VOLUME F2

VOLUME

A Film Beginnings, 1893–1910
F1 Feature Films, 1911–1920
★ F2 FEATURE FILMS, 1921–1930
F3 Feature Films, 1931–1940
F4 Feature Films, 1941–1950
F5 Feature Films, 1951–1960
F6 Feature Films, 1961–1970
S1 Short Films, 1911–1920
S2 Short Films, 1921–1930
S3 Short Films, 1931–1940
S4 Short Films, 1941–1950
S5 Short Films, 1951–1960
S6 Short Films, 1961–1970
N1 Newsreels, 1908–1920
N2 Newsreels, 1921–1930
N3 Newsreels, 1931–1940
N4 Newsreels, 1941–1950
N5 Newsreels, 1951–1960
N6 Newsreels, 1961–1970

THE AMERICAN FILM INSTITUTE CATALOG

OF MOTION PICTURES PRODUCED IN THE UNITED STATES

★ FEATURE FILMS 1921-1930

KENNETH W. MUNDEN
Executive Editor

R. R. BOWKER COMPANY New York & London, 1971

LIBRARY OF CONGRESS CATALOG CARD NO. 79-128587
ISBN 0-8352-0440-5

★ *To the men and women whose work was making motion pictures in the 1920's*

Board of Trustees of THE AMERICAN FILM INSTITUTE June 1967 – June 1971

FOREWORD

★ When the history of the twentieth century in America is written it will include as one of its highlights the growth and flowering of a new art form—one which began as a kind of toy and grew into a device for communication, art, and industry whose dimensions and significance continue to expand.

In fact, in the early days, films grew so fast that there was little time for looking back. Allan Dwan, a director of the 20's and 30's, wrote me recently saying that he never dreamed that another generation would have an interest in his work and consequently he kept no prints or scripts of his films. So records of this past have been sparse, and so too the surviving films.

More than half of the pictures made in the United States had been lost or destroyed and two-thirds of the twentieth century had passed when the American Film Institute came into being in 1967. One task of the Institute is to recover the surviving films—nearly 4,500 are already in the AFI Collection at the Library of Congress—and another is to recover and organize the data which can document the history of an art.

The present volume is the centerpiece of a comprehensive reference work on American cinema. Though not the first in the order in which the complete set of volumes will stand on the shelf, it is nevertheless a fine choice to introduce the work. It describes films of a decade that witnessed the zenith of the silent film and the introduction of sound.

The Credit Index chronicles the founding of thousands of careers in meticulous detail. Every credit of men and women like William Wellman, Mary Pickford, Frank Capra, and Harold Lloyd is listed whether the credit was as actor or writer, as director or assistant. And every career is included whether the assistant remained an assistant or went on to greater things. This information has been compiled by a small staff that has been rigorous in its attention to accuracy and completeness of information; no credit is too small, no career too brief. The same is true of the corporate structures that came into being. The giants are here – M-G-M, Fox, Paramount, United Artists – with every film they produced, and so are hundreds of will-o'-the-wisp companies that failed to survive their first film and vanished without a trace except the film that bears their name.

This volume reflects a great era in human creativity. A decade of adventure for thousands of artists and craftsmen who invested their lives to creating moving pictures. They did it well. It is to their memory that this volume is dedicated.

GEORGE STEVENS, JR.
DIRECTOR, THE AMERICAN FILM INSTITUTE

CONTENTS

INTRODUCTION

★ This volume of *The American Film Institute Catalog* describes United States feature motion pictures that were released between 1 January 1921 and 31 December 1930. With respect to those films the release dates of which are unrecorded, the dates of their copyright registration, trade or public showings, or licensing by state motion picture commissions have determined their inclusion in the volume. Feature films, for the purpose of this volume, are those that are 4,000 ft. or more in length or, in cases where exact or approximate footage is unknown, of 4 or more reels. Other films of the decade here covered are described in companion volumes devoted respectively to short films and newsreels. Feature films of earlier and subsequent decades are described in separate volumes of the *Catalog.*

The films described are those produced or "manufactured" by United States firms, societies or associations, institutions, public (including governmental) agencies, and private individuals that had, or were intended to have, public showings. Since many such films were made, in whole or in part, outside the continental limits of the United States and its territories and possessions, many films that *appear* to be United States productions have actually a doubtful origin. Films of this class, whenever entered in the *Catalog,* are annotated to suggest the possibility of foreign origin.

Each film of concern to this volume is given a separate entry and is arranged by its title in alphabetical sequence with all other entries. Films known by, originally released under, copyrighted by, or re-released under titles other than those chosen to head the descriptive entries in the *Catalog* are cross-referenced from these alternative titles. Besides having an alphabetical arrangement, the entries are numerically arranged, beginning with 0001, with the prefix F2 identifying the series of volumes describing feature films and the volume number of the present work within that series. The use of the entry number in facilitating the use of the accompanying Credit Index and Subject Index is discussed in the introductions to those indexes (pages 937 and 1471); its relevance to a projected cumulative index to the *Catalog* as a whole is obvious.

As applicable and to the extent that data are available, a descriptive entry gives the following information in this order:

IDENTIFICATION AND PHYSICAL DESCRIPTION. The first name appearing after the film title (and its series title, if any) is that of the production company or individual. Any sponsoring company or individual is then named, and the original distributor (if determined, and if different from the production company or individual) is given. The date appearing first is that of release unless otherwise qualified; the copyright date is differentiated from other dates by the prefix "c" and is followed immediately by the copyright dossier number. There then follow data on audio aspects (silent, sound, sound effects), color, gauge, and length.

PRODUCTION CREDITS. Each person, group of persons, firm, institution, or agency involved in the production is named, with the credited function preceding the name in abbreviated form and in italic.

CAST CREDITS. The players, listed by name, include named animals and each group or ensemble; and the role played is stated parenthetically and in italic after each name, or group of names if applicable.

DESCRIPTION OF CONTENTS. Following an indication of genre (expressed usually in the vernacular of the 1920's), the literary, dramatic, or other original source of the film is stated with, whenever possible, full bibliographical citation. There follows a summary of the action depicted, a statement of the situation presented and its manner of resolution, or (in the case of nondramatic films) an explanation of the purpose and scope. At the end of the summary appears the list of subject terms under which the film is indexed in the accompanying Subject Index.

To many entries are added special notes, which serve especially the purpose of calling attention to the inability of the compilers to make conclusive judgments when confronted with conflicting "evidence." For, as is well known, many films accounted for in this *Catalog* are not extant, and many more are not available for screening. Actual screen credits, moreover, are often incomplete and sometimes suspect. Few printed and documentary sources give all the essentials, with the result that only for a relative handful of films has it been possible to find all the data needed in a single source; and the greater the number of sources used in arriving at a description of a given film, the greater the number of discrepancies encountered.

Whenever possible, however, the present work has been based solidly on primary sources and from that point of departure has proceeded to discover the additional, though often conflicting, data published contemporaneously with the release of a film. Two bodies of archives have been thoroughly examined: the records of film copyright application maintained by the Copyright Office, and the licensing application files of the Motion Picture Division (formerly the Motion Picture Commission) of New York State. The records of a number of studios or production companies (among them, Universal Pictures, Paramount Pictures, and Warner Brothers) have constituted a third major category of original documentation made available to the compilers.

The several classes of copyright application dossiers are arranged numerically, and therefore chronologically, by copyright registration number; this number appears in each entry of the *Catalog of Copyright Entries: Motion Pictures 1912-1939* (Washington, 1951) and, as noted above, is repeated for convenience of reference in the present *Catalog*. The absence of copyright information indicates that the film described in the entry was not copyrighted; and for information concerning the considerable number of uncopyrighted features the American Film Institute is indebted especially to the Manuscripts and History Library of the New York State Library, which has custody of the records of the former New York State Motion Picture Division.

Printed materials indispensable to the research for this volume, beyond those found in the copyright application dossiers, include significantly the following serials: *Exhibitors Trade Review, Film Daily, Film Daily Directors' Annual and Production Guide, Film Year Book, Motion Picture Almanac, Motion Picture News, Motion Picture News Booking Guide, Motion Picture News Blue Book, Motion Picture Studio Directory and Trade Annual, Motion Picture Trade Directory, Moving Picture World, National Board of Review Magazine, Photoplay Magazine,* and *Variety*. Among newspaper reviews consulted those published in the *New York Times* have been especially helpful.

Because the publications now controlled by the Quigley Publishing Company are vital to film research, the American Film Institute is particularly indebted to Martin Quigley, Jr., for permission to use them extensively. Four significant Quigley publications of the 1920's– *Exhibitors Herald, Motion Picture News, Motion Picture News Booking Guide,* and *Moving Picture World*–were consolidated in 1931 and are now published by Quigley as *Motion Picture Herald*. Also consolidated in 1931, as *Motion Picture Daily,* were the Quigley publications *Exhibitors Trade Review, Exhibitors Daily Review,* and *Motion Pictures Today*.

Through the generosity of the Librarian of Congress the American Film Institute Catalog project is provided working space in the Motion Picture Section of the Library's Prints and Photographs Division. The Motion Picture Section's film holdings, which include The American Film Institute Collection, and its extensive finding aids and other research materials have been made freely available to the Catalog staff; and for these services and the concomitant administrative support the Institute is most grateful to Edgar Breitenbach and Alan M. Fern, Chief and Assistant Chief, respectively, of the Prints and Photographs Division, and John B. Kuiper, Head of the Motion Picture Section.

Institutions other than those named above whose assistance in the preparation of this volume has been material include the George Eastman House, the Museum of Modern Art (New York City), the Academy of Motion Picture Arts and Sciences, the Special Collections Department of the Library of the University of California at Los Angeles, the National Film Collection of the Public Archives of Canada, the Canadian Film Institute, and the United States National Archives. To these institutions and to the following individuals who voluntarily have contributed important data in significant amounts the American Film Institute is greatly indebted: Harriet Aveney, Geoffrey Bell, John Cocchi, Walter Dean, Kent D. Eastin, Lewis Flacks, George Geltzer, William T. Leonard, Andrew C. McKay, Stephen Manes, Carlton Moss, David Parker, Frank B. Pascoe, Barbara A. Ringer, Samuel K. Rubin, Anne Schlosser, Patrick J. Sheehan, Glenn Shipley, Paul Spehr, and Juliet C. Wolohan.

The American Film Institute is a private, non-profit organization established by the National Council on the Arts in June 1967 and received its initial grants from the National Endowment for the Arts, The Ford Foundation, and the Motion Picture Association of America. Inspiration for undertaking the *Catalog* project was initially provided by Richard Kahlenberg of the AFI staff in consultation with Frances Thorpe, then of the British National Film Catalogue, and the work has gone forward under the general direction of Sam Kula, AFI Archivist. The manuscript was typed for computer input by Symarion Maloushawa Davis, Judith Gerber, Beatrice Ott, Gelah Penn, and Lynn Ruben. Bibliographical citations were checked by Constance Szostak. All details of developing the special computer technology for processing the data have been in the capable hands of Bruce B. Warren of Auto-Graphics, Inc., which has produced the indexes and by photocomposition has presented both the catalog proper and the indexes in camera-ready form for publication.

KENNETH W. MUNDEN

ABBREVIATIONS

This list, with a few exceptions, is confined to abbreviations denoting motion picture credits. Other abbreviations appearing in this work conform to standard practices.

Adapt adaptation, adapter
Adv adviser
Anim animation, animator
Arr arranged, arranger
Auth author
b&w black and white
c copyright
ca about
Camera cameraman
Choreog choreographer, choreography
Cinematog cinematographer, cinematography
Col color
Comp composed, composer
Cons consultant
Cont continuity
Coöp cooperator, cooperation
Cost costume, costumes
Decor decoration, decorator
Dial dialog
Dir director, direction
Dist distributor
Dsgn design, designer
Ed editor, editorial
Eff effects
Elec electrical
Electrn electrician
Engr engineer
Exec executive
Lyr lyrics
Mix mixing
mm millimeters
Mus music
Orch orchestra, orchestration
Photog photographer, photographic
Pres presented, presentor
Prod producer, production, produced
Prop property, properties
Rec recorder, recording
Res research
Scen scenario, scenarist
Sd sound
Si silent
Sets sets, settings
Sp special
Stgd staged
Supv supervisor, supervision
Tech technical, technician
Titl titler, titles
Vers version
Writ written, writer

FEATURE FILMS 1921-1930

ABIE'S IMPORTED BRIDE F2.0001

Temple Theater Amusement Co. *Dist* Trio Productions. c15 Jun **1925** [LP21570]. Si; b&w. 35mm. 7 reels.

Dir-Writ Roy Calnek.

Comedy. When Abie Lavinsky, the son of the owner of the prosperous Lavinsky woolen mills, learns of the plight of Jews starving in Russia, he sets out to collect money to help alleviate their hunger and suffering. He asks the workers at his father's factory to contribute and then, at the sarcastic urging of his father, arranges a charity ball at which he raises $100,000 from his jazz-minded friends. Abie is then elected to go to Russia with the money, and he makes plans to depart immediately. Max Rosenthal, a professional matchmaker, interests the elder Lavinsky in a young girl in Russia, and Abie violently opposes the match. His father is unmoved by Abie's pleas to be reasonable, and Abie is delegated to make the arrangements to bring the young girl to the United States to be wed to the elder Lavinsky. Abie falls in love with her himself, and they decide to be married, fully expecting Abie to be disinherited by his father. When they return to the United States, however, the elder Lavinsky greets them with love, showing Abie a telegram from Max, "Your plan worked fine. Abie swallowed it hook, line and sinker; no danger from flappers now; Abie safely married and on way home." After a few minutes of chagrin, Abie is reconciled with his father. *Jews. Matchmakers. Filial relations. Charity. Famine. Mills. Wool. Russia.*

Note: This film was produced in Philadelphia in October and November of 1924.

ABIE'S IRISH ROSE F2.0002

Paramount Famous Lasky Corp. 5 Jan **1929** [c8 Jan 1929; LP25986]. Talking sequences, sd eff, & mus score (Movietone); b&w. 35mm. 12 reels, 10,471 ft. [Also si; 10,187 ft.]

Assoc Prod B. P. Schulberg. *Dir* Victor Fleming. *Titl* Anne Nichols, Herman Mankiewicz, Julian Johnson. *Adapt* Jules Furthman. *Photog* Harold Rosson. *Film Ed* Eda Warren. *Songs: "Rosemary," "Little Irish Rose"* J. S. Zamecnik.

Cast: Charles Rogers *(Abie Levy)*, Nancy Carroll *(Rosemary Murphy)*, Jean Hersholt *(Solomon Levy)*, J. Farrell MacDonald *(Patrick Murphy)*, Bernard Gorcey *(Isaac Cohen)*, Ida Kramer *(Mrs. Isaac Cohen)*, Nick Cogley *(Father Whalen)*, Camillus Pretal *(Rabbi Jacob Samuels)*, Rosa Rosanova *(Sarah)*.

Drama. Source: Anne Nichols, *Abie's Irish Rose; a Comedy in Three Acts* (New York, 1924). During World War I, Abie Levy, a soldier in the A. E. F., is wounded in combat and, recovering in a hospital, meets Rosemary Murphy, an entertainer. They fall in love and, returning to the United States, they are married in an Episcopal church in Jersey City. Abie then takes Rosemary to his home and introduces her as his sweetheart, Rosie Murpheski; they are then married by a rabbi. Mr. Murphy arrives with a priest and, amid discord and discontent, the young people are married again, this time by the priest. Disowned by both families, Rosemary and Abie are befriended only by the Cohens. On Christmas Eve, the Cohens and their rabbi persuade Solomon to see his son and his new grandchildren; the priest urges Mr. Murphy to do the same. This surprise visit begins in acrimony but ends peacefully as Rosemary presents her newborn twins: Patrick Joseph (named for her father) and Rebecca (named for Abie's dead mother). *Soldiers. Veterans. Entertainers. Jews. Irish. Rabbis. Priests. Marriage—Mixed. Weddings. Prejudice.*

THE ABLEMINDED LADY F2.0003

Pacific Film Co. 1 Jan **1922**. Si; b&w. 35mm. 5 reels, ca4,800 ft.

Dir Ollie Sellers. *Dir? (see note)* Don Gamble.

Cast: Henry B. Walthall *(Breezy Bright)*, Elinor Fair *(Daphne Meadows)*, Helen Raymond *(Widow McGee)*.

Western comedy-drama. Source: William R. Leighton, "The Able-minded Lady," in *Saturday Evening Post*. "An easy-going cowboy bachelor [Breezy Bright] works on a ranch for a three-time widow [Widow McGee]. She is the 'able-minded lady' who keeps reminding him that her late husbands were all lovable gentlemen. He brings a romance between two young people to a happy conclusion. Captures a supposed bandit and finally capitulates to the matrimonial designs of the 'able-minded lady.'" (*Motion Picture News Booking Guide*, 2:9, Apr 1922.) *Widows. Bachelors. Ranches.*

Note: One source credits Don Gamble with direction and Ollie Sellers with photography.

ABOUT TRIAL MARRIAGE *see* **TRIAL MARRIAGE**

ABRAHAM LINCOLN F2.0004

Rockett-Lincoln Film Co. *Dist* Associated First National Pictures. 21 Jan **1924** [New York premiere; released 2 Feb; c2 May 1924; LP20136]. Si; b&w. 35mm. 12 reels, 11,380 ft.

Prod Al Rockett, Ray Rockett. *Dir* Phil Rosen. *Scen* Frances Marion. *Photog* Robert Kurrle, Lyman Broening.

Cast—Kentucky and Indiana Period: Fay McKenzie *(Sarah Lincoln)*, Westcott B. Clarke *(Thomas Lincoln, father)*, Irene Hunt *(Nancy Hanks Lincoln, mother)*, Charles French *(Isom Enlow, neighbor)*, Calvert Carter *(Mr. Gollaher, neighbor)*, Madge Hunt *(Mrs. Gollaher)*, Raymond Lee *(Austin Gollaher, boy chum)*, Ida McKenzie *(Sarah Lincoln, 10 years old)*, Danny Hoy *(Abraham Lincoln, 7 years old)*.

Cast—The New Salem Period: George A. Billings *(Abraham Lincoln, as a young man)*, Ruth Clifford *(Ann Rutledge, first sweetheart)*, Ed Burns *(John McNeil)*, Pat Hartigan *(Jack Armstrong, leader of Clary Grove Gang)*, Otis Harlan *(Denton Offut, employer of Lincoln)*, Jules Hanft *(James Rutledge)*, Julia Hesse *(Mrs. Rutledge)*, Louise Fazenda *(Sally, a country girl)*, Robert Bolder *(a country politician)*, William Humphrey

(Stephen A. Douglas), William McIllwain *(Dr. Allen)*, Fred Kohler *(auctioneer at New Orleans slave market)*, Robert Milasch *(southern planter)*, George Reehm *(another southern planter)*.

Cast—The Springfield Period: George A. Billings *(Abraham Lincoln)*, Nell Craig *(Mary Todd, afterward Mrs. Lincoln)*, Genevieve Blinn *(Mary Todd's sister, Mrs. Ninian Edwards)*, Mickey Moore *(Willie Lincoln)*, Newton Hall *(Tad Lincoln)*, Francis Powers *(Richard J. Oglesby)*.

Cast—The Washington Period: George A. Billings *(Abraham Lincoln, President)*, Nell Craig *(Mrs. Abraham Lincoln)*, Homer Willits *(John Hay, Secretary to the President)*, Jim Blackwell *(Tom, colored servant)*, Eddie Sutherland *(William Scott, Union soldier)*, Frances Raymond *(Scott's mother)*, Jack Rollings *(Union sentry)*, William McCormick *(corporal of guard)*, Frank Newburg *(Bixby, Union soldier)*, William Moran *(John Wilkes Booth)*, John Steppling *(chairman of delegation)*, Wanda Crazer *(a dancer)*, Walter Rogers *(Gen. U. S. Grant)*, Alfred Allen *(Gen. George Meade)*, James Welch *(Gen. Robert E. Lee)*, Miles McCarthy *(Major, afterward General, Anderson)*, Earl Schenck *(Colonel Rathbone)*, Dolly McLean *(Miss Harris)*, Cordelia Callahan *(Mrs. Surratt)*, Dallas Hope *(stable boy)*, Dick Johnson *(bartender)*, Jack Winn *(Ned Spangler)*, Lawrence Grant *(actor at Ford's)*, Ivy Livingston *(actress at Ford's)*, Kathleen Chambers *(another actress)*, Henry Rattenbury *(stagehand)*, W. L. McPheeters *(Allan Pinkerton, Chief of Secret Service)*.

Cast—President Lincoln's Cabinet: Willis Marks *(William H. Seward, Secretary of State)*, Nick Cogley *(Simon Cameron, Secretary of War)*, Charles Smiley *(Salmon P. Chase, Secretary of Treasury/Hugh McCulloch, Secretary of Treasury)*, R. G. Dixon *(Gideon Welles, Secretary of Navy)*, Harry Kelsey *(Caleb B. Smith, Secretary of Interior)*, Joseph Mills *(Montgomery Blair, Postmaster-General)*, Fred Manly *(Edward Bates, Attorney-General)*, William von Hardenburg *(James Speed, Attorney-General)*, R. J. Duston *(William Dennison, Postmaster-General)*.

Biographical drama. Episodes recording the life of Abraham Lincoln from birth to death: saving of his life as an infant, his boyhood years down through his romance with Ann Rutledge, his career as a lawyer and legislator, his nomination and election, the war years, and his assassination. *United States—History—Civil War. Abraham Lincoln. Ann Rutledge. Stephen Arnold Douglas. John Milton Hay. John Wilkes Booth. Ulysses Simpson Grant. George Gordon Meade. Robert Edward Lee. Robert Anderson.*

Note: Original release title: *The Dramatic Life of Abraham Lincoln.*

ABRAHAM LINCOLN **F2.0005**

Feature Productions. *Dist* United Artists. 25 Aug **1930** [New York premiere; released 8 Nov; c1 Sep 1930; LP1585]. Sd (Movietone); b&w. 35mm. 10 reels, 8,704 ft.

Pres by Joseph M. Schenck. *Story and Prod Adv* John W. Considine, Jr. *Dir* D. W. Griffith. *Assoc Dial Dir* Harry Stubbs. *Cont-Dial* Stephen Vincent Benét, Gerrit Lloyd. *Adapt* Stephen Vincent Benét. *Photog* Karl Struss. *Art Dir* William Cameron Menzies, Park French. *Film Ed* James Smith, Hal C. Kern. *Mus Arr* Hugo Riesenfeld. *Sd Rec* Harold Witt. *Prod Mgr* Orville O. Dull. *Prod Staff* Raymond A. Klune, Herbert Sutch. *Cost* Walter J. Israel.

Cast: Lucille La Verne *(Mid-Wife)*, W. L Thorne *(Tom Lincoln)*, Helen Freeman *(Nancy Hanks Lincoln)*, Otto Hoffman *(Offut)*, Walter Huston *(Abraham Lincoln)*, Edgar Deering *(Armstrong)*, Una Merkel *(Ann Rutledge)*, Russell Simpson *(Lincoln's employer)*, Charles Crockett *(Sheriff)*, Kay Hammond *(Mary Todd Lincoln)*, Helen Ware *(Mrs. Edwards)*, E. Alyn Warren *(Stephen A. Douglas)*, Jason Robards *(Herndon)*, Gordon Thorpe *(Tad Lincoln)*, Ian Keith *(John Wilkes Booth)*, Cameron Prudhomme *(John Hay, Secretary to Lincoln)*, James Bradbury, Sr. *(General Scott)*, James Eagle *(Young Soldier)*, Fred Warren *(General Grant)*, Oscar Apfel *(Secretary of War)*, Frank Campeau *(General Sheridan)*, Hobart Bosworth *(General Lee)*, Henry B. Walthall *(Colonel Marshall)*, Hank Bell, Carl Stockdale, Ralph Lewis, George MacQuarrie, Robert Brower.

Historical drama. After a brief scene depicting the circumstances of Lincoln's birth in 1809, we find him at the age of 22, "the ugliest and smartest man in New Salem, Ill." and a clerk in D. Offut's general store. In the spring of 1834, Abe is courting Ann Rutledge when she dies abruptly of fever, causing him great suffering. After 3 years of fighting in the Indian war as Captain of Volunteers, Abe begins his law practice. At a ball given by former Governor Edwards, the awkward lawyer meets Mary Todd and later, despite misgivings, marries her. His reputation as a debater wins him the Republican nomination to the Presidency, and he is elected. John Brown and the Abolitionists capture the armory at Harper's Ferry, and John Wilkes Booth, a fanatic exhorter, cries out for volunteers to avenge the act; thus the Civil War begins—Fort Sumter, Bull Run, then Washington is threatened. Lincoln makes a personal visit to a battlefield and comes upon a court-martial in progress; he asks the defendant to explain his actions, pardons him, and orders him back to his regiment. The signing of the Emancipation Proclamation intensifies the struggle, and Lincoln is encouraged by Congress to end the war. Lincoln selects Grant to lead Union forces; while conferring with Stanton, the President receives word of Sheridan's defeat; he tells Stanton of his vision of a ship with white sails before each victory. ... The last of the Confederate forces under Lee are defeated and the war is over. On the night of April 14, 1865, Lincoln speaks from a box at Ford's Theatre, and just after the play has begun, he is shot by John Wilkes Booth; the resulting uproar gives way to the sobbing of an unseen multitude, and a voice calls out: "Now he belongs to the ages." *Lawyers. Abolitionists. Rural life. Courtship. Elections. Illinois. United States—History—Civil War. Emancipation Proclamation. Ford's Theatre. Abraham Lincoln.*

ABSENT **F2.0006**

Rosebud Film Corp. **1928.** Si; b&w. 35mm. 6 reels, 5,046 ft.

Supv-Dir Harry A. Gant. *Photog* Harry A. Gant.

Cast: Clarence Brooks, George Reed, Virgil Owens, Rosa Lee Lincoln, Floyd Shackelford, Clarence Williams.

Melodrama. A shell shocked Negro veteran drifts into a mining camp and is given sustenance by an old miner and his daughter. He later regains his memory in a fight and is given a fresh start by the American Legion. *Veterans. Miners. Amnesia. Shell shock. Negro life. American Legion.*

THE ABYSMAL BRUTE (Universal-Jewel) **F2.0007**

Universal Pictures. 15 Apr **1923** [c30 Mar 1923; LP18834]. Si; b&w. 35mm. 8 reels, 7,373 ft.

Dir Hobart Henley. *Scen* A. P. Younger. *Photog* Charles Stumar.

Cast: Reginald Denny *(Pat Glendon, Jr.)*, Mabel Julienne Scott *(Marion [Maude?] Sangster)*, Charles French *(Pat Glendon, Sr.)*, Hayden Stevenson *(Sam Stubener)*, David Torrence *(Mortimer Sangster)*, George Stewart *(Wilfred Sangster)*, Buddy Messinger *(Buddy Sangster)*, Crauford Kent *(Deane Warner)*, Dorothea Wolbert *(Mrs. MacTavish)*, Julia Brown *(Violet MacTavish)*, Harry Mann *(Abe Levinsky)*, Kid Wagner *(Battling Levinsky)*, Jack Herrick *(Rough House Ratigan)*, Irene Haisman *(Gwendolyn)*, Nell Craig *(Daisy Emerson)*, Will R. Walling *(Farrell)*.

Melodrama. Source: Jack London, *The Abysmal Brute* (New York, 1913). Reared in the California mountains by his father, an ex-prizefighter, Pat Glendon shows great skill and strength but is terribly shy of women. When he finally enters competition in San Francisco, he achieves success and the title "The Abysmal Brute." One day he rescues a man from drowning, meets socialite Maude Sangster as a result, and falls in love with her at first sight. He keeps her in ignorance of his profession, and though Pat is handicapped by his lack of knowledge of social niceties, they see each other often. When Maude does learn of Pat's prizefighting she repudiates him, but Pat is persistent and finally wins her from his rival. *Prizefighters. Socialites. Manners. Mountain life. California. San Francisco.*

ACCORDING TO HOYLE **F2.0008**

David Butler Productions. *Dist* Western Pictures Exploitation Co. 6 May **1922** [New York State license]. Si; b&w. 35mm. 5 reels.

Pres by Louis Burston. *Dir* W. S. Van Dyke. *Scen* John B. Clymer. *Story* Clyde C. Westover, Lottie Horner. *Photog* Arthur Todd.

Cast: David Butler *("Boxcar" Simmons)*, Helen Ferguson *(Doris Mead)*, Phil Ford *(Jim Mead)*, Fred J. Butler *(Dude Miller)*, Harry Todd *(Jim Riggs)*, Buddy Ross *(Silent Johnson)*, Hal Wilson *(hotel bellboy)*.

Comedy. "'Boxcar' Simmons, a tramp, represents himself as a mining millionaire in a small town. The population accepts him at his own valuation, and two of the town's 'slickers' make desperate efforts to 'take him for his roll.' One of their schemes is to sell him a worthless ranch, but he turns the tables on them by making them believe that the ranch is a veritable bed of silver ore, and then, after they buy it he presents the major part of the proceeds to the girl who owns the place and with whom he had fallen in love." (*Moving Picture World*, 24 Jun 1922, p736.) *Tramps. Millionaires. Wealth. Fraud. Ranches.*

ACCUSED **F2.0009**

Independent Pictures. 3 Dec **1925** [New York State license]. Si; b&w. 35mm. 5 reels, 4,800 ft.

Dir Dell Henderson.

Cast: Dorothy Drew *(Helen)*, Eric Mayne *(Cyrus Braidwood)*, Charles

Delaney *(Steve Randall)*, Charles Gerrard *(Lait Rodman)*, Miss Du Pont *(Rose Bailey)*, Sheldon Lewis *(Bull McLeod)*, Spottiswoode Aitken *(Eagle Eye)*.

Melodrama. Helen is reared by Cyrus Braidwood as his daughter, but, as a young woman, she discovers that her true father is Lait Rodman, against whom Braidwood holds a written confession of murder. Rodman retrieves the confession, and Helen goes to his apartment looking for it, there meeting Steve Randall, a young bachelor. They mistake each other for crooks and are soon imprisoned in an underground thieves' den. The den is flooded, and the two barely escape. Everything works out in the end, and Steve and Helen agree to wed. *Thieves. Bachelors. Parentage. Documentation.*

ACE OF ACTION **F2.0010**

Action Pictures. *Dist* Associated Exhibitors. 28 Nov **1926** [c10 Nov 1926; LU23318]. Si; b&w. 35mm. 5 reels, 4,447 ft.

Pres by Lester F. Scott, Jr. *Dir* William Bertram. *Story-Scen* Betty Burbridge. *Photog* Ray Ries.

Cast: Wally Wales *(Wally Rand)*, Alma Rayford *(June Darcy)*, Charles Colby *(Farber)*, Hank Bell, Charles Whitaker, Fanny Midgley, William Hayes, Frank Ellis.

Western melodrama. A feud develops between the Waltons and the Darcys over the possession of a valuable waterhole. Old John Walton believes the dispute should be settled by an outside party, and Farber, an eastern attorney, decides to impersonate Walton's missing heir. Wally Rand, a young cowboy who falls in love with June Darcy, is mistaken for the rightful heir, and Farber is arrested as an imposter. Lafe Darcy plots with Farber to kidnap Wally, but he is freed by June and after fighting Lafe settles the family feud. *Cowboys. Lawyers. Inheritance. Feuds. Water rights. Imposture.*

ACE OF CACTUS RANGE **F2.0011**

Feature Pictures. *Dist* Aywon Film Corp. Apr **1924.** Si; b&w. 35mm. 5 reels, 4,800 ft.

Dir Denver Dixon, Malon Andrus. *Titl* Al Martin. *Adapt* Nellie Whitefield. *Story* Irving Goldstein. *Photog* Jack Fuqua. *Tech Dir* Marvin G. Bradley.

Cast: Art Mix *(U. S. Marshal Bob Cullen)*, Virginia Warwick *(Virginia Marsden)*, Clifford Davidson *(Bull Davidson)*, Harvey Stafford *(Randolph Truthers)*, Dorothy Chase *(Cleora)*, Charles Colby *(Sheriff Buck Summers)*, H. Paul Walsh *(Markes)*, A. W. Dearie *(Sam)*, Charles Mears *(Quosmo)*.

Western melodrama. "The story is concerned with the activities of a gang of diamond thieves, who respect no law. One of them, Bull Davidson attacks a girl, Virginia Marsden, whose father has discovered their activities and whom they have threatened to kill. She flees to a cabin. They follow her – Bull annoys her – and Bob Cullen, a Secret Service man in disguise overturns a lamp to effect escape. During their ride the horse has an unfortunate fall, after which he is seen limping and Bob and Virginia are forced to spend the night on the plains. They are again overpowered by the gang, who lasso the hero and swing him in the air, suspended from a tree. They then make off with the girl and her helpless father and throw him out of the wagon with intent to kill him. Subsequently the girl is brought to camp and again treated with indignity and there are several fights between the various factions." (Examiner's report, New York State license records.) *United States marshals. Gangs. Disguise. Secret service. Kidnaping. Diamonds.*

THE ACE OF CADS **F2.0012**

Famous Players–Lasky. *Dist* Paramount Pictures. 11 Oct **1926** [c15 Oct 1926; LP24007]. Si; b&w. 35mm. 8 reels, 7,786 ft.

Pres by Adolph Zukor, Jesse L. Lasky. *Assoc Prod* William Le Baron. *Dir* Luther Reed. *Adapt-Screenplay* Forrest Halsey. *Photog* J. Roy Hunt.

Cast: Adolphe Menjou *(Chappel Maturin)*, Alice Joyce *(Eleanour)*, Norman Trevor *(Sir Guy de Gramercy)*, Philip Strange *(Basil de Gramercy)*, Suzanne Fleming *(Joan)*.

Romantic drama. Source: Michael Arlen, "The Ace of Cads," in *Everybody's Magazine* (50:90–100, Jun 1924). Chappel Maturin and Basil de Gramercy, officers in the British Guards, are both in love with the same girl; when Basil betrays his friend by having him compromised with another woman, Maturin takes to drink and is discharged from the service as the result of a drunken brawl. Twenty years later, Basil, who has married Eleanour, has been killed in the trenches; and Joan, an only child, remains Eleanour's sole interest. Maturin, struck by her resemblance to her mother, falls in love with her, but Sir Guy and Eleanour persuade him to discourage the girl. Maturin, therefore, tells Joan the story of his betrayal by Basil, but he reverses their roles. Joan rightly refuses to believe him a wastrel and effects a reconciliation between Maturin and Eleanour. *Courtship. Perfidy. Friendship. Alcoholism. World War I. Paris. Great Britain—Army.*

THE ACE OF CLUBS **F2.0013**

Anchor Film Distributors. *Dist* Rayart Pictures. 14 Aug **1926** [New York State license]. Si; b&w. 35mm. 5 reels.

Dir J. P. McGowan. *Story* G. A. Durlam. *Photog* Robert Cline. *Film Ed* Thelma Smith. *Asst Dir* Mack V. Wright.

Cast: Al Hoxie *(Jack Horton)*, Minna Redman *(the widow Horton)*, Andrew Waldron *(Sandy McGill)*, Peggy Montgomery *(June, McGill's niece)*, Jules Cowles *(Jake McGill)*, Mutt *(a dog)*.

Western melodrama. No information about the precise nature of this film has been found.

THE ACE OF HEARTS **F2.0014**

Goldwyn Pictures. ca17 Sep **1921** [Omaha premiere; released Oct; c9 Sep 1921; LP16948]. Si; b&w. 35mm. 6 reels, 5,883 ft.

Dir Wallace Worsley. *Scen* Ruth Wightman. *Story* Gouverneur Morris. *Photog* Don Short.

Cast: Leatrice Joy *(Lilith)*, John Bowers *(Forrest)*, Lon Chaney *(Farralone)*, Hardee Kirkland *(Morgridge)*, Raymond Hatton *(The Menace)*, Roy Laidlaw *(doorkeeper)*, Edwin Wallock *(chemist)*.

Drama. The members of a radical secret society decide that a wealthy citizen whom they despise must be disposed of. Cards are drawn, and the fatal ace of hearts falls to a young man named Forrest, who is in love with Lilith, a society member who is interested only in the cause but who nevertheless promises to marry him. Discovering that she actually loves him, Lilith begs him to flee, but he returns to the society declaring his inability to fulfill his task because he would have caused the death of two young lovers in the vicinity. The members meet to decide their fate, and Farralone, who has promised Lilith to save her husband, sets off a bomb, which kills the conspiratorial band. *Socialites. Radicalism. Secret societies. Assassination. Murder. Bombs.*

ACE OF THE LAW **F2.0015**

Anchor Film Distributors. 3 Nov **1924** [New York State license]. Si; b&w. 35mm. 5 reels, 4,681 ft.

Cast: Bill Patton *(Bill Kennedy)*, Peggy O'Day *(Mildred Mitchell)*, Lew Meehan *("Black" Muller)*.

Western melodrama. "Black" Muller makes off with Mildred Mitchell and a herd of cattle but is thwarted by Bill Kennedy, who retrieves both the pretty girl and the next fortnight's supper-on-the-hoof. *Cowboys. Rustlers. Kidnaping.*

THE ACQUITTAL (Universal-Jewel) **F2.0016**

Universal Pictures. 19 Nov **1923** [c13 Oct 1923; LP19548]. Si; b&w. 35mm. 7 reels, 6,523 ft.

Dir Clarence Brown. *Scen* Jules Furthman. *Adapt* Raymond L. Schrock. *Cont (see note)* Dale Van Every, John Huston, Tom Reed, Tom KilPatrick, Anthony Veiller, Jules Furthman. *Photog* Silvano Balboni.

Cast: Claire Windsor *(Madeline Ames)*, Norman Kerry *(Robert Armstrong)*, Richard Travers *(Kenneth Winthrop)*, Barbara Bedford *(Edith Craig)*, Charles Wellesley *(Andrew Prentice)*, Frederick Vroom *(Carter Ames)*, Ben Deeley *(The Butler)*, Harry Mestayer *(The District Attorney)*, Emmett King *(The Minister)*, Dot Farley *(The Maid)*, Hayden Stevenson *(The Taxi Driver)*.

Mystery melodrama. Source: Rita Weiman, *The Acquittal* (New York opening: 5 Jan 1920). A wealthy man's adopted sons are suspected of killing him. One is accused; he is proven innocent, then later confesses. *Adoption. Patricide.*

Note: Company records credit the individuals named with continuity.

ACQUITTED **F2.0017**

Columbia Pictures. 15 Nov **1929** [c10 Dec 1929; LP910]. Sd (Movietone); b&w. 35mm. 7 reels, 5,711 ft. [Also si.]

Prod Harry Cohn. *Dir* Frank R. Strayer. *Dial Dir* James Seymour. *Scen-Dial* Keene Thompson. *Photog* Ted Tetzlaff. *Art Dir* Harrison Wiley. *Film Ed* David Berg. *Ch Sd Mixer* John Livadary. *Sd Mixing Engr* G. R. Cooper. *Asst Dir* Charles Stallings.

Cast: Lloyd Hughes *(Dr. Bradford)*, Margaret Livingston *(Marian)*, Sam Hardy *(Egan)*, Charles West *(McManus)*, George Rigas *(Tony)*,

Charles Wilson *(Nelson)*, Otto Hoffman *(Smith)*.

Crime melodrama. While serving a term in an eastern penitentiary, Marian falls in love with Bradford, a physician serving a life sentence for a murder of which she believes him to be innocent. Frank Egan, an underworld leader who has unsuccessfully sought Marian's love, operates a hotel that serves as a blind for his operations and meets Marian when she is released. To her surprise Egan offers to free Bradford and force Smith, who needs money desperately, to confess to the crime; after securing Bradford's release, Egan holds him and threatens his life unless Marian will allow him (Egan) to make love to her; she refuses and shoots him, but when Bradford gives him medical aid, the gang leader repents and confesses to the crime for which Bradford was convicted. *Physicians. Murder. Prisons. Injustice. Hotels.*

ACROSS THE ATLANTIC **F2.0018**

Warner Brothers Pictures. 25 Feb **1928** [c11 Feb 1928; LP24992]. Si; b&w. 35mm. 7 reels, 6,052 ft.

Dir Howard Bretherton. *Adapt* Harvey Gates. *Story* John Ransom. *Photog* Barney McGill. *Asst Dir* Henry Blanke.

Cast: Monte Blue *(Hugh Clayton)*, Edna Murphy *(Phyllis Jones)*, Burr McIntosh *(John Clayton)*, Robert Ober *(Dan Clayton)*.

Romantic drama. Two brothers, Hugh and Dan Clayton, love their father's secretary, Phyllis Jones. She chooses Hugh, and they marry before he goes to war as an airplane pilot. Shot down in France, he loses his memory and becomes a drifter. Eight years later, Phyllis, resigned to her fate, promises to marry Dan after a visit to the place in France where Hugh was last seen. Meanwhile, Hugh, back in America, is working at his father's aircraft plant. While he is test-flying an airplane, his memory returns. He crashes and is taken to an asylum because of his insistence that he is Clayton's son. He escapes the asylum, steals an experimental trans-Atlantic airplane, and flies it to Paris to be reunited with his family. *Wanderers. Brothers. Air pilots. Airplane factories. Amnesia. World War I. France.*

ACROSS THE BORDER *see* **A CALIFORNIA ROMANCE**

ACROSS THE BORDER **F2.0019**

Charles R. Seeling Productions. *Dist* Aywon Film Corp. 15 Jan **1922.** Si; b&w. 35mm. 5 reels.

Dir-Writ Charles R. Seeling.

Cast: Big Boy Williams *(Andy Fowler)*, Patricia Palmer *(Margie Landers)*, William McCall *(Phillip Landers)*, Chet Ryan *(Jim)*.

Western melodrama. Out of gratitude for rescuing a member from a burning cave, a rustling gang makes Andy Fowler one of its number and signifies that fact by allowing him to wear a green band on his arm. Margie Landers, despite her love for Andy, reports the band to Sheriff Lenoir when her father's cattle are stolen. Lenoir, who is really the rustlers' leader, forgets his obligation to Andy out of passion for Margie and pursues the hero; but Andy establishes his innocence in a series of escapades. Lenoir is apprehended; Margie and Andy are left to live in happiness. *Sheriffs. Rustling.*

ACROSS THE CONTINENT **F2.0020**

Famous Players–Lasky. *Dist* Paramount Pictures. ca29 Apr **1922** [New York premiere; released 4 Jun; c26 Apr 1922; LP17830]. Si; b&w. 35mm. 6 reels, 5,502 ft.

Pres by Jesse L. Lasky. *Dir* Philip E. Rosen. *Story-Scen* Byron Morgan. *Photog* Charles Edgar Schoenbaum.

Cast: Wallace Reid *(Jimmy Dent)*, Mary MacLaren *(Louise Fowler)*, Theodore Roberts *(John Dent)*, Betty Francisco *(Lorraine Tyler)*, Walter Long *(Dutton Tyler)*, Lucien Littlefield *(Scott Tyler)*, Jack Herbert *(Art Roget)*, Guy Oliver *(Irishman)*, Sidney D'Albrook *(Tom Bryce)*.

Comedy-melodrama. John Dent, an automobile manufacturer, produces an inexpensive but effective car. His son, Jimmy, rebels when Dent orders all his employees to drive Dent cars. Moreover, Lorraine, daughter of Dutton Tyler, Dent's competitor, induces Jimmy to buy one of *her* father's expensive roadsters. Later, however, when Jimmy learns that Tyler has plotted to wreck a Dent entry in a transcontinental race, he gives up his roadster and agrees to drive his father's car in another race. Louise, his father's secretary, tries to warn him of a sabotage attempt and intervenes by disguising herself as a mechanic; together, they barely escape the path of a train in a railroad tunnel, and Jimmy wins the race and Louise. *Filial relations. Automobile manufacture. Automobile racing.*

ACROSS THE DEAD-LINE (Universal Special) **F2.0021**

Universal Film Manufacturing Co. 9 Jan **1922** [c3 Jan 1922; LP17435]. Si; b&w. 35mm. 5 reels, 4,886 ft.

Pres by Carl Laemmle. *Dir* Jack Conway. *Scen* George C. Hull. *Story* Clarence Budington Kelland. *Photog* Leland Lancaster.

Cast: Frank Mayo *(John Kidder)*, Russell Simpson *(Enoch Kidder)*, Wilfred Lucas *(Aaron Kidder)*, Lydia Knott *(Charity Kidder)*, Molly Malone *(Ruth)*, Frank Thorwald *(Lucas Courtney)*, Josef Swickard *(Abel)*, William Marion *(Gillis)*.

Melodrama. Gilead, a northwestern lumber town, is divided on the one side by Enoch Kidder, his son John, and his puritanical family, and on the other by Aaron Kidder, Enoch's vengeful brother, and Aaron's followers in pleasure and lust. An old feud culminates when Aaron tries to lure John over to his side and revenge himself on Enoch. A girl who has lost her memory is kidnaped and held by Aaron, and John, determined to protect her, follows. The death of one of the brothers brings about a termination of the old family feud, and John succeeds in restoring the girl's dormant memory. *Brothers. Filial relations. Lumber industry. Feuds. Amnesia.*

ACROSS THE DEADLINE **F2.0022**

William Steiner Productions. 26 Apr **1925** [c5 Dec, 8 Dec 1924; LU20855]. Si; b&w. 35mm. 5 reels, 5,000 ft.

Dir Leo Maloney. *Story* Ford I. Beebe. *Photog* Ben Bail, Jacob A. Badaracco.

Cast: Leo Maloney *(Clem Wainright)*, Josephine Hill *(Shirley Revelle)*, Thomas Lingham *(Martin Revelle)*, Bud Osborne *(Ben Larrago)*, Florence Lee *(Mrs. Revelle)*, Rulon Slaughter *(Rance Revelle)*, Pat Rooney *(Shifty Sands)*.

Western melodrama. Despite a feud of 30 years' standing between the Revelle and Wainright families, Shirley Revelle and Clem Wainright fall in love. They are discovered meeting by Clem's rival, Ben Larrago, who informs Shirley's father of their romantic activities. The elder Revelle forbids Shirley to see Clem, and Clem goes out to the Revelle ranch, deliberately riding his horse across the property line. Only the iron will of Shirley's father can keep her brother, Rance, from shooting Clem on the spot, but after the elder Revelle forces Clem to ride off, Rance shoots at him from ambush. Clem is not hurt; Rance, however, takes one of Clem's bullets in the arm. When the stage is held up by Larrago and Shifty Sands, Rance's wound is used by the sheriff to implicate the hot-headed boy in the robbery. He is about to be lynched by an angry mob, when Clem stops the hanging and clears Rance of all suspicion of guilt by pointing out that he himself had wounded Rance before the time of the holdup. Sands and Larrago are captured, and a grateful Martin removes his opposition to the marriage of Clem and Shirley. *Filial relations. Brother-sister relationship. Feuds. Robbery. Lynching.*

ACROSS THE DIVIDE **F2.0023**

G. & J. Photoplay Co. *Dist* Playgoers Pictures. 9 Oct **1921** [c12 Oct 1921; LU17077]. Si; b&w. 35mm. 6 reels, 5,500 ft.

Dir John Holloway. *Scen* Beatrice Frederick. *Photog* A. Quarrier Thompson.

Cast: Rex Ballard *(Kenneth [Buck] Layson)*, Rosemary Theby *(Rosa)*, Ralph Fee McCullough *(Wallace Layson)*, Thomas Delmar *(Dago)*, Gilbert Clayton *(Newton)*, Dorothy Manners *(Helen)*, Flora Hollister *(White Flower)*.

Western melodrama. Wallace Layson, left by his dying mother in the care of Buck, a halfbreed, has no knowledge of his true identity. Layson's father returns to cheat his own son out of a ranch, which he will inherit on his 21st birthday, and induces Rosa, a dancehall girl, to marry young Layson, who is in love with Helen. Buck tells him that the real heir has died and persuades him to pose as the heir, thus foiling the plans of his father and securing a home for young Layson and Helen. Buck then reveals the boy's identity and departs without revealing that he is the boy's half brother. *Brothers. Halfcastes. Dancehall girls. Fatherhood. Personal identity. Impersonation.*

Note: Licensed in New York State as *Across the Great Divide.*

ACROSS THE GREAT DIVIDE *see* **ACROSS THE DIVIDE**

ACROSS THE PACIFIC **F2.0024**

Warner Brothers Pictures. 2 Oct **1926** [c20 Sep 1926; LP23141]. Si; b&w. 35mm. 7 reels, 6,954 ft. [Copyrighted as 8 reels.]

Dir Roy Del Ruth. *Adapt* Darryl Francis Zanuck. *Camera* Byron Haskins. *Asst Camera* Frank Kesson. *Asst Dir* Ross Lederman.

Cast: Monte Blue *(Monte)*, Jane Winton *(Claire Marsh)*, Myrna Loy *(Roma)*, Charles Stevens *(Aguinaldo)*, Tom Wilson *(Tom, Monte's colored servant)*, Walter McGrail *(Captain Grover)*, Herbert Pryor *(Colonel Marsh)*, Ed Kennedy *(Corporal Ryan)*, Theodore Lorch, Sojin *(confidential agents of Aguinaldo)*.

War melodrama. Source: Charles E. Blaney, *Across the Pacific* (New York, 1904). Upon discovering his father's disgrace from the reading of his will, Monte leaves his sweetheart, Claire Marsh, and enlists to fight in the Spanish-American war. Under the leadership of Aguinaldo, their guerilla chieftain, the Filipinos swear death to the American invaders. As a last resort, Monte is ordered to ingratiate himself with Roma, a halfcaste who follows the troops of Aguinaldo; soon she becomes infatuated with Monte. Colonel Marsh and his daughter, Claire, arrive at the post; and Roma, who finds a picture of Claire in Monte's effects, makes passionate love to Monte in Claire's presence. After a series of adventures, Monte obtains the directions to Aguinaldo's camp and brings about the defeat of the insurrectionists. The grief-stricken Claire has agreed to marry Grover, but Monte returns to denounce him as a traitor. Monte and Claire are reunited. *Soldiers. Halfcastes. Wills. Philippines. United States—History—War of 1898. Philippine Insurrection. Emilio Aguinaldo.*

ACROSS THE PLAINS **F2.0025**

Robert J. Horner Productions. *Dist* Associated Independent Producers. 27 Jun **1928** [New York State license]. Si; b&w. 35mm. 5 reels, 4,350 ft.

Dir-Scen Robert J. Horner. *Titl* Royal Brown. *Photog* Jack Draper. *Film Ed* William Austin.

Cast: Pawnee Bill Jr. *(Jim Blake)*, Ione Reed *(Helen Williams)*, Jack Richardson *(Joe Steward)*, Martha Barclay *(Sally Howard)*, Boris Bullock *(Walla Walla Slim)*, Cliff Lyons *(Chuck Lang)*.

Western melodrama(?). No information about the nature of this film has been found.

ACROSS THE WORLD WITH MR. AND MRS. JOHNSON **F2.0026**

Martin Johnson Productions. *Dist* Talking Picture Epics. 20 Jan **1930** [New York premiere]. Sd; b&w. 35mm. 9 reels, 8,860 ft.

Dir J. Leo Meehan. *Dial (see note)* Martin Johnson, J. Leo Meehan, Terry Ramsaye. *Photog* Russell Shields. *Film Ed* Russell Shields.

Personages: Martin Johnson, Osa Johnson, George Eastman, Al Kayser.

Travelog. As if they were showing their film to a few friends in their home, the Johnsons describe their trip across the world, which begins in the South Pacific islands of Hawaii, Samoa, Australia, the Solomons (where they seek and find cannibals), and New Hebrides. Thence on to Africa via the Indian Ocean, Suez Canal, North Africa, and the Nile River to lion country in Tanganyika. (They are briefly joined in Khartum by George Eastman and Dr. Al Kayser.) Taking a safari in the Congo, the Johnsons see animals and pygmies, and travel back to Uganda, British East Africa, and Kenya. *Cannibals. Pygmies. Safaris. Hawaii. Samoa. Australia. Solomon Islands. Tanganyika. Congo. Kenya.*

Note: Later made into a serial of 20-minute episodes. Although Johnson received credit, according to *Motion Picture News* (25 Jan 1930, p42), J. Leo Meehan and Terry Ramsaye were actually responsible for the dialog.

ACROSS TO SINGAPORE **F2.0027**

Metro-Goldwyn-Mayer Pictures. 7 Apr **1928** [c7 Apr 1928; LP25174]. Si; b&w. 35mm. 7 reels, 6,805 ft.

Dir William Nigh. *Cont* Richard Schayer. *Titl* Joe Farnham. *Adapt* Ted Shane. *Photog* John Seitz. *Set Dsgn* Cedric Gibbons. *Film Ed* Ben Lewis. *Wardrobe* David Cox.

Cast: Ramon Novarro *(Joel Shore)*, Joan Crawford *(Priscilla Crowninshield)*, Ernest Torrence *(Capt. Mark Shore)*, Frank Currier *(Jeremiah Shore, father)*, Dan Wolheim *(Noah Shore)*, Duke Martin *(Matthew Shore)*, Edward Connelly *(Joshua Crowninshield)*, James Mason *(Finch)*.

Drama. Source: Ben Ames Williams, *All the Brothers Were Valiant* (New York, 1919). Joel, youngest son of a seafaring family, loves Priscilla, betrothed against her wishes to Mark, his eldest brother. Mark, a ship's captain, sails to Singapore, accompanied by Joel and his brothers. Mark drinks heavily during the voyage, and he is drunk when a conspiratorial crew led by Finch sails from Singapore without him. Joel is put in irons. Reaching home, Joel is freed; he finds Priscilla, and, taking her with him, he returns to Singapore for Mark. There Mark sees that Priscilla does not love him, and he steps aside for his brother. *Sea captains. Brothers. Seafaring life. Drunkenness. Mutiny. Singapore.*

ACTION **F2.0028**

Universal Film Manufacturing Co. 12 Sep **1921** [c25 Aug 1921; LP16889]. Si; b&w. 35mm. 5 reels, 4,509 ft.

Dir Jack Ford. *Scen* Harvey Gates. *Photog* Jack Brown.

Cast: Hoot Gibson *(Sandy Brouke)*, Francis Ford *(Soda Water Manning)*, J. Farrell MacDonald *(Mormon Peters)*, Buck Connors *(Pat Casey)*, Clara Horton *(Molly Casey)*, William Robert Daly *(J. Plimsoll)*, Dorothea Wolbert *(Mirandy Meekin)*, Byron Munson *(Henry Meekin)*, Charles Newton *(Sherriff Dipple)*, Jim Corey *(Sam Waters)*, Ed "King Fisher" Jones *(Art Smith)*.

Western melodrama. Source: J. Allen Dunn, "The Mascotte of the Three Star," in *Short Stories* (95:3–94, Feb 1921). Molly, an orphan, is heir to a ranch and mine and falls under the influence of saloon-owner Plimsoll, who schemes to deprive her of the inheritance. Sandy Brouke and his pals, Soda Water Manning and Mormon Peters, wander off the range and champion the girl's interests. Sandy falls in love with the girl. The partners succeed in getting the mine from the conspirators and working it themselves while sending Molly off to school. Plimsoll frames Sandy and his men, however, and she returns to find them in jail. Through Molly's efforts Sandy is released, and ultimately the crooks are defeated. *Orphans. Saloon keepers. Inheritance. Frameup. Ranches. Mines.*

Note: Working title: *Let's Go.*

THE ACTION CRAVER **F2.0029**

Ben Wilson Productions. *Dist* Rayart Pictures. Feb **1927.** Si; b&w. 35mm. 5 reels, 4,546 ft.

Dir Victor Potel. *Photog* Eddie Linden.

Cast: Dick Hatton.

Western melodrama. "War veteran gets job on ranch but foreman dislikes him because owner's niece is enamored. Calf is found shot dead and vet is accused by foreman; also telegram from woman to vet leads to assumption he had deserted wife. It is found that foreman had shot calf and was also instigator of telegram." (*Motion Picture News Booking Guide,* 12:17, Apr 1927.) *Ranch foremen. Veterans. Ranches.*

ACTION GALORE **F2.0030**

Action Pictures. *Dist* Weiss Brothers Artclass Pictures. 3 Nov **1925.** Si; b&w. 35mm. 5 reels, 4,752 ft.

Dir Robert Eddy.

Cast: Buddy Roosevelt *(Bud Lavrie)*, Toy Gallagher *(Betty McLean)*, Charles Williams *(Luke McLean)*, Joe Rickson *(Gil Kruger)*, Jack O'Brien *(Strike Carney)*, Raye Hamilton *(Ma Kruger)*, Ruth Royce *(Kate Kruger)*.

Western melodrama. "... in which hero, a ranger, sets out to capture notorious criminal, is shot at by girl who mistakes him for claim jumper, is left in burning cabin with girl by villain, escapes and captures villain after fight in deserted mine shaft." (*Motion Picture News Booking Guide,* 10:21, Apr 1926.) *Rangers. Property rights. Fires. Mines.*

THE ACTRESS **F2.0031**

Metro-Goldwyn-Mayer Pictures. 28 Apr **1928** [c28 Apr 1928; LP25200]. Si; b&w. 35mm. 7 reels, 6,998 ft. [Copyrighted as 8 reels.]

Dir Sidney Franklin. *Scen* Albert Lewin, Richard Schayer. *Titl* Joe Farnham. *Photog* William Daniels. *Set Dsgn* Cedric Gibbons. *Film Ed* Conrad A. Nervig. *Asst Dir* Hugh Boswell. *Wardrobe* Gilbert Clark.

Cast—Theatrical: Norma Shearer *(Rose Trelawney)*, Owen Moore *(Tom Wrench)*, Gwen Lee *(Avonia)*, Lee Moran *(Colpoys)*, Roy D'Arcy *(Gadd)*, Virginia Pearson *(Mrs. Telfer)*, William Humphrey *(Mr. Telfer)*, Effie Ellsler *(Mrs. Mossop)*.

Cast—Nontheatrical: Ralph Forbes *(Arthur Gower)*, O. P. Heggie *(Vice-Chancellor Sir William Gower)*, Andrée Tourneur *(Clara de Foenix)*, Cyril Chadwick *(Captain de Foenix)*, Margaret Seddon *(Miss Trafalgar Gower)*.

Comedy-drama. Source: Arthur Wing Pinero, *Trelawney of the "Wells"; a Comedietta in Four Acts* (New York, 1898). Rose Trelawney, a popular actress, marries Arthur Gower, of noble birth, and is brought into his austere household. She leaves when her in-laws insult her theater friends. Still in love with Gower, Rose loses her desire to act and faces poverty. Gower's father, Sir Arthur, attempts to help her by backing a play of hers. Unknown to Rose, Gower plays opposite her. The play is a success, and the family achieves harmony. *Actors. Theatrical backers. In-laws. Nobility. Theater. Family life.*

Note: Published copyright information indicating that the film has sound has not been verified. Continuity sheets show that the final 145 feet of the film are in Technicolor, but that fact, also, has not been verified.

ADAM AND EVA **F2.0032**

Cosmopolitan Productions. *Dist* Paramount Pictures. 11 Feb **1923** [New York premiere; released 12 Mar; c31 Jan 1923; LP18656]. Si; b&w. 35mm. 8 reels, 7,153 ft.

Dir Robert Vignola. *Scen* Luther Reed. *Photog* Harold Wenstrom. *Adtl Photog* Tony Gaudio. *Set Dsgn* Joseph Urban.

Cast: Marion Davies *(Eva King)*, T. Roy Barnes *(Adam Smith)*, Tom Lewis *(James King)*, William Norris *(Uncle Horace)*, Percy Ames *(Lord Andrew Gordon)*, Leon Gordon *(Clinton Dewitt)*, Luella Gear *(Julie Dewitt)*, William Davidson *(Dr. Delamater)*, Edward Douglas *(Lord Andrew's secretary)*, Bradley Barker, John Powers *(Eva's admirers)*, Horace James *(gardener)*.

Society comedy. Source: Guy Bolton and George Middleton, *Adam and Eva*, in *Polly With a Past and Adam and Eva; Two Comedies* (New York, 1923). Unable to curb his daughter Eva's extravagance or to rid himself of Eva's parasitic suitors, wealthy James King throws up his hands in despair, turns his family and business over to employee Adam Smith, and goes to South America. Adam's solution is to announce that King is ruined, his fortune, lost. Eva rises to the occasion and inspires the family to move to a farm, work hard, and change its ways. King returns unexpectedly and is angry at Adam's deception, but he is pleased to find that Eva has learned her lesson while falling in love with Adam. *Fatherhood. Self-reliance. Finance—Personal. Family life. South America.*

ADAM AND EVIL **F2.0033**

Metro-Goldwyn-Mayer Pictures. 27 Aug **1927** [c17 Aug 1927; LP24293]. Si; b&w. 35mm. 7 reels, 6,793 ft.

Dir Robert Z. Leonard. *Orig Screenplay* F. Hugh Herbert, Florence Ryerson. *Titl* Ralph Spence. *Photog* André Barlatier. *Art Dir* Cedric Gibbons, Richard Day. *Film Ed* Leslie F. Wilder. *Wardrobe* René Hubert.

Cast: Lew Cody *(Adam Trevelyan/Allan Trevelyan)*, Aileen Pringle *(Evelyn Trevelyan)*, Gwen Lee *(Gwen de Vere)*, Gertrude Short *(Dora Dell)*, Hedda Hopper *(Eleanor Leighton)*, Roy D'Arcy *(Mortimer Jenkins)*.

Domestic farce. When Adam Trevelyan learns that his twin brother, Allan, is to arrive in town, Adam poses in his stead and finds relief from married life in flirtatious escapades with Gwen de Vere, a gold digger. When Adam's wife, Evelyn, learns of his unfaithfulness, Allan arrives, and a series of complications follow. Adam, by making unusually passionate advances to his wife, convinces her that he is actually his brother, and when he comes home intoxicated, she refuses to let him in. Evelyn leaves him, and a hotel clerk innocently puts her in the same suite with Allan, to whom she makes advances, thereby hoping to make her husband jealous. ... *Twins. Brothers. Gold diggers. Marriage. Infidelity. Hotels.*

ADAM'S RIB **F2.0034**

Famous Players–Lasky. *Dist* Paramount Pictures. 4 Feb **1923** [Los Angeles premiere; released 5 Mar; c7 Feb 1923; LP18658]. Si; b&w with col sequence. 35mm. 10 reels, 9,526 ft.

Pres by Jesse L. Lasky. *Dir* Cecil B. De Mille. *Story-Scen* Jeanie Macpherson. *Photog* Alvin Wyckoff, Guy Wilky.

Cast: Milton Sills *(Michael Ramsay)*, Elliott Dexter *(Prof. Nathan Reade)*, Theodore Kosloff *(Monsieur Jaromir, King of Morania)*, Anna Q. Nilsson *(Mrs. Michael Ramsay)*, Pauline Garon *(Mathilda Ramsay)*, Julia Faye *("The Mischevous One")*, Clarence Geldert *(James Kilkenna)*, George Field *(Minister to Morania)*, Robert Brower *(Hugo Kermaier)*, Forrest Robinson *(Kramar)*, Gino Corrado *(Lieutenant Braschek)*, Wedgewood Nowell *(secretary to minister)*, Clarence Burton *(cave man)*.

Society drama. Mrs. Michael Ramsay, neglected by her Chicago wheatbroker husband and her daughter, Mathilda, meets and falls in love with Monsieur Jaromir, the deposed King of Morania. Although Mathilda is in love with Professor Reade, she tries to save her mother by luring away the king and finds herself in compromising circumstances, while Michael Ramsay arranges to buy Morania's wheat if the king should return to the throne. Mrs. Ramsay realizes the impropriety of her conduct and returns to her husband; Reade perceives the truth and is gladly reunited with Mathilda; Jaromir returns to his throne; and failure of the American wheat crop brings a fortune to Ramsay. A similar story is worked out in prehistoric settings. *Brokers. Royalty. Filial relations. Imaginary kingdoms. Wheat. Prehistory. Chicago.*

ADIÓS *see* **THE LASH**

THE ADORABLE CHEAT **F2.0035**

Chesterfield Motion Picture Corp. 15 Aug **1928.** Si; b&w. 35mm. 6 reels, 5,084-5,400 ft.

Supv Lon Young. *Dir* Burton King. *Scen* Arthur Hoerl. *Titl* De Leon Anthony. *Photog* M. A. Anderson. *Film Ed* De Leon Anthony.

Cast: Lila Lee *(Marian Dorsey)*, Cornelius Keefe *(George Mason)*, Burr McIntosh *(Cyrus Dorsey)*, Reginald Sheffield *(Will Dorsey)*, Gladden James *(Howard Carver)*, Harry Allen *("Dad" Mason)*, Alice Knowland *(Mrs. Mason)*, Virginia Lee *(Roberta Arnold)*, Rolfe Sedan *(card-playing guest)*.

Comedy-drama. "Daughter [Marian Dorsey] of wealthy manufacturer falls in love with his shipping clerk [George Mason] and unknown to her father gets a job as shipping clerk's assistant under an assumed name. The romance ripens and he is invited for a week-end party to her home, where her weakling brother through heavy gambling losses, rifles the father's safe and suspicion is turned on the shipping clerk. He proves his innocence, wins the place of the wealthy man's general manager and also the girl." (*Motion Picture News*, 21 Apr 1928, p1273.) *Manufacturers. Shipping clerks. Theft. Brother-sister relationship. Gambling.*

THE ADORABLE DECEIVER **F2.0036**

R-C Pictures. *Dist* Film Booking Offices of America. 24 Oct **1926** [c28 Sep 1926; LP23148]. Si; b&w. 35mm. 5 reels, 4,879 ft.

Pres by Joseph P. Kennedy. *Dir* Phil Rosen. *Cont* Doris Anderson. *Photog* Roy Klaffki. *Asst Dir* James Dugan.

Cast: Alberta Vaughn *(Princess Sylvia)*, Dan Makarenko *(King Nicholas)*, Harlan Tucker *(Tom Pettibone)*, Frank Leigh *(Jim Doyle)*, Jane Thomas *(Flo Doyle)*, Cora Williams *(Mrs. Pettibone)*, Rosa Gore *(Mrs. Schrapp)*, Sheila Hayward *(Bellona)*.

Romantic Comedy. Source: Harry O. Hoyt, "Triple Trouble" (publication undetermined). King Nicholas of the Balkan state of Santa Maria flees to the United States with his daughter, Sylvia, to avoid revolutionary schemers. Although Sylvia pawns the crown jewels, the royal exiles are soon reduced to poverty; and their landlady, Mrs. Schrapp, gets the king a job. Revolutionaries frighten Sylvia, who flees and spends the night in an automobile showroom; the indignant manager sends her to sell a car to *nouveau riche* Tom Pettibone, who introduces her to society as an Albanian princess. At the country club she meets two crooks masquerading as the king and princess of Santa Maria. Sylvia pursues the phony princess when she steals some jewels, and after an attempted assassination by the revolutionaries, she retrieves the gems and wins Tom. *Royalty. Thieves. Landladies. Revolutions. Exile. Impersonation. Imaginary kingdoms. Automobile agencies. Balkans.*

ADORATION **F2.0037**

First National Pictures. 2 Dec **1928** [c19 Nov 1928; LP25848]. Mus score (Vitaphone); b&w. 35mm. 7 reels, 6,609 ft. [Also si; 6,360 ft.]

Pres by Richard A. Rowland. *Supv* Ned Marin. *Dir* Frank Lloyd. *Scen* Winifred Dunn. *Titl* Garrett Graham. *Story* Lajos Biró. *Photog* John Seitz. *Film Ed* John Rawlins, Frank Stone.

Cast: Billie Dove *(Elena)*, Antonio Moreno *(Serge)*, Emile Chautard *(Murajev)*, Lucy Dorraine *(Ninette)*, Nicholas Bela *(Ivan)*, Nicholas Soussanin *(Vladimir)*, Winifred Bryson *(baroness)*, Lucien Prival *(baron)*.

Drama. On the eve of the Russian Revolution, Prince Serge Orloff mistakenly comes to believe that his wife, Elena, is having an affair with Vladimir. Before Serge can confront Elena with his suspicions, however, fighting breaks out and they are forced to flee separately to Paris; Elena becomes a model, and when he is not too drunk, Serge works as a waiter. Elena finds Serge, but he refuses to believe that she was not Vladimir's mistress. In desperation, Elena goes to Vladimir and pleads with him to tell Serge the truth; he refuses, but Serge, who has followed Elena, overhears the conversation and at last is convinced of her innocence. *Aristocrats. Waiters. Models. Infidelity. Russia—History—1917–21 Revolution. Paris.*

ADVENTURE **F2.0038**

Famous Players–Lasky. *Dist* Paramount Pictures. 27 Apr **1925** [c28 Apr 1925; LP21412]. Si; b&w. 35mm. 7 reels, 6,602 ft.

Pres by Adolph Zukor, Jesse L. Lasky. *Dir* Victor Fleming. *Screenplay* A. P. Younger, L. G. Rigby. *Photog* C. Edgar Schoenbaum.

Cast: Tom Moore *(David Sheldon)*, Pauline Starke *(Joan Lackland)*, Wallace Beery *(Morgan)*, Raymond Hatton *(Raff)*, Walter McGrail *(Tudor)*, Duke Kahanamoku *(Noah Noa)*, James Spencer *(Adam)*, Noble Johnson *(Googomy)*.

Melodrama. Source: Jack London, *Adventure* (London, 1911). David

Sheldon, the owner of a plantation in the Solomon Islands, loses many of his field hands to blackwater fever, finally becoming ill himself. Joan Lackland, a distaff soldier of fortune, arrives by schooner in the islands and, with the help of her Kanaka crew, protects David from attack by natives under the leadership of Googomy. Joan nurses David back to health and goes into partnership with him, protecting his mortgaged property from two avaricious moneylenders. In order to revenge themselves, the moneylenders incite the natives to revolt. David's plantation is set afire, and Joan is kidnaped by the moneylenders and taken aboard their schooner. David saves Joan from the moneylenders, and she realizes that love is the greatest adventure of all. *Soldiers of fortune. Moneylenders. Planters. Revolts. Abduction. Plantations. Blackwater. Solomon Islands. Fires.*

THE ADVENTURER **F2.0039**

Metro-Goldwyn-Mayer Pictures. 14 Jul **1928** [c14 Jul 1928; LP25461]. Si; b&w. 35mm. 5 reels, 4,187 or 4,713 ft.

Dir Viachetslav Tourjansky. *Scen* Jack Cunningham. *Titl* Ruth Cummings. *Story* Leon Abrams. *Photog* Clyde De Vinna. *Set Dsgn* Alexander Toluboff. *Film Ed* Sam S. Zimbalist. *Wardrobe* Lucia Coulter.

Cast: Tim McCoy *(Jim McClellan)*, Dorothy Sebastian *(Dolores de Silva)*, Charles Delaney *(Barney O'Malley)*, George Cowl *(Estaban de Silva)*, Michael Visaroff *(Samaroff)*, Gayne Whitman *(The Tornado)*, Alex Melesh *(John Milton Gibbs)*, Katherine Block *(duenna)*.

Action melodrama. American mining engineer Jim McClellan is in love with Dolores de Silva, daughter of the deposed president of a Latin American country. He becomes involved in the revolution when he attempts to help the president regain power. After many dangerous adventures, including a narrow escape from a rebel firing squad, McClellan succeeds in restoring Silva to office and winning the girl. *Engineers—Mining. Presidents. Revolutions. Latin America.*

ADVENTURES IN PYGMY LAND *see* **BY AEROPLANE TO PYGMYLAND**

ADVENTURES IN THE FAR NORTH **F2.0040**

Capt. F. E. Kleinschmidt–Max Fleischer. *Dist* Lee-Bradford Corp. 1 Sep **1923**. Si; b&w. 35mm. 5 reels, 4,900 ft. [Later changed to 4 reels, 3,100 ft.]

Participants: Capt. F. E. Kleinschmidt, Mrs. F. E. Kleinschmidt.

Travel documentary. "A consistent digest of the travels of Captain and Mrs. Kleinschmidt through the inner passage to Alaska, which extended over a distance of 5,000 miles from Seattle and return. ... The trip was made on a former submarine chaser, which Capt. Kleinschmidt now calls the 'Silver Screen,' with him supervising the work of several camera men who made the picture. The trip began in May, 1922, and lasted seven months. ... Scenes in Glacier Bay show the breaking up of a 40-foot sea wall and the huge waves caused by the collapse, the capture of a school of whales and the disposition of their carcasses at the whaling station. ... A thrilling scene is where Capt. Kleinschmidt, his wife and a camera man are adrift on an ice floe and forced to seek refuge on the top of a giant iceberg." (*Variety*, 13 Sep 1923, p30.) *Ice floes. Alaska. Whales. Seals. Polar bears. Walruses.*

Note: First reviewed as *Captain Kleinschmidt's Adventures in the Far North*.

AN ADVENTURESS *see* **THE ISLE OF LOVE**

THE ADVENTUROUS SEX **F2.0041**

Howard Estabrook Productions. *Dist* Associated Exhibitors. 12 Jun **1925** [New York showing]. Si; b&w. 35mm. 6 reels.

Dir Charles Giblyn. *Scen* Carl Stearns Clancy. *Story* Hamilton Mannin. *Photog* George Peters. *Sets* Tec-Art Studios.

Cast: Clara Bow *(The Girl)*, Herbert Rawlinson *(Her Sweetheart)*, Earle Williams *(The Adventurer)*, Harry T. Morey *(Her Father)*, Mabel Beck *(Her Mother)*, Flora Finch *(The Grandmother)*, Joseph Burke.

Melodrama. When a man spends too much time tinkering with his airplane, his sweetheart gives him the air and begins to enjoy the wild life, taking up with a lecherous charmer. This adventurer forces his way into her hotel room and then calls to his buddies to come on in, badly compromising the girl's reputation. Highly distraught, she jumps into the river above Niagara Falls, over which she is about to be swept to her death when she is spotted by her former sweetheart. He swims out to her, and they climb to safety up a rope ladder hanging from an airplane. The boy and the girl are reconciled, and the charmer is socked in the face. *Flappers. Lechery. Reputation. Suicide. Airplanes. Niagara Falls.*

THE ADVENTUROUS SOUL **F2.0042**

Hi-Mark Productions. Nov **1927**. Si; b&w. 35mm. 6 reels, 5,420 ft.

Supv-Dir-Scen (see note) Harriet Virginia. *Dir (see note)* Gene Carroll. *Scen (see note)* William Holmes, Bennett Graham. *Story* John J. Moreno. *Photog (see note)* Jerry Fairbanks, Lew Lang.

Cast: Mildred Harris *(Miriam Martin)*, Jimmy Fulton *(Dick Barlow)*, Tom Santschi *(Captain Svenson)*, Arthur Rankin *(Glenn Martin)*, Charles K. French *(John Martin)*.

Drama. A desperate father arranges to have his worthless son, Glenn, shanghaied and treated roughly on one of his ships, skippered by the hard Captain Svenson. The son overhears the plan and escapes, and his sister Miriam's sweetheart, shipping clerk Dick Barlow, is taken instead. The clerk makes good under the brother's name, but a visit by Miriam clarifies who is who and who did what. *Ne'er-do-wells. Shipping clerks. Sea captains. Fatherhood. Manhood. Shanghaiing.*

Note: Sources disagree in crediting director, scenarist, and photographer.

AN AFFAIR OF THE FOLLIES **F2.0043**

Al Rockett Productions. *Dist* First National Pictures. 13 Feb **1927** [c27 Jan 1927; LP23598]. Si; b&w. 35mm. 7 reels, 6,433 ft.

Prod Al Rockett. *Dir* Millard Webb. *Scen* June Mathis. *Scen? (see note)* Carey Wilson. *Photog* Tony Gaudio. *Film Ed* Hugh Bennett.

Cast: Lewis Stone *(Hammersley)*, Billie Dove *(Tamara)*, Lloyd Hughes *(Jerry)*, Arthur Stone *(Sam the Waiter)*, Arthur Hoyt *(The Inventor)*, Bertram Marburgh *(Lew Kline [see note])*.

Romantic drama. Source: Dixie Willson, "Here Y'Are, Brother," in *Best Love Stories of 1924–25* (Muriel Miller Humphrey, ed.; Boston, 1925). An inventor, who has been desperately trying to see Hammersley, a millionaire, to sell him an invention, is about to despair over his failure to reach him. Jerry, a clerk, has lost his job; his wife, Tamara, has rejoined the Follies, causing them to separate though they still love each other; and Hammersley, chancing to meet Tamara, has become infatuated. Jubilant at her acceptance of a dinner invitation, Hammersley tells Jerry, who informs him of his own troubles; he advises Jerry to return to his wife and the inventor to go to the millionaire's home. Hammersley tries to win Tamara's love, but finding she is Jerry's wife, he brings them together and accepts the inventor's project. *Chorus girls. Inventors. Clerks. Millionaires. Follies. Florenz Ziegfeld.*

Note: Copyright records credit Carey Wilson with the scenario. The character name Lew Kline was originally Ziegfeld.

THE AFFAIRS OF ANATOL **F2.0044**

Famous Players–Lasky. *Dist* Paramount Pictures. 25 Sep **1921** [c11 Sep 1921; LP16961]. Si; b&w. 35mm. 9 reels, 8,806 ft.

Pres by Jesse L. Lasky. *Dir* Cecil B. De Mille. *Scen* Jeanie Macpherson. *Photog* Alvin Wyckoff, Karl Struss.

Cast: Wallace Reid *(Anatol De Witt Spencer)*, Gloria Swanson *(Vivian, his wife)*, Elliott Dexter *(Max Runyon)*, Bebe Daniels *(Satan Synne)*, Monte Blue *(Abner Elliot)*, Wanda Hawley *(Emilie Dixon)*, Theodore Roberts *(Gordon Bronson)*, Agnes Ayres *(Annie Elliot)*, Theodore Kosloff *(Nazzer Singh)*, Polly Moran *(orchestra leader)*, Raymond Hatton *(Hoffmeier)*, Julia Faye *(Tibra)*, Charles Ogle *(Dr. Bowles)*, Winter Hall *(Dr. Johnson)*.

Comedy-drama. Source: Arthur Schnitzler, *Anatol* (1893). Anatol and his wife, Vivian, come to the Green Fan Cafe, where Anatol recognizes Emilie, a former school companion, with Bronson, a wealthy rake, and persuades her to leave him. Emilie deceives him, however, by failing to throw her diamonds into the river, and out of anger Anatol wrecks her apartment. On the way to the country, Anatol saves Annie Elliot from drowning herself after she is repudiated by her husband for stealing church funds; Annie then steals Anatol's purse and kisses him as Vivian returns with a doctor. At a society gathering, Vivian is hypnotized by a magician, and Anatol, in disgust, seeks out Satan Synne, supposedly New York's wickedest woman. He discovers, however, that Satan is actually the loving wife of a disabled soldier in need of an operation. She obtains the money from Anatol after he learns the truth; disgusted, he returns home to make peace with Vivian. *Philanderers. Marriage. Suicide. Theft. Hypnotism.*

Note: Working titles: *Anatol; Five Kisses.*

AFFINITIES **F2.0045**

Ward Lascelle Productions. *Dist* W. W. Hodkinson Corp. 24 Sep or 15 Oct **1922**. Si; b&w. 35mm. 6 reels, 5,484 ft.

Pres by Ward Lascelle. *Dir* Ward Lascelle. *Scen* H. Landers Jackson. *Photog? (see note)* Joe Scholz, Abe Scholtz.

Cast: John Bowers *(Day Illington)*, Colleen Moore *(Fanny Illington)*, Joe Bonner *(Ferd Jackson)*, Grace Gordon *(Ida Jackson)*, Pietro Sosso *(Professor Savage)*.

Comedy-drama. Source: Mary Roberts Rinehart, "Affinities," in *Affinities, and Other Stories* (New York, 1920). Day and Fanny Illington and Ferd and Ida Jackson spend their considerable amount of leisure time at their country club. An avid golfer, Day leaves Fanny alone for long periods, and she soon falls prey to Ferd's self-appointed companionship. At Ferd's suggestion, there is an "affinity" party for all the men and women who are neglected by their spouses. Ferd and Fanny are accidentally left on an island, but they struggle back to the mainland, where Fanny learns that Day has been having an affinity party of his own with Ida. Fanny and Day realize their error, apologize, and resolve to have no future affinities. *Marriage. Golf. Country clubs.*

Note: Some reviews credit photography to Abe Schultz, which is also spelled Scholtz.

AFLAME IN THE SKY **F2.0046**

R-C Pictures. *Dist* Film Booking Offices of America. 28 Nov **1927** [c28 Nov 1927; LP24689]. Si; b&w. 35mm. 6 reels, 6,034 ft.

Pres by Joseph P. Kennedy. *Dir* J. P. McGowan. *Cont* Ewart Adamson. *Story* Mary Roberts Rinehart. *Camera* Joe Walker. *Asst Dir* James Dugan.

Cast: Sharon Lynn *(Inez Carillo)*, Jack Luden *(Terry Owen)*, William Humphreys *(Major Savage)*, Robert McKim *(Joseph Murdoch)*, Billy Scott *(Saunders)*, Charles A. Stevenson *(grandfather)*, Bill Franey *(Cookie)*, Mark Hamilton *(Slim)*, Walter Ackerman *(Desert Rat)*, Jane Keckley *(Cordelia Murdoch)*, Ranger *(himself, a dog)*.

Action melodrama. Aviators Terry Owen and Major Savage meet in the New Mexico desert to experiment with gas for night skywriting, and there they rescue Inez Carillo, who is being pursued by horsemen. She tells them of her grandfather, who is chronically ill, and of Murdoch, a renegade foreman who wants to marry her to gain control of their hacienda and is actually poisoning her grandfather. Upon returning home, she agrees to marry Murdoch to prolong her grandfather's life. When she overhears a plan to poison Terry's water, she sends him a warning. Terry signals Savage, who gets aid from border police. Murdoch's men are captured; Murdock escapes into the desert but dies of thirst. Free again to wed, Inez accepts Terry. ... *Aviators. Grandfathers. Ranch foremen. Border police. Deserts. Skywriting. Thirst. New Mexico. Dogs.*

AFRAID TO FIGHT **F2.0047**

Universal Film Manufacturing Co. 24 Jul **1922** [c5 Jul 1922; LP18030]. Si; b&w. 35mm. 5 reels, 4,600 ft.

Dir William Worthington. *Scen* Charles Sarver. *Story* Leete Renick Brown. *Photog* Arthur Reeves.

Cast: Frank Mayo *(Tom Harper)*, Lillian Rich *(Harriet Monroe)*, Peggy Cartwright *(Sally Harper)*, Lydia Knott *(Mrs. Harper)*, W. S. McDunnough *(Dr. Butler)*, Tom McGuire *("Big Jim" Brandon)*, Harry Mann *(Leonard)*, Wade Boteler *(Phillip Brand)*, Al Kaufman *("Slick" Morrisey)*, Roscoe Karns *(Bertie)*, Guy Tiney *(fat boy)*, Charles Haefeli *(Johnny Regan)*, Tom Kennedy *(Battling Grogan)*, James Quinn *(Slim Dawson)*.

Melodrama. Tom Harper, a former A. E. F. boxing champion who suffered gas poisoning, is sent to the mountains to regain his health so that he can reenter the ring and earn the money needed for his crippled sister's operation. Under strict orders not to exert himself, Tom allows himself to be beaten up by Phillip Brand, the town bully, in front of his girl, Harriet Monroe. Winning the championship from Slick Morrisey, he returns to take care of the bully and reclaim the girl. *Veterans. Bullies. Brother-sister relationship. Boxing.*

AFRAID TO LOVE **F2.0048**

Paramount Famous Lasky Corp. 9 Apr **1927** [c2 Apr 1927; LP23860]. Si; b&w. 35mm. 7 reels, 6,199 ft.

Pres by Adolph Zukor, Jesse L. Lasky. *Assoc Prod* B. P. Schulberg. *Dir* E. H. Griffith. *Screenplay* Doris Anderson, Joseph Jackson. *Titl* Alfred Hustwick. *Adapt* Doris Anderson. *Photog* J. O. Taylor.

Cast: Florence Vidor *(Katherine Silverton)*, Clive Brook *(Sir Reginald Belsize)*, Norman Trevor *(John Travers)*, Jocelyn Lee *(Helen de Semiano)*, Arthur Lubin *(Rafael)*.

Farce. Source: Mme. Fred De Gresac and F. De Croisset, *La Passerelle* (Adapted as *The Marriage of Kitty* by C. Gordon Lennox; New York, 1909). Sir Reginald Belsize's eccentric uncle dies leaving him his fortune on the condition that he give up Helen, with whom he is infatuated, and marry another girl within 24 hours. His lawyer, John Travers, who is also counselor for Katherine Silverton, at the moment in financial straits, proposes to marry Katherine to the Belsize fortune; Helen agrees to this arrangement provided that the girl, whom she has not seen, is less attractive than herself. Katherine, therefore, adopts a plain appearance, but on the train to Paris, Belsize discovers that she is a beautiful and cultured young lady. A wire from Travers informs him that a detective with a black moustache is following him, forcing him to make open demonstrations of affection to his bride; to complicate matters, Katherine hires eight men with black moustaches to follow them. The intrigue of Helen and Rafael, her former lover, is exposed after amusing complications, and Belsize and Katherine realize their mutual love. *Lawyers. Inheritance. Marriage. Trains. London. Paris.*

AFRICA SPEAKS **F2.0049**

Colorado African Expedition, Inc. *Dist* Columbia Pictures. 15 Sep **1930** [c17 Oct 1930; LP1651]. Narration, mus score, & sd eff (Movietone); b&w. 35mm. 8 reels, 7,054 ft.

Prod Paul L. Hoefler. *Dial* Walter Futter. *Film Ed* Walter Futter. *Rec Engr* Bruce Piersall.

Exploration documentary. "From the Atlantic Ocean to the Indian Ocean the path of the story stretches—across the black throbbing heart of the untouched Congo. Weird customs, wild dances—age-old rituals of worship to the gods of fertility, of love—flame in the background, accenting the panorama of cruelty, sensuality, and amazing feats of heroism." (Studio pressbook.) The expedition, under explorer Paul L. Hoefler, centers around the region of Kiya Be. The customs and rites of the Wasara people are explained, particularly that of the women who insert large wooden discs in their lower lips, distorting themselves in order to avoid being enslaved by marauding Bedouin chiefs. With respect to the pygmies, it is noted that trial marriage has been perfected "to a state that would shock the sensitive and fascinate the modern mind." Natives are shown struggling with lions; women dance to a jazz phonograph record; and a swarm of locusts covers and devours the African jungle. *Pygmies. Wasara. Bedouins. Exploration. Jungles. Phonographs. Congo. Africa. Locusts. Lions.*

AFTER A MILLION **F2.0050**

Sunset Productions. 15 Apr **1924** [scheduled release]. Si; b&w. 35mm. 5 reels, ca4,900 ft.

Dir Jack Nelson.

Cast: Kenneth McDonald *(Gregory Maxim)*, Ruth Dwyer *(Countess Olga)*, Alphonse Martell *(Ivan Senine)*, Joe Girard, Hal Craig, Jay Hunt, Stanley Bingham, Ada Bell.

Comedy-drama. "Beautiful young Russian Countess is told she must marry an American within given time to secure large fortune. Coincidentally a young American must reach a certain bank within given time also to secure a fortune. The latter overcomes attempts to thwart him by jumping from a railway trestle, climbing a skyscraper and similar stunts. He reaches his destination and saves both fortunes by marrying the Countess." (*Motion Pictures News Booking Guide*, [7]:7, Oct 1924.) *Russians. Nobility. Fortune hunters. Stunts.*

AFTER BUSINESS HOURS **F2.0051**

Columbia Pictures. 15 Jun **1925** [New York premiere; c22 Apr 1925; LP21394]. Si; b&w. 35mm. 6 reels, 5,600 ft.

Dir Mal St. Clair. *Scen* Douglas Doty. *Titl* Walter Anthony. *Photog* Dewey Wrigley. *Film Ed* Errol Taggart.

Cast: Elaine Hammerstein *(June King)*, Lou Tellegen *(John King)*, Phyllis Haver *(Sylvia Vane)*, John Patrick *(Richard Downing)*, Lillian Langdon *(Mrs. Wentworth)*, William Scott *(James Hendricks)*, Lee Moran *(Jerry Stanton)*.

Society melodrama. Source: Ethel Watts Mumford, "Everything Money Can Buy," in *Hearst's International* (46:22–27, Aug 1924). John King, a wealthy young man, marries June with the expressed determination that he will give her everything that money can buy. John does not, however, allow her to have any money of her own, trusting to his own generosity to supply her every want and need. June later gets into a "friendly" bridge game and loses heavily, desperately pawning a pin to pay off her debt. To obtain money to get her pin out of hock, June gambles at a party given by Richard Downing and again loses heavily, using her pearls as security. Her chauffeur, Hendricks, then blackmails her, and she is forced to steal a pin belonging to Mrs. Wentworth in order to pay him off. Downing learns of the theft and also blackmails June, forcing her to come to his apartment as the price for not informing the police of her activities. John learns of the situation and goes to Downing's apartment, giving him a severe thrashing and getting back June's pearls. June tells John everything; he realizes the error of his ways and promises that in the future she will have enough money of her own to meet her wants. *Chauffeurs. Theft. Blackmail. Gambling. Finance—Personal. Bridge.*

AFTER DARK **F2.0052**

Jack Noble. *Dist* Lee-Bradford Corp. 21 May **1923** [New York State license application]. Si; b&w. 35mm. 5 reels.

Melodrama. "This is the story of a law abiding, prosperous citizen of a community, [who] for no reason that the story shows is persecuted by an organization of men wearing hoods and masks, [who] order him to leave his home and family and get out of town—nothing in the plot indicates any reason justified or otherwise for this demand, [other] than that he is of another faith. He refuses and is abducted and is viciously and brutally mistreated by this hooded mob. While lashed to a post and tormented by men in hoods and masks he tears the mask from the man nearest him and finds that it is one, Burton, also a prominent member of the same community. Because he has discovered the identity of the wearer of the mask he is condemned to die and is shot and left wounded, tied to a post. All characters of the story are members of three distinct and different faiths." (New York State license records.) A member of the mob goes on trial for attempted murder. The picture's end reveals all of the foregoing to have been a dream. *Religious persecution. Secret societies. Dreams.*

Note: Release title may have been *The Hooded Mob, Men in Masks,* or *Law and Order.*

AFTER DARK **F2.0053**

William Steiner Productions. *Dist* Hurricane Film Corp. 15 Dec **1924** [c1 Nov 1924; LU20726]. Si; b&w. 35mm. 5 reels.

Dir James Chapin. *Story-Screenplay* J. F. Natteford.

Cast: Charles Hutchison *(Billy Fisk)*, Mary Beth Milford *(Little Eva?)*.

Comedy-drama. "Little Eva" Nelson is abandoned atop a ladder by two fellow burglars when they hear Billy Fisk approach. Billy rescues her from a window ledge, believes her story about incriminating letters she is trying to recover, and enters the apartment to look for the letters. He is caught by another girl, who summons the police, and he learns that the "letters" are valuable bonds. To save this girl's reputation, when the policeman arrives, Billy accounts for his presence at that late hour by claiming that he and she are secretly married. The arrival of the girl's aunt and uncle further complicates matters. Billy finally escapes from the apartment as the burglars are making another attempt to seize the bonds, and he spots them making a getaway. A wild chase to the waterfront and an exciting fight occur before the culprits are brought to justice and Billy wins the girl. (The actors playing Dapper Dan Clark, The Girl, The Uncle, The Aunt, a butler, and various crooks and policemen have not been identified.) *Uncles. Aunts. Burglars. Reputation. Chases.*

AFTER MARRIAGE **F2.0054**

Sun Motion Pictures. *For* Mayer & Quinn. *Dist* Madoc Sales. Sep **1925** [c28 Dec 1923; LP19781]. Si; b&w. 35mm. 5 reels, 4,960 ft.

Pres by J. G. Mayer. *Dir-Writ* Norman Dawn.

Cast: Margaret Livingston *(Alma Lathrop)*, George Fisher *(David Morgan)*, Helen Lynch *(Lucille Spencer)*, Herschel Mayall *(James Morgan)*, Annette Perry *(Mrs. George Spencer)*, Mary Young *(Mrs. James Morgan)*, Arthur Jasmine *(Bob Munro)*.

Domestic melodrama. David Morgan marries Lucille Spencer, a poor girl, and is disinherited by his wealthy father, James Morgan, who is carrying on an affair with actress Alma Lathrop. David becomes tired of domestic life and succumbs to Alma's fascinations. Ignorant of her relationship to his father, David meets him aboard the yacht that he (James) gave Alma. A quarrel ensues, and David leaves. James Morgan is killed, and David is suspected; but it develops that Alma is guilty. David and Lucille are reconciled. *Actors. Filial relations Social classes. Wealth. Murder. Disinheritance.*

Note: Apparently intended for release by Mayer & Quinn in 1923. The presenter credit for J. G. Mayer may not have been used in the film as finally released by Madoc Sales Co.

AFTER MIDNIGHT **F2.0055**

Selznick Pictures. *Dist* Select Pictures. 10 Sep **1921** [c9 Sep 1921; LP16978]. Si; b&w. 35mm. 5 reels.

Pres by Lewis J. Selznick. *Dir* Ralph Ince. *Scen* Edward J. Montagne. *Story* John Lynch. *Photog* Jacob A. Badaracco.

Cast: Conway Tearle *(Gordon Phillips/Wallace Phillips)*, Zena Keefe *(Mrs. Gordon Phillips)*, Warren Black *(Mock Sing)*.

Melodrama. "Stranger in an opium joint is asked to impersonate a dying man, whom he recognizes as his twin brother and consents. Taken to his brother's home, he meets and falls in love with the latter's wife. Blackmailer endeavors to get bonds but the stranger thwarts him. In revenge, the wife is kidnapped. The stranger rescues her and the husband is killed by the blackmailer, thus leaving them free to marry and find happiness together." (*Motion Pictures News Booking Guide,* 2:11, Apr 1922.) *Twins. Brothers. Chinese. Impersonation. Opium. Blackmail.*

AFTER MIDNIGHT **F2.0056**

Metro-Goldwyn-Mayer Pictures. 20 Aug **1927** [c17 Aug 1927; LP24413]. Si; b&w. 35mm. 7 reels, 6,312 ft.

Dir-Story Monta Bell. *Scen* Lorna Moon. *Titl* Joe Farnham. *Photog* Percy Hilburn. *Sets* Cedric Gibbons, Richard Day. *Film Ed* Blanche Sewell. *Wardrobe* René Hubert.

Cast: Norma Shearer *(Mary)*, Lawrence Gray *(Joe Miller)*, Gwen Lee *(Maizie)*, Eddie Sturgis *(Red Smith)*, Philip Sleeman *(Gus Van Gundy)*.

Society drama. Joe Miller, a robber, holds up Mary, a nightclub hostess. After knocking him unconscious, she sympathetically cares for him, and under her guidance he decides to reform and marry her. Mary skimps and saves to buy a $1,000 Liberty Bond while Joe saves to invest in a taxicab; then Maizie, Mary's gold-digging, irresponsible sister, returns home with a similar bond given as a favor at a wild party. Depressed at the futility of her efforts, Mary cashes her bond and buys a fancy wardrobe, then accepts an invitation to a party, where she becomes intoxicated after having seen Joe drinking with his former cronies. While returning from the party with her sister, Mary causes an accident, and Maizie is killed. Realizing their error, Mary and Joe plan to start anew. *Robbers. Taxi drivers. Criminals—Rehabilitation. Sisters. Nightclub hostesses. Jazz life. Liberty bonds.*

AFTER THE BALL **F2.0057**

Renco Film Co. *Dist* Film Booking Offices of America. 27 Jan **1924** [c29 Dec 1923; LP19780]. Si; b&w. 35mm. 7 reels, 6,500 ft.

Dir Dallas M. Fitzgerald. *Scen* James Colwell. *Story* Charles K. Harris. *Photog* Ross Fisher.

Cast: Gaston Glass *(Arthur Trevelyan)*, Miriam Cooper *(Lorraine Trevelyan, his sister)*, Thomas Guise *(Mark Trevelyan, his father)*, Robert Frazer *(The District Attorney, Lorraine's fiancé)*, Edna Murphy *(Arthur's wife)*, Eddie Gribbon *(a crook)*.

Melodrama. Source: Charles K. Harris, "After the Ball" (waltz song; Milwaukee, 1892). A fun-loving husband is mistaken for a bandit and sent to prison. He allows everyone, including his wife, to think he has died. Years later, he escapes prison and is reunited with his wife and child after the real criminal admits to the crime for which he was convicted. *Bandits. Prison escapees. Mistaken identity. Injustice.*

AFTER THE FOG **F2.0058**

Beacon Productions. 15 Dec **1929.** Sd (Photophone); b&w. 35mm. 5 reels, 4,915-5,200 ft. [Also si.]

Prod Robert S. Furst. *Dir* Leander De Cordova. *Scen* George Terwilliger. *Story-Dial* Arthur F. Statter, George Terwilliger. *Photog* Charles Boyle. *Monitor Man* Ernest Rovere.

Cast: Mary Philbin *(Faith Barker)*, Russell Simpson *(Joshua Barker)*, Edmund Burns *(John Temple)*, Carmelita Geraghty *(Winifred Blake)*, Margaret Seddon *(Letitia Barker)*, Allan Simpson *(Phil Langhorne)*, Joseph Bennett *(Bill Reynolds)*.

Melodrama. Hoping to continue his family tradition of caring for the Sentinel Light, Joshua Barker suggests that his daughter, Faith, marry Bill Reynolds, a local fisherman. Faith, on the other hand, hates the lighthouse and longs for pretty things and bright lights. Soon after she rebuffs Bill's shy proposal, John Temple's yacht stops at the lighthouse, and there is an instant and obvious attraction between John and Faith, to the annoyance of both her father and Winifred Blake. Over Joshua's violent objections

Faith soon marries John, and family strife and news of John's slipping into his old ways cause Faith's mother, Letitia, to grieve, languish, and die. Losing his last grip on reason, Joshua attacks Faith with an ax; she shoots him, and with this shock come remorse and a happy reconciliation among father, daughter, and son-in-law. *Yachtsmen. Fishermen. Family life. Parenthood. Filial relations. Lighthouses.*

AFTER THE SHOW **F2.0059**

Famous Players–Lasky. *Dist* Paramount Pictures. ca9 Oct **1921** [Seattle premiere; released 30 Oct; c30 Oct 1921; LP17172]. Si; b&w. 35mm. 6 reels, 5,884 ft. [Copyrighted as 7 reels.]

Pres by Jesse L. Lasky. *Dir* William De Mille. *Scen* Hazel Christie MacDonald, Vianna Knowlton. *Photog* Guy Wilky.

Cast: Jack Holt *(Larry Taylor)*, Lila Lee *(Eileen)*, Charles Ogle *(Pop O'Malley)*, Eve Southern *(Naomi Stokes)*, Shannon Day *(Lucy)*, Carlton King *(Mr. McGuire)*, Stella Seager *(Vera)*, Ethel Wales *(landlady)*.

Melodrama. Source: Rita Weiman, "The Stage Door," in *More Aces* (New York, 1925). Pop O'Malley, a former actor now stage doorkeeper, takes a paternal interest in Eileen, a struggling young chorus girl, and takes her into his home. Larry Taylor, millionaire backer of the show, is attracted to Eileen, and against Pop's warnings and objections she falls in love with him. Pop overhears her accepting an invitation from Larry to a party at his summer home and follows her there. When she refuses his entreaties to leave with him, Pop slashes his wrist with a broken bottle, and to save his life Larry offers a transfusion of his own blood. Pop, recovering, is furious, but he relents when he learns that Larry plans to marry Eileen. *Stage doormen. Theatrical backers. Millionaires. Chorus girls. Theater.*

AFTER THE STORM **F2.0060**

Columbia Pictures. 19 Apr **1928** [c19 May 1928; LP25271]. Si; b&w. 35mm. 6 reels, 5,459 ft.

Prod Harry Cohn. *Dir* George B. Seitz. *Adapt-Cont* Will M. Ritchey. *Story* Harold Shumate. *Photog* Joe Walker. *Art Dir* Robert E. Lee. *Film Ed* Arthur Roberts. *Asst Dir* Joe Nadel.

Cast: Hobart Bosworth *(Martin Dane)*, Eugenia Gilbert *(Joan Wells/Mary Brian)*, Charles Delaney *(Joe Dane)*, Maude George *(Molly O'Doon)*, George Kuwa *(A. Hop)*, Linda Loredo *(Malay dancer)*.

Melodrama. Believing his wife, Molly, to be unfaithful, a ship's captain takes his young son, Joe, and quits San Francisco. Twenty years later they return. Molly, whom Captain Dane has taught his son to hate, stows away to be with her son. Also on board is Joan Wells, daughter of a woman Dane once loved. During the trip, Mrs. Dane wins her son's love and her husband's forgiveness. Joan and Joe marry; and Captain Dane, repenting his harsh desertion, sacrifices his life during a storm to save the young couple. *Sea captains. Filial relations. Infidelity. Seafaring life. San Francisco.*

AFTER YOUR OWN HEART **F2.0061**

Fox Film Corp. 7 Aug **1921** [c7 Aug 1921; LP16853]. Si; b&w. 35mm. 5 reels, 4,244 ft.

Pres by William Fox. *Dir* George E. Marshall. *Scen* John Montague. *Adapt* Tom Mix. *Photog* Ben Kline.

Cast: Tom Mix *(Herbert Parker)*, Ora Carew *(Loretta Bramley)*, George Hernandez *(Luke Bramley)*, William Buckley *(Peter Ruddock)*, Sid Jordan *(Tex Marole)*, E. C. Robinson *(aviator)*, Bill Ward *(Fighting Kid)*.

Western melodrama. Source: William Wallace Cook, "After His Own Heart," in *Top-Notch Magazine* (43:1–52, 1 Oct 1920). Herbert Parker, college athlete and rancher, arrives from the East to take over his Arizona ranch and discovers that Luke Bramley, owner of an adjoining ranch, is contesting the rights to a valuable watering spot. Smitten with Loretta Bramley, Parker accepts a job on Bramley's ranch and makes an enemy of Tex Marole, the Bramley foreman, who plans to kidnap the girl with aid of desperadoes. A battle ensues between Parker's men and the gang, the former employing automobiles to attack the villains. When Tex is about to gain his ends, Parker, with the aid of a lasso and car, and Bramley, dropping dynamite from an airplane, manage to rout the outlaws. Parker invites Bramley to live with him and weds Bramley's daughter. *Ranchers. Ranch foremen. Water rights. Airplanes. Arizona. Air stunts.*

AGAINST ALL ODDS **F2.0062**

Fox Film Corp. 27 Jul **1924** [c27 Jul 1924; LP20468]. Si; b&w. 35mm. 5 reels, 4,809 ft.

Pres by William Fox. *Dir* Edmund Mortimer. *Scen* Frederic Chapin. *Photog* Joseph Brotherton.

Cast: Charles "Buck" Jones *(Chick Newton)*, Dolores Rousse *(Judy Malone)*, Ben Hendricks, Jr. *(Jim Sawyer)*, William Scott *(Bill Warner)*, Thais Valdemar *(Olivetta)*, William N. Bailey *(Tom Curtis)*, Bernard Siegel *(Lewis)*, Jack McDonald *(Warner's uncle)*.

Western melodrama. Source: Max Brand, "Cuttle's Hired Man," in *Western Story Magazine* (41:1–38, Mar 1924). Chick Newton's friend, Bill Warner, is arrested for murdering his uncle. However, Bill has been framed by a blackmailer who has plotted with the uncle to have him disappear in order to avoid creditors and collect insurance. Newton unmasks Tom Curtis as the culprit and rescues Warner from a lynching. *Uncles. Blackmail. Murder. Fraud. Lynching.*

THE AGE OF DESIRE **F2.0063**

Arthur H. Jacobs Corp. *Dist* Associated First National Pictures. Sep **1923** [premiere; general release Dec; c20 Sep 1923; LP19416]. Si; b&w. 35mm. 6 reels, 5,174 ft.

Pres by Arthur H. Jacobs. *Dir* Frank Borzage. *Scen* Mary O'Hara. *Titl* Lenore J. Coffee. *Adapt* Dixie Willson. *Photog* Chester Lyons. *Art Sets* Frank Ormston.

Cast: Joseph Swickard *(Marcio)*, William Collier, Jr. *(Ranny at 21)*, Frank Truesdell *(Malcolm Trask, millionaire husband)*, Bruce Guerin *(Ranny at 3)*, Frankie Lee *(Ranny at 13)*, J. Farrell MacDonald *(Dan Reagan)*, Mary Jane Irving *(Margy at 10)*, Myrtle Stedman *(Janet Loring)*, Aggie Herring *(Ann Reagan)*, Mary Philbin *(Margy at 18)*, Edithe Yorke *(Gran'ma)*.

Melodrama. Young widow Janet Loring marries millionaire Malcolm Trask, keeping her former marriage secret and deserting her son Ranny. Ranny becomes a street urchin, eventually joining the household of a bookseller and her granddaughter, Margy. Janet regrets her desertion of the boy and advertises for his return. Marcio, a notorious blackmailer, sends Ranny to pose as her son, unaware that he really is the one. Ranny takes money from his mother to buy a cottage for his fiancée, Margy, but becomes conscience-stricken and admits that he is an impostor. When Janet convinces him that he actually is her son, Trask welcomes the boy as his own, and Ranny marries his sweetheart. *Millionaires. Street urchins. Widows. Waifs. Motherhood. Imposture.*

THE AGE OF INNOCENCE **F2.0064**

Warner Brothers Pictures. 1 Nov **1924** [c3 Nov 1924; LP20739]. Si; b&w. 35mm. 7 reels, 6,700 ft.

Dir Wesley Ruggles. *Cont* Olga Printzlau.

Cast: Edith Roberts, Elliott Dexter, Willard Louis, Fred Huntley, Gertrude Norman, Sigrid Holmquist, Beverly Bayne, Stuart Holmes.

Society drama. Source: Edith Wharton, *The Age of Innocence* (New York, 1920). Countess Ellen Olenska leaves her brutish husband in Poland and returns to her socially prominent New York family, which is concerned lest there be scandal. Thus, there is a reception for Ellen, at which is announced the engagement of Ellen's cousin, May Mingott, and Newland Archer. Several men, including Newland, are attracted to Ellen, and the countess later finds it easy to lead a gay life with bohemian friends. A passionate love springs up between Ellen and Newland, despite the resistance of both to it. Newland marries May and hopes to forget Ellen, but in a subsequent meeting they decide to go away together. Visiting Ellen, May shares a confidence that causes the countess to decide to return to her husband. Ellen bids farewell to Newland with the suggestion that he can learn the reason from his wife. Receiving the news that May expects a child, Newland repents and resolves to be worthy of his wife. *Nobility. Cousins. Bohemianism. Scandal. Infidelity. Poland. New York City.*

AHEAD OF THE LAW **F2.0065**

B. A. Goodman Productions. *Dist* A. G. Steen. 28 Oct **1926** [New York State license]. Si; b&w. 35mm. 5 reels.

Dir Forrest Sheldon.

Cast: Bruce Gordon, Doris Prince.

Western melodrama. "... of Texas Ranger assigned to clean up town, who uncovers intrigues of rustler posing as business man, and saves girl's ranch coveted by rustlers. His heroism and valor in behalf of girl wins her love." ("Motion Picture News Booking Guide," in *Motion Picture News*, 8 May 1926, p21.) *Texas Rangers. Rustlers. Imposture. Ranches.*

AIN'T LOVE FUNNY? **F2.0066**

R-C Pictures. *Dist* Film Booking Offices of America. 10 Apr **1927** [c19 Dec 1926; LP23826]. Si; b&w. 35mm. 5 reels, 4,745 ft.

Pres by Joseph P. Kennedy. *Dir* Del Andrews. *Adapt-Cont* Doris

Anderson. *Story* Kay Clement, Lela Gidley. *Photog* Allen Siegler. *Gag Man* Jack Collins.

Cast: Alberta Vaughn *(Helena Brice)*, Thomas Wells *(Bob Kenwood)*, Syd Crossley *(Spike Murphy)*, Babe London *(Daisy Dooley)*, Johnny Gough *(Saunders)*, Charles Hill Mailes *(John Brice)*.

Comedy. Helena, daughter of John Brice, an airplane manufacturer, breaks off her engagement to Bob Kenwood when he refuses to enlist in the war. Brice soon finds his mansion converted into a recreation center for doughboys and is forced to move to a hotel until the troops leave. Each soldier considers Helena his sweetheart, since she gives them all autographed photos, and she is later forced to send a blanket refusal to their respective proposals of marriage; Bob enlists, but Helena returns his ring when he is detailed to factory duty. To evade her suitors Helena claims to be engaged to Murphy, her maid's beau whom she believes to be dead, but he appears and claims her. Bob pursues them in his roadster, followed by Brice and Daisy, the maid. In a final free-for-all Daisy subdues Murphy and Bob wins Helena. *Soldiers. Housemaids. Courtship. Airplane manufacture. World War I.*

THE AIR CIRCUS **F2.0067**

Fox Film Corp. 30 Sep **1928** [c1 Sep 1928; LP25586]. Talking sequences, sd eff, & mus score (Movietone); b&w. 35mm. 8 reels, 7,702 ft.

Pres by William Fox. *Dir* Howard Hawks, Lewis Seiler. *Dial Dir* Charles Judels. *Scen* Norman Z. McLeod, Seton I. Miller. *Dial* Hugh Herbert. *Titl* William Kernell. *Story* Graham Baker, Andrew Bennison. *Photog* Dan Clark. *Film Ed* Ralph Dixon. *Asst Dir* William Tummel.

Cast: Louise Dresser *(Mrs. Blake)*, David Rollins *(Buddy Blake)*, Arthur Lake *(Speed Doolittle)*, Sue Carol *(Sue Manning)*, Charles Delaney *(Charles Manning)*, Heinie Conklin *(Jerry McSwiggin)*, Earl Robinson *(Lieutenant Blake)*.

Drama. Buddy Blake and Speed Doolittle set out for the Pacific School of Aviation with all the confidence of youth, meeting on the way Sue Manning, a pretty aviatrix. Once at the school, the boys lose their conceit and set about learning to fly. On his first solo flight, however, Buddy has a sudden attack of fear and almost kills himself and his instructor. Buddy despairs of becoming an aviator, and his mother comes to comfort him. Sue and Speed take off in a plane with defective landing gear, and Buddy, overcoming his fear, pilots another plane and prevents Speed from landing until he and Sue have fixed the defective part. *Aviators. Aviation. Motherhood. Acrophobia.*

THE AIR HAWK **F2.0068**

Van Pelt–Wilson Productions. *Dist* Film Booking Offices of America. 21 Dec **1924** [c18 Nov 1924; LP20786]. Si; b&w. 35mm. 5 reels, 4,860 ft.

Ernest Van Pelt Production. *Dir* Bruce Mitchell. *Story* George W. Pyper. *Photog* Bert Longenecker. *Film Ed* Della M. King.

Cast: Al Wilson *(Al Parker/The Air Hawk)*, Webster Cullison *(Major Thomas)*, Frank Tomick *(Major Falles)*, Emmett King *(John Ames)*, Virginia Brown Faire *(Edith, his daughter)*, Lee Shumway *(Robert McLeod)*, Frank Rice *(Higgins, Hank)*, Leonard Clapham *(Kellar)*.

Western melodrama. On the Mexican-American border, Al Parker, an aviator and Secret Service agent, is assigned to investigate a gang of bandits who have been robbing a platinum mine. When John Ames, the superintendent of the mine, discovers a secret passage used by the bandits, he is killed; and his daughter, Edith, with whom Al has fallen in love, assumes the running of the mine. Edith is kidnaped by McLeod, the leader of the gang, who makes his escape in a waiting airplane. Al, "The Air Hawk," gives chase, leaping between the planes in flight and beating McLeod in a desperate struggle. Al and Edith are happily reunited. *Aviators. Secret service. Mining. Kidnaping. Platinum. Mexican border. Air stunts.*

THE AIR LEGION **F2.0069**

FBO Pictures. *Dist* RKO Productions. 6 Jan **1929** [c6 Jan 1929; LP25973]. Si; b&w. 35mm. 7 reels, 6,361 ft.

Dir Bert Glennon. *Cont* Fred Myton. *Titl* Randolph Bartlett. *Story* James Ashmore Creelman. *Photog* Paul Perry. *Film Ed* Archie Marshek. *Asst Dir* Charles Kerr.

Cast: Antonio Moreno *(Steve)*, Ben Lyon *(Dave)*, Martha Sleeper *(Sally)*, John Gough *(McGonigle)*, Colin Chase *(field manager)*.

Melodrama. Airmail pilot Steve Rogers takes under his wing young Dave Grayson, the son of Steve's late commander in the Army Air Corp. Dave proves to be a coward during a rough flight, but Steve covers for him and wins him another chance. Dave later turns yellow for a second time and attempts to shoot himself in the leg to avoid flying supplies to the victims of a tornado. With Steve's help, Dave regains his courage, however, and later saves Steve's life. Dave wins the love of Steve's girl, Sally, and Steve gives them his blessing. *Aviators. Cowardice. Postal service. Tornadoes.*

THE AIR MAIL **F2.0070**

Famous Players–Lasky. *Dist* Paramount Pictures. 16 Mar **1925** [c17 Mar 1925; LP21257]. Si; b&w. 35mm. 8 reels, 6,976 ft.

Pres by Adolph Zukor, Jesse L. Lasky. *Dir* Irvin Willat. *Screenplay* James Shelley Hamilton. *Photog* Alfred Gilks.

Cast: Warner Baxter *(Russ Kane)*, Billie Dove *(Alice Rendon)*, Mary Brian *(Minnie Wade)*, Douglas Fairbanks, Jr. *(Sandy)*, George Irving *(Peter Rendon)*, Richard Tucker *(Jim Cronin)*, Guy Oliver *(Bill Wade)*, Lee Shumway *(Scotty)*, Jack Byron *(René Lenoir)*, John Webb Dillon *(Donald McKee)*, Lloyd Whitlock *(Speck)*.

Melodrama. Source: Byron Morgan, "The Air Mail" (publication undetermined). Russ Kane obtains work as a pilot in the airmail service with the purpose of robbing the mails. However, during his training period at the Reno field, he becomes imbued with the spirit of the service and dedicates himself to getting the mail through. Russ is forced to make an emergency landing near a ghost town, where he meets Alice Rendon and her invalid father, who is badly in need of medicine. Russ repairs his plane and promises to return on the following day with the elder Rendon's medicine. Making good on his promise, Russ returns, carrying with him a valuable mail shipment and his friend, Sandy. The plane is attacked by two planes belonging to a gang that smuggles dope and aliens across the Mexican border. Sandy makes a parachute jump with the mail sack, and Russ maneuvers his craft so that the pursuing planes are forced to crash. Russ then lands his plane, only to discover that the Rendons have been captured by three escaped convicts. Russ manages to bring the men to justice, winning the gratitude and love of Alice. Sandy realizes the crowning ambition of his young life and delivers the mail. *Aviators. Invalids. Smugglers. Prison escapees. Mail theft. Postal service. Parachuting. Narcotics. Mexican border.*

THE AIR MAIL PILOT **F2.0071**

Superlative Pictures. *Dist* Hi-Mark Productions. 11 Feb **1928.** Si; b&w. 35mm. 6 reels, 5,435 ft.

Dir Gene Carroll. *Scen* Harriet Virginia. *Photog* Lew Lang.

Cast: James F. Fulton *(Jimmie Dean)*, Earl Metcalfe *(Tom Miller)*, Blanche Mehaffey *(Ruth Ross)*, De Witt Jennings *(Robert Ross)*, Max Hawley *(Hap Lester)*, Carl Stockdale *(Addison Simms)*.

Action melodrama. "Young air mail pilot arouses wrath of father of girl he loves, result being that he is forbidden to see her. However, he finds that his rival plans to rob the air mail. Villain makes haul, tries to shift blame on others but airman and girl pursue him and bring him down to earth where he gets his just deserts." (*Motion Picture News Booking Guide*, [14]:233, 1929.) The airplane pursuit climaxes in hero's jumping from one in-flight airplane to another and his fight with the villain on the wings of the latter's airplane. *Postal service. Air pilots. Mail theft. Air stunts.*

THE AIR PATROL (Universal-Thrill Feature) **F2.0072**

Universal Pictures. 1 Jan **1928** [c19 Oct 1927; LP24539]. Si; b&w. 35mm. 5 reels, 4,259 ft.

Pres by Carl Laemmle. *Dir* Bruce Mitchell. *Scen* William Lester. *Titl* Gardner Bradford. *Story* Al Wilson. *Photog* William S. Adams. *Film Ed* De Leon Anthony.

Cast: Al Wilson *(Al Langdon)*, Elsa Benham *(Mary Lacy)*, Jack Mower *(Michael Revere)*, Frank Tomick *(Kelly)*, Monte Montague *(Sid Swivel)*, Taylor Duncan *(Captain Carter)*, Art Goebel, Frank Clark *(aviators)*.

Melodrama. Captain Langdon of the Air Patrol forces Kelly, a suspected diamond smuggler, to land, but when he proves to be the wrong man, Langdon's suspicion is directed toward Michael Revere as leader of the gang. During an outing with his neighbor Mary Lacy, Revere finds Langdon parachuting from a plane in an apparently drunken state; in spite of Mary's intercession in his behalf, Langdon is dismissed and later offers his services to Revere as a ruse to aid in capturing the gang. Langdon is captured through Mary's innocent revelation of a secret message, but she discovers Revere's perfidy and Langdon's real purpose; they are captured, and Mary is forced to escape with Revere; but Langdon is freed by an erstwhile detective and overpowers the smugglers in his airplane. *Smugglers. Parachuting. Airplanes. Air patrol.*

AL CHRISTIE'S "MADAME BEHAVE" *see* **MADAME BEHAVE**

THE ALASKAN F2.0073

Famous Players–Lasky. *Dist* Paramount Pictures. ca14 Sep **1924** [New York premiere; released 22 Sep; c17 Sep 1924; LP20578]. Si; b&w. 35mm. 7 reels, 6,736 ft.

Pres by Adolph Zukor, Jesse L. Lasky. *Dir* Herbert Brenon. *Scen* Willis Goldbeck. *Titl* H. H. Caldwell. *Photog* James Howe.

Cast: Thomas Meighan *(Alan Holt)*, Estelle Taylor *(Mary Standish)*, John Sainpolis *(Rossland)*, Frank Campeau *(Stampede Smith)*, Anna May Wong *(Keok)*, Alphonz Ethier *(John Graham)*, Maurice Cannon *(Tautuk)*, Charles Ogle *(The Lawyer)*.

Melodrama. Source: James Oliver Curwood, *The Alaskan* (New York, 1923). Unable to obtain help from the government when his father is murdered by henchmen of a big business syndicate in Alaska headed by John Graham, Alan Holt decides to fight the combination alone. Returning home, he befriends Mary Standish, who seeks refuge from the mistreatment of Graham. Eventually Graham is killed when he falls over a precipice, and Alan and Mary are free to marry. *Syndicates. Murder. Filial relations. Alaska.*

ALASKAN ADVENTURES F2.0074

John Morton Allen. *Dist* Pathé Exchange. 17 Oct **1926** [c22 Oct 1926; MU3616]. Si; b&w with col sequences. 35mm. 6 reels, 5,673 ft.

Prod C. C. Griffin. *Dir* Capt. Jack Robertson. *Titl* Paul D. Hugon. *Photog* Wylie Wells Kelly, Capt. Jack Robertson. *Film Ed* Paul D. Hugon.

Personages: Arthur H. Young, Capt. Jack Robertson, Wrongstart *(a mongrel pup)*.

Travelog. Capt. Jack Anderson and Arthur Young, a champion archer, set out to explore the wilds of Alaska and Siberia, relying for meat upon Young's skill with bow and arrow. Among the sights they see: the breaking-up of the ice in the Yukon River, salmon fighting their way up river to their breeding grounds, the valley of the 10,000 volcanoes, and a variety of wildlife including kodiak bears, mountain sheep, and deer. *Archery. Hunting. Yukon River. Volcanoes. Alaska. Siberia. Dogs. Salmon. Deer. Sheep.*

THE ALBANY NIGHT BOAT F2.0075

Tiffany-Stahl Productions. 20 Jul **1928** [c1 Sep 1928; LP25597]. Si; b&w. 35mm. 6 reels, 5,884 ft.

Dir Alfred Raboch. *Story-Cont* Wellyn Totman. *Titl (see note)* Al Martin, Frederick Hatton, Fanny Hatton. *Photog* Ernest Miller. *Film Ed* Byron Robinson.

Cast: Olive Borden *(Georgie)*, Ralph Emerson *(Ken)*, Duke Martin *(Steve)*, Nellie Bryden *(Mother Crary)*, Helen Marlowe *(The Blonde)*.

Melodrama. Ken, the assistant searchlight operator on the Albany night boat, rescues Georgie from drowning after she jumps overboard from a yacht to avoid a lecherous yachtsman. Ken falls in love with her, and they are married shortly thereafter. They share a house overlooking the Hudson with Steve, Ken's friend and fellow searchlight operator, who makes repeated attempts to seduce Georgie. Ken leaves Georgie alone with Steve one night, and he attacks her. On his way up the Hudson, Ken shines the searchlight on his own house and sees Georgie struggling with Steve. He swims to shore and, scaling the Palisades, reaches his home in time to protect Georgie by pressing a hot iron to Steve's face. Steve goes from their life forever, and Georgie and Ken are content with each another. *Searchlight operators. Seduction. Hudson River.*

Note: Despite Martin's screen credit, Frederick and Fanny Hatton are also credited with writing the titles.

ALEX THE GREAT F2.0076

FBO Pictures. 13 May **1928** [c19 Mar 1928; LP25073]. Si; b&w. 35mm. 7 reels, 5,872 ft.

Dir-Scen Dudley Murphy. *Titl* Randolph Bartlett. *Camera* Virgil Miller. *Film Ed* Ann McKnight.

Cast: Richard "Skeets" Gallagher *(Alex)*, Albert Conti *(Ed)*, Patricia Avery *(Muriel)*, Ruth Dwyer *(Alice)*, Charles Byer *(Brown)*, J. Barney Sherry *(Smith)*.

Comedy. Source: Harry Charles Witwer, *Alex the Great* (Boston, 1919). Alex, a courageous youngster from a small town, setting out to conquer New York City, wins a general sales manager job and a wealthy manufacturer's daughter by recognizing a picture of a pet cow, "Betsy Ross." *Sales managers. New York City. Cows.*

ALIAS FRENCH GERTIE F2.0077

RKO Productions. 20 Apr **1930** [c20 Apr 1930; LP1273]. Sd (Photophone); b&w. 35mm. 7 reels, 6,416 ft.

Assoc Prod Henry Hobart. *Dir* George Archainbaud. *Screenplay-Dial* Wallace Smith. *Photog* J. Roy Hunt. *Rec Engr* Clem Portman.

Cast: Bebe Daniels *(Marie)*, Ben Lyon *(Jimmy)*, Robert Emmett O'Connor *(Kelcey)*, John Ince *(Mr. Matson)*, Daisy Belmore *(Mrs. Matson)*, Betty Pierce *(Nellie)*.

Crime melodrama. Source: Bayard Veiller, *The Chatterbox* (a play; c1948). Marie, posing as a French maid, is about to enter her employer's safe when light-fingered Jimmy Hartigan surprises her and lifts the jewels. He is about to divide the spoils with her at gunpoint when the police arrive; and hiding Marie, he takes the rap. After his release from prison, he and Marie, now known as Gertie the Gun, form a partnership. In a grand apartment she cultivates society friends, including the elderly Mr. and Mrs. Matson, while Jimmy robs banks. At last she induces him to go straight and invest their savings in Mr. Matson's concern, but Jimmy is doublecrossed and determines to return to safecracking. He goes to her former employer's home to steal the jewels, but she wounds him. Kelcey, a detective tipped off by Marie, bids them to go free and reform. *Safecrackers. Housemaids. Socialites. Criminals—Rehabilitation. Bank robberies. Impersonation.*

ALIAS JIMMY VALENTINE F2.0078

Metro-Goldwyn-Mayer Pictures. 26 Jan **1929** [c21 Jan 1929; LP36]. Talking sequences, mus score, & sd eff (Movietone); b&w. 35mm. 8 reels, 7,803 ft. [Also si; 8 reels, 7,142 ft.]

Dir Jack Conway. *Cont* Sarah Y. Mason. *Titl* Joe Farnham. *Adapt* A. P. Younger. *Photog* Merritt B. Gerstad. *Sets* Cedric Gibbons. *Film Ed* Sam S. Zimbalist. *Song: "Love Dreams"* William Axt, Mort Harris, Raymond Klages, David Mendoza. *Wardrobe* David Cox.

Cast: William Haines *(Jimmy Valentine)*, Lionel Barrymore *(Doyle)*, Leila Hyams *(Rose)*, Karl Dane *(Swede)*, Tully Marshall *(Avery)*, Howard Hickman *(Mr. Lane)*, Billy Butts *(Bobby)*, Evelyn Mills *(Little Sister)*.

Crime melodrama. Source: Paul Armstrong, *Alias Jimmy Valentine* (a play; publication undetermined). Safecracker Jimmy Valentine and his pal Swede are in the process of planning a "bank job" with Avery and other thieves, but Jimmy falls in love with Rose. Deciding to go straight under the name of Randall, he retires to the small town where she lives with her father. His cohorts try to dissuade him, and Doyle, a police detective who suspects his motives, tracks him down; but finding him on the level and about to marry Rose, Doyle relents. When Jimmy risks suspicion by opening his employer's safe to rescue a child, Doyle is certain he has reformed. *Safecrackers. Detectives. Criminals—Rehabilitation. Bank robberies.*

ALIAS JULIUS CAESAR F2.0079

Charles Ray Productions. *Dist* Associated First National Pictures. Jul **1922** [c3 Aug 1922; LP18189]. Si; b&w. 35mm. 5 reels, 5,240 ft.

Pres by Arthur S. Kane. *Dir* Charles Ray. *Titl* Edward Withers. *Story* Richard Andres. *Photog* George Rizard. *Art Dir* Howard Berbeck. *Film Ed* Harry Decker. *Asst Dir* Al Ray, Irven H. Ford.

Cast: Charles Ray *(Billy Barnes)*, Barbara Bedford *(Helen)*, William Scott *(Harry)*, Robert Fernandez *(Tom)*, Fred Miller *(Dick)*, Eddie Gribbon *("Nervy" Norton)*, Tom Wilson *(Mose)*, Harvey Clark *(M. Dumas)*, Gus Thomas *(Harrington Whitney)*, Milton Ross *(police sergeant)*, S. J. Bingham *(detective)*, Phillip Dunham *(Billy's valet)*, Bert Offord *(janitor)*.

Farce. Friends lock Billy Barnes in the shower and take away his clothes, but he escapes wrapped in the shower curtain. The police take him for a lunatic and put him in jail, where he meets a jewel thief. They escape together and go to a party. The thief steals a considerable amount of jewelry, tries to implicate Billy, but is finally exposed by him. *Thieves. Insanity.*

ALIAS LADYFINGERS F2.0080

Metro Pictures. 31 Oct **1921** [c7 Dec 1921; LP17322]. Si; b&w. 35mm. 6 reels, 5,304 ft. [Copyrighted as 5 reels.]

Dir Bayard Veiller. *Adapt* Lenore J. Coffee. *Photog* Arthur Martinelli. *Art Dir* A. E. Freuderman.

Cast: Bert Lytell *(Robert Ashe [Ladyfingers])*, Ora Carew *(Enid Camden)*, Frank Elliott *(Justin Haddon)*, Edythe Chapman *(Rachel Stetherill)*, De Witt Jennings *(Lieutenant Ambrose)*, Stanley Goethals *(Robert Ashe, at age of 4)*.

Comedy-drama. Source: Jackson Gregory, *Ladyfingers* (New York,

1920). Five years after Rachel Stetherill has disowned her only daughter because of her marriage, the girl, widowed with one child, is killed. Her boy falls in with a safecracker and soon becomes adept at the profession. Twenty years later, Haddon, the Stetherill lawyer, learns that Ladyfingers, a noted thief, bears a close resemblance to Mrs. Stetherill's husband. Ladyfingers, having fallen in love with Enid, Mrs. Stetherill's ward, attends a charity ball at the old lady's home, and while he is engaged in a conversation with her, a string of pearls disappears; the police accuse Ladyfingers, but the pearls are found and the case is dismissed. He accepts an invitation to visit her, but realizing he cannot win Enid's love he departs, leaving a note in the safe. When Rachel informs him that he is her grandson, Ladyfingers confesses his crimes, and after a 2-year prison term, he takes up farming and is happily married to Enid. *Safecrackers. Grandmothers. Criminals—Rehabilitation. Farmers. Parentage.*

Note: Initially reviewed and released under the title *Ladyfingers.* Described also under that title in Entry F2.2948.

ALIAS MARY FLYNN **F2.0081**

Film Booking Offices of America. 3 May **1925** [c3 May 1925; LP21457]. Si; b&w. 35mm. 6 reels, 5,559 ft.

Dir Ralph Ince. *Scen* Frederick Myton. *Scen? (see note)* Luella Bender. *Story* Frederick Myton, Edward J. Montagne. *Photog* Silvano Balboni. *Asst Dir* Pan Berman.

Cast: Evelyn Brent *(Mary Flynn)*, Malcolm McGregor *(Tim Reagan)*, William V. Mong *(John Reagan)*, Gladden James *(Picadilly Charlie)*, Lou Payne *(Jason Forbes)*, Wilson Benge *(Maurice Deperre)*, John Gough *(Mickey)*, Jacques D'Auray *(chief of crooks)*.

Melodrama. Mary Flynn, a girl thief hunted by the police, takes refuge in the car of John Reagan to break loose from her underworld associates. John gives Mary a fresh start in life, and his son, Tim, an assistant district attorney, soon falls in love with her. A jewel collector named Forbes, who knows that the elder Reagan's past was a little shady, blackmails him into stealing a valuable diamond. In order to protect her mentor, Mary steals the jewel. Piccadilly Charlie, Mary's old accomplice, wants the stone also and kills Forbes in an attempt to get it. John is found with the body and is arrested for the murder. Mary sets a trap for Charlie, using the diamond as bait. Charlie returns for the stone, and Mary captures him, handing him over to the police. John is released from jail, and Mary marries Tim. *District attorneys. Police. Collectors. Theft. Criminals—Rehabilitation. Murder.*

Note: Luella Bender is also credited with the scenario in some sources.

ALIAS PHIL KENNEDY (Entertainment Series) **F2.0082**

Long Beach Motion Pictures. *Dist* Wid Gunning, Inc. Apr **1922.** Si; b&w. 35mm. 5 reels, 5,022 ft.

Dir William Bertram.

Cast: William Patton, Dixie Lamont.

Mystery melodrama(?). "Thrilling mystery in the golden California hills" (New York State license application). *California.*

ALIAS THE DEACON (Universal-Jewel) **F2.0083**

Universal Pictures. 22 Jan **1928** [c2 May 1927; LP23924]. Si; b&w. 35mm. 7 reels, 6,869 ft.

Pres by Carl Laemmle. *Dir* Edward Sloman. *Adapt-Cont* Charles Kenyon. *Titl* Walter Anthony. *Photog* Gilbert Warrenton, Jackson Rose. *Film Ed* Byron Robinson.

Cast: Jean Hersholt *(The Deacon)*, June Marlowe *(Nancy)*, Ralph Graves *(John Adams)*, Myrtle Stedman *(Mrs. Clark)*, Lincoln Plummer *(Cunningham)*, Ned Sharks *("Slim" Sullivan)*, Tom Kennedy *("Bull" Moran)*, Maurice Murphy *(Willie Clark)*, George West *(George)*.

Melodrama. Source: John B. Hymer and Leroy Clemens, *Alias the Deacon, a Comedy in a Prologue and Three Acts* (London, 1928). The Deacon, a professional cardsharp and gambler, meets John Adams, a young hobo, and Nancy, a girl hitching freight trains, disguised as a boy, when he saves Nancy from other tramps who discover she is a girl. In the next town, Nancy works as a hotel clerk and John as a garageman. The Deacon, recognizing Nancy as his daughter whom he has not seen since her childhood, stays at the hotel to protect her. John takes a beating in the prize ring, hoping to start a home for Nancy, but Cunningham, the fight promoter, refuses to pay, and before his wedding John is arrested on a trumped-up charge; but he is bailed out by the hotel proprietress. When Cunningham threatens the hotel owner, the Deacon strips him of his cash in poker and the fight manager confesses to the frame-up. The Deacon turns in the villain, gives the reward to the young couple, and "skips" town to avoid the authorities. *Fight promoters. Hotel clerks. Garagemen. Swindlers. Hotelkeepers. Cardsharps. Gamblers. Hoboes. Disguise. Parentage.*

ALIAS THE LONE WOLF **F2.0084**

Columbia Pictures. 22 Aug **1927** [c14 Sep 1927; LP24404]. Si; b&w. 35mm. 7 reels, 6,843 ft.

Prod Harry Cohn. *Dir* Edward H. Griffith. *Scen* Dorothy Howell, Edward H. Griffith. *Photog* J. O. Taylor. *Art Dir* Robert E. Lee. *Asst Dir* Joe Cook.

Cast: Bert Lytell *(Michael Lanyard)*, Lois Wilson *(Eve de Montalais)*, William V. Mong *(Whitaker Monk)*, Ned Sparks *(Phinuit)*, James Mason *(Popinot)*, Paulette Duval *(Liane Delorme)*, Ann Brody *(Fifi)*, Alphonz Ethier *(Inspector Crane)*.

Mystery melodrama. Source: Louis Joseph Vance, *Alias the Lone Wolf* (Garden City, New York, 1921). Eve de Montalais plans to smuggle her jewels into the United States. On her ship are a gang of thieves, among whom are Liane Delorme and her companion, Phinuit, who plan to steal the jewels. Michael Lanyard, alias The Lone Wolf, upsets the scheming of Popinot, and Eve seeks his aid in getting the gems past customs officials. At a New York nightclub, Liane informs Eve that Lanyard is The Lone Wolf. Whitaker Monk assumes the role of a customs officer and induces Eve to turn over the jewels, and she escapes upon discovering the deception. Lanyard is overpowered by the crooks but manages to free himself and declares the jewels to customs officials, who then summarily arrest the thieves. Eve is relieved to find that Lanyard is a Secret Service agent, and the lovers are reunited. *Thieves. Smuggling. Imposture. Ocean liners. Secret service. Customs (tariff). New York City.*

ALIAS THE NIGHT WIND **F2.0085**

Fox Film Corp. 19 Aug **1923** [c19 Aug 1923; LP19335]. Si; b&w. 35mm. 5 reels, 4,145 ft.

Pres by William Fox. *Dir* Joseph Franz. *Scen* Robert N. Lee. *Photog* Ernest Miller.

Cast: William Russell *(Bing Howard)*, Maude Wayne *(Katherine Maxwell)*, Charles K. French *(Amos Chester)*, Wade Boteler *(Thomas Clancy)*, Donald MacDonald *(Clifford Rushton)*, H. Milton Ross *(R. J. Brown)*, Charles Wellesley *(Police Commissioner)*, Mark Fenton *(The Nurse)*, Otto Matieson, Bob Klein, Bert Lindley *(detectives)*.

Mystery melodrama. Source: Varick Vanardy, *Alias the Night Wind* (New York, 1913). Former stockbroker Bing Howard is called the "Night Wind" because he is a fugitive from justice, constantly being trailed by Clifford Rushton, a private detective who has framed Howard on a bond robbery. Rushton's failure to catch Howard forces the chief to turn the case over to Detective Katherine Maxwell, alias "Lady Kate," whose brother was sent to prison for bond robbery on the same evidence Rushton has brought against Howard. Lady Kate provides a temporary hideout for Howard, then proves that Rushton is guilty of both crimes. *Stockbrokers. Detectives. Fugitives. Frameup. Injustice.*

ALIBI **F2.0086**

Feature Productions. *Dist* United Artists. 20 Apr **1929** [c1 May 1929; LP394]. Sd (Movietone); b&w. 35mm. 10 reels, 8,167 ft. [Also si; 7,263 ft.]

Pres by Joseph M. Schenck. *Prod-Dir* Roland West. *Scen-Titl-Dial* Roland West, C. Gardner Sullivan. *Photog* Ray June. *Art Dir* William Cameron Menzies. *Film Ed* Hal Kern. *Mus Arr* Hugo Riesenfeld. *Dances arranged by* Fanchon.

Cast: Chester Morris *(Chick Williams)*, Harry Stubbs *(Buck Bachman)*, Mae Busch *(Daisy Thomas)*, Eleanor Griffith *(Joan Manning)*, Irma Harrison *(Toots, cabaret dancer)*, Regis Toomey *(Danny McGann)*, Al Hill *(Brown, a crook)*, James Bradbury, Jr. *(Blake, a crook)*, Elmer Ballard *(Soft Malone, cab driver)*, Kernan Cripps *(Trask, plainclothesman)*, Purnell B. Pratt *(Pete Manning, police sergeant)*, Pat O'Malley *(Tommy Glennon, detective)*, De Witt Jennings *(O'Brien, policeman)*, Edward Brady *(George Stanislaus David)*, Edward Jardon, Virginia Flohri *(singers in theater)*.

Underworld drama. Source: John Griffith Wray, J. C. Nugent and Elaine S. Carrington, *Nightstick* (New York opening: 10 Nov 1927). Joan Manning, the daughter of a police sergeant, secretly marries Chick Williams, a gangleader who convinces her that he is leading an honest life. Chick attends the theater with Joan and, at the intermission, sneaks away, committing a robbery during which a policeman is killed. Chick is suspected of the crime but is able to use Joan to substantiate his alibi. The police plant Danny McGann, an undercover agent, in Chick's gang; but he is discovered, and Chick murders him. Chick is later cornered by the police in his own home. *Police. Detectives. Marriage. Robbery. Murder.*

ALICE ADAMS **F2.0087**
Encore Pictures. *Dist* Associated Exhibitors. 8 Apr **1923** [c22 Mar 1923; LU18796]. Si; b&w. 35mm. 6 reels, 6,361 ft.

Pres by King Vidor. *Dir-Adapt* Rowland V. Lee. *Photog* George Barnes.

Cast: Florence Vidor *(Alice Adams)*, Claude Gillingwater *(Virgil Adams)*, Harold Goodwin *(Walter Adams)*, Margaret McWade *(Mrs. Adams)*, Thomas Ricketts *(J. A. Lamb)*, Margaret Landis *(Henrietta Lamb)*, Gertrude Astor *(Mildred Palmer)*, Vernon Steele *(Arthur Russell)*.

Domestic drama. Source: Booth Tarkington, *Alice Adams* (New York, 1921). Unsatisfied with her family's modest means, embarrassed by her headstrong brother, and nagged by her mother, Alice Adams builds romantic dreams and tries to give the impression of wealth to her friends, especially Arthur Russell. During a dinner in the Adams home Arthur discovers Alice's pretense, and she finally realizes she is fooling only herself. Alice decides to go to work to help her father, whose business has failed. *Filial relations. Smalltown life. Family life. Middle classes.*

ALIMONY **F2.0088**
R-C Pictures. *Dist* Film Booking Offices of America. 3 Feb **1924** [c3 Feb 1924; LP20262]. Si; b&w. 35mm. 7 reels, 6,917 ft.

Dir James W. Horne. *Adapt* Wyndham Gittens, E. Magnus Ingleton. *Story* Ashley T. Locke. *Photog* Joseph Dubray, Pierre Collings.

Cast: Grace Darmond *(Marion Mason)*, Warner Baxter *(Jimmy Mason)*, Ruby Miller *(Gloria Du Bois)*, William A. Carroll *(Philip Coburn)*, Jackie Saunders *(Betty Coburn)*, Clyde Fillmore *(Granville)*, Herschel Mayall *(Blake)*, Alton Brown *(Grey)*.

Domestic drama. Having helped her husband from their days of poverty to a period of unexpected wealth, Marion Mason sees other women entering his life. Misunderstanding leads to divorce, but she insists on a large alimony, which she uses to save him after the other woman has wrecked his fortune. He asks her forgiveness, and they are remarried. *Marriage. Divorce. Alimony. Poverty. Wealth.*

ALL ABOARD **F2.0089**
B & H Enterprises. *Dist* First National Pictures. 1 May **1927** [c22 Mar 1927; LP23767]. Si; b&w. 35mm. 7 reels, 6,300 ft.

Pres by C. C. Burr. *Dir* Charles Hines. *Story* Matt Taylor. *Photog* George Peters.

Cast: Johnny Hines *(Johnny)*, Edna Murphy *(May Brooks)*, Dot Farley *(Aunt Patsy)*, Henry Barrows *(Thomas Brooks)*, Frank Hagney *(Ali Ben Ome)*, Babe London *(Princess)*, Sojin *(Prince)*, James Leonard *(El Humid)*.

Comedy. Because of his bad memory, Johnny is discharged from his job as a shoe clerk but is hired as a guide for an Egypt-bound tourist party led by Thomas Brooks, father of May, with whom Johnny falls in love. In Egypt Johnny meets a sheik who wishes to escape his marriage to a fat princess; he induces Johnny to exchange clothes with him; and Johnny, to his dismay, finds himself married to the fat girl. Then he learns that his beloved, May, has been captured by desert bandits. After a struggle, he escapes from his predicament and rescues May during a sandstorm. Later, he discovers that his unfortunate marriage is not valid and that he is free to marry May. *Shoeclerks. Guides. Tourists. Sheiks. Sandstorms. Egypt.*

THE ALL AMERICAN *see* **THE OLYMPIC HERO**

ALL AROUND FRYING PAN **F2.0090**
R-C Pictures. *Dist* Film Booking Offices of America. 8 Nov **1925** [c23 Nov 1925; LP22133]. Si; b&w. 35mm. 6 reels, 5,519 ft.

Dir-Script David Kirkland. *Story* Frank Richardson Pierce. *Photog* Ross Fisher.

Cast: Fred Thomson *(Bart Andrews)*, James Marcus *(sheriff)*, William Courtwright *(All Around Austin)*, John Lince *(Jim Dawson)*, Clara Horton *(Jean Dawson)*, Monte Collins *(Mike Selby)*, Elmo Lincoln *(Foreman Slade)*, Newton Barbar *(Ruddy Logan)*.

Western melodrama. Bart Andrews, a drifting cowboy, is arrested for vagrancy by a sheriff who needs men for the state road gang. On the way to jail, the sheriff stops off at a rodeo, allowing Bart the chance to ride a wild bronc. Bart tames the horse, and, at the urging of some cowboys, the sheriff allows Bart to go to work on the Lawrence ranch. Bart falls in love with Jean Dawson, the ranch manager's daughter, and prevents the theft of a trainload of çattle. Bart later suprises the foreman in the act of robbing the safe at the express office; the men fight, the station agent is killed, and Bart is accused of the crime. He frees himself, brings the foreman to justice, and reveals himself to be the real owner of the Lawrence ranch. *Ranchers. Cowboys. Vagabonds. Sheriffs. Ranch foremen. Station agents. Robbery. Rodeos.*

ALL AT SEA **F2.0091**
Metro-Goldwyn-Mayer Pictures. 9 Feb **1929** [c5 Mar 1929; LP184]. Si; b&w. 35mm. 6 reels, 5,345 ft.

Dir Alf Goulding. *Scen* Ann Price, Byron Morgan. *Titl* Robert Hopkins. *Story* Byron Morgan. *Photog* Arthur Reed. *Art Dir* Cedric Gibbons. *Film Ed* Basil Wrangell. *Wardrobe* Henrietta Frazer.

Cast: Karl Dane *(Stupid McDuff)*, George K. Arthur *(Rollo the Great)*, Josephine Dunn *(Shirley Page)*, Herbert Prior *(Shirley's father)*, Eddie Baker *(The Marine)*.

Comedy-drama. "Small time vaudeville magician and hypnotist finds himself in trouble when he plays a theatre where sailors and marines are principal patrons. A gob is hypnotised and the comedy follows." ("Motion Picture News Booking Guide," in *Motion Picture News*, 15 Mar 1930, p68.) *Hypnotists. Magicians. Sailors. Vaudeville. United States Marines.*

ALL DOLLED UP **F2.0092**
Universal Film Manufacturing Co. Mar **1921** [c25 Feb 1921; LP16186]. Si; b&w. 35mm. 5 reels, 4,780 ft.

Dir Rollin Sturgeon. *Scen* A. P. Younger. *Story* John Colton. *Photog* Alfred Gosden.

Cast: Gladys Walton *(Maggie Quick)*, Edward Hearn *(James Montgomery Johnson)*, Richard Norton *(Percy Prack)*, Florence Turner *(Eva Bundy)*, Helen Bruneau *(The Widow)*, Fred Malatesta *(Amilo Rodolpho)*, Ruth Royce *(Mademoiselle Scarpa)*, John Goff *(Eddie Bowman)*, Frank Norcross *(Mr. Shankley)*, Muriel Godfrey Turner *(Madame De Jercasse)*, Lydia Yeamans Titus *(landlady)*.

Comedy-melodrama. Eva Bundy, a spinster heiress who is in love with Rodolpho, a swindler after her money, is saved by cashier Maggie Quick from being robbed in a department store. When a jealous rival presents evidence of Rodolpho's previous marriage, Eva is heartbroken and sends her elegant wardrobe to Maggie as a reward. In escaping from an unwelcome admirer, Maggie meets James Montgomery Johnson, whom she believes to be an aristocrat; actually, he is Eva's chauffeur. Together they succeed in averting a blackmail plot against Miss Bundy, and as a result she adopts the couple, who then decide to marry. *Spinsters. Swindlers. Cashiers. Chauffeurs. Marriage. Blackmail.*

Note: Working title: *The Bobbed Squab.*

ALL FOR THE LOVE OF GLORIA *see* **HIS MYSTERY GIRL**

ALL MUST MARRY *see* **WOMAN-PROOF**

ALL NIGHT (Reissue) **F2.0093**
Dist Universal Film Manufacturing Co. Aug **1922.** Si; b&w. 35mm. 5 reels.

Note: Originally released by Bluebird Photoplays on 30 Nov 1918, starring Carmel Myers and M. Rodolpho de Valentina.

ALL QUIET ON THE WESTERN FRONT **F2.0094**
Universal Pictures. 29 Apr **1930** [New York premiere; released 24 Aug; c17 May 1930; LP1323]. Sd (Movietone); b&w. 35mm. 14 reels, 12,423 ft. [Also si with synchronized mus; 15 reels.]

Pres by Carl Laemmle. *Prod* Carl Laemmle, Jr. *Dir* Lewis Milestone. *Dial Dir* George Cukor. *Screenplay* Del Andrews, Maxwell Anderson, George Abbott. *Dial* Maxwell Anderson, George Abbott. *Titl* Walter Anthony. *Photog* Arthur Edeson. *Spec Eff Photog* Frank H. Booth. *Art Dir* Charles D. Hall, William R. Schmidt. *Film Ed* Edgar Adams, Milton Carruth. *Synchronization & Score* David Broekman. *Rec Engr* C. Roy Hunter. *Sd Tech* William W. Hedgecock. *Asst Dir* Nate Watt.

Cast: Louis Wolheim *(Katczinsky)*, Lew Ayres *(Paul Bäumer)*, John Wray *(Himmelstoss)*, Raymond Griffith *(Gerard Duval)*, George "Slim" Summerville *(Tjaden)*, Russell Gleason *(Müller)*, William Bakewell *(Albert)*, Scott Kolk *(Leer)*, Walter Rogers *(Behm)*, Ben Alexander *(Kemmerich)*, Owen Davis, Jr. *(Peter)*, Beryl Mercer *(Mrs. Bäumer)*, ZaSu Pitts *(Mrs. Bäumer [original version; see note])*, Edwin Maxwell *(Mr. Bäumer)*, Harold Goodwin *(Detering)*, Marion Clayton *(Miss Bäumer)*, Richard Alexander *(Westhus)*, G. Pat Collins *(Lieutenant Bertinck)*, Yola D'Avril *(Suzanne)*, Poupée Andriot, Renée Damonde *(French girls)*, Arnold Lucy *(Kantorek)*, William Irving *(Ginger)*, Edmund Breese *(Herr Meyer)*, Heinie Conklin *(Hammacher)*, Bertha Mann *(Sister Libertine)*, Bodil Rosing *(watcher)*, Joan Marsh *(poster girl)*, Tom London *(orderly)*, Vincent Barnett *(cook)*,

Fred Zinnemann *(man)*.

War drama. Source: Erich Maria Remarque, *Im Westen nichts neues* (Berlin, 1929). Paul Bäumer, a young German schoolboy, along with his friends, is inspired by his schoolmaster to "save the Fatherland" and joins the Kaiser's forces. Their illusions are soon dispelled, however, by the cruel realities of battle, relieved only by a brief romantic interlude with some French farm girls and the humorous interjections of Katz and Tjaden. When Paul, the only survivor of the group, returns home, he finds the professor still haranguing his young scholars to join the conflict; and when Paul denounces this attitude, he is procalimed a coward by the youths. Tiring of the false impression of war at home, he returns to the front to instruct his new comrades in warfare. As the sole survivor of this group also, Paul reaches over the top of a trench to catch a butterfly and is killed by an enemy sniper. ... Quiet reigns on the front lines. *Soldiers. Schoolteachers. Germans. French. Patriotism. Friendship. World War I.*

Note: The sequences with ZaSu Pitts were cut (though retained in the silent version) and reshot with Beryl Mercer. The film was reduced to 10 reels for reissue in 1939.

ALL SOULS' EVE **F2.0095**

Realart Pictures. Feb **1921** [c10 Jan 1921; LP16013]. Si; b&w. 35mm. 5-6 reels, 5,778 ft.

Dir Chester Franklin. *Scen* Elmer Harris. *Photog* Faxon Dean. *Asst Dir* Fred J. Robinson.

Cast: Mary Miles Minter *(Alice Heath/Nora O'Hallahan)*, Jack Holt *(Roger Heath)*, Carmen Phillips *(Olivia Larkin)*, Clarence Geldert *(Dr. Sandy McAllister)*, Mickey Moore *(Peter Heath)*, Fanny Midgley *(Mrs. O'Hallahan)*, Lottie Williams *(Belle Emerson)*.

Melodrama. Source: Anne Crawford Flexner, *All Souls' Eve* (New York opening: 12 May 1920). Olivia Larkin, out of unrequited love for sculptor Roger Heath, urges a lunatic to kill his beautiful young wife and tries unsuccessfully to regain his affection. Meanwhile, Nora O'Hallahan, an Irish immigrant girl, has taken a position as nursemaid in Heath's household. After a period of severe depression, Heath realizes that the soul of his departed wife has returned to him in the person of Nora, who rekindles his inspiration. She consents to become his wife and the mother of his little son, Peter. *Sculptors. Widowers. Lunatics. Irish. Reincarnation. All Souls' Eve.*

ALL THE BROTHERS WERE VALIANT **F2.0096**

Metro Pictures. 15 Jan **1923** [c10 Jan 1923; LP18742]. Si; b&w. 35mm. 7 reels, 6,265 ft.

Dir Irvin V. Willat. *Adapt-Scen* Julien Josephson. *Photog* Robert Kurrle.

Cast: Malcolm McGregor *(Joel Shore)*, Billie Dove *(Priscilla Holt)*, Lon Chaney *(Mark Shore)*, William H. Orlamond *(Aaron Burnham)*, Robert McKim *(Finch)*, Robert Kortman *(Varde)*, Otto Brower *(Morrell)*, Curt Rehfeld *(Hooper)*, William V. Mong *(cook)*, Leo Willis *(Tom)*, Shannon Day *(The Brown Girl)*.

Melodrama. Source: Ben Ames Williams, *All the Brothers Were Valiant* (New York, 1919). Joel Shore is made captain of the whaling schooner formerly headed by his courageous and admired brother, Mark, who was lost at sea. Accompanied by his bride, who supects Joel to have a cowardly heart, they set sail for a whale hunt. Mark reappears, tells of hidden pearls, and incites the crew to mutiny when Joel refuses to take his ship off course to recover the treasure. Mark finally comes to Joel's aid but falls overboard; Joel unsuccessfully attempts to rescue him; Priscilla acknowledges her husband's heroism. *Brothers. Whaling. Courage. Treasure. The Sea.*

ALL'S FAIR IN LOVE **F2.0097**

Goldwyn Pictures. Sep **1921** [c27 Jul 1921; LP16788]. Si; b&w. 35mm. 5 reels.

Dir E. Mason Hopper. *Scen* Arthur F. Statter. *Photog* John J. Mescall. *Asst Dir* E. J. Babille.

Cast: May Collins *(Natalie Marshall)*, Richard Dix *(Bobby Cameron)*, Marcia Manon *(Vera)*, Raymond Hatton *(Craigh Randolph)*, Stuart Holmes *(Rogers)*, Andrew Robson *(Marshall)*.

Domestic melodrama. Source: Thompson Buchanan, *The Bridal Path* (New York opening: 18 Feb 1913). While golfing, Natalie Marshall meets and falls in love with Bobby Cameron, and after a brief courtship they are married. Just as they are about to embark on their honeymoon, Vera, a young vamp with designs on Bobby, presents Natalie with a bracelet and an accompanying note and inscription that arouse the wife's jealousy and cause an immediate break between the couple. Following a hysterical exhibition and her refusal to see her husband, she determines to win him back by employing Vera's siren methods. She succeeds, but Bobby insists that he wants a real wife, not a vamp. *Vamps. Marriage. Jealousy. Golf.*

ALMA DE GAUCHO **F2.0098**

Chris Phyllis Productions. 7 Jun **1930**. Sd (in Spanish); b&w. 35mm. 6 reels, 5,325 ft.

Dir Henry Otto. *Dial* Benjamin I. Paralupi. *Story* Paul Ellis. *Photog* Leon Shamroy. *Mus* Benjamin I. Paralupi. *Sd* Ralph M. Like.

Cast: Manuel Granada *(Antonio)*, Mona Rico *(Elsa)*, Francisco Amerise *(Don Alfredo)*, Christina Montt *(Doña Cristina)*, Jorge Rigas *(Don Casimiro)*, Humberto Bonavi *(Arturo)*, Alberto Mendoza *(Carlos)*, Ema Mora *(Monona)*.

Romantic drama. Locating Elsa's lost golf ball, Antonio, a dapper gaucho, immediately falls in love with the wealthy Buenos Aires flirt. Elsa responds, but he overhears her laughingly tell her family how she is leading him on, and Antonio abducts her so that he can express his anger. Later, Antonio is about to leave the country when he hears Elsa calling his name, he rushes to her arms, and Elsa confesses her wrong and her true love for Antonio. (There are incidental songs.) *Gauchos. Flirts. Courtship. Golf. Argentina.*

ALMOST A LADY **F2.0099**

Metropolitan Pictures Corp. of California. *Dist* Producers Distributing Corp. 27 Sep **1926** [c3 Aug 1926; LP22994]. Si; b&w. 35mm. 6 reels, 5,702 ft.

Pres by John C. Flinn. *Dir* E. Mason Hopper. *Screenplay–Ed Supv* F. McGrew Willis. *Adapt* Anthony Coldeway. *Photog* Hal Rosson.

Cast: Marie Prevost *(Marcia Blake, a gownshop model)*, Harrison Ford *(William Duke)*, George K. Arthur *(Bob)*, Trixie Friganza *(Mrs. Reilly)*, John Miljan *(Henri)*, Barney Gilmore *(Mr. Reilly)*.

Romantic comedy. Source: Frank R. Adams, "Skin Deep," in *Cosmopolitan Magazine*. Marcia Blake, employed as a model in the fashionable boutique of Monsieur Henri, displays some gowns to Mrs. Reilly, a social climber; and Mr. Reilly furtively flirts with Marcia, though his wife castigates him for doing so. Later, when her brother, Bob, arrives in a new flivver, Marcia quarrels with him; and Henri receives a tomato in the face when he invites Marcia to a reception at the Reilly home. At the reception, Marcia meets William Duke, a social lion, and is anxious to meet Madame O'Flynn, a famous writer; but when the author fails to arrive, Marcia, over protests, is formally presented as Madame O'Flynn. William is smitten with her; and when he declares his love, Marcia is forced to evade him and later to reveal her imposture. Bob's appearance again causes havoc, and though William is also an imposter he buys out Henri and convinces Marcia of his sincerity. *Social climbers. Fashion models. Authors. Courtship. Mistaken identity. Imposture. Boutiques.*

ALMOST HUMAN **F2.0100**

De Mille Pictures. *Dist* Pathé Exchange. 26 Dec **1927** [c3 Nov 1927; LP24616]. Si; b&w. 35mm. 6 reels, 5,596 ft.

Dir Frank Urson. *Screenplay* Clara Beranger. *Titl* John Krafft, Clara Beranger. *Photog* Lucien Andriot. *Art Dir* Wilfred Buckland. *Film Ed* Adelaide Cannon. *Asst Dir* Roy Burns. *Cost* Adrian.

Cast: Vera Reynolds *(Mary Kelly)*, Kenneth Thomson *(John Livingston)*, Majel Coleman *(Cecile Adams)*, Claire McDowell *(Mrs. Livingston)*, Ethel Wales *(Katie)*, Fred Walton *(doctor)*, Hank *(Pal, a dog)*, Paul *(Regent Royal, a dog)*, Trixie *(Maggie, a dog)*.

Society melodrama. Maggie lures champion Regent Royal from his luxurious surroundings to her humble abode in an old barn, but he later ignores her attempts to see him; later a son, Pal, is born to Maggie, and she leaves him to find a "human." In a park, Pal meets Mary Kelly, a homeless orphan, and is later drawn to Regent Royal, who is walking with his master, John Livingston. When Mary is endangered saving a drowning child, John rescues her and takes her to his residence, to the disapproval of his mother, but Mary is permitted to stay. They fall in love; and though his family refuses to approve their marriage, John and Mary are married and obtain employment in an aristocratic home as chauffeur and housemaid. At a party given by their employers, John meets his former sweetheart, Cecile; and Mary, misunderstanding, leaves him and goes to live and work for a kindly doctor, where she has her child. Meanwhile, Pal, reunited with his mother, Maggie, reunites the couple, who are ultimately accepted by Mrs. Livingston. *Orphans. Chauffeurs. Housemaids. Physicians. Motherhood. Marriage. Dogs.*

Note: Working title: *Beautiful But Dumb.*

ALOMA OF THE SOUTH SEAS **F2.0101**

Famous Players–Lasky. *Dist* Paramount Pictures. 16 May **1926** [New York premiere; released 29 May or 2 Aug; c3 Aug 1926; LP23004]. Si; b&w. 35mm. 9 reels, 8,514 ft.

Pres by Adolph Zukor, Jesse L. Lasky. *Dir* Maurice Tourneur. *Supv Ed* E. Lloyd Sheldon. *Scen* James Ashmore Creelman. *Photog* Harry Fischbeck. *Art Dir* Charles M. Kirk.

Cast: Gilda Gray *(Aloma)*, Percy Marmont *(Bob Holden)*, Warner Baxter *(Nuitane)*, William Powell *(Van Templeton)*, Harry Morey *(Red Malloy)*, Julanne Johnston *(Sylvia)*, Joseph Smiley *(Andrew Taylor)*, Frank Montgomery *(Hongi)*, Madame Burani *(Hina)*, Ernestine Gaines *(Taula)*, Aurelio Coccia *(sailor)*.

Melodrama. Source: John B. Hymer and Leroy Clemens, *Aloma of the South Seas* (New York opening: 20 Apr 1925). Aloma, a beautiful dancer on Paradise Island, is jealously guarded by her lover, Nuitane. When Red Malloy, a dishonest trader, annoys her, Bob Holden, an American seeking to forget an unhappy love affair, defends her and wins her allegiance. Andrew Taylor, learning that his niece, Sylvia, who deserted Bob, is coming to the island with her husband, Van Templeton, sends Bob and Aloma to his plantation, though Nuitane objects. Aloma comes to love Bob but is tricked by Van, a sodden flirt, into "marriage," while Bob realizes that he still loves Sylvia. Bob and Van are lost in a canoe that capsizes during a storm, and the jealous women are drawn together in a common bond of sympathy. Then Bob reappears, announcing that Van has drowned; he is reunited with Sylvia; and Aloma continues her relationship with Nuitane. *Traders. Courtship. Jealousy. South Sea Islands. Puerto Rico. Storms.*

Note: Filmed partly on location in Puerto Rico.

ALONG CAME RUTH **F2.0102**

Metro-Goldwyn Pictures. 3 Nov **1924** [c12 Aug 1924; LP20501]. Si; b&w. 35mm. 5 reels, 5,000 ft.

Dir Edward Cline. *Adapt* Winifred Dunn. *Photog* John Arnold.

Cast: Viola Dana *(Ruth Ambrose)*, Walter Hiers *(Plinty Bangs)*, Tully Marshall *(Israel Hubbard)*, Raymond McKee *(Allan Hubbard)*, Victor Potel *(Oscar Sims)*, Gale Henry *(Min, the hired girl)*, De Witt Jennings *(Captain Miles Standish)*, Adele Farrington *(Widow Burnham)*, Brenda Lane *(Annabelle Burnham)*.

Romantic comedy. Source: Holman Francis Day, *Along Came Ruth, a Comedy in Three Acts* (New York, 1930). Jean François Fonson, *La Demoiselle de Magasin; comédie en trois actes.* Arriving in Action, Maine, Ruth Ambrose finds a room above the furniture store of Israel Hubbard, who is 4 months behind in his rent. When he leaves her in charge, she promotes sales, induces a lively business by dressing up the shop, and becomes romantically involved with the storekeeper's nephew, Allan. *Salesclerks. Furniture business. Maine.*

ALONG CAME YOUTH **F2.0103**

Paramount-Publix Corp. 20 Dec **1930** [c19 Dec 1930; LP1833]. Sd (Movietone); b&w. 35mm. 9 reels, 6,623 ft.

Dir Lloyd Corrigan, Norman McLeod. *Screenplay-Dial* George Marion, Jr. *Scen* Marion Dix. *Photog* Henry Gerrard. *Film Ed* Jane Loring. *Rec Engr* Harry M. Lindgren.

Cast: Charles Rogers *(Larry Brooks)*, Frances Dee *(Elinor Farrington)*, Stuart Erwin *(Ambrose)*, William Austin *(Eustace)*, Evelyn Hall *(Lady Prunella)*, Leo White *(Señor Cortés)*, Mathilde Comont *(Señora Cortés)*, Betty Boyd *(Sue Long)*, Arthur Hoyt *(Adkins)*, Sybil Grove *(maid)*, Herbert Sherwood *(doorman)*, Charles West *(chauffeur)*, Macon Jones, Billy Wheaton, George Ernest, Gordon Thorpe, John Strauss *(The Five Neetsfoot Boys)*.

Romantic comedy. Suggested by: Maurice Bedel, *Molinoff, Indre-et-Loire* (Paris, 1928). Larry Brooks, a young American sportsman stranded in London, takes a job as a sandwich man, advertising for a tailor shop, to keep himself alive, as does his buddy, former horsetrainer Ambrose. By accident he meets Elinor Farrington, daughter of an aristocratic but impoverished British family, and they fall in love. Later, Larry gets a job as chef in the Loamshire mansion of a wealthy South American, Señor Cortés, and his portly wife, with Ambrose as his assistant; learning that Elinor's family lives nearby, he pays them a visit, but thinking he is an imposter, Lady Prunella—her mother—orders him away. When Cortés goes away, Larry gains the good graces of the mistress with his desserts, actually prepared by other kitchen helpers, and she helps him regain his horse, Gangster. On the day of a steeplechase, Larry invites the local aristocrats to a hunt breakfast, but it is interrupted by the return of Señor Cortés, who brands his chef as an imposter; but he rides Gangster in the race, regains his fortune, and claims Elinor. *Sportsmen. Sandwich men. Horsetrainers. Aristocrats. Advertising. Impersonation. Courtship. Steeplechasing. England. Horses.*

THE ALTAR STAIRS **F2.0104**

Universal Film Manufacturing Co. 4 Dec **1922** [c13 Nov 1922; LP18414]. Si; b&w. 35mm. 5 reels, 4,641 ft.

Pres by Carl Laemmle. *Dir* Lambert Hillyer. *Scen? (see note)* George Hively, Doris Schroeder, George Randolph Chester. *Photog* Dwight Warren.

Cast: Frank Mayo *(Rod McLean)*, Louise Lorraine *(Joie Malet)*, Lawrence Hughes *(Tony Heritage)*, J. J. Lanoe *(Capt. Jean Malet)*, Harry De Vere *(Blundell)*, Hugh Thompson *(John Strickland)*, Boris Karloff *(Hugo)*, Dagmar Godowsky *(Parete)*, Nick De Ruiz *(Tulli)*.

Melodrama. Source: G. B. Lancaster, *The Altar Stairs* (New York, 1908). Though Rod McLean has rescued him from savages, Tony Heritage steals from Rod and goes to France, where he marries Joie Malet. Joie's father, Capt. Jean Malet, disapproves, however; takes her to a South Sea island; but is forced to employ Tony when he follows. Rod, who also works for Captain Malet, falls in love with Joie even though he knows she is married to some unknown man. Discovering that Tony is inciting the natives to burn the island's church and that he is Joie's husband, Rod pursues Tony and returns alone to marry Joie. *Theft. Churches. Incendiarism. South Sea Islands. France.*

Note: Some sources credit George Randolph Chester with the scenario, although Universal records give credit to George Hively and Doris Schroeder.

ALTARS OF DESIRE **F2.0105**

Metro-Goldwyn-Mayer Pictures. 5 Feb **1927** [c21 Dec 1926; LP23583]. Si; b&w. 35mm. 7 reels, 6,037 ft.

Dir William Christy Cabanne. *Titl* Ruth Cummings. *Adapt* Alice D. G. Miller, Agnes Christine Johnston. *Story* Maria Thompson Daviess. *Photog* William Daniels. *Sets* Cedric Gibbons, Arnold Gillespie. *Film Ed* George Hively. *Wardrobe* Kathleen Kay, Maude Marsh, André-ani.

Cast: Mae Murray *(Claire Sutherland)*, Conway Tearle *(David Elrod)*, Robert Edeson *(John Sutherland)*, Maude George *(Kitty Pryor)*, André Beranger *(Count André D'Orville)*.

Romantic drama. Claire Sutherland, an unsophisticated girl, is sent by her father to Paris to acquire some social polish; she returns with a bevy of fashionable clothes, some new ideas, and a Parisian count with whom she has become infatuated. Claire soon becomes interested, however, in young David Elrod because of his apparent indifference to her. When she discovers that the count is married, and realizes that her happiness actually lies with David, all ends happily. *Nobility. Fashion. Paris.*

ALWAYS RIDIN' TO WIN **F2.0106**

William Steiner Productions. Feb **1925** [c19 Dec 1924; LU20925]. Si; b&w. 35mm. 5 reels.

Dir Forrest Sheldon.

Cast: Pete Morrison.

Western melodrama. "... concerning the competition of two cattle towns to land the railroad terminal which is to be built. In the plotting the hero is falsely accused of horse-stealing, the villain posing as the hero. Things are straightened out when hero proves he is Hackamore by defeating Gus in a riding competition at the rodeo." (*Motion Picture News Booking Guide,* 8:9, Apr 1925.) *Horsethieves. Impersonation. Railroads. Rodeos.*

ALWAYS THE WOMAN **F2.0107**

Betty Compson Productions. *Dist* Goldwyn Distributing Corp. Jul **1922** [c22 Jul 1922; LP18333]. Si; b&w. 35mm. 6 reels, 5,462 ft.

Dir-Writ Arthur Rosson. *Story* Perley Poore Sheehan. *Photog* Ernest G. Palmer.

Cast: Betty Compson *(Celia Thaxter)*, Emory Johnson *(Herbert Boone)*, Doris Pawn *(Adele Boone)*, Gerald Pring *(Reginald Stanhope)*, Richard Rosson *(Mahmud)*, Arthur Delmore *(Gregory Gallup)*, Macey Harlam *(Kelim Pasha)*.

Romantic melodrama. A Cairo-bound steamer has among its passengers Reginald Stanhope, a wealthy playboy; vaudeville dancer Celia Thaxter and her manager, Gregory Gallup, who together are maneuvering Reginald into marrying Celia; Herbert Boone, a drug addict, and his nagging wife, Adele; Kelim Pasha, an Egyptian prince who attracts Adele's affections; and Mahmud, an Egyptian ascetic who insists that Celia and Boone are the reincarnations of the ancient Egyptian queen and priest who sacrificed themselves for their love and that he himself is the reincarnation of the priest who betrayed her. Upon their arrival, the group sets out across the desert in search of the queen's legendary treasure. Kelim Pasha discloses his evil designs on Celia and the treasure and brings the whole party under his power; Reginald admits that he is only an agent of Kelim Pasha, leaves for help, and dies; a rehabilitated Boone shows his love for Celia and tries to protect her. When they arrive at the queen's tomb, Mahmud reveals that there is no treasure but rather atonement for the queen; Kelim Pasha falls to his death in a pit; a grief-stricken Adele falls after him; and Celia and Boone are left free to pursue their happiness. *Royalty. Dancers. Reincarnation. Treasure. Narcotics. Egypt.*

AN AMATEUR DEVIL **F2.0108**

Famous Players–Lasky. *Dist* Paramount Pictures. Jan **1921** [12 Nov 1920; LP15799]. Si; b&w. 35mm. 5 reels, 4,464 ft.

Dir Maurice Campbell. *Scen* Douglas Bronston. *Story* Jessie Henderson, Henry J. Buxton. *Photog* H. Kinley Martin.

Cast: Bryant Washburn *(Carver Endicott)*, Charles Wingate *(his father)*, Ann May *(his sweetheart)*, Sidney Bracey *(his valet)*, Graham Pettie *(Farmer Brown)*, Christine Mayo *(Mrs. Brown)*, Norris Johnson *(her daughter)*.

Farce. Carver Endicott, a young sophisticate, is rejected by his fiancée for being too foppish and dull. When she feigns an interest in his father, Carver attempts to disgrace his family name by working as a farmhand and later as a busboy in a hotel. However, the newspapers only praise him for his self-sacrificing principles; and finding that he cannot bring shame to the family through menial labor, he takes up with a notorious actress. But when this maneuver also fails, he returns to his former fiancée, who has no further complaint about his being an inexperienced dullard. *Dandies. Actors. Busboys. Farmers. Hotels. Courtship.*

THE AMATEUR GENTLEMAN **F2.0109**

Inspiration Pictures. *Dist* First National Pictures. 15 Aug **1926** [New York premiere; released 29 Aug; c16 Aug 1926; LP23029]. Si; b&w. 35mm. 8 reels, 7,790 ft.

Dir Sidney Olcott. *Scen* Lillie Hayward. *Titl* Tom Miranda. *Photog* David W. Gobbett. *Sets* Tec-Art Studios. *Film Ed* Tom Miranda. *Film Cutter* Jeanne Spencer. *Tech Adv* Col. G. L. McDonell.

Cast: Richard Barthelmess *(Barnabas Barty)*, Dorothy Dunbar *(Lady Cleone Meredith)*, Gardner James *(Ronald Barrymaine)*, Nigel Barrie *(Sir Mortimer Carnaby)*, Brandon Hurst *(Peterby)*, John Miljan *(Viscount Devenham)*, Edwards Davis *(John Barty)*, Billie Bennett *(Duchess of Camberhurst)*, Herbert Grimwood *(Jasper Gaunt)*, Gino Corrado *(Prince Regent)*, Sidney De Gray *(Captain Chumley)*, John Peters *(Captain Slingsby)*.

Romantic costume drama. Source: Jeffery Farnol, *The Amateur Gentleman* (Boston, 1913). Barnabas Barty, the son of an innkeeper who was formerly a pugilist, inherits a fortune and sets out for London to become a gentleman. En route, he encounters Lady Cleone and falls madly in love with her, thus incurring the enmity of Sir Mortimer, his rival. In London he becomes friendly with Viscount Devenham and from him purchases a spirited horse, which he enters in a steeplechase. He meets Ronald, Cleone's derelict brother, and offers him money to repay his debts but is refused because of Mortimer's treachery. The steeplechase becomes a contest between Mortimer and Barnabas, the latter winning not only the race but also social standing. When Mortimer buys Ronald's notes and has the creditor threaten him with prison, Ronald kills the creditor in desperation; he then follows Barnabas to Mortimer's country house, where Ronald and Mortimer kill each other. Discouraged and disillusioned, Barnabas returns to his village home. Cleone follows him there, and they are united by love. *Nobility. Social classes. Inheritance. Steeplechasing. Murder. Debt. Great Britain—History—Regency. London.*

AMAZING LOVERS **F2.0110**

A. H. Fischer, Inc. *Dist* Jans Film Service. 15 Sep **1921.** Si; b&w. 35mm. 6 reels.

Dir B. A. Rolfe. *Story* Charles A. Logue.

Cast: Diana Allen, Marc MacDermott.

Crook melodrama. "Plot laid in America, the thread begins in Paris, where the Government is seeking to stop the influx of counterfeit notes which are being made in America. Agent of band is a beautiful French girl who negotiates deal with 'Master Mind' in America. Romance develops between the girl and one of our returned soldiers, who has personal grudge against a member of the band. Girl, later, proves to be Secret Service agent and marries the hero." (*Motion Picture News Booking Guide*, 2:12, Apr 1922.) *Bankers. Apaches—Paris. Secret service. Disguise. Counterfeiting. Murder. Paris.*

THE AMAZING VAGABOND **F2.0111**

FBO Pictures. *Dist* RKO Productions. 7 Apr **1929** [c7 Apr 1929; LP287]. Si; b&w. 35mm. 6 reels, 5,081 ft.

Dir Wallace W. Fox. *Story-Cont* Frank Howard Clark. *Titl* Helen Gregg. *Photog* Virgil Miller. *Film Ed* Della M. King.

Cast: Bob Steele *(Jimmy Hobbs)*, Tom Lingham *(George Hobbs)*, Jay Morley *(Bill Wharton)*, Perry Murdock *(Haywire)*, Lafe McKee *(Phil Dunning)*, Thelma Daniels *(Alice Dunning)*, Emily Gerdes *(Myrtle)*.

Western melodrama. Jimmy Hobbs, the son of a wealthy lumberman, has an unhealthy penchant for stunt flying and blondes. To teach the boy a lesson, his father has him abducted and taken to a lumber camp out west. Jimmy falls in love with the superintendent's daughter and uncovers a plot whereby the mill foreman is selling timber on the sly. *Fatherhood. Aviation. Theft. Abduction. Air stunts. Lumber camps.*

AMBUSHED **F2.0112**

Anchor Film Distributors. 28 Aug **1926** [New York State license]. Si; b&w. 35mm. 5 reels.

Cast: Bob Reeves.

Western melodrama(?). No information about the nature of this film has been found.

AMERICA **F2.0113**

D. W. Griffith, Inc. *Dist* United Artists. 21 Feb **1924** [New York premiere; released 15 Aug; c1 May 1924; LP20288]. Si; b&w. 35mm. 15 reels, 14,700 ft. [Copyrighted as 14 reels. Later cut to 13 reels, 12,600 ft, and then to 11 reels, 11,000 ft.]

Pres by D. W. Griffith. *Prod-Dir* D. W. Griffith. *Scen* John L. E. Pell. *Story* Robert W. Chambers. *Photog* G. W. Bitzer, Marcel Le Picard, Hendrik Sartov, Hal Sintzenich. *Art Dir* Charles M. Kirk. *Film Ed* Rose Smith, James Smith. *Mus Arr* Joseph Carl Breil. *Asst Dir* Herbert Sutch. *Construction Dir* William J. Bantel.

Cast: Neil Hamilton *(Nathan Holden)*, Erville Alderson *(Justice Montague)*, Carol Dempster *(Miss Nancy Montague)*, Charles Emmett Mack *(Charles Philip Edward Montague)*, Lee Beggs *(Samuel Adams)*, John Dunton *(John Hancock)*, Arthur Donaldson *(King George III)*, Charles Bennett *(William Pitt)*, Frank McGlynn, Jr. *(Patrick Henry)*, Frank Walsh *(Thomas Jefferson)*, Lionel Barrymore *(Capt. Walter Butler)*, Arthur Dewey *(George Washington)*, Sydney Deane *(Sir Ashley Montague)*, W. W. Jones *(General Gage)*, Harry O'Neill *(Paul Revere)*, Henry Van Bousen *(John Parker, Captain of Minutemen)*, Hugh Baird *(Major Pitcairn)*, James Milady *(Jonas Parker)*, Louis Wolheim *(Captain Hare)*, Riley Hatch *(Chief of Mohawks, Joseph Brant)*, Emil Hoch *(Lord North)*, Lucille La Verne *(A Refugee Mother)*, Downing Clarke *(Lord Chamberlain)*, P. R. Scammon *(Richard Henry Lee)*, Ed Roseman *(Captain Montour)*, Harry Semels *(Hikatoo, Chief of Senecas)*, H. Koser *(Colonel Prescott)*, Michael Donovan *(Major General Warren)*, Paul Doucet *(Marquis de Lafayette)*, W. Rising *(Edmund Burke)*, Daniel Carney *(personal servant of Miss Montague)*, E. Scanlon *(household servant at Ashley Court)*, Edwin Holland *(Major Strong)*, Milton Noble *(An Old Patriot)*.

Historical drama. The romance of Nathan Holden, a Boston patriot, with the aristocratic daughter of a Virginia Tory is set against the background of the Revolutionary War, showing the events that led to the conflict and terminating in the surrender at Yorktown. *United States—History—Revolution. Boston. Virginia. George Washington. Thomas Jefferson. George III (England). Samuel Adams. John Hancock. William (the Elder) Pitt. Patrick Henry.*

AMERICAN ARISTOCRACY (Reissue) **F2.0114**

Fine Arts Pictures. *Dist* Film Distributors League. 18 Sep **1921.** Si; b&w. 35mm. 5 reels.

Note: A Douglas Fairbanks film originally released by Triangle Film Corp. on 12 Nov 1916.

AMERICAN BEAUTY **F2.0115**

First National Pictures. 9 Oct **1927** [c21 Sep 1927; LP24431]. Si; b&w. 35mm. 7 reels, 6,333 ft.

Pres by Richard A. Rowland. *Prod-Scen* Carey Wilson. *Dir* Richard Wallace. *Titl* Robert Hopkins. *Photog* George Folsey.

Cast: Billie Dove *(Millicent Howard)*, Lloyd Hughes *(Jerry Booth)*, Walter McGrail *(Claverhouse)*, Margaret Livingston *(Mrs. Gillespie)*, Lucien Prival *(Gillespie)*, Al St. John *(waiter)*, Edythe Chapman *(Madame O'Riley)*, Alice White *(Claire O'Riley)*, Yola D'Avril *(telephone girl)*.

Romantic drama. Source: Wallace Irwin, "American Beauty," in *Saturday Evening Post* (199:16–17, 8 Jan 1927). Millicent Howard, a young girl of no means but of great beauty, keeps up an appearance of wealth by clever ruses, hoping to catch a millionaire husband, although she lives at a cheap boardinghouse with her mother. While she is being wooed by Jerry, a young chemist, Millicent meets Archibald Claverhouse, a wealthy young man who becomes infatuated with her and proposes marriage; but she is undecided which to choose. When she is invited to dinner by Claverhouse, Milly spoils her gown and decides to wear one owned by Mrs. Gillespie, sent to her mother's cleaning shop; but unfortunately the lady is present and denounces her for stealing the gown. Humiliated and defeated, Millicent admits her fakery to Claverhouse and goes home. There she finds that Jerry has accepted a job in South America, and she catches him after a mad dash to the station. *Chemists. Drycleaners. Appearances. Wealth. Boardinghouses. Laundries.*

AMERICAN MANNERS **F2.0116**

Richard Talmadge Productions. *For* Truart Film Corp. *Dist* Film Booking Offices of America. 24 Aug **1924** [c20 Aug 1924; LP20521]. Si; b&w. 35mm. 6 reels, 5,200 ft.

Pres by A. Carlos. *Dir* James W. Horne. *Scen* Frank Howard Clark. *Titl* Joseph W. Farnham. *Photog* William Marshall, Jack Stevens.

Cast: Richard Talmadge *(Roy Thomas)*, Mark Fenton *(Dan Thomas)*, Lee Shumway *(Clyde Harven)*, Helen Lynch *(Gloria Winthrop)*, Arthur Millett *(Conway, Secret Service)*, William Turner *(Jonas Winthrop)*, Pat Harmon *(Mike Barclay)*, George Warde *(Bud, The Waif)*.

Action melodrama. Returning to the United States from his studies in Paris, Roy Thomas assumes a new identity in order to catch smugglers operating from one of his father's boats. He joins the crew, and after a series of tremendous obstacles he overpowers the villain, Clyde Harven, clears his father's name, and wins the girl. *Filial relations. Secret service. Smuggling. Ships.*

AMERICAN PLUCK **F2.0117**

Chadwick Pictures. ca12 Sep **1925** [Houston premiere; released 15 Oct; c31 Oct 1925; LP21958]. Si; b&w. 35mm. 6 reels, 5,900 ft.

Pres by I. E. Chadwick. *Dir* Richard Stanton. *Scen-Titl* Ralph Spence. *Photog Eff* Lyman Broening.

Cast: George Walsh *(Blaze Derringer)*, Wanda Hawley *(Princess Alicia)*, Sidney De Grey *(Count Birkhaff)*, Frank Leigh *(Count Verensky)*, Tom Wilson *(Jefferson Lee)*, Leo White *(Lord Raleigh)*, Dan Mason *(American Consul)*.

Melodrama. Source: Eugene P. Lyle, Jr., *Blaze Derringer* (New York, 1910). Blaze Derringer, son of a wealthy cattle king, is sent out into the world by his father with the injunction not to return until he has earned $5,000. Blaze avails himself of the accommodations of a "side door pullman" and falls in with two hoboes, Lord Raleigh and Jefferson Lee. Lord Raleigh becomes his fight manager when Blaze engages in a prizefight with Hard Boiled Perry. He wins the bout but hits Perry so hard that doctors are required, and the mob turns on him. He escapes with the aid of Princess Alicia of Bargonia. The princess is on a diplomatic mission to raise funds to pay off Count Verensky, who is trying to force her into a marriage. Blaze returns with Alicia to Bargonia and wins her heart with his daring deeds. Verensky kidnaps her on the day of her coronation, but Blaze rescues her and Verensky is imprisoned. Blaze wins a wife and a throne. *Tramps. Prizefighters. Fight managers. Royalty. Imaginary kingdoms.*

THE AMERICAN VENUS **F2.0118**

Famous Players–Lasky. *Dist* Paramount Pictures. 25 Jan **1926** [c25 Jan 1926; LP22325]. Si; b&w with col sequences (Technicolor). 35mm. 8 reels, 7,931 ft.

Pres by Adolph Zukor, Jesse L. Lasky. *Dir* Frank Tuttle. *Scen* Frederick Stowers. *Story* Townsend Martin. *Photog* J. Roy Hunt. *Art Dir* Frederick A. Foord.

Cast: Esther Ralston *(Mary Gray)*, Lawrence Gray *(Chip Armstrong)*, Ford Sterling *(Hugo Niles)*, Fay Lanphier *(Miss Alabama)*, Louise Brooks *(Miss Bayport)*, Edna May Oliver *(Mrs. Niles)*, Kenneth MacKenna *(Horace Niles)*, William B. Mack *(John Gray)*, George De Carlton *(Sam Lorber)*, W. T. Benda *(artist)*, Ernest Torrence *(King Neptune)*, Douglas Fairbanks, Jr. *(Triton)*.

Comedy. Mary Gray, whose father manufactures cold cream, is engaged to sappy Horace Niles, the son of Hugo Niles, the elder Gray's most competitive rival in the cosmetics business. Chip Armstrong, a hot-shot public relations man, quits the employ of Hugo Niles and goes to work for Gray, persuading Mary to enter the Miss America contest at Atlantic City, with the intention of using her to endorse her father's cold cream should she win. Mary breaks her engagement with Horace. When it appears that she will win the contest, Hugo lures her home on the pretext that her father is ill, and she misses the contest. Chip and Mary return to Atlantic City, discovering that the new Miss America has told the world that she owes all her success to Gray's cold cream. On this note, Chip and Mary decide to get married. *Business competition. Beauty contests. Publicity. Cosmetics. Atlantic City.*

THE AMERICANO (Reissue) **F2.0119**

Fine Arts Pictures. *Dist* Tri-Stone Pictures. c21 Aug **1923** [LP19328]. Si; b&w. 35mm. 5 reels.

Note: A "re-edited and re-titled" Douglas Fairbanks film originally released by Triangle Film Corp. on 28 Jan 1917.

AMERICA'S BIGGEST CIRCUS **F2.0120**

Raymond Forest Bashford. c2 Nov **1925** [MU3223]. Si; b&w. 35mm. 6 reels.

Documentary. Records a performance of the Wallace and Hagenbeck Circus beginning with advance publicity, the arrival of the circus, a parade, and the assembling of the tents. Following the grand entry there are clowns, wire walkers, animals, trapeze performers, jugglers, more animals, wrestling, and specialty acts. *Circus. Wallace and Hagenbeck Circus.*

ANATOL *see* **THE AFFAIRS OF ANATOL**

THE ANCIENT HIGHWAY **F2.0121**

Famous Players–Lasky. *Dist* Paramount Pictures. 8 Nov **1925** [New York premiere; released 16 Nov; c16 Nov 1925; LP22006]. Si; b&w. 35mm. 7 reels, 6,034 ft.

Pres by Adolph Zukor, Jesse L. Lasky. *Dir* Irvin Willat. *Screenplay* James Shelley Hamilton, Eve Unsell. *Photog* Alfred Gilks.

Cast: Jack Holt *(Cliff Brant)*, Billie Dove *(Antoinette St. Ives)*, Montagu Love *(Ivan Hurd)*, Stanley Taylor *(Gaspard St. Ives)*, Lloyd Whitlock *(John Denis)*, William A. Carroll *(Ambrose)*, Marjorie Bonner *(Angel Fanchon)*, Christian J. Frank *(George Bolden)*.

Adventure melodrama. Source: James Oliver Curwood, *The Ancient Highway; a Novel of High Hearts and Open Roads* (New York, 1925). Clifton Brant, long thought dead, returns after adventuring around the world to his native town along the St. Lawrence River, Canada, to beat up millionaire Ivan Hurd, who cheated his father. Hurd sends the police after him, and Cliff takes to "The Ancient Highway." He meets and falls in love with Antoinette St. Ives, who is also being victimized by Hurd. Together they plan to thwart Hurd. Finally, after numerous adventures, Cliff dynamites the log jam caused by Hurd and effects his defeat. Cliff and Antoinette marry. *Millionaires. Filial relations. Lumbering. Revenge. Saint Lawrence River. Canada.*

THE ANCIENT MARINER **F2.0122**

Fox Film Corp. 27 Dec **1925** [c13 Dec 1925; LP22283]. Si; b&w. 35mm. 6 reels, 5,548 ft.

Pres by William Fox. *Dir* Henry Otto, Chester Bennett. *Titl* Tom Miranda. *Modern Story* Eve Unsell. *Photog* Joseph August. *Asst Dir* James Tinling.

Cast—Modern Sequences: Clara Bow *(Doris)*, Earle Williams *(Victor Brant)*, Leslie Fenton *(Joel Barlowe)*, Nigel De Brulier *(The Skipper)*.

Cast—Ancient Mariner Sequences: Paul Panzer *(The Mariner)*, Gladys Brockwell *(Life in Death)*, Robert Klein *(Death)*.

Fantasy-drama. Source: Samuel Taylor Coleridge, *The Rime of the Ancient Mariner* (London, 1857). Doris Matthews, a beautiful, innocent young girl, forsakes her sweetheart, Joel Barlowe, in favor of Victor Brant, a wealthy roué. On the night before they are to elope, an old sailor gives Brant a strange potion to drink and then unfolds before his eyes "The Rime of the Ancient Mariner." Deeply touched by this story about the consequences of the wanton destruction of innocent beauty, Brant leaves without Doris. After some time, he returns and finds to his pained satisfaction that Doris, having overcome her infatuation for him, has again turned her tender attentions toward Joel. *Sailors. Rakes. Infidelity. Supernatural.*

ANGEL CITIZENS **F2.0123**

William M. Smith Productions. *Dist* Merit Film Corp. Jul **1922.** Si; b&w. 35mm. 5 reels, 4,200 ft.

Dir Francis Ford. *Photog* Reginald Lyons.

Cast: Franklyn Farnum *(Frank Bartlett)*, Al Hart *(London Edwards)*, "Shorty" Hamilton *("Smoky" Nivette)*, Peggy O'Day *(Isabelle Bruner)*, Max Hoffman *(The Doctor)*, Terris Hoffman *(his wife)*, Smoky *(a horse)*.

Western melodrama. Source: William Patterson White, unidentified story in *Everybody's Magazine.* "Angel City is a misnomer. A gang of outlaws is largely in control and when Isabelle Bruner's father is mysteriously killed the sheriff decides to get busy. Frank Bartlett, an idler who could afford to be idle, appeared in town and took Isabelle to the country ball. In search of a new thrill, he decides to aid the sheriff, and the first thing he does is to scare away the would-be robbers of the stage coach. This is only the beginning of a dramatic career which ends in his bringing home the honors, and winning the girl." (*Moving Picture World,* 5 Aug 1922, p450.) *Idlers. Outlaws. Sheriffs. Murder. Stagecoach robberies. Horses.*

THE ANGEL OF BROADWAY **F2.0124**

De Mille Pictures. *Dist* Pathé Exchange. 3 Oct **1927** [c28 Sep 1927; LP24455]. Si; b&w. 35mm. 7 reels, 6,574 ft.

Pres by William Sistrom. *Dir* Lois Weber. *Story-Scen* Lenore J. Coffee. *Titl* John Krafft. *Photog* Arthur Miller. *Art Dir* Mitchell Leisen. *Film Ed* Harold McLernon. *Asst Dir* Fred Tyler. *Prod Mgr* Harry Poppe. *Cost* Adrian.

Cast: Leatrice Joy *(Babe Scott)*, Victor Varconi *(Jerry Wilson)*, May Robson *(Big Bertha)*, Alice Lake *(Goldie)*, Elsie Bartlett *(Gertie)*, Ivan Lebedeff *(Lonnie)*, Jane Keckley *(Captain Mary)*, Clarence Burton *(Herman)*.

Drama. Babe Scott, a cabaret dancer who is constantly searching for sensational material to shock her customers, conceives of burlesquing a Salvation Army girl and attends mission meetings on the East Side for atmosphere. There she meets Jerry Wilson, an honest truckdriver and friend of the Army captain. Although the act is a success, Babe is disillusioned to find Lonnie, a fellow worker who has been romancing her, stealing her money and making overtures to Big Bertha, the hard-boiled club hostess. Babe realizes the bad taste of her impersonation, and mutual recriminations follow when Jerry encounters her at the club; but when he finds Babe at the bedside of Gertie, a girl of the streets who, dying, seeks someone to pray for her, Jerry perceives her sincerity, and they are reunited. *Dancers. Truckdrivers. Prostitutes. Religion. Cabarets. New York City. Salvation Army.*

THE ANGEL OF CROOKED STREET **F2.0125**

Vitagraph Co. of America. 23 Apr **1922** [c4 Apr 1922; LP17723]. Si; b&w. 35mm. 5 reels, 5,280 ft.

Pres by Albert E. Smith. *Dir* David Smith. *Scen* C. Graham Baker. *Story* Harry Dittmar. *Photog* Stephen Smith, Jr.

Cast: Alice Calhoun *(Jennie Marsh)*, Ralph McCullough *(Schuyler Sanford)*, Scott McKee *("Silent" McKay)*, Rex Hammel *("Kid Glove" Thurston)*, William McCall *("Cap" Berry)*, Nellie Anderson *("Mother" De Vere)*, Martha Mattox *(Mrs. Phineas Sanford)*, Mary Young *(Mrs. Marsh)*, George Stanley *(Stoneham)*, Walter Cooper *(Dan Bolton)*.

Crook melodrama. Jennie Marsh, who works as a maid to support her mother, is escorted home from a dance by Dan Bolton. He robs the house of her employer, Mrs. Sanford, while she is making a call there, and unjustly accused of the theft, she is sent to a reformatory. When her mother dies, Jennie becomes embittered against the world and swears vengeance on the woman who treated her unjustly. Upon her release she goes to the city, where she is aided by "Silent" McKay, a burglar who takes her to Mother De Vere's boardinghouse, a hangout for criminals. There she meets young Sanford and plans to frame him for a robbery as her revenge. Eventually, she falls in love with young Sanford, relents when he is falsely accused of murder, and forgives his mother. *Housemaids. Robbery. Injustice. Revenge. Reformatories.*

ANIMAL CRACKERS **F2.0126**

Paramount-Publix Corp. 29 Aug **1930** [New York opening; released 6 Sep; c6 Sep 1930; LP1546]. Sd (Movietone); b&w. 35mm. 10 reels, 8,897 ft.

Dir Victor Heerman. *Screenplay* Morris Ryskind. *Cont* Pierre Collings. *Photog* George Folsey. *Songs: "Why Am I So Romantic?" "Hooray for Captain Spalding"* Bert Kalmar, Harry Ruby. *Song: "Collegiate"* Moe Jaffe, Nat Bonx. *Song: "Some of These Days"* Sheldon Brooks. *Mus Arr* John W. Green. *Rec Engr* Ernest F. Zatorsky.

Cast: Groucho Marx *(Capt. Jeffrey Spaulding)*, Harpo Marx *(professor)*, Chico Marx *(Signor Emanuel Ravelli)*, Zeppo Marx *(Horatio Jamison)*, Lillian Roth *(Arabella Rittenhouse)*, Margaret Dumont *(Mrs. Rittenhouse)*, Louis Sorin *(Roscoe Chandler)*, Hal Thompson *(John Parker)*, Margaret Irving *(Mrs. Whitehead)*, Kathryn Reece *(Grace Carpenter)*, Richard Greig *(Hives)*, Edward Metcalf *(Hennessey)*, The Music Masters *(Six Footmen)*.

Farce. Source: George S. Kaufman, Bert Kalmar, Morris Ryskind and Harry Ruby, *Animal Crackers* (New York opening: 23 Oct 1928). At the estate of Mrs. Rittenhouse, Jeffrey Spaulding, an African explorer, and Horatio, his secretary, become social lions at a house party in progress; and on their heels are the professor and Signor Ravelli, musicians. Arabella, the hostess' daughter, is in love with John Parker, an unknown artist; and Roscoe Chandler, an art connoisseur, arrives with a valuable master painting, of which John had made a pastiche while a student. Arabella persuades the musicians to substitute the copy for the original, and recognizing the art patron as a former fish peddler, they blackmail him. But a rival society matron, whose daughter has copied the same painting, plots a similar substitution to embarrass Mrs. Rittenhouse. Later, during a thunderstorm, the musicians steal the painting, but Hives, the butler, replaces it with the other pastiche, and at the unveiling the plot is exposed. *Explorers. Secretaries. Musicians. Artists. Socialites. Butlers. Peddlers. Blackmail. Paintings.*

ANKLES PREFERRED **F2.0127**

Fox Film Corp. 27 Feb **1927** [c27 Feb 1927; LP23756]. Si; b&w. 35mm. 6 reels, 5,498 ft.

Pres by William Fox. *Dir* J. G. Blystone. *Scen* James Shelley Hamilton. *Story* Kenneth Hawks, J. G. Blystone, Philip Klein. *Photog* Glen MacWilliams. *Asst Dir* Jasper Blystone.

Cast: Madge Bellamy *(Nora)*, Lawrence Gray *(Barney)*, Barry Norton *(Jimmy)*, Allan Forrest *(Hornsbee)*, Marjorie Beebe *(Flo)*, J. Farrell MacDonald *(McGuire)*, Joyce Compton *(Virginia)*, William Strauss *(Mr. Goldberg)*, Lillian Elliott *(Mrs. Goldberg)*, Mary Foy *(Mrs. McGuire)*.

Comedy-drama. Nora, a department store clerk, is determined to succeed on the basis of her brain power despite her attractive ankles. She gets a job as model at the shop of McGuire and Goldberg, and they announce that Nora may be given a trip abroad if she persuades their financer to lend the partners additional funds. The financer, Hornsbee, becomes presumptuous, leading to an encounter between him and Barney, Nora's young suitor; and she is ultimately glad to accept Barney's modest attentions. *Salesclerks. Fashion models. Modistes. Millionaires. Department stores.*

ANNA ASCENDS **F2.0128**

Famous Players–Lasky. *Dist* Paramount Pictures. 19 Nov **1922** [c20 Nov 1922; LP18598]. Si; b&w. 35mm. 6 reels, 5,959 ft.

Pres by Adolph Zukor. *Dir* Victor Fleming. *Scen* Margaret Turnbull. *Photog* Gilbert Warrenton.

Cast: Alice Brady *(Anna Ayyob)*, Robert Ellis *(Howard Fisk)*, David Powell *(The Baron)*, Nita Naldi *(Countess Rostoff)*, Charles Gerrard *(Count Rostoff)*, Edward Durand *(Siad Coury)*, Florence Dixon *(Bessie Fisk)*, Grace Griswold *(Miss Fisk)*, Frederick Burton *(Mr. Fisk)*.

Melodrama. Source: Harry Chapman Ford, *Anna Ascends* (New York opening: 22 Sep 1920). While working in a coffeehouse, Syrian immigrant Anna Ayyob falls in love with Howard Fisk and discovers that her employer ("The Baron") is involved with Count and Countess Rostoff in smuggling jewels. Anna has an encounter with the baron and, thinking she has killed him, disappears. Later, after writing a widely popular novel, Anna again meets Howard and, to save Howard's sister from marrying Count Rostoff, exposes the count and confesses to the baron's murder. Investigation discloses the baron to be alive; Anna and Howard marry. *Syrians. Immigrants. Novelists. Nobility. Brother-sister relationship. Murder. Smuggling. Coffeehouses.*

ANNA CHRISTIE **F2.0129**

Thomas H. Ince Corp. *Dist* Associated First National Pictures. 28 Nov **1923** [New York showing; released 3 Dec 1923; c26 Nov 1923; LP19652]. Si; b&w. 35mm. 8 reels, 7,631 ft.

Pres by Thomas H. Ince. *Dir* John Griffith Wray. *Scen* Bradley King. *Photog* Henry Sharp.

Cast: Blanche Sweet *(Anna Christie)*, William Russell *(Matt Burke)*, George F. Marion *("Chris" Christopherson)*, Eugenie Besserer *(Marthy)*, Ralph Yearsley *(The Brutal Cousin)*, Chester Conklin *(Tommy)*, George Siegmann *(Anna's uncle)*, Victor Potel, Fred Kohler.

Melodrama. Source: Eugene Gladstone O'Neill, *Anna Christie* (New York opening: 1922). Chris Christopherson, an old skipper, is determined to keep his daughter, Anna, away from the sea. Brought up by cousins on a farm in Minnesota, Anna is treated badly by her relatives, and she runs away to Chicago where she soon becomes a streetwalker. Anna visits her father in New York City, hoping he will provide the peace and shelter she needs. The old man, ignorant of her previous life, invites Anna to live on the coal barge he commands. During one trip Anna meets a sailor and, to her father's regret, falls in love. The two men argue Anna's future. Finally, Anna reveals her past life and both men, angry and hurt, leave—to return several days later for a reconciliation. *Prostitutes. Sea captains. Sailors. Seafaring life. Barges. Waterfront. Chicago. New York City.*

ANNA CHRISTIE **F2.0130**

Metro-Goldwyn-Mayer Pictures. 21 Feb **1930** [c10 Feb 1930; LP1062]. Sd (Movietone); b&w. 35mm. 10 reels, 6,700 ft. [Also si.]

Dir Clarence Brown. *Adtl Dir (see note)* Jacques Feyder. *Titl* Madeleine Ruthven. *Adapt* Frances Marion. *Photog* William Daniels. *Art Dir* Cedric Gibbons. *Film Ed* Hugh Wynn. *Rec Engr* G. A. Burns, Douglas Shearer. *Gowns* Adrian.

Cast: Greta Garbo *(Anna)*, Charles Bickford *(Matt)*, George F. Marion *(Chris)*, Marie Dressler *(Marthy)*, James T. Mack *(Johnny the Harp)*, Lee Phelps *(Larry)*.

Drama. Source: Eugene Gladstone O'Neill, *Anna Christie* (New York opening: 1922). Anna Christie was a child relegated by her sailor father to cruel relatives on a farm. Finally leaving the place as a young woman, Anna fends for herself as a prostitute until she decides it is time to go to her father. After taking care of him on his barge and becoming fond of him, they take in a young seaman named Matt, who falls in love with Anna. Unable to keep her previous life a secret any longer, Anna confesses her actions, whereupon Matt leaves her. He returns, however, knowing that he cannot live without her, and after affirming her love by oath on a cross, Anna is content with the prospect of becoming a sailor's wife. *Prostitutes. Sea captains. Sailors. Seafaring life. Waterfront. Barges. Chicago. New York City.*

Note: Swedish and German versions were directed by Jacques Feyder. For additional information on the German version, see separate entry.

ANNA CHRISTIE **F2.0131**

Metro-Goldwyn-Mayer Pictures. **1930.** Sd; b&w. 35mm. 10 reels.

Dir Jacques Feyder.

Cast: Greta Garbo *(Anna Christie)*, Hans Junkermann *(Matt)*, Salka Viertel *(Marthy)*, Theo Shall *(Chris)*.

Drama. Source: Eugene Gladstone O'Neill, *Anna Christie* (New York opening: 1922). German-language version of the 1930 *Anna Christie*, q. v. *Prostitutes. Sea captains. Sailors. Seafaring life. Waterfront. Barges. Chicago. New York City.*

ANNABEL LEE **F2.0132**

Joe Mitchell Chopple. *Dist* Joan Film Sales. **1921.** Si; b&w. 35mm. 5 reels, 4,800 ft.

Dir William J. Scully. *Scen* Arthur Brilliant.

Cast: Jack O'Brien *(David Martin)*, Lorraine Harding *(Annabel Lee)*, Florida Kingsley *(Mother Martin)*, Louis Stearns *(Colonel Lee)*, Ben Grauer *(David Martin, as a child)*, Arline Blackburn *(Annabel Lee, as a child)*, Ernest Hilliard *(David Grainger)*.

Romantic drama. Inspired by: Edgar Allan Poe, "Annabel Lee." Wealthy Colonel Lee disapproves of marriage between his daughter, Annabel, and David Martin, a young village fisherman, but he agrees to the match if David goes away for a year and their love remains true. En route to the South Seas in search of sunken treasure, David and his friend, the Chinese cook, are set off their ship by a mutinous crew. David survives on a desert island, finally hails a passing ship, and returns home to find Annabel waiting for him. *Fishermen. Chinese. Treasure. Courtship. Mutiny. South Seas.*

ANNAPOLIS **F2.0133**

Pathé Exchange. 18 Nov **1928** [c18 Oct 1928; LP25725]. Sd eff & mus score (Photophone); b&w. 35mm. 8 reels, 7,957 ft. [Also si; 7,008 ft.]

Prod-Writ F. McGrew Willis. *Dir* Christy Cabanne. *Titl* John Krafft. *Story* Royal S. Pease. *Photog* Arthur Miller. *Art Dir* Edward Jewell. *Film Ed* Claude Berkeley. *Song: "My Annapolis and You"* Charles Weinberg, Irving Bibo. *Asst Dir* Fred Tyler.

Cast: John Mack Brown *(Bill)*, Hugh Allan *(Herbert)*, Jeanette Loff *(Betty)*, Maurice Ryan *(Fat)*, William Bakewell *(Skippy)*, Byron Munson *(first classman)*, Charlotte Walker *(aunt)*, Hobart Bosworth *(father)*.

Drama. After an initial period of hostility, Bill and Herbert, classmates at the United States Naval Academy, become the best of friends. When Herbert is confined to quarters for dereliction of duty, Bill falls in love with Herbert's fiancée, Betty, who has arrived in Annapolis for the Commencement Ball. Learning of the flirtation, Herbert goes off limits and quarrels with Betty. He returns to base that night and slugs a guard; Bill is unjustly blamed for the assault and ordered to face a court-martial. Herbert confesses to the crime, however, and Bill is free to find happiness with Betty. *Courts-martial. United States Naval Academy.*

ANNE AGAINST THE WORLD (Famous Authors) **F2.0134**

Trem Carr Productions. *Dist* Rayart Pictures. 11 Apr or 1 May **1929.** Si; b&w. 35mm. 6 reels, 5,731 ft.

Dir Duke Worne. *Scen* Arthur Hoerl. *Photog* Hap Depew. *Film Ed* J. S. Harrington.

Cast: Shirley Mason *(Anne)*, Jack Mower *(John Forbes)*, James Bradbury, Jr. *(Eddie)*, Billy Franey, Isabelle Keith *(Teddy)*, Belle Stoddard, Tom Curran *(Emmett)*, Henry Roquemore *(Folmer)*.

Drama. Source: Victor Thorne, *Anne Against the World* (New York, 1925). Surrounded by admirers and pursued by a despicable producer, Anne, a musical comedy star, easily falls for John Forbes, who is tall, handsome, and rolling in wealth. They are married; but the producer will not leave Anne alone, and John tests her by pretending that he is only a penniless namesake of John Forbes. Anne waivers and returns to the old life; but true love triumphs, and the couple are reconciled. *Dancers. Theatrical producers. Wealth. Marriage. Musical revues.*

ANNE OF LITTLE SMOKY **F2.0135**

Wistaria Productions. *Dist* Playgoers Pictures. 20 Nov **1921** [c6 Dec 1921; LU17300]. Si; b&w. 35mm. 5 reels, 5,000 ft.

Dir-Story Edward Connor. *Scen* Frank Beresford. *Photog* John S. Stumar.

Cast: Winifred Westover *(Anne)*, Dolores Cassinelli *(Gita)*, Joe King *(Bob Hayne)*, Frank Hagney *(Ed Brockton)*, Ralph Faulkner *(Tom Brockton)*, Harold Callahan *(Buddy)*, Alice Chapin *(Mrs. Brockton)*, Frank Sheridan *("The" Brockton)*, Edward Roseman *(Sam Ward)*.

Rural melodrama. The Brocktons claim the Little Smoky region as their own when the Government turns it into a forest and game preserve and challenges their rights to use the area as they please. Bob Hayne, a forest ranger, loves Anne, daughter of the Brockton clan leader; but Anne is jealous when Bob defends Gita, a Gypsy princess, from unwelcome attentions and when the Gypsy later saves his life. Bob arrests Anne's father for breaking the game laws, but Brockton is acquitted when Anne steals the evidence. In a row following the trial, Bob is trailed by hounds when he is believed to have killed Ed Brockton. Anne dresses in Bob's clothes to mislead the hounds, and during a storm she finds Ed alive in Bob's cabin. Tom, Anne's brother who was shell-shocked in France, saves the Gypsy, whom he loves, from a renegade Indian, and both couples are happily united. *Mountaineers. Forest rangers. Gypsies. Indians of North America. Veterans. Brother-sister relationship. Land rights. Game preserves.*

ANNIE LAURIE **F2.0136**

Metro-Goldwyn-Mayer Pictures. 11 May **1927** [New York premiere; released 17 Sep; c27 May 1927; LP24122]. Si; b&w. 35mm. 9 reels, 8,730 ft.

Dir John S. Robertson. *Story-Scen* Josephine Lovett. *Titl* Marian Ainslee, Ruth Cummings. *Photog* Oliver Marsh. *Art Dir* Cedric Gibbons, Merrill Pye. *Film Ed* William Hamilton. *Wardrobe* André-ani.

Cast: Lillian Gish *(Annie Laurie)*, Norman Kerry *(Ian MacDonald)*, Creighton Hale *(Donald)*, Joseph Striker *(Alastair)*, Hobart Bosworth *(The MacDonald Chieftain)*, Patricia Avery *(Enid)*, Russell Simpson *(Sandy)*, Brandon Hurst *(The Campbell Chieftain)*, David Torrence *(Sir Robert Laurie)*, Frank Currier *(Cameron of Lochiel)*.

Romantic melodrama. In the Scottish highlands where the MacDonald and Campbell clans are constantly feuding, the body of a MacDonald is sent to the enemy chieftain; that night, the MacDonalds raid the Campbell grounds. Alastair captures Enid, daughter of the Campbell chieftain, and when a truce is declared she decides to remain with her new husband. The King of England attempts to end the clan warfare by peace treaties. Meanwhile, Ian MacDonald begins to court Annie Laurie, the governor's daughter, who has a natural preference for the more refined Donald Campbell. The MacDonalds are tricked into housing Campbell troops, and the bridge to the beacon light is destroyed. Annie gives her aid in lighting the beacon, thus siding with Ian and the MacDonalds, who take revenge on their enemies. *Feuds. Courtship. Scotland.*

ANOTHER MAN'S BOOTS **F2.0137**

Ivor McFadden Productions. *Dist* Anchor Film Distributors. 1 Sep **1922.** Si; b&w. 35mm. 5 reels, 4,587 ft.

Dir William J. Craft. *Story* Daniel F. Whitcomb. *Photog* Edward Estabrook.

Cast: Francis Ford *("The Stranger")*, Harry Smith *(Ned Hadley)*, Elvira Weil *(Nell Hadley)*, Frank Lanning *("Injun Jim")*, Robert Kortman *("Sly" Stevens)*.

Western melodrama. The Stranger complies with the request of his friend, Ned Hadley, to assume the latter's identity when he is badly wounded by outlaws. Accepted by Ned's blind father and his sister, Nell, The Stranger's ruse is successful until Sly Stevens, who has designs on Mr. Hadley's property, accuses "Ned" of being an imposter and has him charged with murder. The real Ned's arrival saves The Stranger from the gallows and allows him to pursue his interest in Nell. *Strangers. Imposture. Blindness. Murder.*

ANOTHER MAN'S SHOES **F2.0138**

Universal Film Manufacturing Co. 6 Nov **1922** [c18 Oct 1922; LP18339]. Si; b&w. 35mm. 5 reels, 4,251 ft.

Pres by Carl Laemmle. *Dir* Jack Conway. *Scen? (see note)* Victor Bridges, Raymond L. Schrock, Arthur F. Statter. *Photog* Ben Reynolds.

Cast: Herbert Rawlinson *(Stuart Granger/Jack Burton)*, Barbara Bedford *(Mercia Solano)*, Una Trevelyn *(Grace Burton)*, Nick De Ruiz *(Ropal)*, Josef Swickard *(Gouret)*, Jean De Briac *(John Alvara)*, Harry Carter *(Lawrence)*, Nelson McDowell *(Milford)*, Lillian Langdon *(Mrs. Chetwell)*, Jessie Deparnette *(duenna)*.

Comedy-melodrama. Source: Victor Bridges, *Another Man's Shoes* (New York, 1913). To evade a gang conspiring to assassinate him, wealthy businessman Stuart Granger induces his unsuspecting cousin, Jack Burton, to impersonate him. Jack survives several attempts on his life, gradually realizes what is happening, and falls in love with Mercia Solano, the leader of the gang. Stuart, however, is killed, and Mercia is happy to learn Jack's identity. *Businessmen. Cousins. Gangs. Impersonation.*

Note: Most sources give Arthur F. Statter credit for scenario, Universal records name Bridges and Schrock.

ANOTHER MAN'S WIFE **F2.0139**

Regal Pictures. *Dist* Producers Distributing Corp. 7 Sep **1924** [c20 Jun 1924; LP20333]. Si; b&w. 35mm. 5 reels, 5,015 ft.

Dir Bruce Mitchell. *Story* Bruce Mitchell, Elliott Clawson. *Photog* Steve Norton.

Cast: James Kirkwood *(John Brand)*, Lila Lee *(Helen Brand)*, Wallace Beery *(Captain Wolf)*, Matt Moore *(Phillip Cockran)*, Zena Keefe *(dancer)*, Chester Conklin *(rumrunner)*.

Society melodrama. Pursued by her vengeful husband when she is kidnaped, Helen Brand finds herself deserted in Mazatlán, aboard a ship. The injured husband is taken aboard the same boat, which sinks in a collision with a rumrunner's craft; on the other craft there is a reconciliation, following a fight between the captain and the husband for his wife. *Rumrunners. Kidnaping. Ships. Mazatlán (Mexico).*

ANOTHER SCANDAL **F2.0140**

Tilford Cinema Corp. *Dist* W. W. Hodkinson Corp. 22 Jun **1924** [c22 Jun 1924; LP20416]. Si; b&w. 35mm. 8 reels, 7,322 ft.

Dir Edward H. Griffith. *Adapt* G. Marion Burton. *Photog* Dal Clawson.

Cast: Lois Wilson *(Beatrix Franklin)*, Herbert Holmes *(Pelham Franklin)*, Ralph Bunker *(Malcolm Fraser)*, Flora Le Breton *(May Beamish)*, Ralph W. Chambers *(Valentine Beamish)*, Hedda Hopper *(Elizabeth MacKenzie)*, Zeffie Tilbury *(Brownie)*, Bigelow Cooper *(Mitchell Burrows)*, Allan Simpson *(Alec Greenwood)*, Harry Grippe *('Arry 'Arris)*.

Society drama. Source: Cosmo Hamilton, *Another Scandal* (Boston, 1924). Beatrix Franklin, about to become a mother, is persuaded to send her husband on a cruise. There he meets May Beamish, who tries, unsuccessfully, to capture him. Piqued at hearing of the attentions paid him, the wife provokes a quarrel and separation by staying out with Alec Greenwood, a former admirer. The vamp seeks to force the husband to a divorce, but she is outsmarted by Beatrix. *Vamps. Pregnancy. Marriage. Divorce.*

ANY NIGHT **F2.0141**

Amalgamated Producing Corp. *Dist* East Coast Productions. Jan **1922.** Si; b&w. 35mm. 5 reels, 4,500 ft.

Supv G. M Anderson. *Dir* Martin Beck. *Photog* Arthur Reeves. *Tech Dir* George Cleethorpe. *Film Ed* Walter A. Rivers.

Cast: Tully Marshall *(Jerry Maguire, "The Weasel")*, Robert Edeson *(Jim Barton?)*, Lila Leslie *(Mrs. Ann Barton)*, Gordon Sackville *(Rev. John Matthew)*, William Courtleigh *(Dr. LeRoy Clifford)*.

Melodrama. Mrs. Ann Barton, a former smalltime criminal, has reformed in order to bring up her son as a fine, honest boy. Her husband, however, is persuaded by "The Weasel" to remain on the crooked path. The two men set off to rob slum doctor LeRoy Clifford's wife of her jewels, but at the doctor's home the two see Barton's boy critically injured after an automobile accident. Jim Barton decides then that he will go straight if the boy lives. His son recovers, and he and his wife reunite with the prospect of an honest life before them. *Thieves. Physicians. Criminals—Rehabilitation. Automobile accidents.*

ANY WIFE **F2.0142**

Fox Film Corp. 1 Jan **1922** [c1 Jan 1922; LP17464]. Si; b&w. 35mm. 5 reels, 4,597 ft.

Pres by William Fox. *Dir* Herbert Brenon. *Story-Scen* Julia Tolsva. *Photog* Tom Malloy.

Cast: Pearl White *(Mrs. John Hill [Myrtle])*, Holmes Herbert *(Philip Gray)*, Gilbert Emery *(Mr. John Hill)*, Lawrence Johnson *(Cyril Hill)*, Augustus Balfour *(Dr. Gaynor)*, Eulalie Jensen *(Louise Farrata)*.

Domestic melodrama. *Growing discontented with the routine of married life and household duties, Myrtle declines her husband's invitation to accompany him on a business trip, and during his absence she accepts the attentions of Philip Gray, her husband's business assistant. Returning unexpectedly, Hill witnesses a love scene between Myrtle and Gray; justly indignant, Hill gets a divorce. Myrtle marries her lover, but when the marriage is a failure Myrtle in desperation commits suicide by drowning.* ... Awakening from this dream, Myrtle is freed from her unhappiness, resolves to devote herself to her husband, and goes on the trip with him as he has desired. *Marriage. Infidelity. Divorce. Suicide. Dreams.*

ANY WOMAN **F2.0143**

Famous Players–Lasky. *Dist* Paramount Pictures. 4 May **1925** [c8 May 1925; LP21441]. Si; b&w. 35mm. 6 reels, 5,963 ft.

Pres by Robert Kane. *Dir* Henry King. *Scen* Jules Furthman, Beatrice Van. *Story* Arthur Somers Roche. *Photog* Ernest Hallor, William Schurr.

Cast: Alice Terry *(Ellen Linden)*, Ernest Gillen *(Tom Galloway)*, Margarita Fisher *(Mrs. Rand)*, Lawson Butt *(James Rand)*, Aggie Herring *(Mrs. Galloway)*, James Neill *(William Linden)*, De Sacia Mooers *(Mrs. Phillips)*, Henry Kolker *(Egbert Phillips)*, Thelma Morgan *(Alice Cartwright)*, George Periolat *(Robert Cartwright)*, Lucille Hutton *(Agnes Young)*, Arthur Hoyt *(Jones)*, Malcolm Denny *(Lord Brackenridge)*.

Drama. Ellen Linden returns home from finishing school and discovers that her father has lost his fortune; she is forced to find a job and becomes a secretary in the brokerage firm of Phillips and Rand. Both men are attracted to her: Phillips makes rough advances, and Rand flatters her. Ellen falls in love with Tom Galloway, inventor of a soft drink called 'Here's How" in which Ellen attempts to interest the brokers. Phillips later tricks Ellen into spending the night on Rand's yacht, but Mrs. Rand sees to it that Galloway leaves by boat for Hawaii. Ellen is reunited with Galloway on the high seas; Rand agrees to back Galloway's soft drink as his wedding present to the reconciled couple. *Inventors. Brokers. Secretaries. Soft drinks.*

ANY WOMAN'S MAN *see* **WOMEN MEN LIKE**

ANYBODY HERE SEEN KELLY? **F2.0144**

Universal Pictures. 9 Sep **1928** [c13 Apr 1928; LP25163]. Si; b&w. 35mm. 6 or 7 reels, 6,243 ft.

Dir William Wyler. *Scen* John B. Clymer. *Titl* Walter Anthony, Albert De Mond. *Adapt? (see note)* Joseph Franklin Poland, James Gruen, John B. Clymer, Rob Wagner, Earl Snell, Samuel M. Pike. *Story* Leigh Jason. *Photog* Charles Stumar. *Film Ed* George McGuire.

Cast: Bessie Love *(Mitzi Lavelle)*, Tom Moore *(Pat Kelly)*, Kate Price *(Mrs. O'Grady)*, Addie McPhail *(Mrs. Hickson)*, Bruce Gordon *(Mr. Hickson)*, Alfred Allen *(Sergeant Malloy)*, Tom O'Brien *(Buck Johnson)*, Wilson Benge *(butler)*, Rosa Gore *(French mother)*, Dorothea Wolbert *(slavey)*.

Comedy-drama. Mitzi Lavelle, in love with carefree Pat Kelly, a member of the A. E. F. in France, follows him to America as a stewardess on a liner. Arriving in New York, Mitzi is met by Buck Johnson, once a rival for her hand, now a customs official. He promises to extend her leave if she will spend it with him. Mitzi rejects him, finds Kelly directing traffic at 42d Street and Broadway (where he is stationed as a traffic policeman), and proceeds to settle down with him. Johnson attempts to have Mitzi deported while Kelly is held in jail for assaulting the customs official. Assisted by an Irish sergeant, Kelly claims Mitzi before the ship departs and marries her, thus forever thwarting Johnson's intentions to eject her. *Customs officers. Police. Immigration. Deportation. World War I. France. American Expeditionary Force.*

Note: The following were not given screen credit for adaptation: Joseph Franklin Poland, James Gruen, John B. Clymer, Rob Wagner, Earl Snell, and Samuel M. Pike.

ANYBODY'S WAR **F2.0145**

Paramount-Publix Corp. 10 Jul **1930** [New York opening; released 2 Aug; cl Aug 1930; LP1460]. Sd (Movietone); b&w. 35mm. 10 reels, 8,120 ft.

Dir Richard Wallace. *Screenplay* Lloyd Corrigan. *Adtl Dial* Walter Weems. *Adapt* Hector Turnbull. *Photog* Allen Siegler. *Film Ed* Otto Levering. *Rec Engr* M. M. Paggi.

Cast: George Moran *(Willie)*, Charles E. Mack *(Amos Crow)*, Joan Peers *(Mary Jane Robinson)*, Neil Hamilton *(Ted Reinhardt)*, Walter Weems *(Sergeant Skipp)*, Betty Farrington *(Camilla)*, Walter McGrail *(Captain Davis)*.

Comedy. Source: Charles E. Mack, *The Two Black Crows in the A. E. F.* (Indianapolis, 1928). At the time of the United States' entry into the European conflict, Amos Crow is dogcatcher in the little river town of Buford, Tennessee, and is so kind-hearted that he boards all his captive canines rather than kill them. His pal, Willie, decides to join his friends who have enlisted after being chided for their lack of patriotism by Camilla, cook in the home of Mary Jane Robinson, daughter of an aristocratic family. Amos is rejected by the Army because of his feet but manages to get in line with recruits bound for France, along with his dog, Deep Stuff. At a camp in France, Mary Jane, now a Y. M. C. A. hostess, breaks off with Captain Davis, who is unmasked as a German spy, and Amos and Willie promise to find Ted for her. In rescuing Ted from a dugout, they learn of a surprise attack and send Deep Stuff back with a message, but he is missing upon their return—after the war, he returns with a dachshund "war bride" and six pups. *Dogcatchers. Negroes. Soldiers. Spies. Courtship. World War I. Tennessee. France. United States Army. Young Men's Christian Association.*

ANYBODY'S WOMAN **F2.0146**

Paramount-Publix Corp. 15 Aug **1930** [New York premiere; released 30 Aug; c31 Aug 1930; LP1531]. Sd (Movietone); b&w. 35mm. 9 reels, 7,243 ft.

Dir Dorothy Arzner. *Screenplay* Zoë Akins, Doris Anderson. *Dial* Zoë Akins. *Photog* Charles Lang. *Film Ed* Jane Loring. *Rec Engr* J. A. Goodrich.

Cast: Ruth Chatterton *(Pansy Gray)*, Clive Brook *(Neil Dunlap)*, Paul Lukas *(Gustav Saxon)*, Huntly Gordon *(Grant Crosby)*, Virginia Hammond *(Katherine Malcolm)*, Tom Patricola *(Eddie Calcio)*, Juliette Compton *(Ellen)*, Cecil Cunningham *(Dot)*, Charles Gerrard *(Walter Harvey)*, Harvey Clark *(Mr. Tanner)*, Sidney Bracy *(butler)*, Gertrude Sutton *(maid)*.

Society melodrama. Source: Gouverneur Morris, "The Better Wife" (publication undetermined). Showgirl Pansy Gray, who ekes out an existence with the help of Dot, another chorus girl, is aided by lawyer Gustav Saxon when she is arrested for indecent exposure and is defended by attorney Neil Dunlap. Later, Dunlap's wife deserts him for another man, and he goes on a prolonged drinking binge. At the apartment of his friend Eddie Calcio they see Pansy and Dot, *en déshabillé*, across the courtyard, and invite them over for a party. Not remembering her, Neil perceives in Pansy a wistful charm, and the next morning he awakens to find they were married the night before; resigned to the situation, he allows her to live with him. His business friends desert him, and he continues drinking heavily; under Pansy's care he is again successful, but when Saxon tries to seduce her and she resists, Neil is indignant at her offending his client. She leaves him and goes away with Saxon, but eventually she returns to Neil and their mutual love is reaffirmed. *Showgirls. Lawyers. Drunkenness. Indecent exposure. Seduction. Marriage.*

ANYTHING ONCE **F2.0147**

Classplay Picture Corp. *Dist* Aywon Film Corp. 21 Jun **1925**. Si; b&w. 35mm. 5 reels, 4,900 ft.

Prod Jack Weinberg. *Dir? (see note)* James McHenry, Justin H. McCloskey. *Scen* Harry Chandlee. *Story* Nate H. Edwards. *Photog* Charles Murphy.

Cast: Tully Marshall, Gladys Walton, Harold Austin, Mathilde Brundage, Francis McDonald, Arko *(a dog)*.

Comedy-drama. A sailor recently discharged from the Navy has only his dog and $2 for company. He acquires a suit of English cut and a turned-down hat and is mistaken by a wealthy old man for the Prince of Wales. The old man invites the sailor to his home and introduces him to his daughter. The girl, who had been recently infatuated with a phony duke, spots the sailor for a ringer and denounces him. The sailor, to make amends, then captures the phony duke, who is a crook, and marries the girl. *Sailors. Mistaken identity. Imposture. Dogs.*

Note: Sources disagree in crediting direction.

THE APACHE *see* **A MAN'S MATE**

THE APACHE **F2.0148**

Columbia Pictures. 19 Nov **1928** [cl Feb 1929; LP90]. Si; b&w. 35mm. 6 reels, 5,789 ft.

Prod Jack Cohn. *Dir* Philip Rosen. *Adapt* Harriet Hinsdale. *Story* Ramon Romero. *Camera* Ted Tetzlaff. *Art Dir* Harrison Wiley. *Asst Dir* Buddy Coleman.

Cast: Margaret Livingston *(Sonya)*, Warner Richmond *(Gaston Laroux)*, Don Alvarado *(Pierre Dumont)*, Philo McCullough *(Monsieur Chautard)*.

Melodrama. A Marseilles cafe performer involved with a pack of thieves is rescued from her criminal life by a police official who sends her lover and partner in a knife-throwing act to jail and then tries to seduce her. Not submitting to the official's advances, she falls in love with an apache in Paris and works with him, holding her other admirer at a distance. The official is mysteriously killed, presumably by her lover, but the real murderer is her former partner, now out of jail. She frees her lover by forcing a confession from her old partner. *Apaches—Paris. Entertainers. Police. Thieves. Seduction. Murder. Paris. Marseilles.*

THE APACHE DANCER **F2.0149**

Charles R. Seeling Productions. *Dist* Aywon Film Corp. Dec **1923**. Si; b&w. 35mm. 5 reels, ca4,800 ft.

Dir Charles R. Seeling.

Cast: George Larkin, Ollie Kirby.

Melodrama. After saving the life of an American girl in a Paris cafe, an apache dancer inherits a fortune and goes to America to persuade the girl to marry him. His suit is temporarily threatened by some evildoers who would like to discredit him, but he emerges the winner after a terrific fight. *Apaches—Paris. Dancers. Inheritance. Paris.*

THE APACHE KID'S ESCAPE **F2.0150**

Robert J. Horner Productions. 22 Nov **1930** [New York State license]. Sd; b&w. 35mm. 5 reels, 4,600 ft.

Cast: Jack Perrin *(The Apache Kid/Jim)*, Starlight *(a horse)*.

Western melodrama. Following a narrow escape from a trap set by the sheriff, the Apache Kid (who poses as Jim, a cowhand) takes on the romantic problems of Ted Conway. Informed by King Conway that Ted is not really his son but rather an orphan picked up on the plains after an Indian attack, Wilson rejects Ted's request to marry his daughter, Jane, and accepts King's offer to destroy Wilson's note and pay him a large sum of money in return for Jane's hand. When Ted is jailed for robbing a stage, the Apache Kid returns the money to the bank and obtains the notes from Conway. Ted is released; the Apache Kid throws the sheriff off his trail, says goodby to his gal, and moves on. *Cowboys. Sheriffs. Outlaws. Orphans. Disguise. Courtship. Stagecoach robberies. Horses.*

THE APACHE RAIDER **F2.0151**

Leo Maloney Productions. *Dist* Pathé Exchange. 12 Feb **1928** [c24 Jan 1928; LP24909]. Si; b&w. 35mm. 6 reels, 5,755 ft.

Dir Leo D. Maloney. *Scen* Ford I. Beebe. *Photog* Edward A. Kull.

Cast: Leo Maloney *("Apache" Bob)*, Eugenia Gilbert *(Dixie Stillwell)*, Don Coleman *(Dal Cartwright)*, Tom London *(Griffin Dawson)*, Jack Ganzhorn *("Breed" Artwell)*, Frederick Dana *("Bit" Ward)*, Joan Renee *(Juanita Wharton)*, William Merrill McCormick *(Ray Wharton)*, Robert C. Smith *("Beaze" La Mare)*, Walter Shumway *("Fang" Jaccard)*,

Murdock MacQuarrie *(Don Felix Beinal)*, Whitehorse *(Ed Stillwell)*, Robin Williamson, Dick La Reno, Robert Burns, Allen Watt.

Western melodrama. Source: William Dawson Hoffman, "The Border Raider" (publication undetermined). Regarded as a bandit, "Apache" Bob actually is stealing his cattle from Griffin Dawson, a rancher who in turn obtained them illegally. Bob discovers that Dawson is a crook who operates through a gang of hired gunmen and scheming politicians. Dawson succeeds in arousing the townspeople to lynch Bob, but at the crucial moment the crowd turns against Dawson; he and Bob shoot it out, and Bob becomes hero of the community. *Politicians. Ranchers. Lynching. Rustling.*

THE APE **F2.0152**

Milt Collins. *Dist* Collwyn Pictures. 28 Mar **1928** [New York State license]. Si; b&w. 35mm. 5 reels.

Dir B. C. Rule.

Cast: Gladys Walton, Ruth Stonehouse, Basil Wilson, Bradley Barker.

Mystery drama(?). "Claimed to be based on actual police record." (*Variety,* 2 May 1928, p26.) No further information about the nature of this film has been found.

APE MAN ISLAND *see* **BALI, THE UNKNOWN; OR, APE MAN ISLAND**

APPEARANCES (United States/ Great Britain) **F2.0153**

Famous Players–Lasky British Producers. *Dist* Paramount Pictures. 12 Jun **1921** [c14 Jun 1921; LP16669]. Si; b&w. 35mm. 5 reels, 4,410 ft.

Dir Donald Crisp. *Adapt* Margaret Turnbull. *Story* Edward Knoblock. *Photog* Hal Young. *Asst Dir* Claude Mitchell.

Cast: David Powell *(Herbert Seaton)*, Mary Glynne *(Kitty Mitchell)*, Langhorne Burton *(Sir William Rutherford)*, Mary Dibley *(Lady Rutherford)*, Marjorie Hume *(Agnes, Kitty's sister)*, Percy Standing *(Dawkins)*.

Society melodrama. Kitty Mitchell, secretary to Sir William Rutherford, marries Herbert Seaton, an architect who promises her more than he is able to provide. Finding it increasingly difficult to keep up appearances, Seaton engages in speculation, while his wife, against his wishes, does some secretarial work for Sir William, who sends her a $25 check. To prevent her cashing it, Seaton changes it to read $2,500. After Dawkins, a promoter, obtains the altered check and cashes it, Sir William destroys it, and Kitty, who has left Seaton because of his drinking, attempts to explain matters. Herbert, however, admits the truth, and the couple decide to begin a new life in Canada. *Secretaries. Architects. Documentation. Speculation. Alcoholism.*

APPLAUSE **F2.0154**

Paramount Famous Lasky Corp. ca9 Oct **1929** [New York premiere; released 30 Aug 1930; c3 Jan 1930; LP969]. Sd (Movietone); b&w. 35mm. 9 reels, 7,357 ft. [Also si; 6,896 ft.]

Assoc Prod Monta Bell. *Dir* Rouben Mamoulian. *Adapt-Dial* Garrett Fort. *Photog* George Folsey. *Film Ed* John Bassler. *Song: "What Wouldn't I Do for That Man"* E. Y. Harburg, Jay Gorney. *Song: "Yaaka Hula Hickey Dula"* E. Ray Goetz, Joe Young, Pete Wendling. *Song: "Give Your Little Baby Lots of Lovin'"* Dolly Morse, Joe Burke. *Song: "I've Got a Feelin' I'm Fallin'"* Billy Rose, Harry Link, "Fats" Waller. *Rec Engr* Ernest F. Zatorsky.

Cast: Helen Morgan *(Kitty Darling)*, Joan Peers *(April Darling)*, Fuller Mellish, Jr. *(Hitch Nelson)*, Jack Cameron *(Joe King)*, Henry Wadsworth *(Tony)*, Dorothy Cumming *(Mother Superior)*.

Drama. Source: Beth Brown, *Applause* (New York, 1928). Kitty Darling, an aging Broadway burlesque queen who still believes in a "big-time" future, has cultural ambitions for April, her 5-year-old daughter, and sends her to a convent for schooling. Years later, blunted by drink and lack of affection, Kitty falls under the influence of Hitch, an unscrupulous comedian who persuades Kitty to bring her daughter to the city to earn her living in the show. Influenced by April's sense of propriety, Kitty marries her worthless consort. Nauseated by the pathetic falseness of her mother's life, April becomes defensive as a result of Hitch's covert advances, but when Tony, a sailor, meets her on the street, their common loneliness blossoms into love. April becomes engaged; but when she overhears Hitch call her mother a "has-been," she declines to marry Tony and instead joins the chorus. Thinking that her daughter is happily married, Kitty takes poison and dies alone in her dressing room; Tony refuses to accept April's rejection, and they are reunited after she performs in her mother's place. *Chorus girls. Sailors. Burlesque. Motherhood. Courtship. Suicide. Convents. New York City—Broadway.*

APRIL FOOL **F2.0155**

Chadwick Pictures. 15 Nov **1926.** Si; b&w. 35mm. 7 reels, 7,100 ft.

Dir Nat Ross. *Scen* Zion Myer. *Titl* James Madison. *Photog* L. William O'Connell.

Cast: Alexander Carr *(Jacob Goodman)*, Duane Thompson *(Irma Goodman)*, Mary Alden *(Amelia Rosen)*, Raymond Keane *(Leon Steinfield)*, Edward Phillips *(Joseph Applebaum)*, Snitz Edwards *(Mr. Applebaum)*, Nat Carr *(Moisha Ginsburg)*, Baby Peggy, Pat Moore, Leon Holmes *(The Children)*.

Comedy. Source: Edgar Allan Woolf and Alexander Carr, *An April Shower* (a play in one act; c21 Aug 1915). A discharged pants-presser makes a fortune in the umbrella business. His daughter is to marry the nephew of a newly-rich neighbor, until her intended is accused by his uncle of stealing a sum of money that was, in fact, stolen by the man's own son. The marriage is called off until the former pants-presser gives up his fortune to assure his daughter's happiness. *Pants-pressers. Nouveaux riches. Jews. Theft. Umbrellas.*

APRIL SHOWERS **F2.0156**

Preferred Pictures. 21 Oct **1923** [c4 Sep 1923; LP19377]. Si; b&w. 35mm. 6 reels, 6,350 ft.

Pres by B. P. Schulberg. *Prod* B. P. Schulberg. *Dir* Tom Forman. *Story-Scen* Hope Loring, Louis D. Lighton. *Photog* Harry Perry.

Cast: Colleen Moore *(Maggie Muldoon)*, Kenneth Harlan *(Danny O'Rourke)*, Ruth Clifford *(Miriam Welton)*, Priscilla Bonner *(Shannon O'Rourke)*, Myrtle Vane *(Mrs. O'Rourke)*, James Corrigan *(Matt Gallagher)*, Jack Byron *(Flash Irwin)*, Ralph Faulkner *(Champ Sullivan)*, Tom McGuire *(Lieutenant Muldoon)*, Kid McCoy, Danny Goodman *(The Ring Managers)*.

Melodrama. Danny O'Rourke, the son of an Irish-American policeman who dies a hero, is training to join the force. His sweetheart, Maggie, is the daughter of a police lieutenant. When society girl Miriam Welton arrives in their slum neighborhood to do social work, she nearly causes a split between the two lovers. Danny takes his final examination and thinks he has failed. At the same time, Danny's sister Shannon is caught shoplifting. Danny enters a prizefighting contest to raise money to save his sister. He loses the fight but discovers that an error in the scoring of his examination makes him eligible to join the police force. *Irish. Police. Social workers. Brother-sister relationship. Shoplifting. Prizefighting.*

Note: Copyright material states that Al Lichtman Corp. was distributor, but the exact date of the merger between Preferred Pictures, Inc., and Al Lichtman Corp. has not been determined.

THE ARAB **F2.0157**

Metro-Goldwyn Pictures. 21 Jul **1924** [c16 Jul 1924; LP20401]. Si; b&w. 35mm. 7 reels, 6,710 ft.

Dir-Writ Rex Ingram. *Photog* John F. Seitz.

Cast: Ramon Novarro *(Jamil Abdullah Azam)*, Alice Terry *(Mary Hilbert)*, Maxudian *(The Governor)*, Jean De Limur *(Hossein, his aide)*, Paul Vermoyal *(Iphraim)*, Adelqui Millar *(Abdullah, see note)*, Alexandresco *(Oulad Nile)*, Justa Uribe *(Myrza)*, Gerald Robertshaw *(Dr. Hilbert)*, Paul Francesci *(Marmount)*, Giuseppe De Compo *(Selim)*.

Melodrama. Source: Edgar Selwyn, *The Arab, a Play* (New York opening: Sep 1911). Jamil, son of a Bedouin tribe leader, is disowned by his father for a desert raid at the time of the Feast of Ramadan. He becomes a guide in a Turkish city, where he falls in love with Mary, the daughter of a Christian missionary. The governor's attempt to massacre the Christians is foiled by Jamil when he calls the Bedouins to his aid. Following the death of his father, he is made leader of his tribe, and he accepts the girl's promise to return to him as she departs for America. *Guides. Arabs. Bedouins. Missionaries. Ramadan. Christianity. Turkey.*

Note: Actor Adelqui Millar may be an erroneous rendition of Adolph Millar.

ARABIA **F2.0158**

Fox Film Corp. 5 Nov **1922** [c14 Nov 1922; LP19209]. Si; b&w. 35mm. 5 reels, 4,448 ft.

Pres by William Fox. *Dir-Scen* Lynn Reynolds. *Titl* Hettie Grey Baker. *Story* Tom Mix, Lynn Reynolds. *Photog* Don Clark. *Film Ed* Hettie Grey Baker.

Cast: Tom Mix *(Billy Evans)*, Barbara Bedford *(Janice Terhune)*,

George Hernandez *(Arthur Edward Terhune)*, Norman Selby *(Pussy Foot Bogs)*, Edward Piel *(Ibrahim Bulamar)*, Ralph Yearsley *(Waldmar Terhune)*, Hector Sarno *(Ali Hasson)*.

Action comedy. Dashing horseman Billy Evans, entrepreneur of a tourist's ranch, swings from an overhanging cliff and ropes a snarling wildcat while acting as guide for Janice Terhune and her father, whose specialization in dead languages soon leads them to Arabia. Billy declines to follow, preferring to rest easy in his hammock, until an Arabian prince roars through the ranch in a roadster, bumping Billy from his sleep. The adventurous cowboy swaps clothes with his highness, who is being pursued by the sultan's agents, bent upon thwarting his plans to marry a "follies" beauty. The car chase ends when Billy drives into the Pacific Ocean and is overtaken and abducted to Arabia, where he ousts a powerful pretender to the throne, restores the sultan to his palace, and rescues Janice Terhune, whose flashy eyes had precipitated her abduction by the evil counterfeit prince. *Linguists. Royalty. Dude ranches. Mistaken identity. Arabia. Pacific Ocean. Chases.*

Note: Also reviewed under the title: *Tom Mix in Arabia.*

ARABIAN LOVE **F2.0159**

Fox Film Corp. 9 Apr **1922** [c9 Apr 1922; LP17824]. Si; b&w. 35mm. 5 reels, 4,440 ft.

Pres by William Fox. *Dir* Jerome Storm. *Story-Scen* Jules Furthman. *Photog* Joe August.

Cast: John Gilbert *(Norman Stone)*, Barbara Bedford *(Nadine Fortier)*, Barbara La Marr *(Themar)*, Herschel Mayall *(The Sheik)*, Robert Kortman *(Ahmed Bey)*, William H. Orlamond *(Dr. Lagorio)*.

Melodrama. Following her marriage, Nadine Fortier is called to the bedside of her mother in a distant city. She then joins her husband, and while her caravan is crossing the desert, she is taken prisoner by bandits. Through a game of chance she becomes the property of Norman Stone, an American fugitive from justice who has joined the band, and he escorts her to safety. She learns that her husband has been killed and offers a reward for the capture of the murderer. Stone falls in love with her, and Themar, the sheik's daughter, out of jealousy tells Nadine that Stone is the murderer. Stone tells her that her husband had arranged clandestine meetings with his sister and that when he confronted him, Fortier's revolver was accidentally discharged. Then, in order to clear his sister, he fled. Realizing her deep love for Stone, Nadine asks his forgiveness and leaves with him for America. *Fugitives. Bandits. Murder. Jealousy. Deserts. Arabia.*

ARE CHILDREN TO BLAME? **F2.0160**

Chopin Features. *Dist* Certified Pictures. 3 Oct **1922** [New York State license]. Si; b&w. 35mm. 5 reels.

Dir-Writ Paul Price.

Cast: Em Gorman *(Little Rosalind)*, Alex K. Shannon *(David Granger)*, Joseph Marquis *(Robert Brown)*, George Henry *(Judge Brown)*, Gordon Standing *(Caleb Hands)*, Tatjena Rirah *(Becky Small)*, Frances Eldridge *(Alice Hawthorne)*, Emma Tausey *(Mrs. Winslow)*, Robert Tausey *(Albert Winslow)*.

Drama. Suggested by: George Eliot, *Silas Marner.* "Brown ... keeps the secret of his wife and baby from his parents. News comes that his wife has died, but that his child, Rosalind, is being cared for by his wife's sister. Brown is called upon to send more and more money for this purpose. Finally he robs the blacksmith, who is called the village miser. The woman who is caring for Rosalind is really an impostor ... Brown is urged to marry respectably ... and on the night of the wedding Rosalind's guardian determines to make a scene by interrupting the wedding. She ... is thwarted by a sudden ... illness, which proves fatal. The child comes into the home of the blacksmith, and when the others find the dead woman and trace the child they attempt to take her away from him. But the miser, who has lost everything he prizes but the child, begs to keep her. It proves to be a mistake that she is Brown's so he is privileged to keep his new-found treasure." *(Moving Picture World,* 2 Dec 1922, p457.) *Students. Blacksmiths. Misers. Children. Robbery.*

Note: Known also as *Are the Children To Blame?*

ARE PARENTS PEOPLE? **F2.0161**

Famous Players–Lasky. *Dist* Paramount Pictures. 1 Jun **1925** [c5 Jun 1925; LP21538]. Si; b&w. 35mm. 7 reels, 6,586 ft.

Pres by Adolph Zukor, Jesse L. Lasky. *Dir* Malcolm St. Clair. *Screenplay* Frances Agnew. *Photog* Bert Glennon.

Cast: Betty Bronson *(Lita Hazlitt)*, Florence Vidor *(Mrs. Hazlitt)*, Adolphe Menjou *(Mr. Hazlitt)*, André Beranger *(Maurice Mansfield)*, Lawrence Gray *(Dr. Dacer)*, Mary Beth Milford *(Aurella Wilton)*, Emily Fitzroy *(Margaret)*, William Courtwright *(Freebody)*.

Comedy. Source: Alice Duer Miller, "Are Parents People?" in *Are Parents People?* (New York, 1924). Mr. and Mrs. Hazlitt believe themselves to be victims of incompatability and begin divorce proceedings. This separation weighs heavily on their daughter, Lita, who is sent back to boarding school when she refuses to live with either of her parents. While there, she learns that parents can only be reunited by a common concern for the welfare of their children. Lita is expelled when she assumes the blame for a romantic letter written by her sentimental roommate to a vain movie star; she decides to use this as a means to reunite her parents and goes to find the movie star on location. Lita's resulting expulsion from school brings her parents together, and she decides to cause them concern once more by running away. She innocently spends the night in the apartment of Dr. Dacer, a young surgeon who has caught her fancy. While Lita comfortably sleeps unnoticed in an easy chair in the doctor's office, her parents spend the night in pacing and recrimination. Lita returns home in the morning, reunites her parents, and wins for herself the affections of the doctor. *Surgeons. Parenthood. Filial relations. Divorce. Boarding schools.*

ARE THE CHILDREN TO BLAME? *see* **ARE CHILDREN TO BLAME?**

ARE YOU A FAILURE? **F2.0162**

Preferred Pictures. *Dist* Al Lichtman Corp. 15 Mar **1923** [c20 Feb 1923; LP18894]. Si; b&w. 35mm. 6 reels, 5,700 ft.

Pres by B. P. Schulberg. *Dir* Tom Forman. *Scen* Eve Unsell. *Story* Larry Evans. *Photog* Harry Perry.

Cast: Madge Bellamy *(Phyllis Thorpe)*, Lloyd Hughes *(Oliver Wendell Blaine)*, Tom Santschi *(Killdevil Brenon)*, Hardee Kirkland *(Gregory Thorpe)*, Jane Keckley *(Aunt Emily)*, Hallam Cooley *(Emmett Graves)*, Sam Allen *(Thaddeus Crane)*, Myrtle Vane *(Aunt Charlotte)*, Sport *(a dog)*.

Drama. Coddled by his maiden aunts and apparently unable to make decisions, Oliver Wendell Blaine signs up for a mail-order course in "Success." Oliver follows the instructions step by step, builds his self-confidence, and proves himself a hero when a log jam threatens the town. He is made river boss and marries Phyllis Thorpe, daughter of the owner of the lumbermill. *Aunts. River bosses. Self-confidence. Correspondence courses. Lumbering. Dogs.*

ARE YOU THERE? **F2.0163**

Fox Film Corp. 30 Nov **1930** [c27 Oct 1930; LP1701]. Sd (Movietone); b&w. 35mm. 6 reels, 5,400 ft.

Dir Hamilton MacFadden. *Story-Dial* Harlan Thompson. *Photog* Joseph Valentine. *Art Dir* Stephen Goosson, Duncan Cramer. *Film Ed* Al De Gaetano. *Songs: "Lady Detectives," "Bagdad Daddies" "Queen of the Hunt Am I"* Grace Henry, Morris Hamilton. *Mus Dir* Arthur Kay. *Choral Dir* Frank Tresselt. *Dance Dir* Edward Dolly. *Sd Rec* W. W. Lindsay. *Asst Dir* Sam Wurtzel. *Cost* Sophie Wachner.

Cast: Beatrice Lillie *(Shirley Travis)*, John Garrick *(Geoffry)*, Olga Baclanova *(Countess Helenka)*, George Grossmith *(Duke of St. Pancras)*, Roger Davis *(barber)*, Jillian Sand *(Barbara Blythe)*, Gustav von Seyffertitz *(barber)*, Nicholas Soussanin *(barber)*, Richard Alexander, Henry Victor *(international crooks)*, Lloyd Hamilton *(hostler)*, Paula Langlen *(page)*.

Musical comedy. Shirley Travis, a lady detective who never fails to solve her case, is approached by Geoffry, son of the Duke of St. Pancras, with the intention of blocking the marriage of his father with the Countess Helenka. Shirley takes the case and goes to the family castle as Lady Diana Drummond, a big game hunter. Ultimately, she exposes the countess as a crook and wins the love of the duke. *Detectives. Hunters. Nobility. Marriage. Filial relations.*

ARGENTINE LOVE **F2.0164**

Famous Players–Lasky. *Dist* Paramount Pictures. 29 Dec **1924** [c2 Dec 1924; LP20844]. Si; b&w. 35mm. 6 reels, 5,970 ft.

Pres by Adolph Zukor, Jesse L. Lasky. *Dir* Allan Dwan. *Scen* Gerald Duffy. *Adapt* John Russell. *Story* Vicente Blasco-Ibáñez. *Photog* Roy Hunt.

Cast: Bebe Daniels *(Consuelo García)*, Ricardo Cortez *(Juan Martin)*, James Rennie *(Philip Sears)*, Mario Majeroni *(Senator Cornejo)*, Russ Whital *(Emanuel García)*, Alice Chapin *(Madame García)*, Julia Hurley *(La Mosca)*, Mark Gonzales *(Rafael Cornejo)*, Aurelio Coccia *(Pedro)*.

Melodrama. While his daughter, Consuelo, is visiting the United States, Emanuel García, the Mayor of Alcorta in the Argentine, arranges for her marriage to Juan Martin, in return for Martin's financial assistance. On her return, Consuelo, who is in love with Philip Sears, an American engineer working in Argentina, refuses Juan but gives no reason. Juan is furious with outraged pride and soon kills Rafael Cornejo, the son of a senator, when he flirts with Consuelo. The people of Alcorta hold her apparently willful refusal of Juan responsible for the killing; they tie her to a cart and beat her. When she is rescued by Philip, Consuelo, fearing that Juan will kill Philip if she betrays her lover for the American, feigns love for the touchy Latin and asks Philip to help them elope. Philip gallantly assists them to the border and returns to Alcorta; Consuelo tells Juan that she will still consent to marriage but that she can never love him, since she loves Philip instead. Not to be shamed by Philip's gallantry, Juan decides to step aside. He is returning to Alcorta to give himself up when he is shot by Senator Cornejo. *Mayors. Engineers. Murder. Self-sacrifice. Argentina.*

THE ARGYLE CASE **F2.0165**

Warner Brothers Pictures. 17 Aug **1929** [c21 Jul 1929; LP535]. Sd (Vitaphone); b&w. 35mm. 9 reels, 7,794 ft. [Also si, 5 Oct 1929; 5,407 ft.]

Dir Howard Bretherton. *Scen-Dial* Harvey Thew. *Titl* De Leon Anthony. *Photog* James C. Van Trees. *Film Ed* Thomas Pratt.

Cast: Thomas Meighan *(Alexander Kayton)*, H. B. Warner *(Hurley)*, Lila Lee *(Mary Morgan)*, John Darrow *(Bruce Argyle)*, ZaSu Pitts *(Mrs. Wyatt)*, Bert Roach *(Joe)*, Wilbur Mack *(Sam)*, Douglas Gerrard *(Finley)*, Alona Marlowe *(Kitty)*, James Quinn *(Skidd)*, Gladys Brockwell *(Mrs. Martin)*, Lew Harvey.

Mystery drama. Source: Harriet Ford and Harvey J. O'Higgins, *The Argyle Case; a Drama in Four Acts* (New York, c1927). Bruce Argyle hires famous detective Alexander Kayton to investigate the murder of his father, John Argyle, a capitalist. Argyle's adopted daughter, Mary Morgan, is suspected until Kayton's investigation reveals that Hurley, a former confidential attorney for Argyle, is actually Kreisler, a notorious counterfeiter who was imprisoned 20 years previously. Threatened with exposure to the police, Hurley, still involved in criminal activities, murders Argyle. *Capitalists. Detectives. Lawyers. Counterfeiters. Murder.*

ARIZONA BOUND **F2.0166**

Famous Players–Lasky. *Dist* Paramount Pictures. 9 Apr **1927** [c9 Apr 1927; LP23859]. Si; b&w. 35mm. 5 reels, 4,912 ft.

Pres by Adolph Zukor, Jesse L. Lasky. *Dir* John Waters. *Screenplay* John Stone, Paul Gangelin. *Titl* Alfred Hustwick. *Adapt* Marion Jackson. *Story* Richard Allen Gates. *Photog* C. Edgar. Schoenbaum.

Cast: Gary Cooper *(Dave Saulter)*, Betty Jewel *(Ann Winslow)*, El Brendel *("Oley Smoke" Oleson)*, Jack Dougherty *(Buck Hanna)*, Christian J. Frank *(Texas Jack)*, Charles Crockett *(John Winslow)*, Joe Butterworth *(Tommy Winslow)*, Guy Oliver *(sheriff)*, Flash *(himself, a horse)*.

Western melodrama. In the little mining town of Mesquite lives Dave Saulter, a ne'er-do-well whose prime interests are Flash, his white horse, and Ann Winslow, who objects to his irresponsible ways. Ann agrees to attend a dance with Buck Hanna, but Dave playfully ensnares her partner just as he is about to commence the first dance. Buck plots to steal the local gold shipment entrusted to him; Dave, desperate for a job as guard, ties up a man and goes in his place. The coach is waylaid by Texas Jack and his gang, and Dave is knocked unconscious. Buck and his pals throw suspicion on Dave, but Oleson, a blundering Swede, accidentally finds the cache of gold. When Betty learns of Buck's guilt, he kidnaps her in a coach, but Dave follows and overpowers him, thus winning the reward and the girl. *Ne'er-do-wells. Swedes. Bandits. Mining towns. California. Horses.*

ARIZONA CYCLONE **F2.0167**

Universal Pictures. 6 May **1928** [c20 Oct 1927; LP24566]. Si; b&w. 35mm. 5 reels, 4,976 ft.

Pres by Carl Laemmle. *Dir* Edgar Lewis. *Story-Cont* William Lester. *Titl* Gardner Bradford. *Photog* Eddie Linden, Bill Cline. *Art Dir* David S. Garber. *Film Ed* Jack Jackson.

Cast: Fred Humes *(Larry Day/Tom Day)*, George K. French *(John Cosgrave)*, Margaret Gray *(Kathleen Cosgrave)*, Cuyler Supplee *(Mel Craven)*, Pee Wee Holmes *(Pee Wee)*, Benny Corbett *(Benny)*, Dick L'Estrange *(Lazy Lester)*, Scotty Mattraw *(Scotty)*.

Western melodrama. Larry Day, foreman of the Triple X Ranch, has a cousin known as the "Night Hawk," to whom he bears a close resemblance. John Cosgrave, Larry's boss, sells stock to Mel Craven and is paid in cash, thus arousing suspicion. Larry, meanwhile, is summoned to help his cousin and is made prisoner by Craven while his cousin (Tom) takes his place and returns to the ranch. During the night a pet monkey takes the money from a desk; when Tom later asks for the money and finds it missing, he causes a disturbance. Larry escapes and after confronting Tom turns him over to the sheriff. The money is recovered. *Ranch foremen. Cousins. Doubles. Impersonation. Fraud. Monkeys.*

ARIZONA DAYS **F2.0168**

El Dorado Productions. *Dist* Syndicate Pictures. 1 Aug **1928.** Si; b&w. 35mm. 5 reels, 4,139 or 4,192 ft.

Dir J. P. McGowan. *Scen* Mack V. Wright. *Story* Brysis Coleman. *Photog* Paul Allen.

Cast: Bob Custer *(Chuck Drexel)*, Peggy Montgomery *(Dolly Martin)*, John Lowell Russell *([Dolly's father])*, J. P. McGowan *([villain])*, Mack V. Wright *([villain])*, Jack Ponder *([detective])*.

Western melodrama. Pretending to join a gang of rustlers in exchange for protection of his herd, Dolly Martin's father is really spying for the cattlemen's association. Chuck Drexel happens along on a similar mission. Dolly believes him to be a gang member, but he shows his true colors by rescuing her father and arresting the leader of the gang (played by J. P. McGowan). *Ranchers. Rustlers. Gangs. Protective associations.*

THE ARIZONA EXPRESS **F2.0169**

Fox Film Corp. 23 Mar **1924** [c13 Mar 1924; LP19989]. Si; b&w. 35mm. 7 reels, 6,316 ft.

Pres by William Fox. *Dir* Thomas Buckingham. *Scen* Fred Jackson, Robert N. Lee. *Story* Lincoln J. Carter. *Photog* Starke Wagner,.

Cast: Pauline Starke *(Katherine Keith)*, Evelyn Brent *(Lola Nichols)*, Anne Cornwall *(Florence Brown)*, Harold Goodwin *(David Keith)*, David Butler *(Steve Butler)*, Francis McDonald *(Victor Johnson)*, Frank Beal *(Judge Ashton)*, William Humphrey *(Henry MacFarlane)*.

Melodrama. David Keith is railroaded to prison for allegedly killing his uncle, a bank president, and he is sentenced to die. His sister Katherine proves that a member of a gang plotting to rob the bank is guilty. Aided by Steve Butler, a railroad mail clerk, she reaches the governor in time to save David. She and Steve find romance. *Mail clerks. Brother-sister relationship. Gangs. Murder. Bank robberies. Capital punishment.*

THE ARIZONA KID **F2.0170**

J. Charles Davis Productions. 1 Apr **1929.** Si; b&w. 35mm. 5 reels, 4,311 ft.

Pres by W. T. Lackey. *Dir-Writ* Horace B. Carpenter.

Cast: Art Acord *(Bill Strong, "The Arizona Kid")*, Cliff Lyons *(Ned Hank)*, Bill Conant *(Sheriff Morton)*, Carol Lane *(Mary Grant)*, George Hollister *(Mandel Labor)*, Lynn Sanderson *(Bud Jenkins)*, James Tromp *(Postman Stebbins)*, Horace B. Carpenter *(Jake Grant, her father)*, Star *(a horse)*, Rex *(a dog)*.

Western melodrama. Bandits rob the mail and express stage and hold the guard and his daughter as hostages. A United States marshal, disguised as a dude, joins the gang, rescues the victims, and sends the bad men to jail. *Bandits. Hostages. Stagecoach robberies. Disguise. Dogs.*

THE ARIZONA KID **F2.0171**

Fox Film Corp. 27 Apr **1930** [c12 Apr 1930; LP1257]. Sd (Movietone); b&w. 35mm. 9 reels, 7,902 ft. [Also si.]

Pres by William Fox. *Dir* Alfred Santell. *Story-Scen-Dial* Ralph Block. *Photog* Glen MacWilliams. *Sets* Joseph Wright. *Film Ed* Paul Weatherwax. *Sd Engr* George Leverett. *Asst Dir* Marty Santell. *Wardrobe* Sophie Wachner.

Cast: Warner Baxter *(The Arizona Kid)*, Mona Maris *(Lorita)*, Carol Lombard *(Virginia Hoyt)*, Theodore von Eltz *(Nick Hoyt)*, Arthur Stone *(Snakebit Pete)*, Solidad Jiminez *(Pulga)*, Walter P. Lewis *(Sheriff Andrews)*, Jack Herrick *(The Hoboken Hooker)*, Wilfred Lucas *(his manager)*, Hank Mann *(Bartender Bill)*, James Gibson *(stagedriver)*, De Sacia Mooers *(Molly)*, Larry McGrath *(Homer Snook)*.

Western melodrama. Posing as a wealthy and carefree Mexican miner, The Arizona Kid is loved by many señoritas, including Lorita, while carrying out his mission as bandit-hero. Their romance is interrupted, however, by the arrival of Virginia, an eastern girl accompanied presumably by her brother, Dick (actually her husband). While The Kid falls for the blonde and she makes a play for him, the sheriff becomes suspicious of his absence. Eventually, The Kid's mine, worked in secret, is raided and his two coworkers are killed. With the help of Lorita, The Kid learns that Dick and Virginia are the culprits; and after a showdown in which Dick is killed, The Kid escapes with Lorita at his side. *Bandits. Mexicans. Miners. Courtship.*

ARIZONA NIGHTS **F2.0172**

R-C Pictures. *Dist* Film Booking Offices of America. 28 Aug **1927** [c10 Jun 1927; LP24188]. Si; b&w. 35mm. 7 reels.

Pres by Joseph P. Kennedy. *Dir* Lloyd Ingraham. *Adapt-Cont* Hal Conklin. *Story* Stewart Edward White. *Photog* Mack Stengler. *Asst Dir* Douglas Dawson.

Cast: Fred Thomson *(Fred Coulter)*, Nora Lane *(Ruth Browning)*, J. P. McGowan *(Jeff Decker)*, William Courtright *(Bill Barrow)*, Lottie Williams *(Aunt Agatha)*, William McCormick *(Speed Lester)*, Dan Peterson *(Red Dog)*, Silver King *(himself, a horse)*.

Western melodrama. Jeff Decker, with the aid of Red Dog, an Indian leader, continually raids the town of Coldwater and plans to buy up all the horses while instigating a false rumor of a gold strike outside town. Fred Coulter, who unsuccessfully works a nearby mining claim, is hired to buy the horses. Decker, after concluding the deal, tries unsuccessfully to induce Ruth Browning, the niece of Aunt Agatha, owner of the lunchroom, to leave town with him. Fred learns from her of the falsity of the rumor and rides to inform the miners. To ward off an Indian attack, the remaining populace gathers in the general store. Silver King rides to warn Fred, and Fred cleverly sets them to rout. After a struggle with Decker, Fred falls into Ruth's waiting arms. *Swindlers. Indians of North America. Gold mines. Restaurants. General stores. Arizona. Horses.*

THE ARIZONA ROMEO **F2.0173**

Fox Film Corp. 4 Jan **1925** [c28 Dec 1924; LP20973]. Si; b&w. 35mm. 5 reels, 4,694 ft.

Pres by William Fox. *Dir* Edmund Mortimer. *Scen* Charles Kenyon. *Story* Charles Kenyon, Edmund Mortimer.

Cast: Buck Jones *(Tom Long)*, Lucy Fox *(Sylvia Wayne)*, Maine Geary *(Richard Barr)*, Thomas R. Mills *(Sam Barr)*, Hardee Kirkland *(John Wayne)*, Marcella Daly *(Mary)*, Lydia Yeamans *(Martha)*, Harvey Clark *(The Sheriff)*, Hank Mann *(deputy)*.

Western melodrama. John Wayne and Sam Barr, two New York financiers, plan to merge their holdings by means of the marriage of Wayne's daughter, Sylvia, to Barr's son, Richard. When Sylvia refuses, the elder Barr, wise in the ways of women, decides that the best way to make her change her mind is to oppose Richard as a suitor. Sylvia immediately runs away to Arizona, where she arranges to meet Richard, and, to pass the time, opens a manicure parlor in the barbershop. When Tom Long, a local rancher, discovers that all his men are getting manicured, he rides into town to put a stop to the practice. At the barbershop, he defends Sylvia from the advances of a tough, and he falls in love with her. Richard arrives from the East, closely followed by a telegram from Sylvia's father offering a reward for the prevention of the marriage. Thinking Sylvia truly in love with Richard, Tom helps them elude the sheriff, but, when he accidently learns that Sylvia is marrying Richard only to spite her father, he chases after the train carrying the eloping couple, jumps aboard from his galloping horse, and declares his love to Sylvia. She realizes that she truly loves him, rather than Richard, and they make plans to be married. *Financiers. Ranchers. Manicurists. Filial relations. Barbershops. Arizona. New York City. Stunts. Chases.*

ARIZONA SPEED **F2.0174**

Associated Independent Producers. 9 Apr **1928** [New York State license]. Si; b&w. 35mm. 5 reels, 5 ft, 4,425 min.

Dir-Scen Robert J. Horner. *Titl* Jack Erwing. *Photog* Paul Allen. *Film Ed* Joe O'Hara.

Cast: Pawnee Bill Jr.

Western melodrama(?). No information about the nature of this film has been found.

THE ARIZONA STREAK **F2.0175**

Film Booking Offices of America. 7 Mar **1926** [c7 Mar 1926; LP22493]. Si; b&w. 35mm. 5 reels, 4,640 ft.

Dir Robert De Lacy. *Cont* Lanier Bartlett. *Story* F. A. E. Pine. *Photog* John Leezer. *Asst Dir* John Burch.

Cast: Tom Tyler *(Dandy Darrell)*, Alfred Hewston *(Smiling Morn)*, Ada Mae Vaughn *(Ruth Castleman)*, Frankie Darro *(Mike)*, Dave Ward *(Denver)*, LeRoy Mason *(Velvet Hamilton)*, Ed Smith *(Jim)*.

Western melodrama. Dandy Darrell wins the Bar C from Rufus Castleman in a card game, and Castleman dies of a heart attack brought on by the shock. Dandy takes possession of his new property and immediately and forcibly removes Black Duff, the drunken foreman. Rufus' daughter, Ruth, returns and, not knowing that her father lost the ranch, assumes Dandy to be the foreman. Dandy does not enlighten her, and they get along fine until Black Duff tells Ruth that Dandy killed her father. Dandy later prevents Black Duff from stealing a herd of cattle, however, and reinstates himself in Ruth's affections. *Ranchers. Ranch foremen. Rustling. Gambling.*

THE ARIZONA SWEEPSTAKES (Universal-Jewel) **F2.0176**

Universal Pictures. 10 Jan **1926** [c7 Oct 1925; LP21886]. Si; b&w. 35mm. 6 reels, 5,418 ft.

Dir Clifford S. Smith. *Scen* Isadore Bernstein. *Story* Charles Logue. *Photog* Harry Neumann.

Cast: Hoot Gibson *(Coot Cadigan)*, Helen Lynch *(Nell Savery)*, Philo McCullough *(Jonathan Carey)*, George Ovey *(Stuffy McGee)*, Emmett King *(Col. Tom Savery)*, Tod Brown *(detective)*, Kate Price *(Mrs. McGuire)*, Jackie Morgan, Billy Kent Schaeffer, Turner Savage *(McGee children)*.

Western melodrama. Coot Cadigan, an Arizona cowpuncher, goes to San Francisco and gets to know Stuffy McGee, a petty crook who stages phony fights for the edification of tourists in Chinatown. A man is killed, and Coot is blamed for the crime. He hides out with Stuffy, but when the latter is arrested, Coot is forced to return to Arizona, taking the three little McGee children with him. Coot enters the Arizona Sweepstakes, on which the future of Colonel Savery's ranch depends. Coot wins the race, Savery's ranch is saved, and Nell Savery, the colonel's daughter, becomes Coot's partner for life. A telegram arrives and absolves Coot of all suspicion of guilt in the Chinatown murder. *Cowboys. Ranchers. Children. Murder. Injustice. Horseracing. Arizona. San Francisco—Chinatown.*

THE ARIZONA WHIRLWIND **F2.0177**

Myron Selznick. *Dist* Pathé Exchange. 27 Mar **1927** [c5 Mar 1927; LU23725]. Si; b&w. 35mm. 5 reels, 4,134 ft.

Dir William J. Craft. *Story-Scen* Carl Krusada. *Photog* Art Reeves.

Cast: Bill Cody *(Bill Farley)*, Margaret Hampton *(Helen Dykeman)*, David Dunbar *(Bert Hawley)*, Hughie Mack *(Gonzales)*, Clark Comstock.

Western melodrama. Bill's father is murdered by Hawley, one of Dykeman's henchmen, who steals a map proving Farley's claim to rich gold claims. Bill, who is engaged to Helen, Dykeman's daughter, routs the gang when they try to dispossess settlers and subsequently eludes a large posse. Later, when Hawley steals a gold shipment, Bill captures him and returns the gold to the Blue Ridge settlers; he is then accused of the robbery, but again he escapes. Disguised as a Spaniard, Bill meets Hawley and discovers him to be his father's murderer; a fight ensues, and Hawley recovers the map and kidnaps Helen in a stagecoach. Bill gives chase, overpowers the villain, and rescues Helen from the burning stagecoach. *Gangs. Posses. Mine claims. Murder. Kidnaping. Robbery. Disguise. Arizona. Documentation.*

THE ARIZONA WILDCAT **F2.0178**

Fox Film Corp. 20 Nov **1927** [c7 Nov 1927; LP24643]. Si; b&w. 35mm. 5 reels, 4,665 ft.

Pres by William Fox. *Dir* R. William Neill. *Scen* John Stone. *Story* Adela Rogers St. Johns. *Photog* Dan Clark. *Asst Dir* Wynn Mace.

Cast: Tom Mix *(Tom Phelan)*, Dorothy Sebastian *(Regina Schyler)*, Ben Bard *(Wallace Van Acker)*, Gordon Elliott *(Roy Schyler)*, Monte Collins, Jr. *(Low Jack Wilkins)*, Cissy Fitzgerald *(Mother Schyler)*, Doris Dawson *(Marie)*, Marcella Daly *(Helen Van Acker)*, Tony *(himself, a horse)*.

Western melodrama. Tom Phelan meets the sweetheart of his boyhood days and finds her the prospective victim of two eastern swindlers. When her brother's polo team is on the verge of defeat through the machinations of one of the society crooks, an attempt is made to deny Tom access to the polo field in Santa Barbara; but with the aid of his faithful Tony he thwarts the plan and arrives in time to win the game and save Regina from the villains. *Cowboys. Swindlers. Brother-sister relationship. Polo. Santa Barbara. Horses.*

THE ARMS AND THE GIRL *see* **THE HEART RAIDER**

AROUND THE CORNER **F2.0179**

Columbia Pictures. 25 Apr **1930** [c17 May 1930; LP1309]. Sd (Movietone); b&w. 35mm. 7 reels, 6,419 ft.

Prod Harry Cohn. *Dir* Bert Glennon. *Dial Dir* Patterson McNutt. *Story-Cont-Dial* Jo Swerling. *Photog* Joe Walker. *Art Dir* Harrison Wiley. *Film Ed* Gene Milford. *Ch Sd Engr* John Livadary. *Sd Mixing Engr* Harry Blanchard. *Asst Dir* David Selman.

Cast: George Sidney *(Kaplan)*, Charlie Murray *(O'Grady)*, Joan Peers *(Rosie O'Grady)*, Larry Kent *(Tommy Sinclair)*, Charles Delaney *(Terry Callahan)*, Jess Devorska *(Moe Levine)*, Fred Sullivan *(Sinclair, Sr.)*, Harry Strang *(Mac)*.

Comedy-drama. O'Grady, an Irish policeman, and Kaplan, a Jewish pawnbroker, bring up a child found on their doorstep; 18 years later, Rosie is in love with prizefighter Terry Callahan, although her guardians prefer Moe Levine as a prospective match for her. A disputation is settled when Rosie declares that the rivals may both escort her to a dress ball; there she meets Tommy Sinclair, a young socialite. O'Grady and Kaplan, resenting Tommy's affections for the girl, pay Sinclair, Sr., a visit, and as a result Tommy chooses to leave home rather than give up Rosie. He arranges a match between himself and Terry; and to everyone's surprise, he wins the fight. When Rosie's guardians see that she has won $25,000 for them, they welcome Tommy as their son-in-law. *Police. Pawnbrokers. Foundlings. Guardians. Socialites. Prizefighters. Irish. Jews. Courtship.*

AROUND THE WORLD IN THE SPEEJACKS **F2.0180**

Famous Players–Lasky. *Dist* Paramount Pictures. 2 Dec **1923.** Si; b&w. 35mm. 7 reels, 6,358 ft.

Camera Ira J. Ingraham.

Personages: Commodore A. Y. Gowen, Mrs. A. Y. Gowen.

Travelog. "A honeymoon cruise among the South Sea Islands as undertaken by Commodore and Mrs. A. Y. Gowen brings the spectator face to face with some new degrees of savagery and many interesting sights. Commodore Gowen of Cleveland, Ohio, made this sixteen months' trip, encircling the globe in a 98-foot motor boat. Although the trip included a visit to a number of points that are centers of civilization, the main emphasis is upon the extreme savage types. Some of these are weird and terrifying in the extreme. For the average person these types seem to have a compelling fascination. Others, probably comprising a smaller class, will find more entertainment in the shots of Java for instance. ... A dance by small native girls is one of the most colorful scenes in the film and by far the most charming." (*Moving Picture World,* 1 Dec 1923, p494.) *Motorboats. Honeymoons. Samoa. Tahiti. Tuamotu Archipelago. Java. Genoa. New Guinea. South Sea Islands.*

AROUND THE WORLD VIA GRAF ZEPPELIN **F2.0181**

Metro-Goldwyn-Mayer Pictures. *For* Hearst Newspapers. 2 Nov **1929** New York showing]. Talking sequences (Movietone); b&w. 35mm. 5,200 ft.

Camera Robert Hartman. *Song: "Singing in the Rain"* Arthur Freed, Nacio Herb Brown.

Participants: Lt. Comdr. Charles L. Rosendahl, USN *(narrator)*, Dr. Hugo Eckener, Lady Drummond Hay.

Travelog. A compilation of sights and incidents of the *Graf Zeppelin*'s tour around the world. The vessel is shown leaving Lakehurst, New Jersey, sailing over Germany, leaving the hangar at Friedrichshafen, flying over Russia, and landing in Japan. We see the passengers in the *Graf Zeppelin*'s dining room enjoying music from a phonograph while looking out on floating clouds and the shimmering sea. A narrator describes what happened on the world tour aboard the dirigible and the experiences of the passengers going through an electric storm over the Pacific. At the end of the voyage, Lady Drummond Hay, the only woman aboard, talks about her experiences while traveling on the craft. *Zeppelins. New Jersey. Germany. Japan. Russia. "Graf Zeppelin".*

Note: The film combines newsreel shots with the record of a trip made by an M-G-M photographer aboard the *Graf Zeppelin.*

AROUND THE WORLD WITH BURTON HOLMES **F2.0182**

Burton Holmes Lectures. 6 May **1922** [trade review]. Si; b&w. 35mm. 11 reels, 11,500 ft.

Travelog. "Sailing from New York harbor, the circuit of eleven countries is made, the return trip being by way of the Pacific" (*Moving Picture World,* 6 May 1922, p90).

ARREST NORMA MACGREGOR **F2.0183**

World Film Corp. *Dist* Rialto Productions. 30 Nov **1921** [New York State license]. Si; b&w. 35mm. 5 reels.

Cast: Joe Moore, Eileen Sedgwick.

Underworld drama. No information about the specific nature of this film has been found.

AS A MAN LIVES **F2.0184**

Achievement Films. *Dist* American Releasing Corp. 21 Jan **1923.** Si; b&w. 35mm. 6 reels, 5,800 ft.

Prod Gilbert E. Gable. *Dir* J. Searle Dawley. *Scen* William Dudley Pelley. *Story* Bob Dexter. *Photog* Bert Dawley. *Asst Dir* Walter Lang.

Cast: Robert Frazer *(Sherry Mason)*, Gladys Hulette *(Nadia Meredith)*, Frank Losee *(Dr. Ralph Neyas)*, J. Thornton Baston *(La Chante)*, Alfred E. Wright *(Henri Camion)*, Kate Blanke *(Mrs. John Mason)*, Tiny Belmont *(Babette)*, Charles Sutton *(Atwill Meredith)*.

Melodrama. Sherry Mason, the wastrel son of wealthy and indulgent parents, almost takes a turn toward reformation when he meets Nadia Meredith, a bookseller's daughter, but she refuses his marriage proposal because of a hint of evil she senses in his face. Sherry goes to Paris with his father's no-good partner, Henri Camion, and gets involved in a cafe fight with an apache, La Chante, who kills his girl friend, Babette. La Chante and Sherry each seek the skill of plastic surgeon Ralph Neyas, who alters La Chante's face (to protect him from the police) and undertakes to remold Sherry's character. The scene abruptly shifts to the American West, where Nadia is hurled into a mine shaft by an explosion set off by Camion. La Chante sacrifices his life to save Nadia, who finds happiness with Sherry. *Idlers. Apaches—Paris. Reformation. Wealth. Plastic surgery. Murder. Explosions. Paris.*

Note: Working title: *Hearts and Faces.*

AS A MAN THINKETH *see* **WHILE JUSTICE WAITS**

AS MAN DESIRES **F2.0185**

First National Pictures. 11 Jan **1925** [c5 Jan 1925; LP20983]. Si; b&w. 35mm. 8 reels, 7,790 ft.

Supv Earl Hudson. *Dir* Irving Cummings. *Ed Dir* Marion Fairfax. *Scen* Marion Orth. *Adapt* Earl Hudson. *Photog* Roy Carpenter. *Art Dir* Milton Menasco. *Film Ed* Charles Hunt.

Cast: Milton Sills *(Maj. John Craig)*, Viola Dana *(Pandora La Croix)*, Ruth Clifford *(Gloria Gordon)*, Rosemary Theby *(Evelyn Beaudine)*, Irving Cummings *(Major Singh)*, Paul Nicholson *(Colonel Carringford)*, Tom Kennedy *(Gorilla Bagsley)*, Hector Sarno *(Toni)*, Lou Payne *(Major Gridley)*, Anna May Walthall *(The Duchess)*, Edneh Altemus *(Camille)*, Frank Leigh *(Watkins)*.

Melodrama. Source: Gene Wright, *Pandora La Croix* (Philadelphia, 1924). Unjustly accused of the murder of Colonel Carringford, Maj. John Craig deserts his post as a surgeon in the British Army in India and drifts to the South Seas, where he soon becomes wealthy by pearl fishing. Afer a boat captained by Gorilla Bagsley poaches on Craig's private pearl beds, Craig searches him out and finds him molesting Pandora, a native dancing girl. Craig overcomes Gorilla in a fight, and Pandora, who thinks that Craig has fought for her, insists on becoming his woman. The first mate of Craig's schooner discovers that there is a reward posted for his captain and sends word of Craig's whereabouts to Watkins, an agent of the British Government. When Watkins arrives on the island, he is stricken with appendicitis; Craig operates on him, saving his life. Gloria Gordon, Craig's onetime love who has accompanied Watkins to the island, informs Craig that he has been cleared of any suspicion of guilt in Carringford's murder. Gorilla attempts to shoot Craig, but Pandora steps between Craig and death, giving up her life to save his. Craig apprehends the brute, and Craig and Gloria make plans to return together to his regiment in India. *Surgeons. Murder. Pearl fishing. Appendicitis. Great Britain—Army. India. South Sea Islands.*

AS THE WORLD ROLLS ON **F2.0186**

Andlauer Productions. *Dist* Elk Photo Plays. 10 Sep **1921** [New York State]. Si; b&w. 35mm. 7 reels, 5,600 ft.

Photog W. A. Andlauer.

Cast: Jack Johnson, Blanche Thompson.

Drama. Tom Atkins and his gang set upon Joe Walker, a small youth who is Tom's rival for the affections of Molly Moran. Jack Johnson hears Joe's call for help and routs the gang of rowdies. Taken with the boy's pluck, Jack accompanies him to a gym and teaches him the fistic art. Jack also teaches Joe how to play baseball, and Joe later helps the Kansas City Monarchs win an important baseball game. In the spirit of revenge, Tom frames Joe and Molly for a robbery. During the trial, a small boy implicates Tom as the true thief, and Tom tries to escape. Joe follows him and subdues him in a fight. Joe marries Polly, and Jack gives them his blessing. *Children. Juvenile delinquents. Negro life. Boxing. Baseball.*

Kansas City Monarchs.
Note: Advertised as featuring "a guaranteed all star colored cast."

ASHAMED OF PARENTS **F2.0187**
Warner Brothers Pictures. 25 Dec **1921** [c21 Nov 1921; LP17220]. Si; b&w. 35mm. 5 or 6 reels.
Dir Horace G. Plympton. *Photog* Jack Brown.
Cast: Charles Eldridge *(Silas Wadsworth)*, Jack Lionel Bohn *(Arthur Wadsworth)*, Edith Stockton *(Marian Hancock)*, Walter McEvan *(Albert Grimes)*, W. J. Gross *(Peter Trotwood)*.
Melodrama. Source: Charles K. Harris, "What Children Will Do" (publication undetermined). Silas Wadsworth, a shoemaker, with the help of two faithful friends, sends his son Arthur to college, where the boy gains fame as a football star and falls in love with Marian Hancock, a young society girl. When they become engaged, Arthur sends an announcement to his parents but wires his father not to come to the reception. Silas and his friends arrive, however, and learn that Arthur is ashamed of them. Marian secretly goes to Arthur's hometown to meet his parents and comes to love Silas. When the latter becomes ill, Arthur is called home and is happily reconciled with his sweetheart. *Cobblers. Fatherhood. Filial relations. Football. Social classes. College life.*

ASHES **F2.0188**
Amalgamated Producing Corp. *Dist* East Coast Productions. 24 Feb **1922** [New York State license]. Si; b&w. 35mm. 5 reels, 4,500 ft.
Dir G. M. Anderson. *Story* Charles Munson. *Photog* Arthur Reeves.
Cast: William Courtleigh *(Mr. DeCourcey)*, Leona Anderson *(Mrs. DeCourcey)*, Margaret Landis *(Madeline DeCourcey)*, Myrtle Stedman *(Mrs. Crafton)*, Wedgewood Nowell *(Mr. Crafton)*, George Howard *(Arthur Spencer)*, Carrie Clark Ward *(Mrs. Van Stuyhl)*, Stanton Heck *(hotel detective)*.
Drama. "A young man in financial difficulties persuades his wife to help him blackmail a supposedly wealthy man. While waiting she reads a magazine story telling how Mr. and Mrs. Crafton ... set out to extort money from DeCourcey. ... Mr. Crafton leaving the room, Mrs. Crafton saying she is in financial difficulties, tries to borrow money. DeCourcey refuses. Mrs. Crafton then makes a scene, her husband enters, she accuses DeCourcey of seeking to attack her. ... DeCourcey, who has remained smoking, shows the ashes remaining on his cigar [to the hotel detective] as evidence that there has been no struggle. The detective believes his accusation of blackmail against the pair and they are arrested. After reading the story the young wife leaves a note saying she has gone back to her home in the country. The intended victim arrives and turns out to be a detective. After reading the note, he takes the penitent young husband to the railroad station and sends him back to his wife." (*Moving Picture World,* 1 Apr 1922, p551.) *Detectives. Blackmail. Finance—Personal.*

ASHES OF VENGEANCE **F2.0189**
Norma Talmadge Film Co. *Dist* Associated First National Pictures. ca18 Aug **1923** [New York premiere; released 1 Oct; c30 Aug 1923; LP19346]. Si; b&w. 35mm. 10 reels, 9,893 ft.
Pres by Joseph M. Schenck. *Prod* Joseph M. Schenck. *Dir-Adapt* Frank Lloyd. *Photog* Tony Gaudio.
Cast: Norma Talmadge *(Yolande de Breux)*, Conway Tearle *(Rupert de Vrieac)*, Wallace Beery *(Duc de Tours)*, Josephine Crowell *(Catherine de Medicis)*, Betty Francisco *(Margot de Vancoire)*, Claire McDowell *(Margot's aunt)*, Courtenay Foote *(Comte de la Roche)*, Howard Truesdell *(Vicomte de Briège)*, Jeanne Carpenter *(Yolande's invalid sister, Anne)*, Forrest Robinson *(Father Paul)*, James Cooley *(Paul)*, Boyd Irwin *(Duc de Guise)*, Winter Hall *(The Bishop)*, William Clifford *(André)*, Murdock MacQuarrie *(Carlotte)*, Hector V. Sarno *(Gallon)*, Earl Schenck *(Blais)*, Lucy Beaumont *(Charlotte)*, Mary McAllister *(Denise)*, Kenneth Gibson *(Phillipe)*, Carmen Phillips *(Marie)*, Rush Hughes *(soldier boy)*, Frank Leigh *(Lupi)*, André de Beranger *(Charles IX)*.
Melodrama. Source: H. B. Somerville, *Ashes of Vengeance, a Romance of Old France* (New York, 1914). When 16th-century France is troubled with intense politico-religious rivalry and Catherine de Medicis launches her attack on the Huguenots, the Comte de la Roche spares the life of his enemy, Rupert de Vrieac, a Huguenot, by making him an indentured servant. At the Roche castle, Rupert falls in love with the count's sister, Yolande, who treats him coldly. When the despicable Duc de Tours attempts to force himself on Yolande by threatening to torture Rupert, Yolande yields. Fortunately, Rupert's men arrive in time to kill Lupi, the torturer. The duke dies following a duel with Rupert, and Yolande persuades her brother to release Rupert from his bondage. *Indentured servants. Nobility. Huguenots. France—History—House of Valois. Charles IX (France). Catherine de Medicis.*

ASÍ ES LA VIDA **F2.0190**
Sono-Art Productions. 1 Jun **1930.** Sd; b&w. 35mm. 7 reels, 6,486 ft.
Pres by O. E. Goebel, George W. Weeks. *Pers Supv* O. E. Goebel. *Dir* George J. Crone. *Dial* Jorge Juan Crespo. *Adapt* Tom Gibson. *Photog* Arthur Todd. *Tech Dir* Charles Cadwallader. *Film Ed* Arturo Tavares. *Mus Dir* Carlos Molina. *Songs: "Son cosas de la vida," "Que tienes en la mirada," "Mi princesita"* Eva Bohr, José Bohr. *Sd* J. G. Greger. *Prod Mgr* J. R. Crone. *Prod Asst* A. S. Black.
Intérpretes: José Bohr *(José Rolan)*, Delia Magana *(Luisa Franklyn)*, Lola Vendrill *(Blanca Franklyn)*, César Vanoni *(Manuel, the butler)*, Enrique Acosta *(Mr. Franklyn)*, Marcela Nivon *(Mrs. Franklyn)*, Tito Davidson *(Jorge Franklyn)*, Myrta Bonillas *(The Countess)*, Julian Rivero *(Calton)*, Ernesto Piedra *("Sapo" [Toad])*, Rosita Gil *(Cora)*.
Comedy. Source: E. J. Rath, *The Dark Chapter* (New York, 1924). Courtenay Savage, *They All Want Something; a Comedy in a Prologue and Three Acts* (New York, 1927). A Spanish-language version of *What a Man*, q. v. *Hoboes. Chauffeurs. Butlers. Bootleggers. English. Canadians.*

AT DEVIL'S GORGE **F2.0191**
Ashton Dearholt. *Dist* Arrow Film Corp. 1 Nov **1923** [c22 Oct 1923; LP19525]. Si; b&w. 35mm. 5 reels, 4,557 ft.
Dir Ashton Dearholt. *Scen* Daniel F. Whitcomb.
Cast: Edmund Cobb *(Paul Clayton)*, Helene Rosson *(Mildred Morgan)*, Wilbur McGaugh *(Clayton's partner, "Dav")*, William White *(Pop Morgan)*, Max Ascher *(Tobias Blake)*, Ashton Dearholt *(a stranger in town)*.
Western melodrama. "Two partners, in love with the same girl, work gold claim. Crooked partner proposes that they play cards to see which one clears out. They do so, but when other partner wins, crooked man imprisons him and robs girl's father. Through help of a man he has aided, hero rights matters." (*Motion Picture News Booking Guide,* 6:10, Apr 1924.) *Miners. Gold mining. Gambling.*

AT THE CROSSROADS **F2.0192**
Dist American Releasing Corp. Nov **1922.** Si; b&w. 35mm. 6 reels.
Cast: Seena Owen.
Melodrama(?). No information about the nature of this film has been found.

AT THE END OF THE WORLD **F2.0193**
Famous Players-Lasky. *Dist* Paramount Pictures. 11 Sep **1921** [c20 Sep 1921; LP16973]. Si; b&w. 35mm. 6 reels, 5,729 ft.
Dir Penrhyn Stanlaws. *Scen* Edfrid A. Bingham. *Adapt* Adelaide Heilbron. *Photog* Paul Perry.
Cast: Betty Compson *(Cherry O'Day)*, Milton Sills *(Gordon Deane)*, Mitchell Lewis *(Donald MacGregor)*, Casson Ferguson *(Harvey Gates)*, Spottiswoode Aitken *(Terence O'Day)*, Joseph Kilgour *(William Blaine)*, Goro Kino *(Uang)*.
Melodrama. Source: Ernest Klein, *At the End of the World* (a play; publication undetermined). Terence O'Day and his daughter, Cherry, operate a gambling establishment, "The Paper Lantern," in Shanghai. She is loved by sailor Donald MacGregor, who leaves, expecting to return and marry her, and by novelist Gordon Deane, who also departs. The death of her father brings about Cherry's marriage to banker William Blaine—an unhappy union, troubled by the attentions of Harvey, her husband's clerk, who steals bank funds to buy her gifts. Meanwhile, Deane recruits Harvey and MacGregor to accompany him to a lonely lighthouse where he plans to work. When Blaine demands a divorce, Cherry consents and starts out to search for Deane; and when wrecked near the lighthouse, she is saved by Deane. A quarrel between the sailor and the clerk results in their both falling to their deaths, but Cherry and Deane return to civilization and happiness. *Sailors. Novelists. Bankers. Fatherhood. Gambling. Divorce. Lighthouses. Shanghai.*

AT THE SIGN OF THE JACK O'LANTERN **F2.0194**
Renco Film Co. *Dist* W. W. Hodkinson Corp. 22 Jan **1922** [c21 Feb 1922; LP17587]. Si; b&w. 35mm. 6 reels, 5,193 ft.
Pres by H. J. Reynolds. *Dir* Lloyd Ingraham. *Adapt* Lloyd Ingraham, David Kirkland.
Cast: Betty Ross Clark *(Mrs. Carr)*, Earl Schenck *(Harlan Carr)*, Wade

Boteler *(Dick)*, Victor Potel *(The Poet)*, Clara Clark Ward *(Mrs. Dodd)*, Monte Collins *(Jeremiah Bradford)*, William Courtwright *(Uncle Skyles)*, Mrs. Raymond Hatton *(Mrs. Holmes)*, Newton Hall *(Willie)*, Zella Ingraham *(Elaine)*.

Mystery-comedy. Source: Myrtle Reed, *At the Sign of the Jack O'Lantern* (New York, 1905). A country residence in New England and the sum of $600 are left to Harlan Carr by the terms of his uncle's will, which further provides that a future legacy will come to him if he properly entertains a number of guests, all married relations of the uncle. Carr and his wife take up residence in the old homestead, where all manner of ghostly events take place. In due course the guests arrive and make life thoroughly miserable for the couple, who tolerate their unpleasantness for fear of losing the legacy. At last Harlan loses all patience and orders them from the house. Then, unexpectedly, the family lawyer informs the Carrs that having done exactly as their uncle wished, they will be rewarded with the remainder of the old man's money. *Wills. Inheritance. Haunted houses. New England.*

AT THE STAGE DOOR **F2.0195**

R-C Pictures. 11 Dec **1921** [c11 Dec 1921; LP17365]. Si; b&w. 35mm. 6 reels, 5,600 or 6,300 ft.

Dir-Writ William Christy Cabanne.

Cast: Frances Hess *(Helen Mathews)*, Elizabeth North *(Helen Mathews, later)*, Miriam Battista *(Mary Mathews)*, Billie Dove *(Mary Mathews, later)*, Margaret Foster *(Mrs. Mathews)*, William Collier, Jr. *(Arthur Bates)*, C. Elliott Griffin *(George Andrews)*, Myrtle Maughan *(Grace Mortimer)*, Charles Craig *(John Brooks)*, Viva Ogden *(Mrs. Reade)*, Billy Quirk *(Harold Reade)*, Huntly Gordon *(Philip Pierce)*, Katherine Spencer *(Alice Vincent)*, Doris Eaton *(Betty)*.

Romantic drama. As a child, Helen Mathews is selfish, and her sister, Mary, gives up everything for her; later, when Helen steals Mary's sweetheart, Mary leaves home to become a chorus girl in New York, and soon she achieves stardom. Philip Pierce, a young millionaire, is attracted to her, but, preferring the simple life, Mary declines his invitation—to the amusement of the other chorus girls. In order to avoid a wild party, however, she allows him to take her home, and she soon falls in love with him. She accepts his proposal but is heartbroken to discover that he is betrothed to a society girl. Later, however, Philip explains that he is not in love with his fiancée and breaks the engagement, reassuring Mary of his love for her. *Sisters. Chorus girls. Millionaires. Vaudeville. Courtship. New York City.*

AT YALE *see* **HOLD 'EM YALE!**

ATTA BOY **F2.0196**

Monty Banks Enterprises. *Dist* Pathé Exchange. 10 Oct **1926** [c4 Oct 1926; LU23179]. Si; b&w. 35mm. 6 reels, 5,775 ft.

Pres by A. MacArthur. *Dir* Edward H. Griffith. *Story-Cont* Charles Horan, Alf Goulding. *Titl* Harold Christie. *Photog* William Reese, Ted Tetzlaff, Blake Wagner. *Tech Dir* Jack Mintz. *Asst Dir* Sherry Hall.

Cast: Monty Banks *(Monty Milde)*, Virginia Bradford *(The Girl)*, Ernie Wood *(Craven, star reporter)*, Fred Kelsey *(detective)*, Virginia Pearson *(Madame Carlton)*, Henry A. Barrows *(Mr. Harrie)*, Earl Metcalf *(his brother)*, Mary Carr *(Grandmother)*, Jimmie Phillips *(Millionaire Kid)*, Alfred Fisher, George Periolat, America Chedister, William Courtwright, Lincoln Plummer, Kewpie Morgan.

Comedy. As a practical joke on his birthday, Monty Milde, copy boy on a large daily newspaper, is told by star reporter Craven that he has been promoted to reporter. Having written a story about a Mr. Smith whose baby has been kidnaped and thus infuriated the man, Craven sends Monty to interview him. Monty encounters all sorts of difficulties at the hotel getting to Mr. Smith, who has detectives on guard, and finally he goes home discouraged; then, discovering a ransom note from the kidnaper left at Smith's room, he trails the kidnaper to a private gambling club. Posing as a waiter, Monty gains entrance to the private rooms of the owner, and there he finds the kidnaper. The den is raided, and Monty rushes off to the office with the baby and collects the reward from Mr. Smith. *Copy boys. Reporters. Infants. Kidnaping.*

ATTA BOY'S LAST RACE (Reissue) **F2.0197**

Fine Arts Pictures. *Dist* Tri-Stone Pictures. **1924.** Si; b&w. 35mm. 5 reels.

Note: A "re-edited and re-titled" Dorothy Gish film originally released by Triangle Film Corp. on 5 Nov 1916.

THE ATTIC OF FELIX BAVU *see* **BAVU**

THE AUCTION BLOCK **F2.0198**

Metro-Goldwyn-Mayer Pictures. 1 Feb **1926** [c1 Mar 1926; LP22467]. Si; b&w. 35mm. 7 reels, 6,239 ft.

Dir Hobart Henley. *Scen* Frederic Hatton, Fanny Hatton. *Photog* John Arnold.

Cast: Charles Ray *(Bob Wharton)*, Eleanor Boardman *(Lorelei Knight)*, Sally O'Neil *(Bernice Lane)*, Ernest Gillen *(Carter Lane)*, Charles Clary *(Homer Lane)*, David Torrence *(Robert Wharton, Sr.)*, James Corrigan *(Mr. Knight)*, Forrest Seabury *(Edward Blake)*, Ned Sparks *(Nat Saluson)*.

Comedy-drama. Source: Rex Beach, *The Auction Block, a Novel of New York Life* (New York, 1916). Lorelei Knight, the pride of Palmdale, South Carolina, wins a beauty contest and becomes the toast of New York, where she meets wealthy Bob Wharton at a charity ball. They fall in love and are married 2 days later. Bob takes her home to meet his father, who quickly disillusions her about Bob's character. Lorelei returns to Palmdale and tells no one of her marriage. Bob follows and finds work in a shoestore, quickly becoming successful and attracting every girl in town. Bernice Lane, a baby vamp and love pirate, deliberately compromises the innocent and protesting Bob by stranding him all night on a country road. As she expected, her father then attempts to make Bob marry her. Mr. Lane soon learns that Bob is already married and goes gunning for him. Lorelei makes Bernice tell her father that Bob was innocent of all wrongdoing and thereby saves Bob's life. Bob and Lorelei are reconciled. *Shoeclerks. Vamps. Smalltown life. Beauty contests. New York City. South Carolina.*

Note: This is a remake of a 1917 film of the same title produced by Goldwyn Pictures.

AUCTION OF SOULS **F2.0199**

Dist Associated First National Pictures. c7 Feb **1922** [LP17531]. Si; b&w. 35mm. 8 reels.

Dir Oscar Apfel. *Scen* Frederic Chapin.

Cast: Aurora Mardiganian *(herself)*.

Documentary. Source: Aurora Mardiganian, *Ravished Armenia; the Story of Aurora Mardiganian, the Christian Girl, Who Lived Through the Great Massacres ...* (interpreted by H. L. Gates; New York, 1918). During World War I, the Turks accuse the Armenians of secretly supporting the Russians, and despite the pleas of American Ambassador Henry Morgenthau the Armenians are rounded up to be sent south. Families are broken up as the men and women are separated; many men are massacred; and the refugees are forced to march across the desert without food or water. At night, only those girls who are buried in the sand by older women are able to escape the "infamy" of the Turks. Against this background is told the story of Aurora Mardiganian, the daughter of a prosperous Armenian family of Harpout, in the shadow of Mt. Ararat. Passelt Pasha, the Turkish governor, demands her hand in marriage, but her father refuses since she would have to deny her Christian faith. Miss Graham, an English girl who teaches at the mission, feeling an obligation to her students, disguises herself as an Armenian and joins the refugees. Miss Graham and Aurora, with the aid of Andranik, a young shepherd attracted to Aurora, escape but are captured by Kurds, violated, and sold into a harem. They are sent to a slave market, after trying to escape, where Andranik buys them. They are captured again by Turks, who have pursued them into a monastery. As a warning against further escape attempts they are shown "a supreme horror—The Cult of the Germans": a long line of naked girls who have been crucified. However, they do manage to escape again, making their way to the American mission. *Armenians. Kurds. Religious persecution. Slavery. World War I. Turkey. United States—Diplomatic and consular service. Henry Morgenthau. Aurora Mardiganian.*

THE AUCTIONEER **F2.0200**

Fox Film Corp. 16 Jan **1927** [c16 Jan 1927; LP23669]. Si; b&w. 35mm. 6 reels, 5,500 ft.

Pres by William Fox. *Dir* Alfred E. Green. *Scen* L. G. Rigby, John Stone. *Photog* George Schneiderman. *Asst Dir* Jack Boland.

Cast: George Sidney *(Simon Levi)*, Marion Nixon *(Ruth Levi)*, Gareth Hughes *(Richard Eagan)*, Doris Lloyd *(Esther Levi)*, Ward Crane *(Paul Groode)*, Sammy Cohen *(Mo)*, Claire McDowell *(Mrs. Tim Eagan)*.

Comedy-drama. Source: Charles Klein and Lee Arthur, *The Auctioneer* (New York opening: 30 Sep 1913). Simon, a Jewish immigrant, adopts the child of a woman dying at sea, and in New York's East Side he builds up a successful pawnbroking-auctioneering business. The girl, Ruth, falls in love with Richard, who is admitted to a bond-brokerage firm when his prospective father-in-law invests his entire fortune in the firm. Owing to the evil machinations of broker Paul Groode, Simon loses everything and is forced to start over again as a peddler. Eventually he catches the crooked broker and regains his money. All ends happily with the lovers united. *Pawnbrokers. Auctioneers. Brokers. Peddlers. Jews. Courtship. Adoption. New York City—East Side.*

AVALANCHE **F2.0201**

Paramount Famous Lasky Corp. 10 Nov **1928** [c9 Nov 1928; LP25814]. Si; b&w. 35mm. 6 reels, 6,099 ft.

Dir Otto Brower. *Scen* Sam Mintz, Herman Mankiewicz, J. Walter Ruben. *Titl* Herman Mankiewicz. *Adapt* J. Walter Ruben, Sam Mintz. *Photog* Roy Clark. *Film Ed* Jane Loring.

Cast: Jack Holt *(Jack Dunton)*, Doris Hill *(Kitty Mains)*, Baclanova *(Grace Stillwell)*, John Darrow *(Verde)*, Guy Oliver *(Mr. Mains)*, Dick Winslow *(Jack Dunton, age 12)*.

Western melodrama. Source: Zane Grey, "Avalanche" (publication undetermined). Jack Dunton, an honest gambler, discovers that his ward, Verde, wants to study mine engineering, and he begins to cheat at cards in order to finance the boy's education. Returning from school 3 years later, Verde begins to lose himself in the wild life of the town, and Jack, determined to get them both out of town, breaks off with his mistress, Grace. In revenge, Grace vamps Verde, and the two old friends come to blows; Verde and Grace elope, and Jack goes after them, saving their lives in an avalanche. This near catastrophe brings everyone to his senses: Verde goes back to Kitty, a storekeeper's pert daughter, and Grace and Jack renew their relationship. *Gamblers. Wards. Storekeepers. Engineers—Mining. Elopement. Avalanches.*

THE AVENGER **F2.0202**

Charles R. Seeling Productions. *Dist* Aywon Film Corp. Jan **1924.** Si; b&w. 35mm. 5 reels, ca4,700 ft.

Dir Charles R. Seeling.

Cast: Big Boy Williams *(Nat Sherwood?)*.

Western melodrama. "A beautiful girl is the object of some villainous schemes to force her into marrying the crooked real estate dealer. His intrigue to make the girl's brother appear a thief is exposed by Nat Sherwood, the hero." *(Motion Picture News Booking Guide,* 6:11, Apr 1924.) *Real estate business. Brother-sister relationship.*

AVENGING FANGS **F2.0203**

Chesterfield Motion Picture Corp. *Dist* Pathé Exchange. 5 Jun **1927** [c10 May 1927; LU23949]. Si; b&w. 35mm. 5 reels, 4,335 ft.

Dir Ernest Van Pelt. *Story-Scen* George Pyper. *Photog* James Brown.

Cast: Kenneth McDonald *(Dick Mansfield)*, Helen Lynch *(Mary Kirkham)*, Jack Richardson *(Trigger Kincaid)*, Max Asher *(sheriff)*, Sandow *(himself, a dog)*.

Action melodrama. Sandow's master is killed by robbers in his home, and a note indicates that the crooks will continue their operations in the West. Dick Mansfield, accompanied by Sandow, succeeds in tracing the leader, Robert Ludlow, and his confederate, Trigger Kincaid. Trigger is captured by the sheriff, but Ludlow convinces him that Dick is the master crook and he also is jailed. Ludlow frees Trigger, and Dick escapes and arrives with the sheriff at Ludlow's cabin; a girl whom the villain has jilted identifies him as one of the murderers. Dick reveals himself as the slain man's brother and takes Mary for his bride. *Brothers. Sheriffs. Murder. Robbery. Dogs.*

THE AVENGING RIDER **F2.0204**

FBO Pictures. 7 Oct **1928** [c7 Oct 1928; LP25925]. Si; b&w. 35mm. 6 reels, 4,785 ft.

Dir Wallace Fox. *Scen* Frank Howard Clark. *Titl* Randolph Bartlett. *Story* Adele Buffington. *Photog* Nick Musuraca. *Film Ed* Della M. King.

Cast: Tom Tyler *(Tom Larkin)*, Florence Allen *(Sally Sheridan)*, Frankie Darro *(Frankie Sheridan)*, Al Ferguson *(Bob Gordon)*, Bob Fleming *(sheriff)*, Arthur Thalasso *(dance professor)*.

Western melodrama. By the will of John Long, a mysteriously murdered ranchman, his estate is jointly shared by Tom Larkin, his ranch foreman, and Sally Sheridan, a niece at school in the East. Sally comes west with all of her classmates, and she and Tom take an instant dislike to each other. Tom is framed for Long's murder by Gordon and arrested by the sheriff. He escapes, proves Gordon to be the murderer, and brings him to justice. Tom and Sally form a mutual admiration society. *Ranchers. Sheriffs. Students. Ranch foremen. Frameup. Injustice. Murder.*

THE AVENGING SHADOW **F2.0205**

Fred J. McConnell Productions. *Dist* Pathé Exchange. 29 or 30 Apr **1928** [c18 Apr 1928; LP25166]. Si; b&w. 35mm. 5 reels, 4,293 ft.

Dir Ray Taylor. *Story-Cont* Bennett Cohen. *Titl* Ray Doyle. *Photog* Harry Cooper, David Smith. *Film Ed* Thomas Malloy.

Cast: Ray Hallor *(James Hamilton, a young bank clerk)*, Wilbur Mack *(Worthington, his assistant cashier)*, Clark Comstock *(Sheriff Apling)*, Howard Davies *(Tom Sommers, the prison warden)*, Margaret Morris *(Marie, his daughter)*, LeRoy Mason *(George Brooks, a deputy warden)*, Grey Boy *(Klondike, a dog)*.

Melodrama. Having been convicted of stealing the factory payroll, bank clerk James Hamilton is railroaded to prison. The guilty persons are Brooks, a deputy warden at the prison where Hamilton is to serve his term, and Worthington, the bank's assistant cashier. The star of the film is Klondike, "a doughty police dog" who remains useful and loyal to Hamilton throughout. Both Hamilton and Klondike figure in a thrilling chase, and Klondike extracts the confession from Brooks that exonerates Hamilton. *Bank clerks. Bankers. Prison wardens. Injustice. Theft. Prisons. Chases. Police dogs.*

THE AVERAGE WOMAN **F2.0206**

C. C. Burr Pictures. 1 Mar **1924** [c10 Feb 1924; LP19920]. Si; b&w. 35mm. 6 reels, 6,021 ft.

Dir William Christy Cabanne. *Scen* Raymond S. Harris. *Photog* Jack Brown, Neil Sullivan.

Cast: Pauline Garon *(Sally Whipple)*, David Powell *(Rudolph Van Alten)*, Harrison Ford *(Jimmy Munroe)*, Burr McIntosh *(Judge Whipple)*, De Sacia Mooers *(Mrs. La Rose)*, William Tooker *(Colonel Crosby)*, Russell Griffin *("Tike" La Rose)*, Coit Albertson *(Bill Brennon)*.

Melodrama. Source: Dorothy De Jagers, "The Average Woman," in *Saturday Evening Post* (194:10–11, 8 Apr 1922). Jimmy Munroe, a newspaper reporter writing an article on "the average woman," encounters Sally Whipple in the library and follows her for material. Sally, whose father is a judge, has the reporter arrested and "sentences" him to visit her once a week. Meanwhile, she is being courted by Van Alten, secret owner of one of the city's most disreputable roadhouses. He forces Sally to agree to marry him by presenting a packet of letters, written by her mother, which he believes to be evidence to embarrass the judge. Whipple deems the letters of no importance: Sally is released from her promise and marries Munroe. *Judges. Reporters. Blackmail. Roadhouses. Documentation.*

THE AVIATOR **F2.0207**

Warner Brothers Pictures. 14 Dec **1929** [c26 Nov 1929; LP872]. Sd (Vitaphone); b&w. 35mm. 7 reels, 6,743 ft. [Also si.]

Dir Roy Del Ruth. *Scen-Dial* Robert Lord, Arthur Caesar. *Titl* De Leon Anthony. *Photog* Chick McGill. *Film Ed* William Holmes.

Cast: Edward Everett Horton *(Robert Street)*, Patsy Ruth Miller *(Grace Douglas)*, Johnny Arthur *(Hobart)*, Lee Moran *(Brown)*, Edward Martindel *(Gordon)*, Armand Kaliz *(Maj. Jules Gaillard)*, Kewpie Morgan *(Sam Robinson)*, Phillips Smalley *(John Douglas)*, William Norton Bailey *(Brooks)*.

Comedy. Source: James Montgomery, *The Aviator* (New York opening: 6 Dec 1910). Wishing to assure the sale of a book of wartime experiences written by an anonymous aviator, Brooks, a publisher, and Brown, his publicist, decide to credit authorship to Robert Street, a highly successful writer. Though he detests aviation, knows nothing about the book in question, and finds the situation socially embarrassing, Street agrees to lend his name to the publication; he then retreats to a fashionable resort. Brown arrives, however, with Street's friends John and Grace Douglas, and he is thoroughly lionized; Street consents to pose for photographs in an airplane on the flying field. Frightened by the camera-flash, he accidentally starts the plane, creating an incredible demonstration landing in a haystack. A race is arranged between Street and Gaillard, a French flyer, and after a series of hair-raising and hilarious complications, Street gives up his pose for the charms of Grace. *Publicists. Authors. Publishers. Aviation. Airplane racing. World War I.*

THE AWAKENING **F2.0208**

Samuel Goldwyn, Inc. *Dist* United Artists. 17 Nov **1928** [c5 Dec 1928; LP25887]. Mus score & sd eff (Movietone); b&w. 35mm. 9 reels, 8,081 ft. [Also si; 7,972 ft.]

Pres by Samuel Goldwyn: *Dir* Victor Fleming. *Scen* Carey Wilson. *Titl*

Katherine Hilliker, H. H. Caldwell. *Story* Frances Marion. *Photog* George Barnes. *Art Dir* William Cameron Menzies. *Film Ed* Viola Lawrence, Katherine Hilliker, H. H. Caldwell. *Mus Score* Hugo Riesenfeld. *Song: "Marie"* Irving Berlin.

Cast: Vilma Banky *(Marie Ducrot)*, Walter Byron *(Count Karl von Hagen)*, Louis Wolheim *(Le Bête)*, George Davis *(The Orderly)*, William H. Orlamond *(Grandfather Ducrot)*, Carl von Hartmann *(Lieut. Franz Geyer)*.

Drama. In Alsace just before the World War, Marie Ducrot, a beautiful and virtuous peasant who falls in love with Count Karl von Hagen—a lieutenant in the German Army—is seen visiting Karl in his quarters, and an angry mob of townspeople hurl stones and curses at her. Marie, mistakenly reported dead, becomes a novice in a religious order. War breaks out, and von Hagen is injured in fighting near Marie's convent; he is cared for by Marie and persuades her to return to Germany with him. Le Bête, a French Army sergeant of their acquaintance, helps them to reach the German lines and safety. Le Bête is killed by a sniper's bullet, and Marie and Karl prepare for a brighter future. *Nobility. Peasants. Soldiers. Novices. Reputation. Convents. World War I. Germany—Army. Alsace.*

AWAY IN THE LEAD **F2.0209**

Goodwill Pictures. 8 Oct **1925** [New York State license]. Si; b&w. 35mm. 5 reels, 4,681 ft.

Cast: Francis X. Bushman, Jr..

Melodrama(?). No information about the nature of this film has been found.

THE AWFUL TRUTH **F2.0210**

Peninsula Studios. *Dist* Producers Distributing Corp. 6 Apr **1925** [c23 Apr 1925; LP21392]. Si; b&w. 35mm. 6 reels, 5,917 ft.

Pres by Elmer Harris. Frank E. Woods Production. *Dir* Paul Powell. *Adapt-Scen* Elmer Harris. *Photog* Joseph A. Dubray.

Cast: Agnes Ayres *(Lucy Slatterley)*, Warner Baxter *(Norman Slatterley)*, Phillips Smalley *(Kempster)*, Raymond Lowney *(Danny Leeson)*, Winifred Bryson *(Josephine)*, Carrie Clark Ward *(Mrs. Leeson)*.

Comedy. Source: Arthur Richman, *The Awful Truth* (New York opening: 18 Sep 1922). Lucy Slatterley flirts with other men to the intense discomfort of her jealous husband, Norman, who resents in particular the attentions of a rounder named Kempster. Kempster makes Norman an irresistible proposal to take over a mining operation, however, and Norman leaves town to investigate the proposition. Kempster then makes advances toward Lucy, who, to avoid him, moves in with her friend, Josephine, a resident of the same apartment building in which Kempster lives. A fire breaks out in the building, and Lucy and Kempster meet in nightclothes on the fire escape just as Norman returns from his business trip. Norman refuses to accept her explanations and obtains a divorce. A year later, Josephine persuades Lucy to accept the proposal of Danny Leeson, a millionaire fop who dotes on her. Norman and Lucy become friendly again, however, but he still believes her to have been unfaithful. Lucy then arranges a meeting with Kempster in a mountain lodge, and Norman comes to her rescue (as she had fully intended). Norman then confesses to Lucy how much he has missed her, and Lucy tells him that there can be no love without trust. Norman finally decides to take Lucy back, trusting to love to see them through. *Millionaires. Flirtation. Marriage. Divorce. Jealousy. Mining. San Francisco. Fires.*

Note: Exteriors shot in San Francisco and Bay area.

THE AWFUL TRUTH **F2.0211**

Pathé Exchange. 10 Aug **1929** [c9 Nov 1929; LP844]. Sd (Photophone); b&w. 35mm. 8 reels, 6,129 ft.

Prod Maurice Revnes. *Dir* Marshall Neilan. *Dial Dir* Rollo Lloyd. *Scen-Dial* Arthur Richman, Horace Jackson. *Camera* David Abel. *Film Ed* Frank E. Hull. *Sd Tech* Earl A. Wolcott. *Prod Mgr* George Webster.

Cast: Ina Claire *(Lucy Warriner)*, Henry Daniel *(Norman Warriner)*, Theodore von Eltz *(Edgar Trent)*, Paul Harvey *(Dan Leeson)*, Blanche Frederici *(Mrs. Leeson)*, Judith Vosselli *(Josephine Trent)*, John Roche *(Jimmy Kempster)*.

Domestic comedy. Source: Arthur Richman, *The Awful Truth* (New York opening: 18 Sep 1922). Shortly after their marriage, Norman Warriner and his wife, Lucy, quarrel over her friendship with Jimmy Kempster, resulting in an interlocutory decree of divorce to be granted within a year unless the couple become reconciled. At a charity bazaar, Lucy dances with Dan Leeson, an oil magnate, who repeatedly proposes to her; and annoyed by her husband's dancing with another woman, Lucy absentmindedly accepts Dan's offer. Finding herself the subject of scandalous gossip, Lucy urges Dan and his aunt to listen to her husband's story; he denies the truth of the rumors and exonerates her, then plans to leave for Europe. Lucy breaks her engagement to Dan and is happily reunited with her husband when he learns that Kempster had only asked his wife for a kiss—which she had refused him! *Marriage. Divorce. Gossip. Bazaars.*

BABBITT **F2.0212**

Warner Brothers Pictures. 15 Jun **1924** [c4 Jun 1924; LP20275]. Si; b&w. 35mm. 8 reels, 7,914 ft.

Dir Harry Beaumont. *Adapt* Dorothy Farnum. *Photog* David Abel.

Cast: Willard Louis *(George F. Babbitt)*, Mary Alden *(Mrs. Myra Babbitt)*, Carmel Myers *(Tanis Judique)*, Raymond McKee *(Theodore Roosevelt Babbitt)*, Maxine Elliott Hicks *(Verona Babbitt)*, Virginia Loomis *(Tina Babbitt)*, Robert Randall *(Paul Reisling)*, Cissy Fitzgerald *(Mrs. Zilla Reisling)*, Gertrude Olmstead *(Eunice Littlefield)*, Lucien Littlefield *(Edward Littlefield)*, Dale Fuller *(Tillie, the maid)*, Kathleen Myers *(Miss McGoun)*, Frona Hale *(Mrs. Littlefield)*.

Drama. Source: Sinclair Lewis, *Babbitt* (New York, 1922). George F. Babbitt, middle-aged, respectable, a prosperous real estate man in the city of Zenith, tired of the routine of family life, finds he has let life slip by. In an attempt to renew his youth he begins an affair with Tanis Judique, an alluring young woman, with whom he plans to leave town; at the pleas of his son, however, he returns to his sick wife, confesses his foolishness, and resumes the happiness of family life. *Real estate business. Middle age. Family life. Social conformity. Babbittry.*

BABE COMES HOME **F2.0213**

First National Pictures. 22 May **1927** [c28 Apr 1927; LP23893]. Si; b&w. 35mm. 6 reels, 5,761 ft.

Prod Wid Gunning. *Dir* Ted Wilde. *Scen* Louis Stevens. *Photog* Karl Struss.

Cast: "Babe" (George Herman) Ruth *(Babe Dugan)*, Anna Q. Nilsson *(Vernie)*, Louise Fazenda *(laundry girl)*, Ethel Shannon *(Georgia)*, Arthur Stone *(laundry driver)*, Lou Archer *(Peewee, third baseman)*, Tom McGuire *(Angel team manager)*, Mickey Bennett *(mascot)*, James Bradbury, Big Boy Williams, James Gordon *(baseball players)*.

Comedy. Source: Gerald Beaumont, "Said With Soap," in *Red Book* (44:52–55, Apr 1925). Babe Dugan, star player of the Angel baseball team, chews tobacco and gets his uniform dirtier than any other player. Vernie, the laundress who cleans his uniform every week, becomes concerned over his untidiness; Babe calls to apologize for unintentionally striking her with a ball during a game; and his pal, Peewee, falls in love with Vernie's friend, Georgia. On an outing to an amusement park, a roller coaster throws Vernie into Babe's arms; soon they are engaged, and Vernie plans to reform him. Scores of tobacco cubes and spittoons are pre-wedding gifts, and they precipitate a lovers' quarrel. But Babe takes the reform idea seriously, though his game slumps and he is put on the bench. At a crucial moment, Vernie relents and throws him a plug of tobacco; and consequently he delivers a four-base blow. *Laundresses. Baseball. Tobacco. Courtship. Amusement parks.*

THE BABY CYCLONE **F2.0214**

Metro-Goldwyn-Mayer Pictures. 27 Sep **1928** [New York showing; c3 Nov 1928; LP25906]. Si; b&w. 35mm. 7 reels, 5,053 ft.

Dir Edward Sutherland. *Adapt-Cont* F. Hugh Herbert. *Titl* Robert Hopkins. *Photog* André Barlatier. *Sets* Cedric Gibbons. *Film Ed* Carl L. Pierson. *Wardrobe* Gilbert Clark.

Cast: Lew Cody *(Joe Meadows)*, Aileen Pringle *(Lydia)*, Robert Armstrong *(Gene)*, Gwen Lee *(Jessie)*, Nora Cecil *(Mrs. Crandall)*, Fred Esmelton *(Mr. Webster)*, Clarissa Selwynne *(Mrs. Webster)*, Wade Boteler *(Bill)*.

Comedy. Source: George Michael Cohan, *The Baby Cyclone; a New American Farce in Three Acts* (New York, c1929). "Lest you think this picture is a mystery thriller you should know that the baby cyclone is a dog—assuming that a Pekingese is really an honest to goodness dog. Neither the husband nor the fatal stepper, who wants to be one, would call him a dog and what they would call him isn't fit to be told. Wife and fiancée, on the other hand, think him an angel pet and what with each of them trying to have him for her very own and the two men co-operating in vain to exterminate the pest you have the making of a lively farce."

(*National Board of Review Magazine*, Oct 1928, p6.) *Vamps. Marriage. Dogs.*

BABY MINE F2.0215

Metro-Goldwyn-Mayer Pictures. 7 Jan **1928** [New York premiere; released 21 Jan 1928; c21 Jan 1928; LP25249]. Si; b&w. 35mm. 6 reels, 5,139 ft.

Dir Robert Z. Leonard. *Scen* F. Hugh Herbert, Lew Lipton. *Titl* Ralph Spence. *Adapt* Sylvia Thalberg. *Photog* Faxon Dean. *Set Dsgn* Cedric Gibbons, Frederic Hope. *Film Ed* Sam S. Zimbalist. *Wardrobe* Gilbert Clark.

Cast: Karl Dane *(Oswald Hardy)*, George K. Arthur *(Jimmy Hemingway)*, Charlotte Greenwood *(Emma)*, Louise Lorraine *(Helen)*.

Farce. Source: Margaret Mayo, *Baby Mine; Domestic Farce in Three Acts* (New York opening: 23 Aug 1910). Tricked into marrying a big, ungainly girl, Oswald Hardy, a student chiropractor, leaves his new wife, Emma, the following morning. A year later Oswald returns, summoned by the news of an addition to the family. A musical chairs sequence involving three babies and a cigar-smoking midget dressed in swaddling clothes suggests to Oswald that he has been tricked again, but he forgives his wife and friends and decides to stay home for a while. *Chiropractors. Infants. Midgets. Marriage. Desertion.*

THE BABY MOTHER *see* **NO BABIES WANTED**

BACHELOR BRIDES F2.0216

De Mille Pictures. *Dist* Producers Distributing Corp. 10 May **1926** [New York premiere; released 4 Jul; c10 Apr 1926; LP22590]. Si; b&w. 35mm. 6 reels, 6,612 ft.

Pres by Cecil B. De Mille. *Dir* William K. Howard. *Scen* Garrett Fort, C. Gardner Sullivan. *Photog* Lucien Andriot. *Art Dir* Max Parker. *Asst Dir* Henry Hathaway.

Cast: Rod La Rocque *(Percy Ashfield)*, Eulalie Jensen *(Lady Ashfield)*, Elinor Fair *(Mary Bowing)*, George Nichols *(Henry Bowing)*, Julia Faye *(Pansy)*, Lucien Littlefield *(Beamish)*, Sally Rand *(maid)*, Eddie Gribbon *(Glasgow Willie)*, Paul Nicholson *(Strang)*.

Comedy–mystery melodrama. Source: Charles Horace Malcolm, *Bachelor Brides* (a play; c13 Aug 1925). Percy Ashfield and Mary Bowing, an American heiress, are about to be married in Duncraggen Towers Castle in Scotland, though Mary's father is opposed to the marriage. While Percy is displaying the family pearls, Pansy, a strange woman, bursts in with a child in her arms and declares that Percy is the child's father by a secret marriage. Percy denies the charge; Dr. Strang arrives and declares the woman insane; then a supposed inspector from Scotland Yard enters saying he has been hired to guard the jewels, but Percy discovers his duplicity. Ultimately, the real detective appears to explain that he has substituted fake jewels for the real ones, and that the doctor, the woman, and the pseudodetective are notorious thieves. Bowing decides that Percy has proved himself and is worthy of his daughter. *Thieves. Detectives. Fatherhood. Weddings. Scotland. Scotland Yard.*

THE BACHELOR DADDY F2.0217

Famous Players–Lasky. *Dist* Paramount Pictures. ca29 Apr **1922** [New York premiere; released 28 May; c6 May 1922; LP17871]. Si; b&w. 35mm. 7 reels, 6,229 ft.

Pres by Adolph Zukor. *Dir* Alfred Green. *Scen* Olga Printzlau. *Photog* William Marshall, Gilbert Warrenton.

Cast: Thomas Meighan *(Richard Chester)*, Leatrice Joy *(Sally Lockwood)*, Maude Wayne *(Ethel McVae)*, Adele Farrington *(Mrs. McVae)*, J. Farrell MacDonald *(Joe Pelton)*, Laurance Wheat *(Charles Henley)*, Charlotte Jackson *(Nita)*, Barbara Maier *(Buddie)*, Bruce Guerin *(Toodles)*, De Briac Twins *(David and Donald)*.

Comedy-drama. Source: Edward Henry Peple, "The Bachelor Daddy" (publication undetermined). Richard Chester, a mineowner in the South, is engaged to Ethel McVae, a poor girl. He is secretly loved, however, by Sally Lockwood, his secretary. Chester's mine is threatened by bandits, and his foreman, Joe Pelton, who cares for five motherless children, saves Chester's life but is himself mortally wounded; and his dying request is that Chester adopt his children. Since Chester's fiancée does not agree to the adoption, he places the children in schools except for the baby, which is cared for by Sally. The day before the wedding, Chester and baby contract mumps, and when Ethel finds Sally nursing them both, she breaks the engagement. Chester gathers the children and plans to be a bachelor daddy, but finding that he needs Sally's help, he falls in love with her and marries her. *Mine foremen. Bachelors. Children. Bandits. Adoption. Courtship. Mumps. United States—South.*

THE BACHELOR GIRL F2.0218

Columbia Pictures. 20 May **1929** [c18 Jun 1929; LP486]. Talking sequences & mus score (Movietone); b&w. 35mm. 7 reels, 5,927 ft. [Also si; 6,245 ft.]

Prod Harry Cohn. *Dir* Richard Thorpe. *Story-Cont* Jack Townley. *Dial* Frederic Hatton, Fanny Hatton. *Titl* Weldon Melick. *Photog* Joseph Walker. *Art Dir* Harrison Riley. *Film Ed* Ben Pivar. *Asst Dir* George Rhein.

Cast: William Collier, Jr. *(Jimmy)*, Jacqueline Logan *(Joyce)*, Edward Hearn *(Campbell)*, Thelma Todd *(Gladys)*.

Society drama. Joyce, a beautiful and efficient young secretary in a business office, and Jimmy, a handsome and shiftless stock clerk, are in love, but because of the boy's inability to get ahead, they are forced to postpone marriage. When he loses his job through carelessness, she gets him another, unknown to him. Just as she believes he is about to propose, he asks her to work for him, and hiding her disappointment, she consents. Joyce handles his customers with the tact and ability he lacks, giving the impression that Jimmy is doing well, and he soon begins to pursue the night life with his boss's sister, Gladys, neglecting his work and Joyce. Joyce covers for him when he fails to show up for a conference, but he arrives later, upbraids her for usurping his position, and is fired on the spot. Two years later, Jimmy is on the downward path and Joyce is a successful bachelor girl; but through a chance meeting, their old love is revived and he promises to make himself worthy of her. *Secretaries. Stock clerks. Businesswomen. Business management. Courtship.*

THE BACHELOR'S BABY F2.0219

Columbia Pictures. 20 Feb **1927** [c11 Feb 1927; LP23674]. Si; b&w. 35mm. 6 reels, 5,260 ft.

Supv Harry Cohn. *Dir* Frank R. Strayer. *Screenplay* Julien Sands. *Story* Garrett Elsden Fort. *Photog* J. O. Taylor.

Cast: Helene Chadwick *(Eleanor Carter)*, Harry Myers *(Bill Taylor)*, Midget Gustav *(Mr. Boppo)*, Edith Yorke *(Mrs. Carter)*, Blanche Payson *(Mrs. Boppo)*, Pat Harmon *("Hardboiled" Hogan)*, James Marcus *(Colonel Carter)*.

Comedy-melodrama. Eleanor Carter smiles at a child in a resort hotel, and Bill Taylor, thinking her attention is directed to him, incurs her indignant wrath. Following her in an automobile, Bill saves Eleanor from an accident, but she is stopped for speeding by "Hard-Boiled" Hogan; Eleanor tells him that she and her "husband" are racing home to their "sick baby," and the officer follows them to Eleanor's apartment to see the baby. While Eleanor stalls Hogan, Bill experiences a series of wild adventures searching for an infant, and finally he prevails upon Mr. Boppo, a midget, to impersonate a baby. All goes well until Eleanor's parents arrive and Mr. Boppo returns to his jealous wife. Bill and Eleanor are forced to escape in an airplane, and they are about to be married by a minister when the pursuit is resumed. But all ends happily. *Bachelors. Infants. Midgets. Police. Mistaken identity. Airplanes. Chases.*

THE BACHELOR'S CLUB F2.0220

Oscar Price. *Dist* Parthenon Pictures. 5 Jan **1929.** Mus score b&w. 35mm. 6 reels, 6,022 ft. [Also si; 5,587 or 5,699 ft.]

Dir Noel Mason. *Scen* Betty Moore. *Titl* Al Martin. *Photog* Harry Cooper, William Wheeler. *Film Ed* Martin Obzina.

Cast: Richard Talmadge, Barbara Worth, Edna Murphy, Edna Ellsmere, V. Talbot Henderson, Herbert Hayes, Barry Palmer.

Action comedy(?). "Attempt made to make something out of a president of a bachelor's club going goofy over a girl and then having the club mete out punishment of him for breaking the very rule he established." (*Variety*, 4 Sep 1929, p24.) *Bachelors. Clubs.*

BACHELOR'S PARADISE F2.0221

Tiffany-Stahl Productions. 15 Mar **1928** [c10 Apr 1928; LP25147]. Si; b&w. 35mm. 7 reels, 6,147 ft.

Dir George Archainbaud. *Titl* Harry Braxton. *Adapt* Frances Guihan, Vera Clark. *Story* Curtis Benton. *Photog* Chester A. Lyons. *Art Dir* Hervey Libbert. *Film Ed* Robert J. Kern.

Cast: Sally O'Neill *(Sally O'Day)*, Ralph Graves *(Joe Wallace)*, Eddie Gribbon *(Terry Malone)*, Jimmy Finlayson *(Pat Malone)*, Sylvia Ashton *(Mrs. Malone)*, Jean Laverty *(Gladys O'Toole)*.

Drama. "Pugilist sprains ankle during a street brawl and is taken care of by girl who loves him. Believing her love is returned, she makes preparations for their marriage. Deserting girl at altar, fighter realizes love for girl when her vision appears to him, while down for count in ring, and [this] enables him to win battle." (*Motion Picture News Booking Guide*, [14]:234, 1929.) *Boxers. Visions.*

BACK FIRE **F2.0222**

Sunset Productions. *Dist* Aywon Film Corp. 1 Nov **1922**. Si; b&w. 35mm. 5 reels, 4,628 ft.

Pres by Anthony J. Xydias. *Dir-Writ* Alvin J. Neitz.

Cast: Jack Hoxie.

Western melodrama. "'Lightning' Carson and a chance acquaintance, Jim Hampton, drift into a little town in the West. Desperately in need of money, Jim suggests that they hold up the Wells-Fargo office. The suggestion is overheard. By chance, the express office is robbed and the two are suspected. Hampton is thrown into jail and 'Lightning' pursued by the Sheriff. He meets Jim's sister and falls in love with her. When the Sheriff finally traps 'Lightning' it is found he is a Texas Ranger. They join forces and a battle follows between them and the real outlaws. When the bandits are captured 'Lightning' claims Jim's sister Betty." (*Motion Picture News Booking Guide*, 4:29, Apr 1923.) *Sheriffs. Texas Rangers. Wells Fargo & Co.. Robbery.*

Note: Reissued in 1929 (New York State license: 14 Nov 1929).

BACK FROM SHANGHAI **F2.0223**

Richard Talmadge Productions. *Dist* Parthenon Pictures, General Pictures. 21 Mar **1929** [New York showing; released 1 Aug 1929]. Mus score & sd eff; b&w. 35mm. 5 reels, 4,700-5,400 ft. [Also si.]

Dir Noel Mason. *Story-Scen* Betty Moos. *Titl* Edward Curtiss. *Photog* Reginald Lyons, Anthony Urgin. *Film Ed* Martin Obzina.

Cast: Leonard St. Leo, Vera Reynolds, Sojin, Joseph W. Girard, Henry Sedley.

Action melodrama. "The plot concerns a sacred vase stolen from a Buddhist temple by an American curio dealer, who is trailed to America and threatened with death if he does not return it. When he cannot buy it back from the man to whom he disposed of it, he tries to steal it and is caught. ... Its action involves gunplay, furious villain-chasing, a fair amount of suspense and no end of personal encounters." (*Film Daily*, 23 Mar 1930, p10.) *Antique dealers. Religious objects. Robbery. Buddhism.*

BACK HOME AND BROKE **F2.0224**

Famous Players–Lasky. *Dist* Paramount Pictures. 24 Dec **1922** [New York premiere; released 25 Dec; c23 Dec 1922; LP18563]. Si; b&w. 35mm. 8 reels, 7,814 ft.

Pres by Adolph Zukor. *Dir* Alfred E. Green. *Scen* J. Clarkson Miller. *Story-Adapt* George Ade. *Photog* Henry Cronjager.

Cast: Thomas Meighan *(Tom Redding)*, Lila Lee *(Mary Thorne)*, Frederick Burton *(Otis Grimley)*, Cyril Ring *(Eustace Grimley)*, Charles Abbe *(H. H. Hornby)*, Florence Dixon *(Olivia Hornby)*, Gertrude Quinlan *(Aggie Twaddle)*, Richard Carlyle *(John Thorne)*, Maude Turner Gordon *(Mrs. Redding)*, Laurance Wheat *(Billy Andrews)*, Ned Burton *(Horace Beemer)*, James Marlowe *(policeman)*, Eddie Borden *(collector)*.

Comedy-drama. Tom Redding is deserted by all save Mary Austin when his apparently wealthy father dies and leaves only debts. Desperate, he goes west and successfully develops an oil well. With the aid of Billy Andrews, Tom returns home in the guise of poverty while a "Mr. Keane" buys up property. At a banquet Tom discloses his ruse and his engagement to Mary, while assuring the townspeople they may retain control of their businesses. *Businessmen. Poverty. Inheritance. Oil wells.*

BACK PAY **F2.0225**

Cosmopolitan Productions. *Dist* Paramount Pictures. 8 Jan **1922** [c8 Jan 1922; LP17459]. Si; b&w. 35mm. 7 reels, 6,460 ft.

Dir Frank Borzage. *Scen* Frances Marion. *Photog* Chester Lyons. *Set Dsgn* Joseph Urban.

Cast: Seena Owen *(Hester Bevins)*, Matt Moore *(Jerry Newcombe)*, J. Barney Sherry *(Charles G. Wheeler)*, Ethel Duray *(Kitty)*, Charles Craig *("Speed")*, Jerry Sinclair *(Thomas Craig)*.

Society melodrama. Source: Fannie Hurst, "Back Pay," in *The Vertical City* (New York, 1922). Country girl Hester Bevins, although in love with Jerry Newcombe, a delivery boy, cannot bring herself to settle down for life in the humdrum town in which they live. In New York she falls in with a fast set, headed by Charles G. Wheeler, a wealthy businessman, and she learns the ways of the city from her companions, Kitty and "Speed." Later, Hester learns that Jerry has been seriously wounded in the war in France, and finding him blinded and with only a few weeks to live, she decides to make his remaining days happy. After a struggle with Wheeler, she brings Jerry to New York and marries him. When Jerry dies, Hester has visions of him calling her from her surroundings, and consequently she leaves her life of luxury with Wheeler, gets a job, rents a furnished room, and finds comfort in her new life. *Smalltown life. Blindness. Hallucinations. World War I. New York City.*

BACK PAY **F2.0226**

First National Pictures. 1 Jun **1930** [c9 Jun 1930; LP1351]. Sd (Vitaphone); b&w. 35mm. 7 reels, 5,672 ft.

Prod Walter Morosco. *Dir* William Seiter. *Scen-Dial* Francis E. Faragoh. *Photog* John Seitz. *Film Ed* Ray Curtiss.

Cast: Corinne Griffith *(Hester Bevins)*, Grant Withers *(Gerald Smith)*, Montagu Love *(Charles Wheeler)*, Hallam Cooley *(Al Bloom)*, Vivian Oakland *(Kitty)*, Geneva Mitchell *(Babe)*, William Bailey *(Ed)*, Virginia Sale *(Wheeler's secretary)*, Dee Loretta *(Aggie Simms)*, James Marcus *(judge)*, Louise Carver *(masseuse)*, Louise Beavers *(Hester's maid)*.

Society melodrama. Source: Fannie Hurst, "Back Pay," in *The Vertical City* (New York, 1922). Hester Bevins, tiring of the humdrum existence of salesclerk in a smalltown department store and deaf to the proposal of bookkeeper Gerald Smith, flees to New York City with Al Bloom, a traveling salesman. There she travels the primrose path to luxury under the "protection" of Charles Wheeler; and though she renews her acquaintance with Gerald, she refuses his proposal because of her present situation. When Gerald loses his eyesight and suffers lung injury in the war, Hester goes to see him; and realizing she owes him something, she persuades Wheeler to agree to her marrying Gerald before he dies. Unexpectedly, she finds happiness and peace in the relationship; and after Gerald's death, she decides to leave Wheeler and return to work. *Salesclerks. Mistresses. Veterans. Traveling salesmen. Smalltown life. Blindness. Wealth. Courtship. Marriage.*

BACK TO GOD'S COUNTRY (Universal-Jewel) **F2.0227**

Universal Pictures. 4 Sep **1927** [c7 Jul 1927; LP24164]. Si; b&w. 35mm. 6 reels, 5,751 ft.

Pres by Carl Laemmle. *Dir* Irvin Willat. *Adapt-Scen* Charles Logue. *Titl* Walter Anthony. *Photog* George Robinson.

Cast: Renée Adorée *(Renée Debois)*, Robert Frazer *(Bob Stanton)*, Walter Long *(Blake)*, Mitchell Lewis *(Jean Debois)*, James Mason *(Jacques Carbeau)*, Walter Ackerman *(clerk)*, Adolph Milar, Flying Eagle.

Northwest melodrama. Source: James Oliver Curwood, *Back to God's Country and Other Stories* (New York, 1920). Trapper Jean Debois, accompanied by his daughter, Renée, arrives with his annual catch of pelts at Carbeau's trading post, and when the wily trader tries to swindle and kill Jean, he is himself killed in the struggle. Blake, a sea captain, fired with rum, threatens to have Jean arrested for murder unless the girl becomes his wife. To save her father, Renée pretends to love Blake, but Bob Stanton, a young engineer, attacks Blake and agrees to help Jean. Aboard ship, Blake creates an "accident" that kills Jean and wounds Bob; when they arrive at the cove, Renée escapes with Bob by sled, pursued by Blake; they are halted by a blizzard, but Blake falls to his death when attacked by a dog. *Trappers. Engineers. Sea captains. Courtship. Trading posts. Canadian Northwest. Blizzards. Dogs.*

BACK TO LIBERTY **F2.0228**

Excellent Pictures. 15 Nov **1927** [c31 Oct 1927; LP24605]. Si; b&w. 35mm. 6 reels, 5,980 ft. [Copyrighted as 7 reels.]

Pres by Samuel Zierler. *Dir* Bernard McEveety. *Story-Cont* Arthur Hoerl. *Titl* Harry Chandlee. *Photog* Marcel Le Picard.

Cast: Jean Del Val *(Rudolph Gambier)*, George Walsh *(Jimmy Stevens)*, Edmund Breese *(Tom Devon/Reginald Briand)*, De Sacia Mooers *(Nina Burke)*, Dorothy Hall *(Gloria Briand)*.

Mystery melodrama. Tom Devon, known to his society friends as Reginald Briand, is the mastermind behind an organization of gentlemen crooks, including Jimmy Stevens and Rudolph Gambier. His pretty daughter, Gloria, unaware of her father's underworld associations, meets Jimmy when he saves her from an embarrassing scene in a restaurant, and they fall in love. Devon, discovering Jimmy's attentions to his daughter and noting his resolve to reform, pays off Gambier and tries to persuade Jimmy to stop seeing Gloria; Gambier returns, thinking himself cheated, and kills Devon. Although Jimmy is arrested and convicted of the murder, Gloria is convinced of his innocence. When Gambier returns for the remainder of the spoils, Gloria intervenes, herself pretending to be a thief; and after winning his affections, she tricks him into confessing the crime. Gambier is mortally wounded by the police, and Jimmy is pardoned by the governor. *Gentlemen crooks. Murder. Circumstantial evidence.*

BACK TO LIFE **F2.0229**

Postman Pictures. *Dist* Associated Exhibitors. 22 Feb **1925** [c12 Feb 1925; LP21129]. Si; b&w. 35mm. 6 reels, 5,826 ft.

Dir Whitman Bennett. *Scen* Harry Chandlee. *Photog* Edward Paul.

Cast: Patsy Ruth Miller *(Margaret Lothbury)*, David Powell *(John Lothbury)*, Lawford Davidson *(Wallace Straker)*, Mary Thurman *(June Porter)*, George Stewart *(Arthur Lothbury)*, Frederick Burton *(Henry Porter)*, Frankie Evans *(Sonny Lothbury)*.

Melodrama. Source: Andrew Soutar, *Back From the Dead* (London, 1920). During the World War, John Lothbury joins the French Air Force as a pilot and is later reported dead by the French Government. John's brother, who has embezzled $10,000 from Wallace Straker, blames the theft on John, and John's widow, Margaret, marries Straker in order to avoid a posthumous scandal involving John. With Margaret still secretly mourning him, John escapes from a German prison camp and returns to the United States. Going back to his small hometown, he discovers that his wife has remarried. He calls on her, introducing himself as a friend of her late husband. Margaret does not recognize him, for his face was blown off in the war and plastic surgery has given him a completely changed appearance. John eventually works himself into the presidency of an aircraft company that is a rival to Straker's firm, and, when Straker finds himself in financial difficulties, John helps him out in order to protect Margaret. Straker finds out John's true identity and, in a state of rage and drunkeness, gets a gun and goes after him. He is about to shoot, when a life of dissipation takes its toll and he dies of a heart attack. John and Margaret are reunited, and John is cleared of all guilt in the theft of Straker's money. *Brothers. Prisoners of war. Plastic surgery. Embezzlement. Airplane manufacture. World War I. Germany. France—Air Force.*

BACK TO OLD VIRGINIA **F2.0230**

Primrose Pictures. 19 Sep **1923** [New York State license]. Si; b&w. 35mm. 5 reels, 4,500 ft.

Cast: Judith Jordan.

Drama(?). No information about the nature of this film has been found. *Virginia.*

BACK TO YELLOW JACKET **F2.0231**

Ben Wilson Productions. *Dist* Arrow Film Corp. 14 Mar **1922** [c25 Mar 1922; LP17669]. Si; b&w. 35mm. 6 reels, 5,901 ft.

Prod-Dir Ben Wilson. *Adapt* J. Grubb Alexander. *Photog* Harry Gersted.

Cast: Roy Stewart *(Jim Ballantyne)*, Kathleen Kirkham *(Carmen, his wife)*, Earl Metcalfe *(Flush Kirby)*, Jack Pratt *(William Carson)*.

Western melodrama. Source: Peter Bernard Kyne, "Back to Yellow Jacket," in *Soldiers, Sailors, and Dogs* (New York, 1936). Carmen, wife of Sunny Jim Ballantyne, a prospector, dissatisfied with life in the wilderness, defies her husband and attends a public dance with Flush Kirby, a gambler. Following a quarrel, she implores William Carson, an old flame, to take her east. Ballantyne battles with Kirby, then discovers that Carmen has disappeared and retreats to the desert where he forms a partnership with Carson in the goldfields. The two men are amiable until Jim finds that Carson offered his wife the shelter of his home; and returning to Yellow Jacket, Jim informs Carmen, now a dancehall girl, that he has set an explosion to kill Carson. She declares Carson is innocent, and although Carson is rescued, Jim is injured by the explosion but is later reconciled with Carmen. *Prospectors. Dancehall girls. Gamblers. Desertion.*

THE BACK TRAIL **F2.0232**

Universal Pictures. 16 Jun **1924** [c20 May 1924; LP20216]. Si; b&w. 35mm. 5 reels, 4,615 ft.

Dir Clifford Smith. *Scen* Isadore Bernstein. *Story* Walter J. Coburn. *Photog* Harry Neumann.

Cast: Jack Hoxie *(Jeff Prouty)*, Alton Stone *(The Tramp)*, Eugenia Gilbert *(Ardis Andrews)*, Claude Payton *("Gentleman Harry" King)*, William Lester *(Jim Lawton)*, William McCall *(Judge Talent)*, Buck Connors *(Shorty)*, Pat Harmon *(Curry)*.

Western melodrama. Jeff Prouty loses his memory as a result of war injuries and is made to believe he has committed past crimes. He is induced to break his father's will to gain his foster sister's estate, but when his identity is established he foils the crooks and wins the girl. *Veterans. Swindlers. Inheritance. Amnesia.*

BACKBONE **F2.0233**

Distinctive Pictures. *Dist* Goldwyn Distributing Corp. 30 Apr **1923** [c26 Apr 1923; LP18899]. Si; b&w. 35mm. 7 reels, 6,821 ft.

Dir Edward Sloman. *Adapt-Scen* Charles E. Whittaker. *Photog* Harry A. Fischbeck. *Art Dir* Clark Robinson.

Cast: Edith Roberts *(Yvonne de Mersay/Yvonne de Chausson)*, Alfred Lunt *(John Thorne/André de Mersay)*, William B. Mack *(Anthony Bracken)*, Frankie Evans *(Doc Roper)*, James D. Doyle *(Colonel Tip)*, L. Emile La Croix *(André de Mersay)*, Charles Fang *(The Chinaman)*, Marion Abbott *(Mrs. Whidden)*, Frank Hagney *(The Indian)*, Sam J. Ryan *(Paddy)*, George MacQuarrie *(The Constable of France)*, William Walcott *(Count de Chausson)*, J. W. Johnston *(Captain of the Guards)*, Adolph Milar *(The Jailer)*, Hugh Huntley *(King)*.

Romantic drama. Source: Clarence Budington Kelland, "Backbone," in *Saturday Evening Post* (195, 30 Sep–4 Nov 1922). As has his family for generations, André de Mersay rules the little town of St. Croix, Maine, and its surrounding lumber interests. While thinking of his granddaughter, Yvonne, who is returning from France, André recalls the story of his namesake ancestor who, in the time of Louis XV of France, was cruelly separated from his sweetheart, Yvonne de Chausson, and exiled to America. When Yvonne arrives she is told by Anthony Bracken, de Mersay's business manager, that her grandfather is seriously ill and may see no one. The arrival of John Thorne and his efforts to open up a tract of lumber long intended to be worked by the de Mersays further infuriate Yvonne. After much conflict and danger to Yvonne and John, it is revealed that de Mersay died sometime ago; that Bracken and his partner, Doc Roper, were embezzling de Mersay funds; and that John Thorne is descended from Yvonne de Chausson. Yvonne and John are united, thus fulfilling a promise centuries old. *French. Lumbering. Embezzlement. Exile. Maine. Louis XV (France).*

BACKSTAGE **F2.0234**

Tiffany Productions. 1 Apr **1927** [c9 Jun 1927; LP24066]. Si; b&w. 35mm. 6 reels, 5,784 ft.

Dir Phil Stone. *Scen* John F. Natteford. *Story* Sarah Y. Mason. *Photog* Joseph A. Dubray, Earl Walker. *Art Dir* George E. Sawley. *Film Ed* Leroy O. Lodwig.

Cast: William Collier, Jr. *(Owen Mackay)*, Barbara Bedford *(Julia Joyce)*, Alberta Vaughn *(Myrtle McGinnis)*, Eileen Percy *(Fanny)*, Shirley O'Hara *(Jane)*, Gayne Whitman *(Frank Carroll)*, Jocelyn Lee *(Flo)*, Guinn Williams *(Mike Donovan)*, Jimmy Harrison *(Charlie)*, Brooks Benedict *(Harry)*, Lincoln Plummer *(Mr. Durkin)*, Marcia Harris *(landlady)*, Louise Carver *(referee)*, John Batten *(Eddie)*.

Comedy-drama. Julia, Myrtle, Fanny, and Jane—all chorus girls—after weeks of rehearsing for a show, find themselves stranded when the manager is broke. Evicted for not paying the rent, they try various schemes to get food and lodging. Julia meets the manager, Carroll, and by accident he takes her to his own apartment, where she decides to remain. Owen, her sweetheart, misunderstands and refuses to accept her explanation until the backer of the show claims the apartment as his own. After a series of amusing complications, Owen and Julia are reconciled. *Chorus girls. Theatrical backers. Courtship. Eviction.*

BAD COMPANY **F2.0235**

St. Regis Pictures. *Dist* Associated Exhibitors. 15 Feb **1925** [c9 Feb 1925; LU21117]. Si; b&w. 35mm. 6 reels, 5,551 ft.

Dir E. H. Griffith. *Cont* Arthur Hoerl. *Adapt* George V. Hobart. *Photog* Marcel Picard, Walter Arthur. *Sets* Tec-Art Studios.

Cast: Madge Kennedy *(Gloria Waring)*, Bigelow Cooper *(Peter Ewing)*, Conway Tearle *(James Hamilton)*, Lucille Lee Stewart *(Teddy Lamont)*, Charles Emmett Mack *(Dick Reynolds)*.

Romantic melodrama. Source: John C. Brownell, "The Ultimate Good" (publication undetermined). Shortly after the death of her father, Gloria Waring discovers that her brother, who stands to inherit the family fortune, is about to marry a notorious gold digger, Teddy Lamont; to prevent the marriage, Gloria openly steals the unopened will from the lawyer, James Hamilton. When Gloria later meets Hamilton at a reception, he recognizes her and confronts her with her crime. Gloria admits to the theft and explains its purpose to Hamilton, who is extremely sympathetic. Hamilton offers to help Gloria, but he is unsuccessful, for he had an affair with Teddy Lamont and she no longer respects him. By the day of the wedding,

Gloria still cannot dissuade her brother from the marriage, and she accompanies him to a justice of the peace in Connecticut. As the ceremony is about to take place, Hamilton steps forward and declares Teddy to be his common-law wife. Gloria's brother is disillusioned by this terrible confession and calls off the wedding. Hamilton decides to go to Europe; and Gloria, who has unexpectedly inherited the family fortune, goes with him. *Gold diggers. Lawyers. Brother-sister relationship. Marriage—Common law. Inheritance. Wills. Connecticut.*

THE BAD LANDS **F2.0236**

Hunt Stromberg Corp. 15 Jul **1925** [cl Aug 1925; LP23195]. Si; b&w. 35mm. 6 reels, 4,956 ft.

Pers Supv Hunt Stromberg. *Dir* Dell Henderson. *Adapt* Harvey Gates. *Story* Kate Corbaley. *Photog* Sol Polito, George Benoit.

Cast: Harry Carey *(Patrick Angus O'Toole)*, Wilfred Lucas *(Colonel Owen)*, Lee Shumway *(Captain Blake)*, Gaston Glass *(Hal Owen)*, Joe Rickson *(Charlie Squirrel)*, Trilby Clark *(Mary Owen)*, Buck Black *(Freckles)*.

Western melodrama. Hal Owen, late of West Point, is on his way in a wagon train to join his father's regiment at Fort Sumner, in the Bad Lands, when a lone rider tries to warn the wagon train of an impending Indian attack. Owen, struck with cowardice, escapes on the rider's horse, leaving others to battle the Indians. After the battle only Freckles, the young son of a pioneer family, and Patrick Angus O'Toole, the lone rider, survive. O'Toole, known in the Army as "Famous Sergeant O'Toole," is also on his way to Fort Sumner and is assigned to clear up a smuggling situation prevailing there. Because of his unsoldierly appearance, O'Toole has difficulty in gaining the troops' confidence. His difficulties increase when he thrashes Captain Blake for forcing his attentions on Mary Owen, the colonel's daughter, whom he silently admires. Incensed, Blake vents his anger on her brother, Hal, by giving him only 24 hours to pay some gambling debts. Owen attempts to hold up the Pony Express, but O'Toole is arrested. Owen is left in charge of the fort while the garrison is out to reconnoiter; the Indians attack, and during the excitement Freckles frees O'Toole, who finds Owen hiding in a corner, trembling in fear. O'Toole finally gets him to fight, and Owen fights like a demon until he is fatally wounded. The garrison returns to turn the tide of battle, and Charlie Squirrel, a halfbreed, is captured and confesses to smuggling guns and liquor with the aid of Blake, the leader of the band. Young Owen, on his deathbed, confesses to the robbery, clearing O'Toole. Mary and O'Toole are united. *Halfcastes. Indians of North America. Smuggling. Cowardice. Wagon trains. Pony Express. Bad lands of Dakota. Fort Sumner. United States Army—Cavalry.*

THE BAD MAN **F2.0237**

Edwin Carewe Productions. *Dist* Associated First National Pictures. 8 Oct **1923** [c5 Oct 1923; LP19472]. Si; b&w. 35mm. 7 reels, 6,404 ft.

Pres by Edwin Carewe. *Dir* Edwin Carewe. *Photog* Sol Polito. *Prod Mgr* John Lynch.

Cast: Holbrook Blinn *(Pancho López)*, Jack Mulhall *(Gilbert Jones)*, Walter McGrail *(Morgan Pell)*, Enid Bennett *(Mrs. Morgan Pell)*, Harry Myers *(Red Giddings)*, Charles A. Sellon *(Uncle Henry)*, Stanton Heck *(Jasper Hardy)*, Teddy Sampson *(Angela Hardy)*, Thomas Delmar *(Captain Blake)*, Frank Lanning *(Indian cook)*, Peter Vanzuella *(Pedro)*.

Western melodrama. Source: Porter Emerson Browne, *The Bad Man, a Play in Three Acts* (New York, 1926). Notorious Mexican bandit Pancho López recognizes Gilbert Jones as the man who once saved his life; therefore, when Jones is in danger of losing his ranch for default of mortgage payment, López determines to help him. At the same time, Morgan Pell, intending to swindle Jones out of his potentially oil-rich property, offers him a sum of money, which Jones conditionally accepts. When López discovers that Jones and Mrs. Pell are in love he has Pell shot, then robs a local bank, pays the mortgage, and returns the cattle he has stolen. With Mr. Pell out of the way and the ranch secure, Jones and Mrs. Pell are free to marry. *Mexicans. Bandits. Swindlers. Ranches. Oil lands. Murder.*

Note: Remade in 1930 under the same title, q. v.

THE BAD MAN **F2.0238**

First National Pictures. 13 Sep **1930** [cl Sep 1930; LP1576]. Sd (Vitaphone); b&w. 35mm. 9 reels, 7,124 ft.

Dir Clarence Badger. *Screenplay-Dial* Howard Estabrook. *Photog* John Seitz. *Film Ed* Frank Ware. *Sd Tech* Glenn E. Rominger.

Cast: Walter Huston *(Pancho López)*, Dorothy Revier *(Ruth Pell)*, James Rennie *(Gilbert Jones)*, O. P. Heggie *(Henry Taylor)*, Sidney Blackmer *(Morgan Pell)*, Marion Byron *(Angela Hardy)*, Guinn Williams *(Red Giddings)*, Arthur Stone *(Pedro)*, Edward Lynch *(Bradley)*, Harry Semels *(José)*, Erville Alderson *(Hardy)*.

Western melodrama. Source: Porter Emerson Browne, *The Bad Man, a Play in Three Acts* (New York, 1926). A remake of the 1923 version, q. v. *Mexicans. Bandits. Swindlers. Ranches. Oil lands. Murder.*

BAD MAN FROM BODIE **F2.0239**

Charles R. Seeling Productions. *Dist* Aywon Film Corp. 7 Apr **1925** [New York State license]. Si; b&w. 35mm. 5 reels, 4,850 ft.

Cast: Big Boy Williams.

Western melodrama(?). No information about the nature of this film has been found.

BAD MAN'S BLUFF **F2.0240**

Action Pictures. *Dist* Associated Exhibitors. 26 Dec **1926** [c10 Dec 1926; LP23415]. Si; b&w. 35mm. 5 reels, 4,441 ft.

Pres by Lester F. Scott, Jr. *Dir* Alvin J. Neitz. *Cont* Betty Burbridge. *Story* Paul M. Bryan.

Cast: Buffalo Bill Jr. *(Zane Castleton)*, Molly Malone *(Alice Hardy)*, Frank Whitson *(Dave Hardy)*, Robert McKenzie *(Hank Dooley)*, Wilbur McGaugh *(Joe Slade)*.

Western melodrama. Zane Castleton goes west with his movie-struck pal, Hank Dooley, in a dilapidated Ford, but the car breaks down on a hill near Cactus, Arizona. Alice Hardy, a young ranchowner, offers to tow the car with her horse and is herself "dethroned" from the saddle. Zane drives her home. It develops that Dave Hardy, her newly appointed guardian, has conspired with Joe Slade to have Slade masquerade as Zane, whose late father was once half owner of the ranch; for Zane does not know that he will be joint owner if he marries Alice before she is 21. Alice is suspicious of Slade, who steals an agreement made between the former partners, and when she refuses his offer he kidnaps her. Zane intercepts the preacher and a bandit, taking the latter's place; Hank arrives with the sheriff, identifying Zane, and the bandits are captured. Alice agrees to marry the real Zane. *Ranchers. Guardians. Impersonation. Kidnaping. Ford automobiles. Motion pictures. Arizona. Documentation.*

BAD MAN'S MONEY *see* **BAD MEN'S MONEY**

BAD MEN'S MONEY **F2.0241**

J. Charles Davis Productions. *Dist* Bell Pictures. ca31 Mar **1929**. Si; b&w. 35mm. 5 reels, 4,850 ft.

Dir-Story-Scen J. P. McGowan. *Photog* George Hollister.

Cast: Yakima Canutt, Peggy Montgomery, John Lowell, J. P. McGowan, Charles Whittaker, Bud Osborne.

Western melodrama. No information about the precise nature of this film has been found.

Note: Also reviewed as *Bad Man's Money.*

THE BAD ONE **F2.0242**

United Artists. 3 May **1930** [c22 May 1930; LP1314]. Sd (Movietone); b&w. 35mm. 8 reels, 6,673 ft.

Pres by Joseph M. Schenck. *Supv* John W. Considine, Jr. *Dir* George Fitzmaurice. *Scen-Dial* Carey Wilson, Howard Emmett Rogers. *Story* John Farrow. *Photog* Karl Struss. *Sets* William Cameron Menzies. *Asst Art Dir* Park French. *Film Ed* Donn Hayes. *Mus Arr* Hugo Riesenfeld. *Rec Engr* Frank Grenzbach. *Asst Dir* Walter Mayo. *Cost* Alice O'Neill.

Cast: Dolores Del Rio *(Lita)*, Edmund Lowe *(Jerry Flanagan)*, Don Alvarado *(Spaniard)*, Blanche Frederici *(Madame Durand)*, Adrienne D'Ambricourt *(Madame Pompier)*, Ullrich Haupt *(Pierre Ferrande)*, Mitchell Lewis *(Borloff)*, Ralph Lewis *(Blochet)*, Charles McNaughton *(Petey)*, Yola D'Avril *(Gida)*, John St. Polis *(judge)*, Henry Kolker *(prosecuting attorney)*, George Fawcett *(warden)*, Victor Potel, Harry Stubbs, Tommy Dugan *(sailors)*.

Romantic melodrama. Lita, a Spanish dancer in a Marseilles cafe, causes American sailor Jerry Flanagan to leave his ship and set out to conquer her, which he does after considerable effort and misunderstanding. On their wedding day, Olaf Swenson claims her; and in a fight the Swede dies as a result of Jerry's blow. Jerry is sentenced to prison as a result of Lita's testimony at the trial and refuses to see her, believing she deceived him. In despair, she makes the acquaintance of Pierre, a brutal prison guard, and becomes engaged to him, hoping thus to see Jerry. Madame Durand, the warden's wife, senses the situation and informs Jerry of her plan; he sends word to Lita to desist, but his message is intercepted by Pierre. Blochet, a prisoner, instigates a prison revolt; Jerry takes over and thwarts his plans but is wounded by the guards. The prisoners surrender; Jerry is awarded a pardon and is reunited with his wife. *Sailors. Dancers. Spanish. Swedes. French. Marriage. Manslaughter. Prisons. Marseilles.*

BAFFLED **F2.0243**
Independent Pictures. Feb **1924**. Si; b&w. 35mm. 6 reels, 5,078 ft.
Pres by Jesse J. Goldburg. *Dir* J. P. McGowan. *Story* James Ormont. *Photog* Walter Griffin.
Cast: Franklyn Farnum, Alyce Mills, Harold Austin, Andrew Waldron.
Western melodrama. "Hero, a rancher, battles lawless elements. Villain, secretly at head of gang of cattle rustlers, tries to get possession of heroine's ranch. Hero is discredited, and villain nearly accomplishes designs, but in the end the hero triumphs." (*Motion Picture News Booking Guide*, 6:11, Apr 1924.) *Ranchers. Rustlers.*

BAG AND BAGGAGE **F2.0244**
Finis Fox Corp. *Dist* Selznick Distributing Corp. 17 or 24 Nov **1923** [c6 Nov 1923; LP19568]. Si; b&w. 35mm. 6 reels, 6,388 ft.
Dir Finis Fox. *Scen* Lois Zellner. *Story* Finis Fox, Lois Zellner. *Photog* Hal Mohr. *Art Dir* Danny Hall.
Cast: Gloria Grey *(Hope Anthony)*, John Roche *(Hal Tracy)*, Carmelita Geraghty *(Lola Cooper)*, Paul Weigel *(Philip Anthony)*, Adele Farrington *(Mrs. Cooper)*, Arthur Stuart Hull *(Jathrow Billings)*, Fred Kelsey *(Fred)*, Harry Dunkinson *(The Hotel Detective)*, R. D. MacLean *(Cyrus Irwin)*, Doreen Turner *(The Girl)*, Ned Grey *(The Boy)*.
Romantic comedy-drama. Country girl Hope Anthony follows Hal Tracy to the city and becomes involved in a jewel theft when Billings, a crook, mistakes her handbag for a satchel of jewels he stole from wealthy Mrs. Cooper. Hal Tracy solves the mystery and keeps Hope out of jail. *Thieves. Hotels.*

THE BAIT (Paramount-Artcraft) **F2.0245**
Hope Hampton Productions. *Dist* Paramount Pictures. 2 Jan **1921** [c1 Sep 1920; LP15636]. Si; b&w. 35mm. 5 reels, 5,289 ft.
Dir Maurice Tourneur. *Scen* John Gilbert. *Photog* Alfred Ortlieb.
Cast: Hope Hampton *(Joan Grainger)*, Harry Woodward *(John Warren, The Fish)*, Jack McDonald *(Bennett Barton, The Fisherman)*, James Gordon *(John Garson, The Game Warden)*, Rae Ebberly *(Dolly, The Hooked)*, Joe Singleton *(Simpson, The Bait-catcher)*, Poupée Andriot *(Madeline, The Minnow)*, Dan Crimmins, Jr. *(Jimmy, The Bullfish)*.
Crook melodrama. Source: Sidney Toler, *The Tiger Lady* (a play; publication undetermined). Joan Grainger, a salesgirl in a jewelry store, is framed for robbery by the floorwalker, Simpson, a member of a gang led by Bennett Barton, and by Dolly, another salesgirl. Barton rescues her from prison and takes her to Paris, where he intends to use her to blackmail millionaires. At the Folies-Bergère, Joan is rescued from an escaped lioness by wealthy John Warren. They return on the same boat to America and fall in love. In New York, Warren obtains a confession from Dolly. Barton tries to obtain the confession but is killed by Simpson, who is also after the paper. Joan is finally exonerated, and Warren wins her hand. *Salesclerks. Floorwalkers. Millionaires. Gangs. Blackmail. Frameup. Folies-Bergère. Paris. New York City. Documentation.*
Note: The copyright material suggests that the film's full title could have been *The Bait, or Human Bait.*

BAITED TRAP **F2.0246**
Ben Wilson Productions. *Dist* Rayart Pictures. Sep **1926**. Si; b&w. 35mm. 5 reels, 4,358 ft.
Dir Stuart Paton. *Story-Scen* George W. Pyper. *Photog* Joseph Walker.
Cast: Ben Wilson *(Jim Banning, Secret Service man)*, Neva Gerber *(Helen Alder)*, Al Ferguson *(Robert Barton, the bandit)*, Monty O'Grady *(Bobbie, the boy)*, Ashton Dearholt *("Red" Killifer)*, Lafe McKee *(Bobbie's father)*, Fang *("Czar")*.
Western melodrama. "City youth sets out for West to avenge father's murder. Arrives in town where killer lives and after a series of fights he accomplishes his purpose. Falls in love with school teacher and resolves to stay in town." (*Motion Picture News Booking Guide*, 12:19, Apr 1927.) *Schoolteachers. Revenge. Dogs.*

BALI, THE UNKNOWN; OR, APE MAN ISLAND **F2.0247**
Harold H. Horton. *Dist* Prizma, Inc. Feb **1921** [New York premiere]. Si; col (Prizma Color). 35mm. 5 reels.
Dir Harold H. Horton.
Travelog. Film dealing with caste, customs, living conditions and industries of Bali with titles relating to prehistoric possibilities of "Ape Man" civilization. *Prehistory. Bali.*
Note: May also have been released about the same time in a 1-reel version. Licensed in New York State as 4 reels, 2 Aug 1927.

THE BALLYHOO BUSTER **F2.0248**
Action Pictures. *Dist* Pathé Exchange. 8 Jan **1928** [c18 Jan 1928; LP24881]. Si; b&w. 35mm. 5 reels, 4,805 ft.
Pres by Lester F. Scott, Jr. *Dir* Richard Thorpe. *Cont* Frank L. Inghram. *Story* Robert Wallace. *Photog* Ray Reis.
Cast: Buffalo Bill Jr. *(Bob Warner)*, Peggy Shaw *(Molly Burnett)*, Nancy Nash *(Dorothy)*, Albert Hart *(medicine show proprietor)*, Floyd Shackleford, Lafe McKee, George Magrill *(Brooks Mitchell)*, Jack Richardson *(Jim Burnett)*, Walter Brennan, Al Taylor.
Western melodrama. Bob Warner sells some cattle to two men who later drug him and rob him of the sale money. He takes a job with a medicine show as a barker, offering a reward to any spectator to last three rounds in fighting him. While in the ring, he notices in the audience the two men who stole his money. He knocks out his contestant, pursues the crooks, and recovers the money. *Barkers. Robbery. Medicine shows. Boxing.*

THE BANDIT BUSTER **F2.0249**
Action Pictures. *Dist* Associated Exhibitors. 19 Dec **1926** [c10 Dec 1926; LU23414]. Si; b&w. 35mm. 5 reels, 4,468 ft.
Pres by Lester F. Scott, Jr. *Dir-Cont* Richard Thorpe. *Story* Frank L. Inghram.
Cast: Buddy Roosevelt *(Buddy Miller)*, Molly Malone *(Sylvia Morton)*, Lafe McKee *(Henry Morton)*, Winifred Landis *(Mrs. Morton)*, Robert Homans *(Romeo)*, Charles Whitaker *(Steve)*, Al Taylor *(hotel clerk)*.
Western melodrama. Sylvia Morton, daughter of Henry Morton, a prominent banker, meets Buddy Miller and his pal, Romeo, and plots with them to kidnap her father and take him to a mountain cabin for an enforced rest, though he is on the brink of an important stock transaction. Morton's clerks appeal to Mrs. Morton to advise them whether they should hold or sell his steel stock, and Romeo discovers the plan without disclosing it to Morton. An inn clerk, overhearing the conversation, learns Morton's whereabouts and arranges to have him kidnaped and held for a large ransom. When Mrs. Morton receives a ransom note, she and Sylvia think that Buddy—who actually tracks down the bandits—has tricked them. Morton's rescue finds him a millionaire, and he retires to a life of camping and fishing. Buddy and Sylvia find happiness together. *Bandits. Bankers. Millionaires. Filial relations. Resorts. Kidnaping. Stock market.*

THE BANDIT TAMER **F2.0250**
Independent Pictures. 2 Jul **1925** [New York State license]. Si; b&w. 35mm. 5 reels, 4,800 ft.
Cast: Franklyn Farnum.
Western melodrama(?). No information about the nature of this film has been found.

THE BANDIT'S BABY **F2.0251**
R-C Pictures. *Dist* Film Booking Offices of America. 17 May **1925** [c24 May 1925; LP21530]. Si; b&w. Kirby, David Bill Henry 5 reels, 5,291 ft.
Dir James P. Hogan. *Scen* Marion Jackson. *Story* Leete Renick Brown. *Photog* Ross Fisher. *Asst Dir* Al Werker.
Cast: Fred Thomson *(Tom Bailey)*, Helen Foster *(Esther Lacy)*, Harry Woods *(Matt Hartigan)*, Mary Louise Miller *(baby)*, Clarence Geldert *(sheriff)*, Charles W. Mack *(doctor)*.
Western melodrama. Tom Bailey is forced to hide in the hills when he is unjustly accused of robbery and murder. He is, however, granted amnesty for a day in order to ride in a rodeo and judge a baby contest. Tom awards the prize to the baby brother of Esther Lacy, whose drunken stepfather, Matt Hartigan, is the real murderer. Later in the day, Tom wins a horserace and eludes the trap set for him by the sheriff. Esther goes to visit her brother in Carson City, and Tom takes care of the baby. Hartigan ascertains when Esther and her brother are expected to return and takes steps to wreck the train by running an unscheduled freight on the main line. An alert station agent switches the freight onto a siding, preventing a crash; the freight then derails and kills Hartigan. Esther's brother proves that his late stepfather actually committed the crimes of which Tom has been accused, clearing the way for Tom to find happiness with Esther.

Sheriffs. Stepfathers. Infants. Station agents. Robbery. Murder. Horseracing. Rodeos. Train wrecks.

BANDITS OF THE AIR **F2.0252**

Bear Productions. *Dist* Aywon Film Corp. 30 Apr **1925.** Si; b&w. 35mm. 5 reels.

Cast: Melbourne MacDowell, Jane Starr.

Melodrama(?). No information about the nature of this film has been found.

THE BANDIT'S SON **F2.0253**

FBO Pictures. 20 Nov **1927** [c2 Feb 1928; LP24949]. Si; b&w. 35mm. 5 reels, 4,789 ft.

Dir Wallace W. Fox. *Story-Cont* Frank Howard Clark. *Photog* Nick Musuraca. *Asst Dir* Richard Easton.

Cast: Bob Steele *(Bob McCall)*, Tom Lingham *(Dan McCall)*, Hal Davis *(Matt Bolton)*, Stanley Taylor *(Rufe Bolton)*, Anne Sheridan *(Helen Todd)*, Bobby Mack *(Jake Kirby)*, Barney Gilmore *(Amos Jordan)*, Finch Smiles *(Reverend Todd)*.

Western melodrama. Bob McCall saves his father, an ex-gunman, from being lynched for a crime he did not commit and captures the real culprit, Rufe Bolton, son of the local sheriff, who owed a gambling debt. His name restored to good standing, Bob marries parson's daughter Helen Todd. *Sheriffs. Clergymen. Filial relations. Lynching.*

THE BANDOLERO **F2.0254**

Metro-Goldwyn Pictures. 20 Oct **1924** [c14 Oct 1924; LP20655]. Si; b&w. 35mm. 8 reels, 6,994 ft.

Pres by Louis B. Mayer. *Dir-Adapt* Tom Terriss. *Photog* George Peters. *Sets* Tec-Art Studios. *Film Ed* Winchell Smith, Don Bartlett. *Asst Dir* Rodney Hickok. *Art Titl* H. E. R. Studios.

Cast: Pedro De Cordoba *(Dorando, the Bandolero)*, Gustav von Seyffertitz *(Marquês de Bazán)*, Manuel Granado *(Ramón, his son)*, Gordon Begg *(Padre Domingo)*, Arthur Donaldson *(Juan)*, José De Rueda *(El Tuerte)*, Renée Adorée *(Petra)*, Dorothy Rush *(Concha)*, Marie Valray *(Maria)*.

Romantic drama. Source: Paul Gwynne, *The Bandolero* (New York, 1904). Dorando, a Spanish Army officer, becomes a notorious bandit leader (known as El Bandolero) when his wife is killed by his commanding officer, the Marqués de Bazán, and he gets his revenge by kidnaping the marqués' young son, Ramón. Years later, Ramón and Dorando's daughter, Petra, fall in love, but confronted with Dorando's extreme displeasure, he leaves and becomes a famous matador. Ramón is gored when Concha, a vamp who was unable to win his love, persuades the marqués to order the matador to kill the bull before it is tired. The marqués learns that Ramón is his son and is reconciled with Dorando; both fathers approve the marriage of Ramón and Petra. *Bullfighters. Vamps. Bandits. Kidnaping. Revenge. Spain.*

THE BANTAM COWBOY **F2.0255**

FBO Pictures. 12 Aug **1928** [c12 Aug 1928; LP25528]. Si; b&w. 35mm. 6 reels, 4,893 ft.

Supv Robert N. Bradbury. *Dir* Louis King. *Titl* Frank T. Daugherty. *Adapt* Frank Howard Clark. *Orig Story* Robert North Bradbury. *Photog* Roy Eslick. *Film Ed* Della M. King. *Asst Dir* Jack Murton.

Cast: Buzz Barton *(David "Red" Hepner)*, Frank Rice *(Sidewinder Steve)*, Tom Lingham *(John Briggs)*, Dorothy Kitchen *(Nan Briggs)*, Bob Fleming *(Jason Todd)*, Bill Patton *(Chuck Rogers)*, Sam Nelson *(Jim Thornton)*.

Western melodrama. Learning that a railroad is planning to build a spur line through Briggs's ranch, Jason Todd, Briggs's half brother, and Chuck Roberts, the ranch foreman, kidnap Briggs and his daughter, Nan, taking them to a deserted cabin. Todd and Chuck plan to kill Briggs and take Nan with them into Mexico, but before they can do so David Hepner, a pint-sized cowboy, and his buddy, Steve, come to the rescue. After many adventures, Dan and Steve ride on, having saved Briggs's ranch and reunited Nan with her sheriff sweetheart. *Cowboys. Ranchers. Ranch foremen. Sheriffs. Kidnaping. Railroads.*

BAR L RANCH **F2.0256**

F. E. Douglas. *Dist* Big 4 Film Corp. 28 Jul or 4 Aug **1930.** Sd (Powers Cinephone); b&w. 35mm. 6 reels, 5,700 ft.

Pres by F. E. Douglas. *Dir* Harry Webb. *Scen* Carl Krusada. *Story* Bennett Cohen. *Photog* William Nobles. *Film Ed* Fred Bain. *Sd* George Lowerry.

Cast: Buffalo Bill Jr. *(Bob Tyler)*, Yakima Canutt *(Steve)*, Betty Baker *(Gene Polk)*, Wally Wales *(Frank Kellogg)*, Ben Corbett *(Barney McCool)*, Fern Emmett.

Western melodrama. Bob Tyler has rustler trouble while driving a herd of cattle to its new owner, but he refuses to turn it over to Frank Kellogg. He has a chance meeting and a run-in with Gene Polk, a very stubborn woman, later discovers that she is the owner of the cattle, and is fired. Charging his friend Barney to keep an eye on things, Bob snoops around until he proves that Kellogg is responsible for the rustling. Gene changes her mind about Bob. *Ranchers. Rustlers. Cowboys.*

BAR NOTHIN' **F2.0257**

Fox Film Corp. 2 Oct **1921** [c2 Oct 1921; LP17206]. Si; b&w. 35mm. 5 reels, 4,311 ft.

Pres by William Fox. *Dir* Edward Sedgwick. *Scen* Jack Strumwasser. *Story* Jack Strumwasser, Clyde C. Westover. *Photog* Frank B. Good.

Cast: Buck Jones *(Duke Smith)*, Ruth Renick *(Bess Lynne)*, Arthur Carew *(Stinson)*, James Farley *(Bill Harliss)*, William Buckley *(Harold Lynne)*.

Western melodrama. Bess Lynne and her invalid brother, Harold, own a ranch and seek the services of a competent foreman. Duke Smith, foreman of the "Bar Nothin'" ranch, rides into town with his men and after a shooting spree applies for the job and is accepted. Harliss and Stinson, crooked cattle buyers, try to force the Lynnes to sell out; Duke hears of their schemings and forces them to buy the Lynnes' cattle. Later, Stinson robs Duke and leaves him in the desert to die, but Duke catches a stray horse and returns to the ranch. When Harold becomes ill, the Lynnes, believing that Duke has deserted them, return to the East. But Duke arrives in time to prevent Bess's marriage to Stinson and win her himself. *Invalids. Ranch foremen. Brother-sister relationship. Ranches.*

THE BAR-C MYSTERY **F2.0258**

Pathé Exchange. 14 Mar **1926.** Si; b&w. 35mm. 5 reels, 4,756 ft.

Prod C. W. Patton. *Dir* Robert F. Hill. *Scen* William Sherwood.

Cast: Dorothy Phillips *(Jane Cortelyou)*, Wallace MacDonald *(Nevada)*, Ethel Clayton *(Mrs. Lane)*, Philo McCullough *(Robbins)*, Johnny Fox *(Tommy)*, Violet Schram *(Wanda)*, Fred De Silva *(Grisp)*.

Western melodrama. Source: Raymond Spears, "Janie of the Waning Glories" (publication undetermined). "The action concerns a hidden gold mine belonging to a westerner, owner of the Bar-C ranch who left for dead, wills the secret of the mine to Jane, a girl in New York. Going west she meets Robbins, who poses as the agent of the miner, but is in reality seeking to get the mine for himself and his partner, Mrs. Lane, a cabaret owner. A cowboy called Nevada comes to Jane's rescue and she discovers he is really the supposedly dead miner who has shaved off his beard. When Robbins gets hold of the secret of the mine, Jane and Nevada beat them to the mine and thwart their attempts to kill them by blowing up the entrance. The conspirators are finally arrested and Nevada wins Jane." (*Moving Picture World*, 27 Mar 1926, p285.) *Cowboys. Gold mines. Disguise. Wills. Cabarets.*

Note: Cut down from a 10-episode serial, which was released a month later.

BARB WIRE **F2.0259**

Sunset Productions. *Dist* Aywon Film Corp. Jun **1922.** Si; b&w. 35mm. 5 reels, 4,800 ft.

Pres by Anthony J. Xydias. *Dir* Frank Grandon. *Story* William Lester, Marin Sais. *Photog* William Nobles.

Cast: Jack Hoxie *(Jack Harding)*, Jean Porter *(Joan Lorne)*, Olah Norman *(Martha Harding)*, William Lester *(Bart Moseby)*, Joe McDermott *(Nick Lazarre)*, Jim Welsh *(Bob Lorne)*.

Western melodrama. "Jack Harding defies a villainous gang by fencing in his claim with barbed wire. Headed by Bart Moseby the gang plans to get him. Harding hides in his sweetheart's room to overhear their plans but is doublecrossed by one of them who commits a crime and leaves Harding's hat and gun as evidence. To save her son at the trial, Harding's mother holds up the court while her son leaps from the window to his horse. A fight between Harding and Moseby follows, ending in the latter's death and Harding's freedom." (*Moving Picture World*, 7 Oct 1922, p506.) *Gangs. Motherhood. Trials. Land claims.*

Note: May also be known as *Barbed Wire*.

BARBARA FRIETCHIE **F2.0260**

Regal Pictures. *Dist* Producers Distributing Corp. 26 Sep **1924** [New York premiere; released 26 Oct; c16 Sep 1924; LP20577]. Si; b&w. 35mm. 8 reels, 7,179 ft.

Pers Supv Thomas H. Ince. *Dir* Lambert Hillyer. *Adapt* Lambert Hillyer, Agnes Christine Johnston. *Photog* Henry Sharp.

Cast: Florence Vidor *(Barbara)*, Edmund Lowe *(Captain Trumbull)*, Emmett King *(Colonel Frietchie)*, Joe Bennett *(Jack Negly)*, Charles Delaney *(Arthur Frietchie)*, Louis Fitzroy *(Colonel Negly)*, Gertrude Short *(Sue Royce)*, Mattie Peters *(Mammy Lou)*, Slim Hamilton *(Fred Gelwek)*, Jim Blackwell *(Rufus)*, George Billings *(Abraham Lincoln)*.

Historical romance. Source: Clyde Fitch, *Barbara Frietchie, the Frederick Girl; a Play* (New York, 1900). Barbara Frietchie, daughter of a patriotic family of the South, falls in love with Trumbull, her brother's friend from the North. When war is declared, Trumbull returns to the North and leads a force that captures Frederickstown (Maryland), where the Frietchies live. Although their love overcomes all differences, the Confederate advance prevents their marriage. After 4 years of discouragement and despair, the lovers are reunited. *United States—History—Civil War. Maryland. Abraham Lincoln. Barbara Frietchie.*

THE BARBARIAN **F2.0261**

Monroe Salisbury. *Dist* Pioneer Film Corp. 30 Apr **1921** [c29 Sep 1920; LU15733]. Si; b&w. 35mm. 6 reels.

Dir Donald Crisp. *Scen* E. P. Heath.

Cast: Monroe Salisbury *(Eric Straive)*, George Burrell *(Elliott Straive)*, Barney Sherry *(James Heatherton)*, Elinor Hancock *(Mrs. Heatherton)*, Jane Novak *(Floria Heatherton)*, Anne Cudahy *(Sylvia Heatherton)*, Michael Cudahy *(Roswell Heatherton)*, Alan Hale *(Mark Brant)*, Milton Markwell *(Mainhall)*, Lillian Leighton *(Redwing)*.

Northwest melodrama. Source: Theodore Seixas Solomons, "The Barbarian" (publication undetermined). Eric Straive, reared in the Canadian Northwest and educated by his erudite father, is a child of nature. His father dies as he reaches manhood. Capitalists use a forged document to claim rights over Eric's estate. Eric meets a white woman for the first time when James Heatherton brings his daughter, Floria, to camp nearby while he investigates mineral deposits. Eric is attracted to Floria, but she spurns him as a barbarian. When Heatherton's representative, Brant, calls upon Eric's lawyer to complete the deal, Eric exposes the forgery through Redwing, who was present when the elder Straive died. Enraged, Eric nearly kills Brant but is calmed by Floria. Eric gives his estate to found a conservatory where the poor may be taught to sing, thus making possible Floria's ambition. *Capitalists. Inheritance. Forgery. Land rights. Conservatories (schools). Canadian Northwest. Documentation.*

BARBED WIRE *see* **BARB WIRE**

BARBED WIRE **F2.0262**

Paramount Famous Lasky Corp. 6 Aug **1927** [New York premiere; released 10 Sep; c10 Sep 1927; LP24408]. Si; b&w. 35mm. 7 reels, 6,951 ft.

Pres by Adolph Zukor, Jesse L. Lasky. *Prod* Erich Pommer. *Assoc Prod* B. P. Schulberg. *Dir* Rowland V. Lee. *Screenplay* Jules Furthman, Rowland V. Lee. *Adapt* Jules Furthman. *Photog* Bert Glennon.

Cast: Pola Negri *(Mona)*, Clive Brook *(Oskar)*, Einar Hanson *(The Brother)*, Claude Gillingwater *(The Father)*, Gustav von Seyffertitz *(The Neighbor)*, Charles Lane *(The Commandant)*, Clyde Cook *(Hans)*, Ben Hendricks, Jr. *(The Sergeant)*.

War drama. Source: Hall Caine, *The Woman of Knockaloe, a Parable* (New York, 1923). In pastoral Normandy the peaceful harvest is broken by the call to colors in 1914, and Mona, a peasant girl, is left to take care of the farm for her father and brother. When the farm is confiscated by French authorities for a prison camp, Mona and her father are forced to assume a mortgage to buy additional stock. Although she despises the Germans, Mona becomes attracted to Oskar, a young prisoner who works at the farm. A French sergeant attempts to force his way into Mona's house, and Oskar, in coming to her aid, is charged with assault; at his trial, however, Mona defends the young German though she is branded as a traitor. After the Armistice, the camp is ordered cleared, but the villagers refuse to harbor the boy; then Mona's blinded brother returns from the war and shames the people with an impassioned plea for love and forgiveness. *Soldiers. Prisoners of war. Germans. Farming. Blindness. World War I. Normandy.*

BARBER JOHN'S BOY *see* **STREET GIRL**

BARBER JOHN'S BOY *see* **MAN TO MAN**

BARDELYS THE MAGNIFICENT **F2.0263**

Metro-Goldwyn-Mayer Pictures. 30 Sep **1926** [Los Angeles premiere; released 21 Nov; c23 Sep 1926; LP23140]. Si; b&w. 35mm. 9 reels, 8,536 ft.

Dir King Vidor. *Adapt* Dorothy Farnum. *Photog* William Daniels. *Sets* Cedric Gibbons, James Dasevi, Richard Day. *Wardrobe* André-ani, Lucia Coulter.

Cast: John Gilbert *(Bardelys)*, Eleanor Boardman *(Roxalanne de Lavedan)*, Roy D'Arcy *(Chatellerault)*, Lionel Belmore *(Vicomte de Lavedan)*, Emily Fitzroy *(Vicomtesse de Lavedan)*, George K. Arthur *(St. Eustache)*, Arthur Lubin *(King Louis XIII)*, Theodore von Eltz *(Lesperon)*, Karl Dane *(Rodenard)*, Edward Connelly *(Cardinal Richelieu)*, Fred Malatesta *(Castelroux)*, John T. Murray *(Lafosse)*, Joseph Marba *(innkeeper)*, Daniel G. Tomlinson *(Sergeant of Dragoons)*, Emile Chautard *(Anatol)*, Max Barwyn *(Cozelatt)*.

Romantic costume drama. Source: Rafael Sabatini, *Bardelys the Magnificent* (Boston & New York, 1905). King Louis XIII sends Chatellerault to win Roxalanne de Lavedan, hoping to keep the girl's fortune within the kingdom. When Chatellerault reports that Roxalanne is unapproachable, Bardelys, a courtier, wagers his entire estate against Chatellerault's that he will capture the girl within 3 months. En route, Bardelys finds a dying man and is given a miniature and some letters bearing the name Lesperon, whose identity he assumes. Finding that Lesperon is a traitor, he seeks shelter in the Lavedan estate, and though she is frightened, Roxalanne allows him to court her. Another suitor, St. Eustache, warns her that Lesperon is engaged to Mademoiselle Mersac. Bardelys is arrested for treason, but the arrival of the king saves him from execution. Roxalanne marries Chatellerault to save Bardelys' life, but Chatellerault is killed in a duel with the courtier, who is thereafter joined with his beloved. *Royalty. Disguise. Treason. Wagers. France—History—Bourbons. Louis XIII (France). Cardinal Richelieu.*

BARE KNEES **F2.0264**

Gotham Productions. *Dist* Lumas Film Corp. 1 Feb **1928** [c2 Feb 1928; LP24941]. Si; b&w. 35mm. 6 reels, 5,268 or 5,800 ft.

Pres by Sam Sax. *Dir* Erle C. Kenton. *Supv-Adapt* Harold Shumate. *Titl* Casey Robinson. *Story* Adele Buffington. *Photog* James Diamond. *Film Ed* Donn Hayes. *Asst Dir* Donn Diggins. *Prod Mgr* Carrol Sax.

Cast: Virginia Lee Corbin *(Billie Durey)*, Donald Keith *(Larry Cook)*, Jane Winton *(Jane Longworth)*, Johnnie Walker *(Paul Gladden)*, Forrest Stanley *(John Longworth)*, Maude Fulton *(Bessie)*.

Comedy-drama. Billie Durey, a flapper, arrives in Portersville, Virginia, to visit her married sister, Jane Longworth, the wife of the district attorney. She arrives in the middle of Jane's birthday party and causes a sensation with her bare knees, cigarettes, and other flapper accouterments. Larry Cook, an apprentice lawyer in Longworth's office, takes an immediate liking to Billie, seeing in her a kindred spirit. Billie wakes up the sleepy town by encouraging the girls' baseball team to don some new, zippy uniforms. Result: the men's team is so busy looking at the girls that they lose their own game. Billie soon discovers that Jane is having an affair with Paul Gladden, a friend of her husband's. She prevents Jane from eloping with Gladden and helps Longworth to realize that he has been neglecting his wife. Then, after having first refused Larry Cook's marriage proposal, she perceives his sterling worth when he rescues her from a burning roadhouse located on a pier, and she accepts him. *Flappers. Sisters. Lawyers. District attorneys. Smalltown life. Infidelity. Roadhouses. Virginia. Fires.*

BARE KNUCKLES **F2.0265**

Fox Film Corp. 20 Mar **1921** [c20 Mar 1921; LP16324]. Si; b&w. 35mm. 5 reels.

Pres by William Fox. *Dir-Scen* James P. Hogan. *Story* A. Channing Edington. *Photog* George Schneiderman.

Cast: William Russell *(Tim McGuire)*, Mary Thurman *(Lorraine Metcalf)*, Correan Kirkham *(Fern)*, George Fisher *(Haines)*, Edwin B. Tilton *(Benham)*, Charles Gorman *(Leek)*, Jack Roseleigh *(Harris)*, John Cook *(Old Soaky)*, Joe Lee *(Abie)*, Charles K. French *(Metcalf)*, Jack Stevens *(Shadow)*.

Melodrama. Tim McGuire, although renowned as "The Brute" in the San Francisco underworld, has an adopted family including Abie (his boyhood friend), a former professor, and the latter's daughter. When he rescues a visitor, Lorraine Metcalf, from a gang of hoodlums, her father awards him a position as construction supervisor for a dam project in the Sierras. The company is opposed by a rival gang aided by a dishonest employee who kidnaps Lorraine during a gang fight. Tim saves the camp from a dynamite explosion and wins the girl. *Gangs. Dams. San Francisco. Sierras.*

BAREE, SON OF KAZAN **F2.0266**

Vitagraph Co. of America. 19 Apr **1925** [c11 Apr 1925; LP21355]. Si; b&w. 35mm. 7 reels, 6,800 ft.

Dir David Smith. *Scen* Jay Pilcher. *Photog* Steve Smith, David Smith.

Cast: Anita Stewart *(Nepeese)*, Donald Keith *(Jim Carvel)*, Jack Curtis *(Bush McTaggart)*, Joe Rickson *(Pierre Eustach)*, Wolf *(Baree)*.

Northwest melodrama. Source: James Oliver Curwood, *Baree, Son of Kazan* (Garden City, New York, 1917). When Jim Carvel's father is killed, Jim takes the law into his own hands and shoots the murderer. Believing the man to be dead, Jim heads for the Northwest, where he breaks his leg chasing a small puppy through the woods and meets Pierre Eustach and his daughter, Nepeese. When Jim's leg heals, he and the dog, called Baree, travel on. McTaggart, the factor, takes an interest in Nepeese and asks for her hand in marriage; she refuses, and McTaggart kills her father in an attempt to take her by force. Nepeese escapes by jumping off a cliff into a raging stream. Jim finds a wounded member of the Mounties, learning from him that the man he shot has recovered and confessed to the murder of the elder Carvel. Jim returns to search for Nepeese, and, with the efforts of Baree, he finds her in the care of a friendly Indian who saved her from the rapids. Baree attacks McTaggart and puts him out of the way, removing the last block to the future happiness of Jim and Nepeese. *Factors. Indians of North America. Murder. Revenge. Northwest Mounted Police. Rapids. Dogs.*

THE BAREFOOT BOY **F2.0267**

Mission Film Corp. *Dist* C. B. C. Film Sales. 1 Sep **1923** [c5 May 1924; LP20174]. Si; b&w. 35mm. 6 reels, 5,943 ft.

Dir David Kirkland. *Story* Wallace Clifton. *Photog* David Abel.

Cast: John Bowers *(Dick Alden)*, Marjorie Daw *(Mary Truesdale)*, Sylvia Breamer *(Milicent Carter)*, George McDaniel *(Rodman Grant)*, Raymond Hatton *(Deacon Halloway)*, Tully Marshall *(Tom Adams)*, George Periolat *(Si Parker)*, Virginia True Boardman *(Mrs. Blake)*, Brinsley Shaw *(Josiah Blake)*, Harry Todd *(Bill Hawkins)*, Otis Harlan *(Wilson)*, Frankie Lee *(Dick Alden, child)*, Gertrude Messinger *(Mary Truesdale, child)*, Lottie Williams.

Rural drama. Source: John Greenleaf Whittier, "The Barefoot Boy." Mistreated by his stepfather and the villagers and wrongly accused of setting fire to the schoolhouse, 12-year-old Dick Alden runs away vowing to revenge himself on his accusers. Years later he returns, determined to close the mill he has inherited; but the love of his childhood sweetheart, Mary, alters his decision, and he resolves to build a new life. *Stepfathers. Childhood. Village life. Revenge. Arson.*

THE BARGAIN (Reissue) **F2.0268**

New York Motion Picture Corp. *Dist* Tri-Stone Pictures. Sep **1923** [c12 Oct 1923; LP19493]. Si; b&w. 35mm. 5 reels.

Note: Originally released by Paramount Pictures, 3 Dec 1914 (c3 Dec 1914; LP5157), 7 reels. Provided with new titles and reedited.

BARGAINS **F2.0269**

Burr Nickle. Apr **1923** [scheduled release]. Si; b&w. 35mm. 6 reels.

Drama(?). No information about the nature of this film has been found.

THE BARKER **F2.0270**

First National Pictures. 19 Dec **1928** [c27 Aug 1928; LP25564]. Mus score (Vitaphone); b&w. 35mm. 8 reels, 7,870 ft. [Also si; 7,137 ft.]

Pres by Richard A. Rowland. *Prod* Al Rockett. *Dir* George Fitzmaurice. *Adapt-Screenplay* Benjamin Glazer. *Dial* Joseph Jackson. *Titl* Herman Mankiewicz. *Photog* Lee Garmes. *Film Ed* Stuart Heisler. *Mus Score* Louis Silvers. *Cost* Max Ree.

Cast: Milton Sills *(Nifty Miller)*, Douglas Fairbanks, Jr. *(Chris Miller)*, George Cooper *(Hap Spissel)*, John Erwin *(Sailor West)*, S. S. Simon *(Colonel Gowdy)*, Dorothy Mackaill *(Lou)*, Betty Compson *(Carrie)*, Sylvia Ashton *(Ma Benson)*.

Drama. Source: Kenyon Nicholson, *The Barker; a Play of Carnival Life in Three Acts* (New York, 1917). Nifty Miller, the greatest carnival barker in the world, sends his son, Chris, to law school in the hope that the boy will find in professional life a more settled and prosperous life than that of the sideshow. During one of his summer vacations, Chris finds work with the carnival, and Nifty breaks off his relationship with Carrie, a hula dancer who, seeking revenge for this slight, pays another carnival girl, Lou, to vamp the innocent boy; Lou, however, genuinely falls in love with Chris. When his father finds out that they are in love, Chris defiantly announces his intention to marry the girl. Seeing his ambitious plans for his son seemingly collapse, Nifty quits the carnival and turns to drink. He later finds out that Chris has returned to law school at Lou's urging. Offered a partnership in the carnival, Nifty returns to his former life as a barker. *Barkers. Dancers. Students. Fatherhood. Carnivals. Sideshows.*

THE BARNSTORMER **F2.0271**

Charles Ray Productions. *Dist* Associated First National Pictures. Jan **1922** [c20 Feb 1922; LP17558]. Si; b&w. 35mm. 6 reels, 5,300 ft.

Pres by Arthur S. Kane. *Dir* Charles Ray. *Titl* Edward Withers. *Story* Richard Andres. *Photog* George Rizard. *Asst Camera* Ellsworth H. Rumer. *Tech Dir* Richard Bennett. *Film Ed* Harry L. Decker. *Asst Dir* Albert Ray, Charles Van Deroef.

Cast: Charles Ray *(Joel, "Utility")*, Wilfred Lucas *(leading man)*, Florence Oberle *(leading lady)*, Lionel Belmore *(manager)*, Phillip Dunham *(stage carpenter)*, Gus Leonard *(theater owner)*, Lincoln Plumer *(druggist)*, Charlotte Pierce *(Emily)*, George Nichols *(Joel's father)*, Blanche Rose *(his mother)*, Bert Offord *(The Nut)*.

Comedy-drama. Joel Matthews, the son of a prosperous farmer, is discontented with rustic life and longs for a career on the stage. When an acting troupe comes to town, he is given a job by the manager as a utility man—hustling trunks, distributing handbills, and performing bit parts. Joel develops a great admiration for the leading man, and when he is finally given a few speaking lines, he proudly invites his girl, Emily, to the performance. During the show, a masked and armed holdup man appears and forces Joel to take a hat and collect from his victims; after the robber's exit, Joel follows him, discovers him to be (alas!) the leading man, and at gunpoint forces him to return his plunder. Joel confesses to Emily that life with her might be more exciting than success on the stage. *Barnstormers. Farmers. Robbers. Theatrical troupes. Rural life.*

BARNUM WAS RIGHT **F2.0272**

Universal Pictures. 22 Sep **1929** [c13 Sep 1929; LP696]. Sd (Movietone); b&w. 35mm. 5 reels, 5,140 ft. [Also si; 4,477 ft.]

Dir Del Lord. *Adapt* Arthur Ripley, Ewart Adamson. *Story* Hutchinson Boyd. *Photog* Jerome Ash.

Cast: Glenn Tryon *(Freddie Farrell)*, Merna Kennedy *(Miriam Locke)*, Otis Harlan *(Samuel Locke)*, Basil Radford *(Standish)*, Clarence Burton *(Martin)*, Lew Kelly *(Harrison)*, Isabelle Keith *(Phoebe O'Dare)*, Gertrude Sutton *(Sarah)*.

Comedy-drama. Source: Philip Bartholomae and John Meehan, *Barnum Was Right* (New York opening: 12 Mar 1923). Samuel Locke, a businessman, promises to give his daughter, Miriam, in marriage to Freddie Farrell if he will fulfill his promise to make Locke mansion, an aging estate in the middle of a swamp, into a profitable investment. Farrell turns the place into a high-priced hotel and revives the legend that there is buried treasure on the property. Finally, he relaxes and watches the guests tear the place apart. An explosion set by one of the visitors lifts the roof off the mansion, revealing the "treasure" (a box of jewels hidden for safekeeping by a burglar). The explosion and the continual digging around the place cause the ocean to enter and create valuable shoreline property out of the Locke estate. *Businessmen. Hotel management. Real estate. Treasure. Swamps.*

THE BARRICADE **F2.0273**

Robertson-Cole Co. *Dist* R-C Pictures. 2 Oct **1921** [c2 Oct 1921; LP17108]. Si; b&w. 35mm. 6 reels, 5,700 ft.

Dir William Christy Cabanne. *Story* Daniel Carson Goodman. *Photog* Philip Armond, William Tuers.

Cast: William H. Strauss *(Jacob Solomon)*, Katherine Spencer *(Jane Stoddard)*, Kenneth Harlan *(Robert Brennon)*, Eugene Borden *(Sam Steiner)*, Dorothy Richards *(Doris Solomon)*, James Harrison *(Phillip Stoddard)*, John O'Connor *(Tim)*.

Melodrama. On New York's East Side, Jacob Solomon and Michael Brennon are partners in a cigar store. Michael dies, and his son, Robert, is adopted by Jacob and becomes a successful physician in the neighborhood. He meets and falls in love with Jane Stoddard, a wealthy society girl, and after their marriage she induces him to forsake his East Side friends and open a Fifth Avenue practice. Jacob is heartbroken when he is snubbed by Robert and does not reveal that he mortgaged his home to pay for Robert's education. Robert and his wife quarrel when her friends discover that Jacob is the young physician's foster father; and returning to his home, Robert finds that Jacob has lost everything. There is a reconciliation between them, and Robert moves back to the East Side. His wife acknowledges the mistake she has made and is forgiven by Robert. *Jews. Irish. Tobacconists. Physicians. Social classes. New York City—East Side.*

THE BARRIER **F2.0274**

Metro-Goldwyn-Mayer Pictures. 8 Mar **1926** [c5 Apr 1926; LP22600]. Si; b&w. 35mm. 7 reels, 6,480 ft.

Dir George Hill. *Scen* Harvey Gates. *Photog* Max Fabian, Ira H. Morgan.

Cast: Norman Kerry *(Meade Burrell)*, Henry B. Walthall *(Gale [Gaylord])*, Lionel Barrymore *(Stark Bennett)*, Marceline Day *(Necia)*, George Cooper *(Sergeant Murphy)*, Bert Woodruff *(No Creek Lee)*, Princess Neola *(Alluna)*, Mario Carillo *(Poleon)*, Pat Harmon *(first mate)*, Shannon Day *(Necia's Indian mother)*.

Northwest melodrama. Source: Rex Beach, *The Barrier, a Novel* (New York, 1908). During a storm off the coast of Alaska, Bennett, a brutal sea captain, forces his wife to assist his men, and she is fatally hurt in an accident. Seaman Gaylord thereupon agrees to take her child from the influence of its father. Seventeen years later, Gale (*i.e.,* Gaylord) is a storekeeper at Flambeau, Alaska. He has reared the child, Necia, as his daughter in ignorance of her halfcaste parentage. Although she is loved by Poleon Doret, a halfbreed, she falls under the influence of Lieut. Meade Burrell, a Virginia aristocrat stationed in the North. When Bennett's ship comes into the port, he reveals the truth about the girl's parentage, and Burrell is stunned. Necia resolves to leave with her brutish father without seeing Meade again. When their ship is ice-jammed, the crew deserts, but Burrell arrives over the ice, leaves the captain unconscious, and rescues Necia; Bennett is destroyed in an ice floe, and the lovers are happily united. *Sea captains. Traders. Halfcastes. Indians of North America. Virginians. Parentage. Alaska. Ice floes.*

BARRIERS AFLAME *see* **WHY WOMEN LOVE**

BARRIERS BURNED AWAY **F2.0275**

Encore Pictures. *Dist* Associated Exhibitors. 4 Jan **1925** [c9 Dec 1924; LU20783]. Si; b&w. 35mm. 7 reels, 6,474 ft.

Pres by Arthur F. Beck. *Dir* W. S. Van Dyke. *Story-Scen* Leah Baird. *Photog* André Barlatier.

Cast: Mabel Ballin *(Christine Randolph)*, Eric Mayne *(Mark Randolph)*, Frank Mayo *(Wayne Morgan)*, Wanda Hawley *(Molly Winthrop)*, Wally Van *(Gale Winthrop)*, Arline Pretty *(Mildred McCormick)*, Lawson Butt *(Earl of Tarnsey)*, Tom Santschi *(Hon. Bill Cronk)*, Harry T. Morey *(Howard Mellon)*, James Mason *("Slim" Edwards)*, J. P. Lockney *(Patrick Leary)*, Mrs. Charles Craig *(Mrs. Leary)*, William V. Mong *(Peg-Leg Sullivan)*, Pat Harmon *(Halstead Street Terror)*, Frankie Mann *(Kitty)*.

Melodrama. Source: Edward Payson Roe, *Barriers Burned Away* (New York, 1872). When a valuable painting by an Old Master is stolen from his mother, Wayne Morgan, an artist himself, attempts to find it by taking a menial position as a porter in the Randolph Art Shop. Mark Randolph, the wealthy owner of the store, hopes that his proud and spoiled daughter, Christine, will marry the Earl of Tarnsey, but she will consent only if a copy of an old masterpiece, on which she is working, is accepted by the Academy of Design. Wayne recognizes Christine's painting as a copy of his mother's Old Master and accuses Mellon, the manager of the art store, of its theft. Mellon is jailed, and, on Wayne's advice, the judges at the academy dismiss Christine's copy as lacking in inspiration. In an attempt to revenge herself on Wayne, Christine leads him on and then dumps him. When the Chicago fire breaks out, however, Wayne rescues her, and, together, they help to protect her father's store from looters. They are later separated, and, after days of desperate searching, Wayne finds her among the ruins, praying for him. They declare their mutual love. *Porters. Artists. Art. Looting. Theft. Chicago—Fire of 1871.*

BARRIERS OF FOLLY **F2.0276**

Clinton Productions. *Dist* Russell Productions. Nov **1922.** Si; b&w. 35mm. 5 reels, 4,800 ft.

Dir Edward Kull. *Cont* Thomas Berrien. *Story* Theodore Rockwell.

Cast: George Larkin *(Jim Buckley)*, Eva Novak *(May Gordon)*, Wilfred Lucas *(Wallace Clifton)*, Lillian West *(Madge Spencer)*, Bud Osborne *(Perry Wilson)*, Karl Silvera *(Wong Foo)*.

Western melodrama. Made suspicious by the substantial sum Wallace Clifton has offered for the neighboring ranches owned by Jim Buckley and May Gordon, Jim urges May not to sell until he can investigate. But May is tired of ranch life and attracted to Clifton's suave, city ways, and she consents to go on a motor trip with him. Jim learns that there is oil on their properties, he goes in search of May, and they both have exciting adventures in Chinatown (city unknown) while escaping from Clifton. In the end, May gladly returns to the ranch as Jim's wife. *Ranch life. Oil. Chinatown.*

BARRIERS OF THE LAW **F2.0277**

Independent Pictures. 27 Mar **1925** [New York showing]. Si; b&w. 35mm. 5 reels, 4,960 ft.

Pres by Jesse J. Goldburg. *Dir* J. P. McGowan. *Scen* William Lester. *Story* Travers Vale. *Photog* Walter Griffin.

Cast: J. P. McGowan *(Steve Redding)*, Helen Holmes *(Rita Wingate)*, William Desmond *(Rex Brandon)*, Albert J. Smith *(Redding's aide)*, Norma Wills *(Annie)*, Marguerite Clayton *(Leila Larkin)*.

Melodrama. When revenue officers are about to capture a scow loaded with bootleg whisky, Rita Wingate, one of the bootleggers, destroys the boat. She escapes, but her father, the captain of the tug pulling the scow, is captured. Steve Redding, the leader of the bootleggers, refuses to help Rita's father, and she quits the gang. To keep her quiet, Steve has her put in a house of ill repute, from which she quickly escapes. Running from the gang, Rita takes refuge in the apartment of Rex Brandon, the revenue chief; she and Rex fall in love and are soon married. When Rex is about to arrest Steve, a bootlegger tells him of Rita's stay in the whorehouse. Rex resigns from the department rather than involve Rita in scandal; Rita rejoins the gang in an attempt to obtain evidence with which to arrest them. Rex learns that Rita was innocent and vows to redeem himself, going after a load of bootleg whisky stored in railroad cars. During the raid, Rita, who tipped off Rex, is locked in a flaming boxcar—but Rex saves her after a wild chase. Rex and Rita are reunited, and Rex assumes his old place in the law enforcement community. *Revenue agents. Bootleggers. Criminals—Rehabilitation. Tugboats. Whorehouses. Railroads. Chases.*

BASHFUL BUCCANEER **F2.0278**

Harry J. Brown Productions. *Dist* Rayart Pictures. 7 Nov **1925** [New York State license]. Si; b&w. 35mm. 5 reels, 5,200 ft.

Dir Harry J. Brown. *Scen* Krag Johnson, Burke Jenkins.

Cast: Reed Howes *(Jerry Logan)*, Dorothy Dwan *(Nancy Lee)*, Sheldon Lewis *(first mate)*, Bull Montana *(second mate)*, Jimmy Aubrey *(cook)*, Sam Allen *(Captain)*, George French *(Clipper Jones)*, Sailor Sharkey, "Gunboat" Smith.

Comedy-melodrama. Jerry Logan, who writes lurid stories of sailors and the sea, has never been aboard a ship in his life and decides, therefore, to go to sea. Two sailors, who want to lift the mortgage on the boat of a sweet orphan named Nancy Lee, tell Jerry a completely fictitious tale of buried treasure and charter Nancy's schooner to him. Jerry hires a crew of ruffians and sets sail to find the pirate gold, only to find himself with a mutiny on his hands. The schooner lands on a location where a film company is shooting a picture, and a fight takes place. Jerry finally marries Nancy and writes new stories of the sea. *Authors. Sailors. Orphans. The Sea. Treasure. Mutiny. Mortgages. Motion pictures. Schooners.*

THE BAT **F2.0279**

Feature Productions. *Dist* United Artists. ca14 Mar **1926** [New York premiere; c23 Mar 1926; LP22528]. Si; b&w. 35mm. 9 reels, 8,219 ft.

Prod-Dir-Adapt Roland West. *Scen* Julien Josephson. *Titl* George Marion, Jr. *Photog* Arthur Edeson. *Art Dir* William Cameron Menzies. *Prod Asst* Frank Hall Crane, Thornton Freeland, Hal C. Kern, Ned Herbert Mann.

Cast: André de Beranger *(Gideon Bell)*, Charles W. Herzinger *(Man in Black Mask)*, Emily Fitzroy *(Miss Cornelia Van Gorder)*, Louise Fazenda *(Lizzie Allen)*, Arthur Houseman *(Richard Fleming)*, Robert McKim *(Dr. Wells)*, Jack Pickford *(Brooks Bailey)*, Jewel Carmen *(Miss Dale Odgen)*, Kamiyama Sojin *(Billy)*, Tullio Carminati *(Moletti)*, Eddie Gribbon *(Detective Anderson)*, Lee Shumway *(The Unknown)*.

Mystery melodrama. Source: Mary Roberts Rinehart and Avery Hopwood, *The Bat, A Play of Mystery in Three Acts* (New York, 1926). A master crook, known as "The Bat" because of his disguise, announces a jewel theft in advance but is foiled by a rival crook at the scene of the crime. Their trail leads to the Courtleigh Fleming estate, now leased to Cornelia Van Gorder, a wealthy spinster. The reported death of banker

Fleming and the disappearance of Brooks Bailey, a young cashier in love with Dale (Miss Van Gorder's niece), add to the complications of a $200,000 bank robbery. Brooks, masquerading as a gardener, remains concealed in the house, hoping to unravel the mystery. Lizzie, a servant, suspects everyone, including Dr. Wells, the butler, and Detective Moletti. The Bat, who has killed Moletti and is impersonating him, is finally captured in a beartrap. *Spinsters. Domestics. Thieves. Disguise. Fear. Murder. Bank robberies.*

THE BAT WHISPERS **F2.0280**

Art Cinema Corp. *Dist* United Artists. 29 Nov **1930** [c24 Nov 1930; LP1761]. Sd (Movietone); b&w. 35mm & 65mm. 10 reels, 7,991 ft.

Pres by Joseph M. Schenck. *Dir-Adapt-Dial* Roland West. *Photog* Ray June. *Photog 65mm vers* Robert H. Planck. *Sets* Paul Crawley. *Film Ed* James Smith. *Rec Engr* Oscar Lagerstrom. *Prod Asst* Roger H. Heman, Charles H. Smith, Ned Herbert Mann, Helen Hallett.

Cast: Chester Morris *(Detective Anderson/The Bat)*, Una Merkel *(Dale Van Gorder)*, Chance Ward *(police lieutenant)*, Richard Tucker *(Mr. Bell)*, Wilson Benge *(butler)*, De Witt Jennings *(police captain)*, Sidney D'Albrook *(police sergeant)*, S. E. Jennings *(man in black mask)*, Grayce Hampton *(Cornelia Van Gorder)*, Maude Eburne *(Lizzie Allen)*, Spencer Charters *(caretaker)*, William Bakewell *(Brook)*, Gustav von Seyffertitz *(Dr. Venrees)*, Hugh Huntley *(Richard Fleming)*, Charles Dow Clark *(Detective Jones)*, Ben Bard *(the unknown)*.

Mystery melodrama. Source: Mary Roberts Rinehart and Avery Hopwood, *The Bat; a Play of Mystery in Three Acts* (New York, 1926). A sound version of the play, following the same general story outline of the 1926 version, entitled *The Bat. Thieves. Millionaires. Domestics. Detectives. Bankers. Robbery. Murder.*

THE BATTLE OF PARIS **F2.0281**

Paramount Famous Lasky Corp. 30 Nov **1929** [c29 Nov 1929; LP877]. Sd (Movietone); b&w. 35mm. 8 reels, 6,218 ft.

Dir Robert Florey. *Story-Dial* Gene Markey. *Photog* Bill Steiner. *Songs: "They All Fall in Love," "Here Comes the Band Wagon," "Housekeeping," "What Makes My Baby Blue"* Cole Porter.

Cast: Gertrude Lawrence *(Georgie)*, Charles Ruggles *(Zizi)*, Walter Petrie *(Tony)*, Gladys Du Bois *(Suzanne)*, Arthur Treacher *(Harry)*, Joe King *(Jack)*.

War drama. Georgie, a singer and music vendor on the streets of Paris, teams with Zizi, a pickpocket, and in the scurry before a police raid she meets Tony, a young American artist. Returning his wallet the next day, Georgie is persuaded to remain and model for him, and as a result they fall in love. When war is declared, Tony enlists and Georgie keeps his apartment for him. While nursing in a large hospital in Paris, Georgie becomes pals with three "musketeers" of the Paris underworld; when Tony fails to meet her on his leave, she finds him in the arms of Suzanne, a cafe waitress; with her friends she monopolizes their attention with her musical talent. Later, Suzanne lures her from the apartment and has her imprisoned. Tony joins the friends in their search for her; and after a battle with the villains, the lovers are reunited. *Singers. Models. Pickpockets. Artists. Nurses. World War I. Paris.*

THE BATTLE OF THE SEXES **F2.0282**

Art Cinema Corp. *Dist* United Artists. 12 Oct **1928** [New York premiere; c17 Oct 1928; LP25734]. Sd eff & mus score (Movietone); b&w. 35mm. 10 reels, 8,180 ft.

Pres by Joseph M. Schenck. *Dir* D. W. Griffith. *Adapt-Titl* Gerrit Lloyd. *Photog* Karl Struss, Billy Bitzer. *Film Ed* James Smith. *Mus Score* R. Schildkret, Hugo Riesenfeld.

Cast: Jean Hersholt *(Judson)*, Phyllis Haver *(Marie Skinner)*, Belle Bennett *(Mrs. Judson)*, Don Alvarado *(Babe Winsor)*, Sally O'Neil *(Ruth Judson)*, William Bakewell *(Billy Judson)*, John Batten *(friend of the Judsons)*.

Domestic drama. Source: Daniel Carson Goodman, "The Single Standard" (publication undetermined). Marie Skinner, a young, beautiful gold digger who sets her sights on J. C. Judson, a wealthy family man who likes nothing better than to warm himself at the domestic hearth, rents the apartment next to his. The two soon meet, and J. C. falls for Marie in a big way. One evening, J. C.'s wife and children find him dancing suggestively with Marie at a nightclub, and J. C. leaves home the next day. J. C. later learns that Marie has another fellow who has been forcing her to dupe him; he quickly leaves her and contritely returns to his wife and children. *Gold diggers. Marriage. Family life. Nightclubs.*

THE BATTLER **F2.0283**

Bud Barsky Corp. 15 Sep **1925** [New York State license]. Si; b&w. 35mm. 5 reels.

Dir-Scen Robert N. Bradbury.

Cast: Kenneth McDonald.

Melodrama(?). No information about the nature of this film has been found.

BATTLIN' BILL **F2.0284**

William (Bill) Mix Productions. 1 Jun **1927** [New York State license]. Si; b&w. 35mm. 5 reels.

Cast: Dick Carter, Gene Crosby.

Western melodrama(?). No information about the nature of this film has been found.

BATTLIN' BUCKAROO **F2.0285**

Dist Anchor Film Distributors. 1 Feb **1924** [scheduled release]. Si; b&w. 35mm. 5 reels.

Cast: Bill Patton, Peggy O'Day.

Western melodrama(?). No information about the nature of this film has been found.

BATTLING BATES **F2.0286**

Ashton Dearholt. *Dist* Arrow Film Corp. 15 Dec **1923.** Si; b&w. 35mm. 5 reels, 4,167 ft.

Dir Webster Cullison. *Story-Scen* Daniel F. Whitcomb.

Cast: Edmund Cobb *(Fred Porter)*.

Western melodrama. Young rancher Fred Porter loves local beauty Betty Bolton. When Porter refuses the affection of Zora Rosario, a female maverick, she sends her gang to kill him. They waylay Porter, but before they can kill him, a stranger comes to the rescue. Then the gang captures Betty. The stranger, a Secret Service agent in search of the gang, intercedes again and rescues both youngsters. *Ranchers. Gangs. Secret service.*

BATTLING BOOKWORM **F2.0287**

Balshofer Productions. *Dist* Biltmore Pictures. 1 Jun **1928** [New York State license]. Si; b&w. 35mm. 5 reels, 4,800 ft.

Cast: William Barrymore.

Action melodrama(?). No information about the precise nature of this film has been found. *Prizefighters. Bookworms.*

BATTLING BUDDY **F2.0288**

Approved Pictures. *Dist* Weiss Brothers Artclass Pictures. 15 Aug **1924** [c22 Jul 1924; LU20418]. Si; b&w. 35mm. 5 reels, 4,600 ft.

Prod Lester F. Scott, Jr. *Dir* Richard Thorpe. *Story* Elizabeth Burbridge. *Photog* George Meehan.

Cast: Buddy Roosevelt *(Buddy West)*, Violet La Plante *(Dorothy Parker)*, William Lowery *(Pete Hall)*, Kewpie King *(Ginger)*, Shorty Hendrix *(Fred Burrows)*, Charles E. Butler *(Sam White)*, Pardner *(himself, a horse)*.

Western melodrama. Young Buddy West inherits a ranch from his uncle, but a clause in the will stipulates that the property shall go to the foreman, Pete Hall, if Buddy should be found incompetent. The foreman has him captured and put in an asylum, but he escapes and returns to outwit his enemies, rescue his uncle's daughter from the foreman, and gain clear title to the ranch. *Cowboys. Ranch foremen. Inheritance. Insane asylums. Horses.*

BATTLING BUNYON **F2.0289**

Crown Productions. *Dist* Associated Exhibitors. 18 Jan **1925** [c17 Nov, 20 Nov, 26 Dec 1924; LU20805, LU20941]. Si; b&w. 35mm. 5 reels, 4,900 ft.

Dir Paul Hurst. *Scen* Jefferson Moffitt. *Titl* Ford Beebe. *Photog* Frank Cotner. *Film Ed* Fred Burnworth.

Cast: Wesley Barry *(["Aiken"] Battling Bunyon)*, Molly Malone *(Molly Coshgan)*, Frank Campeau *(Jim Canby)*, Harry Mann *(manager)*, Johnny Relasco *(Johnny Prentiss)*, Landers Stevens *(Pierson)*, Jackie Fields *(Sailor Levinsky)*, Pat Kemp *("The Trained Seal")*, Chester Conklin *(a stranger)*, Al Kaufman *(referee)*.

Comedy. Source: Raymond Leslie Goldman, "Battling Bunyon Ceases To Be Funny," in *Saturday Evening Post* (196:30–31, 15 Mar 1924). If Aiken Bunyon can raise $1,000, he will be able to buy a partnership in the garage in which he works as a mechanic. When the lightweight boxing champion makes a pass at Aiken's girl, Molly, Aiken tries ineffectually to fight him; and Jim Canby, a local fight promotor who witnesses the incident, immediately signs up Bunyon as a fighter, thinking to use his lack of experience as comic effect in the ring. Bunyon wins his first fight and then agrees to fight the lightweight champ in a comedy bout, getting $200 for each round that he can stay in the ring. Bunyon fights with great spirit but is badly beaten and can last only four rounds. After the fight, however, the champ makes another pass at Molly, and Bunyon then gives him the drubbing of his life. Impressed by Bunyon's grit and determination, Canby gives Bunyon a full thousand dollars, and Molly and Aiken make plans for their future. *Mechanics. Fight promoters. Prizefighting. Garages.*

BATTLING BURKE **F2.0290**

Dist Krelbar Pictures, Collwyn Pictures. 19 Mar **1928** [New York State license]. Si; b&w. 35mm. 5 reels.

Cast: Al Hoxie.

Western melodrama(?). No information about the nature of this film has been found.

Note: May have been produced in 1926 by Anchor Film Distributors.

BATTLING BUTLER **F2.0291**

Buster Keaton Productions. *Dist* Metro-Goldwyn-Mayer Distributing Corp. 22 Aug **1926** [New York premiere; released 4 or 19 Sep; c30 Aug 1926; LP23068]. Si; b&w. 35mm. 7 reels, 6,970 ft.

Pres by Joseph M. Schenck. *Dir* Buster Keaton. *Screen Adapt* Paul Gerard Smith, Al Boasberg, Charles Smith, Lex Neal. *Photog* Dev Jennings, Bert Haines.

Cast: Buster Keaton *(Alfred Butler)*, Sally O'Neil *(The Girl)*, Snitz Edwards *(His Valet)*, Francis McDonald *(Alfred "Battling Butler")*, Mary O'Brien *(His Wife)*, Tom Wilson *(His Trainer)*, Eddie Borden *(His Manager)*, Walter James *(The Girl's Father)*, Bud Fine *(The Girl's Brother)*.

Farce. Source: Stanley Brightman, Austin Melford, Douglas Furber and Philip Brabham, *Battling Butler* (a musical play; lyrics, Furber; music, Brabham; publication undetermined). Indolent and wealthy Alfred Butler, accompanied by Martin, his valet, goes on a camping excursion in his Rolls-Royce with all the accouterments of luxury. He meets Sally and gets up enough ambition to propose marriage, but her husky father and brother persuade him to withdraw his suit. When Martin tells Sally's family that Alfred is actually "Battling Butler," a championship boxer, Alfred is welcomed as a prospective suitor and later is proclaimed a hero for purportedly winning a fight. Then the real Butler appears with his spouse; he decides to humiliate the imposter by having him fight one "Alabama Murderer" and has him trained by his managers. Alfred locks up his bride to keep her from seeing his disgrace but finds that the real "Battling Butler" has already won the fight. Then the boxer begins to fight with Alfred, who finally summons his courage and beats the champion. *Idlers. Boxers. Fight managers. Courtship. Impersonation. Cowardice. Rolls-Royce automobiles.*

THE BATTLING FOOL **F2.0292**

Perfection Pictures. *Dist* C. B. C. Film Sales. 1 Aug **1924** [c30 Jun 1924; LP20364]. Si; b&w. 35mm. 5 reels, 4,978 ft.

Dir W. S. Van Dyke.

Cast: William Fairbanks *(Mark Jenkins)*, Eva Novak *(Helen Chadwick)*, Fred J. Butler *(Hiram Chadwick)*, Laura Winston *(Mrs. Chadwick)*, Mark Fenton *(Rev. Josiah Jenkins)*, Catherine Craig *(Madeline Le Bertin)*, Jack Byron *(Clarence Lorraine)*, Pat Harmon *(Jerry Sullivan)*, Andy Waldron *(Reuben, Chief of Police)*, Ed Kennedy *(Dan O'Leary)*.

Melodrama. Mark Jenkins, a minister's son, realizes his ability as a fighter while defending Helen Chadwick from a crowd of hoodlums. Taken in hand by Jerry Sullivan, ex-prizefighter, he develops into a world champion. While frustrating an attempted embezzlement, he rescues Helen from a burning building. *Prizefighters. Embezzlement Fires.*

BATTLING KID **F2.0293**

Bud Barsky Productions. 15 Oct **1926**. Si; b&w. 35mm. 5 reels.

Dir Paul Hurst.

Cast: Al Hoxie.

Western melodrama. "Not knowing his boss is endeavoring by crooked means to secure possession of neighbor's ranch, hero is model superintendent until he discovers the treachery. He then throws his lot with heroine's father in battle against such foul play and succeeds in foiling his former boss's purposes." (*Motion Picture News Booking Guide*, 12:19, Apr 1927.) *Ranch managers. Property rights.*

BATTLING KING **F2.0294**

P. D. Sargent–William J. Otts. *Dist* Clark-Cornelius Corp. 1 Mar **1922**. Si; b&w. 35mm. 5 reels, 4,809 ft.

Dir P. D. Sargent.

Cast: William J. Otts, Nevada Grey.

Western melodrama. "A pugilist, after his manager skips the town, is stranded in a western hamlet. Through the influence of friends he makes, he is made a sergeant of the state police, and comes into conflict with the crooked gang that controls the town. He is in love with the daughter of the district attorney, but she believes him her father's enemy. A hold-up is staged, and every obstacle placed in the hero's way when he attempts to round up the guilty parties. He puts up a fight, however, and eventually triumphs, practically singlehanded." (*Motion Picture News Booking Guide*, 3:9, Oct 1922.) *Prizefighters. Police. District attorneys. Gangs. Smalltown life.*

BATTLING MASON **F2.0295**

Hercules Film Productions. *Dist* Bud Barsky Corp. 24 Dec **1924** [New York State license]. Si; b&w. 35mm. 5 reels, 4,800 ft.

Dir? (see note) Jack Nelson, William James Craft. *Writ for the screen by* William E. Wing.

Cast: Frank Merrill *(Mason)*, Eva Novak, Billy Elmer, Dick Sutherland, Milburn Morante.

Comedy-melodrama. Mason, a young New York gentleman who is good with his fists, runs for public office under the terms of an agreement that forbids him to fight during the pre-election period. During this time, his rich uncle comes east and soon expresses great disappointment in Mason, who refuses to fight after the worst of provocations and insults. During a political speech in the gashouse district, Mason is set upon by a gang of ruffians, and he runs for his life. The brutes then attack Mason's girl, however, and Mason quickly shows them what getting hit by a ton of bricks feels like. Mason later wins the election, marries the girl, and gains the affection of his wealthy uncle. *Uncles. Politics. Elections. Boxing. New York City.*

Note: Sources disagree in crediting direction.

THE BATTLING ORIOLES **F2.0296**

Hal E. Roach Studios. *For* Pathé Exchange. *Dist* Associated Exhibitors. 26 Oct **1924** [c25 Sep 1924; LP20608]. Si; b&w. 35mm. 6 reels, 5,600 ft.

Pres by Hal Roach. *Dir* Ted Wilde, Fred Guiol. *Story* Hal Roach. *Photog* Floyd Jackman, George Stevens. *Asst Dir* Bert Currigan.

Cast: Glenn Tryon *(Tommy Roosevelt Tucker)*, Blanche Mehaffey *(Hope Stanton)*, John T. Prince *("Cappy" Wolfe)*, Noah Young *(Sid Stanton)*, Sam Lufkin *(Jimmy)*, Robert Page *(Inspector Joslin)*.

Comedy. The members of the once-famous and scrappy Battling Orioles baseball team are now rich, old, and grouchy and belong to the National Club. Their president, "Cappy" Wolfe, discovers barber Tommy Roosevelt Tucker to be a son of a former Oriole and invites him to come to the city and work in the club. Jubilant because his sweetheart, Hope Stanton, is also in the city, Tommy tries to cheer up the old fellows. He only incurs their wrath, but the group rises to the Battling Orioles tradition in order to help Tommy rescue Hope from her Uncle Sid Stanton, who is trying to involve her in a confidence scheme. The film "opens with some excellent comedy depicting base ball as it was played in 1870" (*Moving Picture News*, 23 Aug 1924). *Barbers. Confidence men. Baseball. Clubs.*

BAVU (Universal-Jewel) **F2.0297**

Universal Pictures. 15 Apr or 7 May **1923** [c5 Apr 1923; LP18860]. Si; b&w. 35mm. 8 reels, 6,968 ft.

Dir Stuart Paton. *Scen* Raymond L. Schrock, Albert Kenyon. *Photog* Allen Davey.

Cast: Wallace Beery *(Felix Bavu)*, Estelle Taylor *(Princess Annia)*, Forrest Stanley *(Mischa Vleck)*, Sylvia Breamer *(Olga Stropik)*, Josef Swickard *(Prince Markoff)*, Nick De Ruiz *(Kuroff)*, Martha Mattox *(Piplette)*, Harry Carter *(Shadow)*, Jack Rollens *(Michael Revno)*.

Melodrama. Source: Earl Carroll, *Bavu* (New York opening: 25 Feb 1922). Bavu, an illiterate, uncouth brute, rises to power during the Russian Revolution, plots to wreak vengeance on all who cross him, and incites the peasantry to burn the city. Mischa Vleck, on the other hand, is a more humane official who decides to protect Princess Annia, whom he loves and whose house he once served. Mischa tries to trick Bavu into signing papers permitting Annia and him to marry and leave the country, but Bavu's faithful Olga reveals their contents. Mischa and Bavu fight, and Bavu seals a passage in which he believes Mischa to be hiding. To his horror, Bavu too late realizes that he has trapped Olga, while Mischa and Annia have escaped. *Political refugees. Royalty. Murder. Russia—History—1917–21 Revolution.*

Note: Working title: *The Attic of Felix Bavu.*

BE MY WIFE **F2.0298**

Max Linder Productions. *Dist* Goldwyn Distributing Corp. Dec **1921** [c23 Nov 1921; LP17233]. Si; b&w. 35mm. 5 reels, 4,650 ft.

Prod-Dir-Writ Max Linder. *Photog* Charles J. Van Enger.

Cast: Alta Allen *(The Girl)*, Caroline Rankin *(The Aunt)*, Lincoln Stedman *(Archie)*, Rose Dione *(Madame Coralie)*, Charles McHugh *(Mr. Madame Coralie)*, Viora Daniels *(Mrs. Du Pont)*, Arthur Clayton *(Mr. Du Pont)*, Pal *(The God)*, Max Linder *(The Fiancé)*.

Farce. Max, the fiancé, after he is accepted by his sweetheart, successfully obstructs the machinations of a rival for the girl's favor but has great difficulty in winning over her aunt to his side. After the wedding, when a divorce is pending, he accomplishes the latter feat and at the same time causes his wife to respect him the more. *Aunts. Courtship. Divorce.*

BE YOURSELF! **F2.0299**

United Artists. 8 Feb **1930** [c8 Feb 1930; LP1098]. Sd (Movietone); b&w. 35mm. 9 reels, 6,900 ft.

Pres by Joseph M. Schenck. *Dir* Thornton Freeland. *Adapt* Max Marcin, Thornton Freeland. *Photog* Karl Struss, Robert H. Planck. *Sets* William Cameron Menzies, Park French. *Film Ed* Robert J. Kern. *Song: "When a Woman Loves a Man"* Billy Rose, Ralph Rainger. *Song: "Cooking Breakfast for the One I Love"* Billy Rose, Henry Tobias. *Songs: "Kicking a Hole in the Sky," "Sasha the Passion of the Pascha"* Billy Rose, Ballard MacDonald, Jesse Greer. *Mus Arr* Hugo Riesenfeld. *Dance Dir* Maurice L. Kusell. *Rec Engr* Harold Witt. *Asst Dir* Roger H. Heman. *Cost* Alice O'Neill.

Cast: Fanny Brice *(Fannie Field)*, Robert Armstrong *(Jerry Moore)*, Harry Green *(Harry Field)*, G. Pat Collins *(McCloskey)*, Gertrude Astor *(Lillian)*, Budd Fine *(Step)*, Marjorie "Babe" Kane *(Lola)*, Rita Flynn *(Jessica)*, Jimmy Tolson *(himself)*.

Musical melodrama. Source: Joseph Jackson, "The Champ" (publication undetermined). Fannie, a nightclub entertainer, befriends Jerry Moore, a luckless prizefighter, and is discussing his attempts to break into the big time when McCloskey, heavyweight champion, provokes a quarrel and lays Jerry out on the floor. Fannie induces Jerry to appoint her his manager; after 6 weeks of intensive training, she warns him against his habit of claiming fouls; he promises to win his test fight; and, goaded on by Fannie, he finally wins the championship from McCloskey. Fannie's chief rival, Lillian, dazzles Jerry with her attentions, and to save him Fannie arranges a rematch with McCloskey, though Jerry has just had his nose straightened. Jerry reproaches her for the doublecross when he loses the fight, but he forgives her when he realizes her motive. *Entertainers. Prizefighters. Fight managers. Vamps. Courtship. Nightclubs.*

BEACH OF DREAMS (Robertson-Cole Super Special) **F2.0300**

Haworth Studios. *Dist* Robertson-Cole Distributing Corp. 8 May **1921** [c7 Sep 1920; LU15514]. Si; b&w. 35mm. 5 reels, 5,005 ft.

Dir William Parke. *Scen* E. Richard Schayer, Nan Blair. *Photog (see note)* Felix Schoedsack.

Cast: Edith Storey *(Cleo de Bromsart)*, Noah Beery *(Jack Raft)*, Sidney Payne *(La Touche)*, Jack Curtis *(Bompard)*, George Fisher *(Maurice Chenet)*, Joseph Swickard *(Monsieur de Brie)*, Margarita Fisher *(Madame de Brie)*, W. Templar Powell *(Prince Selm)*, Gertrude Norman *(La Comtesse de Warens)*, Cesare Gravina *(Professor Epnard)*.

Adventure melodrama. Source: Henry de Vere Stacpoole, *The Beach of Dreams, a Romance* (New York, 1919). Parisian society girl Cleo de Bromsart, who is engaged to Maurice Chenet, is bored with her life and decides to accept the invitation of Prince Selm to join his yachting party. The cruise ends in disaster, and Cleo is stranded on a desert island with two sailors. One sailor drowns in quicksand, and Cleo kills the other when he tries to rape her. Several weeks later, Raft, a derelict, is washed ashore. He finds her ill and nurses her back to health. Raft effects their rescue by overpowering a gang of Chinese seal poachers. Back in Paris, given the choice between her fiancé, whom her parents approve, and Raft, whom Cleo has grown to respect, she decides not to marry either. *Socialites. Sailors. Poachers. Chinese. Sealing. Rape. Paris. Shipwrecks.*

Note: The photographer's name is given as *Fred* Schoedsack in *Film Year Book.*

THE BEARCAT **F2.0301**

Universal Film Manufacturing Co. 3 Apr **1922** [c24 Mar 1922; LP17689]. Si; b&w. 35mm. 5 reels, 4,550 ft.

Pres by Carl Laemmle. *Dir* Edward Sedgwick. *Scen* George Hively. *Story* Frank R. Buckley. *Photog* Charles Kaufman.

Cast: Hoot Gibson *(The Singin' Kid)*, Lillian Rich *(Alys May)*, Charles French *(Sheriff Bill Garfield)*, Joe Harris *(Doc Henderson)*, Alfred Hollingsworth *(John P. May)*, Harold Goodwin *(Peter May)*, William Buckley *(Archer Aitken)*, Fontaine La Rue *(Mary Lang)*, James Alamo *(Henry)*, J. J. Allen *(Jake Hensen)*, Stanley Fitz *(Cut Face)*, Joe De La Cruz *(One Eye)*, Sam Pobo *(Pining Willis)*.

Western melodrama. The Bearcat, alias The Singin' Kid, crosses the Rio Grande into Three Pines, singing bloodthirsty verses, but in spite of these he makes friends with Sheriff Bill Garfield and likewise with Alys May, daughter of cattle rancher John P. May, by saving her from a runaway. As a reward he gets a job on the ranch and falls in love with Alys, though warned she is engaged to Aitken, her brother's college chum. Aitken and Peter return from college, and Aitken becomes involved in an affair with Mary Lang, a former sweetheart in a neighboring town, who wants a payment to forget the flirtation. The Kid keeps Aitken from paying, and when Mary's accomplice is murdered he takes the blame, but later he proves himself innocent. Aitken departs for the East, leaving the field free to the Kid and Alys. *Cowboys. Sheriffs. Ranchers. Brother-sister relationship. Courtship. Blackmail. Mexican border.*

THE BEAST *see* **THE WOLF MAN**

BEATEN **F2.0302**

Premium Picture Productions. *Dist* Independent Pictures. Jan **1924.** Si; b&w. 35mm. 5 reels, 4,321 or 4,800 ft.

Dir H. G. Moody.

Cast: Jack Livingston.

Western melodrama. "Hero is sent from the east to check up shortage on mine. Foreman, who is stealing the gold, covets girl with whom hero falls in love. Foreman sends landslide on hero, and later blows up mine when hero and girl are in it, but they escape, and matters are righted." (*Motion Picture News Booking Guide*, 6:12, Apr 1924.) *Mine foremen. Gold mines. Landslides.*

BEATING THE GAME **F2.0303**

Goldwyn Pictures. Sep **1921** [c27 Jul 1921; LP16790]. Si; b&w. 35mm. 6 reels, 5,558 ft.

Dir Victor Schertzinger. *Story-Scen* Charles Kenyon. *Photog* Ernest Miller. *Art Dir* Cedric Gibbons. *Asst Dir* Wyatt Brewster.

Cast: Tom Moore *("Fancy Charlie")*, Hazel Daly *(Nellie Brown)*, De Witt Jennings *(G. B. Lawson)*, Dick Rosson *(Ben Fanchette)*, Nick Cogley *("Slipper Jones")*, Tom Ricketts *(Jules Fanchette)*, Lydia Knott *(Madame Fanchette)*, William Orlamond *(bank president)*, Lydia Yeamans Titus *(Angelica, his wife)*.

Crook melodrama. "Fancy Charlie," an expert safecracker, gains entrance to the apartment of criminologist Lawson and mistakenly assumes he has robbed one of his own profession; Lawson, who believes in "honesty among thieves" and wants to test Charlie, gives him some money with instructions to establish an honest business in the small town of Plumfield and at the end of a year to divide the profits with him. Charlie successfully enters business with the Fanchettes and falls in love with Nellie, the bookkeeper. At the end of the year Charlie decides to go straight and offers to return Lawson's investment, but Lawson refuses the offer. When promoted as a candidate for mayor, Charlie publicly confesses his past, but he is met with cheers; and after Lawson's explanation, he settles down to a happy life with Nellie. *Criminologists. Safecrackers. Criminals—Rehabilitation. Bookkeepers. Mayors.*

BEAU BANDIT **F2.0304**

RKO Productions. 2 Mar **1930** [c2 Mar 1930; LP1179]. Sd (Photophone); b&w. 35mm. 8 reels, 6,169 ft. [Also si.]

Prod William Le Baron. *Assoc Prod* Henry Hobart. *Dir* Lambert Hillyer. *Screenplay* Wallace Smith. *Photog* Jack MacKenzie. *Art Dir* Max Ree. *Film Ed* Archie F. Marshek. *Rec Engr* Clarence M. Wickes.

Cast: Rod La Rocque *(Montero)*, Mitchell Lewis *(Coloso)*, Doris Kenyon *(Helen Wardell)*, Walter Long *("Bob Cat" Manners)*, Charles Middleton *(Perkins)*, George Duryea *(Howard)*, James Donlan *(Buck)*, Charles Brinley *(Slim)*, Barney Furey *(Logan)*, Bill Patton *(Texas)*, Kenneth Cooper, Bob Erickson, Hank Potts, Gordon Jones, Buff Jones,

Walt Robbins, Ben Corbett *(cowhands)*.

Western melodrama. Source: Wallace Smith, "Strictly Business," in *Hearst's International Cosmopolitan* (86:74–77, Apr 1929). Montero, a killer, and his aide Coloso, a vicious deafmute, are pursued through the sand dunes of Arizona by "Bob Cat" Manners and his posse. Montero plans to rob the bank of skinflint Perkins but is sidetracked by singing teacher Helen Wardell; he learns that Perkins has marital designs on her and holds a $3,000 mortgage on the ranch of her fiancé, Howard. Perkins, recognizing Montero as a wanted man, offers him money to kill Howard, but Montero merely fakes the murder. Prepared for a doublecross, Montero takes the posse prisoners and collects the blood money from Perkins, who as justice of the peace is forced to marry Helen and Howard. *Vocal instructors. Fugitives. Deafmutes. Skinflints. Posses. Bandits. Mortgages. Arizona.*

BEAU BROADWAY **F2.0305**

Metro-Goldwyn-Mayer Pictures. 29 Sep **1928** [c29 Sep 1928; LP25668]. Si; b&w. 35mm. 7 reels, 6,037 ft.

Dir-Story Malcolm St. Clair. *Cont* George O'Hara. *Titl* Ralph Spence. *Adapt* F. Hugh Herbert. *Photog* André Barlatier. *Art Dir* Cedric Gibbons. *Film Ed* Harry Reynolds. *Wardrobe* Gilbert Clark.

Cast: Lew Cody *(Jim Lambert)*, Aileen Pringle *(Yvonne)*, Sue Carol *(Mona)*, Hugh Trevor *(Killer Gordon)*, Heinie Conklin *(Dijuha)*, Kit Guard *(Professor Griswold)*, Jack Herrick *(Dr. Monahan)*, James J. Jeffries *(Gunner O'Brien)*.

Romantic drama. Jim Lambert, a fight promoter and gambler, grants Gunner O'Brien his dying wish and agrees to care for Gunner's granddaughter, Mona, believing her to be a child. Mona turns out to be a beautiful young woman, however, and Jim overnight stops drinking and chasing skirts, becoming a devoted family man. Killer Gordon, one of Jim's fighters, becomes friendly with Mona, and Jim, believing that she loves Killer in return, himself turns for consolation to his former mistress, Yvonne, whom he asks to marry him. She refuses, telling Jim that she is engaged to Killer; Jim is skeptical, and Mona, overhearing the conversation, runs to her room in tears. Jim follows and learns to his delight that it is he himself whom Mona loves. *Fight promoters. Gamblers. Prizefighters. Wards. Mistresses.*

BEAU BRUMMELL **F2.0306**

Warner Brothers Pictures. ca30 Mar **1924** [New York premiere; released 15 Mar or 12 Apr; c14 Mar 1924; LP19998]. Si; b&w. 35mm. 10 reels, 9,900 ft.

Dir Harry Beaumont. *Adapt* Dorothy Farnum. *Photog* David Abel.

Cast: John Barrymore *(George Bryan Brummell)*, Mary Astor *(Lady Margery Alvanley)*, Willard Louis *(Prince of Wales)*, Carmel Myers *(Lady Hester Stanhope)*, Irene Rich *(Frederica Charlotte, Duchess of York)*, Alec B. Francis *(Mortimer)*, William Humphreys *(Lord Alvanley)*, Richard Tucker *(Lord Stanhope)*, André de Beranger *(Lord Byron)*, Clarissa Selwynne *(Mrs. Wertham)*, John J. Richardson *("Poodles" Byng)*, Claire De Lorez *(Lady Manly)*, Michael Dark *(Lord Manly)*, Templar Saxe *(Desmond Wertham)*, James A. Marcus *(Snodgrass, an English innkeeper)*, Betty Brice *(Mrs. Snodgrass)*, Roland Rushton *(Mr. Abrahams)*, Carol Holloway *(Kathleen, a maid)*, Kate Lester *(Lady Miora)*, Rose Dione *(Madame Bergère)*.

Historical drama. Source: Clyde Fitch, *Beau Brummell, a Play in Four Acts* (New York opening: 24 Apr 1916). British Army officer George Bryan Brummell decides to become a "beau" and lead a reckless bachelor's life after he sees his sweetheart, Lady Margery, forced to marry Lord Alvanley. He wins the friendship of the Prince of Wales, leaves his regiment, and becomes one of Europe's taste-makers. His insolence and his indiscretions with the ladies of the court make enemies, and he falls into disfavor. After escaping his creditors to France, he eventually dies there in poverty, deserted by all but his servant, Mortimer. *Dandies. England. France. George Bryan Brummell. George Prince of Wales. George Gordon Byron. Hester Lucy Stanhope.*

BEAU GESTE **F2.0307**

Famous Players–Lasky. *Dist* Paramount Pictures. 25 Aug **1926** [New York premiere; released 1 Aug 1927; c1 Aug 1927; LP24265]. Si; b&w with col sequences (Technicolor). 35mm. 10-11 reels, 10,600 ft.

Pres by Adolph Zukor, Jesse L. Lasky. *Dir* Herbert Brenon. *Screenplay* Paul Schofield. *Adapt* John Russell, Herbert Brenon. *Photog* J. Roy Hunt. *Art Dir* Julian Boone Fleming. *Mus Score* Hugo Riesenfeld. *Asst Dir* Ray Lissner.

Cast: Ronald Colman *(Michael "Beau" Geste)*, Neil Hamilton *(Digby Geste)*, Ralph Forbes *(John Geste)*, Alice Joyce *(Lady Brandon)*, Mary Brian *(Isobel)*, Noah Beery *(Sergeant Lejaune)*, Norman Trevor *(Major de Beaujolais)*, William Powell *(Boldini)*, George Rigas *(Maris)*, Bernard Siegel *(Schwartz)*, Victor McLaglen *(Hank)*, Donald Stuart *(Buddy)*, Paul McAllister *(St. André)*, Redmond Finlay *(Cordère)*, Ram Singh *(Prince Ram Singh)*, Maurice Murphy *("Beau")*, Philippe De Lacey *(Digby)*, Mickey McBan *(John)*.

Romantic adventure drama. Source: Percival Christopher Wren, *Beau Geste* (New York, 1925). A relief detachment of the French Foreign Legion arrives at a remote fort in the African desert to find the garrison manned by a force of dead men; a major finds an adjutant's body pierced by a French bayonet near a dead legionnaire; as an Arab attack begins, the bodies disappear and the story shifts to England. *As a boy, Michael "Beau" Geste overhears his aunt, Lady Brandon, telling of a sapphire heirloom, replaced by an imitation; when the gem disappears, Beau, Digby, and John—the three brothers—disappear, each leaving a note assuming the guilt. They join the Foreign Legion, Beau and John serving under brutal Sergeant Lejaune, and Digby, as trumpeter at another post. The men revolt against Lejaune's cruelty, and he determines to get the jewel Beau is rumored to carry, but the garrison is attacked by Arabs and Beau is killed; John revenges his brother by killing Lejaune, and Digby provides Beau with a Viking funeral.* Digby also is killed, and John returns home to Isobel, his fiancée. *Brothers. Arabs. Revenge. Theft. Heirlooms. France—Army—Foreign Legion. Africa. Sahara. England.*

BEAU REVEL **F2.0308**

Thomas H. Ince Productions. *Dist* Paramount Pictures. 20 Mar **1921** [c21 Feb 1921; LP16170]. Si; b&w. 35mm. 6 reels, 5,293 ft.

Pers Supv Thomas H. Ince. *Dir* John Griffith Wray. *Scen* Luther Reed. *Story* Louis Joseph Vance. *Photog* Henry Sharp.

Cast: Lewis S. Stone *(Lawrence "Beau" Revel)*, Florence Vidor *(Nellie Steel)*, Lloyd Hughes *(Dick Revel)*, Kathleen Kirkham *(Alice Latham)*, Richard Ryan *(Rossiter Wade)*, Harlan Tucker *(Will Phyfe)*, William Conklin *(Fred Lathom)*, Lydia Yeamans Titus *(Ma Steel)*, William Musgrave *(Bert Steel)*, Joe Campbell *(butler)*.

Society drama. Lawrence Revel, celebrated in society circles for his success with women, is devoted to his son Dick and objects to his marrying Nellie, a cabaret dancer. To prove her unworthiness, Beau asks his son not to see her for 2 weeks. Unwittingly, Beau falls in love with the girl, but his attentions are refused. When Nellie's brother gets involved with the law, she seeks Beau's aid, but Dick arrives and a stormy scene ensues. Following his son's reproach, Beau leaps from the window to his death, and Dick seeks Nellie's forgiveness. *Dancers. Fatherhood. Family life. Suicide.*

BEAU SABREUR **F2.0309**

Paramount Famous Lasky Corp. 7 Jan **1928** [c7 Jan 1928; LP24838]. Si; b&w. 35mm. 7 reels, 6,704 ft.

Pres by Adolph Zukor, Jesse L. Lasky. *Dir* John Waters. *Titl* Julian Johnson. *Adapt* Tom J. Geraghty. *Photog* C. Edgar Schoenbaum. *Film Ed* Rose Lowenger.

Cast: Gary Cooper *(Major Henri de Beaujolais)*, Evelyn Brent *(Mary Vanbrugh)*, Noah Beery *(Sheikh El Hammel)*, William Powell *(Becque)*, Roscoe Karns *(Buddy)*, Mitchell Lewis *(Suleman the Strong)*, Arnold Kent *(Raoul de Redon)*, Raoul Paoli *(Dufour)*, Joan Standing *(Maudie)*, Frank Reicher *(General de Beaujolais)*, Oscar Smith *(Djikki)*.

Romantic drama. Source: Percival Christopher Wren, *Beau Sabreur* (New York, 1926). Legionnaires Henri de Beaujolais, Raoul de Redon, and Dufour overstay their leave in Algiers and are thrown into jail. There Henri earns the title "Beau Sabreur," given him by his uncle, General Beaujolais, when he wins a duel with a traitor, Becque. The general, who has plans for the Sahara, entreats Henri to forsake women for France, sending him first to the desert to learn the customs of the people, then to Zaguig, where he meets American journalist Mary Vanbrugh, whom he snubs, remembering his vow. Becque, hearing that Henri has orders to visit Sheikh El Hammel at a distant oasis to discuss a treaty, and hoping to prevent his departure, attacks Zaguig, but Henri escapes with Mary, her maid, and his aides. Out of distrust for Becque, the sheikh agrees to a treaty with the French, and they resist an attack led by the vengeful Becque. Henri kills Becque in a duel and, having accomplished his task for France, confesses he loves Mary. *Journalists. Sheiks. Revolts. Colonial administration. France—Army—Foreign Legion. Algeria. Duels.*

THE BEAUTIFUL AND DAMNED **F2.0310**
Warner Brothers Pictures. 10 Dec **1922** [New York premiere; released 1 Jan 1923; c1 Dec 1922; LP18672]. Si; b&w. 35mm. 7 reels.

Dir William A. Seiter. *Adapt* Olga Printzlau.

Cast: Marie Prevost *(Gloria)*, Kenneth Harlan *(Anthony)*, Harry Myers *(Dick)*, Tully Marshall *(Adam Patch)*, Louise Fazenda *(Muriel)*, Cleo Ridgely *(Dot)*, Emmett King *(Mr. Gilbert)*, Walter Long *(Hull)*, Clarence Burton *(Bloeckman)*, Parker McConnell *(Maury)*, Charles McHugh *(Shuttlesworth)*, Kathleen Key *(Rachel)*, George Kuwa *(Tanner)*.

Society drama. Source: F. Scott Fitzgerald, *The Beautiful and Damned* (New York, 1922). After spending most of her father's money Gloria marries Tony, and the two continue their reckless, spendthrift ways. When Tony's grandfather, Adam Patch, dies and leaves Tony nothing but his blessing, the couple try unsuccessfully to work, then return to their frantic pursuit of pleasure. A near collision with a train brings Gloria to her senses, but Tony takes a while longer to decide to end his worthlessness. They break Adam's will and sail for Europe resolved to make good. *Spendthrifts. Jazz life. Wealth.*

BEAUTIFUL BUT DUMB *see* **ALMOST HUMAN**

BEAUTIFUL BUT DUMB **F2.0311**
Tiffany-Stahl Productions. 1 Aug **1928** [c1 Sep 1928; LP25598]. Si; b&w. 35mm. 7 reels, 6,157 ft.

Dir Elmer Clifton. *Story-Cont* J. F. Natteford. *Titl* Frederick Hatton, Fanny Hatton. *Photog* Guy Wilky. *Film Ed* Desmond O'Brien. *Asst Dir* Arthur Rose.

Cast: Patsy Ruth Miller *(Janet Brady)*, Charles Byer *(James Conroy)*, George E. Stone *(Tad)*, Shirley Palmer *(Beth)*, Greta Yoltz *(Mae)*, William Irving *(Ward)*, Harvey Clark *(Broadwell)*.

Romantic comedy. "... of a steno's successful crusade to snare her boss. She learns her personality has no appeal, so she drops her mannish clothes and blossoms forth as a simpering flapper. She develops sex appeal plus and though her boss is nonplussed for a time she wins him in the end." (*Motion Picture News Booking Guide*, [14]:103, 1929.) *Stenographers. Flappers.*

THE BEAUTIFUL CHEAT (Universal-Jewel) **F2.0312**
Universal Pictures. 21 Feb **1926** [c2 Feb 1926; LP22359]. Si; b&w. 35mm. 7 reels, 6,583 ft.

Dir Edward Sloman. *Scen* A. P. Younger, Olga Printzlau. *Photog* Jackson J. Rose.

Cast: Laura La Plante *(Mary Callahan/Maritza Chernovska [Callahansky])*, Harry Myers *(Jimmy Austin)*, Bertram Grassby *(Marquis de la Pontenac)*, Alexander Carr *(Al Goldringer)*, Youcca Troubetzkoy *(Herbert Dangerfield)*, Helen Carr *(Lady Violet Armington)*, Robert Anderson *(Dan Brodie)*.

Comedy-drama. Source: Nina Wilcox Putnam, "Doubling for Cupid," in *Saturday Evening Post* (197:18–19, 13 Dec 1924). A motion picture producer has press agent Jimmy Austin take Mary Callahan, a pretty shopgirl, to Europe. After an extensive publicity campaign, Mary returns to the United States as Maritza Callahansky, a Russian actress owning the crown jewels. To add support to her newly established identity, Maritza gives a party in a Long Island mansion in the rightful owner's absence. The owners return to find their home taken over by strangers and are about to call the police when it is discovered that they are the parents of one of the extras in the company. The owners not only dismiss charges of housebreaking but finance a film in which Maritza will star. Austin marries Maritza. *Shopgirls. Motion picture producers. Press agents. Actors. Imposture. Motion pictures. Russia. Long Island.*

THE BEAUTIFUL CITY **F2.0313**
Inspiration Pictures. *Dist* First National Pictures. 25 Oct **1925** [c26 Oct 1925; LP21930]. Si; b&w. 35mm. 7 reels, 6,466 ft.

Dir Kenneth Webb. *Scen-Titl* Don Bartlett, C. Graham Baker. *Adapt* Violet E. Powell. *Writ* Edmund Goulding. *Photog* Roy Overbaugh, Stuart Kelson. *Sets* Tec-Art Studios. *Film Ed* William Hamilton. *Art Titl* H. E. R. Studios.

Cast: Richard Barthelmess *(Tony Gillardi)*, Dorothy Gish *(Mollie)*, William Powell *(Nick Di Silva)*, Frank Puglia *(Carlo Gillardi)*, Florence Auer *(Mamma Gillardi)*, Lassie Bronte *(The Dog)*.

Melodrama. Tony Gillardi, a young Italian flower vender, makes a poor living when compared by his mother with her favorite, his brother Carlo. Only Mollie O'Connor, his little Irish sweetheart, believes in him. Carlo's source of income, however, is not within the law, for he is dominated by gangster Nick Di Silva, who operates a Chinese theater as a front. Rather than hurt his mother's feelings, Tony takes the blame for a robbery Nick and Carlo committed. After serving a term "up the river," Tony finds out that Carlo is still under Nick's domination and sets out to get him. In a fight between Nick and Tony, Nick accidentally shoots Mamma Gillardi. Nick falls to his death while escaping, the mother recovers, and Tony and Mollie marry. While making a trip around the Battery to Coney Island with Mollie, Tony comes to see, once again, the beauty of his city. *Italians. Irish. Flower vendors. Gangsters. Scapegoats. Family life. Theater—Chinese. New York City. Dogs.*

THE BEAUTIFUL GAMBLER (Universal Special) **F2.0314**
Universal Film Manufacturing Co. Jun **1921** [c25 May 1921; LP16591]. Si; b&w. 35mm. 5 reels, 4,458 ft.

Dir William Worthington. *Scen* Hope Loring. *Story* Peter B. Kyne. *Photog* George Barnes.

Cast: Grace Darmond *(Molly Hanlon)*, Jack Mower *(Miles Rand)*, Harry Van Meter *(Lee Kirk)*, Charles Brinley *(Jim Devlin)*, Herschel Mayall *(Judge Rand)*, Willis Marks *(Mark Hanlon)*.

Western melodrama. After Mark Hanlon gambles away his fortune and his equity in his house, his daughter Molly marries Kirk, proprietor of the gambling hall; and as mistress of the gaming tables she meets young Miles Rand, exiled to the West for his reckless behavior. He falls in love with Molly and protects her from Kirk until the latter apparently dies in a saloon fire. Two years later, however, Kirk finds Molly and Miles in New York and is himself fatally shot in a fight. Miles is arrested and is about to be convicted for the murder when Devlin, Kirk's former handyman, admits to the crime. *Gamblers. Murder. New York City.*

THE BEAUTIFUL LIAR **F2.0315**
Preferred Pictures. *Dist* Associated First National Pictures. 26 Dec **1921** [c27 Dec 1921; LP17386]. Si; b&w. 35mm. 6 reels, 5,236 ft. [Copyrighted as 5 reels.]

Pres by B. P. Schulberg. *Dir* Wallace Worsley. *Scen* Ruth Wightman. *Photog* Joseph Brotherton.

Cast: Katherine MacDonald *(Helen Haynes/Elsie Parmelee)*, Charles Meredith *(Bobby Bates)*, Joseph J. Dowling *(MacGregor)*, Kate Lester *(Mrs. Van Courtlandt–Van Allstyn)*, Wilfred Lucas *(Gaston Allegretti)*.

Comedy-drama. Source: George Marion, Jr., "Peachie" (publication undetermined). The guests at a summer resort hotel, headed by Mrs. Van Courtlandt–Van Allstyn, are preparing to stage a charity performance of a farce, and Gaston Allegretti, threatened with dismissal by the owners, has promised to obtain the services of Broadway star Elsie Parmelee. When the actress refuses, Gaston, in despair, enlists the aid of Helen Haynes, who works in a broker's office and resembles the actress. With MacGregor, a Scottish bookkeeper, she goes to the resort for what she supposes to be a vacation and is reluctant to accept an acting role until she finds that young millionaire Bobby Bates, with whom she is in love, is engaged to play opposite her; although awkward in the part, she is hailed as a great comedienne. Bobby proposes and Helen accepts, thinking he knows her true identity. Later, he learns of the real Elsie Parmelee and is disillusioned, but MacGregor admits his duplicity and all ends well. *Actors. Millionaires. Bookkeepers. Doubles. Impersonation. Theater—Amateur. Resorts.*

THE BEAUTIFUL SINNER **F2.0316**
Perfection Pictures. *Dist* Columbia Pictures. 1 or 15 Oct **1924** [c30 Oct 1924; LP20719]. Si; b&w. 35mm. 5 reels, 4,345 or 4,744 ft.

Dir W. S. Van Dyke. *Story* Wilfred Lucas.

Cast: William Fairbanks *(Henry Avery)*, Eva Novak *(Alice Carter)*, George Nichols *(Benson)*, Kate Lester *(Mrs. Cornelius Westervelt)*, Carmen Phillips *(Carmen De Santas)*, Edward Borman *("Blinky")*, Carl Stockdale *(Bill Parsons)*.

Crook melodrama. Consenting to aid secret serviceman Bill Parsons in recapturing the Benson gang, Henry Avery, wealthy young criminologist, sends Blinky, his assistant, to the waterfront to watch for the thieves while he attends a reception at the home of Mrs. Cornelius Westervelt. There Avery meets Alice Carter, whom he recognizes as a member of the Benson gang. Avery gains possession of the gang's loot (for which they attempt to eliminate him), is captured, and then is freed by Blinky in time to prevent the gang's robbery of Mrs. Westervelt. Benson goes over a cliff in an exciting chase; and Avery is pleased to learn that Alice is really Parson's daughter working to capture the gang. *Criminologists. Gangs. Secret service. Robbery. Chases.*

BEAUTY AND BULLETS **F2.0317**
Universal Pictures. 16 Dec **1928** [c20 Sep 1928; LP25638]. Si; b&w. 35mm. 5 reels, 4,197 ft.

Dir Ray Taylor. *Scen* George Plympton. *Titl* Val Cleveland. *Story* Carl Krusada, Vin Moore. *Photog* Joseph Brotherton. *Film Ed* Gene Havlick.

Cast: Ted Wells *(Bill Allen)*, Duane Thompson *(Mary Crawford)*, Jack Kenney *(Joe Kemp)*, Wilbur Mack *(Frank Crawford)*.

Western melodrama. Bill Allen breaks up an attempt by Joe Kemp and his gang to rob the express company payroll and recognizes one of the bandits as Frank Crawford, his sweetheart's brother. Bill takes the payroll home with him for safekeeping, and Kemp's gang knocks him out and makes off with the money. Bill eventually brings the gang before the bar of justice and arranges for the repentant Frank to be paroled in his custody. *Bandits. Robbery.*

BEAUTY AND THE BAD MAN **F2.0318**
Peninsula Studios. 29 Mar **1925** [c24 Apr 1925; LP21402]. Si; b&w. 35mm. 6 reels, 5,794 ft.

Frank E. Woods Production. *Dir* William Worthington. *Adapt* Frank E. Woods.

Cast: Mabel Ballin *(Cassie)*, Forrest Stanley *(Madoc Bill)*, Russell Simpson *(Chuckwalla Bill)*, André de Beranger *(L. I. B. [Liberty] Bell)*, Edna Mae Cooper *(Mayme)*, James Gordon *(Gold Hill Cassidy)*.

Western melodrama. Source: Peter Bernard Kyne, "Cornflower Cassie's Concert," in *Cosmopolitan* (76:24–29, Feb 1924). Cassie, an orphan who sings angelically in a smalltown church, marries the organist, L. I. B. Bell, when he promises to obtain singing lessons for her. They go to San Francisco, where Cassie leaves Bell within the hour when she discovers his low nature. Answering an advertisement in the paper, Cassie gets a job singing in a mining town dancehall. There she charms everyone with her voice, including Madoc Bill, who, having just won a large sum of money at faro, writes her a check for $10,000 and sends her abroad to study voice. Cassie soon becomes a successful diva, singing in the Grand Opera at Moscow, while Madoc Bill serves 4 years in jail for murder. During Madoc's incarceration, his partner, Chuckwalla Bill, strikes it rich. When Madoc is released from jail, he and Chuckwalla build a house for Cassie, who has just returned to the United States after a triumphant continental tour. Her husband, Bell, suffering from consumption, comes to the mining town, and Cassie nurses him back to health. When Bell learns of Cassie's devotion to Madoc Bill, he attempts to kill him and is himself killed. Cassie marries Madoc, and they settle down in the house he built for her. *Orphans. Singers. Organists. Murder. Smalltown life. Opera. Dancehalls. Gambling. Mining towns. Tuberculosis.*

THE BEAUTY PRIZE **F2.0319**
Metro-Goldwyn Pictures. 22 Dec **1924** [c26 Dec 1924; LP20997]. Si; b&w. 35mm. 6 reels, 5,750 ft.

Dir Lloyd Ingraham. *Cont* Winifred Dunn. *Story* Nina Wilcox Putnam. *Photog* John Arnold.

Cast: Viola Dana *(Connie Du Bois)*, Pat O'Malley *(George Brady)*, Eddie Phillips *(Eddie Schwartz)*, Eunice Vin Moore *(Madame Estelle)*, Edward Connelly *(Pa Du Bois)*, Edith Yorke *(Ma Du Bois)*, Joan Standing *(Lydia Du Bois)*, Frederick Truesdell *(Eric Brandon)*.

Comedy-melodrama. Connie Du Bois, a young and beautiful Manhattan manicurist, is asked by one of her wealthy customers to watch over her mansion on Fifth Avenue while she is in Europe. Connie is then persuaded by a smooth-talking salesman friend, Eddie Schwartz, to enter the annual beauty contest in Atlantic City, and Eddie leads the newspapers to believe that she is a society debutante. Connie wins the contest but refuses the prize money and the title, disclosing her lowly station in life. One of the judges later discovers Connie in her hometown and persuades her to broadcast her experiences on the radio. During the transmission, Connie tells of her mistakes and tearfully cries out the name of her former sweetheart, George Brady, who hears the broadcast and returns to her. Connie and George are reconciled and make plans to be married. *Manicurists. Salesmen. Beauty contests. Radio. Atlantic City. New York City—Fifth Avenue.*

THE BEAUTY SHOP **F2.0320**
Cosmopolitan Productions. *Dist* Paramount Pictures. 14 May **1922** [c16 May 1922; LP17909]. Si; b&w. 35mm. 7 reels, 6,536 ft.

Dir Edward Dillon. *Scen* Doty Hobart. *Photog* Harold Wenstrom. *Set Dsgn* Joseph Urban.

Cast: Raymond Hitchcock *(Dr. Arbutus Budd, a beauty doctor)*, Billy B. Van *(Sobini, an undertaker)*, James J. Corbett *(Panatella, an innkeeper)*, Louise Fazenda *(Cremo Panatella, his daughter)*, Madeline Fairbanks *(Coca)*, Marion Fairbanks *(Cola)*, Diana Allen *(Anna Budd, the doctor's ward)*, Montagu Love *(Maldonado, a bad man)*, Laurance Wheat *(Phil Briggs, Budd's attorney)*.

Comedy. Source: Channing Pollock and Rennold Wolf, *The Beauty Shop, a Musical Comedy* (New York production: 13 Apr 1914). Dr. Arbutus Budd, a New York beauty specialist, does a thriving business but is dogged by creditors. He obtains the crest of a forgotten baron of Bolognia and uses it as a trademark on bottles of beauty lotion; when the crest is recognized, Sobini, an undertaker, is commissioned to bring back the "baron" (Budd) to Bolognia. Expecting to inherit a fortune, Dr. Budd takes his attorney, Phil Briggs, and Anna, his ward, with him. His only legacy, however, is a duel with Maldonado, a notorious badman; moreover, Cremo Panatella, a hideously ugly girl, falls in love with him. He gives her some beauty preparations, which she applies and is unable to remove. Budd flees with Cola, a dancer with whom he has fallen in love, but is captured; he removes the paste from Cremo's face, and she is revealed as strikingly beautiful. The duel is canceled, and they all sail to America. *Undertakers. Cosmetology. Beauty shops. Imaginary kingdoms. Mistaken identity.*

BEAUTY SHOPPERS **F2.0321**
Tiffany Productions. 15 Apr **1927** [c13 Jun 1927; LP24077]. Si; b&w. 35mm. 6 reels, 5,669 ft.

Dir Louis J. Gasnier. *Cont* John F. Natteford. *Story* Travers Lane. *Photog* Joseph A. Dubray, Stephen Norton. *Art Dir* Edwin B. Willis. *Film Ed* James C. McKay.

Cast: Mae Busch *(Mabel Hines)*, Doris Hill *(Peggy Raymond)*, Ward Crane *(Sloane Maddox)*, Thomas Haines *(Dick Merwin)*, Cissy Fitzgerald *(Mrs. Schuyler)*, James A. Marcus *(Sam Billings)*, Leo White *(Achille)*, Dale Fuller *(Olga)*, William A. Carroll *(Mr. Schuyler)*, Luca Flamma *(artist)*.

Society comedy-drama. Peggy Raymond, a country girl, comes to New York with plans for a career in art and is taken by mistake to a Fifth Avenue address where she meets Dick Merwin, the scion of a wealthy family, whom she mistakes for her cousin. Later, in Brooklyn, she finds that her relatives have moved, and Mabel Hines takes her in and gets her a job. By necessity, Peg is forced to demonstrate fat-reducing rollers in a shop window, where she is unfavorably viewed by Mrs. Schuyler and her husband. She is admired by Sam Billings, a wealthy old bachelor, and becomes involved with Maddox, who affects an interest in her paintings. But through a series of reversals and complications, Peg is made to realize that Dick is the worthier man. *Artists. Models. Demonstrators—Commercial products. New York City. New York City—Brooklyn.*

BEAUTY'S WORTH **F2.0322**
Cosmopolitan Productions. *Dist* Paramount Pictures. ca18 Mar **1922** [New York premiere; released 14 May; c5 Apr 1922; LP17726]. Si; b&w. 35mm. 7 reels, 6,751 ft.

Dir Robert G. Vignola. *Scen* Luther Reed. *Photog* Ira H. Morgan. *Set Dsgn* Joseph Urban.

Cast: Marion Davies *(Prudence Cole)*, Forrest Stanley *(Cheyne Rovein)*, June Elvidge *(Amy Tillson)*, Truly Shattuck *(Mrs. Garrison)*, Lydia Yeamans Titus *(Jane)*, Hallam Cooley *(Henry Garrison)*, Antrim Short *(Tommy)*, Thomas Jefferson *(Peter)*, Martha Mattox *(Aunt Elizabeth Whitney)*, Aileen Manning *(Aunt Cynthia Whitney)*, George Dooley *(Doll)*.

Society melodrama. Source: Sophie Kerr, "Beauty's Worth," in *Saturday Evening Post* (192:10–11+, 14 Feb 1920). Prudence Cole, a Quaker brought up by two conservative aunts, Elizabeth and Cynthia Whitney, is happy in her demure unsophistication until Henry Garrison and his mother, formerly neighbors and friends of her family, visit the Whitneys. Henry, snobbish and flirtatious, trifles with her affections and secretly despises her manner of dress. Mrs. Garrison invites Prudence for a visit to a fashionable seaside resort, and Henry, ashamed of her appearance, neglects her for Amy Tillson. To amuse themselves, the girls and boys appoint Prudence to persuade Cheyne Rovein, an artist, to stage a charade at the hotel. She succeeds in doing so, and to their amazement she is chosen for the leading role. Her stunning appearance causes Henry to renew his interest in Prudence, but she chooses Rovein instead. *Artists. Social classes. Resorts. Charades. Society of Friends.*

BECKY **F2.0323**
Cosmopolitan Productions. *Dist* Metro-Goldwyn-Mayer Distributing Corp. 12 Nov **1927** [c12 Oct 1927; LP24500]. Si; b&w. 35mm. 7 reels, 6,433 ft.

Dir John P. McCarthy. *Scen* Marian Constance Blackton. *Titl* Joe Farnham. *Story* Raynor Selig. *Photog* John Arnold. *Sets* Cedric Gibbons, Frederic Hope. *Film Ed* John W. English. *Wardrobe* André-ani.

Cast: Sally O'Neil *(Rebecca O'Brien McCloskey)*, Owen Moore *(Dan Scarlett)*, Harry Crocker *(John Carroll Estabrook)*, Gertrude Olmstead *(Nan Estabrook)*, Mack Swain *(Irving Spiegelberg)*, Claude King *(Boris Abelard)*.

Comedy-drama. Becky McCloskey, a salesgirl at Stacy's Department Store, is discharged for insulting customers. She loses her last dollar to a pickpocket but accepts a dinner invitation from "Broadway Dan" Scarlett, who promises to get her a job in a musical revue. Spiegelberg, the stage director, gives her a role in a satirical version of *Faust* in which she plays "Maggy" and is kicked around the stage, though she aspires to singing. At a theatrical party she meets wealthy and aristocratic young John Estabrook, whose attempts to refine her rough manners cause her to fall in love with him. Meanwhile, Dan, who reveals himself to be a jewel thief, courts Nan Estabrook, but when rejected by her, Dan finds happiness with Becky, who is misjudged by her wealthy suitor. *Salesclerks. Thieves. Social classes. Musical revues. Courtship. "Faust".*

THE BEDROOM WINDOW **F2.0324**
Famous Players–Lasky. *Dist* Paramount Pictures. 15 Jun **1924** [c18 Jun 1924; LP20309]. Si; b&w. 35mm. 7 reels, 6,550 ft.

Pres by Adolph Zukor, Jesse L. Lasky. *Dir* William De Mille. *Story-Scen* Clara Beranger. *Photog* L. Guy Wilky.

Cast: May McAvoy *(Ruth Martin)*, Malcolm McGregor *(Frank Armstrong)*, Ricardo Cortez *(Robert Delano)*, Robert Edeson *(Frederick Hall)*, George Fawcett *(Silas Tucker)*, Ethel Wales *(Matilda Jones, alias Rufus Rome)*, Charles Ogle *(butler)*, Medea Radzina *(Sonya Malisoff)*, Guy Oliver *(detective)*, Lillian Leighton *(Mammy)*.

Mystery melodrama. When Thomas Martin is murdered, his daughter's suitor, Robert Delano, discovers the body and is arrested on suspicion. Matilda Jones, an eccentric relative who is a mystery novelist, comes to the girl's aid and unravels the crime, thus establishing the innocence of the young suspect and trapping the real assassin, the family lawyer. *Novelists. Lawyers. Murder.*

BEFORE MIDNIGHT **F2.0325**
Banner Productions. *Dist* Henry Ginsberg Distributing Corp. 21 Aug **1925** [New York showing; c11 Jul 1925; LP21645]. Si; b&w. 35mm. 5 reels, 4,895 ft.

Dir John Adolfi. *Story* Jules Furthman. *Photog* Dewey Wrigley.

Cast: William Russell *(Tom Galloway)*, Barbara Bedford *(Helene Saldivar)*, Brinsley Shaw *(Dobbs, the valet)*, Alan Roscoe *(J. Dallas Durand)*, Rex Lease *(Julio Saldivar)*.

Melodrama. In order to save her brother from going to prison on a forgery charge, Helene Salvidar agrees to shadow Tom Galloway, who is suspected of smuggling emeralds. Helene and Tom meet at a weekend party and fall in love. J. Dallas Durand, the detective who has forced Helene to watch Tom, finds Tom with an emerald, and Tom bribes him with a large sum of money to keep quiet. After Durand accepts the money, Tom reveals himself to be the head of the detective agency for which Durand works. Tom fires Durand and helps Helene keep her brother out of jail. *Detectives. Forgery. Smuggling. Bribery. Brother-sister relationship.*

BEGGAR ON HORSEBACK **F2.0326**
Famous Players–Lasky. *Dist* Paramount Pictures. 24 Aug **1925** [c15 Sep 1925; LP21822]. Si; b&w. 35mm. 7 reels, 7,197 ft.

Pres by Adolph Zukor, Jesse L. Lasky. *Dir* James Cruze. *Screenplay* Walter Woods. *Photog* Karl Brown.

Cast: Edward Everett Horton *(Neil McRae)*, Esther Ralston *(Cynthia Mason)*, Erwin Connelly *(Mr. Cady)*, Gertrude Short *(Gladys Cady)*, Ethel Wales *(Mrs. Cady)*, Theodore Kosloff *(prince)*, James Mason *(Homer Cady)*, Frederick Sullivan *(Dr. Rice)*.

Comedy. Source: George S. Kaufman and Marc Connelly, *Beggar on Horseback, a Play in Two Parts* (New York, 1924). Neil McRae, an impecunious composer of serious music, is forced to orchestrate jazz scores to make a living. Although he is in love with Cynthia, a lovely and equally impoverished painter, he gives in to the urging of Dr. Rice and proposes to Gladys Cady, a rich girl whom he instructs in music. She accepts. On the verge of psychological collapse, Neil is given medication and goes to sleep. He then has a nightmare in which the vulgarity of the Cady family is greatly magnified. When he awakens, Neil gratefully returns to Cynthia. *Composers. Painters. Physicians. Poverty. Dreams.*

BEGGARS OF LIFE **F2.0327**
Paramount Famous Lasky Corp. 22 Sep **1928** [c21 Sep 1928; LP25642]. Talking sequences, mus score, & sd eff (Movietone); b&w. 35mm. 9 reels, 7,560 ft. [Also si; 7,504 ft.]

Pres by Adolph Zukor, Jesse L. Lasky. *Supv* Benjamin Glazer. *Dir* William A. Wellman. *Scen* Benjamin Glazer, Jim Tully. *Titl* Julian Johnson. *Photog* Henry Gerrard. *Film Ed* Alyson Shaffer.

Cast: Wallace Beery *(Oklahoma Red)*, Louise Brooks *(Nancy)*, Richard Arlen *(Jim)*, Edgar Washington Blue *(Mose)*, H. A. Morgan *(Skinny)*, Andy Clark *(Skelly)*, Mike Donlin *(Bill)*, Roscoe Karns *(Hopper)*, Robert Perry *(Arkansas Snake)*, Johnnie Morris *(Rubin)*, George Kotsonaros *(Baldy)*, Jacques Chapin *(Ukie)*, Robert Brower *(Blind Sims)*, Frank Brownlee *(Farmer)*.

Drama. Source: Jim Tully, *Beggars of Life* (New York, 1924). Nancy lives in mortal fear of her foster father and, when he attacks her, she kills him in a moment of panic. The murder is discovered by Jim, a young hobo, who helps her to escape. Nancy dresses in men's rough clothes, and she and Jim hop a freight; thrown off by the brakeman, they take refuge in a hobo camp, the leadership of which is bitterly contested between Arkansas Snake and Oklahoma Red. The encampment is broken up by detectives, and Jim and Nancy take refuge with Mose and a seriously ill tramp in an abandoned shack. Red unexpectedly shows up with a stolen car and women's clothing for Nancy, helping her and Jim to escape in the car. The sick tramp dies, and Red, dressing him in Nancy's rough clothes, places his body in a lumber car which he sets aflame. The pursuing detective kills Red, and Jim and Nancy (who is declared to be officially dead by the police) hop a passenger train for Canada. *Tramps. Detectives. Foster fathers. Murder. Disguise. Railroads.*

BEHIND CLOSED DOORS **F2.0328**
Columbia Pictures. 24 Feb **1929** [c20 May 1929; LP409]. Si; b&w. 35mm. 6 reels, 5,779 ft.

Prod Harry Cohn. *Dir* R. William Neill. *Scen* Howard J. Green. *Story* Lillian Ducey, H. Milner Kitchin. *Photog* Ted Tetzlaff. *Art Dir* Harrison Wiley. *Film Ed* Ben Pivar. *Asst Dir* Tenny Wright.

Cast: Virginia Valli *(Nina Laska)*, Gaston Glass *(Fred Baher)*, Otto Matiesen *(Max Randolph)*, André De Segurola *(Henrick Schield)*, Fanny Midgley *(Mother Schield)*, Torben Meyer *(Captain von Gilden)*, Broderick O'Farrell *(John Barton)*.

Mystery melodrama. A foreign embassy in Washington is agog over activities of a group of royalists attempting to raise funds to aid a revolution and restore the deposed emperor in a new republic, and within the embassy a mysterious individual known as "The Eagle" is at work. Secret Service agent Fred Baher is assigned to intercept an important document being sent to a group of American financiers. Every act of Henrick Schield and his aristocratic mother is under suspicion, as are the activities of Under Secretary Max Randolph and singer Nina Laska, his companion. At a reception given for Captain von Gilden, who bears the document, Fred is deeply impressed with Nina, but after the murder of a suspect, he secures evidence against her. Randolph admits he is working for the Secret Service and is about to reveal The Eagle's identity when he, too, is shot; Nina learns the document is to change hands at midnight and arranges to intercept it. She learns that Mother Schield is The Eagle but refuses to divulge her identity to Fred; Mother Schield, however, commits suicide, and Fred agrees not to disclose the identity of The Eagle. *Secret service. Royalists. Singers. Personal identity. Revolutions. Suicide. Washington (District of Columbia). United States—State Department. Documentation.*

BEHIND MASKS **F2.0329**
Famous Players–Lasky. *Dist* Paramount Pictures. 24 Jul **1921** [c21 Jul 1921; LP16782]. Si; b&w. 35mm. 5 reels, 4,147 ft.

Dir Frank Reicher. *Scen* Katherine Stuart. *Photog* Gilbert Warrenton.

Cast: Dorothy Dalton *(Jeanne Mesurier)*, Frederick Vogeding *(Andrew Bourne)*, William P. Carleton *(Maj. Nigel Forrest)*, Julia Swayne Gordon *(Madame Ena Delore)*, Gladys Valerie *(Kate Cansard)*, Kempton Greene *(Cecil Bourne)*, Lewis Broughton *(Ronald Engleton)*, Alex Kaufman *(Maurice Bresnault)*.

Melodrama. Source: Edward Phillips Oppenheim, *Jeanne of the Marshes*

(Boston, 1908). Jeanne Mesurier, an orphaned heiress and ward of Madame Delore, rejects the latter's plan to marry her to impoverished Maurice Bresnault. Visiting the estate of Cecil Bourne, who is infatuated with her, Madame Delore and Major Forrest are in league to swindle the unwary at cards. Cecil aids Madame Delore in robbing Ronald Engleton, who is hidden in a smuggler's cave under the house. Meanwhile, Jeanne, who has fallen in love with Andrew, Bourne's brother, discovers the criminals at work and follows them to the cave, where she is locked in with Engleton. Finding an opening to the sea, she succeeds in swimming to Andrew's island. The conspirators are driven from the island, and Andrew claims Jeanne as his wife. *Wards. Heiresses. Cardsharps. Smugglers. Robbery.*

BEHIND THAT CURTAIN **F2.0330**

Fox Film Corp. 30 Jun **1929** [c28 Jun 1929; LP506]. Sd (Movietone); b&w. 35mm. 10 reels, 8,320 ft. [Also si.]

Pres by William Fox. *Dir* Irving Cummings. *Scen* Sonya Levien, Clarke Silvernail. *Titl* Wilbur Morse, Jr. *Photog* Conrad Wells, Dave Ragin, Vincent Farrar. *Film Ed* Alfred De Gaetano. *Sd Rec* George P. Costello. *Asst Dir* Charles Woolstenhulme.

Cast: Warner Baxter *(John Beetham)*, Lois Moran *(Eve Mannering)*, Gilbert Emery *(Sir Frederic Bruce)*, Claude King *(Sir George Mannering)*, Philip Strange *(Eric Durand)*, Boris Karloff *(Soudanese servant)*, Jamiel Hassen *(Habib Hanna)*, Peter Gawthorne *(Scotland Yard inspector)*, John Rogers *(Alf Pornick)*, Montague Shaw *(Hilary Galt)*, Finch Smiles *(Galt's clerk)*, Mercedes De Valaco *(Nunah)*, E. L. Park *(Charlie Chan)*.

Mystery melodrama. Source: Earl Derr Biggers, "Behind That Curtain," in *Saturday Evening Post* (vol 200, 31 Mar–5 May 1928). Eve Mannering, daughter of a wealthy Englishman, marries Eric Durand, a fortune hunter, who kills the investigator hired by her father to examine his past. Upon discovering the plot, Eve leaves him and joins an old family friend on a desert expedition. Later, fearing she will implicate him in her affairs, Eve deserts him and comes to San Francisco. Sir Frederic Bruce, of Scotland Yard, is attracted to the case by a mysterious pair of Chinese slippers found on the victim's body—a gift from the explorer, John Beetham. His investigation leads to a lecture hall where Beetham is speaking, and there Durand is revealed to be the murderer and is killed evading the law, leaving Eve to a happy future with the explorer. *Explorers. Guardians. Fortune hunters. Detectives. Murder. Marriage. Deserts. England. San Francisco. Scotland Yard.*

BEHIND THE CURTAIN **F2.0331**

Universal Pictures. 15 Jul **1924** [New York showing; released 21 Jul; c27 Jun 1924; LP20358]. Si; b&w. 35mm. 5 reels, 4,875 ft.

Dir Chester M. Franklin. *Scen* Emil Forest, Harvey Gates. *Story* William J. Flynn. *Photog* Jackson Rose.

Cast: Lucille Ricksen *(Sylvia Bailey)*, Johnny Harron *(Hugh Belmont)*, Winifred Bryson *(Laura Bailey)*, Charles Clary *(George Belmont)*, Eric Mayne *(Professor Gregorius)*, George Cooper *("Slug" Gorman)*, Clarence Geldert *(district attorney)*, Pat Harmon *("Spike")*.

Mystery melodrama. When his son, Hugh, elopes with the sister of his mistress, George Belmont breaks off with Laura Bailey, claiming a frameup. He attempts to buy off Sylvia and is murdered. Laura and "Slug" Gorman, a crook, are arrested on circumstantial evidence and convicted of the crime, but, at the last minute, Professor Gregorius, a fake spiritualist, is exposed as the assassin. *Fatherhood. Spiritualism. Murder.*

BEHIND THE FRONT **F2.0332**

Famous Players–Lasky. *Dist* Paramount Pictures. 22 Feb **1926** [c24 Feb 1926; LP22417]. Si; b&w. 35mm. 6 reels, 5,555 ft.

Pres by Adolph Zukor, Jesse L. Lasky. *Dir* Edward Sutherland. *Screenplay* Ethel Doherty. *Adapt* Monte Brice. *Photog* Charles Boyle.

Cast: Wallace Beery *(Riff Swanson)*, Raymond Hatton *(Shorty McGee)*, Mary Brian *(Betty Bartlett-Cooper)*, Richard Arlen *(Percy Brown)*, Hayden Stevenson *(Captain Bartlett-Cooper)*, Chester Conklin *(Scottie)*, Tom Kennedy *(Sergeant)*, Frances Raymond *(Mrs. Bartlett-Cooper)*, Melbourne MacDowell *(Mr. Bartlett-Cooper)*.

Comedy. Source: Hugh Wiley, "The Spoils of War," in *Saturday Evening Post* (197:26–27, 9 May 1925). Riff Swanson has his pocket picked by light-fingered Shorty McGee and chases him into the Bartlett-Cooper mansion, where Betty Bartlett-Cooper is recruiting soldiers for the war in France. Betty persuades each of them in turn that she loves only him, and they both enlist. They are sent to France and become buddies, distinguishing themselves not at all and spending their time either in the guardhouse or on lunatic patrols in no man's land. After the war they return to the United States in time to see their mutual sweetheart married to Percy Brown, the son of the hardtack king! *Pickpockets. Hardtack. World War I. France. United States Army–Recruiting.*

BEHIND THE MAKE-UP **F2.0333**

Paramount Famous Lasky Corp. 11 Jan **1930** [c8 Jan 1930; LP981]. Sd (Movietone); b&w. 35mm. 8 reels, 6,364 ft.

Dir Robert Milton. *Adapt-Dial* George Manker Watters, Howard Estabrook. *Photog* Charles Lang. *Film Ed* Doris Drought. *Songs: "My Pals," "Say It With Your Feet," "I'll Remember, You'll Forget"* Leo Robin, Sam Coslow, Newell Chase. *Rec Engr* Harry D. Mills.

Cast: Hal Skelly *(Hap Brown)*, William Powell *(Gardoni)*, Fay Wray *(Marie)*, Kay Francis *(Kitty Parker)*, E. H. Calvert *(Dawson)*, Paul Lukas *(Boris)*, Agostino Borgato *(chef)*, Jacques Vanaire *(valet)*, Jean De Briac *(sculptor)*.

Romantic drama. Source: Mildred Cram, "The Feeder," in *Red Book* (47:83–87, May 1926). Hap Brown, an easygoing, happy-go-lucky actor, falls in love with Marie, a waitress in the French Quarter of New Orleans and befriends Gardoni, a fallen actor with whom he forms a partnership. They soon fall out, however, when Gardoni insists on dominating the act; and Hap takes a job with the cafe where Marie works. When he and Gardoni team up again, Marie is taken with the Italian and they are soon married, leaving Hap hurt and rejected. Overwhelmed by a brilliant Broadway reception, Gardoni neglects his wife for Kitty Parker, an adventuress, and though Hap knows of it, he does not tell Marie; then, scorned by Kitty, Gardoni dies tragically. Hap turns to Marie for support, and under her guidance he proves himself to be a brilliant comedian. *Actors. Waitresses. Italians. Adventuresses. Jealousy. Marriage. Vaudeville. New Orleans. New York City—Broadway.*

BEHIND TWO GUNS **F2.0334**

Sunset Productions. 15 May or 1 Jun **1924.** Si; b&w. 35mm. 5 reels, 4,800-4,902 ft.

Pres by Anthony J. Xydias. *Dir-Story* Robert N. Bradbury. *Titl* Enoch O. Van Pelt. *Photog* Bert Longenecker. *Film Ed* Della M. King.

Cast: J. B. Warner *(Dr. Elijah Carter)*, Hazel Newman *(Jessie Nash)*, Marin Sais *(Mrs. Baxter)*, Jay Morley *(Ward Baxter)*, Jim Welch *(Scout Nash)*, Otto Lederer *(Olaf Ludovic/Dr. Betz)*, William Calles *(Eagle Slowfoot)*, Jack Waltemeyer *(Sheriff Joe Haynes)*, Emily Gerdes *(Esmeralda Parker)*, Bartlett A. Carré *(Jake Watkins)*, Robert North Bradbury *(bit part)*.

Western melodrama. The Baxters, finding Olaf Ludovic stranded on the California desert, take him in, unaware that he is actually Dr. Betz. He hypnotizes Mrs. Baxter and hides her in the boot of Nash's stage with a command to heist the padlocked gold box. Dr. Carter, a Secret Service agent, and his Indian companion Slowfoot respond to Jessie's pleas to vindicate her grandfather, Scout Nash, who was arrested when the theft was discovered. Carter and Slowfoot uncover Betz's hideout, where the villain has hidden the still-captive Mrs. Baxter in the trunk of a car. Carter frees her, takes her place, and kills Betz in the ensuing confrontation, thus precipitating Jessie's grateful love. *Hypnotists. Indians of North America. Secret service. Stagecoach robberies. Kidnaping. Deserts. California.*

BEHOLD THE MAN (United States/France) **F2.0335**

Pathé Exchange–Selwyn Pictures. *Dist* Pathé Exchange. 28 Jan **1921** [trade review]. Si; b&w with col sequences (Pathécolor). 35mm. 6 reels.

Dir of Modern Episode Spencer Gordon Bennett. *Titl* Arthur F. Warde. *Adapt* Harding O. Martin. *Art Dir* Maryan F. Broada.

Cast of Modern Episode: H. O. Pettibone *(The Father)*, Sybil Sheridan *(The Mother)*, Richard Ross *(The Son)*, Violet Axzelle *(The Daughter)*.

Cast of the Bible Story: Monsieur Moreau *(St. Joseph)*, Madame Moreau *(The Virgin Mary)*, Le Petit Briand *(The Boy Christ)*, Monsieur Normand *(The Adult Christ)*, Monsieur Jacquinet *(Judas Iscariot)*.

Biblical drama. A mother tells the Bible Story to her children: The life of Christ from the Annunciation to the Ascension. As the mother tells the story, the film fades into a picturization and periodically fades back to show the children's interests and reactions. *The Bible. Christianity. Religion. Jesus. Virgin Mary. Joseph. Judas Iscariot.*

Note: A reedited version with new footage added ("Modern Episode") to the 1914 Pathé version of the Passion Play entitled *Life of Our Saviour* or *La Passion*, a French production done in color. The modern episode is filmed in the United States in black and white.

BEHOLD THIS WOMAN F2.0336

Vitagraph Co. of America. 3 Aug **1924** [c30 Jun 1924; LP20363]. Si; b&w. 35mm. 7 reels, 6,425 ft.

Pres by Albert E. Smith. *Dir* J. Stuart Blackton. *Scen* Marian Constance. *Photog* L. William O'Connell, Ernest Smith.

Cast: Irene Rich *(Louise Maurel)*, Marguerite De La Motte *(Sophie)*, Charles A. Post *(John Strangeway)*, Harry Myers *(Eugène de Seyre)*, Rosemary Theby *(Calavera)*, Anders Randolph *(Stephen Strangeway)*.

Melodrama. Source: Edward Phillips Oppenheim, *The Hillman* (Boston, 1917). John Strangeway, a young cattleman, falls in love, against his will, with screen star Louise Maurel. When his brother urges him to demand an explanation of her relations with a rich idler, Eugène de Seyre, he is disillusioned by her confession and leaves the city. After accepting Seyre's proposal of marriage, Louise seeks out John to ask his forgiveness. *Actors. Brothers. Marriage. Motion pictures.*

BEING RESPECTABLE F2.0337

Warner Brothers Pictures. 1 Jul **1924** [c1 Jul 1924; LP20365]. Si; b&w. 35mm. 8 reels, 7,500 ft.

Dir Philip Rosen. *Scen* Dorothy Farnum. *Photog* Lyman Broening.

Cast: Marie Prevost *(Valerie Winship)*, Monte Blue *(Charles Carpenter)*, Louise Fazenda *(Deborah Carpenter)*, Irene Rich *(Suzanne Schuyler)*, Theodore von Eltz *(Stephen O'Connell)*, Frank Currier *(Darius Carpenter)*, Eulalie Jensen *(Louise Carpenter)*, Lila Leslie *(Mrs. Winship)*, Sidney Bracey *(Philip Deaby)*.

Society drama. Source: Grace Hodgson Landrau, *Being Respectable* (New York, 1923). Through the scheming of his respectable and wealthy family, Charles Carpenter is obliged to marry Suzanne, although he is in love with young flapper Valerie Winship. Years later, when Valerie is back in town, they renew the affair and Carpenter plans to leave his wife and child for her, but in the end he yields to family duty and respectability. *Flappers. Wealth. Infidelity. Family life.*

BELL BOY 13 F2.0338

Thomas H. Ince Productions. *Dist* Associated First National Pictures. Jan **1923** [c8 Jan 1923; LP18557]. Si; b&w. 35mm. 5 reels, 4,940 ft.

Pres by Thomas H. Ince. *Dir* William Seiter. *Scen* Violet Clark. *Story* Austin Gill. *Photog* Bert Cann. *Spec Orchestration* Sol Cohen.

Cast: Douglas MacLean *(Harry Elrod)*, Margaret Loomis *(Kitty Clyde)*, John Steppling *(Uncle Ellery Elrod)*, Jean Walsh *("Pink")*, Eugene Burr *(The Mystery Man)*, William Courtright *(Reverend Fish)*, Emily Gerdes *(Angela Fish)*.

Farce. Harry Elrod takes a job as a bellboy when he is disinherited by his uncle and fails in his efforts to elope with actress Kitty Clyde. He causes so much confusion that Uncle Elrod buys the hotel so that he may fire Harry. But Harry induces the other employees to strike until Uncle Elrod consents to Harry's marriage to Kitty. *Actors. Bellboys. Uncles. Disinheritance. Hotels. Strikes.*

BELLA DONNA F2.0339

Famous Players–Lasky. *Dist* Paramount Pictures. 1 Apr **1923** [c21 Mar 1923; LP18836]. Si; b&w. 35mm. 8 reels, 7,895-7,903 ft.

Pres by Adolph Zukor. *Dir* George Fitzmaurice. *Scen* Ouida Bergère. *Story* Robert Smythe Hichens. *Photog* Arthur Miller. *Tech Dir* Dudley Stuart Corlett. *Special Tech Adv* Dudley Stuart Corlett.

Cast: Pola Negri *(Bella Donna)*, Conway Tearle *(Mahmoud Baroudi)*, Conrad Nagel *(Nigel Armine)*, Adolphe Menjou *(Mr. Chepstow)*, Claude King *(Dr. Meyer Isaacson)*, Lois Wilson *(Patricia)*, Macey Harlam *(Ibrahim)*, Robert Schable *(Dr. Hartley)*.

Romantic drama. Source: Robert Smythe Hichens, *Bella Donna* (Philadelphia, 1909). After her husband is convicted of throwing one of her suitors into a Venetian canal, adventuress Bella Donna (Mrs. Ruby Chepstow) marries engineer Nigel Armine. They travel to Egypt, where Bella Donna comes under the spell of Mahmoud Baroudi, who persuades her to poison Nigel. He is already seriously ill when a friend diagnoses his trouble, accuses Bella Donna, and brings Nigel back to health. Bella Donna flees to Baroudi's tent but finds him occupied with another woman and having no intention of openly interfering with an Englishman's marriage. Returning to Nigel, she sees her husband in the care of Patricia, a former sweetheart. Bella Donna turns and wanders into a desert sandstorm alone. *Adventuresses. Engineers. Infidelity. Sahara. Egypt.*

BELLAMY TRIAL F2.0340

Metro-Goldwyn-Mayer Pictures. 23 Jan **1929** [New York premiere; c10 Dec 1928; LP25905]. Talking sequences, sd eff, & mus score (Movietone); b&w. 35mm. 8 reels, 8,268 ft. [Also si; 7,524 ft.]

Dir-Scen Monta Bell. *Dial-Titl* Joe Farnham. *Photog* Arthur Miller. *Sets* Cedric Gibbons. *Film Ed* Frank Sullivan. *Wardrobe* Gilbert Clark.

Cast: Leatrice Joy *(Sue Ives)*, Betty Bronson *(girl reporter)*, Edward Nugent *(boy reporter)*, George Barraud *(Pat Ives)*, Margaret Livingston *(Mimi Bellamy)*, Kenneth Thomson *(Stephen Bellamy)*, Margaret Seddon *(Mother Ives)*, Charles Middleton *(district attorney)*, Charles Hill Mailes *(defense attorney)*, William Tooker *(Judge Carver)*.

Drama. Source: Frances Noyes Hart, *The Bellamy Trial* (New York, 1927). When Mimi Bellamy, a young wife whose conduct is not entirely above reproach, is murdered, two persons are placed on trial: her husband, Stephen; and Sue Ives, a beautiful young girl. The two suspects are brutally cross-examined by the district attorney, but the jury finds them not guilty. A man not previously heard in the trial then comes forward and testifies; this witness is a married high school teacher who had been philandering on the night of the murder and whose testimony clears Stephen and Sue of the slightest suspicion of guilt. *District attorneys. Schoolteachers. Philanderers. Marriage. Murder. Trials.*

BELLE OF ALASKA F2.0341

Chester Bennett Productions. *Dist* American Releasing Corp. 5 Mar **1922**. Si; b&w. 35mm. 5 reels, 4,611 or 4,891 ft.

Dir Chester Bennett. *Story-Scen* J. Grubb Alexander, Harvey Gates. *Photog* Jack MacKenzie.

Cast: J. Frank Glendon *("Lucky" Vail)*, Jane Novak *(Ruth Harkin)*, Noah Beery *(Wade Harkin)*, Florence Carpenter *("Chicago Belle")*, Leslie Bates *(Dugan)*.

Northwest melodrama. En route to Alaska in search of gold, Kansas farmers Wade and Ruth Harkin are stranded in Seattle. Wade deserts Ruth, but she finds a protector in gambler Lucky Vail. When Lucky hires Dugan to feign an attack on Ruth, she shoots the degenerate, escapes to Alaska in fear of prosecution, and poses as Lucky's "lady friend," notorious dancehall character Chicago Belle, when the latter drowns. First Lucky, then Harkin, come seeking Belle and recognize Ruth. Realizing that he loves Ruth, Lucky fights Harkin, who is about to deliver the victorious blow when he is shot by an onlooker. *Farmers. Dancehall girls. Gamblers. Kansans. Gold. Desertion. Impersonation. Seattle. Alaska.*

THE BELLE OF BROADWAY F2.0342

Columbia Pictures. 15 Aug **1926** [c5 Oct 1926; LP23184]. Si; b&w. 35mm. 6 reels, 5,877 ft.

Prod Harry Cohn. *Dir* Harry O. Hoyt. *Story-Scen* J. Grubb Alexander, Jean Peary. *Photog* J. O. Taylor.

Cast: Betty Compson *(Marie Duval)*, Herbert Rawlinson *(Paul Merlin)*, Edith Yorke *(Madame Adèle)*, Armand Kaliz *(Count Raoul de Parma)*, Ervin Renard, Max Berwyn, Albert Roccardi, Edward Warren, Tom Ricketts, Edward Kipling, Wilfrid North, August Tollaire.

Romantic melodrama. Adèle, the idol of the Paris theater in 1896, is jealously guarded by her husband from the open admiration of the Count Raoul de Parma; but he deserts her, taking with him their only child, Paul. Years later, earning a meager living, Adèle meets a young American, Marie Duval, who performs in a revue. In a moment of caprice, Marie tries on Adèle's old costume for *Du Barry;* a plan is then devised whereby Marie, under the tutelage of Adèle, becomes the darling of Paris and is presented as the rejuvenated actress. Paul Merlin, now grown to manhood, falls deeply in love with Marie, and the count reenacts his passionate declaration. The count invites Marie to his apartment for dinner, discovers her masquerade, and forces his attentions on her; but she is rescued at the last minute by Paul, who, following a harmless duel, is reunited with his mother and Marie. *Actors. Theater. Desertion. Rejuvenation. Motherhood. Impersonation. Paris. New York City—Broadway.*

THE BELLS F2.0343

Chadwick Pictures. 30 Jul **1926** [New York State license]. Si; b&w. 35mm. 7 reels, 6,300 ft.

Pres by I. E. Chadwick. *Dir* James Young. *Photog* L. William O'Connell.

Cast: Lionel Barrymore *(Mathias)*, Fred Warren *(Kowelski)*, Boris Karloff *(Mesmerist)*, Gustav von Seyffertitz *(Frantz)*, Lola Todd *(Annette)*, Eddie Phillips *(Christian)*.

Melodrama. Source: Alexandre Chatrian and Émile Erckmann, *Le Juif polonais; drame en trois actes et cinq tableaux* (Paris, 1869). Unable to pay his debts, Mathias, an Alsatian innkeeper, murders a rich traveler and takes his gold. Mathias is not suspected of the crime; he is, however, tormented by an avenging conscience. He hears the bells that rang as his victim lay dying and has visions of a courtroom and of the bloody hands of the slain traveler. Mathias finally sees the ghost of the traveler and dies in spiritual agony, his secret unconfessed. *Innkeepers. Jews. Poles. Visions. Conscience. Bells. Murder. Alsace.*

BELLS OF SAN JUAN **F2.0344**

Fox Film Corp. 15 Oct **1922** [c15 Oct 1922; LP19126]. Si; b&w. 35mm. 5 reels, 4,587 ft.

Pres by William Fox. *Dir* Scott Dunlap. *Scen* Rex Taylor. *Photog* Dev Jennings.

Cast: Charles Jones *(Roderick Norton)*, Fritzi Brunette *(Dorothy Page)*, Claude Peyton *(Jim Garson)*, Harry Todd *(John Engel)*, Kathleen Key *(Florrie Engel)*, William Steele *(Kid Rickard)*, Otto Matieson *(Antone)*, Sid Jordan *(Tom Cutter)*.

Western melodrama. Source: Jackson Gregory, *Bells of San Juan* (New York, 1919). Sheriff Rod Norton, determined to capture his father's murderer, suspects Jim Garson, owner of a saloon, but has no evidence to convict him. The Rickard brothers, in league with Garson, kidnap Norton's sweetheart, Dorothy, hoping to lure Norton into a trap. Norton trails them, rescues Dorothy, and captures the outlaws. Later Garson inflicts a head injury on Norton, causing him to commit robbery and turn against his friends. He is cured by an operation: recovered, he extracts a confession from the Rickard brothers that allows him to arrest Garson. *Sheriffs. Brothers. Murder. Robbery. Kidnaping. Mental illness. Saloons.*

THE BELOVED BRUTE **F2.0345**

Vitagraph Co. of America. ca9 Nov **1924** [New York premiere; released 30 Nov; c12 Nov 1924; LP20760]. Si; b&w. 35mm. 7 reels, 6,719 ft.

Pres by Albert E. Smith. *Prod-Dir* J. Stuart Blackton. *Photog* L. W. O'Connell, Ernest Smith.

Cast: Marguerite De La Motte *(Jacinta)*, Victor McLaglen *(Charles Hinges)*, William Russell *(David Hinges)*, Stuart Holmes *(China Jones)*, Frank Brownlee *(Phil Beason)*, Wilfrid North *(Fat Milligan)*, Ernie Adams *(Swink Tuckson)*, D. D. McLean *(Peter Hinges)*, William Moran *(Sheriff Swanson)*, George Ingleton *(Peg Reverly)*, Jess Herring *(Hump Domingo)*.

Western melodrama. Source: Kenneth Perkins, *The Beloved Brute* (New York, 1923). Chafing under his dying father's prediction that he is just a fighter without a soul who someday will be beaten by his long-lost brother, brutish Charles Hinges heads west with Jacinta, a dancehall girl, and Augustina, a fortune-teller. They tour frontier towns, with Charles taking on all challengers in no-holds-barred wrestling matches. Charles is undefeated until he engages his brother, David, the town reformer. In his humiliation, Charles feels he has finally found his soul, fears that Jacinta admires him only for his strength, and sends her to David. Meanwhile, Jacinta has been the object of the unwelcome attentions of halfcaste China Jones. Jones is killed, and saloon keeper Phil Beason fastens the blame on David, who is about to be lynched when Charles claims the guilt. Jacinta saves both brothers from the rope with the timely arrival of a posse and Augustina's confession to Jones's murder. Charles reveals himself to David and is reunited with Jacinta. *Brothers. Reformers. Dancehall girls. Fortune-tellers. Saloon keepers. Halfcastes. Wrestling. Murder. Lynching.*

THE BELOVED ROGUE **F2.0346**

Feature Productions. *Dist* United Artists. 12 Mar **1927** [c23 Feb 1927; LP23689]. Si; b&w. 35mm. 10 reels, 9,264 ft.

Dir Alan Crosland. *Story-Scen* Paul Bern. *Titl* Walter Anthony. *Photog* Joe August. *Art Dir* William Cameron Menzies.

Cast: John Barrymore *(François Villon)*, Conrad Veidt *(Louis XI)*, Marceline Day *(Charlotte de Vauxcelles)*, Henry Victor *(Thibault d'Aussigny)*, Lawson Butt *(John, Duke of Burgundy)*, Mack Swain *(Nicholas)*, Slim Summerville *(Jehan)*, Otto Matieson *(Olivier, the king's barber)*, Rose Dione *(Margot)*, Bertram Grassby *(Duke of Orléans)*, Lucy Beaumont *(Villon's mother)*, Angelo Rossitto *(Beppo, a dwarf)*, Jane Winton *(The Abbess)*, Martha Franklin *(maid)*, Nigel De Brulier *(astrologer)*, Dick Sutherland *(Tristan l'Hermite)*.

Romantic costume drama. François Villon, poet and ardent patriot, is selected by the mob as the king of fools for All Fools' Day. When he makes a witty jest at the expense of the Duke of Burgundy, Louis XI banishes him from Paris. He steals a wagon loaded with food, distributes it to the poor, and is accidentally thrown into the rooms of Charlotte, the king's ward, who is to be forced into marriage with one of the duke's men. When captured, Villon plays on the king's superstition and becomes a court favorite. Charlotte is kidnaped by Burgundy's men, and Villon, who unmasks the schemes perpetrated against the king, follows them and is subjected to torture. In disguise, the king, with his warriors, rescues Villon and Charlotte and consents to their marriage. *Poets. Superstition. All Fools' Day. France—History—House of Valois. François Villon. Louis XI (France).*

BELOW THE DEAD LINE **F2.0347**

Ascher Productions. 6 Nov **1921** [trade review]. Si; b&w. 35mm. 5 reels.

Dir J. P. McGowan. *Story* Arthur Henry Gooden.

Cast: H. B. Warner *(Joe Donovan)*, Lillian Biron *(Alice Elliot)*, Bert Sprotte *(Buck Elliot)*, Robert Anderson *("Hot Dog Heine")*.

Melodrama. Buck Elliot, wharfmaster, is leader of a band of murderous crooks. The gang shoots down a policeman in a wharfside scuffle, and Detective Donovan vows vengeance upon the murderer. He follows Elliot home, where Elliot persuades his wife (previously unaware of her husband's underground life) to alibi for him. When Mrs. Elliot is later brought to police headquarters, incriminating evidence indicating Elliot's complicity in a scheme for a train robbery is disclosed. Under Donovan's leadership, the police catch the thieves in the act. Elliot, not among those arrested, is later caught by Donovan, who comes to realize his own love for Mrs. Elliot. *Wharfmasters. Detectives. Gangs. Murder. Train robberies.*

BELOW THE DEADLINE **F2.0348**

Chesterfield Motion Picture Corp. 1 Jan **1929.** Si; b&w. 35mm. 6 reels, 5,554 ft.

Pers Supv Lon Young. *Dir* J. P. McGowan. *Story-Scen* Arthur Hoerl. *Titl* Lee Authmar. *Photog* M. A. Anderson, Jack Jackson. *Film Ed* James Sweeney.

Cast: Frank Leigh *("Beau" Nash)*, Barbara Worth *(Claire)*, Arthur Rankin *(Jimmy)*, Walter Merrill *(Donald Cornwall)*, J. P. McGowan *(Taggart)*, Mike Donlin *("Sandy")*, Virginia Sale *("Mother" Biblow)*, Lou Gory *(Stella)*, Bill Patton *(Johnston)*, Tiny Ward *("Tubby")*, Charles Hickman *(police captain)*, Fred Walton *(Festenberg)*.

Crook melodrama. "It concerns the operations of a gang of clever crooks below the deadline set by the police and their robbery of a jewelry establishment. In order to get even with the detective who arrests one of the gang, they use the girl as a decoy. The hero, manager of the jewelry store, is framed for the robbery of his employer's place. The detective, who is his buddy, allows him to escape imprisonment so that he can go out and get the evidence on the crooks. This he does with the help of the girl. So the tables are turned very neatly on the head of the gang who is shot." (*Film Daily*, 23 Jun 1929, p12.) *Jewelers. Police. Detectives. Gangs. Robbery.*

BELOW THE LINE **F2.0349**

Warner Brothers Pictures. 26 Sep **1925** [c20 Aug 1925; LP21757]. Si; b&w. 35mm. 7 reels, 6,053 ft.

Dir Herman Raymaker. *Story* Charles A. Logue. *Photog* John Mescall. *Adtl Photog* Bert Shipman. *Asst Dir* Irving Asher.

Cast: Rin-Tin-Tin *(himself, a dog)*, John Harron *(Donald Cass)*, June Marlowe *(May Barton)*, Pat Hartigan *(Jamber Niles)*, Victor Potel *("Cuckoo" Niles)*, Charles Conklin *(deputy sheriff)*, Gilbert Clayton *(Reverend Barton)*, Edith Yorke *(Mrs. Cass)*, Taylor Duncan *(sheriff)*.

Melodrama. Rin-Tin-Tin, a famous fighting dog, falls off a train and is found by Donald Cass, a sweet-tempered village youth who gains the dog's intense loyalty by his acts of kindness. A wealthy woman is murdered by Jamber Niles, a reprobate who later attacks Donald in an effort to seize the church funds. Jamber is choking Donald to death when the dog intervenes and kills Jamber. Rin-Tin-Tin later saves Donald and his sweetheart, May, when they are attacked by a pack of bloodhounds belonging to "Cuckoo" Niles. The murder of the woman is traced to the late Jamber Niles, and Donald looks forward to a happy future with May. *Murder. Village life. Churches. Dogs.*

BELOW THE RIO GRANDE **F2.0350**

William Steiner Productions. 15 Oct **1923** [New York premiere; released Jun; c24 Aug 1923; LU19344]. Si; b&w. 35mm. 5 reels, ca5,000 ft.

Dir-Adapt Neal Hart. *Photog* Harry McGuire. *Assembled by* Fred Burnworth.

Cast: Neal Hart *(King Calhoun)*.

Western melodrama. Source: H. A. Halbert, Jr., "The Fighting Pedagogue" (publication undetermined). Pierre Jacques, French Canadian fugitive from justive, rules a town on the Mexican side of the border. Chuck Watson, his thieving confederate, frames Texas cowboy King Calhoun on a cattle-running charge. King persuades the sheriff to let him prove his innocence by leading the sheriff to Watson and Pierre Jacques. Meanwhile the Northwest Mounted Police and the Mexican Rurales have heard of the outlaws' whereabouts. The three-cornered chase ends in the capture of the bandits and the liberation of King, who finds romance with Pierre Jacques' adopted daughter, Jean. *Cowboys. Rurales. French Canadians. Rustling. Mexican border. Northwest Mounted Police.*

BEN-HUR **F2.0351**

Metro-Goldwyn-Mayer Pictures. 30 Dec **1925** [New York premiere; released 8 Oct 1927; c8 Oct 1927; LP24477]. Si; b&w with col sequences (Technicolor). 35mm. 12 reels, 11,693 ft.

Prod Louis B. Mayer, Samuel Goldwyn, Irving Thalberg. *Dir* Fred Niblo. *Adtl Dir* Ferdinand P. Earle. *2d Unit Dir* Reaves Eason. *Scen* Bess Meredyth, Carey Wilson. *Titl* Katherine Hilliker, H. H. Caldwell. *Adapt* June Mathis. *Photog* René Guissart, Percy Hilburn, Karl Struss, Clyde De Vinna. *Adtl Photog* E. Burton Steene, George Meehan. *Trick Photog* Paul Eagler. *Sets* Cedric Gibbons, Horace Jackson, Arnold Gillespie. *Art Eff* Ferdinand P. Earle. *Film Ed* Lloyd Nosler. *Asst Film Ed* Basil Wrangell, William Holmes, Harry Reynolds, Ben Lewis. *Mus Score* William Axt, David Mendoza. *Asst Dir* Charles Stallings. *Prod Mgr* Harry Edington. *Prod Asst* Silas Clegg, Alfred Raboch, William Wyler. *Wardrobe* Hermann J. Kaufmann. *Traveling Mattes* Frank D. Williams.

Cast: Ramon Novarro *(Ben-Hur)*, Francis X. Bushman *(Messala)*, May McAvoy *(Esther)*, Betty Bronson *(Mary)*, Claire McDowell *(Princess of Hur)*, Kathleen Key *(Tirzah)*, Carmel Myers *(Iras)*, Nigel De Brulier *(Simonides)*, Mitchell Lewis *(Sheik Ilderim)*, Leo White *(Sanballat)*, Frank Currier *(Arrius)*, Charles Belcher *(Balthasar)*, Dale Fuller *(Amrah)*, Winter Hall *(Joseph)*.

Religious spectacular. Source: Lew Wallace, *Ben-Hur, a Tale of the Christ* (1880). In Jerusalem, oppressed by the power of Imperial Rome, Ben-Hur, of the Jewish house of Hur, develops a friendship with Messala, a Roman centurion, which turns to enmity when he learns of Messala's egotism and hatred of the Jews; to please the governor, Messala arrests the entire family when a loose tile falls from their house, killing a general. Sentenced as a galley slave and driven into the desert, Ben-Hur meets the Christ, who gives him water and refreshes his spirit; when he saves the life of Arrius, the ship commander, he is adopted by Arrius and becomes popular and wealthy as a charioteer. In a competition against Messala, he satisfies his revenge by defeating him, and after being recognized by Esther and Simonides, Ben-Hur acquires great wealth. In Jerusalem, where Jesus is crucified, Ben-Hur is recognized by his leprous mother and sister and learns of Jesus' mission to save mankind; Esther takes them to be cured; and, reunited, the family returns to the palace of Hur. *Jews. Centurions. Charioteers. Galley slaves. Revenge. Christianity. Friendship. Leprosy. Rome—History—Empire. Jerusalem.*

Note: The Nativity sequence, filmed in color, is directed by Ferdinand P. Earle. The film was reissued in 1931 in an abbreviated version with synchronized music.

THE BENSON MURDER CASE **F2.0352**

Paramount Famous Lasky Corp. 12 Apr **1930** [c11 Apr 1930; LP1223]. Sd (Movietone); b&w. 35mm. 7 reels, 5,794 ft.

Dir Frank Tuttle. *Dial Dir* Perry Ivins. *Scen-Dial* Bartlett Cormack. *Photog* A. J. Stout. *Film Ed* Doris Drought. *Sd Rec* Harold M. McNiff.

Cast: William Powell *(Philo Vance)*, Natalie Moorhead *(Fanny Del Roy)*, Eugene Pallette *(Sergeant Heath)*, Paul Lukas *(Adolph Mohler)*, William Boyd *(Harry Gray)*, E. H. Calvert *(John F.-X. Markham)*, Richard Tucker *(Anthony Benson)*, May Beatty *(Mrs. Paula Banning)*, Mischa Auer *(Albert)*, Otto Yamaoka *(Sam)*, Charles McMurphy *(Burke)*, Dick Rush *(Welch)*.

Mystery melodrama. Source: S. S. Van Dine, *The Benson Murder Case* (New York, 1926). Anthony Benson, wealthy stockbroker, to escape the threats and pleas of numerous friends he sold out in the market crash, motors to his hunting lodge near New York, accompanied by Harry Gray, a Broadway gambler and one of those he sold out. Benson is followed by three others who have threatened to kill him: Adolph Mohler, whose forged check Benson holds; Mrs. Paula Banning, a widow, in love with Mohler, whose assets have been wiped out; and Fanny Del Roy, a Broadway actress, who claims that the pearls held in lieu of Mohler's check were stolen from her. During a visit by District Attorney Markham and amateur detective Philo Vance, Benson is murdered. While the police stumble on many conflicting clues, Vance pieces them together, reenacts the crime, and proves Gray's guilt; he is shot attempting to escape. *Detectives. District attorneys. Stockbrokers. Actors. Depression—Financial. Murder.*

Note: This film was also produced in a Spanish-language version.

BERTHA, THE SEWING MACHINE GIRL **F2.0353**

Fox Film Corp. 19 Dec **1926** [c19 Dec 1926; LP23469]. Si; b&w. 35mm. 6 reels, 5,245 ft.

Pres by William Fox. *Dir* Irving Cummings. *Scen* Gertrude Orr. *Photog* Abe Fried. *Asst Dir* Charles Woolstenhulme.

Cast: Madge Bellamy *(Bertha Sloan)*, Allan Simpson *(Roy Davis)*, Sally Phipps *(Jessie)*, Paul Nicholson *(Jules Morton)*, Anita Garvin *(Flo Mason)*, J. Farrell MacDonald *(Sloan)*, Ethel Wales *(Mrs. Sloan)*, Arthur Housman *(salesman)*, Harry Bailey *(Sam Ginsberg)*.

Society melodrama. Source: Theodore Kremer, *Bertha, the Sewing Machine Girl* (a play; publication undetermined). Bertha Sloan loses her job as a sewing-machine girl and subsequently is employed as telephone girl with a lingerie manufacturing company. Bertha falls in love with the assistant shipping clerk, Roy Davis, and soon is promoted to chief model for the firm, owing to the patronage of Morton, the wealthy and dastardly manager. Bertha is about to take a position in Paris as designer when Morton lures her to his home. He takes her aboard his yacht, but she is rescued in the nick of time in a thrilling motorboat chase by Roy—who, it develops, is the real owner of the company. *Seamstresses. Telephone operators. Fashion models. Shipping clerks. Sewing machines. Clothing manufacture. Lingerie. Chases.*

THE BEST BAD MAN **F2.0354**

Fox Film Corp. 29 Nov **1925** [c15 Nov 1925; LP22023]. Si; b&w. 35mm. 5 reels, 4,983 ft.

Pres by William Fox. *Dir* J. G. Blystone. *Scen* Lillie Hayward. *Photog* Dan Clark. *Asst Dir* Jasper Blystone.

Cast: Tom Mix *(Hugh Nichols)*, Buster Gardner *(Hank Smith)*, Cyril Chadwick *(Frank Dunlap)*, Clara Bow *(Peggy Swain)*, Tom Kennedy *(Dan Ellis)*, Frank Beal *(Mr. Swain)*, Judy King *(Molly Jones)*, Tom Wilson *(Sam, the butler)*, Paul Panzer *(sheriff)*, Tony *(himself, a horse)*.

Western comedy-melodrama. Source: Max Brand, "Señor Jingle Bells," in *Argosy All Story Weekly* (167:161–180, 364–384, 530–549, 732–750, 919–938, 7 Mar–4 Apr 1925). Hugh Nichols, an absentee ranchowner, visits his Colorado properties in the guise of a peddler of musical instruments. He finds that his agent, Frank Dunlap, has been cheating him and obstructing the construction of a dam Hugh's father had promised the ranchers. Dunlap has also been trying to ruin Old Man Swain, whose daughter, Peggy, he covets. Hugh falls in love with Peggy, who is the leader of the irate ranchers. Dunlap dynamites the dam, trapping Peggy in the resulting flood. Hugh rescues Peggy with the aid of his horse, Tony, and Dunlap is arrested. *Ranchers. Peddlers. Disguise. Dams. Colorado. Floods. Horses.*

THE BEST PEOPLE **F2.0355**

Famous Players–Lasky. *Dist* Paramount Pictures. 9 Nov **1925** [c28 Dec 1925; LP22169]. Si; b&w. 35mm. 6 reels, 5,700 ft.

Pres by Adolph Zukor, Jesse L. Lasky. *Dir* Sidney Olcott. *Screenplay* Bernard McConville. *Photog* James Howe.

Cast: Warner Baxter *(Henry Morgan)*, Esther Ralston *(Alice O'Neil)*, Kathlyn Williams *(Mrs. Lenox)*, Edwards Davis *(Bronson Lenox)*, William Austin *(Arthur Rockmere)*, Larry Steers *(Uncle Throckmorton)*, Margaret Livingston *(Millie Montgomery)*, Joseph Striker *(Bertie Lenox)*, Margaret Morris *(Marian Lenox)*, Ernie Adams *(taxi driver)*.

Romantic comedy. Source: David Gray and Avery Hopwood, *The Best People* (New York opening: 19 Aug 1924). Wealthy Mrs. Lenox intends that her son and daughter shall marry into their own class; the children, Bertie and Marian, plan otherwise: Marian is in love with Henry Morgan, the sensible family chauffeur, and Bertie loves Sally O'Neil, a chorus girl. Arthur Rockmere, Marian's anemic, sometime fiancé, arranges with Marian's father and her uncle, Throckmorton, to meet with Alice and Millie (one of Alice's friends) in order to buy off Alice. Bertie learns of the meeting and tries to disrupt it, landing in jail in the company of Alice, Millie, and Throckmorton. Millie bails them out; Bertie marries Alice, Marian marries Henry, and Uncle Throckmorton, the self-styled social arbiter, marries Millie. *Chauffeurs. Chorus girls. Uncles. Courtship. Social classes. Marriage. Filial relations.*

BETRAYAL **F2.0356**

Paramount Famous Lasky Corp. 11 May **1929** [c11 May 1929; LP365]. Mus score & sd eff (Movietone); b&w. 35mm. 8 reels, 6,614 ft. [Also si; 6,492 ft.]

Dir Lewis Milestone. *Screenplay* Hans Kraly. *Titl* Julian Johnson. *Story* Victor Schertzinger, Nicholas Soussanin. *Photog* Henry Gerrard. *Art Dir* Hans Dreier. *Film Ed* Del Andrews. *Song: "Under the Weather"* J. S. Zamecnik.

Cast: Emil Jannings *(Poldi Moser)*, Esther Ralston *(Vroni, his wife)*, Gary Cooper *(André Frey)*, Jada Weller *(Hans)*, Douglas Haig *(Peter)*, Bodil Rosing *(André's mother)*.

Drama. André Frey, a bohemian artist, woos and wins a rustic Swiss maid, promising to return to her after a visit to the city. The girl, Vroni, finds herself pregnant and is forced by her father to marry Poldi Moser, the mayor of the small Swiss town. Moser and Vroni are happy together, and two sons are born to them. André returns to the village periodically and finally asks Vroni to go away with him. She refuses, and he writes her an angry note. That evening, Vroni and André are involved in a toboggan accident; Vroni is killed outright, and André is fatally injured. Moser finds André's note and goes to him, demanding of the dying man to know which of the boys is in fact André's child. Thinking to protect his own son, André informs Moser that Moser's own son is his (André's) son. Moser swears vengeance on the child but relents when he realizes that he loves both boys equally. *Artists. Mayors. Fatherhood. Parentage. Bohemianism. Toboggans. Switzerland. Sierras.*

Note: Sequences were filmed on location at Lake Tahoe, in the California Sierras.

BETSY'S BURGLAR (Reissue) **F2.0357**

Fine Arts Pictures. *Dist* Tri-Stone Pictures. **1924.** Si; b&w. 35mm. 5 reels.

Note: A "re-edited and re-titled" Constance Talmadge film originally released by Triangle Film Corp. on 5 Mar 1917.

BETTER DAYS **F2.0358**

Pacific Pictures. *Dist* First Division Pictures, Trinity Pictures. 23 Sep **1927** [New York State license]. Si; b&w. 35mm. 7 reels, 6,660 ft.

Dir Frank S. Mattison. *Cont* Betty Garnet. *Titl* Pinto Colvig, Earle Emlay. *Adapt* Cecil Burtis-Hill. *Photog* Earle Emlay, Ernest Depew, Bert Longenecker. *Tech Dir* Ernest Hickson. *Film Ed* Della King.

Cast: Dorothy Devore, Mary Carr, Gareth Hughes, Gaston Glass, Jay Hunt, Reata Hoyt, Jimmy Aubrey, Sidney M. Goldin, George Ovey, Arthur Hotaling, Billy Bletcher, Sam Sidman.

Melodrama. Source: Willis P. Ellery, unidentified story. No information about the nature of this film has been found.

Note: A New York State license was issued to First Division Pictures, but the *Film Year Book* gives the release year as 1928 and the distributor as Trinity Pictures.

THE BETTER MAN **F2.0359**

Selig-Rork Productions. *Dist* Aywon Film Corp. 1 Nov **1921** [New York State; general release: 1 Jan 1922]. Si; b&w. 35mm. 5 reels, ca4,500 ft.

Dir Wilfred Lucas.

Cast: Snowy Baker *(John Harland)*, Brownie Vernon *(Muriel Hammond)*, Charles Villiers *(Martin Giles)*, Wilfred Lucas *(Red Jack Braggan)*.

Melodrama. For his modern tendencies and methods, Rev. John Harland, an ex-prizefighter, receives the disapproval of his congregation and a transfer by his bishop. John resolves to protect Muriel Hammond—whose ranch, Worangi, is near his new parish—from the fraud and the wooing of her manager, Martin Giles; but Muriel considers John a coward for his refusal to stand up to Red Jack Braggan, who threatens to shoot John if he holds services. John discovers that Braggan is a cattle thief and goes to Muriel's ranch in time to rescue her from Giles's forceful marriage proposal. *Prizefighters. Clergymen. Ranchers. Fraud. Australia.*

Note: Filmed in Australia.

THE BETTER MAN **F2.0360**

Richard Talmadge Productions. *For* Carlos Productions. *Dist* Film Booking Offices of America. 6 Jun **1926** [c6 Jun 1926; LP22802]. Si; b&w. 35mm. 5 reels, 4,703 ft.

Dir Scott R. Dunlap. *Cont* Arthur Statter. *Story* Clifford Howard, Burke Jenkins. *Photog* Jack Stevens. *Film Ed* Doane Harrison. *Asst Dir* Albert Metzetti.

Cast: Richard Talmadge *(Lord Hugh Wainwright)*, Ena Gregory *(Nancy Burton)*, John Steppling *(Phineas Ward)*, Margaret Campbell *(Mrs. Ward)*, Herbert Prior *(John Knowlton)*, Charles Hill Mailes *(Charles Clifton)*, Percy Williams *(Hawkins)*.

Comedy. Lord Hugh Wainwright, en route to California to attend a land-inheritance ceremony, misses his boat in rescuing Nancy Burton, a young American girl, from a brutal peddler. Interested in the girl, he obtains employment with her Uncle Phineas Ward as a valet and comes to America with them, though Nancy is aloof because of his low station. Mrs. Ward decides to have Hawkins (really Hugh) pose as Lord Tatterton. Ward takes him into his confidence, revealing his plans to get the Wainwright (Hugh's own) property; but he declares his love for Nancy. When Hugh announces he is Lord Wainright, the Wards send for officers from the insane asylum. Hugh, however, leads a wild chase and abducts Nancy. He is identified by the British consul, and all ends well. *English. Nobility. Valets. Impersonation. Land rights. Personal identity. California. Chases.*

THE BETTER MAN WINS **F2.0361**

Sanford Productions. 1 Sep **1922.** Si; b&w. 35mm. 5 reels.

Dir-Writ Marcel Perez, Frank S. Mattison.

Cast: Pete Morrison *(Bill Harrison)*, Dorothy Woods *(Nell Thompson)*, E. L. Van Sickle *(Hugh Thompson)*, Jack Walters *(Dick Murray)*, Gene Crosby *(Grace Parker)*, Tom Bay *(Dr. Gale)*.

Western melodrama. Refusing Bill Harrison's offers of love and help, Nell is determined to run her ailing father's ranch herself. Dick, a city cabaret proprietor, and Grace, his star performer, become Nell's guests when they have an accident in which Grace sprains her ankle; Grace soon captivates Bill; and Dick encourages Nell to work for him. Bill accompanies Dick and Grace back to the city, but he learns Grace's true nature and returns west to Nell, who has realized the extent of her affection for Bill. *Dancers. Ranchers. Filial relations.*

THE BETTER 'OLE **F2.0362**

Warner Brothers Pictures. 7 Oct **1926** [New York premiere; released 23 Oct; c4 Sep 1926; LP23073]. Si; b&w. 35mm. 9 reels, 8,469 ft.

Dir Charles Reisner. *Titl* Robert Hopkins. *Adapt* Charles Reisner, Darryl Francis Zanuck. *Camera* Ed Du Par. *Asst Camera* Walter Robinson. *Asst Dir* Sandy Roth.

Cast: Syd Chaplin *(Old Bill)*, Doris Hill *(Joan)*, Harold Goodwin *(Bert)*, Theodore Lorch *(Gaspard)*, Ed Kennedy *(Corporal Quint)*, Charles Gerrard *(The Major)*, Tom McGuire *(The English General)*, Jack Ackroyd *(Alf)*, Tom Kennedy *(The Blacksmith)*, Kewpie Morgan *(General Von Hinden)*, Arthur Clayton *(The Colonel)*.

Comedy-drama. Source: Bruce Bairnsfather and Arthur Eliot, *The Better 'Ole, or The Romance of Old Bill* (New York opening: 19 Oct 1918). Old Bill, a jovial Limey sergeant, discovers that the major of his regiment is a German spy in collusion with Gaspard, the local innkeeper. The spies mistrust him and poison his wine; but it spills and eats a hole in the floor through which Gaspard falls into the cellar. Trying to rescue him, Bill discovers a cote of carrier pigeons. Tipped off by the major, the Germans bomb an opera house where Bill and Alf are performing; they escape, however, in their impersonation of a horse and later pose as German soldiers in a German regiment. Bill manages to get a photograph of the major greeting the German general, but it falls into the hands of Joan, a prisoner of war. Bill is forced to join a German attack against the British, and though he saves his own regiment, he is shot as a German spy. An old friend, however, has substituted blank cartridges for the real ones, and Bill is pardoned when Joan and his friend Bert arrive with the incriminating photograph. *English. Germans. Spies. Prisoners of war. Theater—Amateur. World War I. France. Pigeons.*

THE BETTER WAY **F2.0363**

Columbia Pictures. 5 Dec **1926** [c27 Dec 1926; LP23467]. Si; b&w. 35mm. 6 reels, 5,532 ft.

Supv Harry Cohn. *Dir* Ralph Ince. *Cont* Dorothy Howell. *Story* Harry O. Hoyt. *Photog* J. O. Taylor.

Cast: Dorothy Revier *(Betty Boyd)*, Ralph Ince *(Billie Woods)*, Eugene Strong, Armand Kaliz, Hazel Howell.

Romantic drama. Unattractive Betty Boyd, a stenographer for broker Franklyn Collins, is admired by bookkeeper Billie Woods, though she secretly admires her employer. While taking dictation she overhears a market tip from a business associate; investing in the stock herself, she reaps a small fortune, and after a trip to the beauty experts, she is appropriately transformed. Against the advice of Billie, she continues to follow Collins' tips. Billie, jealous of Collins' attentions, reverses her investments, hoping to bring her to her senses through financial ruin, but the plan backfires and they both become wealthy. In desperation, he follows her to Collins' apartment, and there he saves the terrified Betty from Collins' advances and convinces her of his love. *Stenographers. Brokers. Speculation.*

BETWEEN DANGERS **F2.0364**

Action Pictures. *Dist* Pathé Exchange. 13 Feb **1927** [c4 Feb 1927; LU23634]. Si; b&w. 35mm. 5 reels, 4,533 ft.

Pres by Lester F. Scott, Jr. *Dir-Cont* Richard Thorpe. *Photog* Ray Reis.

Cast: Buddy Roosevelt *(Tom Rawlins)*, Alma Rayford *(Sue Conway)*, Rennie Young *(Santine)*, Al Taylor *(Charlie)*, Charles Thurston *(sheriff)*, Allen Sewall, Edward W. Borman, Hank Bell.

Western melodrama. Source: Walter J. Coburn, "Ride 'im Cowboy," in *Action Stories Magazine*. Tom Rawlins is informed by his lawyer that he has fallen heir to the Cross P Ranch, but he is held up and his identification papers are stolen. Arriving in Cactus City, he is innocently involved in a bank robbery and is unable to prove his identity, though Sheriff Conway and his daughter, Sue, believe him. Santine, the crooked foreman who wants to use the ranch for his own purposes, conspires with the lawyer and Chicago Charlie (who is posing as Tom) to incite the townspeople against Tom; but Tom escapes and with the aid of Bill, a ranch hand, rescues Sue from Charlie and the lawyer. In a climactic fight, Santine is killed falling over a cliff, and Tom regains his ranch. *Ranch foremen. Sheriffs. Lawyers. Imposture. Inheritance. Bank robberies.*

BETWEEN FRIENDS **F2.0365**

Vitagraph Co. of America. 11 May **1924** [c8 Apr 1924; LP20116]. Si; b&w. 35mm. 7 reels, 6,936 ft.

Pres by Albert E. Smith. *Dir* J. Stuart Blackton. *Scen* Robert W. Chambers. *Photog* Stephen Smith, Jr.

Cast: Lou Tellegen *(David Drene)*, Anna Q. Nilsson *(Jessica Drene)*, Norman Kerry *(Jack Greylock)*, Alice Calhoun *(Cecile White)*, Stuart Holmes *(Quair)*, Henry Barrows *(Guilder)*.

Melodrama. Source: Robert William Chambers, *Between Friends* (New York, 1914). When Jack Greylock elopes with Jessica, wife of his lifelong friend David Drene, they are taken with remorse and she commits suicide. Later, Jack falls in love with Cecile, David's model, who loves Drene. A jealous rival, Quair, informs David about the elopement with Jessica, and to satisfy David's vengeance Jack proposes to kill himself. By mental telepathy, David prevents the tragedy and forgives him. *Infidelity. Suicide. Mental telepathy.*

BETWEEN THE WORLDS *see* **BORDERLAND**

BETWEEN TWO HUSBANDS **F2.0366**

Mark M. Dintenfass. *Dist* Alexander Film Corp. 23 Oct **1922** [New York State license; New York showing 8 Aug 1924]. Si; b&w. 35mm. 5 reels.

Cast: Jean Gabriel, Arline Pretty.

Melodrama. "... concerning the country maid betrayed by the wayward son and left stranded in the big city. The wayward's brother, a minister, marries the girl to give her child a name, while his villainous twin stumbles downstairs and kills himself during an attempt to abduct the infant." (*Variety,* 20 Aug 1924, p22.) Jean Gabriel portrays both twin brothers. *Clergymen. Twins. Brothers. Illegitimacy. Seduction. Abduction.*

BEVERLY OF GRAUSTARK **F2.0367**

Cosmopolitan Productions. *Dist* Metro-Goldwyn-Mayer Distributing Corp. 22 Mar **1926** [c5 Apr 1926; LP22562]. Si; b&w with col sequence. 35mm. 7 reels, 6,710 or 6,977 ft.

Dir Sidney Franklin. *Titl* Joe Farnham. *Adapt* Agnes Christine Johnston. *Photog* Percy Hilburn. *Art Dir* Cedric Gibbons, Richard Day. *Film Ed* Frank Hull. *Wardrobe* Kathleen Kay, Maude Marsh, André-ani.

Cast: Marion Davies *(Beverly Calhoun)*, Antonio Moreno *(Danton)*, Creighton Hale *(Prince Oscar)*, Roy D'Arcy *(General Marlanx)*, Albert Gran *(Duke Travina)*, Paulette Duval *(Caslotta)*, Max Barwyn *(Saranoff)*, Charles Clary *(Mr. Calhoun)*.

Romantic comedy-drama. Source: George Barr McCutcheon, *Beverly of Graustark* (New York, 1904). Beverly Calhoun, discovering that her Cousin Oscar is the heir to the throne of Graustark, a European kingdom, joins him there. They are met by the Duke Travina, the temporary regent. General Marlanx, pretender to the throne, learning of the young prince's arrival, plots with Saranoff to assassinate him. In the Alps, Oscar is injured while skiing, and the duke suggests that Beverly wear Oscar's uniform and impersonate him until he recovers; Saranoff's plot is thwarted by Danton, leader of a group of shepherds. Danton becomes her constant companion and guard, and she obtains women's clothing to charm him. Confusing her as a rival to the "prince," Danton jealously challenges the prince to a duel. Oscar reveals the impersonation to Marlanx, but Danton, acknowledging himself to be the prince of a nearby kingdom, exposes the pretender's plot and wins the hand of Beverly. *Cousins. Royalty. Shepherds. Skiers. Impersonation. Imaginary kingdoms. Alps.*

Note: The final sequence is in color.

BEWARE OF BACHELORS **F2.0368**

Warner Brothers Pictures. 27 Oct **1928** [c15 Oct 1928; LP25682]. Talking sequences (Vitaphone); b&w. 35mm. 6 reels, 5,778 ft. [Also si, 1 Dec 1928; 5,278 ft.]

Dir Roy Del Ruth. *Scen-Dial* Robert Lord. *Titl* Joseph Jackson. *Photog* Norbert Brodin, Frank Kesson. *Film Ed* Ralph Dawson.

Cast: Audrey Ferris *(May, the wife)*, William Collier, Jr. *(Ed, the husband)*, Clyde Cook *(Joe Babbitt)*, André Beranger *(Claude de Brie)*, Dave Morris *(detective)*, Margaret Livingston *(Miss Pfeffer, the vamp)*.

Comedy. Source: Mark Canfield, "Beware of Bachelors" (publication undetermined). Miss Pfeffer makes a pass at Ed, a handsome doctor, and Ed's wife, May, chooses to misunderstand, reciprocating by picking up Claude de Brie, a perfumer. Ed and May make up, but they are soon quarreling again: May finds Ed with Miss Pfeffer at a cafe and goes off with Claude to a wild party. May finally walks out on Ed, but, when love proves stronger than jealousy, she returns to him ... until the next quarrel. *Physicians. Perfumers. Vamps. Marriage. Jealousy.*

BEWARE OF BLONDES **F2.0369**

Columbia Pictures. 1 Jul **1928** [c15 Aug 1928; LP25532]. Si; b&w. 35mm. 6 reels, 5,649 ft.

Prod Harry Cohn. *Dir* George B. Seitz. *Cont* Peter Milne. *Story* Harvey Thew, George C. Hull. *Photog* Joe Walker. *Art Dir* Joseph Wright. *Film Ed* James McKay. *Asst Dir* Joe Nadel.

Cast: Dorothy Revier *(Mary)*, Matt Moore *(Jeffrey)*, Roy D'Arcy *(Harry)*, Robert Edeson *(Costigan)*, Walter P. Lewis *(Tex)*, Hazel Howell *(Blonde Mary)*, Harry Semels *(Portugee Joe)*.

Melodrama. Jeffrey Black, a clerk in a jewelry store, prevents a robbery there and, as a reward, is given a vacation in Honolulu, provided that he transport a valuable emerald to the Islands. On the boat, he meets Mary, a blonde, and having been warned against a thief called Blonde Mary, he regards her every action with suspicion while simultaneously falling in love with her. Mary, who is in reality a detective, sees that the emerald arrives safely at its destination and brings the real Blonde Mary and a thief named Harry to justice. *Salesclerks. Jewelers. Detectives. Thieves. Robbery. Ocean liners. Honolulu.*

BEWARE OF MARRIED MEN **F2.0370**

Warner Brothers Pictures. 14 Jan **1928** [c7 Jan 1928; LP24833]. Mus score (Vitaphone); b&w. 35mm. 6 reels, 5,421 ft. [Also si.]

Dir Archie L. Mayo. *Screenplay* E. T. Lowe, Jr. *Titl* Joseph Jackson. *Photog* Frank Kesson. *Film Ed* Ralph Dawson. *Asst Dir* Joe Barry.

Cast: Irene Rich *(Myra Martin)*, Clyde Cook *(Botts)*, Audrey Ferris *(Helene Martin)*, Myrna Loy *(Juanita Sheldon)*, Richard Tucker *(Leonard Gilbert)*, Stuart Holmes *(Huntley Sheldon)*, Hugh Allan *(Ralph)*, Rush Hughes.

Farce. Myra Martin, in love with her boss, a noted divorce lawyer, attempts to save her younger sister, Helene, from an attentive married man. The younger sister elopes with her best boyfriend and returns to find Myra being molested by the married man. When the lawyer and the married man's wife arrive, all is straightened out. *Lawyers. Sisters. Infidelity. Divorce.*

BEWARE OF THE LAW **F2.0371**

Dist Jawitz Pictures. 7 Sep **1922** [New York State license]. Si; b&w. 35mm. 5 reels, 4,600-4,800 ft.

Dir W. A. S. Douglas. *Story* Frank S. Beresford. *Photog* Seymour Spiegel, Frank Zukor.

Cast: Marjorie Payne *(Rose LeBarbe)*, William Coughey *(Jean LeBarbe)*, Henry Van Bousen *(Jules Grandin)*, Ann Deering *(Ann LeBarbe)*, D. W. Reynolds *(Jimmy Harvey, alias The Kid)*, John Altieri *(Three-Star Kelly)*, Willard Cooley *(William McRae)*.

Melodrama. "Jules Grandin, a woodsman, finds McRae, a prohibition agent, seriously wounded. He calls for help in taking care of him, from Rose LeBarbe, sister to Ann, his sweetheart. Unknown to Rose, her father is making daily visits to the rum-runners' secret storehouse. When they discover that much of their goods is missing, they determine to get him and dispose of him, as they have of several others in their way. McRae recovers from his wound in time to be of service in saving the girls' father, and Ann who has doublecrossed Jules, repents and goes back to him. McRae, of course, has fallen in love with Rose." (*Moving Picture World,* 11 Nov 1922, p183.) *Rumrunners. Revenue agents. Filial relations. Prohibition.*

Note: Formerly titled *Watered Stock,* but no evidence has been found that this film was ever released under that title.

BEWARE OF WIDOWS (Universal-Jewel) **F2.0372**

Universal Pictures. 23 May **1927** [New York showing; released 19 Jun; c20 Apr 1927; LP23890]. Si; b&w. 35mm. 6 reels, 5,777 ft.

Pres by Carl Laemmle. *Dir* Wesley Ruggles. *Scen-Cont* Beatrice Van. *Photog* Gilbert Warrenton.

Cast: Laura La Plante *(Joyce Bragdon),* Bryant Washburn *(Dr. John Waller),* Paulette Duval *(Mrs. Paula Warren),* Walter Hiers *(William Bradford),* Tully Marshall *(Peter Chadwick),* Kathryn Carver *(Ruth Chadwick),* Heinie Conklin *(Captain),* Otto Hoffman *(Mr. Warren).*

Farce. Source: Owen Moore, *Beware of Widows, a Comedy in Three Acts* (New York, 1930). Joyce Bragdon is engaged to John Waller, a young doctor who is popular with the ladies, and they go to a resort hotel to be married. Paula, one of John's married admirers, feigns illness and brings him to her room; consequently, Joyce breaks the engagement. Later, Paula is divorced and John plans to marry Ruth, a friend of William Bradford, John's pal, aboard Peter Chadwick's houseboat. Joyce wrecks her car nearby and is carried aboard; she sets the houseboat adrift in a storm. Joyce tells Peter that Paula loves him, and when the boat strikes a rock Peter saves Paula. All but John and Joyce flee to safety in a lifeboat. The morning finds Paula comfortably in the arms of Peter and John succumbing to the charms of Joyce. *Physicians. Jealousy. Divorce. Resorts. Houseboats. Shipwrecks. Storms.*

BEWARE THE WOMAN *see* **UNTAMED YOUTH**

BEYOND **F2.0373**

Famous Players–Lasky. *Dist* Paramount Pictures. 30 Oct **1921** [c30 Oct 1921; LP17173]. Si; b&w. 35mm. 5 reels, 5,248 ft.

Pres by Jesse L. Lasky. *Dir* William D. Taylor. *Scen* Julia Crawford Ivers.

Cast: Ethel Clayton *(Avis Langley),* Charles Meredith *(Geoffrey Southerne),* Earl Schenck *(Alec Langley),* Fontaine La Rue *(Mrs. Langley),* Winifred Kingston *(Viva Newmarch),* Lillian Rich *(Bessie Ackroyd),* Charles French *(Samuel Ackroyd),* Spottiswoode Aitken *(Rufus Southerne),* Herbert Fortier *(Dr. Newmarch).*

Spiritualist melodrama. Source: Henry Arthur Jones, *The Lifted Veil* (a play; publication undetermined). On her deathbed, the mother of Avis Langley begs her to watch over her wayward twin brother, Alec. Just before Avis is to be married to Geoffrey Southerne, Alec disappears, and the spirit of Mrs. Langley appears to Avis to remind her of her promise. Samuel Ackroyd, from New Zealand, calls to explain that Alec, who is engaged to his daughter, has disappeared; Avis goes to New Zealand, finds Alec, persuades him to reform and marry Bessie, and then sails for home. En route, the steamer is wrecked, and Avis, being the only survivor, is washed up on the shore of a small island. Geoffrey, believing her dead, marries Viva Newmarch, whom he does not love. After a year, Avis returns, and her mother's spirit comes to console her. She declines to reveal that she is alive, however, until the accidental death of Viva creates the possibility of her reunion with Geoffrey. *Twins. Brother-sister relationship. Ghosts. England. New Zealand. Shipwrecks.*

BEYOND ALL ODDS **F2.0374**

H. T. Henderson Productions. *Dist* Chesterfield Motion Picture Corp. Feb or 15 Jun **1926.** Si; b&w. 35mm. 5 reels, 4,324 ft.

Pres by Joseph Kline. *Dir-Writ* Alvin J. Neitz. *Photog* Bert Baldridge. *Film Ed* Ralph Dietrich.

Cast: Eileen Sedgwick *(Betty Mason),* Carlos Silvera *(George Baker),* Ray Childs *("Casino" Joe),* Theodore Henderson *(Dan Mason),* Les Bates *("Ritch" Walker),* Lew Meehan *(Cory Forbes),* Alfred Hewston *(sheriff),* D. Maley *("Hard Rock" Jordan).*

Western melodrama. "Girl avenges death of brother and abduction of sweetheart by killing villains instrumental in causing both crimes." (*Motion Picture News Booking Guide,* 11:20, Oct 1926.) *Revenge. Abduction. Brother-sister relationship.*

BEYOND LONDON LIGHTS **F2.0375**

FBO Pictures. 18 Mar **1928** [c5 Mar 1928; LP25036]. Si; b&w. 35mm. 6 reels, 5,583 ft.

Dir Tom Terriss. *Screenplay* Jean Dupont. *Titl* George Arthur. *Adapt* Beatrice Burton. *Photog* Robert De Grasse. *Film Ed* Pandro S. Berman. *Asst Dir* Ray McCarey.

Cast: Adrienne Dore *(Kitty Carstairs),* Lee Shumway *(John Risk),* Gordon Elliott *(Colin Drummond),* Herbert Evans *(Symington),* Jacqueline Gadsden *(Lady Dorothy),* Florence Wix *(Mrs. Drummond),* Templar Saxe *(Stephen Carstairs),* Blanche Craig *(Mrs. Bundle),* Katherine Ward *(The Landlady).*

Society drama. Source: John Joy Bell, *Kitty Carstairs* (London, 1917). To put her at a disadvantage, wealthy Mrs. Drummond hires postmaster's daughter Kitty Carstairs, to whom her son Colin is engaged, as a maid in her household. Simultaneously, Mrs. Drummond invites Lady Dorothy, a beautiful heiress, to visit, hoping to lure Colin away from Kitty. Made miserable, Kitty leaves the Drummonds and meets artist John Risk, a friend of theirs. With his assistance Kitty goes to London and becomes a model in a modiste shop. Drummond comes to his senses and breaks his engagement to Dorothy, but it is too late to make amends; Kitty and John have fallen in love. *Artists. Housemaids. Nobility. Fashion models. Postmasters. Modistes. Social classes. London.*

BEYOND PRICE **F2.0376**

Fox Film Corp. 8 May **1921** [c8 May 1921; LP16581]. Si; b&w. 35mm. 5-6 reels.

Pres by William Fox. *Dir* J. Searle Dawley. *Story-Scen* Paul H. Sloane. *Photog* Joseph Ruttenberg.

Cast: Pearl White *(Sally Marrio),* Vernon Steel *(Philip Marrio),* Nora Reed *(Valicia),* Arthur Gordini *(Lester Lawton),* Louis Haines *(J. Peter Weathersby),* Maude Turner Gordon *(Mrs. Florence Weathersby),* Byron Douglas *(Norbert Temple),* Ottola Nesmith *(Mrs. Temple),* Dorothy Walters *(Mrs. Dusenberry),* Dorothy Allen *(Lizzie),* J. Thornton Baston *(Mrs. Temple's friend),* Charles Sutton *(cobbler).*

Society melodrama. Sally Marrio, neglected wife of a prominent shoe designer, has three wishes: to be a millionaire's wife, to be famous, and to have a child. When she is sent to deliver two pairs of shoes—one to Valicia, a dancer, and the other to Mrs. Weathersby, a banker's wife—she leaves a note saying she will not return. Before leaving the Weathersby mansion, she has passed herself off as the millionaire's wife, has saved him from paying blackmailer Lawton, and has been handed a fur coat by mistake. At an art exhibit where the dancer is to appear she is mistaken for a guest and is voted the most handsome woman present, but she barely escapes involvement in a murder triangle. Discovering that her husband has not read the note, she is happily reconciled with him when he plans to adopt a child. *Shoe designers. Marriage. Ambition. Adoption.*

BEYOND THE BORDER **F2.0377**

Rogstrom Productions. *Dist* Producers Distributing Corp. 2 Mar **1925** [c1 Mar 1925; LP21573]. Si; b&w. 35mm. 5 reels, 4,469 ft.

Pres by Hunt Stromberg. *Supv* Hunt Stromberg. *Dir* Scott R. Dunlap. *Adapt* Harvey Gates. *Photog* Sol Polito, George Benoit. *Art Dir* Edward Withers. *Film Ed* Lou Ostrow.

Cast: Harry Carey *(Bob Smith),* Mildred Harris *(Molly Smith),* Tom Santschi *(Nick Perdue),* Jack Richardson *(Brick Dawson),* William Scott *(Moore).*

Western melodrama. Source: Meredith Davis, "When Smith Meets Smith." Sheriff Bob Smith catches Moore, an innocent man who has been unjustly accused of having committed a crime, and discovers that his prisoner is none other that the brother of Molly Smith, Bob's sweetheart. During Bob's absence from town, Brick Dawson defames his character and has himself elected sheriff in Bob's place. Bob returns with Moore, who is sentenced to jail, asking Bob to look after Molly. Bob takes good care of the girl and also clears Moore of the charges against him by exposing the wrongdoings of an outlaw gang led by Perdue. Dawson is convicted along with the Perdue gang, and Bob gets back his job as sheriff. *Sheriffs. Brother-sister relationship. Gangs. Injustice.*

BEYOND THE CROSSROADS **F2.0378**

Pioneer Film Corp. 27 Jan **1922** [trade review]. Si; b&w. 35mm. 5 reels, 4,903 ft.

Dir Lloyd Carleton. *Story* Bradley King.

Cast: Ora Carew *(Leila Wilkes)*, Lawson Butt *(John Pierce/James Fordham)*, Melbourne MacDowell *(David Walton/Truman Breese)*, Stuart Morris *(Charles Wilkes)*.

Melodrama. James Fordham returns home after a 6 months' absence to find that his wife has left him for another man. She returns, asking for forgiveness, but dies shortly thereafter. James swears to avenge her death and sets out to find the man who has wronged her. After changing his name, he discovers that the young girl with whom he is falling in love is engaged to the low fellow who stole his wife. He wins out by proving her fiancé is involved in a crooked business deal. *Businessmen. Swindlers. Desertion. Infidelity. Personal identity.*

BEYOND THE LAW *see* **FLYING HOOFS**

BEYOND THE LAW **F2.0379**

Raytone Talking Pictures. *Dist* Syndicate Pictures. 15 Aug or 1 Oct **1930.** Sd; b&w. 35mm. 6 reels, 4,930-5,700 ft.

Dir J. P. McGowan. *Story* G. A. Durlam. *Photog* Frank Newman. *Film Ed* Arthur Brooks.

Cast: Robert Frazer *(Dan Wright)*, Louise Lorraine *(Barbara Reingold)*, Jimmy Kane *(Ted)*, Lane Chandler *(Jack-Knife)*, Charles L. King *(Brand)*, Edward Lynch *(Slade)*, William Walling *(Reingold)*, George Hackathorne *(Monty)*, Franklyn Farnum *(Lieutenant)*, Robert Graves *(Stone)*.

Western melodrama. Ranchers on the California-Nevada border are harrassed beyond endurance by the combined efforts of Slade, leader of a gang of rustlers, and Brand, who runs a "Protective Association"; and Reingold, the leader of the holdouts, finally goes to the capital for help. Happy-go-lucky drifters Dan Wright and Jack-Knife arrive on the scene in time to prevent Brand's capture of Reingold, and they generally frustrate the rustlers until the Cavalry arrives to round up the gang. *Ranchers. Vagabonds. Rustlers. Protective associations. Extortion. California. Nevada. United States Army—Cavalry.*

Note: Songs: "Soup," "We're Cavalry Men," "Marching Song."

BEYOND THE RAINBOW **F2.0380**

R-C Pictures. 19 Feb **1922** [c19 Feb 1922; LP17703]. Si; b&w. 35mm. 7 reels, 6,500 ft. [Also 6 reels.]

Dir William Christy Cabanne. *Adapt* Eustace Hale Ball, Loila Brooks. *Photog* William Tuers, Philip Armand. *Art Dir* Frank Champury.

Cast: Harry Morey *(Edward Mallory)*, Billie Dove *(Marion Taylor)*, Virginia Lee *(Henrietta Greeley)*, Diana Allen *(Frances Gardener)*, James Harrison *(Louis Wade)*, Macey Harlam *(Count Julien de Brisac)*, Rose Coghlan *(Mrs. Burns)*, William Tooker *(Dr. Ramsey)*, George Fawcett *(Mr. Gardener)*, Marguerite Courtot *(Esther)*, Edmund Breese *(Inspector Richardson)*, Walter Miller *(Robert Judson)*, Charles Craig *(Col. Henry Cartwright)*, Clara Bow *(Virginia Gardener)*, Huntly Gordon *(Bruce Forbes)*.

Society melodrama. Source: Solita Solano, "The Price of Feathers" (publication undetermined). Marion Taylor, secretary to Edward Mallory, a Wall Street magnate, supports her invalid brother, Tommy, who is ordered to the mountains by his doctor. Marion has resisted her employer's advances, but she resolves to seek his aid. Frances Gardener, daughter of a prominent society couple, is admired by Louis Wade, an old friend, and by Count de Brisac. Wade, intent on making Frances jealous, meets Marion and persuades her to come to the ball in the role of Miss Chandler, a famous belle, agreeing to pay her the $250 needed to send Tommy to the mountains. She is a sensation at the ball; meanwhile, Virginia, Frances' younger sister, who has been forbidden to attend the ball, sends anonymous messages among the guests, telling each that his secret is known. When the lights are extinguished, Mallory is shot. The police suspect Bruce Forbes, but the guilty man proves to be Robert Judson. Mallory recovers, and Marion finds happiness with Forbes and her cured brother, Tommy. *Secretaries. Invalids. Sisters. Brother-sister relationship.*

BEYOND THE RIO GRANDE **F2.0381**

Biltmore Productions. *Dist* Big 4 Film Corp. 12 Apr **1930.** Sd (Cinephone); b&w. 35mm. 6 reels, 5,400 ft.

Pres by John R. Freuler. *Dir* Harry Webb. *Story-Scen-Dial* Carl Krusada. *Photog* William Nobles. *Film Ed* Frederick Paine. *Theme Song: "Beyond the Rio Grande"* Henry Taylor. *Sd Engr* William Garrity, George Lowerry.

Cast: Jack Perrin *(Bert Allen)*, Franklyn Farnum *(Joe Kemp)*, Charline Burt *(Betty Burke)*, Emma Tansey *(Mrs. Burke)*, Buffalo Bill Jr. *(Bill)*, Pete Morrison *(Al Mooney)*, Henry Roquemore *(sheriff)*, Edmund Cobb *(Dick)*, Henry Taylor *(doctor)*, Starlight *(himself, a horse)*.

Western melodrama. Having quit their gang and gone straight, Bert Allen and Joe Kemp finally own their own ranch after 3 years, but Joe robs the Riverton bank of the Green River Dam payroll—using Bert's horse, gun, and gloves, and leaving behind Bert's hat. Bert escapes across the Mexican border and there falls in love with Betty Burke. While Bill, Al, and Dick pursue the loot and the $5,000 reward for Bert's capture, Bert offers to surrender if the reward money will be spent on surgery for Betty's blind mother. Joe confesses when the sheriff tells him of Bert's plan, and happiness is complete when Mrs. Burke regains her sight. (Locale: Arizona.) *Criminals—Rehabilitation. Bank robberies. Blindness. Dams. Mexican border. Arizona. Horses.*

Note: *Film Daily* credits *Jack* Nobles with photography.

BEYOND THE ROCKIES **F2.0382**

Independent Pictures. *Dist* Film Booking Offices of America. 21 Feb **1926** [c21 Feb 1926; LP22423]. Si; b&w. 35mm. 5 reels, 4,851 ft.

Prod Jesse J. Goldburg. *Dir* Jack Nelson. *Adapt-Cont* William E. Wing. *Story* J. Edward Leithead.

Cast: Bob Custer *(Con Benteen)*, Eugenie Gilbert *(Flossie)*, David Dunbar *(Cottle)*, Bruce Gordon *(Monte Lorin)*, Milton Ross *(Tex Marcy)*, Eddie Harris *(Sartwell)*, Max Holcomb *(Dunc James)*, Roy Laidlaw *(Dave Heep)*, Max Asher *(Mayor Smithson)*.

Western melodrama. Con Benteen, an undercover agent for the Cattlemen's Protective Association, rides into a lawless town to investigate a band of cattle rustlers known as the Cloaked Riders. He joins the gang and gets the goods on Cottle, the gang's leader. Benteen is eventually identified as a legal officer and tied up in a shack containing live explosives. He escapes and rounds up the rustlers, winning for himself the love of Flossie, a dancehall girl. *Dancehall girls. Rustlers. Protective associations.*

BEYOND THE ROCKS **F2.0383**

Famous Players–Lasky. *Dist* Paramount Pictures. 7 May **1922** [c17 May 1922; LP17892]. Si; b&w. 35mm. 7 reels, 6,740 ft.

Pres by Jesse L. Lasky. *Dir* Sam Wood. *Adapt* Jack Cunningham. *Photog* Alfred Gilks.

Cast: Gloria Swanson *(Theodora Fitzgerald)*, Rodolph Valentino *(Lord Bracondale)*, Edythe Chapman *(Lady Bracondale)*, Alec B. Francis *(Captain Fitzgerald)*, Robert Bolder *(Josiah Brown)*, Gertrude Astor *(Morella Winmarleigh)*, Mabel Van Buren *(Mrs. McBride)*, Helen Dunbar *(Lady Ada Fitzgerald)*, Raymond Blathwayt *(Sir Patrick Fitzgerald)*, F. R. Butler *(Lord Wensleydon)*, June Elvidge *(Lady Anningford)*.

Society melodrama. Source: Elinor Glyn, *Beyond the Rocks* (New York, 1906). To please her father, Theodora Fitzgerald marries Josiah Brown, an elderly millionaire. When she slips over a precipice while climbing the Alps, Theodora is saved by Lord Bracondale; in Paris they meet again, fall in love, and agree to part forever. They do meet, however, at the residence of Lady Anningford in London; again Bracondale declares his love; she resists him, however, but sends him a note confessing her feelings. Morella Winmarleigh, who loves Bracondale, redirects a letter for Brown to Bracondale and the love note to Brown. After a confrontation, Brown decides to sacrifice himself for his wife and accompanies an exploring party to Arabia. His party is attacked by bandits, and he is fatally wounded just as Bracondale, Theodora, her father, and an escort arrive. Before he dies, Brown wishes the lovers happiness. *Millionaires. Infidelity. Mountain climbing. England. Arabia. Alps. Paris.*

BEYOND THE SIERRAS **F2.0384**

Metro-Goldwyn-Mayer Pictures. 15 Sep **1928** [c15 Sep 1928; LP25727]. Si; b&w. 35mm. 6 reels, 5,896 ft.

Dir Nick Grinde. *Screenplay* Robert Lord. *Titl* Ruth Cummings. *Story* John Thomas Neville. *Photog* Arthur Reed. *Film Ed* William Le Vanway. *Wardrobe* Lucia Coulter.

Cast: Tim McCoy *(The Masked Stranger)*, Sylvia Beecher *(Rosa)*, Roy D'Arcy *(Owens)*, Polly Moran *(Inez)*, Richard R. Neill *(Carlos)*, J. Gordon Russell *(Wells)*.

Western melodrama. "Story of a well-known type, including the masked avenger, claim jumpers, banditry, duels, pistol battles, horse riding, fist fights and so on. Pretty scenic decorations." (*Variety*, 12 Dec 1928, p31.) *Claim jumpers. Revenge. Duels.*

BEYOND THE TRAIL **F2.0385**
Sierra Pictures. *Dist* Chesterfield Motion Picture Corp. Sep **1926.** Si; b&w. 35mm. 5 reels, 3,572-4,300 ft.

Prod George R. Batcheller. *Dir* Al Herman. *Film Ed* Joe Basil, Sam Winston.

Cast: Bill Patton *(Bill, a hired hand)*, Eric Mayne *(ranchowner)*, Janet Dawn *(Mary, his daughter)*, Sheldon Lewis *(Cal, foreman)*, Stuart Holmes *(Archibald Van Jones)*, Clara Horton *(Clarabelle Simpkins)*, James F. Fulton *(Buck, ranchhand)*.

Western melodrama. During a welcome-home party for Mary, the daughter of a rancher, the payroll is spirited away from the rancher's desk by Black Mike, a desperado who has received information about the payroll from Cal, the ranch foreman. The pursuing posse includes Bill (the butt of many practical jokes), who separates from the group to practice shooting and accidentally finds Black Mike's gang. Given credit for the deaths of two robbers, who shot each other, Bill is sent to a cabin to capture a third, and he rescues Mary from Cal with hand-to-hand combat. *Ranchers. Ranch foremen. Desperadoes. Posses. Robbery.*

BIFF BANG BUDDY **F2.0386**
Approved Pictures. *Dist* Weiss Brothers Artclass Pictures. 15 Sep **1924** [c25 Aug 1924; LU20512]. Si; b&w. 35mm. 5 reels, 4,500 ft.

Dir Frank L. Inghram. *Story* Reginald C. Barker. *Photog* Irving Ries.

Cast: Buddy Roosevelt *(Buddy Walters)*, Jean Arthur *(Bonnie Norton)*, Buck Connors *(Dad Norton)*, Robert Fleming *(Shane McCune)*, Al Richmond *(Nachez)*.

Western melodrama. Buddy rescues Bonnie Norton and is rewarded with a job on her father's ranch. When he is captured by Nachez' outlaw band and is left tied to a train track, he is rescued by McCune, another bandit. They both escape, and though Buddy is mistakenly identified with the outlaws, he vindicates himself by capturing Nachez. *Cowboys. Ranchers. Outlaws.*

THE BIG ADVENTURE **F2.0387**
Universal Film Manufacturing Co. Apr **1921** [c1 Apr 1921; LP16348]. Si; b&w. 35mm. 5 reels, 4,589 ft.

Dir Reeves Eason. *Scen* George W. Pyper. *Story* James Edward Hungerford. *Photog* Virgil Miller.

Cast: Breezy Eason, Jr. *(Patches)*, Fred Herzog *(Old Whiskers)*, Lee Shumway *(John Wellborn)*, Molly Shafer *(Mrs. Lane)*, Gertrude Olmstead *(Sally)*.

Rural melodrama. Patches, a kindhearted orphan of the slums, finds life unbearable under the cruel abuse of his stepfather, Old Whiskers, for whose support he is forced to steal. Stowing away in a freight car with his dog, he escapes to a neighboring town where he is given a home by Mrs. Lane, sister of the town judge. The stepfather, having turned hobo, kidnaps the boy and holds captive Sally, the judge's daughter, when she finds him. But Patches escapes and returns with a posse to the rescue. *Orphans. Stepfathers. Tramps. Posses. Slums. Kidnaping. Dogs.*

BIG BOY **F2.0388**
Warner Brothers Pictures. 6 Sep **1930** [c5 Aug 1930; LP1465]. Sd (Vitaphone); b&w. 35mm. 9 reels, 6,275 ft.

Dir Alan Crosland. *Screenplay-Dial* William K. Wells, Perry Vekroff, Rex Taylor. *Photog* Hal Mohr. *Film Ed* Ralph Dawson. *Song: "What Will I Do Without You?"* Al Dubin, Joe Burke. *Songs: "Liza Lee," "Tomorrow Is Another Day"* Bud Green, Sammy Stept. *Song: "Down South"* Sigmund Spaeth, George Middleton. *Song: "The Handicap March"* Dave Reed, Jr., George Rosey. *Rec Engr* Hal Bumbaugh.

Cast: Al Jolson *(Gus)*, Claudia Dell *(Annabel)*, Louise Closser Hale *(Mrs. Bedford)*, Lloyd Hughes *(Jack)*, Eddie Phillips *(Coley Reed)*, Lew Harvey *(Doc Wilbur)*, Franklin Batie *(Jim)*, John Harron *(Joe)*, Tom Wilson *(Tucker)*, Carl White *(song director)*, Colin Campbell *(Steve Leslie)*, Noah Beery *(Bagley)*, The Monroe Singers.

Musical comedy-drama. Source: Harold Atteridge, *Big Boy* (New York opening: 7 Jan 1925). Hoping to recoup the family fortune, the Bedfords stake their hopes on Big Boy, a horse trained for the Kentucky Derby by the ever-singing Gus, their faithful Negro jockey. Shortly before the race, Jack and Annabel return from eastern schools, bringing with them Coley Reid, Doc Wilbur (his confidant), and Steve Leslie, an English jockey. Reid persuades Jack to urge Mrs. Bedford to entrust the race to Steve, but she declines, saying Gus has served the family for generations and telling them a story (incorporated in the film and providing the opportunity for the singing of Negro spirituals) of how Gus's grandfather saved Annabel's grandmother from kidnapers in 1870. Threatening Jack with a forged check, Reid forces him to have Gus break training rules, and the trainer is dismissed. But Joe becomes suspicious and learns that Dolly, Reid's wife, is plotting against Annabel, of whom she is jealous, and that Steve plans to "throw" the race; but Gus appears, outsmarts the crooks, and wins the race. Jolson appears without blackface at the end of the film to sing "Tomorrow Is Another Day." *Jockeys. Horsetrainers. Negroes. Horseracing. Courtship. Forgery. Kentucky Derby. Horses.*

BIG BROTHER **F2.0389**
Famous Players–Lasky. *Dist* Paramount Pictures. 23 Dec **1923** [c19 Dec 1923; LP19768]. Si; b&w. 35mm. 7 reels, 7,080 ft.

Pres by Adolph Zukor, Jesse L. Lasky. *Dir* Allan Dwan. *Scen* Paul Sloane.

Cast: Tom Moore *(Jimmy Donovan)*, Edith Roberts *(Kitty Costello)*, Raymond Hatton *(Cokey Joe Miller)*, Joe King *(Big Ben Murray)*, Mickey Bennett *(Midge Murray)*, Charles Henderson *("Father Dan" Marron)*, Paul Panzer *(Mike Navarro)*, Neill Kelley *(Monk Manelli)*, William Black *(Loman Duryea, probation officer)*, Martin Faust *(Spike Doyle)*, Milton Herman *(Izzy)*, Florence Ashbrook *(Mrs. Sheean)*, Yvonne Hughes *(Navarro's girl, "Fly By Night")*, Charles Hammond *(judge)*.

Crook melodrama. Source: Rex Beach, "Big Brother," in *Big Brother, and Other Stories* (New York, 1923). When gangster Jimmy Donovan is made guardian of Midge, the 7-year-old brother of his friend Big Ben Murray, he decides to reform and rear Midge properly. The court takes custody of Midge, but Donovan proves himself by recovering a payroll stolen by some of his ex-colleagues, thereby winning Midge and Kitty, his girl. *Criminals—Rehabilitation. Guardians. Children.*

THE BIG CITY **F2.0390**
Metro-Goldwyn-Mayer Pictures. 18 Feb **1928** [c18 Feb 1928; LP25205]. Si; b&w. 35mm. 7 reels, 6,838 ft. [Copyrighted as 8 reels.]

Dir-Writ Tod Browning. *Scen* Waldemar Young. *Titl* Joe Farnham. *Photog* Henry Sharp. *Set Dsgn* Cedric Gibbons. *Film Ed* Harry Reynolds. *Wardrobe* Lucia Coulter.

Cast: Lon Chaney *(Chuck)*, Marceline Day *(Sunshine)*, James Murray *(Curly)*, Betty Compson *(Helen)*, Matthew Betz *(Red)*, John George *(The Arab)*, Virginia Pearson *(Tennessee)*, Walter Percival *(Grogan)*, Lew Short *(O'Hara)*, Eddie Sturgis *(Blinkie)*.

Crook melodrama. Chuck Collins, owner of a cabaret and master criminal, notices that a rival gang is fleecing his patrons of their jewels and cash. Chuck tricks them into handing the loot over to members of his own gang. Chuck's accomplice, Helen, owns a costume shop that is used as a blind for the gang's activity; there, real jewels can be left about in boxes and containers as if they were paste. Helen's employee, Sunshine, a candid ingenue, persuades the group—Chuck, his partner Curly, and Helen—to reform, while members of the other gang, led by a man named Red, are brought to justice. *Costumers. Criminals—Rehabilitation. Gangs. Theft. Jewels. Cabarets.*

Note: Published copyright information showing that the film has sound has not been verified.

BIG DAN **F2.0391**
Fox Film Corp. 14 Oct **1923** [c14 Oct 1923; LP19539]. Si; b&w. 35mm. 6 reels, 5,934 ft.

Pres by William Fox. *Dir* William A. Wellman. *Story-Scen* Frederick Hatton, Fanny Hatton. *Photog* Joseph August.

Cast: Charles Jones *(Dan O'Hara)*, Marian Nixon *(Dora Allen)*, Ben Hendricks *(Cyclone Morgan)*, Trilby Clark *(Mazie Williams)*, Jacqueline Gadsden *(Nellie McGee)*, Charles Coleman *(Doc Snyder)*, Lydia Yeamans Titus *(Aunt Kate Walsh)*, Monte Collins *(Tom Walsh)*, Charles Smiley *(Father Quinn)*, Harry Lonsdale *(Stephen Allen)*, Mattie Peters *(Ophelia)*, J. P. Lockney *(Pat Mayo)*, Jack Herrick *(Muggs Murphy)*.

Melodrama. Dan O'Hara, known as "Big Dan," returns from the war, and finding that his wife has left him, turns his home into a boys' camp and begins to train boxers. He meets Dora Allen, rescues her from an unwanted suitor, and gives her shelter in the camp. For a time, their relationship, which has become serious, is complicated by the intrusion of another suitor and by a woman who informs Dora that O'Hara is already married. The wife dies, however, and O'Hara wins Dora. *Veterans. Children. Social service. Boxing.*

THE BIG DIAMOND ROBBERY **F2.0392**

FBO Pictures. *Dist* RKO Productions. 13 May **1929** [c13 May 1929; LP529]. Si; b&w. 35mm. 7 reels, 6,114 ft.

Dir-Story Eugene Forde. *Screenplay* John Stuart Twist. *Titl* Randolph Bartlett. *Story* Frank Howard Clark. *Photog* Norman Devol.

Cast: Tom Mix *(Tom Markham)*, Kathryn McGuire *(Ellen Brooks)*, Frank Beal *(George Brooks)*, Martha Mattox *(Aunt Effie)*, Ernest Hilliard *(Rodney Stevens)*, Barney Furey *(Barney McGill)*, Ethan Laidlaw *(Chick)*, Tony *(himself, a horse)*.

Western melodrama. Tom Markham, foreman of an Arizona dude ranch, arrives in a metropolis to confer with George Brooks, owner of the ranch, and to accompany Brooks's daughter, Ellen, on the return trip; the night before the departure, conversation centers on the Regent diamond, which Brooks has set in a ring for Ellen. Her friend Rodney Stevens (actually leader of a gang of thieving thugs) later has his men steal the gem. After a series of encounters, Tom regains the jewel and returns it to Ellen. Later, near the ranch, Tom, disguised as a bandit, holds up the coach, and Ellen refuses to leave the vehicle; Tom pursues the runaway coach and rescues her. In making a search for the diamond, Stevens stumbles on Tom's bandit costume and informs Ellen of his masquerade, proposing that she wear the diamond so that Tom can be induced to abduct her. The plan is carried out, but Tom pursues the gang's car, disposes of the gang, and is reunited with Ellen. *Ranch foremen. Bandits. Imposture. Disguise. Courtship. Stagecoach robberies. Dude ranches. Arizona. Horses.*

THE BIG DRIVE **F2.0393**

J. P. Bohr. *Dist* Bohr Films. Apr **1928** [New York State license]. Si; b&w. 35mm. 7 reels.

Cast: Jack Harris.

Educational film(?). Although no precise information about the nature of this film has been found, there is some evidence that it is concerned with World War I. *World War I.*

Note: Country of origin undetermined.

THE BIG FIGHT **F2.0394**

James Cruze Productions. *Dist* Sono Art–World Wide Pictures. 1 Sep **1930** [c27 Dec 1930; LP1857]. Sd; b&w. 35mm. 7 reels, 5,850 ft.

Supv James Cruze. *Dir* Walter Lang. *Cont–Screen Adapt* Walter Woods. *Photog* Jackson Rose. *Mus & Lyr* Lynn Cowan, Paul Titsworth. *Rec Engr* Fred J. Lau, W. C. Smith.

Cast: Lola Lane *(Shirley)*, Ralph Ince *(Chuck)*, Guinn Williams *(Tiger)*, Stepin Fetchit *(Spot)*, Wheeler Oakman *(Steve)*, James Eagle *(Lester)*, Robert E. O'Connor *(detective)*, Edna Bennett *(Winnie)*, Tony Stabeneau *(Battler)*, Larry McGrath *(Pinkie)*, Frank Jonasson *(Berrili)*.

Melodrama. Source: Milton Herbert Gropper and Max Marcin, *The Big Fight* (New York opening: 18 Sep 1928). Shirley, a manicurist, is in love with Tiger, a famous prizefighter, though Steve, his manager, creates mistrust between the two. Shirley discovers that her brother, Lester, has lost a large bet to gangster leader Chuck and that he will be killed unless he pays off. She appeals to Tiger; he offers him the money, but Shirley refuses to accept it. At Chuck's nightclub, he is told that Lester has killed Whitey, Chuck's bodyguard, and Chuck, in league with Steve, informs Shirley that he will not frame Lester if she will visit Tiger's dressing room before the fight and offer him some drugged water; when she fails to do so, Steve delivers the potion to the ringside. During the fight, Chuck and his gang are pursued by the police, and he is fatally shot. To her joy, Shirley finds that Tiger has won the fight and that pure water was substituted accidentally by Spot, the waterboy. *Manicurists. Prizefighters. Fight managers. Brother-sister relationship. Gangsters.*

BIG GAME **F2.0395**

Metro Pictures. 16 Aug **1921** [c11 Aug 1921; LP16863]. Si; b&w. 35mm. 6 reels.

Dir Dallas M. Fitzgerald. *Adapt* Edward T. Lowe, Jr. *Photog* Jackson Rose. *Art Dir* Sidney Ullman.

Cast: May Allison *(Eleanor Winthrop)*, Forrest Stanley *(Larry Winthrop)*, Edward Cecil *(Jean St. Jean)*, Zeffie Tilbury *(Aunt Sarah Winthrop)*, William Elmer *("Spike" McGafney)*, Sidney D'Albrook *(Henri Baptiste)*.

Society melodrama. Source: Willard Robertson and Kilbourne Gordon, *Big Game* (New York opening: 21 Jan 1920). Larry Winthrop, the pampered son of an aristocratic Boston family, is loved by his wife, Eleanor, but she wants him to prove himself to her as a man. She accompanies him when he is called to Canada on business and there meets Jean St. Jean, a Canadian guide who fancies himself irresistible to the ladies. Hoping to make her husband jealous, Eleanor engages Jean to go with them to a cabin in the woods. The three are snowbound there, and when Jean defies Larry and seizes Eleanor, the husband loses all signs of cowardice and finds himself. Jean is whipped, and Eleanor is delighted that Larry is at last a "real man." *Bostonians. Aristocrats. Guides. Cowardice. Canadian Northwest.*

BIG GAME HUNTING **F2.0396**

Chester Educational Productions. *Dist* Bell Pictures. 10 Dec **1929** [New York State license]. Si; b&w. 35mm. 6 reels.

Travelog(?). No information about the precise nature of this film has been found. *Big game.*

THE BIG HOP **F2.0397**

Buck Jones Productions. 31 Aug **1928**. Sd eff; b&w. 35mm. 7 reels, 6,550-6,750 ft. [Also si.]

Dir James W. Horne. *Story-Scen* J. B. Mack. *Titl* Donn McElwaine. *Photog* Al Siegler. *Film Ed* Donn McElwaine.

Cast: Buck Jones *(Buck Bronson)*, Jobyna Ralston *(June Halloway)*, Ernest Hilliard *(Ben Barnett)*, Charles K. French *(Buck's father)*, Charles Clary *(June's father)*, Duke Lee *(ranch foreman)*, Edward Hearne *(pilot)*, Jack Dill *(mechanic)*.

Action melodrama. "Buck starts out as a failure as a ranch hand and winds up a failure as an aviator, but only because of the dire villainy of his society rival for the girl's hand. This girl, who meets Buck as he descends from a parachute jump immediately becomes interested in him and persuades her wealthy father to back Buck and his pal in the Honolulu [airplane] race. The Villainous rival sees to it that the pilot pal is drugged just before the race starts, so Buck, an inexperienced pilot is compelled to handle the ship on the perilous journey. A feed pipe goes amiss a thousand miles at sea and Buck and his pal crash. They are picked up by a passing ship, but the pal is quite dead. Buck, given up for lost, returns unexpectedly, routs the villain and wins the girl." (*Motion Picture News*, 6 Oct 1928, p1097.) *Aviators. Parachuting. Sea rescue. Airplanes. Airplane racing. Honolulu.*

THE BIG HOUSE **F2.0398**

Cosmopolitan Productions. *Dist* Metro-Goldwyn-Mayer Distributing Corp. 21 Jun **1930** [c19 Jun 1930; LP1367]. Sd (Movietone); b&w. 35mm. 10 reels, 7,901 ft.

Dir George Hill. *Dir Foreign Versions* Paul Fejos, Ward Wing. *Story-Scen-Dial* Frances Marion. *Adtl Dial* Joe Farnham, Martin Flavin. *Photog* Harold Wenstrom. *Art Dir* Cedric Gibbons. *Film Ed* Blanche Sewell. *Rec Engr* Robert Shirley, Douglas Shearer.

Cast: Chester Morris *(Morgan)*, Wallace Beery *(Butch)*, Lewis Stone *(warden)*, Robert Montgomery *(Kent)*, Leila Hyams *(Anne)*, George F. Marion *(Pop)*, J. C. Nugent *(Mr. Marlowe)*, Karl Dane *(Olsen)*, De Witt Jennings *(Wallace)*, Mathew Betz *(Gopher)*, Claire McDowell *(Mrs. Marlowe)*, Robert Emmett O'Connor *(Donlin)*, Tom Kennedy *(Uncle Jed)*, Tom Wilson *(Sandy)*, Eddie Foyer *(Dopey)*, Roscoe Ates *(Putnam)*, Fletcher Norton *(Oliver)*.

Melodrama. Kent Marlowe, charged with manslaughter while driving in an intoxicated state, becomes cellmate with Butch and Morgan, who are imprisoned, respectively, for homicide and forgery. Morgan manages to escape through the mortuary by taking the place of a convict about to be buried; he finds refuge with Anne, Kent's sister, who operates a bookshop, and gradually they fall in love. He is recaptured and returned to prison, but he determines to go straight for the sake of the girl; unrest and revolt are brewing in the prison, however, as a result of intolerable living conditions, and Morgan learns that Butch is planning a riot but is unsuccessful in dissuading him. The plan is thwarted when Kent tips off the warden; and after a lenthy conflict between prisoners and guards, the riot is quelled by Morgan's intervention and he is paroled. *Convicts. Criminals—Rehabilitation. Prison escapes. Brother-sister relationship. Manslaughter. Prison revolts. Prison escapes. Bookshops.*

Note: German and French versions were directed by Paul Fejos, and Ward Wing directed a Spanish version.

BIG HOUSE **F2.0399**

Cosmopolitan Productions. *Dist* Metro-Goldwyn-Mayer Distributing Corp. **1930.** Sd (Movietone); b&w. 35mm. [Length undetermined.]

Dir Paul Fejos. *Dial* Yves Mirande.

Cast: Charles Boyer *(Fred Morgan)*, André Berley *(Butch)*, André Burgères *(Kent)*, Mona Goya *(Anne)*, George Mauloy *(The Prison Warden)*,

Rolla Norman *(The Chief Trustee)*.

Melodrama. French-language version of *The Big House*, q. v. *Convicts. Brother-sister relationship. Manslaughter. Courtship. Prison revolts. Prison escapes. Bookshops.*

Note: Other production credits are probably the same as for *The Big House*.

THE BIG KILLING **F2.0400**

Paramount Famous Lasky Corp. 19 May **1928** [c19 May 1928; LP25272]. Si; b&w. 35mm. 6 reels, 5,805 or 5,930 ft.

Pres by Adolph Zukor, Jesse L. Lasky. *Prod-Dir* F. Richard Jones. *Assoc Prod* B. P. Schulberg. *Scen* Gilbert Pratt, Frank Butler. *Titl* Herman J. Mankiewicz. *Story* Grover Jones. *Photog* Alfred Gilks. *Ed in Ch* B. F. Zeidman. *Asst Film Ed* William Shea.

Cast: Wallace Beery *(Powder-Horn Pete)*, Raymond Hatton *(Dead-Eye Dan)*, Anders Randolph *(Old Man Beagle)*, Mary Brian *(Beagle's daughter)*, Gardner James *(Jim Hicks)*, Lane Chandler *(George Hicks)*, Paul McAllister *(Old Man Hicks)*, James Mason *(Beagle Son No. 1)*, Ralph Yearsley *(Beagle Son No. 2)*, Ethan Laidlaw *(Beagle Son No. 3)*, Leo Willis *(Beagle Son No. 4)*, Buck Moulton *(Beagle Son No. 5)*, Robert Kortman *(Beagle Son No. 6)*, Walter James *(sheriff)*, Roscoe Ward *(barker)*.

Comedy. Two mountain families, the Beagles and the Hickses, who have had a life long feud, are finally united through the aid of Powder-Horn Pete and Dead-Eye Dan, two ex–circus men hired by the Beagles to shoot up the other family. Afraid of firearms, the "sharpshooters" resort to other tactics to get the families to agree to the marriage of Jim Hicks to Beagle's daughter. The feud is ended with the arbitrators themselves being run out of the valley. *Sharpshooters. Mountain life. Feuds. Circus. Phobias.*

BIG MONEY **F2.0401**

Pathé Exchange. 26 Oct **1930** [c26 Oct 1930; LP1684]. Sd (Photophone); b&w. 35mm. 8 reels, 7,698 ft.

Prod E. B. Derr. *Dir* Russell Mack. *Screenplay-Dial* Walter De Leon, Russell Mack. *Story* Walter De Leon. *Camera* John Mescall. *Art Dir* Carroll Clark. *Film Ed* Joseph Kane. *Mus Dir* Josiah Zuro. *Rec Engr* Charles O'Loughlin, Tom Carman. *Asst Dir* Robert Fellows. *Cost* Gwen Wakeling.

Cast: Eddie Quillan *(Eddie)*, Robert Armstrong *(Ace)*, James Gleason *(Tom)*, Margaret Livingston *(Mae)*, Miriam Seegar *(Joan McCall)*, Robert Edeson *(Mr. McCall)*, Dorothy Christy *(Leila)*, G. Pat Collins *(Smiley)*, Morgan Wallace *(Durkin)*, Myrtis Crinley *(Flora)*, Robert Gleckler *(Monk)*, Charles Sellon *(Bradley)*, Kit Guard *(Lefty)*, Johnny Morris *(Weejee)*, Frank Sabini *(waiter)*, Harry Semels *(waiter)*, Clara Palmer *(society woman)*, Ed Deering *(detective)*, Spec O'Donnell *(elevator boy)*, Mona Rico *(maid)*, Murray Smith *(Izzy)*, Harry Tyler *(Wendell)*, Jack McDonald *(butler)*, Zita Moulton *(Michael)*, Jack Hanlon *(office boy)*, Richard Cramer *(Detroit Dan)*, Lewis Wilder *(Maurice Black)*.

Comedy-drama. Eddie, a messenger boy in the George McCall brokerage house, is dispatched to deliver $50,000 in currency to the bank just before before closing time, but his weakness for tossing the dice results in his arriving too late; unable to return it to the company safe, he is forced to take it home. A jokingly intended dinner invitation extended to the boss's daughter is accepted, and when Joan guides Eddie to a restaurant beyond his means, he is forced to delve into the company funds. On the way home he is waylaid by two crooks, Monk and Lefty, and in the ensuing chase Eddie rides the service elevator of a hotel to a room where he gets involved with Ace Carter, a notorious gambler from whom he wins a large sum. Later, when Joan discovers that Eddie is a gambler, she refuses his marriage proposal. At a poker game, Jim Durkin is shot by Monk, the fourth player; Eddie then decides to reform, refuses to gamble, but is arraigned as a witness to the murder; and Durkin's brother, Skip, comes to get revenge but is apprehended after forcing Monk to confess. Eddie is released and reconciled with Joan. *Messengers. Brokers. Gangsters. Gambling. Embezzlement. Speculation. Murder.*

BIG NEWS **F2.0402**

Pathé Exchange. 7 Sep **1929** [c26 Sep 1929; LP735]. Sd (Photophone); b&w. 35mm. 7 reels, 6,028 ft. [Also si; 6,950 ft.]

Dir Gregory La Cava. *Dial Dir* Frank Reicher. *Screenplay* Walter De Leon. *Dial* Frank Reicher. *Adapt* Jack Jungmeyer. *Story* George Brooks. *Photog* Arthur Miller. *Sd* D. A. Cutler, Clarence M. Wickes. *Asst Dir* Paul Jones. *Prod Mgr* Lucky Humberstone.

Cast: Robert Armstrong *(Steve)*, Carol Lombard *(Marg)*, Tom Kennedy *(Ryan)*, Warner Richmond *(district attorney)*, Wade Boteler *(O'Neil)*, Sam Hardy *(Reno)*, Robert Dudley *(telegraph editor)*, Louis Payne *(Hensel)*, James Donlan *(Deke)*, Cupid Ainesworth *(society editor)*, Fred Bahrle *(elevator man)*, Gertrude Sutton *(Helen)*, Colin Chase *(Birn)*, Charles Sellon *(Addison)*.

Mystery drama. Reporter Steve Banks is fired from his job and threatened with divorce by his wife, Margaret, for inattention. Actually Steve is investigating a dope ring headed, he believes, by Reno, owner of a speakeasy and a friend of Addison, the newspaper owner. Banks elicits a confession from Rose Peretti, one of Reno's agents, and deposits it with Addison. Reno murders Addison, destroys the confession, and leaves evidence that implicates Banks. A Dictaphone record Addison was making when he was struck down exonerates Banks and convicts Reno. Banks is rewarded with restoration of his job and the return of his wife. *Reporters. Gangsters. Murder. Speakeasies. Narcotics. Newspapers. Dictographs. Documentation.*

THE BIG NOISE **F2.0403**

First National Pictures. 25 Mar **1928** [c20 Mar 1928; LP25083]. Si; b&w. 35mm. 8 reels, 7,412 ft.

Pres by Robert T. Kane. *Prod-Dir* Allan Dwan. *Adapt-Scen* Tom J. Geraghty. *Titl* George Marion, Jr. *Story* Ben Hecht. *Camera* Ted Pahle. *Film Ed* Doris Farrington, Terry Morse.

Cast: Chester Conklin *(John Sloval)*, Alice White *(Sophie Sloval)*, Bodil Rosing *(Ma Sloval)*, Sam Hardy *(Philip Hurd)*, Jack Egan *(Bill Hedges)*, Ned Sparks *(William Howard)*, David Torrence *(managing editor)*.

Comedy-drama. John Sloval, a New York subway guard, would like to marry his daughter, Sophie, to Philip Hurd, a Coney Island concessionaire, but she is in love with Bill Hedges, son of an upstate dairy farmer. Sloval arranges a wedding in exchange for a quarter interest in the concession, but preparations are interrupted when he falls off a subway platform and is nearly run over by a train. A newspaper capitalizes on the old man's injury to bring subway reform and to promote its candidate. Sloval goes to campaign headquarters after the newspaper's candidate is elected to find that they merely used him for campaign fodder. Dejected, he returns home to find Sophie and Bill, newly married, inviting him to become assistant manager at the dairy farm. *Subway guards. Concessionaires. Farmers. Subways. Politics. Newspapers. Dairying. New York City. Coney Island.*

BIG PAL **F2.0404**

William Russell Productions. *For* Royal Pictures. *Dist* Henry Ginsberg Distributing Corp. Sep **1925** [c19 Oct 1925; LP21921]. Si; b&w. 35mm. 5 reels, 4,543 ft.

Dir John G. Adolfi. *Story* Jules Furthman. *Descriptive Filmusic Guide* Michael Hoffman.

Cast: William Russell *(Dan Williams)*, Julanne Johnston *(Helen Truscott)*, Mary Carr *(Mary Williams)*, Mickey Bennett *(Johnny Williams)*, Hayden Stevenson *(Tim Williams)*, William Bailey.

Melodrama. Judge Truscott's daughter Helen spurns society life for social work in the settlement districts. She is saved from a runaway horse by heavyweight contender Dan Williams, and they become friends. Dan's nephew Johnny is abducted on the eve of the championship fight and threatened with harm unless Dan stands for a knockout in the fifth round. As the fifth round approaches, Helen appears with Johnny, who has escaped: Dan knocks his opponent out and wins the championship and Helen's hand. *Social workers. Prizefighters. Boxing. Abduction.*

THE BIG PARADE **F2.0405**

Metro-Goldwyn-Mayer Pictures. 5 Nov **1925** [Los Angeles premiere; released 10 Sep 1927; c10 Sep 1927; LP24384]. Si; b&w with col sequences (Technicolor). 35mm. 13 reels, 12,550 ft. [Release version: 12 reels, 11,519 ft.]

Dir King Vidor. *Scen* Harry Behn. *Titl* Joseph W. Farnham. *Story* Laurence Stallings. *Photog* John Arnold. *Art Dir* Cedric Gibbons, James Basevi. *Film Ed* Hugh Wynn. *Mus Score* William Axt, David Mendoza. *Wardrobe* Ethel P. Chaffin.

Cast: John Gilbert *(James Apperson)*, Renée Adorée *(Mélisande)*, Hobart Bosworth *(Mr. Apperson)*, Claire McDowell *(Mrs. Apperson)*, Claire Adams *(Justyn Reed)*, Robert Ober *(Harry)*, Tom O'Brien *(Bull)*, Karl Dane *(Slim)*, Rosita Marstini *(French mother)*.

War drama. Lazy Jim Apperson, denounced by his father, a hard-working southern aristocrat, and coaxed by his sweetheart, Justyn, enlists when war is declared and is billeted overseas with his buddies, Bull and Slim, in a French farmhouse. All three take an interest in Mélisande, the owner's daughter, but romance soon develops between her and Jim. At a party given by the villagers, Jim and his buddies engage in a melee in the wine cellar; the following day, when his company moves out, Mêlisande seeks out Jim in a frenzy of despair to bid him farewell. Slim and Bull are killed in action, and when Jim charges a German, both are wounded; a flare reveals the enemy to be merely a boy, and Jim offers him his canteen. Jim awakens in a hospital to find his leg bandaged, but he escapes to Mêlisande's farm only to find it destroyed. He returns home after the war, finds Justyn involved with his brother, Conrad, and returns to France to find Mêlisande. *Southerners. Friendship. Courtship. World War I. France.*

THE BIG PARTY **F2.0406**

Fox Film Corp. 23 Feb **1930** [c23 Jan 1930; LP1052]. Sd (Movietone); b&w. 35mm. 7 reels, 6,520 ft. [Also si.]

Pres by William Fox. *Dir* John Blystone. *Story-Scen-Dial* Harlan Thompson. *Photog* George Schneiderman. *Sets* Jack Schulze. *Film Ed* Edwin Robbins. *Song: "Nobody Knows But Rosie"* James Hanley, Joseph McCarthy. *Song: "I'm Climbing Up a Rainbow"* Edward G. Nelson, Harry Pease. *Songs: "Bluer Than Blue Over You," "Good For Nothing But Love"* William Kernell, Harlan Thompson. *Rec Engr* W. W. Lindsay. *Asst Dir* Jasper Blystone. *Wardrobe* Sophie Wachner.

Cast: Dixie Lee *(Kitty Collins)*, Frank Albertson *(Jack Hunter)*, Walter Catlett *(Mr. Goldfarb)*, Richard Keene *(Eddie Perkins)*, "Whispering" Jack Smith *(Billy Greer)*, Sue Carol *(Flo Jenkins)*, Douglas Gilmore *(Allen Weatherby)*, Charles Judels *(Dupuy)*, Ilka Chase *(Mrs. Dupuy)*, Elizabeth Patterson *(Mrs. Goldfarb)*, Dorothy Brown *(Virginia Gates)*.

Society comedy-drama. Kitty Collins, who works as a singing sales clerk in the music section of a department store, is dismissed for insulting a customer who annoys her. Through Flo Jenkins she obtains a position in an exclusive dressmaking establishment operated by Mr. Goldfarb and Monsieur Dupuy, married men who are constantly flirting with other women. To the displeasure of her sweetheart, Jack, Kitty is obliged to entertain out-of-town buyers; and though she comes to live in luxury, she finds her new life not worth the price and returns to the boy she loves and a simple life. *Singers. Salesclerks. Modistes. Buyers. Wealth. Department stores.*

THE BIG POND **F2.0407**

Paramount-Publix Corp. 3 May **1930** [c6 May 1930; LP1278]. Sd (Movietone); b&w. 35mm. 8 reels, 6,984 ft.

Prod Monta Bell. *Dir* Hobart Henley. *Stage Dir* Bertram Harrison. *Scen* Robert Presnell, Garrett Fort. *Dial* Preston Sturges. *Camera* George Folsey. *Film Ed* Emma Hill, Emma Hill. *Song: "Livin' in the Sunlight, Lovin' in the Moonlight"* Al Lewis, Al Sherman. *Song: "This Is My Lucky Day"* Lew Brown, B. G. De Sylva, Ray Henderson. *Songs: "Mia Cara," "You Brought a New Kind of a Love to Me"* Irving Kahal, Pierre Norman, Sammy Fain. *Mus Arr* John W. Green. *Rec Engr* Ernest F. Zatorsky.

Cast: Maurice Chevalier *(Pierre Mirande)*, Claudette Colbert *(Barbara Billings)*, George Barbier *(Mr. Billings)*, Marion Ballou *(Mrs. Billings)*, Andrée Corday *(Toinette)*, Frank Lyon *(Ronnie)*, Nat Pendleton *(Pat O'Day)*, Elaine Koch *(Jennie)*.

Comedy-drama. Source: George Middleton and A. E. Thomas, *The Big Pond* (New York opening: 21 Aug 1928). Pierre Mirande, son of an impoverished French family, makes a living by acting as guide to Mrs. Billings and her daughter, Barbara, tourists in Venice. Although Barbara falls in love with him, her suitor (Ronnie) and her father see in him a fortune-hunting foreigner, and accordingly they offer him a job in Mr. Billings' chewing gum factory in New York. Forced to live in a dingy boardinghouse, Pierre is given the toughest work in the plant, but Barbara assures him that bluff and fast thinking are necessities in American business. With his humorous songs, he captivates his landlady, Toinette, and the maid, Jennie, but falls asleep on the night he is expected to attend Barbara's party. Wrongfully accused of spilling rum on some chewing gum samples, Pierre is discharged; but he is reinstated and promoted when he sells the idea of rum-flavored chewing gum with his own advertising lyrics. Insulted, Barbara plans to marry Ronnie, but Pierre kidnaps her aboard a speedboat. ... *Guides. Fortune hunters. Landladies. French. Tourists. Courtship. Business management. Chewing gum. Boardinghouses. Venice.*

Note: Simultaneously, a French version, *La Grande Mare*, q. v., was filmed. In both versions, Chevalier sings "You Brought a New Kind of Love to Me" and "Livin' in the Sunlight, Lovin' in the Moonlight."

THE BIG PUNCH **F2.0408**

Fox Film Corp. 30 Jan **1921** [c30 Jan 1921; LP16427]. Si; b&w. 35mm. 5 reels.

Pres by William Fox. *Dir* Jack Ford. *Story-Scen* Jules G. Furthman. *Photog* Frank B. Good.

Cast: Buck Jones *(Buck)*, Barbara Bedford *(Hope Standish)*, George Siegmann *(Flash McGraw)*, Jack Curtis *(Jed, Buck's brother)*, Jack McDonald, Al Fremont *(Jed's pals)*, Jennie Lee *(Buck's mother)*, Edgar Jones *(The Sheriff)*, Irene Hunt *(The Dance Hall Girl)*, Eleanore Gilmore *(Salvation Army Girl)*.

Melodrama. Buck, who is preparing to enter a theological seminary, aids his brother and some friends who are fleeing from justice, and thus implicated he is sent to prison for 2 years. There he meets again Hope Standish, a Salvation Army girl who had interested him. Returning home, he meets the old district circuit rider and promises to continue the circuit rider's work when he dies. The brother escapes from prison and is converted by Buck, who falls in love with Hope. *Ministerial students. Circuit riders. Brothers. Fugitives. Salvation Army.*

THE BIG SHOT *see* **DOUGHBOYS**

THE BIG SHOW **F2.0409**

Miller Brothers Productions. *Dist* Associated Exhibitors. 11 Apr **1926** [c29 Mar 1926; LU22543]. Si; b&w. 35mm. 6 reels, 5,385 ft.

Dir George Terwilliger. *Story* L. Case Russell. *Photog* David W. Gobbett.

Cast: John Lowell *(Bill)*, Evangeline Russell *(Ruth Gordon)*, F. Serrano Keating *(Norman Brackett)*, Jane Thomas *(Marian Kearney)*, Col. Joseph Miller *(Col. Jim Kearney)*, Dan Dix *(Pedro)*, Alice Lecacheur *(Fifi)*, Madi Blatherwick *(Dolly)*.

Melodrama. Bill, a strong, silent stranger, joins a Wild West show and establishes himself as a hero by saving Ruth Gordon, the elephant girl, from a train fire. Pedro, the clown, is his only enemy. Norman Brackett, young oil millionaire and friend of Kearney, the show manager, wins Ruth's admiration, and she accepts his proposal. Norman recognizes Bill to be his brother, whom he swindled out of his oil lands during the war, but he is unaware that Bill has a confession, exposing his fraud, from a confederate of Norman's. When Norman feeds Ruth's elephant some tobacco, the elephant interrupts a marriage ceremony between Marian Kearney and Norman and then kills Norman. Bill explains Norman's treachery and confesses his love for Ruth, with whom he finds happiness. *Brothers. Clowns. Millionaires. Swindlers. Wild West shows. Oil lands. Elephants.*

BIG STAKES **F2.0410**

Metropolitan Pictures. *Dist* East Coast Productions. 15 Aug **1922.** Si; b&w. 35mm. 5 reels, 4,650 ft.

Pres by Franklyn E. Backer. *Dir* Clifford S. Elfelt. *Scen* Frank Howard Clark.

Cast: J. B. Warner *(Jim Gregory)*, Elinor Fair *(Señorita Mercedes Aloyez)*, Les Bates *("Bully" Brand)*, Willie May Carson *(Mary)*, H. S. Karr *(Skinny Fargo)*, Robert Grey *(El Capitân Montaya)*.

Western drama. Source: Earl Wayland Bowman, "High Stakes," in *American Magazine* (90:57–59, Sep 1920). Although she is betrothed to Captain Montaya, Mercedes Aloyez, the daughter of a wealthy Mexican rancher, shows an interest in newcomer Jim Gregory. The feeling is mutual, and Gregory earns Montaya's enmity. The captain surprises Mercedes and Gregory in a rendezvous, threatens to loose a dangerous reptile on the cowboy, but instead finds himself wagering his life against Gregory's with jumping beans. A victorious Gregory spares Montaya but passes to Mercedes the choice of who will live. This situation is interrupted by a request for help from Mary, a waitress, who has been captured by night riders. Gregory leaves Mercedes and Montaya to rescue and find happiness with Mary. *Cowboys. Mexicans. Waitresses.*

BIG STUNT **F2.0411**

Charles R. Seeling Productions. *Dist* Aywon Film Corp. Nov **1925.** Si; b&w. 35mm. 5 reels, 4,800 ft.

Cast: Big Boy Williams.

Western melodrama. No information about the precise nature of this film has been found.

BIG TIMBER **F2.0412**

Universal Pictures. 7 Sep **1924** [c8 Jul 1924; LP20388]. Si; b&w. 35mm. 5 reels, 4,650 ft.

Dir William J. Craft. *Scen* George Melford. *Scen? (see note)* Wyndham Gittens. *Adapt* Isadore Bernstein. *Photog* Jackson Rose.

Cast: William Desmond *(Walter Sandry)*, Olive Hasbrouck *(Sally O'Hara)*, Betty Francisco *(Poppy Ordway)*, Ivor McFadden *(John Daly)*, Lydia Yeamans Titus *(Ma Daly)*, Albert J. Smith *(Fred Hampden)*.

Melodrama. Source: Vingie E. Roe, *The Heart of the Night Wind* (New York, 1913). Walter Sandry, holder of a mortgage on timber lands in the Pacific Northwest, arrives to claim his property. He comes into conflict with a rival company and with lumberjacks influenced by their foreman, Hampden, whom he later beats in a fight. After putting out a big forest fire, Sandry wins the hand of a local girl, Sally O'Hara. *Pacific Northwest. Lumbering. Mortgages. Forest fires.*

Note: Several sources give Wyndham Gittens as scenarist; Universal records have been followed.

BIG TIME **F2.0413**

Fox Film Corp. ca7 Sep **1929** [New York premiere; released 29 Sep; c14 Sep 1929; LP679]. Sd (Movietone); b&w. 35mm. 8 reels, 7,480 or 7,815 ft.

Pres by William Fox. *Assoc Prod* Chandler Sprague. *Dir* Kenneth Hawks. *Stage Dir* A. H. Van Buren. *Dial* Sidney Lanfield, William K. Wells. *Adapt* Sidney Lanfield. *Photog* L. William O'Connell. *Film Ed* Al De Gaetano. *Song: "Nobody Knows You Like I Do"* Sidney Lanfield. *Sd* Harold Hobson. *Asst Dir* Max Gold. *Cost* Sophie Wachner.

Cast: Lee Tracy *(Eddie Burns)*, Mae Clarke *(Lily Clark)*, Daphne Pollard *(Sybil)*, Josephine Dunn *(Gloria)*, Stepin Fetchit *(Eli)*, John Ford *(himself, a director)*.

Melodrama. Source: William Wallace Smith, "Little Ledna," in *Hearst's International Cosmopolitan* (81:112–114, Aug 1926). The vaudeville husband-and-wife team of Eddie Burns, a comedian, and Lily Clark, a singer, breaks up when a schemer named Gloria slips into the act while Lily is out having a baby. Eddie's act goes from bad to worse, while, on her own, Lily becomes a motion picture star. Eddie drifts to Hollywood, gets into one of Lily's pictures as an extra, and is reunited with her. *Actors. Singers. Vamps. Motion picture extras. Vaudeville. Motion pictures. Hollywood.*

BIG TOWN IDEAS **F2.0414**

Fox Film Corp. 5 Jun **1921** [c5 Jun 1921]. Si; b&w. 35mm. 5 reels, 4,200 ft.

Pres by William Fox. *Dir* Carl Harbaugh. *Story-Scen* John Montague. *Photog* Otto Brautigan.

Cast: Eileen Percy *(Fan Tilden)*, Kenneth Gibson *(Alan Dix)*, Jimmie Parrott *(Spick Sprague)*, Lon Poff *(deputy)*, Laura La Plante *(Molly Dorn)*, Leo Sulky *(George Small)*, Harry De Roy *(bald-headed man)*, Lefty James *(warden)*, Larry Bowes *(governor)*, Paul Kamp *(grocer's boy)*, Paul Cazeneuve *(show manager)*, Wilson Hummell *(chef)*, Jess Aldridge *(governor's bodyguard; see note)*.

Comedy. Fan Tilden, a waitress in a smalltown railway station restaurant, longs for the big city. When a young man, convicted as a bond thief, arrives on his way to prison, Fan decides he is innocent and determines to help him. She gets a job in the chorus of the local prison show and during the performance helps him escape. She then goes after the real crooks, recovers the bonds, foils the warden's searching for the escaped convict, intercedes with the governor for a pardon, and proves the young man's innocence. *Waitresses. Thieves. State governors. Prisons. Smalltown life. Theater—Amateur. Prison escapes.*

Note: It has not been confirmed that Jess Aldridge is the same as Jessie J. Aldriche.

BIG TOWN ROUND-UP **F2.0415**

Fox Film Corp. 26 Jun **1921** [c3 Jul 1921; LP16744]. Si; b&w. 35mm. 5 reels, 4,249 ft.

Pres by William Fox. *Dir-Scen* Lynn Reynolds. *Photog* Ben Kline.

Cast: Tom Mix *(Larry McBride)*, Gilbert Holmes *(Pee Wee, "The Runt")*, Ora Carew *(Alice Beaumont)*, Harry Dunkinson *(Luther Beaumont)*, Laura La Plante *(Mildred Hart)*, William Buckley *(Rodney Curtis)*, William Elmer *(Jerry Casey)*, William Crinley *(Tim Johnson)*.

Melodrama. Source: William MacLeod Raine, *Big-Town Round-Up* (Boston, 1920). Alice Beaumont, daughter of a San Francisco capitalist, captures the attentions of rancher Larry McBride by pretending to have been bitten by a rattlesnake in the Arizona mountains, and they become good friends. On the way to visit Alice, Larry tosses gangster Jerry Casey off the train for forcing his attentions on Mildred Hart, a country girl, and he is later her champion in a San Francisco cabaret. There Larry meets Rodney Curtis, a youth who wants to marry Alice for her money. Collaborating with Casey, they plan to frame Larry on a murder charge, but Alice's father reveals Curtis as the killer. Alice and Larry decide to marry, as do his partner Pee Wee and Mildred. *Ranchers. Gangsters. Murder. Frameup. Snakes. Arizona. San Francisco.*

THE BIG TRAIL **F2.0416**

Fox Film Corp. 24 Oct **1930** [New York premiere; released 1 Nov; c30 Sep 1930; LP1683]. Sd (Movietone); b&w. 35mm and 70mm (Grandeur). 13-14 reels, 14,200 ft. [Grandeur version; 11,314 ft, standard version.]

Dir Raoul Walsh. *Screenplay-Dial* Jack Peabody, Marie Boyle, Florence Postal. *Scen* Fred Serser. *Story* Hal G. Evarts. *Photog* Lucien Andriot, Don Anderson, Bill McDonald, Roger Sherman, Bobby Mack, Henry Pollack. *Grandeur Camera* Arthur Edeson, Dave Ragin, Sol Halprin, Curt Fetters, Max Cohn, Harry Smith, L. Kunkel, Harry Dawe. *Art Dir* Harold Miles. *Film Ed* Jack Dennis. *Incidental Mus* Arthur Kay. *Song: "Song of the Big Trail"* Joseph McCarthy, James F. Hanley. *Ch Sd Tech* Donald Flick, George Leverett. *Sd Rec* Bill Brent, Paul Heihly. *Asst Dir* Ewing Scott, Sid Bowen, Clay Crapnell, George Walsh, Virgil Hart, Earl Rettig. *Prod Mgr* Archibald Buchanan. *Prod Asst* Jack Padgen, Joe Flores. *Master of Wardrobe* Earl Moser. *Makeup* Jack Dawn, Louise Sloane. *Stills* Frank Powolny. *Props* Don Greenwood, Tom Plews. *Ch Tech* Donald Flick, Louis Witte. *Ch Carpenter* Les Shaw. *Ch Electrn* L. E. Barber. *Bus Mgr* Ben Wurtzel, George Busch.

Cast: John Wayne *(Breck Coleman)*, Marguerite Churchill *(Ruth Cameron)*, El Brendel *(Gussie)*, Tully Marshall *(Zeke)*, [Frederick] Tyrone Power *(Red Flack)*, David Rollins *(Dave Cameron)*, Ian Keith *(Bill Thorpe)*, Frederick Burton *(Pa Bascom)*, Russ Powell *(Windy Bill)*, Charles Stevens *(Lopez)*, Louise Carver *(Gussie's mother-in-law)*, William V. Mong *(Wellmore)*, Dodo Newton *(Abigail)*, Ward Bond *(Sid Bascom)*, Marcia Harris *(Mrs. Riggs)*, Marjorie Leet *(Mary Riggs)*, Emslie Emerson *(Sairey)*, Frank Rainboth *(Ohio man)*, Andy Shufford *(Ohio man's son)*, Helen Parrish *(Honey Girl)*, Jack Peabody *(Bill Gillis)*, Gertrude Van Lent, Lucille Van Lent *(sisters from Missouri)*, De Witt Jennings *(boat captain)*, Alphonz Ethier *(Marshall)*.

Western spectacular. A wagon train of eastern pioneers leaves from Westport, Mississippi, to travel the Oregon Trail and to extend the boundaries of the American Republic to the Pacific Northwest. Their leader is scout Breck Coleman, who has pledged to avenge the death of a trapper friend. En route, the travelers experience a buffalo hunt, the treacherous fording of a river, a snowstorm, an Indian attack on the wagons, and the lowering of wagons, cattle, women, and children over a mountainside to pick up the trail to the West. Breck is enamored of Ruth Cameron, though he almost loses her to Bill Thorpe, and gradually establishes that Red Flack is the murderer of his friend; Thorpe, under Red's influence, tries to kill Breck but is himself shot. After reaching the Oregon country, Breck sets out in a snowstorm to avenge his pal's death and ultimately brings the villain to his end. *Pioneers. Scouts—Frontier. Indians of North America. Revenge. Courtship. Oregon Trail. Mississippi. Oregon. Blizzards. Buffalo.*

BIGGER THAN BARNUM'S **F2.0417**

R-C Pictures. *Dist* Film Booking Offices of America. 15 Aug **1926** [c10 Jul 1926; LP22989]. Si; b&w. 35mm. 6 reels, 5,391 ft.

Pres by Joseph P. Kennedy. *Dir* Ralph Ince. *Cont* J. Grubb Alexander. *Story* Arthur Guy Empey. *Camera* J. O. Taylor. *Asst Dir* Doran Cox.

Cast: Ralph Lewis *(Peter Blandin)*, George O'Hara *(Robert Blandin)*, Viola Dana *(Juanita Calles)*, Ralph Ince *(Carl Ravelle)*, Lucille Mendez *(Princess Bonita)*, Dan Makarenko *(Jack Ranglin)*, George Holt *(Bill Hartnett)*, William Knight *(ringmaster)*, Rhody Hathaway *(doctor)*.

Melodrama. To enliven business, a circus manager orders a tightrope troupe, consisting of Peter Blandin, his son Robert, and Juanita Calles, to work without safety nets. When Peter becomes too ill to perform, his son refuses to take his place, not wishing to endanger the life of Juanita, with whom he is in love. The father performs in spite of his illness and is seriously injured by a fall; Robert, branded a coward, leaves and becomes a vagrant, while Carl Ravelle, an arrogant wire walker, takes Blandin's place and forces his attentions on Juanita. When Blandin's hotel catches on fire, Robert, breaking through the firelines, walks across a telegraph wire and rescues his father from the burning building, thus proving his courage and winning the respect and love of Juanita. *Tightrope walkers. Family life. Courage. Courtship. Circus. Fires.*

BILL BARLOW'S CLAIM *see* **THE FIGHTING STRAIN**

BILLY JIM **F2.0418**

Fred Stone Productions. *Dist* R-C Pictures. 29 Jan **1922** [c19 Jan 1922; LP17473]. Si; b&w. 35mm. 5 reels, 4,900 ft.

Prod Andrew J. Callaghan. *Dir* Frank Borzage. *Scen* Frank Howard Clark. *Story* Jackson Gregory.

Cast: Fred Stone *(Billy Jim)*, Millicent Fisher *(Martha Dunforth)*, George Hernandez *(Dudley Dunforth)*, William Bletcher *(Jimmy)*, Marian Skinner *(Mrs. Dunforth)*, Frank Thorne *(Roy Forsythe)*.

Western melodrama. Billy Jim, a wealthy westerner posing as a happy-go-lucky cowboy, gets into a dispute with a man aboard a train. A girl berates him for his actions, and he loses his heart to her; later, while drunk, he finds her bound to a chair in a cabin and after releasing her learns that she is traveling with her father to a resort. Billy Jim holds up a card game, hires a car with the money taken, and arrives at the resort ahead of her. At her father's mining camp Billy Jim succeeds in routing claim jumpers and saving the property. When the sheriff arrives to arrest him for holding up the card game, it is revealed that he is a wealthy cattle owner. Billy Jim departs, but the girl follows to return his gun, and all ends happily. *Cowboys. Claim jumpers. Mining camps. Resorts.*

BILLY THE KID **F2.0419**

Metro-Goldwyn-Mayer Pictures. 18 Oct **1930** [c23 Oct 1930; LP1671]. Sd (Movietone); b&w. 35mm and 70mm (Realife). 11 reels, 8,808 ft.

Dir King Vidor. *Cont* Wanda Tuchock. *Dial* Laurence Stallings. *Adtl Dial* Charles MacArthur. *Photog* Gordon Avil. *Art Dir* Cedric Gibbons. *Film Ed* Hugh Wynn. *Rec Engr* Paul Neal, Douglas Shearer. *Wardrobe* David Cox.

Cast: John Mack Brown *(Billy the Kid)*, Wallace Beery *(Garrett)*, Kay Johnson *(Claire)*, Wyndham Standing *(Tunston)*, Karl Dane *(Swenson)*, Russell Simpson *(McSween)*, Blanche Frederici *(Mrs. McSween)*, Roscoe Ates *(Old Stuff)*, Warner P. Richmond *(Ballinger)*, James Marcus *(Donovan)*, Nelson McDowell *(Hatfield)*, Jack Carlyle *(Brewer)*, John Beck *(Butterworth)*, Christopher Martin *(Santiago)*, Marguerita Padula *(Nicky Whoosiz)*, Aggie Herring *(Mrs. Hatfield)*.

Western drama. Source: Walter Noble Burns, *The Saga of Billy the Kid* (Garden City, New York, 1926). Cattlemen Tunston and McSween arrive in a territory "governed" by Hatfield, and despite his orders that they move on, they decide to remain in the valley. Billy the Kid is caught stealing cattle and is about to be hanged by Tunston when the cattleman decides that he would be a welcome addition to his forces. Billy becomes devoted to Tunston, and when Tunston is killed in an open fight with Ballinger, Hatfield's henchman, the Kid decides to kill every man who took part in the fight, particularly for the sake of Claire, Tunston's intended wife. McSween, Billy, and his friends are trapped by Sheriff Garrett in McSween's house, and after extended gunplay, McSween tries to surrender and is killed; the house is set afire, and only Billy shoots his way clear and escapes. Although General Wallace discusses a treaty with Billy, offering him amnesty, he retreats to a cave in the hills, where he is trapped by Garrett. Billy escapes from jail but is shot by Garrett when he returns to see Claire. ... *Outlaws. Cattlemen. Sheriffs. Revenge. Murder. William H. Bonney. Lew Wallace.*

Note: In its initial showings, the film was shown in a 70mm wide screen process known as *Realife*, developed by the studio.

BING BANG BOOM **F2.0420**

Sol Lesser Productions. *Dist* Western Pictures Exploitation Co. 6 Jan **1922** [New York State license]. Si; b&w. 35mm. 5 reels.

Dir Fred J. Butler. *Scen* Vance Wethered.

Cast: David Butler *(Bertram Bancroft Boom)*, Doris Pawn *(Ruth Warren)*, Edwin Wallock *(Ellis Turner)*, Kate Toncray *(Mrs. Jonas Boom)*, Jack Carlyle *(Paprika Blake)*, Carl Stockdale *(David Hudge)*, William Walling *(Sheriff Warren)*, Bert Hadley *(Fred Patterson)*, William Duvall *(The Mayor)*.

Comedy-drama. Source: Raymond Leslie Goldman, "Bing Bang Boom," in *Argosy All-Story Weekly* (vols 123–124, 31 Jul–28 Aug 1920). "Bertrand Bancroft Boom, nicknamed 'Bing, Bang' Boom, through ill luck has hard time keeping a job. Settlement of a war claim of his grandfather's brings him $20,000 and he is persuaded to buy a country hotel. Visiting the place he finds he has been buncoed, but with the aid of the editor of the village paper he succeeds in finally getting the best of the village boss who has cheated him. He also opens the hotel as a health resort and wins the hand of one of the town's belles after having experienced many difficulties, including a fight with a thug hired to beat him." (*Moving Picture World*, 22 Jul 1922, p308.) *Editors. Political bosses. Smalltown life. War claims. Health resorts. Hotels.*

BIRD MANOR **F2.0421**

T. Walter Weisman. c30 Dec **1925** [MU3294]. Si; b&w. 35mm. 5 reels.

Writ T. Walter Weisman.

Instructional film. Arranged for presentation with an oral lecture, this film allows the audience to accompany a group of children on a guided tour of Bird Manor, a sanctuary housing a great variety of birds. *Birds. Bird sanctuaries.*

BIRDS OF PREY **F2.0422**

Columbia Pictures. 20 Mar **1927** [c22 Mar 1927; LP23788]. Si; b&w. 35mm. 6 reels, 6,008 ft.

Prod Harry Cohn. *Dir* William James Craft. *Scen* Dorothy Howell. *Photog* J. O. Taylor.

Cast: Priscilla Dean *(Helen Wayne)*, Hugh Allan *(Hamilton Smith, Jr.)*, Gustav von Seyffertitz *(Foxy)*, Ben Hendricks, Jr. *(Archie Crossley)*, Sidney Bracey *(Gaston)*, William H. Tooker *(J. Hamilton Smith)*, Fritz Becker *(The Runt)*.

Underworld melodrama. Source: George Bronson Howard, *Birds of Prey: Being Pages from the Book of Broadway* (New York, 1918). Helen Wayne and Archie Crossley, two clever pickpockets, rob J. Hamilton Smith, a well-known metropolitan banker, and he is later recognized by one of their gang as a former prisonmate; they demand a price for their silence, and he is forced to accede. At a ball, where the gang stages a theft, Helen meets and falls in love with Smith, Jr. His father, because of financial difficulties, arranges with the gang to undertake a bank robbery and thus obviate the possibility of discovery of his plight. Helen, learning of Smith, Jr.'s, identity, refuses to join in the robbery and warns young Smith. He, unaware that his father is implicated, locks the bandits in the vault. An earthquake occurs, and only young Smith's heroism saves Helen; the gang and the banker are killed, but Helen and Smith, Jr., look forward to a happy future. *Pickpockets. Bankers. Blackmail. Courtship. Bank robberies. Earthquakes.*

BIRTHRIGHT **F2.0423**

Micheaux Film Corp. 1 Feb **1924** [scheduled release]. Si; b&w. 35mm. 10 reels, 9,500 ft.

Cast: J. Homer Tutt *(Peter Siner)*, Evelyn Preer *(Cissie Deldine)*, Salem Tutt Whitney *(Tump Pack)*, Lawrence Chenault, W. B. F. Crowell.

Drama. Source: Thomas Sigismund Stribling, *Birthright* (New York, 1922). A young and idealistic Negro graduate of Harvard College goes to live in a small southern town, where he encounters the bigotry and brutality of both races. *Race relations. Negro life. Smalltown life. Bigotry. Harvard University.*

THE BISHOP MURDER CASE **F2.0424**

Metro-Goldwyn-Mayer Pictures. 3 Jan **1930** [c5 May 1930; LP1274]. Sd (Movietone); b&w. 35mm. 9 reels, 7,901 ft. [Also si; 5,727 ft.]

Screen Dir Nick Grinde. *Stage Dir* David Burton. *Adapt-Scen-Dial* Lenore J. Coffee. *Titl* Fred Niblo, Jr. *Photog* Roy Overbaugh. *Art Dir* Cedric Gibbons. *Film Ed* William Le Vanway. *Rec Engr (see note)* G. A. Burns, Donald MacKenzie. *Wardrobe* Henrietta Frazer.

Cast: Basil Rathbone *(Philo Vance)*, Leila Hyams *(Belle Dillard)*, Roland Young *(Sigurd Arnesson)*, Alec B. Francis *(Prof. Bertrand Dillard)*, George F. Marion *(Adolph Drukker)*, Zelda Sears *(Mrs. Otto Drukker)*, Bodil Rosing *(Greta Menzel)*, Carroll Nye *(John F. Sprigg)*, Charles Quartermaine *(John Pardee)*, James Donlan *(Ernest Heath)*, Sidney Bracey *(Pyne)*, Clarence Geldert *(John F.-X. Markham)*, Delmer Daves *(Raymond Sperling)*, Nellie Bly Baker *(Beedle)*.

Mystery melodrama. Source: S. S. Van Dine, *The Bishop Murder Case* (New York, 1917). At the home of Professor Dillard, the body of Robin Pyne is discovered on the archery range, and detective Philo Vance is assigned to the case. Gathered at the scene of the crime are John Sprigg, the victim's best friend, who vows to find the killer; Belle, the professor's niece; and Arnesson, her fiancé and the professor's assistant. When Arnesson insists on applying scientific theories in the investigation, Vance goes along with him. Sprigg discovers that Adolph Drukker, a hunchbacked invalid, witnessed the crime, and is himself murdered, with suspicion cast on Arnesson. But when the professor commits suicide by drinking poisoned wine, he is revealed as the diabolical villain, obsessed with hatred of Arnesson for robbing him of fame and the affections of his niece. *Detectives. Professors. Hunchbacks. Murder. Archery. Suicide. Chess.*

Note: Although sources credit actor Donald MacKenzie with sound recording, they may have mistaken him for Frank MacKenzie, a recording engineer.

THE BISHOP OF THE OZARKS **F2.0425**

Cosmopolitan Film Co. *Dist* Film Booking Offices of America. 4 Feb **1923** [c23 Jan 1923; LP18615]. Si; b&w. 35mm. 6 reels, 4,852 ft.

Pres by Milford W. Howard. *Dir-Adapt* Finis Fox. *Story* Milford W. Howard. *Photog* Sol Polito.

Cast: Milford W. Howard *(Roger Chapman/Tom Sullivan)*, Derelys Perdue *(Margery Chapman)*, Cecil Holland *(Dr. Earl Godfrey)*, William Kenton *(Dr. Paul Burroughs)*, R. D. MacLean *(Governor of Alabama)*, Mrs. Milo Adams *(shepherd woman)*, Rosa Melville *(Mrs. Jack Armstead)*, Fred Kelsey *(Mart Stoneman)*, George Reed *(Simon)*.

Melodrama. Escaped convict Tom Sullivan changes clothes with minister Roger Chapman (who is later killed), then takes up the pastor's work in the Ozark mountains and cares for Chapman's daughter, Margery. Tom wins the love and respect of the people and becomes chaplain of the state prison, while Margery acquires two suitors—Dr. Paul Burroughs, who offers her love, and Dr. Earl Godfrey, who has her under his evil influence. Tom is exposed but is pardoned by the governor; Margery chooses Dr. Burroughs. "Mysticism has been resorted to in several instances. There is a spiritual seance, a persistent strain of mental telepathy and a definite instance in which the occult powers of evil are demonstrated." (*Moving Picture World*, 10 Mar 1923.) *Prison escapees. Clergymen. State governors. Good and evil. Mental telepathy. Prisons. Spiritualism. Ozarks.*

A BIT OF HEAVEN **F2.0426**

Excellent Pictures. 15 May **1928** [c26 May 1928; LP25301]. Si; b&w. 35mm. 7 reels, 7,000 ft.

Pres by Samuel Zierler. *Prod* Burton King. *Dir* Cliff Wheeler. *Titl* Harry Chandlee. *Adapt* Elsie Werner. *Story* Roland Kingston. *Photog* Edward Snyder, Walter Haas. *Film Ed* Harry Chandlee. *Choreog* Maurice L. Kusell.

Cast: Washburn, Bryant *(Roger Van Dorn)*, Lila Lee *(Fola Dale)*, Martha Mattox *(Aunt Honoria)*, Lucy Beaumont *(Aunt Priscilla)*, Richard Tucker *(Mark Storm)*, Otto Lederer *(Sam Maltman)*, Jacqueline Gadsdon *(Helen Worl)*, Sybil Grove *(maid)*, Edwin Argus *(comedian)*.

Society drama. Roger Van Dorn marries Fola Dale, dancer in a Broadway revue, against the wishes of his Aunt Honoria, who would have him marry Helen Worl, a girl of his own class. Honoria and Helen make Roger believe that Fola is unfaithful, and, although he still loves her, Roger seeks a divorce in Paris while Fola continues her career on stage. When he returns, divorced, to learn that he has become a father, they are reconciled and remarry. *Dancers. Aunts. Social classes. Musical revues. Divorce. New York City—Broadway. Paris.*

Note: Also reviewed as *Little Bit of Heaven*.

BITS OF LIFE **F2.0427**

Marshall Neilan Productions. *Dist* Associated First National Pictures. 26 Sep **1921** [c25 Oct 1921; LP17129]. Si; b&w. 35mm. 6 reels, 6,339 ft.

Pres by Marshall Neilan. *Dir–Adtl Story* Marshall Neilan. *Scen* Lucita Squier. *Photog* David Kesson. *Asst Dir* James Flood, William Scully.

Cast: Wesley Barry *(Tom Levitt, a boy)*, Rockliffe Fellowes *(Tom Levitt)*, Lon Chaney *(Chin Gow)*, Noah Beery *(Hindoo)*, Anna May Wong *(Chin Gow's wife)*, John Bowers *(dentist's patient)*, Teddy Sampson, Dorothy Mackaill, Edythe Chapman, Frederick Burton, James Bradbury, Jr., Tammany Young, Harriet Hammond, James Neill, Scott Welsh.

Melodrama. Source: Hugh Wiley, "Hop," in *Jade and Other Stories* (New York, 1921). Walter Trumbull, "The Man Who Heard Everything," in *Smart Set* (63?:27, Apr 1921). *Episode 1: The Bad Samaritan.* Tom Levitt, halfbreed son of a Chinese and a white woman, is the victim of brutality during his boyhood and becomes a criminal. A friend, released from jail, tells Tom he is going straight and asks for money to leave town; Tom takes a stolen wallet from another boy. After hearing a preacher tell the story of the Good Samaritan, he goes to aid a man who has been assaulted; facing a 10-year sentence for robbery, he reflects on the irony of his downfall. *Episode 2: The Man Who Heard Everything.* Ed Johnson, who barely makes a living from barbering, is deaf, but he is happy in the belief that the world is good and that he is loved by his wife. Coming into possession of an instrument that restores his hearing, he learns that the persons he has idolized are not to be trusted and that his wife is unfaithful; in despair, he destroys the instrument. *Episode 3: Hop.* As a boy in China, Chin Gow learns that girl infants are undesirable. When a man, he becomes proprietor of several San Francisco opium dens and weds Toy Sing, who bears him a baby girl. Chin Gow beats his wife and vows to slay the child. His wife's friend brings in a crucifix sent by the priest, and as he nails it to the wall, the spike penetrates the skull of Chin Gow lying in a bunk on the other side of the wall and kills him. *Episode 4: The Intrigue.* On a yachting tour of the world, Reginald Vandebrook, reaching a foreign country, falls in love with a girl he has never seen before; he hears her called Princess and follows her into a building. There he is surrounded by East Indians who are about to murder him. He awakens to find himself in a dentist's chair having a tooth extracted. *Barbers. Chinese. Dentists. Halfcastes. Samaritanism. Deafness. Opium. San Francisco—Chinatown. Dreams.*

Note: The film was prefaced by a message from Mr. Neilan explaining the reasons for producing it and introducing the characters of each story. An additional literary source—"The Bad Samaritan," by Thomas McMorrow—has not been identified.

BITTER APPLES **F2.0428**

Warner Brothers Pictures. 23 Apr **1927** [c9 Apr 1927; LP23844]. Si; b&w. 35mm. 6 reels, 5,463 ft.

Dir-Scen Harry O. Hoyt. *Camera* Hal Mohr. *Asst Dir* Ross Lederman.

Cast: Monte Blue *(John Wyncote)*, Myrna Loy *(Belinda White)*, Paul Ellis *(Stefani Blanco)*, Charles Hill Mailes *(Cyrus Thornden)*, Sidney De Grey *(Joseph Blanco)*, Ruby Blaine *(Mrs. Channing)*, Patricia Grey *(Wyncote's secretary)*.

Melodrama. Source: Harold MacGrath, "Bitter Apples," in *Red Book Magazine* (45:39–45, 60–65, 86–92, 80–161, Jul–Oct 1925). Following the demise of his father, John Wyncote, finding himself with a bankrupt business, instructs attorney Thornden to sell all interests. One of the depositors, Joseph Blanco, unable to face financial ruin, commits suicide, leaving a daughter, Belinda, and a son, Stefani. Stefani takes the Sicilian oath to avenge his father's death along with his sister; Belinda agrees to take an assumed name and make John fall in love with her and marry her. After the ceremony, aboard an ocean liner, she denounces him. The ship crashes onto a reef, and the crew is overpowered by rumrunners; Wyncote rescues Belinda from the drunken captain's advances, and they are reconciled after being saved by a U. S. destroyer. *Businessmen. Sicilians. Brother-sister relationship. Bankruptcy. Suicide. Revenge. Courtship. Ocean liners. United States Navy. Shipwrecks.*

BITTER SWEETS **F2.0429**

Dist Peerless Pictures. 5 Sep **1928.** Si; b&w. 35mm. 6 reels, 5,700 ft.

Dir Charles Hutchison. *Cont* Elaine Wilmont. *Titl* Terrence Daugherty. *Story* John C. Brownell. *Photog* Leon Shamroy. *Film Ed* Bernard Ray.

Cast: Barbara Bedford *(Betty Kingston)*, Ralph Graves *(Ralph Horton)*, Crauford Kent *(Paul Gebhardt)*, Joy McKnight *(Diana Van Norton)*, Ethan Laidlaw *(Joe Gorman)*, Frank Crane *(Nick Clayton)*, Richard Belfield *(district attorney)*, John Dillon *(Donovan)*, Oscar Smith *(Jeff Washington)*.

Crime melodrama. "The heroine [Betty Kingston] takes a job to endeavor to secure certain incriminating letters that the heavy [Paul Gebhardt] is using to blackmail a society girl. The heavy is shot by a gangster, and the hero [Ralph Horton] is arrested for the murder. Eventually heroine traps the murderer [after a long auto chase] and clears everything up satisfactorily." (*Film Daily*, 23 Sep 1928, p7.) *Gangsters. District attorneys. Blackmail. Murder. Documentation.*

THE BITTERNESS OF SWEETS *see* **LOOK YOUR BEST**

BITTERSWEET *see* **THE SHOCK**

THE BLACK ACE **F2.0430**

Leo Maloney Productions. *Dist* Pathé Exchange. 2 Sep **1928** [c26 Jul 1928; LP25498]. Si; b&w. 35mm. 6 reels, 5,722 ft.

Dir Leo D. Maloney. *Story-Scen* Ford I. Beebe. *Photog* Edward A. Kull. *Film Ed* Joseph Kane.

Cast: Don Coleman *(Dan Stockton)*, Jeanette Loff, Billy Butts, J. P. McGowan, Noble Johnson, William Steele, Ben Corbett, Edward Jones.

Western melodrama. Doublecrossed by his partner, Cherokee Kaul, Draw Evans, a bandit, decides to reform and become foster father to Dan Stockton, a boy whose father Kaul murdered during a solo raid. Evans becomes an express agent, and Dan becomes a Texas Ranger, determined to find the man who murdered his father. Kaul returns to the neighborhood, commits several crimes, and attempts to frame Evans. Dan unearths the truth after an attempt is made to rob the stagecoach of a valuable shipment of gold. Although Evans stops a bullet meant for Dan, he recovers to see his daughter, Mary, marry Dan. *Bandits. Foster fathers. Texas Rangers. Express agents. Murder. Revenge. Stagecoach robberies. Self-sacrifice.*

THE BLACK BAG **F2.0431**

Universal Film Manufacturing Co. 5 Jun **1922** [c2 Jun 1922; LP17934]. Si; b&w. 35mm. 5 reels, 4,343 ft.

Dir Stuart Paton. *Scen* George Hively. *Adapt* Bernard Hyman. *Photog* Virgil Miller. *Adtl Photog* Irving B. Ruby.

Cast: Herbert Rawlinson *(Billy Kirkwood)*, Virginia Valli *(Dorothy Calender)*, Bert Roach *(Mulready)*, Clara Beyers *(Mrs. Hallam)*, Charles L. King *(Freddie Hallam)*, Herbert Fortier *(Samuel Brentwick)*, Lew Short *(Burgoyne)*, Jack O'Brien *(Martin)*.

Comedy–mystery melodrama. Source: Louis Joseph Vance, *The Black Bag* (Indianapolis, 1908). Young businessman Billy Kirkwood goes to New York for a vacation and meets Dorothy Calender, whom he escorts to a taxi because she is being followed. At her seaside resort, Billy discovers that she has a diamond necklace, which a thief has seen her take from a store, and that this man and his confederates have followed her. Billy recovers the necklace from these thieves after they have stolen it; he hides it in his room; but they again take the necklace and escape with it in a motor yacht. Billy overtakes the thieves and at gunpoint forces them to surrender the necklace and to return with him. Billy is arrested with the thieves; later, in Dorothy's bungalow, he learns that Dorothy had stolen her own necklace to raise money for Martin, her brother. After mutual explanations, Billy wins Dorothy. *Businessmen. Brother-sister relationship. Thieves. Resorts. New York City.*

BLACK BEAUTY **F2.0432**

Vitagraph Co. of America. Jan **1921** [c15 Jan 1921; LP16039]. Si; b&w. 35mm. 7 reels.

Pres by Albert E. Smith. *Dir* David Smith. *Scen* William B. Courtney. *Adapt* Lillian Chester, George Randolph Chester. *Photog* Reginald Lyons.

Cast: Jean Paige *(Jessie Gordon)*, James Morrison *(Harry Blomefield)*, George Webb *(Jack Beckett)*, Bobby Mack *(Derby Ghost)*, John Steppling *(Squire Gordon)*, Capt. Leslie T. Peacock *(Lord Wynwaring)*, Adele Farrington *(Lady Wynwaring)*, Charles Morrison *(John Manly)*, Molly McConnell *(Mrs. Gordon)*, Colin Kenny *(George Gordon)*, Georgia French *(Flora Gordon)*, Robert Bolder *(Vicar Blomefield)*, Margaret Mann *(Mrs. Blomefield)*, George Pierce *(Farmer Grey)*, James Donnelly *(fat bailiff)*, Robert Milasch *(lean bailiff)*, Black Beauty *(himself)*.

Melodrama. Source: Anna Sewell, *Black Beauty* (1877). The famous story of Black Beauty tracing his career from colt to thoroughbred and his various exchanges of hands among English aristocracy, a London cabby, and a kind farmer. Beckett, who has framed George Gordon in a robbery, induces Jessie to marry him when she comes of age, but Harry Blomefield, her childhood sweetheart, has discovered the secret through Derby Ghost and uses Black Beauty to get to Jessie ahead of Beckett and to win the race. The horse finds a home with Harry and Jessie. *Cabbies. Farmers. Horseracing. England. London. Horses.*

THE BLACK BIRD **F2.0433**

Metro-Goldwyn-Mayer Pictures. 11 Jan **1926** [c29 Jan 1926; LP22381]. Si; b&w. 35mm. 7 reels, 6,688 ft.

Dir-Writ Tod Browning. *Scen* Waldemar Young. *Photog* Percy Hilburn. *Set Dsgn* Cedric Gibbons, Arnold Gillespie. *Film Ed* Errol Taggart. *Wardrobe* André-ani.

Cast: Lon Chaney *(The Black Bird/The Bishop of Limehouse)*, Renée Adorée *(Fifi)*, Doris Lloyd *(Polly)*, Andy MacLennan *(Ghost)*, William Weston *(Red)*, Eric Mayne *(sightseer)*, Sidney Bracy *(Bertie's No. 1 Man)*, Ernie S. Adams *(Bertie's No. 2 Man)*, Owen Moore *(West End Bertie)*, Lionel Belmore, Billy Mack, Peggy Best.

Melodrama. The Black Bird is a thief in London's Limehouse district who in another identity is known as his own brother, a crippled keeper of a rescue mission where he is affectionately called "The Bishop." The Black Bird and his rival, West End Bertie, both love the same girl, Fifi, and both promise her a diamond collar owned by a member of London's aristocracy. A contest of wits between the two crooks results in The Black Bird's shooting a Scotland Yard man and having to retreat quickly behind the disguise of The Bishop. But this time—so to speak—his joints permanently lock and he cannot resume his original shape; in atonement for his sins, therefore, he decides to give up his underworld life and live as The Bishop. West End Bertie wins Fifi's love. *Thieves. Cripples. Theft. Murder. Missions. London—Limehouse. Scotland Yard.*

THE BLACK BOOMERANG **F2.0434**

William H. Clifford Photoplay Co. **1925**. Si; b&w. 35mm. [Feature length assumed.]

Prod-Writ William H. Clifford.

Melodrama(?). No information about the precise nature of this film has been found. *Negro life.*

Note: The indicated year of release is approximate.

BLACK BUTTERFLIES **F2.0435**

Dist Quality Distributing Corp. 31 Aug **1928** [c7 Jul 1928; LP25433]. Si; b&w. 35mm. 7 reels, 6,216 or 6,220 ft.

Pres by A. Carlos. *Dir* James W. Horne. *Adapt-Cont* Henry McCarty. *Titl* Pat Sutherland. *Photog* Steve Norton, Max Dupont. *Film Ed* Ralph Dawson. *Mus Program* James C. Bradford.

Cast: Jobyna Ralston *(Dorinda Maxwell)*, Mae Busch *(Kitty Perkins)*, Robert Frazer *(David)*, Lila Lee *(Norma Davis)*, Cosmo Kyrle Bellew *(Judge Davis)*, Robert Ober *(Jimmie)*, Ray Hallor *(Chad)*, George Periolat *(Hatch)*.

Society drama. Source: Elizabeth Jordan, *Black Butterflies* (New York & London, 1927). Dorinda, a wealthy flapper who scorns married life, becomes associated with a fast-moving group, the "Black Butterflies." Threatened with scandal, Dorinda chooses David Goddard, a struggling young law clerk, to marry her for $5,000 a year. After the wedding Goddard chafes under his false position, and they quarrel continuously when alone. Goddard's attempts to win her away from her companions fail. Dorinda is responsible for an automobile accident resulting in temporary blindness for Goddard and serious injuries for the other passengers; this catastrophe jars Dorinda to her senses. She quits the "Black Butterflies" and becomes David's earnest wife. *Flappers. Law clerks. Blindness. Marriage of convenience. Automobile accidents.*

BLACK CYCLONE **F2.0436**

Hal Roach Productions. *Dist* Pathé Exchange. 27 Sep **1925** [c4 May 1925; LU21424]. Si; b&w. 35mm. 5 reels, 5,123 ft.

Pres by Hal Roach. *Dir* Fred Jackman. *Titl* H. M. Walker, Malcolm Stuart Boylan. *Story* Hal Roach. *Photog* Floyd Jackman, George Stevens.

Cast: Rex *(king of the wild horses)*, Lady *(a horse)*, The Killer *(a horse)*, The Pest *(a horse)*, Guinn Williams *(Jim Lawson)*, Kathleen Collins *(Jane Logan)*, Christian Frank *(Joe Pangle)*.

Western melodrama. Rex, an outcast colt, grows to maturity versed in the ways of the wild, eventually winning for himself a mate named Lady. Rex and Lady wander into a valley in which there is a herd of horses belonging to the stallion, Killer, with which Rex must fight; Rex loses the fight, and Lady is forced to join Killer's herd. Jim Lawson and Joe Pangle are rivals for the affections of Jane Logan; Jim is run off by Pangle's gang. Wandering in the hills, he finds Rex caught in quicksand and rescues him. Rex goes to find Lady and rescues her from a pack of wolves. He returns to Jim in time to save him from an attack by a mountain lion. Pangle's gang comes after Jim, and Jane rides to warn him but is spotted by Pangle. Jim sees her danger and goes after Pangle, who shoots Jim's horse. Rex goes to Jim's aid, offering his bare back to the unhorsed rider. Jim catches Pangle and beats him up. Rex bests Killer in a fight. Jim and Jane kiss. Rex and Lady rub noses. *Gangs. Quicksand. Wolves. Lions. Horses.*

THE BLACK DIAMOND EXPRESS **F2.0437**

Warner Brothers Pictures. 4 Jun **1927** [c28 May 1927; LP24013]. Si; b&w. 35mm. 6 reels, 5,803 ft.

Dir Howard Bretherton. *Screenplay* Harvey Gates. *Story* Darryl Francis Zanuck. *Story? (see note)* Mark Canfield. *Camera* David Abel, Conrad Wells. *Asst Dir* Eddie Sowders.

Cast: Monte Blue *(Dan Foster)*, Edna Murphy *(Jeanne Harmon)*, Myrtle Stedman *(Mrs. Harmon)*, Claire McDowell *(Martha, Dan's sister)*, Carroll Nye *(Fred, Dan's brother)*, William Demarest *(fireman)*, J. W. Johnston *(Sheldon Truesdell)*.

Society melodrama. Dan Foster, a conscientious railroad engineer who supports his widowed sister and three small children, meets Jeanne Harmon, a girl of class and wealth, when she races his train and is slightly injured in a collision. Realizing their mutual love, Jeanne breaks her engagement to socialite Sheldon Truesdell, though Dan has neither the money nor position to support her. Persuaded to break off the relationship by her mother, Dan feigns drunkenness at a party, and in disgust Jeanne accepts Truesdell but regrets her marriage when again she sees Dan, who drives the train on her honeymoon trip. Dan, however, rescues Jeanne when robbers attack the train and risks his life attempting to save

Truesdell, who is mortally wounded. Dan's valor wins him a promotion and the love of Jeanne, with whom he is united. *Railroad engineers. Bandits. Socialites. Social classes. Train robberies.*

Note: Evidence in copyright records that Mark Canfield wrote the film story has not been confirmed by other sources.

THE BLACK DOMINO *see* **THE BROADWAY MADONNA**

BLACK FEATHER **F2.0438**

Dailey Productions. May **1928**. Si; b&w. 35mm. 6 reels.

Dir John E. Ince. *Scen* L. V. Jefferson. *Titl* Pat Sutherland. *Photog* Robert Martin. *Film Ed* Dave Rothschild.

Cast: Sally Rand, Allan Forrest, Maurice Costello, Wheeler Oakman, Dot Farley, Dave Morris, Ruth Reavis, John Clayton Pool, George Towne, Edith Saunders, Johnny Sinclair, George Towne Hall.

Melodrama(?). No information about the nature of this film has been found.

BLACK GOLD **F2.0439**

William Steiner Productions. 29 May **1924** [New York State license application; c15 May 1924; LU20208]. Si; b&w. 35mm. 5 reels, 4,697 ft.

Dir Forrest Sheldon. *Photog* Ben Kline.

Cast: Pete Morrison *(Don Endicott)*.

Western melodrama. Don Endicott and his Negro servant, Sam, are thrown off a moving train by three cardsharps who have cheated Don. Without funds, they ask for hospitality at the Atwood Ranch, but the daughter, Millie, has them chased off when Don mentions his name. In town, Don finds the cardsharps and recovers his money. He attempts to aid Millie and her family when he finds them in desperate financial straits, but she refuses his aid, believing him to be Big Tim Endicott, Don's father, the president of the oil syndicate that has been hounding the Atwoods and has burned their oil derrick in an attempt to get their land. The father shows up to close the deal but is frustrated. Endicott's henchman, Boyer, beats Don unconscious in a fight. Boyer relates matters to Endicott, who is disappointed in the apparently cowardly behavior of his son. Don recovers and defeats Boyer in a second fight, winning the respect of his father and approval of his love for Millie. *Syndicates. Cardsharps. Filial relations. Oil lands.*

Note: Story and character names are from shooting script in the copyright files and may be different from the final film.

BLACK GOLD **F2.0440**

Norman Film Manufacturing Co. 7 May **1928** [New York State license]. Si; b&w. 35mm. 6 reels, 5,600 ft.

Cast: Lawrence Corman, Kathryn Boyd.

Melodrama(?). No information about the precise nature of this film has been found. *Negro life.*

BLACK JACK **F2.0441**

Fox Film Corp. 25 Sep **1927** [c18 Sep 1927; LP24432]. Si; b&w. 35mm. 5 reels, 4,777 ft.

Pres by William Fox. *Dir* Orville O. Dull. *Scen* Harold Shumate. *Photog* Reginald Lyons. *Asst Dir* Ted Brooks.

Cast: Buck Jones *(Phil Dolan)*, Barbara Bennett *(Nancy Blake)*, Theodore Lorch *(Sam Vonner)*, George Berrell *(judge)*, Harry Cording *(Haskins)*, William Caress *(first deputy)*, Buck Moulton *(second deputy)*, Murdock MacQuarrie *(Holbrook)*, Frank Lanning *(Kentuck)*, Mark Hamilton *(Slim)*, Sam Allen *(Ed Holbrook)*.

Western melodrama. Source: Johnston McCulley, "The Broken Dollar," in *Far West Illustrated Magazine* (Jan 1927). Phil Dolan, known as Black Jack because of his ability at cards, does a favor for Nancy Blake, a pretty girl in distress. She reciprocates by vamping the judge when Phil is brought before him for shiftlessness. Three pieces of a silver dollar on which is indented the map of a mine are held by the girl, Phil, and a rustler. Phil rescues her from the rustlers, and they visit the leader, from whom Phil obtains his portion of the coin. Subsequently, Phil and Nancy are captured by the gang, but they escape; holding off the rustlers, they make their way to the hidden ore mine, where, at the crucial moment, the sheriff's posse appears to capture the gang. *Gamblers. Rustlers. Judges. Mine claims.*

BLACK LIGHTNING **F2.0442**

Gotham Productions. *Dist* Lumas Film Corp. 8 Dec **1924** [New York showing; c7 Oct 1924; LP20668]. Si; b&w. 35mm. 6 reels, 5,500 ft.

Pres by Samuel Sax. *Dir* James P. Hogan. *Scen* Dorothy Howell. *Story* Frank Foster Davis. *Photog* Jack MacKenzie.

Cast: Clara Bow *(Martha Larned)*, Harold Austin *(Ray Chambers)*, Eddie Phillips *(Ez Howard)*, Joe Butterworth *(Dick Larned)*, Thunder *(himself, a dog)*, Mark Fenton *(doctor)*, John Pringle *(city doctor)*, James P. Hogan *(Frank Larned)*.

Melodrama. Accompanied by Thunder, the dog who rescued him from the firing line in France, World War veteran Ray Chambers goes to the mountains to recover from his war injuries. There he meets Martha Larned, a lonely mountain girl who lives with her little brother, Dick. Ray discovers that Martha is the sister of his dead buddy, Frank Larned, and he decides to stay and protect her from harassment by Jim Howard and his halfwitted brother, Ez. When Dick is hurt in a fall, Ray goes for a doctor; Ez kills Jim and attacks Martha; and Thunder takes care of Ez. Ray and Martha then get married. *Veterans. Brother-sister relationship. Halfwits. Mountain life. Dogs.*

BLACK MAGIC **F2.0443**

Fox Film Corp. 7 Jul **1929** [c5 Jul 1929; LP513]. Mus score & sd eff (Movietone); b&w. 35mm. 7 reels, 5,855 ft. [Also si; 5,833 ft.]

Pres by William Fox. *Supv* Bertram Millhauser. *Dir* George B. Seitz. *Scen* Beulah Marie Dix. *Titl* Katherine Hilliker. *Photog* Glen MacWilliams. *Film Ed* Katherine Hilliker. *Asst Dir* Max Gold.

Cast: Josephine Dunn *(Katherine Bradbroke)*, Earle Foxe *(Hugh Darrell)*, John Holland *(John Ormsby)*, Henry B. Walthall *(Dr. Bradbroke)*, Dorothy Jordan *(Ann Bradbroke)*, Fritz Feld *(James Fraser)*, Sheldon Lewis *(witch-doctor)*, Ivan Linow *(Zelig)*, Blue Washington *(Unit)*.

Melodrama. Source: Walter Archer Frost and Paul Dickey, *Cape Smoke* (New York opening: 16 Feb 1925). Walter Archer Frost, *The Man Between* (Garden City, New York, 1913). On a South Seas island, "three white derelicts drink away memories of the past. After many adventures during which a girl enters the picture, the three are rehabilitated and everything turns out happily." ("Motion Picture News Booking Guide," in *Motion Picture News*, 15 Mar 1930, p70.) *Derelicts. Redemption. South Sea Islands.*

BLACK OXEN **F2.0444**

Frank Lloyd Productions. *Dist* Associated First National Pictures. 29 Dec **1924** [San Francisco premiere; released Jan 1924; c12 Dec 1923; LP19700]. Si; b&w. 35mm. 8 reels, 7,937 ft.

Dir Frank Lloyd. *Photog* Norbert Brodin.

Cast: Corinne Griffith *(Madame Zattiany/Mary Ogden)*, Conway Tearle *(Lee Clavering)*, Thomas Ricketts *(Charles Dinwiddie)*, Thomas Guise *(Judge Gavin Trent)*, Clara Bow *(Janet Oglethorpe)*, Kate Lester *(Jane Oglethorpe)*, Harry Mestayer *(James Oglethorpe)*, Lincoln Stedman *(Donnie Ferris)*, Claire McDowell *(Agnes Trevor)*, Alan Hale *(Prince Rohenhauer)*, Clarissa Selwynne *(Gora Dwight)*, Fred Gambold *(Oglethorpe butler)*, Percy Williams *(Ogden butler)*, Otto Nelson *(Dr. Steinach)*, Eric Mayne *(chancellor)*, Otto Lederer *(Austrian advisor)*, Carmelita Geraghty *(Anna Goodrich)*, Ione Atkinson, Mila Constantin, Hortense O'Brien *(flappers)*.

Melodrama. Source: Gertrude Franklin Atherton, *Black Oxen* (New York, 1923). Playwright Lee Clavering falls in love with a mysterious and beautiful woman. She reveals herself as Austrian Countess Zattiany, formerly New York socialite Mary Ogden, who, by medical means, has had her youth restored. Lee plans to marry the countess, but a former admirer of hers intervenes, points out her folly, and escorts her back to Austria. Lee finds romance with flapper Janet Oglethorpe. *Playwrights. Nobility. Flappers. Rejuvenation. Austria. New York City. Eugen Steinach.*

THE BLACK PANTHER'S CUB **F2.0445**

Ziegfeld Cinema Corp. *Dist* Equity Pictures. 15 May **1921** [c7 Mar 1921; LU16407]. Si; b&w. 35mm. 6-7 reels.

Prod William K. Ziegfeld. *Dir* Emile Chautard. *Adapt* Philip Bartholomae. *Photog* Alfred Ortlieb, Jacques Monteran.

Cast: Florence Reed *(The Black Panther/Mary Maudsley/Faustine, the Empress/Faustine)*, Norman Trevor *(Sir Marling Grayham)*, Henry Stephenson *(Clive, Earl of Maudsley)*, Paul Ducet *(Victim of Chance)*, Don Merrifield *(Sir Charles Beresford)*, Henry Carvill *(Lord Whitford)*, Louis Grisel *(butler)*, Earle Foxe *(Lord Maudsley)*, William Roselle *(Hampton Grayham)*, Paula Shay *(Evelyn Grayham)*, Halbert Brown *(Mr. Laird)*, Charles Jackson *(stable boy)*, Ernest Lambart *(money lender)*, Frank De Vernon *(philanthropist)*, [Frederick] Tyrone Power *(Count Boris Orliff)*, Mademoiselle Dazie *(Mademoiselle Daphney)*.

Melodrama. Source: Ethel Donoher, "The Black Panther's Cub" (publication undetermined). Algernon Charles Swinburne, "Faustine." The situation is liberally drawn from Swinburne's poem. Mary Maudsley, daughter of the Black Panther of Paris—a ruthless destroyer of men and mistress of a gambling house—grows up in the care of her adopted father, who believes that the environment he provides will counteract any tendencies she may have inherited from her mother. Just as she seems about to be led into a career patterned after her mother's she reveals herself to be self-sacrificing and capable of a genuine love. *Adoption. Personality. Gambling. Paris.*

BLACK PARADISE **F2.0446**

Fox Film Corp. 30 May **1926** [c29 May 1926; LP22808]. Si; b&w. 35mm. 5 reels, 4,962 ft.

Pres by William Fox. *Dir* R. William Neill. *Story-Scen* L. G. Rigby. *Photog* George Schneiderman. *Asst Dir* Edward O'Fearna.

Cast: Leslie Fenton *(James Callahan)*, Madge Bellamy *(Sylvia Douglas)*, Edmund Lowe *(Graham)*, Edward Piel *(Murdock)*, Harvey Clark *(Hazy)*, Paul Panzer *(Captain)*, Marcella Daly *(Leona)*, Samuel Blum *(The Half Wit)*, Doris Lloyd *(Lillian Webster)*, Patrick Kelly *(Dr. Murphy)*, Mary Gordon *(Mrs. Murphy)*.

Crook melodrama. Graham, a detective pursuing James Callahan, a criminal, to the open seas is shanghaied by a smuggler and taken to a South Seas island, where he falls in love with Sylvia Douglas, the crook's sweetheart, while Callahan falls for Leona, a native girl. Murdock, the master crook, forces Graham to slave on the gang that hauls a sulfur train from a mine at the brink of the island's volcano. Eventually there is a showdown between Murdock and Graham; and after the latter saves Sylvia from a brutish captain, there is a volcanic eruption that devastates the entire island—with the exception of Sylvia and Graham, who are picked up by an American steamer. *Smugglers. Detectives. Shanghaiing. Sea rescue. Sulfur. Volcanoes. South Sea Islands.*

THE BLACK PEARL (Famous Authors) **F2.0447**

Trem Carr Productions. *Dist* Rayart Pictures. 18 Dec **1928.** Si; b&w. 35mm. 6 reels, 5,134 or 5,261 ft.

Dir Scott Pembroke. *Scen-Titl* Arthur Hoerl. *Photog* Hap Depew. *Film Ed* J. S. Harrington.

Cast: Lila Lee *(Eugenie Bromley)*, Ray Hallor *(Robert Lathrop)*, Carlton Stockdale *(Ethelbert/Bertram Chisolm)*, Howard Lorenz *(Dr. Drake)*, Adele Watson *(Sarah Runyan)*, Thomas Curran *(Silas Lathrop)*, Sybil Grove *(Miss Sheen)*, Lew Short *(Eugene Bromley)*, George French *(Stephen Runyan)*, Baldy Belmont *(Wiggenbottom)*, Art Rowlands *(Claude Lathrop)*.

Mystery melodrama. Source: Mrs. Wilson Woodrow, *The Black Pearl* (New York, 1912). A gem stolen from the brow of a sacred Indian idol brings nothing but trouble to its possessors, especially Silas Lathrop. Constantly receiving death threats pinned by daggers, the old man finally gathers his relatives for the reading of his will. Silas and several of his relatives are killed, but in the climax an investigator masquerading as a butler (Ethelbert?) solves the mystery with the help of Eugenie Bromley. *Detectives. Butlers. Sacrilege. Murder. Disguise. Occult.*

Note: *Film Year Book* gives release dates also as Nov 1928 and 1 Jan 1929.

THE BLACK PIRATE **F2.0448**

Elton Corp. *Dist* United Artists. 8 Mar **1926** [New York premiere; c20 Mar 1926; LP22505]. Si; col (Technicolor). 35mm. 9 reels, 8,490 ft.

Gen Mgr Robert Fairbanks. *Dir* Albert Parker. *Scen Ed* Lotta Woods. *Adapt* Jack Cunningham. *Story* Elton Thomas. *Photog* Henry Sharp. *Technicolor Staff* Arthur Ball, George Cave. *Art Dir* Carl Oscar Borg. *Assoc Artists* Edward M. Langley, Jack Holden. *Set Dsgn* Karl Oscar Borg. *Film Ed* William Nolan. *Mus Score* Mortimer Wilson. *Prod Mgr* Theodore Reed. *Marine Tech* P. H. L. Wilson. *Research Dir* Arthur Woods. *Consult* Dwight Franklin, Robert Nichols.

Cast: Douglas Fairbanks *(The Black Pirate [Michel])*, Billie Dove *(The Princess)*, Anders Randolf *(pirate leader)*, Donald Crisp *(McTavish)*, Tempe Pigott *(duenna)*, Sam De Grasse *(lieutenant)*, Charles Stevens *(powder man)*, Charles Belcher *(chief passenger)*, Fred Becker, John Wallace, E. J. Ratcliffe.

Adventure melodrama. A Spanish vessel is captured on the high seas by pirates who bind the crew and loot and blow up the ship. The only survivors are Michel and his father: they are marooned on a desert island, and when his father dies, Michel swears to avenge his death. He joins a pirate band and proves himself by capturing a merchant ship singlehanded; thereafter, he is known as The Black Pirate. Falling in love with a girl (The Princess) on the captured ship, he saves her by keeping her hostage and holding her for ransom, but he is caught in an attempt to escape and is forced to walk the plank. Swimming ashore, he returns with a boatload of men to rescue The Princess; the crew scuttle the ship, and, swimming underwater, Michel and his men storm the pirate vessel and capture it. Michel reveals that he is a Spanish duke and offers his hand in marriage to The Princess, which she accepts. *Pirates. Nobility. Seafaring life. Ransom. Spain.*

BLACK ROSES **F2.0449**

Hayakawa Feature Play Co. *Dist* Robertson-Cole Distributing Corp. 22 May **1921** [c22 May 1921; LP16700]. Si; b&w. 35mm. 6 reels, 5,700 ft.

Dir Colin Campbell. *Story-Scen* E. Richard Schayer. *Photog* Frank D. Williams. *Art Dir* Robert Ellis.

Cast: Sessue Hayakawa *(Yoda)*, Myrtle Stedman *(Blanche De Vore)*, Tsura Aoki *(Blossom)*, Andrew Robson *(Benson Burleigh)*, Toyo Fujita *(Wong Fu)*, Henry Hebert *("Monocle" Harry)*, Harold Holland *("Detective" Cleary)*, Carrie Clark Ward *(Bridget)*.

Crook melodrama. Yoda, a Japanese architect, takes a job as gardener of the estate of retired criminal Benson Burleigh. Members of Burleigh's former gang—"Monocle" Harry, Blanche De Vore, and Wong Fu—murder Burleigh, frame Yoda for the crime, and kidnap Yoda's wife, Blossom. In prison, a former member of the gang who was betrayed by Blanche aids Yoda's escape and his plot of revenge. Reappearing as a Japanese nobleman, Yoda pretends to be in search of a Japanese girl to impersonate the daughter of a rich merchant and is led to his wife's hiding place. There he entraps the gang, proves that Blanche and Harry were the murderers, and is himself absolved of the charge. *Architects. Gardeners. Gangs. Japanese. Murder. Disguise. Revenge.*

BLACK SHADOWS **F2.0450**

World Tours. *Dist* Pathé Exchange. 20 May **1923** [c12 May 1923; MU2276]. Si; b&w. 35mm. 5 reels.

Dir Edward A. Salisbury.

Exploration documentary. Edward G. Salisbury leads an expedition to the outer reaches of civilization: the South Sea Islands. Departing from San Francisco, the expedition makes its first stop in the Marquesas Islands, where the natives have absorbed some of the customs and manners of civilization, and then steams on to the Samoan Islands. Then come the Fiji and Solomon Islands, where cannibals and headhunters can be found. Accompanying the picturesque scenery are scenes of Robert Louis Stevenson's grave, volcanoes, war dances, and other customs of native life. *Cannibals. Headhunters. Volcanoes. South Sea Islands. Marquesas Islands. Samoa. Fiji Islands. Solomon Islands.*

BLACK SHEEP **F2.0451**

Chaudet-Hurst Productions. *Dist* Pinnacle Pictures. 15 May **1921.** Si; b&w. 35mm. 5 reels.

Dir Paul Hurst.

Cast: Neal Hart *(Rex Carson)*, Ted Brooks *(Al Carson)*, George A. Williams *(Jim Carson)*, Frona Hale *(Mrs. Carson)*, Audrey Chapman *(Molly Morran)*, Otto Nelson *(Cap Morran)*, James McLaughlin *(José)*, Charles Thurston *(Sheriff Summers)*, Harry Bushank *("Bubbles")*, Ben Corbett *(Pete Miller)*, Al Kaufman *(Jim McGowan)*.

Western melodrama. Source: W. C. Tuttle, "Baa, Baa Black Sheep," in *Short Stories* (95:3–22, Jan 1921). The plot line is uncertain, but it apparently involves cattlemen and sheepmen; hero Rex Carson, a stickler for fair play, who is expelled from his home by his father; and a mysterious highwayman. Most of the scenes are outdoors, and a heroine enters the plot in time to straighten out complications and identify the real culprit, a Mexican. *Cattlemen. Sheepmen. Highwaymen. Mexicans. Filial relations.*

BLACK TEARS **F2.0452**

John Gorman Productions. *Dist* Hollywood Pictures. 8 Jun **1927** [New York State license]. Si; b&w. 35mm. 6 reels, 5,700 ft.

Prod-Dir-Writ John Gorman. *Story* Van A. James. *Photog* Ernest Depew.

Cast: Bryant Washburn, Vola Vale, Jack Richardson, Hedda Hopper.

Society drama. "The story opens with a rich man's son introducing a Broadway gold digger to a western gold digger, a gold miner. But it happens that the Broadway gold digger is on the level and only 'digs' when she is out of work and unable to pay her room rent. Her love for the rich lad keeps her straight but it is a long and tedious route she travels before she can convince him that he won't go wrong in picking a show girl for a wife." (*Film Daily*, 3 Jul 1927, p9.) *Gold diggers. Miners. Showgirls. Wealth.*

THE BLACK THUNDERBOLT F2.0453

19 Jun **1922.** Si; b&w. 35mm. 7 reels, 6,600 ft.

Cast: Jack Johnson.

Melodrama. Though the plot of this film has not been determined, New York State license records indicate the depiction of a kidnaping of a baby, chloroforming, and tying someone to a rail. *Kidnaping. Chloroform.*

Note: Producer and national distributor not determined. Distributed in New York, and possibly elsewhere, by Excel Film Exchange or New Douglas Film Exchange.

THE BLACK WATCH F2.0454

Fox Film Corp. 8 May **1929** [Los Angeles premiere; released 2 Jun; c31 May 1929; LP424]. Sd (Movietone); b&w. 35mm. 10 reels, 8,487 ft.

Pres by William Fox. *Dir* John Ford. *Dial Dir* Lumsden Hare. *Scen* John Stone. *Dial* James K. McGuinness. *Photog* Joseph August. *Film Ed* Alexander Troffey. *Song: "Flowers of Delight"* William Kernell. *Rec Engr* W. W. Lindsay. *Asst Dir* Edward O'Fearna.

Cast: Victor McLaglen *(Capt. Donald Gordon King)*, Myrna Loy *(Yasmani)*, David Rollins *(Lieut. Malcolm King)*, Lumsden Hare *(Colonel of the Black Watch)*, Roy D'Arcy *(Rewa Chunga)*, Mitchell Lewis *(Mohammed Khan)*, Cyril Chadwick *(Major Twynes)*, Claude King *(General in India)*, Francis Ford *(Major McGregor)*, Walter Long *(Harrim Bey)*, David Torrence *(field marshal)*, Frederick Sullivan *(general's aide)*, Richard Travers *(adjutant)*, Pat Somerset, David Percy *(Black Watch officers)*, Joseph Diskay *(Muezzin)*, Joyzelle.

Adventure melodrama. Source: Talbot Mundy, *King—of the Khyber Rifles; a Romance of Adventure* (New York, c1916). Captain King of the British Army's Black Watch regiment is assigned to a secret mission in India just as his company is called to France at the outbreak of war; as a result, he is considered a coward by his fellows, a suspicion confirmed by his becoming involved in a drunken brawl in India, in which he apparently kills another officer. But he contrives to avert a revolt by gaining the affection of Yasmani, a girl who is looked upon by tribesmen as their goddess and who is to lead them to victory against unbelievers. He quells the rebellion when the tribesmen, angered by her support of King, kill Yasmani. *Highlanders. Scotch. Cowardice. Cults. Revolts. World War I. Great Britain—Army. India.*

BLACKMAIL *see* **THE WHISPERED NAME**

BLARNEY F2.0455

Metro-Goldwyn-Mayer Pictures. 26 Sep **1926** [c23 Sep 1926; LP23165]. Si; b&w. 35mm. 6 reels, 6,055 ft.

Dir Marcel De Sano. *Titl* Joe Farnham. *Adapt* Albert Lewin, Marcel De Sano. *Photog* Ben Reynolds. *Sets* Cedric Gibbons, Sidney Ullman. *Film Ed* Lloyd Nosler. *Wardrobe* André-ani.

Cast: Renée Adorée *(Peggy Nolan)*, Ralph Graves *(James Carabine)*, Paulette Duval *(Marcolina)*, Malcolm Waite *(Blanco Johnson)*, Margaret Seddon *(Peggy's aunt)*.

Melodrama. Source: Brian Oswald Donn-Byrne, "In Praise of John Carabine," in *Saturday Evening Post* (197:3–5, 9 May 1925). James Carabine comes to New York from Ireland, his fare being paid by Peggy Nolan, a girl from his hometown who harbors an affection for the fighting Irishman. However, he falls for Marcolina, who leaves with him when her husband loses a match as the result of the scheming of Johnson's friends. Then Peggy takes him in and, with the aid of an Irish relative, brings him back to form, so that he gets even with Johnson in a knockout fight. Marcolina is united with Johnson and Carabine with Peggy. *Vamps. Prizefighters. Immigrants. Irish. Flattery. New York City.*

THE BLASPHEMER F2.0456

Catholic Art Association. c15 Oct **1921** [LP17188]. Si; b&w. 35mm. 7 reels.

Dir-Story-Scen O. E. Goebel.

Religious drama. John Harden, who has risen from obscurity to a position of power in the financial world, invites a group of intimate friends to a dinner celebration of a recent financial success on Wall Street while his wife remains home with her children, neglected and forgotten. At the dinner, Harden toasts his success and boasts that he is the master of his fate, the captain of his soul, acknowledging neither God nor the devil. Soon afterward, he suffers a great loss; his family is reduced to poverty; and his friends all desert him. His wife struggles to rear their children, and his mother constantly prays for his salvation; eventually, his childhood faith is restored and Divine Providence leads him home, a broken and changed man. *Financiers. Blasphemy. Redemption. New York City—Wall Street.*

BLASTED HOPES F2.0457

Ashton Dearholt Productions. *Dist* Arrow Film Corp. 15 Mar **1924** [c20 Jan 1924; LP19849]. Si; b&w. 35mm. 5 reels, 4,697 ft.

Dir Arthur Rosson. *Story* Daniel F. Whitcomb.

Cast: Edmund Cobb.

Western melodrama. "Nathan Wagner is sent west by his father [so] that he will not become a weakling. He falls in love with Bella Marshall, who spurns him until he proves his worth. He encounters an old woman, 'Dismal Dora,' whose knowledge of the whereabouts of a neglected mine is tricked from her by Nathan's rival. A fight ensues, Nathan kills the rival, proves his worth and wins the girl." (*Motion Picture News Booking Guide*, 7:11, Oct 1924.) *Filial relations. Manhood. Gold mines.*

BLAZE AWAY F2.0458

Frederick Herbst Productions. *Dist* Di Lorenzo, Inc. Oct **1922.** Si; b&w. 35mm. 5 reels, 4,800 ft.

Dir W. Hughes Curran. *Story-Scen* Bruce Boteler. *Photog* John Stumar.

Cast: Guinn "Big Boy" Williams *("Big Boy")*, Molly Malone *(Molly Melody)*, Hal Wilson *(Pop Melody)*, Ed Burns *(Bill Lang)*, Edward Borman *(Tuck Martin)*, William Curran *(Pablo)*.

Western melodrama. "'Tuck' Martin, a crooked rancher, plots to acquire possession of the neighboring ranch belonging to 'Pop' Melody, whose daughter, Molly, is in love with 'Big Boy.' Bill Lang, the Melody ranchman, is in league with Martin and succeeds in rendering Melody helpless, although he had originally intended to have him killed. An attack on the cottage discloses the double dealing of the foreman, who is finally brought to justice, with nothing but happiness left for 'Big Boy' and Molly." (*Moving Picture World*, 25 Mar 1922, p406.) *Ranchers. Ranch foremen. Land rights.*

BLAZE O' GLORY F2.0459

Sono-Art Productions. 30 Dec **1929** [New York premiere; released 1 Jan 1930]. Sd; b&w. 35mm. 10 reels, 8,333 ft.

Pres by O. E. Goebel, George W. Weeks. *Dir* Renaud Hoffman, George J. Crone. *Scen-Dial* Henry McCarty. *Adapt* Renaud Hoffman. *Photog* Harry Jackson. *Film Ed* Arthur Huffsmith. *Mus* James F. Hanley. *Songs: "Welcome Home," "The Doughboy's Lullaby," "Put a Little Salt on the Bluebird's Tail," "Wrapped in a Red Red Rose"* Eddie Dowling, James Brockman, Ballard MacDonald, Joseph McCarthy. *Sd* Ben Harper.

Cast: Eddie Dowling *(Eddie Williams)*, Betty Compson *(Helen Williams)*, Frankie Darro *(Jean Williams)*, Henry B. Walthall *(Burke)*, William Davidson *(district attorney)*, Ferdinand Schumann-Heink *(Carl Hummel)*, Eddie Conrad *(Abie)*, Frank Sabini *(Tony)*, Broderick O'Farrell, The Rounders.

Drama. Source: Thomas Alexander Boyd, "The Long Shot," in *Points of Honor* (New York, 1925). On trial for the murder of Carl Hummel, Eddie Williams tells his story (in a series of flashbacks), which begins just before the World War. *Eddie, a Broadway star, marries Helen and almost immediately goes to the front. Gassed while saving the life of a German soldier (Hummel), Eddie cannot find work when he returns. Helen finds a job, and Eddie grows more despondent. One day he finds Helen in Hummel's arms, and in his rage Eddie shoots the man.* The trial proceeds with the revelation by Defense Attorney Burke (Eddie's wartime commander) of Helen's secret: *she pretended to be single so as to get work; Hummel, who was searching for Eddie, really loved Helen and was ignorant of her relationship with Eddie.* The jury finds Eddie not guilty. *Actors. Lawyers. Germans. Gas warfare. Infidelity. Murder. Trials. Unemployment. World War I.*

Note: Reduced in length just after its New York premiere; some songs were shortened, while the story remained essentially the same. Also produced in a Spanish version; *Sombras de gloria*, q. v.

BLAZING ARROWS F2.0460

Doubleday Productions. *Dist* Western Pictures Exploitation Co. 18 Oct **1922** [New York premiere]. Si; b&w. 35mm. 5 reels.

Supv Charles W. Mack. *Dir-Story-Scen* Henry McCarty.

Cast: Lester Cuneo *(Sky Fire)*, Francelia Billington *(Martha Randolph)*, Clark Comstock *(Gray Eagle)*, Laura Howard *(Mocking Bird)*, Lafayette McKee *(Elias Thornby)*, Lew Meehan *(Bart McDermott)*, Jim O'Neill *(Scarface)*.

Western melodrama. Sky Fire, a student at Columbia, falls in love with

Martha Randolph, but their engagement is broken when a disappointed suitor reveals Sky Fire's Indian identity. The hero returns west, only to have another run-in with the villain, who murders Martha's guardian. Martha seeks Sky Fire's protection, which leads to a long chase and a general cleanup of numerous scoundrels. Finally, Sky Fire learns that he is really a white man who was adopted and brought up by an Indian. *Students. Indians of North America. Racial prejudice. Murder. Columbia University.*

Note: Working title: *Skyfire.*

BLAZING BARRIERS *see* **JACQUELINE, OR BLAZING BARRIERS**

BLAZING DAYS (Blue Streak Western) **F2.0461**

Universal Pictures. 27 Mar **1927** [c1 Feb 1927; LP23624]. Si; b&w. 35mm. 5 reels, 4,639 ft.

Pres by Carl Laemmle. *Dir* William Wyler. *Scen* George H. Plympton, Robert F. Hill. *Story* Florence Ryerson. *Photog* Al Jones. *Art Dir* David S. Garber.

Cast: Fred Humes *(Smilin' Sam Perry)*, Ena Gregory *(Milly Morgan)*, Churchill Ross *(Jim Morgan)*, Bruce Gordon *("Dude" Dutton)*, Eva Thatcher *(Ma Bascomb)*, Bernard Siegel *(Ezra Skinner)*, Dick L'Estrange *("Turtle-Neck-Pete")*.

Western melodrama. Smilin' Sam Perry is threatened with legal action by Ezra Skinner if he fails to repay a loan. When Sam's money is stolen in a stage robbery, he tracks down "Dude" Dutton, who fits the bandit's description. Dutton agrees to teach Jim Morgan, an invalid, the sheep business, and he takes the boy and his sister, Milly, to a shack on Sam's property. When Sam calls at the shack, Dutton tries to abscond with the stolen money, but Milly shields Dutton from Sam for the sake of her brother, who she believes is implicated in the robbery. Sam moves the boy to Gulch City for medical treatment and lodges Milly in a hotel; he captures Dutton when he escapes with the loot, and Millie accepts Sam's proposal of marriage. *Bandits. Invalids. Brother-sister relationship. Stagecoach robberies. Sheep.*

THE BLAZING TRAIL **F2.0462**

Universal Film Manufacturing Co. May **1921** [c19 Apr 1921; LP16411]. Si; b&w. 35mm. 5 reels, 4,448 ft.

Dir Robert Thornby. *Scen* Lucien Hubbard. *Story* Mann Page, Izola Forrester. *Photog* William Fildew.

Cast: Frank Mayo *(Bradley Yates, known as Pickins)*, Frank Holland *(Dr. Pickney Forbes)*, Verne Winter *("Chipmunk" Grannis)*, Bert Sprotte *("Hank" Millicuddy)*, Madge Hunt *(Ma Millicuddy)*, Mary Philbin *(Talithy Millicuddy)*, Lillian Rich *(Carroll Brown)*, Ray Ripley *(Lewis Van Dusen)*, Joy Winthrop *(Hulda Mews)*, Helen Gilmore *(The Village Talking Machine)*.

Melodrama. Young physician Bradley Yates, on the verge of a nervous collapse in his search for an effective serum to counteract blood poisoning, retires to the Blue Ridge Mountains to regain his health. As a woodsman, he is accepted by his neighbors in a mountain community. When the state enforces the school law and sends a young schoolteacher, a romance develops between her and Yates, but gossip links him with Talithy, a local girl, and he is suspected of seducing her. The arrival of Dr. Forbes, his partner, with the perfected serum and the testimony of an eyewitness clear him, and all ends happily. *Physicians. Schoolteachers. Blood poisoning. Mountain life. Seduction. Blue Ridge Mountains.*

BLIND ALLEYS **F2.0463**

Famous Players–Lasky. *Dist* Paramount Pictures. 26 Feb **1927** [New York showing; released 12 Mar; c12 Mar 1927; LP23760]. Si; b&w. 35mm. 6 reels, 5,597 ft.

Pres by Adolph Zukor, Jesse L. Lasky. *Assoc Prod* William Le Baron. *Dir* Frank Tuttle. *Screenplay* Emmet Crozier. *Story* Owen Davis. *Photog* Alvin Wyckoff.

Cast: Thomas Meighan *(Capt. Dan Kirby)*, Evelyn Brent *(Sally Ray)*, Greta Nissen *(María d'Âlvarez Kirby)*, Hugh Miller *(Julio Lachados)*, Thomas Chalmers *(Dr. Webster)*, Tammany Young *(gang leader)*.

Melodrama. Captain Kirby of the merchant marine arrives in New York with his Cuban bride, María. Leaving his hotel to buy flowers, Dan forgets his billfold but meets Julio Lachados, a former admirer of María's. As Dan crosses the street, he is knocked unconscious by an automobile, and the owner, Dr. Webster, has him taken to a private hospital. Failing to find her husband and learning that an unidentified man has been hospitalized, María becomes innocently involved with two jewel thieves, who kidnap her. Dan, regaining consciousness, leaves the hospital and is nursed by Sally Ray. María, freed from her captors, turns to Julio for help and learns of Dan's relationship with Sally; but Dan perceives Sally's duplicity and is reunited with his bride. *Sea captains. Cubans. Thieves. Kidnaping. Merchant marine. New York City.*

A BLIND BARGAIN **F2.0464**

Goldwyn Pictures. 3 Dec **1922** [New York premiere; released 10 Dec; c21 Nov 1922; LP18423]. Si; b&w with col sequence. 35mm. 5 reels, 4,473 ft.

Dir Wallace Worsley. *Scen* J. G. Hawks. *Photog* Norbert Brodin.

Cast: Lon Chaney *(Dr. Arthur Lamb/The Hunchback)*, Raymond McKee *(Robert Sandell)*, Virginia True Boardman *(Mrs. Sandell)*, Fontaine La Rue *(Mrs. Lamb)*, Jacqueline Logan *(Angela Marshall)*, Aggie Herring *(Bessie)*, Virginia Madison *(Angela's mother)*.

Mystery melodrama. Source: Barry Pain, *The Octave of Claudius* (London, 1897). In return for money and medical aid for his mother, struggling author Robert Sandell agrees to subject himself to some experiments by Dr. Lamb, who believes he can prove the theory of evolution by changing a man into an approximation of his simian ancestors. Robert is strapped to an operating table before he realizes the nature of the experiments but is saved when a hunchback, a previous subject of the surgeon, uncages another victim, an ape-man, who crushes Dr. Lamb to death. *Authors. Scientists. Hunchbacks. Ape-men. Filial relations. Evolution.*

BLIND CIRCUMSTANCES **F2.0465**

Morante Productions. *Dist* Clark-Cornelius Corp. 1 Jun **1922.** Si; b&w. 35mm. 5 reels, 4,800 ft.

Dir Milburn Morante. *Scen* Victor Gibson. *Story* Jay Inman Kane.

Cast: George Chesebro *(Silent Morse)*, Alfred Hewston *(Captain Skag)*, Harry Arras *(Kelly)*, Vivian Rich *(Ruth)*, Frank Caffray *(Pierre)*.

Northwest melodrama. Believing that he has killed a man in a Canadian dockyard, Silent Morse hides from the law in the northwest snow country, where he rescues a stranger with a broken leg. The two become friends, but the stranger eventually reveals himself to be a Mounted Police officer (Kelly?) and arrests Morse, who has been blinded by a gunpowder explosion. Ruth, Morse's sweetheart, rescues the hero from a trapper sent by Captain Skag (who covets Ruth) to kill Morse. It develops that the Mountie, who has lost his memory, is really the man Morse is supposed to have killed. Morse is cleared, and faith restores his sight. (Reviews leave the sequence of these events in doubt.) *Blindness. Circumstantial evidence. Amnesia. Faith cure. Dockyards. Explosions. Canadian Northwest. Northwest Mounted Police.*

THE BLIND GODDESS **F2.0466**

Famous Players–Lasky. *Dist* Paramount Pictures. ca4 Apr **1926** [New York premiere; released 12 Apr; c12 Apr 1926; LP22599]. Si; b&w. 35mm. 8 reels, 7,249 or 7,363 ft.

Pres by Adolph Zukor, Jesse L. Lasky. *Dir* Victor Fleming. *Scen* Gertrude Orr. *Adapt* Hope Loring, Louis Duryea Lighton. *Photog* Alfred Gilks.

Cast: Jack Holt *(Hugh Dillon)*, Ernest Torrence *(Big Bill Devens)*, Esther Ralston *(Moira Devens)*, Louise Dresser *(Mrs. Eileen Clayton)*, Ward Crane *(Tracy Redmond)*, Richard Tucker *(Henry Kelling)*, Louis Payne *(Taylor)*, Charles Clary *(district attorney)*, Erwin Connelly *(chief of detectives)*, Charles Lane *(judge)*.

Society-mystery melodrama. Source: Arthur Chesney Train, *The Blind Goddess* (New York, 1926). Eileen, who deserted New York politician Big Bill Devens 20 years earlier, returns and begs him to take her back; but he refuses because of the effect on Moira, their daughter. Devens' partner, Kelling, arrives after her departure to confess that he has implicated Devens in a political graft, and in a sudden rage Kelling shoots Devens to avoid exposure. All evidence points to Eileen's guilt, and Hugh Dillon, Moira's fiancé, learning that Eileen is her mother, resigns as district attorney to defend her. Dillon discovers a dictaphone record on which Devens has recorded his dying words, branding Kelling as his killer. Mrs. Clayton is acquitted, mother and daughter are reunited, and Moira and Dillon are married. *Politicians. District attorneys. Fatherhood. Murder. Circumstantial evidence. Parentage. Trials. Dictographs. New York City.*

BLIND HEARTS **F2.0467**

Hobart Bosworth Productions. *Dist* Associated Producers. 3 Oct **1921** [c27 Dec 1921; LP17388]. Si; b&w. 35mm. 6 reels, 5,488 ft.

Dir Rowland V. Lee. *Scen* Joseph Franklin Poland. *Photog* J. O. Taylor.

Cast: Hobart Bosworth *(Lars Larson)*, Wade Boteler *(John Thomas)*, Irene Blackwell *(Mrs. Thomas)*, Colette Forbes *(Hilda Larson)*, Madge Bellamy *(Julia Larson)*, Raymond McKee *(Paul Thomas)*, William Conklin *(James Curdy)*, Lule Warrenton *(Rita)*, Henry Hebert *(James Bradley)*.

Melodrama. Source: Emilie Johnson, "Blind Hearts" (publication undetermined). In 1898 partners John Thomas and Lars Larson travel to the Yukon with their wives. In Alaska, a boy is born to Thomas and a girl to Larson. The latter discovers on his daughter's shoulder a birthmark resembling one on the shoulder of Thomas, creating a suspicion for which he plans future revenge. In the course of 20 years Larson's wife dies, and the partners become millionaires. Larson is being cheated by his confidential man, Curdy, who is threatened with exposure by Bradley. Meanwhile, Julia Larson and Paul Thomas wish to wed, but the match is opposed by Larson. When Bradley is killed aboard Larson's yacht, Curdy persuades Larson that he is responsible, and Larson flees to the North. Paul is accused of the murder and sentenced to be hanged, but Larson returns to San Francisco after reading a notice about the trial. Rita, a halfbreed servant, confesses to exchanging the Larson-Thomas babies at birth, as the former wanted a girl and Thomas a boy. Curdy is convicted, and Paul is free to marry Julia. *Revenge. Birthmarks. Personal identity. Murder. Trials. Alaska. Yukon. San Francisco.*

BLIND TRAIL **F2.0468**

Maloford Productions. *Dist* Weiss Brothers Clarion Photoplays. 15 Jan **1926.** Si; b&w. 35mm. 5 reels.

Dir Leo Maloney.

Cast: Leo Maloney *(Bob Carson)*, Josephine Hill *(Alice Bartlett)*, Nelson McDowell *(Hank O'Hara)*, Bud Osborne *(Mort Van Vleck)*, James Corey *(Al Leitz)*, Albert Hart *(William Skinner)*, Whitehorse *(The Sheriff)*, Evelyn Thatcher *(The Cook)*, Monte Cristo *(himself, a horse)*, Bullet *(himself, a dog)*.

Western melodrama. "The easy-going and adventurous hero and his partner enter strange town and become involved in scheme of villainous money lender and henchmen to defraud young girl of property. After being suspected of robbery and murder, hero, aided by dog, defeats plot and wins girl." ("Motion Picture News Booking Guide," in *Motion Picture News*, 8 May 1926, p23.) *Moneylenders. Property rights. Robbery. Murder. Dogs. Horses.*

BLINDFOLD **F2.0469**

Fox Film Corp. 9 Dec **1928** [c26 Nov 1928; LP25860]. Mus score (Movietone); b&w. 35mm. 6 reels, 5,598 ft.

Pres by William Fox. *Dir* Charles Klein. *Scen* Ewart Adamson. *Titl* William Kernell. *Adapt* Robert Horwood. *Story* Charles Francis Coe. *Photog* Lucien Andriot. *Film Ed* Jack Dennis. *Asst Dir* Virgil Hart.

Cast: Lois Moran *(Mary Brower)*, George O'Brien *(Robert Kelly)*, Maria Alba *(Pepita)*, Earle Foxe *(Dr. Cornelius Simmons)*, Don Terry *(Buddy Brower)*, Fritz Feld *(Thomas Bernard)*, Andy Clyde *(Funeral)*, Crauford Kent *(Ackroyd)*, Robert E. Homans *(Captain Jenkins)*, John Kelly *(chauffeur)*, Phillips Smalley *(jeweler)*.

Melodrama. Mary Brower sees her sweetheart shot down by a gangster's bullet and temporarily goes into shock. Dr. Cornelius Simmons, a master criminal, recognizes her distracted condition and persuades her to participate in his nefarious schemes. Robert Kelly, a flatfoot, arrests several prominent citizens, including Dr. Simmons, and is thrown off the force when there is insufficient evidence to keep these people in jail. Kelly goes after the gang on his own time and meets Mary. He shocks her back to normalcy, and together they bring the criminal gang to justice. Kelly is reinstated to the force, and Mary's prognosis is good. *Police. Physicians. Gangsters. Murder. Amnesia.*

BLINKY **F2.0470**

Universal Pictures. 17 Aug **1923** [New York premiere; released 3 Sep; c31 Jul 1923; LP19261]. Si; b&w. 35mm. 6 reels, 5,740 or 5,807 ft.

Dir-Scen Edward Sedgwick. *Photog* Virgil Miller.

Cast: Hoot Gibson *(Geoffrey Arbuthnot Islip [Blinky])*, Esther Ralston *(Mary Lou Kileen)*, Mathilde Brundage *(Mrs. Islip)*, De Witt Jennings *(Col. "Raw Meat" Islip)*, Elinor Field *(Priscilla Islip)*, Donald Hatswell *(Bertrand Van Dusen)*, Charles K. French *(Major Kileen)*, John Judd *(Husk Barton)*, William E. Lawrence *(Lieutenant Rawkins)*, W. T. McCulley *(The Adjutant)*.

Romantic comedy. Source: Gene Markey, "Blinky," in *Blue Book* (36: 140–149, Jan 1923). Blinky, the bespectacled son of Col. "Raw Meat" Islip, is scorned by his fellow cavalrymen stationed on the Mexican border because his previous military experience was as a Boy Scout. He redeems himself, though, rescuing Major Kileen's daughter from kidnapers, following their trail in Boy Scout fashion! *Kidnaping. Mexican border. Boy Scouts. United States Army—Cavalry.*

THE BLOCK SIGNAL **F2.0471**

Gotham Productions. *Dist* Lumas Film Corp. 15 Sep **1926** [c28 Sep 1926; LP23154]. Si; b&w. 35mm. 6 reels, 5,900 ft.

Pres by Sam Sax. *Supv* Renaud Hoffman. *Dir-Writ* Frank O'Connor. *Scen* Edward J. Meagher. *Story* F. Oakley Crawford. *Photog* Ray June.

Cast: Ralph Lewis *("Jovial Joe" Ryan)*, Jean Arthur *(Grace Ryan)*, Hugh Allan *(Jack Milford)*, George Cheeseboro *(Bert Steele)*, Sidney Franklin *("Roadhouse" Rosen)*, Leon Holmes *("Unhandy" Andy)*, "Missouri" Royer *(Jim Brennan)*.

Melodrama. "Jovial Joe" Ryan, a crack railroad engineer for 20 years, discovers during a card game with his pal, "Roadhouse" Rosen, that his eyes are failing him and he is becoming colorblind. Bert Steel, Ryan's fireman, who is in love with his daughter, Grace, is angered when Ryan passes the examination, ruining his chance for promotion and winning Grace. Ryan confides to Bert that he needs his assistance in watching the block signals; and when Bert misinforms him, he is demoted to signalman because of a wreck and Bert is promoted to engineer. Ryan, meanwhile, invents an automatic signaling device; and though Bert attempts to sabotage his plan to test it, the device successfully prevents another train wreck. *Railroad engineers. Railroad firemen. Signalmen. Inventors. Railroads. Color blindness. Train wrecks.*

BLOCKADE **F2.0472**

FBO Pictures. 16 Dec **1928** [c16 Dec 1928; LP24]. Talking sequences (Photophone); b&w. 35mm. 7 reels, 6,409 ft. [Also si.]

Dir George B. Seitz. *Cont* Harvey Thew. *Dial* George Le Maire. *Titl* Randolph Bartlett. *Adapt* John Stuart Twist. *Story* Louis Sarecky, John Stuart Twist. *Camera* Robert Martin. *Film Ed* Archie Marshek. *Asst Dir* Thomas Atkins.

Cast: Anna Q. Nilsson *(Bess)*, Wallace MacDonald *(Vincent)*, James Bradbury, Sr. *(Gwynn)*, Walter McGrail *(Hayden)*.

Adventure melodrama. Pirate chief Bess Maitland preys on rumrunners operating between Nassau and Florida. The rum fleet is run by Arnold Gwynn, who poses as a retired philanthropist, and is commanded by renegade skipper Hayden. During a raid, Bess is taken captive but escapes in an open boat and is rescued by Vincent Goddard, a wealthy young sportsman. Ashore, Bess is recognized by Hayden, who informs Gwynn of her identity. Vincent is suspected of being the mysterious "Agent Caravan," ace of the revenue force. Gwynn and Bess join forces against Vincent, and Bess asks for the privilege of killing him "to even an old score." Bess does not carry out the assignment and with Vincent's aid warns the revenue cutter and the Marines. Several battles ensue in which the Marines route Gwynn's land forces, and a bombing plane and a revenue cutter conquer the pirates. Bess is revealed to be the real "Agent Caravan," but Vincent persuades her to resign from government service and become his wife. *Rumrunners. Revenue agents. Philanthropists. Sportsmen. Piracy. Revenge. Florida. Nassau. United States Marines.*

A BLONDE FOR A NIGHT **F2.0473**

De Mille Pictures. *Dist* Pathé Exchange. 26 Feb **1928** [c20 Feb 1928; LP24993]. Si; b&w. 35mm. 6 reels, 5,927 ft.

Supv F. McGrew Willis. *Dir* E. Mason Hopper. *Scen* F. McGrew Willis, Rex Taylor. *Titl* John Krafft. *Comedy Titl* Betty Browne. *Story* Wilson Collison. *Photog* Dewey Wrigley. *Art Dir* Stephen Goosson. *Film Ed* James Morley. *Asst Dir* E. J. Babille.

Cast: Marie Prevost *(Marie)*, Franklin Pangborn *(Hector)*, Harrison Ford *(Bob)*, T. Roy Barnes *(George)*, Lucien Littlefield *(valet)*.

Comedy. Following an argument with her husband, newlywed Marie Webster dons a blonde wig in a Paris dress shop owned by Hector, a former suitor, and attracts the attention of George Mason, a friend of her husband's who is a buyer for an American department store. Failing to recognize her as Robert's wife, Mason recommends her to him as a "ravishing blonde." Marie tries to test her husband's fidelity when he, Mason, and Hector follow her on the train to Berlin, but he remains faithful to his wife, whom he believes to be in Berlin. With Mason and Hector in pursuit, Marie manages to install herself in her husband's compartment. To save herself from being ousted, she doffs the wig. All ends happily. *Modistes. Disguise. Marriage. Fidelity. Paris. Berlin.*

BLONDE OR BRUNETTE **F2.0474**

Famous Players–Lasky. *Dist* Paramount Pictures. 8 Jan **1927** [New York premiere; released 22 Jan; c21 Jan 1927; LP23581]. Si; b&w. 35mm. 6 reels, 5,872 ft.

Pres by Adolph Zukor, Jesse L. Lasky. *Assoc Prod* B. P. Schulberg. *Dir* Richard Rosson. *Adapt-Screenplay* John McDermott. *Titl* George Marion, Jr. *Photog* Victor Milner.

Cast: Adolphe Menjou *(Henri Martel)*, Greta Nissen *(Fanny)*, Arlette Marchal *(Blanche)*, Mary Carr *(grandmother)*, Evelyn Sherman *(mother-in-law)*, Emile Chautard *(father-in-law)*, Paul Weigel *(butler)*, Henry Sedley *(Turney)*, André Lanoy *(Hubert)*, Henri Menjou *(detective)*.

Romantic comedy. Source: Jacques Bousquet and Henri Falk, "Un Ange passe," in *Les Oeuvres Libres* (no. 39; 1 Sep 1924). Disgusted with the jazz-mad crowd that infests his Paris residence, Henri Martel leaves the city, and in a Breton village he meets a sweet old lady whose demure granddaughter, Fanny, he finds extremely attractive. He marries Fanny, and while away on business, he leaves his new bride in Blanche's care. He returns to find that Fanny is now drinking, smoking, and Charlestoning along with the fast crowd, and a divorce follows, though Fanny says it will break her grandmother's heart. Henri marries Blanche, but he regrets this action when she makes life dull for him. Complications ensue when Fanny and Henri are forced into deceiving Grandma; Henri can't have Fanny and Blanche won't have him; thus, he is driven to sleeping outside Fanny's door, and not to be outdone, she curls up on the other side of the closed door. *Grandmothers. Marriage. Divorce. Jazz life. Paris. Brittany.*

THE BLONDE SAINT **F2.0475**

Sam E. Rork Productions. *Dist* First National Pictures. 20 Nov **1926** [New York premiere; released 5 Dec; c14 Nov 1926; LP23339]. Si; b&w. 35mm. 7 reels, 6,800 ft.

Pres by Sam E. Rork. *Dir* Svend Gade. *Adapt* Marion Fairfax. *Photog* Tony Gaudio.

Cast: Lewis Stone *(Sebastian Maure)*, Doris Kenyon *(Ghirlaine Bellamy)*, Ann Rork *(Fannia)*, Gilbert Roland *(Annibale)*, Cesare Gravina *(Ilario)*, Malcolm Denny *(Vincent Pamfort)*, Albert Conti *(Andreas)*, Vadim Uraneff *(Nino)*, Lillian Langdon *(Anne's aunt)*, Leo White *(Tito)*.

Romantic melodrama. Source: Stephen French Whitman, *The Isle of Life: a Romance* (New York, 1913). Sebastian Maure, a novelist with a reputation for fast living, falls in love with Ghirlaine Bellamy, an American society girl whose puritanical ideals cause her to be known as "The Blonde Saint." At a dinner party, Ghirlaine tells him she is engaged to marry Vincent Pamfort and will leave for England the next day. Sebastian tricks her into meeting him aboard a boat going to Palermo and jumps overboard with her in his arms; they are picked up by a Sicilian fishing boat and taken to a small island, where he repeatedly attempts to win her love and she threatens to kill herself. Cholera breaks out in the village, and Ghirlaine is advised to remain in the villa; but when Fannia is stricken, Ghirlaine goes to Sebastian. Pamfort arrives but sends his valet to see her because of the plague. While departing with the valet, Ghirlaine saves Sebastian from death at the hands of a Camorrist and confesses her love for him at last. *Socialites. Novelists. Camorrists. Courtship. Puritanism. Cholera. Sicily.*

THE BLONDE VAMPIRE (Entertainment Series) **F2.0476**

Wray Physioc Co. *Dist* Wid Gunning, Inc. Apr **1922** [c25 Mar 1922; LP18417]. Si; b&w. 35mm. 6 reels, 5,843 ft.

Dir Wray Physioc.

Cast: De Sacia Mooers *(Marcia Saville)*, Joseph Smiley *(John Saville)*, Charles Craig *(Simon Downs)*, Miriam Battista *(Alice)*, Robert Conville *("Jimmy the Rat")*, Edwin August *(Martin Kent)*, Frank Beamish *("The Chief")*, Mildred Wayne *(Lou)*, Alfred Barrett *("The Snapper" [Tom Smith])*.

Melodrama. Marcia Saville, thought to be a hopeless flirt by her sweetheart, Martin Kent, shows him that she prefers Tom Smith, a man from the underworld, because Tom is more authoritative. Tom is induced to enter a scheme to rob Marcia's father in a crooked deal instigated by Simon Downs. Downs plans to have Tom marry Marcia and divide the spoils, as she is to receive a sum of money when she marries. Tom is too smart for them and refuses to get involved. Meantime, Kent proves his strength of character, and Marcia is won over. Downs is exposed to her father and discharged. *Flirts. Robbery. Manhood.*

BLONDES BY CHOICE **F2.0477**

Gotham Productions. *Dist* Lumas Film Corp. 1 Oct or Nov **1927** [c31 Oct 1927; LP24604]. Si; b&w. 35mm. 6-7 reels, 6,987 ft.

Pres by Sam Sax. *Supv* Samuel Bischoff. *Dir* Hampton Del Ruth. *Story-Cont* Josephine Quirk. *Titl* Paul Perez. *Photog* Ray June. *Film Ed* Edith Wakeling. *Prod Mgr* Carrol Sax. *Comedy Construction* Clarence Hennecke.

Cast: Claire Windsor *(Bonnie Clinton)*, Allan Simpson *(Cliff Bennett)*, Walter Hiers *(Horace Rush)*, Bodil Rosing *(Caroline Bennett)*, Bess Flowers *(Olga Flint)*, Leigh Willard *(Benjamin Flint)*, Jack Gardner *(Jones, the valet)*, Louise Carver *(Miss Perkins)*, Mai Wells *(Miss Terwilliger)*, Alice Belcher *(Miss Wattles)*, Joseph Belmont *(Everett Hollingsworth)*.

Comedy-drama. While he is driving on the outskirts of the village of Clinton Harbor, Clifford Bennett's car breaks down, and he is towed to town by a girl he has passed on the road. He is amused at the indignation expressed by the townspeople at the opening of a beauty shop and learns that the proprietress is Bonnie Clinton, the girl who aided him. In an effort to stimulate business, she bleaches her hair, arousing the ire of the Ladies' Aid Society; but when they call on her, Bonnie orders them out. Benjamin Flint, local bank president, wants to secure ownership of Bonnie's property, on which he already holds a mortgage, but she refuses to sell. A society lady (Cliff's mother) invites Bonnie to a yacht party, and the ladies are amazed to see Bonnie treated as guest of honor, persuading the spinsters that they need beauty embellishments. Bonnie's business flourishes; she pays off the mortgage and accepts Cliff's marriage proposal. *Bankers. Smalltown life. Prejudice. Beauty shops. Mortgages. Ladies' Aid Society.*

BLOOD AND SAND **F2.0478**

Famous Players–Lasky. *Dist* Paramount Pictures. 5 Aug **1922** [Los Angeles premiere; released 10 Sep; c15 Aug 1922; LP18230]. Si; b&w. 35mm. 9 reels, 8,110 ft.

Pres by Jesse L. Lasky. *Dir* Fred Niblo. *Scen* June Mathis. *Photog* Alvin Wyckoff.

Cast: Rodolph Valentino *(Juan Gallardo)*, Lila Lee *(Carmen)*, Nita Naldi *(Doña Sol)*, George Field *(El Nacional)*, Walter Long *(Plumitas)*, Rosa Rosanova *(Señora Augustias)*, Leo White *(Antonio)*, Charles Belcher *(Don Joselito)*, Jack Winn *(Potaje)*, Marie Marstini *(El Carnacione)*, Gilbert Clayton *(Garabato)*, Harry La Mont *(El Pontelliro)*, George Periolat *(Marquise de Guevera)*, Sidney De Gray *(Dr. Ruiz)*, Fred Becker *(Don José)*, Dorcas Matthews *(Señora Nacional)*, William Lawrence *(Fuentes)*.

Drama. Source: Vicente Blasco-Ibáñez, *Sangre y arena* (Buenos Aires, 1908). Tom Cushing, *Blood and Sand* (New York opening: 20 Sep 1921). A young matador, Juan Gallardo, marries Carmen, his childhood sweetheart, while achieving fame throughout Spain. He is happy but succumbs, nevertheless, to the passionate charms of Doña Sol. Carmen accepts the situation but comes to nurse Juan when he is gored. Though his skill has diminished, he refuses her pleas that he quit the bullring; and he meets disaster when, distracted by the sight of a handsome young stranger with Doña Sol at a bullfight, he fails to defend himself from the first charge of the bull. Juan dies in Carmen's arms, in the sound of cheers for a new hero, after assuring her that she has always had his love. (In another version Juan recovers and gives up both bullfighting and Doña Sol for good.) *Bullfighting. Infidelity. Spain.*

BLOOD AND STEEL **F2.0479**

Independent Pictures. c29 May **1925** [LP21513]. Si; b&w. 35mm. 5 reels.

Pres by Jesse J. Goldburg. *Supv* Jesse J. Goldburg. *Dir* J. P. McGowan. *Story* George Plympton. *Photog* Roland Price. *Film Ed* Betty Davis.

Cast: Helen Holmes *(Helen Grimshaw)*, William Desmond *(Gordon Steele)*, Robert Edeson *(W. L. Grimshaw)*, Mack V. Wright *(Devore Palmer)*, Albert J. Smith *(Jurgin)*, Ruth Stonehouse *(Vera)*, C. L. Sherwood *(The Cook)*, Paul Walters *(Tommy)*, Walter Fitzroy *(Mr. Steele)*.

Western melodrama. Devore Palmer, the administrative assistant to W. L. Grimshaw, the president of the Pacific Coast Railroad, is being paid by a rival railroad to delay work on one of Pacific's new main lines. Annoyed by the delays, Grimshaw comes from the East with his daughter, Helen, and quickly hires Gordon Steele, who has just finished supervising work on the construction of a new dam, to see that the railroad line is finished on time. When Gordon realizes that Grimshaw is the man who once fired his father, he vows also to delay work on the railroad; but when he falls in love with Helen, his better nature prevails and he sets about his job with a passion. The work is completed on time, and the angry and humiliated Palmer sets a runaway engine in motion on the main line. Helen learns of this development and rides wildly to a switch in time to divert the engine into a shed, thereby saving the Pacific Limited. *Railroad magnates. Construction foremen. Business competition. Railroads.*

THE BLOOD BOND **F2.0480**
William Steiner Productions. c23 Jul **1925** [LU21667]. Si; b&w. 35mm. 5 reels.
Scen Ford Beebe.
Cast: Leo Maloney *(Burr Evans)*, Josephine Hill *(Martha Hazard)*.
Western melodrama. Burr Evans, who owns a small ranch, falls in love with Martha Hazard and runs afoul of her aristocratic father, Mark, by refusing to join in the old man's range war on nesters. Nathan Hazard, Mark's brother, falls from his horse and becomes lost in the high country. He is found and cared for by a nester who is a distant relative of Burr's. The nester sets out to inform the Hazards of Nathan's accident, and Buck Weaver, Burr's rival for the affections of Martha, rides into the nester camp and, mistaking Nathan for a nester, attempts to kill him. Burr then rides up and fights off Buck, taking Nathan home with him. Buck later attempts to kill them, but they are saved by a posse sent out by Martha after talking to the nester. Martha and Burr make plans to be wed. *Ranchers. Brothers. Squatters.*

THE BLOOD SHIP **F2.0481**
Columbia Pictures. 18 Jul **1927** [New York premiere; released 10 Aug; c7 Jul 1927; LP24173]. Si; b&w. 35mm. 7 reels, 6,843 ft. [Copyrighted as 8 reels.]
Prod Harry Cohn. *Dir* George B. Seitz. *Scen* Fred Myton. *Photog* J. O. Taylor, Harry Davis.
Cast: Hobart Bosworth *(A. Newman)*, Jacqueline Logan *(Mary)*, Richard Arlen *(John)*, Walter James *(Captain Swope)*, Fred Kohler *(mate)*, James Bradbury, Sr. *(The Knitting Swede)*, Arthur Rankin *(Nils)*, Syd Crossley *(Cockney)*, Frank Hemphill *(second mate)*, Chappell Dossett *(Reverend Deaken)*, Blue Washington *(Negro)*.
Sea melodrama. Source: Norman Springer, *The Blood Ship* (New York, 1922). Captain Swope of the *Golden Bough* is dreaded by all seamen because of the cruelty with which he and Fitzgibbons, his first mate, treat their crews. When his ship berths at San Francisco, Newman, whose wife and daughter were kidnaped by Swope years before and who was framed for murder, inquires about the captain at The Knitting Swede's, a lodging house for sailors. Along with Newman, young John Shreve enlists on the vessel to be near Mary, believed to be the captain's daughter but in reality Newman's child. With a shanghaied crew, the ship leaves port; Swope recognizes Newman and has him put in irons. The crew mutinies, and Newman is released by Shreve and Mary, who, Newman learns, is his daughter. In a confrontation with Swope, Newman gets his revenge and Mary finds happiness with John. *Sea captains. Ships. Shanghaiing. Revenge. Mutiny. Injustice. San Francisco.*

BLOOD TEST **F2.0482**
Adventure Productions. Apr **1923** [scheduled release]. Si; b&w. 35mm. 5 reels.
Dir Don Marquis. *Photog* Ray Rennahan. *Film Ed* Fred Bain.
Cast: Dick Hatton, Nelson McDowell, William Moran, Lafayette McKee, Florence Lee, Billie Bennett, Les Bates, Frank Rice.
Western melodrama. "A bandit decides to hang up his guns and go straight. His foster-son falls in love with the daughter of a local estate owner. The dissolute manager of the estate is jealous of this relationship, and he informs her father that the boy is the son of an outlaw. Her father turns him off the ranch. The manager shoots the owner in order to prevent him from discovering mistakes in the books. He accuses the outlaw's son of the crime. The outlaw puts on his guns and goes to his son's aid. The manager is brought to justice and the foster son marries his beloved." (*National Film Archive Catalogue, Part III, Silent Fiction Films, 1895-1930;* The British Film Institute, London, 1966, p255.) *Bandits. Foster fathers. Ranch managers. Embezzlement. Reformation.*

BLOOD WILL TELL **F2.0483**
Fox Film Corp. 13 Nov **1927** [c7 Nov 1927; LP24642]. Si; b&w. 35mm. 5 reels, 4,556 ft.
Pres by William Fox. *Dir* Ray Flynn. *Scen* Paul Gangelin. *Story* Adele Buffington. *Photog* Reginald Lyons. *Asst Dir* Ted Brooks.
Cast: Buck Jones *(Buck Peters)*, Kathryn Perry *(Sally Morgan)*, Lawford Davidson *(Jim Cowen)*, Robert Kortman *(Carloon)*, Harry Gripp *(Sandy)*, Austin Jewel *(Buddy Morgan)*.
Western melodrama. After rescuing Sally Morgan, Buck Peters discovers that she is bound for a ranch in which she has invested her fortune; he says nothing about his ownership of this very property and obtains a job as ranch hand. Some villains plot to oust Buck, thus leaving Sally helpless before the advances of the treacherous foreman. The foreman abducts Sally with her money and heads for the border, but Buck with his faithful horse escapes his bonds and pursues the villain. ... *Cowboys. Ranchers. Ranch foremen. Abduction. Horses.*

THE BLOODHOUND **F2.0484**
Independent Pictures. *Dist* Film Booking Offices of America. 12 Jul **1925** [c12 Jul 1925; LP21651]. Si; b&w. 35mm. 5 reels, 4,800 ft.
Pres by Jesse J. Goldburg. *Dir* William James Craft. *Cont* Adele S. Buffington. *Story* H. H. Van Loan. *Photog* Arthur Reeves.
Cast: Bob Custer *(Belleau/Sgt. Bill McKenna)*, David Dunbar *(Rambo)*, Ralph McCullough *(Constable Ray Fitzgerald)*, Mary Beth Milford *(Marie Rambo)*, Emily Barrye *(Betty Belleau)*.
Northwest melodrama. "Moose" Rambo is killed by an unknown assailant during a barroom brawl, and Belleau is wrongfully accused of the crime. Sergeant McKenna of the Northwest Mounted Police is detailed to go after him, and Constable Fitzgerald, who saw Belleau on the night of the murder, is struck by the resemblance between Belleau and McKenna. Believing them to be the same man, Fitzgerald confides his suspicions to the chief and is detailed to pursue McKenna. McKenna tracks Belleau and learns that he is his own twin brother. Fitzgerald tracks McKenna, and McKenna, in order to protect his brother's wife and child, allows himself to be arrested as Belleau. Belleau's wife, who quickly sees through the deception, eventually tells the police that they are holding the wrong man. McKenna is freed and again tracks down his brother, bringing him back to stand trial. The real murderer, a halfbreed, has confessed, however, and Belleau is freed. McKenna marries Marie Rambo. *Brothers. Twins. Halfcastes. Murder. Impersonation. Northwest Mounted Police.*

THE BLOT **F2.0485**
Lois Weber Productions. *Dist* F. B. Warren Corp. 4 Sep **1921** [c25 Aug 1921; LP16892]. Si; b&w. 35mm. 7 reels, 7,118 ft.
Prod-Dir-Writ Lois Weber. *Photog* Philip R. Du Bois, Gordon Jennings.
Cast: Philip Hubbard *(Professor Griggs)*, Margaret McWade *(his wife)*, Claire Windsor *(his daughter, Amelia)*, Louis Calhern *(his pupil, Phil West)*, Marie Walcamp *(The Other Girl)*.
Society melodrama. Downtrodden Professor Griggs has a daughter, Amelia, a clerk in the public library, who is admired by Phil West, one of her father's pupils; but because he is from a wealthy family she keeps her distance. She is likewise admired by a poor minister and by young Olsen, their neighbor's son. When Amelia is taken ill, her mother is unable to provide her with enough nourishment and steals a chicken from her neighbor's kitchen. Phil West intervenes to help the Griggs family; and after persuading his father, a college trustee, to increase the professor's salary, Amelia and Phil become engaged. Amelia finds that her mother has returned the chicken, and happiness comes to all. *Professors. Librarians. Clergymen. Poverty. Theft.*

BLOW YOUR OWN HORN **F2.0486**
R-C Pictures. *Dist* Film Booking Offices of America. 11 Nov **1923** [c3 Oct 1923; LP19466]. Si; b&w. 35mm. 6 reels, 6,315 ft.
Dir James W. Horne. *Scen* Rex Taylor. *Photog* Joseph Dubray.
Cast: Warner Baxter *(Jack Dunbar)*, Ralph Lewis *(Nicholas Small)*, Derelys Perdue *(Anne Small)*, Eugene Acker *(Augustus Jolyon)*, William H. Turner *(Dinsmore Bevan)*, Ernest C. Warde *(Gillen Jolyon)*, John Fox, Jr. *("Buddy" Dunbar)*, Mary Jane Sanderson *(Julia Yates)*, Eugenie Forde *(Mrs. Jolyon)*, Dell Boone *(Mrs. Gilroy Yates)*, Billy Osborne *(Percy Yates)*, Stanhope Wheatcroft *(Timothy Cole)*.
Comedy-drama. Source: Owen Davis, *Blow Your Own Horn; a Merry Adventure in Three Acts* (New York, 1926). Jack Dunbar, needing a job, meets millionaire Nicholas Small, who gives him advice and presents him as a colleague. Small would like his daughter, Anne, to marry inventor Gillen Jolyon. Dunbar perfects and successfully demonstrates Jolyon's wireless power transmitting device in spite of Small's attempts to sabotage it, and he rescues Anne when she is caught in an electric power fracas caused by her father's villainy. Anne breaks her engagement with Jolyon and marries Dunbar. *Millionaires. Inventors. Filial relations. Electric power. Radio.*

BLUE BLAZES **F2.0487**

Doubleday Productions. *Dist* Western Pictures Exploitation Co. 13 Jan **1922** [trade review]. Si; b&w. 35mm. 5 reels.

Dir (see note) Robert Kelly, Charles W. Mack.

Cast: Lester Cuneo *(Jerry Connors)*, Francelia Billington *(Mary Lee)*, Fannie Midgley *(Mrs. Lee)*, Bert Sprotte *(Black Lanning)*, Roy Watson *(foreman of ranch)*, Phil Gastrock *(lawyer)*.

Western melodrama. "Jerry Connors, tired of the flattery that goes with success as a champion fighter, jumps a train to the West, gets left at a wayside station, is robbed by tramps, and disguised as one of them asks food at a neighboring ranch. He soon finds that the girl and her mother are in trouble over the mortgage and the villain is seeking to force the girl to marry him. He decides to stick, and after the many vicissitudes outlined above, succeeds in getting the best of the villain and winning back the valuable oil property. He then discloses the fact that he is not a tramp but a wealthy pugilist, and all ends happily." (*Moving Picture World*, 21 Jun 1922, p320.) *Prizefighters. Tramps. Mortgages. Oil fields.*

Note: Kelly and Mack are separately credited with the direction.

BLUE BLAZES (Blue Streak Western) **F2.0488**

Universal Pictures. 21 Mar **1926** [c16 Jan 1926; LP22279]. Si; b&w. 35mm. 5 reels, 4,659 ft.

Dir Joseph Franz. *Adapt* Frank Beresford. *Story* Frank C. Robertson. *Photog* Jack Young.

Cast: Pete Morrison *(Dee Halloran)*, Jim Welsh *(McKeller)*, Barbara Starr *(Grace Macy)*, Dick La Reno, Jr. *(Jess Macy)*, Les Bates *(Buck Fitzgerald)*, Jerome La Grasse *(Matt Bunker)*, James Lowe *(Rastus)*.

Western melodrama. Dee Halloran rescues Grace Macy from a runaway stage and learns that her grandfather was murdered before he could divulge the whereabouts of a large sum of money he had hidden from thieves. Buck Fitzgerald, the leader of a gang of desperadoes, weasels himself into Grace's confidence and leads her to believe that McKeller, a friend of Dee's, was responsible for the murder. Thinking that Grace knows the location of her grandfather's money, Fitzgerald later tries by force to make her talk. She gets away from him and flees to her grandfather's cabin in Death Wash. Dee comes to her rescue, subdues Fitzgerald, and finds the missing money—winning Grace's love and trust. *Grandfathers. Gangs. Thieves. Murder.*

BLUE BLOOD **F2.0489**

Vitagraph Co. of America. Jun **1922**. Si; b&w. 35mm. 6 reels.

Cast: Alice Calhoun.

Melodrama(?). No information about the nature of this film has been found.

BLUE BLOOD **F2.0490**

Chadwick Pictures. 1 Dec **1925** [c16 Nov 1925; LP22005]. Si; b&w. 35mm. 6 reels, 5,600 ft.

Dir Scott Dunlap.

Cast: George Walsh *(Robert Chester, a young scientist)*, Cecille Evans *(Geraldine Hicks, daughter of the chewing gum king)*, Philo McCullough *(Percy Horton, a social parasite)*, Joan Meredith *(Delight Burns, society debutante)*, Robert Bolder *(Leander Hicks, a chewing gum king)*, Harvey Clark *(Tim Reilly, a hotel detective)*, G. Howe Black *(Amos Jenkins, scientist's colored servant)*, Eugene Borden *(Charley Stevens, Horton's chauffeur)*.

Society melodrama. Source: Frank Howard Clark, "American Aristocracy" (publication undetermined). Chewing gum king Leander Hicks is trying to persuade his willful daughter, Geraldine, to marry malted milk king Percy Horton. Geraldine meets scientist Robert Chester while he is hunting bugs and butterflies, and they fall in love. Bob discovers that Horton is really the leader of a gang of rum-smugglers. Horton attempts a getaway in his yacht with Geraldine and her father on board. Bob boards the vessel, defeats Horton, and is attacked by the crew; but the police arrive and arrest the gang. The lovers are united. *Entomologists. Rumrunners. Parasites. Chewing gum. Malted milk.*

Note: Copyright title: *The Blue Blood.*

THE BLUE DANUBE **F2.0491**

De Mille Pictures. *Dist* Pathé Exchange. 11 Mar **1928** [c11 Feb 1928; LP24974]. Si; b&w. 35mm. 7 reels, 6,589 ft.

Assoc Prod Ralph Block. *Dir* Paul Sloane. *Scen* Harry Carr, Paul Sloane. *Titl* Edwin Justus Mayer, John Krafft. *Story* John Farrow. *Photog* Arthur Miller. *Art Dir* Anton Grot. *Film Ed* Margaret Darrell. *Asst Dir* William Scully. *Prod Mgr* Harry Poppe. *Cost* Adrian.

Cast: Leatrice Joy *(Marguerite)*, Joseph Schildkraut *(Ludwig)*, Nils Asther *(Erich von Statzen)*, Seena Owen *(Helena Boursch)*, Albert Gran *(Herr Boursch)*, Frank Reicher *(Baron)*.

Romantic melodrama. Marguerite, the beauty of an Austrian village, loves the poverty-stricken Baron Erich von Statzen, although her mother is opposed to the affair, having been made suspicious by the hunchback Ludwig, who is smitten by Marguerite's charms and insanely jealous of Statzen. Statzen's uncle would have him marry Helena Boursch, the local brewer's daughter, to save his dwindling estate. Ordered to the front when war is declared, Statzen is forced to leave without saying goodby to Marguerite. Although she receives no letters from him (Ludwig intercepts them), Marguerite remains faithful to Statzen during his absence. Finally, when the uncle and the brewer trick her into believing that Statzen no longer loves her, she marries Ludwig. Statzen returns on the wedding night and discerns Ludwig's treachery. The frenzied hunchback stabs himself in a fit of rage and falls out of a window overlooking the Danube. *Nobility. Hunchbacks. Brewers. Suicide. Weddings. World War I. Austria. Danube River. Documentation.*

THE BLUE EAGLE **F2.0492**

Fox Film Corp. 12 Sep **1926** [c12 Sep 1926; LP23122]. Si; b&w. 35mm. 7 reels, 6,200 ft.

Pres by William Fox. *Dir* John Ford. *Scen* L. G. Rigby. *Photog* George Schneiderman. *Asst Dir* Edward O'Fearna.

Cast: George O'Brien *(George D'Arcy)*, Janet Gaynor *(Rose Cooper)*, William Russell *(Big Tim Ryan)*, Robert Edeson *(Father Joe)*, David Butler *(Nick Galvani)*, Phil Ford *(Limpy D'Arcy)*, Ralph Sipperly *(Slats Mulligan)*, Margaret Livingston *(Mary Rohan)*, Jerry Madden *(Baby Tom)*, Harry Tenbrook *(Bascom)*, Lew Short *(Captain McCarthy)*.

Melodrama. Source: Gerald Beaumont, "The Lord's Referee," in *Red Book Magazine* (41:45–49, 126–134, Jul 1923). George D'Arcy and Tim Ryan, rival leaders of neighborhood gangs, become stokers and watertenders on a U. S. battleship during the World War. For a time, their rivalry over politics, social affairs, and the same girl—Rose—is held in check by discipline, but their parish priest, Father Joe, the ship's chaplain, finally decides to let them fight it out in the ring. Their fight is interrupted, however, by a submarine attack, which is repelled. After the war the feud continues until narcotics smugglers kill one of George's brothers and shoot Tim's buddy; together they storm the smugglers' stronghold and blow up their submarine. Later, under the supervision of Father Joe, a fight is staged, and George is the victor. *Stokers. Clergymen. Smugglers. Gangs. Submarines. Narcotics. Boxing. World War I. United States Navy.*

BLUE SKIES **F2.0493**

Fox Film Corp. 17 Mar **1929** [c18 Mar 1929; LP218]. Mus score & sd eff (Movietone); b&w. 35mm. 6 reels, 5,408 ft. [Also si; 5,367 ft.]

Pres by William Fox. *Supv* Jeff Lazarus. *Dir* Alfred L. Werker. *Scen* John Stone. *Titl* Malcolm Stuart Boylan. *Photog* L. W. O'Connell. *Songs: "You Never Can Tell," "It's a Fine How D'Ya Do," "How Were We To Know"* Walter Bullock, Lew Pollack. *Asst Dir* Horace Hough.

Cast—First Episode: Carmencita Johnson *(Dorothy May, age 6)*, Freddie Frederick *(Richard Lewis, age 8)*, Ethel Wales *(matron)*.

Cast—Second Episode: Helen Twelvetrees *(Dorothy May)*, Frank Albertson *(Richard Lewis)*, Rosa Gore *(Nellie Crouch [matron])*, William Orlamond *(janitor)*, E. H. Calvert *(Mr. Semple Jones)*, Evelyn Hall *(Mrs. Semple Jones)*, Claude King *(Richard Danforth)*, Adele Watson *(1st assistant matron)*, Helen Jerome Eddy *(2d assistant matron)*.

Drama. Source: Frederick Hazlitt Brennan, "The Matron's Report," in *Cosmopolitan* (Mar 1928). "'Blue Skies' is Fox's kid version of 'Over the Hill.' It's about an orphan asylum instead of a poorhouse, with none of the tears the adult orphan picture possessed. ... Youngsters occupy a reel with close-ups and ice cream. Hack situations of turning the hose on the matron, the fat boy getting a licking by the little boy for eating the tiny girl's ice cream—they're all in it. Then of a sudden it's Frank Albertson wearing overalls and Helen Twelvetrees, the girl. The kids around them are still as young as they were in the first reel, excepting one or two. A rich daddy visits the home and Frank changes his foundling dress for that of the girl's. Off she goes to the wealthy home. Of course a year later an identification card is found, but Frank satisfies daddy and the girl. Marriage does it." (*Variety*, 17 Jul 1929, p53.) *Children. Adoption. Orphanages.*

THE BLUE STREAK **F2.0494**
Richard Talmadge Productions. *Dist* Film Booking Offices of America. 31 Jan **1926** [c28 Dec 1925; LP22471]. Si; b&w. 35mm. 5 reels, 4,954 ft.

Pres by A. Carlos. *Dir* Noel Mason. *Story-Cont* James Bell Smith. *Photog* Jack Stevens, Frank Evans. *Film Ed* Doane Harrison. *Tech Dir* Eugene McMurtrie.

Cast: Richard Talmadge *(Richard Manley)*, Charles Clary *(John Manley)*, Louise Lorraine *(Inez Del Rio)*, Henry Herbert *(Jack Slade)*, Charles Hill Mailes *(Don Carlos)*, Victor Dillingham *(Slade's assistant)*, Tote Du Crow *(Pedro)*.

Action melodrama. "Richard Manley visits El Grande mine in his father's interests, renews acquaintance with Inez Del Rio, niece of Don Carlos, owner of the mine. Jack Slade, superintendent, is the rascal responsible for stopping of the ore shipments to Dick's father. Slade plots to remove Dick, who has evidence of his conspiracy, and kidnaps him. But Dick escapes in time to reach the hacienda and rescue the Don and Inez from Slade. Dick constitutes himself Inez's protector for life." (*Motion Picture News*, 20 Feb 1926, p915.) *Mexicans. Mine superintendents. Kidnaping. Mines.*

BLUE STREAK O'NEIL **F2.0495**
Bud Barsky Productions. 15 Dec **1926** [New York State license]. Si; b&w. 35mm. 5 reels, 4,500 ft.

Dir Paul Hurst.

Cast: Al Hoxie.

Western melodrama. "On mission to discover rustlers of cattle on Britton ranch, hero exposes villains mingling with sheriff's posse. Having won ranch for heroine, he accepts from her a half interest in it, and also the girl." (*Motion Picture News Booking Guide*, 12:21, Apr 1927.) *Rustlers. Sheriffs. Posses. Ranches.*

BLUEBEARD, JR. **F2.0496**
James Livingston. *Dist* American Releasing Corp. 19 Mar **1922** [c20 Apr 1922; LP17764]. Si; b&w. 35mm. 5 reels, 4,140 ft.

Dir Scott Dunlap. *Scen* John W. Grey. *Story* Helen Van Upp. *Photog* Stephen Norton.

Cast: Mary Anderson *(Nan Beech)*, Jack Connolly *(Tom Beech)*, George Hernandez *(The Lawyer)*, Laura Anson *(Lucy Page)*, Lila Leslie *(Mrs. Beach)*.

Domestic comedy. Forced to abandon their apartment because of an exorbitant increase in rent, Tom and Nan Beech take up residence in a cheaper, smaller flat. During a quarrel over their situation, Tom angrily leaves for work, while Nan goes to a friend's home. Tom discovers that he is to receive an inheritance provided that he is settled and is leading a happy home life, which the lawyer insists on investigating for himself. Tom persuades his wife's best friend to act as his "temporary" wife and borrows a rich man's house. The rich man's wife, the "temporary," and Nan all arrive unexpectedly, and the lawyer is convinced that Tom is a regular Bluebeard. Complications ensue, but the owner of the house arrives and all is explained. The Beeches are happily reunited, and Tom receives the inheritance. *Lawyers. Marriage. Housing. Inheritance.*

BLUEBEARD'S 8TH WIFE **F2.0497**
Famous Players–Lasky. *Dist* Paramount Pictures. 5 Aug **1923** [New York premiere; released 9 Sep 1923; c26 Jun 1923; LP19167]. Si; b&w. 35mm. 6 reels, 5,960 ft.

Pres by Jesse L. Lasky. *Dir* Sam Wood. *Scen* Sada Cowan. *Photog* Alfred Gilks. *Wax Sculptress* Milba K. Lloyd. *Hairdresser* Hattie Tabourne.

Cast: Gloria Swanson *(Mona de Briac)*, Huntley Gordon *(John Brandon)*, Charles Green *(Robert)*, Lianne Salvor *(Lucienne)*, Paul Weigel *(Marquis de Briac)*, Frank Butler *(Lord Henry Seville)*, Robert Agnew *(Albert de Marceau)*, Irene Dalton *(Alice George)*, Majel Coleman, Thais Valdemar.

Romantic comedy. Source: Alfred Savoir, *La Huitième Femme de Barbe Bleue* (trans. by Charlton Andrews; New York opening under the title *Bluebeard's 8th Wife:* 1921). Mona de Briac, beautiful daughter of a French nobleman, is induced to marry wealthy American John Brandon because her family needs his money. She learns that her husband has divorced seven wives. This knowledge makes her so angry that she tries to force Brandon, who really loves her, into another divorce. Brandon refuses to release her, and they are finally reconciled. *Nobility. Divorce. Marriage. France.*

BLUEBEARD'S SEVEN WIVES **F2.0498**
First National Pictures. ca13 Jan **1926** [New York showing; c30 Dec 1925; LP22216]. Si; b&w. 35mm. 8 reels, 7,774 ft.

Pres by Robert Kane. *Dir* Alfred Santell. *Titl* Randolph Bartlett. *Story* Blanche Merrill, Paul Schofield. *Photog* Robert Haller. *Art Dir* Robert M. Haas. *Prod Mgr* Joseph C. Boyle.

Cast: Ben Lyon *(John Hart/Don Juan Hartez)*, Lois Wilson *(Mary Kelly)*, Blanche Sweet *(Juliet)*, Dorothy Sebastian *(Gilda La Bray)*, Diana Kane *(Kathra Granni)*, Sam Hardy *(Gindelheim)*, Dick Bernard, Andrew Mack *(film magnates)*, B. C. Duval *(Dan Pennell)*, Wilfred Lytell *(Paris)*, Dorothy Sebastian, Katherine Ray, Ruby Blaine, Lucy Fox, Muriel Spring, Kathleen Martyn, Diana Kane *(Bluebeard's seven wives)*.

Comedy. When his sweetheart, Mary Kelly, insists that he must grow a moustache before she will marry him, John Hart, a plodding bank clerk, becomes so distracted that he ends up short in his accounts. He is fired and, unable to land another job, becomes an extra in the movies. In a fit of temperament, the leading man in a major production refuses to work, and the film's director, in a fit of conceit, decides to prove that he can choose any poor slob to replace the leading man. He picks John. John turns out to be a natural and soon finds himself a star, completely at the mercy of the publicity hacks, who put him through seven marriages in as many weeks, each terminating after the wedding night. John soon tires of his frenetic life, runs away, and marries Mary Kelly. They retire to a farm; and despite the pleas of motion picture magnates, John remains there with Mary and the cows. *Bank clerks. Motion picture extras. Motion picture directors. Actors. Farmers. Marriage. Divorce. Motion pictures. Hollywood.*

BLUFF **F2.0499**
Famous Players–Lasky. *Dist* Paramount Pictures. 12 May **1924** [c21 May 1924; LP20225]. Si; b&w. 35mm. 6 reels, 5,442 ft.

Pres by Adolph Zukor, Jesse L. Lasky. *Dir* Sam Wood. *Scen* Willis Goldbeck. *Story* Rita Weiman, Josephine Quirk. *Photog* Alfred Gilks.

Cast: Agnes Ayres *(Betty Hallowell)*, Antonio Moreno *(Robert Fitzmaurice)*, Fred Butler *("Boss" Mitchell)*, Clarence Burton *(Jack Hallowell)*, Pauline Paquette *(Fifine)*, Jack Gardner *(Dr. Steve Curtiss)*, Arthur Hoyt *(Algy Henderson)*, E. H. Calvert *(Norton Conroy)*, Roscoe Karns *(Jack Hallowell)*.

Society drama. In order to give her brother medical aid, Betty Hallowell represents herself to be fashion designer Nina Loring, who is missing. Although successful, she is arrested as Miss Loring on an embezzlement charge but is rescued by attorney Robert Fitzmaurice, with whom she falls in love. *Couturiers. Lawyers. Brother-sister relationship. Embezzlement. Impersonation.*

THE BLUSHING BRIDE **F2.0500**
Fox Film Corp. 27 Feb **1921** [c27 Feb 1921; LP16266]. Si; b&w. 35mm. 5 reels.

Pres by William Fox. *Dir-Story-Scen* Jules G. Furthman. *Photog* Otto Brautigan.

Cast: Eileen Percy *(Beth Rupert)*, Herbert Heyes *(Kingdom Ames)*, Philo McCullough *(Dick Irving)*, Jack La Reno *(K. Ames)*, Rose Dione *(Mrs. K. Ames)*, Harry Dunkinson *(butler)*, Bertram Johns *(Duke of Downcastle)*, Herschel Mayall *(Lord Landsmere)*, Sylvia Ashton *(Mrs. James Horton-Kemp)*, Earl Crain *(Mr. Scanlon)*, Madge Orlamond *(Mrs. Scanlon)*, Robert Klein *(footman)*.

Comedy. Beth Rupert leaves the follies to take up domestic life as the wife of wealthy suitor Kingdom Ames, who believes that she is the niece of the Duke of Downcastle. At the Ames home, she faints at the sight of the butler, whom she recognizes as her long-lost uncle. Further complications arise with the arrival of the uncle's cousin, who poses as the duke. Following several mixups, the uncle is revealed to be the true duke. *Uncles. Domestics. Aristocrats. Marriage. Impersonation. Follies.*

THE BOASTER **F2.0501**
Paul Gerson Pictures. *Dist* Aywon Film Corp. 14 Dec **1926** [New York State license]. Si; b&w. 35mm. 5 reels, 5,200 ft.

Dir Duke Worne. *Scen* Grover Jones.

Cast: Richard Holt, Gloria Grey.

Comedy. The son of a millionaire, given to fits of boasting, proves himself equal to his estimation of himself. *Millionaires. Braggarts.*

BOB HAMPTON OF PLACER **F2.0502**
Marshall Neilan Productions. *Dist* Associated First National Pictures. May **1921** [c4 May 1921; LP16469]. Si; b&w. 35mm. 7-8 reels, 7,268 ft.

Prod-Dir Marshall Neilan. *Scen* Marion Fairfax. *Photog* Jacques Bizeul, David Kesson. *Art Dir* Ben Carré.

Cast: James Kirkwood *(Bob Hampton)*, Wesley Barry *(Dick)*, Marjorie Daw *(The Kid)*, Pat O'Malley *(Lieutenant Brant)*, Noah Beery *(Red Slavin)*, Frank Leigh *(Silent Murphy)*, Dwight Crittenden *(General Custer)*, Tom Gallery *(Reverend Wyncoop)*, Priscilla Bonner *(schoolteacher)*, Charles West *(Major Brant)*, Bert Sprotte *(sheriff)*, Carrie Clark Ward *(housekeeper)*, Vic Potel *(Willie McNeil)*, Buddy Post *(Jack Moffet)*.

Historical drama. Source: Randall Parrish, *Bob Hampton of Placer* (Chicago, 1910). Bob Hampton, a former captain in the U. S. Army, wrongfully convicted and having served a prison sentence for the killing of Major Brant, becomes notorious as a gambler and gunfighter throughout the West in 1876. Joining a party of settlers, Hampton saves the life of a girl known as "The Kid" from an Indian siege. Lieutenant Brant, son of the major, falls in love with her, and Hampton later discovers that she is his lost daughter. Finding the real murderer, Hampton forces him to confess, then continues his journey and joins Custer's last stand with Dick, a befriended waif, and they go to their death in each other's arms. His daughter learns that her father's name has been cleared, and she marries Lieutenant Brant. *Fatherhood. Murder. Frontier and pioneer life. Custer's Last Stand. Little Big Horn.*

BOBBED HAIR **F2.0503**

Realart Pictures. *Dist* Paramount Pictures. 12 Mar **1922** [c15 Mar 1922; LP17646]. Si; b&w. 35mm. 5 reels, 4,395 ft.

Dir Thomas N. Heffron. *Scen* Harvey Thew. *Story* Hector Turnbull. *Photog* William E. Collins.

Cast: Wanda Hawley *(Polly Heath)*, William Boyd *(Dick Barton)*, Adele Farrington *(Aunt Emily)*, Leigh Wyant *(Zoe Dean)*, Jane Starr *(Evelyn)*, Margaret Vilmore *(Daisy)*, William P. Carleton *(Paul Lamont)*, Ethel Wales *(Mrs. Lamont)*, Junior Coghlan, Robert Kelly *(The Lamont Children)*.

Romantic satire. Polly Heath, objecting to her aunt's attempts to marry her off to Dick Barton, a respectable businessman, runs away to join her friend Zoe Dean in an art colony. Polly becomes fascinated with Paul Lamont, a futuristic poet, who neglects to tell her that he is married and the father of two children. When Lamont invites her to his studio one night, having sent the family away, one of the children arouses his wife's suspicions and she returns home to surprise Lamont making love to Polly. Polly joins Mrs. Lamont in denouncing the philanderer, and Dick, ready to cancel his engagement, accepts Zoe's explanation and the affections of Polly, now reconciled to marry him. *Aunts. Businessmen. Artists. Philanderers. Poets. Courtship. Art colonies.*

BOBBED HAIR **F2.0504**

Warner Brothers Pictures. 25 Oct **1925** [c8 Jul 1925; LP21639]. Si; b&w. 35mm. 6 reels, 5,817 ft.

Dir Alan Crosland. *Scen* Lewis Milestone. *Photog* Byron Haskins. *Adtl Photog* Frank Kesson. *Asst Dir* Gordon Hollingshead.

Cast: Marie Prevost *(Connemara Moore)*, Kenneth Harlan *(David Lacy)*, Louise Fazenda *("Sweetie")*, John Roche *(Saltonstall Adams)*, Emily Fitzroy *(Aunt Celimena Moore)*, Reed Howes *(Bingham Carrington)*, Pat Hartigan *("Swede")*, Walter Long *("Doc")*, Francis McDonald *("Pooch")*, Tom Ricketts *(Mr. Brewster)*, Otto Hoffman *(McTish)*, Kate Toncray *(Mrs. Parker)*, Pal *(a dog)*.

Melodramatic farce. Source: Carolyn Wells, Alexander Woollcott and Louis Bromfield, *et al.*, *Bobbed Hair* (New York, 1925). Connemara Moore, an heiress to millions, cannot decide between two suitors, one of whom wants her hair bobbed, the other of whom does not. To add to her dilemma, Connemara will be disinherited by her wealthy aunt if she bobs her hair. Running away from it all, Connemara gets into a car driven by David Lacy, and, in short succession, becomes involved with bootleggers, wild parties, fights, and love. Connemara marries David, thereby solving her dilemma. *Heiresses. Aunts. Bootleggers. Dogs.*

THE BOBBED SQUAB *see* **ALL DOLLED UP**

BODY AND SOUL **F2.0505**

Micheaux Film Corp. 9 Nov **1925** [New York State license application]. Si; b&w. 35mm. 5 reels.

Cast: Paul Robeson, Julia Theresa Russell, Mercedes Gilbert.

Melodrama. "The story of a man, minister of the gospel, whose habits and manner of life are anything but that of a good man. He associates with the proprietor of a notorious gambling house, extorts money from him, betrays a girl of his parish, forces her to steal from the Bible her mother's savings, forces the girl to leave home, and finally kills the girl's brother when he comes to the sister's protection." (New York State licensing records.) *Clergymen. Negro life. Gambling. Extortion. Theft. Seduction. Murder.*

BODY AND SOUL **F2.0506**

Metro-Goldwyn-Mayer Pictures. 1 Oct **1927** [c12 Oct 1927; LP24499]. Si; b&w. 35mm. 6 reels, 5,902 ft.

Dir Reginald Barker. *Screenplay* Elliott Clawson. *Titl* Joe Farnham. *Photog* Percy Hilburn. *Sets* Cedric Gibbons, Arnold Gillespie. *Film Ed* William Le Vanway. *Asst Dir* Nick Grinde. *Wardrobe* René Hubert.

Cast: Aileen Pringle *(Hilda)*, Norman Kerry *(Ruffo)*, Lionel Barrymore *(Dr. Leyden)*, T. Roy Barnes *(The Postman)*.

Romantic drama. Source: Katharine Newlin Burt, "Body and Soul," in *Everybody's* (vol 40–41, Jan–Jul 1919). Dr. Leyden, a brilliant surgeon driven by drink to disgrace, retires to an Alpine village in Switzerland and there becomes enamored of Hilda, a servant at the inn where he lives. To win her love, he intercepts the letter written to her by Ruffo, a dashing ski jumper; and assuming she has been deserted by her lover, Hilda marries the doctor. When Ruffo returns, Leyden, remorseful and also intensely jealous, takes seriously Ruffo's suggestion that he brand his wife. He sinks lower when Ruffo takes Hilda away, but in the end he saves the life of his rival and is himself killed in a snow avalanche. *Surgeons. Skiers. Chambermaids. Courtship. Marriage. Alcoholism. Branding. Switzerland. Alps. Avalanches.*

THE BODY PUNCH **F2.0507**

Universal Pictures. 14 Jul **1929** [c22 May 1928; LP25294]. Si; b&w. 35mm. 5 reels, 4,786 ft.

Dir Leigh Jason. *Story-Scen* Harry O. Hoyt. *Titl* Gardner Bradford. *Adapt* Clarence J. Marks. *Photog* Joseph Brotherton. *Film Ed* Frank Atkinson.

Cast: Jack Daugherty *(Jack Townsend)*, Virginia Browne Faire *(Natalie Sutherland)*, George Kotsonaros *(Paul Steinert)*, Wilbur Mack *(Peyson Turner)*, Monte Montague *(manager)*, Arthur Millett *(detective)*.

Comedy-drama. Boxer Jack Townsend and wrestler Paul Steinert, at odds with each other, fight a benefit match. During the fight, fortune hunter Peyson Turner, who thinks Townsend is his rival for society girl Natalie Sutherland, seeks to frame Townsend by placing a stolen bracelet in his dressing room. The police capture Townsend when Turner, who was knocked unconscious in Townsend's dressing room, implicates him. Townsend escapes and leads the police to Steinert, the real thief. Turner is revealed to be a cad and Natalie realizes that Townsend is the man of her dreams. *Wrestlers. Boxers. Socialites. Fortune hunters. Frameup.*

LA BOHÈME **F2.0508**

Metro-Goldwyn-Mayer Pictures. 24 Feb **1926** [New York premiere]. Si; b&w. 35mm. 9 reels, 8,781 ft.

Dir King Vidor. *Cont* Ray Doyle, Harry Behn. *Titl* William Conselman, Ruth Cummings. *Story* Fred De Gresac. *Photog* Hendrik Sartov. *Sets* Cedric Gibbons, Arnold Gillespie. *Film Ed* Hugh Wynn. *Mus Score* William Axt.

Cast: Lillian Gish *(Mimi)*, John Gilbert *(Rodolphe)*, Renée Adorée *(Musette)*, George Hassell *(Schaunard)*, Roy D'Arcy *(Vicomte Paul)*, Edward Everett Horton *(Colline)*, Karl Dane *(Benoît)*, Frank Currier *(theater manager)*, Mathilde Comont *(Madame Benoît)*, Gino Corrado *(Marcel)*, Gene Pouyet *(Bernard)*, David Mir *(Alexis)*, Catherine Vidor *(Louise)*, Valentina Zimina *(Phémie)*, Blanche Payson *(factory supervisor)*.

Romantic drama. Source: Henri Murger, *Scènes de la vie de Bohème* (Paris, 1851). Mimi, a poor seamstress in the Latin Quarter, is unable to pay her rent and is about to be evicted, when Rodolphe, a struggling young playwright who admires her fragile beauty, takes her into his circle of bohemian friends. Her gratitude to Rodolphe develops into an idyllic love. As time passes, Rodolphe ekes out a meager existence writing for a newspaper while working on a play, inspired by Mimi. He is discharged, but Mimi keeps him in ignorance of the fact, pretending to deliver his articles and secretly sewing at night to support them both. Paul, a cynical boulevardier attracted to Mimi, is induced by her to take the play to a theater manager, and she accompanies him, in clothes borrowed from her friend, Musette. Rodolphe suspects her of infidelity, and she leaves him. Later, his play is successful, and, at the peak of his fame, Mimi returns to him desperately ill and dies in his arms. *Playwrights. Seamstresses. Men-about-town. Theatrical managers. Poverty. Courtship. Bohemianism. Paris—Quartier Latin.*

THE BOLTED DOOR **F2.0509**
Universal Pictures. 5 Mar **1923** [c14 Feb 1923; LP18668]. Si; b&w. 35mm. 5 reels, 4,126 ft.

Dir William Worthington. *Scen* George Randolph Chester. *Story* George Gibbs. *Photog* Benjamin Kline.

Cast: Frank Mayo *(Brooke Garriott)*, Charles A. Stevenson *(Oliver Judson)*, Phyllis Haver *(Natalie Judson)*, Nigel Barrie *(Rene Deland)*, Kathleen Kirkham *(Natalie's chum)*, Frank Whitson *(Attorney Bronson)*, Anderson Smith *(Attorney Rowe)*, Calvert Carter *(butler)*.

Melodrama. Source: George Gibbs, *The Bolted Door* (New York, 1910). In order to inherit her uncle's fortune Natalie Judson enters a marriage of convenience to mechanic Brooke Garriott, who has long loved her. Natalie pursues her gay life while Brooke plunges himself into his work and successfully perfects an engine. One evening Brooke comes home to find Rene Deland making love to Natalie and shows them a telegram saying that the Judson fortune has been wiped out. Deland is no longer interested in Natalie, who now realizes Brooke's true worth and her love for him. *Inventors. Wealth. Inheritance. Marriage of convenience.*

THE BONANZA BUCKAROO **F2.0510**
Action Pictures. *Dist* Associated Exhibitors. 28 Aug **1926** [c26 Jul 1926; LU22965]. Si; b&w. 35mm. 5 reels, 4,460 ft.

Pres by Lester F. Scott, Jr. *Dir* Richard Thorpe. *Scen* Betty Burbridge. *Story* Barr Cross. *Photog* Ray Reis.

Cast: Buffalo Bill Jr. *(Bill Merritt)*, Harry Todd *(Chewin' Charlie)*, Judy King *(Cleo Gordon)*, Lafe McKee *(Mr. Andrew Gordon)*, Winifred Landis *(Mrs. Andrew Gordon)*, Al Taylor *(Carney)*, Charles Whitaker *(Fraction Jack)*, Dutch Maley *(Spike)*, Emily Barrye *(The Maid)*, Bill Ryno *(The Sheriff)*.

Western comedy-melodrama. Bill Merritt and his pal, Chewin' Charlie, notice a touring car passing them on the road. Soon the car stops, and the party sets out after a jackrabbit wanted by an elderly lady in the car. Bill, realizing the brakes have slipped on a downgrade, rescues the runaway car and its occupant, Mrs. Gordon, and wins the lady's admiration. Invited to the hotel of millionaire mineowner Andrew Gordon, Bill becomes interested in his daughter, Cleo, but is told that the man who aspires to be her husband must possess wealth. That night Bill overhears a plot to take over a strip of land between Gordon's mine and that of his enemy Tom Middleton; Bill and Charlie set out to stake their claim, and after subduing "Fraction" Jack, they register the claim. Bill persuades Gordon to buy out his claim and saves Charlie from claim jumpers. *Cowboys. Millionaires. Claim jumpers. Social classes. Mines. Courtship. Business competition. Jackrabbits.*

THE BOND BOY **F2.0511**
Inspiration Pictures. *Dist* Associated First National Pictures. Oct **1922** [c28 Sep 1922; LP18249]. Si; b&w. 35mm. 7 reels, 6,902 ft.

Pres by Charles H. Duell. *Dir* Henry King. *Scen* Charles E. Whittaker. *Photog* Roy Overbaugh. *Art Dir* Charles Osborne Seessel. *Film Ed* Duncan Mansfield.

Cast: Richard Barthelmess *(Peter Newbolt/Joe Newbolt, his son)*, Charles Hill Mailes *(Isom Chase)*, Ned Sparks *(Cyrus Morgan)*, Lawrence D'Orsay *(Colonel Price)*, Robert Williamson *(Lawyer Hammer)*, Leslie King *(district attorney)*, Jerry Sinclair *(sheriff)*, Thomas Maguire *(Saul Greening)*, Lucia Backus Seger *(Mrs. Greening)*, Virginia Magee *(Alice Price)*, Mary Alden *(Mrs. Newbolt)*, Mary Thurman *(Ollie Chase)*.

Melodrama. Source: George Washington Ogden, *The Bondboy* (Chicago, 1922). For the sake of his impoverished mother, Joe Newbolt bonds himself to harsh Isom Chase. Ollie Chase tires of the difficult life her husband has forced on her and plans to elope with Cyrus Morgan, but Joe's sense of honor forces him to intervene. While Joe is trying to persuade Ollie not to proceed with her plans, Chase discovers him with his wife, misunderstands, reaches for his gun, and is accidentally killed. Joe protects Mrs. Chase, though he is accused of murder, tried, convicted, and sentenced to be hanged. But he escapes, goes to Mrs. Chase, and persuades her to reveal the truth. Joe is restored to his sweetheart and discovers that the Chase farm is rightfully his. *Bondage. Filial relations. Infidelity. Inheritance. Capital punishment.*

Note: Copyright title: *The Bondboy*.

BOND OF FEAR (Reissue) **F2.0512**
Triangle Film Corp. *Dist* Film Distributors League. **1921.** Si; b&w. 35mm. 5 reels.

Note: A Roy Stewart film originally released by Triangle Film Corp. on 23 Sep 1917.

THE BOND OF THE RING *see* **THUNDERING DAWN**

THE BONDED WOMAN **F2.0513**
Famous Players–Lasky. *Dist* Paramount Pictures. 21 Aug **1922** [c8 Aug 1922; LP18172]. Si; b&w. 35mm. 6 reels, 5,486 ft.

Pres by Adolph Zukor. *Dir* Philip E. Rosen. *Adapt* Albert Shelby Le Vino. *Photog* James C. Van Trees.

Cast: Betty Compson *(Angela Gaskell)*, John Bowers *(John Somers)*, Richard Dix *(Lee Marvin)*, J. Farrell MacDonald *(Captain Gaskell)*, Ethel Wales *(Lucita)*.

Romantic drama. Source: John Fleming Wilson, "The Salving of John Somers," in *Everybody's* (43:34–40, Aug 1920). Though wooed by a wealthy shipowner, Angela Gaskell is attracted to Somers, a drunken first mate who rescued her father in a shipwreck. To repay him the Gaskells mortgage their property and thus obtain funds for the bond necessary for Somers to captain a ship of his own. When money is stolen from the ship and Somers disappears, Angela rejects her suitor, Marvin, and goes to the South Seas in search of Somers, her true love. She is able to regenerate him, and the thief is finally revealed. *Shipowners. Ship crews. Alcoholism. Theft. South Seas.*

THE BONNIE BRIER BUSH **F2.0514**
Famous Players–Lasky British Producers. *Dist* Paramount Pictures. 20 Nov **1921** [United States release; c23 Nov 1921; LP17228]. Si; b&w. 35mm. 5 reels, 4,662 ft.

Dir Donald Crisp. *Scen* Margaret Turnbull. *Photog* Claude L. MacDonnell.

Cast: Donald Crisp *(Lachlan Campbell)*, Mary Glynne *(Flora Campbell, his daughter)*, Alec Fraser *(Lord Malcolm Hay)*, Dorothy Fane *(Kate Carnegie)*, Jack East *(Posty)*, Langhorne Burton *(John Carmichael)*, Jerrold Robertshaw *(Earl of Kinspindle)*, Mrs. Hayden-Coffin *(Margaret Howe)*, H. H. Wright *(Dr. William MacClure)*.

Melodrama. Source: Ian MacLaren, *Beside the Bonnie Brier Bush* (London, 1895). Lord Malcolm Hay, heir of the Earl of Kinspindle, is pressed to marry Kate Carnegie, the most beautiful and wealthy girl in the village of Drumtochty, despite the fact that the Reverend John Carmichael quietly loves her. Furthermore, Malcolm is in love with Flora, daughter of Lachlan Campbell, stern deacon of the kirk. By Scottish rite Lord Malcolm declares Flora his wife beside the brier bush, the betrothal being witnessed by Posty, a mail carrier; but Campbell appears and orders Malcolm away. Malcolm leaves for London, whereupon Flora hears of his betrothal to Kate and is turned from her house by her father for writing to him; she obtains work in a shop and becomes seriously ill. Upon Malcolm's return, Kate refuses his suit, declaring her love for Carmichael. Malcolm is also refused admittance to the Campbell home, until Posty announces that he has witnessed the marriage rite and that Malcolm and Flora are happily united. *Clergymen. Churchmen. Mail carriers. Courtship. Rites and ceremonies. Scotland.*

THE BOOB **F2.0515**
Metro-Goldwyn-Mayer Pictures. 17 May **1926** [c19 May 1926; LP22753]. Si; b&w. 35mm. 6 reels, 5,020 ft.

Dir William Wellman. *Titl* Katherine Hilliker, H. H. Caldwell. *Adapt* Kenneth B. Clarke. *Story* George Scarborough, Annette Westbay. *Photog* William Daniels. *Art Dir* Cedric Gibbons, Ben Carré. *Film Ed* Ben Lewis.

Cast: Gertrude Olmsted *(Amy)*, George K. Arthur *(Peter Good)*, Joan Crawford *(Jane)*, Charles Murray *(Cactus Jim)*, Antonio D'Algy *(Harry Benson)*, Hank Mann *(village soda clerk)*, Babe London *(fat girl)*.

Comedy. "Peter Good, an idealistic young farmhand, finds that Amy, the girl of his dreams, does not requite his love, and goes forth in search of adventures. He arrives at a roadhouse to which Amy has been brought by Harry Benson, a young city sport wanted by the authorities for bootlegging, and climbs into the car in which Amy is being abducted. A running fight ensues, which ends when the car crashes, slightly bruising all occupants. Harry is taken into custody by dry agents and reconciliation between Amy and Peter follows." (Studio press book.) *Farmers. Bootleggers. Revenue agents. Courtship. Prohibition.*

THE BOOMERANG **F2.0516**
B. P. Schulberg Productions. 28 Feb **1925.** Si; b&w. 35mm. 7 reels, 6,714 ft.

Dir Louis Gasnier. *Adapt* John Goodrich. *Photog* Joseph Goodrich.

Cast: Anita Stewart *(Virginia Zelva)*, Bert Lytell *(Dr. Sumner)*, Donald Keith *(Budd)*, Mary McAllister *(Grace Tyler)*, Ned Sparks *(Bert Hanks)*, Arthur Edmund Carew *(Poulet)*, Philo McCullough *(DeWitt)*, Winter Hall *(Gordon)*.

Comedy-drama. Source: Winchell Smith and Victor Mapes, *The Boomerang; a Comedy in Three Acts* (New York opening: 10 Aug 1915). Lacking patients, Dr. Sumner sets himself up as a psychologist and opens a sanitarium, becoming quite successful. Virginia Zelva, a clairyovant who wants to get into what she regards as a racket, signs on as his nurse. Sumner falls in love with Virginia and, after numerous complications, wins her for his bride. *Physicians. Psychologists. Clairyovants. Nurses. Sanitariums.*

BOOMERANG BILL **F2.0517**

Cosmopolitan Productions. *Dist* Paramount Pictures. ca15 Jan **1922** [Cincinnati premiere; released 12 Feb; c3 Jan 1922; LP17422]. Si; b&w. 35mm. 6 reels, 5,489 ft.

Dir Tom Terriss. *Scen* Doty Hobart. *Photog* Al Ligouri. *Set Dsgn* Joseph Urban.

Cast: Lionel Barrymore *(Boomerang Bill)*, Marguerite Marsh *(Annie)*, Margaret Seddon *(Annie's mother)*, Frank Shannon *(Terrence O'Malley)*, Matthew Betts *(Tony the Wop)*, Charlie Fong, Harry Lee *(Chinamen)*, Miriam Battista, Helen Kim *(Chinese girls)*.

Underworld melodrama. Source: Jack Boyle, "Boomerang Bill" (publication undetermined). A young man who is about to take part in a robbery is told the story of the career of Boomerang Bill, an ex–holdup man, now a shoestring peddler, by Officer Terence O'Malley: *Bill, a Chicago gunman, drifts to New York in search of work and in a dancehall meets a girl named Annie, whom he defends against the insults of Tony the Wop, a gangster. When they fall in love and he meets her invalid mother, Bill decides to go straight, but he learns that Annie's mother will die unless she can go to the country. Bill robs a bank, then takes refuge in a Chinese laundry; but Tony tips off the police and Bill is sentenced to 10 years' imprisonment. Although she promises to wait for Bill, Annie accepts the proposal of a mining engineer who takes her and her invalid mother to the mountains. Following his release, Bill leaves the couple to their happiness.* On hearing the story the young man resists the temptation to steal and promises O'Malley to obtain honest employment. *Peddlers. Criminals—Rehabilitation. Gangsters. Engineers—Mining. Chinese. Robbery. New York City.*

BOOMERANG JUSTICE **F2.0518**

Russell Productions. Sep **1922.** Si; b&w. 35mm. 5 reels, 4,800 ft.

Dir Edward Sedgwick.

Cast: George Larkin, Fritzi Ridgeway.

Western melodrama(?). No information about the nature of this film has been found.

THE BOOTLEGGERS **F2.0519**

Al Gilbert Film Productions. *For* Producers Security Corp. *Dist* Wid Gunning, Inc. Apr **1922** [c15 Jan 1922; LP17542]. Si; b&w. 35mm. 6 reels, 5,544 ft.

Dir Roy Sheldon. *Story-Scen* Thomas F. Fallon. *Photog* Anthony G. Trigili.

Cast: Walter Miller *(Jack Seville)*, Paul Panzer *(José Fernand)*, Jules Cowles *(The Hermit)*, Hazel Flint *(Olive Wood)*, Norma Shearer *(Helen Barnes)*, Jane Allyn *(Alice Barnes)*, Lucia Backus Seger *(Mrs. Murphy)*.

Melodrama. José Fernand, leader of a gang of bootleggers, has designs on Helen Barnes, a shopgirl who supports her delicate sister, and with the aid of Olive Wood, an adventuress, he lures the sisters to a supposed yachting trip. At sea, Helen is attacked by Fernand and dashes to the wireless operator for assistance, but a storm arises and an SOS is barely sent before the ship sinks. An ocean liner, picking up the call, starts for the rescue, and Jack Seville, Helen's sweetheart, a Navy aviator, comes by plane. The sisters and Fernand are cast up on an island and are there sheltered by a hermit, its only inhabitant. Seville and his pilot make a forced landing, and following a struggle between Seville and Fernand the entire party is rescued by the ocean liner. *Bootleggers. Shopgirls. Sisters. Adventuresses. Hermits. Airplanes. Sea rescue. Shipwrecks.*

THE BOOTLEGGER'S DAUGHTER **F2.0520**

Playgoers Pictures. *Dist* Associated Exhibitors. 6 Oct **1922** [New York license application; c9 Oct 1922; LU18277]. Si; b&w. 35mm. 5 reels.

Dir Victor Schertzinger. *Story* R. Cecil Smith. *Photog* Chester Lyons.

Cast: Enid Bennett *(Nell Bradley)*, Fred Niblo *(Rev. Charles Alden)*, Donald MacDonald *(Charles Fuhr)*, Melbourne MacDowell *(Jim Bradley)*, Virginia Southern *(Amy Robinson)*, Billy Elmer *(Ben Roach)*, J. P. Lockney *(Phil Glass)*, Caroline Rankin *(Matilda Boggs)*, Otto Hoffman *(The Deacon)*, Harold Goodwin *(violinist)*.

Melodrama. Nell Bradley, the daughter of a prosperous bootlegger, is encouraged by Rev. Charles Alden to change her way of life and improve herself with some education. She is finally convinced; saves Amy Robinson from the designs of a New York bootlegger; eventually wins the goodwill of the previously hostile community, which sends her to college; and takes her place as Mrs. Charles Alden. *Bootleggers. Clergymen. Education.*

BOOTS AND SADDLES *see* **QUICKSANDS**

BORDER BLACKBIRDS **F2.0521**

Leo Maloney Productions. *Dist* Pathé Exchange. 28 Aug **1927** [c22 Jul 1927; LU24207]. Si; b&w. 35mm. 6 reels, 5,326 ft.

Dir Leo Maloney. *Story-Scen* Ford I. Beebe. *Photog* Edward Kull.

Cast: Leo Maloney *(Bart Evans)*, Eugenia Gilbert *(Marion Kingsley)*, Nelson McDowell *(Mournful Luke)*, Joseph Rickson *(Suderman)*, Bud Osborne *(McWraight)*, Frank Clark, Morgan Davis, Tom London, Don Coleman, Allen Watt.

Northwest melodrama. Bart and Luke, two wanderers in search of work and adventure, are caught in a blizzard and find shelter in a cabin where they find a murdered man. Bart recognizes him as Kingsley, an old pal, and a note places the blame on the Blackbirds, a gang of border bandits. On the advice of banker Lars Suderman, McWraight, the killer, reports them to the sheriff, and they are arrested while trying to establish contact with Marion Kingsley. Bart breaks jail and forces McWraight's hand. While Luke warns the Mounties of an impending holdup, Bart rescues Marion from the bandits, who are subsequently captured by the Mounties. *Wanderers. Bandits. Bankers. Sheriffs. Murder. Jailbreaks. Northwest Mounted Police. Blizzards.*

THE BORDER CAVALIER (Blue Streak Western) **F2.0522**

Universal Pictures. 18 Sep **1927** [c25 Jul 1927; LP24246]. Si; b&w. 35mm. 5 reels, 4,427 ft.

Pres by Carl Laemmle. *Dir* William Wyler. *Story-Scen* Basil Dickey. *Titl* Gardner Bradford. *Photog* Al Jones. *Art Dir* David S. Garber.

Cast: Fred Humes *(Larry Day)*, Evelyn Pierce *(Anne Martin)*, C. E. "Captain" Anderson *(Beaver Martin)*, Boris Bullock *(Victor Harding)*, Joyce Compton *(Madge Lawton)*, Dick La Reno *(Dave Lawton)*, Dick L'Estrange *(Lazy)*, Gilbert "Pee Wee" Holmes *(Pee Wee)*, Benny Corbett *(Bennie)*.

Western melodrama. Vic Harding, a crooked eastern land speculator, learns of a proposed railroad spur that will increase the value of the Lawton ranch and conspires with Hank Martin to buy the property. Visiting the ranch, he falls in love with Madge, Lawton's daughter, flatters her about her singing, and uses this ingratiation to induce her to sell and move to the city. Larry Day, foreman, suspecting treachery, gives Harding a thrashing, discrediting him and his men in Lawton's eyes; but they detain Lawton until news from the railroad arrives. Madge rides to warn her father of the double-dealing, and Harding attempts to remove her; but Larry and his men attack them and, after a fight and chase, rescue the girl and discomfit the villains. *Ranch foremen. Land speculation. Ranches. Railroads.*

BORDER INTRIGUE **F2.0523**

Independent Pictures. 19 Jan **1925** [New York State license application]. Si; b&w. 35mm. 5 reels.

Pres by Jesse J. Goldburg. *Dir* J. P. McGowan. *Story* James Ormont. *Photog* Walter Griffin.

Cast: Franklyn Farnum *(Tom Lassen)*, Jack Vernon *(Dick Lassen)*, Mathilda Brundage *(Mrs. Lassen)*, Dorothy Wood *(Mrs. Edith Harding)*, Robert E. Cline *(Bull Harding)*, Mack V. Wright *(Juan Verdigo)*, "Slender" Whittaker *(Pedro Gonzales)*, Emily Barrye *(Rita)*, J. P. McGowan *("Tough" Tidings)*, Dot Farley *(Tough's sister)*.

Western melodrama. Juan Verdigo, a Mexican line-runner who wants to buy the Lassen ranch because of its fine water supply, persuades Dick Lassen, a weakling lad, to part with his interest. Before the deal can go through, however, Dick's older brother, Tom, puts a stop to it. Verdigo's men then try to intimidate the Lassens, and Dick, who thinks that he has killed one of them in a fight, rides over the Mexican border and asks

Verdigo for protection. Their mother becomes ill, and Tom goes into Mexico after his brother, finding that he has been ensnared by Rita, an adventuress. Tom breaks up the romance, outwits and outlasts Verdigo, and arranges for Dick to marry Edith Harding, a pure and beautiful American girl. *Brothers. Mexicans. Surveyors. Smugglers. Adventuresses. Filial relations. Manhood. Water rights. Mexican border.*

BORDER JUSTICE **F2.0524**

Independent Pictures. c1 Jul **1925** [LP21632]. Si; b&w. 35mm. 5 reels, 5,432 ft.

Dir Reeves Eason. *Story* William Lester. *Photog* Walter Griffin.

Cast: Bill Cody *(Joseph Welland)*, John Gough *(Phillip Gerard)*, Robert Homans *(Robert Maitland)*, Nola Luxford *(Mary Maitland)*, Mack V. Wright *(Angus Bland)*, Tote Du Crow *(Lone Star)*, Dorothy Ponedel *(Annona Wetona)*.

Western melodrama. Joe Welland, a Texas Ranger, is ordered to bring in Phillip Gerard, who has killed an Indian named Lone Star. The ranger overtakes the fugitive, only to discover that Gerard is his own brother. The outlaw resists arrest and in attempting to escape falls over a cliff, apparently to his death. Joe returns sadly to the ranger station and finds consolation in his growing love for Mary Maitland, the daughter of the captain. Angus Bland, the leader of a notorious gang of smugglers, has advanced Captain Maitland money for Mary's education; and Maitland, who cannot repay the loan, allows Bland to move illegal goods freely across the Mexican border. Joe learns of this arrangement and resigns his commission, going after Bland himself. Mary is kidnaped by the smuggler and taken to a cabin, to which they are trailed by Joe. Bland and Joe fight it out, and Bland accidentally sets off a charge of dynamite that blows up the cabin, killing himself and some of his men. Joe finds his brother, who has become a hopeless maniac as the result of his fall. The brother dies, and Joe and Mary make plans to be wed. *Brothers. Smugglers. Fugitives. Texas Rangers. Indians of North America. Lunatics. Murder. Kidnaping. Explosions.*

THE BORDER LEGION **F2.0525**

Famous Players–Lasky. *Dist* Paramount Pictures. ca19 Oct **1924** [New York premiere; released 27 Oct or 24 Nov; c21 Oct 1924; LP20661]. Si; b&w. 35mm. 7 reels, 7,048 ft.

Pres by Adolph Zukor, Jesse L. Lasky. *Dir* William K. Howard. *Scen* George Hull. *Photog* Alvin Wyckoff.

Cast: Antonio Moreno *(Jim Cleve)*, Helene Chadwick *(Joan Randle)*, Rockliffe Fellowes *(Kells)*, Gibson Gowland *(Gulden)*, Charles Ogle *(Harvey Roberts)*, James Corey *(Pearce)*, Edward Gribbon *(Blicky)*, Luke Cosgrave *(Bill Randle)*.

Western melodrama. Source: Zane Grey, *The Border Legion* (New York, 1916). Provoked by Joan Randle's accusation that he is too lazy even to be bad, Jim Cleve goes west and joins a notorious band of outlaws known as the Border Legion. Joan regrets her action, follows Jim, and is captured by Kells, the legion's chief. She is forced to shoot Kells in self-defense but nurses him back to health, and Kells falls in love with her. Joan and Jim later escape during a raid on a mining camp, but they are among the victims of a stagecoach holdup: Joan is recaptured and Jim is shot. Kells and Gulden cut cards for Joan and the gold, Gulden wins, Jim arrives in a weakened condition and battles for Joan, and Kells gives his life so that Joan can escape from Gulden with Jim. *Outlaws. Robbery. Stagecoach robberies.*

Note: Remade in 1930 under the same title, q. v.

THE BORDER LEGION **F2.0526**

Paramount-Publix Corp. 28 Jun **1930** [c27 Jun 1930; LP1403]. Sd (Movietone); b&w. 35mm. 8 reels, 6,088 ft.

Dir Otto Brower, Edwin H. Knopf. *Screenplay* Percy Heath, Edward E. Paramore, Jr. *Photog* Mack Stengler. *Film Ed* Doris Drought. *Rec Engr* Earl Hayman.

Cast: Richard Arlen *(Jim Cleve)*, Jack Holt *(Jack Kells)*, Fay Wray *(Joan Randall)*, Eugene Pallette *("Bunco" Davis)*, Stanley Fields *(Hack Gulden)*, E. H. Calvert *(Judge Savin)*, Ethan Allen *(George Randall)*, Sid Saylor *(Shrimp)*.

Western melodrama. Source: Zane Grey, *The Border Legion* (New York, 1916). Jack Kells, leader of a band of outlaws known as "The Border Legion," finds the townspeople of Alder Creek, Idaho, irate and about to hang Jim Cleve for the killing of a miner, a crime of which one of Kells's own men is actually guilty; he saves the jobless cowboy, and out of gratitude Jim joins the gang. While they are hiding in the mountains, Hack Gulden kidnaps Joan Randall, and Jim is assigned to guard her; but he threatens Jack when he tries to make advances to the girl and returns to town to organize a posse. Believing an armed posse will come in search of the girl, Jack orders an immediate attack on the town; but the townsmen, not trusting Jim, have imprisoned him and are prepared for the Legion with bullets and dynamite. Jim helps Jack and Bunco Davis escape, but the latter is mortally wounded; when Hack Gulden imperils Jim and the girl, Jack confronts him in a gunbattle in which both men die. *Outlaws. Cowboys. Murder. Courtship. Idaho.*

Note: Remake of the 1924 film of the same title, q. v.

THE BORDER PATROL **F2.0527**

Charles R. Rogers Productions. *Dist* Pathé Exchange. 23 Dec **1928** [c8 Dec 1928; LP25914]. Si; b&w. 35mm. 5 reels, 4,598 ft.

Dir James P. Hogan. *Story-Adapt* Finis Fox. *Photog* Sol Polito. *Film Ed* Harry Marker.

Cast: Harry Carey *(Bill Storm)*, Kathleen Collins *(Beverly Dix)*, Phillips Smalley *(Conway Dix)*, Richard Tucker *(Earl Hanway)*, James Neill *(Lefty Waterman)*, James Marcus *(Captain Bonham)*.

Western melodrama. Texas Ranger Bill Storm is sent to El Paso to ferret out a gang of counterfeiters thought to be working there and, on the way, gives a ride to New York socialite Beverly Dix, whose car has been wrecked on the road to El Paso. Bill quickly comes to suspect Earl Hanway and Lefty Waterman of passing bad bills; taking Beverly's father into his confidence, Bill identifies the counterfeiting plant, arrests Hanway and Waterman, and finds himself with his arms full of Beverly. *Texas Rangers. Socialites. Counterfeiters. El Paso.*

THE BORDER RAIDERS **F2.0528**

Dist Aywon Film Corp. Jan **1921.** Si; b&w. 35mm. 5 reels.

Cast: Ben Hill, Walter Lynch.

Western melodrama. "Sensational melodrama of a gang of Mexican bandits, who smuggle whiskey across the Rio Grande until they bump up against the Texas rangers. Highlights, a terrific fight in the cellar of bandit's house, a chase and pistol duel over the mountains of Arizona, the blowing up of a house by a barrel of powder and a hand-to-hand fight in the bandit's mountain cave." (*Motion Picture News Booking Guide,* 1:16, Dec 1921.) *Bandits. Smugglers. Texas Rangers. Mexicans. Arizona. Rio Grande. Mexican border.*

THE BORDER RIDER **F2.0529**

Essanar Film Co. *Dist* Sierra Pictures. 12 Dec **1924.** Si; b&w. 35mm. 5 reels, 4,582 ft.

Dir Frederick Reel, Jr.

Cast: Al Richmond, Lorraine Eason.

Western melodrama. No information about the precise nature of this film has been found.

BORDER ROMANCE **F2.0530**

Tiffany Productions. 18 May **1930** [c13 May 1930; LP1292]. Sd (Photophone); b&w. 35mm. 7 reels, 5,974 ft. [Also si.]

Prod Lester F. Scott, Jr. *Dir* Richard Thorpe. *Story-Scen* John Francis Natteford. *Photog* Harry Zech. *Sets* Ralph De Lacy. *Film Ed* Richard Cahoon. *Songs: "Song of the Rurales," "The Girl From Topolobombo," "Yo te adoro," "My Desert Rose"* Will Jason, Val Burton. *Mus Dir* Al Short. *Rec Engr* J. Stransky, Jr.

Cast: Armida *(Conchita Cortez)*, Don Terry *(Bob Hamlin)*, Marjorie "Babe" Kane *(Nina)*, Victor Potel *(Slim)*, Wesley Barry *(Victor Hamlin)*, Nita Martan *(Gloria)*, Frank Glendon *(Buck)*, Harry von Meter *(Captain of Rurales)*, William Costello *(Lieutenant of Rurales)*.

Western melodrama. Bob Hamlin, his younger brother, Victor, and their helper, Slim, are engaged in horsetrading in the mountains of Mexico. They meet Buck Adams, a prospective buyer; and at a tavern, Vic antagonizes a big Mexican by trying to dance with a girl and is forced to kill him when he draws a gun. Their horses are stolen, but they evade capture by the *rurales*. While giving chase to Buck, Bob encounters Conchita, whose beauty captivates him; but he courts Gloria, Buck's girl, in order to learn the whereabouts of the villain. He abducts the brokenhearted Conchita and takes her to a mountain hideout, where he convinces her of his innocence of the crime. He surrenders to the *rurales*, who take Buck's men prisoners, and collects the reward for having killed El Gallo, a notorious bandit. *Horsetraders. Brothers. Bandits. Rurales. Mexico.*

THE BORDER SCOUTS F2.0531
Dist Bert Hall. **1922.** Si; b&w. 35mm. [Feature length assumed.]
Dir Bert Hall.
Western melodrama(?). No information about the nature of his film has been found.
Note: Date indicated is approximate.

THE BORDER SHERIFF (Blue Streak Western) F2.0532
Universal Pictures. 25 Apr **1926** [c26 Feb 1926; LP22438]. Si; b&w. 35mm. 5 reels, 4,440 ft.
Dir-Cont Robert North Bradbury. *Photog* William Nobles, Harry Mason.
Cast: Jack Hoxie *(Cultus Collins)*, Olive Hasbrouck *(Joan Belden)*, S. E. Jennings *(Carter Brace)*, Gilbert Holmes *(Tater-Bug Gilbert)*, Buck Moulton *(Limpy Peel)*, Tom Lingham *(Henry Belden)*, Bert De Marc *(Joe Martinez)*, Frank Rice *(Hewitt)*, Floyd Criswell *(Frenchie)*, Leonard Trainer *(sheriff)*, Scout *(a horse)*.
Western melodrama. Source: W. C. Tuttle, "Straight Shooting," in *Short Stories* (108:3–63, 10 Aug 1924). Leaving a conference in Washington on narcotics smuggling, Cultus Collins, the sheriff of Cayuse County, goes to San Francisco where he anonymously rescues wealthy Henry Belden during a fight in a Chinatown dive. Cultus later changes clothes with a well-known bandit, and Belden mistakes him for a criminal. Carter Brace, Belden's business representative, attempts to cheat Belden out of a ranch, but Cultus foils the plot. Cultus later saves Belden's life again. The rugged sheriff eventually links Brace with the dope smugglers and quickly breaks up his gang. *Sheriffs. Ranchers. Smugglers. Narcotics. San Francisco—Chinatown. Washington (District of Columbia). Horses.*

BORDER VENGEANCE F2.0533
Harry Webb Productions. *Dist* Aywon Film Corp. ca12 Aug **1925** [New York showing]. Si; b&w. 35mm. 5 reels, 4,850 ft.
Dir Harry Webb. *Story-Scen* Forrest Sheldon. *Photog* William Thornley.
Cast: Jack Perrin *(Wes Channing)*, Minna Redman *(Mrs. Jackson)*, Vondell Darr *(Bimps Jackson)*, Jack Richardson, Josephine Hill, Leonard Clapham.
Western melodrama. "It has a moderately pretty heroine, four or five heavies, ranging from a misguided weakling to a very demon of a despicable gambler, the proper amount of hard riding and fighting, a three-cornered battle for the girl, a mine that after many disappointments fairly spouts precious ore, and practically no comedy whatsoever" (*Variety*, 12 Aug 1925, p45). *Gamblers. Revenge. Mines.*

THE BORDER WHIRLWIND F2.0534
Independent Pictures. *Dist* Film Booking Offices of America. 15 Nov **1926** [c15 Nov 1926; LP23328]. Si; b&w. 35mm. 5 reels, 4,862 ft.
Pres by Joseph P. Kennedy. *Prod* Jesse J. Goldburg. *Dir* John P. McCarthy. *Cont* Enid Hibbard. *Story* James Ormont. *Photog* Ernest Miller.
Cast: Bob Custer *(Tom Blake, Jr.)*, Sally Long *(Isabella Córdova)*, Josef Swickard *(Señor José Córdova)*, Wilbur Higby *(Tom Blake, Sr.)*, Winifred Landis *(Mrs. Blake)*, Philip Sleeman *(Palo, The Scorpion)*, Bobby Nelson *(Petie)*, Julian Rivero *(Captain Gonzales)*, Evelyn Sherman *(duenna)*.
Western melodrama. Tom Blake, Jr., son of a wealthy Texas rancher, is assigned to track down The Scorpion, a mysterious desperado on the Mexican border, as a result of the appeals of José Córdova, a prominent mineowner and friend of the elder Blake. While attempting to discover the bandits' secret trail, Blake, Sr., is killed, and Tom swears vengeance. In his search, Tom encounters Isabella Córdova at her hacienda, but he finds her being pursued by Palo Hernández; Palo plants a suspicion with the Mexican police that Tom is possibly The Scorpion; and Tom is captured by The Scorpion's men when he learns of their plan to rob the mine. Palo is disclosed as the villain, however, and Tom is happily united with Isabella. *Ranchers. Desperadoes. Filial relations. Revenge. Texas. Mexican border.*

THE BORDER WILDCAT F2.0535
Universal Pictures. 19 May **1929** [c7 Sep 1928; LP25617]. Si; b&w. 35mm. 5 reels, 4,259 ft.
Supv William Lord Wright. *Dir* Ray Taylor. *Story-Cont* Carl Krusada, Vin Moore. *Titl* Val Cleveland. *Photog* Joseph Brotherton. *Film Ed* Gene Havlick.
Cast: Ted Wells *(Bob Shaw)*, Kathryn McGuire *(Mary Bell)*, Tom London *(Joe Kern)*, William Malan *(John Bell)*.
Western melodrama. Bob Shaw, sheriff of Rimrock, raids a gambling joint suspected of serving bootleg hootch. The raid is a failure. Bob later stops a truckload of illegal swill headed for Rimrock, and the driver tells Bob that the rotgut was destined for the gambling joint. John Bell, the father of Bob's fiancée, Mary, shoots Joe Kern, the saloon owner, in self-defense and then runs off, pursued by Kern's men. With his dying words, Kern exonorates Bell; Bob goes after Bell, coming to his rescue just as Kern's irate men are about to do him in. Bob sends the bootleggers packing and returns to town with his grateful friend and future father-in-law. *Sheriffs. Gamblers. Saloon keepers. Bootleggers.*

BORDER WOMEN F2.0536
Phil Goldstone Productions. 15 Aug **1924.** Si; b&w. 35mm. 5 reels, 4,500 ft.
Dir Alvin J. Neitz. *Scen* Keene Thompson.
Cast: William Fairbanks *(Big Boy Merritt)*, Dorothy Revier *(May Prentiss)*, Jack Richardson *(Gentleman Jack)*, Chet Ryan *(Cocas Kid)*, William Franey *(McGilligan)*.
Western melodrama. Big Boy Merritt, a Texas Ranger, goes after The Cocas Kid, the leader of a notorious outlaw gang operating on the Mexican border. Merritt captures Gentleman Jack, one of The Kid's hired guns, but Jack escapes and returns to the gang. Jack later quarrels with The Kid, who shoots him, leaving him to die in the desert. Merritt finds Jack as he lies dying, and Jack then commits his sister, Mary, to the ranger's care. Merritt sets out after The Kid again, breaks up his gang, brings The Kid to justice, and wins the love of Mary. *Texas Rangers. Brother-sister relationship. Gangs. Mexican border. Murder.*

BORDERLAND F2.0537
Famous Players–Lasky. *Dist* Paramount Pictures. 30 Jul **1922** [c26 Jul 1922; LP18095]. Si; b&w. 35mm. 6 reels, ca5,500 ft.
Pres by Adolph Zukor. *Dir* Paul Powell. *Story* Beulah Marie Dix. *Photog* Harry Perry.
Cast: Agnes Ayres *(Spirit/Dora Becket/Edith Wayne)*, Milton Sills *(James Wayne)*, Fred Huntley *(William Beckett)*, Bertram Grassby *(Francis Vincent)*, Casson Ferguson *(Clyde Meredith)*, Ruby Lafayette *(Eileen)*, Sylvia Ashton *(Mrs. Conlon)*, Frankie Lee *(Jimty)*, Mary Jane Irving *(Totty)*, Dale Fuller *(Elly)*.
Supernatural melodrama. Dora, a poor soul wandering through space looking for her lost child, stops at the Well at the World's End where she sees Edith, her great-grandniece, about to ruin her life just as she herself did 70 years before, by abandoning her husband and child for another man. Acting through an aging servant, Dora effects a reconciliation between Edith and her husband, and Dora herself is at last reunited with her lost child. *Ghosts. Marriage. Supernatural.*
Note: Working title: *Between the Worlds.*

BORN RECKLESS F2.0538
Fox Film Corp. 11 May **1930** [c25 Apr 1930; LP1279]. Sd (Movietone); b&w. 35mm. 9 reels, 7,400 ft.
Pres by William Fox. *Assoc Prod* James K. McGuinness. *Dir* John Ford. *Stgd by* Andrew Bennison. *Screenplay-Dial* Dudley Nichols. *Camera* George Schneiderman. *Art Dir* Jack Schulze. *Film Ed* Frank E. Hull. *Sd Engr* W. W. Lindsay. *Asst Dir* Edward O'Fearna.
Cast: Edmund Lowe *(Louis Beretti)*, Catherine Dale Owen *(Jean Sheldon)*, Warren Hymer *(Big Shot)*, Marguerite Churchill *(Rosa Beretti)*, Lee Tracy *(Bill O'Brien)*, William Harrigan *(Good News Brophy)*, Frank Albertson *(Frank Sheldon)*, Paul Page *(Ritzy Reilly)*, Ferike Boros *(Ma Beretti)*, Paul Porcasi *(Pa Beretti)*, Joe Brown *(Needle Beer Grogan)*, Eddie Gribbon *(Bugs)*, Mike Donlin *(Fingy Moscovitz)*, Ben Bard *(Joe Bergman)*, Paul Page *(Ritzy Reilly)*, Pat Somerset *(The Duke)*, J. Farrell MacDonald, Roy Stewart *(District Attorney Cardigan, see note)*, Jack Pennick, Ward Bond *(soldiers)*, Yola D'Avril *(French girl)*.
Crime melodrama. Source: Donald Henderson Clarke, *Louis Beretti* (New York, 1929). Louis Beretti and two of his gang are arrested on a robbery charge. As a result of a newspaper campaign initiated by reporter Bill O'Brien to promote the election of the district attorney, the trio are sent overseas to fight in the war. Back in New York, Beretti drifts into the nightclub business, but he is brought back into contact with the East Side Gang when "Big Shot" settles his account with Ritzy Reilly for squealing. Later, when Sheldon's sister reports her child missing, Beretti effects the rescue and shoots it out with Big Shot, who demands an accounting because he failed to "keep his nose clean," resulting in Beretti's death. *Gangsters. Reporters. District attorneys. Friendship. World War I. New*

York City—East Side.

Note: Sources disagree in crediting the role of the district attorney.

BORN RICH **F2.0539**

Garrick Pictures. *Dist* First National Pictures. 7 Dec **1924** [19 Nov 1924; LP20784]. Si; b&w. 35mm. 8 reels, 7,389 ft.

Prod-Dir Will Nigh. *Titl* Harriet Underhill, Walter De Leon. *Photog* George Folsey. *Art Dir* Clark Robinson.

Cast: Claire Windsor *(Chadyeane Fairfax)*, Bert Lytell *(Jimmy Fairfax)*, Cullen Landis *(Jack Le Moyne)*, Doris Kenyon *(Frances Melrose)*, Frank Morgan *(Eugene Magnin)*, J. Barney Sherry *(Maj. Romayne Murphy)*, Maude Turner Gordon *(Aunt Fairfax)*, Jackie Ott *(Bugsy Fairfax)*, William Burton *(Spinks)*.

Social comedy. Source: Hughes Cornell, *Born Rich* (Philadelphia, c1924). When Chaydeane Fairfax leaves her palatial home and fast friends to visit an aunt in France, her husband, Jimmy, falls for Frances Melrose, a flapper and goodtime girl. When Chad returns, she learns of Jimmy's indiscretions and, in order to excite his jealousy and renew his interest in her, she pretends to be infatuated with Jack Le Moyne, a jazz hound. This attitude serves only to drive Jimmy to drink and further indiscretions. After several years of separation, Jimmy suddenly discovers that he has been cheated by his financial advisor, Magnin, and that he is broke. Filled with renewed purpose rather than remorse, Jimmy is reconciled with Chad, only to discover that he has been saved from bankruptcy by a Major Murphy. *Flappers. Jazz life. Marriage. Alcoholism. Wealth.*

BORN TO BATTLE **F2.0540**

R-C Pictures. *Dist* Film Booking Offices of America. 24 Jan **1926** [c24 Jan 1926; LP22341]. Si; b&w. 35mm. 5 reels, 5,153 ft.

Dir Robert De Lacy. *Story-Scen* William E. Wing. *Photog* David Smith, Harold Wenstrom.

Cast: Tom Tyler *(Dennis Terhune)*, Jean Arthur *(Eunice Morgan)*, Ray Childs *(Moxley)*, Fred Gambold *(Morgan)*, Frankie Darro *(Birdie)*, Buck Black *(Tuffy)*, LeRoy Mason *(Daley)*, Ethan Laidlaw *(Trube)*.

Western melodrama. Dennis Terhune, ranch foreman for John Morgan, an eastern capitalist, discovers that there is oil on Morgan's ranch shortly after Morgan has deeded the ranch to Daley, western manager for the Morgan properties. Dennis rides after Daley and retrieves the deed, saving Morgan's ranch and securing for himself the love of the financier's daughter, Eunice. *Ranch foremen. Financiers. Property rights. Oil.*

BORN TO BATTLE **F2.0541**

Bill Cody Productions. *Dist* Pathé Exchange. 11 Sep **1927** [c17 Sep 1927; LU24417]. Si; b&w. 35mm. 5 reels, 4,875 ft.

Dir Alvin J. Neitz. *Story-Scen* L. V. Jefferson. *Photog* Harold Wenstrom, David Smith.

Cast: Bill Cody.

Western melodrama. Ma Cowan, who believes Luke Barstow shot her husband 20 years earlier, tries to incite her sons to carry on the feud when Billy, the youngest, reaches the age of 21, but to no avail. Hank Tolliver, her unscrupulous brother, though anxious to promote the feud for selfish reasons, declares he wants no part in her revenge. Billy is accused by Tolliver of shooting Luke following a dispute with Luke over a load of hay and his attentions to Barbara, Barstow's daughter. But he eludes the posse and gives rout to Tolliver's men; Barstow reveals Tolliver's treachery, ultimately leading to his arrest. *Brothers. Uncles. Posses. Murder. Revenge. Feuds.*

BORN TO THE SADDLE **F2.0542**

Universal Pictures. 10 Mar **1929** [c17 Oct 1928; LP25750]. Si; b&w. 35mm. 5 reels, 4,126 ft.

Dir Josef Levigard. *Story-Scen* George Plympton, George Mitchell. *Titl* Val Cleveland. *Photog* William Adams. *Film Ed* Ted Kent.

Cast: Ted Wells *(Ted Dorgan)*, Duane Thompson *(Helen Pearson)*, Leo White *(Clyde Montmorency Wilpenny)*, Byron Douglas *(John Pearson)*, Merrill McCormick *(Amos Judd)*, Nelson McDowell *(Pop Healy)*.

Western melodrama. Ted Dorgan, a Chicago millionaire who works as a cowboy, rescues John Pearson and his daughter, Helen, when they are held up by Amos Judd and his men. The Pearson party later goes on a camping trip guided by Ted, and Pearson is kidnaped by Judd. Ted rescues him again. Clyde Wilpenny, a weakling dude in love with Helen, arranges a party at the lodge and invites Ted, hoping to show him up as a rough, uncouth fellow. Ted appears in faultless evening dress and prevents a robbery by Judd. Ted and Helen embrace. *Millionaires. Cowboys. Dudes. Kidnaping. Robbery.*

BORN TO THE WEST **F2.0543**

Famous Players–Lasky. *Dist* Paramount Pictures. 14 Jun **1926** [c16 Jun 1926; LP22818]. Si; b&w. 35mm. 6 reels, 6,042 ft.

Pres by Adolph Zukor, Jesse L. Lasky. *Dir* John Waters. *Adapt-Scen* Lucien Hubbard. *Photog* C. Edgar Schoenbaum.

Cast: Jack Holt *("Colorado" Dare Rudd)*, Margaret Morris *(Nell Worstall)*, Raymond Hatton *(Jim Fallon)*, Arlette Marchal *(Belle of Paradise Bar)*, George Siegmann *(Jesse Fillmore)*, Bruce Gordon *(Bate Fillmore)*, William A. Carroll *(Nell's father)*, Tom Kennedy *(Dinkey Hooley)*, Richard Neill *(Sheriff Haverill)*, Edith Yorke *(Mrs. Rudd)*, E. Alyn Warren *(Sam Rudd)*, Billy Aber *("Colorado" Dare Rudd, as a child)*, Jean Johnson *(Nell Worstall, as a child)*, Joe Butterworth *(Bate Fillmore, as a child)*.

Western melodrama. Source: Zane Grey, "Born to the West" (publication undetermined). In a country schoolyard in Colorado, Dare Rudd and Bate Fillmore quarrel over Nell Worstall, and their dispute culminates in a vicious fight. Years later, Dare, now a rugged cowpuncher, decides to return home and marry Nell but finds that the Worstall and Fillmore families have followed a mining boom to Eureka, Nevada. There he renews his old fight with Fillmore over a dancing girl known as Belle, but Jim Fallon turns up and ends the quarrel. Dare learns that Nell is living with his mother and that her father is in jail on a trumped-up charge made by the Fillmores; Dare gets him released, and Nell is abducted by Fillmore when she refuses to marry him. The miners, cheated by Fillmore, clash with his gang, and Nell escapes the clutches of Fillmore when his sweetheart, Belle, attacks him; a spectacular stagecoach crash ends the fight, and Dare is united with Nell. *Cowboys. Miners. Dancers. Feuds. Childhood. Colorado. Nevada.*

BORROWED FINERY **F2.0544**

Tiffany Productions. Nov **1925** [c26 Oct 1925; LP21946]. Si; b&w. 35mm. 7 reels, 6,500 ft.

Dir Oscar Apfel. *Story* George Bronson Howard.

Cast: Louise Lorraine *(Sheila Conroy)*, Ward Crane *(Channing Maynard)*, Lou Tellegen *(Harlan)*, Taylor Holmes *(Billy)*, Hedda Hopper *(Mrs. Bordon)*, Gertrude Astor *(Maisie)*, Trixie Friganza *(Mrs. Brown)*, Barbara Tennant *(Lilly)*, Otto Lederer.

Society melodrama. Sheila Conroy, a model working "by cloaks and suits," borrows a gown to wear to a millionaire's party. Harlan, a society crook posing as a government agent, offers her a job as his assistant. She accepts the job in order to help her sister, Lilly, and Lilly's husband, Billy. (The latter has embezzled money from his firm and is in danger of discovery.) Her assignment is to obtain the necessary "evidence" on Mrs. Bordon, a wealthy widow who has smuggled a jewel of great value into the country. Channing Maynard, a real government agent who is in love with Sheila, exposes Harlan and takes Sheila as his bride. *Fashion models. Sisters. Government agents. Imposture. Embezzlement. Smuggling.*

BORROWED HUSBANDS **F2.0545**

Vitagraph Co. of America. 13 Apr **1924** [c7 Apr 1924; LP20056]. Si; b&w. 35mm. 7 reels, 6,850 ft.

Pres by Albert E. Smith. *Dir* David Smith. *Scen* C. Graham Baker. *Photog* Steve Smith.

Cast: Florence Vidor *(Nancy Burrard)*, Rockliffe Fellowes *(Dr. Langwell)*, Earle Williams *(Major Desmond)*, Robert Gordon *(Gerald Burrard)*, Kathryn Adams *(Edith Langwell)*, Violet Palmer *(Constance Stanley)*, Alpheus Lincoln *(Reeve Lewis)*, Claire Du Brey *(Peggy Fleurette)*, Charlotte Merriam *(Peggy Lewis)*, J. W. Irving *(Curtis Stanley)*.

Society comedy-drama. Source: Mildred K. Barbour, "Borrowed Husbands" (publication undetermined). While her husband, Gerald, is in South America on an archeological expedition, vivacious Nancy Burrard lightens her boredom with several flirtations. Believing her to be a widow, Major Desmond becomes infatuated with her; he meets Gerald in South America, however, and advises him to hurry home. The Burrards are reconciled, and all ends well (except in the case of Dr. Langwell, another of Nancy's dalliances, who has poisoned his nurse, Peggy Fleurette, and then committed suicide). *Flirts. Physicians. Marriage. Archeology. Murder. Suicide. South America.*

BORROWED WIVES **F2.0546**
Tiffany Productions. 20 Aug **1930** [c18 Aug 1930; LP1508]. Sd (Photophone); b&w. 35mm. 7 reels, 5,997 ft.
Dir Frank Strayer. *Dial Dir* Leander De Cordova. *Screenplay* Scott Darling. *Photog* André Barlatier. *Sets* Ralph De Lacy. *Film Ed* Byron Robinson. *Rec Engr* Buddy Myers.
Cast: Rex Lease *(Peter Foley)*, Vera Reynolds *(Alice Blake)*, Nita Martan *(Julia)*, Paul Hurst *(Bull Morgan)*, Robert Randall *(Joe Blair)*, Charles Sellon *(Uncle Henry)*, Dorothea Wolbert *(Aunt Mary)*, Sam Hardy *(Parker)*, Harry Todd *(Winstead)*, Tom London *(cop)*, Eddie Chandler *(sergeant)*.
Comedy-drama. Peter Foley's grandfather wills him $1 million provided that he gets married. Peter plans to marry Alice Blake as soon as she arrives from Kansas City and to take her to his Uncle Henry's home before midnight. Her airplane is delayed, and Parker, to whom Peter is in debt, insists that his own girl friend, Julia, pose as Peter's wife. Alice is informed by Joe Blair that Peter is actually married to Julia; she agrees to marry Joe if this is true; and they are pursued by Bull, a motorcycle policeman who loves Julia. Complications follow at Uncle Henry's: Lawyer Winstead, who is found bound and gagged, agrees to marry them; the uncle, revealed to be posing as a paralytic, is exposed as a villain; and Peter and Alice are married before the hour appointed in the will. *Uncles. Police. Inheritance. Marriage. Kansas City.*

THE BOSS OF CAMP 4 **F2.0547**
Fox Film Corp. 26 Nov **1922** [c29 May 1923; LP18992]. Si; b&w. 35mm. 5 reels, 4,235 ft.
Pres by William Fox. *Dir* W. S. Van Dyke. *Scen* Paul Schofield. *Photog* Ernest Miller, Dev Jennings.
Cast: Charles Jones *(Chet Fanning)*, Fritzi Brunette *(Iris Paxton)*, G. Raymond Nye *(Dave Miller)*, Francis Ford *(Dude McCormick)*, Sid Jordan *(Warren Zome)*, Milton Ross *(Andrew Paxton)*.
Action melodrama. Source: Arthur Preston Hankins, *The Boss of Camp Four, a Western Story* (New York, 1925). Andrew Paxton hires Chet Fanning among the extra men he needs to complete the construction of a road by the agreed date. Dude McCormick, who regains possession of the land if Paxton fails, discovers coal on the property and bribes some workers to delay the project. Chet rescues Iris Paxton from a falling boulder, prevents an explosion, and otherwise thwarts the villains. The road is completed on time, and Chet wins Iris' love. *Road construction. Coal. Land rights. Bribery.*

THE BOSS OF RUSTLER'S ROOST **F2.0548**
Leo Maloney Productions. *Dist* Pathé Exchange. 22 Jan **1928** [c12 Jan 1928; LP24850]. Si; b&w. 35mm. 5 reels, 4,833 ft.
Prod-Dir Leo Maloney. *Scen* Ford I. Beebe. *Story* W. D. Hoffman. *Photog* Edward A. Kull. *Film Ed* Joseph Kane.
Cast: Don Coleman *("Smiler" Cavanaugh)*, Ben Corbett *("Tip" Reardon)*, Tom London *("Pronto" Giles, the foreman)*, Albert Hart *(Henry Everman)*, Dick Hatton *(Bill Everman)*, Frank Clark *(Jud Porter)*, William Bertram *(Sheriff Drain)*, Chet Ryan *(ranger)*, Eugenia Gilbert *(Fay Everman)*.
Western melodrama. Two friends, Cavanaugh and Reardon, buy Rustler's Roost, a ranch previously used for cattle-rustling operations by a mysterious rustler ("Quien Sabe") still at large. Everman, the owner of the neighboring ranch, and his foreman, Giles, object to their purchase and threaten Cavanaugh and Reardon. Everman's daughter, Fay, believing her father to be Quien Sabe, warns Cavanaugh of his danger. Giles perceives that Cavanaugh threatens to sway Fay's affections from himself. A ranger disguised as an Everman ranch hand exposes Giles as Quien Sabe. Giles tries to escape but is killed in a stampede. Fay is rescued by Cavanaugh. *Ranch foremen. Rangers. Filial relations. Rustling. Stampedes.*

BOSTON BLACKIE **F2.0549**
Fox Film Corp. 6 May **1923** [c6 May 1923; LP19080]. Si; b&w. 35mm. 5 reels, 4,522 ft.
Pres by William Fox. *Dir* Scott Dunlap. *Scen* Paul Schofield. *Photog* George Schneiderman.
Cast: William Russell *(Boston Blackie)*, Eva Novak *(Mary Carter)*, Frank Brownlee *(Warden Benton)*, Otto Matieson *(Danny Carter)*, Spike Robinson *(Shorty McNutt)*, Frederick Esmelton *(John Gilmore)*.
Underworld melodrama. Source: Jack Boyle, "The Water Cross," in *Cosmopolitan Magazine* (67:41–45, 92–100, Nov 1919). Boston Blackie, just released from prison, threatens the warden, Benton, that he will have him removed from his job for using the water cross, a form of torture, on prisoners. Blackie's sweetheart, Mary Carter, helps him avoid this torture after his return to prison. The officers pursue Blackie, capture him, and bring him back to Benton, but Mary reports to the governor, and they arrive in time to save Blackie from further torments by bringing his pardon. Benton is fired. *Prison wardens. State governors. Prison reform. Torture.*

THE BOUDOIR DIPLOMAT **F2.0550**
Universal Pictures. 5 Dec **1930** [New York premiere; released 25 Dec; c5 Dec 1930; LP1785]. Sd (Movietone); b&w. 35mm. 8 reels, 6,093 ft.
Pres by Carl Laemmle. *Prod* Carl Laemmle, Jr. *Dir* Malcolm St. Clair. *Screenplay-Dial* Benjamin Glazer, Tom Reed. *Photog* Karl Freund. *Film Ed* Maurice Pivar. *Rec Engr* C. Roy Hunter.
Cast: Betty Compson *(Helene)*, Mary Duncan *(Mona)*, Ian Keith *(Baron Belmar)*, Lawrence Grant *(Ambassador)*, Lionel Belmore *(War Minister)*, Jeanette Loff *(Greta)*, André Beranger *(Potz)*.
Romantic comedy-drama. Source: Rudolph Lothar and Fritz Gottwald, *The Command To Love.* The ambassador of the Kingdom of Luvaria orders Baron Belmar, his attaché, to win the interest of Mona, wife of the war minister, who opposes a treaty the ambassador very much wants signed. However, his mission is complicated by the fact that Helene, the ambassador's wife, is extremely jealous of every woman he meets, for she was responsible for getting him his appointment as attaché. Belmar, nevertheless, is in love with Greta, who will not marry him until he is proven worthy of her trust. After many narrow escapes from exposure of the personal intrigue, he manages to sway the attentions of Mona, who persuades the war minister to sign the treaty, thus gaining Belmar an appointment as ambassador to Peru and Greta as his wife. *Diplomats. Nobility. Treaties. Imaginary kingdoms. Peru.*

BOUGHT AND PAID FOR **F2.0551**
Famous Players–Lasky. *Dist* Paramount Pictures. ca11 Mar **1922** [New York premiere; released 16 Apr; c22 Mar 1922; LP17693]. Si; b&w. 35mm. 6 reels, 5,601 ft.
Pres by Adolph Zukor. *Dir* William C. De Mille. *Scen* Clara Beranger. *Photog* L. Guy Wilky.
Cast: Agnes Ayres *(Virginia Blaine)*, Jack Holt *(Robert Stafford)*, Walter Hiers *(James Gilley)*, Leigh Wyant *(Fanny Blaine)*, George Kuwa *(Oku)*, Bernice Frank *(maid)*, Ethel Wales *(telegraph girl)*.
Domestic drama. Source: George H. Broadhurst, *Bought and Paid For, a Play in Four Acts* (New York, 1916). Virginia Blaine, a hotel telephone operator—at the urging of her sister Fanny and the latter's fiancé, Jimmy—marries Robert Stafford, a young millionaire, though she does not love him. Stafford lavishes her with every luxury. After 2 years of happiness, however, he frequently comes home drunk and insults her with the remark that she is his property, "bought and paid for." Infuriated, she declares she will leave him unless he stops drinking, and when he refuses, she deserts him. She returns to her life of limited means, and Stafford, though he gives up liquor, is too proud to ask her to return to him. Their reconciliation is brought about by Jimmy, now Fanny's husband. *Telephone operators. Millionaires. Sisters. Marriage. Alcoholism.*

THE BOWERY BISHOP **F2.0552**
Rellimeo Film Syndicate. *Dist* Selznick Distributing Corp. 30 Aug **1924** [c1 Sep 1924; LP20536]. Si; b&w. 35mm. 6 reels, 5,568 ft.
Pres by Orlando Edgar Miller. *Supv* Grace Sanderson Michie. *Dir* Colin Campbell. *Story* Alexander Irvine. *Photog* A. G. Heimerl.
Cast: Henry B. Walthall *(Norman Strong)*, Leota Lorraine *(Sybil Stuyvesant)*, George Fisher *(Philip Foster)*, Lee Shumway *(Tim Brady)*, Edith Roberts *(Venitia Rigola)*, William H. Ryno *(Tony Rigola)*, Norval MacGregor *(Mr. Kindly)*.
Drama. Tim Brady accuses Norman Strong, known as the "Bowery Bishop" because he conducts a mission, of seducing Venitia Rigola, the girl he loves, when he finds her and her illegitimate child living in Strong's mission. Brady wrecks the mission and causes Strong's dismissal when he refuses to deny that it was he who wronged Venitia. Strong returns and is shot in a fight with a gang, but he recovers. A trial reveals that he was protecting Philip Foster, a young lawyer, who admits his mistake and is paroled in Strong's custody. Foster marries Venitia. *Seduction. Illegitimacy. Missions. New York City—Bowery.*

A BOWERY CINDERELLA F2.0553
Excellent Pictures. 1 Nov **1927** [c7 Nov 1927; LP24645]. Si; b&w. 35mm. 7 reels, 6,900 ft.
Pres by Samuel Zierler. *Prod* Harry Chandlee. *Dir* Burton King. *Scen* Adrian Johnson. *Titl* Harry Chandlee. *Story* Melvin Houston. *Photog* Art Reeves.
Cast: Gladys Hulette *(Nora Denahy)*, Pat O'Malley *(Larry Dugan)*, Kate Bruce *(Bridget Denahy)*, Ernest Hilliard *(Ned Chandler)*, Rosemary Theby *(Mrs. Chandler)*, Pat Hartigan *(Pat Denahy)*, Pauline Carr *(Maisie Brent)*, Howard Mitchell, Leo White, John Webb Dillon, Music Box Revue Chorus.
Society melodrama. Nora Denahy, a Bowery girl, works as a modiste, and her sweetheart, Larry Dugan, at a newspaper, with the intent of removing Nora's invalid mother to the country. Ned Chandler, a millioniare theatrical backer and constant philanderer, visits the modiste shop to costume a musical production and offers Nora a position with the company, which she accepts. When Nora is detained at a wild party, her parents are furious, and Mrs. Chandler sends Larry to investigate her husband; finding Nora there in his apartment in a "compromising" situation, he is disillusioned. Nora refuses Chandler's offers until, penniless, she accepts an apartment for her mother and herself. When Nora and Larry are reconciled, Chandler plots with an accomplice to put Nora in financial straits, but when Nora resists his pleas, a struggle ensues, terminated by Larry's arrival. Larry's play is a financial success, and he and Nora are married. *Fashion models. Reporters. Playwrights. Millionaires. Philanderers. Theatrical backers. Theater. Filial relations. New York City.*

BOY CRAZY F2,0554
Hunt Stromberg Productions. *Dist* R-C Pictures. 5 Mar **1922** [c5 Mar 1922; LP17663]. Si; b&w. 35mm. 5 reels, 4,800 ft.
Prod Hunt Stromberg. *Dir* William A. Seiter. *Story* Beatrice Van. *Photog* Bert Cann.
Cast: Doris May *(Jackie Cameron)*, Fred Gambold *(Mr. Cameron)*, Jean Hathaway *(Mrs. Cameron)*, Frank Kingsley *(Tom Winton)*, Harry Myers *(J. Smythe)*, Otto Hoffman *(Mr. Skinner)*, Gertrude Short *(Evelina Skinner)*, Eugenia Tuttle *(Mrs. Winton)*, Ed Brady, James Farley *(The Kidnapers)*.
Romantic comedy. When J. Smythe opens a fashionable women's shop in the little town of Santa Boobara, Jackie Cameron takes over her father's establishment across the street and converts it into an up-to-date haberdashery. Smythe, having fallen for Jackie, gives her preference over all his other customers and persuades her to buy a dress already promised to Evelina Skinner, daughter of the town's richest and meanest man. Two kidnapers, shadowing Evelina, mistake Jackie for her and hold Jackie for ransom. Smythe, learning of Jackie's disappearance and seeing the men enter the Skinner residence, follows them to their cabin and rescues Jackie. They force the kidnapers, who have robbed Skinner, to the sheriff's office, collect Skinner's reward, and decide to enter into a lifetime partnership. *Women's wear. Haberdasheries. Courtship. Mistaken identity. Kidnaping. Smalltown life.*

THE BOY FRIEND F2.0555
Metro-Goldwyn-Mayer Pictures. 14 Aug **1926** [New York showing; released 31 Oct; c26 Jul 1926; LP22985]. Si; b&w. 35mm. 6 reels, 5,529 or 5,584 ft.
Dir Monta Bell. *Adapt* Alice D. G. Miller. *Photog* Henry Sharp. *Sets* Cedric Gibbons, Merrill Pye. *Film Ed* Blanche Sewell. *Wardrobe* Kathleen Kay, Maude Marsh, André-ani.
Cast: Marceline Day *(Ida May Harper)*, John Harron *(Joe Pond)*, George K. Arthur *(book agent)*, Ward Crane *(Lester White)*, Gertrude Astor *(Mrs. White)*, Otto Hoffman *(Mr. Harper)*, Maidel Turner *(Mrs. Wilson)*, Gwen Lee *(Pettie Wilson)*, Elizabeth Patterson *(Mrs. Harper)*, Edgar Norton, Clarence Geldert, Evelyn Atkinson, Aileen Manning, Estelle Clark, Virginia Bradford, André Bushe, Ruth Handforth, Dorothy Seay, Archie Burke.
Society comedy-drama. Source: John Alexander Kirkpatrick, *The Book of Charm* (New York opening: 3 Sep 1925). Ida May Harper is envious of her friend Pettie Wilson, whose letters from New York make Ida want to leave her smalltown milieu. On one of her frequent visits to the drugstore where her boyfriend, Joe Pond, works, Ida May is picked up by Mrs. Willet, who is driving her New York guests, and their talk of New York only convinces her that she is wasting her sweetness on the desert air. She accepts an invitation from the Willets for dinner but discourages Joe from attending because of his improper dress. Joe buys a charm book and coaches the Harpers, who stage a houseparty for Ida May's benefit with humorous results. When Joe becomes passionate with Ida May, then threatens to leave for New York, the lovers are happily reconciled; and Pettie returns home to disclose the tragedy of life in the city. *Drug clerks. Smalltown life. Courtship. Etiquette. Upper classes. New York City.*

A BOY OF FLANDERS F2.0556
Jackie Coogan Productions. *Dist* Metro-Goldwyn Distributing Corp. 7 Apr **1924** [c2 Apr 1924; LP20159]. Si; b&w. 35mm. 7 reels, 7,018 ft.
Supv Jack Coogan, Sr. *Dir* Victor Schertzinger. *Scen* Walter Anthony. *Adapt* Marion Jackson. *Photog* Frank Good, Robert Martin. *Art Dir* J. J. Hughes. *Film Ed* Irene Morra.
Cast: Jackie Coogan *(Nello)*, Nigel De Brulier *(Jehan Daas)*, Lionel Belmore *(Baas Cogez)*, Nell Craig *(Marie Cogez)*, Jean Carpenter *(Alios Cogez)*, Russ Powell *(Baas Kronstadt)*, Aimé Charland *(Dumpert Schimmelpennick)*, Eugene Tuttle *(Vrow Schimmelpennick)*, Lydia Yeamans Titus *(serving maid)*, Larry Fisher *(Herr Logarth)*, Josef Swickard *(Jan Van Dullan)*, Sidney Franklin *(Herr Brinker)*, Monte Collins *(caretaker)*, "Teddy" *(Petrasche, the dog)*.
Comedy-drama. Source: Ouida, *A Dog of Flanders* (London, 1872). Nello, a "little Ardennois," saves the life of a dog but returns home to find his aged grandfather, his last remaining relative, dead. Forced from the cottage, he lives with the dog under a haystack until he is blamed for a fire and is to be sent away. Then an artist, Van Dullan, announces a drawing contest in the village. Nello wins the prize and the affections of the artist, who adopts him. *Waifs. Artists. Childhood. Ardennes. Flanders. Dogs.*

BOY OF MINE F2.0557
J. K. McDonald. *Dist* Associated First National Pictures. 23 Dec **1923** [c31 Dec 1923; LP19783]. Si; b&w. 35mm. 7 reels, 6,935 ft.
Pres by J. K. McDonald. *Dir* William Beaudine. *Scen* Hope Loring, Louis D. Lighton. *Titl* Louis D. Lighton. *Adapt* Lex Neal. *Photog* Ray June, George Richter. *Adtl Photog* Richard Fryer, William Rees. *Film Ed* Robert De Lacy. *Asst Dir* George Webster.
Cast: Ben Alexander *(Bill Latimer)*, Rockliffe Fellowes *(Dr. Robert Mason)*, Henry B. Walthall *(William Latimer)*, Irene Rich *(Ruth Latimer)*, Dot Farley *(Mrs. Pettis)*, Lawrence Licalzi *(Junior Pettis)*.
Juvenile drama. Source: Booth Tarkington, "Boy of Mine" (publication undetermined). A rich middle-aged banker, who is strict and unrelenting with his 9-year-old son, Bill, is turned into a likable person after his wife and son temporarily leave home. *Bankers. Children. Family life. Fatherhood.*

A BOY OF THE STREETS F2.0558
Trem Carr Productions. *Dist* Rayart Pictures. Sep **1927.** Si; b&w. 35mm. 6 reels, 5,059 ft.
Dir Charles J. Hunt. *Scen-Cont* Arthur Hoerl. *Story* Charles T. Vincent. *Photog* Ernest Depew.
Cast: Johnny Walker *(Ned Dugan)*, Mickey Bennett *(Jimmy Dugan)*, Henry Sedley *(Louis Wainright)*, Betty Francisco *(Mary Callahan)*, Charles Delaney *(Patrick Gallagher)*, William H. Armstrong *(Dan Gallagher)*, Edward Gordon, Rags *(a dog)*.
Crook melodrama. Falling into the clutches of a crooked politician, Ned Dugan is obliged to rob a safe in the home of Mary Callahan, who coincidentally has sheltered Ned's injured little brother, Jimmy Dugan. Ned is caught, but Betty saves him from punishment. The young crook repays her by going straight, turning the tables on the politician, and saving her impressionable brother from a blackmailer. *Politicians. Brothers. Criminals—Rehabilitation. Robbery. Dogs.*

THE BOY RIDER F2.0559
FBO Pictures. 23 Oct **1927** [c23 Oct 1927; LP24768]. Si; b&w. 35mm. 5 reels, 4,858 ft.
Dir Louis King. *Story-Cont* Frank Howard Clark. *Photog* E. T. McManigal. *Asst Dir* Arthur Flaven.
Cast: Buzz Barton *(David Hepner)*, Lorraine Eason *(Sally Parker)*, Sam Nelson *(Terry McNeil)*, David Dunbar *(Bill Hargus)*, Frank Rice *(Hank Robbins)*, William Ryno *(Jim Parker)*.
Western melodrama. Separated from his parents, David Hepner meets a band of cattle thieves who ask him to join them, intending to use his youth and innocence for criminal ends. An oldtimer of the plains and sidekick of his father helps the boy escape, and together they rescue Sally Parker, held for ransom by the same group of outlaws. *Rustlers. Kidnaping.*

BOYS WILL BE BOYS **F2.0560**
Goldwyn Pictures. 14 May **1921** [trade review; c27 Jan 1921; LP16077]. Si; b&w. 35mm. 5 reels, 4,300 ft.
Dir Clarence G. Badger. *Scen* Edfrid A. Bingham. *Photog* Marcel Le Picard.
Cast: Will Rogers *(Peep O'Day)*, Irene Rich *(Lucy)*, C. E. Mason *(Tom Minor)*, Sydney Ainsworth *(Sublette)*, Edward Kimball *(Judge Priest)*, H. Milton Ross *(Bagby)*, C. E. Thurston *(Sheriff Breck)*, May Hopkins *(Kitty)*, Cordelia Callahan *(Mrs. Hunter)*, Nick Cogley *(Aunt Mandy)*, Burton Halbert *(Farmer Bell)*.
Comedy-drama. Source: Irvin Shrewsbury Cobb, "Boys Will Be Boys," in *Saturday Evening Post* (190:5–7, 34–46, 20 Oct 1917). Charles O'Brien Kennedy, *Boys Will Be Boys: a Comedy of the Soul of Man Under Prosperity, in Three Acts* (New York, 1925). Peep O'Day, an orphan in a small Kentucky town, falls heir to a small fortune and begins to make up for all the lost pleasure of childhood, but Sublette, a crooked attorney, arranges for an eastern belle to show up as Peep's "niece" to steal his fortune. Peep's efforts to aid schoolteacher Lucy Allen are misconstrued, and Sublette tries to have him declared mentally incompetent, but Judge Priest is not convinced and rules in Peep's favor. Lucy wins the man she loves, and Peep plays Santa Claus to the children of the orphanage. *Orphans. Schoolteachers. Judges. Lawyers. Mental illness. Imposture. Inheritance. Kentucky. Santa Claus.*

BRAND OF COWARDICE **F2.0561**
Phil Goldstone Productions. *Dist* Truart Film Corp. 30 Jun **1925** [New York premiere]. Si; b&w. 35mm. 5 reels, 4,600 ft.
Dir John P. McCarthy. *Story* Roger Pocock, John P. McCarthy.
Cast: Bruce Gordon, Carmelita Geraghty, Cuyler Supplee, Ligio De Colconda, Harry Lonsdale, Charles McHugh, Mark Fenton, Sidney De Grey.
Western melodrama. A United States marshal poses as a bandit in a desperate attempt to capture a gang of thieves who are after the jewels of a wealthy Mexican rancher. The marshal eventually brings the gang to justice and marries the rancher's beautiful daughter. *United States marshals. Bandits. Ranchers. Mexicans. Thieves.*

BRANDED **F2.0562**
Dist Lee & Bradford. 1 Oct **1921** [New York State; general release: 1 Jan 1922]. Si; b&w. 35mm. 5 reels.
Cast: Josephine Earle.
Drama. "A drama of a woman charged with having poisoned her husband who was innocent of the offense & lives down the scandal reflected upon her" (New York State license application). *Murder. Injustice. Scandal.*

BRANDED A BANDIT **F2.0563**
Ben Wilson Productions. *Dist* Arrow Film Corp. 20 Dec **1924** [c18 Dec 1924; LP20971]. Si; b&w. 35mm. 5 reels, 4,729 ft.
Dir-Scen-Story Paul Hurst.
Cast: Yakima Canutt *(Jess Dean)*.
Western melodrama. When he is accused of killing Jim Turner, a successful gold prospector, Jess Dean, a rancher, is chased by the sheriff's posse, who trap him in the attic of a shack. Eluding the lawmen by a daring feat, Jess goes on to prove his innocence when he discovers that Turner is still alive. With the help of the posse, Jess brings to justice Horse Williams, the bandit who framed him. Jess is then happily reunited with Williams' granddaughter, with whom he is in love. *Prospectors. Ranchers. Bandits. Grandfathers. Posses. Frameup.*

BRANDED A THIEF **F2.0564**
William Steiner Productions. c4 Aug **1924** [LU18653]. Si; b&w. 35mm. 5 reels, 5,060 ft.
Pres by William Steiner. *Dir–Prepared for the screen by* Neal Hart.
Cast: Neal Hart *(José León)*.
Melodrama. Source: Neal Hart, *The Devil's Bowl* (screenplay, 1923). José León, foreman of the Toro range in Mexico, is engaged to Conchita Mesa. She breaks the engagement when he refuses to reveal the sender or the contents of a letter he has received from his sister, Lola. Several years before, Andy Walker, an American, had led Lola a life of sin before they married, and then the two disappeared. José goes to "The Devil's Bowl," a notorious hideout for thieves, where he finds Lola ill with tuberculosis. Andy arrives, chased by four American ranchers for cattle rustling. Andy forces José to change clothes, and José is mistaken by the ranchers for Andy. They let José go, after Lola's pleas, but first they brand him on the forehead. A gunfight ensues between José and Andy in which the latter kills Lola. The *rurales* capture José but later collaborate with him in Andy's capture. In the end, José and Conchita are reconciled. *Ranch foremen. Rurales. Ranchers. Rustlers. Brother-sister relationship. Tuberculosis.*
Note: Story and character names are from shooting script in the copyright files and may be different from the final film. This script is almost identical to the one found in the file for *The Devil's Bowl* (1923; see separate entry), except for changes in some character names and locales. One may infer that *Branded a Thief* is either a remake or a reissue of the earlier film.

BRANDED MAN **F2.0565**
Dist Niagara Pictures. 21 Dec **1922** [New York State license]. Si; b&w. 35mm. 5 reels.
Cast: George Waggoner, Fritzi Ridgeway.
Western melodrama(?). No information about the nature of this film has been found.

BRANDED MAN **F2.0566**
Trem Carr Productions. *Dist* Rayart Pictures. May **1928.** Si; b&w. 35mm. 6 reels, 6,089 ft.
Dir Scott Pembroke. *Scen* Tod Robbins, Arthur Hoerl. *Story* Tod Robbins. *Photog* Hap Depew. *Film Ed* Charles A. Post.
Cast: Charles Delaney *(Fred "Deacon" Colgate)*, June Marlowe *(Louise)*, Gordon Griffith *(Bruce)*, George Riley *(Billy)*, Andy Clyde *(Jenkins)*, Erin La Bissoniere *(Eleanor)*, Lucy Beaumont *(The Mother)*, Henry Roquemore *("Hippo")*.
Drama. After suddenly inheriting considerable wealth, Fred Colgate marries a resident of one of his tenements. Her roving eye and infidelity lead to Fred's departure and slow degradation, while his wife and friends think him dead. Eventually, Fred meets a fight trainer in Juarez, becomes a successful prizefighter, and falls in love with a former acquaintance, who has loved him for many years. An old friend finally recognizes him, and Fred is free to marry when his wife is killed by a jealous lover. *Inheritance. Infidelity. Prizefighting. Tenements.*

THE BRANDED SOMBRERO **F2.0567**
Fox Film Corp. 8 Jan **1928** [c21 Dec 1927; LP24771]. Si; b&w. 35mm. 5 reels, 4,612 ft.
Pres by William Fox. *Dir-Scen* Lambert Hillyer. *Titl* James K. McGuinness. *Photog* Reginald Lyons. *Film Ed* J. Logan Pearson. *Asst Dir* Ted Brooks.
Cast: Buck Jones *(Starr Hallett)*, Leila Hyams *(Connie Marsh)*, Eagle *(himself, a horse)*, Jack Baston *(Charles Maggert)*, Stanton Heck *("Honest" John Hallett)*, Francis Ford *(Link Jarvis)*, Josephine Borio *(Rosa)*, Lee Kelly *(Lane Hallett)*.
Western melodrama. Source: Cherry Wilson, "The Branded Sombrero," in *Western Story Magazine* (14 May 1927). A ranchowner, on his deathbed, confesses to his two sons that he rustled cattle in his youth, with the number of head stolen from each outfit "branded" on his sombrero. The elder son repays each outfit and saves his weaker brother from prison. *Brothers. Rustling. Horses.*

BRANDING FIRE **F2.0568**
Anchor Productions. 30 Jun **1930** [New York State license]. Si; b&w. 35mm. 5 reels, 4,500 ft.
Cast: Cheyenne Bill.
Western melodrama(?). No information about the nature of this film has been found.

BRASS **F2.0569**
Warner Brothers Pictures. 4 Mar **1923** [Los Angeles premiere; released 18 Mar; c28 Mar 1923; LP18817]. Si; b&w. 35mm. 9 reels, 8,400 ft.
Prod Harry Rapf. *Dir* Sidney A. Franklin. *Adapt-Scen* Julien Josephson. *Titl* Sada Cowan. *Photog* Norbert Brodin. *Art Dir* Esdras Hartley. *Film Ed* Hal Kern. *Asst Dir* Millard Webb.
Cast: Monte Blue *(Philip Baldwin)*, Marie Prevost *(Marjorie Jones)*, Harry Myers *(Wilbur Lansing)*, Irene Rich *(Mrs. Grotenberg)*, Frank Keenan *(Frank Church)*, Helen Ferguson *(Rosemary Church)*, Miss Du Pont *(Lucy Baldwin)*, Cyril Chadwick *(Roy North)*, Margaret Seddon *(Mrs. Baldwin)*, Pat O'Malley *(Harry Baldwin)*, Edward Jobson *(Judge Baldwin)*, Vera Lewis *(Mrs. Jones)*, Harvey Clark *(George Yost)*, Gertrude Bennett *(Mrs. Yost)*, Ethel Grey Terry *(Leila Vale)*, Bruce Puerin *(Baby Paul)*.

Domestic drama. Source: Charles Gilman Norris, *Brass; a Novel of Marriage* (New York, 1921). Philip Baldwin, superintendent of his father's California fruit ranch, falls in love with Marjorie Jones, who is spending her vacation picking fruit, and jilts Rosemary Church to marry her. The match of business-oriented Philip and fun-seeking, frivolous Marjorie is a bad one, however, and is dissolved shortly after a child is born. Philip engages Mrs. Grotenberg to care for his son, and he falls in love with her in spite of his sister's efforts to interest him in Leila Vale. They are about to be married when Marjorie, whose second marriage also has failed, returns. Mrs. Grotenberg leaves, and the story ends with Philip and his son hoping for the return of "Mama G." *Children. Brother-sister relationship. Marriage. Divorce. Fruit culture. California.*

THE BRASS BOTTLE **F2.0570**

Maurice Tourneur Productions. *Dist* Associated First National Pictures. 2 Jan **1923** [c3 Jul 1923; LP19170]. Si; b&w. 35mm. 6 reels, 5,290 ft.

Pres by M. C. Levee. *Pers Dir* Maurice Tourneur. *Scen* Fred Kennedy Myton. *Photog* Arthur Todd. *Art Dir* Milton Menasco. *Film Ed* Frank Lawrence. *Prod Mgr* Scott R. Beal.

Cast: Harry Myers *(Horace Ventimore)*, Ernest Torrence *(Fakresh-el-Aamash)*, Tully Marshall *(Professor Hamilton)*, Clarissa Selwyn *(Mrs. Hamilton)*, Ford Sterling *(Rapkin)*, Aggie Herring *(Mrs. Rapkin)*, Charlotte Merriam *(Sylvia Hamilton)*, Edward Jobson *(Samuel Wackerbath)*, Barbara La Marr *(The Queen)*, Otis Harlan *(captain of the guard)*, Hazel Keener, Julanne Johnston.

Comedy. Source: F. Anstey, *The Brass Bottle* (London, 1900). London architect Horace Ventimore picks up an ancient brass bottle and is suddenly greeted by a genie who promises to grant the architect's every wish in return for his freedom. The wishes, when granted, however, cause too much trouble, so he tricks the genie back into the bottle and tosses it out to sea. *Architects. Genii. London.*

THE BRASS BOWL **F2.0571**

Fox Film Corp. 16 Nov **1924** [c17 Nov 1924; LP20770]. Si; b&w. 35mm. 6 reels, 5,830 ft.

Pres by William Fox. *Dir* Jerome Storm. *Scen* Thomas Dixon, Jr.

Cast: Edmund Lowe *(Dan Maitland/Anisty)*, Claire Adams *(Sylvia)*, Jack Duffy *(O'Hagan)*, J. Farrell MacDonald *(Hickey)*, Leo White *(taxi driver)*, Fred Butler *(bannerman)*.

Mystery melodrama. Source: Louis Joseph Vance, *The Brass Bowl* (Indianapolis, 1907). Arriving unexpectedly at his country home, Dan Maitland discovers a young woman (Sylvia) attempting to open his safe. She mistakes him for Anisty, a notorious thief who is Dan's double, and he gives her the jewels from the safe. Anisty appears, and there follow confusion and thrilling episodes in which Anisty is captured, escapes, and poses as Dan. Dan finally brings Anisty to justice and declares his love for Sylvia, who confesses she was searching Dan's safe to recover papers that might incriminate her father. *Doubles. Thieves. Robbery. Mistaken identity. Documentation.*

BRASS COMMANDMENTS **F2.0572**

Fox Film Corp. 28 Jan **1923** [c28 Jan 1923; LP19033]. Si; b&w. 35mm. 5 reels, 4,829 ft.

Pres by William Fox. *Dir* Lynn F. Reynolds. *Scen* Charles Kenyon. *Photog* Dev Jennings.

Cast: William Farnum *(Stephen "Flash" Lanning)*, Wanda Hawley *(Gloria Hallowell)*, Tom Santschi *(Campan)*, Claire Adams *(Ellen Bosworth)*, Charles Le Moyne *(Dave De Vake)*, Joe Rickson *(Tularosa)*, Lon Poff *(Slim Lally)*, Al Fremont *(Bill Perrin)*, Joseph Gordon *(Clearwater)*, Cap Anderson *(Bannock)*.

Western melodrama. Source: Charles Alden Seltzer, *Brass Commandments* (New York, 1923). "Flash" Lanning returns to Bozzam City from the East to put an end to cattle rustling. Gloria Hallowell, who has known him by reputation, falls in love with Lanning but believes that he loves Ellen Bosworth, an eastern "lady." Campan, the leader of the rustlers, hoping to lure Lanning into a trap, kidnaps both girls. Lanning rescues the girls, punishes Campan, and indicates to Gloria that she is the girl for him. *Rustling. Kidnaping.*

BRASS KNUCKLES **F2.0573**

Warner Brothers Pictures. 3 Dec **1927** [c27 Nov 1927; LP24701]. Si; b&w. 35mm. 7 reels, 6,330 ft.

Dir Lloyd Bacon. *Scen* Harvey Gates. *Photog* Norbert Brodin. *Asst Dir* Henry Blanke.

Cast: Monte Blue *(Zac Harrison)*, Betty Bronson *(June Curry)*, William Russell *("Brass Knuckles" Lamont)*, Georgie Stone *(Velvet Smith)*, Paul Panzer *(Sergeant Peters)*, Jack Curtis *(Murphy)*.

Crime melodrama. During an attempted prison break, "Fade-away" Joe kills the warden and is sentenced to death. Lamont's term is prolonged, and he swears vengeance on Zac Harrison, who is entrusted with a letter to Joe's daughter, June. Zac and Velvet, when freed, call at an orphanage to see June, who then cherishes the kindness Zac brings her and runs away to join them. Velvet gives in to thievery, but Zac induces him to go straight. On her birthday, Velvet takes June to an underworld cafe in some "grown-up" clothes, provoking Zac's anger but bringing the realization that he loves her. Lamont, released from prison, informs the vice squad of their "immoral" relationship, and Zac is jailed; when released, he finds that Lamont, as her "father," has taken June into his custody. Zac is forced to tell her the truth about her father ... but all ends happily. *Orphans. Criminals—Rehabilitation. Prison wardens. Filial relations. Murder. Revenge. Prisons. Prison escapes. Capital punishment.*

BRAVEHEART **F2.0574**

Cinema Corp. of America. *Dist* Producers Distributing Corp. 27 Dec **1925** [c28 Dec 1925; LP22170]. Si; b&w. 35mm. 7 reels, 7,256 ft.

Pres by Cecil B. De Mille. *Dir* Alan Hale. *Adapt* Mary O'Hara. *Photog* Faxon M. Dean.

Cast: Rod La Rocque *(Braveheart)*, Lillian Rich *(Dorothy Nelson)*, Robert Edeson *(Hobart Nelson)*, Arthur Housman *(Frank Nelson)*, Frank Hagney *(Ki-Yote)*, Jean Acker *(Sky-Arrow)*, [Frederick] Tyrone Power *(Standing Rock)*, Sally Rand *(Sally Vernon)*, Henry Victor *(Sam Harris)*.

Western melodrama. Source: William Churchill De Mille, "Braveheart" (publication undetermined). Braveheart, a young Indian brave, is sent east to study law in order to prepare himself to defend the tribe's hereditary fishing rights, which are endangered by Hobart Nelson, the avaricious president of a fish-canning combine. While at college, Braveheart becomes an outstanding scholar and an All-American football player, but his work there comes to nothing, for, in order to save his friend Frank Nelson, from disgrace, he confesses to selling football signals to an opposing team and is expelled. He is an outcast from his tribe as well, but goes into court and wins the fishing rights for his people. Ki-Yote, a troublemaker, incites the tribe to kidnap Nelson and his daughter, Dorothy, with whom Braveheart is in love. Braveheart rescues the Nelsons, but he denies his love for the white girl and marries one of red blood instead. *Indians of North America. Businessmen. Lawyers. Football. College life. Fishing industry.*

BRAWN OF THE NORTH **F2.0575**

Trimble-Murfin Productions. *Dist* Associated First National Pictures. ca12 Nov **1922** [Los Angeles premiere; released Nov; c1 Nov 1922; LP18350]. Si; b&w. 35mm. 8 reels, 7,759 ft.

Pres by Laurence Trimble, Jane Murfin. *Dir* Laurence Trimble. *Cont* Philip Hubbard. *Story* Laurence Trimble, Jane Murfin. *Photog* Charles Dreyer.

Cast: Irene Rich *(Marion Wells)*, Lee Shumway *(Peter Coe)*, Joseph Barrell *(Howard Burton)*, Roger James Manning *(Lester Wells)*, Philip Hubbard *(The Missionary)*, Jean Metcalf *(The Missionary's Wife)*, Baby Evangeline Bryant *(The Baby)*, Lady Silver *(The Vamp, a dog)*, Strongheart *(Brawn)*.

Northwest melodrama. Marion Wells and the dog Brawn go to Alaska to join her brother, Lester, and Howard Burton, her fiancé. The men quarrel, Burton kills Lester, and Brawn drags Marion through a storm to Peter Coe's cabin. Peter forces marriage on her, but she leaves him and sells Brawn to support herself. When Peter finds the dog mistreated by his new owner, he rescues Brawn and returns him to Marion, who now realizes that she loves Peter. Sometime later, while making a trip into town with their baby, Marion and Peter leave their sled to search for Brawn, who has succumbed to the charms of Lady Silver and followed her. They return to find their baby gone, but later they discover that Brawn came back to save the baby from a pack of wolves and carried her to a missionary's cabin. *Brother-sister relationship. Murder. Alaska. Dogs.*

BREAD **F2.0576**

Metro-Goldwyn Pictures. 4 Aug **1924** [c23 Jul 1924; LP20481]. Si; b&w. 35mm. 7 reels, 6,500 ft.

Pres by Louis B. Mayer. *Dir* Victor Schertzinger. *Cont* Albert Lewin. *Adapt* Lenore Coffee.

Cast: Mae Busch *(Jeanette Sturgis)*, Robert Frazer *(Martin Devlin)*, Pat O'Malley *(Roy Beardsley)*, Wanda Hawley *(Alice Sturgis)*, Eugenie

Besserer *(Mrs. Sturgis)*, Hobart Bosworth *(Mr. Corey)*, Myrtle Stedman *(Mrs. Corey)*, Ward Crane *(Gerald Kenyon)*.

Drama. Source: Charles Gilman Norris, *Bread* (New York, 1923). To relieve the burden placed on their mother, Alice Sturgis marries and has several children, while her independent sister, Jeanette, goes to work as a stenographer. Eventually, she is forced to marry a persistent salesman to avoid a scandal. Becoming disillusioned with married life, Jeanette leaves the salesman, but after 3 years' separation she realizes her need for a family and returns to him. *Sisters. Salesmen. Marriage. Family life. Poverty.*

THE BREAK UP **F2.0577**

Capt. Jack Robertson. *Dist* Talking Picture Epics. 29 Jul **1930** [New York showing]. Sd; b&w. 35mm. 5 reels, 4,761 ft.

Dir Capt. Jack Robertson. *Mus Cond* Nathaniel Shilkret.

Travelog. Capt. Jack Robertson, his dog Skooter, and several others journey to Alaska in winter by steamship via the Inside Passage and Prince William Sound. A smaller boat takes them past Harvard Glacier, Chugash Range, and the Great Divide. Continuing by canoe, raft, and dogsled, the group heads northward past Mt. McKinley. In the spring the breakup of the frozen river permits a 1,200-mile trip on the Tanana and Yukon Rivers to the Bering Sea, visiting Eskimos along the way. Next destination is the Alaska Peninsula, with its Valley of Ten Thousand Smokes and spawning salmon, then a last stop on the Kenai peninsula before the coming of winter and a turn toward home. *Eskimos. Alaska. Mount McKinley. Bering Sea. Yukon River. Tanana River. Salmon. Dogs.*

BREAKFAST AT SUNRISE **F2.0578**

Constance Talmadge Productions. *Dist* First National Pictures. 23 Oct **1927** [c30 Aug 1927; LP24335]. Si; b&w. 35mm. 7 reels, 6,042 or 6,222 ft.

Pres by Joseph M. Schenck. *Dir* Malcolm St. Clair. *Adapt* Gladys Unger. *Screen Story* Fred De Gresac. *Photog* Robert B. Kurrle.

Cast: Constance Talmadge *(Madeleine)*, Alice White *(Loulou)*, Bryant Washburn *(Marquis)*, Paulette Duval *(Georgiana)*, Marie Dressler *(Queen)*, Albert Gran *(Champignol)*, Burr McIntosh *(General)*, David Mir *(Prince)*, Don Alvarado *(Lussan)*, Nellie Bly Baker *(Madeleine's maid)*.

Romantic comedy. Source: André Birabeau, *Le Déjeuner au soleil* (c1925). Madeleine Watteau, a wealthy Parisienne, arrives at the Hotel Splendide coincidentally with the coming of Pierre Lussan, broke and hired for "atmospheric" purposes. Madeleine's fiancé, the Marquis de Cerisey, excuses himself from an engagement with her because of a headache while Pierre telephones Loulou, a dancer, and is refused a proposal of marriage. Madeleine is infuriated to learn that the marquis is in the dining room with another woman, and Pierre sees Loulou with a gay old blade. When placed at the same table, the jilted parties decide to win back their former flames by getting married to each other, after which they will divorce. They soon realize their jealousy of each other's erstwhile partners and realize also that they are meant for each other. *Parisians. Dancers. Nobility. Rakes. Courtship.*

BREAKING HOME TIES **F2.0579**

E. S. Manheimer. *Dist* Associated Exhibitors. 12 Nov **1922** [c11 Nov 1922; LU18390]. Si; b&w. 35mm. 6 reels, 5,622 ft.

Pres by E. S. Manheimer. *Dir-Writ* Frank N. Seltzer, George K. Rolands.

Cast: Lee Kohlmar *(Father Bergman)*, Rebecca Weintraub *(Mother Bergman)*, Richard Farrell *(David Bergman)*, Arthur Ashley *(Paul Zeidman)*, Betty Howe *(Esther)*, Jane Thomas *(Rose Neuman)*, Henry B. Schaffer *(J. B. Martin)*, Maude Hill *(Mrs. Martin)*, Robert Maxmillian *(Moskowitz)*.

Drama. Thinking he has killed his friend Paul Zeidman in a jealous rage, David Bergman flees his native Russia; becomes a successful lawyer in New York; and loses touch with his penniless family, who have followed him to America. At his wedding to Rose, which takes place in a home for the aged to which they have contributed, David recognizes Paul among the musicians; and when the Bergmans, who live in the home, hear Paul's rendition of *Eili, Eili* all are reunited. *Russians. Jews. Lawyers. Musicians. Old age homes.*

BREAKING INTO SOCIETY **F2.0580**

Hunt Stromberg Productions. *Dist* Film Booking Offices of America. 30 Sep **1923** [c30 Aug 1923; LP19362]. Si; b&w. 35mm. 5 reels, 4,112 ft.

Prod-Dir-Writ Hunt Stromberg. *Photog* Irving Reis.

Cast: Carrie Clark Ward *(Mrs. Pat O'Toole)*, Bull Montana *(Tim O'Toole)*, Kalla Pasha *(Pat O'Toole)*, Francis Trebaol *(Marty O'Toole)*, Florence Gilbert *(Yvonne)*, Leo White *(a barber)*, Tiny Sanford *(a chiropractor)*, Stanhope Wheatcroft *(a man of wealth)*, Chuck Reisner *(The "Pittsburgh Kid")*, Gertrude Short *(Sally)*, Rags *(Marty O'Toole's dog)*.

Comedy. The O'Tooles inherit a fortune and move to Pasadena where they try to break into society by having lavish dinner parties. The guests are shocked by the O'Tooles' manners, and they leave when the "Pittsburgh Kid" and his Bowery wife, Yvonne, uninvited guests, arrive. *Irish. Chiropractors. Barbers. Social classes. Social customs. Pasadena. Dogs.*

THE BREAKING POINT **F2.0581**

J. L. Frothingham Productions. *Dist* W. W. Hodkinson Corp. Feb **1921.** Si; b&w. 35mm. 6 reels, 5,788 ft.

Dir Paul Scardon. *Scen* H. H. Van Loan. *Photog* René Guissart.

Cast: Bessie Barriscale *(Ruth Marshall)*, Walter McGrail *(Richard Janeway)*, Ethel Grey Terry *(Lucia Deeping)*, Eugenie Besserer *(Mrs. Janeway)*, Pat O'Malley *(Phillip Bradley)*, Winter Hall *(Dr. Hillyer)*, Wilfred Lucas *(Mortimer Davidson)*, Joseph J. Dowling *(Mrs. Marshall)*, Lydia Knott *(Mrs. Marshall)*, Irene Yeager *(Camilla)*.

Domestic melodrama. Source: Mary Lerner, "The Living Child" (publication undetermined). Ruth Marshall is forced financially to marry wealthy Richard Janeway. Janeway turns out to be a drunken philanderer who, on their honeymoon, renews his relationship with a former flame. The night their child is born, Janeway leaves Ruth for a wild party. At another party 5 years later, Janeway fetches the child to entertain the guests, placing his daughter in his mistress' arms. He later throws his wife out of the house, threatening to give the child to Lucia, his mistress. Ruth flees to Janeway's mother, who sympathizes with her. While she is still there, Dr. Hillyer telephones to say Janeway is dead. Ruth confesses she accidently killed him when he goaded her beyond endurance. Dr. Hillyer arranges the body in such a way that the coroner reports the cause of death as suicide. *Philanderers. Mistresses. Mothers-in-law. Marriage. Infidelity. Alcoholism.*

THE BREAKING POINT **F2.0582**

Famous Players–Lasky. *Dist* Paramount Pictures. 4 May **1924** [c23 Apr 1924; LP20114]. Si; b&w. 35mm. 7 reels, 6,664 ft.

Pres by Adolph Zukor, Jesse L. Lasky. *Dir* Herbert Brenon. *Scen* Edfrid Bingham, Julie Herne. *Photog* James Howe.

Cast: Nita Naldi *(Beverly Carlysle)*, Patsy Ruth Miller *(Elizabeth Wheeler)*, George Fawcett *(Dr. David Livingstone)*, Matt Moore *(Judson Clark)*, John Merkyl *(William Lucas)*, Theodore von Eltz *(Fred Gregory)*, Edythe Chapman *(Lucy Livingstone)*, Cyril Ring *(Louis Bassett)*, W. B. Clarke *(Sheriff Wilkins)*, Edward Kipling *(Joe)*, Milt Brown *(Donaldson)*, Charles A. Stevenson *(Harrison Wheeler)*, Naida Faro *(Minnie)*.

Mystery melodrama. Source: Mary Roberts Rinehart, *The Breaking Point* (New York, 1922). Assuming that he has killed the husband of the woman he also loves, Judson Clark flees through a blizzard to a lonely cabin, where he nearly dies. When he recovers, he has lost his memory and is believed to be dead until an actress recognizes "the young doctor." Following many adventures, the real killer confesses and Clark regains his memory and the woman he loves. *Murder. Amnesia. Blizzards.*

THE BREATH OF SCANDAL **F2.0583**

B. P. Schulberg Productions. 1 Sept **1924** [c4 Mar 1925; LP21212]. Si; b&w. 35mm. 7 reels, 6,900 ft.

Dir Louis Gasnier. *Scen* Eve Unsell. *Photog* Harry Perry.

Cast: Betty Blythe *(Sybil Russell)*, Patsy Ruth Miller *(Marjorie Hale)*, Jack Mulhall *(Bill Wallace)*, Myrtle Stedman *(Helen Hale)*, Lou Tellegen *(Charles Hale)*, Forrest Stanley *(Gregg Mowbry)*, Frank Leigh *(Sybil's husband)*, Phyllis Haver *(Clara Simmons)*, Charles Clary *(Atherton Bruce)*.

Melodrama. Source: Edwin Balmer, *The Breath of Scandal* (Boston, 1922). When Charles Hale is visiting his mistress, Sybil Russell, he is shot in the arm by Sybil's estranged and outraged husband. Hale's daughter, Marjorie, is so shocked to discover in this abrupt fashion her father's philandering that she leaves her wealthy home and goes to the slums to do settlement work. Marjorie, who is engaged to the district attorney, is there placed in a compromising position by her father's assailant, who intends to revenge himself upon the entire Hale family. The district attorney breaks off his engagement with Marjorie. She is reconciled to her father, who has given up Sybil. Mrs. Hale, generally engaged in social activities, returns from a convention and is happily reunited with her husband and daughter. The district attorney learns that Marjorie was the victim of Russell's scheming, and he and Marjorie replight their troth. *District attorneys. Mistresses. Filial relations. Social service. Slums.*

THE BREATHLESS MOMENT F2.0584

Universal Pictures. 3 Feb **1924** [c19 Dec 1923; LP19739]. Si; b&w. 35mm. 6 reels, 5,556 ft.

Dir Robert F. Hill. *Screenplay* Raymond L. Schrock. *Scen* William E. Wing, Harvey Gates. *Story* Raymond L. Schrock, Harvey Gates. *Photog* William Thornley.

Cast: William Desmond *(Billy Carson)*, Charlotte Merriam *(June Smart)*, Alfred Fisher *(David Smart)*, Robert E. Homans *(Detective Quinn)*, Lucille Hutton *(Mildred Day)*, John Steppling *(Banker Day)*, Margaret Cullington *(Evangeline Clementine Jones)*, Harry Van Meter *("Tricks" Kennedy)*, Albert Hart *(Dan Cassidy)*.

Comedy-melodrama. Source: Marguerite Bryant, *Richard* (New York, 1922). Unwilling to arrest Billy Carson, a crook who once befriended him, Officer Quinn forces him and Dan, his confederate, to spend a year in a small town. There, Carson falls in love, reforms, and saves his future father-in-law's business. Dan also settles down and marries. *Police. Criminals—Rehabilitation. Businessmen. Friendship.*

Note: Working title: *Sentenced to Soft Labor*. Company records indicate that Harvey Gates's continuity for *Railroaded* from the novel *Richard* was used for the story.

BRED IN OLD KENTUCKY F2.0585

R-C Pictures. *Dist* Film Booking Offices of America. 14 or 28 Nov **1926** [c15 Nov 1926; LP23329]. Si; b&w. 35mm. 6 reels, 5,285 ft.

Pres by Joseph P. Kennedy. *Dir* Eddie Dillon. *Cont* Gerald C. Duffy. *Story* Louis Weadock, C. D. Lancaster. *Camera* Phil Tannura. *Asst Dir* Wallace Fox.

Cast: Viola Dana *(Katie O'Doone)*, Jerry Miley *(Dennis Reilly)*, Jed Prouty *(Jake Trumbull)*, James Mason *(Tod Cuyler)*, Roy Laidlaw *(Mr. Welkin)*, Josephine Crowell *(landlady)*.

Romantic drama. Katie O'Doone inherits her father's dilapidated Kentucky estate and a racehorse; she mortgages the estate and bets the money on her horse in a race. The jockey of Dennis Reilly, a wealthy turfman, rides his horse into Katie's, and it has to be shot as a result of the injury. Katie then meets Jake Trumbull, a generous but dishonest bookie, and he offers her a commission on all the bets she can get for him. Tod Cuyler, an unscrupulous turfman, conspires with Trumbull to bet on Reilly's horse, then substitute an almost identical horse in the race. Katie consents to spy on Reilly and soon falls in love with him; when she discovers that Reilly was innocent of any connection with the crooked race in which her horse was killed, she takes steps to assure that Reilly's horse will win the race. He persuades her to come back to him, as his wife. *Turfmen. Bookies. Inheritance. Courtship. Horseracing. Kentucky. Horses.*

BREED OF COURAGE F2.0586

R-C Pictures. *Dist* Film Booking Offices of America. 7 Aug **1927** [c7 Aug 1927; LP24269]. Si; b&w. 35mm. 5 reels, 4,910 ft.

Pres by Joseph P. Kennedy. *Dir* Howard Mitchell. *Cont* F. A. E. Pine. *Adapt* Leon D'Usseau. *Story* John Stuart Twist. *Photog* Mack Stengler. *Asst Dir* Ray McCarey.

Cast: Sam Nelson *(Alan Haliday)*, Jeanne Morgan *(Claire Dean)*, Stanton Heck *(Wes McQuinn)*, Ethan Laidlaw *(Brack McQuinn)*, Ranger *(himself, a dog)*, Nitchamoose *(Beauty, a dog)*, Ogoma *(Butch, a dog)*.

Melodrama. With the death of the last male in the Deane family, there is a temporary end to the Deane-McQuinn feud, waged for years in the Cumberland mountain district. The feud is renewed, however, when Claire Deane returns home from school and removes a sign and fence erected on her property by Wes McQuinn; she is aided in her struggle by Ranger, the Deane dog, and his wolf mate, Beauty. Wes plans to put an end to Ranger with his dog, Butch, but the McQuinn dog is killed by Ranger when he attacks Beauty. The McQuinns threaten Claire but are disarmed by Alan Haliday, a stranger. After a series of harrowing escapes, Ranger overtakes Brack, who has kidnaped Claire; and the stranger, who is a Federal agent, wins her love. *Strangers. Government agents. Feuds. Cumberland Mountains. Dogs.*

THE BREED OF THE BORDER F2.0587.

Harry Garson Productions. *Dist* Film Booking Offices of America. 28 Dec **1924** [c28 Dec 1924; LP21194]. Si; b&w. 35mm. 5 reels, 4,930 ft.

Dir Harry Garson. *Cont* Paul Gangelin, Dorothy Arzner. *Photog* William Tuers, Henry Kruse. *Asst Dir* Curley Dresden.

Cast: Lefty Flynn *(Circus Lacey)*, Dorothy Dwan *(Ethel Slocum)*, Louise Carver *(Ma Malone)*, Milton Ross *(Dad Slocum)*, Frank Hagney *(Sheriff Wells)*, Fred Burns *(Deputy Leverie)*, Joe Bennett *(Red Lucas)*, Bill Donovan *(Pablo, the bandit)*.

Western melodrama. Source: William Dawson Hoffman, "The Breed of the Border" (publication undetermined). Following the robbery of the Inspiration Gold Mine, Circus Lacey drifts into the border town of Esmeralda, where he saves Ethel Slocum from the unwanted advances of Red Lucas, a notorious gunman. When Ethel later also refuses to submit to the sheriff's demands, the sheriff frames her father for the mine robbery. Circus saves Pa Slocum from mob violence and captures one of Red's hired gunmen, thereby discovering the secret den of the bandits. Circus is surprised there by Red and forced to surrender, but he escapes, returns to town in time to prevent a bank robbery, proves that the sheriff is one of Red's hirelings, and wins Ethel for his wife. *Sheriffs. Robbery. Gold mines.*

BREED OF THE SEA F2.0588

R-C Pictures. *Dist* Film Booking Offices of America. 7 Nov **1926** [c27 Sep 1926; LP23212]. Si; b&w. 35mm. 6 reels, 5,408 ft. [Also 7 reels; 6,450 ft.]

Pres by Joseph P. Kennedy. *Dir* Ralph Ince. *Cont* J. Grubb Alexander. *Adapt* J. G. Hawks. *Photog* Allen Siegler. *Asst Dir* Wallace Fox.

Cast: Ralph Ince *(Tod Pembroke/Tom Pembroke)*, Margaret Livingston *(Marietta Rawdon)*, Pat Harmon *(Lije Marsh)*, Alphonz Ethier *(Bully Rawden)*, Dorothy Dunbar *(Ruth Featherstone)*, Shannon Day *(Martha Winston)*.

Melodrama. Source: Peter Bernard Kyne, "Blue Blood and the Pirates," in *Saturday Evening Post* (184:10, 30 Mar 1912). Tom and Tod Pembroke, twin brothers and both divinity students, love Ruth Featherstone, the dean's daughter. Tod is expelled despite his brother's attempt to shield him; and seeing that Ruth loves Tom, Tod goes to China. Five years later, Tom, a missionary, is married to Ruth and is on his way to establish a mission at Paroa, in the Java Sea, along with Martha Winston, a deaconess. The ship is captured by Tod, now a notorious pirate; and learning of his brother's intentions, he sails for Paroa, leaving his mate, Lije Marsh, in charge, and there takes the place of his fever-stricken brother. Rawden, a trader, intends to drive out the new missionary, but Tod thrashes him and holds services in the mission. Marietta, Rawden's daughter, falls in love with him and signals the pirate ship to assist him when he is taken by Rawden's men; upon Tom's arrival, Tod leaves and is united with Marietta. *Brothers. Twins. Ministerial students. Missionaries. Deaconesses. Traders. Pirates. Courtship. Java. China.*

BREED OF THE SUNSETS F2.0589

FBO Pictures. 1 Apr **1928** [c5 Mar 1928; LP25039]. Si; b&w. 35mm. 5 reels, 4,869 ft.

Dir Wallace W. Fox. *Adapt-Cont* Oliver Drake. *Titl* Randolph Bartlett. *Story* S. E. V. Taylor. *Photog* Robert De Grasse. *Film Ed* Della M. King. *Asst Dir* Sam Nelson.

Cast: Bob Steele *(Jim Collins)*, Nancy Drexel *(The Spanish Girl)*, George Bunny *(Don Alvaro)*, Dorothy Kitchen *(Marie Alvaro)*, Leo White *(Señor Diego Valdez)*, Larry Fisher *(Hank Scully)*.

Western melodrama. Jim, a young cowboy, in love with a Spanish girl who is promised to an unlikely suitor, disguises himself as a Mexican on the wedding eve and abducts the girl. Her father and a posse give chase, but the father, being sympathetic and admiring the cowboy's courage, consents to their marriage. *Cowboys. Spanish. Abduction.*

BREED OF THE WEST F2.0590

National Players. *Dist* Big 4 Film Corp. 12 Nov **1930.** Sd (Cinephone); b&w. 35mm. 6 reels, 5,400-5,700 ft.

Dir-Scen-Dial Alvin J. Neitz. *Story* Alvin J. Neitz, Henry Taylor. *Photog* William Nobles. *Film Ed* Ethel Davey. *Sd* Homer Ellmaker.

Cast: Wally Wales, Virginia Browne Faire.

Western melodrama. Encountering Jim Bradley, a youth searching for his father, a cowboy (played by Wally Wales) takes the boy back to the ranch and gets him a job as cook's helper. Jim catches the cook and Longrope, the trusted foreman, robbing Colonel Sterner, the ranchowner; the cook shoots Jim; and Sterner confesses to his daughter, Betty, that Jim is his son. Capturing the cook and turning him over to the sheriff, who thereby learns of Longrope's murder of a cattle association man, the hero prevents Longrope's second attempt to rob Sterner and brings him to justice. *Cowboys. Ranchers. Ranch foremen. Cooks. Filial relations. Robbery. Murder.*

BREEZY BILL F2.0591

Big Productions Film Corp. *Dist* Syndicate Pictures. 24 Jan **1930** [New York State license]. Si; b&w. 35mm. 5 reels, 4,667 ft.

Dir J. P. McGowan. *Story-Scen* Sally Winters. *Photog* Hap Depew.

Cast: Bob Steele *(Breezy Bill)*, Alfred Hewston *(Henry Pennypincher)*, George Hewston *(Gabe, his brother)*, Edna Aslin *(Barbara, Gabe's daughter)*, Perry Murdock *(Gabe's son)*, Bud Osborne, Cliff Lyons *(bandits)*, J. P. McGowan *(sheriff)*.

Western melodrama. Two bandits out to get their hands on Henry Pennypincher's stocks and bonds abduct the rancher when he refuses to reveal their location. Pennypincher's adopted son, Breezy Bill, is knocked unconscious for intervening, and he consequently is blamed for Pennypincher's disappearance. With the help of Pennypincher's nephew and niece and a flimsy disguise, Bob trails the bandits and rescues Pennypincher. *Ranchers. Misers. Bandits. Abduction. Disguise.*

BREWSTER'S MILLIONS F2.0592

Famous Players–Lasky. *Dist* Paramount Pictures. Jan **1921** [c4 Jan 1921; LP15988]. Si; b&w. 35mm. 6 reels, 5,502 ft.

Pres by Jesse L. Lasky. *Dir* Joseph Henabery. *Scen* Walter Woods. *Photog* Karl Brown.

Cast: Roscoe "Fatty" Arbuckle *(Monte Brewster)*, Betty Ross Clark *(Peggy)*, Fred Huntley *(Mr. Brewster)*, Marian Skinner *(Mrs. Brewster)*, James Corrigan *(Mr. Ingraham)*, Jean Acker *(Barbara Drew)*, Charles Ogle *(Colonel Drew)*, Neely Edwards *(MacLeod)*, William Boyd *(Harrison)*, L. J. McCarthy *(Ellis)*, Parker McConnell *(Pettingill)*, John MacFarlane *(Blake)*.

Farce. Source: George Barr McCutcheon, *Brewster's Millions* (New York, 1905). Winchell Smith and Byron Ongley, *Brewster's Millions; a Comedy in Four Acts* (New York, 1925). Monte Brewster's inheritance of his Grandfather Brewster's $2 million provokes his Grandfather Ingraham to promise Monte $10 million if he can spend his inheritance in one year and remain unmarried. Monte does his best, but he seems to grow wealthier with each spendthrift scheme, and his friends—especially Peggy Gray—secretly save and invest the money they are supposed to help him spend. A disastrous yachting cruise to Peru finally does the trick. Monte is broke, but he has married Peggy, so neither grandfather is satisfied until the salvaged yacht brings Monte a large sum and Peggy's investment in a Peruvian silver mine proves lucrative. *Millionaires. Grandfathers. Inheritance. Peru.*

A BRIDE FOR A KNIGHT F2.0593

Syracuse Motion Picture Co. *Dist* Renown Pictures. 15 Dec **1923** [scheduled release]. Si; b&w. 35mm. 5 reels.

Cast: Henry Hull *(Jimmy Poe)*, Mary Thurman *(Jean Hawthorne)*, William H. Tooker *(Jean's uncle)*, Nellie Parker Spaulding, Alyce Mills, Charles Craig, Tammany Young, Billy Quirk, Marcia Harris.

Comedy. Jimmy inhales too much gas in a dentist's chair, thinks he is a sleuth, and actually captures thieves robbing Jean's uncle's bank. *Detectives. Bankers. Uncles. Dentists. Bank robberies.*

BRIDE OF HATE *see* **WANTED FOR MURDER, OR BRIDE OF HATE**

THE BRIDE OF HATE (Reissue) F2.0594

Triangle Film Corp. *Dist* Tri-Stone Pictures. c12 Jun **1924** [LP20306]. Si; b&w. 35mm. 5 reels.

Note: A Frank Keenan–Margery Wilson film originally released by Triangle Film Corp. on 14 Jan 1917.

BRIDE OF THE DESERT F2.0595

Trem Carr Productions. *Dist* Rayart Pictures. 4 Sep **1929.** Sd (Filmtone); b&w. 35mm. 6 reels, 5,047 or 5,149 ft. [Also si; 4,816 ft.]

Dir Duke Worne. *Story-Scen-Dial* Arthur Hoerl. *Photog* Ernest Depew. *Film Ed* John S. Harrington.

Cast: Alice Calhoun *(Joanna Benton)*, LeRoy Mason *(fugitive)*, Ethan Laidlaw *(Tom Benton)*, Lum Chan *(Wang)*, Walter Ackerman *(Solomon Murphy)*, Horace Carpenter *(sheriff)*.

Western melodrama. The desperate loneliness of Joanna Benton's life as the wife of desert prospector Tom Benton is interrupted by the appearance of a wounded fugitive eluding a posse. She gives him shelter in a lean-to, into which Benton also invites a peddler to spend the night. When the peddler is robbed and murdered, the fugitive is charged, but Joanna reveals that she nursed the accused in her own room all through the night. Benton's enormous indignation is ended by the fugitive's counteraccusation of the peddler's murder, and evidence on Benton's person proves him guilty. *Prospectors. Fugitives. Strangers. Peddlers. Sheriffs. Murder.*

BRIDE OF THE GODS *see* **SHATTERED IDOLS**

BRIDE OF THE REGIMENT F2.0596

First National Pictures. 21 May **1930** [New York premiere; released 22 Jun; c27 Jun 1930; LP1388]. Sd (Vitaphone); col (Technicolor). 35mm. 12 reels, 7,418 ft.

Assoc Prod Robert North. *Dir* John Francis Dillon. *Screenplay* Humphrey Pearson. *Adapt-Dial* Ray Harris. *Photog* Dev Jennings, Charles E. Schoenbaum. *Film Ed* Leroy Stone. *Adtl Songs: "Broken-Hearted Lover," "Cook's Song," "Dream Away," "Heart of Heaven," "I'd Like To Be a Happy Bride," "One Kiss, Sweetheart, Then Goodbye," "Through the Miracle of Love," "One Life, One Love," "You Still Retain Your Girlish Figure"* Al Bryan, Eddie Ward, Al Dubin. *Dance Dir* Jack Haskell. *Rec Engr* Hal Brumbaugh.

Cast: Vivienne Segal *(Countess Anna-Marie)*, Allan Prior *(Count Adrian Beltrami)*, Walter Pidgeon *(Colonel Vultow)*, Louise Fazenda *(Teresa, the maid)*, Myrna Loy *(Sophie)*, Lupino Lane *(Sprotti, ballet master)*, Ford Sterling *(Tangy, silhouette cutter)*, Harry Cording *(Sergeant Dostal)*, Claude Fleming *(Captain Stogan)*, Herbert Clark *(The Prince)*.

Musical romantic drama. Source: Rudolph Schanzer and Ernst Welisch, *Die Frau im Hermelin* (a play). As they are leaving the church following their wedding, Count Adrian Beltrami and Countess Anna-Marie are told that the Austrians are marching on the town to quell an Italian uprising; the bride and relatives induce the count to flee to his castle, but Tangy, a silhouette cutter, brings word from the revolutionary committee asking him to return; the count goes, asking Tangy to pose as the count and protect Anna-Marie. Vultow, the leader of the Austrians, determined to seduce Anna-Marie, learns of Adrian's identity and orders him shot at sunrise unless she submits. Drunk with champagne, Vultow falls asleep and dreams that Anna-Marie comes to him willingly, and later, believing he has conquered her, he consents to Adrian's freedom. When he learns of this trick of fate, however, a hurried dispatch obliges him to depart, and the count and countess are reunited. *Silhouette cutters. Italians. Nobility. Revolts. Impersonation. Seduction. Weddings. Austria. Italy. Dreams.*

BRIDE OF THE STORM F2.0597

Vitagraph Co. of America. *Dist* Warner Brothers Pictures. 20 Feb **1926** [c27 Feb 1926; LP22430]. Si; b&w. 35mm. 7 reels, 6,826 ft.

Dir J. Stuart Blackton. *Adapt* Marian Constance. *Photog* Nick Musuraca. *Adtl Photog* William Adams. *Asst Dir* Al Zeidman.

Cast: Dolores Costello *(Faith Fitzhugh)*, John Harron *(Dick Wayne)*, Otto Matiesen *(Hans Kroon)*, Sheldon Lewis *(Piet Kroon)*, [Frederick] Tyrone Power *(Jacob Kroon)*, Julia Swayne Gordon *(Faith's mother)*, Evon Pelletier *(Faith, aged 8)*, Ira McFadden *(Heine Krutz)*, Tutor Owen *(Funeral Harry)*, Fred Scott *(Spike Mulligan)*, Donald Stuart *(Angus McLain)*, Walter Tennyson *(Ensign Clinton)*, Larry Steers *(Commander of the U. S. S. "Baltimore")*.

Melodrama. Source: James Francis Dwyer, "Maryland, My Maryland," in *Colliers* (65:7–8, 20 Mar 1920). An American ship is wrecked off the coast of the Dutch East Indies, and little Faith Fitzhugh and her mother are washed ashore on a rocky island that supports only a lighthouse. Faith's mother lives only long enough to inform the three Dutch lighthouse keepers that her daughter is the heiress to a large fortune. Years pass, and Faith grows to womanhood. Jacob Kroon and his son, Piet, then conspire to marry Faith to Piet's idiot son, Hans, in order to bring her fortune into the family. Dick Wayne, a sailor on an American cruiser that is repairing a damaged cable in the waters off the lighthouse, learns of Faith's captivity and comes to her rescue. Piet kills Jacob in a fit of jealousy, and Dick then kills Piet in a fight. Hans sets the lighthouse on fire and incinerates himself. Dick and Faith make it back to the cruiser. *Dutch. Sailors. Heiresses. Idiots. Patricide. Lighthouses. Cruisers. Netherlands. East Indies. Shipwrecks.*

BRIDE OF VENGEANCE F2.0598

Peerless Feature Production Co. 19 Jun **1923** [scheduled release]. Si; b&w. 35mm. 5 reels.

Cast: Ellen Richter.

Drama(?). No information about the precise nature of this film has been found. *Sicilians.*

THE BRIDE'S CONFESSION **F2.0599**

Graphic Film Corp. Dec **1921.** Si; b&w. 35mm. [Feature length assumed.]

Dir Ivan Abramson.

Cast: Leah Baird, Rita Jolivet.

Melodrama(?). No information about the nature of this film has been found.

THE BRIDE'S PLAY **F2.0600**

Cosmopolitan Productions. *Dist* Paramount Pictures. ca17 Dec **1921** [premiere; released 22 Jan 1922; c4 Jan 1922; LP17421]. Si; b&w. 35mm. 7 reels, 6,476 ft.

Dir George W. Terwilliger. *Scen* Mildred Considine. *Photog* Ira H. Morgan. *Set Dsgn* Joseph Urban.

Cast—Medieval Story: Marion Davies *(Enid of Cashel)*, Jack O'Brien *(Marquis of Muckross)*, Frank Shannon *(Sir John Mansfield)*.

Cast—Modern Story: Marion Davies *(Aileen Barrett)*, Wyndham Standing *(Sir Fergus Cassidy)*, Carlton Miller *(Bulmer Meade, a poet)*, Richard Cummings *(John Barrett, Aileen's father)*, Eleanor Middleton *(Bridget)*, Thea Talbot *(Sybil)*, John P. Wade *(Sir Robert Fennell)*, Julia Hurley *(old peasant woman)*, George Spink *(Meade's butler)*.

Historical costume romance. Source: Brian Oswald Donn-Byrne, "The Bride's Play," in *Rivers of Damascus and Other Stories* (London, 1931). According to tradition, the Earl of Kenmare, Sir John Mansfield, selects for his wife Lady Enid of Cashel, though she loves the Marquis of Muckross. At the wedding ceremony she carries out the old custom of "The Bride's Play"—making a round of the guests and asking each man in turn if he is the one she loves best—until, suddenly, the Marquis of Muckross appears and carries her away. Sir Fergus, the earl's descendant, is about to marry Aileen Barrett and agrees that the old custom must be adhered to. At the wedding, Aileen's former lover, Bulmer Meade, a young Dublin poet who proved unworthy and was rejected, appears as she asks the question, but instead of winning her Meade receives a slap from Aileen, who rejoins her husband. *Nobility. Poets. Celtic legends. Courtship. Weddings. Ireland.*

THE BRIDGE OF SAN LUIS REY **F2.0601**

Metro-Goldwyn-Mayer Pictures. 30 Mar **1929** [c1 Apr 1929; LP266]. Talking sequences, mus score, & sd eff (Movietone); b&w. 35mm. 10 reels, 7,890 ft. [Also si; 7,330 ft.]

Dir Charles Brabin. *Titl-Dial* Ruth Cummings, Marian Ainslee. *Adapt* Alice D. G. Miller. *Photog* Merritt B. Gerstad. *Art Dir* Cedric Gibbons. *Film Ed* Margaret Booth. *Mus Score* Carli Elinor. *Gowns* Adrian.

Cast: Lily Damita *(Camila)*, Ernest Torrence *(Uncle Pio)*, Raquel Torres *(Pepita)*, Don Alvarado *(Manuel)*, Duncan Renaldo *(Esteban)*, Henry B. Walthall *(Father Juniper)*, Michael Vavitch *(Viceroy)*, Emily Fitzroy *(Marquesa)*, Jane Winton *(Doña Clara)*, Gordon Thorpe *(Jaime)*, Mitchell Lewis *(Captain Alvarado)*, Paul Ellis *(Don Vicente)*, Eugenie Besserer *(nun)*, Tully Marshall *(townsman)*.

Drama. Source: Thornton Wilder, *The Bridge of San Luis Rey* (New York, 1927). The bridge of San Luis Rey, built by the Incas and blessed by St. Louis, stands guarded by the Cathedral of St. Rose of Lima on the highroad of Peru as a symbol of the villagers' communion with God. On 20 July 1714 the bridge collapses, sending five people to their deaths "like stones into the water." The people interpret this catastrophe, coming on the day of the Feast of St. Louis, as forewarning of their imminent doom, and desperately they come to Father Juniper for spiritual guidance. He must delve into the lives of the five to explain this divine intervention: *The Marquesa de Montemayer has been left lonely and disconsolate by her daughter, who married and moved to Spain. Pepita, the convent-reared ward of the marquesa, finds herself so stirred by Esteban that she is relinquishing her freedom to return to a life devoted to the Almighty. Esteban has witnessed the spiritual and finally corporeal destruction of his beloved twin brother by a wanton, power-mad dancer, La Perichole. Pio is an old man who was the dancer's "uncle," and whose selfless devotion and love were spurned by her lustful recklessness. He is leaving her and taking in his charge her young son, Jaime, whom he has sheltered and cared for throughout her heedless debauchery.* Father Juniper exhorts the villagers in a moving sermon to see God's infinite wisdon, to understand that all five have loved and through suffering have known a deepening of their love. "There is a land of the living and the land of the dead—and the bridge is Love—the only survival, the only meaning." *Priests. Wards. Twins. Dancers. Uncles. Loyalty. Dissipation. Cathedrals. Bridges. Providence.*

THE BRIDGE OF SIGHS **F2.0602**

Warner Brothers Pictures. 1 Jan **1925** [c24 Jan 1925; LP21065]. Si; b&w. 35mm. 7 reels, 6,850 ft.

Dir Phil Rosen. *Scen* Hope Loring, Louis D. Lighton. *Story* Charles K. Harris. *Photog* John Mescall.

Cast: Dorothy Mackaill *(Linda Harper)*, Creighton Hale *(Billy Craig)*, Richard Tucker *(Glenn Hayden)*, Alec B. Francis *(John Harper)*, Ralph Lewis *(William Craig)*, Clifford Saum *(Smithers)*, Fanny Midgley *(Mrs. William Craig)*, Aileen Manning *(Mrs. Smithers)*.

Melodrama. Billy Craig, the son of the wealthy president of a steamship line, falls in love with Linda Harper, whose father works for the elder Craig. When Billy's father refuses to give him enough money to cover a gambling debt, Billy steals it from his father's desk, pays the gambler, and leaves town on a trip. Linda's father is accused of the theft and sent to prison. Billy returns from his trip, learns of Harper's incarceration, and confesses his guilt to his father. To spare his ailing wife the shock of a public confession, the elder Craig has Billy forcefully taken aboard one of the company ships. Billy later escapes from the ship, returns home to find his mother dead, and confesses to Linda's ailing father, who has been freed on parole. Billy offers to go to jail, but Harper requests only that Linda be kept ignorant of the facts. Harper then informs Billy that Linda has gone to see Glenn Hayden in an effort to borrow money. Billy goes after her, arriving just in time to save her from Hayden's unwelcome advances. Billy and Linda are married with their parents' grateful consent. *Filial relations. Theft. Gambling. Injustice. Parole. Ship lines.*

BRIGHT LIGHTS **F2.0603**

Metro-Goldwyn-Mayer Pictures. 15 Nov **1925** [New York premiere; released 29 Nov; c1 Dec 1925; LP22058]. Si; b&w. 35mm. 7 reels, 6,153 ft.

Dir Robert Z. Leonard. *Adapt for the screen by* Jessie Burns, Lew Lipton. *Titl* Joseph W. Farnham, William Conselman. *Photog* John Arnold. *Sets* Cedric Gibbons, Richard Day. *Film Ed* William Le Vanway.

Cast: Charles Ray *(Tom Corbin)*, Pauline Starke *(Patsy Delaney)*, Lilyan Tashman *(Gwen Gould)*, Lawford Davidson *(Marty Loftus)*, Ned Sparks *(Barney Gallagher)*, Eugenie Besserer *(Patsy "Mom")*.

Romantic comedy. Source: Richard Connell, "A Little Bit of Broadway," in *Liberty Magazine* (1:10–16, 57–61, 59–62, 57–60, 6 Sep–27 Sep 1924). Tired of the Great White Way "that $ jack $ built," cabaret girl Patsy Delaney goes home to her mother on the farm. A romance develops between Patsy and Tom Corbin, a wholesome country lad. Tom feels acutely his lack of manners in comparison to those of Patsy's friends, and he imitates the style of a well-dressed loafer with disastrous results for their relationship. Patsy's friend puts Tom wise, and he goes back to his former ways and regains her love. *Entertainers. Farmers. Manners. Rural life. Courtship. New York City—Broadway.*

BRIGHT LIGHTS **F2.0604**

First National Pictures. 21 Sep **1930** [c3 Sep 1930; LP1575]. Sd (Vitaphone); col (Technicolor). 35mm. 10 reels, 6,416 ft.

Assoc Prod Robert North. *Dir* Michael Curtiz. *Adapt-Dial* Humphrey Pearson, Henry McCarthy. *Story* Humphrey Pearson. *Photog* Lee Garmes. *Rec Engr* George R. Groves.

Cast: Dorothy Mackaill *(Louanne)*, Frank Fay *(Wally Dean)*, Noah Beery *(Miguel Parada)*, Inez Courtney *(Peggy North)*, Eddie Nugent *("Windy" Jones)*, Daphne Pollard *(Mame Avery)*, Edmund Breese *(Franklin Harris)*, Philip Strange *(Emerson Fairchild)*, James Murray *(Connie Lamont)*, Tom Dugan *(Tom Avery)*, Jean Bary *(Violet Van Dam)*, Edwin Lynch *(Dave Porter)*, Frank McHugh *(Fish, a reporter)*, Virginia Sale *("Sob Sister," a reporter)*.

Melodrama. When Louanne, star of a Broadway revue, announces her engagement to Emerson Fairchild, a group of reporters come to interview her on the last night of the show. She tells of her childhood on an English farm and how she became a cafe hula dancer in the Kohinoor in Africa, where Wally Dean became her friend and protector, saving her from the attack of Miguel Parada, a Portuguese smuggler. She recalls that while touring with a small-time carnival, Wally protected her from the rubes as he still does. Miguel, recognizing Louanne, comes backstage, and Wally asks his friend Connie Lamont to keep him in the dressing room, where, in a struggle for a gun, Lamont shoots Miguel. The police chief finds Wally and Louanne innocent, and while trying to convince him that Miguel committed suicide to save Connie, Wally admits his love for her. A drunken reporter confirms his story, and no charge is filed. Louanne breaks her engagement to Emerson and is united with Wally. *Showgirls.*

Dancers. Police. Reporters. Smugglers. Portuguese. Carnivals. Vaudeville. Suicide. Africa.

BRIGHT LIGHTS OF BROADWAY **F2.0605**

B. F. Zeidman Productions. *Dist* Principal Pictures. 6 Aug **1923** [c23 Oct 1923; LP19518]. Si; b&w. 35mm. 7 reels, 6,765 ft.

Dir Webster Cambell. *Scen* Edmund Goulding. *Titl* Doris Kenyon, Harrison Ford, Edmund Breese. *Story* Gerald C. Duffy.

Cast in order of appearance: Doris Kenyon *(Irene Marley)*, Harrison Ford *(Thomas Drake)*, Edmund Breese *(Rev. Graham Drake)*, Claire De Lorez *(Connie King)*, Lowell Sherman *(Randall Sherrill)*, Tiller Girls *(entertainers)*, Charlie Murray *(El Jumbo)*, Effie Shannon *(Mrs. Grimm, the landlady)*, [Frederick] Tyrone Power *(John Kirk)*.

Melodrama. Smalltown girl Irene Marley leaves her fiancé, Thomas Drake, a minister, and goes to New York City on the advice of impresario Randall Sherrill, who promises to make her a Broadway star. Sherill, a notorious playboy, has recently cast off Connie King, to whom he had made equally glittering promises. Irene forgets her fiancé and hastily marries Sherrill. Tom, concerned about Irene, arrives at Sherrill's apartment, where Connie is hiding. During a struggle between the two men over Irene, a gun is fired and Connie falls dead from behind a curtain. Sherrill, the killer, allows the court to find Tom guilty of murder, but Irene forces a gunpoint confession from Sherrill and races to the prison, getting there seconds before Tom is to be executed. Sherrill, also racing to the prison to prevent the revelation of his confession, is killed in an automobile accident. *Entertainers. Impresari. Clergymen. Murder. Capital punishment. New York City—Broadway.*

THE BRIGHT SHAWL **F2.0606**

Inspiration Pictures. *Dist* Associated First National Pictures. 9 Apr **1923** [c16 Apr 1923; LP18873]. Si; b&w. 35mm. 8 reels, 7,503 ft.

Pres by Charles H. Duell. *Dir* John S. Robertson. *Adapt* Edmund Goulding. *Photog* George Folsey. *Art Dir* Everett Shinn. *Film Ed* William Hamilton.

Cast: Richard Barthelmess *(Charles Abbott, an American)*, André Beranger *(Andrés Escobar, a young Cuban patriot)*, E. G. Robinson *(Domingo Escobar, his father, also a patriot)*, Margaret Seddon *(Carmenita Escobar, his wife)*, Mary Astor *(Narcissa Escobar, their daughter)*, Luis Alberni *(Vincente Escobar, Andrés' brother)*, Anders Randolf *(César y Santacilla, a Spanish captain)*, William Powell *(Gaspar de Vaca, a Spanish captain)*, Dorothy Gish *(La Clavel, an Andalusian dancer)*, Jetta Goudal *(La Pilar, a spy; a sweetheart of Spain)*, George Humbert *(Jaime Quintara, a friend of the Escobars)*.

Historical melodrama. Source: Joseph Hergesheimer, *The Bright Shawl* (New York, 1922). Charles Abbot, a wealthy young American, goes to Cuba with his friend Andrés Escobar to help the cause of Cuban independence. He falls in love with Andrés' sister, Narcissa, although he spends more time with Spanish dancer La Clavel, who is in love with Charles and gives him information she garners from Spanish officers. La Pilar, a Spanish spy, discovers their scheme and sets a trap for them and the entire Escobar family. La Clavel gives her life to save Charles, but it is a chivalrous whim by a Spanish officer that enables Charles, Narcissa, and Narcissa's mother, Carmenita, to escape to the United States. *Dancers. Spies. Spanish. Cuba—History. Revolutions. Duels.*

Note: Made in Cuba.

BRING HIM IN **F2.0607**

Vitagraph Co. of America. 16 Oct **1921** [c1 Sep 1921; LP16926]. Si; b&w. 35mm. 5 reels, 4,987 ft.

Dir Earle Williams, Robert Ensminger. *Adapt* Thomas Dixon, Jr. *Story* H. H. Van Loan. *Photog* Jack MacKenzie.

Cast: Earle Williams *(Dr. John Hood)*, Fritzi Ridgeway *(Mary Mackay)*, Elmer Dewey *(Baptiste)*, Ernest Van Pelt *(Canby)*, Paul Weigel *(Braganza)*, Bruce Gordon *(McKenna)*.

Melodrama. Dr. John Hood dreams that he shoots and kills Canby, a gambler; awakened by a shot, he finds Canby dead in his living room. Hood escapes to the Northwest, and Sergeant McKenna of the Northwest Mounted is detailed to trail him. Hood saves McKenna from drowning, and the two men develop a strong friendship, each unaware of the other's identity. Hood saves Mary McKay, the factor's daughter, from a halfbreed, and they fall in love. McKenna finally takes his prisoner in, but Mary reveals that her brother slew Canby in a quarrel when the latter had made an appointment at Hood's house. Hood is exonerated and takes Mary for his wife. *Physicians. Gamblers. Factors. Halfcastes. Friendship. Murder. Northwest Mounted Police. Dreams.*

BRINGIN' HOME THE BACON **F2.0608**

Action Pictures. *Dist* Weiss Brothers Artclass Pictures. 15 Nov **1924** [c6 Dec 1924; LU20850]. Si; b&w. 35mm. 5 reels, 4,680 ft.

Pres by W. T. Lackey, Lester F. Scott, Jr. *Dir* Richard Thorpe.

Cast: Buffalo Bill Jr. *(Bill Winton)*, Jean Arthur *(Nancy Norton)*, Bert Lindley *(Joe Breed)*, Lafe McKee *(Judge Simpson)*, George F. Marion *(Noel Simms)*, Wilbur McGaugh *(Jim Allen)*, Victor King *(Rastus)*, Laura Miskin *(Bertha Abernathy)*, Frank Ellis *(The Bandit)*.

Western melodrama. Source: Christopher B. Booth, "Buckin' the Big Four," in *Western Story Magazine*. "Plot concerns happy-go-lucky rancher who decides to spruce up in order to win the affection of a girl. Enemies seeking to have him put out of the way, plan to rob a stagecoach with one man dressed in Bill's clothes. He hears of plot and in vigorous fight with gang he whips them and brings them to justice." (*Motion Picture News Booking Guide*, 8:14, Apr 1925.) *Ranchers. Disguise. Stagecoach robberies.*

BRINGING UP FATHER **F2.0609**

Metro-Goldwyn-Mayer Pictures. 17 Mar **1928** [c17 Mar 1928; LP25177]. Si; b&w. 35mm. 7 reels, 6,344 ft.

Dir Jack Conway. *Cont* Frances Marion. *Titl* Ralph Spence. *Story* George McManus. *Photog* William Daniels. *Set Dsgn* Cedric Gibbons, Merrill Pye. *Film Ed* Margaret Booth. *Wardrobe* Gilbert Clark.

Cast: J. Farrell MacDonald *(Jiggs)*, Jules Cowles *(Dinty Moore)*, Polly Moran *(Maggie)*, Marie Dressler *(Annie Moore)*, Gertrude Olmstead *(Ellen)*, Grant Withers *(Dennis)*, Andres De Segurola *(The Count)*, Rose Dione *(Mrs. Smith)*, David Mir *(Oswald)*, Tenen Holtz *(Ginsberg Feitelbaum)*, Toto *(The Dog)*.

Domestic comedy. Based on: George McManus, "Bringing Up Father" (newspaper cartoon feature). Twenty years ago Jiggs and Maggie agreed to marry—and they have never agreed on anything since. Jiggs buys a luxurious mansion, and there Maggie and her daughter give parties in order to become social successes. Excluded from the gaiety and ignored by Maggie, Jiggs pretends to commit suicide. Maggie repents when she sees her "dead" husband, and they are happily reunited when he reveals his trick. *Shrews. Social climbers. Family life. Fatherhood. Suicide. Dogs.*

BROAD DAYLIGHT **F2.0610**

Universal Film Manufacturing Co. 30 Oct **1922** [c7 Oct 1922; LP18296]. Si; b&w. 35mm. 5 reels, 4,961 ft.

Pres by Carl Laemmle. *Dir* Irving Cummings. *Scen* Harvey Gates. *Story* Harvey Gates, George W. Pyper. *Photog* William Fildew.

Cast: Lois Wilson *(Nora Fay)*, Jack Mulhall *(Joel Morgan)*, Ralph Lewis *(Peter Fay)*, Kenneth Gibson *(Davy Sunday)*, Wilton Taylor *(Detective Marks)*, Ben Hewlett *(Shadow Smith)*, Robert Walker *(The "Scarab")*.

Crime melodrama. Nora Fay is persuaded to marry the son of a well-known man in order to embarrass the latter because of her belief that he sent her father to prison. But the bridegroom turns out to be Joel Morgan, only a friend of the intended one. The "Scarab" and his gang are so angry at the failure of their plan that they beat Joel and dump him by the side of a road. Nora finds him and nurses him to health, but circumstances separate them. Years later, when her father, Peter Fay, is freed, The Scarab persuades him to rob one more safe. When Nora intervenes, it is revealed that The Scarab had caused Peter's imprisonment. The Scarab and Peter both die, and Joel and Nora are reunited. *Gangs. Filial relations. Robbery.*

THE BROAD ROAD **F2.0611**

Associated Authors. *Dist* Associated First National Pictures. 1 Sep **1923**. Si; b&w. 35mm. 6 reels, 5,915 ft.

Dir Edmund Mortimer. *Story* Hapsburg Liebe. *Photog* W. S. Cooper, O. S. Zangrilli.

Cast: Richard C. Travers *("Ten Spot" Tifton)*, May Allison *(Mary Ellen Haley)*, Ben Hendricks, Jr. *(Bud Ashley)*, D. J. Flanagan *(Jim Fanning)*, Mary Foy *("Ma" Fanning)*, Charles McDonald *(Sheriff Bill Emmett)*, L. Emile La Croix *("Old Fuzzy" Lippert)*, Roy Kelly *("Kid" Coppins)*, Alicia Collins *(Mrs. Lippert)*.

Melodrama. "Girl is rescued from the pitfalls of city life and taken to the lumber camp where he [the hero] works. Here villain talks loosely about the girl, and in a battle with hero the latter is knocked out by a foul blow. The youth vows to 'get' the crook, who 'frames' the hero in connection with a shooting. Hero is arrested but makes his getaway. He returns to girl's cottage after holding up some motorists. His enemy is on hand and sees him give girl a wad of money. That night villain enters the cottage and steals the money. A fight occurs between the two. A rifle explodes, killing crook, and all ends well." (*Motion Picture News*, 28 Jul 1923, p418.) *Robbery. Frameup. Lumber camps. Florida.*

BROADWAY (Universal Super-Jewel) **F2.0612**

Universal Pictures. 27 May **1929** [New York premiere; released 15 Sep; c11 Jun 1929; LP459]. Sd (Movietone); b&w with col sequence (Technicolor). 35mm. 12 reels, 9,661 ft. [Also si; 9 reels.]

Pres by Carl Laemmle. *Prod* Carl Laemmle, Jr. *Dir* Paul Fejos. *Scen* Edward T. Lowe, Jr., Charles Furthman. *Dial* Edward T. Lowe, Jr. *Titl* Tom Reed. *Photog* Hal Mohr. *Spec Eff Photog* Frank H. Booth. *Art Dir* Charles D. Hall. *Film Ed* Robert Carlisle, Edward Cahn. *Supv Ed* Maurice Pivar. *Synchronization & Score* Howard Jackson. *Songs: "Broadway," "The Chicken or the Egg," "Hot Footin' It," "Hittin' the Ceiling," "Sing a Little Love Song"* Con Conrad, Archie Gottler, Sidney Mitchell. *Dance Numbers* Maurice L. Kusell. *Sd Engr* C. Roy Hunter. *Sd Syst* Smith, Harold I. Monitor. *Cost Dsgn* Johanna Mathieson.

Cast: Glenn Tryon *(Roy Lane)*, Evelyn Brent *(Pearl)*, Merna Kennedy *(Billie Moore)*, Thomas Jackson *(Dan McCorn)*, Robert Ellis *(Steve Crandall)*, Otis Harlan *("Porky" Thompson)*, Paul Porcasi *(Nick Verdis)*, Marion Lord *(Lil Rice)*, Fritz Feld *(Mose Levett)*, Leslie Fenton *("Scar" Edwards)*, Arthur Housman *(Dolph)*, George Davis *(Joe)*, Betty Francisco *(Mazie)*, Edythe Flynn *(Ruby)*, Florence Dudley *(Ann)*, Ruby McCoy *(Grace)*, Gus Arnheim and His Cocoanut Grove Ambassadors.

Musical melodrama. Source: Jed Harris, Philip Dunning and George Abbott, *Broadway, a Play* (New York, 1927). Roy Lane and Billie Moore, entertainers at the Paradise Nightclub, are in love and are rehearsing an act together. Late to work one evening, Billie is saved from dismissal by Nick Verdis, the club proprietor, through the intervention of Steve Crandall, a suave bootlegger, who desires a liaison with the girl. "Scar" Edwards, robbed of a truckload of contraband liquor by Steve's gang, arrives at the club for a showdown with Crandall and is shot in the back. Crandall gives Billie a bracelet to forget that she has seen him helping a "drunk" from the club. Though Roy is arrested by Dan McCorn, he is later released on Billie's testimony. Steve, in his car, is fired at from a taxi, and overheard by Pearl, he confesses to killing Edwards. Pearl confronts Steve in Nick's office and kills him; and McCorn, finding Steve's body, insists that he committed suicide, exonerating Pearl and leaving Roy and Billie to the success of their act. *Singers. Dancers. Gangsters. Murder. Nightclubs. New York City—Broadway.*

BROADWAY AFTER DARK **F2.0613**

Warner Brothers Pictures. 31 May **1924** [c21 Apr 1924; LP20124]. Si; b&w. 35mm. 7 reels, 6,300 ft.

Harry Rapf Production. *Dir* Monta Bell. *Adapt* Douglas Doty. *Photog* Charles Van Enger. *Asst Dir* Sandy Roth.

Cast: Adolphe Menjou *(Ralph Norton)*, Norma Shearer *(Rose Dulane)*, Anna Q. Nilsson *(Helen Tremaine)*, Edward Burns *(Jack Devlin)*, Carmel Myers *(Lenore Vance)*, Vera Lewis *(Mrs. Smith)*, Willard Louis *("Slim" Scott)*, Mervyn LeRoy *(Carl Fisher)*, Jimmy Quinn *(Ed Fisher)*, Edgar Norton *(The Old Actor)*, Gladys Tennyson *(Vera)*, Ethel Miller *(The Chorus Girl)*, Otto Hoffman *(Norton's valet)*, Lew Harvey *(Tom Devery)*, Michael Dark *(George Vance)*, Fred Stone, Dorothy Stone, Mary Eaton, Raymond Hitchcock, Elsie Ferguson, Florence Moore, James J. Corbett, John Steel, Frank Tinney, Paul Whiteman, Irene Castle, Buster West.

Society melodrama. Source: Owen Davis, *Broadway After Dark* (a play, publication undetermined). Ralph Norton, man-about-town and wealthy favorite in Broadway society circles, is attracted to Helen Tremaine, but her flirtatious behavior causes him to reject the superficial life of his set. He seeks seclusion in a sidestreet roominghouse frequented by theatrical people, and there he meets Rose Dulane, a working girl. When she is fired because of a past jail sentence, Ralph passes her off as his ward in theatrical circles, but she is disillusioned when a detective tries to frame her. Ralph intervenes and decides to take her away and begin a new life. *Guardians. Detectives. Theater. New York City—Broadway.*

BROADWAY AFTER MIDNIGHT **F2.0614**

Krelbar Pictures. Oct or 1 Nov **1927.** Si; b&w. 35mm. 7 reels, 6,199 ft.

Pres by Sherman S. Krellberg. *Dir* Fred Windermere. *Scen* Adele Buffington. *Story* Frederic Bartel. *Photog* Charles Davis.

Cast: Matthew Betz *(Quill Burke)*, Priscilla Bonner *(Queenie Morgan/ Gloria Livingston)*, Cullen Landis *(Jimmy Crestmore)*, Gareth Hughes *(Billy Morgan)*, Ernest Hilliard *(Bodo Lambert)*, Barbara Tennant, William Turner, Hank Mann, Paul Weigel.

Crook-society melodrama. Forced into marrying gangster Quill Burke to protect her brother, nightclub entertainer Queenie Morgan is further pressured into impersonating Gloria Livingston, a society girl who has strayed into the underworld and shot her betrayer, Bodo Lambert. The unfortunate Gloria is killed after the gang attempts to obtain money from her parents, and the police trace both killings to Queenie. At her trial, the jury is about to deliver a verdict of guilty when Queenie's maid rushes in with the whole truth, which releases Queenie to the waiting arms of loyal Jimmy Crestmore. *Entertainers. Socialites. Gangsters. Housemaids. Brother-sister relationship. Impersonation. Murder. Extortion. Trials.*

BROADWAY BABIES **F2.0615**

First National Pictures. 30 Jun **1929** [c8 Jul 1929; LP512]. Sd (Vitaphone); b&w. 35mm. 9 reels, 8,067 ft. [Also si, 28 Jul 1929; 6,690 ft.]

Pres by Richard A. Rowland. *Prod* Robert North. *Dir* Mervyn LeRoy. *Screenplay* Monte Katterjohn. *Dial* Monte Katterjohn, Humphrey Pearson. *Titl* Paul Perez. *Photog* Sol Polito. *Art Dir* Jack Okey. *Film Ed* Frank Ware. *Songs: "Wishing and Waiting for Love," "Jig, Jig, Jigaloo"* Grant Clarke, Harry Akst. *Song: "Broadway Baby Doll"* Al Bryan, George W. Meyer. *Cost* Max Ree.

Cast: Alice White *(Delight Foster)*, Charles Delaney *(Billy Buvanny)*, Fred Kohler *(Percé Gessant)*, Tom Dugan *(Scotty)*, Bodil Rosing *(Sarah Durgen)*, Sally Eilers *(Navarre King)*, Marion Byron *(Florine Chandler)*, Jocelyn Lee *(Blossom Royale)*, Louis Natheaux *(Gus Brand)*, Maurice Black *(Nick)*.

Melodrama. Source: Jay Gelzer, "Broadway Musketeers," in *Good Housekeeping* (87:18–21, Oct 1928). Against the advice of her fellow dancers Florine and Navarre, Delight Foster, a Broadway chorus girl, becomes engaged to Billy Buvanny, the stage manager of her show. Then Percé Gessant, a Canadian, falls in love with her, and when she thinks Billy is unfaithful, Delight decides to marry Percé. Meanwhile he becomes involved with Gus Brand, a gambler and gang leader. On their wedding day, Percé is attending a poker game, while his gunmen hold up Brand and his crowd; en route to the wedding with his bride, Percé is shot by Brand from another car just as Delight informs him she still loves Billy. Percé, dying after a showdown with the gang, with his last words bequeaths his money to Billy and Delight, who use it to finance their own show on Broadway. *Chorus girls. Gamblers. Gangsters. Stage managers. Canadians. Murder. New York City—Broadway.*

BROADWAY BILLY **F2.0616**

Harry J. Brown Productions. *Dist* Rayart Pictures. 3 May **1926** [New York State license]. Si; b&w. 35mm. 5 reels, 5,954 ft.

Dir Harry J. Brown. *Scen* Henry R. Simon.

Cast: Billy Sullivan *(Billy Brookes)*, Virginia Brown Faire *(Phyliss Brookes)*, Jack Herrick *(Ace O'Brien)*, Hazel Howell.

Melodrama. Husband of spendthrift wife boxes for larger and larger stakes in order to pay her bills. When she is injured in a car accident, Billy wins the "big fight" with the support of his friends. *Spendthrifts. Prizefighting. Debt. Automobile accidents.*

BROADWAY BLUES *see* **SYNCOPATING SUE**

THE BROADWAY BOOB **F2.0617**

Associated Exhibitors. 25 Apr **1926** [c23 Jan 1926; LU22304]. Si; b&w. 35mm. 6 reels, 5,683 ft.

Dir Joseph Henabery. *Story* Monte M. Katterjohn. *Photog* Marcel Le Picard.

Cast: Glenn Hunter *(Dan Williams)*, Mildred Ryan *(Mary Abbott)*, Antrim Short *(Jack Briggs)*, Beryl Halley *(Queenie Martine)*, Margaret Irving *(Mabel Golden)*.

Comedy-drama. Leaving his small hometown in disgrace, Daniel Williams lands a small part in a Broadway show, and his press agent releases a story that Dan is making $3,000 a week. Dan's father, a banker, finds himself in serious financial trouble and, faced with a run on his bank, appeals to Dan for help. Dan confesses his true state of financial affairs to his father and then, with the help of the press agent, concocts a scheme to save his father's bank. Having finally won the respect of his fellow townspeople, Dan wins his childhood sweetheart. *Actors. Bankers. Press agents. Smalltown life. Banks. New York City—Broadway.*

BROADWAY BROKE **F2.0618**
Murray W. Garsson Productions. *Dist* Selznick Distributing Corp. 27 Oct **1923** [c13 Oct 1923; LP19563]. Si; b&w. 35mm. 6 reels, 5,923 ft.
Dir J. Searle Dawley. *Scen* John Lynch. *Photog* Bert Dawley. *Prod Mgr* John Lynch.
Cast: Mary Carr *(Nellie Wayne)*, Percy Marmont *(Tom Kerrigan)*, Gladys Leslie *(Mary Karger)*, Dore Davidson *(Lou Gorman)*, Maclyn Arbuckle *(P. T. Barnum)*, Macey Harlam *(Claude Benson)*, Edward Earle *(Charles Farrin)*, Pierre Gendron *(Jack Graham)*, Billy Quirk *(Joe Karger)*, Henrietta Crosman *(Madge Foster)*, Sally Crute *(Augusta Karger)*, Leslie King *(Mark Twain)*, Albert Phillips *(General Grant)*, Frederick Burton *(Augustin Daly)*, Lassie Bronte *("Chum," a dog)*.
Melodrama. Source: Earl Derr Biggers, "Broadway Broke," in *Saturday Evening Post* (195:3–5, 7 Oct 1922). Nellie Wayne, a retired theatrical star, whose family's sole supporter is "Chum," an aging vaudeville dog, saves the family's finances when she sells her plays to film executive Lou Gorman and is rediscovered as a motion picture actress. *Actors. Theater. Vaudeville. Motion pictures. Mark Twain. Phineas Taylor Barnum. Ulysses Simpson Grant. Dogs.*

BROADWAY BUCKAROO **F2.0619**
Western Feature Productions. *Dist* Pioneer Film Corp. Oct **1921** [New York State]. Si; b&w. 35mm. 5 reels.
Cast: William Fairbanks.
Western melodrama(?). No information about the nature of this film has been found.

A BROADWAY BUTTERFLY **F2.0620**
Warner Brothers Pictures. 15 Jan **1925** [c5 Jan 1925; LP20991]. Si; b&w. 35mm. 7 reels, 6,750 ft.
Dir William Beaudine. *Story-Scen* Darryl Francis Zanuck. *Photog* Ray June.
Cast: Dorothy Devore *(Irene Astaire)*, Louise Fazenda *(Cookie Dale)*, Willard Louis *(Charles Gay)*, John Roche *(Crane Wilder)*, Cullen Landis *(Ronald Steel)*, Lilyan Tashman *(Thelma Perry)*, Wilfred Lucas *(stage manager)*, Eugenie Gilbert *(riding mistress)*, Margaret Seddon *(Mrs. Steel)*.
Melodrama. Leaving the small country town in which she grew up, Irene Astaire goes to New York in an attempt to find a career on the legitimate stage. She is befriended by Cookie Dale, a wisecracking chorus girl, who finds Irene a place in the chorus of the show on the Amsterdam Roof. When Irene falls in love with Ronald Steel, Crane Wilder determines to break up the romance and get Irene for his own girl. Wilder's plans are spoiled by Cookie, but not before Ronald has seen Wilder leaving Irene's apartment and suspected the worst. Ronald turns to another chorus girl for consolation, and a discouraged Irene decides to give herself to Wilder. In an attempt to preserve Irene's virtue, Cookie persuades her to become a houseguest at the palatial home of Cookie's parents. Irene and Ronald are later reunited through Cookie's good offices and decide to get married. *Chorus girls. Amsterdam Roof. New York City—Broadway.*

BROADWAY DADDIES **F2.0621**
Columbia Pictures. 7 Apr **1928** [c28 Apr 1928; LP25193]. Si; b&w. 35mm. 6 reels, 5,400–5,537 ft.
Prod Harry Cohn. *Dir* Fred Windemere. *Scen* Anthony Coldeway. *Story* Victoria Moore. *Photog* Silvano Balboni. *Art Dir* Robert E. Lee. *Film Ed* Arthur Roberts. *Asst Dir* C. C. Coleman.
Cast: Jacqueline Logan *(Eve Delmar)*, Alec B. Francis *(John Lambert Kennedy)*, Rex Lease *(Richard Kennedy)*, Phillips Smalley *(James Leech)*, De Sacia Mooers *(Fay King)*, Clarissa Selwynne *(Mrs. Winthrop Forrest)*, Betty Francisco *(Agnes Forrest)*.
Society drama. Nightclub dancer Eve Delmar spurns her wealthy and powerful suitors in favor of Richard Kennedy, whom she believes to be poor but ambitious. Actually, Kennedy, son of a wealthy businessman, is using a worn suit and a slim purse to test the girl's love. A newspaper article in the society page gives him away; and assuming that she has been tricked by Dick, Eve dates Jimmy Leech, the most powerful and wealthy but the most repulsive of all her suitors. Leech makes improper advances, and Eve returns to Dick. *Dancers. Wealth. Disguise. Nightclubs.*

THE BROADWAY DRIFTER **F2.0622**
Samuel Zierler Photoplay Corp. *Dist* Excellent Pictures. 1 Apr **1927** [c10 May 1927; LP23947, LP24064]. Si; b&w. 35mm. 6 reels, 5,912 ft.
Pres by Samuel Zierler. *Dir* Bernard McEveety. *Story-Scen* William B. Laub. *Photog* Marcel Le Picard.
Cast: George Walsh *(Bob Stafford)*, Dorothy Hall *(Eileen Byrne)*, Bigelow Cooper *(Myron Stafford)*, Arthur Donaldson *(Frank Harmon)*, Paul Doucet *(Phil Winston)*, Nellie Savage *(Mignon Renee)*, Gladys Valerie *(Laura Morris)*, Donald Laskley *(Sam)*, George Offerman, Jr. *(Tommy)*.
Society melodrama. Bob Stafford, wayward son of a wealthy father, is disowned because of his extravagant expenditures in Broadway haunts. Determined to free himself of all his former associations, Bob changes his appearance and opens a health school for girls, but he is ultimately exposed by a rival admirer of Eileen Byrne, a wealthy client at the school. Bob gets a job in an airplane factory owned, coincidentally, by Eileen's father, with whom he develops a friendship. His rival infers that Bob has been sent by his father to steal a new airplane invention, but Bob, through his air exploits, confirms his loyalty and reveals the rival's true nature. Bob is finally reunited with his father and wins the love of the girl. *Playboys. Filial relations. Disinheritance. Wealth. Disguise. Health clubs. Airplanes. New York City.*

BROADWAY FEVER **F2.0623**
Tiffany-Stahl Productions. 1 Jan **1929** [c18 Dec 1928; LP25951]. Si; b&w. 35mm. 6 reels, 5,412 ft.
Dir Edward Cline. *Cont* Lois Leeson. *Titl (see note)* Frederick Hatton, Fanny Hatton, Paul Perez. *Story* Viola Brothers Shore. *Photog* John Boyle. *Art Dir* Hervey Libbert. *Set Dressings* George Sawley. *Film Ed* Byron Robinson.
Cast: Sally O'Neil *(Sally McAllister)*, Roland Drew *(Eric Byron)*, Corliss Palmer *(Lila Leroy)*, Calvert Carter *(butler)*.
Comedy. Unable to make an appointment with Eric Byron, New York's leading theatrical producer, stagestruck Sally McAllister answers an advertisement for a maid and discovers that she will be working for none other than Byron himself. Sally falls in love with the eligible bachelor and arranges for Lila Leroy, Byron's leading lady, to take a train to Oakland, California, rather than Oakland, New Jersey. Sally herself goes to Oakland, New Jersey, the site of Byron's latest play, and, donning a blonde wig, she impersonates the missing Lila until the night of dress rehearsal. Her ruse is then discovered, but Eric, who has fallen in love with her, allows her to go on stage. *Theatrical producers. Actors. Housemaids. Bachelors. Impersonation. Theater. New York City. New Jersey.*
Note: Sources disagree is crediting title writer.

THE BROADWAY GALLANT **F2.0624**
Richard Talmadge Productions. *For* Carlos Productions. *Dist* Film Booking Offices of America. 25 Apr **1926** [c30 Apr 1926; LP22670]. Si; b&w. 35mm. 6 reels, 5,510 ft.
Dir Noel Mason. *Story-Scen* Frank Howard Clark. *Photog* Jack Stevens. *Film Ed* Doane Harrison.
Cast: Richard Talmadge *(Monty Barnes)*, Clara Horton *(Helen Stuart)*, Joe Harrington *(Jake Peasley)*, Jack Richardson *(Red Sweeney)*, Cecile Cameron *(Rita Delroy)*, Ford West *(Hiram Weatherby)*.
Action melodrama. Helen Stuart, who is engaged to Monty Barnes, a young roustabout, is in the charge of Jack Peasley, who controls her estate. Peasley, using Helen's money, buys a block of railroad stock from Red Sweeney; when Peasley discovers that the bonds are worthless, Sweeney assures him that if Helen should be married before the age of 21, she would never detect the loss, for in that event the estate would revert to Peasley as guardian and uncle. In a plot to achieve this end, Helen is kidnaped; and Sweeney forces her to marry Monty, who is unaware of her identity. Monty, in trouble with the constable, leads the police a merry chase, while his father finds Peasley's bonds were issued by a railroad line he needs to complete a merger. After an exciting chase, Monty recovers the bonds and returns them to Helen, whom he discovers to be his wife. *Roustabouts. Uncles. Embezzlement. Inheritance. Kidnaping. Marriage. Railroads.*

BROADWAY GOLD **F2.0625**
Edward Dillon Productions. *Dist* Truart Film Corp. 29 Jul **1923** [New York premiere; released Sep; c2 Jun 1923; LP19027]. Si; b&w. 35mm. 7 reels, 6,779 ft.
Dir Edward Dillon, J. Gordon Cooper. *Adapt* Kathryn Harris. *Photog* James R. Diamond. *Art Dir* Cedric Gibbons. *Film Ed* Charles Wolfe.
Cast: Elaine Hammerstein *(Sunny Duane)*, Elliott Dexter *(Eugene Durant)*, Kathlyn Williams *(Jean Valjean)*, Eloise Goodale *(Elinor Calhoun)*, Richard Wayne *(Cornelius Fellowes)*, Harold Goodwin *(Page Poole)*, Henry Barrows *(Jerome Rogers)*, Marshall Neilan *(The Driver)*.
Melodrama. Source: William Carey Wonderly, "Broadway Gold," in

Young's Magazine (44:3–31, Dec 1922). Sunny Duane, a chorus girl, goes out to dinner with Cornelius Fellowes, a wealthy man who is murdered the same night. Anxious to avoid suspicion, she escapes and quickly marries a man who believes he is going to die and wants to leave her his fortune. He recovers but is helplessly crippled. Sunny is about to be arrested and questioned about the Fellowes murder when an old sweetheart comes forward and confesses to the murder. Sunny's husband recovers completely, and she realizes that she loves him. *Chorus girls. Cripples. Inheritance. Murder.*

THE BROADWAY HOOFER **F2.0626**

Columbia Pictures. 15 Dec **1929** [c27 Dec 1929; LP943]. Sd (Movietone); b&w. 35mm. 7 reels, 6,360 ft. [Also si.]

Prod Harry Cohn. *Dir* George Archainbaud. *Dial Dir* James Seymour. *Story-Dial-Titl* Gladys Lehman. *Photog* Joseph Walker. *Art Dir* Harrison Wiley. *Film Ed* Maurice Wright. *Ch Sd Engr* John Livadary. *Sd Mixing Engr* Harry Blanchard. *Asst Dir* David Selman.

Cast: Marie Saxon *(Adele)*, Jack Egan *(Bobby)*, Louise Fazenda *(Jane)*, Howard Hickman *(Larry)*, Ernest Hilliard *(Morton)*, Gertrude Short *(Annabelle)*, Eileen Percy *(Dolly)*, Charlotte Merriam *(Mazie)*, Fred Mackaye *(Billy)*, Billy Franey *(baggage man)*.

Melodrama. Adele Dorey, a Broadway dancing star exhausted from strenuous work, leaves New York without revealing her destination to anyone; her maid, Jane, accompanies her to a country village for a rest. The Gay Girlies Burlesque Co. arrives in the village on a barnstorming tour, creating excitement among the yokels; Bobby Lewis, the company's manager, offers a local girl a place in the show, bringing out a flock of country girls; but he sees in Adele his only possibility. Amused, she pretends to be impressed and introduces Jane as her mother; later, Jane informs Larry, Adele's own manager, of her situation and whereabouts. Adele gets Bobby a Broadway job, but he denounces her, learning of the deception. Through Larry's arrangement the couple are reunited and realize their mutual affections. *Dancers. Smalltown life. Burlesque. New York City—Broadway.*

BROADWAY LADY **F2.0627**

R-C Pictures. *Dist* Film Booking Offices of America. 15 Nov **1925** [c1 Dec 1925; LP22108]. Si; b&w. 35mm. 6 reels, 5,500 ft.

Dir Wesley Ruggles. *Story-Cont* Fred Myton. *Asst Dir* Frank Geraghty.

Cast: Evelyn Brent *(Rosalie Ryan)*, Marjorie Bonner *(Mary Andrews)*, Theodore von Eltz *(Bob Westbrook)*, Joyce Compton *(Phyllis Westbrook)*, Clarissa Selwyn *(Mrs. Westbrook)*, Ernest Hilliard *(Martyn Edwards)*, Johnny Gough *(Johnny)*.

Society melodrama. Rosalie Ryan, a chorus girl, takes the fancy of Bob Westbrook, the aristocratic scion of a wealthy family. He proposes to her, and she initially refuses, fearing the effects of his drinking. When she is openly insulted by his family, however, Rosalie changes her mind and marries him, hoping to distress the family. Bob's sister, Phyllis, is in love with Martyn Edwards, a bounder who once betrayed Mary Andrews, one of Rosalie's close friends. Rosalie learns that Mary is planning to run off with Edwards and goes to her apartment, hoping to prevent the elopement. Edwards is felled by a pistol shot, and Rosalie takes the blame in order, she thinks, to protect Phyllis. Mary later comes forward, however, and confesses that she accidentally shot Edwards during a quarrel. Both girls are set free, and Rosalie returns to Bob. *Chorus girls. Brother-sister relationship. Cads. Social classes. Manslaughter. Alcoholism.*

BROADWAY MADNESS **F2.0628**

Excellent Pictures. 1 Oct **1927** [c3 Oct 1927; LP24474]. Si; b&w. 35mm. 7 reels, 6,300 ft.

Pres by Samuel Zierler. *Prod* Harry Chandlee. *Dir* Burton King. *Story-Scen* Harry Chandlee. *Photog* Art Reeves.

Cast: Marguerite De La Motte *(Maida Vincent)*, Donald Keith *(David Ross)*, Betty Hilburn *(Josie Dare)*, Margaret Cloud *(Mary Vaughn)*, George Cowl *(Henry Ableton)*, Louis Payne *(Jared Ableton)*, Robert Dudley *(Thomas)*, Orral Humphreys *(Larry Doyle)*, Thomas Ricketts *(Lawrence Compton)*, Alfred Fisher *(Ev)*, Jack Haley *(radio announcer)*.

Romantic melodrama. In a small town in New York, David Ross, a young farmer, becomes entranced with Maida Vincent, a Broadway gold digger, as a result of her radio broadcasts; therefore, his granduncle, Henry Ableton, threatens to disinherit David, even if Mary Vaughn, a granddaughter, is not found within 6 months of his demise. Maida and Josie, ignorant of the situation, find Mary ill in the city and write to her grandfather, who, however, has since died. When Thomas, the surviving brother, arrives and finds Mary dead, he persuades Maida to impersonate her and claim the fortune. Maida falls in love with David and, discovering he is the alternate heir, confesses the deception, but David forgives her and they are married. *Farmers. Dancers. Gold diggers. Impersonation. Smalltown life. Inheritance. Radio. New York City—Broadway.*

THE BROADWAY MADONNA **F2.0629**

Quality Film Productions. *Dist* Film Booking Offices of America. 29 Oct **1922** [c9 Nov 1922; LP18382]. Si; b&w. 35mm. 6 reels, 5,602 ft.

Dir Harry Revier.

Cast: Dorothy Revier *(Vivian Collins)*, Jack Connolly *(Tom Bradshaw)*, Harry Van Meter *(Dr. Kramer)*, Eugene Burr *(Slinky Davis)*, Juanita Hansen *(Gloria Thomas)*, Lee Willard *(Judge Bradshaw)*, Lydia Knott.

Society melodrama. Dr. Kramer, secretly married to cabaret dancer Vivian Collins, forces his wife to encourage the attentions of wealthy Tom Bradshaw in order to blackmail Tom's father, Judge Bradshaw. At a masked ball Kramer, costumed like Tom, robs Bradshaw's safe and kills the judge. Mrs. Bradshaw is jailed for the murder, but a suspicious Tom discovers the truth with the aid of Kramer's nurse, Gloria Thomas, with whom he falls in love. *Physicians. Dancers. Nurses. Robbery. Murder. Blackmail. San Francisco. Burlingame.*

Note: Working titles: *The Black Domino, Mothers of Men.* Exteriors shot in San Francisco and on an estate in Burlingame.

THE BROADWAY MELODY **F2.0630**

Metro-Goldwyn-Mayer Pictures. 1 Feb **1929** [Los Angeles premier; released 6 Jun 1929; c5 Mar 1929; LP183]. Sd (Movietone); b&w with col sequences (Technicolor). 35mm. 10 reels, 9,372 ft. [Also si; 5,943 ft.]

Dir Harry Beaumont. *Ensemble numbers stgd by* George Cunningham. *Scen* Sarah Y. Mason. *Dial* Norman Houston, James Gleason. *Titl* Earl Baldwin. *Story* Edmund Goulding. *Photog* John Arnold. *Art Dir* Cedric Gibbons. *Film Ed* Sam S. Zimbalist. *Ed Si Vers* William Le Vanway. *Songs: "The Wedding of the Painted Doll," "Broadway Melody," "Love Boat," "Boy Friend," "You Were Meant for Me"* Nacio Herb Brown, Arthur Freed. *Song: "Give My Regards to Broadway"* George M. Cohan. *Song: "Truthful Deacon Brown"* Willard Robison. *Rec Engr* Douglas Shearer. *Sd* Wesley Miller, Louis Kolb, O. O. Ceccarini, G. A. Burns. *Wardrobe* David Cox.

Cast: Anita Page *(Queenie)*, Bessie Love *("Hank")*, Charles King *(Eddie)*, Jed Prouty *(Uncle Bernie)*, Kenneth Thomson *(Jock)*, Edward Dillon *(stage manager)*, Mary Doran *(blonde)*, Eddie Kane *(Zanfield)*, J. Emmett Beck *(Babe Hatrick)*, Marshall Ruth *(Stew)*, Drew Demarest *(Turpe)*.

Musical comedy-drama. Eddie, a smalltime vaudeville hoofer, writes a hit song and is hired by Broadway producer Zanfield to perform in one of his revues. Having long been in love with "Hank" Mahoney, the older member of a vaudeville sister act, Eddie persuades her to leave her current show and come to New York with her sister, Queenie. Eddie soon transfers his attentions to Queenie, however, and she becomes the mistress of one of Zanfield's backers in order to keep Eddie and Hank together. Hank later discovers that Eddie and her sister are in love and persuades Eddie to take Queenie away from the backer. Eddie and Queenie get together, and Hank, finding a new "sister" for her act, returns to tank-town vaudeville. *Dancers. Sisters. Mistresses. Theatrical producers. Theatrical backers. Vaudeville. New York City—Broadway.*

BROADWAY NIGHTS **F2.0631**

Robert Kane Productions. *Dist* First National Pictures. 15 May **1927** [c3 May 1927; LP23913]. Si; b&w. 35mm. 7 reels, 6,765 ft.

Pres by Robert Kane. *Dir* Joseph C. Boyle. *Adapt* Forrest Halsey. *Story* Norman Houston. *Photog* Ernest Haller. *Prod Mgr* Leland Hayward.

Cast: Lois Wilson *(Fannie Fanchette)*, Sam Hardy *(Johnny Fay)*, Louis John Bartels *(Baron)*, Philip Strange *(Bronson)*, Barbara Stanwyck *(dancer)*, "Bunny" Weldon *(night club producer)*.

Romantic drama. Fannie, an ambitious music hall performer, becomes a success with the help of Johnny Fay, master of ceremonies and an inveterate gambler; he marries her, and 3 years later they have a child. In New York they are engaged at a nightclub where Fannie is seen by Bronson and Baron, musical comedy producers. They offer Fannie a job if she will agree to leave Johnny, but she refuses. Fannie and Johnny are fired when a reformer discovers their child, and Johnny loses their last penny gambling. In desperation, Fannie accepts Bronson's offer, while Johnny gets along singing in a honky-tonk. Fannie decides to divorce him but changes her mind when she hears Johnny singing on the radio. Fannie is a flop until Johnny is engaged to stage the show, for which he has actually written the music, and they are then reconciled. *Entertainers. Theatrical producers. Vaudeville. Marriage. Gambling. Nightclubs. New York City—Broadway.*

BROADWAY OR BUST **F2.0632**

Universal Pictures. 9 Jun **1924** [c17 May 1924; LP20215]. Si; b&w. 35mm. 6 reels, 5,272 ft.

Dir Edward Sedgwick. *Scen* Dorothy Yost. *Story* Edward Sedgwick, Raymond L. Schrock. *Photog* Virgil Miller.

Cast: Hoot Gibson *(Dave Hollis)*, Ruth Dwyer *(Virginia Redding)*, King Zany *(Jeff Peters)*, Gertrude Astor *(Mrs. Dean Smythe)*, Stanhope Wheatcroft *(Freddie)*, Fred Malatesta *(Count Dardanelle)*.

Romantic comedy. Virginia Redding inherits a fortune and goes to New York, leaving behind her suitor Dave, a rancher. Good fortune strikes Dave when radium deposits are discovered on his ranch, and he and his partner sell out, go to New York, and become society sensations. Virginia and Dave are reconciled when he saves her from the advances of lecherous Count Dardanelle. *Ranchers. Wealth. Radium. Lechery. New York City.*

THE BROADWAY PEACOCK **F2.0633**

Fox Film Corp. 19 Feb **1922** [c19 Feb 1922; LP17708]. Si; b&w. 35mm. 5 reels, 4,380 ft.

Pres by William Fox. *Dir* Charles J. Brabin. *Story-Scen* Julia Tolsva. *Photog* George W. Lane.

Cast: Pearl White *(Myrtle May)*, Joseph Striker *(Harold Van Tassel)*, Doris Eaton *(Rose Ingraham)*, Harry Southard *(Jerry Gibson)*, Elizabeth Garrison *(Mrs. Van Tassel)*.

Society melodrama. Myrtle May, a hostess at a Broadway cabaret, becomes infatuated with blueblood aristocrat Harold Van Tassel, but his family is firmly opposed to their marriage. One of her patrons, Jerry Gibson, makes advances to Rose Ingraham, a country girl who has been unable to find employment, and Myrtle, befriending Rose, takes her home and treats her as a sister. When Van Tassel calls at Myrtle's house, Myrtle becomes jealous of his attentions to Rose; and when the girl leaves, Myrtle seeks revenge through Mrs. Van Tassel. The family lawyer, however, induces her to relent, and she renounces her claim, leaving the young couple free to marry. *Cafe hostesses. Social classes. Jealousy. New York City—Broadway.*

BROADWAY ROSE **F2.0634**

Tiffany Productions. *Dist* Metro Pictures. 25 Sep **1922** [c28 Aug 1922; LP18201]. Si; b&w. 35mm. 6 reels, 5,500 ft.

Pres by Robert Z. Leonard. *Dir* Robert Z. Leonard. *Story-Scen* Edmund Goulding. *Photog* Oliver T. Marsh. *Set Dsgn* Tilford Cinema Studios.

Cast: Mae Murray *(Rosalie Lawrence)*, Monte Blue *(Tom Darcy)*, Raymond Bloomer *(Hugh Thompson)*, Ward Crane *(Reggie Whitley)*, Alma Tell *(Barbara Royce)*, Charles Lane *(Peter Thompson)*, Mary Turner Gordon *(Mrs. Peter Thompson)*, Jane Jennings *(Mrs. Lawrence)*, Pauline Dempsey *(colored maid)*.

Romantic drama. Broadway dancing star Rosalie Lawrence meets and falls in love with wealthy Hugh Thompson. Because his parents oppose the match and prefer that he marry Barbara Royce, Rosalie and Hugh wed secretly. But when he reveals to Rosalie that he does not consider her worth the loss of his father's millions, she returns to the country and her childhood sweetheart, Tom Darcy. *Dancers. Wealth. Marriage. New York City—Broadway.*

BROADWAY SCANDALS **F2.0635**

Columbia Pictures. 10 Nov **1929** [c17 Dec 1929; LP931]. Sd (Movietone); b&w. 35mm. 9 reels, 6,950 ft. [Also si; 5,108 ft.]

Prod Harry Cohn. *Dir* George Archainbaud. *Dial Dir* James Seymour, Rufus Le Maire. *Scen* Gladys Lehman. *Dial* Norman Houston, Howard J. Green. *Story* Howard J. Green. *Photog* Harry Jackson. *Art Dir* Harrison Wiley. *Film Ed* Leon Barsha, Ben Pivar. *Song: "What Is Life Without Love?"* Fred Thompson, David Franklin, Jack Stone. *Song: "Does an Elephant Love Peanuts?"* James Hanley. *Song: "Can You Read in My Eyes"* Sam Coslow. *Song: "Love's the Cause of All My Blues"* Joe Trent, Charles Daniels. *Song: "Would I Love To Love You"* Dave Dreyer, Sidney Clare. *Songs: "Rhythm of the Tambourine," "Kickin' the Blues Away"* David Franklin. *Ch Sd Engr* John Livadary. *Sd Mixing Engr* W. Hancock. *Asst Dir* C. C. Coleman.

Cast: Sally O'Neil *(Mary)*, Jack Egan *(Ted Howard)*, Carmel Myers *(Valeska)*, Tom O'Brien *(Bill Gray)*, J. Barney Sherry *(Le Maire)*, John Hyams *(Pringle)*, Charles Wilson *(Jack, radio announcer)*, Doris Dawson *(Bobby)*, Gordon Elliott *(George Halloway)*.

Musical comedy–drama. When his vaudeville revue goes broke in a tank town, song-and-dance man Ted Howard spends his last cent to send his girls back to New York, while Mary, who loves him, remains and suggests they finance a new act with her savings. Established in an actors' boardinghouse in New York, Ted and Mary get only smalltown bookings; then Ted, invited by Jack Lane to sing over the radio, meets musical star Valeska, who decides to make him her leading man. Mary overhears him refuse her offer, decides to leave the act, and joins the chorus of Valeska's show. Through Ted's influence, Mary scores a hit in an impersonation number, arousing Valeska's jealousy; when she has Mary discharged, Ted follows and reorganizes the old act. *Song-and-dance men. Chorus girls. Radio announcers. Musical revues. Vaudeville. Jealousy. Boardinghouses. New York City—Broadway.*

BROKEN BARRIERS **F2.0636**

Metro-Goldwyn Pictures. 18 Aug **1924** [c6 Aug 1924; LP20539]. Si; b&w. 35mm. 6 reels, 5,717 ft.

Dir Reginald Barker. *Scen* Sada Cowan, Howard Higgin. *Photog* Percy Hilburn.

Cast: James Kirkwood *(Ward Trenton)*, Norma Shearer *(Grace Durland)*, Adolphe Menjou *(Tommie Kemp)*, Mae Busch *(Irene Kirby)*, George Fawcett *(Mr. Durland)*, Margaret McWade *(Mrs. Durland)*, Robert Agnew *(Bobbie Durland)*, Ruth Stonehouse *(Ethel Durland)*, Robert Frazer *(John Moore)*, Winifred Bryson *(Mrs. Ward Trenton)*, Vera Reynolds *(Sadie Denton)*, Edythe Chapman *(Beulah Reynolds)*, George Kuwa *(Chang)*.

Society drama. Source: Meredith Nicholson, *Broken Barriers* (New York, 1922). Grace Durland, forced to give up college for work when her father loses his money, accepts an invitation to a house party, where she meets and falls in love with Ward Trenton, who is married. His wife agrees to give him his freedom only after he is badly injured in an automobile accident and when it appears that he will be unable to walk again. Trenton fully recovers, however, and is free to marry Grace. *Poverty. Divorce. Automobile accidents.*

BROKEN BARRIERS **F2.0637**

Excellent Pictures. 1 Dec **1928** [c28 Nov 1928; LP25854]. Si; b&w. 35mm. 6 reels.

Pres by Samuel Zierler. *Dir* Burton King. *Scen-Titl* Isadore Bernstein. *Story* Caroline F. Hayward. *Photog* William Miller, Joseph Walters. *Film Ed* Lee Anthony.

Cast: Helene Costello *(Beryl Moore)*, Gaston Glass *(Charles Hill)*, Joseph Girard *(Stanley Moore)*, Frank Beal *(George Austin)*, Carlton Stockdale *(Thomas Walker)*, Frank Hagney *(James Barker)*.

Melodrama. Faced with a newspaper exposé, weak-willed mayoral candidate George Austin tells political boss Stanley Moore he is quitting the race; Moore threatens him with a gun, and Austin dies of a heart attack. Fearing scandal, Moore arranges for Austin's body to be disposed of in a fake automobile accident. Charles Hill, a crack newspaper reporter, is suspicious of the "accident" and gets a job working for Moore. Hill gets his story, but it is never published; for Thomas Walker, Hill's editor at the paper, kills the story as a wedding present for Hill and Moore's daughter, Beryl, with whom Hill has fallen madly in love. *Reporters. Editors. Political bosses. Political campaigns.*

BROKEN CHAINS **F2.0638**

Goldwyn Pictures. 10 Dec **1922** [New York and Los Angeles premieres; released 24 Dec; c30 Nov 1922; LP18477]. Si; b&w. 35mm. 7 reels, 6,190 ft.

Dir Allen Holubar. *Scen* Carey Wilson. *Story* Winifred Kimball. *Photog* Byron Haskins.

Cast: Malcolm McGregor *(Peter Wyndham)*, Colleen Moore *(Mercy Boone)*, Ernest Torrence *(Boyan Boone)*, Claire Windsor *(Hortense Allen)*, James Marcus *(Pat Mulcahy)*, Beryl Mercer *(Mrs. Mulcahy)*, William Orlamond *(Slog Sallee)*, Gerald Pring *(butler)*, Edward Peil *(burglar)*, Leo Willis *(Gus)*.

Melodrama. Peter Wyndham is unable to come to the aid of Hortense Allen when her jewels are stolen, and, disgusted with his cowardice, he heads west. He is bested by Boyan Boone but later is victorious in a long fight with the brutish Boone, thus freeing Boone's daughter, Mercy, from the chains with which she has been bound. *Cowardice. Theft.*

A BROKEN DOLL F2.0639

Allan Dwan Productions. *Dist* Associated Producers. 12 Jun **1921** [c27 May 1921; LP16584]. Si; b&w. 35mm. 5 reels, 4,594 ft.

Scen-Dir Allan Dwan. *Adapt* Lillian Ducey. *Photog* Lyman Broening, L. W. O'Connell.

Cast: Monte Blue *(Tommy Dawes)*, Mary Thurman *(Harriet Bundy)*, Mary Jane Irving *(Rosemary)*, Les Bates *(Bill Nyall)*, Lizette Thorne *(Mrs. Nyall)*, Arthur Millett *(Sheriff Hugh Bundy)*, Jack Riley *(Knapp Wyant)*.

Rural melodrama. Source: Wilbur Hall, "Johnny Cucabod," in *Saturday Evening Post* (192:5–7, 12 Jun 1920). Tommy Dawes, a ranch hand at Bill Nyall's ranch, is devoted to the owner's little crippled daughter, Rosemary, and when he breaks her favorite doll he borrows a $20 goldpiece from the foreman's mattress and starts for town in the rain. He is set upon and robbed by an escaped convict, Knapp Wyant, and encountering him later in a deserted shack he struggles with and shoots Wyant. Tommy is mistaken for the convict by Sheriff Bundy, but he escapes and with help of the sheriff's daughter, Harriet, buys a new doll. After returning the money, he receives a reward for helping the sheriff and is finally accepted by his sweetheart, Harriet. *Cripples. Sheriffs. Cowboys. Robbery. Dolls. Childhood.*

THE BROKEN GATE F2.0640

Tiffany Productions. 15 Feb **1927** [c23 Mar 1927; LP23776]. Si; b&w. 35mm. 6 reels, 5,600 ft.

Dir James C. McKay. *Scen* John Francis Natteford. *Photog* Joseph A. Dubray, Stephen Norton. *Art Dir* Edwin B. Willis. *Film Ed* Merrill White.

Cast: Dorothy Phillips *(Aurora Lane)*, William Collier, Jr. *(Don Lane)*, Jean Arthur *(Ruth Hale)*, Phillips Smalley *(Judge Lucius Henderson)*, Florence Turner *(Miss Julia)*, Gibson Gowland *(Ephraim Adamson)*, Charles A. Post *(Johnny Adamson)*, Caroline "Spike" Rankin *(Mrs. Ephraim Adamson)*, Vera Lewis *(invalid)*, Jack McDonald *(Sheriff Dan Cummins)*, Charles Thurston *(Constable Joe Tarbush)*, Adele Watson *(gossip)*.

Society melodrama. Source: Emerson Hough, *The Broken Gate* (New York, 1917). In the farming community of Spring Valley, Aurora Lane is suspiciously regarded as a sinful woman, having been compromised by Lucius Henderson 20 years earlier and given birth to his child, which he refused to acknowledge. Don, her son, is cared for by Miss Julia, the town librarian, who pretends to be his aunt; he goes to college and there meets and falls in love with Ruth Hale, Henderson's ward. Don graduates and obtains a position. While visiting his "Aunt Julia," he is reunited with his mother, who operates a millinery shop. Scandalmongers, misconstruing her actions, cause her to be driven from town by the constable. Don is later arrested for the murder of the constable and is about to be lynched when Johnny Adamson, a halfwit, confesses to the crime. *Librarians. Milliners. Wards. Halfwits. Murder. Rural life. Illegitimacy. Parentage. Scandal. Lynching.*

BROKEN HEARTED F2.0641

Trinity Pictures. 15 Feb **1929.** Talking sequences; b&w. 35mm. 6 reels, 5,800 ft. [Also si.]

Dir Frank S. Mattison. *Scen* Cecil Burtis Hill. *Dial-Titl* Arthur Hotaling. *Story* Rachel Barton Butler. *Photog* Jules Cronjager. *Film Ed* Minnie Steppler.

Cast: Agnes Ayres, Gareth Hughes, Eddie Brownell.

Melodrama(?). No information about the nature of this film has been found.

BROKEN HEARTS F2.0642

Jaffe Art Films. 16 Feb **1926** [New York State license]. Si; b&w. 35mm. 8 reels, 8,200 ft.

Pres by Louis N. Jaffe. *Dir* Maurice Schwartz. *Adapt* Frances Taylor Patterson. *Photog* Frank Zucker.

Cast: Maurice Schwartz *(Benjamin Rezanov)*, Lila Lee *(Ruth Esterin)*, Wolf Goldfaden *(Cantor Esterin)*, Bina Abramowitz *(Mama Esterin)*, Isidor Cashier *(Victor Kaplin)*, Anna Appel *(Shprintze)*, Charles Nathanson *(Mr. Kruger)*, Liza Silbert *(Mrs. Kruger)*, Theodore Silbert *(Milton Kruger)*, Miriam Ellias *(Miriam)*, Morris Strassberg *(marriage broker)*, Henrietta Schnitzer *(Esther)*, Betty Ferkauf *(Benjamin's mother)*, Louis Lyman *(Mishka)*, Leonid Snegoff *(cossack captain)*, Julius Adler *(David Adler)*.

Domestic drama. Source: Z. Libin, "Broken Hearts" (publication undetermined). A Russian writer is forced to flee his homeland when the government finds his writings objectionable. He goes to New York where he hears from a friend that his wife, whom he was forced to leave behind in Russia, has died. The writer later meets and marries the daughter of the cantor of an East Side congregation. He is rejected by the girl's family, however, who had wanted her to marry the dumbbell son of a rich cloak-and-suitor. The writer then learns that his first wife is still alive, and he sadly returns to Russia, only to find that while he was on his way to Russia she did die in a government hospital. The writer returns to the United States and is happily reunited with his wife on Yom Kippur. *Jews. Authors. Russians. Immigrants. Cantors. Bigamy. Yom Kippur. Russia. New York City.*

BROKEN HEARTS OF BROADWAY F2.0643

Irving Cummings Productions. Jul **1923.** Si; b&w. 35mm. 7 reels, 6,600 or 6,800 ft.

Prod-Dir Irving Cummings. *Scen* Hope Loring, Louis D. Lighton. *Photog* James Diamond.

Cast: Colleen Moore *(Mary Ellis)*, Johnnie Walker *(George Colton)*, Alice Lake *(Bubbles Revere)*, Tully Marshall *(Barney Ryan)*, Kate Price *(Lydia Ryan)*, Creighton Hale *(an outcast)*, Anthony Merlo *(Tony Guido)*, Arthur Stuart Hull *(Barry Peale)*, Freeman Wood *(Frank Huntleigh)*.

Drama. Source: James Kyrle MacCurdy, *The Broken Hearts of Broadway* (c1917). Stage-struck country girl Mary Ellis arrives in New York and gets a job with a chorus line. She is soon out of work for repulsing the attentions of the showowner. George, a songwriter, befriends her and gets her a job in a Chinese cabaret. By a combination of circumstances, Mary is falsely accused of the murder of the showowner's friend. Mary is freed through the devoted efforts of George, who becomes her husband. They both become successful when George writes a hit play, starring Mary, based on their experiences. *Chorus girls. Gold diggers. Composers. Playwrights. Theatrical backers. Murder. Cabarets. New York City—Chinatown. New York City—Broadway.*

BROKEN HEARTS OF HOLLYWOOD F2.0644

Warner Brothers Pictures. 14 Aug **1926** [c14 Aug 1926; LP23032]. Si; b&w. 35mm. 8 reels, 7,770 ft.

Dir Lloyd Bacon. *Scen* C. Graham Baker. *Story* Raymond L. Schrock, Edward Clark. *Camera* Virgil Miller. *Asst Camera* Walter Robinson. *Film Ed* Clarence Kolster. *Asst Dir* Ted Stevens.

Cast: Patsy Ruth Miller *(Betty Anne Bolton)*, Louise Dresser *(Virginia Perry)*, Douglas Fairbanks, Jr. *(Hal Terwilliger)*, Jerry Miley *(Marshall)*, Stuart Holmes *(McLain)*, Barbara Worth *(Molly)*, Dick Sutherland *(sheriff)*, Emile Chautard *(director)*, Anders Randolf *(district attorney)*, George Nichols *(chief of detectives)*, Sam De Grasse *(defense attorney)*.

Domestic melodrama. Virginia Perry leaves her husband and child to return to Hollywood; but having dissipated her beauty and seeking solace in drink, she soon finds herself another "has been" on the fringe of movie circles. Her daughter, Betty Anne, wins a national beauty contest, and en route to Hollywood she meets Hal, another contest winner; both fail in their first screen attempts and turn to Marshall, an unscrupulous trickster, who enrolls them in his acting school. Molly, a movie extra, induces Betty Anne to attend a wild party; she is arrested in a raid; and Hal, to raise the money for her bail, takes a "stunt" job in which he is badly hurt. Betty Anne seeks the aid of star actor McLain, who obtains for her the leading female role in his next film; Virginia, who is cast as her mother, keeps silent about their relationship until the film is completed. Apprehensive for her daughter's safety, she shoots Marshall while in a drunken stupor and is arrested. At the trial, Betty Anne's testimony saves her mother, who is then happily united with her daughter and Hal. *Actors. Family life. Motion pictures. Beauty contests. Courtship. Alcoholism. Trials. Hollywood. Stunts.*

BROKEN HOMES F2.0645

Macfadden True Story Pictures. 15 Feb **1926** [c23 Mar, 6 Apr 1926; LU22552, LP22578]. Si; b&w. 35mm. 6 reels, 5,800 ft.

Dir Hugh Dierker. *Adapt* Lewis Allen Browne.

Cast: Gaston Glass, Alice Lake, J. Barney Sherry, Jane Jennings, Ruth Stonehouse.

Society melodrama. Julia Merritt runs away with an actor who soon dies, leaving her to care for a little daughter. Julia then places the child in the care of Arline Goodwin (the daughter of the Merritt housekeeper), whom she swears to secrecy regarding the child's identity. Arline returns to the Merritt home, and the deacon of the local church, thinking her to be an unwed mother, makes plans to drive her out of town. John Merritt sees to her protection and then leaves home, going on the stage. Two years pass. Disinherited by his father, John becomes a successful actor, returning to his hometown as the leading actor in a play entitled *Broken Homes.*

There is a fire in the theater, and only John's great heroism prevents loss of life. John's father later learns that Julia's ward is his own granddaughter, and, filled with remorse, he is reconciled with his estranged son. John and Julia make plans to be married. *Actors. Deacons. Wards. Grandfathers. Smalltown life. Personal identity. Filial relations. Theater. Fires.*

THE BROKEN LAW **F2.0646**

Ermine Productions. *Dist* Usla Co. c29 Dec **1924** [LU20999]. Si; b&w. 35mm. 5 reels.

Supv Bernard D. Russell. *Scen* George Hively.

Western melodrama. Losing his last dime at poker, Burt Morgan sets out to find a job. When his horse bolts, Burt is thrown and knocked unconscious. His dog is shot by an Indian, who later regrets the action and gives Burt a bag of gold nuggets as a token of his sorrow. Steve and Hal subsequently beat the Indian and steal his treasure map, leaving him for dead. Burt finds work on the cattle ranch of a woman named Sally, with whom he falls in love. Hal is the foreman of the ranch and informs the sheriff that Burt killed the Indian. The sheriff does not arrest Burt, for Burt has hidden the Indian's nuggets and the body of the Indian has mysteriously disappeared. Hal and Steve attempt to kill Burt, but Sally intervenes and chases them off. Hal and Steve then ride into the desert in search of the Indian's hidden gold hoard. While the badly wounded Indian watches, the two men go to their deaths in a booby-trapped mine. The Indian tells the sheriff that Hal and Steve beat him, and then dies. Sally and Burt are married. *Cowboys. Ranch foremen. Sheriffs. Indians of North America. Treasure. Dogs.*

Note: The film was announced by Ermine as one of a series of six westerns, three others of which starred Jack Meehan.

THE BROKEN LAW **F2.0647**

Goodwill Pictures. 3 May **1926** [New York State license]. Si; b&w. 35mm. 5 reels, 4,329 ft.

Cast: Jack Meehan.

No information about the nature of this film has been found.

BROKEN LAWS **F2.0648**

Thomas H. Ince Corp. *Dist* Film Booking Offices of America. 9 Nov **1924** [12 Oct 1924; LP20788]. Si; b&w. 35mm. 7 reels, 6,413 ft.

Dir R. William Neill. *Adapt* Marion Jackson, Bradley King. *Photog* James R. Diamond.

Cast: Mrs. Wallace Reid *(Joan Allen)*, Percy Marmont *(Richard Heath)*, Ramsey Wallace *(Ralph Allen)*, Jacqueline Saunders *(Muriel Heath)*, Arthur Rankin *(Bobby Allen, age 16)*, Virginia Lee Corbin *(Patsy Heath, age 16)*, Pat Moore *(Bobby Allen, age 8)*, Jane Wray *(Patsy Heath, age 8)*.

Social drama. Source: Adela Rogers St. Johns, "Broken Laws" (publication undetermined). In trouble at school and indulged by his mother, Bobby Allen is, at 8 years, a spoiled and willful child. *Grown to 16, never reprimanded or punished, Bobby continues to be arrogant and lawless. When his mother buys him a Stutz Bearcat, he begins to lead a wild life, accompanied by Patsy Heath, an extravagant flapper neglected by her mother. Returning from a disreputable roadhouse one night, Bobby runs into a wagon and kills an old woman. He is tried and convicted of manslaughter in the first degree. His mother pleads with the judge to let her serve Bobby's term, arguing that her own indulgence was responsible for her son's conduct.* Suddenly, the mother awakens and realizes that it was all a dream. She then gives Bobby (still age 8) a good spanking and makes him return to school to apologize for his poor conduct. *Children. Flappers. Motherhood. Automobile accidents. Manslaughter. Stutz automobiles.*

THE BROKEN MASK **F2.0649**

Morris R. Schlank Productions. *Dist* Anchor Film Distributors. Jan **1928.** Si; b&w. 35mm. 6 reels, 5,600 ft.

Pres by Morris R. Schlank. *Dir* James P. Hogan. *Scen* Adele Buffington. *Titl* De Leon Anthony. *Story* Francis Fenton. *Photog* Edward Gheller, Shirley Williams. *Film Ed* Roy Eiler.

Cast: Cullen Landis *(Pertio)*, Barbara Bedford *(Caricia)*, William V. Mong *(Santo Bendito)*, Wheeler Oakman *(Dr. Gordon White)*, James Marcus *(Maurice Armato)*, Philippe De Lacy *(Pertio, as a boy)*, Ina Anson *(Delores)*, Nanci Price *(Caricia, as a girl)*, Pat Harmon.

Drama. Unsuccessful in his career because of facial scars, Pertio, an Argentine dancer, undergoes plastic surgery at the urging of an Argentine girl, Caricia, whose dancing has made her a star. The dancers team up, enjoy success, and fall in love. However, the surgeon, who also has fallen in love with the girl, gives the hero a treatment that causes the scars to reappear. The heroine remains faithful, and the hero punishes the doctor with a whip. (Locale: New Orleans.) *Argentineans. Dancers. Surgeons. Disfiguration. Plastic surgery. Flagellation. New Orleans.*

THE BROKEN SILENCE **F2.0650**

Pine Tree Pictures. *Dist* Arrow Film Corp. 1 May **1922** [c13 Jul 1922; LP18051]. Si; b&w. 35mm. 6 reels, 5,929 ft.

Dir Del Henderson. *Scen* Thomas F. Fallon. *Photog* Charles Downs.

Cast: Zena Keefe *(Jeanne Marat)*, Robert Elliott *(Bruce Cameron)*, J. Barney Sherry *(Inspector Brandt)*, Jack Hopkins *(Pierre Marat)*, Jack Drumier *(Indian Joe)*, James Milady *(padre)*, Roy Gordon *(Jacques Beauvais)*, Gypsy O'Brien *(Marie Beauvais)*, Dorothy Allen *(Loque)*, Ted Griffen *(White Eagle)*, Joseph Depew *(Pierre Beauvais)*, William Fisher *(orderly)*.

Melodrama. Source: James Oliver Curwood, unidentified story. In the Canadian Northwest, a brother and sister who pose as husband and wife are implicated in the murder of a barracks inspector who caused the death of their parents. The brother admits to the crime to protect the sister, but the real murderer confesses and the sister is free to marry the Mountie officer she loves. *Brother-sister relationship. Murder. Canadian Northwest. Northwest Mounted Police.*

THE BROKEN SPUR **F2.0651**

Ben Wilson Productions. *Dist* Arrow Film Corp. Jul **1921.** Si; b&w. 35mm. 5 reels.

Dir Ben Wilson.

Cast: Jack Hoxie *("Silent" Joe Dayton/Jacques Durand)*, Evelyn Nelson *("Angel" Lambert)*, Jim Welch *(Bill Lambert)*, Wilbur McGaugh *(Pierre LeBac)*, Edward Berman *(John Dexter)*, Harry Rattenberry *(Andy MacGregor)*, Marin Sais *(Ida Hunt)*.

Northwest melodrama. "Silent" Joe Dayton is putting through a railroad in the Canadian Northwest. Jacques Durand, a bandit, resents the intrusion, knowing that with the railroad will come law and order. The fact that Dayton and Durand are look-alikes results in Dayton's getting into trouble with his girl, Angel, who mistakes Durand for Dayton when she sees the former with another girl. Dayton is also accused of being the bandit who robbed the bank. The clue of a broken spur, however, clears Dayton and points to Durand. *Bandits. Doubles. Bank robberies. Railroads. Canadian Northwest.*

THE BROKEN VIOLIN **F2.0652**

Atlantic Features. *Dist* Arrow Film Corp. 10 May **1923** [c26 May 1923; LP19006]. Si; b&w. 35mm. 6 reels.

Dir Jack Dillon. *Scen* L. Case Russell. *Story* George Rogan. *Photog* George Peters.

Cast: Joseph Blake *(Jeremy Ellsworth)*, Warren Cook *(Thomas Kitterly)*, Henry Sedley *(James Gault)*, Sydney Deane *(Dr. Mason)*, Reed Howes *(John Ellsworth)*, Dorothy Mackaill *(Constance Morley)*, Rita Rogan *(Beatrice Ellsworth)*, J. H. Lewis *(Jules Davega)*, Zena Keefe *(The Governess)*, Gladden James *(Phil Carter/Floyd Watson)*, Edward Roseman *("a half-wit")*.

Melodrama. When aged Jeremy Ellsworth decides to settle his fortune on John and Beatrice, the children of his disinherited son, he sends for them to come live with him. Beatrice arrives safely, but James Gault, Ellsworth's secretary, intercepts the letter to John and engages Phil Carter to pose as the heir. John, a lumber camp foreman, hears of the plot, hastens to the Ellsworth home, and is overpowered by ruffians, who also kidnap Beatrice. Escaping his captors, John rescues his sister from a speedboat with the aid of a hydroplane and finds love with Beatrice's governess. *Grandfathers. Governesses. Lumbermen. Brother-sister relationship. Inheritance. Imposture. Hydroplanes.*

THE BROKEN VIOLIN **F2.0653**

Micheaux Film Corp. **1927.** Si; b&w. 35mm. 7 reels.

Pres by Frank G. Kirby. Oscar Micheaux Production.

Cast: J. Homer Tutt, Ardelle Dabney, Alice B. Russell, Ike Paul, Daisy Foster, Gertrude Snelson, Boots Hope, Ethel Smith, W. Hill.

Melodrama. Source: Oscar Micheaux, "House of Mystery" (publication undetermined). Lilia Cooper, a beautiful Negress and violin prodigy, finds romance and success despite the fact that her father is a drunkard and her family poor. *Violinists. Alcoholism. Filial relations. Negro life. Poverty.*

THE BROKEN WING **F2.0654**
B. P. Schulberg Productions. *Dist* Preferred Pictures, Al Lichtman Corp. 19 Aug **1923** [c10 Sep 1923; LP19385]. Si; b&w. 35mm. 6 reels, 6,216 ft.

Pres by B. P. Schulberg. *Dir-Scen* Tom Forman. *Photog* Harry Perry.

Cast: Kenneth Harlan *(Philip Marvin)*, Miriam Cooper *(Inez Villera)*, Walter Long *(Capt. Innocencio Dos Santos)*, Miss Du Pont *(Celia)*, Richard Tucker *(Sylvester Cross)*, Edwin J. Brady *(Bassilio)*, Ferdinand Munier *(Luther Farley)*, Evelyn Selbie *(Quichita)*.

Comedy-drama. Source: Paul Dickey and Charles W. Goddard, *The Broken Wing* (New York opening: 29 Nov 1920). American airplane pilot Philip Marvin crashes into a ranch on the Mexican border. Inez, foster daughter of a Mexican ranchman, nurses him back to health. She has been praying for a husband and thinks Marvin, a victim of amnesia, is the answer to her prayers because he fell through the roof into her house. Revolutionary leader Dos Santos has already claimed Inez. He demands a ransom from Marvin's relatives for Marvin's return, but American Secret Servicemen outwit Dos Santos, and Inez wins Marvin. *Air pilots. Secret service. Amnesia. Ransom. Airplane accidents. Mexican border.*

THE BRONC BUSTER *see* **THE BRONC STOMPER**

THE BRONC STOMPER **F2.0655**
Leo Maloney Productions. *Dist* Pathé Exchange. 26 Feb **1928** [c7 Feb 1928; LP24970]. Si; b&w. 35mm. 6 reels, 5,408 ft.

Dir Leo D. Maloney. *Scen-Titl-Adapt* Ford I. Beebe. *Story* Barr Cross. *Photog* Edward Kull. *Film Ed* Joseph Kane.

Cast: Don Coleman *(Richard Thurston)*, Ben Corbett *(Yea Bo Smith)*, Tom London *(Alan Riggs)*, Bud Osborne *(Slim Garvey)*, Frank Clark *(James Hollister)*, Frederick Dana *(R. M. Thompson, the ranger)*, Whitehorse *(town marshal)*, Ray Walters *(deputy marshal)*, Robert Burns *(rodeo manager)*, Florence Lee *(Mrs. Hollister)*, Eugenia Gilbert *(Daisy Hollister)*.

Western melodrama. Rodeo chairman Alan Riggs prevents Dick Thurston, a champion broncobuster, from entering a rodeo by fabricating a rule that entrants must either own property in New Mexico or be employed on a ranch in the state, thus swindling Thurston out of $500 he has deposited to back up his skill. Riggs does not want to lose the large sum of money he has already bet on local champion Slim Garvey. Thurston gets a job on the Hollister ranch, thus becoming eligible for the rodeo. At Riggs's suggestion, Slim steals money Daisy Hollister has saved for renewal of her father's land-grazing lease, and, in a repeated effort to prevent Thurston from entering the rodeo, plants it in Thurston's room before alerting the sheriff. Thurston and his sidekick, Yea Bo, escape the sheriff in time to enter the race; Thurston wins the purse, recovers his money, and exposes Riggs and Slim as crooks. *Broncobusters. Cowboys. Sheriffs. Rodeos. Theft. New Mexico. Horses.*

Note: Also known as *The Bronc Buster.*

THE BRONCHO BUSTER (Blue Streak Western) **F2.0656**
Universal Pictures. 1 May **1927** [c28 Mar 1927; LP23810]. Si; b&w. 35mm. 5 reels, 4,687 ft.

Pres by Carl Laemmle. *Dir* Ernst Laemmle. *Scen* William B. Lester. *Photog* Al Jones. *Art Dir* David S. Garber.

Cast: Fred Humes *(Charlie Smith)*, Gloria Grey *(Barbara Furth)*, George Connors *(Sourdough Jones)*, Charles Lee Quinn *(Jim Gray)*, David Dunbar *(Curtis Harris)*, William Malan *(Maj. John Furth)*.

Western melodrama. Source: Raymond Cannon, "Loco Weed" (publication undetermined). Col. John Furth, a southern aristocrat and the owner of Blue Bird, a prize racehorse, borrows money from Clinton Harris—who wants to marry the colonel's daughter, Barbara—hoping to recoup the family fortune in an eastern derby. Jim Gray, a crooked trainer recommended by Harris, reports that Blue Bird is a killer and must be shot, but he is stopped in the act by Charlie Smith, a neighboring miner who loves Barbara. Charlie takes the horse to the mine he is working with his partner, Sourdough Jones. Two of Harris' men conspire with Sourdough to steal Charlie's claim, and Harris, threatening the colonel, forces Barbara to accept his marriage proposal. Charlie, however, stops the ceremony and exposes the villain. Sourdough clears the colonel's debts with Harris' own money, and the latter is evicted with a claim to a worthless mine. *Broncobusters. Southerners. Miners. Horsetrainers. Mine claims. Horses.*

THE BRONCHO TWISTER **F2.0657**
Fox Film Corp. 13 Mar **1927** [c13 Mar 1927; LP23769]. Si; b&w. 35mm. 6 reels, 5,435 ft.

Pres by William Fox. *Dir* Orville O. Dull. *Scen* John Stone. *Story* Adela Rogers St. Johns. *Photog* Dan Clark. *Asst Dir* Wynn Mace.

Cast: Tom Mix *(Tom Mason)*, Helene Costello *(Paulita Brady)*, George Irving *(Ned Mason)*, Dorothy Kitchen *(Daisy Mason)*, Paul Nicholson *(Black Jack Brady)*, Doris Lloyd *(Teresa Brady)*, Malcolm Waite *(Dan Bell)*, Jack Pennick *(Jinx Johnson)*, Otto Fries *(sheriff)*, Tony the Wonder Horse *(himself)*.

Western melodrama. Tom Mason, returning home after serving in the United States Marines, finds that a neighboring ranchowner, Brady, is attempting by villainy and intimidation to gain control of his father's ranch. He rescues his father and sister from the villain's gang; later he is captured by the gang and learns that Brady's stepdaughter, Paulita, is being forced into marriage with Bell, one of his henchmen. After numerous exciting adventures, Tom escapes and rescues Paulita from the ranch tower. *Ranchers. Gangs. Filial relations. Brother-sister relationship. United States Marines. Horses.*

THE BRONZE BELL **F2.0658**
Thomas H. Ince Productions. *Dist* Paramount Pictures. 19 Jun **1921** [c9 Jul 1921; LP16742]. Si; b&w. 35mm. 6 reels, 5,507 ft.

Supv Thomas H. Ince. *Dir* James W. Horne. *Scen* Del Andrews, Louis Stevens. *Photog* George Barnes.

Cast: Courtenay Foote *(Har Dyal Rutton/David Amber)*, Doris May *(Sophia Farrell)*, John Davidson *(Salig Singh)*, Claire Du Brey *(Nairaini)*, Noble Johnson *(Chatterji)*, Otto Hoffman *(La Bertouche)*, Gerald Pring *(Captain Darrington)*, C. Norman Hammond *(Colonel Farrell)*, Howard Crampton *(Dogget)*, Fred Huntley *(Maharajah)*.

Romantic melodrama. Source: Louis Joseph Vance, *The Bronze Bell* (New York, 1909). East Indian prince Har Dyal Rutton promises his dying father to lead a revolt against English rule, but having occidental sympathies he flees to America and lives in obscurity. Sophia Farrell, daughter of a British colonel and engaged to Darrington, meets David Amber, who bears a strong resemblance to Har Dyal Rutton. When the prince defies a Hindu messenger who reminds him of his oath, he is mortally wounded, but before he dies he arranges that Amber will return to India posing as the prince. Salig Singh and Nairaini, a princess, know Amber's identity and plan to usurp the throne. Sophia is abducted and taken to the Temple of the Bronze Bell, where Amber denounces the rebellion; and just as the fanatics are about to kill them, British troops arrive. *Royalty. Doubles. Imposture. Filial relations. Hinduism. Colonial administration. India.*

BROODING EYES **F2.0659**
Banner Productions. *Dist* Henry Ginsberg Distributing Corp. 15 Mar **1926** [c22 Mar 1926; LP22509]. Si; b&w. 35mm. 6 reels, 5,763 ft.

Dir Edward J. Le Saint. *Adapt-Scen* Mary Alice Scully, Pierre Gendron.

Cast: Lionel Barrymore *(Slim Jim Carey [Lord Tallbois])*, Ruth Clifford *(Joan Ayre)*, Robert Ellis *(Phillip Mott)*, Montagu Love *(Pat Callaghan)*, William V. Mong *(Slaney)*, Lucien Littlefield *(Bell)*, John Miljan *(Drummond)*, Dot Farley *(Marie De Costa)*, Alma Bennett *(Agnes De Costa)*.

Crook melodrama. Source: John Goodwin, "The Man With the Brooding Eyes" (publication undetermined). Pat Callaghan, a gangleader, informs his henchmen—Slaney, Bell, and Drummond—that their former leader, Slim Jim Carey, was in reality Lord Tallbois and that Joan Ayre, Carey's daughter, is the rightful owner of the Knayth estate. Unknown to the gang, Carey returns to spy on them through the eyes of a portrait of himself on the mantel. At the estate, Phillip Mott, a barrister, is showing Joan the house when Slaney, disguised as a butler, recognizes her. Carey, dressed as a tramp, learns Joan's identity and threatens Slaney, while Bell, posing as an attorney, tells Joan of her parentage and has her sign over money to him. The gang conspires to present Agnes De Costa, daughter of Carey's ex-mistress, as the true heiress, but Carey informs Mott of the truth. At a banquet, Carey is shot by the gang and dies in Joan's arms. Mott finds happiness with the girl. *Gangs. Barristers. Butlers. Tramps. Inheritance. Parentage. Disguise. England.*

BROTHERLY LOVE **F2.0660**
Metro-Goldwyn-Mayer Pictures. 13 Oct **1928** [c13 Oct 1928; LP15]. Talking sequences & sd eff (Movietone); b&w. 35mm. 7 reels, 6,053 ft. [Also si.]

Dir Charles F. Reisner. *Scen* Earl Baldwin, Lew Lipton. *Titl* Robert Hopkins. *Photog* Henry Sharp. *Sets* Cedric Gibbons. *Film Ed* George Hively. *Wardrobe* Henrietta Frazer.

Cast: Karl Dane *(Oscar)*, George K. Arthur *(Jerry)*, Jean Arthur *(Mary)*, Richard Carlyle *(Warden Brown)*, Edward Connelly *(Coggswell)*, Marcia Harris *(Mrs. Coggswell)*.

Comedy-drama. Source: Patterson Margoni, "Big-Hearted Jim," in *Liberty Magazine* (3:24, 20 Nov 1926). Oscar, a burly guard at Newberry Prison, gets into an argument with Jerry, a barber. Jerry tries to run away but is arrested as a fugitive and sent to Newberry. Both men fall in love with Mary, the warden's daughter. Oscar has the smallish Jerry put on the prison's football team to show him up, but he proves instead to be a hero. Oscar runs afoul of the law and is sent to a rival prison. Arthur is released but tries to return to prison so as to play against his rival in the big game. Jerry wins the game and Mary becomes his bride. *Barbers. Prison guards. Prisons. Football.*

BROTHERS (Imperial Photoplays) **F2.0661**

Trem Carr Productions. *Dist* Rayart Pictures. 17 Jan or 1 Feb **1929.** Si; b&w. 35mm. 6 reels, 6,092 ft.

Dir Scott Pembroke. *Scen* Arthur Hoerl. *Story* Ford I. Beebe, Arthur Hoerl. *Photog* Hap Depew. *Film Ed* J. S. Harrington. *Song: "I'm Dreaming"* Dan Dougherty.

Cast: Cornelius Keefe *(Tom Conroy)*, Arthur Rankin *(Bob Conroy)*, Barbara Bedford *(Doris La Rue)*, Richard Carle *(Thomas Blackwood)*, George Chesebro *(Randy)*, Paddy O'Flynn *(Norman)*, James Cain *(Tom Conroy, as a child)*, Edward Anderson *(Bob Conroy, as a child)*.

Drama. Two orphaned brothers are separated when Tom, the elder, escapes from the authorities and Bob is taken into an asylum. As years pass Tom drifts into a life of crime, the proceeds of which he contributes to Bob's college education, and the two eventually meet again—without recognition—when Tom tries to involve Bob in a confidence game. Finally recognizing his brother, Tom takes the blame for a murder, of which Bob is accused; but Bob proves the guilt of Randy and Doris La Rue, both members of Tom's gang. *Brothers. Orphans. Confidence men. Gangs. Murder. Education.*

BROTHERS **F2.0662**

Columbia Pictures. 15 Nov **1930** [c18 Sep 1930; LP1667]. Sd (Movietone); b&w. 35mm. 8 reels, 6,843 ft.

Prod Harry Cohn. *Dir* Walter Lang. *Dial Dir* Stuart Walker. *Dial* Sidney Lazarus. *Adapt-Cont* John Thomas Neville, Charles R. Condon. *Camera* Ira Morgan. *Art Dir* Edward Jewell. *Tech Dir* Edward Shulter. *Film Ed* Gene Havlick. *Sd Rec Engr* Russell Malmgren. *Asst Dir* C. C. Coleman.

Cast: Bert Lytell *(Bob Naughton/Eddie Connolly)*, Dorothy Sebastian *(Norma)*, William Morris *(Dr. Moore)*, Richard Tucker *(prosecuting attorney)*, Maurice Black *(Lorenzo)*, Frank McCormack *(Oily Joe)*, Claire McDowell *(Mrs. Naughton)*, Howard Hickman *(Mr. Naughton)*, Francis McDonald *(Tony)*, Rita Carlyle *(Mag)*, Jessie Arnold *(Maud)*.

Society drama. Source: Herbert Ashton, Jr., *Brothers, a Melodrama in Prologue and Three Acts* (New York, 1934). Orphaned twins are adopted in infancy, one by a washerwoman, the other by a wealthy attorney, and they grow to manhood unaware of their relationship. Eddie becomes a piano player in the backroom of Oily Joe's saloon, while Bob Naughton becomes a brilliant attorney though addicted to drink. Bob is engaged to marry Norma, daughter of the orphanage supervisor, but is also involved with the wife of a criminal whom he defended; in an altercation with the husband, Bob kills the husband in a room at Oily Joe's. Because of his physical resemblance, Eddie is accused of the crime, but Bob clears his brother, then suffers a mental collapse and is taken to a sanitarium. Eddie is asked by Colonel Naughton to impersonate Bob in the household so that Mrs. Naughton will not know of his condition. While doing so he falls in love with Norma; he decides to leave, but learning of Bob's death, he remains and declares his love to the girl. *Twins. Brothers. Lawyers. Pianists. Laundresses. Social classes. Wealth. Poverty. Impersonation. Saloons.*

BROTHERS UNDER THE SKIN **F2.0663**

Goldwyn Pictures. 19 Nov **1922** [c25 Sep 1922; LP18346]. Si; b&w. 35mm. 6 reels, 4,983 or 4,961 ft.

Dir E. Mason Hopper. *Cont* Grant Carpenter. *Titl* Peter Bernard Kyne. *Photog* John J. Mescall.

Cast: Pat O'Malley *(Newton Craddock)*, Helene Chadwick *(Millie Craddock)*, Mae Busch *(Flo Bulger)*, Norman Kerry *(Thomas Kirtland)*, Claire Windsor *(Dorothy Kirtland)*.

Comedy-drama. Source: Peter Bernard Kyne, "Brothers Under Their Skins," in *Cosmopolitan* (71:42–48, Oct 1921). Newton Craddock, a shipping clerk, and Thomas Kirtland, vice president of the same company, have similar marital problems—suspicious, spendthrift wives. Their lives cross when Newton is asked to deliver a letter to Kirtland. Newton witnesses a scene in which Kirtland calls a halt to his wife's behavior: Newton then gains the confidence to do the same with respect to both his own wife and his bullying foreman. Both couples are reconciled, and Newton is promoted. *Shipping clerks. Spendthrifts. Marriage. Self-confidence.*

THE BROWN DERBY **F2.0664**

C. C. Burr Pictures. *Dist* First National Pictures. 4 Jul **1926** [c16 Jun 1926; LP22817]. Si; b&w. 35mm. 7 reels, 6,500 or 6,700 ft.

Pres by C. C. Burr. *Dir* Charles Hines. *Screenplay* Bert Wheeler. *Titl* John McGowan. *Photog* George Peters, Al Wilson, Albert Wetzel. *Film Ed* George Amy. *Asst Dir* Joe Bannon, Charlie Berner. *Prod Mgr* Benny Berk.

Cast: Johnny Hines *(Tommy Burke)*, Diana Kane *(Edith Worthing)*, Ruth Dwyer *(Betty Caldwell)*, Flora Finch *(Aunt Anna)*, Edmund Breese *(John J. Caldwell)*, J. Barney Sherry *(Captain Shay)*, Bradley Barker *(Robert Farrell)*, Herbert Standing *(Adolph Plummer)*, Harold Foshay *(Frank Boyle)*, Bob Slater *(Sam)*.

Comedy. Source: E. S. Merlin and Brian Marlow, *The Brown Derby* (a play; c11 Apr 1925). Tommy Burke, a good-natured young plumber who refers to his monkey wrench as his pipe organ, is unaware of his inferiority complex. One day he learns that an eccentric uncle has died, leaving him a brown derby said to bring good luck to its wearer. Meanwhile Edith Worthing and her Aunt Anna are expecting Edith's wealthy uncle, Adolph Plummer, from Australia. On a call to their house, Tommy is mistaken for the uncle, being announced as "a plumber," and soon a mutual romance develops with Edith. They are wedded by mistake when serving as witnesses to marriage by elopement. Farrell, a rival for Edith, learns of Tommy's deception and persuades Edith to elope with him; but Tommy follows in hot pursuit, in his pajamas and derby. At the last minute, a message arrives telling Edith that she and Tommy are already married. *Plumbers. Australians. Mistaken identity. Inferiority complex. Courtship. Talismans. Elopement.*

BROWN OF HARVARD **F2.0665**

Metro-Goldwyn-Mayer Pictures. 5 Apr **1926** [c19 Apr 1926; LP22793]. Si; b&w. 35mm. 8 reels, 7,941 ft.

Dir Jack Conway. *Screenplay* A. P. Younger. *Titl* Joe Farnham. *Adapt* Donald Ogden Stewart. *Photog* Ira H. Morgan. *Sets* Cedric Gibbons, Arnold Gillespie. *Film Ed* Frank Davis. *Wardrobe* Kathleen Kay, Maude Marsh.

Cast: Jack Pickford *(Jim Doolittle)*, Mary Brian *(Mary Abbott)*, Francis X. Bushman, Jr. *(Bob McAndrews)*, Mary Alden *(Mrs. Brown)*, David Torrence *(Mr. Brown)*, Edward Connelly *(Professor Abbott)*, Guinn Williams *(Hal Walters)*, Ernest Gillen *(Reggie Smythe)*, William Haines *(Tom Brown)*.

Romantic drama. Source: Rida Johnson Young, *Brown of Harvard, a Farce in Four Acts* (New York, 1909). Tom Brown, a breezy, handsome youth with a Don Juan reputation, quickly becomes popular at Harvard but soon is temperamentally opposed to Bob McAndrews, a studious, reserved boy who becomes his chief rival for the affections of Mary Abbott, a professor's daughter. Tom rooms with Doolittle (Doo), an awkward but goodhearted backwoods youth who comes to idolize Tom. At a party, Tom forcibly kisses Mary, and a tussle with McAndrews follows. Later, Tom challenges Mac as stroker on the college rowing team but loses; and when he forces a confession of love from Mary, he takes to drink in shame. When he replaces Mac in a match against Yale, Tom collapses and is disgraced but is persuaded by his father to go out for football. To save his friend's reputation, Doo, who is ill, exposes himself to rain and is hospitalized. Tom plays in a game against Yale and at a crucial moment gives Mac a chance to score for the team; he goes to tell Doo of the victory, but Doo dies shortly afterward. Tom is acclaimed a hero and is happily united with Mary. *College life. Football. Rowing. Courtship. Friendship. Harvard University. Yale University.*

THE BRUTE **F2.0666**

Micheaux Film Corp. **1925.** Si; b&w. 35mm. 7 reels.

Cast: Evelyn Preer, Lawrence Chenault.

Melodrama. No information about the precise nature of this film has been found. *Negro life.*

Note: Indicated year is approximate.

THE BRUTE **F2.0667**

Warner Brothers Pictures. 30 Apr **1927** [c16 Apr 1927; LP23878]. Si; b&w. 35mm. 7 reels, 6,901 ft.

Dir Irving Cummings. *Scen* Harvey Gates. *Photog* Abe Fried. *Asst Dir* Charles Woolstenhulme.

Cast: Monte Blue *("Easy Going" Martin Sondes)*, Leila Hyams *(Jennifer Duan)*, Clyde Cook *(Oklahoma Red)*, Carroll Nye *(The El)*, Paul Nicholson *(Square Deal Felton)*.

Western melodrama. Source: W. Douglas Newton, *The Brute* (New York, 1924). "Easy Going" Martin, a Texas cowhand, saves Jennifer Duan from a poisoned spring in the desert, becomes infatuated with her, but is stunned to find she works for Felton, a corrupt saloon owner. The local community turns against Martin when he is robbed and fails to buy out Felton. Later, in an oil town owned by Felton, Martin accepts an offer to cap a wild gas well. Martin has shielded Little Phil, a fugitive who has attempted to kill Felton; they meet Oklahoma Red, a former pal of Martin's, who pays off an old debt. With the money Martin bargains with Felton for Jennifer, so as to test her character. After a deal is made, she is thrown into the street; in a showdown with Felton and Martin, Oklahoma Red kills the villain, and Martin is united with the girl. *Cowboys. Gamblers. Dancehall girls. Texans. Oil fields.*

BUCK PRIVATES (Universal-Jewel) **F2.0668**

Universal Pictures. 3 Jun **1928** [c8 Sep 1927; LP24392]. Si; b&w. 35mm. 7 reels, 6,171 or 6,551 ft.

Pres by Carl Laemmle. *Dir-Adapt* Melville Brown. *Scen* John B. Clymer. *Titl* Albert De Mond. *Story* Lieut. Stuart N. Lake. *Photog* John Stumar. *Film Ed* Frank Atkinson, Ray Curtiss.

Cast: Lya De Putti *(Annie)*, Malcolm McGregor *(John Smith)*, ZaSu Pitts *(Hulda)*, James Marcus *(Major Hartman)*, Eddie Gribbon *(Sergeant Butts)*, Capt. Ted Duncan *(Captain Marshall)*, Bud Jamison *(Cupid Dodds)*, Les Bates *(Mose Bloom)*.

Comedy. John Smith, an American buck private in an occupied German village, is smitten with Annie, the leading citizen's daughter, who is equally admired by Sergeant Butts, his enemy. John is quartered in Annie's home, and he recognizes her father as an officer he took prisoner under amusing conditions before the Armistice, but he himself is not recognized by the father until decorated for bravery. Army officers issue a general order against fraternizing, with court-martial as a penalty. John and Annie meet secretly in the garden, where they are discovered by Butts; as a result, Annie's indignant father cuts her hair. Butts agrees to cancel the court-martial if Annie marries him; she prevails upon the willing Hulda to take her place in the ceremony, while she and John escape on a motorcycle. ... *Courtship. Fraternization. Military occupation. World War I. Germany. United States Army.*

THE BUCKAROO KID (Universal-Jewel) **F2.0669**

Universal Pictures. 14 Nov **1926** [c19 Oct 1926; LP23263]. Si; b&w. 35mm. 6 reels, 6,167 ft.

Pres by Carl Laemmle. *Dir-Adapt* Lynn Reynolds. *Photog* Harry Neumann.

Cast: Hoot Gibson *(Ed Harley)*, Ethel Shannon *(Lyra Radigan)*, Burr McIntosh *(Henry Radigan)*, Harry Todd *(Tom Darby)*, James Gordon *(Mulford)*, Charles Colby, Joe Rickson, Clark Comstock, Newton House.

Western comedy-drama. Source: Peter Bernard Kyne, "Oh, Promise Me" (publication undetermined). As an orphan boy, Ed Harley is taken in and reared by Jim Mulford, rancher and banker; 8 years later Ed is foreman of Mulford's ranch and is indulged by him as a son. Ed is sent to San Francisco to manage the ranch of Henry Radigan, a grouchy old millionaire who resents Ed's youth and particularly his attempts to court his daughter, Lyra. Ed finally goes to the ranch, introduces himself as the new manager, and enforces his authority at the point of a gun; but Radigan reinstates the former manager and fires Ed, who has become popular with the crew. Radigan, however, is forced to call Ed back. Mulford dies and leaves his ranch to Ed, who resigns; and after numerous difficulties, Ed acquires both a loan from Radigan and the heart of his daughter. *Orphans. Bankers. Ranchers. Ranch foremen. Ranch managers. Courtship. San Francisco.*

BUCKIN' THE WEST **F2.0670**

William Steiner Productions. c17 Oct **1924** [LU20675]. Si; b&w. 35mm. 5 reels.

Story-Scen Forrest Sheldon.

Cast: Pete Morrison *(Cal Edwards)*.

Western melodrama. Xyethia Tomkins, an intrepid archeologist, goes west looking for Aztec treasure and meets Cal Edwards, who, with two other cowhands, bought the ranch formerly owned by Xyethia's brother, who died of snakebite. Jacques Ledoux, an international crook, learns that Xyethia's brother left her a rough map showing the location of the treasure and attempts to take it from her. Cal prevents this robbery, and Xyethia later gives the map to her French maid, Else, for safekeeping. Ledoux sees the transaction, however, and kidnaps Else, taking the map. Ledoux later kidnaps Xyethia. Cal rescues Else and Xyethia, recovers the map, and turns Ledoux over to the law. Cal and Xyethia fall in love. *Archeologists. Cowboys. Housemaids. French. Aztec Indians. Kidnaping. Treasure. Mexico. Documentation.*

BUCKING THE BARRIER **F2.0671**

Fox Film Corp. 1 Apr **1923** [c29 May 1923; LP18993]. Si; b&w. 35mm. 5 reels, 4,566 ft.

Pres by William Fox. *Dir* Colin Campbell. *Scen* Jack Strumwasser. *Story* George Goodchild. *Photog* Lucien Andriot.

Cast: Dustin Farnum *(Kit Carew)*, Arline Pretty *(Blanche Cavendish)*, Leon Bary *(Luke Cavendish)*, Colin Chase *(Frank Farfax)*, Hayford Hobbs *(Cyril Cavendish)*, Sidney D'Albrook *(Tyson)*.

Melodrama. Kit Carew leaves his Alaskan mine and journeys to England to take possession of the fortune willed him by his friend Frank Farfax. Kit finds, however, that he must defend himself against Farfax' step-brothers, while at the same time he falls in love with Blanche Cavendish, Farfax' step-sister. Blanche misunderstands Kit's motives; Kit then decides that Blanche doesn't love him and returns to Alaska without his inheritance. Some years later the couple are reunited in Alaska. *Miners. Inheritance. Alaska. England.*

BUCKING THE LINE **F2.0672**

Fox Film Corp. 6 Nov **1921** [c6 Nov 1921; LP17254]. Si; b&w. 35mm. 5 reels, 4,544 ft.

Pres by William Fox. *Dir* Carl Harbaugh. *Photog* Frank B. Good.

Cast: Maurice B. Flynn *(John Montague Smith)*, Molly Malone *(Corona Baldwin)*, Norman Selby *(Jerry, Monty's pal)*, Edwin B. Tilton *(Col. Dexter Baldwin)*, Kathryn McGuire *(Vera Richlander)*, J. Farrell MacDonald *(Dave Kinsey)*, James Farley *(Watrous Dunham)*, Leslie Casey *(Tucker Jibbey)*, George Kerby *(Rand Barlow)*.

Melodrama. Source: Francis Lynde, *The Real Man* (New York, 1915). John Montague Smith, a smalltown bank cashier forced to leave town when he is accused of bad business practices, catches a freight for the West. He rescues Jerry, a tramp, and both apply for work on a railroad construction gang but are refused employment by the foreman, Rand Barlow. John rescues Corona Baldwin from a runaway handcar, and as a result her father gives both men jobs. When John discovers that Barlow and Kinsey are delaying construction work to cause Colonel Baldwin to lose his franchise, he is promoted to foreman; and in spite of obstacles he completes the road. Barlow opens a drawbridge over which John is about to drive the first train, but he is foiled by Jerry. John rescues Kinsey and emerges from the battle victorious with Corona in his arms. *Construction foremen. Railroads. Business management.*

BUCKING THE TIGER **F2.0673**

Selznick Pictures. *Dist* Select Pictures. Apr **1921** [c18 Apr 1921; LP16461]. Si; b&w. 35mm. 6 reels, 5,533-5,550 ft.

Pres by Lewis J. Selznick. *Dir* Henry Kolker. *Scen* Edward J. Montagne. *Photog* Jake Badaracco.

Cast: Conway Tearle *(Ritchie MacDonald)*, Winifred Westover *(Emily Dwyer)*, Gladden James *(Ralph Graham)*, Helene Montrose *(Skaguay Belle)*, Harry Lee *(Andy Walsh)*, George A. Wright *(The Count)*, Templar Saxe *(William Hillyer)*.

Northwest melodrama. Source: Achmed Abdullah, *Bucking the Tiger* (New York, 1917). At Eslick's Grand Palace Hotel in Circle City, Alaska, five Klondike derelicts hold council to decide on some means of recouping their depleted finances. Emily Dwyer, who has come north to marry Graham following news of his success, is discouraged but is saved from suicide by MacDonald, a former football star. At his suggestion, they raise the money for the premium on one insurance policy, to be taken on the life of whoever draws the ace in faro: he would commit suicide at the end of a year, and the other four would become beneficiaries. MacDonald draws the fatal card, then, discovering a gold vein in his mine claim, he abandons the insurance plan. All then find prosperity with MacDonald, who develops a love affair with Emily. *Derelicts. Insurance. Suicide. Mine claims. Alaska.*

BUCKING THE TRUTH (Blue Streak Western) **F2.0674**
Universal Pictures. 18 Jul **1926** [c12 May 1926; LP22723]. Si; b&w. 35mm. 5 reels, 4,305 ft.
Pres by Carl Laemmle. *Dir* Milburn Morante. *Story-Cont* Jay Inman Kane. *Photog* Richard Fryer.
Cast: Pete Morrison *(Slim Duane)*, Brinsley Shaw *("Coarse Gold" Charlie)*, Bruce Gordon *(Matt Holden)*, William La Roche *(Eben Purkiss)*, Charles Whittaker *(Red Sang)*, Ione Reed *(Anne)*, O. Robertson *(Tom Bailey)*, Vester Pegg *(Sheriff Findlay)*.
Western melodrama. Slim Duane, a wandering cowpuncher in search of his stolen horse, is forced by a fugitive to exchange clothes and finds himself stranded and broke in a town. He is seen by Eben Purkiss, who mistakenly identifies him as the fugitive (Matt Holden) and rides for the sheriff. At Ma Findlay's, Holden, identifying himself as Slim Duane, joins the sheriff's posse. Anne, a restaurant owner who gives Slim a meal, warns him of the posse, and he tricks them into following his horse and escapes from Holden. With the aid of "Coarse Gold" Charlie, Slim finds a smugglers' hideout where the real sheriff, Findlay, is being held captive. Slim prevents the lynching of Holden and is happily united with Anne. *Fugitives. Cowboys. Sheriffs. Smugglers. Posses. Personal identity.*

BUFFALO BILL ON THE U. P. TRAIL **F2.0675**
Dist Sunset Productions. 1 Mar **1926**. Si; b&w. 35mm. 6 reels, 5,104 ft.
Pres by Anthony J. Xydias. *Dir* Frank S. Mattison. *Photog* Bert Longenecker. *Tech Dir* Jack Pierce. *Film Ed* Al Martin.
Cast: Roy Stewart *(Buffalo Bill)*, Kathryn McGuire *(Millie)*, Cullen Landis *(Gordon Kent, boyhood sweetheart of Millie)*, Sheldon Lewis *(Maj. Mike Connel, commander of Post Ellsworth)*, Earl Metcalfe *(sheriff)*, Milburn Morante *("Hearts" Farrel, gambler)*, Hazel Howell *(Katy Hale)*, Fred De Silva *(Bill Henry, the "other man")*, Felix Whitefeather *(White Spear, only son of the chief)*, Jay Morley *(Jim Hale, parson of the plains)*, Eddie Harris *(Mose, a runaway slave)*, Dick La Reno *(William Rose, owner of the overland)*, Harry Fenwick *(Dr. Roy Webb, town-locating agent)*.
Western melodrama. Winding its way across western Kansas, a wagon train led by Gordon Kent includes Katy Hale, who is running away from her husband with Bill Henry, and Buffalo Bill, who is seen performing kindnesses for an Indian and for a runaway slave. Six months later Buffalo Bill learns that the railroad is coming through, and he plans with William Rose to build a new town on its route. However, when they refuse train-town locator Roy Webb's offer to "buy in," the latter threatens to change the route, and the entire town moves to a new site, which crosses Kent's property. Enraged, Kent and Buffalo Bill get into a fight with the railroad surveyors, and White Spear starts a buffalo stampede, which endangers Kent's fiancée, Millie. Kent rescues Millie, Buffalo Bill diverts the stampede, Webb agrees to purchase the property rights, and Katy is reunited with her husband. *Indians of North America. Slaves—Runaway. Property rights. Wagon trains. Townsites. William Frederick Cody. Union Pacific Railroad. Stampedes. Buffalo.*
Note: Also known as *With Buffalo Bill on the U. P. Trail.*

THE BUGLE CALL (Reissue) **F2.0676**
Kay-Bee Pictures. *Dist* Tri-Stone Pictures. **1924.** Si; b&w. 35mm. 5 reels.
Note: A "re-edited and re-titled" William Collier, Jr., film originally released by Triangle Film Corp. on 4 Jun 1916.

THE BUGLE CALL **F2.0677**
Metro-Goldwyn-Mayer Pictures. 6 Aug **1927** [c1 Aug 1927; LP24253]. Si; b&w. 35mm. 6 reels, 5,821 ft.
Dir Edward Sedgwick. *Titl* Frederic Hatton, Fanny Hatton. *Adapt* Josephine Lovett. *Story* C. Gardner Sullivan. *Photog* André Barlatier. *Sets* Cedric Gibbons, David Townsend. *Film Ed* Sam S. Zimbalist. *Wardrobe* André-ani.
Cast: Jackie Coogan *(Billy Randolph)*, Claire Windsor *(Alice Tremayne)*, Herbert Rawlinson *(Captain Randolph)*, Tom O'Brien *(Sergeant Doolan)*, Harry Todd *(Corporal Jansen)*, Nelson McDowell *(Luke)*, Sarah Padden *(Luke's wife)*.
Adventure drama. "Romantic tale of Indians and adventure. Deals with life in a frontier cavalry post in the early '70's. Story of the heart of a motherless child, a bugle boy, and a stepmother, who tries to supplant the mother who lived in his memory." (*Motion Picture News Booking Guide*, 13:23, Oct 1927.) *Indians of North America. Orphans. Stepmothers. Frontier and pioneer life. United States Army—Cavalry.*

BUILT FOR RUNNING **F2.0678**
William Steiner Productions. Sep **1924.** Si; b&w. 35mm. 5 reels.
Cast: Leo Maloney.
Western melodrama(?). No information about the nature of this film has been found.

THE BULL DOGGER **F2.0679**
Norman Film Manufacturing Co. **1922.** Si; b&w. 35mm. 5 reels.
Cast: Bill Pickett.
Western melodrama. No information about the precise nature of this film has been found. *Cowboys. Negro life. Bulldogging.*

BULLDOG COURAGE **F2.0680**
Clinton Productions. *Dist* Russell Productions. Aug **1922.** Si; b&w. 35mm. 5 reels, 4,900 ft.
Dir Edward Kull. *Story* Jeanne Poe. *Photog* Harry Neumann. *Art Dir* Louis E. Myers. *Film Ed* Fred Allen.
Cast: George Larkin *(Jimmy Brent)*, Bessie Love *(Gloria Phillips)*, Albert MacQuarrie *(John Morton)*, Karl Silvera *(Smokey Evans)*, Frank Whitman *(Big Bob Phillips)*, Bill Patton *(Sheriff Webber)*, Barbara Tennant *(Mary Allen)*.
Western melodrama. John Morton sends his nephew, college athlete Jimmy Brent, to Wyoming with a promise of $50,000 if he will find and administer a beating to Bob Phillips, Morton's onetime rival for the hand of Mary Allen. Jimmy finds Phillips, but he hesitates to go through with his "job" when he falls in love with the rancher's daughter, Gloria. His way to happiness is blocked, however, by ranch hand Smokey Evans, who causes Phillips to suspect Jimmy of rustling. As a result, Jimmy does get in a fight with Phillips, rounds up Evans and his fellow rustlers, and wins Gloria. *Uncles. Ranchers. Rustling. Wyoming.*

BULLDOG DRUMMOND **F2.0681**
Samuel Goldwyn. *Dist* United Artists. 3 Aug **1929** [c18 Jul 1929; LP593]. Sd (Movietone); b&w. 35mm. 10 reels, 8,376 ft.
Dir F. Richard Jones. *Scen* Wallace Smith, Sidney Howard. *Screen Dial* Sidney Howard. *Photog* George Barnes, Gregg Toland. *Art Dir* William Cameron Menzies. *Film Ed* Viola Lawrence, Frank Lawrence. *Song: "(I Says to Myself Says I) There's the One for Me"* Jack Yellen, Harry Akst. *Asst Dir* Paul Jones.
Cast: Ronald Colman *(Bulldog Drummond)*, Joan Bennett *(Phyllis)*, Lilyan Tashman *(Erma)*, Montagu Love *(Peterson)*, Lawrence Grant *(Dr. Lakington)*, Wilson Benge *(Danny)*, Claude Allister *(Algy)*, Adolph Milar *(Marcovitch)*, Charles Sellon *(Travers)*, Tetsu Komai *(Chong)*.
Action melodrama. Source: "Sapper" and Gerald Du Maurier, *Bulldog Drummond; a Play in Four Acts* (London, 1925). Bored with civilian life in London after World War I, Bulldog Drummond, a young British Army officer, advertises for adventure. His advertisement is answered by Phyllis Benton, a young American who wants Drummond to free her uncle, Hiram J. Travers, from an insane asylum where he is being held prisoner by Dr. Lakington, a sadistic physician, and his confederate, Peterson. Lakington's intention is to torture Travers into signing away his fortune. After several thrilling experiences, Drummond and his friend Algy kidnap Travers, unconscious in a drug-induced coma, and thereby he wins Phyllis' love and Travers' gratitude. *Veterans. Uncles. Physicians. Sadists. Thrill-seeking. Extortion. Insane asylums. Great Britain—Army. London.*

BULLDOG PLUCK **F2.0682**
Bob Custer Productions. *Dist* Film Booking Offices of America. 12 Jun **1927** [c1 Jun 1927; LP24031]. Si; b&w. 35mm. 5 reels, 5,013 ft.
Pres by Joseph P. Kennedy. *Supv* Jesse J. Goldburg. *Dir* Jack Nelson. *Scen* Evanne Blasdale, Madeline Matzen. *Photog* Ernest Miller. *Asst Dir* Paul Stanhope.
Cast: Bob Custer *(Bob Hardwick)*, Viora Daniels *(Jess Haviland)*, Bobby Nelson *(Danny Haviland)*, Richard R. Neill *(Destin)*, Walter Maly *(Gillen)*, Victor Metzetti *(Curley Le Baste)*, Hugh Saxon *("Pa" Haviland)*.
Western melodrama. Source: W. Bert Foster, "Hardwick of Hambone," in *Ace-High Magazine*. The Haviland family, consisting of Pa, Ma, Jess,

and little Dan, are traveling west, and they camp overnight near the town of Hambone. Bob Hardwick, rancher and owner of the Jupiter Pluvious Gambling Hall, compels them to leave but does rescue them from an impending flood. Later, Jess goes to the gambling hall with the family money, and Bob manipulates the game so that she wins heavily. Destin "sells" a ranch he does not own to Jess, and his gang stampede a herd of wild horses, causing the death of Pa Haviland. A vigilante committee headed by Bob and Curley determine to clean out the undesirables, and a bitter fight ensues. Destin wounds Bob in a robbery, but Bob overtakes him and is victorious in the struggle; he is duly united with Jess in marriage. *Ranchers. Homesteaders. Vigilantes. Gambling. Floods. Stampedes.*

THE BULLET MARK **F2.0683**

Fred J. McConnell Productions. *Dist* Pathé Exchange. 25 Mar **1928** [c12 Feb 1928; LP24982]. Si; b&w. 35mm. 5 reels, 4,550 ft.

Dir Stuart Paton. *Scen* Joseph Anthony Roach. *Titl* Jack Kelly. *Story* Harry Wood. *Camera* Allan Davey. *Film Ed* Jack Kelly.

Cast: Joseph W. Girard, Albert J. Smith, Lincoln Plumer, Margaret Gray, Gladys McConnell, Jack Donovan.

Western melodrama. Cal Murdock, a hunter of wild horses, incurs Curly's spite when he takes over his position of ranch foreman. Learning Cal is to deposit the funds from the sale of his herd of horses in the local bank, Curly holds up the bank while Cal is there, leaving Cal in a web of circumstantial evidence. Cal escapes to the Harrington house, where Alice, the ranch owner's daughter, misinforms the posse of his whereabouts. Cal proves his innocence and Curly's guilt and becomes his boss's son-in-law. *Ranch foremen. Posses. Bank robberies. Frameup.*

BULLETS AND JUSTICE **F2.0684**

J. Charles Davis Productions. 18 Feb **1929.** Si; b&w. 35mm. 5 reels, 4,178 ft.

Cast: Art Acord, Carol Lane.

Western melodrama(?). No information about the nature of this film has been found.

BUNTY PULLS THE STRINGS **F2.0685**

Goldwyn Pictures. Jan **1921** [trade review; c28 Nov 1920; LP15851]. Si; b&w. 35mm. 7 reels.

Dir-Supv Reginald Barker. *Scen* J. G. Hawks, Charles Kenyon. *Photog* Percy Hilburn.

Cast: Leatrice Joy *(Bunty)*, Russell Simpson *(Tammas Biggar)*, Raymond Hatton *(Weelum)*, Cullen Landis *(Rab)*, Casson Ferguson *(Jeemy)*, Josephine Crowell *(Susie Simpson)*, Edythe Chapman *(Eelen Dunlap)*, Roland Rushton *(minister)*, Georgia Woodthorpe *(Mrs. Drummon)*, Sadie Gordon *(Maggie)*, Otto Hoffman *(beadle)*.

Comedy-drama. Source: Graham Moffat, *Bunty Pulls the Strings, a Scottish Comedy in Three Acts* (London opening: 4 Jul 1911). Bunty Biggar, sister of Rab and Jeemy and daughter of Tammas, a stern church elder in a small Scotch village, subtly controls all three through diplomatic tactics. Jeemy confesses to having robbed a bank and begs his father to replace the money, which he does with money left with him for safekeeping by Susie Simpson, a spinster interested in Tammas. Susie, who overhears a telephone conversation between Tammas and Eelen, a friend from Tammas' past, hears about the misuse of her money and demands it back; when it is not returned, she disgraces him in church. Bunty intercedes and returns the money by borrowing an equal sum from Weelum, whom she later marries in a double wedding—the other couple: Tammas and Eelen. *Churchmen. Spinsters. Brother-sister relationship. Filial relations. Bank robberies. Weddings. Scotland.*

BURBRIDGE'S AFRICAN GORILLA HUNT *see* **THE GORILLA HUNT**

THE BURDEN OF RACE **F2.0686**

Reol Productions. ca10 Dec **1921** [New York State]. Si; b&w. 35mm. 6 reels.

Cast: Percy Verwayen, Edna Morton, Lawrence Chenault, Elizabeth Williams, Mabel Young, Arthur Ray.

Drama. At a great university, a young Negro, who excels in both academic and athletic pursuits, falls in love with a white girl. After graduation, he becomes extremely successful in the world of business, finding in this girl a constant source of inspiration. *Negroes. Students. Businessmen. Race relations. College life.*

BURIED GOLD **F2.0687**

Anchor Film Distributors. *Dist* Rayart Pictures. Apr **1926.** Si; b&w. 35mm. 5 reels, 4,643 ft.

Dir J. P. McGowan.

Cast: Al Hoxie.

Western melodrama. "Fighting cowpuncher aids ranch owner in recovering gold stolen by discharged ranch foreman and associates. Weds the ranch owner." (*Motion Picture News Booking Guide*, 11:23, Oct 1926.) *Cowboys. Ranchers. Ranch foremen. Gold.*

BURIED TREASURE **F2.0688**

Cosmopolitan Productions. *For* Famous Players–Lasky. *Dist* Paramount Pictures. 10 Apr **1921** [c10 Apr 1921; LP16593]. Si; b&w. 35mm. 6-7 reels, 6,964 ft.

Dir-Writ George D. Baker. *Photog* Hal Rosson. *Set Dsgn* Joseph Urban.

Cast: Marion Davies *(Pauline Vandermuellen)*, Norman Kerry *(Dr. John Grant)*, Anders Randolf *(William Vandermuellen)*, Edith Shayne *(Mrs. Vandermuellen)*, Earl Schenck *(Joeffrey Vandermuellen)*, John Charles *(Duc de Chavannes)*, Thomas Findlay *(The Captain)*.

Fantasy-melodrama. Source: Frederick Britten Austin, "Buried Treasure," in *On the Borderland* (Garden City, New York, 1923). A prolog shows the soul of Pauline Vandermuellen reincarnated in various personalities from one generation to another. In the action proper, Pauline tells her parents, while she is in a trance, of a romance she experienced in Spain years before. Annoyed at his daughter's preference for young Dr. Grant, her father sends her on a Caribbean cruise. During another dream state she describes the general location of a buried treasure; and when her greedy father takes a search party to the island indicated, she misleads him and takes her lover instead to the location revealed in her dream. After finding the treasure, he wins her father's consent to their marriage. *Reincarnation. Treasure. Spain. Caribbean. Trances.*

BURN 'EM UP BARNES **F2.0689**

Mastodon Films. *Dist* Affiliated Distributors. 1 Aug **1921.** Si; b&w. 35mm. 6 reels, 5,600 ft.

Pres by C. C. Burr. *Dir* George André Beranger, Johnny Hines. *Scen* Raymond L. Schrock. *Photog* Ted Beasley, Hal Young, Ned Van Buren.

Cast: Johnny Hines *("Burn 'Em Up Barnes")*, Edmund Breese *("King" Cole)*, George Fawcett *(an eccentric tramp)*, Betty Carpenter *(Madge Thompson)*, J. Barney Sherry *(Whitney Barnes)*, Matthew Betts *(Ed Scott)*, Richard Thorpe *(Stephen Thompson)*, Julia Swayne Gordon *(Mrs. Whitney Barnes)*, Dorothy Leeds *(Betty Scott)*, Harry Fraser *(Francis Jones)*, "Billy Boy" Swinton *(The Baby)*.

Melodramatic farce. "'Burn 'em up Barnes,' the youthful and speed mad son of a millionaire manufacturer of high-powered motor cars, ... leaves home when his father taunts him on his indifference to business and sneers at his ability to do anything useful. A band of crooks waylay him, rob him of his clothes and throw him, unconscious, into an empty freight car, which happens to be carrying a gang of tramps, who adopt him as one of their number. The idea appeals to Barnes and he goes with them on a career of adventure which lands him in a small town where there is a very pretty girl needing his assistance, and he gives it. Of course, there are complications, because the village Beau Brummel pays court to the young lady and resents the intrusion of a tramp; and things look mighty dark for 'Burn 'em up' Barnes when he is arrested for kidnapping a baby. Everything comes out all right in the end but there is a surprise finish." (*Moving Picture World*, 10 Sep 1921, p211.) *Tramps. Automobile manufacturers. Filial relations. Automobile racing. Wealth. Kidnaping.*

BURNING BRIDGES **F2.0690**

Charles R. Rogers Productions. *Dist* Pathé Exchange. 30 Sep **1928** [c10 Sep 1928; LP25609]. Si; b&w. 35mm. 6 reels, 5,400 ft.

Dir James P. Hogan. *Scen* Edward J. Meagher. *Story* Jack Boyle. *Photog* Sol Polito. *Film Ed* Harry Marker.

Cast: Harry Carey *(Jim Whitely/Bob Whitely)*, Kathleen Collins *(Ellen Wilkins)*, William N. Bailey *(Jim Black)*, Dave Kirby *(Crabs)*, Raymond Wells *(Slabs)*, Edward Phillips *(Tommy Wilkins)*, Florence Midgely *(Widow Wilkins)*, Henry A. Barrows *(Ed Wilson)*, Sam Allen *(Zach McCarthy, M. D.)*.

Western melodrama. Bob Whitely, a shell-shocked veteran who has escaped from a sanitarium, holds up the Express, and his twin brother, Jim, is arrested for the crime; in an attempt to find his brother, Jim escapes from jail soon afterward. Jim Black, the sheriff, holds up the local and kills Tommy Wilkins, the brother of Jim's fiancée, Ellen. Jim is thought to be the murderer, and the posse chases him; he makes his escape by a daring leap onto the roof of the Express. A railroad trestle is set afire by Black, and Jim saves the passengers on the train from a terrible fate by uncoupling the engine from the rest of the train. Black is revealed as the real murderer; Bob is cured of his shell shock; and Jim renews his courtship with Ellen. *Veterans. Twins. Brothers. Sheriffs. Shell shock. Amnesia. Murder. Mistaken identity. Jailbreaks. Train robberies.*

BURNING DAYLIGHT **F2.0691**

First National Pictures. 11 Mar **1928** [c14 Mar 1928; LP25063]. Si; b&w. 35mm. 7 reels, 6,500 ft.

Pres by Richard A. Rowland. *Prod* Wid Gunning. *Dir* Charles J. Brabin. *Adapt-Cont* Louis Stevens. *Titl* Dwinelle Benthall, Rufus McCosh. *Camera* Sol Polito. *Film Ed* Frank Ware.

Cast: Milton Sills *(Burning Daylight)*, Doris Kenyon *("The Virgin")*, Arthur Stone *("French Louie")*, Big Boy Williams *("English Harry")*, Lawford Davidson *(Morton)*, Jane Winton *(Martha Fairbee)*, Stuart Holmes *(Blake)*, Edmund Breese *(John Dossett)*, Howard Truesdale *(Letton)*, Frank Hagney *(Johnson)*, Harry Northrup *(The Stranger)*.

Drama. Source: Jack London, *Burning Daylight* (New York, 1910). After making his fortune in Alaskan real estate, Burning Daylight loses it all in San Francisco to a group of investment sharks. He forces them at gunpoint to return his millions, pays off his own small investors, and returns, broke, with his sweetheart to Alaska. *Swindlers. Real estate business. San Francisco. Alaska.*

BURNING GOLD **F2.0692**

Dist Ellbee Pictures. 18 Feb **1927** [New York premiere]. Si; b&w. 35mm. 6 reels, 5,428 ft.

Pres by W. T. Lackey. *Dir* Jack Noble. *Story* Stuart Paton. *Photog* Harry Davis.

Cast: Herbert Rawlinson *(Bob Roberts)*, Shirley Palmer *(Nan Preston)*, Sheldon Lewis *(James Clark)*, Nils Keith *(Preston)*, J. C. Fowler, Mildred Harris.

Melodrama. "The rightful owner of a productive oil field is fleeced by a slick promoter. There is an innocent third party roped into the scheme who, when he learns the true state of affairs, turns the tables on the smart alec and saves the day for the true owner who very appropriately has a good looking daughter to offer as a reward." (*Film Daily*, 27 Feb 1927, p8.) There are some shots of an oil field ablaze apparently excerpted from newsreels. *Oil business. Property rights. Fraud. Fires. Oil fields.*

BURNING SANDS **F2.0693**

Famous Players–Lasky. *Dist* Paramount Pictures. ca3 Sep **1922** [New York premiere; released 15 Oct; c5 Sep 1922; LP18216]. Si; b&w. 35mm. 7 reels, 6,919 ft.

Pres by Jesse L. Lasky. *Dir* George Melford. *Adapt* Olga Printzlau, Waldemar Young. *Photog* Bert Glennon.

Cast: Wanda Hawley *(Muriel Blair, an English girl)*, Milton Sills *(Daniel Lane, a philosopher)*, Louise Dresser *(Kate Bindane, Muriel's friend)*, Jacqueline Logan *(Lizette, a dancer)*, Robert Cain *(Robert Barthampton, an English official)*, Fenwick Oliver *(Mr. Bindane)*, Winter Hall *(governor)*, Harris Gordon *(secretary)*, Albert Roscoe *(Ibrihim, an Arab)*, Cecil Holland *(old sheik)*, Joe Ray *(Hussein)*.

Melodrama. Source: Arthur Weigall, *Burning Sands* (New York, 1921). Daniel Lane, who prefers the desert to living in England, becomes involved in the struggles of an old sheik against the plotting by his son and Robert Barthampton. Muriel meets Lane at an embassy ball and feels compelled to visit him in the desert, partly because she has been told that Lizette is his mistress. On her second visit the oasis camp is attacked, Barthampton forces his attentions on Muriel and is killed by Lane, and Lizette is killed just after she explains that she had seen Lane only to give him helpful information. The British Army comes to the rescue, and Muriel and Lane are reconciled. *Sheiks. Dancers. Filial relations. Deserts. Great Britain—Army.*

BURNING THE WIND **F2.0694**

Universal Pictures. 10 Feb **1929** [c4 May 1928; LP25226]. Si; b&w. 35mm. 6 reels, 5,202 ft.

Dir Henry MacRae, Herbert Blache. *Scen? (see note)* George Plympton, George Morgan, Raymond L. Schrock. *Titl* Gardner Bradford. *Photog* Harry Neumann, Ray Ramsey. *Film Ed? (see note)* Maurice Pivar, Thomas Malloy, Gene Havlick.

Cast: Hoot Gibson *(Richard Gordon, Jr.)*, Virginia Brown Faire *(Maria Valdes)*, Cesare Gravina *(Don Ramón Valdes)*, Boris Karloff *(Pug Doran)*, Pee Wee Holmes *(Peewee)*, Robert Homans *(Richard Gordon, Sr.)*, George Grandee *(Manuel Valdes)*.

Romantic melodrama. Source: William MacLeod Raine, *A Daughter of the Dons; a Story of New Mexico Today* (New York, c1914). Close friends Richard Gordon and Don Ramón Valdes attempt to unite their children—Richard, Jr., and Maria. The old men set a "trap" and wait in seclusion for the results. The youngsters fall into it; and after several complications, including Junior's rescue of Maria when she is kidnaped, wedding bells ring. *Ranchers. Friendship. Ranch life. Marriage—Arranged. New Mexico.*

Note: Sources disagree in crediting film editor and scenarist.

THE BURNING TRAIL **F2.0695**

Universal Pictures. 10 May **1925** [c19 Feb 1925; LP21167]. Si; b&w. 35mm. 5 reels, 4,783 ft.

Dir Arthur Rosson. *Adapt* Isadore Bernstein. *Photog* Gilbert Warrenton.

Cast: William Desmond *("Smiling Bill" Flannigan)*, Albert J. Smith *("Texas")*, Mary McIvor *(Nell Loring)*, James Corey *("Black" Loring)*, Jack Dougherty *(John Corliss)*, Edmund Cobb *(Tommy Corliss)*, Dolores Roussey *(Esther Ramsey)*, Harry Tenbrook *(Reginald Cholmondeley)*.

Western melodrama. Source: Henry Herbert Knibbs, *Sundown Slim* (New York, 1915). "Smiling Bill" Flannigan swears off prizefighting and heads west when his opponent dies after being knocked out. Obtaining a job as a cook on a ranch, he has several run-ins with "Texas," a rough character, which lead to their dismissal. Texas gets a job at John Corliss' ranch, quickly incurring his animosity by showing Tommy, John's younger brother, how to drive cattle over sheepgrazing lands owned by "Black" Loring, whose daughter John loves from afar. Bill arrives at the sheepman's ranch just as Tommy and Texas attack. A fire results, and Bill saves the sheepman's daughter and Corliss' cousin—leading to a double romance. *Prizefighters. Cooks. Ranchers. Cattlemen. Sheepmen. Land rights. Fires.*

BURNING UP **F2.0696**

Paramount Famous Lasky Corp. 1 Feb **1930** [c30 Jan 1930; LP1044]. Sd (Movietone); b&w. 35mm. 6 reels, 5,251 ft. [Also si; 5,338 ft.]

Dir A. Edward Sutherland. *Dial Dir* Perry Ivins. *Story-Scen-Dial* William Slavens McNutt, Grover Jones. *Photog* Allen Siegler. *Film Ed* Richard H. Digges, Jr. *Sd* Earl Hayman.

Cast: Richard Arlen *(Lou Larrigan)*, Mary Brian *(Ruth Morgan)*, Francis McDonald *("Bullet" McGhan)*, Sam Hardy *("Windy" Wallace)*, Charles Sellon *(James R. Morgan)*, Tully Marshall *(Dave Gentry)*.

Action melodrama. Lou Larrigan, employed by Dave Gentry in automobile sales, is ambitious to become a race driver like his partner, "Bullet," who has been barred from the track for causing an accident. When Dave goes broke, he and Bullet accept an offer from "Windy" Wallace, a crooked promoter, to frame a race. Meanwhile, Lou is booked into various races, becomes successful, and wins the love of Ruth Morgan, daughter of the town banker. When Bullet wrecks his car attempting to break a record, a race is arranged between Lou and Bullet; and Windy gets a wealthy man to bet $25,000 on Lou. Learning of the plot, Lou confronts the villains and alarms them by predicting that he will win the race. Bullet deliberately tries to run him off the track, but Lou evades Bullet and in a thrilling finish wins the race. *Salesmen. Swindlers. Automobiles. Automobile racing.*

BURNING UP BROADWAY **F2.0697**

Sterling Pictures. Feb **1928** [New York premiere; c19 Jan 1928; LP24889]. Si; b&w. 35mm. 6 reels, 5,245-6,000 ft. [Also 5 reels, 4,230 ft.]

Prod Joe Rock. *Dir* Phil Rosen. *Scen-Titl* Frances Guihan. *Story* Norman Houston. *Photog* Herbert Kirkpatrick. *Film Ed* Leotta Whytock. *Mus Cues* Michael Hoffman.

Cast: Helene Costello *(Floss)*, Robert Frazer *(Bob Travers)*, Sam Hardy *(Spike)*, Ernest Hilliard *(Harry Wells)*, Max Asher *(Nick)*, Jack Rich *(Slim)*.

Underworld drama. Harry Wells, a New Yorker, takes his friend Bob Travers, a westerner visiting the city, to a cafe for an evening of pleasure. When Bob becomes interested in Floss, the chief chorus girl, he incurs the wrath of Spike, owner of the cafe, who is in love with her. The next night Bob goes again to the cafe, where to their mutual chagrin he meets Harry. Spike, it is revealed, is a bootlegger in partnership with Nick, coowner of the cafe. They find Bob snooping around, knock him out, and, taking Floss, whom they suspect of knowing too much, go off to run a big shipment of liquor. Harry, with a gang of roughnecks in his car, rescues Bob and trails Spike. When the liquor is being unloaded, Harry's men—all revenue agents disguised as hijackers—start a fight, and Bob rescues Floss. It is revealed that Harry and Floss are detectives pursuing Spike and his gang, and Bob and Floss find happiness in each other. *Chorus girls. Detectives. Bootleggers. Revenue agents. Rumrunners. Prohibition. New York City.*

BURNING WORDS **F2.0698**

Universal Pictures. 27 May **1923** [c19 May 1923; LP18977]. Si; b&w. 35mm. 5 reels, 4,944 ft.

Pres by Carl Laemmle. *Dir* Stuart Paton. *Story-Scen* Harrison Jacobs. *Photog* William Thornley.

Cast: Roy Stewart *(David Darby)*, Laura La Plante *(Mary Malcolm)*, Harold Goodwin *(Ross Darby)*, Edith Yorke *(Mother Darby)*, Alfred Fisher *(Father Darby)*, William Welsh *(John Malcolm)*, Noble Johnson *(Bad Pierre)*, Eve Southern *(Nan Bishop)*, Harry Carter *("Slip" Martin)*, George McDaniels *(Sargeant Chase)*.

Melodrama. Keeping in mind that "Greater love hath no man than this, that he lay down his life for a friend" and his mother's admonition to watch over their younger son, David Darby keeps his brother, Ross, out of trouble while both are serving in the Northwest Mounted Police. When Ross is accused of the murder of "Slip" Martin, David takes the blame, but dancehall girl Mary Malcolm proves Ross's guilt. Ross is executed, and David marries Mary. *Brothers. Dancehall girls. Murder. Capital punishment. Northwest Mounted Police.*

BURNT FINGERS **F2.0699**

J. C. Barnstyn Productions. *Dist* Pathé Exchange. 20 Feb **1927** [c31 Jan 1927; LU23608]. Si; b&w. 35mm. 6 reels, 5,854 ft.

Pres by J. C. Barnstyn. *Dir* Maurice Campbell. *Story-Scen* Maurice Campbell, G. Marion Burton. *Photog* Harry Stradling.

Cast: Eileen Percy *(Anne Cabell)*, Ivan Doline *(Stockmar)*, Edna Murphy *(Vera)*, Wilfred Lucas *(Lord Cumberly)*, George O'Hara *(Dick)*, Jane Jennings *(Mrs. Cabell)*, J. Moy Bennett *(Mr. Cabell)*, Jimmie Ward.

Mystery melodrama. Anne Cabell, a popular hostess at the Cafe Justine and the dancing partner of Bernard Stockmar, a ladies' man, learns that her friend Vera fears love letters she wrote to Stockmar will be used to blackmail her; and Anne tries to recover them. Stockmar catches her searching his apartment and is shot by an unknown assailant; a strange neighbor helps her escape from the scene of the murder. Anne is traced by the police, and her fiancé, Dick Farnham, believes her guilty of the crime. Her benefactor, Lord Cumberly of the Foreign Office, provides an alibi for her and proves that the dancer and his murderer were spies for an unfriendly government. The murderer's confession frees Anne, who is happily reunited with Dick. *Cafe hostesses. Spies. Blackmail. Murder. England. Great Britain—Foreign Office.*

THE BUSH LEAGUER **F2.0700**

Warner Brothers Pictures. 20 Aug **1927** [c8 Aug 1927; LP24278]. Si; b&w. 35mm. 7 reels, 6,281 ft.

Dir Howard Bretherton. *Scen* Harvey Gates. *Story* Charles Gordon Saxton. *Camera* Norbert Brodin. *Asst Dir* Eddie Sowders.

Cast: Monte Blue *(Buchanan "Specs" White)*, Clyde Cook *(Skeeter McKinnon)*, Leila Hyams *(Alice Hobbs)*, William Demarest *(John Gilroy)*, Richard Tucker *(Wallace Ramsey)*, Bud Marshall *(Stetson)*, Tom Dempsey *(The "Parson")*, Wilfred North *(Stokes)*, William Wilson *(William [Lefty] Murphy)*, Violet Palmer *(Marie [Alice's maid])*, Rodney Hildebrand *(detective)*.

Comedy-drama. Thomas Buchanan "Specs" White, a garage-owner in an Idaho village and star pitcher on the local ball team, devotes his spare time to the development of an improved gasoline pump. "Lefty" Murphy, a league scout from Los Angeles, offers Specs a position as pitcher, and Specs accepts. Though at first discouraged, Specs is spurred to success by a picture of the girl of his dreams in the newspaper, and manager Gilroy centers his hopes on the rookie pitcher. At his first game Specs suffers from "crowd fright," but the discovery that his girl is Alice Hobbs, owner of the club, adds impetus to his playing. She becomes disillusioned, thinking that Specs has surrendered to the proposal of some rival promoters, but at the last minute he proves his loyalty by blasting a home run. *Garage-keepers. Inventors. Gamblers. Baseball. Idaho. Los Angeles.*

THE BUSHMAN **F2.0701**

Denver African Expedition. *Dist* Players of Boston. 1 Jun **1927** [trade review]. Si; b&w. 35mm. [Feature length assumed.]

Dir C. Ernest Cadle. *Titl* Fred Myton. *Photog* Paul L. Hoefler. *Film Ed* Fred Myton.

Exploration film. The life of the Bushmen in the African interior is shown: their hunting and dancing. There is a scene showing the Bushmen's reaction to a portable phonograph playing an Al Jolson record containing the word "Pickaninny," which the narrator explains is the only word carried over to American idiom by Africans. Atmospheric shots of African coastal towns and long shots of herds of animals are included. *Bushmen. Phonographs. Africa. Al Jolson.*

THE BUSHRANGER **F2.0702**

Metro-Goldwyn-Mayer Pictures. 17 Nov **1928** [c10 Nov 1928; LP25815]. Si; b&w. 35mm. 7 reels, 5,220 ft.

Dir Chet Withey. *Cont* George C. Hull. *Titl* Paul Perez. *Story* Madeleine Ruthven. *Photog* Arthur Reed. *Film Ed* William Le Vanway. *Wardrobe* Lucia Coulter.

Cast: Tim McCoy *(Edward)*, Marian Douglas *(Lucy)*, Russell Simpson *(Sir Eric)*, Arthur Lubin *(Arthur)*, Ed Brady *(Black Murphy)*, Frank Baker *(Blair)*, Dale Austen *(Dale)*, Richard R. Neill *(Colonel Cavendish)*, Rosemary Cooper *(Lady Cavendish)*.

Melodrama. "Story opens in England in the last century. The dastardly brother of the hero kisses the wife of his father's friend near a set of French windows. The horrified husband rushes in to demand vengeance, and the heroic brother takes the blame. A duel results, the foolhardy husband dies and the brave brother is sent to jail for life. Then pass 12 years, the convict has escaped and become a notorious Australian bandit. His father arrives in Australia as the new High Commissioner, and complications result, in which the ward is captured by an opposition gang of robbers and saved by the boy." (*Variety,* 6 Feb 1929, p19.) *Bushrangers. Convicts. Wards. Colonial administration. Penal colonies. Self-sacrifice. England. Australia. Duels.*

THE BUSINESS OF LOVE **F2.0703**

Astor Pictures. 7 Aug **1925** [New York State license]. Si; b&w. 35mm. 6 reels, 5,998 ft.

Dir Irving Reis, Jesse Robbins. *Photog* Irving Reis.

Cast: Edward Everett Horton, Barbara Bedford, ZaSu Pitts, Tom Ricketts, Dorothy Wood, Carl Stockdale, Tom Murray, James Kelly, Stanley Taylor, Newton Hall.

Comedy(?). No information about the nature of this film has been found.

Note: This film was started at the Vitagraph Studios in March 1923 under the working title *The Crash.*

THE BUSTER **F2.0704**

Fox Film Corp. 18 Feb **1923** [c11 Feb 1923; LP19079]. Si; b&w. 35mm. 5 reels, 4,587 ft.

Pres by William Fox. *Dir* Colin Campbell. *Scen* Jack Strumwasser. *Photog* David Abel.

Cast: Dustin Farnum *(Bill Coryell)*, Doris Pawn *(Charlotte Rowland)*, Francis McDonald *(Swing)*, Gilbert Holmes *(Light Laurie)*, Lucille Hutton *(Yvonne)*.

Western melodrama. Source: William Patterson White, *The Buster* (Boston, 1920). In an attempt to tame young city girl Charlotte Rowland, Bill Coryell, a young rancher, plans a fake kidnaping party from which he is to rescue her. A bully interferes and incites her against Bill, but Charlotte discovers the ruse in time to save herself and Coryell. *Ranchers. Ranch life. Kidnaping.*

BUSTIN' THRU (Blue Streak Western) **F2.0705**

Universal Pictures. 18 Oct **1925** [c27 Jun 1925; LP21619]. Si; b&w. 35mm. 5 reels, 4,506 ft.

Dir Clifford S. Smith. *Story-Cont* Buckleigh F. Oxford. *Photog* William Nobles.

Cast: Jack Hoxie *(Jack Savage)*, Helen Lynch *(Helen Merritt)*, William Norton Bailey *(Harvey Gregg)*, Alfred Allen *(John Merritt)*, Georgie Grandee *(Rudolph Romano)*.

Western melodrama. Jack Savage, a rancher, refuses to sell his property to John Merritt, a millionaire newly interested in ranching. Jack later meets Helen Merritt and falls in love with her, not knowing that she is the wealthy man's daughter. Harvey Gregg, Merritt's lawyer, learns that there is gold on Jack's land and gains possession of the ranch on a legal technicality. Jack marries Helen and regains possession of the ranch on another technicality. *Ranchers. Millionaires. Lawyers. Gold. Land rights.*

THE BUTTER AND EGG MAN **F2.0706**

First National Pictures. 23 Sep **1928** [c9 Jul 1928; LP25435]. Si; b&w. 35mm. 7 reels, 6,300 ft.

Pres by Richard A. Rowland. *Supv* Ray Rockett. *Dir* Richard Wallace. *Titl* Gene Towne, Jack Jarmuth. *Adapt* Adelaide Heilbron. *Photog* George Folsey. *Film Ed* LeRoy Stone.

Cast: Jack Mulhall *(Peter Jones)*, Greta Nissen *(Mary Martin)*, Sam Hardy *(Joe Lehman)*, William Demarest *(Jack McLure)*, Gertrude Astor *(Fanny Lehman)*.

Comedy-drama. Source: George S. Kaufman, *The Butter and Egg Man, a Comedy in Three Acts* (New York, 1926). Smalltown boy Peter Jones, a clerk in his grandmother's Chillicothe, Ohio, hotel, fulfills his lifelong ambition to become a Broadway producer when shady producer Jack McLure sells him a play that is sure to fail. Jones falls in love with Mary Martin, his leading lady, and the play has a sellout run in New York. Successful and satisfied, Jones sells the production back to McLure and returns to Chillicothe with Mary. *Clerks. Theatrical producers. Actors. Grandmothers. Hotels. New York City—Broadway. Chillicothe (Ohio).*

BUTTERFLIES IN THE RAIN (Universal-Jewel) **F2.0707**

Universal Pictures. 20 Dec **1926** [New York premiere; released 6 Feb 1927; c16 Sep 1926; LP23136]. Si; b&w. 35mm. 8 reels, 7,319 ft.

Pres by Carl Laemmle. *Dir* Edward Sloman. *Scen* Charles Kenyon. *Photog* Gilbert Warrenton.

Cast: Laura La Plante *(Tina Carteret)*, James Kirkwood *(John Humphries)*, Robert Ober *(Emsley Charleton)*, Dorothy Cumming *(Lady Pintar)*, Oscar Beregi *(Lord Purdon)*, Grace Ogden *(Miss Flax)*, Dorothy Stokes *(Miranda)*, Edwards Davis *(Stuart Carteret)*, Edward Lockhart *(Aubrey Carteret)*, James Anderson *(Dennis Carteret)*, Clarence Thompson *(Mr. Sarling)*, Rose Burdick *(Marie Charleton)*, Ruby Lafayette *(Mrs. Humphries)*, Robert Bolder, George Periolat, Grace Gordon.

Romantic society comedy. Source: Andrew Soutar, *Butterflies in the Rain* (a novel; publication undetermined). Tina, from an aristocratic English family, believes in the new freedom for women and is an ardent follower of a group of pseudo-bohemians. While riding through the neighboring estate of John Humphries, a wealthy commoner resented by the Carteret family, she is retrieved from a fall by John and blames him for the accident; the following day, she invites him to dinner, pretending repentance, but taking pleasure in ridiculing his old-fashioned dignity. He refuses to take her to a disreputable nightclub, thus saving her from a raid; and her confidence turns to love. They are married, with the condition that Tina is to have absolute liberty; and on a Spanish holiday with bohemians, she is threatened with blackmail. John, on the brink of financial ruin, nevertheless shields his wife's reputation. At the suggestion of his friend, Lord Purdon, the plotters are brought together and identified as swindlers; Tina proves her innocence, and John is reconciled to her. *Aristocrats. Swindlers. Social classes. Women's rights. Virtue. Blackmail. Bohemianism. England. Spain.*

THE BUTTERFLY *see* **MOONLIGHT FOLLIES**

BUTTERFLY (Universal-Jewel) **F2.0708**

Universal Pictures. 12 Oct **1924** [c12 Aug 1924; LP20496]. Si; b&w. 35mm. 8 reels, 7,472 ft.

Pres by Carl Laemmle. *Dir* Clarence Brown. *Scen* Olga Printzlau. *Photog* Ben Reynolds.

Cast: Laura La Plante *(Dora Collier)*, Ruth Clifford *(Hilary Collier)*, Kenneth Harlan *(Craig Spaulding)*, Norman Kerry *(Konrad Kronski)*, Cesare Gravina *(Von Mandescheid)*, Margaret Livingston *(Violet Van De Wort)*, Freeman Wood *(Cecil Atherton)*, T. Roy Barnes *(Cy Dwyer)*.

Romantic drama. Source: Kathleen Norris, *Butterfly* (New York, 1923). Hilary Collier sacrifices her own career to support the musical education of her younger sister, Dora (Butterfly), even giving up the man she loves to her precocious charge. When Dora decides to leave her husband for an eminent musician, Kronski—who is in love with Hilary—bitter conflict ensues; but disaster is averted when an unexpected event reunites Dora with Craig, leaving Hilary free to marry the musician. *Musicians. Sisters. Marriage.*

THE BUTTERFLY GIRL **F2.0709**

Playgoers Pictures. *Dist* Pathé Exchange. 12 Jun **1921** [c14 May 1921; LU16533]. Si; b&w. 35mm. 5 reels.

Dir-Writ John Gorman. *Photog* René Guissart.

Cast: Marjorie Daw *(Edith Folsom)*, Fritzi Brunette *(Lorna Lear)*, King Baggot *(H. H. Van Horn)*, Jean De Briac *(John Blaine)*, Ned Whitney Warren *(Ned Lorimer)*, Lisle Darnell *(Mary Van Horn)*.

Melodrama. Young and wealthy Edith Folsom, whose highest ambition is to have a score of admirers at her feet, leaves her local boyfriend, Ned Lorimer, for the city. On the train she encounters a schoolmate, Lorna Lear, and Lorna's cousin, John Blaine, who promptly falls for her. On the night of Lorna's ball, Edith meets H. H. Van Horn, an elderly banker who brings her home in his car. Scolded by Lorna, she runs off to a hotel; then, when her money is depleted, she takes a position as Van Horn's secretary. Two days later she meets John, and they are married. When Van Horn declares his love for her and is overheard by his wife, Edith resolves to reform and take an interest in Mrs. Van Horn's social work. *Flirts. Secretaries. Bankers. Infidelity.*

BUTTERFLY RANCH *see* **BUTTERFLY RANGE**

BUTTERFLY RANGE **F2.0710**

William Steiner Productions. Oct **1922** [c18 Sep 1922; LU18227]. Si; b&w. 35mm. 5 reels, 4,526 ft.

Dir-Story-Adapt Neal Hart. *Photog* William Steiner, Jr., Jacob A. Badaracco.

Cast: Neal Hart *(Steve Saunders)*, Hazel Deane.

Western melodrama. "The story is of easterners crossing the plains ... all alone, and reaching the Steve Saunders' range. Saunders acts as their guide. A strain of gold is located on the range by the head of the eastern family, but meantime the younger easterner in love with the girl gets too gay around her. That's when Steve butted in. When the zealous easterner engaged the bandit chief to kidnap the girl Steve frustrated the plan, and very simply, too, even to the point of making a couple of bandits keep on looking the other way while he made off with the gal. And then the eastern father and mother discovered the bandit chief was their long-lost son, so they thanked Steve for uncovering that as well." (*Variety,* 22 Dec 1922, p134.) *Guides. Bandits. Gold mines. Kidnaping. Personal identity.*

Note: Reviewed in *Variety* as *Butterfly Ranch.*

BUTTONS **F2.0711**

Metro-Goldwyn-Mayer Pictures. 24 Dec **1927** [c24 Dec 1927; LP25198]. Si; b&w. 35mm. 7 reels, 6,050 ft.

Dir-Writ George Hill. *Cont* Marian Constance Blackton. *Titl* Ralph Spence. *Adapt* Hayden Talbot. *Photog* Ira Morgan. *Sets* Cedric Gibbons, Arnold Gillespie. *Film Ed* Sam S. Zimbalist. *Wardrobe* Gilbert Clark.

Cast: Jackie Coogan *(Buttons)*, Lars Hanson *(Captain Travers)*, Gertrude Olmstead *(Ruth Stratton)*, Paul Hurst *("Slugger" McGlue)*, Roy D'Arcy *(Henri Rizard)*, Polly Moran *(Polly)*, Jack McDonald *(Hatchet Face)*, Coy Watson, Jr. *(Brutus)*.

Drama. Buttons, a street urchin, becomes a page boy on the transatlantic liner *S. S. Queenland,* commanded by Captain Travers. Buttons and his friend, Slugger, the ship's recreation leader, get into trouble when they try to show the captain that his fiancée, Ruth, is cheating on him with a bounder named Henri Rizard. Perceiving that they, in addition to Ruth, have abused him, Travers has Buttons and Slugger thrown in the brig. During a shipwreck, Buttons shows his loyalty to Travers when he swims to the bridge and declares his intention to go down with the captain. Real tragedy is avoided when Slugger, on a raft, picks up the two after the ship sinks. *Street urchins. Pages. Infidelity. Ocean liners. Shipwrecks.*

Note: Published copyright information indicating that the film has sound has not been verified.

BY AEROPLANE TO PYGMYLAND **F2.0712**

Stirling New Guinea Expedition. 3 Aug **1927.** Si; b&w. 35mm. 7 reels, 6,500 ft.

Participants: Matthew W. Stirling, Stanley A. Hedberg, Richard A. Peck.

Exploration documentary. A film record (from land and air) of Dr. Matthew Stirling's expedition into Dutch New Guinea. *Pygmies. Airplanes. New Guinea.*

Note: Also reviewed in 1928 as *Adventures in Pygmy Land.*

BY DIVINE RIGHT **F2.0713**
Grand-Asher Distributing Corp. *Dist* Film Booking Offices of America. 17 Feb **1924** [c17 Apr 1924; LP20120]. Si; b&w. 35mm. 7 reels, 6,885 ft.
Pres by Harry Asher. *Dir* R. William Neill. *Scen* Josef von Sternberg. *Adapt* Florence Hein. *Photog* Ray June.
Cast: Mildred Harris *(The Girl)*, Anders Randolf *(Trent, "The Boss")*, Elliott Dexter *(Austin Farrol, "The Prince")*, Sidney Bracey *(The Hireling)*, Jeanne Carpenter *(the Trent baby)*, Grace Carlyle *(Mrs. Trent)*, De Witt Jennings *("Tug" Wilson)*.
Melodrama. Source: Adam Hull Shirk, "The Way Men Love" (publication undetermined). Mildred, a young stenographer, seeks protection at the mission run by Austin Farrol, known as "The Prince," when her employer, Trent, an unscrupulous politician, attempts to seduce her. Mildred begins to work at the mission and falls in love with Farrol. Farrol is accused of arson when a fire started by Trent destroys the mission; but he escapes when the train he rides crashes, assumes a disguise, and gets a position in Trent's household. During a party Trent's child falls from a window and is believed to be permanently crippled, but Farrol, with "divine power," is able to cure her. The film is highlighted by a spectacular train crash. *Political bosses. Stenographers. Religion. Faith cure. Arson. Missions. Train wrecks.*
Note: Also reviewed in late 1923 as *The Way Men Love,* in 7,451 ft.

BY RIGHT OF BIRTH **F2.0714**
Lincoln Motion Picture Co. 1 Oct **1921** [New York State]. Si; b&w. 35mm. 6 reels.
Cast: Clarence Brooks, Anita Thompson.
Drama. "Reunion of family; with mother finding child" (New York State license application). *Family life. Motherhood.*

BY WHOSE HAND? **F2.0715**
Columbia Pictures. 15 Sep **1927** [c10 Oct 1927; LP24491]. Si; b&w. 35mm. 6 reels, 5,432 ft.
Prod Harry Cohn. *Dir* Walter Lang. *Story-Scen* Marion Orth. *Photog* J. O. Taylor. *Art Dir* Robert E. Lee. *Asst Dir* Clifford Saum.
Cast: Ricardo Cortez *(Van Suydam Smith)*, Eugenia Gilbert *(Peg Hewlett)*, J. Thornton Baston *(Sidney)*, Tom Dugan *(Rollins)*, Edgar Washington Blue *(Eli)*, Lillian Leighton *(Silly McShane)*, William Scott *(Mortimer)*, John Steppling *(Claridge)*, De Sacia Mooers *(Tex)*.
Crook-society melodrama. Mortimer, alias "Society Charlie," a well-known confidence man, becomes popular in New York nightclub circles, while Agent X-9, posing as Van Suydam Smith, a member of the smart set, is detailed to keep an eye on him. At a nightclub owned by "Tex," Smith meets Peg Hewlett, one of the entertainers, who gets him an invitation to the McShane party on a Long Island estate. During a game of bridge, Peg goes onto the terrace to join Smith; the room is plunged into darkness, and Mrs. McShane's jewels are stolen. After a series of events during which the jewels pass from one hand to another, Mortimer is exposed by Mr. Sidney, an insurance agent; and Smith, who has suspected Peg, realizes her innocence. *Detectives. Confidence men. Entertainers. Insurance agents. Smart set. Theft. Nightclubs. New York City. Long Island.*

BYE-BYE BUDDY **F2.0716**
Hercules Film Productions. *Dist* Trinity Pictures. 25 Mar **1929.** Talking sequences; b&w. 35mm. 6 reels, 5,700 ft. [Also si.]
Dir Frank S. Mattison. *Scen* Barry Barringer. *Dial-Titl* Arthur Hotaling. *Adapt* Barry Barringer, Frank S. Mattison. *Photog* Robert E. Cline. *Film Ed* Minnie Steppler.
Cast: Agnes Ayres *(Glad O'Brien)*, Bud Shaw *(Buddy O'Brien)*, Fred Shanley *(Dandy O'Brien)*, Ben Wilson *(Major Horton)*, John Orlando *(Johnny Cohen)*, Dave Henderson *(Marty Monihan)*, Hall Cline *(attorney)*.
Drama. Source: Ben Hershfield, "Bye-bye Buddy" (publication undetermined). Because she is the proprietress of a nightclub, Glad O'Brien keeps herself unknown to her son. The story has a crook atmosphere and involves the mother watching her son march off to war. *Motherhood. Nightclubs. World War I.*

CABARET **F2.0717**
Famous Players–Lasky. *Dist* Paramount Pictures. 26 Mar **1927** [c26 Mar 1927; LP23791]. Si; b&w. 35mm. 7 reels, 6,947 ft.
Pres by Adolph Zukor, Jesse L. Lasky. *Dir* Robert G. Vignola. *Screenplay* Becky Gardiner. *Titl* Jack Conway (of *Variety*). *Story* Owen Davis. *Photog* Harry A. Fischbeck.
Cast: Gilda Gray *(Gloria Trask)*, Tom Moore *(Tom Westcott)*, Chester Conklin *(Jerry Trask)*, Mona Palma *(Blanche Howard)*, Jack Egan *(Andy Trask)*, William Harrigan *(Jack Costigan)*, Charles Byer *(Sam Roberts)*, Anna Lavsa *(Mrs. Trask)*.
Crook melodrama. Gloria Trask, who has risen from a squalid East Side environment to stardom in Costigan's nightclub, is admired by Tom Westcott, detective, and Sam Roberts, a gangster with whom her brother is involved. Andy, threatened by the gang, is forced to pay off, and in a showdown in Gloria's dressing room, Andy shoots Roberts in self-defense. Gloria helps her brother to leave on a South American liner, while Tom forces Blanche, Roberts' girl friend, to admit to witnessing the crime. Blanche insists that it was murder, but Tom forces her to admit that Roberts had a gun by accusing her of the killing. *Dancers. Gangsters. Detectives. Brother-sister relationship. Murder. Cabarets. New York City.*

THE CACTUS CURE **F2.0718**
Ben Wilson Productions. *Dist* Arrow Film Corp. 17 Jan **1925** [c28 Jan 1925; LP21095]. Si; b&w. 35mm. 5 reels, 4,922 ft.
Dir Ward Hayes.
Cast: Dick Hatton *(Jimmy King)*, Yakima Canutt *(Bud Osborne, the foreman)*, Wilbur McGaugh *(Buck Lowry)*, Marilyn Mills *(Poppy Saunders)*.
Western comedy. Having stayed out all night once too often, Jimmy King, the profligate son of a wealthy father, is sent west in an effort to cure him of his dissolute ways. Before he arrives at his destination, the Flying W Ranch, he is bullied by Bud Osborne and some of the hands from the Flying W. Once at the ranch, Jimmy falls in love with Poppy Saunders, the rancher's beautiful daughter. Jimmy is later forced into a fight with Buck Lowry, a tough cowhand who considers Poppy his girl. Hearing Osborne and the other cowhands plotting to steal the Flying W cattle, Jimmy alerts the sheriff but is discovered by Osborne and tied up. Osborne then kidnaps Poppy, hiding her in the closet of a house believed to be haunted. Jimmy frees himself and rides to the "haunted house," where he stumbles into a sheet hanging on the clothesline and scares off most of the cowboys, who think he is a ghost. Jimmy gets into a fight with Osborne, who has alone remained behind, and, during the struggle, they knock over a lantern, starting a fire. Poppy is rescued by her horse, Jimmy finally whips Osborne, and the sheriff arrests the frightened cowboys. The following morning, Jimmy is told that Poppy has deserted him, and he returns to New York, only to find her waiting for him there. *Filial relations. Ranch foremen. Cowboys. Sheriffs. Ranch life. Kidnaping. Haunted houses. New York City. Fires. Horses.*

CACTUS TRAILS **F2.0719**
Harry Webb Productions. *Dist* Aywon Film Corp. 28 Dec **1925** [New York State license]. Si; b&w. 35mm. 5 reels, 4,800 ft.
Dir Harry Webb. *Photog* Ernest Miller.
Cast: Jack Perrin.
Western melodrama. "... in which hero returns from war to resume cow-punching, rescues beautiful unknown girl in runaway, is jailed for shooting of which he is innocent, rescued by girl's father, attends fiesta in girl's honor and saves her from kidnappers." (*Motion Picture News Booking Guide,* 10:24, Apr 1926.) *Veterans. Cowboys. Injustice. Murder. Kidnaping.*

CACTUS TRAILS **F2.0720**
Bob Custer Productions. *Dist* Film Booking Offices of America. 23 Jan **1927** [c3 Jan 1927; LP23503]. Si; b&w. 35mm. 5 reels, 4,889 ft.
Pres by Joseph P. Kennedy. *Dir* Percy Pembroke. *Scen* Harry P. Crist. *Adapt* George Merrick. *Story* W. Bert Foster. *Photog* Ernest Miller. *Asst Dir* Harry P. Crist.
Cast: Bob Custer *(Ross Fenton)*, Marjorie Zier *(Sally Crater)*, Lew Meehan *(Angel)*, Roy Watson *(Sheriff Upshaw)*, Inez Gomez *(Aunt Crater)*, Roy Laidlaw *(Jeb Poultney)*, Bud Osborne *("Draw" Egan)*, Milburn Morante *(Jack Mason)*.
Western melodrama. Ross Fenton, an oil company representative, arrives in Led Horse, a boom oil town, to investigate conditions and rescues Sally Crater from an assault by Angel, a gambler, who seeks to lease a ranch from Auntie Crater. "Draw" Egan robs the post office with his gang and is pursued by the sheriff and a posse. When the sheriff is wounded, he makes Fenton his deputy; Sally is rescued from the bandits, and all the men but Egan are captured. Fenton proves that Angel's gambling establishment is "fixed," and Angel takes refuge in the Crater ranchhouse, where he is overcome by Fenton. Fenton discovers oil on the land, and to Sally's delight he brings in a gusher. After capturing Egan, he is united with Sally. *Swindlers. Gamblers. Sheriffs. Posses. Oil. Ranches.*

A CAFE IN CAIRO F2.0721

Hunt Stromberg Productions. *Dist* producers Distributing Corp. 7 Dec **1924** [c7 Dec 1924; LP21053]. Si; b&w. 35mm. 6 reels, 5,656 ft.

Pres by Hunt Stromberg, Charles R. Rogers. *Supv* Hunt Stromberg. *Dir* Chet Withey. *Adapt-Scen* Harvey Gates. *Photog* Sol Polito. *Art Dir* Edward Withers. *Film Ed* Harry L. Decker.

Cast: Priscilla Dean *(Naida)*, Robert Ellis *(Barry Braxton)*, Carl Stockdale *(Jaradi)*, Evelyn Selbie *(Batooka)*, Harry Woods *(Kali)*, John Steppling *(Tom Hays)*, Marie Crisp *(Rosamond)*, Carmen Phillips *(Gaza)*, Larry Steers *(Colonel Alastair-Ker)*, Ruth King *(Evelyn)*, Vincente Orona *(Sadek)*.

Melodrama. Source: Izola Forrester, "A Cafe in Cairo," in *Ainslee's Magazine* (vol 52, Oct 1923–Apr 1924). An Arabian desert bandit, Kali, attacks a British camp and kills Colonel Alastair-Ker and his wife, sparing their small daughter on the condition that one day he be given the chance to claim her in marriage. The child, now called Naida, has grown up, believing herself to be an Arab. Her foster father, Jaradi, uses his cafe in Cairo as a cover for political activities. When Kali visits Jaradi to plot a revolt, he sees Nadia and declares he will soon have her for a wife. A confidential document that the natives wish to obtain has been entrusted to an American soldier of fortune, Barry Braxton, and Naida is commissioned by Kali to procure it. She takes it from Barry's room but, having fallen in love with him, she does not give it to Kali. Kali then demands her in marriage, and Naida goes into the customary seclusion, sending for Barry in order to return the document to him. Kali discovers Barry in Naida's quarters and orders him to be bound and thrown into the Nile. Naida rescues Barry and then is forced to fight Kali, who is about to kill her when he is himself killed by Jaradi. Barry and Naida are married and return to England. *Bandits. Soldiers of fortune. Foster fathers. British. Arabs. Cafes. Revolts. Cairo. Nile River.*

CAIN AND MABEL *see* **THE GREAT WHITE WAY**

THE CALGARY STAMPEDE (Universal-Jewel) F2.0722

Universal Pictures. 1 Nov **1925** [c29 Sep 1925; LP21860]. Si; b&w. 35mm. 6 reels, 5,924 ft.

Dir Herbert Blache. *Story* Raymond L. Schrock, Donald W. Lee, E. Richard Schayer. *Photog* Harry Neumann.

Cast: Hoot Gibson *(Dan Malloy)*, Virginia Brown Faire *(Marie La Farge)*, Clark Comstock *(Jean La Farge)*, Ynez Seabury *(Neenah)*, Jim Corey *(Fred Burgess)*, Philo McCullough *(Callahan)*, W. T. McCulley *(Harkness)*, Ena Gregory *(Trixie)*, Charles Sellon *(Regan)*, Tex Young *(cook)*, Bob Gillis *(Morton)*.

Western melodrama. Dan Malloy, champion roman rider of the United States, goes to Canada to see the country and falls in love with Marie La Farge. Dan wants to marry the girl, but her father disapproves of the match. Fred Burgess, a poacher, kills La Farge, and Dan is blamed for the crime. He eludes the Mounties and finds work on a ranch. On the day of the rodeo at Calgary, Dan is identified by the police, but before he is arrested he wins the roman race and uses his winnings to pay off the mortgage on his employer's ranch. A woman who saw the murder puts the finger on the real killer, and Dan is set free to find happiness with Marie. *Roman riders. Poachers. Injustice. Mortgages. Rodeos. Calgary. Northwest Mounted Police.*

CALIBRE 45 F2.0723

Independent Pictures. 14 Aug **1924.** Si; b&w. 35mm. 5 reels, 4,800-5,100 ft.

Pres by Jesse J. Goldburg. *Dir* J. P. McGowan. *Dir? (see note)* Jack Nelson. *Story* Walter Griffin.

Cast: Franklyn Farnum, Dorothy Wood, Cathleen Calhoun.

Western melodrama. "... concerning a character, Yaqui Dan, who is falsely accused of murder and driven to outlawry. Though many of Dan's operations are outside the law he performs many charitable acts for unfortunates about the country. After an eventful period he gains evidence that the murderer is still living in the vicinity of the crime and Dan comes back and proves his innocence." (*Motion Picture News Booking Guide,* [7]: 14, Oct 1924.) *Outlaws. Charity. Murder.*

Note: At least one source credits Jack Nelson as director.

CALIFORNIA F2.0724

Metro-Goldwyn-Mayer Pictures. 7 May **1927** [c23 May 1927; LP24255]. Si; b&w. 35mm. 5 reels, 4,912 ft.

Dir W. S. Van Dyke. *Cont* Frank Davis. *Titl* Marian Ainslee, Ruth Cummings. *Story* Peter B. Kyne. *Photog* Clyde De Vinna. *Sets* Eddie Imazu. *Film Ed* Basil Wrangell. *Wardrobe* André-ani.

Cast: Tim McCoy *(Capt. Archibald Gillespie)*, Dorothy Sebastian *(Carlotta del Rey)*, Marc MacDermott *(Drachano)*, Frank Currier *(Don Carlos del Rey)*, Fred Warren *(Kit Carson)*, Lillian Leighton *(duenna)*, Edwin Terry *(Brig. Gen. Stephen W. Kearny)*.

Western romance. "The war with Mexico serves to bring together American officer and Mexican señorita, the former all ardent and the latter defiant because of the fact that their countries are at war. Coincident with the American victory is the successful conquest by the 'gringo' of the girl's heart." (*Motion Picture News Booking Guide,* 13:23, Oct 1927.) *Courtship. United States—History—Mexican War. Mexico. Kit Carson. Stephen Watts Kearney.*

CALIFORNIA IN '49 F2.0725

Arrow Film Corp. c13 Nov **1924** [LP20846]. Si; b&w. 35mm. 6 reels.

Dir Jacques Jaccard. *Story* Karl Coolidge.

Cast: Edmund Cobb *(Cal Coleman)*, Neva Gerber *(Sierra Sutter)*, Charles Brinley *(John Sutter)*, Ruth Royce *(Arabella Ryan)*, Wilbur McGaugh *(Marsdon)*.

Western melodrama. Captain John Sutter owns a large tract of land near Sacramento, granted him by the Mexican governor of California. Sutter, planning to create an Empire of the Pacific, is joined in his grand schemes by Arabella Ryan, a handsome adventuress, and Marsdon, an unscrupulous soldier of fortune. When Sutter's daughter, Sierra, finds out that her father is in love with Arabella, she denounces him for defiling the sacred memory of her mother. Sutter is overcome with remorse and angrily orders Marsdon and Arabella from his home. Cal Coleman, a frontier guide and scout who is leading the Donner party across the mountains, is forced to ride for help when their wagon train becomes snowbound in a high mountain pass. Weak from cold and hunger, Cal manages to ride as far as Sutter's fort, whence assistance is dispatched to Donner Pass. Cal is nursed back to health by Sierra, with whom he falls in love. When the Mexican-American settlers decide to revolt against the Mexican Government, Cal is elected their leader, and he organizes a successful attack against Fort Sonoma. California is annexed to the United States, Marsdon is killed in a duel with Judge Coleman, Arabella commits suicide, and Cal and Sierra are married. *Adventuresses. Soldiers of fortune. Guides. Duels. Suicide. Wagon trains. California. Sacramento. John Augustus Sutter.*

Note: *California in '49* is the feature version of the serial *Days of '49* (released 15 Mar 1924).

CALIFORNIA IN 1878 *see* **FIGHTING THRU; OR CALIFORNIA IN 1878**

THE CALIFORNIA MAIL F2.0726

First National Pictures. 7 Apr **1929** [c3 Apr 1929; LP282]. Si; b&w. 35mm. 6 reels, 5,446 ft.

Pres by Charles R. Rogers. *Supv* Harry J. Brown. *Dir* Albert Rogell. *Story-Scen* Marion Jackson. *Titl* Lesley Mason. *Photog* Frank Good. *Film Ed* Fred Allen.

Cast: Ken Maynard *(Bob Scott)*, Dorothy Dwan *(Molly Butler)*, Lafe McKee *(William Butler)*, Paul Hurst *(Rowdy Ryan)*, C. E. Anderson *(Butch McGraw)*, Fred Burns *(John Harrison)*, Tarzan *(himself, a horse)*.

Historical drama. During the darkest hour of the American Civil War, the Union desperately needs gold to keep its armies in the field and its credit good. Federal Agent Bob Scott is therefore instructed to clean out the bandit gangs that have been stopping the vital California gold shipments. Bob joins Butch McGraw's gang and later saves Molly Butler when she is taken off a stage by some of McGraw's henchmen. Bob eventually wins Molly's love, rounds up the McGraw gang, and secures safe passage for the gold shipments. *Government agents. Bandits. Kidnaping. Postal service. Gold. United States—History—Civil War. California. Horses.*

CALIFORNIA OR BUST F2.0727

R-C Pictures. *Dist* Film Booking Offices of America. 9 Jan **1927** [c9 Jan 1927; LP23595]. Si; b&w. 35mm. 5 reels, 4,659 ft.

Pres by Joseph P. Kennedy. *Dir* Phil Rosen. *Story-Cont* Byron Morgan. *Titl* Al Boasberg. *Photog* H. Lyman Broening. *Asst Dir* Ray McCarey.

Cast: George O'Hara *(Jeff Daggett [Darman?])*, Helen Foster *(Nadine Holtwood)*, John Steppling *(President Holtwood)*, Johnny Fox *(mechanic)*, Irving Bacon *(Wade Rexton)*.

Comedy-drama. Jeff Daggett, owner of a garage in Rockett, Arizona, neglects his business for work on a new type of automobile motor, while Johnny Fox, his assistant, handles the business. President Holtwood of a motor company and his daughter Nadine are driving to California when their car breaks down near Rockett. Jeff explains the features of his invention to Holtwood, who wires to Rexton, his chief engineer, to come look at the design; Rexton, who sees in Jeff a rival to Nadine, disparages the motor and proposes that Jeff race the car against his own. Rexton is stopped by a highwayman who steals the car, and the three start off in pursuit. Jeff overtakes and overcomes the bandit; subsequently, he accepts Holtwood's offer to work for him. *Mechanics. Inventors. Highwaymen. Courtship. Automobile manufacturers. Arizona.*

A CALIFORNIA ROMANCE **F2.0728**

Fox Film Corp. 24 Dec **1922** [c24 Dec 1922; LP18997]. Si; b&w. 35mm. 5 reels, 3,892 ft.

Pres by William Fox. *Dir* Jerome Storm. *Scen* Charles E. Banks. *Story* Jules G. Furthman. *Photog* Joseph August.

Cast: John Gilbert *(Don Patricio Fernando)*, Estelle Taylor *(Donna Dolores)*, George Siegmann *(Don Juan Diego)*, Jack McDonald *(Don Manuel Casca)*, Charles Anderson *(Steve)*.

Romantic comedy-drama. Patricio Fernando, a handsome son of California, loves Dolores, a loyal daughter of Mexico, but he disagrees with her in his opinion that California should join the United States. Believing Patricio a coward, Dolores pledges herself to Juan Diego, a Mexican Army officer who is really the leader of a band of renegades. Diego proves his falsity, however, and Patricio comes to the gallant defense of Dolores and the band of women who have been imprisoned. *Mexicans. Bandits. Patriotism. California—Mexican period.*

Note: Working title: *Across the Border.*

CALIFORNIA STRAIGHT AHEAD (Universal-Jewel) **F2.0729**

Universal Pictures. 13 Sep **1925** [c27 Aug 1925; LP21750]. Si; b&w. 35mm. 8 reels, 7,238 ft.

Dir Harry Pollard. *Scen* Harry Pollard, Byron Morgan. *Photog* Gilbert Warrenton.

Cast: Reginald Denny *(Tom Hayden)*, Gertrude Olmsted *(Betty Browne)*, Tom Wilson *(Sambo)*, Charles Gerrard *(Creighton Deane)*, Lucille Ward *(Mrs. Browne)*, John Steppling *(Jeffrey Browne)*, Fred Esmelton *(Mr. Hayden)*.

Comedy-drama. Tom celebrates his last night of bachelorhood with a little too much enthusiasm and arrives at his own wedding late and disheveled. His fiancée refuses to marry him, and Tom is disowned by his family. In the company of his Negro valet, Sambo, he drives west in a touring trailer. En route, he meets his former fiancée and her parents, who are stranded in the desert. Tom rescues them from wild animals that have escaped from a circus during a storm; and he elopes with the girl to Los Angeles. He meets up with her parents later and agrees to drive a car owned by the girl's father in an important automobile race. Tom wins the race and receives the blessings of his new in-laws. *Bachelors. Valets. Disinheritance. Elopement. Weddings. Automobile racing. Circus. Deserts. Los Angeles.*

THE CALL FROM THE WILD **F2.0730**

Pacific Film Co. 12 Aug **1921** [trade review]. Si; b&w. 35mm. 5 reels.

Dir-Story Wharton James. *Photog* Floyd Jackman.

Cast: Frankie James *(The Boy)*, Highland Laddie *(The Dog)*.

Melodrama. A young boy saves a collie pup's life when his master is ready to move on and is about to shoot him. The pup is then free to roam the wilderness and must fight for existence along with the wolves. Acquiring wolfish ways, he is hunted throughout the range as the killer wolf. When the boy goes hunting for this killer wolf and stumbles upon the dog (now grown to adulthood) caught in a trap, he sets him free. The wolf-dog and the boy become friends, and when the boy falls into a trap, the dog fetches help. The searchers free the boy and are about to kill the dog but again the boy comes to his rescue, an act resulting in a permanent bond between man and beast. *Childhood. Wolves. Dogs.*

THE CALL OF COURAGE (Blue Streak Western) **F2.0731**

Universal Pictures. 22 Dec **1925** [c24 Aug 1925; LP21748]. Si; b&w. 35mm. 5 reels, 4,661 ft.

Dir Clifford S. Smith. *Story* Harold Shumate. *Photog* Harold Shumate.

Cast: Art Acord *(Steve Caldwell)*, Olive Hasbrouck *(June Hazelton)*, Duke Lee *(Sam Caldwell)*, Frank Rice *(Slim)*, John T. Prince *(Jeff Hazelton)*, Turner Savage *(Jimmy)*, Floyd Shackelford *(cook)*, Mrs. C. Martin *(servant)*.

Western melodrama. Steve Caldwell is accused of the murder of Jeff Hazelton and is arrested by the sheriff. Freed by his dog and horse, Steve hides in the powder magazine of a mine. He finds Hazelton in the mine, learning from him that the real villain is none other than Sam Caldwell, Steve's brother. The two men go after Sam, who is drowned in the river while trying to escape. Steve wins the love of June, Hazelton's beautiful daughter who has always believed in him. *Sheriffs. Brothers. Murder. Injustice. Mines. Horses. Dogs.*

THE CALL OF HIS PEOPLE **F2.0732**

Reol Productions. 14 Jan **1922** [Washington premiere; c14 Sep 1921; LU17503]. Si; b&w. 35mm. 6 reels.

Adapt Aubrey Bowser.

Cast: George Edward Brown, Edna Morton, Mae Kemp, James Steven, Lawrence Chenault, Mercedes Gilbert, Percy Verwayen.

Melodrama. Source: Aubrey Bowser, "The Man Who Would Be White" (publication undetermined). Nelson Holmes, a Negro passing for white who has advanced himself from office boy to the position of general manager of the Brazilian-American Coffee Co., is visited by James Graves, a boyhood friend looking for a job. Nelson agrees to make Graves his private secretary if he will remain quiet about Nelson's true race. Deeply affected by seeing Graves again, Nelson pays a visit to Graves's sister, Elinor, who was his childhood sweetheart. Elinor receives him coldly, however, angered by his denial of his own people. Graves later protects some valuable contracts from being stolen, and Nelson, extremely grateful for his loyalty, finally informs Weathering, the owner of the coffee company, that he has been passing for white. Weathering assures Nelson that it is the quality and not the color of a man that counts, and Nelson asks Elinor for her hand in marriage, once again proud to be black. *Secretaries. Office boys. Business management. Negro life. Coffee. Documentation.*

THE CALL OF HOME **F2.0733**

R-C Pictures. 5 Feb **1922** [c1 Feb 1922; LP17514]. Si; b&w. 35mm. 6 reels, 5,523 ft.

Dir Louis J. Gasnier. *Scen* Eve Unsell. *Photog* Joseph Dubray. *Art Dir* W. L. Heywood. *Asst Dir* Joseph Rothman.

Cast: Leon Barry *(Alan Wayne)*, Irene Rich *(Alix Lansing)*, Ramsey Wallace *(Gerry Lansing)*, Margaret Mann *(Gerry's mother)*, Jobyna Ralston *(Clem)*, Genevieve Blinn *(Nancy Wayne)*, Wadsworth Harris *(Captain Wayne)*, James O. Barrows *(butler)*, Carl Stockdale *(Kemp)*, Emmett King *(Lieber)*, Norma Nichols *(Margarita)*, Sidney Franklin *(priest)*, Harry Lonsdale *(consul)*.

Melodrama. Source: George Agnew Chamberlain, *Home* (New York, 1914). Gerry Lansing, a wealthy young aristocrat, following a series of misunderstandings, deserts his wife, Alix, whom he believes to have eloped with his friend Alan Wayne, and sails for South America, leaving no trace of his whereabouts. There, as a plantation owner, he becomes involved with Margarita, a Spanish girl whom he marries. A great flood destroys his plantation and drowns Margarita, just as Alan, himself stricken with jungle fever, finds Gerry. From Alan he learns that his wife was blameless and is awaiting his return home, where she has given birth to his son. *Planters. Marriage. Desertion. Jealousy. South America. Floods.*

THE CALL OF THE CANYON **F2.0734**

Famous Players–Lasky. *Dist* Paramount Pictures. 16 Dec **1923** [c25 Dec 1923; LP19767]. Si; b&w. 35mm. 7 reels, 6,993 ft.

Pres by Jesse L. Lasky. *Dir* Victor Fleming. *Adapt* Doris Schroeder, Edfrid Bingham. *Photog* James Howe.

Cast: Richard Dix *(Glenn Kilbourne)*, Lois Wilson *(Carley Burch)*, Marjorie Daw *(Flo Hutter)*, Noah Beery *(Haze Ruff)*, Ricardo Cortez *(Larry Morrison)*, Fred Huntley *(Tom Hutter)*, Lillian Leighton *(Mrs. Hutter)*, Helen Dunbar *(Aunt Mary)*, Leonard Clapham *(Lee Stanton)*, Edward Clayton *(Tenney Jones)*, Dorothy Seastrom *(Eleanor Harmon)*, Laura Anson *(Beatrice Lovell)*, Charles Richards *(Roger Newton)*, Ralph Yearsley *(Charlie Oatmeal)*, Arthur Rankin *(Virgil Rust)*, Mervyn LeRoy *(Jack Rawlins)*.

Western melodrama. Source: Zane Grey, *The Call of the Canyon* (New York, 1924). War veteran Glenn Kilbourne goes to Arizona to regain his health and there is nursed to recovery by local girl Flo Hutter. Kilbourne's fiancée, Carley Burch, follows him but soon becomes disillusioned with the West and returns to New York. Flo Hutter is seriously injured in an accident, and Kilbourne, to repay her for restoring his health, proposes marriage. Carley returns to Arizona on the wedding day, seeking Kilbourne. Flo, seeing that the two are still in love, gives up Kilbourne and marries another admirer, Lee Stanton. *Veterans. New Yorkers. Health. Arizona.*

THE CALL OF THE CIRCUS **F2.0735**

Pickwick Pictures. *Dist* C. C. Burr Pictures. 15 Jan **1930.** Sd (Photophone); b&w. 35mm. 6 reels, 5,466 ft.

Dir Frank O'Connor. *Cont* Jack Townley. *Story-Dial* Maxine Alton. *Photog* Louis Physioc. *Mus Score* Ralph J. Nase. *Theme Song: "Life Is Just a Circus"* Maxine Alton, Aubrey Stauffer.

Cast: Francis X. Bushman *(The Man)*, Ethel Clayton *(The Woman)*, Joan Wyndham *(The Girl)*, William Cotton Kirby *(The Boy)*, Dorothy Gay *(The Girl-at-the-well)*, Sunburnt Jim Wilson *(The Shadow)*.

Domestic drama. A retired clown (The Man) tells a girl, whom he meets at a well, that he is looking for a circus, and he goes on to recount the story of his life since leaving the circus with his wife (The Woman): *Things go smoothly for a time; The Boy (The Woman's son by a previous marriage) and The Shadow also leave the circus to live with the couple. But the call of the circus is too strong, and first The Shadow, then The Boy, return. Soon afterward, The Man rescues a young girl (The Girl) from an accident and falls in love with her. Realizing what is happening, The Woman leaves after sending for The Boy, and, as she has anticipated, The Boy and The Girl fall in love.* The Man finally recognizes his "love" as merely an attraction to The Girl's youth, he finds The Woman and makes amends, and they return to the circus together. *Clowns. Circus. Infidelity.*

CALL OF THE DESERT **F2.0736**

Dist Syndicate Pictures. 1 Mar **1930.** Mus score; b&w. 35mm. 5 reels, 4,800 ft. [Also si.]

Dir J. P. McGowan. *Story-Scen* Sally Winters. *Photog* Hap Depew.

Cast: Tom Tyler *(Rex Carson)*, Sheila Le Gay *(Jean Walker)*, Bud Osborne *(Todd Walker)*, Cliff Lyons *(Nate Thomas)*, Bobby Dunn.

Western melodrama. "Story has to do with a chap who gives a villain and accomplice a lacing when they try to steal his father's [mine?] claim. Most of the action takes place out-doors and sets a fast pace." (*Film Daily*, 18 May 1930, p13.) *Filial relations. Mine claims.*

CALL OF THE FLESH **F2.0737**

Metro-Goldwyn-Mayer Pictures. 16 Aug **1930** [c8 Sep 1930; LP1541]. Sd (Movietone); b&w with col sequences (Technicolor). 35mm. 11 reels, 9,178 ft.

Dir Charles Brabin. *Dial* John Colton. *Story* Dorothy Farnum. *Photog* Merritt B. Gerstad. *Art Dir* Cedric Gibbons. *Film Ed* Conrad A. Nervig. *Songs: "Just for Today," "Not Quite Good Enough for Me," "Lonely"* Herbert Stothart, Clifford Grey. *Rec Engr* Ralph Shugart, Douglas Shearer. *Wardrobe* David Cox.

Cast: Ramon Novarro *(Juan)*, Dorothy Jordan *(María)*, Ernest Torrence *(Esteban)*, Nance O'Neil *(Mother Superior)*, Renée Adorée *(Lola)*, Mathilde Comont *(La Rumbarita)*, Russell Hopton *(Enrique)*.

Romantic drama. María, a novice, admires cafe singer Juan, who is attempting to resist the advances of his partner, Lola. After seeing him from atop the wall of the convent, María builds up an aura of romance around him. Escaping from the convent, she meets Juan, who himself is fleeing from the fiesta and the police. Juan responds to her affectionately and is determined to adopt and protect her. With Esteban, his vocal teacher, and María, Juan goes to Madrid to audition for the opera. Having fallen in love with María, Juan becomes engaged to her; the spurned Lola encourages María's brother, Enrique, to separate them, claiming he has taken her from the Church. Juan pretends to reject her, and she returns to the cloister, but Juan is grief-stricken during a triumphant operatic performance. Lola appeals to the mother superior, who releases María, since she has not taken her final vows. ... *Singers. Novices. Vocal instructors. Courtship. Opera. Convents. Spain. Madrid. Seville.*

Note: Initially reviewed as *The Singer of Seville*. Novarro also sings: "Cavatina" from *L'Elisir d'amore* by Donizetti; and "Questa o quella ..." from *Rigoletto* by Verdi.

CALL OF THE HEART **F2.0738**

Universal Pictures. 29 Jan **1928** [c20 Oct 1927; LP24559]. Si; b&w. 35mm. 5 reels, 4,345 ft.

Pres by Carl Laemmle. *Dir* Francis Ford. *Story-Cont* Basil Dickey. *Titl* Gardner Bradford. *Photog* Jerry Ash. *Film Ed* Leon Barsha.

Cast: Dynamite *(himself, a dog)*, Joan Alden *(Molly O'Day)*, Edmund Cobb *(Jerry Wilson)*, William A. Steele *(Dave Crenshaw)*, Maurice Murphy *(Josh [Jack?] O'Day)*, George Plews, Frank Baker, Owen Train.

Western melodrama. Molly O'Day and her kid brother, Josh (Jack?), homestead a western ranch near Dave Crenshaw, a cattleman and leader of a lawless gang determined to drive homesteaders from their land. By courting Molly, Crenshaw hopes to induce her to abandon the homestead. Discouraged in his suit, he commences terrorist tactics. Molly's dog, sensing the man's deception, influences her against him; and the appearance of Wilson, a stranger who wins Molly's confidence, leads Crenshaw to resort to force and intimidation. With the aid of her dog and Wilson, in reality a government agent, the rancher's downfall is brought about, and Wilson wins the hand of Molly. *Strangers. Homesteaders. Government agents. Gangs. Brother-sister relationship. Ranches. Dogs.*

THE CALL OF THE HILLS **F2.0739**

Dist Lee-Bradford Corp. 18 Apr **1923** [scheduled release]. Si; b&w. 35mm. 5 reels.

Dir Fred Hornby.

Cast: Robert Broderick *(Ben Kruger)*, Sally Edwards *(Mary Kruger)*, Maude Malcolm *(Violet)*, Louis J. O'Connor *(Willie Hoyt)*, Alice Allen *(Mrs. Hoyt)*.

Melodrama. Violet Kruger, mistreated by Jed Keith, a bootlegger, and Ben Kruger, a cruel guardian, is rescued, adopted, and sent to a girls' boarding school on the Hudson River. She falls in love with Allen Grey, a student at West Point. Their romance is temporarily threatened by Keith, the bootlegger, whose attempts to claim Violet for himself meet with failure. Finally, Kruger, the guardian, reveals before he dies that Violet is really the daughter of socially prominent and wealthy parents, who lost her to a Gypsy when she was only a child. *Students. Cadets. Bootleggers. Guardians. Gypsies. Parentage. Boarding schools. United States Military Academy. Hudson River.*

THE CALL OF THE KLONDIKE **F2.0740**

Paul Gerson Pictures. *Dist* Rayart Pictures. 25 Jun **1926** [New York State license]. Si; b&w. 35mm. 6 reels, 5,803 ft.

Dir Oscar Apfel. *Scen* J. F. Natteford. *Photog* Alfred Gosden.

Cast: Gaston Glass *(Norton Mitchell)*, Dorothy Dwan *(Violet Kenney)*, Earl Metcalfe *(Petrov)*, Sam Allen *(Burt Kenney)*, William Lowery *(Harkness)*, Olin Francis *(Dolan)*, Harold Holland *(Downing)*, Jimmy Aubrey *(Bowery Bill)*, Lightning Girl *(a dog)*.

Northwest melodrama. When Norton Mitchell, a young engineer, is attacked by thieves, Violet Kenney and her father, Burt, come to his aid. Norton is then separated from the Kenneys, who go to Alaska, where Violet is forced to sing in a dancehall when her father falls ill. Norton goes to Alaska also and becomes the partner of a miner whom he befriends. Violet consents to submit to the advances of the lecherous Petrov, when that villain offers to rush her father to Dawson for a vital operation. Norton's partner is killed, and Norton is unjustly jailed for the crime. Norton escapes, however, and rescues Violet from Petrov, bringing him and his gang to justice with the aid of the sheriff's men and a dog. *Engineers. Miners. Singers. Sheriffs. Thieves. Dancehalls. Murder. Klondike. Alaska. Dogs.*

CALL OF THE MATE **F2.0741**

Phil Goldstone Productions. *Dist* Renown Pictures. 29 Jul **1924** [New York showing]. Si; b&w. 35mm. 5 reels.

Dir Alvin J. Neitz. *Scen* Jules Furthman. *Photog* Roland Price.

Cast: William Fairbanks, Dorothy Revier, Milton Ross, Billie Bennett, Earl Close, Neil Keller, Stanley Bingham, Marguerite Neitz.

Western melodrama. A wronged dancehall girl with an illegitimate child loves a cowhand with the love of a bad woman for a good man. A gambler takes a shot at the fellow, and the dancehall girl steps in the way, taking more than her share of lead. With her last wish, she asks the cowpoke to marry her and give her child a name. They are quickly wed, but the girl unexpectedly recovers, posing quite a problem for the cowhand, who is in love with another woman. When the dancehall girl is later murdered, the cowhand is unjustly suspected of the crime until he proves that the gambler shot the girl out of malice. The cowhand returns to his first love and marries her, despite the interference of her sullen brothers and somewhat irate father. *Cowboys. Dancehall girls. Gamblers. Brother-sister relationship. Illegitimacy. Murder.*

CALL OF THE NIGHT **F2.0742**

Dist Truart Film Corp. 8 Mar **1926** [New York State license]. Si; b&w. 35mm. 5 reels.

Melodrama(?). No information about the nature of this film has been found.

THE CALL OF THE NORTH **F2.0743**

Famous Players–Lasky. *Dist* Paramount Pictures. 27 Nov **1921** [c29 Nov 1921; LP17248]. Si; b&w. 35mm. 5 reels, 4,823 ft.

Pres by Jesse L. Lasky. *Dir* Joseph Henabery. *Adapt* Jack Cunningham. *Photog* Faxon Dean.

Cast: Jack Holt *(Ned Trent)*, Madge Bellamy *(Virginia Albret)*, Noah Beery *(Galen Albret)*, Francis McDonald *(Achille Picard)*, Edward Martindel *(Graham Stewart)*, Helen Ferguson *(Elodie Albret)*, Jack Herbert *(Louis Placide)*.

Northwest melodrama. Source: Stewart Edward White, *Conjuror's House* (New York, 1903). Galen Albret, factor of the Hudson's Bay Co. in the Canadian Northwest, believes Graham Stewart guilty of conspiracy with his wife and sends them into the wilderness, where they die. Years later, Ned, Stewart's son, is a free trader interfering with Galen's trade, though unaware of Galen's connection with his parents' death. Ned is captured, but Galen's daughter, Virginia, helps him to escape. Discovering Ned's identity and that his father was unjustly suspected, Galen offers him an opportunity for revenge, but Virginia intervenes and the factor relents, surrendering his daughter to Ned. *Factors. Traders. Parentage. Revenge. Canadian Northwest. Hudson's Bay Co.*.

CALL OF THE WEST **F2.0744**

Columbia Pictures. 10 May **1930** [c16 May 1930; LP1300]. Sd (Movietone); b&w. 35mm. 7 reels, 6,500 ft. [Also si.]

Prod Harry Cohn. *Dir* Albert Ray. *Cont-Dial* Colin Clements. *Camera* Ben Kline. *Art Dir* Harrison Wiley. *Film Ed* Ray Snyder. *Ch Sd Engr* John P. Livadary. *Sd Mixing Engr* G. R. Cooper. *Asst Dir* Sam Nelson.

Cast: Dorothy Revier *(Violet La Tour)*, Matt Moore *(Lon Dixon)*, Katherine Clare Ward *(Ma Dixon)*, Tom O'Brien *(Bull Clarkson)*, Alan Roscoe *(Maurice Kane)*, Victor Potel *(Trig Peters)*, Nick De Ruiz *(Frijoles)*, Joe De La Cruz *(Mexicali)*, Blanche Rose *(Mrs. Burns)*, Gertrude Bennett *(Kit)*, Connie La Mont *(Doll)*, Buff Jones *(Red)*.

Society-western drama. Source: Florence Ryerson and Colin Clements, "Borrowed Love" (publication undetermined). Enervated by the nightly round of social activities, Violet La Tour, a popular nightclub entertainer, is refused a New York booking by Maurice Kane, her persistent admirer, and her agent procures work for her in a road show. During a performance in Sagebrush, Texas, she collapses and is taken to the ranch of Lon Dixon, where his mother nurses her. A romance develops, and when Lon proposes to her, Violet accepts; but soon after the ceremony, he agrees to join a party of cowboys in a search for rustlers. Finding his departure unpardonable, Violet impulsively returns to New York and is welcomed with open arms by Kane. She resumes her old society life but resists Kane's attempts at love-making, and when Lon comes to the city to claim her, she gladly confirms her love for him. *Entertainers. Cowboys. Courtship. Road shows. New York City. Texas.*

THE CALL OF THE WILD **F2.0745**

Hal Roach Studios. *Dist* Pathé Exchange. 23 Sep **1923** [c11 Aug 1923; LU19295]. Si; b&w. 35mm. 7 reels, 6,725 ft.

Pres by Hal Roach. *Dir-Writ* Fred Jackman. *Photog* Floyd Jackman.

Cast: Buck *(himself, a dog)*, Jack Mulhall *(John Thornton)*, Walter Long *(Hagin)*, Sidney D'Albrook *(Charles)*, Laura Roessing *(Mercedes, Charles's wife)*, Frank Butler *(Hal)*.

Melodrama. Source: Jack London, *The Call of the Wild* (New York, 1903). Buck, a young Saint Bernard, is stolen from his home in England and shipped to Canada where he is used on a dogsled. He is treated badly until John Thornton, a prospector, befriends him. Buck takes the opportunity to rescue Thornton when his life is endangered. Finally, he settles down to the pleasures of family life. *Prospectors. England. Canada. Dogs.*

THE CALL OF THE WILDERNESS **F2.0746**

Dist Associated Exhibitors. 5 Dec **1926** [c10 Dec 1926; LU23413]. Si; b&w. 35mm. 5 reels, 4,218 ft.

Pres by Van Pelt Brothers. *Supv* Joe Rock. *Dir* Jack Nelson. *Story* Earl W. Johnson, Lon Young.

Cast: Sandow *(himself, a dog)*, Lewis Sargent *(Andrew Horton, Jr.)*, Edna Marion *(The Girl)*, Sydney D. Grey *(Andrew Horton, Sr.)*, Al Smith *("Red" Morgan)*, Max Asher *(Joe)*.

Melodrama. Andy Horton, Jr., is turned out of his father's home for his spirited escapades and leaves town with his dog. In a small town out west, Andy meets the land agent's daughter, and to please her he buys a plot of land; "Red" Morgan, a prospector, tries to drive them off, but Andy's dog comes to the rescue. The prospector waylays Andy in his car and causes him to have a wreck; the injured hero sends the dog for help, and the girl hurries to him. The dog chases Morgan, who, fleeing in terror, falls over a cliff to his death. Sandow returns to his master and finds him happily in love. *Prospectors. Claim jumpers. Courtship. Dogs.*

THE CALL OF YOUTH **F2.0747**

Famous Players–Lasky British Producers. *Dist* Paramount Pictures. 13 Mar **1921** [c26 Jan, 14 Mar 1921; LP16051, LP16320]. Si; b&w. 35mm. 4 reels, 3,871 ft.

Dir Hugh Ford. *Scen* Eve Unsell. *Photog* Hal Young.

Cast: Mary Glynne *(Betty Overton)*, Marjorie Hume *(Joan Lawton)*, Jack Hobbs *(Hubert Richmond)*, Malcolm Cherry *(James Agar)*, Ben Webster *(Mark Lawton)*, Gertrude Sterroll *(Mrs. Lawton)*, Victor Humphrey *(Peter Hoskins)*, John Peachey *(Dr. Michaelson)*, Ralph Foster *(minister)*.

Melodrama. Source: Henry Arthur Jones, "James, the Fogy" (publication undetermined). In London Betty Overton meets Hubert Richmond, who returns a slipper she lost in a stream, and they fall in love. Betty's uncle, Mark Lawton, is ruined in a financial panic but is extricated by her admirer, Agar, whom she consents to marry. To eliminate his rival, Agar assigns Richmond to a position in South Africa, but when Betty realizes there would be no love in their marriage, Agar relinquishes her to Richmond. *Finance—Personal. Courtship. London.*

THE CALLAHANS AND THE MURPHYS **F2.0748**

Metro-Goldwyn-Mayer Pictures. 18 Jun **1927** [c11 Jul 1927; LP24254]. Si; b&w. 35mm. 7 reels, 6,126 ft.

Dir George Hill. *Scen* Frances Marion. *Titl* Ralph Spence. *Photog* Ira Morgan. *Sets* Cedric Gibbons, David Townsend. *Film Ed* Hugh Wynn. *Wardrobe* René Hubert.

Cast: Marie Dressler *(Mrs. Callahan)*, Polly Moran *(Mrs. Murphy)*, Sally O'Neil *(Ellen Callahan)*, Lawrence Gray *(Dan Murphy)*, Eddie Gribbon *(Jim Callahan)*, Frank Currier *(Grandpa Callahan)*, Gertrude Olmsted *(Monica Murphy)*, Turner Savage *(Timmy Callahan)*, Jackie Coombs *(Terrance Callahan)*, Dawn O'Day *(Mary Callahan)*, Monty O'Grady *(Michael Callahan)*, Tom Lewis *(Mr. Murphy)*.

Comedy-drama. Source: Kathleen Norris, *The Callahans and the Murphys* (Garden City, New York, 1924). Mrs. Callahan and Mrs. Murphy, who live on opposite sides of a narrow alley in the tenement district, are quarrelsome friends, although their children, Ellen and Dan, are in love. Dan becomes involved with a gang of bootleggers and disappears. Ellen, meanwhile, gives birth to a child which her mother contrives to adopt without knowledge of its origin. When Dan returns, the couple confess to having been secretly married. The Callahans and Murphys once again resume their happy existence, with the mothers arguing over the baby's family resemblance. *Bootleggers. Irish. Family life. Adoption. Tenements.*

CALVERT'S VALLEY **F2.0749**

Fox Film Corp. 8 Oct **1922** [c2 Oct 1922; LP19088]. Si; b&w. 35mm. 5 reels, 4,416 ft.

Pres by William Fox. *Dir* Jack Dillon. *Scen* Jules Furthman. *Photog* Don Short.

Cast: Jack Gilbert *(Page Emlyn)*, Sylvia Breamer *(Hester Rymal)*, Philo McCullough *(James Calvert/Eugene Calvert)*, Herschel Mayall *(Judge Rymal)*, Lule Warrenton *(The Widow Crowcroft)*.

Mystery melodrama. Source: Margaret Prescott Montague, *In Calvert's Valley* (New York, 1908). When James Calvert visits a tract of land with young lawyer Page Emlyn, he is mysteriously pushed off a cliff to his death. An old woman, who witnessed the incident, accuses Emlyn of killing Calvert, but Emlyn, who was drunk, does not recall anything. Emlyn is sent to jail to await trial. Meanwhile he has fallen in love with Hester Rymal, Calvert's ex-sweetheart, who thinks Calvert committed suicide because of unrequited love. Eventually the old woman admits that her halfwitted son killed Calvert. The youngsters are free to find their happiness. *Halfwits. Lawyers. Murder. Drunkenness.*

CAMEO KIRBY **F2.0750**

Fox Film Corp. 21 Oct **1923** [c8 Oct 1923; LP19564]. Si; b&w. 35mm. 7 reels, 6,931 ft.

Pres by William Fox. *Dir* John Ford. *Scen* Robert N. Lee. *Photog*

George Schneiderman.

Cast: John Gilbert *(Cameo Kirby)*, Gertrude Olmstead *(Adele Randall)*, Alan Hale *(Colonel Moreau)*, Eric Mayne *(Colonel Randall)*, William E. Lawrence *(Tom Randall)*, Richard Tucker *(Cousin Aaron Randall)*, Phillips Smalley *(Judge Playdell)*, Jack McDonald *(Larkin Bunce)*, Jean Arthur *(Ann Playdell)*, Eugenie Ford *(Madame Davezac)*.

Melodrama. Source: Booth Tarkington and Harry Leon Wilson, *Cameo Kirby, a Play in 4 Acts* (New York opening: 20 Dec 1909). Gambler Cameo Kirby enters a card game between Colonel John Randall and a crooked gambler named Colonel Moreau. Kirby wins, although Randall loses his property to Moreau. Kirby, intending to return it to Randall, secures the deed, but not before Randall, in desperation, kills himself. Moreau blames Kirby for the death and shoots him. Then Kirby kills Moreau in a duel. Kirby takes refuge in the Randall country home when the heirs of Colonel Randall seek him out for allegedly shooting Moreau in cold blood. Kirby justifies himself with the Randall brothers and marries their sister, Adele. *Gamblers. Brother-sister relationship. Suicide. Mississippi River. Duels.*

Note: Remade in 1929.

CAMEO KIRBY F2.0751

Fox Film Corp. 12 Jan **1930** [c30 Nov 1929; LP924]. Sd (Movietone); b&w. 35mm. 7 reels, 5,910 ft.

Pres by William Fox. *Dir* Irving Cummings. *Adapt-Cont-Dial* Marion Orth. *Photog* L. William O'Connell, George Eastman. *Film Ed* Alex Troffey. *Incidental Mus* George Lipschultz. *Songs: "Romance," "After a Million Dreams," "Home Is Heaven"* Walter Donaldson, Edgar Leslie. *Song: "Drink to the Girl of My Dreams"* L. Wolfe Gilbert, Abel Baer. *Songs: "Tankard and Bowl," "I'm a Peaceful Man"* Fred Strauss, Ed Brady. *Rec Engr* Joseph Aiken. *Asst Dir* Charles Woolstenhulme. *Wardrobe* Sophie Wachner.

Cast: J. Harold Murray *(Cameo Kirby)*, Norma Terris *(Adele Randall)*, Douglas Gilmore *(Jack Moreau)*, Robert Edeson *(Colonel Randall)*, Myrna Loy *(Lea)*, Charles Morton *(Anatole)*, Stepin Fetchit *(Croup)*, George MacFarlane *(George)*, John Hyams *(Larkin Bunce)*, Madame Daumery *(Claire Devezac)*, Beulah Hall Jones *(Poulette)*.

Musical comedy–melodrama. Source: Booth Tarkington and Harry Leon Wilson, *Cameo Kirby* (New York opening: 20 Dec 1909). Cameo Kirby, an honest riverboat gambler who works the Mississippi, rescues a girl from a gang of ruffians in New Orleans, but she disappears after he sings her a love song. He later joins up with Moreau, a rival gambler, who is scheming to fleece a cotton planter of his year's receipts; Kirby wins the deed to the planter's property, but the planter kills himself before Kirby can return it. He discovers the planter's daughter to be Adele, the same girl he rescued, but Moreau has previously poisoned her against him. The townspeople threaten to lynch Kirby when he kills Moreau in a duel, but he is exonerated when he produces the deed to the property and wins over the girl. *Gamblers. Riverboats. Plantations. Suicide. New Orleans. Mississippi River.*

Note: Remake of *Cameo Kirby*, 1923.

THE CAMERAMAN F2.0752

Metro-Goldwyn-Mayer Pictures. 22 Sep **1928** [c15 Sep 1928; LP25722]. Si; b&w. 35mm. 8 reels, 6,995 ft.

Prod Buster Keaton. *Dir* Edward Sedgwick. *Scen* Richard Schayer. *Titl* Joseph Farnham. *Story* Clyde Bruckman, Lew Lipton. *Photog* Elgin Lessley, Reggie Lanning. *Tech Dir* Fred Gabourie. *Film Ed (see note)* Hugh Wynn, Basil Wrangell.

Cast: Buster Keaton *(Luke Shannon [Buster])*, Marceline Day *(Sally)*, Harry Gribbon *(cop)*, Harold Goodwin *(Stagg)*, Sidney Bracy *(editor)*.

Comedy. Tintype photographer Buster falls in love with Sally, a secretary for the Hearst newsreel, and hocks his still camera in order to buy an ancient movie camera. At Sally's urging, Buster photographs news events that may be of interest to the Hearst organization but all of his attempts turn out badly. Sally tips Buster off about an impending tong war in Chinatown, and he covers all the dangerous action only to discover that he had no film in his camera. The following day Buster is filming a regatta and Sally falls overboard from the boat of Stagg, a cowardly Hearst cameraman who deserts her to save himself. Buster rescues Sally and wins her undying love. *Newsreel photographers. Secretaries. Tongs. Boat racing. Chinatown. Hearst News Service.*

Note: Sources disagree in crediting film editor.

CAMILLE F2.0753

Nazimova Productions. *Dist* Metro Pictures. call Sep **1921** [Milwaukee premiere; released 26 Sep; c21 Sep 1921; LP17932]. Si; b&w. 35mm. 6 reels, 5,600 ft.

Dir Ray C. Smallwood. *Scen-Adapt* June Mathis. *Photog* Rudolph Bergquist. *Art Dir* Natacha Rambova.

Cast: Nazimova *(Camille, Marguerite Gautier)*, Rudolph Valentino *(Armand Duval)*, Arthur Hoyt *(Count de Varville)*, Zeffie Tillbury *(Prudence)*, Rex Cherryman *(Gaston)*, Edward Connelly *(Duke)*, Patsy Ruth Miller *(Nichette)*, Consuelo Flowerton *(Olimpe)*, Mrs. Oliver *(Manine)*, William Orlamond *(Monsieur Duval)*.

Romantic drama. Source: Alexandre Dumas, fils, *La Dame aux Camélias* (novel: 1848; play: 1852). Armand Duval, a young and unsophisticated law student, falls passionately in love with Marguerite Gautier, known as Camille, a notorious Parisian courtesan. Armand forsakes his family and career, Marguerite abandons her friends for him, and they pass the days happily in a country retreat. They soon find themselves without money; consequently, Armand arranges for Marguerite to receive his small legacy, and, unknown to him, Marguerite plans to sell her possessions. Armand's father learns of the situation and determines to save the family name from disgrace. He persuades Marguerite to give up Armand, and she reverts to her former life of debauchery. Visiting a gambling house one evening she encounters Armand; believing himself abandoned for the Count de Varville's wealth, he denounces her before the crowd. Abandoned and ill, Marguerite finally dies in her home, clasping Armand's only gift, a copy of *Manon Lescaut. Prostitutes. Filial relations. Paris. "Manon Lescaut".*

CAMILLE F2.0754

Norma Talmadge Productions. *Dist* First National Pictures. 21 Apr **1927** [New York premiere; released 4 Sep; c21 Apr 1927; LP23879]. Si; b&w. 35mm. 9 reels, 8,700 ft.

Pres by Joseph M. Schenck. *Dir* Fred Niblo. *Screen Story* Fred De Gresac. *Adapt-Scen* Olga Printzlau, Chandler Sprague. *Titl* George Marion, Jr. *Photog* Oliver T. Marsh.

Cast: Norma Talmadge *(Marguerite Gautier [Camille])*, Gilbert Roland *(Armand)*, Lilyan Tashman *(Olympe)*, Rose Dione *(Prudence)*, Oscar Beregi *(Count de Varville)*, Harvey Clark *(The Baron)*, Helen Jerome Eddy *(Camille's maid)*, Alec B. Francis *(The Duke)*, Albert Conti *(Henri)*, Michael Visaroff *(Camille's father)*, Evelyn Selbie *(Camille's mother)*, Etta Lee *(Mataloti)*, Maurice Costello *(Armand's father)*.

Romantic drama. Suggested by: Alexandre Dumas, fils, *La Dame aux Camélias.* At an auction of the possessions of the dead Marguerite Gautier, Armand, her lover, bids on her diary and portrait; the spirit of Camille glides to the portrait, opens the diary, and bids him read. ... In the Paris glove shop of Prudence Duvernoy, Marguerite, a clerk infatuated with the Count de Varville, becomes a courtesan; a year later she lives in luxury and shuffles her admirers like a pack of cards, accepting or dismissing attentions at her will. While at the opera with a wealthy old duke, she meets Armand, who leaves the theater when he learns of her profession, though he is as passionately involved as Camille. They are reunited at a party and make a rendezvous, which is rudely interrupted by the count. They retire to the country together, but at the request of Armand's father Camille leaves her lover and dies lonely and unhappy. *Salesclerks. Prostitutes. Courtship. Paris. Documentation.*

CAMILLE OF THE BARBARY COAST F2.0755

Associated Exhibitors. 1 Nov **1925** [c27 Jul 1925; LU21680]. Si; b&w. 35mm. 6 reels, 5,308 ft.

Dir Hugh Dierker. *Scen* Eugene Edward Holland. *Story* Forrest Halsey. *Photog* Frank Zukor.

Cast: Mae Busch *(Camille Balishaw)*, Owen Moore *(Robert Morton)*, Fritzi Brunette *(Maggie Smith)*, Burr McIntosh *(Henry Norton)*, Harry Morey *(Dan McCarthy)*, Tammany Young *(Barbary Bennie)*, Dorothy King *(Dora Malcolm)*, Robert Daly *(Chauncey Hilburn)*, Dagmar Godowsky *(Sonia Ivanoria)*.

Melodrama. For the sake of a woman, Robert Morton does time in jail, and his father disowns him. He is freed after several years and drifts into a dive on the Barbary Coast, where he meets Camille, one of the women. She shelters him and is instrumental in his rehabilitation. Robert gets a job, but he is fired when his prison record becomes known. Camille sticks by him, and they are married. Robert obtains another position and gradually works his way back to self-respect. His father has a change of heart and seeks out Robert, asking him to return home, but without Camille. Robert sticks by his wife; and the old man, realizing the depth of their love and their need for each other, relents. *Criminals—Rehabilitation. Prostitutes. Filial relations. San Francisco—Barbary Coast.*

THE CAMPUS FLIRT **F2.0756**

Famous Players–Lasky. *Dist* Paramount Pictures. 18 Sep **1926** [New York premiere; released 4 Oct; c5 Oct 1926; LP23181]. Si; b&w. 35mm. 7 reels, 6,702 ft.

Pres by Adolph Zukor, Jesse L. Lasky. *Dir* Clarence Badger. *Story-Screenplay* Louise Long, Lloyd Corrigan. *Titl* Rube Goldberg, Ralph Spence. *Photog* H. Kinley Martin.

Cast: Bebe Daniels *(Patricia Mansfield)*, James Hall *(Denis Adams)*, El Brendel *(Knute Knudson)*, Charles Paddock *(himself)*, Joan Standing *(Harriet Porter)*, Gilbert Roland *(Graham Stearns)*, Irma Kornelia *(Mae)*, Jocelyn Lee *(Gwen)*.

Comedy-drama. Patricia Mansfield, a product of wealth and high society, is sent to Colton College by her father, who hopes to eradicate her snobbish veneer. On the train Pat meets Denis Adams, a prominent athlete who is working his way through school as coach of the girls' track team, and he introduces her to track star Charlie Paddock. Through efforts to keep her associates in place, Pat sinks deeper into the mire of antagonism; and her only friends are Harriet Porter and Knute Knudson, the Swedish janitor. Trying to escape from Knute's pet mouse, she passes Paddock like a streak of lightning. Joining the fast set, Pat is soon branded as the campus flirt, and realizing her foolishness she sets out to vindicate herself by joining the track team. Before a meet, Graham Stearns abducts Adams; and Pat, in rescuing him, is herself detained. Knute rescues her in time for the race, and in a screaming finish with chasing policemen, Paddock saves the event by running the last lap. *Flirts. Athletic coaches. Janitors. Swedes. Social classes. College life. Courtship. Snobbery. Track. University of Southern California.*

Note: Filmed in part on location at the University of Southern California.

CAMPUS KNIGHTS **F2.0757**

Chesterfield Motion Picture Corp. 1 Mar or 15 Jun **1929.** Si; b&w. 35mm. 6 reels, 5,474 ft.

Supv Lon Young. *Dir-Story* Albert Kelly. *Scen* Arthur Hoerl. *Titl* Lee Authmar, Lon Young, Hoey Lawlor. *Photog* M. A. Anderson. *Film Ed* Earl Turner.

Cast: Raymond McKee *(Prof. Ezra Hastings/Earl Hastings)*, Shirley Palmer *(Audrey Scott)*, Marie Quillen *(Edna)*, Jean Laverty *(Pearl)*, J. C. Fowler *(Dean Whitlock)*, Sybil Grove *(The Matron)*, P. J. Danby *(The Janitor)*, Leo White *(Pearl's lawyer)*, Lewis Sargent *(The Sport)*.

Comedy. High-stepper Earl Hastings is continually mistaken for his twin brother, Ezra, a meek professor at a girls' seminary, and his constant flirtations in and around the dormitories—most notably with the daughter of the dean—involve Ezra in several compromising situations. Finally, a woman pursuing Earl for breach of promise unscrambles the twins with the help of the dean's daughter. *Professors. Twins. Brothers. College life. Personal identity. Timidity. Breach of promise.*

CAN A WOMAN LOVE TWICE? **F2.0758**

R-C Pictures. *Dist* Film Booking Offices of America. 4 Mar **1923** [c20 Oct 1922; LP20006]. Si; b&w. 35mm. 7 reels, 6,700 ft.

Dir James W. Horne. *Story-Scen* Wyndham Gittens. *Photog* Joseph A. Dubray, Allen Irving. *Art Dir* W. L. Heywood. *Film Ed* James Morley.

Cast: Ethel Clayton *(Mary Grant)*, Muriel Dana *(Thomas Jefferson Grant, Jr.)*, Kate Lester *(Mrs. Grant)*, Fred Esmelton *(Coleman Grant)*, Victory Bateman *(Mary's landlady)*, Wilfred Lucas *(Franklyn Chase)*, Anderson Smith *(Detective Means)*, Al Hart *(Abner Grant)*, Malcolm McGregor *(Abner's son)*, Theodore von Eltz *(Thomas Jefferson Grant)*, Clara Clark Ward *(housekeeper)*, Madge Hunt *(nurse)*.

Drama. War widow Mary Grant is forced to support herself and her child, Tom, by working in a cabaret, because her deceased husband's parents disapprove of her. They wish to adopt Tom, however; and Mary accepts the offer of Abner Grant (who lost in the war a son with the same name as that of Mary's husband) to live with him on his ranch. To everyone's surprise, Abner's son returns very much alive, but Abner's prewar displeasure with his son has not subsided. He is even more angry when he learns that Mary is not actually his daughter-in-law, but finally he relents and Mary gladly accepts young Grant's marriage proposal. *Ranchers. Widows. Veterans. Imposture.*

THE CANADIAN **F2.0759**

Famous Players–Lasky. *Dist* Paramount Pictures. 27 Nov **1926** [New York premiere; released 6 Dec]. Si; b&w. 35mm. 8 reels, 7,753 ft.

Pres by Adolph Zukor, Jesse L. Lasky. *Assoc Prod* William Le Baron. *Dir* William Beaudine. *Prod Ed* J. Clarkson Miller, Ralph Block. *Titl* Julian Johnson. *Adapt* Arthur Stringer. *Photog* Alvin Wyckoff. *Film Ed* Julian Johnson.

Cast: Thomas Meighan *(Frank Taylor)*, Mona Palma *(Nora)*, Wyndham Standing *(Ed Marsh)*, Dale Fuller *(Gertie)*, Charles Winninger *(Pop Tyson)*, Billy Butts *(Buck Golder)*.

Romantic drama. Source: William Somerset Maugham, *The Land of Promise* (a play; London, 1913). Frank Taylor, a Canadian wheat farmer, works on the farm of Ed Marsh, so as to sustain the loss of his own crop. Marsh's sister, Nora, who has lost her wealth in England, comes to make her home with them, and from the moment that Frank meets her at the station, she treats him like a hired man and incurs his cordial dislike. Nora soon clashes with Gertie, Ed's ex-waitress wife, but swallows her distaste for surrounding crudities and tries to be useful. Soon she is forced to remain an unwelcome guest, and learning that Frank needs a wife, she offers herself. At his farm, Frank concentrates on his effort to raise a new crop, and Nora's bitterness gradually turns to secret respect; at harvesting time, he promises to send her back to England, if successful. Then a raging storm ravages Frank's wheat; Nora prepares to leave on her own money, but as time for parting nears, Frank's reserve breaks and they are happily united in spite of the tragedy. *English. Farmers. Brother-sister relationship. Farm life. Marriage. Wheat. Canadian Northwest. Storms.*

Note: Filmed on location in the Canadian Rockies of Alberta.

THE CANARY MURDER CASE **F2.0760**

Paramount Famous Lasky Corp. 16 Feb **1929** [c15 Feb 1929; LP126]. Sd (Movietone); b&w. 35mm. 7 reels, 7,171 ft. [Also si; 6,554 ft.]

Dir Malcolm St. Clair. *Dial* S. S. Van Dine. *Titl* Herman J. Mankiewicz. *Adapt* Florence Ryerson, Albert S. Le Vino. *Photog* Harry Fischbeck. *Film Ed* William Shea.

Cast: William Powell *(Philo Vance)*, James Hall *(Jimmy Spotswoode)*, Louise Brooks *(Margaret O'Dell)*, Jean Arthur *(Alys La Fosse)*, Gustav von Seyffertitz *(Dr. Ambrose Lindquist)*, Charles Lane *(Charles Spotswoode)*, Eugene Pallette *(Ernest Heath)*, Lawrence Grant *(Charles Cleaver)*, Ned Sparks *(Tony Skeel)*, Louis John Bartels *(Louis Mannix)*, E. H. Calvert *(Markham)*, George Y. Harvey, Oscar Smith, Tim Adair.

Detective drama. Source: S. S. Van Dine, *The "Canary" Murder Case; a Philo Vance Story* (New York, 1927). Margaret O'Dell, a blackmailing musical comedy star, is found strangled in her apartment, and four men come under suspicion: Lindquist, a half-mad doctor in love with Margaret; Cleaver, a politician whose career she threatened; Mannix, a fat broker with a jealous wife; and Jimmy Spotswoode, a young society boy Margaret was attempting to blackmail into marriage. Jimmy is arrested, and Philo Vance, a whimsical society man and amateur detective who is a close friend of Jimmy's father, is called in on the case. Vance proves the murderer to have been the elder Spotswoode. *Detectives. Physicians. Brokers. Politicians. District attorneys. Blackmail. Murder.*

THE CANCELLED DEBT **F2.0761**

Banner Productions. *Dist* Sterling Pictures Distributing Corp. 1 Sep **1927** [c26 Sep 1927; LP24447]. Si; b&w. 35mm. 6 reels, 5,200 ft.

Dir Phil Rosen. *Story-Scen* Frances Guihan. *Photog* Herbert Kirkpatrick.

Cast: Rex Lease *(Patrick Burke)*, Charlotte Stevens *(June Butler)*, Florence Turner *(Mrs. Burke)*, Billy Sullivan *(Jimmy Martin)*, James Gordon *(Mr. Butler)*, Ethel Grey Terry *(Mrs. Martin)*.

Melodrama. June Butler, an inveterate speed driver, is overtaken by young Officer Pat Burke, a motorcycle cop, and given a ticket. When Pat catches a thief, Jimmy Martin, trying to steal from the Butler home, June, out of spite, claims that Jimmy is her fiancé; later, she discovers he is pursued by his former gang and is trying to go straight for the sake of his wife and child. She gets him a job in her father's warehouse. When June gets another ticket from Pat for parking near a fire hydrant, she has him demoted to patrolman through her father's influence, but he is reinstated when he saves June from being robbed in the slums. Jimmy and June are cornered by the gang at the warehouse, but Pat subdues them in a fight; Butler proposes to Mrs. Burke, and their respective offspring are united. *Thieves. Gangs. Police. Filial relations. Automobile driving.*

THE CANDY KID **F2.0762**
Dailey Productions. **1928.** Si; b&w. 35mm. 7 reels, 6,200 ft.
Dir-Titl David Kirkland. *Scen* Rex Lease. *Photog* Charles Bottle, Bert Baldridge. *Film Ed* Minnie Steppler.
Cast: Rex Lease, Pauline Garon, Frank Campeau, Harry Woods, Roy Stewart, Charlotte Merriam, Paul Panzer.
Drama(?). No information about the nature of this film has been found.

THE CANVAS KISSER **F2.0763**
Paul Gerson Pictures. 17 Jun **1925** [New York premiere]. Si; b&w. 35mm. 5 reels.
Pres by B. Berger. *Dir* Duke Worne. *Story* Grover Jones. *Photog* Alfred Gosden.
Cast: Richard Holt, Ruth Dwyer, Garry O'Dell, Cecil Edwards.
Action melodrama. A prizefighter of considerable fistic prowess earns an easy living by betting on his opponents and then taking a dive in his fights. He is reformed by the exacting influence of a girl and retires from the ring. The fighter's sudden honesty arouses the suspicion and enmity of his manager, and he finds himself in a lot of trouble. *Prizefighters. Fight managers. Gambling. Honesty.*

CANYON HAWKS **F2.0764**
National Players. *Dist* Big 4 Film Corp. 26 Aug **1930.** Sd (Cinephone); b&w. 35mm. 6 reels, 5,339 ft.
Dir-Scen-Dial Alvin J. Neitz. *Story* Henry Taylor, Alvin J. Neitz. *Photog* William Nobles. *Film Ed* Fred Bain. *Sd* James Lowrie.
Cast: Yakima Canutt *(Jack Benson)*, Buzz Barton *(George Manning)*, Rene Borden *(Mildred Manning)*, Robert Walker *(Steve Knowles)*, Robert Reeves *(Sheriff Jackson)*, Cliff Lyons *(Tom Hardy)*, Wally Wales *(Dick Carson)*, Bobby Dunn *(Shorty)*.
Western melodrama. Driving their herd of sheep through hostile cattle country, Mildred Manning and her brother, George, are befriended by Jack Benson, who gives them shelter and sells them land. Mildred falls into the villainous hands of Steve Knowles when she hears and believes his report of Jack's killing George, but Jack learns of the deception, sends George for the sheriff, and traps the outlaws. *Ranchers. Brother-sister relationship. Sheep. Cattle.*

THE CANYON OF ADVENTURE **F2.0765**
Charles R. Rogers Productions. *Dist* First National Pictures. 22 Apr **1928** [c14 Feb 1928; LP24984]. Si; b&w. 35mm. 6 reels, 5,800 ft.
Supv Harry J. Brown. *Dir* Albert Rogell. *Story-Scen* Marion Jackson. *Titl* Ford Beebe. *Photog* Ted McCord. *Film Ed* Fred Allen.
Cast: Ken Maynard *(Steven Bancroft)*, Virginia Brown Faire *(Dolores Castanares)*, Eric Mayne *(Don Miguel)*, Theodore Lorch *(Don Alfredo Villegas)*, Tyrone Brereton *(Luis Villegas)*, Hal Salter *(Jake Leach)*, Billy Franey *(Buzzard Koke)*, Charles Whitaker *(Slim Burke)*, Tarzan *(himself, a horse)*.
Action melodrama. Don Alfredo, a scheming Spanish nobleman, plans to steal the lands of a neighboring Don Miguel and marry his worthless son, Luis, to Don Miguel's daughter, Dolores. The plan is foiled by Steven Bancroft, a United States land agent engaged in encouraging the grandees of the new State of California to register their land holdings with the government. Accompanied by two friends disguised as caballeros, Bancroft, who has fallen in love with Dolores, raids the hacienda where she is about to be forced into marrige. Freeing Don Miguel (also held captive by Don Alfredo), they turn Don Alfredo and his son over to authorities and continue the wedding with Bancroft taking the place of the bridegroom. *Nobility. Spanish. Land commissioners. Land registration. Marriage—Arranged. California. Horses.*

THE CANYON OF LIGHT **F2.0766**
Fox Film Corp. 5 Dec **1926** [c14 Nov 1926; LP23348]. Si; b&w. 35mm. 6 reels, 5,399 ft.
Pres by William Fox. *Dir* Benjamin Stoloff. *Scen* John Stone. *Titl* William Conselman. *Photog* Dan Clark. *Asst Dir* Wynn Mace.
Cast: Tom Mix *(Tom Mills)*, Dorothy Dwan *(Concha Deane)*, Carl Miller *(Ed Bardin)*, Ralph Sipperly *(Jerry Shanks)*, Barry Norton *(Ricardo Deane)*, Carmelita Geraghty *(Ellen Bardin)*, William Walling *(Cyrus Dean)*, Duke Lee *(Joe Navardo)*, Tony *(The Wonder Horse)*.
Western melodrama. Source: Kenneth Perkins, *The Canyon of Light* (New York, 1932). Tom Mills's buddy, Ricardo Deane, is killed in France during the war, and after the war Tom is invited to visit Deane's family on the Mexican border. There he discovers that Ed Bardin, Deane's brother-in-law, has been unfaithful to his wife, and that he is a bandit, posing as Tom. Following a stage holdup, a runaway rescue, a near hanging, a rodeo, and cliff and river riding, the gang is captured and Tom wins the heart of Concha, his buddy's sister. *Veterans. Bandits. Impersonation. World War I. Mexican border. Horses.*

THE CANYON OF MISSING MEN **F2.0767**
Dist Syndicate Pictures. 1 Feb or 1 Jun **1930.** Mus score; b&w. 35mm. 5 reels, 4,742 ft. [Also si.]
Dir J. P. McGowan. *Story* George H. Williams. *Photog* Hap Depew.
Cast: Tom Tyler *(Dave Brandon)*, Sheila Le Gay *(Inez Sepulveda)*, Tom Forman *(Juan Sepulveda)*, Bud Osborne *(Slug Slagel)*, J. P. McGowan, Cliff Lyons *(Brill Lonergan)*, Bobby Dunn *(Gimpy Lamb)*, Arden Ellis *(Peg Slagel)*.
Western melodrama. Dave Brandon decides to abandon his gang's life of crime and go straight when he meets Inez Sepulveda, the pretty daughter of a ranchowner. Seeking revenge, the gang kidnaps the girl for ransom, then holds her and her father in preparation for rustling the Sepulveda cattle. Dave's arrival on the scene signals the downfall of the gang, rescue of the Sepulvedas, and wedding bells for Inez. *Ranchers. Gangs. Criminals—Rehabilitation. Rustling. Kidnaping. Ransom.*

CANYON OF THE FOOLS **F2.0768**
R-C Pictures. *Dist* Film Booking Offices of America. 21 Jan **1923** [c18 Nov 1922; LP20005]. Si; b&w. 35mm. 6 reels, 5,180 ft.
P. A. Powers Production. *Dir* Val Paul. *Scen* John W. Grey. *Photog* William Thornley, Robert De Grasse.
Cast: Harry Carey *(Bob)*, Marguerite Clayton *(May)*, Fred Stanton *(Jim Harper/Polhill)*, Joseph Harris *(Terazaz)*, Jack Curtis *(Maricopia)*, Carmen Arselle *(Incarnación)*, Charles J. Le Moyne *(Swasey)*, Vester Pegg *(Knute)*, Murdock MacQuarrie *(Sproul)*, Mignonne Golden *(Aurelia)*.
Western melodrama. Source: Richard Matthews Hallet, *The Canyon of the Fools* (New York, 1922). Bob goes west in search of the man who framed him. On the train he meets his former sweetheart, May, who is now engaged to Jim Harper, and learns that they are on their way to a mining camp near Canyon of the Fools. Agreeing to help the sheriff capture some bandits, Bob goes into a mine cave in which some gold has been hidden. He discovers Jim Harper to be the man he has sought, and after many adventures he rescues May and rounds up the gang. He is rewarded with May's love and the gold. *Bandits. Sheriffs. Treasure.*
Note: Reissued 1930. (New York State license issued to Julius Levine 22 Jan 1930.)

CANYON RUSTLERS **F2.0769**
Harry Webb Productions. *Dist* Aywon Film Corp. 18 Mar **1925.** Si; b&w. 35mm. 5 reels, 4,800 ft.
Dir Harry Webb.
Cast: Jack Perrin.
Western melodrama. A mysterious gang of outlaws, the Wolf Riders, attempts to drive the ranchers from their homesteads in a fertile valley. The gang uses first threats and then murder to persuade the reluctant ranchers to vacate their lands. A stranger arrives in town and is admitted to the Wolf Riders, but the gang becomes suspicious of him when he courts the daughter of a rancher who has fought them. The gang attacks the stranger and abducts the girl. The stranger rescues the girl, arrests the members of the gang, and reveals himself to be a Texas Ranger. *Homesteaders. Texas Rangers. Strangers. Gangs. Murder. Abduction.*

CAPITAL PUNISHMENT **F2.0770**
B. P. Schulberg Productions. *Dist* Preferred Pictures. 1 Jan **1925.** Si; b&w. 35mm. 6 reels, 5,950 ft.
Dir James P. Hogan. *Adapt* John Goodrich. *Story* B. P. Schulberg. *Photog* Joseph Goodrich.
Cast of Prolog: Eddie Phillips *(The Boy)*, Alec B. Francis *(The Chaplain)*, Edith Yorke *(The Mother)*, Joseph Kilgour *(The Governor)*, George Nichols *(The Warden)*, John Prince *(The Doctor)*
Cast of Main Story: Elliott Dexter *(Gordon Harrington)*, George Hackathorne *(Danny O'Connor)*, Clara Bow *(Delia Tate)*, Margaret Livingston *(Mona Caldwell)*, Robert Ellis *(Harry Phillips)*, Mary Carr *(Mrs. O'Connor)*, Fred Warren *(pawnbroker)*, Wade Boteler *(Officer Dugan)*.
Melodrama. After a vain attempt to save an innocent man from execution, welfare worker Gordon Harrington arranges with Dan O'Connor for Dan to be framed for a murder that will never occur, telling Dan that, at

the appropriate moment, the hoax will be disclosed and capital punishment will thereby be discredited. Harrington arranges for his friend, Harry Phillips, to go on an extended sea voyage on his yacht and then makes it appear that O'Connor has murdered Phillips. O'Connor is convicted and sentenced to death. Phillips returns home unexpectedly from his cruise, and, in an argument, Harrington inadvertently kills him. Mona Caldwell, Harrington's fiancée, persuades him not to report the murder to the police, allowing O'Connor to go to his doom. O'Connor protests his innocence but Harrington disavows all knowledge of a frameup. O'Connor is about to be executed when Mona has a change of heart and tells the police that Harrington is the man who murdered Phillips. *Social workers. Murder. Frameup. Hoaxes. Capital punishment. Injustice. Yachts.*

CAPPY RICKS **F2.0771**

Famous Players–Lasky. *Dist* Paramount Pictures. 2 Oct **1921** [c19 Oct 1921; LP17111]. Si; b&w. 35mm. 6 reels, 5,962 ft.

Pres by Adolph Zukor. *Dir* Tom Forman. *Scen* Albert Shelby Le Vino, Waldemar Young. *Photog* Harry Perry.

Cast: Thomas Meighan *(Matt Peasley)*, Charles Abbe *(Cappy Ricks)*, Agnes Ayres *(Florrie Ricks)*, Hugh Cameron *(Murphy)*, John Sainpolis *(Skinner)*, Paul Everton *(Captain Kendall)*, Eugenie Woodward *(Mrs. Peasley)*, Tom O'Malley *(Captain Jones)*, Ivan Linow *(Ole Peterson)*, William Wally *(Swenson)*, Jack Dillon *(Larsen)*, Gladys Granger *(Doris)*.

Sea melodrama. Source: Peter Bernard Kyne, *Cappy Ricks* (New York, 1915). Edward E. Rose, *Cappy Ricks; a Play* (New York, 1923). Seaman Matt Peasley drifts into San Francisco with his pal Murphy and rescues Florrie Ricks, daughter of shipowner Cappy Ricks, from a pickpocket. Peasley and his friend are signed on one of Cappy's ships. When the ship's captain is killed by savages, Matt takes command and brings the ship to Samoa; but when the owner informs him that a new captain is arriving, Matt rebels, thrashes the newcomer into submission, and sails for San Francisco. Ricks is furious over his disobedience and enraged to learn that his daughter loves Matt. The old man sends Florrie on a cruise with Skinner, one of his officials, and the ship is stranded in a storm; Matt and Murphy rescue the party in a tug; and realizing Matt's worth, Cappy withdraws his opposition to his marriage to Florrie. *Seamen. Shipowners. Pickpockets. Ships. Seafaring life. Samoa. San Francisco. Storms.*

CAPTAIN APPLEJACK *see* **STRANGERS OF THE NIGHT**

CAPTAIN BLACKBIRD *see* **LOST AND FOUND ON A SOUTH SEA ISLAND**

CAPTAIN BLOOD **F2.0772**

Vitagraph Co. of America. 21 Sep **1924** [c11 Sep 1924; LP20561]. Si; b&w. 35mm. 11 reels, 10,680 ft.

Pres by Albert E. Smith. *Dir* David Smith. *Scen* Jay Pilcher. *Photog* Steve Smith, Jr. *Art Dir* Al Herman. *Film Ed* Albert Jordan. *Asst Dir* William T. Dagwell. *Research* Philip Goodfriend.

Cast: J. Warren Kerrigan *(Captain Blood)*, Jean Paige *(Arabella Bishop)*, Charlotte Merriam *(Mary Traill)*, James Morrison *(Jeremy Pitt)*, Allan Forrest *(Lord Julian Wade)*, Bertram Grassby *(Don Diego)*, Otis Harlan *(Corliss)*, Jack Curtis *(Wolverstone)*, Wilfrid North *(Colonel Bishop)*, Otto Matiesen *(Lord Jeffreys)*, Robert Bolder *(Admiral Van Der Kuylen)*, Templar Saxe *(Governor Steed)*, Henry Barrows *(Lord Willoughby)*, Boyd Irwin *(Levasseur)*, Henry Hebert *(Captain Hobart)*, Miles McCarthy *(Captain Caverly)*, Tom McGuire *(Farmer Baynes)*, Frank Whitson *(Baron de Rivarol)*, Helen Howard *(Mistress Baynes)*, Robert Milash *(Kent)*, William Eugene *(Don Esteban)*, George Williams *(Major Mallard)*, Omar Whitehead *(Don Miguel)*, Muriel Paull *(Mademoiselle d'Ogeron)*, George Lewis *(Henri d'Ogeron)*.

Romantic adventure. Source: Rafael Sabatini, *Captain Blood, His Odyssey* (Boston & New York, 1922). Young Irish physician Peter Blood is exiled as a slave to Barbados, where he and his friend Jeremy are purchased by Colonel Bishop at the behest of his niece Arabella. With other slaves he captures a Spanish galleon and becomes the terror of the Caribbean privateers until offered a commission in the English Navy. He defeats the French at Port Royal, and as a reward he is named governor of Jamaica and marries Arabella. *Physicians. Irish. Exile. Slavery. Privateering. Piracy. Barbados. Jamaica. Caribbean.*

CAPTAIN CARELESS **F2.0773**

FBO Pictures. 26 Aug **1928** [c26 Aug 1928; LP25579]. Si; b&w. 35mm. 6 reels, 4,876 ft.

Dir Jerome Storm. *Screenplay* Perry Murdock, Frank Howard Clark. *Titl* Randolph Bartlett. *Story* Bob Steele, Perry Murdock. *Photog* Virgil Miller. *Film Ed* Jack Kitchen. *Asst Dir* Pierre Bedard.

Cast: Bob Steele *(Bob Gordon)*, Mary Mabery *(Ruth)*, Jack Donovan *(Ralph)*, Barney Furey *(medicine man)*, Perry Murdock *(Perry)*, Wilfred North *(John Forsythe)*.

Melodrama. Bob Gordon learns that Ruth Devere, the girl he loves, has been reported lost in a South Seas yachting accident, and accompanied by his chum, Perry, he sets out for the Pacific in an airplane. Ruth and her fiancé, Ralph, have been washed up on a cannibal isle, and Bob and Perry rescue them just as they are about to be eaten. During the escape, Bob and Perry hold off the natives while Ralph and Ruth are rescued by a lifeboat from a Navy gunship. Ralph convinces the captain that Bob and Perry have been killed, but that dauntless pair make a liar of him by swimming out to the gunboat. *Cannibals. South Sea Islands. United States Navy. Shipwrecks.*

CAPTAIN COWBOY **F2.0774**

J. Charles Davis Productions. 29 May **1929** [New York State license]. Si; b&w. 35mm. 5 reels, 4,850 ft.

Dir-Story J. P. McGowan. *Photog* Paul Allen. *Film Ed* J. P. McGowan.

Cast: Yakima Canutt, Ione Reed, Charles Whittaker, John Lowell, Bobby Dunn, Betty Carter, Lynn Sanderson, Scotty Mattraw, Cliff Lyons.

Western melodrama. "Canutt is a hardboiled hero in this, confronting a gang of crooks to save the ranch of the heroine and her aunt from foreclosure. He battles against heavy odds, a frame-up and cattle rustling but wins out." (*Film Daily*, 4 Aug 1929, p8.) *Rustling. Ranches. Mortgages. Frameup.*

CAPTAIN FLY-BY-NIGHT **F2.0775**

R-C Pictures. *Dist* Film Booking Offices of America. 24 Dec **1922** [c24 Dec 1922; LP18625]. Si; b&w. 35mm. 5 reels, 4,940 ft.

Dir William K. Howard. *Scen* Eve Unsell. *Photog* Lucien Andriot.

Cast: Johnnie Walker *(First Stranger)*, Francis McDonald *(Second Stranger)*, Shannon Day *(Anita)*, Edward Gribbon *(Cassara)*, Victory Bateman *(Señora)*, James McElhern *(Padre Michael)*, Charles Stevens *(Indian)*, Bert Wheeler *(Governor)*, Fred Kelsey *(Gomez)*.

Melodrama. Source: Johnston McCulley, *Captain Fly-by-Night* (London, 1925). First one stranger, then another, arrive at the presidio, each with a government pass and each claiming to have been robbed by the notorious Captain Fly-by-Night and his highwaymen. The soldiers and Señorita Anita believe the first to be Fly-by-Night and the second to be Señor Rocha, Anita's fiancé and emissary of the governor. But the first stranger, to whom Anita is drawn, proves to be on a government mission and exposes the second stranger as Captain Fly-by-Night. *Highwaymen. Government agents. Strangers. California.*

CAPTAIN JANUARY **F2.0776**

Principal Pictures. 6 Jul **1924.** Si; b&w. 35mm. 6 reels, 6,194 ft.

Pres by Sol Lesser. *Dir* Edward F. Cline. *Scen* Eve Unsell, John Grey. *Photog* Glen MacWilliams. *Art Titl* William J. Sackheim.

Cast: Hobart Bosworth *(Jeremiah Judkins)*, Baby Peggy *(Captain January)*, Irene Rich *(Isabelle Morton)*, Lincoln Stedman *(Bob Pete)*, Harry T. Morey *(George Maxwell)*, Barbara Tennant *(Lucy Tripp)*, John Merkyl *(Herbert Morton)*, Emmett King *(John Elliott)*.

Melodrama. Source: Laura Elizabeth Richards, *Captain January* (Boston, 1891). Jeremiah Judkins, a lighthouse keeper, finds a little girl washed ashore tied to a spar. The kindly old man adopts the child, and she assists him in his duties. Jeremiah falls asleep one night, and the light goes out. As a result of this neglect of duty, a yacht is beached near the lighthouse. One of its passengers, Isabelle Morton, then visits the lighthouse and identifies the little girl, known only as Captain January, as the child of a sister who was killed nearby in an accident at sea. Isabelle then takes the child with her, but the little girl is unhappy in her new home. At the first chance, Captain January returns to the lighthouse keeper, and the Mortons realize that the old man and the little girl are inseparable companions. The Mortons then make room for the old man in the child's new home, bringing happiness to all alike. *Waifs. Childhood. Family life. Lighthouses. Shipwrecks.*

CAPTAIN KLEINSCHMIDT'S ADVENTURES IN THE FAR NORTH *see* **ADVENTURES IN THE FAR NORTH**

CAPTAIN LASH **F2.0777**

Fox Film Corp. 6 Jan **1929** [c28 Dec 1928; LP25959]. Mus score & sd eff (Movietone); b&w. 35mm. 6 reels, 5,454 ft. [Also si; 5,376 ft.]

Pres by William Fox. *Dir* John Blystone. *Scen* John Stone, Daniel G. Tomlinson. *Titl* Malcolm Stuart Boylan. *Story* Laura Hasse, Daniel G. Tomlinson. *Photog* Conrad Wells. *Film Ed* James K. McGuinness.

Cast: Victor McLaglen *(Captain Lash)*, Claire Windsor *(Cora Nevins)*, Jane Winton *(Babe)*, Clyde Cook *(Cocky)*, Arthur Stone *(Gentleman Eddie)*, Albert Conti *(Alex Condax)*, Jean Laverty *(Queenie)*, Frank Hagney *(Bull Hawks)*, Boris Charsky *(Condax's servant)*.

Melodrama. Cora Nevins, a classy dame, is visiting the stokehole of an ocean liner when Captain Lash, the boss of the black gang, saves her from being badly burned after a steam valve is broken by a crazed stoker. Cora and Lash are attracted to each other, and she persuades him to take ashore several diamonds recently stolen from a wealthy jewel collector traveling on the liner. Lash meets Cora at her home only to discover that his friend, Cocky, has substituted lumps of coal for the stolen gems; Lash is set upon by Cora's henchmen, but he proves to be too much for them. The police arrest the gang; Cocky returns the stolen jewels; and Lash returns to his waterfront sweetheart. *Stokers. Police. Gangs. Thieves. Ocean liners.*

CAPTAIN OF THE GUARD **F2.0778**

Universal Pictures. 29 Mar **1930** [c27 Mar 1930; LP1182]. Sd (Movietone); b&w. 35mm. 9 reels, 7,519 ft. [Also si; 5,913 ft.]

Pres by Carl Laemmle. *Dir* John S. Robertson, Paul Fejos. *Dial-Titl* George Manker Watters. *Adapt* Arthur Ripley. *Story* Houston Branch. *Photog* Gilbert Warrenton, Hal Mohr. *Film Ed* Milton Carruth. *Mus* Charles Wakefield Cadman. *Songs: "Song of the Guard," "For You," "You, You Alone," "Maids on Parade," "Can It Be?"* William Francis Dugan, Heinz Roemheld. *Rec Engr* C. Roy Hunter.

Cast: Laura La Plante *(Marie Marnay)*, John Boles *(Rouget de l'Isle)*, Sam De Grasse *(Bazin)*, James Marcus *(Marnay)*, Lionel Belmore *(Colonel of Hussars)*, Stuart Holmes *(Louis XVI)*, Evelyn Hall *(Marie Antoinette)*, Claude Fleming *(Magistrate)*, Murdock MacQuarrie *(Pierre)*, Richard Cramer *(Danton)*, Harry Burkhardt *(Materoun)*, George Hackathorne *(Robespierre)*, De Witt Jennings *(Priest)*, Harry Cording *(Le Bruin)*, Otis Harlan *(Jacques)*, Ervin Renard *(lieutenant)*.

Historical melodrama. Marie Marnay, an innkeeper's daughter, refuses to marry Bazin, a secret agent in the service of the king, but when Bazin sends music master Rouget de l'Isle to give her singing lessons, she falls in love and pledges her troth to Rouget. Marie's father refuses to join the revolt against the king and is killed trying to save her from the advances of a soldier; as a result, she joins the revolutionists, giving up her claim to Rouget, who is in the service of the king, and becomes notorious as "The Torch." Using Rouget as bait, Bazin effects a reconciliation, then orders Marie arrested as well as her consort. Charmed by his voice, Marie Antoinette has Rouget released to sing his song "La Marseillaise" for the king; he then renounces the king and escapes Paris; and in Marseilles he organizes an army, marches on Paris, and is reunited with Marie at the outbreak of the Revolution. *Secret agents. Composers. Revolutionaries. Royalists. Courtship. France—History—Revolution. Paris. Marseilles. Louis XVI (France). Marie Antoinette.*

Note: The film was begun as *La Marseillaise* by Paul Fejos with cameraman Hal Mohr; John S. Robertson completed the film and received screen credit.

THE CAPTAIN OF THE HURRICANE *see* **STORMY WATERS**

CAPTAIN SALVATION **F2.0779**

Cosmopolitan Productions. *Dist* Metro-Goldwyn-Mayer Distributing Corp. 14 May **1927** [c17 May 1927; LP23972]. Si; b&w. 35mm. 8 reels, 7,395 ft.

Dir John S. Robertson. *Scen* Jack Cunningham. *Titl* John Colton. *Photog* William Daniels. *Art Dir* Cedric Gibbons, Leo E. Kuter. *Film Ed* William Hamilton. *Wardrobe* André-ani.

Cast: Lars Hanson *(Anson Campbell)*, Marceline Day *(Mary Phillips)*, Pauline Starke *(Bess Morgan)*, Ernest Torrence *(Captain)*, George Fawcett *(Zeke Crosby)*, Sam De Grasse *(Peter Campbell)*, Jay Hunt *(Nathan Phillips)*, Eugenie Besserer *(Mrs. Buxom)*, Eugenie Forde *(Mrs. Bellows)*, Flora Finch *(Mrs. Snifty)*, James Marcus *(Old Sea Salt)*.

Melodrama. Source: Frederick William Wallace, *Captain Salvation* (New York, 1925). Young Anson Campbell returns from a theological seminary to a New England coastal village, where he is swayed by the call of the sea. When the bigoted villagers scorn Bess Morgan, a fallen woman, he champions her, espousing a broad view of Christianity, but is rejected by the puritanical inhabitants. He ships out aboard a convict ship, and discovering the rejected girl aboard, he exacts from her a promise not to revert to her old life. When she can no longer resist the advances of the ship's captain, Bess kills herself, effecting Anson's return to prayer and faith. Anson engages in a battle with the captain atop a mast; and taking over the ship, he converts the convicts and returns home to marry his sweetheart, Mary Phillips. *Ministerial students. Convict ships. Bigotry. Suicide. Religious conversion. The Sea. New England.*

CAPTAIN SWAGGER **F2.0780**

Pathé Exchange. 14 Oct **1928** [c24 Sep 1928; LP25653]. Sd eff & mus score (Photophone); b&w. 35mm. 7 reels, 6,312 ft.

Dir Edward H. Griffith. *Titl* Paul Perez. *Adapt* Adelaide Heilbron. *Story* Leonard Praskins. *Photog* John J. Mescall. *Art Dir* Edward Jewell. *Film Ed* Harold McLernon. *Song: "Captain Swagger, All the Girls Adore You"* Charles Weinberg, Irving Bibo. *Asst Dir* E. J. Babille. *Prod Mgr* R. A. Blaydon.

Cast: Rod La Rocque *(Captain Swagger (Hugh Drummond))*, Sue Carol *(Sue)*, Richard Tucker *(Phil Poole)*, Victor Potel *(Jean)*, Ullrich Haupt *(Von Dictor)*.

Melodrama. Hugh Drummond goes broke from living too high on the hog and turns to the life of crime in order to make a living. On his first holdup, he meets Sue Arnold, an unemployed cabaret dancer, and gallantly escorts her to his apartment rather than robbing her wealthy escort. They become dancing partners in a cafe, and Sue, who falls in love with Hugh, later comes to believe that he has again returned to the life of crime. Hugh clears himself, however, and he and Sue make plans to waltz through life together. *Dancers. Robbery. Cabarets.*

CAPTAIN THUNDER **F2.0781**

Warner Brothers Pictures. 27 Dec **1930** [c19 Nov 1930; LP1755]. Sd (Vitaphone); b&w. 35mm. 7 reels, 5,875 ft.

Dir Alan Crosland. *Screenplay* Gordon Rigby. *Dial* William K. Wells. *Photog* James Van Trees. *Film Ed* Arthur Hilton. *Rec Engr* George R. Groves.

Cast: Fay Wray *(Ynez Domínguez)*, Victor Varconi *(Captain Thunder)*, Charles Judels *(Comandante Ruiz)*, Robert Elliott *(Pete Morgan)*, Don Alvarado *(Juan Sebastián)*, Natalie Moorhead *(Bonita Salazar)*, Bert Roach *(Pablo)*, Frank Campeau *(Hank Riley)*, Robert Emmett Keane *(Don Miguel Salazar)*, John Sainpolis *(Pedro Domínguez)*.

Romantic melodrama. Source: Pierre Couderc and Hal Devitt, "The Gay Caballero" (publication undetermined). El Capitán Tronido, a handsome and reliable Mexican bandit, flaunts his ventures until the people of El Paramo demand that their Comandante Ruiz bring about his capture. Ynez and Juan, a poor but handsome youth, are lovers; but Ynez's father desires his daughter to marry Señor Morgan, a wealthy gringo rancher. Desperate at the thought of losing his Ynez, Juan goes to her hacienda by night and informs her that he plans to collect the reward for Captain Thunder so that they may be married. Meanwhile, Morgan, a rustler, meets up with the notorious bandit, who grants him a favor. Ruiz schemes to capture Thunder by placing bonfires at points where the bandit is seen, and when he goes to pay hommage to the beautiful Ynez, she hopefully lights a signal fire, then, deciding not to turn in the charming man, hides him from the soldiers; at daybreak Juan captures him and makes plans to marry Ynez, but Thunder escapes. Morgan induces him to break up the wedding, and Thunder is compelled to hold to his promise. After being forced to marry Morgan, Ynez hears a pistol shot, and returning to the festive scene, the bandit orders Juan's release and informs Ynez that already she is a widow. *Caballeros. Ranchers. Bandits. Rustlers. Courtship. Weddings. Mexico.*

Note: Working title: *The Gay Caballero.*

A CAPTAIN'S COURAGE **F2.0782**

Ben Wilson Productions. *Dist* Rayart Pictures. 30 Nov **1926** [New York State license; New York City showing: 29 Jan 1927]. Si; b&w. 35mm. 6 reels.

Dir Louis Chaudet. *Scen* George Pyper. *Orig Story* James Oliver Curwood.

Cast: Richard Holt, Eddie Earl, Jack Henderson, Al Ferguson, Lafe McKee, Dorothy Dwan.

Melodrama. "The story is laid in 1853 and the locale is the shores of Lake Michigan. ... At the finish two groups of men meet off-stage somewhere in a hand-to-hand conflict for possession of an island in Lake

Michigan, and the winning faction gets into the picture after all the fighting is over. ... Some of the action takes place on a sailing vessel becalmed in a bay." (*Variety*, 2 Feb 1927, p19.) *Land rights. Lake Michigan.*

THE CAPTIVE GOD (Reissue) **F2.0783**

Triangle Film Corp. *Dist* Tri-Stone Pictures. 22 Jul **1924** [New York State license]. Si; b&w. 35mm. 5 reels.

Note: A William S. Hart film originally released by Triangle Film Corp. on 23 Jul 1916.

THE CARDBOARD LOVER **F2.0784**

Cosmopolitan Productions. *Dist* Metro-Goldwyn-Mayer Distributing Corp. 25 Aug **1928** [c25 Aug 1928; LP25928]. Si; b&w. 35mm. 8 reels, 7,108 ft.

Dir Robert Z. Leonard. *Scen* F. Hugh Herbert. *Titl* Lucille Newmark. *Adapt* Carey Wilson. *Photog* John Arnold. *Sets* Cedric Gibbons. *Film Ed* Basil Wrangell.

Cast: Marion Davies *(Sally)*, Jetta Goudal *(Simone)*, Nils Asther *(André)*, Andres De Segurola *(himself)*, Tenen Holtz *(Albine)*, Pepe Lederer *(Peppy)*.

Comedy. Source: Jacques Deval, *Dans sa candeur naïve, comédie en trois actes* (Paris, 1927). Sally, an American autograph hound grand-touring Europe with some schoolmates, sets her cap for André, a French tennis champion. She discovers that André's sweetheart, Simone, is not on the level; and André, who is unfortunately infatuated with that undulating French coquette, hires Sally to keep him apart from Simone. Sally dogs the pair and never allows them a moment's peace, finally moving into André's house in order to convince Simone that André is through with her. André eventually comes to love the naive but eccentric American girl and takes her for his wife. *Tourists. Autographs. Tennis. Coquetry. France.*

CARDIGAN **F2.0785**

Messmore Kendall. *Dist* American Releasing Corp. 19 Feb **1922** [c17 Mar 1922; LP17655]. Si; b&w. 35mm. 7 reels, 6,788 ft.

Pres by Messmore Kendall. *Dir* John W. Noble. *Adapt* Robert W. Chambers. *Photog* John S. Stumar, Ned Van Buren, Max Schneider.

Cast: William Collier, Jr. *(Michael Cardigan)*, Betty Carpenter *(Silver Heels)*, Thomas Cummings *(Sir William Johnson)*, William Pike *(Captain Butler)*, Charles Graham *(Lord Dunmore)*, Madeleine Lubetty *(Marie Hamilton)*, Hattie Delaro *(Lady Shelton)*, Louis Dean *(Sir John Johnson)*, Colin Campbell *(The Weazel)*, Jere Austin *(Jack Mount)*, Frank Montgomery *(Chief Logan)*, Eleanor Griffith *(Dulcina)*, Dick Lee *(Quider)*, Jack Johnston *(Colonel Cresap)*, Florence Short *(Molly Brandt)*, George Loeffler *(Patrick Henry)*, William Willis *(John Hancock)*, Austin Hume *(Paul Revere)*.

Historical romance. Source: Robert William Chambers, *Cardigan* (New York, 1901). In Johnstown, New York, 2 years before the American Revolution, young Michael Cardigan, an unwilling subject of King George III, falls in love with the English governor's ward, who is known as Silver Heels. At the outbreak of hostilities between the Colonists and the Indians, Michael is sent by Sir William to carry a peace message to the Cayugas but is intercepted by Britishers; he is saved from being burned at the stake by an Indian runner. In Lexington, Cardigan is admitted to the secret councils of the Minute Men, where he meets Patrick Henry, John Hancock, and Paul Revere and joins in the cause for liberty. Following the famous ride of Paul Revere, the Battles of Lexington and Concord prefigure the retreat of the Redcoats; Cardigan rescues his sweetheart from the advances of Captain Butler, then promises to return to her at the end of the war. *Minute Men. Cayuga Indians. Johnstown (New York). Lexington (Massachusetts). Concord (New Hampshire). United States—History—Revolution. William Johnson. Patrick Henry. John Hancock. Paul Revere.*

CAREERS **F2.0786**

First National Pictures. 2 Jun **1929** [c5 Jun 1929; LP510]. Talking & singing sequences (Vitaphone); b&w. 35mm. 10 reels, 8,435 ft. [Also si, 14 Jul 1929; 6,357 ft.]

Pres by Richard A. Rowland. *Prod* Ned Marin. *Dir* John Francis Dillon. *Adapt-Dial* Forrest Halsey. *Titl* Paul Perez. *Photog* John Seitz. *Film Ed* John Rawlins. *Song: "I Love You, I Hate You"* George W. Meyer, Al Bryan.

Cast: Billie Dove *(Hélène Gromaire)*, Antonio Moreno *(Victor Gromaire)*, Thelma Todd *(Hortense)*, Noah Beery *(The President)*, Holmes Herbert *(Carouge)*, Carmel Myers *(The Woman)*, Robert Frazer *(Lavergne Sojin)*, Mademoiselle Kithnou, André De Segurola, Robert Schable, Robert T. Haines, Marte Faust, Crauford Kent.

Melodrama. Source: Alfred Schirokauer and Paul Rosenhayn, *Karriere, Schauspiel in vier Akten* (Berlin, 1924). Angry at not having received the promotion he thinks he deserves, Victor Gromaire, a young French magistrate in Cochin-China, plans a trip to the capital to complain to the governor of the French colony, bypassing his immediate superior, the president. Carouge, a prominent Paris attorney, enlightens Hélène, Victor's wife, that it is because she is too proper that her husband is still a minor official. She consequently calls on the president, inadvertently disclosing her husband's plan; frantic at having endangered her husband's position, Hélène consents to do anything the president wishes if he refrains from calling the governor. Just as he is about to seduce her, a native musician, hiding in the room, is discovered and kills the president, while Hélène protects herself by wounding him. The musician, however, accuses her of the murder; Victor establishes her innocence and, realizing the quality of Hélène's love, promises to start a new career in Paris. *Magistrates. Lawyers. Musicians. French. Parisians. Marriage. Virtue. Diplomacy. Murder. Colonial administration.*

THE CARELESS AGE **F2.0787**

First National Pictures. 15 Sep **1929** [c21 Sep 1929; LP714]. Sd (Vitaphone); b&w. 35mm. 7 reels, 6,308 ft. [Also si, 13 Oct 1929; 6,428 ft.]

Pres by Richard A. Rowland. *Dir* John Griffith Wray. *Dial* Harold Shumate. *Adapt* Harrison Macklyn. *Photog* Alvin Knechtel, Ben Reynolds. *Song: "Melody Divine"* Herman Ruby, Norman Spencer.

Cast: Douglas Fairbanks, Jr. *(Wyn)*, Carmel Myers *(Ray)*, Holmes Herbert *(Sir John)*, Kenneth Thompson *(Owen)*, Loretta Young *(Muriel)*, George Baxter *(Le Grand)*, Wilfred Noy *(Lord Durhugh)*, Doris Lloyd *(Mabs)*, Ilka Chase *(Bunty)*, Raymond Lawrence *(Tommy)*.

Melodrama. Source: John Van Druten, *Diversion; a Play in Three Acts* (New York, c1933). Sir John Hayward, a noted surgeon, decides that his son Wyn, a medical student, needs a vacation as a temporary diversion from his studies. At Como, Wyn meets and falls in love with Rayetta Muir, an unprincipled actress who trifles with him. In London, Rayetta avoids seeing Wyn, ready to forget him. Wyn is crazed when he learns that Rayetta is intimate with both Lord Durhugh, an old roué, and Le Grand, a French boxer; and in a rage he chokes Rayetta and leaves her for dead. He then confesses to his father that he has killed her. Preparing to take the blame, Sir John, accompanied by Wyn, goes to Rayetta's apartment to find that she did not die after all. *Surgeons. Students. English. Actors. Mistresses. Rakes. Boxers. Fatherhood. Jealousy. Como.*

THE CARELESS WOMAN **F2.0788**

Dist Exclusive Features. Jul **1922** [scheduled release]. Si; b&w. 35mm. 5 reels.

Melodrama. "The story tells of a young wife who carries on 'carefully censored' affair with two friends of her husband. One says, 'Be careful how you tempt me, I am a man of fire.' She writes him, 'Am walking in the park and on my way back will stop in to see you – Oh, man of fire!' She acknowledges compromising relations with the other lover and her husband leaves her. Shortly a daughter is born and the young wife dies, leaving an unfinished letter, 'I swear with my dying breath that my daughter is the child of ...' The child grows up and has a lover with a twin brother, exactly like him. The twin brother passes himself off as the other and seduces her. She is about to take poison when her father, led by a dog (which is the reincarnation of one of the mother's deceased lovers) rushes in and prevents her. He hears her story and challenges the young betrayer to a duel in which the young man is mortally wounded. He calls for a priest and marries the girl. Picture closes with girl and her father gazing fondly at her baby." (New York State license records.) *Brothers. Twins. Filial relations. Infidelity. Seduction. Suicide. Reincarnation. Duels.*

THE CARNATION KID **F2.0789**

Christie Film Co. *Dist* Paramount Pictures. 2 Mar **1929** [c1 Mar 1929; LP176]. Talking sequences, sd eff, & mus score (Movietone); b&w. 35mm. 7 reels, 7,267 ft. [Also si; 6,290 ft.]

Pres by Al Christie. *Dir* E. Mason Hopper. *Dir Sd Sequences* A. Leslie Pearce. *Scen* Henry McCarty. *Titl* Arthur Huffsmith. *Story-Dial* Alfred A. Cohn. *Photog* Alex Phillips, Monte Steadman. *Film Ed* Grace Dazey. *Song: "Carnations"* Sterling Sherwin.

Cast: Douglas MacLean *(Clarence Kendall)*, Frances Lee *(Doris Whitely)*, William B. Davidson *(Blythe)*, Lorraine Eddy *(Lucille)*, Charles Hill Mailes *(Crawford Whitely)*, Francis McDonald *(The Carnation Kid)*, Maurice Black *(Tony)*, Ben Swor, Jr. *(Blinkey)*, Carl Stockdale *(Deacon)*.

Comedy-drama. Typewriter salesman Clarence Kendall takes a train for a small town and is forced to change clothes with The Carnation Kid, a gangster on the way to the same town to rub out Crawford Whitely, a crusading district attorney. Arriving at the station, Clarence is mistaken for The Carnation Kid and installed in a swank hotel suite by the local bootleggers. Clarence manages to save Whitely's life, however, and marries his daughter, Doris. The Carnation Kid ends up behind bars. *Traveling salesmen. Gangsters. District attorneys. Smalltown life. Mistaken identity. Typewriters. San Gabriel (California).*

Note: Exterior scenes were filmed on location in San Gabriel, California.

THE CARNIVAL GIRL **F2.0790**

Associated Exhibitors. 18 Jul **1926** [c28 Apr 1926; LU22649]. Si; b&w. 35mm. 5 reels, 4,962 or 5,025 ft.

Pres by Louis Lewyn. *Dir* Cullen Tate. *Titl* Raymond Cannon, Robert Hopkins. *Story* Raymond Cannon. *Photog* Lee Garmes. *Tech Dir* Walter Lang. *Film Ed* Donn Hayes.

Cast: Marion Mack *(Nanette)*, Gladys Brockwell *(her mother)*, Frankie Darro *(her brother)*, George Siegmann *(Sigmund)*, Allan Forrest *(Lieut. Allan Dale)*, Jack Cooper *(Gunner Sergeant Riley)*, Victor Potel *("Slim")*, Max Asher *(The Barker)*.

Melodrama. Orphaned by the death of their mother, Nanette (a tightrope walker) and her brother (who acts as a trained ape) are left under the cruel guardianship of Sigmund, the strongman, who is also a rumrunner. Nanette falls in love with young Lieut. Allan Dale and sees him secretly. When she attends a masquerade ball with Allan, Sigmund discovers her escapade and gives her a severe beating. Allan and his friend Riley, ordered to San Pedro, come to see Nanette in her act and say goodby. Her little brother accidentally exposes Sigmund's fraudulent weights, and in the ensuing struggle Allan and Riley are pitted against Sigmund and his men while Nanette and her brother flee to a tramper bound for San Pedro, which happens to be Sigmund's. Allan's Coast Guard cutter pursues them and drives them on the rocks. Nanette and her brother are attacked by Sigmund; he is killed by Nanette just as Allan arrives to rescue them. *Orphans. Tightrope walkers. Strongmen. Rumrunners. Brother-sister relationship. Carnivals. United States Coast Guard.*

CASCARRABIAS **F2.0791**

Paramount-Publix Corp. 22 Oct **1930** [Buenos Aires showing]. Sd (Movietone); b&w. 35mm. [Length undetermined.]

Cast: Ernesto Vilches, Carmen Guerrero, Della Magana, Barry Norton, Ramon Pereda, Andres De Segurola.

Drama. Source: Horace Hodges and Thomas Wigney Percyval, *Grumpy, a Play in Four Acts* (New York, 1921). The story line is probably the same as *Grumpy* (1930), although this fact has not been verified. *Lawyers. Grandfathers. Courtship. Robbery. London.*

Note: Spanish-language version of *Grumpy*, a remake of a 1923 film of the same title.

THE CASE OF BECKY **F2.0792**

Realart Pictures. *Dist* Paramount Pictures. Oct **1921** [c16 Sep 1921; LP16964]. Si; b&w. 35mm. 6 reels, 5,498 ft.

Dir Chester M. Franklin. *Adapt* J. Clarkson Miller. *Photog* George Folsey.

Cast: Constance Binney *(Dorothy Stone [Becky])*, Glenn Hunter *(John Arnold)*, Frank McCormack *(Dr. Emerson)*, Montague Love *(Professor Balzamo)*, Margaret Seddon *(Mrs. Emerson)*, Jane Jennings *(Mrs. Arnold)*.

Drama. Source: Edward Locke, "The Case of Becky, a Play," in *Hearst's Magazine* (22:113–128, Aug 1912). Balzamo, a traveling magician, visits the town where Dr. Emerson and his young wife live and takes Mrs. Emerson away with him in a state of hypnotic subjection. Years later, feeling her death near, she calls her daughter, Dorothy, and urges her to escape the man's evil influence. Dorothy seeks shelter with Mrs. Arnold and her son, John, in a small town, where she finds happiness; but when she becomes engaged to John she changes into a wildly mischievous person who calls herself Becky. Dr. Emerson, a nerve specialist, takes her to his sanitarium, where Uriah Stone (alias Balzamo) claims her as his daughter; but Emerson suspects that he is the magician who long ago persuaded his wife to go away with him. Unable to control the doctor, Balzamo sees his power broken and the girl's mind restored. John Arnold wins Dorothy for his wife. *Magicians. Neurologists. Dual personality. Hypnotism. Sanitariums.*

THE CASE OF LENA SMITH **F2.0793**

Paramount Famous Lasky Corp. 19 Jan **1929** [c18 Jan 1929; LP321]. Si; b&w. 35mm. 8 reels, 7,229 ft.

Dir Josef von Sternberg. *Screenplay* Jules Furthman. *Titl* Julian Johnson. *Story* Samuel Ornitz. *Photog* Harold Rosson. *Tech Dir* Hans Dreier, Martin Porkay. *Film Ed* Helen Lewis.

Cast: Esther Ralston *(Lena Smith)*, James Hall *(Franz Hofrat)*, Gustav von Seyffertitz *(Herr Hofrat)*, Emily Fitzroy *(Frau Hofrat)*, Fred Kohler *(Stefan)*, Betty Aho *(Stefan's sister)*, Lawrence Grant *(commissioner)*, Leone Lane *(Pepi)*, Kay Deslys *(Poldi)*, Alex Woloshin *(janitor)*, Ann Brody *(janitor's wife)*, Wally Albright, Jr. *(Franz, age 3)*, Warner Klinger *(Franz, age 18)*.

Romantic drama. Lena, a working girl, secretly marries Franz, a student officer in Vienna, and has his child. When Franz's father takes the baby away Franz is unable to help, and he commits suicide. When the court refuses Lena's pleas she steals the baby. The child grows up to march off to war in 1914 from a Hungarian village. *Children. Suicide. Fatherhood. World War I. Austria-Hungary.*

THE CASE OF SERGEANT GRISCHA **F2.0794**

RKO Productions. 23 Feb **1930** [c23 Feb 1930; LP1180]. Sd (Photophone); b&w. 35mm. 10 reels, 8,261 ft. [Also si.]

Prod William Le Baron. *Dir* Herbert Brenon. *Adapt* Elizabeth Meehan. *Photog* Roy Hunt. *Art Dir* Max Ree. *Film Ed* Marie Halvey. *Rec Engr* John Tribby. *Asst Dir* Raul Spindola, Ray Lissner.

Cast: Chester Morris *(Sgt. Grischa Paprotkin)*, Betty Compson *(Babka)*, Alec B. Francis *(General von Lychow)*, Gustav von Seyffertitz *(General Schieffenzahn)*, Jean Hersholt *(Posnanski)*, Paul McAllister *(Corporal Sacht)*, Layland Hodgson *(Lieutenant Winfried)*, Raymond Whitaker *(Aljoscha)*, Bernard Siegel *(Verressjeff)*, Frank McCormack *(Captain Spierauge/Kolja)*, Percy Barbette *(Sergeant Fritz)*, Hal Davis *(Birkholz)*.

War drama. Source: Arnold Zweig, *Der Streit um den Sergeanten Grischa* (Potsdam, 1928). On a winter's night in 1917, Sgt. Grischa Paprotkin of the Russian army escapes from a German prison camp in Poland and goes to see his wife, Babka, and his newborn child. He lives with Babka for a while; but he is dominated by a desire to return to Russia, and Babka aids him by passing him off as a dead soldier. While seeking food from a friend, Grischa is captured and condemned to death as a spy by Schieffenzahn, German commander on the Eastern Front. His true identity is established, and his nephew Winfried and Advocate Posnanski try to have the order reversed, but with no success. Posing as a peddler, Babka plans for his escape, but Grischa places his faith in General von Lychow, who after a stormy confrontation with Schieffenzahn, sends an order to cancel the death sentence; but the telegram fails to arrive because of a storm. Broken in spirit, Grischa willingly goes to his execution, rejecting his friend's attempts to save him. *Prisoners of war. Prison escapees. Spies. Capital punishment. Military occupation. World War I. Poland. Russia. Germany—Army.*

CASEY AT THE BAT **F2.0795**

Famous Players–Lasky. *Dist* Paramount Pictures. 8 Mar **1927** [c5 Mar 1927; LP23753]. Si; b&w. 35mm. 6 reels, 6,040 ft.

Pres by Adolph Zukor, Jesse L. Lasky. *Prod-Story* Hector Turnbull. *Dir* Monte Brice. *Screenplay* Jules Furthman. *Titl* Sam Hellman, Grant Clarke. *Adapt* Reginald Morris, Monte Brice. *Photog* Barney McGill.

Cast: Wallace Beery *(Casey)*, Ford Sterling *(O'Dowd)*, ZaSu Pitts *(Camille)*, Sterling Holloway *(Putnam)*, Spec O'Donnell *(Spec)*, Iris Stuart *(Trixie [Florodora Girl])*, Sidney Jarvis *(McGraw)*, Lotus Thompson, Rosalind Byrne, Anne Sheridan, Doris Hill, Sally Blane *(other Florodora Girls)*.

Farce. Source: Ernest Thayer, "Casey at the Bat," in *Bookman* (28: 434–435, Jan 1909). At the turn of the century in the town of Centerville, Casey, a junk dealer, is the hardest hitter on the village ball club and—next to Putnam, the town barber—the most persistent suitor of Camille. O'Dowd, supposedly a big league scout, arrives in town, and at Putnam's suggestion, he signs Casey with the New York Giants. In New York Casey gains popularity by his willingness to buy drinks, all bills being paid by Putnam; and distraction is provided by Trixie of the Florodora Sextette, all of whom he invites to dinner. The tipsy party embark for Coney Island, and following a wild, abortive ride, Casey and Camille are reconciled at a beer garden. Spec convinces Casey that he has been hoaxed, and when he comes to bat, O'Dowd throws the pitcher a trick ball and Casey strikes out. But the conspiritors are captured and the manager exonerates Casey.

Junk dealers. Barbers. Baseball scouts. Smalltown life. Baseball. New York City. Coney Island. New York Giants. Florodora Sextette.

CASEY JONES **F2.0796**

Trem Carr Productions. *Dist* Rayart Pictures. 20 Dec **1927** [New York showing; released Jan 1928]. Si; b&w. 35mm. 7 reels, 6,673 ft.

Pres by W. Ray Johnston. *Dir* Charles J. Hunt. *Story-Scen* Arthur Hoerl. *Titl* Richard Weil. *Photog* Hap Depew. *Film Ed* J. S. Harrington.

Cast: Ralph Lewis *(Casey Jones)*, Kate Price *(Mrs. Casey Jones)*, Al St. John *(Jock MacTavish)*, Jason Robards *(Casey Jones, Jr.)*, Anne Sheridan *(Peggy Reynolds)*, Brooks Benedict *(Roland Ayres)*, Violet Kane *(Baby Kathleen Jones)*, Jimmy Kane, Charlie Kane.

Melodrama. Source: T. Lawrence Seibert and Eddie Newton, "Casey Jones" (a song; 1909). Both engineer Casey Jones and his son have unfortunate experiences wih the division superintendent (Roland Ayres?): Casey, Sr., is demoted for refusing to carry out some orders, and Casey, Jr., must rescue Peggy Reynolds from Roland's unwelcome attentions. When three bandits steal a train, Casey and his son give chase, capture the outlaws, and save the train from destruction. The villain is a victim of his own trap, and Casey, Jr., finds romance with Peggy. *Railroad engineers. Bandits. Courtship. Railroads.*

THE CAT AND THE CANARY (Universal-Jewel) **F2.0797**

Universal Pictures. 9 Sep **1927** [c31 Mar 1927; LP23813]. Si; b&w. 35mm. 8 reels, 7,713 ft.

Pres by Carl Laemmle. *Dir* Paul Leni. *Adapt-Scen* Robert F. Hill, Alfred A. Cohn. *Titl* Walter Anthony. *Photog* Gilbert Warrenton. *Sets* Charles D. Hall.

Cast: Laura La Plante *(Annabelle West)*, Creighton Hale *(Paul Jones)*, Tully Marshall *(Roger Crosby)*, Forrest Stanley *(Charlie Wilder)*, Gertrude Astor *(Cicily Young)*, Flora Finch *(Susan Sillsby)*, Arthur Edmund Carewe *(Harry Blythe)*, Martha Mattox *("Mammy" Pleasant)*, George Siegmann *(Hendricks)*, Lucien Littlefield *(Dr. Patterson)*, Joe Murphy *(milkman)*, Billy Engle *(taxi driver)*.

Gothic melodrama. Source: John Willard, *The Cat and the Canary; a Melodrama in Three Acts* (New York, 1927). At the hour of midnight, exactly 20 years after the death of Cyrus West, an eccentric and wealthy recluse, his relatives meet in his mansion to hear the reading of the will. The nearest kin are dismayed to learn they have all been disinherited because they considered Cyrus crazy, and that his most distant living relative, Annabelle West, will inherit the estate provided that she is proved to be sane; otherwise a contingent heir will be named. But the lawyer mysteriously disappears, and various unexplained occurences cause the family to doubt Annabelle's sanity. Her cousin, Paul, imprisoned in the walls, is attacked by the "monster," who is ultimately captured by the police and proves to be Charles Wilder, the secondary heir. *Insanity. Murder. Wills. Haunted houses. Inheritance.*

THE CAT CREEPS **F2.0798**

Universal Pictures. 10 Nov **1930** [c23 Oct 1930; LP1672]. Sd (Movietone); b&w. 35mm. 8 reels, 6,493 ft.

Pres by Carl Laemmle. *Dir* Rupert Julian. *Scen* Gladys Lehman. *Dial* Gladys Lehman, William Hurlbut. *Photog* Hal Mohr, Jerry Ash. *Film Ed* Maurice Pivar. *Rec Engr* Edward Wetzel, C. Roy Hunter.

Cast: Helen Twelvetrees *(Annabelle West)*, Raymond Hackett *(Paul)*, Neil Hamilton *(Charles Wilder)*, Lilyan Tashman *(Cicily)*, Jean Hersholt *(Dr. Patterson)*, Montagu Love *(Hendricks)*, Lawrence Grant *(Crosby)*, Theodore von Eltz *(Harry Blythe)*, Blanche Frederici *(Mam' Pleasant)*, Elizabeth Patterson *(Susan)*.

Mystery melodrama. Source: John Willard, *The Cat and the Canary; a Melodrama in Three Acts* (New York, 1927). A remake of *The Cat and the Canary* (1927) along the same dramatic lines as the earlier version. *Lawyers. Wills. Inheritance. Murder. Insanity. Haunted houses.*

CATCH MY SMOKE **F2.0799**

Fox Film Corp. 3 Dec **1922** [c31 Dec 1922; LP19087]. Si; b&w. 35mm. 5 reels, 4,070 ft.

Pres by William Fox. *Dir* William Beaudine. *Scen* Jack Strumwasser. *Photog* Dan Clark.

Cast: Tom Mix *(Bob Stratton)*, Lillian Rich *(Mary Thorne)*, Claude Peyton *(Tex Lynch)*, Gordon Griffith *(Bub Jessup)*, Harry Griffith *(Al Draper)*, Robert Milash *(Frank Hurd)*, Pat Chrisman *(Joe Bloss)*, Cap Anderson *(sheriff)*, Ruby Lafayette *(Mrs. Archer)*.

Western melodrama. Source: Joseph Bushnell Ames, *Shoe Bar Stratton* (New York, 1922). Bob Stratton returns from war in France to find his ranch in the hands of a pretty girl, Mary Thorne, who explains that upon her father's death she became the sole owner. Thorne had been the executor of Stratton's will, and thinking that Bob had been killed, he had appropriated the place for himself. After several escapades with some shady characters who want to take over the ranch, Stratton settles the question of ownership by asking Mary to marry him. *Veterans. Ranchers. Inheritance.*

CATCH-AS-CATCH-CAN **F2.0800**

Gotham Productions. *Dist* Lumas Film Corp. 1 Jun **1927** [c7 Jun 1927; LP24065]. Si; b&w. 35mm. 5 reels, 5,000 ft.

Pres by Sam Sax. *Supv* Sam Bischoff. *Dir* Charles Hutchison. *Story-Scen* L. V. Jefferson. *Photog* James Brown.

Cast: William Fairbanks *(Reed Powers)*, Jack Blossom *(George Bascom)*, Rose Blossom *(Lucille Bascom)*, Larry Shannon *(Phil Bascom)*, Walter Shumway *(Ward Hastings)*, George Kotsonaros *("Butch")*, George Chapman *(Slippery Schnitzel)*.

Melodrama. Reed Powers manages a smalltime baseball team whose star pitcher is Phil Bascom, son of the mayor and brother of Lucille, with whom Reed is in love. Phil plays into the hands of Hastings, a political fixer, and agrees to throw the last game of the season. Reed sees the payoff and is himself accused by Hastings but remains silent to protect Phil. After difficulties, Reed gets work with a newspaper and exposes the efforts of Hastings and "Butch," a heavyweight wrestler, to buck Mayor Bascom. In a climactic chase, Hastings is killed and Reed wins out over the wrestler. Phil confesses his misdeed, Lucille and Reed are reunited, and Reed is appointed chief of police. *Mayors. Police. Wrestlers. Baseball. Political corruption. Chases.*

THE CAT'S PAJAMAS **F2.0801**

Famous Players–Lasky. *Dist* Paramount Pictures. 29 Aug **1926** [New York showing; released 15 Nov; c17 Nov 1926; LP23346]. Si; b&w. 35mm. 6 reels, 5,790 ft.

Pres by Adolph Zukor, Jesse L. Lasky. *Dir* William Wellman. *Screenplay* Hope Loring, Louis D. Lighton. *Story* Ernest Vajda. *Photog* Victor Milner.

Cast: Betty Bronson *(Sally Winton)*, Ricardo Cortez *(Don Cesare Gracco)*, Arlette Marchal *(Riza Dorina)*, Theodore Roberts *(Sally's father)*, Gordon Griffith *(Jack)*, Tom Ricketts *(Mr. Briggs)*.

Comedy-drama. Sally, seamstress for a fashionable modiste, supports a crippled father and adores her kitten, Tommy. Though loved by Jack, a taxi driver, she is infatuated with Don Cesare Gracco, an operatic sensation. Sally attends an opera performance; Tommy escapes from the cloakroom and wanders backstage. Don Cesare, talking to reporters and seeing the cat, says he will marry the first woman it leads him to: Tommy's selection is Riza, a temperamental dancer. The cat becomes a news item, being given a diamond necklace for having led Cesare to his love. Jealous of her fiancé's publicity, Riza decides to postpone the wedding and refuses to try on her wedding dress. Sally then is recruited as a model, and when Cesare proposes to her, she accepts; but after the marriage, she declares she wanted to teach him a lesson and leaves him. Following a series of complications, however, Sally and Cesare are happily reconciled. *Seamstresses. Fashion models. Taxi drivers. Singers. Opera. Weddings. Cats.*

CAUGHT BLUFFING **F2.0802**

Universal Film Manufacturing Co. 18 Sep **1922** [c2 Sep 1922; LP18190]. Si; b&w. 35mm. 5 reels, 4,717 ft.

Pres by Carl Laemmle. *Dir* Lambert Hillyer. *Scen* Charles Sarver. *Photog* Charles Stumar.

Cast: Frank Mayo *(John Oxford)*, Edna Murphy *(Doris Henry)*, Wallace MacDonald *(Wallace Towers)*, Jack Curtis *(Pete Scarr)*, Andrew Arbuckle *(Ham Thomas)*, Ruth Royce *(College Kate)*, "Bull" Durham *(Siwash Sam)*, Jack Walters *(Silk O'Malley)*, Scott Turner *(Jones)*, Martin Best *(Broome)*, Tote Du Crow *(Indian guide)*.

Melodrama. Source: Jack Bechdolt, "Broken Chains," in *Argosy Magazine* (137:480–509, 8 Oct 1921). John Oxford, gambling hall proprietor whose honesty is widely known, finds it necessary to cheat to save the life of Doris Henry, who has come to Alaska to marry Wallace Towers. Though she has wrongly blamed John for Wallace's enormous gambling losses and embezzlement of company funds, she now realizes which man is truly honest. *Honesty. Gambling. Embezzlement. Alaska.*

CAUGHT IN THE FOG **F2.0803**

Warner Brothers Pictures. 25 Aug **1928** [c22 Aug 1928; LP25554]. Talking sequences (Vitaphone); b&w. 35mm. 7 reels, 6,270 ft. [Also si, 22 Sep 1928; 5,429 ft.]

Dir Howard Bretherton. *Scen-Dial* Charles R. Condon. *Titl* Joseph Jackson. *Story* Jerome Kingston. *Photog* Byron Haskin. *Film Ed* Ralph Dawson.

Cast: May McAvoy *(The Girl)*, Conrad Nagel *(Bob Vickers)*, Mack Swain *(Detective Ryan)*, Hugh Herbert *(Detective Riley)*, Charles Gerrard *(crook)*, Emil Chautard *(The Old Man)*, Ruth Cherrington *(The Old Woman)*.

Comedy-melodrama. Wealthy Bob Vickers visits his mother's Florida houseboat in order to remove her jewelry and stumbles upon a bobbedhair bandit and her male accomplice, who mistake him for another burglar. There is a fight that is broken up by the arrival of an elderly couple (still more burglars) who are posing as guests. Bob keeps his identity secret and passes himself off as the butler; the girl and her partner-in-crime pretend to be the maid and the cook, respectively. Riley and Ryan, a couple of idiotic detectives, arrive on the scene, closely followed by a heavy fog. After a night of ghostly apparitions and gunfights, the detectives take away all of the crooks with the exception of the girl, who, having come to steal Bob's jewels, has stolen his heart. *Detectives. Burglars. Butlers. Housemaids. Cooks. Imposture. Houseboats. Florida.*

CAUGHT SHORT **F2.0804**

Cosmopolitan Productions. *Dist* Metro-Goldwyn-Mayer Distributing Corp. 10 May **1930** [c22 May 1930; LP1315]. Sd (Movietone); b&w. 35mm. 8 reels, 6,873 ft.

Dir Charles F. Reisner. *Cont-Dial* Willard Mack, Robert E. Hopkins. *Story* Willard Mack. *Photog* Leonard Smith. *Art Dir* Cedric Gibbons. *Film Ed* George Hively, Harold Palmer. *Song: "Going Spanish"* Dave Snell, Raymond B. Eagan. *Song: "Somebody"* Roy Turk, Fred Ahlert. *Rec Engr* Fred R. Morgan, Douglas Shearer. *Wardrobe* Henrietta Frazer.

Cast: Marie Dressler *(Marie Jones)*, Polly Moran *(Polly Smith)*, Anita Page *(Genevieve Jones)*, Charles Morton *(William Smith)*, Thomas Conlin *(Frankie)*, Douglas Haig *(Johnny)*, Nanci Price *(Priscilla)*, Greta Mann *(Sophy)*, Herbert Prior *(Mr. Frisby)*, T. Roy Barnes *(Mr. Kidd)*, Edward Dillon *(Mr. Thutt)*, Alice Moe *(Miss Ambrose)*, Gwen Lee *(manicurist)*, Lee Kohlmar *(peddler)*, Greta Granstedt *(Fanny Lee)*.

Comedy. Landladies Polly Smith and Marie Jones, who operate boardinghouses on the same side of the street, are afflicted with numerous petty envies and jealousies but nevertheless are the best of friends. Polly invests in the stock market and begins to reap rewards, but she is unable to persuade Marie to use her life's savings to buy shares of American Cheese or Brazilian Bananas. Meanwhile, Marie's daughter, Genevieve, and Polly's son, William, just back from college, fall in love; but an argument between the ladies breaks up the romance; and smarting under Polly's patronizing manner, Marie plunges into the market herself and with the winnings is able to stage a society splurge at a fashionable resort. In their efforts to outdo each other, Polly and Marie inevitably come together, and the reunion of the lovers becomes possible. *Landladies. Courtship. Boardinghouses. Speculation. Stock market. Resorts.*

CAUSE FOR DIVORCE **F2.0805**

Hugh Dierker Productions. *Dist* Selznick Distributing Corp. 27 Sep or 6 Oct **1923** [c21 Sep 1923; LP19419]. Si; b&w. 35mm. 7 reels, 7,132 ft.

Pres by John S. Woody. *Dir* Hugh Dierker. *Scen* Thelma Lanier, Dorothy Yost. *Story* Thelma Lanier. *Photog* Victor Milner.

Cast: Fritzi Brunette *(Laura Parker)*, David Butler *(Tom Parker)*, Charles Clary *(Martin Sheldon)*, Helen Lynch *(Ruth Metcliffe)*, Pat O'Malley *(Howard Metcliffe)*, Peter Burke *("Count" Lorenz)*, Cleve Moore *(Skippy North)*, James O. Barrows *(Professor Williams)*, Harmon MacGregor *(George Angier)*, Junior Coughlan *(Tommie Parker)*.

Melodrama. Two domestic triangles involving young wives whose husbands are neglectful. Tom Parker's wife, Laura, narrowly escapes being involved in a love affair with Martin Sheldon, a wealthy but unsuccessful suitor from her college days. Sheldon's daughter Ruth, married to a young lawyer, plans to elope with "Count" Lorenz, a crook. Ruth has an automobile accident en route and is brought to Laura's house, where she is encouraged to return to her husband. *Lawyers. Infidelity. Marriage. Divorce. Automobile accidents.*

THE CAVALIER **F2.0806**

Tiffany-Stahl Productions. 1 Nov **1928** [c15 Jun 1928; LP25389]. Sd eff (Photophone); b&w. 35mm. 7 reels, 6,775 ft.

Dir Irvin Willat. *Scen* Victor Irvin. *Titl* Walter Anthony. *Photog* Jack Stevens, Harry Cooper. *Set Dsgn* Eugene McMurtrie. *Film Ed* Doane Harrison. *Mus Score* Hugo Riesenfeld. *Song: "My Cavalier"* R. Meredith Willson, Hugo Riesenfeld.

Cast: Richard Talmadge *(El Caballero/Taki)*, Barbara Bedford *(Lucía D'Arquista)*, Nora Cecil *(Lucía's aunt)*, David Torrence *(Ramón Torreno)*, David Mir *(Carlos Torreno)*, Stuart Holmes *(Sgt. Juan Dinero)*, Christian Frank *(Pierre Gaston)*, Oliver Eckhardt *(The Padre)*.

Action melodrama. Source: Max Brand, "The Black Rider" (publication undetermined). El Caballero, a mysterious knight-errant—beloved by the poor, hated by the rich, and feared by the haughty—disguises himself as Taki, an Aztec servant, and rescues Lucía, a Spanish girl of noble birth, from an unhappy marriage with the son of a wealthy Californian. El Caballero, actually a Spanish don, marries Lucía and returns to Spain with her. *Nobility. Aztec Indians. Spanish. Disguise. Marriage—Arranged. California—Spanish era.*

THE CAVE GIRL **F2.0807**

Inspiration Pictures. *Dist* Associated First National Pictures. 26 Dec **1921** [c18 Nov 1921; LP17058]. Si; b&w. 35mm. 5 reels, 4,405 ft.

Dir Joseph J. Franz. *Scen* William Parker. *Titl* Katherine Hilliker. *Photog* Victor Milner.

Cast: Teddie Gerard *(Margot)*, Charles Meredith *(Divvy Bates)*, Wilton Taylor *(J. T. Bates)*, Eleanor Hancock *(Mrs. Georgia Case)*, Lillian Tucker *(Elsie Case)*, Frank Coleman *(Rufus Patterson)*, Boris Karloff *(Baptiste)*, Jake Abrahams *(Prof. Orlando Sperry)*, John Beck *(Rogers)*.

Melodrama. Source: Guy Bolton and George Middleton, *The Cave Girl, an American Comedy in Three Acts* (New York, 1925). Margot Sperry, who keeps house for her guardian, a professor who wants to revert to primitive modes of living, finds it difficult to find food in the winter wilderness and resorts to pilfering from the Bates's winter camp. Divvy, engaged to a girl he does not love, meets Margot on one of her raids and falls in love with her. Baptiste, a halfbreed employed by the Bates family, is discharged for stealing and burns the camp, driving the family to refuge with Margot. Elsie, hoping to regain Divvy's affections, dresses in boyish clothes similar to Margot's. Joining forces with Baptiste, they capture Margot, and Baptiste takes her in a canoe downstream. Realizing her mistake, Elsie warns Divvy, who bests the halfbreed and then rescues Margot from the falls. *Professors. Halfcastes. Primitive life. Hunger. Waterfalls.*

THE CAVEMAN **F2.0808**

Warner Brothers Pictures. 6 Feb **1926** [c29 Jan 1926; LP22337]. Si; b&w. 35mm. 7 reels, 6,741 ft.

Dir Lewis Milestone. *Adapt* Darryl Francis Zanuck. *Photog* David Abel. *Adtl Photog* Frank Kesson. *Asst Dir* Ross Lederman.

Cast: Matt Moore *(Mike Smagg)*, Marie Prevost *(Myra Gaylord)*, John Patrick *(Brewster Bradford)*, Myrna Loy *(maid)*, Phyllis Haver *(Dolly Van Dream)*, Hedda Hopper *(Mrs. Van Dream)*.

Farce. Source: Gelette Burgess, "The Caveman" (publication undetermined). Myra Burgess, a bored society heiress who longs for adventure, throws a note out of her window offering $100 to the person who brings it back to her. Mike Smagg, a coal heaver, finds the note and comes to collect his reward; Myra is taken with him and, rigging him out as a gentleman, introduces him into society as an eccentric professor. Mike's abrupt charm and rough manner endear him to the ladies, and he soon becomes a social lion; when he no longer will submit to Myra's prompting, however, she exposes his lowly origins, leading to his complete expulsion from high society. He returns to his former life for a while, then abducts Myra in his coal wagon and takes her to a minister to be married. *Socialites. Coalmen. Social classes.*

CELEBRITY **F2.0809**

Pathé Exchange. 7 Oct **1928** [c2 Oct 1928; LP25672]. Si; b&w. 35mm. 7 reels, 6,145 ft.

Ralph Block Production. *Dir* Tay Garnett. *Screenplay* Tay Garnett, George Dromgold. *Titl* John Krafft. *Adapt* Anthony Clawson, George Dromgold. *Photog* Peverell Marley. *Art Dir* Mitchell Leisen. *Film Ed* Doane Harrison. *Asst Dir* Robert Fellows. *Prod Mgr* Harry H. Poppe.

Cast: Robert Armstrong *(Kid Reagan)*, Clyde Cook *(Circus)*, Lina Basquette *(Jane)*, Dot Farley *(mother)*, Jack Perry *(Cyclone)*, Otto Lederer

(Cyclone's manager), David Tearle *(reporter)*.

Comedy. Source: William Keefe, *Celebrity* (New York opening: 26 Dec 1927). Circus, the hard-working manager of prizefighter Kid Reagan, hits upon a scheme to publicize his cauliflowered protégé: he engages a hardboiled mother-and-daughter act from vaudeville to play The Kid's sweet mother and sweetheart and then hires an ex-newspaperman to write poems to which The Kid signs his own name. The poems are printed in the society columns of a newspaper, and The Kid is soon sufficiently well known to warrant a try for the title. Circus convinces The Kid's "fiancée," Jane, that she is bad for The Kid, and Jane walks out on him just before the championship fight. Greatly angered by the taunts of the crowd, The Kid wins the fight and, to complete his happiness, finds Jane waiting for him after the match. *Prizefighters. Fight managers. Reporters. Poets. Publicity. Vaudeville.*

A CERTAIN RICH MAN **F2.0810**

Great Authors Pictures. *Dist* W. W. Hodkinson Corp. ca28 May **1921** [Los Angeles premiere; released 18 Sep 1921]. Si; b&w. 35mm. 6 reels, 5,900 ft.

Prod Benjamin B. Hampton. *Assoc Prod* William H. Clifford, Eliot Howe, Jean Hersholt, Elliott J. Clawson. *Dir* Howard Hickman. *Photog* Joseph A. Dubray.

Cast: Carl Gantvoort *(Bob Hendricks)*, Claire Adams *(Molly Culpepper)*, Robert McKim *(John Barclay)*, Jean Hersholt *(Adrian Brownwell)*, Joseph J. Dowling *(Col. Martin Culpepper)*, Lydia Knott *(John Barclay's mother)*, Frankie Lee *(young Neal Ward)*, Mary Jane Irving *(young Janet Barclay)*, Harry Lorraine *(General Hendricks)*, J. Gunnis Davis *(Lige Bemis)*, Charles Colby *(Watts McHurdie)*, Walter Perry *(Jake Dolan)*, Fleming Pitts *(Mose)*, Grace Pike *(Mrs. Colonel Culpepper)*, Eugenia Gilbert *(Janet Barclay)*, Gordon Dumont *(Neal Ward)*, Edna Pennington *(Mrs. Jane Barclay)*.

Drama. Source: William Allen White, *A Certain Rich Man* (New York, ca1909). In the small town of Sycamore Ridge live youthful sweethearts Bob Hendricks and Molly Culpepper; Bob's banker father, General Hendricks; and John Barclay, head of the Golden Belt Wheat Co. When Adrian Brownwell comes to town to publish a newspaper, his cash deposits in Hendricks' bank relieve the banker's worry that an expected bank examiner will discover the shortage in bank funds resulting from Hendricks' support of Barclay. Adrian falls in love with Molly and decides to leave Sycamore Ridge when she refuses to marry him. Barclay threatens Molly with the financial ruin of many whom she holds dear unless she marries Adrian, and Bob returns from the East to find Molly the new Mrs. Brownwell. Twenty years pass, Barclay becomes a financial power, Adrian falls into drunkenness, and Molly supports herself by working on the newspaper, which Bob now controls. In a rage Adrian shoots Bob and flees, and happiness comes to Bob and Molly when word comes of Adrian's death in a railroad accident. The death of Barclay's wife leads the financier to believe that he is being punished for ruthlessly crushing his rivals, and he distributes his fortune to those whose businesses he has ruined. *Bankers. Smalltown life. Newspapers. Alcoholism. Business ethics. Wheat.*

A CERTAIN YOUNG MAN **F2.0811**

Metro-Goldwyn-Mayer Pictures. 19 May **1928** [c19 May 1928; LP25329]. Si; b&w. 35mm. 6 reels, 5,679 ft.

Dir Hobart Henley. *Scen* Donna Barrell. *Titl* Marian Ainslee, Ruth Cummings. *Story* Doris Bureel. *Photog* Merritt B. Gerstad. *Set Dsgn* Cedric Gibbons, Merrill Pye. *Film Ed* Basil Wrangell. *Wardrobe* Gilbert Clark.

Cast: Ramon Novarro *(Lord Gerald Brinsley)*, Marceline Day *(Phyllis)*, Renée Adorée *(Henriette)*, Carmel Myers *(Mrs. Crutchley)*, Bert Roach *(Mr. Crutchley)*, Huntly Gordon *(Mr. Hammond)*, Ernest Wood *(Hubert)*, Willard Louis.

Romantic comedy. Brinsley, an English lord, has a taste for married women that complicates his life. Forced to take a fishing trip to escape the husbands of his conquests, he meets Phyllis Hammond, an American traveling by train with her father, and he falls in love for the first time. Following them to Biarritz, Brinsley cultivates the young lady's affection. The romance is temporarily interrupted by the arrival of Mrs. Crutchley, unhappy at being left alone in London with her husband. Mr. Crutchley's arrival further complicates matters, but eventually all is resolved. *Philanderers. Infidelity. Fishing. London. Biarritz.*

Note: Reliable sources indicate that the film was made in 1926.

CHAIN LIGHTNING **F2.0812**

Ben Wilson Productions. *Dist* Arrow Film Corp. 25 Apr **1922** [c11 Apr 1922; LP17749]. Si; b&w. 35mm. 5 reels, 4,969 ft.

Prod-Dir Ben Wilson. *Scen* J. Grubb Alexander, Agnes Parsons. *Photog* Harry Gersted.

Cast: Norval MacGregor *(Maj. Lee Pomeroy)*, Joseph W. Girard *(Col. George Bradley)*, William Carroll *(Red Rollins)*, Jack Dougherty *(Bob Bradley)*, Ann Little *(Peggy Pomeroy)*.

Melodrama. Major Lee Pomeroy, of an old southern family, is forced to sell his daughter's favorite racehorse to extricate himself from financial difficulties. Peggy returns home from school to find that Chain Lightning is now in the possession of Colonel Bradley, a longtime enemy of her father and a former suitor of her mother's. Pomeroy falls ill and bets his remaining funds on Chain Lightning in an impending race; meanwhile, Red Rollins, the horse's jockey, makes advances to Peggy, who repulses him but later pretends to agree to his proposition in return for his winning the race on Chain Lightning. An automobile accident allows Peggy to escape, and on the day of the race she dons the jockey's clothes and rides Chain Lightning to victory. The major recovers and is reconciled with Bradley, while Peggy becomes engaged to the colonel's nephew, Bob. *Jockeys. Finance—Personal. Horseracing. Disguise. Wagers. United States–South. Automobile accidents.*

CHAIN LIGHTNING **F2.0813**

Fox Film Corp. 14 Aug **1927** [c14 Aug 1927; LP24336]. Si; b&w. 35mm. 6 reels, 5,333 ft.

Pres by William Fox. *Dir-Scen* Lambert Hillyer. *Titl* Malcolm Stuart Boylan. *Photog* Reginald Lyons. *Film Ed* Louis Loeffler. *Asst Dir* Ted Brooks. *Cost* Kathleen Kay.

Cast: Buck Jones *(Steve Lannon)*, Dione Ellis *(Glory Jackson)*, Ted McNamara *(Shorty)*, Jack Baston *(Campan)*, William Welch *(George Clearwater)*, Marte Faust *(Bannack)*, William Caress *(Tom Yeats)*, Gene Cameron *(Binghamwell Stokes Hurlbert)*.

Western melodrama. Source: Charles Alden Seltzer, *The Brass Commandments* (New York, 1923). Rancher Steve Lannon returns home when he learns that a gang of rustlers have been stealing his horses, including Eagle, his favorite. Eventually, he tracks down the rustlers, led by the notorious Campan, and rescues Glory Jackson from the villains, thus winning her love and bringing the gang to justice. *Ranchers. Rustlers. Horses.*

CHALK MARKS **F2.0814**

Peninsula Studios. *Dist* Producers Distributing Corp. 14 Sep **1924** [c15 Sep 1924; LP20702]. Si; b&w. 35mm. 7 reels, 6,711 ft.

Supv-Writ Frank E. Woods. *Dir* John G. Adolfi. *Photog* Joseph Walker, Charles Kaufman.

Cast: Marguerite Snow *(Angelina Kilbourne)*, Ramsey Wallace *(Herbert Thompson)*, June Elvidge *(Ann Morton)*, Lydia Knott *(Mrs. Mary Kilbourne)*, Rex Lease *(Bert Thompson)*, Helen Ferguson *(Virginia Thompson)*, Priscilla Bonner *(Betty Towner)*, Harold Holland *("Red" Doran)*, Verna Mercereau *(Josie Jennings)*, Fred Church *(The Stranger)*, Lee Willard *(hotel guest)*.

Drama. The window of Herbert Thompson's memory reveals the unrequited love of Angelina Kilbourne, whom Herbert discarded in his youth for the wealth and social prominence of Ann Morton. While Angelina pursues the teaching profession and performs many good deeds, Herbert rises to become district attorney and the father of two children, Bert and Virginia. In defense of his sister's honor, Bert kills a man in a notorious roadhouse, and Angelina persuades Herbert to resign his office to defend his son. In later years Bert succeeds in the business world, returns home, and prevents a "progress-minded" school administration from ousting Angelina, now aged. Angelina is further rewarded by the betrothal of Bert to his schooldays' sweetheart, Betty Towner. *Schoolteachers. District attorneys. Brother-sister relationship. Murder. Retirement. Wealth.*

THE CHALLENGE **F2.0815**

Star Productions. *Dist* American Releasing Corp. 26 Nov **1922.** Si; b&w. 35mm. 5 reels, 5,052 ft.

Dir Tom Terriss. *Photog* Hal Sintzenich.

Cast: Rod La Rocque *(Stanley Roberts)*, Dolores Cassinelli *(Barbara Hastings)*, Warner Richmond *(Ralph Westley)*, De Sacia Mooers *(Peggy Royce)*, Jane Jennings *(Mrs. Hastings)*, Frank Norcross *(Mr. Hastings)*.

Domestic drama. Barbara Hastings, a hostess in an Adirondacks resort, settles the rivalry between artist Stanley Roberts and banker Ralph

Westley by choosing Roberts to be her husband. Westley's jealousy will not let him accept the situation, however, and he throws temptation into Roberts' path by anonymously buying the artist's work. Roberts becomes extravagant, and his attention wanders to an attractive widow, but Barbara remains faithful—even when Westley offers her her old job. Finally realizing the futility of his efforts, Westley helps to reunite Roberts with his wife. *Artists. Bankers. Wealth. Marriage. Courtship. Resorts. Adirondack Mountains.*

CHAMPION OF LOST CAUSES **F2.0816**

Fox Film Corp. 22 Jan **1925** [c17 Feb 1925; LP21150]. Si; b&w. 35mm. 5 reels, 5,115 ft.

Dir Chester Bennett. *Scen* Thomas Dixon, Jr. *Photog* Ernest Palmer.

Cast: Edmund Lowe *(Loring)*, Barbara Bedford *(Beatrice Charles)*, Walter McGrail *(Zanten/Dick Sterling)*, Jack McDonald *(Joseph Wilbur)*, Alec Francis *(Peter Charles)*.

Mystery melodrama. Source: Max Brand, "Champion of Lost Causes," in *Flynn's Magazine* (11 Oct–22 Nov 1924). Loring, an author in search of material for an article, visits a gambling resort run by Zanten. There he notices Joseph Wilbur, who is acting strangely and is later murdered. Peter Charles is accused of the murder, and Loring, who secretly loves Peter's daughter, Beatrice, sets out to clear Peter's name. Loring goes to Zanten for help and advice, becoming involved with a gang of thugs who make several attempts on his life. Loring finally discovers that Zanten himself (who is actually Beatrice's unworthy fiancé, Dick Sterling, in disguise) is the real murderer of Wilbur. Beatrice's father is freed, and Beatrice and Loring are wed. *Authors. Gamblers. Filial relations. Murder. Injustice. Disguise.*

CHANG **F2.0817**

Paramount Famous Lasky Corp. 29 Apr **1927** [New York premiere; released 3 Sep; c2 Sep 1927; LP24344]. Si; b&w. 35mm. 8 reels, 6,536 ft.

Pres by Adolph Zukor, Jesse L. Lasky. *Prod-Dir* Merian Cooper, Ernest B. Schoedsack. *Titl* Achmed Abdullah. *Photog* Ernest B. Schoedsack.

Cast: Kru *(The Pioneer)*, Chantui *(His Wife)*, Nah *(Their Little Boy)*, Ladah *(Their Little Girl)*, Bimbo *(The Monkey)*.

Documentary drama. On the jungle frontier of Siam lives Kru, with his family—his pet goat, a gibbon, and a water buffalo among others—laboring to plant and harvest the rice crop, while menaced on all sides by the jungle beasts. A leopard attacks his goat, and a tiger kills his water buffalo; Kru assembles neighboring warriors in an expedition against their predatory enemies, culminating in the kill of a giant tiger. Then Kru is plagued by the invasion of the dreaded Chang (the Siamese term for elephant), who destroy his little hut and the neighboring village. Kru organizes a massive hunt, and after the elephant herd is tracked down, the animals are driven into a corral and gradually domesticated for heavy labor. Kru, once more contented, returns to rebuild his house, though life still remains hazardous. *Rice. Jungles. Siam. Elephants. Apes. Water buffalo. Goats. Leopards. Tigers.*

Note: In its original presentations certain sequences were projected in Magnascope.

CHANGING HUSBANDS **F2.0818**

Famous Players–Lasky. *Dist* Paramount Pictures. 22 Jun **1924** [New York premiere; released 10 Aug; c8 Jul 1924; LP20384]. Si; b&w. 35mm. 7 reels, 6,799 ft.

Pres by Adolph Zukor, Jesse L. Lasky. *Supv* Cecil B. De Mille. *Dir* Frank Urson, Paul Iribe. *Scen* Sada Cowan, Howard Higgin. *Photog* Bert Glennon.

Cast: Leatrice Joy *(Gwynne Evans/Ava Graham)*, Victor Varconi *(Oliver Evans)*, Raymond Griffith *(Bob Hamilton)*, Julia Faye *(Mitzi)*, ZaSu Pitts *(Delia)*, Helen Dunbar *(Mrs. Evans, Sr.)*, William Boyd *(Conrad Bardshaw)*.

Romantic comedy. Source: Elizabeth Alexander, *Rôles* (Boston, 1924). Gwynne Evans, bored with the routine of her life, adopts a stage career with her husband's consent. Gwynne convinces actress Ava Graham, to whom she bears a strong resemblance, that they should exchange places. Complications develop when Evans falls in love with the other woman, and following a divorce they are married, while Ava's fiancé, Bob Hamilton, takes Gwynne as his wife. *Actors. Doubles. Marriage. Divorce.*

CHANNING OF THE NORTHWEST **F2.0819**

Selznick Pictures. *Dist* Select Pictures. 20 Apr **1922** [c30 Apr 1922; LP17816]. Si; b&w. 35mm. 5 reels, 4,725 ft.

Pres by Lewis J. Selznick. *Dir* Ralph Ince. *Scen* Edward J. Montagne. *Story* John Willard. *Photog* Jack Brown.

Cast: Eugene O'Brien *(Channing)*, Gladden James *(Jim Franey)*, Norma Shearer *(Jes Driscoll)*, James Seeley *(Tom Driscoll)*, Pat Hartigan *(Sport McCool)*, Nita Naldi *(Cicily Varden)*, Harry Lee *(McCool's man)*, J. W. Johnston *(Buddy)*, C. Coulter *(Channing's uncle)*.

Northwest melodrama. Channing, who lives the life of a leisured gentleman in London, falls in love with Cicily Varden, a dancer in the Gaiety Revue, but she breaks off the engagement upon learning he is to be disinherited. Channing leaves for Canada and joins the Canadian Northwest Mounted; there he meets Jes Driscoll, who lives with her father, Tom, and her adopted brother, Jim Franey. Sport McCool, owner of the local dancehall, is known to engage in smuggling hooch across the border, and Channing is detailed to investigate his activities—in which Jim is involved. Inflamed with jealousy and taunted by McCool's insinuations, Jim determines to kill Channing, but he hesitates at an opportune moment and shoots McCool. Jim dies from a wound, and Channing and Jes are united. *Dancers. Smugglers. Canadian Northwest. London. Northwest Mounted Police.*

A CHAPTER IN HER LIFE (Universal-Jewel) **F2.0820**

Universal Pictures. 17 Sep **1923** [c9 Aug 1923; LP19309]. Si; b&w. 35mm. 6 reels, 6,330 ft.

Dir Lois Weber. *Adapt* Lois Weber, Doris Schroeder. *Photog* Ben Kline.

Cast: Claude Gillingwater *(Mr. Everingham)*, Jane Mercer *(Jewel)*, Jacqueline Gadsden *(Eloise Everingham)*, Frances Raymond *(Madge Everingham)*, Robert Frazer *(Dr. Ballard)*, Eva Thatcher *(Mrs. Forbes)*, Ralph Yearsley *(Zeke Forbes)*, Fred Thomson *(Nat Bonnell)*, Beth Rayon *(Susan)*.

Drama. Source: Clara Louise Burnham, *Jewel; a Chapter in Her Life* (Boston, 1903). Rich but unhappy Mr. Everingham resents the presence in his home of Madge, his widowed daughter-in-law, and her daughter Eloise until Jewel, Everingham's younger son's daughter, arrives for a visit and brings cheer and harmony to the household. *Widows. Grandfathers. In-laws. Family life.*

CHARGE IT **F2.0821**

Equity Pictures. *Dist* Jans Film Service. ca11 Jun **1921** [San Francisco premiere]. Si; b&w. 35mm. 7 reels, 6,900 ft.

Pres by Harry Garson. *Dir* Harry Garson. *Story* Sada Cowan. *Photog* Jacques Bizeul.

Cast: Clara Kimball Young *(Julia Lawrence)*, Herbert Rawlinson *(Philip Lawrence)*, Edward M. Kimball *(Tom Garreth)*, Betty Blythe *(Mille Garreth)*, Nigel Barrie *(Dana Herrick)*, Hal Wilson *(Robert McGregor)*, Dulcie Cooper *(Rose McGregor)*.

Domestic drama. Young bride Julia Lawrence is granted a charge account by her husband, Philip, and soon accumulates so many bills that Philip must work overtime to keep out of debt. Feeling neglected and misunderstood, Julia quarrels with Philip and succumbs to the attentions of Dana Herrick. Julia's flirtation ends when she discovers Dana with Mille Garreth, and her life begins a downward trend until she is forced to work as a checkgirl in a hotel. Philip, now prosperous, visits the establishment, and is reunited to a sadder but wiser Julia. *Checkgirls. Marriage. Credit. Finance—Personal.*

THE CHARGE OF THE GAUCHOS **F2.0822**

Ajuria Productions. *Dist* FBO Pictures. 16 Sep **1928** [c16 Sep 1928; LP25691]. Si; b&w. 35mm. 6 reels, 5,487 ft.

Dir Albert Kelly. *Scen* W. C. Clifford. *Titl* Garrett Graham. *Story* Julian Ajuria. *Photog* George Benoit, Nick Musuraca. *Film Ed* George Nichols, Jr.

Cast: Francis X. Bushman *(Belgrano)*, Jacqueline Logan *(Monica Salazar)*, Guido Trento *(Monteros)*, Paul Ellis *(Balcarce)*, Henry Kolker *(viceroy)*, Charles Hill Mailes *(Saavedra)*, John Hopkins *(Lezica)*, Charles K. French *(Salazar)*, Olive Hasbrouck *(Mariana)*, Mathilde Comont *(Aunt Rosita)*, Jack Ponder *(George Gordon)*, Ligo Conley *(Gómez)*, Gino Corrado *(Moreno)*, Frank Hagney *(Goyeneche)*.

Biographical drama. Belgrano, "the Washington of the Argentine," leads his people in open revolt against the Spanish, directing an ill-trained and poorly equipped army to victory after victory against the Loyalist forces. Belgrano's sweetheart, Monica, who is the daughter of a loyalist, secretly sends valuable information to Belgrano until she is exposed as a spy and sentenced to be beheaded. Belgrano rides to her rescue at the head of his gaucho cavalry and saves her from the ax. After the revolution,

Belgrano and Monica are married. *Spanish. Spies. Gauchos. Revolutionaries. Argentina—History—Independence. Manuel Belgrano.*

THE CHARLATAN (Universal-Jewel) **F2.0823**
Universal Pictures. 14 Apr **1929** [c29 Mar 1929; LP259]. Talking sequences (Movietone); b&w. 35mm. 7 reels, 6,097 ft. [Also si, 7 Apr 1929; 5,972 ft.]

Dir George Melford. *Scen* J. G. Hawks. *Dial* Jacques Rollens, Tom Reed. *Titl* Tom Reed. *Adapt* Robert N. Lee. *Photog* George Robinson. *Film Ed* Robert Jahns, Maurice Pivar.

Cast: Holmes Herbert *(Count Merlin/Peter Dwight)*, Margaret Livingston *(Florence)*, Rockliffe Fellowes *(Richard Talbot)*, Philo McCullough *(Doctor Paynter)*, Anita Garvin *(Mrs. Paynter)*, Crauford Kent *(Frank Deering)*, Rose Tapley *(Mrs. Deering)*, Fred Mackaye *(Jerry Starke)*, Dorothy Gould *(Ann Talbot)*.

Melodrama. Source: Ernest Pascal and Leonard Praskins, *The Charlatan* (New York opening: 24 Apr 1922). Peter Dwight, a circus clown, is deserted by his wife, Florence, who runs off with wealthy Richard Talbot, taking their little daughter with her. Fifteen years pass. Posing as a Hindu seer, Dwight finds his wife just as she is planning to leave Talbot for another man. On the night of the elopement, Dwight entertains during at society party a which Florence is a guest. Florence is killed, and the district attorney attempts to arrest Dwight. Outsmarting the man, Dwight locks him up and then impersonates him, proving that Talbot murdered Florence to keep her from running out on him. Dwight is cleared of all suspicion and reunited with his daughter. *Clowns. Hindus. Seers. Charlatans. District attorneys. Fatherhood. Desertion. Divorce. Murder.*

CHARLEY'S AUNT **F2.0824**
Christie Film Co. *Dist* Producers Distributing Corp. 2 Feb **1925** [c2 Feb 1925; LP21264]. Si; b&w. 35mm. 8 reels, 7,243 ft.

Pres by Al Christie, Charles Christie. *Dir* Scott Sidney. *Scen* F. McGrew Willis. *Titl* Joseph Farnham. *Photog* Gus Peterson, Paul Garnett.

Cast: Sydney Chaplin *(Sir Fancourt Babberley)*, Ethel Shannon *(Ela Delahay)*, James E. Page *(Spettigue)*, Lucien Littlefield *(Brasset)*, Alec B. Francis *(Mr. Delahay)*, Phillips Smalley *(Sir Francis Chesney)*, Eulalie Jensen *(Donna Lucia D'Alvâdorez)*, David James *(Jack Chesney)*, Jimmy Harrison *(Charley Wykeham)*, Mary Akin *(Amy)*, Priscilla Bonner *(Kitty)*.

Farce. Source: Brandon Thomas, *Charley's Aunt* (London opening: 21 Dec 1892; published 1935). Sir Fancourt Babberly, known affectionately as Babbs, is a student at Oxford University. Two of his friends, Charley and Jack, who wish to propose to their sweethearts, invite the girls to lunch, promising them that Charley's aunt will be present as chaperon. The aunt, Donna Lucia, does not arrive, and Babbs (who is costumed for a student theatrical in which he has the part of an old woman) is pressed into service to impersonate her. Mr. Spettigue, the girl's guardian, unexpectedly shows up, as does Jack's father. Both men flirt with "Charley's aunt," believing her be a woman of great wealth. Donna Lucia then appears but conceals her identity. By accepting Spettigue's proposal of marriage, "Charley's aunt" gains his consent for the two girls to marry Jack and Charley. Babbs then reveals himself; he becomes engaged to his own sweetheart, Ela; and Jack and Charley become engaged to their respective sweethearts. *Students. Guardians. Aunts. Chaperons. Courtship. Female impersonation. College life. Oxford University.*

Note: Remade in 1930 under the same title, q. v.

CHARLEY'S AUNT **F2.0825**
Christie Film Co. *Dist* Columbia Pictures. 25 Dec **1930** [c24 Dec 1930; LP1848]. Sd (Movietone); b&w. 35mm. 9 reels, 7,890 ft.

Prod Al Christie, Charles Christie. *Dir* Al Christie. *Dial Dir* A. Leslie Pearce. *Screenplay-Dial* F. McGrew Willis. *Camera* Gus Peterson, Harry Zech, Leslie Rowson. *Art Dir* Charles Cadwallader. *Rec Engr* R. S. Clayton. *Asst Rec Engr* Ted Murray. *Asst Dir* Art Black.

Cast: Charles Ruggles *(Lord Fancourt Babberly)*, June Collyer *(Amy Spettigue)*, Hugh Williams *(Charlie Wykeham)*, Doris Lloyd *(Donna Lucia D'Alvâdorez)*, Halliwell Hobbes *(Stephen Spettigue)*, Flora Le Breton *(Ela Delahay)*, Rodney McLennon *(Jack Chesney)*, Wilson Benge *(Brassett)*, Flora Sheffield *(Kitty Verdun)*, Phillips Smalley *(Sir Francis Chesney)*.

Comedy. Source: Brandon Thomas, *Charley's Aunt, a Play in Three Acts* (London opening: 21 Dec 1892; published 1935). Remake of the 1925 film of the same title, q. v. *Students. Guardians. Aunts. Chaperons. College life. Courtship. Female impersonation. Oxford University.*

THE CHARM SCHOOL **F2.0826**
Famous Players–Lasky. *Dist* Paramount Pictures. Jan **1921** [c8 Dec 1920; LP15902]. Si; b&w. 35mm. 5 reels, 4,743 ft.

Dir James Cruze. *Photog* C. Edgar Schoenbaum.

Cast: Wallace Reid *(Austin Bevans)*, Lila Lee *(Elsie)*, Adele Farrington *(Mrs. Rolles)*, Beulah Bains *(Susie Rolles)*, Edwin Stevens *(Homer Johns)*, Grace Morse *(Miss Hayes)*, Patricia Magee *(Sally Boyd)*, Lincoln Stedman *(George Boyd)*, Kate Toncray *(Miss Curtis)*, Minna Redman *(Miss Tevis)*, Snitz Edwards *(Mr. Boyd)*, Helen Pillsbury *(Mrs. Boyd)*, Tina Marshall *(Europia)*.

Comedy. Source: Alice Duer Miller, *The Charm School* (New York, 1919). Austin Bevans, a lively car-salesman, suddenly finds himself heir to the Bevans School for Girls. Since Austin feels that acquiring grace and charm are more important to a young girl than acquiring knowledge, academic courses are dropped, and a charm school emerges. He submits to the charms of Elsie, a student at the school, whose grandfather takes him into his employ after a newly discovered will dispossesses him of the school. Elsie resents Austin for accepting a job with those who formerly thought him undesirable, but later she relents and takes him back. *Salesmen. Students. Dispossession. Personality. Boarding schools. Wills.*

THE CHARMER **F2.0827**
Famous Players–Lasky. *Dist* Paramount Pictures. 20 Apr **1925** [c19 Apr 1925; LP21367]. Si; b&w. 35mm. 6 reels, 5,988 ft.

Pres by Adolph Zukor, Jesse L. Lasky. *Dir* Sidney Olcott. *Scen* Sada Cowan. *Photog* James Howe. *Film Ed* Patricia Rooney.

Cast: Pola Negri *(Mariposa)*, Wallace MacDonald *(Ralph Bayne)*, Robert Frazer *(Dan Murray)*, Trixie Friganza *(Mama)*, Cesare Gravina *(Señor Sprott)*, Gertrude Astor *(Bertha Sedgwick)*, Edwards Davis *(Mr. Sedgwick)*, Mathilda Brundage *(Mrs. Bayne)*.

Comedy-drama. Source: Henry Baerlein, *Mariposa* (London, 1924). Mariposa, a wild dancer in a cheap Seville cafe, is taken to New York by Señor Sprott, a prominent theatrical producer. Billed as "The Charmer," Mariposa becomes the toast of two continents. Among her most ardent admirers are Ralph Bayne, a millionaire playboy, and his chauffeur, Dan Murray, both of whom first met her in Spain. Madly in love with Bayne, Mrs. Sedgwick invites Mariposa and her mother to a weekend party in a deliberate attempt to humiliate the beautiful dancer. Bayne quickly realizes that Mariposa is out of place in high society, and, determining to make her his mistress, takes her home with him. Mrs. Sedgwick unexpectedly arrives at Bayne's swank suite (closely followed by her suspicious husband), and Mariposa protects the society woman's reputation at the cost of her own. Murray arrives and attempts at gunpoint to force Bayne to marry Mariposa, but Mariposa objects and declares her intention of marrying Murray instead. *Dancers. Theatrical producers. Chauffeurs. Playboys. Millionaires. Social classes. Reputation. Infidelity. Cafes. Seville.*

THE CHARMING DECEIVER **F2.0828**
Vitagraph Co. of America. Mar **1921** [c25 Mar 1921; LP16315]. Si; b&w. 35mm. 5 reels.

Dir George L. Sargent. *Scen* Fred Schaefer. *Photog* Vincent Scully.

Cast: Alice Calhoun *(Edith Denton Marsden)*, Jack McLean *(Frank Denton)*, Charles Kent *(John Adams Stanford)*, Eugene Acker *(Don Marsden)*, Roland Bottomley *(Richard Walling)*, Robert Gaillard *(Duncan)*.

Melodrama. Source: Mrs. Owen Bronson, "The Charming Deceiver" (publication undetermined). Wealthy and lonely John Stanford sends for Edith Marsden, the child of his disowned daughter, who, unknown to him, has just been evicted from her flat with her husband imprisoned for forgery and her son recovering from war wounds. Edith becomes a favorite of Stanford, who wishes to match her with a neighbor, Walling, who loves her. Meanwhile, Marsden escapes and comes to Edith under the guise of a brother, but in a drunken rage he reveals himself to Walling as her father. When pursued by the police, Marsden falls to his death in a quarry. Edith and Walling are then happily reunited. *Grandfathers. Fatherhood. Family life.*

CHARMING SINNERS **F2.0829**
Paramount Famous Lasky Corp. 24 Aug **1929** [c17 Aug 1929; LP614]. Sd (Movietone); b&w. 35mm. 8 reels, 6,184 ft. [Also si; 6,530 ft.]

Dir Robert Milton. *Adapt-Screenplay* Doris Anderson. *Photog* Victor Milner. *Film Ed* Verna Willis. *Rec Engr* Earl Hayman.

Cast: Ruth Chatterton *(Kathryn Miles)*, Clive Brook *(Robert Miles)*, Mary Nolan *(Anne-Marie Whitley)*, William Powell *(Karl Kraley)*, Laura Hope Crews *(Mrs. Carr)*, Florence Eldridge *(Helen Carr)*, Montagu

Love *(George Whitley)*, Juliette Crosby *(Margaret)*, Lorraine Eddy *(Alice)*, Claude Allister *(Gregson)*.

Drama. Source: William Somerset Maugham, *The Constant Wife* (New York opening: 29 Nov 1926). To regain the affection of her husband, a wealthy doctor, Kathryn Miles pretends to be in love with an old admirer, Karl Kraley, when she discovers Miles is having an affair with her best friend, Anne-Marie Whitley. Kathryn's rational way of dealing with the erring couple when they are forced to admit their indiscretion so astounds Miles that he casts Anne-Marie aside and asks Kathryn's forgiveness. *Physicians. Infidelity. Marriage.*

THE CHASER **F2.0830**

Harry Langdon Corp. *Dist* First National Pictures. 12 Feb **1928** [c23 Jan 1928; LP24902]. Si; b&w. 35mm. 6 reels, 5,744 ft.

Dir Harry Langdon. *Scen* Clarence Hennecke, Robert Eddy, Harry McCoy. *Titl* E. H. Giebler. *Story* Arthur Ripley. *Photog* Elgin Lessley, Frank Evans. *Film Ed* Alfred De Gaetano. *Comedy Construc* Clarence Hennecke.

Cast: Gladys McConnell *(Wife)*, Harry Langdon *(Husband)*, Helen Hayward *(Her Mother)*, Bud Jamieson *(His Buddy)*, Charles Thurston *(The Judge)*.

Domestic comedy. Harry is sentenced to hard labor in the kitchen when he accidentally stabs his mother-in-law with his lodge sword. Seeking suicide by poisoning, he drinks castor oil by mistake. His wife and mother-in-law think he has died when he disappears, but he returns to make them repent their cruelty. *Mothers-in-law. Judges. Marriage. Suicide.*

CHASING RAINBOWS **F2.0831**

Metro-Goldwyn-Mayer Pictures. 10 Jan **1930** [c6 Jan 1930; LP975]. Sd (Movietone); b&w with col sequences (Technicolor). 35mm. 11 reels, 8,100 ft.

Dir Charles F. Reisner. *Story-Cont* Bess Meredyth. *Dial* Charles F. Reisner, Robert Hopkins, Kenyon Nicholson, Al Boasberg. *Adapt* Wells Root. *Photog* Ira Morgan. *Art Dir* Cedric Gibbons. *Film Ed* George Hively. *Songs: "Happy Days," "Poor But Honest," "My Dynamic Personality," "Love Ain't Nothing But the Blues," "Do I Know What I'm Doing," "Lucky Me and Lovable You," "I Got a Feeling For You"* Milton Ager, Jack Yellen. *Mus Cond* Arthur Lange. *Interpolations* Fred Fisher, Louis Alter, Reggie Montgomery, Gus Edwards, Joe Goodwin, George Ward, J. F. Murray. *Rec Engr* Russell Franks, Douglas Shearer. *Sd Asst* Jack Jordon. *Wardrobe* David Cox.

Cast: Bessie Love *(Carlie)*, Charles King *(Terry)*, Jack Benny *(Eddie)*, George K. Arthur *(Loster)*, Polly Moran *(Polly)*, Gwen Lee *(Peggy)*, Nita Martan *(Daphne)*, Eddie Phillips *(Cordova)*, Marie Dressler *(Bonnie)*, Youcca Troubetzkoy *(Lanning)*.

Musical comedy. Carlie and Terry constitute a vaudeville team in a traveling musical show; also in the company are Eddie, the stage manager; Bonnie, a comedienne; and Polly, the wardrobe mistress. Terry's habit of constantly falling in love with the leading lady causes him to marry Daphne, a two-timing songstress. When he finds her with another man, Eddie threatens to kill himself, but his little partner reassures him that "Happy Days Are Here Again," and the show goes on. *Chorus girls. Stage managers. Wardrobe mistresses. Vaudeville. Road shows.*

Note: Initially reviewed as *The Road Show*.

CHASING THE MOON **F2.0832**

Fox Film Corp. 26 Feb **1922** [c26 Feb 1922; LP17636]. Si; b&w. 35mm. 5 reels, 5,092 ft.

Pres by William Fox. *Dir* Edward Sedgwick. *Titl* Ralph Spence. *Story* Tom Mix, Edward Sedgwick. *Photog* Ben Kline. *Film Ed* Ralph Spence.

Cast: Tom Mix *(Dwight Locke)*, Eva Novak *(Jane Norworth)*, William Buckley *(Milton Norworth)*, Sid Jordan *(Velvet Joe)*, Elsie Danbric *(Princess Sonia)*, Wynn Mace *(Prince Albert)*.

Comedy-melodrama. Dwight Locke, a blasé millionaire, gives a party for his ranch hands at a city restaurant. His fiancée, Jane Norworth, sees him there with a chorus girl and later upbraids him for not being a worker like her brother Milton. When Dwight breaks a retort in Milton's shop, cutting his hand, he learns that it contains a poison that will kill in 30 days unless offset by an antidote known only to a professor who has sailed for Russia. Dwight takes up the chase to find the professor within the time limit, with adventures on sea and land. Meanwhile, Milton discovers that the retort did not contain poison and that Dwight will die if he takes the antidote; together with Jane, he pursues Dwight, whom they find in Spain. There the lovers are united. *Ranchers. Millionaires. Brother-sister relationship. Death. Russia. Spain.*

CHASING THROUGH EUROPE **F2.0833**

Fox Film Corp. 4 Aug **1929** [c21 Aug 1929; LP625]. Talking & singing sequences & sd eff (Movietone); b&w. 35mm. 6 reels, 5,581 ft. [Also si; 5,622 ft.]

Pres by William Fox. *Dir* David Butler, Alfred L. Werker. *Story* Andrew Bennison, John Stone. *Photog* Sidney Wagner, Lucien Andriot, L. W. O'Connell.

Cast: Sue Carol *(Linda Terry)*, Nick Stuart *(Dick Stallings)*, Gustav von Seyffertitz *(Phineas Merrill)*, Gavin Gordon *(Don Merrill)*, E. Alyn Warren *(Louise Herriot)*.

Action melodrama. Dick Stallings, a freelance newsreel photographer, meets Linda Terry, a wealthy American in London, when her chauffeur-driven car bumps him. Attracted to Linda, Stallings induces her to come with him when Phineas Merrill, her guardian, attempts to place her in an insane asylum for refusing to marry his nephew, Don. Stallings and Linda travel around Europe photographing famous landmarks—the Eiffel Tower—and important persons such as Mussolini and the Prince of Wales, pursued by Merrill (a smalltime crook) and his accomplices. While Stallings is photographing Vesuvius, Merrill's men force their way into Linda's apartment and attempt to kidnap her. Dick returns, has Merrill arrested, and he and Linda return to the United States to marry. *Newsreel photographers. Guardians. Embezzlement. Insane asylums. London. Vesuvius. Eiffel Tower. Benito Mussolini. David Prince of Wales.*

CHASING TROUBLE (Blue Streak) **F2.0834**

Universal Pictures. 2 May **1926** [c25 Mar 1926; LP22539]. Si; b&w. 35mm. 5 reels, 4,585 ft.

Pres by Carl Laemmle. *Dir* Milburn Morante. *Story-Scen* Frank Beresford. *Photog* Jack Young.

Cast: Pete Morrison *(Ballard)*, Ione Reed *(Emily Gregg)*, Tom London *(Jerome Garrett)*, Roy Watson *(Judge Gregg)*, Frances Friel *(Sal Karney)*, Milton Fahrney *(sheriff)*, Jew Bennett *(Carnegie McCue)*, J. A. Wiley *(Stech)*, Al Richmond *(Jim O'Rielly)*, Skeeter Bill Robbins *(Munn)*, Lilly Harris *(Ma Flaherty)*, Fred Gamble *(bartender)*, Lightning *(Lightning, the horse)*.

Western melodrama. "Blizz" Ballard, summoned by the Homesteaders' League to track down a gang of cattle rustlers, arrives in Paradise Valley. In the saloon he is taunted by Jerome Garrett, who hopes to intimidate him but is himself beaten in a fight. Ballard, after proving himself by riding an outlaw horse, is taken on at the Gregg ranch. Garrett, in the family's favor and admired by Emily, the judge's daughter, accuses Ballard of being a cattle thief, while his accomplices capture and torture the sheriff. Ballard rescues the sheriff and captures his tormentors, but they are released by their cohorts. Ballard then foils a plot to rob the judge, pursues and captures Garrett, and marries Emily. *Homesteaders. Rustlers. Judges. Sheriffs. Horses.*

CHASTITY **F2.0835**

Preferred Pictures. *Dist* Associated First National Pictures. 31 Dec **1923** [c20 Dec 1923; LP19737]. Si; b&w. 35mm. 6 reels, 6,008 ft.

Pres by B. P. Schulberg. *Dir* Victor Schertzinger. *Story* Ernest Pascal. *Photog* Joseph Brotherton, Ernest Miller. *Film Ed* Eve Unsell.

Cast: Katherine MacDonald *(Norma O'Neill)*, J. Gunnis Davis *(Nat Mason)*, J. Gordon Russell *(Sam Wolfe)*, Huntley Gordon *(Darcy Roche, a theatrical producer)*, Frederick Truesdell *(Fergus Arlington)*, Edythe Chapman *(Mrs. Harris)*.

Melodrama. Norma O'Neill, a young and virtuous actress, is financially backed by Fergus Arlington, a friend of her late father. Unsuccessful at first, Norma finally becomes the reigning beauty of Broadway. Producer Darcy Roche is in love with her, but scandalous publicity causes him to believe that Arlington has more than a protective interest in her. Confronted with her alleged treachery, Norma, heartsick, leaves the stage. She is reported killed in an automobile accident. Later, when Roche meets Norma in California, she discloses that it was her understudy who died in the accident, and that she has come to live with her guardians, Fergus Arlington and his wife. The lovers are reunited. *Actors. Theatrical backers. Theatrical producers. Guardians. Virtue. New York City—Broadway. California.*

CHEAP KISSES F2.0836

C. Gardner Sullivan Productions. *Dist* Film Booking Offices of America. 21 Dec **1924** [c8 Nov 1924; LP20743]. Si; b&w. 35mm. 7 reels, 6,538 ft.

Pres by C. Gardner Sullivan. *Dir* John Ince, Cullen Tate. *Story-Scen* C. Gardner Sullivan. *Photog* Jules Cronjager. *Film Ed* Barbara Hunter.

Cast: Lillian Rich *(Ardell Kendall)*, Cullen Landis *(Donald Dillingham)*, Vera Reynolds *(Kitty Dillingham)*, Phillips Smalley *(George Wescott)*, Louise Dresser *(Jane Dillingham)*, Jean Hersholt *(Gustaf Borgstrom)*, Bessie Eyton *(Maybelle Wescott)*, Lincoln Stedman *(Bill Kendall)*, Kathleen Myers *(Mignon De Lisle)*, Sidney De Grey *(Henry Dillingham)*, Michael Dark *(Butterworth Little)*, Tom Ricketts *(The Old Man)*.

Society comedy-drama. Donald Dillingham refuses to join his family in their new social life when Henry Dillingham suddenly becomes wealthy, and he incurs their even greater disapproval for marrying chorus girl Ardell Kendall. Learning that famous sculptor Gustaf Borgstrom wishes to use Ardell as model, the Dillinghams suddenly welcome Donald and Ardell to their estate. Donald succumbs to both the jazzy pleasures and the attentions of Maybelle Wescott, but Ardell remains aloof and in order to pay off Maybelle threatens Mr. Dillingham with exposure of *his* infatuation with a chorus girl. The adventuress breaks her agreement to leave Donald alone, and Ardell reveals the bargain to Donald, who angrily leaves. Ardell sadly returns to the Dillinghams' honeymoon cottage and finds a repentant Donald awaiting her. *Nouveaux riches. Adventuresses. Chorus girls. Sculptors. Blackmail. Jazz life.*

CHEAPER TO MARRY F2.0837

Metro-Goldwyn Pictures. 9 Feb **1925** [c9 Feb 1925; LP21122]. Si; b&w. 35mm. 7 reels, 6,500 ft.

Pres by Louis B. Mayer. *Dir* Robert Z. Leonard. *Scen* Alice D. G. Miller. *Adapt* Frederick Hatton, Fanny Hatton. *Photog* André Barlatier. *Art Dir* Cedric Gibbons. *Asst Dir* David Todd.

Cast: Conrad Nagel *(Dick Tyler)*, Lewis S. Stone *(Jim Knight)*, Paulette Duval *(Evelyn)*, Marguerite De La Motte *(Doris)*, Louise Fazenda *(Flora)*, Claude Gillingwater *(Riddle)*, Richard Wayne *(Dal Whitney)*.

Domestic comedy-melodrama. Source: Samuel Shipman, *Cheaper To Marry* (New York, 1926). Dick Tyler, the junior partner in the law firm of Knight and Tyler, attempts to persuade Jim Knight, his older partner, that it is cheaper to be married than to trifle with love. Knight is infatuated with Evelyn, a gold digger who is making lavish and unreasonable demands on him, but Knight is satisfied and keeps meeting her every desire. Knight's prodigality places the firm close to bankruptcy, and he turns to Evelyn to assist him financially. Evelyn refuses, and Knight kills himself. Dick's wife, Doris, persuades a banker friend to accept Dick's personal note to keep the firm solvent. Evelyn soon finds another lover and spends her new fortune on him. *Lawyers. Gold diggers. Marriage. Suicide. Bankruptcy. Business management.*

THE CHEAT F2.0838

Famous Players–Lasky. *Dist* Paramount Pictures. 27 Aug **1923** [New York premiere; released 30 Sep; c15 Aug 1923; LP19324]. Si; b&w. 35mm. 8 reels, 7,323 ft.

Pres by Adolph Zukor. *Prod-Dir* George Fitzmaurice. *Adapt* Ouida Bergère. *Photog* Arthur Miller.

Cast: Pola Negri *(Carmelita De Córdoba)*, Jack Holt *(Dudley Drake)*, Charles De Roche *(Claude Mace, known as Prince Rao-Singh)*, Dorothy Cumming *(Lucy Hodge)*, Robert Schable *(Jack Hodge)*, Charles Stevenson *(Horace Drake)*, Helen Dunbar *(duenna)*, Richard Wayne *(attorney for defense)*, Guy Oliver *(district attorney)*, Edward Kimball *(judge)*.

Melodrama. South American beauty Carmelita De Córdoba, who is betrothed to an elderly Latin American, elopes with New York broker Dudley Drake; and after being disinherited by her father, she falls into the clutches of Rao-Singh, a crook masquerading as an Indian prince. When Carmelita seeks to repay her debt to him with money, he refuses her check and brands her as a cheat with his family crest. Carmelita retaliates by shooting him, then escapes. Dudley Drake arrives in time to take the rap, but he is acquitted when Carmelita shows the brand on her shoulder, and the courtroom mobs the bogus prince. *Brokers. New Yorkers. Elopement. Gambling. Imposture. Murder. Branding. Trials.*

Note: Remake of *The Cheat* (1915).

CHEATED HEARTS F2.0839

Universal Film Manufacturing Co. 12 Dec **1921** [c6 Dec 1921; LP17325]. Si; b&w. 35mm. 5 reels, 4,415 ft.

Pres by Carl Laemmle. *Dir* Hobart Henley. *Scen* Wallace Clifton. *Photog* Virgil Miller.

Cast: Herbert Rawlinson *(Barry Gordon)*, Warner Baxter *(Tom Gordon)*, Marjorie Daw *(Muriel Beekman)*, Doris Pawn *(Kitty Van Ness)*, Winter Hall *(Nathanial Beekman)*, Josef Swickard *(Col. Fairfax Gordon)*, Murdock MacQuarrie *(Ibrihim)*, Boris Karloff *(Nli Hamed)*, Anna Lehr *(Naomi)*, Al MacQuarrie *(Hassam)*, Hector Sarno *(Achmet)*.

Melodrama. Source: William Farquhar Payson, *Barry Gordon* (New York, 1908). Barry Gordon, the older son of a Virginia colonel, inherits a taste for alcohol—a habit that caused his father's death. His brother, Tom, falls in love with Muriel Beekman, their guardian's daughter. Barry also loves her but feels himself rejected. Three years later, after extended travels, Barry learns that Tom, having been sent to Morocco by Mr. Beekman, has been captured by desert marauders and is being held for ransom. He begins a search for him and in Tangiers encounters the Beekmans and Kitty Van Ness. Barry and Muriel discover their love for each other, but he refuses to commit himself while Tom is still alive. At the bandits' stronghold, he rescues Naomi, a native girl, from the chieftain and is himself captured while effecting Tom's escape. Naomi aids Barry's escape, during which the chieftain is killed and she dies in his arms. Muriel helps Barry conquer his desire for drink and professes her love for him. *Brothers. Virginians. Bandits. Alcoholism. Courtship. Ransom. Deserts. Morocco.*

CHEATED LOVE F2.0840

Universal Film Manufacturing Co. 16 May **1921** [c7 May 1921; LP16494]. Si; b&w. 35mm. 5 reels, 4,820 ft.

Dir King Baggot. *Scen* Lucien Hubbard, Sonya Levien, Doris Schroeder. *Adtl Story* Sonya Levien. *Photog* Bert Glennon.

Cast: Carmel Myers *(Sonya Schonema)*, George B. Williams *(Abraham Schonema)*, Allan Forrest *(David Dahlman)*, John Davidson *(Mischa Grossman)*, Ed Brady *(Scholom Maruch)*, Snitz Edwards *(Bernie)*, Smoke Turner *(Toscha)*, Virginia Harris *(Sophia Kettel)*, Inez Gomez *(Rose Jacobs)*, Clara Greenwood *(Mrs. Breine)*, Meyer Ouhayou *(Sam Lupsey)*, Laura Pollard *(Mrs. Flaherty)*, Rose Dione *(Madame Yazurka)*, Theresa Gray *(Mrs. Leshinsky)*, Fred G. Becker *(Charles Hensley)*.

Romantic melodrama. Sonya, a Jewish girl, comes to the United States as an immigrant and works in her father's ghetto grocery store, where she gains the affections of a young settlement worker, David Dahlman. But she loves Mischa, a young doctor who soon arrives from Odessa, and to aid him financially, she distinguishes herself in the local Yiddish theater. Mischa turns her down for a wealthy heiress, however, and owing to the jealousy of Yazurka, a prominent Polish actress, Sonya is refused an important role. During a performance, attended by David, there is a boiler explosion that causes panic in the theater, and Sonya comes from backstage and calms the crowd. Later, rescued by David, she accepts his admiration and love. *Jews. Grocers. Physicians. Settlement workers. Immigrants. Actors. Explosions. Theater—Yiddish.*

Note: Remake of *The Heart of a Jewess* (United States, 1913), story by Lucien Hubbard and Doris Schroeder, from an idea by John Colton.

THE CHEATER REFORMED F2.0841

Fox Film Corp. 2 Jan **1921** [c9 Jan 1921; LP16063]. Si; b&w. 35mm. 5 reels.

Pres by William Fox. *Dir* Scott Dunlap. *Scen* Jules Furthman, Scott Dunlap. *Story* Jules Furthman. *Photog* Clyde De Vinna.

Cast: William Russell *(Jordan McCall/Dr. Luther McCall)*, Seena Owen *(Carol McCall)*, John Brammall *("Buster" Dorsey)*, Sam De Grasse *(Thomas Edinburgh)*, Ruth King *(Mrs. Edinburgh)*.

Melodrama. Thomas Edinburgh, financial dictator of Marysville, is secretly in love with Carol, wife of the Reverend Luther McCall, and produces evidence that her husband was once an embezzler. Leaving for Cleveland, the minister meets his twin brother, Lefty, the real embezzler, who is evading the law. Luther is killed in a train wreck, and Lefty, assuming Luther's identity and carrying on the latter's ministerial work, brings about his own conversion and that of his former pal, Buster. He thwarts Edinburgh's plans by stealing the prison record, and after learning Lefty's story Carol comes to love him. *Clergymen. Twins. Brothers. Embezzlement. Impersonation. Religion. Documentation.*

CHEATERS F2.0842

Tiffany Productions. 1 Feb **1927** [c2 Mar 1927; LP23710]. Si; b&w. 35mm. 6 reels, 6,023 ft.

Dir Oscar Apfel. *Cont* W. C. Clifford. *Story* Harry D. Kerr. *Photog* Joseph A. Dubray, Allen Davey. *Art Dir* Edwin B. Willis. *Film Ed* James

C. McKay.

Cast: Pat O'Malley *(Allen Harvey)*, Helen Ferguson *(Mary Condon)*, George Hackathorne *(Paul Potter)*, Lawford Davidson *(Jim Kingston)*, Claire McDowell *(Mrs. Robin Carter)*, Helen Lynch *(Marion Carter)*, Heinie Conklin *(Mose Johnston)*, Alphonz Ethier *(McCann)*, Max Davidson *(Michael Cohen)*, Edward Cecil *(detective)*, William O'Brien *(butler)*.

Crook melodrama. Allen Harvey and Mary Condon, former members of a New York gang headed by Jim Kingston, get work in a California hotel in an attempt to go straight. Also in their company are Paul, who has lost his memory from a war injury, and Mose, a Negro porter. Detective McCann suspects their former affiliation with the gang. Kingston arrives, recognizes McCann, and threatens to expose his former associates unless they help him steal some jewels from the hotel safe; and Mary, to prevent Allen from being harmed, agrees to leave with Kingston, who, unknown to her, frames the robbery and the murder of Paul on Allen. Kingston deserts her in a train wreck, and she is cared for by a Mrs. Carter, who believes her son (Paul) was killed in the war. At a Hallowe'en party Allen and Mary are reconciled, and McCann unmasks Kingston, who dies escaping from the police. *Criminals—Rehabilitation. Gangs. Veterans. Porters. Courtship. Amnesia. Murder. Parentage. Hotels. Hallowe'en.*

CHEATING CHEATERS (Universal-Jewel) **F2.0843**

Universal Pictures. 9 Oct **1927** [c20 Jun 1927; LP24117]. Si; b&w. 35mm. 6 reels, 5,623 ft.

Pres by Carl Laemmle. *Dir* Edward Laemmle. *Cont* James T. O'Donohoe. *Titl* Walter Anthony. *Adapt* Charles A. Logue. *Photog* Jackson Rose.

Cast: Betty Compson *(Nan Carey)*, Kenneth Harlan *(Tom Palmer)*, Sylvia Ashton *(Mrs. Brockton)*, Erwin Connelly *(Mr. Brockton)*, Maude Turner Gordon *(Mrs. Palmer)*, E. J. Ratcliffe *(Mr. Palmer)*, Lucien Littlefield *(Lazare)*, Eddie Gribbon *(Steve Wilson)*, Cesare Gravina *(Tony Verdi)*.

Crook melodrama. Source: Max Marcin, *Cheating Cheaters, a Comic Melodrama in Four Acts* (New York, 1932). Nan Carey, a shoplifter, is caught by the police but acquitted through the influence of Lazare, a crooked lawyer, who places her with a gang of crooks. Posing as the Brockton family, they move to a seaside home, where they plan to steal the jewel collection of the Palmers, their neighbors. Nan wins the confidence of the family by flirting with Tom, who becomes infatuated and wants to go away with her, but she refuses him. Tom is caught red-handed in the Brockton mansion attempting to steal their jewels while Nan is making a success of the Palmer robbery. Tom attempts to rescue Nan from detectives, and they are both arrested along with the gangs. When it is revealed that Nan is actually an undercover agent, she induces them to return the stolen jewels and places them under strict parole; she is then united with Tom. *Thieves. Lawyers. Detectives. Secret agents. Shoplifting.*

THE CHECHAHCOS **F2.0844**

Capt. Austin E. Lathrop. *Dist* Associated Exhibitors. 15 May **1924.** Si; b&w. 35mm. 8 reels, 7,600 ft.

Dir-Writ Lewis H. Moomaw. *Titl* Harvey Gates. *Photog* Herbert H. Brownell.

Cast: William Dills *("Horseshoe" Riley)*, Albert Van Antwerp *(Bob Dexter)*, Eva Gordon *(Mrs. Stanlaw)*, Howard Webster *(Professor Stanlaw)*, Alexis B. Luce *(Richard Steele)*, Baby Margie *(Baby Stanlaw)*, Gladys Johnston *(Ruth Stanlaw)*, Guerney Hays *(Pierre)*, H. Mills *(engineer)*.

Melodrama. "Horseshoe" Riley and Bob Dexter save Baby Margie when the Alaska-bound steamer on which she is riding is destroyed by a boiler explosion. A gambler named Steele permits the mother of the child, Mrs. Stanlaw, to believe that her little girl has drowned and then offers her his "protection." Margie grows to young womanhood and marries Bob. Steele buys a gambling house in which Mrs. Stanlaw is forced to sing. Bob and Riley discover the whereabouts of Mrs. Stanlaw and attempt to restore her to her daughter. The resentful Steele binds Bob to a chair and sets the house on fire. Bob escapes and goes after Steele, who is killed by a collapsing glacier. Mother and daughter are reunited. *Singers. Gamblers. Cheechakos. Motherhood. Alaska. Ship fires. Glaciers.*

Note: *The Chechahcos* was filmed entirely on location in Alaska Territory, under the supervision of Captain Lathrop, who had been one of the adventurers drawn to Alaska during the Gold Rush of '98.

CHECK AND DOUBLE CHECK **F2.0845**

RKO Productions. 3 Oct **1930** [New York premiere; released 25 Oct; c8 Oct 1930; LP1616]. Sd (Photophone); b&w. 35mm. 9 reels, 6,923 ft.

Assoc Prod Bertram Millhauser. *Dir* Melville Brown. *Adapt* J. Walter Ruben. *Story* Bert Kalmar, Harry Ruby. *Photog* William Marshall. *Art Dir* Max Ree. *Songs: "Three Little Words," "Ring Dem Bells"* Bert Kalmar, Harry Ruby. *Song: "Old Man Blues"* Irving Mills, Duke Ellington. *Rec Engr* George Ellis. *Asst Dir* Fred Tyler.

Cast: Freeman F. Gosden *(Amos)*, Charles J. Correll *(Andy)*, Sue Carol *(Jean Blair)*, Charles Norton *(Richard Williams)*, Ralf Harolde *(Ralph Crawford)*, Edward Martindel *(John Blair)*, Irene Rich *(Mrs. Blair)*, Rita La Roy *(Elinor Crawford)*, Russell Powell *(Kingfish)*, Duke Ellington and His Band.

Comedy. New York cab drivers Amos 'n' Andy contract with Kingfish to transport Duke Ellington and His Band to the Blair estate, where they meet Richard Williams, son of their former employer, who is in love with Jean Blair. However, Richard is unable to find the deed to the family property, without which he cannot marry Jean. Believing it to be in the deserted family house, he determines to search for it, though Ralph Crawford, a rival suitor, finds it to his advantage to search for the document himself. Meanwhile, Amos 'n' Andy are ordered by their lodge, "The Mystic Knights of The Sea," to spend the night in the haunted house on the same evening they are to take out their girl friends; they find the assigned paper, marked "check and double check," as well as the missing deed. By mistake they give the paper to Crawford, who thinks it is the deed; and all ends well as Richard perceives this stroke of luck and marries Jean. *Taxi drivers. Negroes. Millionaires. Haunted houses. Fraternities. New York City. Documentation.*

THE CHECKERED FLAG **F2.0846**

Banner Productions. 19 Jan **1926** [New York showing; c15 Jan 1926; LP22320]. Si; b&w. 35mm. 6 reels, 6,071 ft.

Dir John G. Adolfi. *Adapt* Frederick Hatton, Fanny Hatton.

Cast: Elaine Hammerstein *(Rita Corbin)*, Wallace MacDonald *(Jack Reese)*, Lionel Belmore *(Joel Corbin)*, Robert Ober *(Marcel Dejeans)*, Peggy O'Neil *(Mary McQuire)*, Lee Shumway *(Ray Barton)*, Flora Maynard *(Elsie)*.

Melodrama. Source: John Mersereau, *The Checkered Flag* (Boston, 1925). Jack Reese, a mechanic at Corbin Motors, falls in love with Rita Corbin, the daughter of the company's president. Ray Barton, the managing director of Corbin Motors, is also in love with Rita; and aggravated by Jack's affection for her, Barton has him fired. Working with his friend Marcel, Jack perfects a design for a new carburetor, which is then stolen from them by some of Barton's henchmen. Jack and Marcel get it back and enter their car in the big race. On the day of the race, Jack and Marcel are forcibly detained by Barton's men, and Rita takes Jack's place, driving his car to victory. As the result of the carburetor's success, Jack gets his job back and wins her father's approval to marry Rita. *Automobile manufacturers. Mechanics. Theft. Automobile racing. Carburetors.*

THE CHEER LEADER **F2.0847**

Gotham Productions. *Dist* Lumas Film Corp. 1 Jan **1928** [c23 Nov 1927; LP24686]. Si; b&w. 35mm. 6 reels, 5,772 ft.

Pres by Sam Sax. *Dir* Alvin J. Neitz. *Titl* Dudley Early. *Adapt* Jack Casey. *Story* Lee Authmar. *Photog* Edward Gheller. *Film Ed* Edith Wakeling. *Prod Mgr* Carroll Sax.

Cast: Ralph Graves *(Jimmy Grant)*, Gertrude Olmstead *(Jean Howard [Patsy])*, Shirley Palmer *(Elizabeth Summers [Pep])*, Ralph Emerson *(Alfred Crandall)*, Harold Goodwin *(Richard Crosby)*, Donald Stuart *(Percival Spivins)*, Duke Martin *(Chuck Casey)*, Harry Northrup *(John Crandall)*, Ruth Cherrington *(Mrs. Crandall)*, James Leonard *(James Grant, Sr.)*, Lillian Langdon *(Mrs. Grant)*, Bobby Nelson *(Chester Grant)*, Charles North *(Dean Sherwood)*.

Romantic drama. Jimmy Grant and Alfred Crandall, two college freshmen, meet Patsy Howard and Pep Summers, co-eds, on the train, along with Richard Crosby, captain of the football team and his "minstrel," Percival Spivins. Crosby arouses the animosity of the two pals by preventing them from accompanying the girls, leading to a fight between Jimmy and Crosby in which Jimmy is victorious. Although Jimmy is selected for the school team, Alfred is left out and quarrels with Jimmy, then embarks on a wild spree. At a fraternity dance before the game, one of the boys dresses like a girl and flirts with Crosby. In the chase that follows, the "girl" hides in Alfred's room, causing him to be expelled. At the game, Jimmy acts as cheerleader for the team, but at the climax of the game both boys are sent out on the field to win the day. *Cheerleaders. College life. Football. Fraternities. Female impersonation.*

CHEER UP AND SMILE F2.0848

Fox Film Corp. 22 Jun or Jul **1930** [c14 May 1930; LP1341]. Sd (Movietone); b&w. 35mm. 7 reels, 5,730 ft.

Pres by William Fox. *Assoc Prod* Al Rockett. *Dir* Sidney Lanfield. *Adapt-Dial* Howard J. Green. *Photog* Joseph Valentine. *Film Ed* Ralph Dietrich. *Songs: "The Shindig," "Where Can You Be?" "The Scamp of the Campus," "When You Look in My Eyes," "You May Not Like It But It's a Great Idea"* Jesse Greer, Raymond Klages. *Rec Engr* Al Bruzlin. *Asst Dir* Ewing Scott.

Cast: Dixie Lee *(Margie)*, Arthur Lake *(Eddie Fripp)*, Olga Baclanova *(Yvonne)*, "Whispering" Jack Smith *(himself)*, Johnny Arthur *(Andy)*, Charles Judels *(Pierre)*, John Darrow *(Tom)*, Sumner Getchell *(Paul)*, Franklin Pangborn *(Professor)*, Buddy Messinger *(Donald)*.

Musical comedy. Source: Richard Connell, "If I Was Alone With You," in *Collier's Magazine* (84:7–9, 30 Nov 1929). As part of his fraternity initiation, Eddie Fripp is directed to kick the first man he meets and kiss the first female: a college professor is the recipient of the kick, and Margie, a salesclerk, is dismayed to see Eddie kiss a young co-ed. Eddie and Margie are separated at the school dance when he is suspended for his actions, and she is left without an explanation. He goes to New York to work as a singer in Pierre's Cafe and incurs the wrath of the owner by distracting his flirtatious wife. On the night of a holdup, "Whispering" Jack Smith is knocked unconscious in the broadcasting room and Eddie is forced to take his place; his quavering voice is a sensation, and Pierre is obliged to retain him. Meanwhile, Eddie makes up with Margie by telephone, and she comes to New York to marry him; but fearing marriage will ruin his career, Pierre plans a frameup to discredit him in her eyes. But Eddie proves himself innocent, and reconciliation follows. *Salesclerks. Students. Singers. College life. Courtship. Radio.*

THE CHEERFUL FRAUD F2.0849

Universal Pictures. 16 Jan **1927** [c6 Dec 1926; LP23400]. Si; b&w. 35mm. 7 reels, 6,945 ft.

Pres by Carl Laemmle. *Dir* William A. Seiter. *Scen* Leigh Jacobson, Sam Mintz, Rex Taylor, William A. Seiter. *Adapt* Harvey Thew. *Photog* Arthur Todd.

Cast: Reginald Denny *(Sir Michael Fairlie)*, Gertrude Olmstead *(Ann Kent)*, Otis Harlan *(Mr. Bytheway)*, Emily Fitzroy *(Mrs. Bytheway)*, Charles Gerrard *(Steve)*, Gertrude Astor *(Rose)*.

Farce. Source: Kenneth Robert Gordon Browne, *The Cheerful Fraud* (New York, 1925). Sir Michael Fairlie meets Ann Kent, a social secretary to the Bytheways, during a rainstorm in London, and though she snubs him, he promptly falls in love. He intercepts Simmons, an employee of the family, and, buying off his job, he introduces himself as Simmons at the Bytheway residence. Steve, an international crook, breaks into Sir Michael's flat, but he manages to evade the police by means of disguise; later, he accepts an invitation sent to Sir Michael by the Bytheways and is introduced to the real Sir Michael, whom he assumes to be another crook. Rose, a blonde blackmailer, is introduced as the wife of Simmons, and, following a series of mixups and complications, Sir Michael reveals his identity and saves the family jewels, thus winning the love of Ann. *Secretaries. Nobility. Courtship. Impersonation. London.*

THE CHEROKEE KID F2.0850

FBO Pictures. 30 Oct **1927** [c13 Oct 1927; LP24725]. Si; b&w. 35mm. 5 reels, 4,837 ft.

Pres by Joseph P. Kennedy. *Dir* Robert De Lacy. *Adapt-Cont* Oliver Drake. *Story* Joseph Kane. *Photog* Nick Musuraca.

Cast: Tom Tyler *(Bill Duncan)*, Sharon Lynn *(Helen Flynne)*, Jerry Pembroke *(Rolphe McPherson)*, Robert Burns *(sheriff)*, Robert Reeves *(Seth Daggart)*, Ray Childs *(Joe Gault)*, James Van Horn *(Red Flynne)*, Carol Holloway *(Rose)*.

Western melodrama. Concealing his identity because of an old feud, Bill Duncan returns to the scene of his childhood and finds himself suspected of murdering a ranchman, Flynne, a former enemy of Bill's father. Flynne's estate has been bequeathed jointly to Rolfe McPherson, his foreman, and Helen, his daughter, who is given to understand that her father wished her to marry McPherson, who actually plotted Flynne's murder. He arouses the sheriff's suspicion of Billy Duncan, whom Helen loves; but Duncan escapes after being arrested. Through the jealousy of Rose, McPherson's housekeeper, his guilt is disclosed to Duncan and Helen; McPherson kidnaps Helen and rides for the border; Duncan rescues Helen, brings McPherson to justice, clears his name, and wins Helen. *Ranch foremen. Housekeepers. Injustice. Murder. Personal identity. Mexican border.*

THE CHEROKEE STRIP F2.0851

Miller Brothers 101 Ranch. *Dist* Oil Field Amusu Co. 28 Mar **1925** [New York State license]. Si; b&w. 35mm. 6 reels.

Cast: Herbert Bethew, Lucille Mulhall.

Western melodrama. No information about the precise nature of this film has been found. *Cherokee Strip.*

Note: Possibly "manufactured" in 1923.

CHEYENNE F2.0852

First National Pictures. 3 Feb **1929** [c7 Feb 1929; LP93]. Si; b&w. 35mm. 6 reels, 5,944 ft.

Pres by Charles R. Rogers. *Supv* Harry J. Brown. *Dir* Albert Rogell. *Scen* Marion Jackson. *Titl* Don Ryan. *Story* Bennett Cohen. *Camera* Frank Good. *Film Ed* Fred Allen.

Cast: Ken Maynard *(Cal Roberts)*, Gladys McConnell *(Violet Wentworth)*, James Bradbury, Jr. *("Slim")*, William Franey *("Judge" Boggs)*, Charles Whittaker *(Klaxton)*, Tarzan *(a horse)*.

Western melodrama. "Cal Roberts can ride anything with four legs. He enters the contests held at big rodeo. He wins all honors and meets a girl who races horses to help her father clear pressing debts. Complications follow, but Cal wins the girl." ("Motion Picture News Booking Guide," in *Motion Picture News*, 15 Mar 1930, p73.) *Cowboys. Filial relations. Rodeos. Horseracing. Debt. Horses.*

CHEYENNE TRAILS F2.0853

Robert J. Horner Productions. *Dist* Associated Independent Producers. ca14 Aug **1928** [New York State license]. Si; b&w. 35mm. 5 reels, 4,275 ft.

Dir-Scen Robert J. Horner. *Titl* Jack Middleton. *Photog* Paul Allen. *Film Ed* William Austin.

Cast: Pawnee Bill Jr., Bud Osborne, Bill Nestel.

Western melodrama(?). No information about the nature of this film has been found.

CHICAGO F2.0854

De Mille Pictures. *Dist* Pathé Exchange. 23 Dec **1927** [New York showing; released 4 Mar 1928; c6 Feb 1928; LP24955]. Si; b&w. 35mm. 9 reels, 9,145 ft.

Dir Frank Urson. *Adapt-Scen* Lenore J. Coffee. *Titl* John Krafft. *Photog* Peverell Marley. *Art Dir* Mitchell Leisen. *Film Ed* Anne Bauchens. *Asst Dir* Roy Burns. *Prod Mgr* E. O. Gurney. *Cost* Adrian.

Cast: Phyllis Haver *(Roxie Hart)*, Victor Varconi *(Amos Hart)*, Eugene Pallette *(Casley)*, Virginia Bradford *(Katie)*, Clarence Burton *(police sergeant)*, Warner Richmond *(district attorney)*, T. Roy Barnes *(reporter)*, Sidney D'Albrook *(photographer)*, Otto Lederer *(Amos' partner)*, May Robson *(matron)*, Julia Faye *(Velma)*, Robert Edeson *(Flynn)*.

Drama. Source: Maurine Watkins, *Chicago* (New York, 1927). Cigarstand owner Amos Hart steals money from the safe of his lawyer, Flynn, an unscrupulous man who, for a large sum of money, promises to get Hart's wife, Roxie, acquitted. She is accused of murdering automobile salesman Casley, her clandestine lover. Returning home after the much publicized trial, they find two detectives waiting to accuse him of the theft, but Kitty, the maid, thwarts them by removing the extra money before they can institute a search. After they leave, Hart declares that he is through with Roxie, who is still basking in the scandalous publicity. He throws her from the house, which he has nearly destroyed in a rage, and finds peace with Kitty. *Lawyers. Housemaids. Infidelity. Theft. Murder. Trials. Cigarstores. Chicago.*

CHICAGO AFTER MIDNIGHT F2.0855

FBO Pictures. 4 Mar **1928** [c10 Feb 1928; LP24978]. Si; b&w. 35mm. 7 reels, 6,249-6,267 ft.

Dir Ralph Ince. *Cont* Enid Hibbard. *Titl* George M. Arthur. *Story* Charles K. Harris. *Photog* J. O. Taylor. *Film Ed* George M. Arthur.

Cast: Ralph Ince *(Jim Boyd)*, Jola Mendez *(Betty Boyd/Mona Gale)*, Lorraine Rivero *(Betty Boyd [baby])*, James Mason *(Hardy)*, Carl Axzelle *(Ike, the Rat)*, Helen Jerome Eddy *(Mrs. Boyd)*, Ole M. Ness *(Tanner)*, Robert Seiter *(Jack Waring)*, Frank Mills *(Frank)*, Christian J. Frank *(Casey)*.

Underworld melodrama. Gangster Jim Boyd serves a 15-year prison term when Hardy, a rival crook, doublecrosses him. On his release from prison, Boyd seeks out Hardy in Chicago, where he runs a cafe and bootleg operation. He makes the acquaintance of Mona Gale, a dancer in Hardy's cafe who is engaged to marry Jack Waring, the orchestra leader. Unaware that Mona is his daughter, Boyd shoots Hardy in a brawl and leaves behind evidence implicating Waring as the murderer. After Hardy's death, Mona joins Boyd's gang to gather evidence proving her fiancé's innocence. The gang members discover that Mona has dealings with the police, and they begin to torture her. Having learned of Mona's relationship to him at the last minute, Boyd arrives at the gang's hideout in time to save her. He confesses to killing Hardy before he dies from a wound inflicted by one of his own gang, thus freeing Waring to marry Mona. *Dancers. Band leaders. Gangsters. Gangs. Fatherhood. Prisons. Murder. Torture. Chicago.*

CHICAGO SAL *see* **ENVIRONMENT**

THE CHICKEN *see* **THE TOWN SCANDAL**

CHICKEN A LA KING **F2.0856**

Fox Film Corp. ca9 Jun **1928** [New York premiere; released 17 Jun; c31 May 1928; LP25308]. Si; b&w. 35mm. 7 reels, 6,417 ft.

Pres by William Fox. *Dir* Henry Lehrman. *Scen* Izola Forrester, Mann Page. *Titl* James A. Starr. *Photog* Conrad Wells. *Film Ed* Frank Hull, Ralph Dietrich. *Asst Dir* Virgil Hart.

Cast: Nancy Carroll *(Maisie DeVoe)*, George Meeker *(Buck Taylor)*, Arthur Stone *(Oscar Barrows)*, Ford Sterling *(Horace Trundle)*, Frances Lee *(Babe Lorraine)*, Carol Holloway *(Effie Trundle)*.

Comedy. Source: Wallace A. Mannheimer, Isaac Paul, and Harry Wagstaff Gribble, *Mr. Romeo* (New York opening: 5 Sep 1927). "Prosperous business man finds himself in the toils of two gold-digging chorus girls when he tires of his drab wife. Wife goes in for modern clothes and spends considerable of his cash to make herself look young again, and wins him back to the family fireside." (*Motion Picture News Booking Guide*, [14]:241, 1929.) *Gold diggers. Chorus girls. Businessmen. Rejuvenation. Marriage.*

THE CHICKEN IN THE CASE (Star Series Release) **F2.0857**

Selznick Pictures. *Dist* Select Pictures. Jan **1921** [c10 Jan 1921; LP16018]. Si; b&w. 35mm. 5 reels, 5,261 ft.

Pres by Lewis J. Selznick. *Dir-Writ* Victor Heerman. *Scen* Sarah Y. Mason. *Asst Dir* Edwin Sturgis.

Cast: Owen Moore *(Steve Perkins)*, Vivian Ogden *(Aunt Sarah)*, Teddy Sampson *(Winnie Jones)*, Edgar Nelson *(Percival Jones)*, Katherine Perry *(Ruth Whitman)*, Walter Walker *(Major Whitman)*.

Farce. Because wealthy Aunt Sarah threatens to cut off his inheritance unless he marries, Steve Perkins introduces Winnie Jones, his friend's wife, as his own. Complications result from Aunt Sarah's attempts to reconcile the apparently troubled couple and Percy's weariness of the masquerade. Meanwhile, Steve falls in love with Ruth Whitman, and he marries her while Aunt Sarah goes off in pursuit of Winnie and Percy. Confessing the hoax to his aunt, Steve receives her forgiveness and continued blessing. *Aunts. Marriage. Inheritance. Hoaxes.*

Note: Working title: *Lend Me Your Wife.*

THE CHICKEN THAT CAME HOME TO ROOST *see* **THE TOWN SCANDAL**

CHICKENS **F2.0858**

Thomas H. Ince Productions. *Dist* Paramount Pictures. 13 Feb **1921** [c29 Jan 1921; LP16082]. Si; b&w. 35mm. 5 reels, 4,753 ft.

Supv Thomas H. Ince. *Dir* Jack Nelson. *Adapt* Agnes Christine Johnston. *Photog* Bert Cann.

Cast: Douglas MacLean *(Deems Stanwood)*, Gladys George *(Julia Stoneman)*, Claire McDowell *(Aunt Rebecca)*, Charles Mailes *(Dan Bellows)*, Edith Yorke *(his wife)*, Raymond Cannon *(Willie Figg)*, Willis Marks *(Philip Thawson)*, Al Filson *(Decker)*.

Rural comedy-drama. Source: Herschel S. Hall, "Yancona Yillies," in *Saturday Evening Post* (192:20–21, 6 Mar 1920). According to a provision in his uncle's will, society man Deems Stanwood is obliged to live in the country. There he decides to raise chickens on a farm adjoining that of Julia Stoneman. When the trustees mismanage his investments and lose the fortune, Deems fails to make the farm pay and is forced to mortgage it to Willie Figg, his young rival for Julia. By chance she discovers the loss of Deems's fortune and takes over the mortgage from Willie, who is about to foreclose. Finding the release papers in his pocket, Deems realizes that she loves him, and she accepts his marriage proposal. *Socialites. Farmers. Courtship. Finance—Personal. Wills. Mortgages. Chickens.*

CHICKIE **F2.0859**

First National Pictures. 10 May **1925** [c21 Apr 1925; LP21371]. Si; b&w. 35mm. 8 reels, 7,600 ft.

Supv Earl Hudson. *Dir* John Francis Dillon. *Scen* Marion Orth. *Photog* James C. Van Trees. *Art Dir* Milton Menasco. *Film Ed* Arthur Tavares.

Cast: Dorothy Mackaill *(Chickie)*, John Bowers *(Barry Dunne)*, Hobart Bosworth *(Jonathan)*, Gladys Brockwell *(Jennie)*, Paul Nicholson *(Jake Munson)*, Myrtle Stedman *(Janina)*, Olive Tell *(Ila Moore)*, Lora Sonderson *(Bess Abbott)*, Louise Mackintosh *(Mrs. Dunne)*.

Melodrama. Source: Elenore Meherin, *"Chickie"; a Hidden, Tragic Chapter From the Life of a Girl of This Strange "Today"* (New York, 1925). Chickie, a poor stenographer, is initiated by a high-stepping girl friend into the speedy circle of millionaire Jake Munson, at whose parties she submits to the advances of Barry Dunne, a young law clerk. Munson later invites her to dinner and takes her to his apartment, where they run into Barry and his companion, Ila, a rich young girl interested in winning Barry's affections. Barry misunderstands Chickie's presence in Munson's apartment and goes to London to work, followed closely by Ila. Munson finally proposes to Chickie, but when she tells him that she is no longer a virgin, he repulses her. Chickie later discovers that she is pregnant and writes to Barry; Ila intercepts the letter and destroys it, falsely writing back that she and Barry are married. Chickie becomes a mother, and Barry, learning of her predicament, returns from London, assures her that he neither received her letter nor married Ila, and leads her to the altar. *Stenographers. Law clerks. Millionaires. Illegitimacy. London.*

A CHILD IN PAWN **F2.0860**

D. W. D. Film Corp. **1921.** Si; b&w. 35mm. [Feature length assumed.]

Melodrama(?). No information about the precise nature of this film has been found. *Negro life.*

A CHILD OF THE PRAIRIE **F2.0861**

Dist Exclusive Features. 22 Dec **1925** [New York State license]. Si; b&w. 35mm. 5 reels, 4,500 ft.

Dir-Writ Tom Mix.

Cast: Tom Mix *(Square Deal Tom)*, Rose Bronson *(Blonde Nell)*, Ed Brady *(Slippery Jim Watson)*, Mort Thompson *(Sam Jones)*, John Maloney *(Red Mike)*, Fay Robinson *(Loretta)*.

Western melodrama. In Red Gulch Tom is married to Nell and has a daughter. He is shot by cardsharp Jim, who runs off with Nell. The little daughter, found wandering on the prairie by two wolf hunters, is adopted and named Prairie Nell. Fifteen years later, she is the pride of Bar X, when Tom returns, shoots Jim, and finds his daughter. *Gamblers. Waifs. Fatherhood. Revenge.*

Note: Expansion of a 2-reeler of the same title (Selig, 1915), using material from another unidentified Mix film.

THE CHILD THOU GAVEST ME **F2.0862**

John M. Stahl Productions. *Dist* Associated First National Pictures. ca20 Aug **1921** [St. Paul premiere; c14 Nov 1921; LP17432]. Si; b&w. 35mm. 6 reels, 6,091 ft.

Pres by Louis B. Mayer. *Dir* John M. Stahl. *Scen* Chester Roberts. *Story* Perry N. Vekroff. *Photog* Ernest Palmer. *Film Ed* Madge Tyrone.

Cast: Barbara Castleton *(Norma Huntley)*, Adele Farrington *(her mother)*, Winter Hall *(her father)*, Lewis Stone *(Edward Berkeley)*, William Desmond *(Tom Marshall)*, Richard Headrick *(Bobby)*, Mary Forbes *(governess)*.

Domestic melodrama. On the day of her wedding, Norma Huntley, who wants to tell her fiancé, Edward Berkeley, a secret from her past, is advised by her mother not to do so. While the wedding is in progress, the woman who is caring for Norma's child (whom she believes to be dead) sends the child to the Huntley home. When Norma tries to explain matters, Edward tells her that he will adopt the child but will seek out and kill the father. Edward invites to their country home Tom Marshall, a friend he suspects of the parentage; during a storm, he finds Tom and Norma together, and he shoots Tom. Norma informs Edward that she was attacked by an unknown soldier while serving as a nurse in Belgium, and Edward recognizes himself as that very soldier. Edward then tries to kill himself, but Norma insists that he live to rear their child; Tom recovers from his wound; and all are reconciled. *Nurses. Marriage. Illegitimacy. Rape. Suicide. Weddings. World War I. Belgium.*

Note: Working title: *Retribution.*

CHILDREN OF DIVORCE **F2.0863**

Famous Players–Lasky. *Dist* Paramount Pictures. 2 Apr **1927** [c2 Apr 1927; LP23820]. Si; b&w. 35mm. 7 reels, 6,662 or 6,871 ft.

Pres by Adolph Zukor, Jesse L. Lasky. *Dir* Frank Lloyd. *Adtl Dir (see note)* Josef von Sternberg. *Screenplay* Hope Loring, Louis D. Lighton. *Photog* Victor Milner.

Cast: Clara Bow *(Kitty Flanders)*, Esther Ralston *(Jean Waddington)*, Gary Cooper *(Ted Larrabee)*, Einar Hanson *(Prince Ludovico de Sfax)*, Norman Trevor *(Duke de Gondreville)*, Hedda Hopper *(Katherine Flanders)*, Edward Martindel *(Tom Larrabee)*, Julia Swayne Gordon *(Princess de Sfax)*, Tom Ricketts *(The Secretary)*, Albert Gran *(Mr. Seymour)*, Iris Stuart *(Mousie)*, Margaret Campbell *(Mother Superior)*, Percy Williams *(Manning)*, Joyce Coad *(Little Kitty)*, Yvonne Pelletier *(Little Jean)*, Don Marion *(Little Ted)*.

Society melodrama. Source: Owen Johnson, *Children of Divorce* (Boston, 1927). Jean Waddington, a childhood friend of Ted Larrabee, later falls in love with him. As he is, like her, the product of a broken home and the child of a dissolute and irresponsible father, Jean tells him he must prove himself before she will accept his marriage offer. Ted opens an office, but when their mutual friend, Kitty, gives a wild party in the building, he forgets business. Prince Ludovico de Sfax, in the charge of his guardian, the Duke de Gondreville, is attracted to Kitty, but the duke forbids his having an affair with her because of her poverty. One evening, on a drunken spree, Ted and Kitty get married, and, heartbroken, Jean goes to Europe. Later, Kitty and Ted arrive with their child and the prince's love is revived. Realizing that no bond of affection exists between her and Ted, Kitty takes poison, and Ted is reunited with Jean. *Royalty. Friendship. Marriage. Divorce. Suicide.*

Note: Josef von Sternberg, at this time an assistant director at Paramount, is reputed to have directed some sequences of this film.

CHILDREN OF DUST **F2.0864**

Arthur H. Jacobs Corp. *Dist* Associated First National Pictures. 4 Jun **1923** [c11 Jun 1923; LP19077]. Si; b&w. 35mm. 7 reels, 6,228 ft.

Pres by Arthur H. Jacobs. *Dir* Frank Borzage. *Scen* Agnes Christine Johnston. *Adapt* Frank Dazey. *Photog* Chester Lyons. *Art Settings* Frank Ormston. *Film Ed* H. P. Bretherton.

Cast: Bert Woodruff *(Old Archer)*, Johnnie Walker *(Terwilliger as a man)*, Frankie Lee *(Terwilliger as a boy)*, Pauline Garon *(Helen Raymond as a woman)*, Josephine Adair *(Helen Raymond as a girl)*, Lloyd Hughes *(Harvey Livermore as a man)*, Newton Hall *(Harvey Livermore as a boy)*, George Nichols *(Terwilliger's stepfather)*.

Melodrama. Source: Tristram Tupper, "Terwilliger," in *Lucky Star* (New York, 1929). Old Archer, caretaker of Gramercy Park in New York City, is adopted by Terwilliger, an orphan, as his "father" after the old man is arrested for beating the boy when he picked a flower for his dead mother. Terwilliger falls in love with Helen Raymond, a neighborhood girl, but has a rival in Harvey Livermore. When war is declared both boys join the service, and in action Terwilliger saves Harvey's life. On the boys' return Helen marries Terwilliger. *Orphans. Caretakers. Childhood. World War I. New York City.*

CHILDREN OF FATE **F2.0865**

Ivan Abramson Productions. 26 Sep **1926.** Si; b&w. 35mm. 7 reels, 6,600 ft.

Cast: Joseph Shoengold, Betty Hilburn.

Melodrama(?). No information about the nature of this film has been found.

CHILDREN OF FATE **F2.0866**

Colored Players Film Corp. 27 Jan **1928** [New York State license]. Si; b&w. 35mm. 8 reels, 7,500 ft.

Cast: Harry Henderson, Shingzie Howard, Lawrence Chenault, Arline Mickey, William A. Clayton, Jr., Howard Augusta, Alonzo Jackson.

Drama(?). No information about the specific nature of this film has been found. *Negro life.*

CHILDREN OF JAZZ **F2.0867**

Famous Players–Lasky. *Dist* Paramount Pictures. 8 Jul **1923** [c11 Jul 1923; LP19201]. Si; b&w. 35mm. 6 reels, 6,080 ft.

Pres by Jesse L. Lasky. *Dir* Jerome Storm. *Adapt* Beulah Marie Dix. *Photog* Dev Jennings.

Cast: Theodore Kosloff *(Richard Forestall)*, Ricardo Cortez *(Ted Carter)*, Robert Cain *(Clyde Dunbar)*, Eileen Percy *(Babs Weston)*, Irene Dalton *(Lina Dunbar)*, Alec B. Francis *(John Weston)*, Frank Currier *(Adam Forestall)*, Snitz Edwards *(Blivens)*, Lillian Drew *(Deborah)*.

Comedy-melodrama. Source: Harold Brighouse, *Other Times* (a play; publication undetermined). Babs Weston becomes engaged to adventurer Richard Forestall before his hasty departure, accepting his ring and promising to be faithful. When he returns he finds that his fiancée has become a "victim of jazz" and is engaged to two other men, one not yet divorced. He leaves Babs and visits his parents on their island in the Caribbean, where, by coincidence, Babs and some of her thrill-seeking friends become stranded. Forestall, by putting these individuals to useful occupations, reforms them and wins Babs over to a more healthful life. *Jazz life. Infidelity. Caribbean.*

CHILDREN OF PLEASURE **F2.0868**

Metro-Goldwyn-Mayer Pictures. 26 Apr **1930** [c21 Apr 1930; LP1236]. Sd (Movietone); b&w. 35mm. 9 reels, 6,400 ft. [Probably also si.]

Dir Harry Beaumont. *Scen* Richard Schayer. *Dial* Crane Wilbur. *Photog* Percy Hilburn. *Art Dir* Cedric Gibbons. *Film Ed* Blanche Sewell, George Todd. *Songs: "Leave It That Way," "Dust," "Girl Trouble"* Andy Rice, Fred Fisher. *Song: "A Couple of Birds With the Same Thought in Mind"* Howard Johnson, George Ward, Reggie Montgomery. *Dances stgd by* Sammy Lee. *Rec Engr* Douglas Shearer. *Wardrobe* David Cox.

Cast: Lawrence Gray *(Danny Regan)*, Wynne Gibson *(Emma Gray)*, Helen Johnson *(Pat Thayer)*, Kenneth Thompson *(Rod Peck)*, Lee Kohlmar *(Bernie)*, May Boley *(Fanny Kaye)*, Benny Rubin *(Andy Little)*.

Musical society drama. Source: Crane Wilbur, *The Song Writer* (New York opening: 13 Aug 1928). Danny Regan, an up-and-coming songwriter, becomes enamoured of Emma Gray, an heiress; but on the night before the wedding, he finds that Emma considers their marriage to be a trial experiment and plans to continue her affair with his understudy. Incensed, he disappears and his office coworker, Pat, who has been his constant friend, agrees to marry him. After a drinking spree, Danny awakens, believing that he is married to Pat; but he discovers that, thinking he still loves Emma, Pat did not go through with the ceremony. Having learned his lesson, however, he finds that Pat is the girl for him, after all. *Composers. Heiresses. Marriage—Trial. Courtship.*

CHILDREN OF THE NIGHT **F2.0869**

Fox Film Corp. 26 Jun **1921** [c26 Jun 1921; LP16745]. Si; b&w. 35mm. 5 reels, 5,011 ft.

Pres by William Fox. *Dir* Jack Dillon. *Scen* John Montague. *Photog* George Schneiderman.

Cast: William Russell *(Jerrold Jarvis Jones)*, Ruth Renick *(Sylvia Ensor)*, Lefty Flynn *(Alexic Trouvaine)*, Ed Burns *(Barry Dunbar)*, Arthur Thalasso *(Vance)*, Wilson Hummell *(Tankerton)*, Helen McGinnis *(Anne Mannister)*, Edwin Booth Tilton *(Mannister, her father)*, Frederick Kirby *(Carver)*, Herbert Fortier *(Zenia)*.

Fantasy-melodrama. Source: Max Brand, "Children of Night," in *All Story Weekly Magazine* (95:177–199, 394–413, 629–644; 96:97–114, 293–308; 22 Mar–19 Apr 1919). Jerrold Jarvis Jones, a lowly shipping clerk, falls asleep on his office stool and has a dream: *He is an aggressive, carefully groomed man of the world who welcomes adventure when an attractive girl addresses him as Tourvaine and takes him on an automobile ride. He is taken to a meeting of a secret criminal society known as "Children of the Night" and is mistaken for a new leader who was to arrive from abroad, a role he assumes until exposed. In a series of fights with the crooks, he rescues Sylvia (in real life a secretary in his office) and mingles in the world of high society.* Awakening from his dream, he is fired with ambition and astonishes everyone by walking out with the stenographer. *Shipping clerks. Secretaries. Secret societies. Ambition. Dreams.*

CHILDREN OF THE RITZ **F2.0870**

First National Pictures. 3 Mar **1929** [c25 Feb 1929; LP163]. Mus score & sd eff (Vitaphone); b&w. 35mm. 7 reels, 6,426 ft. [Also si, 17 Feb 1929; 6,296 ft.]

Pres by Richard A. Rowland. *Dir* John Francis Dillon. *Scen* Adelaide Heilbron. *Titl* Paul Perez. *Photog* James Van Trees. *Film Ed* LeRoy Stone. *Song: "Some Sweet Day"* Lew Pollack, Nathaniel Shilkret.

Cast: Dorothy Mackaill *(Angela Pennington)*, Jack Mulhall *(Dewey Haines)*, James Ford *(Gil Pennington)*, Richard Carlyle *(Mr. Pennington)*, Evelyn Hall *(Mrs. Pennington)*, Kathryn McGuire *(Lyle Pennington)*, Frank Crayne *(The Butler)*, Ed Burns *(Jerry Wilder)*, Doris Dawson *(Margie Haines)*, Aggie Herring *(Mrs. Haines)*, Lee Moran *(Gaffney)*.

Comedy-drama. Source: Cornell Woolrich, "Children of the Ritz," in

College Humor. Angela Pennington, the spoiled, bored daughter of a wealthy man, amuses herself by attempting to seduce Dewey Haines, the rigid family chauffeur. Dewey wins $50,000 at the race track, and Angela's father, despondent over heavy financial loses, attempts to commit suicide. Dewey gives Mrs. Pennington a large portion of his newly acquired fortune and marries Angela. She quickly spends all of Dewey's remaining money, and he is forced to become a cab driver. Angela goes to live with her parents and comes to suspect Dewey of infidelity. Her suspicions prove to be unfounded, however, and she and Dewey are reconciled, with Angela promising to be frugal. *Socialites. Chauffeurs. Taxi drivers. Suicide. Bankruptcy.*

CHILDREN OF THE WHIRLWIND **F2.0871**

Whitman Bennett Productions. *Dist* Arrow Pictures. 15 Aug **1925** [c30 Jun 1925; LP21651]. Si; b&w. 35mm. 7 reels, 6,500 ft.

Dir Whitman Bennett. *Story* Leroy Scott. *Photog* Edward Paul.

Cast: Lionel Barrymore *(Joe Ellison)*, Johnny Walker *(Larry Brainerd)*, Marguerite De La Motte *(Maggie)*, J. R. Roser *(Hunt)*, Marie Haynes *("The Duchess")*, Bert Tuey *(Barney)*, Frank Montgomery *(Carlisle)*, Ruby Blaine *(Isabel Sherwood)*.

Melodrama. When Larry Brainerd is freed from Sing Sing prison on parole and decides to go straight, his old gang accuses him of being a yellow stool pigeon and sets out to get him. Three of the gang members—Maggie, Barney, and Carlisle—plot to blackmail Dick Sherwood, a man who has done much to help Larry set his feet firmly on the path of righteousness. Larry goes to Maggie and tries to persuade her to leave Sherwood alone, but the hardened girl will not listen to him. Joe Ellison, Maggie's father, is also released from stir and sets out to revenge himself on Carlisle, whom he paid well to keep Maggie from the life of crime. Larry frustrates the blackmail plot, and Carlisle and Barney are sent up the river. Joe is reunited with Maggie, who decides to marry Larry and live an honest life. *Criminals—Rehabilitation. Informers. Parole. Blackmail. Sing Sing.*

CHINA BOUND **F2.0872**

Metro-Goldwyn-Mayer Pictures. 18 May **1929** [c4 Dec 1929; LP881]. Si; b&w. 35mm. 7 reels, 5,716 ft.

Dir Charles F. Reisner. *Cont* Peggy Kelly. *Titl* Robert Hopkins. *Story* Sylvia Thalberg, Frank Butler. *Photog* Reggie Lanning. *Art Dir* Cedric Gibbons. *Film Ed* George Hively. *Wardrobe* David Cox.

Cast: Karl Dane *(Sharkey Nye)*, George K. Arthur *(Eustis)*, Josephine Dunn *(Joan)*, Polly Moran *(Sarah)*, Carl Stockdale *(McAllister)*, Harry Woods *(hard-boiled officer)*.

Farce. Eustis, a clerk in a Scotsman's antique shop, is in love with Joan, his employer's daughter; McAllister, displeased with their courtship, fires Eustis and takes his daughter and her maid, Sarah, aboard an ocean liner bound for China. With the aid of the ship stoker, Sharkey Nye, Eustis follows. In China they encounter a revolution in progress and are jailed in different allotments. After numerous misadventures, the boys manage to rescue the girls and the Scotsman. Eustis is happily united with Joan, and they all make the return voyage home. *Salesclerks. Stokers. Scotch. Antique dealers. Courtship. Revolutions. Ocean liners. China.*

CHINA SLAVER **F2.0873**

Trinity Pictures. 25 Jan **1929.** Si; b&w. 35mm. 6 reels, 5,400 ft.

Dir Frank S. Mattison. *Titl* Arthur Hotaling. *Adapt* L. V. Jefferson, Cecil Burtis Hill. *Story* Rupert Hughes, Calvin Holivey. *Photog* Jules Cronjager. *Film Ed* Minnie Steppler.

Cast: Sojin *(Ming Foy/Wing Foy/The Cobra)*, Albert Valentino *(Mark Conover)*, Iris Yamoaka, Iris Shan *(Foo; see note)*, Ben Wilson *(Sam Warren)*, Jimmy Aubrey *(Willie Kegg)*, James B. Leong *(Lee Mandarin)*, Carl Theobald, Bud Shaw, Dick Sutherland, Opal Baker.

Melodrama. "Story deals with the Chinese boss of an island which serves as a base for traffic in narcotics and white slavery. The Cobra, as the menace is designated, is the almighty ruler until a humble Chinese stowaway appears to upset everything. The little stowaway turns out to be a Chinese Secret Service agent." (*Variety*, 22 May 1929, p24.) *Stowaways. Secret service. Chinese. Narcotics. White slave traffic. Slavers.*

Note: The surname of the actress playing *Foo* has not been exactly determined.

CHINATOWN CHARLIE **F2.0874**

First National Pictures. 15 Apr **1928** [c23 Mar 1928; LP25091]. Si; b&w. 35mm. 7 reels, 6,365 ft.

Prod C. C. Burr. *Dir* Charles Hines. *Scen* Roland Asher, John Grey. *Titl* Paul Perez. *Story* Owen Davis. *Photog* William J. Miller, Al Wilson. *Film Ed* George Amy.

Cast: Johnny Hines *(Charlie)*, Louise Lorraine *(Annie Gordon)*, Harry Gribbon *(Red Mike)*, Fred Kohler *(Monk)*, Sojin *(The Mandarin)*, Scooter Lowry *(Oswald)*, Anna May Wong *(The Mandarin's sweetheart)*, George Kuwa *(Hip Sing Toy)*, John Burdette *(Gyp)*.

Comedy. Charlie, a Chinatown tour guide, attempts to protect one of his female passengers from a gang wanting to steal her ring, reputed to have supernatural powers. He rescues the girl after an escapade at a mandarin's palace in which some acrobats form a human chain across the street two floors aboveground. *Guides. Chinese. Tourists. Acrobats. Supernatural.*

CHINATOWN NIGHTS **F2.0875**

Paramount Famous Lasky Corp. 23 Mar **1929** [c23 Mar 1929; LP274]. Talking sequences, sd eff, & mus score (Movietone); b&w. 35mm. 8 reels, 7,481 ft. [Also si; 7,145 ft.]

Assoc Prod David Selznick. *Dir* William A. Wellman. *Screenplay* Ben Grauman Kohn. *Dial* William B. Jutte. *Titl* Julian Johnson. *Adapt* Oliver H. P. Garrett. *Photog* Henry Gerrard. *Tech Dir* Tom Gubbins. *Film Ed* Allyson Shaffer.

Cast: Wallace Beery *(Chuck Riley)*, Florence Vidor *(Joan Fry)*, Warner Oland *(Boston Charley)*, Jack McHugh *(The Shadow)*, Jack Oakie *(The Reporter)*, Tetsu Komai *(Woo Chung)*, Frank Chew *(The Gambler)*, Mrs. Wong Wing *(The Maid)*, Pete Morrison *(The Bartender)*, Freeman Wood *(Gerald)*.

Melodrama. Source: Samuel Ornitz, "Tong War" (publication undetermined). A Chinatown tourist bus is caught in the middle of a tong war, and in the resulting confusion, society woman Joan Fry is left behind. Chuck Riley, the white leader of a tong faction, pulls her from the dangerous streets and keeps her overnight in his apartment. The following morning, Joan leaves, returning later with friends; Chuck again saves her life. Joan falls in love with Chuck and moves in with him, renouncing her former life. She tries to get Chuck to reform, and he throws her out. Joan wanders the streets, and Boston Charley, Chuck's rival, gets her drunk and sends her back to Chuck with a humiliating letter pinned to her frowsy sweater. Chuck is moved by Joan's condition and, wrecking his dancehall, leaves Chinatown with her, looking for a new beginning and a brighter tomorrow. *Tourists. Socialites. Chinese. Tongs. Drunkenness. Chinatown.*

THE CHINESE PARROT (Universal-Jewel) **F2.0876**

Universal Pictures. 23 Oct **1927** [c24 Aug 1927; LP24331]. Si; b&w. 35mm. 7 reels, 7,304 ft.

Pres by Carl Laemmle. *Dir* Paul Leni. *Adapt-Scen* J. Grubb Alexander. *Titl* Walter Anthony. *Photog* Ben Kline.

Cast: Marian Nixon *(Sally Phillimore)*, Florence Turner *(Sally Phillimore, older)*, Hobart Bosworth *(Philip Madden/Jerry Delaney)*, Edward Burns *(Robert Eden)*, Albert Conti *(Martin Thorne)*, K. Sojin *(Charlie Chan)*, Fred Esmelton *(Alexander Eden)*, Ed Kennedy *(Maydorf)*, George Kuwa *(Louie Wong)*, Slim Summerville, Dan Mason *(prospectors)*, Anna May Wong *(Nautch dancer)*, Etta Lee *(gambling den habitué)*, Jack Trent *(Jordan)*.

Mystery melodrama. Source: Earl Derr Biggers, *The Chinese Parrot* (Indianapolis, 1926). Sally Randall, daughter of a wealthy Hawaiian planter, marries Phillimore, the man of her father's choice, though she has sworn her love to Philip Madden; tearing from her throat the priceless pearls given her by her father, Madden declares that one day he will buy her at the same price. Twenty years later, now a widow in financial straits, Sally offers the pearls for sale in San Francisco. Accompanied by her daughter, Sally, she is astonished to discover Madden bargaining for the pearls, which she has entrusted to Chan, a Chinese detective, and the sale is contingent on her delivery of the jewels to his desert home. Madden is taken prisoner by yeggs and is impersonated by Jerry Delaney, who welcomes Sally and Robert Eden, the jeweler's son. While Chan is secretly undertaking an investigation, the jewels are stolen by various parties, but it develops that a Chinese parrot has witnessed the kidnaping and told him about it. *Chinese. Detectives. Planters. Kidnaping. Jewels. Hawaii. San Francisco. Parrots.*

CHIP OF THE FLYING U (Universal-Jewel) **F2.0877**

Universal Pictures. 14 Mar **1926** [c2 Mar 1926; LP22455]. Si; b&w. 35mm. 7 reels, 6,596 ft.

Dir Lynn Reynolds. *Scen* Lynn Reynolds, Harry Dittmar. *Story* B. M.

Bower. *Photog* Harry Neumann.

Cast: Hoot Gibson *(Chip Bennett)*, Virginia Browne Faire *(Dr. Della Whitmore)*, Philo McCullough *(Duncan Whittaker)*, Nora Cecil *(Dr. Cecil Grantham)*, De Witt Jennings *(J. G. Whitmore)*, Harry Todd *(Weary)*, Pee Wee Holmes *(Shorty)*, Mark Hamilton *(Slim)*, Willie Sung *(Chinese cook)*, Steve Clements *(Indian)*.

Western comedy. Chip Bennett of the Flying U Ranch, though a confirmed misogynist, falls in love with Dr. Della Whitmore, the sister of the rancher for whom Chip works. In order to be near her, Chip fakes an accident and claims to have a damaged ankle. The two fall in love, and Della submits several of Chip's highly accomplished cartoons to a receptive publisher. When she later discovers Chip's deception, however, Della gives him the cold shoulder. Chip is at first heartbroken, but, screwing up his courage, he kidnaps the fair doctor from a dance and carries her off to a parson to be married. *Physicians. Cartoonists. Cowboys. Ranchers. Misogynists.*

CHIVALROUS CHARLEY **F2.0878**

Selznick Pictures. *Dist* Select Pictures. 10 Dec **1921** [c23 Nov 1921; LP17245]. Si; b&w. 35mm. 5 reels, 4,543 ft.

Pres by Lewis J. Selznick. *Dir* Robert Ellis. *Scen* Edward J. Montagne. *Story* May Tully. *Photog* Jules Cronjager.

Cast: Eugene O'Brien *(Charles Riley)*, George Fawcett *(his uncle)*, Nancy Deaver *(Alice Sanderson)*, D. J. Flanagan *(her father)*, Huntley Gordon *(Geoffrey Small)*.

Comedy-drama. Charley Riley, who has a temperamental fault of chivalrous conduct toward ladies, is shipped west by his uncle with the expectation that the rough life will stiffen him. Back in New York, however, Charley is involved in two escapades and lands in jail; later, as he is about to enter his apartment, a young lady appeals to him for shelter from her pursuers and he offers her the hospitality of his apartment for the evening. Her father appears the next morning and forces him to marry her. Alice, who is in league with crooks, departs, then, presumably in distress, sends for him. At her home, Charley is set upon by the thugs, but he escapes with the girl and leads his pursuers to the police station. Impressed with his courage and daring, Alice decides to make her marriage actual as well as legal. *Manhood. Marriage. Gangs. New York City.*

THE CHORUS KID **F2.0879**

Gotham Productions. *Dist* Lumas Film Corp. 10 Apr **1928** [c16 Apr 1928; LP25164]. Si; b&w. 35mm. 6 reels, 6,200 ft.

Dir Howard Bretherton. *Scen* Harold Shumate. *Titl* Casey Robinson. *Adapt* Adele Buffington. *Story* Howard Rockey. *Photog* Charles Van Enger. *Film Ed* Donn Hayes. *Prod Mgr* Carroll Sax.

Cast: Virginia Brown Faire *(Beatrice Brown)*, Bryant Washburn *(John Powell)*, Thelma Hill *(Peggy Powell)*, Hedda Hopper *(Mrs. Garrett)*, John Batten *(Jimmy Garrett)*, Tom O'Brien *(Bill Whipple)*, Sheldon Lewis *(Jacob Feldman)*.

Comedy-drama. Beatrice Brown, 22-year-old member of a chorus line, returns to school on a windfall from an oil investment. She chooses the boarding school of Peggy Powell, whose millionaire father Beatrice would like to capture. Masquerading as "Sally May," Beatrice becomes close friends with Peggy. Beatrice, her "guardian," Bill Whipple, Mrs. Garrett, and Jimmy Garrett (who is in love with Peggy) are invited to spend the holidays with the Powells. Eventually Beatrice's ruse is discovered, and after several complications (including the elopement of Peggy and Jimmy) Beatrice and Powell marry. *Millionaires. Chorus girls. Disguise. Wealth. Boarding schools.*

Note: Published copyright information that the film has sound has not been verified.

THE CHORUS LADY **F2.0880**

Regal Pictures. *Dist* Producers Distributing Corp. 23 Nov **1924** [c10 Nov 1924; LP20813]. Si; b&w. 35mm. 7 reels, 6,020 ft.

Dir Ralph Ince. *Adapt* Bradley King. *Photog* Glen Gano.

Cast: Margaret Livingston *(Patricia O'Brien)*, Alan Roscoe *(Dan Mallory)*, Virginia Lee Corbin *(Nora O'Brien)*, Lillian Elliott *(Mrs. Patrick O'Brien)*, Lloyd Ingraham *(Patrick O'Brien)*, Philo McCullough *(Dick Crawford)*, Eve Southern *(Miss Simpson)*, Mervyn LeRoy *("Duke" [the Jockey])*.

Comedy. Source: James Grant Forbes, *The Chorus Lady; a One-Act Comedy of Stage Life* (New York, c1904). Patricia O'Brien, a chorus girl, plans to marry Dan Mallory, but a fire in Dan's stables blinds his prize filly, Lady Belle, and forces him to postpone the wedding. Pat returns to New York with her sister, Nora, and the girls find work in the Follies. In spite of Lady Belle's blindness, Dan enters her in a race, and she wins $20,000. When he arrives in New York to give Patricia the good news, he discovers that she has gone to the apartment of Dick Crawford, a notorious gambler and philanderer. Dan goes to find Patricia and, through a misunderstanding, believes that she is having an affair with Crawford. Dan and Patricia are reconciled, however, when he discovers that she went to Crawford's apartment only to look for Nora, who had become involved with the gambler. Dan and Patricia are soon married. *Chorus girls. Gamblers. Horseracing. Follies. New York City. Fires. Horses.*

THE CHRISTIAN **F2.0881**

Goldwyn Pictures. ca14 Jan **1923** [Kansas City premiere; released 28 Jan; c5 Feb 1923; LP18644]. Si; b&w. 35mm. 8 reels, 8,000 ft.

Dir Maurice Tourneur. *Scen* Paul Bern. *Photog* Charles Van Enger.

Cast: Richard Dix *(John Storm)*, Mae Busch *(Glory Quayle)*, Gareth Hughes *(Brother Paul)*, Phyllis Haver *(Polly Love)*, Cyril Chadwick *(Lord Robert Ure)*, Mahlon Hamilton *(Horatio Drake)*, Joseph Dowling *(Father Lampleigh)*, Claude Gillingwater *(Lord Storm)*, John Herdman *(Parson Quayle)*, Beryl Mercer *(Liza)*, Robert Bolder *(Reverend Golightly)*, Milla Davenport *(matron)*, Alice Hesse *(Mary)*, Aileen Pringle *(Lady Robert Ure)*, Harry Northrup *(Faro King)*, Eric Mayne *(doctor)*, William Moran *(coroner)*.

Drama. Source: Hall Caine, *The Christian; a Story* (London, 1897). Hall Caine, *The Christian; a Drama in Four Acts* (London, 1907). Glory Quayle and John Storm, sweethearts since childhood on the Isle of Man, go to London—Glory to become a nurse and John to enter a monastery. Instead, Glory becomes a theater star, and John renounces his vows because he cannot forget his love for her. Lord Robert Ure, who has already betrayed Glory's friend, Polly Love, incites the London populace against John, claiming that John has predicted that the world will end on the eve of the Epsom Downs Derby. John goes to kill Glory to save her soul, but instead she convinces him of her love. Confused, John wanders into the street, is mortally hurt by an angry mob, then marries Glory before dying in her arms. *Monks. Actors. Religion. Judgment Day. Isle of Man. London.*

CHRISTINA **F2.0882**

Fox Film Corp. 15 Dec **1929** [c18 Apr 1929; LP314]. Sd eff & mus score (Movietone); b&w. 35mm. 8 reels, 7,651 ft. [Also si; 6,955 ft.]

Pres by William Fox. *Dir* William K. Howard. *Scen* Marion Orth. *Dial* S. K. Lauren. *Titl* Katherine Hilliker, H. H. Caldwell. *Story* Tristram Tupper. *Photog* Lucien Andriot. *Film Ed* Katherine Hilliker, H. H. Caldwell. *Song: "Christina"* Con Conrad, Sidney Mitchell, Archie Gottler. *Asst Dir* Phil Ford.

Cast: Janet Gaynor *(Christina)*, Charles Morton *(Jan)*, Rudolph Schildkraut *(Niklaas)*, Harry Cording *(Dick Torpe)*, Lucy Dorraine *(Madame Bosman)*.

Drama. Christina, the daughter of an aged toymaker in Holland, falls in love with Jan, a young man in shining armor who rides a white horse as an advertisement for a traveling carnival. Jan stays behind when the carnival moves on, and Madame Bosman, the carnival owner, becomes jealous and has Jan unjustly arrested for embezzlement. Christina later goes to Amsterdam looking for Jan, and Madame Bosman wounds him to keep Jan and Christina apart. Christina returns home and prepares to marry another. Recovered from his injury, Jan follows her, and they are reunited. *Toymakers. Embezzlement. Carnivals. Netherlands. Amsterdam.*

CHRISTINE OF THE BIG TOPS **F2.0883**

Banner Productions. *Dist* Sterling Pictures Distributing Corp. 1 or 20 Aug **1926** [c23 Aug 1926; LP23042]. Si; b&w. 35mm. 6 reels, 5,316 or 5,800 ft.

Dir Archie Mayo. *Story-Scen* Sonya Levien.

Cast: Pauline Garon *(Christine)*, Cullen Landis *("Bob" Hastings)*, Otto Matiesen *(Hagan)*, Robert Graves *(Pete Barman)*, John Elliott *(Dr. Hastings)*, Martha Mattox *(Mrs. Hastings)*, Betty Noon *(Doris)*.

Romantic melodrama. Dr. Bob Hastings, a young surgeon who loses courage during his first operation, takes refuge from his family by joining a circus as physician and veterinarian. Christine, an orphan of circus parents who has been reared by Hagan, an accident victim, and Barman, the circus owner, falls in love with Bob. Barman, out of jealousy, fires Bob; and Christine, who is a popular trapeze artist, threatens to leave with him; but finding a note to Bob's former sweetheart, she believes he has spurned her love and accepts Barman's marriage offer. Bob leaves but is brought back by Hagan; a storm wrecks the main tent, and Barman is killed, while Christine is badly injured. Through extraordinary surgery, Bob saves Christine, who becomes his wife, and regains his place in the medical world. *Orphans. Surgeons. Veterinarians. Physicians. Trapezists. Circus.*

CHRISTINE OF THE HUNGRY HEART **F2.0884**

Thomas H. Ince Corp. *Dist* First National Pictures. 12 Oct **1924** [c16 Oct 1924; LP20659]. Si; b&w. 35mm. 8 reels, 7,500 ft.

Pres by Thomas H. Ince. *Pers Supv* Thomas H. Ince. *Dir* George Archainbaud. *Scen* Bradley King. *Photog* Henry Sharp.

Cast: Florence Vidor *(Christine Madison)*, Clive Brook *(Dr. Alan Monteagle)*, Ian Keith *(Ivan Vianney)*, Warner Baxter *(Stuart Knight)*, Walter Hiers *(Dan Madison)*, Lillian Lawrence *(Mrs. Michael Knight)*, Dorothy Brock *("Jeffy")*.

Domestic drama. Source: Kathleen Norris, "Christine of the Hungry Heart," in *Hearst's International* (44:12–17, 42–48, 24–29, 56–61, Sep–Dec 1923; 45:52–57, 82–90, 92–97, Jan–Mar 1924). Desiring more love and attention than her drunkard husband, Stuart Knight, gives her, Christine divorces him to marry Dr. Alan Monteagle. They are happy for a time; they have a son, Jeffy; but eventually Alan neglects his wife for his work; and Christine finds the companionship she seeks with author Ivan Vianney. Christine and Jeffy leave Alan for Ivan, but the doctor regains custody of his son, and Christine decides to take care of Stuart, whom she encounters by chance and who is now in a desperate condition. Just before Stuart dies, Alan and Jeffy find Christine and persuade her to come home with them. *Physicians. Authors. Marriage. Divorce. Alcoholism. Motherhood.*

CHRISTINE OF THE YOUNG HEART *see* **HIGH HEELS**

CHRISTMAS EVE AT PILOT BUTTE *see* **DESPERATE TRAILS**

CINDERELLA OF THE HILLS **F2.0885**

Fox Film Corp. 23 Oct **1921** [c23 Oct 1921; LP17203]. Si; b&w. 35mm. 5 reels, 4,800 ft. [Later cut.]

Pres by William Fox. *Dir* Howard M. Mitchell. *Scen* Dorothy Yost. *Photog* George Webber.

Cast: Barbara Bedford *(Norris Gradley)*, Carl Miller *(Claude Wolcott)*, Cecil Van Auker *(Rodney Bates)*, Wilson Hummel *(Peter Poff)*, Tom McGuire *(Giles Gradley)*, Barbara La Marr Deely *(Kate Gradley)*.

Rural melodrama. Source: John Breckenridge Ellis, *Little Fiddler of the Ozarks* (Chicago, 1913). When her father obtains a divorce and marries another woman, Norris Gradley remains with him, hoping to effect a reconciliation. Snubbed and mistreated by her stepmother, she disguises herself as a boy and earns money by playing the violin at dances. Claude Wolcott, who has been engaged by Giles Gradley to sink oil wells, falls in love with Norris and is present when Gradley discovers Bates, a former lover of Mrs. Gradley's, reviving his affections for her. Claude prevents the enraged man from killing his rival, and Mrs. Gradley, in a rage, rushes from the house and is killed falling into an abyss. Norris reunites her parents and is married to Claude. *Violinists. Stepmothers. Divorce. Disguise. Ozarks.*

CIRCE THE ENCHANTRESS **F2.0886**

Tiffany Productions. *Dist* Metro-Goldwyn Distributing Corp. 6 Oct **1924** [c1 Oct 1924; LP20687]. Si; b&w. 35mm. 7 reels, 6,882 ft.

Pres by Robert Z. Leonard. *Dir* Robert Z. Leonard. *Titl* Frederic Hatton, Fanny Hatton. *Adapt* Douglas Doty. *Written especially for Mae Murray by* Vicente Blasco-Ibáñez. *Photog* Oliver T. Marsh. *Art Dir* Cedric Gibbons. *Asst Dir* David Todd.

Cast: Mae Murray *(Circe, mythical goddess/Cecilie Brunne)*, James Kirkwood *(Dr. Wesley Van Martyn)*, Tom Ricketts *(Archibald Crumm)*, Charles Gerard *(Ballard "Bal" Barrett)*, William Haines *(William Craig)*, Lillian Langdon *(Sister Agatha)*, Gene Cameron *("Madame" Ducelle, modiste)*.

Society drama. Circe, enchantress of ancient times, turned men into swine by magic. The modern Circe, Cecilie Brunne, accomplishes similar results by liquor. ... Cecilie, disillusioned at 18 after she leaves a convent school in New Orleans, swears that all men will pay for what she has lost. Untouched by the desire she arouses, she torments her victims and levies tribute. Only one man, Dr. Van Martyn, withstands her charms. Piqued at first, she at last becomes desperate, finds life impossible without his love, and gives a wild party at her Long Island villa. At the height of a drunken, gambling, dancing orgy, Cecilie realizes she cannot go on with this life, and she retires to the New Orleans convent. One day she is run over while saving the life of a child, and it is feared that she will never walk again. When the test comes, Dr. Van Martyn walks into the room, and Cecilie stumbles her way to his arms. *Sorcerers. Physicians. Jazz life. Paralysis. New Orleans. Long Island. Circe. Mythological characters.*

THE CIRCLE *see* **STRICTLY UNCONVENTIONAL**

THE CIRCLE **F2.0887**

Metro-Goldwyn-Mayer Pictures. 2 Dec **1925** [c14 Sep 1925; LP21825]. Si; b&w. 35mm. 6 reels, 5,511 ft.

Dir Frank Borzage. *Adapt* Kenneth B. Clarke. *Photog* Chester A. Lyons. *Art Dir* Cedric Gibbons, James Basevi. *Wardrobe* Ethel P. Chaffin.

Cast: Eleanor Boardman *(Elizabeth)*, Malcolm McGregor *(Edward Lutton)*, Alec Francis *(Lord Clive Cheney)*, Eugenie Besserer *(Lady Catherine)*, George Fawcett *(Portenous)*, Creighton Hale *(Arnold)*, Otto Hoffman *(Dorker)*, Eulalie Jensen *(Mrs. Shenstone)*.

Comedy-drama. Source: William Somerset Maugham, *The Circle, a Comedy in Three Acts* (London, 1921). In the waning years of the last century, Hugh Portenous, who was to have been the best man at the wedding of Lady Catherine to Lord Cheney, persuades Catherine to elope with him instead. Thirty years pass. Elizabeth, the wife of Lady Catherine's son, Arnold, invites Hugh and Catherine to the country for a visit. Elizabeth is thinking of running off with Edward Lutton and wants to see how well the marriage of her husband's parents has survived the years; what she sees drives her to elope with Lutton. Her husband impersonates the chauffeur, drives the couple to a secluded spot, and thrashes Lutton. He and Elizabeth then return home, resuming married life with a new understanding. *Nobility. Chauffeurs. Marriage. Elopement. Impersonation.*

Note: Remade in 1930 as *Strictly Unconventional*, q. v.

CIRCUMSTANTIAL EVIDENCE **F2.0888**

Chesterfield Motion Picture Corp. 1 Apr **1929**. Si; b&w. 35mm. 7 reels, 6,200 ft.

Supv Lon Young. *Dir-Story-Scen* Wilfred Noy. *Titl* Lee Authmar. *Photog* M. A. Anderson. *Film Ed* James Sweeney.

Cast: Cornelius Keefe *(Arthur Rowland)*, Helen Foster *(Jean Benton)*, Alice Lake *(Lucy Bishop)*, Charles Gerrard *(Henry Lord)*, Ray Hallor *(Tony Benton)*, Fred Walton *(judge)*, Jack Tanner *(prosecuting attorney)*.

Melodrama. While concentrating his attentions on stenographer Jean Benton, roué Henry Lord allows his "regular," Lucy Bishop, to get Jean's weak brother, Tony, to forge checks to cover his racing debts. Lord is murdered during an affair at a country lodge, circumstantial evidence points to Jean, but Arthur Rowland takes the blame. During Arthur's trial it is revealed that Lord was actually shot by the discarded Lucy. *Stenographers. Rakes. Brother-sister relationship. Forgery. Murder. Trials. Circumstantial evidence.*

THE CIRCUS **F2.0889**

Charles Chaplin Productions. *Dist* United Artists. 7 Jan **1928** [c6 Jan 1928; LP24830]. Si; b&w. 35mm. 7 reels, 6,400 ft.

Prod-Dir-Writ Charles Chaplin. *Cinematog* Roland H. Totheroh. *Camera* Jack Wilson, Mark Marlatt. *Art Dir* Charles D. Hall. *Film Ed* Charles Chaplin. *Asst Dir* Harry Crocker. *Laboratory Supv* William E. Hinkley.

Cast: Charles Chaplin *(Charlie, a tramp)*, Merna Kennedy *(The Equestrienne)*, Betty Morrissey *(The Vanishing Lady)*, Harry Crocker *(Rex, King of the High Wire)*, Allan Garcia *(The Circus Proprietor)*, Henry Bergman *(The Clown)*, Stanley J. Sanford *(The Head Property Man)*, George Davis *(The Magician)*, John Rand *(The Assistant Property Man)*, Steve Murphy *(The Pick-pocket)*, Doc Stone *(The Prize Fighter)*.

Comedy. Charlie, a wandering tramp, becomes a circus handyman and falls in love with the circus owner's daughter. Unaware of Charlie's affection, the girl falls in love with a handsome young performer. Charlie's versatility makes him star of the show when he substitutes for an ailing tightwire walker. He is discharged from the company when he protects the girl from her father's abuse, but he returns and appeals to the handsome performer to marry the girl. After the wedding the father prevails upon them to rejoin the circus. Charlie is hired again, but he stays behind when the caravan moves on. *Clowns. Tramps. Tightrope walkers. Circus. Wagon shows.*

THE CIRCUS ACE **F2.0890**

Fox Film Corp. 26 Jun **1927** [c12 Jun 1927; LP24099]. Si; b&w. 35mm. 5 reels, 4,810 ft.

Pres by William Fox. *Dir* Ben Stoloff. *Scen* Jack Jungmeyer. *Story* Harold Shumate. *Photog* Dan Clark. *Asst Dir* Wynn Mace.

Cast: Tom Mix *(Tom Terry)*, Natalie Joyce *(Millie Jane Raleigh)*, Jack Baston *(Kirk Mallory)*, Duke Lee *(Job Jasper)*, James Bradbury *(Gus Peabody)*, Stanley Blystone *(boss canvass man)*, Dudley Smith *(Durgan, the miller)*, Buster Gardner *(sheriff)*, Clarence *(a kangaroo)*, Tony the Wonder Horse.

Western comedy-drama. Tom meets his fate when a balloon goes sailing over the ranch: seeing a girl jump with a parachute, he rides to her rescue. Later, during the circus parade, he rides to her assistance, rescuing her from an elephant and thus arousing the ire of the circus manager, whose henchmen begin to chase Tom. Scrambling over the main tent, Tom falls onto the tightrope and lands in a net with the girl while the crowd wildly applauds. Kirk Mallory, who is jealous of Tom's attentions to Millie, frames Tom for a murder; he lands in jail but escapes and reaches Mallory's ranch in time to rescue the girl and administer a thrashing to the villain. *Cowboys. Murder. Frameup. Parachuting. Balloons. Circus. Elephants. Kangaroos.*

THE CIRCUS COWBOY **F2.0891**

Fox Film Corp. 11 May **1924** [c6 May 1924; LP20161]. Si; b&w. 35mm. 5 reels, 4,175 ft.

Pres by William Fox. *Dir* William A. Wellman. *Scen* Doty Hobart. *Story* Louis Sherwin. *Photog* Joseph Brotherton.

Cast: Charles Jones *(Buck Saxon)*, Marian Nixon *(Bird Taylor)*, Jack McDonald *(Ezra Bagley)*, Ray Hallor *(Paul Bagley)*, Marguerite Clayton *(Norma Wallace)*, George Romain *(Slovini)*.

Melodrama. After a 2-year absence, Buck Saxon returns home to find his girl, Norma, married to the town's wealthiest citizen, Ezra Bagley, yet professing to love Buck. Unjustly accused of attempting to murder Bagley, he escapes and joins a circus, where he falls in love with Bird, a tightrope walker, proves his innocence of the charge, and marries Bird. *Cowboys. Tightrope walkers. Murder. Circus.*

THE CIRCUS CYCLONE (Blue Streak Western) **F2.0892**

Universal Pictures. 4 Oct **1925** [c10 Jul 1925; LP21640]. Si; b&w. 35mm. 5 reels, 4,397 ft.

Dir-Story Albert Rogell. *Photog* Pliny Horne.

Cast: Art Acord *(Jack Manning)*, Moe McCrea *(Eczema Jackson)*, Nancy Deaver *(Doraldina)*, Cesare Gravina *(Pepe)*, Albert J. Smith *(Steve Brant)*, Hilliard Karr *(Fatty)*, George Austin *(Joe Dokes)*, Gertrude Howard *(Mrs. Jackson)*, Jim Corey *(Greasey)*, Ben Corbett *(referee)*.

Western melodrama. Steve Brant, an ex-pugilist who owns a small circus, makes crude advances toward Doraldina, a lovely equestrienne; and when she resists him, he angrily beats her horse. Jack Manning, a cowboy who is passing by, prevents Brant from further injuring the horse, and the two men agree to engage in a boxing match, with the winner getting the horse. Jack wins the fight, and Brant, in an effort to get even with Doraldina, arranges for her father, the clown Pepe, to be framed for bank robbery. Pepe is arrested, and the townspeople threaten to lynch him. Eczema, a small Negro boy, discovers the true identity of the robbers and apprises Jack of their identity. Jack rides after the bank robbers, captures them, and recovers the stolen money, returning to town in time to save Pepe from being lynched. *Prizefighters. Cowboys. Equestrians. Negroes. Circus. Bank robberies. Lynching.*

CIRCUS DAYS **F2.0893**

Sol Lesser. *Dist* Associated First National Pictures. 30 Jul **1923** [c10 Jul 1923; LP19194]. Si; b&w. 35mm. 6 reels, 6,183 ft.

Pres by Sol Lesser. *Supv* Jack Coogan, Sr. *Dir* Edward F. Cline. *Titl* Eve Unsell. *Adapt* Edward F. Cline, Harry Weil. *Photog* Frank Good, Robert Martin. *Tech Dir* Fred Gabourie. *Film Ed* Irene Morra. *Asst Dir* Harry Weil.

Cast: Jackie Coogan *(Toby Tyler)*, Barbara Tennant *(Ann Tyler)*, Russell Simpson *(Eben Holt)*, Claire McDowell *(Martha Holt)*, Cesare Gravina *(Luigi, the clown)*, Peaches Jackson *(Jeannette)*, Sam De Grasse *(Mr. Lord)*, De Witt Jennings *(Mr. Daly)*, Nellie Lane *(World's Fattest Woman)*, William Barlow *(World's Skinniest Man)*.

Melodrama. Source: James Otis, *Toby Tyler; or, Ten Weeks With a Circus* (New York, 1881). Toby Tyler runs away from his cruel uncle and joins a circus to work as lemonade boy. Eventually his talent is discovered, and he becomes the star clown. *Clowns. Childhood. Circus.*

CIRCUS JOYS **F2.0894**

Sherwood MacDonald Productions. 28 Dec **1923** [scheduled release]. Si; b&w. 35mm. 5 reels.

Cast: Gloria Joy.

Comedy(?). No information about the specific nature of this film has been found. *Circus.*

THE CIRCUS KID **F2.0895**

FBO Pictures. 7 Oct **1928** [c25 Sep 1928; LP25650]. Talking prolog, sd eff, & mus score (Photophone); b&w. 35mm. 7 reels, 6,085 ft.

Dir George B. Seitz. *Adtl Dir* Josiah Zuro. *Cont* Melville Baker. *Titl* Randolph Bartlett. *Story* James Ashmore Creelman. *Photog* Philip Tannura. *Film Ed* Ann McKnight. *Asst Dir* Charles Kerr.

Cast—Prolog: George Le Maire, William Le Maire, William Haynes.

Cast—Story: Frankie Darro *(Buddy)*, Poodles Hanneford *(Poodles)*, Joe E. Brown *(King Kruger)*, Helene Costello *(Trixie)*, Sam Nelson *(Tad)*, Lionel Belmore *(Beezicks)*, Charles Miller *(Cadwallader)*, Johnny Gough *(Skelly Crosley,)*, Sid Crosley *(Skelly's runner)*, Charles Gemora *(Zozo)*, Frank Hemphill *(officer)*, Clarence Moorehouse.

Melodrama. Buddy, an acrobatic orphan, runs away from the orphanage and joins the circus, becoming a member of a comic riding act. Tad, a lion tamer, and Kruger, a once great lion tamer trying to make a comeback after being ravaged by a killer lion, are rivals for the love of Trixie, a pretty equestrienne. During an evening show, a killer lion gets loose and attacks Tad; Kruger finds his nerve at last and fights the beast with his bare hands. The lion is shot, but not before Kruger dies, having with his last breath given his blessing to the love between Trixie and Tad. *Orphans. Lion tamers. Equestrians. Acrobats. Circus. Lions.*

Note: The comic prolog ("Sure Shot Dick") and the synchronized score were added after the completion of the main part of the film.

CIRCUS LURE **F2.0896**

Sanford Productions. 15 Jun **1924.** Si; b&w. 35mm. 6 reels, 5,400 ft. [Later reduced to 5 reels.]

Dir Frank S. Mattison.

Cast: Matty Mattison, Lorraine Eason.

Melodrama. "Joe Henry, head of a one-ring circus, plays a small town and after the departure of the troupe a young girl, fascinated by the prospects of being a star, follows. She is engaged and her presence causes jealousy on the part of Joe's sweetheart. When the girl is injured it is revealed that she is the sister of the manager, who lost track of his mother and baby sister years ago. This brings a happy conclusion. Circus stunts are a feature of the picture." (*Motion Picture News Booking Guide*, [7]:16, Oct 1924.) *Brother-sister relationship. Circus.*

CIRCUS ROOKIES **F2.0897**

Metro-Goldwyn-Mayer Pictures. 31 Mar **1928** [c31 Mar 1928; LP25176]. Si; b&w. 35mm. 6 reels, 5,661 ft.

Dir Edward Sedgwick. *Cont* Richard Schayer. *Titl* Robert Hopkins. *Story* Edward Sedgwick, Lew Lipton. *Photog* Merritt B. Gerstad. *Set Dsgn* Cedric Gibbons. *Film Ed* Frank Sullivan. *Wardrobe* David Cox.

Cast: Karl Dane *(Oscar Thrust)*, George K. Arthur *(Francis Byrd)*, Louise Lorraine *(La Belle)*, Sidney Jarvis *(Mr. Magoo)*, Fred Humes *(Bimbo, a gorilla [?])*.

Comedy. Oscar Thrust, trainer of a gorilla billed as "Bimbo, the Man-Eating Ape," takes a disliking to Francis Byrd. Fired from his job as a newspaper reporter, Byrd wants to join the circus to be near La Belle, a trapeze artist. Thrust fouls all of Byrd's attempts to prove himself worthy of the circus, causing La Belle, the daughter of circus-owner Magoo, to believe that Byrd is a coward. Finally, practical joker Thrust puts Bimbo in Byrd's berth on the train. Bimbo gets loose and chases La Belle to the train roof, frightens the engineer into jumping off, speeds up the train, and breaks the whistle. Francis comes to the rescue, stops the train from ramming a freight ahead, and saves everyone from sure destruction. Bimbo gives Thrust a good thrashing. *Reporters. Trapezists. Circus. Trains. Apes.*

THE CITY **F2.0898**

Fox Film Corp. 14 Nov **1926** [c14 Nov 1926; LP23395]. Si; b&w. 35mm. 6 reels, 5,508 ft.

Pres by William Fox. *Dir* R. William Neill. *Scen* Gertrude Orr. *Photog* James Diamond. *Asst Dir* R. Lee Hough.

Cast: Nancy Nash *(Cicely Rand)*, Robert Frazer *(George Rand, Jr.)*, George Irving *(George Rand, Sr.)*, Lillian Elliott *(Mrs. Rand)*, Walter McGrail *(Jim Hannock)*, Richard Walling *(Chad Morris)*, May Allison

(Elinor Vorhees), Melbourne MacDowell *(Vorhees)*, Bodil Rosing *(Sarah)*, Fred Walton.

Domestic melodrama. Source: Clyde Fitch, *The City, a Drama* (Boston, 1915). Following the death of Rand, a wealthy reformed criminal, his family moves to the city, and Rand, Jr., becomes a candidate for mayor. Mrs. Rand neglects her family to pursue social ambitions, and Hannock, a dope fiend, dupes Cicely into a marriage. Hannock, who has caused the death of Rand, Sr., and knows of his past, blackmails the politically ambitious son, George. Eventually awakened to his sense of responsibility and self-respect, George faces up to the villain, whose suicide precipitates the family's return to its village environment. *Politicians. Social climbers. Criminals—Rehabilitation. Family life. Narcotics. Blackmail.*

CITY GIRL **F2.0899**

Fox Film Corp. 16 Feb **1930** [c10 Jan 1930; LP984]. Talking sequences & mus score (Movietone); b&w. 35mm. 7 reels, 6,171 ft. [Also si; 8,217 ft.]

Pres by William Fox. *Dir* F. W. Murnau. *Stage Dir (sd vers)* A. H. Van Buren, A. F. Erickson. *Adapt-Scen* Berthold Viertel, Marion Orth. *Dial* Elliott Lester. *Titl* Katherine Hilliker, H. H. Caldwell. *Photog* Ernest Palmer. *Sets* Harry Oliver. *Film Ed* Katherine Hilliker, H. H. Caldwell. *Mus Score* Arthur Kay. *Rec Engr* Harold Hobson. *Asst Dir* William Tummel. *Cost* Sophie Wachner.

Cast—Silent Version: David Torrence *(The Father)*, Edith Yorke *(The Mother)*, Dawn O'Day *(The Little Daughter)*, Charles Farrell *(The Son)*, Mary Duncan *(The Waitress)*, Guinn "Big Boy" Williams, Dick Alexander, Tom Maguire, Jack Pennick, Ed Brady *(reapers)*, Ed Clay, Harry Gripp, Harry Leonard, Werner Klinger, William Sundholm, Helen Lynch, Marjorie Beebe, Joe Brown, Arnold Lucy, Eddie Boland, Ivan Linow.

Cast—Talking Version: Charles Farrell *(Lem Tustine)*, Mary Duncan *(Kate)*, David Torrence *(Tustine)*, Edith Yorke *(Mrs. Tustine)*, Dawn O'Day *(Mary Tustine)*, Tom Maguire *(Matey)*, Dick Alexander *(Mac)*, Pat Rooney *(Butch)*, Ed Brady, Roscoe Ates *(reapers)*.

Rural drama. Source: Elliott Lester, *The Mud Turtle* (New York opening: 20 Aug 1925). Lem Tustine is the son of a Minnesota wheat farmer off for Chicago to sell his father's annual crop, and though caught in a falling market, he meets Kate, who is a waitress in the Windy City, and brings her home as his bride. His father, whose primary ties are to the land which he loves above all else, takes her for a fortune hunter and strongly resents her marriage to his son and belittles her character. Her repeated efforts to win his approval are unsuccessful. A hailstorm necessitates emergency night-harvesting of the crop, and in the confusion the foreman, Lem's brother, hurts his hand in a threshing machine. Coming to have his hand bandaged, he tries to force his attentions on Kate; and though she repulses him, the elder Tustine witnesses the struggle and informs Lem. The foreman threatens to pull out the workers unless Kate will leave with him; she agrees, thinking her marriage is a failure. Lem bests the foreman in a fight and is barely missed by his father's gunfire at the deserting workers. Realizing he has almost killed his son, Tustine relents, and Lem brings back his wife to a humbled and more tolerant father. *Farmers. Farm foremen. Waitresses. Fatherhood. Wheat. Minnesota. Chicago. Oregon. Hailstorms.*

Note: Filmed on locations in Pendleton, Oregon. Working title: *Our Daily Bread.* In the sound version much greater emphasis is placed upon the attempted seduction of the wife by the foreman and the father's antagonism. Following the fight scene, the husband forces the beaten foreman to apologize to his wife and confess that all the advances were on his side. The sequence of the father shooting at his son is missing in the sound version. Murnau was relieved of directorial duties before completion of the film, and the subsequent ending, along with various "comic relief" scenes interjected throughout, were directed by A. F. "Buddy" Erickson.

THE CITY GONE WILD **F2.0900**

Paramount Famous Lasky Corp. 12 Nov **1927** [c12 Nov 1927; LP24657]. Si; b&w. 35mm. 6 reels, 5,408 ft.

Pres by Adolph Zukor, Jesse L. Lasky. *Dir* James Cruze. *Screenplay* Jules Furthman. *Titl* Herman Mankiewicz. *Story* Charles Furthman, Jules Furthman. *Photog* Bert Glennon.

Cast: Thomas Meighan *(John Phelan)*, Marietta Millner *(Nada Winthrop)*, Louise Brooks *(Snuggles Joy)*, Fred Kohler *(Gunner Gallagher)*, Duke Martin *(Lefty Schroeder)*, Nancy Phillips *(Lefty's girl)*, Wyndham Standing *(Franklin Ames)*, Charles Hill Mailes *(Luther Winthrop)*, King Zany *(bondsman)*, "Gunboat" Smith *(policeman)*.

Crime melodrama. With the outbreak of city gang wars between Gunner Gallagher and Lefty Schroeder, criminal lawyer John Phelan, feared in the underworld, brings temporary peace, while district attorney Franklin Ames investigates. Nada Winthrop, daughter of a powerful capitalist, is sought by both men. Though Nada loves John, she disapproves of his criminal practice; and when he frees Gunner Gallagher on bail, she announces her engagement to Ames. When Ames discovers that her father is the secret brain of the underworld activities and Winthrop has him killed, John takes the district attorneyship to avenge his friend. Snuggles, Gunner's girl, threatens to inform on Winthrop unless John releases Gunner, and he concedes; John is about to resign when Snuggles, rejected by her man, confesses. *Gangsters. Lawyers. District attorneys. Gangs.*

CITY OF PURPLE DREAMS (Famous Authors) **F2.0901**

Trem Carr Productions. *Dist* Rayart Pictures. 1 Sep **1928.** Si; b&w. 35mm. 6 reels, 5,804 or 5,937 ft.

Pres by W. Ray Johnston. *Dir* Duke Worne. *Scen* George Pyper. *Photog* Walter Griffin. *Film Ed* J. S. Harrington.

Cast: Barbara Bedford *(Esther Strom)*, Robert Frazer *(Daniel Randolph)*, David Torrence *(Symington Otis)*, Jacqueline Gadsdon *(Kathleen Otis)*, Paul Panzer *("Slug" Nikolay)*, Jack Carlisle *(Kelly)*, Henry Roquemore *(Quigg)*.

Drama. Source: Edwin Baird, *City of Purple Dreams* (Chicago, 1913). Through sheer determination mill workman Daniel Randolph realizes his dreams of becoming a financial power in the wheat market and wins the love of social worker Esther Strom, the daughter of the wheat king. *Social workers. Financiers. Ambition. Wheat. Chicago.*

CITY OF SILENT MEN **F2.0902**

Famous Players–Lasky. *Dist* Paramount Pictures. 1 May **1921** [c29 Apr 1921; LP16434]. Si; b&w. 35mm. 6 reels, 6,326 ft.

Pres by Jesse L. Lasky. *Dir* Tom Forman. *Scen* Frank Condon. *Photog* Harry Perry.

Cast: Thomas Meighan *(Jim Montgomery)*, Lois Wilson *(Molly Bryant)*, Kate Bruce *(Mrs. Montgomery)*, Paul Everton *("Old Bill")*, George MacQuarrie *("Mike" Kearney)*, Guy Oliver *(Mr. Bryant)*.

Crime melodrama. Source: John A. Moroso, *The Quarry* (Boston, 1913). Smalltown boy Jim Montgomery is framed by a pair of burglars, arrested for murder, and sentenced to Sing Sing for life. There he makes friends with "Old Bill," his cellmate. When news arrives of Jim's mother's illness, Bill helps him escape, and after attending her funeral Jim goes to California. He becomes an officer in a prosperous company and falls in love with the owner's daughter, Molly Bryant. Despite his past she believes him to be innocent, and they are married. A detective finds Jim but decides to leave matters as they stand; later, he is cleared by a criminal's last-minute confession. *Filial relations. Injustice. Prisons. Sing Sing. California.*

Note: Copyright title: *The City of Silent Men.*

THE CITY THAT NEVER SLEEPS **F2.0903**

Famous Players–Lasky. *Dist* Paramount Pictures. ca28 Sep **1924** [New York premiere; released 1 Dec; c31 Oct 1924; LP20737]. Si; b&w. 35mm. 6 reels, 6,097 ft.

Pres by Adolph Zukor, Jesse L. Lasky. *Dir* James Cruze. *Scen* Walter Woods, Anthony Coldeway. *Photog* Karl Brown.

Cast: Louise Dresser *(Mother O'Day)*, Ricardo Cortez *(Mark Roth)*, Kathlyn Williams *(Mrs. Kendall)*, Virginia Lee Corbin *(Molly Kendall)*, Pierre Gendron *(Cliff Kelley)*, James Farley *(Mike)*, Ben Hendricks *(Tim O'Day)*, Vondell Darr *(Baby Molly)*.

Melodrama. Source: Leroy Scott, "Mother O'Day," in *McCall's Magazine* (51:10–12, Jul 1924). Mother O'Day continues to run her Bowery saloon after her husband, Tim, is killed in a barroom brawl, but wishing a better environment for her daughter, Molly, she has her placed in the home of Mrs. Kendall, a refined society woman. Years later, in the prohibition era, Mother O'Day's saloon has become a cabaret frequented by Molly—now a selfish, snobbish flapper—and her set, which includes adventurer Mark Roth. Mother O'Day knows Roth to be a crook and with the aid of reporter Cliff Kelley, Molly's childhood sweetheart, exposes him to Molly, who finally recognizes her mother and is gladly reunited with her. *Flappers. Reporters. Adventurers. Motherhood. Cabarets. Saloons. Prohibition. New York City—Bowery.*

CIVILIZATION (Reissue) **F2.0904**

Thomas H. Ince Corp. *Dist* American Trading Association. 10 Oct **1930** [New York State license]. Mus score & talking sequences (Chromotone); b&w. 35mm. 7 reels, 6,665 ft.

Note: The 1916 film with some alteration, in both English and Spanish versions. As if the film were a radio program, it is introduced by a short discussion of civilization and includes song interludes.

CLANCY IN WALL STREET **F2.0905**

Edward Small Productions. *Dist* Aristocrat Pictures. 15 Mar **1930.** Sd (Photophone); b&w. 35mm. 8 reels, 7,127 ft.

Dir Ted Wilde. *Dial* William Francis Dugan. *Story* Ralph Bell, Jack Wagner. *Photog* Harry Jackson. *Art Dir* Charles Cadwallader. *Film Ed* Phil Cahn. *Sd* Jack Gregor.

Cast: Charles Murray *(Michael Clancy)*, Aggie Herring *(Mrs. Clancy)*, Lucien Littlefield *(Andy MacIntosh)*, Edward Nugent *(Donald MacIntosh)*, Miriam Seegar *(Katie Clancy)*, Reed Howes *(Freddie Saunders)*.

Comedy. While measuring pipe in the stock exchange, plumber Michael Clancy accidentally buys some stock and makes a quick $200 on a 20 percent margin. Clancy wishes to pursue this line of moneymaking, though his thrifty partner, Andy MacIntosh, refuses to participate. Clancy makes a fortune, leaves his business, and moves uptown. Making ludicrous attempts to enter high society, Clancy snubs MacIntosh and urges his daughter, Katie, to reject the MacIntosh son in favor of Freddie Saunders. Katie leaves home, the stock market crashes, and Clancy—a sadder but wiser man—returns to a forgiving MacIntosh. *Plumbers. Businessmen. Partnerships. Wealth. Stock market. Snobbery. Social classes. New York City—Wall Street.*

CLANCY'S KOSHER WEDDING **F2.0906**

R-C Pictures. *Dist* Film Booking Offices of America. 17 Sep **1927** [c19 Aug 1927; LP24310]. Si; b&w. 35mm. 6 reels, 5,700 ft.

Pres by Joseph P. Kennedy. *Dir* Arvid E. Gillstrom. *Screenplay* J. G. Hawks. *Adapt* Curtis Benton, Gilbert Pratt. *Story* Al Boasberg. *Ch Camera* Charles Boyle. *Asst Dir* Ken Marr.

Cast: George Sidney *(Hyman Cohen)*, Will Armstrong *(Timothy Clancy)*, Ann Brody *(Mamma Cohen)*, Mary Gordon *(Molly Clancy)*, Sharon Lynn *(Leah Cohen)*, Rex Lease *(Tom Clancy)*, Ed Brady *(Izzy Murphy)*.

Comedy. Hyman Cohen and Tim Clancy are established as proprietors of adjacent clothing stores, and each resents the fact that their children, Leah and Tom, are exceedingly fond of each other, the Cohens favoring Izzy Murphy, a Jewish prizefighter. At a picnic, Izzy and Tom engage in combat, agreeing that the loser will surrender Leah's hand; and Tim and Hyman wager their savings on the fight. Leah, told that Tom's probable victory will cause her father to lose everything, tries to persuade Tom to desist; but learning of his father's wager, he topples Izzy. The Cohens are dispossessed, and Hyman is forced to become a peddler; missing their old friends, the Clancys take them in as equal partners in business. *Prizefighters. Irish. Jews. Peddlers. Partnerships. Clothing business. Wagers.*

CLARENCE **F2.0907**

Famous Players–Lasky. *Dist* Paramount Pictures. 15 Oct **1922** [New York premiere; released 19 Nov; c14 Oct 1922; LP18328]. Si; b&w. 35mm. 7 reels, 6,146 ft.

Pres by Adolph Zukor. *Dir* William C. De Mille. *Adapt-Scen* Clara Beranger. *Photog* Guy Wilky.

Cast: Wallace Reid *(Clarence Smith)*, Agnes Ayres *(Violet Pinney)*, May McAvoy *(Cora Wheeler)*, Kathlyn Williams *(Mrs. Wheeler)*, Edward Martindel *(Mr. Wheeler)*, Robert Agnew *(Bobby Wheeler)*, Adolphe Menjou *(Hubert Stem)*, Bertram Johns *(Dinwiddie)*, Dorothy Gordon *(Della)*, Mayme Kelso *(Mrs. Martin)*.

High comedy. Source: Booth Tarkington, *Clarence; a Comedy in Four Acts* (New York, 1921). Mr. Wheeler, the head of a temperamental family, hires a former soldier, Clarence, to do odd jobs around his house. Clarence immediately falls in love with Violet Pinney, the governess, who is suspected by Mrs. Wheeler to be the object of her husband's affections and resented by Cora. When Clarence and Violet prevent Cora from eloping with money-seeking Hubert Stem, Mr. Wheeler's private secretary, Stem finds a clipping about Charles Smith, a deserter. He shows it to Mr. Wheeler and insists that Charles Smith and Clarence are one and the same. Wheeler is inclined to believe Stem, since he has noticed his wife's admiring glances toward Clarence. But a letter arrives revealing Clarence to be a university professor about to regain his position; Violet accepts him, and all are reconciled. *Veterans. Governesses. Professors. Secretaries. Family life.*

CLASH OF THE WOLVES **F2.0908**

Warner Brothers Pictures. 17 Nov **1925** [New York premiere; released 28 Nov; c26 Oct 1925; LP21953]. Si; b&w. 35mm. 7 reels, 6,800 ft.

Dir Noel Mason Smith. *Story-Scen* Charles A. Logue. *Photog* Joe Walker. *Film Ed* Clarence Kolster.

Cast: Rin-Tin-Tin *(Lobo, leader of the wolves)*, June Marlowe *(May Barstowe)*, Charles Farrell *(Dave Weston)*, Heinie Conklin *(Alkali Bill)*, Will Walling *(Sam Barstowe)*, Pat Hartigan *(Borax Horton)*.

Western melodrama. Lobo, half dog and half wolf, is the leader of a wolf pack, and the ranchers have put a price on his head. David Weston, a young borax prospector, befriends him after removing a thorn from his paw. Dave and his sweetheart, May Barstowe, disguise Lobo with beard and boots. He repays his new master's kindness by defending him against the attacks of chemist Borax Horton, who covets Dave's claim and sweetheart. When Horton attacks Dave again and leaves him for dead, Lobo takes a message from Dave to May. On the way, he successfully evades a posse that is hunting him and at the same time decoys it to Dave. Lobo kills Horton, and the ranchers learn that Lobo is man's friend. Dave and May get married, and Lobo settles down with them. *Prospectors. Chemists. Ranchers. Posses. Borax. Disguise. Wolves. Dogs.*

CLASSIFIED **F2.0909**

Corinne Griffith Productions. *Dist* First National Pictures. 11 Oct **1925** [c28 Sep 1925; LP21856]. Si; b&w. 35mm. 7 reels, 6,927 ft.

Dir Alfred Santell. *Dial Dir* Perry Ivins. *Ed Dir–Screenplay* June Mathis. *Titl* Ralph Spence. *Photog* Harold Rosson. *Art Dir* E. J. Shulter. *Film Ed* Cyril Gardner. *Asst Dir* Scott R. Beal.

Cast: Corinne Griffith *(Babs Comet)*, Jack Mulhall *(Lloyd Whiting)*, Ward Crane *(Spencer Clark)*, Carroll Nye *(Mart Comet)*, Charles Murray *(Old Man Comet)*, Edythe Chapman *("Maw" Comet)*, Jacqueline Wells *(Jeanette)*, George Sidney *(Weinstein)*, Bernard Randall *(Bernstein)*.

Comedy. Source: Edna Ferber, "Classified," in *Mother Knows Best* (Garden City, New York, 1927). Babs Comet, whose family lives on the West Side of Manhattan, works in the classified advertising section of a Gotham daily. Determined to put her good looks to use, she flirts openly with every wealthy man she meets. By chance, she meets Lloyd Whiting, a garage owner, and falls in love with him. Angered at Lloyd's failure to keep a date, Babs goes for a ride with wealthy Spencer Clark and ends up walking home from the country. She arrives at her parents' home at 7 o'clock in the morning, and they suspect the worst. Lloyd has faith in her, however, and persuades Clark to explain matters to her parents. The contrite millionaire asks Babs to marry him, but she refuses, telling him that she loves only Lloyd. *Millionaires. Newspapers. Advertising. Garages. New York City.*

CLASSMATES **F2.0910**

Inspiration Pictures. *Dist* First National Pictures. 23 Nov **1924** [c11 Nov 1924; LP20752]. Si; b&w. 35mm. 7 reels, 6,992 ft.

Dir John S. Robertson. *Scen* Josephine Lovett. *Photog* Roy Overbaugh, John F. Seitz. *Settings* Tec-Art Studios. *Film Ed* William Hamilton. *Tech Adv* Major Henry B. Lewis. *West Point scenes by authority of* United States Military Academy. *Art Titl* H. E. R. Studios.

Cast: Claude Brooke *(Duncan Irving, Sr.)*, Richard Barthelmess *(Duncan Irving, Jr.)*, Charlotte Walker *(Mrs. Stafford)*, Madge Evans *(Sylvia, her niece)*, Reginald Sheffield *(Bert Stafford, her son)*, Beach Cooke *("Bubby" Dumble)*, James Bradbury, Jr. *("Silent" Clay)*, Major Henry B. Lewis *(Major Lane, officer in charge)*, Richard Harlan *(a halfbreed)*, Chief Tony Tommy *(an Indian guide)*, Antrim Short *(Jones)*, Herbert Corthell *(drummer)*.

Drama. Source: Margaret Turnbull and William C. De Mille, *Classmates; a Play in Four Acts* (New York opening: 29 Aug 1907). Duncan Irving, Jr., a poor boy from a small southern town who loves aristocratic Syliva Randolph, receives an appointment to West Point. In Duncan's final year Sylvia's cousin, Bert Stafford, also enters the academy and resents having to take orders from upperclassman Duncan, whom Bert considers his social inferior. Duncan finally strikes Bert in retaliation for his many insults and consequently is expelled from the Point. When Bert is lost in the jungles of South America, Duncan heads an expedition to rescue his enemy, who finally divulges the truth. Duncan is reinstated at the academy and marries Sylvia upon his graduation. *Southerners. Cadets. Social classes. Jungles. South America. United States Military Academy.*

Note: Major Henry B. Lewis is identified in the film as Adjutant of the Military Academy.

THE CLAW (Universal-Jewel) **F2.0911**

Universal Pictures. 9 May **1927** [New York premiere; released 12 Jun; c20 Apr 1927; LP23883]. Si; b&w. 35mm. 6 reels, 5,252 ft.

Pres by Carl Laemmle. *Dir* Sidney Olcott. *Adapt* Charles A. Logue. *Photog* John Stumar.

Cast: Norman Kerry *(Maurice Stair)*, Claire Windsor *(Dierdre Saurin)*, Arthur Edmund Carewe *(Maj. Anthony Kinsella)*, Tom Guise *(Marquis of Stair)*, Helene Sullivan *(Judy Saurin)*, Nelson McDowell *(Scout Mac Bourney)*, Larry Steers *(Captain Rockwood)*, J. Gordon Russell *(Wagon-driver)*, Myrta Bonillas *(Saba Rockwood)*, Jacques D'Auray *(Richard Saurin)*, Pauline Neff *(Nonie Valetta)*, Bertram Johns *(Dr. Harriatt)*, Billie Bennett *(Mrs. Harriatt)*, Annie Ryan *(Mrs. Mac Bourney)*, Dick Sutherland *(Chief Logenbuela)*.

Romantic drama. Source: Cynthia Stockley, *The Claw* (New York, 1911). Dierdre Saurin, an English girl, becomes infatuated with Major Kinsella while he is on leave to England from his post in East Africa, and when he returns to duty she follows on the pretext of seeing her brother. Maurice Stair, son of the marquis and insanely jealous of Dierdre, is sent to the village by his father and plans revenge. Dierdre refuses to drop Kinsella even when she learns he is married. The major organizes his men to meet a horde of warring Africans on the veldt, while Maurice remains at the settlement; he convinces Dierdre that Kinsella has been killed in the battle, and she finally marries him. Maurice ultimately confesses his deception and after great hardship rescues Kinsella; Dierdre realizes her love for Maurice. *Brother-sister relationship. Revenge. England. East Africa. Great Britain—Army.*

CLAY DOLLARS **F2.0912**

Selznick Pictures. *Dist* Select Pictures. 20 Oct **1921** [c8 Oct 1921; LP17089]. Si; b&w. 35mm. 5 reels.

Pres by Lewis J. Selznick. *Dir* George Archainbaud. *Story-Scen* Lewis Allen Browne. *Photog* Jules Cronjager.

Cast: Eugene O'Brien *(Bruce Edwards)*, Ruth Dwyer *(June Gordon)*, Frank Currier *(Sam Willetts)*, Arthur Houseman *(Ben Willetts)*, Jim Tenbrooke *(Lafe Gordon)*, Florida Kingsley *(Mrs. Gordon)*, Tom Burke *(Buck Jones)*, Jerry Devine *(Peter)*, Bruce Reynolds *(village cut-up)*.

Comedy-melodrama. Bruce Edwards returns to his hometown to take possession of an estate willed him by his father but finds that according to documentary proof exhibited by Squire Willetts the estate has been traded for worthless swampland by his father. Bruce takes a job in the village tavern and romances June Gordon, whose mother suspects Willetts of foul play; he is falsely accused of theft by the squire but escapes and not only makes the squire believe that the swampland is valuable for manufacturing purposes but succeeds in regaining his rightful estate. He and June then leave for their honeymoon. *Swindlers. Smalltown life. Inheritance. Marshes. Documentation.*

THE CLEAN HEART **F2.0913**

Vitagraph Co. of America. ca15 Sep **1924** [New York premiere; released 26 Oct; c16 Sep 1924; LP20583]. Si; b&w. 35mm. 8 reels, 8,000 ft.

Pres by Albert E. Smith. *Dir* J. Stuart Blackton. *Scen* Marian Constance. *Photog* Stephen Smith, Jr.

Cast: Percy Marmont *(Philip Wriford)*, Otis Harlan *(Puddlebox)*, Marguerite De La Motte *(Essie Bickers)*, Andrew Arbuckle *(Bickers)*, Martha Petelle *(Mrs. Bickers)*, Violet La Plante *(Brida)*, George Ingleton, Anna Lockhardt.

Drama. Source: Arthur Stuart-Menteth Hutchinson, *The Clean Heart* (Boston, 1914). Newspaper editor and successful novelist Philip Wriford suffers a mental breakdown from overwork and worry over having to support orphaned children. To get away from the "other self" he imagines is following him, he wanders into the country and befriends Puddlebox, a philosophical tramp, who sacrifices his own life to save Philip. While recovering in a hospital, he meets Essie, a simple and romantic girl, who eventually restores him to health and happiness. *Philosophers. Novelists. Editors. Tramps. Orphans. Mental illness.*

THE CLEAN UP **F2.0914**

Dist Western Feature Productions. Jul **1922.** Si; b&w. 35mm. 5 reels.

Cast: William Fairbanks.

Western melodrama(?). No information about the nature of this film has been found.

THE CLEAN UP **F2.0915**

Universal Pictures. 24 Sep **1923** [c6 Sep 1923; LP19384]. Si; b&w. 35mm. 5 reels, 5,051 ft.

Dir William Parke. *Scen* Harvey Gates, Eugene B. Lewis. *Adapt* Raymond L. Schrock. *Story* H. H. Van Loan. *Photog* Richard Fryer.

Cast: Herbert Rawlinson *(Montgomery Bixby)*, Claire Adams *(Phyllis Andrews)*, Claire Anderson *(Mary Reynolds)*, Herbert Fortier *(Robert Reynolds)*, Margaret Campbell *(Mrs. Reynolds)*, Frank Farrington *(Amos Finderson)*.

Comedy. Monte Bixby's grandfather leaves a will providing each native-born citizen of his small town with $50,000 while giving Monte one dollar. Monte's society fiancée, Mary Reynolds, abandons him, but grandfather Bixby's pretty young secretary, Phyllis Andrews, resolves to help him. Meanwhile life in the town is chaotic as the legatees begin to spend their money. Monte becomes concerned, appoints himself mayor, and restores order. Finally he learns that his inheritance was a trick to teach him the value of money. A real fortune awaits him, and he wins Phyllis. *Mayors. Secretaries. Inheritance. Smalltown life. Wills.*

Note: Working title: *Upside Down.*

THE CLEAN-UP **F2.0916**

Excellent Pictures. 20 Jan **1929** [c11 Feb 1929; LP118]. Si; b&w. 35mm. 6 reels, 5,660 ft.

Pres by Samuel Zierler. *Supv* Burton King. *Dir* Bernard F. McEveety. *Screenplay* Carmelita Sweeney. *Story-Titl* Isadore Bernstein. *Photog* William J. Miller, Walter Haas. *Film Ed* Betty Davis. *Tech Dir* Robert Stevens.

Cast: Charles Delaney *(Oliver Brooks)*, Betty Blake *(Susan Clancy)*, Bruce Gordon *(Hard Boiled Foley)*, Rags *(a dog)*, Lewis Sargent *(Hunch)*, Harry Myers *(Jimmy)*, J. P. McGowan *(Frank Lawrence)*, Charles Hickman *(Captain Clancy)*.

Melodrama. Oliver Brooks, the editor of a newspaper, and Captain Clancy of the metropolitan police set about cleaning up the bootleggers and racketeers who have made the streets of their city unsafe. Foley's gang guns down Clancy, and Brooks and Clancy's sister, Susan, go after Foley. Foley kidnaps Susan, and Brooks rescues her, bringing Foley to justice. *Editors. Police. Bootleggers. Racketeers. Murder. Kidnaping. Dogs.*

THE CLEAN-UP MAN (Universal Thrill Feature) **F2.0917**

Universal Pictures. 12 Feb **1928** [c19 Oct 1927; LP24533]. Si; b&w. 35mm. 5 reels, 4,232 ft.

Pres by Carl Laemmle. *Dir* Ray Taylor. *Story-Cont* George Morgan, Lola D. Moore. *Titl* Gardner Bradford. *Photog* John Hickson, Milton Bridenbecker. *Art Dir* David S. Garber. *Film Ed* Ben Pivar.

Cast: Ted Wells *(Steve Banning or Johnny Parker)*, Peggy O'Day *(Jane Brooks/"Professor" Brooks)*, Henry Hebert *(The Hawk/mysterious stranger)*, George Reed *(Sambo)*, Tom Carter *(sheriff)*.

Western melodrama. Johnny Parker, the new owner of the Banning Ranch, is suspected of being the mysterious "Hawk," a notorious road agent; and determined to clear his name, he and his men disperse bandits from a stage robbery. Banning, who is actually the "Hawk," orders his men to hide in a cave while he changes into his usual ministerial disguise. Jane Brooks, a pretty girl disguised as a bespectacled professor, pretends to be interested in minerology and goes to inspect the caves while Johnny, hearing they are haunted, goes there to satisfy his curiosity. Banning catches her out of disguise, forces her into an automobile, and drives toward the border. Johnny heads off the fugitive and battles Banning in the car to a finish. *Bandits. Professors. Clergymen. Disguise. Stagecoach robberies. Minerology.*

CLEAR THE DECKS (Universal-Jewel) **F2.0918**

Universal Pictures. 3 Mar **1929** [c31 Jan 1929; LP87]. Si; b&w. 35mm. 6 reels, 5,792 ft. [Also si; 5,740 ft.]

Dir Joseph E. Henabery. *Adapt-Cont* Earl Snell, Gladys Lehman. *Titl* Albert De Mond, Charles H. Smith. *Camera* Arthur Todd. *Film Ed* Jack English, B. W. Burton.

Cast: Reginald Denny *(Jack Armitage)*, Olive Hasbrouck *(Miss Bronson)*, Otis Harlan *(Pussyfoot)*, Lucien Littlefield *(Plinge)*, Collette Marten *(Blondie)*, Robert Anderson *(mate)*, Elinor Leslie *(aunt)*, Brooks Benedict *(Trumbull)*.

Romantic comedy. Source: E. J. Rath, *When the Devil Was Sick* (New York, 1926). In order to follow a girl to whom he has been attracted, Jack Armitage embarks on an ocean voyage, using the ticket and assuming the name of a friend who was ordered to take the trip for his health. On the liner, his every attempt to make contact with the girl is thwarted by a male nurse who insists that he remain in his bed and subsist on a diet of goat's milk. But Jack manages to escape from his cabin and in so doing unwittingly assists in the capture of jewel thieves. This act puts him in a favorable light with the girl, the male nurse, and everyone else aboard. *Male nurses. Invalids. Thieves. Ocean liners. Mistaken identity.*

CLEARING THE TRAIL (Universal-Jewel) **F2.0919**

Universal Pictures. 7 Oct **1928** [c10 Jul 1928; LP25453]. Si; b&w. 35mm. 6 reels, 5,311 ft.

Dir Reaves Eason. *Adapt-Scen* John F. Natteford. *Titl* Harold Tarshis. *Story* Charles Maigne. *Photog* Harry Neumann. *Art Dir* David S. Garber. *Film Ed* Gilmore Walker.

Cast: Hoot Gibson *(Pete Watson)*, Dorothy Gulliver *(Ellen)*, Fred Gilman *(Steve Watson)*, Cap Anderson *(Dan Talbot)*, Philo McCullough *(Silk Cardross)*, Andy Waldron *(Judge Price)*, Duke Lee *(cook)*, Monte Montague *(tramp)*, Universal Ranch Riders *(cowboys)*.

Western melodrama. Ex-sheriff Pete Watson comes to Lone Pine to help his brother, Steve, regain their deceased father's ranch, taken over by a murderous gang of horsethieves led by Dan Talbot, owner of a neighboring ranch. Pete gets a job with Talbot and gathers evidence against the gang by establishing a reputation as a bungler. With the assistance of Judge Price, Pete pins a number of crimes on the Talbot gang. Finally, Steve, having rounded up his own boys, engages in a fracas with Talbot and his men and defeats them. Talbot's niece, Ellen, realizes her uncle's perfidy and helps Pete and Steve defeat them; then she returns to Arizona with Pete. *Sheriffs. Brothers. Gangs. Horsethieves. Ranches.*

CLICKING HOOFS **F2.0920**

Dist Truart Film Corp. 27 Feb **1926** [New York State license]. Si; b&w. 35mm. 5 reels.

Western melodrama(?). No information about the nature of this film has been found.

THE CLIMAX **F2.0921**

Universal Pictures. 26 Jan **1930** [c4 Jan 1930; LP978]. Sd (Movietone); b&w. 35mm. 6 reels, 5,846 ft. [Also si; 5,013 ft.]

Pres by Carl Laemmle. *Dir* Renaud Hoffman. *Scen-Adapt* Julian Josephson, Lillian Ducey. *Dial-Titl* Clarence Thompson, Leslie Mason. *Photog* Jerry Ash. *Film Ed* Bernard Burton. *Song: "You, My Melody of Love"* Victor Schertzinger. *Rec Engr* C. Roy Hunter.

Cast: Jean Hersholt *(Luigi Golfanti)*, Kathryn Crawford *(Adella Donatelli)*, LeRoy Mason *(Dr. Gardoni)*, John Reinhardt *(Pietro Golfanti)*, Henry Armetta *(Anton Donatelli)*.

Romantic melodrama. Source: Edward Locke, *The Climax* (London opening: 5 Mar 1910). Adella, a beautiful young Italian girl, aspires to achieve the operatic fame of her mother; and her grandfather, Anton, arranges for her to study under Luigi Golfanti, who coached her mother. While studying with Luigi, she and his son, Pietro, fall in love, and Pietro writes a love song for her. Luigi arranges for her to sing for Bellini, an American impresario; but she goes to her grandfather's deathbed, then sings for Bellini, who suggests a slight operation to improve her voice. Luigi sacrifices to have the surgery performed, but Dr. Gardoni, jealous of Pietro, sprays her throat with a medicine that causes her to lose her voice entirely; Luigi persuades Pietro to give her up in Gardoni's favor. At the wedding ceremony, Pietro plays on the organ the love song he composed for her; and overcome, Adella regains her voice and breaks into song. Conscience-stricken, Gardoni leaves the church. *Singers. Composers. Physicians. Italians. Impresari. Marriage. Opera.*

THE CLIMBERS **F2.0922**

Warner Brothers Pictures. 14 May **1927** [c7 May 1927; LP23936]. Si; b&w. 35mm. 7 reels, 6,631 ft.

Dir Paul L. Stein. *Screenplay* Tom Gibson. *Camera* Frank Kesson. *Asst Dir* George Webster.

Cast: Irene Rich *(Duchess of Arrogan)*, Clyde Cook *(Pancho Mendoza)*, Forrest Stanley *(Duke Córdova/El Blanco)*, Flobelle Fairbanks *(Laska, the Duchess' daughter)*, Myrna Loy *(Countess Veya)*, Anders Randolf *(Martínez)*, Dot Farley *(Juana, the Duchess' maid)*, Rosemary Cooper *(Queen)*, Nigel Barrie *(Duke of Arrogan)*, Joseph Striker *(Ensign Carlos)*, Hector Sarno *(Miguel)*, Max Barwyn *(King Ferdinand VII)*, Martha Franklin *(Clotilda)*.

Romantic melodrama. Source: Clyde Fitch, *The Climbers* (a play; New York, 1905.). At the court of King Ferdinand VII of Spain, the Duke of Arrogan [*sic*], Prime Minister, carries on a liaison with the Countess Veya, a climber seeking favor in high places. The countess, jealous of the duke's wife, plots to disgrace her in the eyes of the king by having Córdova, a political prisoner, hidden in the duchess' boudoir; as a result, both victims are exiled to Porto Rico. The duchess, swearing vengeance on all men, becomes cruel and ruthless, amassing great wealth on her plantation, while Córdova gains notoriety as El Blanco, a pillaging bandit, who begins an affair with the duchess and prevents a riot of the workers on her rancho. Laska, her daughter, commanded to wed the dissolute Prince Treván, escapes to join her mother upon the death of her father. After a battle with the bandits, who have captured Laska, the duchess is reunited with her daughter and Córdova. *Nobility. Bandits. Treason. Revenge. Puerto Rico. Spain. Ferdinand VII (Spain).*

THE CLINGING VINE **F2.0923**

De Mille Pictures. *Dist* Producers Distributing Corp. 6 Sep **1926** [c21 Jul 1926; LP22929]. Si; b&w. 35mm. 7 reels, 6,400 ft.

Supv C. Gardner Sullivan. *Dir* Paul Sloane. *Screenplay* Jack Jevne. *Titl* John Krafft. *Adapt* Rex Taylor. *Photog* Arthur Miller. *Art Dir* Max Parker. *Asst Dir* William Scully.

Cast: Leatrice Joy *(Antoinette Allen)*, Tom Moore *(Jimmy Bancroft)*, Toby Claude *(Grandma Bancroft)*, Robert Edeson *(T. M. Bancroft)*, Dell Henderson *(B. Harvey Phillips)*, Snitz Edwards *(A. Tutweiler)*.

Comedy. Source: Zelda Sears, *The Clinging Vine* (New York, c1922; New York opening: 25 Dec 1922). Antoinette Allen, secretary to T. M. Bancroft, president of a paint company, is the actual brains of the organization; known as A. B., she buys an option on a deposit of "emeraldite," a previously imported mineral, without bothering to consult the board of directors. Bancroft's grandson, Jimmy, who dislikes A. B.'s mannish qualities and hopes to get rich on a patented egg beater, is informed by A. B. that he is fired. When her employer is taken ill, A. B., now nicknamed Ann, is induced by Grandma to feminize herself and flirt with men, and Jimmy falls in love with her. Phillips, a swindler, induces several people to invest in "emeraldite," on which he claims an option, but Ann forces Bancroft to invest in his son's egg beater and manages to save Jimmy's money by playing Phillips off against Bancroft. *Secretaries. Businesswomen. Flirts. Swindlers. Mannishness. Inventions. Paint.*

CLOSE HARMONY **F2.0924**

Paramount Famous Lasky Corp. 13 Apr **1929** [c12 Apr 1929; LP304]. Sd (Movietone); b&w. 35mm. 7 reels, 6,271 ft.

Dir John Cromwell, Edward Sutherland. *Dial* John V. A. Weaver, Percy Heath. *Adapt* Percy Heath. *Story* Elsie Janis, Gene Markey. *Photog* J. Roy Hunt. *Film Ed* Tay Malarkey. *Songs: "She's So, I Dunno," "I Want To Go Places and Do Things," "I'm All A-twitter, I'm All A-twirl"* Richard A. Whiting, Leo Robin. *Ch Rec Engr* Franklin Hansen.

Cast: Charles (Buddy) Rogers *(Al West)*, Nancy Carroll *(Marjorie Merwin)*, Harry Green *(Max Mindel)*, Jack Oakie *(Ben Barney)*, Richard "Skeets" Gallagher *(Johnny Bey)*, Matty Roubert *(Bert)*, Ricca Allen *(Mrs. Prosser)*, Wade Boteler *(Kelly, the cop)*, Baby Mack *(Sybil, the maid)*, Oscar Smith *(George Washington Brown)*, Greta Granstedt *(Eva Larue)*, Gus Partos *(Gustav)*, Jesse Stafford and His Orchestra.

Musical comedy-drama. Marjorie, a song-and-dance girl in the stage show of a palatial movie theater, becomes interested in Al West, a warehouse clerk who has put together an unusual jazz band, and uses her influence to get him a place on one of the programs. Max Mindel, the house manager, has a yen for Marjorie and, discovering that she is in love with Al, gives the band notice and hires harmony singers Barney & Bey as a replacement. Marjorie makes up to both men and soon breaks up the team. Al learns of her scheme, however, and makes her confess to the singers. Barney and Bey make up, and Max gives Al and his band one more chance. Al is a sensation, and Max offers him a contract for $1,000 a week. *Singers. Dancers. Band leaders. Clerks. Motion picture theaters.*

CLOSED DOORS **F2.0925**

Vitagraph Co. of America. Jul **1921** [c27 May 1921; LP16590]. Si; b&w. 35mm. 5 reels.

Dir G. V. Seyffertitz. *Scen* William B. Courtney. *Story* Harry Dittmar. *Photog* Arthur Ross.

Cast: Alice Calhoun *(Dorothy Brainerd)*, Harry C. Browne *(Jim Ranson)*, Bernard Randall *(Rex Gordon)*, A. J. Herbert *(Muffler Mike)*, Betty Burwell *(Jane)*, Charles Brook *(Dan Syrles)*.

Melodrama. When Dan Syrles kills a man who threatens to break up his marriage, Jim Ranson, who believes in the sanctity of the home, helps him escape. Years later, Jim, rising to power and wealth in an eastern city, marries Dorothy, his best friend's daughter, but while he is increasingly involved with business she becomes lonely. While motoring, she meets Rex Gordon, a clever crook who woos her, but when rejected he plots to steal her jewels. Warned of the affair, Ranson sets a trap for Gordon but is prevented from murder by Syrles, posing as a detective. Ranson admits his mistake and is reconciled to his wife. *Businessmen. Thieves. Marriage. Infidelity.*

CLOSED GATES **F2.0926**

Sterling Pictures. 1 Jun **1927** [cJun 1927; LP24050]. Si; b&w. 35mm. 6 reels, 5,503 ft.

Dir Phil Rosen. *Scen* Frances Guihan. *Story* Manfred B. Lee. *Photog* Herbert Kirkpatrick.

Cast: Johnny Harron *(George Newell, Jr.)*, Jane Novak *(Alice Winston)*, Lucy Beaumont *(Mary Newell)*, Sidney De Grey *(George Newell, Sr.)*, LeRoy Mason *(Harvey Newell)*, Rosemary Cooper *(Martha Roberts)*, Ruth Handforth *(Bridget)*, Bud Jamison *(Pat)*.

Melodrama. George Newell, Jr., son of a millionaire, is a constant source of worry to his father and invalid mother. When he is injured in an automobile accident and his girl companion is killed, his mother dies of the shock and Newell, Sr., sends him from home. George goes to war and loses his memory as a result of shell shock. Alice Winston, a nurse, brings him back to health, and their friendship develops into love and marriage. He collapses from overwork while working in a shipyard, and Alice takes him to a sanitarium. While convalescing he is recognized by Newell and his nephew, Harvey; they fail to acknowledge the fact, however, to avoid changing the family will. But through Bridget, the maid, Alice brings George back home, and in his mother's room the sight of the wheelchair restores his memory; he then is reconciled with his father. *Millionaires. Invalids. Housemaids. Amnesia. Shell shock. Fatherhood. Personal identity. Sanitariums. World War I.*

CLOSEUPS OF CHINA **F2.0927**

Burton Holmes Lectures. 20 Mar **1927.** Si; b&w. 35mm. 5 reels.

Travelog. No information about the precise nature of this film has been found. *China.*

CLOTHES **F2.0928**

Cunninghams: Photographers of Commerce. 22 Oct **1924** [New York State license]. Si; b&w. 35mm. 4 reels.

Cast: James O'Leary, Doris C. Mallory.

Comedy(?). No information about the precise nature of this film has been found. *Clothes.*

CLOTHES MAKE THE PIRATE **F2.0929**

Sam E. Rork Productions. *Dist* First National Pictures. 29 Nov **1925** [c23 Nov 1925; LP22025]. Si; b&w. 35mm. 9 reels, 8,000 ft.

Pres by Sam E. Rork. *Supv-Adapt-Scen* Marion Fairfax. *Dir* Maurice Tourneur. *Photog* Henry Cronjager, Louis Dunmyre. *Art Dir* Charles O. Seessel. *Tech Dir* Jack Pringle. *Film Ed* Patricia Rooney. *Asst Dir* Ben Silvey.

Cast: Leon Errol *(Tremble-at-Evil Tidd)*, Dorothy Gish *(Betsy Tidd, his wife)*, Nita Naldi *(Madame De La Tour)*, George F. Marion *(Jennison, first mate on pirate ship)*, Tully Marshall *(Scute, The Baker)*, Frank Lawler *(Crabb, The Innkeeper)*, Edna Murphy *(Nancy Downs)*, James Rennie *(Lieutenant Cavendish)*, Walter Law *(Dixie Bull, The Pirate)*, Reginald Barlow *(Captain Montague)*.

Adventure burlesque. Source: Holman Francis Day, *Clothes Make the Pirate* (New York, 1925). Tremble-at-Evil Tidd, a henpecked Boston tailor of the 1750's, is ridiculed by his neighbors for his timidity. He dreams of being a pirate on the Spanish Main; one night, he dresses up as a pirate, scaring his wife and alarming the neighbors. Tidd hides out in a rowboat where he is mistaken by buccaneers for Dixie Bull, a notorious pirate. Tidd takes command of the pirate vessel, where he finds Scute and other neighbors who have joined the crew to seek their fortune; because of his disguise, however, they do not recognize him. He defeats a British frigate, and for the first time in his life he asserts himself and has the captured women turned over to him. In an attack on a small town, Tidd captures the real Dixie Bull and becomes a hero in the eyes of his wife and all Boston. *Tailors. Pirates. Bakers. Boston. Spanish Main. United States—History—Colonial period.*

CLOTHES MAKE THE WOMAN **F2.0930**

Tiffany-Stahl Productions. 1 May **1928** [c3 May 1928; LP25203]. Si; b&w. 35mm. 6 reels, 5,209 ft.

Dir-Writ Tom Terriss. *Titl* Lesley Mason. *Photog* Chester Lyons. *Art Dir* Hervey Libbert. *Set Dsgn* George Sawley. *Film Ed* Desmond O'Brien.

Cast: Eve Southern *(Princess Anastasia)*, Walter Pidgeon *(Victor Trent)*, Charles Byer *(The Director)*, George E. Stone *(Assistant Director)*, Adolph Millar *(Bolshevik leader)*, Duncan Renaldo, Gordon Begg, Catherine Wallace, Corliss Palmer, Margaret Selby, H. D. Pennell.

Romantic drama. Princess Anastasia of Russia is saved from execution by a young revolutionary who risks his life to help her escape. Years later they meet in Hollywood. Overnight he has become Victor Trent, a popular movie star, and she, having been discovered among the extras, is hired to play the part she once lived. Trent accidentally shoots Anastasia in a reenactment of the execution of the czar with his family, but she recovers and they marry. *Actors. Motion pictures. Russia—History—1917–21 Revolution. Hollywood. Romanov dynasty. Grand Duchess Anastasia.*

THE CLOUD DODGER **F2.0931**

Universal Pictures. 30 Sep **1928** [c28 Dec 1927, 9 May 1928; LP25232, LP24812]. Si; b&w. 35mm. 5 reels, ca4,200 ft.

Dir Bruce Mitchell. *Titl* Gardner Bradford. *Story-Adapt* William B. Lester. *Photog* William Adams. *Film Ed* Jack Bruggy.

Cast: Al Wilson *(Al Williams)*, Gloria Grey *(Sylvia LeMoyne)*, Joe O'Brien *(Stanton Stevens)*, Julia Griffith *(Mrs. LeMoyne/Aunt Myrtle)*, Gilbert "Pee Wee" Holmes *(Joe Merriman)*, George Chandler *(Post Commander)*.

Comedy-drama. Al Williams, an aviator whose sweetheart has left him for Stanton Stevens, a wealthy clubman, interrupts their wedding and chases them in his plane. Climbing onto Stanton's plane, Williams snatches Sylvia from her seat and transfers her to his plane, fully equipped with a minister and witnesses. *Aviators. Airplanes. Abduction. Weddings. Chases. Air stunts.*

THE CLOUD RIDER **F2.0932**

Van Pelt–Wilson Productions. *Dist* Film Booking Offices of America. 15 Feb **1925** [c5 1925; LP21101]. Si; b&w. 35mm. 5 reels, 5,070 ft.

Supv Ernest Van Pelt. *Dir* Bruce Mitchell. *Scen* L. V. Jefferson. *Story* Al Wilson. *Photog* Lige Zerr.

Cast: Al Wilson *(Bruce Torrence)*, Virginia Lee Corbin *(Blythe Wingate)*, Harry von Meter *(Juan Lascelles)*, Helen Ferguson *(Zella Wingate)*, Frank Rice *(Hank Higgins)*, Melbourne MacDowell *(David Torrence)*, Brinsley Shaw *(Peter Wingate)*, Frank Tomick, Boyd Monteith, Frank Clark *(pilots)*.

Melodrama. Bruce Torrence, an aviator and Secret Service agent, is assigned to bring to justice Juan Lascelles, who owns a fleet of airplanes used to smuggle drugs. Suspecting Bruce's purposes, Juan loosens the wheel on Bruce's plane, intending for him to crash; but Zella Wingate, a girl in whom both men are interested, takes the plane up instead of Bruce. Bruce sees the wheel fall off, straps a spare to his back, gives aerial chase to her plane, transfers to it in midair, and bolts the spare wheel in place. Bruce later discovers Zella in Juan's embrace and quickly realizes that he is really in love with Zella's sister, Blythe. Bruce and Blythe are kidnaped by Juan, who takes Blythe off in his plane. Bruce frees himself and gives chase. Blythe tampers with the controls of Juan's plane, and it crashes into the ocean. Bruce jumps into the water from his plane, captures Juan, and rescues the girl. Bruce and Blythe are married and leave on an aerial honeymoon. *Sisters. Secret service. Aviation. Smuggling. Narcotics. Air stunts.*

CLOUDBURST **F2.0933**

Dist Lee-Bradford Corp. Feb **1922.** Si; b&w. 35mm. 5 reels, 4,800 ft.

Cast: Billy Wells.

Melodrama(?). No information about the nature of this film has been found.

A CLOUDED MIND *see* **A CLOUDED NAME**

A CLOUDED NAME **F2.0934**

Logan Productions. *Dist* Playgoers Pictures. 18 Feb **1923** [c17 Feb 1923; LU18681]. Si; b&w. 35mm. 5 reels, 4,885 ft.

Dir Austin O. Huhn. *Story* Tom Bret. *Photog* Jean Logan.

Cast: Norma Shearer *(Marjorie Dare)*, Gladden James *(Jim Allen)*, Yvonne Logan *(Smiles)*, Richard Neill *(Stewart Leighton)*, Charles Miller

(Sam Slocum), Frederick Eckhart *(Ben Tangleface)*.

Melodrama. To avoid seeing Marjorie Dare, Jim Allen visits Stewart Leighton at the latter's country home. (Five years earlier Jim's engagement to Marjorie Dare was broken when her mother was killed and his father disappeared.) Through certain circumstance Marjorie also becomes Leighton's guest, and Jim moves out into the woods. There he meets Smiles, a little girl in the care of strange old Ben Tangleface. Leighton wishes to wed Marjorie for her money and is trying forcefully to persuade her to accept him when Jim comes to the rescue. But Ben, his memory stirred by the sight of Leighton, kills him. Explanations reveal Smiles to be Dorothy's sister and Ben, Jim's father. He was wounded while defending Marjorie's mother, whom Leighton killed. *Sisters. Filial relations. Murder. Personal identity.*

Note: Also reviewed as *A Clouded Mind.*

THE CLOWN F2.0935

Columbia Pictures. 20 Jun **1927** [c29 Jun 1927; LP24133]. Si; b&w. 35mm. 6 reels, 5,470 ft.

Prod Harry Cohn. *Dir* William James Craft. *Cont* Harry O. Hoyt. *Story* Dorothy Howell. *Photog* Norbert Brodin.

Cast: Dorothy Revier *(Fanchon)*, Johnnie Walker *(Bob Stone)*, William V. Mong *(Albert Wells)*, John Miljan *(Bert Colton)*, Barbara Tennant *(Corinne)*, Charlotte Walker.

Melodrama. Circus owner Albert Wells, after inspecting the animal tents during a storm, returns to find his wife, Corinne, in the arms of lion tamer Bert Colton, and in the ensuing struggle Corinne is accidentally killed. Wells is arrested on Colton's accusation, is tried, and is sentenced to life imprisonment for murder. His child, Fanchon, grows up to become an aerial star, believing her parents are dead. Wealthy young Bob Stone loves her—to the disapproval of Colton. Wells sees her at a prison performance and escapes in a clown disguise; when Colton plots to break up the lovers' engagement, Wells turns a lion on him; he then rescues Fanchon from the path of an elephant stampede but is himself killed. *Clowns. Trapezists. Lion tamers. Circus. Parentage. Disguise. Injustice. Prisons. Stampedes. Elephants.*

THE CO-RESPONDENT *see* **THE WHISPERED NAME**

THE COAST OF FOLLY F2.0936

Famous Players–Lasky. *Dist* Paramount Pictures. 21 Sep **1925** [c23 Sep 1925; LP21840]. Si; b&w. 35mm. 7 reels, 6,974 ft.

Pres by Adolph Zukor, Jesse L. Lasky. *Dir* Allan Dwan. *Screenplay* Forrest Halsey. *Adapt* James Ashmore Creelman. *Photog* George F. Webber.

Cast: Gloria Swanson *(Nadine Gathway/Joyce Gathway)*, Anthony Jowitt *(Larry Fay)*, Alec Francis *(Count de Tauro)*, Dorothy Cumming *(Constance Fay)*, Jed Prouty *(Cholly Knickerbocker)*, Eugenie Besserer *(Nanny)*, Arthur Housman *(reporter)*, Lawrence Gray *(bather)*.

Society melodrama. Source: Conigsby William Dawson, *The Coast of Folly* (New York, 1924). Nadine Gathway, unable to abide her priggish husband, leaves home and drops out of sight for 20 years. When Mr. Gathway dies, he leaves his huge fortune to his daughter, Joyce, on the condition that she never become involved in scandal. Joyce becomes interested in Larry Fay, whose wife sues her for alienation of affections. In Paris, Nadine, who has become the Countess de Tauro, hears of the scandal and returns to the United States, intent on helping the daughter she once deserted. Nadine involves Mrs. Fay in a wild and compromising party and "blackmails" her into withdrawing her suit. Nadine then returns to her understanding husband, and Joyce awaits Larry, who is divorcing his wife. *Heiresses. Marriage. Divorce. Scandal. Blackmail. Inheritance. Motherhood. Paris.*

THE COAST PATROL F2.0937

Bud Barsky Corp. 20 Mar **1925** [New York showing]. Si; b&w. 35mm. 5 reels.

Dir Bud Barsky. *Scen* William E. Wing.

Cast: Kenneth McDonald *(Dale Ripley)*, Claire De Lorez *(Valerie Toske)*, Fay Wray *(Beth Slocum)*, Spottiswoode Aitken *(Captain Slocum)*, Geno Corrado *(Eric Marmont)*.

Melodrama. A revenue agent is assigned to stop the activities of a gang of smugglers operating out of a small town on the coast of Maine. The ringleader of the smugglers sets a romantic trap for the beautiful protégée of an old lighthouse keeper and almost ruins her life. With the help of a reformed vamp, who was the ringleader's accomplice, the revenue agent captures the smugglers. The ringleader commits suicide by jumping overboard from a ship, and the revenue officer wins the girl. *Smugglers. Vamps. Revenue agents. Suicide. Lighthouses. Maine.*

COBRA F2.0938

Ritz-Carlton Pictures. *Dist* Paramount Pictures. 30 Nov **1925** [c3 Dec 1925; LP22071]. Si; b&w. 35mm. 7 reels, 6,895 ft.

Dir Joseph Henabery. *Screenplay* Anthony Coldewey. *Photog* J. D. Jennings, Harry Fischbeck. *Set Dsgn* William Cameron Menzies. *Gowns* Gilbert Adrian.

Cast: Rudolph Valentino *(Count Rodrigo Torriani)*, Nita Naldi *(Elise Van Zile)*, Casson Ferguson *(Jack Dorning)*, Gertrude Olmstead *(Mary Drake)*, Hector V. Sarno *(Victor Minardi)*, Claire De Lorez *(Rosa Minardi)*, Eileen Percy *(Sophie Binner)*, Lillian Langdon *(Mrs. Porter Palmer)*, Henry Barrows *(store manager)*, Rosa Rosanova *(Marie)*.

Society drama. Source: Martin Brown, *Cobra* (New York opening: 22 Apr 1924). Count Rodrigo Torriani, a young Italian, has inherited a debt-ridden palace on the Bay of Naples and a fondness for women. He accepts the offer of New York antique dealer Jack Dorning to work in his shop, and there he falls genuinely in love with Jack's secretary, Mary Drake. Rodrigo is pursued by Elise Van Zile, a worldly-wise woman ambitious to marry him for his money—until she learns that Rodrigo is penniless. Elise turns her attentions, successfully, to Jack, and they get married. She tries to have an affair with Rodrigo on the side, but he at first rejects her. Later, Elise meets Rodrigo at a hotel, but he becomes conscience-stricken and leaves. The hotel burns down, killing Elise. Jack becomes frantic about his wife's disappearance, but Rodrigo leaves town, saying nothing. He returns a year later, learns that Jack knows the truth about Elise, and notes that Jack has regained his equanimity under Mary's care. Although he realizes that Mary's love is his for the asking, he treats their relationship casually and sails away, leaving Jack and Mary to their happiness. *Italians. Nobility. Antique dealers. Infidelity. Friendship. Naples.*

COCK O' THE WALK F2.0939

James Cruze Productions. *Dist* Sono Art–World Wide Pictures. 11 Apr **1930** [New York premiere; released 15 May; c22 Dec 1930; LP1829]. Sd (Photophone); b&w. 35mm. 7 reels, 7,200 ft.

Supv James Cruze. *Dir* R. William Neill, Walter Lang. *Scen* Nagene Searle, Frances Guihan. *Dial* Brian Marlow, Ralph Bell. *Song: "Play Me a Tango Tune"* Paul Titsworth.

Cast: Joseph Schildkraut *(Carlos López)*, Myrna Loy *(Narita)*, Philip Sleeman *(José)*, Edward Peil *(Ortega)*, John Beck *(cafe manager)*, Olive Tell *(Rosa Vallejo)*, Wilfred Lucas *(Señor Vallejo)*, Frank Jonasson *(Pedro)*, Sally Long *(Paulina Castra)*, Natalie Joyce *(María)*.

Romantic drama. Source: Arturo S. Mom, "Un Seguro sobre la dicha," in *La Estrella polar y otros cuentos* (Buenos Aires, 1927). Carlos López, a cafe violinist who preys upon married women, saves Narita from a suicide attempt on his way to work; later, at the cafe, having left the girl at his home, he engages in a flirtation with Paulina Castra but is disturbed by the appearance of Señor Vallejo with his wife, also enamored of Carlos. After beating the insolent Ortega, he and Paulina retire to his home, but she leaves, angered by the presence of Narita. Driven from the house, Narita threatens another suicide attempt; Carlos prevails upon her to postpone it for a year, proposing a marriage that would involve an insurance policy, payments from which would finance his violin studies; and she accepts the offer. While Rosa Vallejo awaits Carlos in Paris, her husband arrives to see him, but Narita manages to avert a disaster by protecting her husband from Ortega; ultimately, there is a confrontation in which Ortega is killed and Carlos arrested; but he escapes jail and again saves Narita from suicide, assuring her of his love. *Violinists. Philanderers. Spanish. Manslaughter. Insurance. Suicide. Infidelity. Paris.*

THE COCK-EYED WORLD F2.0940

Fox Film Corp. 3 Aug **1929** [New York premiere; released 20 Oct; c12 Aug 1929; LP586]. Sd (Movietone); b&w. 35mm. 12 reels, 10,611 ft. [Also si, 5 Oct 1929; 8,217 ft.]

Pres by William Fox. *Dir-Scen* Raoul Walsh. *Dial* William K. Wells. *Titl* Wilbur Morse, Jr. *Photog* Arthur Edeson. *Song: "Semper Fidelis"* John Philip Sousa. *Song: "Over There"* George M. Cohan. *Song: "Rose of No Man's Land"* James Caddigan, James Brennan. *Song: "Ka-Ka-Ka-Katy"* Geoffrey O'Hara. *Song: "Hinky Dinky Parley Voo"* Al Dubin, Irving Mills, Jimmy McHugh. *Songs: "So Long," "So Dear to Me"* Sidney Mitchell, Archie Gottler, Con Conrad. *Song: "You're the Cream in My Coffee"* Lew Brown, B. G. De Sylva, Ray Henderson. *Song:*

"Glorianna" Sidney Clare, Lew Pollack. *Sd* Edmund H. Hansen. *Asst Dir* Archibald Buchanan.

Cast: Victor McLaglen *(Top Sergeant Flagg)*, Edmund Lowe *(Sgt. Harry Quirt)*, Lily Damita *(Elenita)*, Lelia Karnelly *(Olga)*, El Brendel *(Olson)*, Bob Burns *(Connors)*, Jeanette Dagna *(Katinka)*, Joe Brown *(Brownie)*, Stuart Erwin *(Buckley)*, Ivan Linow *(Sanovich)*, Jean Bary *(Fanny)*, Solidad Jiminez *(innkeeper)*, Albert Dresden *(O'Sullivan)*, Joe Rochay *(Jacobs)*.

Musical comedy-drama. Source: Laurence Stallings and Maxwell Anderson, "Tropical Twins" (unpublished play). Two marines, Top Sergeant Flagg and Sgt. Harry Quirt, are continually falling out over their women. In Russia they meet a firebrand named Katinka, in Brooklyn a wise-cracking flapper from Coney Island, and in the tropics a Spanish siren named Elenita. The two pals are separated when Flagg goes on a reconnaissance mission by plane, leaving Quirt, who has contracted fever, behind. After a battle episode in which Flagg leads his troops to victory, he and Quirt, now fully recovered, argue about which of them is the father of Elenita's child. That settled, the regiment (and Flagg and Quirt) prepare to return to the States. *Russia. New York City—Brooklyn. Tropics. World War I. United States Marines.*

Note: Sequel to *What Price Glory.*

THE COCOANUTS **F2.0941**

Paramount Famous Lasky Corp. 3 Aug **1929** [c2 Aug 1929; LP576]. Sd (Movietone); b&w. 35mm. 10 reels, 8,613 ft.

Dir Joseph Santley, Robert Florey. *Adapt* Morris Ryskind. *Photog* George Folsey. *Song: "When My Dreams Come True"* Irving Berlin.

Cast: Groucho Marx *(Hammer)*, Harpo Marx *(Harpo)*, Chico Marx *(Chico)*, Zeppo Marx *(Jamison)*, Mary Eaton *(Polly)*, Oscar Shaw *(Bob)*, Katherine Francis *(Penelope)*, Margaret Dumont *(Mrs. Potter)*, Cyril Ring *(Yates)*, Basil Ruysdael *(Hennessey)*, Sylvan Lee *(bell captain)*, Alan K. Foster Girls, Gamby-Hall Girls *(dancing bellhops)*.

Comedy. Source: George S. Kaufman and Irving Berlin, *The Cocoanuts* (New York opening: 8 Dec 1925). Hammer, the stogey-chewing, mustachioed entrepreneur of the Hotel de Cocoanut, moonlights as an auctioneering real estate speculator during the Florida Land Boom of the Twenties. Though his 600-room establishment is filled with an assortment of guests, only one, the haughtily stuffed Mrs. Potter, is paying any rent. Meanwhile, her lovely daughter Polly is paying court to hotel clerk Bob Shaw, whose own ambitions towards architectural fame and love's reward are chronicled in the Irving Berlin tune, "When My Dreams Come True." Hammer's financial throes abound, precipitating ever more ingenious and whacky plots to salvage his position, the most ardently pursued of which is the wooing of the wealthy Mrs. Potter. The rascal even exhorts his employees to labor gratis in order to free themselves from "wage slavery." Guests Chico and Harpo, unable to pay their bill, cascade through the hotel, mischievously bent upon larcenous chicanery, stealing silverware, evading Hammer, fumbling uproariously with stock hotel props such as bellboys, luggage, roomkeys, and mailbins. Among Hammer's other guests are Harvey Yates and Penelope, two somewhat more dedicated miscreants who have designs on Mrs. Potter's lucre, plotting to purloin her precious necklace. She remains in the dark as to their devilish deviousness, duped to the point of promoting a match between the lovely Polly and Harvey, whom she regards as "one of the Boston Yates." The stolen necklace is discovered by Harpo, who cleverly produces it from the stump of a tree on the lot that Shaw buys at Hammer's auction. Bob is tossed into jail, later to be freed by Chico and Harpo, while the precious Polly has so infatuated Yates that he is tricked into revealing the true tale of the theft. The jig finally up, the engagement party continues with only the substitution of Shaw as the prospective groom needed to change pretty Polly's perilous predicament to one of anticipated paradise. *Hotelkeepers. Hotel clerks. Theft. Land speculation. Hotels. Auctions. Florida.*

CODE OF HONOR (Reissue) **F2.0942**

Mark M. Dintenfass. *Dist* Alexander Film Corp. 6 Nov **1922** [New York State license]. Si; b&w. 35mm.

Note: Originally released by United Picture Theatres as *Her Code of Honor,* Mar 1919.

CODE OF HONOR **F2.0943**

G. A. Durlam Productions. *Dist* Syndicate Pictures. 1 Oct **1930.** Sd (Cinephone); b&w. 35mm. 6 reels, 5,605 ft.

Dir J. P. McGowan. *Story* G. A. Durlam. *Photog* Otto Himm. *Film Ed* Arthur Brooks.

Cast: Mahlon Hamilton *(Jack Cardigan)*, Doris Hill *(Doris Bradfield)*, Robert Graves, Jr. *(Jed Harden)*, Stanley Taylor *(Tom Bradfield)*, Lafe McKee *(Dad Bradfield)*, Jimmy Aubrey *(Nosey)*, Harry Holden, William Dyer.

Western melodrama. Jack Cardigan, a cardsharp wanted for murder, decides to go straight when he meets Doris Bradfield, but he finds it necessary to use his skills one more time on behalf of her father. Dad Bradfield has finally established his ownership of his ranch (a Spanish grant later purchased by his grandfather), but the title falls into the hands of Jed Harden through the weaknesses of his son, Tom Bradfield, who has fallen into debt to Harden. Jack wins the title from Harden with some well-timed cheating, and the sheriff reports that a confession has cleared Jack of the murder charge. (Songs: "The Roundup's Done," "He's Only a Cowboy.") *Cardsharps. Criminals—Rehabilitation. Murder. Property rights. Land grants. Documentation.*

CODE OF THE AIR **F2.0944**

Bischoff Productions. Oct **1928.** Si; b&w. 35mm. 6 reels, 5,700 ft.

Dir James P. Hogan. *Titl* De Leon Anthony. *Story* Barry Barringer. *Photog* William Miller. *Film Ed* De Leon Anthony.

Cast: Kenneth Harlan *(Blair Thompson)*, June Marlowe *(Helen Carson)*, Arthur Rankin *(Alfred Clark)*, William V. Mong *(Professor Ross)*, Paul Weigel *(Doc Carson)*, James Bradbury, Jr. *(Stuttering Slim)*, Silverstreak *(himself, a dog)*, Edna Mae Cooper.

Melodrama. "It revolves around the work of a gang to rob a fleet of commercial planes carrying stocks and bonds. A criminal inventor heads the gang with his death ray that can be trained on an airplane and bring it down in flames. ... All the good old hokum is dragged in including the police dog who helps foil the villains. A pleasing love triangle is interwoven." (*Film Daily,* 16 Dec 1928, p9.) *Inventors. Air pilots. Robbery. Death rays. Police dogs.*

CODE OF THE COW COUNTRY **F2.0945**

Action Pictures. *Dist* Pathé Exchange. 19 Jun **1927** [c10 May 1927; LU23950]. Si; b&w. 35mm. 5 reels, 4,512 ft.

Pres by Lester F. Scott, Jr. *Dir* Oscar Apfel. *Scen* Betty Burbridge. *Story* Wilton West. *Photog* Ray Ries.

Cast: Buddy Roosevelt *(Jim West)*, Hank Bell *(Red Irwin)*, Elsa Benham *(Helen Calhoun)*, Melbourne MacDowell *(John Calhoun)*, Sherry Tansey *(Ted Calhoun)*, Richard Neill *(Bill Jackson)*, Walter Maly *(Dutch Moore)*, Frank Ellis *(Tallas)*, Ruth Royce *(Dolores)*.

Western melodrama. Jim West, foreman of John Calhoun's ranch, falls in love with Helen, the boss's daughter, after rescuing her from a runaway horse. Her brother, Ted, falls into the companionship of Bill Jackson, a notorious gambler and saloon keeper, who persuades Ted to sign I. O. U.'s while under the influence of alcohol. Jim, in company with Red Irwin, a tough deputy sheriff, confronts the gambler and forces a confession. Jackson plans a raid on the Calhoun cattle, forcing Ted to be his ally. Dolores, a dancehall girl, overhears the plot and tells Jim, causing Helen to misunderstand his motives. Jim's men capture the bandits, and Ted is forgiven by his father when he is wounded in a fight with Jackson. Jim is reunited with Helen after explaining his relation to Dolores. *Ranch foremen. Sheriffs. Gamblers. Dancehall girls. Saloon keepers. Brother-sister relationship.*

CODE OF THE NORTHWEST **F2.0946**

Chesterfield Motion Pictures. *Dist* Associated Exhibitors. 25 Jul **1926** [c4 Oct 1926; LU23180]. Si; b&w. 35mm. 4 reels, 3,965 ft.

Pres by Van Pelt Brothers. *Dir-Story* Frank S. Mattison. *Photog* Elmer G. Dyer.

Cast: Sandow *(himself, a dog)*, Richard Lang *(Sgt. Jerry Tyler)*, Tom London *(Pvt. Frank Stafford)*, Frank Austin *(Sandy McKenna)*, Shirley Palmer *(Lorna McKenna)*, Billy Franey *(Posty McShanigan)*, Eddie Brownell *(Clay Hamilton)*, Loraine Lamont *(Jeanie McKenna)*, Jack Richardson *(Donald Stafford)*.

Northwest melodrama. Pvt. Frank Stafford of the Northwest Mounted Police is sent to bring in his brother, Donald, who is wanted for murder and wife desertion. The trail leads toward the cabin of Sandy McKenna, a blind old widower who lives with his daughter, Lorna, and Jeanie, who has married Donald against McKenna's wishes. McKenna, however, welcomes Clay Hamilton, Lorna's sweetheart, accompanied by Sandow, his police dog, who rescues Jeanie from attempted suicide. Donald evades the police but is found by Sandow and brought to Jeanie's cabin. Pursued by Clay, Donald overcomes him, but Sandow unbinds his master and rescues him after saving Jeanie from the rapids. Frank and Donald fight aboard a raft heading for the rapids; Donald is killed when thrown from the raft, but Frank makes it to shore. *Brothers. Murder. Suicide. Desertion. Northwest Mounted Police. Rapids. Police dogs.*

CODE OF THE RANGE **F2.0947**

Morris R. Schlank Productions. *Dist* Rayart Pictures. 6 May **1927** [New York showing]. Si; b&w. 35mm. 5 reels, 4,747 ft.

Pres by W. Ray Johnston. *Dir* Bennett Cohn, Morris R. Schlank. *Story* Cleve Meyer. *Photog* William Hyer.

Cast: Jack Perrin, Nelson McDowell, Pauline Curley, Lew Meehan, Chic Olsen, Starlight, Rex.

Western melodrama. "Perrin is a cowpuncher out for revenge on the gent who seduced his sister into a dance hall by advertising for a school teacher and then finished her off before he blew town." (*Variety,* 11 May 1927, p20–21.) Rex and Starlight do their part in Perrin's victory over the villain and his assistant. *Cowboys. Dancehall girls. Revenge. Brother-sister relationship. Seduction. Horses. Dogs.*

THE CODE OF THE SCARLET **F2.0948**

Charles R. Rogers Productions. *Dist* First National Pictures. 1 Jul **1928** [c13 Jun 1928; LP25350]. Si; b&w. 35mm. 6 reels, 5,600 ft.

Dir Harry J. Brown. *Scen* Forrest Sheldon. *Titl* Ford I. Beebe. *Story* Bennett Cohen. *Photog* Ted McCord. *Film Ed* Fred Allen.

Cast: Ken Maynard *(Bruce Kenton)*, Gladys McConnell *(Helen Morgan)*, Ed Brady *(Paddy Halloran)*, J. P. McGowan *(Blake)*, Dot Farley *(Widow Malone)*, Sheldon Lewis *(bartender)*, Hal Salter *(comic)*, Joe Rickson *(Pete)*, Robert Walker *(Frank Morgan)*.

Northwest melodrama. Royal Canadian Northwest Mounted Policemen Bruce Kenton and Paddy Halloran rescue Helen Morgan when a gang they have been sent to capture ambushes her wagon destined for nearby lawless community Caribou Flats. Blake, proprietor of the Caribou Flats trading post and leader of the gang, hires Kenton when he is apparently dismissed from the service for shooting Helen Morgan's brother. While in Blake's employ, Kenton discovers that Blake shot Helen's brother and furthermore that he is guilty of committing a crime for which the brother has been accused. Kenton captures Blake and his gang after a fearful fight and reinstates himself with Helen. *Gangs. Brother-sister relationship. Factories. Trading posts. Northwest Mounted Police.*

CODE OF THE SEA **F2.0949**

Famous Players–Lasky. *Dist* Paramount Pictures. 2 Jun **1924** [c4 Jun 1924; LP20273]. Si; b&w. 35mm. 6 reels, 6,038 ft.

Pres by Adolph Zukor, Jesse L. Lasky. *Dir* Victor Fleming. *Scen* Bertram Millhauser. *Story* Byron Morgan. *Photog* Charles Edgar Schoenbaum.

Cast: Rod La Rocque *(Bruce McDow)*, Jacqueline Logan *(Jenny Hayden)*, George Fawcett *(Captain Hayden)*, Maurice B. Flynn *(Ewart Radcliff)*, Luke Cosgrave *(Captain Jonas)*, Lillian Leighton *(Mrs. McDow)*, Sam Appel *(John Swayne)*.

Melodrama. Bruce McDow, son of a skipper, believes he has inherited the cowardice of his father and loses the respect of his associates. Jenny, who loves and believes in him, gets him a job as mate of the lightship, and during an ensuing storm he proves his courage by saving her life and averting disaster to an endangered ship. *Seafaring life. Manhood. Lightships.*

CODE OF THE WEST **F2.0950**

Famous Players–Lasky. *Dist* Paramount Pictures. 6 Apr **1925** [c10 Apr 1925; LP21345]. Si; b&w. 35mm. 7 reels, 6,777 ft.

Pres by Adolph Zukor, Jesse L. Lasky. *Dir* William K. Howard. *Scen* Lucien Hubbard. *Photog* Lucien Andriot.

Cast: Owen Moore *(Cal Thurman)*, Constance Bennett *(Georgie May Stockwell)*, Mabel Ballin *(Mary Stockwell)*, Charles Ogle *(Henry Thurman)*, David Butler *(Bid Hatfield)*, George Bancroft *(Enoch Thurman)*, Gertrude Short *(Mollie Thurman)*, Lillian Leighton *(Ma Thurman)*, Edward Gribbon *(Tuck Merry)*, Pat Hartigan *(Cal Bloom)*, Frankie Lee *(Bud)*.

Western melodrama. Source: Zane Grey, *Code of the West* (New York, 1934). Georgie May Stockwell, a young and willful New York flapper, visits the Thurman ranch and vamps every man on the place, including Cal Thurman, who falls hard for the pert easterner. Valuable ranch land is opened by the government, and Cal beats Hatfield in a hot race for the best homesteading site. Georgie carries on a flirtation with Hatfield, who tries to get rough with her until he is roundly trounced by Cal. Tuck Merry, a local character, advises Cal to assert himself with Georgie, and Cal takes the advice to heart, kidnaping her and forcing her to marry him. Cal takes Georgie to his cabin in the woods, and they are most unhappy with each other until they come to realize their mutual love when faced with the hazards of a forest fire. *Homesteaders. Vamps. Jazz life. Abduction. Forest fires.*

CODE OF THE WEST **F2.0951**

Dist Syndicate Pictures. Nov **1929.** Si; b&w. 35mm. 5 reels, 4,800 ft.

Dir J. P. McGowan. *Story-Scen-Titl* Sally Winters. *Photog* Hap Depew.

Cast: Bob Custer *(Jack Hartley)*, Vivian Bay *(Phyllis)*, Bobby Dunn, Martin Cichy, Bud Osborne, Cliff Lyons, Tom Bay, Buck Bucko.

Western melodrama. "All about a gang in a Western town who are working a racket to steal insured packages from the railroad station agent [Shorty] and collect the insurance. Bob is sent as a special investigator by the railroad to catch the thieves. Working with the station agent, a dumb but honest gent, he pins the thefts on a gang who are operating a dive on railroad property. He serves notice on the leader [Leary] to close up the joint at midnight, or he will run him out of town. Then ... a finish fight in which Bob beats the leader and runs him out. Then an anti-climax with the rest of the gang caught red-handed robbing the night train." (*Film Daily,* 27 Jul 1930, p11.) *Station agents. Investigators. Gangs. Mail theft. Postal service. Insurance.*

CODE OF THE WILDERNESS **F2.0952**

Vitagraph Co. of America. 6 Jul **1924** [c25 Jun 1924; LP20332]. Si; b&w. 35mm. 7 reels, 6,480 ft.

Pres by Albert E. Smith. *Dir* David Smith. *Scen* Jay Pilcher. *Story* Charles Alden Seltzer.

Cast: John Bowers *(Rex Randerson)*, Alice Calhoun *(Ruth Harkness)*, Alan Hale *(Willard Masten)*, Charlotte Merriam *(Hagar)*, Otis Harlan *(Uncle Jephon)*, Kitty Bradbury *(Aunt Martha)*, Joseph Rickson *(Tom Chavis)*, Cliff Davidson *(Jim Picket)*.

Western melodrama. Ruth Harkness, inheriting an uncle's ranch, comes west to take possession. Though attracted to her foreman, Randerson, she cannot accept his ideas of frontier justice when he is forced to shoot a man. Ultimately forced to defend herself against a villain with a gun, she begins to understand Randerson's point of view and accepts his love. *Ranch foremen. Inheritance. Frontier and pioneer life.*

THE COHENS AND KELLYS (Universal-Jewel) **F2.0953**

Universal Pictures. 28 Feb **1926** [c13 Feb 1926; LP22400]. Si; b&w. 35mm. 8 reels, 7,774 ft.

Prod E. M. Asher. *Adapt-Dir* Harry Pollard. *Scen* Alfred A. Cohn. *Photog* Charles Stumar. *Art Dir* Charles D. Hall.

Cast: Charlie Murray *(Patrick Kelly)*, George Sidney *(Jacob Cohen)*, Vera Gordon *(Mrs. Cohen)*, Kate Price *(Mrs. Kelly)*, Olive Hasbrouck *(Nannie Cohen)*, Nat Carr *(Milton Katz)*, Mickey Bennett *(Milton J. Katz)*.

Comedy. Source: Aaron Hoffman, *Two Blocks Away; a Play in Three Acts* (New York, 1925). Jacob Cohen, who owns a drygoods store, and Patrick Kelly, an Irish cop, are constantly at loggerheads, feuding over anything and everything. Kelly's son, Tim, and Cohen's daughter, Nannie, fall in love despite the bickering of their parents and when they cannot get parental consent for their marriage are secretly wed. Cohen inherits a fortune and moves to the upper East Side, taking Nannie with him. Sometime later, Nannie gives birth to a child, and when her parents will not let any of the Kelly clan see the child, Nannie leaves home and goes to live with the Kellys; Mrs. Cohen soon joins her. Cohen then discovers that Kelly is the rightful heir to the fortune that he himself has inherited and, moved by honesty, he goes to the burly cop and tells him so. The men are reconciled and decide to go into partnership together. *Irish. Jews. Police. Merchants. Inheritance. Marriage. Partnerships. Drygoods stores. New York City—East Side.*

THE COHENS AND KELLYS IN AFRICA **F2.0954**

Universal Pictures. 19 Dec **1930** [New York premiere; released 19 Jan 1931; c24 Dec 1930; LP1837]. Sd (Movietone); b&w. 35mm. 8 reels, 7,225 ft.

Dir Vin Moore. *Scen* William K. Wells. *Dial* William K. Wells, Maurice Pivar. *Story* Vin Moore, Edward Luddy. *Photog* Hal Mohr. *Rec Engr* C. Roy Hunter.

Cast: George Sidney *(Mr. Cohen)*, Charles Murray *(Mr. Kelly)*, Vera Gordon *(Mrs. Cohen)*, Kate Price *(Mrs. Kelly)*, Frank Davis *(Windjammer Thorn)*, Lloyd Whitlock *(sheik)*, Nick Cogley *(guide)*, Eddie Kane *(chief [Sam Ginsberg])*, Renée Marvelle, Georgette Rhodes *(dancing girls)*.

Comedy. In need of a supply of ivory for their piano-manufacturing business, the Cohens and the Kellys journey to Africa under the guidance of Windjammer Thorn. Cohen and Kelly soon are separated from their wives, who wind up in the custody of a desert sheik, and they themselves seek refuge from an elephant herd in a native village, which they find under the control of their old friend Sam Ginsberg. Defeating Ginsberg in a game of miniature golf, Cohen and Kelly leave the village with an ample supply of ivory, retrieve their reluctant wives from the sheik's harem, and return home. *Irish. Jews. Sheiks. Guides. Partnerships. Pianos. Ivory. Miniature golf. Harems. Deserts. Africa.*

THE COHENS AND KELLYS IN ATLANTIC CITY **F2.0955**

Universal Pictures. 17 Mar **1929** [c4 Mar 1929; LP189]. Talking sequences & mus score (Movietone); b&w. 35mm. 8 reels, 7,401 ft. [Also si; 7,752 ft.]

Dir William James Craft. *Adapt-Cont* Earl Snell. *Dial-Titl* Albert De Mond. *Story* Jack Townley. *Photog* Al Jones. *Film Ed* Charles Craft, Richard Cahoon.

Cast: George Sidney *(Mr. Cohen)*, Vera Gordon *(Mrs. Cohen)*, Mack Swain *(Mr. Kelly)*, Kate Price *(Mrs. Kelly)*, Cornelius Keefe *(Pat Kelly)*, Nora Lane *(Rose Cohen)*, Virginia Sale *(Miss Rosenberg)*, Tom Kennedy *(crook)*.

Comedy. After 30 years in the bathing suit business, Cohen and Kelly have fallen on hard times; their merchandise and their business methods are both out of date. While they are away on a selling trip, Cohen's daughter, Rosie, and Kelly's son, Pat, introduce a new line of merchandise into the family business and to promote it plan a beauty contest to be held at Atlantic City. Cohen and Kelly return in a rage, and the children sneak off to Atlantic City to avoid involving their parents in the contest. After numerous complications, Rosie wins the contest, the family business is saved, and a happy reunion of the two families occurs. *Irish. Jews. Businessmen. Beauty contests. Bathing suits. Business management. Publicity. Atlantic City.*

Note: Some scenes were filmed on location in Atlantic City.

THE COHENS AND THE KELLYS IN PARIS (Universal Super-Jewel) **F2.0956**

Universal Pictures. 15 Jan **1928** [c3 Jan 1928; LP24820]. Si; b&w. 35mm. 8 reels, 7,481 ft.

Pres by Carl Laemmle. *Screen Supv* Joseph Poland. *Dir* William Beaudine. *Story-Cont* Alfred A. Cohn. *Titl* Albert De Mond. *Photog* Charles Stumar. *Film Ed* Frank Atkinson, Robert Carlisle.

Cast: George Sidney *(Nathan Cohen)*, J. Farrell MacDonald *(Patrick Kelly)*, Vera Gordon *(Mrs. Cohen)*, Kate Price *(Mrs. Kelly)*, Charles Delaney *(Patrick Kelly)*, Sue Carol *(Sadye Cohen)*, Gertrude Astor *(Paulette)*, Gino Corrado *(Pierre, Paulette's husband)*, Charlie Murray.

Comedy. Nathan Cohen and Patrick Kelly, two quarreling business partners—one Irish and the other Jewish—board a liner for France with their wives to forestall a marriage between their son and daughter, Patrick and Sadye. Upon arrival in Paris they find their children already married and nearly divorced. Paulette, an artist's model whom Pat is painting in the nude, is the bone of contention between the newlyweds. Visiting Paulette, Cohen and Kelly quarrel with her husband, Pierre, an apache, and nearly wreck the Café Diable. Pierre challenges Cohen and Kelly to a duel, but the wives rescue their husbands in an airplane; once in the air, the two families make up their differences. *Apaches—Paris. Artists. Models. Irish. Jews. Businessmen. Partnerships. Paris.*

THE COHENS AND THE KELLYS IN SCOTLAND **F2.0957**

Universal Pictures. 17 Mar **1930** [c6 Mar 1930; LP1129]. Sd (Movietone); b&w. 35mm. 8 reels, 7,600 ft. [Also si; 6,584 ft.]

Pres by Carl Laemmle. *Dir* William James Craft. *Scen-Dial* Albert De Mond. *Story* John McDermott. *Photog* C. Allen Jones. *Film Ed* Harry Lieb. *Rec Engr* Joseph R. Lapis, C. Roy Hunter.

Cast: George Sidney *(Cohen)*, Charles Murray *(Kelly)*, Vera Gordon *(Mrs. Cohen)*, Kate Price *(Mrs. Kelly)*, E. J. Radcliffe *(McPherson)*, William Colvin *(McDonald)*, Lloyd Whitlock *(Prince)*.

Farce. Accompanied by their respective spouses, Cohen and Kelly go to Scotland to buy plaids, each having received a tip that the Prince of Morania, a style dictator, is to have a plaid motif in his spring collection. Cohen buys all the plaids of McPherson, while Kelly purchases those of McDonald. Cohen gets into trouble with a stranger on the golf course and is horrified to find that he has insulted the prince; they attend the races where the prince is expected to show himself in plaids, but they are covered by his raincoat. Thinking themselves ruined, each decides to commit suicide; but when Cohen tries to drown himself, Kelly rescues him. They astound McPherson and McDonald by asking them to buy back the plaids, but when the prince is seen wearing them in a parade, the Scotsmen gladly pay them a fortune. *Irish. Jews. Couturiers. Clothes. Plaids. Golf. Scotland.*

COINCIDENCE **F2.0958**

Metro Pictures. May **1921** [c13 May 1921; LP16561]. Si; b&w. 35mm. 5 reels.

Dir Chet Withey. *Scen* Brian Hooker. *Story* Howard E. Morton. *Photog* Louis C. Bitzer.

Cast: Robert Harron *(Billy Jenks)*, June Walker *(Phoebe Howard)*, Bradley Barker *("Handsome Harry" Brent)*, William Frederic *(Stephen Fiske)*, Frank Belcher *(John Carter)*, June Ellen Terry *(Dorothy Carter)*.

Comedy. Smalltown bank clerk Billy Jenks comes to New York in search of greater opportunity and becomes a cashier in a department store, where he meets stenographer Phoebe Howard. When both lose their jobs, Billy wires his aunt, but he learns that she has died and left him a fortune in bonds. The couple then plan to marry, and on a bus their conversation is overheard by Harry Brent, a crook who arranges to "help" them. When, however, the bonds are stolen by John Carter, who is desperately in debt, Billy mistakes Fiske, his creditor, for the thief. In a series of chases, notes and bonds are exchanged to the satisfaction of all parties. *Cashiers. Confidence men. Inheritance. Department stores. New York City. Chases.*

COLD FURY **F2.0959**

Art Mix Productions. *Dist* Aywon Film Corp. 5 Feb **1925**. Si; b&w. 35mm. 5 reels, 4,800 ft.

Cast: Jack Richardson, Ora Carew.

Western melodrama(?). No information about the nature of this film has been found.

COLD NERVE **F2.0960**

Independent Pictures. 8 Jun **1925** [New York State license]. Si; b&w. 35mm. 5 reels, 4,792 ft.

Pres by Jesse J. Goldburg. *Dir* J. P. McGowan. *Scen* William Lester. *Photog* Walter Griffin. *Film Ed* Betty Davis.

Cast: Bill Cody, Ena Gregory, Joe Bennett, Arthur Morrison, Joan Lowell, Edward Coxen, Monte Collins.

Western melodrama. "The integrity of a young cowboy, Grit, proves unassailable when he is cheated of his property, accused of stealing and murder. His enemies are finally brought to justice and he wins the girl he loves." (*National Film Archive Catalogue, Part III, Silent Fiction Films, 1895–1930;* The British Film Institute, London, 1966, p258.) *Cowboys. Murder. Injustice.*

COLD STEEL *see* **THE TRAIL TO RED DOG**

COLD STEEL **F2.0961**

L. J. Meyberg. *Dist* Robertson-Cole Distributing Corp. 29 May **1921** [c29 May 1921; LP16657]. Si; b&w. 35mm. 6 reels, 5,800 ft.

Prod L. J. Meyberg. *Dir* Sherwood MacDonald. *Adapt* Monte Katterjohn. *Photog* Ernest Depew, John Thompson.

Cast: J. P. McGowan *(Steele Weir)*, Kathleen Clifford *(Janet Hosmer)*, Stanhope Wheatcroft *(Ed Sorenson)*, Arthur Millett *(Mr. Sorenson)*, Charles E. Insley *(Vose)*, Milt Brown *(Burkhart)*, Nigel De Brulier *(Martinez)*, George Clair *(Gordon)*, Andy Waldron *(Johnson)*, Elinor Fair *(Mary Johnson)*, V. L. Barnes *(bartender)*.

Action melodrama. Source: George Clifford Shedd, *In the Shadow of the Hills* (New York, 1919). On his deathbed Steele Weir's father tells his son of a band of criminals who framed him for murder and robbed him of valuable land in the West. Under contract to build a dam, Steele goes to the headquarters of the gang; and becoming aware of his identity, they plot against him with the services of lawyer Martinez. He, however, proves to be Steele's friend and obtains evidence against the gang. When Ed Sorenson, the leader's son, steals the evidence, Steele's sweetheart, Janet, outwits the enemies, and after many adventures the bandits are convicted and Steele wins the girl. *Lawyers. Gangs. Filial relations. Land rights. Dams.*

COLLEEN **F2.0962**

Fox Film Corp. 3 Jul **1927** [c23 Jul 1927; LP24150]. Si; b&w. 35mm. 6 reels, 5,301 ft.

Pres by William Fox. *Dir* Frank O'Connor. *Story-Scen* Randall H. Faye. *Photog* George Schneiderman. *Asst Dir* A. F. Erickson.

Cast: Madge Bellamy *(Sheila Kelly)*, Charles Morton *(Terry O'Flynn)*, J. Farrell MacDonald *(Mr. O'Flynn)*, Tom Maguire *(Sheridan McShane Kelly)*, Sammy Cohen *(son of pawnbroker)*, Marjorie Beebe *(Kitty)*, Ted McNamara *(groom of O'Flynn)*, Tom McGuire *(police lieutenant)*, Sarah Padden *(wife of police lieutenant)*, Sidney Franklin *(pawnbroker)*, Carl Stockdale *(bailiff)*.

Comedy-drama. "A story of Irish hearts and racing horses. Deals with the son of impoverished lord who is in love with the daughter of wealthy neighbors. Their love making under difficulties and constant squabbles form basis of action." (*Motion Picture News Booking Guide*, 13:25, Oct 1927.) *Irish. Horseracing. Courtship.*

COLLEEN OF THE PINES **F2.0963**

Chester Bennett Productions. *Dist* Film Booking Offices of America. 9 Jul **1922** [c9 Jul 1922; LP18055]. Si; b&w. 35mm. 5 reels, 4,738 ft.

Dir Chester Bennett. *Story-Scen* J. Grubb Alexander. *Photog* Jack MacKenzie.

Cast: Jane Novak *(Joan Cameron)*, Edward Hearn *(Barry O'Neil)*, Alfred Allen *(Duncan Cameron)*, J. Gordon Russell *(Paul Bisson)*, Charlotte Pierce *(Esther Cameron)*, Ernest Shields *(Jules Perrault)*, "Smoke" Turner *(Jerry-Jo)*.

Northwest melodrama. Joan Cameron is engaged against her will to Paul Bisson, the trading post factor. While her father and Bisson are away, Joan's sister, Esther, elopes with trapper Jules Perrault, and Joan meets Barry O'Neil, a dashing Northwest Mounted Police officer who falls in love with her and departs, promising to return. Months later, Esther, bearing a child, returns. Cameron and Bisson also show up unexpectedly, and Joan claims the child as her own to save Esther from Cameron's wrath. In pursuit of Esther (who he believes murdered Perrault), O'Neil chases Joan, unaware that she is his "Colleen," when she flees with the child in a canoe during a raging forest fire, assisted by Jerry-Jo, the halfbreed. Bisson, enraged, also gives chase, kills Jerry-Jo, and then dies when the halfbreed's dog attacks him. Joan and O'Neil return to the post to find Perrault, still alive, planning to marry Esther. *Sisters. Trappers. Factors. Halfcastes. Illegitimacy. Northwest Mounted Police. Forest fires. Dogs.*

Note: In the copyright version Esther apparently does kill the trapper but is exonerated of the murder, as justifiable homicide.

COLLEGE **F2.0964**

Joseph M. Schenck Productions. *Dist* United Artists. 10 Sep **1927** [New York premiere; released Nov; c10 Sep 1927; LP24409]. Si; b&w. 35mm. 6 reels, 5,916 ft.

Pres by Joseph M. Schenck. *Supv* Harry Brand. *Dir* James W. Horne. *Story-Scen* Carl Harbaugh, Bryan Foy. *Photog* Dev Jennings, Bert Haines. *Tech Dir* Fred Gabourie. *Film Ed* J. S. Kell.

Cast: Buster Keaton *(The Boy)*, Anne Cornwall *(The Girl)*, Flora Bramley *(her friend)*, Harold Goodwin *(a rival)*, Buddy Mason, Grant Withers *(his friends)*, Snitz Edwards *(The Dean)*, Carl Harbaugh *(crew coach)*, Sam Crawford *(baseball coach)*, Florence Turner *(a mother)*, Paul Goldsmith, Morton Kaer, Bud Houser, Kenneth Grumbles, Charles Borah, Leighton Dye, Lee Barnes, "Shorty" Worden, Robert Boling, Erick Mack *(themselves)*, University of Southern California Baseball Team.

Comedy. The Boy graduates from high school with interscholastic honors, and as class orator he speaks on "Brains vs. Brawn," demeaning athletics, thereby winning the favor of the pedagogs but not that of the students. His college sweetheart requires that he become an athlete, so he spends his savings and tries out for all sports and is a perfect flop. He goes to work to pay his way through school, but every job adds to his blunders. His rival takes delight in maneuvering The Girl to his place of employment and further humiliating him. Then the college dean takes an interest in The Boy and insists that the varsity coach give him a chance; through coincidence, he thwarts a plot against him and wins a race. Learning that his rival has locked The Girl in the dormitory, The Boy goes to the rescue, performing all the athletic feats he dreamed about, and knocks the rival cold; thus the weakling becomes the college idol. *College life. Courtship. Track. Baseball.*

THE COLLEGE BOOB **F2.0965**

Harry Garson Productions. *Dist* Film Booking Offices of America. 15 Aug **1926** [c15 Aug 1926; LP23059]. Si; b&w. 35mm. 6 reels, 5,340 ft.

Pres by Joseph P. Kennedy. *Dir* Harry Garson. *Screen Adapt* Gerald C. Duffy. *Story* Jack Casey. *Photog* James Brown.

Cast: Lefty Flynn *(Aloysius Appleby)*, Jean Arthur *(Angela Boothby)*, Jimmy Anderson *(Horatio Winston, Jr.)*, Bob Bradbury, Jr. *(Shorty Buzelle)*, Cecil Ogden *(Smacky McNeil)*, Dorothea Wolbert *(Aunt Polly)*, William Malan *(Uncle Lish)*, Raymond Turner *(Whitewings Washington)*.

Comedy-drama. Aloysius Appleby, known as Ally, leaves his small town for Baldwin College and promises his Aunt Polly and Uncle Lish that he will not indulge in sports. Horatio Winston, a senior at the college, becomes jealous of Ally's powerful physique and plans to make him the college boob. Ally meets Angela Boothby (Horatio's girl), is immediately smitten, and pesters his roommate, Shorty Buzelle, for information about her. At a "pep" dance, the boys dress Ally in a ridiculous manner: he is severely ridiculed, and, at Angela's insistence, he promotes some respect with his fists. Pop Warren, the football coach, encourages him to try out for the team, in spite of his promise, and he is the hero of the first game. Later, when Ally refuses to play, Angela explains the importance of his playing to his aunt and uncle. They come to the game, and Ally goes in in time to save the team. *Students. Athletic coaches. Aunts. Uncles. College life. Football.*

THE COLLEGE COQUETTE **F2.0966**

Columbia Pictures. 5 Aug **1929** [c3 Sep 1929; LP671]. Sd (Movietone); b&w. 35mm. 6 reels, 6,149 ft. [Also si; 5,566 or 6,215 ft.]

Prod Harry Cohn. *Dir* George Archainbaud. *Dial Dir* James Seymour. *Screenplay-Dial* Norman Houston. *Story* Ralph Graves. *Photog* Jackson Rose. *Art Dir* Harrison Wiley. *Film Ed* Gene Havlick. *Asst Dir* Eugene De Rue.

Cast: Ruth Taylor *(Betty Forrester)*, William Collier, Jr. *(Tom Marion)*, Jobyna Ralston *(Doris Marlowe)*, John Holland *(Coach Harvey Porter)*, Adda Gleason *(Ethel Forrester)*, Gretchen Hartman *(Mrs. Marlowe)*, Frances Lyons *(Edna)*, Edward Piel, Jr. *(Slim)*, Edward Clayton *(Ted)*, Maurice Murphy *(Jimmy Doolittle)*, Billy Taft *(boy with ukelele)*.

Melodrama. Betty Forrester, a college flirt who is determined to attract Harvey Porter, the school coach, starts playing around to make him jealous. Her roommate, Doris Marlowe, is a naive girl who falls madly in love with Tom, a sophisticated playboy who leads Doris on until he tires of her. At this point Doris pleads with Tom to love her, but he refuses. Betty, afraid for Doris' welfare, tries to save her from Tom by falsely attracting him to herself. Doris, crestfallen, leaves them and accidentally tumbles into an elevator shaft and dies. Harvey is furiously jealous and determines never to see Betty again until he learns the real reason for her actions with Tom; then he asks her to marry him. *Flirts. Athletic coaches. Playboys. College life. Jealousy.*

Note: Theme song: "I Want To Be Good and Bad."

COLLEGE DAYS **F2.0967**

Tiffany Productions. 15 Oct **1926** [c21 Oct 1926; LP23249]. Si; b&w. 35mm. 8 reels, 7,300 ft.

Supv-Story-Scen A. P. Younger. *Dir* Richard Thorpe. *Photog* Milton Moore, Mack Stengler. *Art Dir* Edwin B. Willis. *Film Ed* James C. McKay.

Cast: Marceline Day *(Mary Ward)*, Charles Delaney *(Jim Gordon)*, James Harrison *(Larry Powell)*, Duane Thompson *(Phyllis)*, Brooks Benedict *(Kenneth Slade)*, Kathleen Key *(Louise)*, Edna Murphy *(Bessie)*, Robert Homans *(Mr. Gordon)*, Crauford Kent *(Kent)*, Charles Wellesley *(Bryson)*, Gibson Gowland *(Carter)*, Lawford Davidson *(Professor Maynard)*, Pat Harmon *(coach)*, William A. Carroll *(dean)*.

Romantic comedy-drama. Jim Gordon, the son of a proud and loving father, enters the University of California as a student. There he meets Mary Ward, a campus coed who captures his heart on the first day. He becomes close friends with Larry Powell, his roommate, but incurs the wrath of Kenneth Slade, who is unable to take a practical joke. Jim and Larry attend a campus dance with Bessie and Phyllis, two vamps, and through a series of romantic complications Jim tries to convince Mary of his love for her. Later, Louise successfully waylays Jim on his way from the training field and the sight of them disillusions Mary; trying to repair matters in a classroom, Jim is reprimanded, is physically punished by Professor Maynard, and is expelled. Later he is reinstated by the dean and plans to join the football squad against Stanford, but the day of the game finds him again in disgrace because he has gone to a roadhouse to protect Mary from her jazzy companions, and then to assist her after an accident. At the last minute, he is called into the game, and his team wins. *College life. Jazz life. Football. University of California. Stanford University.*

THE COLLEGE HERO **F2.0968**

Columbia Pictures. 9 Oct **1927** [c4 Nov 1927; LP24627]. Si; b&w. 35mm. 6 reels, 5,628 ft.

Prod Harry Cohn. *Dir* Walter Lang. *Story-Screenplay* Dorothy Howell. *Camera* Joseph Walker. *Film Ed* Arthur Roberts. *Asst Dir* Max Cohn. *Tech Dir* Charles Paddock.

Cast: Bobby Agnew *(Bob Cantfield)*, Pauline Garon *(Vivian Saunders)*, Ben Turpin *(The Janitor)*, Rex Lease *(Jim Halloran)*, Churchill Ross *(Sampson Saunders)*, Joan Standing *(Nellie Kelly)*, Charles Paddock *(The Coach)*.

Romantic comedy-drama. Bob Cantfield, a freshman at Carver College, averts the hazing committee with the aid of his tin lizzie but is chagrined when the car falls apart while he is escorting Vivian Saunders to her dormitory. Bob is assigned to room with Jim Halloran, and after an initial scrap they become pals. Bob agrees to escort the sister of Sampson Saunders to a prom, and the evening launches a romance between Bob and Vivian, with the faithful Jim as a secret rival. As Bob becomes the hero of the football team, Jim's jealousy and envy cause him to deliberately trip Bob on the practice field, causing him injury; later, conscience-stricken, Jim drowns his grief in drink and is knocked out by Bob in a confrontation. In spite of his injury, Bob scores a spectacular touchdown and wins a game for Carver. At the hospital Jim confesses, and Bob, consoled by Vivian, forgives his friend. *Janitors. College life. Football. Friendship. Drunkenness. Automobiles.*

COLLEGE LOVE (Universal-Jewel) **F2.0969**

Universal Pictures. 7 Jul **1929** [c13 Jun 1929; LP468]. Sd (Movietone); b&w. 35mm. 8 reels, 6,864 ft. [Also si; 6,145 ft.]

Pres by Carl Laemmle. *Prod* Carl Laemmle, Jr. *Dir* Nat Ross. *Scen* John B. Clymer, Pierre Couderc. *Titl* Albert De Mond. *Story-Dial* Leonard Fields. *Photog* George Robinson. *Film Ed* Ted Kent, Richard Cahoon. *Songs: "It's You," "Oh, How We Love Our College"* Dave Silverstein, Lee Zahler. *Sd Rec* C. Roy Hunter.

Cast: George Lewis *(Bob Wilson)*, Eddie Phillips *("Flash" Thomas)*, Dorothy Gulliver *(Dorothy May)*, Churchill Ross *(Jimmie Reed)*, Hayden Stevenson *(Coach Jones)*, Sumner Getchell *(Fat)*.

Comedy-drama. At Caldwell College, "Flash" Thomas, captain of the football team, is in love with Dorothy May, who is infatuated with Bob Wilson, without whose help Thomas would not be such an outstanding player. Broken-hearted, Thomas tries to laugh it off, then against rules accepts an invitation to a roadhouse party. Wilson, discovering he is missing, hides in Thomas' bed to fool the coach, then tries to persuade him to leave the party; when they return, however, the coach discovers the ruse and puts Wilson, who shields Thomas, out of the game. Dorothy asks for an explanation and, receiving none, returns Thomas' fraternity pin. At the last minute, Wilson is rushed into the game and Thomas plays to redeem himself; Wilson scores a touchdown, is proclaimed a hero, and wins the love of Dorothy. *Athletic coaches. College life. Football. Roadhouses. Courtship.*

COLLEGE LOVERS **F2.0970**

First National Pictures. 5 Oct **1930** [c3 Oct 1930; LP1601]. Sd (Vitaphone); b&w. 35mm. 6 reels, 5,633 ft.

Dir John G. Adolfi. *Scen-Dial* Douglas Doty. *Story* Earl Baldwin. *Photog* Frank Kesson. *Film Ed* Frederick Y. Smith. *Songs: "Up and At 'Em," "One Minute of Heaven"* Ned Washington, Herb Magidson, Michael Cleary. *Rec Engr* Cal Applegate.

Cast: Jack Whiting *(Frank Taylor)*, Marion Nixon *(Madge Hutton)*, Frank McHugh *(Speed Haskins)*, Guinn Williams *(Tiny Courtley)*, Russell Hopton *(Eddie Smith)*, Wade Boteler *(Coach Donovan)*, Phyllis Crane *(Josephine Crane)*, Richard Tucker *(Gene Hutton)*, Charles Judels *(spectator)*.

Romantic comedy. Tiny Courtley plans to leave college because the girl he loves has eloped with another boy. As he is being driven to the station by Eddie, Frank Taylor plots with Madge Hutton to fake a suicide on a bridge; Tiny saves her, but Eddie intrudes and he and Tiny both fall in love with her, though she actually loves Frank. On the night before an important football game, Tiny and Eddie engage in a heated argument, and Frank suggests that Madge send each a love note that he is the favored one. At the half, they accuse each other of stealing their notes, and their fighting causes them to be put on the bench. Frank proposes that Madge tell the boys about their engagement to marry, and friends again, the boys are reinstated to lead the team to victory. *Courtship. College life. Football. Jealousy. Suicide. Friendship.*

THE COLLEGE WIDOW **F2.0971**

Warner Brothers Pictures. 15 Oct **1927** [c10 Oct 1927; LP24496]. Si; b&w. 35mm. 7 reels, 6,616 ft.

Dir Archie L. Mayo. *Titl* Jack Jarmuth. *Adapt* Paul Schofield, Peter Milne. *Camera* Barney McGill. *Film Ed* Clarence Kolster. *Asst Dir* Henry Blanke.

Cast: Dolores Costello *(Jane Witherspoon)*, William Collier, Jr. *(Billy Bolton)*, Douglas Gerrard *(Professor Jelicoe)*, Anders Randolf *(Hiram Bolton)*, Charles Hill Mailes *(Professor Witherspoon)*, Robert Ryan *(Jack Larrabee)*, Sumner Getchell *(Jimmie Hopper)*, Big Boy Williams *(Don White)*, Grace Gordon *(Flora)*, Jess Hibbs.

Romantic comedy. Source: George Ade, *The College Widow, a Pictorial Comedy in Four Acts* (New York, 1924). Following another instance of the perennial defeat of the Atwater College football team, President Witherspoon is told that unless better athletes can be induced to come to Atwater, he will be asked to resign. Acting upon the suggestion of Professor Jelicoe, Jane, the professor's beautiful daughter, uses her personal charm to draw noted football stars from neighboring schools by a series of ruses at a vacationing spot. Billy Bolton, son of a financial magnate, falls for Jane and to prove himself registers under another name and works his way through school, attaining scholastic and athletic honors. Through the jealousy of another girl, Billy learns of Jane's trickery and persuades the athletes not to play; Jane finds them at a notorious roadhouse, and, after explaining her father's position, wins them over, though she denounces Billy. His athletic prowess, however, wins the game for Atwater and the approval of his father and Jane. *Professors. Athletes. College life. Football. Resorts.*

COLLEGIATE **F2.0972**

R-C Pictures. *Dist* Film Booking Offices of America. 29 Aug **1926** [c29 Aug 1926; LP23444]. Si; b&w. 35mm. 5 reels, 4,718 ft.

Pres by Joseph P. Kennedy. *Dir* Del Andrews. *Adapt* James Gruen. *Story* Jean Dupont. *Photog* Jules Cronjager. *Asst Dir* Doran Cox.

Cast: Alberta Vaughn *(Patricia Steele)*, Donald Keith *(Jimmy Baxter)*, John Steppling *(Mr. Steele)*, Alys Murrell *(Iris Vale)*, William Austin *(G. Horace Crumbleigh)*, Frankie Adams *(Bumper Smith)*, Charles Cruz *(Piggy)*.

Romantic comedy. Patricia Steele, madcap daughter of a millionaire, is ordered to college by her father as an alternative to marrying G. Horace Crumbleigh. Pursued by Steele and Crumbleigh, she leaps onto a float of bathing girls in a competition and when adjudged winner is compelled to appear in a department store window with football hero Jimmy Baxter, who persuades her to go to college. Knowing that Jimmy is working his way, Pat gets a job as a waitress. She repulses the advances of Piggy Fordyce, a rich loafer engaged to Iris Vale, the dean's secretary; Fordyce cheats on an examination but casts suspicion on Jimmy, causing him to be barred from a game. Pat is locked in the dormitory for betting on the team but escapes and, to clear Jimmy, says she is the guilty one. Bumper forces a confession from Iris and Fordyce, and Pat is happily reconciled with Jimmy. *Millionaires. College life. Flirtation. Beauty contests. Football.*

COLORADO **F2.0973**

Universal Film Manufacturing Co. 14 Feb **1921** [c5 Feb 1921; LP16142]. Si; b&w. 35mm. 5 reels, 4,875 ft.

Pres by Carl Laemmle. *Dir* Reaves Eason. *Scen* Wallace Clifton, Eleanor Fried. *Photog* Virgil Miller.

Cast: Frank Mayo *(Frank Austin)*, Charles Newton *(Tom Doyle)*, Gloria Hope *(Kitty Doyle)*, Lillian West *(Mrs. Doyle)*, Charles Le Moyne *(James Kincaid)*, Leonard Clapham *(David Collins)*, Dan Crimmins *(Lem Morgan)*, Rosa Gore *(Salla Morgan)*.

Melodrama. Source: Augustus Thomas, *Colorado* (New York opening: 18 Nov 1901). While awaiting his discharge at an eastern Army camp, Lieut. Frank Hayden thrashes Captain Kincaid for attacking a girl, and to avoid court-martial he deserts. In the desert, he rescues Tom Doyle from dying of thirst and takes him home, where he falls in love with Tom's daughter, Kitty, and assumes the name of Austin. When he and Doyle become partners and discover a vein of gold, David Collins, a jealous rival, informs Kincaid, who arrives and recognizes Hayden. Threats of disclosure cause Hayden to relinquish his share, but when he saves Kincaid from a mine flood, Kincaid clears Hayden of guilt. *Mining. Partnerships. Colorado. United States Army—Desertion. Floods. Deserts.*

COLORADO PLUCK **F2.0974**

Fox Film Corp. 1 May **1921** [c1 May 1921; LP16486]. Si; b&w. 35mm. 5 reels, 4,700 ft.

Pres by William Fox. *Dir-Writ* Jules G. Furthman. *Photog* George Schneiderman.

Cast: William Russell *(Colorado Jim)*, Margaret Livingston *(Angela Featherstone)*, William Buckley *(Reggie Featherstone)*, George Fisher *(Philip Meredith)*, Helen Ware *(Lady Featherstone)*, Bertram Johns *(Lord Featherstone)*, Ray Berger *(butler)*.

Domestic melodrama. Source: George Goodchild, *Colorado Jim; or The Taming of Angela* (London, 1920). Colorado Jim, who has just become a millionaire, meets in New York young Englishman Reggie Featherstone, with whom he eventually goes to London. There he meets the Featherstone family, which is in financial distress. He falls in love with Angela, and, yielding to family pressure, she accepts Jim but informs him she will be his wife in name only. After she has depleted his money, he takes her back to Colorado, and they are followed by Philip Meredith, who also loves her. In evicting three men from his ranch, Jim is wounded, and while nursing him to health Angela finally realizes her love for him. *Millionaires. Ranchers. Marriage. London. Colorado.*

COLUMBUS (Chronicles of America Series) **F2.0975**

Chronicles of America Pictures. *For* Yale University Press. *Dist* Pathé Exchange. 7 Oct **1923** [c2 Apr 1923; LP18848]. Si; b&w. 35mm. 5 reels.

Dir Edwin L. Hollywood. *Adapt* Arthur E. Krows.

Cast: Fred Eric *(Christopher Columbus)*, Paul McAllister *(King John II of Portugal)*, Howard Truesdell *(The Bishop of Ceuta)*, Leslie Stowe *(Juan Pérez, prior of La Rábida)*, Dolores Cassinelli *(Queen Isabella)*, Robert Gaillard *(King Ferdinand)*.

Historical drama. Source: Irving Berdine Richman, *The Spanish Conquerors; a Chronicle of the Dawn of Empire Overseas* (New Haven, 1919). King John of Portugal continually puts off Christopher Columbus' plans to sail west in an effort to find a new route to India. After 4 years of waiting, however, Columbus discovers that the king has sent out his own men, who report no discovery of land. He goes to Spain, where he is again rebuffed, but the intercession of a former confessor of Queen Isabella results in an audience before the royal court. The queen is in sympathy with Columbus, and she secretly sells her jewels to finance his exploration. He sails with three ships and in October 1492 lands on an island in the West Indies. *America—Discovery and exploration. Portugal. Spain. Christopher Columbus. Isabella I (Castile and Aragon). Ferdinand V (Castile). John II (Portugal). Juan Pérez.*

THE COMBAT (Universal-Jewel) **F2.0976**

Universal Pictures. 28 Mar **1926** [c8 Feb 1926; LP22388]. Si; b&w. 35mm. 7 reels, 6,714 ft.

Dir Lynn Reynolds. *Screenplay* J. G. Hawks. *Story* J. G. Hawks, Edward J. Montagne. *Photog* Charles Stumar.

Cast: House Peters *(Blaze Burke)*, Wanda Hawley *(Ruth Childers)*, Walter McGrail *(Milton Symmons)*, C. E. Anderson *(Red McLaughlin)*, Charles Mailes *(Jerry Flint)*, Steve Clemento *(halfbreed)*, Howard Truesdale *(sheriff)*.

Melodrama. Blaze Burke, rough-and-ready lumberjack, is promised the job of camp boss if he eliminates a gang of lumber poachers. He is doublecrossed and the job goes to Milton Symmons, the employer's nephew. Blaze persuades Ruth Childers, Symmons' girl, to accompany him to a desolate cabin where they are followed by Red McLaughlin, deposed leader of the poachers, who after wounding Blaze is thrown to his death. Ruth returns to Symmons but transfers her love to Blaze when, during a forest fire, Symmons runs away and Blaze dashes through the flames to save her. *Lumberjacks. Lumber camps. Poaching. Forest fires.*

COMBAT **F2.0977**

Burton King Productions. *Dist* Pathé Exchange. 23 Oct **1927** [c29 Sep 1927; LU24457]. Si; b&w. 35mm. 6 reels, 5,100 ft.

Dir Albert Hiatt. *Story-Scen* William B. Laub. *Photog* Marcel Le Picard.

Cast: George Walsh *(Jack Hammond)*, Bradley Barker *(Capt. Samuel Yearkes)*, Claire Adams *(Wanda, his ward)*, Gladys Hulette *(Risa Bartlett)*, Dex Reynolds *(Craig Gordon)*.

Adventure melodrama. As Jack Hammond succeeds in perfecting his invention of a valuable formula, his uncle, Mark Hammond, for whom he has been working, declares it to be his own. Jack decides to fight him in court, but the uncle hires Capt. Samuel Yearkes, a desperado living on the Florida Keys, to do away with Jack. Risa Bartlett, a cafe hostess and admirer of Jack's, decides to lend him the money for a legal battle, but he is lured away to Tostado Island by a bodyguard position offered by Yearkes. There he falls in love with Wanda, Yearkes's ward, but Yearkes tries to influence her against the boy. Meanwhile Risa learns that Jack has been framed by his uncle and flies to Tostado with Craig Gordon, a millionaire suitor, and lands on a pretext. Yearkes's plan to kill Jack is foiled when they escape in his boat; Wanda decides to join them at the last minute. *Inventors. Uncles. Cafe hostesses. Millionaires. Bodyguards. Wards. Florida Keys.*

COME ACROSS **F2.0978**

Universal Pictures. 30 Jun **1929** [c8 Jun 1929; LP460]. Talking sequences (Movietone); b&w. 35mm. 6 reels, 5,330 ft. [Also si; 5,593 ft.]

Pres by Carl Laemmle. *Dir* Ray Taylor. *Adapt-Cont* Peter Milne. *Dial* Jacques Rollens, Monte Carter, Ford I. Beebe. *Titl* Ford I. Beebe. *Photog* Frank Redman. *Film Ed* Thomas Malloy. *Sd Rec* C. Roy Hunter.

Cast: Lina Basquette *(Mary Houston)*, Reed Howes *(Harry Fraser)*, Flora Finch *(Cassie)*, Crauford Kent *(George Harcourt)*, Gustav von Seyffertitz *(Pop Hanson)*, Clarissa Selwynne *(Harriet Houston)*.

Crook melodrama. Source: William Dudley Pelley, "The Stolen Lady" (publication undetermined). Desiring to see how the other half live, Mary Houston, a Long Island society girl, gets a dancing job at the Sphinx Night Club. Gang leader Pop Hanson, who owns the club, is scheming in tandem with Cassie and "Gentleman" Harry Fraser to swindle a Montana millionaire by having Harry pose as his long-lost brother. Harry falls for Mary and saves her during a police raid. Finding herself interested in Harry, Mary agrees to pose as his wife, though she is startled to learn the swindlers will use the temporarily deserted mansion of her aunt as base of operations. Mary asks George Harcourt, one of her admirers, to impersonate the intended victim; enraged by jealousy, Harcourt accuses Harry of being a fortune-hunting crook and summons the police. Pop and Cassie are arrested, and it develops that Harry is actually a playwright researching material for one of his stories. *Socialites. Dancers. Gangsters. Playwrights. Millionaires. Montanans. Impersonation. Courtship. Nightclubs.*

COME AND GET IT **F2.0979**

FBO Pictures. 3 Feb **1929** [c10 Jan 1929; LP25995]. Si; b&w. 35mm. 6 reels, 5,164 ft.

Dir Wallace Fox. *Scen* Frank Howard Clark. *Photog* Virgil Miller. *Film Ed* Della King. *Asst Dir* Richard Easton.

Cast: Bob Steele *(Breezy Smith)*, Jimmy Quinn *(Butch Farrel)*, Betty Welsh *(Jane Elliott)*, Jay Morley *(Tout Regan)*, James B. Leong *(Singapore Joe)*, Harry O'Connor *(Breezy's father)*, Marin Sais *(Breezy's mother)*, William Welsh *(Judge Elliott, Jane's father)*.

Melodrama. Breezy Smith, Navy lightweight boxing champion, is discharged from the service and, as he is leaving the docks, is attacked by Regan and Singapore Joe, a couple of crooks. Smith gets away from them, and the crooks trail him to his parents' home where Regan kills Judge Elliott, one of the Smith family's neighbors. Breezy's father is accused of the crime. Singapore Joe has a falling out with Regan and offers to get the goods on Regan in return for $1,000. Breezy wins the money in a prizefight and sees that Regan is brought to justice. *Prizefighters. Judges. Sailors. Informers. Injustice. Murder.*

COME ON COWBOYS! **F2.0980**

Ben Wilson Productions. *Dist* Arrow Film Corp. 6 Dec **1924** [c10 Dec 24; LP20900]. Si; b&w. 35mm. 5 reels, 4,641 ft.

Dir Ward Hayes. *Story-Cont* Ward Hayes, Dick Hatton.

Cast: Dick Hatton *(Jim Cartwright, top cowhand)*, Marilyn Mills *(Priscilla Worden, Rampart's ward)*, Harry Fenwick *(Wallace Rampart, Priscilla's uncle)*, Philip Sleeman *(F. Richard Worthington, Priscilla's suitor)*, Beverly *(herself, a horse)*.

Western melodrama. F. R. Worthington, a wealthy New Yorker, wants to marry popular Priscilla Worden, but she refuses; her uncle, Wallace Rampart, who is her legal guardian, owes Worthington a large sum of money and daily encourages his stubborn ward to accept the suit. Finally, out of desperation, Uncle Wallace, hoping to remove Priscilla from other and more attractive suitors, arranges for the three of them to visit the family ranch in Arizona, but his plan fails when, once out west, Priscilla falls in love with Jim Cartwright. Three cattle thieves, whom Worthington hires to kill Jim, throw him from a cliff into a deep ravine; Jim survives, however, and is rescued by Beverly, his educated horse. Jim then evens the score with the three men, but Priscilla must return to New York. She soon wires Jim that she is being forced into marriage with Worthington. Taking a few of his trusted men with him, Jim goes to New York. There the dauntless cowboys ride up Park Avenue to a last-minute rescue, and Jim and Priscilla make plans for an immediate marriage. *Cowboys. Uncles. Rustlers. Debt. New York City. Arizona. Horses.*

COME ON OVER **F2.0981**

Goldwyn Pictures. ca11 Mar **1922** [Los Angeles, Chicago, and Cleveland premieres; c25 Feb 1922; LP17582]. Si; b&w. 35mm. 6 reels, 5,556 ft.

Dir Alfred E. Green. *Story-Scen* Rupert Hughes. *Photog* L. William O'Connell. *Art Dir* Cedric Gibbons.

Cast: Colleen Moore *(Moyna Killiea)*, Ralph Graves *(Shane O'Mealia)*, J. Farrell MacDonald *(Michael Morahan)*, Kate Price *(Delia Morahan)*, James Marcus *(Carmody)*, Kathleen O'Connor *(Judy Dugan)*, Florence Drew *(Bridget Morahan)*, Harold Holland *(Myle Morahan)*, Mary Warren *(Kate Morahan)*, Elinor Hancock *(Mrs. Van Dusen)*, Monte Collins *(Dugan)*, C. E. Mason *(Barney)*, C. B. Leasure *(priest)*.

Comedy. Shane O'Mealia emigrates from Ireland to the United States, having promised to send for his sweetheart, Moyna Killiea, when he has earned money for her passage. He lives with the Morahans in New York, where he is unlucky in finding jobs and is constantly seen with Judy Dugan, for whose father he finds a job and whom he induces to take the temperance pledge. Secretly, Morahan goes to Ireland and brings back Moyna and her mother. As a result of a misunderstanding, Moyna believes that Shane and Judy are engaged to be married, and she vanishes. When found, she refuses to see Shane until his employer's sister, Mrs. Van Dusen, gives her a frock to wear to a party. At first Shane does not recognize her in her finery, but when he dances into her arms they are happily reunited. *Immigrants. Irish. Temperance. New York City.*

Note: Working title: *Darling*.

COME TO MY HOUSE **F2.0982**

Fox Film Corp. 25 Dec **1927** [c12 Dec 1927; LP24742]. Si; b&w. 35mm. 6 reels, 5,430 ft.

Pres by William Fox. *Dir* Alfred E. Green. *Scen* Marion Orth. *Titl* Malcolm Stuart Boylan. *Adapt* Philip Klein. *Photog* Joseph August. *Asst Dir* Jack Boland.

Cast: Olive Borden *(Joan Century)*, Antonio Moreno *(Floyd Bennings)*, Ben Bard *(Fraylor)*, Cornelius Keefe *(Murtaugh Pell)*, Doris Lloyd *(Renee Parsons)*, Richard Maitland *(Jimmy Parsons)*.

Society melodrama. Source: Arthur Somers Roche, *Come to My House* (New York, 1927). Joan Century, a carefree society girl, agrees to marry her persistent suitor, Murtaugh Pell, though she is not really in love with him; then, at a party, she meets Floyd Bennings, a woman-hating lawyer, and accepts his invitation to go to his house. She is seen by a blackmailer and is threatened with exposure unless she pays. Bennings agrees to take care of the blackmailer and when brought to trial for murder refuses to reveal the reason for his crime. Joan confesses at the last moment, risking her reputation to free him, and though she becomes a social outcast, she finds happiness in marriage with Bennings. *Socialites. Lawyers. Misogynists. Murder. Blackmail. Trials.*

COMING AN' GOING **F2.0983**

Action Pictures. *Dist* Weiss Brothers Artclass Pictures. 13 Mar **1926**. Si; b&w. 35mm. 5 reels, 4,800 ft.

Dir Richard Thorpe. *Scen* Frank L. Inghram.

Cast: Buffalo Bill Jr. *(Bill Martin)*, Belva McKay *(Rose Brown)*, Harry Todd *(Andy Simms)*, Hal Thompson *(James Bryce Brown)*, Mathilde Brundage *(Mrs. Brown)*.

Western melodrama. "Cowpuncher awakes in hotel of daughter of banker and is forced to marry her, though thought inferior by girl's mother. Saves mother from fire and she reverses her opinion." (*Motion Picture News Booking Guide*, 11:25, Oct 1926.) *Cowboys. Reputation. Hotels. Fires.*

THE COMING OF AMOS **F2.0984**

Cinema Corp. of America. *Dist* Producers Distributing Corp. 6 Sep **1925** [c5 Sep 1925; LP21791]. Si; b&w. 35mm. 6 reels, 5,677 ft.

Pres by Cecil B. De Mille. *Dir* Paul Sloane. *Prod Ed* Elmer Harris. *Adapt* James Ashmore Creelman, Garrett Fort. *Photog* Arthur Miller. *Art Dir* Chester Gore. *Asst Dir* William J. Scully.

Cast: Rod La Rocque *(Amos Burden)*, Jetta Goudal *(Princess Nadia Ramiroff)*, Noah Beery *(Ramón García)*, Richard Carle *(David Fontenay)*, Arthur Hoyt *(Bendyke Hamilton)*, Trixie Friganza *(Dowager Duchess of Parth)*, Clarence Burton *(Pedro Valdez)*, Ruby Lafayette *(nurse)*.

Romantic melodrama. Source: William John Locke, *The Coming of Amos* (London, 1924). Amos Burden, an Australian sheep rancher, fulfills a promise to his deceased mother and goes to visit his Uncle David, an artist, who lives on the Riviera. Despite his lack of polish and finesse, Amos attracts the attention of Nadia, an exiled Russian princess, and the two soon fall madly in love. Nadia then tells Amos that she is married to Ramón García, an unprincipled scoundrel who forced her into marriage by promising to save her family from the Russian reign of terror. García later kidnaps Nadia and takes her to an island fortress, attempting to have his way with her by locking her in a dungeon that is rapidly filling with water. Amos follows them to the island and rescues Nadia. Foiled by his own devious design, García himself drowns in the dungeon. *Sheepmen. Uncles. Artists. Royalty. Russians. Spanish. Australians. Torture. Riviera.*

COMING THROUGH **F2.0985**

Famous Players–Lasky. *Dist* Paramount Pictures. 26 Jan **1925** [c17 Feb 1925; LP21172]. Si; b&w. 35mm. 7 reels, 6,522 ft.

Pres by Adolph Zukor, Jesse L. Lasky. *Dir* Edward Sutherland. *Screenplay* Paul Schofield. *Photog* Faxon M. Dean.

Cast: Thomas Meighan *(Tom Blackford)*, Lila Lee *(Alice Rand)*, John Miltern *(John Rand)*, Wallace Beery *(Joe Lawler)*, Laurance Wheat *(Munds)*, Frank Campeau *(Shackleton)*, Gus Weinberg *(Dr. Rawls)*, Alice Knowland *(Mrs. Rawls)*.

Melodrama. Source: Jack Bethea, *Bed Rock* (Boston & New York, 1924). Tom Blackford is counting upon a promised promotion to enable him to marry Alice Rand, the daughter of a mine president; the appointment goes instead to Rand's nephew. Tom marries Alice anyway, much to the distress of her father, who discredits Tom in Alice's eyes by quoting to her Tom's incautious remark that the road to advancement seems to lie through relationship. Rand appoints Tom to be superintendent of his toughest mining camp, instructing his other executives that he wants Tom to fail at the job. Alice accompanies Tom to the camp, but she remains his wife in name only. Joe Lawler, the assistant foreman, working with the owner of a local saloon, foments trouble among the workers, and their joint efforts soon result in a strike. Tom destroys the saloon after a drunken engineer nearly kills some of the mine workers. Tom later discredits Lawler when he discloses that Lawler has been cheating the miners with crooked scales. Tom kills Lawler in a fight, and Tom and Alice are truly united at last. *Mine foremen. Saloon keepers. Mining camps. Strikes. Marriage—Companionate. Ambition.*

COMMON CLAY **F2.0986**

Fox Film Corp. 1 Aug **1930** [New York premiere; released 13 Aug; c14 Jun 1930; LP1369]. Sd (Movietone); b&w. 35mm. 9 reels, 7,961 ft.

Pres by William Fox. *Dir* Victor Fleming. *Screenplay-Dial* Jules Furthman. *Camera* Glen MacWilliams. *Sets* William Darling. *Film Ed* Irene Morra. *Rec Engr* B. J. Kroger, Eugene Grossman. *Asst Dir* William Tummel. *Cost* Sophie Wachner.

Cast: Constance Bennett *(Ellen Neal)*, Lew Ayres *(Hugh Fullerton)*, Tully Marshall *(W. H. Yates)*, Matty Kemp *(Arthur Coakley)*, Purnell B. Pratt *(Richard Fullerton)*, Beryl Mercer *(Mrs. Neal)*, Charles McNaughton *(Edwards)*, Hale Hamilton *(Judge Samuel Filson)*, Genevieve Blinn *(Mrs. Fullerton)*, Ada Williams *(Hugh's sister)*.

Society drama. Source: Cleves Kincaid, *Common Clay* (New York, 1917). Ellen Neal, after being arrested in a nightclub raid, follows the advice of the judge and determines to start a new life. She obtains a position as maid in the Fullerton home, where everyone from the butler to young Hugh Fullerton tries to engage her attentions; her affair with Hugh culminates in due course when their child is born. When Ellen refuses to accept a monetary settlement from the socially elite family, they investigate her past: it develops that she is herself illegitimate and that her mother had committed suicide to prevent the father's disgrace; but later her father is revealed to be none other than Fullerton's lawyer. Finally Hugh changes his judgment of her, and they are reunited. *Housemaids. Lawyers. Judges. Social classes. Seduction. Illegitimacy.*

THE COMMON LAW **F2.0987**

Selznick Pictures. 30 Aug **1923** [c26 Jul 1923; LP19245]. Si; b&w. 35mm. 8 reels, 7,527 ft.

Supv Myron Selznick. *Dir* George Archainbaud. *Adapt* Edward J. Montagne.

Cast: Corinne Griffith *(Valerie West)*, Conway Tearle *(Louis Neville)*, Elliott Dexter *(José Querida)*, Hobart Bosworth *(Henry Neville)*, Lillian

Lawrence *(Martha Neville)*, Bryant Washburn *(John Burleson)*, Doris May *(Stephanie)*, Harry Myers *(Cardemon)*, Miss Du Pont *(Lily Neville)*, Phyllis Haver *(Rita Terris)*, Wally Van *(Samuel Ogilvy)*, Dagmar Godowsky *(Mazie)*.

Society melodrama. Source: Robert William Chambers, *The Common Law* (New York, 1911). Valerie West, an artist's model, falls in love with Louis Neville, an aristocratic artist. His family, scorning Valerie, elicits her promise that she won't marry him. Valerie promises Neville that she will become his common-law wife on a certain date the next summer. Before that time arrives, the fiancé of Neville's sister forces his attentions on Valerie, but she escapes to Neville's home and wins his father's consent to their marriage. *Artists. Models. Social classes. Marriage—Common law.*

THE COMMON SIN *see* **FOR YOUR DAUGHTER'S SAKE**

THE COMPANIONATE MARRIAGE **F2.0988**

C. M. Corp. *Dist* First National Pictures. 21 Oct **1928** [c25 Aug, 11 Oct 1928; LP25570, LP25703]. Si; b&w. 35mm. 7 reels, 6,132 ft.

Supv Harold Shumate. *Dir* Erle C. Kenton. *Screenplay* Beatrice Van. *Scen* Benjamin Barr Lindsey, Wainwright Evans. *Titl* Casey Robinson. *Photog* Ray June. *Film Ed* Donn Hayes.

Cast: Betty Bronson *(Sally Williams)*, Alec B. Francis *(Judge Meredith)*, William Welsh *(Mr. Williams)*, Edward Martindel *(James Moore)*, Sarah Padden *(Mrs. Williams)*, Hedda Hopper *(Mrs. Moore)*, Richard Walling *(Donald Moore)*, Arthur Rankin *(Tommy Van Cleve)*, Ruth Moore *(June Nash)*.

Drama. Source: Benjamin Barr Lindsey and Wainwright Evans, *The Companionate Marriage* (New York, 1927). Sally Williams, the product of poverty and a broken home, works as a secretary for wealthy James Moore, whose son, Donald, falls in love with her and proposes marriage. Embittered and cynical, Sally wants no part of marriage and turns Donald down. Ruth Moore, Donald's sister, impulsively marries Tommy Van Cleve during a drunken party at a roadhouse and is herself quickly disillusioned about matrimony; after the birth of a baby, Tommy deserts her, and she commits suicide. Moved by Donald's grief and anger, Sally offers to marry him. He refuses until Judge Meredith, a family friend, draws up a legal contract whereby if, at the end of a stipulated period, either party is dissatisfied, the marriage is legally abrogated. Several years pass, and Donald and Sally find nothing but happiness and joy together. *Secretaries. Judges. Brother-sister relationship. Marriage. Marriage—Companionate. Suicide. Roadhouses.*

COMPASSION **F2.0989**

Victor Adamson Productions. 24 Dec **1927** [New York State license]. Si; b&w. 35mm. 6 reels, 5,800 ft.

Prod Denver Dixon. *Dir* Victor Adamson, Norval MacGregor. *Photog* Jack Fuqua.

Cast: Gaston Glass *(David Stanley)*, Alma Bennett *(Judith Deering)*, Josef Swickard *(Judge Henning)*, J. Frank Glendon, Dorise Lee *(Little Jester)*, Grace Dalton *(Gloria)*, Lillian Langdon *(Madame Gabrielle)*, Rolfe Sedan, Ernest Hilliard *(Carter)*.

Society drama(?). Source: Beth Slater Whitson, "Wings" (publication undetermined). No information about the precise nature of this film has been found. *Artists.*

Note: Also shown in New York (outside of New York City) in 5 reels.

COMPLETELY AT SEA *see* **OUT ALL NIGHT**

COMPROMISE **F2.0990**

Warner Brothers Pictures. 24 Oct **1925** [c2 Oct 1925; LP21873]. Si; b&w. 35mm. 7 reels, 6,789 ft.

Dir Alan Crosland. *Screenplay* Edward T. Lowe, Jr. *Photog* David Abel.

Cast: Irene Rich *(Joan Trevore)*, Clive Brook *(Alan Thayer)*, Louise Fazenda *(Hilda)*, Pauline Garon *(Nathalie)*, Raymond McKee *(Cholly)*, Helen Dunbar *(Aunt Catherine)*, Winter Hall *(Joan's father)*, Edward Martindel *(Commodore Smithson)*, Lynn Cowan *(James)*, Frank Butler *(Ole)*, Muriel Frances Dana *(Nathalie, as a child)*.

Drama. Source: Jay Gelzer, *Compromise* (New York, 1923). Joan Trevore, a woman of high ideals, expects to find in her marriage to Alan Thayer the happiness that has long eluded her. She and Alan are still on their honeymoon, however, when Nathalie Trevore, Joan's spoiled and selfish younger sister, sets her cap for Alan and successfully vamps him. Alan later boards a yacht for a business appointment and is "shaghaied" by Nathalie and her friends, who take him ashore so that Nathalie may triumph over Joan at the honeymoon cottage. Joan horsewhips Nathalie. A cyclone wrecks the cottage, and Alan saves Joan's life, leading to a reconciliation between them. *Sisters. Vamps. Brides. Marriage. Infidelity. Honeymoons. Flagellation. Yachts. Cyclones.*

COMRADES **F2.0991**

James Ormont Productions. *Dist* First Division Distributors. 1 Jan or 10 Feb **1928.** Si; b&w. 35mm. 6 reels, 5,400 ft.

Dir Cliff Wheeler. *Scen* Ruth Todd. *Titl* Jean Plannette. *Story* William Gilbert. *Photog* Ted Tetzlaff. *Film Ed* Gene Milford.

Cast: Donald Keith *(Perry O'Toole)*, Helene Costello *(Helen Dixon)*, Gareth Hughes *(Bob Dixon)*, Lucy Beaumont *(Mrs. Dixon)*, Joseph Swickard *(John Burton)*, James Lloyd *("Tommy")*.

Drama. Military school cadets Perry O'Toole and Bob Dixon agree to exchange names so that Perry, the younger and braver of the two, may enlist in the war effort. Bob's sister, Helen, believes Perry to be a coward, and returns his engagement ring. The soldier performs many feats of valor, which are attributed to the other boy, but the girl finally learns the truth while serving as a Red Cross nurse. Later her brother overcomes his cowardice and shields his friend from a bullet fired by a man deranged by the loss of his sons in the war. *Nurses. Brother-sister relationship. Cowardice. Military schools. World War I. Red Cross.*

CONCEIT **F2.0992**

Selznick Pictures. *Dist* Select Pictures. 20 Dec **1921** [c10 Dec 1921; LP17405]. Si; b&w. 35mm. 5 reels, 4,700 ft.

Pres by Lewis J. Selznick. *Dir* Burton George. *Scen* Edward J. Montagne. *Titl* Randolph Bartlett. *Story* Michael J. Phillips. *Photog* Alfred Gondolfi. *Film Ed* Cyril Gardner.

Cast: William B. Davidson *(William Crombie)*, Hedda Hopper *(Mrs. Crombie)*, Charles Gerard *(Hurt Kilstrom)*, Betty Hilburn *(Jeanette)*, Maurice Costello *(Barbe la Fleche)*, Pat Hartigan *(Bowles)*, Warren Cook *(McBain)*, Red Eagle *(Indian trapper)*.

Melodrama. William Crombie, a wealthy man of weak character, becomes lost in the wilderness on a hunting trip and is sheltered by a rough woodsman (Bowles) who lives with a pretty girl named Jeanette. Crombie becomes infatuated with her but is afraid to fight the woodsman for her, and she views him with contempt. Returning home, Crombie finds his neglected wife involved in an affair and decides to make a man of himself; after developing himself physically, he thrashes his wife's lover. He then seeks the woodsman to accept his challenge, but finding him near death, he pays for his medical care. Then, seeing that Jeanette really loves Bowles, he paves their way to a happy future. Returning to his hunting lodge, Crombie is surprised to find his wife awaiting his return. *Marriage. Cowardice. Manhood. Canadian Rockies.*

THE CONCENTRATIN' KID **F2.0993**

Hoot Gibson Productions. *Dist* Universal Pictures. 26 Oct **1930** [c10 Oct 1930; LP1631]. Sd (Movietone); b&w. 35mm. 6 reels, 5,148 ft.

Pres by Carl Laemmle. *Dir* Arthur Rosson. *Scen-Dial* Harold Tarshis. *Story* Harold Tarshis, Charles Gordon Saxton. *Photog* Harry Neumann. *Film Ed* Gilmore Walker. *Rec Engr* C. Roy Hunter.

Cast: Hoot Gibson *(Concentratin' Kid)*, Kathryn Crawford *(Betty Lou Vaughn)*, Duke R. Lee *(Moss Blaine)*, James Mason *(Campbell)*, Robert E. Homans *(C. C. Stile)*.

Western melodrama. A cowboy, known as The Concentratin' Kid, becomes enamoured of Betty Lou Vaughn, a radio singer whom he has never seen, and is inveigled into a wager with his friends whereby he loses a radio if he is not successful in winning her hand. Moss Blaine, foreman of the Bar Q Ranch, is in league with rustlers along with Campbell, whose friend Stile brings a group of showgirls to the town, including Betty Lou. She refuses the Kid's proposal after learning of the wager, and dejected, he returns to the ranch to find the cattle have been rustled while the hands were attending the show. He rides to head off the gang and meets Campbell, who has kidnaped Betty Lou; the Kid scatters the rustlers, rescues the girl, and marries her, thus winning the bet. *Cowboys. Singers. Showgirls. Rustlers. Ranch foremen. Wagers. Radio.*

THE CONCERT **F2.0994**

Goldwyn Pictures. 27 Feb **1921** [trade review; c21 Jan 1921; LP16041]. Si; b&w. 35mm. 6 reels.

Dir Victor Schertzinger. *Scen* J. E. Nash. *Photog* George Webber. *Asst Dir* Wyatt Brewster.

Cast: Lewis S. Stone *(Augustus Martinot)*, Myrtle Stedman *(Mary, his wife)*, Raymond Hatton *(Dr. Hart)*, Mabel Julienne Scott *(Delphine, his wife)*, Gertrude Astor *(Eva)*, Russ Powell *(Pollinger)*, Lydia Yeamans Titus *(Mrs. Pollinger)*, Frances Hall *(secretary)*, Louie Cheung *(Chinese servant)*.

Romantic comedy. Source: Hermann Bahr, *The Concert* (adapted by L. J. Ditrichstein; New York opening: 4 Oct 1910). Augustus Martinot, at 43 a renowned pianist fascinated by women but with an understanding wife, meets Delphine Hart, impressionable wife of a physician. In the mutual agreement that they are soul mates she induces him to take her to his mountain cabin for a weekend. Dr. Hart and Mrs. Martinot follow, and pretending to agree to the exchange of partners they shock Martinot and Delphine into reality. Each couple is reconciled. *Pianists. Physicians. Marriage. Mate swapping.*

Note: This film was remade in 1929 under the title *Fashions in Love*, q. v.

CONDEMNED **F2.0995**

Ben Wilson Productions. *Dist* Grand-Asher Distributing Corp. Dec **1923** [c6 Feb 1924; LP19887]. Si; b&w. 35mm. 6 reels, 6,000 ft. [Also 6,197 ft.]

Dir Arthur Rosson. *Story* Jules Furthman.

Cast: Mildred Davis *(The Girl)*, Carl Miller *(The Man)*.

Comedy-drama. Unable to pay the extra fare, The Girl—returning home after failing to make good in the city—bundles her pet dog to look like a baby. On the train the dog is mistaken for a kidnaped baby, and The Girl is left with the real baby. The presence of the baby coupled with the extraordinary explanation causes The Girl's guardians to doubt her and the town to ring with gossip. The original kidnapers, who have followed her home, attempt to retrieve the baby, and The Girl, discovered fainting in the arms of The Man who befriended her on the train, is turned out of her home. The Man loses his job for shielding The Girl. Just as they are being marched to the outskirts of town to be tarred and feathered, the guardians arrive with the real parents to claim the baby. The Girl marries her protector. *Guardians. Infants. Kidnaping. Gossip. Dogs.*

CONDEMNED **F2.0996**

Samuel Goldwyn, Inc. *Dist* United Artists. 3 Nov **1929** [New York premiere; released 16 Nov; c1 Dec 1929; LP912]. Sd (Movietone); b&w. 35mm. 10 reels, 8,300-9,000 ft. [Also si.]

Prod Samuel Goldwyn. *Dir* Wesley Ruggles. *Dial Dir* Dudley Digges. *Screenplay-Dial* Sidney Howard. *Photog* George Barnes, Gregg Toland. *Set Dsgn* William Cameron Menzies. *Film Ed* Stuart Heisler. *Song: "Song of the Condemned"* Jack Meskill, Pete Wendling.

Cast: Ronald Colman *(Michel)*, Ann Harding *(Madame Vidal)*, Dudley Digges *(Vidal)*, Louis Wolheim *(Jacques)*, William Elmer *(Pierre)*, Albert Kingsley *(Félix)*, William Vaughn *(Vidal's orderly)*.

Melodrama. Source: Blair Niles, *Condemned to Devil's Island* (New York, 1928). Michel, a debonair young thief, and Jacques, an unscrupulous murderer, are sent to Devil's Island, the French penal colony, where Vidal, the dictatorial warden, rules with an iron hand. His beautiful young wife, Madame Vidal, repelled by the island, becomes dangerously attracted to Michel when he is made her house servant, thus severing his friendship with Jacques. When Vidal hears gossip about his wife and Michel, he confronts his wife, then Michel, with jealous accusations; frenzied, his wife turns on him, swearing Michel is innocent though she loves him. Michel is sent to solitary confinement on the dreaded island of St. Joseph. Learning Vidal plans to send her back to France, Madame Vidal communicates through Jacques with Michel, who effects an escape and conspires to meet her aboard a steamer. In the escape attempt, Vidal is drowned and Jacques is fatally shot; Michel surrenders but exchanges an oath of eternal fidelity with the lady. *French. Convicts. Friendship. Jealousy. Penal colonies. Prison escapes. Devil's Island.*

CONDUCTOR 1492 **F2.0997**

Warner Brothers Pictures. 12 Jan **1924** [c25 Dec 1923; LP20761]. Si; b&w. 35mm. 7 reels, 6,500 ft.

Dir Charles Hines, Frank Griffin. *Story* Johnny Hines. *Photog* Charles E. Gilson. *Film Ed* Clarence Kolster.

Cast: Johnny Hines *(Terry O'Toole, "Conductor 1492")*, Doris May *(Noretta Connelly)*, Dan Mason *(Mike O'Toole)*, Ruth Renick *(Edna Brown)*, Robert Cain *(Richard Langford)*, Fred Esmelton *(Denman Connelly)*, Byron Sage *(Bobby Connelly)*, Michael Dark *(James Stoddard)*, Dorothy Burns *(Mrs. Brown)*.

Comedy-drama. Terry O'Toole, a young Irishman, arrives in America and gets a job as a streetcar conductor. He rescues the son of company president Denman Connelly; foils the attempts of crooks to gain control of the company; and marries Connelly's daughter, Noretta. *Irish. Immigrants. Streetcar conductors. Streetcars.*

CONEY ISLAND **F2.0998**

FBO Pictures. 13 Jan **1928** [c13 Jan 1928; LP24950]. Si; b&w. 35mm. 7 reels, 6,385 ft.

Dir Ralph Ince. *Screenplay* Enid Hibbard. *Scen* Joseph Jefferson O'Neil. *Titl* Dorothy Herzog, Jack Conway (of *Variety*). *Story* Joseph Jefferson O'Neil, Adele Buffington, Maxine Alton. *Photog* J. O. Taylor, Robert Martin. *Film Ed* George M. Arthur.

Cast: Lois Wilson *(Joan Wellman)*, Lucilla Mendez *(Joy Carroll)*, Eugene Strong *(Tammany Burke)*, Rudolph Cameron *(Bob Wainwright)*, William Irving *(Hughey Cooper)*, Gus Leonard *(Jingles Wellman)*, Orlo Sheldon *(Cooper's aide)*, Carl Axzelle *(Grimes)*.

Romantic drama. Tammany Burke, young owner of a giant roller coaster, is fighting heavy odds against a syndicate led by financial baron Hughey Cooper. Assisted by his sweetheart, Joan, and her father, Jingles Wellman, formerly a clown, Burke prepares for a sabotage of his machine by syndicate hirelings. In the midst of a great battle the riot squad arrives to arrest the troublemakers, and Burke and his sweetheart are left in happy possession of their roller coaster. *Clowns. Concessionaires. Financiers. Syndicates. Roller coasters. Amusement parks. Coney Island.*

CONFESSION (Reissue) **F2.0999**

Dist George H. Davis. 3 May **1927** [New York showing]. Si; b&w. 35mm. 7 reels.

Note: Originally produced and distributed by National Film Co., caMar 1920.

CONFESSIONS OF A QUEEN **F2.1000**

Metro-Goldwyn Pictures. 30 Mar **1925** [c25 Mar 1925; LP21273]. Si; b&w. 35mm. 7 reels, 5,820 ft.

Pres by Louis B. Mayer. *Dir* Victor Seastrom. *Adapt* Agnes Christine Johnston. *Photog* Percy Hilburn. *Art Dir* Cedric Gibbons, James Basevi. *Film Ed* Hugh Wynn. *Cost* Ethel P. Chaffin.

Cast: Alice Terry *(Frederika/The Queen)*, Lewis Stone *(The King)*, John Bowers *(Prince Alexei)*, Eugenie Besserer *(Elanora)*, Helena D'Algy *(Sephora)*, Frankie Darro *(Prince Zara)*, Joseph Dowling *(Duke of Rosen)*, André de Beranger *(Lewin)*, Bert Sprotte *(revolutionary leader)*, Wilbur Higby *(revolutionary officer)*, Otto Hoffman *(king's valet)*, Frances Hatton *(queen's maid)*, James McElhern *(king's Parisian valet)*.

Drama. Source: Alphonse Daudet, *Les Rois en exil; roman parisien* (Paris, 1879). King Christian of Illyria, a small and decadent empire, spends all his time with his voluptuous mistress, Sephora, on the days immediately preceding his marriage to Princess Frederika, a beautiful and highly spiritual young noblewoman. Prince Alexei, the king's cousin, entertains Frederika, and the two become greatly attracted to each other. After the royal marriage, a child is born to the queen, but the king is interested only in a new mistress, with whom he openly rides in the streets. The populace becomes discontented, a revolution breaks out, and the king abdicates, escaping with his wife and child to Paris, where they finally come to love each other. Alexei works for the king's reinstatement, but the closeness between Frederika and the prince provokes the king to jealousy, and he turns to rowdy companions for solace. The king later secures the throne for Alexei, who then plots to poison him. Frederika learns of the plot and finds her husband just in time to save his life. Alexei ascends the unhappy throne of Illyria, while the former king and his family live in happy exile in Paris. *Mistresses. Royalty. Revolutions. Infidelity. Imaginary kingdoms. Paris.*

CONFESSIONS OF A WIFE **F2.1001**

Excellent Pictures. 10 Dec **1928** [c18 Dec 1928; LP25935]. Si; b&w. 35mm. 6 reels, 6,047 ft.

Pres by Samuel Zierler. *Supv* Burton King. *Dir* Albert Kelly. *Photog* M. A. Anderson, Louis Dengel.

Cast: Helene Chadwick *(Marion Atwell)*, Arthur Clayton *(Paul Atwell)*, Ethel Grey Terry *(Mrs. Livingston)*, Walter McGrail *(Henri Duval)*, Carl Gerard *(Handsome Harry)*, Clarissa Selwynne *(Mrs. Jonathan)*, Sam Lufkin *(Bumby Lewis)*, De Sacia Mooers *(Dupree)*, Suzanne Rhoades

(Annette Pringle).

Society melodrama. Source: Owen Davis, *Confessions of a Wife; or From Mill to Millions* (c1904). Marion Atwell, a compulsive gambler who loses a large sum of money at bridge, becomes increasingly indebted to Henri Duval, a shill for a gang of thieves and murderers who prey on the idle rich. Duval offers to free Marion of all her debts if she will gain his gang's admittance to Mrs. Jonathan's Jewel Ball, a social occasion at which all of the guests wear their best gems. Marion notifies the detectives instead, and Duval and his men are arrested. Marion tells her pathetic story to the guests at the ball and is forgiven by friend and family alike. *Gamblers. Socialites. Idle rich. Detectives. Robbery. Blackmail.*

CONFIDENCE **F2.1002**

Universal Film Manufacturing Co. 25 Sep **1922** [c13 Sep 1922; LP18224]. Si; b&w. 35mm. 5 reels, 4,787 ft.

Pres by Carl Laemmle. *Dir* Harry Pollard. *Scen* Raymond L. Schrock. *Story* Bernard Hyman. *Photog* Howard Oswald.

Cast: Herbert Rawlinson *(Bob Mortimer)*, Harriet Hammond *(Miriam Wiggins)*, Lincoln Plummer *(Professor Lang)*, William A. Carroll *(Homer Waldron)*, Otto Hoffman *(Josiah Wiggins)*, William Robert Daly *(Ephraim Bates)*, Hallam Cooley *(Elmer Tuttle)*, John Steppling *(Henry Tuttle)*, Melbourne MacDowell *(J. D. Sprowl)*, Gerald Pring *(Henry Taylor)*, Robert Milasch *(Bige Miller)*, Margaret Campbell *(Mrs. Waldron)*, Sam Allen *(Constable Kittering)*.

Rural comedy. Bob Mortimer, an unsuccessful traveling salesman, picks up the wrong valise and finds it full of money. This gives him the confidence, which he has previously lacked, to convince the townspeople to invest in a new factory, prevent Josiah Wiggins from absconding with the invested funds, and marry Miriam Wiggins. *Traveling salesmen. Self-confidence. Factories.*

Note: Working title: *Rainbow Chasers.*

THE CONFIDENCE MAN **F2.1003**

Famous Players–Lasky. *Dist* Paramount Pictures. 20 Apr **1924** [c30 Apr 1924; LP20134]. Si; b&w. 35mm. 8 reels, 7,304 ft.

Pres by Adolph Zukor, Jesse L. Lasky. *Dir* Victor Heerman. *Scen* Paul Sloane. *Titl* George Ade. *Story* Laurie York Erskine, Robert Hobart Davis. *Photog* Henry Cronjager.

Cast: Thomas Meighan *(Dan Corvan)*, Virginia Valli *(Margaret Leland)*, Laurence Wheat *(Larry Maddox)*, Charles Dow Clark *(Godfred Queritt)*, Helen Lindroth *(Mrs. Bland)*, Jimmie Lapsley *(Jimmie Bland)*, Margaret Seddon *(Mrs. X)*, George Nash *(Wade)*, Dorothy Walters *(Mrs. O'Brien)*, David Higgins *(The Minister)*.

Crook melodrama. Source: Laurie York Erskine, *The Confidence Man* (New York, 1925). Dan Corvan and Larry Maddox, salesmen for promoters of phony oil stock, endear themselves to the people of Fairfield, Florida, in an attempt to fleece skinflint Godfrey Queritt. When they are at the point of success, an old lady asks Corvan to restore some money her son has stolen, and touched by the trust of local girl Margaret Leland, Corvan decides to go straight. *Confidence men. Criminals—Rehabilitation. Skinflints. Smalltown life. Florida.*

THE CONFLICT (Universal-Jewel) **F2.1004**

Universal Film Manufacturing Co. 7 Nov **1921** [c22 Oct 1921; LP17123]. Si; b&w. 35mm. 7 reels, 6,205 ft.

Pres by Carl Laemmle. *Dir* Stuart Paton. *Scen* George C. Hull. *Photog* Harold Janes.

Cast: Priscilla Dean *(Dorcas Remalie)*, Edward Connelly *(John Remalie)*, Hector Sarno *(Buck Fallon)*, Martha Mattox *(Miss Labo)*, Olah Norman *(Letty Piggott)*, Herbert Rawlinson *(Jevons)*, L. C. Shumway *(Mark Sloane)*, Sam Allen *(Orrin Lakin)*, C. E. Anderson *(Ovid Jenks)*, Knute Erickson *(Hannibal Ginger)*, Bill Gillis *(Hasdrubel Ginger)*.

Melodrama. Source: Clarence Budington Kelland, *Conflict* (New York, c1922). Society girl Dorcas Remalie, to fulfill the dying request of her father, goes to live in the northwoods home of her Uncle John, a sinister and dictatorial lumber baron whose household is managed by the forbidding Miss Labo. While the uncle is away, Miss Labo tries to poison Dorcas, and Dorcas seeks safety with Jevons, a young man who is fighting her uncle for land rights. Learning that Jevons is in captivity and danger, Dorcas assumes his place and leads his lumbermen to a fight with Remalie's men. She is forced to dynamite a dam, thus creating a torrent that floods a dry streambed. Learning that Jevons is trapped in the flood's path, she rescues him before he reaches the falls. The uncle repents, and Jevons and Dorcas become engaged. *Socialites. Uncles. Lumbering. Land rights. Dams. Floods.*

THE CONJURE WOMAN **F2.1005**

Micheaux Film Corp. **1926.** Si; b&w. 35mm. [Feature length assumed.]

Cast: Evelyn Preer, Percy Verwayen.

Melodrama(?). No information about the precise nature of this film has been found. *Conjurers. Negro life.*

A CONNECTICUT YANKEE AT KING ARTHUR'S COURT **F2.1006**

Fox Film Corp.–Mark Twain Co. 11 Sep **1921** [c20 Dec 1920; LP16111]. Si; b&w. 35mm. 8 reels, 8,291 ft.

Pres by William Fox. *Dir* Emmett J. Flynn. *Adapt* Bernard McConville. *Photog* Lucien Andriot. *Art Dir* Ralph De Lacy. *Film Ed* C. R. Wallace. *Asst Dir* Ray Flynn.

Cast: Harry Myers *(The Yankee/Martin Cavendish)*, Pauline Starke *(Sandy [Betty?])*, Rosemary Theby *(Queen Morgan le Fay)*, Charles Clary *(King Arthur)*, William V. Mong *(Merlin the Magician)*, George Siegmann *(Sir Sagramore)*, Charles Gordon *(The Page, Clarence)*, Karl Formes *(Mark Twain)*, Herbert Fortier *(Mr. Cavendish)*, Adele Farrington *(Mrs. Cavendish)*, Wilfred McDonald *(Sir Lancelot)*.

Satire. Source: Mark Twain, *A Connecticut Yankee at King Arthur's Court* (1889). Wealthy young Martin Cavendish, whose mother wants him to marry Lady Gordon, is in love with Betty, his mother's secretary. One night, while reading about the Age of Chivalry, he is knocked unconscious by a burglar: *In a dream he finds himself in sixth-century England and is taken to the castle of King Arthur. His use of American slang complicates matters; Merlin, the king's magician, suggests that he be burned at the stake, but he escapes death by predicting accurately an eclipse of the sun. Martin is knighted as Sir Boss and proceeds to provide the castle with the latest (1921) improvements: telephones, plumbing, and tin lizzies. After rescuing a damsel from the wicked Queen Morgan le Fay, Martin accepts a challenge with Sir Sagramore in a tournament in which he is victorious with his lariat.* He awakens from his trance and elopes with his mother's secretary. *Secretaries. Filial relations. Age of Chivalry. Connecticut. Mark Twain. King Arthur. Dreams.*

THE CONQUERING POWER (Metro Special) **F2.1007**

Metro Pictures. ca8 Jul **1921** [New York premiere; c28 Nov 1921; LP17258]. Si; b&w. 35mm. 7 reels.

Prod-Dir Rex Ingram. *Adapt* June Mathis. *Photog* John F. Seitz. *Tech Dir* Ralph Barton, Amos Myers.

Cast: Alice Terry *(Eugénie Grandet)*, Rudolph Valentino *(Charles Grandet)*, Eric Mayne *(Victor Grandet)*, Ralph Lewis *(Père Grandet)*, Edna Demaurey *(his wife)*, Edward Connelly *(Notary Cruchot)*, George Atkinson *(his son)*, Willard Lee Hall *(The Abbé)*, Mark Fenton *(Monsieur des Grassins)*, Bridgetta Clark *(his wife)*, Ward Wing *(Adolph)*, Mary Hearn *(Nanon)*, Eugène Pouyet *(Cornoiller)*, Andrée Tourneur *(Annette)*.

Drama. Source: Honoré de Balzac, *Eugénie Grandet* (1883). Monsieur Grandet, the wealthiest man in his province, forces his wife and daughter, Eugénie, to submit to the regime of mean poverty. Because of her wealth, Eugénie attracts aspiring suitors Cruchot de Bonfons, a minor magistrate, and Alphonse des Grassins, son of a local banker. Grandet's nephew Charles, a wealthy young dandy, arrives from Paris with news of his father's suicide and falls in love with Eugénie, with whom he exchanges vows before leaving for Martinique to repair his fortune. Père Grandet intercepts their letters and locks up Eugénie after learning that she has lent Charles money for his voyage. His mind affected by the death of his wife, Grandet is trapped while contemplating his money and in his efforts to escape is killed by a chest of gold. Eugénie is about to sign a marriage contract with Cruchot when Charles arrives to claim her. *Misers. Dandies. Wealth. Suicide. Family life. Courtship. France. Martinique.*

CONQUERING THE WOMAN **F2.1008**

King W. Vidor Productions. *Dist* Associated Exhibitors. 10 Dec **1922** [c11 Nov 1922; LU18394]. Si; b&w. 35mm. 6 reels, 5,887 ft.

Dir King Vidor. *Scen* Frank Howard Clark. *Photog* George Barnes.

Cast: Florence Vidor *(Judith Stafford)*, Bert Sprotte *(Tobias Stafford)*, Mathilde Brundage *(Aunt Sophia)*, David Butler *(Larry Saunders)*, Roscoe Karns *(Shorty Thompson)*, Peter Burke *(Count Henri)*, Harry Todd *(Sandy MacTavish)*.

Romantic drama. Source: Henry Cottrell Rowland, "Kidnapping Coline," in *Everybody's* (29:312–327, 494–509, 644–659, 845–857; 30:123–135; Sep 1913–Jan 1914). Spoiled society girl Judith Stafford accepts the proposal of Count Henri, while acquiring a foreign manner and scorn for American "barbarians." Her displeased father, Tobias Stafford, contrives to have Judith and his cowboy friend, Larry Saunders, marooned on a South Sea isle to break her spirit. Harsh treatment has no effect, but gentler methods cause a change and the couple fall in love. The count kidnaps Judith, but Tobias arrives in time to retrieve her for Larry. *Cowboys. Socialites. Filial relations. South Sea Islands.*

THE CONQUEROR (Reissue) **F2.1009**

Fox Film Corp. 14 Sep **1924.** Si; b&w. 35mm. 6 reels.

Note: Originally released by Fox (16 Sep 1917; c9 Sep 1917; LP11362) in 8 reels, starring William Farnum in the role of Sam Houston.

CONQUEST **F2.1010**

Warner Brothers Pictures. 22 Dec **1928** [c18 Dec 1928; LP25927]. Sd (Vitaphone); b&w. 35mm. 8 reels, 6,729 ft. [Also si, 19 Jan 1929; 4,700 ft.]

Dir Roy Del Ruth. *Screenplay* C. Graham Baker. *Dial* Jackson Rose. *Titl* Joseph Jackson. *Adapt* Eve Unsell. *Photog* Barney McGill. *Film Ed* Jack Killifer. *Asst Dir* Joe Barry. *Cost* Earl Luick.

Cast: Monte Blue *(Donald Overton)*, H. B. Warner *(James Farnham)*, Lois Wilson *(Diane Holden)*, Edmund Breese *(William Holden)*, Tully Marshall *(Dr. Gerry)*.

Melodrama. Source: Mary Imlay Taylor, "Conquest" (publication undetermined). Attempting to fly an airplane to the South Pole, James Farnham and Donald Overton crash in the Antarctic wastes. Donald's leg is broken, and Farnham leaves him to die, returning to civilization and marrying Donald's former fiancée, Diane Holden, who takes pity on him. Donald is rescued by the crew of a whaler and, scarred and crazed, returns to civilization looking for revenge. He persuades Diane's father, the sponsor of the first flight, to finance another one and again takes Farnham with him as copilot. Again they crash, and this time Farnham's leg is broken. Donald cannot bring himself to leave him, and together they make their way to safety. On the way back to civilization, Farnham asks Donald's forgiveness and then kills himself, freeing Donald to find happiness with Diane. *Explorers. Aviators. Sea rescue. Revenge. Suicide. Whaling ships. Antarctic regions. Airplane accidents.*

THE CONQUEST OF CANAAN **F2.1011**

Famous Players–Lasky. *Dist* Paramount Pictures. 21 Aug **1921** [c20 Aug 1921; LP16883]. Si; b&w. 35mm. 7 reels.

Pres by Adolph Zukor. *Dir* R. William Neill. *Scen* Frank Tuttle. *Photog* Harry Perry.

Cast: Thomas Meighan *(Joe Louden)*, Doris Kenyon *(Ariel Taber)*, Diana Allen *(Mamie Pike)*, Ann Egleston *(Mrs. Louden)*, Alice Fleming *(Claudine)*, Charles Abbe *(Eskew Arp)*, Malcolm Bradley *(Jonas Taber)*, Paul Everton *(Happy Farley)*, Macey Harlam *(Nashville Cory)*, Henry Hallam *(Colonel Flintcroft)*, Louis Hendricks *(Judge Pike)*, Charles Hartley *(Peter Bradbury)*, Jed Prouty *(Norbert Flintcroft)*, Cyril Ring *(Gene Louden)*, J. D. Walsh *(Squire Buckelew)*, Riley Hatch *(Mike Sheenan)*.

Drama. Source: Booth Tarkington, *The Conquest of Canaan* (1905). Joe Louden's defiance of conventions and his knowledge of corrupt political leaders in the town of Canaan stamp him as an outcast of polite society. His friend Ariel Taber, who becomes wealthy when her uncle dies, leaves town, advising him to make good; and he begins to study law. Later, after Ariel's return, he opens a law office in Beaver Beach, a hotbed of political scandals. Happy Farley kills Nashville Cory because of the latter's attentions to his wife, and Joe defends him. His prime witness reveals in anger that Judge Pike, the social and political ruler of the town, is the owner of the beach, and Farley defends the judge against the mob. Farley is acquitted; Joe wins Ariel and is proclaimed the next mayor of Canaan. *Nonconformists. Lawyers. Judges. Mayors. Political corruption. Smalltown life. Murder.*

CONSPIRACY **F2.1012**

RKO Productions. 3 or 10 Aug **1930** [c27 Jul 1930; LP1452]. Sd (Photophone); b&w. 35mm. 7 reels, 6,480 ft.

Prod William Le Baron. *Assoc Prod* Bertram Millhauser. *Dir* Christy Cabanne. *Screenplay-Dial* Beulah Marie Dix. *Photog* Nick Musuraca. *Art Dir* Max Ree. *Film Ed* Arthur Roberts, Sam White. *Rec Engr* John Tribby. *Asst Dir* Dewey Starkey.

Cast: Bessie Love *(Margaret Holt)*, Ned Sparks *(Winthrop Clavering)*, Hugh Trevor *(John Howell)*, Rita La Roy *(Nita Strong)*, Ivan Lebedeff *(Butch Miller)*, Gertrude Howard *(Martha)*, Otto Matieson *(James Morton [Marco])*, Jane Keckley *(Rose Towne)*, Donald MacKenzie *(Captain McLeod)*, George Irving *(Mark Holt)*, Bert Moorehouse *(Victor Holt)*, Walter Long *(Weinberg)*.

Mystery melodrama. Source: Robert Melville Baker and John Emerson, *Conspiracy* (New York, 1913). Margaret Holt and her brother Victor set out to smash a narcotics ring responsible for their father's death: Victor becomes a district attorney and weaves a net around the gang and its leader Marco, alias James Morton, while Margaret becomes Marco's secretary. Marco soon discovers her duplicity and is about to have his henchmen kill her brother when she stabs him with a paper cutter; but she is too late to save Victor. In desperation, she goes to apply for shelter and meets John Howell, a young reporter looking for a story, who promises to help. Winthrop Clavering, an eccentric author of mystery stories, employs Margaret as his secretary and unravels the truth about the murder. Meanwhile, Howell learns that Victor is being held prisoner by the gangsters. Learning the identity of Margaret, Clavering summons the gang to his apartment, where they are arrested; Howell rescues Victor and wins Margaret. *Secretaries. District attorneys. Gangsters. Reporters. Novelists. Brother-sister relationship. Murder. Narcotics.*

CONTRABAND **F2.1013**

Famous Players–Lasky. *Dist* Paramount Pictures. 16 Feb **1925** [c10 Feb 1925; LP21107]. Si; b&w. 35mm. 7 reels, 6,773 ft.

Pres by Adolph Zukor, Jesse L. Lasky. *Dir* Alan Crosland. *Screenplay* Jack Cunningham. *Photog* Al Siegler.

Cast: Lois Wilson *(Carmel Lee)*, Noah Beery *(Deputy Jenney)*, Raymond Hatton *(Launcelot Bangs)*, Raymond McKee *(Evan B. Pell)*, Charles Ogle *(Sheriff Churchill)*, Luke Cosgrave *(Tubal)*, Edwards Davis *(Abner Fownes)*, Johnny Fox *(Simmy)*, Victor Potel *(George Bogardus)*, Alphonse Ethier *(Jared Whitfield)*, Cesare Gravina *(Pee Wee Bangs)*, Lillian Leighton *(Mrs. Churchill)*.

Melodrama. Source: Clarence Budington Kelland, *Contraband* (New York & London, c1923). Carmel Lee inherits a newspaper in a small country town and leaves her home in the city to take charge of it. She soon discovers that the town is terrorized by a band of bootleggers, who abduct and later kill the local sheriff. With the aid of Professor Pell, who has been recently fired as school superintendent, Carmel makes a public issue of the sheriff's murder, editorializing in her paper for justice and reform. Pell and Carmel are kidnaped by the bootleggers, but Carmel escapes and alerts the police. The bootleggers are arrested, the sheriff's murder in solved, and Abner Fownes, a politician and one of the town's leading citizens, is uncovered as the leader of the gang. *Bootleggers. Sheriffs. Professors. Politicians. Murder. Abduction. Newspapers.*

CONTRE-ENQUÊTE **F2.1014**

Warner Brothers Pictures. 5 Dec **1930** [Paris premiere]. Sd (Vitaphone); b&w. 35mm. 7 reels.

Dir Jean Daumery.

Cast: Daniel Mendaille *(Joe)*, Suzy Vernon *(Nora)*, Jeanne Helbling *(Betty)*, Georges Mauloy *(Dan)*, Rolla Norman *(Benson)*, Louis Mercier *(Tonio)*, Frank O'Neil *(Fred)*, Emile Chautard *(O'Brien)*.

Underworld melodrama. Source: George Kibbe Turner, "Those Who Dance" (publication undetermined). A French-language version of *Those Who Dance,* q. v. *Gangsters. Molls. Detectives. State governors. Brother-sister relationship. Imposture. Frameup. Dictographs.*

THE CONVICT'S CODE **F2.1015**

W. Ray Johnston. *Dist* Syndicate Pictures. Aug **1930.** Sd; b&w. 35mm. 7 reels, 6,500 ft. [Also 6 reels, 5,600 ft.]

Dir Harry Revier. *Story-Scen-Dial* Mabel Z. Carroll, Vincent Valentini. *Photog* George Peters, Al Harsten. *Sd* George Luckey, T. Dewhurst.

Cast: Cullen Landis *(Kenneth Avery)*, Eloise Taylor *(Nan Perry)*, William Morris *(Theodore Perry)*, Robert Cummings *(Governor Johnson)*, Lyle Evans *(Robert Shannon)*, Mabel Z. Carroll *(Mazie Lawrence)*, John Irwin *(a lifer)*, John Burkell *(trusty)*.

Mystery drama. Just before the scheduled electrocution of stockbroker Kenneth Avery for the murder of Mazie Lawrence, Nan Perry makes one last plea to the governor for a stay of execution and relates the incidents that led to Mazie's death: *Maneuvering Kenneth to his apartment, Mazie gives him every opportunity to alleviate her unhappiness with her husband, but he refuses to succumb to her advances. Nan and Shannon, Kenneth's lawyer and rival, enter; there is a shot and a scream; and Mazie is dead. Believing Kenneth guilty, Nan testifies against him at the trial.* The governor refuses her plea, but a prison break interrupts Kenneth's execution and results in a fatal wound to Shannon, who, dying, confesses to Mazie's murder. *Stockbrokers. Lawyers. State governors. Murder. Capital punishment. Prison escapes. Trials.*

CONVOY **F2.1016**

Robert Kane Productions. *Dist* First National Pictures. 24 Apr **1927** [c11 Apr 1927; LP23841]. Si; b&w. 35mm. 8 reels, 7,724 ft.

Pres by Robert Kane. *Assoc Prod* Victor Hugo Halperin, Edward R. Halperin. *Dir* Joseph C. Boyle. *Scen* Willis Goldbeck. *Photog* Ernest Haller. *Prod Mgr* Leland Hayward.

Cast: Lowell Sherman *(Ernest Drake)*, Dorothy Mackaill *(Sylvia Dodge)*, William Collier, Jr. *(John Dodge)*, Lawrence Gray *(Eugene Weyeth)*, Ian Keith *(Smith)*, Gail Kane *(Mrs. Weyeth)*, Vincent Serrano *(Mr. Dodge)*, Donald Reed *(Smith's assistant)*, Eddie Gribbon *(Eddie)*, Jack Ackroyd *(Jack)*, Ione Holmes *(Ione)*.

War melodrama. Source: John Taintor Foote, *The Song of the Dragon* (New York, 1923). Sylvia Dodge is engaged to Eugene Weyeth, best friend of her brother, John, when war is declared; and both young men enlist in the Navy. Smith, a secret service operative, informs Sylvia that Ernest Drake, one of her most persistent admirers, is the leader of a German spy ring and persuades her to encourage his companionship so as to learn his contacts and methods. Found in Drake's apartment by her brother and fiancé, Sylvia is disowned by her family; and when Drake is arrested, she leaves home. Attempting to learn the location of her brother from sailors at the Navy Yard, Sylvia is arrested as a streetwalker and sentenced to a year on Blackwells Island. In a great naval conflict, combined British and American fleets repell the Germans in Keil Harbor, and John is killed. After the Armistice, Sylvia is reunited with Eugene at her brother's grave. *Prostitutes. Germans. Secret service. Spies. Naval battles. World War I. Kiel. Blackwells Island. United States Navy.*

THE COP **F2.1017**

De Mille Pictures. *Dist* Pathé Exchange. 20 Aug **1928** [c11 Jul 1928; LP25458]. Si; b&w. 35mm. 8 reels, 7,054 ft.

Prod Ralph Block. *Dir* Donald Crisp. *Scen* Tay Garnett. *Titl* John Krafft. *Story* Elliott Clawson. *Photog* Arthur Miller. *Art Dir* Stephen Goosson. *Film Ed* Barbara Hunter. *Asst Dir* Emile De Ruelle. *Prod Mgr* Harry Poppe. *Tech Adv* Schuyler E. Grey.

Cast: William Boyd *(Pete Smith)*, Alan Hale *(Mather)*, Jacqueline Logan *(Mary Monks)*, Robert Armstrong *(Scarface Marcas)*, Tom Kennedy *(Sergeant Coughlin)*, Louis Natheaux *(Louie)*, Phil Sleeman *(Lord Courtney)*.

Underworld melodrama. Pete Smith, a rookie cop, is assigned to run down Scarface Marcas, a crook leader whom he once befriended. (A friendship that developed between the two when Smith, caretaker of a drawbridge, nursed Marcas, wounded in a gun battle, quickly terminated when Marcas secretly left, taking with him Smith's overcoat and bankroll.) Smith doubles his efforts when his best friend, Sergeant Coughlin, dies in a gun battle with Marcas. Dressed in plain clothes, Smith finds Marcas, shoots him, and rescues Mary Monks, a girl who was in Marcas' power. *Police. Friendship. Murder.*

COQUETTE **F2.1018**

Pickford Corp. *Dist* United Artists. 12 Apr **1929** [c30 Mar 1929; LP560]. Sd (Movietone); b&w. 35mm. 9 reels, 6,993 ft.

Dir-Dial Sam Taylor. *Adapt* John Grey, Allen McNeil. *Photog* Karl Struss. *Song: "Coquette"* Irving Berlin.

Cast: Mary Pickford *(Norma Besant)*, John Mack Brown *(Michael Jeffrey)*, Matt Moore *(Stanley Wentworth)*, John Sainpolis *(Dr. John Besant)*, William Janney *(Jimmy Besant)*, Henry Kolker *(Jasper Carter)*, George Irving *(Robert Wentworth)*, Louise Beavers *(Julia)*.

Melodrama. Source: George Abbott and Anne P. Bridgers, *Coquette; a Play in Three Acts* (New York, 1928). Norma Besant, a heartless belle of a southern town, falls in love with Michael Jeffrey, a crude and prideful mountaineer. Her father, a physician, is so displeased that he refuses to allow them to marry, orders Jeffrey out of his house, and, half-crazed, shoots and kills Jeffrey to preserve his family's good name. While he is awaiting his trial Besant commits suicide in a final effort to atone to his daughter for her unhappiness. *Mountaineers. Physicians. Filial relations. Coquetry. Murder. Suicide. Trials. United States—South.*

CORDELIA THE MAGNIFICENT **F2.1019**

Samuel Zierler Photoplay Corp. *Dist* Metro Pictures. 30 Apr **1923** [c11 Jun 1923; LP19379]. Si; b&w. 35mm. 7 reels, 6,800 ft.

Dir George Archainbaud. *Scen* Frank S. Beresford. *Photog* Charles Richardson.

Cast: Clara Kimball Young *(Cordelia Marlowe)*, Huntley Gordon *(D. K. Franklin)*, Carol Halloway *(Esther Northworth)*, Lloyd Whitlock *(Jerry Plimpton)*, Jacqueline Gadsden *(Gladys Northworth)*, Lewis Dayton *(James Mitchell Grayson, the butler)*, Mary Jane Irving *(François)*, Catherine Murphy *(Jackie Thorndyke)*, Elinor Hancock *(Mrs. Marlowe)*.

Society mystery melodrama. Source: Leroy Scott, *Cordelia the Magnificent* (New York, 1923). Cordelia Marlowe, a society girl whose family fortune is depleted, becomes the tool of D. K. Franklin, a dishonest lawyer whose business is blackmail. She is innocently involved in a scheme to extract money from a family friend, but she realizes her mistake and attempts to get out of the deal. *Socialites. Lawyers. Blackmail.*

CORNERED **F2.1020**

Warner Brothers Pictures. 1 Aug **1924** [c9 Aug 1924; LP20480]. Si; b&w. 35mm. 7 reels, 6,500 ft.

Dir William Beaudine. *Scen* Hope Loring, Louis Duryea Lighton. *Photog* Ray June.

Cast: Marie Prevost *(Mary Brennan/Margaret Waring)*, Rockliffe Fellowes *(Jerry, the Gent)*, Raymond Hatton *(Nick, the Dope)*, John Roche *(George Wells)*, Cissy Fitzgerald *(Lola Mulvaney)*, Vera Lewis *(Mrs. Wells)*, George Pearce *(Brewster)*, Bartine Burkett *(The Bride)*, Billy Fletcher *(The Groom)*, Ruth Dwyer *(Mrs. Webster)*, Bertram Johns *(Webster)*, Wilfred Lucas *(Updike)*.

Crook melodrama. Source: Dodson Mitchell and Zelda Sears, *Cornered* (New York opening: Dec 1920). Two thieves, discovering that their accomplice, Mary Brennan, is a double for heiress Margaret Waring, place her in the Waring home during Margaret's absence. Margaret returns as they are about to rob the safe and is shot; however, a detailed police investigation establishes the identity of the real heiress. *Thieves. Doubles. Imposture.*

CORPORAL KATE **F2.1021**

De Mille Pictures. *Dist* Producers Distributing Corp. 6 Dec **1926** [c29 Nov 1926; LP23383]. Si; b&w. 35mm. 8 reels, 7,460 ft.

Supv C. Gardner Sullivan. *Dir* Paul Sloane. *Scen* Albert Shelby Le Vino. *Titl* John Krafft. *Story* Zelda Sears, Marion Orth. *Photog* Henry Cronjager.

Cast: Vera Reynolds *(Kate)*, Julia Faye *(Becky)*, Majel Coleman *(Evelyn)*, Kenneth Thompson *(Jackson)*, Fred Allen *(Williams)*.

Comedy-drama. Kate and Becky, Brooklyn manicurists, work up a song-and-dance act and through the influence of a friend are assigned to the French front to entertain the troops. Both girls fall in love with Jackson Clark, a society man, and he in turn falls for Kate. The Germans advance, and Becky is killed, dying contentedly in Jackson's arms. Kate loses her arm in a selfless and heroic action, and Jackson, still greatly in love with her, proposes that they spend the rest of their lives together. *Manicurists. Entertainers. World War I. France.*

THE COSSACKS **F2.1022**

Metro-Goldwyn-Mayer Pictures. ca23 Jun **1928** [New York premiere; released Jun; c23 Jun 1928; LP25438]. Si; b&w. 35mm. 10 reels.

Dir George Hill. *Adapt-Cont* Frances Marion. *Titl* John Colton. *Photog* Percy Hilburn. *Sets* Cedric Gibbons, Alexander Toluboff. *Film Ed* Blanche Sewell. *Wardrobe* David Cox. *Tech Adv* Theodore Lodi.

Cast: John Gilbert *(Lukashka)*, Renée Adorée *(Maryana)*, Ernest Torrence *(Ivan)*, Nils Asther *(Prince Olenin)*, Paul Hurst *(Sitchi* [*or Zarka*]*)*, Dale Fuller *(Maryana's mother, Ulitka)*, Mary Alden *(Lukashka's mother)*, Josephine Borio *(Stepka)*, Yorke Sherwood *(Uncle Eroshka)*, Joseph Mari *(Turkish spy)*, Neil Neely *(see note)*.

Melodrama. Source: Leo Nikolaevich Tolstoy, *The Cossacks* (1862). Lukashka humiliates his father, Ivan, by refusing to participate in the Cossack preoccupation—killing Turks. The townspeople brand him a coward, and his behavior elicits the disapproval of Maryana, his favorite pastime. The escape of several Turkish prisoners arouses his fighting spirit; he becomes a real warrior and returns from battle proudly displaying a mouth wound (a heroic injury, yielding status). When his pride causes him to be aloof with Maryana, she accepts the marriage proposal of visiting Prince Olenin. Lukashka chases the couple, already on their way to the capital, kidnaps Maryana, and leaves the royal party to a band of marauding Turks. *Cossacks. Turks. Royalty. Russia. Cowardice.*

Note: Some sources suggest that Neil Neely plays the part of Prince Olenin.

THE COSTELLO CASE **F2.1023**

James Cruze Productions. *Dist* Sono Art–World Wide Pictures. 15 Oct **1930** [c7 Nov 1930; LP1711]. Sd; b&w. 35mm. 7 reels, 7,200 ft.

Prod James Cruze, Samuel Zierler. *Dir* Walter Lang. *Story-Scen-Dial* F. McGrew Willis. *Photog* Harry Jackson. *Art Dir* Robert E. Lee. *Ch Sd Rec* W. C. Smith. *Asst Dir* Bernard F. McEveety.

Cast: Tom Moore *(Mahoney)*, Lola Lane *(Mollie)*, Roscoe Karns *(Blair)*, Wheeler Oakman *(Mile-Away-Harry)*, Russell Hardie *(Jimmie)*, William Davidson *(Saunders)*, Dorothy Vernon *(Landlady)*, Jack Richardson *(Donnelly)*, William Lawrence *(Babe)*, M. K. Wilson *(Henderson)*.

Crime melodrama. Patrolman Mahoney reports the discovery of the body of Costello, robbed and murdered in his funeral parlor, to Captain Saunders; Mile-Away-Harry is suspected but released after cross-examination. Meanwhile Mollie and Jimmie are picked up at a train station but are released when they insist they are elopers. Jimmie confesses to Mollie that he robbed the Costello safe and also saw the murderer; still pretending to be married, they go with Officer Mahoney to his boardinghouse. Mahoney is cornered by Harry and his gang, who plan to force him to resign before killing him; but his life is spared by the arrival of the police, who were tipped off by Blair, a newspaperman. Although Mahoney suspects Jimmie, he gets him a job, and Jimmie plans to return the money and go straight; but Harry, Mollie's former sweetheart, threatens Jimmie and is exposed as the murderer. Harry is killed in a confrontation with Mahoney, and after hearing Jimmie's confession, Mahoney sends them off to be married. ... *Gangsters. Police. Undertakers. Murder. Robbery. Courtship.*

COTTON AND CATTLE **F2.1024**

Westart Pictures. 30 Jun **1921** [Brooklyn showing]. Si; b&w. 35mm. 5 reels.

Dir Leonard Franchon. *Writ* W. M Smith. *Photog* A. H. Vallet.

Cast: Al Hart *(Bill Carson)*, Jack Mower *(Jack Harding)*, Robert Conville *(Buck Garrett)*, Edna Davies *(Edna Harding)*, Ethel Dwyer *(Ethel Carson)*.

Western melodrama. Because Buck Garrett threatens to foreclose the mortgage on her father's cotton plantation, Ethel Carson enlists the aid of her sweetheart, rancher Jack Harding, and his cowboys in quickly picking the crop for market. Garrett gets an idea from a newspaper, and the next day Carson receives a note from "the night rider" warning him to cease harvesting. Carson stubbornly refuses, and his harassment begins: the Negro pickers are frightened away by hooded men, their huts are burned, Carson is kidnaped. Donning the cloak of a felled "night rider," Jack finds Carson, subdues the band's leader, and unmasks Garrett. (Locale: Oklahoma.) *Ranchers. Cowboys. Farmers. Negroes. Terrorists. Cotton. Plantations. Mortgages. Oklahoma.*

COUNSEL FOR THE DEFENSE **F2.1025**

Burton King. *Dist* Associated Exhibitors. 6 Dec **1925** [c6 Nov 1925; LU21981]. Si; b&w. 35mm. 7 reels, 6,622 ft.

Pers Supv Edward S. Silton. *Dir* Burton King. *Screenplay* Arthur Hoerl. *Photog* Ned Van Buren, George Porter.

Cast: Jay Hunt *(Doc West [Dr. David West])*, Betty Compson *(Katherine West)*, House Peters *(Arnold Bruce)*, Rockliffe Fellowes *(Harrison Blake)*, Emmett King *(Harvey Sherman)*, Bernard Randall *(Stephen Marcy)*, George MacDonald *(Hosea Hollingsworth)*, George MacDowell *(see note)*, William Conklin *(Thomas Burke)*, Joan Standing *(printer's devil)*.

Melodrama. Source: Leroy Scott, *Counsel for the Defense* (New York, 1912). Typhoid specialist Doc West has fought long and hard for the construction of the new municipal waterworks. Harrison Blake, the town's leading lawyer and banker, conspires to have the waterworks put into private hands and frames West for accepting a bribe. As none of the town's lawyers will take the case, Katherine, West's daughter and a recent law school graduate, accepts her first client in her father. The circumstantial evidence, however, is too great, and West is convicted and sent to jail. Blake bribes a worker to sabotage the waterworks, causing a public clamor for their takeover by private interests. Katherine, with the aid of newspaper editor Arnold Bruce, uncovers the conspiracy after the outbreak of a typhoid epidemic. West is freed, and Katherine weds Arnold. *Lawyers. Editors. Circumstantial evidence. Typhoid. Epidemics. Public utilities. Bribery.*

Note: At least one source gives the actor playing Hosea Hollingsworth as George MacDowell. Copyright records have been followed.

THE COUNT OF LUXEMBOURG **F2.1026**

Chadwick Pictures. 1 Feb **1926** [c14 Dec 1925; LP22116]. Si; b&w. 35mm. 7 reels, 6,400 ft.

Supv Hampton Del Ruth. *Dir* Arthur Gregor. *Adapt* John F. Natteford, Arthur Gregor. *Photog* Stephen Smith, Jr.

Cast: George Walsh *(René Duval)*, Helen Lee Worthing *(Angele Didier)*, Michael Dark *(Duke Rutzinoff)*, Charles Requa *(secretary)*, James Morrison *(Anatole)*, Lola Todd *(Juliette)*, Joan Meredith *(Yvonne)*.

Romantic drama. Source: Franz Lehár, *Der Graf von Luxemburg* (Vienna, 1909). Duke Rutzinoff is prevented from marrying Angele Didier, an actress, by her lack of title. To obtain a title for her, the duke persuades her to marry the impoverished Count of Luxembourg by proxy, preparing to divorce him immediately afterward, still sight unseen. Angele becomes the Countess of Luxembourg and goes to the Riviera, where she awaits the final decree. She meets the count there, and they fall in love. The enraged duke, thinking himself to have been betrayed, lets Angele know that the man with whom she has fallen in love is the same man who married her for selfish gain. Angele walks out on the count, but when she learns that he sold his title only in order to pay for a friend's operation, she returns to him and they are reconciled. *Royalty. Marriage—Proxy. Divorce. Luxembourg. Riviera.*

THE COUNT OF TEN (Universal-Jewel) **F2.1027**

Universal Pictures. 10 Mar **1928** [New York premiere; released 17 Jun; c20 Oct 1927; LP24557]. Si; b&w. 35mm. 6 reels, 5,557 ft.

Pres by Carl Laemmle. *Dir* James Flood. *Cont* Harry O. Hoyt. *Titl* Albert De Mond. *Photog* Virgil Miller, Ben Kline. *Film Ed* George McGuire.

Cast: Charles Ray *(Johnny McKinney)*, James Gleason *(Billy Williams)*, Jobyna Ralston *(Betty)*, Edythe Chapman *(Mother)*, Arthur Lake *(Brother)*, Charles Sellon *(Boland)*, George Magrill *(Cleaver)*, Jackie Coombs *(Baby McKinney)*.

Melodrama. Source: Gerald Beaumont, "Betty's a Lady," in *Red Book* (45:80–83, May 1925). Johnny McKinney, an ambitious young prizefighter, meets Betty behind a glove counter in a department store and falls in love. His manager returns from a business trip to find him idolized by Betty, her father, and her younger brother; when Johnny and Betty are married, the brother and father move in with them, and the financial burden is such that Johnny is forced to fight too frequently. In a charity bout Johnny sustains a fractured hand, and he is ordered out of the ring for 3 months. When Betty's brother needs a large sum to cover a worthless check, she tells Johnny she is expecting a baby, but his manager refuses his request for funds. Johnny suffers a crushing defeat in the ring and is embittered toward his wife upon learning of her deception, but they are reconciled when the manager orders her relatives out. *Salesclerks. Prizefighters. Fight Managers. In-laws. Marriage. Finance—Personal. Department stores.*

COUNTERFEIT LOVE **F2.1028**

Murray W. Garsson. *Dist* Playgoers Pictures. 10 Jun **1923** [c6 Jun 1923; LP19042]. Si; b&w. 35mm. 6 reels, 4,550 ft.

Prod Murray W. Garsson. *Dir* Roy Sheldon, Ralph Ince. *Story* Thomas F. Fallon, Adeline Leitzbach. *Photog* William J. Black.

Cast: Joe King *(Richard Wayne)*, Marian Swayne *(Mary Shelly)*, Norma Lee *(Rose Shelly)*, Jack Richardson *(Roger Crandall)*, Irene Boyle *(Miss Ferris)*, Isabel Fisher *(Mabel Ford)*, Alexander Giglio *(George Shelly)*, Danny Hayes *(Bill Grigg)*, Frances Grant *(Mandy)*, William Jenkins *(Mose)*.

Melodrama. Mary Shelly, sole supporter of her brother and sister, both invalids, is being courted by a mysterious stranger who urges her to marry and thus resolve her financial difficulties. Interest on the mortgage is due, and when her brother produces some money she applies part of it to the mortgage, then finds that the money, wrongfully obtained, is counterfeit. Betting the rest on a horserace, Mary loses it all. Brokenhearted, the girl is about to marry the stranger, who turns out to be the leader of the counterfeit gang, when Secret Service agent Richard Wayne, with whom Mary has fallen in love, exposes the mystery man and earns himself a wife. *Invalids. Brother-sister relationship. Secret service. Counterfeiting. Horseracing. Gambling.*

THE COUNTRY BEYOND **F2.1029**

Fox Film Corp. 17 Oct **1926** [c17 Oct 1926; LP23223]. Si; b&w. 35mm. 6 reels, 5,363 ft.

Pres by William Fox. *Dir* Irving Cummings. *Scen* Irving Cummings,

Ernest Maas. *Titl* Katherine Hilliker, H. H. Caldwell. *Photog* Abe Fried.

Cast: Olive Borden *(Valencia)*, Ralph Graves *(Roger McKay)*, Gertrude Astor *(Mrs. Andrews)*, J. Farrell MacDonald *(Sergeant Cassidy)*, Evelyn Selbie *(Martha Leseur)*, Fred Kohler *(Joe Leseur)*, Lawford Davidson *(Henry Harland)*, Alfred Fisher *(Father John)*, Lottie Williams *(Valencia's maid)*.

Northwest melodrama. Source: James Oliver Curwood, *The Country Beyond; a Romance of the Wilderness* (New York, 1922). Roger McKay, who has looted a trader's store to feed some starving Indians, is sought by Sergeant Cassidy of the Northwest Mounted Police, and while hiding out he falls in love with Valencia, a backwoods girl, who he believes is guilty of murdering a white slaver. He takes the blame for her supposed crime; and Valencia, who has a talent for dancing, travels to New York and on Broadway becomes a successful theatrical entertainer. Learning of Roger's sacrifice, she returns to the Northwest; Roger is cleared by a confession of the murdered man's wife, however, and the lovers are happily reunited. *Actors. Injustice. Hunger. Canadian Northwest. New York City—Broadway. Jasper National Park. Northwest Mounted Police.*

Note: Photographed on locations in Jasper National Park, Canada.

THE COUNTRY DOCTOR **F2.1030**

De Mille Pictures. *Dist* Pathé Exchange. 22 Aug **1927** [c6 Sep 1927; LP24376]. Si; b&w. 35mm. 8 reels, 7,500 ft.

Supv Bertram Millhauser. *Dir* Rupert Julian. *Screenplay* Beulah Marie Dix. *Photog* Peverell Marley. *Art Dir* Anton Grot. *Film Ed* Claude Berkeley. *Asst Dir* Leigh Smith. *Cost* Adrian.

Cast: Rudolph Schildkraut *(Amos Rinker)*, Junior Coghlan *(Sard Jones)*, Sam De Grasse *(Ira Harding)*, Virginia Bradford *(Opal Jones)*, Gladys Brockwell *(Myra Jones)*, Frank Marion *(Joe Harding)*, Jane Keckley *(Abbie Harding)*, Louis Natheaux *(Sidney Fall)*, Ethel Wales *(Redora Bump)*.

Drama. Source: Izola Forrester and Mann Page, unidentified stories. In the rural community where Dr. Amos Rinker practices, the affections of Opal Jones and Joe Harding are opposed by the boy's father, Ira, who scorns Opal's mother as a sinful woman. Believing herself a handicap, the woman commits suicide; Ira then threatens to place Opal and her brother Sard in the poorhouse, but Amos takes them into his home, thus incurring the displeasure of Ira. Although Amos greatly desires a position at a new hospital, Ira's influence crushes all his hopes. Meanwhile, Joe is injured by a falling tree; Sard is dispatched for help in a blizzard; and when the city physician refuses to go, Amos braves the storm. Joe is trapped by a fire in the cabin, but Amos rescues him and performs a successful operation. With the coming of spring, Amos recovers from his arduous experience and the young couple find happier days. *Physicians. Rural life. Self-sacrifice. Fatherhood. Blizzards.*

THE COUNTRY FLAPPER **F2.1031**

Dorothy Gish Productions. *Dist* Producers Security Corp. 29 Jul **1922** [c19 Jul 1922; LP18060]. Si; b&w. 35mm. 5 reels, 5,000 ft.

Dir F. Richard Jones. *Scen* Harry Carr. *Titl* Joseph W. Farnham. *Cinematog* Fred Chaston. *Film Ed* Joseph W. Farnham.

Cast: Dorothy Gish *(Jolanda, The Flapper)*, Glenn Hunter *(Nathaniel Huggins, The Boy)*, Mildred Marsh *(The Other Flapper)*, Harlan Knight *(Ezra Huggins, The Boy's Father)*, Tom Douglas *(Lemuell Philpotts, The Bashful Boy)*, Raymond Hackett *(one brother)*, Albert Hackett *(another brother)*, Kathleen Collins *(The Sister)*.

Farce. Source: Nalbro Isadorah Bartley, "Cynic Effect," in *Redbook* (34:34–38, 162–173, Feb 1920). Jolanda, a country girl, in order to win her beau, Nathaniel Huggins, back from another girl (The Other Flapper) just returned from the city, blackmails his father—druggist, churchman, and the village "moonshiner"—into consenting to their marriage. The girl gets caught in a fire and is rescued by the bashful boy, who has loved her all along. *Pharmacists. Churchmen. Bootleggers. Courtship. Blackmail. Rural life.*

THE COUNTRY KID **F2.1032**

Warner Brothers Pictures. 4 Nov Oct **1923** [c9 Oct 1923; LP19483]. Si; b&w. 35mm. 6 reels, 5,686 ft.

Dir William Beaudine. *Story* Julien Josephson. *Photog* E. B. Du Par. *Film Ed* Clarence Kolster.

Cast: Wesley Barry *(Ben Applegate)*, Spec O'Donnell *(Joe Applegate)*, Bruce Guerin *(Andy Applegate)*, Kate Toncray *(Mrs. Grimes)*, Helen Jerome Eddy *(Hazel Warren)*, George Nichols *(Mr. Grimes)*, Edward Burns *(Arthur Grant)*, George C. Pearce *(The County Judge)*.

Melodrama. Ben Applegate, eldest of three orphans, runs the farm his father left him and takes charge of younger brothers Joe and Andy. Their Uncle Grimes, legal guardian eager to take possession of the farm, declares Ben incompetent and sends Joe and Andy to an orphanage. When a helpful judge relieves Grimes of his duties, the youngsters are restored to the farm and adopted by an affectionate neighbor and his new wife. *Orphans. Guardians. Brothers. Farming. Orphanages.*

COURAGE **F2.1033**

Sidney A. Franklin Productions. *Dist* Associated First National Pictures. May **1921** [c2 Jun 1921; LP16598]. Si; b&w. 35mm. 6 reels, 6,244 ft.

Prod Albert A. Kaufman. *Dir* Sidney A. Franklin. *Scen* Sada Cowan. *Story* Andrew Soutar. *Photog* David Abel. *Film Ed* William Shea. *Asst Dir* Frederic Leahy.

Cast: Naomi Childers *(Jean Blackmoore)*, Sam De Grasse *(Stephan Blackmoore)*, Lionel Belmore *(Angus Ferguson)*, Adolphe Menjou *(Bruce Ferguson)*, Lloyd Whitlock *("Speedy" Chester)*, Alec B. Francis *(McIntyre)*, Ray Howard *(Stephan Blackmoore, Jr.)*, Gloria Hope *(Eve Hamish)*, Charles Hill Mailes *(Oliver Hamish)*.

Drama. Stephan, a young father and husband who has left his former position with Angus Ferguson, owner of a Scotch steel mill, is struggling with a new invention. He visits Ferguson to collect money owed him. Before his arrival, Ferguson is killed by his son, Bruce, in an attempted robbery. Stephan is convicted for the murder and imprisoned, but his wife, Jean, continues the work of perfecting his invention and remains faithful to him though courted by a man of wealth and position. When she has all but despaired, the confession of the actual murderer of Ferguson brings Stephan's release and their reunion. *Inventors. Scotch. Patricide. Injustice. Steel industry.*

COURAGE **F2.1034**

Independent Pictures. Dec **1924.** Si; b&w. 35mm. 5 reels, 4,750-4,850 ft.

Pres by Jesse J. Goldburg. *Dir* J. P. McGowan. *Story* James Ormont.

Cast: Franklyn Farnum, Dorothy Wood.

Western melodrama. No information about the specific nature of this film has been found.

COURAGE **F2.1035**

Warner Brothers Pictures. 22 May **1930** [New York premiere; released 7 Jun; c12 May 1930; LP1288]. Sd (Vitaphone); b&w. 35mm. 8 reels, 6,630 ft.

Dir Archie Mayo. *Screenplay-Dial* Walter Anthony. *Rec Engr* Clare A. Riggs.

Cast: Belle Bennett *(Mary Colbrook)*, Marion Nixon *(Muriel Colbrook)*, Rex Bell *(Lynn Willard)*, Richard Tucker *(James Rudlin)*, Leon Janney *(Bill Colbrook)*, Carter De Haven, Jr. *(Reginald Colbrook)*, Blanche Frederici *(Aunt Caroline)*, Charlotte Henry *(Gwendolyn Colbrook)*, Dorothy Ward *(Gladys Colbrook)*, Byron Sage *(Richard Colbrook)*, Don Marion *(Vincent Colbrook)*.

Domestic melodrama. Source: Tom Barry, *Courage* (New York & Los Angeles, 1929). Mary Colbrook, a widowed mother with seven children, through poor business management is faced with poverty though she is determined to educate her children and give them every advantage. In her absence, Muriel and Reginald, the eldest, are besieged by creditors; but Mary arrives with money from Rudlin, a banker of bad reputation, and partially clears her debts. Muriel, engaged to marry Lynn Willard, a well-to-do youth, is shocked at her mother's actions and plans to sacrifice herself to Rudlin to clear their obligation. Caroline, the sister of Mary's husband, arrives, and by cold scheming turns the children against their mother, with the exception of young Bill, who inherits the fortune of a neighboring spinster, Miss Crosby. Mary discovers noble qualities in Rudlin; and after convincing Muriel of her foolishness, she accepts him as her future husband. *Widows. Bankers. Children. Family life. Poverty. Debt. Motherhood.*

COURAGE OF WOLFHEART **F2.1036**

Charles R. Seeling Productions. *Dist* Aywon Film Corp. 24 Sep **1925** [New York State license]. Si; b&w. 35mm. 5 reels, 4,850 ft.

Cast: Big Boy Williams, Wolfheart *(a dog)*.

Western melodrama(?). No information about the nature of this film has been found. *Dogs.*

THE COURAGEOUS COWARD **F2.1037**

Sable Productions. *Dist* Usla Co. c6 Oct, 1 Nov **1924** [LU20728]. Si; b&w. 35mm. 5 reels, 4,652 ft.

Supv-Story Bernard D. Russell. *Dir* Paul Hurst.

Cast: Jack Meehan *(Jimmy Reed)*, Jackie Saunders *(Doris Hilton)*, Mary MacLaren *(Jerry Luther)*, Earl Metcalf *(J. Roger Dawson)*, Bruce Gordon *(Dave Morgan)*, James Gordon *(Charles Reed)*.

Melodrama. "Jimmy Reed had everything but courage, so his father shipped him off to work under Roger Dawson, engineer, on a big dam the elder Reed was building. There Jimmy is the under dog in several affairs of the fists but stays on the job because of his interest in Jerry Luther, daughter of 'Dad' Luther, a foreman. It develops that Dawson is double-crossing the elder Reed and Jimmy suddenly finds himself and prevents the wrecking of the dam. Then Jerry accepts his suit and Jimmy's father rejoices in an upstanding, fearless son." *(Moving Picture World,* 6 Dec 1924, p547.) *Engineers—Civil. Fatherhood. Cowardice. Dams.*

COURAGEOUS FOOL **F2.1038**

Harry J. Brown Productions. *Dist* Rayart Pictures. 6 Jul **1925** [New York State license]. Si; b&w. 35mm. 5 reels, 4,800 ft.

Cast: Reed Howes.

Action melodrama(?). No information about the nature of this film has been found.

COURT-MARTIAL **F2.1039**

Columbia Pictures. 12 Aug **1928** [c24 Sep 1928; LP25644]. Si; b&w. 35mm. 7 reels, 6,014 ft.

Prod Harry Cohn. *Dir* George B. Seitz. *Cont* Anthony Coldeway. *Titl* Morton Blumenstock. *Story* Elmer Harris. *Photog* Joe Walker. *Art Dir* Robert E. Lee. *Film Ed* Arthur Roberts. *Asst Dir* Max Cohn.

Cast: Jack Holt *(Capt. James Camden)*, Betty Compson *(Belle Starr)*, Pat Harmon *("Bull")*, Doris Hill *(general's daughter)*, Frank Lackteen *("Devil" Dawson)*, Frank Austin *(Abraham Lincoln)*, George Cowl *(Gen. Robert Hackathorne)*, Zack Williams *(Negro)*.

Historical drama. James Camden, a Union officer with a fine combat record, is ordered by President Lincoln to break up a Confederate guerrilla band led by Belle Starr. Camden joins the band by posing as a western gunman and soon falls in love with Belle, a charming southern girl intent on avenging the slaughter of her father. During a cavalry attack, Camden saves Belle's life, and she returns the favor when, after discovering Camden's true identity, her gang wants to lynch him. Camden finally returns to the Union Army without Belle and is sentenced to face a firing squad. Belle again saves Camden's life by giving herself up voluntarily, dying shortly thereafter from a gunshot wound inflicted by one of her discontented followers. *Spies. Guerrillas. Revenge. United States—History—Civil War. Belle Starr. Abraham Lincoln.*

COURTIN' WILDCATS **F2.1040**

Universal Pictures. 22 Dec **1929** [c9 Dec 1929; LP904]. Sd (Movietone); b&w. 35mm. 6 reels, 5,118 ft. [Also si; 5,142 ft.]

Pres by Carl Laemmle. *Dir* Jerome Storm. *Scen-Dial* Dudley McKenna. *Photog* Harry Neumann. *Film Ed* Gilmore Walker.

Cast: Hoot Gibson *(Clarence Butts)*, Eugenia Gilbert *(Calamity Jane)*, Harry Todd *(McKenzie)*, Joseph Girard *(Mr. Butts)*, Monty Montague *(McLaren)*, John Oscar *(Quid Johnson)*, Jim Corey *(The Fugitive)*, James Farley *(The Doctor)*, Pete Morrison *(Huxley)*, Joe Bonomo *(Gorilla)*.

Comedy-drama. Source: William Dudley Pelley, "Courtin' Calamity" (publication undetermined). Clarence Butts, a college student pretending to be a weakling to avoid being put to work in his father's steel foundry, leads a wild life, culminating in a chase and a fight with a policeman. The family doctor, perceiving his subterfuge, has Clarence placed with a Wild West show, where he courts destruction by flirting with Calamity Jane, a broncho-rider who dislikes men because a man once robbed her and her father of their fortune. When the villain appears at the show, Jane shoots him and rides away; Clarence helps her elude the police in his car; and as they face danger together, she realizes his fondness for her. She consents to marry him, and they set out to find a handy minister. *Students. Man-haters. Foundries. Steel industry. Wild West shows.*

THE COURTSHIP OF MILES STANDISH **F2.1041**

Charles Ray Productions. *Dist* Associated Exhibitors. 30 Dec **1923** [c8 Dec 1923; LU19681]. Si; b&w. 35mm. 9 reels.

Dir Frederick Sullivan. *Scen* Al Ray. *Photog* George Rizard.

Cast: Charles Ray *(John Alden)*, Enid Bennett *(Priscilla Mullens)*, E. Alyn Warren *(Miles Standish)*, Joseph Dowling *(Elder Brewster)*, Sam De Grasse *(John Carver)*, Norval MacGregor *(William Bradford)*, Thomas Holding *(Edward Winslow)*, Frank Farrington *(Isaac Allerton)*, William Sullivan *(John Howland)*, Marian Nixon *(see note)*.

Historical drama. Source: Henry Wadsworth Longfellow, "The Courtship of Miles Standish" (1858). Based on Longfellow's famous poem, this film depicts the Pilgrims' journey across the Atlantic, the landing at Plymouth, the hardships of this first year, and the romance between John Alden and Priscilla Mullens. *Pilgrim Fathers. Miles Standish. John Alden. Priscilla Mullens. William Brewster. John Carver. William Bradford. Edward Winslow. Isaac Allerton. "Mayflower"*

Note: Some sources indicate that Marian Nixon is also in the cast.

COUSIN KATE (Alice Joyce Productions) **F2.1042**

Vitagraph Co. of America. Jan **1921** [c8 Dec 1920; LP15899]. Si; b&w. 35mm. 5 reels, 4,800 ft.

Pres by Albert E. Smith. *Dir* Mrs. Sidney Drew. *Adapt* L. Case Russell. *Photog* Joe Shelderfer.

Cast: Alice Joyce *(Kate Curtis)*, Gilbert Emery *(Heath Desmond)*, Beth Martin *(Amy Spencer)*, Inez Shannon *(Mrs. Spencer)*, Leslie Austin *(Rev. James Bartlett)*, Freddie Verdi *(Bobby)*, Frances Miller Grant *(Jane)*, Henry Hallam *(Bishop)*.

Romantic comedy. Source: Hubert Henry Davies, *Cousin Kate; a Comedy in Three Acts* (Boston, 1910). Amy Spencer is engaged to artist Heath Desmond, a nature worshiper who shuns organized religion. James Bartlett, a minister in love with Amy, influences her against Heath, and they break up. Cousin Kate Curtis, a novelist whose views on love are considered by her relatives to be unconventional, is called in to smooth matters over. She meets Heath on the train, and the two, not knowing each other's identity, apparently fall in love. Kate takes refuge in Heath's house in a storm; Amy arrives; and Kate, to Heath's dismay, confesses that she was only indulging in a flirtation. Bartlett arrives and successfully proposes to Amy, and Heath and Kate are reunited. *Clergymen. Novelists. Flirts. Naturalism.*

THE COVERED TRAIL **F2.1043**

Sunset Productions. 16 May **1924** [New York showing; New York State license 29 Apr 1924]. Si; b&w. 35mm. 5 reels, 4,900 ft.

Dir Jack Nelson.

Cast: J. B. Warner *(Bill Keats)*, Robert McKenzie *(sheriff)*, Ruth Dwyer.

Western melodrama. "Keats, in an effort to save his wayward weakling brother from the influence of a gang of rustlers and bad men, is compromised and suspected as one of the gang. He is captured by the vigilantes and about to be hung when the local sheriff ... liberates him through a ruse. Keats is recaptured and lodged in the local jail but escapes just in time to foil a lynching party and to interrupt a robbery of the Wells Fargo office by the local gang. He and the local sheriff capture the band. Subsequently, a confession from the dying brother, who has been shot by one of his old gang, exonerates Keats." *(Variety,* 21 May 1924, p25.) *Gangs. Vigilantes. Brothers. Lynching. Wells Fargo & Co..*

THE COVERED WAGON **F2.1044**

Famous Players–Lasky. *Dist* Paramount Pictures. 16 Mar **1923** [New York premiere; released 8 Sep 1924; c14 Mar 1923; LP18770]. Si; b&w. 35mm. 10 reels, 9,407 ft.

Pres by Jesse L. Lasky. *Also Pres by* Adolph Zukor *(see note)*. *Prod-Dir* James Cruze. *Scen* Jack Cunningham. *Camera* Karl Brown. *Film Ed* Dorothy Arzner. *Mus Arr* Hugo Riesenfeld. *Adv* Col. T. J. McCoy.

Cast: Lois Wilson *(Molly Wingate)*, J. Warren Kerrigan *(Will Banion)*, Ernest Torrence *(Jackson)*, Charles Ogle *(Mr. Wingate)*, Ethel Wales *(Mrs. Wingate)*, Alan Hale *(Sam Woodhull)*, Tully Marshall *(Bridger)*, Guy Oliver *(Kit Carson)*, John Fox *(Jed Wingate)*.

Epic western. Source: Emerson Hough, *The Covered Wagon* (New York, 1922). Two wagon trains—one led by Wingate, the other by Will Banion—in 1848 travel from Westport Landing (Kansas City) over the Oregon Trail to California and Oregon. Their major adventures include the crossing of the Platte River, an Indian attack, and a prairie fire. The narrative revolves around Will Banion and Wingate's daughter, Molly. Her scoundrel fiancé, Sam Woodhull, works constantly to discredit Banion, with the eventual result that Banion and his wagons are banished from the train and follow the lure of gold to California. Molly learns the truth through Kit Carson and Bridger and sends Jackson for Banion. They are married after Jackson saves Banion from being murdered by Woodhull. *Pioneers. Indians of North America. Westport Landing. Oregon Trail.*

Platte River. Fort Bridger. Kit Carson. James Bridger.

Note: Adolph Zukor was later added as Presenter with Jesse L. Lasky. "'The Covered Wagon' ... is dedicated to the memory of Theodore Roosevelt" (souvenir program). The cast of 3,000 people includes 1,000 Indians brought from reservations in Wyoming, New Mexico, and other States under the direction of Col. T. J. McCoy.

COVERED WAGON TRAILS **F2.1045**

Dist Syndicate Pictures. 1 Feb **1930.** Mus score; b&w. 35mm. 5 reels, 4,617 ft. [Also si.]

Dir J. P. McGowan. *Story-Scen* Sally Winters. *Photog* Hap Depew.

Cast: Bob Custer *("Smoke" Sanderson)*, Phyllis Bainbridge *(Wanda Clayton)*, Perry Murdock *(Chet Clayton)*, Charles Brinley *(Sheriff Brunton)*, Martin Cichy *(Brag Vogel)*, J. P. McGowan *(King Kincaid)*.

Western melodrama. "Smoke" Sanderson "is after a gang of smugglers operating at the border, and as deputy [sheriff?] he rides into all kinds of trouble and excitement before he finally lands the gang. Of course there is the girl whose brother is working with the gang." (*Film Daily*, 18 May 1930, p12.) *Sheriffs. Smugglers. Gangs. Brother-sister relationship.*

THE COWARD (Reissue) **F2.1046**

Kay-Bee Pictures. *Dist* Tri-Stone Pictures. **1924.** Si; b&w. 35mm. 5 reels.

Note: A "re-edited and re-titled" Charles Ray–Frank Keenan film originally released by Triangle Film Corp. on 14 Nov 1915 (c29 Oct 1915; LU6808).

THE COWARD **F2.1047**

R-C Pictures. *Dist* Film Booking Offices of America. 21 Aug **1927** [c21 Aug 1927; LP24466]. Si; b&w. 35mm. 6 reels, 5,093 ft.

Pres by Joseph P. Kennedy. *Dir* Alfred Raboch. *Cont* Edfrid Bingham, Enid Hibbard. *Adapt* J. G. Hawks. *Photog* Jules Cronjager. *Asst Dir* William T. Dagwell.

Cast: Warner Baxter *(Clinton Philbrook)*, Sharon Lynn *(Alicia Van Orden)*, Freeman Wood *(Leigh Morlock)*, Raoul Paoli *(Pierre Bechard)*, Byron Douglas *(Darius Philbrook)*, Charlotte Stevens *(Marie)*, Hugh Thomas *(Maitland)*.

Society melodrama. Source: Arthur Stringer, "The Coward," in *Hearst's International* (43:60–65, Mar 1923). Clinton Philbrook, a wealthy young idler, is in love with aristocratic Alicia Van Orden, but she refuses to marry him until he proves his worth. When Clinton's rival, Leigh Morlock, insults him at an exclusive club, Clinton strikes Morlock but is himself given a severe beating; Alicia refuses to see him again because of the resulting scandal. In despair, Clinton goes to a Canadian lumber town, and thence on a trapping expedition with Pierre Bechard, a woodsman. When Morlock is lost on a hunting trip, Clinton finds him in the mountains, treats his wounds, and carries him back to the lodge. Alicia admits her love for Clinton but exacts a promise that he not fight Morlock; he agrees, but when taunted by his former rival, Clinton gives him a sound trouncing, winning Alicia's admiration and love. *Idlers. Upper classes. Manhood. Cowardice. Hunting. Clubs. Canadian Northwest.*

A COWBOY ACE **F2.1048**

Westart Pictures. 26 Mar **1921** [trade review; Woodhaven, N. Y., showing: 3 Jul 1921]. Si; b&w. 35mm. 5 reels.

Dir Leonard Franchon. *Writ* W. M. Smith. *Photog* A. H. Vallet.

Cast: Al Hart *(Pete Filson)*, Jack Mower *(Bill Gaston)*, Robert Conville *("Snake" Bullard)*, Ethel Dwyer *(Ethel Filson)*, Red Bush *(himself)*.

Western melodrama. Returning from her eastern school to her father's ranch, Ethel Filson meets and falls in love with Bill Gaston. She learns that Red Bush badly needs the $1,000 in a roundup contest and persuades Bill to allow Red to win. Red later returns the favor by using his airplane to help Bill find Ethel, who has been kidnaped by Snake Bullard. Bill punishes Snake, and all hands agree that Red's purchase of his airplane with his prize money was "a good buy." *Cowboys. Roundups. Contests. Kidnaping. Airplanes.*

THE COWBOY AND THE COUNTESS **F2.1049**

Fox Film Corp. 31 Jan **1926** [c4 Jan 1926; LP22218]. Si; b&w. 35mm. 6 reels, 5,345 ft.

Pres by William Fox. *Dir* R. William Neill. *Scen* Charles Darnton. *Story* Maxine Alton, Adele Buffington. *Photog* Reginald Lyons.

Cast: Buck Jones *(Jerry Whipple)*, Helen D'Algy *(Countess Justina)*, Diana Miller *(Nanette)*, Harvey Clark *(Edwin Irving Mansfield)*, Monte Collins, Jr. *(Slim)*, Fletcher Norton *(Duke de Milos)*, Chappell Dossett *(Alexis Verlaine)*, Jere Austin *(Bozarri)*, White Eagle *(a horse)*.

Western melodrama. While touring the American West, Countess Justina of Belgravia is involved in an automobile accident. Jerry Whipple, a devil of the range, comes to her aid, and the two become friends. Justina returns to her kingdom and reluctantly prepares for her state marriage to Duke de Milos; Jerry joins a Wild West show and, while on tour, comes to Belgravia. Jerry learns that the duke is secretly the leader of a gang of thieves and abducts Justina to save her from the duke's evil. Jerry then defeats the duke and his men and returns to the palace with Justina, where they are wed in a formal ceremony. *Cowboys. Thieves. Nobility. Abduction. Wild West shows. Imaginary kingdoms. Automobile accidents. Horses.*

THE COWBOY AND THE FLAPPER **F2.1050**

Phil Goldstone Productions. *Dist* Truart Film Corp. 25 Aug **1924.** Si; b&w. 35mm. 5 reels.

Dir Alvin J. Neitz. *Story* Jefferson Moffitt. *Photog* Roland Price.

Cast: William Fairbanks *(Dan Patterson)*, Dorothy Revier *(Alice Allison)*, Jack Richardson *(Red Carson)*, Milton Ross *(Colonel Allison)*, Morgan Davis *(Deputy Jack Harrison)*, Andrew Waldron *(Al Lyman, veterinary)*, Fred Haynes *(Handsome Ed Burns)*.

Western melodrama. Marshal Dan Patterson, posing as a badman, joins the Carson gang. Their captive, Alice Allison, not knowing who he is, doesn't know if she should trust him. Dan has to fight the whole gang before help comes. *United States marshals. Cowboys. Flappers. Disguise.*

Note: Reissued as *The Sheriff's Lone Hand*.

THE COWBOY AND THE LADY **F2.1051**

Famous Players–Lasky. *Dist* Paramount Pictures. ca15 Oct **1922** [Cleveland premiere; released 22 Oct; c24 Oct 1922; LP18344]. Si; b&w. 35mm. 5 reels, 4,918 ft.

Pres by Jesse L. Lasky. *Dir* Charles Maigne. *Adapt* Julian Josephson. *Photog* Faxon M. Dean.

Cast: Mary Miles Minter *(Jessica Weston)*, Tom Moore *(Teddy North)*, Viora Daniels *(Molly X)*, Patricia Palmer *(Midge)*, Robert Schable *(Weston)*, Guy Oliver *(Ross)*, Leonard Clapham *(Joe)*, Robert Mack *(justice of the peace)*.

Western melodrama. Source: Clyde Fitch, *The Cowboy and the Lady; a Comedy in Three Acts* (New York, 1908). Disgusted by her husband's philandering, Jessica Weston goes to her Wyoming ranch. Weston accompanies her and promptly starts a flirtation with Molly, a saloon proprietress, and consequently angers Ross, their ranch foreman. Jessica and Teddy North, a gentleman rancher who mounts his hands on motorcycles, fall in love. When Weston is killed, Jessica and Teddy each suspects the other, but Teddy accepts the guilt to protect Jessica. His trial is nearly over when Jessica learns from Molly that Ross committed the murder, and the lovers are then united. *Ranchers. Ranch foremen. Infidelity. Ranch life. Saloons. Murder. Wyoming.*

THE COWBOY AND THE OUTLAW **F2.1052**

Big Productions Film Corp. *Dist* Syndicate Pictures. Oct **1929.** Mus score & sd eff; b&w. 35mm. 5 reels. [Also si.]

Dir J. P. McGowan. *Story* Sally Winters. *Photog* Hap Depew.

Cast: Bob Steele *(George Hardcastle)*, Edna Aslin *(Bertha Bullhead)*, Bud Osborne *(Lefty Lawson)*, Thomas G. Lingham *(Tom Bullhead)*, Cliff Lyons *(Slim Saxon)*, J. P. McGowan *(Pepper Hardcastle)*, Alfred Hewston *(Walter Driver)*.

Western melodrama. "The plot revolves around the attempt to capture the slayer of a ranch owner killed on his way from the bank. After a number of exciting encounters the slain ranchman's son trails the murderer by means of a coat button picked up at the scene of the crime. The lad knows that if he finds the coat minus the button the rest will be easy. How he comes into possession of the garment makes a thrilling story." (*Film Daily*, 23 Feb 1930, p8.) *Cowboys. Outlaws. Ranchers. Filial relations. Murder.*

THE COWBOY CAVALIER **F2.1053**

Action Pictures. *Dist* Pathé Exchange. 29 Jan **1928** [c18 Jan 1928; LP24879]. Si; b&w. 35mm. 5 reels, 4,526 ft.

Dir Richard Thorpe. *Adapt* Frank L. Inghram. *Story* Betty Burbridge. *Photog* Ray Reis.

Cast: Buddy Roosevelt, Olive Hasbrouck, Charles K. French, Fannie Midgley, Robert Walker, Bob Clark, William Ryno.

Mystery drama. A girl loses her memory when she witnesses her uncle's murder. The murderer, to obtain a written confession from her that she killed her uncle, kidnaps the girl. A young deputy, assigned to the case, discovers that the girl's cousin, expecting to inherit his uncle's ranch, hired the killer. The deputy solves the mystery, rescues the girl, who has regained her memory, and marries her. *Cowboys. Amnesia. Inheritance. Murder.*

COWBOY CAVALIER **F2.1054**

William M. Pizor Productions. 14 Jun **1929** [New York State license]. Si; b&w. 35mm. 5 reels.

Cast: Montana Bill.

Western melodrama(?). No information about the nature of this film has been found.

THE COWBOY COP **F2.1055**

R-C Pictures. *Dist* Film Booking Offices of America. 11 Jul **1926** [c11 Jul 1926; LP22892]. Si; b&w. 35mm. 5 reels, 4,385 ft.

Pres by Joseph P. Kennedy. *Dir* Robert De Lacey. *Cont* F. A. E. Pine. *Story* Frank Richardson Pierce. *Photog* John Leezer. *Asst Dir* John Burch.

Cast: Tom Tyler *(Jerry McGill)*, Jean Arthur *(Virginia Selby)*, Irvin Renard *(Count Mirski)*, Frankie Darro *(Frankie)*, Pat Harmon *(Dago Jack, first crook)*, Earl Haley *(second crook)*, Beans *(himself, a dog)*.

Action melodrama. Jerry McGill, an Arizona cowpuncher, arrives in Los Angeles, is robbed by a stranger in a taxi, and is stranded. He is befriended by Frankie, a newsboy, who buys his dinner and becomes his pal. Jerry joins the police force as a mounted policeman and, while patroling a wealthy residential district, thwarts a holdup perpetrated on heiress Virginia Selby by her companion, Count Mirski, who has hired two crooks. To Frankie's sorrow, Jerry and Virginia become fast friends. She invites Jerry to a dinner party, where the count plots to rob the Selby safe; but when Virginia interrupts the crooks she is kidnaped. Jerry, warned by Frankie's dog, pursues the crooks in a car; when ditched, he follows on a motorcycle and subdues the count and his men. Virginia's father invites Jerry to his ranch, and he is united with Virginia. *Cowboys. Police. Newsboys. Arizonans. Robbery. Los Angeles. Dogs.*

COWBOY COURAGE **F2.1056**

Robert J. Horner Productions. *Dist* Aywon Film Corp. 6 Nov **1925** [New York State license]. Si; b&w. 35mm. 5 reels, 4,800 ft.

Dir Robert J. Horner.

Cast: Kit Carson *(Bud Austin)*, Pauline Curley *(Ruth Dawson)*, Gordon Sackville *(Tex Miller)*.

Western melodrama(?). No information about the nature of this film has been found. *Cowboys.*

COWBOY GRIT **F2.1057**

Lariat Productions. *Dist* Vitagraph Co. of America. c14 Aug **1925** [LP21728]. Si; b&w. 35mm. 5 reels.

Story-Cont Victor Roberts.

Cast: Pete Morrison.

Western melodrama. A cowboy saves a girl named Betty from being trampled to death in a cattle stampede, thereby winning her love. A gang of desperadoes later try to force him from his ranch, but the tall Arizonan stands firm: he defeats the desperadoes, saves his ranch, and wins Betty's love for life. *Ranchers. Cowboys. Arizonans. Desperadoes. Stampedes.*

THE COWBOY KID **F2.1058**

Fox Film Corp. 15 Jul **1928** [c5 Jul 1928; LP25418]. Si; b&w. 35mm. 5 reels, 4,293 ft.

Pres by William Fox. *Dir* Clyde Carruth. *Scen* James J. Tynan. *Titl* Delos Sutherland. *Story* Harry Sinclair Drago, Seton I. Miller. *Photog* Sol Halprin. *Film Ed* Milton Carruth. *Asst Dir* David Todd.

Cast: Rex Bell *(Jim Barrett)*, Mary Jane Temple *(Janet Grover)*, Brooks Benedict *(Trig Morgan)*, Alice Belcher *(Lilly Langton)*, Joseph De Grasse *(John Grover)*, Syd Crossley *(sheriff)*, Billy Bletcher *(deputy sheriff)*.

Western comedy. "... young cowboy becomes entangled in the affairs of a girl. The latter's father is the town banker and the victim of various bank robberies. The cowboy captures the thieves, saves the father from financial ruin and wins the girl." (*Motion Picture News Booking Guide*, [14]:243–4, 1929.) *Cowboys. Bankers. Thieves. Smalltown life.*

THE COWBOY KING **F2.1059**

Charles R. Seeling Productions. *Dist* Aywon Film Corp. May **1922**. Si; b&w. 35mm. 5 reels, 4,900 ft.

Dir Charles R. Seeling.

Cast: Big Boy Williams *(Dud Smiley)*, Patricia Palmer *(Ethel Dunlap)*, Elizabeth De Witt *(Mrs. Stacey)*, William Austin *(Wilbur)*, Chet Ryan *(Lije Butters)*, Bill Dyer *(Bart Hadley)*, Mae Summers *(Norma)*.

Western melodrama. "Hadley, owner of a nearby ranch, had fenced off a water hole belonging to Miss Dunlap, thus depriving her stock of water. Undaunted, the young Eastern woman and her two-fisted fighting foreman went at it for all they were worth, and after risking their lives and going through gun fights and other trying events won out at last." (*Moving Picture World*, 21 Apr 1923, p850.) *Ranch foremen. Ranchers. Water rights.*

THE COWBOY MUSKETEER **F2.1060**

R-C Pictures. *Dist* Film Booking Offices of America. 13 Dec **1925** [c13 Dec 1925; LP22244]. Si; b&w. 35mm. 5 reels, 4,500 ft.

Dir Robert De Lacy. *Story* Buckleigh Fritz Oxford. *Photog* John Leezer.

Cast: Tom Tyler *(Tom Latigo)*, Jim London *(Joe Dokes)*, Frances Dare *(Leila Gordon)*, David Dunbar *(Tony Vaquerrelli)*, Frankie Darro *(Billy)*, Beans *(a dog)*.

Western melodrama. Leila Gordon's father dies before he can tell her the location of the map to his hidden gold mine. Joe Dokes, the foreman of the Gordon ranch, wants to get the map for himself and hires Tony Vaquerrelli to give him a hand. Tom Latigo, a bashful but resourceful cowpoke, learns of Leila's plight and decides to help her out. He poses as a notorious thug, finds the map, outwits Dokes, and wins Leila for his wife. *Cowboys. Ranch foremen. Impersonation. Gold mines. Documentation.*

THE COWBOY PRINCE **F2.1061**

Ben Wilson Productions. *Dist* Arrow Film Corp. 1 Sep **1924** [c16 Sep 1924; LP20585]. Si; b&w. 35mm. 5 reels, 4,410 ft.

Dir Francis Ford.

Cast: Ashton Dearholt.

Western melodrama. Count Arcata, who covets the throne of Darius, ruler of San Gordio, spreads false rumors about Darius' birthright. Darius and the princess flee to the United States to find his birth certificate. They are pursued by Robert and his sister Carmelita, agents of the count, but are able to obtain the document and return to their native land with the aid of cowboy friends. The cowboys, fearing for the safety of their new friends, follow and arrive in time to help Darius secure the throne from Count Arcata's followers. In the end, Paula is made Darius' queen and the cowboys find jobs in San Gordio. *Cowboys. Royalty. Imaginary kingdoms. Documentation.*

THE COWBOY PRINCE **F2.1062**

Anchor Productions. 26 Jul **1930** [New York State license]. Si; b&w. 35mm. 5 reels, 4,500 ft.

Cast: Cheyenne Bill.

Western melodrama(?). No information about the precise nature of this film has been found. *Cowboys.*

COYOTE FANGS **F2.1063**

Harry Webb Productions. *Dist* Aywon Film Corp. 21 Aug **1924** [New York State license]. Si; b&w. 35mm. 5 reels, 4,700 ft.

Dir Harry Webb. *Photog* William Thornley.

Cast: Jack Perrin *(Jack Burroughs)*, Josephine Hill *(Sylvia Dodge)*.

Western melodrama. "A jealous suitor fires a shot at Jack Burroughs and Sylvia Dodge as they are embracing. The bullet strikes the girl. The would-be assassin escapes and then accuses Jack of the act. Organizing a posse, the jealous man sets out to lynch Jack, but their plot is frustrated by the arrival of another group of cowboys. It is later revealed that Jack is innocent and the guilty man discovered, following which there is a happy ending." (*Motion Picture News Booking Guide*, [7]:18, Oct 1924.) *Cowboys. Lynching. Jealousy.*

CRACK O' DAWN **F2.1064**

Harry J. Brown Productions. *Dist* Rayart Pictures. 21 Aug **1925** [New York State license application]. Si; b&w. 35mm. 5 reels, 5,236 ft.

Dir Albert Rogell. *Scen* Henry Roberts Symonds, John Wesley Grey. *Photog* Lee Garmes.

Cast: Reed Howes *(Earle Thorpe, Jr.)*, J. P. McGowan *(Earle Thorpe, Sr.)*, Ruth Dwyer *(Etta Thompson)*, Henry A. Barrows *(Henry Thompson)*, Eddie Barry *(Toby Timkins)*, Tom O'Brien *(Stanley Steele)*, Ethan Laidlaw *(Red Riley)*.

Action melodrama. Henry Thompson and Earle Thorpe, Sr., who are partners in an automobile manufacturing concern, quarrel over the design of a new racing car and part company. Their children, Etta and Earle, are in love, and together they build a racing car patterned on the once-successful design used by their parents' firm. Shortly before the big race, one of Thompson's men recognizes young Thorpe at the track, and numerous attempts are made to prevent him from entering the race. Earle wins the race in his special car. The fathers are reconciled, and the lovers are happy. *Automobile manufacture. Automobile racing. Partnerships. Filial relations.*

THE CRACKERJACK **F2.1065**

East Coast Films. 8 May **1925** [New York showing; c8 May 1925; LP21442]. Si; b&w. 35mm. 7 reels, 6,500 ft.

Pres by C. C. Burr. *Dir* Charles Hines. *Scen* Victor Grandin, Argyll Campbell. *Titl* John Krafft. *Story* Richard M. Friel. *Photog* Charles E. Gilson, John Geisel, Al Wilson.

Cast: Johnny Hines *(Tommy Perkins)*, Sigrid Holmquist *(Rose Bannon)*, Henry West *(General Bannon)*, Bradley Barker *(Alonzo López)*, J. Barney Sherry *(Colonel Perkins)*.

Comedy. Crackerjack Perkins works his way through college with his skill of flipping flapjacks. After graduation, Crackerjack goes south to manage his uncle's pickle factory. On a sales trip near the Mexican border, he meets Rose Bannon, an old college sweetheart, to whose father he sells a large order of pickles. The elder Bannon and his manager, López, plan to conceal bullets in the pickles and ship them to revolutionaries south of the border. Crackerjack learns of the plan and replaces the bullets with cheese. He later finds himself in the middle of the revolution and, after many adventures and tribulations, ends up selling his uncle's pickles to government and insurgents alike. *Salesmen. Students. College life. Revolutions. Smuggling. Pickles. Flapjacks. Mexico.*

THE CRADLE **F2.1066**

Famous Players–Lasky. *Dist* Paramount Pictures. ca4 Mar **1922** [Baltimore premiere; released 9 Apr; c28 Dec 1921; LP17460]. Si; b&w. 35mm. 5 reels, 4,698 ft.

Pres by Jesse L. Lasky. *Dir* Paul Powell. *Scen* Olga Printzlau. *Photog* Hal Rosson.

Cast: Ethel Clayton *(Margaret Harvey)*, Charles Meredith *(Dr. Robert Harvey)*, Mary Jane Irving *(Doris Harvey)*, Anna Lehr *(Lola Forbes)*, Walter McGrail *(Courtney Webster)*, Adele Farrington *(Mrs. Mason)*.

Domestic melodrama. Source: Eugène Brieux, *Le Berceau, comédie en trois actes* (Paris, 1908). Dr. Robert Harvey, under the stress of financial difficulties, yields to the charms of Lola Forbes, who becomes enamored of him when he calls to attend her. Because he has neglected his wife, Margaret, and his daughter, rumors link Robert's name with Lola, and he soon obtains a divorce from Margaret and marries her, while Margaret consents to marry Webster, one of her former admirers. The child, Doris, who spends a half year with each parent, is resented by Webster, and Lola clearly prefers her Pekinese. When Lola beats the child and she is stricken with a serious illness, Harvey takes her to her mother; and realizing their mistakes, the couple are reunited. *Children. Parenthood. Marriage. Finance—Personal. Divorce. Dogs.*

THE CRADLE BUSTER **F2.1067**

Patuwa Pictures. *Dist* American Releasing Corp. 19 Mar **1922** [c25 Mar 1922; LP17665]. Si; b&w. 35mm. 5 or 6 reels, 5,200-5,947 ft.

Prod Frank Tuttle, Fred Waller, Jr. *Dir-Story-Scen* Frank Tuttle. *Photog* Fred Waller, Jr. *Film Ed* Cecil R. Snape.

Cast: Glenn Hunter *(Benjamin Franklin Reed)*, Marguerite Courtot *(Gay Dixon)*, Mary Foy *(Melia Prout)*, William H. Tooker *("Blarney" Dixon)*, Lois Blaine *(PollyAnn Parsons)*, Osgood Perkins *(Crack "Spoony")*, Townsend Martin *(Holcomb Berry)*, Beatrice Morgan *(Mrs. Reed)*.

Comedy-drama. Benjamin Franklin Reed, otherwise known as Sweetie, resents being tied to his mother's apron strings and on the occasion of his 21st birthday decides to assert his adult independence. He begins by smoking a cigar, swearing mildly, and taking a drink. Later, he becomes enamored of a cabaret performer, kisses her passionately before the audience, then goes to her dressing room to apologize and to find that she takes a sympathetic interest in him. The pair decide to elope to Boston, but Benjamin loses his money, and his bride is snatched from him by an irate father. Benjamin learns of a cabaret clown's plot on the girl's life, and following a struggle with the clown, he rescues the girl as the villain falls to his death from a stage platform. Now proved to be a man, "The Cradle Buster" embarks on his honeymoon. *Entertainers. Clowns. Filial relations. Manhood. Cabarets.*

THE CRADLE OF THE WASHINGTONS **F2.1068**

Thompson & Branscombe Manufacturing Co. *Dist* H. W. Thompson. 21 Jun **1922** [New York State license]. Si; b&w. 35mm. 4 reels.

Educational drama(?). No information about the nature of this film has been found.

THE CRADLE SNATCHERS **F2.1069**

Fox Film Corp. 28 May **1927** [New York premiere; released 5 Jun; c24 Apr 1927; LP23985]. Si; b&w. 35mm. 7 reels, 6,281 ft.

Pres by William Fox. *Dir* Howard Hawks. *Scen* Sarah Y. Mason. *Titl* Malcolm Stuart Boylan. *Photog* L. William O'Connell. *Asst Dir* James Tinling.

Cast: Louise Fazenda *(Susan Martin)*, J. Farrell MacDonald *(George Martin)*, Ethel Wales *(Ethel Drake)*, Franklin Pangborn *(Howard Drake)*, Dorothy Phillips *(Kitty Ladd)*, William Davidson *(Roy Ladd)*, Joseph Striker *(Joe Valley)*, Nick Stuart *(Henry Winton)*, Arthur Lake *(Oscar)*, Dione Ellis *(Ann Hall)*, Sammy Cohen *(Ike Ginsberg)*, Tyler Brook *(Osteopath)*.

Farce. Source: Russell G. Medcraft and Norma Mitchell, *Cradle Snatchers, a Farce-Comedy in Three Acts* (New York, c1931). To cure their flirtatious husbands of consorting with flappers, three wives—Susan Martin, Ethel Drake, and Kitty Ladd—arrange with three college boys—Henry Winton, Oscar, and Joe Valley—to flirt with them at a house party. Joe Valley, who poses as a hot-blooded Spaniard, is vamped by Ginsberg in female attire, and Oscar, a bashful Swede, uses caveman methods when aroused. During a rehearsal of the party, the three husbands arrive, followed by their flapper friends, leading to comic complications that are resolved. *Flappers. Students. Flirtation. Jealousy. Marriage.*

Note: Remade in 1929 by Fox in a musical version under the title *Why Leave Home.*

CRAIG'S WIFE **F2.1070**

Pathé Exchange. 16 Sep **1928** [c5 Sep 1928; LP25585]. Si; b&w. 35mm. 7 reels, 6,670 ft.

Dir William C. De Mille. *Adapt* Clara Beranger. *Photog* David Abel. *Art Dir* Edward Jewell. *Film Ed* Anne Bauchens. *Asst Dir* Morton S. Whitehill. *Prod Mgr* Morton S. Whitehill.

Cast: Irene Rich *(Mrs. Craig)*, Warner Baxter *(Mr. Craig)*, Virginia Bradford *(Ethel)*, Carroll Nye *(John Fredericks)*, Lilyan Tashman *(Mrs. Passmore)*, George Irving *(Mr. Passmore)*, Jane Keckley *(Miss Austen)*, Mabel Van Buren *(Mrs. Frazer)*, Ethel Wales *(Eliza)*, Rada Rae *(Mary)*.

Drama. Source: George Edward Kelly, *Craig's Wife; a Drama* (Boston, 1926). Mrs. Craig is a fastidious and efficient tyrant in her own home, intolerant of dirt and disorder, egocentric, iron-willed, and intolerable. Her younger sister, Ethel, falls in love with a young professor at college, and Mrs. Craig, disapproving of the match, goes to Ethel and makes her promise to end the affair and return home. While Mrs. Craig is away, her husband comes to be suspected of a double murder, and, returning home, she does everything in her power to thwart the police and avert scandal. Mr. Craig is eventually cleared of suspicion in the murder (discovered to have been a murder-suicide) and, realizing at last the selfishness of his frigid wife, he leaves home, taking Ethel with him and encouraging her to return to college and love. *Professors. Sisters. Murder. Suicide. Scandal. Marriage. College life. Frigidity.*

THE CRASH *see* **THE BUSINESS OF LOVE**

THE CRASH **F2.1071**

First National Pictures. 7 Oct **1928** [c12 Jun 1929; LP457]. Si; b&w. 35mm. 8 reels, 6,225 ft.

Pres by Richard A. Rowland. *Dir* Eddie Cline. *Cont* Charles Kenyon. *Titl* Dwinelle Benthall, Rufus McCosh. *Photog* Ted McCord. *Film Ed* Al Hall.

Cast: Milton Sills *(Jim Flannagan)*, Thelma Todd *(Daisy McQueen)*, Wade Boteler *(Pat Regan)*, William Demarest *(Louie)*, Fred Warren *(Corbett)*, Sylvia Ashton *(Mrs. Carleton)*, De Witt Jennings *(Superintendent Carleton)*.

Melodrama. Source: Frank L. Packard, "The Wrecking Boss," in *The Night Operator* (New York, 1919). Jim Flannagan, a two-fisted, hard-fighting Irishman, returns from the war to White Cloud, a railroad junction high in the Sierras, and is put in charge of a wrecking crew. He becomes fascinated with Daisy, soubrette of a traveling theatrical troupe, and she accepts his offer of marriage. Although she is a good cook and housekeeper, her free and easy ways arouse Jim's suspicious jealousy; and a fight with Louie, manager of the show troupe, causes Daisy to leave him. Jim takes to drinking and misses a call to clear a wreck, and he is discharged. Then Regan, a friend, sends for Daisy, and she returns with their child, a baby girl; although overjoyed, Jim's old jealous doubt returns, and, her pride offended, Daisy returns to the city. Her train collides with a fast freight, and against orders Jim joins the crew and retrieves the miraculously unharmed Daisy from the wreck. They are thus reunited. *Veterans. Irish. Railroad wrecking crews. Theatrical troupes. Drunkenness. Marriage. Jealousy. Sierras. Train wrecks.*

CRASHIN' THROUGH **F2.1072**

Robert J. Horner Productions. *Dist* Anchor Film Distributors. 10 Sep **1924** [New York State license]. Si; b&w. 35mm. 5 reels.

Pres by Morris R. Schlank. *Dir-Writ* Alvin J. Neitz. *Photog* Paul Allen. *Asst Dir* W. L. Guthrie.

Cast: Jack Perrin *(Jack Lawton)*, Jack Richardson *(Scarface Jordan)*, Steve Clements *(Pedro)*, Dick La Reno *(Mr. Rankin)*, Jean Riley *(Eloise Hackle Penny)*, Taylor Graves *(Freddy, her brother)*, Peggy O'Day *(see note)*.

Western melodrama. No information about the precise nature of this film has been found.

Note: New York State licensing records show Peggy O'Day in cast, but this information has not been verified.

CRASHIN' THRU **F2.1073**

R-C Pictures. *Dist* Film Booking Offices of America. 1 Apr **1923** [c16 Mar 1923; LP18773]. Si; b&w. 35mm. 6 reels, 6,500 ft.

Dir Val Paul. *Adapt* Beatrice Van. *Photog* William Thornley, Robert De Grasse.

Cast: Harry Carey *(Blake)*, Cullen Landis *(Cons Saunders)*, Myrtle Stedman *(Celia)*, Vola Vale *(Diane)*, Charles Le Moyne *(Saunders)*, Winifred Bryson *(Gracia)*, Joseph Harris *(Holmes)*, Donald MacDonald *(Allison)*, Charles Hill Mailes *(Benedict)*.

Western melodrama. Source: Elizabeth Dejeans, "If a Woman Will," in *Blue Book Magazine* (28:1–19, 106–123, 106–119; Feb–Apr 1919). Gracia, a halfbreed Indian girl, plots with Cons Saunders to steal cattle from Blake because he is oblivious to her charms. With his stock gone, he cannot repay the money he owes his Uncle Benedict, and when Benedict is murdered, Blake is suspected. Because Blake has taken care of Saunders (Cons's father) for the many years he has been without the use of his legs, the latter is finally conscience-stricken and confesses to the crime, thus freeing Blake to marry Diana. *Halfcastes. Invalids. Rustling. Debt. Murder.*

Note: Working title: *The One Man.*

CRASHING COURAGE **F2.1074**

Premium Picture Productions. *Dist* Independent Pictures. Jul **1923.** Si; b&w. 35mm. 5 reels.

Dir Harry Moody.

Cast: Edith Hall, Jack Livingston.

Melodrama. "Story deals with the efforts of a star of the Ranger troop to prevent smugglers from taking contraband goods [drugs] across the border, and track down the leader of the smugglers [Steve], who had abducted the girl [Letitia Houston] he loved." (*Motion Picture News Booking Guide,* 5:16, Oct 1923.) *Smugglers. Smuggling. Narcotics.*

CRASHING THROUGH **F2.1075**

Liberty Pictures. *Dist* Pathé Exchange. 5 Feb **1928** [c24 Jan 1928; LP24907]. Si; b&w. 35mm. 5 reels, 4,480-4,580 ft.

Dir Thomas Buckingham. *Scen* Wyndham Gittens. *Titl* F. Anderson. *Story* Jack Stevens. *Photog* Harry Davis, M. A. Anderson.

Cast: Jack Padjan *("Tex" Belden)*, Sally Rand *(Rita Bayne)*, William Eugene *(Jim Bayne)*, Buster Gardner *("Slim")*, Tom Santschi *(Bart Ramy)*, Duke R. Lee *(sheriff)*, Jack Livingston, Mary Wynn *(see note)*.

Western melodrama. Brother and sister Jim and Rita Bayne own a ranch. Jim, a confirmed gambler, loses his share in a crooked card game with Bart Ramy. Unaware that Ramy now owns part of the ranch, Rita asks her brother to hire Tex Belden, a stranger who saved her life by stopping a runaway team of horses. Taking an immediate dislike to the stranger, Ramy accuses Tex of cattle rustling. At the same time Ramy incites Jim to rob the stagecoach. Jim is shot during the robbery, and Ramy escapes with the money. A confession from the dying boy saves Tex from being hanged. Tex proves Ramy's guilt and helps the posse capture him. *Ranchers. Gamblers. Posses. Brother-sister relationship. Rustling. Stagecoach robberies. Capital punishment.*

Note: At least one source includes Jack Livingston and Mary Wynne in the cast.

CRAZY THAT WAY **F2.1076**

Fox Film Corp. 30 Mar **1930** [c10 Mar 1930; LP1177]. Sd (Movietone); b&w. 35mm. 6 reels, 5,800 ft. [Also si.]

Pres by William Fox. *Assoc Prod* George Middleton. *Dir* Hamilton MacFadden. *Screenplay-Dial* Hamilton MacFadden, Marion Orth. *Photog* Joseph Valentine. *Art Dir* Duncan Cramer. *Film Ed* Ralph Dietrich. *Sd* Alfred Bruzlin. *Asst Dir* Sam Wurtzel. *Cost* Sophie Wachner.

Cast: Kenneth MacKenna *(Jack Gardner)*, Joan Bennett *(Ann Jordan)*, Regis Toomey *(Robert Metcalf)*, Jason Robards *(Frank Oakes)*, Sharon Lynn *(Marion Sears)*, Lumsden Hare *(Mr. Jordan)*, Baby Mack *(Julia)*.

Comedy. Source: Vincent Lawrence, *In Love With Love, a Play in Three Acts* (New York, 1927). Ann Jordan, who is engaged to Frank Oakes, is constantly pursued by young Robert Metcalf at the local country club—in fact, wherever she and her fiancé go—much to Frank's displeasure. When she at last becomes exasperated by their continuous wrangling, she begins to notice her father's friend, Jack Gardner, an engineer to whose charming presence she has hitherto remained oblivious. When the boys virtually wreck her garden, they find that she has fallen in love with Jack. *Engineers. Courtship. Gardening. Country clubs.*

CRAZY TO MARRY **F2.1077**

Famous Players–Lasky. *Dist* Paramount Pictures. 28 Aug **1921** [c28 Aug 1921; LP16974]. Si; b&w. 35mm. 5 reels, 4,693 or 5,402 ft.

Dir James Cruze. *Scen* Walter Woods. *Story* Frank Condon. *Photog* Karl Brown.

Cast: Roscoe "Fatty" Arbuckle *(Dr. Hobart Hupp)*, Lila Lee *(Annabelle Landis)*, Laura Anson *(Estrella De Morgan)*, Edwin Stevens *(Henry De Morgan)*, Lillian Leighton *(Sarah De Morgan)*, Bull Montana *(Dago Red, a crook)*, Allen Durnell *(Arthur Simmons)*, Sidney Bracey *(Colonel Landis)*, Genevieve Blinn *(Mrs. Landis)*, Clarence Burton *(Gregory Slade, a lawyer)*, Henry Johnson *(Norman Gregory, his son)*, Charles Ogle *(cement man)*, Jackie Young *(Cupid)*, Lucien Littlefield *(minister)*.

Farce. Dr. Hobart Hupp, who believes he can cure criminals by surgery, is about to experiment on Dago Red, who has been promised freedom if the operation is successful, when he is reminded that it is his wedding day. Estrella De Morgan, daughter of a socially prominent family, is waiting to become his bride, although she is actually in love with young Arthur Simmons. En route, Hupp is mistaken by the charming Annabelle Landis for her chauffeur, and deciding to desert the waiting bride, he drives Annabelle to her home, 300 miles away. There she is halted by her parents, who want her to marry another man. Dago Red now appears to rescue the doctor, and with a minister and Annabelle they row to an island. There they find Estrella, who has eloped with Arthur, and the parents arrive to find them all married. *Surgeons. Socialites. Criminals—Rehabilitation. Clergymen. Weddings.*

CREAM OF THE EARTH *see* **RED LIPS**

THE CREED THAT WEAKENS *see* **THE GALLOPING ACE**

THE CRICKET ON THE HEARTH **F2.1078**

Paul Gerson Pictures. *Dist* Selznick Distributing Corp. 11 Aug **1923** [c11 Aug, 5 Oct 1923; LP19311, LP19473]. Si; b&w. 35mm. 7 reels.

Dir Lorimer Johnston. *Scen* Caroline Frances Cooke.

Cast: Josef Swickard *(Caleb Plummer)*, Fritzi Ridgeway *(Bertha Plummer)*, Paul Gerson *(John Perrybingle)*, Virginia Brown Faire *(Dot Marley)*, Paul Moore *(Edward Plummer)*, Lorimer Johnston *(Josiah Tackleton)*, Margaret Landis *(May Fielding)*, Joan Standing *(Tillie Slowboy)*.

Domestic comedy-drama. Source: Charles Dickens, *The Cricket on the Hearth* (1845). In a small village in England, John Perrybingle, the mail carrier, a bachelor, pays court to and marries Dot, whom he takes to his home. The livingroom contains a large hearth, with a kettle hung over the fire, and with great glee Dot spies on the hearth a cricket, which is supposed to be a sign of happiness. The story is of the life of John and Dot, and of the trust that is shaken but restored through the singing of the cricket. *Mail carriers. Marriage. Village life. England.*

THE CRIMSON CANYON **F2.1079**

Universal Pictures. 14 Oct **1928** [c3 Aug 1928; LP25511]. Si; b&w. 35mm. 5 reels, 4,201 ft.

Supv William Lord Wright. *Dir* Ray Taylor. *Story-Cont* Hugh Nagrom.

Titl Val Cleveland. *Photog* Joseph Brotherton. *Film Ed* Gene Havlick.

Cast: Ted Wells *(Phil "Six Gun" Lang)*, Lotus Thompson *(Daisy Lanning)*, Wilbur Mack *(Sam Slade)*, Buck Connors *("Dad" Packard)*, George Atkinson *(Abner Slade)*, Henri De Velois.

Western melodrama. Phil Lang, a cowhand, helps Dad Packard pay off the $1,000 loan advanced to him by Abner Slade. Phil then rescues Daisy Lanning from a runaway wagon only to discover that he has interrupted the filming of a motion picture sequence. Phil invites Daisy to a dance, where he is knocked out by Sam Slade, Abner's son, who spirits Daisy away by means of a ruse. Phil revives, rescues Daisy, and reunites her with Dad Packard, her grandfather. *Cowboys. Actors. Grandfathers. Abduction. Motion pictures.*

THE CRIMSON CHALLENGE F2.1080

Famous Players–Lasky. *Dist* Paramount Pictures. ca2 Apr **1922** [New York premiere; released 23 Apr; c4 Apr 1922; LP17725]. Si; b&w. 35mm. 5 reels, 4,942 ft.

Pres by Adolph Zukor. *Dir* Paul Powell. *Scen* Beulah Marie Dix. *Photog* Harry Perry.

Cast: Dorothy Dalton *(Tharon Last)*, Jack Mower *(Billy)*, Frank Campeau *(Buck Courtrey)*, Irene Hunt *(Ellen Courtrey)*, Will R. Walling *(Jim Last)*, Howard Ralston *(Clive)*, Clarence Burton *(Black Bart)*, George Field *(Wylackie)*, Mrs. Dark Cloud *(Anita)*, Fred Huntly *(Confora)*.

Western melodrama. Source: Vingie E. Roe, *Tharon of Lost Valley* (New York, 1919). In the cattle town of Lost Valley, Buck Courtrey, saloon owner and political boss, covets Tharon, daughter of Jim Last, a small rancher; and when rebuffed, he has Last killed. Tharon swears revenge with her father's own guns and organizes a vigilante band to check Courtrey's activities. Learning that she loves Billy, a cowpuncher, Courtrey kidnaps and threatens to kill him unless Tharon agrees to marry Courtrey following his divorce from Ellen. Courtrey's wife informs Tharon of Billy's whereabouts, and she rescues him in time to join the townspeople attacking Courtrey's gang. Courtrey is pursued by Tharon, who kills him and returns to become Billy's wife. *Ranchers. Cowboys. Political bosses. Vigilantes. Revenge.*

THE CRIMSON CITY F2.1081

Warner Brothers Pictures. 7 Apr **1928** [c3 Apr 1928; LP25117]. Si; b&w. 35mm. 6 reels, 5,388 ft.

Dir Archie Mayo. *Titl* James A. Starr. *Story* Anthony Coldeway. *Photog* Barney McGill. *Asst Dir* Gordon Hollingshead.

Cast: Myrna Loy *(Onoto)*, John Miljan *(Gregory Kent)*, Leila Hyams *(Nadine Howells)*, Matthew Betz *("Dagger" Foo)*, Anders Randolf *(Major Howells)*, Sojin *(Sing Yoy)*, Anna May Wong *(Su)*, Richard Tucker *(Richard Brand)*.

Melodrama. Young English aristocrat Gregory Kent is wrongfully wanted for embezzlement, but unable to prove his innocence he flees to China. There fear prevents his seeking out Nadine Howells, the girl he loves, who with her father is staying with oil magnate Richard Brand. When papers proving Kent's innocence arrive from England, Brand, who has been courting Nadine, makes a deal with Ronald Foo, owner of a notorious waterfront den, to steal them. Unaware of the contents, Kent offers to steal the documents if Foo will free Onoto, a Chinese girl about to be sold into slavery. Onoto, who has grown to love Kent, discovers the nature of the papers. Realizing that she may lose him, she switches the contents, replacing a blank paper for the pardon. When Kent discovers that he has stolen his own ticket to freedom, he recovers from Foo what he believes to be his pardon and goes to Brand's house to prove his innocence to Nadine's father. The envelope he presents to Major Howells contains only blank paper. Onoto arrives, and seeing the futility of her love for Kent, she hands the authentic papers over to Nadine. *Embezzlement. Slavery. China. Documentation.*

CRIMSON CLUE F2.1082

Dist Clark-Cornelius Corp. 9 Oct **1922.** Si; b&w. 35mm. 5 reels, 3,655 or 3,811 ft.

Cast: Jack Richardson, Josephine Sedgwick.

Western melodrama. "José is discharged by Marion Gray from ranch for beating horse. Marion goes looking for new foreman. Benson, neighboring rancher, connives with José to kidnap Marion. 'Bash' Dixon, itinerant cowboy, witnesses José's attempt to abduct Marion and rescues her. Benson contrives to get a handkerchief embroidered for 'Bash,' the new foreman, by Marion. José steals horses from Marion's ranch and dropping handkerchief centers suspicion on 'Bash.' Marion, certain of 'Bash's' innocence, arranges scheme to get real culprit. José is captured in stealing more horses from Marion's ranch; Benson is also involved; and all ends well for 'Bash' and Marion." (*Motion Picture News Booking Guide*, 4: 39–40, Apr 1923.) *Ranch foremen. Cowboys. Horsethieves. Ranch life. Horses.*

THE CRIMSON CROSS F2.1083

Fanark Corp. *Dist* Pioneer Film Corp. 22 Apr **1921** [trade review; c17 Mar 1921; LU16560]. Si; b&w. 35mm. 5 reels.

Pres by D. J. H. Levett. *Prod-Dir* George Everett. *Story-Scen* N. Brewster Morse.

Cast: Van Dyke Brooks *(Richard Gromley)*, Edward Langford *(Buddy Billings)*, Marian Swayne *(Mary Wallace)*, Eulalie Jensen *(Mrs. Otto Fischer)*, William E. Hallman *(Otto Fischer)*, Augustus Phillips *(Bill Billings)*, Archie Clark *(Jim Hawkins)*.

Melodrama. Buddy Billings, adopted son of the dean of detectives, uses hypnotism to extract confessions. Richard Gromley, a welfare worker who has redeemed many prisoners through love and kindness, warns Buddy against the use of hypnotism. Buddy does not listen and uses his power to make Mrs. Otto Fischer, an anarchist, confess. Mr. Fischer, furious over his wife's treatment, reveals that Buddy has just convicted his own mother and father and proves it by the crimson cross on Buddy's arm. Fischer escapes, and Buddy becomes depressed to the point of almost committing suicide. Gromley, however, using a divine power, redeems Fischer, who reveals that Gromley is Buddy's real father and that he had stolen the baby to revenge Gromley's use of hypnotism to get a confession. Buddy becomes convinced of his past errors and all ends happily. *Social workers. Detectives. Faith healers. Anarchists. Hypnotism. Parentage. Birthmarks.*

CRIMSON GOLD F2.1084

East Coast Productions. 30 Jun **1923.** Si; b&w. 35mm. 5 reels, 4,900 ft.

Prod-Dir Clifford S. Elfelt. *Story* Frank Howard Clark. *Photog* Clyde De Vinna, Robert Newhard.

Cast: J. B. Warner *(Larry Crawford)*, Edith Sterling *(Grace Miller)*, Martha McKay *(Virginia Farley)*, George Burrell *(Jake Higgins)*, Ferri Remand *(Martha Parsons)*, Albert MacQuarrie *(David Ellis)*, Jay Morley *(Clem Bisbee)*, George Stanley *(Ike Slade)*.

Comedy-drama(?). No information about the nature of this film has been found.

THE CRIMSON RUNNER F2.1085

Hunt Stromberg Corp. *Dist* Producers Distributing Corp. 2 Mar **1925** [c24 Apr 1925; LP21401]. Si; b&w. 35mm. 6 reels, 4,775 ft.

Pres by Hunt Stromberg, Charles R. Rogers. *Pers Supv* Hunt Stromberg. *Dir* Tom Forman. *Story-Scen* Harvey Gates. *Photog* Sol Polito. *Art Dir* W. L. Heywood. *Film Ed* William Decker.

Cast: Priscilla Dean *(Bianca Schreber)*, Bernard Siegel *(Alfred Schreber)*, Alan Hale *(Gregory [later Krutz])*, Ward Crane *(Count Meinhard von Bauer)*, James Neill *(Baron Rudolph)*, Charles Hill Mailes *(Baron Semlin)*, Ilsa De Lindt *(Princess Cecile)*, Mitchell Lewis *(Conrad, the Black)*, Taylor Holmes *(Bobo, the valet)*, Arthur Millett *(captain of police)*.

Melodrama. In Vienna after the war, Professor Schreber and his daughter, Bianca, are reduced to poverty. Gregory, the janitor of the apartment house in which they live, assaults the girl, and her father sets fire to the building in order to preserve his daughter's honor, himself dying in the flames. Bianca escapes from the burning building and devotes herself to avenging the rich, from whom she, disguised as the Crimson Runner, and her band of daredevil thieves continually steal. Among those who suffer from the gang's depredation is the handsome Count Meinhard, a gallant nobleman who later shields Bianca from the police when she take refuge in his apartment. Meinhard falls in love with the lovely thief, and she eventually comes to return his affection. Under the assumed name of Krutz, Gregory has been elevated from janitor to chief of police; he falls into Bianca's power, and Meinhard kills him in a duel. Bianca is later pardoned for her crimes, and she and Meinhard find happiness in the halls of royalty. *Professors. Police. Janitors. Thieves. Nobility. Poverty. Revenge. Vienna. Fires. Duels.*

THE CRIMSON SKULL F2.1086

Norman Film Manufacturing Co. **1921** [New York State release: 20 Apr 1922]. Si; b&w. 35mm. 6 reels, 5,934 ft.

Cast: Anita Bush, Lawrence Chenault, Bill Pickett, Steve Reynolds.

Western melodrama. No information about the precise nature of this film has been found. *Cowboys. Oklahoma.*

Note: Cast includes "30 colored cowboys" (advertising poster). Filmed in Boley, Oklahoma.

CRINOLINE AND ROMANCE **F2.1087**

Metro Pictures. 5 Feb **1923** [c7 Feb 1923; LP18737]. Si; b&w. 35mm. 6 reels, 6,740 ft.

Dir Harry Beaumont. *Story-Scen* Bernard McConville. *Photog* John Arnold.

Cast: Viola Dana *(Miss Emmy Lou)*, Claude Gillingwater *(Col. Charles E. Cavanaugh)*, John Bowers *(Davis Jordan)*, Allan Forrest *(Augustus Biddle)*, Betty Francisco *(Kitty Biddle)*, Mildred June *(Birdie Bevans)*, Lillian Lawrence *(Mrs. Kate Wimbleton)*, Gertrude Short *(Sibil Vane)*, Lillian Leighton *(Abigail)*, Nick Cogley *(Uncle Mose)*.

Comedy-drama. Brought up by her grandfather, Col. Charles E. Cavanaugh, in a secluded area of North Carolina, Emmy Lou lives in ignorance of the outside world. When she visits Mrs. Kate Wimbleton still wearing her crinolines, she is a great success with the men, especially Davis Jordan and Augustus Biddle. Emmy Lou quickly takes to the jazz ways of the young people gathered at the Wimbletons', but she returns to her grandfather when she hears of his illness. Both Jordan and Biddle follow her, and Emmy Lou is unable to decide between them until Colonel Cavanaugh stages a pistol duel. Biddle cheats, and Emmy Lou chooses to marry Jordan. *Grandfathers. Jazz life. North Carolina. Duels.*

CROOKED ALLEY **F2.1088**

Universal Pictures. 7 Nov **1923** [New York showing; released 19 Nov or 2 Dec; c24 Oct 1923; LP19545]. Si; b&w. 35mm. 5 reels, 4,900 ft.

Dir Robert F. Hill. *Scen* Adrian Johnson. *Adapt* Robert F. Hill. *Story* Jack Boyle. *Photog* Harry Fowler.

Cast: Thomas Carrigan *(Boston Blackie)*, Laura La Plante *(Norine Tyrell/Olive Sloan)*, Tom S. Guise *(Judge Milnar)*, Owen Gorine *(Rudy Milnar)*, Albert Hart *(Kaintuck)*.

Crook melodrama. Reformed crook Boston Blackie takes revenge on a judge who refused to arrange a pardon for a dying friend: he hires Norine, the dying man's daughter, to "get" the judge through his son Rudy Milnar. A romance between the two prevents the plan from succeeding. *Judges. Criminals—Rehabilitation. Revenge.*

Note: Working title: *The Daughter of Crooked Alley.*

CROOKS CAN'T WIN **F2.1089**

FBO Pictures. 7 Apr **1928** [c7 Mar 1928; LP25149]. Si; b&w. 35mm. 7 reels, 6,291 ft.

Dir George M. Arthur. *Titl* Randolph Bartlett. *Adapt* Enid Hibbard. *Story* Joseph Jefferson O'Neil. *Photog* Robert Martin. *Film Ed* George M. Arthur. *Asst Dir* Thomas Atkins.

Cast: Ralph Lewis *(Dad Gillen)*, Thelma Hill *(Mary Gillen)*, Sam Nelson *(Danny Malone)*, Joe Brown *(Jimmy Wells)*, Eugene Strong *(Alfred Dayton, Jr.)*, James Eagle *(Dick Malone)*, Charles Hall *("Bull" Savage)*.

Underworld melodrama. "Bull" Savage, leader of a gang of silk thieves, lures police officer Danny Malone away from his post outside a silk warehouse by tricking him into thinking that his estranged brother, Dick Malone, another member of the gang (but not a hardened criminal), is in danger. The chief inspector, upon finding Danny away from his post after the crime has been committed, suspects him of complicity. Danny's reluctance to mention his long-lost brother costs him his job. Wells, a newspaper reporter, believing Danny (now working as a truckdriver) to be innocent, assists him in capturing the silk thieves the next time they stage a holdup. *Brothers. Reporters. Truckdrivers. Police. Gangs. Silk.*

A CROOK'S ROMANCE **F2.1090**

American Film Co. **1921.** Si; b&w. 35mm. 5 reels.

Cast: Helen Holmes, J. P. McGowan.

Western melodrama(?). No information about the nature of this film has been found.

CROSS BREED **F2.1091**

Bischoff Productions. 30 Nov **1927** [New York showing]. Si; b&w. 35mm. 6 reels, 5,900 ft.

Dir Noel Mason Smith. *Scen* Bennett Cohen. *Story* Welles W. Ritchie. *Photog* Ray June.

Cast: Johnnie Walker *(Andy Corwin)*, Gloria Heller *(Marie Dumont)*, Charles K. French *(John Corwin)*, Frank Glendon *(Jacques Berreau)*, Henry Hebert *(Sam Cranister)*, Joseph Mack *(George Dumont)*, Olin Francis *(Poleon)*, Silverstreak *(Commanche, a dog)*.

Melodrama. Andy Corwin, a war veteran, is still suffering from shock and is branded a coward. He and his dog, Commanche, are finally goaded into action by the efforts of various villains to drive him off of his valuable timberland. They defend each other against the attacks of bullies and eventually emerge triumphant. *Veterans. Cowardice. Timberlands. Dogs.*

CROSS ROADS **F2.1092**

William M. Smith Productions. *Dist* Merit Film Corp. Dec **1922.** Si; b&w. 35mm. 5 reels, 4,500 ft.

Dir? (see note) Francis Ford.

Cast: Franklyn Farnum *(The Hero)*, Shorty Hamilton *(Onate)*, Al Hart *(The Yaqui)*, Genevieve Bert *(Jackie)*.

Western melodrama. "A young Westerner on the Mexican border is prevented from being made sheriff by a cunning Mexican, Onate, who forges the papers and makes himself sheriff. He immediately starts proceedings against the real sheriff and forces him to kill a man in his own defense. The Westerner escapes and is befriended by a lonely girl, Jackie, whom everyone shuns because of a belief that she brings bad luck. He is pursued and imprisoned by Onate's men, but Jackie obtains a pardon from the governor and Onate's faithful servant, the Indian, turns traitor for the sake of his American friend. Onate is punished, the sheriff's commission is restored to the right man, and Jackie finds that her curse has finally been removed." (*Moving Picture World,* 6 Jan 1923, p61.) *Sheriffs. Yaqui Indians. Mexicans. Superstition.*

Note: Probably directed by Francis Ford, who directed several other Farnum features for Smith in this period. *The Lariat Thrower* (licensed in New York State 2 Dec 1922, produced by William M. Smith Productions in 5 reels, and starring Franklyn Farnum) may be the same film.

CROSSED SIGNALS **F2.1093**

Morris R. Schlank Productions. *Dist* Rayart Pictures. 28 Sep **1926.** Si; b&w. 35mm. 5 reels, 4,318 ft.

Prod Morris R. Schlank. *Dir* J. P. McGowan. *Adtl Dir* Mack V. Wright. *Story* George Saxton. *Photog* Robert Cline. *Film Ed* Thelma Smith.

Cast: Helen Holmes *(Helen Wainwright)*, Henry Victor *(Jack McDermott)*, Georgie Chapman *(Overland Ike)*, William Lowery *(George Harvey)*, Milla Davenport *(Mother Slattery)*, Nelson McDowell *(Mike Bradley)*, Clyde McAtee *(T. P. Steele)*.

Melodrama. "Woman station agent is unknowingly dupe of counterfeiters. Federal agent succeeds with her help in rounding up criminals after combat on fast train. Money is recovered and station agent is freed of blame, with Federal agent claiming her for his own." (*Motion Picture News Booking Guide,* 11:25, Oct 1926.) *Station agents. Government agents. Counterfeiters. Railroads.*

CROSSED TRAILS **F2.1094**

Independent Pictures. 8 Apr **1924** [New York showing; released May 1924]. Si; b&w. 35mm. 5 reels, ca4,880 ft.

Pres by Jesse J. Goldburg. *Dir* J. P. McGowan. *Story* James Ormont. *Photog* Walter Griffin.

Cast: Franklyn Farnum *(Tom Dawson)*, William Buehler *(J. M. Anders)*, V. L. Barnes *(George Moran)*, Mack V. Wright *(Buck Sloman)*, Alyce Mills *(Mary Morgan)*, Buck Black *(Tom Dawson, 8 years old)*, Billie Bennett *(Alice Dawson)*, J. P. McGowan *("Pepper" Baldwin/Bandy Dawson)*.

Western melodrama. "Tom Dawson learns that the father of the girl he loves is a bandit and though reluctant to be the cause of sorrow to the girl, the depredations of the bandit soon become so outrageous that he is forced to expose the man. Lynching is proposed, but Tom protects 'Pepper' Baldwin against the mob, but the wounds the bandit received in the fight leading to his capture prove fatal, and Tom eventually wins the girl of his heart." (*Motion Picture News Booking Guide,* [7]:18, Oct 1924.) *Bandits. Lynching.*

CROSSED WIRES *see* **DAUGHTERS OF THE NIGHT**

CROSSED WIRES **F2.1095**

Universal Pictures. 14 May **1923** [c4 May 1923; LP18931]. Si; b&w. 35mm. 5 reels, 4,705 ft.

Pres by Carl Laemmle. *Dir* King Baggot. *Scen* Hugh Hoffman. *Story* King Baggot, Raymond Schrock. *Photog* Ben Kline.

Cast: Gladys Walton *(Marcel Murphy)*, George Stewart *(Ralph Benson)*, Tom S. Guise *(Bellamy Benson)*, Lillian Langdon *(Mrs. Margaret Benson)*, William Robert Daly *(Pat Murphy)*, Kate Price *(Nora Murphy)*, Eddie

Gribbon *(Tim Flanagan)*, Marie Crisp *(Madalyn Van Ralston Kemp)*, Eloise Nesbit *(Annie)*, Helen Broneau *(Fannie)*, Lewis Mason *(Cyril Gordon)*.

Comedy. Marcel Murphy, a telephone operator with society aspirations, overhears Mrs. Benson's conversation describing a party she is planning for her son, Ralph, and wangles an invitation by imitating Mrs. Benson's voice. At the party a maid accuses Marcel of the theft of another guest's jewelry, but she appeals to Mr. Benson, who covers up for her by describing Marcel as the daughter of an old friend and by secretly installing her in a hotel suite. Complications reach a climax when Ralph, Mrs. Benson, and Marcel's parents arrive at the hotel at the same time and find Marcel alone with Mr. Benson. Matters are explained, and Ralph asks Marcel to be his wife. *Telephone operators. Social climbers. Upper classes. Theft.*

CROSSING TRAILS **F2.1096**

Cliff Smith Productions. *Dist* Associated Photoplays. 23 Nov **1921** [New York State]. Si; b&w. 35mm. 5 reels, 4,800 ft.

Dir Cliff Smith. *Adapt* L. V. Jefferson, Alvin J. Neitz. *Story* L. V. Jefferson. *Photog* John Thompson.

Cast: Pete Morrison *(Jim Warren)*, Esther Ralston *(Helen Stratton)*, John Hatton *(Buster Stratton)*, Lew Meehan *("Red" Murphy)*, Floyd Taliaferro *(Peter Marcus)*, J. B. Warner *("Bull" Devine)*, Billie Bennett *(Mrs. Warren)*.

Western melodrama. Unjustly accused of murder, Helen Stratton flees with her brother, Buster, but is overtaken by her accuser, Bull Devine, and his henchmen, Red Murphy and Peter Marcus. Devine has the sheriff believing that his purpose is to bring Helen to justice, but his true intention is to force marriage upon her because she is an heiress. Jim Warren happens along at the right time to rescue Helen from Devine's clutches; she changes hands several times; and the sheriff finally learns what Helen has known all along—Devine committed the murder for which the heroine has been sought. *Heiresses. Brother-sister relationship. Murder.*

THE CROSSROADS OF NEW YORK **F2.1097**

Mack Sennett Productions. *Dist* Associated First National Pictures. 21 May **1922** [New York premiere; released May 1922; c9 Jul 1922; LP18091]. Si; b&w. 35mm. 6 reels, 6,292 ft.

Pres by Mack Sennett. *Dir* F. Richard Jones. *Story-Scen* Mack Sennett. *Photog* Homer Scott, Fred W. Jackman, Robert Walters. *Elec Eff* Paul Guerin. *Tech Dir* Ed Holmgren.

Cast: George O'Hara *(Michael Flint)*, Noah Beery *(James Flint)*, Ethel Grey Terry *(Grace St. Clair)*, Ben Deely, Billy Bevan *(press agents)*, Herbert Standing *(John D. Anthony)*, Dot Farley *(landlady)*, Eddie Gribbon *(star boarder)*, Kathryn McGuire *(Ruth Anthony)*, Robert Cain *(Garrett Chesterfield)*, Mildred June *(waitress)*, Raymond Griffith *(a Wall Street "wolf")*, Charles Murray *(a judge)*, James Finlayson *(a lawyer)*.

Melodrama. Country boy Michael Flint arrives in the big city with a letter of introduction to his wealthy uncle, who secures for Michael a job with a uniform—streetcleaning. He is immediately pursued by a variety of ladies, including his landlady, and the volume increases when Uncle James Flint's reported death makes Michael an heir. Meanwhile, he has lost his heart to Ruth Anthony. Life grows more complicated, but the unexpected return of James Flint resolves a breach of promise suit brought against Michael by Grace St. Clair, Broadway actress and the elder Flint's old girl friend, and Michael traces a sudden drop in the stock market to the abduction of Ruth and her father. Rescued, Mr. Anthony acknowledges Michael's worthiness of Ruth. *Streetcleaners. Uncles. Actors. Kidnaping. Stock market. Breach of promise. Courtship.*

Note: "This Mack Sennett production was made about a year ago and originally shown in Los Angeles at Sennett's Mission theatre under another title [and has] since ... undergone some changes" (*Variety*, 26 May 1922, p33). Original title: *For Love or Money.*

THE CROWD **F2.1098**

Metro-Goldwyn-Mayer Pictures. ca18 Feb **1928** [New York premiere; released 3 Mar; c3 Mar 1928; LP25202]. Si; b&w. 35mm. 9 reels, 8,538-8,548 ft.

Dir-Story King Vidor. *Scen* King Vidor, John V. A. Weaver, Harry Behn. *Titl* Joe Farnham. *Photog* Henry Sharp. *Set Dsgn* Cedric Gibbons, Arnold Gillespie. *Film Ed* Hugh Wynn.

Cast: Eleanor Boardman *(Mary)*, James Murray *(John)*, Bert Roach *(Bert)*, Estelle Clark *(Jane)*, Daniel G. Tomlinson *(Jim)*, Dell Henderson *(Dick)*, Lucy Beaumont *(Mother)*, Freddie Burke Frederick *(Junior)*, Alice Mildred Puter *(Daughter)*.

Drama. Mary, a working girl, meets John Sims, a dreamer who believes that luck will eventually bring him success. They marry after their first date—to Coney Island—and honeymoon at Niagara Falls. After 5 years and two children, John, who works as a clerk, has not distinguished himself from the rest of the "crowd." Winning $500 in a slogan contest brightens their lives, but the death of the younger child causes John to become despondent. He and Mary quarrel; he loses his job and becomes a door-to-door salesman; and Mary follows her family's advice to leave him. John is at the point of committing suicide when consideration for his son prevents him. They go home together to find that Mary could not stay away. (A happy ending, not approved by Vidor, was added: John's knack for slogans gets him a position with an advertising firm. The family prospers and is shown in the final scene gathered around a glittering Christmas tree.) *Clerks. Salesmen. In-laws. Family life. Luck. Advertising. Christmas. New York City. Niagara Falls. Coney Island.*

THE CROWDED HOUR **F2.1099**

Famous Players–Lasky. *Dist* Paramount Pictures. 20 Apr **1925** [c23 Apr 1925; LP21389]. Si; b&w. 35mm. 7 reels, 6,558 ft.

Pres by Adolph Zukor, Jesse L. Lasky. *Dir* E. Mason Hopper. *Scen* John Russell. *Photog* J. Roy Hunt.

Cast: Bebe Daniels *(Peggy Laurence)*, Kenneth Harlan *(Billy Laidlaw)*, T. Roy Barnes *(Matt Wilde)*, Frank Morgan *(Bert Caswell)*, Helen Lee Worthing *(Grace Laidlaw)*, Armand Cortez *(Captain Soulier)*, Alice Chapin *(Grand'mère Buvasse)*, Warner Richmond *(operator)*.

War drama. Source: Channing Pollock and Edgar Selwyn, *The Crowded Hour* (New York opening: 22 Nov 1918). Peggy Laurence, a telephone operator, puts on an act with Matt Wilde at a Bowery amateur night and is seen by Billy Laidlaw, who becomes convinced of her talents. Billy subsequently arranges for the Broadway debut of the act and falls in love with Peggy, who wholeheartedly returns his affection. When the World War breaks out, Billy remains unconcerned until his younger brother is killed in action. Billy then immediately enlists and is sent to France; Peggy joins the Red Cross to be with him, and Grace Laidlaw, Billy's wife, also goes to France, working with the Y. M. C. A. Billy is assigned to destroy an ammunition dump, and Peggy learns, after he has left on the mission, that he has been recalled. The phone lines are down, and Peggy volunteers to go after Billy herself. She is soon faced with having to decide between his life and the lives of a whole battalion. She chooses to sacrifice him and is herself temporarily blinded as a consequence. Peggy is nursed back to health by Grace, who wins her sympathy and respect. When Billy unexpectedly shows up unharmed, Peggy sends him back to his wife, giving up her happiness for that of the couple she has come to love. *Telephone operators. Self-sacrifice. Marriage. World War I. New York City—Bowery. France. Young Men's Christian Association. Red Cross.*

THE CROWN OF LIES **F2.1100**

Famous Players–Lasky. *Dist* Paramount Pictures. ca27 Mar **1926** [New York premiere; released 12 Apr; c12 Apr 1926; LP22598]. Si; b&w. 35mm. 5 reels, 5,016 ft.

Pres by Adolph Zukor, Jesse L. Lasky. *Dir* Dimitri Buchowetski. *Scen* Hope Loring, Louis Duryea Lighton. *Story* Ernest Vajda. *Photog* Bert Glennon.

Cast: Pola Negri *(Olga Kriga)*, Noah Beery *(Count Mirko)*, Robert Ames *(John Knight)*, Charles A. Post *(Karl)*, Arthur Hoyt *(Fritz)*, Mikhael Vavitch *(Vorski)*, Cissy Fitzgerald *(Leading Lady)*, May Foster *(Landlady)*, Frankie Bailey *(Actress)*, Edward Cecil *(Leading Man)*, Erwin Connelly *(Stage Manager)*.

Romantic drama. Olga Kriga, a boardinghouse girl who dreams of becoming a great actress, is turned down by a theater manager because of the jealousy of the leading lady. She then accompanies her admirer, John Knight, a young flivver salesman, when he accepts an agency offered in a small Balkan country. Karl, an alien, avows that Olga is his beloved "Queen" and begs her to return with him to Sylvania; at the hotel, Count Mirko and his ministers greet her. Count Mirko perceives the resemblance and quickly formulates a scheme to gain wealth and power in the country with Olga posing as the lost queen returning to free the people from tyranny. Accompanied by John, Olga arrives in Sylvania, where the uneasy tyrant, Vorski, agrees to pay for her removal; but after revolt she ascends the throne. Happiness restored, Olga returns to New York with John. *Royalty. Mistaken identity. Impersonation. Automobile agencies. Imaginary kingdoms. Balkans. New York City.*

THE CROW'S NEST **F2.1101**

Sunset Productions. *Dist* Aywon Film Corp. 15 Sep **1922.** Si; b&w. 35mm. 5 reels, 4,403-4,700 ft.

Pres by Anthony J. Xydias. *Dir* Paul Hurst. *Story* William Lester. *Photog* William Nobles.

Cast: Jack Hoxie *(Esteban)*, Ruddel Weatherwax *(Esteban, as a boy)*, Evelyn Nelson *(Patricia Benton)*, Tom Lingham *(Beaugard)*, William Lester *(Pecos)*, William Dyer *(Timberline)*, Mary Bruce *(Margarita)*, Bert Lindley *(John Benton)*, Augustina Lopez *(The Squaw)*.

Western melodrama. Esteban (a white boy) is reared by an Indian squaw, whom he believes to be his mother and from whom Beaugard steals the papers documenting Esteban's birth and his right to inherit a ranch. When he is grown, Esteban falls in love with Patricia Benton, Beaugard "exposes" Esteban to Patricia, and the villain taunts the lad that he has no right to a white woman. After a series of adventures in which Esteban recovers Patricia from Beaugard's grasp, the couple happily learn the truth from Esteban's "mother." *Indians of North America. Inheritance. Racial prejudice. Parentage. Documentation.*

THE CRUEL TRUTH **F2.1102**

Sterling Pictures. 10 Jul **1927** [c25 Jul 1927; LP24226]. Si; b&w. 35mm. 6 reels, 5,167 ft.

Dir Phil Rosen. *Story-Scen* Frances Guihan. *Photog* Herbert Kirkpatrick.

Cast: Hedda Hopper *(Grace Sturdevant)*, Constance Howard *(Helen Sturdevant)*, Hugh Allan *(Reggie Copeley)*, Frances Raymond *(Mrs. Copeley)*, Ruth Handforth *(maid)*.

Romantic drama. Under the watchful eye of Mrs. Copeley, who defends him from a horde of feminine admirers, wealthy young Reggie Copeley sees one woman at the beach whose attractiveness seems different from that of the others. He thus falls prey to the charms of Grace Sturdevant, many years his senior, though she manages to preserve her youth through beauty treatments. Grace is disturbed by the appearance of Helen, her daughter, and forces her to remain in the background, while she continues to entertain Reggie. But Reggie, by chance, saves Helen from drowning, and they soon fall in love. Grace is at first miserably unhappy but decides to forego her own welfare for the sake of the young lovers. *Courtship. Youth. Motherhood.*

THE CRUISE OF THE HELLION (Rayart-Imperial Photoplay) **F2.1103**

Duke Worne Productions. *Dist* Rayart Pictures. 10 Sep **1927.** Si; b&w. 35mm. 7 reels, 6,089 ft.

Pres by W. Ray Johnston. *Dir* Duke Worne. *Story-Scen* George W. Pyper. *Photog* Walter Griffin.

Cast: Donald Keith *(Jack Harlan)*, Edna Murphy *(Diana Drake)*, Tom Santschi *(Kilroy)*, Sheldon Lewis *(Captain Drake)*, Sailor Sharkey *(Reid)*, Charles K. French *(John Harlan)*, Francis Ford *(Peg-leg)*, Martin Turner.

Melodrama. John Harlan has his son, Jack, shanghaied in the hope that a cruise aboard the *Hellion* will make a man of him. Jack finds a brutal crew led by Kilroy, the first mate; a loyal old salt in Peg-leg; a captain who only occasionally lapses into sobriety; and a single ray of sunshine in Diana Drake, the captain's daughter. The crew mutinies to gain possession of the *Hellion*'s cargo of gold, but Jack gamely allies himself with Drake to put down the rebellion and is rewarded with Diana's love. *Sailors. Ship crews. Manhood. Fatherhood. Seafaring life. Mutiny. Gold. Drunkenness. Shanghaiing.*

THE CRUISE OF THE JASPER B **F2.1104**

De Mille Pictures. *Dist* Producers Distributing Corp. 13 Dec **1926** [c7 Dec 1926; LP23406]. Si; b&w. 35mm. 6 reels, 5,780 ft.

Supv William Sistrom. *Dir* James W. Horne. *Titl* John Krafft. *Adapt* Zelda Sears, Tay Garnett. *Photog* Lucien Andriot. *Art Dir* John Hughes. *Cutter* Jack Dennis. *Asst Dir* Arthur Flaven. *Unit Mgr* E. O. Van Pelt. *Script Girl* Reine Serviss.

Cast: Rod La Rocque *(J. Clement Cleggett)*, Mildred Harris *(Agatha Fairhaven)*, Jack Ackroyd *(Wiggins)*, Snitz Edwards *(Reginald Maltravers)*, Otto Lederer *(auctioneer)*, James Mack *(assistant auctioneer)*.

Romantic comedy. Source: Don Marquis, *The Cruise of the Jasper B* (New York, 1916). Jerry Cleggett, descendant of a seafaring, buccaneering family, in order to inherit the family fortune, must marry on the deck of the *Jasper B*, now rotting on the docks. Aided by an overzealous valet, Jerry looks over a large number of prospective partners; then Agatha Fairhaven, trying to save a fortune of her own, enters his house—seeking protection just as the entire house is being auctioned off. Jerry and Agatha fall instantly in love, and with Jerry dressed in pirate regalia they proceed to the ancestral ship. When their taxicab goes on a wild, driverless spree, the couple are joined by a trio of bandits who have just held up a mailtruck; and they are pursued by local, state, and Federal authorities. Aboard ship, the crew escape the authorities as, following a furious battle, a bomb jars the vessel from her concrete bed and into the water. *Valets. Pirates. Bandits. Ships. Inheritance. Courtship. Auctions.*

CRUSADE OF THE INNOCENT **F2.1105**

2 Feb **1922** [New York State license application]. Si; b&w. 35mm. 5 reels.

Drama. "A story of leprosy (or syphilis), seduction, murder, and cruelty and final redemption—with closeups of Jesus in all the art titles" (New York State license records). *Leprosy. Venereal disease. Murder. Seduction. Redemption. Jesus.*

Note: Production and distribution companies not determined. Distribution in New York handled by Popular Film Co. or Jawitz Pictures Corp.

THE CRUSADER **F2.1106**

Fox Film Corp. 10 Sep **1922** [c10 Sep 1922; LP19156]. Si; b&w. 35mm. 5 reels, 4,780 ft.

Pres by William Fox. *Dir* Howard M. Mitchell. *Scen* William K. Howard, Jack Strumwasser. *Photog* David Abel.

Cast: William Russell *(Peter Brent)*, Gertrude Claire *(Mrs. Brent)*, Helen Ferguson *(Mary)*, Fritzi Brunette *(Alice)*, George Webb *(James Symonds)*, Carl Grantvoort *(Bob Josephson)*.

Western melodrama. Source: Alan Sullivan, "The Crusader," in *Popular Magazine* (40:1–69, 20 Mar 1916). Peter Brent discovers silver in the Cobalt mining district and sends for Jim Symonds, an acquaintance, to assist in developing the vein. Although the mine proves to be worthless, Symonds sells stock to exploit the local citizens. Brent is buried in a cave-in caused by one of Symond's crooked pals, but a neighbor and her father rescue Brent and he arrives in time to force Symonds to return the citizens' money. *Swindlers. Silver mines.*

CRUSADERS OF THE WEST **F2.1107**

Anchor Productions. 28 Jul **1930** [New York State license]. Si; b&w. 35mm. 5 reels, 4,500 ft.

Cast: Cliff (Tex) Lyons.

Western melodrama(?). No information about the nature of this film has been found.

THE CRYSTAL CUP **F2.1108**

Henry Hobart Productions. *Dist* First National Pictures. 16 Oct **1927** [c13 Sep 1927; LP24396]. Si; b&w. 35mm. 7 reels, 6,386 ft.

Prod Henry Hobart. *Dir* John Francis Dillon. *Adapt-Scen* Gerald C. Duffy. *Titl* Mort Blumenstock. *Photog* James Van Trees.

Cast: Dorothy Mackaill *(Gita Carteret)*, Rockliffe Fellowes *(John Blake)*, Jack Mulhall *(Geoffrey Pelham)*, Clarissa Selwynne *(Mrs. Pleyden)*, Jane Winton *(Polly Pleyden)*, Edythe Chapman *(Mrs. Carteret)*.

Romantic drama. Source: Gertrude Franklin Atherton, *The Crystal Cup* (New York, 1925). As the result of an early and brutal seduction, Gita Carteret, a wealthy young heiress, develops an intense dislike for men. She dresses in clothes of extreme masculine cut, wears short hair, and abandons all feminine mannerisms. Fulfilling a promise to her dying grandmother, Gita attends a fashionable ball at the Pleydens, clad in proper feminine attire, where she finds herself the object of the attentions of John Blake, a successful novelist, and his friend Dr. Geoffrey Pelham. Warned by Mrs. Pleyden of gossip associating Gita with Blake, Gita decides to marry him "in name only," and he reluctantly agrees. While Blake is working on a novel, she develops an intimate friendship with Pelham but is frightened by her attraction to him. Blake's longing overwhelms his former caution in winning her love, and when he enters her room at night, the terrified Gita shoots him. Dying, he realizes that Pelham is the only man who can awaken the feminine in her nature and asks him to marry her. *Novelists. Heiresses. Man-haters. Marriage of convenience. Seduction. Mannishness. Reputation.*

THE CUB REPORTER **F2.1109**

Phil Goldstone Productions. Aug **1922.** Si; b&w. 35mm. 5 reels.

Dir Jack Dillon. *Scen* George Elwood Jenks. *Photog* Harry Fowler.

Cast: Richard Talmadge *(Dick Harvey)*, Jean Calhoun *(Marion Rhodes)*, Edwin B. Tilton *(Harrison Rhodes)*, Wilson Hummel *(mandarin)*, Lewis

Mason, Ethel Hallor *(crooks)*.

Action melodrama. "Harvey, of the Morning Times, is called upon to do one daredevil stunt after another in his efforts to recover the Sacred Jewel of Buddha. ... He dives head first through a skylight into the den of the Tong and gets away with the Jewel. Then he braves the underground passages of the Chinese underworld to rescue the girl stolen by the Tong and held as hostage for the return of the jewel. He proves too much for a whole squad of Chinamen and escapes with the beautiful girl." *(Moving Picture World*, 30 Sep 1922, p396.) *Reporters. Chinese. Hostages. Tongs. Stunts.*

THE CUCKOOS **F2.1110**

RKO Productions. 4 May **1930** [c4 May 1930; LP1331]. Sd (Photophone); b&w. 35mm. 11 reels, 9,170 ft.

Supv Louis Sarecky. *Dir* Paul Sloane. *Adapt* Cyrus Wood. *Photog* Nicholas Musuraca. *Art Dir* Max Ree. *Film Ed* Arthur Roberts. *Songs: "I Love You So Much," "Knock Knees," "Looking for the Lovelight in Your Eyes"* Bert Kalmar, Harry Ruby. *Song: "Wherever You Are"* Charles Tobias, Cliff Friend. *Song: "If I Were a Traveling Salesman"* Al Dubin, Joe Burke. *Mus Dir* Victor Baravalle. *Dance Dir* Pearl Eaton. *Rec Engr* John Tribby.

Cast: Bert Wheeler *(Sparrow)*, Robert Woolsey *(Professor Bird)*, June Clyde *(Ruth)*, Hugh Trevor *(Billy)*, Dorothy Lee *(Anita)*, Ivan Lebedeff *(The Baron)*, Marguerita Padula *(Gypsy Queen)*, Mitchell Lewis *(Julius)*, Jobyna Howland *(Fannie Furst)*, Raymond Maurel.

Musical comedy. Source: Guy Bolton, Harry Ruby and Bert Kalmar, *The Ramblers* (a musical play). Professor Bird, a fortune-teller, and his assistant, Sparrow, are stranded at a border resort. There Sparrow has fallen in love with Anita, an American girl who lives with a band of Gypsies, though he is threatened by Julius, leader of the band. Baron de Camp loves Ruth Chester, who has been in flight from her aunt, Fannie Furst, who wants to separate her from Billy Shannon, an aviator; but Billy soon arrives in Mexico. Fannie invites the professor and Sparrow to a party; Julius' men kidnap Ruth, and the fortune-tellers promise Fannie they will rescue her. Billy finds Ruth and with the assistance of the professor and Sparrow overcomes the baron and his gang. The happy group return to Fannie's home in San Diego. *Fortune-tellers. Gypsies. Kidnaping. Courtship. Mexican border. San Diego.*

THE CUP OF LIFE **F2.1111**

Thomas H. Ince Productions. *Dist* Associated Producers. 7 Aug **1921** [c24 Aug 1921; LP16890]. Si; b&w. 35mm. 6 reels.

Pres by Thomas H. Ince. *Supv* Thomas H. Ince. *Dir* Rowland V. Lee. *Scen* Joseph Franklin Poland. *Story* Carey Wilson. *Photog* J. O. Taylor.

Cast: Hobart Bosworth *("Bully" Brand)*, Madge Bellamy *(Pain)*, Niles Welch *(Roy Bradley or Warren Bradford)*, Tully Marshall *(Chan Chang)*, Monte Collins *(Larry Donovan)*, May Wallace *(Mollie)*.

Melodrama. Bully Brand, a notorious Singapore smuggler, refuses to sell a wonderful pearl, coveted by Chinese merchant Chan Chang for the necklace of his adopted white daughter, Pain. Brand's son, Warren Bradford, who believes that Brand is merely his guardian, returns from college and falls in love with Pain. Learning of the necklace, he persuades his father to give him the pearl, which he presents to Pain. Recognizing the pearl, Chang angrily believes that Brand has wronged her and demands that Brand marry her under penalty of death. Brand attempts to escape, and Warren, ignorant of the bridegroom's identity, tries to prevent the ceremony. Chang, seeking double revenge, plays one against the other. Following a fight in the darkened wedding room, Brand discovers his assailant's identity, brings Chang to account, and arranges the marriage of Warren and Pain. *Smugglers. Personal identity. Pearls. Singapore.*

CUPID'S BRAND **F2.1112**

Unity Photoplays. *Dist* Arrow Film Corp. Apr **1921.** Si; b&w. 35mm. 6 reels, 4,751 ft.

Ben Wilson Production. *Dir* Rowland V. Lee.

Cast: Jack Hoxie *(Reese Wharton)*, Wilbur McGaugh *("Spike" Crowder)*, Charles Force *("Bull" Devlin)*, Mignon Anderson *(Neva Hedden)*, William Dyer *(Slade Crosby)*, A. T. Van Sicklen *(Steve Heden)*.

Melodrama. Warton, an ex-convict, and Crowder and Devlin, both counterfeiters, join forces to set up an operation in a small western town on the edge of the desert. The town's sheriff, wanting to cut into the deal, offers them protection in return for a rakeoff. The trio, not agreeable to this arrangement, incurs his enmity; and the sheriff retaliates by trying to have them hanged. All looks dim for the three when chased into the desert by the sheriff's men, but they escape. *Counterfeiters. Sheriffs. Graft. Deserts.*

CUPID'S FIREMAN **F2.1113**

Fox Film Corp. 16 Dec **1923** [c8 Dec 1923; LP19711]. Si; b&w. 35mm. 5 reels, 4,204 ft.

Pres by William Fox. *Dir* William A. Wellman. *Scen* Eugene B. Lewis. *Story* Richard Harding Davis. *Photog* Joseph August.

Cast: Charles Jones *(Andy McGee)*, Marian Nixon *(Agnes Evans)*, Brooks Benedict *(Bill, Agnes' husband)*, Eileen O'Malley *(Elizabeth Stevens)*, Lucy Beaumont *(Mother)*, Al Fremont *(fire chief)*, Charles McHugh *(Old Man Turner)*, Mary Warren *(Molly Turner)*, L. H. King *(veteran)*.

Melodrama. Source: Richard Harding Davis, "Andy M'Gee's Chorus Girl" in *Van Bibber, and Others* (New York, 1892). Andy McGee becomes a fireman against his mother's wishes. He meets a beautiful woman, rescues her from a burning house, and marries her when she becomes a widow. *Firemen. Widows. Filial relations. Fires.*

CUPID'S KNOCKOUT **F2.1114**

Hercules Film Productions. 1 Aug **1926** [c3 Aug 1926; LP23005]. Si; b&w. 35mm. 5 reels, 4,814 ft.

Pres by Peter Kanellos. *Dir* Bruce Mitchell. *Story-Scen* Grover Jones.

Cast: Frank Merrill *(Frank Gibson)*, Andrée Tourneur *(Sally Hibbard)*, Donald Fullen *(David Manning)*, Marco Charles *("Measles" Martin)*, George French *(George Hibbard)*, Mathilde Brundage *(Mrs. Hibbard)*, William Hayes *("Rubber Chin" Smith)*, George Kotsonaros.

Comedy-drama. Wealthy town "boss" David Manning has everything he desires except Sally Hibbard, and he plots to "rescue" Sally and her parents from a situation and thus put her under an obligation to him. Sally, however, meets Frank Gibson when they find themselves photographed together by a "picture machine." Later, Manning's henchmen attack Frank and his pal, "Rubber Chin" Smith, but the gang gets the worst of it. While on his milk delivery route, Frank overhears Manning's plotting and by accident finds himself at the Hibbard home, where Sally invites him to join a party. The party is invited to a tavern, where Frank follows and frustrates Manning's scheme to stage a police raid by substituting milk for the liquor on the guests' tables. Frank turns out to be the governor's son and is betrothed to Sally. *Milkmen. Courtship. Prohibition. Photography.*

CUPID'S RUSTLER **F2.1115**

Dearholt Productions. *Dist* Arrow Film Corp. 1 Jun **1924** [c25 May 1924; LP20240]. Si; b&w. 35mm. 5 reels, 4,590 ft.

Dir-Writ Francis Ford.

Cast: Edmund Cobb *(a victim of a crooked card game [Jim])*, Florence Gilbert *(another victim of circumstances)*, Clark Coffey *(The Sheriff)*, Ashton Dearholt *(Harry)*, Wilbur McGaugh *(foreman of the Jones Ranch)*.

Western melodrama. Jim, in order to help a dancehall girl start a new life, agrees to help make her ranch pay an income. He steals 200 horses from an adjoining ranch, and when the sheriff comes for him the girl hides him in a deserted cabin. Harry, the owner of the saloon, has become tired of his own girl and turns his attentions to the dancehall girl. Jim beats Harry in a fight, and the sheriff returns; but Jim reveals himself as the wealthy owner of the ranch from which the horses were stolen. Harry goes back to his former sweetheart. *Dancehall girls. Ranchers. Horsethieves. Saloons.*

CURLYTOP **F2.1116**

Fox Film Corp. 28 Dec **1924** [30 Nov 1924; LP20907]. Si; b&w. 35mm. 6 reels, 5,828 ft.

Pres by William Fox. *Dir* Maurice Elvey. *Adapt-Scen* Frederick Hatton, Fanny Hatton. *Photog* Joseph Valentine.

Cast: Shirley Mason *(Curlytop)*, Wallace MacDonald *(Bill Branigan)*, Warner Oland *(Shanghai Dan)*, Diana Miller *(Bessie)*, George Kuwa *(Wang Toy)*, Ernest Adams *(Sproggs)*, Nora Hayden *(Hilda)*, La Verne Lindsay *(Annie)*.

Romantic melodrama. Source: Thomas Burke, "Twelve Golden Curls," in *More Limehouse Nights* (New York, c1921). Curlytop, an attractive, naive girl who works in Sprogg's department store in the Limehouse district of London, meets Bill Branigan, a charming but feckless young man, and falls in love with him. Bill casts aside his sweetheart, Bessie, and, reformed by Curlytop's love, goes to Hammersmith to find work. In his absence, Bessie gets Curlytop drunk and cuts off her twelve golden curls. Shanghai Dan, a sinister, halfcaste Chinese mesmerist, then hires the shorn Curlytop as a waitress on his floating barge-restaurant. Bill returns; but not finding Curlytop, he renews his relationship with Bessie, until, by chance, he discovers the golden curls among Bessie's belongings. Forcing her to tell him where he can find his lost love, Bill arrives on the waterfront just as Dan's barge is sinking after a collision with a schooner. Bill rescues Curlytop from the water, but Dan, who at the time of the accident was below decks hypnotizing the unwilling girl in a locked cabin, is lost in the Thames. *Salesclerks. Waitresses. Mesmerists. Halfcastes. Chinese. Hypnotism. London—Limehouse.*

THE CURSE OF DRINK **F2.1117**

Weber & North. Oct **1922** [c18 May 1922; LP17894]. Si; b&w. 35mm. 6 reels, 5,900 ft.

Dir-Scen Harry O. Hoyt. *Photog* Harry Fischbeck.

Cast: Harry T. Morey *(Bill Sanford)*, Edmund Breese *(John Rand)*, Marguerite Clayton *(Ruth Sanford)*, George Fawcett *(Ben Flartey)*, Miriam Battista *(Baby Betty)*, Brinsley Shaw *(Sam Handy)*, Alice May *(Mother Sanford)*, Albert L. Barrett *(Harry Rand)*, June Fuller *(Margaret Sanford)*.

Melodrama. Source: Charles E. Blaney, *The Curse of Drink; a Melodrama in Four Acts* (c20 Jan 1904). Bill Sanford, once a first-rate railroad engineer and happy father, is victimized by bootleggers and soon becomes known as the village drunkard. His daughter, Ruth, a stenographer, is in love with her employer's son, Harry, but his father, Rand, opposes the match, though he consents to it when Sanford seems to reform. Ruth's mother arranges a celebration dinner, but Sam Handy, a rival for Ruth, tempts the father with bootleg liquor; he becomes intoxicated, breaks up the gathering, and brings about his discharge. To revenge himself on Rand, he mounts an engine attached to his special car with the intention of wrecking it. The lovers pursue in another engine, and Ruth effects a rescue. The reconciliation of the families and the arrest of the bootleggers resolve the situation. *Railroad engineers. Stenographers. Bootleggers. Alcoholism. Fatherhood. Railroads.*

THE CUSTARD CUP **F2.1118**

Fox Film Corp. 1 Jan **1923** [c31 Dec 1922; LP18996]. Si; b&w. 35mm. 7 reels, 6,166 ft.

Pres by William Fox. *Dir* Herbert Brenon. *Scen* G. Marion Burton. *Titl* Ralph Spence. *Photog* Tom Malloy.

Cast: Mary Carr *(Mrs. Penfield ["Penzie"])*, Myrta Bonillas *(Gussie Bosley)*, Miriam Battista *(Lettie)*, Jerry Devine *(Crink)*, Ernest McKay *(Thad)*, Peggy Shaw *(Lorene Percy)*, Leslie Leigh *(Mrs. Percy)*, Frederick Esmelton *(Jeremiah Winston)*, Henry Sedley *(Frank Bosley)*, Louis Hendricks *(Alderman Curry)*, Edward Boring *(Mr. Wopple)*, Emily Lorraine *(Perennial Prue)*, Ben Lyon *(Dick Chase)*, Richard Collins *(counterfeiter)*, Nick Hollen *(detective)*.

Drama. Source: Florence Bingham Livingston, *The Custard Cup* (New York, 1921). The "Custard Cup," a tenement neighborhood, is the home of Mrs. Penfield, an elderly widow who is mother to three adopted children, and of counterfeiters Mr. and Mrs. Frank Bosley. During a boat excursion hosted by an alderman, a fire results from Bosley's efforts to destroy the counterfeit money in his pocket. Mrs. Penfield and the children are rescued, but she is accused of passing phony bills. A detective proves her to be an unwitting dupe, and the Bosleys are apprehended. *Widows. Counterfeiters. Motherhood. Tenements. Ship fires.*

CUSTER'S LAST FIGHT (Reissue) **F2.1119**

Dist Quality Amusement Corp. **1925** [c1 Jun 1925; LP21952]. Si; b&w. 35mm. 5 reels.

Note: This is a reissue of a Thomas Ince film written by Richard V. Spencer and edited and titled by Inez A. Ridgeway.

CYCLONE BLISS **F2.1120**

Unity Photoplays. *Dist* Arrow Film Corp. Jan **1921.** Si; b&w. 35mm. 5 reels.

Prod Ben Wilson. *Dir* Francis Ford. *Photog* William Nobles.

Cast: Jack Hoxie *(Jack Bliss)*, Frederick Moore *(Bill Turner)*, Evelyn Nelson *(Helen Turner)*, Fred Kohler *(Jack Hall)*, Steve Clemento *(Pedro)*, William Dyer *(Slim)*, James Kelly *(Jimmie Donahue)*.

Western melodrama. Quiet and fairminded Jack Bliss traces his missing father to Hell's Hole, where he meets Helen Turner and Jack Hall, the leader of an outlaw gang rendezvousing at Hell's Hole. Hall kills Helen's father but fails in his attempts to get rid of Bliss and Helen, and Bliss, singlehanded, takes on the gang while the neighboring ranchers, settlers, and herders unite to clean out the outlaws. They arrive in time to save Bliss and Helen and to hear Hall's confession to the murder of Bliss's father. *Ranchers. Gangs. Murder. Filial relations.*

CYCLONE BOB **F2.1121**

Larry Wheeler Productions. *Dist* Anchor Film Distributors. 23 Jun **1926** [New York State license]. Si; b&w. 35mm. 5 reels.

Dir J. P. McGowan.

Cast: Bob Reeves *(Cyclone Bob Flemming)*, Tex Starr *("Spook" Nelson)*, D. Maley *("Skeeter" Thompson)*, Alma Rayford *(Molly Mallory)*, Leon De La Mothe *(Bert Rodgers)*, Percy Challenger *(Malcomb Mallory)*, Fred Hank *(Sheriff Hodges)*.

Western melodrama(?). No information about the nature of this film has been found.

CYCLONE BUDDY **F2.1122**

Approved Pictures. *Dist* Weiss Brothers Artclass Pictures. 15 Dec **1924** [c6 Dec 1924; LU20849]. Si; b&w. 35mm. 5 reels, 4,850 ft.

Pres by Lester F. Scott, Jr. *Story-Dir* Alvin J. Neitz. *Photog* Irving Ries, Phillip Tannura.

Cast: Buddy Roosevelt *(Buddy Blake)*, Norma Conterno *(Doris Martin)*, Alfred Hewston *(Judd Martin)*, Bud Osborne *(Steve Noels)*, J. P. Lockney *(Luke Noels)*, Chet Ryan *(Sheriff Brady)*, Shorty Hendrix *(Shorty)*.

Western melodrama. Unjustly accused of murder, Buddy Blake escapes from the courtroom where he is on trial for his life and rounds up the Raiders, an outlaw gang, secretly led by Luke Noels, that has been attempting to drive Buddy's boss, Martin, from his ranch on Granite Range. Buddy and Doris Martin then receive her father's permission to be married. *Ranchers. Murder. Injustice. Trials.*

CYCLONE CAVALIER **F2.1123**

Harry J. Brown Productions. *Dist* Rayart Pictures. caSep **1925.** Si; b&w. 35mm. 5 reels, 4,928 ft.

Dir Albert Rogell. *Scen* Krag Johnson, Burke Jenkins. *Photog* Lyman Broening. *Adtl Photog* William Tuers.

Cast: Reed Howes *(Ted Clayton)*, Carmelita Geraghty *(Rosita Gonzales)*, Wilfred Lucas *(Hugh Clayton)*, Eric Mayne *(President Gonzales)*, Jack Mower *(El Diablo)*, Johnny Sinclair *(Mickey)*, Ervin Renard *(Van Blatten)*.

Comedy-melodrama. Ted Clayton, a live wire who thirsts for adventure and trouble, is sent to Costa Blanca, a Central American republic, on his father's business. En route, he falls in love with Rosita Gonzales and runs afoul of her father, President of Costa Blanca. Once in the country, Ted accidentally overhears the plans of Gonzales' secretary, El Diablo, to overthrow the government. Ted then obtains an audience with the president, persuades him of his friendship, and informs him of El Diablo's plans. Ted later helps defend the palace against the revolutionaries until the loyal troops arrive, thus winning the love of Rosita and her father's gratitude. *Thrill-seeking. Imaginary republics. Revolutions. Central America.*

THE CYCLONE COWBOY **F2.1124**

Action Pictures. *Dist* Pathé Exchange. 2 Jan **1927** [c31 Dec 1926; LP23488]. Si; b&w. 35mm. 5 reels, 4,447 ft.

Pres by Lester F. Scott, Jr. *Dir* Richard Thorpe. *Story* Tommy Gray. *Photog* Ray Reis.

Cast: Wally Wales *(Wally Baxter)*, Violet Bird *(Norma)*, Raye Hampton *(Ma Tuttle)*, Richard Lee *(Gerald Weith)*, Ann Warrington *(Laura Tuttle)*, George Magrill.

Western melodrama. Rancher Ma Tuttle, who wants her top hand, Wally, for a son-in-law, is annoyed when her daughter, Norma, writes that she is engaged to Gerald Weith, a city slicker. Ma takes Wally and goes to the city to rescue Norma, who suggests they take Gerald back to the ranch. Gerald fails to adjust to the rugged western life and suggests an elopement to which Norma consents, despite her admiration for Wally. A storm overtakes Norma, Gerald, and Wally, and they seek refuge in a shack that houses a gang of rustlers. Gerald proves to be a coward, and Norma, in danger, turns instinctively to Wally. With the help of Ma and her men, the thieves are rounded up, and Gerald surrenders the girl to Wally. *Cowboys. Rustlers. Ranchers. Courtship. Cowardice.*

CYCLONE JONES **F2.1125**

Charles R. Seeling. *Dist* Aywon Film Corp. Sep **1923.** Si; b&w. 35mm. 5 reels, ca4,800 ft.

Dir Charles R. Seeling. *Story* John F. Natteford. *Photog* Marcel Le Picard.

Cast: Big Boy Williams *(Cyclone Jones)*, Bill Patton *(Kirk Davis)*, J. P.

McKee *(John Billings)*, Kathleen Collins *(Sylvia Billings)*, Fatty Alexander *(Fatty Wirthing)*, Fred Burns *(Jack Thompson)*.

Western melodrama. Cyclone Jones falls in love with Sylvia Billings, who, with her father, a sheep rancher, has recently arrived in a western town. Sylvia rejects Jones's attentions until he saves her from a runaway horse and protects Billings from local hostile cattle ranchers. *Ranchers. Cattle. Sheep.*

CYCLONE OF THE RANGE **F2.1126**

FBO Pictures. 24 Apr **1927** [c18 Apr 1927; LP23876]. Si; b&w. 35mm. 5 reels, 4,818 ft.

Dir Robert De Lacy. *Cont* Arthur Statter, F. A. E. Pine. *Story* Oliver Drake. *Photog* Nick Musuraca. *Asst Dir* William Cody.

Cast: Tom Tyler *(Tom Mackay)*, Elsie Tarron *(Mollie Butler)*, Harry O'Connor *(Seth Butler)*, Richard Howard *(Jake Dakin)*, Frankie Darro *(Frankie Butler)*, Harry Woods *(The Black Rider/Don Alvarado)*, Beans *(himself, a dog)*.

Western melodrama. Cowboy Tom Mackay, who takes a job on the Butler ranch, is out looking for an outlaw who murdered his brother. Tom falls in love with the rancher's daughter, Mollie, finding a rival in foreman Dakin, who attempts to get rid of Tom by alleging he is the notorious outlaw, the "Black Rider." Making a deal with the real Black Rider, Dakin attempts to frame Tom. Just as the crowd is about to lynch Tom, Dakin doublecrosses the Black Rider and receives a bullet for his efforts. The Black Rider is captured trying to escape. Satisfied that the Black Rider killed his brother, Tom settles down with Mollie. *Cowboys. Ranch foremen. Outlaws. Murder. Lynching. Dogs.*

THE CYCLONE RIDER **F2.1127**

Fox Film Corp. 14 Sep **1924** [c6 Aug 1924; LP20472]. Si; b&w. 35mm. 7 reels, 6,472 ft.

Dir-Scen Thomas Buckingham. *Story* Lincoln J. Carter. *Photog* Sidney Wagner.

Cast: Reed Howes *(Richard Armstrong)*, Alma Bennett *(Doris Steele)*, William Bailey *(Reynard Trask)*, Margaret McWade *(Mrs. Armstrong)*, Frank Beal *(Robert Steele)*, Evelyn Brent *("Weeping Wanda")*, Eugene Pallette *(Eddie)*, Ben Deeley *("Silent Dan")*, Charles Conklin *(Remus)*, Bud Jamison *(Romulus)*, Ben Hendricks, Jr. *(taxi driver)*.

Action melodrama. Richard Armstrong, inventor of a carburetor that will make his car a sure winner in a road race, works on a skyscraper for Richard Steele and falls in love with his daughter, Doris. Though Steele prefers Trask, an underworld king, he agrees to discuss marriage if Armstrong wins the prize money. Though losing the race, Armstrong averts Trask's efforts to kill him and wins the girl. *Inventors. Automobile racing.*

CYTHEREA **F2.1128**

Madison Productions. *Dist* Associated First National Pictures. 4 May **1924** [c24 Apr 1924; LP20119]. Si; b&w with col sequence (Technicolor). 35mm. 8 reels, 7,400 ft.

Pres by Samuel Goldwyn. *Dir* George Fitzmaurice. *Adapt* Frances Marion. *Photog* Arthur Miller. *Tech Dir* Ben Carré. *Film Ed* Stuart Heisler.

Cast: Irene Rich *(Fanny Randon)*, Lewis Stone *(Lee Randon)*, Norman Kerry *(Peyton Morris)*, Betty Bouton *(Claire Morris)*, Alma Rubens *(Savina Grove)*, Charles Wellesley *(William Grove)*, Constance Bennett *(Annette Sherwin)*, Peaches Jackson *(Randon child)*, Mickey Moore *(another Randon child)*, Hugh Saxon *(butler in Randon home)*, Lee Hill *(butler in Grove home)*, Lydia Yeamans Titus *(laundress)*, Brandon Hurst *(Daniel Randon)*.

Romantic drama. Source: Joseph Hergesheimer, *Cytherea, Goddess of Love* (New York, 1922). Lee Randon, weary of business duties and a conventional home life, acquires a long-lost sense of excitement and romance with young flapper Claire Morris. When he meets her married aunt, Savina Grove, she appears to be the woman he imagines whenever he gazes at a doll he has christened Cytherea, goddess of love. Breaking past ties, he and Savina begin an intense affair, and their search for a romantic paradise in Cuba leads to Savina's tragic death. Lee returns home, repents, and is reunited with his wife and children. *Businessmen. Flappers. Aunts. Infidelity. Dolls. Cuba. Calypso.*

Note: Cuban sequence is in color.

THE CZAR OF BROADWAY **F2.1129**

Universal Pictures. 25 May **1930** [c9 May 1930; LP1291]. Sd (Movietone); b&w. 35mm. 8 reels, 7,314 ft. [Also si; 7,106 ft.]

Pres by Carl Laemmle. *Dir* William James Craft. *Story-Cont-Dial* Gene Towne. *Photog* Hal Mohr. *Film Ed* Harry Lieb. *Mus Arr* Lou Handman. *Rec Engr* C. Roy Hunter.

Cast: John Wray *(Morton Bradley)*, Betty Compson *(Connie Colton)*, John Harron *(Jay Grant)*, Claude Allister *(Francis)*, Wilbur Mack *(Harry Foster)*, King Baggot *(Dane Harper)*, Edmund Breese *(McNab)*.

Crime melodrama. Mort Bradley, New York political boss and underworld czar, controls not only the city's most popular nightclub but also much of the press; however, the managing editor of the *Times* is determined to expose him. Jay Grant, a San Francisco reporter, is assigned to investigate Mort, who believes Jay to be a country boy and is delighted to see him fall in love with Connie Colton, of whom Mort has tired. Dismayed to learn that Jay is a reporter, Mort plans to have his gunman, Francis, kill him, but both Mort and Francis are shot by rival gangsters. Jay, believing that Mort will recover, rushes to the newspaper with an exposé, but while writing it he learns of Mort's death and decides their friendship would not permit him to submit the story. He leaves his paper and embarks on a new life with Connie. *Political bosses. Gangsters. Reporters. San Franciscans. Nightclubs. Newspapers. Courtship. Friendship. New York City. Arnold Rothstein.*

Note: The story is based on the life of Arnold Rothstein.

D. W. GRIFFITH'S "THAT ROYLE GIRL" *see* **"THAT ROYLE GIRL"**

DADDIES **F2.1130**

Warner Brothers Pictures. 9 Feb **1924** [c6 Feb 1924; LP19900]. Si; b&w. 35mm. 7 reels, 6,500-6,800 ft.

Dir William A. Seiter. *Scen* Julien Josephson. *Photog* John Stumar.

Cast: Mae Marsh *(Ruth Atkins)*, Harry Myers *(Robert Audrey)*, Claude Gillingwater *(James Crockett)*, Crauford Kent *(William Rivers)*, Claire Adams *(Bobette Audrey)*, Willard Louis *(Henry Allen)*, Boyce Combe *(Nicholson Walters)*, Georgia Woodthorpe *(Mrs. Audrey)*, Otto Hoffman *(Parker)*, Priscilla Moran *(Alice)*, De Briac Twins, King Evers *(The Triplets)*, Milla Davenport *(Katie)*, Muriel Frances Dana *(Lorrie)*, Monte Blue *(see note)*.

Comedy. Source: John L. Hobble, *Daddies, a Comedy in Four Acts* (New York, c1929). Five confirmed bachelors, comprising a club of woman-haters, adopt war orphans. Bob Audrey's orphan turns out to be 18-year-old Ruth Atkins. They fall in love and marry. The other bachelors also obtain wives to be mothers to their children. *Bachelors. Orphans. Misogynists. Adoption. Marriage. Fatherhood.*

Note: According to a dialog cutting continuity, Monte Blue was to play Robert Audrey; Harry Myers to play Henry Allen; Boyce Combe, Billy Rivers; and Willard Louis, Nicholson Walters.

DADDY **F2.1131**

Jackie Coogan Productions. *Dist* Associated First National Pictures. 26 Mar **1923** [c6 Mar 1923; LP18750]. Si; b&w. 35mm. 6 reels, 5,738 ft.

Pres by Sol Lesser. *Prod* Sol Lesser. *Pers Supv* Jack Coogan, Sr. *Dir* E. Mason Hopper. *Story* Mr. and Mrs. Jack Coogan. *Photog* Frank B. Good, Robert Martin. *Film Ed* Irene Morra. *Lighting Eff* James Buchanan.

Cast: Jackie Coogan *(Jackie Savelli/Jackie Holden)*, Arthur Carewe *(Paul Savelli)*, Josie Sedgwick *(Helene Savelli)*, Cesare Gravina *(Cesare Gallo)*, Bert Woodruff *(Eben Holden)*, Anna Townsend *(Mrs. Holden)*, Willard Louis *(impresario)*, George Kuwa *(valet)*, Mildred *(herself)*.

Melodrama. Believing her husband to be unfaithful, Helene Savelli takes her son, Jackie, to the Holdens' farm and dies shortly afterward. The Holdens keep Jackie, but he eventually goes to the city when the elderly couple lose their farm and retire to the poorhouse. Jackie next is befriended by Cesare Gallo, a sidewalk musician who was also the teacher of Paul Savelli—now a famous violinist. A chance meeting with Savelli by Jackie reunites him with Gallo just before the old man dies. Savelli takes Jackie home with him, happily discovers the boy to be his son, and restores the farm to the Holdens. *Musicians. Orphans. Violinists. Farmers. Parentage.*

DADDY'S GONE A-HUNTING **F2.1132**

Metro-Goldwyn Pictures. 8 Mar **1925** [c9 Mar 1925; LP21218]. Si; b&w. 35mm. 6 reels, 5,851 ft.

Pres by Louis B. Mayer. *Dir* Frank Borzage. *Adapt* Kenneth B. Clarke. *Photog* Chester Lyons. *Sets* Cedric Gibbons. *Film Ed* Frank Sullivan. *Asst*

Dir Bunny Dull.

Cast: Alice Joyce *(Edith)*, Percy Marmont *(Julian)*, Virginia Marshall *(Janet)*, Helena D'Algy *(Olga)*, Ford Sterling *(Oscar)*, Holmes Herbert *(Greenough)*, Edythe Chapman *(Mrs. Greenough)*.

Drama. Source: Zoë Akins, *Daddy's Gone a-Hunting* (New York, 1923). After several years of marriage, Julian's life with Edith has dulled his artistic inspiration, and he persuades her to take a menial position in order to finance his art studies abroad. Julian spends a year in Paris and returns home with bohemian attitudes and desires. He and Edith move into an artists' colony, and she soon realizes that his affection for her has waned. Edith's only consolations are her small daughter and her friendship with Greenough, who offers to marry her. Julian stands aside gladly, but he later recognizes his loss and paints a picture entitled "Realization," which wins him international acclaim. An accident to his daughter, Janet, brings Julian to her bedside in time to watch her die, after which he and Edith decide to start their life together anew. *Artists. Parenthood. Bohemianism. Divorce. Manslaughter. Paris.*

DADDY'S LOVE **F2.1133**

Dist R. H. Klumb. Jun **1922.** Si; b&w. 35mm. [Feature length assumed.]

Melodrama(?). No information about the nature of this film has been found.

DAMAGED HEARTS **F2.1134**

Pilgrim Pictures. *Dist* Film Booking Offices of America. ca21 Feb **1924** [New York showing; released 3 Mar; c17 Feb 1924; LP19921]. Si; b&w. 35mm. 6-7 reels, 6,154 ft.

Prod-Dir T. Hayes Hunter. *Adapt* Barbara Kent. *Story* Basil King. *Photog* Abe Scholtz.

Cast: Mary Carr *(The Mother)*, Jerry Devine *(David [The Boy])*, Helen Rowland *(The Girl)*, [Frederick] Tyrone Power *(Sandy)*, Jean Armour *(Celia Stevens)*, Thomas Gillen *(Hugh Winfield)*, Edmund Breese *(The Innkeeper)*, Effie Shannon *(his wife)*, Rolinda Bainbridge *(The Florida "Cracker")*, Eugene Strong *(David [The Man])*, Florence Billings *(Mrs. Langham)*, Sara Mullon *(Edwina Winfield)*, Charles Deforrest *(The Cripple)*, Brian Donlevy *(Jim Porter, Mrs. Langham's brother)*.

Melodrama. Two orphans, brother and sister, are sent to different foster homes, and both are abused. When David's sister dies from neglect, he vows vengeance on the adopting family. He grows up to become an outlaw, and when the opportunity arises, he captures the wife of Hugh Winfield, who, as a boy, was partially responsible for the children's suffering. David intends to kill her but falls in love with and marries her when Winfield dies from a stab wound inflicted by a hunchback during an underwater fight. *Orphans. Brother-sister relationship. Hunchbacks. Adoption. Revenge.*

DAMAGED LOVE **F2.1135**

Superior Talking Pictures. *Dist* Sono Art–World Wide Pictures. 15 Dec **1930** [c9 Mar 1931; LP2027]. Sd (Phonofilm); b&w. 35mm. 6,333 ft.

Pres by Louis Weiss. *Dir* Irvin Willat. *Dial* Thomas William Broadhurst. *Adapt* Frederic Hatton, Fanny Hatton. *Song: "In Each Other's Arms"* Milton H. Pascal, M. Homer Pearson.

Cast: June Collyer *(Nita Meredith)*, Charles R. Starrett *(Jim Powell)*, Eloise Taylor *(Rose Powell)*, Betty Garde *(Madge Sloan)*, Charles Trowbridge *(Ned Endicott)*.

Romantic drama. Source: Thomas William Broadhurst, *Our Pleasant Sins* (New York opening: 21 Apr 1919). The newlywed bliss of Jim and Rose Powell begins to disintegrate with the arrival of their daughter, Ruth, and Rose's increasing concentration on motherhood leaves Jim susceptible to the charms of lovely Nita Meredith. Their chance meeting develops into a love affair, and Rose is unable to reach Jim on the night that Ruth falls ill and dies. Following the advice of Jim's sister, Madge, who has confronted them with their responsibilities, Nita accepts the inevitable, and Jim asks Rose's forgiveness. *Marriage. Motherhood. Parenthood. Brother-sister relationship. Infidelity.*

DAME CHANCE **F2.1136**

David Hartford Productions. *Dist* American Cinema Association. 23 Sep **1926** [c2 Dec 1926; LP23390]. Si; b&w. 35mm. 7 reels, 6,769 ft.

Supv David Hartford. *Dir* Bertram Bracken. *Story-Adapt* Frances Nordstrom. *Photog* Walter Griffin.

Cast: Julanne Johnston *(Gail Vernon)*, Gertrude Astor *(Nina Carrington)*, Robert Frazer *(Lloyd Mason)*, David Hartford *(Craig Stafford)*, Lincoln Stedman *(Bunny Dean)*, Mary Carr *(Mrs. Vernon)*, John T. Prince *(Sims)*.

Romantic drama. Actress Gail Vernon receives an enticing proposal from businessman Craig Stafford, who offers to support her until she attains success in her profession, but she declines. After 6 years of struggle and hardship, Gail accepts his offer to provide her mother with a crucial operation. Though her mother dies, she fulfills her obligation and then is introduced to Lloyd Mason, a prominent playwright who becomes increasingly fond of her. Craig desists in view of Lloyd's love for the girl, but Lloyd decides not to marry her, realizing that she loves Craig. Gail learns from a servant that Craig has been disillusioned by his wife's infidelity and that subsequently she died in an asylum fire. Gail and Craig are at last happily united. *Actors. Businessmen. Playwrights. Filial relations.*

DAMES AHOY! **F2.1137**

Universal Pictures. 9 Feb **1930** [c28 Jan 1930; LP1035]. Sd (Movietone); b&w. 35mm. 6 reels, 5,773 ft. [Also si; 5,271 ft.]

Pres by Carl Laemmle. *Dir* William James Craft. *Scen* Matt Taylor. *Dial-Titl* Albert De Mond, Matt Taylor. *Story* Sherman Lowe. *Photog* C. Allen Jones. *Film Ed* Harry Lieb. *Rec Engr* C. Roy Hunter.

Cast: Glenn Tryon *(Jimmy Chase)*, Helen Wright *(Mabel McGuire)*, Otis Harlan *(Bill Jones)*, Eddie Gribbon *(MacDougal)*, Gertrude Astor *(The Blonde)*.

Comedy. Three sailors—Jimmy, Bill, and Mac—on shore leave set out to find the blonde who tricked Bill into drawing half his pay from the Navy, claiming to be his wife. After several adventures in which they look for an identifying strawberry birthmark on the legs of many girls, Bill remembers that he met her a dancehall. There, Jimmy and his partner, Mabel, win first prize and, provided that they marry, a furnished bungalow; Jimmy decides to marry her and buy off Bill's wife, and Mabel agrees in order to get the bungalow. Afterwards, the young couple find themselves in love, and Jimmy, to the disgust of his friends, resolves not to reenlist; but Mabel succeeds in dominating the whole group. *Sailors. Dancehalls. Marriage. Birthmarks.*

DANCE HALL **F2.1138**

RKO Productions. 14 Dec **1929** [New York premiere; released 27 Dec; c14 Dec 1929; LP935]. Sd (Photophone); b&w. 35mm. 7 reels, 5,700 ft. [Also si.]

Prod Henry Hobart. *Dir* Melville Brown. *Scen-Dial* Jane Murfin, J. Walter Ruben. *Photog* Jack MacKenzie. *Art Dir* Max Ree. *Film Ed* Ann McKnight.

Cast: Olive Borden *(Gracie Nolan)*, Arthur Lake *(Tommy Flynn)*, Margaret Seddon *(Mrs. Flynn)*, Ralph Emerson *(Ted Smith)*, Joseph Cawthorn *(Bremmer)*, Helen Kaiser *(Bee)*, Lee Moran *(Ernie)*, Tom O'Brien *(truckdriver)*.

Melodrama. Source: Viña Delmar, "Dance Hall," in *Liberty Magazine* (6:7, 16 Mar 1929). Tommy Flynn loves Gracie Nolan, a blonde hostess at the Paradise Dance Hall. One evening she is annoyed by a drunken truckdriver, and Ted Smith, a handsome young aviator, intervenes. Tommy, grateful for Ted's help, allows him to dance the prize contest with Gracie. Gracie falls madly in love with the glamorous aviator, to Tommy's despair. When Ted's plane crashes on a coast-to-coast flight, Gracie goes into a state of shock, then calls for Ted. Tommy learns that Ted is not seriously interested in Gracie and that actually he refuses to see her; Tommy then is badly beaten in a fight. Gracie realizes the extent of Tommy's sacrifice, and after their reunion they are married. *Dancehall hostesses. Aviators. Truckdrivers. Dancehalls.*

DANCE MADNESS **F2.1139**

Metro-Goldwyn-Mayer Pictures. 4 Jan **1926** [c29 Jan 1926; LP22352]. Si; b&w. 35mm. 7 reels, 6,393 ft.

Dir Robert Z. Leonard. *Scen* Frederica Sagor. *Story* S. Jay Kaufman. *Photog* John Arnold, William Daniels. *Sets* Cedric Gibbons, James Basevi. *Film Ed* William Le Vanway. *Wardrobe* Kathleen Kay, Maude Marsh, André-ani.

Cast: Conrad Nagel *(Roger Halladay)*, Claire Windsor *(May Anderson)*, Douglas Gilmore *(Bud)*, Hedda Hopper *(Valentina)*, Mario Carillo *(Strokoff)*.

Farce. Roger Halladay has a weakness for drink and dancers. He falls madly in love with May Anderson, a classical dancer, after a brief and inebriated encounter; he finally wins her; and they go to live in Paris. After a year his love wanes, and he becomes infatuated with a masked Russian dancer, Valentina. May, sensing the involvement, visits Valentina to appeal to her sense of honor and finds that Valentina's husband, Strokoff, is her old dance instructor. The three decide to have fun at Roger's expense and perhaps cure him of his infatuation. May masquerades successfully as Valentina for several days, then is found out when her mask slips off. Roger, however, tries to convince her he knew it was she all along. *Dancers. Russians. Dance teachers. Marriage. Impersonation. Alcoholism. Paris.*

DANCE MAGIC **F2.1140**

Robert Kane Productions. *Dist* First National Pictures. 12 Jun **1927** [c11 Jun 1927; LP24068]. Si; b&w. 35mm. 7 reels, 6,588 ft.

Pres by Robert Kane. *Dir* Victor Halperin. *Scen* Adelaide Heilbron, Earle Roebuck. *Photog* Ernest Haller. *Prod Mgr* Leland Hayward.

Cast: Pauline Starke *(Jahala Chandler)*, Ben Lyon *(Leach Norcutt)*, Louis John Bartels *(Jed Brophy)*, Isabel Elson *(Selma Bundy)*, Harlan Knight *(Jahala's father)*, Judith Vosselli *(her mother)*.

Society melodrama. Source: Clarence Budington Kelland, *Dance Magic* (New York, 1927). Jahala Chandler, who lives in a religious community in New England, is forbidden to dance by her stern and bigoted father. Unable to brook her father's narrow views, she runs away to the city for a career on the Broadway stage. There, she meets theatrical producer Jed Brophy and Leach Norcutt, a theater angel. Leach falls in love with her, but Jed, promising her stardom, casts off his former sweetheart, Selma, and hopes to win her submission. When Jahala finds Jed murdered in his apartment, she suspects Leach; thinking she has committed the crime, Leach makes a confession to the police, which is, however, repudiated by Selma, who surrenders. Jahala returns to her rural home, broken by the events. Leach, who realizes his love for her, comes to claim her. *Dancers. Theatrical producers. Theatrical backers. Filial relations. Rural life. Bigotry. Theater. New York City—Broadway. New England.*

THE DANCE OF LIFE **F2.1141**

Paramount Famous Lasky Corp. 16 Aug **1929** [New York premiere; released 7 Sep; c7 Sep 1929; LP672]. Sd (Movietone); col sequences (Technicolor). 35mm. 13 reels, 10,619 ft. [Also si; 7,488 ft.]

Assoc Prod David Selznick. *Dir* John Cromwell, Edward Sutherland. *Screenplay* Benjamin Glazer. *Dial* George Manker Watters. *Titl* Julian Johnson. *Photog* J. Roy Hunt. *Film Ed* George Nichols, Jr. *Songs: "True Blue Lou," "King of Jazzmania," "Cuddlesome Baby," "Flippity Flop," "Ladies of the Dance," "The Mightiest Matador" "Sweet Rosie O'Grady," "In the Gloaming," "Sam, the Accordian Man"* Richard Whiting, Leo Robin, Sam Coslow. *Choreog* Earl Lindsay. *Rec Engr* Harry D. Mills. *Lighting* Earl Miller.

Cast: Hal Skelly *(Ralph "Skid" Johnson)*, Nancy Carroll *(Bonny Lee King)*, Dorothy Revier *(Sylvia Marco)*, Ralph Theodore *(Harvey Howell)*, Charles D. Brown *(Lefty)*, Al St. John *(Bozo)*, May Boley *(Gussie)*, Oscar Levant *(Jerry)*, Gladys Du Bois *(Miss Sherman)*, James Quinn *(Jimmy)*, James Farley *(Champ Melvin)*, George Irving *(minister)*, Gordona Bennet, Miss La Reno, Cora Beach Shumway, Charlotte Ogden, Kay Deslys, Madga Blom *(Amazon chorus girls)*, Thelma McNeal *(gilded girl, "Lady of India")*, John Cromwell *(doorkeeper)*, Edward Sutherland *(theater attendant)*.

Musical comedy-melodrama. Source: George Manker Watters and Arthur Hopkins, *Burlesque* (London opening: 3 Dec 1928). Skid, a burlesque entertainer, and Bonny, a specialty dancer, meet, fall in love, and marry. As a comedy-dance team they play the circuit until Skid gets an offer from a Broadway talent scout. Bonny remains "on the road" while Skid, a sensation in New York, resumes an affair with Sylvia Marco, an old flame in the same show. Aware that Skid is unfaithful, Bonny decides to divorce him and marry wealthy rancher Harvey Howell. Unable to go on without Bonny, Skid begins to drink heavily, and he loses his job. Bonny returns and helps Skid walk through the first performance of his new job. *Actors. Dancers. Flirts. Talent scouts. Ranchers. Burlesque. Infidelity. Divorce. Alcoholism. New York City—Broadway.*

THE DANCER OF PARIS **F2.1142**

First National Pictures. 28 Feb **1926** [c2 Mar 1926; LP22431]. Si; b&w. 35mm. 7 reels, 6,220 ft.

Pres by Robert Kane. *Dir* Alfred Santell. *Photog* Ernest Haller. *Art Dir* Robert M. Haas. *Prod Mgr* Joseph C. Boyle.

Cast: Conway Tearle *(Noel Anson)*, Dorothy Mackaill *(Consuelo Cox)*, Robert Cain *(Sir Roy Martel)*, Henry Vibart *(Doctor Frank)*, Paul Ellis *(Cortez)*, Frances Miller Grant *(Mammy)*.

Drama. Source: Michael Arlen, "The Dancer of Paris," in *World's Best Short Stories of 1925* (New York, 1926). In Florida, Consuelo Cox falls in love with Sir Roy Martel, a wealthy Englishman, and accepts his proposal of marriage. Quickly discovering that Roy's love is of the basest kind, however, Consuelo breaks off the engagement and goes to Paris, where she becomes a dancer and falls in love with Noel Anson. Sir Roy, also in Paris, becomes jealous and blackmails Consuelo's dancing partner into injuring her during one of their dance routines. As if this were not enough, Sir Roy then dupes Consuelo into visiting the apartment of a notorious roué, arranging for Noel to be there as well. Noel believes in Consuelo's innocence, however, and takes her away from the wild party. Sir Roy goes mad, and Consuelo comforts him in his dying hours, herself finding sustenance in Noel's love. *Aristocrats. Dancers. Rakes. Blackmail. Jealousy. Reputation. Paris. Florida.*

THE DANCER OF THE NILE **F2.1143**

William P. S. Earle Productions. *Dist* Film Booking Offices of America. 28 Oct **1923** [c18 Oct 1923; LP19515]. Si; b&w. 35mm. 6 reels, 5,787 ft.

Dir-Adapt William P. S. Earle. *Story* Blanche Taylor Earle. *Photog* Jules Cronjager.

Cast: Carmel Myers *(Arvia)*, Malcolm McGregor *(Karmet)*, Sam De Grasse *(Pasheri)*, Bertram Grassby *(Prince Tut)*, June Eldridge *(The Princess)*, Iris Ashton *(Mimitta)*.

Melodrama. An Egyptian princess falls in love with Karmet, prince of a neighboring kingdom, who loves Arvia, a dancing girl. The princess orders Arvia killed, but Arvia's father, a high priest, saves her for Karmet. The princess finds another prince and marries him. *Royalty. Dancers. Egypt.*

THE DANCERS **F2.1144**

Fox Film Corp. 4 Jan **1925** [c11 Jan 1925; LP21098]. Si; b&w. 35mm. 7 reels, 6,583 ft.

Pres by William Fox. *Dir* Emmett J. Flynn. *Scen* Edmund Goulding. *Photog* Ernest G. Palmer, Paul Ivano.

Cast: George O'Brien *(Tony)*, Alma Rubens *(Maxine)*, Madge Bellamy *(Una)*, Templar Saxe *(Fothering)*, Joan Standing *(Pringle)*, Alice Hollister *(Mrs. Mayne)*, Freeman Wood *(Evan Caruthers)*, Walter McGrail *(The Argentine)*, Noble Johnson *(Ponfilo)*, Tippy Grey *(Captain Bassil)*.

Melodrama. Source: Hubert Parsons, *The Dancers* (New York, 1923). Unable to make a living in crowded London, Tony goes to South America. There he becomes owner of a saloon and dancehall. One of the dancers, Maxine, falls in love with him, but he remains true to the memory of Una, his childhood sweetheart. Una lives a life of mad parties and champagne, forgets Tony, and finally yields to the embraces of an admirer. Tony unexpectedly becomes heir to a title and a fortune and returns to London, becoming immediately engaged to Una. She keeps her indiscretion secret until the night before the wedding, when she tells Tony of her slip from virtue. Tony forgives her, but she has taken poison and dies. Tony returns to South America and finds solace in a marriage with Maxine. *Fidelity. Saloons. Dancehalls. Suicide. London. South America.*

THE DANCERS **F2.1145**

Fox Film Corp. 9 Nov **1930** [c14 Oct 1930; LP1694]. Sd (Movietone); b&w. 35mm. 9 reels, 7,500 ft.

Dir Chandler Sprague. *Adapt* Edwin Burke. *Ch Camera* Arthur Todd. *Art Dir* David Hall. *Film Ed* Alexander Troffey. *Song: "Love Has Passed Me By"* Jimmy Monaco, Cliff Friend. *Rec Engr* Alfred Bruzlin. *Asst Dir* Horace Hough. *Cost* Sophie Wachner.

Cast: Lois Moran *(Diana)*, Phillips Holmes *(Tony)*, Walter Byron *(Berwin)*, Mae Clarke *(Maxine)*, Tyrrell Davis *(Archie)*, Mrs. Patrick Campbell *(Aunt Emily)*.

Society melodrama. Source: Gerald Du Maurier and Viola Tree, *The Dancers* (New York, 1923). A remake of the silent 1925 version, with the change of locations from South America to Canada. *Socialites. Dancehall girls. Courtship. Wealth. Marriage. Lumber camps. Canada. London.*

THE DANCING CHEAT **F2.1146**

Universal Pictures. 7 Apr **1924** [c14 Mar 1924; LP19996]. Si; b&w. 35mm. 5 reels, 4,727 ft.

Dir Irving Cummings. *Adapt* Raymond L. Schrock. *Photog* William Thornley.

Cast: Herbert Rawlinson *(Brownlow Clay)*, Alice Lake *("Poppy" Marie Andrews)*, Robert Walker *(Bobby Norton)*, Jim Blackwell *(Mose)*, Edwin J. Brady *("Denker" Eddie Kane)*, Harmon MacGregor *("Moron Mike" Downs)*.

Melodrama. Source: Calvin Johnston, "Clay of Ca'lina," in *Saturday Evening Post* (195:16–18, 113, 117–118, 120, 124, 7 Apr 1923). Gambler Eddie Kane induces his estranged wife, "Poppy" Marie Andrews, to help him blackmail Brownlow Clay, owner of a Mexican gambling hall, when Clay refuses entrance to Kane. According to the plan, Kane finds Poppy in Clay's apartment and demands hush money. Poppy, ashamed of her part in the scheme and genuinely in love with Clay, doublecrosses her husband and later marries Clay. *Gambling. Blackmail. Mexico.*

DANCING DAYS **F2.1147**

Preferred Pictures. 1 Sep **1926** [c10 Sep 1926; LP23090]. Si; b&w. 35mm. 6 reels, 5,900 ft.

Pres by J. G. Bachmann. *Dir* Albert Kelley. *Adapt* Dorothy Cairns. *Photog* H. Lyman Broening.

Cast: Helene Chadwick *(Alice Hedman)*, Forrest Stanley *(Ralph Hedman)*, Gloria Gordon *(a maid)*, Lillian Rich *(Lillian Loring)*, Robert Agnew *(Gerald Hedman)*, Thomas Ricketts *(Stubbins)*, Sylvia Ashton *(Katinka)*.

Domestic drama. Source: John Joy Bell, "Dancing Days" (publication undetermined). After 10 years of marriage, Ralph Hedman takes his wife, Alice, and his comfortable home for granted; and when Gerald, his brother, introduces him to Lillian Loring, Ralph accepts an invitation to attend a party at her apartment, though Alice is unable to attend. Alice's suspicions are aroused when she later finds him lunching with Lillian; consequently, she rearranges their bedroom; but refusing to divorce him, she gives him a year to make up his mind. Caught up in the constant whirl of Lillian's social set, Ralph becomes ill, and when the crisis passes, Alice invites Lillian to stay with them until his recovery is complete. Lillian introduces a jazz treatment of the patient (dancing the Charleston and playing the saxophone), and at last Alice is compelled to admit defeat. Ralph then leaves home in disgust, but when their cars accidentally collide, Alice and Ralph are brought to a mutual reconciliation. *Marriage. Infidelity. Jazz life. Charleston (dance).*

DANCING MOTHERS **F2.1148**

Famous Players–Lasky. *Dist* Paramount Pictures. 1 Mar **1926** [c3 Mar 1926; LP22441]. Si; b&w. 35mm. 8 reels, 7,169 ft.

Pres by Adolph Zukor, Jesse L. Lasky. *Dir* Herbert Brenon. *Scen* Forrest Halsey. *Photog* J. Roy Hunt. *Art Dir* Julian Boone Fleming.

Cast: Alice Joyce *(Ethel Westcourt)*, Conway Tearle *(Jerry Naughton)*, Clara Bow *(Kittens Westcourt)*, Donald Keith *(Kenneth Cobb)*, Dorothy Cumming *(Mrs. Massarene)*, Elsie Lawson *(Irma)*, Norman Trevor *(Hugh Westcourt)*.

Society drama. Source: Edgar Selwyn and Edmund Goulding, *Dancing Mothers* (New York opening: 11 Aug 1924). Ethel Westcourt discovers that her husband is having an affair with another woman and that her daughter, Kittens, is seeing too much of Jerry Naughton. In an effort to break up the relationship between Naughton and Kittens, Ethel goes to see Naughton at his apartment and falls in love with him. Her husband discovers Ethel's new love and begs her to return to him. Ethel refuses and takes a boat to Paris, intending to start a new life there. *Motherhood. Marriage. Infidelity. Paris.*

DANCING SWEETIES **F2.1149**

Warner Brothers Pictures. 19 Jul **1930** [c1 Jul 1930; LP1390]. Sd (Vitaphone); b&w. 35mm. 7 reels, 5,656 ft.

Dir Ray Enright. *Adapt-Dial* Gordon Rigby, Joseph Jackson. *Photog* Robert Kurrle. *Song: "Wishing and Waiting for Love"* Grant Clarke, Harry Akst. *Song: "Hullabaloo"* Bobby Dolan, Walter O'Keefe. *Song: "I Love You I Hate You"* Al Bryan, Joseph Meyer. *Song: "The Kiss Waltz"* Al Dubin, Joe Burke. *Rec Engr* David Forrest.

Cast: Grant Withers *(Bill Cleaver)*, Sue Carol *(Molly O'Neill)*, Eddie Phillips *(Needles Thompson)*, Edna Murphy *(Jazzbo Gans)*, Sid Silvers *(Jerry Browne)*, Tully Marshall *(Pa Cleaver)*, Margaret Seddon *(Mrs. Cleaver)*, Kate Price *(Mrs. O'Neill)*, Vincent Barnett *(Ted Hoffman)*, Dora Dean *(Nellie O'Neill)*, Ada Mae Vaughn *(Emma O'Neill)*, Eddie Clayton *(Onions)*, Joe Young *(Pat)*, Billy Bletcher *(Bud)*, Barnett and Clark *(dancers)*.

Romantic comedy-drama. Source: Harry Fried, "Three Flights Up" (publication undetermined). An evening at Hoffman's Parisian Dance Palace offers a dance contest with the added attraction of a free public wedding and a furnished home for a bridal couple. Tall and handsome Bill Cleaver and gum-chewing, wise-cracking Jazzbo Gans, usual dance partners, are amused to hear "Needles" Thompson, an overly dressed sheik, declare he will win the cup. But when Bill sees Molly, Thompson's partner, he schemes to meet her; after some effort he manages to win her attention; and in a secluded booth they discuss their mutual problems, leaving Needles and Jazzbo to their devices. Later they are induced to substitute for the bridal couple, asserting their independence. Mrs. O'Neill is shocked to learn that Bill is only a soda jerk, but Mrs. Cleaver is sympathetic. Their happiness is threatened when Jazzbo lures Bill to another dance contest; but they are reconciled after Needles wins a cup with Jazzbo. *Soda clerks. Dandies. Courtship. Dancehalls. Dance contests. Weddings.*

DANGER **F2.1150**

Clifford S. Elfelt Productions. ca7 Jul **1923** [New York showing]. Si; b&w. 35mm. 6 reels. [Later cut to 5 reels.]

Dir Clifford S. Elfelt. *Story* Frank Howard Clark. *Photog* Joseph Walker.

Cast: J. B. Warner *(Dave Collins)*, Lillian Hackett *(Nan Higgins)*, June La Vere *(Dolores)*, Edith Sterling *(Judy)*, Mary Wynn *(Phyllis Baxter)*, William Merrill McCormick *(Jose)*, Charles Newton *(Dry Walsh Jake)*, Bert Apling *(Norton)*, B. F. Blinn *(Mark Baxter)*, Billie Ralt *(Mrs. Meehan)*, A. Knott *(Blance)*, B. Brady *(Tom Blake)*.

Melodrama. "David Collins, a westerner, in search of a 'silhouette girl' with whom he has fallen in love under mysterious circumstances, is appointed guardian to Nan Higgins, an orphan. He entrusts her to a neighbor, who maltreats her. In his business ventures Dave has run across a gang of crooks who swear to get him and come within an ace of doing so, but for the timely interference of Nan, ... the conqueror of his heart." (*Moving Picture World,* 7 Jul 1923, p63.) *Orphans. Guardians.*

DANGER AHEAD **F2.1151**

Universal Film Manufacturing Co. 8 Aug **1921** [c21 Jul 1921; LP16779]. Si; b&w. 35mm. 5 reels, 4,353 ft.

Pres by Carl Laemmle. *Dir* Rollin Sturgeon. *Scen* A. P. Younger.

Cast: Mary Philbin *(Tressie Harlow)*, James Morrison *(Norman Minot)*, Jack Mower *(Robert Kitteridge)*, Minna Redman *(Deborah Harlow)*, George Bunny *(Nate Harlow)*, George B. Williams *(Mr. Minot)*, Jane Starr *(Dolly Demere)*, Emily Rait *(Mrs. Della Mayhew)*, Helene Caverly *(Dora Mayhew)*.

Melodrama. Source: Sara Ware Bassett, *The Harbor Road* (Philadelphia, 1919). When the Harlow family is forced to take in summer boarders, young Tressie welcomes the change and promptly falls in love with Boston society youth Norman Minot, who returns her affection; but prospects are clouded by the arrival of a fortune-hunting mother and daughter. Kitteridge, an artist friend of Minot's, takes an interest in Tressie, and while they are sailing one evening their boat is rammed by a steamer. They are rescued and put ashore in Boston the next morning. In his studio, the artist tries to make love to Tressie, but Dolly, an athletic vaudeville actress, intervenes and thrashes him. Norman, warned of the disappearance, arrives to take Tressie home, and they announce their engagement. *Artists. Fortune hunters. Actors. Family life. Boardinghouses. Boston.*

DANGER AHEAD **F2.1152**

Phil Goldstone Productions. Sep **1923** [scheduled release]. Si; b&w. 35mm. 5 reels.

Dir William K. Howard. *Story* Keene Thompson. *Photog* Reginald Lyons.

Cast: Richard Talmadge *(Bruce Randall)*, Helen Rosson *(Mrs. Randall)*, J. P. Lockney *(Todd)*, David Kirby *(Mahoney)*, Fred Stanton *(Mortimer)*.

Crime melodrama. "Bruce Randall is injured after a fight with Mortimer, who has attempted to rob his home, and is reported dead by the police. They bury a man they believe to be Bruce, while Bruce wanders about, unable to recall his past. Two crook lawyers find him, hire him to impersonate Bruce so as to get some pearls in the Randall mansion, and Mrs. Randall believes he is really her husband. He regains his memory in time to defeat the crooks and save his wife's happiness." (*Moving Picture World,* 29 Dec 1923, p825.) *Mistaken identity. Robbery. Impersonation. Amnesia.*

THE DANGER GIRL **F2.1153**

Metropolitan Pictures. *Dist* Producers Distributing Corp. 31 Jan **1926** [c23 Jan 1926; LP22321]. Si; b&w. 35mm. 6 reels, 5,660 ft.

Pres by John C. Flinn. *Dir* Edward Dillon. *Adapt* Finis Fox. *Photog* Georges Benoit. *Prod Mgr* George Bertholon.

Cast: Priscilla Dean *(Marie Duquesne)*, John Bowers *(Wilson Travers)*, Gustav von Seyffertitz *(James, the butler)*, Cissy Fitzgerald *(Henrietta Travers)*, Arthur Hoyt *(Mortimer Travers)*, William Humphreys *(Pelham)*, Clarence Burton *(organ man)*, Erwin Connelly *(Henderson)*.

Melodrama. Source: George Middleton and Stuart Olivier, *The Bride*

(New York, 1926). Wilson Travers and his brother, Mortimer, live singular lives, interested only in their respective hobbies of collecting rare gems and even rarer tropical fish. The police learn that jewel thieves are planning to knock over the Wilson gem collection, and the brothers take precautions. One evening, Marie Duquesne, dressed as a bride, appeals to the brothers to help her avoid a distasteful marriage to an old man. The brothers let her stay the night; Mortimer resents her presence, but Wilson falls in love with her. The following morning, the butler tells Wilson that, suspicious of Marie's nocturnal prowling, he has called the police; and a policeman soon arrives and takes her into custody. That night the butler is prevented from looting the safe by Marie, who has returned to the house. Marie, who is a detective, sees to the arrest of the butler and then turns her attentions to Wilson. *Collectors. Detectives. Thieves. Butlers. Brides. Robbery. Disguise. Gems. Tropical fish.*

DANGER LIGHTS **F2.1154**

RKO Radio Pictures. 21 Aug **1930** [standard vers; 15 Nov, wide screen vers; c15 Dec 1930; LP1786]. Sd (Photophone); b&w. 35mm and 65mm (Spoor-Berggren Natural Vision Process). 8 reels, 6,550 ft.

Prod William Le Baron. *Assoc Prod* Myles Connolly. *Dir* George B. Seitz. *Dial Dir* Hugh Herbert. *Story-Adapt-Dial* James Ashmore Creelman. *Photog* Karl Struss, John Boyle. *Film Ed* Archie Marshek. *Sd Rec* Clem Portman.

Cast: Louis Wolheim *(Dan Thorn)*, Robert Armstrong *(Larry Doyle)*, Jean Arthur *(Mary Ryan)*, Frank Sheridan *(Ed Ryan)*, Robert Edeson *(engineer)*, Hugh Herbert *(professor)*, James Farley *(Joe Geraghty)*, Alan Roscoe *(general manager)*, William P. Burt *(chief dispatcher)*.

Melodrama. A landslide on the Chicago, Milwaukee, St. Paul & Pacific Railroad ties up traffic and throws employees into confusion until Dan Thorn, division superintendent, sets about clearing the debris. Enlisting a group of hoboes from a boxcar for the work, Dan spots Larry Doyle, previously an engineer but discharged for insubordination, and succeeds in putting him to work as a fireman. Larry meets Mary Ryan, engaged to Thorn, and they fall in love; he plans to marry her when he is given a vacation; but on the night he is to announce their plans, there is a washout on the line. Notified of the lovers' elopement, Dan saves Larry from an oncoming express when his foot is caught in an electric switch, but Dan suffers a brain injury. Larry drives a fast train to Chicago, where an operation saves Dan; and upon his recovery, he gives his blessing to Mary and Larry. *Railroad engineers. Tramps. Courtship. Railroad accidents. Landslides.*

THE DANGER LINE **F2.1155**

R-C Pictures. *Dist* Film Booking Offices of America. 26 May **1924** [c17 May 1924; LP20210]. Si; b&w. 35mm. 6 reels, 5,800 ft.

Dir E. E. Violet. *Scen* Margaret Turnbull. *Photog* Asselin, Dubais, Quintin.

Cast: Sessue Hayakawa *(Marquis Yorisaka)*, Tsuru Aoki *(Marquise Yorisaka)*, Gina Palerme *(Mrs. Hockey)*, Cady Winter *(Miss Vane, her secretary)*, Felix Ward *(Captain Fergan)*.

Melodrama. Source: Claude Farrère, *La Bataille* (Paris, 1908). While her husband is away on a secret mission, the Marquise Yorisaka is Americanized by Mrs. Hockey and becomes the object of Captain Fergan's affections. Warned of the captain's activities, the marquis obtains a post for him on his battleship and forces him to take command when he himself is wounded. The death of the captain brings about a reconciliation of the couple and resumption of a life in keeping with their tradition. *Nobility. Americanization. Japan. Japan—Navy.*

THE DANGER MAN **F2.1156**

Cosmos Pictures. 20 May **1930.** Mus score & sd eff; b&w. 35mm. 6 reels, 5,500 or 6,516 ft. [Also si.]

Dir-Scen-Titl Bud Pollard. *Story* Charles Hutchinson. *Photog* Charles Levine. *Film Ed* Bud Pollard. *Sd* D. Castagnaro.

Cast: Charles Hutchinson *(Tom Manning)*, Edith Thornton *(Betty Blair)*, Virginia Pearson *(Mrs. Blair)*, Sheldon Lewis, Eddie Phillips *(blackmailers)*, Violet Schram *(Renée)*, LeRoy Mason *(Harold Wright)*, William St. James.

Melodrama. "The plot revolves around the attempt of a secret service man to capture a group of blackmailers. Land, water and aircraft figure in the pursuit." (*Film Daily*, 27 Apr 1930, p13.) *Secret service. Blackmail. Stunts.*

Note: A feature version of the 1926 serial *Lightning Hutch*, which was produced by the Hurricane Film Corp. and directed by Charles Hutchinson from the scenario by John Francis Natteford. Cosmos may have added a prolog of its own making.

DANGER PATROL **F2.1157**

Duke Worne Productions. *Dist* Rayart Pictures. Apr **1928.** Si; b&w. 35mm. 6 reels, 6,076 ft.

Dir Duke Worne. *Scen* H. H. Van Loan, Arthur Hoerl. *Story* H. H. Van Loan. *Photog* Walter Griffen. *Film Ed* Malcolm Sweeney.

Cast: William Russell *(Sgt. John Daley)*, Virginia Browne Faire *(Céleste Gambier)*, Wheeler Oakman *(George Gambier)*, Rhea Mitchell *(Gladys Lawlor)*, Ethan Laidlaw *("Regina Jim" Lawlor)*, S. D. Wilcox *(André)*, Napoleon Bonaparte *(the dog)*.

Northwest melodrama. Forced into a marriage of convenience by her grasping mother, Céleste Gambier escapes to the frozen North to join her father. She finds him accused of murder and in the custody of a snowblinded Mountie, Sergeant Daley. The prisoner escapes, Céleste nurses Daley back to health, and the two fall in love. Three murders prove both the innocence of Céleste's father and the rascality of her husband. *Filial relations. Marriage of convenience. Murder. Snow blindness. Northwest Mounted Police. Dogs.*

THE DANGER POINT **F2.1158**

Halperin Productions. *Dist* American Releasing Corp. 24 Dec **1922** [c11 Nov 1922; LP18624]. Si; b&w. 35mm. 6 reels, 5,807 ft.

Dir Lloyd Ingraham. *Titl* Adelaide Heilbron. *Story* Victor Hugo Halperin. *Photog* Ross Fisher. *Tech Dir* Albert Rogell.

Cast: Carmel Myers *(Alice Torrance)*, William P. Carleton *(James Benton)*, Vernon Steel *(Duncan Phelps)*, Joseph J. Dowling *(Benjamin)*, Harry Todd *(Sam Biggs)*, Margaret Joslin *(Elvira Hubbard)*.

Rural comedy-drama. James Benton marries Alice Torrance, a much younger girl from the city, but she finds it difficult to adjust to the small town and Benton's preoccupation with his oil wells. She finally leaves Benton while he is away. Duncan Phelps, a longtime admirer, appears in her train compartment, and Alice repulses him just as there is a train wreck. Benton finds Alice's farewell note at the moment he hears of the wreck, but when Alice returns on the rescue train they have a reconciliation. *Marriage. Smalltown life. Oil wells. Train wrecks.*

Note: *Film Year Book* gives release date as 3 Nov 1922.

DANGER QUEST **F2.1159**

Harry J. Brown Productions. *Dist* Rayart Pictures. 9 Jan **1926** [New York State license]. Si; b&w. 35mm. 5 reels, 5,392 ft.

Dir Harry J. Brown. *Story-Scen* Henry Roberts Symonds.

Cast: Reed Howes *(Rob Rollins)*, Ethel Shannon *(Nan Colby)*, J. P. McGowan *(Colonel Spiffy)*, David Kirby *(Spatz Barrett)*, Billy Franey *(Roll Royce)*, Fred Kohler *(Otto Shugars)*, George Reed *(Umhatten)*, Rodney Keyes *(inspector)*.

Action melodrama. A handsome American adventurer goes into the interior of Africa on a quest for the great starfire diamond. After much action and adventure, he obtains the diamond and rescues the girl he loves from a band of hostile natives. *Adventurers. Diamonds. Africa.*

DANGER RIDER (Reissue) **F2.1160**

Dist Aywon Film Corp. 19 Feb **1925** [New York State license application]. Si; b&w. 35mm. 5 reels, 4,900 ft.

Note: This film is a reissue of an earlier Selig film with Tom Mix; original title and year of release have not been determined.

THE DANGER RIDER (Universal-Jewel) **F2.1161**

Universal Pictures. 18 Nov **1928** [c23 Oct 1928; LP25769]. Si; b&w. 35mm. 6 reels, 5,357 ft.

Dir Henry MacRae. *Adapt-Scen* Arthur Statter. *Titl* Harold Tarshis. *Story* Wynn James. *Photog* Harry Neumann. *Art Dir* David S. Garber. *Film Ed* Gilmore Walker.

Cast: Hoot Gibson *(Hal Doyle)*, Eugenia Gilbert *(Mollie Dare)*, Reeves Eason *(Tucson Joe)*, Monty Montague *(Scar Bailey)*, King Zany *(Blinky Ben)*, Frank Beal *(Warden Doyle)*, Milla Davenport *(housekeeper)*, Bud Osborne *(sheriff)*.

Western melodrama. Hal Doyle, the son of a prison warden, falls in love with Mollie Dare, who conducts a reformatory for ex-convicts, and to be near her impersonates Tucson Joe, a notorious outlaw. The real Tucson Joe soon arrives at the reformatory and, with Scar Bailey's assistance, plots to rob the safe. Hal prevents the robbery and hands Tucson Joe over to the authorities. Hal's true identity is revealed, and he and Mollie embrace. *Prison wardens. Sheriffs. Impersonation. Robbery. Reformatories.*

THE DANGER SIGNAL **F2.1162**

Columbia Pictures. 1 Jul **1925** [c7 Jul 1925; LP21636]. Si; b&w. 35mm. 6 reels, 5,502 ft.

Dir Erle C. Kenton. *Story* Douglas Z. Doty. *Photog* Dewey Wrigley.

Cast: Jane Novak *(Mary Browning)*, Dorothy Revier *(Laura Whitman)*, Robert Edeson *(Cyrus Browning)*, Gaston Glass *(Ralph Browning)*, Robert Gordon *(Robert Browning)*, Mayme Kelso *(Mrs. Whitman)*, Lee Shumway *(John Moran)*, Lincoln Stedman *(Pudgy)*.

Melodrama. Mary Browning, the widow of the disinherited son of wealthy Cyrus Browning, is the mother of twin boys. Browning, who believes that he has only one grandchild, offers to adopt him and give him the best that money can buy. Mary sadly gives up Ralph, keeping Robert, the other son. Ralph grows up a wastrel, while Robert turns out to be a sterling young fellow, who finds work with his grandfather's railroad. The boys fall in love with the same girl, Laura Whitman; and Ralph, thinking to belittle Robert in her eyes, has him fired. Robert saves the mails from robbery and later saves his grandfather's private car from being wrecked. Cyrus Browning finally meets Mary, whom he has not seen for many years, and she introduces him to his second grandson. The old man realizes the faultiness of his attitude and promises to make amends for the hardships of Mary's life. Robert wins Laura, and Mary's gentle influence makes a man of Ralph. *Widows. Twins. Brothers. Grandfathers. Wastrels. Motherhood. Disinheritance. Railroads. Train robberies. Postal service.*

DANGER STREET **F2.1163**

FBO Pictures. 26 Aug **1928** [c26 Aug 1928; LP25574]. Si; b&w. 35mm. 6 reels, 5,621 ft.

Dir Ralph Ince. *Screenplay-Titl* Enid Hibbard. *Photog* Robert Martin. *Film Ed* George M. Arthur. *Asst Dir* Thomas Atkins.

Cast: Warner Baxter *(Rolly Sigsby)*, Martha Sleeper *(Kitty)*, Duke Martin *(Dorgan)*, Frank Mills *(Bull)*, Harry Tenbrook *(Borg)*, Harry Allen Grant *(Bauer)*, Ole M. Ness *(Cloom)*, Spec O'Donnell *(Sammy)*.

Underworld melodrama. Source: Harold MacGrath, "The Beautiful Bullet," in *Red Book* (50:88–92, Nov 1927). Rolly Sigsby, a society clubman bitterly weary of life, wanders into the middle of a gunfight between the Dorgan and Borg gangs on the Lower East Side in the hope that he will be killed by a stray bullet. To his disappointment, he emerges unscathed and later goes into Bauer's chop house, the hangout of the neighborhood thugs, where he meets Kitty, the cashier, to whom he is attracted. Rolly sets out to antagonize both of the local gangs and, in the expectation of his quick demise, marries Kitty, leaving everything to her in his will. Dorgan takes a shot at Rolly, and Kitty steps in front of him, thereby herself getting shot. She recovers from this wound, and Rolly, realizing how much he has come to love her, regains his love of life. *Socialites. Cashiers. Gangsters. Suicide. Self-sacrifice. New York City—Lower East Side.*

THE DANGER TRAIL (Reissue) **F2.1164**

24 May **1927** [New York State license]. Si; b&w. 35mm.

Note: A Selig film originally released in 1917 with H. B. Warner.

DANGER TRAIL **F2.1165**

Dist General Pictures. **1928.** Si; b&w. 35mm. 6 reels, 5,200 ft.

Dir Noel Mason. *Photog* Harry Cooper.

Cast: Barbara Bedford, Stuart Holmes.

Western melodrama(?). No information about the nature of this film has been found.

DANGER VALLEY **F2.1166**

Pinnacle Productions. *Dist* Independent Film Assn. 3 Jun **1921** [trade review]. Si; b&w. 35mm. 5 reels.

Cast: Neal Hart *(Doug McBride)*.

Melodrama. Goulding, a wealthy man with a pretty daughter, Eileen, invests all his money in a mine, the map of which has been stolen. He sends for McBride, a mining engineer, to help him locate the mine. Van Zant, who wants to ruin Goulding so that his daughter will be forced to marry him, resents McBride's interference. McBride goes west, followed by Goulding and Eileen. After McBride saves an Indian's life in a saloon scuffle, the Indian guides him to the mine. At the same time, Van Zant and Goulding have become lost while searching for the mine. But McBride rides to the rescue, and after a long struggle all ends well for everyone—except Van Zant. *Engineers—Mining. Indians of North America. Mines.*

THE DANGER ZONE **F2.1167**

Bud Barsky Corp. 22 Dec **1925** [New York State license]. Si; b&w. 35mm. 5 reels, 4,900 ft.

Dir Robert N. Bradbury.

Cast: Kenneth McDonald *(Reggie Collins)*, Frances Dair *(Diana Horton)*, Hal Waters *(Jimmy Duff)*, Bruce Gordon *(Paul Taylor)*, Charles Gaskill *(Colonel Horton)*.

Melodrama. Reggie Collins wins a bet that he will capture a notorious crook and his gang. *Gangs. Wagers.*

A DANGEROUS ADVENTURE **F2.1168**

Warner Brothers Pictures. 1 or 15 Nov **1922.** Si; b&w. 35mm. 7 reels, 6,500 ft.

Dir Sam Warner, Jack Warner. *Photog* John W. Boyle, André Barlatier, Floyd Jackson, W. R. Griffin.

Cast: Philo McCullough *(MacDonald Hayden)*, Grace Darmond *(Marjorie Stanton)*, Derelys Perdue *(Edith Stanton)*, Robert Agnew *(Jimmy Morrison)*, Jack Richardson *(Herbert Brandon)*.

Adventure melodrama. Source: Frances Guihan, "A Dangerous Adventure" (publication undetermined). "Marjorie and Edith Stanton, accompanied by their uncle are in quest of a treasure chest left by their uncle hidden in a Central African town. The crafty uncle agrees to return Marjorie to the jungle chief in return for a caravan. MacDonald Hayden, in love with Marjorie, and a chum, decide to go to her rescue. In a terrific storm the natives flee the caravan and the uncle is killed. Several adventures precede the rescue of the girls by the American pair." (*Motion Picture News Booking Guide,* 4:41, Apr 1923.) *Sisters. Uncles. Jungles. Treasure. Africa.*

Note: Also issued as a 15-episode serial in 1922 under the same title.

THE DANGEROUS AGE **F2.1169**

Louis B. Mayer Productions. *Dist* Associated First National Pictures. ca26 Nov **1922** [Chicago premiere; released 20 Jan 1923; c6 Nov 1922; LP18374]. Si; b&w. 35mm. 7 reels, 7,145 ft.

Pres by Louis B. Mayer. *Dir* John M. Stahl. *Scen* J. G. Hawks, Bess Meredyth. *Story* Frances Irene Reels. *Photog* Jackson J. Rose, Al Siegler. *Asst Dir* Sidney Algier.

Cast: Lewis Stone *(John Emerson)*, Cleo Madison *(Mary Emerson)*, Edith Roberts *(Ruth Emerson)*, Ruth Clifford *(Gloria Sanderson)*, Myrtle Stedman *(Mrs. Sanderson)*, James Morrison *(Bob)*, Helen Lynch *(Bebe Nash)*, Lincoln Stedman *(Ted)*, Edward Burns *(Tom)*, Richard Tucker *(Robert Chanslor)*.

Domestic drama. Married 22 years, Mary Emerson treats her husband, John, more like a son than a husband. He is stung by her rebuffs and, therefore, succumbs to the youthful charms of Gloria Sanderson, whom he meets on a business trip. But just after he mails a letter to Mary telling her that he will not return, John finds Gloria in the arms of her fiancé. Realizing his foolishness, he races to the train in an effort to retrieve the letter. He fails, and Mary receives and reads the letter; but she too has seen her error, conceals her knowledge of the letter's contents, and accepts John's professions of love. *Marriage. Middle age. Documentation.*

THE DANGEROUS BLONDE **F2.1170**

Universal Pictures. 19 May **1924** [c22 Apr 1924; LP20107]. Si; b&w. 35mm. 5 reels, 4,919 ft.

Dir Robert F. Hill. *Scen* Hugh Hoffman. *Photog* Jackson Rose.

Cast: Laura La Plante *(Diana Faraday)*, Edward Hearn *(Royall Randall)*, Arthur Hoyt *(Mr. Faraday)*, Philo McCullough *(Gerald Skinner)*, Rolfe Sedan *(Henry)*, Eve Southern *(Yvette)*, Margaret Campbell *(Mrs. Faraday)*, Dick Sutherland *(The Cop)*, Frederick Cole *(Roger)*.

Romantic comedy. Source: Hulbert Footner, "A New Girl in Town," in *Argosy All-Story Magazine* (145:801–819, 23 Sep 1922; 146:43–60, 226–242, 432–450, 613–633, 778–791, 30 Sep–28 Oct 1922). Colonel Faraday asks his daughter, Diana, to recover some letters he wrote to Yvette, an adventuress, when she tries to blackmail him. Diana is vamping Gerald Skinner, Yvette's partner, so as to get the letters when a football hero in love with her, Royall Randall, piqued at being stood up, bursts into the cafe, starts a fight, and manages to recover the letters. *Students. Adventuresses. Vamps. Blackmail. Football. College life. Documentation.*

DANGEROUS BUSINESS *see* **PARTY GIRL**

THE DANGEROUS COWARD F2.1171

Monogram Pictures. *Dist* Film Booking Offices of America. 26 May **1924** [c17 May 1924; LP20211]. Si; b&w. 35mm. 5 reels, 4,830 ft.

Prod Harry J. Brown. *Dir* Albert Rogell. *Story* Marion Jackson. *Photog* Ross Fisher.

Cast: Fred Thomson *(Bob Trent, "The Lightning Kid")*, Hazel Keener *(Hazel McGuinn)*, Frank Hagney *(Wildcat Rea)*, Andrew Arbuckle *(David McGuinn)*, David Kirby *(Red O'Hara)*, Al Kaufman *(Battling Benson)*, Lillian Adrian *(Conchita)*, Jim Corey *("The Weazel")*, Silver King *(himself, a horse)*.

Western melodrama. Believing that he has crippled The Weazel, his opponent in a prizefight, The Lightning Kid goes west under the name of Bob Trent, vowing never again to fight. Discovering that The Weazel is only pretending, he enters the ring to defeat Battling Benson, recovers his bet on the fight, and wins the villain's girl. *Prizefighters. Horses.*

DANGEROUS CURVE AHEAD (Eminent Authors) F2.1172

Goldwyn Pictures. Oct **1921** [c27 Jul 1921; LP16785]. Si; b&w. 35mm. 6 reels, 5,503 ft.

Dir E. Mason Hopper. *Cont* Julian Josephson. *Story* Rupert Hughes. *Photog* John Mescall. *Asst Dir* William J. Reiter.

Cast: Helene Chadwick *(Phoebe Mabee)*, Richard Dix *(Harley Jones)*, Maurice B. Flynn *(Anson Newton)*, James Neill *(Mr. Mabee)*, Edythe Chapman *(Mrs. Mabee)*, Kate Lester *(Mrs. Noxon)*.

Domestic melodrama. Though engaged to Harley Jones, Phoebe Mabee flirts with Anson Newton. She and Harley, as a result, break their engagement, but within 6 months they are reconciled and married. Phoebe becomes a mother, and when Harley is sent abroad by his business firm she and her two children go to a summer resort where she renews her romance with Newton. Harley returns unexpectedly and finds Phoebe about to keep a dinner appointment with Mrs. Noxon, Newton's aunt, with Newton as her escort; and although Harley is indignant and one of their children is ill, she insists on attending. At dinner she is reminded of her sick child and hurries home in time to calm it; husband and wife are then happily reconciled. *Flirts. Marriage. Infidelity. Motherhood.*

Note: Working title: *Mr. and Miserable Jones.*

DANGEROUS CURVES F2.1173

Paramount Famous Lasky Corp. 13 Jul **1929** [c12 Jul 1929; LP528]. Sd (Movietone); b&w. 35mm. 9 reels, 7,287 ft. [Also si; 7,395 ft.]

Supv B. F. Zeidman. *Dir* Lothar Mendes. *Screenplay* Donald Davis, Florence Ryerson. *Dial* Viola Brothers Shore. *Titl* George Marion, Jr. *Story* Lester Cohen. *Photog* Harry Fischbeck. *Film Ed* Eda Warren.

Cast: Clara Bow *(Pat Delaney)*, Richard Arlen *(Larry Lee)*, Kay Francis *(Zara Flynn)*, David Newell *(Tony Barretti)*, Anders Randolf *(Col. P. P. Brock)*, May Boley *(Ma Spinelli)*, T. Roy Barnes *(Pa Spinelli)*, Joyce Compton *(Jennie Silver)*, Charles D. Brown *(Spider)*, Stuart Erwin *(first Rotarian)*, Jack Luden *(second Rotarian)*, Oscar Smith *(Negro porter)*.

Comedy-drama. Pat, a circus bareback rider, loves Larry, the star tightrope walker, who is infatuated with his partner, Zara Flynn, who in turn loves Tony Barretti of Larry's act. Pat tells Larry of Zara's duplicity, and as a result he sustains an injury in a fall from the wire. He takes to drinking heavily, but Pat persuades him to return to the circus; and in order to bolster his confidence, she works with him in a comic act. To Pat's dismay, however, he again falls under her spell. Meanwhile, Zara and Tony have been secretly married, but they fail to get bookings and Zara rejoins Larry in the tightrope act; to Pat's dismay he again falls under her spell. However, when Larry learns Zara is married, he again takes to the bottle, and Pat is forced into a scheme whereby she saves his reputation, though it costs her her own job. At last, realizing her sacrifice, Larry discovers that he loves Pat. *Roman riders. Tightrope walkers. Alcoholism. Reputation. Circus.*

THE DANGEROUS DUB F2.1174

Action Pictures. *Dist* Associated Exhibitors. 4 Jul **1926** [c6 Jul 1926; LU22873]. Si; b&w. 35mm. 5 reels, 4,472 ft.

Pres by Lester F. Scott, Jr. *Dir* Richard Thorpe. *Scen* Frank L. Inghram. *Story* James Madison.

Cast: Buddy Roosevelt *(Buddy Martin)*, Peggy Montgomery *(Rose Cooper)*, Joseph Girard *(W. J. Cooper)*, Fanny Midgley *(Mrs. Cooper)*, Al Taylor *("Scar-Face" Hanan)*, Curley Riviere *(The Law)*.

Western melodrama. Buddy Martin, a cowpuncher, falls in love with Rose Cooper, whom he meets in a Chinese restaurant in Omaha, and frustrates a plot between Bill Cooper, her stepfather, and Scar-Face Hanan, a notorious criminal. At Rose's insistence, Buddy is given a job on their ranch. Buddy overhears Cooper conspiring with Scar-Face to rustle his own (Cooper's) herd until he can persuade Rose's mother to sell the ranch; when Buddy discovers the rustlers at work, Cooper accuses him of being a rustler and sends him off the ranch, and disguised with a beard, he finds refuge in a camp maintained by Scar-Face. When the sale of the ranch is imminent, Buddy circumvents the bandits, takes the money from Cooper, and notifies the sheriff. In a series of chases on horseback and by train, Buddy overcomes Scar-Face and then marries Rose. *Ranchers. Rustlers. Cowboys. Omaha. Nebraska. Chases.*

THE DANGEROUS DUDE F2.1175

Harry J. Brown Productions. *Dist* Rayart Pictures. 25 Jun **1926** [New York State license]. Si; b&w. 35mm. 5 reels, 5,087 ft.

Dir Harry J. Brown. *Scen* Henry Roberts Symonds. *Photog* Ben White.

Cast: Reed Howes *(Bob Downs)*, Bruce Gordon *(Harold Simpson)*, Dorothy Dwan *(Janet Jordan)*, Billy Franey, Dave Kirby, Richard Travers.

Action melodrama. When a builder receives a contract for the construction of a large dam, his business rival sets out to blacken his good name by substituting inferior cement while the dam is being built. Bob Downes, a bright young man who hates his soft job, learns of the plot to ruin the dam and lends his considerable energy to defeating the conspirators, thereby saving the power project and winning the love of the builder's beautiful daughter. *Contractors. Reputation. Business competition. Dams. Construction materials.*

DANGEROUS FISTS F2.1176

Harry Webb Productions. *Dist* Rayart Pictures. 27 Nov **1925** [New York State license]. Si; b&w. 35mm. 5 reels, 4,800 ft.

Cast: Jack Perrin.

Western melodrama(?). No information about the nature of this film has been found.

THE DANGEROUS FLIRT F2.1177

Gothic Pictures. *Dist* Film Booking Offices of America. 19 Oct **1924** [c19 Oct 1924; LP20795]. Si; b&w. 35mm. 6 reels, 5,297 ft.

Dir Tod Browning. *Adapt* E. Richard Schayer. *Photog* Lucien Andriot, Maynard Rugg. *Asst Dir* Fred Tyler.

Cast: Evelyn Brent *(Sheila Fairfax)*, Edward Earle *(Dick Morris)*, Sheldon Lewis *(Don Alfonso)*, Clarissa Selwynne *(Aunt Prissy* [*Priscilla Fairfax*]*)*, Pierre Gendron *(Captain José Gonzales)*.

Romantic melodrama. Source: Julie Herne, "The Prude" (publication undetermined). Sheila Fairfax, brought up by a strict and puritanical spinster aunt, is the innocent victim of a scandal caused by an all-night escapade with José Gonzales. In spite of her undeserved reputation, Dick Morris, a mining engineer, marries her. On their wedding night, she is so filled with fear of Dick's embraces that she repulses him. Thinking that Sheila does not love him, Dick goes to South America in order to buy a mine from Don Alfonso. Sheila follows, hoping to win him back, realizing that the influence of her repressed aunt is responsible for the false modesty that has separated them. Dick and Sheila become the guests of Don Alfonso, uncle of José Gonzales. Don Alfonso and José vie for her regard, and Alfonso kills José in a fight. Dick faces a firing squad under Alfonso's orders, but Sheila saves him by a ruse and they escape, happily reunited. *Flirts. Aunts. Engineers—Mining. Scandal. Frigidity. Mining. South America.*

Note: Working title: *The Prude.*

DANGEROUS FRIENDS F2.1178

Banner Productions. *Dist* Sterling Pictures Distributing Corp. 30 Oct **1926** [c17 Nov 1926; LP23344]. Si; b&w. 35mm. 6 reels, 5,087 ft.

Dir Finis Fox. *Story-Scen* Charles A. Logue. *Photog* Harry Davis.

Cast: T. Roy Barnes *(Augustus Gale)*, Marjorie Gay *(Honey Gale)*, Arthur Hoyt *(Frederick Betts)*, Gertrude Short *(Linda Betts)*, Burr McIntosh *(Mr. Barker)*, Mathilde Brundage *(Mrs. Barker)*.

Comedy-drama. On the morning of his first wedding anniversary, Augustus Gale, known as "Gusty" to his friends, awakes with a headache from an evening spent with Linda Betts, wife of Frederick Betts, his wealthy neighbor. Gusty sells 10 blocks of Peerless Park real estate in exchange for 20 blocks of Paradise Garden, a bit of worthless swampland; and his employer is so enraged that he gives Gusty the swampland in lieu of a commission. Following an amusing sequence with Mr. and Mrs. Barker, his wife's parents, Gusty again goes out with Linda, while his wife (Honey) and Betts spend the evening together listening to the radio. Following matrimonial recriminations, Barker offers to buy Gusty's land, which he needs for the right-of-way of his railroad. The couple are happily reconciled. *In-laws. Real estate business. Infidelity. Wedding anniversaries. Railroads.*

A DANGEROUS GAME **F2.1179**

Universal Pictures. 17 Dec **1922** [New York premiere; released 25 Dec; c5 Dec 1922; LP18466]. Si; b&w. 35mm. 5 reels, 5,087 ft.

Pres by Carl Laemmle. *Dir* King Baggot. *Scen* Hugh Hoffman. *Photog* Victor Milner.

Cast: Gladys Walton *(Gretchen Ann Peebles)*, Spottiswoode Aitken *(Edward Peebles)*, Otto Hoffman *(Uncle Stillson Peebles)*, Rosa Gore *(Aunt Constance)*, William Robert Daly *(Bill Kelley)*, Kate Price *(Mrs. Kelley)*, Robert Agnew *(John Kelley)*, Edward Jobson *(Pete Sebastian)*, Anne Schaefer *(Stella Sebastian)*, Christine Mayo *(Madame Gaunt)*, Harry Carter *(her manager)*, Bill Gibbs *(butler)*.

Drama. Source: Louis Dodge, "Gret'n Ann," in *Ladies Home Journal* (39:3–5, 22–23, 24–26, May–Jul 1922). Gretchen Ann runs away from her foster parents but is sheltered first by Bill Kelley, a train brakeman, then by elderly oilman Pete Sebastian. After Gretchen keeps Sebastian from being duped by a medium, he sends her to a fashionable school, asking that she agree to marry him when she returns. She accepts the condition, but Sebastian releases her from the commitment when he realizes that Gretchen loves John Kelley. *Railroad brakemen. Oilmen. Mediums. Adolescence. Spiritualism.*

DANGEROUS HOUR **F2.1180**

Cliff Reid. 12 Dec **1923** [New York premiere]. Si; b&w. 35mm. 5 reels, 4,900 ft.

Johnnie Walker Production. *Dir* William Hughes Curran. *Story* Rena Parker.

Cast: Eddie Polo *(himself)*, Jack Carlisle *(Jim Crawley)*, George A. Williams *("Dad" Carson)*, Catherine Bennett *(Anita Carson)*.

Comedy-drama. Making a film on location in Arizona, Polo learns of the oppression of the miners by Jim Crawley. Back in Hollywood, news of a mine disaster causes him to return to Arizona and right the wrongs done to the town. *Actors. Miners. Motion pictures. Arizona. Hollywood.*

DANGEROUS INNOCENCE (Universal-Jewel) **F2.1181**

Universal Pictures. 12 Apr **1925** [c12 Mar 1925; LP21243]. Si; b&w. 35mm. 7 reels, 6,759 ft.

Dir William A. Seiter. *Scen* James O. Spearing. *Adapt* Lewis Milestone. *Photog* Richard Fryer, Merritt Gerstad. *Art Dir* Leo E. Kuter.

Cast: Laura La Plante *(Ann Church)*, Eugene O'Brien *(Major Seymour)*, Jean Hersholt *(Gilchrist)*, Alfred Allen *(Captain Rome)*, Milla Davenport *(stewardess)*, Hedda Hopper *(Muriel Church)*, William Humphrey *(John Church)*, Martha Mattox *(aunt)*.

Comedy-melodrama. Source: Pamela Wynne, *Ann's an Idiot* (London, 1923). Ann Church, a 19-year-old girl who looks much younger, meets Major Seymour on a boat sailing from Liverpool to Bombay. Ann falls in love with the handsome young military man and makes numerous innocent advances toward him, but he remains unmoved, deterred both by her youth and by the fact that he once was in love with her mother. When Gilchrist, another passenger, takes advantage of the girl's innocence and places her in a compromising position, Major Seymour, in an effort to save the girl's reputation, asks her to marry him. Ann accepts, but when they arrive in Bombay, Gilchrist tells Ann that Seymour had an affair with her mother, and Ann breaks off the engagement. Seymour then follows Gilchrist to his apartment and thrashes him. Ann prepares to return to England alone, and Seymour forces Gilchrist to tell the girl that his relationship with her mother was purely platonic. The lovers are reunited and are later married by the ship's captain on the high seas. *Platonic love. Reputation. Ships. Great Britain—Army. Bombay. Liverpool.*

DANGEROUS LIES (United States/Great Britain) **F2.1182**

Famous Players–Lasky British Producers. *Dist* Paramount Pictures. 18 Sep **1921** [United States release; c20 Sep 1921; LP16975]. Si; b&w. 35mm. 6 reels, 5,355 ft.

Dir Paul Powell. *Adapt* Mary Hamilton O'Connor.

Cast: David Powell, Mary Glynne.

Melodrama. Source: Edward Phillips Oppenheim, "Twice Wed" (publication undetermined). When their father dies, Joan and Olive, daughters of the Reverend Farrant, are left in poverty as a result of being swindled by Londoner Leonard Pearce, who has courted Joan. Olive becomes a nurse but loses her position, and Joan agrees to marry Pearce provided that he take Olive into his home. Olive learns of Pearce's swindle, and Joan leaves him and goes to London, where she becomes secretary to Sir Henry Bond, a book collector, who falls in love with her and proposes. She refuses at first, but hearing that Pearce has died she accepts Sir Henry's offer; Pearce returns quite alive, however, and finding her married, he drops dead in a fit of rage. *Sisters. Swindlers. Nurses. Bibliophiles. London.*

THE DANGEROUS LITTLE DEMON (Universal Special) **F2.1183**

Universal Film Manufacturing Co. 27 Mar **1922** [c14 Mar 1922; LP17643]. Si; b&w. 35mm. 5 reels, 4,751 ft.

Pres by Carl Laemmle. *Dir* Clarence G. Badger. *Scen* Doris Schroeder. *Story* Mildred Considine. *Photog* Ben Bail.

Cast: Marie Prevost *(Teddy Harmon)*, Jack Perrin *(Kenneth Graham)*, Robert Ellis *(Gary McVeigh)*, Anderson Smith *(Demy Baker)*, Fontaine La Rue *(Helene Westley)*, Edward Martindel *(Harmon)*, Lydia Knott *(Aunt Sophia)*, Herbert Prior *(Jay Howard)*.

Comedy-melodrama. Teddy Harmon, a society girl preoccupied with pleasure, is persuaded by her father's serious-minded secretary that she is in love with him, but meeting his family, she becomes bored and seeks the society of Gary McVeigh, a wealthy neighbor. At a gambling house, she finds her father with a dashing young widow, and later, the proprietor, though ostensibly a friend, tries to force his attentions on her and she is taken to jail in a raid. She is rescued by Gary, and the secretary, learning of her father's financial difficulties, breaks the engagement. Her father is saved by a loan from Gary, and, realizing her mistake, Teddy gladly accepts the latter's attentions. *Socialites. Gamblers. Secretaries. Filial relations. Wealth. Courtship.*

THE DANGEROUS MAID **F2.1184**

Joseph M. Schenck Productions. *Dist* Associated First National Pictures. 19 Nov **1923** [c25 Oct 1923; LP19530]. Si; b&w. 35mm. 8 reels, 7,337 ft.

Pres by Joseph M. Schenck. *Dir* Victor Heerman. *Scen* C. Gardner Sullivan. *Photog* Glen MacWilliams.

Cast: Constance Talmadge *(Barbara Winslow)*, Conway Tearle *(Capt. Miles Prothero)*, Morgan Wallace *(Col. Percy Kirk)*, Charles Gerrard *(Sir Peter Dare)*, Marjorie Daw *(Cecelie Winslow)*, Kate Price *(Jane, the cook)*, Tully Marshall *(Simon, the peddler)*, Lou Morrison *(Corporal Crutch)*, Phillip Dunham *(Private Stich)*, Otto Matiesen *(Judge George Jeffreys)*, Wilson Hummel *(Jewars, Jeffreys' secretary)*, Thomas Ricketts *(John Standish Lane)*, Ann May *(Prudence Lane)*, Ray Hallor *(Rupert Winslow)*, Lincoln Plummer *(The Farmer)*.

Historical melodrama. Source: Elizabeth Ellis, *Barbara Winslow—Rebel* (New York, 1906). A melodramatic romance of 17th-century England during the Duke of Monmouth rebellion in which Barbara Winslow, affianced to Sir Peter Dare, attempts to save her cousin, Rupert, a fugitive rebel, from the king's officers and incidentally falls in love with Miles Prothero, a captain in the king's army. *Great Britain—History—Stuarts. Monmouth Rebellion.*

THE DANGEROUS MOMENT **F2.1185**

Universal Film Manufacturing Co. Apr **1921** [c29 Mar 1921; LP16346]. Si; b&w. 35mm. 5 reels, 4,850 ft.

Pres by Carl Laemmle. *Dir* Marcel De Sano. *Scen* William Clifton. *Story* Douglas Z. Doty. *Story? (see note)* John Colton. *Photog* Bert Glennon.

Cast: Carmel Myers *(Sylvia Palprini)*, Lule Warrenton *(Mrs. Tarkides)*, George Rigas *(Movros Tarkides)*, W. T. Fellows *(Jack Reeve)*, Billy Fay *(Collins)*, Bonnie Hill *(Marjory Blake)*, Herbert Heyes *(George Duray)*, Fred G. Becker *(Henry Trent)*, Marian Skinner *(Aunt Cynthia Grey)*, Smoke Turner *(Trotsky)*.

Melodrama. Sylvia Palprini is a waitress at The Black Beetle, a restaurant considered to be the leading bohemian resort of Greenwich Village. Among the extremely varied customers is an artist whom she fancies. A jealous suitor, Movros Tarkides, threatens Sylvia, and when he is killed she is accused of the murder. The police find her hiding in the artist's studio, but the confession of the real murderer proves her innocent and she wins the artist's love. *Artists. Waitresses. Bohemianism. Murder. New York City—Greenwich Village.*

Note: Working title: *Dangerous Moments.* Universal records indicate that John Colton may have been author of the original story.

DANGEROUS MONEY **F2.1186**

Famous Players–Lasky. *Dist* Paramount Pictures. ca12 Oct **1924** [New York premiere; released 20 Oct; c14 Oct 1924; LP20662]. Si; b&w. 35mm.

Pres by Adolph Zukor, Jesse L. Lasky. *Dir* Frank Tuttle. *Scen* Julie Herne. *Adapt* John Russell. *Photog* Roy Hunt.

Cast: Bebe Daniels *(Adele Clark)*, Tom Moore *(Tim Sullivan)*, William Powell *(Prince Arnolfo da Pescia)*, Dolores Cassinelli *(Signorina Vitale)*, Mary Foy *("Auntie" Clark)*, Edward O'Connor *(Sheamus Sullivan)*, Peter Lang *(Judge Daniel Orcutt)*, Charles Slattery *(O'Hara)*, Diana Kane.

Society drama. Source: Robert Herrick, *Clark's Field* (New York, 1914). Boardinghouse drudge Adele Clark is unexpectedly awarded the ownership of a certain piece of New York City property known as Clark's Field. The trustees send her to a finishing school, whose headmistress, Signorina Vitale, persuades Adele and her sweetheart, Tim Sullivan, that she should travel in Europe. Adele's new riches cause her to lose her sense of proportion, and she soon is involved with a fast set indulging in the jazz life. Even Tim cannot curb Adele's extravagance, and he returns to America while Adele marries Italian fortune-hunter Prince Arnolfo da Pescia. When a will is discovered naming Tim as the rightful heir to Clark's Field, Adele and Arnolfo hurry to New York, and Arnolfo tries to steal the will, then dies in a hotel fire. All dispute over the land is ended when Tim and Adele are united. *Drudges. Irish. Italians. Nobility. Inheritance. Wealth. Jazz life. Property rights. Boardinghouses. Boarding schools.*

DANGEROUS NAN MCGREW **F2.1187**

Paramount-Publix Corp. 20 Jun **1930** [New York premiere; released 5 Jul; c6 Jul 1930; LP1408]. Sd (Movietone); b&w. 35mm. 7 reels, 6,571 ft.

Dir Malcolm St. Clair. *Screenplay* Paul Gerard Smith, Pierre Collings. *Story* Charles Beahan, Garrett Fort. *Photog* George Folsey. *Film Ed* Helene Turner. *Songs: "Dangerous Nan McGrew," "I Owe You"* Don Hartman, Al Goodhart. *Song: "Aw! C'mon, Whatta Ya Got To Lose?"* Leo Robin, Richard A. Whiting. *Song: "Once a Gypsy Told Me (You Were Mine)"* Sammy Fain, Irving Kahal, Pierre Norman. *Rec Engr* Edwin Schabbehar, C. A. Tuthill.

Cast: Helen Kane *(Dangerous Nan McGrew)*, Victor Moore *(Doc Foster)*, James Hall *(Bob Dawes)*, Stuart Erwin *(Eustace Macy)*, Frank Morgan *(Muldoon)*, Roberta Robinson *(Clara Benson)*, Louise Closser Hale *(Mrs. Benson)*, Allan Forrest *(Godfrey Crofton)*, John Hamilton *(Grant)*, Robert Milash *(Sheriff)*.

Comedy-drama. Nan McGrew and Doc Foster, star and owner respectively of a medicine show, are stranded near the town of Wagontrack in the Candian Northwest and there meet Muldoon, who, Helen learns, is about to divide the spoils of a bank robbery. During the performance in Wagontrack, Nan captures the heart of Eustace Macy, who hires the show as entertainment for his Aunt Clara Benson's Christmas Eve party. Muldoon, disguised as Santa Claus, captures Bob Dawes, an officer in the Royal Mounted; but Nan shoots and disarms the villain, who has a price on his head. Muldoon manages to escape from Eustace, a saxophonist. By chance, Doc Foster and Muldoon both appear at the carnival in the guise of Buster Brown; and Crofton, the master criminal, gives the loot to Foster by mistake. Nan recognizes Muldoon, however, and following his pursuit and capture, she wins Eustace as her husband as well as a $10,000 reward. The lovers—Bob and Clara—are united. *Singers. Bank robberies. Saxophonists. Santa Claus. Medicine shows. Christmas. Canadian Northwest. Northwest Mounted Police.*

DANGEROUS ODDS **F2.1188**

Independent Pictures. 7 Apr **1925** [New York State license]. Si; b&w. 35mm. 5 reels, 4,800 ft.

Cast: Bill Cody.

Western melodrama(?). No information about the nature of this film has been found.

DANGEROUS PARADISE **F2.1189**

Paramount Famous Lasky Corp. 22 Feb **1930** [c23 Feb 1930; LP1103]. Sd (Movietone); b&w. 35mm. 6 reels, 5,244 ft. [Also si; 5,343 ft.]

Dir William Wellman. *Screenplay-Dial* William Slavens McNutt, Grover Jones. *Photog* Archie J. Stout. *Song: "Smiling Skies"* Leo Robin, Richard Whiting.

Cast: Nancy Carroll *(Alma)*, Richard Arlen *(Heyst)*, Warner Oland *(Schomberg)*, Gustav von Seyffertitz *(Mr. Jones)*, Francis McDonald *(Ricardo)*, George Kotsonaros *(Pedro)*, Dorothea Wolbert *(Mrs. Schomberg)*, Clarence H. Wilson *(Zangiacomo)*, Evelyn Selbie *(his wife)*, Willie Fung *(Wang)*, Wong Wing *(his wife)*, Lillian Worth *(Myrtle)*.

Melodrama. Suggested by: Joseph Conrad, *Victory* (1915). Alma, a member of Zangiacomo's all-female orchestra, playing at Schomberg's hotel in Sourabaya, is frightened by the men's advances; attracted by the kindness of Heyst, a hotel guest, she hides on his boat to escape her tormentors. Heyst, who has retreated to a remote island following an unhappy love affair, discovers her and grudgingly allows her to remain at his cabin. Meanwhile Zangiacomo and Schomberg fight over her, resulting in Zangiacomo's death; Schomberg is then held prisoner by Mr. Jones, Ricardo, and Pedro, three desperadoes, who convert the hotel into a gambling house. To divert them, Schomberg tells them of gold on the island; and after killing and robbing Schomberg, the men depart. In a desperate confrontation with Heyst, Pedro and Ricardo are killed and Alma is wounded; but Heyst is grateful for the awakening of courage and love. *Violinists. Desperadoes. Gambling. Seduction. Murder. Hotels. South Sea Islands.*

Note: Working title: *Flesh of Eve.*

DANGEROUS PASTIME **F2.1190**

Louis J. Gasnier Productions. 4 Feb **1922** [trade review]. Si; b&w. 35mm. 5 reels.

Dir James W. Horne. *Scen* H. Tipton Steck. *Story* Wyndham Martin.

Cast: Lew Cody *(Barry Adams)*, Cleo Ridgely *(Mrs. Stowell)*, Elinor Fair *(Celia)*, Mrs. Irving Cummings *(Mrs. Gregor)*.

Drama. Barry Adams proposes to Celia in 57 ways but is always refused because she believes he is too fond of adventure to settle down. After the 58th refusal, he starts out in search of the adventure he has been accused of wanting. He receives a mysterious note from a previous love who is trying to reestablish their relationship. When he resists her charms, she drugs him and takes him to an isolated country place. He manages to escape and returns to Celia assuring her that adventure no longer intrigues him. *Thrill-seeking. Courtship.*

DANGEROUS PATHS **F2.1191**

Berwilla Film Corp. *Dist* Arrow Film Corp. Jul **1921** [c27 Jul 1921; LP16798]. Si; b&w. 35mm. 5 reels, 5,000 ft.

Prod Ben Wilson. *Dir* Duke Worne. *Story-Scen* Joseph W. Girard.

Cast: Neva Gerber *(Ruth Hammond)*, Ben Wilson *(John Emerson)*, Edith Stayart *(Violet Benson)*, Joseph W. Girard *(Silas Newton)*, Henry Van Sickle *(Noah Hammond)*, Helen Gilmore *(Deborah Hammond)*.

Society melodrama. Rather than be forced by her shrewish stepmother into marriage to wealthy but cruel Silas Newton, Ruth Hammond leaves her country home and goes to the city, where she is aided by Violet Benson. Newton finds her there and tries to force his attentions on her, but she has him thrown out of her hotel. Newton spreads false rumors and scandal in the country village, while Pastor Emerson, who loves Ruth, takes Ruth and Violet into his home. In a sermon he denounces Ruth's vilifiers, and the stepmother admits her shortcomings and welcomes the girls back to her home. *Shrews. Stepmothers. Clergymen. Village life. Slander.*

DANGEROUS PLEASURE **F2.1192**

Independent Pictures. 11 Feb **1925** [New York State license]. Si; b&w. 35mm. 6 reels, 5,800 ft.

Dir Harry Revier.

Cast: Niles Welch, Dorothy Revier.

Melodrama. "This story deals with a man, who causes his wife great jealousy on account of his relation to other women, yet who regards himself as a man of destiny in settling others unhappy marital relations. He is named co-respondent in a suit - leaves town - takes a house in a smaller village - picks up a little girl on the street in his car and drives into the country. She leaves his car and walks home. He meets a beautiful woman whose husband, unjustly jealous of her is hiring men to 'get something on her.' He sends for his own wife to come and frame this man. The wife, posing as an agent for beauty preparations, vamps the man and makes an appointment with him. While they are at supper his car is tampered with. He and the woman come out - he very drunk or drugged - and get into the car. There is a long struggle in which the woman is badly bruised. The man becomes unconscious and the car is wrecked. He awakens in a hut with a broken arm and is led to believe that he has killed the girl. Then a man of destiny blackmails him - gets a check for $50,000 which he gives to the injured wife and she marries the boy of whom her husband was jealous." (New York State license records.) *Infidelity. Jealousy. Divorce. Blackmail. Marriage.*

DANGEROUS TOYS F2.1193

Bradley Feature Film Corp. *Dist* Federated Film Exchange. Aug **1921.** Si; b&w. 35mm. 7 reels, 6,000 ft.

Dir Samuel Bradley. *Story* Edmund Goulding. *Photog* Don Canady.

Cast: Frank Losee *(Hugo Harman)*, Marion Elmore *(Mrs. Harman)*, Marguerite Clayton *(Louise Malone)*, William Desmond *(Jack Gray)*, Frances Devereaux *(Mrs. Malone)*, Lillian Greene *(Phyllis Harman)*.

Domestic melodrama. "Because his wife left him for another man, Harman, a banker, loses faith in women. Twenty years later he has stifled his grief and thinks women playthings. He takes deep interest in his clerk, Jack Gray, but, on finding him married, seeks to cause his wife to leave him, believing she is a hindrance to his ambitions. He places her in an apartment, gives her plenty of money without any conditions for three weeks, and also seeks to get Gray interested in other women. Scheme fails, as Mrs. Gray learns the emptiness of such a life. Husband, regardless of appearances, believes in her and takes her back. Broken in spirit and realizing there is true love, Harman is forgiven by the Grays and they bring about a reconciliation with his wife, who is living in poverty." (*Motion Picture News Booking Guide*, 1:27, Dec 1921.) *Bankers. Bank clerks. Infidelity. Desertion. Marriage.*

Note: Also reviewed as *Don't Leave Your Husband.*

DANGEROUS TRAFFIC F2.1194

Otto K. Schreier Productions. *Dist* Goodwill Pictures. 7 Jun **1926** [New York State license]. Si; b&w. 35mm. 5 reels, 4,300 ft.

Dir-Writ Bennett Cohn. *Photog* Dwight Warren. *Film Ed* Fred Bain.

Cast: Francis X. Bushman, Jr. *(Ned Charters)*, Jack Perrin *(Tom Kennedy)*, Mildred Harris *(Helen Leonard)*, Tom London *(Marc Brandon)*, Ethan Laidlaw *(Foxy Jim Stone)*, Hal Walters *(Harvey Leonard)*.

Melodrama. Ned Charters, a reporter for the *Seaside Record*, takes over the investigation of the activities of a band of smugglers after Tom Kennedy, a revenue agent, is wounded by one of the gang members. Helen Leonard, whose brother's death was caused by the smugglers, works as a cigarette girl at the Surfridge Inn, hoping to obtain evidence to bring the gang to justice. Tom joins the smugglers and is instrumental in arresting the gang. *Smugglers. Reporters. Revenue agents. Cigarette girls. Inns.*

DANGEROUS TRAILS F2.1195

Rocky Mountain Productions. *Dist* Anchor Productions. 10 Jan **1923** [scheduled release]. Si; b&w. 35mm. 6 reels.

Pres by Morris R. Schlank. *Dir* Alvin J. Neitz.

Cast: Irene Rich *(Grace Alderson)*, Tully Marshall *(Steve Bradley)*, Noah Beery *(Inspector Criswell)*, Allan Penrose *(Roland St. Clair)*, William Lowery *(Jean Le Fere)*, Jack Curtis *(Wang)*, Jane Talent *(Beatrice Layton)*.

Northwest melodrama. Northwest Mounted Policeman Roland St. Clair falls for resort entertainer Grace Alderson while tracking down some opium smugglers. Grace's fiancé, Steve Bradley, a dancehall proprietor, is revealed to be in league with Jean Le Fere and Wang, both known smugglers. A wild chase follows the smugglers' futile attempts to escape St. Clair's scrutiny. Grace, a secret service employee, marries St. Clair. *Entertainers. Smugglers. Secret service. Opium. Resorts. Northwest Mounted Police.*

A DANGEROUS WOMAN F2.1196

Paramount Famous Lasky Corp. 18 May **1929** [c17 May 1929; LP391]. Sd (Movietone); b&w. 35mm. 8 reels, 6,643 ft.

Assoc Prod Louis D. Lighton. *Dir* Rowland V. Lee. *Adtl Dir* Gerald Grove. *Dial* Edward E. Paramore, Jr. *Adapt* John Farrow. *Photog* Harry Fischbeck. *Set Dsgn* Hans Dreier.

Cast: Baclanova *(Tania Gregory)*, Clive Brook *(Frank Gregory)*, Neil Hamilton *(Bobby Gregory)*, Clyde Cook *(Tubbs)*, Leslie Fenton *(Peter Allerton)*, Snitz Edwards *(Chief Macheria)*.

Melodrama. Source: Margery H. Lawrence, "A Woman Who Needed Killing," in *Hearst's International Cosmopolitan* (82:90–93, Apr 1927). Frank Gregory, the British representative in Central East Africa, loves his Russian wife, Tania, despite the fact that she is repeatedly unfaithful to him. Frank's assistant, Peter Allerton, commits suicide for love of Tania, and Frank's younger brother, Bobby, is sent out to replace him. Tania makes eyes at the young fellow, and Frank places deadly poison in her nightly glass of lime juice. Tubbs, Frank's faithful cockney servant, removes the lime juice, however, and places a poisonous snake in her bed instead. Tania dies, and the Gregory brothers return to England. *Russians. British. Murder. Infidelity. Suicide. British East Africa. Snakes.*

Note: Known also as *The Woman Who Needed Killing.*

DANIEL BOONE THRU THE WILDERNESS F2.1197

Sunset Productions. 1 May **1926.** Si; b&w. 35mm. 6 reels, 5,587 ft.

Dir? (see note) Frank S. Mattison, Robert N. Bradbury. *Photog* James Brown.

Cast: Roy Stewart, Kathleen Collins.

Historical drama(?). No information about the precise nature of this film has been found. *Daniel Boone.*

Note: The two directors named are each given credit for this film by different sources.

DANTE'S INFERNO F2.1198

Fox Film Corp. 7 Sep **1924** [c30 Jun 1924; LP20370]. Si; b&w. 35mm. 6 reels, 5,484 ft.

Pres by William Fox. *Dir* Henry Otto. *Adapt* Edmund Goulding. *Story* Cyrus Wood. *Photog* Joseph August.

Cast: Lawson Butt *(Dante)*, Howard Gaye *(Virgil)*, Ralph Lewis *(Mortimer Judd)*, Pauline Starke *(Marjorie Vernon)*, Josef Swickard *(Eugene Craig)*, Gloria Grey *(Mildred Craig)*, William Scott *(Ernest Judd)*, Robert Klein *(fiend)*, Winifred Landis *(Mrs. Judd)*, Lorimer Johnston *(doctor)*, Lon Poff *(secretary)*, Bud Jamison *(butler)*.

Allegorical drama. Ruthless millionaire Mortimer Judd refuses to repair his tenements and declines to give financial aid to his friend Craig. Craig sends him a copy of *The Inferno*, accompanied by a curse; and as Judd reads, in a delirious dream he envisions Dante's tour of hell and scenes of punishment for his own sins. Awakening, he seeks to make amends for his past injustices. *Millionaires. Hell. Housing. Dante Alighieri. Vergil. Dreams.*

DAPHNE AND THE PIRATE (Reissue) F2.1199

Fine Arts Pictures. *Dist* Tri-Stone Pictures. **1924.** Si; b&w. 35mm. 5 reels.

Note: A "re-edited and re-titled" Lillian Gish film originally released by Triangle Film Corp. on 5 Mar 1916 (c28 Feb 1916; LP8165).

DAREDEVIL'S REWARD F2.1200

Fox Film Corp. 15 Jan **1928** [c27 Jan 1928; LP24917]. Si; b&w. 35mm. 5 reels, 4,987-5,000 ft.

Pres by William Fox. *Dir* Eugene Forde. *Story-Scen* John Stone. *Photog* Dan Clark. *Asst Dir* Clay Crapnell.

Cast: Tom Mix *(Tom Hardy)*, Natalie Joyce *(Ena Powell)*, Lawford Davidson *(Foster)*, Billy Bletcher *(Slim)*, Harry Cording *(Second Heavy)*, William Welch *(James Powell)*, Tony the Wonder Horse *(himself)*.

Western melodrama. "Western in which the Texas Ranger rounds up a band of desperate highwaymen, headed by the uncle of the girl with whom he eventually falls in love. She is abducted by the bandits after her uncle is shot and is rescued by the hero in a mad plunge down the mountainside in an uncontrollable automobile." (*Motion Picture News Blue Book*, 1929, p245.) *Texas Rangers. Uncles. Highwaymen. Automobiles. Abduction. Horses.*

Note: Also copyrighted 6 Jan 1928, LP24826, as *$5,000 Reward.*

DARING CHANCES F2.1201

Universal Pictures. 19 Oct **1924** [c19 Jul 1924; LP20409]. Si; b&w. 35mm. 5 reels, 4,543 ft.

Dir Clifford S. Smith. *Cont* Wyndham Gittens. *Story* Isadore Bernstein. *Photog* Harry Neumann.

Cast: Jack Hoxie *(Jack Armstrong)*, Alta Allen *(Agnes Rushton)*, Claude Payton *(Sampson Burke)*, Jack Pratt *(Joe Slavin)*, Catherine Wallace *(Ethel Slavin)*, Doreen Turner *(Bebe Slavin)*, Genevieve Danninger *(Roberta Simpson)*, Newton Campbell *(Bill)*, William McCall *(sheriff)*, Scout *(himself, a horse)*.

Western melodrama. When his sister, who is married to saloon keeper Joe Slavin, dies, Jack Armstrong takes in her little daughter, Bebe. Sampson Burke, his rival for schoolteacher Agnes Rushton, conspires with Slavin to have Jack arrested for abduction, but Jack is released to participate in a rodeo. The child and the gate receipts are stolen by Slavin, but he is killed, the child is rescued, and the teacher is won by Jack. *Children. Schoolteachers. Saloon keepers. Abduction. Rodeos.*

Note: Working title: *His Trust.*

DARING DANGER F2.1202

Cliff Smith Productions. *For* Associated Photoplays. *Dist* American Releasing Corp. 5 Mar **1922** [c25 Mar 1922; LP17666]. Si; b&w. 35mm. 5 reels, 4,669 ft.

Prod-Dir Cliff Smith. *Story-Scen* L. V. Jefferson.

Cast: Pete Morrison *(Cal Horton)*, Esther Ralston *(Ethel Stanton)*, Bill Ryno *(Bill Stanton)*, Lew Meehan *(Steve Harris)*, Bob Fleming *(Bull Weaver)*.

Western melodrama. Cal Horton, a rancher who has suffered considerably at the hands of cattle rustlers who have become a menace to local life and property, is called on by the United States Government to track down the outlaws. Horton visits his sweetheart, Ethel Stanton, informs her of his mission, and bids her goodby. The foreman of a neighboring ranch, noted for his "churchly" qualities but actually in league with the cattle thieves, seeks the hand of Ethel, and suggests to her that Horton is an outlaw, causing her to break the engagement. Meanwhile, Horton travels day and night to overtake the rustlers, and although placed in many perilous encounters manages to escape his enemies; soon the sheriff and his men come to his rescue, and the guilty foreman is punished. Horton is rewarded by the government and marries Ethel. *Ranchers. Ranch foremen. Churchmen. Rustlers.*

DARING DAYS (Blue Streak Western) **F2.1203**

Universal Pictures. 8 Nov **1925** [c24 Oct 1925; LP21941]. Si; b&w. 35mm. 5 reels, 4,622 ft.

Pres by Carl Laemmle. *Dir* John B. O'Brien. *Story* George Hull. *Photog* Benjamin Kline.

Cast: Josie Sedgwick *(Eve Underhill)*, Edward Hearne *(Catamount Carson)*, Frederick Cole *(Henry Sheldon)*, Zama Zamoria *(Lucille Somers)*, Harry Rattenberry *(Uncle Johnny Catter)*, Ted Oliver *(Boggs)*, Harry Todd *(Hank Skinner)*, T. C. Jack *(Eli Carson)*, Ben Corbett *(Ambrose Carson)*.

Western melodrama. Eve Underhill quits her job in the "want ad" department of a San Francisco newspaper and heads for Eden, Arizona, to answer its advertisement for a lady mayor. Upon her arrival, the womanless town hails her as boss, and she initiates a cleanup campaign. A romance develops between her and Catamount Carson, mayor of the rival town of Catamount. Complications revolve about the efforts of Catamount Carson's evil cousin, Ambrose Carson, to inflame a dispute between the two towns over water rights. Henry Sheldon, jealous of Eve's attentions to Catamount, is brought into the plot but is killed by Ambrose. Catamount pursues Ambrose, and in a fight both fall from a canyon wall: Eve ropes Catamount's fast-disappearing foot, saving his life, but Ambrose falls to his death. *Mayors. Women in public office. Reformers. Water rights. Smalltown life. Arizona.*

DARING DEEDS **F2.1204**

Duke Worne Productions. *Dist* Rayart Pictures. May **1927.** Si; b&w. 35mm. 5 reels, 5,101 ft.

Dir Duke Worne. *Scen* George W. Pyper. *Photog* Ernest Smith.

Cast: Billy Sullivan *(William Gordon, Jr.)*, Molly Malone *(Helen Courtney)*, Earl Metcalfe *(Rance Sheldon)*, Thomas Lingham *(William Gordon, Sr.)*, Robert Walker *(Walter Sarles)*, Lafe McKee *(John Courtney)*, Milburn Morante *("Smudge" Rafferty)*, Robert Littlefield *(mysterious stranger)*.

Comedy-drama. "Young flyer displeases his dad, an aeroplane manufacturer. The youth leaves home in search of adventure. Develops romance with daughter of an inventor, and saves her father from a man bent on ruining him. He wins airplane race and government contract." (*Motion Picture News Booking Guide*, 13:25, Oct 1927.) *Aviators. Inventors. Airplanes. Airplane manufacture. Airplane racing.*

DARING LOVE **F2.1205**

Hoffman Productions. *Dist* Truart Film Corp. 15 Jun **1924** [c1 Jul 1924; LP20379]. Si; b&w. 35mm. 6 reels, 5,006 ft.

Pres by M. H. Hoffman. *Dir* Roland G. Edwards. *Scen* Hope Loring, Louis D. Lighton. *Adapt* Roland West, Willard Mack. *Photog* Oliver T. Marsh, James R. Diamond. *Art Dir* W. L. Heywood. *Asst Dir* A. Carle Palm. *Gowns* Sophie Wachner.

Cast: Elaine Hammerstein *(Bobo)*, Huntly Gordon *(John Stedman)*, Walter Long *(Red Bishop)*, Gertrude Astor *(Mrs. John Stedman)*, Johnny Arthur *("Music")*, Cissy Fitzgerald *(Queenie)*, Morgan Wallace *(Jerry Hayden)*.

Society melodrama. Source: Albert Payson Terhune, "Driftwood," in *Red Book* (31:89–94, Sep 1918). When his wife threatens to leave him because of his weakness for drink, John Stedman, finding her with another man, provides grounds for divorce in an open affair with Bobo, a dive entertainer. Later, Stedman is nursed back to health by Bobo. He returns from wartime service, marries her, and becomes governor, despite efforts of his former wife to win him back. *Veterans. Entertainers. State governors. Divorce. Alcoholism. Politics.*

THE DARING YEARS **F2.1206**

Daniel Carson Goodman Corp. *Dist* Equity Pictures. 15 Sep **1923** [c14 Aug 1923; LP19306]. Si; b&w. 35mm. 7 reels, 6,782 ft.

Prod-Story-Adapt Daniel Carson Goodman. *Dir* Kenneth Webb.

Cast: Mildred Harris *(Susie La Motte)*, Charles Emmett Mack *(John Browning)*, Clara Bow *(John's sweetheart, Mary)*, Mary Carr *(Mrs. Browning)*, Joe King *(Jim Moran, a pugilist)*, [Frederick] Tyrone Power *(James La Motte)*, Skeets Gallagher *(The College Boy)*, Jack Richardson *(Flaglier, cabaret owner)*, Joseph Depew, Helen Rowland *(La Motte children)*, Sam Sidman *(Curly, Moran's manager)*, Sherman Sisters *(Moran girls)*.

Melodrama. Although Susie La Motte, a cabaret dancer, loves boxer Jim Moran, she vamps young, idealistic John Browning. Moran accidently shoots himself during a fight with the jealous Browning, and Susie, out of malice, accuses Browning of murder. Browning is sentenced to death by electrocution, but a power failure and a last-minute confession from Susie save him. *Dancers. Boxers. Murder. Capital punishment.*

DARING YOUTH **F2.1207**

B. F. Zeidman. *Dist* Principal Pictures. 1 Feb **1924.** Si; b&w. 35mm. 6 reels, 5,795 ft.

Dir William Beaudine. *Scen* Alexander Neal. *Story* Dorothy Farnum. *Photog* Charles J. Van Enger. *Art Dir* Joseph Wright. *Film Ed* Edward McDermott.

Cast: Bebe Daniels *(Miss Alita Allen)*, Norman Kerry *(John J. Campbell)*, Lee Moran *(Arthur James, the rival)*, Arthur Hoyt *(Winston Howell)*, Lillian Langdon *(Mrs. Allen)*, George Pearce *(Mr. Allen)*.

Comedy-drama. Suggested by: William Shakespeare, *Taming of the Shrew*. On the eve of the marriage of her daughter, Alita, Mrs. Allen, unhappily married for 25 years, advocates writer Fannie Hurst's widely publicized mode of living with her husband: only two breakfasts a week together and complete freedom otherwise. Alita marries John Campbell on condition that she enjoy similar independence, but after a few weeks the idea begins to pall. Her husband's willingness to continue the arrangement infuriates her. She is about to elope with Arthur James, a "boob-admirer," when Campbell asserts himself, beats up the rival, and takes charge of his wife, who is overjoyed to lead a conventional life. *Shrews. Women's rights. Fannie Hurst.*

THE DARK ANGEL **F2.1208**

Samuel Goldwyn Productions. *Dist* First National Pictures. 27 Sep **1925** [c14 Sep 1925; LP21814]. Si; b&w. 35mm. 8 reels, 7,311 ft.

Pres by Samuel Goldwyn. *Dir* George Fitzmaurice. *Scen* Frances Marion. *Photog* George Barnes.

Cast: Ronald Colman *(Capt. Alan Trent)*, Vilma Banky *(Kitty Vane)*, Wyndham Standing *(Capt. Gerald Shannon)*, Frank Elliott *(Lord Beaumont)*, Charles Lane *(Sir Hubert Vane)*, Helen Jerome Eddy *(Miss Bottles)*, Florence Turner *(Roma)*.

Drama. Source: H. B. Trevelyan, *The Dark Angel, a Play of Yesterday and To-day* (London, 1928). Ordered unexpectedly back into action, Captain Trent is unable to obtain a marriage license and, without benefit of clergy, must spend the night with his fiancée, Kitty Vane, in an English inn. Trent is blinded in battle and taken prisoner by the Germans. He is reported to be dead, and his friend, Captain Shannon, discreetly woos Kitty, seeking to soothe her grief with his gentle love. After the war, Shannon finds Trent in a remote corner of England, writing children's stories for a living. Loyal to his former comrade in arms, Shannon informs Kitty of Trent's reappearance. She goes to him, and he conceals his blindness, telling Kitty that he no longer cares for her. She sees through his deception, however, and they are reunited. *Authors. Prisoners of war. Friendship. Blindness. World War I. England.*

DARK SECRETS **F2.1209**

Famous Players–Lasky. *Dist* Paramount Pictures. 21 Jan **1923** [New York premiere; released 5 Feb; c17 Jan 1923; LP18636]. Si; b&w. 35mm. 6 reels, 4,337 ft.

Pres by Adolph Zukor. *Dir* Victor Fleming. *Story-Scen* Edmund Goulding. *Photog* Hal Rosson.

Cast: Dorothy Dalton *(Ruth Rutherford)*, Robert Ellis *(Lord Wallington)*, José Ruben *(Dr. Mohammed Ali)*, Ellen Cassidy *(Mildred Rice)*, Pat

Hartigan *(Biskra)*, Warren Cook *(Dr. Case)*, Julia Swayne Gordon *(Mrs. Rutherford)*.

Melodrama. Long Island socialite Ruth Rutherford, crippled as a result of being thrown from a horse, breaks her engagement to Lord Wallington. Dejected, Wallie returns to his regiment in Egypt and sinks into dissipation. Ruth hears of his plight and also goes to Egypt, where she meets Dr. Mohammed Ali. Ali cures her lameness in return for Ruth's agreeing to become his wife, but Biskra, Ruth's servant, kills Ali before he can collect. Even from death Ali's power over Ruth returns her to her wheelchair until she jumps up to save Wallington from an attack feigned by Biskra. *Physicians. Socialites. Cripples. Autosuggestion. Long Island. Egypt.*

DARK SKIES **F2.1210**

Biltmore Productions. 10 Dec **1929** [New York showing; released 1 Jan 1930]. Sd (Telefilm); b&w. 35mm. 8 reels, 6,400 ft.

Dir Harry S. Webb. *Dir? (see note)* Harry O. Hoyt. *Story* John Francis Natteford. *Photog* Ray Reis, Harry Fowler. *Song: "Juanita"* Walter Sheridan, Lee Zahler. *Sd* Ralph M. Like.

Cast: Wallace MacDonald *(Capt. Pedro Real)*, Shirley Mason *(Juanita Morgan)*, Evelyn Brent *(see note)*, William V. Mong *(Mr. Morgan)*, Tom O'Brien *(Pete)*, Josef Swickard *(Señor Moreno)*, Larry Steers *(Captain Nelson)*, Tom Wilson *(Mike)*.

Melodrama. Juanita Morgan's life of drudgery (renting beach umbrellas for her uncle, Mr. Morgan) is brightened when she meets Capt. Pedro Real during one of his visits to her southern California town. They fall in love, but Juanita refuses to marry Pedro until he quits his successful rumrunning business. Promising to go straight after one more trip, Pedro persuades Juanita to give a warning light should she see Captain Nelson, the government agent and Pedro's friend. Morgan discovers the plan and prevents Juanita from signaling Nelson's presence to Pedro, but she persuades Mike to hijack Pedro's boat. Nelson finds Mike in possession of the rum boat outside the 12-mile limit. *Government agents. Rumrunners. Hijackers. Uncles. Territorial waters. California.*

Note: Two sources give the title as *Darkened Skies* and credit direction to Harry O. Hoyt and the female lead (expressed as Juanita *Moore*) to Evelyn Brent.

DARK STAIRWAYS (Universal-Jewel) **F2.1211**

Universal Pictures. 22 Jun **1924** [c4 Jun 1924; LP20268]. Si; b&w. 35mm. 5 reels, 5,030 ft.

Dir Robert F. Hill. *Adapt* L. G. Rigby. *Story* Marion Orth. *Photog* William Thornley.

Cast: Herbert Rawlinson *(Sheldon Polk)*, Ruth Dwyer *(Sunny Day)*, Hayden Stevenson *(Frank Farnsworth)*, Robert E. Homans *("Dippy" Blake)*, Walter Perry *(Chris Martin)*, Bonnie Hill *(Rita Minar)*, Kathleen O'Connor *(Geraldine Lewis)*, Dolores Rousse *(Madge Armstrong)*, Emmett King *(Henry Polk)*, Lola Todd *(stenographer)*, Tom McGuire *(police chief)*.

Mystery-melodrama. Sheldon Polk's father, a wealthy banker, agrees to make a loan to Frank Farnsworth. Sheldon is robbed while delivering the money and is arrested for theft on circumstantial evidence. He escapes from prison to establish his innocence and discovers that Farnsworth is the leader of the criminals who committed the robbery and the murder of his father. *Bankers. Robbery. Murder. Circumstantial evidence. Prison escapes.*

DARK STREETS **F2.1212**

First National Pictures. 11 Aug **1929** [c30 Aug 1929; LP730]. Sd (Vitaphone); b&w. 35mm. 6 reels, 5,416 ft. [Also si, 8 Sep 1929; 5,514 ft.]

Prod Ned Marin. *Dir* Frank Lloyd. *Adapt-Dial* Bradley King. *Story* Richard Connell. *Photog* Ernest Hallor. *Film Ed* Edward Schroeder.

Cast: Jack Mulhall *(Pat McGlone/Danny McGlone)*, Lila Lee *(Katie Dean)*, Aggie Herring *(Mrs. Dean)*, Earl Pingree *(Cuneo)*, Will Walling *(police captain)*, E. H. Calvert *(police lieutenant)*, Maurice Black *(Beefy Barker)*, Lucien Littlefield *(census taker)*, Pat Harmon.

Crook melodrama. Of twin brothers, Pat and Danny McGlone, one is a policeman, the other, a crook. Both love Katie, daughter of their foster mother, Mrs. Dean. During a raid on a silk warehouse, Pat shoots the driver of the getaway truck as it passes him, and he notices Danny in the truck. When the gang tells Danny that they plan to kill Pat, he finds Pat on his beat, knocks him unconscious, exchanges clothes with him, and accepts the bullets meant for his brother. *Twins. Brothers. Foster mothers. Police. Gangs. Self-sacrifice.*

THE DARK SWAN **F2.1213**

Warner Brothers Pictures. Nov **1924** [New York premiere; released 7 Dec; c1 Nov 1924; LP20762]. Si; b&w. 35mm. 7 reels, 6,700 ft.

Dir Millard Webb. *Adapt* Fred Jackson. *Photog* David Abel, Millard Webb.

Cast: Marie Prevost *(Eve Quinn)*, Monte Blue *(Lewis Dike)*, Helene Chadwick *(Cornelia Quinn)*, John Patrick *(Wilfred Meadows)*, Lilyan Tashman *(Sybil Johnson)*, Vera Lewis *(Mrs. Quinn)*, Carlton Miller *(Tim Fontanelle)*, Mary MacLaren *(Mary Robinson)*, Arthur Rankin *(Clifford Raynes)*.

Drama. Source: Ernest Pascal, *The Dark Swan* (New York, 1924). "Because she is a clever vamp, Eve Quinn has generally had her way with men, while her sister Cornelia, a quiet, deep-thinking girl, cannot bring herself to deliberately pursue them. So Eve wins Lewis Dike, whom Cornelia loves. Immediately after her marriage Eve begins a series of dangerous adventures with Wilfred Meadows. Lewis learns of them and endeavors to reason with his wife, but she will not listen to him. As Cornelia is sailing for Europe, Lewis meets her at the dock, tells her that he has made a mistake in marrying Eve, that they are to be divorced and that he loves Cornelia. They part with mutual assurances of a future meeting." (*Moving Picture World,* 29 Nov 1924, p545.) *Sisters. Flappers. Marriage. Infidelity. Divorce.*

DARKENED ROOMS **F2.1214**

Paramount Famous Lasky Corp. 23 Nov **1929** [c22 Nov 1929; LP870]. Sd (Movietone); b&w. 35mm. 7 reels, 6,066 ft. [Also si.]

Dir Louis Gasnier. *Titl* Richard H. Digges, Jr. *Adapt-Dial* Patrick Kearney, Melville Baker. *Photog* Archie J. Stout. *Film Ed* Frances Marsh.

Cast: Evelyn Brent *(Ellen)*, Neil Hamilton *(Emory Jago)*, Doris Hill *(Joyce Clayton)*, David Newell *(Billy)*, Gale Henry *(Madame Silvara)*, Wallace MacDonald *(Bert Nelson)*, Blanche Craig *(Mrs. Fogarty)*, E. H. Calvert *(Mr. Clayton)*, Sammy Bricker *(sailor)*.

Mystery melodrama. Source: Philip Hamilton Gibbs, "Darkened Rooms," in *Cosmopolitan Magazine* (vol 84, Mar–Jun 1928). Emory Jago, a boardwalk photographer who makes false photographs for Madame Silvara, a fake seeress, wants himself to benefit from the profits of spiritualism. Ellen, an unemployed chorus girl, faints from exhaustion when she visits his studio, and he engages her to act as his "medium." Madame Silvara arranges an appointment for a seance at the home of wealthy Mr. Clayton; they learn that his daughter, Joyce, now engaged to Billy, once loved an aviator who died in a crash; and gaining her confidence, Emory lures her to his studio, but Billy intervenes and takes her away. When the girl returns for another seance, Ellen, determined to queer Emory's game, engages Bert Nelson, an actor friend, to pose as the dead lover, and in sepulchral tones he announces Emory to be a fake. Emory is reconciled with Ellen, unaware of her spurious cure. *Photographers. Seers. Chorus girls. Actors. Spiritualism. Divination.*

DARKENED SKIES *see* **DARK SKIES**

DARKNESS AND DAYLIGHT **F2.1215**

Dist Bancroft. **1923.** Si; b&w. 35mm. [Feature length assumed.]

Dir Albert Plummer.

Melodrama(?). No information about the nature of this film has been found.

DARLING *see* **COME ON OVER**

THE DARLING OF NEW YORK (Universal-Jewel) **F2.1216**

Universal Pictures. 3 Dec **1923** [c24 Oct 1923; LP19546]. Si; b&w. 35mm. 6 reels, 6,260 ft.

Dir King Baggot. *Scen* Raymond L. Schrock. *Story* King Baggot, Raymond L. Schrock. *Cont* Adrian Johnson. *Photog* John Stumar.

Cast: Baby Peggy Montgomery *(Santussa)*, Sheldon Lewis *(Giovanni)*, Gladys Brockwell *(Light Fingered Kitty)*, Pat Hartigan *(Big Mike)*, Frank Currier *(Grandfather Van Dyne)*, Junior Coughlan *(The Ross Kid)*, Dorothy Hagan *(Mrs. Ross)*, Estelle Goulder *(governess)*, Carl Stockdale *(Soulful Sid)*, William H. Turner *(Close, The Master Mind)*, Jose Devere *(Florrie)*, William Jack Quinn *(Ice Malone)*, Max Davidson *(Solomon Levinsky)*, Emma Steele *(Mrs. Levinsky)*, Walter "Spec" O'Donnell *(Willie)*, Frederick Esmelton *(Norwood)*, Betty Francisco *(Frances)*, Anderson Smith *(Bice)*.

Melodrama. Santussa, an orphan who becomes separated from her nurse en route to America to live with her grandfather, is cared for by gangsters who hide their stolen jewels in her ragdoll. In New York, Big Mike, finding

Santussa a nuisance, dumps her and the doll in a trash can, where a newsboy finds her. After several adventures, Santussa finds her grandfather, the jewels are handed over to customs officials, and the gang of crooks is reformed. *Orphans. Gangs. Criminals—Rehabilitation. Smuggling. Dolls. New York City.*

Note: Working title: *Wanted, a Home.*

THE DARLING OF THE RICH **F2.1217**

B. B. Productions. 6 Dec **1922** [New York opening; released 15 Jan 1923]. Si; b&w. 35mm. 6 reels, 6,144 ft.

Prod Whitman Bennett. *Dir* John G. Adolfi. *Adapt-Scen* Dorothy Farnum. *Photog* Edward Paul.

Cast: Betty Blythe *(Charmion Winship)*, Gladys Leslie *(Lizzie Callahan)*, Jane Jennings *(Jane Winship)*, Montague Love *(Peyton Martin)*, Charles Gerard *(Torrence Welch)*, Leslie Austin *(Mason Lawrence)*, Julia Swayne Gordon *(Dippy Helen)*, Albert Hackett *(Fred Winship)*, Walter Walker *(Mike Callahan)*, A. Gowin *(detective)*, Rita Maurice *(The Baby)*.

Melodrama. Source: Leonard Merrick and Michael Morton, *The Imposter; a Drama* (New York opening: 20 Dec 1910). Charmion Winship is left penniless by her father. She goes to New York and there is hired by a gang of crooks to pose as a princess who is selling her jewels for relief money. A rich suitor and former admirer are rivals, and the latter, who once saved her life, wins her hand. *Gangs. Imposture. Poverty. Wealth. New York City.*

DARWIN WAS RIGHT **F2.1218**

Fox Film Corp. 26 Oct **1924** [c26 Oct 1924; LP20750]. Si; b&w. 35mm. 5 reels, 4,992 ft.

Pres by William Fox. *Dir* Lewis Seiler. *Story-Scen* Edward Moran. *Photog* Jay Turner.

Cast: Nell Brantley *(Alice)*, George O'Hara *(Robert Lee)*, Stanley Blystone *(Courtney Lawson)*, Dan Mason *(Henry Baldwin)*, Lon Poff *(Egbert Swift)*, Bud Jamison *(Alexander)*, Myrtle Sterling *(Liza)*, Nora Cecil *(Aunt Priscilla)*, David Kirby *(The Crook)*.

Farce. Just as he is about to experiment with an elixir of youth, Prof. Henry Baldwin is kidnaped by Courtney Lawson with his secretary, Egbert Swift, and his butler, Alexander, and placed in an asylum. A runaway dogcart deposits three babies in the house, and three escaped chimpanzees take their place. As a result, Alice and Priscilla Baldwin are led to believe that the professor has taken an overdose and has proved that Darwin was correct in theorizing that man is descended from the monkey. There are merry chases when the researchers escape and are pursued by asylum attendants. The villains and the chimpanzees are finally routed. *Scientists. Infants. Evolution. Insane asylums. Charles Darwin. Chimpanzees.*

DASHING THRU **F2.1219**

Hercules Film Productions. *Dist* Bud Barsky Corp. 26 Jun **1925** [New York State license]. Si; b&w. 35mm. 5 reels, 4,900 ft.

Cast: Frank Merrill, Kathryn McGuire, James Mason, Emily Gerdes, Harry McCoy.

Melodrama(?). No information about the nature of this film has been found.

THE DAUGHTER OF CROOKED ALLEY *see* **CROOKED ALLEY**

THE DAUGHTER OF DAWN **F2.1220**

Chief Buffalo Bear–Princess Buffalo Bear. 2 Apr **1924** [New York State license]. Si; b&w. 35mm. 5 reels.

Drama(?). No information about the nature of this film has been found. *Indians of North America.*

DAUGHTER OF DEVIL DAN **F2.1221**

Buffalo Motion Picture Co. 22 Jul **1921** [trade review]. Si; b&w. 35mm. [Feature length assumed.]

Cast: Irma Harrison, Kempton Greene.

Melodrama. "High-spirited daughter of Louisville gentleman with gray moustache and imperiale married 'Devil Dan' against her father's wishes and Dan is killed by a moonshiner. Young wife is seen on her deathbed, unforgiven by irate father. She gives villainous attorney 'the papers' and her seven-year-old daughter. He steals the fortune and takes the child to the moonshiner's hut. Ten years pass. Child is young girl, uncouth and unkempt, but buxom. Dashing young revenue officer appears. She saves his life and escapes disguised as a boy. Young revenue officer visits girl's grandfather (son of his old schoolmate stuff). They walk on street and find girl as newsboy in a fight. They take her home, old colonel wants to adopt her. She explores garret in colonial home, finds crinoline dress her mother wore, dons it, old colonel sees resemblance to his daughter, cries 'My search for my granddaughter has ended.' Villainous lawyer and moonshiner kidnap girl. ... Young revenue officer to the rescue, villain-lawyer (who turns out to be hero's uncle) is shot in the melee, confesses and the clinch is finally arrived at." (*Variety,* 22 Jul 1921, p36.) *Moonshiners. Revenue agents. Grandfathers. Lawyers. Personal identity. Disguise. Louisville (Kentucky).*

A DAUGHTER OF LUXURY **F2.1222**

Famous Players–Lasky. *Dist* Paramount Pictures. 4 Dec **1922** [New York premiere; released 25 Dec; c2 Dec 1922; LP18671]. Si; b&w. 35mm. 5 reels, 4,538 ft.

Pres by Adolph Zukor. *Dir* Paul Powell. *Scen* Beulah Marie Dix. *Photog* Bert Baldridge.

Cast: Agnes Ayres *(Mary Fenton)*, Tom Gallery *(Blake Walford)*, Edith Yorke *(Ellen Marsh)*, Howard Ralston *(Bill Marsh)*, Edward Martindel *(Loftus Walford)*, Sylvia Ashton *(Mrs. Walford)*, Clarence Burton *(Red Conroy)*, ZaSu Pitts *(Mary Cosgrove)*, Robert Schable *(Charlie Owen)*, Bernice Frank *(Winnie)*, Dorothy Gordon *(Genevieve Fowler)*, Muriel McCormac *(Nancy)*.

Society comedy-drama. Source: Leonard Merrick and Michael Morton, *The Imposter* (New York opening: 20 Dec 1910). A lawsuit temporarily reduces Mary Fenton to poverty, and circumstances result in her posing as heiress Mary Cosgrove in the Walford mansion. The real Mary Cosgrove arrives and demands Mary's arrest. There are explanations, Mary foils an attempted jewel robbery, and the matter is happily resolved by the marriage of Mary and Blake Walford. *Poverty. Impersonation. Robbery. Lawsuits.*

A DAUGHTER OF THE CONGO **F2.1223**

Micheaux Pictures. 5 Apr **1930** [New York showing]. Talking sequences & mus score; b&w. 35mm. 9 reels, 7,934 ft. [Also si.]

Cast: Kathleen Noisette, Loretta Tucker, Clarence Reed, Willor Lee Guilford.

Melodrama(?). No information about the precise nature of this film has been found. *Negro life.*

THE DAUGHTER OF THE DON **F2.1224**

Sun Films. *Dist* Arrow Film Corp. Nov **1921.** Si; b&w. 35mm. 6 reels, 5,970 ft.

Cast: Hal Cooley *(Lieutenant Merritt)*, Marie McKeen *(Ysabel Carrillo)*, V. O. Whitehead *(Don José Carrillo)*, William Ramón Ehfe, Grant Churchill *(Eugene McNamara)*.

Historical romance. Source: Winifield Hogaboom, "Daughter of the Don" (publication undetermined). "The story deals with the love affair of a young American lieutenant and the daughter of a wealthy ranch owner in the days of 1847. The young couple have declared their love and the fortunes of war cause them to be separated for what seems forever. The shadows of war enter and the little valley near Los Angeles is in a turmoil. A British secret agent is eventually exposed and the two factions, the Americans and the native Californians, again declare peace." (*Moving Picture World,* 15 Apr 1922, p764.) *Secret agents. California—Mexican period. Los Angeles.*

Note: Country of origin undetermined.

A DAUGHTER OF THE LAW **F2.1225**

Universal Film Manufacturing Co. 15 Jul **1921** [c1 Aug 1921; LP16835]. Si; b&w. 35mm. 5 reels, 4,752 ft.

Dir Jack Conway. *Scen* Harvey Gates. *Photog* Bert Glennon.

Cast: Carmel Myers *(Nora Hayes)*, Jack O'Brien *(Jim Garth)*, Fred Kohler *(George Stacey)*, Jack Walters *(Slim Dolan)*, Dick La Reno *(Pata Marlowe)*, Charles Arling *(Inspector Hayes)*, Joe Bennett *(Eddie Hayes)*.

Crook melodrama. Source: Wadsworth Camp, "The Black Cap," in *Collier's* (65:10–11, 24 Jan 1920). Nora, daughter of Inspector Hayes, attempts to retrieve her erring brother Eddie from the underworld gang of George Stacey and to warn him of an impending roundup by the police. Nora is trapped and held prisoner, however, while Eddie is forced into a job with the gang. Nora escapes and informs her father of Eddie's predicament; Chief Detective Garth, who is in love with Nora, surrounds the gang with his men, and in the battle Eddie is killed by Stacey. The leader and his henchmen are convicted on Nora's testimony, but they escape and capture Nora, holding her for ransom and threatening to blind her with vitriol. Garth is captured, Nora bargains for his life, and eventually she gains possession of the vitriol. The gangsters are taken into custody, while Garth and Nora are united. *Brother-sister relationship. Detectives. Gangs. Police. Ransom. Kidnaping.*

A DAUGHTER OF THE SIOUX **F2.1226**
Davis Distributing Division. c28 Dec **1925** [LP22182]. Si; b&w. 35mm. 5 reels, 4,700 ft.

Dir Ben Wilson. *Adapt* George W. Pyper. *Photog* William Fildew. *Asst Dir* Archie Ricks.

Cast: Ben Wilson *(John Field)*, Neva Gerber *(Nanette)*, Robert Walker *(Eagle Wing)*, Fay Adams *(Trooper Kennedy)*, William Lowery *(Big Bill Hay)*, Rhody Hathaway *(Maj. John Webb)*.

Western melodrama. Source: Gen. Charles King, *A Daughter of the Sioux, a Tale of the Indian Frontier* (New York, 1903). John Field, a government surveyor, suspects that Nanette, known at Fort Frayne as the "daughter of the Sioux," is giving information about the fort's defenses to the Indians. Eagle Wing, a renegade, incites the Sioux to attack a number of isolated settlers, and John rides after him, bringing him back to the fort. An old scout recognizes Nanette, apparently an Indian squaw, as a white child stolen long ago by the Sioux. Nanette admits this truth and further reveals that Eagle Wing is, in actuality, the son of Big Bill Hay. John, who has fallen in love with the dark-browed Nanette, declares his love for her. *Surveyors. Scouts—Frontier. Spies. Sioux Indians. Parentage. Forts.*

DAUGHTERS OF DESIRE **F2.1227**
Excellent Pictures. 1 Mar **1929** [c27 Dec 1928; LP25954]. Si; b&w. 35mm. 6 reels.

Dir Burton King. *Scen-Titl* Isadore Bernstein. *Story* Janet Vale. *Photog* William Miller, Joseph Walters. *Film Ed* Betty Davis.

Cast: Irene Rich, Richard Tucker, June Nash, Julius Molnar, Jr., Jackie Searle, William Scott.

Melodrama. Bernice Burke accidentally kills Del Livingston when he becomes too friendly in a parked car. Louise Burke, Bernice's stepmother, assumes the blame for the shooting and is sentenced to 10 years in jail. She begins to serve her time, but Bernice, who has always resented Louise for marrying her father, has a change of heart and confesses her own guilt. Bernice is placed on probation and at last comes to love Louise as much as she loved her own mother. *Stepmothers. Manslaughter. Injustice.*

DAUGHTERS OF PLEASURE **F2.1228**
B. F. Zeidman. *Dist* Principal Pictures. 29 Feb **1924.** Si; b&w. 35mm. 6 reels.

Dir William Beaudine. *Titl* Harvey Thew. *Adapt* Eve Unsell. *Story* Caleb Proctor. *Photog* Charles Van Enger. *Art Dir* Joseph Wright. *Film Ed* Edward McDermott.

Cast: Marie Prevost *(Marjory Hadley)*, Monte Blue *(Kent Merrill)*, Clara Bow *(Lila Millas)*, Edythe Chapman *(Mrs. Hadley)*, Wilfred Lucas *(Mark Hadley)*.

Domestic melodrama. Newly rich Mark Hadley drifts from his old-fashioned wife into a secret liason with Lila Millas, a pretty French girl. At the same time, he advises his daughter, Marjory, to break her ties with Kent Merrill, a "chippy-chasing young rounder." Marjory visits Lila, who was her school friend in Paris, and is shocked to find her father there. She upbraids him and, heedless of his previous advice, goes with Merrill to his summer place. En route, they are sobered by an automobile accident, and they get married. Hadley confesses his misdeeds to his wife and is forgiven. *Nouveaux riches. Cads. French. Family life. Fatherhood. Automobile accidents.*

DAUGHTERS OF THE NIGHT **F2.1229**
Fox Film Corp. 9 Nov **1924** [c26 Oct 1924; LP20722]. Si; b&w. 35mm. 6 reels, 5,470 or 5,740 ft.

Pres by William Fox. *Dir* Elmer Clifton. *Story-Scen* Willard Robertson. *Story? (see note)* R. T. Barrett.

Cast: Orville Caldwell *(Billy Roberts)*, Alyce Mills *(Betty Blair)*, Phelps Decker *(Doc Long)*, Alice Chapin *(Grandma Backer)*, Warner Richmond *(Lawyer Kilmaster)*, Bobbie Perkins *(Eloise Dabb)*, Clarice Vance *(Mrs. Dabb)*, Claude Cooper *(Mr. Dabb)*, Willard Robertson *(Professor Woodbury)*, Charles Slattery *(Dick Oliver)*, Henry Sands *(Jimmy Roberts)*.

Crook melodrama. Disinherited by their father when they are arrested for brawling, Jimmy Roberts joins his crook friends, and Billy Roberts decides to go straight, gets a job as a telephone lineman, and falls in love with Betty Blair, a telephone operator. In making a getaway from a bank robbery, Jimmy ducks into the telephone building, which catches on fire. The gang cut the wires, but Betty stays at her post until Billy repairs them and rescues her. Jimmy, however, perishes in the fire. Billy and Betty return to his forgiving family. *Brothers. Telephone operators. Linemen. Bank robberies. Fires.*

Note: Working title: *Crossed Wires*. Copyright records credit R. T. Barrett with story.

DAUGHTERS OF THE RICH **F2.1230**
B. P. Schulberg Productions. *Dist* Al Lichtman Corp. 15 Jun **1923** [c15 Jun 1923; LP19112]. Si; b&w. 35mm. 6 reels, 6,073 ft.

Pres by B. P. Schulberg. *Dir* Louis Gasnier. *Adapt* Olga Printzlau, Josephine Quirk. *Photog* Karl Struss.

Cast—Released Version: Miriam Cooper *(Maud Barhyte)*, Gaston Glass *(Gerald Welden)*, Ethel Shannon *(Mademoiselle Giselle)*, Ruth Clifford *(Sally Malakoff)*, Josef Swickard *(Maud's father)*, Truly Shattuck *(Sally's mother)*.

Cast—Copyright Version: Gaston Glass *(Gerard Walden)*, Ruth Clifford *(Sally Malakoff)*, Ethel Shannon *(Mademoiselle Giselle)*, Marjorie Daw *(Maud Barhyte)*, Stuart Holmes *(Count Malakoff)*.

Society melodrama. Source: Edgar Saltus, *Daughters of the Rich* (New York, 1900). Maud Barhyte visits Paris with her fiancé, Gerald Welden, and her father. Sally Malakoff, Welden's childhood sweetheart whose marriage to the Duke Malakoff was arranged by her ambitious and title-hungry mother, entertains the three as her guests. By a series of misunderstandings Sally disrupts relations between Welden and his fiancée, causing Maud to return to America. Sally divorces the duke, and Welden, thinking Maud no longer loves him, marries Sally. Later, Welden discovers Sally's maneuverings and denounces her. Now an unhappy drug addict, Sally commits suicide, sending confessions to Maud exonerating Welden, already imprisoned on suspicion of murdering his wife. Maud presents the papers to police authorities, freeing Welden. *Nobility. Divorce. Narcotics. Wealth. Suicide. Murder. Paris.*

Note: Explanation of the difference in cast between the copyright version and the final release version is that the emphasis of the story had been shifted from showing Sally Malakoff, played by Ruth Clifford, as the female lead to presenting Miriam Cooper, playing Maud Barhyte, in the leading role. In the copyright material Marjorie Daw plays Maud Barhyte as the second leading lady and Miriam Cooper does not appear in the cast.

DAUGHTERS OF TODAY **F2.1231**
Sturgeon-Hubbard Co. *Dist* Selznick Distributing Corp. 2 Feb **1924** [c2 Feb 1924; LP19990]. Si; b&w. 35mm. 7 reels, ca7,300 ft.

Dir Rollin Sturgeon. *Story* Lucien Hubbard. *Photog* Milton Moore.

Cast: Patsy Ruth Miller *(Lois Whittall)*, Ralph Graves *(Ralph Adams)*, Edna Murphy *(Mabel Vandegrift)*, Edward Hearn *(Peter Farnham)*, Philo McCullough *(Reggy Adams)*, George Nichols *(Dirk Vandegrift)*, Gertrude Claire *(Ma Vandegrift)*, Phillips Smalley *(Leigh Whittall)*, ZaSu Pitts *(Lorena)*, H. J. Herbert *(Calnan)*, Fontaine La Rue *(Mrs. Mantell)*, Truman Van Dyke *(Dick)*, Dorothy Wood *(Flo)*, Marjorie Bonner *(Maisie)*.

Society melodrama. Country girl Mabel Vandegrift enrolls in a fashionable city college and there she joins a fast-moving crowd. During a houseparty Reggy Adams tries to force his attentions on her, but she escapes. Later, when he is found dead, she is accused of murdering him. Her country sweetheart, Peter Farnham, solves the mystery, and all ends happily. *Jazz life. College life. Murder.*

Note: Originally released in May 1923 as *What's Your Daughter Doing.*

DAUGHTERS WHO PAY **F2.1232**
Banner Productions. 10 May **1925** [c6 Mar 1925; LP21211]. Si; b&w. 35mm. 6 reels, 5,700 ft.

Dir George Terwilliger. *Story* William B. Laub. *Photog* Edward Paul, Charles Davis, Murphy Darling.

Cast: Marguerite De La Motte *(Sonia/Margaret Smith)*, John Bowers *(Dick Foster)*, Barney Sherry *(Foster, Sr.)*.

Melodrama. Margaret Smith leads a double life: during the week she is "Sonia," a Russian cafe dancer, and on Sundays she returns to her house in the suburbs, where she is known as "Miss Smith." Dick Foster, the son of a millionaire, is infatuated with "Sonia"; Bob Smith, Margaret's brother, is employed by the elder Foster and is weak enough to embezzle $10,000 from him. Margaret goes to old man Foster and begs him to be lenient with Bob; when he refuses, she returns as "Sonia" and makes a deal with him: she will disillusion Foster's son if he will let her brother go. Margaret is later responsible for the wholesale arrest of a gang of Red agents by the Secret Service. She then reveals her deception to the Fosters, and she and Dick decide to be married. *Dancers. Communists. Secret service. Brother-sister relationship. Embezzlement. Dual lives.*

DAVY CROCKETT AT THE FALL OF THE ALAMO **F2.1233**

Sunset Productions. 1 Aug **1926.** Si; b&w. 35mm. 6 reels, 5,540 ft.

Dir Robert North Bradbury. *Titl* Clover Roscoe. *Adapt* Ben Ali Newman. *Photog* William Brown, Jr., Elvert M. McManigal. *Art Dir* Wilson Silsby, Paul Cosgrove. *Film Ed* Della M. King. *Asst Dir* Jack Pierce, William Dagnell.

Cast: Cullen Landis *(Davy Crockett)*, Kathryn McGuire *(Alice Blake)*, Joe Rickson *(Colonel Travis)*, Bob Fleming *(Colonel Bowie)*, Ralph McCullough *(Colonel Bonham)*, Fletcher Norton *(General Santa Anna)*, Anne Berryman *(Kate Kennedy)*, Jay Morley *(Zachary Kennedy)*, Thomas Lingham *("Dandy Dick" Heston)*, Frank Rice *(Lige Beardsley)*, Betty Brown *(Myra Winkler)*, Bob Bradbury, Jr. *("Pinky" Smith)*, Steve Clemento *(Mose)*.

Western historical drama. No information about the precise nature of this film has been found. *Texas. Alamo. David Crockett. Antonio López de Santa Anna. William Barret Travis. James Bowie.*

Note: Also known as *With Davy Crockett at the Fall of the Alamo.*

THE DAWN OF A TOMORROW **F2.1234**

Famous Players–Lasky. *Dist* Paramount Pictures. ca23 Mar **1924** [New York premiere; released 14 Apr; c8 Apr 1924; LP20055]. Si; b&w. 35mm. 6 reels, 6,084 ft.

Pres by Adolph Zukor, Jesse L. Lasky. *Dir* George Melford. *Scen* Harvey Thew. *Photog* Charles G. Clarke.

Cast: Jacqueline Logan *(Glad)*, David Torrence *(Sir Oliver Holt)*, Raymond Griffith *(The Dandy)*, Roland Bottomley *(Arthur Holt)*, Harris Gordon *(Nod)*, Guy Oliver *(Black)*, Tempe Piggot *(Ginney)*, Mabel Van Buren *(Bet)*, Marguerite Clayton *(Madge)*, Alma Bennett *(Polly)*, Warren Rodgers *(Barney)*.

Crook melodrama. Source: Frances Hodgson Burnett, *The Dawn of a Tomorrow* (New York, 1906). Frances Hodgson Burnett, *The Dawn of a Tomorrow; a Play in Three Acts* (New York opening: 25 Jan 1909). Expecting to die soon or to go insane, Sir Oliver Holt disappears into the London slums intending to commit suicide; but he is dissuaded by Glad, a cheerful girl whose sweetheart (a burglar called "The Dandy") Sir Oliver has sent to obtain money from his safe. The Dandy discovers Arthur Holt, Sir Oliver's nephew, already looting the safe; and he (The Dandy) is framed for the murder of a policeman. When Glad appeals to Arthur for help, he attacks her, but The Dandy comes to the rescue, followed by the police. Sir Oliver arrives, establishes The Dandy's innocence, and makes the crook and Glad his wards. *Criminals—Rehabilitation. Robbery. Murder. Insanity. Suicide. Frameup. Slums. London.*

DAWN OF REVENGE **F2.1235**

Charles E. Bartlett Productions. *Dist* Aywon Film Corp. 1 Oct **1922.** Si; b&w. 35mm. 5 reels, ca4,800 ft.

Pres by Nathan Hirsh. *Dir* Bernard Sievel.

Cast: Richard C. Travers *(Judson Hall)*, Muriel Kingston *(Sherry Miles)*, Charles Graham *("Ace" Hall)*, Florence Foster *(Alice Blake Miles)*, Louis Dean *(Nelson Miles)*, May Daggert *(Baba)*.

Melodrama. "Ace" Hall is a bitter, half-crazed cripple as a result of losing Alice Blake to Nelson Miles and going over a cliff in a fight with Miles. He kidnaps the Mileses' infant son and rears the boy (Judson) as his own and later discovers that there is also a beautiful Miles daughter (Sherry). Plotting his final revenge, Hall maneuvers Judson into marriage to his own sister. At the wedding ceremony Alice learns Judson's identity, but she then reveals that Sherry was adopted. The young couple finds happiness; Hall dies in an explosion. *Cripples. Revenge. Incest. Kidnaping. Weddings.*

DAWN OF THE EAST **F2.1236**

Realart Pictures. *Dist* Paramount Pictures. Oct **1921** [c20 Sep 1921; LP16972]. Si; b&w. 35mm. 5 reels, 5,392 ft.

Dir E. H. Griffith. *Story-Scen* E. Lloyd Sheldon. *Photog* Gilbert Warrenton. *Asst Dir* J. Malcolm Dunn.

Cast: Alice Brady *(Countess Natalya)*, Kenneth Harlan *(Roger Strong)*, Michio Itow *(Sotan)*, America Chedister *(Mariya)*, Betty Carpenter *(Sonya)*, Harriet Ross *(Mrs. Strong)*, Sam Kim *(Wu Ting)*, Frank Honda *(Liang)*, H. Takemi *(Kwan)*, Patricio Reyes *(Chang)*.

Melodrama. Countess Natalya, a Russian refugee, supports herself and her invalid sister, Sonya, by dancing and singing in a Shanghai cafe. Eager to escape this life, she falls into the net of Sotan, who pretends friendship for her and arranges an official betrothal between Natalya and wealthy Wu Ting. With the betrothal money Natalya and Sonya escape to the United States, where Natalya marries American diplomat Roger Strong. Later, Sotan, who is secretly plotting to restore the Russian monarchy, follows her to America and attempts to blackmail her unless she gives information about Strong's mission to Pekin. But she denounces Sotan to Wu Ting, who, learning of Sotan's monarchist plot, kills him and, in gratitude, destroys the evidence of his marriage to Natalya. *Sisters. Diplomats. Monarchists. Entertainers. Political refugees. Blackmail. Shanghai.*

THE DAWN PATROL **F2.1237**

First National Pictures. 10 Jul **1930** [New York opening; released 20 Aug; c25 Aug 1930; LP1547]. Sd (Vitaphone); b&w. 35mm. 12 reels, 9,500 ft.

Prod Robert North. *Dir* Howard Hawks. *Adapt-Dial* Howard Hawks, Dan Totheroh, Seton I. Miller. *Photog* Ernest Haller. *Film Ed* Ray Curtiss.

Cast: Richard Barthelmess *(Dick Courtney)*, Douglas Fairbanks, Jr. *(Douglas Scott)*, Neil Hamilton *(Major Brand)*, William Janney *(Gordon Scott)*, James Finlayson *(field sergeant)*, Clyde Cook *(Bott)*, Gardner James *(Ralph Hollister)*, Edmund Breon *(Lieutenant Bathurst)*, Frank McHugh *(Flaherty)*, Jack Ackroyd, Harry Allen *(mechanics)*.

War melodrama. Source: John Monk Saunders, "The Flight Commander" (publication undetermined). Major Brand, squadron commander of the 59th British Squadron in France, fears he is becoming an executioner of his young fliers who are being sent to their deaths in inferior planes. Brand breaks off relations with ace Dick Courtney when he and his best friend, Scott, defy orders to go over German lines. After a narrow escape, Courtney is made squadron commander by Brand, who is relieved at that time. Under the strain of his new responsibility, Courtney begins to drink. Scott's younger brother, Gordon, arrives as a flier with the new replacements, and when Courtney sends him to his death, Scott holds him personally responsible and their friendship is broken. Brand, assigned to blow up a munition dump behind German lines, returns to the squadron. Scott demands to go on the one-man mission, and Courtney agrees but plies him with liquor and goes out himself to avenge Gordon's death. The mission is successful, but Courtney is killed; and that night a German flier drops the information to Scott, who is waiting for his friend's return. *Aviators. Brothers. Friendship. Revenge. World War I. Great Britain—Royal Flying Corps.*

THE DAWN TRAIL **F2.1238**

Columbia Pictures. 28 Nov **1930** [c16 Dec 1930; LP1818]. Sd (Movietone); b&w. 35mm. 7 reels, 5,850 ft.

Prod Harry Cohn. *Dir* Christy Cabanne. *Adapt* John Thomas Neville. *Story* Forrest Sheldon. *Photog* Ted McCord. *Film Ed* James Sweeney. *Sd Engr* Bruce Piersall.

Cast: Buck Jones *(Larry)*, Miriam Seegar *(June)*, Charles Morton *(Mart)*, Erville Alderson *(Denton)*, Edward Le Saint *(Amos)*, Charles L. King *(Skeets)*, Hank Mann *(Cock Eye)*, Vester Pegg *(Mac)*, Slim Whittaker *(Steve)*, Charles Brinley *(Nestor)*, Inez Gomez *(Maria)*, Bob Burns *(Settler)*, Robert Fleming *(Henchman)*, Violet Axzelle *(Molly)*, Buck Connors *(Jim Anderson)*, Jack Curtis *(Hank)*.

Western melodrama. Dissension arises between cattlemen in Osage County, Texas, and sheepherders who have settled there and use the same watering stream in the center of the homesteaders' settlement. Mart Denton, son of a wealthy cattleman, quarrels with and kills one of the homesteaders, thus placing Sheriff Larry Williams in a delicate position; for he is Mart's best friend and is engaged to Mart's sister, June. However, he arrests Mart, incensing the other cattlemen, who help him escape, wounding Larry. June rescues him and takes him to the Denton home, concealing him in her room; in a confrontation with Mart, Larry subdues the cattlemen. Denton, mistaking his son for a sheepherder, kills him. His death brings about peace in Osage County, and June, realizing that Larry merely had done his duty, assures him of her love. *Cattlemen. Sheepherders. Homesteaders. Sheriffs. Water rights. Friendship. Fatherhood. Texas.*

THE DAY OF FAITH **F2.1239**

Goldwyn Pictures. *Dist* Goldwyn-Cosmopolitan Distributing Corp. 21 Oct **1923** [c11 Nov 1923; LP19742]. Si; b&w. 35mm. 7 reels, 6,557 ft.

Dir Tod Browning. *Adapt* June Mathis, Katharine Kavanaugh. *Photog*

William Fildew.

Cast: Eleanor Boardman *(Jane Maynard)*, [Frederick] Tyrone Power *(Michael Anstell)*, Raymond Griffith *(Tom Barnett)*, Wallace MacDonald *(John Anstell)*, Ford Sterling *(Montreal Sammy)*, Charles Conklin *(Yegg Darby)*, Ruby Lafayette *(Granny Maynard)*, Jane Mercer *(Red Johnston's child)*, Edward Martindel *(Uncle Mortimer)*, Winter Hall *(Bland Hendricks)*, Emmett King *(Simmons)*, Jack Curtis *(Red Johnson)*, Frederick Vroom *(Marley Maynard)*, John Curry *(Isaac)*, Henry Herbert *(Samuel Jackson)*, Myles McCarthy *(Kelly)*, Robert Dudley *(Morris)*.

Melodrama. Source: Arthur Somers Roche, *The Day of Faith* (Boston, 1921). Jane Maynard opens a mission in memory of philanthropist Bland Hendricks. John Anstell, son of a powerful and selfish millionaire, Michael Anstell, falls in love with Jane, to the old man's disapproval. Anstell tries to undermine Jane's work by hiring reporter Tom Barnett to write an unfavorable story about the mission. After a visit, Barnett is so convinced, by Jane's sincerity, of the value of the endeavor that he volunteers his help. Anstell pretends to support the mission to gain public favor, but a mob seeking revenge for wrongs done by Anstell attacks the son, John, and beats him to death. Anstell sees his mistakes, awakens to the real purpose of Jane's work, and reforms. Jane and Barnett continue together at the mission. *Social workers. Millionaires. Reporters. Revenge. Philanthropy. Missions.*

DAYTIME WIVES **F2.1240**

R-C Pictures. *Dist* Film Booking Offices of America. 2 Sep **1923** [c7 Aug 1923; LP19280]. Si; b&w. 35mm. 7 reels, 6,651 ft.

Dir Emile Chautard. *Adapt* Wyndham Gittens, Helmer Bergman. *Story* Lenore Coffee, John Goodrich. *Photog* Lucien Andriot.

Cast: Derelys Perdue *(Ruth Holt)*, Wyndham Standing *(Elwood Adams)*, Grace Darmond *(Francine Adams)*, William Conklin *(Amos Martin)*, Edward Hearn *(Ben Branscom)*, Katherine Lewis *(Betty Branscom)*, Kenneth Gibson *(Larry Gilfeather)*, Christina Mott *(Celeste)*, Jack Carlyle *(Jack Jagner)*, Craig Biddle, Jr. *(a laborer)*.

Melodrama. Ruth Holt, secretary to architect Elwood Adams, assists him during a business crisis and effects a reconciliation between him and his estranged wife, Francine. *Secretaries. Architects. Marriage.*

DEAD GAME **F2.1241**

Universal Pictures. 23 or 24 Apr **1923** [New York premiere; released 23 May; c27 Mar 1923; LP18815]. Si; b&w. 35mm. 5 reels, 4,819 ft.

Dir-Story-Scen Edward Sedgwick. *Photog* Charles Kaufman.

Cast: Ed (Hoot) Gibson *("Katy" Didd)*, Robert McKim *(Prince Tetlow)*, Harry Carter *(Jenks)*, Laura La Plante *(Alice Mason)*, William Welsh *(Harlu)*, Tony West *(Hiram)*, William A. Steele *(Sam Antone)*.

Western melodrama. "Katy" Didd holds up the stage in which his sweetheart, Alice Mason, is traveling to her wedding to Prince Tetlow, to whom her guardian insists that she be married. Katy hides her at his ranch, but Tetlow finds her and abandons Katy in the desert. He finds his way back, however, carries Alice from the church just as she is repeating her wedding vows, and convinces the townspeople that they should rid themselves of Tetlow and his henchmen. *Guardians. Royalty. Ranchers. Weddings. Deserts.*

Note: Working title: *Katy Didd.*

THE DEAD LINE **F2.1242**

Independent Pictures. *Dist* Film Booking Offices of America. 27 Jun **1926** [c19 Jun 1926; LP22829]. Si; b&w. 35mm. 5 reels, 5,200 ft.

Prod Jesse J. Goldburg. *Dir* Jack Nelson. *Story-Cont* Barr Cross. *Photog* Art Reeves.

Cast: Bob Custer *(Sonora Slim)*, Nita Cavalier *(Alice Wilson)*, Robert McKim *("Silver Sam" McGee)*, Tom Bay *(Snake Smeed)*, Marianna Moya *(Lolita)*, Billy Franey *("Extra" Long)*, Gino Corrado *(Juan Álavarez)*.

Western melodrama. Sonora Slim discovers Dry Wash Wilson dying in the desert and learns he has discovered a mine and has been shot by a bandit. Sonora is arrested by two rangers, but he disarms them and rides on killer Snake Smeed's trail. Smeed joins his partner, Silver Sam McGee, in San Blas, across the border, while Sonora confides in Juan Álvarez, captain of the *rurales*, about the killing; but Juan breaks with Sonora when he learns that Lolita, his beloved, is in love with him. Meanwhile, Alice Wilson, daughter of the slain man, and "Extra" Long are on their way to the mine and believe Sonora to be the wanted man. Lolita overhears McGee and Smeed plot to capture Sonora and warns Álvarez. Sonora saves the lives of Alice and Extra when their buckboard crashes over a cliff, and they are ambushed by the bandits but rescued by the *rurales*. *Miners. Rurales. Bandits. Murder. Texas. Mexican border.*

DEAD MAN'S CURVE **F2.1243**

FBO Pictures. 15 Jan **1928** [c15 Jan 1928; LP24865]. Si; b&w. 35mm. 6 reels, 5,511 ft.

Dir Richard Rosson. *Titl* Randolph Bartlett. *Adapt* Ewart Adamson. *Photog* Phillip Tannura. *Film Ed* Ewart Adamson. *Asst Dir* James Dugan.

Cast: Douglas Fairbanks, Jr. *(Vernon Keith)*, Sally Blane *(Ethel Hume)*, Charles Byer *(George Marshall)*, Arthur Metcalfe *(Fergus Hume)*, Kit Guard *(Goof Goober)*, Byron Douglas *(Benton)*, James Mason *(Derne)*.

Action drama. Vernon Keith, racing driver for Aladdin Motors, has finished third in a race and contends that the car's design is faulty. George Marshall, chief engineer of the company and Vernon's rival for the affections of Ethel Hume, daughter of the company's president, defends his model and blames Keith's cowardice for the loss of first place. Keith redesigns the engine on his own and offers to sell it to Aladdin Motors. When Mr. Hume refuses to purchase it, Keith quits his job to find a backer for the design. Ethel Hume, aware of Keith's need for a backer, secretly arranges to finance the project. Keith enters a new race, wins it, and at the finish discovers that Ethel has backed him. The final scene finds them in each other's arms. *Engineers. Automobile racing. Automobiles.*

DEAD OR ALIVE **F2.1244**

Unity Photoplays. *Dist* Arrow Film Corp. Mar **1921.** Si; b&w. 35mm. 5 reels.

Ben Wilson Production. *Dir* Dell Henderson.

Cast: Jack Hoxie *(Jack Stokes)*, Joseph Girard *(Sheriff Lamar)*, Marin Sais *(his wife)*, C. Ray Florhe *(Nate Stratton)*, Wilbur McGaugh *(Tom Stone)*, Evelyn Nelson *(Beulah, his sister)*.

Western melodrama. "Tom Stone assumes the name of his dead pal, Jim Bland, and then our hero comes along and assumes the name of Tom Stone. With a sheriff after both, there are many thrilling encounters, due to the mix-up of identities. Hard riding, plenty of action and small love interest are embodied in western of present day." (*Motion Picture News Booking Guide,* 1:28, Dec 1921.) *Cowboys. Sheriffs. Personal identity.*

DEADSHOT CASEY **F2.1245**

Dist Krelbar Pictures, Collwyn Pictures. 21 Jul **1928** [New York State license]. Si; b&w. 35mm. 5 reels.

Cast: Al Hoxie, Al Richmond, Chris Allen, Berth Rae.

Western melodrama(?). No information about the nature of this film has been found.

Note: May have been produced by Anchor Film Distributors in 1926.

THE DEADWOOD COACH **F2.1246**

Fox Film Corp. 7 Dec **1924** [c6 Dec 1924; LP20874]. Si; b&w. 35mm. 7 reels, 6,346 ft.

Pres by William Fox. *Dir-Scen* Lynn Reynolds. *Photog* Dan Clark.

Cast—The Prolog: Frank Coffyn *(Walter Gordon)*, Jane Keckley *(Mrs. Gordon)*, Ernest Butterworth *(Jimmie Gordon)*.

Cast—The Play: Tom Mix *(The Orphan)*, George Bancroft *(Tex Wilson)*, De Witt Jennings *(Jim Shields)*, Buster Gardner *(Bill Howland)*, Lucien Littlefield *(Charlie Winter)*, Doris May *(Helen Shields)*, Norma Wills *(Mrs. Shields)*, Sid Jordan *(Need)*, Nora Cecil *(Matilda Shields)*.

Western melodrama. Source: Clarence E. Mulford, *The Orphan* (New York, 1908). When he was a boy, growing up in the Bad Lands of Dakota Territory, Jimmie Gordon's parents were killed by Tex Wilson, a brutal bandit. Jimmie swore vengeance, and, known only as The Orphan, he has spent the subsequent years looking for Wilson. At last, hot on the trail of the Wilson gang, The Orphan prevents a holdup of the Deadwood Stage but loses Wilson. He meets one of the passengers on the stage, Helen Shields, the daughter of the local sheriff, and accompanies her to town, only to discover that her father is an old friend whom he once saved from the Indians. As the men talk, Helen learns of The Orphan's tragic past, and the two are soon in love. On their wedding day, the venomous Wilson interrupts the ceremony, insults the unarmed bridegroom, and kidnaps Helen. Wilson makes his escape in the Deadwood Coach, closely followed by The Orphan. When the coach breaks down, Wilson abandons the unharmed girl and tries to escape on foot. The Orphan and Wilson fight it out on the edge of a precipice, and Wilson is thrown to his death. *Orphans. Gangs. Indians of North America. Stagelines. Revenge. Dakota Territory. Bad Lands of Dakota.*

Note: Exteriors were shot on location in the Dakota Bad Lands.

DEARIE **F2.1247**
Warner Brothers Pictures. 18 Jun **1927** [c11 Jun 1927; LP24072]. Si; b&w. 35mm. 6 reels, 5,897 ft.
Dir Archie Mayo. *Scen* Anthony Coldewey. *Titl* Jack Jarmuth. *Story* Carolyn Wells. *Camera* David Abel. *Asst Dir* Henry Blanke.
Cast: Irene Rich *(Sylvia Darling)*, William Collier, Jr. *(Stephen, her son)*, Edna Murphy *(Ethel Jordan)*, Anders Randolf *(Samuel Manley)*, Richard Tucker *(Luigi)*, Arthur Rankin *(Paul)*, David Mir *(Max)*, Douglas Gerrard *(Manley's friend)*, Violet Palmer *(Sylvia's maid)*.
Society melodrama. Finding herself in dire circumstances, the widowed Sylvia Darling determines that her son, Stephen, will complete his college education and develop his supposed literary talents; thus, she accepts a contract as singer in a Broadway nightclub, billed as "Dearie," and becomes an immediate sensation. Samuel Manley, a wealthy publisher who is attracted to Sylvia, allows her to entertain in his home, escorted by Luigi, the club proprietor. At college, Stephen and his self-styled roommates, Paul and Max, are expelled; and he romances Edna, the publisher's niece, who promises to promote his book with her uncle. Unimpressed by the egotistical youth, Manley rejects his work, and enraged, Stephen accidentally wounds his mother; furthermore, he denounces her when he learns that she is a cabaret entertainer, but he repents and is forgiven. Sylvia marries Luigi. *Widows. Egotists. Singers. Authors. Publishers. College life. Motherhood. Nightclubs. New York City—Broadway.*

DEATH VALLEY **F2.1248**
Furst Wells Productions. *Dist* First Division Distributors. 1 Sep **1927.** Si; b&w. 35mm. 6 reels, 5,960 ft.
Pres by I. E. Chadwick. *Dir* Paul Powell. *Story* Raymond Wells. *Photog* Frank Heisler, Clifton Maupin, Joseph Walker.
Cast: Carroll Nye *(boy)*, Rada Rae *(girl)*, Sam Allen *(her father)*, Raymond Wells *(man)*, Grace Lord *(woman)*, Rex *(dog)*.
Drama. A boy finds gold in Death Valley. The villain, knowing of the boy's good fortune, is determined to steal his gold; but too cowardly to do the job himself, he forces a woman to take the gold. Later he kills the woman only to meet his own death in the desert. The boy and his dog, Rex, find the body of the man along with the gold and take it to the girl and her father living in a deserted settlement. *Children. Greed. Murder. Deserts. Gold. Dogs.*

A DEBTOR TO THE LAW **F2.1249**
Norman Film Manufacturing Co. **1924.** Si; b&w. 35mm. 6 reels.
Cast: Henry Starr.
Western melodrama(?). No information about the precise nature of this film has been found. *Negro life.*

DECEIT **F2.1250**
Micheaux Film Corp. 1 Mar **1923** [scheduled release]. Si; b&w. 35mm. 6 reels.
Pres by Oscar Micheaux.
Cast: Evelyn Preer *(Doris Rutledge/Evelyn Bently)*, William E. Fontaine, George Lucas, Narmon Johnston *(Alfred DuBois/Gregory Wainwright)*, A. B. De Comatheire *(Reverend Bently)*, Cleo Desmond *(Charlotte Chesbro)*, Louis De Bulger *(Mr. Chesbro)*, Mabel Young *(Mrs. Levine)*, Cornelius Watkins *(Gregory Wainwright, as a boy)*, Mrs. Irvin C. Miller *(Mrs. Wainwright)*, Ira O. McGowan *(Mr. Wainwright)*, Lewis Schooler *(actor)*, Jerry Brown *(actress)*, James Carey *(banker)*, Viola Miles, Mary Watkins *(teachers)*, J. Coldwell, F. Sandfier, Jesse Billings, Allen Dixon *(preachers)*, Leonard Galezio, William Petterson, Sadie Grey *(censors)*, William Petterson, Melton Henry *(rescue party)*.
Melodrama(?). No information about the precise nature of this film has been found. *Clergymen. Actors. Bankers. Schoolteachers. Censors. Negro life.*

THE DECEIVERS *see* **WHY ANNOUNCE YOUR MARRIAGE?**

DÉCLASSÉE *see* **HER PRIVATE LIFE**

DÉCLASSÉE **F2.1251**
Corinne Griffith Productions. *Dist* First National Pictures. 12 Apr **1925** [c20 Mar 1925; LP21250]. Si; b&w. 35mm. 8 reels, 7,733 ft.
Dir Robert Vignola. *Screenplay* Charles E. Whittaker, Bradley King. *Photog* Gaetano Gaudio. *Art Dir* J. J. Hughes. *Film Ed* Cyril Gardner. *Asst Dir* Philip Carle.
Cast: Lloyd Hughes *(Ned Thayer)*, Corinne Griffith *(Lady Helen Haden)*, Clive Brook *(Rudolph Solomon)*, Rockliffe Fellowes *(Sir Bruce Haden)*, Lilyan Tashman *(Mrs. Leslie)*, Hedda Hopper *(Lady Wildering)*, Bertram Johns *(Sir Emmett Wildering)*, Gale Henry *(Timmins)*, Louise Fazenda *(Mrs. Walton)*, Eddie Lyons *(Mr. Walton)*, Mario Carillo *(hotel manager)*, Paul Weigel *(Henri)*.
Drama. Source: Zoë Akins, *Déclassée* (New York, 1923). Lady Helen Haden, the last of the impulsive Varicks, is married to Sir Bruce Haden, a brute who treats her shamefully. She falls in love with Ned Thayer, a young American, but refuses to divorce her husband beause of the attendant scandal and disgrace. Sir Bruce gains possession of a love letter written to Ned by Lady Helen and divorces her. Ned goes to Africa, and Lady Helen comes to the United States, where she encounters Rudolph Solomon, an art collector who wants her to become his mistress. The noblewoman at first refuses, but when her money runs out, she agrees to the proposal and attends a party at his home. Ned, who has learned of the divorce, comes looking for Helen and meets her at Solomon's party. Lady Helen is so humiliated and ashamed that she rushes from the house and throws herself in front of an automobile. She is not badly injured, and Ned reaffirms his love for her. *Collectors. Aristocrats. Mistresses. Marriage. Divorce. Documentation.*
Note: Known also as *The Social Exile,* this film was remade in 1929 under the title *Her Private Life.*

DEEDS OF DARING **F2.1252**
Charles R. Seeling Productions. *Dist* Aywon Film Corp. Jan **1924.** Si; b&w. 35mm. 5 reels, ca4,800 ft.
Dir Charles R. Seeling.
Cast: George Larkin.
Melodrama. A girl traveling in the Sierras with her father and an artist whom she loves meets a guide, who falls in love with her and becomes jealous of her sweetheart. The guide's plot to collect ransom from the girl, after he has kidnaped the young man, is foiled by the artist—proof that he is a man of courage and daring. *Guides. Artists. Kidnaping. Courage. Sierras.*

THE DEERSLAYER **F2.1253**
Mingo Pictures. *Dist* Cameo Distributing Co. 24 Aug **1923** [New York State license]. Si; b&w. 35mm. 5 reels.
Educational-historical drama. No information about the precise nature of this film has been found.

DEFEND YOURSELF **F2.1254**
W. T. Lackey Productions. *Dist* Ellbee Pictures. 28 Jun **1925.** Si; b&w. 35mm. 5 reels, 4,700 ft.
Dir Dell Henderson. *Story* Frank Beresford.
Cast: Dorothy Drew *(Louise Nolan)*, Miss Du Pont *(The Mouse)*, Robert Ellis *(Dr. Poole)*, Sheldon Lewis *(Smiley Bill Curtain)*.
Melodrama. After her father is murdered, Louisa Nolan goes to work as a masked dancer in a sporting cafe in order to support her crippled brother. When a girl called The Mouse is hurt, Smiley Bill Curtain, the sugardaddy who killed Louisa's father, calls in Poole, a physician who has been treating Louisa's brother. Poole arouses Curtain's jealousy, and Curtain orders the doctor to be forcibly detained, simultaneously announcing his own marriage to an unwilling and surprised Louisa. In a fit of anger, The Mouse kills Curtain; Poole escapes and takes Louisa with him, obtaining her promise to become his wife. *Dancers. Physicians. Brother-sister relationship. Murder. Cafes.*

DEFYING DESTINY **F2.1255**
Rellimeo Film Syndicate. *Dist* Selznick Distributing Corp. 29 Sep **1923** [c29 Sep 1923; LP19567]. Si; b&w. 35mm. 6 reels, 5,663 ft.
Dir Louis Chaudet. *Story* Grace Sanderson Michie. *Photog* Lenwood Abbott.
Cast: Monte Blue *(Jack Fenton)*, Irene Rich *(Beth Alden)*, Tully Marshall *(Dr. Gregory)*, Jackie Saunders *(Mrs. Harris)*, Z. Wall Covington *(Sam Harris)*, Russell Simpson *(Mr. Wilkens)*, James Gordon *(Mr. Alden)*, Frona Hale *(Mrs. Alden)*, Laura Ames *(Jack Fenton's aunt)*, George Reehm *(The Promoter)*.
Melodrama. Jack Fenton, wrongfully accused of stealing bank funds, is acquitted by a court but driven from town by public opinion. In the city to which he flees he has an accident and is sent to a hospital. There a plastic surgeon pays Jack $5,000 for the privilege of operating on his face, scarred earlier by a fire in his hometown from which he had rescued Beth Alden, his sweetheart and the daughter of the bank president. The operation is

successful; Jack returns home, make a wise investment, earns the respect of the townspeople, and marries Beth. *Theft. Plastic surgery. Banks. Fires.*

DEFYING THE LAW **F2.1256**

Robert J. Horner Productions. Jun **1922** [scheduled release]. Si; b&w. 35mm. 5 reels.

Dir Robert J. Horner.

Cast: Monte Montague, Ena Gregory.

Melodrama(?). No information about the nature of this film has been found.

Note: The New York State license for this film was "abandoned."

DEFYING THE LAW **F2.1257**

William B. Brush Productions. *Dist* Gotham Productions. 3 Jun **1924** [New York premiere; c15 Apr 1924; LP20115]. Si; b&w. 35mm. 5 reels.

Dir Bertram Bracken. *Titl* Andrew Bennison. *Story* Bertram Bracken, John T. Prince. *Photog* Gordon Pollock. *Film Ed* Leonard Wheeler.

Cast: Lew Cody *(Pietro Savori)*, Renée Adorée *(Lucia Brescia)*, Josef Swickard *(Michelo Brescia)*, Charles "Buddy" Post *(Francisco)*, Naldo Morelli *(Guido Savori)*, Dick Sutherland *(Luigi Bevani)*, James B. Leong *(Dr. Chong Foo)*, Evelyn Adamson *(Maria Baretto)*, Kathleen Chambers *(Sylvia Baretto)*, Marguerite Kosik *(Alicia Bevani)*.

Melodrama. Discouraged with life, Michelo throws his daughter Lucia into the sea, but she falls into a fisherman's boat and is taken to a fishing village. Francisco kidnaps her and takes her to the headquarters of Dr. Chong Foo, a smuggler, which is in a studio occupied by Pietro Savori, an unwilling partner. Chong Foo kills Savori to gain the girl for himself, but Bevani comes to the rescue and saves Lucia for her sweetheart, Guido. *Fishermen. Smugglers. Chinese. Kidnaping. Fatherhood.*

THE DELIGHTFUL ROGUE **F2.1258**

RKO Productions. 22 Sep **1929** [c22 Sep 1929; LP810]. Sd (Photophone); b&w. 35mm. 7 reels, 6,532 ft. [Also si; 6,274 ft.]

Prod William Le Baron. *Dir* Lynn Shores. *Dial Dir* A. Leslie Pearce. *Adapt-Dial* Wallace Smith. *Art Dir* Max Ree. *Mus* Oscar Levant. *Lyr* Sidney Clare.

Cast: Rod La Rocque *(Lastro)*, Rita La Roy *(Nydra)*, Charles Byer *(Harry Beall)*, Ed Brady *(MacDougal)*, Harry Semels *(Hymie)*, Sam Blum *(Junipero)*, Bert Moorehouse *(Nielson)*.

Romantic melodrama. Source: Wallace Smith, "A Woman Decides," in *Cosmopolitan Magazine.* Lastro, a languid Latin who prides himself on his villainy, seizes a yacht and turns pirate on the tropical seas. Wanted for murder, arson, and robbery, Lastro sails into Tapit, where he encounters Junipero, a native leader, and proffers a better photograph than the one on the handbill offering a reward for his capture. In a cafe he meets Nydra, an American dancer sought after by Harry Beall, scion of a wealthy family, and when Lastro becomes interested, his audacity amuses the girl; Lastro flings Beall aside in a skirmish and vanquishes Junipero and his police. Later, Lastro kidnaps Beall, and Nydra comes to plead for her lover's freedom. Lastro agrees but insists that she spend the night in his cabin, and behind locked doors they talk the night away. Beall's indignant attitude at her actions causes Nydra to leave him in disgust and sail away with the pirate. *Pirates. Dancers. Kidnaping. Tropics.*

DELIVERANCE **F2.1259**

Stanley Advertising Co. 24 May **1928** [New York State license application; c29 Jun 1928; LP25431]. Si; b&w. 35mm. 6 reels.

Dir B. K. Blake. *Scen* Duncan Underhill.

Drama. Source: Irving Fisher, *Prohibition at Its Worst* (New York, 1926). Irving Fisher, *Prohibition Still at Its Worst* (New York, 1928). Newspaper publisher and United States Senator Grayson asks his chief reporter, George Meredith, to conduct a survey of the effects of prohibition before he votes on the 18th Amendment. He is motivated in part by the fact that his automobile has nearly collided with one driven by his managing editor, Patton, obviously intoxicated. Believing that the survey will favorably affect passage of the bill, lobbyists against prohibition approach Patton, owner of a large bootlegging interest, and reveal their plan to bribe Grayson. Anticipating an illegal offer when the lobbyists make an appointment to see him, the senator installs a dictograph in his office and records the conversation. Through the efforts of Meredith and Madeline, Grayson's daughter, the bribery offer and the results of the survey are published simultaneously; Patton is fired, and Meredith becomes Grayson's son-in-law. *Publishers. Reporters. Bootleggers. Lobbyists. Bribery. Prohibition. Newspapers. Dictographs. United States Congress.*

Note: Produced for Robert E. Corradini.

THE DEMI-BRIDE **F2.1260**

Metro-Goldwyn-Mayer Pictures. 19 Feb **1927** [c2 Mar 1927; LP23717]. Si; b&w. 35mm. 7 reels, 6,886 ft.

Dir Robert Z. Leonard. *Story-Cont* F. Hugh Herbert, Florence Ryerson. *Titl* Paul Perez, Terrence Daugherty. *Photog* Percy Hilburn. *Sets* Cedric Gibbons, Arnold Gillespie. *Film Ed* William Le Vanway. *Wardrobe* André-ani.

Cast: Norma Shearer *(Criquette)*, Lew Cody *(Philippe Levaux)*, Lionel Belmore *(Monsieur Girard)*, Tenen Holtz *(Gaston)*, Carmel Myers *(Madame Girard)*, Dorothy Sebastian *(Lola)*, Nora Cecil *(schoolteacher)*.

Farce. Vivacious young Criquette becomes enamored of Parisian dandy Philippe, and upon discovering that he is carrying on an affair with Madame Girard, her stepmother, she uses the information as a means of tricking him into marrying her. Philippe demurs but soon is captivated by her charm. Then Lola, a former sweetheart of the bridegroom, becomes intoxicated and goes to sleep in his bed; and Gaston, his valet, attempts to eject this woman and secretly notify the husband of the embarrassing situation. But Philippe is so convinced of his love for Criquette that he forgives Lola her indiscretion. *Dandies. Stepmothers. Valets. Drunkenness. Courtship. Paris.*

THE DEMON (Blue Streak Western) **F2.1261**

Universal Pictures. 31 Jan **1926** [c9 Dec 1925; LP22097]. Si; b&w. 35mm. 5 reels, 4,539 ft.

Pres by Carl Laemmle. *Dir* Cliff Smith. *Cont* Buckleigh F. Oxford. *Story* William C. Beale. *Story? (see note)* Buckleigh F. Oxford, Alvin J. Neitz. *Photog* William Nobles.

Cast: Jack Hoxie *(Dane Gordon)*, Lola Todd *(Goldie Fleming)*, William Welsh *(Percival Wade)*, Jere Austin *(Bat Jackson)*, Al Jennings *(Dan Carroll)*, Georgie Grandee *(The Secretary)*, Harry Semels *(Joseph Lomax)*, Scout *(himself, the horse)*.

Western melodrama. A band of marauders are burning the property of ranchers in Slocum Valley. Dane Gordon, Percival Wade's silent partner, poses as an ex-convict, joins the gang, and falls in love with Goldie Fleming, stenographer to Bat Jackson, the brains of the gang. He learns that the raids are conducted for the purpose of depreciating the properties so that they can be purchased for a song. The gang learns Dane's real identity and plots to blow him up. Dane, however, successfully leads a posse to round up all the outlaws save Bat. Bat is just about to shoot Dane when he himself is mysteriously shot. Dane finds that Goldie is largely responsible for their success. She admits her love for Dane. *Swindlers. Stenographers. Gangs. Posses. Land speculation. Imposture. Horses.*

Note: Most sources give story credit to Buck Oxford and Alvin J. Neitz, but copyright records have been followed.

THE DEMON RIDER (Ken Maynard Series) **F2.1262**

Dist Davis Distributing Division. Nov-Dec? **1925** [c3 Dec 1925; LP22068]. Si; b&w. 35mm. 5 reels, 4,950 ft.

Dir Paul Hurst. *Story* Jay Inman Kane. *Photog* Frank Cotner.

Cast: Ken Maynard *(Billy Dennis)*, Alma Rayford *(Mary Bushman)*, Fred Burns *(Jim Lane)*, Tom London *(Black Hawk)*, James Lowe *(cook)*, Tarzan *(himself, a horse)*, Hollywood Beauty Sextette *(tourists)*.

Western melodrama. Billy Dennis, foreman of the B-Star Ranch, captures the mysterious "Black Hawk" and his outlaw gang singlehanded. He leaves them tied up in a cabin while he goes to return the gold. The sheriff and his posse, accompanied by Billy's fiancée, Mary Bushman, arrive on the scene. One of the outlaws takes advantage of the sheriff's suspicions of the horseman just departed to declare Billy the real "Black Hawk." Billy gets in a scuffle with two deputies, not realizing who they are, and the bag of gold is accidentally picked up by the ranch's Negro cook. Mary warns Billy, and he takes to the hills until he can find the gold. The sheriff abandons his less "important" prisoners to go after Billy. Black Hawk and his men also take to the hills, and there they commandeer a car driven by some female tourists. Billy ropes the gang just as their car is going off the cliff, but the sheriff arrives to arrest him. Matters are finally cleared up when the cook arrives. *Ranch foremen. Outlaws. Sheriffs. Cooks. Horses.*

THE DENIAL **F2.1263**

Metro-Goldwyn Pictures. 22 Mar **1925** [c9 Mar 1925; LP21220]. Si; b&w. 35mm. 5 reels, 4,791 ft.

Pres by Louis B. Mayer. *Dir* Hobart Henley. *Adapt* Agnes Christine Johnston. *Photog* Benjamin F. Reynolds. *Art Dir* Cedric Gibbons, Joseph Wright. *Film Ed* Frank Davis.

Cast: Claire Windsor *(Mildred)*, Bert Roach *(Arthur)*, William Haines *(Lyman)*, Lucille Rickson *(Dorothy)*, Robert Agnew *(Bob)*, Emily Fitzroy *(Rena)*, William Eugene *(Eugene)*, Estelle Clark *(Rosie)*, Vivia Ogden *(Effie)*.

Drama. Source: Lewis Beach, *The Square Peg, a Play in Three Acts* (Boston, 1925). *In 1897 Mildred Huckins is a beautiful young girl in love with Lyman Webb. Her austere and inexorable mother is opposed to the match and would marry her to an adipose millionaire. Lyman then joins the Rough Riders and goes off to fight in the Spanish-American War. Mildred's mother intercepts his letters, and Lyman's affection for Mildred cools. So tyrannical and dictatorial is Mildred's mother that Mildred's brother, Gene, goes to the bad and gets in trouble with a woman. Mildred's father, in an attempt to avert disgrace, then steals money from the bank in which he works. Gene extricates himself from his difficulties, but his father commits suicide. Lyman is killed in action, and Mildred finally marries Arthur; but their life together is a drab one.* Years later, Mildred's daughter, Dorothy, falls in love with a promising young man and asks her mother's consent to marry. Mildred at first refuses her permission, but when she reflects on her own shattered romance, she relents and gives the children her blessing. *Millionaires. Filial relations. Embezzlement. Suicide. United States—History—War of 1898. Rough Riders.*

THE DENVER DUDE (Universal-Jewel) **F2.1264**

Universal Pictures. 13 Feb **1927** [c9 Feb 1927; LP23650]. Si; b&w. 35mm. 6 reels, 5,292 ft.

Pres by Carl Laemmle. *Dir* B. Reeves Eason. *Adapt* Carl Krusada, William B. Lester. *Story* Earle Snell. *Photog* Harry Neumann. *Art Dir* David S. Garber.

Cast: Hoot Gibson *(Rodeo Randall)*, Blanche Mehaffey *(Patricia La Mar)*, Robert McKim *(Bob Flint)*, George Summerville *(Slim Jones)*, Glenn Tryon *(Percy, the Dude)*, Howard Truesdell *(Colonel La Mar)*, Mathilde Brundage *(Mrs. Phipps)*, Rolfe Sedan *(Henry Bird)*, Grace Cunard *(Mrs. Bird)*, Buck Carey *(Red Quincy)*, Pee Wee Holmes *(Shorty Dan)*.

Western melodrama. Rodeo Randall, a broncobuster, returns home after some years' absence. His father sells a prize bull to Colonel La Mar, a neighbor, but demands a cash payment, and the money is to be delivered by Henry Bird, a dude from Denver, who occupies the homebound stage with Rodeo. The cowboy falls in love with a newspaper picture of La Mar's daughter, Patricia, but is assured by Bird that she will demand "class." When they are held up, Bird flees in terror while Rodeo puts the bandits to rout and discovers the loot. Dolling himself up in Bird's spare clothes and appropriating his letter of recommendation, he gets a job with La Mar. Rodeo is framed by the ranch foreman for robbery, but he escapes, pursues the bandits to their hideout, and returns La Mar's money, thus winning Patricia. *Broncobusters. Ranch foremen. Dandies. Bandits. Stagecoach robberies.*

DERELICT **F2.1265**

Paramount-Publix Corp. 22 Nov **1930** [c21 Nov 1930; LP1749]. Sd (Movietone); b&w. 35mm. 8 reels, 6,702 ft.

Dir Rowland V. Lee. *Screenplay* William Slavens McNutt, Grover Jones. *Photog* Archie J. Stout. *Film Ed* George Nichols, Jr. *Song: "Over the Sea of Dreams"* Leo Robin, Jack King. *Rec Engr* Eugene Merritt.

Cast: George Bancroft *(Bill Rafferty)*, Jesse Royce Landis *(Helen Lorber)*, William Boyd *(Jed Graves)*, Donald Stuart *(Fin Thomson)*, James Durkin *(Jameson)*, William Stack *(Travis)*, Wade Boteler *(Captain Gregg)*, William Walling *(Captain Hogarth)*, Paul Porcasi *(Masoni)*, Brooks Benedict *(McFall)*.

Adventure melodrama. Bill Rafferty and Jed Graves, rival first mates on the Batson freighter line, come into open conflict when they fall in love with the same girl, Helen Lorber, a cafe entertainer in Havana. When Bill offers to take Helen to Rio aboard his ship, she accepts and leaves her job; but, unexpectedly, Bill is made captain of another freighter and maliciously chooses Jed as his mate. Unwilling to risk taking a woman aboard, Bill calls off his offer, and Helen angrily appeals to Jed, who smuggles her into a cabin. Disaster is narrowly avoided when the ship collides with another vessel in the dense fog; and Bill is relieved of command for neglect of duty, while Jed takes his place and beats him in a fight. Helen goes with Bill, and he furiously blames her for the loss of his command; he ships on a tramp steamer bound for Rio and guides it through a tropical storm in a drunken state; when Jed's ship sends up a distress signal, Bill goes to his aid with the steamer. For his heroism, Bill is restored to his command, and realizing that Helen has stood by him, giving up her chance to go to Rio, he is happily reunited with her. *Sea captains. Entertainers. Singers. Freighters. Havana. Shipwrecks.*

DESERT BLOSSOMS **F2.1266**

Fox Film Corp. 13 Nov **1921** [c13 Nov 1921; LP17253]. Si; b&w. 35mm. 5 reels, 4,500 ft.

Pres by William Fox. *Dir* Arthur Rosson. *Scen* Arthur J. Zellner. *Story* Kate Corbaley. *Photog* Ross Fisher.

Cast: William Russell *(Stephen Brent)*, Helen Ferguson *(Mary Ralston)*, Wilbur Higby *(James Thornton)*, Willis Robards *(Henry Ralston)*, Margaret Mann *(Mrs. Thornton)*, Dulcie Cooper *(Lucy Thornton)*, Charles Spere *(Bert Thornton)*, Gerald Pring *(Mr. Joyce)*.

Melodrama. Steve Brent, a construction engineer with an excellent reputation, is blamed for having used inferior materials on a bridge that collapses. Bert Thornton, his employer's son, is actually responsible, but not wishing to expose him, Brent surrenders his position. Assuming another name, he goes west to work on a desert irrigation project where the manager's daughter, Mary Ralston, recognizes him but keeps his secret. Ralston is informed by an enemy of Steve's, but Mary helps to protect Steve's name until he is exonerated and becomes free to marry her. *Engineers—Civil. Bridges. Irrigation. Deserts.*

THE DESERT BRIDE **F2.1267**

Columbia Pictures. 26 Mar **1928** [c19 Apr 1928; LP25167]. Si; b&w. 35mm. 6 reels, ca5,400 ft.

Prod Harry Cohn. *Dir* Walter Lang. *Scen* Elmer Harris. *Adapt* Anthony Coldeway. *Photog* Ray June. *Art Dir* Robert E. Lee. *Film Ed* Arthur Roberts. *Asst Dir* Max Cohn.

Cast: Betty Compson *(Diane Duval)*, Allan Forrest *(Capt. Maurice de Florimont)*, Edward Martindel *(Colonel Sorelle)*, Otto Matiesen *(Kassim Ben Ali)*, Roscoe Karns *(Private Terry)*, Frank Austin *(beggar)*.

Melodrama. Source: Ewart Adamson, "The Adventuress" (publication undetermined). Maurice de Florimont, an officer with the intelligence department of the French Army, is captured by Arab nationalists while on a mission of espionage. His sweetheart, Diane Duval, is also taken prisoner when she comes to the fortress in search of Florimont. Kassim Ben Ali, leader of the Arab nationalists, tortures both, but they refuse to divulge information. Finally, they are rescued by French troops who storm the fortress and kill Kassim. *Spies. Arabs. Torture. France—Army—Intelligence service.*

A DESERT BRIDEGROOM **F2.1268**

Ben Wilson Productions. *Dist* Arrow Film Corp. 28 May **1922** [c24 Mar 1922; LP17670]. Si; b&w. 35mm. 5 reels, 4,784 ft.

Dir-Story Roy Clements.

Cast: Jack Hoxie *(Jack Harkins)*, Evelyn Nelson.

Western melodrama. Jack Harkins, sheriff of Stony Ridge, goes in search of Red Saunders, who caused the death of Jack's sister, and incurs the enmity of the townsmen in Cactus Center. Saunders, who is forcing his attentions on Matilda Ann Carter, a wealthy young heiress, is frightened by the approach of Harkins. Ann shields him from his pursuers and leads him to Saunders, to whom he gives a fierce beating. Saunders feigns death, and Harkins is sought for murder but manages to expose the ruse. All ends happily. *Sheriffs. Brother-sister relationship. Revenge.*

THE DESERT DEMON **F2.1269**

Action Pictures. *Dist* Weiss Brothers Artclass Pictures. 4 Oct **1925.** Si; b&w. 35mm. 5 reels, 5,012 ft.

Dir Richard Thorpe. *Scen* Alex McLaren. *Photog* Ray Ries.

Cast: Buffalo Bill Jr. *(Bill Davis)*, Betty Morrissey *(Nita Randall)*, Frank Ellis *(Jim Slade)*, Harry Todd *(Snitz Doolittle)*, Jack O'Brien *(Bugs)*, Frank Austin *(Dad Randall)*, Margaret Martin *(squaw)*.

Western melodrama. Bill Davis saves an Indian woman from attack by Jim Slade. Bill later gets lost in the desert, where his horse dies from thirst. Nita Randall, whose father operates a mine on the edge of the desert, finds Bill in time to prevent him from suffering a similar fate. Jim Slade plots to get control of the Randall mine; Randall kills one of Slade's men and himself dies of an injury. Bill takes the blame, and Nita turns against him. She later forgives him after he beats up Slade. Nita and Bill are united. *Indians of North America. Thirst. Deserts. Mines. Horses.*

DESERT DRIVEN **F2.1270**

R-C Pictures. *Dist* Film Booking Offices of America. 8 Jul **1923** [c8 Jul 1923; LP19212]. Si; b&w. 35mm. 6 reels, 5,840 ft.

Dir Val Paul. *Adapt* Wyndham Gittens. *Photog* William Thornley, Robert De Grasse.

Cast: Harry Carey *(Bob)*, Marguerite Clayton *(Mary)*, George Waggner *(Craydon)*, Charles J. Le Moyne *(Leary)*, Alfred Allen *(Yorke)*, Camille Johnson *(Ge-Ge)*, Dan Crimmins *(Brown)*, Catherine Kay *(wife)*, Tom Lingham *(sheriff)*, Jack Carlyle *(Warden)*, Jim Wang *(cook)*, Ashley Cooper *(Kendall)*.

Western melodrama. Source: Wyndham Martin, "The Man From the Desert," in *Action Story Magazine*. Bob, wrongfully accused of murder, escapes from prison, takes to the desert, and gets a job on a ranch owned by Yorke, who conceals Bob's identity and assists him in proving his honesty. Bob falls in love with Yorke's daughter, who saves him from being sent back to prison by finding a confession that exonerates him. *Ranchers. Prison escapees. Murder. Injustice.*

Note: Reissued 1930. (New York State license issued to Julius Levine ca16 Jan 1930.)

DESERT DUST **F2.1271**

Universal Pictures. 18 Dec **1927** [c20 Oct 1927; LP24558]. Si; b&w. 35mm. 5 reels, 4,349 ft.

Pres by Carl Laemmle. *Dir* William Wyler. *Story-Scen* William B. Lester. *Titl* Gardner Bradford. *Photog* Milton Bridenbecker. *Art Dir* David S. Garber.

Cast: Ted Wells *(Frank Fortune)*, Lotus Thompson *(Helen Marsden)*, Bruce Gordon *("Butch" Rorke)*, Jimmy Phillips *(The Rat)*, Charles (Slim) Cole *(The Parson)*, George Ovey *(Shorty Benton)*, Dick L'Estrange *(Slim Donovan)*.

Western melodrama. Frank Fortune, a young rancher, is jailed along with two of his men for fighting with rival ranchers. Helen Marsden, daughter of a wealthy senator who is interested in prison reform, prevails on the judge to parole them into her custody and work at her ranch. Frank falls in love and, so as to stay on at the ranch, convinces her he is a notorious criminal. When the senator visits her with a large sum of money belonging to the state, three "reformed" crooks on the premises plan to steal it. Fortune's friends learn of the plot and decide to take the money for safekeeping, but Fortune intervenes; the real crooks do steal the funds, however, and depart with Helen in an automobile. Fortune overtakes the speeding car and rescues Helen. *Cowboys. Ranchers. Politicians. Criminals—Rehabilitation. Prison reform. Parole. Theft.*

THE DESERT FLOWER **F2.1272**

First National Pictures. 21 Jun **1925** [c1 Jun 1925; LP21514]. Si; b&w. 35mm. 7 reels, 6,383 ft.

Dir Irving Cummings. *Ed Dir–Scen* June Mathis. *Photog* T. D. McCord. *Art Dir* Edward Shulter. *Film Ed* George McGuire.

Cast: Colleen Moore *(Maggie Fortune)*, Lloyd Hughes *(Rance Conway)*, Kate Price *(Mrs. McQuade)*, Geno Corrado *(José Lee)*, Fred Warren *(Dizzy)*, Frank Brownlee *(Mike Dyer)*, Isabelle Keith *(Inga Hulverson)*, Anna May Walthall *(Flozella)*, William Norton Bailey *(Jack Royal)*, Monte Collins *(Mr. McQuade)*, Ena Gregory *(Fay Knight)*.

Western melodrama. Source: Don Mullally, *The Desert Flower* (New York opening: 18 Nov 1924). Maggie Fortune, who lives in a boxcar near a railroad line being built through the desert, is cruelly treated by Mike Dyer, her stepfather, and goes to the mining town of Bullfrog, where she encounters Rance Conway, a young derelict addicted to drink. Maggie attempts to get Rance to stop drinking, but he repeatedly falls off the wagon, until finally she shames him into accepting a grubstake from her. Rance goes prospecting and returns just as Mike Dyer arrives in town. Dyer is shot by an unknown assailant, and Rance takes the blame in order to protect Maggie; Maggie also confesses to the crime (to protect Rance), and the puzzled sheriff finally calls Dyer's death a suicide. Having cured himself of drunkenness, Rance, who turns out to be the son of wealthy parents, asks Maggie to marry him. *Stepfathers. Derelicts. Prospectors. Sheriffs. Alcoholism. Murder. Suicide. Mining towns. Railroads.*

DESERT GOLD **F2.1273**

Famous Players–Lasky. *Dist* Paramount Pictures. ca21 Mar **1926** [New York premiere; released 19 Apr; c20 Apr 1926; LP22626]. Si; b&w. 35mm. 7 reels, 6,900 ft.

Pres by Adolph Zukor, Jesse L. Lasky. *Supv* Hector Turnbull, B. P. Schulberg. *Dir* George B. Seitz. *Scen* Lucien Hubbard. *Photog* Charles Edgar Schoenbaum.

Cast: Neil Hamilton *(George Thorne)*, Shirley Mason *(Mercedes Castanada)*, Robert Frazer *(Dick Gale)*, William Powell *(Landree)*, Josef Swickard *(Sebastián Castanada)*, George Irving *(Richard Stanton Gale)*, Eddie Gribbon *(One Round Kelley)*, Frank Lackteen *(Yaqui)*, Richard Howard *(sergeant)*, Bernard Siegel *(goat herder)*, George Rigas *(Verd)*, Ralph Yearsley *(halfwit)*, Aline Goodwin *(Alarcon's wife)*.

Western melodrama. Source: Zane Grey, *Desert Gold, a Romance of the Border* (New York, 1913). Dick Gale, the fun-loving son of a respectable eastern family, is evicted and goes west to aid his friend Lieutenant Thorne on the border. Landree, an unscrupulous outlaw and killer, plunders the villa of Don Sebastián Castanada and attempts to capture his daughter, Mercedes, whom Thorne loves; she escapes disguised as a peon boy. Guided by a Yaqui, Dick and Mercedes flee into the desert. There a sandstorm turns back the villains, their horses are lost, and the Indian guide is injured. Thorne, injured in rescuing the girl, returns to the fort unaware of their plight. They are tracked down by Landree's men; the Yaqui precipitates a landslide, which blocks their path but costs him his life. Thorne rescues the party, and realizing the love of Dick and Mercedes, he relinquishes his own claim on her. *Outlaws. Yaqui Indians. The Painted Desert. Mexican border. Sandstorms.*

DESERT GREED **F2.1274**

Dist Goodwill Pictures. **1926.** Si; b&w. 35mm. 5 reels.

Dir Jacques Jaccard.

Cast: Yakima Canutt.

Western melodrama(?). No information about the nature of this film has been found.

THE DESERT HAWK **F2.1275**

Berwilla Film Corp. *Dist* Arrow Film Corp. 25 Oct **1924** [c22 Jul 1924; LP20412]. Si; b&w. 35mm. 5 reels, 4,828 ft.

Prod Ben Wilson. *Dir* Leon De La Mothe. *Cont* Daniel F. Whitcomb. *Story* Jay Inman Kane, Robert McKenzie.

Cast: Ben Wilson *(Hollister, the fugitive from justice)*, Mildred Harris *(Marie Nicholls, an eastern girl)*, William Bailey *(Tex Trapp)*, Louise Lester *(Bridget, a relic of the past)*, Yakima Canutt *(a handy man to the foreman of the Mirage Ranch)*, Ed La Niece *(Sheriff Carson)*, Leon De La Mothe *(Sheriff Jackson)*, Helen Broneau *(Mercedes Nicholls)*.

Western melodrama. "Hawk" Hollister, wanted for killing the sheriff's brother, decides to assist Marie Nicholls, who has fallen from a passing train, get to the ranch she has inherited from her uncle. He discovers that Marie alone knows the whereabouts of her uncle's treasure, sought by Trapp, foreman of the ranch. Hawk is arrested, but the sheriff releases him to rescue Marie when she falls into the clutches of Trapp's gang. Meanwhile, the sheriff learns that his own wife really killed his brother. Trapp is arrested, the uncle's disinherited wife is remunerated, and Hawk selects a ring for his bride-to-be from the uncle's treasure. *Fugitives. Sheriffs. Brothers. Murder. Treasure. Inheritance.*

DESERT MADNESS **F2.1276**

Harry Webb Productions. *Dist* Aywon Film Corp. 13 Jan **1925** [New York State license]. Si; b&w. 35mm. 5 reels, 4,800 ft.

Dir Harry Webb.

Cast: Jack Perrin.

Western melodrama. "Old miner is killed after finding gold vein. His daughter is protected by Jack Powell, who files claim in her name. Murderer who converts [*sic*] mine tries to get rid of Jack and his Sweetheart Mary, who is abducted, but the hero administers sound trouncing to villain and save the girl." (*Motion Picture News Booking Guide*, 8:23, Apr 1925.) *Miners. Murder. Abduction. Gold.*

DESERT MAN (Reissue) **F2.1277**

28 Mar **1927** [New York State license]. Si; b&w. 35mm.

Note: A William S. Hart western, first released by Triangle Film Corp., 22 Apr 1917.

DESERT NIGHTS **F2.1278**

Metro-Goldwyn-Mayer Pictures. 9 Mar **1929** [c11 Mar 1929; LP199]. Mus score & sd eff (Movietone); b&w. 35mm. 7 reels, 7,177 ft. [Also si.]

Dir William Nigh. *Scen* Lenore Coffee, Willis Goldbeck. *Titl* Marian Ainslee, Ruth Cummings. *Adapt* Endre Bohem. *Story* John Thomas Neville, Dale Van Every. *Photog* James Howe. *Art Dir* Cedric Gibbons. *Film Ed* Harry Reynolds. *Wardrobe* Henrietta Frazer.

Cast: John Gilbert *(Hugh Rand)*, Ernest Torrence *(Lord Stonehill)*, Mary Nolan *(Lady Diana)*.

Melodrama. Posing as Lord and Lady Stonehill, two diamond thieves hold up the main offices of a South African diamond mine and make off with a fortune in uncut stones, taking with them mine manager Hugh Rand as a hostage. The thieves attempt to make an escape across the desert and become lost in the hot and trackless wastes. They release Hugh from his shackles, and he leads them to safety. The girl reforms, and the man is arrested by the authorities. Hugh and "Lady" Diana fall in love. *Hostages. Robbery. Diamond mines. Deserts. South Africa.*

Note: This film was reviewed in *Motion Picture News* under the title *Thirst.*

THE DESERT OF THE LOST **F2.1279**

Action Pictures. *Dist* Pathé Exchange. 18 Dec **1927** [c28 Nov 1927; LP24704]. Si; b&w. 35mm. 5 reels, 4,993 ft.

Pres by Lester F. Scott, Jr. *Dir* Richard Thorpe. *Scen* Frank L. Inghram. *Story* Walter J. Coburn. *Photog* Ray Ries.

Cast: Wally Wales *(Jim Drake)*, Peggy Montgomery *(Dolores Wolfe)*, William J. Dyer *(Steve Wolfe)*, Edward Cecil, Richard Neill, Kelly Cafford, Ray Murro, George Magrill, Charles Whitaker.

Western melodrama. Jim Drake, who has shot a man in self-defense and is unable to prove it, flees to Mexico and is followed by Murray, a detective. Jim is befriended by Dolores Wolfe, the daughter of Steve Wolfe, a renegade American innkeeper; she is being forced to marry El Chino, a halfbreed Chinese bandit who keeps a secret gold mine. Jim defends the girl against her own father and the bandit, and when trapped by Dolores' father, he discovers the mine and cleverly captures the gang. Murray finds Jim through following Dolores and tells him the charges have been dropped against him; Jim returns home accompanied by the girl. *Fugitives. Cowboys. Detectives. Bandits. Innkeepers. Halfcastes. Chinese. Manslaughter. Gold mines. Mexico.*

THE DESERT OUTLAW **F2.1280**

Fox Film Corp. 24 Aug **1924** [c24 Aug 1924; LP20528]. Si; b&w. 35mm. 6 reels, 5,576 ft.

Pres by William Fox. *Dir* Edmund Mortimer. *Story-Scen* Charles Kenyon. *Photog* Joseph Brotherton.

Cast: Buck Jones *(Sam Langdon)*, Evelyn Brent *(May Halloway)*, De Witt Jennings *(Doc McChesney)*, William Haynes *(Tom Halloway)*, Claude Payton *(Black Loomis)*, William Gould *(The Sheriff)*, Bob Klein *(Mad McTavish)*.

Western melodrama. Tom Halloway, compelled through circumstances to become an outlaw, robs the express office on the day of his sister's arrival from the East and is seen at the scene of the crime by McTavish, a religious fanatic. Accompanying Tom in his escape from the posse is Sam Langdon, a prospector charged with McTavish's murder. He clears up the situation, wins a pardon for Tom, and wins May, Tom's sister. *Outlaws. Fanatics. Murder. Robbery. Brother-sister relationship.*

THE DESERT PIRATE **F2.1281**

FBO Pictures. 25 Dec **1927** [c26 Dec 1927; LP24876]. Si; b&w. 35mm. 5 reels.

Dir James Dugan. *Adapt-Cont* Oliver Drake. *Story* Frank Howard Clark.

Cast: Tom Tyler *(Tom Corrigan)*, Frankie Darro *(Jimmy Rand)*, Duane Thompson *(Ann Farnham)*, Edward Hearne *(Norton)*, Tom Lingham *(Shorty Gibbs)*.

Western melodrama. Sheriff Tom Corrigan gives up his guns and adopts the orphaned son of a suicidal bandit he has trailed. He falls in love with Ann, a neighborhood girl whose father is in the clutches of gamblers. When the gamblers try to frame the sheriff on a murder charge, he successfully vindicates himself, clears Ann's father, and wins the girl. *Sheriffs. Gamblers. Adoption.*

DESERT RIDER **F2.1282**

Sunset Productions. Jun **1923** [scheduled release]. Si; b&w. 35mm. 5 reels, 4,700 ft.

Dir Robert North Bradbury. *Story* Frank Howard Clark. *Photog* Bert Longenecker. *Asst Dir* Jack Pierce.

Cast: Jack Hoxie *(Jack Sutherland, ranch owner)*, Frank Rice *(Toby Jones, his pard)*, Evelyn Nelson *(Carolyn Grey from Kentucky)*, Claude Peyton *(Rufe Kinkaid, trickster)*, Tom Lingham *(Dan Baird)*, Walter Wilkinson *(his motherless son, Mickey)*.

Western melodrama. No information about the precise nature of this film has been found. *Ranchers. Children. Kentuckians.*

THE DESERT RIDER **F2.1283**

Metro-Goldwyn-Mayer Pictures. 11 May **1929** [c8 Aug 1929; LP286]. Si; b&w. 35mm. 6 reels, 4,943 ft.

Dir Nick Grinde. *Screenplay* Oliver Drake. *Titl* Harry Sinclair Drago. *Story* Ted Shane, Milton Bren. *Photog* Arthur Reed. *Film Ed* William Le Vanway. *Wardrobe* Lucia Coulter.

Cast: Tim McCoy *(Jed Tyler)*, Raquel Torres *(Dolores)*, Bert Roach *(Friar Bernardo)*, Edward Connelly *(Padre Quintada)*, Harry Woods *(Williams)*, Jess Cavin *(Black Bailey)*.

Western melodrama. "Bandit gang robs rider of pony express of government land grant belonging to Mexican girl. Jed Tyler tracks down the bandits and saves the ranch for the girl." ("Motion Picture News Booking Guide," in *Motion Picture News*, 15 Mar 1930, p77.) *Bandits. Mexicans. Pony Express. Land rights.*

THE DESERT SECRET **F2.1284**

H. & B. Film Co. *Dist* Madoc Sales. 24 May **1924** [New York State license]. Si; b&w. 35mm. 5 reels.

Dir Frederick Reel, Jr.

Cast: Bill Patton.

Western melodrama. "Two partners in a prospecting deal locate 'pay dirt.' One has a weakness for drink and while intoxicated tells the location of his discovery. A rush to file claims starts, and the other partner believing himself done out of his land disappears for a time. Later when he returns, however, he finds that the land has been secured to him by Peggy Madison, a girl he loved and who was the first to file a claim on the land." (*Motion Picture News Booking Guide*, 7:201, Oct 1924.) *Prospectors. Drunkenness. Mine claims.*

THE DESERT SHEIK **F2.1285**

Truart Film Corp. *Dist* Film Booking Offices of America. 21 Jul **1924** [c14 Jun 1924; LP20307]. Si; b&w. 35mm. 6 reels, 5,700 ft.

A. C. Bromhead Production. *Dir* Tom Terriss. *Scen* Alicia Ramsey. *Titl* Arthur Hoerl. *Photog* A. St. A. Brown, H. W. Bishop. *Film Ed* Arthur Hoerl.

Cast: Wanda Hawley *(Corinne Adams)*, Nigel Barrie *(Major Egerton)*, Pedro De Cordoba *(Prince Ibrahim)*, Edith Craig *(Miss Adams)*, Arthur Cullen *(Sir Charles Roden)*, Stewart Rome *(The Reverend Roden)*, Douglas Munro *(Mansoor)*, Percy Standing *(Stephen Belmont)*, Cyril Smith *(Lord Howard Cecil)*, Hamed El Gabrey *(Emir, Desert Sheik)*.

Romantic drama. Source: Arthur Conan Doyle, *A Desert Drama, Being The Tragedy of the Korosko* (London, 1898). At the time Corinne Adams, an American girl, arrives in Egypt, Major Egerton, who is suffering from a terminal illness, goes to Cairo with some English friends. They meet and fall in love. During a trip into the desert, the party is attacked by Bedouins, the women are captured, and Egerton is struck down and left for dead. All are rescued by British troops, while Egerton is cured by a dervish's blow and is free to declare himself to Corinne. *Bedouins. Dervishes. Egypt. Sahara. Great Britain—Army.*

THE DESERT SONG **F2.1286**

Warner Brothers Pictures. 8 Apr **1929** [New York premiere; c6 May 1929; LP358]. Sd (Vitaphone); b&w. 35mm. 13 reels, 11,034 ft.

Dir Roy Del Ruth. *Scen-Dial* Harvey Gates. *Photog* Bernard McGill. *Film Ed* Ralph Dawson. *Songs: "Riff Song," "French Military Marching Song," "Then You Will Know," "Love's Dear Yearning," "Desert Song," "Song of the Brass Key," "One Flower Grows Alone in Your Garden," "Sabre Song," "Romance"* Oscar Hammerstein, II, Sigmund Romberg. *Rec Engr* George R. Groves. *Cost* Earl Luick.

Cast: John Boles *(The Red Shadow/Pierre Birbeau)*, Carlotta King *(Margot)*, Louise Fazenda *(Susan)*, Johnny Arthur *(Bennie Kid, a reporter)*, Edward Martindel *(General Birbeau)*, Jack Pratt *(Pasha)*, Otto Hoffman *(Hasse)*, Robert E. Guzman *(Sid El Kar)*, Marie Wells *(Clementina)*, John Miljan *(Captain Fontaine)*, Del Elliott *(rebel)*, Myrna Loy *(Azuri)*.

Operetta. Source: Otto Harbach, Frank Mandel, and Oscar Hammerstein, II, *The Desert Song; a Musical Play in Two Acts* (New York, 1932). The Red Shadow, the leader of a tribe of Riff horsemen, is in actuality Pierre Birbeau, the seemingly weak and simple-minded son of the commandant of French forces in the Moroccan desert. Pierre's father champions a marriage between Margot and Paul, and Pierre, who loves the girl passionately, dons his disguise and kidnaps her, taking her to the desert palace of Ali Ben Ali. The commandant follows with a troop of men and challenges The Red Shadow (his own son) to a duel. The Red Shadow refuses the challenge and is disgraced in front of his men, losing their respect. The Red Shadow goes off into the desert, then, dropping his disguise, returns to the fort to be greeted warmly by his father and Margot, who have learned that Pierre and The Red Shadow are one and the same! *Riffs. Filial relations. Disguise. Kidnaping. Deserts. Morocco. France—Army—Foreign Legion. Duels.*

DESERT VALLEY **F2.1287**

Fox Film Corp. 26 Dec **1926** [c12 Dec 1926; LP23439]. Si; b&w. 35mm. 5 reels, 4,731 ft.

Pres by William Fox. *Dir* Scott R. Dunlap. *Scen* Randall H. Faye. *Photog* Reginald Lyons. *Asst Dir* Virgil Hart.

Cast: Buck Jones *(Fitzsmith)*, Virginia Brown Faire *(Mildred Dean)*, Malcolm Waite *(Jeff Hoades)*, J. W. Johnston *(Timothy Dean)*, Charles Brinley *(sheriff)*, Eugene Pallette *(deputy)*.

Western melodrama. Source: Jackson Gregory, *Desert Valley* (New York, 1921). Montgomery Wilson Fitzsmith, a roaming cowboy, wanders into Desert Valley and finds the ranchers are losing their cattle because Jefferson Hoades has cornered the water supply. He saves some cattle on the Dean ranch from dying, and there he is jailed for stealing some pie from a windowsill. Fitzsmith escapes and goes into the desert where he again encounters Mildred Dean, the rancher's daughter, whom he saves from the advances of a water profiteer. He learns that Dean is accused of breaking the pipeline and is being tried for the offense; returning to town, he tells the true story, and a chase ensues. Fitzsmith bests Hoades in a fight, and the ranchers drive the villain from the land. *Cowboys. Water rights. Courtship.*

DESERT VULTURES **F2.1288**

Art Mix Productions. 25 Apr **1930** [New York State license]. Si; b&w. 35mm. 5 reels.

Cast: Art Mix.

Western melodrama(?). No information about the nature of this film has been found.

DESERTED AT THE ALTAR **F2.1289**

Phil Goldstone Productions. 1 Dec **1922.** Si; b&w. 35mm. 7 reels, 6,850 ft.

Pres by Phil Goldstone. *Dir* William K. Howard, Al Kelley. *Adapt* Grace Miller White. *Photog* Glen MacWilliams, John Meigle.

Cast: Tully Marshall *(Squire Simpson)*, Bessie Love *(Anna Moore, The Country Girl)*, William Scott *(Bob Crandall, The City Chap)*, Barbara Tennant *(Nell Reed, The Other Woman)*, Eulalie Jensen *(The Teacher)*, Fred Kelsey *(The Other Man)*, Frankie Lee *(Tommy Moore, The Boy)*, Wade Boteler *(John Simpson, The Minister)*, Les Bates *(The Mob Leader)*, Edward McQuade *(The Sheriff)*, Helen Howard *(The Gossip)*, Queenie *(The Dog)*.

Melodrama. Source: Pierce Kingsley, *Deserted at the Altar* (a play; cMay 1922). Anna Moore, a poor orphaned country girl, and her little brother, Tommy, live with hypocritical Squire Simpson, who conspires with his son to acquire the inheritance due the girl. When Bob Crandall comes from the city and the girl falls in love with him, the squire approves of the marriage. The ceremony is interrupted, however, by a strange woman who describes the bridegroom as the father of the baby in her arms. The girl goes home broken-hearted, and the townspeople rise against Bob, but the woman finally exonerates him and reveals the squire's nefarious scheme. *Orphans. Parentage. Inheritance. Weddings. Dogs.*

THE DESERT'S CRUCIBLE **F2.1290**

Ben Wilson Productions. *Dist* Arrow Film Corp. 23 Apr **1922** [c1 Mar 1922; LP17589]. Si; b&w. 35mm. 5 reels, 4,749 ft.

Prod Ben Wilson. *Scen-Dir* Roy Clements.

Cast: Jack Hoxie *(Jack Hardy, Jr./Deerfoot)*, Claude Payton *(Tex Fuller)*, Andrée Tourneur *(Miss Benson)*.

Western melodrama. "Jack Hardy, Sr., sends his son West to make a man of him. Jack falls in love with Miss Benson, ranch secretary. Taunted by the girl, he breaks an intractable horse to prove his courage. When Tex Fuller and his gang try to get Jack, Deerfoot, his half-breed brother, takes the missiles intended for his brother. Jack fights the gang and brings them to justice. But Miss Benson is not yet won. She thinks of the girl back East to whom Jack was engaged. Jack's father arrives and announces that he is engaged to the Eastern girl. Miss Benson surrenders." (*Motion Picture News Booking Guide*, 3:16, Oct 1922.) *Secretaries. Halfcastes. Manhood. Ranch life. Horses.*

THE DESERT'S PRICE **F2.1291**

Fox Film Corp. 13 Dec **1925** [c13 Dec 1925; LP22129]. Si; b&w. 35mm. 6 reels, 5,709 ft.

Pres by William Fox. *Dir* W. S. Van Dyke. *Scen* Charles Darnton. *Photog* Reginald Lyons. *Asst Dir* Mike Miggins.

Cast: Buck Jones *(Wils McCann)*, Florence Gilbert *(Julia)*, Edna Marion *(Nora)*, Ernest Butterworth *(Phil)*, Arthur Houseman *(Tom Martin)*, Montague Love *(Jim Martin)*, Carl Stockdale *(Gitner)*, Harry Dunkinson *(sheriff)*, Henry Armetta *(shepherd)*.

Western melodrama. Source: William MacLeod Raine, *The Desert's Price* (Garden City, New York, 1924). During a range war between sheepmen and cattle ranchers, Julia Starke's father is brutally murdered by the Martin brothers. Wils McCann, a decent cattle rancher, takes pity on the girl and goes to work for her tending sheep. Sam Martin tries to force his attentions on Peggy Starke and inadvertently injures the girl. An enraged Julia takes a shot at Sam and wounds him; Julia's brother, Phil, later kills him in self-defense. Jim Martin has Julia arrested for Sam's murder and then incites a mob to attempt a lynching. Wils's men break up the mob, and Jim Martin is brought before the court to stand trial for the murder of Julia's father. *Sheepmen. Ranchers. Sisters. Brother-sister relationship. Range wars. Murder. Lynching.*

THE DESERT'S TOLL **F2.1292**

Metro-Goldwyn-Mayer Pictures. 14 Nov **1926** [c21 Dec 1926; LP23610]. Si; b&w. 35mm. 6 reels, 5,376 ft.

Pres by The Big Horn Ranch. *Dir* Clifford Smith. *Titl* Gardner Bradford. *Photog* George Stevens, Jack Roach. *Film Ed* Richard Currier.

Cast: Kathleen Key *(Muriel Cooper)*, Chief Big Tree *(Red Eagle)*, Anna May Wong *(Oneta)*, Francis McDonald *(Frank Darwin)*, Tom Santschi *(Jasper)*, Lew Meehan, Guinn Williams.

Western melodrama. Simon Cooper, an old miner, makes a valuable strike but is murdered by bandits who want to discover the location of his mine. Before his death, Cooper confides in Frank Darwin, who frustrates the bandit's efforts. Muriel, the miner's niece, arrives in search of her uncle, and Jasper Martin, the bandit, tells her Darwin is his murderer. Ultimately she learns the truth, marries Darwin, and becomes heir to the mine. *Miners. Uncles. Bandits. Mine claims. Murder.*

Note: Also reviewed under the title *The Devil's Toll.*

DESIRE **F2.1293**

Metro Pictures. 1 Oct **1923** [c17 Sep 1923; LP19414]. Si; b&w. 35mm. 7 reels, 6,500 ft.

Pres by Louis Burston. *Dir* Rowland V. Lee. *Story-Scen (see note)* John B. Clymer, Henry R. Symonds. *Photog* George Barnes. *Art Dir* J. J. Hughes.

Cast: Marguerite De La Motte *(Ruth Cassell)*, John Bowers *(Bob Elkins)*, Estelle Taylor *(Madalyn Harlan)*, David Butler *(Jerry Ryan)*, Walter Long *(Bud Reisner)*, Edward Connelly *(Rupert Cassell)*, Ralph Lewis *(De Witt Harlan)*, Chester Conklin *(Oland Young)*, Vera Lewis *(Mrs. De Witt Harlan)*, Nick Cogley *(Patrick Ryan)*, Sylvia Ashton *(Mrs. Patrick Ryan)*, Frank Currier *(Mrs. Elkins)*, Lars Landers *(The Best Man)*.

Melodrama. Society children Madalyn Harlan and Bob Elkins separate the day they are to be married. Madalyn marries her chauffeur, Jerry, while Bob falls in love with unsophisticated Ruth Cassell and, after careful consideration, marries her. Madalyn's marriage is unhappy, ending in a double suicide after Madalyn's parents disown her and Jerry's family proves to be lower class. *Social classes. Parenthood. Marriage. Suicide.*

Note: Copyright records suggest that scenario was written by John B. Clymer alone.

THE DESIRED WOMAN **F2.1294**

Warner Brothers Pictures. 27 Aug **1927** [c20 Aug 1927; LP24330]. Si; b&w. 35mm. 7 reels, 6,408 ft.

Dir Michael Curtiz. *Scen* Anthony Coldewey. *Story* Mark Canfield. *Camera* Conrad Wells. *Asst Dir* Henry Blanke.

Cast: Irene Rich *(Diana Maxwell)*, William Russell *(Captain Maxwell)*, William Collier, Jr. *(Lieut. Larry Trent)*, Douglas Gerrard *(Fitzroy)*, Jack Ackroyd *(Henery)*, John Miljan *(Lieutenant Kellogg)*, Richard Tucker *(Sir Sydney Vincent)*.

Romantic melodrama. The beautiful and cultured Lady Diana Whitney marries Captain Maxwell of the British Army. When he is transferred to the Sahara, life at his remote post becomes one trial after another for Diana. Then Larry Trent, a young lieutenant, arrives to provide a pleasant reminder of days past, but Maxwell, in a jealous rage over their innocent companionship, sends Trent to a distant village. Moreover, fearing the attentions being paid his wife by Lieutenant Kellogg, he assigns Kellogg a torturous desert patrol. Larry finds Kellogg suffering from sunstroke and brings him to the post; he persuades Diana to elope with him, but she repents her action and returns to her husband. Larry shoots Kellogg to preserve the girl's honor and is sentenced to prison. Diana returns to London, divorces Maxwell, and marries Sir Sydney, a former suitor, who obtains a pardon for Larry. *Murder. Jealousy. Divorce. Deserts. Sahara. Great Britain—Army.*

Note: Some sources suggest that the location of the film story is India instead of North Africa.

A DESPERATE ADVENTURE **F2.1295**

Independent Pictures. 20 Jun or 29 Sep **1924.** Si; b&w. 35mm. 5 reels, ca4,880 ft.

Pres by Jesse J. Goldburg. *Dir* J. P. McGowan. *Story* James Ormont. *Photog* Walter Griffin.

Cast: Franklyn Farnum, Marie Walcamp, Priscilla Bonner.

Western drama. "... involving a Secret Service agent's adventures in running down a band of smugglers. The love romance develops along with the mystery plot by having the father of the heroine become involved with the 'Black Pete gang.' The difficulties facing the hero are smoothed out, however, and he performs his duty as a Government agent and brings his suit for the girl's hand to a successful issue." (*Motion Picture News Booking Guide,* [7]:20, Oct 1924.) *Smugglers. Secret service.*

DESPERATE CHANCE **F2.1296**

Anchor Film Distributors. *Dist* Rayart Pictures. Mar **1926.** Si; b&w. 35mm. 5 reels, 4,462 ft.

Prod Morris R. Schlank. *Dir* J. P. McGowan. *Story* Charles Saxton.

Cast: Bob Reeves, Ione Reed, Leon De La Mothe, Charles Whittaker, Gypsy Clarke, Harry Hurley.

Western melodrama. "Girl's father in sore financial straits because of corporation man is aided by stranger who reveals that his father was ruined same way by the same person. When this man is found dead suspicion falls on girl's father but the employer of murdered man confesses." (*Motion Picture News Booking Guide,"* 11:26, Oct 1926.) *Businessmen. Strangers. Finance—Personal. Murder.*

DESPERATE COURAGE **F2.1297**

Action Pictures. *Dist* Pathé Exchange. 15 Jan **1928** [c12 Jan 1928; LP24851]. Si; b&w. 35mm. 5 reels, 4,398 ft.

Dir Richard Thorpe. *Scen* Frank L. Inghram. *Story* Grant Taylor. *Photog* Ray Reis.

Cast: Wally Wales *(Jim Dane)*, Olive Hasbrouck *(Ann Halliday)*, Tom Bay *(Colonel Halliday)*, Lafe McKee, Fanchon Frankel, Bill Dyer *(the Brannon brothers)*, Charles Whitaker, Al Taylor, S. S. Simon.

Western melodrama. Jim Dane, arriving at the Halliday ranch to see Ann, his sweetheart, finds the Brannon brothers persecuting Ann's father, Colonel Halliday. They have already taken Halliday's cattle, which they claim according to a Spanish land grant, and are about to take the horses when Jim drives them away. The case comes to trial, and Brannon, presenting the fake land grant, thinks he has won. When a fire starts in the building, however, the document is destroyed. The Brannon gang, realizing that Dane is a threat to their plans, try to kill him, but he frustrates them. The Brannons take Ann prisoner, but Dane comes to the rescue and holds off the gang until help arrives. *Ranchers. Brothers. Land rights. Documentation.*

THE DESPERATE GAME (Blue Streak Western) **F2.1298**

Universal Pictures. 14 Feb **1926** [c22 Jan 1926; LP22318]. Si; b&w. 35mm. 5 reels, 4,400 ft.

Dir Joseph Franz. *Story* George C. Jenks. *Photog* William Thornley.

Cast: Pete Morrison *(Jim Wesley)*, Dolores Gardner *(Marguerite Grayson)*, James Welsh *(Jim's father)*, Jere Austin *(Mel Larrimer)*, J. P. Lockney *(Adam Grayson)*, Al Richmond *(Montana McGraw)*, Virginia Warwick *(Belle Deane)*, Lew Meehan *(Bat Grayson)*, Milburn Morante *(Shinney)*, William Merrill McCormick *(Luke Grayson)*.

Western melodrama. Jim Wesley returns from college with a silk shirt and eastern ways, earning the contempt of the cowpunchers on his father's ranch. With a little hard riding and fancy roping, however, Jim proves himself to be a regular guy. Jim's father is involved in a dispute over water rights with Adam Grayson, a neighboring rancher, and the two men decide to settle the disagreement by a marriage between Jim and Grayson's daughter, Marguerite. The young people refuse, but when Marguerite is attacked by a rejected suitor, Jim comes quickly to her rescue. When a fight later breaks out between the men from the neighboring ranches, Marguerite steps in and puts an end to it. Having fallen in love, Jim and Marguerite decide to wed. *Cowboys. Ranchers. Water rights.*

A DESPERATE MOMENT (Royal Production) **F2.1299**

Banner Productions. *Dist* Henry Ginsberg Distributing Corp. 19 Jan **1926** [New York showing; c25 Jan 1926; LP22322]. Si; b&w. 35mm. 6 reels, 5,781 ft.

Dir Jack Dawn. *Titl* Bertha M. Price. *Story* Coral Burnette. *Photog* Roland Price. *Film Ed* Joe Basil. *Asst Dir* Joe Basil.

Cast: Wanda Hawley *(Virginia Dean)*, Theodore von Eltz *(Capt. John Reynolds)*, Sheldon Lewis *(Blackie Slade)*, Leo White *(Percy Warren)*, Dan Mason *(Jim Warren)*, James Neill *(Peter Dean)*, Bill Franey *(Sam)*.

Melodrama. While on a yachting trip with her father, Virginia Dean falls in love with the vessel's captain, John Reynolds. The yacht is seized by a gang of criminals that have stowed away, and Virginia's father and the crew are set adrift in a small boat. John and Virginia are kept on board the yacht, which soon catches fire. All aboard abandon ship and take refuge on a nearby tropical island. Blackie, the leader of the thugs, incites the natives to attack the others; Blackie is slain, and the rest are rescued by a passing steamer. John and Virginia are united. *Sea captains. Yachtsmen. Ship fires. Tropics.*

DESPERATE ODDS **F2.1300**

H. Jane Raum Productions. *Dist* Sierra Pictures. 15 Feb **1925** [or May 1926]. Si; b&w. 35mm. 5 reels, 4,360 ft.

Dir Horace B. Carpenter.

Cast: Bob Burns, Dorothy Donald.

Western melodrama. "Cowboy riding about looking for a job meets adventure when an attack by bandits on a widow's home affords opportunity for a lively scrap in which he triumphs. The bandits abduct the girl the cowboy met when he first came to town, and this gives him another chance at the bad men. His bravery in her behalf wins the love of the girl." (*Motion Picture News Booking Guide,* 8:23, Apr 1925.) *Cowboys. Widows. Bandits. Abduction.*

DESPERATE TRAILS **F2.1301**

Universal Film Manufacturing Co. Jun **1921** [c11 Jun 1921; LP16667]. Si; b&w. 35mm. 5 reels, 4,577 ft.

Pres by Carl Laemmle. *Dir* Jack Ford. *Scen* Elliott J. Clawson. *Photog* Harry Fowler, Robert De Grasse.

Cast: Harry Carey *(Bart Carson)*, Irene Rich *(Mrs. Walker)*, Georgie Stone *(Dannie Boy)*, Helen Field *(Carrie)*, Edward Coxen *(Walter A. Walker)*, Barbara La Marr *(Lady Lou)*, George Siegmann *(Sheriff Price)*, Charles E. Insley *(Doc Higgins)*.

Western melodrama. Source: Courtney Ryley Cooper, "Christmas Eve at Pilot Butte," in *Redbook* (36:59–63, Jan 1921). Bart Carson believes himself to be in love with Lady Lou and is persuaded by her to assume the guilt for her "brother," who has deserted his wife and children and robbed the train. In prison Bart learns that the "brother," Walker, is actually Lou's lover, and he escapes to kill him, then goes to the Walker home on Christmas Eve. So that Mrs. Walker will receive the reward, he gives himself up as the prisoner of her young son, but the sheriff informs him that Lou has confessed her perfidy and that justice will prevail. *Prison escapees. Infidelity. Revenge. Christmas.*

Note: Working title: *Christmas Eve at Pilot Butte.*

DESPERATE YOUTH **F2.1302**

Universal Film Manufacturing Co. 25 Apr **1921** [c7 Apr 1921; LP16376]. Si; b&w. 35mm. 5 reels, 4,505 ft.

Dir Harry B. Harris. *Scen* George C. Hull, A. P. Younger. *Photog* Earl M. Ellis.

Cast: Gladys Walton *(Rosemary Merridew)*, J. Farrell MacDonald *("Mendocino" Bill)*, Lewis Willoughby *("Alabam" Spencer Merridew/ Henry Merridew)*, Muriel Godfrey Turner *(Mrs. Merridew)*, Hazel Howell *(Pauline Merridew)*, Harold Miller *(Dr. Tom Dowling)*, Lucretia Harris *(Aunt Chlordiny)*, Jim Blackwell *(Sam)*.

Melodrama. Source: Francis Hopkinson Smith, "A Kentucky Cinderella" (publication undetermined). A claim jumper kills "Alabam"; and his partner, "Mendocino," sends Rosemary to his brother, Henry, in a southern city. Henry welcomes her, but his wife and daughter, Pauline, see her as an intruder, especially when young Tom Dowling, whom Mrs. Merridew seeks to match with her daughter, falls in love with Rosemary. Through efforts of the Negro servants, Chlo and Sam, Rosemary and Tom are united. Mendocino, who has struck it rich, comes to the wedding. *Orphans. Domestics. Claim jumpers. Youth. United States—South.*

DESTINY *see* **A WOMAN OF PARIS**

DESTINY'S ISLE **F2.1303**

William P. S. Earle Pictures. *Dist* American Releasing Corp. 30 Apr **1922** [c30 Apr 1922; LP18108]. Si; b&w. 35mm. 6 reels, 5,496 ft.

Pres by William P. S. Earle. *Dir* William P. S. Earle. *Story* Margery Land May. *Photog* William S. Adams.

Cast: Virginia Lee *(Lola Whitaker)*, Ward Crane *(Tom Proctor)*, Florence Billings *(Florence Martin)*, Arthur Housman *(Arthur Randall)*, George Fawcett *(Judge Richard Proctor)*, William B. Davidson *(Lazus)*, Mario Majeroni *(Dr. Whitaker)*, Ida Darling *(Mrs. Pierpont)*, Albert Roccardi *(Mrs. Ripp)*, Pauline Dempsey *(Mammy)*.

Romantic society drama. Feeling jilted after seeing his sweetheart, Florence, in his rival's arms, Tom is injured and cast ashore on an island near the Florida coast when his motorboat is struck by lightning. There he is nursed by Lola, a doctor's daughter; and to allay the suspicions of Florence and her guardian, Tom declares that Lola is his wife. In her pique, Florence tries to implicate Tom in a crime, but Lola accepts the blame instead. The rival exposes Florence's trickery, and Tom marries his island girl. *Physicians. Breach of promise. Motorboats. Florida.*

THE DESTROYING ANGEL **F2.1304**

Arthur F. Beck. *Dist* Associated Exhibitors. 19 Aug **1923** [c11 Aug 1923; LU19297]. Si; b&w. 35mm. 6 reels, 5,640 ft.

Dir W. S. Van Dyke. *Scen* Leah Baird. *Photog* André Barlatier.

Cast: Leah Baird *(Mary Miller/Sara Law)*, John Bowers *(Hugh Miller Whittaker)*, Noah Beery *(Curtis Drummond)*, Ford Sterling *(Max Weil)*, Mitchell Lewis *("Strangler" Olsen)*.

Romantic comedy. Source: Louis Joseph Vance, *The Destroying Angel* (Boston, 1912). Hugh Whittaker, who believes he has only a few months to live, meets a girl who has been deserted by her lover and marries her to prevent a scandal when she returns home. He goes to Europe, recovers his health, and returns to New York where he meets and falls in love with Sara Law, an actress. Sara recognizes Hugh as her husband but she becomes the victim of kidnapers and is not reunited with Hugh until he trails her; then she reveals herself as his wife. *Actors. Death. Marriage. Kidnaping.*

DETECTIVES **F2.1305**

Metro-Goldwyn-Mayer Pictures. 9 Jun **1928** [c9 Jun 1928; LP25391]. Si; b&w. 35mm. 7 reels, 5,838 or 5,842 ft.

Dir Chester M. Franklin. *Story-Cont* Robert Lord, Chester M. Franklin. *Titl* Robert Hopkins. *Photog* John Arnold. *Film Ed* Frank Sullivan. *Wardrobe* David Cox.

Cast: Karl Dane *(house detective)*, George K. Arthur *(bellhop)*, Marceline Day *(Lois)*, Tenen Holtz *(Orloff)*, Felicia Drenova *(Mrs. Winters)*, Tetsu Komai *(Chin Lee)*, Clinton Lyle *(Roberts)*.

Comedy-drama. ". . . house detective and bellhop are rivals for the love of the public stenographer. Burglary is committed in hotel and reward offered for return of stolen jewels. Girl promised to marry bellhop if he wins reward. After many exciting episodes, he runs down the burglar and outwits the house detective in gaining the reward." (*Motion Picture News Booking Guide*, [14]:245, 1929.) *Detectives. Bellboys. Burglars. Stenographers. Hotels.*

DETERMINATION **F2.1306**

United States Moving Picture Corp. *Dist* Lee-Bradford Corp. Jan or Mar **1922**. Si; b&w. 35mm. 10 reels, 8,807-11,500 ft.

Pres by James W. Martin. *Dir* Joseph Levering. *Adtl Dir* Garfield Thompson, James W. Martin, George McCutchin, H. McRae Webster. *Scen* Garfield Thompson. *Story* Captain Stoll. *Photog* William L. Crolly. *Art Dir* Herbert L. Messmore.

Cast: Alpheus Lincoln *(John Morton Jr./James Melvale)*, Corinne Uzzell *(Madge Daley)*, Irene Tams *(Lucky)*, Maurice Costello *(Putnam)*, Walter Ringham *(Lord Warburton)*, Gene Burnell *(Frances Lloyd)*, Mabel Allen *(Lady Dalton)*, Byron Russell *(Lord Dalton)*, Nina Herbert *(Whitechapel Mary)*, Charles Ascott *(dopefiend)*, Hayden Stevenson *(Sport Smiler)*, Bernard Randall, Louis Wolheim.

Melodrama. London settlement worker John Morton, Jr., is unaware of the existence of his twin brother, James Melvale, a Paris man-about-town. Frances Lloyd, the wealthy daughter of an American senator, becomes interested in John's work and falls in love with him; but his rival, Lord Warburton, makes Frances believe that John is also James. After many adventures in the underworlds of London and Paris, Warburton is exposed as an imposter and leader of crooks; the brothers are reunited; James reforms; and John finds happiness with Frances. *Settlement workers. Twins. Brothers. Men-about-town. Wealth. Narcotics. Imposture. Slums. London. Paris.*

Note: Mabel Allen may actually be Mabel Adams.

DEUCE HIGH **F2.1307**

Action Pictures. *Dist* Weiss Brothers Artclass Pictures. 22 Apr **1926**. Si; b&w. 35mm. 5 reels, 4,550 ft.

Dir Richard Thorpe. *Scen* Walter J. Coburn.

Cast: Buffalo Bill Jr. *(Ted Crawford)*, Alma Rayford *(Nell Clifton)*, Robert Walker *(Ranger McLeod)*, J. P. Lockney *(Mandell Armstrong)*, Harry Lord *(Jim Blake)*.

Western melodrama. "Cowpuncher, thinking he is a murderer and no longer caring for life for this reason, risks his life to save ranch. Discovers that man supposedly murdered was only stunned." (*Motion Picture News Booking Guide*, 11:27, Oct 1926.) *Cowboys. Murder. Ranches.*

THE DEUCE OF SPADES **F2.1308**

Charles Ray Productions. *Dist* First National Exhibitors Circuit. May **1922** [c5 May 1922; LP17827]. Si; b&w. 35mm. 5 reels, 4,505 ft.

Pres by Arthur S. Kane. *Dir* Charles Ray. *Scen* Andres Richard. *Titl* Edward Withers, Alfred W. Alley. *Photog* George Rizard. *Adtl Photog* Ellsworth H. Rumer. *Art Dir* Wilfred Buckland. *Film Ed* Harry L. Decker. *Asst Dir* Albert Ray, Charles Van Deroef.

Cast: Charles Ray *(Amos)*, Marjorie Maurice *(Sally)*, Lincoln Plumer *(Elkhorn Jenkins)*, Phillip Dunham *(Edwin Dobbs)*, Andrew Arbuckle *(Fat Ed)*, Dick Sutherland *(bouncer)*, Jack Richardson *(Hawk-nose)*, J. P. Lockney *(restaurant owner)*, Gus Leonard *(peddler)*, Bert Offord *(The Sponge)*, William Courtwright *(Driver Bill)*.

Comedy-drama. Source: Charles E. Van Loan, "The Weight of the Last Straw" (publication undetermined). Amos, an unsophisticated Bostonian, goes west to Little Butte, Montana, a relic of the mining days, where the town restaurant is turned over to him at gunpoint. With the help of Sally, the waitress, Amos converts the establishment into a model of cleanliness, and his business prospers so that he is able to return to Boston. At the railroad station Amos is victimized by an old card trick; this error costs him his savings, and returning to the town he finds that his restaurant has been decorated with deuces of spades. In a wild fury, he shoots up the town, and when the gamblers who fleeced him stop in he forces them to eat a special deuce-of-spades sandwich, recovers his losses from them, and chases them out of town. *Restaurateurs. Bostonians. Gamblers. Swindlers. Montana.*

THE DEVIL **F2.1309**

Associated Exhibitors. *Dist* Pathé Exchange. 16 Jan **1921** [New York premiere; released Feb; c22 Dec 1920; LU15953]. Si; b&w. 35mm. 6 reels, 5,682 ft.

Prod Harry Leonhardt, Andrew J. Callaghan. *Dir* James Young. *Story-Scen* Edmund Goulding. *Photog* Harry A. Fischbeck. *Art Dir* Charles O. Seessel. *Art Work* Frederick E. Triebel. *Architect & Tech* Clark Robinson.

Cast: George Arliss *(Dr. Muller)*, Sylvia Breamer *(Mimi)*, Lucy Cotton *(Marie Matin)*, Mrs. George Arliss *(her aunt)*, Edmund Lowe *(Paul de Veaux)*, Roland Bottomley *(Georges Roben)*.

Satiric drama. Source: Ferenc Molnár, *Az ördög; vigjáték három felvonásban* (Budapest, 1908; adapted by Oliver Herford as *The Devil; a Comedy in Three Acts* [New York, 1908]). Dr. Muller, a friend to all, finds pleasure in turning the goodness in people to evil ends. He meets Marie Matin and her fiancé, Georges Roben, while viewing a new painting, "The Martyr—Truth Crucified by Evil." Marie declares that the picture was wrong—evil could never triumph over truth—and though Muller says he agrees with her, he plots to prove otherwise. To this end, he entangles Marie with artist Paul de Veaux, Georges's best friend, causing the latter's model, Mimi, to become jealous. Georges, believing that he is standing between Paul and Marie, releases Marie from her engagement. Marie finds Paul with Mimi and turns back to Georges, whom she marries. This does not discourage Muller, who but for Marie's purity almost succeeds in his evil designs. As a last resort, Muller lures Marie to his apartment. There she prays for help; a vision of a shining cross appears; and Muller is consumed in flames. Marie and Georges are happily reunited. *Artists. Models. Demonology. Good and evil. Infidelity.*

THE DEVIL DANCER **F2.1310**

Samuel Goldwyn, Inc. *Dist* United Artists. 3 Nov **1927** [Los Angeles premiere; released 19 Nov; c29 Dec 1927; LP24804]. Si; b&w. 35mm. 8 reels, 7,600 ft.

Dir Fred Niblo. *Dir (see note)* Alfred Raboch, Lynn Shores. *Scen* Alice D. G. Miller. *Titl* Edwin Justus Mayer. *Story* Harry Hervey. *Cinematog* George Barnes, Thomas Brannigan. *Set Dsgn* Willy Pogany, Harold Grieve. *Film Ed* Viola Lawrence. *Asst Dir* H. B. Humberstone.

Cast: Gilda Gray *(Takla, The Devil Dancer)*, Clive Brook *(Stephen Athelstan)*, Anna May Wong *(Sada)*, Serge Temoff *(Beppo)*, Michael Vavitch *(Hassim)*, Sojin *(Sadik Lama)*, Ura Mita, Ann Schaeffer *(Tana, see note)*, Albert Conti *(Arnold Guthrie)*, Clarissa Selwynne, Martha Mattox *(Isabel, see note)*, Kalla Pasha *(Toy)*, James B. Leong *(The Grand Lama)*, William H. Tooker *(Lathrop)*, Claire Du Brey *(Audrey)*, Nora Cecil *(Julia)*, Barbara Tennant *(The White Woman)*.

Romantic melodrama. Takla, a white orphan brought up and kept captive in a Himalayan monastery, is rescued by Althestan, an adventurous Englishman who falls in love with her. His sister, displeased with her brother's choice, arranges to have Takla kidnaped. Althestan searches for her and eventually finds her with a troupe of itinerant Muslim entertainers. *Brother-sister relationship. Muslims. Islam. Monasteries. Himalayan Mountains.*

Note: According to *Variety* (9 Nov 1927) Alfred Raboch began the film with Lynn Shores as his assistant. Then Lynn Shores became director, and Alfred Raboch became his assistant. Finally, Fred Niblo took over, finished the film, and received sole screen credit. Press sheet credits Ura Mita and Clarissa Selwynne with roles of Tana and Isabel, while trade reviews credit Ann Schaeffer and Martha Mattox.

DEVIL DOG DAWSON **F2.1311**

Unity Photoplays. *Dist* Arrow Film Corp. May **1921.** Si; b&w. 35mm. 5 reels.

Ben Wilson Production. *Story* Carl Coolidge.

Cast: Jack Hoxie, Helen Rosson, Evelyn Selbie, Wilbur McGaugh, Arthur Mackley.

Northwest melodrama. "Hero (title name) in full cowboy attire and equipment, blows into Bartlett's camp, a little combination lumbering and mining settlement in Northwest. In the town, living alone, is Widow Larson, a long resident, but whose past history is unknown. A robbery occurs, and melodrama gets under way. Incidental love interest." (*Motion Picture News Booking Guide,* 1:29, Dec 1921.) *Lumbering. Mining. Robbery.*

DEVIL DOGS **F2.1312**

Morris R. Schlank Productions. *Dist* Anchor Film Distributors, Crescent Pictures. 23 Aug **1928** [New York showing; New York State license: 13 Aug 1927]. Si; b&w. 35mm. 6 reels, 5,361 ft.

Dir Fred Windermere. *Cont* Maxine Alton. *Titl* Al Martin. *Adapt* Adele Buffington. *Photog* Robert E. Cline. *Film Ed* L. Rosen.

Cast: Alexander Alt *(Archie Van Stratten)*, Pauline Curley *(Joyce Moore)*, Stuart Holmes *(Sgt. Gordon White)*, Ernest Hilliard *(Lieutenant Holmes)*, J. P. McGowan *(Captain Standing)*.

Comedy. "Story is of two boys [Archie Van Stratten and Gordon White] who join the army and go to the front. Both after the same girl. One of the boys has a mustache. The other gets into jams with the captain and is sent to jail. He comes out of jail. And so on ... to the end." (*Variety,* 29 Aug 1928, p28.) *Soldiers. World War I. United States Army.*

THE DEVIL HORSE **F2.1313**

Hal Roach Productions. *Dist* Pathé Exchange. 12 Sep **1926** [c6 Mar 1926; LU22462]. Si; b&w. 35mm. 6 reels, 5,853 ft.

Dir Fred Jackman. *Story* Hal Roach. *Photog* Floyd Jackman, George Stevens.

Cast: Rex *(The Devil Horse)*, The Killer *(A Black and White [horse])*, Lady *(herself, a horse)*, Yakima Canutt *(Dave Garson)*, Gladys Morrow *(Marion Marrow)*, Robert Kortman *(Prowling Wolf)*, Roy Clements *(Major Morrow)*, Master Fred Jackson *(Young Dave)*.

Western melodrama. A wagon train of Montana settlers is attacked by Indians, and all but young Dave Garson are slaughtered. Years pass, and Dave grows to manhood hating the Indians and shouting for the cavalry. Prowling Wolf, a renegade Indian, kidnaps the major's daughter, and Dave, riding the much-feared Devil Horse, rescues her. The following day, the Indians attack the fort and destroy the ammunition stores. Daves rides for help and, reaching a wagon train, sends shells and powder back to the fort. *Settlers. Indians of North America. Wagon trains. Forts. Montana. United States Army—Cavalry. Horses.*

A DEVIL WITH WOMEN **F2.1314**

Fox Film Corp. 18 Oct **1930** [New York premiere; released 16 Nov; c7 Oct 1930; LP1649]. Sd (Movietone); b&w. 35mm. 7 reels, 5,750 ft.

Pres by William Fox. *Assoc Prod* George Middleton. *Dir* Irving Cummings. *Screenplay-Dial* Dudley Nichols, Henry M. Johnson. *Photog* Arthur Todd, Al Brick. *Art Dir* William Darling. *Film Ed* Jack Murray. *Song: "Amor Mio"* Cliff Friend, Jimmy Monaco. *Rec Engr* George P. Costello, E. Clayton Ward, Harry Leonard. *Asst Dir* Charles Woolstenhulme. *Cost* Sophie Wachner.

Cast: Victor McLaglen *(Jerry Maxton)*, Mona Maris *(Rosita Fernández)*, Humphrey Bogart *(Tom Standish)*, Luana Alcaniz *(Dolores)*, John St. Polis *(Don Diego)*, Michael Vavitch *(Morloff)*, Solidad Jiminez *(duenna)*, Mona Rico *(Alicia)*, Robert Edeson *(General García)*, Joe De La Cruz *(Juan)*.

Adventure melodrama. Source: Clements Ripley, "Dust and Sun," in *Adventure Magazine* (15 Dec 1928). En route to Central America, Tom Standish makes futile advances toward Alicia, who is detained by seaport customs officials for smuggling guns to revolutionaries. Jerry, on his way to capture Morloff, the revolutionary leader, encounters Tom and Alicia, now friends, and great rivalry springs up between the two men. At Del Rio, Alicia meets Dolores, also working for Morloff, and they plan to detain Jerry until Morloff arrives. At Dolores' apartment, Jerry is overpowered and thrown into jail, where he is held for ransom. By a ruse, Jerry and Tom escape and rescue Rosita and her duenna from the villains. But both fall in love with Rosita, who returns Tom's affections, while her father thinks she loves Jerry. When the bandits attack the hacienda, Jerry goes for aid and appoints Tom in charge, but he returns with the disarmed Morloff, who is killed by his own men in an escape attempt. Jerry gives Tom and Rosita his blessings and sets out in search of another war. *Soldiers of fortune. Revolutionaries. Vamps. Bandits. Courtship. Central America.*

Note: Initially reviewed as *On the Make.*

THE DEVIL WITHIN **F2.1315**

Fox Film Corp. 20 Nov **1921** [c20 Nov 1921; LP17287]. Si; b&w. 35mm. 6 reels, 5,997 ft.

Pres by William Fox. *Dir* Bernard J. Durning. *Scen* Arthur J. Zellner. *Photog* Don Short.

Cast: Dustin Farnum *(Captain Briggs)*, Virginia Valli *(Laura)*, Nigel De Brulier *(Dr. Philiol)*, Bernard Durning *(Hal)*, Jim Farley *(Scurlock)*, Tom O'Brien *(Wansley)*, Bob Perry *(Crevay)*, Charles Gorman *(Bevins)*, Otto Hoffman *(Ezra)*, Kirk Incas *(cabin boy)*, Evelyn Selbie *(witch)*, Hazel Deane *(juvenile witch)*.

Sea melodrama. Source: George Allan England, *Cursed* (Boston, 1919). Captain Briggs, a drunkard and a tyrannical brute, while cruising in the South Seas in the 1870's, steals an idol from some islanders and thereby provokes an attack on his ship; the natives are beaten, and their witch calls down a curse on the captain. In port Briggs sells his opium cargo, becomes wealthy, and marries. In time, the captain's wife and child die, and his nephew Hal becomes a sailor. In a drunken brawl, Hal steals the captain's savings and arouses the fear of his sweetheart, Laura. In a battle, Hal is wounded with a poisonous Malay sword, and Dr. Philiol succeeds in mixing the indicated remedy just in time to save his life. After a long illness, Hal reforms, regains the love of his aged uncle, and wins the hand of Laura. *Sea captains. Uncles. Sailors. Witches. Theft. Opium. South Sea Islands.*

DEVIL-MAY-CARE **F2.1316**

Metro-Goldwyn-Mayer Pictures. 27 Dec **1929** [c13 Jan 1930; LP989]. Sd (Movietone); b&w. 35mm. 11 reels, 8,782 ft.

Dir Sidney Franklin. *Stage Dir* J. Clifford Brooke. *Scen* Hans Kraly. *Dial* Zelda Sears. *Adapt* Richard Schayer. *Photog* Merritt B. Gerstad. *Art Dir* Cedric Gibbons. *Film Ed* Conrad A. Nervig. *Ballet Mus* Dimitri Tiomkin. *Songs: "The Old Guard Song," "The Gang Song," "Why Waste Your Charms?" "Madame Pompadour," "Charming," "If He Cared," "Shepherd's Serenade"* Herbert Stothart, Clifford Grey. *Ballet Dir*

Albertina Rasch. *Rec Engr* Ralph Shugart, Douglas Shearer. *Sd Asst* Jack Jordon. *Gowns* Adrian.

Cast: Ramon Novarro *(Armand)*, Dorothy Jordan *(Léonie)*, Marion Harris *(Louise)*, John Miljan *(De Grignon)*, William Humphrey *(Napoleon)*, George Davis *(Groom)*, Clifford Bruce *(Gaston)*.

Musical costume drama. Source: Augustin Eugène Scribe and Ernest Legouvé, *La Bataille de dames, ou un duel en amour* (Paris, 1851). When Napoleon is banished to Elba, Armand, one of his daring young followers, escapes death and makes his way to his cousin's home in the south of France. En route, he is forced to enter a house to escape pursuing Royalist soldiers, and there he encounters Léonie. Upon learning he is a Bonapartist, she attempts to turn him over to the Royalists, but he escapes. Later, at the home of his cousin, De Grignon, disguised as a butler, he again meets and falls in love with Léonie. With the return of Napoleon, Léonie capitulates and admits her love for Armand. *Bonapartists. Royalists. Disguise. Napoleonic Wars. Elba. France. Napoleon I.*

DEVIL'S ANGEL **F2.1317**

Dist Clark-Cornelius Corp. 3 Jan **1922** [New York State license]. Si; b&w. 35mm. 5 reels.

Dir Lejaren a'Hiller.

Cast: Helen Gardner *(Cymba Roget)*, Templar Saxe *(The Hindoo Hypnotist)*, Peggy O'Neil *(artist's model)*, C. D. Williams, Lejaren a'Hiller, Marc Connelly.

Melodrama. Escaping from a hypnotist's influence, Cymba becomes a model for three bohemian artists. *Hypnotists. Artists. Models. Bohemianism.*

THE DEVIL'S APPLE TREE **F2.1318**

Tiffany-Stahl Productions. 20 Feb **1929** [c11 Feb 1929; LP111]. Si; b&w. 35mm. 7 reels, 6,430 ft.

Dir Elmer Clifton. *Story-Cont* Lillian Ducey. *Titl* Frederick Hatton, Fanny Hatton. *Photog* Ernest Miller. *Film Ed* Frank Sullivan.

Cast: Dorothy Sebastian *(Dorothy Ryan)*, Larry Kent *(John Rice)*, Edward Martindel *(Colonel Rice)*, Ruth Clifford *(Jane Norris)*, George Cooper *(Cooper)*, Cosmo Kyrle Bellew *(The Roué)*.

Melodrama. Dorothy Ryan, traveling steerage to a tropical island to marry Cooper, a man to whom she has become engaged through a matrimonial agency, assumes the identity of wealthy Jane Norris, a young woman who appears to be dying from smallpox. Arriving on the island, Dorothy slights Cooper and goes to live with Colonel Rice, falling in love with his son, John. Jane Norris, fully recovered, appears, and Dorothy is exposed as a fraud. Dorothy then wanders distractedly into the jungle and is captured by the natives, who make plans to burn her alive. Though Cooper rescues her, John kills Cooper in a fight. John and Dorothy declare their renewed love for each other. *Matrimonial agencies. Impersonation. Human sacrifice. Smallpox. South Sea Islands.*

THE DEVIL'S BOWL **F2.1319**

William Steiner Productions. 15 Mar **1923** [c10 Feb 1923; LU18653]. Si; b&w. 35mm. 5 reels.

Dir-Prepared for the screen by Neal Hart. *Photog* Jake Badaracco.

Cast in order of appearance: Catherine Bennett *(Helen Hand)*, W. J. Allen *(Jim Sands)*, Fonda Holt *(his wife)*, Neal Hart *(Sam Ramsey)*, William McLaughlin *(Sgt. Jerry O'Neill)*, John Beck *(Andy Walker)*, Gertrude Ryan *(Mary Walker)*.

Western melodrama. Source: Philip Le Noir, "The Man Who Wouldn't Take Off His Hat," in *Argosy All Story Weekly* (145:27–46, 19 Aug 1922). Sam Ramsey, a ranch foreman, is engaged to Helen Hand, who has a jealous disposition. She becomes furious and leaves him when he receives a letter in a woman's handwriting. He quits his job and leaves the ranch in response to the letter, which is later revealed to have been written by his sister, Mary, who had married Andy Walker, a horsethief. He finds her in a place called "The Devil's Bowl," in the Mexican badlands, where her husband has taken her. Walker gets the drop on Sam, compelling him to change clothes, and Sam is captured and branded on his forehead as a thief. Later, when Sam and his sister attempt to get out of Mexico, she is ambushed and killed by Walker. The Mexican authorities accuse Sam of the murder, but he finds the real culprit, then returns to patch up his engagement. *Ranch foremen. Horsethieves. Brother-sister relationship. Murder. Branding. Mexico.*

Note: Also advertised under its working title: *In the Devil's Bowl.* Remade or reissued in 1924 under the title *Branded a Thief* (see separate entry). Some plot details have been derived from the shooting script in the copyright files.

THE DEVIL'S CAGE **F2.1320**

Chadwick Pictures. 5 Jun **1928.** Si; b&w. 35mm. 6 reels, 5,400-5,800 ft.

Prod I. E. Chadwick. *Dir* Wilfred Noy. *Story-Scen-Titl* Isadore Bernstein. *Photog* Ted Tetzlaff. *Film Ed* Gene Milford.

Cast: Pauline Garon *(Eloise)*, Ruth Stonehouse *(Marcel)*, Donald Keith *(Franklyn)*, Armand Kaliz *(Pierre)*, Lincoln Stedman *(Maurice)*.

Melodrama. Forced to find work as a dancer in an underworld dive, Eloise, a French girl, again meets Franklyn, an American artist who once saved her from a beating. The cafe's owner, Pierre, becomes insanely jealous when the girl rebuffs him and displays an obvious interest in the artist, and he becomes an apache and swears vengeance. Pierre attacks Franklyn but flees when Eloise feigns death. *Dancers. Apaches—Paris. Artists. Jealousy.*

THE DEVIL'S CARGO **F2.1321**

Famous Players–Lasky. *Dist* Paramount Pictures. 2 Feb **1925** [c27 Jan 1925; LP21073]. Si; b&w. 35mm. 8 reels, 7,980 ft.

Pres by Adolph Zukor, Jesse L. Lasky. *Dir* Victor Fleming. *Screenplay* A. P. Younger. *Story* Charles E. Whittaker. *Photog* C. Edgar Schoenbaum.

Cast: Wallace Beery *(Ben)*, Pauline Starke *(Faro Sampson)*, Claire Adams *(Martha Joyce)*, William Collier, Jr. *(John Joyce)*, Raymond Hatton *(Mate)*, George Cooper *(Jerry Dugan)*, Dale Fuller *(Millie)*, Spec O'Donnell *(Jimmy)*, Emmett C. King *(Square Deal Sampson)*, John Webb Dillon *(Farwell)*, Louis King *(Briggs)*.

Melodrama. Arriving in Sacramento during the Gold Rush of 1849, John Joyce becomes the editor of a newspaper that crusades stridently for the reformation of the manners and morals of Sacramento's citizens. John meets Faro Sampson, whom he believes to be the daughter of a minister; he later discovers that her father is a notorious gambler and that she is the chief attraction of a gambling casino. John spurns Faro, but a group of vigilantes, inspired largely by John's editorial policy, later find him in her room and denounce him as a hypocrite. John and Faro are then herded with the other disreputables of the town onto a cargo ship, to be taken to the East. The deportees overpower the ship's crew and take charge, but a boiler explodes and the ship drifts out into the open sea. A rugged seaman named Ben assumes command and attempts to molest John's sister, who had been put on the boat by accident. John rescues his sister, "the Devil's cargo" are rescued by another ship, and John is reconciled with Faro, finding love more rewarding than reform. *Editors. Vigilantes. Brother-sister relationship. Reformation. Gambling. Newspapers. Gold rushes. California. Sacramento. Ship explosions.*

DEVIL'S CHAPLAIN (Famous Authors) **F2.1322**

Trem Carr Productions. *Dist* Rayart Pictures. 2 or 15 Mar **1929.** Si; b&w. 35mm. 6 reels, 5,451 ft.

Dir Duke Worne. *Scen* Arthur Hoerl. *Photog* Hap Depew. *Film Ed* J. S. Harrington.

Cast: Cornelius Keefe *(Yorke Norray)*, Virginia Brown Faire *(Princess Therese)*, Josef Swickard *(The King)*, Boris Karloff *(Boris)*, Wheeler Oakman *(Nicholay)*, Leland Carr *(Ivan)*, George McIntosh *(The Prince)*.

Romantic melodrama. Source: George Bronson Howard, *Devil's Chaplain* (New York, 1922). A revolution in his Balkan kingdom brings the young heir to the throne to the United States seeking refuge, while his betrothed, Princess Therese, pretends to be a revolutionary in hopes of saving the prince. Stepping in to uncover the international spies involved, U. S. Secret Service agent Yorke Norray takes the prince under his protection and sees him restored to the throne. By this time, Princess Therese realizes her affections lie elsewhere, and she leaves the prince for the American. *Political refugees. Royalty. Secret service. Spies. Imaginary kingdoms. Revolutions. Balkans.*

THE DEVIL'S CIRCUS **F2.1323**

Metro-Goldwyn-Mayer Pictures. 15 Feb **1926** [c1 Mar 1926; LP22466]. Si; b&w. 35mm. 7 reels, 6,750 ft.

Story-Scen-Dir Benjamin Christensen. *Photog* Ben Reynolds.

Cast: Norma Shearer *(Mary)*, Charles Emmett Mack *(Carlstop)*, Carmel Myers *(Yonna)*, John Miljan *(Lieberkind)*, Claire McDowell *(Mrs. Peterson)*, Joyce Coad *(Little Anita)*.

Drama. Mary falls in love with Richard Carlstop, a handsome young pickpocket who takes the innocent young girl into his home and offers her his protection. Richard is then arrested and sent to jail. Desperate for money, Mary finds work with an aerial act that performs its most dangerous stunt over an open lioncage. Lieberkind, the lion tamer, becomes infatuated with Mary and crudely forces his attentions on her. Yonna, his mistress, becomes wild with jealousy and tampers with Mary's trapeze, causing her to fall and severely injure herself. Seven years pass. Richard is released from prison and becomes a shoemaker; he finds Mary, and they are married. Richard later learns about Lieberkind's treatment of Mary and goes after him in a homicidal rage, but his anger turns to pity when he discovers that, wounded in the war, Lieberkind has become a blind beggar. *Lion tamers. Trapezists. Pickpockets. Cobblers. Beggars. Cripples. Rape. Blindness. Circus.*

THE DEVIL'S CONFESSION **F2.1324**
Dist Circle Film Attractions. 5 Mar **1921** [trade review]. Si; b&w. 35mm. 5 reels.
Dir John S. Lopez. *Photog* Frank Perugini.
Cast: Frank Williams *(Bob Perry)*, Lillian Ward *(Kate Perry)*, Mary Eberle *(Ma Perry)*, Louise Lee *(Rose)*, Harold Foshay *(Neil Drake)*.
Melodrama. Bob Perry loses his temper and threatens to kill a scandalmonger who is spreading gossip about the affections paid by Neil Drake to Bob's girl, Rose Hill. When the man is found dead, Bob is arrested and convicted for murder while the actual killer, Neil Drake, goes free. The sentence of death is about to be executed when two children find Drake's cap in a nearby brook. Kate, Bob's sister, feeling certain that Drake is the murderer, entices him to use a Ouija board and forces a confession through its revelations. She rushes the written confession to the governor, who at the last minute pardons Bob. *State governors. Brother-sister relationship. Murder. Capital punishment. Occult. Injustice. Ouija boards. Mental telepathy.*

DEVIL'S DICE **F2.1325**
Banner Productions. *Dist* Sterling Pictures Distributing Corp. 5 Oct **1926** [c12 Oct 1926; LP23211]. Si; b&w. 35mm. 6 reels, 5,377 ft.
Dir Tom Forman. *Adapt* Charles A. Logue. *Photog* Harry Davis.
Cast: Barbara Bedford *(Helen Paine)*, Robert Ellis *(Larry Bannon)*, Josef Swickard *(Judge Casper Paine)*, Tom Forman *(Oberfield)*, James Gordon *(Martin Godfrey)*, Jack Richardson *(Weary)*.
Melodrama. Source: Frank R. Adams, "Devil's Dice" (publication undetermined). Larry Bannon, a young mining engineer, gets into a dice game in a San Francisco gambling establishment and is so successful that the proprietor tries to cheat him. Attempting to escape with his winnings, Bannon wounds a man planted to intercept his flight and is arrested; Judge Casper Paine is unsympathetic to his pleas and sentences him to 3 years' imprisonment. At the time of Bannon's release, Paine, who now operates a mine, is being ruined by Oberfield, his foreman, who is being bribed by Godfrey, a syndicate representative. Paine advertises for an investor, and Bannon responds to his offer under an assumed name. Although he is softened by Helen, the ex-judge's daughter, Bannon is bent on revenge; but after saving him from a mine accident, she tells him about the plotters. After subduing Oberfield and Godfrey in a fight, Bannon is trapped with Helen in a mine flood; but they are rescued at the last minute and find happiness together. *Engineers—Mining. Judges. Gambling. Injustice. Revenge. Courtship. Mines. San Francisco. Floods.*

THE DEVIL'S DISCIPLE **F2.1326**
Micheaux Film Corp. **1926.** Si; b&w. 35mm. [Feature length assumed.]
Cast: Evelyn Preer, Lawrence Chenault.
Comedy. No information about the precise nature of this film has been found. *Negro life.*

THE DEVIL'S DOORYARD **F2.1327**
Ben Wilson Productions. *Dist* Arrow Film Corp. 15 Feb **1923** [c12 Feb 1923; LP18661]. Si; b&w. 35mm. 5 reels, 4,838 ft.
Dir Lewis King.
Cast: William Fairbanks *(Paul Stevens)*, Ena Gregory *(Mary Jane Haley)*, Joseph Girard *(Snag Thorn)*, Bob McKenzie *(Windy Woods)*, Claude Payton *(Fred Bradley)*, Wilbur McGaugh *(Bill Bowers)*, William White *(Sheriff Allen)*.
Western melodrama. Source: W. C. Tuttle, "The Devil's Doooryard," in *Adventure Magazine* (29:149–170, 3 May 1921). "Paul Stevens catches three men in the act of hiding money which they have stolen. He takes the money after they have disappeared and plans to find the real owner. He discovers that he has been murdered and that the money belongs to a relative who is not in town. Paul sends for the relative, known as M. J. Haley, and is surprised to find that M. J. stands for Mary Jane. The thieves attempt to get Paul out of the way, but in a thrilling battle for Mary and himself he holds his own until the sheriff arrives." (*Moving Picture World*, 25 Aug 1923, p658.) *Thieves. Detectives. Murder. Inheritance.*

THE DEVIL'S GHOST **F2.1328**
Dist Western Pictures Exploitation Co. 10 Nov **1922** [New York State license]. Si; b&w. 35mm. 5 reels.
Western melodrama(?). No information about the nature of this film has been found.

THE DEVIL'S GULCH **F2.1329**
R-C Pictures. *Dist* Film Booking Offices of America. 8 Aug **1926** [c24 Jul 1926; LP22961]. Si; b&w. 35mm. 5 reels.
Pres by Joseph P. Kennedy. *Dir* Jack Nelson. *Cont* Barr Cross. *Story* Arthur Preston Hankins.
Cast: Bob Custer *(Ace Remsen, alias I. Nesmer/Deuce Remsen, twin brother)*, Hazel Deane *(Merrill Waverly)*, Charles Belcher *(Max Crew)*, Pat Beggs *(Bill Griggs)*, Roy Laidlaw *(Seth Waverly)*, Mark Hamilton *(sheriff)*, Buck Molton, Tom Bay *(heavies)*.
Western melodrama. Deuce Remsen, a mine guard, is found dead, evidently from a rattlesnake bite, but a message indicates he was murdered by "Twin Hand," a notorious bandit who, because of a nervous condition, must use both hands together; furthermore, Twin Hand has robbed the bullion vault. Deuce's twin brother, Ace, determines to avenge Deuce's death, and a small clue leads him to Gaileyville, where he meets Merrill, a town girl, and Max Crew, a local politician who wants to marry her. Under an alias, Ace gets work as a cowpuncher and suspects Crew because he always keeps his hands in his pockets, while Crew notes Ace's resemblance to Deuce and orders his men to get him. Merrill, riding out to see Ace with Bill Briggs, an orphan friend, stalls the men's attempt to lure Ace into a trap. Ace, by a ruse making them follow him, captures them. After employing a rattlesnake to force a confession from Crew, Ace is united with Merrill. *Cowboys. Brothers. Twins. Murder. Robbery. Neurological disorders. Snakes.*

THE DEVIL'S HOLIDAY **F2.1330**
Paramount-Publix Corp. 9 May **1930** [c23 May 1930; LP1326]. Sd (Movietone); b&w. 35mm. 9 reels, 6,743 ft.
Dir-Story-Scen Edmund Goulding. *Photog* Harry Fischbeck. *Film Ed* George Nichols, Jr. *Mus Score* Edmund Goulding. *Song: "You Are a Song"* Leo Robin, Edmund Goulding. *Rec Engr* Harry D. Mills.
Cast: Nancy Carroll *(Hallie Hobart)*, Phillips Holmes *(David Stone)*, James Kirkwood *(Mark Stone)*, Hobart Bosworth *(Ezra Stone)*, Ned Sparks *(Charlie Thorne)*, Morgan Farley *(Monkey McConnell)*, Jed Prouty *(Kent Carr)*, Paul Lucas *(Dr. Reynolds)*, ZaSu Pitts *(Ethel)*, Morton Downey *(Freddie, the tenor)*, Guy Oliver *(Hammond)*, Jessie Pringle *(Aunt Betty)*, Wade Boteler *(house detective)*, Laura La Varnie *(Madame Bernstein)*.
Romantic drama. Hallie Hobart, a man-hating manicurist in a western hotel, builds up a small fortune through side deals with farm machinery salesmen; thus she meets David Stone, the unsophisticated young son of Ezra, a wealthy wheat farmer, and leads him into falling in love with her. But his brother Mark comes to the city to save him from her intrigues, and enraged by his branding her a cheat, she plots revenge. When David proposes marriage, she accepts him; at the farm, Stone forces Mark to be polite; but Ezra is incensed to learn she does not love his son, and she exacts a price to leave them. Later, he appears at her hotel, where she is holding a farewell party, and she begins to regret her action. When David begins to suffer from mental strain, Hallie returns the money, seeking his forgiveness, and they are reconciled. *Manicurists. Farmers. Man-haters. Brothers. Wheat. Revenge. Marriage.*

DEVIL'S ISLAND **F2.1331**
Chadwick Pictures. 20 Jul **1926** [New York State license]. Si; b&w. 35mm. 7 reels, 6,900 ft.
Dir Frank O'Connor. *Story-Scen* Leah Baird. *Photog* André Barlatier.
Cast: Pauline Frederick *(Jeannette Picto)*, Marion Nixon *(Rose Marie)*, George Lewis *(Léon Valyon)*, Richard Tucker *(Jean Valyon)*, William Dunn *(Guillet)*, Leo White *(Chico)*, John Miljan *(André Le Fèvier)*, Harry Northrup *(The Commandant)*.
Romantic melodrama. After spending 7 years on Devil's Island, a French penal colony off the coast of French Guiana, Valyon, a once-great Paris surgeon, is transferred to the prison city of Cayenne, where he is permitted to marry Jeanette, his faithful mistress, and to cultivate a small piece of land. They become the parents of a son, Léon, who, grown to manhood,

also becomes a surgeon. After the death of his father, Léon arranges for his mother to be released from Cayenne. *Surgeons. Filial relations. Penal colonies. Devil's Island. Cayenne.*

THE DEVIL'S MASTERPIECE **F2.1332**

Sanford F. Arnold. 29 Apr **1927** [New York showing]. Si; b&w. 35mm. 6 reels.

Pres by Sanford F. Arnold. *Dir* John P. McCarthy. *Story* Mason Harbringer. *Photog* Lyman Broening.

Cast: Virginia Browne Faire, Gordon Brinkley, Fred Kohler *(Reckless Jim Regan [villain])*.

Northwest melodrama. "A melodramatic plot with a background of Royal mounted cops and dope smugglers. ... The leading man ... on the trail of the man who murdered his father is unable to explain to the girl he meets and loves that he is a mountie working in civilian clothes to trap the dope gang. She misunderstands and believes him one of the gang." (*Variety,* 11 May 1927, p21.) *Detectives. Gangs. Narcotics. Smuggling. Revenge. Northwest Mounted Police.*

THE DEVIL'S MATCH **F2.1333**

Jan Strasser. *Dist* American Colored Film Exchange. 9 Mar **1923** [New York State license]. Si; b&w. 35mm. 5 reels.

Comedy-drama. No information about the precise nature of this film has been found. *Negro life.*

THE DEVIL'S NEEDLE (Reissue) **F2.1334**

Fine Arts Pictures. *Dist* Tri-Stone Pictures. c2 Nov **1923** [LP19559]. Si; b&w. 35mm. 5 reels, 4,800 ft.

Note: A "re-edited and re-titled" Norma Talmadge film originally released by Triangle Film Corp. on 13 Aug 1916.

THE DEVIL'S PARTNER **F2.1335**

Iroquois Productions. *Dist* Independent Pictures. Jun **1923.** Si; b&w. 35mm. 5 reels, 4,800 ft.

Dir Caryl S. Fleming.

Cast: Norma Shearer *(Jeanne)*, Charles Delaney *(Pierre [Sergeant Drummond])*, Henry Sedley *(Henri, Jeanne's father)*, Edward Roseman *(Jules Payette)*, Stanley Walpole.

Northwest melodrama. The story concerns "two young lovers in primitive Canadian village, whose happiness is ever threatened by the plots of a smuggler known as 'The Devil's Partner' [Jules Payette], who holds the girl's father in his power. Happiness comes to the young couple when the man meets his death." (*Motion Picture News Booking Guide,* 5:18, Oct 1923.) *Smugglers. Village life. Canada.*

THE DEVIL'S PARTNER **F2.1336**

Dist Truart Film Corp. 6 Mar **1926** [New York State license]. Si; b&w. 35mm. 5 reels.

Melodrama(?). No information about the nature of this film has been found.

Note: Possibly a reissue of the same title produced by Iroquois Productions, 1923.

THE DEVIL'S PIT **F2.1337**

Universal Pictures. 9 Mar **1930** [c25 Feb 1930; LP1123]. Mus score (Movietone); b&w. 35mm. 6 reels, 6,642 ft. [Also si, 24 Nov 1929; 5,597 ft.]

Pres by Carl Laemmle. *Dir-Writ* Lew Collins. *Titl* Walter Anthony. *Photog* Wilfred Cline, Howard Smith. *Film Ed* Hugh Hoffman. *Mus Arr* Bathie Stuart.

Cast: Patiti Warbrick *(Patiti)*, Witarina Mitchell *(Miro)*, Hoana Keeha *(Rangi)*, Ani Warbrick *(Anu)*, Apirlhana Wiari *(Te Kahu)*, Te Paiaha *(Paiaka)*, Paora Tomati *(Tamanui, the fat carver)*, Ewa Tapiri *(Wura, the carver's wife)*.

Folk drama. The Maori tribe, the Ariki, separated from its enemy, the Watee, by a volcano known as the Dragon Pit, wages war with its neighbors for centuries until Chief Pakura of the Ariki asks that his daughter, Miro, be offered in marriage to Prince Patiti of the Watee, if he proves his supremacy in the Contest of the Spears; if he fails, Miro is to be given to Rangi, of the Ariki. The sullen and vain Rangi discards his mistress, Anu, determined to win Miro; and through an unfair trick, he is victor in the contest. Miro is put into the taboo house, where no man may touch her until her wedding day, but she secretly meets the prince in the sea-caves. One night, Rangi follows her; and to prevent his informing the tribe, Patiti throws him into the volcano. Just as war is declared, the volcano erupts and Te Kahu and the Watee chief are killed. Patiti succeeds his father and makes peace with the Ariki; he finds happiness with Miro. *Maori. Ariki. Watee. Spears. Volcanoes. New Zealand.*

Note: Filmed entirely on location in New Zealand, with a cast composed of Maori tribesmen. Originally reviewed in 1929 as a silent film entitled *Under the Southern Cross.*

THE DEVIL'S SADDLE **F2.1338**

Charles R. Rogers Productions. *Dist* First National Pictures. 10 Jul **1927** [c11 Jul 1927. LP24160]. Si; b&w. 35mm. 6 reels, 5,488 ft.

Pres by Charles R. Rogers. *Dir* Albert Rogell. *Adapt* Marion Jackson, Charles R. Rogers. *Photog* Ross Fisher.

Cast: Ken Maynard *(Harry Morrel)*, Kathleen Collins *(Jane Grey)*, Francis Ford *(Pete Hepburn)*, Will Walling *(Sheriff Morrel)*, Earl Metcalfe *("Gentle" Ladley)*, Tarzan *(a horse)*, Paul Hurst *("Swig" Moran)*.

Western melodrama. Source: Kenneth Perkins, "The Devil's Saddle," in *Argosy All-Story Weekly* (181:481–502, 687–706, 889–909, 30 Oct–13 Nov 1926; 182:259–279, 443–462, 20 Nov–4 Dec 1926). "Concerns the early lives of Hopi Indians. Evolves around the invasion of their lands by prospectors. Hero is center of plot of gang of lawless whites to convice Indians he killed one of their number. Finally clears himself." (*Motion Picture News Booking Guide,* 13:27, Oct 1927.) "The strongest situations are those near the end where the hero corners the villain, hog-ties him and delivers him to the Indians ... the Indians are seen setting fire to the hero's father's home in revenge for the father's failure to punish the son whom they had thought guilty of the murder; they had demanded the same law for the whites as for the Indians." (*Harrison's Reports,* 13 Aug 1927, p130.) *Prospectors. Hopi Indians. Murder. Filial relations. Law.*

THE DEVIL'S SKIPPER **F2.1339**

Tiffany-Stahl Productions. 1 Feb **1928** [c28 Feb 1928; LP25015]. Si; b&w. 35mm. 6 reels, 5,510 ft.

Prod Roy Fitzroy. *Dir* John G. Adolfi. *Scen* John Francis Natteford. *Titl* Harry Braxton, Viola Brothers Shore. *Adapt* Robert Dillon. *Photog* Ernest Miller. *Film Ed* Desmond O'Brien.

Cast: Belle Bennett *(The Devil Skipper)*, Montagu Love *(first mate)*, Gino Corrado *(Philip La Farge)*, Mary McAllister *(Marie La Farge)*, Cullen Landis *(John Dubray)*, G. Raymond Nye *(Nick the Greek)*, Pat Hartigan *(Captain McKenna)*, Adolph Millar *(Mate Cornish)*, Caroline Snowden *(slave)*, Stepin Fetchit *(her husband)*.

Drama. Source: Jack London, "Demetrios Contos," in *Tales of the Fish Patrol* (New York, 1905). A female commander of a slave ship discovers that the man responsible for her suffering is a Louisiana planter named La Farge. Under the pretext of selling him slaves, she lures La Farge to her cabin and tells him the story of a woman whose husband shanghais her to a hell ship and has her child killed in her presence. She tortures La Farge and abandons to her drunken crew a young girl he has brought aboard. When La Farge tells her that the girl is her daughter, The Devil Skipper pulls her away from a Greek sailor who has fought for her. Dying from a stab wound inflicted by the Greek, The Devil Skipper has her husband and daughter led safely ashore, and she collapses in the arms of her loyal first mate. He puts her in her bunk and goes to kill the Greek. *Slavers. Planters. Ship crews. Motherhood. Torture. Louisiana.*

THE DEVIL'S TOLL *see* **THE DESERT'S TOLL**

DEVIL'S TOWER **F2.1340**

Trem Carr Productions. *Dist* Rayart Pictures. Jun **1928.** Si; b&w. 35mm. 5 reels, 4,533 ft.

Dir J. P. McGowan. *Scen* Victor Rousseau, J. P. McGowan. *Story* Victor Rousseau. *Photog* Ernest Depew. *Film Ed* Erma Horsley.

Cast: Buddy Roosevelt *(James Murdock)*, Frank Earle *(Tom Murdock)*, J. P. McGowan *(George Stilwell)*, Thelma Parr *(Doris Stilwell)*, Art Rowlands *(Phillip Wayne)*, Tommy Bay *(Dutch Haynes)*.

Western melodrama. A tool of a gang of thieves, Tom Murdock threatens contractor George Stilwell that he will seek compensation for damage to grazing land he claims to have resulted from Stilwell's new dam. Mudock's son, James, enters the conflict and, after preventing destruction of the dam by the crooks, receives Stilwell's permission to marry his daughter, Doris. *Contractors. Ranchers. Gangs. Filial relations. Dams.*

THE DEVIL'S TRADEMARK F2.1341

FBO Pictures. 7 Apr or 28 May **1928** [c14 May 1928; LP25246]. Si; b&w. 35mm. 6 reels, 5,984 ft.

Dir Leo Meehan. *Scen* Dorothy Yost. *Titl* Randolph Bartlett. *Photog* Al Siegler. *Film Ed* Edward Schroeder. *Asst Dir* Charles Kerr.

Cast: Belle Bennett *(Millie Benton)*, William V. Mong *(Fred Benton)*, Marian Douglas *(Mona Benton)*, William Bakewell *(Tom Benton)*, Patrick Cunning *(Algernon Gray)*, William Desmond *(Morgan Gray)*, Olin Francis *(Milt Soreley)*.

Melodrama. Source: Calvin Johnston, "Pedigree" (publication undetermined). Two thieves, a man and his wife, decide to go straight for the sake of their children. The husband, believing that criminal tendencies are inherited, feels that the effort is useless, but he agrees to refrain from stealing, at least until the children prove themselves to be innately dishonest. He resists the final temptation to hurl himself back into a life of crime when he discovers that his daughter, who, he thought, had stolen some money, actually received it from her fiancé to pay off the mortgage on her parents' house. *Thieves. Criminals—Rehabilitation. Heredity. Parenthood.*

THE DEVIL'S TWIN F2.1342

Leo Maloney Productions. *Dist* Pathé Exchange. 11 Dec **1927** [c26 Oct 1927; LP24575]. Si; b&w. 35mm. 6 reels, 5,478 ft.

Dir Leo Maloney. *Story-Scen* Ford I. Beebe. *Photog* Edward Kull. *Art Dir* Ernest Hickson. *Prod Mgr* Don F. Osborne.

Cast: Leo Maloney *(Honest John Andrews/George Andrews)*, Josephine Hill *(Alice Kemper)*, Don Coleman *(Bud Kemper)*, Albert Hart *(Uriah Hodge)*, Joseph Rickson *(Carl Blackburn)*, Tom London *(Otis Dilbre)*, Whitehorse *(Solon Kemper)*, Bud Osborne *(Tom Todd)*, Bert Apling *(sheriff)*, William Rhine *(hotel clerk)*.

Western melodrama. Honest John Andrews, an itinerant horse trader, arrives at the ranch of Solon Kemper, a retired Federal judge who has just sold his cattle to clear his debts. Kemper, a cripple, has just signed over the check to Uriah Hodge when two gamblers present a bill of sale, signed by Kemper's son, Bud, which they claim to have won at cards, but young Kemper claims he did not sign the note. Bud and Alice go to Hodge's office to seek a renewal on the loan, while Honest John follows and finds traces of attempted forgeries. Warned of his peril by the judge's daughter, John contrives to impersonate an alleged "twin brother," who is a notorious criminal, but Hodge and the gamblers soon catch on to the ruse, frame him for murdering his "twin," and persuade the judge to relinquish his ranch. But John escapes jail and proves that Hodge is seeking revenge for a sentence the judge passed on his son. *Ranchers. Judges. Cripples. Gamblers. Twins. Brothers. Forgery. Revenge. Personal identity. Jailbreaks.*

DEVOTION F2.1343

Associated Producers. 24 Jul **1921** [c9 Jul 1921; LP16741]. Si; b&w. 35mm. 6 reels, 5,669 ft.

Dir Burton George. *Titl* Eve Unsell. *Story* A. J. Bimberg. *Photog* Ollie Leach. *Film Ed* Eve Unsell.

Cast: Hazel Dawn *(Ruth Wayne)*, E. K. Lincoln *(Robert Trent)*, Violet Palmer *(Marian Wayne)*, Renita Randolph *(Lucy Marsh)*, Bradley Barker *(Stephen Bond)*, Henry G. Sell *(James Marsh)*, Wedgewood Nowell *(Teddy Grandin)*.

Society melodrama. Wealthy Mrs. Wayne announces her daughter Marian's marriage to Grandin, a man of position, and hopes that Ruth, another daughter, will marry wealthy Stephen Bond, but Ruth chooses Robert Trent, a poor man. Escaped convict Jim Marsh finds his wife, Lucy, remarried to a wealthy man, and she agrees to hide him if he does not harm her child. Meanwhile, Bob loses his position, and finding Ruth expensively attired as a result of Marian's plotting, he accuses Ruth of being unfaithful with Bond. At the moment the police shoot Marsh, Lucy hurries to Bob's apartment, where she names Bond as the father of her child. Realizing Ruth's devotion, Bob forgives her; and both couples are reconciled. *Sisters. Prison escapees. Wealth. Marriage. Infidelity.*

THE DIAMOND BANDIT F2.1344

Ben Wilson Productions. *Dist* Arrow Film Corp. 15 Oct **1924** [c9 Oct 1924; LP20683]. Si; b&w. 35mm. 5 reels, 4,698 ft.

Dir-Writ Francis Ford.

Cast: Arthur George *(Father Cantos)*, Florence Gilbert *(The Mission Waif)*, Frank Baker *(Jaspaz Lorenzo [The Bull])*, Robert McGowan *(his lieutenant)*, Ashton Dearholt *(Juan López/Pinto Pete)*, Harry Dunkinson *(Friar Michael)*, Francis Ford *(Friar Aluviscious)*.

Melodrama. Oppressed by their tax-greedy *comandante*, Jaspaz Lorenzo, the Indians of the mountain village of Pala look for aid to Pinto Pete, a masked man whom they know as village idler Juan López. When tax time comes, Father Cantos is attacked by Lorenzo's soldiers. Pinto Pete, with his famed bullwhip, routs the soldiers, but the padre dies after sending Juan to Pinto Pete with a request to look after the mission's welfare. Pinto Pete is finally captured by Lorenzo; but he escapes in a friar's robe, rallies his forces to overwhelm Lorenzo, and is proclaimed governor, with the mission waif as his wife. *Priests. Indians of South America. Missions. Taxes.*

DIAMOND CARLISLE F2.1345

Milburn Morante. *Dist* Clark-Cornelius Corp. 1 Mar or 1 Jun **1922**. Si; b&w. 35mm. 5 reels, 4,685 ft.

Dir Milburn Morante.

Cast: George Chesebro *("Diamond" Carlisle)*, Iva Brown *(Mae Boyd)*, Virginia Morante *(Virginia Boyd)*, Alfred Hewston *(Lopez)*, Milburn Morante *("Black" Meyer)*, Peggy Weightman *(Belle)*, Frank Caffray *(Dick Boyd)*, Mary Hawley *(Mrs. Boyd)*.

Northwest melodrama. Daring bandit Diamond Carlisle and Lopez, a murderer, cleverly escape from a posse and cross the border into Canada. Abandoned by Lopez, Carlisle is hired by gambler and saloonkeeper Black Meyer to use his skill with cards to bankrupt Dick Boyd, who owns valuable timberland. Carlisle proceeds successfully until he falls in love with Dick's sister, Mae. He then has a change of heart and returns his winnings to Dick. Lopez reappears, fights with Carlisle, and is killed. Carlisle exchanges clothes with him, thus satisfying the Northwest Mounted Police, when they find the body, and leaving Carlisle free to marry Mae. *Bandits. Gamblers. Murder. Lumbering. Northwest Mounted Police.*

Note: Working title: *Solace of the Woods.*

DIAMOND HANDCUFFS F2.1346

Cosmopolitan Productions. *Dist* Metro-Goldwyn-Mayer Distributing Corp. 5 May **1928** [c5 May 1928; LP25253]. Si; b&w. 35mm. 7 reels, 6,057 or 6,070 ft.

Dir John P. McCarthy. *Cont* Bradley King. *Titl* Joe Farnham. *Adapt* Willis Goldbeck. *Story* Carey Wilson. *Photog* Henry Sharp. *Set Dsgn* Alexander Toluboff. *Film Ed* Sam S. Zimbalist. *Wardrobe* David Cox.

Cast—Act I: Lena Malena *(Musa)*, Charles Stevens *(Niambo)*.

Cast—Act II: Lena Malena *(Musa [as a maid])*, Conrad Nagel *(The Husband, John)*, Gwen Lee *(The Wife, Cecile)*, John Roche *(The Friend, Jerry Fontaine)*.

Cast—Act III: Lena Malena *(Musa [as a cafe dancer])*, Eleanor Boardman *(Tillie)*, Lawrence Gray *(Larry)*, Sam Hardy *(Spike)*.

Drama. Source: Henry C. Vance, "Pin Money," in *Snappy Stories* (63: 95–104, 2 Dec 1921). Three stories dealing with the pursuit of a diamond that brings only misfortune to its owner: I. In South Africa, a mineworker loses his life for stealing a diamond he has found. Before he dies he gives the stone to Musa, a local girl. II. The gem becomes known as the Shah diamond and ends up in a New York City jewelry store window, where Cecile, an upper-class matron, admires it. Her husband leaves her when he discovers that Jerry, a family friend, has given Cecile the diamond, under the pretense that it is a glass trinket. Musa, now Cecile's maid, is again the recipient of the gem. III. The diamond is stolen by a gang of thieves. Tillie, the roughly treated "woman" of Spike, cafe owner and gangster, admires the diamond. Larry, who really loves her, secretly gives her money to go to a sanitarium in order to cure her lung disease. Instead, Tillie uses the money to buy the diamond. That night, Spike is killed when police raid his cafe, and a Negro dancer named Musa dies from a bullet wound she receives while trying to retrieve the diamond. Tillie accepts a modest diamond from Larry and becomes his wife. *Housemaids. Negroes. Dancers. Gangsters. Occult. Diamonds. Tuberculosis. South Africa. New York City.*

DIAMONDS ADRIFT F2.1347

Vitagraph Co. of America. Jan **1921** [c24 Dec 1920; LP15960]. Si; b&w. 35mm. 5 reels, 4,424 or 5,006 ft.

Pres by Albert E. Smith. *Dir* Chester Bennett. *Story-Scen* Frederick J. Jackson. *Photog* Jack MacKenzie.

Cast: Earle Williams *(Bob Bellamy)*, Beatrice Burnham *(Consuela Velasco)*, Otis Harlan *("Brick" McCann)*, George Field *(Don Manuel Morales)*, Jack Carlisle *("Home Brew" Hanson)*, Hector Sarno *(Señor Rafael Velasco)*, Melbourne MacDowell *(James Bellamy)*, Omar *(himself, the cat)*.

Romantic comedy. Wealthy shipowner James Bellamy decides to punish his carefree son, Bob, by forcing him to pay his $5,000 in debts by working as a $50-a-month supercargo. In a card game, Bob wins a runaway Persian cat, which is wearing a $30,000 diamond bracelet. Not realizing their value, he gives both cat and bracelet to Consuela Velasco, a girl he meets in Mexico. Back in San Francisco, he learns the true value of the bracelet and returns to Mexico just as Consuela is about to marry against her will. Bob carries off the girl, cat, and bracelet; gets the reward; and is reconciled with his father. *Ship crews. Filial relations. Debt. Merchant ships. Mexico. Cats.*

DIANE OF STAR HOLLOW **F2.1348**

C. R. Macauley Photo Plays. *Dist* Producers Security Corp. Mar **1921.** Si; b&w. 35mm. 6 reels.

Dir Oliver L. Sellers. *Scen* Joseph Farnham. *Photog* Lucien Tainguy.

Cast: Bernard Durning *(Sgt. Pat Scott)*, Evelyn Greeley *(Diane Orsini)*, George Majeroni *(Alessandro Orsini)*, Fuller Mellish *(Father Lorenzo)*, George E. Romain *(D. Crispi)*, Freeman Wood *(Dick Harrison)*, Al Hart *(Hanscom)*, Louis J. O'Connor *(sheriff)*, Joseph Gramby *(Pietro)*, Sonia Marcelle *(Carlotta Orsini)*, Charles Mackay *(Dr. Ogden)*, May Hopkins *(Jessie)*, Julia Neville *(Jessie's mother)*.

Underworld melodrama. Source: David Potter, "Diane of Star Hollow" (publication undetermined). Patrick Scott, local chief of state constabulary, loves Diane Orsini, whose father, a rich Italian, is suspected of being head of the Black Hand. Scott is detailed to obtain evidence and capture the gang and its leader. This investigation results in several tense situations—the last one an all-out gun fight in which Pat is injured and Orsini's henchmen are killed. Pat later recovers both his health and Diane, and Orsini, having incurred his daughter's animosity and seen his empire destroyed, commits suicide. *Italians. Constabularies. Suicide. Secret societies. Black Hand.*

THE DICE WOMAN **F2.1349**

Metropolitan Pictures Corp. of California. *Dist* Producers Distributing Corp. 27 Jun **1927** [c25 May 1926; LP22764]. Si; b&w. 35mm. 6 reels, 5,614 ft.

Pres by John C. Flinn. *Dir* Edward Dillon. *Story-Scen* Percy Heath. *Cinematog* George Benoit. *2d Cinematog* William Coopersmith. *Art Dir* Charles Cadwallader. *Asst Dir* Edward Bernoudy. *Prod Mgr* George Bertholon. *Asst Prod Mgr* Bert Gilroy.

Cast: Priscilla Dean *(Anita Gray)*, John Bowers *(Hamlin)*, Gustav von Seyffertitz *(Datto of Mandat)*, Lionel Belmore *(Rastillac)*, Phillips Smalley *(Mr. Gray)*, Malcolm Denny *(Satterlee)*, William Humphrey *(ship captain)*, George Kuwa *(steward)*.

Comedy-melodrama. Anita Gray, the spoiled daughter of an American millionaire, is lucky with dice. She gives a ride to a jewel thief and is implicated in a robbery he perpetrates. Pursued to the docks, she boards a steamer and is forced to work her passage to China. There she bribes a Chinese steward with a diamond ring to disguise her as an Oriental, and she escapes to the mainland. Her father, learning of her plight, cables $1,000 for her to Hamlin, an agent in China, and when she denies her identity, Hamlin seeks the aid of the police commissioner, Satterlee. She repulses the advances of Rastillac, the hotel owner, but agrees to work as his "dice woman." Hamlin tells her of her father's cable and becomes infatuated, but so does the Datto of Mandat, a potentate who pays off Rastillac, then hypnotizes and kidnaps her. Hamlin tries to rescue her and is himself captured, but they are both freed by Satterlee and find happiness on their voyage to the United States. *Thieves. Police. Luck. Disguise. Gambling. Kidnaping. Hypnotism. Circumstantial evidence. Steamboats. China.*

DICK TURPIN **F2.1350**

Fox Film Corp. 1 Feb **1925** [c1 Feb 1925; LP21086]. Si; b&w. 35mm. 7 reels, 6,716 ft.

Pres by William Fox. *Dir* John G. Blystone. *Scen* Charles Kenyon. *Story* Charles Darnton, Charles Kenyon. *Photog* Dan Clark.

Cast: Tom Mix *(Dick Turpin)*, Kathleen Myers *(Alic Brookfield)*, Philo McCullough *(Lord Churlton)*, James Marcus *(Squire Crabstone)*, Lucille Hutton *(Sally, the maid)*, Alan Hale *(Tom King)*, Bull Montana *(Bully Boy)*, Fay Holderness *(barmaid)*, Jack Herrick *(Bristol Bully)*, Fred Kohler *(Taylor)*.

Costume adventure. Dick Turpin, an English highwayman who robs from the rich and gives to the poor, holds up the coach of Lord Churlton. Sometime later, in aiding a coach attacked by ruffians, Dick meets aristocratic Alice Brookfield, who is being forced by her family to marry Churlton. Dick offers to assist her to avoid the unwanted marriage, and they travel to London together, with Alice disguised as a boy. Churlton pursues them, and, after several narrow escapes, Dick is captured by the royal guards and sentenced to be hanged. On the scaffold, Dick is told by his friend, Tom King, who has taken the hangman's place, that the crowd is sympathetic; and Dick makes his escape, riding his horse to York. Dick finds the house where Alice is being held prisoner, kills Churlton, and escapes to France with Alice, whom he marries. Dick gives up his profession and settles down to family life. *Aristocrats. Highwaymen. Robbery. Disguise. Capital punishment. England. London. France.*

THE DICTATOR **F2.1351**

Famous Players–Lasky. *Dist* Paramount Pictures. 25 Jun **1922** [Los Angeles premiere; released 7 Aug; c11 Jul 1922; LP18045]. Si; b&w. 35mm. 6 reels, 5,221 ft.

Pres by Jesse L. Lasky. *Dir* James Cruze. *Adapt* Walter Woods. *Photog* Karl Brown.

Cast: Wallace Reid *(Brooke Travers, who is better versed in flappers than in fruit)*, Theodore Kosloff *(Carlos Rivas, exiled from San Mañana for politico-bananico reasons)*, Lila Lee *(Juanita, his daughter)*, Kalla Pasha *(General Campos, ... president of San Mañana)*, Sidney Bracey *(Henry Bolton, political agent ...)*, Fred Butler *(Sam Travers, the Banana King ...)*, Walter Long *(Mike "Biff" Dooley, taxi driver)*, Alan Hale *(Sabos, an amateur Sherlock but professional Don Juan)*.

Adventure comedy. Source: Richard Harding Davis, *The Dictator; a Farce in Three Acts* (promptbook; New York, 1904). Pursued by a cab driver for an unpaid fare, a millionaire's son, Brooke Travers, hides on a steamer, and both men find themselves en route to South America, where they are caught up in a revolution. Brooke falls in love with Juanita, then learns that she is the daughter of the leader of the revolution and his father's enemy. Although his father's business interests control the country, Brooke helps the revolutionary forces to victory and earns his father's respect. *Millionaires. Taxi drivers. Revolutions. South America.*

DIPLOMACY **F2.1352**

Famous Players–Lasky. *Dist* Paramount Pictures. 20 Sep **1926** [c21 Sep 1926; LP23132]. Si; b&w. 35mm. 7 reels, 6,950 ft.

Pres by Adolph Zukor, Jesse L. Lasky. *Dir* Marshall Neilan. *Screenplay* Benjamin Glazer. *Photog* David Kesson, Donald Keyes.

Cast: Blanche Sweet *(Dora)*, Neil Hamilton *(Julian Weymouth)*, Arlette Marchal *(Countess Zicka)*, Matt Moore *(Robert Lowry)*, Gustav von Seyffertitz *(Baron Ballin)*, Earle Williams *(Sir Henry Weymouth)*, Arthur Edmund Carew *(Count Orloff)*, Julia Swayne Gordon *(Marquise de Zares)*, David Mir *(Reggie Cowan)*, Charles "Buddy" Post *(baron's secretary)*, Mario Carillo *(John Stramir)*, Sojin *(Chinese diplomat)*, Edgar Norton, Linda Landi *(servants)*.

Mystery melodrama. Source: Victorien Sardou, *Diplomacy* (New York opening: 1 Apr 1878). At Deauville, an informal conference of diplomatic powers is attended by: Julian Weymouth and his brother Sir Henry, of the British Diplomatic Service; Count Orloff, a young Russian royalist; the Marquise de Zares and her daughter, Dora; and Countess Zicka, who sells political secrets to Baron Ballin, reputedly an agent of the Bolshevik Government. Count Orloff, believing that Dora has been responsible for his arrest in Russia, hastens to warn his friends at the British Embassy, unaware that Julian and Dora, who have just been married, are leaving for London with a treaty from the Chinese delegation. Julian's trust in Dora is shattered when the document is stolen. Julian and Sir Henry make a desperate effort to regain the lost treaty, addressed in Dora's handwriting to Ballin. With the aid of Robert Lowry, an American, Zicka is tricked into admitting her guilt. Julian and Dora renew their vows of love. *Chinese. Russians. British. Bolshevists. Diplomacy. Espionage. Treaties. Deauville. Documentation.*

THE DISCIPLE (Reissue) **F2.1353**

Kay-Bee Pictures. *Dist* Tri-Stone Pictures. 3 Jul **1924** [New York State license]. Si; b&w. 35mm. 5 reels.

Note: A "re-edited and re-titled" William S. Hart film originally released by Triangle Corp. on 21 Nov 1916.

DISCONTENTED HUSBANDS **F2.1354**

Columbia Pictures. *Dist* C. B. C. Film Sales. 15 Jan **1924** [c7 Feb 1924; LP19897]. Si; b&w. 35mm. 6 reels, 5,421 ft.

Prod Harry Cohn. *Dir* Edward J. Le Saint. *Story* Evelyn Campbell.

Cast: James Kirkwood *(Michael Frazer)*, Cleo Madison *(Jane Frazer)*, Grace Darmond *(Emily Ballard)*, Arthur Rankin *(Dick Everton)*, Vernon

Steele *(Jack Ballard)*, Carmelita Geraghty *(Marcia Frazer)*, Baby Muriel McCormac *(Baby Ballard)*.

Domestic melodrama. Michael Frazer, newly rich from his invention of a can-opener, has drifted away from Jane, his wife, who persists in her old-fashioned ways. He advises his daughter Marcia to marry "someone congenial so that when love goes you will have common interests." Neighboring architect Jack Ballard obtains the contract to design Frazer's house through the friendship of his attractive wife, Emily, with Frazer. Emily and Frazer become intimate friends, arousing the concern of Mrs. Frazer and Jack Ballard. Determined to teach his wife a lesson and win her back, Jack asks Marcia Frazer to run away with him. She consents but later reconsiders and they return home. Frazer realizes that Mrs. Ballard meant nothing to him, and Jack is reunited with his wife. *Nouveaux riches. Inventors. Architects. Marriage. Infidelity.*

DISCONTENTED WIVES **F2.1355**

Herald Productions. *Dist* Playgoers Pictures. 25 Sep **1921** [c7 Sep 1921; LU16944]. Si; b&w. 35mm. 5 reels, 4,[illegible]50 ft.

Dir J. P. McGowan. *Auth* Fred Windermere. *Photog* Ben Bail.

Cast: J. P. McGowan *(John Gaylord)*, Fritzi Brunette *(Ruth Gaylord)*, Jean Perry *(Kirk Harding)*, Andy Waldron *(a desert rat)*.

Melodrama. Ruth Gaylord gives up her home in New York to marry John Gaylord but grows discontented with the loneliness and desolation of life in the West and leaves her husband. *After returning home, she hears that he has struck one of the richest gold veins in California. A letter surrendering her interests in the mine falls into the hand of Kirk Harding, an eastern capitalist; and John, tricked into surrendering his rights and discovering the truth, struggles with Harding.* Ruth awakens, discovering it was all a dream, and decides not to leave her dedicated husband after all. *Capitalists. Property rights. Marriage. California. New York City. Dreams.*

DISRAELI **F2.1356**

Distinctive Productions. *Dist* United Artists. Aug **1921** [c25 Aug 1921; LP16895]. Si; b&w. 35mm. 7 reels, 6,800 ft.

Dir Henry Kolker. *Scen* Forrest Halsey. *Photog* Harry A. Fischbeck. *Art Dir* Charles O. Seessel.

Cast: George Arliss *(The Honourable Benjamin Disraeli, M. P.)*, Mrs. George Arliss *(Lady Beaconsfield)*, Margaret Dale *(Mrs. Noel Travers)*, Louise Huff *(Clarissa)*, Reginald Denny *(Charles, Viscount Deeford)*, E. J. Ratcliffe *(Hugh Meyers)*, Henry Carvill *(Duke of Glastonbury)*, Grace Griswold *(Duchess of Glastonbury)*, Noel Tearle *(Foljambe)*, Fred Nicholls *(butler at Glastonbury Towers)*.

Historical drama. Source: Louis Napoleon Parker, *Disraeli* (New York, 1911). Disraeli, Prime Minister of England under Queen Victoria, attempts to secure possession of the Suez Canal for his country, a project opposed by Russia. At a reception given by the Duke of Glastonbury, Disraeli confers with Sir Michael Probert, who, influenced by Lady Travers in the employ of the Russian ambassador, refuses to advance funds to purchase the canal. Charles becomes Disraeli's secretary, and Meyers, a banker, negotiates a South American loan to cover the transaction, but saboteurs sink the shipment of gold. The bankruptcy of Meyers forces Disraeli to seek fresh credit and Sir Michael to advance the credit, averting the closing of the Bank of England. The Queen holds a reception at which Charles receives the Ribbon of the Bath, while Disraeli and Lady Beaconsfield pay homage. *Banks. Diplomacy. Great Britain—History—19th Century. Suez Canal. Benjamin Disraeli. Queen Victoria.*

DISRAELI **F2.1357**

Warner Brothers Pictures. 2 Oct **1929** [New York premiere; released 1 Nov; c8 Oct 1929; LP756]. Sd (Vitaphone); b&w. 35mm. 9 reels, 8,044 ft. [Also si.]

Dir Alfred E. Green. *Scen-Dial* Julian Josephson. *Titl* De Leon Anthony. *Photog* Lee Garmes. *Film Ed* Owen Marks. *Mus Arr* Louis Silvers.

Cast: George Arliss *(Disraeli)*, Joan Bennett *(Lady Clarissa Pevensey)*, Florence Arliss *(Lady Beaconfield)*, Anthony Bushell *(Charles—Lord Deeford)*, David Torrence *(Lord Probert)*, Ivan Simpson *(Hugh Meyers)*, Doris Lloyd *(Mrs. Travers)*, Gwendolen Logan *(Duchess of Glastonbury)*, Charles E. Evans *(Potter)*, Cosmo Kyrle Bellew *(Mr. Terle)*, Jack Deery *(Bascot)*, Michael Visaroff *(Count Bosrinov)*, Norman Cannon *(Foljambe)*, Henry Carvill *(Duke of Glastonbury)*, Shayle Gardner *(Dr. Williams)*, Powell York *(Flookes)*, Margaret Mann *(Queen Victoria)*.

Historical drama. Source: Louis Napoleon Parker, *Disraeli, a Play* (New York, 1911). British Prime Minister Benjamin Disraeli is stymied by Liberal opponent Gladstone in an attempt to appropriate an unusually large slice of power and financial credit, and, feeling "bound to furnish [his] antagonists with arguments, but not with comprehension," he retires to his country estate, Hughenden, amidst public agitation. A mysterious Mrs. Travers, whom Disraeli knows to be a Russian spy, learns of Disraeli's intention to buy the Suez Canal from Egypt and ensure England's Indian Empire, when the prime minister receives a coded telegram indicating Egyptian khedive Ismail Pasha's immediate financial throes and his susceptibility to an offer. Unable to obtain credit from the Bank of England, he arranges through international Jewish banker Hugh Meyers for funding and dispatches Charles (Lord Deeford) with Meyer's check to Cairo. Charles arrives ahead of Foljambe, Mrs. Travers' accomplice, and obtains the controlling shares in the Canal, but Disraeli's elation is shortlived as Meyers informs him of his firm's bankruptcy. Disraeli bluffs the reluctant Bank of England manager, Lord Probert, into honoring the check, and Queen Victoria later graces a reception at Downing Street honoring Disraeli, who has made her "Empress of India." *Prime ministers. Bankers. Diplomats. Spies. Jews. Great Britain—History—19th Century. Egypt. Benjamin Disraeli. Queen Victoria. Suez Canal.*

THE DIVINE LADY **F2.1358**

First National Pictures. 31 Mar **1929** [c28 Mar 1929; LP285]. Singing sequences (Vitaphone); b&w. 35mm. 12 reels, 9,914 ft. [Also si, 14 Apr 1929; 8,993 ft.]

Pres by Richard A. Rowland. *Assoc Prod* Walter Morosco. *Dir* Frank Lloyd. *Cont* Agnes Christine Johnston. *Titl* Harry Carr, Edwin Justus Mayer. *Adapt* Forrest Halsey. *Photog* John F. Seitz. *Art Dir* Horace Jackson. *Film Ed* Hugh Bennett. *Song: "Lady Divine"* Joseph Pasternac, Richard Kountz. *Cost* Max Ree. *Makeup* Fred C. Ryle.

Cast: Corinne Griffith *(Emma, Lady Hamilton)*, Victor Varconi *(Lord Nelson)*, H. B. Warner *(Sir William Hamilton)*, Ian Keith *(Greville)*, William Conklin *(Romney)*, Marie Dressler *(Mrs. Hart)*, Michael Vavitch *(King of Naples)*, Evelyn Hall *(Duchess of Devonshire)*, Montague Love *(Captain Hardy)*, Helen Jerome Eddy *(Lady Nelson)*, Dorothy Cumming *(Queen of Naples)*.

Historical drama. Source: E. Barrington, *The Divine Lady; a Romance of Nelson and Emma Hamilton* (New York, 1924). Emma Hart, the daughter of Charles Greville's cook, marries William, Lord Hamilton, the British ambassador at the Court of Naples. Years later, Emma falls in love with Capt. Horatio Nelson and, during the Napoleonic wars, is instrumental in gaining royal permission for him to take on badly needed water and provisions at Naples. Nelson then annihilates the French Fleet on the Nile and bottles up Napoleon in Egypt. Nelson and Lady Hamilton later return to England; and when she is snubbed by proper society everywhere, they retire to his country estate. Duty later calls Nelson away from her, and he is killed at Trafalgar, having again defeated the French Fleet. *Cooks. Nobility. Royalty. Napoleonic Wars. Great Britain—Diplomatic and consular service. England. Naples. Trafalgar. Horatio Nelson. Emma Hamilton.*

DIVINE SINNER (Blue Ribbon) **F2.1359**

Trem Carr Productions. *Dist* Rayart Pictures. Jul **1928.** Si; b&w. 35mm. 6 reels, 5,683 ft.

Dir Scott Pembroke. *Story-Scen* Robert Dillon. *Photog* Hap Depew. *Film Ed* J. S. Harrington.

Cast: Vera Reynolds *(Lillia Ludwig)*, Nigel De Brulier *(Minister of Police)*, Bernard Seigel *(Johann Ludwig)*, Ernest Hilliard *(Prince Josef Miguel)*, John Peters *(Luque Bernstorff)*, Carol Lombard *(Millie Claudert)*, Harry Northrup *(Ambassador D'Ray)*, James Ford *(Heinrich)*, Alphonse Martel *(Paul Coudert)*.

Romantic drama. To aid her destitute family in Austria, Lillia Ludwig goes to Paris after the war to find work and falls in with a forger. They are arrested, and the police trade their freedom for Lillia's agreement to make love to Prince Josef Miguel as part of a "diplomatic" plot. Lillia successfully vamps the prince and then falls in love with him. When Josef's father dies and the prince is informed of his succession to the throne, the plot thickens, but Josef has the final word: he abdicates for his lady love. *Royalty. Police. Diplomats. Forgery. Paris. Austria.*

THE DIVINE WOMAN **F2.1360**

Metro-Goldwyn-Mayer Pictures. 14 Jan **1928** [c14 Jan 1928; LP25398]. Si; b&w. 35mm. 8 reels, 7,300 ft.

Dir Victor Seastrom. *Scen* Dorothy Farnum. *Titl* John Colton. *Treatment* Gladys Unger. *Photog* Oliver Marsh. *Sets* Cedric Gibbons, Arnold Gillespie. *Film Ed* Conrad A. Nervig.

Cast: Greta Garbo *(Marianne)*, Lars Hanson *(Lucien)*, Lowell Sherman

(Monsieur Legrande), Polly Moran *(Madame Pigonier)*, Dorothy Cumming *(Madame Zizi Rouck)*, John Mack Brown *(Jean Lery)*, Cesare Gravina *(Gigi)*, Paulette Duval *(Paulette)*, Jean De Briac *(stage director)*.

Romantic drama. Source: Gladys Unger, *Starlight* (New York opening: 3 Mar 1925). Scorned by her pleasure-loving mother, Marianne is reared by peasants in Brittany. Ten years later, in Paris, she falls in love with Lucien, a soldier, and enters the realm of the theater with the help of Legrande, a theatrical producer and former suitor of Marianne's mother. Lucien, a deserter, is jailed when he steals a dress for Marianne. Although she promises to wait for Lucien, Marianne succumbs to Legrande and his wealth; but ultimately she relinquishes fame and recognition and nearly commits suicide for the love of Lucien. They marry when he is released from jail and settle down to a farm life. *Actors. Peasants. Soldiers. Theatrical producers. Deserters—Military. Motherhood. Paris. Brittany.*

DIVORCE **F2.1361**

Dist Film Booking Offices of America. 10 Jun **1923** [c10 Jun 1923; LP20001]. Si; b&w. 35mm. 6 reels, 5,900 ft.

Dir Chester Bennett. *Story* Andrew Bennison. *Photog* Jack MacKenzie.

Cast: Jane Novak *(Jane Parker)*, John Bowers *(Jim Parker)*, James Corrigan *(George Reed)*, Edythe Chapman *(Mrs. George Reed)*, Margaret Livingston *(Gloria Gayne)*, Freeman Wood *(Townsend Perry)*, George McGuire *(Tom Tucker)*, George Fisher *(Winthrop Avery)*, Philippe De Lacy *("Dicky" Parker)*.

Domestic drama. While Jane and Jim Parker witness the divorce proceedings of Jane's parents, the George Reeds, they resolve that such a disaster will never occur in their happy lives. But when Jim achieves success in Reed's company, he becomes increasingly interested in his new fast friends, especially vamp Gloria Gayne; and he asks Jane for a divorce. At Jane's request, Reed fires his son-in-law, and Jim finds himself deserted by his friends. He returns home, repentant, to his forgiving wife. *Vamps. Divorce. Marriage.*

DIVORCE AMONG FRIENDS **F2.1362**

Warner Brothers Pictures. 13 or 27 Dec **1930** [c4 Dec 1930; LP1787]. Sd (Vitaphone); b&w. 35mm. 9 reels, 6,076 ft.

Dir Roy Del Ruth. *Scen-Dial* Harvey Thew, Arthur Caesar. *Adapt* Harvey Thew. *Story* Jack Townley. *Photog* Dev Jennings. *Film Ed* Owen Marks.

Cast: James Hall *(George Morris)*, Irene Delroy *(Helen Morris)*, Lew Cody *(Paul Wilcox)*, Natalie Moorhead *(Joan Whitley)*, Edward Martindel *(Tom)*, Margaret Seddon *(maid)*.

Domestic comedy. George Morris, who is constantly inventing excuses to cover up his philandering escapades, is about to separate again from his wife, Helen; but as George is leaving, a party of guests arrive, led by Paul Wilcox, a hard-drinking bachelor who greatly admires Helen; and by the end of the evening, husband and wife are reconciled. Later, at a gas station, George meets young Joan Whitley, and she insists on taking a cigarette lighter that Helen has recently given him. That evening, at a dinner party, Helen introduces George to her former roommate at school, who happens to be Joan, though she fails to recognize him. George implores the girl to return the lighter in the darkened library, but Helen finds it and takes her place; complications ensue when Paul, Joan's friend, occupies Helen's bedroom. Helen plans to get a divorce on grounds of desertion. George's car is stuck during a rainstorm, the presence of Paul and Helen in the back seat is revealed, and they are all robbed by thieves—eventually there is a return to marital bliss. *Bachelors. Vamps. Marriage. Infidelity. Divorce. Drunkenness.*

DIVORCE COUPONS **F2.1363**

Vitagraph Co. of America. ca2 Jul **1922** [Washington premiere; released 31 Aug; c22 Jun 1922; LP17991]. Si; b&w. 35mm. 6 reels, 5,249 ft. [Also 5 reels.]

Pres by Albert E. Smith. *Dir* Webster Campbell. *Scen* William B. Courtney. *Photog* Joe Shelderfer.

Cast: Corinne Griffith *(Linda Catherton)*, Holmes E. Herbert *(Roland Bland)*, Mona Lisa *(Ishtar Lane)*, Diana Allen *(Teddy Beaudine)*, Cyril Ring *(Conrad Fontaine)*, Vincent Coleman *(Buddy)*.

Society melodrama. Sourc : Ethel Watts Mumford, "Divorce Coupons" (publication undetermined). Linda Catherton, a poor smalltown girl in search of a wealthy suitor, meets Roland Bland, a man of notorious reputation, at the wedding of her friend Teddy Beaudine. Although she does not love him, Linda accepts his marriage proposal, believing that alimony will compensate her eventually for the unhappy experiment; but following their honeymoon she acknowledges their mutual love and affection. Fontaine, Teddy's husband, who is in debt, discovers a letter from Linda indicating her real intentions in marriage and sends it to Roland, who then gives his wife grounds for a divorce but threatens to kill the informer. When Fontaine is killed, Linda and Roland suspect each other, but it develops that Ishtar Lane, who formerly loved Roland, committed the murder, hoping thus to assure his own happiness. Ishtar dies, and the couple are reconciled. *Fortune hunters. Social classes. Divorce. Alimony. Murder.*

DIVORCE MADE EASY **F2.1364**

Christie Film Co. *Dist* Paramount Famous Lasky Corp. 6 Jul **1929** [c6 Jul 1929; LP520]. Sd (Movietone); b&w. 35mm. 6 reels, 5,386 ft. [Also si; 5,270 ft.]

Prod Al Christie. *Dir Sd Vers* Walter Graham. *Dir Si Vers* Neal Burns. *Adapt-Dial* Alfred A. Cohn. *Titl* Garrett Graham. *Photog* Gus Peterson, Alex Phillips, William Wheeler.

Cast: Douglas MacLean *(Billy Haskell)*, Marie Prevost *(Mabel Deering)*, Johnny Arthur *(Percy Deering)*, Frances Lee *(Eileen Stanley)*, Dot Farley *(Aunt Emma)*, Jack Duffy *(Uncle Todd)*, Buddy Wattles *(Jerry)*, Hal Wilson *(Parkins)*.

Farce. Source: Wilson Collison, *Divorce Made Easy* (a play; publication undetermined). When his aunt disapproves of his marriage to Mabel Deering and threatens to disinherit him, Percy elicits the aid of his buddy Billy Haskell, who is engaged to Eileen Stanley. It is arranged that Billy and Mabel be found together in compromising circumstances by Percy and his aunt, but matters are complicated by the arrival of Billy's uncle in the city, and Aunt Emma becomes very fond of him. All is subsequently explained and thoughts of "divorce" are smoothed away as Uncle Todd couples up with Aunt Emma, and Billy and Eileen, and Percy and Mabel, reinstitute their carefree engagements. *Aunts. Uncles. Disinheritance. Courtship.*

Note: Marie Prevost sings the theme song, "So Sweet."

A DIVORCE OF CONVENIENCE **F2.1365**

Selznick Pictures. *Dist* Select Pictures. May **1921** [c8 May 1921; LP16545]. Si; b&w. 35mm. 5 reels, 4,995 ft.

Dir Robert Ellis. *Scen* Sarah Y. Mason. *Story* Victor Heerman. *Photog* Alfred Gondolfi.

Cast: Owen Moore *(Jim Blake)*, Katherine Perry *(Helen Wakefield)*, George Lessey *(Senator Wakefield)*, Nita Naldi *(Tula Moliana)*, Frank Wunderley *(Blinkwell Jones)*, Dan Duffy *(Mr. Hart)*, Charles Craig *(Mr. Holmes)*.

Domestic comedy. Spanish coquette Tula Moliana finds herself encumbered with two husbands, and in order to get a divorce from the first, Senator Wakefield, she engages Jim Blake, the fiancé of Helen, the senator's daughter, to be her corespondent. Jim agrees to help her but finds himself entangled in a web of deceit and has difficulty in making excuses to Helen for the numerous adventures in which he becomes involved, especially when his life is threatened by a jealous rival pursuing Tula. Matters are cleared up when Helen discovers he has been victimized, and Tula accepts her first husband. *Spanish. Divorce. Bigamy. United States Congress.*

THE DIVORCÉE **F2.1366**

Metro-Goldwyn-Mayer Pictures. 19 Apr **1930** [c23 Apr 1930; LP1244]. Sd (Movietone); b&w. 35mm. 9 reels, 7,533 ft. [Also si.]

Dir Robert Z. Leonard. *Cont-Dial* John Meehan. *Treatment* Nick Grinde, Zelda Sears. *Photog* Norbert Brodin. *Art Dir* Cedric Gibbons. *Film Ed* Hugh Wynn, Truman K. Wood. *Sd Engr* J. K. Brock, Douglas Shearer. *Gowns* Adrian.

Cast: Norma Shearer *(Jerry)*, Chester Morris *(Ted)*, Conrad Nagel *(Paul)*, Robert Montgomery *(Don)*, Florence Eldridge *(Helen)*, Helene Millard *(Mary)*, Robert Elliott *(Bill)*, Mary Doran *(Janice)*, Tyler Brooke *(Hank)*, Zelda Sears *(Hannah)*, George Irving *(Dr. Bernard)*, Helen Johnson *(Dorothy)*.

Romantic drama. Source: Katherine Ursula Parrott, *Ex-Wife* (New York, 1929). Jerry marries Ted, a newspaperman, and they settle down to 3 years of marital bliss. On their third wedding anniversary, when he is leaving for Chicago, she learns that Ted has been having an affair with another woman. Disillusioned, although before her marriage she had agreed on a liberal attitude, she turns to Don, her husband's best friend, for comfort. Ted refuses to accept her having affairs with other men; consequently, they obtain a divorce and go separate ways. After numerous affairs, Jerry meets Paul, who had loved her before her marriage, vacations on his yacht, and decides to accompany him to Japan as his wife; but his wife, Helen, makes a plea for her husband, and realizing she does not love him, Jerry returns to Paris. There, on New Year's Eve, she is reconciled with Ted. *Reporters. Marriage. Infidelity. Divorce. Wedding anniversaries. New Year's Eve. Paris.*

DIXIANA **F2.1367**

RKO Productions. 1 Aug **1930** [c16 Aug 1930; LP1530]. Sd (Photophone); b&w with col sequences (Technicolor). 35mm. 12 reels, 8,908 ft.

Prod William Le Baron. *Dir-Adapt* Luther Reed. *Photog* Roy Hunt. *Art Dir* Max Ree. *Mus Dir* Victor Baravalle. *Songs: "Here's to the Old Days," "A Tear, a Kiss, a Smile," "My One Ambition Is You," "A Lady Loved a Soldier," "Mr. and Mrs. Sippi," "Guiding Star"* Anne Caldwell, Harry Tierney. *Song: "Dixiana"* Benny Davis. *Orch Arr* Max Steiner. *Dance Dir* Pearl Eaton. *Rec Engr* Hugh McDowell. *Asst Dir* Frederick Fleck.

Cast: Bebe Daniels *(Dixiana)*, Everett Marshall *(Carl Van Horn)*, Bert Wheeler *(Peewee)*, Robert Woolsey *(Ginger)*, Joseph Cawthorn *(Cornelius Van Horn)*, Jobyna Howland *(Mrs. Van Horn)*, Dorothy Lee *(Poppy)*, Ralf Harolde *(Royal Montague)*, Edward Chandler *(Blondell)*, George Herman *(contortionist)*, Raymond Maurel *(Cayetano)*, Bruce Covington *(company porter)*, Bill Robinson *(specialty dancer)*, Eugene Jackson *(cupid)*.

Musical costume drama. Source: Harry Tierney and Anne Caldwell, "Dixiana" (publication undetermined). In New Orleans in the 1840's, Dixiana, a singer and dancer, is the captivating star of the Cayetano Circus Theatre, rendezvous of the southern aristocracy, and is sought by Royal Montague, a powerful southern gambler. She falls in love with Carl Van Horn, scion of a wealthy southern family, and agrees to forsake her career to marry him. Taking with her Peewee and Ginger, her faithful circus friends, she goes with Carl to visit the elder Van Horns on their Louisiana plantation. A great ball is held in her honor, but her friends divulge the secret that she is a circus performer and Mrs. Van Horn forces their departure. Refused reemployment by Cayetano, the trio takes work at Montague's gambling establishment, and Dixiana becomes instrumental in Montague's plan to ruin Carl financially; she is made Queen of the Mardi Gras but is abducted by Montague, whom Carl challenges to a duel. Dixiana, after detaining Carl, disguises herself and goes to duel in his stead and to expose Montague's treachery; later, the lovers are reconciled. *Singers. Dancers. Gamblers. Aristocrats. Circus. Plantations. New Orleans. Louisiana. Duels. Mardi Gras.*

THE DIXIE FLYER **F2.1368**

Trem Carr Productions. *Dist* Rayart Pictures. 29 Jul **1926** [New York State license]. Si; b&w. 35mm. 6 reels, 5,274 ft.

Dir Charles J. Hunt. *Story-Scen* H. H. Van Loan. *Photog* William Tuers, Joseph Walker.

Cast: Cullen Landis, Eva Novak, Pat Harmon.

Action melodrama. "Vice-president of railroad seeks removal of president and stirs up insurrection in ranks with exception of young foreman. President's daughter seeks to find trouble and meets foreman. Between the two they defeat attempts of vice-president and find mutual love." (*Motion Picture News Booking Guide*, 12:26, Apr 1927.) *Railroad magnates. Railroad foremen. Labor. Railroads.*

THE DIXIE HANDICAP **F2.1369**

Metro-Goldwyn Pictures. 12 Jan **1925** [c5 Jan 1925; LP21018]. Si; b&w. 35mm. 7 reels, 6,509 ft.

Pres by Louis B. Mayer. *Dir* Reginald Barker. *Adapt* Waldemar Young. *Photog* Percy Hilburn. *Art Dir* Cedric Gibbons. *Film Ed* Daniel J. Gray. *Asst Dir* Harry Schenck.

Cast: Claire Windsor *(Virginia)*, Frank Keenan *(Judge Roberts)*, Lloyd Hughes *(Johnny Sheridan)*, John Sainpolis *(Dexter)*, Otis Harlan *(Noah)*, Joseph Morrison *(Bubbles)*, Otto Hoffman *(The Major)*, Edward Martindel *(Mr. Bosworth)*, Ruth King *(Mrs. Bosworth)*, William Quirk *(a tout)*, James Quinn *(a tout)*, Loyal Underwood *(Losing Jones)*, Bert Lindley *(conductor)*, William Orlamond *(sheriff)*, Milton Ross *(constable)*, J. P. Lockney *(milkman)*.

Melodrama. Source: Gerald Beaumont, "Dixie," in *Red Book* (43:62–66, Sep 1924). Though greatly reduced in circumstances, Judge Roberts hides his true financial condition from his daughter, Virginia, whom he brings up in luxury by selling his estate a little at a time. After years of living this magnificent lie, the judge is left with only the family homestead and a horse named Southern Melody. The horse dies shortly after foaling, but her filly, Dixie, shows great speed and promise when she is trained by Johnny Sheridan, the judge's partner and friend. The superintendent of an adjoining stable tells Virginia of her father's reduced circumstances and offers to help the judge financially if she will marry him. Virginia consents, but the judge hears of it, sells Dixie, continues with his deception, and sends Virginia abroad. The judge's fortunes soon hit rock bottom: he loses his home, is defeated for reelection, and becomes a drunken derelict. Dixie is injured in the Belmont Stakes; Johnny buys her back, takes her to Kentucky, nurses her back to health, and enters her in the Derby. Virginia returns shortly before the race and learns of her father's poverty. The colt wins the race and a prize of $50,000. The old estate is restored to the judge, and Virginia asks the bashful Johnny to marry her. *Judges. Fatherhood. Horseracing. Finance—Personal. Kentucky Derby. Belmont Park. Horses.*

THE DIXIE MERCHANT **F2.1370**

Fox Film Corp. 7 Mar **1926** [c7 Mar 1926; LP22604]. Si; b&w. 35mm. 6 reels, 5,126 ft.

Pres by William Fox. *Dir* Frank Borzage. *Scen* Kenneth B. Clarke. *Photog* Frank B. Good. *Asst Dir* Bunny Dull.

Cast: J. Farrell MacDonald *(Jean Paul Fippany)*, Madge Bellamy *(Aida Fippany)*, Jack Mulhall *(Jimmy Pickett)*, Claire McDowell *(Josephine Fippany)*, Harvey Clark *(Baptiste)*, Edward Martindel *(John Pickett)*, Evelyn Arden *(Minnie Jordan)*, Onest Conly *(Eph)*, Paul Panzer *(Whitcomb)*.

Comedy-drama. Source: John Barry Benefield, *The Chicken-Wagon Family* (New York, 1925). Easygoing J. P. Fippany loses his home and takes to the road on a chickenwagon with his wife and daughter. The wagon is wrecked in an automobile collision involving Jimmy Pickett, who falls in love with daughter Aida, and through a misunderstanding involving Marseillaise, Fippany's racehorse, his wife Josephine and Aida go to live with relatives. The disconsolate Fippany sells Marseillaise to Jimmy's father, sends the money to his wife, then disappears. Meanwhile, Jimmy finds Aida and convinces her of his love. Marseillaise, badly driven in a race, loses a heat, but Fippany emerges and rides her to victory, following which there is a reconciliation between husband and wife. *Vagabonds. Family life. Courtship. Automobile accidents. Horseracing. United States—South. Horses.*

DO AND DARE **F2.1371**

Fox Film Corp. 1 Oct **1922** [c1 Oct 1922; LP19258]. Si; b&w. 35mm. 5 reels, 4,744 ft.

Pres by William Fox. *Dir-Scen* Edward Sedgwick. *Titl* Ralph Spence. *Story* Marion Brooks. *Photog* Dan Clark. *Film Ed* Ralph Spence.

Cast: Tom Mix *(Kit Carson Boone/Henry Boone)*, Dulcie Cooper *(Mary Lee)*, Claire Adams *(Juanita Sánchez)*, Claude Peyton *(Córdoba)*, Jack Rollins *(José Sánchez)*, Hector Sarno *(General Sánchez)*, Wilbur Higby *(Col. "Handy" Lee)*, Bob Klein *(Yellow Crow)*, Gretchen Hartman *(Zita)*.

Melodrama. When Henry Boone hears his grandfather's stories of his youth as a pioneer and scout, he is gripped by the fires of romance and decides to hunt adventure. Boone finds himself in an airplane carrying a military message to a leader of a revolution in a South American country. He is arrested as a spy but escapes and saves the ruler's daughter from the revolutionaries. *Grandfathers. Scouts—Frontier. Spies. Revolutions. South America.*

Note: Working title: *A Kiss in the Dark.*

DO IT NOW **F2.1372**

Phil Goldstone Productions. *Dist* Renown Pictures. 1 Feb **1924** [Scheduled release]. Si; b&w. 35mm. 6 reels.

Dir Duke Worne. *Story* Malcolm S. White. *Photog* Roland Price, Edgar Lyons.

Cast: William Fairbanks, Alec B. Francis, Madge Bellamy, Arthur Hoyt, John Fox, Jr., G. Raymond Nye, Dorothy Revier.

Action melodrama. At the urgings of his sweetheart, Rosemary Smith, a man (played by William Fairbanks) leaves his soft job in the east and goes west to settle a dispute over oil lands owned by Rosemary's father. This man evicts the wrong party and later must return west in order to set things right, protecting the honor of a girl from the advances of the crooked foreman. *Ranch foremen. Dudes. Eviction. Oil lands.*

DO THE DEAD TALK? **F2.1373**

Ebony Film Corp. *Dist* Arista Film Corp. 20 Nov **1922** [New York State]. Si; b&w. 35mm. 5 reels.

Dir-Writ Jack MacCullough.

Cast: Willard Burt, Hermina France, Grant Fohrman.

Drama(?). No information about the nature of this film has been found.

DO YOUR DUTY F2.1374

First National Pictures. 14 Oct **1928** [c9 Oct 1928; LP25702]. Si; b&w. 35mm. 7 reels, 5,996 ft.

Pres by Richard A. Rowland. *Dir* William Beaudine. *Scen* Vernon Smith. *Titl* Gene Towne, Casey Robinson. *Story* Julian Josephson. *Photog* Michael Joyce. *Film Ed* Stuart Heisler.

Cast: Charlie Murray *(Tim Maloney)*, Lucien Littlefield *(Andy McIntosh)*, Charles Delaney *(Danny Sheehan, Jr.)*, Edward Brady *(Ritzy Dalton)*, Blue Washington *(Dude Jackson)*, Doris Dawson *(Mary Ellen Maloney)*, Aggie Herring *(Mrs. Maloney)*, George Pierce *(Capt. Dan Sheehan)*.

Comedy-drama. Just before a robbery, Sgt. Tim Maloney, one of New York's Finest, is knocked cold by the Dalton gang, and a bottle of whisky is poured over him. Still dizzy, Tim regains consciousness and goes out to the street; suspected of being drunk while on duty, he is demoted to private. Tim's daughter, Mary Ellen, is to be married to patrolman Danny Sheehan at the station house, but Tim is too ashamed to attend. Tim brings in the Dalton gang on his own, however, and is made a lieutenant in time to give the bride away. *Police. Gangs. Robbery. Weddings. New York City.*

THE DOCKS OF NEW YORK F2.1375

Paramount Famous Lasky Corp. 29 Sep **1928** [c29 Sep 1928; LP2566]. Si; b&w. 35mm. 8 reels, 7,202 ft.

Assoc Prod J. G. Bachmann. *Dir* Josef von Sternberg. *Titl* Julian Johnson. *Adapt* Jules Furthman. *Story* John Monk Saunders. *Photog* Harold Rosson. *Set Dsgn* Hans Dreier. *Film Ed* Helen Lewis.

Cast: George Bancroft *(Bill Roberts)*, Betty Compson *(Sadie)*, Baclanova *(Lou)*, Clyde Cook *(Sugar Steve)*, Mitchell Lewis *(third engineer)*, Gustav von Seyffertitz *(Hymn Book Harry)*, Guy Oliver *(The Crimp)*, May Foster *(Mrs. Crimp)*, Lillian Worth *(Steve's girl)*.

Drama. Bill Roberts, a stoker on a tramp steamer, comes ashore for 8 hours' leave and saves the life of Sadie, a bitter waterfront tramp who, tired of her sordid life in sailors' dancehalls, throws herself into the water. That evening Bill gets drunk and marries Sadie in a ceremony presided over by Hymn Book Harry, a mission worker; the following morning Bill leaves her without a word and returns to his ship. The third engineer tries to make love to Sadie and is killed by his wife, Lou; Sadie is blamed for the crime, but Lou comes forward and confesses. As the steamer is leaving New York harbor, Bill realizes that he loves Sadie and jumps ship, swimming to shore. Sadie has been taken into court for stealing the clothes Bill had given her to be married in, and he confesses to the theft, promising to return to Sadie after his 60 days in jail. *Sailors. Stokers. Prostitutes. Marine engineers. Mission workers. Marriage. Murder. Suicide. Theft. Docks.*

DOCTOR JACK F2.1376

Hal E. Roach Studios. *Dist* Associated Exhibitors. 26 Nov **1922** [c9 Oct 1922; LU18289]. Si; b&w. 35mm. 5 reels, 4,700 ft.

Prod Hal Roach. *Dir* Fred Newmeyer. *Scen* Thomas J. Crizer. *Story* Hal Roach, Sam Taylor, Jean Havez. *Photog* Walter Lundin.

Cast: Harold Lloyd *(Dr. Jackson, "Dr. Jack" for short)*, Mildred Davis *(The Sick-Little-Well-Girl)*, John T. Prince *(Her Father)*, Eric Mayne *(Dr. Ludwig von Saulsbourg)*, C. Norman Hammond *(The Lawyer)*, Anna Townsend *(His Mother)*, Mickey Daniels.

Comedy. Dr. Jack, who often prescribes sunshine, good cheer, and commonsense, is called in to consult with Dr. Ludwig von Saulsbourg on the health of an invalid girl. Since in Dr. Jack's opinion she needs excitement, he dresses and acts like an escaped lunatic, to the delight of the girl but creating an uproar in the household. The girl is cured and loses her heart to Dr. Jack, while Saulsbourg makes an undignified retreat. *Invalids. Physicians. Insanity.*

DR. JIM F2.1377

Universal Film Manufacturing Co. 28 Nov **1921** [c18 Nov 1921; LP17212]. Si; b&w. 35mm. 5 reels, 4,474 ft.

Pres by Carl Laemmle. *Dir* William Worthington. *Scen* Eugene B. Lewis. *Story* Stuart Paton. *Photog* Leland Lancaster.

Cast: Frank Mayo *(Dr. Jim Keene)*, Claire Windsor *(Helen Keene)*, Oliver Cross *(Kenneth Cord)*, Stanhope Wheatcroft *(Bobby Thorne)*, Robert Anderson *(Tom Anderson)*, Herbert Heyes *(Captain Blake)*, Gordon Sackville *(assistant doctor)*.

Society melodrama. Dr. Jim Keene, a great surgeon whose professional life occupies most of his time, loves his wife, Helen, but she resents his devotion to his work. When he suffers a nervous collapse, the couple go on a sea voyage; Helen is the only woman aboard a ship manned by roughnecks and skippered by a hulking brute. She is attracted to the captain's virility, and a quarrel ensues between the captain and Jim during a storm; the captain is injured, and Jim is forced to operate to save his life. With the aid of the crew, Jim makes Helen realize the captain's bestiality, and in a final battle Jim is able to beat him. Jim and Helen are reconciled, and she understands his love for her and learns to respect his profession. *Surgeons. Ship crews. Marriage. Manhood.*

THE DOCTOR'S SECRET F2.1378

Paramount Famous Lasky Corp. 26 Jan **1929** [c25 Jan 1929; LP66]. Sd (Movietone); b&w. 35mm. 6 reels, 5,832 ft.

Dir-Adapt William C. De Mille. *Photog* J. Roy Hunt. *Film Ed* Merrill White. *Ch Rec Engr* Franklin Hansen.

Cast: Ruth Chatterton *(Lillian Garson)*, H. B. Warner *(Richard Garson)*, John Loder *(Hugh Paton)*, Robert Edeson *(Dr. Brodie)*, Wilfred Noy *(Mr. Redding)*, Ethel Wales *(Mrs. Redding)*, Nancy Price *(Susie)*, Frank Finch Smiles *(Wethers)*.

Society melodrama. Source: James Matthew Barrie, "Half an Hour," in *The Plays of J. M. Barrie* (New York, 1929). A girl of the English nobility, Lillian has been forced to marry wealthy commoner Richard Garson, but she decides to elope with Hugh Paton, a man of her own station. He is killed in an automobile accident, and she returns home. A doctor who has witnessed the accident shows up for dinner and arouses the husband's suspicions, but he is convinced otherwise. *Physicians. Nobility. Social classes. Automobile accidents. England.*

Note: Also produced in a French-language version, *Le Secret du docteur*, q. v.

DOES IT PAY? F2.1379

Fox Film Corp. 7 Oct **1923** [c1 Sep 1923; LP19410]. Si; b&w. 35mm. 7 reels, 6,652 ft.

Pres by William Fox. *Dir* Charles Horan. *Scen* Howard Irving Young. *Story* Julius Steger. *Story? (see note)* Bernice Dovskie. *Photog* Joseph Ruttenberg.

Cast: Hope Hampton *(Doris Clark)*, Robert T. Haines *(John Weston)*, Florence Short *(Martha Weston)*, Walter Petri *(Jack Weston)*, Peggy Shaw *(Alice Weston)*, Charles Wellesley *(Senator Delafield)*, Mary Thurman *(Marion)*, Claude Brooke *(Attorney Alden)*, Pierre Gendron *(Harold Reed)*, Roland Bottomley *(François Chavelle)*, Marie Shotwell *(Mrs. Clark)*, Bunny Grauer *(The Boy)*.

Melodrama. John Weston is lured away from his wife and children by Doris Clark, a youthful adventuress and employee in the Weston household. Weston divorces his wife and marries Miss Clark. One evening he suffers a nervous breakdown when he finds his bride in her boudoir embracing her music teacher, François Chavelle. Weston loses his memory and is taken to the first Mrs. Weston, who, with her daughter, welcomes him and promises to restore his health. *Adventuresses. Music teachers. Infidelity. Amnesia. Divorce.*

Note: Some sources credit Bernice Dovskie with story.

DOG JUSTICE F2.1380

FBO Pictures. 10 Jun **1928** [c14 May 1928; LP25240]. Si; b&w. 35mm. 6 reels, 5,043 ft.

Dir Jerome Storm. *Story-Scen* Ethel Hill. *Titl* Randolph Bartlett. *Photog* Nick Musuraca. *Film Ed* Jack Kitchen. *Asst Dir* James Dugan.

Cast: Ranger *(himself, a dog)*, Edward Hearn *(Jimmie O'Neil)*, Nita Martan *(Babbette)*, James Welsh *(Baptiste, her grandfather)*, Al Smith *(Pierre La Grande, prospector)*, John Northpole *(Flint, mineowner)*.

Northwest melodrama. Trooper O'Neil thinks his sweetheart, Babbette, committed a murder. She escapes as he is about to arrest her. Later, Babbette finds O'Neil snowblind from exposure and she nurses him back to health. Ranger, O'Neil's dog, helps him find the true murderer, Pierre La Grande, who shot mineowner Flint in a dispute over a gold mine. *Murder. Snow blindness. Northwest Mounted Police. Dogs.*

DOG LAW F2.1381

FBO Pictures. 2 Sep **1928** [c2 Sep 1928; LP25589]. Si; b&w. 35mm. 6 reels, 4,802 ft.

Dir Jerome Storm. *Screenplay* Frank Howard Clark. *Titl* Helen Gregg. *Story* S. E. V. Taylor. *Photog* Sam De Grasse. *Film Ed* Della M. King. *Asst Dir* Sam Nelson.

Cast: Ranger *(a dog)*, Robert Sweeney *(Jimmy)*, Jules Cowles *(Hawkins)*, Walter Maly *(McAllister)*, Mary Mabery *(Jean Larson)*.

Melodrama. Jim Benson loses all his money in a crooked card game with a gambler named McAlister, and when McAlister is murdered by Hawkins, Jim is accused of the crime on circumstantial evidence. With the help of his girl, Jean, Jim clears himself of suspicion, and his dog, Ranger, drives Hawkins off a cliff to a just doom. *Gamblers. Murder. Circumstantial evidence. Dogs.*

A DOG OF THE REGIMENT **F2.1382**

Warner Brothers Pictures. 29 Oct **1927** [c20 Oct 1927; LP24546]. Si; b&w. 35mm. 5 reels, 5,003 ft.

Dir Ross Lederman. *Scen* Charles R. Condon. *Photog* Ed Du Par. *Film Ed* Clarence Kolster. *Asst Dir* Joe Barry.

Cast: Rin-Tin-Tin *(Rinty)*, Dorothy Gulliver *(Marie von Waldorf)*, Tom Gallery *(Richard Harrison)*, John Peters *(Eric von Hager)*.

War melodrama. Source: Albert S. Howson, "A Dog of the Regiment" (publication undetermined). Dick Harrison, a young American lawyer, goes to Germany to represent the settlement of the Waldorf estate, while the heiress, Marie, retains for her legal counsel Eric von Hagar because of his long association with the family. Dick accuses Hagar of furthering his own interests in the settlement, thus incurring his enmity, but winning the admiration of Marie and her dog Rinty. At the outbreak of war, Marie becomes a nurse and remains indifferent to Eric's advances, though he is now a captain. Dick's plane is downed nearby, Rinty extricates him from the wreckage, but Dick is captured. Eric orders him executed, forging the general's signature, but Dick and Rinty escape. Following the peace settlement, they are reunited with Marie. *Heiresses. Lawyers. Nurses. World War I. Germany. Dogs.*

DOLLAR DEVILS **F2.1383**

Victor Schertzinger. *Dist* W. W. Hodkinson Corp. 28 Jan **1923**. Si; b&w. 35mm. 6 reels, 5,600 ft.

Dir Victor Schertzinger. *Scen* Louis Stevens. *Photog* John Stumar.

Cast: Joseph Dowling *(Zannon Carthy)*, Miles McCarthy *(Hal Andrews)*, May Wallace *(Mrs. Andrews)*, Eva Novak *(Amy)*, Hallam Cooley *(Bruce Merlin)*, Cullen Landis *(Jim Biggers)*, Lydia Knott *(Mrs. Biggers)*, Neyneen Farrell *(Helen Andrews)*.

Melodrama. A small New England town loses its head over the discovery of oil just outside the town by Bruce Merlin, a dapper young man from the city. With the exception of Zannon Carthy, the town patriarch, everyone invests in the venture. Jim Biggers, who is studying engineering with Carthy's financial assistance, saves the community by exposing Merlin as a swindler. Jim loses his sweetheart, Helen Andrews, to Merlin, but later he finds that her sister, Amy, is a better bet. *Swindlers. Engineers. Sisters. Smalltown life. Oil. New England.*

DOLLAR DOWN **F2.1384**

Co-Artists Productions. *Dist* Truart Film Corp. Sep **1925** [c19 Oct 1925; LP21917]. Si; b&w. 35mm. 6 reels, 6,318 ft.

Dir Tod Browning. *Adapt for the screen by* Fred Stowers. *Story* Jane Courthope, Ethel Hill. *Photog* Allen Thompson.

Cast: Ruth Roland *(Ruth Craig)*, Henry B. Walthall *(Alec Craig)*, Maym Kelso *(Mrs. Craig)*, Earl Schenck *(Grant Elliot)*, Claire McDowell *(Mrs. Meadows, Craig's sister)*, Roscoe Karns *(Gene Meadows, her son)*, Jane Mercer *(Betty Meadows, her daughter)*, Lloyd Whitlock *(Howard Steele)*, Otis Harlan *(Norris)*, Edward Borman *(Tilton)*.

Melodrama. Although Alec Craig has a good position in a manufacturing company, he is brought close to financial ruin by his wife and daughter, who live beyond their means and who have fallen prey to instalment sharks. Grant Elliot, an aviator, loves Ruth and waits for the day when his invention will be a success so that they can marry. To stave off an instalment collector, Ruth illegally pawns a ring that is not yet paid for. She is tricked by society parasite Howard Steele, an agent of real estate speculators, into divulging information on the location of a valuable site on which the company has taken an option. The company blames Craig for the leak, and he is fired. The collector calls for the ring and finds that it has been pawned. Ruth, realizing she has been tricked, gets even with Steele by taking him up and making him stay up in an airplane past the time when the option expires. Craig's widowed sister and her son, Gene, redeem the ring and make Ruth and her mother promise never to fall prey to instalment sharks again. Ruth's flight has proved the value of Grant's invention, and their future is assured. *Aviators. Inventors. Parasites. Instalment buying. Finance—Personal. Real estate. Thrift.*

THE DOLLAR-A-YEAR MAN **F2.1385**

Famous Players–Lasky. *Dist* Paramount Pictures. 3 Apr **1921** [c3 Apr 1921; LP16383]. Si; b&w. 35mm. 5 reels, 4,606 ft.

Dir James Cruze. *Story-Scen* Walter Woods. *Photog* Karl Brown.

Cast: Roscoe "Fatty" Arbuckle *(Franklin Pinney, a laundryman)*, Lila Lee *(Peggy Bruce)*, Winifred Greenwood *(Kate Connelly)*, J. M. Dumont *(Tipson Blair, a Socialist)*, Edward Sutherland *(The Prince)*, Edwin Stevens *(Colonel Bruce, a Secret Service agent)*, Henry Johnson *(General Oberano)*.

Farce. Laundryman Franklin Pinney, the owner of the only speedboat of the Santa Vista Yacht Club, is requested not to attend the club's reception for a visiting prince. Franklin meets the prince in a haunted house after a band of anarchists have plotted to kidnap him and have absconded with a South American diplomat by mistake. Discovering that his sweetheart's father is a Secret Service man on the track of the anarchists and is detailed to act as bodyguard to the prince, Franklin and the prince overcome the blackguards, and, invited to the reception, the laundryman is welcomed as a hero and son-in-law by his sweetheart's father. *Laundrymen. Secret service. Royalty. Anarchists. Socialists. Diplomats. Kidnaping. Boat clubs. Haunted houses.*

A DOLL'S HOUSE **F2.1386**

Nazimova Productions. *Dist* United Artists. 12 Feb **1922** [c13 Feb 1922; LP17555]. Si; b&w. 35mm. 7 reels, 6,650 ft.

Dir Charles Bryant. *Scen* Peter M. Winters. *Photog* Charles Van Enger.

Cast: Alan Hale *(Torvald Helmer)*, Alla Nazimova *(Nora, his wife)*, Nigel De Brulier *(Dr. Rank)*, Elinor Oliver *(Anna, a nurse)*, Wedgewood Nowell *(Nils Krogstad)*, Cara Lee *(Ellen, a maid)*, Florence Fisher *(Mrs. Linden)*, Philippe De Lacy *(Ivar)*, Barbara Maier *(Emmy)*.

Drama. Source: Henrik Ibsen, *A Doll's House* (1879). In order that her husband may retire and recover his health, Nora Helmer goes to Krogstad, a moneylender, and forges her father's name to a note. Six years later, Torvald, her husband, has risen to managership in a bank but refuses to retain Krogstad in his employ; the latter threatens Nora with exposure unless she uses her influence in his behalf. In spite of Nora's efforts, her husband denounces Krogstad as a criminal, and in desperation he sends Torvald a letter exposing Nora's forgery. Instead of shielding his wife, Torvald is infuriated at the blow to his reputation; however, influenced by Mrs. Linden, Krogstad relents and withdraws his accusation, and all is well. Nora, finding her illusions about her marriage shattered, perceives the truth about her doll-like existence and asserts her right to live her own life. *Moneylenders. Marriage. Forgery. Blackmail. Women's rights. Sweden.*

DOMESTIC MEDDLERS **F2.1387**

Tiffany-Stahl Productions. 15 Aug **1928** [c19 Nov 1928; LP25849]. Si; b&w. 35mm. 6 reels, 5,632 ft.

Dir James Flood. *Story-Cont* Wellyn Totman. *Titl* Frederick Hatton, Fanny Hatton. *Photog* Ernest Miller. *Film Ed* Byron Robinson.

Cast: Claire Windsor *(Claire)*, Lawrence Gray *(Walter)*, Roy D'Arcy *(Lew)*, Jed Prouty *(Jonsey)*.

Comedy-drama. Lew, a philandering, debonair braggart, invites his partner, Walter, and Walter's wife, Claire, to dine with him. Walter falls asleep during the meal, and Lew and Claire go dancing on a nearby roof garden; Jonsey, an out-of-town buyer and one of Lew and Walter's best customers, sees Lew dancing with Claire, and the next day Walter hears office gossip that mistakenly makes him believe his wife has been unfaithful to him. Lew again invites them to dinner, and Walter pretends to fall asleep on the couch; Lew attempts to kiss Claire, and she fends him off with her fists. With his faith in Claire renewed, Walter bullwhips Lew and returns home with Claire. *Buyers. Infidelity. Gossip. Partnerships. Flagellation.*

DOMESTIC RELATIONS **F2.1388**

Preferred Pictures. *Dist* Associated First National Pictures. 4 Jun **1922** [New York premiere; released Jun 1922; cll Jul 1922; LP18041]. Si; b&w. 35mm. 6 reels, 5,192 ft.

Pres by B. P. Schulberg. *Dir* Chet Withey. *Story-Scen* Violet Clark. *Photog* Joseph Brotherton. *Camera? (see note)* Bert Glennon. *Sets* Frank Ormston. *Art Titl* Ferdinand P. Earle.

Cast: Katherine MacDonald *(Barbara Benton)*, William P. Carleton *(Judge James Benton, her husband)*, Frank Leigh *(Joe Martin)*, Barbara La Marr *(Mrs. Martin)*, Gordon Mullen *(Sandy, a neighbor of the Martins)*, George Fisher *(Pierre, an artist)*, Lloyd Whitlock *(Dr. Chester Brooks)*.

Domestic drama. Though Judge Benton unhesitatingly sentences laborer Joe Martin to a year in prison for beating his wife, he thoughtlessly abandons his own faithful wife to the attentions of an artist and demands a divorce when he suspects her of wrongdoing. Through coincidence Barbara Benton and Mrs. Martin become friends, and Barbara learns of Joe's desire for revenge. She warns her husband and makes him realize that his treatment of her is no different from Joe's behavior toward his wife; both parties are reconciled. *Judges. Artists. Marriage. Revenge.*

Note: One source credits Bert Glennon with photography.

DOMESTIC TROUBLES **F2.1389**

Warner Brothers Pictures. 24 Mar **1928** [c16 Mar 1928; LP25068]. Mus score (Vitaphone); b&w. 35mm. 6 reels, 5,164 ft. [Also si.]

Dir Ray Enright. *Story-Scen* C. Graham Baker. *Titl* Joseph Jackson. *Photog* Charles Van Enger. *Film Ed* George Marks. *Asst Dir* Chauncy Pyle.

Cast: Clyde Cook *(James Bullard/Horace Bullard)*, Louise Fazenda *(Lola)*, Betty Blythe *(Carrie)*, Jean Laverty *(Grace)*, Arthur Rankin *(Meredith Roberts)*.

Comedy. Twin brothers James and Horace Bullard have opposite personalities: James, a gay dandy, marries a clubwoman; Horace, straitlaced, introverted, and prudish, draws a butterfly for a wife. While Carrie is away, Horace takes a joyride with an old sweetheart, is arrested for speeding, and sent to jail. At James's request, Horace impersonates his brother when Carrie returns. They meet Grace, Horace's wife, at a cabaret, and having admired her high-stepping brother-in-law, Grace accepts his invitation to come home with them. Flirting with "James," Grace discovers a small birthmark on his neck—the same as her husband's. James appears in the midst of Horace's dilemma, and Carrie never learns of the escapade. *Twins. Brothers. Clubwomen. Dandies. Prudes. Impersonation. Birthmarks.*

DON DARE DEVIL **F2.1390**

Universal Pictures. 18 Jul **1925** [c10 Apr 1925; LP21352]. Si; b&w. 35mm. 5 reels.

Dir Clifford S. Smith. *Story-Scen* Wyndham Gittens. *Photog* Harry Neumann.

Cast: Jack Hoxie *(Jack Bannister)*, Cathleen Calhoun *(Ynez Remado)*, Duke Lee *(Bud Latham)*, William Welch *(José Remado)*, Thomas G. Lingham *(Felipe Berengo)*, Evelyn Sherman *(Señora Berengo)*, William A. Steele *(Benito Menocal)*, Cesare Gravina *(Esteban Salazar)*, Tommy Grime *(Texas)*, Demetrius Alexis *(Parader)*.

Melodrama. Jack Bannister returns to his home in South America, bringing with him some Wyoming cowboys. At a fiesta, he meets Menocal, an old friend, who is murdered moments later by Bud Latham, an American bandit under the protection of the local sheriff, a rascal named Berengo. Jack sets out after Latham and finds the killer trailing another outlaw, José Remado. Jack catches up with Latham and whips him in a brutal fight. The following day, Remado is jailed by Berengo, and Jack is persuaded by Remado's beautiful daughter, Ynez, to help her father escape from jail. Jack disguises himself as a peon, slips into Berengo's office, and frees Remado. In the meantime, Latham and his gang kidnap Ynez. Jack gives chase to the bandits with his Wyoming buddies, and there is a great revolver battle with the desperadoes. Jack rescues Ynez after a tough fight with Latham in a cave. *Cowboys. Desperadoes. Sheriffs. Wyomingites. Murder. South America.*

DON DESPERADO **F2.1391**

Leo Maloney Productions. *Dist* Pathé Exchange. 8 May **1927** [c1 Apr 1927; LU23806]. Si; b&w. 35mm. 6 reels, 5,804 ft.

Dir Leo Maloney. *Story-Scen* Ford I. Beebe. *Photog* Ben White.

Cast: Leo Maloney *(Leo McHale)*, Eugenia Gilbert *(Doris Jessup)*, Frederick Dana *(Nathan Jessup)*, Charles Bartlett *(Aaron Blaisdell)*, Whitehorse *(Ables)*, Bud Osborne *(Frenchy)*, Allen Watt *(agent)*, Morgan Davis *(Joe Jessup)*, Harry W. Ramsey *(Dr. Wilder)*.

Western melodrama. A western mining town is besieged by the Black Bandit, who repeatedly robs the stagecoach; and amidst talk of ousting the sheriff, deputy sheriff Leo McHale brings in Frenchy, a local layabout whom he suspects. The miners and townsmen, headed by Nathan Jessup, want a lynching, but McHale effects a clever escape with his prisoner. Blaisdell, a lawyer who agrees to help, lets Frenchy escape, claiming to have been overpowered by him. After a mob has almost lynched Jessup's innocent son following another stagecoach robbery, McHale proves that Blaisdell is backing the bandit and wins the hand of Doris, Jessup's daughter. *Bandits. Sheriffs. Lawyers. Stagecoach robberies. Lynching. Mining towns.*

DON JUAN **F2.1392**

Warner Brothers Pictures. 6 Aug **1926** [New York premiere; released 19 Feb 1927; c9 Jun 1926; LP22815]. Sd eff & mus score (Vitaphone); b&w. 35mm. 10 reels, 10,018 ft.

Dir Alan Crosland. *Screenplay* Bess Meredyth. *Titl* Walter Anthony, Maude Fulton. *Photog* Byron Haskins. *Asst Camera* Frank Kesson. *Art Dir* Ben Carré. *Film Ed* Harold McCord. *Orig Mus* William Axt. *Mus Arr* Maj. Edward Bowes, David Mendoza, William Axt. *Bacchanalian Art Dancing* Marion Morgan. *Rec Engr* George R. Groves. *Asst Dir* Gordon Hollingshead. *Elec Eff* F. N. Murphy. *Master of Prop* A. C. Wilson. *Art Titl* Victor Vance.

Cast: John Barrymore *(Don Juan/Don José)*, Mary Astor *(Adriana Della Varnese)*, Willard Louis *(Pedrillo)*, Estelle Taylor *(Lucretia Borgia)*, Helene Costello *(Rena, Adriana's maid)*, Myrna Loy *(Maia, Lucretia's maid)*, Jane Winton *(Beatrice)*, John Roche *(Leandro)*, June Marlowe *(Trusia)*, Yvonne Day *(Don Juan, 5 years old)*, Philippe De Lacey *(Don Juan, 10 years old)*, John George *(hunchback)*, Helena D'Algy *(murderess of José)*, Warner Oland *(Caesar Borgia)*, Montagu Love *(Donati)*, Josef Swickard *(Duke Della Varnese)*, Lionel Braham *(Duke Margoni)*, Phyllis Haver *(Imperia)*, Nigel De Brulier *(Marquis Rinaldo)*, Hedda Hopper *(Marquise Rinaldo)*, Helen Lee Worthing *(Eleanora)*, Emily Fitzroy *(The Dowager)*, Gustav von Seyffertitz *(alchemist)*, Sheldon Lewis, Gibson Gowland, Dick Sutherland *(gentlemen of Rome)*.

Romantic drama. Inspired by: George Gordon Byron, *Don Juan*. In the prolog, Don José, warned of his wife's infidelity, seals his wife's lover alive in his hiding place and drives her from the castle; abandoned to his lust, he is stabbed by his last mistress, and with his dying words he implores his son, Juan, to take all from women but yield nothing. Ten years later, young Don Juan is famous as a lover and pursued by many women, including the powerful Lucretia Borgia, who invites him to her ball; his contempt for her incites her hatred of Adriana, the daughter of the Duke Della Varnese, with whom he is enraptured; and Lucretia plots to marry her to Donati and poison the duke. Don Juan intervenes and thwarts the scheme, winning the love of Adriana, but the Borgia declare war on the duke's kinsmen, offering them safety if Adriana marries Donati; Don Juan is summoned to the wedding, but he prefers death to marriage with Lucretia. He escapes and kills Donati in a duel; the lovers are led to the death-tower, but while Adriana pretends suicide, he escapes; and following a series of battles, he defeats his pursuers and is united with Adriana. *Rakes. The Renaissance. Italy. Rome. Lucrezia Borgia. Cesare Borgia.*

DON JUAN OF THE WEST **F2.1393**

Dist Anchor Film Distributors. 11 Oct **1928** [New York State license]. Si; b&w. 35mm. 5 reels, 4,800 ft.

Cast: Cheyenne Bill.

Western melodrama(?). No information about the nature of this film has been found.

DON JUAN'S THREE NIGHTS **F2.1394**

Henry Hobart Productions. *Dist* First National Pictures. 4 Sep **1926** [New York premiere; released 3 Oct; c12 Aug 1926; LP23015]. Si; b&w. 35mm. 7 reels, 6,374 ft.

Pres by Henry Hobart. *Dir* John Francis Dillon. *Screenplay* Clara Beranger. *Titl* Gerald C. Duffy. *Photog* James C. Van Trees.

Cast: Lewis Stone *(Johann Aradi)*, Shirley Mason *(Ninette Cavallar)*, Malcolm McGregor *(Giulio Roberti)*, Myrtle Stedman *(Madame Cavallar)*, Betty Francisco *(Madame de Courcy)*, Kalla Pasha *(Monsieur de Courcy)*, Alma Bennett *(Carlotta)*, Natalie Kingston *(Vilma Theodori)*, Mario Carillo *(Count di Bonito)*, Jed Prouty *(Lippi)*, Madeline Hurlock *(Louise Villate)*, Gertrude Astor *(Baroness von Minden)*.

Romantic drama. Source: Ludwig Biró, *Don Juans drei Nächte* (Berlin, 1917). Johann Aradi, a famous concert pianist with a reputation of being a great lover, is delighted to learn that Ninette Cavallar, the youthful daughter of his salon hostess, has fallen in love with him, but discovering that Ninette is only 16, he discourages her love and tries to promote the suit of Giulio Roberti, her youthful admirer. Ninette continues to cherish her love for Aradi, however, and to discourage Roberti. Aradi gives a wild party, to which he invites Ninette, and he succeeds in making himself disgusting to her by his actions during a drunken orgy. Roberti arrives to rescue Ninette from Aradi's passionate advances and challenges him to a duel in which Aradi allows himself to be wounded in the hand. Ninette realizes her love for Roberti, while Aradi, unable thereafter to play the piano, finds solace in his lady friends. *Pianists. Courtship. Self-sacrifice. Duels.*

DON MIKE **F2.1395**

R-C Pictures. *Dist* Film Booking Offices of America. 25 Jan or 27 Feb **1927** [c27 Jan 1927; LP23596]. Si; b&w. 35mm. 6 reels, 5,723 ft.

Pres by Joseph P. Kennedy. *Dir-Cont* Lloyd Ingraham. *Story* Frank M. Clifton. *Photog* Ross Fisher. *Asst Dir* Douglas Dawson.

Cast: Fred Thomson *(Don Miguel Arguella)*, Silver King *(Rey de Plata, a horse)*, Ruth Clifford *(Mary Kelsey)*, Noah Young *(Reuben Pettingill)*, Albert Prisco *(Don Luis Ybara)*, William Courtright *(Gômez)*, Tom Bates *(Jason Kelsey)*, Norma Marie *(Dolores)*, Carmen Le Roux *(Carmen)*.

Romantic melodrama. Don Miguel Arguella, owner of a vast California estate, is holding a fiesta when message arrives of a lost party in the desert; he rescues the pioneers, headed by Reuben Pettingill and including Jason Kelsey and his daughter Mary, to whom Don Mike is attracted. The *alcalde*, Don Luis Ybara, is embittered because of Don Miguel's interference in his persecution of Carmen, a girl on the estate. Pettingill, learning that "Don Mike" has neglected to record the boundaries of his land, files claim to the greater part of the estate and persuades Kelsey to promise him Mary. Don Luis is found murdered, and Pettingill offers a reward for the capture of Don Mike. General Frémont hears of the incident and sends a group of soldiers to the rancho, while Don Mike, dressed as a monk, attends the wedding as the officiating priest. A struggle ensues, and Pettingill is unmasked as the murderer and usurper. *Spanish. Mayors. Land rights. Murder. Courtship. Frontier and pioneer life. California. Horses.*

DON Q, SON OF ZORRO **F2.1396**

Elton Corp. *Dist* United Artists. 20 Sep **1925** [c8 Jul 1925; LP21637]. Si; b&w. 35mm. 11 reels, 10,264 ft.

Dir Donald Crisp. *Scen Ed* Lotta Woods. *Photoplay* Jack Cunningham. *Photog* Henry Sharp. *Adtl Photog* E. J. Vallejo. *Supv Art Dir* Edward M. Langley. *Asst Art Dir* Francesc Cugat, Anton Grot, Harold Miles. *Consulting Artist* Harry Oliver. *Research Dir* Arthur Woods. *Film Ed* William Nolan. *Mus Score* Mortimer Wilson. *Asst Dir* Frank Richardson. *Prod Mgr* Theodore Reed. *Gen Mgr* Robert Fairbanks. *Wardrobe* Paul Burns. *Tech Eff* Ned Mann. *Master of Prop* Howard MacChesney. *Lighting Eff* William S. Johnson.

Cast: Douglas Fairbanks *(Don César de Vega/Zorro)*, Mary Astor *(Dolores de Muro)*, Jack McDonald *(General de Muro)*, Donald Crisp *(Don Sebastian)*, Stella De Lanti *(The Queen)*, Warner Oland *(The Archduke)*, Jean Hersholt *(Don Fabrique)*, Albert MacQuarrie *(Colonel Matsado)*, Lottie Pickford Forrest *(Lola)*, Charles Stevens *(Robledo)*, Tote Du Crow *(Bernado)*, Martha Franklin *(The Duenna)*, Juliette Belanger *(dancer)*, Roy Coulson *(her admirer)*, Enrique Acosta *(Ramón)*.

Costume drama. Source: Hesketh Prichard and Kate Prichard, *Don Q's Love Story* (New York, 1925). Don César de Vega, a dashing young Californian, is sent by his father, Zorro, to Spain in order to broaden himself as is the tradition of the family. There he falls in love with a beauty named Dolores and also, owing to his prowess, gains favor with the Spanish court and the visiting Austrian Archduke. When the archduke is assassinated by one of the queen's guards and Don César is accused, the only witness refuses to clear Don César. So as to gain time to unmask the real criminals, Don César then feigns suicide, and with the help of his father, who has come to Spain, he succeeds in solving the mystery. His reward is the love of Dolores. *Royalty. Assassination. Suicide. Spain. California.*

DON QUICKSHOT OF THE RIO GRANDE **F2.1397**

Universal Pictures. 4 Jun **1923** [c2 Jun 1923; LP19053]. Si; b&w. 35mm. 5 reels, 4,894 ft.

Pres by Carl Laemmle. *Dir* George E. Marshall. *Scen* George Hively. *Photog* Charles Kaufman.

Cast: Jack Hoxie *("Pep" Pepper)*, Emmett King *(Jim Hellier)*, Elinor Field *(Tulip [Virginia?] Hellier)*, Fred C. Jones *(George Vivian)*, William A. Steele *(Bill [Joe?] Barton)*, Bob McKenzie *(Sheriff Littlejohn)*, Harry Woods *(a knight)*, Hank Bell, Ben Corbett *(henchmen)*, Skeeter Bill Robbins *(barfly)*, Scout *(himself, a horse)*.

Western melodrama. Source: Stephen Chalmers, "Don Quickshot of the Rio Grande," in *Short Stories Magazine* (25 Oct 1921). "Pep" Pepper, a romantic cowboy whose faculty for dreaming loses him his job, tries to emulate Don Quixote's courage after reading the Spanish classic. He intervenes in a saloon quarrel; a knife is thrown, killing the proprietor; and Pep is blamed. He escapes by leaping from a window to his horse. In his wanderings he meets and falls in love with Tulip Hellier, daughter of a wealthy cattleman. Pep rescues Tulip from a bandit gang and exonerates himself from the charge of killing the bartender. *Cowboys. Bartenders. Courage. Don Quixote. Horses.*

DON X **F2.1398**

A. G. Steen. *Dist* B. A. Goodman Productions. 11 Jul **1925** [review date]. Si; b&w. 35mm. 5 reels.

Dir-Writ Forrest Sheldon.

Cast: Bruce Gordon *(Frank Blair/Don X)*, Josephine Hill *(Gladys Paget)*, Boris Bullock *(Perez Blake)*, Victor Allen *(Pecos Pete)*, Milburn Morante *(Frank Paget)*, Robert Williamson *(Red)*.

Western melodrama. Perez Blake, apparently a decent rancher, is, in fact, the head of a gang of cattle rustlers. Frank Paget, a rancher much preyed upon by Blake's men, goes to the Cattlemen's Protective Association and asks for help. Frank Blair, the head of the association, appears at the ranch, disguised as Don X, a Mexican cattle buyer. Blair soon breaks up the gang and brings Blake to justice, winning for himself the love of Gladys Paget, the rancher's beautiful daughter. *Ranchers. Rustlers. Protective associations. Disguise.*

THE DONOVAN AFFAIR **F2.1399**

Columbia Pictures. 11 Apr **1929** [c10 May 1929; LP381]. Sd (Movietone); b&w. 35mm. 8 reels, 7,140 ft. [Also si; 7,189 ft.]

Prod Harry Cohn. *Dir* Frank R. Capra. *Scen* Dorothy Howell. *Dial-Titl* Howard J. Green. *Photog* Teddy Tetzlaff. *Art Dir* Harrison Wiley. *Film Ed* Arthur Roberts. *Asst Dir* Tenny Wright.

Cast: Jack Holt *(Inspector Killian)*, Dorothy Revier *(Jean Rankin)*, William Collier, Jr. *(Cornish)*, Agnes Ayres *(Lydia Rankin)*, John Roche *(Jack Donovan)*, Fred Kelsey *(Carney)*, Hank Mann *(Dr. Lindsey)*, Wheeler Oakman *(Porter)*, Virginia Browne Faire *(Mary Mills)*, Alphonse Ethier *(Capt. Peter Rankin)*, Edward Hearn *(Nelson)*, Ethel Wales *(Mrs. Lindsey)*, John Wallace *(Dobbs)*.

Mystery melodrama. Source: Owen Davis, *The Donovan Affair; a Play in Three Acts* (New York, 1930). Gambler and philanderer Jack Donovan is killed with a carving knife at a dinner party, and police inspector Killian at first suspects Porter, a sometime criminal present at the affair. Porter denies his accusation, however, and is about to tell Killian whom he suspects of the murder when he is himself murdered. After following several false scents, Killian discovers that Donovan and Porter were killed by Nelson, the butler, who was angry with Donovan for playing around with Mary Mills, a servant in the Donovan residence. *Philanderers. Gamblers. Police. Butlers. Murder.*

DON'T **F2.1400**

Metro-Goldwyn-Mayer Pictures. 15 Nov **1925** [c11 Jan 1926; LP22351]. Si; b&w. 35mm. 6 reels, 5,529 ft.

Dir Alf Goulding. *Adapt-Scen* Agnes Christine Johnston. *Photog* Max Fabian.

Cast: Sally O'Neil *(Tracey Moffat)*, John Patrick *(Gilbert Jenkins)*, Bert Roach *(Uncle Nat)*, James Morrison *(Abel)*, Estelle Clark *(Jane)*, De Witt Jennings *(Mr. Moffat)*, Ethel Wales *(Mrs. Moffat)*, Johnny Fox *(Horace Moffat)*, Dorothy Seay *(Nettie Moffat)*, Evelyn Pierce *(Marian Jenkins)*, Helen Hoge *(The Child)*, Brinsley Shaw *(The Tramp)*.

Comedy. Source: Rupert Hughes, "Don't You Care!" in *Saturday Evening Post* (4 Jul 1914). Tracey Moffat, a schoolgirl flapper, makes a bid for her freedom by rejecting the man her father has chosen for her to marry and instead chooses fun-loving Gilbert Jenkins. Her parents' interference proves to be more than Tracey can bear, and she threatens to leave home. Mr. and Mrs. Moffat reevaluate their position, however, and decide to support their daughter's decision. Free to go, Tracey nevertheless decides to stay home and marry Gilbert. *Flappers. Parenthood. Family life. Marriage—Arranged.*

DON'T CALL IT LOVE **F2.1401**

Famous Players–Lasky. *Dist* Paramount Pictures. 6 Jan **1924** [c5 Jan 1924; LP19801]. Si; b&w. 35mm. 7 reels, ca6,450 ft.

Pres by Adolph Zukor. *Dir* William C. De Mille. *Scen* Clara Beranger. *Photog* Guy Wilky.

Cast: Agnes Ayres *(Alice Meldrum)*, Jack Holt *(Richard Parrish)*, Nita Naldi *(Rita Coventry)*, Theodore Kosloff *(Luigi Busini)*, Rod La Rocque *(Patrick Delaney)*, Robert Edeson *(Henry Van Courtlandt)*, Julia Faye *(Clara Proctor)*.

Romantic comedy-drama. Source: Julian Leonard Street, *Rita Coventry* (Garden City, New York, 1922). Hubert Osborne, *Rita Coventry* (New York opening: 19 Feb 1923). Prima donna Rita Coventry charms Richard

Parrish from his fiancée, Alice Meldrum. Tiring of Parrish, Miss Coventry casts him aside and begins a flirtation with Patrick Delaney, a piano tuner of some musical talent. Parrish attempts to return to Alice, who, on the advice of a girl friend, rebuffs him; later she agrees to become his wife. *Flirts. Singers. Piano tuners. Opera.*

DON'T CALL ME LITTLE GIRL **F2.1402**

Realart Pictures. Jun **1921** [c28 Apr 1921; LP16436]. Si; b&w. 35mm. 5 reels, 4,212 ft.

Dir Joseph Henabery. *Scen* Edith Kennedy. *Photog* Faxon M. Dean. *Asst Dir* Dick Johnston.

Cast: Mary Miles Minter *(Jerry)*, Winifred Greenwood *(Harriet Doubleday)*, Ruth Stonehouse *(Joan Doubleday)*, Jerome Patrick *(Monty Wade)*, Edward Flanagan *(Peter Flagg)*, Fannie Midgley *(Mrs. Doubleday)*.

Comedy. Source: Catherine Chisholm Cushing, *Jerry; a Comedy in Three Acts* (New York, 1930). Shy and spinsterish Joan Doubleday, who has been engaged to Monty Wade for 12 years, is secretly adored by Peter Flagg. Her young niece, Jerry, arrives and sets out to capture Monty. On the wedding day, Jerry announces that the grooms have exchanged places and that Peter will marry Joan. A quarrel suspends preparations for the wedding, but Jerry finally convinces Joan that she was meant for Peter. *Spinsters. Aunts. Weddings. Courtship.*

DON'T DOUBT YOUR HUSBAND **F2.1403**

Metro Pictures. *Dist* Metro-Goldwyn Distributing Corp. 24 Mar **1924** [c26 Mar 1924; LP20030]. Si; b&w. 35mm. 6 reels, 5,517 ft.

Dir Harry Beaumont. *Story-Scen* Sada Cowan, Howard Higgin. *Photog* John Arnold.

Cast: Viola Dana *(Helen Blake)*, Allan Forrest *(Richard Blake)*, Winifred Bryson *(Alma Lane)*, John Patrick *(Reginald Trevor)*, Willard Louis *(Mr. Ruggles)*, Adele Watson *(Mrs. Ruggles)*, Robert Dunbar *(Mr. Clinton)*.

Domestic farce. "Helen Blake, wed six months, is unduly jealous of husband Dick. She is especially suspicious of pretty Alma Lane, hired to decorate the Blake home. Various incidents arise to fan the flame of Helen's jealousy. She threatens to divorce Dick. Finding him in a seemingly compromising position with Alma is the final straw. But Alma's fiancé arrives, explains everything satisfactorily, and the Blakes are reconciled." (*Exhibitors Trade Review*, 5 Jul 1924, p75.) *Interior decorators. Jealousy. Marriage.*

DON'T DOUBT YOUR WIFE **F2.1404**

Leah Baird Productions. *Dist* Associated Exhibitors. 12 Mar **1922** [c8 Feb 1922; LU17535]. Si; b&w. 35mm. 5 reels, 4,742 ft.

Prod Arthur F. Beck. *Dir* James W. Horne. *Story-Scen* Leah Baird. *Photog* Charles Stumar.

Cast: Leah Baird *(Rose Manning)*, Edward Peil *(John Manning)*, Emory Johnson *(Herbert Olden)*, Mathilde Brundage *(Mrs. Evanston)*, Katherine Lewis *(Marie Braban)*.

Domestic melodrama. Rose Manning, on her way home, is overtaken by a storm and compelled to take refuge in a roadhouse with Herbert Olden. When the lodge is raided by prohibition enforcement agents, Rose leaves by a window only partially clothed and escapes with Herbert. Reaching home, she finds her husband, John, waiting for her; and seeing her wearing Olden's coat, he assumes the worst and orders her from the house. Olden's mother, knowing her to be innocent, persuades her to see John again, which she does but to no avail. In despair, Rose accepts Herbert's proposal of marriage, following her divorce from John, but when Herbert discovers that Rose is about to become a mother, he resolves to effect a reconciliation and informs John of her condition. On their wedding night, John appears and repudiates his hasty conclusion. There is a mutual reconciliation. *Motherhood. Divorce. Pregnancy. Prohibition.*

DON'T GET PERSONAL (Universal Special) **F2.1405**

Universal Film Manufacturing Co. ca1 Jan **1922** [New York premiere; released 16 Jan; c5 Jan 1922; LP17439]. Si; b&w. 35mm. 5 reels, 4,783 ft.

Pres by Carl Laemmle. *Dir* Clarence G. Badger. *Scen* Doris Schroeder. *Story* I. R. Ving. *Photog* Milton Moore.

Cast: Marie Prevost *(Patricia Parker)*, George Nichols *(Silas Wainwright)*, Daisy Robinson *(Emily Wainwright)*, Roy Atwell *(Horace Kane)*, T. Roy Barnes *(John Wainwright)*, G. Del Lorice *(Maisie Morrison)*, Sadie Gordon *(Arabella New)*, Alida B. Jones *(Jane New)*, Ralph McCullough *(Jimmie Barton)*.

Comedy. Patricia Parker, on the advice of her father, leaves her life as a chorus girl for the bucolic surroundings of Silas Wainwright, an old friend of her father's. She immediately sides with Horace, a suitor to Emily, Wainwright's daughter; and her efforts to disentangle Horace from his clinging vine, Maisie Morrison, the village vamp, result in the jealous concern of John Wainwright, a declared woman-hater. Seeing Patricia drag Horace from the vamp's bridal party, John mistakes the escape for an elopement and strikes Horace. In his fury Silas orders her back to Broadway, but John overrules his father; Horace and Emily are reunited; and Wainwright finally gives his blessing to both couples. *Chorus girls. Vamps. Misogynists. Fatherhood. Brother-sister relationship. Smalltown life.*

DON'T LEAVE YOUR HUSBAND *see* **DANGEROUS TOYS**

DON'T MARRY **F2.1406**

Fox Film Corp. 13 Jun **1928** [c16 May 1928; LP25264]. Si; b&w. 35mm. 6 reels, 5,708 ft.

Pres by William Fox. *Dir* James Tinling. *Adapt-Scen* Randall H. Faye. *Titl* William Kernell. *Story* Philip Klein, Sidney Lanfield. *Photog* Joseph August. *Asst Dir* Leslie Selander.

Cast: Lois Moran *(Priscilla Bowen/Betty Bowen)*, Neil Hamilton *(Henry Willoughby)*, Henry Kolker *(General Willoughby)*, Claire McDowell *(Aunt Abigail Bowen)*, Lydia Dickson *(Hortense)*.

Comedy. To capture straitlaced Henry Willoughby, a young lawyer with old-fashioned ideas about women, flapper Priscilla Bowen masquerades as her Victorian "cousin," playing the harp and dressing in clothes from the nineties. Willoughby quickly sees his error when he is humiliated at a party by this girl, and he returns to the flapper. *Flappers. Lawyers. Puritanism. Disguise.*

DON'T MARRY FOR MONEY **F2.1407**

Weber & North Productions. ca19 Aug **1923** [New York premiere; released 25 Aug; c30 Aug 1923; LP19363]. Si; b&w. 35mm. 6 reels, 5,563 ft.

B. P. Fineman Production. *Dir* Clarence L. Brown. *Story* Hope Loring, Louis D. Lighton.

Cast: House Peters *(Peter Smith)*, Rubye De Remer *(Marion Whitney)*, Aileen Pringle *(Edith Martin)*, Cyril Chadwick *(Crane Martin)*, Christine Mayo *(Rose Graham)*, Wedgewood Nowell *(The Inspector)*, George Nichols *(Amos Webb)*, Hank Mann *(an explorer)*, Charles Wellesley *(Alec Connor)*.

Melodrama. Marion Whitney marries millionaire Peter Smith and finds that life is not sufficiently romantic. She has a flirtation with Crane Martin, who makes a living by compromising wives of wealthy men, then blackmailing them. Clever Peter quietly exposes Martin's trickery to Marion, and she returns to her trusting husband. *Millionaires. Flirtation. Blackmail.*

DON'T NEGLECT YOUR WIFE **F2.1408**

Goldwyn Pictures. 31 Jul **1921** [c2 Feb 1921; LP16086]. Si; b&w. 35mm. 6 reels, 5,574 ft.

Supv-Dir Wallace Worsley. *Scen* Louis Sherwin. *Story* Gertrude Franklin Atherton. *Photog* Don Short. *Asst Dir* A. Channing Edington.

Cast: Mabel Julienne Scott *(Madeline)*, Lewis S. Stone *(Langdon Masters)*, Charles Clary *(Dr. Howard Talbot)*, Kate Lester *(Mrs. Hunt McLane)*, Arthur Hoyt *(Ben Travers)*, Josephine Crowell *(Mrs. Abbott)*, Darrel Foss *(Holt)*, Norma Gordon *(Sybyl Geary)*, Richard Tucker *(George Geary)*, R. D. MacLean *(Mr. Hunt McLane)*.

Romantic drama. In 1876 Dr. Howard Talbot and his beautiful wife, Madeline, move in the best circles of San Francisco society, but when neglected by her husband she seeks the friendship of brilliant young newspaperman Langdon Masters. Realizing where their mutual love is leading them, they decide to part; and scandal provokes Talbot to ask Masters to leave town. Abandoning his career, Masters drifts to New York's notorious "Five Points," where he becomes an alcoholic. In despair, Madeline leaves her husband and obtains a divorce; then, with the help of a mutual friend, she reclaims Masters from his degradation. *Reporters. Infidelity. Alcoholism. Divorce. San Francisco. New York City.*

DON'T SHOOT **F2.1409**

Universal Film Manufacturing Co. 21 Aug **1922** [c28 Jul 1922; LP18099]. Si; b&w. 35mm. 6 reels, 5,130 ft.

Pres by Carl Laemmle. *Dir* Jack Conway. *Scen* George Hively. *Story* George Bronson Howard. *Photog* Virgil Miller.

Cast: Herbert Rawlinson *(James Harrington Court)*, William Dyer

(Boss McGinnis), Harvey Clarke *(Honest John Lysaght)*, Wade Boteler *(Buck Lindsay)*, Margaret Campbell *(Mrs. Van Deek)*, Edna Murphy *(Velma Gay)*, George Fisher *(Archie Craig)*, Tiny Sanford *(Jim)*, Duke Lee *(Pete)*, Mrs. Bertram Grassby *(Mrs. Ransom)*, Fred Kelsey *(police officer)*, L. J. O'Connor *(Larry the Dip)*.

Crook drama. Court, a crook, is forced to marry Velma by her enraged fiancé, who mistakes him for her clandestine suitor. Velma tries to reform Court but is hindered by the machinations of Boss McGinnis until alderman Honest John Lysaght lends a hand. Finally Court beats up the boss's gang and wins the favor of Velma's family. *Criminals—Rehabilitation. Political corruption.*

Note: Remake of *Come Through,* 1917, 7 reels, directed by Jack Conway, starring Herbert Rawlinson. The rest of the cast, except for William Dyer, has been changed.

DON'T TELL EVERYTHING **F2.1410**

Famous Players–Lasky. *Dist* Paramount Pictures. ca13 Nov **1921** [Des Moines premiere; released 11 Dec; c15 Nov 1921; LP17186]. Si; b&w. 35mm. 5 reels, 4,939 ft.

Pres by Jesse L. Lasky. *Supv* Thompson Buchanan. *Dir* Sam Wood. *Scen* Albert Shelby Le Vino. *Story* Lorna Moon. *Photog* Al Gilks. *Asst Dir* A. R. Hamm.

Cast: Wallace Reid *(Cullen Dale)*, Gloria Swanson *(Marian Westover)*, Elliott Dexter *(Harvey Gilroy)*, Dorothy Cumming *(Jessica Ramsey)*, Genevieve Blinn *(Mrs. Morgan)*, Baby Gloria Wood *(Cullen's niece)*, De Briac Twins *(Morgan Twins)*.

Comedy-drama. Marian Westover is loved by wealthy young Cullen Dale and his best friend, Harvey Gilroy, but the latter's loyalty to Dale keeps him silent. After they both sustain injuries in a polo game, Cullen shows particular solicitude in caring for his friend. Cullen proposes to and is accepted by Marian, but she becomes jealous of his former girl friends, and when Jessica Ramsey arrives and tries to capture Cullen, Marian fails in emulating her athletic prowess. Jessica invites the couple to a mountain lodge, but when Marian refuses to go Cullen sweeps her into an automobile and has a marriage ceremony performed. She returns home, and Cullen goes on to the lodge, keeping his marriage secret. A storm prevents Cullen from returning home, and Marian, in alarm, enlists the aid of Gilroy; at the lodge everything is explained to the satisfaction of all but Jessica. *Athletes. Courtship. Friendship. Marriage. Polo.*

DON'T TELL THE WIFE **F2.1411**

Warner Brothers Pictures. 22 Jan **1927** [c27 Jan 1927; LP23618]. Si; b&w. 35mm. 7 reels, 6,972 ft.

Dir Paul Stein. *Screenplay* Rex Taylor. *Camera* David Abel. *Asst Dir* Henry Blanke.

Cast: Irene Rich *(Mrs. Cartier)*, Huntly Gordon *(Jacques Cartier)*, Lilyan Tashman *(Suzanna)*, Otis Harlan *(magistrate)*, William Demarest *(Ray Valerian)*.

Romantic comedy. Source: Victorien Sardou and Émile de Najac, *Cyprienne* or *Divorçons* (Paris, 1883). Having become restless after 7 years of married life, Jacques Cartier welcomes a flirtation by the flippant Suzanna. Suspicious of her husband's numerous "business appointments," Madame Cartier invites Ray, Suzanna's fiancé, to accompany her to a ball where she is convinced her husband and Suzanna have gone. Cartier is informed by a magistrate of his wife's presence, and later he returns home in a jealous rage. Ray, slightly enamored of his companion, agrees to marry Madame Cartier when her husband insists on a divorce. The magistrate processes a fake divorce and then marries both couples; later, discovering they have each embarked on honeymoons, he locates them with some difficulty at the Cartiers' summer lodge, where each pair has gone unknown to the other, and performs a legal marriage for Ray and Suzanna. (Locale: Paris and nearby countryside.) *Flirts. Magistrates. Marriage. Divorce. Paris.*

DON'T WRITE LETTERS **F2.1412**

S-L Pictures. *Dist* Metro Pictures. 15 May **1922** [c10 May 1922; LP17867]. Si; b&w. 35mm. 5 reels, 4,800 ft.

Dir-Scen George D. Baker. *Photog* Rudolph Bergquist. *Art Dir* E. J. Shulter.

Cast: Gareth Hughes *(Robert W. Jenks)*, Bartine Burkett *(Anna May Jackson)*, Herbert Hayes *(Richard W. Jenks)*, Harry Lorraine *(The Father)*, Margaret Mann *(Aunt Jane)*, Lois Lee *(The Sweetheart)*, Victor Potel *(The Lover)*.

Comedy-drama. Source: Blanche Brace, "The Adventure of a Ready Letter Writer," in *Saturday Evening Post* (193:18–19, 13 Nov 1920). At the outbreak of World War I, Bobby Jenks enlists in the Army, and as he is undersized, he finds himself assigned as cook in the supply department. In the pocket of an oversized shirt, given to him by a practical joker, he finds a letter from Anna May Jackson, a Brooklyn factory girl, who expresses her admiration for big westerners. Bobby begins a correspondence with the girl, exaggerating his muscular development, proposes marriage by proxy, and is accepted. Returning home, he passes himself off as Richard Jenks, the pal of Robert Jenks, her correspondent; then the genuine Richard Jenks arrives, and Bobby induces him to carry out the deception. After many complications, the truth is revealed, and Anna May confesses her love for Bobby, despite his handicap. *Soldiers. Cooks. Factory workers. World War I. New York City—Brooklyn.*

DOOMSDAY **F2.1413**

Paramount Famous Lasky Corp. 18 Feb **1928** [c18 Feb 1928; LP25000]. Si; b&w. 35mm. 6 reels, 5,652 ft.

Pres by Adolph Zukor, Jesse L. Lasky. *Dir* Rowland V. Lee. *Scen* Donald W. Lee. *Titl* Julian Johnson. *Adapt* Doris Anderson. *Photog* Henry Gerrard. *Film Ed* Robert Bassler. *Wardrobe* Travis Banton.

Cast: Florence Vidor *(Mary Viner)*, Gary Cooper *(Arnold Furze)*, Lawrence Grant *(Percival Fream)*, Charles A. Stevenson *(Capt. Hesketh Viner)*.

Drama. Source: George Warwick Deeping, *Doomsday* (London, 1927). Forced to choose between two suitors—Percival Fream, a rich landowner, and Arnold Furze, a handsome farmer—Mary Viner, daughter of a retired English sea captain, selfishly marries Fream to escape the poverty she has known, although she really loves Furze. Leaving her father in the care of a nurse, Mary and her husband live abroad for a year. Her experience teaches her that money can't buy happiness; she gets an annulment, marries Furze, and moves to his family farm, "Doomsday." *Farmers. Drudges. Sea captains. English. Poverty. Wealth. Marriage—Annulment.*

THE DOORWAY TO HELL **F2.1414**

Warner Brothers Pictures. 18 Oct **1930** [c6 Oct 1930; LP1614]. Sd (Vitaphone); b&w. 35mm. 8 reels, 7,092 ft.

Dir Archie Mayo. *Screenplay-Dial* George Rosener. *Photog* Barney McGill. *Film Ed* Robert Crandall.

Cast: Lew Ayres *(Louis Ricardo)*, Charles Judels *(Sam Margoni)*, Dorothy Mathews *(Doris)*, Leon Janney *(Jackie Lamarr)*, Robert Elliott *(Captain O'Grady)*, James Cagney *(Steve Mileaway)*, Kenneth Thomson *(captain of military academy)*, Jerry Mandy *(Joe)*, Noel Madison *(Rocco)*, Eddie Kane *(Dr. Morton)*, Edwin Argus *(midget)*.

Underworld melodrama. Source: Rowland Brown, "A Handful of Clouds" (publication undetermined). Louis Ricardo, a handsome young gang leader, becomes the underworld boss of an entire city, dividing the territory into zones confined to the rackets of separate mobs that pay him for protection. He meets Doris, a gold digger, whom he marries, unaware that she loves his best pal, Mileaway. Despite the warnings of his men, Louis takes his bankroll and bride and leaves for Florida, stopping off at a military school to see his kid brother, Jackie, of whom he is fond. With Mileaway in charge of the city mobs, chaos reigns among rival factions, but Louis refuses to return to his life of crime. Two mobsters plan to kidnap Jackie and thus force Louis to return to the underworld, but Jackie is accidentally killed by their truck. Louis swears revenge on the killers and is arrested by O'Grady; he learns of a plan to spring him from prison, and after the break he is machine-gunned by the gang responsible for his brother's death. *Gangsters. Racketeers. Gold diggers. Brothers. Friendship. Infidelity. Murder. Extortion. Revenge. Prison escapes.*

DOROTHY VERNON OF HADDON HALL **F2.1415**

Mary Pickford Productions. *Dist* United Artists. 15 Mar **1924** [c16 Apr 1924; LP20113]. Si; b&w. 35mm. 10 reels, 9,351 ft.

Dir Marshall Neilan. *Scen* Waldemar Young. *Photog* Charles Rosher.

Cast: Mary Pickford *(Dorothy Vernon)*, Anders Randolph *(Sir George Vernon)*, Marc MacDermott *(Sir Malcolm Vernon)*, Carrie Daumery *(Lady Vernon)*, Allan Forrest *(Sir John Manners)*, Wilfred Lucas *(Earl of Rutland)*, Clare Eames *(Queen Elizabeth)*, Estelle Taylor *(Mary, Queen of Scots)*, Courtenay Foote *(Earl of Leicester)*, Colin Kenny *(Dawson)*, Lottie Pickford Forrest *(Jennie Faxton)*.

Historical romance. Source: Charles Major, *When Knighthood Was in Flower* (Indianapolis, 1898). Dorothy, the willful and rebellious daughter of Sir George Vernon, is pledged to marry her cousin on her 18th birthday. Risking parental wrath, she meets and falls in love with Sir John Manners, a childhood playmate, who is a member of the enemy house and faces treachery and intrigue before he wins her. She is accused of treason but saves Queen Elizabeth's life, and after being pardoned she leaves for Wales with Sir John. *Parenthood. Treason. Great Britain—History—Tudors. Elizabeth I (England). Mary Stuart.*

THE DOTTED LINE *see* **LET WOMEN ALONE**

DOUBLE ACTION DANIELS (Thunderbolt Thrillers) **F2.1416**
Action Pictures. *Dist* Weiss Brothers Artclass Pictures. c8 May **1925** [LU21445]. Si; b&w. 35mm. 5 reels, 4,650 ft.
Pres by Lester F. Scott, Jr. *Dir* Richard Thorpe. *Story* Elizabeth Burbridge. *Photog* Ray Ries.
Cast: Buffalo Bill Jr. *(Double Action Daniels)*, Lorna Palmer *(Ruth Fuller)*, Edna Hall *(Mother Rose Daniels)*, J. P. Lockney *(Old Bill Daniels)*, Edward Piel *(Jack Monroe)*, D'Arcy Corrigan *(Richard Booth)*, N. E. Hendrix *(Davis)*, Lafe McKee *(The Banker)*, Harry Belmore *(The Hotelkeeper)*, Clyde McClary *(The Sheriff)*, William Ryno *(The Wop)*, Cy Belmore *(The Kid)*, Sammy Thomas *(Sammy)*.
Western melodrama. Young Bill Daniels, known as "Double Action," goes into town with the cowboys from his father's ranch to see a traveling show. The sheriff attempts to stop the show, and Bill throws him off the stage. The show closes, however, and Bill gets the leading lady, Ruth Fuller, a job working on his father's spread. Old Bill later learns that she is an actress and fires her. Young Bill then leaves the ranch, taking most of the hands with him. Old Bill soon loses his ranch, when Jack Monroe, a real smooth talker, cheats him into signing away his land rights. Old Bill, homeless, comes to town and discovers that Mother Rose, the character actress of the stranded company who is scrubbing floors in the hotel, is in fact his wife, who ran away years before to become an actress. Young Bill gives Monroe a sound beating, and Monroe has him put in jail. Mother Rose tells Ruth that there is a deed, giving her the ranch, hidden in the newel post of the stairway at the ranch, and Rose goes there to get it, pretending that she came to see Monroe. Young Bill's buddies blast him out of jail, and he goes to his father's ranch, finding Ruth there. He rides away in dejection but quickly returns when he hears Ruth scream for help. Young Bill beats Monroe in a fight and acquires the true deed to his father's ranch. Old Bill and Rose are reconciled, and Young Bill asks Ruth to be his wife. *Actors. Theatrical troupes. Cowboys. Ranchers. Jailbreaks. Documentation.*

DOUBLE CROSS ROADS **F2.1417**
Fox Film Corp. 20 Apr **1930** [c22 Mar 1930; LP1206]. Sd (Movietone); b&w. 35mm. 6 reels, 5,800 ft. [Also si.]
Pres by William Fox. *Dir* Alfred L. Werker. *Staged by* Melville Burke. *Screenplay-Dial* Howard Estabrook. *Adapt* George Brooks. *Photog* Joseph August, Sol Halprin. *Art Dir* Joseph Wright. *Film Ed* Jack Dennis. *Songs: "My Lonely Heart," "Show Me the Way"* Charles Wakefield Cadman, William Kernell. *Ch Sd Rec* Al Protzman. *Asst Dir* William Tummel. *Cost* Sophie Wachner.
Cast: Robert Ames *(David Harvey)*, Lila Lee *(Mary Carlyle)*, Edythe Chapman *(Mrs. Carlyle)*, Montagu Love *(Gene Dyke)*, Ned Sparks *(Happy Max)*, Thomas Jackson *(Deuce Wilson)*, Charlotte Walker *(Mrs. Tilton)*, George MacFarlane *(warden)*, William V. Mong *(Caleb)*, Thomas Jefferson *(caretaker)*.
Melodrama. Source: William Lipman, *Yonder Grow the Daisies* (New York, 1929). David Harvey, an ex-convict, determines to go straight and retires to a country town where he meets and falls in love with Mary Carlyle. The mob attempts to induce him to participate in another robbery—of a wealthy woman in a nearby town—but he puts them off until he discovers that Mary is part of the gang; then, disillusioned, he goes through with it. Mary agrees provided that Happy Max lets David go, but she is doublecrossed. Another gang invades the house during a party and forces David to turn over the jewels, but he gives them paste imitations. The two gangs shoot it out from speeding automobiles, and ultimately the path to romance is cleared for the young couple. *Criminals—Rehabilitation. Gangs. Courtship. Smalltown life. Robbery.*

DOUBLE DARING **F2.1418**
Action Pictures. *Dist* Weiss Brothers Artclass Pictures. 11 Jun **1926**. Si; b&w. 35mm. 5 reels, 4,797 ft.
Dir Richard Thorpe. *Cont* Frank L. Inghram. *Story* Betty Burbridge.
Cast: Wally Wales *(Wally Meeker)*, J. P. Lockney *(Banker Wells)*, Jean Arthur *(Marie Wells, the banker's daughter)*, Hank Bell *(Lee Falcon, a mysterious bandit)*, Charles Whittaker *(Blackie Gorman, bandit leader)*, Toby Wing *(Nan, an orphaned child)*, N. E. Hendrix *(The Law)*.
Western melodrama(?). No information about the nature of this film has been found.

DOUBLE DEALING **F2.1419**
Universal Pictures. 21 May **1923** [c11 May 1923; LP18966]. Si; b&w. 35mm. 5 reels, 5,105 ft.
Pres by Carl Laemmle. *Dir-Story* Henry Lehrman. *Scen* George C. Hull. *Story? (see note)* George W. Pyper. *Photog* Dwight Warren.
Cast: Hoot Gibson *(Ben Slowbell)*, Helen Ferguson *(The Slavey)*, Betty Francisco *(Stella Fern)*, Eddie Gribbon *(Alonzo B. Keene)*, Gertrude Claire *(Mother Slowbell)*, Otto Hoffman *(Uriah Jobson)*, Frank Hayes *(The Sheriff)*, Jack Dillon *(Jobson's assistant)*.
Rural comedy. After failing in several businesses, Ben Slowbell is threatened with foreclosure of his latest mortgage when Alonzo B. Keene, a shady character from the city working in collusion with village skinflint Uriah Jobson, persuades Ben with promises of oil to buy some worthless property. But the property proves to be valuable to another man, and Ben sells it for a tidy sum, thanks to the clever bargaining by a servant girl (The Slavey), whom Ben realizes to be his "one and only." *Drudges. Skinflints. Real estate. Fraud. Mortgages.*
Note: Working titles: *The Poor Worm, The Knocker.* Certain Universal records credit George W. Pyper with story, although the Story Department credits Lehrman.

DOUBLE FISTED **F2.1420**
Harry Webb Productions. *Dist* Rayart Pictures. 9 Jul **1925** [New York State license]. Si; b&w. 35mm. 5 reels, 4,800 ft.
Dir Harry Webb.
Cast: Jack Perrin.
Western melodrama(?). No information about the nature of this film has been found.

THE DOUBLE O **F2.1421**
Ben Wilson Productions. *Dist* Arrow Film Corp. 29 Nov **1921** [c3 Dec 1921; LP17272]. Si; b&w. 35mm. 5 reels.
Dir-Scen Roy Clements. *Photog* King Gray.
Cast: Jack Hoxie *(Happy Hanes)*, Steve Clemento *(Cholo Pete)*, William Lester *(Mat Haley)*, Ed La Niece *(Jim)*, Evelyn Nelson *(Frances Powell)*.
Western melodrama. Happy Hanes, foreman of the Double O Ranch (which is near the Mexican border), and his pal, Jim, incur the enmity of the ranch manager and Cholo Pete, who are in league with cattle rustlers. He insults the new ranch owner, Frances Powell, by offering to "sell" Pete for a kiss from her (saying he won Pete in a game), and she dismisses him. Mat Haley, the manager, angered by Frances' refusal to marry him, has Pete kidnap her, but Happy rescues her. Mexican bandits capture Happy and hold him for ransom, but Frances rescues him and the two are happily married. *Ranch foremen. Ranch managers. Rustlers. Mexicans. Ransom. Kidnaping. Mexican border.*

DOUBLE-BARRELED JUSTICE **F2.1422**
Independent Pictures. 17 Oct **1925** [New York State license]. Si; b&w. 35mm. 5 reels, 4,800 ft.
Cast: Franklyn Farnum.
Western melodrama(?). No information about the nature of this film has been found.

DOUBLING FOR ROMEO **F2.1423**
Goldwyn Pictures. Jan **1922** [c2 Nov 1921; LP17141]. Si; b&w. 35mm. 6 reels, 5,304 ft.
Dir Clarence Badger. *Scen* Bernard McConville. *Story* Elmer Rice. *Photog* Marcel Le Picard.
Cast: Will Rogers *(Sam [Romeo])*, Sylvia Breamer *(Lulu [Juliet])*, Raymond Hatton *(Steve Woods [Paris])*, Sydney Ainsworth *(Pendleton [Mercutio])*, Al Hart *(Big Alec [Tybalt])*, John Cossar *(Foster [Capulet])*, C. E. Thurston *(Duffy Saunders [Benvolio])*, Cordelia Callahan *(Maggie [maid])*, Roland Rushton *(minister [friar])*, Jimmy Rogers *(Jimmie Jones)*, William Orlamond *(movie director)*.
Burlesque. Remote derivation: William Shakespeare, *Romeo and Juliet.* Arizona cowpoke Sam Cody is in love with Lulu Foster but has a rival in Steve Woods, a handsome soda jerk in the village drugstore. As a remedy for his awkwardness, Sam is advised to study techniques of making love in the movies. In Hollywood, he gets work as a double for the villain, and

having been battered before the camera in a fight, he resigns at the mention of a retake. Then, given the part of a lover, he fails and is dismissed. Back in Arizona, he has nothing to show for the trip, and Lulu orders him away until he can love her as Romeo loved Juliet. He acquires a copy of Shakespeare's play, and, falling asleep, has a dream in which he and his friends take on character parts with swashbuckling sword fights and strenuous wooing scenes. Awakening, he mingles the eloquence of Romeo with brute strength and sweeps Lulu off her feet. *Cowboys. Soda clerks. Motion pictures. Arizona. Hollywood. "Romeo and Juliet"*

DOUBLING WITH DANGER **F2.1424**

Richard Talmadge Productions. *For* Carlos Productions. *Dist* Film Booking Offices of America. 18 Jul **1926** [c18 Jul 1926; LP22960]. Si; b&w. 35mm. 5 reels.

Pres by A. Carlos. *Dir* Scott R. Dunlap. *Scen* Grover Jones. *Film Ed* Doane Harrison.

Cast: Richard Talmadge *(Dick Forsythe)*, Ena Gregory *(Madeline [Margaret?] Haver)*, Joseph Girard *(Elwood Haver)*, Fred Kelsey *(Avery McCade)*, Harry Dunkinson *(Detective McCade [see note])*, Douglas Gerrard *(Malcolm Davis)*, Paul Dennis *(Arthur Channing)*, Herbert Prior *(Manning Davis)*, Joseph Harrington *(Morton Stephens)*.

Mystery melodrama. While Elwood Haver is visiting an inventor who is working on a special airplane for the government, the inventor is killed and Haver guards his papers carefully. Retiring to his country mansion, Haver puts himself under the protection of eccentric detective Avery McCade. At a houseparty, Malcolm Davis and Arthur Channing are among the guests; the latter romances Madeline, Haver's daughter, but to no avail. McCade accuses his secretary, Dick, of being a criminal, but Dick explains that he has a twin brother whom he himself brought to justice; Haver, disbelieving him, dispenses with his services. Overhearing Channing and a servant arranging a meeting, Dick follows them, assumes the role of his twin brother, and is engaged to steal the papers from Haver. He succeeds in acquiring the papers, but he will not surrender them until he is paid; Madeline is abducted, but following a series of fights and chases, Dick, Haver, and McCade capture the crooks. *Inventors. Twins. Brothers. Detectives. Airplanes. Impersonation. Abduction. Documentation.*

Note: Some sources credit Fred Kelsey in the role of McCade while others credit Harry Dunkinson.

DOUGHBOYS **F2.1425**

Metro-Goldwyn-Mayer Pictures. 30 Aug **1930** [c8 Sep 1930; LP1540]. Sd (Movietone); b&w. 35mm. 9 reels, 7,325 ft.

Dir Edward Sedgwick. *Scen* Richard Schayer. *Dial* Al Boasberg, Richard Schayer. *Story* Al Boasberg, Sidney Lazarus. *Photog* Leonard Smith. *Art Dir* Cedric Gibbons. *Film Ed* William Le Vanway. *Songs: "Military Man," "Sing"* Edward Sedgwick, Howard Johnson, Joseph Meyer. *Dance Dir* Sammy Lee. *Rec Engr* Karl E. Zint, Douglas Shearer. *Wardrobe* Vivian Baer.

Cast: Buster Keaton *(Elmer Stuyvesant)*, Sally Eilers *(Mary)*, Cliff Edwards *(Nescopeck)*, Edward Brophy *(Sergeant Brophy)*, Victor Potel *(Svedenburg)*, Arnold Korff *(Gustave)*, Frank Mayo *(Captain Scott)*, Pitzy Katz *(Abie Cohn)*, William Steele *(Lieutenant Randolph)*.

Comedy. Wealthy Elmer Stuyvesant tries to court an unwilling shopgirl during a recruiting parade, and his chauffeur decides to join the Army. While trying to hire a new chauffeur, Elmer stumbles upon a recruiting office; and before he can protest, he is being given an induction physical. His aristocratic hauteur is soon flattened by a tough sergeant, Brophy, but he finds solace in the charms of Mary, a canteen girl; and when sent to the front, he becomes a hero by accident. *Soldiers. Shopgirls. Chauffeurs. World War I. France. United States Army—Recruiting.*

Note: Initially reviewed as *The Big Shot.*

DOUGLAS FAIRBANKS IN ROBIN HOOD *see* **ROBIN HOOD**

THE DOVE **F2.1426**

Norma Talmadge Productions. *Dist* United Artists. 31 Dec **1927** [New York premiere; released 7 Jan; c16 Jan 1928; LP24864]. Si; b&w. 35mm. 9 reels, 9,100 ft.

Pres by Joseph M. Schenck. *Dir* Roland West. *Cont* Wallace Smith, Paul Bern. *Titl* Wallace Smith. *Adapt* Roland West, Wallace Smith, Willard Mack. *Photog* Oliver Marsh. *Art Dir* William Cameron Menzies. *Film Ed* Hal Kern.

Cast: Norma Talmadge *(Dolores)*, Noah Beery *(Don José María y Sandoval)*, Gilbert Roland *(Johnny Powell)*, Eddie Borden *(Billy)*, Harry Myers *(Mike)*, Michael Vavitch *(Gómez)*, Brinsley Shaw *(The Patriot)*, Kalla Pasha *(The Comandante)*, Charles Darvas *(The Comandante's Captain)*, Michael Dark *(Sandoval's Captain)*, Walter Daniels *(The Drunk)*.

Romantic melodrama. Source: Willard Mack, *The Dove, a Play in Three Acts* (New York opening: Feb 1925). Gerald Beaumont, *The Dove* (New York, 1925). Dolores, a dancehall girl known as "The Dove," is in love with a gambler named Johnny Powell. Don José, a wealthy caballero smitten by Dolores' beauty, frames Powell on a murder charge. Dolores bargains with Don José to release Powell in exchange for her freedom; but on the eve of her marriage to Don José, Powell returns from exile to claim Dolores. After an unsuccessful escape, Powell and Dolores are about to be shot when a crowd of bystanders forces Don José to release them. He relents, frees the prisoners, and gives them his carriage in which to depart. *Dancehall girls. Caballeros. Gambling. Frameup. Murder.*

DOWN BY THE RIO GRANDE **F2.1427**

Phil Goldstone Productions. 20 May **1924** [New York State license]. Si; b&w. 35mm. 5 reels, 4,800 ft.

Dir Alvin J. Neitz. *Scen* Donald Fitch. *Story* Julio Sabello. *Photog* Roland Price.

Cast: William Fairbanks, Dorothy Revier, Andrew Waldron, Olive Trevor, Jack Richardson, Milton Ross.

Melodrama. "The script ... [tells] of a Spanish family who own an extensive ranch, with the deed to the property ultimately finding its way to the rightful owner, the unspoken-of relative (Fairbanks), after a villainous cousin has possessed the papers and stated marriage to the daughter as the price of his silence." (*Variety,* 18 Jun 1924, p23.) *Spanish. Ranches. Property rights. Rio Grande. Documentation.*

THE DOWN GRADE **F2.1428**

Gotham Productions. *Dist* Lumas Film Corp. c25 Jul **1927** [LP24237]. Si; b&w. 35mm. 5 reels, 5,000 ft.

Pres by Sam Sax. *Dir* Charles Hutchison. *Story-Scen* Welles W. Ritchie. *Photog* James Brown.

Cast: William Fairbanks *(Ted Lanning)*, Alice Calhoun *(Molly Crane)*, Charles K. French *(Mr. Lanning)*, Big Boy Williams *(Ed Holden)*, Jimmy Aubrey *(The Runt)*.

Action melodrama. In an effort to report to his father's office on the B & R Railroad, Ted Lanning covers 50 miles in 50 minutes via a freight car that ends with a wild crash that loses him his job and his fiancée. Later, Ted is held up in the freight yard by some yeggs who throw him into the river. Making his way on foot to a mining town, Ted goes to Molly Crane's lunchroom, saves her from the unwelcome attentions of Big Ed Holden, and discovers a clue to the railroad robberies. He obtains an incriminating telegram, and Holden's men kidnap him. Molly frees him, and they go after the bandits. Holden warns Ted of trouble on the main line, and Ted prevents the Limited from being wrecked. *Bandits. Kidnaping. Train robberies. Railroads. Train wrecks. Documentation.*

DOWN THE STRETCH (Universal-Jewel) **F2.1429**

Universal Pictures. 29 May **1927** [c13 Dec 1926; LP23430]. Si; b&w. 35mm. 7 reels, 6,910 ft.

Pres by Carl Laemmle. *Dir* King Baggot. *Adapt-Cont* Curtis Benton. *Photog* John Stumar.

Cast: Robert Agnew *(Marty Kruger)*, Marian Nixon *(Katie Kelly)*, Virginia True Boardman *(Mrs. Kruger)*, Lincoln Plummer *(Devlin)*, Jack Daugherty *(Tupper)*, Ward Crane *(Conlon)*, Ben Hall *(Pee Wee)*, Otis Harlan *(Babe Dilley)*, Ena Gregory *(Marion Hoyt)*.

Melodrama. Source: Gerald Beaumont, "The Money Rider," in *Red Book* (43:53–57, Aug 1924). Against the wishes of his mother, Marty Kruger becomes a jockey, like his father, and soon gains an outstanding reputation. He joins the Tupper stables and, despite the tyranny of trainer Hippo Devlin, finds happiness in his work and falls in love with Katie Kelly, a lunchroom waitress. They are engaged at the time Marty is laid up by an accident, and as he returns to the track overweight, Devlin forces him to reduce to the point of endangering his health. "Silk" Conlon, representing betting interests, wants the Tupper entry to lose the race and tries to bribe Marty into eating a square meal; but he refuses for fear of disgrace, and though he wins the race, he faints from weakness. Tupper thrashes the trainer and fires him, and when Marty and Katie are married, Marty is made Devlin's successor. *Jockeys. Waitresses. Horsetrainers. Horseracing. Courtship. Bribery. Diet.*

DOWN TO THE SEA IN SHIPS F2.1430

Whaling Film Corp. *Dist* W. W. Hodkinson Corp. Nov **1922** [Providence, Rhode Island, premiere; released 4 Mar 1923;]. Si; b&w. 35mm. 12 reels. [Also 9 reels, 8,900 ft.]

Pres by Elmer Clifton. *Dir* Elmer Clifton. *Story-Scen* John L. E. Pell. *Photog* Alexander G. Penrod. *Adtl Photog* Paul Allen, Maurice E. Kains, Albert Doubrava. *Mus Score Dsgnd by* Henry F. Gilbert. *Adv* James F. Avery, Benjamin D. Cleveland, Antonoe T. Edwards, Henry J. Mandly, Antone J. Mandly, William J. Shockley, George F. Tilton, James Tilton. *Staff* P. Major, Leigh R. Smith, Phelps Decker, Paul F. Maschke, Harry Thompson, Elizabeth Musgrave.

Cast in order of appearance: William Walcott *(Charles W. Morgan)*, William Cavanaugh *(Henry Morgan)*, Leigh R. Smith *("Scuff" Smith)*, Elizabeth Foley *(Baby Patience Morgan)*, Thomas White *(Baby Tommy Dexter)*, Juliette Courtot *("Judy" Peggs)*, Clarice Vance *(Nahoma)*, Curtis Pierce *(The Town Crier)*, Ada Laycock *("Henny" Clark)*, Marguerite Courtot *(Patience Morgan)*, Clara Bow *("Dot" Morgan)*, James Turfler *("Jimmy")*, Pat Hartigan *(Jake Finner)*, Capt. James A. Tilton *(Captain of the "Morgan")*, J. Thornton Baston *(Samuel Siggs)*, Raymond McKee *(Thomas Allan Dexter)*.

Melodrama. Though Patience Morgan is sought by many suitors, her father, Charles, insists that she marry a man who is both Quaker and whaleman. Because Samuel Siggs convincingly poses as both, he is favored by Charles Morgan—despite the fact that Patience loves Allan Dexter, who is neither. Allan embraces the Quaker faith, proves himself worthy as a whaleman when he is shanghaied and tossed by stormy seas, and returns to New Bedford just as she is about to marry Siggs. *Whaling. Filial relations. Shanghaiing. Society of Friends. New Bedford (Massachusetts).*

DOWN UPON THE SUWANNEE RIVER F2.1431

Royal Palm Productions. *Dist* Lee-Bradford Corp. 21 Oct **1925.** Si; b&w. 35mm. 6 reels, 5,700 ft.

Dir Lem F. Kennedy. *Scen* Hapsburg Liebe.

Cast: Charles Emmett Mack *(Bill Ruble)*, Mary Thurman *(Mary Norwood)*, Arthur Donaldson *(Dais Norwood)*, Wally Merrill *(Herbert Norwood)*, Walter Lewis *(Rev. John Banner)*, Blanche Davenport *(Old Mag)*, Charles Shannon *(Hoss-Fly Henson)*.

Melodrama. Bill Ruble, whose atheism earns him the dislike of his fellow townspeople, elopes with Mary Norwood. Bill is falsely accused of theft and leaves town, signing up as a deckhand on a ship sailing around the world. A baby is born to Mary in Bill's absence, and she is disowned by friend and neighbor alike. She attempts to drown herself in the river, but an old Negro rescues her. Mary returns home and finds Bill there. He has become a true believer and a member of the church during his travels, and he and Mary are happily reunited. *Sailors. Negroes. Religion. Atheism. Elopement. Suicide. Smalltown life. Suwannee River.*

DRAG F2.1432

First National Pictures. 21 Jul **1929** [c10 Aug 1929; LP585]. Sd (Vitaphone); b&w. 35mm. 9 reels, 7,642 ft. [Also si, 11 Aug 1929; 5,633 ft.]

Pres by Richard A. Rowland. *Dir* Frank Lloyd. *Adapt-Dial* Bradley King. *Photog* Ernest Hallor. *Songs: "My Song of the Nile," "I'm Too Young To Be Careful"* Al Bryan, George W. Meyer.

Cast: Richard Barthelmess *(David Carroll)*, Lucien Littlefield *(Pa Parker)*, Katherine Ward *(Ma Parker)*, Alice Day *(Allie Parker)*, Tom Dugan *(Charlie Parker)*, Tom Dugan *(Charlie Parker)*, Lila Lee *(Dot)*, Margaret Fielding *(Clara)*.

Drama. Source: William Dudley Pelley, *Drag; a Comedy* (Boston, 1925). Young David Carroll takes over the publication of a local Vermont newspaper. Although he is attracted to Dot, "the most sophisticated girl in town," he marries Allie Parker, daughter of the couple who run the boardinghouse where he lives. Inseparable from her parents, Allie remains at home when David goes to New York City to sell a musical he has written. There, Dot, now a successful costume designer, uses her influence to get David's play produced. David and Dot fall in love, but she leaves for Paris when David indicates he will remain true to Allie. He sends for Allie; but when she arrives with her whole family, he decides to follow Dot to Paris. *Publishers. Playwrights. Costumers. In-laws. Newspapers. Boardinghouses. New York City. Paris. Vermont.*

DRAG HARLAN (Reissue) F2.1433

Fox Film Corp. Feb **1925.** Si; b&w. 35mm. 5 reels.

Note: A William Farnum western originally released by Fox in Oct 1920 (c24 Oct; LP15737).

THE DRAGNET F2.1434

Paramount Famous Lasky Corp. 26 May **1928** [c26 May 1928; LP25299]. Si; b&w. 35mm. 8 reels, 7,720-7,866 ft.

Dir Josef von Sternberg. *Scen* Jules Furthman, Charles Furthman. *Titl* Herman J. Mankiewicz. *Adapt* Jules Furthman. *Story* Oliver H. P. Garrett. *Photog* Harold Rosson. *Set Dsgn* Hans Dreier. *Film Ed* Helen Lewis.

Cast: George Bancroft *(Two-Gun Nolan)*, Evelyn Brent *(The Magpie)*, William Powell *(Dapper Frank Trent)*, Fred Kohler *("Gabby" Steve)*, Francis McDonald *(Sniper Dawson)*, Leslie Fenton *(Shakespeare)*.

Underworld melodrama. Hardboiled detective Two-Gun Nolan resigns from the force, a broken man, when he shoots his partner, Shakespeare, during a battle with a gang of hijackers whose leader, Dapper Frank Trent, Nolan was attempting to capture. "The Magpie," Trent's correspondent, informs Nolan that Trent killed Shakespeare, thus raising Nolan from his alcoholic depression. Trent shoots The Magpie; Nolan kills Trent, then returns to the force and marries The Magpie after she recovers. *Gangsters. Detectives. Police. Hijackers. Murder. Alcoholism.*

THE DRAGON HORSE *see* **THE SILK BOUQUET**

THE DRAKE CASE F2.1435

Universal Pictures. 1 Sep **1929** [c14 Aug 1929; LP604]. Sd (Movietone); b&w. 35mm. 7 reels, 6,448 ft. [Also si; 6,644 ft.]

Dir Edward Laemmle. *Scen* J. G. Hawks. *Dial* J. G. Hawks, Charles Logue. *Titl* Dudley Early. *Story* Charles Logue. *Photog* Jerome Ash. *Film Ed* Ted Kent.

Cast: Gladys Brockwell *(Lulu Marks)*, Forrest Stanley *(district attorney)*, Robert Frazer *(Roger Lane)*, James Crane *(Hugo Jepson)*, Barbara Leonard *(Mrs. Drake)*, Doris Lloyd *(Georgia)*, Bill Thorne *(Captain Condon)*, Edward Hearn *(Edmonds)*, Tom Dugan *(Bill)*, Byron Douglas *(judge)*.

Mystery melodrama. Lulu Marks, disguised as a maid, comes to the home of her divorced husband, believed to be deceased, and is accused of murdering Mrs. Drake, her husband's second wife. Lulu has discovered that Mrs. Drake wished to make her stepdaughter, Georgia, a dope addict so that she and someone else might gain possession of her estate. Lulu keeps quiet as to the identity of the "someone else" until it is proved in court that the coconspirator and murderer of Mrs. Drake is none other than her husband, who has concealed his identity so well that he has become Georgia's fiancé. *Drug addicts. Housemaids. Stepmothers. Murder. Disguise.*

THE DRAMATIC LIFE OF ABRAHAM LINCOLN *see* **ABRAHAM LINCOLN**

THE DREAM MELODY F2.1436

Excellent Pictures. 25 Jan **1929** [c11 Feb 1929; LP119]. Si; b&w. 35mm. 6 reels, 5,050 ft.

Pres by Samuel Zierler. *Dir* Burton King. *Scen-Titl* Isadore Bernstein, Carmelita Sweeney. *Adapt* Hazel Jamieson. *Story* Lenore Gray. *Photog* William J. Miller, Walter Haas. *Film Ed* Betty Davis. *Sp Eff* Robert Stevens.

Cast: John Roche *(Richard Gordon)*, Mabel Julienne Scott *(Mary Talbot)*, Rosemary Theby *(Alicia Harrison)*, Robert Walker *(George Monroe)*, Adabelle Driver *(Nora Flanigan)*, Adolph Faylor *(Signor Malesco)*, Elinor Leslie *(Mrs. Chance)*.

Drama. Richard Gordon, an impoverished composer, writes a hauntingly beautiful song, and Mary Talbot finds him working in the cabaret where she sings. Alicia Harrison, a rich widow, becomes infatuated with Richard and appoints herself as his patroness, promising to introduce him to Signor Malesco, a prominent impresario. The introduction does not take place, and loyal Mary persuades Richard to approach Malesco on his own. Malesco is impressed with Richard's talent and promises him a great future. Richard at last realizes his love for Mary and asks her to share his success and happiness. *Composers. Impresari. Widows. Singers. Cabarets.*

DREAM OF LOVE F2.1437

Metro-Goldwyn-Mayer Pictures. 1 Dec **1928** [c17 Dec 1928; LP25919]. Si; b&w. 35mm. 6 reels, 5,764 ft. [Copyrighted as 9 reels.]

Dir Fred Niblo. *Screenplay* Dorothy Farnum. *Titl* Marian Ainslee, John Howard Lawson, Ruth Cummings. *Photog* Oliver Marsh, William Daniels. *Art Dir* Cedric Gibbons. *Film Ed* James McKay. *Asst Dir* Harold S. Bucquet. *Gowns* Adrian.

Cast: Nils Asther *(Mauritz)*, Joan Crawford *(Adrienne)*, Aileen Pringle *(duchess)*, Warner Oland *(duke)*, Carmel Myers *(countess)*, Harry Reinhardt *(count)*, Harry Myers *(baron)*, Alphonse Martell *(Michonet)*, Fletcher Norton *(Ivan)*.

Drama. Source: Augustin Eugène Scribe and Ernest Legouvé, *Adrienne Lecouvreur; comédie-drame en cinq actes en prose* (Paris, 1849). Adrienne, a Gypsy girl performing in a traveling carnival, falls in love with Mauritz, the crown prince, who is traveling incognito, but they must part when, for diplomatic reason, he is called upon to make love to the rich wife of an influential man. Adrienne later becomes a great dramatic actress and again meets the prince at a time when he is struggling to win his throne from a usurping dictator. With Adrienne's help, the prince becomes king, but she and Mauritz must again go their separate ways, he to the palace and she to the theater. *Actors. Royalty. Dictators. Disguise. Diplomacy. Theater. Carnivals.*

DREAM STREET F2.1438

D. W. Griffith, Inc. *Dist* United Artists. 12 Apr **1921** [New York premiere; released 25 Apr; c14 Jun 1921; LP16672]. Si; b&w. 35mm. 11,000 ft. [Premiere showing: 10 reels; released and copyrighted as 9 reels.]

Pres by D. W. Griffith. *Prod-Dir* D. W. Griffith. *Scen* Roy Sinclair. *Photog* Hendrik Sartov. *Set Dsgn* Charles M. Kirk. *Film Cont* James Smith, Rose Smith. *Mus Arr* Louis Silvers. *Tech Supt* Frank Wortman.

Cast: Carol Dempster *(Gypsy Fair)*, Ralph Graves *(James Spike McFadden)*, Charles Emmett Mack *(Billy McFadden)*, Edward Peil *(Swan Way)*, W. J. Ferguson *(Gypsy's father)*, Porter Strong *(Samuel Jones)*, George Neville *(Tom Chudder)*, Charles Slattery *(Police Inspector)*, [Frederick] Tyrone Power *(A Preacher of the Streets)*, Morgan Wallace *(The Masked Violinist)*.

Allegorical melodrama. Source: Thomas Burke, "Gina of Chinatown" and "The Lamp in the Window," in *Limehouse Nights* (London, 1916). Gypsy Fair, a music hall dancer, is admired by Spike McFadden, a swaggering bully with a golden voice, and his brother, Billy, a timid and frail composer and poet. She is also coveted by Swan Way, a Chinaman who seeks vengeance when Gypsy not only rejects him but reveals his secret gambling den. One of Swan Way's followers attempts to rob Billy, and when the boy kills him, Spike assumes guilt for the crime and Swan Way makes it appear that Gypsy has betrayed him to the police. At the inquest, Billy saves Spike by a last-minute confession and is acquitted on a verdict of self-defense. Billy achieves fame as a composer, while Spike and Gypsy sign a contract with an important theatrical production. *Dancers. Brothers. Singers. Composers. Poets. Chinese. Music halls. Gambling. London—Limehouse.*

Note: Following the New York opening, Griffith offered a showing at Town Hall with an experimental sound-on-disc process developed by Orlando Kellum for several sequences.

DREARY HOUSE F2.1439

Andrew L. Stone. 12 Jul **1928** [New York State license]. Si; b&w. 35mm. 8 reels, 7,300 ft.

Drama(?). No information about the nature of this film has been found.

DRESS PARADE F2.1440

De Mille Pictures. *Dist* Pathé Exchange. 29 Oct **1927** [New York premiere; released 11 Nov; c27 Oct 1927; LP24576]. Si; b&w. 35mm. 7 reels, 6,599 ft.

Pres by William Sistrom. *Dir* Donald Crisp. *Screenplay* Douglas Z. Doty. *Titl* John Krafft. *Photog* Peverell Marley. *Art Dir* Mitchell Leisen. *Film Ed* Barbara Hunter. *Asst Dir* Emile De Ruelle. *Prod Mgr* E. O. Gurney. *Cost* Adrian. *Tech Adv* Schuyler E. Grey.

Cast: William Boyd *(Vic Donovan)*, Bessie Love *(Janet Cleghorne)*, Hugh Allan *(Stuart Haldane)*, Walter Tennyson *(Dusty Dawson)*, Maurice Ryan *(Mealy Snodgrass)*, Louis Natheaux *(Patsy Dugan)*, Clarence Geldert *(Commandant)*.

Romantic drama. Source: Major Alexander Chilton, Major Robert Glassburn, and Herbert David Walter, "Raw Material" (publication undetermined). Vic Donovan, an amateur middleweight champion en route to a training camp, stops at West Point to see dress parade and falls for the commandant's daughter, Janet Cleghorne, who snubs him; and he is rebuked by Stuart Haldane, a cadet, for forcing his attentions on her. During the training period, Vic studies diligently and through political influence wins an appointment to the Academy, where he assumes a patronizing attitude; however, he is soon put in place by upperclassmen Dusty Dawson and Mealy Snodgrass as an ordinary plebe. An intense rivalry ensues for the attentions of Janet between Vic and Haldane, and when the latter is injured in a sham battle, Vic saves his life. Haldane is subject to dismissal, but Vic admits his responsibility for the accident and is given another chance, thus winning the heart of the girl. *Boxers. Cadets. United States Military Academy.*

DRESSED TO KILL F2.1441

Fox Film Corp. 18 Mar **1928** [c13 Mar 1928; LP25058]. Si; b&w. 35mm. 7 reels, 6,566 ft.

Pres by William Fox. *Dir* Irving Cummings. *Scen* Howard Estabrook. *Titl* Malcolm Stuart Boylan. *Story* William M. Conselman, Irving Cummings. *Photog* Conrad Wells. *Camera? (see note)* Charles Woolstenhulme. *Film Ed* Frank Hull. *Asst Dir* Charles Woolstenhulme.

Cast: Edmund Lowe *("Mile-Away Barry")*, Mary Astor *(Jeanne)*, Ben Bard *(Nick)*, Robert Perry *(Ritzy Hogan)*, Joe Brown *(himself)*, Tom Dugan *(Silky Levine)*, John Kelly *(Biff Simpson)*, Robert E. O'Connor *(Detective Gilroy)*, R. O. Pennell *("Professor")*, Ed Brady *("Singing Walter")*, Charles Morton *(Jeanne's sweetheart)*.

Underworld melodrama. "Mile-Away Barry," a "gentleman" gangleader, falls in love with Jeanne, a girl who has sought his help in releasing her sweetheart, a bank officer, from prison. He pays a heavy penalty for his kindness when members of his own gang shoot him down for his chivalry. *Gentlemen crooks. Bankers. Gangs. Parole.*

Note: Some sources show Charles Woolstenhulme as cameraman.

THE DRESSMAKER FROM PARIS F2.1442

Famous Players–Lasky. *Dist* Paramount Pictures. 30 Mar **1925** [c3 Apr 1925; LP21320]. Si; b&w. 35mm. 8 reels, 7,080 ft.

Pres by Adolph Zukor, Jesse L. Lasky. *Dir* Paul Bern. *Scen* Adelaide Heilbron. *Story* Adelaide Heilbron, Howard Hawks.

Cast: Leatrice Joy *(Fifi)*, Ernest Torrence *(Angus McGregor)*, Allan Forrest *(Billy Brent)*, Mildred Harris *(Joan McGregor)*, Lawrence Gray *(Allan Stone)*, Charles Crockett *(mayor)*, Rosemary Cooper *(mayor's daughter)*, Spec O'Donnell *(Jim)*.

Romance. Billy Brent meets and falls in love with Fifi in France during the Great War, but they are parted by the fighting and go their separate ways. By 1925, Billy is the manager of a clothing store in a staid midwestern town, greatly dissatisfied with the old-fashioned merchandising ideas of the store's owner, Angus McGregor. Taking advantage of McGregor's absence, Billy invites a famous dressmaker from Paris to put on a fashion show in the store, only to discover when she arrives that the designer is none other than his lost love, Fifi. McGregor returns in time to witness the fashion show, which proceeds despite the protests of local reformers and is a great success. Fifi and Billy end up at the altar. *Couturiers. Clothing business. Smalltown life. Fashion shows. Business management. World War I. France.*

THE DRIFTER *see* **THE GALLOPING ACE**

THE DRIFTER F2.1443

FBO Pictures. *Dist* RKO Productions. 18 Mar **1929** [c25 Feb 1929; LP145]. Si; b&w. 35mm. 6 reels, 5,896 ft.

Dir Robert De Lacy. *Cont* George W. Pyper. *Titl* Randolph Bartlett. *Story* Oliver Drake, Robert De Lacy. *Photog* Norman Devol. *Film Ed* Tod Cheesman. *Asst Dir* James Dugan.

Cast: Tom Mix *(Tom McCall)*, Dorothy Dwan *(Ruth Martin)*, Barney Furey *(Happy Hogan)*, Al Smith *(Pete Lawson)*, Ernest Wilson *(Uncle Abe)*, Frank Austin *(Seth Martin)*, Joe Rickson *(Hank)*, Wynn Mace *(henchman)*.

Western melodrama. Tom McCall, a deputy marshal, is detailed to hunt for narcotics smugglers and heads into the California Sierras where he buys an old white mule and goes to work for Ruth Martin, the owner of the Lazy M. The mule belonged to Ruth's recently murdered grandfather and is the only living being knowing the way to his hidden gold mine. Lawson, a narcotics smuggler, attempts unsuccessfully to steal the mule and later, when the mule finds the mine, tries to forestall Ruth's filing a claim. Tom arrests Lawson and files the claim for Ruth, whom he intends to make his bride. *Ranchers. United States marshals. Smugglers. Murder. Mines. Narcotics. California. Sierras. Mules.*

DRIFTIN' SANDS **F2.1444**

FBO Pictures. 1 Jan **1928** [c1 Jan 1928; LP24869]. Si; b&w. 35mm. 5 reels, 4,770 ft.

Dir Wallace W. Fox. *Adapt-Cont* Oliver Drake. *Titl* Frank T. Daugherty. *Photog* Allan Siegler. *Film Ed* Oliver Drake.

Cast: Bob Steele *(Driftin' Sands)*, Gladys Quartaro *(Nita Aliso)*, William H. Turner *(Don Roberto Aliso)*, Gladden James *(Benton)*, Jay Morley, Carl Axzelle.

Western melodrama. Source: W. C. Tuttle, "Fate of the Wolf," in *Short Stories* (111:68–77, 25 Jun 1925). Don Roberto Aliso, a wealthy Mexican rancher, concerned about the safety of his daughter, Nita, hires Driftin' Sands to protect her, but when they fall in love he forbids them to meet. Later, when outlaws attack the ranch, Driftin' Sands proves his worth and obtains Don Roberto's consent to the marriage. *Mexicans. Bodyguards. Outlaws. Fatherhood.*

DRIFTIN' THRU **F2.1445**

Charles R. Rogers Productions. *Dist* Pathé Exchange. 21 Feb **1926** [c23 Jan 1926; LU22305]. Si; b&w. 35mm. 5 reels, 4,820 ft.

Pres by Charles R. Rogers. *Dir* Scott R. Dunlap. *Scen* Harvey Gates. *Story* Basil Dickey, Harry Haven. *Photog* Sol Polito.

Cast: Harry Carey *(Daniel Brown)*, Stanton Heck *(Bull Dunn)*, Ruth King *(Stella Dunn)*, G. Raymond Nye *(Joe Walters)*, Joseph Girard *(sheriff)*, Harriet Hammond *(The Girl)*, Bert Woodruff *(Joshua Reynolds)*.

Western melodrama. Drifting through the Southwest, Daniel Brown is unjustly accused of the murder of a gambler. Escaping from the sheriff, Dan boards a train and is hidden by a girl in her Pullman compartment. Dan later takes refuge with a prospector and learns that the girl who so generously helped him on the train owns a nearby ranch, on which, unknown to her, there are rich gold deposits. Joe Walters, the foreman of the ranch, is plotting with Stella Dunn (the widow of the murdered gambler) to buy the girl's ranch for a pittance. Dan prevents the sale, and, when he is about to be arrested by the sheriff, the widow Dunn confesses to having murdered her husband. *Prospectors. Gamblers. Ranch foremen. Wanderers. Widows. Sheriffs. Injustice. Murder.*

DRIFTING (Universal Jewel) **F2.1446**

Universal Pictures. 19 Aug **1923** [New York premiere; released 26 Aug; c31 Jul 1923; LP19262]. Si; b&w. 35mm. 7 reels, 7,394 ft.

Pres by Carl Laemmle. *Dir* Tod Browning. *Scen* Tod Browning, A. P. Younger. *Titl* Gardner Bradford. *Photog* William Fildew. *Film Ed* Errol Taggart.

Cast: Priscilla Dean *(Cassie Cook/Lucille Preston)*, Matt Moore *(Capt. Arthur Jarvis)*, Wallace Beery *(Jules Repin)*, J. Farrell MacDonald *(Murphy)*, Rose Dione *(Madame Polly Voo)*, Edna Tichenor *(Molly Norton)*, William V. Mong *(Dr. Li)*, Anna May Wong *(Rose Li)*, Bruce Guerin *(Billy Hepburn)*, Marie De Albert *(Mrs. Hepburn)*, William Moran *(Mr. Hepburn)*, Frank Lanning *(Chang Wang)*.

Melodrama. Source: John Colton and Daisy H. Andrews, *Drifting* (New York opening: 2 Jan 1922). Cassie Cook, an American girl in China, is smuggling opium under secret surveillance of Captain Jarvis, a government agent posing as a mining engineer. Cassie and Jules Repin, her confederate, try to kill Jarvis, but Cassie falls in love with Jarvis and reforms. *Smugglers. Engineers—Mining. Criminals—Rehabilitation. Opium. China.*

THE DRIFTING KID **F2.1447**

Dist Rayart Pictures. 27 Apr **1928** [New York State license]. Si; b&w. 35mm. 5 reels, 4,800 ft.

Cast: Tex Maynard, Betty Caldwell.

Western melodrama(?). No information about the nature of this film has been found.

Note: Other Tex Maynard films in this period were produced by Trem Carr Productions.

DRIFTING ON **F2.1448**

Dist Hollywood Pictures. 2 Feb **1927** [New York State license]. Si; b&w. 35mm. 5 reels, 4,900 ft.

Cast: Tom Bay.

Western melodrama(?). No information about the nature of this film has been found.

DRIFTWOOD **F2.1449**

F. C. F. Feature Corp. *Dist* Aywon Film Corp. 15 Oct **1924** [New York State license]. Si; b&w. 35mm. 5 reels, 4,700 ft.

Cast: Al Ferguson, Virginia Abbot.

Melodrama(?). No information about the nature of this film has been found.

DRIFTWOOD **F2.1450**

Columbia Pictures. 15 Oct **1928** [c8 Nov 1928; LP25817]. Si; b&w. 35mm. 7 reels, 6,267 ft.

Prod Jack Cohn. *Dir* Christy Cabanne. *Adapt-Cont* Lillie Hayward. *Titl* Morton Blumenstock. *Photog* Joe Walker. *Art Dir* Harrison Wiley. *Film Ed* Ben Pivar. *Asst Dir* Tenny Wright.

Cast: Don Alvarado *(Jim Curtis)*, Marceline Day *(Daisy Smith)*, Alan Roscoe *(Johnson)*, J. W. Johnston *(Barlow)*, Fred Holmes *(Doc Prouty)*, Fritzi Brunette *(Lola)*, Nora Cecil *(Mrs. Prouty)*, Joe Mack *(Johnson's henchman)*.

Melodrama. Source: Richard Harding Davis, "Driftwood" (publication undetermined). When Barlow, an amorous yachtsman, becomes too demanding, Daisy Smith, a proud woman of easy virtue, abandons ship off the island of Luna and swims to shore, where she meets Jim Curtis, an alcoholic American beachcomber. Johnson, the rough island superintendent, quickly attempts to force Daisy to submit to his foul embraces by threatening to deport her for having no visible means of support; when she is unable to find work, Daisy gives the drunken Jim $10 to marry her. When Jim sobers up the following day, he regains his sense of pride and goes to work loading steamers on the docks. Johnson later abducts him, and Daisy comes to his rescue. Jim and Daisy leave the island together, searching for a new start and a better tomorrow. *Prostitutes. Yachtsmen. Beachcombers. Alcoholism. Yachts. South Seas.*

DRINK *see* **THE FACE ON THE BARROOM FLOOR**

DRIVEN **F2.1451**

Charles J. Brabin. *Dist* Universal Film Manufacturing Co. 5 Mar **1923.** Si; b&w. 35mm. 6 reels, 5,400 ft.

Dir Charles J. Brabin. *Scen* Alfred Raboch. *Photog* George W. Lane. *Sets* Tec-Art Studios.

Cast: Emily Fitzroy *(Mrs. Tolliver)*, Burr McIntosh *(Mr. Tolliver)*, Charles Emmett Mack *(Tom Tolliver)*, George Bancroft *(Lem Tolliver)*, Fred Koser, Ernest Chandler *(Tolliver sons)*, Leslie Stowe *(John Hardin)*, Elinor Fair *(Essie Hardin)*.

Rural melodrama. Source: Jay Gelzer, "The Flower of the Flock," in *Cosmopolitan Magazine* (61:73–78, Aug 1921). Essie Hardin, resident of a southern mountain hamlet, moves in with the Tolliver family when revenue agents (she believes) kill her father. She falls in love with Tom, the youngest son in the family of bootleggers. Another son, Lem, the murderer of John Hardin, also wants Essie. Tom is badly beaten in a fight with Lem, who, following the fight, announces his intention of marrying Essie. Mrs. Tolliver attempts to thwart Lem by telling the revenue officers the whereabouts of the Tolliver still. She then collects the reward and sends Tom and Essie on their way with it. *Bootleggers. Brothers. Murder. Mountain life.*

DRIVEN FROM HOME **F2.1452**

Chadwick Pictures. 15 Jan **1927.** Si; b&w. 35mm. 7 reels, 6,800 ft.

Pres by Jesse J. Goldburg. *Dir* James Young. *Scen* Enid Hibbard, Ethel Hill. *Photog* Ernest Miller.

Cast: Ray Hallor, Virginia Lee Corbin, Pauline Garon, Sojin, Anna May Wong, Melbourne MacDowell, Margaret Seddon, Sheldon Lewis, Virginia Pearson, Eric Mayne, Alfred Fisher.

Drama. Source: Hal Reid, unidentified play. "Poor little girl [played by Virginia Lee Corbin] turned out by an irate papa [played by Melbourne MacDowell] because she eloped with his good looking but poor secretary [played by Ray Hallor] while papa had a titled foreigner all signed to the dotted line. But that isn't all. The complications are many and lurid. A subsea tunnel cave-in, a Chinese hop joint, a scheming housekeeper, and troubles without end pile on." (*Film Daily,* 6 Feb 1927, p12.) When things are blackest for the couple, the father relents, and happiness comes to all. *Secretaries. Housekeepers. Chinese. Fatherhood. Elopement. Opium.*

THE DRIVIN' FOOL **F2.1453**

Regent Pictures. *Dist* W. W. Hodkinson Corp. 12 Sep **1923** [c1 Oct 1923; LP19706]. Si; b&w. 35mm. 6 reels, 5,700 ft.

Dir Robert T. Thornby. *Titl* Walter Anthony. *Adapt* H. H. Van Loan. *Photog* A. J. Stout, Steve Rounds. *Asst Dir* Emile De Ruelle.

Cast: Alec B. Francis *(John Moorhead)*, Patsy Ruth Miller *(Sylvia Moorhead, his daughter)*, Wilton Taylor *(Henry Locke)*, Wally Van *(Hal Locke, his speed-mad son)*, Ramsey Wallace *(Richard Brownlee)*, Wilfred North *(Howard Grayson)*, Jessie J. Aldriche *(Horatio Jackson Lee St. Albans)*, Kenneth R. Bush *(John Lawson)*.

Action comedy. Source: William F. Sturm, "The Drivin' Fool," in *Blue Book Magazine* (34:23–38, Apr 1922). Speed-mad Hal Locke saves his father's business and the family fortune by driving his car from San Francisco to New York City in the face of insurmountable odds to deliver a check within the required time limit. He thereby thwarts Richard Brownlee, a scheming Wall Street broker, who, through a technicality, plans to take over the business. *Brokers. Swindlers. Automobiles. San Francisco. New York City—Wall Street.*

THE DROP KICK **F2.1454**

First National Pictures. 25 Sep **1927**. Si; b&w. 35mm. 7 reels, 6,819 or 6,900 ft.

Dir Millard Webb. *Adapt* Winifred Dunn. *Photog* Arthur Edeson, Alvin Knechtel.

Cast: Richard Barthelmess *(Jock Hamill)*, Barbara Kent *(Cecily Graves)*, Dorothy Revier *(Eunice Hathaway)*, Eugene Strong *(Brad Hathaway)*, Alberta Vaughn *(Molly)*, James Bradbury, Jr. *(Bones)*, Brooks Benedict *(Ed Pemberton)*, Hedda Hopper *(Mrs. Hamill)*, Mayme Kelso *(Mrs. Graves)*, George Pearce *(The Dean)*.

Drama. Source: Katherine Brush, *Glitter* (New York, 1926). Serious complications result for college football star Jock Hamill when he is vamped by his coach's wife, Eunice Hathaway, a former sweetheart. The coach commits suicide after his wife's extravagance drives him to embezzlement, Eunice tricks Jock into promising marriage, and Jock is suspected of murdering the coach. Greatly worried and shunned by his fellow students, Jock nearly loses the big game; but he finally comes through with a timely drop kick, his mother exposes the truth, and Jock is reunited with his true love, Cecily Graves. *Athletic coaches. College life. Football. Suicide. Embezzlement.*

Note: Cast also includes 10 college football stars (University of Southern California, Stanford, etc.).

THE DRUG MONSTER **F2.1455**

Warning Films. 2 Mar **1923** [New York State license]. Si; b&w. 35mm. 5 reels.

Melodrama(?). No information about the precise nature of this film has been found except that it includes a scene depicting the smoking of opium. *Narcotics. Opium.*

DRUG STORE COWBOY **F2.1456**

Independent Pictures. 1 Jun **1925**. Si; b&w. 35mm. 5 reels, 4,356 ft.

Dir Park Frame.

Cast: Franklyn Farnum *(Marmaduke Grandon)*, Robert Walker *(Gentleman Jack)*, Jean Arthur *(Jean)*, Malcolm Denny *(Wilton)*, Ronald Goetz *(director)*, Dick La Reno *(sheriff)*.

Comedy-melodrama. Marmaduke Grandon, a clerk in a drugstore, wants to get into the movies and is given the chance when an actor dies suddenly during the shooting of a film. Marmaduke is hired to take his place, but he never gets in front of the cameras, for on his way to work the first day, dressed in cowboy duds, he is forced to exchange clothes with Gentleman Jack, a crook on the lam. Jack takes Marmaduke's place with the movie company until Marmaduke shows up and runs him off, ruining the heroine's big scene. Later, during the filming of a scene at a local bank, Jack uses the company as a diversion and robs the bank. Marmaduke again intervenes, captures Jack, ruins the picture, and ties up the leading lady for life. *Soda clerks. Actors. Bank robberies. Motion pictures. Impersonation. Drugstores.*

THE DRUG TRAFFIC **F2.1457**

Irving Cummings. Mar **1923** [scheduled release]. Si; b&w. 35mm. 5 reels.

Pres by Sol Lesser. *Dir* Irving Cummings. *Story* Harvey Gates.

Cast: Bob Walker *(Willie Shade)*, Gladys Brockwell *(Edna Moore)*, Barbara Tennant *(Mary Larkin)*.

Melodrama. "... the story of a successful surgeon [Dr. Steve Maison] who, trying to burn the candle at both ends through keeping up his professional activities and also keeping abreast of his social obligations to please his fiancée, resorts to a drug to stimulate him as he is about to perform an operation. This leads to a shot now and again, and soon he is an addict, giving up his profession and sinking to the slums, until he is thrown into jail. He escapes and returns to his humble abode, burglarizes the hospital where he was formerly an attaché to obtain a supply of drug, and then when he is brought to a realization of the uselessness of it all he puts up a fight to get away from his habit, but although he spends a night of terror fighting off his desire his victory against the drug brings death." (*Variety*, 26 Apr 1923, p26.) The names of the actors who play the roles of Dr. Steve Maison and George Wallace have not been determined. *Drug addicts. Surgeons. Narcotics. Burglary.*

DRUMS OF DESTINY *see* **DRUMS OF FATE**

DRUMS OF FATE **F2.1458**

Famous Players–Lasky. *Dist* Paramount Pictures. 14 Jan **1923** [New York premiere; released 18 Feb 1923; c27 Dec 1922; LP18584]. Si; b&w. 35mm. 6 reels, 5,716 ft.

Pres by Adolph Zukor. *Dir* Charles Maigne. *Scen* Will M. Ritchey. *Photog* James Howe.

Cast: Mary Miles Minter *(Carol Delliver)*, Maurice B. Flynn *(Laurence Teck)*, George Fawcett *(Felix Brantome)*, Robert Cain *(Cornelius Rysbroek)*, Casson Ferguson *(David Verne)*, Bertram Grassby *(Hamoud Bin-Said)*, Noble Johnson *(native king)*.

Romantic drama. Source: Stephen French Whitman, *Sacrifice* (New York, 1922). Believing her husband, Laurence Teck, to be dead in the African jungle, Carol marries musician David Verne. Laurence does come home, but, thinking it best for Carol, he returns to the jungle. The shock kills David, and Carol sets out in search of Laurence, has many adventures, and finally finds him with the friendly native king who saved him. *Musicians. Bigamy. Jungles. Africa.*

Note: Working title: *Drums of Destiny*.

THE DRUMS OF JEOPARDY **F2.1459**

Hoffman Productions. *Dist* Truart Film Corp. Nov **1923** [c10 Mar 1924; LP19983]. Si; b&w. 35mm. 7 reels, 6,529 ft.

Pres by M. H. Hoffman. *Supv* Roland G. Edwards. *Dir* Edward Dillon. *Titl* Alfred A. Cohn, A. Carle Palm. *Adapt* Arthur Hoerl. *Photog* James Diamond. *Art Dir* Horace Jackson. *Film Ed* Alfred A. Cohn, A. Carle Palm.

Cast: Elaine Hammerstein *(Dorothy Burrows)*, Jack Mulhall *(Jerome Hawksley)*, Wallace Beery *(Gregor Karlov)*, David Torrence *(Cutty)*, Maude George *(Olga Andrevich)*, Eric Mayne *(Banker Burrows)*, Forrest Seabury *(Stefani)*.

Mystery melodrama. Source: Harold MacGrath, *The Drums of Jeopardy* (New York, 1920). Grand Duke Alexis of Russia gives to his private secretary, Jerome Hawksley, two priceless emeralds, set in the heads of drums, which allegedly exert a sinister power over their owner. Gregor Karlov notes their value and attempts to steal them in New York City, where they have been sent for safekeeping. Karlov kills Banker Burrows, the man to whom the jewels were entrusted, and kidnaps Hawksley. Burrows' daughter, Dorothy, and Cutty, a secret service man, trace Karlov to a cafe, and there Karlov is killed in a fight. Hawksley marries Dorothy, and the jewels are returned to him. *Secretaries. Royalty. Russians. Occult. Kidnaping. Theft. New York City.*

DRUMS OF LOVE **F2.1460**

United Artists. 24 Jan **1928** [New York premiere; released 31 Mar; c13 Apr 1928; LP25144]. Si; b&w. 35mm. 9 reels, 8,350 ft.

Pres by D. W. Griffith. *Prod-Dir* D. W. Griffith. *Adapt-Titl* Gerrit Lloyd. *Photog* Karl Struss. *Asst Camera* Harry Jackson, Billy Bitzer. *Set Dsgn* William Cameron Menzies. *Film Ed* James Smith. *Mus Score* Charles Wakefield Cadman, Sol Cohen, Wells Hively. *Cost* Alice O'Neill.

Cast: Mary Philbin *(Princess Emanuella)*, Lionel Barrymore *(Duke Cathos de Alvia)*, Don Alvarado *(Count Leonardo de Alvia)*, Tully Marshall *(Bopi)*, William Austin *(Raymond of Boston)*, Eugenie Besserer *(Duchess de Alvia, Aunt to Cathos and Leonardo)*, Charles Hill Mailes *(Duke de Granada)*, Rosemary Cooper *(The Maid)*, Joyce Coad *(The Little Sister)*.

Historical drama. Based on a "historical incident" in the life of Francesca da Rimini. To save her father's life and diminishing estates, Emanuella marries Duke Cathos de Alvia, a grotesque hunchback, although she loves Leonardo, his handsome younger brother. Emanuella and Leonardo continue their affair after the wedding until they are discovered "flagrante delicto" by Cathos after he is informed of their unfaithfulness by Bopi, a malicious court jester. Having stationed himself at the place of rendezvous, Cathos slays both, kissing each one before the fatal stabbing. In an alternative ending Bopi and Cathos stab each other to death and the lovers are forgiven by the dying hunchback. *Hunchbacks. Court jesters. Brothers. Infidelity. Rimini. Francesca da Rimini. Paolo Malatesta. Giovanni Malatesta.*

DRUMS OF THE DESERT **F2.1461**

Paramount Famous Lasky Corp. 4 Jun **1927** [c4 Jun 1927; LP24049]. Si; b&w. 35mm. 6 reels, 5,907 ft.

Pres by Adolph Zukor, Jesse L. Lasky. *Dir* John Waters. *Screenplay* John Stone. *Photog* C. Edgar Schoenbaum.

Cast: Warner Baxter *(John Curry)*, Marietta Millner *(Mary Manton)*, Ford Sterling *(Perkins)*, Wallace MacDonald *(Will Newton)*, Heinie Conklin *(Hi-Lo)*, George Irving *(Prof. Elias Manton)*, Bernard Siegel *(Chief Brave Bear)*, Guy Oliver *(Indian agent)*.

Western drama. Source: Zane Grey, "Desert Bound" (publication undetermined). At the Navajo reservation Chief Brave Bear and his people gather to meet an issue foisted on them by a group of men, headed by Will Newton, who seek to force them off their desert lands. Perkins and Hi-Lo meet the exploring party of Elias Manton and his daughter, Mary; and posing as desert rats, they are hired as guides. They encounter John Curry, a friend of the Indians whose cordiality arouses their suspicion; Newton tries, unsuccessfully, to dissuade them from continuing their work in the desert and casts aspersions on Curry. Manton is kidnaped by Newton's men, but Curry rescues him after a search. Newton starts for the oil claims, while the Navajo prepare to defend their sacred altars. Curry tries unsuccessfully to placate the Indians and is shot by Newton, who fails to listen to reason. United States Cavalry arrive and place Newton's men under arrest; and Mary realizes the worth of her protector. *Navajo Indians. Land rights. Oil lands. Arizona. United States Army—Cavalry.*

Note: Photographed on location at an Arizona Navajo reservation.

DRUSILLA WITH A MILLION **F2.1462**

Associated Arts Corp. *Dist* Film Booking Offices of America. 18 Jun **1925** [c18 Jun 1925; LP21653]. Si; b&w. 35mm. 7 reels, 7,391 ft.

Supv Ludwig G. B. Erb. *Dir* F. Harmon Weight. *Scen* Lois Zellner. *Photog* Lyman Broening. *Asst Dir* Thornton Freeland.

Cast: Mary Carr *(Drusilla Doane)*, Priscilla Bonner *(Sally May Ferris)*, Kenneth Harlan *(Colin Arnold)*, Henry Barrows *(Elias Arnold)*, William Humphreys *(John Thornton)*, Claire Du Brey *(Daphne Thornton)*.

Drama. Source: Elizabeth Cooper, *Drusilla With a Million* (New York, 1916). Drusilla Doane, a charity patient in a home for the aged, inherits a mansion and a million dollars from a distant relative and turns her new home into an orphanage, thereby infuriating her haughty neighbors. Colin Arnold, the disinherited son of the man who left Drusilla the money, is involved in an automobile accident, and Sally May, an orphan, saves his life, nursing him back to health. Colin and Sally May are married and find happiness together until Daphne Thornton, a gold digger, convinces Sally May that she is ruining Colin's chances of disputing his father's will. Sally May leaves Colin and, reduced to poverty, gives birth to a baby, which she attempts to leave on Drusilla's doorstep. She is arrested on a complaint filed by Drusilla's neighbors, who want to stop Drusilla's private charities. Colin and Sally May are reunited in court and go to live with Drusilla, who continues her good deeds. *Gold diggers. Inheritance. Automobile accidents. Orphanages. Old age homes. Wills.*

DRY MARTINI **F2.1463**

Fox Film Corp. 7 Oct **1928** [c24 Sep 1928; LP25646]. Mus score (Movietone); b&w. 35mm. 7 reels, 7,176 ft. [Also si; 6,828 ft.]

Pres by William Fox. *Dir* H. D'Abbadie D'Arrast. *Scen-Titl* Douglas Z. Doty. *Photog* Conrad Wells. *Film Ed* Frank E. Hull. *Mus Score* Erno Rapee, S. L. Rothafel. *Asst Dir* Ray Flynn.

Cast: Mary Astor *(Elisabeth Quimby)*, Matt Moore *(Freddie Fletcher)*, Jocelyn Lee *(Lina)*, Sally Eilers *(Lucille Grosvenor)*, Albert Gran *(Willoughby Quimby)*, Albert Conti *(Conway Cross)*, Tom Ricketts *(Joseph)*, Hugh Trevor *(Bobbie Duncan)*, John Webb Dillon *(Frank)*, Marcelle Corday *(Mrs. Koenig)*.

Comedy-drama. Source: John Thomas, *Dry Martini: a Gentleman Turns to Love* (New York, 1926). Willoughby Quimby, a divorced American in Paris, receives a wire from his ex-wife informing him that his daughter, Elisabeth, will soon arrive in France on a visit. Anticipating a prim and proper young lady, Will gives up his mistress and dry martinis, but he needn't have bothered, for Elisabeth is in search of a wild time. She quickly becomes involved with a French artist and considers entering into a companionate marriage with him. Freddie Fletcher, Will's boon drinking companion, tries to keep Elisabeth away from the artist and is soundly drubbed for his troubles. Elisabeth is at first sympathetic to Freddie and later loving, eventually returning with him to the United States. Will again takes up residence at his old place in Harry's American Bar. *Artists. Expatriates. Thrill-seeking. Marriage—Companionate. Fatherhood. Divorce. Harry's American Bar. Paris.*

DU BARRY, WOMAN OF PASSION **F2.1464**

Art Cinema Corp. *Dist* United Artists. 11 Oct **1930** [c10 Nov 1930; LP1708]. Sd (Movietone); b&w. 35mm. 10 reels, 8,110 ft.

Pres by Joseph M. Schenck. *Dir-Adapt* Sam Taylor. *Stage Dir* Earle Browne. *Photog* Oliver Marsh. *Art Dir* William Cameron Menzies, Park French. *Film Ed* Allen McNeil. *Sd Rec* Frank Grenzbach. *Asst Dir* Walter Mayo. *Prod Mgr* Orville O. Dull.

Cast: Norma Talmadge *(Jeannette Vaubernier)*, William Farnum *(Louis XV, King of France)*, Conrad Nagel *(Cosse de Brissac)*, Hobart Bosworth *(Duc de Brissac)*, Ullrich Haupt *(Jean Du Barry)*, Alison Skipworth *(La Gourdan)*, E. Alyn Warren *(Denys)*, Edgar Norton *(Renal)*, Edwin Maxwell *(Maupeou)*, Henry Kolker *(D'Aiguillon)*.

Romantic costume-melodrama. Source: David Belasco, "Du Barry," in *Six Plays* (Boston, 1928; New York opening: 29 Sep 1902). Jeannette Vaubernier, an impulsive shopgirl en route to deliver a hat, dreams of luxury and position as she saunters through the woods, and attracted by a pool of water, she disrobes and plunges in. Cosse de Brissac, a handsome private in the King's Guards, comes to her rescue and they become sweethearts. Meanwhile, Jean Du Barry, a shrewd roué, takes note of her at the millinery shop and tricks her into staying at La Gourda's, where she soon becomes a favorite among the men. Louis XV, seeing her at the opera, arranges a meeting; and just as she is about to elope with young Brissac, the king offers her all she desires. She is admitted to court, where her marriage to Du Barry is arranged, though she still loves Brissac and is upbraided by the king for her lack of gratitude. The Pacte de Famine forces the people to pay high prices for grain, causing a revolt; meanwhile, the king orders a lavish feast in Jeannette's honor. Brissac, leading the mob, seeks revenge on the king, but he is captured and ordered executed; just before the command to fire, Jeannette opens the gates, and the people storm the palace. As a result, Jeannette is taken to prison with the cry, "The guillotine for Du Barry"; and though Brissac pleads for her life, the revolutionists are obdurate. Reaffirming their mutual love, Brissac renounces the revolutionary cause and prepares to die with her. *Shopgirls. Mistresses. Royalty. France—History—Revolution. Paris. Marie Jeanne Bécu Du Barry. Louis XV (France). Pacte de Famine.*

THE DUCHESS OF BUFFALO **F2.1465**

Constance Talmadge Productions. *Dist* First National Pictures. 8 Aug **1926** [New York premiere; released 5 Sep; c4 Oct 1926; LP23186]. Si; b&w. 35mm. 7 reels, 6,940 ft.

Pres by Joseph M. Schenck. *Dir* Sidney Franklin. *Screenplay* Hans Kraly. *Titl* George Marion, Jr. *Photog* Oliver Marsh.

Cast: Constance Talmadge *(Marian Duncan)*, Tullio Carminati *(Lieut. Vladimir Orloff)*, Edward Martindel *(Grand Duke Gregory Alexandrovich)*, Rose Dione *(Grand Duchess Olga Petrovna)*, Chester Conklin *(hotel manager)*, Lawrence Grant *(commandant)*, Martha Franklin *(maid)*, Jean De Briac *(adjutant)*.

Romantic comedy. Source: Max Bordy and Franz Martos, *Sybil* (a play; publication undetermined). Marian Duncan, an American dancer, climaxes her theatrical success in Russia by becoming the fiancée of Vladimir Orloff, a young army officer, unaware that the Grand Duke Alexandrovich is also in love with her. Marian refuses the nobleman's gifts and advances; and enraged over his rival, the grand duke has the lieutenant arrested. Marian flees to another city, but Orloff escapes and follows her. The citizens and soldiers believe Marian and Orloff to be a grand duchess and her adjutant, and the pair accept the people's homage. The grand duke arrives, and instead of denouncing her imposture, he insists on accompanying her to her suite, where Orloff is hiding. Then the real grand duchess arrives, and Alexandrovich, afraid of his jealous spouse, is forced to forgive Orloff and to sanction his marriage to the American dancer. *Royalty. Dancers. Jealousy. Imposture. Russia.*

THE DUCHESS OF LANGEAIS *see* **THE ETERNAL FLAME**

DUCKS AND DRAKES F2.1466

Realart Pictures. Feb **1921** [c29 Jan 1921; LP16087]. Si; b&w. 35mm. 5 reels, 4,876 ft.

Pres by Bebe Daniels. *Supv* Elmer Harris. *Dir* Maurice Campbell. *Story-Scen* Elmer Harris. *Photog* H. Kinley Martin. *Art Dir* Una Hopkins.

Cast: Bebe Daniels *(Teddy Simpson)*, Jack Holt *(Rob Winslow)*, Mayme Kelso *(Aunty Weeks)*, Edward Martindel *(Dick Chiltern)*, William E. Lawrence *(Tom Hazzard)*, Wade Boteler *(Colonel Tweed)*, Maurie Newell *(Cissy)*, Elsie Andrean *(Mina)*.

Society farce. Teddy Simpson, a spoiled young lady who lives with her straitlaced aunt and is engaged to Rob Winslow, carries on telephone flirtations with Dick Chiltern and Tom Hazzard, fellow clubmen of her fiancé. Overhearing a conversation at the club, the trio with the aid of Colonel Tweed proceed to teach her a lesson: she is coaxed into visiting a hunting camp, where she and Hazzard are surprised by Tweed, posing as an escaped convict, who forces his attentions on her and locks her in a room. Following her escape, Rob finds her subdued and ready to marry him. *Flirts. Aunts. Prison escapees. Disguise. Clubs.*

THE DUDE COWBOY F2.1467

Independent Pictures. *Dist* Film Booking Offices of America. 31 Oct **1926** [c15 Oct 1926; LP23218]. Si; b&w. 35mm. 5 reels, 4,593 or 4,953 ft.

Pres by Joseph P. Kennedy. *Prod* Jesse J. Goldburg. *Dir* Jack Nelson. *Cont* Paul M. Bryan. *Story* James Ormont. *Photog* Ernest Miller. *Asst Dir* Archie Ricks.

Cast: Bob Custer *(Bob Ralston)*, Flora Bramley *(Doris Wrigmint)*, Billy Bletcher *(Shorty O'Day)*, Howard Truesdell *(Amos Wrigmint)*, Bruce Gordon *(Carl Kroth)*, Amber Norman *(Mable La Rue)*, Sabel Johnson *(Aver Du Pais?)*, Edward Gordon *(Count Duse)*.

Western melodrama. Bob Ralston, with Shorty O'Day and a group of trusted cowpunchers, sets out to assume charge of his dude ranch in Arizona. En route they rescue Amos Wrigmint and his daughter, Doris, from a bandit attack, and learning that they are bound for the ranch, Bob joins them as a chauffeur-valet to be near the girl. Later, Shorty discovers evidence connecting two ranch hands with the bandits and becomes suspicious of the foreman, Kroth; and Bob overhears Kroth planning to rob the guests at a dance. With the help of his friends, Bob drives off the outlaws from the dance and rescues Doris from the foreman; he then discloses his identity as the owner of the ranch, and all ends happily. *Cowboys. Ranch foremen. Bandits. Chauffeurs. Valets. Impersonation. Dude ranches. Arizona.*

THE DUDE WRANGLER F2.1468

Sono-Art Productions. 1 Jun **1930** [c12 Dec 1930; LP1814]. Sd; b&w. 35mm. 6 reels, 6,200 ft.

Pres by Mrs. Wallace Reid, Cliff Broughton. *Dir* Richard Thorpe. *Adapt-Dial* Robert N. Lee.

Cast: Lina Basquette *(Helen Dane)*, George Duryea *(Wally McCann)*, Clyde Cook *(Pinkey Fripp)*, Francis X. Bushman *(Canby)*, Margaret Seddon *(Aunt Mary)*, Ethel Wales *(Mattie)*, K. Sojin *(Wong)*, Wilfred North *(The "Snorer")*, Alice Davenport, Virginia Sale, Julia Swayne Gordon, Louis Payne, Fred Parker, Aileen Carlyle, Jack Richardson *(dude guests)*.

Western comedy. Source: Caroline Lockhart, *The Dude Wrangler* (Garden City, New York, 1921). Tied to his Aunt Mary's apron strings, Wally McCann is a spineless, effeminate youth who spends his time designing embroidery patterns, and though Helen Dane, who breeds polo ponies, is fond of him, she cold-shoulders him, hoping thus to make a man of him. Determined to make good as a farmer, Wally buys some land in Wyoming, near Helen's farm, and arrives in cowboy attire with his handyman, Pinkey Fripp. Wally is literally washed out by a cloudburst and is jailed for fighting while on a drunken spree. Later, he borrows money from the bank to purchase a dude ranch. Among the guests is Canby, who is in love with Helen and resents Wally's interference; plotting with Wong, the Chinese cook, Candy plans a series of mishaps which frighten the other guests and give Wally the opportunity to rescue a lady from a stampede. Enraged at Canby's perfidy, Wally fights him and compels him to take over the ranch, thus winning the admiration and love of Helen. *Chinese. Dudes. Cooks. Ranchers. Farmers. Horsebreeders. Drunkenness. Effeminacy. Courtship. Dude ranches.*

DUGAN OF THE DUGOUTS F2.1469

Morris R. Schlank Productions. *Dist* Anchor Film Distributors. 15 Apr **1928.** Si; b&w. 35mm. 6 reels, 5,600 ft.

Dir-Story Robert Ray. *Scen* J. P. McGowan. *Titl* Al Martin. *Photog* Robert E. Cline. *Film Ed* William Holmes.

Cast: Pauline Garon *(Betty)*, Danny O'Shea *(Danny Dugan)*, Ernest Hilliard *(Sergeant Davis)*, J. P. McGowan *(Captain von Brinken)*, Sid Smith *(Danny's buddy)*, Alice Knowland.

Comedy. "This [action] centers around the usual dance hall lad who gets into the uniform because his dame likes the setup of a sergeant. ... The sergeant turns out [to be] a spy and the mick hero [Danny Dugan] is roped in by the enemy with his girl [Betty] as well, who affords the Red Cross angle. Laughing gas not only comes to the rescue of the couple but also gets the enemy into such a hilarious mood that the Yanks have to carry them off to the brig." (*Variety*, 22 Aug 1928, p34.) *Dancers. Spies. Laughing gas. United States Army. Red Cross.*

THE DUKE OF CHIMNEY BUTTE F2.1470

Fred Stone Productions. *Dist* R-C Pictures. 4 Dec **1921** [c4 Dec 1921; LP17383]. Si; b&w. 35mm. 5 reels, 4,600 ft.

Prod Andrew J. Callaghan. *Dir* Frank Borzage. *Scen* Marian Ainslee. *Photog* Jack MacKenzie.

Cast: Fred Stone *(Jeremeah Lambert)*, Vola Vale *(Vesta Philbrook)*, Josie Sedgwick *(Grace Kerr)*, Chick Morrison *(Kerr, the son)*, Buck Connors *(Taters)*, Harry Dunkinson *(Jedlick)*.

Western melodrama. Source: George Washington Ogden, *The Duke of Chimney Butte* (Chicago, 1920). While trying to sell a mechanical contrivance that peels potatoes, opens cans, pulls nails, etc., young Lambert stumbles on a band of cowboys at supper on a cattle ranch. He quickly wins their admiration by his valorous feats and becomes one of their leaders, revealing himself as an expert horseman. He obtains a job as aide and protector of Vesta Philbrook, who is trying to manage a ranch despite the constant raids of cattle rustlers. "The Duke," however, launches a campaign against the cattle thieves, and in a series of hair-raising adventures, with the aid of his friend Taters, he breaks up the gang and kills the leaders, headed by Kerr, then captures the love of Vesta. *Cowboys. Peddlers. Rustlers. Ranches.*

THE DUKE STEPS OUT F2.1471

Metro-Goldwyn-Mayer Pictures. 16 Mar **1929** [c16 Jul 1929; LP525]. Mus score & sd eff (Movietone), b&w. 35mm. 8 reels, 6,236 ft. [Also si; 6,201 ft.]

Dir James Cruze. *Adapt-Cont* Raymond Schrock, Dale Van Every. *Titl* Joe Farnham. *Story* Lucian Cary. *Photog* Ira Morgan. *Art Dir* Cedric Gibbons. *Film Ed* George Hively. *Song: "Just You"* William Axt, David Mendoza. *Wardrobe* David Cox.

Cast: William Haines *(Duke)*, Joan Crawford *(Susie)*, Karl Dane *(Barney)*, Tenen Holtz *(Jake)*, Edward Nugent *(Tommy Wells)*, Jack Roper *(Poison Kerrigan)*, Delmer Daves *(Bossy Edwards)*, Luke Cosgrave *(Professor Widdicomb)*, Herbert Prior *(Mr. Corbin)*.

Comedy-drama. Duke, the pampered son of a millionaire, decides to prove to his father that he can be a success on his own and takes up prizefighting. On his way to an important match, he sees Susie on a train with a group of college youths and falls in love, deciding to return to college. Although he is determined to compel her to accept him, she consistently refuses his attentions. When at length he wins her admiration, he is obliged to forego a meeting with her so as to fill a Decoration Day fighting engagement in San Francisco. She believes there is an ulterior motive in his absence, but hearing the fight on the radio, she realizes her mistake. *Students. Prizefighters. Filial relations. College life. Decoration Day. San Francisco.*

DULCY *see* **NOT SO DUMB**

DULCY F2.1472

Constance Talmadge Film Co. *Dist* Associated First National Pictures. 27 Aug **1923** [c21 Aug 1923; LP19322]. Si; b&w. 35mm. 7 reels, 6,859 ft.

Dir Sidney A. Franklin. *Scen* Anita Loos, John Emerson. *Cont* C. Gardner Sullivan. *Photog* Norbert Brodin.

Cast: Constance Talmadge *(Dulcy)*, Claude Gillingwater *(Mr. Forbes)*, Jack Mulhall *(Gordon Smith)*, May Wilson *(Mrs. Forbes)*, Johnny Harron *(Billy Parker)*, Anne Cornwall *(Angela Forbes)*, André Beranger *(Vincent Leach)*, Gilbert Douglas *(Schuyler Van Dyke)*, Frederick Esmelton *(Blair Patterson)*, Milla Davenport *(Matty, Dulcy's companion)*.

Comedy-drama. Source: George S. Kaufman and Marc Connelly, *Dulcy, a Comedy in Three Acts* (New York, 1921). Dulcy, a devoted but scatterbrained bride, tries to improve her absent husband's finances by inviting two of his business prospects to dinner. Though at first thoroughly confusing the deal, she does get her husband a bigger share than he bargained for. *Businessmen. Brides.*

Note: This film was remade in 1930 under the title *Not So Dumb*, q. v.

DUMBBELLS IN ERMINE F2.1473

Warner Brothers Pictures. 10 May **1930** [c23 Apr 1930; LP1251]. Sd (Vitaphone); b&w. 35mm. 7 reels, 6,300 ft. [Also si.]

Dir John G. Adolfi. *Screenplay* Harvey Thew. *Dial* James Gleason. *Photog* Dev Jennings. *Sd Engr* Mel Le Mon.

Cast: Robert Armstrong *(Jerry Malone)*, Barbara Kent *(Faith Corey)*, Beryl Mercer *(Grandma Corey)*, James Gleason *(Mike)*, Claude Gillingwater *(Uncle Roger)*, Julia Swayne Gordon *(Mrs. Corey)*, Arthur Hoyt *(Siegfried Strong)*, Mary Foy *(Mrs. Strong)*, Charlotte Merriam *(Camilla)*.

Society drama. Source: Lynn Starling, *Weak Sisters* (New York opening: 13 Oct 1925). In a small town in Virginia, Faith Corey, daughter of a socially prominent family, meets and falls in love with Jerry Malone, a prizefighter, though her straitlaced mother wants her to marry Siegfried, a spellbinding "missionary reformer." Though Grandma Corey promotes the romance with the prizefighter, Mike, the fighter's hardboiled, wisecracking manager, tries to keep them apart; following a quarrel, Faith reconciles herself to marrying Siegfried, but when he invites a group of "weak sisters" to a revival meeting, he is disgraced when one accuses him of her downfall. Finally, with Mike's advice, Jerry wins back Faith and they are united with the family's blessings. *Prizefighters. Fight managers. Socialites. Grandmothers. Evangelists. Courtship. Smalltown life. Revivals. Virginia.*

THE DUMMY F2.1474

Paramount Famous Lasky Corp. 9 Mar **1929** [c8 Mar 1929; LP206]. Sd (Movietone); b&w. 35mm. 6 reels, 5,357 ft.

Supv Hector Turnbull. *Dir* Robert Milton. *Adapt-Dial* Herman J. Mankiewicz. *Photog* J. Roy Hunt. *Film Ed* George Nichols, Jr.

Cast: Ruth Chatterton *(Agnes Meredith)*, Fredric March *(Trumbell Meredith)*, John Cromwell *(Walter Babbing)*, Fred Kohler *(Joe Cooper)*, Mickey Bennett *(Barney Cook)*, Vondell Darr *(Peggy Meredith)*, Jack Oakie *(Dopey Hart)*, ZaSu Pitts *(Rose Gleason)*, Richard Tucker *(Blakie Baker)*, Eugene Pallette *(Madison)*.

Comedy melodrama. Source: Harvey J. O'Higgins and Harriet Ford, *The Dummy; a Detective Comedy in Four Acts* (New York, 1925). Barney Cook, a bright Bowery youngster, gets a job with a detective agency and is used by his employer in a plan to trap a gang of kidnapers who have abducted the small daughter of the Merediths, an estranged wealthy couple: pretending to be deaf and dumb, Barney deliberately gets himself abducted by the gang. His ruse is later discovered but he gets word to the agency, and the kidnapers are rounded up. Little Peggy Meredith is returned to her parents, who have been brought back together by sharing worry on account of their daughter. *Detectives. Deafmutes. Kidnaping. Parenthood. New York City—Bowery.*

Note: This film is a remake of a 1917 Paramount film of the same title with Jack Pickford in the role of Barney Cook.

DUNDEE-CRIQUI BOXING EXHIBITION F2.1475

Leon D. Britton. *Dist* Penser's Productions. 31 Jul **1923** [scheduled release]. Si; b&w. 35mm. 4 reels.

Boxing film. On 26 Jul 1923 Johnny Dundee, an Italian-American from New York City's West Side, beats Eugène Criqui, France's spectacular featherweight boxer, in a 15-round battle at the Polo Grounds. *John Dundee. Eugène Criqui. Boxing. New York City—Polo Grounds.*

THE DUNGEON F2.1476

Micheaux Film Corp. 22 May **1922** [scheduled release]. Si; b&w. 35mm. 7 reels, ca6,300 ft.

Cast: William E. Fountaine, Shingzie Howard, J. Kenneth Goodman, W. B. F. Crowell, Earle Browne Cook, Blanche Thompson.

Bluebeard melodrama. "The story treats of Gyp Lassiter, a villainous wretch, who employs a drug fiend to hypnotize a woman whom he wants to get possession of. The drug fiend brings the woman to Gyp who marries her while she is in a hypnotic condition. Gyp then takes her to a house which has been the scene of the murder of eight of his previous wives. By nature a killer, he then proceeds to asphyxiate her in a dungeon. From the clutches of death, she is rescued by a former lover who then kills Gyp." (New York State license records.) *Drug addicts. Hypnotism. Murder.*

DUPED F2.1477

Independent Pictures. 1 Apr **1925**. Si; b&w. 35mm. 5 reels, 5,400 ft.

Dir J. P. McGowan. *Story* John Clymer.

Cast: William Desmond *(John Morgan)*, Helen Holmes *(Dolores Verdiego, last of the Benevidas)*, J. P. McGowan *("Hard Rock" Ralston)*, Dorothea Wolbert *(Sweet Marie)*, George Magrill *(George Forsyth, superintendent of the Golden Gate Mine)*, Ford West *(marshal)*, James Thompson *(A-1, who does everything but take a job)*.

Melodrama(?). No information about the precise nature of this film has been found. *Mine superintendents. United States marshals.*

DURAND OF THE BAD LANDS F2.1478

Fox Film Corp. 1 Nov **1925** [c6 Sep 1925; LP21955]. Si; b&w. 35mm. 6 reels, 5,844 ft.

Pres by William Fox. *Dir-Adapt-Scen* Lynn Reynolds. *Story* Maibelle Heikes Justice. *Photog* Allan Davey. *Asst Dir* Leslie Selander, Harry Welfar.

Cast: Buck Jones *(Dick Durand)*, Marion Nixon *(Molly Gore)*, Malcolm Waite *(Clem Allison)*, Fred De Silva *(Pete Garson)*, Luke Cosgrave *(Kingdom Come Knapp [Preacher Knapp])*, George Lessey *(John Boyd)*, Buck Black *(Jimmie)*, Seesel Ann Johnson *(Clara Belle)*, James Corrigan *(Joe Gore)*, Carol Lombard *(Ellen Boyd)*.

Western melodrama. Dick Durand, deciding to move to Mexico, sells his ranch and belongings to Sheriff Clem Allison, and Pete Garson, one of Allison's henchman, uses Durand's regalia to commit a number of crimes. Durand returns to vindicate himself and falls in love with Molly Gore, who with her invalid father is struggling to make out on a small ranch. She spurns him at first but softens after he returns with three children, the survivors of a raid on a wagon carrying gold for banker John Boyd. Durand finally establishes his innocence, rescues Boyd's daughter, who is imprisoned in the mine by Pete, and wins Boyd's gratitude and Molly's love. *Ranchers. Outlaws. Bankers. Mistaken identity.*

Note: Story first filmed in 1917 under the same title.

DUSK TO DAWN F2.1479

Florence Vidor Productions. *Dist* Associated Exhibitors. 2 Sep **1922** [c9 Aug 1922; LU18125]. Si; b&w. 35mm. 6 reels, 5,200 ft.

Dir King Vidor. *Scen* Frank Howard Clark. *Photog* George Barnes.

Cast: Florence Vidor *(Marjorie Latham/Aziza)*, Jack Mulhall *(Philip Randall)*, Truman Van Dyke *(Ralph Latham)*, James Neill *(John Latham)*, Lydia Knott *(Mrs. Latham)*, Herbert Fortier *(Mark Randall)*, Norris Johnson *(Babette)*, Nellie Anderson *(Marua)*, Sidney Franklin *(Nadar Gungi)*.

Drama. Source: Katherine Hill, *The Shuttle Soul.* Marjorie has nightly dreams wherein she enacts the life of Aziza, a beggar girl in India. To save her brother from imprisonment for forgery, Marjorie agrees to break up an affair between the bank president's son and a notorious dancer, the real forger. But it is not until Majorie's dream counterpart dies and frees her from her double life that she finds happiness in her love for the banker's son. *Bankers. Dancers. Forgery. India. Dreams.*

THE DUST FLOWER F2.1480

Goldwyn Pictures. ca2 Jul **1922** [c8 Jul 1922; LP18040]. Si; b&w. 35mm. 6 reels, 5,651 ft.

Dir Rowland V. Lee. *Story* Basil King. *Photog* Max Fabian.

Cast: Helene Chadwick *(Letty Gravely)*, James Rennie *(Rashleigh Allerton)*, Claude Gillingwater *(Steptoe)*, Mona Kingsley *(Barbara Wallbrook)*, Edward Peil *(Judson Flack)*, George Periolat *(Ott)*.

Society drama. Trying to escape her miserable existence, Letty attempts suicide but is stopped by Rashleigh Allerton, a millionaire, who asks her to be his wife to spite his fiancée who has just jilted him. The irate ex-fiancée succeeds in breaking up the new marriage. Rash, realizing his love for Letty, rescues her from the cafe where her cruel stepfather has forced her to work. *Millionaires. Poverty. Wealth. Marriage. Suicide.*

DUTY FIRST F2.1481

Sanford Productions. 1 Dec **1922**. Si; b&w. 35mm. 5 reels.

Dir Marcel Perez.

Cast: Pete Morrison.

Northwest melodrama. "A band of opium smugglers, with the exception of their leader, is captured by the betrayal of a dance hall girl to a private in the mounted police. The latter is ordered to get the leader and the chase proceeds to New York, where, after an exciting episode the leader again escapes to the Canadian woods. He is eventually taken in the cabin of the girl with whom the officer is in love, from which incident the title of the story is taken." (*Motion Picture News Booking Guide*, 4:44, Apr 1923.) *Smugglers. Dancehall girls. Narcotics. Canada. New York City. Northwest Mounted Police.*

DUTY'S REWARD **F2.1482**

Ellbee Pictures. 10 Jun **1927** [New York showing]. Si; b&w. 35mm. 6 reels, 5,345 ft.

Dir Bertram Bracken. *Story-Scen* A. B. Barringer. *Photog* Ernest Depew, Robert Cline.

Cast: Allan Roscoe *(Richard Webster)*, Eva Novak *(Dorothy Thompson)*, Lou Archer *("Peek" Harvey)*, Edward Brownell *(Spencer Haynes)*, George Fawcett *(James Thompson)*.

Melodrama. "The melodramatic kick is centered on the big building which is built of very bad cement, a condition understood by those in on the villainy side of the film. Of course, it collapses, the hero [Spencer Haynes] saves the heroine [Dorothy Thompson] and all ends well. There's a stretch of comedy by-play through the efforts of a newspaper man ['Peek' Harvey] to run down the deep-dyed villain [Richard Webster] who stalks through the picture. The dashing young hero, however, is a motorcycle cop." (*Variety*, 15 Jun 1927, p25.) *Reporters. Police. Construction materials. Cement.*

DYNAMITE **F2.1483**

Metro-Goldwyn-Mayer Pictures. 13 Dec **1929** [c23 Sep 1929; LP704]. Sd (Movietone); b&w. 35mm. 14 reels, 11,584 ft. [Also si; 10,771 ft.]

Prod-Dir Cecil B. De Mille. *Screenplay* Jeanie Macpherson. *Dial* John Howard Lawson, Gladys Unger, Jeanie Macpherson. *Photog* Peverell Marley. *Art Dir* Cedric Gibbons, Mitchell Leisen. *Film Ed* Anne Bauchens. *Mus* Herbert Stothart. *Theme Song: "How Am I To Know?"* Dorothy Parker, Jack King. *Rec Engr* J. K. Brock, Douglas Shearer. *Asst Dir* Mitchell Leisen. *Gowns* Adrian.

Cast: Conrad Nagel *(Roger Towne)*, Kay Johnson *(Cynthia Crothers)*, Charles Bickford *(Hagon Derk)*, Julia Faye *(Marcia Towne)*, Joel McCrea *(Marco, her boyfriend)*, Muriel McCormac *(Katie Derk)*, Robert Edeson, William Holden, Henry Stockbridge *(Three Wise Fools)*, Leslie Fenton, Barton Hepburn *(Young "Vultures")*, Tyler Brooke *(The Life of the Party)*, Ernest Hilliard, June Nash, Nancy Dover, Neely Edwards, Jerry Zier, Rita LeRoy *(Good Mixers)*, Clarence Burton, James Farley *(officers)*, Robert T. Haines *(The Judge)*, Douglas Frazer Scott *(Bobby)*, Jane Keckley *(his mother)*, Fred Walton *(The Doctor)*, Ynez Seabury, Blanche Craig, Mary Gordon *(neighbors)*, Scott Kolk *(radio announcer)*, Russ Colombo *(Mexican prisoner)*.

Society melodrama. Society girl Cynthia Crothers marries Hagon Derk, a miner sentenced to be executed for murder, to fulfill the terms of her grandfather's will. The miner is found innocent at the last minute, dashing Cynthia's hope of marrying her lover, Roger, a man whose wife refuses to divorce him. Advised by her lawyers that she should live with her husband so as to obtain her money, Cynthia goes to the mining town and lives the life of a miner's wife. There she realizes the futility of her former life when a mine disaster threatens to take both Hagon and Roger away from her. After Roger is killed in a dynamite explosion while helping them escape, Cynthia finds happiness with the miner. *Socialites. Coal miners. Wills. Marriage of convenience. Mine disasters. Capital punishment.*

DYNAMITE ALLEN **F2.1484**

Fox Film Corp. 20 Feb **1921** [c20 Feb 1921; LP16268]. Si; b&w. 35mm. 5 reels.

Pres by William Fox. *Dir* Del Henderson. *Story-Scen* Thomas F. Fallon. *Photog* Charles E. Gilson.

Cast: George Walsh *("Dynamite" Allen)*, Edna Murphy *(Betty Reed)*, Dorothy Allen *(Jenny Allen)*, Carola Parsons *(Sue Bennett)*, Byron Douglas *("Bull" Snide)*, J. Thornton Baston *(Howard Morton)*, Nellie Parker Spaulding *(Mrs. Roger Pitney)*, Mrs. Lottie Ford *(Mrs. Sid Allen)*, Brigham Royce *(Sid Allen)*, Frank Nelson *(Lawyer Smoot)*, Billy Gilbert *("Simp" Hallett)*.

Melodrama. Betty Reed, a blind child, is the sole witness to the murder of mine owner Roger Pitney, and her mistaken testimony convicts Sid Allen, her benefactor. Years later, her sight restored, Betty returns to the mining town and meets with timely aid from the condemned man's son, "Dynamite" Allen, who saves her from kidnapers headed by "Bull" Snide, the guilty one. Allen uncovers the facts about the murder, exposes the perpetrators, and falls in love with Betty. *Coal miners. Blindness. Kidnaping. Murder. Pennsylvania.*

DYNAMITE DAN **F2.1485**

Sunset Productions. *Dist* Aywon Film Corp. 3 Oct **1924** [New York showing]. Si; b&w. 35mm. 5 reels, 4,850 ft.

Pres by Anthony J. Xydias. *Dir-Scen* Bruce Mitchell. *Photog* Bert Longenecker.

Cast: Kenneth McDonald *(Dan)*, Frank Rice *(Boss)*, Boris Karloff *(Tony)*, Eddie Harris *(Sherlock Jones)*, Diana Alden *(Helen)*, Harry Woods *(Brute Lacy)*, Jack Richardson *(fight manager)*, Emily Gerdes, Jack Waltemeyer, Max Ascher, Frank Rice.

Action melodrama. Dan, a gallant hod carrier, finds the heavyweight champ and his manager insulting Helen, Dan's sweetheart and the belle of an exclusive finishing school. Dan's left hook to the jaw floors the champ for the count, and the manager doesn't require half that much. Dan then becomes a pugilist and wins his first 21 fights in the first round by knockouts. Dan is matched with the champ and takes his crown in a brutal match. *Hod carriers. Prizefighters. Fight managers. Boarding schools.*

DYNAMITE SMITH **F2.1486**

Thomas H. Ince Corp. *Dist* Pathé Exchange. 12 Oct **1924** [c8 Sep 1924; LP20552]. Si; b&w. 35mm. 7 reels, 6,400 ft.

Dir Ralph Ince. *Story-Scen* C. Gardner Sullivan. *Photog* Henry Sharp.

Cast: Charles Ray *(Gladstone Smith)*, Jacqueline Logan *("Kitty" Gray)*, Bessie Love *(Violet)*, Wallace Beery *("Slugger" Rourke)*, Lydia Knott *(Aunt Mehitabel)*, S. D. Wilcox *(Marshall)*, Russell Powell *(Colin MacClintock)*, Adelbert Knott *(Dad Gray)*.

Melodrama. Timid San Francisco news reporter Gladstone Smith, assigned to a murder case, sympathizes with the wife of the killer, Rourke, and flees with her to Alaska. When Rourke finds them, Smith escapes with her baby to a settlement where he meets restaurant cashier Kitty Gray. Again Rourke interferes, but Smith manages to capture him in a bear trap and Rourke dies in a dynamite explosion. *Reporters. Cashiers. San Franciscans. Murder. Alaska.*

EAGER LIPS **F2.1487**

Chadwick Pictures. *Dist* First Division Distributors. 15 Jul or 15 Aug **1927.** Si; b&w. 35mm. 7 reels, 6,208 ft.

Dir Wilfred Noy. *Story-Scen* Adele Buffington. *Photog* Ted Tetzlaff, Ernest Miller.

Cast: Pauline Garon *(Mary Lee)*, Betty Blythe *(Paula)*, Gardner James *(Bill Armstrong)*, Jack Richardson *(Tony Tyler)*, Evelyn Selbie *(Miss Lee)*, Fred Warren *(Clancy)*, Erin La Bissoniere *(Charmonta)*.

Drama. Paula, worldly-wise owner of a Coney Island show, promises to take under her protection the innocent daughter of a dying actress. Mary Lee, a dancer, is headstrong, however, and good advice doesn't keep her from falling under the influence of Tony Tyler, the oily, philandering owner of a neighboring show, who promises marriage to the girl. The elder woman does some private vamping of her own, the scoundrel shows his true colors, and the girl returns to Bill Armstrong, who loves her. *Dancers. Philanderers. Coney Island.*

THE EAGLE **F2.1488**

Art Finance Corp. *Dist* United Artists. 8 Nov **1925** [c16 Nov 1925; LP22011]. Si; b&w. 35mm. 7 reels, 6,755 ft.

Pres by John W. Considine, Jr. *Dir* Clarence Brown. *Screenplay* Hans Kraly. *Titl* George Marion, Jr. *Photog* George Barnes, Dev Jennings. *Art Dir* William Cameron Menzies. *Film Ed* Hal C. Kern. *Asst Dir* Charles Dorian. *Cost* Adrian. *Tech Adv* Michael Pleschkoff.

Cast: Rudolph Valentino *(Vladimir Dubrovsky)*, Vilma Banky *(Mascha Troekouroff)*, Louise Dresser *(The Czarina)*, Albert Conti *(Kuschka)*, James Marcus *(Kyrilla Troekouroff)*, George Nichols *(judge)*, Carrie Clark Ward *(Aunt Aurelia)*, Michael Pleschkoff *(Captain Kuschka of the Cossack Guard)*, Spottiswoode Aitken *(Dubrovsky's father)*, Gustav von Seyffertitz, Mario Carillo, Otto Hoffman, Eric Mayne, Jean De Briac.

Romantic comedy. Source: Aleksander Sergeevich Pushkin, "Dubrovsky," in *Prose Tales of Alexander Poushkin* (translated from the Russian by T. Keane; London, 1894). Vladimir Dubrovsky, a young and inexperienced Cossack lieutenant, spurns the amorous advances of the Czarina, Katherine II, and flees to his barracks. There he finds a letter from his father asking him to plead with the czarina to intercede on his behalf lest a neighbor, Kyrilla Troekouroff, seize his estate and castle. Returning to the imperial castle, he discovers that there is a price on his head. Dubrovsky returns home to find his father dying in a peasant's hut; he swears vengeance against Kyrilla and becomes The Eagle—leader of a bandit gang which befriends the poor and oppressed. He enters Kyrilla's home in the guise of his daughter's French tutor. Dubrovsky falls in love with the daughter (Mascha) and drops his plans for revenge. He is arrested by the czarina's troops and sentenced to be executed. Mascha marries him in prison, but the czarina relents, stages a fake execution, and allows the newlyweds to leave the country. *Cossacks. Bandits. Land rights. Revenge. Imposture. Russia. Catherine the Great.*

Note: Working title: *The Lone Eagle.*

THE EAGLE OF THE SEA **F2.1489**

Famous Players–Lasky. *Dist* Paramount Pictures. 18 Oct **1926** [c22 Oct 1926; LP23266]. Si; b&w. 35mm. 8 reels, 7,250 ft.

Pres by Adolph Zukor, Jesse L. Lasky. *Assoc Prod* B. P. Schulberg. *Dir* Frank Lloyd. *Screenplay* Julien Josephson. *Photog* Norbert Brodin.

Cast: Florence Vidor *(Louise Lestron)*, Ricardo Cortez *(Captain Sazarac)*, Sam De Grasse *(Colonel Lestron)*, André de Beranger *(John Jarvis)*, Mitchell Lewis *(Crackley)*, Guy Oliver *(Beluche)*, George Irving *(Gen. Andrew Jackson)*, James Marcus *(Dominique)*, Ervin Renard *(Don Robledo)*, Charles Anderson *(Bohon)*.

Adventure melodrama. Source: Charles Tenney Jackson, *Captain Sazarac* (Indianapolis, 1922). Captain Sazarac—actually the notorious buccaneer Jean Lafitte—saves Louise Lestron from harm while attending a masked ball in New Orleans, being given in honor of Gen. Andrew Jackson. The hall is invaded by John Jarvis and a band of mock pirates, among them Sazarac; Jarvis unmasks the buccaneer, and General Jackson gives him until dawn to leave town. Colonel Lestron, a French patriot, wishes to send the *Seraphine* to rescue Napoleon from St. Helena and invites Lafitte to lead the ship; but he declines and exposes her uncle's plans to Louise. When she is sent away on another ship, Lafitte abducts her, but in New Orleans, Crackley, leader of the insurgents, imprisons Lafitte and his followers. The *Seraphine* is captured by a Spanish man-o'-war on which the colonel has followed; and with the aid of Louise, Lafitte and his men are freed. *Pirates. Naval battles. New Orleans. Jean Lafitte. Andrew Jackson. Napoleon I.*

THE EAGLE'S CLAW **F2.1490**

Charles R. Seeling Productions. *Dist* Aywon Film Corp. Feb **1924.** Si; b&w. 35mm. 5 reels, 4,700 ft.

Dir Charles R. Seeling.

Cast: Big Boy Williams.

Western melodrama. "A mine inherited by the hero makes him the object of repeated attacks on the part of an old enemy. The rightful mine owner, however, triumphs in the end and he wins the girl of his heart." (*Motion Picture News Booking Guide*, 6:24, Apr 1924.) *Miners. Inheritance. Mines.*

THE EAGLE'S FEATHER (Metro Special) **F2.1491**

Metro Pictures. 15 Oct **1923** [c5 Sep 1923; 19401]. Si; b&w. 35mm. 7 reels, 6,500 ft.

Dir Edward Sloman. *Scen* Winifred Dunn. *Story* Katharine Newlin Burt.

Cast: Mary Alden *(Delia Jamieson)*, James Kirkwood *(John Trent)*, Lester Cuneo *(Jeff Carey)*, Elinor Fair *(Martha)*, George Siegmann *(Van Brewen)*, Crauford Kent *(Count De Longe)*, John Elliott *(Parson Winger)*, Charles McHugh *(The Irishman)*, William Orlamond *(The Swede)*, Jim Wang *(Wing Ling)*.

Western romance. Hardy ranchowner Delia Jamieson hires John Trent as her foreman after he befriends her niece Martha. Jeff Carey, jealous of Trent's friendship with Martha, plants some stolen gold in his room and reveals this act to Delia, who visits Trent privately. Trent tries to tell Delia of his love for Martha, but she misunderstands him, thinking he is in love with her. When Delia does understand, however, she sends Martha away and orders the boys to whip Trent. She repents in time, sacrificing herself for her niece's happiness. *Ranch foremen. Aunts. Jealousy. Theft.*

THE EARLY BIRD **F2.1492**

East Coast Films. 1 Jan **1925** [c10 Dec 1924; LP20901]. Si; b&w. 35mm. 7 reels, 6,700 ft.

Pres by C. C. Burr. *Dir* Charles Hines. *Scen* Victor Grandin, Argyll Cambell. *Titl* Ralph Spence. *Story* Richard M. Friel. *Photog* Charles E. Gilson, Neil Sullivan, John Geisel. *Sets* Tec-Art Studios.

Cast: Johnny Hines *(Jimmy Burke)*, Sigrid Holmquist *(Jean Blair)*, Wyndham Standing *(George Fairchild)*, Edmund Breese *(The Great La Tour)*, Maude Turner Gordon *(Jean's aunt)*, Bradley Barker *(Fairchild's accomplice)*, Flora Finch *(Miss Quincy)*, Jack De Lacey *("Flyn")*.

Comedy-melodrama. Jimmy Burke, an idealistic young milkman, organizes the independent deliverers to combat the trust. While on his rounds one morning, he meets Jean Blair, president of the milk trust, who is returning home from a costume party disguised as a maid. Jimmy offers her a ride in his wagon, and they fall in love. Jimmy later discovers that George Fairchild, the manager of the milk guild, is conspiring to fix the price. Jimmy goes to the trust building and finds out that the president of the milk trust is the pretty "domestic" with whom he has fallen in love. He believes that she has been using him, but Jean is innocent of the price-fixing, and she immediately fires Fairchild. Jean then discovers that Fairchild has poisoned the independent milk supply. She alerts Johnny, who destroys the bad milk. Jean is kidnaped by Fairchild's men, who lock her in a refrigerator room. Jimmy saves her from death by an ice-cutting machine and fights off the villains. Jimmy and Jean make plans to merge the independents and the trust by means of their marriage. *Milkmen. Trusts. Food poisoning. Price control. Disguise. Milk.*

EARLY TO WED **F2.1493**

Fox Film Corp. 25 Apr **1926** [c18 Apr 1926; LP22658]. Si; b&w. 35mm. 6 reels, 5,912 ft.

Pres by William Fox. *Dir* Frank Borzage. *Scen* Kenneth B. Clarke. *Photog* Ernest G. Palmer. *Asst Dir* Lew Borzage.

Cast: Matt Moore *(Tommy Carter)*, Kathryn Perry *(Daphne Carter)*, Albert Gran *(Cassius Hayden)*, Julia Swayne Gordon *(Mrs. Hayden)*, Arthur Housman *(Art Nevers)*, Rodney Hildebrand *(Mike Dugan)*, ZaSu Pitts *(Mrs. Dugan)*, Belva McKay *(Mrs. Nevers)*, Ross McCutcheon *(Bill Dugan)*, Harry Bailey *(Pelton Jones)*.

Domestic comedy-drama. Source: Evelyn Campbell, "Splurge," in *McCall's Magazine* (52:20, Nov 1924). Tommy and Daphne Carter, a young married couple, following the advice of a pretentious friend, decide to impress their friends by appearing to be prosperous. Their efforts end in disillusionment when Tommy loses his job and their furniture is collected for nonpayments. However, by feasting a millionaire with a borrowed dinner and accommodating him for the night in a borrowed bed, they gain his sympathy; and he offers the young husband a substantial position. *Millionaires. Appearances. Instalment buying.*

THE EARTH WOMAN **F2.1494**

Mrs. Wallace Reid Productions. *Dist* Associated Exhibitors. 4 Apr **1926** [c29 Mar 1926; LU22542]. Si; b&w. 35mm. 6 reels, 5,830 ft.

Prod Mrs. Wallace Reid. *Dir* Walter Lang. *Story* Norton S. Parker. *Photog* Milton Moore.

Cast: Mary Alden *(Martha Tilden, "The Earth Woman")*, Priscilla Bonner *(Sally, the apple of her eye)*, Russell Simpson *(Ezra Tilden, shiftless "head of the family")*, Carroll Nye *(Steve Tilden, a stalwart son)*, Joe Butterworth *(Joe Tilden, demon of mischief)*, John Carr *(Simon, an accident of birth)*, Johnny Walker *(John Mason, frontier sheriff)*, William Scott *(Mark McWade, profligate son of wealth)*.

Melodrama. When Ezra Tilden, a shiftless husband and notorious alcoholic, is accused of murdering Mark McWade, the community sets out to lynch him, but his courageous and strong-willed wife, Martha, admits to the crime. She tells the crowd how young McWade enticed her daughter, Sally, to a secret rendezvous; warned by Simon, she followed and horsewhipped the scoundrel, who, enraged, confessed to murdering her son, and in a scuffle, McWade was killed. John Mason, the sheriff, who is in love with Sally, appears to take Martha's part, and suddenly, Simon, a halfwitted, deformed lad who has witnessed the struggle and who is dying from a fall, crawls into the crowd and confesses that he shot the villain to save Martha. Sally finds happiness with Sheriff Mason. *Homesteaders. Halfwits. Family life. Lynching. Revenge. Alcoholism.*

EAST IS WEST **F2.1495**

Constance Talmadge Productions. *Dist* Associated First National Pictures. ca15 Oct **1922** [Cleveland and Des Moines premieres; released Oct; c7 Nov 1922; LP18405]. Si; b&w. 35mm. 8 reels, 7,737 ft.

Prod Joseph M. Schenck. *Dir* Sidney Franklin. *Adapt-Scen* Frances Marion. *Photog* Antonio Gaudio. *Art Dir* Stephen Goosson.

Cast: Constance Talmadge *(Ming Toy)*, Edward Burns *(Billy Benson)*, E. A. Warren *(Lo Sang Kee)*, Warner Oland *(Charley Yong)*, Frank Lanning *(Hop Toy)*, Nick De Ruiz *(Chang Lee)*, Nigel Barrie *(Jimmy Potter)*, Lillian Lawrence *(Mrs. Benson)*, Winter Hall *(Mr. Benson)*, Jim Wang *(proprietor of love boat)*.

Melodrama. Source: Samuel Shipman and John B. Hymer, *East Is West; a Comedy in Three Acts and a Prologue* (New York, 1924). Ming Toy, the eldest of Hop Toy's many children, is rescued from the auction block by Billy Benson and sent to the United States in the care of Lo Sang Kee. There she continues her interest in western ways and attracts the attention of a powerful Chinatown figure, Charley Yong. When Charley Yong demands the hand of Ming Toy, she is again rescued by Benson. There ensues a chase, Billy takes Ming Toy to his home and declares his love, and Charley Yong acquiesces when it is revealed that Ming Toy, as a baby, was kidnaped from American parents. *Chinese. Kidnaping. San Francisco—Chinatown.*

EAST IS WEST **F2.1496**

Universal Pictures. 23 Oct **1930** [c11 Oct 1930; LP1628]. Sd (Movietone); b&w. 35mm. 8 reels, 6,683 ft.

Pres by Carl Laemmle. *Assoc Prod* E. M. Asher. *Dir* Monta Bell. *Screenplay-Adtl Dial* Tom Reed. *Adapt* Winifred Eaton. *Photog* Jerry Ash. *Spec Eff Photog* Frank H. Booth. *Film Ed* Harry Marker. *Rec Engr* C. Roy Hunter.

Cast: Lupe Velez *(Ming Toy)*, Lew Ayres *(Billy Benson)*, Edward G. Robinson *(Charlie Yong)*, Mary Forbes *(Mrs. Benson)*, E. Alyn Warren *(Lo Sang Kee)*, Henry Kolker *(Mr. Benson)*, Tetsu Komai *(Hop Toy)*, Edgar Norton *(Thomas)*, Charles Middleton *(Dr. Fredericks)*.

Romantic drama. Source: Samuel Shipman and John B. Hymer, *East Is West, a Comedy in Three Acts and a Prologue* (New York, 1924). The plot is essentially the same as that of the 1922 Constance Talmadge Production of the same title, q. v. *Chinese. Kidnaping. San Francisco—Chinatown.*

Note: Also made in a Spanish-language version.

EAST LYNNE **F2.1497**

Hugo Ballin Productions. *Dist* W. W. Hodkinson Corp. Mar **1921.** Si; b&w. 35mm. 7 reels, 6,634 ft.

Dir-Scen Hugo Ballin. *Photog* William S. Adams.

Cast: Edward Earle *(Archibald Carlyle)*, Mabel Ballin *(Isabel Vane)*, Gladys Coburn *(Barbara Hare)*, Gilbert Rooney *(Richard Hare)*, Henry G. Sell *(Francis Levison)*, Nellie Parker Spaulding *(Miss Cornelia)*, Doris Sheerin *(Afy Hallijohn)*.

Drama. Source: Mrs. Henry Wood, *East Lynne* (1861). Happily married to Archibald Carlyle and the proud mother of a son, Isabel Vane leads a life of bliss at the family estate, East Lynne, until she suspects her husband of infidelity with Barbara Hare, who has come to East Lynne to seek Archibald's legal advice. Isabel succumbs to the persuasions of Francis Levison, and she leaves her family to marry him. When Levison abandons Isabel and their daughter, she sets out for East Lynne to ask Archibald's forgiveness but is seriously injured in a train wreck. Finally arriving at her destination, Isabel dies before she learns that Archibald—believing her dead—has married Barbara Hare. *Marriage. Infidelity. Bigamy. Train wrecks.*

EAST LYNNE **F2.1498**

Fox Film Corp. 23 Nov **1925** [c9 Aug 1925; LP21835]. Si; b&w. 35mm. 9 reels, 8,975 ft.

Pres by William Fox. *Dir* Emmett Flynn. *Adapt* Lenore J. Coffee, Emmett Flynn. *Photog* Ernest G. Palmer.

Cast: Alma Rubens *(Lady Isabel)*, Edmund Lowe *(Archibald Carlyle)*, Lou Tellegen *(Sir Francis Levison)*, Frank Keenan *(Chief Justice Hare)*, Marjorie Daw *(Barbara Hare)*, Leslie Fenton *(Richard Hare)*, Belle Bennett *(Afy Hallijohn)*, Paul Panzer *(Mr. Hallijohn)*, Lydia Knott *(Mrs. Hare)*, Harry Seymour *(Mr. Dill)*, Richard Headrick *(Willie Carlyle)*, Virginia Marshall *(Little Isabel)*, Martha Mattox *(Cornelia Carlyle)*, Eric Mayne *(Earl of Mount-Severn)*.

Melodrama. Source: Mrs. Henry Wood, *East Lynne* (1861). When Archibald Carlyle, a wealthy young Englishman, buys the debt-ridden estate of Lord Mount-Severn, he persuades the late lord's daughter, Lady Isabel, to marry him. Years pass. A villager (the father of a wayward girl) is murdered, and Richard Hare, the brother of Barbara, Archibald's onetime sweetheart, is accused. Barbara meets Archibald privately to seek his intercession on her brother's behalf, and Sir Francis persuades Isabel that the two are lovers. Francis and Isabel go abroad together, but Francis soon casts her off, and Isabel returns to England, being reported dead in an automobile accident. Archibald marries Barbara. One of Isabel's children becomes ill, and, disguised as a nurse, she goes to him and saves his life. Isabel herself becomes ill and dies, being recognized, at last, by Archibald, who keeps her secret. *Landed gentry. Nurses. Nobility. Brother-sister relationship. Motherhood. Marriage. Disguise. Village life. England.*

EAST OF BROADWAY **F2.1499**

Encore Pictures. *Dist* Associated Exhibitors. 23 Nov **1924** [c11 Dec 1924; LU20888]. Si; b&w. 35mm. 6 reels, 5,785 ft.

Dir William K. Howard. *Adapt-Scen* Paul Schofield. *Photog* Lucien Andriot.

Cast: Owen Moore *(Peter Mullaney)*, Marguerite De La Motte *(Judy McNulty)*, Mary Carr *(Mrs. Morrisey)*, Eddie Gribbon *(Danny McCabe)*, Francis McDonald *(Professor Mario)*, Betty Francisco *(Diana Morgan)*, George Nichols *(Officer Gaffney)*, Ralph Lewis *(Commissioner)*.

Comedy-melodrama. Source: Richard Connell, "Tropic of Capricorn," in *The Sins of Monsieur Pettipon, and other Humorous Tales* (New York, 1922). Peter Mullaney, the son of Irish immigrants living on the East Side of Manhattan, has one ambition in life: to become one of New York's Finest. He goes to the Police Training School and is about to be rejected for not meeting the height qualification when he demonstrates his prowess in a fight. The commissioner then decides to give Peter a chance to make the force, if he scores well on the written examination. Peter declares the Tropic of Capricorn to be in the Bronx and fails to pass; the commissioner, however, allows him to wear the uniform for one night in order not to disappoint Peter's girl, Judy McNulty. Walking the beat with Officer Gaffney, he becomes involved in preventing a robbery, during which Gaffney is shot. Peter comes to his aid and captures the robbers, being himself hurt in the process. In the hospital, the commissioner, on account of his bravery, pins a shield on him, and Peter and Judy make plans to be married. *Irish. Police. Robbery. New York City—East Side.*

EAST OF SUEZ **F2.1500**

Famous Players–Lasky. *Dist* Paramount Pictures. 12 Jan **1925** [13 Jan 1925; LP21010]. Si; b&w. 35mm. 7 reels, 6,716 ft.

Pres by Adolph Zukor, Jesse L. Lasky. *Dir* Raoul Walsh. *Scen* Sada Cowan. *Photog* Victor Milner.

Cast: Pola Negri *(Daisy Forbes)*, Edmund Lowe *(George Tevis)*, Rockliffe Fellowes *(Harry Anderson)*, Noah Beery *(British Consul)*, Kamiyama Sojin *(Lee Tai)*, Mrs. Wong Wing *(Amah)*, Florence Regnart *(Sylvia Knox)*, Charles Requa *(Harold Knox)*, E. H. Calvert *(Sidney Forbes)*.

Melodrama. Source: William Somerset Maugham, *East of Suez; a Play in Seven Scenes* (London, 1922). After being educated in England, Daisy Forbes returns to China, the country of her birth, and discovers that her father has recently died and that she has become a social outcast, owing to the public revelation that the oriental nurse who raised her was actually her mother. Daisy is in love with George Tevis, the nephew of the British consul, but she is disappointed by George when he is persuaded by his uncle to renounce her in favor of a diplomatic career. Lee Tai, a sinister mandarin, kidnaps Daisy with the aid of drugs and hypnotism; she is rescued by Harry Anderson, a rotter whom she soon marries out of desperation. When Anderson discovers that Daisy is an ostracized halfcaste, he bitterly regrets their marriage. Not knowing of the marriage, George searches her out, only to find her a married woman. Anderson forbids George to see Daisy again, but George defies the ban and meets her at her house to say goodby. Before he can shoot George, Anderson drinks wine poisoned by Lee Tai—and dies. Tevis takes Daisy back to England, and Lee Tai is executed according to Chinese law. *Halfcastes. Narcotics. Hypnotism. Kidnaping. Capital punishment. China. England. Great Britain—Diplomatic and consular service.*

EAST SIDE SADIE **F2.1501**

Dist Worldart Film Co. 20 May **1929** [New York showing]. Mus score & talking sequences; b&w. 35mm. 6 reels, 5,500-6,100 ft. [Also si.]

Dir-Story Sidney M. Goldin. *Titl* Sam Citen. *Photog* Frank Zucker. *Film Ed* Sam Citen.

Cast: Bertina Goldin, Jack Ellis, Boris Rosenthal, Lucia Backus Seger, Abe Sinkoff, John Halliday, Al Stanley, Maechivinko, Mark Schweid.

Drama. A Jewish sweatshop seamstress contributes her meager earnings to her boyfriend's college education, but he falls into the hands of a marriage broker, who matches him with a wealthy girl. Given a beating by the seamstress' brother just before the wedding, the boy awakens to the girl's sacrifices and is reunited with her. (Sources are somewhat confusing about the story line. The boy may be Irish and have a Jewish stepfather. There is also a vague reference to a comedy scene on a tenement roof involving some Italians. Sound sequences include singing children, a cantor singing a wedding prayer, and some shouting during the wedding.) *Jews. Italians. Irish. Seamstresses. Marriage brokers. Education. Brother-sister relationship. Sweatshops. Weddings. New York City—East Side.*

EAST SIDE, WEST SIDE F2.1502
Fox Film Corp. 9 Oct **1927** [c9 Oct 1927; LP24479]. Si; b&w. 35mm. 9 reels, 8,154 ft.
Pres by William Fox. *Dir-Adapt* Allan Dwan. *Photog* George Webber. *Asst Dir* Arthur Cozine.
Cast: George O'Brien *(John Breen)*, Virginia Valli *(Becka Lipvitch)*, J. Farrell MacDonald *(Pug Malone)*, Dore Davidson *(Channon Lipvitch)*, Sonia Nodalsky *(Mrs. Lipvitch)*, June Collyer *(Josephine)*, John Miltern *(Gerrit Rantoul)*, Holmes Herbert *(Gilbert Van Horn)*, Frank Dodge *(Judge Kelly)*, Dan Wolheim *(Grogan)*, Johnny Dooley *(one of Grogan's gang)*, John Kearney *(policeman)*, Edward Garvey *(second)*, Frank Allsworth *("Flash")*, William Fredericks *(Breen)*, Jean Armour *(Mrs. Breen)*, Gordon McRae, Harold Levett *(engineers)*.
Society melodrama. Source: Felix Riesenberg, *East Side, West Side* (New York, 1927). After his mother and stepfather have been killed in a barge accident, John Breen is rescued from some East Side toughs by the Lipvitches. He remains in the city, determined to find his real father, who rejected his mother; and after some success as a prizefighter, he is virtually adopted by Van Horn, a millionaire who actually is his father. Becka Lipvitch renounces his love when Pug Malone advises her that their marriage would endanger his future. John becomes engaged to Josephine, Van Horn's ward, and rejects the boxing ring for an engineering career. While returning from Europe, Van Horn is drowned when his ship sinks; Josephine and Rantoul, finding consolation in each other's love, are rescued and are married. Meanwhile, John rescues Becka from Flash, a nightclub owner and narcotics peddler, and they are reconciled. *Millionaires. Boxers. Engineers. Filial relations. Social classes. Narcotics. New York City—East Side. New York City—West Side. Shipwrecks.*

EAST SIDE—WEST SIDE F2.1503
Principal Pictures. Apr or 30 Jun **1923** [c26 Dec 1923; LP19760]. Si; b&w. 35mm. 6 reels, ca6,000 ft.
Pres by Irving Cummings. *Prod-Dir* Irving Cummings. *Adapt* Hope Loring, Louis D. Lighton. *Photog* Arthur Martinelli.
Cast: Kenneth Harlan *(Duncan Van Norman)*, Eileen Percy *(Lory James)*, Maxine Elliott Hicks *(Kit Lamson)*, Lucille Hutton *(Eunice Potter)*, Lucille Ward *(Mrs. Cornelia Van Norman)*, John Prince *(Paget)*, Betty May *(Amy Van Norman)*, Charles Hill Mailes *(Dr. Ernest Shepley)*, Wally Van *(Skiddy Stillman)*.
Drama. Source: Leighton Osmun and Henry Hull, *East Side—West Side* (unpublished play). Wealthy young author Duncan Van Norman falls in love with his secretary, Lory James, a poor girl from New York's East Side. Van Norman's socially conscious mother dismisses Lory when she hears of the budding romance, but the unhappiness she causes the household makes Mrs. Van Norman seek out Lory to ask her forgiveness. *Authors. Secretaries. Social classes. Motherhood. New York City—East Side. New York City—West Side.*

EASY COME, EASY GO F2.1504
Paramount Famous Lasky Corp. 21 Apr **1928** [c21 Apr 1928; LP25171]. Si; b&w. 35mm. 6 reels, 5,364 ft.
Pres by Adolph Zukor, Jesse L. Lasky. *Dir* Frank Tuttle. *Scen* Florence Ryerson. *Titl* George Marion, Jr. *Photog* Edward Cronjager. *Film Ed* Otto Lovering. *Rec Engr* R. H. Quick.
Cast: Richard Dix *(Robert Parker)*, Nancy Carroll *(Babs Quayle)*, Charles Sellon *(Jim Bailey)*, Frank Currier *(Mr. Quayle)*, Arnold Kent *(Winthrop)*, Christian J. Frank, Joseph J. Franz *(detectives)*, Guy Oliver *(conductor)*.
Farce. Source: Owen Davis, *Easy Come, Easy Go; a Farce in Three Acts* (New York, c1926). Robert Parker, an honest young man temporarily out of work, innocently becomes the accomplice of Jim Bailey, a veteran thief. When he learns the truth, Parker attempts to shield Bailey and at the same time to return the stolen payroll to Mr. Quayle, president of the robbed bank. *Bankers. Thieves. Unemployment. Bank robberies.*

EASY GOING F2.1505
Action Pictures. *Dist* Weiss Brothers Artclass Pictures. 22 May **1926.** Si; b&w. 35mm. 5 reels, 4,900 ft.
Dir Richard Thorpe.
Cast: Buddy Roosevelt.
Western melodrama. "Wealthy girl is saved from machinations of suave villain by son of her lawyer. Develops romance with son. Mountain resort locale." (*Motion Picture News Booking Guide,* 11:27, Oct 1926.) *Lawyers. Wealth. Resorts.*

EASY GOING GORDON F2.1506
Paul Gerson Pictures. 6 Aug **1925** [New York State license]. Si; b&w. 35mm. 5 reels.
Pres by B. Berger. *Dir* Duke Worne. *Scen* Grover Jones.
Cast: Richard Holt *(Gordon Palmer)*, Kathryn McGuire *(Aileen Merton)*, Gordon Russell *(Slung Williams)*, Fernando Galvez *(Beef O'Connell)*, Roy Cushing *(Judson)*, Harris Gordon *(George Elvin)*.
Action melodrama. Gordon Palmer, the son of a rich man, is the epitome of sloth until he and his sweetheart are held up by two thieves who take, among other valuables, her engagement ring. Gordon, aroused at last from lethargy, pursues the men and scares them into returning the jewelry. When his father is later faced with financial ruin, Gordon saves the family business by stealing proxies from his father's partners with the help of the two crooks who once robbed him. Gordon's unorthodox business methods work, and his father is saved from ruin. Gordon then weds Aileen. *Idle rich. Business management. Robbery. Documentation.*

EASY MONEY F2.1507
Reol Productions. 29 Mar **1922** [New York State license application; c3, 6 Mar 1922; LU17737]. Si; b&w. 35mm. 6 reels, 5,500 ft.
Copyright Auth J. Rufus Hill.
Cast: Edna Morton, H. L. Pryor, Inez Clough, Sherman H. Dudley, Jr., Alex K. Shannon, Percy Verwayen.
Comedy-melodrama. Source: J. Rufus Brown, unidentified story. Andy Simpson, constable, blacksmith and all-round mechanic of Millbrook, a thrifty little southern town, is looked upon as slow, plodding, and lacking in ambition by all save Margie Watkins, his sweetheart and daughter of the bank president. Margie, however, becomes attracted to J. Overton Tighe (a partner of James Bradford, notorious promoter of "wildcat" investments), who is newly arrived in town in an expensive car. Despite Andy's warnings, the townspeople eagerly buy shares in a phony stock promoted by Tighe. Mrs. Watkins even persuades her husband to invest some of the bank's funds in the enterprise. Even after he finds conclusive evidence, Andy hesitates to arrest Tighe, for an arrest would mean the ruin of Margie's father. Margie, apparently disregarding Andy's advice, continues her affair with Tighe, and they become engaged. Tighe finds oil on Andy's land and buys it for a song. Andy finally exposes Tighe's real business in Millbrook (which is more serious than swindling), arrests Tighe, and in the end turns the tables on the shrewd promoter and himself gets the easy money. *Swindlers. Constables. Blacksmiths. Mechanics. Bankers. Speculation. Smalltown life. United States—South.*

EASY MONEY F2.1508
Harry J. Brown Productions. *Dist* Rayart Pictures. 1 Jan **1925.** Si; b&w. 35mm. 6 reels, 6,067 ft.
Pres by W. Ray Johnston. *Dir* Albert Rogell. *Scen* Marion Jackson. *Story* Sam Mintz. *Photog* Ross Fisher.
Cast: Cullen Landis *(Bud Parsons)*, Mildred Harris *(Blanche Amory)*, Mary Carr *(Mrs. Hale)*, Crauford Kent *(Lewis)*, Gertrude Astor, Gladys Walton, Rex Lease, David Kirby, Joseph Swickard, Wilfred Lucas.
Melodrama. A boy, who turns to larceny to satisfy the expensive whims of a cabaret dancer, is apprehended by the authorities. He then becomes involved with a crooked attorney, who persuades him to impersonate the missing heir of a wealthy family. The boy falls in love with the beautiful daughter of the family. The real son returns and is framed for burglary. The boy confesses to his deception and is forgiven by the family. The real son is restored to his rightful place, and the boy marries the girl. *Dancers. Lawyers. Theft. Impersonation. Inheritance.*

EASY PICKINGS F2.1509
First National Pictures. 20 Feb **1927** [c7 Feb 1927; LP23636]. Si; b&w. 35mm. 6 reels, 5,400 ft.
Prod Frank Griffin. *Dir* George Archainbaud. *Scen* Louis Stevens. *Auth? (see note)* William A. Burton. *Photog* Charles Van Enger.
Cast: Anna Q. Nilsson *(Mary Ryan)*, Kenneth Harlan *(Peter Van Horne)*, Philo McCullough *(Stewart)*, Billy Bevan *(The Detective)*, Jerry Miley *(Tony)*, Charles Sellon *(Dr. Naylor)*, Zack Williams *(Remus)*, Gertrude Howard *(Mandy)*.
Mystery melodrama. Source: Paul A. Cruger, *Easy Pickings, a Mystery-Comedy in Three Acts* (San Francisco, 1929). Simeon Van Horne is poisoned by Stewart, his lawyer, who hopes to get a part of the estate to be divided between young Peter Van Horne and Dolores, Peter's cousin. Knowing that Dolores is dead, Stewart, who catches Mary Ryan burglarizing the Van Horne home, induces her to pose as Dolores. Mary's

companion, Tony, is pulled into a secret passage; Van Horne's body disappears; Remus, the colored servant, sees a black-hooded figure; the lights go off and on; and a detective is the object of many hoaxes perpetrated by the mysterious figure. When the figure (played alternately by Tony and Dr. Naylor) discloses the features of Van Horne, he frightens a confession from Stewart, then discloses himself as Peter's "chauffeur." Peter discovers that Mary deserves a part of the fortune and convinces her of his love. *Detectives. Lawyers. Thieves. Murder. Imposture. Inheritance.*

Note: Copyright records also credit William A. Burton with authorship.

THE EASY ROAD **F2.1510**

Famous Players–Lasky. *Dist* Paramount Pictures. 13 Feb **1921** [New York premiere; released Feb; c14 Dec 1920; LP15938]. Si; b&w. 35mm. 5 reels, 4,982 ft.

Dir Tom Forman. *Scen* Beulah Marie Dix. *Photog* Harry Perry. *Asst Dir* Harold Schwartz.

Cast: Thomas Meighan *(Leonard Fayne)*, Gladys George *(Isabel Grace)*, Grace Goodall *(Katherine Dare)*, Arthur Carew *(Heminway)*, Lila Lee *(Ella Klotz)*, Laura Anson *(Minnie Baldwin)*, Viora Daniels *(Laura)*.

Melodrama. Source: Blair Hall, "Easy Street," in *Snappy Stories*. Leonard Fayne, sailor and novelist, marries wealthy Isabel Grace. Isabel's attitude and her silly associates hamper Leonard's creative faculties. On the suggestion of Katherine Dare, a sculptress friend, Isabel goes to Europe, leaving her husband with instructions to use her bank account. He refuses her money, gradually drifts downward, and is on the verge of suicide when he meets Ella Klotz, a waif, who is about to kill herself because she is going blind. He takes Ella to his studio to care for her, and believing he owes his life to her, he once again begins to write. Meanwhile, Isabel, who is being pursued by Heminway, an old suitor, realizes her love for her husband and returns from Europe. Heminway tries unsuccessfully to keep the couple apart. *Authors. Waifs. Marriage. Blindness.*

EASY STREET **F2.1511**

Micheaux Pictures. 1 Aug **1930** [New York State license]. Sd? b&w. 35mm. 5 reels, 4,974 ft.

Cast: Richard B. Harrison, Alice B. Russell.

Melodrama(?). No information about the precise nature of this film has been found. *Negro life.*

EBB TIDE **F2.1512**

Famous Players–Lasky. *Dist* Paramount Pictures. 19 Nov **1922** [New York premiere; released 4 Dec; c8 Nov 1922; LP18457]. Si; b&w. 35mm. 8 reels, 7,336 ft.

Pres by Jesse L. Lasky. *Prod Supv* Tom Geraghty. *Dir* George Melford. *Adapt-Scen* Waldemar Young. *Photog* Bert Glennon.

Cast: Lila Lee *(Ruth Attwater)*, James Kirkwood *(Robert Herrick)*, Raymond Hatton *(J. L. Huish)*, George Fawcett *(Captain Davis)*, Noah Beery *(Richard Attwater)*, Jacqueline Logan *(Tehura)*.

Adventure melodrama. Source: Robert Louis Stevenson and Lloyd Osbourne, *The Ebb-Tide; a Trio and Quartette* (1894). Captain Davis, Robert Herrick, and J. L. Huish—three failures on a derelict ship—visit an island on which pearl concessionaire Richard Attwater and his daughter, Ruth, are the only white inhabitants. Davis and Huish plan to steal Attwater's pearls while Herrick falls in love with Ruth, but they all meet Attwater's wrath when he becomes aware of their intentions. Huish is consumed in flames; a mast crushes Attwater; Herrick and Ruth escape both a burning ship and an octopus attack. *Pearl fisheries. Papeete. South Sea Islands. Octopi.*

EDEN AND RETURN **F2.1513**

Hunt Stromberg Productions. *Dist* R-C Pictures. 25 Dec **1921** [c25 Dec 1921; LP17456]. Si; b&w. 35mm. 5 reels, 4,600 ft.

Dir William A. Seiter. *Scen* Beatrice Van. *Story* Ralph E. Renaud. *Photog* Bert Cann. *Art Dir* W. L. Heywood. *Asst Dir* Ralph Walters.

Cast: Doris May *(Betty Baylock)*, Emmett King *(Robert Baylock)*, Margaret Livingston *(Connie Demarest)*, Earl Metcalfe *(John [Jack] Grey)*, Margaret Campbell *(Aunt Sarah)*, Buddy Post *(Sam Padgett)*, Frank Kingsley *(Dempsey Chubbs)*.

Comedy-drama. After buying a wishing rug from a peddler, Betty wishes for a dark-haired, blue-eyed man, hoping to rid herself of three pestiferous suitors. When her father decrees that she marry immediately, instead of choosing among them she dismisses them all. Her father becomes furious when she becomes friendly with Jack Grey, who has squandered a fortune, and when they are married he ousts them, ordering Jack to earn back the money he has lost. Learning that Baylock writes stock tips on his shirt cuffs, Jack copies the notations and makes a fortune on the market. He offers Baylock a tip on the stock, and after he admits his methods, there is a reconciliation. *Fatherhood. Courtship. Speculation. Stock market.*

THE EDUCATION OF ELIZABETH **F2.1514**

Famous Players–Lasky. *Dist* Paramount Pictures. 16 Jan **1921** [c28 Dec 1920; LP15980]. Si; b&w. 35mm. 5 reels, 4,705 ft.

Dir Edward Dillon. *Scen* Elmer Harris. *Photog* George Folsey.

Cast: Billie Burke *(Elizabeth Banks)*, Lumsden Hare *(Thomas)*, Edith Sharpe *(Lucy Fairfax)*, Donald Cameron *(Harry)*, Frederick Burton *(Middleton)*.

Comedy. Source: Roy Horniman, unidentified play. A follies girl is courted by the son of an aristocratic family. The presence of this rough and ready showgirl in such sedate surroundings creates amusing situations. She brings with her to the household a sympathetic pet—a goldfish—to which she confides her troubles. When her wealthy suitor is called away on business, she learns of his younger brother, who, though he appears to be absorbed in his books, is more her type. She transforms him into her ideal and alienates the elder brother; her own wit brings about a happy ending in her prospective marriage to the younger brother. *Brothers. Chorus girls. Aristocrats. Courtship. Follies. Goldfish.*

THE EINSTEIN THEORY OF RELATIVITY **F2.1515**

Premier Productions. 8 Feb **1923** [trade review; c25 Apr 1923; MP2271]. Si; b&w. 35mm. 4 reels, 4,000 ft. [Also 2 reels.]

Pres by Edwin Miles Fadman. *Supv* S. F. Nicolai, H. W. Kornblum, C. Bueck. *Drawings & Animated Diagrams* Max Fleischer. *Film Ed* Garrett P. Serviss.

Educational film. An attempt to translate Einstein's Theory of Relativity into nonscientific terms with the use of illustrations. By using simple parallels from everyday life, the theory regarding the relativity of time, space, and distance is explained. One illustration demonstrates that if a man aboard a ship walks toward the stern at the same speed the ship is moving away from the shore, the man is standing still in relation to the shore but moving backward in relation to the boat. The fourth dimension and the bending of light rays are briefly touched upon. *Theory of Relativity. Albert Einstein.*

Note: The 2-reel version was for commercial theater use; 4-reel version, use in schools and colleges.

EK *see* **ONE GLORIOUS DAY**

THE ELEVENTH HOUR **F2.1516**

Fox Film Corp. 20 Jul **1923** [New York premiere; released 2 Sep; c1 Aug 1923; LP19412]. Si; b&w. 35mm. 7 reels, 6,820 ft.

Pres by William Fox. *Dir* Bernard J. Durning. *Scen* Louis Sherwin. *Photog* Don Short.

Cast: Shirley Mason *(Barbara Hackett)*, Charles Jones *(Brick McDonald)*, Richard Tucker *(Herbert Glenville)*, Alan Hale *(Prince Stefan de Bernie)*, Walter McGrail *(Dick Manley)*, June Elvidge *(Estelle Hackett)*, Fred Kelsey *(The Submarine Commander)*, Nigel De Brulier *(Mordecai Newman)*, Fred Kohler *(Barbara's uncle)*.

Action melodrama. Source: Lincoln J. Carter, "The Eleventh Hour" (unpublished and uncopyrighted play). Mad Prince Stefan intends to take over the world as soon as he acquires a new explosive developed at a plant owned by Barbara Hackett. By blackmailing them, Stefan wins the cooperation of Barbara's uncle and the dishonest executive, Glenville, who would like to marry Barbara. Brick McDonald, an employee of Prince Stefan's, wins Barbara's confidence and after many complications—wild chases involving motor boats, airplanes, and submarines; fights with lions; and a rescue from a threatened descent into a pit of molten steel—he frustrates Prince Stefan's plans and reveals himself as the Chief of the U. S. Secret Service. *Royalty. Explosives. Secret service. Blackmail. Insanity. Chases.*

ELLA CINDERS **F2.1517**

John McCormick Productions. *Dist* First National Pictures. 6 Jun **1926** [c27 May 1926; LP22779]. Si; b&w. 35mm. 7 reels, 6,540 ft.

Pres by John McCormick. *Dir* Alfred E. Green. *Scen* Frank Griffin, Mervyn LeRoy. *Titl* George Marion, Jr. *Photog* Arthur Martinelli. *Art Dir* E. J. Shulter. *Film Ed* Robert J. Kern.

Cast: Colleen Moore *(Ella Cinders)*, Lloyd Hughes *(Waite Lifter)*, Vera Lewis *("Ma" Cinders)*, Doris Baker *(Lotta Pill)*, Emily Gerdes *(Prissy*

Pill), Mike Donlin *(Film Studio Gateman)*, Jed Prouty *(The Mayor)*, Jack Duffy *(The Fire Chief)*, Harry Allen *(The Photographer)*, D'Arcy Corrigan *(The Editor)*, Alfred E. Green *(The Director)*, Harry Langdon, E. H. Calvert, Chief Yowlache, Russell Hopton.

Romantic comedy. Source: William Conselman and Charles Plumb, "Cinderella in the Movies," a syndicated comic strip. Ella, who slaves in the Cinders household to ensure the comfort of her stepsisters Lotta and Prissy Pill, has only one joy in life—the smile of Waite Lifter, the local iceman. When a movie contest is announced, Ella has herself photographed as an entry; she goes to the ball dressed in one of Lotta's gowns and her stepmother's piano scarf as a drape but is dragged home by an indignant Ma Cinders. They are all disgusted when Ella wins the contest and is sent to Hollywood. There she finds herself jobless, and after a chase with a gateman, she gains entry to a studio and disrupts numerous productions. Finally, caught in a fire scene and thinking it is real, Ella is awarded a contract for her splendid acting. Waite, who has promised to marry Ella, leaves for Hollywood, claiming he is broke (he is really wealthy), and is happily united with Ella in a desert town. *Drudges. Stepsisters. Stepmothers. Actors. Icemen. Talent contests. Motion pictures. Hollywood.*

ELOPE IF YOU MUST **F2.1518**

Fox Film Corp. 2 Apr **1922** [c2 Apr 1922; LP17823]. Si; b&w. 35mm. 5 reels, 4,995 ft.

Pres by William Fox. *Dir* C. R. Wallace. *Scen* Joseph Franklin Poland. *Photog* Otto Brautigan.

Cast: Eileen Percy *(Nancy Moore)*, Edward Sutherland *(Jazz Hennessy)*, Joseph Bennett *(Willie Weems)*, Mildred Davenport *(Elizabeth Magruder)*, Mary Huntress *(Mrs. Magruder)*, Harvey Clarke *(Mr. Magruder)*, Larry Steers *(Warren Holt)*.

Farce. Source: E. J. Rath, *Elope If You Must* (New York, 1926). Nancy Moore and Jazz Hennessy, two members of a theatrical troupe, are stranded in a small town and board the train for the city. En route Nancy meets Mr. Magruder, who offers her $10,000 if she will prevent his daughter Elizabeth from marrying Willie Weems and bring about her marriage to Warren Holt. While engaged as a maid in his home, Nancy overhears Elizabeth's plans to elope with Willie. Jazz abducts Willie in his car and leaves him in the country, but the irrepressible Willie returns. Not until he is locked in the attic are the barnstormers able to get Elizabeth and Holt together for a marriage ceremony. *Theatrical troupes. Marriage. Elopement.*

EMBARRASSING MOMENTS (Universal-Jewel) **F2.1519**

Universal Pictures. 2 Feb **1930** [c8 Oct 1929; LP757]. Sd (Movietone); b&w. 35mm. 6 reels, 5,230 ft. [Also si; 5,821 ft.]

Pres by Carl Laemmle. *Dir* William James Craft. *Scen* Earl Snell, Gladys Lehman. *Titl* Albert De Mond. *Story* Earl Snell. *Camera* Arthur Todd. *Film Ed* Duncan Mansfield. *Rec Engr* C. Roy Hunter.

Cast: Reginald Denny *(Thaddeus Cruikshank)*, Merna Kennedy *(Marion Fuller)*, Otis Harlan *(Adam Fuller)*, William Austin *(Jasper Hickson)*, Virginia Sale *(Aunt Prudence)*, Greta Granstedt *(Betty Black)*, Mary Foy *(Mrs. Hickson)*.

Comedy-drama. Marion Fuller returns home after studying art in New York City and finds that her Aunt Prudence and her fiancé, Jasper Hickson, are suspicious of the influence of city life on her. Weary of her fiancé's attitude, she tells her family that she has engaged in a "trial marriage" in New York with Thaddeus Cruikshank, a name she remembers as the author of a book she has read. Her father wires Cruikshank, demanding that he come to Fullervale, and thinking that an imposter is using his name, Thaddeus obeys the summons; finding Marion to his liking, he is not disturbed when Fuller insists upon an immediate marriage. Complications ensue as the family tries to keep them apart until after the ceremony. Marion wilfully declines to marry him, but Thaddeus "compromises" her to such an extent that she consents. *Students. Authors. Aunts. Marriage—Trial. Smalltown life. Art.*

EMBLEMS OF LOVE **F2.1520**

Progress Productions. 8 Feb **1924** [New York State license]. Si; b&w. 35mm. 7 reels, 6,800 ft.

Cast: Jack Drumier, Jane Jennings, Charles Delaney, Grace Cunard, Jane Thomas, Bernard Siegel, James West, Jack Driscoll, John Flowers.

Melodrama(?). No information about the nature of this film has been found.

EMPIRE BUILDERS **F2.1521**

Phil Goldstone. *Dist* Capital Film Co. Mar **1924** [scheduled release]. Si; b&w. 35mm. 5 reels.

Cast: Snowy Baker.

Drama(?). No precise information about the nature of this film has been found. As submitted for licensing, the film included sequences showing shooting of British officers and the beating of a Negro slave. *Slavery.*

THE EMPTY CRADLE **F2.1522**

State Pictures. *Dist* Truart Film Corp. 1 May **1923** [c18 Mar 1923; LP18789]. Si; b&w. 35mm. 7 reels, 6,984 ft.

Dir Burton King.

Cast: Mary Alden *(Alice Larkin)*, Harry T. Morey *(John Larkin)*, Mickey Bennett *(Buddy Larkin)*, Edward Quinn *(Frankie Larkin)*, Helen Rowland *(Baby Louise)*, Coit Albertson *(Robert Lewis)*, Madeline La Varre *(Ethel)*, Rica Allen *(Martha Blake)*.

Domestic melodrama. Source: Leota Morgan, "Cheating Wives" (publication undetermined). *Disowned by her family for marrying John Larkin, Alice lives in poverty with her husband and children. Wealthy Ethel Lewis, on the other hand, is separated from her husband because she refuses to have children. Ethel sends a lawyer to Alice with the offer of $50,000 in exchange for the adoption of one of her children (Louise) and, when Alice reluctantly accepts, tells her husband that the child is their own. Alice visits the Lewis home frequently to be near her daughter, thereby rekindling Robert Lewis' old interest in her. In his jealousy, John shoots at Robert but hits Louise. Both women confess their actions.* At this point Alice awakes to find this all a horrible dream. She refuses the lawyer's offer just as her Aunt Martha enters with apologies and Christmas presents. *Lawyers. Filial relations. Motherhood. Christmas. Social classes. Poverty. Adoption. Jealousy. Christmas. Dreams.*

EMPTY HANDS **F2.1523**

Famous Players–Lasky. *Dist* Paramount Pictures. 17 Aug **1924** [New York showing; released 13 Oct; c26 Aug 1924; LP20522]. Si; b&w. 35mm. 7 reels, 6,976 ft.

Pres by Adolph Zukor, Jesse L. Lasky. *Dir* Victor Fleming. *Scen* Carey Wilson. *Photog* Charles Edgar Schoenbaum.

Cast: Jack Holt *(Grimshaw)*, Norma Shearer *(Claire Endicott)*, Charles Clary *(Robert Endicott)*, Hazel Keener *(Mrs. Endicott)*, Gertrude Olmstead *(Gypsy)*, Ramsey Wallace *(Montie)*, Ward Crane *(Milt Bisnet)*, Charles Stevens *(Indian guide)*, Hank Mann *(Spring Water Man)*, Charles Green *(butler)*.

Romantic drama. Source: Arthur Stringer, *Empty Hands* (Indianapolis, 1924). Shocked by his daughter's flirtatious behavior at a party in his home, Robert Endicott takes her on a trip to the Canadian Northwest. While fishing, she is unwittingly drawn into the rapids, and Grimshaw, her father's engineer, attempts to rescue her. They both reach safety in an inaccessible basin, where a romance develops before they are rescued. *Engineers. Flirts. Rapids. Canadian Northwest.*

EMPTY HEARTS **F2.1524**

Banner Productions. 15 Sep **1924** [c10 Sep 1924; LP20562]. Si; b&w. 35mm. 6 reels.

Prod Ben Verschleiser. *Dir* Al Santell. *Scen* Adele Buffington. *Photog* Ernest Haller.

Cast: John Bowers *(Milt Kimberlin)*, Charles Murray *(Joe Delorme)*, John Miljan *(Frank Gorman)*, Clara Bow *(Rosalie)*, Buck Black *(Val Kimberlin)*, Lillian Rich *(Madeline)*, Joan Standing *(Hilda, the maid)*.

Domestic melodrama. Source: Evelyn Campbell, "Empty Hearts," in *Metropolitan* (59:64–68, Sep 1924; 60:68–77, Oct 1924). Milt Kimberlin meets Rosalie, a cabaret entertainer, and marries her. In a streak of bad luck he loses all his money, and his wife dies. Later, he becomes wealthy, marries Madeline, but longs for the happiness of his former marriage. He realizes his mistake when Madeline leaves him as the result of the implications of a forged letter "proving" Rosalie's infidelity. The blackmailer is unmasked, however, and the couple find new happiness together. *Entertainers. Marriage. Infidelity. Blackmail. Finance—Personal.*

THE EMPTY SADDLE **F2.1525**

Lariat Productions. *Dist* Vitagraph Co. of America. 28 Mar **1925** [LP21287]. Si; b&w. 35mm. 5 reels.

Dir Harry S. Webb. *Story* Forrest Sheldon.

Cast: Pete Morrison *(Bob Kingston)*, Betty Goodwin *(Mary Manning)*.

Western melodrama. Bob Kingston and Frank Carson are partners with

Jimmie Manning in a mining operation that has made them all rich; both Bob and Frank are also in love with Jimmie's sister, Mary. Jimmie, who is a weakling and a drunk, sneaks into town and starts on a binge. Bob goes after him and is forced to knock him cold in order to quiet him. Bob takes the inert Jimmie back to a hotel room, where, the next morning, Jimmie is found dead. Bob is blamed for the crime and almost lynched by a hysterical mob; the sheriff, however, manages to get him into the comparative safety of the jail. Frank, despite his past friendship for Bob, again incites the mob to violence; for it is he who killed Jimmie, after the boy discovered that he had been having an affair with a Mexican whore. Bob is moved to the state penitentiary for his own safety, and the Mexican woman tells Mary of Bob's innocence. Bob is freed and goes after Frank, bringing him to justice after a savage fight. Bob marries Mary. *Prostitutes. Mexicans. Brother-sister relationship. Murder. Lynching. Mines.*

THE ENCHANTED COTTAGE **F2.1526**

Inspiration Pictures. *Dist* Associated First National Pictures. 24 Mar **1924** [c24 Mar 1924; LP20022]. Si; b&w. 35mm. 7 reels, 7,120 ft.

Dir John S. Robertson. *Adapt-Scen* Josephine Lovett. *Titl* Gertrude Chase. *Photog* George Folsey. *Film Ed* William Hamilton.

Cast: Richard Barthelmess *(Oliver Bashforth)*, May McAvoy *(Laura Pennington)*, Ida Waterman *(Mrs. Smallwood)*, Alfred Hickman *(Rupert Smallwood)*, Florence Short *(Ethel Bashforth)*, Marion Coakley *(Beatrice Vaughn)*, Holmes E. Herbert *(Major Hillgrove)*, Ethel Wright *(Mrs. Minnett)*, Harry Allen.

Drama. Source: Arthur Wing Pinero, *The Enchanted Cottage, a Fable in Three Acts* (London, 1922). Left a physical wreck by the war, Oliver Bashforth leaves his family and moves into a lonely cottage in search of solitude. He meets Laura Pennington—a plain, lonely, and unattractive woman— and marries her, primarily to escape from his energetic sister, Ethel. In their unhappy marriage they allow their ugliness to suppress romance, but their mutual admiration grows and becomes love, manifested by recognition of inner beauty and faith that their children will possess the physical perfection denied them. *Veterans. Brother-sister relationship. Marriage. Ugliness.*

THE ENCHANTED HILL **F2.1527**

Famous Players–Lasky. *Dist* Paramount Pictures. 18 Jan **1926** [c25 Jan 1926; LP22326]. Si; b&w. 35mm. 7 reels, 6,326 ft.

Pres by Adolph Zukor, Jesse L. Lasky. *Dir* Irvin Willat. *Screenplay* James Shelley Hamilton. *Photog* Al Gilks.

Cast: Jack Holt *(Lee Purdy)*, Florence Vidor *(Gail Ormsby)*, Noah Beery *(Jake Dort)*, Mary Brian *(Hallie Purdy)*, Richard Arlen *(Link Halliwell)*, George Bancroft *(Ira Todd)*, Ray Thompson *(Tommy Scaife)*, Brandon Hurst *(Jasper Doak)*, Henry Hebert *(Bud Shannon)*, George Kuwa *(Chan)*, Mathilde Comont *(Conchita)*, Willard Cooley *(Curley MacMahon)*, George Magrill *(first killer)*.

Western melodrama. Source: Peter Bernard Kyne, *The Enchanted Hill* (New York, 1924). Lee Purdy, the owner of a ranch on "Enchanted Hill," is subjected to repeated attacks by unknown assailants. He meets Gail Ormsby, the owner of the neighboring Box K Ranch, and the two are immediately attracted to each other. Ira Todd, Gail's crooked foreman, fills her head with lies about Lee, whom she unjustly comes to hate. In a pitched battle between the men from Enchanted Hill and those from the Box K, Todd's men are routed. Lee then learns that Todd (in league with a banker who knows that there is gold on Lee's land) has attempted to frighten him off by means of the repeated attacks. The law steps in, and Lee and Gail renew their courtship. *Ranchers. Ranch foremen. Bankers. Gold.*

THE ENCHANTED ISLAND **F2.1528**

Tiffany Productions. 15 Mar **1927** [c14 May 1927; LP23962]. Si; b&w. 35mm. 6 reels, 5,100 ft. [Also 5 reels, 4,857 ft.]

Dir? (see note) William G. Crosby, Allan Dale. *Screenplay* Kay Sherwood. *Story* John Thomas Neville. *Photog* Joseph A. Dubray, Stephen Norton. *Art Dir* George E. Sawley.

Cast: Henry B. Walthall *(Tim Sanborn)*, Charlotte Stevens *(Alice Sanborn)*, Pierre Gendron *(Bob Hamilton)*, Pat Hartigan *("Red" Blake)*, Floyd Shackleford *(Ulysses Abraham Washington)*.

Melodrama. Tim Sanborn and his daughter Alice are stranded on a tropical island, along with many trained animals, for 15 years. Their enchanted life is interrupted by wealthy young Bob Hamilton, "Red" Blake, a vicious brute, and Ulysses Abraham Washington, a Negro cook—all of whom are survivors of shipwreck. Tim disguises his daughter as a boy and introduces her as "Al." She is befriended by Bob, who tells her of the outside world, and when he learns "he" is actually a girl, he falls in love with her, saving her from the lustful glances of Blake. In a quarrel with Blake, Tim is killed. During a volcanic eruption, Ulysses engages in a fight with the villainous Blake, and both die in the molten lava; the lovers escape from the island and are rescued by a cruiser. *Cooks. Male impersonation. Courtship. Tropics. Shipwrecks. Volcanoes. Animals.*

Note: Copyright records incorrectly credit direction of this film to Allan Dale.

ENCHANTMENT **F2.1529**

Cosmopolitan Productions. *Dist* Paramount Pictures. 30 Oct **1921** [New York premiere; released 20 Nov; c23 Oct 1921; LP17199]. Si; b&w. 35mm. 6-7 reels, 6,982 ft.

Dir Robert G. Vignola. *Scen* Luther Reed. *Photog* Ira H. Morgan. *Set Dsgn* Joseph Urban.

Cast: Marion Davies *(Ethel Hoyt)*, Forrest Stanley *(Ernest Eddison)*, Edith Shayne *(Mrs. Hoyt)*, Tom Lewis *(Mr. Hoyt)*, Arthur Rankin *(Tommy Corbin)*, Corinne Barker *(Nalia)*, Maude Turner Gordon *(Mrs. Leigh)*, Edith Lyle *(The Queen [in fairy tale])*, Huntley Gordon *(The King [in fairy tale])*.

Comedy-drama. Source: Frank Ramsay Adams, "Manhandling Ethel," in *Cosmopolitan* (70:29, Jan 1921). Ethel Hoyt, the only child of wealthy parents, surrounds herself with six young college men and spends her time dancing and dining with them, causing her parents to become alarmed. On her father's birthday, they attend a performance of *The Taming of the Shrew* in which Ernest Eddison is starred, and Mr. Hoyt decides that Eddison would be just the man to tame Ethel and makes the proper arrangements with the star. After they meet, a friend of Eddison's produces *The Sleeping Beauty*, and he suggests Ethel for the leading role. She accepts; but at rehearsals she stubbornly insists that her boyfriends be allowed to attend. Eddison gives in, but during the action of the play, he kisses her energetically and she is indignant until he is about to leave her; then, she admits her love for him. *Shrews. Actors. Wealth. Family life. Theater. "Taming of the Shrew". "Sleeping Beauty".*

THE END OF THE ROAD *see* **LOVEBOUND**

THE END OF THE ROAD **F2.1530**

Saul Burstein. 27 Oct **1923** [New York State license application]. Si; b&w. 35mm. 7 reels.

No information about the nature of this film has been found.

END OF THE ROPE **F2.1531**

Charles R. Seeling Productions. *Dist* Aywon Film Corp. Oct **1923.** Si; b&w. 35mm. 5 reels, 4,700 ft.

Dir Charles R. Seeling. *Photog* Vernon Walker.

Cast: Big Boy Williams.

Western melodrama. "Brothers resembling each other in appearance but not character are mistaken for each other repeatedly; the good suffering for the faults of the bad. The love romance ends happily, however, when the criminally inclined brother is killed." (*Motion Picture News Booking Guide,* 6:24–25, Apr 1924.) *Brothers. Mistaken identity.*

END OF THE TRAIL (Reissue) **F2.1532**

Fox Film Corp. Oct **1924.** Si; b&w. 35mm. 5 reels.

Note: A William Farnum feature originally released by Fox (7 Aug 1916; c6 Aug 1916; LP8878).

ENEMIES OF CHILDREN **F2.1533**

Fisher Productions. *Dist* Mammoth Pictures. 13 Dec **1923** [c9 Oct 1923; LP19487]. Si; b&w. 35mm. 6 reels, 5,800 ft.

Prod Victor B. Fisher. *Dir-Adapt* Lillian Ducey, John M. Voshell.

Cast: Anna Q. Nilsson, George Siegmann, Claire McDowell, Lucy Beaumont, Joseph Dowling, Raymond Hatton, Ward Crane, Charles Wellesley, Virginia Lee Corbin, Kate Price, Boyd Irwin, Eugenie Besserer, William Boyd, Mary Anderson.

Melodrama. Source: George Gibbs, *Youth Triumphant* (New York, 1921). "A street waif of questionable parentage through circumstances is taken into a wealthy home where she is adopted and cared for until her marriage, which follows the successful attempt to expose the mystery of her birth" (*Variety,* 20 Dec 1923, p26). *Waifs. Adoption. Parentage. Personal identity.*

THE ENEMIES OF WOMEN **F2.1534**

Cosmopolitan Productions. *Dist* Goldwyn Distributing Corp. ca15 Apr **1923** [New York premiere; released 2 Sep; c21 May 1923; LP19004]. Si; b&w. 35mm. 11 reels, 10,501 ft.

Dir Alan Crosland. *Scen* John Lynch. *Photog* Ira Morgan. *Sets* Joseph Urban. *Prod Mgr* John Lynch. *Cost* Gretl Urban.

Cast: Lionel Barrymore *(Prince Lubimoff)*, Alma Rubens *(Alicia)*, Pedro De Cordoba *(Atilio Castro)*, Gareth Hughes *(Spadoni)*, Gladys Hulette *(Vittoria)*, William Thompson *(Colonel Marcos)*, William Collier, Jr. *(Gaston)*, Mario Majeroni *(Duke de Delille)*, Betty Bouton *(Alicia's maid)*, Madame Jean Brindeau *(Madame Spadoni)*, Ivan Linow *(terrorist)*, Paul Panzer *(Cossack)*.

Romantic drama. Source: Vicente Blasco-Ibáñez, *Los Enemigos de la mujer* (trans. by Irving Brown; New York, 1920). After killing a Cossack in a duel, middle-aged libertine Prince Lubimoff flees Russia with the aid of Alicia, in whom he has taken great interest. In Paris, however, Lubimoff mistakes Alicia's son, Gaston, for a young lover and leaves her. They next meet in Monte Carlo, where Alicia is desperately trying to earn money for Gaston (now a captured soldier) at the gaming tables. In the meanwhile, Lubimoff, who has lost most of his fortune during the revolution in Russia, has formed a small group called "Enemies of Women." Circumstances bring about a duel between Lubimoff and Gaston, who dies of heart failure. Lubimoff learns the truth and, chastened, leaves to serve in the war. He later finds Alicia serving as a Red Cross nurse, and they seek consolation in each other's love. *Rakes. Nurses. Misogynists. Russia—History—1917–21 Revolution. World War I. Monte Carlo. Red Cross. Duels.*

ENEMIES OF YOUTH **F2.1535**

Atlas Educational Film Co. *Dist* Moeller Theater Service. c6 Mar **1925** [LP21234]. Si; b&w. 35mm. 6 reels, 5,187 ft.

Dir Arthur Berthelet. *Story* Stacey A. Van Petten.

Cast: Mahlon Hamilton, Gladys Leslie, J. Barney Sherry, Jack Drumier, Jane Jennings, Burr McIntosh, Charles Delaney, Gladys Walton.

Drama. For many years, the destinies of the sleepy town of Arcadia have been controlled by a group of its inhabitants who insist on legislating morality into the local citizens. The town is so uninviting and unattractive that James Rutledge, an industrial magnate, refuses to locate a new factory there. Tom Raymond, the prosecuting attorney of Arcadia, is nominated for mayor on the platform of rigid law enforcement, but he declines to run and the nomination goes instead to Robert Lawton, the father of Alice, Tom's fiancée. Lawton's son gets into trouble in a neighboring town, and Tom decides that Arcadia should have some healthful recreational facilities. He then runs independently for mayor on a platform that will bring innocent fun for the young people back to Arcadia. The governor of the state speaks in Tom's behalf, and this appeal assures Tom's election. A recreation center is erected, Rutledge decides to erect his factory in Arcadia, and Tom and Alice make plans to be married. *Lawyers. Mayors. Reformers. State governors. Elections.*

THE ENEMY **F2.1536**

Metro-Goldwyn-Mayer Pictures. Dec **1927** [New York premiere; released 18 Feb 1928; c18 Feb 1928; LP25197]. Si; b&w. 35mm. 9 reels, 8,189 ft.

Dir Fred Niblo. *Cont* Willis Goldbeck, Agnes Christine Johnston. *Titl* John Colton. *Adapt* Willis Goldbeck. *Photog* Oliver Marsh. *Set Dsgn* Cedric Gibbons, Richard Day. *Film Ed* Margaret Booth. *Asst Dir* Harold S. Bucquet. *Wardrobe* Gilbert Clark.

Cast: Lillian Gish *(Pauli Arndt)*, Ralph Forbes *(Carl Behrend)*, Ralph Emerson *(Bruce Gordon)*, Frank Currier *(Professor Arndt)*, George Fawcett *(August Behrend)*, Fritzi Ridgeway *(Mitzi Winkelmann)*, John S. Peters *(Fritz Winkelmann)*, Karl Dane *(Jan)*, Polly Moran *(Baruska)*, Billy Kent Schaefer *(Kurt)*.

War melodrama. Source: Channing Pollock, *The Enemy; a Play in Four Acts* (New York opening: 20 Oct 1925). Young Austrians Carl Behrend and Pauli Arndt marry as the World War breaks out. Carl is drafted immediately. Pauli and her baby nearly starve to death when her grandfather, a professor, loses his job for speaking out against war. Carl is reported killed en route home for a 10-day furlough, and the baby dies in spite of Pauli's resorting to prostitution to keep him alive. Eventually, Carl does return from the war, Arndt is reinstated, and happiness is restored to the unfortunate family. *Pacifists. Military life. Motherhood. Starvation. Prostitution. World War I. Vienna.*

Note: Published copyright information showing that the film has sound has not been verified.

AN ENEMY OF MEN **F2.1537**

Columbia Pictures. 1 Jul **1925** [c20 Jul 1925; LP21658]. Si; b&w. 35mm. 6 reels.

Dir Frank R. Strayer. *Story* Douglas Bronston. *Photog* Frank B. Good.

Cast: Cullen Landis, Dorothy Revier, Charles Clary.

Melodrama. Since the death of their parents, Norma Bennett has assumed the responsibility for looking after her younger sister, Janet. Political boss John Hurd marries Janet on the sly and then deserts her. Never telling Norma her husband's name, Janet dies while giving birth to a baby, and Norma takes a vow to make all men suffer for her sister's death. Norma becomes the toast of New York nightclubs; men pay heavily and receive only a mocking smile in return. Norma opens The Janet Bennett Home for Girls and falls in love with Doctor Phil, a fine young fellow whom she adamantly refuses to marry. Norma learns that Hurd was Janet's husband and sets out to kill him. She is forestalled, however, when Hurd is shot to death by the brother of one of his many victims. Putting aside her vengeance, Norma is finally free to find happiness with Doctor Phil. *Sisters. Man-haters. Physicians. Political bosses. Murder. Marriage. Desertion. Revenge. Nightclubs. New York City.*

THE ENEMY SEX **F2.1538**

Famous Players–Lasky. *Dist* Paramount Pictures. 25 Aug **1924** [c15 Jun 1924; LP20397]. Si; b&w. 35mm. 8 reels, 7,919 ft.

Dir James Cruze. *Scen* Walter Woods, Harvey Thew. *Photog* Karl Brown.

Cast: Betty Compson *("Dodo" Baxter)*, Percy Marmont *(Garry Lindaberry)*, Sheldon Lewis *(Albert Edward Sassoon)*, Huntley Gordon *(Judge Massingale)*, De Witt Jennings *(Harrigan Blood)*, William H. Turner *(Blainey)*, Dot Farley *(Ida Summers)*, Ed Faust *(Comte de Joncy)*, Pauline Bush *(Miss Snyder)*, Kathlyn Williams *(Mrs. Massingale)*.

Comedy-drama. Source: Owen Johnson, *The Salamander* (Indianapolis, 1914). Chorus girl "Dodo" Baxter is invited to a party given by millionaire Albert Sassoon. There she meets five wealthy and worldly-wise men who attempt various schemes to add her to their conquests. But she beats them all at their own game and declines offers of a stage career, wealth, and position in favor of restoring the health of an alcoholic, Garry Lindaberry. *Chorus girls. Millionaires. Alcoholism.*

L'ENIGMATIQUE MONSIEUR PARKES **F2.1539**

Paramount Famous Lasky Corp. 17 Oct **1930** [Paris premiere]. Sd (Movietone); b&w. 35mm. 7 reels, 6,204 ft.

Dir Louis Gasnier. *Screenplay-Dial* Henri Bataille. *Story* Percy Heath. *Photog* Allen Siegler. *Film Ed* Henri Bataille.

Cast: Adolphe Menjou *(Courtenay Parkes)*, Claudette Colbert *(Lucy de Stavrin)*, Emile Chautard *(H. Sylvester Corbett)*, Adrienne D'Ambricourt *(Mrs. Corbett)*, Sandra Ravel *(Edith Corbett)*, Armand Kaliz *(Malatroff)*, Frank O'Neill *(Jimmy Weyman)*, André Cheron *(Commissaire de Police)*, Jacques Jou-Jerville.

Society melodrama. A French-language version of *Slightly Scarlet*, q. v. *Socialites. Nouveaux riches. Thieves. Courtship. Paris. Nice.*

ENTER MADAME **F2.1540**

Samuel Zierler Photoplay Corp. *Dist* Metro Pictures. 13 Nov **1922** [c5 Dec 1922; LP18471]. Si; b&w. 35mm. 7 reels, 6,500 ft.

Prod Harry Garson. *Dir* Wallace Worsley. *Scen* Frank Beresford. *Story* Gilda Varesi, Dolly Byrne. *Photog* L. William O'Connell.

Cast: Clara Kimball Young *(Prima Donna Lisa Della Robia [Mrs. Gerald Fitzgerald])*, Elliott Dexter *(Gerald Fitzgerald)*, Louise Dresser *(Mrs. Flora Preston)*, Lionel Belmore *(Archimede)*, Wedgewood Nowell *(doctor)*, Rosita Marstini *(Bice)*, Ora Devereaux *(Miss Smith)*, Arthur Rankin *(John Fitzgerald)*, Mary Jane Sanderson *(Aline Chalmers)*, George Kuwa *(Tomamoto)*.

Romantic comedy-drama. Source: Gilda Varesi and Dolly Byrne, *Enter Madame; a Play in Three Acts* (New York, 1924). Upon receiving a request for divorce from her husband, impulsive opera star Lisa Della Robia causes a flurry by suddenly returning to New York in the middle of an Italian tour. She at first refuses to see her husband, then uses her woman's wiles to regain his love and eliminate her rival. *Singers. Divorce. Opera. New York City. Italy.*

ENTICEMENT **F2.1541**

Thomas H. Ince Corp. *Dist* First National Pictures. 1 Feb **1925** [c19 Jan 1925; LP21037]. Si; b&w. 35mm. 7 reels, 6,407 ft.

Pers Supv Thomas H. Ince. *Dir* George Archainbaud. *Adapt* Bradley

King. *Photog* Henry Sharp.

Cast: Mary Astor *(Leonore Bewlay)*, Clive Brook *(Henry Wallis)*, Ian Keith *(Richard Valyran)*, Louise Dresser *(Mrs. Samuel Murray)*, Edgar Norton *(William Blake)*, Vera Lewis *(Mrs. Blake)*, Lillian Langdon *(Mrs. Edward Merley)*, Lorimer Johnston *(Edward Merley)*, Maxine Elliott Hicks *(Olive Merley)*, Fenwick Oliver *(Mr. Kerry)*, Florence Wix *(Mrs. Kerry)*, George Bunny *(The Bishop)*, Roland Bottomley *(Bevington)*, Aileen Manning *(The Old Maid)*.

Melodrama. Source: Clive Arden, *Enticement* (Indianapolis, c1924). Leonore Bewlay meets her old friend Richard Valyran in Switzerland 2 years after the Great War, during which they did relief work together in Belgium. Previously their friendship was platonic, but Richard now finds Leonore sexually attractive. On their way to an inn high in the Alps, they are caught in a snowslide and Leonore's leg is injured. Val carries her to the inn, helps remove her clothes, and, overcome with lust, kisses her madly. This display of passion effectively destroys their friendship. Leonore soon marries Henry Wallis, whom she truly loves, and returns with him to his home in London where she is unpopular with his conservative family, who consider her too outspoken and independent. When Leonore is named as the corespondent in a divorce suit filed by Richard's estranged wife, Henry loses faith in her. When she goes to Richard for consolation, he perceives that she still loves Henry and deliberately walks in front of an oncoming car. As he lies dying in a hospital, Richard has the final satisfaction of seeing Henry and Leonore reconciled, to be saved from the consequences of scandal by his imminent death. *Divorce. Suicide. Platonic love. World War I. Switzerland. London. Commission for Relief in Belgium. Avalanches.*

ENVIRONMENT **F2.1542**

Irving Cummings. *Dist* Principal Pictures. 1 Dec **1922**. Si; b&w. 35mm. 6 reels, 5,700 ft.

Dir Irving Cummings. *Story* Harvey Gates.

Cast: Milton Sills *(Steve MacLaren)*, Alice Lake *(Sally Dolan, known as "Chicago Sal")*, Ben Hewlett *("Willie Boy" Toval)*, Gertrude Claire *(Grandma MacLaren)*, Richard Headrick *("Jimmie," Steve's adopted boy)*, Ralph Lewis *("Diamond Jim" Favre)*.

Crook melodrama. The rehabilitaton of "Chicago Sal," a lady crook, is seemingly realized when probation officers send her to the country home of Steve MacLaren to work off money stolen from him by her partner. She falls in love with MacLaren and is accepted as a member of the household. Unable to resist the temptation, however, she leaves the farm with two former colleagues when they come to visit her. MacLaren follows her to the city. She commits a crime; he helps her escape but is himself arrested for vagrancy and sent to jail. Sal returns to the country and promises to wait for him. *Criminals—Rehabilitation. Farmers. Probation.*

Note: Working title: *Chicago Sal.*

EQUATORIAL AFRICA; ROOSEVELT'S HUNTING GROUNDS **F2.1543**

c15 Dec **1924** [and c26 Feb 1925; MU2929]. Si; b&w. 35mm. 7 reels.

Photog A. J. Klein.

Travelog. Leaving the British colony of Kenya, the expedition enters Tanganyika Territory, crossing Lake Victoria, traverses Uganda to Lakes Edward and Albert, and finishes on the Nile. En route there are scenes of a Kikuyu harvest celebration; a forest fire; animals—zebra, topi, gazelles, impala, lions; vermin and insects; Masai life; more animals—birds, waterbucks, warthogs, antelope, rhinoceros, baboons, hippopotami; the ascent of Mt. Ruwenzori through lush jungle to splendid glaciers over 12,000 feet high; and elephants, of course, at home in the equatorial forest. *Kikuyu. Masai. Forest fires. Jungles. Glaciers. Africa. Kenya. Tanganyika. Uganda. Nile River.*

Note: Production and distributing companies have not been established. Christian Thams was copyright claimant.

ERIK THE GREAT *see* **THE LAST PERFORMANCE**

ERMINE AND RHINESTONES **F2.1544**

Jans Productions. 1 Oct **1925** [c23 Nov 1925; LP22044]. Si; b&w. 35mm. 6 reels, 5,800 ft. [Later cut to 5 reels.]

Prod Herman F. Jans. *Dir* Burton King. *Cont-Titl* William B. Laub. *Story* Louise Winter. *Film Ed* William B. Laub. *Furs dsgnd by* Hickson of Fifth Avenue.

Cast: Edna Murphy *(Minnette Christie)*, Niles Welch *(Billy Kershaw)*, Ruth Stonehouse *(Peggy Rice)*, Coit Albertson *(Pierce Ferring)*, Sally Crute *(Alys Ferring)*, Bradley Barker *(Jim Gorman)*, Marguerite McNulty *(Nita Frost)*.

Society melodrama. Billy, the son of a manufacturer in a small western town, comes to New York on business. He becomes engaged to Peggy Rice, a member of the modern jazz set. Sometime before, Billy had sent Jim Gorman to jail for theft, causing Gorman's girl, Minette Christie, to leave town. At a fashion show, Peggy persuades Billy to buy her an ermine wrap, trimmed with rhinestones, which is modeled by a girl who turns out to be Minette. Billy realizes that Peggy is no more than a gold digger and breaks the engagement. Gorman shows up and attempts to kill Minette, for he believes she turned him in. Billy, however, defeats Gorman in a fight and saves Minette in the nick of time from being gassed to death in her apartment. Billy comes to realize that Minette is the girl for him. *Gold diggers. Models. Jazz life. Revenge. New York City.*

THE ESCAPE (Blue Streak Western) **F2.1545**

Universal Pictures. 6 Jun **1926** [c23 Apr 1926; LP22637]. Si; b&w. 35mm. 5 reels, 4,500 ft.

Pres by Carl Laemmle. *Dir* Milburn Morante. *Scen* Frank Beresford. *Story* L. V. Jefferson. *Photog* Jack Young.

Cast: Pete Morrison *(Johnny Bowers)*, Barbara Starr *(Evelyn Grant)*, Frank Norcross *(Jeremiah Grant)*, Bruce Gordon *(Howard Breen)*, Elmer Dewey *(Silas Peele)*, Jane Arden *(Flossie Lane)*, Tex (Shorty) Young *(Manuel Estrada)*, Lightning *(Johnny's horse)*.

Western melodrama. Johnny Bowers, of the Rockin' P Ranch, while riding to meet Evelyn Grant, daughter of the rancher and banker, Jeremiah Grant, interrupts a gang of train robbers headed by Wingo Wade. Later, Wingo and Howard Breen, who has his eye on Evelyn and who admits to being short in his bank account, plot to waylay a stage that is bringing a consignment of money to the bank. Though Johnny and his pals have been jailed, they trick the constable and escape with his badge, rob the stage, deliver the money to the bank, and return to jail. In desperation, Wingo's gang handcuffs the sheriff and robs the bank; Johnny and his pals pursue them. Johnny engages in a fight with Breen, who falls to his death, leaving Johnny free to marry Evelyn. *Ranchers. Sheriffs. Train robberies. Stagecoach robberies. Bank robberies. Horses.*

THE ESCAPE **F2.1546**

Fox Film Corp. 29 Apr **1928** [c23 Apr 1928; LP25173]. Si; b&w. 35mm. 6 reels, 5,109 ft.

Dir Richard Rosson. *Scen* Paul Schofield. *Titl* Garrett Graham. *Photog* H. Kinley Martin. *Photog? (see note)* Kenneth Hawks. *Film Ed* J. Logan Pearson, Edwin Robbins.

Cast: William Russell *(Jerry Magee [Martin])*, Virginia Valli *(May Joyce)*, Nancy Drexel *(Jennie Joyce)*, George Meeker *(Dr. Don Elliott)*, William Demarest *(Trigger Caswell)*, James Gordon *(Jim Joyce)*.

Melodrama. Source: Paul Armstrong, *The Escape* (New York opening: 20 Sep 1913, 26 Oct 1927). Jerry Magee, a hospital intern, falls in love with May Joyce, a poor girl whose father is a bootlegger. May gets a job in a nightclub when her father is killed in a raid. There she works for the man responsible for her father's death. Magee loses his job, begins to drink heavily, and becomes a bootlegger. One night he makes a delivery to the place where May works. In the last few scenes Magee, May, and her sister escape from the nightclub just before the police break in for a raid. *Bootleggers. Hospital interns. Nightclubs. Alcoholism.*

Note: There is some doubt about the credit for Kenneth Hawks.

THE ESCAPED CONVICT (Reissue) **F2.1547**

10 Nov **1927** [New York State license]. Si; b&w. 35mm. 6 reels, 5,800 ft.

Note: A Broncho Billy Anderson film, the original release date of which has not been determined. Possibly a changed title. Distributed in New York State (1927) by George Cranfield.

ESTRELLADOS *see* **FREE AND EASY**

THE ETERNAL CITY **F2.1548**

Madison Productions. *Dist* Associated First National Pictures. 17 Dec **1923** [New York premiere; released Jan 1924; c31 Dec 1923; LP19782]. Si; b&w. 35mm. 8 reels, 7,800 ft. [Also 7,929 ft.]

Pres by Samuel Goldwyn. *Dir* George Fitzmaurice. *Scen* Ouida Bergère. *Photog* Arthur Miller.

Cast: Barbara La Marr *(Donna Roma)*, Bert Lytell *(David Rossi)*, Lionel Barrymore *(Baron Bonelli)*, Richard Bennett *(Bruno)*, Montagu Love

(Minghelli).

Historical melodrama. Remote source: Hall Caine, *The Eternal City* (New York, 1901). David Rossi, an Italian orphan, is cared for by Bruno, a tramp. Dr. Roselli, a pacifist, adopts him and rears him together with Roma, his daughter. They grow up and pledge their love. Dr. Roselli dies, David and Bruno join the army after war breaks out, and Roma becomes a famous sculptor with the financial assistance of Baron Bonelli, the secret leader of the Communist party. David joins the Fascists and becomes Mussolini's righthand man. He meets Roma and denounces her as Bonelli's mistress; then he leads the Fascists against the Bolshevists and kills Bonelli. Roma takes the blame for Bonelli's murder, thereby convincing David that she had not betrayed him. (Climaxes with a view of Mussolini on the balcony of the royal palace, beside the king, reviewing the entrance of his troops into the city.) *Orphans. Tramps. Sculptors. Fascists. Bolshevists. Pacifists. World War I. Italy. Rome. Benito Mussolini.*

THE ETERNAL FLAME **F2.1549**

Norma Talmadge Film Co. *Dist* Associated First National Pictures. Sep **1922** [c16 Aug 1922; LP18154]. Si; b&w. 35mm. 8 reels, 7,453 ft.

Pres by Joseph M. Schenck. *Dir* Frank Lloyd. *Adapt* Frances Marion. *Photog* Tony Gaudio. *Art Dir* Stephen Goosson. *Cost* Walter J. Israel.

Cast: Norma Talmadge *(Duchesse de Langeais)*, Adolphe Menjou *(Duc de Langeais)*, Wedgewood Nowell *(Marquis de Ronquerolles)*, Conway Tearle *(Général de Montriveau)*, Rosemary Theby *(Madame de Serizy)*, Kate Lester *(Princess de Vlamont-Chaurray)*, Thomas Ricketts *(Vidame de Pameir)*, Otis Harlan *(Abbé Conrand)*, Irving Cummings *(Count de Marsay)*.

Historical drama. Source: Honoré de Balzac, *La Duchesse de Langeais*. In the period of Louis XVIII, while her self-centered husband is away with his troops, the Duchesse de Langeais is pursued by many men. When the famous Général de Montriveau arrives, her flirting turns to love for him, and although gossip says otherwise he believes her to be sincere until he learns that the duchesse has boasted of her conquest. He abducts her, but, unable to bring himself to inflict the torture he has planned, he releases her. A year of unanswered letters convinces the duchesse that her love is in vain, and she enters a convent. The general relents, however, and goes to her just before she is to take her final vows. *Nobility. Convents. France—History—Restoration. Paris.*

Note: Working title: *The Duchess of Langeais.*

ETERNAL FOOLS (EWIGE NARANIM) **F2.1550**

Judea Films. 23 Sep **1930** [c4 Oct 1930; LU1640]. Sd; b&w. 35mm. 8 reels, 6,120 ft.

Dir Sidney M. Goldin. *Scen-Dial* H. Kalmonowitz. *Photog* Charles Levine, Sam Schwartz. *Film Ed* Louis Schwartz. *Rec Engr* Douglas Shearer.

Cast: Yudel Dubinsky *(Grandfather)*, Jehuda Bleich *(Morris Rothstein, father)*, Bella Gudinsky *(Mother)*, Seymour Rechtzeit *(Son)*, Isadore Meltzer *(Comedian)*, Charlotte Goldstein *(Daughter)*, Beatrice Miller *(Son's Wife)*, Eddie Friedlander, Gertie Krause *(Babies)*.

Domestic drama. Source: H. Kalmonowitz, "Ewige Naranim" (Yiddish play; publication undetermined). Morris Rothstein, a factory worker of ordinary means, makes many sacrifices in order that his children may reap the benefit of his labor. In later years, when he has attained wealth and a comfortable position, he finds that his children no longer consider him in their plans, and his daughter-in-law takes over the management of the household. Completely disillusioned, Rothstein decides to destroy the fruit of all his labor, but his father stops him by reminding him that his children's behavior is no different from that of his own and that he too once treated his father in the same manner. He affirms that "we must not destroy what we have built. We must go on." *Fatherhood. Children. Jews. Family life. Self-sacrifice. Filial relations.*

Note: The entire film employs Yiddish dialog.

ETERNAL LOVE **F2.1551**

Feature Productions. *Dist* United Artists. 11 May **1929** [c15 May 1929; LP530]. Mus score & sd eff (Movietone); b&w. 35mm. 9 reels, 6,515 ft. [Also si; 6,498 ft.]

Pres by Joseph M. Schenck. *Assoc Prod* John W. Considine, Jr. *Dir* Ernst Lubitsch. *Adapt-Scen* Hans Kraly. *Titl* Katherine Hilliker, H. H. Caldwell. *Photog* Oliver Marsh. *Sets* Walter Reimann. *Film Ed* Andrew Marton. *Mus Arr* Hugo Riesenfeld. *Asst Dir* George Hippard. *Cost* Walter Reimann.

Cast: John Barrymore *(Marcus Paltram)*, Camilla Horn *(Ciglia)*, Victor Varconi *(Lorenz Gruber)*, Hobart Bosworth *(Reverend Tass)*, Bodil Rosing *(Housekeeper)*, Mona Rico *(Pia)*, Evelyn Selbie *(Pia's mother)*.

Romantic drama. Source: Jakob Christoph Heer, *Der König der Bernina, Roman aus dem Schweizerischen Hochgebirge* (Stuttgart, 1928). Ordered by an invading army to surrender their firearms, the liberty-loving mountaineers of a Swiss village capitulate only through the efforts of their pastor. Marcus Paltram, however, a reckless hunter, defies the order. Though loved by Ciglia, who is also sought by Lorenz Gruber, Marcus is obsessively adored by Pia, a wild mountain girl, who hates Ciglia and awaits an opportunity to separate her from Marcus. At a masquerade party in the village inn, Ciglia invites him home in a drunken state; Pia, in disguise, follows and makes him a victim of her wiles. Later, when Pia's mother demands that justice be done to her daughter, Marcus disconsolately marries her, while Ciglia and Gruber soon marry. During a storm, Marcus is endangered, and Pia persuades the villagers to go on a rescue expedition. Infuriated by his wife's continuing love for Marcus, Gruber offers Marcus a bribe to leave the village. Marcus spurns the proposition and is forced to shoot Gruber in self-defense. Accused of murder, Marcus flees into the mountains with Ciglia. Resolving never again to be separated, they walk into the path of an avalanche. *Mountaineers. Hunters. Clergymen. Military occupation. Courtship. Drunkenness. Seduction. Jealousy. Alps. Switzerland.*

THE ETERNAL MOTHER **F2.1552**

Pioneer Film Corp. c30 Mar **1921** [LU16338]. Si; b&w. 35mm. [Feature length assumed.]

Prod A. J. Bimberg. *Dir* William Davis. *Writ* John K. Holbrook.

Cast: Florence Reed.

Melodrama. Shortly before her marriage to Howard Hollister, socialite Laura West meets Stephen Rhodes, who introduces her to the cult of the East Indian goddess Gaia—the personification of Nature, the Eternal Mother. Though Laura is fascinated, she shies away from Rhodes's efforts to initiate her and make her his earthly personification of Gaia. Laura and Howard marry, and they spend happy newlywed days, but Laura's continued interest in Gaia and frequent daydreams of herself leading the cult upset Howard, who angrily urges Laura to return to reality and her work in the tenement slums. Falling asleep after their quarrel, Laura dreams: *she becomes queen of the cult—richly adorned and ardently worshiped. She comes to realize that Rhodes's purpose is his own sensual gratification and decides that life is no longer worth living. Rhodes's attempts against the life of her child cause Laura to awaken, screaming.* Howard comforts Laura, who assures him that her only desires are motherhood and his love. *Socialites. Social workers. Motherhood. Cults. Suicide. Dreams.*

ETERNAL PEACE **F2.1553**

Dist Webster Pictures. 20 Jun **1922** [New York State license application]. Si; b&w. 35mm. 6 reels.

Cast: Betty Harte.

Melodrama. "This is a story in three episodes of the evils of Kaiserism. The first incident is the tale of a German spy who comes to a Viking's court disguised as a Prince. He pursues the Princess with insulting proposals and then tries to abduct her. The Viking forthwith throws the daughter into the sea as a human sacrifice. The second tale shows an English soldier who has become a German spy. He tries to betray the Arabian sweetheart of a superior officer and is killed in the attempt. The third incident depicts a young American soldier, married to a German girl. Upon discovering the girl's father is a German spy, the young soldier murders him." (New York State license records.) *Germans. Kaiserism. Vikings. Spies.*

Note: Country of origin not determined.

THE ETERNAL STRUGGLE **F2.1554**

Louis B. Mayer Productions. *Dist* Metro Pictures. 8 Oct **1923** [c5 Sep 1923; LP19403]. Si; b&w. 35mm. 8 reels, 7,374 ft.

Pres by Louis B. Mayer. *Prod* Louis B. Mayer. *Dir* Reginald Barker. *Scen* Monte M. Katterjohn. *Adapt* J. G. Hawks. *Photog* Percy Hilburn. *Film Ed* Robert J. Kern.

Cast: Renée Adorée *(Andrée Grange)*, Earle Williams *(Sgt. Neil Tempest)*, Barbara La Marr *(Camille Lenoir)*, Pat O'Malley *(Bucky O'Hara)*, Wallace Beery *(Barode Dukane)*, Josef Swickard *(Pierre Grange)*, Pat Harmon *(Oily Kirby)*, Anders Randolf *(Capt. Jack Scott)*, Edward J. Brady *(Jean Cardeau)*, Robert Anderson *(Olaf Olafson)*, George Kuwa *(Wo Long)*.

Melodrama. Source: G. B. Lancaster, *The Law-Bringers* (New York, 1913). Northwest Mounted Policeman Bucky O'Hara is attracted to a cafe owner's daughter, Andrée Grange, who falls in love with him although O'Hara has a rival in his colleague, Sgt. Neil Tempest. Believing that she is responsible for the death of would-be seducer Barode Dukane, Andrée flees to northern Canada, taking refuge aboard a whaling ship. Both men pursue her—Tempest to aid in her escape, O'Hara to bring her to justice. After O'Hara captures Andrée, the real killer is apprehended, and the romance continues. *Courtship. Whaling ships. Murder. Canada. Northwest Mounted Police.*

Note: Possible working title: *The Man Thou Gavest Me.*

THE ETERNAL THREE **F2.1555**

Goldwyn Pictures. *Dist* Goldwyn-Cosmopolitan Pictures. 23 Sep **1923** [c23 Sep 1923; LP19510]. Si; b&w. 35mm. 7 reels, 6,854 ft.

Dir Marshall Neilan, Frank Urson. *Scen* Carey Wilson. *Story* Marshall Neilan. *Photog* David Kesson.

Cast: Hobart Bosworth *(Dr. Frank R. Walters)*, Claire Windsor *(Mrs. Frank R. Walters)*, Raymond Griffith *(Leonard Foster)*, Bessie Love *(Hilda Gray)*, George Cooper *(Bob Gray)*, Tom Gallery *(Tommy Tucker)*, Helen Lynch *(Miriam Barnes)*, Alec Francis *(Dr. Steven Browning)*, William Orlamond *(owner of hacienda)*, Charles West *(butler)*, Maryon Aye *(maid)*, William Norris *(old roué)*, James F. Fulton *(governor)*, Irene Hunt *(governor's wife)*, Peaches Jackson *(governor's child)*, Victory Bateman *(Mrs. Tucker)*, Billie Bennett *(Mrs. Tucker's friend)*, Lillian Leighton *(housekeeper)*.

Melodrama. A busy brain surgeon's neglected young wife becomes attracted to Leonard Foster, her husband's adopted son, an uncontrollable youth who is injured in an automobile accident following the seduction of his foster father's secretary. The doctor, naturally, operates, cures the boy, and sends him with a sound thrashing, after he has regained his health, to Europe; then he vows to pay more attention to his wife. *Surgeons. Adoption. Automobile accidents. Seduction. Marriage.*

THE ETERNAL WOMAN **F2.1556**

Columbia Pictures. 18 Mar **1929** [c14 Jun 1929; LP470]. Si; b&w. 35mm. 6 reels, 5,812 ft.

Prod Harry Cohn. *Dir* John P. McCarthy. *Screenplay* Wellyn Totman. *Photog* Joseph Walker. *Art Dir* Harrison Wiley. *Film Ed* Ben Pivar. *Asst Dir* Charles C. Coleman.

Cast: Olive Borden *(Anita)*, Ralph Graves *(Hartley Forbes)*, Ruth Clifford *(Doris Forbes)*, John Miljan *(Gil Martin)*, Nina Quartaro *(Consuelo)*, Josef Swickard *(Ovaldo)*, Julia Swayne Gordon *(Mrs. Forbes)*.

Melodrama. Source: Wellyn Totman, "The Wildcat" (publication undetermined). Amidst the mountains of Argentina, Doris Forbes, wife of a wealthy American, seeks her lover, Gil Martin, a supposed friend of her husband's, while Hartley, her husband, is loved by Consuelo, a native girl. The father of two Argentine girls is killed by Martin, and Anita, the elder of the daughters, seeks revenge. After the wreck of a steamer bound for the United States, on which she is a stowaway, Anita saves Hartley from drowning in a storm. She later comes to love him, though she is unaware of his identity. In his home, she discovers a picture of his wife, remembers her as the wife of her father's murderer, and suspects that her sweetheart murdered her father. She renounces love for revenge, but her attempt to kill him is frustrated; at length, she learns her error, and the real culprit is exposed. *Sisters. Marriage. Infidelity. Murder. Mistaken identity. Revenge. Buenos Aires. Argentina. Shipwrecks.*

EVANGELINE **F2.1557**

Edwin Carewe Productions–Feature Productions. *Dist* United Artists. 27 Jul **1929** [New York opening; released 24 Aug; c1 Jul 1929; LP531]. Mus score & sd eff (Movietone); b&w. 35mm. 9 reels, 8,268 ft. [Also si; 7,862 ft.]

Dir Edwin Carewe. *Screenplay-Titl* Finis Fox. *Photog* Robert B. Kurrle, Al M. Green. *Lighting Engr* C. P. Drew. *Sets* Stephen Goosson. *Film Ed* Jeanne Spencer. *Mus Synchronization* Hugo Riesenfeld. *Asst Dir* Jack Boland. *Prod Mgr* Louis M. Jerome. *Ch Prod Aide* Wallace Fox. *Master of Wardrobe* Charles Huber. *Tech Aide* Eugene Hornbostel. *Master of Properties* Gene Rossi. *Historian* Finis Fox.

Cast: Dolores Del Rio *(Evangeline)*, Roland Drew *(Gabriel)*, Alec B. Francis *(Father Felician)*, Donald Reed *(Baptiste)*, Paul McAllister *(Benedict Bellefontaine)*, James Marcus *(Basil)*, George Marion, Sr. *(René La Blanc)*, Bobby Mack *(Michael)*, Lou Payne *(Governor-General)*, Lee Shumway *(Colonel Winslow)*.

Historical drama. Source: Henry Wadsworth Longfellow, *Evangeline, A Tale of Acadie* (1847). In the quiet Nova Scotian village of Grand-Pré lives the fair, beloved Evangeline with her father, Benedict Bellefontaine, a prosperous and honored farmer of the Acadian community. Though she admires and is loved by Baptiste, son of the notary, she is pledged to Gabriel, son of Basil, the village smith. Before they can be married, France and England declare war, and the Acadians, bound by allegiance to England and by ties of kinship to France, refuse to take up arms against France and as a result are ordered deported. As the men are herded aboard a British man-o'-war, the governor-general sets fire to the village of Grand-Pré. Suffering from exposure and broken by the sight, Benedict dies in the arms of Evangeline, who departs for unknown lands with Father Felician. They arrive at Bayou Têche, Louisiana (just missing Gabriel), where former residents of Grand Pré have established a settlement. Through the wilds of the gulf coast, Evangeline suffers many hardships in search of her beloved, refusing the offer of Baptiste, who has meanwhile become a prosperous land owner. Basil offers to aid her in her search for Gabriel, but they are separated by a storm on the rapids. Traveling alone through unexplored country, Evangeline arrives at a settlement of Jesuits where she becomes a Sister of Mercy, though ever hopeful of finding Gabriel. At the termination of the war, Evangeline is sent to Philadelphia to care for the maimed and friendless, and in an almshouse, she is at last reunited with her long-sought beloved. *Farmers. Cajuns. Courtship. Village life. Colonial administration. French and Indian War. Acadia (Nova Scotia). Acadia (Louisiana). Philadelphia. Society of Jesus.*

EVENING CLOTHES **F2.1558**

Famous Players–Lasky. *Dist* Paramount Pictures. 19 Mar **1927** [c19 Mar 1927; LP23777]. Si; b&w. 35mm. 7 reels, 6,287 ft.

Pres by Adolph Zukor, Jesse L. Lasky. *Assoc Prod* B. P. Schulberg. *Dir* Luther Reed. *Screenplay* John McDermott. *Titl* George Marion, Jr. *Photog* Hal Rosson. *Film Ed* Eda Warren.

Cast: Adolphe Menjou *(Lucien D'Artois)*, Virginia Valli *(Germaine)*, Noah Beery *(Lazarre)*, Louise Brooks *(Fox Trot)*, Lido Manetti *(Henri)*, André Cheron *(Germaine's father)*.

Society comedy. Source: André Picard and Yves Mirande, *L'Homme en habit; piece en trois actes* (Paris, 1922). Lucien D'Artois, a wealthy French farmer fond of raising horses, is married to Germaine, according to the terms of a marriage contract. When she finds his rustic interests unbearable, she leaves him. Determined to become a polished Parisian, Lucien goes to the city and assiduously studies fencing and dancing but is unable to gain her favor. He embarks on a life of frivolity and free spending and to demonstrate his powers with women deliberately steals Fox Trot, a nightclub girl, from Lazarre. When his fortune is depleted, his entire possessions are confiscated with the exception of a suit of evening clothes. Living by his wits, Lucien imagines himself still a popular and wealthy count, and returning to his bare flat, he finds his wife returned to him. *Farmers. Dancers. Nobility. Marriage. Poverty. Fencing. France. Paris.*

EVER SINCE EVE **F2.1559**

Fox Film Corp. 28 Aug **1921** [c28 Aug 1921; LP16950]. Si; b&w. 35mm. 5 reels.

Pres by William Fox. *Dir* Howard M. Mitchell. *Scen* Dorothy Yost. *Story* Joseph Ernest Peat. *Photog* Glen MacWilliams.

Cast: Shirley Mason *(Célestine Le Farge)*, Herbert Heyes *(Carteret)*, Eva Gordon *(Lorita)*, Mrs. Vin Moore *(Svenson)*, Charles Spere *(Percy Goring)*, Frances Hancock *(Mrs. Kerry)*, Ethel Lynn *(The Stranger)*, Louis King *(Lieut. Gerald O'Connor)*.

Romantic comedy. Carteret, an artist, adopts Célestine, a French orphan, who makes evasive replies to inquiries about a certain young "man," her close acquaintance. A detective watches the movements of Célestine and the mysterious stranger, whom he believes to be implicated in a murder case. The artist, realizing he is in love with his adopted daughter, is about to propose to her when she "elopes" with the stranger, who, it develops, is actually the girl he had adopted and who has married an army officer, Célestine acting as her proxy. Delighted with the turn of events, Carteret decides to marry Célestine at once. *Detectives. Artists. Strangers. Mistaken identity. Adoption.*

THE EVERLASTING WHISPER **F2.1560**

Fox Film Corp. 11 Oct **1925** [c4 Oct 1925; LP21874]. Si; b&w. 35mm. 6 reels, 5,611 ft.

Pres by William Fox. *Dir* J. G. Blystone. *Scen* Wyndham Gittens. *Photog* Dan Clark.

Cast: Tom Mix *(Mark King)*, Alice Calhoun *(Gloria Gaynor)*, Robert Cain *(Gratton)*, George Berrell *(Old Honeycutt)*, Walter James *(Aswin*

Brody), Virginia Madison *(Mrs. Gaynor)*, Karl Dane *(Jarrold)*.

Western melodrama. Source: Jackson Gregory, *The Everlasting Whisper, a Tale of the California Wilderness* (New York, 1922). Mark King, a prospector who prefers the everlasting whisper of the pines to the roar of city streets, rescues Gloria Gaynor, a society heiress, when her horse runs away with her. Mark later protects Old Honeycutt from the scheming of Gratton, who wants to discover the location of Old Honeycutt's mine. Gratton tries to force Gloria into marriage, but Tom forestalls him by marrying Gloria himself. Gloria soon longs for city life and, resenting Mark for the abrupt manner of their marriage, returns to San Francisco. Gloria later realizes the depth of her love for Mark, and they are reunited under the whispering pines. *Prospectors. Heiresses. Marriage. Forests. Mines. San Francisco.*

EVERY MAN'S WIFE **F2.1561**

Fox Film Corp. 7 Jun **1925** [c31 May 1925; LP21548]. Si; b&w. 35mm. 5 reels, 4,365 ft.

Pres by William Fox. *Dir* Maurice Elvey. *Scen* Lillie Hayward. *Story* Ethel Hill, Enid Hibbard.

Cast: Elaine Hammerstein *(Mrs. Randolph)*, Herbert Rawlinson *(Mr. Randolph)*, Robert Cain *(Mr. Bradin)*, Diana Miller *(Emily)*, Dorothy Phillips *(Mrs. Bradin)*.

Domestic drama. Mr. and Mrs. Randolph are newly wed, and she, being of a jealous nature, is looking for the slightest hint of infidelity in her husband. One morning, he leaves for the office early and sees a cat, which closely resembles one that lately ran away from his wife. He follows the cat and discovers that it belongs to Mrs. Bradin, a comely neighbor, with whom he briefly chats. Mrs. Randolph sees them together and suspects her husband of infidelity, soon making his life so miserable that he takes up residence at his club. Mrs. Randolph, convinced of the righteousness of her wrath, then invites both her husband and the Bradins to a party, hoping to catch Mr. Randolph making love to Mrs. Bradin. Randolph proves himself to be the model of fidelity and attentiveness, and Mr. Bradin tries to seduce his own wife, mistaking her for Mrs. Randolph in the half light. Mr. and Mrs. Randolph are reunited, renewing their marriage on a better foundation of trust and understanding. *Marriage. Infidelity. Jealousy. Seduction. Clubs. Cats.*

EVERY WOMAN'S HUSBAND (Reissue) **F2.1562**

Triangle Film Corp. *Dist* Tri-Stone Pictures. 25 Mar **1925** [New York State license]. Si; b&w. 35mm.

Note: A Gloria Swanson film originally released by Triangle Film Corp. on 7 Jul 1918.

EVERY WOMAN'S PROBLEM **F2.1563**

Plymouth Pictures. 19 Mar **1921** [trade review]. Si; b&w. 35mm. 5 reels.

Dir Willis Robards. *Scen* J. F. Natteford. *Story* Hal Reid. *Film Ed* Martin G. Cohn.

Cast: Dorothy Davenport *(Clara Madison)*, Willis Robards *(Grant Williams)*, Maclyn King *("Big Bill" Deavitt)*, Wilson Du Bois *(Dan Channing)*.

Melodrama. "Clara Madison, a lawyer, is nominated by the woman's party for a judgeship and is elected. A yellow newspaper opposes her to such an extent that her husband threatens the life of the editor. Bootleggers whom the paper has also opposed concoct a scheme by which the newspaper office is destroyed by a bomb and the editor killed. Circumstantial evidence overwhelmingly points to the guilt of Clara's husband and with the two bootleggers, he is sentenced to death. Clara, in the meantime, is elected governor and is now faced with the question of allowing the law to take its course or of pardoning her husband, whom she dearly loves. She decides on the former course, but he is saved by the last minute confession of one of the bootleggers." *(Moving Picture World*, 19 Mar 1921, p312.) *Lawyers. Judges. Editors. Bootleggers. State governors. Women in public office. Yellow journalism. Murder. Capital punishment. Circumstantial evidence.*

EVERYBODY'S ACTING **F2.1564**

Famous Players–Lasky. *Dist* Paramount Pictures. 8 Nov **1926** [c17 Nov 1926; LP23345]. Si; b&w. 35mm. 7 reels, 6,139 ft.

Pres by Adolph Zukor, Jesse L. Lasky. *Dir-Story* Marshall Neilan. *Screenplay* Benjamin Glazer. *Titl* George Marion, Jr. *Photog* David Kesson, Donald Keyes.

Cast: Betty Bronson *(Doris Poole)*, Ford Sterling *(Michael Poole)*, Louise Dresser *(Anastasia Potter)*, Lawrence Gray *(Ted Potter)*, Henry Walthall *(Thorpe)*, Raymond Hitchcock *(Ernest Rice)*, Stuart Holmes *(Clayton Budd)*, Edward Martindel *(Peter O'Brien)*, Philo McCullough *(Paul Singleton)*, Jed Prouty *(Bridewell Potter)*, Jocelyn Lee *(Barbara Potter)*.

Comedy-drama. Doris Poole, orphaned daughter of traveling actors, is adopted by four members of the company and a newspaper reporter, Peter O'Brien. In 1926 the "family" settles in San Francisco, and Betty becomes the ingenue of a stock company. She falls in love with Ted Potter, a taxicab driver (in reality the son of Anastasia Potter, a wealthy and domineering businesswoman) who is working on a novel. Anastasia, opposed to her son's attachment to a common actress, investigates the girl's past and uncovers information about her father's execution for murdering his wife. To outwit her, the five "fathers" urge Ted to accept a position in the Orient his mother has offered him, and they secretly book passage on the same steamer for Betty; the lovers are thus happily united, and Anastasia, realizing her defeat, sends her blessing. *Orphans. Actors. Reporters. Taxi drivers. Novelists. Businesswomen. Social classes. Adoption. Courtship. San Francisco.*

EVERYMAN'S PRICE **F2.1565**

J. W. Film Corp. 14 Oct **1921** [trade review; c3 Jun 1921; LU16720]. Si; b&w. 35mm. 5 reels.

Dir Burton King. *Story* F. McGrew Willis. *Photog* L. D. Littlefield.

Cast: Grace Darling *(Ethel Armstrong)*, E. J. Radcliffe *(Henry Armstrong)*, Charles Waldron *(Bruce Steele)*, Bud Geary *(Jim Steele)*.

Comedy-drama. Bruce Steele, the district attorney, is concerned about the extent of profiteering in foodstuff. He assigns men to investigate the problem, then dashes off to propose marriage to Ethel Armstrong, who accepts but later breaks the engagement when the investigators report that her father is a profiteer. Bruce interrupts her father's trial, dismissing the case for lack of evidence. Grateful, Mr. Armstrong arranges to get Bruce and Ethel together again by a plot involving his son and Bruce's brother in a forgery case. The plot proves successful, everyone involved is proven innocent, and Bruce and Ethel rediscover their love. *Investigators. Profiteers. District attorneys. Forgery. Frameup. Trials. Foodstuff.*

EVERYTHING FOR SALE **F2.1566**

Realart Pictures. *Dist* Paramount Pictures. ca25 Sep **1921** [Pittsburgh premiere; released Sep; c25 Aug 1921; LP16893]. Si; b&w. 35mm. 5 reels, 5,091 ft.

Dir Frank O'Connor. *Story-Scen* Hector Turnbull. *Photog* Hal Rosson. *Asst Dir* Fred J. Robinson.

Cast: May McAvoy *(Helen Wainwright)*, Eddie Sutherland *(Donald Scott)*, Kathlyn Williams *(Mrs. Wainwright)*, Edwin Stevens *(Mr. Wainwright)*, Richard Tucker *(Lee Morton)*, Betty Schade *(Lillian Lord)*, Dana Todd *(Billy Mitchell)*, Jane Keckley *(Sarah Calmm)*.

Society drama. Helen Wainwright goes to live with her aunt after leaving finishing school, and Mrs. Wainwright plans to marry her to young millionaire Lee Morton, on whom Helen makes a dazzling impression. Meanwhile, Helen renews acquaintance with her childhood sweetheart, Donald Scott. Morton parts with his mistress, Lillian Lord, and becomes engaged to Helen. On the day Helen is to wed, Scott returns from a business trip and takes Helen on a boating excursion; they are stranded on an island and compelled to remain there overnight. Angrily, Morton breaks the engagement and returns to Lillian, while the lovers are free to wed. *Millionaires. Aunts. Mistresses. Courtship.*

EVE'S LEAVES **F2.1567**

De Mille Pictures. *Dist* Producers Distributing Corp. 13 Jun **1926** [c10 May 1926; LP22698]. Si; b&w. 35mm. 7 reels, 6,754 ft.

Pres by Cecil B. De Mille. *Dir* Paul Sloane. *Prod Ed–Adapt* Elmer Harris. *Cont* Jack Jevne. *Titl* John Krafft. *Photog* Arthur Miller. *Art Dir* Max Parker. *Asst Dir* William Scully.

Cast: Leatrice Joy *(Eve Corbin)*, William Boyd *(Bob Britton)*, Robert Edeson *(Captain Corbin)*, Walter Long *(Chang Fang)*, Richard Carle *(Thomas Britton)*, Arthur Hoyt *(a missionary)*, Sojin *(Lee Sing)*, Nambu *(The Executioner)*.

Romantic comedy. Source: Harry Chapman Ford, *Eve's Leaves* (New York opening: 26 Mar 1925). Eve, the boyish daughter of a freighter captain stationed in a Chinese port, is addicted to dime novels and romantic daydreams. Going ashore with her father, she meets Bob Britton, the son of a wealthy teaplanter, who teases her, thinking she is a boy. When Chang Fang, a Chinese pirate, stages a raid on the town, Eve uses the situation to shanghai Bob aboard her father's vessel, which is then taken by the pirates. Bob is taken to Chang's stronghold with Eve, who conceals herself in a large rug; when she reveals herself, Chang orders the room cleared, but she binds him hand and foot, as she did earlier to Bob. Eve and Bob escape, pursued by the pirate band. Chang is popped into a jar and ejected from a window by a missionary, who then reads psalms to Chang while Eve ropes *him;* drawn up to the window, Bob and Eve compel the missionary to marry them ... . *Tomboys. Chinese. Pirates. Missionaries. Courtship. Shanghaiing. Reading. China.*

EVE'S LOVER **F2.1568**

Warner Brothers Pictures. 6 Jul **1925** [c3 Apr 1925; LP21321]. Si; b&w. 35mm. 7 reels, 7,237 ft.

Dir Roy Del Ruth. *Adapt* Darryl Francis Zanuck. *Photog* George Winkler.

Cast: Irene Rich *(Eve Burnside)*, Bert Lytell *(Count Leon Molnar)*, Clara Bow *(Rena D'Arcy)*, Willard Louis *(Austin Starfield)*, John Steppling *(Burton Gregg)*, Arthur Hoyt *(Amos Potts)*, Lew Harvey *(agitator)*.

Melodrama. Source: W. K. Clifford, "Eve's Lover," in *Eve's Lover, and Other Stories* (New York, 1924). Eve Burnside's steel mill is coveted by Austin Starfield, a business rival who persuades an impoverished count, Leon Molnar, to attempt to persuade Eve to marry him and thereby gain control of her business. The count, who has given a bad check to Starfield, succeeds in marrying Eve but meanwhile falls in love with her and breaks off dealings with Starfield. Rena D'Arcy, a flapper and sometime sweetheart of Leon, arrives in town and tells Eve that Leon married her only for money, thereby disrupting relations between Eve and Leon. Starfield foments labor disputes at the Burnside mill by hiring agitators to start a strike, but the count intercedes at a crucial moment and saves the day. Leon regains Eve's affections, and Starfield is arrested for consiracy. *Businessmen. Nobility. Flappers. Steel industry. Strikes. Marriage.*

EVE'S SECRET **F2.1569**

Famous Players–Lasky. *Dist* Paramount Pictures. 11 May **1925** [15 May 1925; LP21465]. Si; b&w. 35mm. 6 reels, 6,305 ft.

Pres by Adolph Zukor, Jesse L. Lasky. *Dir* Clarence Badger. *Scen* Adelaide Heilbron. *Photog* H. Kinley Martin.

Cast: Betty Compson *(Eve)*, Jack Holt *(Duke of Poltava)*, William Collier, Jr. *(Pierre)*, Vera Lewis *(Duchess)*, Lionel Belmore *(Baron)*, Mario Carillo *(Prince Boris)*.

Romantic comedy. Source: Zoë Akins and Lajos Biró, *The Moon-Flower* (1924?). Having no use for women of his own rank, the Duke of Poltava falls in love with Eve, a peasant girl whom he sends to Paris to be educated preparatory to becoming his duchess. Having learned all the secrets of femininity in the shops and salons of the French capital, Eve joins the Duke at the Villa d'Or on the Riviera, where the duke, made suspicious by Eve's poise and beauty, attempts to keep other men away from her. Pierre then arrives on the beach, intent on going through the small fortune left him by his uncle. Pierre meets Eve, and it is love at first sight. He soon angers the duke, and they fight a duel, with Pierre wounding the duke. Pierre then goes to Eve and claims her for his own, but she rejects him and returns to the duke, to whom she expresses her undying love. *Peasants. Royalty. Jealousy. Paris. Riviera. Duels.*

EVIDENCE **F2.1570**

Selznick Pictures. *Dist* Select Pictures. 5 May **1922** [c5 May 1922; LP17845]. Si; b&w. 35mm. 5 reels, 4,642 ft.

Pres by Lewis J. Selznick. *Dir* George Archainbaud. *Story-Scen* Edward J. Montagne. *Photog* Jack Brown, Jules Cronjager.

Cast: Elaine Hammerstein *(Florette)*, Niles Welsh *(Phillip Rowland)*, Holmes Herbert *(Judge Rowland)*, Constance Bennett *(Edith)*, Marie Burke *(Mrs. Bascom)*, Matilda Metevier *(Louise)*, Ernest Hilliard *(Walter Stanley)*.

Society melodrama. When Florette, a popular actress, and her friend Edith become rivals for the love of Walter Stanley, a leading man, Florette sacrifices her feelings for the other girl. Three years later, Phillip Rowland, a young aristocrat, falls in love with Florette. When Edith intrudes in her affairs, Florette—although she fears unhappiness will result because of their differing social positions—decides to marry Rowland regardless of the consequences. Rowland stands by his wife, although she is snubbed by his family, but when Edith conspires with Walter Stanley to place Florette in a compromising position, Judge Rowland accepts circumstantial evidence as truth and plans for a divorce. Florette, however, cleverly puts her brother-in-law on the defensive; making amends, he has her reinstated in the family's good graces. *Actors. Social classes. Marriage. Jealousy.*

EVIDENCE **F2.1571**

Warner Brothers Pictures. 5 Oct **1929** [c26 Sep 1929; LP716]. Sd (Vitaphone); b&w. 35mm. 8 reels, 7,152 ft. [Also si.]

Dir John G. Adolfi. *Scen-Dial* J. Grubb Alexander. *Titl* De Leon Anthony. *Photog* Barney McGill. *Film Ed* Robert Crandall. *Song: "Little Cavalier"* Al Dubin, M. K. Jerome.

Cast: Pauline Frederick *(Myra Stanhope)*, William Courtenay *(Cyril Wimborne)*, Conway Tearle *(Harold Courtenay)*, Lowell Sherman *(Norman Pollock)*, Alec B. Francis *(Harbison)*, Freddie Burke Frederick *(Kenyon Wimborne)*, Madeline Seymour *(Mrs. Debenham)*, Ivan Simpson *(Peabody)*, Myrna Loy *(native girl)*, Lionel Belmore *(innkeeper)*.

Society melodram. Source: J. Du Rocher MacPherson, *Evidence* (New York opening: 7 Oct 1914). Lord Cyril Wimborne, a barrister, divorces his wife, Myra, and takes custody of their child, Kenyon, when he finds her name linked with the profligate Major Pollock. Myra goes into seclusion while Pollock, intending to conceal Myra's innocence, goes to Burma. A few years later Myra sees Kenyon in the park with Mrs. Debenham, a widow with designs on Wimborne. Noting the resemblance between the lady in the park (whom he calls his "princess") and a photograph of his mother, Kenyon invites Myra to dinner at a time when his father, who has curtailed the visits to the park, plans to be away. At the same time Harold Courtenay, an old family friend, sees an opportunity to reunite the estranged couple. Myra and Wimborne are reunited when Pollock commits suicide, leaving a note completely exonerating her from the charge of adultery. *Barristers. Rakes. Nobility. Infidelity. Divorce. Suicide. England. Burma.*

THE EVIL HALF *see* **WOLVES OF THE NORTH**

EVOLUTION **F2.1572**

Red Seal Pictures. 1 Jun **1923** [New York State license]. Si; b&w. 35mm. 6 reels.

Ed? Max Fleischer.

Scientific film. The film begins with a series of shots showing how man has controlled his environment by the use of mechanical devices and proceeds to put forth a theory of the birth of the earth. The development of cellular life, fish, and reptiles is all preliminary to the major part of the picture, which deals with the evolution of man. Various stages of monkey groups are shown to progress in their development until the final point in the argument is demonstrated—the evolution of modern man. *Evolution. Monkeys.*

EWIGE NARANIM *see* **ETERNAL FOOLS (EWIGE NARANIM)**

EX-FLAME **F2.1573**

Liberty Productions. 19 Nov **1930** [New York State license]. Sd; b&w. 35mm. 8 reels, 6,480 or 6,698 ft.

Supv M. H. Hoffman, Edward R. Halperin. *Dir-Story* Victor Halperin. *Dial Dir* Herbert Farjeon. *Adapt-Dial* George Draney. *Photog* Ernest Miller. *Art Dir* Charles Cadwallader. *Film Ed* Donn Hayes. *Rec Engr* Harold Hobson. *Asst Dir* Gordon Cooper. *Prod Mgr* George Bertholon.

Cast: Neil Hamilton *(Sir Carlisle Austin)*, Marian Nixon *(Lady Catherine)*, Judith Barrie *(Barbara Lacey)*, Norman Kerry *(Beaumont Winthrop)*, Snub Pollard *(Boggins)*, Roland Drew *(Umberto)*, José Bohr *(Argentinean)*, Joan Standing *(Kilmer)*, Cornelius Keefe *(Keith)*, May Beatty *(Lady Harriett)*, Lorimer Johnson *(Colonel Lacey)*, Joseph North *(Wilkins)*, Charles Crockett *(Parson)*, Billy Hagerty *(Master Stuart Austin)*, Louis Armstrong and His Band.

Domestic-society drama. Source: Mrs. Henry Wood, *East Lynn* (1861). After 4 years of wedded bliss at the Austin family estate, Kitty (Lady Catherine) becomes jealous of her husband's ex-flame, Barbara Lacey, who has divorced her American husband and is visiting a neighboring estate with Beaumont Winthrop, an ex-flame of Kitty's. Incensed at Carlisle's attention to Barbara, Kitty leaves home with her baby and later is visited by Beau, who has a short time to live and wishes to declare his love for her. Bidding Kitty goodby late at night, Beau collapses; Kitty then calls a doctor, and a scandal ensues. As a result, Kitty loses custody of her son, and she begins resort-hopping with one man after another. Reading of Carlisle's engagement to Barbara, Kitty returns to England bent on kidnaping her son, but Carlisle finds her hiding in a closet, and they are reconciled. (There are incidental songs.) *Nobility. Infidelity. Divorce. Jealousy. Kidnaping. Reputation. England.*

THE EXALTED FLAPPER **F2.1574**

Fox Film Corp. 9 Jun **1929** [c6 Jun 1929; LP444]. Synchronized mus score (Movietone); b&w. 35mm. 6 reels, 5,806 ft. [Also si; 5,790 ft.]

Pres by William Fox. *Supv* Kenneth Hawks. *Dir* James Tinling. *Scen* Matt Taylor. *Titl* H. H. Caldwell. *Adapt* Ray Harris. *Photog* Charles Clarke. *Asst Photog* Don Anderson. *Film Ed* H. H. Caldwell. *Mus Score* Arthur Kay. *Asst Dir* William Tinling.

Cast: Sue Carol *(Princess Izola)*, Barry Norton *(Prince Boris of Dacia)*, Irene Rich *(Queen Charlotte of Capra)*, Albert Conti *(King Alexander of Capra)*, Sylvia Field *(Majorie)*, Stuart Erwin *(Bimbo Mehaffey)*, Lawrence Grant *(Premier Vadisco of Dacia)*, Charles Clary *(Dr. Nicholas)*, Michael Visaroff *(Old Fritz)*.

Romantic comedy. Source: Will Irwin, "The Exalted Flapper," in *American Weekly Sunday Magazine* (12 Aug–14 Oct 1925). Princess Izola, a flapper princess of a foreign kingdom, refuses to marry Prince Boris of Dacia, whom she has never seen; but when she meets him traveling incognito, the princess falls in love. The Queen of Capra, unaware of his identity, has him shanghaied, but he is rescued by the princess. The two countries then become stronger allies, and in due course Izola and Boris are married. *Royalty. Flappers. Personal identity. Courtship. Shanghaiing. Imaginary kingdoms.*

EXCESS BAGGAGE **F2.1575**

Metro-Goldwyn-Mayer Pictures. 8 Sep **1928** [c8 Sep 1928; LP25612]. Sd eff & mus score (Movietone); b&w. 35mm. 8 reels, 7,182 ft. [Also si.]

Dir James Cruze. *Cont* Frances Marion. *Dial-Titl* Ralph Spence. *Photog* Ira Morgan. *Sets* Cedric Gibbons. *Film Ed* George Hively. *Wardrobe* David Cox.

Cast: William Haines *(Eddie Kane)*, Josephine Dunn *(Elsa McCoy)*, Neely Edwards *(Jimmy Dunn)*, Kathleen Clifford *(Mabel Ford)*, Greta Granstedt *(Betty Ford)*, Ricardo Cortez *(Val D'Errico)*, Cyril Chadwick *(Crammon)*.

Comedy-drama. Source: John Wesley McGowan, *Excess Baggage* (New York opening: 26 Dec 1927). Eddie Kane, a brash vaudeville juggler and acrobat, falls in love with Elsa McCoy, one of Dunn's Dancing Dames. After they are married, Elsa becomes a success in the movies. Eddie remains in vaudeville and, chafing at his lack of advancement, comes to believe that Elsa has been unfaithful to him with Val D'Errico, a handsome actor. Eddie and Elsa separate, and he takes a bad fall during a high wire act. During a later comeback attempt, Eddie loses his nerve until unexpectedly Elsa appears onstage and assures him of her continuing love and fidelity. Eddie completes his act, and he and Elsa are reunited. *Jugglers. Acrobats. Actors. Dancers. Aerialists. Marriage. Infidelity. Vaudeville. Motion pictures.*

EXCHANGE OF WIVES **F2.1576**

Metro-Goldwyn-Mayer Pictures. 4 or 23 Oct **1925** [c5 Nov 1925; LP21984]. Si; b&w. 35mm. 7 reels, 6,300 ft.

Dir Hobart Henley. *Adapt-Titl* Frederic Hatton, Fanny Hatton. *Camera* Ben Reynolds. *Art Dir* Cedric Gibbons.

Cast: Eleanor Boardman *(Margaret Rathburn)*, Lew Cody *(John Rathburn)*, Renée Adorée *(Elise Moran)*, Creighton Hale *(Victor Moran)*.

Domestic comedy. Source: Cosmo Hamilton, *Exchange of Wives* (New York opening: 26 Sep 1919). Two couples, John and Margaret Rathburn and Victor and Elise Moran, have been married a year and live next door to each other. Margaret is an excellent cook and housekeeper but is not very affectionate, while Elise is very affectionate but cannot cook. Circumstances throw the couples together as Elise vamps John and Victor falls in love with Margaret. Margaret, determined to keep John, arranges for the four to go to a mountain lodge where the husbands and wives would live in separate cabins and each wife would cook for the other's husband. In the end John is glad to return to Margaret, and a sudden reversion to caveman tactics brings Elise to Victor's arms. *Marriage. Mate swapping.*

Note: Copyright title: *An Exchange of Wives*

EXCITEMENT **F2.1577**

Universal Pictures. 13 Apr **1924** [c4 Mar 1924; LP19967]. Si; b&w. 35mm. 5 reels, 4,913 ft.

Pres by Carl Laemmle. *Dir* Robert F. Hill. *Scen* Hugh Hoffman. *Story* Crosby George. *Photog* Jackson Rose.

Cast: Laura La Plante *(Nila Lyons)*, Edward Hearn *(Arthur Drew)*, William Welsh *(Hiram Lyons)*, Frances Raymond *(Mrs. Lyons)*, Fred De Silva *(Eric Orton)*, Margaret Cullington *(Violet Smith)*, Albert Hart *(Abner Smith)*, Rolfe Sedan *(Willie Winkle)*, Bert Roach *(Toby)*, Stanley Blystone *(Freddie)*, Lon Poff *(Roger Cove)*, George Fisher *(Chester Robbins)*, Fay Tincher *("Mammy")*.

Comedy-melodrama. Newlywed Nila Drew is cured of thrill-seeking when she is finally rescued by her husband after being kidnaped, stuffed into a mummy case, and shipped to an Egyptian who calls her the Queen of Pharaoh and threatens to put her back into the tomb. Her husband, Arthur, arrives in time to save her and reveals that it was all a trick to cure Nila of her desire for excitement. *Egyptians. Thrill-seeking. Hoaxes. Mummies.*

Note: Working title: *The Thrill Girl.*

THE EXCITERS **F2.1578**

Famous Players–Lasky. 3 Jun **1923** [c3 Jun 1923; LP19025]. Si; b&w. 35mm. 6 reels, 5,939 ft.

Pres by Adolph Zukor. *Dir* Maurice Campbell. *Scen* John Colton, Sonya Levien. *Photog* George Webber.

Cast: Bebe Daniels *(Ronnie Rand)*, Antonio Moreno *(Pierre Martel)*, Burr McIntosh *(Rackham, The Lawyer)*, Diana Allen *(Ermintrude)*, Cyril Ring *(Roger Patton)*, Bigelow Cooper *(Hilary Rand)*, Ida Darling *(Mrs. Rand)*, Jane Thomas *(Della Vaughn)*, Allan Simpson *(The Mechanician)*, George Backus *(The Minister)*, Henry Sedley *("Gentleman Eddie")*, Erville Alderson *("Chloroform Charlie")*, Tom Blake *("Flash")*.

Melodrama. Source: Martin Brown, *The Exciters* (production and publication undetermined). Ronnie Rand, obliged to marry before she is 21 or lose her inheritance, meets Pierre Martel, member of a gang of crooks, and, convinced that he is a "real man," she marries him. Pierre's confederates attempt to blackmail Ronnie, and when she refuses to sign a check they try to kill Pierre; but police arrive in time to save him. Pierre is revealed to be a U. S. Intelligence Service agent. Ronnie, though somewhat disappointed that her husband is not at all a crook, accepts the situation. *Intelligence agents. Gangs. Inheritance. Blackmail.*

EXCLUSIVE RIGHTS **F2.1579**

Preferred Pictures. 15 Dec **1926** [c17 Dec 1926; LP23494]. Si; b&w. 35mm. 6 reels, 6,087 ft.

Pres by J. G. Bachmann. *Dir* Frank O'Connor. *Adapt* Eve Unsell. *Photog* André Barlatier.

Cast: Gayne Whitman *(Stanley Wharton)*, Lillian Rich *(Catherine Courtwright)*, Gloria Gordon *(Mae Morton)*, Raymond McKee *(Mack Miller)*, Gaston Glass *(Flash Fleming)*, Grace Cunard *(nightclub hostess)*, Sheldon Lewis *(Bickel)*, Charles Mailes *(Boss Morris)*, Shirley Palmer *(Sadie Towner)*, James Bradbury, Jr. *(Bat Hoover)*, Fletcher Norton *(Garth)*, Jimmy Savo *(specialty dancer)*.

Crook melodrama. Source: Jerome N. Wilson, "Invisible Government" (publication undetermined). Stanley Wharton, war hero and candidate for governor, is the avowed enemy of Al Morris, boss of crooks and politicians constituting an invisible government, and when elected to office he allows the death sentence of Bickel, a gang member, for murder, to stand. In cooperation with Catherine Courtwright, Wharton's fiancée, Morris champions a new bill for the abolition of capital punishment, then frames Mack Miller, Wharton's war buddy, with the murder of Bat Hoover at the Elite Club, a gang rendezvous. Torn between friendship and duty, Governor Wharton refuses to sign the bill though Catherine breaks the engagement. Sadie, secretly Mack's wife, obtains a confession from Flash Fleming, but Fleming is killed before he signs it. Wharton tricks Morris into believing that Mack has been executed, thereby forcing the hand of the corrupt ringleader and obtaining a statement from Bickel. *Political bosses. Veterans. State governors. Blackmail. Murder. Capital punishment. Friendship.*

EXCUSE ME **F2.1580**

Metro-Goldwyn Pictures. 19 Jan **1925** [c29 Jan 1925; LP21084]. Si; b&w. 35mm. 6 reels, 5,747 ft.

Pres by Louis B. Mayer. *Dir* Alf Goulding. *Adapt-Scen* Rupert Hughes. *Photog* John Boyle. *Art Dir* Cedric Gibbons. *Asst Dir* Nick Grinde.

Cast: Norma Shearer *(Marjorie Newton)*, Conrad Nagel *(Harry Mallory)*, Renée Adorée *(Francine)*, Walter Hiers *(Porter)*, John Boles *(Lieutenant Shaw)*, Bert Roach *(Jimmy Wellington)*, William V. Mong *(Rev. Dr. Temple)*, Edith Yorke *(Mrs. Temple)*, Gene Cameron *(Lieutenant Hudson)*, Fred Kelsey *(George Ketchem)*, Paul Weigel *(Rev. Job Wales)*, Mai Wells *(Mrs. Job Wales)*.

Farce. Source: Rupert Hughes, *Excuse Me* (New York, c1911). When Lieutenant Mallory is ordered to report immediately for duty in Honolulu, he persuades his fiancée, Marjorie Newton, a beautiful society debutante, to marry him immediately, enabling them to spend their honeymoon in the Islands. Mallory and Marjorie attempt without success to find a minister to marry them on such short notice, but, as they are about to part at the station, Mallory sees a minister getting aboard the train he is to take, and he and Marjorie quickly decide to be married on the train. Once underway, they cannot find the minister, though they discover that the bridal compartment has been reserved for them. To avoid sleeping together, they stage a terrible argument, and Mallory spends the night in the washroom. The following day, Mallory and Marjorie have a genuine misunderstanding over the attentions of a French girl to Mallory. After reconciliation, Mallory gets off the train at a village in which there is a minister's convention, but, before he can return to the train, it leaves without him. Mallory hires a plane to follow the train, sees that a bridge ahead of it is on fire, makes a daring transfer from the plane to the train, and alerts the engineer in time to avoid disaster. Mallory and Marjorie are finally married in San Francisco and catch a boat to Honolulu for their honeymoon. *Socialites. Clergymen. Weddings. Trains. San Francisco. Honolulu. Air stunts.*

EXILED *see* **THE JILT**

THE EXILES **F2.1581**

Fox Film Corp. 14 Oct **1923** [c14 Oct 1923; LP19565]. Si; b&w. 35mm. 5 reels, 4,719 ft.

Pres by William Fox. *Dir* Edmund Mortimer. *Scen* Fred Jackson. *Adapt* John Russell.

Cast: John Gilbert *(Henry Holcombe)*, Betty Bouton *(Alice Carroll)*, John Webb Dillon *(Wilhelm von Linke)*, Margaret Fielding *(Rose Ainsmith)*, Fred Warren *(Dr. Randolph)*.

Melodrama. Source: Richard Harding Davis, *The Exiles, and Other Stories* (New York, 1894). Alice Carroll, involved in a murder mystery, flees to Tangiers where District Attorney Henry Holcombe, who has discovered that she is innocent, finds her. Holcombe kidnaps Alice, newly fallen prey to Wilhelm von Linke, owner of a gambling den. After a struggle with Linke, Holcombe takes Alice back to the States with him. Romance buds. *District attorneys. Murder. Gambling. Tangiers. Africa.*

EXIT SMILING **F2.1582**

Metro-Goldwyn-Mayer Pictures. 6 Nov **1926** [New York premiere; released 14 Nov; c29 Nov 1926; LP23377]. Si; b&w. 35mm. 7 reels, 6,461 ft.

Dir Sam Taylor. *Scen* Sam Taylor, Tim Whelan. *Titl* Joe Farnham. *Story* Marc Connelly. *Photog* André Barlatier. *Sets* Cedric Gibbons, Frederic Hope. *Film Ed* Daniel J. Gray. *Wardrobe* André-ani.

Cast: Beatrice Lillie *(Violet)*, Jack Pickford *(Jimmy Marsh)*, Doris Lloyd *(Olga)*, De Witt Jennings *(Orlando Wainwright)*, Harry Myers *(Jesse Watson)*, Tenen Holtz *(Tod Powell)*, Louise Lorraine *(Phyllis Tichnor)*, Franklin Pangborn *(Cecil Lovelace)*, D'Arcy Corrigan *(Macomber)*, William Gillespie *(Jack Hastings)*, Carl Richards *(Dave)*.

Comedy-drama. Jimmy Marsh, a bank teller, is in love with Phyllis, daughter of the bank president. Jesse Watson, vice president and cashier, who also seeks the hand of Phyllis, considers investing in a roadhouse owned by bootlegger Tod Powell. Seeing Jimmy intoxicated there, Watson gets Powell to forge Jimmy's name to a gambling note and later has him discharged. Jimmy falls in with a repertory company and, thanks to Violet—the utility woman and wardrobe mistress—is hired as a stagehand; then, coached by Violet, he becomes the understudy for the villain. When the show plays in his hometown, Violet dons male attire and plays the villain herself. Violet learns that Powell has threatened Watson with exposure; and through her scheming, Jimmy is cleared of the charge and is reunited with Phyllis. *Bankers. Bank clerks. Bootleggers. Actors. Wardrobe mistresses. Courtship. Theater. Roadhouses.*

EXIT THE VAMP **F2.1583**

Famous Players–Lasky. *Dist* Paramount Pictures. ca6 Nov **1921** [Washington premiere; released 4 Dec; c12 Nov 1921; LP17187]. Si; b&w. 35mm. 5 reels, 4,554 ft.

Pres by Jesse L. Lasky. *Dir* Frank Urson. *Story-Adapt* Clara Beranger. *Photog* Charles Edgar Schoenbaum. *Asst Dir* Harold Schwartz.

Cast: Ethel Clayton *(Marion Shipley)*, T. Roy Barnes *(John Shipley)*, Fontaine La Rue *(Mrs. Willy Strong)*, Theodore Roberts *(Old Man Shipley)*, William Boyd *(Robert Pitts)*, Mickey Moore *(Junior Shipley)*, Mattie Peters *(Colored Mammy)*.

Comedy-drama. Marion Shipley is happily devoted to her husband until Mrs. Willy Strong, a thorough coquette, succeeds in capturing the affections of John Shipley. When John vouches for Mrs. Strong's credit in obtaining a diamond necklace, the salesman, who is a friend of Marion's, informs her of the intrigue. She goes to a restaurant where John and Mrs. Strong are dining and sees the vamp give him the key to her apartment. Obtaining entrance to her rival's room, Marion transforms herself with the siren's clothes and makeup, and when Shipley arrives he is unable in the dim light to distinguish her identity. Marion is in his arms when Mrs. Strong arrives, and he denounces her for his wife. *Vamps. Marriage. Infidelity.*

EXPERIENCE **F2.1584**

Famous Players–Lasky. *Dist* Paramount Pictures. 7 Aug **1921** [New York premiere; released 23 Oct; c23 Oct 1921; LP17160]. Si; b&w. 35mm. 7 reels, 6,560 ft.

Pres by Adolph Zukor. *Dir* George Fitzmaurice. *Scen* Waldemar Young. *Photog* Arthur Miller.

Cast: Richard Barthelmess *(Youth)*, John Miltern *(Experience)*, Marjorie Daw *(Love)*, E. J. Radcliffe *(Ambition)*, Betty Carpenter *(Hope)*, Kate Bruce *(Mother)*, Lilyan Tashman *(Pleasure)*, R. Senior *(Opportunity)*, Joseph Smiley *(Chance)*, Fred Hadley *(Tout)*, Harry J. Lane *(Despair)*, Helen Ray *(Intoxication)*, Jed Prouty *(Good Nature)*, Barney Furey *(Poverty)*, Charles Stevenson *(Wealth)*, Edna Wheaton *(Beauty)*, Yvonne Routon *(Fashion)*, Ned Hay *(Sport)*, Sibyl Carmen *(Excitement)*, Robert Schable *(Conceit)*, Nita Naldi *(Temptation)*, Frankie Evans *(Work)*, Frank McCormack *(Delusion)*, Louis Wolheim *(Crime)*, Agnes Marc *(Habit)*, Mrs. Gallagher *(Degradation)*, Florence Flinn *(Frailty)*, Mac Barnes *(Makeshift)*, Leslie King *(Gloom)*.

Allegorical drama. Source: George V. Hobart, *Experience, a Morality Play of Today* (New York, 1915). Youth leaves his mother at the behest of Ambition and with Love and Hope goes to the city, where he encounters Pleasure and asks Opportunity to wait; but she refuses and leaves him. At the Primrose Path (a cabaret), Pleasure introduces him to Beauty, Wealth, Fashion, and Temptation. Youth's mother dies, and Love sends him a telegram, which is intercepted by Temptation; and when Love comes to the city, she is turned away from the Primrose Path. Chance directs Youth to a gambling house where he loses everything but the ring given him by Love, and he is haunted by Poverty and Delusion. With the exception of Temptation, all have forgotten him. He meets Vice and Habit and finally consents to go with Crime to rob Wealth's house. On the way he hears a church choir singing and decides to go home; with Experience he returns where Love and Hope await him. Ambition again seeks Youth, who with Love at his side starts a new life. *Personification.*

THE EXQUISITE SINNER **F2.1585**

Metro-Goldwyn-Mayer Pictures. 28 Mar **1926** [c19 Apr 1926; LP22777]. Si; b&w. 35mm. 6 reels, 5,977 or 5,844 ft.

Dir (see note) Josef von Sternberg, Phil Rosen. *Titl* Joe Farnham. *Adapt* Josef von Sternberg, Alice D. G. Miller. *Photog* Maximilian Fabian. *Art Dir* Cedric Gibbons, Joseph Wright. *Film Ed* John W. English. *Asst Dir* Robert Florey. *Wardrobe* André-ani.

Cast: Conrad Nagel *(Dominique Prad)*, Renée Adorée *(The Gypsy Maid, Silda)*, Paulette Duval *(Yvonne)*, Frank Currier *(Colonel)*, George K. Arthur *(His Orderly)*, Matthew Betz *(The Gypsy Chief, Secchi)*, Helena D'Algy, Claire Du Brey *(Dominique's sisters)*, Myrna Loy *(The Living Statute)*.

Romantic melodrama. Source: Alden Brooks, *Escape* (New York, 1924). Dominique Prad, a wounded soldier convalescing at a French resort with his fiancée, determines to escape the conventions of society when he sees a group of Gypsies in the town. A wire from Paris urges him to return and take charge of his uncle's business, but at his uncle's funeral he finds that his sisters have inherited the estate. Though made manager of a silk mill, he spends his time painting. His sisters and brother-in-law destroy his paintings and denounce him as a loafer; infuriated, he goes to a doctor, who, to his chagrin, declares him well. As a result, he attempts suicide. Thinking him insane, his family tie him to the bedpost, but he escapes in a colonel's uniform and joins a Gypsy band. Silda, a Gypsy maid, learning of a reward for his capture, flees the camp and Secchi, her lover, with Dominique; and they are befriended by a Breton mayor. Secchi discovers them at the mayor's about to be married; Dominique denounces his family and fiancée and insults the colonel; and a bloodless duel ensues. To the approval of the Bretons, he departs with the Gypsy girl. *Artists. Gypsies. Brother-sister relationship. Social conformity. Insanity. Inheritance. Factory* *management. Silk. Brittany. France.*

Note: Sternberg was replaced during filming, and Rosen completed the film.

EXTRA! EXTRA! **F2.1586**

Fox Film Corp. 5 Mar **1922** [c5 Mar 1922; LP17682]. Si; b&w. 35mm. 5 reels, 4,160 ft.

Pres by William Fox. *Dir* William K. Howard. *Scen* Arthur J. Zellner. *Story* Julien Josephson. *Photog* George Webber.

Cast: Edna Murphy *(Myra Rogers)*, Johnnie Walker *(Barry Price)*, Herschel Mayall *(Edward Fletcher)*, Wilson Hummell *(Jim Rogers)*, John Steppling *(Haskell)*, Gloria Woodthorpe *(Mrs. Rogers)*, Theodore von Eltz *(Fordney Stowe)*, Edward Jobson *(Alvin Stowe)*.

Romantic adventure. Barry Price, cub reporter at the *Morning Sun,* is assigned to assist Jim Rogers in getting a story from Edward Fletcher regarding the merger of Fletcher's and Stowe's firms. When Rogers fails to get aboard Fletcher's yacht, Barry feigns drowning and obtains the interview. Rogers is discharged, and his daughter, Myra, secretary to Stowe, although she knows of the consolidation plans, cannot divulge them to her father. Barry—then assigned to interview Stowe, who dislikes reporters—assumes the guise of a butler and learns that written proof is to be found in the house safe, but he finds that Stowe's nephew, Fordney, who is in debt, and Myra, who hopes to help her father, are after the papers. Stowe steals the papers, however, but Barry and Myra follow him and recover them. Rogers is given back his job, and Barry and Myra are happily united. *Reporters. Filial relations. Business combinations. Documentation.*

THE EXTRA GIRL **F2.1587**

Mack Sennett Productions. *Dist* Associated Exhibitors. 28 Oct **1923** [c9 Nov 1923; LU19583]. Si; b&w. 35mm. 6-7 reels.

Dir F. Richard Jones. *Scen* Bernard McConville. *Story* Mack Sennett. *Photog* Homer Scott, Eric Crockett.

Cast: Mabel Normand *(Sue Graham)*, Ralph Graves *(Dave Giddings)*, George Nichols *(Pa Graham)*, Anna Hernandez *(Ma Graham)*, Vernon Dent *(Aaron Applejohn)*, Ramsey Wallace *(Phillip Hackett)*, Charlotte Mineau *(Belle Brown)*, Mary Mason, Max Davidson, Louise Carver, William Desmond, Carl Stockdale, Harry Gribbon, Billy Bevan, André Beranger.

Comedy-drama. Hometown girl Sue Graham wins a movie contest and goes to Hollywood when her parents forbid her to marry Dave Giddings, her father's garage mechanic. Arriving in Hollywood, Sue finds that there is no work except in the wardrobe department. She falls into the clutches of an oil swindler named Hackett. When Sue's parents lose their fortune to Hackett, Sue determines to recover the money. She does that, returns home, and marries Dave, now the family hero. *Swindlers. Mechanics. Motion pictures. Smalltown life. Talent contests. Hollywood.*

EXTRAVAGANCE **F2.1588**

Metro Pictures. 7 Mar **1921** [c7 Mar 1921; LP16237]. Si; b&w. 35mm. 6 reels.

Dir Philip E. Rosen. *Scen* Edward T. Lowe, Jr. *Photog* Rudolph Bergquist. *Art Dir* Sidney Ullman.

Cast: May Allison *(Nancy Brown)*, Robert Edeson *(Richard Vane)*, Theodore von Eltz *(Dick Vane)*, William Courtwright *("Pa" Brown)*, Grace Pike *("Ma" Brown)*, Lawrence Grant *(Uncle Mark)*.

Society melodrama. Source: Ben Ames Williams, "More Stately Mansions," in *Good Housekeeping* (71:18–22, 34–37, Oct, Nov 1920). Young lawyer Dick Vane, after marrying Nancy Brown, discovers that her extravagant tastes are beyond his means. When she acquires an expensive gown Dick demands its return, but at a wild party the gown is ruined. Then, though he cannot afford it, Dick consents to buy a new house, and to raise the money he forges his father's signature on a check. Vane blames Nancy for his son's dishonor, and realizing the consequences of her actions, she repents; she and Dick are then forgiven. *Lawyers. Forgery. Finance—Personal.*

EXTRAVAGANCE **F2.1589**

Tiffany Productions. 10 Oct **1930** [c18 Sep 1930; LP1668]. Sd (Photophone); b&w. 35mm. 7 reels, 5,892 ft.

Dir Phil Rosen. *Cont-Dial* Adele Buffington, Frances Hyland, Phil Rosen. *Story (see note)* A. P. Younger, M. B. Deering. *Photog* Max Dupont. *Sets* Ralph De Lacy. *Film Ed* Charles K. Harris. *Rec Engr* Buddy Myers.

Cast: June Collyer *(Alice Kendall)*, Lloyd Hughes *(Fred Garlan)*, Owen Moore *(Jim Hamilton)*, Dorothy Christy *(Esther Hamilton)*, Jameson Thomas *(Morrell)*, Gwen Lee *(Sally)*, Robert Agnew *(Billy)*, Nella Walker *(Mrs. Kendall)*, Martha Mattox, Arthur Hoyt *(guests)*, Davis Hawthorne, Lawrence Baskcomb.

Domestic drama. Alice Kendall, who has always indulged her extravagant tastes, marries Fred Garlan, who after a year is fighting to keep his business financed and meet the constant expenses of his wife. He refuses her nothing—until she asks for a sable coat. Their best friend, Jim Hamilton, brags about his wife Esther's thrift, unaware that she has been given a sable coat by her wealthy lover, Harrison Morrell. When Alice and Fred quarrel over her new dress, she goes to a bridge party and he leaves on business. At the party Alice wins a large sum, receiving the flattery and indulgence of Morrell. Later, she buys a sable coat with money Morell has invested for her and joins Esther and Morrell at a restaurant. Fred sees Esther and Morrell together and warns Alice against her friend, then, discovering her coat, denounces her as a cheat. She decides to divorce him, but Esther's disillusionment and suicide lead to Alice's reconciliation with Fred and a realization of her thoughtless extravagance. *Businessmen. Spendthrifts. Marriage. Gambling. Infidelity. Divorce. Suicide. Clothes.*

Note: Conflicting sources indicate that *either* Younger or Deering wrote the original story, not both.

EYES OF HOLLYWOOD **F2.1590**

Chesterfield Motion Pictures. 3 Sep **1925** [New York State license]. Si; b&w. 35mm. 5 reels, 4,492 ft.

Cast: Ward Wing, Priscilla Bonner.

Comedy(?). No information about the precise nature of this film has been found. *Hollywood.*

Note: May have been "manufactured" in 1923.

EYES OF THE DESERT **F2.1591**

Dist Sierra Pictures. Feb **1926** [Deferred New York State license: 13 Jun 1929]. Si; b&w. 35mm. 5 reels, 4,500 ft.

Dir Frederick Reel, Jr.

Cast: Al Richmond, Dorothy Donald.

Western melodrama(?). No information about the nature of this film has been found.

EYES OF THE FOREST **F2.1592**

Fox Film Corp. 30 Dec **1923** [c28 Dec 1923; LP19775]. Si; b&w. 35mm. 5 reels, 4,408 ft.

Pres by William Fox. *Dir* Lambert Hillyer. *Scen* LeRoy Stone. *Story* Shannon Fife. *Photog* Daniel Clark.

Cast: Tom Mix *(Bruce Thornton)*, Pauline Starke *(Ruth Melier)*, Sid Jordan *(Horgan)*, Buster Gardner *(sheriff)*, J. P. Lockney *(Jaol Fierro)*, Tom Lingham *(Dr. Jerry MacGinnity)*, Edwin Wallock *(Julius Duval)*, Tony *(himself, a horse)*.

Western melodrama. Bruce Thornton, a forest ranger pilot, captures Ruth Melier, accused of murdering her stepfather. She claims that her husband, Horgan, a brutal timber thief, is the murderer. The ranger pilot, assisted by another pilot, rounds up Horgan and his gang of timber thieves and establishes Ruth's innocence. *Forest rangers. Air pilots. Thieves. Murder. Horses.*

EYES OF THE TOTEM **F2.1593**

H. C. Weaver Productions. *Dist* Pathé Exchange. 15 May **1927** [c5 Mar 1927; LU23726]. Si; b&w. 35mm. 7 reels, 6,228 ft.

Dir W. S. Van Dyke. *Adapt* E. C. Maxwell. *Story* W. W. Dickson. *Photog* Abe Scholtz.

Cast: Wanda Hawley *(Mariam Hardy)*, Tom Santschi *(Philip La Rue)*, Anne Cornwall *(Betty Hardy)*, Gareth Hughes *(Bruce Huston)*, Bert Woodruff *(Toby)*, Monte Wax *(Jim Hardy)*, Violet Palmer *(Stella Haynes)*, Mary Louise Jones *(Mrs. Francis Huston)*, Dorothy Llewellyn *(Peggy Huston)*, Nell Barry Taylor *(Bessie Snyder)*.

Melodrama. Mariam Hardy persuades her husband to sell his rich Alaska claim and return to civilization for the sake of her child, Betty, but before they arrive a strange man stabs her husband and steals his money. Friendless and without funds, she and the child walk the streets of Tacoma; Uncle Toby, a "blind" beggar, saves the child from a runaway team and persuades Mariam to disguise herself as a blind beggar; and at the bench under a vast totem pole, she awaits the sight of the murderer's eyes. With her earnings, years later, she is able to send Betty to a fashionable seminary. Mariam recognizes Philip La Rue, operator of a cafe, as the villain; through a faked accident he meets Betty and Bruce Huston, her beau. Betty accepts an invitation to tea, but Bruce and the police arrive in time to save her from his attack; La Rue is killed, and Mariam is happily reunited with her daughter. *Beggars. Blindness. Motherhood. Murder. Totems. Alaska. Tacoma.*

Note: Working title: *The Totem Pole Beggar.* Also known as *The Eyes of Totem.*

EYES OF THE UNDERWORLD F2.1594

Universal Pictures. 28 Apr **1929** [c16 Oct 1928; LP25743]. Si; b&w. 35mm. 5 reels, 4,208 ft.

Dir Leigh Jason, Ray Taylor. *Story-scen* Leigh Jason, Carl Krusada. *Titl* Val Cleveland. *Photog* Al Jones, Frank Redman.

Cast: Bill Cody *(Pat Doran)*, Sally Blane *(Florence Hueston)*, Arthur Lubin *(gang leader)*, Harry Tenbrook *(Gimpy Johnson)*, Charles Clary *(John Hueston)*, Monty Montague *(gardener)*.

Melodrama. John Hueston, a wealthy newspaper publisher, plans to publish an exposé of a criminal gang but is silenced by a bullet. Pat Doran, rich sportsman, is consoling Hueston's daughter at her home when members of the gang break into the house in an effort to put their hands on the incriminating evidence accumulated by Florence's father. Pat chases the crooks off and follows them to their hideout; they capture him, and he is imprisoned on a deserted island. Pat escapes, rounds up the gang, and wins Florence's love. *Publishers. Sportsmen. Gangs. Murder. Newspapers. Documentation.*

THE EYES OF THE WORLD F2.1595

Inspiration Pictures. *Dist* United Artists. 30 Aug **1930** [c30 Aug 1930; LP1549]. Sd (Movietone); b&w. 35mm. 8 reels, 7,272 ft.

Prod Sol Lesser. *Dir* Henry King. *Screenplay* N. Brewster Morse. *Adapt-Dial* Clarke Silvernail. *Photog* Ray June, John Fulton. *Film Ed* Lloyd Nosler. *Sd Rec* Ernest Rovere.

Cast—Prolog: Eulalie Jensen *(Mrs. Rutledge)*, Hugh Huntley *(James Rutledge)*, Myra Hubert *(Myra)*, Florence Roberts *(maid)*.

Cast—Story: Una Merkel *(Sybil)*, Nance O'Neil *(Myra)*, John Holland *(Aaron King)*, Fern Andra *(Mrs. Taine)*, Hugh Huntley *(James Rutledge)*, Frederic Burt *(Conrad LaGrange)*, Brandon Hurst *(Mr. Taine)*, William Jeffrey *(Bryan Oakley)*.

Melodrama. Source: Harold Bell Wright, *The Eyes of the World* (Chicago, 1914). As an unsophisticated young girl, Myra Willard is seduced into "marrying" James Rutledge and bears his child, Gertrude; but his legal wife in a fit of rage disfigures Myra's face with acid and leaves marks on the child, causing Myra to retreat from the eyes of the world to a mountain village. Thirty years later, she arranges her daughter's marriage to Edward Taine, a rich, elderly man. Later, in Paris, Gertrude meets and falls in love with Aaron King, a young artist, and induces her husband to help him. Hoping to break up the relationship, Taine has Aaron, Gertrude, and young James Rutledge, Jr., accompany him to his camp in the mountains. There, Aaron meets Sybil, daughter of novelist Conrad LaGrange, and falls in love with her. But when she is humiliated by Gertrude, Sybil allows James, Jr., to accompany her home, where he attempts to seduce her. The disfigured Myra enters and, recognizing Rutledge's son, is about to kill him, but he is saved by the arrival of Gertrude and Aaron; Myra reveals her identity, and Sybil learns that Gertrude's flirtation with Aaron is innocent, thus effecting a reconciliation between the two. ... *Artists. Novelists. Children. Motherhood. Disfiguration. Seduction. Marriage. Bigamy. Mountain life. Paris.*

THE EYES OF TOTEM *see* **EYES OF THE TOTEM**

EYES RIGHT! F2.1596

Otto K. Schreier Productions. *Dist* Goodwill Pictures. 29 Jun **1926** [New York State license]. Si; b&w. 35mm. 5 reels, 4,500 ft.

Dir Louis Chaudet. *Adapt* Leslie Curtis. *Story* Ernest Grayman. *Photog* Allen Davey. *Asst Dir* Dick Sherer.

Cast: Francis X. Bushman, Jr. *(Ted Winters)*, Flobelle Fairbanks *(Betty Phillips)*, Dora Dean *(Alice Murdock)*, Larry Kent *(Major Snodgrass)*, Frederick Vroom *(Col. Thomas A. Davis)*, Robert Hale *(Lieutenant Smith)*.

Melodrama. Ted Winters, a star football player who is unable to raise enough money to enroll in the San Diego Army and Navy Academy, gets a job in the academy kitchen washing dishes. Ted soon proves his skill on the gridiron, and Colonel Davis, the commandant, arranges for Ted to become a cadet. Ted falls in love with Betty Phillips, the commandant's niece, and thereby incurs the wrath of Cadet-Major Snodgrass, who discredits the innocent Ted in a prearranged scandal at a roadhouse. Ted is barred from the big game, and the team seems headed for certain defeat. Betty, however, convinces her uncle of Ted's good character; and he is sent into the game, leads the team to victory, wins Betty's love, and has the pleasure of seeing Snodgrass expelled. *Students. Football. Scandal. Frameup. Military schools. Roadhouses. San Diego.*

THE FACE BETWEEN F2.1597

Metro Pictures. 17 Apr **1922** [c24 Apr 1922; LP17800]. Si; b&w. 35mm. 5 reels, 4,997 ft.

Dir Bayard Veiller. *Adapt* Lenore J. Coffee. *Photog* Arthur Martinelli. *Art-Tech Dir* A. F. Mantz.

Cast: Bert Lytell *(Tommy Carteret, Sr./Tommy Carteret, Jr.)*, Andrée Tourneur *(Sybil Eliot)*, Sylvia Breamer *(Marianna Canfield)*, Hardee Kirkland *(Mr. Hartwell)*, Gerard Alexander *(Mrs. Eliot)*, Frank Brownlee *(Joe Borral)*, Burwell Hamrick *(Jared)*, Joel Day *(Mr. Canfield)*, De Witt Jennings *(The Doctor)*.

Melodrama. Source: Justus Miles Forman, "The Carterets" (publication undetermined). On the night of his engagement to Sybil Eliot, young Tommy Carteret realizes that his father is guilty of intruding on a neighbor's household. Taking the blame on himself, he consents to go with Hartwell, the man who preferred charges against him, and live in a desolate mountain cabin. There he meets Marianna, the daughter of a poor family, who is pursued by Joe Borral though she does not love him. Joe threatens the intruder, and when Marianna goes to warn him and is found in his cabin, she declares that Tommy is to marry her, and in a confused state, Tommy agrees. En route to the minister, Tommy learns that Hartwell has died and that his fiancée has forgiven him, but Joe shoots Marianna and wounds Tommy. He is taken home to Sybil, and from time to time he suffers hallucinations in which Marianna comes between them; but eventually he improves and is free to marry Sybil. *Mountain life. Mental illness. Hallucinations.*

THE FACE IN THE FOG F2.1598

Cosmopolitan Productions. *Dist* Paramount Pictures. 8 Oct **1922** [c27 Sep 1922; LP18332]. Si; b&w. 35mm. 7 reels, 6,095 ft.

Dir Alan Crosland. *Scen* John Lynch, Jack Boyle. *Photog* Ira H. Morgan, Harold Wenstrom. *Prod Mgr* John Lynch.

Cast: Lionel Barrymore *(Boston Blackie Dawson, a reformed crook)*, Seena Owen *(Grand Duchess Tatiana, a Russian refugee)*, Lowell Sherman *(Count Alexis Orloff, a Russian nobleman)*, George Nash *(Huck Kant, a detective)*, Louis Wolheim *(Petrus, a revolutionist)*, Mary MacLaren *(Mary Dawson, Blackie's wife)*, Macey Harlam *(Count Ivan, a renegade)*, Gustav von Seyffertitz *(Michael, a family servant)*, Joe King *(Detective Wren)*, Tom Blake *(Surtep)*, Marie Burke *(Olga)*, Joseph Smiley *(police captain)*, Martin Faust *(Ivan's valet)*, Mario Majeroni *(Grand Duke Alexis)*.

Mystery melodrama. Source: Jack Boyle, "The Face in the Fog," in *Cosmopolitan* (68:65–70, 96–102, May 1920). Boston Blackie Dawson, a reformed crook, accidentally comes into possession of the Romanov jewels, which the Grand Duchess Tatiana and her friends have brought to the United States for safety. Terrorists in search of the jewels transfer their attention to Dawson, but he is able to capture them with the aid of new electronic equipment and to expose Count Ivan as their leader. When Dawson gives paste copies to the U. S. Government, which also seeks the smuggled jewels, and returns the originals to their owner, Tatiana and Count Orloff are free to find happiness. *Bolshevists. Nobility. Smuggling. Romanov dynasty.*

FACE OF THE WORLD F2.1599

Willat Productions. *Dist* W. W. Hodkinson Corp. Aug **1921** [New York State]. Si; b&w. 35mm. 6 reels, 5,800 ft.

Dir Irvin V. Willat. *Scen* Dwight Cleveland, L. V. Jefferson. *Photog* Clyde De Vinna. *Art Dir* Harry Oliver. *Asst Dir* John Waters.

Cast: Edward Hearn *(Harold Mark)*, Barbara Bedford *(Thora)*, Harry Duffield *(Grandfather)*, Lloyd Whitlock *(Monsieur Duparc)*, Gordon Mullen *(Ivar Holth)*, J. P. Lockney *(Dr. Prahl)*, Fred Huntley *(Attorney Gundahl)*.

Melodrama. Source: Johan Bojer, *Verdens ansigt* (Copenhagen, 1917). Harold Mark marries Thora after treating her injured grandfather, then migrates to the city with his young wife in order to study surgery. While Harold devotes himself to his studies and to social problems, Thora seeks expression with a wild set in Greenwich Village and falls prey to the flattery of sculptor Duparc, who convinces Thora that she is neglected by her husband. The Marks separate, Harold rises to become the head of the hospital, and Thora spends a year as the guest of Duparc's aunt. On his way to persuade Harold to divorce Thora, Duparc is injured in an automobile accident. Harold unselfishly operates to save Duparc (in the midst of a fire set by a patient) and returns to Thora's country home. Thora follows, and they are reconciled. *Surgeons. Sculptors. Arson. Marriage. Automobile accidents. New York City—Greenwich Village.*

THE FACE ON THE BARROOM FLOOR **F2.1600**

Fox Film Corp. 1 Jan **1923** [c31 Dec 1922; LP19137]. Si; b&w. 35mm. 6 reels, 5,787 ft.

Pres by William Fox. *Dir* Jack Ford. *Scen* G. Marion Burton, Eugene B. Lewis. *Adtl Story* G. Marion Burton. *Photog* George Schneiderman.

Cast: Henry B. Walthall *(Robert Stevens)*, Ruth Clifford *(Marion Trevor)*, Walter Emerson *(Dick Von Vleck)*, Frederick Sullivan *(Thomas Waring)*, Alma Bennett *(Lottie)*, Norval MacGregor *(Governor)*, Michael Dark *(Henry Drew)*, Gus Saville *(fisherman)*.

Melodrama. Partial source: Hugh Antoine D'Arcy, "The Face Upon the Floor." As a derelict paints the face of a girl on a barroom floor, the plot is developed in a series of flashbacks: *Robert Stevens, an artist engaged to marry Marion, a society girl, becomes charmed with a fisherman's daughter who poses for him. The society girl's brother brings dishonor upon the fisherman's daughter, and when she commits suicide the artist shields the brother. Stevens is blamed by his fiancée, who terminates their engagement. The artist becomes a derelict and is wrongfully imprisoned.* Eventually Stevens is exonerated and reunited with Marion. *Artists. Derelicts. Alcoholism. Suicide. Injustice. Saloons.*

Note: Working title: *Drink*. Burton and Lewis apparently wrote separate scenarios, Burton adapting his own story and Lewis the D'Arcy poem.

FACE TO FACE **F2.1601**

Reginald Warde Productions. *Dist* Playgoers Pictures. 17 Sep **1922** [c12 Aug 1922; LU18142]. Si; b&w. 35mm. 5 reels, 4,587 ft.

Dir-Story-Scen Harry Grossman.

Cast: Marguerite Marsh *(Helen Marsley)*, Edna Holman *(Grace Weston)*, Richard Stewart *(John W. Weston)*, Coit Albertson *(Jack Weston)*, Joseph Marba *(Martin Hartley)*, Frances White *(Cleo Rand)*, William Kendall *(Bert Manners)*, Edna Holman.

Mystery drama. Just as John Weston is committing suicide a would-be burglar, Bert Manners, is startled by and shoots at his own reflection in a mirror. Bert is caught with the gun and is accused of murder. Helen, a school chum of Weston's daughter, finds the evidence that acquits Bert and causes Hartley to confess his keeping the suicide secret in order to hide his theft of Weston's bonds. *Burglars. Suicide. Theft.*

FACE VALUE **F2.1602**

Sterling Pictures. 1 Aug **1927** [c16 Aug 1927; LP24302]. Si; b&w. 35mm. 5 reels, 4,393 ft. [Copyrighted as 6 reels.]

Dir Robert Florey. *Story-Scen* Frances Guihan. *Photog* Herbert Kirkpatrick.

Cast: Fritzi Ridgeway *(Muriel Stanley)*, Gene Gowing *(Howard Crandall)*, Betty Baker *(Clara)*, Paddy O'Flynn *(Bert)*, Jack Mower *(Arthur Wells)*, Edwards Davis *(Crandall, Sr.)*, Joe Bonner *(butler)*.

Romantic drama. Howard Crandall, Jr., son of a wealthy family, forms a secret society in Paris after the war, composed of men who have been facially marred in military action. Crandall, Jr., who has been afraid to inform his father or his sweetheart, Muriel Stanley, of his disfigurement, decides at last to go home. Although shocked at his appearance, they try to make him happy. He is revolted by Muriel's pity; and when Arthur Wells, a persistent admirer in Howard's absence, calls and receives Muriel's intimate greeting, Howard seeks out Bert, an old Army buddy, and they go on a spree. Howard finds some satisfaction in reuniting Bert with his girl, Clara; but on returning home in a drunken state, he releases Muriel altogether. Thinking he does not love her, Muriel accepts Wells; and Howard returns to his comrades in Paris. But as a result of Clara's intervention, Muriel learns the truth and follows him to Paris. ... *War heroes. Veterans. Disfiguration. Secret societies. Courtship. World War I. Paris.*

FAGASA **F2.1603**

Dist First Division Distributors. 10 Apr **1928.** Si; b&w. 35mm. 6 reels, 5,600 ft.

Dir-Scen Raymond Wells. *Titl* Jack Kelly. *Photog* M. A. Anderson.

Cast: George Kelley, Grace Lord, Gael Kelton, Raymond Wells.

Western melodrama(?). No information about the nature of this film has been found.

FAINT PERFUME **F2.1604**

B. P. Schulberg Productions. 1 Jun **1925.** Si; b&w. 35mm. 6 reels, 6,186 ft.

Dir Louis Gasnier. *Adapt* John Goodrich. *Photog* Allen Siegler.

Cast: Seena Owen *(Richmiel Crumb)*, William Powell *(Barnaby Powers)*, Alyce Mills *(Ledda Perrin)*, Mary Alden *(Ma Crumb)*, Russell Simpson *(Grandpa Crumb)*, Betty Francisco *(Pearl Crumb)*, Jacqueline Saunders *(Tweet Crumb)*, Philo McCullough *(Richmiel's lover)*, Ned Sparks *(Orrin Crumb)*, Dicky Brandon *(Oliver Powers)*, Joan Standing *(The Hired Girl)*.

Domestic drama. Source: Zona Gale, *Faint Perfume* (New York, 1923). After 6 years of marriage, Barnaby Powers divorces his wife, Richmiel, and she returns home, taking their small boy, Oliver, with her. Barnaby soon follows after her to ask for possession of the child and falls in love with Ledda, Richmiel's sensitive cousin. Richmiel at first agrees to give up the child but spitefully changes her mind when she discovers that Barnaby and Ledda are in love. Oliver almost dies in an accident, however, and the neglectful Richmiel, who wants to go off with a new lover, finally agrees to give custody of the child to Barnaby and Ledda. *Children. Cousins. Marriage. Divorce. Motherhood.*

THE FAIR CHEAT **F2.1605**

R-C Pictures. *Dist* Film Booking Offices of America. 16 Sep **1923** [c24 Sep 1923; LP19453]. Si; b&w. 35mm. 6 reels, 5,652 ft.

Dir Burton King. *Story-Cont* William B. Laub. *Photog* Alfred Ortlieb. *Art Dir* Joseph Clement.

Cast: Edmund Breese *(Morgan Van Dam)*, Wilfred Lytell *(John Hamilton)*, Dorothy Mackaill *(Camilla)*, Marie White *(Gloria Starke)*, William Robyns *(Rutledge Stone)*, Harold Foshay *(Crittenden Scott Buckley)*, Bradley Barker *(Sloman Zeigler)*, Jack Newton *(Sam Hiller)*, Tom Blake *("Bunk" Willis)*.

Comedy-drama. Camilla Van Dam is in love with her rich father's poor employee, John Hamilton. Van Dam is against their marriage but proposes an arrangement to which Camilla agrees. Van Dam goes abroad with the understanding that she will not marry for a year or reveal her whereabouts to Hamilton. Announcing to the press that she is accompanying her father, Camilla instead gets a job as a chorus girl, takes an apartment, and supports herself. Hamilton finds her and joins in the deception until Van Dam's secretary tries to make off with the fortune on hearing the false rumor of Van Dam's death. Van Dam consents readily to his daughter's marriage when he returns. *Chorus girls. Fatherhood. Marriage. Wealth. Self-reliance.*

THE FAIR CO-ED **F2.1606**

Metro-Goldwyn-Mayer Pictures. 15 Oct **1927** [c20 Oct 1927; LP24527]. Si; b&w. 35mm. 7 reels, 6,408 ft.

Dir Sam Wood. *Adapt-Cont* Byron Morgan. *Titl* Joe Farnham. *Photog* John Seitz. *Art Dir* Cedric Gibbons, Arnold Gillespie. *Film Ed* Conrad A. Nervig. *Wardrobe* Gilbert Clark.

Cast: Marion Davies *(Marion)*, John Mack Brown *(Bob Dixon)*, Jane Winton *(Betty)*, Thelma Hill *(Rose)*, Lillian Leighton *(housekeeper)*, Gene Stone *(Herbert)*.

Comedy. Source: George Ade, *The Fair Co-ed, a Play* (New York opening: 1 Feb 1909). Marion, who is firmly opposed to attending college, agrees to go to Bingham College only after making the acquaintance of Bob, who is working his way through school as basketball coach. Marion joins the team, becomes a star player, but, piqued at Bob's coolness, caused by a misunderstanding, deserts the team on the eve of an important game. When the team loses the game, Marion becomes the object of her fellow students' scorn. Realizing her lack of sportsmanship, she joins in the second game and scores the winning points at the last minute. She regains her popularity and wins the love of Bob. *Athletic coaches. College life. Basketball. Sportsmanship.*

FAIR LADY **F2.1607**

Bennett Pictures. *Dist* United Artists. 19 Mar **1922** [c18 Mar 1922; LP17661]. Si; b&w. 35mm. 7 reels, 6,400 ft.

Prod Whitman Bennett. *Dir* Kenneth Webb. *Scen* Dorothy Farnum. *Photog* Harry Stradling, Edward Paul.

Cast: Betty Blythe *(Countess Margherita)*, Thurston Hall *(Caesar Maruffi)*, Robert Elliott *(Norvin Blake)*, Gladys Hulette *(Myra Nell Drew)*, Florence Auer *(Lucrezia)*, Walter James *(Gian Norcone)*, Macey

Harlam *(Count Modena)*, Henry Leone *(Riccardo)*, Effingham Pinto *(Count Martinello)*, Arnold Lucy *(Uncle Bernie Drew)*.

Underworld melodrama. Source: Rex Beach, *The Net* (New York, 1912). In Sicily, Cardi, a Mafia leader of unknown identity, sends warnings to Countess Margherita that she must not marry Count Martinello. En route to the wedding Martinello is murdered by Cardi's band, and Norvin Blake, a wounded young American, makes his way to the countess and breaks the news, and she swears to avenge the death of her beloved. Several years later, in New Orleans, Margherita, posing as a nurse, meets Blake, and he declares his love for her. Recognizing Norcone, a giant laborer, as the leader of the band that killed Martinello, Blake has him arrested after engaging him in a hand-to-hand fight. Maruffi, a suitor for the hand of Margherita, is discovered to be Cardi. The Italian-Sicilian colony is aroused against him, and during a fight between Blake and Cardi, the latter is stabbed by Margherita's maid; Blake finally wins Margherita. *Nobility. Nurses. Italians. Mafia. Revenge. New Orleans. Sicily.*

FAIR PLAY **F2.1608**

William Steiner Productions. caFeb **1925** [c2 Apr 1925; LU21325]. Si; b&w. 35mm. 5 reels, 5,035 ft.

Supv Charles Hutchinson. *Dir* Frank Crane. *Story* John Francis Natteford. *Photog* Ernest Miller.

Cast: Edith Thornton *(Norma Keith)*, Lou Tellegen *(Bruce Elliot)*, Gaston Glass *(Dickie Thane)*, Betty Francisco *(Rita Thane)*, David Dunbar *(Bull Mong)*, Simon Greer *(Charlie Morse)*.

Melodrama. Norma Keith, an industrious secretary, helps Bruce Elliot rise from obscurity to a position of increasing prominence as a criminal lawyer. Norma's devotion goes unnoticed, however, and Bruce marries a mercenary blonde schemer named Rita Thane. When Rita is accidentally killed, Bruce is convicted of murdering her on damaging circumstantial evidence. Norma then scouts around in the underworld and finds evidence to set Bruce free, earning his love and gratitude. *Secretaries. Lawyers. Gold diggers. Murder. Circumstantial evidence.*

FAIR WEEK **F2.1609**

Famous Players–Lasky. *Dist* Paramount Pictures. 16 Mar **1924** [c25 Mar 1924; LP20028]. Si; b&w. 35mm. 5 reels, 4,636 ft.

Pres by Adolph Zukor, Jesse L. Lasky. *Dir* Rob Wagner. *Scen* Tom Geraghty. *Story* Walter Woods. *Photog* Bert Baldridge.

Cast: Walter Hiers *(Slim Swasey)*, Constance Wilson *(Ollie Remus)*, Carmen Phillips *(Madame Le Grande)*, J. Farrell MacDonald *(Jasper Remus)*, Bobby Mack *(Dan Hogue)*, Mary Jane Irving *(Tinkle)*, Earl Metcalf *("Sure Thing" Sherman)*, Knute Erickson *(Isadore Kelly)*, Jane Keckley *(Mary Ellen Allen)*.

Rural comedy-melodrama. "Sure Thing" Sherman, masquerading as an evangelist, and Isadore Kelly arrive in Rome, Missouri, during the county fair, intending to rob the bank while fellow conspirator Madame Le Grande performs her balloon stunt. Their scheme is upset by rotund village jack-of-all-trades Slim Swasey, and he wins Ollie Remus, who was on the verge of eloping with Sherman. It develops that Tinkle, a child whom Slim has found and cared for, is the daughter of Madame Le Grande. *Balloonists. Evangelists. Foundlings. Robbery. Fairs. Missouri.*

FAITH FOR GOLD **F2.1610**

Mission Film Society. c22 Apr **1930** [LU1242]. Si; b&w. 35mm. 9 reels.

Religious melodrama. In the Burg household, Alice rejects a life of comfort and social splendor to join the life of the cloister, though her decision is bitterly resented by her brother, Joseph, an aspiring young pianist. Because she donates her part of the family fortune to the Church, he denounces her and forbids mention of the Church or religion in the home. Fifteen years later, having achieved fame and fortune, Joseph is apparently lost aboard a sinking ocean liner; and his wife (Emily?) at the insistence of their son, Johnny, turns to God for strength and guidance. Although Joseph does return safely, he remains adamantly against God and the Church in spite of the entreaties of Father Thomas, a friend of Johnny's. When Johnny is injured in a fall, Alice comes to nurse him; and Emily, in despair, asks for a divorce but is denied it by "the law of God and the Church." However, through Father Thomas' guidance, the couple are reconciled; and Joseph realizes his error in giving up "faith for gold." *Pianists. Nuns. Clergymen. Brother-sister relationship. Religion. Mammon. Catholic Church.*

THE FAITH HEALER **F2.1611**

Famous Players–Lasky. *Dist* Paramount Pictures. 3 Apr **1921** [c3 Apr 1921; LP16382]. Si; b&w. 35mm. 7 reels, 6,346 ft.

Dir George Melford. *Scen* Mrs. William Vaughn Moody, Z. Wall Covington. *Photog* Harry Perry.

Cast: Milton Sills *(Michaelis)*, Ann Forrest *(Rhoda Williams)*, Fontaine La Rue *(Mary Beeler)*, Frederick Vroom *(Matthew Beeler)*, Loyola O'Connor *(Martha Beeler)*, May Giraci *(Little Annie)*, John Curry *(Uncle Abe, a Negro)*, Adolphe Menjou *(Dr. Littlefield)*, Edward Vroom *(Dr. Sanchez)*, Robert Brower *(Dr. Martin)*, Winifred Greenwood *(a mother)*.

Inspirational melodrama. Source: William Vaughn Moody, *The Faith Healer, a Play* (New York, 1910). Rhoda Williams, an orphan who is the mistress of Dr. Littlefield, sees a crippled man restored to health by Michaelis, a young shepherd who has the power of divine healing, and flees to the home of her invalid aunt, Mary Beeler. She summons Michaelis, who cures the woman of her paralysis, and Rhoda tells him of her wasted life. Michaelis falls in love with her, but when called to cure a woman's sick baby he fails and attributes his loss of power to Rhoda. Ultimately, she convinces him that his failure was the result of his lack of faith in the strength of love, and he is then able to restore the baby to health. *Orphans. Mistresses. Physicians. Aunts. Religion. Miracles. Paralysis. Faith cure.*

FAITH OF MILLIONS **F2.1612**

Chester Productions. c26 Apr **1927** [MP3970]. Si; col (Technicolor); 35mm. 6 reels.

Ed-Titl Jean Conover.

Participants: John Cardinal Bonzano, Patrick Cardinal O'Donnell, Patrick Joseph Cardinal Hayes, Alfred Emanuel Smith *(Governor of New York)*, James John Walker *(Mayor of New York City)*, William Emmett Dever *(Mayor of Chicago)*, James John Davis *(Secretary of Labor)*, Bishop Edward Francis Hoban.

Documentary. A filmed account of the 28th Eucharistic Congress held in Chicago, 20–24 June 1926. A pilgrimage of 750,000 people journey to the Seminary of Saint Mary of the Lake in Mundelein, Illinois, for the great pageant of the Eucharistic Procession. Cardinal Bonzano is shown officiating at the high mass at an altar erected before the Church of the Immaculate Conception with 11 other cardinals in attendance. Children's day is celebrated in Soldiers Field with a children's choir of 62,000. *Eucharistic Congresses. Chicago. Mundelein (Illinois). Catholic Church.*

FAITHFUL WIVES **F2.1613**

Platinum Pictures. 25 Nov **1926**. Si; b&w. 35mm. 6 reels, 5,800 ft.

Dir Norbert Myles.

Cast: Wallace MacDonald *(Tom Burke)*, Edythe Chapman *(The Mother)*, Doris May *(Tom's sister)*, Niles Welch *(Charles Austin)*, Philippe De Lacy *(The Child)*, Myrda Dagmarna *(Tom's wife)*, Dell Boone *(The Widow)*, William Lowery *(Buck Randall)*, William Conklin *(Governor Turner)*, Bill Brown *(The Lawyer)*, Alec B. Francis, Kate Price.

Melodrama. An innocent man sentenced to die in the electric chair is saved in the 11th hour by a pardon from the governor. The film is based on a story, "The Faithful Sex," the authorship of which has not been determined. *State governors. Fidelity. Capital punishment.*

FAITHLESS LOVER **F2.1614**

Krelbar Pictures. Jan **1928**. Si; b&w. 35mm. 6 reels, 5,450-5,626 ft. ft.

Supv Sherman S. Krellberg. *Dir* Lawrence Windom. *Scen* Jack Murray. *Titl* Sam Sherman. *Photog* Frank Zucker. *Film Ed* K. Brownell. *Prod Mgr* Benny Berk.

Cast: Eugene O'Brien *(Austin Kent)*, Gladys Hulette *(Mary Callender)*, Raymond Hackett *(Harry Ayres)*, Jane Jennings *(Mrs. Seeton)*, James S. Barrett *(Bert Rogers)*, George De Carlton *(Charles Dunbar)*.

Drama. Source: Baroness D'Arville, "Faithless Lover" (publication undetermined). Construction engineer Austin Kent falls in love with Mary Callender, a society girl who loves the somewhat worthless Harry Ayres. Austin even presents Harry with a considerable sum of money, enabling him to marry Mary. The bursting of Austin's dam leads to the revelation of Harry's cowardice, Austin's daring rescue of Mary, and the realization of true love between Mary and Austin. *Socialites. Engineers—Civil. Cowardice. Dams. Floods.*

Note: Also reviewed as *The Pasteboard Lover.*

THE FAITHLESS SEX **F2.1615**

Signet Films. 20 May **1922** [trade review]. Si; b&w. 35mm. 5 reels.

Dir Henry J. Napier. *Story-Scen* Herbert Hall Winslow.

Cast: Frances Nelson *(Violet)*, Leonore Harris *(Aunt Kitty)*, Gladden James *(Monte Pym)*, Robert Frazer *(Latimer)*, Frank Beamish *(The Black Duke)*.

Melodrama. "James Lenox, known as the 'Black Duke' on Broadway, calls upon Kitty Langdon to help him to fleece the wealthy young Latimer who comes to play cards in the Black Duke's den. Latimer loses interest in the place because of losing so much and Lenox thinks up a scheme to keep him. They send for Kitty's niece, Violet, who wants to come to New York. She innocently exposes her aunt's dishonesty after she becomes acquainted with Latimer, who has grown to trust her. Lenox locks her in her room for punishment. She escapes and Latimer finds a place for her to stay. They are both inveigled in a crime, of which both are innocent, and succeed in proving this and tracing the real criminal, a pal of Kitty's." *(Moving Picture World,* 20 May 1922, p341.) *Gamblers. Aunts. New York City.*

THE FAKER **F2.1616**

Columbia Pictures. 2 Jan **1929** [c22 Mar 1929; LP238]. Si; b&w. 35mm. 6 reels, 5,538 ft.

Prod Harry Cohn. *Dir* Phil Rosen. *Story-Scen* Howard J. Green. *Photog* Teddy Tetzlaff. *Art Dir* Harrison Wiley. *Tech Dir* Edward Shulter. *Film Ed* William Hamilton. *Asst Dir* Tenny Wright.

Cast: Jacqueline Logan *(Rita Martin)*, Charles Delaney *(Bob Williams)*, Warner Oland *(Hadrian, the faker)*, Charles Hill Mailes *(John Clayton)*, Gaston Glass *(Frank Clayton)*, Flora Finch *(Emma)*, David Mir *(believer)*, Lon Poff *(Hadrian's aid)*, Fred Kelsey *(detective)*.

Melodrama. Rita Martin, the partner of a phony spiritualist who uses information supplied by her to gull and astonish the rubes, gets work as private secretary to John Clayton, a wealthy man who has just disinherited his worthless son, Frank, and left his entire fortune to his upright stepson, Bob Williams. At Frank's request, the spiritualist later performs for the elder Clayton a seance during which Rita impersonates the late Mrs. Clayton and arranges for a reconciliation between Frank and his father. Rita falls in love with Bob, however, and, in order to protect Bob's interests against Frank's, exposes the spiritualist as a faker. Frank is disgraced in his father's eyes, and Bob quickly forgives Rita for her past complicity in Frank's schemes. *Spiritualists. Secretaries. Filial relations. Inheritance.*

THE FALL GUY **F2.1617**

RKO Productions. 15 Jun **1930** [c15 Jun 1930; LP1397]. Sd (Photophone); b&w. 35mm. 7 reels, 6,175 ft.

Prod William Le Baron. *Assoc Prod* William Sistrom. *Dir* A. Leslie Pearce. *Screenplay-Dial* Tim Whelan. *Photog* Leo Tover. *Art Dir* Max Ree. *Film Ed* Archie Marshek. *Rec Engr* George Ellis.

Cast: Jack Mulhall *(Johnny Quinlan)*, Mae Clarke *(Bertha Quinlan)*, Ned Sparks *(Dan Walsh)*, Pat O'Malley *(Charles Newton)*, Thomas Jackson *("Nifty" Herman)*, Wynne Gibson *(Lottie Quinlan)*, Ann Brody *(Mrs. Bercowich)*, Elmer Ballard *("Hutch")*, Alan Roscoe *(Detective Keefe)*.

Melodrama. Source: George Abbott and James Gleason, *The Fall Guy, a Comedy in Three Acts* (New York, 1928). Johnny Quinlan, who loses his job as a drug clerk, finally agrees to work for racketeer "Nifty" Herman, whom he believes to be a bootlegger; and he accepts for safekeeping a suitcase, which he takes home. Although he hides the suitcase under a chair, his inquisitive wife, Lottie, discovers it, and Newton, his sister's sweetheart, who is a government agent, recognizes it as a "hot" grip that he and his associates have been trailing in their pursuit of a narcotics gang. Newton is obliged to accuse Johnny, but as he is about to take him to jail, Nifty arrives, and Johnny tricks him into revealing that he (Johnny) was unaware of the contents of the suitcase. He thus exposes Nifty as the leader of the narcotics gang; Newton captures his man and awards Johnny with a job as his assistant. *Drug clerks. Racketeers. Government agents. Scapegoats. Narcotics. Circumstantial evidence.*

THE FALL OF EVE **F2.1618**

Columbia Pictures. 17 Jun **1929** [New York premiere; released 25 Jun; c25 Jul 1929; LP579]. Sd (Movietone); b&w. 35mm. 6 reels, 6,245 ft. [Also si; 5,799 ft.]

Prod Harry Cohn. *Dir* Frank R. Strayer. *Dial* Frederic Hatton, Fanny Hatton. *Adapt* Gladys Lehman. *Story* Anita Loos, John Emerson. *Photog* Teddy Tetzlaff. *Art Dir* Harrison Wiley. *Asst Dir* George Rhein.

Cast: Patsy Ruth Miller *(Eve Grant)*, Ford Sterling *(Mr. Mack)*, Gertrude Astor *(Mrs. Ford)*, Arthur Rankin *(Tom Ford, Jr.)*, Jed Prouty *(Tom Ford, Sr.)*, Betty Farrington *(Mrs. Mack)*, Fred Kelsey *(cop)*, Bob White *(Hank Mann)*.

Farce. Tom Ford, Jr., keeps secret his romance with his father's secretary, Eve Grant. Ford, Sr., enlists Eve to entertain out-of-town buyer Mr. Mack. When Mack's wife insists on joining the nightclub party, Eve is introduced as Mrs. Ford. A radio broadcast from the nightclub alerts the vacationing Mrs. Ford that something is amiss when she hears that a certain dance tune has been requested by "Mr. and Mrs. Tom Ford." Ford calls his son to help extricate him from his difficulties with the boorish couple. Ford, Jr., agrees to come if Ford, Sr., will consent to his marriage. The party returns to the Ford home. The intoxicated Mr. Mack and his corpulent wife, having decided to stay the night, are about to go to bed when Mrs. Ford returns and calls the police, having seen an unfamiliar figure raiding her icebox. Ford, Jr., explains the situation to everyone's satisfaction and introduces Eve as his bride. *Businessmen. Secretaries. Buyers. Filial relations. Radio.*

FALLEN ANGELS *see* **MAN, WOMAN, AND WIFE**

THE FALSE ALARM **F2.1619**

Columbia Pictures. 20 Sep **1926** [c13 Oct 1926; LP23235]. Si; b&w. 35mm. 6 reels, 5,235 ft.

Prod Harry Cohn. *Dir* Frank O'Connor. *Story-Scen* Leah Baird. *Photog* Faxon M. Dean.

Cast: Ralph Lewis *(Fighting John Casey)*, Dorothy Revier *(Mary Doyle)*, John Harron *(Joe Casey)*, Mary Carr *(Mrs. Casey)*, George O'Hara *(Tim Casey)*, Priscilla Bonner *(Bessie Flannigan)*, Lillian Leighton *(Mrs. Flannigan)*.

Melodrama. Fireman Joe Casey, failing to rescue his father from a burning building because of his fear of fire, is branded a coward by his father, "Fighting John," and driven from home. Joe takes a job in a steel mill, and in rescuing a fellow worker, he overcomes his fear of flames. He returns home, is reinstated in his job, but finds that his brother, Tim, is forcing his attentions on Mary Doyle, an orphan girl, who is Joe's sweetheart. Bessie Flannigan, who has been engaged to Tim, denounces him when she finds him with Mary. During a fight over the girls between Joe and Tim, a building is set afire; Joe rescues Mary and his brother; but Bessie perishes. Later, Joe and Mary are married. *Firemen. Steelworkers. Brothers. Filial relations. Cowardice. Family life. Pyrophobia.*

FALSE BRANDS **F2.1620**

World Film Corp. *Dist* Pacific Film Co. 14 Feb **1922** [New York State license]. Si; b&w. 35mm. 5 reels, 4,400 ft.

Dir-Story William J. Craft. *Scen* Harry Chandlee, William B. Laub. *Photog* Joseph Mayer.

Cast: Joe Moore *(Joe Sullivan)*, Eileen Sedgwick *(Eileen Morgan)*, C. W. Williams *(Sam Morgan)*, Robert Kentman *(Max Shultz)*.

Western melodrama. Sent home from college for playing pranks, Joe Sullivan goes to his father's western ranch to take the place of the deceased superintendent and is reunited with the decedent's daughter, Eileen Morgan, his college sweetheart. Joe is suspected of cattle rustling and accused of a murder committed by foreman Max Shultz, but he vindicates himself—despite his "greenness"—and tricks Shultz into a confession. *Ranch managers. Ranch foremen. Rustling. Murder.*

FALSE COLORS *see* **TRUE HEAVEN**

FALSE FATHERS **F2.1621**

El Dorado Productions. *Dist* J. Charles Davis Productions. 28 Apr **1929** [New York showing]. Si; b&w. 35mm. 5 reels, 4,377 ft.

Dir Horace B. Carpenter. *Photog* Harry Neumann.

Cast: Noah Beery *(parson)*, Horace B. Carpenter, Francis Pomerantz, E. A. Martin.

Western melodrama. Approaching a mining town under attack by Indians, two gold prospectors rout the assailants with dynamite. A dog leads them to a baby, whose care they undertake to the best of their ability. One of the men, who is wanted for murder (of which he is innocent), saves the life of the detective pursuing him, thus learning that the real murderer has confessed. It develops that the baby belongs to one of the men, but the authorities take it away. A parson persuades the officials that the baby belongs with its father, and there is a happy reunion. *Prospectors. Detectives. Infants. Clergymen. Fatherhood. Dogs.*

FALSE FRIENDS **F2.1622**

Goodwill Pictures. 27 Dec **1926** [New York State license]. Si; b&w. 35mm. 5 reels, 4,400 ft.

Dir Francis Ford. *Photog* Alfred Gosden.
Cast: Jack Mower, Florence Ulrich.
Melodrama(?). No information about the nature of this film has been found.

FALSE FRONTS **F2.1623**
Herold Brothers. *Dist* American Releasing Corp. 30 Apr **1922** [c30 Apr 1922; LP18197]. Si; b&w. 35mm. 5 reels, 5,044 ft.
Dir Samuel R. Bradley. *Story-Scen* S. Barrett McCormick. *Photog* Don Canady.
Cast: Edward Earle *(Keith Drummond)*, Madelyn Clare *(Marjorie Kemble)*, Frank Losee *(John Lathrop)*, Barbara Castleton *(Helen Baxter)*, Bottles O'Reilly *(Jackie Parker)*.
Society drama. Keith Drummond, a penniless youth from a well-known family, is advised by John Lathrop to put on a wealthy front and work hard in order to be successful. With money borrowed from Lathrop, Keith takes only the first part of the advice and plunges into a social whirl. He marries *nouveau riche* Helen Baxter, but one day he denounces his whole way of life and leaves to work in the western oil fields. They are reunited when Keith establishes himself and Helen is reduced to poverty. *Poverty. Wealth. Oil fields.*

FALSE KISSES **F2.1624**
Universal Film Manufacturing Co. 21 Nov **1921** [c15 Nov 1921; LP17197]. Si; b&w. 35mm. 5 reels, 4,335 ft.
Pres by Carl Laemmle. *Dir* Paul Scardon. *Scen* Wallace Clifton. *Adapt* Winifred Reeve. *Photog* Ben Reynolds.
Cast: Miss Du Pont *(Jennie)*, Pat O'Malley *(Paul)*, Lloyd Whitlock *(Jim)*, Camilla Clark *(Pauline)*, Percy Challenger *(John Peters)*, Madge Hunt *(Mrs. Simpson)*, Fay Winthrop *(Mrs. Glimp)*, Joseph Hazelton *(Mr. Glimp)*, Mary Philbin *(Mary)*.
Melodrama. Source: Wilbur Daniel Steele, "Ropes [a Play in One Act]," in *Harper's Magazine* (142:193–208, Jan 1921). Jennie Blake, a schoolteacher from the city, comes between Paul Whalen and Jim Payne, fishing partners in the seaport town of Rocky Point, and is unable to decide which one she loves until Jim loses his temper and is beaten in a fight by Paul; she then marries Paul. Jim enters lighthouse service and 5 years later returns as coast inspector, finds Paul out of work, and sends the couple to a lonely and depressing lighthouse. On Jim's monthly visit to the light, Jennie is at times tempted by his amorous attentions. Paul loses his sight in a fall, and on Jim's next visit the blind husband suspects his wife and friend of infidelity. A fight ensues, and a blow restores Paul's sight. Jennie confesses that she has kissed Jim, but she declares that she has remained a faithful wife. *Schoolteachers. Blindness. Friendship. Lighthouses.*
Note: Working title: *Ropes*.

FALSE MORALS **F2.1625**
Dist Hi-Mark Productions. 21 Apr **1927.** Si; b&w. 35mm. 6 reels, 5,900 ft.
Cast: Gaston Glass, Joseph Swickard, Duane Thompson, Mary Carr.
Society drama(?). No information about the nature of this film has been found.

FALSE PLAY *see* **THE LONE HAND**

FALSE PRIDE **F2.1626**
Macfadden True Story Pictures. c23 Mar, 6 Apr **1926** [LU22551, LP22580]. Si; b&w. 35mm. 6 reels, 5,700 ft.
Dir Hugh Dierker. *Scen* Lewis Allen Browne.
Cast: Owen Moore.
Melodrama. James Mason Ardsley, a young lawyer of good family, is retained by wealthy Julia Kingsley to go to the exclusive Cranston School for Girls and investigate the conduct of Mary Sargent, the daughter of Mrs. Kingsley's deceased half sister. Ardsley gets a job as the Cranston chauffeur and falls in love with Mary, who is a housekeeper at the school. Willis Herbert, a bounder, arrives at the school and persuades Mary to go to the city with him, falsely promising her a good job. Ardsley goes after them. Herbert attacks Mary in his apartment, and she hits him with a bronze bookend. Herbert is found stabbed to death, and Ardsley is accused of the crime on circumstantial evidence. He is sentenced to be executed, but at the last moment, Norma (a woman badly wronged by Herbert) comes forward and confesses that, finding Herbert unconscious from the blow struck by Mary, she finished him off with a knife. Ardsley and Mary make plans to wed. *Lawyers. Chauffeurs. Housekeepers. Murder. Injustice. Boarding schools. Capital punishment.*

FALSE TRAILS **F2.1627**
William Steiner Productions. Oct **1924** [c12 Sep 1924; LU20588]. Si; b&w. 35mm. 5 reels.
Writ Forrest Sheldon.
Cast: Pete Morrison *(Stewart [Wolf] Larsen ["The Son of the Wolf"])*.
Western melodrama. Stewart Larsen's son, Bud, is killed by Chet Ogden, foreman of El Cajón Rancho and veterinarian of the Cattlemen's Association, who has falsely told Larsen that his cattle were infected. Ogden plans to sell the cattle in Mexico. Larsen blames Don Felipe Ortega, owner of El Cajón and president of the association, and swears vengeance. Years later, Larsen, now known as "The Son of the Wolf," menaces the countryside with his gang. His foster son, Jim, is wounded and captured by Ortega and is nursed back to health by Ortega's daughter, Ynez. Hearing a report that Jim is turning traitor, Larsen goes after Ortega, but Jim prevents Larsen from killing him. Jim and Larsen attempt to escape, but Larsen is fatally wounded by Ogden. Jim chases Ogden, who falls to his death during a fight. Ogden's accomplice, Hippy Jake, confesses to the dying Larsen Ogden's guilt in starting the feud. Larsen dies, and all parties are recónciled. *Ranch foremen. Veterinarians. Gangs. Cattle—Diseases. Protective associations.*
Note: Story and character names are from shooting script in copyright files and may differ from the final film.

FALSE WOMEN **F2.1628**
Pandora Productions. *Dist* Aycie Pictures. 24 May **1921** [Brooklyn showing]. Si; b&w. 35mm. 5 reels, 4,464 ft.
Dir-Writ R. Dale Armstrong. *Photog* C. J. Barber.
Cast: Sheldon Smith *(Fred Bentley)*, Audrey Chapman *(Marion Carroll)*, Catherine Bradley *(Mrs. Carroll)*, Antonio Corsi *(Father Felix)*, Wheeler Dryden *(Richard Lane)*.
Romantic drama. While studying for the priesthood under the guidance of Father Felix, Fred Bentley falls in love with Marion Carroll. He gives up his studies at the mission and enters a secular college, but happiness slips from his grasp: his roommate becomes a rival for Marion's affections, and Marion's girl friend opposes her union with Fred. Distraught at his troubles, Fred is driven to steal deadly poison from the laboratory, but—before using it on his enemies—he comes to his senses. Renouncing worldly pleasures, he returns to Father Felix and the mission, and after his ordination he performs the wedding ceremony for Marion and Richard Lane. (Locale: Southern California.) *Ministerial students. Clergymen. Courtship. College life. Missions. Murder. Weddings. California.*

THE FAMILY CLOSET **F2.1629**
Ore-Col Film Corp. *Dist* Playgoers Pictures. 18 Sep **1921** [c7 Sep 1921; LU16945]. Si; b&w. 35mm. 6 reels.
Dir John B. O'Brien. *Photog* Lawrence E. Williams.
Cast: Holmes Herbert *(Alfred Dinsmore)*, Alice Mann *(Louise Dinsmore)*, Kempton Greene *(Ned Tully)*, Byron Russell *(J. Wesley Tully)*, Josephine Frost *(Mrs. Tully)*, Walter Ware *(Charles Purcell)*, John Dillon *(Denis J. McMurty)*, Verne Layton *(Lowell Winthrope)*, Walter Lewis *(John Colby)*, May Kitson *(Mrs. Dinsmore)*.
Mystery melodrama. Source: Will J. Payne, "Black Sheep," in *Saturday Evening Post*. When Alfred Dinsmore refuses to withdraw his libel suit against *The Leader*, editor Charles Purcell hires McMurty to obtain evidence against his opponent. A man recognizes Dinsmore as one Tom Wilson, who took part in a bank robbery and was known to have a scar on his chin: although Dinsmore wears a beard, the resemblance is exact. Dinsmore agrees to withdraw his suit, but Purcell demands blackmail; Purcell is forced to relent when Dinsmore establishes his innocence by removing his beard. The opponents decide to overlook their political differences when their children, who are in love, are reunited despite parental objections. *Editors. Libel. Mistaken identity. Politics. Blackmail. Robbery. Newspapers.*

THE FAMILY SECRET (Universal-Jewel) **F2.1630**
Universal Pictures. 4 Sep **1924** [New York showing; released 28 Sep; c4 Jun 1924; LP20265]. Si; b&w. 35mm. 6 reels, 5,676 ft.
Pres by Carl Laemmle. *Dir* William Seiter. *Scen* Lois Zellner. *Photog* John Stumar.
Cast: Baby Peggy Montgomery *(Baby Peggy Holmes)*, Gladys Hulette *(Margaret Selfridge)*, Edward Earle *(Garry Holmes)*, Frank Currier *(Sim*

Selfridge), Cesare Gravina *(fruit vendor)*, Martin Turner *(Uncle Rose)*, Elizabeth Mackey *(Aunt Mandy)*, Martha Mattox *(nurse)*, Lucy Beaumont *(Miss Abigail)*.

Melodrama. Source: Frances Hodgson Burnett, *Editha's Burglar, a Story for Children* (Boston, 1878). Augustus Thomas, *Editha's Burglar, a Dramatic Sketch in One Act* (New York, 1932). Garry Holmes, who is secretly married to Margaret Selfridge and disliked by her father, is arrested as a burglar when he comes to see his baby and is sent to prison. Following his release, Baby Peggy wanders from home and is found by Garry, who does not recognize her, and he takes her to a police station. Persuaded by necessity to join in a robbery, Garry finds himself unwittingly in the Selfridge home, where he is shot in an attempt to escape, but later he is forgiven and reunited with his wife and child. *Children. Criminals—Rehabilitation. Fatherhood. Family life. Robbery.*

THE FAMILY UPSTAIRS **F2.1631**

Fox Film Corp. 29 Aug **1926** [c24 Jul 1926; LP22957]. Si; b&w. 35mm. 6 reels, 5,971 ft.

Pres by William Fox. *Dir* J. G. Blystone. *Scen* L. G. Rigby. *Photog* Reginald Lyons.

Cast: Virginia Valli *(Louise Heller)*, Allan Simpson *(Charles Grant)*, J. Farrell MacDonald *(Joe Heller)*, Lillian Elliott *(Emma Heller)*, Edward Piel, Jr. *(Willie Heller)*, Dot Farley *(Mademoiselle Clarice)*, Cecille Evans *(see note)*, Jacqueline Wells *(Annabelle Heller)*.

Comedy-drama. Source: Harry Delf, *The Family Upstairs, a Comedy of Home Life* (New York, 1926). Louise, a quiet and refined girl, is taunted by her mother, brother, and sister because she has no sweetheart. Finally a bank teller, Charles Grant, falls in love with her and insists upon visiting her family in their apartment. Mrs. Heller drives him away by her talk of the luxury to which her daughter is accustomed, and when he departs Louise accuses her family of spoiling her one chance for romance. Impulsively, she takes a taxi to Coney Island to lose herself in the crowds but is followed by Charles, who has seen through the family's pretense. There she meets two boys who work in her office; and when Charles tries to talk to her, they resent his interference, assuming him to be a masher. Charles is struck down by her companions, but as a result Louise and Charles are happily reconciled. *Bank clerks. Filial relations. Family life. Courtship. Coney Island. New York City.*

Note: Some sources show Cecille Evans in the role of Mademoiselle Clarice.

THE FAMOUS MRS. FAIR **F2.1632**

Louis B. Mayer Productions. *Dist* Metro Pictures. 19 Feb **1923** [c6 May 1923; LP18791]. Si; b&w. 35mm. 8 reels, 7,775 ft.

Pres by Louis B. Mayer. *Prod* Louis B. Mayer. *Dir* Fred Niblo. *Adapt-Scen* Frances Marion. *Photog* Charles J. Van Enger. *Art Dir* Howard Higgin. *Film Ed* Lloyd Nosler.

Cast: Myrtle Stedman *(Mrs. Fair)*, Huntly Gordon *(Jeffrey Fair)*, Marguerite De La Motte *(Sylvia Fair)*, Cullen Landis *(Alan Fair)*, Ward Crane *(Dudley Gillette)*, Carmel Myers *(Angy Brice)*, Helen Ferguson *(Peggy)*, Lydia Yeamans Titus, Dorcas Matthews, Frankie Bailey, Josephine Kirkwood, Muriel Beresford, Eva Mudge, Kathleen Chambers, Peggy Blackwood *(Buddies)*, Coast Artillery Corps Soldiers—Fort MacArthur.

Domestic melodrama. Source: James Grant Forbes, *The Famous Mrs. Fair*, in *The Famous Mrs. Fair and Other Plays* (New York, 1920). Highly decorated for her service as a wartime nurse, Mrs. Nancy Fair returns home after the hostilities to find her family falling apart. Nevertheless, she goes on a lecture tour in hopes of doing more good. Her second homecoming finds Mr. Fair involved in an affair with Angy Brice, a neighboring widow; her son, Alan, married and in bad company; and her daughter, Sylvia, eloped. The search for Sylvia brings Mrs. Fair to her senses and reunites the family. *Nurses. Lecturers. World War I. Family life.*

FANCY BAGGAGE **F2.1633**

Warner Brothers Pictures. 26 Jan **1929** [c19 Jan 1929; LP33]. Talking sequences, mus score, & sd eff (Vitaphone); b&w. 35mm. 8 reels, 6,447 ft. [Also si, 23 Feb 1929; 5,983 ft.]

Dir John G. Adolfi. *Adapt-Scen* C. Graham Baker. *Titl-Dial* James A. Starr. *Story* Jerome Kingston. *Photog* William Reis. *Film Ed* Owen Marks.

Cast: Audrey Ferris *(Naomi Iverson)*, Myrna Loy *(Myrna)*, George Fawcett *(Iverson)*, Hallam Cooley *(Dickey)*, Wallace MacDonald *(Ernest Hardin)*, Edmund Breese *(John Hardin)*, Eddie Gribbon *(Steve)*, Burr McIntosh *(Austin)*, Virginia Sale *(Miss Hickey?)*.

Drama. Naomi Iverson learns that her father has assumed the blame for engaging in an illegal stock pool and is to be sentenced by the Federal Government to 5 years in prison. In return, Iverson will receive a check for $1 million from John Hardin, his former partner and now his bitterest enemy. She appropriates the check and goes to Hardin's yacht hoping to recover the written "confession." There she meets and falls in love with Hardin's son, Ernest. Complications set in when Iverson arrives and is set adrift by Tony, leader of a gang of rumrunners. Tony, who covets Naomi, gets involved in a fight with Ernest; Tony corners her, but she is rescued by Ernest. The revenue officers seize the rum boat and arrest the two old men as bootleggers. When Naomi and Ernest confront their fathers with their love, the fathers bow to necessity and once again become friends. *Rumrunners. Scapegoats. Revenue agents. Filial relations. Friendship. Fraud. Documentation.*

FANGS OF DESTINY **F2.1634**

Universal Pictures. 4 Dec **1927** [c20 Oct 1927; LP24562]. Si; b&w. 35mm. 5 reels, 4,295 ft.

Pres by Carl Laemmle. *Dir* Stuart Paton. *Story-Scen* George Morgan. *Titl* Gardner Bradford. *Photog* Jerry Ash.

Cast: Dynamite *(himself, the dog)*, Edmund Cobb *(Jerry Matthews)*, Betty Caldwell *(Rose Shelby)*, George Periolat *(Colonel Shelby)*, Carl Sepulveda *(Hank Mitchell)*, Al Ferguson *(Thomas Shields)*, Joan Hathaway *(Sally Ann)*, Brick Cannon *(sheriff)*.

Western melodrama. Jerry Matthews is hired by Colonel Shelby to replace Hank Mitchell, whom Shelby suspects of being in league with rustlers. Shields, a neighboring rancher who holds a note on Shelby's stock, plots with the rustlers to ruin Shelby so as to foreclose on the ranch, where he (Shields) has discovered oil. Dynamite, Jerry's constant companion, is instrumental in revealing to Jerry the presence of oil on the land, and consequently Jerry is captured by the gang. Dynamite confronts Shields and takes his gun to Rose Shelby, the colonel's daughter, then returns and frees Jerry; a fierce fight ensues, and the rustlers are routed. Jerry arrives to prevent the sheriff from dispatching the foreclosure and exposes Shields's plotting. *Ranchers. Rustlers. Sheriffs. Mortgages. Oil lands. Ranches. Dogs.*

FANGS OF FATE **F2.1635**

H. B. Carpenter Productions. *Dist* Chesterfield Motion Pictures. 9 Dec **1925** [New York State license]. Si; b&w. 35mm. 5 reels.

Dir-Writ Horace B. Carpenter. *Photog* Paul Allen.

Cast: Bill Patton *(Bob Haynes, a Black Raider)*, Dorothy Donald *(Azalia Bolton)*, Ivor McFadden *(Dan Dodo Briggs, the sheriff)*, Beatrice Allen *(Azalia's mother)*, William Bertram *(Judge Harcourt)*, Merrill McCormick *("Red Mack," the renegade)*, Tex Starr *(Bill)*, Carl Silvera *(Lew Sontag)*.

Western melodrama(?). No information about the nature of this film has been found.

FANGS OF FATE **F2.1636**

Fred J. McConnell Productions. *Dist* Pathé Exchange. 24 Jun **1928** [c25 Jun 1928; LP25413]. Si; b&w. 35mm. 5 reels, 4,476 ft.

Dir Noel Mason Smith. *Scen* Jack Kelly. *Dial* Arthur Q. Hagerman. *Story* Earl W. Johnson. *Photog* Edward Snyder. *Film Ed* William Austin.

Cast: Arnold Gray *(Arnold Barcklay)*, Henry Hebert *(Eli Hargraves)*, Robert Reault *(Robert Winter)*, Kathleen Collins *(Dorothy Winter, his sister)*, Alfred Fisher *(Jed Morgan)*, Klondike *(himself, a dog)*.

Melodrama. Hargraves, the village Shylock, murders his ward, Robert Winters, on his 21st birthday when he learns that corporation representative Arnold Barcklay would like to purchase Robert's valuable invention. Hargraves' attempts to shift the blame for Robert's death onto Barcklay are thwarted by the dead man's faithful dog, Klondike, who drags into the courtroom Hargraves' jacket containing the missing blueprints for Robert's invention. Exonerated, Barcklay remains in town to pursue his romance with Robert's sister, Dorothy. *Inventors. Moneylenders. Guardians. Wards. Businessmen. Murder. Trials. Dogs. Documentation.*

FANGS OF JUSTICE **F2.1637**

Samuel Bischoff Productions. 23 Dec **1926** [New York State license]. Si; b&w. 35mm. 6 reels.

Dir Noel Mason Smith. *Story* Adele De Vore. *Photog? (see note)* James B. King, James Brown.

Cast: Silverstreak *(himself, a dog)*, Johnny Walker *(Terry Randall)*, Wheeler Oakman *(Paul Orr)*, June Marlowe *(Janet Morgan)*, Frank Hagney

(Walter Page), Freddie Frederick *(Sonny, the boy)*, Cecile Cameron *(Trixie)*, George Irving.

Melodrama. A brave and faithful dog saves his master from an unscrupulous man who plots to deprive him of his rightful inheritance. *Inheritance. Dogs.*

Note: Sources disagree in crediting photography.

FANGS OF THE WILD **F2.1638**

FBO Pictures. 5 Feb **1928** [c1 Feb 1928; LP24932]. Si; b&w. 35mm. 5 reels, 4,578 ft.

Dir Jerome Storm. *Scen* Ethel Hill, Dwight Cummins. *Titl* Randolph Bartlett. *Story* Dorothy Yost, Dwight Cummins. *Photog* Robert De Grasse. *Film Ed* Pandro S. Berman. *Asst Dir* Jack Murton.

Cast: Ranger *(himself, a dog)*, Dorothy Kitchen *(Blossom Williams)*, Sam Nelson *(Larry Holbrook)*, Tom Lingham *(Pap Williams)*, Syd Crossley *(Rufe Anderson)*.

Action melodrama. Blossom, a girl of the Kentucky hills, has a drunkard father who forces her to accept the attentions of oafish Rufe Anderson, a superstitious mountain man who hates and fears Blossom's dog, Ranger. Anderson fails at his several attempts to do away with Ranger; each time Anderson feels safe in attacking Blossom, Ranger appears, having escaped his peril, to save her. Larry Holbrook, representative of a railroad, arrives to purchase Blossom's land for his company, and he falls in love with her. Anderson steals the cash payment from Larry before he has a chance to deliver it, then hurls him over a cliff. Ranger saves Larry and recovers the money, while Blossom's father comes to his senses and sends Anderson packing. *Alcoholism. Mountain life. Superstition. Fatherhood. Railroads. Kentucky. Dogs.*

FANGS OF THE WOLF **F2.1639**

Clarion Photoplays. *Dist* Weiss Brothers Artclass Pictures. 15 Sep **1924.** Si; b&w. 35mm. 5 reels.

Dir (see note) Harry O. Hoyt, Joseph A. Golden.

Cast: Charles Hutchison.

Western melodrama(?). No information about the nature of this film has been found.

Note: Sources disagree in crediting direction.

FANGS OF WOLFHEART **F2.1640**

Charles R. Seeling Productions. *Dist* Aywon Film Corp. 2 Mar **1925** [New York State license]. Si; b&w. 35mm. 5 reels, 4,900 ft.

Cast: Big Boy Williams, Wolfheart *(a dog)*.

Western melodrama(?). No information about the nature of this film has been found. *Dogs.*

THE FAR CALL **F2.1641**

Fox Film Corp. 28 Apr **1929** [c27 Apr 1929; LP336]. Mus score & sd eff (Movietone); b&w. 35mm. 6 reels, 5,313 ft. [Also si; 5,282 ft.]

Pres by William Fox. *Dir* Allan Dwan. *Scen* Seton I. Miller. *Titl* H. H. Caldwell. *Adapt* Walter Woods. *Photog* Hal Rosson. *Film Ed* H. H. Caldwell. *Asst Dir* William Tummel.

Cast: Charles Morton *(Pal Loring)*, Leila Hyams *(Hilda Larsen)*, Arthur Stone *(Schmidt)*, Warren Hymer *(Soup Brophy)*, Dan Wolheim *(Black O'Neil)*, Stanley J. Sandford *(Captain Storkerson)*, Ullrich Haupt *(London Nick)*, Charles Middleton *(Kris Larsen)*, Pat Hartigan *(Lars Johannson)*, Charles Gorman *(Haycox)*, Ivan Linow *(Red Dunkirk)*, Harry Gripp *(Pete)*, Sam Baker *(Tubal)*, Bernard Siegel *(Aleut chief)*, Willie Fung *(Wing)*, Frank Chew *(Ling Fu)*, Randolph Scott *(Helms)*.

Melodrama. Source: Edison Marshall, "The Far Call," in *Good Housekeeping* (vol 85–86, Aug 1927–Jan 1928). Pal Loring is making plans to rob the seal hatchery on St. Paul Island in the Bering Sea and goes to the island to reconnoiter, there meeting Hilda Larsen, the daughter of the island's governor. Hilda later discovers Pal to be the long-lost son of Paul Webber, who, while living, was a greatly respected member of the island community. Pal then decides not to go through with the robbery. Pal's former henchman, London Nick, sets out to rob the seal hatchery, and Pal fights him off, protecting the baby seals and winning himself a respected place in society. *Criminals—Rehabilitation. Seal hatcheries. Bering Sea. Saint Paul Island.*

THE FAR CRY **F2.1642**

First National Pictures. 14 Feb **1926** [c17 Feb 1926; LP22404]. Si; b&w. 35mm. 8 reels, 6,868 ft.

Dir Silvano Balboni. *Ed Dir* June Mathis. *Adapt* Katharine Kavanaugh. *Photog* John Boyle. *Art Dir* E. J. Shulter. *Film Ed* Al Hall.

Cast: Blanche Sweet *(Claire Marsh)*, Jack Mulhall *(Dick Clayton)*, Myrtle Stedman *(Louise Marsh)*, Hobart Bosworth *(Julian Marsh)*, Leo White *(Max Fraisier)*, Julia Swayne Gordon *(Helen Clayton)*, William Austin *(Eric Lancefield)*, John Sainpolis *(Count Filippo Sturani)*, Dorothy Revier *(Yvonne Beaudet)*, Mathilde Comont *(maid)*.

Society drama. Source: Arthur Richman, *The Far Cry* (New York opening: 30 Sep 1924). Dick Clayton and Claire Marsh fall in love in Paris, and their respective parents come to the Continent to break up the match. Mrs. Clayton is so insulting in her determination to save Dick from Claire that Claire decides to teach her a lesson: she lures Dick into proposing in the hearing of Mrs. Clayton and then turns him down. Dick goes to Venice to paint and forget; Claire quickly follows him, and they make up. Dick becomes jealous of one of Claire's admirers, they quarrel again, and Claire returns to Paris. Dick soon follows and saves her from a fire. They make plans to be married. *Artists. Aristocrats. Parenthood. Paris. Venice. Fires.*

FAR WESTERN TRAILS **F2.1643**

Associated Independent Producers. 20 May **1929.** Si; b&w. 35mm. 5 reels, 4,315 ft.

Dir-Scen Robert J. Horner. *Titl* Jack Erwing. *Photog* John Jenkins. *Film Ed* William Austin.

Cast: Ted Thompson, Bud Osborne, Lew Ames, Betty O'Doan.

Western melodrama(?). No information about the nature of this film has been found.

THE FARMER'S DAUGHTER **F2.1644**

Fox Film Corp. 14 Oct **1928** [c5 Oct 1928; LP25716]. Si; b&w. 35mm. 6 reels, 5,148 ft.

Pres by William Fox. *Dir (see note)* Norman Taurog, Arthur Rosson. *Scen (see note)* Gilbert W. Pratt, Frederica Sagor. *Titl* Garrett Graham. *Story (see note)* Lou Breslow, Henry M. Johnson, Harry Brand. *Photog* Joseph August. *Film Ed* J. Logan Pearson. *Asst Dir* Edmund Grainger.

Cast: Marjorie Beebe *(Margerine Hopkins)*, Frank Albertson *(Allan Boardman, Jr.)*, Arthur Stone *(J. Langley Smythe)*, Lincoln Stedman *(Noah Busby)*, Jimmie Adams *(Cicero Hopkins)*, Charles Middleton *(Hiram Flint)*.

Comedy. "City slicker tries to 'put something over' in a hick town. Country girl falls for him, passing up her country suitor, an inventor. When a milk baron comes to town he sees a fortune in the inventor's machine and the country girl goes back to her rural boy, the city slicker getting the air." ("Motion Picture News Booking Guide," in *Motion Picture News*, 15 Mar 1930, p78.) *Inventors. Smalltown life. Milk.*

Note: Sources disagree in crediting direction, scenario, and story.

FASCINATING YOUTH **F2.1645**

Famous Players–Lasky. *Dist* Paramount Pictures. 17 Mar **1926** [New York special showing; released 23 Aug; c23 Aug 1926; LP23043]. Si; b&w. 35mm. 7 reels, 6,882 ft.

Pres by Adolph Zukor, Jesse L. Lasky. *Dir* Sam Wood. *Scen* Paul Schofield. *Story* Byron Morgan. *Photog* Leo Tover.

Cast: Charles Rogers *(Teddy Ward)*, Ivy Harris *(Jeanne King)*, Jack Luden *(Ross Page)*, Walter Goss *(Randy Furness)*, Claud Buchanan *(Bobby Stearns)*, Mona Palma *(Dotty Sinclair)*, Thelma Todd *(Lorraine Lane)*, Josephine Dunn *(Loris Lane)*, Thelda Kenvin *(Betty Kent)*, Jeanne Morgan *(Mae Oliver)*, Dorothy Nourse *(Mary Arnold)*, Irving Hartley *(Johnnie)*, Gregory Blackton *(Frederick Maine)*, Robert Andrews *("Duke" Slade)*, Charles Brokaw *(Gregory)*, Iris Gray *(Sally Lee)*, Ralph Lewis *(John Ward)*, Joseph Burke *(Ward's secretary)*, James Bradbury, Sr. *(The Professor)*, Harry Sweet *(The Sheriff)*, William Black *(deputy sheriff)*, Richard Dix, Adolphe Menjou, Clara Bow, Lois Wilson, Percy Marmont, Chester Conklin, Thomas Meighan, Lila Lee, Lewis Milestone, Malcolm St. Clair *(themselves)*.

Society drama. Teddy Ward, son of a wealthy hotel owner, falls in love with Jeanne King, a Greenwich Village sketch artist, though his father favors a match with Loris Lane, a society girl. On the condition that he is successful in reviving business at his father's mountain resort, he may, however, marry the girl of his choice. With the aid of his friends, Teddy launches an advertising stunt involving an iceboat contest, but the plan is opposed by his father; then, in desperation, he invites a group of movie stars to the hotel. When the stars plead previous engagements, his friends try to help by disguising themselves as stars, but Jeanne, who has been sketching at a studio, arrives with half a dozen famous actors. Although

Teddy's father has refused to pay the prize money, the iceboat race takes place; and Teddy is forced to race against Slade, a champion, and win his own race to save face. Mr. Ward forgives him and announces his approval of Jeanne. *Artists. Actors. Hotel management. Motion pictures. Resorts. Boat racing. Iceboats. New York City—Greenwich Village.*

Note: The "stars" of the film include the 1926 graduating class of the first Paramount School for Stars, known as the Junior Stars of 1926.

FASCINATION **F2.1646**

Tiffany Productions. *Dist* Metro Pictures. 10 Apr **1922** [c12 Apr 1922; LP17758]. Si; b&w. 35mm. 8 reels, 7,940 ft.

Prod-Dir Robert Z. Leonard. *Story-Scen* Edmund Goulding. *Photog* Oliver T. Marsh. *Art Sets* Charles Cadwallader.

Cast: Mae Murray *(Dolores de Lisa)*, Creighton Hale *(Carlos de Lisa, her brother)*, Charles Lane *(Eduardo de Lisa, her father)*, Emily Fitzroy *(The Marquesa de Lisa, her aunt)*, Robert Frazer *(Carrita, a toreador)*, Vincent Coleman *(Ralph Kellogg, an American)*, Courtenay Foote *(The Count de Morera)*, Helen Ware *(Parola, a dancer)*, Frank Puglia *(Nema)*.

Melodrama. Dolores de Lisa, an impulsive American girl living with her aunt in Spain, disguises herself in a holiday costume and slips away to a bullfight during Easter celebration. She is fascinated by the toreador Carrita, and an introduction is offered by Count de Morera, provided that she attend a party at his home that evening. There she captures the heart of Carrita by her interpretation of "La Danza del Toro," while her aunt receives word of the arrival of her father, brother, and fiancé from America. Her father finds her in the company of Parola, a cabaret entertainer, with whom he had previously been linked, and Parola attempts to blackmail him, telling Dolores that he is Carrita's father. Carrita, in an attempt to revenge his wrongs, tries to kill him, but Dolores receives the toreador's knife, though the wound does not prove fatal. Parola confesses her mendacity, and Dolores begs Ralph, her sweetheart, to help her overcome her fascination with the exotic. *Bullfighters. Entertainers. Blackmail. Jealousy. Disguise. Easter. Spain.*

FASHION MADNESS **F2.1647**

Columbia Pictures. 8 Dec **1928** [c13 Jan 1928; LP24855]. Si; b&w. 35mm. 6 reels, 5,513 ft.

Prod Harry Cohn. *Dir* Louis J. Gasnier. *Adapt* Olga Printzlau. *Story* Victoria Moore. *Photog* J. O. Taylor. *Art Dir* Robert E. Lee. *Film Ed* Arthur Roberts. *Asst Dir* Clifford Saum.

Cast: Claire Windsor *(Gloria Vane)*, Reed Howes *(Victor Redding)*, Laska Winters *(Tanaka)*, Donald McNamee *(Bill)*, Boris Snegoff *(Count Costano)*.

Romantic drama. Gloria Vane, a young, headstrong debutante, is in love with Victor Redding, but she is another Katherine who needs a Petruchio to tame her. She is indignant when Redding takes her on his yacht and then to his cabin in the Canadian wilds. In the woods she sees her worthlessness, but when Redding is in danger of dying from an infected wound she drags him on a sled to the nearest settlement 10 miles away. The ordeal transforms her. *Shrews. Fashion. Courage. Canada.*

FASHION ROW **F2.1648**

Tiffany Productions. *Dist* Metro Pictures. 3 Dec **1923** [c5 Dec 1923; LP19732]. Si; b&w. 35mm. 7 reels, 7,300 ft.

Prod M. Leonard. *Dir* Robert Z. Leonard. *Scen* Sada Cowan, Howard Higgin. *Titl* Alfred A. Cohn. *Photog* Oliver T. Marsh. *Art Dir* Horace Jackson.

Cast: Mae Murray *(Olga Farinova/Zita, her younger sister)*, Earle Foxe *(James Morton)*, Freeman Wood *(Eric Van Corland)*, Mathilde Brundage *(Mrs. Van Corland)*, Elmo Lincoln *(Kaminoff)*, Sidney Franklin *(Papa Levitzky)*, Madame Rosa Rosanova *(Mama Levitzky)*, Craig Biddle, Jr. *(a press agent)*.

Melodrama. Two peasant sisters flee Russia during the revolution and sail to America. One, Olga Farinova, masquerades as a princess, becomes a noted actress, and marries a millionaire's son. Olga repudiates her sister, Zita, who has no illusions about her past life or present poverty. When Olga is shot by Kaminoff, a rejected suitor, Zita is adopted into the husband's family. *Peasants. Political refugees. Actors. Sisters. Millionaires. Imposture. Russia—History—1917–21 Revolution.*

FASHIONABLE FAKERS **F2.1649**

R-C Pictures. *Dist* Film Booking Offices of America. 16 Dec **1923** [c16 Dec 1923; LP19851]. Si; b&w. 35mm. 5 reels, 4,869 ft.

Dir William Worthington. *Adapt* Melville Brown. *Story* Frederick Stowers. *Photog* William O'Connell.

Cast: Johnnie Walker *(Thaddeus Plummer)*, Mildred June *(Clara Ridder)*, George Cowl *(Creel)*, J. Farrell MacDonald *(Pat O'Donnell, alias Abdul Ishmid)*, Lillian Lawrence *(Mrs. Ridder)*, Robert Balder *(Mr. Carter)*, George Rigas *(A. Turk)*.

Comedy-drama. Thaddeus Plummer, whose nickname is "The Worm" because his job is to bore holes into furniture to make it look antique, buys an oriental rug and nearly loses his job when his employer, Pat O'Donnell, alias Abdul Ishmid, deems it worthless. Plummer, having heard that it is a "wishing rug," makes a wish over it and becomes very lucky. He wishes to see his sweetheart and is rewarded; then he sells the rug for $1,000. Finally, the antique shop becomes his and he marries the girl. *Superstition. Antiques. Rugs.*

FASHIONS FOR WOMEN **F2.1650**

Famous Players–Lasky. *Dist* Paramount Pictures. 26 Mar **1927** [c2 Apr 1927; LP23822]. Si; b&w. 35mm. 7 reels, 6,296 ft.

Pres by Adolph Zukor, Jesse L. Lasky. *Dir* Dorothy Arzner. *Screenplay* Percy Heath. *Titl* George Marion, Jr. *Adapt* Jules Furthman, Herman J. Mankiewicz. *Photog* H. Kinley Martin.

Cast: Esther Ralston *(Céleste de Givray/Lola Dauvry)*, Raymond Hatton *(Sam Dupont)*, Einar Hanson *(Raoul de Bercy)*, Edward Martindel *(Duke of Arles)*, William Orlamond *(roué)*, Agostino Borgato *(Monsieur Alard)*, Edward Faust *(Monsieur Pattibone)*, Yvonne Howell *(Mimi)*, Maude Wayne *(The Girl)*, Charles Darvas *(restaurant manager)*.

Society drama. Source: Gladys Unger, *The Girl of the Hour* (from the French of Paul Armont and Léopold Marchand). Céleste de Givray, whose social success is the result of the audacity of her press agent, Sam Dupont, is persuaded to retreat from public life and to have her face lifted. Lola Dauvry, a cigarette girl at the Café Pierre, who loves Raoul de Bercy, a former aviator, is hired by Sam to pose as the new Céleste in a fashion show while Raoul is hired as Céleste's private aviator. While Raoul is waiting for Lola at Céleste's apartment, the Duke of Arles, one of Céleste's sweethearts, arrives; in despair, Lola begs Sam to inform Raoul of her identity, but he refuses. At the fashion show, Céleste appears and declares Lola an impostor, but the latter is declared "the best dressed woman" by the judges. Raoul, realizing that Lola has been faithful, returns to her at the cafe and they are happily reunited. *Fashion models. Cigarette girls. Press agents. Aviators. Plastic surgery. Impersonation. Fashion shows. Paris.*

Note: Varying sources render the cigarette girl's name as Lolo Dulay and Lulu Duffy.

FASHIONS IN LOVE **F2.1651**

Paramount Famous Lasky Corp. 29 Jun **1929** [c28 Jun 1929; LP509]. Sd (Movietone); b&w. 35mm. 8 reels, 6,592 ft. [Also si; 6,024 ft.]

Dir Victor Schertzinger. *Screenplay* Louise Long. *Adapt-Dial* Melville Baker. *Titl* Richard H. Digges, Jr. *Photog* Edward Cronjager. *Film Ed* George Nichols, Jr. *Songs: "Delphine," "I Still Believe in You"* Leo Robin, Victor Schertzinger.

Cast: Adolphe Menjou *(Paul de Remy)*, Fay Compton *(Marie de Remy)*, Miriam Seegar *(Delphine Martin)*, John Miljan *(Dr. Martin)*, Joan Standing *(Miss Weller)*, Robert Wayne *(Levisohn)*, Russ Powell *(Joe)*, Billie Bennett *(Jane)*, Jacques Vanaire *(valet)*.

Musical comedy. Source: Hermann Bahr, *The Concert* (New York opening: 4 Oct 1910). This is a remake of the 1921 film, *The Concert*, q. v. *Pianists. Physicians. Marriage. Infidelity. Courtship.*

FAST AND FEARLESS **F2.1652**

Action Pictures. *Dist* Weiss Brothers Artclass Pictures. 15 Sep **1924** [c12 Sep 1924; LU20560]. Si; b&w. 35mm. 5 reels, 4,600 ft.

Dir Richard Thorpe. *Photog* Irving Ries.

Cast: Buffalo Bill Jr. *(Lightning Bill Lewis)*, Jean Arthur *(Mary Brown)*, William Turner *(Judge Brown)*, George Magrill *(Pedro Gómez)*, Julian Rivero *(Captain Duerta)*, Emily Barrye *(Blanca)*, Kewpie King *(Fatty Doolittle)*, Steve Clemento *(Gonzales)*, Victor Allen *(Sheriff Hawkins)*.

Western melodrama. Bill Lewis sets out to capture Gómez, leader of a gang that has been terrorizing a border town. He prevents Gómez from kidnaping his girl, Mary, but Gómez escapes. With the aid of Captain Duerta, Bill pursues the gang, and when it is captured by Mexican soldiers he is free to marry. *Gangs. Kidnaping. Mexican border. Mexico—Army.*

FAST AND FURIOUS **F2.1653**

Universal Pictures. 12 Jun **1927** [c27 May 1927; LP24012]. Si; b&w. 35mm. 6 reels, 5,684 ft.

Pres by Carl Laemmle. *Dir* Melville W. Brown. *Adapt* Raymond Cannon. *Story* Reginald Denny. *Photog* Arthur Todd.

Cast: Reginald Denny *(Tom Brown)*, Barbara Worth *(Ethel)*, Claude Gillingwater *(Smithfield)*, Armand Kaliz *(Dupont)*, Lee Moran *(Joe)*, Charles K. French *(Hodge)*, Wilson Benge *(coachman)*, Robert E. Homans *(doctor)*, Kingsley Benedict *(Shorty)*, Edgar Norton *(Englishman)*.

Farce. Tom Brown, a wealthy young bachelor fond of speeding, wrecks his car and is aided by Smithfield, whereupon he instantly becomes enamored of the latter's daughter, Ethel. After recuperating from the accident, Tom embarks for California to find the Smithfields. During a traffic jam, he and Smithfield get into an altercation, which results in Tom's tweaking Smithfield's nose; at the Smithfield residence, Tom visits Ethel, who is supervising the creation of a statue dedicated by her father to racing drivers. Only Ethel's and the sculptor's combined efforts prevent a battle with Smithfield. Tom agrees to impersonate Billings, a racing champion, who is to pose for the sculptor and appear at the dedication, and is forced to complete the deception by driving in a race. After numerous adventures he wins the race and the love of Ethel. *Bachelors. Sculptors. Automobile racing. Impersonation. Reckless driving. Automobile accidents.*

FAST AND LOOSE **F2.1654**

Paramount-Publix Corp. 8 Nov **1930** [c11 Nov 1930; LP1737]. Sd (Movietone); b&w. 35mm. 7 reels, 6,384 ft.

Dir Fred Newmeyer. *Dial Dir* Bertram Harrison. *Screenplay* Doris Anderson, Jack Kirkland. *Adtl Dial* Preston Sturges. *Photog* William Steiner. *Rec Engr* C. A. Tuthill.

Cast: Miriam Hopkins *(Marion Lenox)*, Carol Lombard *(Alice O'Neil)*, Frank Morgan *(Bronson Lenox)*, Charles R. Starrett *(Henry Morgan)*, Henry Wadsworth *(Bertie Lenox)*, Winifred Harris *(Carrie Lenox)*, Herbert Yost *(George Crafton)*, David Hutcheson *(Lord Rockingham)*, Ilka Chase *(Millie Montgomery)*, Herschel Mayall *(Judge Summers)*.

Romantic comedy. Source: David Gray and Avery Hopwood, *The Best People* (New York opening: 19 Aug 1924). Marion and Bertie Lenox are representatives of the fast younger generation in a wealthy, tradition-bound Long Island family of which Bronson and Carrie Lenox are the heads. When Bronson is informed by his brother-in-law that his son Bertie is involved with a chorus girl, Bronson determines to investigate the matter, as his wife insists on keeping the family among only "the best people." At the cabaret where she works, Bronson is forced to admit that Alice is a fine girl and also discovers that his daughter Marion is in love with Henry Morgan, an automobile mechanic. Bronson later attempts to iron out the difficulties to the tune of hysterics from his wife and ranting by George, the brother-in-law. When it develops that Alice's friend, Millie, is opposed to her marrying, and when Morgan, interviewed as to his intentions, wants to test Marion before contemplating marriage, the family begins to promote rather than denounce the situation, resulting in a double wedding with blessings on all sides. *Socialites. Chorus girls. Mechanics. Courtship. Wealth. Weddings. New York City. Long Island.*

FAST COMPANY **F2.1655**

Paramount Famous Lasky Corp. 14 Sep **1929** [c13 Sep 1929; LP683]. Sd (Movietone); b&w. 35mm. 8 reels, 6,863 ft. [Also si; 6,459 ft.]

Dir A. Edward Sutherland. *Screenplay* Florence Ryerson, Patrick Kearney, Walton Butterfield. *Dial* Joseph L. Mankiewicz. *Adapt* Patrick Kearney, Walton Butterfield. *Photog* Edward Cronjager. *Film Ed* Jane Loring. *Song: "You Want Lovin', I Want Love"* Sam Coslow. *Rec Engr* Eugene Merritt.

Cast: Evelyn Brent *(Evelyn Corey)*, Jack Oakie *(Elmer Kane)*, Richard "Skeets" Gallagher *(Bert Wade)*, Sam Hardy *(Dave Walker)*, Arthur Housman *(Barney Barlow)*, Gwen Lee *(Rosie La Clerq)*, Chester Conklin *(C. of C. President)*, E. H. Calvert *(Platt)*, Eugenie Besserer *(Mrs. Kane)*, Bert Rome *(Hank Gordon)*, Irish Meusel, Arnold "Jigger" Statz, Truck Hannah, Gus Sanberg, Ivan Olson, Wally Rehg, Jack Adams, George Boehler, Howard Burkett, Red Rollings, Frank Greene, Lez Smith *(themselves, baseball players)*.

Comedy-romance. Source: Ring Lardner and George M. Cohan, *Elmer The Great* (New York opening: 24 Sep 1928). Elmer Kane, a village baseball hero turned professional, loves vampish vaudeville actress Evelyn Corey, who thinks he is a hick. At training camp Yankee scout Bert Wade sends him love letters signed by Evelyn to make Elmer perform well. During the World Series games with Pittsburgh Elmer discovers the deception. Then some crooked gamblers try to bribe Elmer to throw the game. The final deciding game goes badly because Elmer is in a slump over Evelyn. Wade sends Evelyn in to cheer him. While she is with him she finds she really loves him—Elmer bangs out the home run that wins the World Series. *Actors. Gamblers. Baseball scouts. Baseball. Vaudeville. Bribery. World Series. New York Yankees. Pittsburgh Pirates.*

FAST FIGHTIN' **F2.1656**

Approved Pictures. *Dist* Weiss Brothers Artclass Pictures. 15 Feb **1925** [c11 Mar 1925; LU21231]. Si; b&w. 35mm. 5 reels, 4,800 ft.

Pres by Lester F. Scott, Jr. *Dir* Richard Thorpe. *Story* A. E. Serrao. *Photog* Ray Ries.

Cast: Buddy Roosevelt *(The Cowboy)*, Nell Brantley *(The Girl)*, Joe Rickson *(The Man)*, Emily Barrye *(The Other Woman)*, Sherry Tansey *(The Boy)*, Emma Tansey *(The Mother)*, Leonard Trainor *(The Sheriff)*.

Western melodrama. The Cowboy works on the ranch owned by The Girl. Her brother, in the clutches of a crook, attempts to steal money from The Girl: blame for the theft is laid on The Cowboy. The Cowboy learns of the plot of The Man, another rancher, to steal The Girl's money. The Cowboy prevents the theft, captures The Man, and wins The Girl. *Cowboys. Ranchers. Brother-sister relationship. Theft.*

THE FAST FREIGHT **F2.1657**

Famous Players–Lasky. *Dist* Paramount Pictures. **1921** [scheduled release]. Si; b&w. 35mm. 5 reels.

Dir James Cruze. *Story* Curtis Benton.

Cast: Roscoe Arbuckle.

Comedy.

Note: Made but never released in the United States. Also known as *Freight Prepaid*, *Via Fast Freight*.

FAST LIFE **F2.1658**

First National Pictures. 15 Aug **1929** [New York premiere; released 1 Sep; c18 Sep 1929; LP741]. Sd (Vitaphone); b&w. 35mm. 9 reels, 7,541 ft. [Also si, 29 Sep 1929; 6,702 ft.]

Pres by Richard A. Rowland. *Dir* John Francis Dillon. *Scen-Dial-Titl* John F. Goodrich. *Photog* Faxon Dean. *Film Ed* Ralph Holt. *Song: "Since I Found You"* Ray Perkins.

Cast: Douglas Fairbanks, Jr. *(Douglas Stratton)*, Loretta Young *(Patricia)*, William Holden *(governor)*, Frank Sheridan *(warden)*, Chester Morris *(Paul Palmer)*, Ray Hallor *(Rodney Hall)*, John St. Polis *(Andrew Stratton)*, Purnell Pratt *(Berton Hall)*.

Melodrama. Source: Samuel Shipman and John B. Hymer, *Fast Life* (New York opening: 26 Sep 1928). Douglas Stratton and Patricia Mason, secretly married, are preparing for bed when unsuccessful suitor Rodney Hall disturbs them by climbing through the window. A struggle follows; Rodney is killed; and Douglas is sentenced to die in the electric chair. It is revealed that Paul Palmer, son of the governor and nephew of the prison warden, actually killed Rodney and is remaining silent, hoping to marry Patricia when Douglas is out of the way. The warden, protective of his brother's political career, determines to let Douglas die and swears Paul to silence. At the last minute, the warden weakens and orders Douglas' release. Paul commits suicide rather than face his father. Douglas and Pat are reunited. *State governors. Prison wardens. Filial relations. Murder. Injustice. Capital punishment. Suicide.*

THE FAST MAIL **F2.1659**

Fox Film Corp. 20 Aug **1922** [c20 Aug 1922; LP19207]. Si; b&w. 35mm. 6 reels.

Pres by William Fox. *Dir* Bernard J. Durning. *Scen* Agnes Parsons, Jacques Jaccard. *Photog* George Schneiderman, Don Short.

Cast: Charles Jones *(Stanley Carson)*, Eileen Percy *(Virginia Martin)*, James Mason *(Lee Martin)*, William Steele *(Pierre La Fitte)*, Adolphe Menjou *(Cal Baldwin)*, Harry Dunkinson *(Harry Joyce)*.

Action melodrama. Source: Lincoln J. Carter, *The Fast Mail* (unpublished play). Cowboy Stanley Carson is visiting Virginia Martin in a southern city when her brother and his gambler friends try to disgrace her. Then Carson is tricked out of winning a horserace by crooked gamblers who abduct Virginia. He chases them by jumping into a boat, swimming ashore, and leaping aboard a fast train. Jumping from the train into a moving automobile, he arrives at the hotel where Virginia is held captive. Here he pauses to rescue a family from a fire and then proceeds to save Virginia. *Cowboys. Gamblers. Horseracing. Abduction. Automobiles. Fires. Stunts.*

THE FAST SET F2.1660

Famous Players–Lasky. *Dist* Paramount Pictures. 20 Oct **1924** [c22 Oct 1924; LP20699]. Si; b&w. 35mm. 8 reels, 6,754 ft.

Pres by Adolph Zukor, Jesse L. Lasky. *Dir* William De Mille. *Scen* Clara Beranger. *Photog* L. Guy Wilky.

Cast: Betty Compson *(Margaret Sones)*, Adolphe Menjou *(Ernest Steele)*, Elliott Dexter *(Richard Sones)*, ZaSu Pitts *(Mona)*, Dawn O'Day *(Little Margaret Sones)*, Grace Carlyle *(Jane Walton)*, Claire Adams *(Fay Collen)*, Rosalind Byrne *(Connie Gallies)*, Edgar Norton *(Archie Wells)*, Louis Natheaux *(Billy Sommers)*, Eugenio De Liguoro *(Walters)*, Fred Walton *(Simpson)*.

Domestic comedy-drama. Source: Frederick Lonsdale, *Spring Cleaning, a Comedy in Three Acts* (New York, 1925). Novelist Richard Sones enjoys the company of his books and intellectual friends, while his wife, Margaret, prefers the jazz life of a fast set. Adept at sympathizing with neglected wives, Ernest Steele finds Margaret receptive to his flattering phrases. Richard, realizing that he must take drastic action, invites Mona, a girl of the streets, to accompany him to one of Margaret's parties and there describes her as a professional in the game they play as amateurs. Margaret decides upon a divorce, but Steele fears for his freedom and brings about a reconciliation between the Soneses. *Novelists. Prostitutes. Jazz life. Marriage. Divorce.*

THE FAST WORKER (Universal-Jewel) F2.1661

Universal Pictures. 26 Oct **1924** [c15 Sep 1924; LP20580]. Si; b&w. 35mm. 7 reels, 6,896 ft.

Pres by Carl Laemmle. *Dir* William Seiter. *Scen* Beatrice Van, Raymond L. Schrock. *Photog* Ben Reynolds.

Cast: Reginald Denny *(Terry Brock)*, Laura La Plante *(Connie)*, Ethel Grey Terry *(Edith Medcroft)*, Muriel Frances Dana *(Toodles)*, Lee Moran *(Freddie)*, Richard Tucker *(Roxbury Medcroft)*, Margaret Campbell *(Mrs. Rodney)*, Betty Morrisey *("Kath" Rodney)*, Mildred Vincent *(nurse)*, John Steppling *(Mr. Rodney)*, T. D. Crittenden *(Mr. O'Dell Carney)*, Clarissa Selwynne *(Mrs. O'Dell Carney)*.

Comedy. Source: George Barr McCutcheon, *Husbands of Edith* (New York, 1908). Roxbury persuades his architect friend, Terry, to assume his identity and go to Catalina on a vacation with his wife, Edith, and daughter, Toodles. Terry falls in love with Edith's sister, Connie, and when a scandal arises at the hotel resort, a police force, a truck, and a yacht are needed to extricate Terry from the ensuing trouble. *Architects. Sisters. Impersonation. Catalina.*

THE FATAL KISS *see* **THE FATAL MISTAKE**

THE FATAL MARRIAGE (Reissue) F2.1662

Dist R-C Pictures. Jun **1922** [c18 Jun 1922; LP17972]. Si; b&w. 35mm. 5 reels, 4,630 ft. [Original length: 4 reels.]

Note: Retitled adaptation of Tennyson's poem "Enoch Arden," produced in 1915 by Majestic and supervised by D. W. Griffith.

THE FATAL MISTAKE F2.1663

Perfection Pictures. c10 Dec **1924** [LP20904]. Si; b&w. 35mm. 5 reels.

Dir Scott Dunlap. *Photog* Allen Thompson.

Cast: William Fairbanks *(Jack Darwin)*, Eva Novak *(Ethel Bennet)*, Wilfred Lucas, Dot Farley, Bruce Gordon, Harry McCoy, Paul Weigel, Frank Clark.

Melodrama. After the attempted theft of the Rigo jewels from the mansion of wealthy Helen Van Dyke, a socialite engaged to Prince Rigo, Jack Darwin, a cub reporter of the *Star*, determines to obtain a picture of Miss Van Dyke, who has never been photographed. Jack goes to the mansion and there snaps a shot of a young woman in a wedding gown, but, after the photograph has been featured in a special edition, the city editor discovers that it is merely a picture of Ethel Bennet, a maid employed by Miss Van Dyke. Fired, Jack visits an employment agency, where he meets Ethel, who also has lost her job. Together they return to the Van Dyke mansion, hoping to get an exclusive that will win him back his job. They separate, and Jack witnesses a robbery and kidnaping; after a wild car chase, he subdues both of the malefactors. The kidnaped woman—Ethel—informs him that she is an undercover agent for the police, assigned to protect the Rigo jewels. Jack files the story, gets his job back, and marries Ethel. *Socialites. Housemaids. Reporters. Photographers. Newspapers. Kidnaping. Robbery. Chases.*

Note: Working title: *The Fatal Kiss.*

THE FATAL PLUNGE F2.1664

Dist Weiss Brothers Artclass Pictures. 23 Dec **1924** [New York State license application]. Si; b&w. 35mm. 5 reels.

Dir Harry O. Hoyt.

Cast: Charles Hutchison, Ann Luther, Laura La Plante.

Society melodrama. This film contains elements of blackmail, murder, blackjacking, second-story work, extortion, and safe-cracking. *Safecrackers. Blackmail. Murder. Extortion.*

Note: This film was cut down from a 15-episode serial, *The Great Gamble*, produced by Western Photoplays and released by Pathé in 1919. The serial was written and directed by Joseph A. Golden, and it seems likely that Harry O. Hoyt supervised the reshaping of the original film for his version.

THE FATAL 30 F2.1665

Pacific Film Co. 1 Dec **1921**. Si; b&w. 35mm. 5 reels.

Dir John J. Hayes.

Cast: John J. Hayes, Fritzi Ridgeway, Lillian West, Carl Stockdale, Al Fremont.

Melodrama. "A melodrama that deals with a religious cult of sun-worshippers and their belief of human sacrifice to the sun. Love interest is introduced between young newspaper reporter and his sweetheart, and shows their search for a lost chart revealing untold wealth, which takes them through many dives of the underworld and eventually to a happy ending." *(Motion Picture News Booking Guide, 2:25, Apr 1922.) Reporters. Cults. Human sacrifice. Treasure. Documentation.*

FATE F2.1666

W. E. Weathers. *Dist* Master Photo Drama Co. Aug **1921**. Si; b&w. 35mm. 8 reels, 7,600 ft.

Cast: John Ince, Clara Smith Hamon.

Drama. Middle-aged Jacob L. Hamon (played by John Ince) strikes up an acquaintance with Clara Smith, an innocent young high school girl, offers her financial assistance for her education, and employs her as a confidential secretary. Although Hamon is married, an intimate relationship springs up between the wealthy man and Clara, which leads Hamon to arrange a marriage of convenience between Clara and his nephew, F. L. Hamon. (This arrangement allows Clara and Hamon to travel together as Mr. and Mrs. Hamon.) Hamon strikes oil and rises to influence in both the political and business worlds, while his excessive drinking results in increasing debauchery and in brutality to Clara and his business associates. On one occasion Hamon is particularly violent to Clara, and she shoots him. After a few days, Hamon dies, and Clara flees to Texas, thence to Mexico. She later surrenders, returns to Oklahoma, and is tried for murder but is acquitted to the joy of the courtroom audience. *Secretaries. Infidelity. Marriage of convenience. Alcoholism. Murder. Trials. Oklahoma. Texas. Mexico. Clara Smith Hamon. Jacob L. Hamon.*

Note: This film is purported to be based on actual events in the life of Clara Smith Hamon, who was tried for and acquitted of the murder of Jacob L. Hamon in 1921.

THE FATE OF A FLIRT F2.1667

Waldorf Pictures. *Dist* Columbia Pictures. 15 Nov **1925** [c28 Dec 1925; LP22171]. Si; b&w. 35mm. 6 reels, 5,793 ft.

Prod Harry Cohn. *Dir* Frank R. Strayer. *Cont* Albert Lewin. *Titl* Malcolm S. Boylan. *Story* Janet Crothers. *Photog* Sam Landers. *Film Ed* Charles J. Hunt.

Cast: Dorothy Revier *(Mary Burgess)*, Forrest Stanley *(James)*, Thomas Ricketts *(Uncle John Burgess)*, Phillips Smalley *(Sir Horace Worcester)*, William Austin *(Riggs)*, Clarissa Selwynne *(Aunt Louise Burgess)*, Charles West *(Eddie Graham)*, Louis Payne *(Simpson)*.

Romantic comedy. James, a young English lord, takes a job as the chauffeur of the wealthy Burgess family in order to be near Mary Burgess, a girl with whom he is in love. The romance scandalizes Mary's relatives; and James, in order to gain their consent to marry Mary, resorts to blackmail: he arranges for one of his friends to romance innocently Mary's aunt and then, if her aunt will not give her consent, threaten to expose this harmless but humiliating intrigue to the world. A real blackmailer turns up, but Jimmy soon has him on the run. Jimmy's high birth becomes public knowledge, and he and Mary are wed with the proud blessing of the entire Burgess clan. *Flirts. Nobility. Aunts. Chauffeurs. Social classes. Disguise. Courtship. Blackmail.*

FATHER AND SON **F2.1668**

Columbia Pictures. 13 May or 5 Jun **1929** [c12 Jun 1929; LP464]. Talking sequences, mus score, & sd eff (Movietone); b&w. 35mm. 7 reels, 6,310 ft. [Also si; 6,765 ft.]

Prod Harry Cohn. *Dir* Erle C. Kenton. *Cont* Jack Townley. *Dial-Titl* Frederic Hatton, Fanny Hatton. *Story* Elmer Harris. *Photog* Ted Tetzlaff. *Art Dir* Harrison Wiley. *Mus Score* Constantin Bakaleinikoff. *Asst Dir* Tenny Wright.

Cast: Jack Holt *(Frank Fields)*, Dorothy Revier *(Grace Moore)*, Helene Chadwick *(Miss White)*, Mickey McBan *(Jimmy Fields)*, Wheeler Oakman *(Anton Lebau)*.

Domestic drama. Wealthy businessman and widower Frank Fields departs for Europe, leaving his son Jimmy in the charge of Miss White, a nextdoor neighbor. Fields meets the fascinating Grace Moore (in reality a notorious adventuress) and falls in love with her; but she is living with Anton Lebau, a confidence man sought by the authorities. When Lebau objects to her relationship with Fields, she betrays him to the police. Unprepared for a stepmother, Jimmy takes an intense dislike to his father's new wife, who deliberately causes friction between father and son. She destroys a letter for Fields from Lebau, and when Fields finds the partially burned envelope in Jimmy's stamp album and reprimands him, the boy leaves home. Meanwhile Fields discovers his wife's s duplicity and quarrels with her; complications ensue when Jimmy returns home for his possessions and Lebau is killed in the library; Jimmy and his father each think the other committed the crime, but Jimmy's recordograph reveals the guilty party. *Businessmen. Widowers. Children. Confidence men. Filial relations. Stepmothers. Documentation. Recordographs.*

FATHER TOM **F2.1669**

O'Brien Productions. *Dist* Playgoers Pictures. 13 Nov **1921** [c2 Nov 1921; LU17155]. Si; b&w. 35mm. 5 reels.

Dir John B. O'Brien. *Scen Ed* Rodney Hickok. *Story* Carl Krusada. *Photog* Lawrence E. Williams.

Cast: Tom Wise *(Father Tom)*, James Hill *(Jim Colby)*, May Kitson *(Mary)*, Myra Brooks *(Mrs. Martin)*, Ray Allen *(Mrs. Wellington)*, Harry Boler *(H. C. Dalton)*, Alexander Clark *(Bob Wellington)*, James Wallace *(The Constable)*, Nancy Deaver *(Margie)*.

Rural melodrama. Bob Wellington, distressed by his mother's infatuation for Mr. Dalton, whom he distrusts, seeks the help of Father Tom, adored by the villagers for his acts of kindness, and Father Tom agrees to help. Margie, orphaned and with only a horse for companionship, comes to town; Father Tom finds a home for her, and soon she and Tom fall in love. Mrs. Wellington, however, disapproves, and blames Father Tom, at the same time refusing to renew the mortgage she holds on his church. To obtain the church money, Bob and Margie plan to enter the horse in a race, and though Colby, the owner of a notorious roadhouse, steals the horse, Father Tom retrieves it in time for the race. When Dalton is unmasked as a masher, Mrs. Wellington forgives Bob and accepts Margie. *Orphans. Clergymen. Motherhood. Horseracing. Churches. Horses.*

FAZIL **F2.1670**

Fox Film Corp. 4 Jun **1928** [c14 Nov 1927; LP24650]. Mus score & sd eff (Movietone); b&w. 35mm. 7 reels, 7,217 ft. [Also si.]

Pres by William Fox. *Dir* Howard Hawks. *Scen* Seton I. Miller. *Adapt* Philip Klein. *Photog* L. William O'Connell. *Asst Dir* James Tinling.

Cast: Charles Farrell *(Prince Fazil)*, Greta Nissen *(Fabienne)*, Mae Busch *(Helene Debreuze)*, Vadim Uraneff *(Ahmed)*, Tyler Brooke *(Jacques Debreuze)*, Eddie Sturgis *(Rice)*, Josephine Borio *(Aicha)*, John Boles *(John Clavering)*, John T. Murray *(Gondolier)*, Erville Alderson *(Iman Idris)*, Dale Fuller *(Zouroya)*, Hank Mann *(Ali)*.

Romantic drama. Source: Pierre Frondaie, "L'Insoumise," in *La Petite Illustration's Library of Plays*, no. 80 (Paris, 1922). Prince Fazil, an Arab chieftain, marries Fabienne, a carefree Parisienne, but once she is subjected to the rigors of desert life, she rebels and in doing so precipitates a quarrel. Prince Fazil leaves her for his beloved desert and establishes a harem. Her jealousy aroused, Fabienne returns to him and compels the desert maidens to disperse. The prince denounces her actions, and when a rescue party arrives to save Fabienne, he is mortally wounded; but before dying he poisons her, and they are united in death. *Arabs. Parisians. Marriage. Suicide. Harems. Deserts.*

THE FEAR FIGHTER **F2.1671**

Harry J. Brown Productions. *Dist* Rayart Pictures. ca30 Sep **1925** [New York premiere]. Si; b&w. 35mm. 5 reels, 4,800 ft.

Dir Albert Rogell. *Story* Grover Jones. *Photog* Ross Fisher.

Cast: Billy Sullivan *(Billy Griffin)*, Ruth Dwyer *(Catherine Curtis)*, J. P. McGowan *(James Curtis)*, "Gunboat" Smith *(prison inmate)*, Phil Salvadore, Spike Robinson, Jack Herrick, Billy Franey.

Comedy. Billy Griffin, who is in love with Catherine Curtis, the daughter of a fight promoter, must fight her father in order to win her hand in marriage. Billy puts on the gloves and is knocked senseless by the elder Curtis, losing his memory in the process. Billy is later sentenced to 90 days in jail, where his cellmate, a former boxer, teaches him the fistic art. After he is released from jail, Billy becomes a boxer and is soon successful enough in the ring to be matched with the light heavyweight champion. Billy then regains his memory and remembers nothing of his days as a fighter. He enters the ring with the champ, and for several rounds he is badly beaten. Finally Catherine calls him yellow, and Billy, greatly angered, handily wins the fight. He also wins Catherine for his bride. *Fight promoters. Courage. Prizefighting. Amnesia. Jails.*

FEAR-BOUND **F2.1672**

Nigh-Smith Pictures. *Dist* Vitagraph Co. of America. 18 Jan **1925** [c17 Jan 1925; LP21056]. Si; b&w. 35mm. 6 reels, 5,877 ft.

Dir-Writ Will Nigh. *Sets* Tec-Art Studios.

Cast: Marjorie Daw *(Falfi Tumble)*, Will Nigh *(Jim Tumble)*, Niles Welch *(Tod Vane)*, Louise Mackintosh *(Ma Tumble)*, Edward Roseman *(Pa Tumble)*, James Bradbury, Jr. *(Luke Tumble)*, Warner Richmond *(Ed Tumble)*, Dexter McReynolds *(Alkali Red)*, Jean Jarvis *(Fluffy Ralston)*, Frank Conlon *(Cooky)*.

Western melodrama. Deserted by her husband and three sons, Ma Tumble supports herself and her small daughter, Falfi, by farming. Fifteen years later, her youngest son, Jim, returns to her, wanted by the law for his part in a bank robbery. At Falfi's insistence, Ma hides Jim from the sheriff's posse and later moves with her family to another town, where she opens a restaurant. Jim gets a job guarding payrolls and ore shipments at a local mine. Recently released from jail, Pa Tumble and the other sons find Ma Tumble and, discovering Jim's job, force him to help them rob an ore shipment. After the robbery, Ma calls Jim a vile coward and forbids him to return until he proves himself a man. Brought to his senses, Jim kills one of his brothers and brings his father and other brother to justice. Jim is then welcomed back by his mother and sister and acclaimed a hero by the grateful populace. *Brothers. Guards. Motherhood. Robbery. Mining. Cowardice. Filial relations. Farming. Fratricide. Restaurants.*

FEARLESS DICK **F2.1673**

Prairie Productions. 9 Sep **1922** [New York State license]. Si; b&w. 35mm. 5 reels.

Cast: Dick Hatton.

Western melodrama(?). No information about the nature of this film has been found.

THE FEARLESS LOVER **F2.1674**

Perfection Pictures. 1 Feb **1925** [c2 Mar 1925; LP21191]. Si; b&w. 35mm. 5 reels, 4,656 ft.

Dir Henry MacRae. *Story* Scott Dunlap. *Photog* Allen Thompson.

Cast: William Fairbanks *(Patrick Michael Casey)*, Eva Novak *(Enid Sexton)*, Tom Kennedy *(Tom Dugan)*, Lydia Knott *(Mrs. James Sexton)*, Arthur Rankin *(Ted Sexton)*, Frankie Darrow *(Frankie)*.

Melodrama. Patrick Michael Casey, a young patrolman and the second generation of his family on the force, arrests the brother of Enid Sexton, the girl with whom he is in love. Patrick learns that the boy was forced into a life of crime by Tom Dugan, notorious crook, and determines to bring Dugan to justice. Patrick succeeds in arresting Dugan and thus effects the release of Enid's brother from jail. Enid and Patrick make plans to pound the beat of life together. *Police. Irish. Brother-sister relationship.*

THE FEARLESS RIDER **F2.1675**

Universal Pictures. 15 Jan **1928** [c20 Oct 1927; LP24568]. Si; b&w. 35mm. 5 reels, 4,173 ft.

Pres by Carl Laemmle. *Dir* Edgar Lewis. *Story-Cont* Basil Dickey. *Titl* Gardner Bradford. *Photog* Wilfred Cline. *Art Dir* David S. Garber. *Film Ed* Jack Jackson, Harry Marker.

Cast: Fred Humes *(Larry Day)*, Barbara Worth *(Kate Lane)*, Ben Corbett *(Two-Spot Tommy)*, Pee Wee Holmes *(Hank Hook)*, Buck Connors *(Jeff Lane)*, William Steele *(Dr. Lucifer Blade)*.

Western melodrama. Larry Day, owner of the Triple D Ranch, and his foreman are called to the claim of Jeff Lane, a gold prospector who has been reported injured in a mine explosion. Although Jeff is unhurt, Doc Blade recommends to Kate, Lane's daughter, that he be hospitalized; becoming suspicious, Larry stays with the girl to watch the mine. Doc Blade makes Lane a prisoner and gathers his men to raid the mine, but he is stopped by Larry, who follows him to his cabin, where Kate also has been made prisoner; after freeing her and her father, Larry and his men capture the outlaws. *Prospectors. Physicians. Filial relations. Claim jumpers. Gold mines.*

FEEL MY PULSE **F2.1676**

Paramount Famous Lasky Corp. 25 Feb **1928** [c25 Feb 1928; LP25002]. Si; b&w. 35mm. 6 reels, 5,808 ft.

Pres by Adolph Zukor, Jesse L. Lasky. *Dir* Gregory La Cava. *Scen* Keene Thompson, Nick Barrows. *Titl* George Marion, Jr. *Story* Howard Emmett Rogers. *Photog* J. Roy Hunt. *Ed in Ch* E. Lloyd Sheldon.

Cast: Bebe Daniels *(Barbara Manning)*, Melbourne MacDowell *(Her Uncle Wilburforce)*, George Irving *(Her Uncle Edgar)*, Charles Sellon *(Her Sanitarium's Caretaker)*, Heinie Conklin *(Her Patient)*, William Powell *(Her Nemesis)*, Richard Arlen *(Her Problem)*.

Comedy. Barbara Manning, a girl who since childhood has been made to believe she is sickly, visits an island sanitarium inherited from her Uncle Edgar. The cowardly caretaker has turned the place over to a gang of rumrunners to use as their headquarters and battleground to oppose their enemies, the hijackers. Barbara believes that the rumrunners and an undercover newspaper reporter (played by Richard Arlen), disguised as one of the gang, are patients. The reporter, having fallen in love with Barbara, asks her to leave because he is afraid she will be harmed. She refuses and comes to his aid when the gang, suspecting he has informed Barbara of their activities, attack him. Barbara fends them off with chloroform and surgical instruments, discovering that she is not sickly after all. Another uncle, concerned about her health, arrives on the island to find Barbara robustly healthy, holding the rumrunners prisoner. *Invalids. Uncles. Rumrunners. Hijackers. Reporters. Sanitariums.*

FEET FIRST **F2.1677**

Harold Lloyd Corp. *Dist* Paramount-Publix Corp. 8 Nov **1930** [c11 Nov 1930; LP1738]. Sd (Movietone); b&w. 35mm. 10 reels, 8,100 ft.

Dir Clyde Bruckman. *Screenplay-Dial* Felix Adler, Lex Neal, Paul Gerard Smith. *Story* John Grey, Al Cohn. *Photog* Walter Lundin, Henry Kohler. *Film Ed* Bernard Burton. *Rec Engr* William R. Fox.

Cast: Harold Lloyd *(Harold Horne)*, Robert McWade *(John Tanner)*, Lillian Leighton *(Mrs. Tanner)*, Barbara Kent *(Mary)*, Alec B. Francis *(Old Timer, Mr. Garson)*, Noah Young *(ship's officer)*, Henry Hall *(Endicott)*, Arthur Housman *(clubman)*, Sleep 'n' Eat *(himself)*.

Comedy. Harold Horne, an apprentice clerk in a Honolulu shoe store, is ambitious and hopes to rise in John Tanner's organization, but his nervousness at waiting on Mary, a lady customer, causes numerous distractions, including the loss of her dog in the street, resulting in amusing complications with taxi drivers. As social secretary to wealthy Mrs. Tanner, Mary declares her confidence in the enterprising Harold, while he confides to Mr. Carson, a roomer in his boardinghouse, that he will take a correspondence course to become rich and worthy of Mary. Harold crashes a series of society gatherings and boasts of his prowess at polo and other pastimes of the wealthy, but later he makes a general botch of Mrs. Tanner's shoes and stockings at the store, trying to elude Mary's glance. In delivering shoes to an ocean liner, Harold is forced to remain aboard; he discovers Mary is only a secretary. To escape being caught, Harold hides in a mail bag and in a series of maneuvers ends up flying to San Francisco, where he delivers an urgent bid for Tanner, saving Mary her job, and winning himself a promotion as well as a wife. *Shoeclerks. Secretaries. Taxi drivers. Social classes. Courtship. Ocean liners. Airplanes. Honolulu. San Francisco. Dogs.*

FEET OF CLAY **F2.1678**

Famous Players–Lasky. *Dist* Paramount Pictures. 22 Sep **1924** [c24 Sep 1924; LP20598]. Si; b&w. 35mm. 10 reels, 9,746 ft.

Pres by Adolph Zukor, Jesse L. Lasky. *Dir* Cecil B. De Mille. *Scen* Beulah Marie Dix, Bertram Millhauser. *Photog* Peverell Marley, Archibald Stout. *Tech Dir* Roy Pomeroy.

Cast: Vera Reynolds *(Amy Loring)*, Rod La Rocque *(Kerry Harlan)*, Ricardo Cortez *(Tony Channing)*, Robert Edeson *(Dr. Fergus Lansell)*, Julia Faye *(Bertha Lansell)*, Theodore Kosloff *(Bendick)*, Victor Varconi *(The Bookkeeper)*.

Society drama. Source: Margaretta Tuttle, *Feet of Clay* (Boston & New York, 1923). After being injured in a battle with a shark, Kerry Harlan is unable to work, and his youthful wife, Amy, becomes a fashion model. While she is away, his surgeon's wife, Bertha, tries to force her attentions on Kerry and is accidentally killed in an attempt to evade her husband. Amy is courted by Tony Channing following the scandal, but she returns to her husband and finds him near death from gas fumes. As they both attempt suicide, their spirits are rejected by "the other world," and learning the truth from Bertha's spirit they fight their way back to life. *Fashion models. Supernatural. Suicide. Ghosts. Sharks.*

THE FEMALE **F2.1679**

Famous Players–Lasky. *Dist* Paramount Pictures. ca31 Aug **1924** [New York premiere; released 29 Sep 1924; c3 Sep 1924; LP20537]. Si; b&w. 35mm. 7 reels, 6,167 ft.

Dir Sam Wood. *Scen* Agnes Christine Johnston. *Photog* Alfred Gilks.

Cast: Betty Compson *(Dalla)*, Warner Baxter *(Colonel Valentia)*, Noah Beery *(Barend de Beer)*, Dorothy Cumming *(Clodah Harrison)*, Freeman Wood *(Clon Biron)*, Helen Butler *(Laura Alcutt)*, Pauline French *(Mrs. Castigne)*, Edgar Norton *(Clyde Wiel)*, Florence Wix *(Lady Malete)*.

Romantic drama. Source: Cynthia Stockley, *Dalla, the Lion Cub* (New York, 1924). Although she is attracted to Colonel Valentia, a hunter, Dalla, an impetuous South African orphan, accepts the offer of her benefactor, Barend de Beer, to marry him after she visits England. The visit transforms her into a polished lady. On a lion hunt Beer is killed by Clon Biron, a jealous rival. Dalla is accused, but the truth is established and she is free to live a happy life with Valentia. *Hunters. South Africa. Big game.*

UNE FEMME A MENTI *see* **THE LADY LIES**

THE FEUD WOMAN **F2.1680**

Sierra Pictures. Dec **1926**. Si; b&w. 35mm. 6 reels.

Dir R. E. Williamson. *Photog* King Gray.

Melodrama(?). No information about the nature of this film has been found.

Note: *The Feud Woman,* released by Pizor Productions in 1928, was probably a reissue of this film.

FIFTH AVENUE **F2.1681**

Belasco Productions. *Dist* Producers Distributing Corp. 24 Jan **1926** [c11 Jan 1926; LP22260]. Si; b&w. 35mm. 6 reels, 5,503 ft.

Prod A. H. Sebastian. *Dir* Robert G. Vignola. *Screenplay* Anthony Coldewey. *Titl* Frederick Hatton, Fanny Hatton. *Photog* James C. Van Trees. *Art Dir* Charles L. Cadwallader. *Asst Art Dir* T. E. Dickson. *Asst Dir* Philip Carle.

Cast: Marguerite De La Motte *(Barbara Pelham)*, Allan Forrest *(Neil Heffner)*, Louise Dresser *(Claudine Kemp)*, William V. Mong *(Peter Heffner)*, Crawford Kent *(Allan Trainor)*, Lucille Lee Stewart *(Natalie Van Loon)*, Anna May Wong *(Nan Lo)*, Lillian Langdon *(Mrs. Van Loon)*, Josephine Norman, Sally Long *(Greenwich Village girls)*, Flora Finch *(Mrs. Pettygrew)*.

Society drama. Source: Arthur Stringer, "Fifth Avenue," in *Saturday Evening Post* (198:12–13, 19 Sep 1925). When her cotton crop is burned, Barbara Pelham, a beautiful southern girl, comes to New York to find work as a fashion designer, staying with Mrs. Kemp, a woman she meets on the northbound train. In Mrs. Kemp's house, Barbara encounters Peter Heffner, a wealthy stockbroker, and discovers from him that she has taken up residence in a whorehouse. There is a police raid, but Barbara escapes arrest and returns home. Heffner's son, Neil, goes south to inspect some family property and there meets Barbara, with whom he falls in love. They decide to be married, and she accompanies him to New York, where she meets the elder Heffner for a second time. He denounces her as a whore, but Barbara goes to Mrs. Kemp, who explains the misunderstanding to everyone's satisfaction. *Southerners. Couturiers. Madams. Stockbrokers. Police. Reputation. Whorehouses. New York City.*

FIFTH AVENUE MODELS (Universal-Jewel) **F2.1682**

Universal Pictures. 26 Apr **1925** [c30 Dec 1924; LP20979]. Si; b&w. 35mm. 7 reels, 6,581 ft.

Pres by Carl Laemmle. *Dir* Svend Gade. *Adapt* Olga Printzlau. *Photog* Charles Stumar.

Cast: Mary Philbin *(Isoel Ludant)*, Norman Kerry *(Francis Doran)*, Josef Swickard *(Joseph Ludant)*, William Conklin *(Abel von Groot)*, Rosemary Theby *(Tory Serecold)*, Rose Dione *(Mademoiselle Suze)*,

Robert Brower *(art salesman)*, Betty Francisco *(Rosalie)*, Helen Lynch *(maid)*, George B. Williams *(Van der Frift)*, Jean Hersholt *(crook)*, Bob McKenzie *(Mr. Fisk)*, Ruth Stonehouse *(Mrs. Fisk)*, Lee Moran *(Mrs. Frisk's lover)*, Mike Donlin *(crook's henchman)*, Cesare Gravina, Dorothy Seastrom.

Melodrama. Source: Muriel Hine Coxen, *The Best in Life* (New York, 1918). Isoel Ludant, the beautiful daughter of a talented but unsuccessful artist, supports both her father and herself by working in the shop of a fashionable modiste, where she is occasionally required to act as a model. When she attracts the attention of Francis Doran, an art dealer and connoisseur of women, another of the models makes a cutting remark to her, and Isoel attacks the girl furiously. Isoel is discharged and informed that her father, Joseph, will be arrested unless she pays $150 for a dress she ruined in the fight. When Joseph learns of this, he determines to get the money and agrees to accompany some crooks on a job in order to identify a painting they want to steal. The gang is arrested, and Joseph is sentenced to 3 years in Sing Sing. Unable to find any other work, Isoel is forced to become Doran's secretary, a position that places her in many embarrassing and compromising situations. Knowing nothing of her father's disgrace, Doran professes his love, but Isoel believes his intentions to be strictly dishonorable. Joseph is released from jail, one of his paintings is acclaimed a masterpiece, and the yellow press headlines the news that he is an ex-con. Doran stands by Isoel in her time of disgrace and wins her grateful love. *Artists. Fashion models. Modistes. Art dealers. Secretaries. Filial relations. Theft. Yellow journalism. Sing Sing. New York City—Fifth Avenue.*

THE FIFTH COMMANDMENT **F2.1683**

Dist Kaufman Film Co. 6 Apr **1927** [New York State license]. Si; b&w. 35mm. 6 reels.

Cast: Miss Dubinsky.

Drama(?). No information about the precise nature of this film has been found. *Filial relations.*

Note: Country of origin undetermined.

THE FIFTH HORSEMAN **F2.1684**

E. M. McMahon. cl Sep **1924** [LP21581]. Si; b&w. 35mm. 7 reels.

Story E. M. McMahon.

Cast: Cornelius Keefe *(John Franklin)*, Una Merkel *(Dorothy)*, Joseph Depew *(Sonny)*, Charles Brook *(Tom Mather)*, Alice May *(Jane Mather)*, Leslie Stowe *(Colonel Woodson)*, Horace Haine *(Red Hogan)*, William Black *(Bill Gorman)*, Al H. Stewart *(Buck Daniels)*, Louis Reinhard *(Pete Orloff)*, Philip Van Loan *(St. John the Divine)*, Gregory Blackton *(The Fifth Horseman)*.

Melodrama. John Franklin, a young American involved in social work, and Colonel Woodson, a veteran of both the War Between the States and the Ku Klux Klan, separately help Tom Mather find the road to redemption. The colonel imbues Tom's boy, Sonny, with a love for God, home, and country, and John helps Tom's daughter find a cure for the lameness that has haunted her since birth. John also helps extricate Tom from a band of radicals who are involved in bootlegging and city politics. *Social workers. Veterans. Cripples. Bootlegging. Religion. Patriotism. Apocalypse. United States—History—Civil War. John the Divine. Ku Klux Klan.*

THE FIFTH YEAR **F2.1685**

Friends of Soviet Russia. 1 Jun **1923** [scheduled release]. Si; b&w. 35mm. 9 reels, 8,800 ft.

Documentary. Historical, news, scenic, educational film depicting actual events in the Soviet Union, chiefly during 1922. *Union of Soviet Socialist Republics.*

Note: Country of origin undetermined.

FIFTY CANDLES **F2.1686**

Willat Productions. *Dist* W. W. Hodkinson Corp. 11 Dec **1921.** Si; b&w. 35mm. 5 reels.

Dir Irvin V. Willat.

Cast: Bertram Grassby *(Hung Chin Chung)*, Marjorie Daw *(Mary-Will Tellfair)*, Ruth King *(Carlotta Drew)*, Wade Boteler *(Mark Drew)*, William Carroll *(Henry Drew)*, George Webb *(Dr. Parker)*, Dorothy Sibley *(Mah Li)*, Edward Burns *(Ralph Coolidge)*.

Mystery melodrama. Source: Earl Derr Biggers, *Fifty Candles* (Indianapolis, 1926). Sentenced to be deported from Hawaii, Hung Chin Chung pledges 20 years of service to Henry Drew to escape the certain death that awaits him in China. Rage at his humiliation and inability to marry as a free man smolders in him throughout his servitude, near the end of which he sails to San Francisco with the Drew family. Also on board is Ralph Coolidge, who tries to retrieve from Drew his share of their gold mine, and who loves Drew's secretary, Mary-Will Tellfair. Shortly after their arrival, Henry Drew is murdered; suspicion falls on Ralph, the owner of the murder weapon, a curious Chinese dagger; but subsequent events lead Hung Chin Chung to confess to the crime. *Chinese. Secretaries. Bondage. Murder. Deportation. Hawaii. San Francisco.*

50–50 (Reissue) **F2.1687**

Fine Arts Pictures. *Dist* Tri-Stone Pictures. **1924.** Si; b&w. 35mm. 5 reels.

Note: A "re-edited and re-titled" Norma Talmadge film originally released by Triangle Film Corp. on 22 Oct 1916.

$50,000 REWARD **F2.1688**

Clifford S. Elfelt Productions. *Dist* Davis Distributing Division. Dec **1924** [c23 Nov 1925; LP22040]. Si; b&w. 35mm. 5 reels, 4,950 ft.

Pers Supv-Dir Clifford S. Elfelt. *Story* Frank Howard Clark. *Photog* Bert Longenecker.

Cast: Ken Maynard *(Tex Sherwood)*, Tarzan *(himself, a horse)*, Esther Ralston *(Carolyn Jordan)*, Bert Lindley *(Anthony Jordan)*, Edward Peil *(Buck Schofield)*, Lillian Leighton *(Mrs. Miller)*, Charles Newton *(Pa Miller)*, Frank Whitson *(Asa Holman)*.

Western melodrama. Texas cowboy Tex Sherwood arrives in Belmont, Montana, to register his title to land he has inherited. Banker Asa Holman, Buck Schofield, and their cohorts are determined to stop him, however, because of a large reclamation project and a million-dollar dam financed by Holman on Tex's property. Tex eludes Schofield's ruffians; sparks a romance with Carolyn Jordan, who is in charge of the dam's construction for her injured father; and arrives at the courthouse in time to foil the gang. More complications follow, but Tex eventually receives $5 million for his land, Carolyn finishes the dam on time to earn a bonus, and the pair leave for Texas together. *Texans. Cowboys. Bankers. Land reclamation. Dams. Montana. Documentation. Horses.*

FIFTY-FIFTY **F2.1689**

Encore Pictures. *Dist* Associated Exhibitors. 15 Nov **1925** [c29 May 1925; LU21509]. Si; b&w. 35mm. 5 reels.

Prod-Dir Henri Diamant Berger. *Story* Allan Dwan. *Photog* Henry Cronjager.

Cast: Hope Hampton *(Ginette)*, Lionel Barrymore *(Frederick Harmon)*, Louise Glaum *(Nina Olmstead)*, J. Moy Bennett *(Charles O'Malley)*, Arthur Donaldson *(Grand Duke Popovitch)*, Jean Del Val *(Jean)*.

Melodrama. During a business trip to Paris, Frederick Harmon, a wealthy American, meets beautiful Ginette, a fashion model by day and apache dancer by night. In a nightclub fight, he saves her from two apaches only to discover later that both the nightclub and fight were phony, existing only in order to amuse and fleece gullible American tourists. Frederick marries Ginette and returns with her to New York, where he soon becomes involved with Nina Olmstead, a scheming divorcee. Ginette learns of the affair and decides to win her husband back by flirting with Jean, an old flame. Nina learns of Ginette's flirtation and uses it to widen the breach between the Harmons. Frederick learns of Nina's perfidy and is gratefully reconciled with Ginette, whose loyalty he has come to trust implicitly. *Dancers. Fashion models. Infidelity. Apaches—Paris. Nightclubs. New York City. Paris.*

Note: A remake of a Triangle film with Norma Talmadge.

THE FIFTY-FIFTY GIRL **F2.1690**

Paramount Famous Lasky Corp. 12 May **1928** [c12 May 1928; LP25237]. Si; b&w. 35mm. 7 reels, 6,402 ft.

Dir Clarence Badger. *Scen* Ethel Doherty. *Adapt* Lloyd Corrigan. *Story* John McDermott. *Photog* J. Roy Hunt. *Wardrobe* Travis Banton.

Cast: Bebe Daniels *(Kathleen O'Hara)*, James Hall *(Jim Donahue)*, William Austin *(engineer)*, George Kotsonaros *(Buck, the Gorilla Man)*, Johnnie Morris *(Oscar, a thug)*, Alfred Allen *(Kathleen's uncle)*, John O'Hara.

Comedy-drama. Kathleen O'Hara, a headstrong girl who believes in equality of sexes, makes a pact with her sweetheart, Jim Donahue, when they become joint owners of a California gold mine. According to the agreement, Donahue will do the housekeeping while Kathleen runs the mine; the first to call for help loses his share of the mine. When they arrive, they find Morgan, owner of a neighboring mine, working their claim. Failing in his attempts to drive the couple away, then to kill them, Morgan persuades his workers to attack Kathleen. She calls for help, and Jim arrives. *Claim jumpers. Gold mines. Women's rights. California.*

FIG LEAVES **F2.1691**

Fox Film Corp. 22 Aug **1926** [c3 Jul 1926; LP22885]. Si; b&w with col sequence (Technicolor). 35mm. 7 reels, 6,498 ft.

Pres by William Fox. *Supv* Winfield R. Sheehan. *Dir-Story* Howard Hawks. *Scen* Hope Loring, Louis D. Lighton. *Photog* Joe August. *Asst Dir* James Tinling. *Cost* Adrian.

Cast: George O'Brien *(Adam Smith)*, Olive Borden *(Eve Smith)*, Phyllis Haver *(Alice Atkins)*, André de Beranger *(Josef André)*, William Austin *(André's assistant)*, Heinie Conklin *(Eddie McSwiggen)*, Eulalie Jensen *(Madame Griswald)*.

Comedy-drama. In a prolog, Adam and Eve live in a primitive apartment. Adam, with his morning paper (a stone slab with the latest news engraved on it), has to rush to catch the morning commuter train (a cart with strap hangers pulled by a dinosaur), while Eve, though she has an extensive wardrobe, declares she has "nothing to wear" and prates about a sale on "fig leaves," causing the serpent to tempt her. In modern New York, Adam is a plumber struggling for an existence, and Eve, discontented with her lot, longs for luxury. An automobile accident brings her to the attention of a Fifth Avenue shop, where she is engaged as a model under the egis of Josef André. The serpent emerges as a blonde seductress living across the hallway from the couple, and when Adam encounters his wife modeling, comic complications arise; eventually Eve spurns the advances of André and is reconciled with Adam. *Plumbers. Fashion models. Marriage. Automobile accidents. Women's wear. Prehistory. New York City. Biblical characters.*

A FIGHT FOR HONOR **F2.1692**

Perfection Pictures. *Dist* C. B. C. Film Sales. 1 Aug **1924** [c28 Aug 1924; LP20535]. Si; b&w. 35mm. 5 reels, 4,570 ft.

Dir Henry MacRae. *Story* H. W. George.

Cast: Eva Novak *(Margaret Hill)*, William Fairbanks *(Jack Adams)*, Claire McDowell *(Mrs. Hill)*, Jack Byron *(Walter Bradson)*, Marion Harlan *(Mary Hill)*, Derry Welford *(Gertie Gilson)*, Wilfred Lucas *(Tom Grady)*, Pal *(himself, a dog)*.

Melodrama. Two malcontents attempt to avenge their dismissal from the railroad by robbing the station at Warwick, which is manned by Margaret Hill. Her fiancé, Jack Adams, arrives and after a violent fight drives them off. Frustrated, the two men plan to blow up a railroad bridge. Tom Grady, the foreman, discovers the plot and tells Margaret to warn the train, which is being driven by Jack and has her mother as passenger. However, Pal, her pet dog, arrives with evidence that her sister Mary is in danger. She rushes home and finds Walter Bradson, Mary's "suitor," trying to force himself on Mary. At gunpoint, Margaret forces him to desist and compels him to drive her to the station. Exhausted, she falls on the track in front of the onrushing train, but Jack manages a daring rescue to save her and stops the train. *Sisters. Robbery. Seduction. Railroads. Dogs.*

Note: Copyright title: *The Fight for Honor.*

A FIGHT TO THE FINISH **F2.1693**

Columbia Pictures. 1 or 15 Nov **1925** [c3 Dec 1925; LP22074]. Si; b&w. 35mm. 5 reels, 4,603 ft.

Dir Reeves Eason. *Story* Dorothy Howell. *Photog* George Meehan.

Cast: William Fairbanks *(Jim Davis)*, Phyllis Haver *(Mary Corbett)*, Tom Ricketts *(Cyrus J. Davis)*, Pat Harmon *(Pat O'Brien)*, William Bolder *(Henry McBride)*, Leon Beauman *(Battling Wilson)*.

Melodrama. Millionaire Cyrus J. Davis is in despair at the antics of his playboy son, Jim. At the suggestion of Henry McBride, an old crony, he tells Jim he has lost his fortune. Confronted with this news, Jim declares his intention of getting a job to support his "poor old father." However, Jim finds it difficult to find work. He knocks out a tough who has insulted a girl, Mary Corbett. Mary reveals that he has just whipped Battling Wilson, the state champion, and offers to train Jim for a professional match with Wilson. Jim accepts but is drugged on the night of the fight, and he loses the match. Afterwards, in the dressing room, he beats Wilson up with his bare fists, becomes reconciled with his father, and introduces Mary as his future bride. *Millionaires. Prizefighters. Filial relations.*

Note: The press sheet refers to the character played by Leon Beauman alternately as Battling Wilson *and* as Knockout Riley.

THE FIGHTER **F2.1694**

Selznick Pictures. *Dist* Select Pictures. Jul **1921** [c20 Jul 1921; LP16850]. Si; b&w. 35mm. 5 reels, 4,943 ft.

Pres by Lewis J. Selznick. *Dir* Henry Kolker. *Scen* R. Cecil Smith.

Cast: Conway Tearle *(Caleb Conover)*, Winifred Westover *(Dey Shevlin)*, Arthur Housman *(Blacardo)*, Ernest Lawford *(Caine)*, George Stewart *(Jack Standish)*, Warren Cook *(Senator Burke)*, Helen Lindroth *(Mrs. Hawarden)*.

Melodrama. Source: Albert Payson Terhune, *The Fighter* (New York, 1909). Following the death of her father, Dey Shevlin becomes the ward of Caleb Conover, a railroad president. His enemy Jimmy Blacardo induces a country club's officials to challenge his right to membership in the organization; Dey persuades him to fight back, and he defeats his accusers. Newspapers then reveal a scandal involving the late Tom Shevlin's shady dealings, and though Conover takes the blame, Dey accuses him of using her father as a shield. In a mountain retreat, she discovers the truth from Caine, and Conover comes to her declaring his love, then returns to fight his enemies. When he hears later that Dey has drowned in a canoe accident, Conover banishes the doctor from the room and restores the girl by mental effort. He returns to the city on a locomotive that falls through a burning bridge, but he survives to triumph over his enemies. *Railroad magnates. Wards. Scandal. Mental healing. Country clubs. Train wrecks.*

FIGHTERS OF THE SADDLE **F2.1695**

J. Charles Davis Productions. 12 Aug **1929.** Si; b&w. 35mm. 5 reels, 4,156 ft.

Photog Paul Allen.

Cast: Art Acord *(Dick Weatherby)*, John Lowell *(Henry "Bulldog" Weatherby)*, Tom Bay *(Dick's cousin, Pete)*, Peggy Montgomery *(Nesta)*, Jack Ponder *(her brother, Tom Wayne)*, Betty Carter *(Patty Wayne)*, Lynn Sanderson *(Art Wayne)*, Cliff Lyons *(member of Weatherby's gang)*.

Western melodrama(?). No information about the precise nature of this film has been found. *Cowboys.*

Note: Known also as *Fighters in the Saddle.*

FIGHTER'S PARADISE **F2.1696**

Phil Goldstone Productions. 28 Jun **1924** [New York State license]. Si; b&w. 35mm. 5 reels, 4,800 ft.

Dir Alvin J. Neitz. *Scen* J. F. Natteford.

Cast: Rex (Snowy) Baker, Andrew Waldron, Dick Sutherland, Jack Curtis, Harry Burns, Kenneth Benedict, Margaret Landis.

Western melodrama. A young man who jerks sodas in a smalltown ice cream parlor is at heart a coward. He is mistaken for Cyclone Carter, a famous pug, and forced into a fight. A fortuitous blow on the head changes him into a fighting demon, and he wins the admiration of the townspeople and the love of his girl. *Soda clerks. Smalltown life. Cowardice. Prizefighting.*

THE FIGHTIN' COMEBACK **F2.1697**

Action Pictures. *Dist* Pathé Exchange. 3 Apr **1927** [c1 Apr 1927; LU23807]. Si; b&w. 35mm. 5 reels, 4,415 ft.

Pres by Lester F. Scott, Jr. *Dir* Tenny Wright. *Cont* Frank L. Inghram. *Photog* Ray Ries.

Cast: Buddy Roosevelt *(Jim Jones)*, Clara Horton *(Goldie Lamont)*, Sidney M. Goldin *(Sam Phillips)*, Richard Neill *(Three-Card Spencer)*, Robert Homans *(Sheriff Beasley)*, Charles Thurston *(Boulder City Sheriff)*, Richard Alexander *(Red Pollock)*.

Western melodrama. Source: Walter J. Coburn, "The Sun Dance Kid" (publication undetermined). Jim Jones, cheated by Three-Card Spencer, a gambler in Red Dog, Arizona, steals the money and escapes to Mexico. There he joins a band of outlaws and becomes their leader; eventually he persuades them to return to Arizona and give themselves up. In Boulder City Jim meets Goldie, a stranded chorus girl working as a waitress, and she resolves to help him. She goes to Red Dog, returns the gamblers' stolen money, and tells Jim's story to the sheriff, but she is herself arrested; Jim cleverly eludes the sheriff of Red Dog, but the Boulder City sheriff proves that the stolen money is counterfeited, and Three-Card is convicted. Jim gets a reward and wins Goldie. *Gamblers. Chorus girls. Waitresses. Counterfeiters. Sheriffs. Arizona. Mexico.*

FIGHTIN' DEVIL **F2.1698**

W. B. M. Photoplays. *Dist* Sanford Productions. 1 Sep **1922.** Si; b&w. 35mm. 5 reels.

Dir Robert McKenzie.

Cast: Olin Francis.

Western melodrama. "Plot concerns a foreman who is, in reality, a cattle rustler, whose villainy is invariably exposed by the hero. In desperation the villain kidnaps the heroine, who subsequently is rescued by the hero after a terrific battle. Picture is enlivened by lively fight sequences with the struggle on the edge of an abyss the particular thriller. Considerable comedy is interspersed." (*Motion Picture News Booking Guide,* 4:48, Apr 1923.) *Ranch foremen. Rustling.*

FIGHTIN' MAD **F2.1699**

William Desmond Productions. *Dist* Metro Pictures. 5 Dec **1921** [c6 Dec 1921; LP17329]. Si; b&w. 35mm. 6 reels, 5,436 ft.

Supv Robert Brunton. *Dir* Joseph J. Franz. *Story-Scen* H. H. Van Loan. *Photog* Harry Gersted.

Cast: William Desmond *(Bud McGraw)*, Virginia Brown Faire *(Peggy Hughes)*, Doris Pawn *(Eileen Graham)*, Rosemary Theby *(Nita de Garma)*, Joseph J. Dowling *(James McGraw)*, William Lawrence *(Francisco Lazaro)*, Emmett C. King *(Howard Graham)*, Jack Richardson *(Amos Rawson)*, William J. Dyer *(Obadiah Brennan)*, Bert Lindley *(Micah Higgins)*, George Stanley *(Colonel Gates)*, Vernon Snively *(Captain Farley)*.

Western comedy-melodrama. Returning to his father's cattle ranch after the excitement of serving in combat overseas, Bud McGraw becomes restless, and his father decides to send him to an old friend who commands the Border Police in Texas. On the way he meets Peggy Hughes, accompanying her Uncle Graham, a customs inspector, and he retrieves her hat from the rails of a train. At the headquarters, numerous scrapes and fights win him the admiration of, and friendship with, the men. Lazaro, a Secret Service agent, invites Mrs. Graham and Peggy, who are staying at the border station, for an automobile ride, and they are captured by bandits and held for ransom. Bud and his pals deliver the ransom and discover that Lazaro is the bandit chief. Lazaro refuses to release Peggy, but a jealous rival, Nita de Garma, causes his downfall and shoots him as the Border Police arrive to rescue the party. *Veterans. Bandits. Border police. Secret service. Ransom. Customs (tariff). Texas.*

FIGHTIN' ODDS **F2.1700**

Anchor Film Distributors. 8 Jan **1925** [New York State license]. Si; b&w. 35mm. 5 reels, 4,200 ft.

Supv B. A. Goodman. *Dir-Writ* Bennett Cohn. *Photog* Ralph Staub.

Cast: Bill Patton *(Bruce Martin)*, Doris Dare *(Helen Morrison)*, Jack House *("Flash" Lamore)*, Jack Ganzhorn *(Dave Ormsby)*, Hugh Saxon *(Judge Mayhew)*, Alfred Hewston *(Sam Winton)*, Edmund Burns *(Sheriff Lane)*.

Western melodrama. "The entire picture is the story of a villain, Ormsby, who connives with a judge and sheriff to kill the heir to an estate and seize his ranch. The many closeups of guns pointed from behind trees, of men with guns on each other, of blows and blood stained faces, add to the criminal effect of the picture. Twice Bruce, the heir, is kicked senseless by his assailants and bound, head down to a horse and driven off into the woods. Ormsby is in love with Bruce's sweetheart. He attacks her, kidnaps and carries her kicking and struggling into a cabin where Bruce discovers him and a fierce fight ensues. Ormsby's entire gang attacks Bruce who engages them all in a fierce and brutal fight. Ormsby is knocked senseless and dragged out. There are closeups of choking and nose pulling—but all the gang is overcome, carried out, tied face downward to horses and driven off out of the picture." (New York State licensing records.) *Judges. Sheriffs. Gangs. Inheritance. Ranches. Property rights. Inheritance.*

THE FIGHTIN' REDHEAD **F2.1701**

FBO Pictures. 1 Jul **1928** [c1 Jul 1928; LP25436]. Si; b&w. 35mm. 5 reels, 4,758 ft.

Dir Louis King. *Cont* Frank Howard Clark. *Titl* Frank T. Daugherty. *Story* E. A. Patterson. *Photog* Roy Eslick. *Film Ed* Della M. King. *Asst Dir* Sam Nelson.

Cast: Buzz Barton *(Red Hepner)*, Duane Thompson *(Jane Anderson)*, Milburn Morante *(Sidewinder Steve)*, Bob Fleming *(Bob Anderson)*, Edmund Cobb *(Tom Reynolds)*, Edward Hearn *(Jim Dalton)*.

Western melodrama. In the western town of Shady Bend, blacksmith Tom Reynolds and poolroom proprietor Jim Dalton are rivals for Jane Anderson, the sheriff's daughter. Arriving in Shady Bend, Red Hepner and his sidekick, Steve, are attracted to a $1,000 reward offered to the captor of a "mysterious bandit" who has been terrorizing the community. Red and Steve help the sheriff and his deputy ferret out the mysterious bandit (Dalton) when Dalton tries to pin a recent bank robbery on Tom Reynolds. Red stops Dalton with his slingshot when he tries to slip out of town with Jane and the stolen money after convincing Jane that Tom is the culprit. Red and Steve give the reward to Tom and Jane as a housewarming gift before they leave Shady Bend to continue their wandering. *Wanderers. Blacksmiths. Bandits. Frameup. Bank robberies. Billiard parlors.*

FIGHTIN' THRU **F2.1702**

H. & B. Film Co. *Dist* Madoc Sales. 18 Jul **1924** [New York State license]. Si; b&w. 35mm. 5 reels, 4,800 ft.

Dir Roy M. Hughes.

Cast: Bill Patton, Donna Hale.

Western melodrama. "... in which young cowpuncher wins gratitude of wealthy ranch owner and is given latter's property when owner is driven away by bandit gang. Bandits attempt to steal property by falsifying tax records with assistance of youth in tax office who is brother of girl loved by hero. After desperate fight bandits are subdued and the property and girl won by cowpuncher." (*Motion Picture News Booking Guide,* [7]:20, Oct 1924.) *Cowboys. Bandits. Ranches. Property rights. Tax records. Documentation.*

THE FIGHTING ACE *see* **FLYING ACE**

THE FIGHTING AMERICAN (Universal-Jewel) **F2.1703**

Universal Pictures. 23 Jun **1924** [c23 May 1924; LP20236]. Si; b&w. 35mm. 6 reels, 5,251 ft.

Pres by Carl Laemmle. *Dir* Tom Forman. *Scen* Harvey Gates. *Adapt* Raymond L. Schrock. *Story* William Elwell Oliver. *Photog* Harry Perry.

Cast: Pat O'Malley *(Bill Pendleton)*, Mary Astor *(Mary O'Mallory)*, Raymond Hatton *(Danny Daynes)*, Warner Oland *(Fu Shing)*, Edwin J. Brady *(Quig Morley)*, Taylor Carroll *(W. F. Pendleton)*, Clarence Geldert *(William A. Pendleton)*, Alfred Fisher *(Mr. O'Mallory)*, Jack Byron *(Alfred Rutland)*, James Wang *(Lee Yong)*, Emmett King *(college professor)*, Jane Starr *(Lizzie)*, Frank Kingsley *(Harry March)*.

Romantic comedy. On the wager that he will propose marriage to any girl selected by his fraternity brothers, Bill Pendleton finds himself making love to Mary O'Mallory, an old-fashioned girl who is secretly in love with him. Disillusioned upon discovering his deceit, she joins her missionary father in China, where the hero follows and rescues her from revolutionists. *Fraternities. Marriage. Wagers. Revolutions. China.*

Note: Raymond Hatton is credited by at least one source as playing also the part of Po-Hsing-Chien.

THE FIGHTING BLADE **F2.1704**

Inspiration Pictures. *Dist* Associated First National Pictures. 10 Sep **1923** [c25 Sep 1923; LP19446]. Si; b&w. 35mm. 9 reels, 8,729 ft.

Pres by Charles H. Duell. *Dir* John S. Robertson. *Scen* Josephine Lovett. *Titl* Don Bartlett. *Photog* George Folsey. *Art Dir* Everett Shinn. *Tech Dir* William B. Ihnen. *Ed* William Hamilton.

Cast: Richard Barthelmess *(Karl Van Kerstenbroock)*, Lee Baker *(Earl of Staversham)*, Morgan Wallace *(Lord Robert Erisey)*, Bradley Barker *(Watt Musgrove)*, Frederick Burton *(Cromwell)*, Stuart Sage *(Viscount Carisford)*, Philip Tead *(Lord Trevor)*, Walter Horton *(Bob Ayskew)*, Dorothy Mackaill *(Thomsine Musgrove)*, Allyn King *(Charlotte Musgrove)*, Marcia Harris *(Joan Laycock)*.

Romantic drama. Source: Beulah Marie Dix, *The Fighting Blade* (New York, 1912). Karl Van Kerstenbroock, a famous Flemish soldier of fortune, trails Basil Dormer to England, where, to avenge his sister's death, he challenges and kills him. Royalist Watt Musgrove, hearing of his friend's death, challenges Van Kerstenbroock to a duel. To save his life, Watt's sister, Thomsine, who is betrothed to Viscount Carisford, disguises herself as a boy and pleads with Van Kerstenbroock to cancel the duel. When Watt fails to appear, Van Kerstenbroock escapes arrest by Royalist guards and falls into the hands of Cromwell, whose forces he joins, leading them against Charles II. Acting as a spy, Van Kerstenbroock visits Staversham, the home of the father of Thomsine's fiancé. Thomsine hides Van Kerstenbroock in her room when his life is in danger. After she helps him escape, he leads a battalion to dethrone the king, then rescues Thomsine. *Soldiers of fortune. Flemings. Royalists. Roundheads. Puritans. Great Britain—History—Civil War and Commonwealth. Charles II (England). Oliver Cromwell.*

THE FIGHTING BOOB **F2.1705**

R-C Pictures. *Dist* Film Booking Offices of America. 4 Apr **1926** [c5 Apr 1926; LP22589]. Si; b&w. 35mm. 5 reels, 4,549 ft.

Dir Jack Nelson. *Scen* Jack Nelson, James Ormont. *Story* William

Lester. *Photog* Arthur Reeves.

Cast: Bob Custer *(The Tiger)*, Frank Whitson *(Clayton)*, Sherry Tansey *(Timothy Raymond)*, Hugh Saxon *(Jasper Steele)*, Violet Palmer *(Helen Hawksby)*, Andrew Arbuckle *(Old Man Hawksby)*, Sam Lufkin *(Jeff Randall)*, Tom Bay *(Bowers)*, Joan Meredith *(Dolores)*, Bobby Nelson *(Bobby)*, Artie Ortega *(Ortega)*.

Western melodrama. Jasper Steele, a wealthy rancher on the border, sends for Timothy, his nephew, to assist him in a feud with Hawksby, a rival rancher. The Tiger, a former war buddy of Timothy's, holds up his stagecoach and persuades his friend—ill from being gassed in the war—to go into seclusion while he poses as the nephew. The Tiger learns that Randall and Clayton, a heavy, are plotting to kidnap Helen (Hawksby's granddaughter) and Timothy to gain possession of the property. While Randall is forcing Hawksby and Steele to sign over their ranches, The Tiger, aided by Romero and his men, liberate the prisoners. The Tiger gets Helen with her grandfather's blessing, and Timothy finds love with Dolores, Romero's daughter. *Ranchers. Uncles. Veterans. Feuds. Gas warfare. Impersonation. Mexican border.*

THE FIGHTING BREED **F2.1706**

Selig-Rork Productions. *Dist* Aywon Film Corp. 1 Sep **1921.** Si; b&w. 35mm. 5 reels.

Dir Wilfred Lucas. *By* Wilfred Lucas, Bess Meredyth.

Cast: Snowy Baker *(Brian O'Farrell)*, Wilfred Lucas *(John MacDonald)*, Ethel Payton *(Enid MacDonald)*, Brownie Vernon *(see note)*.

Western melodrama. Wealthy young Australian Brian O'Farrell, the last of the "Fighting O'Farrells," resolves to be worthy of his forbears and visits his ranch in the guise of a tenderfoot. He wins the admiration of his employees and the love of settlement worker Enid MacDonald, the daughter of his neighbor, while seeing plenty of action both in the Bush Country and the city slums. *Cowboys. Settlement workers. Slums. Australia. Kangaroos.*

Note: Filmed in Australia. There is some doubt that Brownie Vernon is in the cast.

THE FIGHTING BUCKAROO **F2.1707**

Fox Film Corp. 4 Apr **1926** [c28 Mar 1926; LP22605]. Si; b&w. 35mm. 5 reels, 5,095 ft.

Pres by William Fox. *Dir* R. William Neill. *Scen* Charles Darnton. *Story* Frank Howard Clark. *Photog* Reginald Lyons. *Asst Dir* Mike Miggins.

Cast: Buck Jones *(Larry Crawford)*, Sally Long *(Betty Gregory)*, Lloyd Whitlock *(Glenmore Bradley [or Bradshaw])*, Frank Butler *(Percy M. Wellington)*, E. J. Ratcliffe *(Judge Richard Gregory)*, Ben Hendricks, Jr. *(first crook)*, Ray Thompson *(second crook)*, Frank Rice *(Andy Parker)*.

Comedy-melodrama. Larry Crawford, who hopes to purchase a ranch on which gold is discovered just before the option expires, hurries to Los Angeles with two pals, pursued by an unscrupulous promoter who enlists the aid of a gang of thugs. In a traffic accident, Larry meets Betty Gregory, with whom he becomes infatuated, but whose father, Judge Gregory, he contrives constantly to offend. His attempts to meet the girl and the villain's efforts to outwit him and steal the girl's necklace afford a rapid succession of comic situations, including a chase after a speeding train on a motorcycle, the kidnaping of the girl, Larry's encounter with the thugs, and, in the end, his winning of the girl. *Broncobusters. Judges. Gangs. Gold. Land options. Los Angeles. Chases. Automobile accidents.*

THE FIGHTING CHEAT **F2.1708**

Action Pictures. *Dist* Weiss Brothers Artclass Pictures. 11 Feb **1926.** Si; b&w. 35mm. 5 reels, 4,626 ft.

Dir Richard Thorpe. *Scen* Betty Burbridge.

Cast: Wally Wales *(Wally Kenyon)*, Jean Arthur *(Ruth Wells)*, Ted Rackerby *(Lafe Wells)*, Fanny Midgley *(Mrs. Wells)*, Charles Whitaker *(Jud Nolan)*, V. L. Barnes *(doctor)*, Al Taylor *(cook)*.

Western melodrama. Lafe Wells, a member of a bandit gang, is wounded and left for dead by his companions. Wally Kenyon finds Lafe; and the outlaw, believing himself to be close to death, then asks Wally to take some money to his mother. Wally does as the bandit asks and meets Lafe's sister, Ruth. Lafe recovers; later, when Wally and Ruth are ambushed by outlaws, he brings the sheriff's men to their aid. Wally and Ruth then get married. *Bandits. Filial relations. Brother-sister relationship.*

FIGHTING COURAGE **F2.1709**

Clifford S. Elfelt Productions. *Dist* Davis Distributing Division. c4 Dec **1925** [LP22079]. Si; b&w. 35mm. 5 reels.

Dir Clifford S. Elfelt. *Story* Frank Howard Clark. *Photog* Joseph Walker.

Cast: Ken Maynard *(Richard Kingsley)*, Peggy Montgomery *(Marjorie Crenshaw)*, Melbourne MacDowell *(Kingsley, Sr.)*, Frank Whitson *(Mark Crenshaw)*, Henry Ward *(Bert Kinkaid)*, Gus Saville *(Luke Collins)*, James Barry, Jr. *(Sambo)*.

Melodrama. Richard Kingsley, son of a financier, trying to aid Marjorie Crenshaw and her sister during a raid on a New York roadhouse, is arrested. His father, enraged by the bad publicity, threatens to disinherit him if he doesn't go to Colorado in search of a mine. While traveling west, Richard meets a group of chorus girls and has his pocket picked by their manager. Without funds, he continues on foot; he meets Kinkaid, a bandit who has stolen $5,000 from Marjorie Crenshaw's father. Richard recognizes that Kinkaid's horse is the one stolen from his father and demands it be returned. Kinkaid gives him the horse but forces Richard to exchange clothes with him. Now mistaken for Kinkaid, Richard must flee from the posse but first uses altruistically the $5,000 he finds in Kinkaid's clothing. Kinkaid, missing the money, backtracks in search of Dick but instead meets Marjorie, whom he tries to seduce. Richard arrives in time to save her and takes her home, where her father believes him to be the bandit who robbed him. All complications are straightened out when Richard's father arrives and identifies his son; Dick discovers the mine; and Marjorie discovers that she loves Dick. *Financiers. Chorus girls. Bandits. Pickpockets. Mistaken identity. Mines. Colorado.*

THE FIGHTING COWARD **F2.1710**

Famous Players–Lasky. *Dist* Paramount Pictures. 16 Mar **1924** [New York premiere; released 30 Mar; c1 Apr 1924; LP20039]. Si; b&w. 35mm. 7 reels, 6,501 ft.

Pres by Adolph Zukor, Jesse L. Lasky. *Dir* James Cruze. *Scen* Walter Woods. *Photog* Karl Brown.

Cast: Ernest Torrence *(Gen. Orlando Jackson)*, Mary Astor *(Lucy)*, Noah Beery *(Captain Blackie)*, Cullen Landis *(Tom Rumford)*, Phyllis Haver *(Elvira)*, G. Raymond Nye *(Major Patterson)*, Richard R. Neill *(Joe Patterson)*, Carmen Phillips *(Mexico, an octoroon)*, Bruce Covington *(General Rumford)*, Helen Dunbar *(Mrs. Rumford)*, Frank Jonasson *(Rumbo)*.

Comedy-drama. Source: Booth Tarkington, *The Magnolia* (New York opening: 27 Aug 1923). Tom Rumford, a southerner reared by Quaker relatives in the North, has been taught not to fight, and consequently he incurs the disfavor of his family when he refuses to duel with Major Patterson for the favor of his (Tom's) Cousin Elvira. Because everyone except Elvira's sister, Lucy, regards Tom as a coward, he secretly learns from General Jackson all he can about the use of swords and guns. Under the name of Colonel Blake, Tom cows bully Captain Blackie and revenges himself on Major Patterson. Tom wins Lucy's love when he explains that the affair was all a bluff. *Cowardice. United States—South. Society of Friends. Duels.*

FIGHTING COWBOY **F2.1711**

Dist Krelbar Pictures. 14 Mar **1930** [New York State license]. Si; b&w. 35mm. 5 reels, 4,500 ft.

Cast: Al Hoxie.

Western melodrama(?). No information about the precise nature of this film has been found. *Cowboys.*

Note: May have been produced by Anchor Film Distributors in 1926.

THE FIGHTING CUB **F2.1712**

Crown Productions. *Dist* Truart Film Corp. 27 Jul **1925** [New York premiere; c21 Jan 1925; LU21055]. Si; b&w. 35mm. 6 reels, 5,800 ft.

Phil Goldstone Production. *Dir* Paul Hurst. *Story* Adele Buffington. *Photog* Frank Cotner, Lee Humiston.

Cast: Wesley Barry *(Thomas Patrick O'Toole)*, Mildred Harris, Pat O'Malley, Mary Carr, George Fawcett, Stuart Holmes.

Melodrama. Thomas Patrick O'Toole, a copy boy on the *Daily News*, wants desperately to become a cub reporter and hourly approaches Jack Turner, the city editor, on the subject of a raise and a promotion. Turner finally tells Tom that he can become a reporter if he obtains an interview with a publicity-shy philanthropist, J. William Toler. With the help of Toler's daughter, Margie, Tom gets both the interview and the promotion. Later, Tom accidentally discovers the hideout of a notorious gang of thieves, the Owls, and tells Turner of his find. Tom is overheard by Bull Conner, the *News* police reporter, who is in league with the Owls. Conner decides to pull out and anonymously informs the police of the Owls' hideout. Tom goes to the thieves' den for a story, only to discover that the mysterious leader of the Owls is none other than Toler. Toler has decided to give up his life of crime and disband the gang, but, at that moment, the police raid the hideout and arrest them all. Tom manages to clear Toler, by explaining the philanthropist's reformation, and does not file the story. *Reporters. Editors. Copy boys. Philanthropists. Criminals—Rehabilitation. Newspapers.*

THE FIGHTING DEACON **F2.1713**

Ike Weber–Walk Miller. *Dist* Theatrical Owners Booking Association. c3 Aug **1926** [MU3529]. Si; b&w. 35mm. 5 reels.

Prod-Writ Walk Miller.

Personages: Theodore "Tiger" Flowers, Walk Miller.

Documentary. Episodes from the boyhood and early manhood of Theodore Flowers are presented, including his experiences in the United States Army during World War I. Following the Armistice, Flowers turns to boxing and, under the training of Walk Miller, becomes the middleweight champion, beating Harry Greb for the title. *Boxers. Deacons. Fight managers. Prizefighting. World War I. Theodore Flowers. Harry Greb. Walk Miller.*

Note: Also known as *The Life of Tiger Flowers.*

THE FIGHTING DEMON **F2.1714**

Richard Talmadge Productions. *Dist* Film Booking Offices of America. 24 May **1925** [c19 May 1925; LP21510]. Si; b&w. 35mm. 6 reels, 5,470 ft.

Pres by A. Carlos. *Dir* Arthur Rosson. *Cont* James Bell Smith. *Story* Charles Metz. *Photog* William Marshall, Jack Stevens. *Tech Dir* Eugene McMurtrie. *Film Ed* Doane Harrison. *Stunts conceived by* Richard Talmadge.

Cast: Richard Talmadge *(John Drake)*, Lorraine Eason *(Dolores Darcy)*, Dick Sutherland *(Dynamite Díaz)*, Peggy Shaw *(Mrs. Díaz)*, Herbert Prior *(Jackson Pierce)*, Charles Hill Mailes *(Señor Darcy)*, Stanton Heck *(Isaac Belding)*, Jack Hill *(Professor)*, Dave Morris *(Kid Price)*, André Cheron *(Slippery Logan)*, Frank Elliott *(Arnold Malvin)*.

Melodrama. John Drake, a college athlete, starts for South America, where he has been promised a good job on the strength of his knowledge of the construction of safes and vaults. Aboard ship, he falls in love with Dolores Darcy, the daughter of a leading Latin American banker. Arriving in South America, John discovers that he has been made the dupe of criminals, who want him to open the vault in Señor Darcy's bank. John refuses, and his passport and wallet are stolen. In desperation, he signs up to fight an exhibition bout with Dynamite Díaz, the South American boxing champion. Isaac Belding, the leader of the criminals, has John kidnaped, forcing him to open the Darcy vault. John locks the gang in the vault, telling the police of his actions on the way to the bout. John beats Díaz and then captures Pierce, the banker's secretary, who is in league with Belding. John becomes the hero of the town, and Dolores declares her love for him. *Athletes. Bankers. Boxers. Police. Kidnaping. Robbery. Ships. Passports. Prizefighting. Banks. Safes. Vaults. South America. Stunts. Documentation.*

THE FIGHTING DOCTOR **F2.1715**

Hercules Film Productions. 1 Jul **1926** [c22 Jun 1926; LP22840]. Si; b&w. 35mm. 5 reels, 4,900 ft.

Pres by Peter Kanellos. *Dir* Robert North Bradbury. *Story-Scen* Grover Jones.

Cast: Frank Merrill *(Dr. Frank Martin)*.

Action melodrama. Dr. Frank Martin, just as he is opening office for the day, meets "Chug" Wilson, owner of the local gymnasium, and George Stafford, who demands that the doctor make a call at the Sanders house. There he finds Malcolm Sanders and his daughter, Susie, caring for Jimmy, a cripple suffering from measles. Stafford resents the fact that Susie and Frank are attracted to each other; and as the two men are coming to blows, Wilson invites them to the gym to fight it out. Jimmy's measles are cured, and with exercise in the gym, his leg begins to mend under Frank's care. Stafford schemes with "Scissors" Lomski, a professional wrestler, to stage a match, designates Sanders as trustee of the prize money, but substitutes old paper for the money. Frank learns of the swindle and proceeds to thrash the culprits but is downed by foul play. At the wrestling contest, while Lomski is being beaten, Stafford abducts Susie, and Frank pursues in a car, then in a speedboat, to rescue her. *Physicians. Cripples. Wrestlers. Swindlers. Wrestling. Measles. Gymnasiums. Chases.*

THE FIGHTING EAGLE **F2.1716**

De Mille Pictures. *Dist* Pathé Exchange. 29 Aug **1927** [c9 Aug 1927; LP24283]. Si; b&w. 35mm. 8 reels, 8,002 ft. [Copyrighted as 9 reels.]

Supv C. Gardner Sullivan. *Dir* Donald Crisp. *Adapt-Cont* Douglas Z. Doty. *Titl* John Krafft. *Photog* Arthur Miller. *Art Dir* Mitchell Leisen. *Film Ed* Barbara Hunter. *Asst Dir* Emile De Ruelle. *Cost* Adrian.

Cast: Rod La Rocque *(Étienne Gerard)*, Phyllis Haver *(Countess de Launay)*, Sam De Grasse *(Talleyrand)*, Max Barwyn *(Napoleon)*, Julia Faye *(Josephine)*, Sally Rand *(Fräulein Hertz)*, Clarence Burton *(Colonel Neville)*, Alphonse Ethier *(Major Oliver)*.

Romantic melodrama. Source: Arthur Conan Doyle, *The Exploits of Brigadier Gerard* (London, 1896). Napoleon sends for Talleyrand, Minister of Foreign Affairs, and informs him that the Countess de Launay is returning with war communiques from Spain, instructing him to seek Russia's support. Talleyrand accepts a bribe from the Spanish Ambassador to arrest the countess. At an inn in the Pyrenees, Étienne Gerard, as he witnesses the arrival of the countess, longs to serve with Napoleon. When she is arrested, Gerard, who has fallen in love, aids her escape and drives her to Paris, where he is made a captain. In thwarting Talleyrand's attempts to arrest the countess, Gerard hides himself in a chest, and the countess secretes some important papers in his cap, which Gerard tosses away when he is arrested as a deserter; in recovering the cap he poses as Napoleon's guard and kidnaps the emperor, but the countess arrives with the documents just as Gerard is about to face a firing squad. *Bribery. Imposture. Documentation. France. Paris. Pyrenees. Napoleon I. Joséphine de Beauharnais. Charles Maurice de Talleyrand-Périgord.*

THE FIGHTING EDGE **F2.1717**

Warner Brothers Pictures. 8 Jan **1926** [c7 Jan 1926; LP22238]. Si; b&w. 35mm. 7 reels, 6,369 ft.

Dir Henry Lehrman. *Adapt* Edward T. Lowe, Jr., Jack Wagner. *Photog* Allan Thompson. *Adtl Photog* Robert Laprell. *Film Ed* Clarence Kolster. *Asst Dir* Sandy Roth.

Cast: Kenneth Harlan *(Juan de Dios O'Rourke)*, Patsy Ruth Miller *(Phoebe Joyce)*, David Kirby *(Gilette)*, Charles Conklin *(Chuck)*, Pat Hartigan *(Taggert)*, Lew Harvey *(Bailey)*, Eugene Pallette *(Simpson)*, Pat Harmon *(Hadley)*, W. A. Carroll *(Joyce)*.

Melodrama. Source: William MacLeod Raine, *The Fighting Edge* (Boston & New York, 1922). A government agent named Joyce is imprisoned in a ranch house by a gang of smugglers. Juan O'Rourke, another agent, is then assigned to the case, going across the Mexican border disguised as a halfbreed. He meets Joyce's daughter, Phoebe, and together they work their way into the smugglers' ranch house. With the aid of the cook, they free Joyce and make a break for the U. S. border. The smugglers follow, and the four take refuge in a deserted house. They are surrounded, but before they are finished off, the United States Army arrives and drives off the smugglers. Phoebe and Juan are married. *Government agents. Cooks. Smugglers. Halfcastes. Disguise. Mexican border. United States Army.*

THE FIGHTING FAILURE **F2.1718**

Alpine Productions. *Dist* Hollywood Pictures. 2 Dec **1926** [New York State license]. Si; b&w. 35mm. 6 reels.

Dir E. G. Boyle. *Story* Mary Eunice McCarthy.

Cast: Cullen Landis *(Denny O'Brien)*, Peggy Montgomery, Lucy Beaumont, Sidney Franklin, Ernest Hilliard.

Western melodrama. Denny O'Brien, a champion prizefighter, is falsely accused of cowardice and goes west to live down his humiliation. He falls in love with a beautiful ranchowner and saves her from the double dealing of her foreman. *Prizefighters. Ranchers. Ranch foremen. Cowardice.*

FIGHTING FATE **F2.1719**

Harry J. Brown Productions. *Dist* Rayart Pictures. 9 Oct **1925** [New York State license]. Si; b&w. 35mm. 5 reels.

Dir Albert Rogell. *Story-Scen* Henry R. Symonds, John W. Grey. *Photog* Lyman Broening.

Cast: Billy Sullivan *(The Fighter)*, Johnny Sinclair *(The Manager)*, Nancy Deaver *(The Girl)*, Tom McGuire.

Action melodrama. A prizefighter from a small town tries to break into the big time, but he is doped during his first professional fight and is later barred from the ring by the boxing commission on the charge of throwing the match. The fighter attempts to prove his innocence with the help both of his loyal manager and of the girl he loves, the daughter of a man who is about to lose his beanery to the sheriff for nonpayment of a mortgage note. The fighter eventually clears his name and wins his second professional fight, earning enough money to pay off his future father-in-law's mortgage. *Prizefighters. Fight managers. Mortgages. Restaurants.*

FIGHTING FOR JUSTICE **F2.1720**

J. Joseph Sameth. *Dist* Madoc Sales. 1 Apr **1924.** Si; b&w. 35mm. 5 reels, 5,000 ft.

Dir Walter De Courcy. *Scen* Joseph Anthony Roach.

Cast: Art Acord *(Bullets Bernard)*, Vane Truant *(Shirley Payton)*, Paul Weigel *(Sam Culvert)*.

Western melodrama. Bullets Bernard is wrongly accused of a holdup. In jail he meets an ex-lawyer who offers to plead his case and at the same time advises Bernard to escape. Bernard gets out just in time to see one of the real outlaws skipping town with his sweetheart. He lassoes the man, hauls him into court, and proves his own innocence. *Outlaws. Lawyers. Robbery. Prison escapes.*

FIGHTING FURY **F2.1721**

Universal Pictures. 24 Aug **1924** [c2 Jul 1924; LP20375]. Si; b&w. 35mm. 5 reels, 4,491 ft.

Dir Clifford S. Smith. *Scen* Isadore Bernstein. *Photog* Harry Neumann.

Cast: Jack Hoxie *(Clay Hill, Sr./Clay Hill, Jr.)*, Helen Holmes *(June Sanford)*, Fred Kohler *("Two-finger" Larkin)*, Duke R. Lee *("Scarface" Denton)*, Bert De Marc *("Crooked Nose" Evans)*, Al Jennings *(Splain)*, George Connors *(Shorty)*, Art Manning *(Ike Niber)*.

Western melodrama. Source: Walter J. Coburn, "Triple Cross for Danger" (publication undetermined). Clay Hill, Jr., a Spanish-American boy reared by his Mexican servant, vows vengeance on three disfigured ranchers who murdered his parents. He hunts down "Two-finger" Larkin, "Scarface" Denton, and "Crooked Nose" Evans, eliminates them, and, after saving June Sanford's cattle from being rustled, gets a job and settles down on her ranch. *Ranchers. Rustlers. Revenge. Murder.*

THE FIGHTING GOB **F2.1722**

Bear Productions. *Dist* Aywon Film Corp. 25 Mar **1926** [New York State license]. Si; b&w. 35mm. 5 reels, 4,850 ft.

Dir Harry L. Fraser.

Cast: Gordon Clifford, Charlotte Pierce.

Melodrama(?). No information about the specific nature of this film has been found. *Sailors.*

THE FIGHTING GUIDE **F2.1723**

Vitagraph Co. of America. 15 Oct **1922** [c15 Aug 1922; LP18151]. Si; b&w. 35mm. 5 reels, 4,890 ft.

Dir William Duncan, Don Clark. *Story-Scen* Bradley J. Smollen. *Photog* George Robinson.

Cast: William Duncan *(Ned Lightning)*, Edith Johnson *(Ethel MacDonald)*, Harry Lonsdale *(Lord Chumleigh Winston)*, William McCall *(Tubbs)*, Sidney D'Albrook *(Grant Knowles)*, Charles Dudley *(John MacDonald)*, Fred De Silva *("Indian Bill")*, Mrs. Harry Burns *(Mrs. Carmody)*.

Northwest melodrama. While impersonating Lord Winston, his client, Ned Lightning, a guide, discovers a plot to pin a charge of murder on John MacDonald and to deprive his daughter, Ethel, of her valuable land. Ned investigates, finds the evidence to free MacDonald, exposes Grant Knowles as swindler and murderer, and is made the new manager of Lord Winston's trading company as a reward. *Guides. Traders. Swindlers. Murder. Impersonation.*

A FIGHTING HEART **F2.1724**

Hercules Film Productions. *Dist* Bud Barsky Corp. 28 Jul **1924** [New York State license]. Si; b&w. 35mm. 6 reels, 5,800 ft.

Dir-Story Jack Nelson.

Cast: Frank Merrill *(Jack Melford)*, Margaret Landis *(Rae Davis)*, Milburn Morante *("Cloudy Day")*, May Sherman *(Julia Cunningham)*, Otto Lederer *(Dr. Logan)*, Alphonse Martell *(Dr. Dehli)*, Kathleen Calhoun *(Blanche Renault)*.

Action melodrama. Jack Melford, the prize hurdler at a small college, wins a big race and learns immediately afterward that his father is near death. He returns home to find his father dead and himself penniless, his father having left everything to Dr. Dehli, the foreign specialist who treated him. Jack later discovers that the same Dr. Dehli is caring for Julia Cunningham, the aunt of his orphaned sweetheart, Rae Davis. Jack eventually exposes the doctor as a charlatan, revealing Dehli's plans to hypnotize Rae's aunt and force her to disinherit the girl. Jack also rounds up the crooks who worked with Dehli, winning for himself the love of Rae and the gratitude of her aunt. *Hurdlers. Physicians. Charlatans. Orphans. Aunts. College life. Disinheritance. Wills. Hypnotism.*

THE FIGHTING HEART **F2.1725**

Fox Film Corp. 18 Oct **1925** [c24 May 1925; LP21571]. Si; b&w. 35mm. 7 reels, 6,978 ft.

Pres by William Fox. *Dir* John Ford. *Scen* Lillie Hayward. *Photog* Joe August.

Cast: George O'Brien *(Denny Bolton)*, Billie Dove *(Doris Anderson)*, J. Farrell MacDonald *(Jerry)*, Victor McLaglen *(Soapy Williams)*, Diana Miller *(Helen Van Allen)*, Bert Woodruff *(Grandfather)*, Francis Ford *(Town Fool)*, Hazel Howell *(Oklahoma Kate)*, Edward Piel *(Flash Fogarty)*, James Marcus *(Judge Maynard)*.

Drama. Source: Larry Evans, *Once to Every Man* (New York, 1913). Denny Bolton, who comes from a long line of men who have drunk themselves to death, discovers Soapy Williams, a tough bootlegger, selling bootleg hootch to his grandfather and gives Williams a sound thrashing. Denny's grandfather later dies, and Denny is suspected of excessive drinking, deeply feeling the scorn of his townspeople. When Doris Anderson, his sweetheart, also turns against him, Denny leaves for New York, hoping to get a chance to fight Soapy Williams, who has become the heavyweight champion. Denny gets a tryout at Flash Fogarty's gym and does well enough to be matched eventually against Williams. Helen Van Allen, an ardent follower of Williams, vamps Denny and causes him to break training. This relaxation undermines his constitution, and he loses the fight. Denny later meets Williams and Helen in front of a nightclub and, goaded by the champ's taunts, defeats him in a rough-and-tumble street fight. Denny then returns home to the welcoming arms of Doris. *Prizefighters. Bootleggers. Vamps. Alcoholism. Smalltown life. Nightclubs. Prizefighting. New York City.*

FIGHTING HEARTS **F2.1726**

Western Feature Productions. 23 Aug **1922** [New York State license]. Si; b&w. 35mm. 5 reels.

Cast: William Fairbanks.

Comedy-drama(?). No information about the nature of this film has been found.

THE FIGHTING HOMBRE **F2.1727**

Bob Custer Productions. *Dist* Film Booking Offices of America. 1 May **1927** [c16 Apr 1927; LP23875]. Si; b&w. 35mm. 5 reels, 4,624 ft.

Pres by Joseph P. Kennedy. *Supv* Jesse J. Goldburg. *Dir* Jack Nelson. *Scen* Evanne Blasdale, Madeline Matzen. *Camera* Ernest Miller.

Cast: Bob Custer *(Bob Camp)*, Mary O'Day *(Rose Martin)*, Bert Sprotte *(Henry Martin)*, David Dunbar *("Goldstud" Hopkins)*, Carlo Schipa *(Tony Mendoza)*, Zita Makar *(Marie Mendoza)*, Walter Maly *(Lone Badger)*, Jack Anthony *(The Sheriff)*.

Western melodrama. Source: Estrella Warde, "Cherokee Rose," in *Ace-High Magazine.* Bob Camp, a ranch foreman, saves his choreboy, Tony Mendoza, from a beating at the hands of "Goldstud" Hopkins; Lone Badger, a renegade Indian, intervenes and holds them up, and Goldstud escapes. Having wronged Marie, Tony's sister, the gambler attempts to win the favor of Rose Martin, daughter of the ranchowner, who is loved by Bob. While Bob is deputized to search for Lone Badger, Marie tries to induce Goldstud to marry her; when Tony attacks the gambler, Rose accidentally kills Goldstud. Bob suspects Marie, but he is interrupted by a battle between the posse and the cornered Lone Badger. Marie confesses to killing the unfaithful Goldstud but is freed by the "unwritten law." *Ranch foremen. Cowboys. Ranchers. Brother-sister relationship. Indians of North America. Murder.*

FIGHTING JACK **F2.1728**

Goodwill Pictures. 4 Jun **1926** [New York State license]. Si; b&w. 35mm. 4 reels.

Dir Louis Chaudet. *Story* Peggene Olcott. *Photog* Allen Davey.

Cast: Bill Bailey *(Jack Rhodes)*, Hazel Deane *(Betty Bingham)*, Frona Hale *(Jack's mother)*, John Byron *(José Cortez)*, Sailor Sharkey *(Pedro Sánchez)*, Herma Cordova *(María Sánchez)*.

Western melodrama(?). No information about the nature of this film has been found.

FIGHTING JIM GRANT **F2.1729**
Ward Lascelle Productions. c28 Dec **1923** [LP19802]. Si; b&w. 35mm. 5 reels, ca4,800 ft.
Dir-Writ W. Adcook.
Cast: Lester Cuneo, Alma Deer.
Western melodrama. Rancher Jim Grant breaks a vow made to his mother (that he will not fight) to protect his sweetheart, Alma Jepson, when three heavies, who claim to be relatives of her dead father, try to overrun her ranch. *Ranchers. Pacifists. Filial relations.*

THE FIGHTING KID **F2.1730**
Robert J. Horner Productions. *Dist* Bell Pictures. 22 Nov **1922** [New York State license]. Si; b&w. 35mm. 5 reels, 4,500 ft.
Western melodrama(?). No information about the nature of this film has been found.

THE FIGHTING LEGION **F2.1731**
Ken Maynard Productions. *Dist* Universal Pictures. 6 Apr **1930** [c8 Mar 1930; LP1133]. Sd (Movietone); b&w. 35mm. 8 reels, 6,763 ft. [Also si; 6,937 ft.]
Pres by Carl Laemmle. *Dir* Harry J. Brown. *Story-Scen* Bennett Cohen. *Dial* Bennett Cohen, Leslie Mason. *Titl* Leslie Mason. *Photog* Ted McCord. *Film Ed* Fred Allen. *Rec Engr* C. Roy Hunter.
Cast: Ken Maynard *(Dave Hayes)*, Dorothy Dwan *(Molly Williams)*, Ernie Adams *(Jack Bowie)*, Stanley Blystone *(Burl Edwards)*, Frank Rice *(Cloudy Jones)*, Harry Todd *(Dad Williams)*, Bob Walker *(Tom Dawson)*, Jack Fowler *(John Blake)*, Les Bates *(Fred Hook)*, Bill Nestel *(Ed Hook)*, Charles Whittaker *(Red Hook)*, Tarzan *(himself, a horse)*.
Western melodrama. A Texas Ranger pursuing Dave Hayes and Cloudy Jones for disturbing the peace in a camp is injured when his horse falls; the two men aid him, and, in gratitude, he lets them off; but as he rides away he is shot by an unknown assailant. Dave and Cloudy ride to Bowden to turn in his badge; and Dave, mistaken for a ranger, becomes interested in Molly Williams. Blake, a banker, and Edwards, a cattle buyer, determine to dispose of Dave by accusing him of murdering the ranger; but before the mob can lynch him, Dave escapes to another town. Dave then appears in a saloon at midnight, and just as the guilty man is about to confess, he is shot by Edwards, who imprisons Molly in a nearby building. Dave confronts Edwards in a fight and subdues him. With peace restored to the town, Dave and Molly are united. *Cowboys. Texas Rangers. Lynching. Courtship. Horses.*

FIGHTING LOVE **F2.1732**
De Mille Pictures. *Dist* Producers Distributing Corp. 14 Feb **1927** [c25 Jan 1927; LP23579]. Si; b&w. 35mm. 7 reels, 7,017 ft.
Supv Bertram Millhauser. *Dir* Nils Olaf Chrisander. *Adapt* Beulah Marie Dix. *Photog* Henry Cronjager.
Cast: Jetta Goudal *(Donna Vittoria)*, Victor Varconi *(Gabriel Amari)*, Henry B. Walthall *(Filipo Navarro)*, Louis Natheaux *(Dario Niccolini)*, Josephine Crowell *(Princess Torini)*.
Romantic melodrama. Source: Rosita Forbes, *If the Gods Laugh* (London, 1925). Discovering her fiancé, Dario Niccolini, kissing a servant, Donna Vittoria appeals to her grandmother, the Princess Torini, to be freed from her betrothal and is refused. Nevertheless, Vittoria marries Count Filipo Navarro, an old family friend, on the condition that he take her with him to Africa. Owing to the malicious machinations of Dario, Navarro is called to Tripoli and is dispatched to the desert on a false rumor of uprising. Vittoria is accompanied to her husband's camp by Gabriel Amari, a handsome young soldier, and they gradually fall in love, though the preoccupied Navarro is blind to their feelings. Following a report of Navarro's death they are married by an Arab ceremony; then, learning the report to be false, Vittoria goes to join her first husband; in desperation over his defeat by the Bedouins, he slays himself, leaving her free to marry Gabriel. *Bedouins. Nobility. Marriage. Infidelity. Bigamy. Courtship. Sahara. Italy. North Africa.*

THE FIGHTING LOVER **F2.1733**
Universal Film Manufacturing Co. 13 Jun **1921** [c2 Jun 1921; LP16638]. Si; b&w. 35mm. 5 reels, 4,040 ft.
Pres by Carl Laemmle. *Dir* Fred Leroy Granville. *Scen* Harvey Gates. *Photog* Leland Lancaster.
Cast: Frank Mayo *(Andrew Forsdale)*, Elinor Hancock *(Mrs. Lydia Graham)*, Gertrude Olmsted *(Jean Forsdale)*, Jackson Read *(Ned Randolph)*, Colin Kenny *(Vic Ragner)*, Jacqueline Logan *(Helen Leigh)*, Joe Singleton *(Quig Munday)*, Gordon Sackville *(Barclay)*, Jean Calhoun *(Julia Gunther)*, Ruth Ashby *(Anna Hughes)*, Fred G. Becker *(Dr. Munro)*, Robert Bolder *(valet)*.
Comedy-mystery. Source: Ben Ames Williams, "Three in a Thousand," in *All-Story Weekly* (20 Oct 1917). Andrew Forsdale bets his friend Ned Randolph $10,000 that Ned will fall in love with one of three girls within 30 days. Vic Ragner, a mutual friend, is to be stakeholder and judge. The girls are obtained through advertising, and Andrew unexpectedly falls for Helen, one of them. Helen, Ann, and Julia are in turn suspected of being in league with thieves who have stolen a valuable diamond from the house safe and have killed Ragner. Julia is revealed to be the confederate; Helen and Andrew are united; and Ned wins Ann but loses his bet to Andrew. *Wagers. Theft.*

FIGHTING LUCK **F2.1734**
Anchor Film Distributors. *Dist* Rayart Pictures. 14 Dec **1926** [New York State license]. Si; b&w. 35mm. 5 reels.
Prod-Dir J. P. McGowan.
Cast: Bob Reeves *(Tiger Slauson)*, Ione Reed *(Texas Houston)*, Bill Ryno *(Silver Houston)*, Lew Meehan *(Dude Slade, The Coyote)*.
Western melodrama. On his way to the Houston ranch, Tiger Slauson, a hired gunman, is wounded by The Coyote and his gang. At the ranch, Tiger gets into a fight with Dude over Texas, the rancher's daughter. Dude, who is in actuality The Coyote, kidnaps Texas, and Tiger goes to her rescue, roping Dude and pulling him from the wagon to certain death. *Ranchers. Gangs.*

THE FIGHTING MARINE **F2.1735**
Pathé Exchange. 24 Oct **1926** [c26 Oct 1926; LU23261]. Si; b&w. 35mm. 7 reels, 6,977 ft.
Dir Spencer Gordon Bennett. *Story* Frank Leon Smith. *Photog* Edward Snyder.
Cast: Gene Tunney, Marjorie Gay, Walter Miller, Virginia Vance, Sherman Ross, Mike Donlin, Wally Oettel, Jack Anthony, Anna May Walthall, Frank Hagney.
Melodrama. Answering an advertisement in the newspaper, reporter Dick Farrington becomes the champion and guardian of Lady Chatfield, who, in order to inherit vast mining properties in the American West, must occupy them without interruption for 6 months. Under the terms of the eccentric will, if Lady Chatfield leaves the property for even a day, the land will be inherited by the miners and the mine superintendent. Lady Chatfield is sorely beset by troubles that result from the devious plottings of the mine superintendent, but Farrington comes to her aid again and again, and she satisfies the terms of the will, inheriting the property. Lady Chatfield and Dick fall in love. *Reporters. Mine superintendents. Miners. Aristocrats. Inheritance. Wills. Land rights.*
Note: This is a feature version of a 10-reel serial released by Pathé in 1926.

THE FIGHTING PEACEMAKER (Blue Streak Western) **F2.1736**
Universal Pictures. 7 Jul **1926** [c6 May 1926; LP22684]. Si; b&w. 35mm. 5 reels, 4,500 or 4,080 ft.
Pres by Carl Laemmle. *Dir* Clifford S. Smith. *Scen* Alvin J. Neitz, Harrison Jacobs. *Photog* William Nobles.
Cast: Jack Hoxie *(Peace River Parker)*, Lola Todd *(Jess Marshall)*, Ted Oliver *(Jefferson Crane)*, William A. Steele *(Clell Danert)*, Robert McKenzie *(Hanna)*, Clark Comstock *(Marshall)*, Frank Rice *(sheriff)*.
Western melodrama. Source: W. C. Tuttle, "Peace Medicine" (publication undetermined). Peace River Parker, foreman of the Cross L Ranch and engaged to Jess, the daughter of the owner, is railroaded into a prison term by the false witness of Jefferson Crane, who covets the ranch and Jess. Through the complicity of Clell Danert, a villainous foreman who also desires Jess, Crane arranges to ruin the Marshall ranch by driving a herd of sheep onto the cattle range. Peace, released on good behavior, learns of the plot from Danert, who takes him for a hobo and hires him to herd the sheep. Peace informs Jess, who rides to protect her father's ranch but is captured by Crane's men; Crane proposes marriage; but Jess gains the upper hand and forces him to confess to the crime for which Peace was convicted. Jess and the Marshall ranchmen arrive in time to save Peace from a lynching and clear his name. *Ranch foremen. Ranchers. Injustice. Parole. Lynching. Cattle. Sheep.*

THE FIGHTING RANGER F2.1737

Bill Miller Productions. 13 Jun **1922** [New York State license application]. Si; b&w. 35mm. 5 reels.

Cast: Bill Miller *(Ranger Bill, watchman)*, May Carson *(Ruth)*.

Melodrama. "The story tells of a gentleman thug in love with a young girl, who tries to possess her by reducing her old drunken father to the lowest forms of degradation. The girl is protected by a watchman working at a gold mine. The thug and his gang plot to rob the mine, kill the watchman and abduct the girl. Their plans carry, the gold is stolen and the mine owner is killed. The watchman is falsely accused of the murder. In order to rescue the girl who is held captive, he breaks jail after practically killing his jailer. He hastens to save the girl and arrives just as the thug and gang are struggling to possess her. A terrific fight ensues, he chokes the thug into insensibility and rescues the girl." (Examiner's report, New York State license records.) *Rangers. Watchmen. Gold mines. Drunkenness. Theft. Murder. Jailbreaks.*

FIGHTING RANGER F2.1738

Bud Barsky Productions. 15 Sep **1926.** Si; b&w. 35mm. 5 reels, 4,900 ft.

Dir Paul Hurst.

Cast: Al Hoxie.

Western melodrama. "Ranger inherits uncle's ranch and is threatened by enemies who do not desire his presence. He sustains all their attempts to remove him, captures mysterious ghost of range, and rustlers who are after his cattle. He also wins the girl in the case, a sister of a member of the outlaw gang who had reformed." *(Motion Picture News Booking Guide,* 12:28, Apr 1927.) *Rangers. Rustlers. Gangs. Inheritance. Brother-sister relationship. Ranches. Ghosts.*

THE FIGHTING ROMEO F2.1739

J. J. Fleming Productions. *Dist* Davis Distributing Division. 21 Jul **1925** [New York State license]. Si; b&w. 35mm. 5 reels.

Dir Al Ferguson. *Story* J. J. Fleming.

Cast: Al Ferguson *(Dave Mathews)*, Elaine Eastman *(Helen McMasters)*, Paul Emery *(Buck Conners)*, George Routh *(Henry Warner)*, F. Schumann-Heink *(James Warner)*, William Dills *(Gerald Mertagh)*.

Western melodrama. Dave Mathews, the foreman of Helen McMaster's ranch, travels east with a shipment of cattle and there discovers Jim Warner, the son of an old friend, in the act of stealing money from his father's safe to pay gambling debts. Dave protects the boy from the consequences of his action and takes him west to make a man of him. Buck Conners, whom Dave suspects of cattle rustling, abducts Helen, and Jim rides to her rescue. Jim later saves Dave from Buck's gang. The gang is finally captured, Jim has become a man, and Dave and Helen make plans to ride the range of life together. *Ranch foremen. Theft. Gambling. Rustling. Abduction. Manhood.*

THE FIGHTING SAP F2.1740

Monogram Pictures. *Dist* Film Booking Offices of America. 30 Jun **1924** [c19 Jun 1924; LP20323]. Si; b&w. 35mm. 6 reels, 5,138 ft.

Prod Harry J. Brown. *Dir* Albert Rogell. *Story* Marion Jackson. *Photog* Ross Fisher.

Cast: Fred Thomson *(Craig Richmond)*, Hazel Keener *(Marjorie Stoddard)*, Wilfred Lucas *(Charles Richmond)*, George Williams *(Walter Stoddard)*, Frank Hagney *(Nebraska Brent)*, Ralph Yearsley *("Twister")*, Bob Williamson *(Chicago Kid)*, Robert Fleming *(sheriff)*, Silver King *(himself, a horse)*.

Western melodrama. Craig Richmond, rejected by his father, engages in geological research at his father's gold mine and discovers a plot among the workmen to steal bullion. After many narrow escapes and rescues, he thwarts their plans, wins the love of the superintendent's daughter, and is reconciled to his father. *Geologists. Mining. Filial relations. Horses.*

THE FIGHTING SHERIFF F2.1741

Independent Pictures. 17 May **1925** [26 Nov 1924; LP20812]. Si; b&w. 35mm. 5 reels.

Prod Jesse J. Goldburg. *Dir* J. P. McGowan. *Story* George W. Pyper. *Photog* Al Siegler.

Cast: Bill Cody *(Larry O'Donnell, the fighting sheriff)*, Frank Ellis *(Jeff Bains)*, Walter Shumway *(G. Smiley, the mine superintendent)*, Hazel Holt *(Madge Blair, the postmistress)*.

Western melodrama. A gang of bandits known as the Wolf Pack is prevented by Larry O'Donnell, the fighting sheriff, from robbing a packtrain loaded with platinum. Larry puts the precious metal in a jail cell for safekeeping, but he is overpowered and the sacks of ore are stolen. When Larry pursues the bandits out of town, he is struck on the head by one of them; and for several months he loses his memory. Using Larry's disappearance as proof of guilt, Jeff Bains, the real leader of the Wolf Pack, convinces the townspeople that Larry is a criminal and has himself elected sheriff. When Larry regains his memory, he obtains documentary proof of Bains's guilt and seals it in an envelope, which he gives to Madge Blair, the postmistress from the East, with instructions to mail it to the governor. Discovering the existence of the letter, Bains orders his men to rob the mail stage, but the resourceful Madge has telegraphed the information incriminating Bains to the State Capitol, instead of mailing it, and the bandits are captured. Larry is reinstated as sheriff, and things look good for his future with Madge. *Sheriffs. Postmistresses. Robbery. Telegraph. Platinum. Amnesia. Documentation.*

THE FIGHTING SMILE F2.1742

Independent Pictures. 4 Aug **1925** [New York State license]. Si; b&w. 35mm. 5 reels, 4,564 ft.

Pres by Jesse J. Goldburg. *Dir* Jay Marchant. *Scen* William A. Burton, Harry J. Brown. *Photog* Harry J. Brown.

Cast: Bill Cody *(Bud Brant)*, Jean Arthur *(Rose Craddock)*, Charles Brinley, George Magrill, Billie Bennett.

Western melodrama. "Bud Brant returns to his father's ranch to find that his father's helper, Shorty, is rustling cattle for a neighbouring rancher. Shorty, an old friend of Bud's tries to get out of the gang, but is shot. Before he dies, he draws Bud a map of the rustler's camp; Bud takes the sheriff there, and the rustlers are rounded up." *(National Film Archive Catalogue, Part III, Silent Fiction Films, 1895–1930;* The British Film Institute, London, 1966, p259.) *Outlaws. Sheriffs. Rustling. Documentation.*

THE FIGHTING STALLION F2.1743

Dist Goodwill Pictures. **1926.** Si; b&w. 35mm. 5 reels.

Dir Ben F. Wilson.

Cast: Yakima Canutt.

Western melodrama(?). No information about the nature of this film has been found.

THE FIGHTING STRAIN F2.1744

William Steiner Productions. 13 Sep **1923** [New York premiere; c6 Aug 1923; LU19277]. Si; b&w. 35mm. 5 reels.

Dir-Story-Scen-Titl Neal Hart. *Photog* Harry McGuire Stanley.

Cast: Neal Hart *(Jack Barlow)*, Beth Mitchell *(Bess Barlow)*, William Quinn *(Jim Black)*, Bert Wilson *(John Canfield)*, Gladys Gilland *(Miss Canfield)*.

Western melodrama. Soldier Jack Barlow returns home to find that his sister, Bess, has been kidnaped by Jim Black, a scoundrel who cheated Mr. Canfield, the father of Jack's sweetheart, by means of some fake mine stock. Jack goes to Canada, nails Black, and after releasing Bess and Miss Canfield (who are imprisoned by Black), marries Miss Canfield and arranges for Bess to marry his sweetheart's brother, John. *Veterans. Brother-sister relationship. Swindlers. Mining. Canada.*

Note: Working title: *Bill Barlow's Claim.*

THE FIGHTING STRANGER F2.1745

William N. Selig. *Dist* Canyon Pictures. c25 Jan **1921** [LU16048]. Si; b&w. 35mm. 5 reels.

Dir Webster Cullison.

Cast: Franklyn Farnum *("Australia Joe")*, Flora Hollister *(Madeline Ayre)*, W. A. Alleman *(Winthrop Ayre)*, Vester Pegg *(Joe Kilburn)*, W. A. Bartlett *("Laughing" Bill)*, Churchill Scott *(Bob Scarritt)*, Emma Burns *(Mrs. Ayre)*.

Western melodrama. Source: William E. Wing, "Danger" (publication undetermined). "Australia Joe," after being released from prison, attempts a bank robbery and escapes. Out west, his gang robs the townhall and steals papers for some mysterious person "higher up." Joe learns the identity of this man and prevents his marriage to the daughter of a man he has framed. To the surprise of all, Joe discloses himself to be a Secret Service agent rather than a notorious bandit. *Secret service. Gangs. Robbery. Frameup. Documentation.*

THE FIGHTING STREAK F2.1746

Fox Film Corp. 14 May **1922** [c14 May 1922; LP17905]. Si; b&w. 35mm. 5 reels, 4,888 ft.

Pres by William Fox. *Dir-Scen* Arthur Rosson. *Photog* Dan Clark.

Cast: Tom Mix *(Andrew Lanning)*, Patsy Ruth Miller *(Ann Withero)*, Gerald Pring *(Charles Merchant)*, Al Fremont *(Jasper Lanning)*, Sidney Jordan *(Bill Dozier)*, Bert Sprotte *(Hal Dozier)*, Robert Fleming *(Chick Heath)*.

Western melodrama. Source: George Owen Baxter, *Free Range Lanning* (New York, 1921). Andy Lanning, a peace-loving blacksmith, rescues Ann, the fiancée of Charles Merchant, from a runaway team. When the town bully picks a fight with Andy, he knocks him unconscious, and (thinking he has killed him) Andy rides into the hills. Merchant, jealous of Ann's admiration for Andy, bribes the sheriff to kill Andy, who has joined a band of outlaws in the wastelands. Forced to defend himself, Andy kills the sheriff, but later he saves the new sheriff's life and forces him to hear his story when he is placed in jeopardy by the outlaw band. Meanwhile, Ann, who has broken her engagement to Merchant, engages a lawyer to clear Andy, and he returns to find her awaiting him. *Blacksmiths. Sheriffs. Outlaws. Peace.*

THE FIGHTING TERROR **F2.1747**

J. P. McGowan Productions. *Dist* Syndicate Pictures. Aug **1929.** Si; b&w. 35mm. 5 reels.

Dir J. P. McGowan. *Story* Sally Winters. *Photog* Hap Depew.

Cast: Bob Custer, Bud Osborne, Hank Bell, J. P. McGowan, Adabelle Driver, Hazel Mills, Cliff Lyons, Tom Bay.

Western melodrama. "Custer, known as the Fighting Terror, is out to avenge the shooting of his brother by a gang of outlaws. The action takes place on the border of the states of California and Nevada. With the help of a crooked sheriff, the gang makes use of the border line to jump across and prevent pursuit by the posse who are out to get them." (*Film Daily*, 8 Dec 1929, p9.) *Outlaws. Brothers. Sheriffs. Posses. State boundaries. Revenge. California. Nevada.*

FIGHTING THE FLAMES **F2.1748**

Columbia Pictures. c3 Apr **1925** [LP21322]. Si; b&w. 35mm. 6 reels, 5,800 ft.

Dir Reeves Eason. *Story-Scen* Douglas Z. Doty. *Titl* Walter Anthony. *Photog* Dewey Wrigley. *Film Ed* Viola Lawrence.

Cast: William Haines *(Horatio Manly, Jr.)*, Dorothy Devore *(Alice Doran)*, Frankie Darro *(Mickey)*, David Torrence *(Judge Manly)*, Sheldon Lewis *(Big Jim)*, William Welsh *(Charlie Ryan)*, Charles Murray *(pawnbroker)*.

Melodrama. Horatio Manly, the only son of Judge Manly, is disowned by his father when he is thrown in the drunk tank for obstructing the work of several firemen during a hotel blaze. When Horatio is released the following day, he meets Mickey, a street urchin, whose father has been arrested as a sneak thief. Horatio and Mickey become fast friends, and Horatio joins the fire department. When a fire breaks out in the city jail, Mickey's father escapes, begins searching for his child, and finds him in a beanery having lunch with Alice, a friend of Horatio's. Mickey's father tries to grab the child, but Alice prevents this seizure by pushing him against a hot stove. Alice and the boy escape from the badly burned father, but the degraded fellow follows Mickey back to Alice's boardinghouse, where he traps both Alice and the boy in her room. A fire breaks out in the building, trapping all three of them on the top floor. Horatio's company is called to the scene, and he rescues Alice and the boy and captures Mickey's father. *Firemen. Street urchins. Judges. Thieves. Disinheritance. Fatherhood. Fire departments. Jails. Fires.*

FIGHTING THOROBREDS **F2.1749**

Harry J. Brown Productions. *Dist* Rayart Pictures. 6 May **1926** [New York State license]. Si; b&w. 35mm. 5 reels.

Dir Harry J. Brown.

Cast: Billy Sullivan.

Melodrama(?). No information about the nature of this film has been found.

THE FIGHTING THREE (Blue Streak Western) **F2.1750**

Universal Pictures. 3 Jul **1927** [c21 May 1927; LP24008]. Si; b&w. 35mm. 5 reels, 4,108 or 4,167 ft.

Pres by Carl Laemmle. *Dir* Albert Rogell. *Story-Scen* William Lester. *Photog* William Nobles. *Art Dir* David S. Garber.

Cast: Jack Hoxie *(Jack Conway)*, Olive Hasbrouck *(Jeanne D'Arcy)*, Marin Sais *(Clara Jones)*, Fanny Warren *(widow)*, William Malan *(John D'Arcy)*, Buck Connors *(Marshall Skinner)*, William Dyer *(Timothy)*, Henry Roquemore *(Revere)*, William Norton Bailey *(Steve Clayton)*, Scout *(himself, a horse)*, Bunk *(a dog)*.

Western melodrama. Mademoiselle Jeanne D'Arcy, the soubrette in a Parisian Follies company, meets Jack Conway, a good-natured cowhand, when he tows their stalled truck across the county line. While they are playing the local opera house, John Dorsey is writing his last will in favor of Jeanne, his missing daughter. Dorsey's ne'er-do-well nephew, Steve Clayton, demands money from him and tries to force a revision of the will. Jack hears Dorsey's call for help and is framed by Clayton for Dorsey's murder. Jack escapes and finds refuge in Jeanne's dressing room, where she disguises him as a mystic. Clayton persuades her that Conway is her father's murderer, forcing Jack to abduct her to a mountain shack. The report of Dorsey's death proves erroneous as he returns with the accusatory finger pointed at Clayton. *Cowboys. Actors. Uncles. Ne'er-do-wells. Follies. Wills. Horses. Dogs.*

FIGHTING THRU; OR CALIFORNIA IN 1878 **F2.1751**

Tiffany Productions. 16 Dec **1930** [c7 Jan 1931; LP1883]. Sd (Photophone); b&w. 35mm. 7 reels, 5,200 ft.

Dir William Nigh. *Screenplay* John Francis Natteford. *Photog* Arthur Reed. *Film Ed* Earl Turner.

Cast: Ken Maynard *(Dan Barton)*, Jeanette Loff *(Alice Malden)*, Wallace MacDonald *(Tennessee Malden)*, Carmelita Geraghty *(Queenie)*, William L. Thorne *(Ace)*, Charles L. King *(Fox Tyson)*, Fred Burns *(sheriff)*.

Western melodrama. Dan Barton, a recruit of the '49 gold miners, returns to his cabin to find that his partner, Tennessee Malden, has departed to meet his sister, Alice, and rushes to town to stop him. He finds him playing cards with Fox Tyson, a gambler, Queenie, a tavern girl, and the tavern owner, Ace Brady, who are out to swindle his partner. At their cabin, Tennessee is killed by Fox, who makes it appear that Dan is the guilty party, and he is accused by Alice and Ace. Dan escapes and learns that Ace and Queenie plan to obtain a power of attorney so as to divert Tennessee's interests from Alice; he convinces Alice that he is innocent, saves her from a stagecoach disaster, and subdues Ace in a saloon melee. The sheriff arrives to vindicate Dan, having heard Fox's dying confession at the wrecked stagecoach. Ace shoots Dan, but he recovers and marries Alice. *Goldminers. Gamblers. Murder. Brother-sister relationship. Frameup. Circumstantial evidence. Gold rushes. California.*

FIGHTING YOUTH **F2.1752**

Perfection Pictures. *Dist* Columbia Pictures. 1 Jul **1925** [c27 Jun 1925; LP21609]. Si; b&w. 35mm. 5 reels.

Dir Reeves Eason. *Adapt* Dorothy Howell. *Story* Paul Archer. *Photog* George Meehan.

Cast: William Fairbanks *(Dick Covington)*, Pauline Garon *(Jean Manley)*, George Periolat *(Judge Manley)*, William Norton Bailey *(Harold Brennty)*, Pat Harmon *(Paddy O'Ryan)*, Frank Hagney *("Murdering" Mooney)*, Tom Carr *(gangster)*, Jack Britton *(referee)*.

Action melodrama. Dick Covington, a young society man with a quick temper and quicker fists, becomes involved in so many public scrapes that his fiancée, Jean Manley, threatens to break off their engagement if he ever fights again. Dick promises to be peaceful, but, the following day, Jean's father, Judge Manley, talks him into fighting in a charity bout to aid the milk fund. Jean breaks off the engagement, and Dick goes into training with Paddy O'Ryan. "Murdering" Mooney, Dick's opponent in the charity match, is involved in a minor automobile accident in which a car driven by Jean's younger brother backs into his car; Mooney knocks Jean's brother brutally to the ground, and Jean goes to Dick, asking to be forgiven and encouraging Dick to make hash of Mooney. On the day before the fight, Dick is kidnaped by Harold Brennty, the judge's junior partner, who hopes that, if Dick misses the match, Jean will turn from Dick to him. Dick escapes from his captors and arrives at the ring just in time for round one. Dick is being badly beaten when Jean exhorts him to do his best; he thereupon lays out the champ in short order. *Judges. Boxers. Kidnaping. Brother-sister relationship. Automobile accidents. Charity. Prizefighting.*

FIGURES DON'T LIE **F2.1753**

Paramount Famous Lasky Corp. 8 Oct **1927** [c8 Oct 1927; LP24493]. Si; b&w. 35mm. 6 reels, 5,280 ft.

Pres by Adolph Zukor, Jesse L. Lasky. *Assoc Prod* B. P. Schulberg. *Dir* Edward Sutherland. *Screenplay* Ethel Doherty, Louise Long. *Titl* Herman Mankiewicz. *Adapt* Grover Jones. *Story* B. F. Zeidman. *Photog* Alfred Gilks.

Cast: Esther Ralston *(Janet Wells)*, Richard Arlen *(Bob Blewe)*, Ford Sterling *("Howdy" Jones)*, Doris Hill *(Mamie)*, Blanche Payson *(Mrs. Jones)*, Natalie Kingston *(Dolores)*.

Romantic comedy. Janet Wells, the efficient and beautiful secretary of "Howdy" Jones, finds it difficult to conduct office affairs because of the attitude of her employer's violently jealous wife. Janet becomes diverted, however, by the attentions of the new sales manager, Bob Blewe, though she considers him to be fresh. When she refuses his invitation to the office picnic, Bob takes Dolores, a pretty but emptyheaded stenographer, provoking Janet's jealousy and causing her to play up to Mr. Jones; but when Janet gets entangled in seaweed during a swim, she is rescued by Bob. Later, the enraged Mrs. Jones finds Janet and her husband in a compromising situation; but Bob thwarts her plan to shoot Janet, and all ends happily. *Secretaries. Sales managers. Marriage. Jealousy. Swimming.*

THE FINAL EXTRA **F2.1754**

Gotham Productions. *Dist* Lumas Film Corp. 7 Feb **1927** [cl Feb 1927; LP23664]. Si; b&w. 35mm. 6 reels, 6,000 ft.

Pres by Sam Sax. *Dir* James P. Hogan. *Story-Scen* Herbert C. Clark. *Camera* Ray June. *Film Ed* Edith Wakeling. *Prod Mgr* Glenn Belt.

Cast: Marguerite De La Motte *(Ruth Collins)*, Grant Withers *(Pat Riley)*, John Miljan *(Mervin Le Roy)*, Frank Beal *(Tom Collins)*, Joseph W. Girard *(Editor Williams)*, Billy "Red" Jones *(Buddy Collins)*, Leon Holmes *(The Copyboy)*.

Melodrama. Pat Riley, an aspiring young newspaper columnist, envies the big assignments given to Tom Collins, who is working on a bootlegging story. Pat is sent to get a story on a new musical revue being produced by Mervin Le Roy, a well-known impresario of doubtfui reputation, and meets Tom's daughter, Ruth, who is a chorus girl. Later he learns that Tom has been killed by the bootleggers; and swearing revenge on Tom's killers, Pat manages to take over Tom's assignment. Ruth is to dance at a large houseparty given by Le Roy, who has designs on her, but the appearance of Pat makes him hesitate; his men capture Pat after a fight, but he escapes and reveals the identity of the gang leader to the police. He rescues Ruth from the clutches of Le Roy, who is arrested as the murderer of her father. *Reporters. Columnists. Chorus girls. Bootleggers. Theatrical producers. Musical revues. Murder.*

FIND THE WOMAN **F2.1755**

Cosmopolitan Productions. *Dist* Paramount Pictures. 2 Apr **1922** [c8 Feb 1922; LP17547]. Si; b&w. 35mm. 6 reels, 5,144 ft.

Dir Tom Terriss. *Scen* Doty Hobart. *Photog* Ira H. Morgan. *Set Dsgn* Joseph Urban.

Cast: Alma Rubens *(Sophie Carey)*, Eileen Huban *(Clancy Deane)*, Harrison Ford *(Philip Vandevent)*, George MacQuarrie *(Judge Walbrough)*, Norman Kerry *(Marc Weber)*, Ethel Duray *(Fay Weber)*, Arthur Donaldson *(Morris [Maurice?] Beiner)*, Henry Sedley *(Don Carey)*, Sydney Deane *(Spofford)*, Emily Fitzroy *(Mrs. Napoli)*.

Mystery melodrama. Source: Arthur Somers Roche, *Find the Woman* (New York, 1921). Clancy Deane, who leaves her home in Ohio for a career on the New York stage, makes the acquaintance of the Webers, tools of Maurice Beiner, a blackmailer operating under the cover of a theatrical agency. While in Beiner's office seeking an engagement, Clancy witnesses his being stunned by a fall over a table. She leaves by a window, and on the fire escape she encounters Mrs. Carey, who wants to secure some letters. When Beiner's murder is investigated, Mrs. Carey is implicated but is released after examination. Judge Walbrough is knocked out by an unknown assailant, whose fingerprints are identical with those on the knife that killed Beiner. Following numerous complications, Don Carey, a dissolute alcoholic who kills himself, is revealed as the murderer. Clancy marries Philip Vandevent, and Judge Walbrough wins Sophie Carey. *Actors. Ohioans. Judges. Theatrical agents. Blackmail. Alcoholism. Suicide. Theater. Murder. Documentation.*

FIND YOUR MAN **F2.1756**

Warner Brothers Pictures. 1 Sep **1924** [c18 Aug 1924; LP20505]. Si; b&w. 35mm. 7 reels, 6,800 ft.

Dir Mal St. Clair. *Story-Adapt-Scen* Darryl Francis Zanuck. *Photog* Lee Garmes.

Cast: Rin-Tin-Tin *(Buddy, a dog)*, June Marlowe *(Carolina Blair)*, Eric St. Clair *(Paul Andrews)*, Charles Mailes *(Gregory Mills)*, Pat Hartigan *(Martin Dains)*, Fred Stanton *(sheriff)*, Lew Harvey *(half-breed)*, Charles Conklin *(lumberjack)*.

Melodrama. Returning from the wartime service, Paul Andrews sets out to find his missing sweetheart with the aid of Buddy, his dog. They hop a freight to a lumber camp, and upon rescuing a girl from Martin Dains they discover her to be his sweetheart, Caroline. When Martin kills the girl's stepfather suspicion falls on Paul, but a confession is wrested from the villain by Buddy. *Veterans. Lumbering. Dogs.*

FINDERS KEEPERS **F2.1757**

Art-O-Graph Productions. *Dist* Pioneer Pictures. 18 Feb **1921** [trade review]. Si; b&w. 35mm. 6 reels, 6,003 ft.

Dir Otis B. Thayer. *Story* Robert Ames Bennett.

Cast: Violet Mersereau *(Amy Lindel)*, Edmund Cobb *(Paul Rutledge)*, Dorothy Simpson *(Oliva Satterlee)*, Verne Layton *(Hobart Keith)*, S. May Stone *(Mrs. Satterlee)*.

Melodrama. Amy Lindel, who sang in the church choir until she went to the city to make a fortune with her voice, finds cabaret singing is the best she can do. She charms one man, is admired by another less honorable man who plants stolen diamonds on her. He then has the police break into her boyfriend's house in order to search Amy. But Amy, distraught with the thought of the threatened arrest and with the shame of being turned away from her boardinghouse, has thrown herself into a lake. Her sweetheart saves her, clears her name, and then makes her his wife. *Singers. Thieves. Frameup. Suicide. Cabarets.*

FINDERS KEEPERS (Universal-Jewel) **F2.1758**

Universal Pictures. 11 Mar **1928** [c17 Jan 1928; LP24886]. Si; b&w. 35mm. 6 reels, 6,081 ft.

Dir Wesley Ruggles. *Scen* Beatrice Van. *Titl* Tom Reed. *Photog* Virgil Miller. *Film Ed* Leon Halen.

Cast: Laura La Plante *(Barbara Hastings)*, John Harron *(Carter Brooks)*, Edmund Breese *(Colonel Hastings)*, William Gorman *(Bozo)*, Eddie Phillips *(Kenneth)*, Arthur Rankin *(Percy)*, Joe Mack *(chaplain)*.

Comedy. Source: Mary Roberts Rinehart, "Make Them Happy," in *Saturday Evening Post* (4 Oct 1919). Barbara, a colonel's daughter, falls in love with Carter, one of the soldiers in her father's training camp. On the day that the two decide to get married the regiment is ordered overseas. Unable to get into camp as a civilian, but determined to be near Carter, Barbara dresses in a soldier's uniform and joins the ranks. Her father perceives her disguise but gives the couple permission to marry before the regiment leaves for the front. *Soldiers. Military life. Disguise. Male impersonation. World War I.*

FINE CLOTHES **F2.1759**

Louis B. Mayer Productions. *Dist* First National Pictures. 9 Aug **1925** [c27 Jul 1925; LP21674]. Si; b&w. 35mm. 8 reels, 6,971 ft.

Pres by Louis B. Mayer. *Dir* John M. Stahl. *Adapt* Benjamin Glazer. *Photog* Ernest Palmer. *Col Cons* James Basevi. *Art Dir* Cedric Gibbons. *Film Ed* Margaret Booth, Robert Kern. *Asst Dir* Sidney Algier.

Cast: Lewis Stone *(Earl of Denham)*, Percy Marmont *(Peter Hungerford)*, Alma Rubens *(Paula)*, Raymond Griffith *(Oscar)*, Eileen Percy *(Adele)*, William V. Mong *(Philip)*, John Merkyl *(receiver)*, Otis Harlan *(Alfred)*.

Comedy-drama. Source: Ferenc Molnár, *Fashions for Men*, in *Fashions for Men and The Swan; Two Plays* (English texts by Benjamin Glazer; New York, 1922). Peter Hungerford, the kindhearted proprietor of a London clothing store, loses both his wife and his business when she takes all of his savings and runs off with Oscar, the clerk. Forced into bankruptcy, Peter takes a position as the manager of a cheese business owned by his patron, the Earl of Denham. The earl also hires Paula, Peter's former cashier; and Peter, aware of the earl's amorous intentions, keeps strict watch over the girl. The earl, finally driven to distraction, fires Peter, but, overtaken by remorse, he soon rehires him. The creditors who put Peter's store into receivership request that he return as manager, and he leaves the estate, upbraiding Paula for her announced intentions of staying on as the earl's companion. Paula then realizes that she loves Peter and follows him back to the shop, where she takes charge of him and his affairs on a permanent basis. *Nobility. Cashiers. Receivership. Desertion. Divorce. Bankruptcy. Clothing business. Cheese. London.*

FINE FEATHERS **F2.1760**

Metro Pictures. 20 Jun **1921** [c20 Jun 1921; LP16696]. Si; b&w. 35mm. 6 reels.

Supv Maxwell Karger. *Dir* Fred Sittenham. *Scen* Lois Zellner. *Adapt* Eugene Walter. *Photog* Arthur A. Cadwell. *Art Dir* Lester J. Vermilyea.

Cast: Eugene Pallette *(Bob Reynolds)*, Claire Whitney *(Jane Reynolds)*, Thomas W. Ross *(Dick Meade)*, Warburton Gamble *(John Brand)*, June

Elvidge *(Mrs. Brand)*.

Society melodrama. Source: Eugene Walter, *Fine Feathers* (New York opening: 21 Jan 1920). Young construction engineer Bob Reynolds, in financial difficulty, is persuaded by John Brand to use an inferior cement in the construction of a dam. In an attempt to ruin Reynolds, Brand then cajoles him into buying worthless stock, and in desperation Reynolds forges a check in Brand's name. When the dam breaks under high pressure, Reynolds, suspected by the authorities, sends his wife to Brand for money, which she obtains through the innocent intervention of Mrs. Brand. Reynolds becomes frantic over the dam disaster and the consequent loss of life, and believing that his wife is conspiring with Brand he kills him and then commits suicide. *Engineers—Civil. Finance—Personal. Forgery. Suicide. Murder. Dams.*

FINE MANNERS **F2.1761**

Famous Players–Lasky. *Dist* Paramount Pictures. 16 Aug **1926** [c16 Aug 1926; LP23028]. Si; b&w. 35mm. 7 reels, 6,435 ft.

Pres by Adolph Zukor, Jesse L. Lasky. *Dir* Richard Rosson. *Screenplay* James Ashmore Creelman. *Story* James Ashmore Creelman, Frank Vreeland. *Photog* George Webber.

Cast: Gloria Swanson *(Orchid Murphy)*, Eugene O'Brien *(Brian Alden)*, Helen Dunbar *(Aunt Agatha)*, Walter Goss *(Buddy Murphy)*, John Miltern *(Courtney Adams)*.

Society comedy-drama. Orchid, a New York chorus girl, lives in a cheap tenement with her brother Buddy, who jealously guards his sister against wealthy men who might plot to corrupt her. Young Brian Alden, an uptown society man, bored with a New Year's Eve party, joins the merrymakers in Times Square and finds himself thrown against Orchid, who is on her way to a public dancehall; separated from Buddy, she strikes up an acquaintance with Alden, whom she takes to be a waiter. Amused by the girl's vibrant personality, Alden seeks her out the following night, and Buddy is informed that he is an uptown "swell." Although arousing her brother's suspicions, Orchid consents to Alden's plan that she study social etiquette with his Aunt Agatha during his business travels. Disappointed at finding Orchid transformed into an artificial society flower, Alden admits his mistake; and Orchid, after assuring her jealous brother that Alden will marry her, accepts Alden's apology and proposal. *Chorus girls. Aunts. Brother-sister relationship. Wealth. Courtship. Etiquette. New Year's Eve. New York City.*

FINGER PRINTS **F2.1762**

Dist Hyperion Pictures. 19 Jan **1923** [trade review]. Si; b&w. 35mm. [Feature length assumed.]

Dir Joseph Levering. *Story* Alton Floyd.

Cast: Violet Palmer.

Mystery melodrama. A string of valuable pearls provides the motivation for the killing of a man, who intended them for his motherless daughter's homecoming. Finding her father's financial affairs in a terrible state, the girl is comforted by her father's friend, while her fiancé works diligently to identify the murderer. The butler acts suspiciously, but the true criminal is finally revealed (the father's friend?). *Butlers. Guardians. Filial relations. Murder. Finance—Personal.*

FINGER PRINTS **F2.1763**

Warner Brothers Pictures. 8 Jan **1927** [c25 Dec 1926; LP23486]. Si; b&w. 35mm. 7 reels, 7,031 ft.

Dir Lloyd Bacon. *Scen* Graham Baker, Edward Clark. *Camera* Virgil Miller. *Asst Camera* Edward Cronewealth. *Asst Dir* Ted Stevens.

Cast: Louise Fazenda *(Dora Traynor)*, John T. Murray *(Homer Fairchild)*, Helene Costello *(Jacqueline Norton)*, Myrna Loy *(The Vamp)*, George Nichols *(S. V. Sweeney)*, Martha Mattox *(Mother Malone)*, Franklin Pangborn *(The Bandoline Kid)*, William Demarest *(Cuffs Egan)*, Robert Perry *(Hard-Boiled Ryan)*, Ed Kennedy *(O. K. McDuff)*, Jerry Miley *(Chicago Ed)*, Joseph B. (Doc) Stone *(Cabbage Head McCarthy)*, Warner Richmond *("Annie Laurie" Andy Norton)*, Lew Harvey *(Secret Service man)*.

Comedy-melodrama. Source: Arthur Somers Roche, "Finger Prints" (publication undetermined). Andy Norton, chief of a gang of mail thieves, is captured and imprisoned, though he does not reveal to the other gang members the hiding place of the loot. They plot to obtain the secret from him, but to no avail. Inspector Sweeney of the Post Office Department, posing as a criminal, suspects that the stolen property is hidden in the house of Mother Malone, a clairvoyant. There he finds the gang members who have escaped and who threaten Norton's daughter, Jacqueline, thus forcing Norton to divulge the secret. After a series of mysterious and comic adventures, the gang is arrested with the aid of Dora, a servant who turns out to be a Secret Service agent, and the booty is retrieved. *Thieves. Clairvoyants. Postal inspectors. Secret service. Mail theft.*

FINNEGAN'S BALL **F2.1764**

Graf Brothers Studio. *Dist* First Division Pictures. 15 Sep **1927**. Si; b&w. 35mm. 7 reels, 6,200-6,700 ft.

Supv-Scen Max Graf. *Dir* James P. Hogan. *Photog* Blake Wagner.

Cast: Blanche Mehaffey *(Molly Finnegan)*, Mack Swain *(Patrick Flannigan)*, Cullen Landis *(Flannigan, Jr.)*, Aggie Herring *(Maggie Finnegan)*, Charles McHugh *(Danny Finnegan, Sr.)*, Westcott B. Clarke *(Lawyer O'Connell)*, Kewpie Morgan *(Judge Morgan)*, Mimi Finnegan *(Danny Finnegan, Jr.)*.

Comedy. Source: George H. Emerick, *Finnegan's Ball; a Comedy in Three Acts* (c1894). The Finnegans follow the Flannigans to America, Mr. Finnegan goes to work for Mr. Flannigan, and Molly and Jimmy are reunited. A feud between the families breaks out, however, which results in the Finnegans snubbing the Flannigans when the former fall heir to a fortune. But the inheritance proves to be an error, and the Finnegans are reduced to their earlier position. The Flannigans forgive them, and amity between the families is assured by the marriage of Molly and Jimmy. *Irish. Immigrants. Family life. Inheritance. Wealth. Courtship. Feuds.*

FIRE AND STEEL **F2.1765**

Dist Ellbee Pictures. 1 Jul **1927** [New York showing]. Si; b&w. 35mm. 6 reels, 5,600 ft.

Pres by W. T. Lackey. *Dir* Bertram Bracken. *Story* A. B. Barringer. *Photog* Robert Cline, Joseph Walker.

Cast: Jack Perrin *(Terry O'Farrell)*, Philo McCullough *(Tom Welbourne)*, Mary McAllister *(Ann McGreagor)*, Burr McIntosh *(Sandy McGreagor)*, Cissy Fitzgerald *(Mary O'Farrell)*, Frank Newburg *(G. W. Bronson)*.

Action drama. Terry O'Farrell pulls off several rescues in the course of the plot, whose locale is a steel mill, and Ann McGreagor uses her common sense to expose the villain's trickery and save the day for her sweetheart. *Steel industry.*

THE FIRE BRIDE (Entertainment Series) **F2.1766**

Wid Gunning, Inc. *Dist* R-C Pictures. Mar **1922** [c18 Mar 1922; LP18310]. Si; b&w. 35mm. 5 reels, 4,928 ft.

Prod W. F. Alder, S. M. Unander. *Dir* Arthur Rosson. *Story* W. F. Alder. *Photog* Arthur Ross.

Cast: Ruth Renick *(Lois Markham)*, Edward Hearn *(Steve Maitland)*, Walt Whitman *(Captain Markham)*, Fred Stanton *(Captain Blackton)*, Paki *(Atel)*, Taura *(Kalom)*.

Adventure melodrama. Captain Markham charters the boat of the evil Captain Blackton to search for a treasure he once buried on a South Sea island. Accompanying him are his daughter, Lois, and first mate Steve Maitland. They arrive at the island in time to witness a native ceremony of choosing the Fire Bride for sacrifice to the gods. Blackton accompanies Markham to the island to search for the gold, kills him when they find it, and reports to Lois and Steve that they were attacked by natives. Blackton goes ashore to bury Markham but incurs the natives' wrath when he dishonors Atel, the Fire Bride. Steve warns Blackton but, when he learns that the villain caused the death of his sister, helps the natives subdue him. *Murder. Rites and ceremonies. Treasure. Tahiti. South Sea Islands.*

Note: Filmed in Tahiti.

THE FIRE BRIGADE **F2.1767**

Metro-Goldwyn-Mayer Pictures. 20 Dec **1926** [New York premiere; released 12 Feb 1927; c10 Jan 1927; LP23573]. Si; b&w with col sequences (Technicolor). 35mm. 9 reels, 8,716 ft. [Copyrighted as 10 reels.]

Dir William Nigh. *Titl* Lotta Woods. *Adapt* Robert N. Lee. *Photog* John Arnold. *Sets* Cedric Gibbons, Paul Crawley. *Film Ed* Harry L. Decker. *Wardrobe* Kathleen Kay, Maude Marsh, André-ani.

Cast: May McAvoy *(Helen Corwin)*, Charles Ray *(Terry O'Neil)*, Holmes Herbert *(James Corwin)*, Tom O'Brien *(Joe O'Neil)*, Eugenie Besserer *(Mrs. O'Neil)*, Warner P. Richmond *(Jim O'Neil)*, Bert Woodruff *(Captain O'Neil)*, Vivia Ogden *(Bridget)*, De Witt Jennings *(Fire Chief Wallace)*, Dan Mason *(Peg Leg Murphy)*, Erwin Connelly *(Thomas Wainright)*.

Melodrama. Source: Kate Corbaley, "The Fire Brigade" (publication undetermined). Retired fire captain Grandpop O'Neil conducts a rookie school, which includes his grandson Terry. The blaze in which Jim O'Neil,

Terry's father, loses his life leads to an investigation and the discovery by Fire Chief Wallace that the building was flimsily erected by Corwin, a contractor favored in bidding for city jobs. When he protests the contractor's working on a new orphanage, the chief is removed by the town political boss. Terry discovers that the father of the girl he loves, Helen Corwin, is guilty of conspiring with the town boss and denounces him. A gigantic fire sweeps the city, and Terry is called into action with the antiquated horse-drawn equipment. He makes a valiant rescue of a child from a burning roof, though his brother, Joe, dies from the flames. *Firemen. Contractors. Political bosses. Family life. Fires.*

THE FIRE CAT **F2.1768**

Universal Film Manufacturing Co. Feb **1921** [cl Feb 1921; LP16089]. Si; b&w. 35mm. 5 reels, 4,785 ft.

Pres by Carl Laemmle. *Dir-Story* Norman Dawn. *Scen* Philip Hurn. *Photog* Thomas Rae.

Cast: Edith Roberts *(Dulce)*, Walter Long *(Gringo Burke)*, William Eagle Eye *(Cholo Pete)*, Olga D. Mojean *(Mother Alvarez)*, Beatrice Dominguez *(Margarita)*, Arthur Jasmine *(Pancho)*, Wallace MacDonald *(David Ross)*.

Melodrama. Dulce, last of the Alvarez family, lives with her mother in the Andes and is worshipped by Pancho, a halfcaste. Gringo Burke, an American renegade, robs and kills her mother. Accusing Pancho of cowardice, Dulce vows to seek revenge. As a cafe dancer she meets Burke, and David Ross, an American derelict, defends her against him. The eruption of Cotopaxi finishes off Burke and his gang, who have come to steal ore in the mines, and Dulce saves Ross from the burning lava. *Halfcastes. Dancers. Traitors. Revenge. Volcanoes. Andes. Cotopaxi.*

THE FIRE EATER (Universal Special) **F2.1769**

Universal Film Manufacturing Co. 24 Dec **1921** [c16 Dec 1921; LP17373]. Si; b&w. 35mm. 5 reels, 4,341 ft.

Pres by Carl Laemmle. *Dir* Reaves Eason. *Scen* Harvey Gates. *Photog* Alfred H. Lathem.

Cast: Hoot Gibson *(Bob Corey)*, Louise Lorraine *(Martha McCarthy)*, Walter Perry *(Jim O'Neil)*, Tom Lingham *(Jacob Lemar)*, Fred Lancaster *(Wolf Roselli)*, Carmen Phillips *(Marie Roselli)*, George Berrell *(Dad McCarthy)*, W. Bradley Ward *(Marty Frame)*, George A. Williams *(Mort Frame)*.

Western melodrama. Source: Ralph Cummins, "The Badge of Fighting Hearts," in *Short Stories* (96:13–153, Jul 1921). "Smilin" Bob Corey and his partner Jim O'Neil, forest rangers, are sent to make a peaceful "penetration" into Paradise Valley, which is to be incorporated into a national park. They meet a sullen reception from the people but manage to obtain supplies from Marie Roselli, an Italian girl whose brother, Wolf, owns a cattle ranch. Corey rescues Martha McCarthy from the advances of Lemar, who, he learns, is cutting timber illegally; Corey falls in love with Martha but is dismissed from the house by her father when he discovers that Bob is a forest ranger. Lemar tries to frame Corey for the murder of Wolf and kidnaps Martha. Bob rescues her from the path of a raging forest fire, and they are both rescued by the rangers. *Forest rangers. Ranchers. Italians. Land rights. Forest fires. National parks.*

THE FIRE PATROL **F2.1770**

Hunt Stromberg Productions. *Dist* Chadwick Pictures. 15 Aug or 15 Sep **1924** [cl Aug 1924; LP20493]. Si; b&w. 35mm. 7 reels, 6,600 ft.

Dir Hunt Stromberg. *Scen* Garrett Elsden Fort. *Photog* Silvano Balboni.

Cast: Anna Q. Nilsson *(Mary Ferguson)*, William Jeffries *(Capt. John Ferguson, prolog)*, Spottiswoode Aitken *(Capt. John Ferguson, later)*, Jack Richardson *("Butch" Anderson)*, Madge Bellamy *(Molly Thatcher)*, Helen Jerome Eddy *(Emma Thatcher)*, Dicky Brandon *(Colin Ferguson, prolog)*, Johnny Harron *(Colin Ferguson, later)*, Gale Henry *(Alice Masters)*, Frances Ross *(village belle)*, Chester Conklin, Bull Montana *(firemen)*, Charlie Murray.

Melodrama. Source: James W. Harkins, Jr., and Edwin Barbour, *The Fire Patrol* (a play; Worcester, 1891). In the midst of a romantic entanglement between Colin and Molly Thatcher, Capt. John Ferguson—blinded and cast adrift from his wife by sea pirate "Butch" Anderson 18 years earlier—stumbles on the villain when he is rescued from a wrecked ship by the fire patrol and takes his vengeance. *Blindness. Seafaring life. Revenge. Fireboats.*

THE FIREBRAND **F2.1771**

Phil Goldstone Productions. 15 Dec **1922.** Si; b&w. 35mm. 5 reels.

Dir Alvin J. Neitz. *Photog* Edgar Lyons.

Cast: Franklyn Farnum *(Bill Holt)*, Ruth Langdon *(Alice Acker)*, Fred Gamble *(Judd Acker)*, Pat Harmon *(Hank Potter)*, William Lester *(Sheriff Harding)*, Tex Keith *(Buck Knowles)*.

Western melodrama. Nester Bill Holt is beset from all sides, but he manages to maintain his hold on his small homestead. Meanwhile, he helps the sheriff round up a gang of rustlers. Bill has his final triumph when he informs his neighbor and chief opponent, Judd Acker, that he has been married to Acker's daughter, Alice, for a year. *Squatters. Homesteaders. Ranchers. Sheriffs. Rustlers.*

FIREBRAND JORDAN **F2.1772**

National Players. *Dist* Big 4 Film Corp. 28 Jan **1930.** Sd (Cinephone); b&w. 35mm. 6 reels, 5,400 ft.

Supv Henry Taylor. *Dir* Alvin J. Neitz. *Story-Scen-Dial* Carl Krusada. *Photog* William Nobles. *Sd* William Garrity.

Cast: Lane Chandler *(Firebrand Jordan)*, Aline Goodwin *(Joan Howe)*, Yakima Canutt *(Red Carson)*, Sheldon Lewis *(David Hampton)*, Marguerite Ainslee *(Peggy Howe)*, Tom London *(Ed Burns)*, Lew Meehan *(Spike)*, Frank Yaconelli *(Tony)*, Alfred Hewston *(Ah Sing)*, Fred Harvey *(Judd Howe)*, Cliff Lyons *(Pete)*.

Western melodrama. Assigned to help the sheriff find a gang of counterfeiters, Firebrand Jordan happens upon the difficulties of Joan and Peggy Howe, whose father, Judd, has disappeared from their ranch. David Hampton, who always seems to have a lot of money, very smoothly suggests to Joan that he will forget Judd's debts in return for her favors, and Joan gladly accepts this condition. After numerous changes in Firebrand's fortunes, he finally discovers Hampton to be the source of the counterfeit money and the man responsible for Judd Howe's abduction. *Sisters. Counterfeiters. Ranchers. Sheriffs. Abduction. Debt.*

FIREMAN, SAVE MY CHILD **F2.1773**

Paramount Famous Lasky Corp. 1 Aug **1927** [cl Aug 1927; LP24266]. Si; b&w. 35mm. 6 reels, 5,399 ft.

Pres by Adolph Zukor, Jesse L. Lasky. *Assoc Prod* B. P. Schulberg. *Dir* Edward Sutherland. *Story-Screenplay* Monty Brice, Tom Geraghty. *Photog* H. Kinley Martin.

Cast: Wallace Beery *(Elmer)*, Raymond Hatton *(Sam)*, Josephine Dunn *(Dora Dumston)*, Tom Kennedy *(Captain Kennedy)*, Walter Goss *(Walter)*, Joseph Girard *(Chief Dumston)*.

Farce. "Elmer and Sam, childhood chums, meet later in life and by a trick of fate become members of the fire department. They manage to rescue a parrot, prized possession of the Chief's daughter, Dora, and later, when an alarm rings for a second fire in the Chief's home, they succeed in effecting the rescue of a figure wrapped in a blanket—Captain Kennedy." (*Moving Picture World,* 10 Dec 1927, p41.) *Firemen. Children. Fires. Parrots.*

FIRES OF YOUTH **F2.1774**

Ed Schlortzer. *Dist* Reputable Pictures. 28 Mar **1924** [New York State license]. Si; b&w. 35mm. 5 reels, 4,557 ft.

Cast: Ted Edwards, Billie Rhodes.

Comedy-drama(?). No information about the nature of this film has been found.

Note: Ed Schlortzer is listed as "manufacturer" on New York State license application.

THE FIRST AUTO **F2.1775**

Warner Brothers Pictures. 27 Jun **1927** [New York premiere; released 18 Sep; c26 May 1927; LP24006]. Si; b&w. 35mm. 7 reels, 6,767 ft.

Dir Roy Del Ruth. *Scen* Anthony Coldewey. *Titl* Jack Jarmuth. *Story* Darryl Francis Zanuck. *Camera* David Abel. *Asst Dir* Ross Lederman.

Cast: Barney Oldfield *(himself, The Master Driver)*, Patsy Ruth Miller *(Rose Robbins)*, Charles Emmett Mack *(Bob Armstrong)*, Russell Simpson *(Hank Armstrong)*, Frank Campeau *(Mayor Jim Robbins)*, William Demarest *(Dave Doolittle)*, Paul Kruger *(Steve Bentley)*, Gibson Gowland *(The Blacksmith)*, E. H. Calvert *(Elmer Hays, The Inventor)*, Douglas Gerrard *(Banker Stebbins)*.

Comedy-drama. Hank Armstrong, an essentially old-fashioned man, is a lover of horses and resents the new invention of the "horseless carriage" for which his son, Bob, has a particular fondness. When his son takes an interest in automobile racing, Hank disowns him and tinkers with a racing car so that it will explode, not knowing his son is to be the driver. Although Bob is not seriously hurt, Hank is cured of his hatred of automobiles, while Bob wins the love of Rose, the girl of his dreams. *Horseless carriages. Automobile racing. Filial relations. Courtship. Horses.*

THE FIRST BORN **F2.1776**

Hayakawa Feature Play Co. *Dist* Robertson-Cole Distributing Corp. 30 Jan **1921** [c22 Nov 1920, 30 Jan 1921; LU15817, LU16178]. Si; b&w. 35mm. 5 or 6 reels.

Dir Colin Campbell. *Scen* Fred Stowers. *Photog* Frank D. Williams.

Cast: Sessue Hayakawa *(Chan Wang)*, Helen Jerome Eddy *(Loey Tsing)*, "Sonny Boy" Warde *(Chan Toy)*, Goro Kino *(Man Low Tek)*, Marie Pavis *(Chan Lee)*, Wilson Hummel *(Kuey Lar)*, Frank M. Seki *(Hop Lee)*.

Romantic melodrama. Source: Francis Powers, *The First Born; a Chinese Drama in One Act* (New York production: 5 Oct 1897). Chan Wang, boatman on the Hoang-Ho, is forced to marry Chan Lee, when his beloved, Loey Tsing, is sold to Kuey Lar, a rich merchant in San Francisco. Soon a son, Chan Toy, is born to Chan Lee. In San Francisco Wang meets his former sweetheart and arouses the jealousy of her owner, who entices Chan's wife and son to his home. There the child falls from a window and is killed. In revenge, Wang kills the abductor of his former love and the destroyer of his firstborn; then, in final submission, he returns to his native land with Loey Tsing. *Boatmen. Merchants. China. Yellow River. San Francisco.*

THE FIRST DEGREE **F2.1777**

Universal Pictures. 30 Jan **1923** [New York premiere; released 5 Feb; c24 Jan 1923; LP18617]. Si; b&w. 35mm. 5 reels, 4,395 ft.

Pres by Carl Laemmle. *Dir* Edward Sedgwick. *Scen* George Randolph Chester. *Photog* Benjamin Kline.

Cast: Frank Mayo *(Sam Bass)*, Sylvia Breamer *(Mary)*, Philo McCullough *(Will Bass)*, George A. Williams *(sheriff)*, Harry Carter *(district attorney)*.

Rural melodrama. Source: George Patullo, "The Summons," in *Saturday Evening Post* (186:10, 14 Feb 1914). Sam Bass receives a summons to testify before a grand jury, and not realizing that the matter concerns sheep-stealing he assumes it to concern the murder of his brother, Will. Conscience-stricken, Sam relates a long tale about how Will had framed him for bank robbery, then blackmailed him. Sam further confesses that he killed Will in a fight. However, the jury is sympathetic and refuses to indict Sam. The next witness is Will, very much alive, who is eventually convicted of both sheep-stealing and blackmail. *Brothers. Frameup. Grand juries. Murder. Blackmail. Sheep.*

THE FIRST KISS **F2.1778**

Paramount Famous Lasky Corp. 25 Aug **1928** [c25 Aug 1928; LP25566]. Si; b&w. 35mm. 6 reels, 6,134 ft.

Pres by Adolph Zukor, Jesse L. Lasky. *Dir* Rowland V. Lee. *Titl* Tom Reed. *Adapt* John Farrow. *Photog* Alfred Gilks.

Cast: Fay Wray *(Anna Lee)*, Gary Cooper *(Mulligan Talbot)*, Lane Chandler *(William Talbot)*, Leslie Fenton *(Carol Talbot)*, Paul Fix *(Ezra Talbot)*, Malcolm Williams *("Pap")*, Monroe Owsley *(other suitor)*.

Drama. Source: Tristram Tupper, "Four Brothers," in *Saturday Evening Post* (200:8–10, 7 Apr 1928). The Talbots, formerly one of the Eastern Shore's first families, have gone to seed: Pap is a drunk, soddenly decaying in his ruined ancestral home, and three of his sons (William, Carol, and Ezra) are lazy, shiftless young men. Mulligan, Pap's second son who supports the entire family by oyster fishing, falls in love with wealthy Anna Lee, but when he first kisses her, she calls him "white trash." Pap dies, and Mulligan, determined that the Talbot name will again be a respected one, turns to robbing ships in the Chesapeake Bay in order to finance educations for his three brothers. Six years pass: William becomes a minister, Carol a lawyer, and Ezra a doctor. Mulligan then sells a ship that he built with his own hands and pays back all those he robbed, thereby bringing about his own arrest. Placed on trial for piracy, Anna and his brothers come to his defense; found guilty, he is paroled in Anna's care. *Brothers. Fishermen. Clergymen. Lawyers. Physicians. Fatherhood. Piracy. Social classes. Family life. Alcoholism. Maryland—Eastern Shore. Chesapeake Bay.*

FIRST LOVE **F2.1779**

Realart Pictures. *Dist* Paramount Pictures. Dec **1921** [c22 Nov 1921; LP17229]. Si; b&w. 35mm. 5 reels, 4,862 ft.

Dir Maurice Campbell. *Scen* Percy Heath, Aubrey Stauffer. *Story* Sonya Levien. *Photog* H. Kinley Martin.

Cast: Constance Binney *(Kathleen O'Donnell)*, Warner Baxter *(Donald Holliday)*, George Webb *(Harry Stanton)*, Betty Schade *(Yvette De Vonne)*, George Hernandez *(Tad O'Donnell)*, Fannie Midgley *(Mrs. O'Donnell)*, Edward Jobson *(Peter Holliday)*, Agnes Adams *(icecream-cone girl)*, Maxine Elliott Hicks *(Speeder)*, Dorothy Gordon *(Elsie Edwards)*.

Romantic comedy. Kathleen O'Donnell, a young factory worker, falls in love with Harry Stanton, an ambulance driver who convinces her that he is a struggling medical student. She leaves home when her father, who knows something of Stanton's character, forbids her to invite him to the house. She takes up residence in a boardinghouse and gives Harry her spare wages to buy schoolbooks. Donald Holliday, the factory owner, realizing her folly and being in love with her himself, tries to warn her about Harry, but she resents his interference and goes to work in a restaurant where she is completely disillusioned when Harry brings another girl to dinner. As a result she falls ill, and during her convalescence she finds a worthy affection in Holliday. *Ambulance drivers. Students. Waitresses. Courtship. Duplicity. Factories.*

Note: Working title: *The Heart of Youth.* New York State license application title: *Her First Love.*

THE FIRST NIGHT **F2.1780**

Tiffany Productions. 1 Jan **1927** [c3 Feb 1927; LP23630]. Si; b&w. 35mm. 6 reels, 5,500 ft.

Dir Richard Thorpe. *Cont* Esther Shulkin. *Story* Frederica Sagor. *Photog* Milton Moore, Mack Stengler. *Art Dir* Edwin B. Willis. *Film Ed* James C. McKay.

Cast: Bert Lytell *(Dr. Richard Bard)*, Dorothy Devore *(Doris Frazer)*, Harry Myers *(hotel detective)*, Frederic Kovert *(Mimi/Jack White)*, Walter Hiers *(Mr. Cleveland)*, Lila Leslie *(Mrs. Cleveland)*, James Mack *(The Drunk)*, Hazel Keener *(Miss Leeds)*, Joan Standing *(Mrs. Miller)*.

Bedroom farce. Following the announcement of her engagement to Dr. Richard Bard, Doris Frazer receives a letter from Jack White, to whom she was formerly engaged, threatening to prevent her marriage; and Mimi, an adventuress, calls on Dr. Bard with proof that he married her in France. Consequently, Doris and Richard decide to elope and are married. Complications ensue when Mrs. Cleveland, one of the doctor's patients, feigns sickness, and when Mimi arrives to claim the doctor as her husband. It is revealed, however, that Mimi is actually Jack White, Doris' ex-fiancé, in female attire. Doris and Dick admit their former affairs and swear their mutual devotion. *Physicians. Adventuresses. Elopement. Female impersonation.*

THE FIRST NOTCH *see* **NOTCH NUMBER ONE**

THE FIRST WOMAN **F2.1781**

D. & M. Films. *Dist* R-C Pictures. 30 Apr **1922** [c25 Apr 1922; LP17780]. Si; b&w. 35mm. 5 reels, 4,950 ft.

Dir-Writ Glen Lyons. *Photog* Alvin Knechtel.

Cast: Percy Marmont *(Paul Marsh)*, Lloyd Hammond *(Jack Gordon)*, Donald Blakemore *(Tom Markham)*, Oliver La Baddie *(Professor Bazzufi)*, Wallace Baker *(Eloysius Bangs)*, Andrew Hicks *(Mr. Sham)*, J. A. West *(Judge Stone)*, Joseph G. Portell *(Jacquis)*, Hubert La Baddie *(Murat)*, Corydon W. Hatt *(The Priest)*, Walter Orr *(James)*, Ernest Blasdell *(detective)*, Stephen Geitz *(police sergeant)*, Mrs. J. Montgomery *(Mrs. Giggleton)*, Betty Hall *(Marie)*, Flora Arline Arle *(Elsa)*, Mildred Harris *(The Girl)*.

Melodrama. Playwright Paul Marsh is displeased with the selection (by his manager, Tom Markham) of Billie Mayo for the leading lady in his new play. Returning home, he finds a strange girl playing the violin in his apartment, and when a detective comes to arrest her, she persuades Marsh and his sister to protect her. She confides that she has come from Canada to avenge the betrayal of her sister and the murder of her father. When Paul's sister, Elsa, finds the girl in her fiancé's arms, there is a scene, and the girl leaves. Paul later receives a note stating that Jack (Elsa's fiancé) is the man she is seeking and that she is now about to kill him; Paul and Elsa arrive at Jack's home just in time to see her stab him; suddenly Jack begins laughing and Elsa embraces the girl, who is actually Billie Mayo. Billie has staged a role to prove her dramatic abilities to Paul. He forgives her for the hoax and becomes engaged to her. *Playwrights. Actors. Brother-sister relationship. Hoaxes.*

THE FIRST YEAR **F2.1782**

Fox Film Corp. 24 Jan **1926** [c10 Jan 1926; LP22272]. Si; b&w. 35mm. 6 reels, 6,038 ft.

Pres by William Fox. *Dir* Frank Borzage. *Scen* Frances Marion. *Photog* Chester Lyons. *Asst Dir* Bunny Dunn.

Cast: Matt Moore *(Tom Tucker)*, Kathryn Perry *(Grace Livingston)*, John Patrick *(Dick Loring)*, Frank Currier *(Dr. Livingston)*, Frank Cooley *(Mr. Livingston)*, Virginia Madison *(Mrs. Livingston)*, Carolynne Snowden *(Hattie)*, J. Farrell MacDonald *(Mr. Barstow)*.

Comedy. Source: Frank Craven, *The First Year, a Comic Tragedy of Married Life, in Three Acts* (New York, c1921). Tom Tucker, an easygoing, bashful type, marries Grace Livingston and moves with her to a small country town. During the first year of their marriage, Grace, who is more ambitious for Tom than he is for himself, becomes discontented and restless. Tom, who finally works up a deal with a railroad company from which he stands to make a lot of money, invites the principals in the deal, Mr. and Mrs. Barstow, to dinner. The dinner is a disaster: the maid is inexperienced and clumsy; Grace lets slip an unfortunate remark; and Dick Loring, once a rival for Grace's love, drops in unexpectedly. When Grace realizes that Tom may spoil the deal, she goes to her mother's house. While she is gone, Tom signs the final papers and goes after Grace. They are reconciled, and Tom learns that she is going to have a baby. *Businessmen. Newlyweds. Marriage. Smalltown life. Railroads.*

FIVE AND TEN CENT ANNIE **F2.1783**

Warner Brothers Pictures. 26 May **1928** [c24 May 1928; LP25292]. Sd eff (Vitaphone); b&w. 35mm. 5 reels, 4,914 ft. [Copyrighted as 6 reels.]

Dir Roy Del Ruth. *Scen* Charles R. Condon, Robert Lord. *Titl* Joe Jackson. *Story* Leon Zurade. *Photog* Norbert Brodin. *Film Ed* Ralph Dawson. *Asst Dir* Joe Barry.

Cast: Louise Fazenda *(Annie)*, Clyde Cook *(Elmer Peck)*, William Demarest *(Briggs)*, Gertrude Astor *(Blonde)*, Tom Ricketts *(Adam Peck)*, Douglas Gerrard *(judge)*, André Beranger *(orchestra leader)*, Eddie Haffner *(midget)*, Flora Finch, Sunshine Hart, Bill Franey *(guests)*.

Slapstick comedy. Elmer Peck, a streetcleaner who loves Annie, salesgirl in a five-and-ten-cent store, inherits a large fortune from an eccentric uncle. In a special provision, the uncle requests that the fortune revert to Briggs, his faithful servant, in the event that Peck dies without marrying. Briggs shanghais Peck to prevent his marriage to Annie, but she thwarts Briggs by slipping aboard as a crewman, then rescues Peck with the aid of the Coast Guard. *Streetcleaners. Salesclerks. Valets. Inheritance. Disguise. Shanghaiing. Five-and-ten-cent stores. United States Coast Guard.*

FIVE DAYS TO LIVE **F2.1784**

R-C Pictures. 8 Jan **1922** [c8 Jan 1922; LP17455]. Si; b&w. 35mm. 6 reels, 5,210 ft.

Dir Norman Dawn. *Adapt* Eve Unsell, Garrett Elsden Fort.

Cast: Sessue Hayakawa *(Tai Leung)*, Tsuru Aoki *(Ko Ai)*, Goro Kino *(Chong Wo)*, Misao Seki *(Li)*, Toyo Fujita *(Young Foo)*, George Kuwa *(Hop Sing)*.

Oriental melodrama. Source: Dorothy Goodfellow, "The Street of the Flying Dragon," in *Romance* (2:126–132, Sep 1920). Tai Leung, a dreamer and a carver of ivory images, falls in love with Ko Ai, who is overworked and mistreated by her foster father Chong Wo, a restaurant owner; and she becomes radiantly happy under the influence of Tai Leung's love. Determined to take her away from her life of drudgery, he wins the father's consent by promising a vast sum of money; Tai Leung learns that The Wolf, a pirate who has been sentenced to hang, will pay a substitute handsomely; and Tai Leung agrees to take his place. The marriage of the young couple follows, and Ko Ai is happy, ignorant of the terms of her husband's agreement. At the stipulated time, Tai Leung presents himself at the prison to be executed and learns that the convict has died and justice is satisfied. Returning to his wife, he finds that she has inhaled poisonous incense, but he is able to revive her and they are happily united. *Sculptors. Poverty. Capital punishment. China.*

Note: Working title: *The Street of the Flying Dragon.*

THE FIVE DOLLAR BABY **F2.1785**

Metro Pictures. ca25 Jun **1922** [New York premiere; released 4 Sep; c29 Jul 1922; LP18123]. Si; b&w. 35mm. 6 reels, 5,990 ft.

Prod-Dir Harry Beaumont. *Scen* Rex Taylor. *Story* Irvin S. Cobb. *Photog* John Arnold. *Art & Tech Dir* A. F. Mantz.

Cast: Viola Dana *(Ruth)*, Ralph Lewis *(Ben Shapinsky)*, Otto Hoffman *(The Solitary Kid)*, John Harron *(Larry Donovan)*, Tom McGuire *(Mr. Donovan)*, Arthur Rankin *(Bernie Riskin)*, Marjorie Maurice *(Esther Block)*, Ernst Pasque *(Isadore)*.

Comedy-drama. The Solitary Kid, a tramp, finds a waif, Ruth, on a doorstep with a note promising a rich reward when the child becomes 18. He "hocks" her for $5 with a Jewish pawnbroker, who rears her as his own daughter. When she becomes 18, The Solitary Kid learns that his reward is one that he will receive in heaven and tries to blackmail the pawnbroker. Ruth overhears the proposition and informs the police, The Solitary Kid is arrested, and Ruth marries an Irish youth who was her childhood sweetheart. *Jews. Irish. Waifs. Pawnbrokers. Blackmail.*

FIVE KISSES *see* **THE AFFAIRS OF ANATOL**

FIVE-THOUSAND-DOLLAR REWARD *see* **DAREDEVIL'S REWARD**

THE FLAME OF LIFE (Universal-Jewel) **F2.1786**

Universal Pictures. 5 Feb **1923** [c5 Jan 1923; LP18561]. Si; b&w. 35mm. 7 reels, 5,780 ft.

Pres by Carl Laemmle. *Dir* Hobart Henley. *Scen* Elliott J. Clawson. *Photog* Virgil Miller.

Cast: Priscilla Dean *(Joan Lowrie)*, Robert Ellis *(Fergus Derrick)*, Kathryn McGuire *(Alice Barholm)*, Wallace Beery *(Dan Lowrie)*, Fred Kohler *(Spring)*, Beatrice Burnham *(Liz)*, Emmett King *(Barholm)*, Frankie Lee *(Jud)*, Grace De Garro *(Mag)*, Dorothy Hagan *(Baroness)*, Evelyn McCoy *(Fauntleroy)*.

Melodrama. Source: Frances Hodgson Burnett, *That Lass o' Lowrie's* (London, 1877). Joan Lowrie and her brutal father, Dan, labor in the English coal mines of the 1870's. Fergus Derrick, a new over-man, attempts to make his workers' lives more bearable but incurs Lowrie's wrath when he fires him for smoking in the mine. Bent on vengeance, Lowrie is beaten when he picks a fight with Fergus, then defiantly smokes in a mine tunnel. There is an explosion, Joan rescues Fergus, and their love triumphs over their class barriers. *Coal mining. Safety—Industrial. Mine disasters. Social classes. Smoking. England.*

Note: Also advertised in 1922 under its working title, *That Lass o' Lowrie's.*

FLAME OF THE ARGENTINE **F2.1787**

R-C Pictures. *Dist* Film Booking Offices of America. 11 Jul **1926** [c11 Jul 1926; LP22891]. Si; b&w. 35mm. 5 reels, 5,004 ft.

Pres by Joseph P. Kennedy. *Dir* Edward Dillon. *Cont* Ewart Adamson. *Story* Burke Jenkins, Krag Johnson. *Camera* Roy Klaffki. *Asst Dir* Doran Cox.

Cast: Evelyn Brent *(Inez Remírez)*, Orville Caldwell *(Dan Prescott)*, Frank Leigh *(Emilio Tovar)*, Dan Makarenko *(Marsini)*, Rosita Marstini *(Madame Marsini)*, Evelyn Selbie *(Nana)*, Florence Turner *(Doña Aguila)*.

Action melodrama. Doña Aguila, owner of a vast ranch and a valuable emerald mine in the Argentine, longs for her lost daughter, Conchita, and is victimized by her manager, Emilio Tovar, who is secretly stealing gems. Tovar goes to New Orleans to dispose of some emeralds, and persuading cabaret pianist Inez Remírez to impersonate the dead daughter, he schemes to divide her inheritance. Dan Prescott, a stranger, forces himself into their confidence and accompanies the couple on their return voyage. Doña Aguila's kindness causes Inez to repent and to refuse to carry out the plan; Tovar and his men attack the rancho to acquire an emerald necklace, and Inez rides for aid. Prescott, revealing himself to be an insurance agent, wins the heart of Inez, and Doña Aguila adopts her as her legal daughter. *Ranchers. Thieves. Pianists. Insurance agents. Impersonation. Emeralds. Argentina. New Orleans.*

THE FLAME OF THE YUKON (Reissue) **F2.1788**

Kay-Bee Pictures. *Dist* Tri-Stone Pictures. **1923.** Si; b&w. 35mm. 5 reels.

Note: A "re-edited and re-titled" Dorothy Dalton film originally released by Triangle Film Corp. on 1 Jul 1917 (c1 Jul 1917; LP11889).

THE FLAME OF THE YUKON **F2.1789**

Metropolitan Pictures Corp. of California. *Dist* Producers Distributing Corp. 30 Aug **1926** [c22 Jun 1926; LP22841]. Si; b&w. 35mm. 6 reels, 5,800 ft.

Dir George Melford. *Scen* Will M. Ritchey. *Adapt* Finis Fox. *Story* Monte Katterjohn. *Photog* David Kesson.

Cast: Seena Owen *(The Flame)*, Arnold Gray *(George Fowler)*, Matthew Betz *(Black Jack Hovey)*, Jack McDonald *(Sour Dough Joe)*, Vadim Uraneff *(Solo Jim)*, Winifred Greenwood *(Dolly)*.

Melodrama. During the gold rush in Alaska, Flame, a pretty dancing girl, is the chief attraction at a popular saloon in Hope City and is jealously guarded by Black Jack Hovey, the proprietor. George Fowler, a tenderfoot from the States, and Sour Dough Joe visit the saloon, and Joe warns Fowler to conceal a bulging money belt; but Black Jack, seeing the belt, directs Flame to acquire it at first opportunity. Finding Fowler broke, she reviles him, but he promises to return with a rich strike. Later, Flame discovers he has taken a job washing windows and develops an interest in him, and when he departs for the gold fields, she announces her intention of living straight. Fowler strikes it rich but is robbed in a faro game by Black Jack. Flame wins a large sum with money borrowed from Sour Dough, and when Black Jack tries to deprive her of the money, Fowler fights with him in her behalf. Flame mistakenly believes that Fowler is married but is relieved to find herself in error, and they are happily united. *Dancehall girls. Saloon keepers. Reformation. Gambling. Gold rushes. Alaska. Yukon.*

FLAMES **F2.1790**

Associated Exhibitors. 15 Sep **1926** [c17 May 1926; LU22727]. Si; b&w. 35mm. 6 reels, 5,888 ft.

Dir Lewis H. Moomaw. *Story-Scen* Alfred A. Cohn. *Photog* King Gray, Herbert H. Brownell. *Tech Dir* Lee Lawson. *Film Ed* Frank Lawrence. *Asst Dir* Eddie Sowders.

Cast: Eugene O'Brien *(Herbert Landis)*, Virginia Valli *(Anne Travers)*, Jean Hersholt *(Ole Bergson)*, Bryant Washburn *(Hilary Fenton)*, Cissy Fitzgerald *(Mrs. Edgerton)*, George Nichols *(James Travers)*, Boris Karloff *(Blackie Blanchette)*.

Melodrama. Herbert Landis, who secretly loves Anne Travers, is sent by her father to supervise construction of a bridge in Oregon. Anne insists that Hilary Fenton, a society man, join the party, and as a result Landis broods in his cabin, which he shares with Ole Bergson, his foreman. Ole, who claims to know all about love, disguises himself as Blackie Blanchette, a well-known desperado, and kidnaps the girl, leaving a note urging Landis to "rescue" her; however, Ole is captured by the real Blackie. While a raging forest fire breaks out, Landis rides to the cabin and confronts Blackie; as the fire reaches the cabin, Blackie meets a fiery death while Landis and Anne stagger through the flames to the river. The other suitor, finding country customs too rough, departs, leaving Anne to discover her true love. *Construction foremen. Desperadoes. Courtship. Disguise. Bridges. Oregon. Forest fires.*

FLAMES OF DESIRE **F2.1791**

Fox Film Corp. 30 Nov **1924** [c2 Nov 1924; LP20763]. Si; b&w. 35mm. 6 reels, 5,439 ft.

Pres by William Fox. *Dir* Denison Clift. *Scen* Denison Clift, Reginald G. Fogwell. *Photog* Ernest G. Palmer.

Cast: Wyndham Standing *(Daniel Strathmore)*, Diana Miller *(Marion Vavasour)*, Richard Thorpe *(Dick Langton)*, Frank Leigh *(Ferand Vavasour)*, George K. Arthur *(Lionel Caryll)*, Jackie Saunders *(Viola Lee)*, Frances Beaumont *(Lucille Errol)*, Hayford Hobbs *(secretary)*, Charles Clary *(Clive Errol)*, Eugenia Gilbert *(Mrs. Courtney Ruhl)*.

Drama. Source: Ouida, *Strathmore* (a play; Philadelphia, 1866). "The locale is Washington and the central character, Daniel Strathmore, has wealth and influence. He forms an infatuation for a beautiful adventuress and when a friend interferes he fights him and the friend is accidentally killed. Strathmore takes care of the friend's daughter, who later falls in love with him. She forgives the past and they marry." (*Motion Picture News Booking Guide*, 8:30, Apr 1925.) *Adventuresses. Friendship. Marriage. Washington (District of Columbia).*

FLAMES OF PASSION **F2.1792**

Premium Picture Productions. *Dist* Independent Pictures. 1 Mar **1923.** Si; b&w. 35mm. 5 reels, 4,700 ft.

Dir H. G. Moody. *Story* George Hively. *Photog* H. C. Cook.

Cast: Frank Whitson *(John Markham)*, Al Ferguson *(Lew Harkness)*, George Larkin *(Grant Whitney)*, Frank Whitlock *(Brute Turner)*, Laura Anson *(Alys Markham)*, Ruth Stonehouse *(Jimmie)*, Karl Silvera *(Victor Lonsdale)*.

Northwest melodrama. Grant Whitney, manager of a lumber camp, discovers a plot to delay a shipment of logs. Lew Harkness, a foreman, is in league with a rival lumber company, and he is the cause of the delay. On his dismissal, Harkness causes trouble between Whitney and Brute Turner, the father of Jimmie, with whom Whitney is in love. Turner accuses Whitney of trifling with his daughter's affections, but Whitney proves his seriousness when he rescues both from a forest fire. *Fatherhood. Lumbering. Forest fires.*

FLAMES OF WRATH **F2.1793**

Western Film Producing Co. **1923.** Si; b&w. 35mm. 5 reels.

Scen Samuel Ellison.

Cast: Roxie Mankins *(Pauline Keith)*, John Burton *(William Jackson)*, Charles Pearson *(Guy Braxton)*, Anna Kelson *(Flora Fulton)*, John Lester Johnson *(Frank Keith)*, Frank Colbert *(C. Dates)*.

Melodrama. Pauline Keith, a young Negress who works as a stenographer for William Jackson, an unscrupulous lawyer, learns of his plan to steal a diamond of great value that is owned by Guy Braxton, a prosperous drygoods merchant. When he finds that several incriminating documents are missing, Jackson fires Pauline, and she immediately goes to work for Braxton and prevents the theft of the diamond. Jackson is later elected district attorney and orders the arrest of Braxton. Pauline obtains evidence of Braxton's innocence and saves him from a long prison term. *Stenographers. Lawyers. Merchants. District attorneys. Negro life. Trials. Documentation.*

FLAMING BARRIERS **F2.1794**

Famous Players–Lasky. *Dist* Paramount Pictures. 27 Jan **1924** [c16 Jan 1924; LP19838]. Si; b&w. 35mm. 6 reels, 5,821 ft.

Pres by Adolph Zukor, Jesse L. Lasky. *Dir* George Melford. *Adapt* Harvey Thew. *Story* Byron Morgan. *Photog* Charles G. Clarke.

Cast: Jacqueline Logan *(Jerry Malone)*, Antonio Moreno *(Sam Barton)*, Walter Hiers *(Henry Van Sickle)*, Charles Ogle *(Patrick Malone)*, Robert McKim *(Joseph Pickens)*, Luke Cosgrave *(Bill O'Halloran)*, Warren Rogers *(Mayor Steers)*, Claribel Campbell.

Melodrama. Patrick Malone, inventor of a fire-fighting apparatus, seeks financial aid from local banker Joseph Pickens, who, hoping to control the manufacture of these machines, sends for a man to assist him. Sam Barton arrives. He is impressed with Malone's machine, falls in love with Jerry, Malone's daughter, and refuses to enter into Pickens' scheme. During a visit of neighboring fire chiefs, a fire breaks out, and Sam and Jerry are able to prove the value of the apparatus by dousing a burning bridge, thereby saving the lives of hundreds of people. This act promotes the sale of a number of firetrucks and brings happiness to Malone, his daughter, and Sam. *Bankers. Inventors. Fire departments.*

THE FLAMING CRISIS **F2.1795**

Monarch Productions. *Dist* Mesco Production. 21 Aug **1924** [New York State license application]. Si; b&w. 35mm. 6 reels, 4,400 ft.

Prod Lawrence Goldman.

Cast: Calvin Nicholson, Dorothy Dunbar.

Western melodrama. A young Negro newspaperman is convicted of murder on circumstantial evidence and sentenced to prison. He escapes and makes his way to the southwestern cattle country, where he falls in love with Tex Miller, a beautiful cowgirl. Having rid the territory of an outlaw band, he gives himself up to the law, thinking he will be sent back to prison. He discovers, however, that the real murderer has confessed, and he returns to Tex and the country he has come to love. *Negroes. Reporters. Fugitives. Outlaws. Murder. Injustice. Circumstantial evidence.*

THE FLAMING FOREST **F2.1796**

Cosmopolitan Productions. *Dist* Metro-Goldwyn-Mayer Distributing Corp. 21 Nov **1926** [c29 Nov 1926; LP23376]. Si; b&w with col sequences (Technicolor). 35mm. 7 reels, 6,567 ft.

Dir Reginald Barker. *Scen* Waldemar Young. *Titl* Lotta Woods. *Photog* Percy Hilburn. *Sets* Cedric Gibbons, B. H. Martin. *Film Ed* Ben Lewis. *Asst Dir* Harry Schenck. *Prod Mgr* John Lynch. *Wardrobe* André-ani.

Cast: Antonio Moreno *(Sgt. David Carrigan)*, Renée Adorée *(Jeanne-Marie)*, Gardner James *(Roger Audemard)*, William Austin *(Alfred Wimbledon)*, Tom O'Brien *(Mike)*, Emile Chautard *(André Audemard)*, Oscar Beregi *(Jules Lagarre)*, Clarence Geldert *(Maj. Charles McVane)*, Frank Leigh *(Lupin)*, Charles Ogle *(Donald McTavish)*, Roy Coulson *(François)*, D'Arcy McCoy *(Bobbie)*, Claire McDowell *(Mrs. McTavish)*, Bert Roach *(Sloppy)*, Mary Jane Irving *(Ruth McTavish)*.

Northwest melodrama. Source: James Oliver Curwood, *The Flaming Forest, a Novel of the Canadian Northwest* (New York, 1921). Jules Lagarre, a halfbreed brigand, undertakes to dominate the Canadian Northwest with the aid of Indians and cutthroats. André Audemard, a trading post merchant, appeals to the government for help and is murdered by Lagarre's henchmen, Lupin and François, leaving his children, Jeanne-Marie and Roger. Lagarre attempts to establish himself as head of a provisional republic, but the Canadian government forms the Northwest Mounted Police to establish law and order. Jeanne-Marie persuades the settlers to remain, and she falls in love with Sergeant Carrigan. Roger murders Lupin and François in a rage, for the killing of his parents, and Carrigan comes to arrest him; as a result, Jeanne-Marie turns against him. Lagarre organizes an Indian attack on the post and orders the forest set afire to hem off the Mounted Police; however, the rescue is effected. Roger dies protecting Jeanne, and she is reconciled with Carrigan. *Bandits. Halfcastes. Murder. Courtship. Canadian Northwest. Montana. Northwest Mounted Police. Forest fires.*

Note: Exteriors filmed in Canada and Montana.

THE FLAMING FORTIES **F2.1797**

Stellar Productions. *Dist* Producers Distributing Corp. 21 Dec **1924** [c30 Dec 1924; LP20972]. Si; b&w. 35mm. 6 reels, 5,770 ft.

Pres by Hunt Stromberg. *Pers Supv* Hunt Stromberg. *Dir* Tom Forman. *Cont* Harvey Gates. *Story* Elliott J. Clawson. *Photog* Sol Polito. *Art Dir* Edward Withers. *Film Ed* Robert De Lacy.

Cast: Harry Carey *(Bill Jones, Tennessee's Pardner)*, William Norton Bailey *(Desparde)*, Jacqueline Gadsdon *(Sally)*, James Mason *(Jay Bird Charley)*, Frank Norcross *(Colonel Starbottle)*, Wilbur Higby *(The Sheriff)*.

Western melodrama. Source: Bret Harte, "Tennessee's Pardner," in *Booklovers Magazine* (Jul 1903). Bill Jones, who lives on the banks of the Sacramento River, saves Jack Desparde from drowning after Desparde jumps from the steamboat taking him to be hanged at Sandy Bar. Bill later helps the outlaw escape. When Sally Corbin, a beautiful southerner, arrives in Sandy Bar looking for her husband, she discovers that he is the man known as Desparde—and takes to drink. Bill's cabin is attacked by Indians, but he is saved from sure death by Desparde. Bill prevents Sally from running off with Jay Bird Charley, a cowardly bandit who once rode with Desparde. Riding into Sandy Bar, Desparde is surprised by the sheriff's men and barricades himself in the saloon. Bill again helps him to escape. The angry townspeople are about to hang Bill, when Desparde plunges his horse over an embankment, killing himself to save Bill. Bill and Sally look to each other for consolation and a brighter future together. *Southerners. Outlaws. Sheriffs. Bandits. Indians of North America. Lynching. Sacramento River.*

THE FLAMING FRONTIER (Universal-Jewel) **F2.1798**

Universal Pictures. 12 Sep **1926** [c13 Feb 1926; LP22401]. Si; b&w. 35mm. 9 reels, 8,828 ft.

Story-Dir Edward Sedgwick. *Scen* Edward J. Montagne, Charles Kenyon. *Adapt* Raymond L. Schrock. *Photog* Virgil Miller.

Cast: Hoot Gibson *(Bob Langdon)*, Anne Cornwall *(Betty Stanwood)*, Dustin Farnum *(General Custer)*, Ward Crane *(Sam Belden)*, Kathleen Key *(Lucretia)*, Eddie Gribbon *(Jonesy)*, Harry Todd *(California Joe)*, Harold Goodwin *(Lawrence Stanwood)*, George Fawcett *(Senator Stanwood)*, Noble Johnson *(Sitting Bull)*, Charles K. French *(Senator Hargess)*, William Steele *(Penfield)*, Walter Rodgers *(President Grant)*, Ed Wilson *(Grant's secretary)*, Joe Bonomo *(Rain in the Face)*.

Western epic. Through the influence of Senator Stanwood, Bob Langdon, a Pony Express rider, is admitted to West Point. Bob falls in love with the senator's daughter, Betty, and to protect the senator's son from a scandal involving a woman Bob assumes the blame himself. Thrown out of the academy, Bob returns to the command of General Custer. Custer is attacked at the Little Big Horn, and Bob rides for help. Bob later brings Belden, a crooked Indian agent, before the bar of justice and, his reputation cleared, returns to the Military Academy. *Indians of North America. Indian agents. Pony Express. Little Big Horn. Ulysses Simpson Grant. George Armstrong Custer. Sitting Bull. United States Military Academy. United States Congress.*

FLAMING FURY **F2.1799**

R-C Pictures. *Dist* Film Booking Offices of America. 5 Dec **1926** [c5 Dec 1926; LP23416]. Si; b&w. 35mm. 5 reels, 4,464 ft.

Pres by Joseph P. Kennedy. *Dir* James P. Hogan. *Scen* Ewart Adamson. *Photog* Joe Walker. *Asst Dir* John Burch.

Cast: Ranger *(himself, a dog)*, Charles Delaney *(Dan Duval)*, Betty May *(Jeanette Duval)*, Boris Karloff *(Gaspard)*, Eddie Chandler *(Bethune)*.

Melodrama. Source: Ewart Adamson, "The Scourge of Fate" (publication undetermined). Dan Duval, who lives in the north woods with his wife, Jeanette, is plotted against by Bethune and Gaspard, the former a disappointed suitor of Jeanette. Ranger, Dan's dog, attacks Gaspard when he finds him hiding, and Dan mistakenly considers the attack unwarranted and drives Ranger into the woods, where he earns the reputation of "killer." Later, Dan discovers Bethune's perfidy and moves to another district. Bethune and Gaspard unwittingly dynamite a cave where Ranger's mate and pups are hiding, and Ranger takes the one surviving pup to Dan's cabin, where he is adopted. When Jeanette becomes ill, Dan sends the pup with a note to the doctor; Bethune, crazed by Ranger's unremitting attacks, kills Gaspard and goes to the cabin. Ranger intercepts the puppy and delivers the note to the doctor; he returns in time to kill Bethune and save Jeanette. *Perfidy. Murder. Explosives. Dogs.*

FLAMING HEARTS **F2.1800**

Metropolitan Pictures. *Dist* East Coast Productions. 1 Nov **1922.** Si; b&w. 35mm. 5 reels.

Dir Clifford S. Elfelt.

Cast: J. B. Warner, Kathleen Myers, Alma Bennett, George Hernandez, Frankie Lee.

Western melodrama. "Jeff Hartman, society lap-dog, goes West to make a man of himself. En route aboard box-car [he] captures two tramps who have stolen payroll. Hands them over to sheriff and gets himself in solid. Tenderfoot develops after much adversity into cowboy. At county fair Hartman wins raffle, the reward being a kiss from Marion Barrows, the sheriff's daughter. Hartman, fearful of taking the privilege, flees. Sheriff and daughter angered by insult. Fair receipts missing. Suspicion centers on Hartman. Marion discovers Jeff in shack and at point of gun leads him to her father. Revealed that sheriff's little nephew has taken bag holding Fair's receipts to play with them. Jeff and Marion reunited." (*Motion Picture News Booking Guide,* 4:49, Apr 1923.) *Sheriffs. Cowboys. Manhood. Fairs.*

THE FLAMING HOUR **F2.1801**

Universal Pictures. 12 Dec **1922** [New York premiere; released 31 Dec; c5 Dec 1922; LP18462]. Si; b&w. 35mm. 5 reels, 4,508 ft.

Pres by Carl Laemmle. *Dir* Edward Sedgwick. *Scen* George Randolph Chester. *Story* Lillian Chester. *Photog* Ben Kline.

Cast: Frank Mayo *(Bruce Henderson)*, Helen Ferguson *(Lucille Danby)*, Melbourne MacDowell *(John Danby)*, Charles Clary *(Richard Mower)*, Albert MacQuarrie *(Jones)*, Tom Kennedy *(Ben)*.

Melodrama. Lucille Danby marries Bruce Henderson after her father, John Danby, fires him, but she leaves him when Bruce's quick temper flares at seeing her with his old rival, Richard Mower. Disconsolate yet determined to alert Danby to Mower's thievery, Bruce collects evidence while disguised as a bum. Mower discovers Bruce and shoots at him, thus causing a chain of explosions in the fireworks factory. Danby and his daughter are trapped until they are rescued by Bruce. *Fireworks. Disguise. Theft. Marriage.*

Note: Working title: *The Hot-head.*

FLAMING PASSION *see* **LUCRETIA LOMBARD**

FLAMING WATERS **F2.1802**

Associated Arts Corp. *Dist* Film Booking Offices of America. 13 Dec **1925** [c13 Dec 1925; LP22243]. Si; b&w. 35mm. 7 reels, 6,591 ft.

Dir F. Harmon Weight. *Cont* Frederick Myton. *Story* E. Lloyd Sheldon. *Photog* William Marshall.

Cast: Malcolm McGregor *(Dan O'Neil)*, Pauline Garon *(Doris Laidlaw)*, Mary Carr *(Mrs. O'Neil)*, John Miljan *(Jasper Thorne)*, Johnny Gough *(Midge)*, Mayme Kelso *(Mrs. Rutherford)*.

Melodrama. Danny O'Neil returns from the sea to discover that his mother has been cheated out of her life savings by Jasper Thorne, an unscrupulous promoter of oil stocks. Going after Thorne, Danny takes his mother to the oil fields, where he meets Doris Laidlaw, a society girl with whom he falls in love. Danny catches up with Thorne and, after a little quick thinking, gets back his mother's money. Danny invests the cash in another well and strikes oil. Thorne learns of the strike and starts a fire near the well. Danny rescues Doris from a path of burning oil, and Thorne perishes in the fire he started. Doris and Danny seem destined for wedlock. *Sailors. Socialites. Filial relations. Oil business. Fraud. Oil wells. Fires.*

FLAMING YOUTH **F2.1803**

Associated First National Pictures. 12 Nov **1923** [c14 Dec 1923; LP19712]. Si; b&w. 35mm. 9 reels, 8,434 ft.

Dir John Francis Dillon. *Scen* Harry O. Hoyt.

Cast: Colleen Moore *(Patricia Fentriss)*, Milton Sills *(Cary Scott)*, Elliott Dexter *(Dr. Bobs)*, Sylvia Breamer *(Dee Fentriss)*, Myrtle Stedman *(Mona Fentriss)*, Betty Francisco *(Connie Fentriss)*, Phillips Smalley *(Ralph Fentriss)*, Walter McGrail *(Jamieson James)*, Ben Lyon *(Monty Standish)*, George Barraud *(Fred Browning)*, John Patrick *(Warren Graves)*, Geno Corrado *(Leo Stenak)*, Gertrude Astor *(Annie)*, Michael Dark *(Sidney*

Rathbone).

Melodrama. Source: Warner Fabian, *Flaming Youth* (New York, 1923). Discouraged by the unhappy marriages in her family, Patricia Fentriss refuses Cary Scott's proposal and allows herself to be charmed by Leo Stenak, a musician, into joining a yachting party to the tropics. Patricia escapes by jumping overboard when Stenak tries to force his attentions upon her. Rescued, she is carried home and is reunited with Cary Scott. *Musicians. Marriage. Jazz life. Youth. Yachts. Tropics.*

FLAPPER WIVES **F2.1804**

Laurence Trimble and Jane Murfin Productions. *Dist* Selznick Distributing Corp. 23 Feb **1924** [c25 Feb 1924; LP19971]. Si; b&w. 35mm. 7 reels, 6,864 ft.

Dir Jane Murfin, Justin H. McCloskey. *Story* Jane Murfin. *Photog* King Grey, Connie De Roo.

Cast: May Allison *(Claudia Bigelow)*, Rockliffe Fellowes *(Stephen Carey)*, Vera Reynolds *(Sadie Callahan)*, Edward Horton *(Vincent Platt)*, Harry Mestayer *(Charles Bigelow)*, William V. Mong *(Enoch Metcalf)*, Edward Phillips *(Tony)*, Tom O'Brien *(Tim Callahan)*, Evelyn Selbie *(Hulda)*, Robert Dudley *(Lem)*, Stanley Goethals *(Jimsy)*, J. C. Fowler *(Dr. Oliver Lee)*, Brawn (son of Strongheart) *(Wolf)*.

Melodrama. Stephen Carey, a broadminded rector, is ousted from his church by the vestrymen. He befriends Claudia Bigelow, a young divorcée who defended his position in the church. Claudia's carelessness in leaving a cigarette burning causes Jimsy, the son of the housekeeper, to go blind. Stephen's prayers restore the boy's sight, and a happy future is predicted for all. *Clergymen. Vestrymen. Flappers. Blindness. Smoking. Fires. Dogs.*

THE FLASH **F2.1805**

Clinton Productions. *Dist* Russell Productions. Jan **1923**. Si; b&w. 35mm. 5 reels, 4,788 ft.

Dir William J. Craft. *Story* George Hively.

Cast: George Larkin, Ruth Stonehouse.

Melodrama. "The story tells of the head of the police department starting on a campaign to clean up a city, arousing the ire of the gambling and political element; the frame to get the daughter involved to make the chief lay off and the boy reporter always thwarting the enemies of noble ideals." (*Variety*, 25 Jan 1923, p40.) The melodrama is heightened by automobile chases and the hero's rescue of the heroine, who has been abandoned by the villain in a rowboat surrounded by rapids. *Reformers. Police. Reporters. Political corruption. Gambling. Frameup. Chases. Rapids.*

FLASH O' LIGHTNING **F2.1806**

William Steiner Productions. c22 May **1925** [LU21489]. Si; b&w. 35mm. 5 reels.

Dir Leo Maloney. *Scen* Ford I. Beebe.

Cast: Leo Maloney *(Flash Lightnin'/Richard Coakley)*, Josephine Hill *(Edith Willett)*, Evelyn Thatcher *(Aunt M'liss)*, Whitehorse *(Caleb Flint)*, Bud Osborne *(Ed Wiley)*, Bullet *(a dog)*, Senator *(a horse)*.

Western melodrama. Bad guy "Breed" Saunders carries a tattoo on his right forearm and a $1,000 price on his hide. About to be captured by a pursuing posse, he steals the horse of good-natured "Flash Lightnin'," who is playing with his dog. Flash gives chase on Saunders' foaming steed, but the posse chases Flash to the ranch of crooked skinflint Caleb Flint. Flint is looking for an impersonator to pose as Richard Coakley, the rightful heir to a ranch where a gold vein has been uncovered. When the sheriff and his posse arrive, Flint and henchman Ed Wiley blackmail Flash into posing as Coakley and send him to the ranch where "Ol' Man" Coakley's pretty ward, Edith Willett, and her stern nursemaid, Aunt M'liss, are in residence. Breed turns up at Flint's place, with the saddlebags full of letters to the real Coakley, and is taken for the rightful heir. The three nefarious gents confront Flash and Edith with their ruse, but Flash reveals himself to be the *real* Richard Coakley, and packs Saunders and Co. off to jail, sticking around to see just what kind of girl his father reared, while Bullet keeps Aunt M'liss' censorial tendencies at bay. *Ranchers. Sheriffs. Posses. Fraud. Impersonation. Blackmail. Mistaken identity. Documentation. Tattoos. Dogs.*

FLASH OF THE FOREST **F2.1807**

William M. Pizor Productions. **1928** [New York State license: 3 Apr 1930]. Si; b&w. 35mm. 5 reels, 4,500 ft.

Cast: Braveheart *(a dog)*.

Melodrama(?). No information about the precise nature of this film has been found. *Dogs.*

FLASHES OF ACTION **F2.1808**

United States Army Signal Corps. 17 Aug **1925** [New York State license]. Si; b&w. 35mm. 5 reels.

Documentary. This film is a record both of civilian life and of military action during the period of the First World War. *World War I.*

FLASHING FANGS **F2.1809**

R-C Pictures. *Dist* Film Booking Offices of America. 5 Sep **1926** [c5 Sep 1926; LP23092]. Si; b&w. 35mm. 5 reels, 4,853 ft.

Pres by Joseph P. Kennedy. *Dir* Henry McCarthy. *Story-Cont* Ewart Adamson. *Photog* Glen Gano, B. P. Carpenter. *Asst Dir* John Burch.

Cast: Ranger *(himself, a dog)*, Robert Ramsey *(Dan Emory)*, Lotus Thompson *(Bessie Lang)*, Eddie Chandler *("Red" Saunders)*, Clark Comstock *(Andrew Lang)*, Ada Mae Vaughn *(June)*, George Reehm *(sheriff)*, Mary Dow *(baby)*.

Melodrama. Dan Emory, a miner in the Sierras, tries to beat "Red" Saunders for mistreating his dog, Ranger; but Saunders bests him and turns the dog on the beaten man; the dog instinctively protects Dan and afterwards takes up with the miner. Dan arouses the interest of Bessie, daughter of Andrew Lang, a local farmer, though Lang is doubtful about him. When Dan is injured in a mine explosion, he sends Ranger for help, and Bessie protects the dog from settlers who think he has assaulted a child. Later, Dan strikes ore, and Saunders tries to steal the claim but is beaten by Dan. Saunders kills Lang in an argument; and Dan, accused of the crime, is about to be lynched when Ranger arrives with a note from Bessie, who has been kidnaped; Bessie is rescued from the villain's clutches and reunited with Dan. *Miners. Farmers. Bullies. Injustice. Murder. Lynching. Kidnaping. Sierras. Dogs.*

FLASHING HOOFS **F2.1810**

Dist Anchor Film Distributors. 1 Nov **1928** [New York State license]. Si; b&w. 35mm. 5 reels.

Cast: Cliff (Tex) Lyons.

Western melodrama(?). No information about the nature of this film has been found.

FLASHING SPURS **F2.1811**

Independent Pictures. *Dist* Film Booking Offices of America. 14 Dec **1924** [c29 Dec 1924; LP21004]. Si; b&w. 35mm. 5 reels, 5,068 ft.

Pres by Jesse J. Goldburg. *Dir* Reeves Eason. *Story-Cont* William Lester. *Photog* Walter Griffen.

Cast: Bob Custer *(Sergeant Stuart of the Rangers)*, Edward Coxen *(Steve Clammert, "The Spider")*, Marguerite Clayton *(Ruth Holden/Rena Holden)*, Joe Bennett *(Butch Frazier)*, William Hayes *(Scarbee)*, William Malan *(John Holden)*, Andy Waldron *(Flynn)*, Park Frame *(Bill Carbee)*.

Western melodrama. While visiting New York City, Ranger Sergeant Stuart becomes involved in an unequal fight with two gunmen, escaping from them by hiding in the hotel room of Rena Holden, to whom he is greatly attracted. When Rena later mysteriously disappears, Stuart finds evidence among her things that she is a member of the Clammert gang, which is planning to rob the safe of Rena's father, John Holden. Stuart goes west to the Holden mine, where he sees Ruth Holden, Rena's twin sister, whom he mistakes for Rena and publicly denounces as a thief and a liar. Stuart is captured by Clammert's men, tied to a rock, and dynamited. He escapes injury, joins forces with a repentant Rena, rides to Clammert's cabin, and saves Ruth from injurious attack. Rena is hurt in the struggle and explains to Stuart that she was forced to help Clammert by the threat of blackmail. Stuart forgives her, and Rena consents to marry the burly ranger. *Rangers. Twins. Sisters. Mining. Blackmail. Robbery. New York City.*

FLASHING STEEDS **F2.1812**

H. B. Carpenter Productions. *Dist* Chesterfield Motion Picture Corp. 1 Nov **1925**. Si; b&w. 35mm. 5 reels.

Dir H. B. Carpenter.

Cast: Bill Patton *(Bill Swift)*, Dorothy Donald *(Helen Randall)*, Merrill McCormick *(Lord Rathburne)*, Ethel Childers *(Lady Rathburne)*, Alfred Hewston *(Shorty)*, Dick La Reno *(Captain Randall)*, Harry O'Connor *(Joe Stern)*.

Western melodrama. Disguised as a cowhand, government agent Bill Swift gains the confidence of Lord and Lady Rathburne, a couple of international swindlers attempting to steal a valuable black pearl belonging to Bill's employer, Randall, a retired sea captain doing all his sailing on prairie schooners. Swift thwarts the schemes of the swindlers and marries

Randall's daughter, Helen. *Government agents. Cowboys. Swindlers. Sea captains. English. Disguise.*

FLATTERY **F2.1813**

Mission Film Corp. *Dist* Chadwick Pictures. 15 Feb **1925.** Si; b&w. 35mm. 6 reels, 5,600 ft.

Supv Norman Walker. *Dir* Tom Forman. *Story* H. H. Van Loan. *Photog* King Gray. *Adtl Photog* Harry Perry.

Cast: John Bowers *(Reginald Mallory)*, Marguerite De La Motte *(Betty Biddle)*, Alan Hale *(Arthur Barrington)*, Grace Darmond *(Allene King)*, Edwards Davis *(John Biddle)*, Louis Morrison *(mayor)*, Larry Steers *(district attorney)*.

Melodrama. Petted and pampered all his life, Reginald Mallory has grown to manhood easily swayed by flattery. On the verge of an outstanding career in civil engineering, he is appointed city engineer by a corrupt cartel of politicians and contractors, who use his vanity to further their crooked ends. Mallory is wheedled into signing a contract for the construction of a new city hall that will provide the minimum of quality at the maximum of cost. Everyone loses faith in Mallory except Betty Biddle, his sweetheart, who is the daughter of the president of a construction company. Mallory appears to have turned crooked, but he finally demonstrates his honesty—first by producing enough documentary evidence to convict the cartel of fraud and then by blowing up the partly finished city hall to demonstrate its substandard construction. *Engineers—Civil. Politicians. Contractors. Construction. Cartels. Flattery. Vanity. Honesty. Documentation.*

THE FLEET'S IN **F2.1814**

Paramount Famous Lasky Corp. 15 Sep **1928** [c20 Sep 1928; LP25632]. Mus score (Movietone); b&w. 35mm. 8 reels, 6,918 ft.

Dir Malcolm St. Clair. *Titl* George Marion. *Story-Scen* Monte Brice, J. Walter Ruben. *Photog* Harry Fischbeck. *Film Ed* B. F. Zeidman.

Cast: Clara Bow *(Peaches Deane)*, James Hall *(Eddie Briggs)*, Jack Oakie *(Searchlight Doyle)*, Bodil Rosing *(Mrs. Deane)*, Eddie Dunn *(Al Pearce)*, Jean Laverty *(Betty)*, Dan Wolheim *(Double-Duty Duffy)*, Richard Carle *(Judge Hartley)*, Joseph Girard *(commandant)*.

Comedy-drama. The Pacific Fleet comes into port, and the girls from the Roseland Dance Hall come dockside to wish the boys welcome. Eddie Briggs, a self-styled sailor sheik, is greatly attracted by Peaches Deane, a dime-a-dance girl with a heart of gold. That evening, Eddie goes to Roseland, and he and Peaches win a dance contest. He takes her home, gets fresh, and is shown the gate. Back on board ship, Eddie realizes that he loves Peaches and returns to Roseland to find her wearing Doyle's ring. There is a brawl, and Eddie is arrested. Peaches takes the blame for the fight, however, and Eddie is freed. He must leave immediately with the fleet, but he promises to return for her. *Sailors. Dancehall girls. United States Navy.*

FLEETWING **F2.1815**

Fox Film Corp. 24 Jun **1928** [c24 Jun 1928; LP25417]. Si; b&w. 35mm. 5 reels, 4,939 ft. [Copyrighted as 6 reels.]

Pres by William Fox. *Dir* Lambert Hillyer. *Scen* Elizabeth Pickett. *Story* Lambert Hillyer, Elizabeth Pickett. *Photog* Frank Good. *Film Ed* Alexander Troffey. *Asst Dir* Virgil Hart.

Cast: Barry Norton *(Jaafor [Ami])*, Dorothy Janis *(Thurya)*, Ben Bard *(Metaab [Zeki])*, Robert Kortman *(Auda)*, Erville Alderson *(Trad Ben Sabam)*, James Anderson *(Mansoni)*, Arabian Horse *(The Simoon Fleetwing)*, Blanche Frederici *(Furja)*.

Melodrama. "Capturing a beautiful horse and a slave girl, young Arab's happiness is short lived when girl is sold to a cruel sheik. He escapes with her on horse and is captured. The attack on an enemy tribe saves him, sheik is slain and youth's tribe celebrates his nuptials with the slave girl." (*Motion Picture News Booking Guide*, [14]:250, 1929.) *Sheiks. Slavery. Arabia. Horses.*

FLESH *see* **THE MIDNIGHT GUEST**

FLESH AND BLOOD **F2.1816**

Dist Western Pictures Exploitation Co. Jul **1922.** Si; b&w. 35mm. 6 reels, 5,300 ft.

Pres by Irving Cummings. *Dir* Irving Cummings. *Story* Louis Duryea Lighton.

Cast: Lon Chaney *(David Webster)*, Edith Roberts *(The Angel Lady)*, De Witt Jennings *(Detective Doyle)*, Noah Beery *(Li Fang)*, Ralph Lewis *(Fletcher Burton)*, Jack Mulhall *(Ted Burton)*, Togo Yamamoto *(The Prince)*, Kate Price *(The Landlady)*, Wilfred Lucas *(The Policeman)*.

Drama. Unjustly imprisoned for 15 years, David Webster, hoping to visit his wife, escapes; but he arrives in time only to see her funeral procession. The convict receives shelter from Li Fang, a Chinese politician; disguises himself as a crippled beggar to escape the police; and meets his daughter, the Angel Lady, to whom he does not reveal his identity. Determined to have revenge on Fletcher Burton, the man who sent him to prison, Webster finally corners his enemy and obtains a signed confession. At that moment, Webster's daughter enters the room, and he learns of her desire to marry Burton's son, Ted. In exchange for Burton's approval of the marriage Webster destroys the confession and returns to prison satisfied with the knowledge of his daughter's happiness. *Prison escapees. Cripples. Chinese. Revenge. Fatherhood.*

Note: "There is a bit of inserted action, illustrating a tale related to the impatient Webster by the philosophic Li Fang, which is told in color with Chinese players." (*Exhibitors Trade Review,* 19 Aug 1922, p806.)

FLESH AND SPIRIT **F2.1817**

United States Moving Picture Corp. *Dist* Lee-Bradford Corp. Jun **1922.** Si; b&w. 35mm. 6 reels, 5,500 ft.

Dir Joseph Levering. *Story* Garfield Thompson. *Photog* Joseph Levering.

Cast: Belle Bennett *(Truth Eldridge)*, Walter Ringham *(Donald Wallace)*, Denton Vane *(James Dale)*, James McDuff *(Rev. Howard Renfield)*, Rita Rogan *(Peggy)*, Logan Paul *(Peters Roberts)*, Jean Robertson *(Paula Roberts)*, May Kitson *(Mrs. Wallace)*, Hayden Stevenson *(The Gardener)*, Mary Rehan *(his wife)*.

Drama. "Donald Wallace is an atheist, who believes that all religion is a farce and that science is the only God. He is loved by his cousin, but is too self centered and too attentive to his scientific experiments to notice the girl's affection. She is killed through the mistake of one of Wallace's enemies, who had planned to murder the scientist in an insane rage at the way Wallace treats the girl. Shortly after her death the girl returns in spirit form and frequently appears in the man's vision, finally convincing him that there is a God." (*Moving Picture World,* 15 Apr 1922, p762.) *Ghosts. Atheists. Scientists. Religion. Murder.*

FLESH AND THE DEVIL **F2.1818**

Metro-Goldwyn-Mayer Pictures. 25 Dec **1926** [c10 Jan 1927; LP23514]. Si; b&w. 35mm. 9 reels, 8,759 ft.

Dir Clarence Brown. *Screenplay* Benjamin F. Glazer. *Titl* Marian Ainslee. *Photog* William Daniels. *Sets* Cedric Gibbons, Frederic Hope. *Film Ed* Lloyd Nosler. *Asst Dir* Charles Dorian. *Wardrobe* André-ani.

Cast: John Gilbert *(Leo von Sellenthin)*, Greta Garbo *(Felicitas von Kletzingk)*, Lars Hanson *(Ulrich von Kletzingk)*, Barbara Kent *(Hertha Prochvitz)*, William Orlamond *(Uncle Kutowski)*, George Fawcett *(Pastor Brenckenburg)*, Eugenie Besserer *(Leo's mother)*, Marc MacDermott *(Count von Rhaden)*, Marcelle Corday *(Minna)*.

Romantic drama. Source: Hermann Sudermann, *Es war; Roman in zwei Bänden* (Stuttgart, 1893). Leo von Sellenthin and Ulrich von Kletzingk, two boys who have grown up together, swear eternal friendship through a blood bond. They attend military school together, and at home on annual holiday, Leo meets the entrancing Felicitas at a ball. When her husband discovers Leo with her in her boudoir, a duel is called and the husband is killed; forced into foreign service, Leo asks his friend Ulrich to console the widow. Three years later Leo is pardoned by the emperor and returns to find that Felicitas has married Ulrich. Vainly he seeks to escape her attempts to revive their former affair. Ultimately, the two men resort to a duel, each unable to fire the fatal shot. Hurrying to the scene of the duel, Felicitas falls through an ice floe to her death, removing the spell cast upon their lives and reuniting the friends. *Widows. Friendship. Infidelity. Courtship. Military schools. Ice floes. Duels.*

FLESH OF EVE *see* **DANGEROUS PARADISE**

FLIGHT **F2.1819**

Columbia Pictures. 18 Sep **1929** [New York premiere; released 1 Nov; c4 Dec 1929; LP884]. Sd (Movietone); b&w. 35mm. 12 reels, 10,670 ft. [Also si; 9,005 ft.]

Prod Harry Cohn. *Dir* Frank R. Capra. *Scen* Howard J. Green. *Dial* Frank R. Capra. *Story* Ralph Graves. *Camera* Joseph Walker, Joe Novak. *Asst Camera* Elmer Dyer, Paul Perry. *Art Dir* Harrison Wiley. *Film Ed* Ben Pivar, Maurice Wright, Gene Milford. *Tech Sd Engr* John Livadary. *Sd Mixing Engr* Harry Blanchard. *Sd Syst* Hahn, Eddie. *Asst Dir* Buddy

Coleman. *Adv* Capt. Francis E. Pierce. *Sd Equip Supv* Ellis Gray.

Cast: Jack Holt *(Panama Williams)*, Lila Lee *(Elinor)*, Ralph Graves *("Lefty" Phelps)*, Alan Roscoe *(Major)*, Harold Goodwin *(Steve Roberts)*, Jimmy De La Cruze *(Lobo)*.

Adventure melodrama. "Lefty" Phelps, who misplays in a Harvard-Yale football match because of a nervous reaction, joins the flying squad of the Marines. Williams, who was present at the game, sympathizes with the boy and becomes his pal; thus, when Lefty falls in love with Elinor, a nurse, and later discovers that Williams claims her, he treats the girl with indifference. On the day of his first solo flight, Lefty loses control of his plane and crashes, escaping with only minor injuries; but Williams requests that he be made his mechanic, and together they leave for Nicaragua to assist in quelling a revolutionary uprising. When Williams asks Lefty to propose to Elinor for him, he does so, but she confesses that she loves him and not Williams; a fight results in Lefty's transfer; but when Lefty is lost in the jungle, Williams flies to his rescue and is injured. Lefty flies him to the landing base, thus winning his flying insignia; and with the approval of his pal, he is united with Elinor. *Aviators. Mechanics. Nurses. Football. Aviation. Revolutions. Friendship. Nicaragua. United States Marines. Harvard University. Yale University.*

THE FLIGHT OF THE SOUTHERN CROSS; OR, THE FOUR HUMAN EAGLES **F2.1820**

G. Allan Hancock. c5 Feb **1929** [MP462]. Si; b&w. 35mm. 4 reels.

In-flight Photog Capt. Charles E. Kingsford-Smith, Capt. Charles T. P. Ulm.

Participants: G. Allan Hancock *(flight sponsor)*, Lieut. Harry W. Lyons *(navigator)*, James Warner *(radio operator)*, Capt. Charles E. Kingsford-Smith *(flight commander)*, Capt. Charles T. P. Ulm *(relief pilot)*.

Documentary. An account of the flight of the trimotor *Southern Cross* from Oakland, California, to Australia (31 May–9 Jun 1928), including scenes of preparation of the machine, takeoff, flight above the Pacific Ocean, Hawaii, Fiji Islands, Sydney, the fliers' welcome at Brisbane, and homecoming of Lyons and Warner at San Francisco. *Air pilots. Airplanes. Pacific Ocean. Hawaii. Australia. Oakland (California). San Francisco. "Southern Cross".*

FLINTS OF STEEL *see* **TWO-FISTED JEFFERSON**

THE FLIRT (Universal-Jewel) **F2.1821**

Universal Pictures. 24 Dec **1922** [New York premiere; released Dec; c16 Dec 1922; LP18526]. Si; b&w. 35mm. 8 reels.

Pres by Carl Laemmle. *Dir* Hobart Henley. *Scen-Adapt* A. P. Younger. *Photog* Charles Kaufman.

Cast: George Nichols *(Papa Madison)*, Lydia Knott *(Mama Madison)*, Eileen Percy *(Cora Madison)*, Helen Jerome Eddy *(Laura Madison)*, Buddy Messenger *(Hedrick Madison)*, Harold Goodwin *(Jimmy Madison)*, Nell Craig *(Della Fenton)*, Tom Kennedy *(Sam Fenton)*, Lloyd Whitlock *(Valentine Corliss)*, Edward Hearn *(Richard Lindley)*, Bert Roach *(Wade Trumble)*, William Welsh *(George Carroll)*, Dorothea Wolbert *(The Cook)*.

Domestic comedy-drama. Source: Booth Tarkington, *The Flirt* (New York, 1913). Treats of the average, smalltown, middleclass family life. Flirtatious Cora Madison is engaged to Richard Lindley but is attracted to Val Corliss, who has come to town to promote oil stock. When Cora's father refuses to become involved, she forges his name on some papers, thus enabling Corliss to sell many shares. Corliss absconds with the funds; Mr. Madison takes the blame; Richard marries Cora's sister, Laura; and Cora confesses to her deception. Corliss is caught, and Cora settles down with her new husband, Wade Trumble. *Flirts. Family life. Middle classes. Smalltown life. Forgery. Embezzlement.*

THE FLIRTING WIDOW **F2.1822**

First National Pictures. 11 May **1930** [c7 Jun 1930; LP1352]. Sd (Vitaphone); b&w. 35mm. 8 reels, 6,664 ft.

Dir William Seiter. *Scen-Dial* John F. Goodrich. *Photog* Sid Hickox. *Film Ed* John F. Goodrich.

Cast: Dorothy Mackaill *(Celia)*, Basil Rathbone *(Colonel Smith)*, Leila Hyams *(Evelyn)*, William Austin *(James Raleigh)*, Claude Gillingwater *(Faraday)*, Emily Fitzroy *(Aunt Ida)*, Flora Bramley *(Phyllis)*, Anthony Bushell *(Bobby)*, Wilfred Noy *(Martin)*.

Romantic comedy-drama. Source: Alfred Edward Woodley Mason, *Green Stockings, a Comedy in Three Acts* (New York & London, 1909). Eccentric and headstrong, Sir William Farady refuses to allow his daughter Phyllis to marry Bobby Tarver until Celia, his oldest daughter, is married. When Celia returns to London from a vacation, she announces her engagement to a Colonel Smith, who she says has sailed for Arabia, hoping thereby to help Bobby and Phyllis. The family is elated, and at her sister Evelyn's insistence, Celia writes a love letter that she intends to destroy but which is accidentally posted. It happens that there is actually in Arabia a Colonel Smith, who is amused by the letter. When Celia publishes his obituary in the *Times*, however, he decides to visit her, claiming to be a friend of the deceased. After making her thoroughly uncomfortable, he reveals his identity, and they find a mutual affection growing. ... *Sisters. Fatherhood. Courtship. Hoaxes. London.*

FLIRTING WITH LOVE **F2.1823**

First National Pictures. 17 Aug **1924** [c19 Aug 1924; LP20500]. Si; b&w. 35mm. 7 reels, 6,926 ft.

Supv Earl Hudson. *Dir* John Francis Dillon. *Ed Dir* Marion Fairfax. *Scen* Joseph Poland. *Photog* T. D. McCord. *Art Dir* Milton Menasco. *Film Ed* LeRoy Stone. *Cost* Clare West.

Cast: Colleen Moore *(Gilda Lamont)*, Conway Tearle *(Wade Cameron)*, Winifred Bryson *(Estelle Van Arden)*, Frances Raymond *(Mrs. Cameron)*, John Patrick *(Dickie Harrison)*, Alan Roscoe *(Franklyn Stone)*, William Gould *(John Williams)*, Marga La Rubia *(Henderson)*.

Drama. Source: Leroy Scott, "Counterfeit" (publication undetermined). When Wade Cameron, chairman of the Better Plays Society, halts the production of actress Gilda Lamont's first stage success, she attempts to revenge herself by feigning another personality and gaining his confidence. He assigns her a role in an improvised production of a new play as an unknown actress, thwarts her attempt to expose him, and ends by capturing her heart. *Actors. Censorship. Theater.*

THE FLOATING COLLEGE **F2.1824**

Tiffany-Stahl Productions. 10 Nov **1928** [c29 Oct 1928;LP25772]. Si; b&w. 35mm. 6 reels, 5,477 ft.

Dir George J. Crone. *Story-Cont* Stuart Anthony. *Titl* Paul Perez. *Photog* Harry Jackson. *Film Ed* Desmond O'Brien.

Cast: Sally O'Neil *(Pat Bixby)*, William Collier, Jr. *(George Dewey)*, Georgia Hale *(Frances Bixby)*, Harvey Clark *(The Dean)*, Georgie Harris *(Snug)*, E. J. Ratcliffe *(Nathan Bixby)*, Virginia Sale *(Miss Cobbs)*.

Comedy-melodrama. Frances and Pat Bixby, rich sisters, both fall in love with George Dewey, a swimming instructor. To get Pat out of the way, Frances contrives for her to be enrolled in a floating college. George is an instructor on the ship, however, and Frances soon joins her sister on the high seas. In a Chinese port, Frances locks Pat in a hotel closet and returns to the ship only to discover that there has been a native rebellion. Frances tells George of Pat's captivity, and he rescues her; they are married on the way back to the ship. *Athletic coaches. Sisters. Students. Revolts. Swimming. College life. Ships. China.*

FLOODGATES **F2.1825**

Lowell Film Productions. 29 Feb **1924** [c25 Feb 1924; LP19988]. Si; b&w. 35mm. 7 reels, ca6,400 ft.

Dir George Irving. *Story-Scen* L. Case Russell. *Photog* Joseph Settle.

Cast: John Lowell *(Dave Trask)*, Evangeline Russell *(Ruth Trask)*, Jane Thomas *(Alice Trask)*, Baby Ivy Ward *(Peggy Trask)*, William Calhoun *(Lem Bassett)*, F. Serrano Keating *(Tom Bassett)*, William Kavanaugh *(Morton)*, Frank Montgomery *(Jeff)*, J. N. Bradt *(Sliver)*, Homer Lind *(Dr. Vedos)*, Arthur Ludwig *(Regan)*, Hap Hadley *(Ladus)*.

Rural melodrama. Millowner Lem Bassett uses his foreman, Dave Trask, whose power among the people in the neighborhood is great, to obtain their land so that he can build a bigger dam for water power, flooding the lands above it. One of these people finds that Bassett has tricked him, and he demands recompense. When it is refused, Dave leads a group of men to dynamite the dam. In the path of the waters is Bassett's home, where Dave's crippled daughter has been taken so that a famous specialist retained by Tom Bassett, nephew of Lem (who loves Dave's sister), may operate. Dave saves the child and Tom, and Bassett agrees to surrender. *Swindlers. Dams. Power projects. Land rights. Water power. Floods.*

THE FLORODORA GIRL **F2.1826**

Metro-Goldwyn-Mayer Pictures. 31 May **1930** [c3 Jun 1930; LP1339]. Sd (Movietone); b&w with col sequence (Technicolor). 35mm. 9 reels, 7,260 ft. [Also si.]

Dir Harry Beaumont. *Scen-Dial* Gene Markey. *Adtl Dial* Ralph Spence, Al Boasberg, Robert Hopkins. *Photog* Oliver T. Marsh. *Art Dir* Cedric

Gibbons. *Film Ed* Carl L. Pierson. *Songs: "My Kind of Man," "Pass the Beer and Pretzels"* Herbert Stothart, Clifford Grey, Andy Rice. *Rec Engr* Paul Neal, Douglas Shearer. *Gowns* Adrian.

Cast: Marion Davies *(Daisy)*, Lawrence Gray *(Jack)*, Walter Catlett *(De Boer)*, Louis John Bartels *(Hemingway)*, Ilka Chase *(Fanny)*, Vivian Oakland *(Maud)*, Jed Prouty *(Old Man Dell)*, Claud Allister *(Rumblesham)*, Sam Hardy *(Fontaine)*, Nance O'Neil *(Mrs. Vibart)*, Robert Bolder *(Commodore)*, Jane Keithly *(Constance)*, Maude Turner Gordon *(Mrs. Caraway)*, George Chandler *(Georgie Smith)*, Anita Louise, Mary Jane Irving *(Vibart children)*.

Romantic costume drama. Source: Gene Markey, "The Gay Nineties" (publication undetermined). Daisy, a Florodora girl, who is too man-shy to go after a husband, is taken into hand by her sisters and embarks on an affair with young millionaire Jack Vibart, whose mother has already planned his marriage. She falls in love, although her friends warn her of his dishonorable intentions; realizing that he loves her, he proposes, but the marriage is opposed by his mother when he loses the family fortune. Daisy marries him, nevertheless, and he finally makes good in the new automobile business and comes to carry her off during the Florodora act. *Florodora Sextette. Millionaires. Courtship. Gay Nineties. Family life. Vaudeville. Automobiles.*

FLOWER OF DARKNESS *see* **THE NIGHT ROSE**

FLOWER OF NIGHT **F2.1827**

Famous Players–Lasky. *Dist* Paramount Pictures. 18 Oct **1925** [New York premiere; released 2 Nov; c5 Nov 1925; LP21972]. Si; b&w. 35mm. 7 reels, 6,374 ft.

Pres by Adolph Zukor, Jesse L. Lasky. *Dir* Paul Bern. *Screenplay* Willis Goldbeck. *Story* Joseph Hergesheimer. *Photog* Bert Glennon. *Gambling Adv* Scott Turner. *Coöp* Mexican Government.

Cast: Pola Negri *(Carlota y Villalon)*, Joseph Dowling *(Don Geraldo y Villalon)*, Youcca Troubetzkoy *(John Basset)*, Warner Oland *(Luke Rand)*, Edwin J. Brady *(Derck Bylandt)*, Eulalie Jensen *(Mrs. Bylandt)*, Cesare Gravina *(servant)*, Gustav von Seyffertitz *(vigilante leader)*, Helen Lee Worthing *(Josefa)*, Thais Valdemar, Manuel Acosta, Frankie Bailey.

Melodrama. In the California of 1856, Don Geraldo y Villalon, descendant of Spanish grandees, has had the Flor de Noche goldmine wrested from him by dishonest Americans. Carlota, his daughter, falls in love with John Basset, the new assistant superintendent at the mine, and goes to a dance, against her father's wishes, to be near him. Mine superintendent Derck Bylandt, who has had too much to drink, dies of a heart attack when he tries to force Carlota to dance with him. Disgusted with the scene, Basset ignores her. She confesses to her father that she has disgraced the Villalon name, and he commits suicide. She then goes to San Francisco and becomes a dancehall girl. Stung by Basset's contempt, she accepts the offer of infatuated Luke Rand, the sinister head of the Vigilance Committee, to help her recover the mine. She recants when she realizes that Basset's life is in danger. In the end, Basset kills Rand; and he and Carlota realize their mutual love. *Spanish. Dancehall girls. Vigilantes. Suicide. Mines. California. San Francisco.*

Note: Musical theme and prolog entitled "Magic Love."

FLOWER OF THE NORTH **F2.1828**

Vitagraph Co. of America. 4 Dec **1921** [c7 Nov 1921; LP17165]. Si; b&w. 35mm. 7 reels, 7,130 ft.

Pres by Albert E. Smith. *Dir* David Smith. *Scen* Bradley J. Smollen. *Photog* Stephen Smith, Jr.

Cast: Henry B. Walthall *(Philip Whittemore)*, Pauline Starke *(Jeanne D'Arcambal)*, Harry Northrup *(Thorpe)*, Joe Rickson *(Pierre)*, Jack Curtis *(Blake)*, Emmett King *(D'Arcambal)*, Walter Rodgers *(MacDougal)*, William McCall *(Cassidy)*, Vincent Howard *(Sachigo)*.

Melodrama. Source: James Oliver Curwood, *The Flower of the North* (New York, 1912). In the Canadian forest lives D'Arcambal with his daughter Jeanne (known as "The Flower of the North") and a halfbreed servant, Pierre. Philip Whittemore, a young American, arrives and forms the Northern Fish and Development Company, backed by Brokaw, a New York capitalist. Brokaw, however, sends Thorpe, an unscrupulous associate, with instructions to delay the work of the company, and D'Arcambal revokes Whittemore's right-of-way through his holdings. Thorpe convinces Jeanne, who is unaware that her mother eloped with a lover before she was born, that he is her father. Whittemore rescues Jeanne from drowning, and when Thorpe and his gang attack Whittemore's camp Jeanne brings a band of friendly Indians to Whittemore's aid. Thorpe is defeated, Jeanne learns that D'Arcambal is really her father, and she is united with Philip. *Indians of North America. Filial relations. Fisheries. Land rights. Canadian Northwest.*

FLOWING GOLD **F2.1829**

Westart Pictures. 13 Jul **1921** [Brooklyn showing]. Si; b&w. 35mm. 5 reels.

Dir Leonard Franchon. *Writ* W. M. Smith. *Photog* A. H. Vallet.

Cast: Al Hart, Jack Mower, Robert Conville.

Western melodrama. No information about the precise nature of this film has been found.

FLOWING GOLD **F2.1830**

Richard Walton Tully Productions. *Dist* Associated First National Pictures. 1 Mar **1924** [c13 Feb 1924; LP19910, LP19964]. Si; b&w. 35mm. 8 reels, 8,005 or 8,076 ft.

Pres by Richard Walton Tully. *Dir* Joseph De Grasse. *Scen* Richard Walton Tully. *Photog* Gilbert Warrenton, Roy Carpenter. *Art Dir* William S. Hinshelwood. *Tech Artist* Conrad Tritschler. *Film Ed* LeRoy Stone. *Asst Dir* George Reehm.

Cast: Anna Q. Nilsson *(Allegheny Briskow)*, Milton Sills *(Calvin Gray)*, Alice Calhoun *(Barbara Parker)*, Crauford Kent *(Henry Nelson)*, John Roche *(Buddy Briskow)*, Cissy Fitzgerald *(The Suicide Blonde)*, Josephine Crowell *(Ma Briskow)*, Bert Woodruff *(Pa Briskow)*, Charles Sellon *(Tom Parker)*.

Melodrama. Source: Rex Beach, *Flowing Gold* (New York, 1922). Soldier of fortune Calvin Gray find work in a Texas oil town aiding the Briskows, a family of homesteaders who have become rich from the discovery of oil on their property. The Briskows allow Gray to manage their investments, and he thwarts the evil plans of Henry Nelson, a banker who (as an officer in the Army) persecuted him. Gray then prevents an adventuress, "The Suicide Blonde," from swindling Buddy, the Briskows' son; and finally he marries daughter Allegheny Briskow after she saves his life during a fire and flood caused by a thunderstorm. *Soldiers of fortune. Bankers. Adventuresses. Swindlers. Homesteaders. Wealth. Oil wells. Texas. Fires. Floods. Storms.*

THE FLYIN' COWBOY (Universal-Jewel) **F2.1831**

Universal Pictures. 12 May **1928** [New York premiere; released 1 Jul; c24 Mar 1928; LP25096]. Si; b&w. 35mm. 6 reels, 5,109 ft.

Dir-Cont Reaves Eason. *Story-Adapt* Arthur Statter. *Titl* Harold Tarshis. *Photog* Harry Neumann. *Art Dir* David S. Garber. *Film Ed* Gilmore Walker.

Cast: Hoot Gibson *(Bill Hammond)*, Olive Hasbrouck *(Connie Lamont)*, Harry Todd *(Tom Gordon)*, William Bailey *(James Bell)*, Buddy Phillips *("Chuck" Ward)*, Ann Carter *(Alice Gordon)*.

Western melodrama. A cowboy, invited to a dude ranch to stage Wild West shows, arrives by parachuting into the swimming pool. Meanwhile, two gangsters staying at the ranch are trying to appropriate the jewels of the guests. The cowboy apprehends the bandits and recovers the jewelry. *Cowboys. Gangsters. Parachuting. Dude ranches. Wild West shows.*

FLYIN' THRU (Aviation Aces Series) **F2.1832**

Al Wilson Pictures. *Dist* Davis Distributing Division. Dec? **1925** [c3 Dec 1925; LP22073]. Si; b&w. 35mm. 6 reels, 5,800 ft.

Dir Bruce Mitchell. *Scen* George W. Pyper. *Story* Al Wilson.

Cast: Al Wilson *(Lieutenant Wilson)*, Elinor Fair *(Anne Blair)*, George French *(Judson Blair)*, James McElhern *(Jim Willis)*, Clarence Burton *(Melvin Parker)*, Fontaine La Rue *(Sybil)*, Garry O'Dell *(Bill Goofus)*.

Melodrama. Aviator Al Willis returns home from combat duty in France to find his father, a cotton farmer, in jail for the murder of neighbor Jud Blair—a crime actually committed by dancehall proprietor Parker. Al becomes partners with an ex-sergeant he knew in France, and they buy a plane with which they go barnstorming around the country, all the while looking for clues to reveal the real murderer. At a bullfight across the border, Sybil, Parker's dancehall sweetheart, becomes infatuated with Al and betrays Parker. Parker flees in an automobile, but Al flies after him, leaps from his airplane into the speeding automobile, and overcomes Parker. His father is set free, and Al weds Ann, Blair's daughter, in an airplane far above the clouds. *Veterans. Farmers. Aviators. Filial relations. Airplanes. Murder. Cotton. Bullfighting. Barnstorming. Mexican border.*

FLYING ACE **F2.1833**

Norman Film Manufacturing Co. 19 May **1928** [New York State license]. Si; b&w. 35mm. 6 reels, 5,600 ft.

Cast: Lawrence Corman, Kathryn Boyd, J. Lawrence Criner.

Melodrama(?). No information about the precise nature of this film has been found. *Pilots. Negro life. Airplanes.*

Note: May also be known as *The Fighting Ace.*

THE FLYING BUCKAROO **F2.1834**

Action Pictures. *Dist* Pathé Exchange. 25 Nov **1928** [c18 Oct 1928; LP25778]. Si; b&w. 35mm. 5 reels, 4,571 ft.

Pres by Lester F. Scott, Jr. *Dir* Richard Thorpe. *Cont* Betty Burbridge. *Story* Frank L. Inghram. *Photog* Ray Reis.

Cast: Wally Wales *(Bill Mathews)*, Jack D'Oise *(Henry Mathews)*, J. P. Lockney *(Mr. Mathews)*, Fanny Midgley *(Mrs. Mathews)*, Duane Thompson *(Sally Brown)*, Mabel Van Buren *(Mrs. Brown)*, Charles K. French *(Banker Brown)*, Charles Whitaker *(Delno, the bandit)*, Helen Marlowe *(city girl)*, Bud McLure *(sheriff)*.

Western melodrama. Bill Mathews mistakenly comes to believe that his sweetheart, Sally Brown, prefers the company of his brother, Henry, to that of his own and dejectedly goes to the city, where he finds work driving a truck. Six months later Bill returns home; that very day, the Delno gang robs the bank and kidnaps Sally. Bill follows the outlaws in a plane and parachutes into their mountain hideout; he captures Delno's men and rescues Sally, who quickly convinces him that she has never loved another. *Truckdrivers. Brothers. Bank robberies. Kidnaping. Airplanes. Parachuting.*

THE FLYING DUTCHMAN **F2.1835**

R-C Pictures. *Dist* Film Booking Offices of America. 29 Jul **1923** [c29 Jul 1923; LP19264]. Si; b&w. 35mm. 6 reels, 5,800 ft.

Dir-Adapt Lloyd B. Carleton. *Photog* André Barlatier.

Cast: Lawson Butt *(Philip Vanderdecker)*, Nola Luxford *(Melissa)*, Ella Hall *(Zoe)*, Edward Coxen *(Robert)*, Walter Law *(Peter Van Dorn)*.

Romantic fantasy. Source: Richard Wagner, *Der fliegende Holländer* (1841). Philip Vanderdecker falls asleep while reading *The Flying Dutchman* and dreams about Peter Van Dorn, burgomaster of a small Dutch seacoast town, telling the legend to his two daughters, Melissa and Zoe. Vanderdecker imagines that he is The Flying Dutchman, condemned by God for blaspheming during a storm to roam the seas in a phantom ship and to reach port only once every 7 years. His only salvation is in finding a woman who will be faithful to him. If he finds such a woman the curse will be lifted. While the burgomaster is telling the story, a stranger comes to the inn. He falls in love with Melissa, but is blind to Zoe, who recognizes him as The Flying Dutchman. Melissa promises to be faithful and sends her former fiancé on a sea voyage from which she hopes he will never return. When Melissa cannot keep her promise, Zoe, who is revealed as Philip Vanderdecker's wife, declares her love and saves The Flying Dutchman just as he is about to embark on another 7-year voyage. *Blasphemy. Curses. Phantoms. The Sea. Netherlands. Dreams.*

THE FLYING FLEET **F2.1836**

Metro-Goldwyn-Mayer Pictures. 19 Jan **1929** [c16 Jan 1929; LP37]. Synchronized mus score (Movietone); b&w. 35mm. 11 reels, 9,044 ft. [Also si.]

Dir George Hill. *Screenplay* Richard Schayer. *Titl* Joe Farnham. *Story* Lieut. Comdr. Frank Wead, U. S. N. *Photog* Ira Morgan. *Air Photog* Charles A. Marshall. *Art Dir* Cedric Gibbons. *Film Ed* Blanche Sewell. *Song: "You're the Only One for Me"* William Axt, David Mendoza. *Wardrobe* David Cox. *Prod with the sanction of the* United States Navy.

Cast: Ramon Novarro *(Tommy)*, Ralph Graves *(Steve)*, Anita Page *(Anita)*, Edward Nugent *(Dizzy)*, Carroll Nye *(Tex)*, Sumner Getchell *(Kewpie)*, Gardner James *(Specs)*, Alfred Allen *(Admiral)*, The Three Sea Hawks.

Drama. Six graduates of the Naval Academy, after attending the Naval Flying School, successfully undertake a flight from San Diego to Honolulu. The film includes considerable background material concerning test flying and gives a detailed account of what aspirants for flying berths must endure to get their wings. *Aviators. Aviation. San Diego. Honolulu. United States Naval Academy.*

Note: "Dedicated to the officers and men of NAVAL AVIATION whose splendid co-operation made this production possible."

FLYING FOOL **F2.1837**

Sunset Productions. *Dist* Aywon Film Corp. 3 Sep **1925** [New York State license]. Si; b&w. 35mm. 5 reels, 4,870 ft.

Pres by Anthony J. Xydias. *Dir* Frank S. Mattison. *Titl* Ralph Spence. *Photog* Bert Longenecker, Gus Boswell. *Art Dir* Milton Fowler.

Cast: Gaston Glass *(Jack Bryan)*, Dick Grace *(Donald Daring)*, Wanda Hawley *(The Bride)*, Mary Land *(bride's mother)*, Dorothy Vernon *(Mrs. Gibbs)*, Dick Sutherland *(skipper of Jack's yacht)*, Eddie Harris *(Phinneas Gibbs)*, Milburn Morante.

Melodrama. Source: Putnam Hoover, "The Ace and the Queen" (publication undetermined). Donald Daring is late for his own wedding, and his piqued bride leaves the church, accompanied by best man Jack Bryan. At the bride's home her mother puts the jewels back in the safe. Donald arrives at the house and, refused admission, enters by an upstairs window. A policeman, thinking Donald a burglar, knocks him out, and Jack takes the jewels from the safe, planting them on Donald's person. Donald is arrested as a thief, and Jack persuades Donald's fiancée to fly to San Diego with him. Donald is bailed out of jail and, learning of the elopement, gives chase, rescuing his disillusioned fiancée from Jack's lecherous clutches. Donald is cleared of all suspicion of wrongdoing, and he and his intended are finally married. *Burglars. Weddings. Airplanes. San Diego.*

THE FLYING FOOL **F2.1838**

Pathé Exchange. 23 Jun **1929** [c26 Jul 1929; LP549]. Sd (Photophone); b&w. 35mm. 7 reels, 6,720 ft. [Also si; 5,715 ft.]

Supv William Sistrom. *Dir* Tay Garnett. *Dial* James Gleason. *Story-Adapt* Elliott Clawson, Tay Garnett. *Photog* Arthur Miller. *Song: "If I Had My Way," "I'm That Way About Baby"* George Waggner, George Green. *Rec Engr* Ben Winkler, Earl A. Wolcott. *Asst Dir* Leigh Smith. *Prod Mgr* John Rohlfs. *Prop Man* Allen Smiley.

Cast: William Boyd *(The Flying Fool)*, Marie Prevost *(Pat)*, Russell Gleason *(Jimmy Taylor)*, Tom O'Brien *(Tom Dugan)*.

Melodrama. Bill Taylor, an ace pilot known as the "Flying Fool" in the World War, falls in love with his brother's girl, Pat, a singer, when he visits her to find out what kind of girl she is. To his surprise he discovers that she is a "smalltown girl," decent and likable. The brothers take to their airplanes to decide which of them wins Pat. After a thrilling air "battle," Bill and Jimmy land safely: Pat decides she loves Bill, and Jimmy transfers his affections to another pretty thing. *Aviators. Veterans. Brothers. Singers. Air stunts.*

FLYING HIGH **F2.1839**

Camera Pictures. *Dist* Lumas Film Corp. 20 Dec **1926** [c31 Jan 1927; LP23607]. Si; b&w. 35mm. 5 reels, 5,000 ft.

Pres by Sam Sax. *Prod* Samuel Bischoff. *Dir* Charles Hutchinson. *Story-Scen* L. V. Jefferson. *Photog* James Brown. *Film Ed* Edward Curtiss.

Cast: William Fairbanks *(Roy Cummins)*, Alice Calhoun *(Patricia Barton)*, Frank Rice *(Haines, the mechanic)*, LeRoy Mason *(Lester Swope)*, Jimmy Anderson *(Carson)*, Cecile Cameron *(Vera Owens)*, Joseph W. Girard *(Col. Rockliffe Owens)*, James Gordon *(V. E. Martin)*.

Action melodrama. Roy Cummins, an ex–army aviator, who runs exhibition passenger flights at a summer resort, earns $500 by carrying a passenger to a steamer offshore. As he returns he is met by Patricia Barton, who warns him not to accept the money; for she has learned that the passenger, Swope, is a criminal with stolen goods. Cummins takes her for an aerial ride, and they see a commercial express plane being attacked by another plane with a machine gun; Roy saves the express plane, and as a result he is engaged by the company as a commercial pilot. Colonel Stone (Owens?), who is in league with the bandits, sends Vera Owens to vamp Roy and learn his plans to capture the gang. Roy foils the plot, discovers the bandits' hiding place, and in a sensational air battle captures the gang. *Aviators. Resorts. Air pirates. Air stunts.*

FLYING HOOFS **F2.1840**

Universal Pictures. 8 Feb **1925** [c2 Dec 1924; LP20481]. Si; b&w. 35mm. 5 reels, 4,274 ft.

Dir Clifford S. Smith. *Story* Clee Woods. *Photog* Harry Neumann.

Cast: Jack Hoxie *(Frank Moody)*, Bartlett A. Carré *(Henry Moody)*, William Welsh *(Banker Conner)*, Gordon Russell *(James Perdee)*, Charlotte Stevens *(Emily Perdee)*, Alys Murrell *(Mary Conner)*, Duke R. Lee *(The Raven)*.

Western melodrama. Sheriff Frank Moody has sworn to bring to justice a notorious bandit known only as The Raven, but, as he hunts for the unknown outlaw, circumstantial evidence and village gossip suggest that Henry Moody, the sheriff's kid brother, may be the bandit. Henry compounds his difficulties when he openly threatens the town banker, who has recently foreclosed on the Moody ranch. When the bank is robbed, the innocent Henry is arrested, given a hasty trial, and sentenced to be hanged. His identity hidden by the hangman's hood, Frank takes his brother's place on the scaffold, but at the last moment he is rescued by The Raven's men, who will not let an innocent man die. The sheriff captures The Raven, who turns out to be the bank manager, and Henry is cleared of all guilt. *Sheriffs. Brothers. Bankers. Bandits. Circumstantial evidence. Capital punishment.*

Note: Working title: *Beyond the Law.*

THE FLYING HORSEMAN **F2.1841**

Fox Film Corp. 5 Sep **1926** [c29 Aug 1926; LP23146]. Si; b&w. 35mm. 5 reels, 4,971 ft.

Pres by William Fox. *Dir* Orville O. Dull. *Scen* Gertrude Orr. *Photog* Joe August.

Cast: Buck Jones *(Mark Winton)*, Gladys McConnell *(June Savary)*, Bruce Covington *(Colonel Savary)*, Walter Percival *(Bert Ridley)*, Silver Buck *(White Eagle)*, Hank Mann *(Newton Carey)*, Harvey Clark *(Happy Joe)*, Vester Pegg, Joseph Rickson.

Western melodrama. Source: Max Brand, "Dark Rosaleen," in *Country Gentleman* (vol 89–90, 27 Dec 1924–24 Jan 1925). Mark Winton, a wandering cowboy en route to a cross-country race, takes up the cause of a group of children who are bullied by Bert Ridley, buys Boy Scout outfits for them, and teaches them scouting. June, the daughter of Colonel Savary, enters her horse in the race to pay off the ranch mortgage, but she is thwarted by Ridley, who wants her father's property *and* the girl. Mark is framed for murder when he intervenes, but he returns to do a favor for the girl and is arrested. With the aid of his horse, he breaks jail, wins the race, saves the colonel's ranch, and brings the gang to justice. *Ranchers. Cowboys. Children. Swindlers. Horseracing. Murder. Mortgages. Frameup. Jailbreaks. Boy Scouts. Horses.*

FLYING LUCK **F2.1842**

Monty Banks Enterprises. *Dist* Pathé Exchange. 4 Dec **1927** [c30 Oct 1927; LP24641]. Si; b&w. 35mm. 7 reels, 6,403 ft.

Prod Monty Banks. *Dir* Herman C. Raymaker. *Scen* Charles Horan, Matt Taylor. *Titl* Paul Perez. *Story* Charles Horan, Monty Banks. *Photog* James Diamond. *Asst Camera* Stanley Norsley. *Film Ed* William Holmes. *Asst Dir* Ray McDevitt, Arthur Varney.

Cast: Monty Banks *(The Boy)*, Jean Arthur *(The Girl)*, J. W. Johnston *(The Colonel)*, Kewpie Morgan *(The Sergeant)*, Eddie Chandler *(The Corporal)*, Silver Harr *(The Orderly)*.

Comedy. With Lindbergh as his hero, young Monty (The Boy) buys a junked airplane, rebuilds it, and studies flying in "Ten Easy Lessons by Mail." His premiere exhibition ends in a crash through the roof of an Army recruiting office, where he is inspired to enlist. En route to the training camp, a series of mixups results in his arrival in the entourage of a foreign dignitary; and he is accepted as a friend of the foreigner, who does not speak English. The error is discovered at a banquet, and he is turned over to the sergeant, who puts him to work in the stables. A romance develops when Monty discovers that his suitcase has been delivered to the colonel's governess. He is tricked into joining an air meet in honor of the visitor, and his air stunts win him the prize and the girl's admiration. *Aviators. Governesses. Military life. Correspondence courses. United States Army—Recruiting. Charles Augustus Lindbergh. Air stunts.*

THE FLYING MAIL **F2.1843**

Al Wilson Productions. *Dist* Associated Exhibitors. 10 Sep **1926** [c26 Oct 1926; LU23254]. Si; b&w. 35mm. 5 reels, 4,500 ft.

Pres by A. Carlos. *Dir* Noel Mason. *Story* Frank Howard Clark.

Cast: Al Wilson *(Sherry Gillespie)*, Joseph W. Girard *(Martin Hardwick)*, Kathleen Myers *(Alice Hardwick)*, Carmelita Geraghty *(Cleo Roberts)*, Harry Van Meter *(Bart Sheldon)*, Eddie Gribbon *("Gluefoot" Jones)*, Frank Tomick *(Tom Corrigan)*.

Action melodrama. Following a party, Sherry Gillespie, a U. S. Mail flyer, awakes to find himself in a strange apartment and is shown evidence by Cleo Roberts that they were married the previous evening. Bart Sheldon, a crook, plots with an associate to pilot Sherry's plane and cautions Cleo not to let the pilot escape. When Sherry escapes and returns to the flying field, he is suspended, then estranged from Alice, his fiancée, by the appearance of Cleo, who is scheming with Sheldon to obtain part of an inheritance that Sherry is to receive if he earns $10,000 in a year. Following a series of fast complications, Sherry tracks down the gang: swinging from a motorcycle to a rope ladder, he mounts a plane, encounters the robber's plane, and fights with the villains. He and Sheldon parachute to the ground, and Sherry is finally vindicated in the eyes of his girl and his employer. *Aviators. Gangs. Postal service. Inheritance. Marriage—Fake. Air stunts.*

THE FLYING MARINE **F2.1844**

Columbia Pictures. 5 Jun **1929** [c12 Jun 1929; LP527]. Sd (Movietone); b&w. 35mm. 6 reels, 5,951 ft. [Also si; 5,736 ft.]

Prod Harry Cohn. *Dir* Albert Rogell. *Story-Cont* John Francis Natteford. *Titl* Weldon Melick. *Photog* Ted Tetzlaff. *Art Dir* Harrison Wiley. *Film Ed* William Hamilton. *Asst Dir* Tenny Wright.

Cast: Ben Lyon *(Steve Moran)*, Shirley Mason *(Sally)*, Jason Robards *(Mitch Moran)*.

Drama. Mitch Moran, a commercial flyer, takes under his wing his young brother, Steve, who has been discharged from the Marines. Sally, with whom Mitch is in love, carried away by the glamour surrounding Steve, also an aviator, promises to be his wife. However, she soon discovers him to be irresponsible and that it is actually Mitch she loves. About to break her engagement, Sally receives word that Steve has been injured in an accident resulting from stunt work for a movie director. She and Mitch agree that their love must be kept from Steve, who loses his hearing as a result of the injury. Steve, however, learns of their sacrifice when they raise the money for an operation that cures his affliction. He regains their money by further stunt flying but is killed in the effort. *Aviators. Brothers. Motion picture directors. Courtship. Deafness. United States Marines. Air stunts.*

FLYING ROMEOS **F2.1845**

First National Pictures. 26 Feb **1928.** Si; b&w. 35mm. 7 reels, 6,184 or 6,845 ft.

Prod E. M. Asher. *Dir* Mervyn LeRoy. *Story-Scen* John McDermott. *Titl* Sidney Lazarus, Gene Towne, Jack Conway (of *Variety*). *Photog* Dev Jennings. *Film Ed* Paul Weatherwax.

Cast: Charlie Murray *(Cohan)*, George Sidney *(Cohen)*, Fritzi Ridgeway *(Minnie)*, Lester Bernard *(Goldberg)*, Duke Martin *(The Aviator)*, James Bradbury, Jr. *(The Nut)*, Belle Mitchell *(Mrs. Goldberg)*.

Comedy. Barbers Cohen and Cohan both love their manicurist, who has a fondness for aviators. Therefore, they sign up for flying lessons and accidentally find themselves performing some fancy stunts in an airplane. Its impressed owner persuades the duo to make an overseas flight, which makes for more hi-jinks; and on their return Cohen and Cohan find their manicurist married to a pilot. *Barbers. Manicurists. Air pilots. Jews. Irish. Airplanes. Air stunts.*

THE FLYING U RANCH **F2.1846**

R-C Pictures. *Dist* Film Booking Offices of America. 4 Sep **1927** [c4 Sep 1927; LP24421]. Si; b&w. 35mm. 5 reels, 4,924 ft.

Pres by Joseph P. Kennedy. *Dir* Robert De Lacy. *Cont* Oliver Drake. *Photog* Joe Walker. *Asst Dir* William Cody.

Cast: Tom Tyler *(Señor Miguel García)*, Nora Lane *(Sally Denson)*, Bert Hadley *(Chip Bennett)*, Grace Woods *(The Little Doctor)*, Frankie Darro *(Chip, Jr.)*, Beans *(Sitting Bull)*, Olin Francis *(Dunk Whitaker)*, Barney Furey *(Pink)*, Dudley Hendricks *(Weary)*, Bill Patton *(Happy Jack)*.

Western melodrama. Source: B. M. Bower, *The Flying U Ranch* (New York, 1914). Miguel García, a supercilious Spaniard, fails to impress the residents of the Flying U Ranch, with the exception of the owner's young son, Chip. Dunk Whitaker, a neighboring rancher, who has been rustling Bennett's cattle, manages to steal the contract guaranteeing Flying U's rights to a waterhole and tries to force his attentions on Sally, Bennett's niece. Miguel rescues her and takes her to a dance, incurring Dunk's wrath. Sally agrees to Dunk's proposal of marriage in order to save the ranch, and Miguel is captured by Dunk's henchmen. He escapes and confronts the villain and the girl on a lake; Dunk is drowned; Miguel is revealed to be an undercover agent; and, as such, he wins the heart of Sally. *Ranchers. Spanish. Secret agents. Rustlers. Water rights. Documentation.*

THE FOG **F2.1847**

Max Graf Productions. *Dist* Metro Pictures. 18 Jun **1923** [c9 Jul 1923; LP19195]. Si; b&w. 35mm. 7 reels, 6,737 ft.

Prod under pers supv of Max Graf. *Dir* Paul Powell. *Scen* Winifred Dunn. *Adapt* H. H. Van Loan. *Photog* John Arnold.

Cast: Mildred Harris *(Madelaine Theddon)*, Louise Fazenda *(Millie Richards)*, Louise Dresser *(Mrs. Theddon)*, Marjorie Prevost *(Edith Forge)*, Ann May *(Carol Gardner)*, Ethel Wales *(Mrs. Forge)*, Cullen Landis *(Nathan Forge)*, Ralph Lewis *(Johnathan Forge)*, David Butler *(Si Plumb)*, Frank Currier *(Caleb Gridley)*, Edward Phillips *(Gordon Ruggles)*, Charles Anderson.

Melodrama. Source: William Dudley Pelley, *The Fog* (Boston, 1921). Nathan Forge, romantic son of a cruel businessman, publishes in a local newspaper a poem about a girl who once befriended him. The girl, a student in a nearby school, reads the poem and recognizes herself. Years pass, and Nathan goes through various hardships, including an unhappy marriage, imprisonment, and the war. Then in Siberia, working for the International Red Cross, he meets the girl who is the subject of his poem and thus achieves happiness. (The title could have either or both of two explanations: the protagonists "spend their youth in a fog, battling against the tyranny, ignorance and obscurity of their situations"; or their eventful meeting takes place on a foggy hilltop.) *Poetry. World War I. Siberia. San Francisco. Red Cross.*

Note: Exteriors shot in San Francisco Bay area.

FOG BOUND **F2.1848**

Famous Players–Lasky. *Dist* Paramount Pictures. 27 May **1923** [c22 May 1923; LP18982]. Si; b&w. 35mm. 6 reels, 5,692 ft.

Pres by Adolph Zukor. *Dir* Irvin Willat. *Scen* Paul Dickey. *Photog* Henry Cronjager.

Cast: Dorothy Dalton *(Gale Brenon)*, David Powell *(Roger Wainright)*, Martha Mansfield *(Mildred Van Buren)*, Maurice Costello *(Deputy Brown)*, Jack Richardson *(Sheriff Holmes)*, Ella Miller *(Mammy)*, Willard Cooley *(Deputy Kane)*, William David *(Gordon Phillips)*, Warren Cook *(Revenue Officer Brenon)*.

Melodrama. Source: Jack Bechdolt, "Fog Bound," in *Argosy* (137: 738–746, 22 Oct 1921). Mutual interest springs up between Roger Wainright, a wealthy New York idler visiting his Florida estate, and Gale Brenon, daughter of a Federal revenue agent. In a raid on a fashionable gambling resort where liquor is served, Mr. Brenon is killed, and suspicion fastens on Roger, who escapes to Gale's home. Gale helps Roger get away into the swamp but joins the search for him when she learns of Brenon's death. Gale weakens when she finds him, but Roger decides to surrender. Mildred Van Buren exposes Deputy Brown to be Brenon's murderer. *Revenue agents. New Yorkers. Idlers. Prohibition. Murder. Swamps. Florida Everglades.*

FOLKS FROM WAY DOWN EAST **F2.1849**

Emmons Film Corp. *Dist* Joy Film Distributing Co. 24 Apr **1924** [New York State license]. Si; b&w. 35mm. 5 reels.

Cast: Violet Horner.

Melodrama(?). No information about the nature of this film has been found. The New York State licensing records suggest that another title used for this film was *Ten Nights in a Barroom*.

FOLLOW THE LEADER **F2.1850**

Paramount-Publix Corp. 5 Dec **1930** [New York premiere; released 13 Dec; c12 Dec 1930; LP1809]. Sd (Movietone); b&w. 35mm. 9 reels, 6,851 ft.

Dir Norman Taurog. *Dial Dir* Albert Parker. *Screenplay* Gertrude Purcell, Sid Silvers. *Photog* Larry Williams. *Film Ed* Barney Rogan. *Song: "Broadway, the Heart of the World"* Lew Brown, B. G. De Sylva, Ray Henderson. *Song: "Brother Just Laugh It Off"* E. Y. Harburg, Arthur Schwartz. *Song: "Satan's Holiday"* Irving Kahal, Sammy Fain. *Rec Engr* Ernest F. Zatorsky.

Cast: Ed Wynn *(Crickets)*, Ginger Rogers *(Mary Brennan)*, Stanley Smith *(Jimmy Moore)*, Lou Holtz *(Sam Platz)*, Lida Kane *(Ma Brennan)*, Ethel Merman *(Helen King)*, Bobby Watson *(George White)*, Donald Kirke *(R. C. Black)*, William Halligan *(Bob Sterling)*, Holly Hall *(Fritzie Devere)*, Preston Foster *(Two-Gun Terry)*, James C. Morton *(Mickie)*.

Comedy. Source: William K. Wells, George White, Buddy De Sylva, Lew Brown, and Ray Henderson, *Manhattan Mary*. Crickets, a timorous former acrobat and comedian, works as waiter in Ma Brennan's restaurant, where Mary, the owner's stage-struck daughter, is in love with Jimmy Moore, a saxophonist. Sam Platz, a theatrical press agent, recognizes Crickets as an old acquaintance and promises to promote Mary's career. At the same time, Two-Gun Terry, a neighborhood gangster, kills the leader of the Hudson Dusters, a rival gang, and the leaderless gang takes refuge in the restaurant, followed by Terry; terrified, Crickets tries to serve him and accidentally knocks him unconscious; hailed as a hero, he is elected to head the Dusters and is assigned to force a manager to give Mary a chance on the stage. He succeeds in getting her the job of understudy in George White's Scandals by locking the star in her apartment. Mary sings the role and is hailed by the critics though rebuffed by Jimmy; but Crickets effects their reconciliation after she has risen to stardom, giving them his patented mosquito exterminator for a wedding present. *Saxophonists. Waiters. Gangsters. Press agents. Singers. Kidnaping. Musical revues. New York City—Broadway. George White's Scandals.*

Note: Only one song, "Satan's Holiday," sung by Ethel Merman, was retained from the musical comedy source.

FOLLOW THRU **F2.1851**

Paramount-Publix Corp. 27 Sep **1930** [c26 Sep 1930; LP1593]. Sd (Movietone); col (Technicolor). 35mm. 10 reels, 8,386 ft.

Prod Laurence Schwab, Frank Mandel. *Dir-Screenplay* Laurence Schwab, Lloyd Corrigan. *Photog* Henry Gerrard, Charles Boyle. *Film Ed* Alyson Shaffer. *Song: "A Peach of a Pair"* George Marion, Jr., Richard Whiting. *Song: "It Must Be You"* Elwood Eliscu, Manning Sherwin. *Songs: "You Wouldn't Fool Me, Would You?"* Lew Brown, B. G. De Sylva, Ray Henderson. *Song: "I'm Hard To Please"* Lorenz Hart, Richard Rodgers. *Rec Engr* Harry M. Lindgren.

Cast: Charles Rogers *(Jerry Downs)*, Nancy Carroll *(Lora Moore)*, Zelma O'Neal *(Angie Howard)*, Jack Haley *(Jack Martin)*, Eugene Pallette *(J. C. Effingham)*, Thelma Todd *(Ruth Van Horn)*, Claude King *(Mac Moore)*, Kathryn Givney *(Mrs. Bascomb)*, Margaret Lee *(Babs Bascomb)*, Don Tomkins *(Dinty Moore)*, Albert Gran *(Martin Bascomb)*.

Musical comedy. Source: Lew Brown, B. G. De Sylva, Ray Henderson, and Laurence Schwab, *Follow Thru* (New York opening: 9 Jan 1929). Lora Moon, runner-up for the women's golf title of the Mission Country Club, loses to Ruth Van Horn. During the championship match, Lora falls in love with Jerry Downs, golf instructor to Jack Martin, a girl-shy young millionaire. Jerry arouses Ruth's jealousy by offering to coach Lora's game, but the attentions of Angie Howard, Lora's friend, cause young Martin to cut short his stay. Angie, however, with a mysterious love perfume, vamps Martin into remaining; and finding his ring, she refuses to return it. When Lora hears that Jerry is going to Ruth's house, she challenges her rival to a match the following day. Lora takes the lead; but at Angie's urging, Jerry takes the place of Lora's caddie, and she wins the match. Lora and Jerry and Angie and Martin plan a double wedding. *Athletic coaches. Millionaires. Courtship. Golf. Country clubs.*

THE FOLLY OF VANITY **F2.1852**

Fox Film Corp. 21 Dec **1924** [c25 Jan 1925; LP21130]. Si; b&w. 35mm. 6 reels, 5,250 ft.

Pres by William Fox. *Dir of Modern Story* Maurice Elvey. *Fantasy Creations* Henry Otto. *Scen* Edfrid Bingham. *Story* Charles Darnton. *Photog* G. O. Post, Joe August, Joseph Valentine.

Cast—Modern sequence: Billie Dove *(Alice)*, Jack Mulhall *(Robert)*, Betty Blythe *(Mrs. Ridgeway)*, John Sainpolis *(Ridgeway)*, Fred Becker *(The Banker)*, Otto Matiesen *(Frenchman)*, Byron Munson *(Old Johnny)*, Edna Mae Cooper *(Russian vamp)*, Fronzie Gunn *(Scandinavian type)*, Marcella Daly *(French woman)*, Lotus Thompson *(Blond gold digger)*.

Cast—Fantasy: Consuelo *(Thetis)*, Jean La Motte *(Lorelei)*, Bob Klein *(Neptune)*, Ena Gregory *(The Siren)*, Lola Drovnar *(The Witch)*, Paul Weigel *(old roué)*, Billie Dove.

Domestic melodrama. A young husband and wife, Alice and Robert, attend an extravagant party given by one of Robert's wealthy clients, Ridgeway. At the party Alice accepts a gift of a pearl necklace from her wealthy host and in consequence has a misunderstanding with Robert. All of Ridgeway's guests are invited on a yachting cruise during which Ridgeway is attentive to Alice, while Robert flirts with a wealthy widow. One night, Alice dreams that, *when Ridgeway tries to attack her, she jumps into the sea and is carried to Neptune's court. There a festival is held in her honor, and she is shown the most beautiful of the sea's sirens. When a witch discovers that the pearl necklace has made a mark of vanity on Alice's neck, Neptune orders her from the deep.* Alice awakens, returns the necklace to Ridgeway, and is reconciled with Robert. *Marriage. Vanity. Mythological characters. Legendary characters. Neptune. Dreams.*

FOLLY OF YOUTH **F2.1853**

Sable Productions. c7 Feb **1925** [LU21182]. Si; b&w. 35mm. 5 reels. *Scen* George Hively.

Melodrama. Evelyn Cartwright becomes dangerously ill from poisoned liquor, and her brother Robert determines to put a stop to the local traffic in bootleg booze. He forces Jimmy Adler, who bought the bad bottle at a small restaurant, to put a finger on the man from whom he bought it. Robert takes the man to the Cartwright house at the point of a gun and soon discovers the man's source: the landlady at the Rex apartments. Robert rents a room there and discovers the warehouse where the stuff is made and bottled. Robert then captures one of the bootleggers, a beautiful woman named Leona, who has been forced into a life of crime by her husband, Lee Haynes. Robert takes Leona to his home and confronts her with his desperately ill sister. Leona repents of her life of crime and offers to help Robert bring the bootleggers to justice. The man held prisoner in the Cartwright home escapes and alerts Haynes. Robert and Leona are captured and tied up; but Leona with a knee motion sends a message by wireless, and the gang is captured by the police. Haynes is killed by the harbor police, and Evelyn soon recovers enough to see Leona and Robert married. *Criminals—Rehabilitation. Police. Landladies. Brother-sister relationship. Bootlegging. Radio.*

THE FOOD GAMBLERS (Reissue) **F2.1854**

Dist Tri-Stone Pictures. **1923**. Si; b&w. 35mm. 5 reels.

Note: A "re-edited and re-titled" Wilfred Lucas film originally released by Triangle Film Corp. on 5 Aug 1917.

THE FOOL **F2.1855**

Fox Film Corp. 15 Nov **1925** [c29 Mar 1925; LP21448]. Si; b&w. 35mm. 10 reels, 9,453 ft.

Pres by William Fox. *Dir* Harry Millarde. *Scen* Edmund Goulding. *Photog* Joseph Ruttenberg. *Asst Dir* Nick Hollen.

Cast: Edmund Lowe *(Daniel Gilchrist)*, Raymond Bloomer *(Jerry)*, Henry Sedley *(Stedman)*, Paul Panzer *(Umanski)*, A. J. Herbert *(Hennig)*, Downing Clarke *(Rev. Everett Wadham)*, George Lessey *(Goodkind)*, Blanche Craig *(Mrs. Henry Gilliam)*, Fred C. Jones *(poor man)*, Rose Blossom *(Dilly Gilliam)*, Anne Dale *(Mary Margaret)*, Helena D'Algy *(Mrs. Thornbury)*, Mary Thurman *(Pearl)*, Lucille Lee Stewart *(society lady)*, Brenda Bond *(Clare)*, Marie Shaffer *(Mrs. Tice)*, Joseph Burke *(Mr. Barnsby, sexton)*.

Drama. Source: Channing Pollock, *The Fool; a Play in Four Acts* (New York, 1922). Daniel Gilchrist, an assistant rector in a fashionable church, preaches a sermon in which he exhorts his congregation to emulate the life of Christ by giving up worldy possessions in order to find spiritual happiness. Because of this radical point of view, Gilchrist is dismissed from his post and deserted by his fiancée, Clare, who soon marries Jerry Goodkind, the son of a millionaire. Daniel starts a mission, and there Clare, who has been badly hurt by the open and callous infidelity of her husband, comes to do volunteer work. Jerry accuses Clare of infidelity, and she comes to Daniel to seek solace; Daniel then bids her return to her husband and find solace through service to Christ. A distraught miner, Henning, who believes that Daniel seduced his wife, incites a mob to burn the mission; Daniel is beaten by the mob, whose fury abates only when Pearl, Hennig's wife, confesses that the man who seduced her was Jerry Goodkind. A small child, crippled since birth, sees Daniel lying on the ground, bleeding from the fury of the mob's unthinking blows, and haltingly walks to him; the crowd declares that it has seen a miracle. Jerry is emotionally shaken by the events, and his wealthy father comes to see that a truly Christian life is the only path to happiness on this earth. *Millionaires. Clergymen. Christianity. Infidelity. Missions. Miracles.*

A FOOL AND HIS MONEY **F2.1856**

Columbia Pictures. 1 Jan **1925** [c24 Jan 1925; LP21067]. Si; b&w. 35mm. 6 reels, 5,801 ft.

Dir Erle C. Kenton. *Cont* Dorothy Howell. *Titl* Walter Anthony. *Adapt* Douglas Z. Doty. *Film Ed* Jack Kelly.

Cast: Madge Bellamy *(Countess von Pless)*, William Haines *(John Smart)*, Stuart Holmes *(Count von Pless)*, Alma Bennett *(Annette Ritazi)*, Charles Conklin, Lon Poff, Carrie Clark Ward *(Mrs. Schmick)*, Eugenie Besserer *(mother)*, Edwards Davis, Baby Billie Jean Phyllis.

Melodrama. Source: George Barr McCutcheon, *A Fool and His Money* (New York, c1913). John Smart, a hack writer, inherits a fortune from a distant uncle and buys a castle in Laupheim from Count von Pless. Arriving in Laupheim, John, who is received coldly by the count's former retainers, is informed that the castle is haunted. John later sees what appears to be the ghost of a beautiful young woman and pursues it, discovering that the "ghost" is the estranged wife of the count, hidden with her child at the castle by devoted servants. The woman tells John of her husband's cruelty, and John vows to protect her. When the count discovers that John is harboring his wife, he returns to the castle with soldiers and attempts to abduct her by force. John fights off the count until the girl and her child have had time to escape by airplane. Smart is convicted of obstructing justice, his castle is confiscated, and he is deported to the United States. Unknown to John, his valet has discovered a hidden fortune at the castle and brought it back to America. This fortune enables John to marry the divorced countess. *Nobility. Authors. Inheritance. Divorce. Abduction. Haunted houses.*

A FOOL THERE WAS **F2.1857**

Fox Film Corp. ca18 Jun **1922** [Los Angeles premiere; released 10 Sep; c10 Sep 1922; LP18991]. Si; b&w. 35mm. 7 reels, 6,604 ft.

Pres by William Fox. *Dir* Emmett J. Flynn. *Scen* Bernard McConville. *Photog* Lucien Andriot.

Cast: Estelle Taylor *(Gilda Fontaine)*, Lewis Stone *(John Schuyler)*, Irene Rich *(Mrs. Schuyler)*, Muriel Dana *(Muriel Schuyler)*, Marjorie Daw *(Nell Winthrop)*, Mahlon Hamilton *(Tom Morgan)*, Wallace MacDonald *(Avery Parmelee)*, William V. Mong *(Boggs)*, Harry Lonsdale *(Parks)*.

Drama. Source: Porter Emerson Browne, *A Fool There Was* (New York opening: 24 Mar 1909). Rudyard Kipling, *The Vampire; A Poem* (New York, 1898). On a trip to Europe, financier John Schuyler meets Gilda Fontaine, the cause of his business partner's suicide, and falls prey to her evil charm. He forsakes his wife and daughter to be with Gilda and soon falls into remorse and drunkenness, while Gilda takes another lover. John and his wife are about to be reconciled through the efforts of Tom Morgan when Gilda reappears and John again weakens. Realizing that only her death will free him, John attempts to strangle Gilda, but he himself falls and dies. *Financiers. Vamps. Infidelity. Alcoholism.*

THE FOOLISH AGE **F2.1858**

Hunt Stromberg Productions. *Dist* Robertson-Cole Distributing Corp. 16 Oct **1921** [c16 Oct 1921; LP17234]. Si; b&w. 35mm. 5 reels, 4,500 ft.

Prod-Story Hunt Stromberg. *Dir* William A. Seiter. *Scen* William A. Seiter, Violet Clark. *Photog* Bert Cann. *Art Dir* W. L. Heywood. *Asst Dir* Lewis Milestone.

Cast: Doris May *(Margie Carr)*, Hallam Cooley *(Homer Dean Chadwick)*, Otis Harlan *("Old Top" Carr)*, Arthur Hoyt *(Lester Hicks)*, Lillian Worth *(Flossy)*, Bull Montana *(Bubbs)*, Billy Elmer *(Cauliflower Jim)*, "Spike" Robinson *(Todd)*.

Comedy. Margie Carr, the only daughter of wealthy Tom Carr, obsessed with aiding less fortunate people, opens an office, advertises for secretarial applicants, and hires Bubbs, a roughneck gangster who bounces the other applicants. Her sweetheart, Homer, tries to disguise himself as a tough and romance her, but he is evicted by Bubbs and seeks the aid of his friend Lester Hicks, who convinces Margie that he has suicidal tendencies. Margie agrees to go to his rescue at any hour of the day or night. When Margie goes to the theater and sees her sweetheart there with an ex-chorus girl, Flossie, on his arm, a riot ensues, and Margie decides to marry Hicks; he, however, decides to take the chorus girl. Realizing the folly of her schemes, she agrees to be the wife of Homer Dean Chadwick. *Philanthropists. Chorus girls. Gangsters.*

FOOLISH LIVES **F2.1859**

Young Producers Filming Co. **1922.** Si; b&w. 35mm. [Feature length assumed.]

Cast: Frank Chatman, Henry Harris, Frank Carter, Jewell Cox, Marguerite Patton, Jonella Patton.

Melodrama(?). No information about the precise nature of this film has been found. *Negro life.*

THE FOOLISH MATRONS **F2.1860**

Maurice Tourneur Productions. *Dist* Associated Producers. 19 Jun **1921** [c7 Jun 1921; LP16654]. Si; b&w. 35mm. 6-7 reels, 6,544 ft.

Dir Maurice Tourneur, Clarence L. Brown. *Scen* Wyndham Gittens. *Photog* Charles Van Enger, Kenneth Gordon MacLean.

Cast: Hobart Bosworth *(Dr. Ian Fraser)*, Doris May *(Georgia Wayne)*, Mildred Manning *(Sheila Hopkins)*, Kathleen Kirkham *(Annis Grand)*, Betty Schade *(The Mysterious Woman)*, Margaret McWade *(Mrs. Eugenia Sheridan)*, Charles Meredith *(Lafayette Wayne)*, Wallace MacDonald *(Anthony Sheridan)*, Michael Dark *(Chester King)*, Frankie Lee *(Bobby)*.

Melodrama. Source: Brian Oswald Donn-Byrne, *The Foolish Matrons* (New York, 1920). Three women, each living in a separate social sphere, work out their destinies in New York. Annis Grand, who has achieved great success on the stage, meets Ian Fraser as the result of an automobile accident, and when he is overworked and resorts to drugs after their marriage she gives up her career for their mutual happiness. Georgia Wayne, from a small southern town, marries a plodding young lawyer, Lafayette Wayne; then, compromised by wealthy promoter Chester King, she is discarded by both men. Sheila Hopkins, a young newspaperwoman who marries to escape being an old maid, is selfishly concerned only with her career; and lacking sympathy for her sensitive husband, Tony Sheridan, she drives him to drink. Returning to his hometown, he dies, leaving her to realize her loss. *Actors. Lawyers. Reporters. Physicians. Marriage. Narcotics. Alcoholism. New York City.*

FOOLISH MONTE CARLO (Entertainment Series) **F2.1861**

Wid Gunning, Inc. *Dist* R-C Pictures. Mar **1922** [c15 Apr 1922; LP18311]. Si; b&w. 35mm. 5 reels, 4,235 ft.

Dir William Humphrey. *Scen* William Humphrey, George Edwardes-Hall.

Cast: Mary Clare *(Angela Brentwood)*, Sam Livesey *(Reggie Cosway)*, Robert Corbins *(Archie Lowndes)*, Betty Hall *(Irene Carfour)*, Hayden Coffin *(Lord Carfour)*, Adeline Coffin *(Lady Carfour)*.

Mystery melodrama. Source: Carlton Dawe, *The Black Spider* (London, 1911). The perpetrator of a series of robberies in Monte Carlo leaves his calling card, on which a black spider is drawn, at the scene of each robbery. Suspects include Irene Carfour and Archie Lowndes, who is in love with Angela Brentwood, although her guardians, the Carfours, insist that she marry one Beauvais. Charming but muddleheaded Reggie Cosway maintains that he can solve the mystery and accuses Archie of the latest theft. Angela defends Archie, explaining that she took the necklace as a joke. Cosway then accuses Angela, but a detective arrives with Beauvais, who confesses to the crimes—thus freeing Angela to marry Archie. *Guardians. Robbery. Monte Carlo.*

FOOLISH MOTHERS **F2.1862**

Corona Cinema Corp. 12 Jan **1923** [New York State license]. Si; b&w. 35mm. 6 reels, 5,540 ft.

Cast: Edward Coxen, Enid Markey.

Melodrama(?). No information about the nature of this film has been found.

Note: Local New York State distribution was by Webster Pictures.

THE FOOLISH TWINS **F2.1863**

Dist Lee-Bradford Corp. caJan **1923**. Si; b&w. 35mm. 5 reels.

Cast: Terry Twins.

Melodrama(?). No information about the nature of this film has been found.

THE FOOLISH VIRGIN **F2.1864**

Columbia Pictures. *Dist* C. B. C. Film Sales. 15 Aug **1924** [c6 Aug 1924; LP20474]. Si; b&w. 35mm. 6 reels, 5,900 ft.

Dir George W. Hill. *Adapt-Cont* Lois Zellner. *Photog* Norbert Brodin. *Asst Dir* Frank O'Neil.

Cast: Elaine Hammerstein *(Mary Adams)*, Robert Frazer *(Jim Owens/ Eiphan Owens)*, Gladys Brockwell *(Nance Owens)*, Phyllis Haver *(Jane Sanderson)*, Lloyd Whitlock *(Charles Spencer)*, Irene Hunt *(Mrs. Dawson)*, Howard Truesdell *(Dr. Dawson)*, Jack Henderson *(Sam Allen)*, Roscoe Karns *(Chuck Brady)*, Oliver Cross *(Lawson Howard)*, Edward Borman *(Dan O'Leary)*, Spec O'Donnell *(little boy)*.

Melodrama. Source: Thomas Dixon, *The Foolish Virgin: A Romance of Today* (New York & London, 1915). Jim Owens, son of a brutal father, grows to manhood as a reformed thief and successful inventor. At a jazz party he meets quiet and refined Mary Adams, who loves him until she learns the truth about his past. When he rescues her from a forest fire, however, their mutual love is confirmed. *Criminals—Rehabilitation. Inventors. Jazz life. Forest fires.*

FOOLISH WIVES (Universal Super-Jewel) **F2.1865**

Universal Film Manufacturing Co. 11 Jan **1922** [New York premiere; released 8 May; c11 Feb 1922; LP17550]. Si; b&w. 35mm. 14 reels, 14,120 ft. [Release version: 10 reels.]

Pres by Carl Laemmle. *Dir-Story-Scen* Erich von Stroheim. *Titl* Marian Ainslee, Erich von Stroheim. *Photog* Ben Reynolds, William Daniels. *Ch Engr Illumination & Lighting Eff* Harry J. Brown. *Art Dir* E. E. Sheeley, Richard Day. *Scenic Artist* Van Alstein. *Tech Dir* William Meyers, James Sullivan, George Williams. *Mus Score* Sigmund Romberg. *Asst Dir* Edward Sowders, Jack R. Proctor. *Wardrobe* Western Costuming Co. *Sculpture* Don Jarvis. *Master of Prop* C. J. Rogers.

Cast: Rudolph Christians *(Andrew J. Hughes)*, Miss Du Pont *(Helen, his wife)*, Maude George *(Princess Olga Petschnikoff)*, Mae Busch *(Princess Vera Petschnikoff)*, Erich von Stroheim *(Count Sergius Karamzin [Captain, 3d Hussars, Imperial Russian Army])*, Dale Fuller *(Maruschka, a maid)*, Al Edmundsen *(Pavel Pavlich, a butler)*, Cesare Gravina *(Caesare Ventucci, a counterfeiter)*, Malvine Polo *(Marietta, his daughter)*, Louis K. Webb *(Dr. Judd)*, Mrs. Kent *(his wife)*, C. J. Allen *(Albert I, Prince of Monaco)*, Edward Reinach *(Secretary of State of Monaco)*.

Society melodrama. Count Sergius Karamzin, an adventurer, and his two cousins, Olga and Vera, lease a villa at Monte Carlo and cultivate the friendship of American envoy Andrew J. Hughes and his wife, Helen, who is flattered by the flirtations of the count. While strolling in the country, the count and Helen take refuge from a storm in a hut, and though they are obliged to remain overnight the arrival of an old monk keeps the count from revealing his intentions. At the casino the diplomat's wife wins, and when the party retires to the count's villa for poker, Mrs. Hughes, in response to a secret note from the count, meets him in the tower, where he wheedles her out of her money and begins to seduce her. Meanwhile, Hughes, having discovered the cousins cheating at the casino, returns to the hotel. The count's maid, a victim of his lechery, becomes desperately jealous, sets fire to the villa, and leaps into the sea. The count and Mrs. Hughes are saved by jumping into a life net, and Hughes, becoming aware of the count's intrigue, attacks him and arranges a duel for the following morning. Infuriated by his folly, the "Princesses" drive the count from the villa; at the house of Ventucci, for whom he has been passing counterfeit money, the count attacks Ventucci's halfwitted daughter; later, Ventucci kills him and drops his body in a sewer. Returning from the dueling place, Hughes finds that his wife has given premature birth to a child, and they are reconciled. *Diplomats. Gambling. Suicide. Murder. Lechery. Monte Carlo. Albert I (Monaco). Fires. Duels.*

FOOLS AND RICHES **F2.1866**

Universal Pictures. 7 May **1923** [c30 Apr 1923; LP18929]. Si; b&w. 35mm. 5 reels, 4,904 ft.

Dir Herbert Blache. *Scen* Charles Kenyon, George Hull. *Story* Frederick J. Jackson. *Photog* Allen Davey.

Cast: Herbert Rawlinson *(Jimmy Dorgan)*, Katherine Perry *(Nellie Blye)*, Tully Marshall *(John Dorgan)*, Doris Pawn *(Bernice Lorraine)*, Arthur S. Hull *(Dick McCann)*, Nicholas De Ruiz *(Frasconi)*, Roy Laidlaw *(lawyer)*, John Cossar *(president of the railroad)*.

Drama. During his lifetime John Dorgan is unsuccessful in his attempts to cure his son, Jimmy, of his spendthrift ways, but his will leaves only a part of his fortune to Jimmy, while explaining where to dig for the rest. With the help of his friends, Jimmy rapidly goes broke. Nellie Blye stands by him, however, and encourages him to get a job. While working as a waiter, he overhears information with which he prevents a railroad from being taken over and is rewarded with a position in the company. He follows his father's directions, finds the rest of his inheritance, and marries Nellie. *Spendthrifts. Waiters. Inheritance. Railroads. Wills.*

Note: Working title: *Twenty Dollars.*

A FOOL'S AWAKENING **F2.1867**

Metro Pictures. 28 Jan **1924** [c13 Feb 1924; LP19941]. Si; b&w. 35mm. 6 reels, ca5,760 ft.

Dir Harold Shaw. *Adapt-Cont* Tom J. Hopkins. *Photog* Allen Siegler. *Art Dir* J. J. Hughes.

Cast: Harrison Ford *(John Briggs)*, Enid Bennett *(Olivia Gale)*, Alec Francis *(Major Oliphant)*, Mary Alden *(Myra)*, Lionel Belmore *(Herbert Lorington)*, Harry Northrup *(Hargrave Mavenna)*, Evelyn Sherman *(Miss Oliphant)*, John Sainpolis *(Lieutenant Wedderburn)*, Pauline French *(Lady Ordwynne)*, Edward Connelly *(Blandon)*, D. R. O. Hatswell *(Bobby Walton)*, Mark Fenton *(Wainwright)*, Arline Pretty *(Lydia Mainwaring)*, Lorimer Johnston *(Colonel Onslow)*.

Society melodrama. Source: William John Locke, *The Tale of Triona* (London, 1912). While escaping Russia during the Revolution, John Briggs, an Englishman employed as a chauffeur to a nobleman, discovers a diary on the dead body of an officer identified as Alexis Triona. The diary describes the man's thrilling exploits among the Bolshevists. Briggs returns to England, continues to work as a chauffeur, and writes stories in his spare time. Following the rejection by publishers of his manuscripts, Briggs uses the stories in Triona's diary, and suddenly he becomes famous. Posing as Triona, he weds Olivia Gale, a beautiful heiress. Eventually, his wife learns his true identity and leaves him. Years later they are reunited.

Authors. Bolshevists. Chauffeurs. Impersonation. Plagiarism. England. Russia—History—1917–21 Revolution. Documentation.

FOOLS FIRST **F2.1868**

Marshall Neilan Productions. *Dist* Associated First National Pictures. ca27 May **1922** [Dallas premiere; c19 Jun 1922; LP17992]. Si; b&w. 35mm. 6 reels, 5,773 ft.

Prod-Dir Marshall Neilan. *Scen* Marion Fairfax. *Titl* Hugh Wiley. *Photog* David Kesson, Karl Struss. *Film Ed* Daniel J. Gray. *Asst Dir* Thomas Held.

Cast: Richard Dix *(Tommy Frazer)*, Claire Windsor *(Ann Whittaker)*, Claude Gillingwater *(Denton Drew)*, Raymond Griffith *(Tony, the Wop)*, George Siegmann *(Spud Miller)*, Helen Lynch *("Blondie" Clark)*, Shannon Day *("Cutie" Williams)*, George Dromgold *(Skinny, the Hick)*, Leo White *(Geffy, the Dope)*, Robert Brower *(The Butler)*.

Crime melodrama. Source: Hugh MacNair Kahler, "Fool's First," in *Saturday Evening Post* (193:12–13, 20 Nov 1920). Tommy Frazer, a product of Hell's Kitchen, is sentenced to a prison term for forgery; upon his release, he meets Ann Whittaker, a bank clerk, and they decide to rob the bank where she works. She obtains references whereby Tommy is also employed there, and banker Denton Drew trusts them implicitly. When an unusually large deposit is made, Tommy takes the money and meets Ann at a railroad station, only to find that he is unable to go through with his plan. With Ann's consent he sets out to return the money but is waylaid by his former gang associates. Drew, however, has arranged a fake deposit as a test for Tommy; and when the latter confesses, Drew feels that Tommy has proved himself and marks him for a promotion. Tommy and Ann set out on a fresh path together. *Criminals—Rehabilitation. Bankers. Forgery. Robbery. New York City—Hell's Kitchen.*

FOOLS FOR LUCK **F2.1869**

Paramount Famous Lasky Corp. 7 May **1928** [c5 May 1928; LP25220]. Si; b&w. 35mm. 6 reels, 5,758 ft.

Dir Charles Reisner. *Adapt-Scen* Sam Mintz, J. Walter Ruben. *Story* Harry Fried. *Photog* William Marshall.

Cast: W. C. Fields *(Richard Whitehead)*, Chester Conklin *(Samuel Hunter)*, Sally Blane *(Louise Hunter)*, Jack Luden *(Ray Caldwell)*, Mary Alden *(Mrs. Hunter)*, Arthur Houseman *(Charles Grogan)*, Robert Dudley *(Jim Simpson)*, Martha Mattox *(Mrs. Simpson)*.

Comedy. Richard Whitehead plays the bumpkin when convenient—as on entering Huntersville, where Samuel Hunter reigns supreme on the pool table and promotes a match, offering to wield the cue with a single hand; Whitehead soon ruffles Hunter's feathers. He goes on to concoct a scheme promoting some suspect oil fields and diverts suspicion by hiring Ray Caldwell, scion of a prominent town family, whose gullible but ingenuous nature is adored by Hunter's daughter, Louise. Hunter is thus forced to legitimize Whitehead's larceny even to the point of promoting sale of the stock. He then secretly buys the real deed to the property and starts a rumor that the black gold has indeed come through. His ruse prompts the original swindler, the wheedling Mr. Whitehead, to buy back his fraudulent stock. The tables turn once when oil really does come in and then again when Whitehead is informed who really owns the land. *Confidence men. Social classes. Fraud. Smalltown life. Billiard parlors. Oil wells.*

FOOLS' HIGHWAY (Universal Super-Jewel) **F2.1870**

Universal Pictures. 3 or 9 Mar **1924** [c13 Feb 1924; LP19911]. Si; b&w. 35mm. 7 reels, 6,800 ft.

Pres by Carl Laemmle. *Dir* Irving Cummings. *Scen* Lenore J. Coffee, Harvey Gates. *Adapt* Emil Forst. *Photog* William Fildew.

Cast: Mary Philbin *(Mamie Rose)*, Pat O'Malley *(Mike Kildare)*, William Collier, Jr. *(Max Davidson)*, Lincoln Plummer *(Mike Flavin, The Boss)*, Edwin J. Brady *(Jackie Doodle)*, Max Davidson *(Old Levi)*, Kate Price *(Mrs. Flannigan)*, Charles Murray *(Mamie's father)*, Sherry Tansey *(Ole Larsen)*, Steve Murphy *(Chuck Connors)*, Tom O'Brien *(Philadelphia O'Brien)*.

Romantic melodrama. Source: Owen Frawley Kildare, *My Mamie Rose; the Story of My Regeneration* (New York, 1903). Mike Kildare, a swaggering youth from New York City's Bowery at the turn of the century, loves Mamie Rose, a mender in a secondhand clothing shop. Mamie is fascinated by Kildare's brute strength, but she is also attracted to a kind and gentle Jewish boy. Kildare's gang, which he forsakes to prove his love to Mamie, waylays and beats him (Kildare) in an underground den. He takes the severe punishment, reforms, wins Mamie, and joins the police force. *Seamstresses. Police. Irish. Jews. Gangs. Clothing business. New York City—Bowery.*

FOOLS IN THE DARK **F2.1871**

R-C Pictures. *Dist* Film Booking Offices of America. 4 Aug **1924** [c16 Jul 1924; LP20399]. Si; b&w. 35mm. 8 reels, 7,702 ft.

Dir Al Santell. *Story-Scen* Bertram Millhauser. *Photog* Leon Eycke, Blake Wagner.

Cast: Patsy Ruth Miller *(Ruth Rand)*, Matt Moore *(Percy Schwartz)*, Bertram Grassby *(Kotah)*, Charles Belcher *(Dr. Rand)*, Tom Wilson *(Diploma)*, John Steppling *(Julius Schwartz)*.

Comedy. When he asks his sweetheart's father for consent to marry her, young Percy finds himself a prisoner of a mad scientist. Assisted by Diploma, a Negro streetcleaner, he makes his escape and then rescues Ruth from the plotters with the aid of a seaplane and the timely assistance of marines. *Scientists. Streetcleaners. Insanity. Seaplanes. United States Marines.*

FOOLS OF FASHION **F2.1872**

Tiffany Productions. 1 Oct **1926** [c15 Sep 1926; LP23108]. Si; b&w. 35mm. 7 reels, 6,484 ft.

Dir James C. McKay. *Scen* Sarah Y. Mason. *Photog* Faxon Dean, Al M. Green. *Art Dir* Edwin B. Willis.

Cast: Mae Busch *(Enid Alden)*, Marceline Day *(Mary Young)*, Theodore von Eltz *(Matthew Young)*, Robert Ober *(Joe Alden)*, Hedda Hopper *(Countess de Fragni)*, Rose Dione *(Francine)*, James Mack *(pawnbroker)*, Albert Roccardi *(William Norris)*.

Society drama. Source: George Randolph Chester, *The Other Woman* (a novel; publication undetermined). Mary Young, a young wife who longs for beautiful clothes, is invited by her friend Enid to shop at Madame Francine's, where she meets the Countess de Fragni, an artist, and Mr. Norris, an elderly roué. Mary, persuaded by Enid, buys an expensive fur coat with money she wins in a poker game and tells her husband that she won it with a pawn ticket; she agrees to earn back the money by posing for the countess, and her husband, Matthew, unexpectedly finds her there in a compromising situation with Norris. Joe, Enid's husband, also suspects his wife of infidelity and follows her to the countess' house, where Enid falls to her death from the balcony. Mary goes to Norris' apartment to prevent Matthew from killing Norris, and having been convinced that he has been ungenerous with his wife, he repents. *Artists. Rakes. Marriage. Clothes. Fashion. Infidelity. Suicide.*

FOOLS OF FORTUNE **F2.1873**

Golden State Films. *Dist* American Releasing Corp. 24 Sep or 5 Oct **1922** [c5 Jul, 7 Sep 1922; LU18203]. Si; b&w. 35mm. 6 reels, 5,609 ft.

Prod A. Byron Davis. *Dir* Louis Chaudet. *Scen* Wilbur C. Tuttle. *Photog* King Gray.

Cast: Frank Dill *(Chuck Warner)*, Russell Simpson *(Magpie Simpkins)*, Tully Marshall *(Scenery Sims)*, Frank Brownlee *(Ike Harper)*, Thomas Ricketts *(Milton DePuyster)*, Lillian Langdon *(Mrs. DePuyster)*, Marguerite De La Motte *(Marion DePuyster)*.

Western comedy. Source: Wilbur C. Tuttle, "Assisting Ananias," in *Adventure* (25:119–131, 1 Apr 1920). Chuck Warner and three friends go east and try to pass Chuck off as the long-lost son of millionaire Milton DePuyster. When DePuyster avers that he never had a son, the group causes a commotion sufficient to bring out the police. Chuck admits his ruse, but he is revealed to be Mrs. DePuyster's son by an earlier marriage. *Millionaires. Parentage. Imposture.*

FOOL'S PARADISE **F2.1874**

Famous Players–Lasky. *Dist* Paramount Pictures. 9 Dec **1921** [New York premiere; released 19 Mar 1922; c23 Dec 1921; LP17420]. Si; b&w. 35mm. 9 reels, 8,681 ft.

Pres by Jesse L. Lasky. *Dir* Cecil B. De Mille. *Scen* Beulah Marie Dix, Sada Cowan. *Photog* Karl Struss, Alvin Wyckoff.

Cast: Dorothy Dalton *(Poll Patchouli)*, Mildred Harris *(Rosa Duchêne)*, Conrad Nagel *(Arthur Phelps)*, Theodore Kosloff *(John Rodriguez)*, John Davidson *(Prince Talaat-Noi)*, Julia Faye *(Samaran, his chief wife)*, Clarence Burton *(Manuel)*, Guy Oliver *(Briggs)*, Kamuela C. Searle *(Kay)*, Jacqueline Logan *(Girda)*.

Melodrama. Source: Leonard Merrick, "Laurels and the Lady," in *The Man Who Understood Women, and Other Stories* (London, 1908). Phelps, an ex-service man who has suffered an eye injury, falls in love with Rosa Duchêne, a French dancer, but in a Mexican bordertown he meets Poll

Patchouli, also a dancer. When he rejects Poll's advances, she tricks him with an explosive cigar that blinds him. Later, he hears Poll mimicking Rosa's voice, and believing her to be his beloved, he tells her about the accident; Poll resolves to atone and begs him to marry her, and he consents. She takes him to a surgeon who restores his sight, but discovering her deception, Phelps leaves her in search of Rosa. At last he finds Rosa living with a prince in Siam; unable to decide which one she loves, Rosa throws her glove into a crocodile pit, promising to take the man who retrieves it. The prince is almost killed by the reptiles, but Phelps saves him. Rejecting Rosa, nevertheless, Phelps returns to Poll but finds her engaged to Rodríguez. In a quarrel, Poll is injured and Phelps carries her from the dancehall. Following her recovery they get married. *Veterans. Dancers. Royalty. Blindness. Jealousy. Mexico. Siam. Crocodiles.*

A FOOL'S PROMISE **F2.1875**

White Film Corp. **1921**. Si; b&w. 35mm. [Feature length assumed.]

Melodrama(?). No information about the precise nature of this film has been found. *Negro life.*

FOOTFALLS **F2.1876**

Fox Film Corp. Nov **1921** [c3 Sep 1921; LP17005]. Si; b&w. 35mm. 8 reels, 8,068 ft.

Pres by William Fox. *Dir-Scen* Charles J. Brabin. *Photog* George W. Lane.

Cast: [Frederick] Tyrone Power *(Hiram Scudder)*, Tom Douglas *(Tommy, his son)*, Estelle Taylor *(Peggy Hawthorne)*, Gladden James *(Alec Campbell)*.

Melodrama. Source: Wilbur Daniel Steele, "Footfalls," in *Tower of Sand and Other Stories* (New York, 1929). Hiram Scudder, a blind cobbler, lives with his son, Tommy, and Alec Campbell, a lodger of whom Tommy becomes jealous when he overhears him paying attentions to his sweetheart, Peggy. The two fight, and one is killed, while the other attempts to escape with a satchel of money. The murderer is seized by the cobbler, who retains the money but is unable to prevent his escape. Meanwhile, an overturned lamp sets fire to the room, and the killer's victim is burned beyond recognition, although a pocketbook later identifies him as the lodger. For 3 years the cobbler waits for the murderer to return, and the villagers believe him mad. Finally, one night he does return and is strangled by the cobbler, whose revenge is complete when he is assured that his victim is Campbell. *Cobblers. Fatherhood. Blindness. Murder. Revenge.*

THE FOOTLIGHT RANGER **F2.1877**

Fox Film Corp. 14 Jan **1923** [c14 Jan 1923; LP19172]. Si; b&w. 35mm. 5 reels, 4,729 ft.

Pres by William Fox. *Dir* Scott Dunlap. *Scen* Dorothy Yost. *Story* William Branch. *Photog* Dev Jennings.

Cast: Charles Jones *(Bill Moreland)*, Fritzi Brunette *(Janet Ainslee)*, James Mason *(Al Brownley)*, Lillian Langdon *(Nellie Andrews)*, Lydia Yeamans Titus *(Miss Amelia)*, Henry Barrows *(David Marsh)*.

Western melodrama. Cowboy Bill Moreland meets and falls in love with Janet Ainslee, a stranded actress. He sells his prize dogs to pay her way back to New York and eventually follows her to the city, where he rescues her from a producer who is willing to back her if she will pay the price. Moreland and Janet marry and return west. *Cowboys. Actors. Theatrical producers. Dogs.*

FOOTLIGHTS **F2.1878**

Famous Players–Lasky. *Dist* Paramount Pictures. 2 Oct **1921** [c5 Oct 1921; LP17034]. Si; b&w. 35mm. 7 reels, 7,078 ft.

Pres by Adolph Zukor. *Dir* John S. Robertson. *Scen* Josephine Lovett. *Photog* Roy Overbaugh. *Art Dir* Robert M. Haas.

Cast: Elsie Ferguson *(Lisa Parsinova/Lizzie Parsons)*, Reginald Denny *(Brett Page)*, Marc MacDermott *(Oswald Kane)*, Octavia Handworth *(Etta)*.

Drama. Source: Rita Weiman, "Footlights," in *Saturday Evening Post* (191:53–54, 17 May 1919). Lizzie Parsons scores a success in vaudeville impersonations and attracts the attention of Oswald Kane, a theatrical promoter, who trains her and introduces her to the New York stage as Lisa Parsinova, a famous Russian actress. Later she falls in love with wealthy Brett Page and begins to despise the personas of her new self: therefore, in agreement with Kane, at the close of the season, an empty boat is found containing the garments of Lisa. Brett searches in vain for the "drowned" actress and finally meets Lizzie as her ordinary American self in a railroad restaurant, where they decide to marry. *Actors. Vaudeville. Theater. Impersonation. Personality.*

FOOTLIGHTS AND FOOLS **F2.1879**

First National Pictures. 4 Nov **1929** [c12 Nov 1929; LP856]. Sd (Vitaphone); b&w with col sequences (Technicolor). 35mm. 8 reels, 6,952 ft.

Pres by John McCormick. *Dir* William A. Seiter. *Screenplay* Tom Geraghty. *Dial* Carey Wilson. *Photog* Sidney Hickox, Henry Freulich. *Songs: "You Can't Believe My Eyes," "If I Can't Have You"* Ray Perkins, Norman Spencer, Herman Ruby.

Cast: Colleen Moore *(Fifi D'Auray)*, Raymond Hackett *(Jimmy Willet)*, Fredric March *(Gregory Pyne)*, Virginia Lee Corbin *(Claire Floyd)*, Mickey Bennett *(Call Boy)*, Edward Martindel *(Chandler Cunningham)*, Adrienne D'Ambricourt *(Jo)*, Frederick Howard *(Treasurer)*, Sidney Jarvis *(Stage Manager)*, Cleve Moore *(Press Agent)*, Andy Rice, Jr. *(Stage Plugger)*, Ben Hendricks, Jr. *(Stage Doorman)*, Larry Banthim *(Bud Burke)*.

Society melodrama. Source: Katherine Brush, "Footlights and Fools" (publication undetermined). Fifi D'Auray, the sensation of "The Sins of 1930," is actually Betty Murphy, who from her chorus days has been in love with Jimmy Willet, a gambling youth, though she refuses to marry him until he gets a job. Gregory Pyne, a wealthy young bachelor, becomes infatuated with Fifi and bribes his friend Claire to bring her to supper. There she quarrels with him and leaves in a feigned huff; and to make amends, Gregory agrees to give Jimmy a job as treasurer of the theater. When Jimmy declares he has been accused of complicity in a robbery and a warrant is issued for his arrest, Fifi accuses Pyne of framing him; then Jimmy defiantly reveals their marriage to Pyne, who is completely disillusioned. But when Fifi learns of Jimmy's guilt, she sends him away and makes plans for a divorce. *Chorus girls. Gamblers. Theater. Marriage. Divorce. Frameup.*

FOOTLOOSE WIDOWS **F2.1880**

Warner Brothers Pictures. 19 Jun **1926** [c18 Jun 1926; LP22825]. Si; b&w. 35mm. 7 reels, 7,163 ft.

Dir Roy Del Ruth. *Scen* Darryl Francis Zanuck. *Photog* David Abel. *Asst Camera* Charles Van Enger. *Asst Dir* William McGann.

Cast: Louise Fazenda *(Flo)*, Jacqueline Logan *(Marian)*, Jason Robards *(Jerry)*, Arthur Hoyt *(Henry)*, Neely Edwards *("The Senator")*, Jane Winton *(Mrs. Drew)*, Mack Swain *(Marian's husband-in-retrospect)*, John Miljan *(Mr. Smith)*, Eddie Phillips *("Tuxedo" Eddie)*, Henry Barrows *(hotel manager)*.

Farce. Source: Beatrice Burton, *Footloose* (Gerrard, Douglas Mr. Dunn). New York models Flo and Marian entice their employer to give them each a fine wardrobe for a party, then slip off to Florida and install themselves in a luxury hotel, posing as two wealthy widows. While Flo captures the fancy of "The Senator," a solid citizen, she has Marian plot to ensnare a Mr. Smith, supposedly a millionaire, but Marian accidentally meets Jerry, a personable and charming young man (actually Mr. Smith) and falls in love with him. Under pressure from Flo, Marian finally accepts Smith's ardent proposal of marriage, each supposing the other to be wealthy; but Dunn, the girls' employer, arrives and has them arrested. Jerry, disillusioned, pays their hotel bills; Marian returns his gift of $1,000 and declares her love for him. The two are married, and Flo continues her interrupted courtship with "The Senator." *Fashion models. Millionaires. Courtship. Imposture. Florida.*

Note: The copyright title, recorded in error, is *Footloose Windows.*

FOR ALIMONY ONLY **F2.1881**

De Mille Pictures. *Dist* Producers Distributing Corp. 20 Sep **1926** [New York premiere; released 8 Nov; c30 Aug 1926; LP23058]. Si; b&w. 35mm. 7 reels, 6,400 ft.

Pres by John C. Flinn. *Dir* William De Mille. *Story-Cont* Lenore J. Coffee. *Photog* Arthur Miller. *Art Dir* Max Parker. *Film Ed* Adelaide Cannon. *Unit Mgr* George Hippard. *Cost* Adrian.

Cast: Leatrice Joy *(Mary Martin Williams)*, Clive Brook *(Peter Williams)*, Lilyan Tashman *(Narcissa Williams)*, Casson Ferguson *(Bertie Waring)*, Toby Claude *(The Maid)*.

Domestic drama. A stormy marriage of 6 months between Narcissa and Peter Williams ends in a bitter quarrel, and to gain his freedom Peter offers her more alimony than he can afford. Then he meets Mary Martin, who restores his faith in marriage. With business reverses, Peter falls behind in his alimony payments and neglects his new wife. Narcissa, however, manages to support Bertie Waring, a young sofa-hound; but she protests the delayed alimony and Mary is forced to take a job with an interior decorating establishment. Peter goes to Narcissa to appeal to her generosity, at the moment when Mary (unaware of Narcissa's identity as her husband's first wife) is working in Narcissa's apartment; seeing them together, Mary leaves in humiliation and accepts an invitation from Bertie. Determined to take revenge on the woman who has "stolen her sweetheart," Narcissa follows the couple to a roadhouse; Peter arrives, and during a police raid Mary suggests that Narcissa is engaged to Bertie. Rather than face jail, they get married, thus cutting off their means of support—alimony. *Interior decorators. Marriage. Divorce. Alimony. Personal identity.*

FOR ANOTHER WOMAN **F2.1882**

Rayart Pictures. 1 Nov **1924** [c1 Dec 1924; LP20923]. Si; b&w. 35mm. 6 reels, 5,637 ft.

Pres by W. Ray Johnston. Frank Talbot Production. *Dir* David Kirkland. *Scen* Agnes Christine Johnston, Frank Dazey. *Photog* Horace G. Plympton.

Cast: Kenneth Harlan, Florence Billings, Henry Sedley, Mary Thurman, Kathryn Riddell, Arnold Daly, Alan Hale, [Frederick] Tyrone Power.

Melodrama. Source: Pearl Doles Bell, "Just Mary" (publication undetermined). Upon his death, the estate of Richard Winthrop, the *maître* of a French Canadian village, is inherited by his American nephew, Stephen Winthrop, who continues to live a wild life in New York and neglects the responsibilities of his new position. Unknown to Stephen, Frank Garson, the family attorney, bans all hunting on the Winthrop lands, depriving the villagers of their livelihood. Mary Cartier, the goddaughter of the blind village priest, comes to New York and informs Stephen of Garson's actions. Stephen returns with her and lifts the ban, deciding to stay in Canada. Linked romantically with Stephen in village gossip, Mary again comes to New York to try to help Garson's abandoned and ailing wife, Felice, but to no avail. Felice dies, and Mary returns to Canada with Felice's newborn baby. The villagers suppose her to be a fallen woman, and an angry mob forms to drive her from the village. She is saved from this ugly expulsion when she explains the parentage of the baby. Garson is exposed as a cad and a schemer, and Mary and Stephen declare their love for each other. *French Canadians. Lawyers. Village life. Gossip. Hunting. Inheritance. Canada. New York City.*

FOR BIG STAKES **F2.1883**

Fox Film Corp. 18 Jun **1922** [c18 Jun 1922; LP18340]. Si; b&w. 35mm. 5 reels, 4,378 ft.

Pres by William Fox. *Dir-Writ* Lynn Reynolds. *Titl* Ralph Spence. *Photog* Dan Clark. *Film Ed* Ralph Spence.

Cast: Tom Mix *("Clean-up" Sudden)*, Patsy Ruth Miller *(Dorothy Clark)*, Sid Jordan *(Scott Mason)*, Bert Sprotte *(Rowell Clark)*, Joe Harris *(Ramon Valdez)*, Al Fremont *(Sheriff Blaisdell)*, Earl Simpson *(Tin Horn Johnnie)*, Tony *(himself, a horse)*.

Western melodrama. "Clean-up" Sudden, a stranger in town, incurs the wrath of Scott Mason and wins the love of Dorothy Clark while punishing a crooked sheriff and cleaning up the ranch of Rowell Clark, Dorothy's father. Mason ties Dorothy to a tree, sets fire to the ranch, and dies in that fire. Clean-up rescues the girl, though he cannot save the buildings, and reveals himself to be the rightful owner of the ranch. *Sheriffs. Political corruption. Incendiarism. Ranches. Horses.*

FOR HEAVEN'S SAKE **F2.1884**

Harold Lloyd Corp. *Dist* Paramount Pictures. 5 Apr **1926** [c6 Apr 1926; LP22577]. Si; b&w. 35mm. 6 reels, 5,356 ft.

Dir Sam Taylor. *Titl* Ralph Spence. *Story* John Grey, Ted Wilde, Clyde Bruckman. *Photog* Walter Lundin. *Asst Camera* Henry Kohler. *Art Dir* Liell K. Vedder. *Tech Dir* William MacDonald. *Film Ed* Allen McNeil. *Asst Dir* Robert A. Golden. *Prod Mgr* John L. Murphy.

Cast: Harold Lloyd *(The Uptown Boy [J. Harold Manners])*, Jobyna Ralston *(The Downtown Girl [Hope])*, Noah Young *(The Roughneck)*, James Mason *(The Gangster)*, Paul Weigel *(The Optimist [Brother Paul])*.

Comedy. J. Harold Manners (The Uptown Boy), a debonair young millionaire in search of a downtown restaurant, passes an evangelist's coffee stand and accidentally starts a fire; Harold contributes a thousand dollars for damages, which the evangelist uses to open a mission named for the donor. Coming to protest this honor, Harold meets Hope, the evangelist's daughter, and offers to help her bring in the poolroom toughs and gangsters. He draws them into a chase, and with the aid of the police, he retrieves the property they have stolen. Harold's club friends abduct him to prevent his marriage to Hope, but his slum cronies come to the club and rescue him. The race back to the mission turns into a melee of trials and tribulations for Harold as his inebriated friends wreak havoc; and at the mission Hope and Harold are married amidst the cheers of the converts. *Millionaires. Evangelists. Gangsters. Slums. Missions. Chases.*

FOR HIS MOTHER'S SAKE **F2.1885**

Blackburn-Velde Pictures. *Dist* Fidelity Pictures. 1 Jan **1922** [New York State]. Si; b&w. 35mm. 6 reels, 5,400 ft.

Cast: Jack Johnson, Mattie Wilkes.

Melodrama. For the sake of his mother, a son must endure hardship and misfortune. *Filial relations.*

FOR HIS SAKE **F2.1886**

Dist Zerner Film Co. Apr **1922** [New York State]. Si; b&w. 35mm. 5 reels, 4,850 ft.

Dir-Story-Scen John S. Lawrence.

Cast: John Dillon *(Sidney Bentham)*, Hilda Nord *(Ethel Dean)*, Charles Jackson *(Jimmie)*, Mrs. Coller *(Mrs. Dean)*, Jane Jennis *(Aunt Elizabeth)*.

Drama. "Ethel Dean is left an orphan when her mother dies of consumption, because of insufficient care. Her mother's brother, Sidney Bentham, is a wealthy financier, but has isolated himself from all his relatives. Ethel and her pal, Jimmy, the newsie, set out to find Bentham. They happen to arrive at his home, and Bentham, who has heard of his sister's death, repents sufficiently to take Ethel into his home. Jimmie, too, finds shelter there and the two plot to reform Bentham, who is bent on destroying his brother in the stock market. The two children plan a clever campaign and succeed in restoring the friendship between the two brothers." *(Moving Picture World,* 10 Jun 1922, p577.) *Orphans. Children. Financiers. Newsboys. Brothers. Stock market. Tuberculosis.*

FOR LADIES ONLY **F2.1887**

Columbia Pictures. 20 Jul **1927** [c22 Aug 1927; LP24328]. Si; b&w. 35mm. 6 reels, 5,507 ft.

Prod Harry Cohn. *Dir* Scott Pembroke, Henry Lehrman. *Scen* Robert Lord. *Adapt? (see note)* Ernest S. Pagano, Albert Payson Terhune. *Photog* J. O. Taylor.

Cast: John Bowers *(Cliff Coleman)*, Jacqueline Logan *(Ruth Barton)*, Edna Marion *(Gertie Long)*, Ben Hall *(Joe Decker)*, William H. Strauss *(Mr. Ginsberg)*, Templar Saxe, Kathleen Chambers, Henry Roquemore.

Romantic comedy. Source: George Frank Worts, "Down With Women" (publication undetermined). Clifford Coleman decides that women, because of their excessive concern with perfume and hosiery, are an impediment to business and discharges all his female help. Ruth Barton, the manager's secretary, warns him that once she has left, she will exact a price for any information he needs from her. Later, a buyer closes a deal, adding that he will get his usual "rake-off," and Coleman is forced to consult Ruth; she forces him to pay $500 to learn that the "rake-off" is a 5-lb. box of candy. Coleman concedes her outwitting him but is unconvinced of her sales abilities until she intercepts a large order and offers it to a rival concern. Ruth agrees to return to work on condition that all the other girls are reinstated, but Coleman refuses—that is, until she tells a female buyer that he discriminates against women. Coleman surrenders and soon discovers that he loves Ruth. *Businessmen. Office clerks. Secretaries. Buyers. Women's rights. Employment—Women. Bribery.*

Note: Sources disagree on adaptation credit.

FOR LOVE OF SERVICE **F2.1888**

Dist Clark-Cornelius Corp. 1 Apr **1922.** Si; b&w. 35mm. 5 reels.

Prod Milburn Morante.

Cast: George Chesebro.

Northwest melodrama. "... dealing with man falsely accused of murder who escapes from prison, goes to Canada, and becomes member of the Mounted Police. Learning that his two former enemies, whom he believes committed murder of which he is accused, are in Canada, he starts after them. Girl who aided his escape falls in clutches of these two. One double-crosses the other, and leaves with girl. Hero obtains confession from other, and starts after man and girl. Falling tree strikes him, but he struggles on on foot. Meantime, his captain has learned of charge against him and arrests him, but he has rescued girl and confession clears him." (*Motion Picture News Booking Guide,* 3:26, Oct 1922.) *Prison escapees. Murder. Injustice. Canada. Northwest Mounted Police.*

FOR LOVE OR MONEY *see* **THE CROSSROADS OF NEW YORK**

FOR SALE **F2.1889**

Associated First National Pictures. 15 Jun **1924** [c16 Jun 1924; LP20311, LP20484]. Si; b&w. 35mm. 8 reels, 7,840 ft.

Pers Supv–Story Earl Hudson. *Dir* George Archainbaud. *Ed Dir* Marion Fairfax. *Scen* Fred Stanley. *Photog* T. D. McCord. *Architecture* Milton Menasco. *Film Ed* George McGuire.

Cast: Claire Windsor *(Eleanor Bates)*, Adolphe Menjou *(Joseph Hudley)*, Robert Ellis *(Allan Penfield)*, Mary Carr *(Mrs. Harrison Bates)*, Tully Marshall *(Harrison Bates)*, John Patrick *(Cabot Stanton)*, Vera Reynolds *(Betty Twombly-Smith)*, Jule Power *(Mrs. Twombly-Smith)*, Lou Payne *(Mr. Twombly-Smith)*, Phillips Smalley *(Mr. Winslow)*, Christine Mayo *(Mrs. Winslow)*, Jean Vachon *(The Flapper)*, George Irving *(Eric Porter, journalist)*, Frank Elliott *(Sir John Geddes, English explorer)*, Finch Smiles *(butler)*, Marga La Rubia *(demimondaine)*.

Society melodrama. Eleanor Bates, the daughter of a socially prominent family, agrees to her parents' firm request that she not marry her sweetheart, Allan Penfield, until he makes good financially. Eleanor's father, faced with economic ruin, then makes illicit use of funds belonging to Joseph Hudley and, to save himself from disgrace, persuades Eleanor to marry Cabot Stanton, a wealthy young man. Before the wedding, however, Cabot is killed in an automobile accident; Hudley himself then takes an interest in Eleanor, persuading her to become engaged to him. Eleanor sees Allan again, however, and the old love flares up. She asks Hudley to free her, but he refuses; overcome by grief, she takes poison. Allan saves her life, and Hudley, impressed with the depth of Eleanor's love for Allan, disavows his claims against the elder Bates, leaving Eleanor free to marry Allan. *Embezzlement. Finance—Personal. Filial relations. Automobile accidents. Suicide.*

FOR THE DEFENSE **F2.1890**

Famous Players–Lasky. *Dist* Paramount Pictures. ca4 Jun **1922** [Los Angeles premiere; released 9 Jul; c21 May 1922; LP17893]. Si; b&w. 35mm. 5 reels, 4,905 ft.

Pres by Jesse L. Lasky. *Dir* Paul Powell. *Adapt* Beulah Marie Dix. *Photog* Hal Rosson.

Cast: Ethel Clayton *(Anne Woodstock)*, Vernon Steele *(Christopher Armstrong)*, ZaSu Pitts *(Jennie Dunn)*, Bertram Grassby *(Dr. Joseph Kasimir)*, Maym Kelso *("Smith")*, Sylvia Ashton *(Signora Bartoni)*, Mabel Van Buren *(Cousin Selma)*.

Mystery melodrama. Source: Elmer Rice, *For the Defense, a Drama* (New York production: 19 Dec 1919). Anne Woodstock, a singer, is engaged to district attorney Christopher Armstrong and is a patient of Dr. Kasimir, a Hindu hypnotist-physician, who presumably restores her voice. By a ruse, he lures Anne to his office and hypnotizes her; the next day, Anne, who remembers nothing of the occurrence, leaves for Europe and Kasimir is found murdered in his office. His attendant, Jennie Dunn, who possesses money taken from the safe, is accused of the crime. "Smith," another member of Kasimir's household, identifies a pin found near the body and swears it was worn by Jennie; Anne, returning from her trip, remembers that she was present on the fatal night and insists on her guilt. Jennie then confesses, but Smith explains that she killed Kasimir in a jealous rage. *Singers. District attorneys. Physicians. Hindus. Hypnotism. Murder. Trials.*

FOR THE DEFENSE **F2.1891**

Paramount-Publix Corp. 26 Jul **1930** [c25 Jul 1930; LP1444]. Sd (Movietone); b&w. 35mm. 7 reels, 5,670 ft.

Dir John Cromwell. *Scen-Dial* Oliver H. P. Garrett. *Story* Charles Furthman. *Photog* Charles Lang. *Film Ed* George Nichols, Jr. *Rec Engr* Harold M. McNiff.

Cast: William Powell *(William Foster)*, Kay Francis *(Irene Manners)*, Scott Kolk *(Defoe)*, William B. Davidson *(District Attorney Stone)*, John Elliott *(McGann)*, Thomas Jackson *(Daly)*, Harry Walker *(Miller)*, James Finlayson *(Parrott)*, Charles West *(Joe)*, Charles Sullivan *(Charlie)*, Ernest Adams *(Eddie Withers)*, Bertram Marburgh *(Judge Evans)*, Edward Le Saint *(Judge)*.

Melodrama. William Foster, an eminently successful criminal defense lawyer under investigation by Daly, a particularly shrewd detective, loves Irene Manners, an actress, but refuses to marry her, declaring he is not the marrying kind. To arouse his jealousy, Irene makes a play for Defoe, a society idler; she is at the wheel of his car as they are returning from a roadhouse, and the car strikes and kills a pedestrian. Defoe takes the blame for the accident, and though Foster defends him, the trial goes badly for the defense; and when Foster learns Irene is, in fact, guilty, he becomes unnerved and, under the influence of alcohol, agrees to bribe a juror to hang the case. Daly extracts a confession from the juror, and Foster is arrested for bribery. Irene tells her story to the district attorney and is about to confess when Foster goes to the stand to plead guilty himself; she promises to be waiting for him upon his release from prison. *Lawyers. Actors. Detectives. Socialites. Automobile accidents. Manslaughter. Courtship. Bribery. Trials.*

FOR THE FREEDOM OF IRELAND **F2.1892**

Dist Creation Pictures. **1921** [New York State license: 12 Nov 1927]. Si; b&w. 35mm. 5 reels.

Drama(?). No information about the precise nature of this film has been found. *Ireland.*

Note: Country of origin undetermined. May have been released in 1920.

FOR THE LOVE O' LIL **F2.1893**

Columbia Pictures. 29 Aug **1930** [c24 Sep 1930; LP1599]. Sd (Movietone); b&w. 35mm. 7 reels, 6,606 ft.

Prod Harry Cohn. *Supv* William Conselman. *Dir* James Tinling. *Screenplay* Dorothy Howell. *Adapt-Dial* Bella Cohen, Robert Bruckner. *Photog* Ted Tetzlaff. *Art Dir* Edward Jewell. *Tech Dir* Edward Shulter. *Film Ed* Edward Curtiss. *Rec Engr* G. R. Cooper. *Asst Dir* David Selman.

Cast: Jack Mulhall *(Wyn Huntley)*, Elliott Nugent *(Sandy Jenkins)*, Sally Starr *(Lil)*, Margaret Livingston *(Eleanor Cartwright)*, Charles Sellon *(Mr. Walker)*, Julia Swayne Gordon *(Mrs. Walker)*, Billy Bevan *(Edward O. Brooks)*, Claire Du Brey *(Mrs. Gardner)*, Joan Standing *(chambermaid)*.

Romantic drama. Source: Leslie Thrasher, "For the Love o' Lil," in *Liberty Magazine.* Although he is very much in love with Lil, girl-shy Sandy Jenkins lacks the courage to propose; but his rival, Wyn Huntley, having both money and leisure, gives numerous parties designed to impress Lil. At Huntley's suggestion, Eleanor, an old flame, vamps Sandy, but Lil upsets the scheme by staging a drowning act and is rescued by Sandy; in the pool he proposes, and she accepts. As they are preparing to spend their wedding night, Wyn interferes and later chooses their apartment and friends for a housewarming. Prospects seem brighter when Mr. Walker, senior partner in a brokerage firm, agrees to give Sandy a promotion for aiding in an oil merger; on the strength of this, Sandy makes plans for a suburban home, but at the housewarming, under the influence of liquor, he orders Wyn from the house, smashes the furniture, and alienates his wife. A divorce is averted when Lil effects a reconciliation. *Socialites. Courtship. Marriage. Timidity. Business combinations.*

FOR THE LOVE OF MIKE **F2.1894**

Robert Kane Productions. *Dist* First National Pictures. 31 Jul **1927** [c1 Aug 1927; LP24252]. Si; b&w. 35mm. 7 reels, 6,588 ft.

Pres by Robert Kane. *Dir* Frank Capra. *Scen* J. Clarkson Miller. *Photog* Ernest Haller.

Cast: Claudette Colbert *(Mary)*, Ben Lyon *(Mike)*, George Sidney *(Abraham Katz)*, Ford Sterling *(Herman Schultz)*, Hugh Cameron *(Patrick O'Malley)*, Richard "Skeets" Gallagher *("Coxey" Pendleton)*, Rudolph Cameron *(Henry Sharp)*, Mabel Swor *(Evelyn Joyce)*.

Romantic drama. Source: John Moroso, "Hell's Kitchen" (publication undetermined). As a baby, Mike is abandoned on the doorstep of a tenement in Hell's Kitchen, and is reared by Herman Schultz, Abie Katz, and Patrick O'Malley, who support him through high school and plan a college career for him. With the persuasion of Mary, a pretty Italian cashier in Schultz's delicatessen, Mike enters Yale, where he distinguishes himself socially and athletically. The "fathers" plan a 21st birthday banquet above their store, inviting prominent community members; Mike, however, is coaxed into inebriation at a cocktail party by a girl friend and arrives to insult the guests. Returning to college, he begins to worry about his finances and becomes involved with a crooked gambler who threatens to have him arrested unless he throws a race. Mike rows the Yale team to victory, and the "fathers" throttle the gambler's protests. All is forgiven and he wins the heart of Mary. *Foundlings. Gamblers. Irish. Jews. Italians. College life. Courtship. Rowing. Tenements. Delicatessens. New York City—Hell's Kitchen. Yale University.*

FOR THOSE WE LOVE **F2.1895**

Betty Compson Productions. *Dist* Goldwyn Pictures. Sep **1921** [c27 Jul 1921; LP16786]. Si; b&w. 35mm. 6 reels, 5,752 ft.

Prod Betty Compson. *Dir-Adapt* Arthur Rosson. *Story* Perley Poore Sheehan.

Cast: Betty Compson *(Bernice Arnold)*, Richard Rosson *(Jimmy Arnold)*, Camille Astor *(Vida)*, Bert Woodruff *(Dr. Bailee)*, Harry Duffield *(George

Arnold), Walter Morosco *(Johnny Fletcher)*, George Cooper *(Bert)*, Frank Campeau *(Frank)*, Lon Chaney *(Trix Ulner)*.

Rural melodrama. Trix Ulner, who deals stud poker at Frank's smalltown gambling resort, rescues Bernice Arnold from drowning, and her subsequent acquaintance with him causes scandal and annoys her sweetheart, Johnny Fletcher. When her brother, Jimmy, steals money from his father and loses it in a game with Trix and Frank, Bernice attempts to convince her father that he has mislaid the money and begs Frank for its return, but nevertheless the father tries to have Jimmy arrested. Bernice hides him in the home of Vida Brown, and when it burns they all find shelter in the Arnold house. Bert, Jimmy, and Trix rob Frank's house to retrieve the money, and in the process Frank shoots and kills Jimmy. When Trix threatens him, Frank swears that the boy died while trying to capture some burglars. Bernice weds Fletcher. *Gambling. Fatherhood. Filial relations. Brother-sister relationship. Theft.*

FOR WIVES ONLY **F2.1896**

Metropolitan Pictures Corp. of California. *Dist* Producers Distributing Corp. 8 Nov **1926** [c20 Oct 1926; LP23234]. Si; b&w. 35mm. 6 reels, 5,800 ft.

Pres by John C. Flinn. *Dir* Victor Heerman. *Ed Supv* F. McGrew Willis. *Adapt* Anthony Coldeway. *Photog* Hal Rosson.

Cast: Marie Prevost *(Laura Rittenhaus)*, Victor Varconi *(Dr. Rittenhaus)*, Charles Gerrard *(Dr. Carl Tanzer)*, Arthur Hoyt *(Dr. Fritz Schwerman)*, Claude Gillingwater *(Prof. von Waldstein)*, Josephine Crowell *(housekeeper)*, Dorothy Cumming *(Countess von Nessa)*, William Courtright *(butler)*.

Domestic farce. Source: Rudolph Lothar and Hans Bachwitz, *The Critical Year* (publication undetermined). Dr. Josef Rittenhaus, a popular young society physician of Vienna, at the behest of his friend Waldstein, goes to consider a proposal by Countess von Nessa to donate a site and funds for the erection of a new sanitarium. His wife, Laura, piqued by his apparent indifference, is left in the hands of Carl Tanzer, supposedly the doctor's best friend, whose advances she rejects. Laura contrives to make her husband jealous with a bogus letter, but to no avail; later, escaping from a masher, she meets her husband's friend Fritz Schwerman, from whom she escapes after accepting a luncheon offer. While Laura tries to vamp her husband's other friends at a card game, the countess tries to make love to the doctor. Rittenhaus returns home in disgust and is happily reconciled with his wife. *Physicians. Marriage. Philanthropy. Jealousy. Flirtation. Sanitariums. Vienna.*

FOR WOMAN'S FAVOR **F2.1897**

Lund Productions. *Dist* Lee-Bradford Corp. 1 Aug **1924.** Si; b&w. 35mm. 6 reels, 5,600 ft.

Dir Oscar Lund. *Photog* Marcel Le Picard. *Adtl Photog* Robert A. Olssen.

Cast: Seena Owen *(June Paige)*, Elliott Dexter *(Howard Fiske)*, Wilton Lackaye *(Bracken)*, Irma Harrison *(The Lamb)*, Henry Hull *(The Fool/The Lover)*, Paul McAllister *(The Wolf)*, Arthur Donaldson *(The Brother)*.

Melodrama. Howard Fiske must watch impotently as his sweetheart, June Paige, is forced by her scheming family into marriage with a millionaire whom she does not love. Howard is in debt to Bracken, an old acquaintance who hounds him for money, forcing him to blackmail June for $10,000 by threatening to show her old, undated love letters to the millionaire. Bracken sends June to Howard's house by promising her the letters on payment of the money. Before she arrives, Howard picks up a volume of Boccaccio and reads "The Falcon," which recounts the tale of a selfless lover who sacrifices his dearest possession to satisfy the desire of his lady love. As Howard finishes the story, June appears and asks for the letters. Howard quickly realizes that she has been sent by Bracken and seeks to relieve her fear of exposure by throwing the letters in the fire. June realizes the true depth of Howard's love and gives herself to him, saying with the girl in "The Falcon": "You have always possessed me with your love." *Millionaires. Debt. Blackmail. Giovanni Boccaccio. Documentation.*

FOR YOU MY BOY **F2.1898**

Rubicon Pictures. 15 Jul **1923.** Si; b&w. 35mm. 6 reels.

Dir-Writ William L. Roubert. *Photog* Richard Fryer.

Cast: Ben Lewin *(John Austin)*, Louis Dean *(Grant Melford)*, Matty Roubert *(Jack Melford)*, Schuyler White *(Jack Austin)*, Jean Armour *(Mrs. Melford)*, Gladys Grainger *(The Girl)*, Scott Hinchman *(George Harvey)*, Franklin Hanna *(The Girl's father)*.

Melodrama. The motherless child of a bank clerk is adopted by the Melfords, a wealthy couple, who rear him as their son. Years pass. Jack, a young man, takes the blame for a bank theft committed by Melford, whom he believes to be his father. Melford dies; Jack goes to jail and after several years is released. Jack discovers that Austin is his real father, and eventually they are reunited. *Bank clerks. Fatherhood. Adoption. Parentage. Theft.*

FOR YOUR DAUGHTER'S SAKE (Reissue) **F2.1899**

Burton King Productions. *Dist* J. W. Film Corp. Jan **1922** [c8 Nov, 17 Nov 1921; LU17208]. Si; b&w. 35mm. 5 reels, 4,950 ft.

Note: Originally released as *The Common Sin* by Hallmark Pictures in 1920 (6 reels). Possibly reissued also under the same title.

FORBIDDEN CARGO **F2.1900**

Gothic Productions. *Dist* Film Booking Offices of America. 22 Feb **1925** [c22 Feb 1925; LP21295]. Si; b&w. 35mm. 5 reels, 4,850 ft.

Dir Thomas Buckingham. *Story-Scen* Fred Kennedy Myton. *Photog* Silvano Balboni.

Cast: Evelyn Brent *(Polly O'Day)*, Robert Ellis *(Jerry Burke)*, Boris Karloff *(Pietro Castillano)*.

Melodrama. A beautiful and spirited young woman known only as Captain Joe captains a rumrunner operating between the Bahamas and the United States. Jerry Burke, a Secret Service agent assigned to the Bahamas to halt this illegal trade in rum, meets Captain Joe, whom he knows as Peggy O'Day, and falls in love with her, arousing the antipathy of Pietro, Peggy's first mate. Pietro later learns that Jerry is a government agent and kidnaps him, hiding him on Peggy's boat. Making a delivery to the mainland, the boat is then attacked by hijackers led by Pietro, who wound Peggy and take her boat, leaving behind Jerry and Peggy. Taking the hijackers' craft to a small island, Jerry sends a radio message for help to Peggy's father, a cashiered naval officer; Pietro intercepts the radio message, goes to the island, and forces Peggy and Jerry aboard the rumrunner. Peggy manages to send an S. O. S. signal to a U. S. warship before Pietro dynamites the boat. Peggy and Jerry survive the explosion and are picked up by a Navy warship; Pietro is captured, and Jerry uses his influence to have the elder O'Day cleared of the false charges that led to his disgrace. Peggy and Jerry make plans to be wed. *Rumrunners. Hijackers. Abduction. Secret service. Bahamas. United States Navy.*

FORBIDDEN FRUIT **F2.1901**

Famous Players–Lasky. *Dist* Paramount Pictures. 23 Jan **1921** [New York premiere; released Feb 1921; c6 Jan 1921; LP16001]. Si; b&w. 35mm. 8 reels, 7,804 ft.

Pres by Jesse L. Lasky. *Supv* Howard Higgin. *Prod-Dir* Cecil B. De Mille. *Story* Jeanie Macpherson. *Photog* Alvin Wyckoff. *Wardrobe* Theodore Kosloff.

Cast: Agnes Ayres *(Mary Maddock)*, Clarence Burton *(Steve Maddock)*, Theodore Roberts *(James Harrington Mallory)*, Kathlyn Williams *(Mrs. Mallory)*, Forrest Stanley *(Nelson Rogers)*, Theodore Kosloff *(Pietro Giuseppe)*, Shannon Day *(Nadia Craig)*, Bertram Johns *(John Craig)*, Julia Faye *(maid)*.

Society drama. Forced to work because her wastrel husband, Steve, prefers to gamble, seamstress Mary Maddock agrees to substitute for an ailing debutante at Mrs. Mallory's dinner in honor of oil magnate Nelson Rogers. She makes a hit, and—angered at Steve—she accepts Mrs. Mallory's invitation to visit for a few days. Steve persuades Pietro, the Mallory butler, to help him rob the Mallory safe; and Mary's scream of recognition awakes Nelson, who releases Steve and pays him blackmail money because he is Mary's husband. A quarrel between Steve and Pietro leads to Steve's death, Pietro's arrest, and future happiness for Mary and Nelson. *Seamstresses. Gamblers. Butlers. Oil magnates. Blackmail. Robbery.*

FORBIDDEN GRASS **F2.1902**

Oscar Price. *Dist* General Pictures. 15 Oct **1928.** Si; b&w. 35mm. 5 reels, 4,100 ft.

Dir E. M. Eldridge. *Story* A. Ashley. *Photog* M. A. Anderson, L. De Angelis. *Film Ed* Roy Eiler.

Cast: William Anderson, Evelyn Nicholas, Jack Padjan, Otto Meek, Walter Long, Elsie Duane, Billy Nichols.

Western melodrama. "An effort to recount the story of the action taken by the state of Utah a few years ago to rid the plains of wild horses and save the grass for the sheep herds. The rascally rancher who has the commission from the state government to do the dirty work in the mountain section is shown with his gang rounding up the horses and running them into corrals. The hero is concerned with saving a private herd that the agent tries to stampede. This is accomplished with the aid of the heroine's horse." (*Film Daily,* 28 Oct 1928, p9.) *Ranches. Grasslands. Utah. Horses. Sheep.*

FORBIDDEN HOURS **F2.1903**

Metro-Goldwyn-Mayer Pictures. 16 Jun **1928** [c16 Jul 1928; LP25396]. Si; b&w. 35mm. 6 reels, 4,987 or 5,011 ft.

Dir Harry Beaumont. *Story-Scen* A. P. Younger. *Titl* John Colton. *Photog* Merritt B. Gerstad. *Sets* Richard Day. *Prod Dsgn* Cedric Gibbons. *Film Ed* William Hamilton.

Cast: Ramon Novarro *(His Majesty, Michael IV)*, Renée Adorée *(Marie de Floriet)*, Dorothy Cumming *(Queen Alexia)*, Edward Connelly *(Prime Minister)*, Roy D'Arcy *(Duke Nicky)*, Mitzi Cummings *(Princess Ena)*, Alberta Vaughn *(Nina)*.

Romantic melodrama. Michael, young ruler of the small kingdom of Balanca, falls in love with Marie de Floriet, niece of his prime minister, and abdicates so as to marry her. His family, however, would have him marry Ena, a rich and eligible visiting princess, and the prime minister and Nicky, Michael's cousin, scheme to show Marie in a compromising situation to quell his passion. Marie agrees to the scheme, convinced that the kingdom is more important than her love. Michael "surprises" Nicky and Marie in bed together; he denounces her and tosses her to his officers as he leaves the inn. Subsequently Michael returns and, determined to renounce his crown, flees to the border with Marie. The border guards request the young couple to return to the palace, however, when the people demand Michael and Marie as their monarchs. *Royalty. Prime ministers. Abdication. Imaginary kingdoms.*

Note: Copyright indication that the film has sound has not been confirmed.

FORBIDDEN LOVE **F2.1904**

Wistaria Productions. *Dist* Playgoers Pictures. 17 Jul **1921** [c7 Jun 1921; LU16651]. Si; b&w. 35mm. 6 reels.

Prod Thomas De Vassey. *Dir* Philip Van Loan. *Adapt-Story* Edward Russell. *Photog* Louis Geleng, Richard Fryer. *Film Ed* Bernard Hays Connor.

Cast: Creighton Hale *(Harold Van Zandt)*, George MacQuarrie *(Peter Van Zandt)*, Marguerite Clayton *(Eileen Arden)*, Thomas Cameron *(John Van Zandt)*, Peggy Shaw *(Muriel Martin)*, Harold Thomas *(Charlie Lee)*, Baby Ivy Ward *(Little Anne)*.

Melodrama. Harold and Peter Van Zandt, sons of a seafaring father, are in love with Eileen Arden, who favors Harold, the younger and gentler brother. Peter tells her that Harold is circulating false rumors about her, persuades Harold to go to Boston, and wins over the girl. Years later, when their father's illness necessitates Harold's return, Peter becomes jealous and in a drunken frenzy causes the death of his child. After confessing to his previous scheming, Peter visits Harold in the lighthouse at the height of a storm, and during a struggle Peter falls into the sea. *Brothers. Filial relations. Seafaring life. New England. Lighthouses.*

Note: Copyright title: *Women Who Wait.* The release date and the distributor given above apply to the film under the copyright title.

FORBIDDEN LOVER **F2.1905**

Sierra Pictures. *Dist* Selznick Distributing Corp. 28 Jul **1923.** Si; b&w. 35mm. 5 reels, 4,283 or 4,825 ft.

Dir Nat Deverich.

Cast: Noah Beery, Barbara Bedford, Elliott Sparling.

Melodrama. "Yankee sea captain lands on the coast during the old Spanish days to trade with the ranch owners. He meets a girl who is betrothed to a man she loathes. After a series of adventures and narrow escapes he shows up the unscrupulous ranch owner and wins the girl." (*Motion Picture News Booking Guide,* 6:22, Oct 1923.) *Sea captains. Ranchers. Traders. California—Spanish era.*

FORBIDDEN PARADISE **F2.1906**

Famous Players–Lasky. *Dist* Paramount Pictures. 16 Nov **1924** [New York premiere; released 24 Nov; c21 Nov 1924; LP20776]. Si; b&w. 35mm. 8 reels, 7,543 ft.

Pres by Adolph Zukor, Jesse L. Lasky. *Dir* Ernst Lubitsch. *Screenplay* Agnes Christine Johnston, Hans Kraly. *Photog* Charles J. Van Enger. *Set Dsgn* Hans Dreier.

Cast: Pola Negri *(The Czarina)*, Rod La Rocque *(Alexei)*, Adolphe Menjou *(Chancellor)*, Pauline Starke *(Anna)*, Fred Malatesta *(French ambassador)*, Nick De Ruiz *(general)*, Madame Daumery *(lady-in-waiting)*, Clark Gable.

Costume comedy-drama. Source: Lajos Biró and Menyhért Lengyel, *A cárnő szinmu: három felvonásban* (Budapest, 1913). "Alexei, a young officer, saves the Czarina of a small European kingdom from revolutionary conspirators and is rewarded with her love. Infatuated, he deserts his sweetheart, Anna, the Czarina's lady-in-waiting, only to discover that his Queen is far from true to him. Desperate, he joins the revolutionists and plots against her. The Czarina pleads that she loves only him, and he swears no harm will befall her. Meantime the chancellor nips the revolution in the bud, and the Czarina orders Alexei's arrest. But she causes herself such unhappiness in doing so that she releases him from prison, relinquishes him to Anna, and seeks solace in a new affair with the French Ambassador." (*Exhibitors Trade Review,* 6 Dec 1924, p51.) *Royalty. Revolutions. Imaginary kingdoms. France—Diplomatic and consular service.*

THE FORBIDDEN RANGE **F2.1907**

William Steiner Productions. 15 Jul **1923** [c6 Jun 1923; LU19035]. Si; b&w. 35mm. 5 reels.

Dir-Story-Adapt Neal Hart. *Photog* Jack Specht, William Steiner, Jr.

Cast: Neal Hart *(Jack Wilson)*, Yakima Canutt *(Buck Madison)*.

Western melodrama. "In the interests of fair play, ... [Jack Wilson, a square-dealing cowman] elects to champion the cause of sheepmen who have lately invaded the cow country. The rest of the cowmen, abetted by their scheming, vicious leader [Buck Madison], are in favor of burning the sheepmen's ranches, and then of stampeding them and their live stock. The hero has many a rough and tumble fight with the opposing gang's leader, but triumphs in the end. In addition to winning for his bride [Mary Brodie] the attractive young daughter of [John Brodie] one of the sheepmen, he rightly earns the gratitude and esteem of all those he had befriended." (*Harrison's Reports,* 21 Jul 1923.) *Cowboys. Sheepmen.*

Note: Character names are from shooting script in copyright files and may be different from the final film.

THE FORBIDDEN TRAIL **F2.1908**

Sunset Productions. 1 Feb **1923.** Si; b&w. 35mm. 5 reels, 4,721 or 4,800 ft.

Dir-Auth-Titl Robert North Bradbury. *Photog* Jack Brown. *Film Ed* Robert North Bradbury.

Cast: Jack Hoxie *(Jack Merriwell/Col. Jim Merriwell)*, Evelyn Nelson *(Isobel Lorraine)*, Frank Rice *(Toby Jones)*, William Lester *(Rufe Trent)*, Joe McDermott *(Red [Hawk] Dugan)*, Tom Lingham *(John Anthony Todd)*, Steve Clemento *(Mose)*.

Western melodrama. "Jack Merriwell goes west in a search for the slayer of his father. In his pursuits he meets Isobel. The girl is the supposed daughter of 'Red Hawk' Dugan, and she is forced by him to assist the notorious gang, of which he is the head, in their raids and crooked deals. Jack learns that Dugan is the man he seeks. A series of fights and escapes follow. It is established that Isobel is no relation to Dugan and the lovers prepare to start home." (*Motion Picture News Booking Guide,* 4:50, Apr 1923.) *Gangs. Parentage. Revenge.*

FORBIDDEN TRAILS **F2.1909**

Associated Independent Producers. 26 Nov **1928** [New York State license]. Si; b&w. 35mm. 5 reels.

Dir-Scen Robert J. Horner. *Titl* William Harris. *Photog* Jack Draper. *Film Ed* William Austin.

Cast: Pawnee Bill Jr., Bud Osborne, Kit Carson *(see note)*.

Melodrama(?). No information about the nature of this film has been found.

Note: *Film Daily Yearbook* gives Kit Carson as the star.

FORBIDDEN WATERS **F2.1910**

Metropolitan Pictures. *Dist* Producers Distributing Corp. 21 Mar **1926** [c5 Mar 1926; LP22444]. Si; b&w. 35mm. 6 reels, 5,335 ft.

Pres by John C. Flinn. *Dir* Alan Hale. *Adapt* Charles A. Logue. *Story* Percy Heath. *Photog* George Benoit. *2d Photog* William Coopersmith. *Art Dir* Charles Cadwallader. *Asst Dir* Jack McKeown. *Prod Mgr* George Bertholon.

Cast: Priscilla Dean *(Nancy)*, Walter McGrail *(J. Austin Bell)*, Dan Mason *(Nugget Pete)*, Casson Ferguson *(Sylvester)*, De Sacia Mooers *(Ruby)*.

Comedy. After divorcing her husband in Reno, Nancy Bell is arrested for speeding and thrown into jail. Unable to pay the fine, she wires her former husband, J. Austin, for help; he comes to Nevada and gets her out of the clink. A blonde crook named Ruby becomes enamored of J. Austin, and Nancy, who still loves her former husband, does everything within her power to prevent J. Austin from falling in love with the gold digger. Eventually Ruby is arrested by the police, and Nancy and J. Austin are remarried by a bemused preacher. *Gold diggers. Automobile driving. Divorce. Reno.*

THE FORBIDDEN WOMAN **F2.1911**

De Mille Pictures. *Dist* Pathé Exchange. 29 Oct **1927** [New York premiere; released 7 Nov; c1 Nov 1927; LP24593]. Si; b&w. 35mm. 7 reels, 6,568 ft.

Supv William C. De Mille. *Dir* Paul L. Stein. *Adapt-Cont* Clara Beranger. *Photog* David Abel. *Art Dir* Mitchell Leisen, Wilfred Buckland. *Asst Dir* Curt Rehfeld. *Cost* Adrian.

Cast: Jetta Goudal *(Zita)*, Ivan Lebedeff *(Sheik)*, Leonid Snegoff *(Sultan)*, Josephine Norman *(Zita's maid)*, Victor Varconi *(Colonel Gautier)*, Joseph Schildkraut *(Jean La Coste)*.

Melodrama. Source: Elmer Harris, "Brothers" (publication undetermined). Zita, a beautiful spy for the Sultan of Morocco, is commissioned to obtain military secrets from the French troops, and the Sultan cleverly arranges a meeting of Zita and Col. Pierre Gautier. The meeting leads to their marriage, and this alliance enables Zita to gain valuable information, which she transmits through her maid, an accomplice. Shortly after the wedding, Colonel Gautier is called to Paris, and Zita follows by boat to join him in France, where she meets Jean La Coste, an internationally famous violinist, and they fall desperately in love. In Paris, Zita is shocked to learn that Jean is Pierre's younger brother, and both despair over the situation. When they are surprised in a compromising situation by Pierre, Jean is sent to join the army in Morocco. Finding her love for Jean hopeless, Zita frames him as a spy, but Jean's confession of love prompts her to admit her guilt; the reunited brothers witness her execution. *Spies. Violinists. Brothers. Royalty. Capital punishment. Morocco. France—Army—Foreign Legion. Paris.*

FOREIGN DEVILS **F2.1912**

Metro-Goldwyn-Mayer Pictures. 3 Sep **1927** [c17 Aug 1927; LP24294]. Si; b&w. 35mm. 5 reels, 4,658 ft.

Dir W. S. Van Dyke. *Scen* Marian Ainslee. *Titl* Marian Ainslee, Ruth Cummings. *Story* Peter Bernard Kyne. *Photog* Clyde De Vinna. *Art Dir* Cedric Gibbons, David Townsend. *Film Ed* Sam S. Zimbalist. *Wardrobe* René Hubert.

Cast: Tim McCoy *(Capt. Robert Kelly)*, Claire Windsor *(Lady Patricia Rutledge)*, Cyril Chadwick *(Lieut. Lord Vivien Cholmondeley)*, Frank Currier *(U. S. Minister Conger)*, Emily Fitzroy *(Mrs. Conger)*, Lawson Butt *(Sir Claude)*, Sojin *(Lama Priest)*, Frank Chew *(Prince Tuan)*.

Action melodrama. "Attaché at American Embassy in Peking at the time of the Boxer Rebellion (Captain Robert Kelly) becomes attached to an English lady (Lady Patricia Rutledge). He rescues her from the hands of the priests of a Chinese temple which she has gone to visit, entrusts her to a friend to carry her to safety to the barricade and alone battles the Chinese until they have made their escape. Later on, he brings news to the barricade of the approach of the allies and subsequently wins the girl." (*Motion Picture News*, 28 Apr 1928, p1348.) *China—History—Boxer Rebellion. Peking. United States—Diplomatic and consular service. Edwin Hurd Conger.*

THE FOREIGN LEGION **F2.1913**

Universal Pictures. 23 Jun **1928** [New York premiere; released 1 Jul or 23 Sep; c18 Mar 1928; LP25168]. Si; b&w. 35mm. 8 reels, 7,828 ft.

Dir Edward Sloman. *Adapt-Scen* Charles Kenyon. *Titl* Jack Jarmuth. *Photog* Jackson Rose. *Film Ed* Ted Kent.

Cast: Norman Kerry *(Richard Farquhar)*, Lewis Stone *(Colonel Destinn)*, Crauford Kent *(Captain Arnaud)*, Mary Nolan *(Sylvia Omney)*, June Marlowe *(Gabrielle)*, Walter Perry *(Corporal Gotz)*.

Melodrama. Source: Ida Alexa Ross Wylie, *The Red Mirage* (London, 1913). Richard Farquhar, falsely accused of a crime, is forced to resign his commission in the army. Remaining silent to protect Arnaud, the husband of his former fiancée, Sylvia, Farquhar joins the Foreign Legion in Algeria and there serves under his father, whom he has not seen since he was a child. After a time Farquhar meets Arnaud and Sylvia again, and the result is trouble. Destinn, the commanding officer, is forced to sentence Farquhar to die, but when he learns that Farquhar is his son, he sacrifices himself so that Farquhar and his sweetheart, Gabrielle, may escape. *Fatherhood. Self-sacrifice. France—Army—Foreign Legion. Algeria.*

Note: Working title: *The Red Mirage.*

THE FOREMAN OF BAR Z RANCH **F2.1914**

Dist Aywon Film Corp. 24 Dec **1924** [New York State license]. Si; b&w. 35mm. 5 reels, 4,800 ft.

Cast: Tom Mix.

Note: Expansion of a 1-reeler of the same title (Selig, 1915).

FOREST HAVOC **F2.1915**

Ellbee Pictures. 15 Nov **1926** [New York State license]. Si; b&w. 35mm. 6 reels, 5,650 ft.

Dir Stuart Paton. *Story-Scen* Roy O. Reilly. *Photog* William Tuers.

Cast: Forrest Stanley, Peggy Montgomery, Martha Mattox, Ernest Hilliard, Sidney De Grey.

Action melodrama. A man rescues the girl he loves from a forest fire and, as a result, goes blind. He attempts to hide his blindness from the girl and eventually recovers his sight. *Blindness. Forest fires.*

THE FOREST KING **F2.1916**

Pacific Film Co. 17 Mar **1922** [trade review]. Si; b&w. 35mm. 5 reels, 5,000 ft.

Dir F. G. Hartman. *Story* L. V. Jefferson. *Photog* Ralph Hawkins, E. C. Peters.

Cast: L. M. Wells *(Martin Webb)*, Virginia Ware *(Mrs. Webb)*, Reed Chapman *(Bob Lanier)*, Dahlia Pears *(Evelyn Webb)*, Lillian Hall *(Leslie Houston)*, Arthur Millett *(Eugene Stratton)*, Joe Ray *(Steve Hawkin)*.

Melodrama. Bob Lanier is given half ownership of a lumbermill by Martin Webb, who believes him to be in love with his daughter, Evelyn. Martin dies, and his manager plots to gain complete control by arousing the jealousy of Evelyn when Bob helps Leslie Houston, who is the sole support of her invalid father. Leslie falls in love with Bob but is kidnaped by a lumberjack at the orders of Evelyn. The scheming manager, his plans defeated, attempts to rob the office safe by putting dynamite in Bob's desk so arranged that a footfall on a loose board will set it off. The scheme backfires when the kidnaping lumberjack and the manager, left in the office to quarrel about the money in the safe, step on the loose board. The landscape spouts up in flames, Evelyn repents, and Bob and Leslie seek each other's embrace. *Invalids. Lumberjacks. Lumbering. Kidnaping. Explosions. Forest fires.*

FOREVER **F2.1917**

Famous Players–Lasky. *Dist* Paramount Pictures. ca16 Oct **1921** [New York premiere; released 5 Mar 1922; c5 Mar 1922; LP17662]. Si; b&w. 35mm. 7 reels, 7,236 ft.

Pres by Adolph Zukor. *Dir* George Fitzmaurice. *Scen* Ouida Bergère. *Photog* Arthur Miller. *Art Dir* Robert M. Haas.

Cast: Wallace Reid *(Peter Ibbetson)*, Elsie Ferguson *(Mimsi)*, Montagu Love *(Colonel Ibbetson)*, George Fawcett *(Major Duquesnois)*, Dolores Cassinelli *(Dolores)*, Paul McAllister *(Monsieur Seraskier)*, Elliott Dexter *(Monsieur Pasquier)*, Barbara Dean *(Madame Pasquier)*, Nell Roy Buck *(The Child Mimsi)*, Charles Eaton *(The Child Gogo)*, Jerome Patrick *(Duke of Towers)*.

Romantic drama. Source: George Du Maurier, *Peter Ibbetson* (1891). John Nathan Raphael, *Peter Ibbetson, a Play in Four Acts* (New York, 1934). Gogo Pasquier, the small son of a Parisian chemist and the sweetheart of Mimsi Seraskier, is adopted by Colonel Ibbetson, an English rake, following the death of his father and mother. In England, as Peter Ibbetson, he grows up in a dissolute environment and is repulsed by the colonel. One night, at the theater, he meets Mimsi and learns that she is now the Duchess of Towers. In the dressing room of a dancer, Peter quarrels with his uncle, who asserts that Peter is, in fact, his son, and in a later encounter Peter kills him in self-defense. Although he is tried and sentenced to be hanged, Peter's sentence is commuted through the influence of the Duchess of Towers to life imprisonment. Both grow old, but their dream life continues; Mimsi perishes while rescuing children from a burning orphanage, her soul returns to Peter when he dies, and the two are reunited in spiritual bonds. *Orphans. Rakes. Courtship. Theater. Manslaughter. Immortality. France. England. Fires.*

Note: Working title: *The Great Romance.* Initially released and reviewed as *Peter Ibbetson.*

FOREVER AFTER **F2.1918**
First National Pictures. 24 Oct **1926** [c30 Sep 1926; LP23163]. Si; b&w. 35mm. 7 reels, 6,330 ft.

Dir F. Harmon Weight. *Scen* Paul Gangelin. *Adapt* Julian Josephson. *Photog* Karl Struss. *Prod Mgr* B. P. Fineman.

Cast: Lloyd Hughes *(Theodore Wayne)*, Mary Astor *(Jennie Clayton)*, Hallam Cooley *(Jack Randall)*, David Torrence *(Clayton)*, Eulalie Jensen *(Mrs. Clayton)*, Alec Francis *(Wayne)*, Lila Leslie *(Mrs. Wayne)*.

Romantic drama. Source: Owen Davis, *Forever After* (New York, 1928). Theodore Wayne, an infantry captain wounded at the front, recalls the highlights of his earlier life: *As a schoolboy in an old New England town, he meets Jennie Clayton, daughter of a wealthy family, and they become constant sweethearts. Jack Randall, scion of a wealthy family, is the suitor favored by Jennie's mother, who wants her to marry for wealth and position. For Jennie's sake, Ted goes to Harvard, though his father, an impractical lawyer, makes vital sacrifices to meet the expense; after his father's death, he is forced to return home and support his mother. Convinced by Mr. Clayton, Ted gives up Jennie and leaves with his mother in an effort to forget. Jennie refuses to marry Randall and joins the Red Cross in France.* There in a hospital, she is reunited with Ted and nurses him back to health. Their love is thus reaffirmed. *Nurses. Filial relations. Courtship. Social classes. World War I. New England. Harvard University.*

FORGET-ME-NOT **F2.1919**
Louis Burston Productions. *Dist* Metro Pictures. ca23 Jul **1922** [New York premiere; released 2 Oct; c14 Aug 1922; LP18153]. Si; b&w. 35mm. 6-7 reels.

Dir W. S. Van Dyke. *Adapt* John B. Clymer. *Story* Henry R. Symonds. *Photog* Arthur L. Todd.

Cast: Irene Hunt *(Mary Gordon, The Mother)*, William Machin *(The Father)*, Bessie Love *(Ann, The Girl)*, Gareth Hughes *(Jimmy, The Boy)*, Otto Lederer *(Rodolfo, The Musician)*, Myrtle Lind *(The Other Girl)*, Hal Wilson, Gertrude Claire, Sam Allen, William Lawrence, Queenie *(just a dog)*.

Society melodrama. Poverty causes Mary to leave her infant daughter (Ann) at the door of an orphanage. Fifteen years later Mary returns and, unable to recognize Ann, adopts Ann's sweetheart, Jimmy, while Ann is adopted by a musician and becomes a fine violinist through his teaching. Among her performances is one at Jimmy's wedding to another girl. After Jimmy's wife dies, he recognizes Ann's picture on a concert poster. Ann is reunited with Jimmy and, with the aid of an old janitor, her mother. *Foundlings. Violinists. Music teachers. Janitors. Motherhood. Dogs.*

FORGIVE AND FORGET **F2.1920**
Columbia Pictures. *Dist* C. B. C. Film Sales. 15 Sep **1923** [c20 Feb 1924; LP19952]. Si; b&w. 35mm. 6 reels, ca5,877 ft.

Prod Harry Cohn. *Dir* Howard M. Mitchell. *Scen* Jack Strumwasser. *Story* Charles Furthman. *Photog* King Gray.

Cast: Estelle Taylor *(Mrs. Cameron)*, Pauline Garon *(Virginia Clark)*, Philo McCullough *(Blake)*, Josef Swickard *(John Standing)*, Wyndham Standing *(Mr. Cameron)*, Raymond McKee *(Dick Merrill)*, Vernon Steele *(Ronnie Sears)*, Lionel Belmore *(butler)*.

Society drama. Mrs. Cameron ends her affair with Ronnie Sears following a visit to his apartment. She had been summoned there by Ronnie's roommate, Blake, who intends to blackmail her with a packet of letters she wrote to Ronnie. Ronnie arrives and is killed during a quarrel with Blake. Mr. Cameron follows his wife to the apartment and is arrested for Ronnie's murder, but Mrs. Cameron obtains Blake's confession before he falls to his death from an open window. *Infidelity. Blackmail. Murder. Documentation.*

FORGOTTEN FACES **F2.1921**
Paramount Famous Lasky Corp. 11 Aug **1928** [c11 Aug 1928; LP25520]. Si; b&w. 35mm. 8 reels, 7,640 ft.

Pres by Adolph Zukor, Jesse L. Lasky. *Supv* David Selznick. *Dir* Victor Schertzinger. *Scen* Howard Estabrook. *Titl* Julian Johnson. *Adapt* Oliver H. P. Garrett. *Photog* J. Roy Hunt. *Film Ed* David Selznick, George Nichols, Jr.

Cast: Clive Brook *(Heliotrope Harry Harlow)*, Mary Brian *(Alice Deane)*, Baclanova *(Lilly Harlow)*, William Powell *(Froggy)*, Fred Kohler *(Number 1309)*, Jack Luden *(Tom)*.

Melodrama. Source: Richard Washburn Child, "Whiff of Heliotrope," in *Famous Story Magazine* (1:390–400, Dec 1925). Heliotrope Harry Harlow finds his wife making cheatie with another man and sends him to hell. Before surrendering to the police, Harry leaves his infant daughter on the doorstep of a wealthy couple who take the child in and treat her as their own. Fifteen years pass. Harry's wife discovers the girl's whereabouts and goes to see Harry in prison, cruelly informing him of her intention to see the girl. Harry is fortuitously released on parole and obtains a position as butler in the house in which his daughter has been brought up. He forestalls two attempts by his wife to see the girl and finally provokes her into mortally harming him. She is convicted and sent to prison, and Harry dies happy in the knowledge that his daughter is safe from the evil influence of her mother. *Butlers. Convicts. Fatherhood. Murder. Infidelity. Adoption. Prisons.*

THE FORGOTTEN LAW **F2.1922**
Graf Productions. *Dist* Metro Pictures. ca5 Nov **1922** [San Francisco premiere; released 20 Nov; c13 Nov 1922; LP18407]. Si; b&w. 35mm. 7 reels, 6,900 ft.

Prod under supv of Max Graf. *Dir* James W. Horne. *Adapt* Joseph Franklin Poland. *Photog* John Stumar. *Art Dir* Earl Sibley.

Cast: Milton Sills *(Richard Jarnette)*, Jack Mulhall *(Victor Jarnette)*, Cleo Ridgely *(Margaret)*, Alec B. Francis *(Judge Kirtley)*, Muriel Dana *(Muriel)*, Alice Hollister *(Rosalie)*, Edneh Altemus *(Flo)*, Lucretia Harris *(Mammy Cely)*, Walter Law *(detective)*.

Domestic melodrama. Source: Caroline Abbot Stanley, *A Modern Madonna* (New York, 1906). When Margaret Jarnette confronts her husband, Victor, with his infidelity, he is enraged and has his lawyer construct his will so that his brother, Richard, will be declared guardian of his (Victor's) daughter, Muriel, in case of his death. Victor is killed, and Richard, ignorant of his brother's true character and believing Margaret to be guilty of the murder, takes Muriel into his home. When the truth is revealed to Richard and Victor's murderer makes a deathbed confession, Richard comes to understand the situation and marries Margaret. *Brothers. Guardians. Infidelity. Murder. Wills.*

FORGOTTEN WOMAN **F2.1923**
Pioneer Film Corp. 26 Jul **1921** [Port Washington, N. Y., showing]. Si; b&w. 35mm. 5 reels.

Dir Park Frame. *Scen* Catherine Carr. *Story* Evelyn Campbell.

Cast: Pauline Starke *(Dixie LaRose)*, J. Frank Glendon *(Julian LaRose)*, Allan Forrest *(Keith Demming)*, Laura Winston *("Sis" Maloney)*, Roy Coulson *(Joe Maloney)*, L. M. Wells *(Colonel Demming)*.

Melodrama. "Dixie, a water waif, is 'adopted' by wretched Mrs. Maloney and her son, Joe, both of whom make her life miserable, finally fooling her into a marriage with Joe. He is arrested on his wedding night and sent to prison. Sometime later Dixie is found by Keith Demming, who falls in love with her and takes her to the first party. That night Joe returns, but the unexpected appearance of Dixie's father saves Dixie from a life with Joe. He is accidentally killed and she is free to marry Keith." (*Moving Picture World,* 4 Feb 1922, p552.) *Waifs. Waterfront. Parentage.*

FORLORN RIVER **F2.1924**
Famous Players–Lasky. *Dist* Paramount Pictures. 27 Sep **1926** [c24 Sep 1926; LP23151]. Si; b&w. 35mm. 6 reels, 5,992 ft.

Pres by Adolph Zukor, Jesse L. Lasky. *Dir* John Waters. *Screenplay* George C. Hull. *Photog* C. Edgar Schoenbaum.

Cast: Jack Holt *(Nevada)*, Raymond Hatton *(Arizona Pete)*, Arlette Marchal *(Ina Blaine)*, Edmund Burns *(Ben Ide)*, Tom Santschi *(Bill Hall)*, Joseph Girard *(Hart Blaine)*, Christian J. Frank *(Les Setter)*, Albert Hart *(Sheriff Stroble)*, Nola Luxford *(Magda Lee)*, Chief Yowlache *(Modoc Joe)*, Jack Moore *(deputy)*.

Western melodrama. Source: Zane Grey, *Forlorn River* (New York, 1927). Nevada, a fugitive from justice, is left by his companion, Bill Hall, to die on the range and is rescued by Ben Ide, a young rancher. Ina Blaine, daughter of a neighboring rancher, discovers that she loves Nevada instead of Ben, but Nevada's loyalty to his friend causes him to send her away. Ina falls into the clutches of Bill Hall, now a rustler king associated with Les Setter, who poses as an honest cattleman. Nevada learns of the girl's plight and invades the rustler stronghold; Setter kills Hall, and Nevada kills Setter, while Ina's father and Ben arrive with a posse of ranchers. Nevada takes refuge with Ina on a ledge, and Ben, believing him to be a rustler, shoots at him. Later, Nevada is cleared and is united with Ina. *Fugitives. Rustlers. Ranchers. Posses. Courtship. Friendship. Utah.*

Note: Exteriors filmed in Zion National Park and Bryce Canyon in Utah.

FORSAKING ALL OTHERS F2.1925

Universal Pictures. 10 Dec **1922** [c23 Nov 1922; LP18431]. Si; b&w. 35mm. 5 reels, 4,462 ft.

Pres by Carl Laemmle. *Dir* Emile Chautard. *Scen* Doris Schroeder. *Story* Mary Lerner. *Photog* Charles Stumar.

Cast: Colleen Moore *(Penelope Mason)*, Cullen Landis *(Oliver Newell)*, Mrs. Wallace *(Mrs. Newell)*, Sam De Grasse *(Dr. Mason)*, June Elvidge *(Enid Morton)*, David Torrence *(Mr. Morton)*, Melbourne MacDowell *(Cyrus K. Wharton)*, Elinor Hancock *(Mrs. Wharton)*, Lucille Rickson *(May Wharton)*.

Drama. Jealous of her son Oliver's interest in Penelope Mason, Mrs. Newell takes him to a resort where he is easy prey for designing Enid Morton. After some near-disastrous situations with Enid's suspicious husband, Penelope comes to Oliver's rescue at Mrs. Newell's request. There is a surprise ending. *Vamps. Motherhood. Resorts.*

FORT FRAYNE F2.1926

Davis Distributing Division. c11 Jan **1926** [LP22249]. Si; b&w. 35mm. 5 reels.

Dir Ben Wilson. *Adapt* George W. Pyper. *Photog* Alfred Gosden.

Cast: Ben Wilson *(Capt. Malcolm Teale)*, Neva Gerber *(Helen Farrar)*, Ruth Royce *(Mrs. Daunton)*, Bill Patton *(Royle Farrar/Graice)*, Lafe McKee *(Col. John Farrar)*.

Western melodrama. Source: Gen. Charles King, *Fort Frayne* (Philadelphia, 1901). Captain Teale, stationed at Fort Frayne, a small garrison in Indian country, falls in love with Helen Farrar, the daughter of the colonel commanding the cavalry troop. During a skirmish with the Indians, Colonel Farrar is mortally wounded and with his dying words confides to Teale that his son, Royle, thought dead by Mrs. Farrar and Helen, has become a renegade. After the colonel's death, the Farrars go east, returning in a year's time with Mrs. Daunton as their companion. Mrs. Daunton immediately recognizes Graice, one of the new recruits, as the man who several years before deserted her shortly after their marriage; Graice kills an Indian in a saloon brawl and is confined to the guardhouse. When the Indians attack the fort in reprisal, Graice is mortally wounded, confessing before he dies that he is Royle Farrar; he is forgiven by both his wife and mother and dies at peace with God and himself. *Traitors. Indians of North America. Personal identity. Desertion. Saloons. United States Army—Cavalry.*

THE 40TH DOOR F2.1927

Pathé Exchange. 17 Aug **1924**. Si; b&w. 35mm. 6 reels, 6,000 ft.

Prod C. W. Patton. *Dir* George B. Seitz. *Scen* Frank Leon Smith. *Photog* Vernon Walker.

Cast: Allene Ray *(Aimee)*, Bruce Gordon *(Jack Ryder)*, David Dunbar *(Andy McLean)*, Anna May Wong *(Zira)*, Frances Mann *(Jimmy Jeffries)*, Frank Lackteen *(Hamid Bey)*, Lillian Gale *(Miriam)*, Bernard Seigel *(Tew Fick Pasha)*, Whitehorse *(Sheik Hassan)*, Omar Whitehead *(Paul Delcarte)*, Scott McGee *(Commissioner of Police)*, Eli Stanton *(Ali)*.

Adventure melodrama. Source: Mary Hastings Bradley, *The Fortieth Door* (New York, 1920). Plenty of adventure in the desert, with "villains dashing madly across deserts with the lives of both the hero and the heroine at stake, ... long underground avenues, trick doors, trap doors and many ways of the unwily villuns to torture the innocent. ... Allene Ray plays the daughter of a Mohammedan desert merchant, and the discovery that she is really French furthers her romance with the hero. Also featured are archeological diggings and rescue by the British Army." (*Variety*, 20 Aug 1924, p22.) *French. Archeology. Deserts. Islam. Great Britain—Army.*

Note: Feature version of a serial by the same title released in May 1924.

THE FORTUNE HUNTER F2.1928

Warner Brothers Pictures. 7 Nov **1927** [c15 Aug 1927; LP24289]. Mus score (Vitaphone); b&w. 35mm. 7 reels, 6,639 ft. [Also si.]

Dir Charles F. Reisner. *Scen* Bryan Foy, Robert Dillon. *Camera* Ed Du Par. *Asst Dir* Sandy Roth.

Cast: Syd Chaplin *(Nat Duncan)*, Helene Costello *(Josie Lockwood)*, Clara Horton *(Betty Graham)*, Duke Martin *(Handsome Harry West)*, Thomas Jefferson *(Sam Graham)*, Erville Alderson *(Blinky Lockwood)*, Paul Kruger *(Roland)*, Nora Cecil *(Betty Carpenter)*, Louise Carver *(drygoods store owner)*, Bob Perry *(sheriff)*, Babe London *(waitress)*.

Comedy-drama. Source: Winchell Smith, *The Fortune Hunter, a Play* (c1909). Nat Duncan, a cafe bouncer, is astonished to see his old panhandling pal, Handsome Harry, visiting the cabaret in the company of a bejeweled matron. Harry persuades Nat that he too can marry money and agrees to support him in the venture for a share of the profit; he supplies him with clothes and a ticket for Radville, a hick town. There Nat leads a model existence as a churchman and man of means, literally having to fight off the women, including Josie Lockwood, the town banker's daughter. He meets Betty Graham, whose father has neglected his drugstore in his efforts to make gasoline out of crude oil. Nat comes to the rescue and revives the business. Later, Harry arrives, having depleted his wife's fortune, and tries to force Nat into marrying Josie. But Nat, with the aid of a wax model, creates the impression of being fickle, thus breaking the engagement so as to marry Betty. *Bouncers. Churchmen. Pharmacists. Fortune hunters. Smalltown life. Courtship. Gasoline.*

FORTUNE'S MASK F2.1929

Vitagraph Co. of America. Oct **1922** [c18 Aug 1922; LP18171]. Si; b&w. 35mm. 5 reels, 5,000 ft.

Dir Robert Ensminger. *Scen* C. Graham Baker. *Photog* Steve Smith.

Cast: Earle Williams *(Ramón Olivarra, alias "Dicky Maloney")*, Patsy Ruth Miller *(Pasa Ortiz)*, Henry Hebert *(Losada)*, Milton Ross *(General Pilar)*, Eugenie Ford *(Madame Ortiz)*, Arthur Tavares *(Vicenti)*, Frank Whitson *(Espiración)*, Oliver Hardy *(Chief of Police)*, William McCall *(Captain Cronin)*.

Romantic drama. Source: O. Henry, "Fortune's Mask," in *Cabbages and Kings* (New York, 1904). Dicky Maloney, an Irish newcomer to a Central American town, wins the hearts of the people and the love of Pasa Ortiz with his charm and daring deeds against the army. He finally reveals himself as the son of a deposed president, successfully leads a revolution, and becomes president himself. *Irish. Revolutions. Central America.*

FORTY WINKS F2.1930

Famous Players–Lasky. *Dist* Paramount Pictures. 2 Feb **1925** [c3 Feb 1925; LP21097]. Si; b&w. 35mm. 7 reels, 6,293 ft.

Pres by Adolph Zukor, Jesse L. Lasky. *Dir* Frank Urson, Paul Iribe. *Screenplay* Bertram Millhauser. *Photog* Peverell Marley.

Cast: Viola Dana *(Eleanor Butterworth)*, Raymond Griffith *(Lord Chumley)*, Theodore Roberts *(Adam Butterworth)*, Cyril Chadwick *(Gasper Le Sage)*, Anna May Wong *(Annabelle Wu)*, William Boyd *(Lieut. Gerald Hugh Butterworth)*.

Comedy melodrama. Source: Cecil B. De Mille and David Belasco, *Lord Chumley* (New York, 1888). Gaspar Le Sage, the Butterworth family attorney and a suitor for the hand of Eleanor Butterworth, persuades a beautiful Eurasian adventuress, Annabelle Wu, to help him steal the official plans for the coastal defense of California from Eleanor's brother, Lieutenant Butterworth. Annabelle gets the susceptible lieutenant drunk at a roadhouse, steals his keys, and gets the plans. Blame for the theft is placed on Lord Chumley, a British secret service agent engaged to Eleanor, who immediately sets out to clear his own name and save the family honor. He prevents young Butterworth from killing himself, recovers the documents, and saves Eleanor, who has been kidnaped, in desperation, by Le Sage. *Halfcastes. Adventuresses. Lawyers. British. Brother-sister relationship. Secret service. Suicide. Defense—National. California. Documentation.*

45 CALIBRE WAR F2.1931

Leo Maloney Productions. *Dist* Pathé Exchange. 17 Feb **1929** [c30 Jan 1929; LP68]. Si; b&w. 35mm. 5 reels, 4,790 ft.

Pres by Leo Maloney. *Dir* Leo Maloney. *Story-Scen-Titl* Ford I. Beebe. *Photog* Edward A. Kull. *Film Ed* Joseph Kane.

Cast: Don Coleman *(Reed Lathrop)*, Ben Corbett *("Toad" Hunter)*, Al Hart *(Reverend Mr. Simpson)*, Edward Jones *(Sheriff Henshaw)*, Duke R. Lee *(Nick Darnell)*, Floyd Ames *(Jim Walling)*, Jeanette Loff *(Ruth Walling)*, Murdock MacQuarrie *(Mark Blodgett)*, Orin Jackson *(Dr. Sprague)*.

Western melodrama. Reed Lathrop, in response to a letter from Ruth Walling, returns to his old home, accompanied by his friend, "Toad" Hunter, to investigate an undercover attempt to force the ranchers to sell their property for practically nothing. Finding the ranchers demoralized, he organizes a vigilance committee and enlists the aid of the local circuit rider. Darnell, the owner of the saloon, and Blodgett, a local dealer in ranchlands, are revealed to be the arch-conspirators. After a battle in the street, the ranchers win the day and the outlaws are sent to prison. *Ranchers. Vigilantes. Circuit riders. Saloon keepers. Property rights.*

40-HORSE HAWKINS **F2.1932**

Universal Pictures. 21 Apr **1924** [c28 Mar 1924; LP20038]. Si; b&w. 35mm. 6 reels, 5,419 ft.

Dir Edward Sedgwick. *Story-Scen* Edward Sedgwick, Raymond L. Schrock. *Photog* Virgil Miller.

Cast: Hoot Gibson *(Luke [Bud] Hawkins)*, Anne Cornwall *(Mary Darling)*, Richard Tucker *(Rudolph Catalina)*, Helen Holmes *(Sylvia Dean)*, Jack Gordon Edwards *(Johnny)*, Ed Burns *(sheriff)*, Edward Sedgwick *(stage manager)*, John Judd *(Wild Bill Bailey)*.

Comedy. Luke Hawkins, the jack-of-all-trades of the western town of Lariat, falls in love with Mary Darling, the leading lady in a traveling theatrical troupe (of the old-fashioned "mortgage melodrama" variety). He follows her to New York, takes another series of jobs, and finally works as an extra in Mary's new production. Just as the play is about to flop, Luke recognizes Mary, and his rush to take her in his arms turns the show into a hit. *Actors. Handymen. Theatrical troupes. Theater. New York City.*

THE FORWARD PASS **F2.1933**

First National Pictures. 10 Nov **1929** [c12 Nov 1929; LP855]. Sd (Vitaphone); b&w. 35mm. 7,246 ft. [Also si, 1 Dec 1929; 4,920 ft.]

Dir Eddie Cline. *Scen-Dial-Titl* Howard Emmett Rogers. *Story* Harvey Gates. *Photog* Arthur Todd. *Film Ed* Ralph Holt. *Songs: "One Minute of Heaven," "H'lo Baby," "I Gotta' Have You," "Huddlin"* Herb Magidson, Ned Washington, Michael H. Cleary.

Cast: Douglas Fairbanks, Jr. *(Marty Reid)*, Loretta Young *(Patricia Carlyle)*, Guinn Williams *(Honey Smith)*, Marion Byron *(Mazie)*, Phyllis Crane *(Dot)*, Bert Rome *(Coach Wilson)*, Lane Chandler *(Assistant Coach Kane)*, Allan Lane *(Ed Kirby)*, Floyd Shackleford *(trainer)*, University of Southern California Football Team.

Romantic sports drama. Marty Reid, the star quarterback at Sanford College, is constantly singled out by the opposition for punishment, and he swears to his pal, Honey Smith, and to Coach Wilson that he will quit the game forever. Ed Kirby, who dislikes Reid, calls him yellow; and Wilson gets Patricia Carlyle, the college vamp, to induce Reid to play. At a sorority dance, where only football players can cut in, Kirby persecutes Reid by dancing with Pat, and as a result Reid does apply to play in the game. When he learns of her trickery, however, Reid fumbles in the game, and both he and Kirby are withdrawn and start a fight in the locker room. Convinced that Reid is no coward, Kirby joins him and they win the game. *Vamps. Football. College life. Sororities. University of Southern California.*

Note: Filmed on locations at the University of Southern California campus.

FOUND GUILTY **F2.1934**

15 Aug **1922** [New York State license application]. Si; b&w. 35mm. 5 reels.

Cast: Tom Santschi.

Melodrama(?). "The picture opens with a speech, by a person supposed to be a representative of Congress, against capital punishment. There then follow scenes of beheading people, hanging, electrocuting and killing them by means of the guillotine, which scenes are supposed to be founded upon historical facts. The film also has several dance-hall scenes, showing a girl living with a man without being married and finally where he deserts her and marries another. There is also shown a murder of a girl by her sister and subsequent trial of an innocent man for the murder, at which he is found guilty. Scenes are shown in detail leading up to his electrocution." (New York State license records.) *Capital punishment. Murder. United States Congress.*

Note: Production and distribution companies not determined. Released in New York State by Anthony Moratto.

FOUR DEVILS **F2.1935**

Fox Film Corp. 15 Sep **1929** [c1 Oct 1928; LP25737]. Sd eff, mus score, and talking sequences (Movietone); b&w. 35mm. 12 reels, 9,496 ft. [Also si, 22 Dec 1929; 9,295 ft.]

Pres by William Fox. *Dir* F. W. Murnau. *Stgd by* A. H. Van Buren, A. F. Erickson. *Scen* Carl Mayer. *Dial* John Hunter Booth. *Adapt* Berthold Viertel, Marion Orth. *Photog* Ernest Palmer, L. W. O'Connell. *Film Ed* Harold Schuster. *Mus Score* S. L. Rothafel. *Song: "Marion"* Erno Rapee, Lew Pollack. *Rec Engr* Harold Hobson. *Asst Dir* A. F. Erickson.

Cast—First Sequence: Farrell MacDonald *(The Clown)*, Anders Randolf *(Cecchi)*, Claire McDowell *(woman)*, Jack Parker *(Charles, as a boy)*, Philippe De Lacy *(Adolf, as a boy)*, Dawn O'Day *(Marion, as a girl)*, Anita Fremault *(Louise, as girl)*, Wesley Lake *(old clown)*.

Cast—Second Sequence: Janet Gaynor *(Marion)*, Charles Morton *(Charles)*, Nancy Drexel *(Louise)*, Barry Norton *(Adolf)*, Mary Duncan *(The Lady)*, Michael Visaroff *(circus director)*, George Davis *(mean clown)*, André Cheron *(old roué)*.

Drama. Source: Herman Joachim Bang, *De Fire Djaevle; excentrisk novelle* (Kristiania, 1895). A kindly old clown rescues four children (Charles, Adolf, Marion, and Louise) from the brutal tutelage of a circus owner and brings up the quartet himself, training them to be acrobats. Years pass, and the children form a successful trapeze act known as the Four Devils. Charles and Marion are engaged, but while at the Cirque Olympia in Paris, Charles becomes infatuated with a beautiful vamp. Marion learns of the affair and becomes distracted; working without a net for a dangerous finale, she falls. Marion is not killed, however, and Charles is brought to his senses by the near tragedy. *Acrobats. Clowns. Trapezists. Circus. Paris. Cirque Olympia.*

THE FOUR FEATHERS **F2.1936**

Paramount Famous Lasky Corp. 12 Jun **1929** [New York premiere; released 28 Dec; c27 Dec 1929; LP945]. Mus score & sd eff (Movietone); b&w. 35mm. 8 reels, 7,472 ft. [Also si.]

Assoc Prod David Selznick. *Dir* Merian C. Cooper, Ernest B. Schoedsack, Lothar Mendes. *Screenplay* Howard Estabrook. *Titl* Julian Johnson, John Farrow. *Adapt* Hope Loring. *Photog* Robert Kurrle, Merian C. Cooper, Ernest B. Schoedsack. *Film Ed* Ernest B. Schoedsack. *Mus Score* William Frederick Peters. *Asst Dir* Ivan Thomas.

Cast: Richard Arlen *(Harry Feversham)*, Fay Wray *(Ethne Eustace)*, Clive Brook *(Lieutenant Durrance)*, William Powell *(Captain Trench)*, Theodore von Eltz *(Lieutenant Castleton)*, Noah Beery *(slave trader)*, Zack Williams *(Idris)*, Noble Johnson *(Ahmed)*, Harold Hightower *(Ali)*, Philippe De Lacy *(Harry, as a boy of 10)*, E. J. Radcliffe *(Colonel Eustace)*, George Fawcett *(Colonel Feversham)*, Augustin Symonds *(Colonel Sutch)*.

Adventure melodrama. Source: Alfred Edward Woodley Mason, *The Four Feathers* (London, 1902). Harry Feversham, a British regimental officer, fears the consequences of war. When his regiment is sent to active duty in the Sudan, he leaves the military service to marry Ethne Eustace. His companions, Durrance, Trench, and Castleton, learn he has actually resigned out of cowardice, and each sends him a white feather, symbolizing a disgrace that causes his father's death. Determined to redeem himself, he leaves England and becomes an African wanderer. Learning that Trench is imprisoned in a native fortress, he goes there but is himself captured; they are sold to a slave trader, but Harry kills him and they are pursued by tribesmen; a jungle fire and a herd of hippopotami prevent their escape across the Nile, but they are rescued by British soldiers in the Sudan, where Harry returns feathers to Durrance and Trench. The outpost is besieged by fuzzy-wuzzies, but a relief column under Castleton saves the British and Harry proves his bravery by killing the native chieftain. Later, the last feather is redeemed to Ethne, and the four comrades are decorated in England. *Fuzzy-wuzzies. Cowardice. Colonialism. Slavery. Jungles. Sudan. Great Britain—Army. Hippopotami.*

Note: Filmed on locations in Africa, including the Egyptian Sudan.

THE FOUR FROM NOWHERE **F2.1937**

Goodwill Pictures. 6 Nov **1925** [New York State license]. Si; b&w. 35mm. 5 reels, 4,395 ft.

Prod-Dir-Writ Francis Ford. *Scen* Peggy O'Day. *Camera* Mark Thwaites.

Cast: Francis Ford, Peggy O'Day, Phil Ford, Billie Ford, George Rheam.

Melodrama. Snowed in for the winter, four inhabitants of a cabin have only copies of *The Count of Monte Cristo* and the Bible for a diversion. The four decide to read the former, allowing for a tableau of highlights from Dumas' story. *"Count of Monte Cristo" The Bible.*

FOUR HEARTS **F2.1938**

Dist Western Pictures Exploitation Co. 13 May **1922** [trade review]. Si; b&w. 35mm. 5 reels.

Dir Leonard Wheeler. *Story-Scen* Dick Hatton, Leonard Wheeler.

Cast: Dick Hatton *(Dick Reynolds)*, Nell Spaugh *(Mary Reynolds)*, Carmen Arselle *(Marion Berkley)*, Bud Geary *(Bob Berkley)*, Lucille Du Bois *(Betty Davis)*, Barney Furey *(Gordon Ferris)*, Ed Fitzharis *(Jim Hawkins)*.

Western melodrama. Taking test samples of dye deposit from his western land (not yet paid for) to New York, Dick Reynolds meets his war buddy, Bob Berkley, who is in ill health, and Dick takes Bob and his sister, Marion, back home with him. The sample tester follows them and does all in his power to gain possession of Dick's land, and Dick is even jailed under charges of murder. Setting out to prove Dick's innocence, Marion, Bob, and Bob's sweetheart join in the search for the murderer; and Marion vamps the ranch foreman into a confession that implicates the chemist and another man. Freed, Dick gives the villain a beating and lands him in the sheriff's office. *Sheriffs. Veterans. Ranch foremen. Chemists. Property rights. Murder. Injustice. Dye.*

THE FOUR HORSEMEN OF THE APOCALYPSE **F2.1939**

Metro Pictures. 6 Mar **1921** [New York premiere; c24 Mar 1921; LP16308]. Si; b&w. 35mm. 11 reels.

Dir Rex Ingram. *Adapt* June Mathis. *Photog* John F. Seitz. *Asst Photog* Starret Ford, Walter Mayo. *Art Dir* Joseph Calder, Amos Myers. *Film Ed* Grant Whytock. *Mus* Louis F. Gottschalk. *Asst Dir* Walter Mayo. *Art Titl* Jack W. Robson.

Cast: Rodolph Valentino *(Julio Desnoyers)*, Alice Terry *(Marguerite Laurier)*, Pomeroy Cannon *(Madariaga, the Centaur)*, Josef Swickard *(Marcelo Desnoyers)*, Brinsley Shaw *(Celendonio)*, Alan Hale *(Karl von Hartrott)*, Bridgetta Clark *(Doña Luisa)*, Mabel Van Buren *(Elena)*, Nigel De Brulier *(Tchernoff)*, Bowditch Turner *(Argensola)*, John Sainpolis *(Laurier)*, Mark Fenton *(Senator Lacour)*, Virginia Warwick *(Chichi)*, Derek Ghent *(René Lacour)*, Stuart Holmes *(Captain von Hartrott)*, Jean Hersholt *(Professor von Hartrott)*, Henry Klaus *(Heinrich von Hartrott)*, Edward Connelly *(lodgekeeper)*, Georgia Woodthorpe *(lodgekeeper's wife)*, Kathleen Key *(Georgette)*, Wallace Beery *(Lieutenant-Colonel von Richthoffen)*, Jacques D'Auray *(Captain d'Aubrey)*, Curt Rehfeld *(Major Blumhardt)*, Harry Northrup *(The Count)*, Claire De Lorez *(Mademoiselle Lucette, the model)*, Bull Montana *(the French butler)*, Isabelle Keith *(the German woman)*, Jacques Lanoe *(her husband)*, Noble Johnson *(Conquest)*, Minnehaha *(The Old Nurse)*, Arthur Hoyt *(Lieutenant Schnitz)*, Beatrice Dominguez *(dancer)*.

Epic drama. Source: Vicente Blasco-Ibáñez, *The Four Horsemen of the Apocalypse* (trans. by Charlotte Brewster Jordan of *Los cuatros jinetes del Apocalipsis;* New York, 1918). Madariaga, a wealthy old cattle owner of Argentina who despises his German son-in-law, lavishes all his affections on Julio. After Madariaga's death, the estate is divided and all the family disperse to Europe: the von Hartrotts to Germany and the Desnoyers to Paris. Julio buys a castle on the Marne and opens a studio, where he entertains, paints pictures, and soon falls desperately in love with Marguerite Laurier, youthful wife of a jurist. War comes, Marguerite joins the Red Cross, and her husband enlists. Finding him blinded, she determines to resist the attentions of Julio. Spurred on by the words of a stranger, who invokes the Four Horsemen—War, Conquest, Famine, and Death—Julio enlists, and after distinguishing himself for bravery he is killed in an exchange with his cousin, an officer in the German Army. *Ranchers. Artists. Blindness. World War I. Apocalypse. Argentina. France. Germany. Red Cross.*

THE FOUR HUMAN EAGLES *see* **THE FLIGHT OF THE SOUTHERN CROSS; OR, THE FOUR HUMAN EAGLES**

FOUR SEASONS (Urban Popular Classic) **F2.1940**

Kineto Co. of America. ca8 Oct **1921** [New York premiere]. Si; b&w. 35mm. 4 reels.

Pres by Charles Urban. *Prod-Dir* Raymond L. Ditmars. *Film Ed* Charles Urban.

Documentary. "One reel is devoted to each season ... and with the successive seasons the unfolding of plant and animal life, its adolescence, full growth and then the period of death or dormancy that comes with the snows of winter are graphically shown by well chosen examples" (*Moving Picture World,* 8 Oct 1921, p694). *Nature. Spring. Summer. Autumn. Winter. Plant life. Animal life.*

FOUR SONS **F2.1941**

Fox Film Corp. 13 Feb **1928** [c6 Feb 1928; LP24963]. Mus score & sd eff (Movietone); b&w. 35mm. 9-10 reels, 8,962-9,412 ft. [Copyrighted as 11 reels.]

Pres by William Fox. *Dir* John Ford. *Adapt-Cont* Philip Klein. *Titl* Katherine Hilliker, H. H. Caldwell. *Photog* George Schneiderman, Charles G. Clarke. *Film Ed* Margaret V. Clancey. *Theme Song: "Little Mother"* Erno Rapee, Lew Pollack. *Mus Arr* S. L. Rothafel. *Asst Dir* Edward O'Fearna.

Cast: James Hall *(Joseph Bernle)*, Margaret Mann *(Grandma Bernle)*, Earle Foxe *(Von Stomm)*, Charles Morton *(Johann Bernle)*, Francis X. Bushman, Jr. *(Franz Bernle)*, George Meeker *(Andres Bernle)*, Albert Gran *(letter carrier)*, Frank Reicher *(schoolmaster)*, Hughie Mack *(innkeeper)*, Michael Mark *(Von Stomm's orderly)*, August Tollaire *(burgomaster)*, June Collyer *(Ann, the American girl)*, Wendell Phillips Franklin *(James Henry)*, Ruth Mix *(Johann's girl)*, Jack Pennick *(Joseph's American friend)*, Leopold Archduke of Austria *(German captain)*, Robert Parrish *(child)*, L. J. O'Connor *(Aubergiste)*, Capt. John Porters, Ferdinand Schumann-Heink, Carl Boheme, Constant Franke, Hans Furberg, Tibor von Janny, Stanley Blystone, Lieut. George Blagoi *(officers)*.

Drama. Source: Ida Alexa Ross Wylie, "Grandmother Bernle Learns Her Letters," in *Saturday Evening Post* (199:8–9, 11 Sep 1926). A Bavarian widow with four sons loses them in the war one by one until only Joseph is left. Having migrated to America, Joseph marries, opens a delicatessen, starts a family, and survives the war fighting on the Allied side. After the war, Joseph returns to America and invites his mother to live with him and his family. *Widows. Soldiers. Motherhood. Delicatessens. World War I. Bavaria. Germany.*

FOUR WALLS **F2.1942**

Metro-Goldwyn-Mayer Pictures. 11 Aug **1928** [c4 Aug 1928; LP25604]. Si; b&w. 35mm. 8 reels, 6,620 ft.

Dir William Nigh. *Cont* Alice D. G. Miller. *Titl* Joe Farnham. *Photog* James Howe. *Sets* Cedric Gibbons. *Film Ed* Harry Reynolds. *Wardrobe* David Cox.

Cast: John Gilbert *(Benny)*, Joan Crawford *(Frieda)*, Vera Gordon *(Mrs. Horowitz)*, Carmel Myers *(Bertha)*, Robert E. O'Connor *(Sullivan)*, Louis Natheaux *(Monk)*, Jack Byron *(Duke Roma)*.

Underworld melodrama. Source: Dana Burnet and George Abbott, *Four Walls* (New York opening: 19 Sep 1927). Benny Horowitz, an East Side gang leader, kills another gangster in self-defense and is sentenced to prison on the charge of manslaughter. Having served out his term, Benny decides to go straight and finds work in a garage. His old girl, Frieda, wants to resume their former intimacy, but although he still loves her, Benny turns instead to Bertha, a plain girl who befriended his mother while he was in jail. He later attends a party at which Monk, the new gangleader, is accidentally killed in a fall. Sullivan, the detective who sent Benny up the first time, at first suspects him of having murdered Monk; eventually Benny is cleared of suspicion, inviting Frieda to share a new life with him. *Gangsters. Detectives. Criminals—Rehabilitation. Murder. New York City—East Side.*

THE FOUR-FOOTED RANGER **F2.1943**

Universal Pictures. 25 Mar **1928** [c20 Oct 1927; LP24560]. Si; b&w. 35mm. 5 reels, 4,426 ft.

Pres by Carl Laemmle. *Dir* Stuart Paton. *Story-Cont* Paul M. Bryan. *Titl* Gardner Bradford. *Adapt* Cromwell Kent. *Photog* Jerry Ash. *Film Ed* Thomas Malloy.

Cast: Dynamite *(The Dog)*, Edmund Cobb *(Jack Dunne)*, Marjorie Bonner *(Katy Pearl Lee)*, Pearl Sindelar *(Mary Doolittle)*, Francis Ford *(Brom Hockley)*, Pat Rooney *(Bull Becker)*, Frank M. Clark *(Handsome Thomas)*, Carl Sepulveda *(Jake)*, Lee Lin *(Chinese cook)*.

Western melodrama. Goaded to action by a gang of cattle rustlers, a group of ranchers organize and enlist the services of Jack Dunne, a Texas Ranger, assisted by his police dog; they also call on Brom Hockley, who is managing the K. P. Lee ranch while its owner is in the East, and who is actually leader of the rustlers, aided and abetted by Bull Becker. Jones and the cattlemen meet Jack on his way to the ranch; he is introduced as Jones's nephew and is given a letter purloined from Hockley by Handsome, a loyal hand on the Lee ranch. Gaining their trust, he goes to the ranch and impersonates Lee, Jr., unaware that K. P. Lee, Jr., is the *female* heiress of the ranch. She duly arrives with her spinster aunt, Mary Ann Doolittle. Following a sequence of plot and counterplot, interspersed with fast action, the hero and heroine are united and the villains brought to justice. *Ranchers. Rustlers. Texas Rangers. Impersonation. Police dogs.*

THE FOURFLUSHER (Universal-Jewel) **F2.1944**

Universal Pictures. 8 Jan **1928** [c4 Nov 1927; LP24629]. Si; b&w. 35mm. 6 reels, 6,193 ft.

Pres by Carl Laemmle. *Dir* Wesley Ruggles. *Adapt-Cont* Earl Snell. *Titl* Albert De Mond. *Photog* Ben Reynolds. *Film Ed* Robert Carlisle.

Cast: George Lewis *(Andy Wittaker)*, Marion Nixon *(June Allen)*, Eddie Phillips *(Robert Riggs)*, Churchill Ross *(Jerry)*, Jimmie Ayre *(Toni)*, Burr McIntosh *(Ira Wittaker)*, Otto Hoffman *(Mr. Riggs)*, Wilfred North *(Mr. Stone)*, Knute Erickson *(jeweler)*, Patricia Caron *(cashier)*, Mariam

Fauche, Hayden Stevenson.

Comedy-drama. Source: Cesar Dunn, *The Four-Flusher, an American Comedy in Three Acts* (New York, 1925). Andy Wittaker, an ambitious shoeclerk who has invented an unmarketed arch supporter, meets June Allen on the street and pretends he is an important businessman. Later, she comes to the shop and forgives his deception, but when Robert Riggs, the owner's son, catches him dancing with her, Andy has to resign. Andy obtains a loan from a trust fund established for him by his uncle, but en route to a party, he hits the uncle with his new car, and therefore the uncle decides to cancel the trust fund. Andy is then hounded by creditors for the return of a ring he has bought for June, and he goes away in disgrace. Meanwhile, he opens a shoestore so as to sell his arch supporters, and June hires an actor to make a fictitious offer for the marketing rights in the presence of the creditors; but Andy sells the rights at a high price to a bona fide buyer. He and June then find happiness in their success. *Shoeclerks. Inventors. Bankers. Uncles. Debt. Automobile accidents.*

THE FOURTEENTH LOVER **F2.1945**

Metro Pictures. 9 Jan **1922** [c4 Jan 1922; LP17442]. Si; b&w. 35mm. 5 reels, 5,180 ft.

Dir Harry Beaumont. *Scen* Edith Kennedy. *Photog* John Arnold. *Art Dir* A. F. Mantz.

Cast: Viola Dana *(Vi Marchmont)*, Jack Mulhall *(Richard Hardy)*, Theodore von Eltz *(Clyde Van Ness)*, Kate Lester *(Aunt Letitia)*, Alberta Lee *(Mrs. Hardy)*, Frederick Vroom *(Mr. Marchmont)*, Fronzie Gunn *(maid)*.

Comedy. Source: Alice D. G. Miller, "The Fourteenth Lover" (publication undetermined). Vi Marchmont, who has 13 suitors and is becoming interested in No. 14, is ordered by her father and Aunt Letitia to call a halt. With the aid of the family doctor, Vi convinces the family that she has a heart ailment and is sent to the country to recuperate. There she takes an interest in Richard Hardy, the gardener on her father's estate. Hardy is discharged by Vi's aunt when she discovers Vi's infatuation with him, and Van Ness, a wealthy young suitor, tries to convince Vi that Hardy is married; Vi, however, learns housekeeping, confident that Hardy will return. Hardy obtains a landscaping job, but in his unhappiness he confides in his mother, who visits Vi. In spite of Hardy's objections, Vi spends the night at his house, while he sleeps in her roadster. The following morning Vi informs him that she will not be happy until they are married, and they agree to elope. *Gardeners. Aunts. Courtship. Motherhood.*

THE FOURTH ALARM **F2.1946**

Continental Talking Pictures. 25 Oct **1930** [c1 Nov 1930; LP1963]. Sd (Photophone); b&w. 35mm. 6 reels, 5,494 ft.

Pres by W. Ray Johnston. *Dir* Phil Whitman. *Story-Scen-Dial* Scott Littleton. *Photog* Herbert Kirkpatrick. *Film Ed* Carl Himm. *Sd* Neil Jack.

Cast: Nick Stuart *(Dick Turner)*, Ralph Lewis *(Chief Turner)*, Tom Santschi *(Benjamin Griffith)*, Ann Christy *(Helen Griffith)*, Harry Bowen *(Mac)*, Jack Richardson *(fireman)*.

Melodrama. Following in his father's footsteps, Dick Turner becomes a fireman, but he breaks his leg in a firetruck-auto collision with wealthy, speed-crazy Helen Griffith. They fall in love during his stay in the hospital, and Helen's father sees in this development a perfect opportunity to keep secret his clandestine manufacture and storage of nitroglycerin by having Dick appointed fire inspector. The upstanding lad puts duty before love, but his report is countered by an accusation of solicitation of bribery. Just then, a fire breaks out in Griffith's warehouse; Dick is detailed to the station house, but he finally bolts to the fire in time to rescue Helen, who was trapped in a storeroom. *Firemen. Fire inspectors. Filial relations. Bribery. Nitroglycerin. Automobile accidents. Fires.*

THE FOURTH COMMANDMENT (Universal-Jewel) **F2.1947**

Universal Pictures. 20 Mar **1927** [c14 Oct 1926; LP23239]. Si; b&w. 35mm. 8 reels, 7,560 ft. [Release version: 7 reels, 6,863 ft.]

Pres by Carl Laemmle. *Dir-Adapt* Emory Johnson. *Titl* Carroll Owen. *Photog* Arthur Todd.

Cast: Henry Victor *(Gordon Graham)*, June Marlowe *(Marjorie Miller)*, Belle Bennett *(Virginia)*, Leigh Willard *(Edmund Graham)*, Mary Carr *(Mrs. Graham)*, Brady Cline *(Ray Miller)*, Catherine Wallace *(Mrs. Miller)*, Frank Elliott *(Frederick Stoneman)*, Knute Erickson *(John Malloy)*, Kathleen Myers *(Mrs. Smith)*, Robert Agnew *(Sonny)*, Wendell Phillips Franklin *(Sonny, as a little boy)*, Lorraine Rivero *(Marjorie, as a little girl)*, Malcolm Jones *(Gordon, as a little boy)*, Stanley Taylor *(Count Douglas Von Rosen)*.

Domestic melodrama. Source: Emilie Johnson, "The Fourth Commandment" (publication undetermined). Following a reversal in the Graham family fortune, a childhood love affair between Gordon Graham and Marjorie Miller is frustrated by the socially ambitious Mrs. Miller. After graduation from college, Gordon marries Virginia; and 4 years after the birth of their child, Virginia, eager to return to work, accepts her mother-in-law's offer to live with them and care for Sonny. Jealous of Mrs. Graham for stealing her child's affections, she reproaches her and leaves with Sonny. Virginia then marries Stoneman, her employer, but when he is imprisoned on embezzlement charges, she is left destitute. Taken in by Sonny and his wife, she in turn excites the young wife's jealousy; and when the couple move to Paris, Virginia decides to pass out of their lives. While attending an architectural convention in Paris, Gordon and Marjorie (now his wife) are recognized by the haggard woman, but she dies in the street before she can reach them. *Mothers-in-law. Architects. Wealth. Poverty. Marriage. Motherhood. Jealousy. Embezzlement. Paris.*

THE FOURTH MUSKETEER **F2.1948**

R-C Pictures. *Dist* Film Booking Offices of America. 25 Mar **1923** [c18 Mar 1923; LP20149]. Si; b&w. 35mm. 6 reels, 5,800 ft.

Prod J. G. Caldwell. *Dir* William K. Howard. *Adapt* Paul Schofield. *Photog* William O'Connell.

Cast: Johnnie Walker *(Brian O'Brien)*, Eileen Percy *(Mrs. Brian O'Brien)*, Eddie Gribbon *(Mike Donovan)*, William Scott *(Joe Tracy)*, Edith Yorke *(Mrs. Tracy)*, Georgie Stone *(Jimmy Tracy)*, James McElhern *(Don O'Reilly)*, Philo McCullough *(Gerald Van Sicklen)*, Kate Lester *(Mrs. Rector)*.

Melodrama. Source: Harry Charles Witwer, "The Fourth Musketeer," in *Cosmopolitan* (73:51–55, Sep 1922). Successful pugilist Brian O'Brien quits the ring to become a mechanic. He lends his winnings to a rival and opens his garage with a bank note. Meanwhile, his wife neglects him for a high society type, but she finally realizes her place with him when he recovers some stolen jewels and is acclaimed as a hero. *Prizefighters. Mechanics. Marriage. Theft.*

THE FOX (Universal-Jewel) **F2.1949**

Universal Film Manufacturing Co. 31 Oct **1921** [c12 Nov 1921; LP17181]. Si; b&w. 35mm. 7 reels, 6,941 ft.

Pres by Carl Laemmle. *Dir* Robert Thornby. *Scen* Lucien Hubbard. *Story (see note)* Arthur Henry Gooden. *Photog* William Fildew.

Cast: Harry Carey *(Ol' Santa Fe)*, George Nichols *(Sheriff Mart Fraser)*, Gertrude Olmsted *(Stella Fraser)*, Betty Ross Clark *(Annette Fraser)*, Johnny Harron *(Dick Farwell)*, Gertrude Claire *(Mrs. Farwell)*, Alan Hale *(Rufus B. Coulter)*, George Cooper *(K. C. Kid)*, Breezy Eason, Jr. *(Pard)*, Charles Le Moyne *(Black Mike)*, C. E. Anderson *(Rollins)*, Harley Chambers *(Hubbs)*.

Western melodrama. Santa Fe, a tramp, is saved from a jeering mob in the desert town of Caliente by Annette, the sheriff's daughter; and after adopting Pard he gets a job as porter in the bank. Santa Fe learns that the leading banker, Coulter, is in league with a band of outlaws, and when Coulter frames Dick Farwell, Annette's fiancé, Dick is suspected of robbery and is captured by the outlaws. Santa Fe saves the sheriff from death in a sandstorm but is himself captured; he escapes with Dick by a subterranean river and arrives in town in time to save the sheriff from a mob and to reveal himself as a special agent sent to catch Coulter. Aided by the U. S. Cavalry and a posse, he leads an attack on the outlaw stronghold and takes Coulter. Santa Fe wins the love of Annette. *Porters. Sheriffs. Tramps. Outlaws. Posses. Secret service. Banks. United States Army—Cavalry.*

Note: Working title: *Partners.* Harry Carey received screen credit for the story, but Universal records indicate that it was written by Arthur Henry Gooden.

FOX MOVIETONE FOLLIES OF 1929 **F2.1950**

Fox Film Corp. 25 May **1929** [c8 May 1929; LP402]. Sd (Movietone); b&w with col sequence (Technicolor). 35mm. 14 reels, 8,291 ft.

Pres by William Fox. *Dir-Story* David Butler. *Revue Dir* Marcel Silver. *Dial* William K. Wells. *Photog* Charles Van Enger. *Film Ed* Ralph Dietrich. *Songs: "Walking With Susie," "Why Can't I Be Like You?" "Legs," "The Breakaway," "That's Your Baby," "Look What You've Done to Me," "Big City Blues," "Pearl of Old Japan"* Con Conrad, Sidney Mitchell, Archie Gottler. *Mus Cond* Arthur Kay. *Ensembles* Archie Gottler, Fanchon & Marco. *Rec Engr* Joseph E. Aiken. *Cost* Sophie Wachner, Alice O'Neill.

Linda time to go to South America with an understanding Brian. *Detectives. Poverty. Larceny. Insurance. Monte Carlo.*

THE GILDED HIGHWAY **F2.2070**

Warner Brothers Pictures. 13 Mar **1926** [c15 Mar 1926; LP22514]. Si; b&w. 35mm. 7 reels, 6,927 ft.

Dir J. Stuart Blackton. *Adapt* Marian Constance. *Photog* Nicholas Musuraca. *Asst Camera* William S. Adams. *Asst Dir* Walter Mayo.

Cast: Dorothy Devore *(Primrose Welby)*, John Harron *(Jack Welby)*, Maclyn Arbuckle *(Jonathan Welby)*, Myrna Loy *(Irene Quartz)*, Florence Turner *(Mrs. Welby)*, Sheldon Lewis *(Uncle Nicholas Welby)*, Andrée Tourneur *(Amabel)*, Gardner James *(Hugo Blythe)*, Mathilde Comont *(Sarah)*, Thomas Mills *(Adolphus Faring)*.

Society melodrama. Source: William Babington Maxwell, *A Little More* (London, 1921). Both Jack Welby and his sister, Primrose, of a happy, contented middleclass family, are in love and considering marriage. Suddenly, their father's wealthy uncle, Nicholas, dies leaving the family his entire fortune. Intoxicated by riches, the Welbys immediately rush into extravagance, forsaking their home—which Sarah, their faithful servant, converts into a boardinghouse—for a magnificent estate. With the rise of jealousy, bickering, insincerity, and acrimony in the household, Jack neglects Amabel, his sweetheart, and Primrose looks scornfully on Hugo, her former fiancé. At the height of a lavish charity ball, Jack receives a note from Amabel, intimating suicide, and coming to his senses, he decides to marry her. Finally, the family are stunned to find that their fortune has been lost in speculation. Poverty soon engulfs them, and the parents seek aid at the poorhouse but find shelter in their old home with Sarah. Primrose is reunited with Hugo, and happiness returns to their home. *Nouveaux riches. Family life. Wealth. Inheritance.*

GILDED LIES **F2.2071**

Selznick Pictures. Mar **1921** [c14 Mar 1921; LP16291]. Si; b&w. 35mm. 5 reels, 4,496 ft.

Dir William P. S. Earle. *Scen* R. Cecil Smith. *Story* John Lynch. *Photog* Jules Cronjager.

Cast: Eugene O'Brien *(Keene McComb)*, Martha Mansfield *(Hester Thorpe)*, Frank Whitson *(Martin Ward)*, George Stewart *(Andrew Scott)*, Arthur Donaldson *(Major Burns)*.

Melodrama. When Keene McComb, a young explorer on an expedition to the North Pole, is given up for lost, his fiancée, Hester Thorpe, is coerced by an ambitious aunt into marrying Martin Ward, a man of reputed wealth. McComb survives, however, and returns to New York a few hours after the marriage. Later, Hester seeks his protection when Ward strikes her because of her refusal to ask McComb for money, and when it appears that Ward has committed suicide she and McComb are married. Ward is still alive, however, but he meets his death on a rocky precipice. *Explorers. Aunts. Bigamy. Suicide. Arctic regions.*

THE GILDED LILY **F2.2072**

Famous Players–Lasky. *Dist* Paramount Pictures. 27 Mar **1921** [c27 Mar 1921; LP16329]. Si; b&w. 35mm. 7 reels, 6,060 ft.

Pres by Adolph Zukor. *Dir* Robert Z. Leonard. *Titl* Tom McNamara. *Story* Clara Beranger. *Photog* Ernest Haller. *Art Dir* Robert M. Haas.

Cast: Mae Murray *(Lillian Drake)*, Lowell Sherman *(Creighton Howard)*, Jason Robards *(Frank Thompson)*, Charles Gerard *(John Stewart)*, Leonora Ottinger *(Mrs. Thompson)*.

Society melodrama. Lillian Drake, a Broadway cafe hostess, is a well-known figure with many suitors, including Creighton Howard, wealthy man-about-town, and a country boy, Frank Thompson. Frank becomes infatuated with her, and in spite of his mother's objections he marries her. Lily gives up her work and plans to lead a quiet life, but Frank begins drinking and encourages her to return to her former life, which she does. Collapsing on the dance floor, she is rescued by Creighton, who then is shot at by Frank. Later, at his home, Creighton introduces the girl to his mother as his fiancée. *Cafe hostesses. Dissipation. Marriage. New York City—Broadway.*

GIMME **F2.2073**

Goldwyn Pictures. 14 Jan **1923** [New York premiere; released 21 Jan; c2 Jan 1923; LP18565]. Si; b&w. 35mm. 6 reels, 5,769 ft.

Dir-Scen Rupert Hughes. *Story* Rupert Hughes, Adelaide Hughes. *Photog* John J. Mescall. *Art Dir* Cedric Gibbons.

Cast: Helene Chadwick *(Fanny Daniels)*, Gaston Glass *(Clinton Ferris)*, Kate Lester *(Mrs. Roland Ferris)*, Eleanor Boardman *(Clothilde Kingsley)*, David Imboden *(Claude Lambert)*, May Wallace *(Mrs. Cecily McGimsey)*, Georgia Woodthorpe *(Annabel Wainwright)*, H. B. Walthall *(John McGimsey)*, Jean Hope *(Lizzie)*.

Domestic comedy-drama. Fanny Daniels borrows $500 from Claude Lambert, her employer, for the trousseau for her marriage to Clinton Ferris. When Lambert asks for the money, Fanny draws a check on Clinton's account because she dislikes having to ask her husband for money. There is a row when Clinton finds out; Fanny leaves him and returns to work for Lambert. Clinton then realizes his wife's attitude and agrees to "live 50-50" with her. *Debt. Marriage. Finance—Personal.*

THE GINGHAM GIRL **F2.2074**

R-C Pictures. *Dist* Film Booking Offices of America. 16 Jul **1927** [New York premiere; released 2 Oct; c16 Jul 1927; LP24361]. Si; b&w. 35mm. 7 reels, 6,257 ft.

Pres by Joseph P. Kennedy. *Dir* David Kirkland. *Cont* Ewart Adamson. *Adapt* David Kirkland, Rex Taylor. *Photog* Jules Cronjager. *Asst Dir* Bill Dagwell.

Cast: Lois Wilson *(Mary Thompson)*, George K. Arthur *(Johnny Cousins)*, Charles Crockett *(Pat O'Day)*, Hazel Keener *(Letty O'Day)*, Myrta Bonillas *(Sonia Mason)*, Jerry Miley *(Harrison Bartlett)*, Betty Francisco *(Mazie Le Lewer)*, Derelys Perdue *(Mildred Ripley)*, Jed Prouty *(Hayden)*, Maude Fulton *(Mrs. Trask)*.

Comedy-drama. Source: Daniel Kussell, *The Gingham Girl, a Musical Comedy in Three Acts* (New York, 1932). Mary Thompson, a smalltown girl, ekes out an existence through the sale of home-baked cookies to Pat O'Day, owner of a local store. His daughter, Letty, is smitten by the metropolitan air of Hayden, a salesman, who gives Johnny Cousins, one of Mary's admirers, the addresses of Mazie and Sonia, two city girls. After meeting Bartlett, son of a biscuit king, Mary becomes interested in enlarging her business; Johnny then leaves for New York, where he models for Sonia, a Greenwich Village artist. Mary arrives but is estranged from Johnny over a misunderstanding. He later finds employment in the Bluebird Cookie Factory, where Mary and Bartlett have built up a thriving business; the lovers are reconciled, and Bartlett retires, leaving the business to them. *Businesswomen. Salesmen. Artists. Models. Smalltown life. Business management. Bakeries. New York City—Greenwich Village.*

GINSBERG THE GREAT **F2.2075**

Warner Brothers Pictures. 26 Nov **1927** [c17 Nov 1927; LP24670]. Si; b&w. 35mm. 6 reels, 5,390 ft.

Dir Byron Haskin. *Story-Scen* Anthony Coldewey. *Camera* Conrad Wells. *Film Ed* Clarence Kolster. *Asst Dir* Henry Blanke.

Cast: George Jessel *(Johnny Ginsberg)*, Audrey Ferris *(Mary)*, Gertrude Astor *(Sappho)*, Douglas Gerrard *(Sam Hubert)*, Jack Santoro *(Hawkins)*, Theodore Lorch *(Charles Wheeler)*, Jimmie Quinn *(crook)*, Stanley J. Sanford *(Hercules)*, Akka *(a chimpanzee)*.

Comedy-drama. Johnny Ginsberg, a tailor's apprentice who aspires to be a famous magician, joins a carnival troupe that stops in the town and doubles for sideshow attractions. The troupers, actually a gang of thieves, direct their chimpanzee to pick the pockets of Sam Hubert, a theatrical magnate who is in the audience, but Johnny recovers the wallet. Sappho, an Oriental dancer, learning that Hubert has purchased the Russian crown jewels, vamps Johnny into taking her to his home; and with the aid of the gang, she steals the jewels. Overhearing the gang quarreling over the spoils, Johnny tries to make a getaway with the gems, knocking out each member of the gang separately and affixing to each of them a tag signed "Ginsberg the Great." Hawkins, a newspaperman, publicizes the event, and Johnny consequently receives a reward and a contract from Hubert. *Tailors. Magicians. Dancers. Reporters. Thieves. Carnivals. Sideshows. Publicity. Chimpanzees.*

THE GIRL AND THE GOOSE *see* **THE SMART SEX**

THE GIRL FROM CHICAGO **F2.2076**

Warner Brothers Pictures. 19 Nov **1927** [c29 Oct 1927; LP24589]. Si; b&w. 35mm. 6 reels, 5,798 ft. [Copyrighted as 7 reels.]

Dir Ray Enright. *Scen* Graham Baker. *Photog* Hal Mohr. *Asst Dir* Frank Shaw.

Cast: Conrad Nagel *(Handsome Joe)*, Myrna Loy *(Mary Carlton)*, William Russell *("Big Steve" Drummond)*, Carroll Nye *(Bob Carlton)*, Paul Panzer *(Dopey)*, Erville Alderson *(Colonel Carlton)*.

Crime melodrama. Source: Arthur Somers Roche, "Business Is Best" (publication undetermined). Mary Carlton, who lives with her invalid father on a cotton plantation, receives a letter from Bob, her brother, in New York, stating that he faces death in the electric chair for a crime of which he claims to be innocent. Determined to save him, she goes there, learns of his association with an underworld gang, and begins to suspect Handsome Joe of a connection with the crime. Posing as a Chicago moll, she makes the acquaintance of Joe and his friend Drummond. Drummond throws a wild party for her at a cabaret, but Handsome Joe protects her from his friend's attentions. Mary succeeds in eliciting a confession of guilt from Drummond in a fit of anger and learns that Joe is an undercover detective. In a gun battle with the gang, Joe, with the help of policemen summoned by Mary, forces their surrender. *Molls. Gangsters. Detectives. Murder. Circumstantial evidence. Brother-sister relationship. Capital punishment. Plantations. Cotton. New York City.*

THE GIRL FROM CONEY ISLAND *see* **JUST ANOTHER BLONDE**

THE GIRL FROM GAY PAREE **F2.2077**

Tiffany Productions. 15 Sep **1927** [c17 Sep 1927; LP24425]. Si; b&w. 35mm. 6 reels, 5,233 ft.

Dir Phil Stone. *Story-Scen* Violet Clark. *Photog* Max Dupont, Earl Walker, George Stevens. *Art Dir* George E. Sawley. *Film Ed* Martin G. Cohn.

Cast: Lowell Sherman *(Robert Ryan)*, Barbara Bedford *(Mary Davis)*, Malcolm McGregor *(Kenneth Ward)*, Betty Blythe *(Mademoiselle Fanchon)*, Walter Hiers *(Sam)*, Margaret Livingston *(Gertie)*, Templar Saxe *(Wayne)*, Leo White *(Monsieur Logier)*.

Farce. Mary Davis, alone and destitute in the big city, fleeces a meal out of a restaurant, and pursued by police, she seeks refuge in the Cafe Royalle, where she is shuffled along a line of girls waiting for job interviews. In desperation, Mary agrees to impersonate a Mademoiselle Fanchon of the Folies-Bergère who has failed to keep her contract. The *New York Star* sends Kenneth Ward to interview the famous wild Frenchwoman; and through a mistake in cues, she rushes wildly into his arms. Mary's picture appears and is seen by Robert Ryan, a bachelor friend of the real Fanchon, and he comes to investigate. In repelling Ryan's advances, Mary believes she has killed him; then the real Fanchon appears and threatens to kill Ryan. Mary's sweetheart, Kenneth, following a series of amusing complications, comes to her aid, and they are united. *Entertainers. Reporters. Parisians. Cafes. Poverty. Impersonation. Folies-Bergère.*

THE GIRL FROM GOD'S COUNTRY **F2.2078**

Nell Shipman Productions. *Dist* F. B. Warren Corp. 18 Sep **1921** [c25 Sep 1921; LP17007]. Si; b&w. 35mm. 7 reels, 6,957 ft.

Pres by W. H. Clune. *Dir* Nell Shipman, Bert Van Tuyle. *Story-Scen* Nell Shipman. *Photog* Joseph Walker.

Cast: Nell Shipman *(Neeka Le Mort/Marion Carslake)*, Edward Burns *(Owen Glendon)*, Al Filson *(J. Randall Carslake)*, George Berrell *(Pierre Le Mort)*, Walt Whitman *(The Old Inventor)*, C. K. Van Auker *(Otto Kraus)*, Lillian Leighton *(Notawa)*, L. M. Wells *(Sandy McIntosh)*, Milla Davenport *(Mrs. Kraus)*.

Melodrama. Carslake, a millionaire airplane manufacturer, his daughter, Marion, and her fiancé are on a hunting party in the North. There they meet Neeka, a halfbreed girl who saves Carslake from the wrath of her grandfather, who recognizes him as the betrayer of her mother. Unaware that she is actually his daughter, Carslake adopts the girl and takes her to California. Otto Kraus, Carslake's competitor in a trans-Pacific flight, enlists Neeka's sympathies for his efforts when she and Marion quarrel over social blunders, and he obtains the secret of a "solidified gasoline," which Carslake himself has gained fraudulently from a demented inventor. The inventor's mind is restored when a hangar is set afire, and Neeka, realizing she has been duped, rescues him. Carslake's pilot is injured, but Neeka aids her sweetheart, a blinded aviator; Kraus is defeated in the competition and drowns after a fight with Neeka. *Millionaires. Inventors. Halfcastes. Hunting. Parentage. Aviation. Gasoline. California.*

THE GIRL FROM HAVANA **F2.2079**

Fox Film Corp. 22 Sep **1929** [c6 Sep 1929; LP661]. Sd (Movietone); b&w. 35mm. 6 reels, 5,986 ft. [Also si, 29 Dec 1929; 6,545 ft.]

Pres by William Fox. *Dir* Benjamin Stoloff. *Stage Dir* Edwin Burke. *Titl* Edwin Burke. *Story* John Stone. *Photog* Joseph A. Valentine. *Film Ed* Paul Weatherwax. *Song: "Time Will Tell"* L. Wolfe Gilbert, Abel Baer. *Mus Arr* S. L. Rothafel. *Sd* Willard W. Starr. *Asst Dir* Sam Wurtzel.

Cast: Lola Lane *(Joan Anders)*, Paul Page *(Allan Grant)*, Kenneth Thompson *(William Dane)*, Natalie Moorhead *(Lona Martin)*, Warren Hymer *(Spike Howard)*, Joseph Girard *(Dougherty)*, Adele Windsor *(Babe Hanson)*, Marcia Chapman *(Sally Green)*, Dorothy Brown *(Toots Nolan)*, Juan Sedillo *(detective)*, Raymond Lopez *(Joe Barker)*, The Roxyettes.

Crook melodrama. Joan Anders, a girl detective for a jewelers' protective association, poses as a chorus girl in a musical comedy troupe to capture a gang of jewel thieves. On a steamer from Los Angeles to Havana, Joan falls in love with Allan Grant, one of the suspected crooks. After the gang has been apprehended, Grant is revealed to be the son of a murdered jeweler who fell in with the gang to track down the murderer. *Detectives. Chorus girls. Thieves. Jewelers. Murder. Protective associations. Ocean liners. Los Angeles. Havana.*

THE GIRL FROM MONTMARTRE **F2.2080**

Associated Holding Corp. *Dist* First National Pictures. 31 Jan **1926** [c27 Jan 1926; LP22332]. Si; b&w. 35mm. 6 reels, 6,200 ft.

Arthur H. Sawyer Production. *Dir* Alfred E. Green. *Ed Dir* June Mathis. *Cont* Eve Unsell. *Titl* George Marion, Jr. *Photog* Rudolph Berquist. *Art Dir* E. J. Shulter. *Film Ed* Al Hall.

Cast: Barbara La Marr *(Emilia)*, Lewis Stone *(Jerome)*, Robert Ellis *(Ewing)*, William Eugene *(Rodney)*, E. H. Calvert *(Robert Hautrive)*, Mario Carillo *(Lawrence Faneaux)*, Mathilde Comont *(Carmenata)*, Edward Piel *(messenger)*, Nicholas De Ruiz *(Don Angel)*, Bobby Mack *(cab driver)*.

Romantic melodrama. Source: Anthony Pryde, *Spanish Sunlight* (New York, 1925). During the World War, Emilia, a Spanish girl of good family, dances in a Paris cafe in order to provide small luxuries for her brothers, who are fighting for the Allied cause. After the Armistice, Emilia returns to her home on the island of Majorca, taking up her old life. Jerome, an English officer who knew Emilia during the war, comes to Majorca and renews his acquaintance with her. Ewing, a crooked thespian, persuades Emilia that she cannot marry Jerome because of her high social station, and she takes a job dancing in a low dive in order to discourage the romantic Englishman. Ewing abducts Emilia, and Jerome rescues her, wounding Ewing. Jerome and Emilia are married. *Dancers. Actors. Soldiers. Abduction. Cabarets. World War I. Majorca. Paris—Montmartre.*

THE GIRL FROM NOWHERE **F2.2081**

Selznick Pictures. *Dist* Select Pictures. Jun **1921** [c1 Jun 1921; LP16634]. Si; b&w. 35mm. 5 reels, 5,161 ft.

Pres by Lewis J. Selznick. *Dir* George Archainbaud. *Scen* Sarah Y. Mason. *Story* Bradley King. *Photog* William Wagner.

Cast: Elaine Hammerstein *(Mavis Cole)*, William B. Davidson *(Jimmy Ryder)*, Huntley Gordon *(Herbert Whitman)*, Louise Prussing *(Dorothy Grosscup)*, Colin Campbell *(Samuel Grosscup)*, Al H. Stewart *(Steve La Marche)*, Warren Cook *(Judge Cole)*, Vera Conroy *(Grace Parker)*.

Melodrama. Mavis defies her grandfather and runs away with Herbert Whitman, a man of social standing but of poor character. He plants a stolen necklace on her and attempts to have her arrested when he comes under suspicion. She then seeks refuge with young Jimmy Ryder; and after she claims to be Mrs. Ryder, Jimmy agrees to make the title legal. Gradually, he comes to love her. Meanwhile, Whitman bribes ex-convict La Marche to steal a jewel from his sister, Dorothy. Jimmy captures the thief, who at first refuses to confess; Dorothy then accuses Mavis of the theft, but she is cleared by La Marche and Whitman is punished. *Thieves. Marriage. Brother-sister relationship.*

THE GIRL FROM PORCUPINE **F2.2082**

Pine Tree Pictures. *Dist* Arrow Film Corp. 26 Oct **1921** [c29 Nov 1921; LP17244]. Si; b&w. 35mm. 6 reels.

Dir Dell Henderson. *Story-Scen* James Oliver Curwood. *Photog* Lucien Tainguy, Charles Downs.

Cast: Faire Binney *(Hope Dugan)*, William (Buster) Collier, Jr. *(Jim McTavish)*, Jack Drumier *(Bill Higgins)*, James Milady *(Sam Hawks)*, Adolph Milar *(Red McTavish)*, Tom Blake *(Dugan)*, Marcia Harris *(schoolteacher)*, Jack Hopkins *(her brother)*, Sam J. Ryan *(Brandt)*, Gus Pixley *(Miller)*, Marie Malatesta *(Mrs. Miller)*, Tom Wallace *(first holdup man)*, Ben Lewis *(second holdup man)*, Lassie *(The Dog)*.

Melodrama. Hope Dugan rescues young Jim McTavish from a beating at the hands of his cruel father, who then is himself beaten in a fight with Hope's father. Seeking revenge, Red kills Dugan and is hanged, leaving Jim and Hope orphaned. They are adopted by two old miners, Sam Hawks and Bill Higgins, who later sell their mine in order to send Hope to school but are robbed of the money by Brandt, who has offered to buy the claim. Jim learns of Brandt's treachery and recovers the money in a holdup but is arrested. Hope returns to find that Sam has died, and she believes that Jim also is dead until Bill tells her he is being framed for robbery. She and Bill hold up the stagecoach and rescue Jim, pretending to shoot him. United and free again, Hope and Jim face a happy life together. *Orphans. Miners. Fatherhood. Adoption. Robbery. Capital punishment. Dogs.*

THE GIRL FROM RIO **F2.2083**

Gotham Productions. *Dist* Lumas Film Corp. 1 Sep **1927** [c6 Sep 1927; LP24385]. Si; b&w with col sequences (Technicolor). 35mm. 6 reels, 5,960 ft. [Also 6,710 ft.]

Pres by Sam Sax. *Prod* Sam Bischoff. *Dir-Adapt* Tom Terriss. *Cont-Titl* Pauline Forney. *Story* Norman Kellogg. *Photog* Ray June. *Prod Mgr* Carroll Sax.

Cast: Carmel Myers *(Lola)*, Walter Pidgeon *(Paul Sinclair)*, Richard Tucker *(Antonio Santos)*, Henry Herbert *(Farael Fuentes)*, Mildred Harris *(Helen Graham)*, Edouard Raquello *(Raoul, the dancer)*.

Romantic drama. Paul Sinclair, engaged to Helen Graham, represents a large coffee concern in Rio de Janeiro and while visiting with the American consul is taken by the beauty of Lola, a cafe dancer. Learning that she is the undisputed object of the affections of Antonio Santos, Paul obtains an introduction and dances with her, much to Santos' dissatisfaction. Soon Paul falls in love with her, and after a quarrel she breaks with Santos, who seeks revenge by having Paul's coffee orders canceled. When Paul bargains directly with the planters he again thwarts Santos' sabotage attempts. Raoul, Lola's dancing partner, in a jealous frenzy, fires at Paul, and Paul kills him; Santos reports the events to the police, swearing a warrant for Paul's arrest. Lola appeals to Santos to spare him; and realizing that his own love for her is futile, he relents. Learning that his former fiancée has married, Paul finds happiness with Lola. *Dancers. Planters. Courtship. Jealousy. Manslaughter. Coffee. Rio de Janeiro. United States—Diplomatic and consular service.*

THE GIRL FROM ROCKY POINT **F2.2084**

Pacific Film Co. 1 Feb **1922**. Si; b&w. 35mm. 5 reels.

Dir Fred G. Becker. *Scen* Sherwood MacDonald. *Photog* John Thompson.

Cast: Milton Ross *(Samuel Hayden)*, Ora Carew *(Betty)*, Gloria Joy *(Corrine)*, Charles Spere *(Daniel Williams)*, E. G. Davidson *(Timothy Smith)*, Theodore von Eltz *(Robert Giffing)*, Verna Brooks *(Mignon)*, Walt Whitman *(The Devil)*.

Melodrama. Betty falls in love with Samuel Hayden, who was washed ashore after having survived a shipwreck. The self-acclaimed most religious man in town accuses a kindly man, whom he calls "The Devil," of robbing Samuel. Soon becoming bored with this slander, he attempts to break up the romance between Betty and Samuel, contriving to have her turned out by her stern father. Samuel is later discovered to be an escaped convict. This disclosure results in a series of escapades during which the true character of the village hypocrite and "The Devil" are revealed, showing the former to be vicious and the latter to be generous and benevolent. *Prison escapees. Hypocrisy. Religion. Robbery. Slander. Maine.*

GIRL FROM THE WEST **F2.2085**

Sam Warner. *Dist* Aywon Film Corp. Sep **1923**. Si; b&w. 35mm. 5 reels, 4,700 ft.

Dir Wallace MacDonald. *Story* Carter De Haven.

Cast: Jack Richardson, Juanita Hansen, Edward Sutherland.

Western melodrama. "At an eastern college the girl meets a boy who loves her. But the girl thinks continually of a boy who lives out west. The easterner goes out west and shows his mettle, living down the reputation of tenderfoot and capturing the cattle rustlers as well." (*Motion Picture News Booking Guide*, 6:31, Apr 1924.) *Students. Rustlers. Manhood.*

THE GIRL FROM WOOLWORTH'S **F2.2086**

First National Pictures. 27 Oct **1929** [c14 Dec 1929; LP915]. Sd (Vitaphone); b&w. 35mm. 7 reels, 6,171 ft. [Also si; 5,008 ft.]

Pres by Richard A. Rowland. *Dir* William Beaudine. *Story-Scen* Adele Commandini. *Dial* Richard Weil, Edward Luddy. *Titl* Richard Weil. *Photog* Jackson Rose. *Film Ed* Terry Morse. *Song: "Crying for Love"* Al Bryan, George W. Meyer.

Cast: Alice White *(Daisy King)*, Charles Delaney *(Bill Harrigan)*, Wheeler Oakman *(Lawrence Mayfield)*, Ben Hall *(Jerry Donnelly)*, Rita Flynn *(Tillie Hart)*, Gladden James *(Dowling)*, Bert Moorehouse *(Dave)*, Patricia Caron *(Cleo)*, William Orlamond *(Pa Donnelly)*, Milla Davenport *(Ma Donnelly)*.

Romantic comedy-drama. Daisy King, a singing clerk at Woolworth's, meets Bill Harrigan, a subway guard, at a party, each boasting another job. He recovers her handbag from the subway and invites her to dinner. Lawrence Mayfield, the owner of the Mayfield Club, offers Daisy a job as entertainer there, and though Bill is displeased, Daisy is delighted. After having accepted Bill's proposal of marriage, Daisy reports to Mayfield's club, and Tillie Hart, her roommate, explains her absence to Bill, who then is injured in a wreck on his way to the club. Daisy learns of the accident but is forced to go through with her act; later, Mayfield tries to detain her in the dressing room, but Bill, with his face and arm bandaged, enters, and Daisy is happy to forego her career for him. *Salesclerks. Singers. Entertainers. Subway guards. F. W. Woolworth & Co. Five-and-ten-cent stores. Nightclubs.*

THE GIRL HE DIDN'T BUY **F2.2087**

Dallas M. Fitzgerald Productions. *Dist* Peerless Pictures. 15 Apr **1928**. Si; b&w. 35mm. 6 reels, 5,390-5,600 ft.

Dir Dallas M. Fitzgerald. *Story-Cont* Gladys Gordon, Ada McQuillan. *Titl* Gardner Bradford. *Photog* Milton Moore. *Film Ed* Otto Ludwig.

Cast: Pauline Garon *(Ruth Montaigne)*, Allan Simpson *(Edward Edinburg)*, William Eugene *(Philip D'Arcy)*, Gladden James *(Hal De Forrest)*, Rosemary Cooper *(Maizie Dupont)*, May Prestelle *(Martha)*, James Aubrey *(Hans)*.

Comedy-drama. Aspiring Broadway actress Ruth Montaigne refuses to submit to a philandering backer in return for stardom, but she does agree to marry him at the end of a year. In Havana she meets an upstanding Englishman, Edward Edinburg, to whom she is attracted, and when left alone on a small boat they are married by the captain of their ship. The backer and a jealous showgirl try to frame the couple, with scandalous circumstances regarding the marriage, but the situation is resolved satisfactorily for all parties. *Actors. Theatrical backers. Philanderers. Showgirls. English. Theater. Reputation. Frameup. New York City—Broadway. Havana.*

THE GIRL I LOVED **F2.2088**

Charles Ray Productions. *Dist* United Artists. 15 Feb **1923** [c3 Jan 1923; LP18627]. Si; b&w. 35mm. 8 reels, 7,100 ft.

Dir Joseph De Grasse. *Film Cont* Harry L. Decker. *Titl* Edward Withers. *Adapt* Albert Ray. *Photog* George Rizard. *Asst Photog* George Meehan. *Art Dir* Robert Ellis. *Cost* Stanley Partridge. *Sp Eff* Edward Withers.

Cast: Charles Ray *(John Middleton)*, Patsy Ruth Miller *(Mary)*, Ramsey Wallace *(Willy Brown)*, Edythe Chapman *(Mother Middleton)*, William Courtwright *(Neighbor Silas Gregg)*, Charlotte Woods *(Betty Short)*, Gus Leonard *(Neighbor Perkins)*, F. B. Phillips *(hired man)*, Lon Poff *(minister [circuit rider])*, Jess Herring *(Hiram Lang)*, Ruth Bolgiano *(Ruth Lang)*, Edward Moncrief *(The Judge)*, George F. Marion *(The Organist)*, Billie Latimer *(a spinster)*.

Rural drama. Source: James Whitcomb Riley, *The Girl I Loved* (Indianapolis, c1910). An only child, John Middleton at first resents Mary, an orphan adopted by his mother, then gradually becomes resigned, feels brotherly affection, and finally falls in love with her. But before John can bring himself to propose to Mary, she announces her engagement to Willy Brown. With difficulty John reconciles himself to his loss, keeps it to himself, and gives the bride away to Willy. *Orphans. Filial relations. Rural life. Adoption. Indiana.*

A GIRL IN EVERY PORT **F2.2089**

Fox Film Corp. 26 Feb **1928** [c20 Feb 1928; LP24994]. Si; b&w. 35mm. 6 reels, 5,500 ft.

Pres by William Fox. *Dir* Howard Hawks. *Scen* Seton I. Miller. *Titl* Malcolm Stuart Boylan. *Orig Story* Howard Hawks. *Screen Story* James K. McGuinness. *Photog* L. W. O'Connell, Rudolph Berquist. *Film Ed* Ralph Dixon. *Asst Dir* William Tummell.

Cast: Victor McLaglen *(Spike Madden)*, Maria Casajuana *(Chiquita)*, Natalie Joyce, Dorothy Mathews, Elena Jurado *(girls in Panama)*, Louise Brooks *(Marie, girl in France)*, Francis McDonald *(gang leader)*, Phalba Morgan *(Lena, girl in Holland)*, Felix Valle *(Lena's husband)*, Greta Yoltz *(other girl in Holland)*, Leila Hyams *(the sailor's wife)*, Robert Armstrong *(Salami)*, Sally Rand *(girl in Bombay)*, Natalie Kingston *(girl in South Sea Islands)*, Caryl Lincoln *(girl from Liverpool)*.

Comedy. Sailor Spike Madden, a gay Lothario, finds that another sailor is a rival for his girl friends in various ports of call. He finally overtakes Salami, the other sailor, and they become fast friends. Spike believes he has fallen in love with Marie, an especially attractive gold digger in France, but his friend dissuades him and they continue their merry way. *Sailors.*

Gold diggers. Panama. Netherlands. France. South Sea Islands. Bombay. Liverpool.

THE GIRL IN HIS ROOM **F2.2090**

Vitagraph Co. of America. 4 Jun **1922** [c5 May 1922; LP17844]. Si; b&w. 35mm. 5 reels, 4,523 ft.

Pres by Albert E. Smith. *Dir* Edward José. *Scen* C. Graham Baker, Harry Dittmar. *Photog* Ernest Smith.

Cast: Alice Calhoun *(Myra Pendleton)*, Warner Baxter *(Kirk Waring)*, Robert Anderson *(Paul Duprez)*, Faye O'Neill *(Molly Maguire)*, Eve Southern *(Elinor Larrimore)*.

Melodrama. Source: J. Raleigh Davies, "Locked Out" (publication undetermined). Myra Pendleton returns from college to meet her father, whom she has never seen, in a new home he has purchased for her. Finding he has been called away, she takes over the management of the house. Kirk Waring, the estate's former owner, returns from Europe, unaware that his home has been sold, and finds it occupied by Myra. Needing money, and discovering that Paul Duprez, who holds the power of attorney, has sold the estate and disappeared, Waring enters the house to obtain some hidden bonds. Myra recognizes him but allows his escape; then, followed by Kirk, she goes to her father's secretary and discovers him to be Duprez, the man who robbed Waring—and her own father! After explanations, Waring forgives Duprez, proposes to Myra, and is accepted. *Students. Secretaries. Inheritance. Parentage. Personal identity.*

Note: Working title: *Locked Out.*

THE GIRL IN THE GLASS CAGE **F2.2091**

First National Pictures. 23 Jun **1929** [c8 Jul 1929; LP511]. Talking sequences & mus score (Vitaphone); b&w. 35mm. 8 reels, 7,159 ft. [Also si; 6,705 ft.]

Pres by Richard A. Rowland. *Prod* Ned Marin. *Dir* Ralph Dawson. *Screenplay* James Gruen. *Dial-Titl* Paul Perez. *Photog* Ernest Haller. *Art Dir* John J. Hughes. *Film Ed* Terry Morse.

Cast: Loretta Young *(Gladys Cosgrove)*, Carroll Nye *(Terry Pomfret)*, Mathew Betz *("Doc" Striker)*, Lucien Littlefield *(Sheik Smith)*, Ralph Lewis *(John Cosgrove)*, George Stone *(Carlos)*, Julia Swayne Gordon *(Mrs. Pomfret)*, Majel Coleman *(Isabelle Van Court)*, Charles Sellon *(Prosecutor Dan Jackson)*, Robert T. Haines *(Pomfret, the attorney)*.

Melodrama. Source: George Kibbe Turner, *The Girl in the Glass Cage* (New York, 1927). In a squalid manufacturing town in New York State, Gladys Cosgrove, who lives with her bachelor uncle, court reporter John Cosgrove, sells tickets at the Elysium Theater, suffering the insults and smirks of the town loafers and wise guys, particularly Striker, owner of the speakeasy, his halfwit friend, Carlos, and Sheik Smith. She is saved from embarrassment one night by Terry Pomfret, a wealthy young college student, promised to Isabelle Van Court, and despite her uncle's determination to prevent it, a romance develops. Terry's mother disapproves of Gladys and prevails upon her to persuade him to return to school. Learning of Striker's decadent behavior toward Gladys, Terry whips him. Smith is killed, and Gladys, believing Terry guilty, confesses to the crime, claiming to have had an affair with Smith. Later, she exacts a confession from her uncle that he killed Smith, mistaking him for Terry. Her uncle then kills both Striker and himself, while Terry wins forgiveness and his family's consent to marriage with Gladys. *Cashiers. Students. Reporters. Smalltown life. Courtship. Murder. Trials. Motion picture theaters. New York State.*

THE GIRL IN THE LIMOUSINE **F2.2092**

Chadwick Pictures. *Dist* Associated First National Pictures. 20 Jul **1924** [c25 Jul 1924; LP20420]. Si; b&w. 35mm. 6 reels, 5,630 ft.

Dir Larry Semon. *Scen* Graham Baker. *Photog* H. F. Koenekamp.

Cast: Larry Semon *(Tony)*, Claire Adams *(The Girl)*, Charles Murray *(The Butler)*, Lucille Ward *(Aunt Cicily)*, Larry Steers *(Dr. Jimmy)*, Oliver Hardy *(Freddie)*.

Farce. Source: Avery Hopwood and Wilson Collison, *The Girl in the Limousine, a Farce* (New York opening: 6 Oct 1919). Bashful Tony, having lost the girl he loves to a rival, wanders down the street after the wedding ceremony and is kidnaped by two crooks in a limousine, one disguised as a girl. They overpower him and hide him in the girl's bedroom, dressed in her pajamas. Complications result from his efforts to dodge the husband and various guests, and when the crooks steal the girl's jewels, he overtakes them and becomes a hero. *Theft. Weddings. Disguise.*

THE GIRL IN THE PULLMAN **F2.2093**

De Mille Pictures. *Dist* Pathé Exchange. 31 Oct **1927** [c20 Oct 1927; LP24528]. Si; b&w. 35mm. 6 reels, 5,867 ft.

Supv-Adapt-Cont F. McGrew Willis. *Dir* Erle Kenton. *Photog* Dewey Wrigley. *Art Dir* Charles Cadwallader. *Film Ed* James Morley. *Asst Dir* C. C. Coleman. *Prod Mgr* John Rohlfs. *Cost* Gwen Wakeling.

Cast: Marie Prevost *(Hazel Burton)*, Harrison Ford *(Dr. Donald Burton)*, Franklin Pangborn *(Hector Brooks)*, Kathryn McGuire *(Dollie Jones)*, Ethel Wales *(Mrs. Jones)*, Harry Myers *(Jerry Mason)*.

Comedy. Source: Wilson Collison, *The Girl in Upper C* (c1926). Dr. Donald Burton, a successful neurologist awaiting his final divorce decree, becomes engaged to Dollie Jones, a social climber who does not love him. Burton is treating a patient when his fiancée arrives and informs him that they are to have lunch with her mother; Jerry Mason, Burton's lawyer, interrupts to tell him that Hazel, the wife he is divorcing, is in town. Dollie knows nothing about Hazel, and, unfortunately, they lunch at the hotel where Hazel is staying, and where she is looked upon with scorn. In passing their table, Hazel stumbles over Burton's foot and pretends to have been injured. Complications ensue when Hector Brooks, a patient with a nervous ailment, is confronted by Dollie, who has jilted him; Dollie marries the doctor in haste, but the court nullifies their marriage; everyone meets in the pullman car of a train, and the couples are respectively reconciled when the car is wrecked. *Neurologists. Social climbers. Lawyers. Divorce. Marriage. Pullman cars. Train wrecks.*

GIRL IN THE RAIN **F2.2094**

Carloma Productions. *Dist* Kerman Films. 25 Feb **1927** [New York showing]. Si; b&w. 35mm. 5 reels.

Cast: David Butler, Claribel Campbell, Hale Hamilton.

Western melodrama. Although it is known that Butler plays a dual role, no information about the precise nature of this film has been found.

THE GIRL IN THE SHOW **F2.2095**

Metro-Goldwyn-Mayer Pictures. 31 Aug **1929** [c9 Sep 1929; LP663]. Sd (Movietone); b&w. 35mm. 9 reels, 7,574 ft. [Also si.]

Dir–Adapt–Adtl Dial Edgar Selwyn. *Titl* Joe Farnham. *Photog* Arthur Reed. *Art Dir* Cedric Gibbons. *Film Ed* Harry Reynolds, Truman K. Wood. *Rec Engr* Russell Franks. *Wardrobe* David Cox.

Cast: Bessie Love *(Hattie Hartley)*, Raymond Hackett *(Mal Thorne)*, Edward Nugent *(Dave Amazon)*, Mary Doran *(Connie Bard)*, Jed Prouty *(Newton Wampler)*, Ford Sterling *(Ed Bondell)*, Nanci Price *(Oriole)*, Lucy Beaumont *(Lorna Montrose)*, Richard Carlyle *(Leon Montrose)*, Alice Moe *(Grace Steeple)*, Frank Nelson *(Tracy Boone)*, Jack McDonald *(Ernest Beaumont)*, Ethel Wales *(Mrs. Truxton)*, John F. Morrissey *(Jess Morrissey)*.

Comedy-melodrama. Source: Kenyon Nicholson and John Golden, *Eva the Fifth; the Odyssey of a Tom Show in Three Acts* (New York, 1928). An *Uncle Tom's Cabin* troupe traveling through Kansas is left high and dry by their manager, Ed Bondell, when he absconds with their meager stake. Hattie Hartley, the fifth in a line of thespian Little Evas, falls for Mal Thorne, another member of the troupe, but it appears that she will marry local undertaker Newton Wampler, whose wealth will keep the show alive and send her sister Oriole to school. When Thorne secures the act a billing, the altar-bound Hattie is replaced as Eva by Oriole, and so desirous of regaining her old part is she that a lethal dose of candy to her sister does she feed. The sweet supper takes its toll midway through the show, allowing Hattie to step into her old shoes, and Thorne and her to marry. *Actors. Theatrical managers. Sisters. Undertakers. Marriage. Kansas. "Uncle Tom's Cabin".*

THE GIRL IN THE TAXI **F2.2096**

Carter De Haven Productions. *Dist* Associated First National Pictures. Apr **1921** [c26 Apr 1921; LP16424]. Si; b&w. 35mm. 6 reels, 5,420 ft.

Pres by Carter De Haven. *Dir* Lloyd Ingraham. *Adapt* Bob McGowan. *Photog* Ross Fisher. *Art Dir* Milton Menasco. *Film Ed* George J. Crone.

Cast: Mrs. Carter De Haven *(Mignon Smith)*, Carter De Haven *(Bertie Stewart)*, King Baggot *(Maj. Frederick Smith)*, Grace Cunard *(Marietta)*, Otis Harlan *(Alexis)*, Tom McGuire *(John Stewart)*, Margaret Campbell *(Clara Stewart)*, Lincoln Plumer *(Percy Peters)*, Freya Sterling *(Mary Peters)*, John Gough *(Dr. Paul)*.

Comedy. Source: Stanislaus Strange, *The Girl in the Taxi; a Farce* (New York production: 24 Oct 1910). John Stewart considers his son Bertie a mollycoddle. Refused an increased allowance, Bertie pawns his father's best clothes and while hiding in a waiting taxi is suddenly whirled away with a strange, beautiful young lady. Later, Bertie recognizes her at a party at his house, and meeting her for lunch he gains his father's esteem. Matters are complicated by the intervention of the lady's husband, Major Smith. *Self-confidence. Fatherhood.*

THE GIRL OF GOLD **F2.2097**

Regal Pictures. *Dist* Producers Distributing Corp. 16 Feb **1925** [c12 Feb 1925; LP21133]. Si; b&w. 35mm. 6 reels, 4,969 ft.

Dir John Ince. *Scen* Eve Unsell. *Adapt* Kate Corbaley.

Cast: Florence Vidor *(Helen Merrimore)*, Malcolm McGregor *(Schuyler Livingstone)*, Alan Roscoe *(Ned Loring)*, Bessie Eyton *(Ada Tremaine)*, Claire Du Brey *(Edith Loring)*, Charles French *(Lucius Merrimore)*.

Society melodrama. Source: Cleveland Moffatt and Anna Chapin, "The Girl of Gold," in *Snappy Stories* (vol 47–49, 2 Dec 1919–1 Mar 1920). Helen Merrimore, the daughter of a mine owner, is snubbed by New York society. Weary of being courted for her wealth, she attends under an assumed name a houseparty being given by Ned and Edith Loring. There she falls in love with Schuyler Livingstone, the impoverished heir of the elite Livingstone line. Edith Loring, who secretly loves Schuyler, arranges to have dinner with him at a questionable roadhouse. They are discovered by Edith's husband, Ned, but Helen, who has happened to come there, protects the innocent Schuyler by telling Ned that she herself arranged the dinner meeting to announce her engagement to Schuyler. Helen later learns that Schuyler earlier has been persuaded by her father to marry her—sight unseen, buying Schuyler's name with Merrimore money. The estranged but still engaged couple give a ball in Merrimore's mine, during which there is a cave-in. She and Schuyler come to recognize their true love just as they are rescued. *Wealth. Poverty. Roadhouses. Mine disasters. New York City.*

THE GIRL OF THE GOLDEN WEST **F2.2098**

Associated First National Pictures. 3 May **1923** [c25 May 1923; LP18987]. Si; b&w. 35mm. 7 reels, 6,800 ft.

Pres by Edwin Carewe. *Prod* Robert North. *Dir* Edwin Carewe. *Adapt* Adelaide Heilbron. *Photog* Sol Polito, Thomas Storey. *Art Dir* Milton Menasco. *Film Ed* Robert De Lacy. *Asst Dir* Wallace Fox.

Cast: Sylvia Breamer *(The Girl)*, J. Warren Kerrigan *(Ramerrez)*, Russell Simpson *(Jack Rance)*, Rosemary Theby *(Nina Micheltorena)*, Wilfred Lucas *(Ashby)*, Nelson McDowell *(Sonora Slim)*, Charles McHugh *(Trinidad Joe)*, Hector V. Sarno *(Castro)*, Jed Prouty *(Nick)*, Cecil Holland *(Antonio)*, Thomas Delmar *(Handsome Harry)*, Fred Warren *(Old Jed Hawkins)*, Sam Appel *(Pedro Micheltorena)*, Minnie Prevost *(The Squaw)*.

Western melodrama. Source: David Belasco, *The Girl of the Golden West, a Play in Four Acts* (New York, c1933). The Girl, owner of the Polka Saloon, falls in love with Ramerrez, whom she later discovers to be a bandit. When a snowstorm forces Ramerrez to stay the night with The Girl, jealousy drives dancer Nina Micheltorena to reveal his identity and whereabouts to Sheriff Jack Rance, who also loves The Girl. She denies Ramerrez's presence, the bandit is shot when he tries to escape, and she once again shelters him. This time, drops of blood prove The Girl wrong, but she wins Ramerrez's and her own freedom in a poker game with the sheriff. Stirred by Nina, vigilantes are about to lynch Ramerrez when the sheriff interferes, explains his bargain, and restores him to The Girl. *Saloon keepers. Sheriffs. Bandits. Miners. Gambling. Poker. Jealousy. Saloons.*

Note: Remade under the same title in 1930, q. v.

THE GIRL OF THE GOLDEN WEST **F2.2099**

First National Pictures. 12 Oct **1930** [c5 Oct 1930; LP1611]. Sd (Vitaphone); b&w. 35mm. 10 reels, 6,750 or 7,276 ft.

Assoc Prod Robert North. *Dir* John Francis Dillon. *Screenplay-Dial* Waldemar Young. *Photog* Sol Polito.

Cast: Ann Harding *(Minnie)*, James Rennie *(Dick Johnson)*, Harry Bannister *(Jack Rance)*, Ben Hendricks, Jr. *(Handsome Charlie)*, J. Farrell MacDonald *(Sonora Slim)*, George Cooper *(Trinidad Joe)*, Johnny Walker *(Nick)*, Richard Carlyle *(Jim Larkins)*, Arthur Stone *(Joe Castro)*, Arthur Houseman *(Sidney Dick)*, Norman McNeil *(Happy Holiday)*, Fred Warren *(Jake Wallace)*, Joe Girard *(Ashby)*, Newton House *(Pony Express rider)*, Pincess Noola *(Wowkle)*, Chief Yowlache *(Billy Jackrabbit)*.

Western melodrama. Source: David Belasco, *The Girl of the Golden West* (Boston, 1925). Remake of the 1923 film of the same title, q. v. *Saloon keepers. Sheriffs. Miners. Bandits. Gambling. Poker. Saloons. Jealousy.*

Note: "The dialog version is practically the stage piece [1905] in unchanged transcription, even to the arrangement of scenes—Polka saloon for the first act, the girl's shack for the second act and a place in the woods for the third. Such an arrangement only emphasizes the mechanical limitations of the stage and calls attention to the artificiality of the whole affair." (*Variety,* 29 Oct 1930, p27.)

A GIRL OF THE LIMBERLOST **F2.2100**

Gene Stratton Porter Productions. *Dist* Film Booking Offices of America. 28 Apr **1924** [c18 Apr 1924; LP20104]. Si; b&w. 35mm. 6 reels, 5,943 ft.

Dir James Leo Meehan. *Scen* Gene Stratton Porter. *Photog* Howard Anderson, Henry Sharp.

Cast: Gloria Grey *(Elnora Comstock)*, Emily Fitzroy *(Kate Comstock)*, Arthur Currier *(Robert Comstock)*, Raymond McKee *(Philip Amon)*, Arthur Millett *(Philip Amon, Sr.)*, Cullen Landis *(Hart Henderson)*, Gertrude Olmstead *(Edith Carr)*, Alfred Allen *(Wesley Sinton)*, Virginia Boardman *(Margaret Sinton)*, Myrtle Vane *(Elvira Carney)*, Jack Daugherty *(Freckles)*, Ruth Stonehouse *(Freckles' wife)*, Baby Pat O'Malley *(Freckles' baby)*, Buck Black *(Billy, aged 5 years)*, Newton Hall *(Billy, aged 9 years)*, Lisamae Grey *(The Bird-Woman)*, Snap *(himself, a dog)*.

Melodrama. Source: Gene Stratton Porter, *A Girl of the Limberlost.* (New York, 1909). Because her husband died tragically in the quicksands of the Limberlost when her daughter Elnora was born, Kate Comstock has an aversion to the child. Later, when she discovers that he had been unfaithful to her, she comes to love the girl. At high school, Philip Amon, who is engaged to Edith Carr, falls in love with Elnora, who leaves him upon discovering his betrothal. When Philip is taken ill, however, she returns to him and helps him regain his health. Edith then leaves them free to marry. *Infidelity. Motherhood. Adolescence. High school life. Quicksand. Marshes. Dogs.*

GIRL OF THE PORT **F2.2101**

RKO Productions. 2 Feb **1930** [c2 Feb 1930; LP1113]. Sd (Photophone); b&w. 35mm. 8 reels, 6,174 ft. [Also si.]

Dir Bert Glennon. *Screenplay* Beulah Marie Dix. *Dial* Frank Reicher. *Photog* Leo Tover. *Art Dir* Max Ree. *Sd* Clarence M. Wickes.

Cast: Sally O'Neil *(Josie)*, Reginald Sharland *(Jim)*, Mitchell Lewis *(McEwen)*, Duke Kahanamoku *(Kalita)*, Donald MacKenzie *(MacDougal)*, Renée Macready *(Enid)*, Arthur Clayton *(Burke)*, Gerald Barry *(Cruce)*, Barrie O'Daniels *(Blair)*, John Webb Dillon *(Cole)*, William Burt *(Toady)*, Hugh Crumplin *(Wade)*.

Romantic melodrama. Source: John Russell, "The Fire-walker," in *Far Wandering Men* (New York, c1929). Josie, a showgirl stranded in Suva, Fiji, is befriended by Kalita, who gets her a job as barmaid in a local cabaret. There she meets Jim, an English war veteran, who has become an alcoholic and is haunted by a fear of fire as a result of his war experiences. Their attachment enrages McEwen, a wealthy halfcaste posing as white, and their quarreling results in a fight in which Jim leaves the impression of being a coward. Josie learns the truth about his war experiences, and under her care he begins to recover. McEwen, however, lures Jim away to Benga Island, where he plans to torture him, and Josie follows to be near Jim; McEwen forces Jim to emulate the natives in their fire-walking rite, and in so doing he loses his fear and soundly thrashes the villainous rival, winning the admiration of his bride-to-be. *Barmaids. Veterans. English. Halfcastes. Pyrophobia. Courtship. Regeneration. Alcoholism. Rites and ceremonies. Fiji Islands.*

GIRL OF THE WEST **F2.2102**

H. T. Henderson. *Dist* Chesterfield Motion Pictures. 1 Dec **1925.** Si; b&w. 35mm. 5 reels.

Dir Alvin J. Neitz.

Cast: Eileen Sedgwick.

Western melodrama. "Girl, educated in East, returns to ranch inherited from father, finding it apparently mortgaged to limit. She and her sweetheart suspect holder of mortgage, their suspicions being confirmed when he resorts to violence in effort to obtain property. Girl and sweetheart triumph." ("Motion Picture News Booking Guide," in *Motion Picture News,* 8 May 1926, p29.) *Ranchers. Mortgages. Inheritance.*

THE GIRL ON THE BARGE (Universal-Jewel) **F2.2103**

Universal Pictures. 3 Feb **1929** [c22 Nov 1928; LP25857]. Talking sequences (Movietone); b&w. 35mm. 8 reels, 7,510 ft. [Also si; 6,908 ft.]

Dir Edward Sloman. *Story Supv* Edward J. Montagne. *Adapt-Cont* Charles Kenyon, Nan Cochrane. *Dial* Tom Reed, Charles H. Smith. *Titl* Tom Reed. *Photog* Jackson Rose. *Film Ed* Edward Cahn. *Song: "When You're in Love With No One But Me"* Roy Turk, Fred Ahlert, Joseph Cherniavsky.

Cast: Jean Hersholt *(McCadden)*, Sally O'Neill *(Erie McCadden)*,

Malcolm McGregor *(Fogarty)*, Morris McIntosh *(Huron McCadden)*, Nancy Kelly *(Superior McCadden)*, George Offerman, Jr *(Ontario McCadden)*, Henry West *(tug captain)*, J. Francis Robertson *(engineer)*, Rex *(dog)*.

Melodrama. Source: Rupert Hughes, "The Girl on the Barge," in *Hearst's International Cosmopolitan* (83:50–53, Oct 1927). Erie McCadden, the daughter of a mean, hard-drinking barge captain, falls in love with Fogarty, a tugboat pilot who teaches her to read. McCadden finds them together and fires Fogarty, who then defiantly takes Erie to a fair. McCadden beats her on her return, and Fogarty attempts to elope with her. McCadden knocks him unconscious and takes his barge downriver. Months later, the barge breaks loose from its Hudson River mooring in a storm and drifts out to sea; Fogarty goes after it in his tug and manages to throw the McCaddens a line. He is knocked unconscious by a falling lamp, and Erie crawls along the rope and pilots the tug to shore. Two years pass. McCadden swears off drink, and Erie and Fogarty present him with a grandson. *Sea captains. Pilots. Illiteracy. Drunkenness. Elopement. Barges. Tugboats. Fairs. Hudson River. Dogs.*

THE GIRL ON THE STAIRS **F2.2104**

Peninsula Studios. *Dist* Producers Distributing Corp. 16 Nov **1924** [c20 Nov 1924; LP20969]. Si; b&w. 35mm. 7 reels, 6,214 ft.

Pres by Elmer Harris. Frank E. Woods Production. *Supv-Adapt* Elmer Harris. *Dir* William Worthington. *Photog* Joseph Walker, Charles Kaufman.

Cast: Patsy Ruth Miller *(Dora Sinclair)*, Frances Raymond *(Agatha Sinclair)*, Arline Pretty *(Joan Wakefield)*, Shannon Day *(Mañuela Sarmento)*, Niles Welch *(Frank Farrell)*, Freeman Wood *(Dick Wakefield)*, Bertram Grassby *(José Sarmento)*, Michael Dark *(Wilbur)*, George Periolat *(Dr. Bourget)*.

Mystery melodrama. Source: Winston Bouve, "The Girl on the Stairs," in *Ainslee's Magazine* (53:1–52, Mar 1924). Discovering that Dick Wakefield, with whom she has been carrying on a flirtation, is married, Dora Sinclair becomes engaged to Frank Farrell, a rising young attorney. Wakefield refuses to return her love letters, and his wife walks out on him. While sleepwalking one evening, Dora enters the Wakefield home in an unsuccessful and unconscious effort to retrieve the letters. The following morning Wakefield is found murdered, and Joan is accused of the crime. Farrell undertakes her defense and calls Dr. Bourget to the stand. Bourget hypnotizes her, and she recalls the events of the night of the crime, revealing that she had seen José Sarmento, an insanely jealous South American, kill Wakefield for flirting with Señora Sarmento. Dora is freed, and she and Dick marry. *Flirts. Lawyers. Physicians. Somnambulism. Hypnotism. Murder. Infidelity. Trials. Documentation.*

GIRL OVERBOARD **F2.2105**

Universal Pictures. 28 Jul **1929** [c15 Jul 1929; LP533]. Talking sequences & mus score (Movietone); b&w. 35mm. 8 reels, 7,362 ft. [Also si.]

Supv Harry L. Decker. *Dir* Wesley Ruggles. *Scen* Paul Schofield. *Dial* Walter Anthony, Charles H. Smith. *Titl* Walter Anthony. *Story* John B. Clymer. *Photog* John Stumar. *Film Ed* Ray Curtiss. *Song: "Today and Tomorrow"* Roy Turk, Fred Ahlert, Joseph Cherniavsky.

Cast: Mary Philbin *(Joan)*, Fred Mackaye *(Denton Ford, Jr.)*, Otis Harlan *(Joe Evans)*, Francis McDonald *(Francisco)*, Edmund Breese *(Jim Keefe)*, Wilfred North *(judge)*, Mary Alden.

Melodrama. Denton Ford, Jr., sentenced to prison for a crime committed by his father, is paroled after a year with the provision that, if he marries within 8 years, he must return to prison for 8 years. Denton goes to live with Joe Evans on an old schooner and saves Joan from drowning in a river. The homeless girl takes up residence on the schooner as well, and she and Denton are married. Jim Keefe, the parole officer, learns of the marriage but allows the couple to stay together, realizing their great love for each other. *Parole officers. Sea captains. Marriage. Parole. Schooners.*

Note: Known also as *Port of Dreams* and *Salvage*.

THE GIRL SAID NO **F2.2106**

Metro-Goldwyn-Mayer Pictures. 15 Mar **1930** [c10 Mar 1930; LP1137]. Sd (Movietone); b&w. 35mm. 10 reels, 8,382 ft. [Also si; 5,772 ft.]

Dir Sam Wood. *Dial* Charles MacArthur. *Adapt* Sarah Y. Mason. *Story* A. P. Younger. *Photog* Ira Morgan. *Art Dir* Cedric Gibbons. *Film Ed* Frank Sullivan, Truman K. Wood, George Boemler. *Song: "I Don't Want Your Kisses If I Can't Have Your Love"* Martin Broones, Fred Fisher. *Rec Engr* Robert Shirley, Douglas Shearer. *Wardrobe* David Cox.

Cast: William Haines *(Tom Ward)*, Leila Hyams *(Mary Howe)*, Polly Moran *(Hildegarde)*, Marie Dressler *(Hettie Brown)*, Francis X. Bushman, Jr. *(McAndrews)*, Clara Blandick *(Mrs. Ward)*, William Janney *(Jimmie Ward)*, William V. Mong *(Mr. Ward)*, Junior Coghlan *(Eddie Ward)*, Phyllis Crane *(Alma Ward)*.

Farce. Tom Ward, a cocky young football hero, returns home after graduation determined to conquer the world. He begins a flirtation with Mary Howe, secretary to his rival, McAndrews, and in a restaurant he bribes a waiter to spill soup on her employer. Although offered a local banking job, Tom stakes his fortunes on a scheme to sell bonds to wealthy old Hattie Brown, a befuddled spinster, and achieves the difficult task while posing as a doctor by getting her drunk. Finally, desperate over Mary's engagement to McAndrews, Tom kidnaps her from the altar. In a chase finale she is convinced that he loves her. *Bond salesmen. Secretaries. Spinsters. Ambition. Courtship. Football. Chases.*

GIRL SHY **F2.2107**

Harold Lloyd Corp. *Dist* Pathé Exchange. 28 Mar **1924** [New York trade showing; released 20 Apr; c12 Mar 1924; LU19987]. Si; b&w. 35mm. 8 reels, 7,457 ft.

Dir Fred Newmeyer, Sam Taylor. *Story* Sam Taylor, Ted Wilde, Tim Whelan, Tommy Gray. *Photog* Walter Lundin, Henry Kohler.

Cast: Harold Lloyd *(The Poor Boy)*, Jobyna Ralston *(The Rich Girl)*, Richard Daniels *(The Poor Man)*, Carlton Griffin *(The Rich Man)*.

Romantic comedy. En route to the city to find a publisher for his book, a collection of romances in which he plays the amorous hero, The Poor Boy, a shy tailor's apprentice, meets The Rich Girl and helps conceal her toy dog from the train conductor. The publisher rejects his manuscript, and The Poor Boy, disappointed at his failure, gives up The Rich Girl. Following a change of mind, the publisher sends The Poor Boy an advance of $3,000, thereby provoking him to pursue his true love, who is about to marry a man who already has a wife. In a wild chase, The Poor Boy, using an automobile, motorcycles, horses, and a trolley car, arrives at the church in time to halt the wedding. Tonguetied, he picks up the girl and carries her out of the church. *Tailors. Authors. Publishers. Wealth. Poverty. Weddings. Chases.*

THE GIRL WHO CAME BACK **F2.2108**

B. P. Schulberg Productions. *Dist* Preferred Pictures. 15 Apr **1923** [c18 Jun 1923; LP19144]. Si; b&w. 35mm. 6 reels, 6,100 ft.

Pres by B. P. Schulberg. *Dir* Tom Forman. *Adapt* Evelyn Campbell. *Photog* Harry Perry.

Cast: Miriam Cooper *(Sheila)*, Gaston Glass *(Ray Underhill)*, Kenneth Harlan *(Martin Norries)*, Fred Malatesta *(Ramon Valhays)*, Joseph Dowling *("Old 565")*, Ethel Shannon *(Belle Bryant)*, Mary Culver *(Mayme Miller)*, ZaSu Pitts *(Anastasia Muldoon)*.

Crook melodrama. Source: Samuel Ruskin Golding and Charles E. Blaney, *The Girl Who Came Back* (Hoboken production: 1920). Ray, a car thief, inveigles Sheila, a country girl, into a fake marriage, and both are arrested as thieves. Sheila serves a 2-year sentence and is released. Ray and Martin Norries, another convict, escape, and when Ray goes to Sheila's boardinghouse he is rearrested. He gives her Norries' address, suggesting that she steal the fortune hidden there. She follows his advice and flees to South Africa, but there she encounters Norries. She confesses the theft: they fall in love and marry, Sheila believing Ray to be dead. They return to the United States, and Sheila learns that her marriage to Ray was a fake. *Thieves. Prison escapees. Marriage—Fake. South Africa.*

THE GIRL WHO RAN WILD **F2.2109**

Universal Film Manufacturing Co. 9 Oct **1922** [c25 Sep 1922; LP18251]. Si; b&w. 35mm. 5 reels, 4,506 ft.

Dir Rupert Julian. *Scen* Rupert Julian, George C. Hull. *Photog* Allen Davey.

Cast: Gladys Walton *(M'liss)*, Marc Robbins *("Bummer" Smith)*, Vernon Steele *(The Schoolmaster)*, Joseph Dowling *(Calaveras John)*, William Burress *(Johnny Cake)*, Al Hart *(preacher)*, Nelson McDowell *(Deacon McSnagley)*, Lloyd Whitlock *(Jack Velvet)*, Lucille Ricksen *(Clytie)*.

Western melodrama. Source: Bret Harte, "M'liss; an Idyl of Red Mountain," in *The Luck of Roaring Camp, and Other Sketches*. M'liss, raised in the mountains as an unruly tomboy, is orphaned and is offered "protection" by Calaveras John and Johnny Cake, friends of her father's murderer. She shows no interest in anything until the new schoolmaster persuades her to tidy herself and get some education. Believing the schoolmaster to be in love with some other girl, M'liss decides to run off with another man. The schoolmaster finally fights his rival to convince her of his sincerity in wanting her to stay. *Tomboys. Schoolteachers. Adolescence. Mountain life. Education.*

THE GIRL WHO WOULDN'T WORK **F2.2110**

B. P. Schulberg Productions. 18 Aug **1925**. Si; b&w. 35mm. 6 reels, 5,979 ft.

Dir Marcel De Sano. *Adapt* Lois Hutchinson. *Photog* Allen Siegler.

Cast: Lionel Barrymore *(Gordon Kent)*, Marguerite De La Motte *(Mary Hale)*, Henry B. Walthall *(William Hale)*, Lilyan Tashman *(Greta Verlaine)*, Forrest Stanley *(William Norworth)*, Winter Hall *(district attorney)*, Thomas Ricketts *(The Rounder)*.

Drama. Source: Gertie Wentworth-James, *The Girl Who Wouldn't Work* (London, 1913). Tired of a dull job and an even duller fiancé, Mary Hale flirts with Gordon Kent, a rich philanderer, and loses her job. Quarreling with her father, Mary leaves home, and Kent lets her stay in his apartment, arranging to sleep at his club. Greta Verlaine, an actress and formerly Kent's mistress, visits Kent's apartment and throws Mary out. Mary's distraught father traces her to Kent's apartment, goes there, and shoots Greta, whom he mistakes for his erring daughter. Kent initially takes the blame for the murder, but Mary's father comes forward and confesses. Kent spends his entire fortune in Hale's defense and wins an acquittal. Mary and Kent are married, and Kent settles down to work for a living. *Philanderers. Mistresses. Actors. Murder. Fatherhood. Reputation.*

THE GIRL WITH A JAZZ HEART **F2.2111**

Goldwyn Pictures. 7 Jan **1921** [trade review; c14 Aug 1920; LP15436]. Si; b&w. 35mm. 5 reels.

Dir Lawrence C. Windom. *Scen* Philip Lonergan, George Mooser. *Story* Robert Terry Shannon. *Photog* George Peters.

Cast: Madge Kennedy *(Kittie Swasher/Miriam Smith)*, Joe King *(Miles Sprague)*, Leon Guerre Gendron *(Tommie Fredericks)*, William Walcott *(Miriam's uncle)*, Helen Du Bois *(Miriam's aunt)*, Robert Vaughn *(Simeon Althoff)*, Emil Hoch *(Dectective Quinn)*, Lillian Worth *(Camille)*, Robert Tansey *(Jimmie)*, Dorothy Haight *(Mamie)*.

Comedy-drama. Miriam, a village heiress, is being forced into marriage with a local hobbledehoy for whom she has no love. Her guardians' expressed reason for urging this step is to prevent her fortune from corrupting her soul, while their real purpose is to gain control of her money. In pursuit of a matrimonial-bureau advertiser, Miriam goes to New York. There she meets Camille, who loves jazz and cabarets, and Miles Sprague, with whom she falls in love. The schemers at home inform the New York police that she is a runaway and have her picked up and returned home, where she is locked in her room. Her erstwhile fiancé breaks into the room, not content to wait one more day, when they would be married. Miles, Camille, and the latter's sweetheart come to the rescue; after a rough and tumble, the village lover is put to flight and Miriam is carried off by her mail-order husband. *Heiresses. Guardians. Marriage—Arranged. Matrimonial agencies. Village life. Jazz life. New York City.*

THE GIRL-SHY COWBOY **F2.2112**

Fox Film Corp. 12 Aug **1928** [c21 Aug 1928; LP25551]. Si; b&w. 35mm. 5 reels, 4,404 ft.

Pres by William Fox. *Dir* R. Lee Hough. *Scen* James J. Tynan. *Titl* Garrett Graham. *Story* Seton I. Miller. *Photog* Sol Halprin. *Film Ed* J. Logan Pearson. *Asst Dir* Louis Lambermont.

Cast: Rex Bell *(Joe Benson)*, George Meeker *(Harry Lasser)*, Patsy O'Leary *(Alice Weldon)*, Donald Stuart *(Red Harden)*, Margaret Coburn *(Eve Adams)*, Betty Caldwell *(Gladys Ward)*, Joan Lyons *(Alice Mervin)*, Ottola Nesmith *(girl's college teacher)*.

Western melodrama. Joe Benson and Harry Lasser, a couple of cowboy buddies, come to blows and a parting of the ways when they both fall in love with Alice Weldon, a pretty eastern girl who has come west with a group of classmates. Red Harden, the leader of an outlaw gang, has something on Harry and forces him to agree to rob the schoolgirls; Joe helps his pal go straight and breaks up the outlaw gang, winning Alice for his wife. *Cowboys. Robbery. Blackmail.*

GIRLS' CLUB WORK FILM *see* **WHAT A GIRL CAN DO**

A GIRL'S DECISION *see* **NINE POINTS OF THE LAW**

A GIRL'S DESIRE **F2.2113**

Vitagraph Co. of America. 10 Sep **1922** [c1 Aug 1922; LP18098]. Si; b&w. 35mm. 5 reels, 4,950 ft.

Dir David Divad. *Scen* J. Raleigh Davies. *Story-Scen? (see note)* C. Graham Baker, Bradley J. Smollen. *Photog* Steve Smith, Jr.

Cast: Alice Calhoun *(Elizabeth Browne)*, Warner Baxter *("Jones" [Lord Dysart])*, Frank Crane *("Lord" Cecil Dysart)*, Lillian Lawrence *(Lady Dysart)*, Victory Bateman *(Mrs. Browne)*, James Donnelly *(H. Jerome Browne)*, Sadie Gordon *(Miss Grygges)*, Charles Dudley *(Perkins)*, Lydia Yeamans Titus *(cook)*, Harry Pringle *(solicitor)*.

Society comedy-drama. Mrs. H. Jerome Browne, wife of a wealthy American, sends her daughter, Elizabeth, to a boarding school and goes to England to "find" a family tree, a title, and some heirlooms to go with them. Lady Dysart, widow of Lord Dysart, sells the heirlooms of the Dysart castle to obtain money to send her son, Cecil, to America so that he may marry well. Cecil and Elizabeth meet and are about to marry when Richard Jones, the real heir to the Dysart title masquerading as a journalist, intercepts the elopement and reveals Cecil, Lady Dysart's son from a former marriage, to be an impostor. *Nouveaux riches. Nobility. Wealth. Genealogy. Impersonation.*

Note: Several sources credit C. Graham Baker with story and scenario, while another credits Bradley J. Smollen.

GIRLS DON'T GAMBLE **F2.2114**

D. N. Schwab, Inc. *Dist* Jans Film Service. Feb **1921**. Si; b&w. 35mm. 5 reels.

Dir Fred J. Butler. *Photog* Robert Martin.

Cast: David Butler, Harry Todd, Elinor Field, Elsie Bishop, Rhea Haines, Alice Knowland, Margaret Joslin, Elmer Dewey, Rex Zane, Jack Cosgrave, Wilbur Higby.

Comedy. Source: George Weston, "Girls Don't Gamble Anymore," in *Saturday Evening Post* (192:8–10, 24 Apr 1920). "The hero, with a penchant for machinery, leaves home, enters the employ of a department store as a chauffeur, comes in contact with a Cinderella-type of maiden, is 'framed' by co-workers, foils them after they rob his ex-employer's department store, and receives the blessing of all" (*Variety*, 62:40, 4 Mar 1921). *Mechanics. Chauffeurs. Drudges. Robbery. Frameup. Department stores.*

GIRLS GONE WILD **F2.2115**

Fox Film Corp. 24 Mar **1929** [c16 Mar 1929; LP219]. Sd eff & mus score (Movietone); b&w. 35mm. 6 reels, 5,305 ft. [Also si; 5,227 ft.]

Pres by William Fox. *Dir* Lewis Seiler. *Scen* Beulah Marie Dix. *Titl* Malcolm Stuart Boylan. *Story* Bertram Millhauser. *Photog* Arthur Edeson, Irving Rosenberg.

Cast: Sue Carol *(Babs Holworthy)*, Nick Stuart *(Buck Brown)*, William Russell *(Dan Brown)*, Roy D'Arcy *(Tony Morelli)*, Leslie Fenton *(Boots)*, Hedda Hopper *(Mrs. Holworthy)*, John Darrow *(Speed Wade)*, Matthew Betz *(Augie Sten)*, Edmund Breese *(Judge Elliott)*, Minna Ferry *(Grandma)*, Louis Natheaux *(Dilly)*, Lumsden Hare *(Tom Holworthy)*.

Melodrama. Wealthy Babs Holworthy falls in love with Buck Brown but gives him up when she discovers that his father is the motorcycle cop who once would not let her father "fix" her speeding ticket, taking her to court instead. She attends a street dance in a tough neighborhood and is dancing with a notorious bootlegger when he is bumped off by members of a rival gang. Buck is in the crowd and gets Babs into his car. The killers kidnap them and force Buck to help them get away. Buck's father gives chase and is shot; Buck is then thrown out of the car. He takes his father's gun, rescues Babs, and brings the killers to justice. Babs learns to love Buck a little. *Police. Bootleggers. Filial relations. Murder. Kidnaping. Automobile driving.*

GIRLS MEN FORGET **F2.2116**

Principal Pictures. 27 July **1924**. Si; b&w. 35mm. 6 reels, 5,116 ft.

Dir Maurice Campbell. *Scen* Percy Heath, Maurice Campbell. *Photog* Allen Siegler. *Adtl Photog* Glenn Kershner.

Cast: Johnnie Walker *(Russell Baldwin)*, Patsy Ruth Miller *(Kitty Shayne)*, Alan Hale *(Jimmy Masson)*, Mayme Kelso *(Lucy)*, Carrie Clark Ward *(Aunt Clara)*, Wilfred Lucas *(Michael Shayne)*, Frances Raymond *(Mrs. Baldwin)*, Shannon Day *(Ruby Thomas)*.

Comedy-melodrama. Source: Fannie Kilbourne, "The Girl Who Was the Life of the Party," in *American Magazine* (96:8–10, Dec 1923). Kitty Shayne, a cut-up who is the life of every party she attends, discovers that the men in her life invariably pass her up in order to marry timid and retiring girls. Kitty then goes to live with an aunt in a distant town, assuming there the role of a modest young woman in order to find herself a husband. She soon meets and falls in love with Russell Baldwin, a proper young man who hates jazz babies. When she and Russell become engaged, Mrs. Baldwin gives a party to celebrate the occasion, but the affair is a dull one until Kitty risks her romance to save her future mother-in-law from the heartbreak of social embarrassment; Kitty once again becomes the life of the party, and Mrs. Baldwin's gathering becomes an instant success. Russell is disgusted with Kitty until she explains that she became gay only to please his mother. Russell and Kitty are reconciled. *Flappers. Jazz life. Smalltown life.*

GIRLS WHO DARE **F2.2117**

Trinity Pictures. 1 Jan **1929.** Si; b&w. 35mm. 6 reels, 5,400-5,600 ft.

Dir Frank S. Mattison. *Scen* Cecil Burtis Hill. *Titl* Arthur Hotaling. *Story* Frank S. Mattison, Ben Hershfield. *Photog* Jules Cronjager. *Film Ed* Minnie Steppler.

Cast: Rex Lease *(Chet Randolf)*, Priscilla Bonner *(Sally Casey)*, Rosemary Theby *("Alabam" Kenyon)*, Ben Wilson *(Robert Randolf)*, Steve Hall *(Dick Burke)*, Eddie Brownell *(Pat Moran)*, Sarah Roberts *(Mrs. Randolf)*, May Hotely *(Miss Casey, Sally's aunt)*, Hall Cline.

Drama. A wealthy man who is playing around with nightclub hostess "Alabam" Kenyon refuses to allow his son, Chet Randolf, to marry chorus girl Sally Casey. Sally nearly marries a policeman, but he dies in an automobile accident, and she finally weds Chet—with parental permission. *Nightclub hostesses. Chorus girls. Police. Filial relations. Courtship. Automobile accidents.*

GIVE AND TAKE (Universal-Jewel) **F2.2118**

Universal Pictures. 23 Dec **1928** [c8 Aug 1928; LP25524]. Talking sequences, sd eff, and mus score (Movietone); b&w. 35mm. 7 reels, 7,098 ft. [Also si; 6,552 ft.]

Dir William Beaudine. *Dial Dir* A. B. Heath. *Adapt-Scen* Harvey Thew. *Dial* Albert De Mond. *Adapt (see note)* Harry O. Hoyt. *Photog* Charles Van Enger. *Film Ed* Robert Carlisle. *Mus Score* Joseph Cherniavsky.

Cast: Jean Hersholt *(John Bauer)*, George Sidney *(Albert Kruger)*, George Lewis *(Jack Bauer)*, Sharon Lynn *(Marion Kruger)*, Sam Hardy *(Craig)*, Rhoda Cross *(Nancy)*, Charles Mailes *(Drumm)*.

Comedy-drama. Source: Aaron Hoffman, *Give and Take* (New York, 1926). Jack Bauer returns from college and immediately begins to organize the workers in his father's fruit cannery into an Industrial Democracy, thereby precipitating a strike. Jack's father, in debt to the bank for $25,000, seems on the edge of financial ruin until he receives an order from Craig, a financier, for a large consignment of canned goods; Bauer then finds out that Craig is insolvent, having recently escaped from a mental hospital. Deprived of the expected payroll, the workers riot. Craig reappears, however, and exhibits court papers that prove him to be both sane and solvent. Bauer's business is saved, and Jack resumes his courtship with Marion Kruger, the daughter of the factory foreman. *Financiers. Factory management. Strikes. Canneries.*

Note: Sources disagree in crediting adaptation.

THE GLAD RAG DOLL **F2.2119**

Warner Brothers Pictures. 4 May **1929** [c29 Apr 1929; LP341]. Sd (Vitaphone); b&w. 35mm. 8 reels, 6,885 ft. [Also si, 8 Jun 1929; 5,449 ft.]

Dir Michael Curtiz. *Scen-Titl-Dial* Graham Baker. *Story* Harvey Gates. *Photog* Byron Haskins. *Song: "Glad Rag Doll"* Milton Ager, Dan Dougherty, Jack Yellen. *Asst Dir* Cliff Salm.

Cast: Dolores Costello *(Annabel Lea)*, Ralph Graves *(John Fairchild)*, Audrey Ferris *(Bertha Fairchild)*, Albert Gran *(Nathan Fairchild)*, Maude Turner Gordon *(Aunt Fairchild)*, Tom Ricketts *(admiral)*, Claude Gillingwater *(Sam Underlane)*, Arthur Rankin *(Jimmy Fairchild)*, Dale Fuller *(Miss Peabody)*, Douglas Gerard *(butler)*, André Beranger *(Barry, an actor)*, Lee Moran *(press agent)*, Tom Kennedy *(manager)*, Louise Beavers *(Hannah)*, Stanley Taylor *(chauffeur)*.

Farce. Jimmy Fairchild, the youngest son of an old Philadelphia family, falls in love with Annabel Lea, the star of a Broadway revue, and John Fairchild, Jimmy's unbending older brother, has her fired from the show. Seeking revenge, Annabel goes to Philadelphia and uses a stack of Jimmy's compromising love letters to blackmail John into allowing her to spend the weekend as a houseguest. Annabel then learns some interesting things about the Fairchild family: Aunt Fairchild is a kleptomaniac; Uncle Nathan is having an affair with the housekeeper; and Bertha Fairchild, John's sister, is secretly married to the chauffeur. John and Annabel fall in love. Jimmy receives word that he has written $10,000 in bad checks, and to cover him Annabel arranges with the Fairchild family lawyer to exchange the love letters for that sum. John is at first heartbroken to find that Annabel seems to be a gold digger; but when he learns that she took the money to help out Jimmy, he forgives her, making her his bride. *Actors. Chauffeurs. Housekeepers. Brothers. Social classes. Kleptomania. Blackmail. Philadelphia. New York City—Broadway.*

Note: Louise Beavers sings "Some of These Days."

GLASS HOUSES **F2.2120**

Metro Pictures. 6 Mar **1922** [c13 Mar 1922; LP17696]. Si; b&w. 35mm. 5-6 reels.

Dir Harry Beaumont. *Adapt* Edith Kennedy. *Story* Clara Genevieve Kennedy. *Photog* John Arnold. *Art Dir* A. F. Mantz. *Prod Mgr* David H. Thompson.

Cast: Viola Dana *(Joy Duval)*, Gaston Glass *(Billy Norton)*, Maym Kelso *(Aunt Harriet)*, Helen Lynch *(Cicily Duval)*, Claire Du Brey *(Mrs. Vicky)*, Ellsworth Gage *(Orville King)*, John Steppling *(The Lawyer)*.

Romantic comedy. When Joy Duval and her sister, Cicily, lose their inheritance and are faced with the necessity of working, Joy applies at an employment agency disguised as a prim old-fashioned working girl and is hired by Aunt Harriet as a companion. She is primarily concerned with the reform of Billy Norton, Harriet's nephew. The young couple are discovered in the garage of a wealthy relative, where they spend the night unaware of each other's presence; and it is assumed that they have eloped. Harriet is delighted when they are married, and Billy is happy to find that his wife is actually a chic beauty. Through a misunderstanding, his wife is mistaken for Angel Face Ann, a notorious thief, but all ends well when the real lady crook is captured. *Aunts. Sisters. Inheritance. Disguise.*

GLEAM O'DAWN **F2.2121**

Fox Film Corp. 8 Jan **1922** [c22 Jan 1922; LP17602]. Si; b&w. 35mm. 5 reels, 4,178 ft.

Pres by William Fox. *Dir* Jack Dillon. *Scen* Jules G. Furthman. *Photog* Don Short.

Cast: John Gilbert *(Gleam O'Dawn)*, Barbara Bedford *(Nini)*, James Farley *(Caleb Thomas)*, John Gough *(Gordon Thomas, his son)*, Wilson Hummel *(Pierre)*, Edwin Booth Tilton *(Silas Huntworth)*.

Melodrama. Source: Arthur Frederick Goodrich, *Gleam O'Dawn* (New York, 1908). Gleam O'Dawn, an artist living in the Canadian woods, encounters Silas Huntworth and his adopted daughter, Nini; and they become his friends. A daily visitor to the Huntworth cabin is Pierre, a demented halfbreed fiddler who confides to Gleam that Huntworth, who deserted his wife years before, is actually Gleam's father. Pierre, who was in love with Gleam's mother, incites him to face Huntworth with the accusation and to take revenge on him. Huntworth confesses that he was married but was taken ill with fever while searching for gold and was later unable to find his adopted son, left homeless by the death of his wife. Realizing his failure to obtain revenge, Pierre leaves Silas, Gleam, and Nini to their happiness. *Artists. Violinists. Halfcastes. Revenge. Canada.*

GLENISTER OF THE MOUNTED **F2.2122**

Harry Garson Productions. *Dist* Film Booking Offices of America. 23 May **1926** [c18 May 1926; LP22750]. Si; b&w. 35mm. 6 reels, 5,480 ft.

Prod-Dir Harry Garson. *Cont* William E. Wing. *Story* Arthur Guy Empey. *Photog* James Diamond.

Cast: Lefty Flynn *(Sgt. Richard Glenister)*, Bess Flowers *(Elizabeth Danrock)*, Lee Shumway *(Jack Danrock)*, Walter James *(Thorald)*, James Gibson *(Rafferty)*, Arthur Millett *(Sgt. Major Willis)*.

Northwest melodrama. Sergeant Glenister of the Mounted Police, caught in the snows of the Northwest, is tended in a semiconscious state by Jack and Betty Danrock, who are fleeing from the police; at Rafferty's trading post Glenister again encounters the pair, but Betty disclaims having met him and poses as Jack's wife. Later, Dick is assigned to track down the murderers of Thorald's partner and captures the couple. Returning, they are caught in a forest fire, and Glenister is injured rescuing Jack; when he revives, the prisoners tell him their story and convince him of their innocence. Glenister discovers that Jack was tricked by an ingeniously placed mirror and that Thorald, the partner, is the murderer. Glenister forces him to confess. *Fugitives. Canadian Northwest. Northwest Mounted Police. Forest fires.*

THE GLIMPSES OF THE MOON F2.2123

Famous Players–Lasky. *Dist* Paramount Pictures. 25 Mar **1923** [c20 Mar 1923; LP18808]. Si; b&w. 35mm. 7 reels, 6,502 ft.

Pres by Jesse L. Lasky. *Dir* Allan Dwan. *Scen* E. Lloyd Sheldon, Edfrid Bingham. *Photog* Hal Rosson.

Cast: Bebe Daniels *(Susan Branch)*, Nita Naldi *(Ursula Gillow)*, David Powell *("Nick" Lansing)*, Maurice Costello *(Fred Gillow)*, Rubye De Remer *(Mrs. Ellie Vanderlyn)*, Charles Gerard *("Streffy" [Lord Altringham])*, William Quirk *(Bob Fulmer)*, Pearl Sindelar *(Grace Fulmer)*, Beth Allen, Mrs. George Peggram, Dolores Costello, Millie Muller, Beatrice Coburn, Fred Hadley, Robert Lee Keeling, Barton Adams, Freddie Veri.

Drama. Source: Edith Wharton, *The Glimpses of the Moon* (New York, 1922). Although Susan Branch is herself without finances, she has many wealthy friends who supply her with clothes and gay times. She is in love with struggling author Nick Lansing, who also attracts the interests of Susan's chief patron, Ursula Gillow, and is persuaded by Ellie Vanderlyn to marry him for at least a year's happiness. Their marriage falls apart when their wedding gifts are spent; they become involved with the Vanderlyns' domestic affairs; and Ursula decides she wants Nick for herself. However, the lawyer handling the Lansings' divorce proceedings brings them back together, and Nick sells his novel. *Novelists. Lawyers. Marriage. Divorce.*

GLORIFYING THE AMERICAN GIRL F2.2124

Paramount Famous Lasky Corp. 7 Dec **1929** [c7 Dec 1929; LP905]. Sd (Movietone); b&w with col sequences (Technicolor). 35mm. 9-10 reels, 8,071 ft. [Also si; 6,786 ft.]

Supv Florenz Ziegfeld. *Dir* Millard Webb. *Revue Dir* John Harkrider. *Story* Joseph Patrick McEvoy, Millard Webb. *Photog* George Folsey. *Mus Dir* Frank Tours. *Song: "Blue Skies"* Irving Berlin. *Song: "I'm Just a Vagabond Lover"* Rudy Vallee, Leon Zimmerman. *Song: "What Wouldn't I Do for That Man"* E. Y. Harburg, Jay Gorney. *Songs: "At Sundown," "Beautiful Changes"* Walter Donaldson. *Ballet Ensembles* Ted Shawn.

Cast: Mary Eaton *(Gloria Hughes)*, Edward Crandall *(Buddy)*, Olive Shea *(Barbara)*, Dan Healy *(Miller)*, Kaye Renard *(Mooney)*, Sarah Edwards *(Mrs. Hughes)*, Eddie Cantor, Helen Morgan, Rudy Vallee, Mr. & Mrs. Florenz Ziegfeld, Adolph Zukor, Otto Kahn, Mayor and Mrs. James Walker, Ring Lardner, Noah Beery, Texas Guinan, Norman Brokenshire, Johnny Weismuller *(themselves)*.

Musical revue–drama. As a child, Gloria Hughes cherishes the ambition of becoming a Ziegfeld revue girl, and at 17 she sings in the music department of a store where Buddy, who loves her, accompanies her on the piano. At the annual company picnic, Buddy takes her canoeing and proposes, but she rejects him, saying the stage is her greatest love. When the Miller-Mooney dancing act falls apart as the result of a quarrel, Miller takes on Gloria as his partner; in New York he makes objectionable advances, but she does obtain a Ziegfeld contract. Barbara, who loves Buddy, comes with him to see Gloria, and when Barbara is injured in a street accident, Buddy realizes that he loves her. At Gloria's debut, many celebrities are introduced; the show opens with Rudy Vallee and his orchestra, followed by a blues song from Helen Morgan, and Eddie Cantor does his "Cheap Charlie" skit; then Gloria appears as the premiere danseuse and is a sensation; her triumph is lessened by news of Buddy and Barbara's marriage, but she finds contentment in the applause. *Singers. Pianists. Dancers. Ambition. Vaudeville. Ziegfeld Follies.*

THE GLORIOUS ADVENTURE (United States/Great Britain) **F2.2125**

J. Stuart Blackton. *Dist* Allied Producers and Distributors. 23 Apr **1922** [New York premiere; released 27 Aug; c15 Sep 1922; LP18472]. Si; col (Prizma); 35mm. 7 reels, 6,600 ft.

Prod-Dir-Writ J. Stuart Blackton. *Scen* Felix Orman. *Photog* William T. Crespinel.

Cast: Diana Manners *(Lady Beatrice Fair)*, Gerald Lawrence *(Hugh Argyle)*, Alice Crawford *(Stephanie Dangerfield)*, Cecil Humphreys *(Walter Roderick)*, William Luff *(King Charles II)*, Lennox Pawle *(Samuel Pepys)*, Rosalie Heath *(Catherine of Braganza)*, Lois Sturt *(Nell Gwyn)*, Elizabeth Beerbohm *(Barbara Castlemaine)*, Flora Le Breton *(Rosemary)*, Victor McLaglen *(Bulfinch)*, Rudolph De Cordova *(Thomas Unwin)*, Gertrude Sterroll *(Duchess of Moreland)*, Fred Wright *(Humpty)*, Violet Virginia Blackton *(Lady Beatrice, as a child)*, Tom Heselwood *(Solomon Eagle)*.

Costume melodrama. Walter Roderick conspires with Bulfinch to impersonate Hugh Argyle in order to acquire his title, fortune, and childhood sweetheart, Lady Beatrice Fair. She, however, is heavily in debt from being cheated at the gaming table and, to absolve herself, she follows the custom of marrying a condemned criminal, who turns out to be Bulfinch. But Bulfinch escapes and hides his bride when the Great Fire of London sweeps the city. Hugh reappears and rescues Beatrice, while Bulfinch is reclaimed by his deserted wife. *Nobility. Gambling. Impersonation. Great Britain—History—Stuarts. London. Charles II (England). Samuel Pepys. Nell Gwyn. Catherine of Braganza. Barbara Villiers. Fires.*

GLORIOUS BETSY F2.2126

Warner Brothers Pictures. 26 Apr **1928** [New York premiere; released 9 Jun; c5 Apr 1928; LP25131]. Talking sequences (Vitaphone); b&w. 35mm. 7 or 8 reels, 7,091 ft.

Dir Alan Crosland. *Scen* Anthony Coldeway. *Titl* Jack Jarmuth. *Camera* Hal Mohr. *Film Ed* Thomas Pratt. *Rec Engr* George R. Groves. *Asst Dir* Gordon Hollingshead.

Cast: Dolores Costello *(Betsy Patterson)*, Conrad Nagel *(Jérôme Bonaparte)*, John Miljan *(Preston)*, Marc MacDermott *(Colonel Patterson)*, Pasquale Amato *(Napoleon)*, Michael Vavitch *(Captain St. Pierre)*, André De Segurola *(Captain Du Fresne)*, Paul Panzer *(The Ship's Captain)*, Clarissa Selwynne *(Aunt Mary)*, Betty Blythe *(Princess Fredericka)*.

Historical drama. Source: Rida Johnson Young, *Glorious Betsy* (New York opening: 7 Sep 1908). Jérôme Bonaparte visits Baltimore, where he poses as a teacher and wins the love of Elizabeth Patterson, a society girl. After marrying Elizabeth, he reveals himself to be the brother of the Emperor Napoleon Bonaparte. Napoleon refuses to let her land in France, has their marriage annulled, and sends her back to Baltimore. On the eve of his arranged wedding to the Princess of Würtemburg, Jérôme escapes. He returns to Elizabeth shortly after the birth of their son. *Brothers. Marriage. Napoleon I. Jérôme Bonaparte. Elizabeth Patterson Bonaparte. Baltimore.*

THE GLORIOUS FOOL F2.2127

Goldwyn Pictures. ca15 Jan **1922** [Milwaukee premiere; released Sep; c15 Nov 1921; LP17189]. Si; b&w. 35mm. 6 reels, 5,392 ft.

Dir E. Mason Hopper. *Adapt* J. G. Hawks. *Photog* John Mescall.

Cast: Helene Chadwick *(Jane Brown)*, Richard Dix *(Billy Grant)*, Vera Lewis *(Miss Hart)*, Kate Lester *(head nurse)*, Otto Hoffman *(Dummy)*, John Lince *(Jenks)*, Theodore von Eltz *(senior surgical interne)*, Frederick Vroom *(Mr. Lindley Grant)*, Lillian Langdon *(Mrs. Lindley Grant)*, George Cooper *(Al)*.

Comedy-drama. Source: Mary Roberts Rinehart, "In the Pavilion" and "Twenty-two," in *Love Stories* (New York, 1919). Billy Grant, who is jilted by his society sweetheart because of his alcoholism, gets drunk, drives his car into a motor truck, and wakes up in a hospital. Anxious to prevent his relatives from falling heir to his property, he persuades his probationary nurse, Jane Brown, to marry him. Billy recovers, and while convalescent he decides to go home, and although he loves Jane, to free her. When she is threatened with expulsion for being out after hours, Billy discovers that she has gone to comfort a young girl in the maternity ward; he defends Jane, and she promises to live with him as his wife. *Nurses. Alcoholism. Hospitals. Automobile accidents.*

GLORIOUS SWITZERLAND F2.2128

Burton Holmes Lectures. 30 Jan **1924** [scheduled release]. Si; b&w. 35mm. 4 reels.

Travelog. No information about the specific nature of this film has been found. *Switzerland.*

THE GLORIOUS TRAIL F2.2129

Charles R. Rogers Productions. *Dist* First National Pictures. 28 Oct **1928** [c11 Sep 1928; LP25611]. Si; b&w. 35mm. 6 reels, 5,886 ft.

Pres by Charles R. Rogers. *Supv* Harry J. Brown. *Dir* Albert Rogell. *Titl* Don Ryan. *Story* Marion Jackson. *Photog* Frank Good. *Film Ed* Fred Allen.

Cast: Ken Maynard *(Pat O'Leary)*, Gladys McConnell *(Alice Harper)*, Frank Hagney *(Gus Lynch)*, Les Bates *(Horse-Collar Keller)*, James Bradbury, Jr. *(Bill Keller)*, Billy Franey *(Jimmy Bacon)*, Chief Yowlache *(High Wolf)*.

Western melodrama. After a work crew stringing telegraph wires across the Great Plains is slaughtered by Indians, Pat O'Leary, the company superintendent, must take out another supply train to make the dangerous trip across open country. The Indians attack and are driven off. On the day the wires are finally strung, the settlers gather to hear the first message from the East. The Indians (incited by Lynch, a white renegade) attack the settlers, and Pat uses the telegraph to alert a nearby fort. The Indians are driven off; Lynch is killed; and Pat prepares to settle down with Alice Harper. *Linemen. Traitors. Indians of North America. Settlers. Frontier and pioneer life. Telegraph. Great Plains.*

THE GLORY OF CLEMENTINA **F2.2130**

R-C Pictures. 28 May **1922** [c28 May 1922; LP17965]. Si; b&w. 35mm. 6 reels, 5,700 ft.

Dir Emile Chautard. *Scen* E. Richard Schayer, Winifred Dunn. *Photog* Dev Jennings.

Cast: Pauline Frederick *(Clementina Wing)*, Edward Martindel *(Quixtus)*, George Cowl *(Huckaby)*, Lincoln Plummer *(Billiter)*, Edward Hearn *(Tommy Burgrave)*, Jean Calhoun *(Etta Concannon)*, Wilson Hummel *(Vandemeer)*, Louise Dresser *(Lena Fontaine)*, Helen Stone *(Little Sheila)*, Lydia Yeamans Titus *(Shiela's maid)*, Truly Shattuck *(Lady Louise Malling)*.

Melodrama. Source: William John Locke, *The Glory of Clementina* (New York, 1911). Clementina Wing, a successful portrait painter who sacrifices all self-interest to her art, complies with the request of Tommy Burgrave, a fellow artist, that she paint a portrait of Tommy's wealthy Uncle Quixtus, whose unhappy life has made him misanthropic. Quixtus is about to be taken advantage of by Lena Fontaine, an adventuress, when Clem intervenes. At a dinner party given by Quixtus, Clem is transformed from her drab dowdiness into a brillant young woman and impresses Quixtus with her charms. Will Hammersley, an old friend whom Quixtus had suspected of an affair with his wife, dies and entrusts his daughter to Clementina and Quixtus. At first Quixtus declines the responsibility, but the child arouses Clem's instinct of motherhood; she marries Quixtus and they accept the child as their own. *Artists. Uncles. Adventuresses. Misanthropy. Adoption. Motherhood.*

THE GLORY OF LOVE *see* **WHILE PARIS SLEEPS**

GO GET HIM **F2.2131**

Western Feature Productions. *Dist* Pioneer Film Corp. 8 Nov **1921** [New York State]. Si; b&w. 35mm. 5 reels, 4,127 ft.

Cast: William Fairbanks.

Drama. The action would appear to take place in Canada and concern the apprehension of an offender against the law. *Northwest Mounted Police.*

GO STRAIGHT **F2.2132**

Universal Film Manufacturing Co. 17 Oct **1921** [c4 Oct 1921; LP17067]. Si; b&w. 35mm. 5 reels, 4,220 ft.

Dir William Worthington. *Scen* George Hively. *Story* William Harper Dean. *Photog* Leland Lancaster.

Cast: Frank Mayo *(Rev. Keith Rollins)*, Cora Drew *(Mrs. Conners)*, Harry Carter *(Hellfire Gibbs)*, Lillian Rich *(Hope Gibbs)*, George F. Marion *(Jim Boyd)*, Lassie Young *(Laura Boyd)*, Charles Brinley *(Buck Stevens)*.

Melodrama. Young minister Keith Rollins comes to a backwoods community in Kentucky and finds that lawless and political elements are against him and threaten his position with the congregation. His only supporters are his housekeeper and Hope, the daughter of Hellfire Gibbs, a crooked evangelist in league with political boss Jim Boyd. Hope warns Keith of a plot against him, and he beats her father in a fight when he insults her. Later, Keith is lured to her home by a fictitious note and is detained by the hillmen to prevent his attending a town meeting to answer Boyd's challenge. Meanwhile, Hope convinces Buck Stevens of Keith's innocence, and they aid his escape. He returns to expose the political boss and win the love of Hope. *Clergymen. Evangelists. Political bosses. Fatherhood. Kentucky.*

GO STRAIGHT **F2.2133**

B. P. Schulberg Productions. 27 Apr **1925.** Si; b&w. 35mm. 6 reels, 6,107 ft.

Dir Frank O'Connor. *Cont* Agnes Brand Leahy. *Story* Ewart Adamson. *Photog* Harry Perry.

Cast: Owen Moore *(John Rhodes)*, Mary Carr *(Mrs. Rhodes)*, George Fawcett *(Madison)*, Ethel Wales *(Mamie)*, Gladys Hulette *(Gilda Hart)*, Lillian Leighton *(Gilda's aunt)*, Robert Edeson *(The Hawk)*, De Witt Jennings *(The Hunter)*, Francis McDonald *(The Dove)*, Anita Stewart *(herself)*, Larry Semon *(himself)*.

Melodrama. Gilda Hart quits her life of crime and goes to Hollywood with her aunt. She finds work in a bank and falls in love with John Rhodes, the bank president. Her old gang finds her and attempts to talk her into knocking over John's bank. She refuses and personally takes all the money in the vaults to John's house. The gang breaks into the empty bank and is arrested there by the police. Gilda confesses her former life of crime to John, and he quickly forgives her. *Criminals—Rehabilitation. Aunts. Bankers. Gangs. Police. Bank robberies. Hollywood.*

GO WEST **F2.2134**

Buster Keaton Productions. *Dist* Metro-Goldwyn Distributing Corp. 25 Oct **1925** [New York premiere; released 1 Nov; c23 Nov 1925; LP22048]. Si; b&w. 35mm. 7 reels, 6,293 ft.

Pres by Joseph M. Schenck. *Dir-Story* Buster Keaton. *Scen* Raymond Cannon. *Camera* Elgin Lessley, Bert Haines.

Cast: Howard Truesdale *(owner of the Diamond Bar Ranch)*, Kathleen Myers *(his daughter)*, Ray Thompson *(The Foreman)*, Brown Eyes *(herself, a cow)*, Buster Keaton *(Friendless)*.

Western burlesque. Friendless Homer Holiday drifts west and after a variety of adventures finds employment on the Thompson ranch. He befriends Brown Eyes, a cow, who reciprocates by saving his life. When she is included in a shipment of cattle bound for the stockyard, Homer goes along. Tom Jackson, a rival rancher, attacks the train, and while the Thompson and Jackson men are fighting, Homer commandeers the train and after many vicissitudes safely delivers the cattle. In gratitude, Thompson offers him his choice of a reward, and Homer selects Brown Eyes. In the end, Thompson, his daughter Gloria, Homer, and Brown Eyes all drive away in an automobile. *Wanderers. Ranchers. Trains. Stockyards. Cattle. Cows.*

THE GO-GETTER **F2.2135**

Cosmopolitan Productions. *Dist* Paramount Pictures. 8 Apr **1923** [c4 Apr 1923; LP18855]. Si; b&w. 35mm. 8 reels, 7,771 ft.

Dir E. H. Griffith. *Scen* John Lynch. *Photog* Harold Wenstrom. *Prod Mgr* John Lynch. *Adv* William J. MacMillan, Dr. William V. Healey. *Coöp* Curtiss Aeroplane and Motor Corp.

Cast: T. Roy Barnes *(Bill Peck)*, Seena Owen *(Mary Skinner)*, William Norris *(Cappy Ricks)*, Tom Lewis *(Charles Skinner)*, Louis Wolheim *(Daniel Silver)*, Fred Huntley *(Jack Morgan)*, John Carr *(Joe Ryan)*, Frank Currier *(Hugh McNair)*, William J. Sorrelle *(Mayor Healey)*, William J. MacMillan *(pilot)*, Jawn *(dog)*, Jane Jennings.

Comedy. Source: Peter Bernard Kyne, "The Go-Getter," in *Cappy Ricks Comes Back* (New York, 1934). After spending 2 years in a hospital recovering from his war wounds, Bill Peck sets out to succeed as salesman for Cappy Ricks's lumber company. First he must make good with foreman Charles Skinner and overcome many obstacles to purchase a vase for Cappy Ricks. Along the way he wins the heart and support of Mary Skinner and a management position with the firm. *Veterans. Salesmen. Lumber industry. Dogs.*

GOAT GETTER **F2.2136**

Harry J. Brown Productions. *Dist* Rayart Pictures. 25 Aug **1925** [New York State license]. Si; b&w. 35mm. 5 reels, 5,040 ft.

Dir Albert Rogell. *Scen* Grover Jones. *Photog* Lee Garmes.

Cast: Billy Sullivan *(Billy Morris)*, Johnny Sinclair *(Pie-Eye Pickens)*, Kathleen Myers *(Virginia Avery)*, Virginia Vance *(Mamie Arthur)*, Eddie Diggins *(Lightning Bradley)*, William Buckley *(Carter Bond)*, Joe Moore *(Slug Geever)*.

Action melodrama. While making a series of boxing exhibitions, "Lightning" Bradley, the lightweight champion, is matched with Billy Morris in a small western town. Bradley knocks Billy out, and Billy, looking for another chance to fight, follows the champ from town to town, finally drifting into Hollywood, where Bradley is making a picture. Billy gets a chance to box Bradley before the cameras, and news of the bout is leaked to the press. Billy knocks Bradley out, and the sporting extras print the story. Billy also wins Virginia Avery, the star of the film Bradley has been making. *Actors. Reporters. Boxing. Motion pictures. Newspapers. Hollywood.*

GOD GAVE ME TWENTY CENTS **F2.2137**

Famous Players–Lasky. *Dist* Paramount Pictures. 20 Nov **1926** [New York premiere; released 12 Feb 1927; c25 Nov 1926; LP23658]. Si; b&w. 35mm. 7 reels, 6,321 ft.

Pres by Adolph Zukor, Jesse L. Lasky. *Dir* Herbert Brenon. *Scen* Elizabeth Meehan. *Adapt* John Russell. *Photog* Leo Tover. *Asst Dir* Ray

Lissner.

Cast: Lois Moran *(Mary)*, Lya De Putti *(Cassie Lang)*, Jack Mulhall *(Steve Doren)*, William Collier, Jr. *(Barney Tapman)*, Adrienne D'Ambricourt *(Ma Tapman)*, Leo Feodoroff *(Andre Dufour)*, Rosa Rosanova *(Mrs. Dufour)*, Claude Brooke *(a florist)*, Tommy Madden, Phil Bloom, Eddie "Spider" Kelly, Jack "Young" Sharkey, Harry Lewis *(thugs in cafe)*.

Melodrama. Source: Dixie Willson, "God Gave Me Twenty Cents," in *Cosmopolitan Magazine*. Sailors Steve Doren and Barney Tapman ship into New Orleans just in time for the last day of the Mardi Gras. They enter on a boisterous tour of the city, and as they pass a storefront restaurant, Steve's eye falls upon Mary, a fragile flower of a waitress, and the rugged sailor sweeps her onto their float, beginning a whirlwind courtship that leads to the altar in less than a fortnight. Steve's old flame, Cassie, is a worldly woman but cannot accept her lover's hands-off policy. She dares him to toss coins with her for a last fling, and when "heads" come up, Cassie and Steve are off to a cafe, where Steve buys them some coffee and inexplicably rushes out, angrily flinging the coins into the gutter. Apparently deserted, Mary is despondent until, finding two dimes on the dock, she buys a white flower for her hair, hopefully remembering the night she met Steve. She then stumbles upon Barney and Cassie, who have fallen back into larcenous ways and are rifling a safe. Cassie is shot, clears Steve before dying, and sets Mary's heart a-thumping in anticipation of Steve's returning ship. The lovers are happily rejoined, and the erstwhile florist finally shows up with two dimes, each with two heads, and Mary answers Steve's curious entreaties: "I prayed—and God gave me twenty cents." *Sailors. Waitresses. Florists. Robbery. Wagers. Cafes. Mardi Gras. New Orleans.*

GOD OF MANKIND **F2.2138**

H. V. Productions. *Dist* Hi-Mark Productions. Mar **1928.** Si; b&w. 35mm. 5 reels, 4,458 ft.

Dir Grover Jones. *Scen* Adam Hull Shirk. *Titl* John Langford. *Photog* Louis Physioc. *Film Ed* John Langford.

Cast: Emmett King, Eulalie Jensen, Jimmy Fulton, Ralph Faulkner, Winston Miller.

Melodrama. "Grandson of a wealthy old man who cannot trust his heirs, is made beneficiary of grandfather. Goes to live with grandfather and sees him accidentally slay his son. The shock kills the old man and boy inherits money. His aunt tries to kill boy but is prevented by faithful servant." *(Motion Picture News Booking Guide,* [14]:254, 1929.) *Grandfathers. Aunts. Domestics. Inheritance. Family life. Murder.*

THE GODLESS GIRL **F2.2139**

C. B. De Mille Productions. *Dist* Pathé Exchange. 31 Mar **1929** [c23 Aug 1928. LP25553]. Talking sequences (Photophone); b&w. 35mm. 12 reels, 9,328 ft. [Also si; 9,019 ft.]

Dir Cecil B. De Mille. *Story-Cont-Dial* Jeanie Macpherson. *Titl* Beulah Marie Dix, Jeanie Macpherson. *Photog* Peverell Marley. *Adtl Photog* J. F. Westerberg, Franklin McBride. *Art Dir* Mitchell Leisen. *Prop* Roy Burns. *Film Ed* Anne Bauchens. *Asst Dir* Frank Urson, Curt Rehfeld. *Cost* Adrian. *Tech Eng* Paul Sprunck.

Cast: Lina Basquette *(Judith Craig)*, Marie Prevost *(Mame)*, George Duryea *(Bob Hathaway)*, Noah Beery *(head guard)*, Eddie Quillan *("Goat")*, Mary Jane Irving *(victim)*, Clarence Burton, Dick Alexander *(guards)*, Kate Price, Hedwig Reicher *(matrons)*, Julia Faye, Viola Louie, Emily Barrye *(inmates)*, Jimmy Aldine, Vivian Bay, Elaine Bennett, Wade Boteler, Betty Boyd, Julia Brown, Archie Burke, Colin Chase, Cameron Coffey, Cecilia De Mille, Jacqueline Dyris, George Ellis, Anielka Elter, James Farley, Larry Fisher, Evelyn Francisco, May Giraci, Grace Gordon, Milton Holmes, William Humphrey, George Irving, Peaches Jackson, Dolores Johnson, Jane Keckley, Nora Kildare, Richard Lapan, Ida McKenzie, Don Marion, Edith May, Mary Mayberry, Collette Merton, Buddy Messinger, Pat Moore, Jack Murphy, Pat Palmer, Janice Peters, Hortense Petra, Gertrude Quality, Rae Randall, Billie Van Avery, Dorothy Wax.

Melodrama. Judith Craig, the daughter of an atheist, forms a club called The Godless Society in her high school and begins to recruit members. Bob Hathaway, a stalwart Christian lad, incites the students to attack the atheists, and there is a riot. Grace is killed as a direct consequence of this disturbance, and Bob and Judith are sent to the state reformatory. Bob and Judith are badly treated by the head guard, and Bob, attacking the grocery man, escapes with Judith in his wagon. They are quickly recaptured and locked in cells. A fire breaks out, and Bob rescues both Judith and the head guard. As a result of this selfless bravery, Bob and Judith are returned to freedom, facing life with a renewed faith in Divine Providence. *Atheists. Prison guards. High school life. Reformatories. Clubs. Fires.*

GODLESS MEN **F2.2140**

Goldwyn Pictures. 4 Feb **1921** [trade review; c25 Sep 1920; LP15584]. Si; b&w. 35mm. 7 reels.

Dir Reginald Barker. *Scen* J. G. Hawks, Edfrid A. Bingham. *Photog* Percy Hilburn.

Cast: Russell Simpson *("Black" Pawl)*, James Mason *("Red" Pawl)*, Helene Chadwick *(Ruth Lytton)*, John Bowers *(Dan Darrin)*, Alec B. Francis *(Rev. Sam Poor)*, Robert Kortman *(Speiss)*.

Melodrama. Source: Ben Ames Williams, *Black Pawl* (New York, 1922). "Black" Pawl, a sea rover, returns from a cruise with his young son, "Red," to find that his wife has left him for another man. He instills in his son a hatred for humanity resulting in an enmity between father and son so great that Black fears his son may kill him. Years later, Black puts ashore at a South Sea island, and Red is approached by a lovely young girl and a missionary, Reverend Poor, begging to be taken aboard. Red, his lust aroused, consents. When Dan Darrin, second mate, also is attracted to Ruth, there ensues between Black and his son a fight during which the girl's locket reveals that she is Black's daughter. Black relates the story of his life to the missionary, who tries to instill in him a love for God. *Missionaries. Filial relations. Brother-sister relationship. Misanthropy. Seafaring life. Infidelity. Religion. South Sea Islands.*

GOD'S COUNTRY AND THE LAW **F2.2141**

Pine Tree Pictures. *Dist* Arrow Film Corp. Jun **1921** [c19 Jul 1921; LP16766]. Si; b&w. 35mm. 6 reels.

Dir Sidney Olcott. *Scen* Harry O. Hoyt. *Photog* Lucien Tainguy. *Art Dir* Edward Venturini. *Asst Dir* Jack Bedell. *Still Photog* Herman O. Langley.

Cast: Fred C. Jones *(André)*, Gladys Leslie *(Marie)*, William H. Tooker *(Jacques Doré)*, Cesare Gravina *('Poleon)*, Hope Sutherland *(Oachi)*.

Northwest melodrama. Source: James Oliver Curwood, *God's Country and the Woman* (Garden City, New York, 1915). 'Poleon and his daughter Oachi live a happy existence in the North Woods, as do their neighbors, André and Marie Beauvais. Doré, a villainous whisky runner fleeing from the Northwest Mounted Police, is hospitably welcomed by 'Poleon; but when he forces his attentions on Oachi, her father drives him away. Terror-stricken by the loss of his rattlesnake amulet, and thus deprived of communion with the evil spirits, he is welcomed at André and Marie's cabin but is likewise thrashed soundly and sent on his way. Doré returns when Marie is ill, in André's absence, and kidnaps her during a storm; she escapes and leaps over an embankment, there to be found unconscious by Oachi the next day. Doré, driven mad with fear, returns to their home wounded, and a vision of Marie brings his death. *Fugitives. French Canadians. Superstition. Abduction. Canadian Northwest. Northwest Mounted Police.*

GOD'S CRUCIBLE **F2.2142**

Winnipeg Productions. *Dist* W. W. Hodkinson Corp. Sep **1921.** Si; b&w. 35mm. 7 reels.

Pres by Ernest Shipman. *Dir* Henry MacRae. *Scen* Faith Green. *Photog* William Thornley.

Cast: Gaston Glass *(Ivan Kalmar)*, Gladys Coburn *(Marjorie Menzies)*, Wilton Lackaye *(Michael Kalmar)*, Edna Shipman *(Irma Kalmar)*, Ann Sutherland *(Kalmars' servant)*, Bigelow Cooper *(Sir Robert Menzies)*, Bradley Barker *(Mortimer Staunton)*, William Colvin *(Makaroff)*, Robert T. Haines *(Jack French)*, Jules Cowles *(Jack French's servant)*, Edward Elkas *(Portnoff)*, Kate Price *(Nora Fitzpatrick)*.

Melodrama. Source: Ralph Connor, *The Foreigner, a Tale of Saskatchewan* (New York, 1909). While their father, Michael Kalmar, remains in a Siberian prison, political refugees Ivan and Irma Kalmar seek freedom in Canada (Winnipeg). But they again encounter persecution—from their father's enemy, Makaroff—and the prejudice of some of their neighbors. Ivan's violin playing attracts the interest of Marjorie Menzies and—with it—the enmity of District Attorney Mortimer Staunton, who insults Ivan as a "foreigner." When Irma is insulted at a party, her abuser is slain, and Ivan is arrested. Michael, who has escaped from prison and just arrived, confesses to the murder and is jailed. Ivan becomes a foreman in the coal mine that Makaroff is trying to acquire. The villain fails and attempts to destroy the mine and its employees with an explosion, in which he dies. The confession of a long-time servant of the Kalmars frees

Michael, and Ivan wins Marjorie. *Mine foremen. Violinists. Russians. Immigrants. Political refugees. Prejudice. Mine disasters. Winnipeg.*
Note: Country of origin undetermined.

GOD'S GOLD **F2.2143**
Pinnacle Productions. 17 Jun **1921** [trade review]. Si; b&w. 35mm. 5 reels.
Dir Webster Cullison. *Story* Arthur Henry Gooden.
Cast: Neal Hart *(Jack Cameron—The Last of the Camerons)*, Audrey Chapman *(Mary Anson—petted by society)*, James McLaughlin *(Corwin Carson—her fiancé)*, Al Kaufman *(Dan Cuttle—a waterfront bully)*, C. D. Rehfeld *("Bosun" Briggs)*, Jacob Abrams *(Isaac Solomon—ship broker)*, Charles Holly *(Dr. Anson—Mary's father)*, Dick Sutherland *(The "Wolf")*.
Melodrama. Jack Cameron takes charge of a ship that is sailing for the South Seas in search of a buried treasure. The ship is owned by Dr. Anson, whose daughter, Mary, and her fiancé, Corwin Carson, accompany him on the voyage. After a disagreement with Jack, Carson takes command of the ship, but when the crew hears about the buried treasure, there is a mutiny and the ship sinks. Jack displays his courage by getting Mary and Carson ashore on a raft, protecting them from savages, and trapping the mutineers in a cave. The treasure is found, and Jack, who now has the full admiration of Mary, asks her to be his wife. *Physicians. Mutiny. Treasure. Ships. South Sea Islands.*

GOD'S GREAT WILDERNESS **F2.2144**
David M. Hartford Productions. *Dist* American Cinema Association. 15 Jan **1927** [c8 Mar 1927; LP23737]. Si; b&w. 35mm. 6 reels, 5,398 ft.
Dir-Supv David M. Hartford. *Screen Vers* Frances Nordstrom. *Story* Spottiswoode Aitken. *Photog* Walter Griffin. *Film Ed* Walter Griffin. *Asst Dir* Gavin Young.
Cast: Lillian Rich *(Mary Goodheart)*, Joseph Bennett *(Dick Stoner)*, Russell Simpson *(Richard Stoner)*, Mary Carr *(Emma Stoner)*, John Steppling *(Noah Goodheart)*, Rose Tapley *(Susan Goodheart)*, Edward Coxen *(Paul Goodheart)*, Tom Bates *(Peter Marks)*, Wilbur Higby *(Ward Maxwell)*, Roy Laidlaw *(circuit rider)*, Hank *(Bob)*.
Melodrama. Noah Goodheart, a merchant, brings his family to the northern timber country and becomes a competitor of Stoner's, though the latter threatens to put him out of business. The community's unfriendly feeling toward Stoner, because of his abusive treatment of his wife and his son, Dick, is aroused when Stoner ejects from his store a penniless widow seeking food for her starving children; but the Goodhearts come to her rescue, and as a result Stoner loses trade rapidly. Having forbidden Dick's meeting with Mary Goodheart, Stoner is enraged at learning they have been secretly married. He beats the boy into senselessness and causes the death of his invalid mother. Dick wanders in the wilderness until he is recognized and rescued by a clergyman. Then Dick and Mary's brother, Paul, who brings about Stoner's regeneration, ride together through a storm to Mary's bedside. *Merchants. Clergymen. Family life. Fatherhood. Courtship. Regeneration.*

GOD'S PAY DAY *see* **THE WAGES OF SIN**

GOING CROOKED **F2.2145**
Fox Film Corp. 12 Dec **1926** [c5 Dec 1926; LP23440]. Si; b&w. 35mm. 6 reels, 5,345 ft.
Pres by William Fox. *Dir* George Melford. *Scen? (see note)* Keene Thompson, Albert Shelby Le Vino. *Photog* Charles Clarke. *Asst Dir* Ray Flynn.
Cast: Bessie Love *(Marie)*, Oscar Shaw *(Banning)*, Gustav von Seyffertitz *(Mordaunt)*, Ed Kennedy *(detective)*, Leslie Fenton *(Rogers)*, Lydia Knott *(Mother)*, Bernard Siegel *(crook)*.
Crook melodrama. Based on John Golden's production: Winchell Smith and William Collier, *Going Crooked; a Comedy in Three Acts, From a Tale of Hoffman's (Aaron's)* (New York, 1926). Aaron Hoffman, "One Hundred Thousand Dollars Reward" (unpublished play). Disguised as an old woman, Marie assists a gang, headed by Mordaunt, in a daring jewel robbery. A murder is committed during the holdup, and Rogers, a young boy, is held for the crime and sentenced to death. Marie falls in love with Banning, the district attorney who prosecuted the case, and with her help, a last-minute confession is obtained from Mordaunt and Rogers is saved from electrocution. The boy is reunited with his grieving mother, and Marie, because of her aid, is absolved of her part in the robbery. *District attorneys. Injustice. Capital punishment. Robbery. Murder.*
Note: Copyright records credit Le Vino with scenario and Thompson with adaptation, although other sources indicate Thompson wrote the scenario.

GOING STRAIGHT (Reissue) **F2.2146**
Fine Arts Pictures. *Dist* Film Distributors League. **1921.** Si; b&w. 35mm. 5 reels.
Note: A Norma Talmadge film originally released by Triangle Film Corp. on 4 Jun 1916.

GOING THE LIMIT **F2.2147**
Paul Gerson Pictures. 25 May **1925** [New York State license]. Si; b&w. 35mm. 5 reels.
Pres by B. Berger. *Dir* Duke Worne. *Story-Scen* Grover Jones. *Photog* Alfred Gosden.
Cast: Richard Holt, Ruth Dwyer, Garry O'Dell, Miriam Fouche, Robert Cosgrif, Rupert Drum, George Kelley, Hal Stephens.
Melodrama. A criminal gang gains the confidence of a superstitious San Francisco millionaire by posing as clairvoyants. Having acquired his power of attorney, the swindlers then kidnap the millionaire's beautiful daughter. A young man in love with the girl sets out after the kidnapers and, after a wild chase up and down the hills of the city, rescues her and brings the criminals to justice. *Clairvoyants. Millionaires. Gangs. Swindlers. Superstition. Kidnaping. San Francisco. Chases.*

GOING THE LIMIT **F2.2148**
R-C Pictures. *Dist* Film Booking Offices of America. 12 Sep **1926** [c12 Sep 1926; LP23144]. Si; b&w. 35mm. 5 reels, 4,265 or 4,690 ft.
Pres by Joseph P. Kennedy. *Dir* Chet Withey. *Photog* André Barlatier. *Asst Dir* Jimmy Dugan.
Cast: George O'Hara *(Gordon Emery [Harden])*, Sally Long *(Estelle Summers)*, Brooks Benedict *(George Stanways [Tom Stanway])*, Tom Ricketts *(Mortimer Harden)*, Murdock MacQuarrie *(Simson Windsor)*.
Comedy-drama. Source: Arthur Ebenhack, "He Stopped at Murder" (publication undetermined). Young Gordon Emery is in love with wealthy Estelle Summers and is given encouragement to propose at a party; but abashed by the thought of his poverty, he desists. Gordon then learns that he is the sole beneficiary of a $2 million will, but Estelle tells him she will not marry him unless he loses all his money. His partner, Windsor, advises him to get a jail sentence, which would cause his Uncle Mortimer to cut him off. He tries forgery, stealing a motor car, and robbing a bank; but he succeeds only in becoming a hero for capturing some real thieves. In desperation, he tries to burglarize the home of George Stanways; then he learns that his uncle has just willed his money to a new wife. When Gordon and Estelle are about to be married, however, he is arrested, but the complications are ultimately resolved. *Uncles. Courtship. Inheritance. Poverty. Wills.*

GOING UP **F2.2149**
Douglas MacLean Productions. *Dist* Associated Exhibitors. 30 Sep **1923** [c1 Sep 1923; LU19364]. Si; b&w. 35mm. 6 reels, 5,800-6,000 ft.
Dir Lloyd Ingraham. *Scen* Raymond Griffith. *Photog* Ross Fisher.
Cast: Douglas MacLean *(Robert Street)*, Hallam Cooley *(Hopkinson Brown)*, Arthur Stuart Hull *(James Brooks)*, Francis McDonald *(Jules Gaillard)*, Hughie Mack *(Sam Robinson)*, Wade Boteler *(John Gordon)*, John Steppling *(William Douglas)*, Mervyn LeRoy *(The Bellboy)*, Marjorie Daw *(Grace Douglas)*, Edna Murphy *(Madeline Manners)*, Lillian Langdon *(Mrs. Douglas)*.
Farce. Source: Otto Harbach and Louis A. Hirch, *Going Up* (New York opening: 25 Dec 1917). Robert Street, an author of aviation novels, has acquired the reputation of being an expert pilot, though he is without experience and has an unreasonable fear of airplanes. He is challenged to compete with ace pilot Jules Gaillard in a race for Grace Douglas' love. The film climaxes in Street's thrilling victory after his friends vainly attempt to help him duck out of the competition. *Air pilots. Novelists. Acrophobia. Airplane racing.*

GOING WILD **F2.2150**
First National Pictures. 21 Dec **1930** [c27 Dec 1930; LP1897]. Sd (Vitaphone); b&w. 35mm. 7 reels, 6,486 ft.
Dir William A. Seiter. *Screenplay* Humphrey Pearson, Henry McCarty. *Story* Humphrey Pearson. *Photog* Sol Polito. *Film Ed* Peter Fritch. *Rec Engr* Joseph Kane.
Cast: Joe E. Brown *(Rollo Smith)*, Laura Lee *(Peggy)*, Walter Pidgeon *(Ace Benton)*, Frank McHugh *(Ricky Freeman)*, Ona Munson *(Ruth)*,

Lawrence Gray *(Jack Lane)*, May Boley *(May Bunch)*, Johnny Arthur *(Simpkins)*, Anders Randolf *(Edward Howard)*, Arthur Hoyt *(Robert Story)*, Fred Kelsey *(conductor)*, Sam Cantor *(Sammy)*, Harvey Clark *(Herndon Reamer)*, Larry Banthim *(Matt Gore)*.

Farce. Source: James Montgomery, *The Aviator* (New York opening: 6 Dec 1910). A series of coincidences (Rollo Smith's and Jack Lane's stowing away in Robert Story's compartment for lack of train fare, Peggy's efforts to vamp Story, and May Bunch's determination to make Story "do right" by her sister) result in Rollo's being mistaken for Story, a famous aviator. Pleased with the admiration he receives, Rollo accepts the situation and finds himself involved in an air race and a $25,000 wager with Ace Benton. Peggy substitutes herself for the mechanic who was to help Rollo fly the plane, and the pair drive Benton out of the sky with their wild gyrations. Unable to land, Peggy accidentally pulls the parachute ring, and they safely float to earth while Rollo proposes. *Aviators. Stowaways. Airplane racing. Mistaken identity. Wagers. Air stunts.*

GOLD AND GRIT **F2.2151**

Approved Pictures. *Dist* Weiss Brothers Artclass Pictures. 15 Jan **1925** [c24 Dec 1924; LU20940]. Si; b&w. 35mm. 5 reels, 4,623 ft.

Pres by Lester F. Scott, Jr. *Dir* Richard Thorpe. *Story* Ned Nye. *Photog* Irving Ries.

Cast: Buddy Roosevelt *(Buddy)*, Ann McKay *(Helen Mason)*, William H. Turner *(Bill Mason)*, L. J. O'Connor *(Jim Crawford)*, Wilbur Mack *(Jack Crawford)*, Nelson McDowell *(Horatio Jefferson Blaabs)*, Hank Bell *(The Sheriff)*.

Western melodrama. After he stops a runaway stage, Buddy is given the job of replacing its driver, who was just killed in an attempted holdup. When he gets to Mineral City, Buddy is recognized by Blaabs, a stranded Shakespearian actor, who recalls that Buddy was once accused of robbery. Blaabs remains silent, and he and Buddy are soon sharing a cabin near the goldfields. During a storm, Helen Mason and Jack Crawford, the son of the owner of the Golden Eagle Mine, take refuge with Buddy at his cabin. By cheating at cards, Jack forces Helen to accept his proposal of marriage. Buddy then produces proof that Jack is guilty of the crime of which he himself has been wrongly accused. About to strike Buddy with a knife, Jack is struck down by a bolt of lightning. When the elder Crawford is later charged with fraudulent ownership of the mine, he arranges for some of his men to remove most of the gold. Buddy captures the men and returns the stolen ore. Crawford attempts to blow up the mine and is killed in the resulting explosion. Buddy and Helen make plans to be married. *Miners. Actors. Stagecoach drivers. Injustice. Supernatural. Lightning.*

GOLD AND THE GIRL **F2.2152**

Fox Film Corp. 5 Apr **1925** [c22 Mar 1925; LP21271]. Si; b&w. 35mm. 5 reels, 4,512 ft.

Pres by William Fox. *Dir* Edmund Mortimer. *Story-Scen* John Stone. *Photog* Allen Davey.

Cast: Buck Jones *(Dan Prentiss)*, Elinor Fair *(Ann Donald)*, Bruce Gordon *(Bart Colton)*, Claude Peyton *(Rankin)*, Lucien Littlefield *(Weasel)*, Alphonz Ethier *(Sam Donald)*, Pal *(himself, a dog)*.

Western melodrama. Dan Prentiss, the special undercover agent of a mining company, is assigned to investigate a series of robberies involving gold shipments. He earns the friendship of Ann Donald by saving her life when her horse is frightened by his dog, Pal. Dan also meets both Ann's uncle, Sam, and his partner, Colton, who is one of Ann's suitors. Dan finally decides to trap the unknown robbers by driving the truck carrying the gold shipment himself. After he sets out on this perilous journey, Ann discovers that her uncle and Colton are the bandits and sets out to warn Dan. The sheriff's posse captures all of Sam's gang except Sam and Colton, who head for the hills. Dan tails them and captures Colton; wounded by the posse, Sam kills himself to avoid capture. Ann promises to wait for Buck, who plans to return for her as soon as his work permits. *Investigators. Sheriffs. Bandits. Posses. Mining. Suicide. Gold. Dogs.*

GOLD CHEVRONS **F2.2153**

Dist Big Three Productions. 12 Nov **1927** [New York showing]. Si; b&w. 35mm. 6 reels, 5,500 ft.

Historical documentary. "Collection of official war pictures, taken by the U. S. Signal Corps. Here billed as 'New York Troops in the World War' ... Views deal mostly with the Rainbow Division of New York in their operations at Chateau Thierry and with other New York troops in the Argonne, including the 'Lost Battalion.' ... In connection with the film, Private Clayton K. Slack, one of the 53 soldiers to whom was awarded the Congressional war medal, makes a personal appearance, reciting humorous personal experiences of the war for about 10 minutes. ... Some show the hottest kind of trench action; advances of troops under fire; in one instance what purports to be an actual picture record of an engagement between a German and an American combat plane in the air. Several views show troops advancing under machine-gun and shrapnel fire, and the spectator can readily see men drop wounded. One bit shows a squadron of cavalry rushing across open fields and caught as an enemy shell explodes among them. ... A heightened effect is given to the American advance by the interpolation of film records from the German war office showing the action from the German side." (*Variety*, 23 Nov 1927, p25.) *World War I. Château-Thierry. Argonne. Clayton K. Slack. United States Army—Rainbow (77th) Division.*

THE GOLD DIGGERS **F2.2154**

Warner Brothers Pictures. 22 Sep **1923** [c4 Sep 1923; LP19370]. Si; b&w. 35mm. 8 reels, 5,600 ft.

David Belasco Production. *Dir* Harry Beaumont. *Scen* Grant Carpenter. *Film Ed* Frank Dazey.

Cast: Hope Hampton *(Jerry La Mar)*, Wyndham Standing *(Stephen Lee)*, Louise Fazenda *(Mable Munroe)*, Gertrude Short *(Topsy St. John)*, Alec Francis *(James Blake)*, Jed Prouty *(Barney Barnett)*, Arita Gillman *(Eleanor Montgomery)*, Peggy Browne *(Trixie Andrews)*, Margaret Seddon *(Mrs. La Mar)*, Johnny Harron *(Wally Saunders)*, Anne Cornwall *(Violet Dayne)*, Louise Beaudet *(Cissie Gray)*, Edna Tichenor *(Dolly Baxter)*, Frances Ross *(Gypsy Montrose)*, Marie Prade *(Sadie)*.

Comedy-drama. Source: Avery Hopwood, *The Gold Diggers; a Comedy in Three Acts* (Atlantic City opening: 23 Jun 1919). Stephen Lee objects to the marriage of his nephew, Wally Saunders, to dancer Violet Dayne because he feels that all chorus girls are gold diggers. Violet's friend, Jerry La Mar, who is not a gold digger, decides to vamp Lee so that he will see by comparison what an unselfish girl Violet is. Lee becomes fascinated with Jerry, and although he knows the truth, he marries her, approving at the same time his nephew's choice. *Uncles. Gold diggers. Chorus girls.*

Note: Remade in 1929 as *Gold Diggers of Broadway*.

GOLD DIGGERS OF BROADWAY **F2.2155**

Warner Brothers Pictures. 30 Aug **1929** [New York premiere; released 5 Oct; c12 Sep 1929; LP680]. Sd (Vitaphone); col (Technicolor). 35mm. 10 reels, 9,122 ft. [Copyrighted as 11 reels. Also si, 23 Nov 1929.]

Dir Roy Del Ruth. *Scen-Dial* Robert Lord. *Titl* De Leon Anthony. *Photog* Barney McGill, Ray Rennahan. *Film Ed* William Holmes. *Songs: "The Song of the Gold Diggers," "Painting the Clouds With Sunshine," "Tip-Toe Thru the Tulips," "In a Kitchenette," "Keeping the Wolf From the Door," "Mechanical Man," "Go to Bed," "And They Still Fall in Love," "What Will I Do Without You?" "Poison Kiss of That Spaniard"* Al Dubin, Joe Burke. *Mus Cond* Louis Silvers. *Dance & Stage Presentations* Larry Ceballos. *Rec Engr* George R. Groves. *Asst Dir* Ross Lederman. *Cost* Earl Luick. *Technicians* Lewis Geib, M. Parker, F. N. Murphy, Victor Vance.

Cast: Nancy Welford *(Jerry)*, Conway Tearle *(Stephen Lee)*, Winnie Lightner *(Mable)*, Ann Pennington *(Ann Collins)*, Lilyan Tashman *(Eleanor)*, William Bakewell *(Wally)*, Nick Lucas *(Nick)*, Helen Foster *(Violet)*, Albert Gran *(Blake)*, Gertrude Short *(Topsy)*, Neely Edwards *(stage manager)*, Julia Swayne Gordon *(Cissy Gray)*, Lee Moran *(dance director)*, Armand Kaliz *(Barney Barnett)*.

Musical comedy. Source: Avery Hopwood, *The Gold Diggers; a Comedy in Three Acts* (Atlantic City opening: 23 Jun 1919). This is a remake of *The Gold Diggers* (1923); the story is essentially the same. *Gold diggers. Guardians. Millionaires. Lawyers. Chorus girls. New York City—Broadway.*

GOLD FROM WEEPAH **F2.2156**

Bill Cody Productions. *Dist* Pathé Exchange. 20 Nov **1927** [c14 Nov 1927; LU24660]. Si; b&w. 35mm. 5 reels, 4,968 ft.

Dir William Bertram. *Cont* L. V. Jefferson. *Story* Bill Cody. *Photog* Ernest Smith, David Smith.

Cast: Bill Cody *(Bill Carson)*, Doris Dawson *(Elsie Blaine)*, Dick La Reno, Joe Harrington, Fontaine La Rue, David Dunbar.

Western melodrama. En route to Weepah in search of gold, Jim Blaine and his daughter Elsie meet Bill Carson when he tows their car out of a river ford. Elsie, who is much admired by Bill, plays the violin in the dancehall operated by Steve Morton, who controls a gang of claim jumpers. When Elsie's father is robbed of gold dust by one of Morton's men, Bill recovers it and indicates he knows the culprit. The miners organize against Morton's men but lack evidence until they attack Blaine's claim; the culprits set fire to the record office, but Bill saves the claim files. Pearl, a dancer, angered at Bill's attentions to Elsie, kidnaps her. Bill confronts the villains with strong evidence and rescues Elsie, ensuring the triumph of justice and love. *Miners. Violinists. Claim jumpers. Dancehall girls. Kidnaping. Incendiarism. Records preservation.*

GOLD GRABBERS **F2.2157**

W. M. Smith Productions. *Dist* Merit Film Corp. 21 Nov **1922** [New York premiere]. Si; b&w. 35mm. 5 reels, 4,600 ft.

Dir Francis Ford. *Story* William Wallace Cook. *Photog* Reginald Lyons.

Cast: Franklyn Farnum, Shorty Hamilton, Al Hart, Genevieve Berte.

Western melodrama. "This story is based on the struggle for a mine and a battle between the new manager and a gang of claim jumpers. ... First the heroine's father bought an option. Then he was cheated out of it and it fell into the hands of a Denver promoter, who hired Farnum to operate the property. The original option holder and his daughter somehow managed to support a gang of hirelings to prevent the profitable running of the mine. ... In the end the heroine let Farnum in on a secret ledge of fabulous richness. ... Farnum sent for the Denver sharper, but when he arrived he turned against his own superintendent and tried to kill him. Almost succeeded, too. But when Farnum recovered and gave the Denver man a talking to on the subject of mine business ethics, he was ashamed of himself and immediately signed over a half interest in the property to Chiquita, the heroine." (*Variety*, 24 Nov 1922, p34.) *Denverites. Mine claims. Sabotage. Fraud.*

GOLD HEELS **F2.2158**

Fox Film Corp. 30 Nov **1924** [c11 Jan 1925; LP21112]. Si; b&w. 35mm. 6 reels, 6,020 ft.

Pres by William Fox. *Dir* William S. Van Dyke. *Scen* John Stone, Frederic Chapin. *Photog* Arthur Todd.

Cast: Robert Agnew *(Boots)*, Peggy Shaw *(Pert Barlow)*, Lucien Littlefield *(Push Miller)*, William Norton Bailey *(Kendall, Jr.)*, Carl Stockdale *(Barlow)*, Fred Butler *(Kendall, Sr.)*, Harry Tracey *(Tobe)*, James Douglas, Winifred Landis, Katherine Craig, Buck Black.

Melodrama. Source: Henry Martyn Blossom, *Checkers; a Hard Luck Story* (Chicago, 1896). Following a streak of hard luck at the racetrack, Boots and his pal, Push, are down to their last dime. Boots saves a drunken young man named Kendall from being robbed of his considerable winnings at the roulette table and later drives Kendall back to his small hometown. There Boots meets Pert Barlow and decides to stay near her, taking a job in her father's store. Old Barlow owns a broken-down racehorse named Gold Heels, which Boots buys from him and trains for the big race. At the local orphanage, a child dies because of the dilapidated condition of the building, and Pert raises enough money to build a new orphanage. Old Barlow takes charge of the money, but it is stolen. Boots is accused of the crime and sent to jail. He is sprung by his pals, loads Gold Heels in a horse-trailer, drives to the track, and watches his horse win the big race. Kendall is exposed as the real thief and Boots is reconciled with Pert, whose father gives them his blessing to be married. *Thieves. Gambling. Horseracing. Orphanages. Horses.*

THE GOLD HUNTERS **F2.2159**

Guaranteed Pictures. *Dist* Davis Distributing Division. c28 Dec **1925** [LP22186]. Si; b&w. 35mm. 7 reels, 6,500 ft.

Dir Paul Hurst.

Cast: David Butler *(Roderick Drew)*, Hedda Nova *(Minnetake)*, Mary Carr *(Mary McAllister)*, Bull Montana *("Hairy" Grimes)*, Jimmy Aubrey *(Shorty)*, Al Hallett *(Mukoki)*, Noble Johnson *(Wabigoon)*, Frank Elliott *(Hugh Beresford)*, John T. Prince *(John Ball)*, William Humphrey *(John McAllister)*, Kathryn McGuire *(Miss Drew)*.

Western melodrama. Source: James Oliver Curwood, *The Gold Hunters; a Story of Life & Adventure in the Hudson Bay Wilds* (Indianapolis, 1909). Roderick Drew, a wolf-hunter, discovers a birchbark map loosely gripped in the white fingers of a skeleton. Shortly thereafter, Roderick is almost killed by a golden bullet; he is then endangered by an unexpected avalanche. Roderick is preparing to see where the map leads when it is stolen by Hairy Grimes, a crook who has discovered the map's existence from Roderick's sweetheart, Minnetake. Minnetake tries to warn Roderick and is abducted by Grimes. Roderick learns of Minnetake's danger and goes after Grimes, defeating him and his gang with the help of an unknown ally. This ally turns out to be Minnetake's grandfather, and Roderick wins both the girl and her grateful grandfather's gold. *Hunters. Indians of North America. Grandfathers. Abduction. Treasure. Sequoia National Park. Hudson Bay. Avalanches. Documentation.*

Note: Filmed on location in Sequoia National Park.

THE GOLD LURE (Reissue) **F2.2160**

Leon Victor. May **1923** [scheduled release]. Si; b&w. 35mm. 5 reels.

Note: Originally entitled *Lone Star Rush;* c20 Jan 1915; LU4259.

GOLD MADNESS **F2.2161**

Perfect Pictures. *Dist* Principal Pictures. 2 Oct **1923** [New York showing]. Si; b&w. 35mm. 6 reels, 5,860 ft.

Pres by E. de B. Newman. *Dir* Robert T. Thornby. *Scen* Fred Kennedy Myton.

Cast: Guy Bates Post *(Jim Kendall, alias Calgarth)*, Cleo Madison *(Olga McGee)*, Mitchell Lewis *(Scotty McGee)*, Grace Darmond *(Hester Stanton)*.

Melodrama. Source: James Oliver Curwood, "The Man From Ten Strike" (publication undetermined). Crooked mine dealer Scotty McGee lures away gold prospector Tim Kendal's wife, Olga, who married out of gold madness. Kendall gets revenge when he actually strikes gold, then later, as a member of the police force, arrests McGee and Olga as swindlers. *Prospectors. Police. Swindlers. Gold mines. Greed. Infidelity.*

THE GOLD RUSH **F2.2162**

Charles Chaplin Productions. *Dist* United Artists. 16 Aug **1925** [c16 Aug 1925; LP21805]. Si; b&w. 35mm. 9 reels, 8,555 ft.

Prod-Dir-Writ Charlie Chaplin. *Photog* Roland H. Totheroh. *Camera* Jack Wilson. *Tech Dir* Charles D. Hall. *Asst Dir* Charles F. Reisner, Harry D'Abbadie D'Arrast. *Prod Mgr* Alfred Reeves.

Cast: Charlie Chaplin *(The Lone Prospector)*, Mack Swain *(Big Jim McKay)*, Tom Murray *(Black Larsen)*, Georgia Hale *(The Girl)*, Betty Morrissey *(The Girl's Friend)*, Malcolm Waite *(Jack Cameron)*, Henry Bergman *(Hank Curtis)*.

Comedy-drama. Drawn to the Klondike by the lure of gold, The Lone Prospector takes refuge from a storm in the cabin of Black Larsen, a desperado. Also there is Big Jim McKay, another prospector, who has just struck it rich. Larsen later discovers the location of McKay's claim and knocks him unconscious with a shovel, causing him to lose his memory. Soon afterward, Larsen is killed in an avalanche. The Lone Prospector wanders into a mining town and falls in love with a dancehall girl, who rejects his humble advances. The Lone Prospector runs into McKay and, together, they contrive to find McKay's claim. McKay shares his wealth with The Lone Prospector, who finally wins the love of the dancehall girl. *Prospectors. Desperadoes. Dancehall girls. Amnesia. Gold rushes. Mining towns. Klondike. Avalanches.*

THE GOLDEN BED **F2.2163**

Famous Players–Lasky. 19 Jan **1925** [c21 Jan 1925; LP21054]. Si; b&w. 35mm. 9 reels, 8,584 ft.

Pres by Adolph Zukor, Jesse L. Lasky. *Dir* Cecil B. De Mille. *Screenplay* Jeanie Macpherson. *Photog* Peverell Marley.

Cast: Lillian Rich *(Flora Lee Peake)*, Vera Reynolds *(Margaret Peake)*, Henry Walthall *(Colonel Peake)*, Rod La Rocque *(Admah Holtz)*, Theodore Kosloff *(The Marquis de San Pilar)*, Warner Baxter *(Bunny)*, Robert Cain *(The Duc de Savarac)*, Julia Faye *(Mrs. Amos Thompson)*, Robert Edeson *(Amos Thompson)*, Jacqueline Wells *(Flora, as a child)*, Mary Jane Irving *(Admah as a child)*, Charles Clary *(James Gordon)*.

Society melodrama. Source: Wallace Irwin, "Tomorrow's Bread," in *Pictorial Review* (25:12–17, Jan–Mar 1924). Flora Lee, the spoiled daughter of an aristocratic southern family of rapidly dwindling means, marries the Marquis de San Pilar. Three years pass. Climbing the Jungfrau, the Marquis finds his wife in the arms of another man and kills both that man and himself. Flora Lee returns home and marries Admah Holtz, a self-made young man long in love with her. Flora Lee's extravagance soon brings Admah close to financial ruin, but nevertheless he allows her to give an elaborate ball, using money not entirely his own to finance it. Admah is sent to jail for 5 years, and Flora Lee runs off with Bunny. When Admah is released from jail, he returns home in time to comfort Flora Lee, who has been cast off by Bunny and is dying of pneumonia. Admah rebuilds his business and finds comfort with Margaret, Flora Lee's sister, who has loved him patiently for many years. *Southerners. Sisters. Nobility. Marriage. Infidelity. Bankruptcy. Embezzlement. Suicide. Mountain climbing. Pneumonia. Jungfrau. Switzerland.*

THE GOLDEN CALF **F2.2164**

Fox Film Corp. 16 Mar **1930** [c17 Feb 1930; LP1118]. Sd (Movietone); b&w. 35mm. 8 reels, 6,800 ft.

Pres by William Fox. *Assoc Prod* Ned Marin. *Dir* Millard Webb. *Stgd by* Frank Merlin. *Cont* Marion Orth. *Dial* Harold Atteridge. *Photog* Lucien Andriot. *Film Ed* Alexander Troffey. *Songs: "You Gotta Be Modernistic," "Maybe Someday," "Can I Help It If I'm in Love With You?" "Telling the World About You," "A Picture No Artist Can Paint"* Cliff Friend, Jimmy Monaco. *Ensemble Dir* Earl Lindsay. *Sd* Donald Flick. *Asst Dir* R. L. Hough. *Cost* Sophie Wachner.

Cast: Jack Mulhall *(Philip Homer)*, Sue Carol *(Marybelle Cobb)*, El Brendel *(Knute Olson)*, Marjorie White *(Alice)*, Richard Keene *(Tommy)*, Paul Page *(Edwards)*, Walter Catlett *(master of ceremonies)*, Ilka Chase *(comedienne)*.

Romantic musical comedy. Source: Aaron Davis, "The Golden Calf," in *Liberty Magazine* (3:48–52, 25 Dec 1926). Marybelle Cobb, a plain and old-fashioned girl, is secretary to commercial illustrator Philip Homer, with whom she is secretly in love. When Homer advertises for a girl with perfect leg measurements to be a model for a hosiery manufacturer's advertising, Marybelle, with the aid of her friend Alice, decides to transform herself completely and apply for the job. She wins the much-sought-after appointment against considerable opposition. When Homer's indifference turns to love, Marybelle confesses the deception and all ends well. *Secretaries. Commercial artists. Models. Advertising. Hosiery.*

THE GOLDEN COCOON **F2.2165**

Warner Brothers Pictures. 30 Jan **1926** [c18 Jul 1925; LP21656]. Si; b&w. 35mm. 7 reels, 7,200 ft.

Dir Millard Webb. *Adapt* Hope Loring, Louis D. Lighton. *Photog* Byron Haskins. *Asst Dir* William McGann.

Cast: Huntly Gordon *(Gregory Cochran)*, Helene Chadwick *(Molly Shannon)*, Richard Tucker *(Mr. Renfro)*, Frank Campeau *(Mr. Bancroft)*, Margaret Seddon *(Mrs. Shannon)*, Carrie Clark Ward *(Mrs. Parker)*, Charles McHugh *(Mr. Shannon)*, Violet Kane *(Baby)*.

Melodrama. Source: Ruth Cross, *The Golden Cocoon* (New York & London, 1924). After she is left standing at the altar by Renfro, Molly Shannon walks the streets aimlessly in a blinding rainstorm and faints in front of a sporting house, into which she is taken. Sometime later she meets Gregory Cochran, a wealthy judge with whom she finds true marital happiness. Gregory is being mentioned for the governorship, and a member of the opposition party threatens to nip Gregory's political career in the bud by revealing that he once saw Molly coming from a house of ill repute. Knowing that public mention of the incident will ruin her husband's career, Molly feigns suicide and disappears. On election eve, she is seen by Renfro, who goes to Gregory with the news of his wife's presence in this world. Molly sees Renfro and follows him to his room, where the two scuffle for possession of a gun. The gun accidentally goes off, mortally wounding Renfro. Gregory arrives, and Renfro exonerates Molly. *Judges. Politicians. Suicide. Elections. Whorehouses. Storms.*

GOLDEN DAWN **F2.2166**

Warner Brothers Pictures. 14 Jun **1930** [c5 Jun 1930; LP1355]. Sd (Vitaphone); col (Technicolor). 35mm. 10 reels, 7,447 ft.

Dir Ray Enright. *Screenplay-Dial* Walter Anthony. *Photog* Dev Jennings. *Songs: "My Heart's Love Call," "Africa Smiles No More," "Mooda's Song," "In a Jungle Bungalow"* Grant Clarke, Harry Akst. *Songs: "Whip Song," "Dawn," "My Bwanna," "We Two"* Otto Harbach, Oscar Hammerstein, II, Emmerich Kalman. *Dance Dir* Larry Ceballos. *Rec Engr* Glenn E. Rominger.

Cast: Walter Woolf *(Tom Allen)*, Vivienne Segal *(Dawn)*, Noah Beery *(Shep)*, Alice Gentle *(Mooda)*, Lupino Lane *(Pigeon)*, Marion Byron *(Johanna)*, Lee Moran *(Blink)*, Nigel De Brulier *(Hasmali)*, Otto Matieson *(Captain Eric)*, Dick Henderson *(Duke)*, Nina Quartaro *(maid-in-waiting)*, Sojin *(Piper)*, Julanne Johnston *(Sister Hedwig)*, Nick De Ruiz *(Napoli)*, Edward Martindel *(Colonel Judson)*.

Musical melodrama. Source: Oscar Hammerstein, II, Otto Harbach, Emmerich Kalman and Herbert Stothart, *Golden Dawn* (New York opening: 30 Nov 1927). Dawn, a young white girl who has been kidnaped in infancy and reared by Mooda, an African woman who operates a canteen in the German cantonment, meets and falls in love with Tom Allen, an English rubber planter who is a prisoner of war. Shep Keyes, who has joined the German troops, covets her but realizes he cannot possess her because she is betrothed to the tribal god, Mulunghu; and on the eve of the ceremony he learns of her love for Tom. Tom, meanwhile, is sent back to England, and when the English take the territory from the Germans, Shep tries to incite the natives, who are experiencing a drought, against Dawn because of her love of a mortal. Tom learns from Mooda that Dawn was stolen from a white trader and finds her seeking refuge in a convent. Shep arouses the natives, but Dawn declares her faith in the white man's God and a thunderstorm brings relief to the parched land, after which Tom claims her for his bride. *Planters. Sutlers. Prisoners of war. Germans. Religion. Personal identity. World War I. German East Africa. Drought.*

GOLDEN DREAMS **F2.2167**

Benjamin B. Hampton. *Dist* Goldwyn Distributing Corp. ca4 Jun **1922** [New York premiere; released Jun; c8 Jul 1922; LP18039]. Si; b&w. 35mm. 5 reels, 4,500 ft.

Prod-Dir-Adapt Benjamin B. Hampton. *Assoc Dir* Jean Hersholt, Gus Peterson, Charles O. Rush.

Cast: Rose Dione *(Countess de Elberca)*, Claire Adams *(Mercedes McDonald)*, Norris McKay *(Enrique McDonald)*, Carl Gantvoort *(Sandy Buchanan)*, Audrey Chapman *(Althea Lippincott)*, Ida Ward *(Countess de Elberca's cousin)*, Bertram Grassby *(Duke of Othomo)*, Frank Leigh *(Don Felipe de Cristobal)*, Gordon Mullen *(Pedro)*, Pomeroy Cannon *(Big Bill [foreman])*, Frank Hayes *(circus clown)*, Babe London *(strong woman)*, Jane Irving *(little boy clown)*, Walter Perkins *(circus manager)*, Harry Lorraine *(innkeeper)*, C. B. Murphy *(animal trainer)*, William Orlamond *(schoolmaster)*, D. J. Mitsoras *(majordomo)*.

Adventure melodrama. Suggested by: Zane Grey, unidentified novel. Oil is discovered on the Countess de Elberca's estate in a mythical Spanish American country. Mercedes McDonald, her niece, falls in love with Sandy Buchanan, a young Scotch engineer hired by the countess. Don Felipe, a neighbor in need of money to avoid arrest for embezzlement, conspires with his nephew, the Duke of Othomo, for the latter to wed Mercedes. The aunt approves the suit. Felipe and Othomo attempt to kill Mercedes' sweetheart, but Buchanan, with the aid of her brother and a traveling American circus, foils their plans. Felipe and Othomo are killed by the circus animals, and the aunt consents to Mercedes' marriage to Buchanan. *Aunts. Engineers. Scotch. Embezzlement. Oil. Circus. Imaginary republics. Latin America. Animals.*

THE GOLDEN FLAME **F2.2168**

Prairie Productions. 16 Nov **1923** [New York State license]. Si; b&w. 35mm. 5 reels, 4,800 ft.

Cast: Dick Hatton.

Western melodrama. No information about the nature of this film has been found.

THE GOLDEN GALLOWS (Universal Special) **F2.2169**

Universal Film Manufacturing Co. 27 Feb **1922** [c2 Feb 1922; LP17517]. Si; b&w. 35mm. 5 reels, 4,808 ft.

Pres by Carl Laemmle. *Dir* Paul Scardon. *Scen* Harvey Gates. *Photog* Ben Reynolds.

Cast: Miss Du Pont *(Willow Winters)*, Edwin Stevens *(Leander Sills)*, Eve Southern *(Cleo Twayne)*, Jack Mower *(Peter Galliner)*, George B. Williams *(Mark Buckheim)*, Douglas Gerrard *(Alexander Riche)*, Elinor Hancock *(Mrs. Galliner)*, Barbara Tennant *(Flo)*.

Society melodrama. Source: Victoria Galland, "The Golden Gallows," in *Snappy Stories* (61:5–31, 1 Oct 1921). Leander Sills, wealthy friend of Willow Winters, a chorus girl who has risen to fame as a result of a star's illness, is so impressed by the girl's resistance to his offers of wealth and luxury that he wills her his fortune. When Sills is killed by a former sweetheart, his lawyer gives the matter publicity, with the result that Peter Galliner, who is in love with Willow, believes that Willow's relations with Sills have been improper, denounces her, and leaves town. Under an assumed name, Willow becomes a friend of Peter's mother and wins her respect. Returning home, Peter is still suspicious, but finally he is convinced of her innocence and proceeds to punish the malicious lawyer who is responsible for her "golden gallows." *Chorus girls. Inheritance. Scandal. Murder. Wills.*

THE GOLDEN GIFT **F2.2170**

Metro Pictures. 6 Feb **1922** [c27 Feb 1922; LP17687]. Si; b&w. 35mm. 5 reels, 4,986 ft.

Dir Maxwell Karger. *Scen* Florence Hein. *Story* June Mathis. *Photog* John Boyle. *Art Dir* Joseph Calder. *Prod Mgr* Clifford P. Butler.

Cast: Alice Lake *(Nita Gordon)*, John Bowers *(James Llewelyn)*, Harriet

Hammond *(Edith Llewelyn)*, Joseph Swickard *(Leonati)*, Bridgetta Clark *(Rosana)*, Louis Dumar *(Malcolm Thorne)*, Geoffrey Webb *(Stephen Brand)*, Camilla Clark *(Joy Llewelyn)*.

Society melodrama. After the birth of her child, Nita Gordon, once a successful singer, loses her voice and and—deserted by her husband—is forced to become a Mexican cafe dancer to support herself and the child. Having traced her husband (Malcolm Thorne) to a little oil center in Mexico, Nita finds him married to Edith Llewelyn. She witnesses his death, then leaves her child in a mission. Edith adopts the child but is ignorant of its parentage. Meanwhile, Nita returns to Italy with Leonati, a conductor friend, regains her voice, and becomes a star at the Metropolitan Opera in New York, where James Llewelyn falls in love with her. At the Llewelyn home Nita sees Joy, the child she left behind, and Edith declares that its mother sacrificed her child's love for ambition. Nita confesses to being the child's mother, and Llewelyn threatens to expose her; he relents, however, realizing her love for the child. *Singers. Dancers. Desertion. Motherhood. Mexico. Italy. Metropolitan Opera.*

Note: *Moving Picture World* credits the story as being based on a play entitled "The Claim." No author is mentioned.

THE GOLDEN PRINCESS **F2.2171**

Famous Players–Lasky. *Dist* Paramount Pictures. 5 Oct **1925** [c6 Oct 1925; LP21880]. Si; b&w. 35mm. 9 reels, 8,584 ft.

Pres by Adolph Zukor, Jesse L. Lasky. *Dir* Clarence Badger. *Scen* Frances Agnew. *Photog* H. Kinley Martin.

Cast: Betty Bronson *(Betty Kent)*, Neil Hamilton *(Tennessee Hunter)*, Rockliffe Fellowes *(Tom Romaine)*, Phyllis Haver *(Kate Kent)*, Joseph Dowling *(Padre)*, Edgar Kennedy *(Gewilliker Hay)*, George Irving *(Bill Kent)*, Norma Wills *(Indian squaw)*, Mary Schoene *(Betty, as a child)*, Don Marion *(Tennessee Hunter, age 10)*.

Western melodrama. Source: Bret Harte, "The Golden Princess" (publication undetermined). During the Gold Rush of '49, Tom Romaine kills William Kent and runs off with his wife, Kate, leaving behind Kate's daughter, Betty, who is reared by a priest. Fifteen years later, Betty goes to California and looks up Tennessee, one of her father's friends, who makes her his partner in the Golden Princess Mine. Romaine learns of Betty's whereabouts and, with Kate's help, passes himself off as Betty's father. Tennessee recognizes them both and lets Betty know that Romaine killed her father. Romaine dynamites the mine with Betty and Tennessee inside; and Kate, who has killed Romaine, dies while rescuing them. Tennessee and Betty decide to become partners in marriage. *Prospectors. Miners. Clergymen. Murder. Impersonation. Motherhood. Gold rushes. California.*

GOLDEN SHACKLES **F2.2172**

Dallas M. Fitzgerald Productions. *Dist* Peerless Pictures. 15 Mar **1928.** Si; b&w. 35mm. 6 reels, 5,600 ft.

Dir Dallas M. Fitzgerald. *Scen* Ada McQuillan, Gladys Gordon. *Titl* M. C. Dewar. *Story* G. Marion Burton. *Photog* Milton Moore. *Film Ed* M. C. Dewar.

Cast: Grant Withers *(Frank Fordyce)*, Priscilla Bonner *(Lucy Weston)*, LeRoy Mason *(Herbert Fordyce)*, Ruth Stewart *(Vivi Norton)*.

Drama. Swearing revenge, a nurse, Lucy Weston, marries the young millionaire she believes to be responsible for her father's death, which occurred during his robbery of the millionaire's home. The wealthy youth sends the girl away as a result of a frameup perpetrated by her former sweetheart; but she retaliates by disguising herself, vamping her husband, and casting him aside. She later discovers that her father was killed by one of his confederates, and the couple is reunited. *Millionaires. Nurses. Revenge. Murder. Robbery. Frameup.*

GOLDEN SILENCE **F2.2173**

Sylvanite Productions. *Dist* Kipling Enterprises. 19 Mar **1923** [scheduled release]. Si; b&w. 35mm. 5 reels, 4,800 ft.

Dir Paul Hurst.

Cast: Jack Perrin, Hedda Nova.

Western melodrama. "Sam Corwin, stage line owner and camp bully, makes unwelcome love to Polly, daughter of an old prospector. The old man drives him off the place at gunpoint and Sam conspires to have the old man sent to prison. He stages a fake hold-up, leaving the old man's hat on the scene. This is managed with the connivance of one of Sam's stage drivers. By one of those far-fetched coincidences of the screen the whole plot is unfolded to a stranger in those parts, and he impersonates the hold-up artist, double-crossing the plotters, vindicating the old man, overthrowing the villains, and in the end winning the girl." (*Variety*, 19 Apr 1923, p36.) *Prospectors. Frameup. Stagecoach robberies. Impersonation. Stagelines.*

THE GOLDEN SNARE **F2.2174**

David Hartford Productions. *Dist* Associated First National Pictures. Jul **1921** [c21 Jun 1921; LP16695]. Si; b&w. 35mm. 6 reels, 5,900 ft.

Dir David M. Hartford. *Adapt* James Oliver Curwood, David M. Hartford. *Photog* Walter Griffin.

Cast: Lewis Stone *(Sgt. Philip Raine)*, Wallace Beery *(Bram Johnson)*, Melbourne MacDowell *("Doug" Johnson)*, Ruth Renick *(Celie)*, Wellington Playter *("Black" Dawson)*, De Witt Jennings *("Fighting" Fitzgerald)*, Francis McDonald *(Pierre Thoreau)*, Little Esther Scott *(Baby)*.

Northwest melodrama. Source: James Oliver Curwood, *The Golden Snare* (New York, 1921). Sgt. Philip Raine of the Royal Northwest Mounted Police is sent to the mountains to capture killer Bram Johnson. Raine encounters a dying Frenchman—whom he believes to be Johnson—who gives him a tiny baby and a rabbit snare made of golden hair. Overtaken by a blizzard and set upon by a pack of wolf dogs, he is escorted by Celie, a beautiful blonde, to the stockade where she lives with Johnson. She shields Raine from Johnson, but she and Raine are later captured by "Black" Dawson, a jealous rival. At the critical moment, Bram arrives and saves them. Before dying, he explains the mystery of Celie, who was found as a baby in an explorer's icebound ship. *Foundlings. Arctic regions. Canada. Northwest Mounted Police. Blizzards.*

Note: Reissued by the Aywon Film Corp. in Aug 1927.

THE GOLDEN STRAIN **F2.2175**

Fox Film Corp. 27 Dec **1925** [c27 Dec 1925; LP22166]. Si; b&w. 35mm. 6 reels, 5,989 ft.

Pres by William Fox. *Dir* Victor Schertzinger. *Scen* Eve Unsell. *Photog* Glen MacWilliams. *Asst Dir* William Tummel.

Cast: Hobart Bosworth *(Major Milton Mulford)*, Kenneth Harlan *(Milt Mulford, Jr.)*, Madge Bellamy *(Dixie Denniston)*, Lawford Davidson *(Major Gaynes)*, Ann Pennington *(Lucy Sulter)*, Frank Beal *(Major Denniston)*, Frankie Lee *(Milt, as a boy)*, Coy Watson *(Zeb, as a boy)*, Robert Frazer *(sergeant)*, Oscar Smith *(Snowball)*, George Reed *(butler)*, Grace Morse *(Clara)*, Frank McGlynn, Jr. *(Zeb)*, Larry Fisher *(Captain Powell)*, Lola Mackey *(Arabella)*.

Western melodrama. Source: Peter Bernard Kyne, "Thoroughbreds," in *Hearst's International Cosmopolitan* (79:50–53, Sep 1925). Milt Mulford, a West Point graduate, is commissioned as a lieutenant and assigned to a cavalry outpost near an Apache reservation. The Indians, cheated out of their supplies by Gaynes, a crooked Indian agent, go on the warpath, and Milt takes a detachment of cavalry after them. In his baptism under fire, Milt loses his nerve and fails to lead his men. He is drummed out of the service, and his fiancée, Dixie Denniston, breaks their engagement. Milt later proves both his courage and his qualities of leadership, thereby regaining his commission and Dixie's love. *Indian agents. Indians of North America. Cowardice. United States Army—Cavalry.*

A GOLDEN THOUGHT **F2.2176**

Dist Elvin Film Corp. 6 Dec **1924** [New York State license]. Si; b&w. 35mm. 5 reels.

Cast: Tom Mix.

Note: Expansion of a 2-reeler, *The Golden Thought* (Selig, 1917).

THE GOLDEN TRAIL **F2.2177**

William (Bill) Mix Productions. 16 Sep **1927** [New York State license]. Si; b&w. 35mm. 5 reels.

Cast: Dick Carter, Dorothy Wood.

Western melodrama(?). No information about the nature of this film has been found.

THE GOLDEN WEB **F2.2178**

Gotham Productions. *Dist* Lumas Film Corp. 1 Sep **1926** [c7 Jul 1926; LP22883]. Si; b&w. 35mm. 6 reels, 6,224 ft.

Pres by Sam Sax. *Supv* Renaud Hoffman. *Dir* Walter Lang. *Adapt-Cont* James Bell Smith. *Photog* Ray June. *Prod Mgr* Glenn Belt.

Cast: Lillian Rich *(Ruth Rowan)*, Huntly Gordon *(Roland Deane)*, Jay Hunt *(John Rowan)*, Lawford Davidson *(George Sisk)*, Boris Karloff *(Dave Sinclair)*, Nora Hayden *(Miss Philbury)*, Syd Crossley *(butler)*, Joe Moore *(office boy)*.

Mystery melodrama. Source: Edward Phillips Oppenheim, *The Golden*

Web (Boston, 1910). Roland Deane, president of the International Mining Co., owns a South African mine that suddenly becomes valuable after the partners leave because of earthquakes. One partner, Dave Sinclair, steals a bill of sale covering his share of the mine and threatens Deane, who sends John Rowan, the original owner of the mine (and in financial straits), to confer with him on the matter. Deane is about to become engaged to a society debutante when he hears that Sinclair has been murdered and Rowan arrested; Rowan's daughter, Ruth, learns that her father did not commit the crime and finds the missing deed in Sinclair's coat at the district attorney's office. Deane marries Ruth to atone for her father's predicament but is ruined socially and financially as a result. Rowan is sentenced to death; but at the last minute, Sisk is arrested for trying to steal the deed and confesses to the murder. Deane saves Ruth from suicide because of her father, and they are happily reunited. *Mining. Murder. Capital punishment. Injustice. Documentation. South Africa. Earthquakes.*

THE GOLDEN YUKON **F2.2179**

Sierra Pictures. *Dist* Aywon Film Corp. 24 Oct **1927** [New York State license]. Si; b&w. 35mm. 7 reels, 6,540 ft.

Sam Pisor Production. *Dir* Nell Shipman, Bert Van Tuyle. *Story-Scen* Nell Shipman.

Cast: Nell Shipman, Alfred Allen, Lillian Leighton, Hugh Thompson, Ah Wing, C. K. Van Auker.

Melodrama. "Innocent and trusting girl is taken to Alaska by an unscrupulous gent, who commits bigamy and tries to commit murder. Crazy miner with tales of a bonanza kicked around by the rabble, only to be proven right in the end." (*Variety*, 22 Feb 1928, p25.) *Miners. Bigamy. Alaska.*

THE GOLDFISH **F2.2180**

Constance Talmadge Productions. *Dist* Associated First National Pictures. 30 Mar **1924** [c3 Apr 1924; LP20047]. Si; b&w. 35mm. 7 reels, 7,145 ft.

Pres by Joseph M. Schenck. *Dir* Jerome Storm. *Adapt* C. Gardner Sullivan. *Photog* Ray Binger.

Cast: Constance Talmadge *(Jennie Wetherby)*, Jack Mulhall *(Jimmy Wetherby)*, Frank Elliott *(Duke of Middlesex)*, Jean Hersholt *(Herman Krauss)*, ZaSu Pitts *(Amelia Pugsley)*, Edward Connelly *(Count Nevski)*, William Conklin *(J. Hamilton Powers)*, Leo White *(Casmir)*, Nellie Bly Baker *(Ellen)*, Kate Lester *(Mrs. Bellmore)*, Eric Mayne *(The Prince)*, William Wellesley *(Mr. Crane)*, Jacqueline Gadsden *(Helen Crane)*, Percy Williams *(Wilton)*, John Patrick *(reporter)*.

High comedy. Source: Gladys Unger, *The Goldfish* (New York opening: 17 Apr 1922). Jennie Wetherby and her song-plugging husband, Jimmy, agree that if either ever tires of wedded life, the presentation of a bowl of goldfish to the other will signify the end of their relationship. After Count Nevski convinces Jennie that she could be a great lady if she would choose the right husbands, the Wetherbys quarrel and Jimmy gets the goldfish. Jennie successfully climbs the social ladder by marrying Herman Krauss, then J. Hamilton Powers; and she is about to announce her engagement to the Duke of Middlesex when Jimmy achieves success. Their old love wins out, they are reunited with Krauss's help, and the Duke gets the goldfish. *Marriage. Social climbers. Goldfish.*

GOLF WIDOWS **F2.2181**

Columbia Pictures. 1 May **1928** [c31 May 1928; LP25310]. Si; b&w. 35mm. 6 reels, 5,592 ft.

Prod Harry Cohn. *Dir* Erle C. Kenton. *Scen* W. Scott Darling. *Photog* Arthur Todd. *Art Dir* Joseph Wright. *Asst Dir* Eugene De Rue.

Cast: Vera Reynolds *(Alice Anderson)*, Harrison Ford *(Charles Bateman)*, John Patrick *(Billy Gladstone)*, Sally Rand *(Mary Ward)*, Kathleen Key *(Ethel Dixon)*, Vernon Dent *(Ernest Ward)*, Will Stanton *(John Dixon)*.

Comedy. Two golf widows, Ethel Dixon and Mary Ward, decide to get even with their husbands by going to the Tijuana horseraces with Billy Gladstone, a wealthy broker, and Charles Bateman, an insurance salesman. The quartet is followed across the border by Ward and Dixon in one car and by Alice Anderson, Bateman's fiancée, in another car. Complications follow in rapid succession. Later, in a hotel room, Charles explains to his fiancée and the two husbands that the whole affair was arranged as a lesson to illustrate the danger of neglecting their wives for golf. Alice accepts Bateman's explanation and marries him in Tijuana. *Brokers. Insurance agents. Golf. Marriage. Horseracing. Tijuana (Mexico).*

GOOD AND NAUGHTY **F2.2182**

Famous Players–Lasky. *Dist* Paramount Pictures. 7 Jun **1926** [c9 Jun 1926; LP22809]. Si; b&w. 35mm. 6 reels, 5,503 ft.

Pres by Adolph Zukor, Jesse L. Lasky. *Dir* Malcolm St. Clair. *Screenplay* Pierre Collings. *Photog* Bert Glennon.

Cast: Pola Negri *(Germaine Morris)*, Tom Moore *(Gerald Gray)*, Ford Sterling *(Bunny West)*, Miss Du Pont *(Claire Fenton)*, Stuart Holmes *(Thomas Fenton)*, Marie Mosquini *(Chouchou Rouselle)*, Warner Richmond *("Bad News" Smith)*.

Romantic comedy. Source: René Peter and Henri Falk, *Naughty Cinderella, a Comedy in Three Acts* (as adapted by Avery Hopwood; New York, 1934). Germaine Morris, considered an ugly duckling, is in love with her employer, Gerald Gray, an interior decorator who caters to the smart set, and is concerned over his affair with Claire Fenton, the wife of a wealthy broker. When Claire invites Gerald on a yachting trip to Florida, his friend Bunny West invites showgirl Chouchou Rouselle to pose as Gerald's fiancée, but Germaine determines to substitute her own womanly beauty. In Florida she wins the attentions of all the men, causing a quarrel between Claire and Gerald; and Fenton hopes to obtain a corespondent as grounds for divorce. When Germaine, in her negligee, delivers a pipe to Gerald's room, he proposes; Fenton suggests that he take Germaine, leaving Claire and Gerald to go their way; but Smith, the showgirl's admirer, tries to claim her and is beaten by Gerald, who effects a reconciliation between the Fentons and claims the girl he loves. *Interior decorators. Brokers. Showgirls. Divorce. Yachts. New York City.*

GOOD AS GOLD **F2.2183**

Fox Film Corp. 12 Jun **1927** [c12 Jun 1927; LP24108]. Si; b&w. 35mm. 5 reels, 4,545 ft.

Pres by William Fox. *Dir* Scott Dunlap. *Scen* Jack Jungmeyer. *Photog* Reginald Lyons. *Asst Dir* Virgil Hart.

Cast: Buck Jones *(Buck Brady)*, Frances Lee *(Jane Laurier)*, Carl Miller *(Thomas Tilford)*, Charles French *(Sheriff John Gray)*, Adele Watson *(Timothea)*, Arthur Ludwig *(Henchman)*, Mickey Moore *(Buck Brady as a boy)*.

Western melodrama. Source: Murray Leinster, "The Owner of the Aztec," in *Western Magazine* (5 May 1926). When Buck Brady is a child, his father's mine is stolen, and he grows up planning to revenge the injustice. He finally retaliates by holding up the mine's payroll messengers. He falls in love with Janet Laurier, who, he later learns, is the owner of the mine; Buck saves her from Tilford, the crooked foreman, and fights Tilford on a moving car that finally falls over the edge of a cliff. *Mine foremen. Revenge. Robbery. Filial relations. Mine claims.*

GOOD BAD BOY **F2.2184**

B. F. Zeidman. *Dist* Principal Pictures. 1 Jun **1924.** Si; b&w. 35mm. 5 reels, 5,198 ft.

Dir Eddie Cline.

Cast: Joe Butterworth *(Billy Benson)*, Mary Jane Irving *(Judge Fawcett's daughter)*, Brownie *(himself, a dog)*, Forrest Robinson *(John Benson)*, Lucy Beaumont *(Mrs. Benson)*, Arthur Hull *(Sidney Marvin)*, Richard Wayne *(Walter Howe)*, Edwards Davis *(Judge Fawcett)*.

Juvenile melodrama. John Benson, an unsuccessful inventor, spends half his time violating the Volstead Act. Billy, his only son, has acquired a reputation for belligerence because he defends Benson with his fists. As a result, Billy has few friends: Brownie, his dog, and Judge Fawcett's daughter. Finally, when one of Mr. Benson's inventions proves marketable, Sidney Martin, a crooked lawyer, and his accomplice, Walter Howe, plan to steal it. They trump up a false charge and Benson is railroaded to jail. Mrs. Benson falls ill and has to be hospitalized. During the Bensons' absence, Howe, attempting to steal the blueprints, accidentally sets fire to their house, trapping Judge Fawcett's daughter in it. Billy rescues her and, with his Boy Scout troop, chases Howe, who has fled in Judge Fawcett's car. Howe is captured, Benson is freed, Mrs. Benson recovers, and the townspeople praise Billy. *Inventors. Judges. Alcoholism. Prohibition. Boy Scouts. Documentation. Fires. Dogs.*

THE GOOD BAD MAN (Reissue) **F2.2185**

Fine Arts Pictures. *Dist* Tri-Stone Pictures. c19 Oct **1923** [LP19514]. Si; b&w. 35mm.

Note: A "re-edited and re-titled" Douglas Fairbanks film originally released by Triangle Film Corp. on 7 May 1916.

GOOD FOR NOTHING *see* **POLLY OF THE FOLLIES**

GOOD INTENTIONS F2.2186

Fox Film Corp. 29 Jun **1930** [c19 May 1930; LP1349]. Sd (Movietone); b&w. 35mm. 8 reels, 6,340 ft.

Pres by William Fox. *Dir-Story* William K. Howard. *Stgd by* Henry Kolker. *Scen* George Manker Watters. *Dial* William K. Howard, George Manker Watters. *Photog* George Schneiderman. *Sets* Duncan Cramer. *Film Ed* Jack Murray. *Song: "A Slave to Love"* Cliff Friend, Jimmy Monaco. *Rec Engr* Al Protzman. *Asst Dir* R. L. Hough, Ray Flynn.

Cast: Edmund Lowe *(David Cresson)*, Marguerite Churchill *(Helen Rankin)*, Regis Toomey *(Richard Holt)*, Earle Foxe *("Flash" Norton)*, Eddie Gribbon *(Liberty Red)*, Robert McWade *(Cyrus Holt)*, Georgia Caine *(Miss Huntington)*, Owen Davis, Jr. *(Bud Finney)*, Pat Somerset *(Babe Gray)*, J. Carrol Naish *(Charlie Hatrick)*, Henry Kolker *(butler)*, Hale Hamilton *(Franklin Graham)*.

Society melodrama. David Cresson, the leader of a gang of thieves, passes himself off in society circles as a gentleman and cultivates the romantic inclinations of Helen Rankin, who knows nothing of his criminal activities. When his lieutenant, "Flash" Norton, doublecrosses him and robs the girl of a necklace he has given her, Richard Holt, whom Helen actually loves, is held hostage. Realizing that Helen loves him, David sacrifices his own life to clear Holt. *Gentlemen crooks. Socialites. Hostages. Courtship. Robbery. Self-sacrifice.*

GOOD MEN AND BAD F2.2187

F. W. Kraemer. *Dist* American Releasing Corp. 14 Jul **1923** [c1 Apr 1923; LP19243]. Si; b&w. 35mm. 5 reels, ca4,600 ft.

Dir Merrill McCormick. *Story-Scen* William Lester. *Mus sets arr by* J. Ernest Zivelli.

Cast: Marin Sais *(Felicia)*, Steve Carrie *(Steve Kinnard)*, Merrill McCormick *(Don Pedro Martínez)*, George Guyton *(Don Esteban Valdeo)*, Faith Hope *(Rosalia)*.

Melodrama. Argentinean rancher Don Valdeo has a daughter, Felicia, whom he would like to give away to Don Martínez in payment of a debt. Felicia, however, is in love with Steve Kinnard, an American cowboy visiting Argentina. Felicia announces at a fiesta that she will marry the man who can ride her wild horse. When Martínez refuses to compete, Steve wins by default. *Ranchers. Cowboys. Horsemanship. Argentina.*

Note: Copyright application credits F. W. Kraemer as director.

GOOD MEN AND TRUE F2.2188

R-C Pictures. *Dist* Film Booking Offices of America. 5 Nov **1922** [Omaha premiere; released 12 Nov; c12 Nov 1922; LP18600]. Si; b&w. 35mm. 6 reels, 5,267 ft.

Dir Val Paul. *Adapt-Scen* George Edwardes-Hall. *Story* Eugene Manlove Rhodes. *Photog* William Thornley, Robert De Grasse.

Cast: Harry Carey *(J. Wesley Pringle)*, Vola Vale *(Georgie Hibbler)*, Thomas Jefferson *(Simon Hibbler)*, Noah Beery *(S. S. Thorpe)*, Charles J. Le Moyne *(Bowerman)*, Tully Marshall *(Fite)*, Helen Gilmore *(Mrs. Fite)*.

Western melodrama. So determined is S. S. Thorpe to be elected sheriff that he shoves his favored opponent, J. Wesley Pringle, off a cliff, then frames him for murder. Wesley recovers, however, and returns to bring Thorpe to justice, rescue his sweetheart, Georgie Hibbler, and win the election. *Sheriffs. Elections. Murder.*

Note: Reissued by FBO in 1928 (New York showing: 10 Sep).

GOOD MORNING, JUDGE (Universal-Jewel) F2.2189

Universal Pictures. 29 Apr **1928** [c13 Mar 1928; LP25071]. Si; b&w. 35mm. 6 reels, 5,645 ft.

Dir William A. Seiter. *Story Supv* Joseph Franklin Poland. *Cont* Beatrice Van. *Titl* Tom Reed. *Adapt* Earle Snell. *Story* Harry O. Hoyt. *Photog* Arthur Todd. *Film Ed* Edward McDermott.

Cast: Reginald Denny *(Freddie Grey)*, Mary Nolan *(Julia Harrington)*, Otis Harlan *(Jerry Snoot)*, Dorothy Gulliver *(Ruth Grey)*, William Davidson *(Elton)*, Bull Montana *(first crook)*, William Worthington *(Mr. Grey, Sr.)*, Sailor Sharkey *(second crook)*, Charles Coleman *(butler)*, William H. Tooker *(judge)*.

Comedy. Freddie, a rich young idler, meets Julia Harrington, a wealthy social service worker who runs a haven for reformed criminals. By telling her he is a hardened criminal, he is allowed to stay at the mission. At a charity ball given by his sister in honor of his poor and homeless colleagues, Freddie discovers that some of the men are stealing jewelry from the mission girl's friends. He reveals his true identity, rounds up the thieves, recovers the jewelry, and wins the girl. *Social workers. Idlers. Thieves. Missions. Reformatories.*

GOOD NEWS F2.2190

Metro-Goldwyn-Mayer Pictures. 23 Aug **1930** [c25 Aug 1930; LP1506]. Sd (Movietone); b&w. 35mm. 11 reels, 8,100 ft.

Dir Nick Grinde. *Stage Dir* Edgar J. MacGregor. *Screenplay* Frances Marion. *Dial* Joe Farnham. *Photog* Percy Hilburn. *Art Dir* Cedric Gibbons. *Film Ed* William Le Vanway. *Songs: "He's a Lady's Man," "The Best Things in Life Are Free," "Varsity Drag," "Good News," "Tait Song" "Students Are We"* Buddy De Sylva, Lew Brown, Ray Henderson. *Songs: "If You're Not Kissing Me," "Football"* Arthur Freed, Nacio Herb Brown. *Song: "I Feel Pessimistic"* J. Russell Robinson, George Waggner. *Song: "I'd Like To Make You Happy"* Reggie Montgomery. *Interpolations* Nacio Herb Brown, Arthur Freed, Felix Feist, Jr., Reggie Montgomery. *Dance Dir* Sammy Lee. *Rec Engr* Russell Franks, Douglas Shearer. *Wardrobe* David Cox.

Cast: Mary Lawlor *(Connie)*, Stanley Smith *(Tom)*, Bessie Love *(Babe)*, Cliff Edwards *(Kearney)*, Gus Shy *(Bobby)*, Lola Lane *(Pat)*, Thomas Jackson *(coach)*, Delmer Daves *(Beef)*, Billy Taft *(freshman)*, Frank McGlynn *(Professor Kenyon)*, Dorothy McNulty *(Flo)*, Helyn Virgil, Vera Marsh *(girls)*, Abe Lyman and His Band.

Musical comedy. Source: Laurence Schwab, Lew Brown, Frank Mandel, and B. G. De Sylva, *Good News* (New York opening: 6 Sep 1927). Among the students at Tait College are football star Tom Marlowe, whose neglect of studies threatens the chances of the school team; Bobby, a wise-cracking freshman, who makes a play for the school vamp, Babe, and wins her; and Connie, who falls for Tom. Although they all prefer the Varsity Drag to studying, Tom is finally reinstated with the help of Professor Kenyon. He wins the climactic game as well as the love of Connie. *Professors. Football. College life. Courtship.*

THE GOOD PROVIDER F2.2191

Cosmopolitan Productions. *Dist* Paramount Pictures. ca2 Apr **1922** [New York premiere; released 30 Apr; c19 Apr 1922; LP17819]. Si; b&w. 35mm. 8 reels, 7,753 ft.

Dir Frank Borzage. *Scen* John Lynch. *Photog* Chester Lyons.

Cast: Vera Gordon *(Becky Binswanger)*, Dore Davidson *(Julius Binswanger)*, Miriam Battista *(Pearl Binswanger)*, Vivienne Osborne *(Pearl Binswanger)*, William (Buster) Collier, Jr. *(Izzy Binswanger)*, John Roche *(Max Teitlebaum)*, Ora Jones *(Mrs. Teitlebaum)*, Edward Phillips *(Broadway sport)*, Muriel Martin *(flapper)*, James Devine *(Mr. Boggs)*, Blanche Craig *(Mrs. Boggs)*, Margaret Severn *(specialty dancer)*.

Society melodrama. Source: Fannie Hurst, "The Good Provider," in *Saturday Evening Post* (187:12, 15 Aug 1914). Working as a peddler in a small American town, Julius Binswanger, a poor Jewish immigrant, becomes prosperous; 15 years later, great changes have transformed the community, and Binswanger finds difficulty in competing with the city trade. Since his daughter, Pearl, is in love with Max Teitlebaum, a wealthy New Yorker, and because his children chafe at smalltown life, Binswanger, with the help of their mother, is persuaded to move to New York. Fast life at the Hotel Wellington, with exorbitant prices, appals Julius; yet, he rejects his son Izzy's commericial ideas. Business troubles multiply, and when Izzy requests a loan to take over the business with Max, Julius passionately announces his bankruptcy and plans to take an overdose of sleeping powder. Max, however, explains to Pearl that he will ask no dowry from her and wishes to form a partnership with her father. Becky announces the good news to Julius, Max and Pearl are happily united, and the family returns home. *Immigrants. Jews. Smalltown life. Ghettos. Bankruptcy. New York City.*

GOOD TIME CHARLEY F2.2192

Warner Brothers Pictures. 5 Nov **1927** [c5 Nov 1927; LP24638]. Si; b&w. 35mm. 7 reels, 6,302 ft.

Dir Michael Curtiz. *Scen* Ilona Fulop. *Titl* Jack Jarmuth. *Adapt* Anthony Coldewey, Owen Francis. *Story* Darryl Francis Zanuck. *Camera* Barney McGill.

Cast: Helene Costello *(Rosita Keene)*, Warner Oland *(Good Time Charley [Charles Edward Keene])*, Clyde Cook *(Bill Collins)*, Montagu Love *(John Hartwell)*, Hugh Allan *(John Hartwell, Jr.)*, Julanne Johnston *(Elaine Keene)*.

Melodrama. Song-and-dance man Charles Edward Keene (Good Time Charley) is bereft when his wife, Elaine, dies as a result of a fall incurred trying to evade the advances of Hartwell, her manager. Years later, his daughter, Rosita, becomes an overnight sensation as a result of her cafe act under Hartwell's management, and Charley is given a bit part in the show at her request. Hartwell, Jr., asks his father's permission to marry

Rosita; and when refused, the couple elope, causing Hartwell to dismiss Charley, who is losing his sight and cannot afford eye surgery. Bill Collins, the prop man, mortgages his interest in a theater to get the money for Charley; and disappointed when Charley gives it to the newlyweds, Bill tells him who is responsible for his wife's death. In a rage, Charley shoots at Hartwell's reflection, thinking he has killed him. Rosita is abandoned by Jack, who loses confidence in her, and Charley and Bill are forced to live in an actor's home; but on Christmas Eve, Rosita visits the home with a troupe and is reunited with her father. *Song-and-dance men. Actors. Prop men. Murder. Fatherhood. Revenge. Blindness. Christmas. New York City—Broadway.*

GOOD WOMEN **F2.2193**

Robertson-Cole Pictures. 3 Apr **1921** [c3 Apr 1921; LP16465]. Si; b&w. 35mm. 6-7 reels, 6,300 ft.

Dir Louis J. Gasnier. *Story-Scen* C. Gardner Sullivan. *Photog* Arthur Edeson.

Cast: Rosemary Theby *(Katherine Brinkley)*, Hamilton Revelle *(Nicolai Brouevitch)*, Irene Blackwell *(Inna Brouevitch)*, Earl Schenck *(John Wilmot)*, William P. Carleton *(Sir Richard Egglethorpe)*, Arthur Stuart Hull *(Franklin Shelby)*, Rhea Mitchell *(Natalie Shelby)*, Eugenie Besserer *(Mrs. Emmeline Shelby)*.

Society melodrama. Katherine Brinkley, a rich young woman who delights in challenging conventions, elopes with a married young musician, Nicolai Brouevitch, but when he deserts her she is cast aside by society. Wandering off to Italy, she meets Franklin Shelby, a young American also married, with whom she falls in love. When Shelby and Katherine encounter Brouevitch and his wife, the latter, failing to establish a satisfactory relationship, reveals Katherine's past to Shelby's wife. Shelby defends Katherine, and his mother and wife finally realize that she is a "good woman" when she sends Shelby back to his wife. *Musicians. Infidelity. Good and evil. Social conformity. Italy.*

THE GOOD-BAD WIFE **F2.2194**

Vera McCord Productions. *Dist* Federated Film Exchanges of America. Feb **1921** [c7 Jun 1920; LP15224]. Si; b&w. 35mm. 5 reels, 5,000 ft. [Copyrighted and trade-shown in 6 reels.]

Dir Vera McCord. *Scen* Paul Price. *Photog* Abe Fried.

Cast: Sidney Mason *(William Carter)*, Dorothy Green *(Fanchon La Fare)*, Moe Lee *(Toy To)*, Leslie Stowe *(Johnson Carter)*, Mathilde Brundage *(Mrs. Carter)*, Albert Hackett *(Leigh Carter)*, Beatrice Jordan *(Emily)*, Pauline Dempsey *(Mirandy)*, Wesley Jenkins *(Scipio)*, J. Thornton Baston *(Daniel Carter)*, Erville Alderson *(Colonel Denbigh)*, John Ardizoni *(Aristide Corwin)*.

Society melodrama. Source: Mary Imlay Taylor, *The Wild Fawn* (New York, 1920). William Carter, the eldest son of an aristocratic southern family, marries famed Parisian dancer Fanchon La Fare without his family's consent. Mrs. Carter's attitude annoys Fanchon, and she decides to seek revenge: she smokes cigarettes before the family; performs a dance at a church entertainment in a scanty costume; and flirts with Carter's younger brother, Leigh. Fanchon's ex-husband, Corwin, shows up; he insults her, and Leigh kills him. At the trial, Fanchon's testimony frees Leigh, and the couple are eventually reunited. *Aristocrats. Marriage. Social conformity. Dancers. Trials. United States—South.*

Note: Apparently this film was originally to have been released by Film Booking Offices in 1920, but distribution rights were sold to the Walgreene Film Corp. caOct-Nov 1920; the latter, in turn, assigned distribution rights to the Federated Film Exchanges of America, which released it in Feb 1921. Its New York premiere was probably ca14 Jan 1921.

GOOD-BY GIRLS! **F2.2195**

Fox Film Corp. 11 Mar **1923** [c11 Mar 1923; LP19051]. Si; b&w. 35mm. 5 reels, 4,746 ft.

Pres by William Fox. *Dir* Jerome Storm. *Scen* Joseph Franklin Poland. *Photog* Joe August.

Cast: William Russell *(Vance McPhee)*, Carmel Myers *(Florence Brown)*, Tom Wilson *(Jordan)*, Kate Price *(Sarah)*, Robert Klein *(Batista)*.

Mystery comedy. Source: George Foxhall, "McPhee's Sensational Rest," in *Argosy Magazine* (85:529–592, Jul 1917). Author Vance McPhee goes for a rest to his country home, where he finds a mysterious woman, Florence Brown, pursued by a gang of men. Florence asks his protection without giving a reason. McPhee fights off the assailants and finds that they are seeking a box containing valuable patents belonging to Florence's father. Having fallen in love with Florence, McPhee follows his doctor's advice and marries her. *Authors. Gangs. Filial relations. Documentation.*

THE GOOD-BYE KISS **F2.2196**

Mack Sennett Productions. *Dist* First National Pictures. 8 Jul **1928** [c6 Jun 1928; LP25339]. Mus score & sd eff (Western Electric); b&w. 35mm. 8 reels, 7,300-7,989 ft. [Also si; 9 reels, 8,030 ft.]

Dir Mack Sennett. *Scen* Jefferson Moffitt, Mack Sennett. *Titl* Carl Harbaugh. *Story* Jefferson Moffitt, Phil Whitman, Carl Harbaugh. *Photog* John Boyle. *Film Ed* William Hornbeck.

Cast: Johnny Burke *(Johnny)*, Sally Eilers *(Sally)*, Matty Kemp *(Bill Williams)*, Wheeler Oakman *(Sergeant Hoffman)*, Irving Bacon *(Colonel von Stein)*, Lionel Belmore *(The General)*, Alma Bennett *("Toots")*, Carmelita Geraghty *(Mademoiselle Nannette)*, Eugene Pallette *(The Captain)*, Jean Laverty *(Mademoiselle Jeanne)*, Andy Clyde *(The Grandfather)*.

War comedy. Sally, Bill's fiancée, stows away on his ship to Europe when he is drafted into the A. E. F. Sympathetic Salvation Army workers enlist Sally when she is discovered, and she accompanies Bill's unit when they go to the front. Bill finds he is a coward when faced with combat duty, but Sally shames him into becoming a hero during an air raid on Paris. He ferrets out a German spy and saves his pals from being destroyed by the enemy. *Stowaways. Spies. Cowardice. World War I. Paris. Salvation Army. American Expeditionary Force. Aerial bombardment.*

THE GOOSE HANGS HIGH **F2.2197**

Famous Players–Lasky. *Dist* Paramount Pictures. 30 Mar **1925** [c3 Apr 1925; LP21319]. Si; b&w. 35mm. 6 reels, 6,186 ft.

Pres by Adolph Zukor, Jesse L. Lasky. *Dir* James Cruze. *Scen* Walter Woods, Anthony Coldewey. *Photog* Karl Brown.

Cast: Constance Bennett *(Lois Ingals)*, Myrtle Stedman *(Eunice Ingals)*, George Irving *(Bernard Ingals)*, Esther Ralston *(Dagmar Carroll)*, William R. Otis, Jr. *(Hugh Ingals)*, Edward Peil, Jr. *(Bradley Ingals)*, Gertrude Claire *(Granny)*, James A. Marcus *(Elliott Kimberly)*, Anne Schaefer *(Rhoda)*, Z. Wall Covington *(Noel Derby)*, Cecille Evans *(Mazie)*.

Comedy-drama. Source: Lewis Beach, *The Goose Hangs High, a Play in Three Acts* (Boston, 1924). Bernard Ingals, who holds a municipal position, has almost bankrupted himself sending his three children to college. The youngsters all arrive home for Christmas Eve, and their parents do their utmost to give them a good time, but the thoughtless and selfish children make other plans and go to a party, leaving their parents to a lonely dinner. A member of the common council arrives at the Ingals home and orders Bernard to reinstate a municipal employee who has been dismissed; Bernard refuses and submits his resignation. The grandmother, a strong-minded old lady, then sets out to put things right: she stakes Bernard to his life-long dream, a greenhouse of his own, and then lectures the children on their thoughtless and profligate ways. The children reform and get jobs, and the goose hangs high at last. *Students. Education. Finance—Personal. Family life. Government—Local. Christmas.*

THE GOOSE WOMAN (Universal-Jewel) **F2.2198**

Universal Pictures. 27 Dec **1925** [c18 Jul 1925; LP21557]. Si; b&w. 35mm. 8 reels, 7,500 ft.

Pres by Carl Laemmle. *Dir* Clarence Brown. *Scen* Melville Brown. *Titl* Dwinelle Benthall. *Photog* Milton Moore. *Art Dir* E. E. Sheeley, William R. Schmidt. *Film Ed* Ray Curtiss. *Asst Dir* Charles Dorian.

Cast: Louise Dresser *(Mary Holmes/Marie de Nardi)*, Jack Pickford *(Gerald Holmes)*, Constance Bennett *(Hazel Woods)*, James O. Barrows, Spottiswoode Aitken *(Jacob Riggs [see note])*, George Cooper *(reporter)*, Gustav von Seyffertitz *(Mr. Vogel)*, George Nichols *(Detective Lopez)*, Marc MacDermott *(Amos Ethridge)*.

Drama. Source: Rex Beach, "The Goose Woman," in *The Goose Woman, and Other Stories* (New York & London, 1925). Marie de Nardi, an internationally known opera singer, gives birth to an illegitimate son and, as a consequence, loses her following at the height of her artistic and financial success. Bitter at the neglect of those who once flattered her, she turns to drink and eventually comes to live in seclusion in a tumbledown shack, tending geese for her livelihood. Living under the name of Mary Holmes, she brings up her son, Gerald, with neither love nor affection, blaming him for her decline. Gerald becomes engaged to Hazel Woods, a local actress, and, out of spite, Mary tells him of his illegitimacy. Amos Ethridge, a millionaire who backs the local stock company, is murdered, and Mary sees the chance to be again on the front pages of the world's newspapers. She fabricates a story concerning the murder, with herself as the key witness, only to discover that by chance the circumstances of her story implicate her son. Her long-suppressed love for her son finally bursts forth, and she retracts her testimony. The doorman at the theater confesses that he shot Amos, who had seduced a number of young girls, in order to protect Hazel from his vile advances. *Singers. Actors. Millionaires. Doorkeepers. Opera. Theater. Illegitimacy. Motherhood. Murder. Alcoholism. Geese.*

Note: Spottiswoode Aitken and James O. Barrows are variously credited with the role of Jacob Riggs.

THE GORILLA **F2.2199**

First National Pictures. 13 Nov **1927** [c10 May 1929; LP441]. Si; b&w. 35mm. 8 reels.

Pres by Asher-Small-Rogers. *Dir* Alfred Santell. *Scen* Al Cohn, Henry McCarty. *Titl* Sidney Lazarus, Al Boasberg. *Adapt* James T. O'Donohoe. *Photog* Arthur Edeson. *Rec Engr* Russell S. Hoff. *Prod Mgr* Edward Small.

Cast: Charlie Murray *(Garrity)*, Fred Kelsey *(Mulligan)*, Alice Day *(Alice Townsend)*, Tully Marshall *(William Townsend)*, Claude Gillingwater *(Cyrus Townsend)*, Walter Pidgeon *(Stevens)*, Gaston Glass *(Marsden)*, Brooks Benedict *(The Reporter)*, Aggie Herring *(The Cook)*, Syd Crossley *(The Butler)*, John Gough *(Sailor)*.

Mystery melodrama. Source: Ralph Spence, *The Gorilla, a Mystery Comedy in Three Acts* (New York, 1950). Cyrus Townsend, father of Alice, is mysteriously slain in his home and suspicion centers on Arthur Marsden, his secretary and Alice's sweetheart. The circumstances of the murder are similar to those of numerous unsolved killings believed to have been perpetrated by a gorilla. As Alice, Marsden, and Stevens (a friend of Cyrus) are gathered in the library, a note warns them to leave the house before midnight. Later, they are terrified by the unexpected arrival of Mulligan and Garrity, two callous detectives sent to solve the mystery; subsequently, persons suddenly vanish, strange noises are heard, and lights go off and on. While searching for each other, the detectives discover a gorilla on the premises; a sailor confesses to being the gorilla; but Marsden, who reveals himself also to be a detective, leads them to Stevens, the true culprit. *Secretaries. Detectives. Sailors. Murder. Disguise. Apes.*

Note: Remade in 1930 under the same title, q. v.

THE GORILLA **F2.2200**

First National Pictures. 2 Nov **1930** [c16 Nov 1930; LP1730]. Sd (Vitaphone); b&w. 35mm. 7 reels.

Dir Bryan Foy. *Scen-Dial* Ralph Spence. *Adapt* Harrison Orkow, Herman Ruby. *Photog* Sid Hickox. *Film Ed* George Amy.

Cast: Joe Frisco *(Garrity)*, Harry Gribbon *(Mulligan)*, Walter Pidgeon *(Arthur Marsden)*, Lila Lee *(Alice Denby)*, Purnell Pratt *(The Stranger)*, Edwin Maxwell *(Cyrus Stevens)*, Roscoe Karns *(Simmons)*, William H. Philbrick *(Jeff)*, Landers Stevens *(inspector)*.

Mystery melodrama. A remake of the 1927 silent version, q. v. *Secretaries. Detectives. Sailors. Disguise. Murder. Apes.*

THE GORILLA HUNT **F2.2201**

Ben Burbridge. *Dist* Film Booking Offices of America. 7 Oct **1926** [c7 Nov 1926; MP3669]. Si; b&w. 35mm. 5 reels, 4,362 ft.

Documentary. Ben Burbridge leads an expedition into Africa in search of six gorillas to bring back alive to captivity. On the way to the interior, the Burbridge party meets with a tribe of pygmies, whose friendship is purchased by means of a gift of salt and safety pins. Other events of interest include: the shooting of an elephant and three lions, the strange contortions of a python, the fording of a stream thick with crocodiles, and the eventual capture of the baby gorillas. *Pygmies. Big game. Africa. Crocodiles. Lions. Elephants. Snakes. Apes.*

Note: Known also as *Burbridge's African Gorilla Hunt.*

GOSSIP **F2.2202**

Universal Pictures. 12 Mar **1923** [c20 Feb 1923; LP18710]. Si; b&w. 35mm. 5 reels, 4,488 ft.

Dir King Baggot. *Scen* Hugh Hoffman. *Photog* Victor Milner.

Cast: Gladys Walton *(Caroline Weatherbee)*, Ramsey Wallace *(Hiram Ward)*, Albert Prisco *(John Magoo)*, Freeman Wood *(Robert Williamson)*, Carol Halloway *(Mrs. Boyne)*.

Drama. Source: Edith Barnard Delano, "Gossip" (publication undetermined). Hiram Ward, cynical businessman, is having trouble with his employees when Caroline Weatherbee arrives and claims to be a distant relative. Her natural charm brings about a peaceful settlement of a strike, but she returns to her southern home for fear of bringing scandal to Hiram. He follows and marries her. *Strikes. Business management. Gossip.*

THE GOVERNOR'S LADY **F2.2203**

Fox Film Corp. 28 Oct **1923** [c28 Dec 1923; LP19776]. Si; b&w. 35mm. 8 reels, 7,669 ft.

Pres by William Fox. *Dir* Harry Millarde. *Scen* Anthony Paul Kelly.

Cast: Robert T. Haines *(Daniel Slade)*, Jane Grey *(Mrs. Slade)*, Ann Luther *(Katherine Strickland)*, Frazer Coulter *(George Strickland)*, Leslie Austen *(Robert Hayes)*.

Domestic drama. Source: Alice Bradley, *The Governor's Lady* (1915). Daniel Slade, a miner, becomes wealthy from his investments and acquires enough social position to run for political office. His wife, Mary, unable to adjust to a life of wealth and leisure, embarrasses him in front of his friends. He plans to get a divorce; later, he decides he really loves her. *Miners. State governors. Marriage. Wealth. Politics. Public office. Divorce.*

GOW, THE HEAD HUNTER **F2.2204**

Edward A. Salisbury. 20 Oct **1928** [New York State license]. Si; b&w. 35mm. 7 reels, 6,790 ft.

Photog Merian C. Cooper, Ernest B. Schoedsack.

Travelog. "There is a slight plot toward the conclusion of the picture, where an effort has been made to show the hunters going to war, conquering and then returning with new skulls to add to the shrines at home. For the most part, however, 'Gow' contents itself with showing tribal custom ... with brief hints of what the natives might do were they aroused. By way of contrast the picture starts in Fiji, where Captain Salisbury portrays the effects of seventy-five years' civilization on a people once cannibal. Then it jumps to the Western Solomon Islands, the New Hebrides and the Eastern Solomons." (*New York Times*, 25 Dec 1928, p31.) *Headhunters. Cannibals. Fiji Islands. New Hebrides. Solomon Islands.*

GRAFT *see* **FREEDOM OF THE PRESS**

THE GRAIL **F2.2205**

Fox Film Corp. 14 Oct **1923** [c2 Aug 1923; LP19319]. Si; b&w. 35mm. 5 reels, 4,617 ft.

Pres by William Fox. *Dir* Colin Campbell. *Scen* Charles Kenyon. *Story* George Scarborough. *Photog* Joseph Brotherton.

Cast: Dustin Farnum *(Chic Shelby)*, Peggy Shaw *(Dora Bledsoe)*, Carl Stockdale *(Reverend Bledsoe)*, Frances Raymond *(Mrs. Bledsoe)*, James Gordon *(James Trammel)*, Jack Rollins *(John Trammel)*, Frances Hatton *(Mrs. Trammel)*, Alma Bennett *(Susie Trammel)*, Leon Barry *(Sam Hervey)*.

Western melodrama. Source: George Scarborough, "The Grail" (unpublished and uncopyrighted play). Texas Ranger Chic Shelby is sent to capture James Trammel and his son, John—two outlaws hiding in the mountains who are victims of a cattle war. Shelby tricks John, who has killed a cattleman, into believing he is an itinerant preacher by delivering a sermon on eternal love. John comes forward to be arrested, obviously moved by Shelby's sermon. Meanwhile, Sam Hervey betrays John's sister, Susie. Fearing her father's wrath, Hervey seeks out James Trammel, shoots him, and blames the crime on Shelby. Shelby clears himself by capturing Hervey, John is acquitted, and Susie ends her own life by drowning. *Texas Rangers. Clergymen. Filial relations. Brother-sister relationship. Murder. Religion. Revivalism. Suicide.*

THE GRAIN OF DUST **F2.2206**

Tiffany-Stahl Productions. 10 Jul **1928** [c25 Aug 1928; LP25569]. Si; b&w. 35mm. 7 reels, 6,126 ft.

Dir George Archainbaud. *Cont* Frances Hyland. *Titl* Paul Perez. *Adapt* L. G. Rigby. *Photog* Ernest Miller. *Art Dir* Hervey Libbert. *Set Dressings* George Sawley. *Film Ed* Robert Kern.

Cast: Ricardo Cortez *(Fred Norman)*, Claire Windsor *(Josephine Burroughs)*, Alma Bennett *(Dorothea Hallowell)*, Richard Tucker *(George)*, John St. Polis *(Mr. Burroughs)*, Otto Hoffman *(chief clerk)*.

Melodrama. Source: David Graham Phillips, *The Grain of Dust* (New York, 1911). "A man [Fred Norman] throws away all his prospects of happiness and success when he becomes madly infatuated with a typist [Dorothea Hallowell]. He marries her, neglects his business. Unhappy, his best friend a suicide because of him, the man realizes he's a fool. When his wife leaves him, he returns repentant to the woman who always loved him." (*Motion Picture News Booking Guide*, [14]:123, 1929.) *Businessmen. Typists. Marriage. Infidelity. Suicide.*

THE GRAND DUCHESS AND THE WAITER **F2.2207**

Famous Players–Lasky. *Dist* Paramount Pictures. 8 Feb **1926** [c11 Feb 1926; LP22392]. Si; b&w. 35mm. 7 reels, 6,314 ft.

Pres by Adolph Zukor, Jesse L. Lasky. *Dir* Malcolm St. Clair. *Scen* Pierre Collings. *Adapt* John Lynch. *Camera* Lee Garmes.

Cast: Adolphe Menjou *(Albert Durant)*, Florence Vidor *(Grand Duchess Zenia)*, Lawrence Grant *(Grand Duke Peter)*, André Beranger *(Grand Duke Paul)*, Dot Farley *(Prascovia)*, Barbara Pierce *(Henriette)*, Brandon Hurst *(Matard)*, William Courtright *(Blake)*.

Romantic comedy. Source: Alfred Savoir, *La Grande-duchesse et le garçon d'etage; comédie en trois actes* (Paris, 1924). Albert Durant, a millionaire turfman, becomes infatuated with the Grand Duchess Zenia, a Russian refugee in Paris. Unable to make her acquaintance, he disguises himself as a waiter. His presumptuous manner plus his ineptness so annoy Zenia that she has him hired for her personal staff to do only menial work. Despite herself, she falls in love with him. When she learns his true identity she flees from Paris. Months later, Albert finds her, wealth gone, running a humble roadside inn. Albert offers to take her away from all this life, and of course she happily complies. *Turfmen. Millionaires. Nobility. Russians. Waiters. Disguise. Paris.*

GRAND LARCENY **F2.2208**

Goldwyn Pictures. Jan **1922** [c24 Jan 1922; LP17495]. Si; b&w. 35mm. 6 reels, 5,227 ft.

Dir Wallace Worsley. *Scen* Bess Meredyth, Charles Kenyon. *Story* Albert Payson Terhune. *Photog* Norbert Brodin.

Cast: Claire Windsor *(Kathleen Vaughn)*, Elliott Dexter *(John Annixter)*, Richard Tucker *(Franklin)*, Tom Gallery *(Thad)*, Roy Atwell *(Harkness Boyd)*, John Cossar *(Emerson)*, Lowell Sherman *(Barry Clive)*.

Society melodrama. Source: Albert Payson Terhune, "Grand Larceny," in *Cosmopolitan* (69:37, Dec 1920). John Annixter, a northern corporation lawyer with a stern sense of justice, marries Kathleen, a southern belle and a habitual coquette. Immersed in his work, Annixter allows his wife to pursue a social life under the escort of his friends. Barry Clive, an architect, becomes infatuated with her and mistakes her flirting for genuine passion; Annixter returns home unexpectedly, witnesses Clive embracing his wife, and without hearing any explanation obtains a divorce from Kathleen, declaring her actions to be "grand larceny." She marries Clive but is constantly unhappy because of his jealousy. At a concert, she encounters her first husband, and when the two men develop an argument, Kathleen declares that she will have neither of them, thus asserting her independence. *Lawyers. Flirts. Architects. Southerners. Marriage. Women's rights. Divorce. Larceny.*

THE GRAND PARADE **F2.2209**

Pathé Exchange. 2 Feb **1930** [c11 Mar 1930; LP1143]. Sd (Photophone); b&w. 35mm. 8 reels, 7,450 ft.

Prod-Writ Edmund Goulding. *Dir* Fred Newmeyer. *Stgd by* Frank Reicher. *Photog* David Abel. *Art Dir* Edward Jewell. *Set Dsgn* Ted Dickson. *Songs: "Moanin' for You," "Molly"* Dan Dougherty, Edmund Goulding. *Musical Numbers* Richard Boleslavsky. *Rec Engr* George Ellis, Cliff Stein. *Prod Mgr* Gordon Cooper. *Cost Dsgn* Gwen Wakeling. *Prop Man* Larry Haddock.

Cast: Helen Twelvetrees *(Molly)*, Fred Scott *(Kelly)*, Richard Carle *(Rand)*, Marie Astaire *(Polly)*, Russell Powell *(Calamity Johnson)*, Bud Jamieson *(Honey Sullivan)*, Jimmie Adams *(Jones)*, Lillian Leighton *(Madam Stitch)*, Spec O'Donnell *(Call Boy)*, Sam Blum *(Sam)*, Tom Malone *(Dougherty)*, Jimmy Aubrey *(The Drunk)*.

Romantic drama. Kelly, a minstrel singer known as "Come-back" because of his weakness for liquor, degenerates because of his unhappiness with Polly Malone, a burlesque actress, and finds refuge in a cheap hotel where he is cared for by Molly, a slavey. Rand, producer of the minstrel show to which Kelly was attached, induces him to return to his work; and he is a success when he changes his song hit, "Polly," to "Molly." When Polly returns, Kelly introduces Molly as his wife, and she later consents to marry him. Molly joins the show and leads the grand parade at every performance. But in Detroit, Kelly weakens and goes on a spree with Polly. Rejected, Molly, who is pregnant, contemplates suicide; but realizing the truth, Kelly promises to go straight, and she beseeches God to help them both in their struggle. *Drudges. Minstrel shows. Burlesque. Alcoholism. Courtship. Marriage. Pregnancy. Religion. Detroit.*

LA GRANDE MARE **F2.2210**

Paramount-Publix Corp. ca16 Aug **1930** [New York showing]. Sd (Movietone); b&w. 35mm. 8 reels.

Prod Monta Bell. *Dir* Hobart Henley, Jacques Bataille-Henri. *Adtl Dial* Jacques Bataille-Henri. *Film Ed* Barney Rogan.

Cast: Maurice Chevalier *(Pierre Mirande)*, Claudette Colbert *(Barbara Billings)*, Henry Mortimer *(Mr. Billings)*, Maude Allen *(Mrs. Billings)*, Andrée Corday *(Toinette)*, William Williams *(Ronnie)*, Nat Pendleton *(Pat O'Day)*, Loraine Jaillet *(Jennie)*.

Comedy-drama. Source: George Middleton and A. E. Thomas, *The Big Pond* (New York opening: 21 Aug 1928). French-language version of *The Big Pond*, q. v. *Guides. Fortune hunters. Landladies. French. Tourists. Courtship. Business management. Chewing gum. Boardinghouses. Venice.*

GRANDMA'S BOY **F2.2211**

Hal Roach Studios. *Dist* Associated Exhibitors. ca20 May **1922** [Los Angeles premiere; released 3 Sep; c27 Apr 1922; LU17796]. Si; b&w. 35mm. 5 reels, 4,841 ft.

Pres by Hal Roach. *Dir* Fred Newmeyer. *Scen* Thomas J. Crizer. *Titl* H. M. Walker. *Story* Sam Taylor, Jean Havez, Hal Roach. *Photog* Walter Lundin.

Cast: Harold Lloyd *(The Boy)*, Mildred Davis *(The Girl)*, Anna Townsend *(The Grandmother)*, Charles Stevenson *(The Bully)*, Noah Young *(The Sheriff)*, Dick Sutherland *(The Rolling Stone)*.

Comedy. In the small country town of Blossom Bend lives Grandma's Boy, a meek youth of 19, who is in love but is frightened by his rival, The Bully. They are both paying a visit to The Girl's house when news is received that the local jewelry shop has been robbed. The citizens organize to hunt down the bandit, and The Boy is made a member of the posse. The Boy overcomes his cowardice when his grandmother tells him about his grandfather's fighting prowess and gives him an umbrella handle, a charm guaranteed to make a lion-hearted hero of its possessor. As a result, he captures the bandit (The Rolling Stone), gives The Bully a thrashing, and then induces The Girl to marry him. *Grandmothers. Bandits. Posses. Manhood. Superstition. Smalltown life.*

GRASS; A NATION'S BATTLE FOR LIFE **F2.2212**

Famous Players–Lasky. *Dist* Paramount Pictures. 30 Mar **1925** [New York premiere; c21 Jun 1926; MP3484]. Si; b&w. 35mm. 7 reels.

Pres by Adolph Zukor, Jesse L. Lasky. *Prod-Dir* Merian Cooper, Ernest B. Schoedsack, Marguerite Harrison. *Photog* Ernest B. Schoedsack, Merian Cooper. *Mus Arr* Hugo Riesenfeld.

Personages: Merian Cooper, Ernest B. Schoedsack, Marguerite Harrison, Haidar Khan *(chief of Bakhityari tribe)*, Lufta *(son of Haidar Khan)*.

Documentary. Marguerite Harrison, Merian Cooper, and Ernest B. Schoedsack travel through Asia Minor to reach a tribe of nomads in Iran known as the Bakhityari. They follow the tribesmen on their 48-day trek across deserts, rivers, and mountains to reach summer pasture for their flocks. The hardships and conquests of the 50,000 tribesmen are shown: fording the treacherous waters of the Karun River by floating on rafts buoyed by inflated goatskins; ascending an almost perpendicular mountain only to be confronted by yet another, pathless and covered with deep snow; and finally descending to their goal—a fertile and grassy valley. *Bakhityari. Nomads. Deserts. Mountain climbing. Iraq. Iran. Asia Minor. Karun River.*

Note: Also known as *Grass; The Epic of a Lost Tribe.*

GRASS; THE EPIC OF A LOST TRIBE *see* **GRASS; A NATION'S BATTLE FOR LIFE**

GRAUSTARK **F2.2213**

Joseph M. Schenck Productions. *Dist* First National Pictures. 30 Aug **1925** [c31 Aug 1925; LP21782]. Si; b&w. 35mm. 7 reels, 5,900 ft.

Pres by Joseph M. Schenck. *Dir* Dimitri Buchowetzki. *Adapt* Frances Marion. *Photog* Tony Gaudio.

Cast: Norma Talmadge *(Princess Yetive)*, Eugene O'Brien *(Grenfall Lorry)*, Marc MacDermott *(Prince Gabriel)*, Roy D'Arcy *(Dangloss)*, Albert Gran *(Count Halfont)*, Lillian Lawrence *(Countess Halfont)*, Michael Vavitch *(Captain Quinnox)*, Frank Currier *(King)*, Winter Hall *(Ambassador)*, Wanda Hawley *(Dagmar)*.

Romantic drama. Source: George Barr McCutcheon, *Graustark, The Story of a Love Behind a Throne* (Chicago, 1901). Traveling by train through the West, Grenfall Lorry meets a beautiful girl and falls hopelessly in love with her. The girl, who, unknown to Grenfall, is the Princess Yetive, is called home to the Kingdom of Graustark against her will in order to marry Gabriel, the prince of a neighboring country. Grenfall follows her, and Gabriel orders one of his henchmen, Dangloss, to put him out of the way. The men fight, and Dangloss is wounded. Spiriting Dangloss out of the country, Gabriel has Grenfall tried for his "murder." Yetive frees him and sends him to the border, where he finds Dangloss. Returning with Dangloss just as the wedding ceremony begins, Grenfall discredits Gabriel, who leaves the country in disgrace. Yetive appeals to the populace and wins their approval to marry the American commoner. *Royalty. Murder. Trials. Weddings. Imaginary kingdoms.*

THE GRAY DAWN **F2.2214**

Benjamin B. Hampton Productions. *Dist* W. W. Hodkinson Corp. 5 Feb or 28 May **1922.** Si; b&w. 35mm. 6 reels, 5,600 ft.

Dir? (see note) Benjamin B. Hampton, Charles O. Rush, James Townsend, David Hampton, Eliot Howe, Jean Hersholt. *Scen* E. Richard Schayer, Marie Jenny Howe. *Photog* Gus Peterson, Friend Baker.

Cast: Carl Gantvoort *(Milton Keith)*, Claire Adams *(Nan Bennett)*, Robert McKim *(Ben Sansome)*, George Hackathorne *(Calhoun Bennett)*, Snitz Edwards *(Krafft)*, Stanton Heck *(Casey)*, Omar Whitehead *(Charles Cora)*, Claire McDowell *(Mrs. Bennett)*, Maude Wayne *(Mimi Morrell)*, J. Gunnis Davis *(Mr. Morrell)*, Zack Williams *(Sam)*, Grace Marvin *(Mammy)*, Charles Arling *(Ned Coleman)*, Harvey Clark *(King of William)*, Charles Thurston *(Marshal Richardson)*, Marc Robbins *(Chinaman)*, Charles B. Murphy *(bill collector)*.

Melodrama. Source: Stewart Edward White, *The Gray Dawn* (Garden City, New York, 1915). During a period of lawlessness (ca1856) in San Francisco, District Attorney Milton Keith is prevented by politician Ben Sansome from exerting any control. The murder of U. S. Marshal Richardson, after which Sansome prevents conviction of the murderer, rouses public sentiment against Keith; and vigilantes are organized. Further complications result from the murder of the editor of the newspaper, for which Cal Bennett, the brother of Keith's sweetheart, Nan, is sentenced to be hanged. In desperation Nan appeals to Sansome and is lured away on his boat; Krafft, who has threatened to expose Sansome, uses oriental torture to find the real culprit; and Keith and Cal rescue Nan. *Politicians. United States marshals. District attorneys. Vigilantes. Murder. Torture. Capital punishment. San Francisco.*

Note: Some sources credit Howe and Hersholt; others list the four other names. Also known as *The Grey Dawn.*

GREASED LIGHTNING **F2.2215**

Universal Pictures. 29 Jul **1928** [c20 Oct 1927; LP24561]. Si; b&w. 35mm. 5 reels, 4,600 ft.

Pres by Carl Laemmle. *Dir* Ray Taylor. *Story-Cont* William Lester. *Titl* Gardner Bradford. *Photog* Milton Bridenbecker. *Art Dir* David S. Garber. *Film Ed* Ben Pivar.

Cast: Ted Wells *(Johnny Parker)*, Betty Caldwell *(Diana Standish)*, Walter Shumway *(Dick Merrihew)*, Lon Poff *(Beauty Jones)*, George Dunning *(Mickey Murphy)*, Myrtis Crinley *(Annie Murphy)*, Victor Allen *(Jack Crane)*.

Western melodrama. Diana Standish, a city thoroughbred, falls heir to her grandfather's ranch. Johnny Parker, her foreman, is kept busy pursuing cattle rustlers working for Dick Merrihew, a crooked lawyer in love with Diana. When Johnny leaves for the mountains, Mickey, the ranch protégé, stays behind to protect Diana; refusing Merrihew's proposal because of her love for Johnny, Diana is saved by Mickey's clever thinking, but en route to Johnny's camp they are captured by the outlaws. Mickey escapes and warns Johnny of the danger; Johnny subdues Merrihew's men with the aid of his ranch hands and wins Diana. *Ranch foremen. Lawyers. Rustlers. Inheritance. Ranches.*

THE GREAT ADVENTURE **F2.2216**

Whitman Bennett Productions. *Dist* Associated First National Pictures. Jan **1921** [c6 Jan, 19 Feb; LP16003, LP16153]. Si; b&w. 35mm. 6 reels, 5,627 ft.

Pres by Whitman Bennett. *Dir* Kenneth Webb. *Scen* Dorothy Farnum. *Photog* Harry Stradling, T. L. Griffith.

Cast: Lionel Barrymore *(Priam Farll)*, Doris Rankin *(Alice Challice)*, Octavia Broske *(Lady Sophia Entwhistle)*, Thomas Braidon *(Henry Leek)*, Arthur Rankin *(Leek's son)*, Paul Kelly *(another Leek son)*, Maybeth Carr *(Dorothy, a blind child)*, Charles Land *(Charles Oxford)*, Jed Prouty *(Mr. Witt)*, E. J. Ratcliffe *(Lord Leonard Alcar)*, Ivo Dawson *(Duncan Farll)*, Katherine Stewart *(Mrs. Leek)*.

Romantic comedy. Source: Arnold Bennett, *Buried Alive; a Tale of These Days* (London, 1908). Arnold Bennett, *The Great Adventure, a Play of Fancy in Four Acts* (London, 1913). Hounded by publicity seekers, Priam Farll, the greatest painter of his day, finds the anonymity he seeks by assuming the identity of his deceased valet, Henry Leek. He is ejected from Westminster Abbey for creating a disturbance during his "own" elaborate funeral, and young widow Alice Challice nurses his consequent injuries. Priam marries Alice for her meager income and grows to love her, but he cannot escape fame when he again begins to paint and a dealer identifies his work. Priam finally accepts his fate—happily, with Alice at his side. *Painters. Valets. Recluses. Widows. Impersonation. Funerals. Westminster Abbey.*

THE GREAT ALONE **F2.2217**

West Coast Films. *Dist* American Releasing Corp. 21 May **1922.** Si; b&w. 35mm. 6 reels, 5,912 ft.

Pres by Isadore Bernstein. *Supv Dir* Isadore Bernstein. *Dir* Jacques Jaccard, James Colwell. *Story* Jacques Jaccard. *Photog* Frank B. Good. *Asst Dir* Justin H. McCloskey.

Cast: Monroe Salisbury *(Silent Duval)*, Laura Anson *(Nadine Picard)*, Walter Law *(Winston Sassoon)*, Maria Law *(Mary MacDonald)*, George Waggoner *(Bradley Carstairs)*, Richard Cummings *(MacDonald, the factor)*.

Northwest melodrama. While attending Stanford University, Silent Duval, a halfbreed Indian, is both a football star and the object of scorn by his fellow students—except Mary MacDonald. Duval leaves college in disgust and returns to his Northland home as a secret agent for MacDonald's business firm. Later, Duval learns that Mary has been lost in a violent snowstorm while searching for her father, and he defies death to repay her kindness by rescuing her and teaching her father's enemy, Winston Sassoon, a lesson in the law of the Yukon. Duval rewards the patience of Nadine Picard, also a halfbreed, with his love. *Halfcastes. Indians of North America. Racial prejudice. Football. Yukon. Stanford University. Storms.*

Note: Some snow exteriors filmed at Blairsden, Feather River, California.

THE GREAT AUSTRALIAN BUSH, ITS WONDERS AND MYSTERY **F2.2218**

c8 Aug, 26 Aug **1927** [MU4258]. Si; b&w. 35mm. 6 reels.

Story-Titl Edward Percy Bailey. *Photog* Edward Percy Bailey. *Film Ed* George Scott.

Personages: Edward Percy Bailey, Mrs. [Edward Percy] Bailey.

Travelog. Beginning scenes show the Australian bush country: vast areas of gum trees; giant bush fig trees; fields of orchids; unique vegetation, valley of ferns, vine-clad jungles and thickly wooded hills. Colonel and Mrs. Bailey board the Trans-Australian train and travel through the desert shooting pictures. A variety of bush animals are caught by the close-up lens: platypi, kangaroos (including wallabies), emus. The aborigines are shown constructing a spearhead, and when it is completed the art of throwing spears is displayed; this art is later applied during a kangaroo hunt and in battle. The natives' courtship dance is also shown. *Australian Bush. Hunting. Spears. Emus. Platypi. Kangaroos.*

THE GREAT DAY **F2.2219**

Famous Players–Lasky British Producers. *Dist* Paramount Pictures. 17 Apr **1921** [c17 Apr 1921; LP16409]. Si; b&w. 35mm. 5 reels.

Dir Hugh Ford. *Scen* Eve Unsell. *Photog* Hal Young.

Cast: Arthur Bourchier *(Sir John Borstwick)*, May Palfrey *(Lady Borstwick)*, Marjorie Hume *(Clara Borstwick)*, Bertram Burleigh *(Frank Beresford)*, Mrs. Hayden Coffin *(Mrs. Beresford)*, Percy Standing *(Paul Nikola)*, Meggie Albanesi *(Lillian Leeson)*, Geoffrey Kerr *(Dave Leeson)*, Lewis Dayton *(Lord Medway)*, Mrs. L. Thomas *(Lord Medway's mother)*, L. C. Carelli *(Semki)*.

Melodrama. Source: Louis Napoleon Parker and George Robert Sims, *The Great Day, a Play* (publication undetermined). Frank Beresford, a chemist at the Borstwick Steel Works who invents a carbonizing process that yields a fine grade of steel, meets the owner's daughter, Clara, and they are married, though her father refuses to give his consent. On their wedding day, Frank's wife, Lillian, whom he believes to have been lost, visits him and threatens blackmail. Summoned to Paris, he finds Leeson, Lillian's former husband, believed to have been lost in the Alps after the war; and when approached by a foreign agent, he refuses to sell him the carbonizing process. In consequence, he and Leeson are thrown into a sewer, but they escape. The experience restores Leeson's memory, Lillian is checkmated, and Clara and Frank are reunited. *Chemists. Foreign agents. Steel industry. Bigamy. Amnesia. Blackmail. Paris.*

THE GREAT DECEPTION **F2.2220**

Robert Kane Productions. *Dist* First National Pictures. 25 Jul **1926** [c27 Jul 1926; LP22984]. Si; b&w. 35mm. 6 reels, 5,855 ft. [Copyrighted as 7 reels.]

Pres by Robert Kane. *Dir* Howard Higgin. *Scen* Paul Bern. *Photog* Ernest Haller.

Cast: Ben Lyon *(Cyril Mansfield)*, Aileen Pringle *(Lois)*, Basil Rathbone *(Rizzio)*, Sam Hardy *(Handy)*, Charlotte Walker *(Mrs. Mansfield)*, Amelia Summerville *(Lady Jane)*, Hubert Wilke *(General Von Frankenhauser)*, Lucien Prival *(Von Markow)*, Lucius Henderson *(Burton)*, Mark Gonzales *(Maxwell)*.

Spy melodrama. Source: George Gibbs, *The Yellow Dove* (New York, 1915). Cyril Mansfield, a handsome young Englishman, is associated with the German Secret Service as a spy in England but is loyal to British intelligence, of which he is a member. He is loved by Lois, an American whose favor is sought by Rizzio, also a double agent, who suspects Cyril's disloyalty to Germany. With the intention of conveying false information to the Imperial German Government, Cyril, accompanied by his faithful mechanic, Handy, and by Lois, escapes to Germany, though Lois is herself abducted by Rizzio and brought to headquarters in a U-boat. Innocently, she betrays Cyril, and they are both sentenced to death. On a pretense of aiding Cyril, Rizzio urges Lois to accompany him on a diplomatic mission, but Cyril and Handy overcome their captors; and Lois and Cyril escape to England in his aircraft. *Spies. English. Germans. Submarines. Airplanes. London. Great Britain—Intelligence service. Germany—Intelligence service. World War I.*

THE GREAT DIAMOND MYSTERY **F2.2221**

Fox Film Corp. 5 Oct **1924** [c28 Sep 1924; LP20611]. Si; b&w. 35mm. 5 reels, 5,096 ft.

Pres by William Fox. *Dir* Denison Clift. *Scen* Thomas Dixon, Jr. *Story* Shannon Fife.

Cast: Shirley Mason *(Ruth Winton)*, Jackie Saunders *(Phyllis)*, Harry von Meter *(Murdock)*, John Cossar *(Graves)*, Philo McCullough *(Mallison)*, Hector V. Sarno *(Davis)*, William Collier, Jr. *(Perry Standish)*, Eugenia Gilbert *(Diana)*, Mary Mayo *(see note)*, Hardee Kirkland *(Peter Standish)*.

Mystery melodrama. Ruth Winton, author of *The Great Diamond Mystery*, tests its hypothesis—that a murderer will return to the scene of the crime—when her sweetheart, Perry Standish, is sentenced to death for the murder of his employer (Graves), a diamond merchant with underworld connections. Ruth rents Graves's house; rehires Davis, the butler; and notices that Mallison, Graves's partner, snoops around the house for some missing diamonds. In the climax, the butler is shot and makes a dying confession to Graves's murder; Perry is pardoned at the last minute. *Authors. Publishers. Butlers. Murder. Capital punishment. Diamonds.*

Note: *Variety* credits Mary Mayo in the part of Diana.

THE GREAT DIVIDE **F2.2222**

Metro-Goldwyn Pictures. 15 Feb **1925** [c2 Feb 1925; LP21083]. Si; b&w. 35mm. 8 reels, 7,811 ft.

Pres by Louis B. Mayer. *Produced under supv of* Irving Thalberg. *Dir* Reginald Barker. *Cont* Waldemar Young. *Adapt* Benjamin Glazer. *Photog* Percy Hilburn. *Art Dir* Cedric Gibbons. *Film Ed* Robert Kern. *Asst Dir* Harry Schenck. *Cost* Sophie Wachner.

Cast: Alice Terry *(Ruth Jordan)*, Conway Tearle *(Stephen Ghent)*, Wallace Beery *(Dutch)*, Huntly Gordon *(Philip Jordan)*, Allan Forrest *(Dr. Winthrop Newbury)*, George Cooper *(Shorty)*, ZaSu Pitts *(Polly Jordan)*, William Orlamond *(Lon)*.

Western. Source: William Vaughn Moody, *The Great Divide; a Play in Three Acts* (New York, 1909). Alone and unprotected in an isolated wilderness cabin, Ruth Jordan is discovered by three drunken brutes who begin to barter for her. In desperation, she appeals to Stephen Ghent, the least degraded of the desperadoes, promising herself to him if he saves her from the others. Ghent buys off Shorty with a chain of gold nuggets and knocks Dutch senseless. Ghent then sends Dutch off with Shorty and takes Ruth to the next town, where he forces her to marry him. During the 3-day ride across the desert to Ghent's gold mine, the idealistic Ruth learns that he is a man of rough passions. Ruth, later located by her brother, returns with him to his ranch. Having fallen in love with Ruth, Ghent goes to fetch her; but she refuses to go away with him and becomes desperately ill. Ghent rides to a distant village and gets a doctor; on the return trip, the doctor's horse falls and Stephen gives him his mount, placing himself in dire peril from a flood. A son is born to Ruth, and, when she hears of Stephen's heroic sacrifice, she realizes her love for him, and they are reconciled. *Brother-sister relationship. Desperadoes. Physicians. Deserts. Gold mines. Floods.*

Note: Remade in 1929 by First National under the same title.

THE GREAT DIVIDE **F2.2223**

First National Pictures. 15 Sep **1929** [c30 Sep 1929; LP728]. Sd (Vitaphone); b&w. 35mm. 6,722 reels. [Also si, 27 Oct 1929; 5,989 ft. Copyrighted as 8 reels.]

Pres by Richard A. Rowland. *Prod* Robert North. *Dir* Reginald Barker. *Scen* Fred Myton. *Dial-Titl* Fred Myton, Paul Perez. *Photog* Lee Garmes, Alvin Knechtel. *Song: "The End of the Lonesome Trail"* Herman Ruby, Ray Perkins.

Cast: Dorothy Mackaill *(Ruth Jordan)*, Ian Keith *(Stephen Ghent)*, Myrna Loy *(Manuella)*, Lucien Littlefield *(Texas Tommy)*, Creighton Hale *(Edgar Blossom)*, George Fawcett *(Lon Anderson)*, Claude Gillingwater *(Winthrop Amesbury)*, Roy Stewart *(Joe Morgan)*, Ben Hendricks, Jr. *(Dutch Romero)*, Jean Laverty *(Verna)*.

Western melodrama. Source: William Vaughn Moody, *The Great Divide; a Play in Three Acts* (New York, 1909). Stephen Ghent, a mineowner, falls in love with Ruth Jordan, an arrogant girl from the East, unaware that she is the daughter of his dead partner. Ruth is vacationing in Arizona and Mexico with a fast set of friends, including her fiancé, Edgar. Manuella, a Spanish halfbreed hopelessly in love with Ghent, causes Ruth to return to her fiancé when she insinuates that Ghent belongs to her. Ghent follows Ruth, kidnaps her, and takes her into the wilderness to endure hardship. There she discovers that she loves Ghent, and she discards Edgar in favor of him. *Halfcastes. Flappers. Mining. Jealousy. Kidnaping. Arizona. Mexico.*

THE GREAT GABBO **F2.2224**

James Cruze, Inc. *Dist* Sono Art–World Wide Pictures. 12 Sep **1929** [New York premiere; released 1 Jan 1930; c10 Dec 1930; LP1815]. Sd; b&w with col sequences (Technicolor). 35mm. 10 reels, 8,049 ft.

Pres by Henry D. Meyer, Nat Cordish. *Dir* James Cruze. *Cont-Dial* Hugh Herbert. *Story* Ben Hecht. *Photog* Ira H. Morgan. *Sets* Robert E. Lee. *Songs: "The New Step," "I'm in Love With You," "I'm Laughing," "Ickey," "Every Now and Then," "The Web of Love," "The Ga-Ga Bird"* Paul Titsworth, Lynn Cowan, Donald McNamee, King Zany. *Mus Dir* Howard Jackson. *Dance Dir* Maurice L. Kusell. *Ch Sd Engr* Helmer Bergman. *Prod Mgr* Vernon Keays. *Cost* André-ani.

Cast: Erich von Stroheim *(Gabbo)*, Betty Compson *(Mary)*, Donald Douglas *(Frank)*, Marjorie "Babe" Kane, Otto *(himself, a dummy)*.

Drama. Gabbo, a ventriloquist and a supreme egotist, Mary, his assistant, and Little Otto, Gabbo's dummy, are all performing on a vaudeville circuit; Gabbo constantly finds fault with Mary's efforts to please and insists upon his own greatness. During a performance Mary stumbles and drops a tray, thus infuriating Gabbo, who orders her to her dressing room after the performance, berates her, and finally forces her to leave. Determined to increase his fame, Gabbo becomes featured in The Manhattan Revue, in which Mary is working as a singer and dancer along with her new partner, Frank. More conceited than ever, Gabbo is certain that Mary will return to him. Spying Otto at a cafe, Mary converses with Gabbo through the dummy, and Gabbo realizes that he loves her. Frank sees them together and forbids her to see him again. Learning later of her marriage, Gabbo is driven to madness, and he rushes on stage, disrupting a musical act; during the outburst, he smashes Otto, then realizes him to be his sole object of love and is unable to recognize Mary, who tries to comfort him. He shuffles from the theater with Otto under his arm, shouting hopelessly at the workmen removing the sign advertising "The Great Gabbo." *Dancers. Egotists. Ventriloquism. Insanity. Musical revues. Dummies.*

THE GREAT GATSBY **F2.2225**

Famous Players–Lasky. *Dist* Paramount Pictures. 8 Nov **1926** [c9 Nov, 14 Dec 1926; LP23315, LP23428]. Si; b&w. 35mm. 8 reels, 7,296 ft.

Pres by Adolph Zukor, Jesse L. Lasky. *Dir* Herbert Brenon. *Screenplay* Becky Gardiner. *Adapt* Elizabeth Meehan. *Photog* Leo Tover. *Asst Dir* Ray Lissner.

Cast: Warner Baxter *(Jay Gatsby)*, Lois Wilson *(Daisy Buchanan)*, Neil Hamilton *(Nick Carraway)*, Georgia Hale *(Myrtle Wilson)*, William

Powell *(George Wilson)*, Hale Hamilton *(Tom Buchanan)*, George Nash *(Charles Wolf)*, Carmelita Geraghty *(Jordan Baker)*, Eric Blore *(Lord Digby)*, "Gunboat" Smith *(Bert)*, Claire Whitney *(Catherine)*.

Society drama. Source: F. Scott Fitzgerald, *The Great Gatsby* (1925). Owen Davis, *The Great Gatsby* (a play; 1925). On a summer night in Louisville, in 1917, Jay Gatsby, a young Army officer, falls in love with Daisy Fay, a society belle; before leaving for the war, Gatsby swears that he will raise himself to her social station, and they avow their undying love. Nine years later, Gatsby, through mysterious association with a Charles Wolf, has come to possess great wealth and a Long Island estate, while Daisy, swayed by parental authority, has married Tom Buchanan, a dissolute blueblood, who also maintains an affair with Myrtle Wilson, a garage-keeper's wife. At a party given by Gatsby, Daisy declares that she still cares for him. Later, Tom charges Gatsby with making love to his wife and with bootlegging; and Daisy prepares to leave with Gatsby in his roadster. Wilson upbraids his wife for her infidelity; and dashing onto the road, Myrtle is struck down by Gatsby's car, and he confesses his responsibility to the police. Friendless and alone, Gatsby roams through his garden and is shot by the vengeful Wilson. *Socialites. Veterans. Garage-keepers. Social classes. Wealth. Courtship. Infidelity. Jazz life. Kentucky. Long Island.*

THE GREAT IMPERSONATION **F2.2226**

Famous Players–Lasky. *Dist* Paramount Pictures. 9 Oct **1921** [c10 Oct 1921; LP17066]. Si; b&w. 35mm. 7 reels, 6,658 ft.

Pres by Jesse L. Lasky. *Dir* George Melford. *Scen* Monte M. Katterjohn. *Photog* William Marshall.

Cast: James Kirkwood *(Sir Everard Dominey/Leopold von Ragastein)*, Ann Forrest *(Rosamond Dominey)*, Winter Hall *(Duke of Oxford)*, Truly Shattuck *(Duchess of Oxford)*, Fontaine La Rue *(Princess Eiderstrom)*, Alan Hale *(Gustave Seimann)*, Bertram Johns *(Dr. Eddy Pelham)*, William Burress *(Dr. Hugo Schmidt)*, Cecil Holland *(Roger Unthank)*, Tempe Pigott *(Mrs. Unthank)*, Lawrence Grant *(Emperor William of Germany)*, Louis Dumar *(Prince Eiderstrom)*, Frederick Vroom *(Prince Terniloff)*, Florence Midgely *(Princess Terniloff)*.

Melodrama. Source: Edward Phillips Oppenheim, *The Great Impersonation* (Boston, 1920). Sir Edward Dominey and Baron Leopold von Ragastein, almost identical classmates at Oxford, meet again several years later in German East Africa during the Great War. Von Ragastein is serving as military commandant, and Dominey has left England after being suspected of murdering a man who has interfered with his marriage. Von Ragastein plots to have Dominey poisoned by the natives; and assuming Dominey's name, he proceeds to England to spy for the German Emperor. There he meets Princess Eiderstrom, with whom he has had a previous affair, and she resents his apparent affection for the mentally ill Rosamond. The princess, along with Schmidt, another German spy, accuses him of violating national ethics; it transpires, however, that Ragastein is actually Dominey, who has thwarted his enemies. The princess and Schmidt are arrested, and Rosamond is happily reunited with her husband, whom she had suspected to be an imposter. *Spies. Doubles. Impersonation. World War I. German East Africa. William II (Germany). Oxford University.*

THE GREAT JEWEL ROBBERY **F2.2227**

John Ince Productions. *Dist* Kerman Films. 24 Nov **1925** [New York State license]. Si; b&w. 35mm. 5 reels, 4,800 ft.

Dir John Ince.

Cast: Herbert Rawlinson *(Steve Martindale)*, Grace Darmond *(Doris Dunbar)*, Frank Darmond *(McGroody)*, Carlton Griffin *(Hooper)*, Marcella Daly *(Mrs. Hooper)*, Chester Conklin *(Cootie Joe)*.

Society melodrama. Doris Dunbar, a detective on the trail of stolen jewels, visits the Red Mill Inn, where Hooper (a jewel thief) and Steve Martindale (a man-about-town) are having a drink together. Hooper, who has some hot jewelry on him, puts it in Steve's pocket, fearing to be arrested by Doris. Doris and Steve are later kidnaped by Hooper and held prisoner at his hideout. Steve discovers that Doris is his childhood sweetheart, and they attempt to escape together. Their plans are foiled, but they are rescued by the police and decide to become partners for life. *Detectives. Thieves. Men-about-town. Kidnaping.*

THE GREAT K & A TRAIN ROBBERY **F2.2228**

Fox Film Corp. 17 Oct **1926** [c5 Oct 1926; LP23193]. Si; b&w. 35mm. 5 reels, 4,800 ft.

Pres by William Fox. *Dir* Lewis Seiler. *Scen* John Stone. *Photog* Dan Clark. *Asst Dir* Wynn Mace.

Cast: Tom Mix *(Tom Gordon)*, Dorothy Dwan *(Madge Cullen)*, William Walling *(Eugene Cullen)*, Harry Grippe *(DeLuxe Harry)*, Carl Miller *(Burton)*, Edward Piel *(bandit leader)*, Curtis McHenry *(Cullen's butler)*, Tony *(himself, a horse)*.

Western melodrama. Source: Paul Leicester Ford, *The Great K & A Train Robbery* (New York, 1897). When the K & A Railroad is subjected to a series of mysterious robberies, detective Tom Gordon is detailed to uncover the mystery. Disguised as a bandit, Tom boards the train of K & A President Cullen; but Cullen's daughter, Madge, senses that Tom is not a criminal and soon falls in love with him, though she is sought after by Burton, her father's secretary, who is in league with the bandits. Ultimately Tom discovers his duplicity, and with the aid of Tony, his horse, rounds up the villains, thus winning the hand of Madge. *Bandits. Railroads. Train robberies. Impersonation. Colorado. Horses.*

Note: Photographed in Royal Gorge, Colorado.

THE GREAT LOVE **F2.2229**

Metro-Goldwyn-Mayer Pictures. 27 Dec **1925** [c11 Jan 1926; LP22267]. Si; b&w. 35mm. 6 reels, 4,521 ft.

Dir-Story Marshall Neilan. *Scen* Benjamin F. Glazer.

Cast: Robert Agnew *(Dr. Lawrence Tibbits)*, Viola Dana *(Minette Bunker)*, Frank Currier *(Mr. Bunker)*, ZaSu Pitts *(Nancy)*, Chester Conklin *(Perkins)*, Junior Coughlan *(Patrick)*, Malcolm Waite *(Tom Watson)*, Norma *(an elephant)*.

Comedy. Tibbits, a struggling young doctor in a rural community, cures Norma, a circus elephant, when she is injured in a fire. The circus moves on, but Norma, who has become quite attached to the young doctor, keeps coming back, trampling everything in her way. Minette Bunker, the girl Tibbits loves, is kidnaped by one of her frustrated suitors, and Tibbits goes to the rescue, aided by Norma and 2,000 Boy Scouts. Norma later returns to the circus, and Minette prepares herself for the joys and sorrows of being a country doctor's wife. *Physicians. Boy Scouts. Abduction. Fires. Circus. Rural life. Elephants.*

THE GREAT MAIL ROBBERY **F2.2230**

R-C Pictures. *Dist* Film Booking Offices of America. 19 Jul **1927** [New York premiere; released 15 Aug; c10 Jun 1927; LP24186]. Si; b&w. 35mm. 7 reels, 6,504 ft.

Pres by Joseph P. Kennedy. *Dir* George B. Seitz. *Story-Adapt-Cont* Peter Milne. *Photog* Joe Walker. *Asst Dir* Ray McCarey.

Cast: Theodore von Eltz *(Lieut. Donald Macready)*, Frank Nelson *(Sgt. Bill Smith)*, Jeanne Morgan *(Laura Phelps)*, Lee Shumway *(Philip Howard)*, De Witt Jennings *(Captain Davis)*, Cora Williams *(Mrs. Davis)*, Nelson McDowell *(sheriff)*, Charles Hill Mailes *(Stephen Phelps)*, Yvonne Howell *(Sally)*.

Melodrama. As a result of a series of spectacular railroad robberies, Lieutenant Macready of the U. S. Marines is sent with his company of men to the gold country, aided by Sergeant Smith. Phil Howard, who is actually an undercover agent for the Marines, is accused of stealing bonds and takes refuge with the Davises; Davis, a former sea captain, fully convinced that Howard is a fugitive from justice, reveals himself to be the leader of the mail bandits, whom Howard joins. Davis plans to loot the gold train, but during the robbery, Howard radios the Marine base for help. The bandits seize the gold but are pursued by airplanes and forced to surrender in a canyon. Howard and Laura are happily reunited. *Secret agents. Sea captains. Railroads. Gold. Airplanes. Mail theft. Train robberies. Postal service. United States Marines.*

THE GREAT MOMENT **F2.2231**

Famous Players–Lasky. *Dist* Paramount Pictures. 4 Sep **1921** [c13 Aug 1921; LP16861]. Si; b&w. 35mm. 7 reels, 6,372 ft.

Pres by Jesse L. Lasky. *Dir* Sam Wood. *Scen* Monte M. Katterjohn. *Story* Elinor Glyn. *Photog* Alfred Gilks.

Cast: Gloria Swanson *(Nada Pelham/Nadine Pelham)*, Alec B. Francis *(Sir Edward Pelham)*, Milton Sills *(Bayard Delavel)*, F. R. Butler *(Eustace)*, Arthur Hull *(Hopper)*, Raymond Brathwayt *(Lord Crombie)*, Helen Dunbar *(Lady Crombie)*, Clarence Geldert *(Bronson)*, Julia Faye *(Sadi Bronson)*, Ann Grigg *(Blenkensop)*.

Melodrama. Sir Edward Pelham, who has married a Russian Gypsy, fears that his daughter will follow in her mother's footsteps and arranges a marriage with her cousin, whom she does not love. During a trip to Nevada with her father, she meets engineer Bayard Delavel, who saves her life when she is bitten by a snake; when her father finds her with Bayard in his cabin, he forces them to marry. Believing that Nadine does not love him, Delavel leaves her and prepares to sue for divorce. In Washington Nadine is reconciled with her father and agrees to marry Hopper, a millionaire; she meets Delavel on the night of her engagement ball, however, and the lovers are reunited. *Gypsies. Russians. Engineers. Divorce. Snakes. Nevada. Washington (District of Columbia).*

THE GREAT NIGHT **F2.2232**

Fox Film Corp. 3 Dec **1922** [c3 Dec 1922; LP19114]. Si; b&w. 35mm. 5 reels, 4,346 ft.

Pres by William Fox. *Dir* Howard M. Mitchell. *Story-Scen* Joseph Franklin Poland. *Photog* David Abel.

Cast: William Russell *(Larry Gilmore)*, Eva Novak *(Mollie Martin)*, Winifred Bryson *(Papita Gonzales)*, Henry Barrows *(Robert Gilmore)*, Wade Boteler *(Jack Denton)*, Harry Lonsdale *(Simpkins)*, Earl Metcalfe *(Green)*.

Comedy-melodrama. Larry Gilmore must marry by a certain date to inherit a fortune. He is besieged by women anxious to assist in getting the money. To escape them, he gets a job as a police officer and dons a uniform. He falls in love with Mollie Martin, a waitress who does not know his identity but agrees to marry him. Before the ceremony several complications occur, and Larry rounds up a band of jewel thieves. A few seconds before the expiration date he marries and gets the fortune. *Police. Waitresses. Thieves. Inheritance.*

GREAT POWER **F2.2233**

Franklin Warner. *Dist* Metro-Goldwyn-Mayer Distributing Corp. 23 Mar **1929** [New York premiere]. Sd (Bristolphone); b&w. 35mm. 9 reels.

Dir Joe Rock. *Scen-Dial* Myron C. Fagan. *Film Ed* Myron C. Fagan.

Cast: Minna Gombell *(Joan Wray)*, Herschel Mayall *(John Power)*, Nelan Jaap *(Frank Forrest)*, Alan Birmingham *(Bruce Power)*, Jack Leslie *(Gerald Graves)*, G. Davidson Clark *(Judge Ben Forrest)*, Jack Anthony *(Senator Dick Wray)*, Walter F. Scott *(Jordan, a butler)*, Conway Winafield *(Reverend Dr. Elliott)*, Walter Walker *(Senator Charles Davis)*, Elinor Martin *(maid)*, Helen Shipman *(Peggy Wray)*, Alfred Swenson *(District Attorney Crane)*.

Drama. Source: Myron C. Fagan, *The Great Power* (New York opening: 11 Sep 1928). Wall Street financier John Power, whose influence extends far into the financial and political worlds, becomes involved in Joan Wray's efforts to clear her brother, Senator Dick Wray, of rumored connections with questionable transactions among Frank Forrest (Joan's fiancé), a western oil company official, and two stockbrokers. Joan poses as an assistant to the U. S. Attorney General so as to gain entrance to the Power household and falls in love with Power's son, Bruce, after persuading him to help her. Having discovered Joan's identity and her relationship to Frank Forrest, John Power uses this knowledge to try to antagonize Bruce, but this objective is accomplished instead by Forrest. In a frenzy Joan shoots Forrest, and Bruce takes the blame; in the confusion and explanations that follow it is revealed that Gerald Graves, Power's secretary, actually killed Forrest and that Joan is the daughter of John Power's former sweetheart. Falling ill, Power has feverish dreams, through which pass most of the people he manipulated throughout his life, and upon recovering he has Senator Davis drop impeachment proceedings against Senator Wray and is reconciled with Joan and Bruce, who find happiness in each other's love. *Financiers. Politicians. Brother-sister relationship. Graft. Murder. Oil business. Impeachment. United States Congress. New York City—Wall Street. Dreams.*

Note: A performance of Myron Fagan's Broadway play, with its original cast, which was transported to the Bristolphone factory in Waterbury, Connecticut, for the making of this film.

THE GREAT ROMANCE *see* **FOREVER**

THE GREAT SENSATION **F2.2234**

Columbia Pictures. 1 Oct **1925** [c15 Sep 1925; LP21817]. Si; b&w. 35mm. 5 reels, 4,470 ft.

Dir Jay Marchant. *Story* Douglas Z. Doty. *Photog* George Meehan.

Cast: William Fairbanks *(Jack Curtis)*, Pauline Garon *(Peggy Howell)*, Lloyd Whitlock *(Captain Winslow)*, William Franey *(Harry Ruby)*, Winifred Landis *(Mrs. Franklin Curtis)*, Adelaide Hallock *(Mrs. Howell)*, Pauline Paquette *(maid)*.

Melodrama. Jack Curtis, the scion of a wealthy family, passes himself off as a chauffeur and goes to work for Peggy Howell, a beautiful flapper with whom he has fallen in love. Jack saves her from drowning and recovers her mother's jewels, stolen by Captain Winslow, a society crook. Peggy and Jack make plans to be married. *Chauffeurs. Flappers. Thieves. Disguise.*

THE GREAT WHITE NORTH **F2.2235**

H. A. Snow. *Dist* Fox Film Corp. 25 Jul **1928** [New York premiere; c25 Jul, 28 Dec 1928; MP5226, LP25958]. Sd eff & talking sequence (Movietone); b&w. 35mm. 6 reels, 5,560 ft.

Dir-Story Sydney Snow, H. A. Snow. *Titl* Malcolm Stuart Boylan, Barney Wolf. *Photog* Sydney Snow, H. A. Snow. *Film Ed* Kenneth Hawks.

Cast: Vilhjalmur Stefanson *(speaker in a short prolog to the film)*.

Documentary. This film is a record of some aspects of life in the arctic: there are a walrus hunt; a bear hunt that ends in the capture of the bear in nets; a conspectus of arctic bird life; and a whale hunt in which a whale is harpooned. The film concludes with scenes of Herald Island, where several members of the Stefanson Polar Expedition lost their lives. *Explorers. Arctic regions. Herald Island. Stefanson Polar Expedition. Polar bears. Walruses. Birds. Whales.*

Note: This film was also copyrighted and reviewed under the title *Lost in the Arctic.*

THE GREAT WHITE WAY **F2.2236**

Cosmopolitan Corp. *Dist* Goldwyn-Cosmopolitan Distributing Corp. 3 Jan **1924** [New York premiere; released 17 Feb or 9 Mar; c12 Mar 1924; LP19978]. Si; b&w. 35mm. 10 reels, 9,800 or 10,000 ft.

Dir E. Mason Hopper. *Scen* L. Dayle. *Adapt* Luther Reed. *Photog* Harold Wenstrom, Henry Cronjager. *Sets* Joseph Urban. *Film Ed* Walter Futter. *Asst Dir* E. J. Babille. *Coöp* New York City Fire Department. *Art Titl* Old Master Studio.

Cast: Anita Stewart *(Mabel Vandergrift)*, Tom Lewis *(Duke Sullivan)*, T. Roy Barnes *(Jack Murray)*, Oscar Shaw *(Joe Cain)*, Dore Davidson *(Adolph Blum)*, Ned Wayburn *(himself)*, G. L. (Tex) Rickard *(himself)*, Harry Watson *(city editor)*, Hal Forde *(Brock Morton)*, Olin Howland *(Stubbs)*, Pete Hartley *(English boxing champion)*, Stanley Forde *(Joe's father)*, J. W. McGurk *(himself)*, Fay King *(herself)*, Earle Sande *(himself)*, Kid Broad *(himself)*, Jimmy Stone *(Pete Hartley)*, Johnny Gallagher *(referee)*, Johnny Hennessey *(Cain's second)*, Billy Gould *(Stone's second)*, Frank Wunderley *(McIntyre)*, Joe Humphries *(announcer)*, Jerry Peterson *(Smoke)*, Ziegfeld "Follies" Chorus, Arthur Brisbane, Irvin S. Cobb, Harry Charles Witwer, "Bugs" Baer, Damon Runyon *(themselves, world-famous writers)*, Billy De Beck, George McManus, Winsor McKay, Nell Brinkley, Harry Hirshfield, Hal Coffman *(themselves, newspaper artists)*, Tammany Young.

Comedy-drama. Source: Harry Charles Witwer, "Cain and Mabel" (unidentified magazine story). Jack Murray, a press agent, tries to make popular his two clients—Joe Cain, a prizefighter, and Mabel Vandergrift, a follies dancer—by linking their names romantically. His plan succeeds when they actually fall in love. However, Morton, the jealous owner of the show, threatens to close it if Mabel does not renounce Joe. To save the show and his own reputation, Joe buys out Morton by agreeing to fight the English boxing champion. All ends well when Joe wins the title. The show is saved, and Mabel and Joe return to the West with Joe's father. *Press agents. Authors. Artists. Athletes. Dancers. Theatrical backers. Prizefighters. New York City—Broadway.*

Note: Many cast members play themselves—famous men and women in newspaper work, the sporting world, and the theater. Working title: *Cain and Mabel.*

THE GREATER CLAIM **F2.2237**

Metro Pictures. 21 Jan **1921** [c23 Feb 1921; LP16175]. Si; b&w. 35mm. 6 reels.

Dir Wesley Ruggles. *Scen* Albert Shelby Le Vino. *Story* Izola Forrester, Mann Page. *Photog* Arthur Reeves. *Art Dir* Sidney Ullman.

Cast: Alice Lake *(Mary Smith)*, Jack Dougherty *(Richard Everard [Charlie])*, Edward Cecil *(Abe Dietz)*, De Witt Jennings *(Richard Everard, Sr.)*, Florence Gilbert *(Gwendolyn)*, Lenore Lynard *(Rosie)*.

Domestic drama. Charlie Everard elopes with chorus girl Mary Smith against the will of his father, and Everard, Sr., has his son shanghaied aboard a sailing vessel. Believing herself deserted, Mary joins her chorus friend, Gwen, and refuses an offer from Everard's lawyer to have the marriage annulled. Charlie returns to her but reproaches her for associating with the theater set. After the birth of their child, alone and facing poverty, she surrenders the baby to the grandparents. Three years later, however,

Everhard, Sr., experiences a change of heart, and mother, father, and child are united. *Chorus girls. Family life. Theater. Motherhood. Shanghaiing.*

THE GREATER GLORY **F2.2238**

First National Pictures. 2 May **1926** [New York premiere; c23 Apr 1926; LP22631]. Si; b&w. 35mm. 11 reels, 9,710 ft.

Pres by Richard A. Rowland. *Dir* Curt Rehfeld. *Scen* June Mathis. *Photog* John W. Boyle, Arthur Martinelli. *Art Dir* E. J. Shulter. *Film Ed* George McGuire. *Prod Mgr* Ray Rockett.

Cast: Conway Tearle *(Count Maxim von Hurtig)*, Anna Q. Nilsson *(Fanny)*, May Allison *(Corinne)*, Ian Keith *(Pauli Birbach)*, Lucy Beaumont *(Tante Ilde)*, Jean Hersholt *(Gustav Schmidt)*, Nigel De Brulier *(Dr. Hermann von Berg)*, Bridgetta Clark *(Mizzi, his wife)*, John Sainpolis *(Prof. Leopold Eberhardt)*, Marcia Manon *(Kaethe, his wife)*, Edward Earle *(Otto Steiner)*, Virginia Southern *(Liesel, his wife)*, Isabelle Keith *(Anna, Pauli's wife)*, Kathleen Chambers *(Irma von Berg, the stepmother)*, Hale Hamilton *(Leon Krum)*, Cora Macey *(Marie)*, Carrie Daumery *(Countess von Hurtig)*, Thur Fairfax *(Theodore von Hurtig)*, Boris Karloff *(scissors grinder)*, George Billings *(cross bearer)*, Bess Flowers *(Helga)*, Marcelle Corday *(maid)*.

Epic drama. Source: Edith Louise O'Shaughnessy, *The Viennese Medley* (New York, 1924). Fanny von Berg, daughter of a wealthy Viennese family, is betrothed to the aristocratic Count Maxim von Hurtig, but when she brings disgrace to her family by entering into an escapade to aid a girl in distress, the marriage is canceled. Her sister, Corinne, breaks off with Pauli Birbach as a result, and Fanny becomes an outcast of respectable society. Following the outbreak of war, she is aided by Gustav Schmidt, a dealer in war supplies and owner of a gambling establishment, and is able to give financial aid to her family, now in dire want. Count Maxim, while visiting the gambling resort, meets Fanny again, and his love triumphs over his scruples; but Fanny, at the plea of the count's mother, refuses his suit and finds happiness with Gustav. The Berg family, chastened by war, famine, and death, is again drawn together. *Sisters. Aristocrats. War matériel. Social classes. Family life. Reputation. World War I. Vienna.*

Note: Working title: *The Viennese Medley*.

THE GREATER PROFIT **F2.2239**

Haworth Studios. *Dist* R-C Pictures. Jul **1921** [c6 Apr 1920; LU14973]. Si; b&w. 35mm. 5 reels, 4,220 ft.

Dir William Worthington. *Scen* Bennett Cohen. *Story* Clifford Howard, Burke Jenkins. *Photog* Edward Gheller.

Cast: Edith Storey *(Maury Brady)*, Pell Trenton *(Capt. Ward Ransom)*, Willis Marks *("Nunc" Brady)*, Lloyd Bacon *(Jim Crawkins)*, Bobbie Roberts *("Gimp" the Hunchback)*, Ogden Crane *(Creighton Hardage)*, Lillian Rambeau *(Mrs. Creighton Hardage)*, Dorothy Wood *(Rhoda Hardage)*.

Crook drama. Maury Brady, a product of New York's East Side, has learned the craft of safecracking and shoplifting from her uncle, "Nunc." While "working" a department store, she captures a lost poodle belonging to Mrs. Hardage, wife of a millionaire. When Maury later is caught lifting some lace, Mrs. Hardage vouches for her, takes her into her home, and puts her to work on a crusade against profiteers. The fiancé of Mrs. Hardage's daughter, Captain Ransom, is attracted to Maury, who consequently is asked to leave. Before leaving she takes a paper proving Mr. Hardage to be one of the country's most unlawful profiteers. She shows the paper to Ransom, who, deciding not to join the company, uses the evidence to bring down the cost of foods. Maury says *yes* to Ransom. *Uncles. Profiteers. Safecrackers. Shoplifting. Price control. Department stores. New York City—East Side. Documentation. Dogs.*

GREATER THAN A CROWN **F2.2240**

Fox Film Corp. 12 Jul **1925** [19 Jul 1925; LP21687]. Si; b&w. 35mm. 5 reels.

Pres by William Fox. *Dir* R. William Neill. *Scen* Wyndham Gittens. *Photog* Joseph August.

Cast: Edmund Lowe *(Tom Conway)*, Dolores Costello *(Isabel Francis)*, Margaret Livingston *(Molly Montrose)*, Ben Hendricks *(Tiger Bugg)*, Paul Panzer *(Marquis Ferasti)*, Anthony Merlo *(King Danilo)*, Robert Klein *(Count Seda)*.

Romantic drama. Source: Victor Bridges, *The Lady From Longacre* (New York 1919). Tom Conway, a wealthy American from Yonkers, saves a girl from assailants while in London and, with the help of a friend, Tiger Bugg, finds her lodging for the night with Molly Montrose, their actress friend. The following day, Molly discovers that both her jewels and the girl are missing, and Tom supposes that the strange girl, who gave her name as Isabel Francis, is responsible for the theft. Tom later learns that Isabel is the Princess of Lividia, who has run away from her country rather than marry King Danilo (who has also run away and is in London, paying court to Molly Montrose). Danilo and Isabel are kidnaped by agents of Lividia and taken home to be forcibly wed. Tom and Molly follow them, and Tom prevents the marriage. The king then reveals that he is already married to Molly, and Tom prepares to wed Isabel. *Royalty. Actors. Theft. Marriage. Imaginary kingdoms. London.*

GREATER THAN LOVE **F2.2241**

J. Parker Read, Jr., Productions. *Dist* Associated Producers. 17 Jul **1921** [c9 Jul 1921; LP16740]. Si; b&w. 35mm. 6-7 reels.

Pres by J. Parker Read, Jr. *Dir* Fred Niblo. *Story-Scen* C. Gardner Sullivan. *Photog* Charles J. Stumar.

Cast: Louise Glaum *(Grace Merrill)*, Patricia Palmer *(Elsie Brown)*, Rose Cade *(Maizie)*, Eve Southern *(Clairice)*, Willie May Carson *(Pinkie)*, Betty Francisco *(Helen Wellington)*, Mahlon Hamilton *(Bruce Wellington)*, Donald MacDonald *(Elliott)*, Edward Martindel *(Frank Norwood)*, Gertrude Claire *("Mother" Brown)*, Stanhope Wheatcroft *(The Youth)*.

Society melodrama. Grace Merrill, one of six young girls who idle their lives away staging jazz parties in a New York apartment, advises the youngest, Elsie, who is disillusioned by Frank Norwood, that men are worthless creatures. In a round of revelry Elsie takes her own life. Her mother, a quiet, strong woman, comes to visit the girls, and her fine character impresses them all during her short visit. As a result, Grace perceives the emptiness of her life of selfish pleasure and determines to better herself. Having previously agreed to be Bruce Wellington's corespondent for a sum of money, she declines her part and is welcomed into the home of Elsie's mother. *Jazz life. Motherhood. Redemption. Suicide.*

GREATER THAN MARRIAGE **F2.2242**

Romance Pictures. *Dist* Vitagraph Co. of America. 16 Nov **1924** [c20 Oct 1924; LP20682]. Si; b&w. 35mm. 7 reels, 6,821 ft.

Dir-Screenplay Victor Hugo Halperin. *Titl* Victor Hugo Halperin. *Photog* Edward Paul, Carl Vanderbroch.

Cast: Marjorie Daw *(Joan Thursday)*, Lou Tellegen *(John Masters)*, Peggy Kelly *(Maizie de Noovan)*, [Frederick] Tyrone Power *(Father)*, Mary Thurman *(Venetia)*, Dagmar Godowsky *(Nella Gardrow)*, Raymond Bloomer *(Vincent Marbridge)*, Effie Shannon *(Mother)*, Florence Billings *(Aunt Helena)*, William Ricciardi *(Sam Goldman)*, Ed Roseman *(Charlie Quan)*.

Domestic drama. Source: Louis Joseph Vance, *Joan Thursday* (Boston, 1913). Joan Thursday leaves home because of her father's opposition to her becoming an actress and later marries playwright John Masters, who also disapproves of Joan's pursuing a career outside of home. When John is called to California to supervise rehearsals of his new play, Joan cannot resist the temptation of the stage and accepts backer Vincent Marbridge's offer to star in a new production. Joan is a success, but John's play fails, and he angrily leaves her when he learns of her acting endeavor. John refuses producer Sam Goldman's offer to produce his play with Joan as star, Joan finds Marbridge's attentions increasingly difficult to avoid, and she attempts to jump out of a window. Finally, realizing the truth of her mother's dying admonition—never sacrifice love for a stage career—Joan returns to John. *Actors. Theatrical backers. Playwrights. Theater. Marriage. Suicide. New York City—Broadway. California.*

THE GREATEST LOVE OF ALL **F2.2243**

George Beban Productions. *Dist* Associated Exhibitors. 1 Feb **1925** [c31 Dec 1924; LU20975]. Si; b&w. 35mm. 7 reels, 6,400 ft.

Dir-Story George Beban.

Cast: George Beban *(Joe, the iceman)*, J. W. Johnston *(District Attorney Kelland)*, Wanda Lyon *(Mrs. Godfrey Kelland)*, Baby Evelyn *(their daughter)*, Nettie Belle Darby *(Marie Simpkin, the Maid)*, O. Zangrilli *(The Cobbler)*, Mary Skurkoy *(his daughter, Trina)*, Maria Di Benedetta *(his "Sweetheart")*, William Howatt *(The Presiding Judge)*, John K. Newman *(attorney for the defense)*, George Humbert *(interpreter)*, Robert M. Doll *(court officer)*.

Melodrama. Joe, a poor Italian iceman, saves enough money both to furnish a basement apartment in New York and to arrange passage to America from the old country for his mother. Joe is soon engaged to Trina, and Joe's mother secretly finds work doing laundry in the home of District Attorney Kelland, in order to help them save enough to be married. When a diamond bracelet belonging to Mrs. Kelland disappears, Joe's mother finds it in the dirty linen, but, before she can return it, she is seen with it and arrested as a thief. She is tried, convicted, and sentenced to 3 years in jail. Joe is driven wild with anxiety and joins in a plot to kill the D. A. by putting high explosives in his golf ball. Joe relents and saves the D. A. when Trina proves that the Kellands' daughter was responsible for putting the bracelet in the wash. Joe's mother is released from jail, and she and the young lovers find happiness in a little home in the country. *Italians. Icemen. Laundresses. Immigrants. Filial relations. Motherhood. Injustice. New York City.*

THE GREATEST MENACE **F2.2244**

J. G. Mayer. *Dist* Mayer & Quinn. 19 May **1923** [c27 Mar 1923; LP18818]. Si; b&w. 35mm. 7 reels, ca6,000 ft.

Pres by J. G. Mayer. *Dir-Adapt* Albert Rogell. *Titl* Andrew Bennison. *Story* Angela C. Kaufman. *Photog* Ross Fisher.

Cast: Ann Little *(Velma Wright)*, Wilfred Lucas *(Charles W. Wright)*, Robert Gordon *(Charles W. Wright, Jr.)*, Harry Northrup *(Herbert Van Raalte)*, Jack Livingston *(Douglas Ferguson)*, Rhea Mitchell *(Mary Lewis)*, Andy MacLennan *(The Gopher)*, Mildred June *(Mrs. Charles W. Wright, Jr.)*, "Red" Kirby *(Riley Hogan)*, Gordon Mullen *(Tim)*, Lew Meehan *(Gus)*.

Melodrama. Charles Wright, Jr., the son of the district attorney, wishes to write about life as it really is and especially about evils of drug addiction. To that end and against the advice of Velma Wright, his lawyer sister, he persistently visits the haunts of drug addicts and becomes the constant companion of Mary Lewis, who to ensnare Charles is acting as bait for a drug ring. Mary dies while waiting for Charles to obtain drugs for her, and he is arrested for murder. Velma and her father become interested in prosecuting the case, but she defends Charles when she learns the identity of the accused. He is found not guilty and is reunited with his family. *Lawyers. Authors. District attorneys. Brother-sister relationship. Narcotics.*

THE GREATEST SIN **F2.2245**

Trio Production Co. **1922.** Si; b&w. 35mm. 4 reels.

Cast: Mae Evlyn Lewis, Victor Nix.

Melodrama(?). No information about the precise nature of this film has been found. *Negro life.*

GREECE AND ITS MAGNIFICENT HISTORICAL MONUMENTS **F2.2246**

A. A. Foussianis. 20 Apr **1929** [New York State license]. Si; b&w. 35mm. 11 reels, 10,400 ft.

Travelog(?). No information about the precise nature of this film has been found. *Greece.*

Note: Country of origin undetermined.

GREED **F2.2247**

Metro-Goldwyn Pictures. 26 Jan **1925** [c10 Feb 1925; LP21123]. Si; b&w. 35mm. 10 reels, 10,067 ft.

Pres by Louis B. Mayer. *Adapt-Scen-Dir* Erich von Stroheim. *Titl* June Mathis. *Photog* William Daniels, Ben Reynolds, Ernest B. Schoedsack. *Art Dir* Cedric Gibbons, Richard Day. *Film Ed (see note)* Joseph Farnham, Erich von Stroheim, Rex Ingram, June Mathis. *Asst Dir* Eddy Sowders, Louis Germonprez.

Cast: Gibson Gowland *(McTeague)*, ZaSu Pitts *(Trina)*, Jean Hersholt *(Marcus Schouler)*, Chester Conklin *(Mr. Sieppe)*, Sylvia Ashton *(Mrs. Sieppe)*, Dale Fuller *(Maria)*, Joan Standing *(Selina)*, Austin Jewel *(August Sieppe)*, Oscar Gottell, Otto Gottell *(The Sieppe Twins)*, Frank Hayes *(Old Grannis)*, Fanny Midgley *(Miss Baker)*, Hughie Mack *(Mr. Heise)*, Jack Curtis *(McTeague's father)*, Tempe Pigott *(McTeague's mother)*, James F. Fulton *(sheriff)*, Jack McDonald *(Gribbons)*, Lon Poff *(lottery agent)*, Max Tyron *(Mr. Oelberman)*, Erich von Ritzau *(traveling dentist)*, William Mollenheimer *(The Palmist)*, Hugh J. McCauley *(The Photographer)*, S. S. Simon *(Frena)*, William Barlow *(minister)*, Mrs. E. Jones *(Mrs. Heise)*, Mrs. Reta Rebla *(Mrs. Ryer)*, J. Libbey *(Mr. Ryer)*, James Gibson *(deputy)*.

Drama. Source: Frank Norris, *McTeague; a Story of San Francisco* (New York, 1899). McTeague, a San Francisco dentist, marries Trina, a thrifty woman who has won $5,000 in a lottery. She banks this money and, by scrimping and saving, hoards most of the money her husband makes. Marcus Schouler, Trina's frustrated suitor, discovers that McTeague does not have a license to practice dentistry and causes him to lose his business. McTeague can make only a poor living as a laborer, and he and Trina eventually drift to squalid quarters. Trina hoards money compulsively, and McTeague, crazed with the knowledge of the money, kills her and escapes with the gold, fleeing into Death Valley. Marcus goes after him, and the men fight. McTeague kills Marcus but finds himself handcuffed to the dead man. Unable to find the key to free himself, McTeague dies of thirst. *Hoarders. Dentists. Thrift. Greed. Lotteries. Murder. Thirst. San Francisco. Death Valley.*

Note: Stroheim reduced his initial 42 reels to 24 reels and then refused to further touch the film, asking his friend, Rex Ingram, to work on it. Ingram further cut the film to 18 reels. June Mathis then cut the film to 10 reels and added new titles. Joseph Farnham received screen credit as film editor.

GREEK-TURK WAR IN ASIA MINOR **F2.2248**

Pekras & Phelos. 19 Feb **1922** [New York State]. Si; b&w. 35mm. 6 reels, 5,900 ft.

Documentary(?). No information about the nature of this film has been found. *Greco-Turkish War (1921–22). Greece—History. Turkey—History.*

Note: Country of origin not determined.

THE GREEN GODDESS **F2.2249**

Distinctive Productions. *Dist* Goldwyn-Cosmopolitan Distributing Corp. 14 Aug **1923** [New York premiere; released 16 Sep; c17 Sep 1923; LP19418]. Si; b&w. 35mm. 10 reels. [Released as 8 reels, 8,000 ft.]

Dir Sidney Olcott. *Adapt* Forrest Halsey. *Photog* Harry Fischbeck. *Mus Score* Joseph Carl Breil.

Cast: George Arliss *(Rajah of Rukh)*, Alice Joyce *(Lucilla Crespin)*, David Powell *(Dr. Traherne)*, Harry T. Morey *(Major Crespin)*, Jetta Goudal *(Ayah)*, Ivan Simpson *(Watkins)*, William Worthington *(The High Priest)*.

Melodrama. Source: William Archer, *The Green Goddess; a Play in Four Acts* (New York, 1921). Fleeing a threatened Hindu uprising, Major Crespin and his wife, accompanied by Dr. Traherne, travel by airplane to a distant settlement. The Rajah of Rukh makes them his prisoner-guests when the airplane crashes in his kingdom. He informs the three that they will be killed in retaliation for the approaching execution by the British of his three brothers. Crespin and Traherne bribe the butler to send an appeal for help over the wireless, but he betrays them and loses his life. Crespin gets the message through before the rajah shoots him. British aviators arrive in time to save Traherne and Mrs. Crespin. *Royalty. Hostages. Brothers. Butlers. Hindus. Airplane accidents. Radio. India. Great Britain—Army.*

Note: Remade in 1930 under the same title, q. v.

THE GREEN GODDESS **F2.2250**

Warner Brothers Pictures. 13 Feb **1930** [New York premiere; released 3 or 8 Mar 1930; c7 Sep 1929; LP667]. Sd (Vitaphone); b&w. 35mm. 7 reels, 6,653 ft. [Also si.]

Dir Alfred Green. *Screenplay-Titl-Dial* Julien Josephson. *Photog* James Van Trees. *Film Ed* James Gribbon. *Rec Engr* Joseph Kane.

Cast: George Arliss *(The Raja)*, H. B. Warner *(Crespin)*, Alice Joyce *(Lucilla Crespin)*, Ralph Forbes *(Dr. Traherne)*, David Tearle *(temple high priest)*, Reginald Sheffield *(Lieutenant Cardew)*, Nigel De Brulier *(hermit priest)*, Betty Boyd *(Ayah)*, Ivan Simpson *(Hawkins)*.

Melodrama. Source: William Archer, *The Green Goddess; a Play in Four Acts* (New York, 1921). The plot is essentially that of the 1923 film, *The Green Goddess*, q. v. *Royalty. Hostages. Butlers. Brothers. Hindus. Airplane accidents. Radio. India. Great Britain—Army.*

GREEN GRASS WIDOWS **F2.2251**

Tiffany-Stahl Productions. 10 Jun **1928** [c15 Jun 1928; LP25363]. Si; b&w. 35mm. 6 reels, 5,334 ft.

Dir Alfred Raboch. *Cont* Wellyn Totman. *Titl* Paul Perez. *Story* Viola Brothers Shore. *Photog* Jackson Rose. *Art Dir* Hervey Libbert. *Set Dressings* George Sawley. *Film Ed* Robert J. Kern.

Cast: Walter Hagen *(himself)*, Gertrude Olmstead *(Betty Worthing)*, John Harron *(Del Roberts)*, Hedda Hopper *(Mrs. Worthing)*, Lincoln Stedman *(Fat)*, Ray Hallor *(Cliff)*.

Comedy-drama. Del Roberts, a college youth whose father has gone bankrupt, enters a golf tournament to make money to finish his studies. Golf pro Walter Hagen is his chief competitor. Interested in the boy's welfare, Hagen plays a close game to the last hole, then throws it in favor of Roberts, enabling him to remain in school and marry his sweetheart, Betty Worthing. Surmising that Hagen let him win, Roberts and Betty decide to name their first child for him; accordingly, twins would be called Haig 'n Hagen! *Students. Golf. Sportsmanship. Bankruptcy.*

THE GREEN TEMPTATION F2.2252

Famous Players–Lasky. *Dist* Paramount Pictures. ca18 Mar **1922** [New York premiere; released 2 Apr; c29 Mar 1922; LP17705]. Si; b&w. 35mm. 6 reels, 6,165 ft. [Release version: 5 reels.]

Pres by Adolph Zukor. *Dir* William D. Taylor. *Scen* Monte M. Katterjohn, Julia Crawford Ivers. *Photog* James C. Van Trees.

Cast: Betty Compson *(Genelle/Coralyn/Joan Parker)*, Mahlon Hamilton *(John Allenby)*, Theodore Kosloff *(Gaspard)*, Neely Edwards *(Pitou)*, Edward Burns *(Hugh Duyker)*, Lenore Lynard *(Duchesse de Chazarin)*, Mary Thurman *(Dolly Dunton)*, William von Hardenburg *(Monsieur Jounet)*, Betty Brice *(Mrs. Weedon Duyker)*, Arthur Hull *(Mr. Weedon Duyker)*.

Melodrama. Source: Constance Lindsay Skinner, "The Noose," in *Ainslee's* (46:1–40, Sep 1920). In the days before the Great War, Genelle and Gaspard, apaches, operate a harlequin show in Paris, while Pitou, the clown, robs the audience. Later, as Coralyn, a dancer, the girl meets the Duchesse de Chazarin and Allenby, an Englishman who knows Genelle and Coralyn to be the same person. Genelle steals a famous emerald from the duchess, and, warned by Allenby, she escapes to an apache den. At the outbreak of war, Coralyn becomes a Red Cross nurse under the name of Joan Parker, and the suffering and danger of the battlefield effect a change in her character. To escape the influence of Gaspard, she comes to America to visit with Hugh Duyker, an American soldier, and refuses to aid Gaspard (who arrives posing at Count Oudry) in stealing a jewel from Mrs. Duyker. Genelle attempts to thwart Gaspard's plot and is herself accused; Gaspard escapes with the jewel but is killed by detectives; and Genelle, vindicated, is united with Allenby. *Apaches—Paris. Thieves. Dancers. World War I. Paris. Red Cross.*

THE GREEN-EYED MONSTER F2.2253

Norman Film Manufacturing Co. **1921**. Si; b&w. 35mm. 8 reels.

Cast: Jack Austin, Louise Dunbar.

Melodrama. Two men, Negroes, both in love with the same girl, work for two different railroads that are competing for a contract to carry the Government Fast Mail. In order to establish a basis on which the contract can be awarded, a race is arranged between two trains. The winner of that race also wins the hand of his sweetheart. *Railroads. Negro life. Postal service. Jealousy.*

THE GREENE MURDER CASE F2.2254

Paramount Famous Lasky Corp. 31 Aug **1929** [c31 Aug 1929; LP660]. Sd (Movietone); b&w. 35mm. 8 reels, 6,383 ft. [Also si.]

Dir Frank Tuttle. *Screenplay* Louise Long. *Dial* Bartlett Cormack. *Titl* Richard H. Digges, Jr. *Photog* Henry Gerrard.

Cast: William Powell *(Philo Vance)*, Florence Eldridge *(Sibella Greene)*, Ullrich Haupt *(Dr. Von Blon)*, Jean Arthur *(Ada Greene)*, Eugene Pallette *(Sergeant Heath)*, E. H. Calvert *(John F. X. Markham)*, Gertrude Norman *(Mrs. Tobias Greene)*, Lowell Drew *(Chester Greene)*, Morgan Farley *(Rex Greene)*, Brandon Hurst *(Sproot)*, Augusta Burmeister *(Mrs. Mannheim)*, Marcia Harris *(Hemming)*, Mildred Golden *(Barton)*, Mrs. Wilfred Buckland *(nurse for Mrs. Greene)*, Helena Phillips *(police nurse for Mrs. Greene)*, Shep Camp *(medical examiner)*, Charles E. Evans *(Lawyer Canon)*.

Mystery drama. Source: S. S. Van Dine, *The Greene Murder Case* (New York, 1928). District Attorney John F. X. Markham calls in ace detective Philo Vance when he and his men are unable to solve the death of eccentric Chester Greene, allegedly shot to death by a member of his own family. Vance's investigation reveals an atmosphere of hatred in the Greene household. Two more Greenes are murdered before the mystery is solved when the person least suspected falls to death (while committing another murder) into the icy waters of the East River. *Detectives. District attorneys. Murder. Family life. New York City. East River.*

THE GREY DAWN *see* **THE GRAY DAWN**

THE GREY DEVIL F2.2255

George Blaisdell Productions. *Dist* Rayart Pictures. 14 Aug **1926** [New York State license]. Si; b&w. 35mm. 5 reels, 4,274 ft.

Dir Bennett Cohn. *Story-Scen* Henry Ziegler. *Photog* William Thornley.

Cast: Jack Perrin, Tom London, Lorraine Eason, Andy Waldron, Jerome La Grasse, Milburn Morante, Starlight *(The Grey Devil, a horse)*.

Western melodrama. "Hero is fired from ranch from which cattle are disappearing. He sets out to find rustlers and discovers rival for his girl's hand is man he is looking for. After a series of skirmishes he bests the villain and the girl promises to wed him." (*Motion Picture News Booking Guide*, 12:33, Apr 1927.) *Rustling. Ranches.*

THE GREY STREAK F2.2256

Balshofer Productions. 4 Mar **1927** [New York State license]. Si; b&w. 35mm. 5 reels, 4,800 ft.

Cast: William Barrymore.

Action drama(?). No information about the nature of this film has been found.

THE GREY VULTURE F2.2257

Davis Distributing Division. c11 Jan **1926** [LP22250]. Si; b&w. 35mm. 5 reels.

Dir Forrest K. Sheldon. *Story* George Hively.

Western melodrama. Thinking that he has killed a man, Bart Miller, a courtly westerner, heads for the hills, encountering on the way a driverless stagecoach full of beautiful girls. He accompanies the girls to their destination and falls in love with Betty Taylor, the daughter of the rancher with whom the girls are staying. Luke Hatton, the foreman of the Taylor ranch, runs off with some of Taylor's cattle; Betty discovers the theft and arranges with the sheriff for his arrest. The sheriff informs Bart that the man he thought he had killed has fully recovered, and Bart makes plans to hitch up with Betty. *Sheriffs. Cattlemen. Rustling.*

THE GREYHOUND LIMITED F2.2258

Warner Brothers Pictures. 9 Feb **1929** [c2 Feb 1929; LP74]. Talking sequences, mus score, & sd eff (Vitaphone); b&w. 35mm. 7 reels, 6,114 ft. [Also si, 23 Mar 1929; 4,696 ft.]

Dir Howard Bretherton. *Scen* Anthony Coldeway. *Dial* Robert Lord. *Titl* Joseph Jackson. *Story* Albert S. Howson. *Photog* Ben Reynolds.

Cast: Monte Blue *(Monte)*, Edna Murphy *(Edna)*, Grant Withers *(Bill)*, Lucy Beaumont *(Mrs. Williams, his mother)*, Ernie Shields *(Limpy)*, Lew Harvey *(The Rat)*.

Crime melodrama. Believing that his pal Monte, a railroad engineer, has stolen his girl friend, Edna, Bill leaves town with a crowd of bums. When he reappears with them several weeks later, Bill is falsely accused of a murder. Monte and Edna capture the real murderer just in time to stop Bill's execution. *Railroad engineers. Tramps. Murder. Capital punishment.*

THE GRIM COMEDIAN F2.2259

Goldwyn Pictures. ca13 Nov **1921** [Los Angeles and Omaha premieres; released Nov; c9 Nov 1921; LP17176]. Si; b&w. 35mm. 6 reels, 5,509 ft.

Dir Frank Lloyd. *Scen* Bess Meredyth. *Story* Rita Weiman. *Photog* Norbert Brodin.

Cast: Phoebe Hunt *(Marie Lamonte)*, Jack Holt *(Harvey Martin)*, Gloria Hope *(Dorothy)*, Bert Woodruff *(Old Dad)*, Laura La Varnie *(Gracie Moore)*, May Hopkins *(Billie Page)*, John Harron *(Geoffrey Hutchins)*, Joseph J. Dowling *(Carleton Hutchins)*.

Society melodrama. Musical comedy star Marie Lamonte, the mistress of Harvey Martin, has her daughter, Dorothy, reared in a convent school. Realizing that the daughter is about to come home, Marie gives up her luxurious life with Martin and in maternal devotion retires to humble lodgings. There she is happy with Dorothy, who is in love with young artist Geoffrey Hutchins. Martin, however, lavishes Dorothy with gifts and persuades her to elope with him; learning that Martin has fascinated Dorothy, Marie goes to his apartment to plead with him to give up the girl, who meanwhile is concealed in an adjoining room. Martin refuses, and in desperation Marie shoots at him. In admiration of her courage, Martin changes his mind, telling Dorothy that he never intended to marry her; and when the girl is united with Geoffrey, Marie is at last happy. *Mistresses. Actors. Artists. Motherhood.*

GRINNING GUNS (Blue Streak Western) F2.2260

Universal Pictures. 22 May **1927** [c31 Mar 1927; LP23816]. Si; b&w. 35mm. 5 reels, 4,689 ft.

Pres by Carl Laemmle. *Dir* Albert Rogell. *Story-Scen* Grover Jones. *Photog* William Nobles. *Art Dir* David S. Garber.

Cast: Jack Hoxie *("Grinner" Martin)*, Ena Gregory *(Mary Felden)*, Robert Milasch *(Buckaroo Bill)*, Arthur Morrison *(Harvey Purcell)*, George French *(Amos Felden)*, Dudley Hendricks *(Sheriff)*, Alphonse Martell *(Tony, The Dude)*.

Western melodrama. "Grinner" Martin, an optimistic cowboy whose admiration for the writing of Amos Felden takes him to a western town where the newspaper publisher is fighting off ruffians, rescues Felden and his daughter, Mary, from a gang of bullies. Purcell, the saloon owner and town boss, has Martin and his pal Buckaroo Bill arrested, then incites the mob to lynch them. Tony turns against Purcell and liberates the prisoners, who persuade Felden to publish the names of undesirable citizens. Purcell threatens Felden when he is named and sets fire to the office. Tony is mortally wounded while saving the life of Felden, and Martin fights Purcell to the latter's death in a waterfall. Martin rehabilitates the newspaper office and finds happiness with Mary. *Cowboys. Publishers. Saloon keepers. Gangs. Newspapers.*

THE GRIP OF THE YUKON (Universal-Jewel) **F2.2261**

Universal Pictures. 9 Jul **1928** [New York premiere; released 15 Jul 1928; c28 Dec 1927; LP24809]. Si; b&w. 35mm. 7 reels, 6,599 ft.

Dir Ernst Laemmle. *Adapt-Screenplay* Charles A. Logue. *Titl* Buford Bennett, Tom Reed. *Photog* Jackson Rose. *Film Ed* Maurice Pivar, Ted Kent.

Cast: Francis X. Bushman *(Colby MacDonald)*, Neil Hamilton *(Jack Elliott)*, June Marlowe *(Sheila O'Neil)*, Otis Harlan *(Farrell O'Neil)*, Burr McIntosh *(Chardon, the hotelkeeper)*, James Farley *(sheriff)*.

Melodrama. Source: William MacLeod Raine, *The Yukon Trail, a Tale of the North* (Boston, 1917). Two lost prospectors, MacDonald and Elliott, meet Farrell O'Neil, a hermit who lives in the Yukon. O'Neil, crazed with desire for gold, starts a fight with MacDonald and Elliott, and they accidently kill him. Afraid to confess because they are unknown in the community, the two men take possession of the old man's mine. Sheila, O'Neil's daughter, arrives to find him dead; she soon runs out of funds and is forced to take a job in a dancehall. The two men befriend her, hoping to conceal their slaughter of her father. Both fall in love with her, but when she chooses Elliott, the younger of the two, MacDonald tells the sheriff about their crime. Seeing that it was a clear case of self-defense, the sheriff exonerates them both, and MacDonald leaves the lovers to their happiness. *Miners. Dancehall girls. Manslaughter. Yukon.*

GRIT **F2.2262**

Film Guild. *Dist* W. W. Hodkinson Corp. 7 Jan **1924.** Si; b&w. 35mm. 6 reels, 5,800 ft.

Dir Frank Tuttle. *Scen* James Ashmore Creelman. *Photog* Fred Waller, Jr. *Set Dsgn* Junius Crovins.

Cast: Glenn Hunter *("Kid" Hart)*, Helenka Adamowska *(Annie Hart)*, Roland Young *(Houdini Hart)*, Osgood Perkins *(Boris Giovanni Smith)*, Townsend Martin *(Flashy Joe)*, Clara Bow *(Orchid McGonigle)*, Dore Davidson *(Pop Finkel)*, Martin Broder *(Bennie Finkel)*, Joseph Depew *(Tony O'Cohen)*.

Crook melodrama. Source: F. Scott Fitzgerald, "Grit" (publication undetermined). Kid Hart, whose gangster father is killed by gang leader Boris Smith for attempting to go straight, is brought up by the same East Side gang. As a result of a childhood firearms accident, he becomes a fear-filled coward, unable to break away, until Orchid McGonigle, another member determined to reform, shows him the way. They effect the rescue of Bennie Finkel from the gang and find happiness together. *Criminals—Rehabilitation. Cowardice. Poverty. Childhood. Kidnaping. New York City—East Side.*

GRIT WINS **F2.2263**

Universal Pictures. 27 Jan **1929** [c28 Oct 1928; LP25762]. Si; b&w. 35mm. 5 reels, 4,596 ft.

Supv William Lord Wright. *Dir* Josef Levigard. *Story-Scen* George Plympton. *Titl* Val Cleveland. *Photog* William Adams. *Film Ed* Gene Havlick.

Cast: Ted Wells *(Jack Deering)*, Kathleen Collins *(Nan Pickens)*, Al Ferguson *(Logan)*, Buck Connors *(Ted Pickens)*, Nelson McDowell *(John Deering)*, Edwin Moulton *(Jake)*.

Western melodrama. Logan finds out that there are valuable oil deposits on the ranch of Ted Pickens and frames him for the shooting of John Deering, a long-time enemy; Logan then offers to clear Pickens of the charge against him in return for the rights to his land. Jack Deering, John's forceful son and the sweetheart of Nan Pickens, comes to the rescue: he saves the ranch and pulls Nan and her uncle from a burning farmhouse. *Ranchers. Frameup. Murder. Oil lands. Land rights. Fires.*

GROUNDS FOR DIVORCE **F2.2264**

Famous Players–Lasky. *Dist* Paramount Pictures. 27 Jul **1925** [c10 Jun 1925; LP21546]. Si; b&w. 35mm. 6 reels, 5,692 ft.

Pres by Adolph Zukor, Jesse L. Lasky. *Dir* Paul Bern. *Scen* Violet Clark. *Adapt* Guy Bolton. *Photog* Bert Glennon.

Cast: Florence Vidor *(Alice Sorbier)*, Matt Moore *(Maurice Sorbier)*, Harry Myers *(Count Zapata)*, Louise Fazenda *(Marianne)*, George André Beranger *(Guido)*, Gustav von Seyffertitz *(Labell)*, Edna Mae Cooper *(Marie)*.

Romantic comedy. Source: Ernö Vajda, *Vàlòpörös Hölay* (Budapest, 1923). Maurice Sorbier, one of the most successful divorce lawyers in Paris, is himself divorced by his wife, Alice, when he becomes excessively involved in his work. Alice then marries Count Zapata, greatly disappointing her admirer, Guido, an aviator and ace of hearts. Alice gradually comes to realize that she does not love Zapata, but he refuses to give her a divorce. The attentive Guido suggests that Alice ask Maurice for his professional help, which she does, primarily in order to see him again. Guido takes Zapata for a ride in his plane and, by means of a series of perilous stunts, forces him to sign a divorce agreement. When Guido returns to the ground, expecting to find a waiting Alice, he finds that she and Maurice have run off together. Guido seeks solace in the love of Marianne, a temperamental actress whom he does not much like. *Lawyers. Aviators. Actors. Divorce. Paris. Air stunts.*

GROWING BETTER **F2.2265**

Sanford Productions. Sep **1923** [scheduled release]. Si; b&w. 35mm. 5 reels.

Cast: William Patton.

Comedy-drama(?). No information about the nature of this film has been found.

THE GRUB STAKE **F2.2266**

Nell Shipman Productions. *Dist* American Releasing Corp. 18 Feb **1923.** Si; b&w. 35mm. 6,408 or 8,061 ft.

Dir Bert Van Tuyle. *Story* Nell Shipman. *Photog* Joseph Walker.

Cast: Nell Shipman *(Faith Diggs)*, Hugh Thompson *(Jeb)*, Alfred Allen *(Mark Leroy)*, George Berrell *(Malamute Mike)*, Walt Whitman *(The "Skipper")*, C. K. Van Auker *(The Mounty)*, Ah Wing *(Wong)*.

Northwest melodrama. Faith Diggs, who is caring for her invalid father, meets Mark Leroy, an Alaskan gambler, and he entices her to the Klondike through a fake marriage. She learns the truth about her marriage from Dawson Kate, a dancehall woman, and with her father she flees into the wilderness and becomes stranded without food. Faith encounters wild animals and cares for her now delirious father until Kate's son rescues them. A romance develops between them, and when they find a mine, Mark tries to jump the claim but is repulsed and killed by a fall. *Dancehall hostesses. Invalids. Gamblers. Claim jumpers. Marriage–Fake. Mines. Klondike. Alaska.*

GRUMPY **F2.2267**

Famous Players–Lasky. *Dist* Paramount Pictures. ca 11 Mar **1923** [Los Angeles premiere; released 8 Apr; c28 Mar 1923; LP18835]. Si; b&w. 35mm. 6 reels, 5,621 ft.

Pres by Adolph Zukor. *Dir* William De Mille. *Adapt-Scen* Clara Beranger. *Photog* L. Guy Wilky.

Cast: Theodore Roberts *("Grumpy" [Andrew Bullivant])*, May McAvoy *(Virginia Bullivant)*, Conrad Nagel *(Ernest Heron)*, Casson Ferguson *(Chamberlin Jarvis)*, Bertram Johns *(Keble)*, Charles Ogle *(Ruddock)*, Robert Bolder *(Dawson)*, Charles French *(Wolfe)*, Bernice Frank *(Susan)*, Bertram Frank *(Jarvis' valet)*.

Comedy-drama. Source: Horace Hodges and Thomas Wigney Percyval, *Grumpy; a Play in Four Acts* (New York, 1921). Andrew Bullivant, a retired lawyer known as "Grumpy" for his irascibility, calls on all his experience and powers of deduction to expose Chamberlin Jarvis as the thief of a valuable diamond being transported by Ernest Heron. A gardenia is the clue; and Virginia Bullivant, Ernest's sweetheart, is Jarvis' unwitting dupe. *Lawyers. Detectives. Thieves. Personality.*

Note: Remade in 1930 as *Grumpy* (English language) and *Cascarrabias* (Spanish language).

GRUMPY **F2.2268**

Paramount-Publix Corp. 1 Aug **1930** [New York premiere; released 23 Aug; c22 Aug 1930; LP1511]. Sd (Movietone); b&w. 35mm. 9 reels, 6,651 ft.

Dir George Cukor, Cyril Gardner. *Screenplay–Adtl Dial* Doris Anderson. *Photog* David Abel. *Rec Engr* Harold C. Lewis.

Cast: Cyril Maude *("Grumpy" Bullivant)*, Phillips Holmes *(Ernest Heron)*, Frances Dade *(Virginia)*, Paul Lukas *(Berci)*, Halliwell Hobbes

(Ruddick), Paul Cavanagh *(Jarvis)*, Doris Luray *(Susan)*, Olaf Hytten *(Keble)*, Robert Bolder *(Merridew)*, Colin Kenny *(Dawson)*.

Melodrama. Source: Horace Hodges and Thomas Wigney Percyval, *Grumpy, a Play in Four Acts* (New York, 1921). Grumpy, a retired London criminal lawyer who lives on his country estate with his granddaughter, Virginia, is a witty and lovable, though temperamental, old man. Jarvis, one of Virginia's recent acquaintances, is their houseguest when Ernest Heron, Virginia's sweetheart, returns from South Africa as the secret bearer of a valuable diamond. That night, Ernest is attacked in the library and the diamond is stolen, the only clue being a camellia placed in his hand. Grumpy's sleuthing leads him to suspect Jarvis, and he follows him to London. There he is unable to sell the diamond to Berci, who learns that Jarvis is under suspicion. Terrified by Grumpy's visit to his apartment, Jarvis returns to the country to retrieve the camellia; faced with Grumpy's accusations, he returns the diamond and is arrested. Ernest and Virginia are left to their happiness as the old man grumbles off to bed. *Lawyers. Grandfathers. Courtship. Robbery. London.*

Note: Remake of the 1923 film of the same title; also produced in a Spanish-language version, *Cascarrabias*, in 1930.

GUARDIANS OF THE WILD **F2.2269**

Universal Pictures. 16 Sep **1928** [c11 Jan 1928; LP24857]. Si; b&w. 35mm. 5 reels, 4,868 ft.

Dir Henry MacRae. *Story-Cont (see note)* Basil Dickey, George Morgan. *Titl* Gardner Bradford. *Photog* Virgil Miller, George Robinson. *Film Ed* Thomas Malloy.

Cast: Rex *(himself, a horse)*, Starlight *(herself, a horse)*, Jack Perrin *(Jerry Lane)*, Ethlyne Clair *(Madge Warren)*, Al Ferguson *(Mark Haman)*, Bernard Siegel *(Sing Lo)*.

Western melodrama. Rex, leader of a pack of wild horses, rescues young forest ranger Jerry Lane, his sweetheart Madge Warren, and her father from the machinations of Mark Haman, a horsethief who is trying to take ownership of the Warren ranch. *Forest rangers. Horsethieves. Horses.*

Note: Universal records credit Basil Dickey with story and continuity although other sources give scenario credit to George Morgan.

GUILE OF WOMEN **F2.2270**

Goldwyn Pictures. ca1 Jan **1921** [Los Angeles premiere; c26 Dec 1920; LP15975]. Si; b&w. 35mm. 5 reels, 4,496 ft.

Dir Clarence Badger. *Cont Writ* Edfrid A. Bingham. *Auth* Peter Clark MacFarlane. *Photog* Marcel Picard. *Asst Dir* James Flood.

Cast: Will Rogers *(Yal)*, Mary Warren *(Hulda)*, Bert Sprotte *(Skole)*, Lionel Belmore *(Armstrong)*, Charles A. Smiley *(Captain Larsen)*, Nick Cogley *(Captain Stahl)*, Doris Pawn *(Annie)*, John Lince *(butler)*; Jane Starr *(maid)*.

Comedy-drama. Skole and Hjamlamar (better known as Yal) are sailors aboard the White Bear Line's oil steamer *Almaden*. Yal tells Skole of his unhappy experience with his sweetheart, Hulda, back in Sweden: 5 years ago he sent her $1,000 to come to America, but she never showed up. Despite this experience, Yal has a new girl, Annie, who is his partner in a delicatessen in San Francisco. When they arrive in port, Captain Larsen, president of the company, offers him a promotion and a chance to buy a share in a new ship, the *Hulda*. He goes to tell Annie the news and finds her in Skole's arms. Yal throws him out after a fight. When he tells her about his opportunity, Annie refuses to sell the shop—and he cannot prove that it was bought with his money. Dejected, Yal seeks the docks. Unknown to Yal, Hulda never received the $1,000 he sent her but came to San Francisco anyhow and has been adopted by the Larsens. They meet, and she persuades him to return to work, telling him she is only a maid in the Larsen household. When Larsen dies, she inherits the estate and Yal is made president of the company. *Swedes. Sailors. Ship lines. Delicatessens. San Francisco.*

GUILTY *see* **THRU DIFFERENT EYES**

GUILTY **F2.2271**

Bill Miller Productions. Jun **1922** [scheduled release]. Si; b&w. 35mm. 5 reels.

Cast: Bill Miller, May Carson.

Drama(?). No information about the precise nature of this film has been found. *Northwest Mounted Police.*

Note: The New York State license application for this film was "abandoned."

GUILTY? **F2.2272**

Columbia Pictures. 3 Mar **1930** [c7 Mar 1930; LP1134]. Sd (Movietone); b&w. 35mm. 7 reels, 6,371 ft. [Also si.]

Prod Harry Cohn. *Dir* George B. Seitz. *Dial Dir* Ira Hards. *Story-Dial* Dorothy Howell. *Photog* Ted Tetzlaff. *Art Dir* Harrison Wiley. *Film Ed* Leon Barsha. *Ch Sd Engr* John P. Livadary. *Sd Mixing Engr* E. L. Bernds. *Asst Dir* Sam Nelson.

Cast: Virginia Valli *(Carolyn)*, John Holland *(Bob Lee)*, John St. Polis *(Polk)*, Lydia Knott *(Martha)*, Erville Alderson *(Lee)*, Richard Carlyle *(Dr. Bennett)*, Clarence Muse *(Jefferson)*, Eddie Clayton *(Jerry)*, Robert T. Haines *(prosecuting attorney)*, Frank Fanning *(warden)*, Edward Cecil *(judge)*, Gertrude Howard *(Lucy)*.

Society melodrama. Source: Dorothy Howell, "The Black Sheep" (publication undetermined). Senator Daniel Polk is sentenced to prison for bribery on circumstantial evidence, and as a result his daughter, Carolyn, is ostracized by the young set. Later, she attracts the attention of Bob Lee, son of the judge who convicted Polk, and they fall in love. Polk is released on parole, and Bob and Carolyn become engaged. Judge Lee, now a senator, and Polk quarrel bitterly over the engagement, and Lee threatens to report him unless Carolyn refuses to marry his son; she agrees to do so. Realizing the unhappiness he has caused his daughter, Polk commits suicide with an insecticide purchased by Bob for his daughter; and though the evidence is circumstantial, Bob is convicted on a murder charge. But Carolyn finds her father's confession in a Bible at the last minute and saves the boy from execution. *Judges. Bribery. Murder. Circumstantial evidence. Courtship. Suicide. Parole. United States Congress.*

A GUILTY CONSCIENCE **F2.2273**

Vitagraph Co. of America. 27 Nov **1921** [c8 Dec 1921; LP17327]. Si; b&w. 35mm. 5 reels.

Pres by Albert E. Smith. *Dir* David Smith. *Scen* Jay Pilcher. *Story* George Cameron. *Photog* George Robinson.

Cast: Antonio Moreno *(Gilbert Thurstan)*, Betty Francisco *(Emily Thurstan)*, Harry Van Meter *(Vincent Chalmers)*, Lila Leslie *(Ida Seabury)*, John MacFarlane *(James Roberts)*.

Melodrama. Gilbert Thurstan, deputy inspector of the British Civil Service Commission in India, is warned by his physician that his wife, Emily, cannot remain in the hot climate where he is stationed, and he applies to his superior, Vincent Chalmers, for a transfer. Chalmers, fascinated by Emily, sends Thurstan to a post in Kajra where the previous inspector died of fever, and Thurstan is able to send his wife to Simla, where Chalmers follows. While Chalmers seeks the favor of Mrs. Thurstan, her husband, fighting fever, clashes with Hindu fanatics and manages to quell the natives alone. Chalmers, repulsed by Emily, is conscience-stricken by visions of Thurstan dying and travels to Kajra to relieve him of his appointment. Thurstan is reassigned to another city, where his wife happily awaits him. *Hindus. India. British Civil Service Commission.*

THE GUILTY ONE **F2.2274**

Famous Players–Lasky. *Dist* Paramount Pictures. 8 Jun **1924** [c11 Jun 1924; LP20297]. Si; b&w. 35mm. 6 reels, 5,365 ft.

Pres by Adolph Zukor, Jesse L. Lasky. *Dir* Joseph Henabery. *Scen* Anthony Coldewey. *Photog* Faxon Dean.

Cast: Agnes Ayres *(Irene Short)*, Edward Burns *(Donald Short)*, Stanley Taylor *(Philip Dupre)*, Crauford Kent *(Seaton Davies)*, Cyril Ring *(H. Beverly Graves)*, Thomas R. Mills *(Sam Maynard)*, Catherine Wallace *(Bess Maynard)*, George Siegmann *(captain)*, Clarence Burton *(detective)*, Dorothea Wolbert *(Anne, the maid)*.

Mystery melodrama. Source: Michael Morton and Peter Traill, *The Guilty One* (New York opening: Mar 1914). Thinking she is helping her husband, Donald, Irene continues a friendship with Davies, a man-about-town who promises to help Donald get an architectural contract. Graves, a blackmailing publisher, prints the story of their affair, thereby casting suspicion on Donald and Philip Dupre, Irene's brother, when Davies is murdered. Irene effects their release by extracting a confession from Graves. *Publishers. Architects. Men-about-town. Blackmail. Infidelity. Circumstantial evidence.*

THE GUN FIGHTER (Reissue) **F2.2275**

Kay-Bee Pictures. *Dist* Film Distributors League. 25 Sep **1921**. Si; b&w. 35mm. 5 reels.

Note: A William S. Hart film originally released by Triangle Film Corp. on 11 Feb 1917.

GUN GOSPEL F2.2276

Charles R. Rogers Productions. *Dist* First National Pictures. 6 Nov **1927** [c1 Nov 1927; LP24591]. Si; b&w. 35mm. 7 reels, 6,228 ft.

Pres by Charles R. Rogers. *Dir* Harry J. Brown. *Titl* Don Ryan. *Adapt* Marion Jackson. *Photog* Sol Polito.

Cast: Ken Maynard *(Granger Hume)*, Bob Fleming *(Dad Walker)*, Romaine Fielding *(Richard Carrol)*, Virginia Brown Faire *(Mary Carrol)*, J. P. McGowan *(Bill Brogan)*, Jerry Madden *(orphan)*, Noah Young *(Jack Goodshot)*, Bill Dyer *(sheriff)*, Slim Whittaker *(Brogan's henchman)*, Tarzan *(himself, a horse)*.

Western melodrama. Source: William Dawson Hoffman, *Gun Gospel* (Chicago, 1926). Granger Hume, seeing his name posted for reward, discovers at a masquerade ball—where he meets and falls in love with Mary (or Nancy) Carrol—that Bill (or Badger) Brogan, a wealthy land-baron, seeks the capture of Hume and his partners because of a grudge against Dad Walker. In a confrontation with Brogan's henchmen, Walker is killed; but before dying, he tells Hume that the gospel of the gun is wrong and makes him promise not to avenge his death by shooting Brogan. Disguised as a parson, Hume overhears Brogan's plot to raid neighboring ranches and warns the people, and in self-defense he is forced to break his promise by killing Brogan when he is pursued by his men. Hume is lauded as a hero and wins the love of Mary. *Fugitives. Clergymen. Outlaws. Disguise. Guns. Horses.*

GUN LAW F2.2277

FBO Pictures. *Dist* RKO Productions. 3 Mar **1929** [c3 Mar 1929; LP337]. Si; b&w. 35mm. 6 reels, 4,746 ft.

Dir (see note) Robert De Lacey, John Burch. *Story-Scen* Oliver Drake. *Titl* Helen Gregg. *Photog* Nick Musuraca. *Film Ed* Jack Kitchen.

Cast: Tom Tyler *(Tom O'Brien)*, Barney Furey *(Cy Brown)*, Ethlyne Clair *(Nancy)*, Frankie Darro *(Buster Brown)*, Lew Meehan *(Big Bill Driscoll)*, Tom Brooker *(Surveyor)*, Harry Woods *(Bull Driscoll)*.

Western melodrama. Tom O'Brien asks Nancy Brown to marry him, and she refuses. The boundary lines of the Brown ranch are disputed by Driscoll, and Tom brings in a surveyor to settle the matter. The survey proves that a valuable marble quarry supposedly owned by Brown is in fact owned by no one, and Tom rushes to the land office, filing for the land in Nancy's name. Nancy then repents of her former coldness toward Tom and agrees to marry him. *Surveyors. Property rights. Marble. Quarries.*

Note: Sources disagree in crediting direction.

THE GUN RUNNER F2.2278

Tiffany-Stahl Productions. 20 Nov **1928** [c3 Nov 1928; LP25786]. Si; b&w. 35mm. 6 reels, 5,516 ft.

Dir Edgar Lewis. *Cont* J. F. Natteford. *Titl* Paul Perez. *Photog* Harry Jackson. *Film Ed* Sherman Kell.

Cast: Ricardo Cortez *(Julio)*, Nora Lane *(Inez)*, Gino Corrado *(García)*, John St. Polis *(Presidente)*.

Melodrama. Source: Arthur Stringer, *The Gun Runner* (New York, 1909). The president of a troubled Central American republic entrusts Julio with the capture of García, a gunrunner. Julio rents a room at an inn near the frontier and falls in love with Inez, the innkeeper. Going into the hills, Julio captures García only to lose him soon afterward. When García's men, seeking revenge, are unable to find Julio, the gunrunner himself comes down from the hills to take charge of the search: Julio again captures García and, learning that he is Inez' brother, lets him go in return for García's promise to give up guns and revolutions. Julio becomes a national hero and marries Inez. *Presidents. Innkeepers. Gunrunners. Revolutionaries. Central America.*

GUN SHY F2.2279

Phil Goldstone Productions. Sep **1922**. Si; b&w. 35mm. 5 reels.

Dir Alvin J. Neitz.

Cast: Franklyn Farnum *(James Brown)*, Florence Gilbert *(Betty Benson)*, Andrew Waldron *(Pop Benson)*, Robert Kortman *(Buck Brady)*, George F. Marion *(The Undertaker)*, William Dyer *(Bill Williams)*.

Western melodrama. Repeated raids on a southwestern town by a gang that wishes to appropriate a nearby mine coincide with the arrival of two strangers. James Brown, an easterner, is afraid of his own shadow, but the townspeople believe he is a marshal sent to restore law and order. While looking for an opportunity to escape, James learns that the other visitor, Bill Williams, is the real marshal, and an attempt on James's life spurs him to action. The mine is saved, and the gang leader is brought to justice. *United States marshals. Dudes. Gangs. Mistaken identity. Mine claims.*

GUN-HAND GARRISON F2.2280

Trem Carr Productions. *Dist* Rayart Pictures. Oct **1927**. Si; b&w. 35mm. 5 reels, 4,879 ft.

Dir Edward R. Gordon. *Scen* Arthur Hoerl. *Story* Hamilton. *Photog* Ernest Depew.

Cast: Tex Maynard, Ruby Blaine, Jack Anthony, Charles O'Malley, Charles Schaeffer, Edward Heim, Arthur Witting, Paul Malvern.

Western melodrama. "Stranger joins girl in saving ranch from thieves. In developments, leader of gang is murdered and the stranger, thinking girl's brother guilty, takes blame and rides off. Later he manages to get thieves in tight corner and forces them to divulge identity of real murderer, who happened to be leader's lieutenant." (*Motion Picture News Booking Guide*, [14]:256, 1929.) *Strangers. Gangs. Brother-sister relationship. Murder.*

THE GUNFIGHTER F2.2281

Fox Film Corp. 2 Sep **1923** [c2 Aug 1923; LP19320]. Si; b&w. 35mm. 5 reels, 4,700 ft.

Pres by William Fox. *Dir-Scen* Lynn F. Reynolds. *Photog* Dev Jennings.

Cast: William Farnum *(Billy Buell)*, Doris May *(Nellie Camp)*, L. C. Shumway *(Joe Benchley)*, J. Morris Foster *(Lew Camp)*, Virginia True Boardman *(Marjorie Camp)*, Irene Hunt *(Alice Benchley)*, Arthur Morrison *(Jacob Benchley)*, Cecil Van Auker *(William Camp)*, Jerry Campbell *(Henry Benchley)*.

Melodrama. Source: Max Brand, "Hired Guns," in *Western Story Magazine* (10 Mar 1923). A bitter feud begins in a southern mountain community between the Benchleys and the Camps when Lew Camp learns that his daughter Nell was taken from her mother to replace a dead child in the Benchley family. For years the Camps try to get Nell back; then Billy Buell, a chivalrous stranger, falls in love with her and restores her to her mother. The Benchley clan arrives at the Camp homestead for a shoot-up. The feud is ended, though, when Buell announces that he wishes to marry Nell. *Strangers. Kidnaping. Parentage. Feuds. Mountain life.*

THE GUNSAULUS MYSTERY F2.2282

Micheaux Film Corp. 18 Apr **1921** [New York premiere]. Si; b&w. 35mm. 7 reels.

Pres by Oscar Micheaux. *Prod-Dir-Writ* Oscar Micheaux. *Photog* Leonard Galezio.

Cast: Lawrence Chenault, Evelyn Preer, Edward R. Abrams, Louis De Bulger, Mattie Wilkes, Bessie Bearden, Ethel Williams, Edward Brown, Mabel Young, Hattie Christian, E. G. Tatum, Ethel Watts, George Russel, W. D. Sindle, Alix Kroll.

Melodrama. No information about the precise nature of this film has been found. *Negro life.*

THE GUTTERSNIPE (Universal Special) F2.2283

Universal Film Manufacturing Co. 30 Jan **1922** [c10 Jan 1922; LP17449]. Si; b&w. 35mm. 5 reels, 4,225 ft.

Pres by Carl Laemmle. *Dir* Dallas M. Fitzgerald. *Scen* Wallace Clifton. *Story* Percival Wilde. *Photog* Milton Moore.

Cast: Gladys Walton *(Mazie O'Day)*, Walter Perry *(Dennis O'Day)*, Kate Price *(Mrs. O'Day)*, Jack Perrin *(Tom Gilroy)*, Sidney Franklin *(Sam Rosen)*, Carmen Phillips *(Lady Clarissa)*, Edward Cecil *(Lord Bart)*, Hugh Saxon *(Angus)*, Seymour Zeliff *(Red Galvin)*, Eugene Corey *(Clarence Phillips)*, Lorraine Weiler *(Sally)*, Christian J. Frank *(Gregory)*.

Romantic satire. Mazie, a shopgirl of New York City's Little Ireland, goes to the aid of a young man in formal attire involved in a street fight. Though badly beaten, he bears a strong resemblance to Lord Lytton, the hero of a magazine story Mazie is reading in instalments. Although he is in reality a soda clerk, Mazie permits his attentions, and together they read the "Sloppy Stories" yarn about English nobility. When her beau is arrested as a counterfeiter, Mazie turns to the latest episode of the story for advice; and through this device the ending of their own love story is achieved. *Shopgirls. Irish. Soda clerks. Counterfeiters. Reading. New York City.*

Note: Also known as *The Gutter Snipe.*

GYPSY OF THE NORTH F2.2284

Trem Carr Productions. *Dist* Rayart Pictures. Mar or Apr **1928**. Si; b&w. 35mm. 6 reels, 5,813 or 5,976 ft.

Dir Scott Pembroke. *Scen* Arthur Hoerl. *Story* Howard Emmett Rogers.

Photog Hap Depew. *Film Ed* Charles A. Post.

Cast: Georgia Hale *(Alice Culhane)*, Huntley Gordon *(Steve Farrell)*, Jack Dougherty *(Chappie Evans)*, William Quinn *(Baptiste)*, Hugh Saxon *(Davey)*, Henry Roquemore *(theater manager)*, Erin La Bissoniere *(Jane)*.

Northwest melodrama. Just before she is to go on stage in her greatest role, an actress learns that her brother has been killed in Alaska, reportedly by his best friend. She immediately goes to the frozen North, dons her Gypsy costume, and works as a dancehall girl while searching for her brother's murderer. Eventually, the heroine discovers the guilty party to be the suave owner of the town saloon—not the pal. *Actors. Dancehall girls. Saloon keepers. Brother-sister relationship. Murder. Alaska.*

THE GYPSY ROMANCE **F2.2285**

Samuel Bischoff, Inc. *Dist* Prime Pictures. 22 Dec **1926** [New York State license]. Si; b&w. 35mm. 6 reels.

Cast: Thur Fairfax *(Jaime)*, Shannon Day *(Maya)*.

Melodrama. Maya, betrothed to a treacherous tribesman, is rescued from the wedding by Jaime. Both are caught, however, and are returned to the Gypsy camp where Jaime is sentenced to be burned alive. Maya joins him on the pyre, but both are saved by Maya's father and his men. *Gypsies. Weddings. Capital punishment.*

HAIL THE HERO **F2.2286**

Dist Film Booking Offices of America. 23 Nov **1924**. Si; b&w. 35mm. 5 reels.

Dir James W. Horne.

Cast: Richard Talmadge.

Melodrama(?). No information about the nature of this film has been found.

Note: Because it is unusual to find no information on a Richard Talmadge or an FBO film (the facts reported here are taken from the *Film Year Book*, 1925), it can be concluded that this film was probably also known by another title.

HAIL THE WOMAN **F2.2287**

Thomas H. Ince Productions. *Dist* Associated Producers. 28 Nov **1921** [c8 Dec 1921; LP17324]. Si; b&w. 35mm. 8 reels, 7,222 ft.

Pres by Thomas H. Ince. *Supv* Thomas H. Ince. *Dir* John Griffith Wray. *Story-Scen* C. Gardner Sullivan. *Photog* Henry Sharp.

Cast: Florence Vidor *(Judith Beresford)*, Lloyd Hughes *(David Beresford)*, Theodore Roberts *(Oliver Beresford)*, Gertrude Claire *(Mrs. Beresford)*, Madge Bellamy *(Nan Higgins)*, Tully Marshall *("Odd Jobs Man")*, Vernon Dent *(Joe Hurd)*, Edward Martindel *(Wyndham Gray)*, Charles Meredith *(Richard Stuart)*, Mathilde Brundage *(Mrs. Stuart)*, Eugene Hoffman *(The Baby)*, Muriel Frances Dana *(David, Junior)*.

Melodrama. Oliver Beresford, a bigoted New England farmer, puts women in their place with his uncompromising creed, "Men and their sons first." His son, David, who is studying for the ministry, secretly marries Nan, stepdaughter of the village odd-jobs man, and when Beresford learns that David is responsible for her pregnancy, and Nan does not reveal their marriage, he buys off her father, who drives her from home. She goes to New York, where her child is born, and she and the baby suffer from want and poverty while David maintains a cringing silence. The other daughter, Judith, defends Nan and also is driven from home; in New York she finds Nan, learns of her marriage, and after Nan dies cares for the child. Later, Judith returns with the child to her New England home on the day David is to be ordained as a missionary. Confronted by his child in the presence of the congregation, he confesses his sin and remorsefully acknowledges his son. *Farmers. Clergymen. Sisters. Bigotry. Fatherhood. New England. New York City.*

HAIR TRIGGER BAXTER **F2.2288**

Independent Pictures. *Dist* Film Booking Offices of America. 5 or 19 Sep **1926** [c5 Sep 1926; LP23125]. Si; b&w. 35mm. 5 reels, 4,690 ft.

Pres by Joseph P. Kennedy. *Prod* Jesse J. Goldburg. *Dir* Jack Nelson. *Cont* Paul M. Bryan. *Story* James Ormont. *Photog (see note)* Ernest Miller, Ernest Haller.

Cast: Bob Custer *(Baxter Brant)*, Eugenia Gilbert *(Rose Moss)*, Lew Meehan *(Mont Blake)*, Murdock MacQuarrie *(Joe Craddock)*, Fannie Midgley *(Mrs. Craddock)*, Jim Corey *(Jim Dodds)*, Ernie Adams *(Shorty Hillis)*, Hugh Saxon *(Silas Brant)*.

Western melodrama. Mont Blake, who controls the town of Sundown, is about to hang Shorty Hillis, a jockey who has drugged his racehorse. Rose, the jockey's sister, who is forced by her stepfather, Joe Craddock, to work in Blake's saloon, interferes; but Shorty is saved by Baxter Brant. At Craddock's ranch, Baxter forces the stepfather to protect Shorty and Rose, then proceeds to his father's ranch to help ferret out rustlers. Blake, who is in league with Craddock, forces him to surrender the girl, then is himself killed by Dodds, who kidnaps her. Baxter sends Shorty to bring his father, Silas, to apprehend the rustlers; and after a bitter fight he subdues Dodds and two other men, supposedly the Brants' faithful employees. Hair Trigger Baxter and Rose find happiness together. *Rustlers. Jockeys. Stepfathers. Brother-sister relationship. Lynching. Kidnaping. Saloons.*

Note: Sources disagree on photography credit.

HAIR TRIGGER CASEY (Mutual Masterpictures De Luxe) **F2.2289**

American Film Co. May **1922** [New York State]. Si; b&w. 35mm. 5 reels, 4,600 ft.

Dir Frank Borzage.

Cast: Frank Borzage *(Immediate Lee)*, Ann Little *(Beulah)*, Chick Morrison *(John Masters)*, Jack Richardson *(Kentucky Hurley)*.

Western melodrama. Original version, which may differ from this one (see note, below): Immediate Lee is dismissed from his job on John Masters' ranch through the influence of a fellow employee, who is involved with Masters in a brand-blotting scheme. Lee swears vengeance on brand-blotter Kentucky Hurley when the latter scars Lee's face. Beulah, a dancehall girl who has attracted Hurley's attentions, prefers Lee, but she intercedes for Hurley's life when the two men fight. Hurley is later killed in another skirmish, Lee helps expose and round up the brand-blotters, and Beulah is rewarded with Lee's proposal. *Cowboys. Dancehall girls. Rustling. Revenge. Branding.*

Note: According to advertising in *Motion Picture News* (3 Dec 1921, p2912), this film is a reedited and retitled version of *Immediate Lee*, which was released 16 Nov 1916. Role names may have been changed.

HALDANE OF THE SECRET SERVICE **F2.2290**

Houdini Picture Corp. *Dist* Film Booking Offices of America. 30 Sep **1923**. Si; b&w. 35mm. 6 reels, 5,908 ft.

Dir Harry Houdini. *Photog* Frank Zucker, Irving B. Rubenstein.

Cast: Harry Houdini *(Heath Haldane)*, Gladys Leslie *(Adele Ormsby)*, William Humphrey *(Edward Ormsby)*, Richard Carlyle *(Joe Ivor)*, Jane Jennings *(Mrs. Clara Usher)*, Charles Fang *(Ah Sing)*, Myrtle Morse *(Andrea Dayton)*, Irving Brooks *(Bruce Dayton)*, Edward Bouldin *(Raoul Usher)*.

Crook melodrama. "Houdini as the son of detective slain by gang of counterfeiters swears vengeance. He rescues girl from gang, but is thrown into river by them for dead, escapes, rounds them up after many adventures, brings about their arrest and discovers real leader is father of girl whom he loves." (*Motion Picture News Booking Guide*, 6:33, Apr 1924.) *Secret service. Counterfeiters. Escape artists. Revenge.*

HALF A BRIDE **F2.2291**

Paramount Famous Lasky Corp. 16 Jun **1928** [c16 Jun 1928; LP25385]. Si; b&w. 35mm. 7 reels, 6,238 ft.

Pres by Adolph Zukor, Jesse L. Lasky. *Dir* Gregory La Cava. *Scen* Doris Anderson, Percy Heath. *Titl* Julian Johnson. *Photog* Victor Milner. *Film Ed* Verna Willis.

Cast: Esther Ralston *(Patience Winslow)*, Gary Cooper *(Captain Edmunds)*, William Worthington *(Mr. Winslow)*, Freeman Wood *(Jed Session)*, Mary Doran *(Betty Brewster)*, Guy Oliver *(chief engineer)*, Ray Gallagher *(second engineer)*.

Drama. Source: Arthur Stringer, "White Hands," in *Saturday Evening Post* (vol 200, 30 Jul–20 Aug 1927). Thrill-seeker Patience Winslow hears a radio program on companionate marriage and enters into a trial marriage. It is never consummated, however, because her father breaks up the ill-advised union by kidnaping her and taking her aboard his private yacht. She escapes from the yacht in a launch, but Edmunds, captain of the yacht, jumps overboard after her. A storm arises and they are cast ashore. During the weeks of privation that precede their rescue, Patience learns to love her fellow castaway. Her previous marriage annulled, she marries, with parental enthusiasm, Edmunds. *Sea captains. Castaways. Marriage—Trial. Marriage—Annulment. Fatherhood. Thrill-seeking.*

THE HALF BREED **F2.2292**

Oliver Morosco Productions. *Dist* Associated First National Pictures. Jun **1922** [c15 Nov 1921, 7 Jul 1922; LU17194, LP18037]. Si; b&w. 35mm. 6 reels, 5,484 ft.

Pres by Oliver Morosco. *Dir-Scen* Charles A. Taylor. *Photog* Charles G. Clarke, James C. Hutchinson. *Film Ed* Elmer J. McGovern.

Cast: Wheeler Oakman *(Delmar Spavinaw, the halfbreed)*, Ann May *(Doll Pardeau)*, Mary Anderson *(Evelyn Huntington)*, Hugh Thompson *(Ross Kennion)*, King Evers *(Dick Kennion)*, Joseph Dowling *(Judge Huntington)*, Lew Harvey *(The Snake)*, Herbert Pryor *(Ned Greenwood)*, Sidney De Gray *(Leon Pardeau)*, Nick De Ruiz *(Juan Del Rey)*, Leela Lane *(Isabelle Pardeau)*, Eugenia Gilbert *(Marianne)*, Carl Stockdale *(John Spavinaw)*, Evelyn Selbie *(Mary)*, Dorris Deane *(Nanette)*, Albert S. Lloyd *(Hops)*, George Kuwa *(Kito)*.

Western melodrama. Source: H. D. Cottrell and Oliver Morosco, *Half-Breed; a Tale of Indian Territory; Comedy Drama in Four Acts* (c1906). Delmar Spavinaw, an educated halfbreed, loves Evelyn Huntington, daughter of a racist judge. Evelyn's other suitor is Ross Kennion, a widower with one child, and owner of a vast tract of land which Spavinaw insists belongs to his Indian mother. Spavinaw seeks revenge when Judge Huntington decides to evict the squaw. Assisted by Juan Del Rey, a cattle rustler, Spavinaw steals the title to the land, wounds Kennion, stages a raid on the judge's cattle, and attempts to kidnap Kennion's son and Evelyn. The arrival of the sheriff forces him into flight across the border without his hostages. En route he meets Doll Pardeau, a school friend of Evelyn's, and together they ride for the Mexican border. Caught between a cattle stampede and a sheriff's posse, the couple catch a passing freight train, leaving calamity behind as the train slowly passes. *Squatters. Indians of North America. Halfcastes. Racism. Land rights.*

THE HALF BREED (Reissue) **F2.2293**

Fine Arts Pictures. *Dist* Tri-Stone Pictures. **1924.** Si; b&w. 35mm. 5 reels.

Note: A "re-edited and re-titled" Douglas Fairbanks film originally released by Triangle Film Corp. on 30 Jul 1916.

HALF MARRIAGE **F2.2294**

RKO Productions. 13 Oct **1929** [c13 Oct 1929; LP760, LP897]. Sd (Photophone); b&w. 35mm. 7 reels, 6,501 ft. [Also si; 5,883 ft.]

Prod William Le Baron. *Dir* William J. Cowen. *Scen-Dial* Jane Murfin. *Art Dir* Max Ree. *Film Ed* Archie Marshek. *Song: "After the Clouds Roll By"* Sidney Clare, Oscar Levant.

Cast: Olive Borden *(Judy Page)*, Morgan Farley *(Dick Carroll)*, Ken Murray *(Charles Turner)*, Ann Greenway *(Ann Turner)*, Anderson Lawler *(Tom Stribbling)*, Sally Blane *(Sally)*, Hedda Hopper *(Mrs. Page)*, Richard Tucker *(George Page)*, James Bradbury, Jr. *(Poverty)*, Jack Trent *(Rudy)*, James Eagle *(Matty)*, G. Pat Collins *(Mulhall)*, Gus Arnheim and His Cocoanut Grove Ambassadors.

Romantic drama. Source: George Kibbe Turner, "Half Marriage" (publication undetermined). Following a party at Judy Page's Greenwich Village apartment, she elopes with Dick Carroll, a young architect employed by her father. Later, Judy's mother arrives, insisting that she return to the Page country estate, while Dick hides in the apartment. He visits Judy while her parents are away and quarrels with Tom Stribbling, who monopolizes Judy's attentions at a country club dance. They make an appointment to meet at Judy's apartment, but Tom learns of their plan, sends a telegram to Dick canceling the meeting, and meets the girl himself. Tom attempts to force his attention on her; and, in a struggle outside her window, he falls to his death just as Dick enters the apartment. Dick assumes blame for Tom's death, but investigation reveals that Judy is justified; their secret marriage is revealed, and Judy's parents, after admonishment, give their blessing to the couple. *Architects. Elopement. Marriage. Parenthood. New York City—Greenwich Village.*

HALF SHOT AT SUNRISE **F2.2295**

RKO Productions. 4 Oct **1930** [c25 Sep 1930; LP1588]. Sd (Photophone); b&w. 35mm. 10 reels, 7,059 ft.

Prod William Le Baron. *Assoc Prod* Henry Hobart. *Dir* Paul Sloane. *Story-Scen* James Ashmore Creelman. *Dial* Anne Caldwell, Ralph Spence. *Photog* Nick Musuraca. *Film Ed* Arthur Roberts. *Song: "Nothing But Love"* Anne Caldwell, Harry Tierney. *Dance Dir* Mary Read. *Sd Rec* Hugh McDowell.

Cast: Bert Wheeler *(Tommy)*, Robert Woolsey *(Gilbert)*, Dorothy Lee *(Annette)*, Hugh Trevor *(Lieut. Jim Reed)*, Edna May Oliver *(Mrs. Marshall)*, Eddie De Lange *(military policeman)*, E. H. Calvert *(General Hale)*, Alan Roscoe *(Captain Jones)*, John Rutherford *(M. P. sergeant)*, George MacFarlane *(Colonel Marshall)*, Roberta Robinson *(Eileen)*, Leni Stengel *(Olga)*.

Comedy. Colonel Marshall, with the United States Army in Paris, is charged with the delivery of important orders pertaining to a major offensive, but instead he gets love notes from Olga, a French flirt whom his wife does not appreciate. His daughter, Eileen, loves Lieut. Jim Reed, whom the colonel dislikes. Meanwhile, Tommy and Gilbert, buck privates, go A. W. O. L., and to escape pursuit by military police, they steal the colonel's car, along with Annette, his younger daughter. To win them the colonel's forgiveness, Annette and Olga plan to make the boys heroes by intercepting papers intended for Lieutenant Reed, detailed to the front, and sending the boys on Reed's mission. They are captured, and the colonel threatens to have them shot; but they blackmail him to forgive them with the aid of one of Olga's perfumed love notes. *Soldiers. Flirtation. Blackmail. United States Army—Military Police. World War I. Paris.*

HALF-A-DOLLAR BILL **F2.2296**

Graf Productions. *Dist* Metro Pictures. 14 Jan **1924** [c1 Jan 1924; LP19791]. Si; b&w. 35mm. 6 reels, ca5,800 ft.

Prod-Adapt Max Graf. *Dir* William S. Van Dyke. *Titl* Alfred A. Cohn. *Story* Curtis Benton. *Photog* André Barlatier.

Cast: Anna Q. Nilsson *(The Stranger [Mrs. Webber])*, William P. Carleton *(Captain Duncan McTeague)*, Raymond Hatton *("Noodles," the cook)*, Mitchell Lewis *(Papeete Joe)*, Alec B. Francis *(Judge Norton)*, George MacQuarrie *(Martin Webber)*, Frankie Darro *(Half-a-Dollar Bill)*, Irish, Cameo *(themselves, boston terriers)*, Rosa Gore.

Melodrama. McTeague, captain of the *Grampus*, finds a baby boy with half of a dollar bill pinned to his shirt. An attached note from the mother who abandoned him indicates that she will one day claim her child with the other half of the dollar. The captain calls him Bill, becomes very fond of the child, and protects him from the taunts of Webber, the ship's mate, who is revealed to be the child's father. Webber is fired, kidnaps the boy in revenge, and dies accidentally after a fight with the captain, who marries Bill's mother when she comes to claim her child. *Infants. Foundlings. Parentage. Kidnaping. Seafaring life. Dogs.*

THE HALF-WAY GIRL **F2.2297**

First National Pictures. 16 Aug **1925** [c10 Aug 1925; LP21707]. Si; b&w. 35mm. 8 reels, 7,570 ft.

Supv Earl Hudson. *Dir* John Francis Dillon. *Scen* Joseph Poland, Earl Snell. *Story* E. Lloyd Sheldon. *Photog* George Folsey. *Art Dir* Milton Menasco. *Film Ed* Marion Fairfax.

Cast: Doris Kenyon *(Poppy La Rue)*, Lloyd Hughes *(Philip Douglas)*, Hobart Bosworth *(John Guthrie)*, Tully Marshall *(The Crab)*, Sam Hardy *(Jardine)*, Charles Wellesley *(Gibson)*, Martha Madison *(Miss Brown)*, Sally Crute *(Effie)*.

Melodrama. Disillusioned by war and a faithless woman, Philip Douglas Guthrie, the son of the Superintendent of Singapore Police, gets drunk in a dive and accidentally kills the owner when he attempts to take Philip's wallet. Philip goes into hiding under the name of Douglas and meets Poppy La Rue, a member of a stranded theatrical troupe who has been forced by poverty to become a hostess in a low dive. Poppy and Philip fall in love, and she helps him to find refuge on a steamer bound for Penang. Going back for Philip's luggage, she is discovered by Phillip's father, who mistakes her for an adventuress and sends her into the Singapore red light district. She escapes from a house of ill repute and gets on the steamer. The boat blows up, and, after surviving several hazards, Philip and Poppy are reunited. Philip is reconciled with his father, and Poppy forgives the old man for having misjudged her motives. *Fugitives. Police. Cafe hostesses. Drunkenness. Murder. Whorehouses. Singapore. Ship explosions.*

HALF-WAY TO HEAVEN **F2.2298**

Paramount Famous Lasky Corp. 14 Dec **1929** [c13 Dec 1929; LP919]. Sd (Movietone); b&w. 35mm. 8 reels, 6,254 ft. [Also si; 5,179 ft.]

Dir-Adapt George Abbott. *Titl* Gerald Geraghty. *Photog* Alfred Gilks, Charles Lang. *Film Ed* William Shea. *Song: "Louise"* Leo Robin, Richard Whiting. *Rec Engr* Earl Hayman.

Cast: Charles "Buddy" Rogers *(Ned Lee)*, Jean Arthur *(Greta Nelson)*, Paul Lukas *(Nick)*, Helen Ware *(Madame Elsie)*, Oscar Apfel *(manager)*, Edna West *(Mrs. Lee)*, Irving Bacon *(Slim)*, Al Hill *(Blackie)*, Lucille Williams *(Doris)*, Richard K. French *(Klein)*, Freddy Anderson *(Tony)*, Nestor Aber *(Eric)*, Ford West *(stationmaster)*, Guy Oliver *(farmer)*.

Romantic melodrama. Source: Henry Leyford Gates, *Here Comes the Bandwagon* (New York, 1928). Nick, the "swing" man in a trapeze troupe, loves Greta Nelson, the girl in the act; and Tony, the "flyer," incurs his enmity as Greta seems to favor him; thus Nick fails to catch Tony, and

Tony is killed. Ned Lee, a novice, reports for the next engagement. Meanwhile, Greta discovers that Nick purposely dropped Tony, and, frightened, she seeks refuge with Ned, with whom she falls in love. Greta remains with the act to protect Ned, and when the jealous Nick plots to kill him in a similar manner, Ned swings past him and hangs by his feet. After the show, a fight results in Nick's dismissal and the reunion of the lovers. *Trapezists. Circus. Murder. Jealousy.*

HALLELUJAH **F2.2299**

Metro-Goldwyn-Mayer Pictures. 20 Aug **1929** [c3 Sep 1929; LP652]. Sd (Movietone); b&w. 35mm. 12 reels, 9,711 ft. [Also si; 6,579 ft.]

Story-Dir King Vidor. *Scen* Wanda Tuchock. *Dial* Ransom Rideout. *Titl* Marian Ainslee. *Treatment* Richard Schayer. *Photog* Gordon Avil. *Art Dir* Cedric Gibbons. *Film Ed* Hugh Wynn, Anson Stevenson. *Songs: "Waiting at the End of the Road," "Swanee Shuffle"* Irving Berlin. *Rec Engr* Douglas Shearer. *Asst Dir* Robert A. Golden. *Wardrobe* Henrietta Frazer.

Cast: Daniel L. Haynes *(Zeke)*, Nina Mae McKinney *(Chick)*, William E. Fountaine *(Hot Shot)*, Harry Gray *(Parson)*, Fannie Belle De Night *(Mammy)*, Everett McGarrity *(Spunk)*, Victoria Spivey *(Missy Rose)*, Milton Dickerson, Robert Couch, Walter Tait *(Johnson kids)*, Dixie Jubilee Singers.

Drama. Accompanied by a younger brother, Zeke (a Negro tenant farmer) takes the family cotton crop to market and sells it for nearly $100. Chick, a dancehall temptress, then uses her wiles to lure Zeke into a crap game with her lover, Hot Shot, who cheats Zeke out of his money with loaded dice. Zeke and Hot Shot fight, and Zeke gets possession of Hot Shot's gun, firing point blank into the crowd. Zeke accidentally kills his brother and, in repentance, becomes a preacher. Zeke again meets Chick, and she gets religion, deserting Hot Shot to go with him. Zeke falls for Chick and jilts Missy Rose. Hot Shot returns, and the fickle Chick goes off with him. Zeke gives chase, and Chick is killed when Hot Shot's buggy overturns. Zeke then kills Hot Shot in a swamp and after serving time on the chain gang returns home to the faithful Rose. *Brothers. Tenant farmers. Vamps. Gamblers. Preachers. Gambling. Cotton. Religion. Negro life. Chain gangs.*

Note: Several traditional Negro spirituals are used in the film, including "Goin' Home" and "Swing Low, Sweet Chariot."

HAM AND EGGS AT THE FRONT **F2.2300**

Warner Brothers Pictures. 24 Dec **1927** [c14 Nov 1927; LP24662]. Si; b&w. 35mm. 6 reels, 5,613 ft.

Dir Roy Del Ruth. *Scen* Robert Dillon, James A. Starr. *Story* Darryl Francis Zanuck. *Photog* Charles Clarke. *Asst Dir* Ross Lederman.

Cast: Tom Wilson *(Ham)*, Heinie Conklin *(Eggs)*, Myrna Loy *(Fifi)*, William J. Irving *(von Friml)*, Noah Young *(Sergeant)*, Cameo *(himself, a dog)*.

Comedy. Ham and Eggs, privates in an all-Negro regiment, become buddies while at training camp and are stationed together in a small French village. The innkeeper, Friml, an enemy spy, desirous of learning the number of soldiers in the Negro regiment, has Fifi, his Negro waitress, flirt with the soldiers so as to get this information. Ham and Eggs fall for her flirtation and go to her house that night, each trying to outstay the other. An officer commands the two to force her to disclose the location of Friml and to shoot her if she refuses to talk; she escapes them, but they uncover a coded enemy message. When the pair are sent to the front, Ham is wounded; they are accidentally cast adrift in a balloon; and in parachuting to safety, they "capture" Friml. They are later decorated for their bravery. *Spies. Balloons. World War I. France. United States Army—Negro troops. Dogs.*

Note: Copyright title: *Ham and Eggs.*

HANDCUFFED **F2.2301**

Trem Carr Productions. *Dist* Rayart Pictures. 8 Aug **1929.** Sd; b&w. 35mm. 6 reels, 5,393 ft. [Also si; 5,666 ft.]

Pres by W. Ray Johnston. *Dir* Duke Worne. *Story-Scen-Dial* Arthur Hoerl. *Photog* Hap Depew. *Tech Dir* E. R. Hickson. *Film Ed* John S. Harrington. *Sd Engr* Freeman Lang. *Prod Mgr* Charles R. Post.

Cast: Virginia Brown Faire *(Gloria Randall)*, Wheeler Oakman *(Tom Bennett)*, Dean Jagger *(Gerald Morely)*, James Harrison *(Billy Hatton)*, Broderick O'Farrell *(John Randall)*, George Chesebro *(detective)*, Frank Clark, Charles West.

Mystery melodrama. Gerald Morely's father commits suicide, leaving a note blaming his despair on a stock swindle perpetrated by John Randall. Denying the charge, Randall is himself murdered by Tom Bennett, who then has Deagan (the butler) plant the murder weapon so as to frame Jerry. Posing as her protector, Bennett persuades Randall's daughter, Gloria, to marry him. Meanwhile, Jerry falls in love with Gloria, is arrested, tried for murder, and found guilty. He escapes on Gloria's wedding night and arrives in time to overhear her admit her love for him and Bennett drunkenly confess to Randall's murder. The police join the scene, Bennett dies in a fall, his accomplice confesses, and there is a happy ending for Jerry and Gloria. *Swindlers. Butlers. Murder. Suicide. Trials.*

HANDCUFFS OR KISSES **F2.2302**

Selznick Pictures. *Dist* Select Pictures. 5 Sep **1921** [c10 Sep 1921; LP16953]. Si; b&w. 35mm. 6 reels.

Pres by Lewis J. Selznick. *Dir* George Archainbaud. *Scen* Lewis Allen Browne. *Photog* Jules Cronjager.

Cast: Elaine Hammerstein *(Lois Walton)*, Julia Swayne Gordon *(Mrs. Walton)*, Dorothy Chappell *(Violet)*, Robert Ellis *(Peter Madison)*, Alison Skipworth *(Miss Strodd)*, Florence Billings *(Miss Dell)*, Ronald Schabel *(Leo Carstairs)*, George Lessey *(Elias Pratt)*, Ronald Colman *(Lodyard)*.

Melodrama. Source: Thomas Edgelow, "Handcuffs and Kisses," in *Young's Magazine* (40:3–47, Dec 1920). Orphan Lois Walton is treated unkindly by her aunt, who has her placed in a reformatory. She and the other inmates are badly abused but are afraid to complain, and she remains silent after a riot is subdued. She arouses the sympathy of Peter Madison, a lawyer who conducts an investigation, and is paroled. Placed in a doctor's home, she is frightened by his advances and runs away. Refusing Madison's offer of refuge in his apartment, she becomes social secretary to Miss Dell, operator of a gambling house, who tries to force her into a marriage with wealthy young Leo Carstairs; but she is saved by Madison, who claims her as his own wife. *Orphans. Lawyers. Physicians. Parole. Reformatories. Gambling.*

THE HANDICAP **F2.2303**

Phil Goldstone Productions. 17 Jun **1925** [New York State license]. Si; b&w. 35mm. 5 reels.

Melodrama(?). No information about the nature of this film has been found.

HANDLE WITH CARE **F2.2304**

Rockett Film Corp. *Dist* Associated Exhibitors. 22 Jan **1922** [c31 Dec 1921; LU17415]. Si; b&w. 35mm. 5 reels.

Prod Al Rockett, Ray Rockett. *Dir* Philip E. Rosen. *Scen* Will M. Ritchie. *Photog* Philip Hurn.

Cast: Grace Darmond *(Jeanne Lee)*, Harry Myers *(Ned Picard)*, James Morrison *(Phil Burnham)*, Landers Stevens *(David Norris)*, William Austin *(Peter Carter)*, William Courtleigh *(MacCullough)*, Patsy Ruth Miller *(Marian)*.

Domestic comedy. Source: Charles Belmont Davis, "Handle With Care" (publication undetermined). Although five of her suitors declare they would die for her, Jeanne marries young lawyer David Norris. Two years later, David, absorbed in an important lawsuit, forgets their wedding anniversary, and when reprimanded for his neglect, he agrees to give Jeanne a divorce if any one of her ex-suitors will elope with her. Jeanne picks up Phil Burnham on his morning walk and recalls old times, but when asked to elope, he confesses to being engaged; Ned Picard, although staggered by her proposition, consents, then accepts David's offer of $10,000 to call it off. Jeanne is prepared to relent until she sees David kissing Marian, his pretty ward. David follows Jeanne to the office of Peter Carter, an author of books on marriage, who declares his love for her; but threatened by David with a gun, Peter's cries of mercy prove him unworthy. MacCullough, the last of her ex-suitors, almost carries her off but proves to be Marian's new husband and brings about a reunion of Jeanne with David. *Lawyers. Authors. Marriage. Elopement. Divorce.*

HANDS ACROSS THE BORDER **F2.2305**

R-C Pictures. *Dist* Film Booking Offices of America. 1 May **1926** [c30 Apr 1926; LP22669]. Si; b&w. 35mm. 6 reels, 5,367 ft.

Dir David Kirkland. *Scen* William E. Wing. *Titl* Malcolm Stuart Boylan. *Story* Frank M. Clifton. *Photog* Ross Fisher.

Cast: Fred Thomson *(Fred Drake)*, [Frederick] Tyrone Power *(John Drake)*, Bess Flowers *(Ysabel Castro)*, William Courtwright *(Grimes)*, Clarence Geldert *(Don Castro)*, Tom Santschi *(Breen)*, Silver King *(a horse)*.

Western melodrama. At a horseshow, Fred Drake, son of a wealthy Los

Angeles businessman, sees a beautiful Spanish girl forcibly carried off by automobile. Fred gives chase, pursuing the car through traffic, even across private lawns, but manages to elude the traffic police; at length, he rescues the girl, Ysabel Castro, from a boarding school and delivers her to a speeding express bound for Mexico. Fred's father wishes to send him to the border to investigate narcotic smuggling on his property, and he agrees to go upon discovering that the neighboring ranch belongs to the Castros. In course, Fred ambushes two men who shoot the smugglers' messenger; and impersonating him, he returns to the Castro ranch where he has been courting Ysabel. Soon his ruse is discovered, and he is taken prisoner. He is about to be executed along with Castro and the girl when Silver King brings a detachment of American and Mexican cavalry to the rescue. *Spanish. Smugglers. Narcotics. Horseshows. Mexican border. Los Angeles. United States Army—Cavalry. Chases. Horses.*

THE HANDS OF NARA F2.2306

Samuel Zierler Photoplay Corp. *Dist* Metro Pictures. ca26 Aug **1922** [Atlanta premiere; released 18 Sep; c15 Sep 1922; LP18387]. Si; b&w. 35mm. 6 reels, 6,000 ft. [Copyrighted as 7 reels.]

Pres by Harry Garson. *Dir* Harry Garson. *Photog* L. W. O'Connell.

Cast: Clara Kimball Young *(Nara Alexieff)*, Count John Orloff *(Boris Alexieff)*, Elliott Dexter *(Emlen Claveloux)*, Edwin Stevens *(Connor Lee)*, Vernon Steele *(Adam Pine)*, John Miltern *(Dr. Haith Claveloux)*, Margaret Loomis *(Emma Gammell)*, Martha Mattox *(Mrs. Miller)*, Dulcie Cooper *(Carrie Miller)*, Ashley Cooper *(Gus Miller)*, Myrtle Stedman *(Vanessa Yates)*, Eugenie Besserer *(Mrs. Claveloux)*.

Melodrama. Source: Richard Washburn Child, *The Hands of Nara* (New York, 1922). Nara Alexieff, a Russian refugee from the Bolshevik revolution, comes to New York and is "taken up" by society woman Vanessa Yates. She meets Connor Lee, who convinces Nara that her hands have healing powers; sculptor Adam Pine; and Dr. Emlen Claveloux, who falls in love with Nara but rejects her when he suspects she is involved with Pine. Nara causes several cures, and, when the stories reach Emlen's father, the elder Dr. Claveloux begs Nara to help his wife. When she does so, Emlen reconsiders both his total reliance on science and his opinion of Nara, and they marry. *Russians. Physicians. Sculptors. Refugees. Faith cure.*

HANDS OFF F2.2307

Fox Film Corp. 3 Apr **1921** [c3 Apr 1921; LP16390]. Si; b&w. 35mm. 5 reels, 4,158 ft.

Pres by William Fox. *Dir* George E. Marshall. *Scen* Frank Howard Clark. *Story* William MacLeod Raine. *Photog* Ben Kline.

Cast: Tom Mix *(Tex Roberts)*, Pauline Curley *(Ramona Wadley)*, Charles K. French *(Clint Wadley)*, Lloyd Bacon *(Ford Wadley)*, Frank Clark *(Capt. Jim Ellison)*, Sid Jordan *(Pete Dinsmore)*, William McCormick *(Tony Alviro)*, Virginia Warwick *(Bonita)*, J. Webster Dill *(The Terrible Swede)*, Marvin Loback *(Jumbo)*.

Western melodrama. When Tex Roberts rides into a border town and rescues Ramona Wadley from the unwelcome attentions of Pete Dinsmore, leader of a gang of rustlers, and later snatches her sister from the path of a stampede, he is awarded a job on the Wadley ranch. When the owner sends his son, Ford, who is in league with Dinsmore, to collect money, a fake holdup is staged and Ford is killed. Tex is arrested but clears his name and fights to a showdown with Pete and the gang. *Cowboys. Rustling. Ranches. Stampedes.*

HANDS OFF (Blue Streak Western) F2.2308

Universal Pictures. 19 Jun **1927** [c17 May 1927; LP23993]. Si; b&w. 35mm. 5 reels, 4,773 ft.

Pres by Carl Laemmle. *Dir* Ernst Laemmle. *Scen* William B. Lester, George H. Plympton. *Adapt* Robert F. Hill. *Story* J. Allen Dunn. *Photog* Al Jones. *Art Dir* David S. Garber.

Cast: Fred Humes *(Sandy Loom)*, Helen Foster *(Myra Perkins)*, George Connors *("Stills" Manners)*, Nelson McDowell *(Professor Hawley)*, Bruce Gordon *(Simeon Coe)*, William Dyer *(Judge Emory)*, William Ellingford *(Sheriff Daws)*, Bert Apling *(Bull Duncan)*.

Western melodrama. Sandy Loom, a young drifter, finds prospector Jim Perkins dying and promises to take care of his daughter Myra. Aided by Professor Hawley and "Stills" Manners, he works her father's gold claim. Simeon Coe, a land shark and claim jumper, asks the judge to appoint him the girl's guardian, swearing it was Jim's last request, and though the judge refuses, Coe orders Sandy and his pals off the claim, backed by the sheriff. Sandy is jailed but is released by the judge and corners Coe in a mine shaft, where the latter falls to his death. The gold claim proves worthless, but Sandy finds happiness with Myra. *Prospectors. Wanderers. Guardians. Claim jumpers. Sheriffs. Mine claims. Gold.*

HANDS UP! F2.2309

Famous Players–Lasky. *Dist* Paramount Pictures. 11 Jan **1926** [c11 Jan 1926; LP22253]. Si; b&w. 35mm. 6 reels, 5,883 ft.

Pres by Adolph Zukor, Jesse L. Lasky. *Dir* Clarence Badger. *Scen* Monty Brice, Lloyd Corrigan. *Story* Reginald Morris. *Photog* H. Kinley Martin.

Cast: Raymond Griffith *(Confederate spy)*, Marion Nixon *(The Girl He Loves)*, Virginia Lee Corbin *(The Other Girl He Loves)*, Mack Swain *(mineowner)*, Montague Love *(Union general)*, George Billings *(Abraham Lincoln)*, Noble Johnson *(Sitting Bull)*, Charles K. French *(Brigham Young)*.

Comedy. President Lincoln calls his cabinet into session in order to underline the fact that the fate of the Union depends on finding a new source of finance. He then receives word that a western mineowner will supply the Union with gold, and Lincoln sends a messenger for it. Simultaneously, General Lee sends a Confederate spy to the West to forestall the Union messenger. Eluding death at the hands of firing squads and Indians, the Confederate spy finally locates the stagecoach that is bringing back the Union gold. The spy is caught, and, when he is about to be hanged, the daughters of the mineowner, who have both fallen in love with him, save his life. The war ends, and the spy sets off with both the young girls for Salt Lake City, where he prepares to settle down in bigamy blessed by the Latter-day Saints. *Spies. Funds—Public. Bigamy. United States—History—Civil War. Abraham Lincoln. Robert Edward Lee. Brigham Young. Sitting Bull. Church of Jesus Christ of Latter-day Saints.*

THE HANDSOME BRUTE F2.2310

Columbia Pictures. 1 Dec **1925** [c11 Jan 1926; LP22256]. Si; b&w. 35mm. 5 reels, 4,779 ft.

Dir Robert Eddy. *Scen* Lillian Taft Maize. *Photog* George Meehan.

Cast: William Fairbanks *(Larry O'Day)*, Virginia Lee Corbin *(Nelly Egan)*, Lee Shumway *(John Granger)*, Robert Bolder *(Thomas Egan)*, J. J. Bryson *(captain)*, Daniel Belmont *(watchman)*.

Melodrama. Through misadventure and bad luck, Larry O'Day loses his job on the metropolitan police force. Working on his own initiative, he goes after the Brady gang, a group of notorious thugs. John Granger, an internationally known detective, is called in on the case, and Larry notices that Granger bears a close resemblance to a certain well-known criminal. Larry trails the detective and discovers him in the act of looting a jewelry store owned by Thomas Egan, the father of Larry's sweetheart, Nelly. In a hard-fought fight, Larry subdues Granger and his two accomplices. He is reinstated to the force and marries Nelly. *Police. Jewelers. Detectives. Robbery.*

HANGMAN'S HOUSE F2.2311

Fox Film Corp. 13 May **1928** [c13 May 1928; LP25248]. Si; b&w. 35mm. 7 reels, 6,518 ft.

Pres by William Fox. *Dir* John Ford. *Scen (see note)* Marion Orth, Willard Mack. *Titl* Malcolm Stuart Boylan. *Adapt* Philip Klein. *Photog* George Schneiderman. *Film Ed* Margaret V. Clancey. *Asst Dir* Phil Ford.

Cast: June Collyer *(Connaught O'Brien)*, Larry Kent *(Dermott McDermott)*, Earle Foxe *(John Darcy)*, Victor McLaglen *(Citizen Hogan)*, Hobart Bosworth *(Lord Chief Justice O'Brien)*, Joseph Burke *(Neddy Joe)*, Eric Mayne *(Colonel of Legionnaires)*, Belle Stoddard *(Anne McDermott)*.

Melodrama. Source: Brian Oswald Donn-Byrne, *Hangman's House* (New York & London, 1926). Irish lass Connaught O'Brien is in love with Dermott McDermott, but to please her dying father she marries John Darcy, a drunkard and a wastrel. Darcy meets his death in a duel with soldier of fortune Citizen Hogan, whose sister Darcy wronged, leaving Connaught free to marry her childhood sweetheart. *Irish. Soldiers of fortune. Marriage. Alcoholism. Ireland. Duels.*

Note: Sources disagree in crediting scenarist.

HAPPINESS F2.2312

Metro Pictures. 9 Mar **1924** [c5 Mar 1924; LP20031]. Si; b&w. 35mm. 8 reels, 7,745 ft.

Dir King Vidor. *Adapt-Cont* J. Hartley Manners. *Photog* Chester A. Lyons.

Cast: Laurette Taylor *(Jenny Wreay)*, Pat O'Malley *(Fermoy MacDonough)*, Hedda Hopper *(Mrs. Chrystal Pole)*, Cyril Chadwick

(Philip Chandos), Edith Yorke *(Mrs. Wreay)*, Patterson Dial *(Sallie Perkins)*, Joan Standing *(Jenny)*, Lawrence Grant *(Mr. Rosselstein)*, Charlotte Mineau *(head saleslady)*.

Society drama. Source: J. Hartley Manners, "Happiness," in *Happiness and Other Plays* (New York, 1914). Jenny, a poor New York shopgirl, is befriended by two members of the bored and idle rich, Mrs. Chrystal Pole and Philip Chandos, who through the association deepen their lives. The girl marries Fermoy MacDonough, an electrician, and years later these four principals are able to recount their experience to benefit another waif. *Shopgirls. Electricians. Philanthropy. Poverty. New York City.*

HAPPINESS AHEAD **F2.2313**

First National Pictures. 24 Jun **1928** [c12 Jun 1928; LP25360]. Si; b&w. 35mm. 8 reels, 7,100 ft.

Pres by John McCormick. *Dir* William A. Seiter. *Scen* Benjamin Glazer. *Titl* George Marion. *Story* Edmund Goulding. *Photog* Sid Hickox. *Film Ed* Paul Weatherwax.

Cast: Colleen Moore *(Mary Randall)*, Edmund Lowe *(Babe Stewart)*, Charles Sellon *(Mr. Randall)*, Edythe Chapman *(Mrs. Randall)*, Carlos Durand *(Vargas)*, Lilyan Tashman *(Kay)*, Robert Elliott *(detective)*, Diane Ellis *(Edna)*.

Melodrama. Cardsharp Babe Stewart hides out in upstate New York when his irate partner and mistress, Kay, threatens to turn him over to the police. There he meets Mary, daughter of local hardware store proprietor Randall; marries her; returns to New York City; and obtains a position in a brokerage office. While he is eating his birthday dinner, detectives tipped off by Kay arrive and arrest him for cardsharping. Sentenced to a 6-month prison term, Babe leads Mary to believe that he is going on a business trip to Buenos Aires, and he arranges with a friend to have letters mailed to her periodically from there. Babe tries to tell Mary the truth when he is released, but she will not listen and continues the deception for the sake of their expected child. *Cardsharps. Mistresses. Marriage. Prisons. New York State. New York City. Buenos Aires.*

HAPPY DAYS **F2.2314**

Fox Film Corp. 17 Sep **1929** [New York premiere; released 2 Mar 1930; c23 Dec 1929; LP1009]. Sd (Movietone); b&w. 35mm & 70mm (Grandeur). 9 reels, 7,526 ft.

Pres by William Fox. *Dir* Benjamin Stoloff. *Staged by* Walter Catlett. *Dial* Edwin Burke. *Story* Sidney Lanfield. *Photog* Lucien Andriot, John Schmitz. *Grandeur Camera* J. O. Taylor. *Art Dir* Jack Schulze. *Film Ed* Clyde Carruth. *Songs: "Mona," "Snake Hips," "Crazy Feet"* Con Conrad, Sidney Mitchell, Archie Gottler. *Songs: "Minstrel Memories," "I'm on a Diet of Love,"* L. Wolfe Gilbert, Abel Baer. *Songs: "We'll Build a Little World of Our Own," "A Toast to the Girl I Love," "Dream on a Piece of Wedding Cake"* James Hanley, James Brockman. *Song: "Whispering"* Joseph McCarthy, James Hanley. *Song: "Vic and Eddie"* Harry Stoddard, Marcy Klauber. *Dance Dir* Earl Lindsay. *Rec Engr* Samuel Waite. *Asst Dir* Ad Schaumer, Michael Farley, Lew Breslow. *Cost* Sophie Wachner.

Cast—Principals: Charles E. Evans *(Col. Billy Batcher)*, Marjorie White *(Margie)*, Richard Keene *(Dick)*, Stuart Erwin *(Jig)*, Martha Lee Sparks *(Nancy Lee)*, Clifford Dempsey *(Sheriff Benton)*, Janet Gaynor, Charles Farrell, Marjorie White, Victor McLaglen, El Brendel, William Collier, Sr., Tom Patricola, George Jessel, Dixie Lee, Nick Stuart, Rex Bell, Frank Albertson, Sharon Lynn, "Whispering" Jack Smith, Lew Brice, Farrell MacDonald, Will Rogers, Edmund Lowe, Walter Catlett, Frank Richardson, Ann Pennington, David Rollins, Warner Baxter, J. Harold Murray, Paul Page, The Slate Brothers, Flo Bert, James J. Corbett *(interlocutor)*, George MacFarlane *(interlocutor)*, George Olsen and his Orchestra.

Cast—Gentlemen of the Choral Ensemble: Jack Frost, John Westerfelt, Douglas Steade, Peter Custulovich, John Lockhart, Randall Reynolds, Carter Sexton, Leo Hanly, George Scheller, Kenneth Nordyke, Marius Langan, Ralph Demaree, Glen Alden, Frank McKee, Bob McKee, Joe Holland, Ed Rockwell, Clarence Brown, Jr., Roy Rockwood, Enrico Cuccinelli, Harry Lauder, Ted Waters, Thomas Vartian, J. Harold Reeves, Phil Kolar, Frank Heller, William Hargraves, Ted Smith.

Cast—Young Ladies of the Choral and Dancing Ensembles: Helen Mann, Mary Lansing, Beverly Royed, Joan Navarro, Catherine Navarro, Joan Christensen, Dorothy McNames, Vee Maule, Hazel Sperling, Bo Peep Karlin, Georgia Pembleton, Marbeth Wright, Miriam Hellman, Margaret La Marr, Consuelo De Los Angeles, Lee Auburn, Betty Halsey, Joyde Lorme, Myra Mason, Eileen Bannon, Theresa Allen, Pear La Velle, Barbara La Velle, Gertrude Friedly, Dorothy Kritser, Doris Baker, Melissa Ten Eyck, Kay Gordon, Betty Gordon, Jean De Parva, Joan Gaylord, Charlotte Hamill, Alice Goodsell, Gwen Keate, Virginia Joyce, LaVerne Leonard, Betty Grable, Marjorie Levoe, Pat Hanne, Estella Essex.

Musical revue. Margie is a soubrette on Col. Billy Batcher's Mississippi riverboat, and though she is in love with Dick, the colonel's grandson, she longs to seek her fortune in New York City. When the showboat is in danger of going broke, Margie goes to the city to call on the star troupers who formerly served their apprenticeship under the colonel and asks their aid. All the stars agree to stage a benefit in Memphis, and when they gather for the event Margie is reunited with her sweetheart. *Actors. Singers. Dancers. Sheriffs. Showboats. Musical revues. Memphis. Mississippi River. New York City.*

HAPPY HAWAII **F2.2315**

Burton Holmes Lectures. 8 Jan **1928.** Si; b&w. 35mm. 4 reels.

Travelog. No information about the precise nature of this film has been found. *Hawaii.*

THE HAPPY WARRIOR **F2.2316**

Vitagraph Co. of America. 5 Jul **1925** [c15 Jul 1925; LP21654]. Si; b&w. 35mm. 8 reels, 7,865 ft.

Pres by Albert E. Smith. *Dir* J. Stuart Blackton. *Scen* Marian Constance. *Photog* Paul Allen.

Cast: Malcolm McGregor *(Ralph)*, Alice Calhoun *(Dora)*, Mary Alden *(Aunt Maggie)*, Anders Randolf *(Stingo Hannaford)*, Olive Borden *(Ima)*, Gardner James *(Rollo)*, Otto Matieson *(Egbert)*, Wilfred North *(Mr. Letham)*, Eulalie Jensen *(Mrs. Letham)*, Andrée Tourneur *(Audrey)*, Jack Herrick *(Foxy Pinsent)*, Philippe De Lacy *(Ralph, at 8 years)*, Bobby Gordon *(Rollo, at 10 years)*.

Melodrama. Source: Arthur Stuart-Menteth Hutchinson, *The Happy Warrior* (London, 1912). Lord Bordon dies while traveling abroad, and a distant relative inherits the title. Lady Bordon, whose existence is not known to the world, goes to England to dispute the claim but dies before she can make her presence known. Her sister, Maggie, takes over the care of a surviving son, Ralph, who grows to manhood not knowing that he is a peer. Ralph, a strong lad, gets a job doing exhibition boxing in a circus, where he falls in love with Ima. Ralph meets Rollo, the weak fellow who will become Lord Bordon, and the two become friends. Ralph goes to the Argentine to procure horses and stays there for several years. On the eve of Rollo's wedding to Dora, Ralph returns and learns from his aunt that he is the rightful heir. Ralph at first decides to ruin the wedding by revealing his claim to the title, but his better nature prevails and he does nothing, returning to the circus and Ima, his true love. *Boxers. Nobility. Circus. Inheritance. Weddings. Argentina. England.*

HARBOR PATROL **F2.2317**

F. C. F. Feature Corp. *Dist* Aywon Film Corp. 29 Sep **1924** [New York State license]. Si; b&w. 35mm. 5 reels, 4,530 ft.

Cast: Al Ferguson, Virginia Abbot.

Melodrama. "The entire story has to do with a gang of smugglers, their operations and criminal efforts to elude police. The daughter of the captain, who has been sandbagged and dragged away by smugglers, is kidnapped by the gang whose chief says 'The girl knows too much—we'll take her to headquarters. Plenty of chance to get rid of her there.' She is gagged—taken to office and handed over to Sal, a drug addict who drags her along corridor and pushes her on bed in dirty room, locks door and girl struggles for her life. Revenue officer is attacked by gang, knocked out, taken to water's edge, robbed and kicked in. A raid follows, girl is again attacked and villain finally is drowned." (New York State license records.) *Revenue agents. Drug addicts. Smuggling. Kidnaping.*

HARD BOILED **F2.2318**

Fox Film Corp. 6 Jun **1926** [c29 May 1926; LP22794]. Si; b&w. 35mm. 6 reels, 5,679 ft.

Pres by William Fox. *Dir* J. G. Blystone. *Scen* Charles Darnton, John Stone. *Titl* Ralph Spence. *Story* Shannon Fife. *Photog* Dan Clark. *Asst Dir* Jasper Blystone.

Cast: Tom Mix *(Tom Bouden [or Jeff Boyden])*, Helene Chadwick *(Marjorie Gregg)*, William Lawrence *(Gordon Andrews)*, Charles Conklin *(Bill Grimes)*, Emily Fitzroy *(Abigail Gregg)*, Phyllis Haver *(Justine Morton)*, Dan Mason *(Abrue Boyden)*, Walter "Spec" O'Donnell *(Eddie Blix)*, Ethel Grey Terry *(Mrs. Sarah Morton)*, Edward Sturgis *(first* *crook)*, Eddie Boland *(second crook)*, Emmett Wagner *(third crook)*, Tony *(himself, a horse)*.

Western comedy. Tom Bouden, ordered by his millionaire uncle to help a friend and her niece run a health resort out west, insults the niece before meeting her. Irate, the latter goes west without him. Later Tom and his sidekick disguise themselves in order to elude a posse and wind up at the resort, where Tom is mistaken for a fashionable doctor. Realizing that all the guests want to see the "real" West, "just like in the movies," Tom lets them have it—stagecoaches, Indians, and the rest—and soon the hotel is overflowing. A band of thieves tries to rob the hotel safe, but Tom, aided by the bellhop, rounds up the culprits, retrieves the jewels, and proves himself a man to the girl in question. *Cowboys. Physicians. Bellboys. Mistaken identity. Hotels. Health resorts. Horses.*

HARD FISTS (Blue Streak Western) **F2.2319**

Universal Pictures. 24 Apr **1927** [c10 Mar 1927; LP23758]. Si; b&w. 35mm. 5 reels, 4,387 ft.

Pres by Carl Laemmle. *Dir* William Wyler. *Adapt-Cont* William Lester, George H. Plympton. *Photog* Edwin Linden. *Art Dir* David S. Garber.

Cast: Art Acord *(Art Alvord)*, Louise Lorraine *(Betty Barnes)*, Lee Holmes *(Jed Leach)*, Albert J. Smith *(Charles Crane)*.

Western melodrama. Source: Charles A. Logue, "The Grappler" (publication undetermined). Art Alvord, a fancy-riding ranch hand with a mysteriously shady past, is challenged to a race by a gray-haired colonel, Jed Leach, who wins with dubious tactics. Alvord is provoked to the point of striking Leach, but he is restrained and eventually becomes the evil colonel's protégé, under threat of revelation of a past crime. He is forced to swindle the ranch hands out of their money. Later, in a different town, Art saves the life of an elderly woman who owns a dairy and falls in love with her daughter, Betty. When the colonel repeats his swindling ruse, Art again assists but soon comes to protest the arrangement. Their critical encounter is overheard by Charles Crane, who informs the sheriff that Art is wanted for murder. When the colonel tries to force the mutinous Art's arrest, he accidentally reveals his own disguise and is himself put behind bars. *Blackmail. Extortion. Courtship. Murder. Disguise. Dairying.*

HARD HITTIN' HAMILTON **F2.2320**

Action Pictures. *Dist* Artclass Pictures. 15 Oct **1924** [c23 Oct 1924; LU20685]. Si; b&w. 35mm. 5 reels, 4,600 ft.

Pres by W. T. Lackey, Lester F. Scott, Jr. *Dir* Richard Thorpe.

Cast: Buffalo Bill Jr. *(Bill Hamilton)*, Hazel Keener *(Mary Downing)*, Gordon Russell *(Buck Wilson)*, William Ryno *("Skinflint" Bressler)*, Lafe McKee *(Jim Downing)*.

Western melodrama. Bill Hamilton is on his way to inspect the Lazy-B ranch, which he has inherited, when he collides with the Lazy-B foreman, Buck Wilson, and has a fight with him. Later, while working on Jim Downing's ranch, he foils Wilson's attempts to acquire Downing's mortgage and foreclose. Mary Downing helps by forcing a confession from the man who killed her father, thus clearing Bill of murder charges. Bill protects Mary from Buck just before a rescue party arrives. *Ranch foremen. Ranches. Mortgages. Murder.*

HARD ROCK *see* **THE GALLOPING ACE**

HARD TO GET **F2.2321**

First National Pictures. 4 Aug or 8 Sep **1929** [c16 Sep 1929; LP700]. Sd (Vitaphone); b&w. 35mm. 8 reels, 7,328 ft. [Also si, 15 Sep 1929; 5,981 ft.]

Scen James Gruen. *Dial-Titl* Richard Weil, James Gruen. *Photog* John Seitz. *Film Ed* Stuart Heisler. *Theme Song: "The Things We Want Most Are Hard To Get"* George W. Meyer, Al Bryan, John McLaughlin.

Cast: Dorothy Mackaill *(Bobby Martin)*, Charles Delaney *(Jerry Dillon)*, Jimmy Finlayson *(Pa Martin)*, Louise Fazenda *(Ma Martin)*, Jack Oakie *(Marty Martin)*, Edmund Burns *(Dexter Courtland)*, Clarissa Selwynne *(Mrs. Cortland)*.

Comedy-drama. Source: Edna Ferber, "Classified," in *Mother Knows Best* (Garden City, New York, 1927). Dexter Courtland, a millioniare philanderer, and Jerry Dillon, an automobile mechanic, are rivals for Bobby Martin, a mannequin in a fashionable modiste's shop. Bobby favors Courtland until he makes unwanted advances while they are on a date. Soon Bobby discards her taste for luxury for the sake of the mechanic. *Fashion models. Millionaires. Mechanics. Philanderers. Modistes.*

HARD-BOILED HAGGERTY **F2.2322**

First National Pictures. 21 Aug **1927** [c13 Aug 1927; LP24285]. Si; b&w. 35mm. 8 reels, 7,443 ft.

Pres by Richard A. Rowland. *Prod* Wid Gunning. *Dir* Charles Brabin. *Scen* Carey Wilson. *Photog* Sol Polito. *Cost* Walter Pulunkett.

Cast: Milton Sills *(Hard-Boiled Haggerty)*, Molly O'Day *(Germaine Benoit/Go-Go Benoit)*, Mitchell Lewis *(Major Cotton)*, Arthur Stone *(Klaxon, the mechanic)*, George Fawcett *(brigadier-general)*, Yola D'Avril *(cafe dancer)*.

Comedy-drama. Source: Elliott White Springs, "Belated Evidence," in *Liberty Magazine* (3:43–47, 18 Dec 1926). After bringing down yet another German aviator and escaping uninjured from a burning plane, Haggerty and his buddy, machinist Klaxon, head for Paris without leave of absence. In escaping from M. P.'s, Haggerty takes refuge in a room occupied by Germaine. From her protection springs a love affair, and Haggerty decides to reform, returning to Major Cotton with this resolution. He is unprepared, however, to be awarded a medal for distinguished service. The major, when introduced to Germaine at the officers' ball, recognizes her as Go-Go, a notorious cabaret dancer, and tries to inform Haggerty of her identity. Haggerty knocks him down, and they are both arrested. At the trial, the major tells his story and Germaine confesses. After the Armistice, it develops that Go-Go is actually Germaine's sister, and that Germaine was trying to protect her. The lovers are reunited. *Aviators. Dancers. Machinists. Brother-sister relationship. Mistaken identity. Courts-martial. World War I. Paris.*

HARDBOILED **F2.2323**

FBO Pictures. 3 Feb or 9 Mar **1929** [c3 Jan 1929; LP17]. Si; b&w. 35mm. 7 reels, 5,966 ft.

Dir-Titl Ralph Ince. *Screenplay* Enid Hibbard. *Camera* Robert Martin. *Asst Dir* George Arthur.

Cast: Sally O'Neill *(Teena Johnson)*, Donald Reed *(Kyle Stannard)*, Lilyan Tashman *(Minnie)*, Bob Sinclair *(Scotty)*, Ole M. Ness *(Warren Kennedy)*, Tom O'Grady *(Jerry)*.

Melodrama. Teena Johnson, a Follies showgirl, fulfills her desire to marry for money when she weds Kyle Stannard, the playboy son of an oil millionaire. She refuses his father's offer of $100,000 to give his son a divorce. Kyle is cut off by his father and goes to work for the first time in his life, while Teena returns to the chorus. He incurs large gambling debts, and when his father refuses to help he turns to Teena. She realizes her love for him and voluntarily leaves him; but the father, understanding her sacrifice, effects a reconciliation. *Showgirls. Playboys. Wealth. Marriage. Gambling. Fatherhood. Disinheritance. Follies.*

Note: Credits give titler credit to "Ralph Ince and staff."

HARDBOILED ROSE **F2.2324**

Warner Brothers Pictures. 30 Mar **1929** [c23 Mar 1929; LP231]. Talking sequences, sd eff, & mus score (Vitaphone); b&w. 35mm. 6 reels, 5,610 ft. [Also si, 4 May 1929; 4,875 ft.]

Dir F. Harmon Weight. *Scen-Dial* Robert Lord. *Titl* Joseph Jackson. *Story* Melville Crossman. *Photog* William Reese. *Film Ed* William Holmes.

Cast: Myrna Loy *(Rose Duhamel)*, William Collier, Jr. *(Edward Malo)*, John Miljan *(Steve Wallace)*, Gladys Brockwell *(Julie Malo)*, Lucy Beaumont *(Grandmama Duhamel)*, Ralph Emerson *(John Trask)*, Edward Martindel *(Jefferson Duhamel)*, Otto Hoffman *(Apyton Hale)*, Floyd Shackelford *(butler)*.

Melodrama. Courtly Jefferson Duhamel, partner in a New Orleans banking firm, steals $200,000 in securities to pay off a gambling debt to Julie Malo and then kills himself. John Trask, Duhamel's private secretary, is in love with his late employer's daughter, Rose, and assumes the blame for the theft in order to save the Duhamel family from disgrace. Julie learns of Trask's sacrifice and, donning a worldly dress and sophisticated airs, goes to Julie Malo's gambling casino. Rose vamps Julie's son, Edward, and tricks him into revealing the whereabouts of the securities. Rose eventually recovers the securities; her father's name is thus kept free of scandal, and Trask is released from jail. *Bankers. Gamblers. Secretaries. Theft. Self-sacrifice. Suicide. New Orleans.*

HARMONY AT HOME **F2.2325**

Fox Film Corp. 12 Jan **1930** [c12 Dec 1929; LP942]. Sd (Movietone); b&w. 35mm. 7 reels, 6,295 ft.

Pres by William Fox. *Dir* Hamilton MacFadden. *Adapt-Cont* Clare Kummer, Seton I. Miller, William Collier, Sr., Charles J. McGuirk. *Adtl Dial* Edwin Burke, Elliott Lester. *Photog* Daniel Clark. *Film Ed* Irene

Morra. *Song: "A Little House To Dream by a Mountain Stream"* James Brockman, James Hanley. *Rec Engr* Al Bruzlin. *Asst Dir* Sam Wurtzel.

Cast: Marguerite Churchill *(Louise Haller)*, Rex Bell *(Dick Grant)*, Charlotte Henry *(Dora Haller)*, Charles Eaton *(Willie Haller)*, Dixie Lee *(Rita Joyce)*, William Collier, Sr. *(Joe Haller)*, Elizabeth Patterson *(Emma Haller)*, Dot Farley *(The Modiste)*.

Domestic comedy-drama. Source: Harry Delf, *The Family Upstairs, a Comedy of Home Life* (New York, 1926). When Joe Haller is promoted to superintendent, everyone in his family typically takes advantage of him, with the exception of Louise, his daughter. Mrs. Haller, an ardent matchmaker but overly protective of her daughter, makes the girl's life miserable. One night Louise meets Dick Grant at a concert. They become good friends and have a pleasant time until he visits the Haller home and her mother launches the usual routine; her father takes the situation in hand, however, and all ends well. *Family life. Parenthood.*

Note: A sound version of the 1926 film *The Family Upstairs*, and also known in 1930 as *She Steps Out*.

HAROLD TEEN F2.2326

First National Pictures. 29 Apr **1928** [c24 Apr 1928; LP25184]. Si; b&w. 35mm. 8 reels, 7,541 ft.

Pres by Robert Kane. Allan Dwan Production. *Dir* Mervyn LeRoy. *Scen-Titl* Tom J. Geraghty. *Photog* Ernest Haller. *Film Ed* LeRoy Stone.

Cast: Arthur Lake *(Harold Teen)*, Mary Brian *(Lillums Lovewell)*, Lucien Littlefield *(Dad Jenks)*, Jack Duffy *(Grandpop Teen)*, Alice White *(Giggles Dewberry)*, Jack Egan *(Horace Teen)*, Hedda Hopper *(Mrs. Hazzit)*, Ben Hall *(Goofy)*, William Bakewell *(Percival)*, Lincoln Stedman *(Beezie)*, Fred Kelsey *(Mr. Lovewell)*, Jane Keckley *(Mrs. Teen)*, Ed Brady *(Officer Axel Dewberry)*, Virginia Sale *(Mrs. Schmittenberger)*.

Comedy. Based on: Carl Ed, "Harold Teen" (newspaper comic strip). Farmboy Harold moves to the city and there attends high school. Soon he is very popular, his spirited nature causing much excitement on the campus. He joins a fraternity, goes out for football, and directs his class theatrical effort. Instead of a school play, Harold suggests doing a western motion picture. Part of the plot requires them to blow up the dam that has cut off the water supply to Harold's homestead in the country. After the explosion Harold runs away because he is afraid of being arrested, but he returns just in time to win a football game for his team. *Adolescence. High school life. Motion pictures. Football. Fraternities. Dams. Theater—Amateur.*

A HARP IN HOCK F2.2327

De Mille Pictures. *Dist* Pathé Exchange. 10 Oct **1927** [c10 Oct 1927; LP24480]. Si; b&w. 35mm. 6 reels, 5,996 ft.

Dir Renaud Hoffman. *Screenplay* Sonya Levien. *Photog* Dewey Wrigley. *Art Dir* Charles Cadwallader. *Film Ed* Donn Hayes. *Asst Dir* Glenn Belt. *Cost* Gwen Wakeling.

Cast: Rudolph Schildkraut *(Isaac Abrams)*, Junior Coghlan *(Tommy Shannon)*, May Robson *(Mrs. Banks)*, Bessie Love *(Nora Banks)*, Louis Natheaux *(Nick)*, Elsie Bartlett *(Mrs. Shannon)*, Mrs. Charles Mack *(The Clock Woman)*, Joseph Striker *(Dr. Franz Mueller)*, Adele Watson *(investigator)*, Lillian Harmen *(Sourface)*, Clarence Burton *(plainclothesman)*, Bobby Heck *(Snipe Banks)*.

Melodrama. Source: Evelyn Campbell, "A Harp in Hock" (publication undetermined). Isaac Abrams, a lonely ghetto pawnbroker, is disliked by all his neighbors with the exception of Nora Banks, the landlady's charming daughter, and Mrs. Shannon, a poor scrubwoman who saves to bring her son Tommy from Ireland. On the day the child arrives at Ellis Island, his mother is taken fatally ill and Abrams is forced to take in the child; Tommy, who comes to love Abrams, is taught to care for the shop, barter with the customers, and study. When he beats Snipe Banks, the neighborhood toughie, Mrs. Banks vengefully reports Tommy to the authorities, who remove him to an orphanage and later to an Iowa family. But Tommy escapes and returns to the pawnshop, and when they are faced with another parting, Abrams plans to take him away; Abrams is denounced by Mrs. Banks, precipitating a riot, but Dr. Mueller, Nora's suitor, arrives to straighten out matters and Abrams is permitted to adopt the boy. *Jews. Pawnbrokers. Irish. Charwomen. Orphans. Adoption. New York City. Ellis Island. Iowa.*

THE HARVEST OF HATE F2.2328

Universal Pictures. 4 Aug **1929** [c3 Apr 1928; LP25124]. Si; b&w. 35mm. 5 reels, 4,719 ft.

Dir Henry MacRae. *Cont* George H. Plympton. *Titl* Gardner Bradford. *Story* William Lord Wright, George H. Plympton. *Photog* George Robinson. *Film Ed* Thomas Malloy.

Cast: Rex *(himself, a horse)*, Jack Perrin *(Jack Merritt)*, Helen Foster *(Margie Smith)*, Tom London *(Martin Trask)*, Starlight *(himself, a horse)*.

Western melodrama. Purchasing the Carney Carnival and Road Show, crooked sportsman Martin Trask assumes he has ownership of Rex, the world's greatest trained horse, and its rider, Mademoiselle Estrella (Margie Smith); but the girl releases Rex, flees from Trask in a runaway wagon, and finds shelter with young cowboy farmer Jack Merritt, with whom she falls in love. Trask cancels the mortgage he holds on Jack's property in return for Margie's accompanying him, but Jack learns the truth and pursues them. Rex comes to Margie's aid and kills Trask, while Jack rescues the girl from a tree limb on the side of a cliff. *Equestrians. Sportsmen. Farmers. Cowboys. Carnivals. Mortgages. Horses.*

THE HARVESTER F2.2329

R-C Pictures. *Dist* Film Booking Offices of America. 7 Nov **1927** [New York premiere; released 23 Nov; c3 Nov 1927; LP24633]. Si; b&w. 35mm. 8 reels, 7,045 ft.

Pres by Joseph P. Kennedy. *Dir* Leo Meehan. *Scen* Dorothy Yost. *Titl* Jeanette Porter Meehan. *Camera* Allen Siegler. *2d Camera* James Giridlian. *Asst Dir* Charles Kerr.

Cast: Orville Caldwell *(David Langston)*, Natalie Kingston *(Ruth)*, Will R. Walling *(Henry Jamison)*, Jay Hunt *(Dr. Carey)*, Lola Todd *(nurse)*, Edward Hearn *(Dr. Harmon)*, Fanny Midgley *(Granny Moreland)*.

Domestic melodrama. Source: Gene Stratton Porter, *The Harvester* (Garden City, New York, 1911). David Langston, a harvester of medicinal herbs found in the forest, comes upon Ruth, the reality of a secret vision he has cherished for years, and she accuses him of "stealing" her ginseng. They meet many times, he tells her of his love, but she is overcome by shyness. David rescues her from her uncle's tyranny; they are married; and though she shrinks from his advances, she is overwhelmed by his patience and understanding. When Ruth tells him she had promised to marry Dr. Harmon, she becomes deathly ill, and Harmon comes to care for her; perceiving, however, that he loves the nurse, she feels released from her promise and recovers. A detective hired by David discovers Ruth's wealthy parents, and believing he has failed her, David sends her away; but upon receiving his written declaration of love, she happily returns to him. *Harvesters. Physicians. Nurses. Detectives. Rural life. Parentage. Marriage. Herbs.*

HAS THE WORLD GONE MAD! F2.2330

Daniel Carson Goodman Corp. *Dist* Equity Pictures. 28 Feb **1923** [c12 Mar 1923; LP18768]. Si; b&w. 35mm. 7 reels, 6,047 ft.

Pres by Daniel Carson Goodman. *Dir* J. Searle Dawley. *Story-Scen* Daniel Carson Goodman. *Photographic Staff* Ned Van Buren, Hal Sintzenich, Bert Dawley. *Sets* Tilford Cinema Studios. *Art Titl* Oscar C. Buchheister.

Cast: Robert Edeson *(Mr. Adams)*, Hedda Hopper *(Mrs. Adams)*, Vincent Coleman *(their son)*, Mary Alden *(Mrs. Bell)*, Charles Richman *(Mr. Bell)*, Elinor Fair *(their daughter)*, Lyda Lola *(cabaret dancer)*.

Society drama. Mrs. Adams succumbs to the spirit of jazz, moves into her own apartment, and even has an affair with Mr. Bell, the father of her son's sweetheart. Miss Bell discovers their meetings, and only then does Mrs. Adams realize the unhappiness she has caused. Shortly thereafter, she effects a general reconciliation. *Jazz life. Motherhood. Infidelity.*

HATE F2.2331

Metro Pictures. 20 May **1922** [c20 May 1922; LP17930]. Si; b&w. 35mm. 6 reels, 5,500 ft.

Dir Maxwell Karger. *Adapt* June Mathis. *Photog* Allan Siegler. *Art-Tech Dir* Joseph Calder.

Cast: Alice Lake *(Babe Lennox)*, Conrad Nagel *(Dick Talbot)*, Harry Northrup *(Dave Hume)*, Charles Clary *(Edward Felton)*, John Ince *(Inspector Garth)*.

Crime melodrama. Source: Wadsworth Camp, "Hate," in *The Communicating Door* (Garden City, New York, 1923). Gamblers Dave Hume and Ed Felton are rivals for the love of Babe Lennox, a chorus girl. Hume informs on Felton, and though the latter is arrested he is released on bail, and Talbot, the attorney, warns Hume to stay clear of him. Hume, who is in ill health, determines to commit suicide, making it appear that Felton killed him; and (concealing a record of his plans on a small statuette) he makes a wager with Felton that he can do so. When Hume is found dead, Talbot prosecutes the case against Felton, and just as Felton is about to be electrocuted Babe delivers the statue by which his innocence is proved. Babe, who had denounced Talbot for having convicted Felton, acknowledges her love for him; and all ends well. *Gamblers. Chorus girls. Informers. District attorneys. Suicide. Circumstantial evidence. Capital punishment.*

THE HATE TRAIL **F2.2332**

Milburn Morante. *Dist* Clark-Cornelius Corp. 1 May or 1 Aug **1922.** Si; b&w. 35mm. 5 reels, 4,588 ft.

Dir Milburn Morante.

Cast: George Chesebro *(Sgt. Steve Bain)*, Frank Caffray *(Chief Painting Cougar)*, Alfred Hewston *(Hank Munger)*, Fritzi Ridgeway *(Mary Munger)*, Pearl Barbour *(Moon Face)*, Russell Tizzard *(John Ingless)*, Virginia Morante *(Little Cougar)*.

Northwest melodrama. While tracking border raiders, Steve Bain, a Northwest Mounted Police sergeant, finds a baby girl in a deserted cabin and leaves her in the care of an Indian couple. Later, the baby's mother, Mary Munger, leaves her rumrunner husband, gets lost in the woods, and is also found by the sergeant. Munger kidnaps Mary, who escapes; he then abducts the baby to lure Steve to a cave. Steve and Munger battle, Steve emerges victorious, and Munger takes his own life—leaving Steve and Mary free to marry. *Rumrunners. Infants. Indians of North America. Abduction. Northwest Mounted Police.*

Note: May be the same film as *The Menacing Past,* q.v.

THE HAUNTED HOUSE **F2.2333**

First National Pictures. 4 Nov **1928** [c3 Oct 1928; LP25681]. Sd eff & mus score (Vitaphone); b&w. 35mm. 7 reels, 5,755 ft. [Also si; 5,775 ft.]

Pres by Richard A. Rowland. *Prod* Wid Gunning. *Dir* Benjamin Christensen. *Scen* Richard Bee, Lajos Biró. *Titl* William Irish. *Photog* Sol Polito. *Film Ed* Frank Ware.

Cast: Larry Kent *(Billy)*, Thelma Todd *(The Nurse)*, Edmund Breese *(James Herbert)*, Sidney Bracy *(Tully)*, Barbara Bedford *(Nancy)*, Flora Finch *(Mrs. Rackham)*, Chester Conklin *(Mr. Rackham)*, William V. Mong *(The Caretaker)*, Montague Love *(The Mad Doctor)*, Eve Southern *(sleepwalking girl)*, Johnny Gough *(Jack, the chauffeur)*.

Comedy-melodrama. Source: Owen Davis, *The Haunted House; an American Comedy in Three Acts* (New York, 1926). James Herbert, an eccentric millionaire apparently on the brink of death, sends for his four most likely heirs: Billy, Tully, Nancy, and Mrs. Rackham. He gives each of them a sealed letter with instructions not to open it until his death. All four disregard the old man's wishes and open their letters, learning that Herbert has hidden a fortune in bonds in a haunted house. The four go there and meet with a mad doctor, a caretaker, a sleepwalking girl, and a beautiful nurse. After a night of strange noises, weird happenings, and screams, Herbert appears and explains that the ghosts and ghouls, hired from central casting, were part of a test to discover the true nature of his presumptive heirs. Billy is then designated as the rightful heir. *Physicians. Lunatics. Millionaires. Caretakers. Nurses. Actors. Somnambulism. Inheritance. Ghosts. Haunted houses.*

THE HAUNTED RANCH *see* **THE HAUNTED RANGE**

THE HAUNTED RANGE **F2.2334**

Davis Distributing Division. c11 Jan **1926** [LP22248]. Si; b&w. 35mm. 5 reels.

Dir Paul Hurst. *Story* Frank Howard Clark. *Photog* Frank Cotner.

Cast: Ken Maynard *(Terry Baldwin)*, Alma Rayford *(Judith Kellerd)*, Harry Moody *(Alex Forester)*, Al Hallett *(executor)*, Fred Burns *(Charlie Titus)*, Bob Williamson *(Ralph Kellerd)*, Tarzan *(himself, a horse)*.

Western melodrama. Terry Baldwin inherits a ranch provided that within 6 months he solves the mystery of Haunted Ranch and brings to justice the killer of Kellerd, a neighboring rancher. Terry falls in love with Kellerd's daughter, Alma, and learns that her brother, Ralph, is in the power of Alex Forester, a cattle thief. Terry later finds out that the ghost of Haunted Ranch is one of Forester's men dressed in a sheet, the "haunting" being used as a ruse for cattle rustling. Terry brings Forester and his gang to justice, sees to Ralph's redemption, and marries Alma. *Ranchers. Rustlers. Ghosts. Haunted houses.*

Note: This film was also reviewed under the title *The Haunted Ranch.*

THE HAUNTED SHIP **F2.2335**

Tiffany-Stahl Productions. 1 Dec **1927** [c13 Dec 1927; LP24778]. Si; b&w. 35mm. 5 reels, 4,752 ft.

Prod Roy Fitzroy. *Dir* Forrest K. Sheldon. *Scen* Forrest K. Sheldon, Ben Ali Newman. *Titl* Viola Brothers Shore, Harry Braxton. *Adapt* E. Morton Hough. *Photog* J. O. Taylor, Glenn Kershner. *Film Ed* L. R. Brown.

Cast: Dorothy Sebastian *(Goldie Kane)*, Montagu Love *(Capt. Simon Gant)*, Tom Santschi *(Glenister, first mate)*, Ray Hallor *(Danny Gant)*, Pat Harmon *(mate)*, Alice Lake *(Martha Gant)*, Bud Duncan *(Dinty)*, Blue Washington *(Mose)*, Sojin *(Bombay Charlie)*, Andrée Tourneur *(Goldie's companion)*, William Lowery.

Drama. Source: Jack London, "White and Yellow," in *Tales of the Fish Patrol* (New York, 1905). Believing that his wife, Martha, has been unfaithful, cruel Capt. Simon Gant sets her adrift in a small boat with their son, Danny, whom he suspects to have been fathered by Glenister, his first mate. Gant puts Glenister in chains and tortures him daily to extract a confession of his guilt. Years later, Gant shanghais stranded chorus girl Goldie Kane and a boy he believes to be Danny. Danny has sworn vengeance on his father, but Gant puts him in chains along with Glenister. The ship's crew mutinies, the ship explodes, and all escape except Gant and Glenister. *Chorus girls. Seafaring life. Torture. Infidelity. Mutiny. Revenge. Shanghaiing. Ship explosions.*

HAVOC *see* **THUNDERING DAWN**

HAVOC **F2.2336**

Fox Film Corp. 27 Sep **1925** [c26 Jul 1925; LP21686]. Si; b&w. 35mm. 9 reels, 9,283 ft.

Pres by William Fox. *Dir* Rowland V. Lee. *Scen* Edmund Goulding. *Photog* G. O. Post. *Asst Dir* Daniel Keefe.

Cast: Madge Bellamy *(Tessie Dunton)*, George O'Brien *(Dick Chappel)*, Walter McGrail *(Roddy Dunton)*, Eulalie Jensen *(Alice Deering)*, Margaret Livingston *(Violet Deering)*, Leslie Fenton *(Babe)*, David Butler *(Smithy)*, Harvey Clark *(Biddle)*, Wade Boteler *(Sergeant Major)*, Edythe Chapman *(Mrs. Chappel)*, Capt. E. H. Calvert *(regimental adjutant)*, Bertram Grassby *(Alexi Betskoy)*.

Drama. Source: Henry Wall, "Havoc" (publication undetermined). Roddy Dunton and Dick Chappel, friends and officers in the British Army during the World War, both fall in love with Violet Deering, a heartless flirt. When she jilts Roddy in favor of Dick, Roddy becomes insane with jealous rage and sends Dick to a post in the trenches that means almost certain death. Dick manages to escape with his life, but he is blinded; and Roddy, in a fit of remorse, kills himself. After the war, Dick is jilted by Violet, and he falls in love with Rod's sister, Tessie. Dick's sight is restored, and he marries the faithful and loving Tessie. *Flirts. Friendship. Suicide. Jealousy. Blindness. World War I. Great Britain—Army.*

HAWK OF THE HILLS **F2.2337**

Pathé Exchange. 17 Mar **1929.** Si; b&w. 35mm. 5 reels, 4,840 ft.

Dir Spencer Gordon Bennett. *Story-Scen-Titl* George Arthur Gray. *Photog* Edward Snyder, Frank Redman.

Cast: Allene Ray *(Mary Selby)*, Walter Miller *(Laramie)*, Robert Chandler *(Clyde Selby)*, Jack Ganghorn *(Henry Selby)*, Frank Lackteen *(The Hawk)*, Paul Panzer *(Manson)*, Wally Oettel *(Shorty)*, Harry Semels *(Sheckard)*, Jack Pratt *(Colonel Jennings)*, J. Parks Jones *(Lieutenant MacCready)*, Frederick Dana *(Larry)*, John T. Prince *(The Hermit)*, Chief Whitehorse, George Magrill, Evangeline Russell, Chief Yowlache *(Chief Long Hand)*.

Western melodrama. The story line of this film is similar to that of the serial from which it was taken. The serial deals with the adventures of The Hawk, the halfbreed leader of a band of Indians and renegade whites; prospectors, the objects of The Hawk's treachery; Mary Selby, the daughter of a prospector and the niece of an Indian agent; a stranger (Laramie), who poses as an outlaw, becomes a member of The Hawk's gang, and finally reveals himself to be a government agent; and assorted Indians and troopers. *Indians of North America. Halfcastes. Gangs. Traitors. Prospectors. Indian agents. Government agents. United States Army—Cavalry.*

Note: A feature film version of a 10-episode serial released by Pathé in 1927.

THE HAWK'S NEST **F2.2338**

First National Pictures. 27 May **1928** [c28 May 1928; LP25302]. Si; b&w. 35mm. 8 reels, 7,426 or 7,433 ft.

Pres by Richard A. Rowland. *Dir* Benjamin Christensen. *Scen* James T. O'Donohue. *Titl* Casey Robinson. *Story* Wid Gunning. *Photog* Sol Polito. *Art Dir* Max Parker. *Film Ed* Frank Ware.

Cast: Milton Sills *(The Hawk/John Finchley)*, Montagu Love *(Dan Daugherty)*, Mitchell Lewis *(James Kent)*, Doris Kenyon *(Madelon Arden)*, Stuart Holmes *(Barney McGuire)*, Sojin *(himself)*.

Melodrama. Determined to find the murderer of McGuire, one of his employees, "The Hawk," owner of a Chinatown cafe, has plastic surgery done on his scarred face and masquerades as Finchley, a gangster from Chicago. He thus hopes to save the life of Kent, manager of his cafe, who is being framed on a murder charge. The Hawk gains the confidence of Dan Daugherty, owner of a rival cafe, whom he suspects to be the murderer, and Madelon Arden, a dancer in Daugherty's cafe. When he fails to prove Daugherty's guilt, the council of Chinatown, aware that Daugherty also caused the death of Ching Ling Fu, a Chinatown leader, forces Daugherty to confess to the other killing. The Hawk finds romantic interest in Madelon. *Dancers. Gangsters. Cafes. Plastic surgery. Frameup. San Francisco—Chinatown.*

HAZARDOUS VALLEY **F2.2339**

Dist Ellbee Pictures. 6 Aug **1927** [New York State license]. Si; b&w. 35mm. 6 reels, 5,508 ft.

Dir Alvin J. Neitz. *Story-Scen* A. B. Barringer. *Photog* Harold Wenstrom.

Cast: Vincent Brownell, Virginia Brown Faire, Sheldon Lewis, Pat Harmon, David Torrence, Andrew Arbuckle, Burr McIntosh.

Melodrama. "Story of a youth [played by Vincent Brownell] who goes to his father's lumber camp and personally sees to it that the all-important shipment of logs is delivered on time. The difficulties overcome are fostered by his father's rival, who later sees the light when his own daughter [played by Virginia Brown Faire] is in the arms of the courageous youth." (*Variety*, 30 Nov 1927, p23.) *Filial relations. Business competition. Lumber camps.*

HE KNEW WOMEN **F2.2340**

RKO Productions. 18 Apr **1930** [New York premiere; released 18 May; c18 May 1930; LP1383]. Sd (Photophone); b&w. 35mm. 6,317 ft.

Prod William Le Baron. *Assoc Prod* Myles Connolly. *Dir* Hugh Herbert, Lynn Shores. *Screenplay* William B. Jutte, Hugh Herbert. *Photog* Edward Cronjager. *Art Dir* Max Ree. *Film Ed* Ann McKnight, George Marsh. *Sd Rec* Lambert E. Day.

Cast: Lowell Sherman *(Geoffrey Clarke)*, Alice Joyce *(Alice Frayne)*, David Manners *(Austin Lowe)*, Frances Dade *(Monica Grey)*.

Comedy-drama. Source: S. N. Behrman, *The Second Man* (New York, 1927). Geoffrey Clarke, a poet always in need of money, decides to resolve his financial plight by marrying wealthy widow Alice Frayne, though he is madly pursued by beautiful Monica Grey. He counters Monica's disappointment with the argument that she would be happier married to Austin Lowe, a wealthy young chemist who loves her. Geoffrey arranges for Monica to dine with Austin in his (Geoffrey's) apartment; and though she treats Austin rudely, upon discovering a check that Mrs. Frayne has given Geoffrey she denounces him and agrees to marry Austin. Later, she desperately announces that Geoffrey has compromised her and insists that he marry her; consequently, Mrs. Frayne breaks the engagement. Austin, mortified at Monica's story, tries to shoot Geoffrey; and when she learns of this action, Monica realizes that Austin is her man. Meanwhile, as they sail for Europe, Clarke is reconciled with Mrs. Frayne. *Poets. Widows. Chemists. Fortune hunters. Courtship. Wealth.*

HE WHO GETS SLAPPED **F2.2341**

Metro-Goldwyn-Mayer Corp. *Dist* Metro-Goldwyn Distributing Corp. ca9 Nov **1924** [New York premiere; released 22 Dec; c10 Nov 1924; LP20745]. Si; b&w. 35mm. 7 reels, 6,953 ft.

Pres by Louis B. Mayer. *Prod* Louis B. Mayer. *Dir* Victor Seastrom. *Adapt* Carey Wilson, Victor Seastrom. *Photog* Milton Moore. *Sets* Cedric Gibbons. *Film Ed* Hugh Wynn. *Cost* Sophie Wachner.

Cast: Lon Chaney *("He Who Gets Slapped")*, Norma Shearer *(Consuelo)*, John Gilbert *(Bezano)*, Tully Marshall *(Count Mancini)*, Marc MacDermott *(Baron Regnard)*, Ford Sterling *(Tricaud)*, Harvey Clarke *(Briquet)*, Paulette Duval *(Zinida)*, Ruth King *(He's wife)*, Clyde Cook, Brandon Hurst, George Davis *(clowns)*.

Tragedy. Source: Leonid Nikolaevich Andreyev, *He, the One Who Gets Slapped; a Play in Four Acts* (trans. by Gregory Zilboorg of *Tot, Kto Poluchaet Poshchechiny;* New York, 1921). On the eve of great success, a scientist ("He Who Gets Slapped") loses both his invention and his wife to Baron Regnard, who describes his victim as a fool. He decides to lose himself in the laughter of others and becomes France's most famous clown. Even Consuelo, a bareback rider who loves her partner, Bezano, laughs when He confesses his love for her. Learning that Consuelo's father, Count Mancini, plans her marriage to Baron Regnard, He releases a lion which kills the pair; and, fatally stabbed by Regnard, the clown stumbles and staggers around the circus ring to the delight of the audience. He dies in the arms of Consuelo, who is free to marry Bezano. *Clowns. Roman riders. Scientists. Circus. Revenge. France.*

HE WHO LAUGHS LAST **F2.2342**

Bud Barsky Corp. 11 Jan **1925** [New York State license]. Si; b&w. 35mm. 5 reels, 4,800 ft.

Dir Jack Nelson. *Story* Grover Jones. *Photog* Hal Mohr. *Film Ed* Grace Harrison, June Harrison.

Cast: Kenneth McDonald *(Jimmy Taylor)*, Margaret Cloud *(Janice Marvin)*, David Torrence *(George K. Taylor)*, Gino Corrado *(Elwood Harkness)*, Harry Northrup *(James Marvin)*.

Melodrama. Jimmy Taylor, an adventurous rich kid, is accused of being the notorious "Killer" who has robbed and killed many citizens in the town. He escapes from prison so that he may capture the real criminal, Elwood Harkness, who is also vying for the heart of Janice Marvin. Harkness' game is over when he attempts to sell to Janice's father some stock proxies that he has stolen from Jimmy's father. Jimmy is then cleared, and he and Janice resume a pleasant relationship. *Robbery. Prisons. Prison escapes.*

A HE-MAN'S COUNTRY **F2.2343**

Ben Wilson Productions. *Dist* Rayart Pictures. Nov **1926**. Si; b&w. 35mm. 5 reels, 4,620 ft.

Dir Dick Hatton.

Cast: Dick Hatton.

Western melodrama. "Cowpuncher, in love with sheriff's daughter, becomes deputy with special duty of cleaning up gang. In order to do this he disguises himself as darky and in this manner outwits gang, saving loot and besting the robber chief. He wins the girl." (*Motion Picture News Booking Guide*, 12:33, Apr 1927.) *Cowboys. Sheriffs. Gangs. Disguise.*

HEAD HUNTERS OF THE SOUTH SEAS **F2.2344**

Martin Johnson Film Co. *Dist* Associated Exhibitors. 1 Oct **1922** [c27 Sep 1922; LU18245]. Si; b&w. 35mm. 5 reels, 4,387 ft.

Dir Martin Johnson. *Titl* Arthur Hoerl. *Photog* Martin Johnson. *Film Ed* Arthur Hoerl.

Personages: Nagapate, Martin Johnson, Osa Johnson.

Travel documentary. Mr. and Mrs. Martin Johnson pay a return visit to Nagapate, Chief of the Big Numbers, a tribe of cannibals in the South Sea island of Malekula who had held the Johnsons captive 2 years before. They show him the movie they made of their experience: *Captured by Cannibals.* They also visit the primitive tribes of Santo; the island of Lombumbubu, home of a strange tribe of monkey people who live in trees; and Tomann, where the natives bind their children's heads so that they grow long. Also shown are how human heads are mummified, methods of shark fishing, and the eruption of Lopevi, a volcano. *Cannibals. Headhunters. Motion pictures. Volcanoes. South Sea Islands. Sharks.*

THE HEAD MAN **F2.2345**

First National Pictures. 8 Jul **1928** [c27 Jun 1928; LP25415]. Si; b&w. 35mm. 7 reels, 6,502 ft.

Pres by Richard A. Rowland. *Dir* Eddie Cline. *Cont* Howard Green, Harvey Thew. *Titl* Sidney Lazarus, Gerald Duffy. *Adapt* Harvey Thew. *Story* Harry Leon Wilson. *Photog* Michael Joyce. *Film Ed* Terrell Morse.

Cast: Charlie Murray *(Watts)*, Loretta Young *(Carol Watts)*, Larry Kent *(Billy Hurd)*, Lucien Littlefield *(Ed Barnes)*, E. J. Ratcliffe *(Wareham)*, Irving Bacon *(The Mayor)*, Harvey Clark *(McKugg)*, Sylvia Ashton *(Mrs. Briggs)*, Dot Farley *(Mrs. Denny)*, Martha Mattox, Rosa Gore *(The Twins)*.

Drama. Because he refuses to be a tool for a political mob, Watts, an ex-senator, is relegated to the public wastebasket. When he opposes a rival politician in a mayoral campaign, Watts evokes the public's sympathy and is elected to the mayor's chair, again becoming a power in local politics. *Politicians. Mayors. United States Congress.*

THE HEAD OF THE FAMILY **F2.2346**

Gotham Productions. *Dist* Lumas Film Corp. c8 Nov **1928** [LP25808]. Si; b&w. 35mm. 7 reels, 6,250 ft.

Pres by Sam Sax. *Supv* Casey Robinson. *Assoc Prod* Harold Shumate. *Dir* Joseph C. Boyle. *Screenplay* Peter Milne. *Titl* Casey Robinson. *Photog*

Charles Van Enger. *Film Ed* Donn Hayes. *Prod Mgr* Donn Diggins.

Cast: William Russell *(The Plumber)*, Mickey Bennett *(His Assistant)*, Virginia Lee Corbin *(Alice Sullivan)*, Richard Walling *(Charley Sullivan)*, Alma Bennett *(Mabel Manning)*, William Welsh *(Daniel Sullivan)*, Aggie Herring *(Maggie Sullivan)*.

Comedy. Source: George Randolph Chester, "The Head of the Family," in *Saturday Evening Post* (185:14, 26 Oct 1912). Henpecked Daniel Sullivan, a good provider, leaves for a health cure and puts Eddie the plumber in charge of his nagging wife, Maggie, his flapper daughter, Alice, and his reckless son, Charley. Eddie soon tames Alice and rescues Charley from the machinations of a vamp. Eddie and Alice fall in love, and Dan returns from his cure to a respectful, loving family. *Plumbers. Flappers. Vamps. Family life. Health cures.*

HEAD OVER HEELS **F2.2347**

Goldwyn Pictures. Apr **1922** [c20 Apr 1922; LP17763]. Si; b&w. 35mm. 5 reels, 4,229 ft.

Dir Victor Schertzinger, Paul Bern. *Scen* Julien Josephson, Gerald C. Duffy. *Story* Nalbro Isadorah Bartley. *Photog* George F. Webber.

Cast: Mabel Normand *(Tina)*, Hugh Thompson *(Lawson)*, Russ Powell *(Papa Bambinetti)*, Raymond Hatton *(Pepper)*, Adolphe Menjou *(Sterling)*, Lilyan Tashman *(Babe)*, Lionel Belmore *(Al Wilkins)*.

Comedy-drama. Sterling, a theatrical agent, hires Tina to come to the United States to perform when he sees her in an acrobatic act in Naples. Tina arrives ill-clad and plain. Her guardian, Papa Bambinetti, is "taken in" by Pepper, a press agent, who promises to make Tina a motion picture star. After they drag Tina into a beauty parlor, she emerges, to everyone's surprise, a beautiful young woman. Lawson, a member of the theatrical firm, falls in love with Tina, who cannot decide between him and her career. She decides against both and packs to return to Italy when she spies Lawson with another actress. But when Lawson repents, she chooses in his favor. *Theatrical agents. Press agents. Guardians. Acrobats. Italians. Motion pictures. Naples.*

HEAD WINDS (Universal-Jewel) **F2.2348**

Universal Pictures. 29 Mar **1925** [c9 Mar 1925; LP21242]. Si; b&w. 35mm. 6 reels, 5,486 ft.

Dir Herbert Blache. *Screenplay* Edward T. Lowe, Jr. *Photog* John Stumar.

Cast: House Peters *(Peter Rosslyn)*, Patsy Ruth Miller *(Patricia Van Felt)*, Richard Travers *(John Templeton Arnold)*, Arthur Hoyt *(Winthrop Van Felt)*, William Austin *(Theodore Van Felt)*, Lydia Yeamans Titus *(nurse)*, Togo Yamamoto *(Woo Lang)*, George Kuwa *(Wai Sai)*, K. Nambu *(Foo)*.

Melodrama. Source: A. M. Sinclair Wilt, *Head Winds* (New York, 1923). Peter Rosslyn, a sturdy gentleman yachtsman in love with irresponsible and vivacious Patricia Van Felt, does not propose to her in the hope that with time she will mature. When Peter learns, however, that she is planning to marry Templeton Arnold, a fortune hunter, he arranges for her to be brought aboard his yacht, where he impersonates Arnold by swathing his head in bandages. A minister is brought on board, and Patricia marries Peter, still thinking him to be Arnold. Peter sets sail, taking off his bandages in private. Patricia is stunned to see him, believing herself to have been kidnaped; she tries to escape in a rowboat but is brought back to the yacht by its Chinese crew. She becomes ill and learns from her nurse that she is really married to Peter. When she recovers, she and Peter are reconciled and begin married life in earnest. *Yachtsmen. Fortune hunters. Clergymen. Nurses. Chinese. Impersonation.*

HEADIN' FOR DANGER **F2.2349**

FBO Pictures. *Dist* RKO Productions. 16 Dec **1928** [c16 Dec 1928; LP82]. Si; b&w. 35mm. 6 reels, 5,265 ft.

Dir Robert North Bradbury. *Scen* Frank Howard Clark. *Photog* Virgil Miller. *Film Ed* Della M. King.

Cast: Bob Steele *(Jimmy Marshall)*, Jola Mendez *(Chiquita Ramerez)*, Al Ferguson *(Ed Thorpe)*, Tom Forman *(Bill Braxton/El Toro)*, Frank Rice *(Andy Johnson)*, Harry De Roy *(Pedro)*, Leonard Trainer.

Melodrama. "Jimmy Marshall, an adventurous youth, wanders in disguise into a small Mexican town seeking adventure. Captured by bandits he fights his way to freedom, meets the girl of his dreams." ("Motion Picture News Booking Guide," in *Motion Picture News*, 15 Mar 1930, p83.) *Bandits. Thrill-seeking. Disguise. Mexico.*

HEADIN' NORTH **F2.2350**

Dist Arrow Film Corp. Mar **1921.** Si; b&w. 35mm. 5 reels, 4,257 ft.

Dir Charles Bartlett. *Story-Scen* Barney Furey.

Cast: Pete Morrison *(Bob Ryan)*, Jack Walters *(Arthur Stowell)*, Gladys Cooper *(Madge Mullin)*, Dorothy Dickson *(Frances Wilson)*, William Dills *(Hank Wilson)*, Barney Furey *(The Boob)*, Will Franks *(Madge's father)*.

Western melodrama. Eloping Madge Mullin is killed when thrown from a stagecoach carelessly driven by Arthur Stowell, engineer of a surveying crew. Bashful Bob Ryan, who was also in love with her, swears revenge and follows the engineer, who has taken the alias of Bull Thompson. Bull robs the wagon carrying the payroll to the men, framing Bob, who then is saved by the village fool from being lynched. This man discloses evidence clearing Bob and convicting Thompson, who admits to his former identity. Bob decides to remain in town with his new love, Frances, whom he has saved from a runaway coach. *Engineers. Surveyors. Robbery. Frameup. Revenge. Elopement. Lynching.*

HEADIN' NORTH **F2.2351**

Trem Carr Productions. *Dist* Tiffany Productions. 1 Nov **1930** [c15 Nov 1930; LP1748]. Sd (Photophone); b&w. 35mm. 6 reels, 4,950 ft.

Prod Trem Carr. *Dir-Writ* J. P. McCarthy. *Film Ed* Fred Allen.

Cast: Bob Steele *(Jim Curtis)*, Barbara Luddy *(Mary Jackson)*, Perry Murdock *("Snicker")*, Walter Shumway *(Arnold)*, Eddie Dunn *(announcer)*, Fred Burns *(U. S. marshal)*, Gordon De Main *(foreman)*, Harry Allen, J. Gunnis Davis *(Smith & Smith)*, S. S. Simon *(Palace owner)*, Jack Henderson *(drunk)*, Jim Welsh *(old actor)*.

Western melodrama. Determined to prove his innocence, Jim Curtis, an escaped convict, eludes a posse led by U. S. Marshal Harrison. "Snicker" Kimball, son of a ranchowner, returns to the ranch, sees Jim employed as a new cowhand, and challenges him to fight, losing badly. Consequently, Snicker apologizes, and the two men become fast friends. Later, when the marshal inquires about him, Snicker and Red deny having seen the fugitive, and Jim tells them his story: *His father, an agent for an express company, is persuaded by Arnold, a gambler, to lend him money. Arnold absconds with it; in helping his father across the border, Jim is held as an accomplice; and Mary Jackson has informed him that Arnold is in Gold Creek.* In his search, Jim and Snicker find themselves stranded in a railway station with two actors with whom they exchange identities; contacting Mary Jackson, Jim trails a man named Stanton to a gambling hall and by a ruse forces a confession, proving that Stanton is Arnold. *Fugitives. United States marshals. Ranch foremen. Actors. Gamblers. Impersonation.*

HEADIN' THROUGH **F2.2352**

Maloford Productions. *Dist* Photo Drama Co. **1924** [New York State license application: 20 Dec 1923; c10 Dec 1923; LU19689]. Si; b&w. 35mm. 5 reels.

Dir Leo D. Maloney, Bob Williamson. *Writ* Ford Beebe, Frances Beebe. *Photog* Jake Badaracco. *Ed* Fred Bain.

Cast: Leo D. Maloney *(Bob Baxter)*, Josephine Hill *(Rhoda Hilder)*, Horace Carpenter *("Pop" Hilder)*, Robert Williamson *("The Duke")*, Jim Corey *(Lige Gilson)*, Chet Ryan *(Yuma Kid)*, Leonard Clapham *(Roy Harlan)*, Bullet *(himself, Bob's dog)*.

Western melodrama. Bob Baxter, a man whose past is a closed book, is in love with ranchowner "Pop" Hilder's daughter, Rhoda. Gambler Roy Harlan arrives and attempts to blackmail Bob for $25,000, the reward advertised for the apprehension of Bob under the name "Warner." Rhoda overhears the conversation, but Bob refuses to explain. She finally gets Bob's sidekick, "The Duke," to divulge that Bob took the blame for a shooting done by his brother-in-law. Bob attempts to leave, and Harlan calls for the sheriff and solicits the aid of Lige Gilson and his two buddies, The Yuma Kid and Roxy LaRue, who have a grudge against Bob. Rhoda tries to help Bob but is abducted by Harlan. Bob tracks Harlan to his hideout with the aid of his dog, Bullet. He captures the gang by a ruse and beats up Harlan. The sheriff arrives with the news that Bob's brother-in-law has confessed on his deathbed to the shooting. Bob is free to pursue his romance with Rhoda. *Fugitives. Ranchers. Blackmail. Family life. Dogs.*

Note: Story and character names are from shooting script in copyright files and may differ from the final film. Of the cast (also taken from the shooting script) there is some doubt whether Horace Carpenter, Jim Corey, and Chet Ryan were in the final film.

HEADIN' WEST (Universal Special) **F2.2353**

Universal Film Manufacturing Co. 13 Feb **1922** [c27 Jan 1922; LP17506]. Si; b&w. 35mm. 5 reels, 4,548 ft.

Pres by Carl Laemmle. *Dir* William J. Craft. *Story-Scen* Harvey Gates. *Photog* Alfred H. Lathem.

Cast: Hoot Gibson *(Bill Perkins)*, Gertrude Short *(Potato Polly)*, Charles Le Moyne *(Mark Rivers)*, Jim Corey *(Red Malone)*, Leo White *(Honey Giroux)*, Louise Lorraine *(Ann Forest)*, George A. Williams *(Barnaby Forest)*, Frank Whitson *(Stub Allen)*, Mark Fenton *(Judge Dean)*.

Western melodrama. Bill Perkins, a war veteran bumming his way across the country with an airplane pilot, is forced to disembark via parachute when he arrives at a familiar spot. He lands in the midst of a cattlemen's dispute, gets a job as a dishwasher, and learns of a conspiracy to steal the ranch from its absent heir. The crooked foreman, to get even with Polly, who has high ideals, persuades Bill to impersonate the missing heir. At an opportune moment Bill proves that the ranch gang are cattle rustlers; when he is denounced as an imposter, he proves that he is the rightful heir to the property and wins the love of Polly. *Veterans. Rustlers. Cattlemen. Ranch foremen. Impersonation. Inheritance. Parachuting. Airplanes.*

HEADIN' WESTWARD **F2.2354**

El Dorado Productions. *Dist* Syndicate Pictures. Dec **1928** [or 15 Feb 1929]. Si; b&w. 35mm. 5 reels, 5,008 ft.

Dir J. P. McGowan. *Story-Scen* Sally Winters. *Adapt* Philip Schuyler. *Photog* Paul Allen.

Cast: Bob Custer *(Oklahoma Adams)*, Mary Mayberry *(Mary Benson)*, John Lowell *(Ed Benson)*, J. P. McGowan *(Sneezer Clark)*, Charles Whittaker *(Buck McGrath)*, Mack V. Wright *(Slim McGee)*, Cliff Lyons *(Pat Carle)*, Dorothy Vernon *(Lizzie)*.

Western melodrama. Concern for her father, who is being slowly ruined by cattle rustling, prompts Mary Benson to do some investigating in a distant cattle town, where she briefly encounters drifters Oklahoma Adams and Sneezer Clark. They follow her back to Arizona, go to work on the Benson ranch, and discover the ranch foreman to be responsible for the rustling and the robbery of a rodeo box office. *Ranchers. Ranch foremen. Rustlers. Vagabonds. Robbery. Rodeos. Arizona.*

THE HEADLESS HORSEMAN **F2.2355**

Sleepy Hollow Corp. *Dist* W. W. Hodkinson Corp. 5 Nov **1922.** Si; b&w. 35mm. 7 reels, 6,145 ft.

Dir Edward Venturini. *Adapt* Carl Stearns Clancy. *Photog* Ned Van Buren. *Sets* Tec-Art Studios.

Cast: Will Rogers *(Ichabod Crane)*, Lois Meredith *(Katrina Van Tassel)*, Ben Hendricks, Jr. *("Brom" Bones)*, Mary Foy *(Dame Martling)*, Charles Graham *(Hans Van Ripper)*.

Comedy-drama. Source: Washington Irving, "The Legend of Sleepy Hollow." Ichabod Crane, the lanky new schoolteacher from New York, does not find immediate acceptance in the community, but he does receive attention from Katrina Van Tassel, who cannot resist maintaining her reputation of community belle. Seeing the advantage of marrying into Katrina's wealthy family, Ichabod takes her seriously, thus establishing himself as Brom Bones's rival. The villagers nearly tar and feather Ichabod before they discover that his alleged cruelty to his students is a fabrication; and Brom takes advantage of Ichabod's interest in a legendary headless horseman. Disguising himself as the phantom, Brom encounters Ichabod on a lonely bridge one night, and Ichabod rides away—never to be seen in the village again. *Schoolteachers. New Yorkers. Flirts. Village life. Wealth. Phantoms. Legendary characters.*

HEADLINES **F2.2356**

St. Regis Productions. *Dist* Associated Exhibitors. 16 Jul **1925** [c20 Aug 1925; LU21743]. Si; b&w. 35mm. 6 reels, 5,600 ft.

Dir E. H. Griffith. *Cont* Peter Milne, Arthur Hoerl. *Story? (see note)* Dorian Neve, Olga Printzlau. *Photog* Marcel Picard, Walter Arthur.

Cast: Alice Joyce *(Phyllis Dale)*, Malcolm McGregor *(Lawrence Emmett)*, Virginia Lee Corbin *("Bobby" Dale)*, Harry T. Morey *(Donald Austin)*, Ruby Blaine *(Stella Austin)*, Elliott Nugent *(Roger Hillman)*.

Melodrama. Phyllis Dale, a feature writer on a newspaper, keeps secret the fact that she is the mother of an 18-year-old daughter. This girl, "Bobby," who is a regular jazz baby, is expelled from an exclusive boarding school and returns home, posing as Phyllis' sister. Bobby starts seeing Donald Austin, a wealthy philanderer, and simultaneously falls in love with Lawrence Emmett, her mother's sweetheart. Bobby becomes involved in a scandal, and Phyllis assumes the appearance of guilt in order to save her daughter's reputation. Bobby is greatly chastened and accepts the proposal of Roger Hillman, the easygoing editor of Phyllis' paper. Lawrence and Phyllis clear up their misunderstandings and return to their former intimacy. *Flappers. Reporters. Editors. Philanderers. Motherhood. Reputation. Jazz life. Boarding schools.*

Note: Sources disagree on credit for story.

HEADS UP *see* **SINGLE HANDED**

HEADS UP **F2.2357**

Harry Garson Productions. *Dist* Film Booking Offices of America. 2 Aug **1925** [premiere?; released 25 Oct; c2 Aug 1925; LP21897]. Si; b&w. 35mm. 6 reels, 5,842 or 5,482 ft.

Dir Harry Garson. *Cont* Rob Wagner. *Story* A. B. Barringer.

Cast: Maurice B. Flynn *(Breckenridge Gamble)*, Kathleen Myers *(Angela)*, Kalla Pasha *(Malofich)*, Jean Perry *(Cortez)*, Milton Ross *(Losada)*, Harry McCoy *(Biff)*, Hazel Rogers *(Anita)*, Ray Ripley *(comandante)*, Robert Cautier *(spy)*, Raymond Turner *(Zeke)*.

Adventure comedy-drama. Bored with his daily routine, Breckenridge Gamble accepts a secret mission from some oil magnates to deliver a message to President Losada of the South American Republic of Centralia. Upon his arrival, Gamble learns from Angela, the president's daughter, that her father has been imprisoned by Cortez, the leader of the revolutionaries. Gamble also is imprisoned but frees all the prisoners as well as himself by impersonating the prison *comandante.* After forming an army, Gamble delivers the message—a large money draft sufficient to pay the army and secure President Losada's government—and is rewarded with Angela's love. *Couriers. Revolutionaries. Imaginary republics. Oil business. Prisons. South America.*

HEADS UP **F2.2358**

Paramount-Publix Corp. 3 or 11 Oct **1930** [c10 Oct 1930; LP1635]. Sd (Movietone); b&w. 35mm. 9 reels, 6,785 ft.

Dir Victor Schertzinger. *Screenplay* John McGowan, Jack Kirkland. *Cont* Louis Stevens. *Photog* William Steiner. *Songs: "My Man Is on the Make," "A Ship Without a Sail"* Lorenz Hart, Richard Rodgers. *Song: "If I Knew You Better"* Victor Schertzinger. *Dance Dir* George Hale.

Cast: Charles Rogers *(Jack Mason)*, Victor Moore *(Skippy Dugan)*, Helen Kane *(Betty Trumbull)*, Margaret Breen *(Mary Trumbull)*, Helen Carrington *(Mrs. Trumbull)*, Gene Cowing *(Rex Cutting)*, Billy Taylor *(Georgie)*, Harry Shannon *(Captain Denny)*, C. Anthony Hughes *(Larry White)*, John Hamilton *(Captain Whitney)*, Stanley Jessup *(naval officer)*, Preston Foster *(Blake)*.

Musical comedy. Source: John McGowan, Paul Gerard Smith, Richard Rogers, and Lorenz Hart, *Heads Up* (New York opening: 4 Nov 1929). Jack Mason of the Coast Guard Academy meets Mary at the graduation ball and falls in love with her, though the girl's mother finds wealthy Rex Cutting a more proper choice for her daughter. On a yachting cruise arranged by Mrs. Trumbull, Jack is not invited. Meanwhile, Mary suspects Rex of picking up contraband beyond the 12-mile limit and refuses his proposal of marriage, while Betty, her impish sister, drives Skippy to distraction in the galley, where he has installed an automatic kitchen that does most of his work. Jack smuggles himself aboard but is forcibly ejected at port by a coast guard, and Mrs. Trumbull discourages his attempt to elope with Mary; but on a subsequent cruise, he hides himself in a lifeboat with two aides. When the captain stops to take on a cargo of rum, Jack and his aides take over the vessel, and a battle ensues. The yacht is wrecked on an island, and Jack proves his heroism, while Rex reveals his true colors and is identified as a fugitive bootlegger. *Bootleggers. Smuggling. Courtship. Yachts. United States Coast Guard Academy. New London (Connecticut).*

THE HEART BANDIT **F2.2359**

Metro Pictures. 24 Jan **1924** [c15 Jan 1924; LP19835]. Si; b&w. 35mm. 5 reels, ca4,900 ft.

Dir Oscar Apfel. *Adapt-Cont* Tom J. Hopkins. *Photog* John Arnold.

Cast: Viola Dana *(Molly O'Hara)*, Milton Sills *(John Rand)*, Gertrude Claire *(Mrs. Rand)*, Wallace MacDonald *("Spike" Malone)*, Bertram Grassby *(Ramón Orestes Córdova)*, De Witt Jennings *(Pat O'Connell)*, Nelson McDowell *(Jenks)*, Mathew Betz *(Monk Hinman)*, Edward Wade *(Silas Wetherbee)*.

Underworld melodrama. Source: Fred Kennedy Myton, "Angel-Face Molly" (publication undetermined). Mrs. Rand, a kindly old lady, effects the reform of smalltime crook Molly O'Hara, alias "Angel Face." Mrs. Rand's son, John, is involved in a suspicious financial deal. Through Molly's help, Rand is rehabilitated. He falls in love with Molly and acquires a renewed appreciation of his mother. *Criminals—Rehabilitation. Filial relations. Motherhood.*

THE HEART BUSTER **F2.2360**

Fox Film Corp. 6 Jul **1924** [c20 Jul 1924; LP20499]. Si; b&w. 35mm. 5 reels, 4,500 ft.

Pres by William Fox. *Dir* Jack Conway. *Scen* John Stone. *Story* George Scarborough. *Photog* Daniel Clark.

Cast: Tom Mix *(Tod Walton)*, Esther Ralston *(Rose Hillyer)*, Cyril Chadwick *(Edward Gordon)*, William Courtwright *(justice of the peace)*, Frank Currier *(John Hillyer)*, Tom Wilson *(George)*.

Comedy-melodrama. Tod Walton's childhood sweetheart, Rose, is engaged to Edward Gordon, whose elopement with another girl he assisted 5 years earlier. In spite of Tod's objections, she continues with wedding preparations. Tod abducts the sheriff and several ministers and holds them until he establishes evidence against his rival and thus wins the girl. *Sheriffs. Clergymen. Bigamy. Courtship. Abduction.*

THE HEART LINE **F2.2361**

Leah Baird Productions. *Dist* Pathé Exchange. 5 Jun **1921** [c14 May 1921; LU16532]. Si; b&w. 35mm. 6 reels.

Pres by Arthur F. Beck. *Prod* Arthur F. Beck. *Dir* Frederick A. Thompson. *Scen* George Jenks. *Photog* George Barnes.

Cast: Leah Baird *(Fancy Gray)*, Jerome Patrick *(Francis Granthope)*, Frederick Vroom *(Oliver Payson)*, Ruth Sinclair *(Clytie Payson)*, Ivor McFadden *(Big Dougal)*, Philip Sleeman *(Gay P. Summers)*, Mrs. Charles Craig *(Madame Spoll)*, Martin Best *(Blanchard Cayley)*, Ben Alexander *(The Child)*.

Melodrama. Source: Gelette Burgess, *The Heart Line; a Drama of San Francisco* (Indianapolis, 1907). Madame Spoll, a fake medium, is consulted by Oliver Payson, a wealthy businessman searching for a boy left in his charge 20 years before when his business partner was killed in a railroad accident. His daughter, Clytie, falls in love with Francis Granthope, a clairvoyant who tells his clients what they like to hear. Granthope is also loved by Fancy Gray, who sacrifices her own happiness when she learns of his feelings for the girl and helps him expose the medium. When Granthope is revealed to be the missing boy, he is free to marry Clytie. *Fatherhood. Spiritualism. Clairvoyance. San Francisco.*

HEART O' THE WEST *see* **HEARTS OF THE WEST**

THE HEART OF A COWARD **F2.2362**

Duke Worne Productions. *Dist* Rayart Pictures. 17 Jul **1926** [New York State license]. Si; b&w. 35mm. 5 reels, 5,038 ft.

Pres by W. Ray Johnston. *Dir* Duke Worne. *Photog* Ernest Smith.

Cast: Billy Sullivan, Edith Yorke, Jack Richardson, Myles McCarthy.

Action melodrama. "Boy, writer, is deprived of valuable oil property by schemer acting for publisher. Boy recovers property and publisher discovers his writing ability. They meet and publisher's daughter falls in love with writer and he with her." (*Motion Picture News Booking Guide*, 12:33, Apr 1927.) *Authors. Publishers. Cowardice. Property rights.*

THE HEART OF A FOLLIES GIRL **F2.2363**

First National Pictures. 18 Mar **1928** [c7 Mar 1928; LP25045]. Si; b&w. 35mm. 7 reels, 5,957 ft.

Pres by Richard A. Rowland. *Prod* Sam E. Rork, John Francis Dillon. *Cont* Charles A. Logue. *Titl* Dwinelle Benthall, Rufus McCosh. *Adapt* Gerald C. Duffy. *Story* Adela Rogers St. Johns. *Photog* James Van Trees. *Film Ed* Harold Young.

Cast: Billie Dove *(Teddy O'Day)*, Larry Kent *(Derek Calhoun)*, Lowell Sherman *(Rogers Winthrop)*, Clarissa Selwynne *(Caroline Winthrop)*, Mildred Harris *(Florine)*.

Comedy. Derek Calhoun, a secretary, falls in love with his boss's girl friend, Teddy O'Day, a Follies girl. Ashamed of his poverty, he steals from his employer, Winthrop, to buy her a gift. Discovering the theft and the fact that Calhoun is going out with Teddy, Winthrop has him arrested but later asks that he be pardoned. *Secretaries. Poverty. Theft. Follies.*

HEART OF A FOOL (Reissue) **F2.2364**

15 Nov **1927** [New York State license]. Si; b&w. 35mm.

Note: First released Oct 1920 by First National as *In the Heart of a Fool.*

THE HEART OF A JEWESS *see* **CHEATED LOVE**

HEART OF A SIREN **F2.2365**

Associated Pictures. *Dist* First National Pictures. 15 Mar **1925** [c2 Apr 1925; LP21296]. Si; b&w. 35mm. 7 reels, 6,700 ft.

Supv Arthur H. Sawyer. *Dir* Phil Rosen. *Cont* Arthur Hoerl. *Adapt* Frederick Hatton, Fanny Hatton. *Photog* Rudolph Berquist. *Art Dir* M. P. Staulcup. *Film Ed* Elmer J. McGovern. *Asst Dir* Al Hall. *Prod Mgr* Barney Lubin.

Cast: Barbara La Marr *(Isabella Echevaria)*, Conway Tearle *(Gerald Rexford)*, Harry Morey *(John Strong)*, Paul Doucet *(Mario)*, Ben Finney *(George Drew)*, Florence Auer *(Lisette)*, Ida Darling *(Duchess of Chatham)*, William Ricciardi *(Emilio)*, Clifton Webb *(Maxim)*, Florence Billings *(Lady Calvert)*, Mike Rayle *(Pierre)*, Katherine Sullivan *(Marie)*.

Melodrama. Source: William Hurlbut, *Hail and Farewell* (New York opening: 19 Feb 1923). Isabella Echevaria, whose beauty has won her a legion of disappointed admirers, arrives with her retinue of servants at a fashionable French hotel, and there she encounters Gerald Rexford, a young Briton who remains indifferent to her charms. Isabella becomes determined to bring Gerald to his knees and follows him to Paris, where she arranges a meeting with him through a mutual acquaintance. Gerald falls in love with her, and Isabella finds that she truly loves him in return. They share their idyllic love in a small house in the country until Gerald's mother persuades Isabella that Gerald will never find lasting happiness with her. Isabella then arranges with John Strong to make Gerald jealous by allowing Gerald to find her in John's embrace. Gerald discovers them together, suspects the worst, and leaves Isabella; Strong then has a change of heart and tells Gerald of Isabella's noble deception. Gerald returns to her in time to prevent her from poisoning herself and declares his intention to marry her immediately. *Vamps. Motherhood. Suicide. Jealousy. Paris.*

Note: Copyrighted also as *Heart of a Temptress*, 9 Mar 1925; LP21225.

HEART OF A TEMPTRESS *see* **HEART OF A SIREN**

THE HEART OF A TEXAN **F2.2366**

William Steiner Productions. Apr **1922** [c27 Mar 1922; LU17685]. Si; b&w. 35mm. 5 reels, 4,577 ft.

Prod William Steiner. *Dir-Writ* Paul Hurst. *Story* James Britton. *Photog* Jacob A. Badaracco, Jack Specht.

Cast: Neal Hart *(King Calhoun)*, William Quinn *(Pete Miller)*, Sarah Bindley *(Ma Jackson)*, Hazel Maye *(June Jackson)*, Yakima Canutt *(Link)*, Ben Corbett *(Commanche Horse)*.

Western melodrama. King Calhoun, son of an old Texas ranching family, gives aid to Ma Jackson, who attempts to manage a neighboring ranch after the death of her husband. Her foreman, who wishes to marry her daughter, June, threatens revenge when he is discharged, and enlisting the aid of other men on the ranch, he plans to drive her cattle into Mexico and at the same time to abduct June. Calhoun, however, learns of the plot, and with the aid of the ranchers, he prepares to defend the Jackson home; he misleads the attackers with a dummy and later returns to the ranch to save June as his men rout the outlaws. *Widows. Ranchers. Ranch foremen. Rustlers. Texas.*

HEART OF ALASKA **F2.2367**

Lee-Bradford Corp. 1 Aug **1924.** Si; b&w. 35mm. 5 reels, 4,800 ft.

Prod-Dir Harold McCracken.

Cast: Maurice Costello, Marian Swayne.

Melodrama(?). No information about the nature of this film has been found.

THE HEART OF BROADWAY **F2.2368**

Duke Worne Productions. *Dist* Rayart Pictures. Jan **1928.** Si; b&w. 35mm. 6 reels, 5,853 ft.

Dir Duke Worne. *Story-Scen* Arthur Hoerl. *Photog* Walter Griffen. *Film Ed* Malcolm Sweeney.

Cast: Pauline Garon *(Roberta Clemmons)*, Bobby Agnew *(Billy Winters)*, Wheeler Oakman *("Dandy Jim" Doyle)*, Oscar Apfel *(Dave Richards)*, Duke Lee *(Duke Lee)*.

Melodrama. "Small town girl [Roberta Clemmons] goes to city to become actress after meeting hoofer [Dave Richards]. They get work in a cabaret, but show backer makes life unpleasant for girl. When he is shot by an enemy, hoofer takes blame believing girl committed the murder. When it is proven that a henchman of the crook's was the guilty party the boy is exonerated and marries the girl." (*Motion Picture News Booking Guide*, [14]:257, 1929.) *Actors. Dancers. Theatrical backers. Murder. New York City—Broadway.*

THE HEART OF LINCOLN (Reissue) **F2.2369**

New Era Productions. *Dist* Anchor Film Distributors. 1 Nov **1922.** Si; b&w. 35mm. 5 reels, 4,445 ft.

Prod-Dir Francis Ford.

Cast: Francis Ford *(Abraham Lincoln)*, Grace Cunard *(Betty)*, Ella Hall, William Quinn, Elmer Morrow, Lew Short.

Historical drama. "Character study of the great Emancipator which deals with a few of the incidents in Lincoln's life. The romance features a broken love between a youth who joins the Union forces and the brother of his sweetheart, who joins the Confederate forces. The Southerner is captured, but the Union officer allows him to escape. For doing so he is tried for treason and the death warrant is brought to Lincoln to sign. He pardons the boy, and the youthful sweethearts are happy again." (*Motion Picture News Booking Guide,* 4:57, Apr 1923.) *Military life. Courts-martial. Treason. United States—History—Civil War. Abraham Lincoln.*

Note: A Gold Seal film originally released in 3 reels by Universal, 9 Feb 1915.

THE HEART OF MARYLAND **F2.2370**

Vitagraph Co. of America. May **1921** [c16 Mar 1921; LP16289]. Si; b&w. 35mm. 6 reels.

Dir Tom Terriss. *Scen* William B. Courtney. *Photog* Tom Malloy.

Cast: Catherine Calvert *(Maryland Calvert)*, Crane Wilbur *(Alan Kendrick)*, Felix Krembs *(Col. Fulton Thorpe)*, Ben Lyon *(Bob Telfair)*, William Collier, Jr. *(Lloyd Calvert)*, Warner Richmond *(Tom Boone)*, Bernard Siegel *(Provost-Sergeant Blount)*, Henry Hallam *(General Kendrick)*, Victoria White *(Nanny McNair)*, Marguerite Sanchez *(Phoebe Yance)*, Jane Jennings *(Mrs. Claiborne)*.

Melodrama. Source: David Belasco, *The Heart of Maryland & Other Plays* (Glenn Hughes & G. Savage, eds.; Princeton, N. J., 1941). At the outbreak of the Civil War, Alan Kendrick, an officer in the U. S. Army born in the South, sides with the North, but his sweetheart, Maryland, is for the Southern cause. When Alan is captured by the Confederates near her home she succeeds in halting his execution, then aids his escape by silencing the clapper of the warning church bell. *United States—History—Civil War. Prisoners of War.*

Note: Remade by Warner Brothers in 1927 under the same title, q. v.

THE HEART OF MARYLAND **F2.2371**

Warner Brothers Pictures. 23 Jul **1927** [c2 Jul 1927; LP24142]. Si; b&w. 35mm. 6 reels, 5,868 ft. [Copyrighted as 7 reels.]

Dir Lloyd Bacon. *Scen* Graham Baker. *Camera* Hal Mohr. *Asst Dir* Ross Lederman.

Cast: Dolores Costello *(Maryland Calvert)*, Jason Robards *(Maj. Alan Kendrick)*, Warner Richmond *(Capt. Fulton Thorpe)*, Helene Costello *(Nancy)*, Carroll Nye *(Lloyd Calvert)*, Charles Edward Bull *(Abraham Lincoln)*, Erville Alderson *(Maj. General Kendrick)*, Paul Kruger *(Tom Boone)*, Walter Rodgers *(General Grant)*, James Welch *(General Lee)*, Orpha Alba *(Mammy)*, Myrna Loy *(mulatta)*, Harry Northrup *(Gen. Joe Hooker)*, Nick Cogley *(Negro butler/Eli Stanton)*, Lew Short *(Allan Pinkerton)*, Leonard Mellon *(Young Stewart)*, Madge Hunt *(Mrs. Abraham Lincoln)*, Charles Force *(Colonel Lummon)*, Francis Ford *(Jeff Davis)*, Ruth Cherrington *(Mrs. Gordon, aunt)*, S. D. Wilcox *(General Scott)*.

Historical melodrama. Source: David Belasco, *The Heart of Maryland & Other Plays* (Glenn Hughes & G. Savage, eds.; Princeton, N. J., 1941). At the outbreak of the War Between the States, Maryland Calvert is loved by Maj. Alan Kendrick, son of a Virginia general, and Capt. Fulton Thorpe. Nancy, whom Thorpe has loved unwisely, follows him to Washington and commits suicide when she learns he will not marry her; as a result, Alan is forced to request his resignation. When Fort Sumter is fired upon, Alan, who admires Lincoln's principles, joins the Union Army though his father is among the Secessionist leaders; as a result, he is estranged from Maryland. Thorpe, who has joined the Confederacy as a spy, is responsible for Alan's arrest, but Maryland comes to his aid by ringing the alarm bell, as in the earlier (1921) version. *Spies. Suicide. Filial relations. United States—History—Civil War. Abraham Lincoln. Ulysses Simpson Grant. Robert Edward Lee. Jefferson Davis. Winfield Scott. Allan Pinkerton.*

Note: Remake of a 1921 Vitagraph film of the same title, q. v.

THE HEART OF SALOME **F2.2372**

Fox Film Corp. 8 May **1927** [c8 May 1927; LP24005]. Si; b&w. 35mm. 6 reels, 5,615 ft.

Pres by William Fox. *Dir* Victor Schertzinger. *Scen* Randall H. Faye. *Photog* Glen MacWilliams. *Film Ed* Margaret V. Clancey. *Asst Dir* William Tummel. *Cost* Kathleen Kay.

Cast: Alma Rubens *(Helene)*, Walter Pidgeon *(Monte Carroll)*, Holmes Herbert *(Sir Humphrey)*, Robert Agnew *(Redfern)*, Erin La Bissoniere *(Helene's maid)*, Walter Dugan *(chauffeur)*, Barry Norton *(Henri Bezanne)*, Virginia Madison *(Madame Bezanne)*.

Romantic melodrama. Source: Allen Raymond, *The Heart of Salome* (Boston, c1925). Monte Carroll, while visiting a French province, falls in love with Helene, an American, whom he believes to be a simple country girl. After returning with her to Paris, he comes to scorn her when he finds she has stolen some of his valuable papers. Determined to get revenge, Helene promises to marry her employer, Sir Humphrey, if he will, like the stepfather of Salome of old, take the life of her former lover. She gloats over his predicament as he is manacled and imprisoned in a dungeon; but ultimately she experiences a change of heart, saves him, and effects a a reconciliation. *Thieves. Courtship. Revenge. France. Paris. Salome. Documentation.*

THE HEART OF THE NORTH **F2.2373**

Quality Film Productions. *Dist* C. B. C. Film Sales. 10 Sep **1921** [c1 Sep 1921; LP16928]. Si; b&w. 35mm. 6 reels, 5,800 ft.

Pres by George H. Davis. *Dir* Harry Revier. *Story* Edward Dowling. *Photog* Lee Humiston.

Cast: Roy Stewart *(Sgt. John Whitley/"Bad" Maupome)*, George Morrell *(Father Ormounde)*, Harry von Meter *(De Brac)*, Roy Justi *(Sir Archibald)*, William Lion West *(Mad Pierre Maupome)*, Louise Lovely *(Patricia Graham)*, Betty Marvyn *(Rosa De Brac)*.

Northwest melodrama. Orphan twins found in a snowstorm by Father Ormounde are adopted from a Montreal orphanage by an officer of the Northwest Mounted Police and Pierre Maupome, a leader of desperadoes. Twenty years later, one of them, "Bad" Maupome, has become leader of a gang of thieves, and the other, John, has become a lieutenant in the Northwest Mounted Police. John meets Patricia Graham and falls in love with her after rescuing her from a forest fire. Meanwhile, having directed the looting of an Indian village, "Bad" goes to De Brac's trading post and roughs up the trader when he objects to his seeing his daughter; however, the infatuated Rosa goes to "Bad's" cabin where Father Ormounde discloses the bandit's identity. Maupome steals a police uniform and robs and wounds Miss Graham's father. John is arrested, but he escapes and trails his brother, who is killed by a falling tree in a storm. John is cleared by the girl's testimony, and they are happy together. *Trappers. Twins. Brothers. Bandits. Northwest Mounted Police. Storms. Fires.*

HEART OF THE WEST *see* **HEARTS OF THE WEST**

THE HEART OF THE YUKON **F2.2374**

H. C. Weaver Productions. *Dist* Pathé Exchange. 29 May **1927** [c7 Apr 1927; LU23834]. Si; b&w. 35mm. 7 reels, 6,562 ft.

Dir-Writ W. S. Van Dyke. *Scen* E. C. Maxwell. *Photog* Abe Scholtz, David Smith.

Cast: John Bowers *(Jim Winston)*, Anne Cornwall *(Anita Wayne)*, Edward Hearn *(Jack Waite)*, Frank Campeau *("Old Skin Full")*, Russell Simpson *("Cash" Gynon)*, George Jeske *(bartender)*.

Northwest melodrama. After the death of her mother, Anita Wayne finds herself an heiress and for the first time hears of her father, from whom her mother was separated for many years. He is rumored to be in Alaska. Determined to find him, Anita arrives in a mining town and becomes known to "Cash" Gynon, a notorious saloon keeper. Through a locket in his possession, Gynon learns that Old Skin Full, a drunkard, is her father, but Gynon convinces her that he, himself, is her lost father and takes her into the saloon. Jim Winston, with his partner, who has just discovered a rich gold vein, admires her but is disgusted to find her transformed into a saloon lady. Jim discovers Old Skin Full in the snow, learns Anita is his daughter, and returns to battle the villainous Gynon, who falls to his death. Jim is united with the girl. *Heiresses. Saloon keepers. Impersonation. Parentage. Alcoholism. Mining towns. Alaska. Yukon.*

THE HEART OF YOUTH *see* **FIRST LOVE**

THE HEART RAIDER **F2.2375**

Famous Players–Lasky. *Dist* Paramount Pictures. 10 Jun **1923** [c13 Jun 1923; LP19099]. Si; b&w. 35mm. 6 reels, 5,075 ft.

Pres by Adolph Zukor. *Dir* Wesley Ruggles. *Adapt-Cont* Jack Cunningham. *Story* Harold Riggs Durant, Julie Herne. *Photog* Charles E. Schoenbaum.

Cast: Agnes Ayres *(Muriel Gray, a speed girl)*, Mahlon Hamilton *(John Dennis, a bachelor)*, Charles Ruggles *(Gaspard McMahon, an insurance clerk)*, Frazer Coulter *(Reginald Gray, Muriel's father)*, Marie Burke *(Mrs. Dennis, John's mother)*, Charles Riegal *(Jeremiah Wiggins, captain of yacht)*.

Romantic comedy-drama. Muriel Gray causes her father so much trouble that he takes out an insurance policy that will cover him for any damages she causes. The insurance company, irritated at Muriel's reckless driving habits, sends one of its agents to marry her, but she sets out to win a confirmed bachelor. The insurance agent is the best man at their wedding. *Insurance agents. Bachelors. Automobile driving. Weddings.*

Note: Working title: *The Arms and the Girl.*

THE HEART SPECIALIST **F2.2376**

Realart Pictures. *Dist* Paramount Pictures. 9 Apr **1922** [c28 Mar 1922; LP17704]. Si; b&w. 35mm. 5 reels, 4,768 ft.

Dir Frank Urson. *Scen* Harvey Thew. *Story* Mary Morrison. *Photog* Allen Davey.

Cast: Mary Miles Minter *(Rosalie Beckwith)*, Allan Forrest *(Bob Stratton)*, Roy Atwell *(Winston Gates)*, Jack Matheis *(city editor)*, Noah Beery *(Dr. Thomas Fitch)*, James Neill *(Fernald)*, Carmen Phillips *(Grace Fitch)*.

Melodrama. Rosalie Beckwith, a newspaper writer, is instructed by her editor to gain some insight into the kinds of romances about which she is writing. In Essex, Connecticut, she is mistaken for Madame Murat Bey, a distant relative of Robert Stratton, a war hero, and co-heir of his estate. Accepting the situation, Rosalie discovers that Fitch, the family physician who is caring for Bob, is conspiring with his sister, Grace, to poison Bob before he discovers Fitch's embezzlement of funds belonging to the estate. When they realize that Rosalie has uncovered the plot, they throw her into a well; then Grace, appearing as the real Madame Bey, announces that the girl is an imposter. Rosalie escapes in time to prevent Bob from eating poisoned food, and she exposes Grace and Fitch. The physician is killed by poisonous fumes in his laboratory, Grace is arrested, and Rosalie gives up newspaper work to live with Bob. *Journalists. War heroes. Physicians. Brother-sister relationship. Impersonation. Connecticut.*

THE HEART THIEF **F2.2377**

Metropolitan Pictures Corp. of California. *Dist* Producers Distributing Corp. 2 May **1927** [c21 Apr 1927; LP23884]. Si; b&w. 35mm. 6 reels, 6,035 ft.

Pres by John C. Flinn. *Dir* Nils Olaf Chrisander. *Cont* Sonya Levien. *Titl* Lesley Mason. *Adapt* Gladys Unger. *Photog* Henry Cronjager. *Art Dir* Charles Cadwallader. *Asst Dir* Ed Bernoudy. *Translator* James Burrell.

Cast: Joseph Schildkraut *(Paul Kurt)*, Lya De Putti *(Anna Galambos)*, Robert Edeson *(Count Franz Cserhati)*, Charles Gerrard *(Count Lazlos)*, Eulalie Jensen *(Countess Lazlos)*, George Reehm *(Galambos)*, William Bakewell *(Victor)*.

Romantic drama. Source: Lajos Biró, *A Rablólovag* (Budapest, 1912). Paul Kurt, embittered and disillusioned by war, returns to Budapest and devotes his life to roistering and gambling. He falls in love with Anna Galambos but leaves her when he realizes his unworthiness. She returns to her father, a gamekeeper at the castle of Count Franz, a despotic bachelor whose brothers Lazlos and Michael covet his estate. Disheartened by her shattered romance, Anna accepts the proposal of Franz. The brothers conspire to hire Paul to compromise the girl, but Paul, discovering she is none other than the woman he loves, decides to win her for himself. Paul finally exposes the plot to Franz, and Anna, convinced of his sincerity, is reunited with him after Franz releases her. *Rakes. Brothers. Gamekeepers. Courtship. Nobility. Budapest.*

HEART TO HEART **F2.2378**

First National Pictures. 22 Jul **1928** [c14 Jul 1928; LP25475]. Si; b&w. 35mm. 7 reels, 6,071 ft.

Dir William Beaudine. *Cont* Adelaide Heilbron. *Titl* Dwinelle Benthall, Rufus McCosh. *Story* Juliet Wilbur Tompkins. *Photog* Sol Polito. *Film Ed* Frank Ware.

Cast: Mary Astor *(Princess Delatorre/Ellen Gutherie)*, Lloyd Hughes *(Philip Lennox)*, Louise Fazenda *(Aunt Katie Boyd)*, Lucien Littlefield *(Uncle Joe Boyd)*, Thelma Todd *(Ruby Boyd)*, Raymond McKee *(Milt D'Arcy)*, Virginia Grey *(Hazel Boyd)*, Aileen Manning *(Aunt Meta)*.

Comedy-drama. Princess Delatorre, young and beautiful widow of an Italian scion of royalty, returns with her fortune to the small American town where she grew up as Ellen Gutherie. Arriving by train a few days earlier than she planned, Ellen is mistaken for Mrs. Arden, a seamstress of doubtful repute from a neighboring town. She carries on the deception for fun when her nearsighted Aunt Katie and others believe she is Mrs. Arden. Phil, her old sweetheart, recognizes her, however, and shows her his new invention, a corkscrew that turns itself—a failure because of prohibition. Ellen leaves, having heard how much store is set on her coming; she returns on the proper train, elaborately made up as Princess Delatorre, and the big reception takes place as planned. Then she and Phil return to Italy, where they expect the corkscrew to be a success. *Widows. Royalty. Inventors. Seamstresses. Aunts. Smalltown life. Prohibition. Mistaken identity. Corkscrews. Italy.*

A HEART TO LET **F2.2379**

Realart Pictures. Jul **1921** [c20 Jun 1921; LP16694]. Si; b&w. 35mm. 5 reels, 5,249 ft.

Dir Edward Dillon. *Scen* Clara Beranger. *Photog* George Folsey.

Cast: Justine Johnstone *(Agatha Kent)*, Harrison Ford *(Burton Forbes)*, Marcia Harris *(Zaida Kent)*, Thomas Carr *(Howard Kent)*, Elizabeth Garrison *(Mrs. Studley)*, Winifred Bryson *(Julia Studley)*, Claude Cooper *(Doolittle)*, James Harrison *(Warren)*.

Comedy-melodrama. Source: Harriet Lummis Smith, *Agatha's Aunt* (Indianapolis, 1920). Sidney Toler, *Agatha's Aunt, a Comedy in Three Acts* (New York, 1923). Agatha Kent inherits a southern mansion from her maiden aunt Agatha. When she advertises for boarders, young Burton Forbes, who is blind and alone in the world, recalls his visits to Aunt Agatha as a boy and answers the advertisement. Disguised as her aunt, she welcomes her guest, who is distressed over a broken engagement. His gratitude for her kindness ripens into love, which she returns, but he does not disclose that he has seen through her deception. A lucky turn on the stock market results in the repair of his fortune, but when his former fiancée seeks him out he turns her down for Agatha. *Aunts. Blindness. Impersonation. Finance—Personal. Stock market. United States—South.*

HEART TROUBLE **F2.2380**

Harry Langdon Corp. *Dist* First National Pictures. 21 Jul **1928** [c17 Aug 1928; LP25537]. Si; b&w. 35mm. 6 reels, 5,400 ft.

Dir Harry Langdon. *Scen* Earle Rodney, Clarence Hennecke. *Titl* Gardner Bradford. *Story* Arthur Ripley. *Photog* Frank Evans, Dev Jennings. *Film Ed* Alfred De Gaetano.

Cast: Harry Langdon *(Harry Van Housen)*, Doris Dawson *(The Girl)*, Lionel Belmore *(Adolph Van Housen)*, Madge Hunt *(Mrs. Adolph Van Housen)*, Bud Jamieson *(contractor)*, Mark Hamilton, Nelson McDowell *(conductors)*.

Comedy. Harry Van Housen, the son of German immigrants, desperately wants to enlist in the United States Army during the World War in order to prove to his sweetheart that he is a true blue American. As many times as Harry volunteers for service, that many times he is turned down for unfitness: he is underweight, 4 inches too short, nearsighted, flatfooted, and suffering from dandruff. Unwittingly, he comes across a German base being used to shuttle supplies to submarines off the United States coast and all unknowingly manages to free an American officer, blow up the base, and round up the spies. Harry is given a hero's welcome by his hometown, but he misses it, being too busy courting his girl to care about civic honors. *Immigrants. Spies. Patriotism. Civil defense. World War I.*

HEARTBOUND **F2.2381**

Stereoscopic Productions. *Dist* Ace-High Productions. caFeb **1925.** Si; b&w. 35mm. 5 reels, 4,900 ft.

Dir Glen Lambert.

Cast: Ranger Bill Miller, Bess True.

Western melodrama. "... with a western ranch and New York figuring as the locale. Worthless husband of Beth is believed lost at sea, but later he turns up when she is married again to a ranch foreman, who leaves her, thinking she loves her first husband. The latter, however, comes to grief through his derelictions and Bill regains Beth after saving her from a desperado at the ranch." (*Motion Picture News Booking Guide*, 8:36, Apr 1925.) *Ranch foremen. Bigamy. Ranch life. New York City.*

HEARTLESS HUSBANDS **F2.2382**

Sun Motion Pictures. *Dist* Madoc Sales. 5 Oct **1925** [New York State license]. Si; b&w. 35mm. 5 reels, 4,900 ft.

Dir Bertram Bracken. *Scen* Burl R. Tuttle. *Photog* Gordon Pollock.

Cast: John Prince *(James Carleton)*, Gloria Grey *(Mary Kayne)*, Thomas G. Lingham *(Jackson Cain)*, Vola Vale *(Mrs. Jackson Cain)*, Edna Hall

(Minnie Blake), L. J. O'Connor *(Detective Kelly)*, Waldo Moretti *(Sonny)*.

Melodrama. Sonny Cain, an orphan, is adopted by James Carleton, an ex-convict who sees to it that Sonny treads the straight and narrow path. Carleton is later sent to jail again and is not released until Sonny attains manhood. Sonny falls in love with Mary Kayne and asks permission to marry her, but Mary's father reveals that he himself is Sonny's father. Carleton doubts the story and rifles Kayne's safe to find proof that Kayne is lying. Carleton is surprised by a detective, who shoots him; the wounded Carleton then tells the detective that Kayne is a thief. Kayne is arrested and given truth serum to make him talk. Kayne confesses that he is not indeed Sonny's father, and the lovers are free to marry. *Safecrackers. Orphans. Detectives. Adoption. Parentage. Truth serum.*

HEARTS AFLAME **F2.2383**

Louis B. Mayer Productions. *Dist* Metro Pictures. 1 Jan **1923** [c9 Jan 1923; LP18571]. Si; b&w. 35mm. 9 reels, 8,110 ft.

Pres by Louis B. Mayer. *Dir* Reginald Barker. *Scen* J. G. Hawks, L. G. Rigby. *Photog* Percy Hilburn.

Cast: Frank Keenan *(Luke Taylor)*, Anna Q. Nilsson *(Helen Foraker)*, Craig Ward *(John Taylor)*, Richard Headrick *(Bobby Kildare)*, Russell Simpson *(Black Joe)*, Richard Tucker *(Philip Rowe)*, Stanton Heck *(Jim Harris)*, Martha Mattox *(Aunty May)*, Walt Whitman *(Charley Stump)*, Joan Standing *(Ginger)*, Ralph Cloninger *(Thad Parker)*, Lee Shumway *(Milt Goddard)*, John Dill *(Lucius Kildare)*, Gordon McGee *(sheriff)*, Irene Hunt *(Jennie Parker)*.

Melodrama. Source: Harold Titus, *Timber* (Boston, 1922). Retired lumberman Luke Taylor sends his reluctant son, John, to Michigan to clear a logjam. There he meets and falls in love with Helen Foraker, who refuses to sell her acres of timber unless the buyer promises to replant the trees. Both Luke and uncrupulous Jim Harris try to force her to sell without agreeing to her conditions, and Harris starts a forest fire. After the fire is halted Luke agrees to replant and gives the couple his blessing. *Reforestation. Land rights. Lumbering. Michigan. Forest fires.*

HEARTS AND FACES *see* **AS A MAN LIVES**

HEARTS AND FISTS **F2.2384**

H. C. Weaver Productions. *Dist* Associated Exhibitors. 3 Jan **1926** [c22 Jan 1926; LU22290]. Si; b&w. 35mm. 6 reels, 5,438 ft.

Dir Lloyd Ingraham. *Cont* Paul Schofield. *Photog* Abe Scholtz. *Film Ed* Peter L. Shamray.

Cast: John Bowers *(Larry Pond)*, Marguerite De La Motte *(Alexia Newton)*, Alan Hale *(Preston Tolley)*, Dan Mason *(Tacitus Hopper)*, Lois Ingraham *(Jean Carrol)*, Howard Russell *(Luther Newton)*, Jack Curtis *(Gus Brent)*, Kent Mead *(Egbert Head)*, Charles Mailes *(Bill Fawcett)*.

Melodrama. Source: Clarence Budington Kelland, "Hearts and Fists," in *American Magazine* (vols 96–97, Nov 1923–Apr 1924). Larry Pond inherits an almost bankrupt lumber company from his father and attempts to turn it into a successful operation, taking into partnership his father's loyal clerk and a college friend. Preston Tolley, a rival lumberman, hires a thug to prevent Larry from getting his logs to the mill, but Larry beats the thug in a fight and, commandeering a train and a preacher, marries Alexia Newton, Tolley's former fiancée, en route to the mill with his logs. *Clerks. Preachers. Lumbermen. Railroads. Lumber camps.*

HEARTS AND MASKS **F2.2385**

Federated Productions. *Dist* Film Booking Offices of America. 1 Jul **1921** [trade review; c18 Oct 1920; LP15713]. Si; b&w. 35mm. 5 reels, 5,200 ft.

Dir William A. Seiter. *Adapt-Scen* Mildred Considine. *Photog* Walter Griffin. *Art Dir* Martin J. Doner.

Cast: Elinor Field *(Alice Gaynor)*, Francis McDonald *(Galloping Dick)*, Lloyd Bacon *(Richard Comstock)*, John Cossar *(John Gaynor)*, Molly McConnell *(Mrs. Graves)*.

Romantic comedy. Source: Harold MacGrath, *Hearts and Masks* (Indianapolis, [1905]). Alice, an energetic vixen, lives in a country estate with her gouty uncle, who denies her any companions. She plagues him with pranks until he leaves the estate. Now free to seek adventure, she dresses as a maid and convinces a passer-by, Richard Comstock, a celebrated author, that the estate is a boardinghouse. She has the servants pose as distinguished guests. The uncle returns and spoils the spoof. Later she meets Richard at the hunt club ball, which Galloping Dick, a gentleman burglar, also attends, in a strictly professional capacity. When jewels are discovered missing, Alice, thinking Richard is the thief, hides him in the cellar, where they run into Galloping Dick's accomplice. Alice and Richard are at first denounced as thieves, but the actual culprits are apprehended. *Uncles. Authors. Thieves. Gentlemen crooks. Disguise.*

HEARTS AND SPANGLES **F2.2386**

Gotham Productions. *Dist* Lumas Film Corp. 15 Jun **1926** [c21 Apr 1926; LP22628]. Si; b&w. 35mm. 6 reels, 5,775 or 5,980 ft.

Pres by Sam Sax. *Dir* Frank O'Connor. *Scen* Henry McCarty. *Adapt* James J. Tynan. *Story* Norman Houston. *Photog* Edward Gheller. *Film Ed* Leonard Wheeler. *Asst Dir* Rudolph Bylek.

Cast: Wanda Hawley *(Peg Palmer)*, Robert Gordon *(Steve Carris)*, Barbara Tennant *(Grace Carris)*, Eric Mayne *(Dr. Carris)*, Frankie Darrow *(Bobby)*, Larry Steers *(Peter Carris)*, J. P. Lockney *(Harry Riley)*, George Cheeseboro *(Barclay)*, Charles Force *(Hawkins)*.

Melodrama. Steve Carris, a young medical student, is expelled from college as the result of an escapade and seeks refuge with Hawkins, the owner of a traveling circus; though his sister Marian sides with him, his father and his brother, Peter, do not welcome his return home. Steve takes a job with the circus as canvas man and makes friends with all the troupe, especially Peg Palmer (a riding star), Harry Riley (the clown), and Bobby (his orphan grandchild). Barclay, the ringmaster, who resents Peg's friendship with Steve, becomes Steve's enemy after he receives a thrashing from him. Steve attempts a reconciliation with his family but is unsuccessful and takes Riley's place as the clown. Barclay plans revenge by releasing some wild animals, and Steve is injured in their stampede; Dr. Carris is reconciled with his son and learns that Bobby is the son of Grace, Peter's wife by another marriage; and Steve marries Peg. *Clowns. Ringmasters. Students. Physicians. Filial relations. Brother-sister relationship. Jealousy. Circus. Stampedes.*

HEARTS AND SPURS **F2.2387**

Fox Film Corp. 7 Jun **1925** [c7 Jun 1925; LP21549]. Si; b&w. 35mm. 5 reels, 4,600 ft.

Pres by William Fox. *Dir* William S. Van Dyke. *Scen* John Stone. *Photog* Allan Davey.

Cast: Buck Jones *(Hal Emory)*, Carol Lombard *(Sybil Estabrook)*, William Davidson *(Victor Dufresne)*, Freeman Wood *(Oscar Estabrook)*, Jean La Motte *(Celeste)*, J. Gordon Russell *(Sid Thomas)*, Walt Robbins *(Jerry Clark)*, Charles Eldridge *(sheriff)*.

Western melodrama. Source: Jackson Gregory, *The Outlaw* (New York, 1914). Sybil Estabrook comes west with her maid in order to visit her brother, Oscar, who has been sent to the plains to make a man of himself. Oscar, who has been losing at cards to Victor Dufresne, is forced by him to rob a stagecoach in order to pay off his gambling debts. Hal Emory, an honest cowpoke, rescues Sybil from a landslide, winning her affection. Hal later learns of Oscar's actions and himself takes the blame for the holdup in order to protect the boy. Dufresne plans to kill Oscar, and Hal arrives just in time to prevent the crime. Dufresne is later killed by falling rocks, Oscar settles his account with the law, and Hal wins Sybil's love. *Cowboys. Gamblers. Brother-sister relationship. Debt. Robbery. Manhood. Stagecoach robberies. Landslides.*

HEART'S HAVEN **F2.2388**

Benjamin B. Hampton Productions. *Dist* W. W. Hodkinson Corp. Aug **1922.** Si; b&w. 35mm. 6 reels, 5,275 ft.

Dir-Scen Benjamin B. Hampton. *Photog* Gus Peterson, Friend Baker. *Asst Dir* Eliot Howe, Jean Hersholt.

Cast: Robert McKim *(Adam Breed)*, Claire Adams *(Vivian Breed)*, Carl Gantvoort *(Joe Laird)*, Claire McDowell *(May Caroline)*, Betty Brice *(Gladys Laird)*, Frankie Lee *(Bobbie Laird)*, Mary Jane Irving *(Ella Laird)*, Harry Lorraine *(Dr. Burchard)*, Jean Hersholt *(Henry Bird)*, Frank Hayes *(Pynch)*, Aggie Herring *(Mrs. Harohan)*.

Domestic melodrama. Source: Clara Louise Burnham, *Heart's Haven* (Boston, 1918). Joe Laird, a fine young man, becomes secretary to railroad executive Adam Breed, but his promotion is not appreciated by his rather insensitive wife, Gladys. Soon afterward, May Caroline, Joe's mother, comes to live with the Lairds, their daughter, Ella, and crippled son, Bobby; and she is able to effect a cure of Bobby through her great faith. Meanwhile, Mr. Breed's daughter, Vivian, is seriously injured while trying to rescue Ella from an accident, and Breed asks May Caroline's help. Vivian also is cured, she finds happiness with Joe when Gladys is killed in an automobile accident, and Breed proposes to May Caroline. (The part of Pynch is that of a hypochondriac and is played for comedy.) *Secretaries. Railroad magnates. Hypochondriacs. Cripples. Faith cure. Paralysis.*

Infidelity.
Note: Hampton "and staff" are credited with direction and scenario.

HEARTS IN DIXIE **F2.2389**
Fox Film Corp. 10 Mar **1929** [c16 Mar 1929; LP234]. Si; b&w. 35mm. 8 reels, 6,444 ft.
Pres by William Fox. *Dir* Paul Sloane. *Adtl Dir* A. H. Van Buren. *Story-Scen-Dial* Walter Weems. *Photog* Glen MacWilliams. *Film Ed* Alexander Troffey. *Song: "Hearts in Dixie"* Walter Weems, Howard Jackson. *Choreog* Fanchon & Marco. *Sd* Arthur L. von Kirbach.
Cast: Clarence Muse *(Nappus)*, Eugene Jackson *(Chiquapin)*, Stepin Fetchit *(Gummy)*, Bernice Pilot *(Chloe)*, Clifford Ingram *(Rammey)*, Mildred Washington *(Trailia)*, Zack Williams *(deacon)*, Gertrude Howard *(Emmy)*, Dorothy Morrison *(Melia)*, Vivian Smith *(Violet)*, Robert Brooks *(True Love)*, A. C. H. Billbrew *(voodoo woman)*, Richard Carlyle *(white doctor)*.
Comedy-drama. Nappus, an old Negro who works a farm despite his advanced years, has a daughter, Chloe, married to Gummy, a shiftless young man who does nothing but sun himself while Chloe does both the housework and the manual labor. Gummy and Chloe have two children: Chiquapin and Trailia. Chloe and Trailia are taken ill, and instead of sending for the white doctor, Gummy sends for the voodoo woman. The children die, and Nappus sells his farm and his mule to raise enough money to send Chiquapin north to become a doctor, hoping that the boy will someday return south to help his people. *Farmers. Physicians. Children. Voodoo. Negro life. United States—South. Mules.*

HEARTS IN EXILE **F2.2390**
Warner Brothers Pictures. 14 Sep **1929** [c31 Aug 1929; LP657]. Sd (Vitaphone); b&w. 35mm. 9 reels, 7,877 ft. [Also si, 16 Nov 1929; 5,059 ft.]
Dir Michael Curtiz. *Adapt-Dial* Harvey Gates. *Titl* De Leon Anthony. *Photog* William Rees. *Theme Song: "Like a Breath of Springtime"* Al Dubin, Joe Burke.
Cast: Dolores Costello *(Vera Ivanova)*, Grant Withers *(Paul Pavloff)*, James Kirkwood *(Baron Serge Palma)*, George Fawcett *(Dmitri Ivanov)*, David Torrence *(governor)*, Olive Tell *(Anna Reskova)*, Lee Moran *(Professor Rooster)*, Tom Dugan *(orderly)*, Rose Dione *(Marya)*, William Irving *(rat catcher)*, Carrie Daumery *(Baroness Veimar)*.
Melodrama. Source: John Oxenham, *Hearts in Exile* (New York, 1904). Vera Ivanova, daughter of a Moscow fishmonger, loves dissolute student Paul Pavloff, a boarder in their quarters above the fish market. Paul loves Vera, but he neglects her and his studies to drink and gamble. She marries, at her father's request, Baron Serge Palma, a man with a good name and the means to support Vera. Later, Palma is banished for 20 years to Siberia for alleged involvement in the assassination of the czar's cousin. On the road Palma meets Paul, now a medical doctor, also exiled to Siberia for a minor infraction. Because he is sorry for Vera and her child, Paul exchanges his 2-year sentence for Palma's 20. Vera follows Palma into Siberia with her child, who dies of exposure. Arriving there, she finds Paul and lives with him until her husband comes to help them escape. When Palma senses that Vera and Paul are in love, he kills himself, allowing them to escape to a happier life. (In an alternate ending the two lovers are captured and sent back to Siberia to finish their exile.) *Fishmongers. Students. Nobility. Physicians. Marriage—Arranged. Exile. Suicide. Self-sacrifice. Moscow. Siberia.*

HEARTS O' THE RANGE **F2.2391**
J. Joseph Sameth Productions. *Dist* Forward Film Distributors. 5 Mar **1921** [trade review]. Si; b&w. 35mm. 5 reels, 4,800 ft.
Dir Milburn Morante. *Story-Scen* Victor Gibson. *Photog* H. O. Himm.
Cast: Milburn Morante *(Beldon)*, Alma Rayford *(The Girl)*.
Western melodrama. "Beldon, the new foreman of Squaredeal's ranch, arrives and with his arrival the rustling that terrorized the ranch ceases. Among those under him Beldon recognizes Cole, former manager of the Bar X ranch, whom he catches annoying a servant and knocks him down. Seeking vengeance Cole proceeds to make life troublous for Beldon, who is entrusted with a large sum of money by Squaredeal, to be deposited in the bank. Accompanied by Squaredeal's daughter, Beldon sets out to deposit the money the next morning, is overtaken by Cole and the two are locked in the latter's shack. The disappearance results in a search by Beldon's cowboys. Meanwhile Beldon has freed himself, subdues Cole in a fight, throwing him from a cliff, just as the posse appears. Explanations follow with everybody happy." (*Exhibitor's Trade Review*, 5 Mar 1921, p1336a.) *Ranch foremen. Cowboys. Posses. Rustling.*

HEARTS OF MEN **F2.2392**
Morris R. Schlank Productions. *Dist* Anchor Film Distributors. 15 Feb **1928.** Si; b&w. 35mm. 6 reels, 5,106 or 5,800 ft.
Dir James P. Hogan. *Scen* E. C. Maxwell. *Titl* De Leon Anthony. *Photog* Robert E. Cline. *Film Ed* De Leon Anthony.
Cast: Mildred Harris *(Alice Weston)*, Thelma Hill *(Doris Weston)*, Cornelius Keefe *(John Gaunt)*, Warner Richmond *(William Starke)*, Julia Swayne Gordon *(Mrs. Robert Weston)*, Harry McCoy *(Tippy Ainsworth)*.
Melodrama. Source: James Oliver Curwood, "Hearts of Men" (publication undetermined). "The poor lad thwarts his rich competitor, knocking over barriers of a killing and a burglary, to win the girl." (*Variety*, 6 Jun 1928, p25.) *Courtship. Burglary. Murder.*

HEARTS OF OAK **F2.2393**
Fox Film Corp. 5 Oct **1924** [c8 Sep 1924; P20590]. Si; b&w. 35mm. 6 reels, 5,336 ft.
Pres by William Fox. *Dir* John Ford. *Scen* Charles Kenyon. *Photog* George Schneiderman.
Cast: Hobart Bosworth *(Terry Dunnivan)*, Pauline Starke *(Chrystal)*, Theodore von Eltz *(Ned Fairweather)*, James Gordon *(John Owen)*, Francis Powers *(Grandpa Dunnivan)*, Jennie Lee *(Grandma Dunnivan)*, Francis Ford.
Melodrama. Source: James A. Herne, "Hearts of Oak," in Mrs. James A. Herne, ed., *Shore Acres and Other Plays* (New York, 1928). Chrystal is about to marry her elderly guardian, Terry Dunnivan, a sea captain who adopted her as a child, when Ned Fairweather, her sweetheart who has been missing at sea for 2 years, is rescued from a wrecked steamer. Hearing of their plans, Ned persuades Terry to marry her, but, suspecting Ned's true feelings, the old captain follows him to the Arctic, fills Ned's place aboard ship, and dies several years later, while Ned finds happiness with Chrystal. *Guardians. Seafaring life. Self-sacrifice. New England. Arctic regions.*

HEARTS OF THE WEST **F2.2394**
Ward Lascelle Productions. 20 Jan **1925** [New York State license]. Si; b&w. 35mm. 5 reels, 4,800 ft.
Cast: Lester Cuneo, Annabelle Lee, Charles L. King, Slim Podgett.
Western melodrama. The owner of a ranch fires his foreman for whipping a horse. Embittered, the foreman joins in with rustlers but is saved from a life of crime by his sister, who becomes the sweetheart of the ranchowner. *Ranchers. Ranch foremen. Rustlers. Brother-sister relationship. Horses.*
Note: Known also as *Heart o' the West* and *Heart of the West.*

HEARTS OF THE WOODS **F2.2395**
Supreme Art Productions. **1921.** Si; b&w. 35mm. [Feature length assumed.]
Dir Roy Calnek. *Photog* Jack Specht.
Cast: Clifford Harris, Laurence McGuire, Don Pierson, Anna Lou Allen.
Melodrama(?). No information about the precise nature of this film has been found. *Negro life.*

HEARTS OF YOUTH **F2.2396**
Fox Film Corp. May **1921** [c8 May 1921; LP16579]. Si; b&w. 35mm.
Dir Tom Miranda, Millard Webb. *Adapt* Millard Webb. *Photog* Walter Williams.
Cast: Harold Goodwin *(Ishmael Worth)*, Lillian Hall *(Beatrice Merlin)*, Fred Kirby *(Judge Merlin)*, George Fisher *(Herman Brudenell)*, Iris Ashton *(Mrs. Grey [formerly Hannah Worth])*, Glen Cavender *(Reuben Grey)*, Grace Goodall *(Countess Hurstmonceaus)*, Colin Kenny *(Lord Vincent)*.
Melodrama. Source: E. D. E. N. Southworth, *Ishmael; or, In the Depths* (New York, [1904]). Ishmael Worth renounces his young sweetheart, Beatrice, because he believes himself to be illegitimate and does not want to bring shame to her. Later it is revealed that his mother and father *had* married. His father's previous wife, thought to be dead, turns up to confront him; but the fact that the first wife was a bigamist makes her marriage to Ishmael's father null and void and the marriage between his mother and father therefore valid. Ishmael, having a legitimate father, now can give Beatrice an honest name. *Bigamy. Illegitimacy. Courtship.*

HEAVEN ON EARTH F2.2397

Metro-Goldwyn-Mayer Pictures. 5 Mar **1927** [c28 Mar 1927; LP23780]. Si; b&w. 35mm. 7 reels, 6,301 ft.

Dir Phil Rosen. *Story-Scen* Harvey Gates. *Titl* Lotta Woods. *Photog* John Arnold. *Art Dir* Cedric Gibbons, Arnold Gillespie. *Film Ed* John W. English. *Wardrobe* Kathleen Kay, Maude Marsh, André-ani.

Cast: Renée Adorée *(Marcelle)*, Conrad Nagel *(Edmond Durand)*, Gwen Lee *(Claire)*, Julia Swayne Gordon *(Aunt Emilie)*, Marcia Manon *(Aunt Jeanne)*, Pat Hartigan *(Anton)*.

Romantic drama. Young Edmond Durand has been reared under the autocratic influence of his aunt, who directs a large silk mill in southern France. He revolts against a stifling career planned for him and leaves home with Marcelle, a Gypsy girl. They roam the countryside with a Gypsy caravan in romantic bliss; they are inadvertently separated but at the outbreak of war are reunited. When peace is restored, the lovers find happiness together. *Vagabonds. Gypsies. Aunts. Adolescence. Courtship. Mills. Silk. World War I. France.*

HEEDLESS MOTHS F2.2398

Perry Plays. *Dist* Equity Pictures. 3 Jun **1921** [New York premiere; released 1 Oct; c5 Jun 1921; LP17645]. Si; b&w. 35mm. 6 reels.

Prod George Perry. *Dir-Writ* Robert Z. Leonard. *Staging (tableaux)* David Burton. *Photog* Hal Young. *Prod Interiors* A. B. Viragh Flower. *Stage Settings* Tiffany Studios. *Film Ed* Joseph W. Farnham. *Cost* Lucille Ltd. *Sketching* Henry Clive.

Cast: Holmes E. Herbert *(The Sculptor)*, Hedda Hopper *(His Wife)*, Ward Crane *(The Dilletante)*, Tom Burroughs *(The Sage)*, Audrey Munson *(Audrey Munson)*, Jane Thomas *(Audrey Munson [on screen])*, Henry Duggan *("The Spirit of the Arch")*.

Melodrama. Source: Audrey Munson, "Studio Secrets," "Life Story," etc., in *Hearst's Sunday Magazine.* Audrey Munson, who works as an artist's model, is asked by a Greenwich Village painter to pose for him at night; finding that his intentions are not wholly artistic, she flees from the studio and is found wandering in a storm by a kindly old man who takes her in and introduces her to a celebrated sculptor. Inspired by her, he obtains her consent to pose in the nude for a sculpture to be called "Body and Soul." The sculptor's wife, jealous of his art, falls prey to the attentions of the painter, and a model whom the painter has seduced, intent on killing him, informs the sculptor. Audrey, who has become infatuated with the sculptor, pretends drunkenness; and in disgust he destroys his masterpiece. Ultimately she effects a reconciliation between the sculptor and his wife. *Models. Painters. Sculptors. Seduction. New York City—Greenwich Village.*

Note: At the New York premiere at the Greenwich Village Theatre, a prolog was given by "The Spirit of the Arch," and small side screens were used to show a portion of the action, with cast members enacting stage tableaux of the incidents shown after the main screen was raised.

HEIR-LOONS F2.2399

Spitzer Productions. *Dist* Pathé Exchange. 25 Aug **1925** [New York State license]. Si; b&w. 35mm. 6 reels.

Prod Nat H. Spitzer, Grover Jones. *Dir-Scen* Grover Jones.

Cast: Wallace MacDonald *(George Brockton)*, Edith Roberts *(Mary Dale)*, Cecille Evans *(Marjie Trenton)*, Frank Campeau, Stuart Holmes, Snitz Edwards, Martha Mattox, Emily Gerdes *(The Brockton Family)*, Theodore Lorch, Sam De Grasse, Max Asher, Ralph Lewis, William H. Turner, Harry McCoy.

Comedy(?). No information about the nature of this film has been found.

HELD BY THE LAW (Universal-Jewel) F2.2400

Universal Pictures. 10 Apr **1927** [c10 Jan 1927; LP23543]. Si; b&w. 35mm. 7 reels, 6,929 ft.

Pres by Carl Laemmle. *Dir* Edward Laemmle. *Adapt-Cont* Charles A. Logue. *Story* Bayard Veiller. *Photog* Jackson Rose.

Cast: Ralph Lewis *(George Travis)*, Johnnie Walker *(Tom Sinclair)*, Marguerite De La Motte *(Mary Travis)*, Robert Ober *(Boris Morton)*, Fred Kelsey *(detective)*, Maude Wayne *(Ann)*, E. J. Ratcliffe *(Henry Sinclair)*.

Crime melodrama. At the engagement party of Mary Travis and Tom Sinclair, Tom's cousin, Boris Morton, facing exposure for the theft of a necklace, shoots Tom's father. Tom unconsciously casts suspicion on Mary's father, at whose feet the weapon is found; and Travis is convicted and sentenced to die. Although she has broken their engagement, Mary seeks Tom's aid in saving her father; they induce Morton to accompany Mary to the scene of the crime; and when he attempts to retrieve his gloves from a vase, he is arrested by waiting detectives. Travis is saved from the electric chair, and Mary and Tom are reconciled. *Detectives. Murder. Filial relations. Theft. Capital punishment.*

HELD TO ANSWER F2.2401

Metro Pictures. 22 Nov **1923** [c24 Oct 1923; LP19528]. Si; b&w. 35mm. 6 reels, 5,601 ft.

Dir Harold Shaw. *Adapt-Cont* Winifred Dunn. *Photog* George Rizard.

Cast: House Peters *(John Hampstead)*, Grace Carlyle *(Marian Dounay)*, John Sainpolis *(Hiram Burbeck)*, Evelyn Brent *(Bessie Burbeck)*, James Morrison *(Rollie Burbeck)*, Lydia Knott *(Mrs. Burbeck)*, Bull Montana *("Red" Lizard)*, Gale Henry *(The Maid)*, Thomas Guise *(The Judge)*, Robert Daly *(The Organist)*, Charles West *("Spider" Welch)*, Charles Mailes *(District Attorney Searle)*.

Melodrama. Source: Peter Clark MacFarlane, *Held To Answer* (Boston, 1916). John Hampstead gives up his career as an actor and his actress sweetheart, Marian Dounay, to become a minister in a western town. Marian appears, and failing to win him back she tries to ruin his reputation. Hampstead is accused of stealing some jewelry though actually he is protecting the scapegrace brother of his current sweetheart, Bessie. Hampstead is about to give up his church at the request of his congregation when the brother comes forward to confess. *Clergymen. Actors. Theft. Reputation.*

HELEN OF TROY *see* **THE PRIVATE LIFE OF HELEN OF TROY**

HELEN'S BABIES F2.2402

Principal Pictures. 12 Oct **1924.** Si; b&w. 35mm. 6 reels, 5,620 ft.

Pres by Sol Lesser. *Prod* Sol Lesser. *Dir* William A. Seiter. *Adapt* Hope Loring, Louis D. Lighton. *Photog* William Daniels. *Adtl Photog* Glen MacWilliams. *Film Ed* Owen Marks.

Cast: Baby Peggy *(Toddie)*, Clara Bow *(Alice Mayton)*, Jean Carpenter *(Budge)*, Edward Everett Horton *(Uncle Harry)*, Claire Adams *(Helen Lawrence)*, George Reed *(Rastus)*, Mattie Peters *(housekeeper)*, Richard Tucker *(Tom Lawrence)*.

Comedy-drama. Source: John Habberton, *Helen's Babies* (Boston, c1876). "... concerns a little girl who makes life rather miserable for her bachelor uncle, who is left in charge of the child while her parents tour abroad." (*Motion Picture News Booking Guide*, 8:36, Apr 1925.) *Children. Bachelors. Uncles.*

HELL AND THE WAY OUT F2.2403

James K. Shields. *Dist* League of Nations Non-Partisan Association. 17 Mar **1926** [New York State license]. Si; b&w. 35mm. 5 reels.

Documentary(?). This film advocates the entry of the United States into the League of Nations. *League of Nations.*

THE HELL DIGGERS F2.2404

Famous Players–Lasky. *Dist* Paramount Pictures. 4 Sep **1921** [c25 Aug 1921; LP16896]. Si; b&w. 35mm. 5 reels, 4,277 ft.

Dir Frank Urson. *Scen* Byron Morgan. *Photog* Charles E. Schoenbaum.

Cast: Wallace Reid *(Teddy Darman)*, Lois Wilson *(Dora Wade)*, Alexander Broun *(John Wade)*, Frank Geldert *(Calthorpe Masters)*, Lucien Littlefield *(Silas Hoskins)*, Clarence Geldert *(Silverby Rennie)*, Buddy Post *(fat farmer)*.

Melodrama. Source: Byron Morgan, "The Hell Diggers," in *Saturday Evening Post* (193:8–9, 2 Oct 1920). Teddy Darman, construction superintendent of the Continental Gold Dredging Co., falls in love with Dora Wade, daughter of John Wade, who leads the area's farmers opposing the destruction of their land. At her suggestion, Darman designs a machine that will resoil the land as it digs, and the farmers mortgage their farms to build it. Masters, agent for Continental who lent the money for the dredging operation, causes the machine to be wrecked. A battle with Masters' men ensues, and Teddy and the farmers beat their opponents as the sheriff arrives. Masters agrees to use the new machine, and Ted wins Dora and is made general manager of the company. *Construction crews. Farming. Gold dredging. Soil.*

HELL HARBOR F2.2405

Inspiration Pictures. *Dist* United Artists. 15 Mar **1930** [c26 Feb 1930; LP1097]. Sd (Movietone); b&w. 35mm. 10 reels, 8,354 ft.

Dir Henry King. *Cont-Dial* Clarke Silvernail. *Adapt* Fred De Gresac, N. Brewster Morse. *Photog* John Fulton, Mack Stengler. *Art Dir* Robert M. Haas. *Film Ed* Lloyd Nosler. *Rec Engr* Ernest Rovere.

Cast: Lupe Velez *(Anita)*, Jean Hersholt *(Joseph Horngold)*, John Holland *(Bob Wade)*, Gibson Gowland *(Harry Morgan)*, Al St. John *(Bunion)*, Harry Allen *(Peg-Leg)*, Paul E. Burns *(Blinkey)*, George Book-Asta *(Spotty)*, Rondo Hatton *(dancehall proprietor)*, Habanera Sextette.

Romantic melodrama. Source: Rida Johnson Young, *Out of the Night* (New York, 1925). Anita, the daughter of a descendant of Morgan, the pirate, lives with her unscrupulous father, Harry, on a Caribbean island. Joseph Horngold, a pearl trader, seeing Morgan kill a stranger in the island honky-tonk, bargains with him, proposing that he marry Anita as the price for his silence; but the strong-willed Anita refuses to submit to her father's demands. She tells Bob Wade, an American trader, of her father's plans and warns him of her father and Joseph's treachery; consequently, he agrees to protect her. Anita steals Joseph's pearls; and when he accuses Morgan of the theft, Morgan kills the trader and menaces the girl with a similar fate. Learning of her peril, Wade comes to her aid and charges Morgan with the murder. Ultimately, Wade and Anita are happily reunited. *Traders. Courtship. Pearls. Murder. Florida. Caribbean. Henry Morgan.*

Note: Photographed on locations near Tampa, Florida.

HELL-BENT FER HEAVEN **F2.2406**

Warner Brothers Pictures. 1 May **1926** [c30 Apr 1926; LP22667]. Si; b&w. 35mm. 7 reels, 6,578 ft.

Dir J. Stuart Blackton. *Adapt* Marian Constance Blackton. *Photog* Nicholas Musuraca. *Asst Camera* William Adams. *Asst Dir* William McGann.

Cast: Patsy Ruth Miller *(Jude Lowrie)*, John Harron *(Sid Hunt)*, Gayne Whitman *(Andy Lowrie)*, Gardner James *(Rufe Pryer)*, James Marcus *(Dave Hunt, Sid's grandfather)*, Wilfred North *(Matt Hunt, Sid's father)*, Evelyn Selbie *(Meg Hunt, Sid's mother)*.

Melodrama. Source: Hatcher Hughes, *Hell-Bent fer Heaven, a Play in Three Acts* (New York, 1924). When Sid Hunt returns to his Carolina mountain home from the war and is welcomed as a hero, Rufe Pryer, a hired man who covets Jude Lowrie, Sid's sweetheart, and is envious of Sid's courage and honesty, determines to bring about his downfall. Under the guise of a psalm-singing religious fanatic, Rufe rekindles a feud between the Hunts and Lowries; and when his methods fail to take effect, he proceeds to dynamite a dam. The escaping water floods the local countryside and pours into a cellar where Andy, Jude's brother, is caught along with Sid. When Rufe sees Jude helpless in the water, he frees the men so that they may rescue her, but he himself is swept away by the torrent. Jude and Sid are happily reunited. *Veterans. Brothers. Fanatics. Mountain life. Feuds. North Carolina. Floods.*

HELLHOUNDS OF THE WEST **F2.2407**

Prairie Productions. *Dist* Western Pictures Exploitation Co. **1922** [deferred New York State license 24 Jan 1923]. Si; b&w. 35mm. 5 reels.

Cast: Dick Hatton *(Dick Sinclair)*, Catherine Craig *(Virginia Stacy)*, Frank Thompson *(Frank Sinclair)*, Willie May Carson *(Camille Daggett)*, Frank Lanning *("Black Joe")*, Clark Comstock *(Clayt Stacy)*, Richard De Vilbiss *(Jimmy)*.

Western melodrama. Dick Sinclair, who has always looked after his younger brother, Frank, falls in love with Virginia Stacy, who is also the object of Frank's affection. The younger Sinclair goes west and later sends for Virginia. Deciding that she needs protection, Dick accompanies Virginia and does, indeed, rescue her from an Indian attack on their wagon train. Upon reaching their destination, Dick finds Frank involved with dancehall girl Camille Daggett, quarrels with him, and is nearly stabbed by Frank's ally, Black Joe. Dick, Frank, Joe, and Virginia thereafter engage in a series of dangerous adventures and encounters revolving around Joe's pursuit of Virginia and Frank's desire for her map of a gold mine. Dick scrambles through rapids, fights, and flames to rescue Virginia and kill Joe (who has already killed Frank). *Brothers. Indians of North America. Dancehall girls. Wagon trains. Gold mines. Rapids. Documentation.*

THE HELLION **F2.2408**

Sunset Productions. 15 Jul **1924.** Si; b&w. 35mm. 5 reels, 4,557 or 4,850 ft.

Dir Bruce Mitchell.

Cast: J. B. Warner.

Western melodrama. "... Tex Gardy, handsome young ranchman saves the property of the father of the girl he loves from the Hellion and her band of outlaws, who would seize it as their own. He reforms the Hellion and weds the girl." (*Motion Picture News Booking Guide*, 7:26–27, Oct 1924.) *Ranchers. Gangs.*

Note: Reissued Jan 1930.

HELLO CHEYENNE **F2.2409**

Fox Film Corp. 13 May **1928** [c29 Mar 1928; LP25109]. Si; b&w. 35mm. 5 reels, 4,618 ft.

Pres by William Fox. *Dir* Eugene Forde. *Scen* Fred Kennedy Myton. *Titl* Dudley Early. *Story* Harry Sinclair Drago. *Photog* Dan Clark. *Film Ed* Robert W. Bischoff.

Cast: Tom Mix *(Tom Remington)*, Caryl Lincoln *(Diana Cody)*, Jack Baston *(Buck Lassiter)*, Martin Faust *(Jeff Bardeen)*, Joseph Girard *(Fremont Cody)*, Al St. John *(Zip Coon)*, William Caress *(bus driver)*, Tony the Wonder Horse *(himself)*.

Western melodrama. Two rival telephone crews race to be the first to make connections between Rawhide and Cheyenne. Tom's girl's father is foreman of one of the crews and is depending on this victory to reestablish himself. Jeff Bardeen, rival foreman, kidnaps Tom's sweetheart, stopping at nothing to accomplish his ends. Tom rescues the girl and wins the race for her father. *Linemen. Telephone. Cheyenne. Horses.*

HELLO SISTER **F2.2410**

James Cruze, Inc. *Dist* Sono Art–World Wide Pictures. 15 Feb **1930** [c10 Dec 1930; LP1816]. Sd; b&w. 35mm. 8 reels, 6,200 ft.

Pres by Henry D. Meyer, Nat Cordish. *Supv* James Cruze. *Dir* Walter Lang. *Cont-Dial* Brian Marlow. *Photog* Hal Rosson. *Art Dir* Robert E. Lee. *Mus Comp* Russ Colombo. *Mus Arr* Howard Jackson. *Dance Dir* Maurice L. Kusell.

Cast: Olive Borden *("Vee" Newell)*, Lloyd Hughes *(Marshall Jones)*, George Fawcett *(Fraser Newell)*, Bodil Rosing *(Martha Peddie)*, Norman Peck *("Tivvie" Rose)*, Howard Hickman *(John Stanley)*, Raymond Keane *(Randall Carr)*, Wilfred Lucas *(Dr. Saltus)*, James T. Mack *(Horace Peddie)*, Harry MacDonald *(Appleby Sims)*.

Society drama. Source: Rita Lambert, "Clipped Wings," in *Delineator* (112:8–9, 16–17, Feb–Mar 1928). After a full-blown jazz party, "Vee" Newell, a headstrong, society-mad girl, bids her invalid grandfather adieu before going on to the country club, where Tivvie and Rann get into a fight over her. Returning home later with a jazz band, Vee realizes that her grandfather has died and hysterically drives the crowd from the house. Her grandfather's will provides that she will inherit all his estate if she gives up parties, cocktails, cigarettes, rouge, and lipstick and attends church regularly every Sunday for 6 months. She accepts the challenge and attends church the following Sunday, where she meets young attorney Marshall Jones, who walks her home. An accident at a society bazaar makes her realize that she loves Marshall, but when he refuses her, Vee decides to resume her life of dissipation with her former sweetheart; Marshall then forcibly removes her from a roadhouse, and they are married. Vee learns that she is to receive the inheritance after all, the restrictions having been a test planned by her grandfather. *Grandfathers. Inheritance. Jazz life. Wealth. Courtship. Church attendance. Wills. Bazaars. Roadhouses.*

HELL'S ANGELS **F2.2411**

Caddo Co. *Dist* United Artists. 27 May **1930** [Los Angeles premiere; released 15 Nov; c27 May 1930; LP1363]. Sd (Movietone); b&w with col sequences (Technicolor). 35mm. 14 reels, 10,390 ft. [Copyrighted as 16 reels.]

Prod-Dir Howard Hughes. *Dial Dir* James Whale. *Scen* Harry Behn, Howard Estabrook. *Dial* Joseph Moncure March. *Story* Marshall Neilan, Joseph Moncure March. *Ch Camera* Gaetano Gaudio, Harry Perry. *Asst Photog* E. Burton Steene, Harry Zech, Jockey Feindel, Fred R. Eldridge, Jack MacKenzie, Paul Perry, Roy Greiner, Dewey Wrigley, Elmer Dyer, Pliny Goodfriend, Alvin Wyckoff, Sam Landers, William Tuers, Glenn Kershner, Donald Keyes, Roy Klaffki, Paul Ivano, Charles Boyle, Herman Schoop, L. Guy Wilky, John Silver, Edward Snyder, Edward Kull, Jack Greenhalgh, Henry Cronjager, Edward Cohen, Jack Breamer, Ernest Laszlo. *Art Dir* Julian Boone Fleming, Carroll Clark. *Film Ed* Douglas Biggs, Perry Hollingsworth, Frank Lawrence. *Mus* Hugo Riesenfeld. *Ch Sd Rec* Lodge Cunningham. *Asst Dir* Reginald Callow, William J. Scully, Frederick Fleck. *Prod Mgr* J. W. Engel. *Prod Asst* Charles Stallings. *Tech Engr* E. Roy Davidson. *Ch Elec* Bardwell C., Tom Willette. *Ch of Aeronautics* J. B. Alexander. *German Tech* Julius Schroeder, A. K. Graves, K. Arnstein.

Cast—Principals: Ben Lyon *(Monte Rutledge)*, James Hall *(Roy Rutledge)*, Jean Harlow *(Helen)*, John Darrow *(Karl Armstedt)*, Lucien

Prival *(Baron von Krantz)*, Frank Clark *(Lieutenant von Bruen)*, Roy Wilson *("Baldy")*, Douglas Gilmore *(Captain Redfield)*, Jane Winton *(Baroness von Krantz)*, Evelyn Hall *(Lady Randolph)*, William B. Davidson *(Staff Major)*, Wyndham Standing *(RFC squadron commander)*, Lena Malena *(Gretchen)*, Carl von Haartmann *(Zeppelin commander)*, Stephen Carr *(Elliott)*, Hans Joby *(Von Schieben)*, Pat Somerset *(Marryat)*, Marilyn Morgan *(girl selling kisses)*, F. Schumann-Heink *(1st Officer of Zeppelin)*, William von Brinken *(Von Richter)*.

Additional Cast: Jerry Andrews, C. W. Angel, Bob Blair, E. D. Baxter, Howard Batt, George Berliner, Edward Brownell, J. A. Carmichael, G. G. Calahan, Harry Cameron, Milo Campbell, Thomas Carr, Ben Catlin, Frank Clarke, Ross Cooke, Virgil Cline, Harry Crandall, Ray Crawford, Lawford Davidson, J. Granville Davis, Jack Deery, Vernon Dorrell, C. E. Dowling, B. Foster, Curt Furberg, Frank Goddard, Lisa Gora, Douglas Gordon, Earl W. Gordon, Owen Gorin, V. A. Grant, Ed Greer, Pat Harmon, C. E. Herberger, Joe Henry, George A. Heddinger, Lyn Hayes, Al Johnson, Nelson D. Jenkins, Morey Johnson, H. J. Kelsey, Warner Klinger, H. G. Kraft, Al Lary, Burton Lane, Garland Lincoln, R. S. McCallister, R. P. McDonald, R. B. McGuggin, Lena Malena, Billy Martin, Renée Marvelle, George Maves, Marilyn Morgan, K. Meinard, R. C. Merriam, A. F. Mickel, Jack Miller, Roy Minor, H. F. Murchie, M. H. Murphy, Stuart Murphy, Leo Nomis, L. M. Owen, George H. Parker, R. A. Patterson, Tom Penfield, John Penfield, C. K. Phillips, Thor H. Polson, Dave Postle, John H. Rand, G. P. Reed, George D. Ream, Ira Reed, Georgette Rhodes, Louis Roepke, Rudolph Schad, Jack Schneider, Harry Semels, Robert O. Shallaire, Douglas Schilling, Joan Standing, Ernie Smith, Bob Starkey, Harry Strang, C. F. Sullivan, Gertrude Sutton, S. Sweet, Frank Tomick, Roscoe Turner, Julian Wagy, J. G Walsh, Ted Weaver, George H. Willingham, Al Wilson, Roy Wilson, Dewey Ward.

War melodrama. In Munich, Roy Rutledge, a young Oxford student, is visiting his classmate and friend Karl Arnstedt, along with his pleasure-loving brother, Monte, who is challenged to a duel by the Baron von Kranz, who catches him with his wife. Monte absconds, leaving Roy to take his place. ... Later the boys join their Oxford friends at home, where Roy continues his blind infatuation with Helen, a glittering social butterfly. With the outbreak of war with Germany, Roy enlists in the R. F. C., while the cowardly Monte is accidentally recruited through a kiss. At a charity ball, given by Lady Randolph, Helen snares Monte with her charms, and they begin a clandestine affair; on a mission to bring down a German zeppelin, the brothers barely escape death, unlike their friends Elliott and Karl. They meet Helen again in France, in Lady Randolph's Canteen, and she is exposed as a coldhearted flirt. Monte is openly accused of cowardice by fellow officers, and as a result both brothers volunteer for a mission behind enemy lines. But their planes are captured by the Germans; and when Monte frantically agrees to reveal the English position, Roy tries to effect a desperate plan to save him but at length is obliged to shoot him. When he himself refuses to give information to the enemy, he is ordered before a firing squad; but their sacrifice is not in vain, for the 7th Brigade's attack on the Germans is a complete success. *Students. Brothers. Vamps. Prisoners of war. English. Germans. Cowardice. Aviation. Zeppelins. Munich. World War I. Great Britain—Royal Flying Corps. Oxford University.*

HELL'S BELLES *see* **WOMEN EVERYWHERE**

HELL'S BOARDER *see* **HELL'S BORDER**

HELL'S BORDER **F2.2412**

Western Feature Productions. Jun **1922** [New York State]. Si; b&w. 35mm. 5 reels.

Cast: William Fairbanks.

Western melodrama(?). No information about the nature of this film has been found.

Note: May also be known as *Hell's Boarder.*

HELL'S 400 **F2.2413**

Fox Film Corp. 14 Mar **1926** [c14 Mar 1926; LP22561]. Si; b&w with col sequence (Technicolor). 35mm. 6 reels, 5,582 ft.

Pres by William Fox. *Dir* John Griffith Wray. *Scen* Bradley King. *Photog* Karl Struss. *Asst Dir* Buddy Erickson.

Cast: Margaret Livingston *(Evelyn Vance)*, Harrison Ford *(John North)*, Henry Kolker *(John Gilmore)*, Wallace MacDonald *(Marshall Langham)*, Rodney Hildebrand *(Bill Montgomery)*, Amber Norman *(Vivian)*.

Melodrama. Suggested by: Vaughan Kester, *The Just and the Unjust* (Indianapolis, 1912). "[Chorus girl] Evelyn [Vance] marries the rich Marshall Langham thereby double-crossing Gilmore, her boss, who had employed her to rope Langham into a scandal because of debts he owed Gilmore. The latter is killed and North, district attorney and sworn enemy of Gilmore and his gambling house, is held on circumstantial evidence. Evelyn could clear North but in so doing, she would expose Langham, the guilty one. When he is dying, he clears North who is engaged to his sister. At this point, Evelyn sees a vision in which her sins take the forms of monsters. For a fade-out you have Evelyn waking from a bad dream and all set to go on the iceman's picnic instead of hunting a rich papa." *(Film Daily,* 30 May 1926, p39.) *Gold diggers. Gamblers. District attorneys. Icemen. Circumstantial evidence. Murder. Visions.*

Note: The allegorical dream sequence, in reel 6, is in color.

HELL'S HEROES **F2.2414**

Universal Pictures. 5 Jan **1930** [c19 Dec 1929; LP930]. Sd (Movietone); b&w. 35mm. 7 reels, 6,148 ft. [Also si; 5,836 ft.]

Pres by Carl Laemmle. *Dir* William Wyler. *Adapt-Scen-Dial* Tom Reed. *Photog* George Robinson. *Film Ed* Harry Marker. *Rec Engr* C. Roy Hunter. *Sd Tech* William W. Hedgecock.

Cast: Charles Bickford *(Bob Sangster)*, Raymond Hatton *("Barbwire" Gibbons)*, Fred Kohler *("Wild Bill" Kearney)*, Fritzi Ridgeway, *(mother)*, Maria Alba *(Carmelita)*, José De La Cruz *(José)*, Buck Connors *(Parson Jones)*, Walter James *(sheriff)*.

Western melodrama. Source: Peter Bernard Kyne, *The Three Godfathers* (New York, 1913). While waiting for his three bandit partners in New Jerusalem, Bob Sangster spends some time with a dancehall girl and annoys the sheriff; later, the quartet robs the bank; and Edwards, the cashier, and one of the bandits are killed. Sangster, Kearney, and Gibbons escape, and a sandstorm delays pursuit by the posse. Slowed by Gibbons' serious wound, the bandits discover a woman in a wagon, abandoned, giving birth to a child; before her death she asks them to be the child's godfathers and to take the baby to New Jerusalem to its father. After burying her, they decide to return as promised; both Kearney and Gibbons die from thirst, and Sangster quenches his thirst with poisoned water in order to get to the town; at length, he reaches the church with the baby and dies. *Bandits. Dancehall girls. Sheriffs. Godfathers. Robbery. Childbirth. Thirst. Self-sacrifice. Sandstorms.*

HELL'S HIGHROAD **F2.2415**

Cinema Corp. of America. *Dist* Producers Distributing Corp. 18 Oct **1925** [c17 Aug 1925; LP21770]. Si; b&w. 35mm. 6 reels, 6,084 ft.

Pres by Cecil B. De Mille. *Dir* Rupert Julian. *Adapt* Lenore Coffee, Eve Unsell. *Photog* Peverell Marley.

Cast: Leatrice Joy *(Judy Nichols)*, Edmund Burns *(Ronald McKane)*, Robert Edeson *(Sanford Gillespie)*, Julia Faye *(Anne Broderick)*, Helene Sullivan *(Dorothy Harmon)*.

Society melodrama. Source: Ernest Pascal, *Hell's Highroad* (New York, 1925). Judy Nichols, a poor Chicago secretary, falls in love with Ronald McKane, a struggling young civil engineer, but refuses to marry him and commit herself to a life of poverty. Judy goes to New York, meets financier Sanford Gillespie, a habitual philanderer, and persuades him to advance Ronald's career. Judy and Ronald are married, but he increasingly devotes his time to business, neglecting Judy in favor of the frenzied pursuit of mammon. Ronald meets a millionaire widow and leaves Judy so as to court her. Out of spite and wounded pride, Judy goes to Gillespie and persuades him to ruin Ronald, offering herself to him in return. Ronald's fortune is wiped out the following day, and Ronald goes to the banker's apartment, intent on exacting revenge for Gillespie's action. Ronald finds Judy there and tries to strangle her. Gillespie breaks in, and Ronald and Judy are reconciled. *Secretaries. Engineers—Civil. Financiers. Philanderers. Widows. Marriage. Wealth. Bankruptcy. Chicago. New York City.*

HELL'S HINGES (Reissue) **F2.2416**

Kay-Bee Pictures. *Dist* Tri-Stone Pictures. **1923.** Si; b&w. 35mm. 5 reels.

Note: A "re-edited and re-titled" William S. Hart film originally released by Triangle Film Corp. on 5 Mar 1916.

HELL'S HOLE **F2.2417**

Fox Film Corp. 23 Sep **1923** [c25 Jul 1923; LP19347]. Si; b&w. 35mm. 6 reels, 5,488 ft.

Pres by William Fox. *Dir* Emmett J. Flynn. *Scen* Bernard McConville. *Story* George Scarborough.

Cast: Charles Jones *(Tod Musgrave)*, Maurice B. Flynn *(Dell Hawkins)*,

Eugene Pallette *(Pablo)*, George Siegmann *(Conductor)*, Ruth Clifford *(Dorothy Owen)*, Kathleen Key *(Mabel Grant)*, Hardee Kirkland *(The Warden)*, Charles K. French *(The Sheriff)*, Henry Miller, Jr., Fred Kohler, Dick Sutherland *(prisoners)*.

Western melodrama. A railway conductor throws cowboys Tod Musgrave and Dell Hawkins off the train because they are without tickets. Settling down in a station, Tod dreams: *Dell robs the train and escapes, planting some of the money on him. After an episode of adventure and romance in which Tod is sent to prison, escapes, and finally tracks down the culprit,* Tod awakens to find that Dell is still his jolly companion. *Cowboys. Railroad conductors. Train robberies. Dreams.*

Note: Working title: *Payday.*

HELL'S ISLAND **F2.2418**

Columbia Pictures. 16 Jul **1930** [c17 Jul 1930; LP1432]. Sd (Movietone); b&w. 35mm. 8 reels, 7,462 ft.

Prod Harry Cohn. *Dir* Edward Sloman. *Adapt-Cont-Dial* Jo Swerling. *Story* Thomas Buckingham. *Photog* Ted Tetzlaff. *Art Dir* Harrison Wiley. *Film Ed* Leonard Wheeler. *Sd Rec Engr* G. R. Cooper, John Livadary. *Asst Dir* C. C. Coleman.

Cast: Jack Holt *(Mac)*, Ralph Graves *(Griff)*, Dorothy Sebastian *(Marie)*, Richard Cramer *(Sergeant Klotz)*, Harry Allen *(Bert, the Cockney)*, Lionel Belmore *(Monsieur Dupont)*, Otto Lang *(German legionnaire)*, Carl Stockdale *(colonel)*.

Adventure melodrama. Mac and Griff, two Americans serving in the French Foreign Legion, are friendly rivals until they meet Marie, a cabaret entertainer in the oasis of Bel-Abbas; but they become bitter enemies when Marie favors Griff. During an encounter with Riffs, Mac is shot by a sniper and believes his former pal to be responsible; but Griff refuses to leave him in the desert and is sentenced to Devil's Island for refusing to obey orders. When Mac is discharged, she marries him and persuades him to serve as a guard on Devil's Island so as to be near Griff. Mac, planning revenge, pretends to aid Griff's escape with Marie, but he learns, too late, that his friend did not shoot him; disguised as Griff, he is killed by the prison guards, while Marie and Griff safely escape. *Entertainers. Prison guards. Riffs. Friendship. Courtship. Devil's Island. France—Army—Foreign Legion.*

HELL'S RIVER *see* **THE MAN FROM HELL'S RIVER**

HELLSHIP BRONSON **F2.2419**

Gotham Productions. *Dist* Lumas Film Corp. May **1928** [c12 May 1928; LP25238]. Si; b&w. 35mm. 7 reels, 6,267 ft.

Prod Harold Shumate. *Dir* Joseph E. Henabery. *Scen* Louis Stevens. *Titl* Terrence Daugherty. *Story* Norton S. Parker. *Photog* Ray June. *Film Ed* Donn Hayes.

Cast: Noah Beery *(Capt. Ira Bronson)*, Mrs. Wallace Reid *(Mrs. Bronson)*, Reed Howes *(Tim Bronson)*, Helen Foster *(Mary Younger)*, James Bradbury, Jr. *(The Hoofer)*, Jack Anthony *(Abner Starke)*.

Melodrama. Believing his wife has been unfaithful, Captain Bronson, a sailor, takes Tim, their young son, leaves San Francisco, and finally returns 20 years later. Mrs. Bronson, whom the captain has taught Tim to hate, stows away on the ship to be with her son. Joining her on board is Mary Younger, daughter of a woman whom Bronson once loved. Tim and Mary fall in love, Mrs. Bronson wins her husband's forgiveness, and Captain Bronson, repenting his cruelty, sacrifices himself during a storm to save Tim and Mary. *Sea captains. Stowaways. Seafaring life. Parenthood. Infidelity. Self-sacrifice. San Francisco.*

HER ACCIDENTAL HUSBAND **F2.2420**

Belasco Productions. *Dist* C. B. C. Film Sales. 16 Apr **1923** [New York premiere; released 1 Mar; c10 Apr 1923; LP18870]. Si; b&w. 35mm. 6 reels, 5,800 ft.

Dir Dallas M. Fitzgerald. *Story* Lois Zellner.

Cast: Miriam Cooper *(Rena Goring)*, Mitchell Lewis *("Old Blind Goring," her father)*, Richard Tucker *(Paul Dupré, an artist)*, Forrest Stanley *(Gordon Gray)*, Kate Lester *(his aunt, Mrs. Gray)*, Maude Wayne *(his fiancée, Vera Hampton)*.

Melodrama. While caught in a storm, Rena Goring and her father rescue Gordon Gray from the sea, but "Old Blind Goring" drowns. Rena blames Gordon and insists that he marry her to carry on her father's work—fishing. Gordon complies, but after 6 months of unhappiness he persuades Rena to return to his home and wealthy family. While Rena receives training in etiquette from Gordon's aunt, Paul Dupré tries to break up her marriage. Rena accepts his attentions to spite Gordon, but the Grays come to realize their love for each other—climaxing in an edge-of-a-cliff battle between Gordon and Paul. Paul falls into the sea; the Grays are firmly united. *Sea rescue. Fishing industry. Etiquette. New England.*

HER BIG ADVENTURE **F2.2421**

Kerman Films. *Dist* A. G. Steen. 5 Jan **1926** [New York State license]. Si; b&w. 35mm. 5 reels, 4,800 ft.

Dir John Ince.

Cast: Herbert Rawlinson *(Ralph Merriwell)*, Grace Darmond *(Betty Burton)*, Vola Vale *(Countess Fontaine)*, Carlton Griffin *(Count Fontaine)*, William Turner *(Silas Merriwell)*, Edward Gordon *(Transatlantic Smith)*.

Society melodrama. Ralph Merriwell quarrels with his wealthy father and sets out on his own, taking a job as a bellhop in a Los Angeles hotel. Betty Burton, the beautiful secretary of Ralph's father, gets a $1,000 bonus for an advertisement she devises and takes a week's vacation. She comes to the hotel where Ralph works, poses as the Countess Fontaine, and lives in high style. Ralph falls in love with her, but the course of true love runs roughly, for the real Count and Countess Fontaine turn up. After numerous complications, Ralph is reconciled with his father, and he and Betty make plans to be married. *Secretaries. Bellboys. Nobility. Filial relations. Advertising. Impersonation. Hotels. Los Angeles.*

HER BIG NIGHT (Universal-Jewel) **F2.2422**

Universal Pictures. 5 Dec **1926** [c5 Jun 1926; LP22811]. Si; b&w. 35mm. 8 reels, 7,603 ft.

Pres by Carl Laemmle. *Dir-Adapt* Melville W. Brown. *Scen? (see note)* Rex Taylor, Nita O'Neil. *Photog* Arthur Todd.

Cast: Laura La Plante *(Frances Norcross/Daphne Dix)*, Einar Hansen *(Johnny Young)*, ZaSu Pitts *(Gladys Smith)*, Tully Marshall *(J. Q. Adams, reporter)*, Lee Moran *(Tom Barrett)*, Mack Swain *(Myers)*, John Roche *(Allan Dix)*, William Austin *(Harold Crosby)*, Nat Carr *(Mr. Harmon)*, Cissy Fitzgerald *(Mrs. Harmon)*.

Comedy. Source: Peggy Gaddis, "Doubling for Lora" (publication undetermined). Tom Barrett, a motion picture press agent, noting Frances Norcross' resemblance to film star Daphne Dix, offers her passes to the star's personal appearance. While waiting for her fiancé, Johnny Young, Frances is offered $1,000 to impersonate Daphne and successfully appears in her place, assuaging the fears of Myers, a producer, who knows Daphne is with millionaire Harmon on a yacht. Reporter J. Q. Adams has his suspicions aroused and sends a cub reporter to impersonate Daphne's husband. At Daphne's apartment, Adams arrives and presses Barrett for an interview with the star. Frances is confronted by the reporter and manages to bluff her way; Harmon arrives to ask forgiveness, and he is followed by his wife, then Johnny, both demanding explanations. Frances exchanges places with the real Daphne, and, after she explains, all ends happily. *Actors. Press agents. Millionaires. Doubles. Motion pictures. Impersonation. Mistaken identity.*

Note: One source credits the scenario to Rex Taylor and Nita O'Neil.

HER CODE OF HONOR *see* **CODE OF HONOR**

HER FACE VALUE **F2.2423**

Realart Pictures. *Dist* Paramount Pictures. 13 Oct **1921** [c26 Sep 1921; LP17008]. Si; b&w. 35mm. 5 reels, 4,718 ft.

Dir Thomas N. Heffron. *Scen* Percy Heath. *Photog* William E. Collins.

Cast: Wanda Hawley *(Peggy Malone)*, Lincoln Plummer *(Pop Malone)*, Dick Rosson *(Eddie Malone)*, T. Roy Barnes *(Jimmy Parsons)*, Winifred Bryson *(Laurette)*, Donald MacDonald *(Martin Fox)*, Harvey Clark *(F. B. Sturgeon)*, George Periolat *(James R. Greenwood)*, Eugene Burr *(Jack Darian)*, Ah Wing *(Chinaman)*.

Society melodrama. Source: Earl Derr Biggers, "The Girl Who Paid Dividends," in *Saturday Evening Post* (193:12–13, 23 Apr 1921). Chorus girl Peggy Malone, who supports her shiftless father and brother, marries press agent Jimmy Parsons. All goes well until Pop and Eddie practically move into Jimmy's flat, keeping him away from home and causing Peggy to return to stage work. When his health is jeopardized, Jimmy is sent to Arizona, while Peggy also goes west to accept an offer from the movies. She becomes a star and continues to support her father and brother and to aid Jimmy. Peggy is injured while performing in a dangerous scene and is forced to choose between her wealthy admirer, Martin Fox, and Jimmy, who comes to Los Angeles to fight for her. Her husband has saved the money sent him and has become a successful scenarist; thus, their future is assured. *Chorus girls. Actors. Motion picture scenarists. Press agents. In-laws. Motion pictures. Family life. Hollywood. Arizona.*

HER FATAL MILLIONS **F2.2424**

Metro Pictures. *Dist* Associated First National Pictures. 9 Apr **1923** [c19 Apr 1923; LP18925]. Si; b&w. 35mm. 6 reels, 5,390 ft.

Dir William Beaudine. *Adapt* Arthur Statter. *Story* William Dudley Pelley. *Photog* John Arnold.

Cast: Viola Dana *(Mary Bishop)*, Huntly Gordon *(Fred Garrison)*, Allan Forrest *(Lew Carmody)*, Peggy Browne *(Louise Carmody)*, Edward Connelly *(Amos Bishop)*, Kate Price *(Mary Applewin)*, Joy Winthrop *(landlady)*.

Farce. Jewelry store clerk Mary Bishop receives word that her former sweetheart, Fred Garrison, who has made his fortune in the city, is returning home for a visit and wishes to see her. Believing him married to a society girl and wishing to appear successful, Mary "borrows" jewels and clothes and tells Fred she has married the town's richest citizen. There follows a series of mixups and comedy situations (one of which shows Mary in Chaplin-like makeup and an oversize suit of men's clothes). Finally, Mary admits her bluff, and Fred explains that he is indeed unmarried but wishes Mary to be his wife. *Salesclerks. Wealth. Jewelry trade.*

HER FATHER SAID NO **F2.2425**

R-C Pictures. *Dist* Film Booking Offices of America. 2 Jan **1927** [c24 Dec 1926; LP23468]. Si; b&w. 35mm. 7 reels, 6,808 ft.

Pres by Joseph P. Kennedy. *Dir* Jack McKeown. *Cont-Titl* Al Boasberg. *Story* Harry Charles Witwer. *Photog* Lyman Broening. *Asst Dir* Sam Nelson.

Cast: Mary Brian *(Charlotte Hamilton)*, Danny O'Shea *(Danny Martin)*, Al Cooke *(Al Conklin)*, Kit Guard *(Kit Goodwin)*, John Steppling *(John Hamilton)*, Frankie Darro *(Matt Doe)*, Gene Stone *(Herbert Penrod)*, Betty Caldwell *(Betty Francis)*.

Romantic comedy. While taking a morning workout, young prizefighter Danny Martin encounters Charlotte Hamilton in distress over her balky roadster. Martin wins his fight but is counted a loser by a crooked referee. Later, he is invited to a barbecue at Charlotte's home, but when John Hamilton, who strongly dislikes fighters, learns of Martin's profession, he shows him the door. Danny gives up his career for Charlotte and opens a health resort for obese millionaires. Hamilton and his prospective son-in-law, Penrod, arrive at the resort for treatment, and their indignation and disgust at the treatment provide comic complications. Learning that Danny and Charlotte have already eloped, Hamilton is at first furious, then resigns himself to their happiness. *Prizefighters. Millionaires. Health resorts. Obesity. Courtship. Elopement.*

HER FIRST LOVE *see* **FIRST LOVE**

HER GILDED CAGE **F2.2426**

Famous Players–Lasky. *Dist* Paramount Pictures. ca5 Aug **1922** [New York premiere; released 3 Sep; c9 Aug 1922; LP18134]. Si; b&w. 35mm. 6 reels, 6,338 ft.

Pres by Jesse L. Lasky. *Dir* Sam Wood. *Adapt* Elmer Harris, Percy Heath. *Photog* Alfred Gilks.

Cast: Gloria Swanson *(Suzanne Ornoff, a cabaret dancer)*, David Powell *(Arnold Pell, an American artist)*, Harrison Ford *(Lawrence Pell, his brother)*, Anne Cornwall *(Jacqueline Ornoff, Suzanne's sister)*, Walter Hiers *(Bud Walton, a publicity agent)*, Charles A. Stevenson *(Gaston Petitfils, a French beau)*.

Romantic drama. Source: Anne Nichols, *The Gilded Cage* (New York opening: 10 Oct 1921). A French actress, the daughter of an aristocratic family, in order to aid her impoverished uncle and invalid sister, accepts a press agent's idea that she be billed as "Fleur d'Amour, the favourite of King Fernando." Actually, she has encountered the king only when performing in a cabaret. The tactic, however, is a huge success, but her lover, an American artist, misunderstands. They are later reconciled, and her sister is subsequently cured. *Sisters. Invalids. Press agents. Artists. Entertainers. Cabarets. Paris.*

HER HALF BROTHER *see* **PALS OF THE WEST**

HER HONOR THE GOVERNOR **F2.2427**

R-C Pictures. *Dist* Film Booking Offices of America. ca 17 Jul **1926** [New York premiere; released 17 Oct; c17 Jul 1926; LP22918]. Si; b&w. 35mm. 7 reels, 6,712 ft.

Pres by Joseph P. Kennedy. *Dir* Chet Withey. *Adapt-Cont* Doris Anderson. *Story* Hyatt Daab, Doris Anderson. *Photog* André Barlatier. *Asst Dir* Doran Cox.

Cast: Pauline Frederick *(Adele Fenway)*, Carroll Nye *(Bob Fenway)*, Greta von Rue *(Marian Lee)*, Tom Santschi *(Richard Palmer)*, Stanton Heck *(Jim Dornton)*, Boris Karloff *(Snipe Collins)*, Jack Richardson *(Slade)*, Charles McHugh, Kathleen Kirkham, William Worthington.

Domestic melodrama. Bob Fenway, the only son of Gov. Adele Fenway, is engaged to Marian Lee, and at a dinner Adele announces her intention of giving them a wedding house. Having refused to support a water power bill endorsed by Jim Dornton, the political boss of the state, the governor is threatened. Through Snipe Collins, Dornton discovers that Adele's deceased husband was previously married and that his first wife claims the divorce was not legal. Confronted with the evidence by Dornton, the governor turns to Richard Palmer for aid, but he is unable to find the divorce papers. Bob goes to the Athletic Club to force Dornton's apology; and Snipe Collins, in a fight with Blake, one of Dornton's men, kills him while he (Collins) is to inform the governor by telephone of Dornton's treachery. Unaware of the act, Bob returns home and is arrested for murder. At the trial Mrs. Fenway makes a plea for his innocence and is unable to pardon him when she is impeached by Dornton's scheming; but Old Lem, having overheard incriminating evidence, brings it to bear against Collins. *State governors. Women in public office. Politicians. Murder. Divorce. Filial relations. Water power. State legislatures. Documentation.*

HER HUSBAND'S SECRET **F2.2428**

Frank Lloyd Productions. *Dist* First National Pictures. 22 Feb **1925** [c2 Feb 1925; LP21075]. Si; b&w. 35mm. 7 reels, 6,151 ft.

Dir Frank Lloyd. *Adapt* J. G. Hawks. *Photog* Norbert Brodin.

Cast: Antonio Moreno *(Elliot Owen)*, Patsy Ruth Miller *(Judy Brewster)*, Ruth Clifford *(Mrs. Pearce)*, David Torrence *(Ross Brewster)*, Walter McGrail *(Leon Kent)*, Phyllis Haver *(Pansy La Rue)*, Pauline Neff *(Mrs. Van Tuyler)*, Margaret Fielding *(Irene Farway)*, Edwards Davis *(Tony Van Orien)*, Frank Coffyn, Fred Warren *(brokers)*, Frankie Darro *(young Elliot Owen)*, Frances Teague *(Miss Van Tuyler)*, Lou Salter *(maid)*, Harry Lonsdale *(Brewster butler)*.

Melodrama. Source: May Edginton, "Judgement," in *Saturday Evening Post* (197:37–42, 23 Aug 1924). To relieve the monotony of home life, Leon Kent throws a wild party. Distracted by the noise and drunken revelry, Kent's wife leaves the house with her small son and goes to the house of a sympathetic neighbor, Ross Brewster, a wealthy banker. The following morning, Kent becomes enraged to discover that his wife has spent the night with Brewster; and he divorces her, taking their young son with him. For 25 years, Mrs. Kent, known now by her maiden name, Pearce, and Ross Brewster maintain a beautiful relationship, although they never marry. Brewster's daughter, Judy, returns home with Elliot Owen, a young man whom she introduces as her fiancé. Brewster soon discovers that Owen is guilty of fraudulent investment-promotion, and Owen discloses that he has been married to Judy for 3 months. Brewster refuses to help Owen and hints that the best and most honorable thing for Owen to do would be to kill himself. Owen then reveals that he is the son of Mrs. Pearce. Brewster still refuses to help Owen; Owen is overcome with remorse and jumps over a cliff. He is not killed, however, and Brewster helps him regain spiritual and physical health. Judy gives birth to a child, and Brewster takes Owen into the banking business with him. *Bankers. Divorce. Fraud. Suicide.*

HER HUSBAND'S TRADEMARK **F2.2429**

Famous Players–Lasky. *Dist* Paramount Pictures. ca19 Feb **1922** [New York premiere; released 19 Mar; c14 Feb 1922; LP17562]. Si; b&w. 35mm. 5 reels, 5,101 ft.

Pres by Jesse L. Lasky. *Dir* Sam Wood. *Adapt* Lorna Moon. *Story* Clara Beranger. *Photog* Al Gilks.

Cast: Gloria Swanson *(Lois Miller)*, Richard Wayne *(Allan Franklin)*, Stuart Holmes *(James Berkeley)*, Lucien Littlefield *(Slithy Winters)*, Charles Ogle *(Father Berkeley)*, Edythe Chapman *(Mother Berkeley)*, Clarence Burton *(Mexican bandit)*, James Neill *(Henry Strom)*.

Society melodrama. James Berkeley (who wants to get rich) and Allan Franklin (determined to be a great engineer) are rivals for the hand of Lois Miller. Berkeley marries her, and 15 years later, though he has not realized his ambition, he keeps his wife luxuriously attired as a "trademark" of his prosperity. Allan, who has obtained a large tract of oil land from the Mexican Government, visits the Berkeleys; and James, hoping to profit from his wealth, goes to Mexico with him, accompanied by Lois, who unwillingly agrees to help her husband. When Allan and Lois realize their love for each other, James, refusing to become angry, is denounced by his wife. A band of Mexican bandits attempt to capture Lois, and in the attack James is slain. Allan rescues Lois, and they escape across the border. *Engineers. Bandits. Infidelity. Wealth. Oil lands. Mexico.*

HER INDISCRETIONS **F2.2430**

Dist Jans Productions. 6 Jan **1927** [New York State license]. Si; b&w. 35mm. 6 reels, 5,800 ft.

Cast: Mahlon Hamilton, May Allison.

Society drama(?). No information about the nature of this film has been found.

HER LORD AND MASTER **F2.2431**

Vitagraph Co. of America. Mar **1921** [c3 Mar 1921; LP16226]. Si; b&w. 35mm. 6 reels.

Dir Edward José. *Scen* J. Clarkson Miller. *Photog* Joe Shelderfer.

Cast: Alice Joyce *(Indiana Stillwater)*, Holmes Herbert *(Rt. Hon. Thurston Ralph, Viscount Canning)*, Walter McEwen *(Lord Nelson Stafford)*, Frank Sheridan *(Fred Stillwater)*, Marie Shotwell *(Mrs. Stillwater)*, Louise Beaudet *(Mrs. Chazy Bunker)*, Eugene Acker *(Glen Masters)*, John Sutherland *(Jennings)*, Ida Waterman *(Lady Canning)*.

Comedy-drama. Source: Martha Morton, *Her Lord and Master: A Comedy in Four Acts* (New York, 1912). Indiana Stillwater, spoiled daughter of a wealthy American railroad magnate, marries Viscount Canning and goes to England. Although her husband's family finds her unconventional attire and manners shocking, she is received kindly until Indiana's parents invite her to a Sunday-night supper in their hotel—an arrangement incompatible with her husband's notions of social propriety. She disobeys his order not to attend and, returning home, finds herself locked out, though an old butler admits her. Canning suggests a separation, but his wife repents and they are reconciled. *Railroad magnates. Social customs. Marriage. England.*

HER LOVE STORY **F2.2432**

Famous Players–Lasky. *Dist* Paramount Pictures. 6 Oct **1924** [c30 Sep 1924; LP20597]. Si; b&w. 35mm. 7 reels, 6,750 ft.

Pres by Adolph Zukor, Jesse L. Lasky. *Dir* Allan Dwan. *Scen* Frank Tuttle. *Photog* George Webber.

Cast: Gloria Swanson *(Princess Marie)*, Ian Keith *(Captain Rudi)*, George Fawcett *(Archduke)*, Echlin Gayer *(The King)*, Mario Majeroni *(Prime Minister)*, Sidney Herbert *(Archduke's adviser)*, Donald Hall *(court physician)*, Baroness de Hedemann *(lady-in-waiting)*, Jane Auburn *(Clothilde)*, Bert Wales *(The Boy)*, General Lodijensky *(Minister of War)*.

Romantic drama. Source: Mary Roberts Rinehart, "Her Majesty, the Queen," in *Temperamental People* (New York, 1924). Princess Marie of the Balkan kingdom of Viatavia falls in love with Captain Rudi of the King's Guards, though her father arranges her marriage with the king of a neighboring country. Although Marie and Rudi are secretly wed by a Gypsy, the duke ignores the marriage and exiles Rudi. When a child is born to Marie, she declares to the king that it is Rudi's and is thereafter banished to a convent; however, Rudi returns and helps Marie retrieve her child from the palace, and they find happiness in another land. *Royalty. Marriage. Imaginary kingdoms. Balkans.*

HER MAD BARGAIN **F2.2433**

Anita Stewart Productions. *Dist* Associated First National Pictures. 12 Dec **1921** [c9 Dec 1921; LP17355]. Si; b&w. 35mm. 6 reels, 5,491 ft.

Pres by Louis B. Mayer. *Dir* Edwin Carewe. *Scen* Josephine Quirk. *Story* Florence Auer. *Photog* Robert B. Kurrle. *Art Dir* William Darling. *Asst Dir* Wallace Fox.

Cast: Anita Stewart *(Alice Lambert)*, Arthur Edmund Carew *(Grant Lewis)*, Helen Raymond *(Mrs. Henry Beresford)*, Adele Farrington *(Mrs. Gordon Howe)*, Margaret McWade *(Mrs. Dunn)*, Percy Challenger *(Parsons)*, Walter McGrail *(David Leighton)*, Gertrude Astor *(Ruth Beresford)*, George B. Williams *(Monsieur Armand)*, Ernest Butterworth *(Jerry Dunn, Jr.)*, Will Badger *(Jerry Dunn, Sr.)*.

Society melodrama. Following the death of her benefactress, Mrs. Beresford, Alice Lambert is evicted by Ruth, Mrs. Beresford's jealous niece; and in despair Alice seeks employment as a model. Her refusal to accept the attentions of Monsieur Armand ends in her dismissal, and as an artist's model she has a similarly unpleasant experience with Grant Lewis, from whom she seeks refuge in the studio of sculptor David Leighton. She later attempts suicide but is forestalled by Leighton, who proposes that she insure her life for $35,000 (a portion of which she will receive immediately) and that at the end of 6 months she "accidentally" take her life. She agrees, and Leighton decides to immortalize her hands in a statue and secretly falls in love with her. At a tea given by his aunt, she discovers that her rival is Ruth Beresford and meets Grant Lewis, who slanders her. Alice injures a newsboy, Jerry Dunn, in an accident, and while she is convalescing from the experience Leighton declares his love for her. *Models. Sculptors. Artists. Newsboys. Suicide. Insurance. Jealousy.*

HER MAJESTY **F2.2434**

Playgoers Pictures. *Dist* Associated Exhibitors. 23 Jul **1922** [c20 Jul 1922; LU18072]. Si; b&w. 35mm. 5 reels, 4,331 ft.

Prod Paul Salvin. *Dir* George Irving. *Story-Scen* H. Thompson Rich. *Photog* Walter Arthur.

Cast: Mollie King *(Susan & Rosalie Bowers, twins)*, Creighton Hale *(Ted Harper)*, Rose Tapley *(Aunt Worthington)*, Neville Percy *(Wilfred Parkington)*, Jerome Lawler *("Slick" Harry)*.

Society comedy-drama. Rosalie and Susan, identical orphaned twins, are adopted by two aunts and live in separate households. Susan develops as a poor, wholesome farmgirl, and Rosalie becomes a wealthy snob. Susan's beau, Ted Harper, confuses the girls' identities, but Susan wins his love after preventing Rosalie from eloping with scoundrel "Slick" Harry Ives. *Twins. Sisters. Aunts. Adoption. Class conflict.*

HER MAN **F2.2435**

Phil Goldstone Productions. 20 Jul **1924**. Si; b&w. 35mm. 5 reels.

Cast: William Fairbanks, Tom McGuire, James Pierce, Frank Whitson, Margaret Landis.

Western melodrama. A high-hat debutante accompanies her wealthy father on a business trip to the West. She is soon "kidnaped" by a friendly business rival of her family, who plans to enter into a $1 million wager with her father on the exact time of her return. An outsider spoils the gag by foiling 15 men and rescuing the girl. He turns out to be the son of a successful meatpacker, and he and the chastened deb, with her father's blessing, make plans to be married. *Debutantes. Businessmen. Abduction. Wagers. Meatpacking.*

HER MAN **F2.2436**

Pathé Exchange. 21 Sep **1930** [c21 Sep 1930; LP1664]. Sd (Photophone); b&w. 35mm. 8 reels, 7,508 ft.

Prod E. B. Derr. *Dir* Tay Garnett. *Screenplay* Thomas Buckingham. *Story* Howard Higgin, Tay Garnett. *Photog* Edward Snyder. *Art Dir* Carroll Clark. *Film Ed* Joseph Kane, Doane Harrison. *Mus Dir* Josiah Zuro. *Rec Engr* Earl A. Wolcott, Harold Stine. *Asst Dir* Robert Fellows. *Cost Dsgn* Gwen Wakeling.

Cast: Helen Twelvetrees *(Frankie)*, Marjorie Rambeau *(Annie)*, Ricardo Cortez *(Johnnie)*, Phillips Holmes *(Dan)*, James Gleason *(Steve)*, Harry Sweet *(Eddie)*, Stanley Fields *(Al)*, Mathew Betz *(Red)*, Thelma Todd *(Nelly)*, Franklin Pangborn *(Sport)*, Mike Donlin *(bartender)*, Slim Summerville *(The Swede)*, Sally Ferguson, Blythe Daley, Ruth Hiatt, Edith Rosita, Lelia Karnelly, Peggy Howard *(dancehall girls)*.

Romantic melodrama. At the Thalia, a dancehall in Havana, Frankie, a showgirl, takes the part of Annie, who has been compelled to return to Havana from the States. She gets into an altercation with a patron who accuses her of stealing his bankroll, but Johnnie, her "business" partner, arrives in time to protect her. Red, another rival for her love, quarrels with Johnnie and is killed in the ensuing struggle, witnessed only by Annie. Later, Frankie is attracted by the singing of Dan Keefe, a sailor, on a spree with his buddies, who protects her; she tells him of her longing to quit the life she is leading. Although disgusted with her double-dealing, Dan stays behind and takes Frankie to church for the first time. She confesses that she loves him and plans to elope with him to the States. Johnnie and his henchmen plot to kill Dan, but Johnnie is accidentally killed; Frankie and Dan escape and sail to their happiness. *Showgirls. Sailors. Courtship. Murder. Religion. Dancehalls. Havana.*

HER MAN O' WAR **F2.2437**

De Mille Pictures. *Dist* Producers Distributing Corp. 23 Aug **1926** [c4 Aug 1926; LP23003]. Si; b&w. 35mm. 6 reels, 6,106 ft.

Supv C. Gardner Sullivan. *Dir* Frank Urson. *Scen* Charles Logue. *Photog* Peverell Marley. *Art Dir* Max Parker. *Asst Dir* Roy Burns.

Cast: Jetta Goudal *(Cherie Schultz)*, William Boyd *(Jim Sanderson)*, Jimmie Adams *(Shorty Flynn)*, Grace Darmond *(Countess of Lederbon)*,

Kay Deslys *(Big Bertha)*, Frank Reicher *(Professor Krantz)*, Michael Vavitch *(Colonel Prittwitz)*, Robert Edeson *(Field Marshall)*, Junior Coghlan *(Peterkin Schultz)*.

War melodrama. Source: Fred Jackson, "Black Marriage" (publication undetermined). In a shelltorn German village, deserters Jim Sanderson and Shorty Flynn are questioned by a German colonel, and both give information about the movements of the American Army, but the colonel decides to keep them under surveillance. Jim is assigned to help Cherie Schultz, a German girl who operates a farm, and Shorty is assigned to Big Bertha, whom he manages to boss. While hanging wash on the line, Jim signals an American airplane, thereby obtains a wireless, and is thus able to send a message to his American comrades, who are tunneling to the German headquarters in the castle of the Countess of Lederbon. Cherie informs on him but becomes penitent when she realizes she loves him; and after being betrayed by the colonel, she sends directions to the sappers. All are sentenced to death, but all are saved by the arrival of American troops. *Prisoners of war. Sapping. Radio. World War I. Germany. United States Army. United States Army—Desertion.*

HER MARKET VALUE **F2.2438**

Paul Powell Productions. *Dist* Producers Distributing Corp. 9 Feb **1925** [c9 Feb 1925; LP21262]. Si; b&w. 35mm. 6 reels, 5,931 ft.

Frank E. Woods Production. *Dir* Paul Powell. *Adapt* Olga Printzlau.

Cast: Agnes Ayres *(Nancy Dumont)*, George Irving *(Harvey Dumont)*, Anders Randolf *(Cyrus Hamilton)*, Hedda Hopper *(Mrs. Bernice Hamilton)*, Edward Earle *(Anthony Davis)*, Taylor Holmes *(Courtney Brooks)*, Gertrude Short *(Kitty)*, Sidney Bracy *(Banks)*.

Melodrama. Source: Frances Nordstrom, "Her Market Price" (publication undetermined). Harvey Dumont loses his entire fortune in the stock market and commits suicide, leaving his wife, Nancy, "in trust" to three of his friends: Hamilton, Brooks, and Davis. Following the funeral, the three men meet to decide the fate of the penniless Nancy, and each of them makes a generous contribution to her welfare by buying shares in "the Dumont stock." Nancy uses the $40,000 that she receives to pay off her husband's debts and then takes a job as Hamilton's secretary. Hamilton has a more than friendly interest in the beautiful young woman and seeks to buy out his partners; Davis refuses. Hamilton later discovers Brooks and Nancy in a compromising situation and forces him to part with his share of Dumont stock. Hamilton then sets out to bankrupt Davis by feeding him bad information through a crooked broker, but Davis discovers the plot and makes a killing in the market despite this trickery. Mrs. Hamilton and Brooks arrange for Hamilton to be found in a compromising situation with the innocent Nancy, but Davis learns of the plan and prevents its completion. Davis shoots Hamilton, wounding him slightly; Hamilton is then reconciled to his wife, and Davis buys Hamilton's share of Nancy, with whom he is in love. *Stockbrokers. Widows. Suicide. Reputation. Partnerships. Duplicity. Stock market.*

HER MARRIAGE VOW **F2.2439**

Warner Brothers Pictures. 20 Jul **1924** [c26 Jul 1924; LP20430]. Si; b&w. 35mm. 7 reels, 6,800 ft.

Dir-Scen Millard Webb.

Cast: Monte Blue *(Bob Hilton)*, Willard Louis *(Arthur Atherton)*, Beverly Bayne *(Carol Hilton)*, Margaret Livingston *(Estelle Winslow)*, John Roche *(Ted Lowe)*, Priscilla Moran *(Barbara)*, Mary Grabhorn *(Janey)*, Martha Petelle *(Mrs. Pelham)*, Aileen Manning *(spinster)*, Arthur Hoyt *(Winslow)*.

Society drama. Source: Owen Davis, *At the Switch; or Her Marriage Vow, a Play in Four Acts* (c1920). When neglected by her hard-working husband, Carol Hilton attends a party given by Estelle Winslow and appears to her husband—who watches from their apartment—to be carrying on a flirtation with her former suitor, Ted Lowe. He effects a separation, but her devotion to the children leads to their reconciliation. *Motherhood. Marriage.*

HER NIGHT OF NIGHTS **F2.2440**

Universal Film Manufacturing Co. 26 Jun **1922** [c24 Jun 1922; LP18017]. Si; b&w. 35mm. 5 reels, ca4,500 ft.

Pres by Carl Laemmle. *Dir* Hobart Henley. *Scen* Doris Schroeder. *Photog* Victor Milner.

Cast: Marie Prevost *(Molly May Mahone)*, Edward Hearn *(Jerry Trimble)*, Hal Cooley *(Ted Bradley)*, Betty Francisco *(Myone Madrigal)*, Charles Arling *(Cyrus Bradley)*, Jane Starr *(Lily Everson)*, George B. Williams *(Gus Wimple)*, William Robert Daly *(Pop Mahone)*, Richard Daniels *(Micky Dennis Mahone)*.

Romantic comedy-drama. Source: C. S. Montayne, "Her Night of Nights," in *Snappy Stories* (61:115–116, 10 Oct 1921; 62:111–126, 25 Oct 1921). Molly, a glamorous clothing model in New York, though yearning for a life of luxury, spurns the advances of her boss's son in favor of a shipping clerk, late of the backwoods. Their plans for marriage and a suburban home are nearly ruined by a misunderstanding on her part; Molly is nearly compromised by the boss's son but is brought to her senses and returns to the man she loves. *Fashion models. Shipping clerks. Class conflict. New York City.*

HER NIGHT OF ROMANCE **F2.2441**

Constance Talmadge Productions. *Dist* First National Pictures. Oct **1924** [c27 Oct 1924; LP20693]. Si; b&w. 35mm. 8 reels, 7,211 ft.

Pres by Joseph M. Schenck. *Dir* Sidney A. Franklin. *Story* Hans Kraly. *Photog* Ray Binger, Victor Milner. *Film Ed* Hal Kern.

Cast: Constance Talmadge *(Dorothy Adams)*, Ronald Colman *(Paul Menford)*, Jean Hersholt *(Joe Diamond)*, Albert Gran *(Samuel C. Adams, Dorothy's father)*, Robert Rendel *(Prince George)*, Sidney Bracey *(butler)*, Joseph Dowling *(Professor Gregg)*, Templar Saxe *(Dr. Wellington)*, Eric Mayne *(Dr. Scott)*, Emily Fitzroy *(nurse)*, Clara Bracey *(housekeeper)*, James Barrows *(old butler)*, Claire De Lorez *(artist, Paul's friend)*.

High comedy. Heiress Dorothy Adams disguises her identity while traveling in England with her father and falls in love with Paul Menford, an impoverished nobleman who poses as a doctor in order to meet Dorothy. Unknown to Paul, Mr. Adams buys the Menford estate, and Dorothy is there alone on the same night that Paul, inebriated, also decides to sleep there. They encounter each other in the morning and are discovered by a friend of Paul's, to whom Paul introduces Dorothy as his wife. When the news spreads, they decide to actually marry, but Dorothy changes her mind when she overhears Paul discussing with Joe Diamond his promise to pay the agent a sum upon marrying the Adams heiress. Dorothy's father realizes that Paul was ignorant of Dorothy's identity and successfully contrives to reunite the pair. *Nobility. Heiresses. Imposture. England.*

HER OWN FREE WILL **F2.2442**

Eastern Productions. *Dist* W. W. Hodkinson Corp. 20 Jul **1924** [c20 Jun 1924; LP20432]. Si; b&w. 35mm. 6 reels, 5,959 ft.

Dir Paul Scardon. *Scen* Gerald C. Duffy. *Photog* J. Roy Hunt.

Cast: Helene Chadwick *(Nan Everard)*, Holmes Herbert *(Peter Craddock)*, Allan Simpson *(Jerry Lister)*, George Backus *(Colonel Everard)*, Violet Mersereau *(Mona Everard)*.

Society drama. Source: Ethel May Dell, "Her Own Free Will," in *The Odds and Other Stories* (New York, 1922). To save her father from bankruptcy, Nan Everard marries wealthy Peter Craddock and under protest goes with him to South America. En route she is injured in an automobile wreck, but Peter continues the trip. He returns to find her renewing an old friendship, and though she hopes to obtain a divorce she finally surrenders to his stronger will. *Divorce. Filial relations. Automobile accidents.*

HER OWN MONEY **F2.2443**

Famous Players–Lasky. *Dist* Paramount Pictures. ca15 Jan **1922** [Buffalo premiere; released 19 Feb; c20 Dec 1921; LP17377]. Si; b&w. 35mm. 5 reels, 4,981 ft.

Dir Joseph Henabery. *Scen* Elmer Harris. *Photog* Faxon Dean.

Cast: Ethel Clayton *(Mildred Carr)*, Warner Baxter *(Lew Alden)*, Charles French *(Thomas Hazelton)*, Clarence Burton *(Harvey Beecher)*, Mae Busch *(Flora Conroy)*, Jean Acker *(Ruth Alden)*, Roscoe Karns *(Jerry Woodward)*.

Domestic comedy-drama. Source: Mark Elbert Swan, *Her Own Money, a Comedy in Three Acts* (New York, 1915). Mildred Carr, an efficient and capable businesswoman, falls in love with Lewis Alden, a real estate broker who is inclined to be dictatorial and extravagant. Five years after their marriage, she has secretly saved $2,000 to purchase a home. Finding that he needs the money in order to save himself from financial embarrassment, she schemes to offer him the money through Harvey Beecher, a neighbor. Beecher's jealous wife reveals the secret negotiation between Harvey and Mildred, and when the option lapses Alden leaves home in a rage. Later he sends her an apology and a check for the amount. Mildred finds that the house she wanted has been sold—then is astonished to learn that the owner is Alden, who has paid his debts and bought the house for his wife; she accepts his forgiveness and they are reunited. *Businesswomen. Marriage. Finance—Personal. Real estate business.*

HER OWN STORY F2.2444

Buckley Ferguson Productions. *Dist* American Releasing Corp. 20 Oct **1922** [New York State license]. Si; b&w. 35mm. 5 reels, 4,200 ft.

Cast: Sydney Deane, Mildred Elsie Ferguson.

Melodrama(?). No information about the nature of this film has been found.

HER OWN STORY F2.2445

Dist Goodwill Distributing Corp. **1926.** Si; b&w. 35mm. 5 reels.

Dir Francis Ford. *Photog* Alfred Gosden.

Cast: Jack Mower, Mary Carr.

Drama(?). No information about the nature of this film has been found.

HER PRIVATE AFFAIR F2.2446

Pathé Exchange. 28 Sep **1929** [c24 Sep 1929; LP733]. Talking sequences & sd eff (Photophone); b&w. 35mm. 7 reels, 6,440 ft.

Dir Paul Stein. *Dial Dir* Rollo Lloyd. *Scen-Dial* Francis E. Faragoh. *Adapt* Francis E. Faragoh, Herman Bernstein. *Photog* David Abel, Norbert Brodin. *Rec Engr* W. C. Brown, D. A. Cutler. *Asst Dir* E. J. Babille.

Cast: Ann Harding *(Vera Kessler)*, Harry Bannister *(Judge Kessler)*, John Loder *(Carl Weild)*, Kay Hammond *(Julia Sturm)*, Arthur Hoyt *(Michael Sturm)*, William Orlamond *(Dr. Zeigler)*, Lawford Davidson *(Arnold Hartmann)*, Elmer Ballard *(Grimm)*, Frank Reicher *(state's attorney)*.

Society melodrama. Source: Leo Urvantzov, *Her Private Affair* (a play, publication undetermined). Judge Kessler, a distinguished judge in Vienna, and his wife, Vera, separate for a while after a brief misunderstanding but then reunite. During their separation Vera writes Arnold Hartmann some incriminating letters with which he later blackmails her. She pays Hartmann in his apartment, but he forces unwanted advances on her, and she picks up a revolver which accidentally goes off and kills him. Grimm, the butler, is charged with the murder, though acquitted, but guilt and blood are so much on Vera's mind that she leaves her husband. On New Year's Eve, she meets Grimm, who begs her to prevent his insanity by telling him that he did not commit the murder. She admits to the action; and her husband, overhearing her confession, comes to her and they fall into each other's arms. *Judges. Butlers. Marriage. Blackmail. Murder. Insanity. New Year's Eve. Vienna.*

HER PRIVATE LIFE F2.2447

First National Pictures. 25 Aug or 8 Sep **1929** [c16 Sep 1929; LP739]. Sd (Vitaphone); b&w. 35mm. 8 reels, 6,488 ft. [Also si, 6 Oct 1929; 5,815 ft.]

Pres by Richard A. Rowland. *Prod* Ned Marin. *Dir* Alexander Korda. *Scen-Titl-Dial* Forrest Halsey. *Photog* John Seitz. *Film Ed* Harold Young. *Song: "Love Is Like a Rose"* Al Bryan, George W. Meyer.

Cast: Billie Dove *(Lady Helen Haden)*, Walter Pidgeon *(Ned Thayer)*, Holmes Herbert *(Solomon)*, Montagu Love *(Sir Bruce Haden)*, Thelma Todd *(Mrs. Leslie)*, Roland Young *(Charteris)*, Mary Forbes *(Lady Wildering)*, Brandon Hurst *(Sir Emmett Wildering)*, ZaSu Pitts *(Timmins)*.

Drama. Source: Zoë Akins, *Déclassée* (New York, 1923). Lady Helen Haden, an Englishwoman married to a boor, falls in love with Ned Thayer, an American. The discovery that Thayer has cheated at cards leads to blackmail and an ugly divorce for Lady Haden. She goes to America alone and pawns her jewels to survive there. When wealthy American Rudolph Solomon proposes, Lady Haden accepts, although she still loves Thayer. Solomon steps aside for Thayer, his employee, when Lady Haden learns that Thayer's sister, Mrs. Leslie, not he, cheated at cards. *English. Nobility. Divorce. Cheating. Blackmail.*

Note: Remake of the 1925 film, *Déclassée,* q. v.

HER REPUTATION F2.2448

Thomas H. Ince Corp. *Dist* Associated First National Pictures. Sep **1923** [c21 Aug 1923; LP19321]. Si; b&w. 35mm. 7 reels, 6,566 ft.

Pers Supv Thomas H. Ince. *Dir* John Griffith Wray. *Scen* Bradley King.

Cast: May McAvoy *(Jacqueline Lanier)*, Lloyd Hughes *(Sherwood Mansfield)*, James Corrigan *("Dad" Lawrence)*, Casson Ferguson *(Jack Calhoun)*, Eric Mayne *(Don Andrés Miro)*, Winter Hall *(John Mansfield)*, Louise Lester *(Consuelo)*, Brinsley Shaw *(Clinton Kent)*, George Larkin *(Ramón Cervanez)*, Eugenie Besserer *(Madame Cervanez)*, Jane Miller *(Pepita)*, Jane Wray *(see note)*, Charlie *(himself, a monkey)*, Gus Leonard *(Rodriguez)*.

Melodrama. Source: Talbot Mundy and Bradley King, *Her Reputation* (Indianapolis, 1923). Louisiana plantation owner Don Andrés Miro, knowing he has only a short time to live, arranges to marry his young ward Jacqueline Lanier, intending to leave her his fortune. Unsuccessful suitor Jack Calhoun shoots Miro and commits suicide. Clinton Kent, an ambitious newspaper reporter, writes an account of the slaying, which represents Miro as a victim of Jacqueline's infidelity. Jacqueline runs away to escape notoriety and joins a troupe of dancers. Kent finds her, but Sherwood Mansfield, the newspaper owner's son, falls in love with Jacqueline, vindicates her, and prevents Kent's story from being published. *Reputation. Guardians. Murder. Suicide. Newspapers. Louisiana. Monkeys.*

Note: *Exhibitors Trade Review, Variety,* and *Motion Picture World* claim that Jane Wray plays the part of Pepita.

HER SACRIFICE F2.2449

Sanford Productions. 27 Sep **1926** [New York State license]. Si; b&w. 35mm. 6 reels, 6,100 ft.

Prod Frank M. Sanford. *Dir* Wilfred Lucas. *Adapt* Edwin J. Sullivan. *Photog* Harry Vallejo, Harry Fowler. *Tech Supv* E. J. Vallejo.

Cast: Gaston Glass *(David Orland)*, Bryant Washburn *(Donald Gorham)*, Herbert Rawlinson *(James Romaine)*, Gladys Brockwell *(Mary Cullen)*, Wilfred Lucas *(Edwin Ramsey)*, Ligia Golconda *(Margarita Darlow)*, Gene Crosby *(Waynne Landis)*, Hector Sarno *(Professor Oliver)*, Charles "Buddy" Post *(Ambassador Dupree)*, Barbara Tennant *(Madame Dupree)*, Marshall Ruth *(Cyril)*.

Melodrama. Source: Manuel Acuña, *El Pasado; ensayo dramático en tres actos y en prosa* (México, D. F., 1890). Receiving the news from Professor Oliver that he has won a painting scholarship to study in Paris, David Orland proposes to Margarita Darlow, who refuses him because of her past. (Flashbacks reveal Margarita's earlier seduction by Edwin Ramsey, from whom she had sought aid for her dying mother, and her subsequent cohabitation with him as his "niece.") David's persistence and willingness to forget the past persuade Margarita to reject Ramsey and his friend, Donald Gorham, and they go to Paris. Life is difficult, and Margarita must model to augment David's meager scholarship, but David finally receives a large prize, and they return home. Threatened by Ramsey with exposure of Margarita's past, she intends suicide, but Mary Cullen intercepts her, and David kills Ramsey in a duel. *Painters. Models. Seduction. Suicide. Paris. Duels.*

HER SECOND CHANCE F2.2450

First National Pictures. *Dist* Vitagraph Co. of America. 28 Mar **1926** [c28 Mar 1926; LP22606]. Si; b&w. 35mm. 7 reels, 6,420 ft.

Dir Lambert Hillyer. *Ed Dir* June Mathis. *Cont* Eve Unsell. *Photog* John W. Boyle. *Art Dir* E. J. Shulter. *Film Ed* George McGuire.

Cast: Anna Q. Nilsson *(Mrs. Constance Lee/Caroline Logan)*, Huntly Gordon *(Judge Jeffries)*, Charlie Murray *(Bell)*, Sam De Grasse *(Beachey)*, William J. Kelly *(Gabriel)*, Mike Donlin *(De Vries)*, Dale Fuller *(Delia)*, Jed Prouty *(a darky stable boy)*, Corliss Palmer *(Nancy)*.

Melodrama. Source: Mrs. Wilson Woodrow, *The Second Chance* (New York, 1924). Caroline Logan, a turbulent Kentucky mountain girl, emerges from a reformatory and vows revenge on Judge Jeffries, who sentenced her for shooting a trespasser on her land. As Constance Lee she engages Louis Beachey, a shrewd lawyer, to retrieve some property willed her and incidentally to plot the judge's downfall. Beachey comes upon information that gives him a business advantage over Perry Gabriel, a society "bounder"; Gabriel blames this development on Constance and engages a detective to investigate her. Constance enters her horse in a race to compete against Jeffries' entry, but Gabriel connives to substitute a "ringer" for the judge's horse. Hearing of the substitution, Constance experiences a change of heart but arrives too late to rectify matters; she denounces the plotters, however, and saves the judge from disgrace. *Mountaineers. Judges. Lawyers. Revenge. Horseracing. Kentucky.*

HER SISTER FROM PARIS F2.2451

Joseph M. Schenck Productions. *Dist* First National Pictures. 2 Aug **1925** [c10 Aug 1925; LP21708]. Si; b&w. 35mm. 7 reels, 7,255 ft.

Pres by Joseph M. Schenck. *Dir* Sidney Franklin. *Story* Hans Kraly. *Photog* Arthur Edeson. *Art Dir* William Cameron Menzies. *Asst Dir* Scot R. Beal. *Wardrobe* Adrian.

Cast: Constance Talmadge *(Helen Weyringer/Lola)*, Ronald Colman *(Joseph Weyringer)*, George K. Arthur *(Robert Well)*, Margaret Mann, Gertrude Claire *(Bertha [see note])*.

Comedy. Joseph Weyringer, a celebrated author, loses interest in his wife and finally drives her away. The lady in question, Helen Weyringer, then meets up with her twin sister, Lola, a celebrated dancer and vamp, and Lola decides to help her sister regain Joseph's affections, persuading Helen to assume the identity of Lola and return to her husband. Both Joseph and his friend Robert fall in love with this "Lola," and Joseph attempts to seduce her. She then tells Joseph that she will give herself to him as soon as he declares himself to have been a rotten husband to Helen. Joseph eagerly confesses, and Helen then reveals that he has been making love to his own wife! Joseph and Helen are reconciled and decide to begin life together anew. *Sisters. Twins. Authors. Dancers. Parisians. Marriage. Seduction. Impersonation.*

Note: Gertrude Claire and Margaret Mann are separately credited with the role of Bertha.

HER SOCIAL VALUE **F2.2452**

Katherine MacDonald Pictures. *Dist* Associated First National Pictures. 24 Oct **1921** [c17 Oct 1921; LP17489]. Si; b&w. 35mm. 6 reels, 5,140 ft.

Dir Jerome Storm. *Scen* Gerald Duffy, Jerome Storm. *Story* B. P. Fineman, J. A. Barry. *Photog* Joseph Brotherton. *Adtl Photog* Clarence Brotherton. *Art Dir* Floyd Mueller. *Asst Dir* James Dugan.

Cast: Katherine MacDonald *(Marion Hoyte)*, Roy Stewart *(James Lodge)*, Bertram Grassby *(Clifford Trent)*, Betty Ross Clarke *(Bertha Harmon)*, Winter Hall *(Shipley)*, Joseph Girard *(Joe Harmon)*, Lillian Rich *(Gwendolyn Shipley)*, Vincent Hamilton *(Leroy Howard)*, Helen Raymond *(Ruth Lodge)*, Violet Phillips *(Belle)*, Arthur Gibson *(The Baby)*.

Society melodrama. Salesgirl Marion Hoyte, unlike the other members of her family, seeks to rise from her lowly station in life; thus, when she accidentally becomes acquainted with young architect James Lodge, who clears her of the charge of stealing a customer's purse, Marion accepts his attentions. Leroy, a suitor for Marion, and her sister Bertha object, but Marion soon becomes engaged to James. Shipley, a financier, plans that James will marry his daughter, Gwendolyn, and will be engaged to plan the new state capitol building; but when Marion and James are married, Shipley withdraws his patronage and Marion is ostracized by James's social set. Determined not to ruin her husband's career, Marion arranges a fake elopement with Clifford Trent. When Marion learns that James has been injured in a western mining camp, however, she goes to his aid; and through this twist of fate their love is reawakened. *Architects. Salesclerks. Sisters. Financiers. Social classes. Ambition. Marriage.*

HER STURDY OAK **F2.2453**

Realart Pictures. Jul **1921** [c14 Jul 1921; LP16762]. Si; b&w. 35mm. 5 reels, 4,590 ft.

Dir Thomas N. Heffron. *Story-Scen* Elmer Harris. *Photog* William E. Collins. *Asst Dir* Maynard Laswell.

Cast: Wanda Hawley *(Violet White)*, Walter Hiers *(Samuel Butters)*, Sylvia Ashton *(Belle Bright)*, Mayme Kelso *(Mrs. White)*, Leo White *(Archibald Mellon)*, Frederick Stanton *(ranch foreman)*.

Comedy. Samuel Butters, who is engaged to Belle Bright, a fleshy young woman who wears knickers and rules the ranch with an iron hand, musters up the courage to ask her for money. With $125 he visits a summer hotel and there meets and falls in love with pretty Violet White. They appeal to Belle to break her engagement, and she consents but refuses to allow Samuel his part of the farm investment. The lovers marry, and when twins arrive they have a difficult time, until they discover a cache of honey in the chimney. Belle arrives suddenly and announces that she is foreclosing on the mortgage, but the twins bring about a change of heart and she relents. *Twins. Ranchers. Courtship. Marriage. Mortgages. Resorts. Bees.*

HER SUMMER HERO **F2.2454**

FBO Pictures. 12 Feb **1928** [c30 Jan 1928; LP24923]. Si; b&w. 35mm. 6 reels, 5,146 ft.

Dir James Dugan. *Cont* Jean Dupont. *Titl* Jean Dupont, Randolph Bartlett. *Story* Gertrude Orr. *Photog* Philip Tannura. *Film Ed* Archie F. Marshek.

Cast: Hugh Trevor *(Kenneth Holmes)*, Harold Goodwin *(Herb Darrow)*, Duane Thompson *(Joan Stanton)*, James Pierce *(Chris)*, Cleve Moore *(Al Stanton)*, Sally Blane *(Grace)*.

Comedy-drama. Champion college swimmer and summer lifeguard Ken Holmes saves Joan Stanton from drowning. They are sweethearts until a misunderstanding causes Joan to cast off Ken for his chief competitor, Herb Darrow. Joan promises Herb she will wear his fraternity pin if he wins the big swimming race at the hotel the next day. Despondent over his loss, Ken decides not to enter the race; later, he reconsiders when he learns that Joan is to wear Herb's pin if Herb wins. Ken wins the race and solves his misunderstanding with Joan. *Lifeguards. Swimming. College life. Fraternities. Resorts.*

HER TEMPORARY HUSBAND **F2.2455**

Associated First National Pictures. Dec **1923** [c11 Dec 1923; LP19691]. Si; b&w. 35mm. 7 reels, 6,723 ft.

Dir John McDermott. *Scen* F. McGrew Willis. *Photog* Sam Landers.

Cast: Owen Moore *(Thomas Burton)*, Sydney Chaplin *(Judd)*, Sylvia Breamer *(Blanche Ingram)*, Tully Marshall *(John Ingram)*, Charles Gerrard *(Clarence Topping)*, George Cooper *(Conrad Jasper)*, Chuck Reisner *(Hector)*, John Patrick *(Larry)*.

Comedy-drama. Source: Edward A. Paulton, *Her Temporary Husband; a Comedy in Three Acts* (New York, 1927). Blanche Ingram must marry quickly to inherit her aunt's fortune. She chooses an old man but is tricked into marrying young, handsome Tom Burton, who disguises himself as the invalid groom in hopes of sharing the fortune. Blanche takes the "old man" home, and there his true identity is eventually revealed. He becomes Blanche's permanent husband when she finds she has fallen in love. *Inheritance. Marriage. Impersonation. Weddings.*

HER UNBORN CHILD **F2.2456**

Windsor Picture Plays. 10 Jan **1930** [c20 Dec 1929; LP967]. Sd (De Forest Phonofilm); b&w. 35mm. 9 reels, 7,609 ft.

Dir Albert Ray, Charles McGrath. *Adapt-Dial* Raymond Hatton, Fanny Hatton. *Photog* Tom Malloy, Irving Browning, Buddy Harris.

Cast: Adele Ronson *(Dorothy Kennedy)*, Elisha Cook, Jr. *(Stewart Kennedy)*, Frances Underwood *(Mrs. Kennedy)*, Pauline Drake *("Beth" Gilbert)*, Paul Clare *(Jack Conover)*, Doris Rankin *(his aunt)*, Harry Davenport *(Dr. Remington)*, Elizabeth Wrangle *("Pegs" Kennedy)*, Frances Grant *(Mandy)*.

Social drama. Source: Howard McKent Barnes, *Her Unborn Child* (New York opening: 5 Mar 1928). While youthful, innocent love blossoms between bashful Stew Kennedy and Elizabeth Gilbert, Dorothy Kennedy falls in love with Jack Conover, completely under the domination of his "aunt," who later proves to be his mother. Though he loves Dorothy, Jack resists making a marriage proposal because he thinks he is illegitimate. Meanwhile, Dorothy becomes pregnant, and efforts to inveigle her into an abortion are thwarted by Dr. Remington, the family doctor, who notifies her mother of her condition. When Jack discovers his true parentage, he offers to marry Dorothy; and ultimately she accepts. *Courtship. Illegitimacy. Smalltown life. Motherhood. Abortion. Parentage.*

HER WEDDING NIGHT **F2.2457**

Paramount-Publix Corp. 18 Sep **1930** [c24 Oct 1930; LP1687]. Sd (Movietone); b&w. 35mm. 9 reels, 6,294 ft.

Assoc Prod E. Lloyd Sheldon. *Dir* Frank Tuttle. *Screenplay* Henry Myers. *Photog* Harry Fischbeck. *Film Ed* Doris Drought. *Rec Engr* J. A. Goodrich.

Cast: Clara Bow *(Norma Martin)*, Ralph Forbes *(Larry Charters)*, Charles Ruggles *(Bertie Bird)*, Skeets Gallagher *(Bob Hawley)*, Geneva Mitchell *(Gloria Marshall)*, Rosita Moreno *(Lulu)*, Natalie Kingston *(Eva)*, Wilson Benge *(Smithers)*, Lillian Elliott *(Mrs. Marshall)*.

Romantic comedy. Source: Avery Hopwood, *Little Miss Bluebeard* (New York opening: 28 Aug 1923). Gábor Drégely, *Der Gatte des Fraüleins; Lustspiel in drei Aufzügen* (Wien, 1916). Norma Martin, an American film actress vacationing in Paris, weary of male admirers, leaves with her friend Gloria Marshall for the south of France. On the same train is Larry Charters, a famous composer of popular songs, and his friend, Bob Hawley, Gloria's fiancé; to escape pursuing worshipers, he persuades Bob to exchange identities during the trip. When Norma and Bob are left behind at a station, the mayor mistakes them for two elopers thought to be on the train, and before they know it they are married, Bob still masquerading as Larry. Norma and Bob then arrive at their originally intended destination, and complications ensue when Bertie Bird and Mrs. Marshall take Norma and Larry to be man and wife. In spite of the humorous confusion, they decide to let the marriage remain legal, and Bertie gets to sleep after two nights of farcical madness. *Actors. Composers. Elopement. Impersonation. Courtship. Motion pictures. Paris. France.*

HER WILD OAT **F2.2458**

First National Pictures. 25 Dec **1927** [c23 Dec 1927; LP24795]. Si; b&w. 35mm. 7 reels, 6,118 ft.

Pres by John McCormick. *Dir* Marshall Neilan. *Scen-Adapt* Gerald C. Duffy. *Titl* Gerald C. Duffy, George Marion, Jr. *Story* Howard Irving

Young. *Photog* George Folsey. *Film Ed* Al Hall.

Cast: Colleen Moore *(Mary Brown)*, Larry Kent *(Philip Latour)*, Hallam Cooley *(Tommy Warren)*, Gwen Lee *(Daisy)*, Martha Mattox *(dowager)*, Charles Giblyn *(Duke Latour)*, Julanne Johnston *(Miss Whitley)*.

Comedy. With savings from the operation of a lunch wagon, Mary Brown attempts to enter an exclusive summer resort society. Snubbed by the other guests, she disguises herself (on the suggestion of a story-hungry young reporter) as the Duchesse de Granville, staying at an elegant hotel, and accepting expensive gifts from traveling salesmen. The arrival of Philip Latour, the son of the Duke of Granville, complicates the situation, but they fall in love and Philip extricates Mary from her embarrassing dilemma. *Upper classes. Reporters. Imposture. Lunch wagons. Resorts.*

HER WINNING WAY **F2.2459**

Realart Pictures. *Dist* Paramount Pictures. Sep **1921** [c15 Aug 1921; LP16864]. Si; b&w. 35mm. 5 reels, 4,715 ft.

Dir Joseph Henabery. *Scen* Douglas Doty. *Photog* Faxon Dean.

Cast: Mary Miles Minter *(Ann Annington)*, Gaston Glass *(Harold Hargrave)*, Carrie Clark Ward *(Nora)*, Fred Goodwins *(Sylvester Lloyd)*, Helen Dunbar *(Mrs. Hargrave)*, Grace Morse *(Evangeline)*, John Elliott *(Mallon)*, Omar Whitehead *(Dr. Claude Gravat)*.

Comedy-drama. Source: Lechemere Worrall, *Ann, a Comedy in Three Acts* (New York, 1913). Edgar Jepson, *Ann Annington* (Indianapolis, 1918). Ann Annington, book reviewer for a metropolitan newspaper, is assigned to interview author Harold Hargrave. Knowing that Hargrave has resisted previous attempts, Ann obtains a position in his apartment as a maid and resolves to break up his engagement to Evangeline, a girl chosen for him by his mother. She plants ladies' garments about his room and hairpins in the bed, and Evangeline is indignant. Discovering he has been tricked, Hargrave dismisses Ann. That evening they realize their mutual love, with the result that she does not report the details of his private life to the press. *Authors. Book reviewers. Housemaids. Journalism. Motherhood. Disguise.*

HERE HE COMES **F2.2460**

Sierra Pictures. 26 Oct **1926** [New York State license]. Si; b&w. 35mm. 5 reels.

Dir Travers Corby.

Cast: Earl Douglas.

No information about the nature of this film has been found.

THE HERITAGE OF THE DESERT **F2.2461**

Famous Players–Lasky. *Dist* Paramount Pictures. 20 or 27 Jan **1924** [c30 Jan 1924; LP19874]. Si; b&w with col sequences (Technicolor). 35mm. 6 reels, 5,785 ft.

Pres by Adolph Zukor, Jesse L. Lasky. *Dir* Irvin Willat. *Adapt* Albert Shelby Le Vino. *Photog* Charles E. Schoenbaum.

Cast: Bebe Daniels *(Mescal)*, Ernest Torrence *(August Naab)*, Noah Beery *(Holderness)*, Lloyd Hughes *(Jack Hare)*, Ann Schaeffer *(Mrs. Naab)*, James Mason *(Snap Naab)*, Richard R. Neill *(Dene)*, Leonard Clapham *(Dave Naab)*.

Western melodrama. Source: Zane Grey, *The Heritage of the Desert; a Novel* (New York, 1910). Pioneer rancher August Naab finds easterner Jack Hare in the desert and takes him home. There, Mescal, Naab's Spanish-Indian ward, cares for and falls in love with Jack though she is betrothed to Naab's wayward son, Snap. To avoid marrying Snap, Mescal flees to the desert and there is captured by desert pirate Mal Holderness, a ruthless man who is seeking to control the water rights of the surrounding area by buying or seizing the local ranches. Because Naab has refused to sell, Holderness begins a feud, taking Mescal prisoner and killing Snap, the prospective bridegroom, who has followed Mescal into the desert. As the leader of the law-abiding community, Naab, with a group of sympathetic Indians, burns down the neighboring town serving as a hideout for Holderness and his gang. Mescal is rescued and returned to Jack. *Ranchers. Indians of North America. Halfcastes. Deserts. Water rights.*

THE HERO **F2.2462**

Preferred Pictures. *Dist* Al Lichtman Corp. 1 Jan **1923** [c20 Dec 1922; LP18895]. Si; b&w. 35mm. 7 reels, 6,800 ft.

Pres by B. P. Schulberg. *Dir* Louis J. Gasnier. *Scen* Eve Unsell. *Photog* Karl Struss.

Cast: Gaston Glass *(Oswald Lane)*, Barbara La Marr *(Hester Lane)*, John Sainpolis *(Andrew Lane)*, Martha Mattox *(Sarah Lane)*, Frankie Lee *(Andy Lane)*, David Butler *(Bill Walters)*, Doris Pawn *(Martha)*, Ethel Shannon *(Hilda Pierce)*, Cameo *(a dog)*.

Drama. Source: Gilbert Emery, *The Hero; a Play in Three Acts*, in A. H. Quinn, *Contemporary American Plays* (New York, 1923). Oswald Lane is welcomed by his hometown as a war hero and enjoys recounting his adventures to anyone who will listen. He accepts an invitation to stay in the home of his rather colorless brother, Andrew, and is soon not only making love to Martha, the Belgian maid, but is also finding Andrew's wife, Hester, receptive to his flirting. After stealing money entrusted to Andrew by his church, Oswald is on his way out of town when he passes a school fire, rescues several children, and is himself seriously burned. Andrew offers his own skin for grafting, and Oswald directs Hester to return the money. *Veterans. War heroes. Brothers. Housemaids. Belgians. Theft. World War I. Dogs. Fires.*

A HERO FOR A NIGHT (Universal-Jewel) **F2.2463**

Universal Pictures. 18 Dec **1927** [c15 Nov 1927; LP24672]. Si; b&w. 35mm. 6 reels, 5,711 ft.

Pres by Carl Laemmle. *Dir* William James Craft. *Story-Scen* Harry O. Hoyt. *Titl* Albert De Mond. *Photog* George Robinson.

Cast: Glenn Tryon *(Hiram Hastings)*, Patsy Ruth Miller *(Mary Sloan)*, Lloyd Whitlock *(Fred Knox)*, Burr McIntosh *(Samuel Sloan)*, Robert Milash *(Bill Donovan)*, Ruth Dwyer *(Nurse Mack)*, Bobbie *(himself, a chimp)*.

Comedy. Hiram Hastings, who drives a taxi at an eastern summer resort, takes a correspondence course in aviation and builds his own airplane, hoping to enter a race from New York to Europe. Samuel Sloan, a wealthy soap manufacturer, arrives with his daughter Mary, a trained nurse, and his confidential secretary, the last two secretly plotting to get Sloan's holdings. Hiram, infatuated with Mary, crashes a banquet in honor of a visiting French aviator and takes it upon himself to be speaker of the evening, though he is ejected. Mary learns of the plotting and with the aid of Hiram and his plane sets out for New York, but Hiram pilots them across the ocean into Russia and there makes a forced landing. The success of the flight, however, saves the Sloan fortune. *Taxi drivers. Aviators. Nurses. Swindlers. Resorts. Soap. Correspondence courses. Russia. Chimpanzees.*

A HERO OF THE BIG SNOWS **F2.2464**

Warner Brothers Pictures. 24 Jul **1926** [c10 Jul 1926; LP22902]. Si; b&w. 35mm. 5 reels, 4,582 ft.

Dir Herman C. Raymaker. *Story-Scen* Ewart Adamson. *Camera* Ed Du Par. *Asst Camera* Walter Robinson. *Asst Dir* Gene Anderson.

Cast: Rin-Tin-Tin *(himself)*, Alice Calhoun *(Mary Mallory)*, Don Alvarado *(Ed Nolan)*, Leo Willis *(Black Beasley)*, Mary Jane Milliken *(The Baby)*.

Northwest melodrama. Discouraged and despondent with life among the trappers in the snow country, Ed Nolan finds Black Beasley mistreating a dog at the local trading post and gets in a fight trying to defend it. Rinty, the dog, wins the battle by attacking the cruel trapper and, accepting Ed as his friend, follows him home but refuses to enter the neglected cabin. Ed takes Rinty to Mary Mallory, whom Ed has failed to win, and in their mutual solicitude over the dog, a new understanding is born and Ed emerges from his inertia. Rinty, who has devoted himself to Mary and her little sister, engages in a fight with a black wolf that tries to attack the child in the woods; Mary, finding the child ill from fright, believes the dog has attacked her, and Ed determines to shoot him. When Mary is forced to take the child through a storm to a doctor, a fallen tree capsizes the sled; the faithful Rinty takes a message to Ed, who arrives with a rescue party. *Trappers. Children. Storms. Dogs.*

A HERO ON HORSEBACK (Universal-Jewel) **F2.2465**

Universal Pictures. 10 Jul **1927** [c30 Jun 1927; LP24135]. Si; b&w. 35mm. 6 reels, 5,551 ft.

Pres by Carl Laemmle. *Dir* Del Andrews. *Adapt* Mary Alice Scully, Arthur Statter. *Photog* Harry Neumann. *Art Dir* David S. Garber.

Cast: Hoot Gibson *(Billy Garford)*, Ethlyne Clair *(Ollie Starbuck)*, Edwards Davis *(J. D. Starbuck)*, Edward Hearn *(Harvey Grey)*, Dan Mason *(Jimmie Breeze)*.

Western melodrama. Source: Peter Bernard Kyne, "Bread Upon the Waters," in *Hearst's International* (44:30–35, Sep 1923). Billy Garford, a happy-go-lucky cowboy, loses at the gaming table most of the $500 lent him by rancher J. D. Starbuck and invests $50 for a grubstake with Jimmie Breeze, an old prospector. Billy hires himself out to Starbuck and becomes infatuated with his daughter, Ollie, but is fired when his courtship is discovered. Jimmie returns with a big strike and with Billy buys out a local banker. Billy hires Ollie as secretary, though this riles Harvey Grey, the cashier who considers himself engaged to her. Grey robs the bank, but Billy is suspected on the basis of numerous IOU's. While Billy pursues Grey, Ollie has inadvertently been locked in the bank vault; Billy returns with the money and rescues her. *Cowboys. Prospectors. Bankers. Secretaries. Gambling. Loans. Bank robberies.*

HEROES AND HUSBANDS **F2.2466**

Preferred Pictures. *Dist* Associated First National Pictures. 21 Aug **1922** [c16 Aug 1922; LP18155]. Si; b&w. 35mm. 6 reels, 5,500 ft.

Pres by B. P. Schulberg. *Dir* Chet Withey. *Story-Scen* Charles A. Logue. *Photog* Joseph Brotherton. *Art Dir* Frank Ormston.

Cast: Katherine MacDonald *(Susanne Danbury, a popular novelist)*, Nigel Barrie *(Walter Gaylord, illustrator of Susanne's work)*, Charles Clary *(Hugh Bemis, publisher of her books)*, Charles Gerrard *(Martin Tancray, Susanne's legal advisor)*, Mona Kingsley *(Agatha Bemis, the publisher's wife)*, Ethel Kay *(Annette, a maid)*.

Society drama. Susanne Danbury and Walter Gaylord, the man she loves, are among the weekend guests of her publisher, Hugh Bemis, and his wife, who also loves Walter. While enacting a play Susanne shoots Bemis with a gun she thought to be unloaded. Investigation reveals that Martin Tancray intended the bullet for Gaylord, and Susanne is exonerated. *Novelists. Illustrators. Publishers.*

HEROES IN BLUE **F2.2467**

Duke Worne Productions. *Dist* Rayart Pictures. Nov **1927.** Si; b&w. 35mm. 5 reels, 4,936-5,076 ft.

Pres by W. Ray Johnston. *Dir* Duke Worne. *Scen* George Pyper. *Story* Leota Morgan. *Photog* Walter Griffin.

Cast: John Bowers, Sally Rand, Gareth Hughes, Ann Brody, Lydia Yeamans Titus, George Bunny, Barney Gilmore.

Melodrama. "Around the Dugans and the Kellys is built this meller. Sally Rand of the 'Smoky' Dugan clan is opposite John Bowers, a young cop whose sire is a veteran flat-foot. The Dugan's stepson is a pyromaniac responsible for the series of incendiary fires and simultaneous robberies. A young member of the Kelly tribe, on the detective squad, is killed by the Dugan bad boy, as is Kelly pere. The double murder is avenged by her own father, 'Smoky' Dugan, who dies with the hoodlum in the punch conflagration of the footage." (*Variety,* 8 Feb 1928, p24.) *Irish. Police. Firemen. Pyromaniacs. Murder. Revenge.*

HEROES OF THE NIGHT **F2.2468**

Gotham Productions. *Dist* Lumas Film Corp. 3 Jan **1927** [c15 Jan 1927; LP23546]. Si; b&w. 35mm. 7 reels, 6,500 ft.

Pres by Sam Sax. *Supv* Renaud Hoffman. *Dir* Frank O'Connor. *Adapt-Cont* F. Oakley Crawford. *Story* James J. Tynan. *Photog* Ray June. *Asst Dir* Glenn Belt.

Cast: Cullen Landis *(Joe Riley)*, Marion Nixon *(Mary Allen)*, Rex Lease *(Tom Riley)*, Wheeler Oakman *(Jack Nichols)*, Sarah Padden *(Mrs. Riley)*, J. P. Lockney *(Marty Allen)*, Robert E. Homans *("Bull" Corrigan)*, Lois Ingraham *(Jennie Lee)*.

Melodrama. Policeman Tom Riley rescues Mary Allen from the unwelcome advances of Jack Nichols, a political "fixer"; escorting her home, he wins her friendship. The same evening, his brother, fireman Joe Riley, is introduced to Mary by Marty Allen, and at home each brother tells Mrs. Riley of the wonderful girl he has met, neither realizing she is the same girl. Both boys propose to Mary, who agrees to give her answer at her birthday party; as a result, bad feeling springs up between them. Tom receives a big reward for capturing a criminal and also gets a promotion. Joe, becoming discouraged, quarrels with Mary and resigns from the fire department. The police corner Corrigan and Nichols' headquarters, a fire ensues, and Joe makes a spectacular rescue of Tom. Joe learns that Mary actually loves Tom, and reconciles himself with Jennie, a reporter. *Police. Firemen. Brothers. Reporters. Courtship.*

HEROES OF THE STREET **F2.2469**

Warner Brothers Pictures. ca17 Dec **1922** [New York and Los Angeles premieres; released 24 Dec; c24 Dec 1922; LP18693]. Si; b&w. 35mm. 6 reels.

Prod Harry Rapf. *Dir* William Beaudine. *Adapt* Edmund Goulding, Mildred Considine. *Photog* E. B. Du Par, Floyd Jackman. *Adtl Photog* Max Dupont. *Mus composed and compiled by* Leo Edwards. *Choreog* Ernest Belcher.

Cast: Wesley Barry *(Mickey Callahan)*, Marie Prevost *(Betty Beaton)*, Jack Mulhall *(Howard Lane)*, Philo McCullough *(Gordon Trent)*, Will Walling *(Mike Callahan)*, Aggie Herring *(Mrs. Callahan)*, Wilfred Lucas *(Symes)*, Wedgewood Nowell *(Arthur Graham)*, Phil Ford *(The Kid)*, "Peaches" Jackson *(Peaches Callahan)*, Joe Butterworth *(Joe Callahan)*, Lillian Leeds, Billie Beaudine, Jr. *(Baby Callahan)*, Cameo *(The Dog)*.

Melodrama. Source: Leon Parker, *Heroes of the Street* (a play; publication undetermined). Mike Callahan, one of "New York's finest," is killed in the line of duty, and his murderer is not captured although "The Shadow" is suspected. Mike's young son, Mickey, bravely tries to act as head of the family, and through his friend, Broadway chorus girl Betty Beaton, he gets a job as property boy. Betty is in love with Howard Lane, but to further her career she accepts the attentions of wealthy Gordon Trent, then agrees with him to undergo a phony kidnaping as a publicity stunt. Unwittingly, Mickey tries to rescue Betty, uncovers a blackmail plot against her, and discovers Trent to be not only "The Shadow" but also his father's murderer. *Police. Chorus girls. Kidnaping. Murder. New York City—Broadway.*

THE HEROIC LOVER **F2.2470**

Richard Talmadge Productions. *Dist* Parthenon Pictures, General Pictures. 1 May **1929.** Mus score & sd eff; b&w. 35mm. 6 reels, 5,500 ft. [Also si.]

Dir Noel Mason. *Scen* Betty Moore. *Titl* Al Martin. *Photog* Harry Cooper, William Wheeler. *Film Ed* Martin Obzina.

Cast: Leonard St. Leo, Barbara Bedford, Stuart Holmes, Ted Snell, Hugh Metcalf, William Franey.

Comedy. "The story tells of a pair of vibrator salesmen who happen into a small town at the time of a train robbery and who through a lucky chance bring about the capture of the robbers." (*Film Daily,* 16 Mar 1930, p8.) *Traveling salesmen. Train robberies. Smalltown life. Vibrators.*

HE'S A PRINCE *see* **A REGULAR FELLOW**

HEY! HEY! COWBOY (Universal-Jewel) **F2.2471**

Universal Pictures. 3 Apr **1927** [c22 Mar 1927; LP23787]. Si; b&w. 35mm. 6 reels, 5,378 ft.

Pres by Carl Laemmle. *Story-Scen-Dir* Lynn Reynolds. *Photog* Harry Neumann. *Art Dir* David S. Garber.

Cast: Hoot Gibson *(Jimmie Roberts)*, Nick Cogley *(Julius Decker)*, Kathleen Key *(Emily Decker)*, Wheeler Oakman *(John Evans)*, Clark Comstock *(Joe Billings)*, Monte Montague *(Hank Mander, Decker's foreman)*, Milla Davenport *(Aunt Jane)*, Jim Corey *(Blake)*, Slim Summerville *(Spike Doolin)*.

Western comedy-melodrama. A longstanding friendship between Julius Decker and Joe Billings, neighboring ranchers, is broken by a series of mystifying occurrences, and their relationship ultimately develops into a feud. John Evans, who is engaged to Emily Decker, tries without success to patch up the quarrel. Jimmie Roberts, a detective posing as a hobo, gets work with Decker, falls in love with Emily, and exposes Evans, who is responsible for the trouble. Evans tries to elope with Emily, but Jimmie's friend, Doolin, foils his plan, and Jimmie is united with the girl. *Ranchers. Tramps. Detectives. Friendship. Feuds. Courtship.*

HEY RUBE! *see* **THE WILD WEST SHOW**

HEY RUBE! **F2.2472**

FBO Pictures. 23 Dec **1928** [c4 Dec 1928; LP25885]. Si; b&w. 35mm. 7 reels, 6,290 ft.

Dir George B. Seitz. *Cont* Wyndham Gittens. *Titl* Randolph Bartlett. *Story* Wyndham Gittens, Louis Sarecky. *Photog* Robert Martin. *Film Ed* Ann McKnight. *Asst Dir* Thomas Atkins.

Cast: Hugh Trevor *(String)*, Gertrude Olmstead *(Lutie)*, Ethlyne Clair *(Zelda)*, Bert Moorehouse *(Moffatt)*, Walter McGrail *(Duke)*, James Eagle *(Andy)*.

Melodrama. String Whalen, a wheel-of-fortune operator in a carnival, is greatly attracted to Lutie and gains her gratitude when he recovers her purse from a pickpocket; at a dance that evening, String promises Lutie to forsake his gambling career. He breaks that promise the very next day when he returns to the wheel in an effort to win $1,500 for an operation on his crippled friend, Andy. Zelda, a firediver at the carnival, resents String's attentions to Lutie and, when Lutie goes to the diving platform with Zelda to research a newspaper article, Zelda sets the platform afire. There is a riot at the carnival and, unknown to Zelda, the diving tank is broken. Zelda dives into an empty tank and breaks her neck; String rescues Lutie and is duly rewarded. *Pickpockets. Firedivers. Gambling. Carnivals.*

HI-JACKING RUSTLERS F2.2473

Ben Wilson Productions. *Dist* Rayart Pictures. Nov **1926.** Si; b&w. 35mm. 5 reels, 4,935 ft.

Dir Bennett Cohn.

Cast: Jack Perrin, Josephine Hill, Billy Lamar, Leonard Trainor, Bud Osborne, Al Ferguson, Walter Shumway, Starlight *(a horse)*, Rex *(a dog)*.

Western melodrama. "Hero circumvents cattle rustlers and bank robbers. There is a romance." (*Motion Picture News Booking Guide,* 12:34, Apr 1927.) *Bank robberies. Rustling. Dogs. Horses.*

HICKVILLE TO BROADWAY F2.2474

Fox Film Corp. 28 Aug **1921** [c28 Aug 1921; LP16951]. Si; b&w. 35mm. 5 reels, 4,219 ft.

Pres by William Fox. *Dir-Writ* Carl Harbaugh. *Titl* Ralph Spence. *Photog* Otto Brautigan. *Film Ed* Ralph Spence.

Cast: Eileen Percy *(Anna Mae Neil)*, William Scott *(Virgil Cole)*, Rosemary Theby *(Sibyle Fane)*, John P. Lockney *(Elder Neil)*, Margaret Morris *(Violet Garden)*, Ray Howard *(Pinky Hale)*, Paul Kamp *(helper)*, Ed Burns *(Peter Van Reuter)*.

Comedy. Broadway actress Sibyle Fane visits the home of Anna Mae Neil, daughter of a Hickville farmer, who is engaged to local druggist Virgil Cole. Impressed with Miss Fane, Virgil sells his business and sets out for Broadway. Miss Fane suggests to Anna Mae that she reach New York ahead of Virgil and pass herself off as a city vamp; there she introduces Anna Mae to sculptress Violet Garden and songwriter Pinky Hale, who teach her the latest jazz steps. She flirts with Virgil in a fashionable restaurant and discovers his shifting affections at a party. Convinced of his worthlessness, Anna decides that talented young artist Peter Van Reuter is deserving of her love. *Actors. Pharmacists. Sculptors. Artists. Composers. Smalltown life. New York City.*

HIDDEN ACES F2.2475

Louis T. Rogers. *Dist* Pathé Exchange. 7 Aug **1927** [c19 Jul 1927; LU24190]. Si; b&w. 35mm. 5 reels, 4,620 ft.

Dir Howard Mitchell. *Story-Scen* John F. Natteford. *Photog* Leon Shamroy.

Cast: Charles Hutchison *(Larry Hutchdale)*, Alice Calhoun *(Natalie Kingston)*, Barbara Tennant *(Princess Orloff)*, Paul Weigel *(Serge Demidoff)*, Harry Norcross *(Burke)*, James Bradbury, Jr. *(butler)*, Frank Whitson *(captain)*.

Action melodrama. Princess Orloff and her friend Serge Demidoff arrive in the United States with valuable jewels; and Larry Hutchdale, Serge's secretary (Natalie Kingston), and Burke (a private detective) all plan independently to get possession of them. The police captain accuses Natalie, who steals the jewels from Serge, then makes her getaway in an automobile, followed by Larry on a motorcycle, the police also pursuing. Larry overtakes her, springs from his cycle to her car, and diverts it from the path of an express train. Larry pretends to join her in flight, and when the police arrive, he assumes all blame. It is revealed that the princess has stolen the jewels from a consulate in Shanghai and that Larry and Natalie are both Secret Service agents. *Royalty. Secretaries. Thieves. Detectives. Motorcyclists. Secret service. Chases.*

HIDDEN LOOT (Blue Streak Western) F2.2476

Universal Pictures. 31 Oct **1925** [or Aug 1926; c13 Sep 1926; LP23105]. Si; b&w. 35mm. 5 reels, 4,738 ft.

Pres by Carl Laemmle. *Dir* Robert North Bradbury. *Scen* Harry Dittmar. *Story* William J. Neidig. *Photog* William Nobles,

Cast: Jack Hoxie *(Cranner)*, Olive Hasbrouck *(Anna Jones)*, Edward Cecil *(Dick Jones)*, Jack Kenney *("Big Bill" Angus)*, Buck Connors *(Buck)*, Bert De Marc *(Manning)*, Charles Brinley *(Jordan)*.

Western melodrama. Anna Jones, racing her brother Dick to their ranch, is "rescued" from her fast horse by a stranger (Cranner) whom she indignantly brands a bonehead before riding away. "Big Bill," a ranch employee, steals the payroll bag and joins his gang in the forest, where the stranger sees them hiding the bag in a shack. He investigates and is captured by the gang. His dog, Bunk, however, leaps through a window with the loot, buries it, then returns, frees Cranner by digging a hole under the wall, and keeps the bandits at bay while Cranner escapes. Anna encounters Cranner, and though she believes him guilty, she is so impressed by his gallantry that she falls in love with him and helps him evade Bill and his gang. Cranner follows Anna and rescues her from the clutches of Bill; then the posse arrives, and Anna discovers that the stranger is actually a Texas Ranger. *Ranchers. Bandits. Texas Rangers. Strangers. Dogs.*

THE HIDDEN MENACE F2.2477

William Steiner Productions. Jan **1925** [c23 Jan, 24 Jan 1925; LU21058]. Si; b&w. 35mm. 5 reels.

Dir Charles Hutchison. *Scen* J. F. Natteford.

Cast: Charles Hutchison.

Melodrama. "... with newspaper reporter as hero who wins a girl's love in thrilling rescue. Later she is abducted by demented sculptor, who wants her as a model for a work he thinks will be his masterpiece. Held prisoner and menaced by the lunatic, the girl is about to be sacrificed when hero arrives to save her." (*Motion Picture News Booking Guide,* 8:37, Apr 1925.) *Reporters. Sculptors. Lunatics. Human sacrifice.*

THE HIDDEN WAY F2.2478

Joseph De Grasse. *Dist* Associated Exhibitors. 26 Jul or 16 Aug **1926** [c28 Apr 1926; LU22650]. Si; b&w. 35mm. 6 reels, 5,919 ft.

Dir Joseph De Grasse. *Story-Scen* Ida May Park. *Photog* Joseph Dubray.

Cast: Mary Carr *(Mother)*, Gloria Grey *(Mary)*, Tom Santschi *(Bill)*, Arthur Rankin *(Harry)*, Ned Sparks *(Mulligan)*, Jane Thomas *(The Woman)*, Billie Jeane Phelps *(The Child)*, Wilbur Mack *(Sid Atkins)*, William Ryno *(Samuel Atkins)*.

Crook melodrama. Mary and her mother live in a quiet valley at the foot of a hill on which is located a penitentiary. Three released convicts—Bill, Harry, and Mulligan—all hardened criminals, save Mary from death by intercepting her rearing horse at a railroad crossing. Mary's mother heartily welcomes the men to her home and gives them dinner. The next morning, Mulligan discovers a natural spring on the property and suggests that they doctor the water and pass it off as a life-giving mineral water. Mary sets out to deliver the treated water to a chemist but accidentally spills the container and refills it. Returning home with news that the water is indeed therapeutic, Mary finds that her mother has taken in a poor woman—and her child—who had been betrayed by Sid Atkins, son of the town's wealthiest citizen. Bill becomes attached to this woman, and Harry to Mary. Fearing discovery of his "fraud," Bill convinces Mother that she should sell her house; but later he causes Atkins to rescind the agreement, and all ends happily. *Criminals—Rehabilitation. Motherhood. Fraud. Springs.*

THE HIDDEN WOMAN F2.2479

Nanuet Amusement Corp. *Dist* American Releasing Corp. 2 Apr **1922** [c2 Apr 1922; LP17917]. Si; b&w. 35mm. 5 reels, 4,626 ft.

Prod-Dir Allan Dwan.

Cast: Evelyn Nesbit *(Ann Wesley)*, Crauford Kent *(Bart Andrews)*, Murdock MacQuarrie *(Iron MacLoid)*, Ruth Darling *(Vera MacLoid)*, Albert Hart *(Bill Donovan)*, Russell Thaw *(Johnny Randolph)*, Mary Alden *(Mrs. Randolph)*, Jack Evans *(The Derelict)*.

Society melodrama. Ann Wesley, a well-to-do society girl, is loved by Bart Andrews, who reproaches her for her frivolity and believes that she conceals a better self within her personality. Her fortune is lost in a stock market panic, and she retires to live quietly at a settlement in the Adirondacks. There her unconventionality provokes the wrath of Iron MacLoid, the local reformer and town boss. Ann becomes friends with little Johnny Randolph, whose father is a drunkard; and unknown to her, Bart follows and watches over her every movement. While in the woods with Johnny, Ann is attacked by Bill Donovan, but Randolph comes to her aid and beats Donovan in a fight. After effecting the regeneration of the father and reuniting him with his wife, Ann proves her worth and Bart makes his appearance to claim her. *Socialites. Reformers. Alcoholism. Stock market. New York City—Broadway. Adirondack Mountains.*

HIDE-OUT F2.2480

Universal Pictures. 30 Mar **1930** [c17 Mar 1930; LP1163]. Sd (Movietone); b&w. 35mm. 7 reels, 5,297 ft. [Also si; 5,759 ft.]

Pres by Carl Laemmle. *Dir* Reginald Barker. *Story-Scen* Arthur Ripley, Lambert Hillyer, Lambert Hillyer. *Dial* Matt Taylor. *Photog* Gilbert Warrenton. *Film Ed* Harry Marker. *Song: "Just You and I"* Sam Perry, Clarence J. Marks. *Rec Engr* C. Roy Hunter.

Cast: James Murray *(Jimmy Dorgan/Morley Wallace)*, Kathryn Crawford *(Dorothy Evans)*, Carl Stockdale *(Dorgan)*, Lee Moran *(Joe Hennessey)*, Edward Hearn *(Coach Latham)*, Robert Elliott *(William Burke)*, Jackie Hanlon *(Jerry)*, George Hackathorne *(Atlas)*, Sarah Padden *(Mrs. Dorgan)*, Jane Keckley *(Mrs. Evans)*, Richard Carlyle *(Dean)*, Frank Campeau *(see note)*, Frank De Voe *(see note)*.

Melodrama. Morley Wallace, whose real name is Jimmy Dorgan, returns to Crane University in the South, after escaping from Detective Burke, who has arrested him for illegal liquor activities. Wallace, who is a college hero as a result of his prowess on the boat crew, barely escapes a police raid on a roadhouse, where he goes with co-ed Dorothy Evans; and he decides to repent of his past. The day before a boating race, Burke finds Wallace, and, as a test, threatens to arrest him unless he throws the race. Wallace agrees to the proposition; but finding that he cannot go through with the treachery, he takes a winning lead. Assured of his decision to reform, Burke leaves him free to marry Dorothy. *Racketeers. Athletes. Criminals—Rehabilitation. College life. Courtship. Boat racing.*

Note: Some sources indicate Frank Campeau in the role of Dorgan and Frank De Voe playing Joe Hennessey.

HIGH AND HANDSOME **F2.2481**

R-C Pictures. *Dist* Film Booking Offices of America. 21 Jun **1925** [c21 Jun 1925; LP21775]. Si; b&w. 35mm. 6 reels, 5,669 ft.

Dir Harry Garson. *Scen* Rex Taylor. *Story* Gerald Beaumont. *Photog* Ernest Hallor. *Asst Dir* Ted Butcher.

Cast: Maurice B. Flynn *(Joe Hanrahan)*, Ethel Shannon *(Marie Ducette)*, Tom Kennedy *(Bat Kennedy)*, Ralph McCullough *(Irving Ducette)*, Jean Perry *(Burke)*, Marjorie Bonner *(Myrt Riley)*, John Gough *(Jimmy)*, Lydia Knott *(Mrs. Hanrahan)*.

Melodrama. Joe Hanrahan, a tough patrolman, warns fight promoter Burke to repair the shaky gallery in his arena. Burke does not comply with this order, and Joe is suspended from the force for fighting in public with Battling Kennedy, Joe's rival for the affections of Marie Ducette. Burke then matches Joe and Kennedy in an exhibition bout in his arena. Joe knocks out Kennedy and, when the gallery collapses, injuring several people, arrests Burke. Joe is reinstated on the force and wins Marie. *Police. Prizefighters. Fight promoters. Safety—Buildings. Arenas.*

THE HIGH FLYER **F2.2482**

Harry J. Brown Productions. *Dist* Rayart Pictures. 30 Sep **1926** [New York State license]. Si; b&w. 35mm. 5 reels, 5,610 ft.

Dir Harry J. Brown.

Cast: Reed Howes *(Jim)*, Ethel Shannon *(Winnie)*, James Bradbury *(Dick)*, Ray Hallor *(Tom)*, Paul Panzer *(McGrew)*, Josef Swickard, Cissy Fitzgerald, Ernest Hilliard, Earl Metcalfe, Joseph Girard.

Action melodrama. Source: J. Frank Clark, "The Bird Man" (publication undetermined). "War veteran with plans for new areoplane [*sic*] disappears and his buddy seeks to sell them to rich manufacturer with beautiful daughter. Inventor shows up in time to prevent foreman of manufacturer's plant from stealing plans. Falls in love with daughter and she with him." (*Motion Picture News Booking Guide*, 12:34, Apr 1927.) *Inventors. Veterans. Shop foremen. Airplane manufacture. Airplane factories.*

HIGH GEAR JEFFREY **F2.2483**

American Film Co. c1 Jun **1921** [LP16595]. Si; b&w. 35mm.

Dir Edward Sloman. *Story-Adapt* Jules Furthman.

Cast: William Russell, Francelia Billington, Clarence Burton, Al Ferguson, Harvey Clarke, Lucille Ward, Charles Newton, William Spencer.

Melodrama. Jeffrey Claiborne, the only son of a wealthy father, rescues Betty Jane from the unwelcome attentions of a chauffeur and accepts Betty's offer of a job in her mother's taxicab business. He proposes marriage, but Mother Moir scorns him as a prospective son-in-law. He learns that the mother is threatened with exposure of her past by an underworld gang; and since she is in love with the police captain, she agrees to cooperate with them, but with Jeffrey's help the purpose of the criminals is defeated. He wins the girl. *Businesswomen. Chauffeurs. Taxicabs. Police. Gangs. Blackmail. Social classes.*

Note: "Re-edited" version of *The Frame-up* (Mutual, 1917).

THE HIGH HAND **F2.2484**

Leo Maloney Productions. *Dist* Pathé Exchange. 12 Sep **1926** [c26 Jul 1926; LU22977]. Si; b&w. 35mm. 6 reels, 5,679 ft.

Dir Leo Maloney. *Story-Scen* Ford I. Beebe. *Photog* Hal Mohr.

Cast: Leo Maloney *(Sandy Sands)*, Josephine Hill *(Edith Oaks)*, Paul Hurst *(Chris Doble)*, Murdock MacQuarrie *(Martin Shaler)*, Whitehorse *(John Oaks)*, Gus Saville *(swamper)*, Dick La Reno *(sheriff)*, Florence Lee *(Mrs. Oaks)*.

Western melodrama. The home of John Oaks, an impoverished cattleman hounded by rustlers, is burned down, and Sandy, a lone cowpuncher, arrives and takes it upon himself to round up Oaks's enemies, being won over to the charms of Oaks's daughter, Edith. Adopting the pseudonym "The Collector," he commits apparent depredations but always sends the gains to the sheriff, declaring that they will be accounted for at a later date. Following many raids and battles, some of the town's leading citizens, including the sheriff, are caught in the net of guilt, due reparation is made, and Sandy marries the rancher's daughter. *Ranchers. Rustlers. Cowboys. Sheriffs.*

HIGH HAT **F2.2485**

Robert Kane Productions. *Dist* First National Pictures. 13 Mar **1927** [c8 Mar 1927; LP23738]. Si; b&w. 35mm. 7 reels, 6,161 ft.

Pres by Robert Kane. *Dir* James Ashmore Creelman. *Story-Scen* James Ashmore Creelman, Melville Baker. *Photog* William Schurr. *Prod Mgr* Leland Hayward.

Cast: Ben Lyon *(Jerry)*, Mary Brian *(Millie)*, Sam Hardy *(Tony)*, Lucien Prival *(The Director)*, Osgood Perkins *(The Assistant Director)*, Jack Ackroyd *(The Property Man)*, Iris Gray, Ione Holmes *(The Stars)*.

Comedy-drama. Jerry, a lazy extra on the Superba-Prettygood Pictures lot, is in love with Millie, the wardrobe mistress, who is also being courted by Tony, another extra. Von Strogoff, a temperamental German director making a film on the Russian Revolution, finds Jerry useless, but Millie gets him a "closeup" assignment, the prize of all extras. True to form, Jerry falls asleep on a prop bed and is fired. Tony steals some jewels entrusted to Millie and tries to turn them over to a pair of crooks; Jerry follows and is captured by the crooks, but he escapes and chases Tony to the studio. Jerry's battle with Tony is filmed by mistake for Von Strogoff; when the hero produces the jewels he learns they are paste, but his "closeup" is kept in the picture. *Actors. Wardrobe mistresses. Motion picture directors. Motion pictures. Russia—History—1917–21 Revolution. Chases.*

HIGH HEELS **F2.2486**

Universal Film Manufacturing Co. 24 Oct **1921** [c11 Oct 1921; LP17063]. Si; b&w. 35mm. 5 reels, 4,541 ft.

Dir Lee Kohlmar. *Scen* Wallace Clifton. *Story* Louise B. Clancy. *Photog* Earl Ellis.

Cast: Gladys Walton *(Christine Trevor)*, Frederick Vogeding *(Dr. Paul Denton)*, William Worthington *(Joshua Barton)*, Freeman Wood *(Cortland Van Ness)*, George Hackathorne *(Laurie Trevor)*, Charles De Briac *(Daffy Trevor)*, Raymond De Briac *(Dilly Trevor)*, Milton Markwell *(Douglas Barton)*, Dwight Crittenden *(John Trevor)*, Robert Dunbar *(Robert Graves)*, Ola Norman *(Amelia)*, Leigh Wyant *(Jennie Chubb)*, Jean De Briac *(Armand)*, Hugh Saxon *(Mike [butler])*.

Society drama. Christine Trevor, a spoiled and selfish society girl of 18, neglects her sister and two brothers and merely tolerates her indulgent father. When her father suddenly dies, leaving them virtually penniless, Christine all but deserts the family to marry a social parasite. Dr. Denton, the family physician, prevents the marriage by appealing to her better nature and helps her build a home for the family. She rescues her grouchy old neighbor from his burning house, though he is the very man who is responsible for wrecking the family fortune out of vengeance for a wrong against him years earlier; and he comes to admire her. At last, Christine realizes her love for Dr. Denton, and they are united. *Orphans. Physicians. Family life. Redemption.*

Note: Working title: *Christine of the Young Heart.*

HIGH SCHOOL HERO **F2.2487**

Fox Film Corp. 16 Oct **1927** [c10 Oct 1927; LP24478]. Si; b&w. 35mm. 6 reels, 5,498 ft.

Pres by William Fox. *Dir* David Butler. *Scen* Seton I. Miller. *Titl* Delos Sutherland. *Story* David Butler, William M. Conselman. *Photog* Ernest Palmer. *Asst Dir* Park Frame.

Cast: Nick Stuart *(Pete Greer)*, Sally Phipps *(Eleanor Barrett)*, William N. Bailey *(Mr. Merrill)*, John Darrow *(Bill Merrill)*, Wade Boteler *(Mr. Greer)*, Brandon Hurst *(Mr. Golden)*, David Rollins *(Allen Drew)*, Charles Paddock *(coach)*, Wee Gee *(Greer's dog)*, Pal *(Merrill's dog)*.

Comedy-drama. Pete Greer and Bill Merrill, rivals since childhood, continue feuding in high school, and their natural friction is intensified by each centering his attention on Eleanor Barrett, a new classmate. Amusing complications involve a sequence in which the high school Latin class, under the egis of Mr. Golden, presents what is intended to be a Roman tragedy but develops as a comic farce. The boys' enmity threatens to disrupt the school basketball team, but loyalty to their school compels them to drop their differences. Eleanor incontinently turns to Allen

Drew, a bespectacled, studious type. *Basketball. High school life. Latin language. Theater—Amateur. Dogs.*

HIGH SOCIETY BLUES **F2.2488**

Fox Film Corp. 23 Mar **1930** [c3 Mar 1930; LP1160]. Sd (Movietone); b&w. 35mm. 10 reels, 8,995 ft.

Pres by William Fox. *Assoc Prod* Al Rockett. *Dir* David Butler. *Adapt-Dial* Howard J. Green. *Photog* Charles Van Enger. *Film Ed* Irene Morra. *Songs: "I'm in the Market for You," "Eleanor," "High Society Blues," "Just Like in a Story Book," "The Song I Sing in My Dreams"* Joseph McCarthy, James Hanley. *Rec Engr* Joseph E. Aiken. *Asst Dir* Ad Schaumer. *Cost* Sophie Wachner.

Cast: Janet Gaynor *(Eleanor Divine)*, Charles Farrell *(Eddie Granger)*, William Collier, Sr. *(Horace Divine)*, Hedda Hopper *(Mrs. Divine)*, Joyce Compton *(Pearl Granger)*, Lucien Littlefield *(Eli Granger)*, Louise Fazenda *(Mrs. Granger)*, Brandon Hurst *(Jowles)*, Gregory Gaye *(Count Prunier)*.

Comedy-drama. Source: Dana Burnet, "Those High Society Blues," in *Saturday Evening Post* (197:8–9, 23 May 1925). After selling his business in Iowa, Eli Granger and his family move to an exclusive Scarsdale area in New York, where by chance he occupies a house adjacent to Horace Divine, a wealthy businessman with whom he made his business transaction. Although the Divines scorn their *nouveaux riches* neighbors, the children, Eleanor Divine and Eddie Granger, meet when Eleanor aspires to learn to play the ukelele under Eddie's tuition. Eleanor's mother is arranging to marry her to a foreign count, but she falls in love with Eddie; and while their fathers are warring on Wall Street, the children elope and in the end bring peace and prosperity to both families. *Businessmen. Nouveaux riches. Family life. Courtship. Elopement. Iowa. New York City. New York City—Wall Street.*

HIGH SPEED **F2.2489**

Universal Pictures. 20 May **1924** [New York premiere; released 26 May; c1 May 1924; LP20141]. Si; b&w. 35mm. 5 reels, 4,927 ft.

Dir Herbert Blache. *Scen* Helen Broderick. *Photog* Merritt Gerstad.

Cast: Herbert Rawlinson *(Hi Moreland)*, Carmelita Geraghty *(Marjory Holbrook)*, Bert Roach *(Dick Farrell)*, Otto Hoffman *(Daniel Holbrook)*, Percy Challenger *(Rev. Percy Humphries)*, Jules Cowles *(burglar)*, Cleo Bartlett *(Susanna)*, J. Buckley Russell *(taxi driver)*.

Comedy-melodrama. Source: Fred Jackson, "High Speed," in *Argosy Magazine* (95:413–439, 1 Jun 1918). Handsome athlete Hi Moreland tries to win the hand of the bank president's daughter, Marjory Holbrook, from a wealthy but insipid competitor who is in the father's favor. He eludes the schemes to frame him and following a series of complications marries the girl. *Athletes. Bankers. Courtship.*

HIGH SPEED LEE **F2.2490**

Atlantic Features. *Dist* Arrow Film Corp. 1 Jun **1923** [c9 Mar 1923; LP18765]. Si; b&w. 35mm. 5 reels, 4,816 ft.

Dir-Adapt Dudley Murphy.

Cast: Reed Howes *(James Jefferson Lee)*.

Society comedy-drama. Source: John Phillips Marquand, "Only a Few of Us Left," in *Saturday Evening Post* (194:3–5, 17–19, 14–21, Jan 1922). James Jefferson Lee, a wealthy, idle, adventure-loving young Long Islander, begins a beautiful friendship with Jane when he accepts her dare to jump with her from the roof of the Yacht Club into the sparkling sound below. Displeased with Jimmy's shiftless ways, however, Jane prods him into devoting some time to his business interests, especially the All-American Tire Co., of which his rival, stodgy Harold Polk, is general manager. Jimmy's unconventional methods result in resignations by all the company's executives, but he manfully steers the business to financial success and, meanwhile, rides a dangerous horse—thereby silencing those who scoffed at him and winning Jane's heart. *Wealth. Business management. Tire manufacture. Long Island. Horses.*

HIGH STEPPERS **F2.2491**

Edwin Carewe Productions. *Dist* First National Pictures. 14 Mar **1926** [c12 Apr 1926; LP22607]. Si; b&w. 35mm. 7 reels, 6,136 ft.

Pres by Edwin Carewe. *Dir* Edwin Carewe. *Scen* Lois Leeson. *Adapt* Finis Fox. *Photog* Robert Kurrle.

Cast: Lloyd Hughes *(Julian Perryam)*, Mary Astor *(Audrey Nye)*, Dolores Del Rio *(Evelyn Iffield)*, Rita Carewe *(Janet Perryam)*, John T. Murray *(Cyril Buckland)*, Edwards Davis *(Victor Buckland)*, Alec B. Francis *(Father Perryam)*, Clarissa Selwyn *(Mrs. Perryam)*, Charles Sellon *(Grandpa Perryam)*, John Steppling *(Major Iffield)*, Emily Fitzroy *(Mrs. Iffield)*, Margaret McWade *(Mrs. Clancy)*.

Society melodrama. Source: Philip Hamilton Gibbs, *Heirs Apparent: a Novel* (London, 1923). Expelled from Oxford for his jazz existence, Julian Perryam returns to the family mansion near London. There he finds his sister Janet and his mother equally caught up in a swirl of frivolity and his father (editor of *The Week*, a scandal sheet) too busy to interfere in their diversions. Julian is discouraged, moreover, by the rebuff of Evelyn Iffield, with whom he is in love, and observes that his sister is falling prey to Cyril Buckland, son of his father's publisher. In London he meets Audrey Nye, an intelligent girl expelled with Julian, who gets him a position working with her as a reporter for *The Truth*. He learns that Victor Buckland is stealing from a charity fund and prepares to expose him. As a result, Buckland is killed by a mob, his son flees the country, Evelyn is reconciled with her husband, and Julian marries Audrey, who has aided him in investigating Buckland. *Reporters. Brother-sister relationship. Family life. Jazz life. Scandal sheets. London. Oxford University.*

HIGH VOLTAGE **F2.2492**

Pathé Exchange. 7 Apr **1929** [c3 Jun 1929; LP420]. Sd (Photophone); b&w. 35mm. 6 reels, 5,743 ft. [Also si; 5,118 ft.]

Supv Ralph Block. *Dir* Howard Higgin. *Screenplay* James Gleason, Kenyon Nicholson. *Dial* Elliott Clawson, James Gleason. *Story* Elliott Clawson. *Photog* John Mescall. *Film Ed* Doane Harrison. *Song: "Colleen O'Kildare"* George Green, George Waggner. *Asst Dir* Leigh Smith. *Prod Mgr* Richard Blaydon.

Cast: William Boyd *(Bill Dougherty, lineman)*, Owen Moore *(Detective Dan Egan)*, Carol Lombard *(Billie Davis)*, Diane Ellis *(Diane)*, Billy Bevan *(Gus Engstrom, stage driver)*, Phillips Smalley *(J. Milton Hendricksen, banker)*.

Drama. Through heavy snow in the High Sierras, a motorbus carries an assorted group of passengers, although warned by a gas station attendant that the road is impassable. On the bus are Dan Egan, a deputy sheriff who holds in custody Billie Davis, a girl crook he is taking to prison; J. Milton Hendricksen, a banker with a firm belief in the power of money; and Diane, a girl en route to her wedding. During a blinding snowstorm, the driver loses his way and they are marooned. Reaching a small country church, apparently deserted, they encounter Bill Dougherty, a lineman, who apportions them a small amount of food. Billie falls in love with the lineman, whom she later discovers to be a criminal hiding from the law. For his part, Dan is torn between his duty and his dawning love for her. Billie and Bill plan to escape together, but when the group is rescued, they decide to serve their sentences, hoping for a happy future. *Criminals—Rehabilitation. Sheriffs. Bankers. Linemen. Buses. Churches. Sierras. Storms.*

THE HIGHBINDERS **F2.2493**

Worthy Pictures. *Dist* Associated Exhibitors. 21 Mar **1926** [c12 Mar 1926; LU22473]. Si; b&w. 35mm. 6 reels, 5,486 ft.

Dir George W. Terwilliger. *Scen* Calder Johnstone. *Story* William T. Tilden. *Photog* Walter Blakely.

Cast: William T. Tilden, Marjorie Daw, Ben Alexander, George Hackathorne, Edmund Breese, Walter Long, George F. Marion, Effie Shannon, Hugh Thompson.

Underworld melodrama. Author David Marshall is sandbagged by holdup men and loses his memory. He finds his way to a bookshop run by his friend Ladd, who takes him in with the hope of helping him to regain his memory. David there meets Hope Masterson and falls in love with her. Bill Dorgan, a gangster in love with Hope, kidnaps her, and David comes to her rescue. David is hit again on the head, and this time he regains his memory. He still recognizes Hope, however, and they look forward to a long and happy life together. *Authors. Gangsters. Bookshops. Amnesia.*

THE HIGHEST BIDDER **F2.2494**

Goldwyn Pictures. ca15 Jan **1921** [Detroit and Chicago premieres; c23 Dec 1920; LP15969]. Si; b&w. 35mm. 6 reels, 4,960 ft.

Pres by Samuel Goldwyn. *Dir* Wallace Worsley. *Cont* Lloyd Lonergan. *Camera* George Peters. *Art Dir* Gilbert White. *Asst Dir* Jo Sternberg.

Cast: Madge Kennedy *(Sally Raeburn)*, Lionel Atwill *(Lester)*, Vernon Steele *(Hastings)*, Ellen Cassity *(Fanny de Witt)*, Zelda Sears *(Mrs. Steese)*, Joseph Brennan *(Horace Ashe)*, Reginald Mason *(Mawsby)*, Brian Darley *(Butts)*, William Black *(Mr. Steese)*.

Society melodrama. Source: Maximilian Foster, *The Trap* (New York, 1920). Henry Lester—a millionaire wary of women because he was jilted in early youth by a girl in favor of a man she thought richer than he—meets and falls in love with Sally Raeburn. Sally is chaperoned by her "aunt," Mrs. Steese, a scheming adventuress who rescued her from poverty and has made Sally promise to "marry for money" to repay her. Sally returns Lester's affections, but he discovers the scheme and vows revenge. He rescues a man named Hastings from the gutter and passes him off to Mrs. Steese as a wealthier and more desirable match for Sally. His scheme works too well, and he finds himself jealous. Sally and Lester are reconciled, however, and she agrees to become his wife. *Millionaires. Social classes. Wealth. Marriage.*

THE HIGHEST LAW **F2.2495**

Selznick Pictures. 5 Feb **1921** [trade review; c28 Dec 1920; LP15979]. Si; b&w. 35mm. 6 reels.

Supv-Dir Ralph Ince. *Story* Lewis Allen Browne.

Cast: Ralph Ince *(Abraham Lincoln)*, Robert Agnew *(Bobby Goodwin)*, Margaret Seddon *(Mrs. Goodwin)*, Aleen Burr *(The Girl)*, Cecil Crawford *(Tad)*.

Historical drama. "'The Highest Law' is the law of humanity as opposed to the Army regulations against desertion which Secretary of War Stanton urges President Lincoln to enforce more strictly, declaring that clemency is destroying the morale of the army. Lincoln quietly but firmly declares that as Commander in Chief he will exercise his judgment and conscience, and the cabinet meeting is dismissed with feeling running somewhat high. ... [Lincoln] learns the story of how Bobby Goodwin had been drafted after his two brothers, who had volunteered, had been killed, earlier in the struggle. His fiancée writes him that his dying mother is calling for him, and when leave of absence is refused, he goes without permission. Investigation proves the story to be true and Lincoln again braves Stanton by pardoning the young offender. A part of the story is shown as being told to Tad, the president's little son, but the entire story follows a prologue in which two overseas men, following the 1920 Memorial Day parade engage in conversation a G. A. R. man, who is seated at the base of a Lincoln statue, and comment on the statue leads to the telling of the story which concludes as the little heroine of the Lincoln story, now an aged woman, comes to meet him and he rises with the declaration that he was the boy of the story." (*Moving Picture World*, 5 Feb 1921, p727.) *Memorial Day. Grand Army of the Republic. United States—History—Civil War. United States Army—Desertion. Abraham Lincoln. Edwin McMasters Stanton. Tad Lincoln.*

THE HILL BILLY **F2.2496**

Jack Pickford Productions. *Dist* Allied Producers and Distributors. 15 Mar **1924** [c2 Feb 1924; LP19951]. Si; b&w. 35mm. 6 reels, 5,734 ft.

Dir George Hill. *Scen-Adapt* Marion Jackson. *Titl* Waldemar-Young. *Story* John William Fox. *Photog* David Kesson, Allen Thompson. *Sets* Harry Oliver. *Ed* Margaret Lysaght. *Mus Synop* James C. Bradford.

Cast: Jack Pickford *(Jed McCoy)*, Lucille Ricksen *(Emmy Lou Spence)*, Frank Leigh *("Groundhog" Spence)*, Ralph Yearsley *(Aaron Spence)*, Jane Keckley *(Mother McCoy)*, Snitz Edwards *(Tabb Tafel)*, Malcolm Waite *("Big-Boy")*, Maine Geary *(Sid Stebbins)*, Margaret Caldwell Shotwell *(a courtroom extra)*, Alphie James *(a comic extra)*, Madame de Bodamere *(an extra)*.

Rural melodrama. "Groundhog" Spence slays Jed McCoy's father and marries Mrs. McCoy to obtain her lands rich in coal. Jed loves Spence's niece, Emmy Lou, an attractive orphan who teaches him to read and write. Spence forces Emmy Lou to marry his son Aaron. Someone in an angry mob of hillsmen shoots Aaron while attempting to drive out swindlers who want the coal lands. Jed is charged with the killing but is acquitted. Anticipating an acquittal, Groundhog attempts to escape before Jed is freed, but Jed chases him to a raft on a river, and there Spence is drowned. The raft collapses, and Jed is rescued by Emmy Lou. The last reel contains a thrilling fight scene on board the makeshift raft as it dashes unguided downstream toward the rapids. *Swindlers. Murder. Mountain life. Coal. Land rights. Rapids.*

HILLS OF HATE **F2.2497**

Ben Wilson Productions. *Dist* Arrow Film Corp. Jul **1921.** Si; b&w. 35mm. 5 reels.

Cast: Jack Hoxie.

Western melodrama. "A Western which first depicts hero in business with his father, much sought after by mothers in the city, who have marriageable daughters. To no avail, since young man has already made his choice secretly. His father is involved in financial scandal, innocently enough, through clever crook, and the one girl hero believed would understand refuses to see him. Going West, eventually he finds gold and the girl, who is only too glad to be reunited with rugged, brave lover." (*Motion Picture News Booking Guide*, 1:50, Dec 1921.) *Businessmen. Bachelors. Filial relations. Reputation. Scandal.*

HILLS OF KENTUCKY **F2.2498**

Warner Brothers Pictures. 19 Feb **1927** [c12 Feb 1927; LP23657]. Si; b&w. 35mm. 7 reels, 6,271 ft.

Dir Howard Bretherton. *Scen* Edward Clark. *Camera* Frank Kesson. *Asst Dir* Ted Stevens.

Cast: Rin-Tin-Tin *(The Grey Ghost)*, Jason Robards *(Steve Harley)*, Dorothy Dwan *(Janet)*, Tom Santschi *(Ben Harley)*, Billy Kent Schaeffer *(Little Davey)*, Rin-Tin-Tin Jr. *(puppy)*, Nanette *(herself)*.

Melodrama. Source: Dorothy Yost, "The Untamed Heart" (publication undetermined). In a famine-striken section of Kentucky, the mountain people are forced to turn out their dogs. One dog, which becomes the leader of a foraging dog pack, is known as The Grey Ghost. Ben, a bully, and Steve, his shy and gentle half brother, vie for the attentions of Janet, their new schoolmistress, who likes Steve but considers him cowardly for enduring the childrens' taunts. The Grey Ghost is injured in an attack and hides near a stream where little Davey is fishing. He permits the boy to bathe his wound and feed him. They secretly become friends, and The Grey Ghost saves the boy from an attack by the pack. In a jealous frenzy, Ben turns the farmers against Janet, then ties her to a canoe headed for the rapids. The Grey Ghost saves Steve from an attack by Ben and rescues Janet. All ends happily. *Brothers. Schoolteachers. Children. Famine. Mountain life. Kentucky. Dogs.*

HILLS OF MISSING MEN **F2.2499**

Playgoers Pictures. *Dist* Associated Exhibitors. 26 Feb **1922** [c8 Feb 1922; LU17536]. Si; b&w. 35mm. 5-6 reels.

Dir-Writ J. P. McGowan. *Story* John B. Clymer. *Photog* Ben Bail.

Cast: J. P. McGowan *(The Dragon)*, Jean Perry *(Crando)*, James Wang *(Li Fung)*, Charles Brinley *(Bandini)*, Andrew Waldron *(Buck Allis)*, Florence Gilbert *(Hilma Allis)*, Helen Holmes *(Amy Allis)*.

Adventure melodrama. Crando, who lives like a feudal monarch in a walled castle amid the hills of Baja California, believes himself destined to be an emperor, but to the annoyance of Li Fung, his prime minister, and Bandini, a border bandit, he hesitates because of his love for Hilma Allis, who hates Crando as much as her sister, Amy, loves him. Hilma gives aid to the Dragon, actually Captain Brandt of the United States Army, but Crando and Bandini, learning that the Dragon is a government spy, try to poison him. He is revived by Hilma, and his cavalry troops arrive from the hills and storm the castle. Brandt finds Crando dead by his own hand and rescues Hilma from the clutches of the desperadoes. *Bandits. Sisters. Delusion of grandeur. Baja California. United States Army—Cavalry.*

HILLS OF PERIL **F2.2500**

Fox Film Corp. 1 May **1927** [c1 May 1927; LP24015]. Si; b&w. 35mm. 5 reels, 4,983 ft.

Pres by William Fox. *Dir* Lambert Hillyer. *Scen* Jack Jungmeyer. *Photog* Reginald Lyons. *Asst Dir* Ted Brooks.

Cast: Buck Jones *(Laramie)*, Georgia Hale *(Ellen)*, Albert J. Smith *(Rand)*, Buck Black *(Grimes's boy)*, William Welch *(Grimes)*, Marjorie Beebe *(Sophia)*, Duke Green *(Jake)*, Charles Athloff *(Ezra)*, Robert Kortman *(Red)*.

Western melodrama. Source: Winchell Smith and George Abbott, *The Holy Terror; a None-Too-Serious Drama* (New York, 1926). Laramie, a cowpuncher, wins the confidence of the sheriff when he rescues him from two crooks. In town, he becomes involved with a gang of bootleggers; and after meeting Ellen Wade, who is trying to reactivate an abandoned mine, Laramie decides to stay. Though he joins with the gang, he is actually working for the town authorities. Sensing imminent capture by the local posse, the gang escape from the dancehall, but with Laramie's help they are captured; he is elected sheriff and wins the girl. *Cowboys. Bootleggers. Sheriffs. Posses. Mines.*

HIS BACK AGAINST THE WALL **F2.2501**

Goldwyn Pictures. Jan **1922** [c3 Jan 1922; LP17424]. Si; b&w. 35mm. 5 reels, 4,690 ft.

Dir Rowland V. Lee. *Scen* Julien Josephson. *Story* John Frederick. *Photog* Max Fabian.

Cast: Raymond Hatton *(Jeremy Dice)*, Virginia Valli *(Mary Welling)*,

Will Walling *(Sheriff Lawrence)*, Gordon Russell *(Bronc Lewis)*, W. H. Bainbridge *(Henry Welling)*, Virginia Madison *(Mrs. Welling)*, Fred Kohler *(Arizona Pete)*, Jack Curtis *(Lew Shaler)*, Dudley Hendricks *(Dr. Farley)*, Shannon Day *(Dorothy Petwell)*, Raymond Cannon *(Jimmy Boyle)*, Louis Morrison *(Foutch)*.

Comedy-drama. Jeremy Dice, a finisher in a New York East Side tailor shop who prides himself on being a smart dresser and dancer, proves to be cowardly when he retreats from a bully who gets fresh with his girl, and his employer discharges him. Deciding to go out west, Jeremy is caught hitching the rails and comes upon two outlaws in the desert disputing over booty; they are both killed in a shoot-out, and Jeremy is proclaimed a hero by the sheriff, but he is so frightened that he is unable to tell the truth. He is taken in by Welling, a wealthy rancher, and his daughter Mary, who develops an interest in him. When Jeremy's bravery is publicly discredited and Mary's name is slandered by one of the men, Jeremy lands a punch on the accuser's jaw, reestablishing his popularity and winning the admiration of Mary. *Tailors. Ranchers. Bandits. Cowardice. New York City—East Side. Arizona.*

HIS BROTHER'S KEEPER **F2.2502**

American Cinema Corp. *Dist* Pioneer Film Corp. Feb **1921** [c16 Oct 1920; LP15704]. Si; b&w. 35mm. 6 reels.

Dir Wilfrid North. *Story-Scen* N. Brewster Morse. *Photog* Arthur Quinn, William L. Crolly.

Cast: Albert L. Barrett *(John Bonham)*, Martha Mansfield *(Helen Harding)*, Rogers Lytton *(Rex Radcliffe)*, Frazer Coulter *(William Harding)*, Gretchen Hartman *(Amalita Cordova)*, Gladden James *(Harvey Weer)*, Anne Drew *(Mrs. Harvey Weer)*.

Mystery melodrama. Rex Radcliffe, vice president of the Northern Atlantic Railroad, is opposed by company president William Harding in his desire to put over a deal that would jeopardize the stockholders of the Interstate Railroad. Using thought control, he causes Weer, Harding's discharged secretary, to murder his ex-boss. Weer is arrested for the murder. Radcliffe then puts Harding's daughter, Helen, also under his influence. John Bonham, Interstate president, becomes interested in the case, and with the aid of Mrs. Weer he exposes Radcliffe, who then commits suicide. *Thought transference. Railroads. Business management. Murder. Suicide.*

HIS BUDDY'S WIFE **F2.2503**

Associated Exhibitors. 4 Oct **1925** [c10 Jul 1925; LU21469]. Si; b&w. 35mm. 6 reels, 5,226 ft.

Scen-Dir Tom Terriss. *Photog* Henry Cronjager.

Cast: Glenn Hunter *(Jimmy McMorrow)*, Edna Murphy *(Mary Mullaney)*, Gordon Begg *(Dr. Summerfield)*, Harlan Knight *(Mr. Jones)*, Cora Williams *(Mrs. Jones)*, Flora Finch *(Mirandy)*, Blanche Davenport *(Mother Mullaney)*, Douglas Gilmore *(Bill Mullaney)*.

Melodrama. Source: T. Howard Kelly, "His Buddy's Wife," in *Smart Set*. Jim McMorrow and Bill Mullaney become close friends during the fighting in France, and Bill asks Jim to look after his family if anything should happen to him. Bill does not return from a patrol in no man's land, and Jim goes to the Mullaney farm, taking care of Bill's wife, Mary, and old Mother Mullaney, who dies shortly after Jim arrives. Jim and Mary are left alone on the farm, and the neighbors begin to gossip. Mary decides that she and Jim must be married, but Bill reappears on the eve of the wedding, telling of his capture by the Germans. Jim quickly realizes that Mary still loves Bill and reluctantly passes out of their lives, finding a cup of gall where he expected a wedding feast. *Veterans. Farmers. Prisoners of war. Reputation. World War I*

HIS CAPTIVE WOMAN **F2.2504**

First National Pictures. 2 Apr **1929** [New York showing; c11 Feb 1929; LP105]. Talking sequences, sd eff, & mus score (Vitaphone); b&w. 35mm. 8 reels, 8,305 ft. [Also si, 3 Feb 1929; 7,692 ft.]

Pres by Richard A. Rowland. *Dir* George Fitzmaurice. *Scen* Carey Wilson. *Dial-Titl* Paul Perez. *Photog* Lee Garmes. *Film Ed* Stuart Heisler.

Cast: Milton Sills *(Officer Thomas McCarthy)*, Dorothy Mackaill *(Anna Janssen)*, Gladden James *(Alastair de Vries)*, Jed Prouty *(Fatty Fargo)*, Sidney Bracey *(Means)*, Gertrude Howard *(Lavoris Smythe)*, Marion Byron *(Baby Meyers)*, George Fawcett *(Howard Donegan)*, William Holden *(judge of the court)*, Frank Reicher *(district attorney)*, August Tollaire *(governor of the island)*, Doris Dawson.

Melodrama. Source: Brian Oswald Donn-Byrne, "Changeling," in *Changeling and Other Stories* (New York, 1923). Cabaret dancer Anna Janssen kills her sugardaddy and escapes to a South Seas island on the yacht of a wealthy admirer. Stolid, conscientious Tom McCarthy, a New York detective, is sent after Anna and arrests her, chartering a steamer to bring her back to the United States. The steamer sinks, and Anna and Tom are stranded on a small island. They fall in love, and Tom's influence brings about a benign change in Anna's character. They are rescued, however, and Anna is placed on trial for her life. Tom takes the stand in her defense and informs the judge of Anna's conversion in the solitude of the island. The judge instructs Tom to marry Anna and then sentences them to life—on the island where they found happiness together. *Dancers. Detectives. Judges. Criminals—Rehabilitation. Murder. Trials. South Sea Islands.*

HIS CHILDREN'S CHILDREN **F2.2505**

Famous Players–Lasky. *Dist* Paramount Pictures. 4 Nov **1923** [New York premiere; released 18 Nov; c21 Nov 1923; LP19640]. Si; b&w. 35mm. 8 reels, ca8,300 ft.

Pres by Adolph Zukor. *Dir* Sam Wood. *Scen* Monte M. Katterjohn. *Photog* Alfred Gilks.

Cast: Bebe Daniels *(Diana)*, Dorothy Mackaill *(Sheila)*, James Rennie *(Lloyd Maitland)*, George Fawcett *(Peter B. Kayne)*, Hale Hamilton *(Rufus Kayne)*, Katheryn Lean *(Claudia)*, Mahlon Hamilton *(Larry Devereaux)*, Mary Eaton *(Mercedes)*, Warner Oland *(Dr. Dahl)*, John Davidson *(Florian)*, Sally Crute *(Mrs. Wingate)*, Joseph Burke *(Uncle Billy McGaw)*, Templar Powell *(Lord Harrowdale)*, Lawrence D'Orsay *(Mr. Pepperill)*, Dora Mills Adams *(Mrs. Rufus Kayne)*, H. Cooper Cliffe *(Krabfleisch, an attorney)*.

Society melodrama. Source: Arthur Chesney Train, *His Children's Children* (New York, 1923). Peter Kayne's great wealth exercises a baneful influence on his son, Rufus, and his three granddaughters, Claudia, Sheila, and Diana. Shortly before the "Old Pirate" dies, Rufus, through his association with a chorus girl named Mercedes, is blackmailed; Claudia marries a scoundrel; and Sheila becomes part of a fast-moving set of lounge lizards and flappers. Diana, the sensible daughter, rescues Sheila and marries Maitland, an idealistic young lawyer. While the old man is upstairs dying, his Fifth Avenue home and all its contents are being auctioned. Reviving sufficiently to come downstairs, he sees what is happening and falls dead, tearing from the wall a tapestry concealing the legend "Except the Lord build the house, they labor in vain that build it." *Grandfathers. Chorus girls. Flappers. Lawyers. Wealth. Blackmail. Family life. Auctions.*

HIS DARK CHAPTER *see* **WHAT A MAN**

HIS DARKER SELF **F2.2506**

G. and H. Pictures. *Dist* W. W. Hodkinson Corp. 16 Mar **1924** [c19 Mar 1924; LP20906]. Si; b&w. 35mm. 5 reels.

Pres by Albert L. Grey. *Dir* John W. Noble. *Titl* Ralph Spence. *Story* Arthur Caesar.

Cast: Lloyd Hamilton *(Claude Sappington)*, Tom Wilson *(Bill Jackson)*, Tom O'Malley *(Uncle Eph)*, Lucille La Verne *(Darktown's Cleopatra)*, Edna May Sperl *(Bill Jackson's sweetheart)*, Sally Long *(Claude's sweetheart)*, Kate Bruce *(Claude's mother)*, Warren Cook *(The Governor)*.

Satiric comedy. Thinking that he is hauling crates of bananas, Uncle Eph, an old Negro working for the Sappington family, nightly carts contraband liquor to a dancehall run by Bill Jackson. When the revenue officers stage a raid on the dancehall, Jackson, believing that Eph has squealed, frames him for murder. Assuming that Eph is innocent, Claude Sappington, a mystery-story writer, sets out to prove it: disguised by blackface, he gets a job as a busboy in Jackson's dancehall. When Jackson's jealous girl friend catches the bootlegger visiting Darktown's Cleopatra, she accuses him of the murder for which Eph is charged; Claude overhears the angry remark and immediately tries to apprehend Jackson, who escapes in a speedboat. Claude gives chase and captures him, taking him to the governor in time to save Eph from hanging. While at the state capitol, Claude, who is in love with the governor's daughter, obtains his permission to marry her. *Authors. Negroes. State governors. Revenue agents. Bootlegging. Murder. Injustice. Capital punishment. Frameup. Disguise. Dancehalls.*

HIS DOG **F2.2507**

De Mille Pictures. *Dist* Pathé Exchange. 25 Jul **1927** [c5 Jul 1927; LP24147]. Si; b&w. 35mm. 7 reels, 6,788 ft.

Pres by Walter Woods. *Supv* Walter Woods. *Dir* Karl Brown. *Adapt-Cont* Olga Printzlau. *Titl* John Krafft. *Photog* Fred Westerberg. *Art Dir*

Edward Jewell. *Supv Art Dir* Mitchell Leisen. *Film Ed* Margaret Darrell. *Asst Dir* William Scully. *Cost* Adrian.

Cast: Joseph Schildkraut *(Peter Olsen)*, Julia Faye *(Dorcas)*, Crauford Kent *(Mr. Gault)*, Sally Rand *(Marian Gault)*, Robert Edeson *(Colonel Marsden)*, Annabelle Magnus *(Olive)*, Fred Walton *(Chatham)*.

Melodrama. Source: Albert Payson Terhune, *His Dog* (New York, 1922). Peter Olsen, a young social outcast who lives alone on a rundown farm and raises vegetables for a living, finds his only consolation in liquor, though Dorcas Chatham, daughter of the general store owner, begs him to forego this indulgence. Returning from town, he finds a dog by the roadside, apparently injured by a car, and takes it home. Later, on a drunken spree, Peter is attacked by robbers, but the dog comes to his rescue and frightens the assailants away. Stirred by the unselfish devotion of his dog, Peter gradually regains his self-respect, and Dorcas falls in love with him and accepts his proposal, though she fears the dog. When Peter enters the dog in a show, another exhibitor proves to be its owner, and Peter is first parted from, then reunited with, "his" dog. Dorcas overcomes her fear and is united with Peter. *Truck farmers. Robbers. Alcoholism. Rural life. General stores. Dogs.*

HIS ENEMY'S DAUGHTER (Reissue) **F2.2508**

Dist Candler Pictures. 29 Jan **1921** [trade review]. Si; b&w. 35mm. [Feature length assumed.]

Note: Advertised as a reedited version of *A Modern Monte Cristo* (Pathe, 1917), but there is no apparent difference in story line.

HIS FIRST COMMAND **F2.2509**

Pathé Exchange. 28 Dec **1929** [c2 Feb 1930; LP1046]. Sd (Photophone); b&w with col sequences (Multicolor). 35mm. 7 reels, 5,850 ft. [Also si; 5,577 ft.]

Assoc Prod Ralph Block. *Dir* Gregory La Cava. *Story-Scen-Dial* Jack Jungmeyer, James Gleason. *Photog* Arthur Miller, John J. Mescall. *Art Dir* Edward Jewell. *Film Ed* Doane Harrison. *Rec Engr* Earl A. Wolcott, D. A. Cutler. *Asst Dir* Paul Jones. *Prod Mgr* Harry Poppe. *Tech Dir* Charles Maigne. *Tech Adv* Schuyler E. Grey.

Cast: William Boyd *(Terry Culver)*, Dorothy Sebastian *(Judy Gaylord)*, Gavin Gordon *(Lieutenant Allen)*, Helen Parrish *(Jame)*, Alphonse Ethier *(Colonel Gaylord)*, Howard Hickman *(Major Hall)*, Paul Hurst *(Sergeant Westbrook)*, Jules Cowles *(Corporal Jones)*, Rose Tapley *(Mrs. Pike)*, Mabel Van Buren *(Mrs. Sargent)*, Charles Moore *(Homer)*.

Romantic comedy-drama. Terry Culver, scapegrace son of the wealthy owner of the Culver Rubber Tire Co., is sent to Kansas to assume charge of a branch office, accompanied by Homer, a Negro chauffeur, who is to keep Terry straight and warn him against women. En route, Terry gives aid to Judy Gaylord, daughter of a colonel in the U. S. Cavalry. Later, at a reception, she is offended by his impudence and tells him she confines her romances to Army circles, thus causing him to enlist. Learning that Terry is responsible for the orchids she receives daily, she gives them to an officer to feed to his horse. With the help of Jane, Terry excels in the color guard, earning the secret admiration of Judy; but he incurs the jealousy of Lieutenant Allen and is arrested for striking him. Jane enters the steeplechase and is hurt in a fall; Terry rescues her but is knocked unconscious by another horse, awakening the sympathy of the colonel's daughter. *Soldiers. Chauffeurs. Military life. Horseracing. Automobile tires. Kansas. United States Army—Cavalry.*

HIS FIRST FLAME **F2.2510**

Mack Sennett Productions. *Dist* Pathé Exchange. 3 May **1927** [c6 Feb 1926; LU22377]. Si; b&w. 35mm. 6 reels, 4,700 ft.

Pres by Mack Sennett. *Dir* Harry Edwards. *Scen* Arthur Ripley, Frank Capra. *Photog* William Williams, Ernie Crockett.

Cast: Harry Langdon *(Harry Howells)*, Ruth Hiatt *(Mary Morgan)*, Natalie Kingston *(Ethel Morgan)*, Vernon Dent *(Amos McCarthy)*, Bud Jamieson *(Hector Benedict)*, Dot Farley *(Mrs. Benedict)*.

Farce. Returning home from college, Harry Howells becomes engaged to Mary Morgan, a young girl interested only in his money. Harry's uncle, the fire chief, breaks up the romance, and Helen Morgan, Mary's sister, sets out to win Harry's love. She sets her house on fire, and Harry rescues her. He falls in love with Helen and eventually leads her to the altar. *Firemen. Sisters. Uncles. Incendiarism. Fires.*

HIS FOREIGN WIFE **F2.2511**

William Wallace Cook. *Dist* Pathé Exchange. 27 Nov **1927** [c19 Jul 1927; LU24191]. Si; b&w. 35mm. 5 reels, 4,890 ft.

Dir-Writ John P. McCarthy. *Scen* Albert De Mond.

Cast: Greta von Rue *(Hilda Schultzenbach)*, Edna Murphy *(Mary Jackson)*, Wallace MacDonald *(Johnny Haines)*, Charles Clary *(The Mayor)*, Elsie Bishop *(Frau Schultzenbach)*, Lee Shumway.

Society drama. When the United States is drawn into the European conflict, Joe and Johnny Haines enlist and are sent to the front. Joe is killed, but his brother Johnny falls in love with a German girl while remaining with the United States Occupation Forces, marries her, and brings her to America. To his dismay, he finds that bitter prejudice against Germans makes his father hostile to his wife. When the father, a town official, is assigned to pin a decoration of bravery on his son, before an assembly Johnny denounces his father's sense of false patriotism and his inability to forget the past. Later, the father, realizing his error, forgives his son, and the family is happy once again. *War brides. Brothers. Germans. Prejudice. Chauvinism. Military occupation. World War I.*

HIS FORGOTTEN WIFE **F2.2512**

Palmer Photoplay Corp. *Dist* Film Booking Offices of America. 14 Apr **1924** [c14 Apr 1922; LP20078]. Si; b&w. 35mm. 6 reels, 6,500 ft.

Dir William Seiter. *Story-Screenplay* Will Lambert. *Adapt* Will Lambert, Del Andrews. *Photog* Max Dupont, Abe Fried.

Cast: Madge Bellamy *(Suzanne)*, Warner Baxter *(John Rolfe)*, Maude Wayne *(Corinne McRea)*, Hazel Keener *(Irene Humphrey)*, Tom Guise *(Judge Henry)*, Willis Marks *(Meadows)*, Eric Mayne *(French major)*.

Melodrama. During the World War, Donald Allen is reported killed in action but is really a victim of amnesia. His French nurse, Suzanne, gives him a new identity (John Rolfe), and they marry. Together they get jobs as servants on Donald's estate, now in the hands of Corinne, his ex-fiancée. He is recognized, and after an operation he regains his memory but forgets his wife. Corinne, in the meanwhile, attempts to run off with some of Donald's money but is foiled by Suzanne. Donald finally recognizes his wife. *Veterans. Nurses. Domestics. Personal identity. Amnesia. Brain surgery. World War I.*

Note: Copyright records render the name of the character Suzanne as Jane Loring. Working title: *Lost.*

HIS GLORIOUS NIGHT **F2.2513**

Metro-Goldwyn-Mayer Pictures. 28 Sep **1929** [c4 Nov 1929; LP839]. Sd (Movietone); b&w. 35mm. 9 reels, 7,173 ft. [Also si; 5,353 ft.]

Dir Lionel Barrymore. *Screenplay-Dial* Willard Mack. *Photog* Percy Hilburn. *Art Dir* Cedric Gibbons. *Film Ed* William Le Vanway. *Mus* Lionel Barrymore. *Mus Cond* William Axt. *Sd* Douglas Shearer. *Wardrobe* David Cox.

Cast: John Gilbert *(Captain Kovacs)*, Catherine Dale Owen *(Princess Orsolini)*, Nance O'Neil *(Eugenie)*, Gustav von Seyffertitz *(Krehl)*, Hedda Hopper *(Mrs. Collingswood Stratton)*, Doris Hill *(Priscilla Stratton)*, Tyrrell Davis *(Prince Luigi Caprilli)*, Gerald Barry *(Lord York)*, Madeline Seymour *(Lady York)*, Richard Carle *(Count Albert)*, Eva Dennison *(Countess Lina)*, Youcca Troubetzkoy *(Von Bergman)*, Peter Gawthorne *(General Ettingen)*.

Romantic drama. Source: Ferenc Molnár, *Olympia; vígjáték három felvonásban* (Budapest, c1928). Princess Orsolini, known to maintain an icy demeanor, has a marriage arranged for her by her royal parents, but quite suddenly she falls in love with Kovacs, a cavalry captain known for his mastery of horses and women. Though they meet secretly, her mother advises her to break off the affair, and she reluctantly informs the captain that she cannot love the son of a peasant. Kovacs spreads a rumor that he is is an imposter and swindler to avenge himself on the princess and her mother. Fearing scandal, the queen prevails upon the commissioner to bring him to their apartment so that they may retrieve some love letters written by the princess; but Kovacs names as his price the princess' spending the night in his quarters. He and the princess are reconciled. *Royalty. Imaginary kingdoms. Social classes.*

Note: In addition to original music composed for the film, orchestral selections include: "Light Cavalry Overture," by Franz von Suppé, "Hungarian Comedy Overture," by Keler-Bela, and "Radetzsky March," by Johann Strauss. Also produced in foreign-language versions: *Olimpia* (Spanish), *Olympia* (German), and *Si l'Empereur savait ça!* (French), q. v.

HIS GOOD NAME *see* **TRIFLING WITH HONOR**

HIS GREAT CHANCE **F2.2514**

Ben Strasser Productions. *Dist* North State Film Co. 26 May **1923** [scheduled release]. Si; b&w. 35mm. 5 reels, 4,680 ft.

Cast: Sandy Burns, Fannetta Burns, Bobby Smart, Tim Moore, Gertrude Moore, Fred Hart, Sam Russell, Mark Slater, Walter Long.

Comedy-drama(?). No information about the nature of this film has been found.

HIS GREATEST BATTLE **F2.2515**

Robert J. Horner Productions. *Dist* Aywon Film Corp. May **1925.** Si; b&w. 35mm. 5 reels, 4,900 ft.

Pres by Nathan Hirsh. *Dir* Robert J. Horner.

Cast: Jack Randall, Kit Carson, Jack Richardson, Pauline Curley, John Pringle, Gladys Moore, Louis Moniago.

Western melodrama(?). No information about the nature of this film has been found.

HIS GREATEST SACRIFICE **F2.2516**

Fox Film Corp. 17 Apr **1921** [c17 Apr 1921; LP16474]. Si; b&w. 35mm. 7 reels, 6,295 ft.

Pres by William Fox. *Dir* J. Gordon Edwards. *Story-Scen* Paul H. Sloane. *Photog* Harry L. Keepers.

Cast: William Farnum *(Richard Hall)*, Alice Fleming *(Alice Hall, his wife)*, Lorena Volare *(Grace Hall, his daughter)*, Evelyn Greeley *(Mrs. Oliver)*, Frank Goldsmith *(James Hamilton)*, Charles Wellesley *(John Reed)*, Edith McAlpin Benrimo *(Mrs. Hall, Richard's mother)*, Henry Leone *(Rimini)*.

Domestic tragedy. Richard Hall, a successful writer, is married to a woman intent on a singing career. She meets James Hamilton and through his influence is engaged to sing at the Opéra in Paris. Hall puts their child into his mother's care, but unable to endure the separation, he begs his wife to return. In a jealous rage, he kills Hamilton and is sentenced to life imprisonment. After 20 years, he is paroled and meets his daughter, Grace, secretary to philanthropist John Reed. Refusing aid, he is arrested as a suspicious character and begs to be returned to prison, but he is persuaded to live with his daughter and Reed when they marry. *Authors. Singers. Opera. Marriage. Parenthood. Murder. Parole. Paris.*

HIS HOUR **F2.2517**

Louis B. Mayer Productions. *Dist* Metro-Goldwyn Distributing Corp. 29 Sep **1924** [c23 Sep 1924; LP20635]. Si; b&w. 35mm. 7 reels, 6,300 ft.

Pres by Louis B. Mayer. *Supv* Elinor Glyn. *Dir* King Vidor. *Scen* Elinor Glyn. *Titl* King Vidor, Maude Fulton. *Photog* John Mescall. *Art Dir* Cedric Gibbons. *Asst Dir* David Howard. *Gowns* Sophie Wachner.

Cast: Aileen Pringle *(Tamara Loraine)*, John Gilbert *(Gritzko)*, Emily Fitzroy *(Princess Ardacheff)*, Lawrence Grant *(Stephen Strong)*, Dale Fuller *(Olga Gleboff)*, Mario Carillo *(Count Valonne)*, Jacquelin Gadsdon *(Tatiane Shebanoff)*, George Waggoner *(Sasha Basmanoff)*, Carrie Clark Ward *(Princess Murieska)*, Bertram Grassby *(Boris Varishkine)*, Jill Reties *(Sonia Zaieskine)*, Wilfred Gough *(Lord Courtney [Jack])*, Frederick Vroom *(English Minister)*, Mathilde Comont *(fat harem lady)*, E. Eliazaroff *(Khedive)*, David Mir *(Serge Grekoff)*, Bert Sprotte *(Ivan)*.

Melodrama. Source: Elinor Glyn, *His Hour* (New York, 1910). Tamara Loraine, a beautiful young Englishwoman, is attracted to Russian Prince Gritzko, who is famed for his many romantic affairs, when she meets him in Egypt and again in Russia. Gritzko is attentive, but Tamara remains distant so as not to be numbered among his conquests. When Gritzko wins a duel and the right to accompany Tamara to a ball, she decides to return to England. On their way to the ship during a snowstorm, Gritzko maneuvers Tamara to his lodge for shelter, and she resists his advances until she collapses from exhaustion. Gritzko then leaves her alone, but in the morning Tamara finds her waist opened (Gritzko wanted to know if her heart was beating) and believes that honor dictates that she marry him. After the ceremony, the prince offers to go away until sent for, but Tamara realizes their mutual, sincere love and bids him stay. *English. Nobility. Virtue. Russia. Egypt. Duels.*

HIS JAZZ BRIDE **F2.2518**

Warner Brothers Pictures. 15 Jan **1926** [c12 Dec 1925; LP22121]. Si; b&w. 35mm. 7 reels, 6,420 ft.

Dir Herman C. Raymaker. *Screenplay* Charles A. Logue, Walter Morosco. *Photog* David Abel. *Film Ed* Clarence Kolster.

Cast: Marie Prevost *(Gloria Gregory)*, Matt Moore *(Dick Gregory)*, Gayne Whitman, John Patrick, Mabel Julienne Scott, Stanley Wayburn, Don Alvarado, Helen Dunbar, George Irving, George Seddon.

Society melodrama. Source: Beatrice Burton, *The Flapper Wife* (New York, 1925). Dick Gregory, a young lawyer, is hard pressed to pay the bills of his wife, Gloria, and equally hard pressed to keep up with the frantic pace of her life. Edward Martindel, an attorney who represents a corporation against which Dick is litigating, attempts to bribe Dick with a substantial sum of money; Dick refuses, and Gloria develops a grievance against him on this account. After a particularly bitter argument, Gloria leaves Dick and joins some friends for a moonlight cruise. Alec Seymour, a friend of the Gregorys', tells Dick that the boat on which Gloria is sailing has not met safety standards, and Dick goes after her, saving her life when the boat sinks. Gloria repents of her wild and wicked ways, and she and Dick settle into calm domesticity. *Lawyers. Jazz life. Bribery. Marriage. Shipwrecks.*

HIS LAST BULLET **F2.2519**

Dist Krelbar Pictures, Collwyn Pictures. 19 Mar **1928** [New York State license]. Si; b&w. 35mm. 5 reels.

Cast: Al Hoxie.

Western melodrama(?). No information about the nature of this film has been found.

Note: May have been produced in 1926 by Anchor Film Distributors.

HIS LAST HAUL **F2.2520**

FBO Pictures. 11 Nov **1928** [c5 Nov 1928; LP25797]. Si; b&w. 35mm. 6 reels, 5,797 ft.

Dir Marshall Neilan. *Screenplay* W. Scott Darling. *Adtl Dial* Randolph Bartlett. *Story* Louis Sarecky. *Photog* Phil Tannura. *Film Ed* Mildred Richter. *Asst Dir* James Graham.

Cast: Tom Moore *(Joe Hammond)*, Seena Owen *(Blanche)*, Charles Mason *(Anthony Dugan)*, Al Roscoe *(fly cop)*, Henry Sedley *(blackmailer)*.

Underworld melodrama. Eluding the police, larcenous Joe Hammond joins a Salvation Army gathering, where, under the cold and watchful eye of Dugan the cop, he declares that he has forsaken the life of crime. Blanche, a Salvation Army lass and sometime blackmailer, congratulates Joe on his reformation, little knowing that within days Joe, disguised as Santa Claus, will again be robbing the rich. Joe and Blanche are later separately arrested and taken to the station house; before they are parted by iron bars, however, they make plans for a long, happy, and honest future together. *Police. Criminals—Rehabilitation. Salvation Army. Santa Claus.*

HIS LAST RACE **F2.2521**

Phil Goldstone Productions. Aug **1923** [scheduled release]. Si; b&w. 35mm. 6 reels, 5,800 ft.

Dir Reeves Eason, Howard Mitchell. *Photog* Jackson Rose. *Art Dir* Gustave Ertl.

Cast: Rex (Snowy) Baker *(Carleton)*, Gladys Brockwell *(Mary)*, William Scott *(Stewart)*, Harry Depp *(Denny)*, Pauline Starke *(Denny's wife)*, Robert McKim *(Tim Bresnahan)*, Noah Beery *(Packy Sloane)*, Boomerang *(himself, a horse)*, Tully Marshall *(Mr. Strong)*, King Baggot, Harry Burns, Dick Sutherland, Alec B. Francis *(see note)*.

Melodrama. Rejected suitor Dick Carleton seeks solace in the woods where he and some friends establish a health resort. After a time, Mary, his former sweetheart, arrives. She is now a widow whose son is in bad health. Her situation rekindles Carleton's affection and he enters a horserace to earn money so as to be able to marry her. A plot is formed against Carleton to annex his property and steal his horse. After numerous complications Carleton defeats his enemies, wins the race, and weds Mary. *Widows. Horseracing. Health resorts. Horses.*

Note: Cast *may* include Baggot, Burns, Sutherland, and Francis.

HIS LUCKY DAY **F2.2522**

Universal Pictures. 2 Jun **1929** [c1 Jun 1929; LP433]. Talking sequences (Movietone); b&w. 35mm. 6 reels, 6,731 ft. [Also si; 5,630 ft.]

Pres by Carl Laemmle. *Dir* Edward Cline. *Story-Scen* John B. Hymer, Gladys Lehman. *Titl* Albert De Mond. *Photog* Arthur Todd. *Film Ed* Ted Kent, Harry Marker.

Cast: Reginald Denny *(Charles Blaydon)*, Lorayne Du Val *(Kay Weaver)*, Otis Harlan *(Jerome Van Dyne)*, Eddie Phillips *(Spider)*, Cissy Fitzgerald *(dowager)*, Harvey Clarke *(Weaver)*, Tom O'Brien *(chauffeur)*.

Comedy. Charles Blaydon, a young real estate dealer, rents a fashionable suburban house to Weaver, a wealthy art collector, but is unable to sell it until another buyer purchases the neighboring house. As Charles is in love with Weaver's daughter, he is desperate to find a buyer and mistakes a gang of bank robbers who stop near the house as prospective tenants. That night Weaver invites them to his house, and Charles is horrified to find one of the guests stealing valuable curios, though Weaver is delighted with his new neighbors and will not believe that they are thieves. "Spider," posing as Van Dyne, takes Kay to a gang rendezvous; they are followed by Charles, who starts a row but manages to escape. The gangsters are recognized by the police; Charles, dressed as a black cat, frightens Van Dyne, arousing Kay and Weaver as the police arrive. Weaver agrees to buy both houses, and Charles is united with Kay. *Real estate agents. Art collectors. Thieves. Gangsters. Imposture. Courtship.*

HIS MAJESTY, BUNKER BEAN **F2.2523**

Warner Brothers Pictures. 19 Sep **1925** [c2 Sep 1925; LP21790]. Si; b&w. 35mm. 8 reels, 7,291 ft.

Dir Harry Beaumont. *Scen* Julien Josephson. *Photog* Byron Haskins. *Adtl Photog* Frank Kesson. *Asst Dir* William McGann.

Cast: Matt Moore *(Bunker Bean)*, Dorothy Devore *(Marie Breede)*, David Butler *(Bud Matthews)*, George Nichols *(Jim Breede)*, Helen Dunbar *(Mrs. Breede)*, Frank Leigh *(Professor Balthasar)*, Nora Cecil *(Countess Casanova)*, Henry Barrows *(Reginald Larabee)*, Gertrude Claire *(Grandma Breede)*, Lucille Ward *(Nurse)*, Gayne Whitman *(Bert Hollins)*.

Comedy. Source: Lee Wilson Dodd, *His Majesty, Bunker Bean; a Comedy in Four Acts and Five Scenes* (New York, 1922). Harry Leon Wilson, *Bunker Bean* (Garden City, New York, 1913). Bunker Bean, a poor clerk completely lacking in ambition, is convinced by two phony clairvoyants that he is the reincarnation of Ram Tah, an ancient Egyptian pharaoh. Feeling his own worth for the first time in his life, Bunker buys a phony mummy from the clairvoyants and starts to romance Marie Breede, the beautiful young daughter of his employer. She proposes to him, and they become engaged; but when Bunker's dog tears apart the mummy and reveals it to be a fake, Bunker loses his confidence and wants to call off the nuptials. He keeps his head, however, and gets into a fight with Bert Hollins, his rival for Marie's affections. Bunker wins the fight and, with renewed confidence, prepares to marry Marie, assured of her love and of her father's approval. *Clerks. Clairvoyants. Swindlers. Reincarnation. Courtship. Mummies. Dogs.*

HIS MAJESTY THE OUTLAW **F2.2524**

Ben Wilson Productions. *Dist* Arrow Film Corp. 22 Nov **1924** [29 Oct 1924; LP20809]. Si; b&w. 35mm. 5 reels, 5,089 ft.

Dir-Writ Jacques Jaccard.

Cast: Ben Wilson *(King Carson)*, Violet La Plante.

Western melodrama. King Carson, a rancher near Cochise City, is ordered to leave the Arizona Territory by iron-fisted Jeff Williams, an empire-builder embittered by the desertion of his wife and daughter years earlier. An itinerant theatrical troupe gives a performance in Cochise City, and Carson defiantly attends; when several of Williams' men throw rotten vegetables at the actors, he beats them in a fight. After the performance, Carson befriends a young actress who has fallen ill, taking her to the cave where he is hiding from Williams' gunmen. The girl's condition worsens, and Carson is forced to return to town for a doctor. He is caught by a lynch party led by Williams but escapes with the help of a small Mexican girl. He returns to the cave, followed closely by the mob. He is about to be killed when the young actress is identified as Williams' long-lost daughter. Carson and the grateful Williams are reconciled, and things look good for the honest rancher and the actress. *Ranchers. Actors. Mexicans. Theatrical troupes. Lynching. Arizona.*

HIS MASTER'S VOICE **F2.2525**

Gotham Productions. *Dist* Lumas Film Corp. Sep **1925** [c13 Oct 1925; LP21905]. Si; b&w. 35mm. 6 reels, 5,827 ft.

Pres by Sam Sax. *Dir* Renaud Hoffman. *Scen* Henry McCarty. *Adapt* James J. Tynan. *Story* Frank Foster Davis. *Photog* Jack MacKenzie. *Mus Setting* Joseph E. Zivelli. *Theme Song: "His Master's Voice"* Gus Edwards. *Lyr* Howard Johnson, Irving Bibo.

Cast: Thunder *(The Dog)*, George Hackathorne *(Bob Henley)*, Marjorie Daw *(Mary Blake)*, Mary Carr *(Mrs. Henley)*, Will Walling *(William Marshall)*, Brooks Benedict *(Jack Fenton)*, White Fawn *(The White Dog)*, Flash *("The Pup")*.

Melodrama. The upbringing of Robert Henley, architectural student, has made him a coward. Jack Fenton, his rival for the hand of Mary Blake, forges his name on plans for the new town library, which Bob has submitted in a competition. The World War breaks out, and Bob is sent to the front lines, while his dog, Thunder, is sent over in a Red Cross relief unit. Bob tries to desert, but Thunder finds him and brings him back. Sent on a dangerous mission behind enemy lines to blow up a mine, Bob is wounded; and the mission is completed by Thunder. Through Thunder's heroism, Bob is regenerated, joins the Air Corps, and becomes an aviation ace. Wounded, he meets Mary, who has become a nurse; and they renew their love. On his return home, he discovers Fenton's deception, gives him a sound thrashing, and restores his image in the eyes of the townspeople. *Architects. Nurses. Aviators. Cowardice. Libraries. World War I. Red Cross. United States Army—Air Corps. Dogs.*

HIS MYSTERY GIRL **F2.2526**

Universal Pictures. 4 Dec **1923** [c1 Dec 1923; LP19667]. Si; b&w. 35mm. 5 reels, 4,487 ft.

Dir Robert F. Hill. *Scen* William E. Wing. *Story* Marion Orth. *Photog* William Thornley.

Cast: Herbert Rawlinson *(Kerry Reynolds)*, Ruth Dwyer *(Gloria Bliss)*, Margaret Campbell *(Laurette Sligsby)*, Jere Austin *(Benn Bliss)*, Ralph Fee McCullough *(Dick Reynolds)*, William Quinn *(The Valet)*.

Comedy-melodrama. Kerry Reynolds' prankster friends trick him into thinking he has discovered a distressed damsel. After an adventure involving a diamond necklace he marries the girl, and all ends happily. *Mistaken identity. Hoaxes.*

Note: Working titles: *No Questions Asked; All for the Love of Gloria.*

HIS NEW YORK WIFE **F2.2527**

Preferred Pictures. 1 Nov **1926** [c1 Nov 1926; LP23280]. Si; b&w. 35mm. 6 reels, 5,294 ft.

Pres by J. G. Bachmann. *Dir* Albert Kelley. *Story-Cont* Leon Abrams. *Photog* Nicholas Musuraca.

Cast: Alice Day *(Lila Lake)*, Theodore von Eltz *(Philip Thorne)*, Ethel Clayton *(Alicia Duval)*, Fontaine La Rue *(Julia Hewitt)*, Charles Cruz *(Jimmy Duval)*, Edith Yorke *(Lila's aunt)*.

Romantic drama. Lured to New York with false promises of having her play produced, Lila Lake is forced to accept a secretarial position with Mrs. Julia Hewitt, a dashing young widow secretly married to Jimmy Duval, son of Alice Duval, a prominent society leader. Alice seeks the aid of young lawyer Philip Thorne, who hires detectives to follow Julia; the latter, however, has left town with Jimmy, and Lila has agreed to impersonate her. Thorne, who has previously met Lila, and is unaware of her situation, rescues her from the detectives, and through a misunderstanding they are both arrested and are subsequently disillusioned in each other. Jimmy, however, achieves a reconciliation between his wife and mother, and when Thorne discovers his mistake, he is happily united with Lila. *Playwrights. Secretaries. Lawyers. Detectives. Filial relations. Marriage. Impersonation.*

HIS NIBS **F2.2528**

Exceptional Pictures. *Dist* "His Nibs" Syndicate. 22 Oct **1921** [trade review; c14 Jan 1922; LP17458]. Si; b&w. 35mm. 5 reels, 5,145 ft.

Dir Gregory La Cava. *Titl* Arthur Hoerl. *Photog* William Tuers, A. J. Stout. *Film Ed* Arthur Hoerl.

Cast: Charles (Chic) Sale *(Theo. Bender, "His Nibs"/Wally Craw, local weather prophet/Mr. Percifer, editor of The Weekly Bee/Elmer Bender/Peelee Gear, Jr., boy tenor/Miss Dessie Teed, village organist/The Boy, hero of "He Fooled 'Em All")*, Colleen Moore *(The Girl)*, Joseph Dowling *(The Girl's Father)*, J. P. Lockney *(Old Sour Apples)*, Walt Whitman *(The Boy's Father)*, Lydia Yeamans Titus *(The Boy's Mother)*, Harry Edwards *(First Villain)*.

Rural comedy. At the Slippery Elm Picture Palace, an old-fashioned movie house, various humorous rural types are seen—the girl at the piano, the local editor, the tenor singer, *et al.* "His Nibs," the owner and operator, is at his projection machine and informs the audience that he has cut the titles from the film to be shown but will explain the action as it unfolds in the story "He Fooled 'Em All." *The Boy leaves a small town to get rich in the city, but he is swindled out of his money, his clothes are stolen, and he is forced to become a dishwasher to pay his rent. The city chap persuades The Girl and The Girl's Father to visit the city, hoping to swindle them, but they stay at the hotel where The Boy is working, and he tracks the swindlers and obstructs the plot.* Having eliminated the customary happy ending, "His Nibs" tells the audience that The Boy and The Girl get married just the same. *Motion pictures. Motion picture theaters. Rural life.*

Note: In Oct 1921, during the film's first-run engagements, all United States rights were purchased from Exceptional Pictures by "His Nibs" Syndicate.

HIS OWN LAW **F2.2529**

Sable Productions. c23 Oct, 5 Nov **1924** [LU20741]. Si; b&w. 35mm. 5 reels.

Copyright Auth George Hively.

Cast: Wesley Barry.

Western melodrama. Itinerant photographer Dave Shipley stops at Dad Emerson's sheep ranch and stays to help him and his children, Buddy and Mary, resist Blackie Duncan's efforts to take over the ranch, which is the cattlemen's only access to the border. Buddy falls into Duncan's hands, but he cleverly escapes and warns Dave of the villain's intention to raid the ranch. A pitched battle ensues while Buddy brings friendly cattlemen to the rescue. Dave produces photographs of Duncan and his men rustling cattle, of which Dad Emerson has been accused, and wins Mary as a reward. *Cattlemen. Photographers. Ranchers. Rustling. Mexican border.*

HIS PAJAMA GIRL **F2.2530**

Dist C. B. Price Films. 21 May **1921** [trade review]. Si; b&w. 35mm. 5 reels, 4,500 ft.

Cast: Billie Rhodes *("Dolly" Dodd)*, Harry Rattenberry *(Henry Dodd)*, Harry Edwards *(Blakie Jones)*, George French *(The Deacon)*, Eddie Barry *(Peter Johnson)*, Nigel De Brulier *(Manuel Lopez)*, Harry Hamm *(Harry)*.

Comedy-drama. "Dolly" Dodd's dad forbids her to have gentlemen callers. But Secret Service man Harry, working on a drug smuggling case involving the kidnaping of the Mexican president, manages to meet Dolly, who falls in love with him at first sight. Dolly's father becomes involved when the crooks bribe him to put up money in return for concessions. The scheme fails, and Harry tracks and arrests the crooks, who quickly escape. When Dolly and Harry marry, her friends lure him away and shut her up in a folding bed, which is then sent to Harry's friend Peter. A chaotic chase culminates with Harry and friends falling through a skylight into the crooks' hideout. *Mexicans. Presidents. Secret service. Filial relations. Smuggling. Bribery. Kidnaping. Narcotics. Chases.*

HIS PEOPLE (Universal-Jewel) **F2.2531**

Universal Pictures. 1 Nov **1925** [New York premiere; released 27 Dec; c17 Nov 1925; LP22021]. Si; b&w. 35mm. 9 reels, 8,983 ft.

Pres by Carl Laemmle. *Dir* Edward Sloman. *Adapt-Cont* Charles E. Whittaker, Alfred A. Cohn. *Titl* Alfred A. Cohn. *Story* Isadore Bernstein. *Photog* Max Dupont. *Mus Score* Edward Kilenyi.

Cast: Rudolph Schildkraut *(Rabbi David Cominsky)*, Rosa Rosanova *(Rosie Cominsky)*, George Lewis *(Sammy Cominsky [grown])*, Bobby Gordon *(Sammy Cominsky [child])*, Arthur Lubin *(Morris Cominsky [grown])*, Albert Bushaland *(Morris Cominsky [child])*, Blanche Mehaffey *(Mamie Shannon [grown])*, Jean Johnson *(Mamie Shannon [child])*, Kate Price *(Kate Shannon)*, Virginia Brown Faire *(Ruth Stein)*, Nat Carr *(Chaim Barowitz)*, Bertram Marburgh *(Judge Nathan Stein)*, Edgar Kennedy *(Thomas Nolan)*, Charles Sullivan *(The Champion)*, Sidney Franklin *(Levensky)*.

Domestic melodrama. Rabbi Cominsky, the father of two sons, ekes out a living in New York's Lower East Side as a pushcart peddler. He favors the studious and ambitious Morris, the elder, who wants to be a lawyer, rather than the loyal Sammy, who sells papers and who helps put his older brother through college. Cominsky finds out that Sammy has become a prizefighter under the name "Battling Rooney" and drives him out of the house. Morris demands that his father buy him a dress suit, so Cominsky pawns his overcoat to get one (which Morris throws in an ashcan) and becomes seriously ill from exposure to the cold. Cominsky passes the crisis but is told he must go to a warmer climate. Morris, meanwhile, has become engaged to marry Ruth Stein, his boss's daughter, but is ashamed of his parentage. Cominsky arrives at the engagement party, and Morris refuses to acknowledge his own father. Sammy, after winning the lightweight championship, faces up to his brother, denounces him, and drags him home. Morris, realizing his sin, begs and receives forgiveness. Cominsky acknowledges his gratitude to Sammy and gives his blessing to Sammy's Irish sweetheart, Mamie. *Jews. Irish. Rabbis. Prizefighters. Peddlers. Family life. New York City—Lower East Side.*

Note: Initially shown under the title: *Proud Heart*. Working titles: *The Jew* and *His People*.

HIS PRIVATE LIFE **F2.2532**

Paramount Famous Lasky Corp. 17 Nov **1928** [c16 Nov 1928; LP25841]. Si; b&w. 35mm. 5 reels, 4,690 ft.

Dir Frank Tuttle. *Scen* Ethel Doherty. *Titl* George Marion. *Story* Keene Thompson, Ernest Vajda. *Photog* Henry Gerrard. *Film Ed* Verna Willis.

Cast: Adolphe Menjou *(Georges St. Germain)*, Kathryn Carver *(Eleanor Trent)*, Margaret Livingston *(Yvette Bérgère)*, Eugene Pallette *(Henri Bérgère)*, André Cheron *(Maurice)*, Sybil Grove *(maid)*, Paul Guertzman *(stupid boy)*, Alex Melesh *(salesman)*, Alex Woloshin *(hotel clerk)*.

Romantic comedy. Georges St. Germain, a suave Parisian boulevardier, is attracted to Eleanor Kent, a cute American, and discovers that she is a close friend of Yvette Bérgère, Georges' onetime fiancée and the wife of corpulent, insanely jealous Henri Bérgère. In an effort to be near Eleanor, Georges takes up residence in Bérgère's hotel, leading Yvette to believe that he is attempting to renew their affair. Georges and Eleanor eventually come to love each other, despite the assorted lusts, vanities, and jealousies of the Bérgères. *Men-about-town. Jealousy. Courtship. Paris.*

HIS RISE TO FAME **F2.2533**

Excellent Pictures. 15 Feb **1927** [c4 Feb 1927; LP23656]. Si; b&w. 35mm. 6 reels, 5,790 ft.

Pres by Samuel Zierler. *Dir* Bernard McEveety. *Story* Victoria Moore. *Photog* Marcel Le Picard.

Cast: George Walsh *(Jerry Drake)*, Peggy Shaw *(Laura White)*, Bradley Barker *(Hubert Strief)*, Mildred Reardon *(Helen Lee)*, Martha Petelle *("Ma" Drake)*, William Nally *(Montana Mack)*, Ivan Linow *(Bull Vickers)*.

Melodrama. Jerry, a ne'er-do-well, after losing his latest job, drifts into a cabaret and meets Laura White, a dancer. Hubert Strief, a crooked fight promoter, who also desires Laura, has one of his thugs work over Jerry; as a result the boy shamefully reviews his life—his laziness and neglect of his mother. He obtains a job as helper in Montana Mack's gymnasium and after lengthy training proves himself a skillful fighter; but through the treachery of Strief, he is knocked out and sent to a sanitarium. Regaining his memory, he escapes and thrashes the villains, who are holding Laura against her will. In the climactic fight, Jerry wins the championship and the love of the girl. *Dancers. Ne'er-do-wells. Prizefighters. Fight promoters. Sanitariums. Gymnasiums.*

HIS SECRETARY **F2.2534**

Metro-Goldwyn-Mayer Pictures. 6 Dec **1925** [c11 Jan 1926; LP22258]. Si; b&w. 35mm. 7 reels, 6,433 ft.

Dir Hobart Henley. *Scen* Louis D. Lighton, Hope Loring. *Titl* Joseph W. Farnham. *Story* Carey Wilson. *Photog* Ben Reynolds. *Art Dir* Cedric Gibbons, Richard Day. *Film Ed* Frank Davis. *Wardrobe* Clement Andréani.

Cast: Norma Shearer *(Ruth Lawrence)*, Lew Cody *(David Colman)*, Willard Louis *(John Sloden)*, Karl Dane *(janitor)*, Gwen Lee *(Clara Bayne)*, Mabel Van Buren *(Mrs. Sloden)*, Estelle Clark *(Minnie)*, Ernest Gillen *(head clerk)*.

Comedy. Ruth Lawrence, a plain and severe girl, works as a stenographer for the firm of Colman and Sloden, and quietly she falls in love with David Colman, the handsome junior partner. Sloden's wife catches him flirting with his beautiful secretary, and, as a joke, Colman arranges for Ruth to accompany Sloden on a business trip to Washington. Ruth overhears Colman remark that he would not kiss her for $1,000 and, stung to the quick, goes to a beautician who transforms her into a beautiful young woman. Colman falls for her, and Ruth arranges a little practical joke on him: when he kisses her, she has the janitor walk in on them and claim to be her husband. Ruth extorts $1,000 from Colman and then, letting him in on the fun, declares her love for him. *Stenographers. Janitors. Cosmetologists. Partnerships. Courtship. Washington (District of Columbia).*

HIS SUPREME MOMENT **F2.2535**

Samuel Goldwyn Productions. *Dist* First National Pictures. 3 May **1925** [c15 Apr 1925; LP21360]. Si; b&w with col sequences (Technicolor). 35mm. 8 reels, 6,500 ft.

Pres by Samuel Goldwyn. *Dir* George Fitzmaurice. *Adapt* Frances Marion. *Photog* Arthur Miller.

Cast: Blanche Sweet *(Carla King)*, Ronald Colman *(John Douglas)*, Kathleen Myers *(Sara Deeping)*, Belle Bennett *(Carla Light)*, Cyril Chadwick *(Harry Avon)*, Ned Sparks *(Adrian)*, Nick De Ruiz *(Mueva)*.

Drama. Source: May Edginton, "World Without End" (publication undetermined). John Douglas, a mining engineer who has returned from South America in order to obtain financing for a goldmining venture, attends the theater with Sara Deeping and falls madly in love with Carla King, the star of the play. Sara becomes jealous but nevertheless secretly arranges the financing for John's mine. John proposes to Carla, and she agrees to marry him only if they first live together for a year like brother and sister. John consents, and he and Carla go to South America, where Carla is severely depressed by the rough, isolated surroundings. John finally attempts to embrace her in passion, and the gulf between them widens. Carla saves John's life during a labor dispute and then becomes ill with fever. Sara appears and persuades John and Carla that their platonic experiment has failed; Sara then arranges for them to return to New York, where John becomes infatuated with Sara. Carla agrees to marry a millionaire named Avon in return for Avon's promise to back John. John learns of her noble sacrifice, prevents the marriage to Avon, arranges independent financing for the mine, and returns to South America with Carla. *Engineers—Mining. Actors. Millionaires. Platonic love. Strikes. Gold mines. South America. New York City.*

HIS TIGER LADY **F2.2536**

Paramount Famous Lasky Corp. ca26 May **1928** [New York premiere; released 9 Jun; c9 Jun 1928; LP25353]. Si; b&w. 35mm. 5 reels, 4,998 ft. [Copyrighted as 6 reels, 5,038 ft.]

Pres by Adolph Zukor, Jesse L. Lasky. *Dir* Hobart Henley. *Titl* Herman J. Mankiewicz. *Adapt* Ernest Vajda. *Photog* Harry Fischbeck. *Film Ed* Alyson Shaffer. *Wardrobe* Travis Banton. *Circus Animals* Al G. Barnes.

Cast: Adolphe Menjou *(Henri, the "super")*, Evelyn Brent *(The Tiger Lady)*, Rose Dione *(Madame Duval)*, Emil Chautard *(stage manager)*, Mario Carillo *(The Duke)*, Leonardo De Vesa *(The Count)*, Jules Rancourt *(The Marquis)*, Jewel *(herself, an elephant)*, Pocahontas *(herself, a tiger)*.

Society melodrama. Source: Alfred Savoir, *La Grande-duchesse et le garçon d'etage, comédie en trois actes* (Paris, 1925). Henri, a stage "super," plays an extra in a Folies revue whose job is to sit astride an elephant in a rajah's costume, and he falls in love with a beautiful and haughty duchess, a regular patron who is fascinated with the tigers in the revue. To win her, Henri appears dressed in the rajah's costume at the restaurant that she and her admirers frequent. Henri arouses her interest, then finally her love when he shows tremendous courage before the tigers; then he admits to being a sham and confesses that the tiger whose cage he entered was dead. The next day she proves her love by joining the chorus line. *Stagehands. Actors. Theatrical extras. Nobility. Imposture. Paris. Folies-Bergère. Tigers. Elephants.*

HIS TRUST *see* **DARING CHANCES**

HIS WIFE'S HUSBAND **F2.2537**

Pyramid Pictures. *Dist* American Releasing Corp. 14 May **1922** [c14 Jun 1922; LP18208]. Si; b&w. 35mm. 6 reels, 6,092 ft.

Dir-Adapt Kenneth Webb. *Scen* Dorothy Farnum. *Photog* Harry Stradling.

Cast: Betty Blythe *(Olympia Brewster)*, Huntley Gordon *(George Packard)*, Arthur Carewe *(John Brainerd)*, George Fawcett *(Dominick Duffy)*, Grace Goodall *(Bess)*, Blanche Davenport *(Mrs. Althorpe)*, Rita Maurice *(Baby Packard)*.

Society melodrama. Source: Anna Katharine Green, *The Mayor's Wife* (Indianapolis, 1907). Olympia Brewster marries John Brainerd to escape a life of drudgery and immediately realizes that he does not love her but only desires her physically. She leaves a suicide note, starts for her uncle's home, pausing only to see a woman shoot at her husband, apparently fatally. Some years later she marries George Packard, a successful lawyer who becomes mayor. A private secretary whom he hires turns out to be Brainerd, who blackmails Packard into rejecting a nomination for governor. But just as he is starting his speech, Olympia finds proof that Brainerd was already married when he married her. *Lawyers. Mayors. Politicians. Bigamy. Suicide. Blackmail.*

HIT AND RUN **F2.2538**

Universal Pictures. 10 Aug **1924** [c14 Jul 1924; LP20389]. Si; b&w. 35mm. 6 reels, 5,508 ft.

Dir Edward Sedgwick. *Story-Scen* Edward Sedgwick, Raymond L. Schrock. *Photog* Virgil Miller.

Cast: Hoot Gibson *("Swat" Anderson)*, Marion Harlan *(Joan McCarthy)*, Cyril Ring *(George Collins)*, Harold Goodwin *(Tex Adams)*, De Witt Jennings *(Joe Burns)*, Mike Donlin *(Red McCarthy)*, William A. Steele *(The Gopher)*.

Comedy-drama. Big league baseball scout Red McCarthy signs up "Swat," a bush leaguer from a desert town, and Swat becomes a success because of his exceptional hitting. When Swat begins a romance with the scout's daughter, he and the girl are kidnaped by gamblers intent on winning the series, but the hero escapes in time to score a home run. *Baseball scouts. Gamblers. Baseball.*

HIT OF THE SHOW **F2.2539**

FBO Pictures. 23 Sep **1928** [c4 Sep 1928; LP25580]. Talking sequences (Photophone); b&w. 35mm. 7 reels, 6,476 ft. [Also si.]

Dir Ralph Ince. *Cont* Enid Hibbard. *Dial* Edgar Allan Woolf. *Titl* George Arthur, Jack Conway (of *Variety*). *Photog* Robert Martin. *Film Ed* George Arthur. *Song: "You're in Love and I'm in Love"* Walter Donaldson. *Song: "Waitin' for Katie"* Gus Kahn, Ted Shapiro. *Asst Dir* Thomas Atkins.

Cast: Joe E. Brown *("Twisty")*, Gertrude Olmstead *(Kathlyn Carson)*, William Norton Bailey *(Tremaine)*, Gertrude Astor *(Trece)*, Ole M. Ness *(Goldstein)*, Lee Shumway *(Greening)*, William Francis Dugan *(Teague)*, Ione Holmes *(Charlotte Van)*, LeRoy Mason *(Woody)*, Frank Mills *(Barnes)*, Daphne Pollard *(The Slavey)*, Cosmo Kyrle Bellew *(Mr. Carson)*.

Melodrama. Source: Viola Brothers Shore, "Notices" (publication undetermined). After 15 years of hard work, "Twisty," a stage comedian, finally gets a chance to make the big time when he is called in for an interview with Greening, a prominent theatrical producer. Twisty meets Kathlyn Carson in Greening's office, however, and taken with the girl's charms, forgets about the interview and leaves with her instead. Taking her under his wing, he finds her a place to stay and a part in a show. On the show's opening night, Twisty gets into a fight with the leading man and knocks him cold; the show goes on, however, for Twisty dons the man's makeup and plays his part to perfection. He becomes the hit of the show, but the strain is too much for his weak heart, and he dies shortly after the last curtain. *Actors. Theatrical producers. Theater. Heart disease. New York City—Broadway.*

HIT THE DECK **F2.2540**

RKO Productions. 14 Jan **1930** [New York premiere; released 23 Feb; c13 Jan 1930; LP1083]. Sd (Photophone); b&w with col sequences (Technicolor). 35mm. 12 reels, 9,327 ft.

Dir-Adapt Luther Reed. *Photog* Robert Kurrle. *Set Dsgn* Max Ree. *Mus Dir* Victor Baravalle. *Songs: "Sometimes I'm Happy," "Hallelujah"* Leo Robin, Clifford Grey, Vincent Youmans. *Song: "Keeping Myself for You"* Sidney Clare, Vincent Youmans. *Dance Dir* Pearl Eaton. *Rec Engr* Hugh McDowell. *Asst Dir* Frederick Fleck. *Cost* Max Ree.

Cast: Jack Oakie *(Bilge)*, Polly Walker *(Looloo)*, Roger Gray *(Mat)*, Franker Woods *(Bat)*, Harry Sweet *(Bunny)*, Marguerita Padula *(Lavinia)*, June Clyde *(Toddy)*, Wallace MacDonald *(Lieutenant Allen)*, George Ovey *(Clarence)*, Ethel Clayton *(Mrs. Payne)*, Nate Slott *(Dan)*, Andy Clark *(Dinty)*, Del Henderson *(Admiral)*, Charles Sullivan *(Lieut. Jim Smith)*.

Musical comedy–revue. Source: Vincent Youmans, *Hit the Deck* (New York opening: 25 Apr 1927). Hubert Osborne, *Shore Leave, a Sea-goin' Comedy in Three Acts* (New York opening: 8 Aug 1922). When the U. S. Fleet returns from a cruise, sailors congregate at Looloo's coffeeshop. Mrs. Payne, a wealthy society matron, drops into the shop with Admiral Payne and Lieutenant Allen and shows an interest in Looloo's heirloom necklace. Later, Bilge Smith arrives with Clarence, Lavinia's runaway sweetheart, and promptly falls for Looloo, to whom he reveals his ambitions to captain his own ship; but he is carried off by his shipmates. Looloo sells the necklace to Mrs. Payne to help Bilge; and when the fleet returns, the shop has been converted into a "home." To find her sweetheart, Looloo arranges with Mrs. Payne to give a party for the men. She accepts Bilge's proposal; he is offended at her offering him money to help him obtain his own ship; and he leaves but returns to her after being ousted from the service. When Looloo convinces him that she no longer has any money, they plan to marry. *Sailors. Courtship. Wealth. Coffeeshops. United States Navy.*

HOGAN'S ALLEY **F2.2541**

Warner Brothers Pictures. 12 Dec **1925** [c7 Nov 1925; LP21983]. Si; b&w. 35mm. 7 reels, 6,875 ft.

Dir Roy Del Ruth. *Adapt* Darryl Francis Zanuck. *Camera* Charles Van Enger. *Asst Camera* Willard Van Enger. *Film Ed* Clarence Kolster. *Asst Dir* Ross Lederman.

Cast: Monte Blue *(Lefty O'Brien)*, Patsy Ruth Miller *(Patsy Ryan)*, Willard Louis *(Michael Ryan)*, Louise Fazenda *(Dolly)*, Ben Turpin *(a stranger)*, Charles Conklin *(his friend)*, Max Davidson *(Jewish clothier [Abie O'Murphy])*, Herbert Spencer Griswold *("The Texas Kid")*, Frank Hagney *(Battling Savage)*, Nigel Barrie *(Dr. Emmett Franklin)*, Mary Carr *(Mother Ryan)*, Frank Bond *(Al Murphy)*.

Action melodrama. Source: Gregory Rogers, "Hogan's Alley" (publication undetermined). Lefty O'Brien, a pugilist, becomes engaged to ex-tomboy Patsy Ryan against the wishes of her father, Michael. They both live in an Irish-Jewish neighborhood on New York's East Side known as "Hogan's Alley." Lefty defeats Battling Savage for the championship, breaking his left hand and leaving his opponent close to death. Lefty seeks refuge from apprehension by the police, but Michael turns out both Lefty and Patsy. Patsy is injured, and Michael calls in wealthy Dr. Emmett Franklin, who takes more than a professional interest in Patsy. He invites Michael and Patsy to a dinner that turns into a wild party. Lefty breaks in, and Patsy returns his ring. The doctor invites father and daughter to his mountain lodge, but he leaves Michael stranded at the station. Michael and Lefty pursue the train in an automobile. The car and train collide, and the engineer abandons the train, leaving a part of it to run away. Lefty rescues Patsy with the aid of an airplane; the two settle down to married life and, to Michael's pleasure, make their fortune in plumbing. *Plumbers. Physicians. Irish. Jews. Boxing. New York City—East Side. Train wrecks.*

HOLD 'EM YALE! **F2.2542**

De Mille Pictures. *Dist* Pathé Exchange. 14 May **1928** [c14 Apr 1928; LP25186]. Si; b&w. 35mm. 8 reels, 7,056 ft.

Hector Turnbull Production. *Dir* Edward H. Griffith. *Scen* George Dromgold, Sanford Hewitt. *Titl* John Krafft. *Adapt* George Dromgold. *Photog* Arthur Miller. *Art Dir* Anton Grot. *Film Ed* Harold McLernon. *Asst Dir* Richard Blaydon.

Cast: Rod La Rocque *(Jaime Emmanuel Alvarado Montez)*, Jeanette Loff *(Helen)*, Hugh Allan *(Oscar)*, Joseph Cawthorn *(professor)*, Tom Kennedy *(detective)*, Jerry Mandy *(valet)*.

Farce. Source: Owen Davis, *Life at Yale* (a play; c1906). An Agentinean named Montez goes to Yale with his pet monkey and there he is a great success, especially with one professor's daughter. He becomes a football hero by winning the game against Princeton in the last few minutes of play. Throughout, a halfwitted detective trails Montez because he believes Montez is wanted for something. *Argentineans. Detectives. Halfwits. College life. Football. Yale University. Princeton University. Monkeys.*

Note: Also reviewed as *At Yale.*

HOLD EVERYTHING **F2.2543**

Warner Brothers Pictures. 20 Mar **1930** [New York premiere; released 1 May; c14 Apr 1930; LP1224]. Sd (Vitaphone); col (Technicolor). 35mm. 10 reels, 7,513 ft. [Also si.]

Dir Roy Del Ruth. *Screenplay* Robert Lord. *Photog* Dev Jennings. *Film Ed* William Holmes. *Songs: "Take It On the Chin," "When Little Red Roses Get the Blues for You," "Sing a Little Theme Song," "Physically Fit," "Isn't This a Cock-eyed World?" "Girls We Remember," "All Alone Together"* Al Dubin, Joe Burke. *Rec Engr* Glenn E. Rominger.

Cast: Joe E. Brown *(Gink Schiner)*, Winnie Lightner *(Totts Breen)*, Georges Carpentier *(Georges La Verne)*, Sally O'Neil *(Sue Burke)*, Edmund Breese *(Pop O'Keefe)*, Bert Roach *(Nosey Bartlett)*, Dorothy Revier *(Norine Lloyd)*, Jack Curtis *(Murph Levy)*, Tony Stabeneau *(Bob Morgan)*, Lew Harvey *(Dan Larkin)*, Jimmie Quinn *(The Kicker)*.

Musical comedy. Source: Buddy De Sylva, John McGowan, Ray Henderson, and Lew Brown, *Hold Everything* (New York opening: 10 Oct 1928). At a training camp preparing for a heavyweight championship bout are Georges La Verne with Pop O'Keefe, his manager; Nosey Bartlett, the camp cook; and Gink Schiner, a lazy, second-rate fighter who is to appear in a preliminary before the big fight. Although Georges is pursued by society girl Norine Lloyd, he is more interested in Sue Burke, his advisor and childhood playmate; Toots, Gink's sweetheart, is constantly concerned over Gink's flirting with pretty girls. Larkin, manager of champion Bob Morgan, comes to the camp and attempts to have the fight "fixed," but O'Keefe informs him Georges will do his best. The Kicker is delegated by Larkin to incapacitate Georges at a party with a knockout pill, but Gink switches his drink with Nosey's. To everyone's surprise, Gink wins his bout. Before his fight, Georges is accosted by Morgan, and he fares badly in the ring until, with a change of tactics, he knocks out Morgan and wins the title. *Prizefighters. Cooks. Fight managers. Courtship.*

HOLD THAT LION **F2.2544**

Douglas MacLean Productions. *Dist* Paramount Pictures. 4 Sep **1926** [New York premiere; released 27 Sep; c24 Sep 1926; LP23152]. Si; b&w. 35mm. 6 reels, 5,811 ft.

Pres by Adolph Zukor, Jesse L. Lasky. *Dir* William Beaudine. *Scen* Joseph Franklin Poland. *Story* Rosalie Mulhall. *Photog* Jack MacKenzie.

Cast: Douglas MacLean *(Jimmie [Daniel?] Hastings)*, Walter Hiers *(Dick Warren)*, Constance Howard *(Marjorie Brand)*, Cyril Chadwick *(H. Horace Smythe)*, Wade Boteler *(Andrew MacTavish)*, George C. Pearce *(Professor Brand)*.

Farce. Jimmie Hastings, an impulsively romantic youth, falls madly in love with Marjorie Brand and, accompanied by his pal, Dick Warren, follows her and her father on a round-the-world trip. After many adventures he encounters her in East Africa, and she promises him the first dance at a hotel ball. A rip in his trousers forces him to take cover in a Scottish kilt, and complications follow from his efforts to live up to his disguise. Marjorie invites him to join a "cat" hunt her father has organized, and he happily accepts her invitation. Caught up in a jungle safari, Hastings plays hide-and-seek with hungry lions, ending with his capturing a cat that accidentally gets entangled in a net. Hastings thus proves his "heroism" and wins the girl. *Courtship. Safaris. Big game. Africa. Lions.*

Note: Working titles: *Ladies First, Hunting Trouble*

HOLD YOUR BREATH **F2.2545**

Christie Film Co. *Dist* W. W. Hodkinson Corp. 25 May **1924** [c25 May 1924; LP20299]. Si; b&w. 35mm. 6 reels, 5,900 ft.

Dir Scott Sidney. *Story* Frank Roland Conklin. *Photog* Gus Peterson, Alex Phillips. *Tech Dir* Tom Brierley.

Cast: Dorothy Devore *(The Girl)*, Walter Hiers *(Her Fiancé)*, Tully Marshall *(The Eccentric Collector)*, Jimmie Adams *(beauty parlor proprietor)*, Priscilla Bonner *(The Sister)*, Jimmy Harrison *(Her Husband)*, Lincoln Plumer *(city editor)*, Patricia Palmer *(hairdresser)*, Rosa Gore *(customer)*, Jay Belasco *(another customer)*, George Pierce *(The Mayor)*, Victor Rodman *(oil salesman)*, Budd Fine *(policeman)*, Eddie Baker *(detective)*, Max Davidson *(street merchant)*.

Comedy. When her brother Dick loses his job and she herself is discharged from a beauty parlor, Dorothy decides to take his job as a reporter. After muffing several assignments, she succeeds in interviewing an eccentric collector, who allows her to see a $50,000 bracelet. When a monkey grabs it from a window, she chases him up a skyscraper and recovers the bracelet. *Reporters. Collectors. Brother-sister relationship. Beauty shops. Monkeys.*

HOLD YOUR HORSES **F2.2546**

Goldwyn Pictures. 28 Jan **1921** [trade review; c20 Dec 1920; LP15976]. Si; b&w. 35mm. 5 reels.

Dir E. Mason Hopper. *Scen* Gerald C. Duffy. *Photog* John Mescall.

Cast: Tom Moore *(Daniel Canavan)*, Sylvia Ashton *(Honora Canavan)*, Naomi Childers *(Beatrice Newness)*, Bertram Grassby *(Rodman Cadbury)*, Mortimer E. Stinson *(Jim James)*, Sydney Ainsworth *(Horace Slayton)*.

Comedy. Source: Rupert Hughes, "Canavan, the Man Who Had His Way," in *Long Ever Ago* (New York, 1918). Dan Canavan, a raw immigrant from Ireland, goes from streetcleaner to husband of society belle Beatrice Newness. As a streetcleaner he is trampled by horses drawing the Newness victoria. The accident leaves on his chest a scar in the shape of a horseshoe that perpetually brings him good luck. He finds he can control the world with the wave of a red flag. He makes this power the basis of his philosophy of life, and becoming a politician, he rises quickly to the position of czar of the city. He takes as his wife the woman whose horses once trampled him. When, however, she tires of his boorish, lower class manner and is about to leave him, he again waves the red flag and she is made to see his intrinsic worth beyond superficial manifestation. *Irish. Immigrants. Streetcleaners. Politicians. Socialites. Social classes. Talismans. Victorias. Horses.*

HOLD YOUR MAN **F2.2547**

Universal Pictures. 15 Sep **1929** [c7 Sep 1929; LP676]. Sd (Movietone); b&w. 35mm. 6 reels, 5,794 ft. [Also si; 5,023 ft.]

Dir Emmett J. Flynn. *Cont-Dial* Harold Shumate. *Story* Maxine Alton. *Photog* Gilbert Warrenton. *Film Ed* Jack English.

Cast: Laura La Plante *(Mary)*, Walter (Scott) Kolk *(Jack)*, Eugene Borden *(Beno)*, Mildred Van Dorn *(Rhea)*, Walter F. Scott.

Romantic comedy-drama. Mary Hopkins leaves her husband, Jack, a lawyer, to study painting in Paris. Rhea, Jack's former sweetheart, persuades him to go to Paris for a divorce. In France, Jack decides he wants his wife back after she willingly consents to a divorce and discloses that she had an imaginary affair with a bogus count. Rhea is discredited, and Jack and Mary are reunited. *Artists. Lawyers. Divorce. Paris.*

THE HOLE IN THE WALL F2.2548

Metro Pictures. 12 Dec **1921** [c4 Jan 1922; LP17444]. Si; b&w. 35mm. 6 reels, 6,100 ft.

Dir Maxwell Karger. *Adapt* June Mathis. *Photog* Allen Siegler. *Art Dir* Joseph Calder.

Cast: Alice Lake *(Jean Oliver)*, Allan Forrest *(Gordon Grant)*, Frank Brownlee *(Limpy Jim)*, Charles Clary *(The Fox)*, William De Vaull *(Deagon)*, Kate Lester *(Mrs. Ramsey)*, Carl Gerrard *(Donald Ramsey)*, John Ince *(Inspector of Police)*, Claire Du Brey *(Cora Thompson)*.

Mystery melodrama. Source: Fred Jackson, *The Hole in the Wall* (New York opening: 26 Mar 1920). Madame Mysteria, a fashionable medium, is killed in a train crash, and her three assistants—The Fox, Limpy Jim, and Deagon—each with a criminal record, decide not to identify the body, since the medium had extracted valuable information from her wealthy clients. The Fox produces a substitute—Jean Oliver, who has been framed by wealthy Mrs. Ramsey because of her son Donald's attentions to the girl—and Jean consents to assume the role on the condition that they help her revenge herself by kidnaping Mrs. Ramsey's grandson. Meanwhile, Gordon Grant, whom Jean loves and to whom she was previously engaged, has become an amateur sleuth; in investigating the connection between Madame Mysteria and the robberies perpetrated upon her former clients, he uncovers the swindlers and the missing Ramsey baby. Jean is cleared by a statement from Mrs. Ramsey and is reunited with Gordon. *Mediums. Detectives. Spiritualism. Impersonation. Frameup. Kidnaping. Revenge. Railroad accidents.*

Note: Remade in 1929 under the same title, q. v.

THE HOLE IN THE WALL F2.2549

Paramount Famous Lasky Corp. 27 Apr **1929** [c26 Apr 1929; LP334]. Sd (Movietone); b&w. 35mm. 7 reels, 5,850 ft.

Supv Monta Bell. *Dir* Robert Florey. *Adapt-Dial* Pierre Collings. *Photog* George Folsey. *Film Ed* Morton Blumenstock.

Cast: Claudette Colbert *(Jean Oliver)*, Edward G. Robinson *(The Fox)*, David Newell *(Gordon Grant)*, Nellie Savage *(Madame Mystera)*, Donald Meek *(Goofy)*, Alan Brooks *(Jim)*, Louise Closser Hale *(Mrs. Ramsey)*, Katherine Emmett *(Mrs. Carslake)*, Marcia Kango *(Marcia)*, Barry Macollum *(Dogface)*, George MacQuarrie *(inspector)*, Helen Crane *(Mrs. Lyons)*, Gamby-Hall Girls.

Mystery melodrama. Source: Fred Jackson, *The Hole in the Wall* (New York opening: 26 Mar 1920). Jean Oliver falls in love with a wealthy young man, and his mother, Mrs. Ramsey, sees to it that she is sent to prison on a trumped-up charge. Time passes. Jean is released from stir and throws in with a band of phony spiritualists, donning the robes of Madame Mystera, a crook recently killed in an accident on the elevated. Jean quickly proposes that her new companions in crime kidnap the granddaughter of Mrs. Ramsey and hold the child for ransom. The child is taken, but the police arrest the gang. The Fox, crafty leader of the spiritualists, is the only one who knows the whereabouts of the missing child, however, and he trades this information for immunity *and* a statement from Mrs. Ramsey that Jean had not in fact committed the crime for which she was sent to jail. Jean is freed and reunited with Gordon Grant, her childhood sweetheart, a reporter who has accompanied the police in the raid on the gang. *Reporters. Mediums. Police. Spiritualism. Frameup. Kidnaping. Revenge. Ransom. Prisons. Railroad accidents.*

HOLIDAY F2.2550

Pathé Exchange. 3 Jul **1930** [New York premiere; released 13 Jul; c6 Jun 1930; LP1462]. Sd (Photophone); b&w. 35mm. 9 reels, 8,870 ft.

Prod E. B. Derr. *Dir* Edward H. Griffith. *Screenplay-Dial* Horace Jackson. *Photog* Norbert Brodin. *Art Dir* Carroll Clark. *Film Ed* Daniel Mandell. *Mus Score* Josiah Zuro. *Rec Engr* D. A. Cutler, Harold Stine. *Asst Dir* Paul Jones. *Cost* Gwen Wakeling.

Cast: Ann Harding *(Linda)*, Mary Astor *(Julia Seton)*, Edward Everett Horton *(Nick Potter)*, Robert Ames *(Johnny Case)*, Hedda Hopper *(Susan Potter)*, Monroe Owsley *(Ned)*, William Holden *(Edward Seton)*, Elizabeth Forrester *(Laura)*, Mabel Forrest *(Mary Jessup)*, Creighton Hale *(Pete Hedges)*, Hallam Cooley *(Seton Cram)*, Mary Forbes *(Mrs. Pritchard Ames)*.

Society drama. Source: Philip Barry, *Holiday, a Comedy in Three Acts* (New York, 1929). Wealthy Julia Seton meets Johnny Case at Lake Placid and takes him home, introducing him to her family as her future husband. A poor, struggling young lawyer, Johnny is greeted with kindly tolerance by old Seton and his children, Linda and Ned. Seton finally agrees to Julia's plans and arranges an engagement party; but Linda gives a party of her own at which Nick and Susan Potter are the honored guests. Johnny reveals that he has invested in the stock market and plans to quit work after marriage. When Seton learns of this announcement, he is furious, but Linda, who is taken with Johnny, supports him. Johnny and Julia separate, and he plans to go to Europe with Nick and Susan, but he changes his mind and agrees to work for 3 years before going on holiday. However, he revolts at the idea of Seton's planning his life, and Linda, pleased by his assertion of personal freedom, joins him aboard the steamer. *Lawyers. Sisters. Social classes. Courtship. Wealth. Speculation. Family life. Lake Placid.*

HOLLYWOOD F2.2551

Famous Players–Lasky. *Dist* Paramount Pictures. 19 Aug **1923** [c10 Jul 1923; LP19202]. Si; b&w. 35mm. 8 reels, 8,100 ft.

Pres by Jesse L. Lasky. *Dir* James Cruze. *Adapt* Tom Geraghty. *Story* Frank Condon. *Photog* Karl Brown.

Cast—The Story: Hope Drown *(Angela Whitaker)*, Luke Cosgrave *(Joel Whitaker)*, George K. Arthur *(Lem Lefferts)*, Ruby Lafayette *(Grandmother Whitaker)*, Harris Gordon *(Dr. Luke Morrison)*, Bess Flowers *(Hortense Towers)*, Eleanor Lawson *(Margaret Whitaker)*, King Zany *(Horace Pringle)*, Roscoe Arbuckle *(fat man in casting director's office)*.

Cast—Stars and Celebrities: Gertrude Astor, Mary Astor, Agnes Ayres, Baby Peggy, T. Roy Barnes, Noah Beery, William Boyd, Clarence Burton, Robert Cain, Edythe Chapman, Betty Compson, Ricardo Cortez, Viola Dana, Cecil B. De Mille, William De Mille, Charles De Roche, Dinky Dean, Helen Dunbar, Snitz Edwards, George Fawcett, Julia Faye, James Finlayson, Alec Francis, Jack Gardner, Sid Grauman, Alfred E. Green, Alan Hale, Lloyd Hamilton, Hope Hampton, William S. Hart, Gale Henry, Walter Hiers, Mrs. Walter Hiers, Stuart Holmes, Sigrid Holmquist, Jack Holt, Leatrice Joy, Mayme Kelso, J. Warren Kerrigan, Theodore Kosloff, Kosloff Dancers, Lila Lee, Lillian Leighton, Jacqueline Logan, May McAvoy, Robert McKim, Jeanie Macpherson, Hank Mann, Joe Martin, Thomas Meighan, Bull Montana, Owen Moore, Nita Naldi, Pola Negri, Anna Q. Nilsson, Charles Ogle, Guy Oliver, Kalla Pasha, Eileen Percy, Carmen Phillips, Jack Pickford, Chuck Reisner, Fritzi Ridgeway, Will Rogers, Sennett Girls, Ford Sterling, Anita Stewart, George Stewart, Gloria Swanson, Estelle Taylor, Ben Turpin, Bryant Washburn, Maude Wayne, Claire West, Laurence Wheat, Lois Wilson.

Comedy-drama. Angela Whitaker and her grandfather Joel visit Hollywood—the grandfather to regain his health, and Angela to get into the movies. But Joel gets the offers. Then Angela's sweetheart Lem and the rest of Angela's family, hearing of grandfather Joel's debut, come to Hollywood to rescue him from "evil influences" and find themselves drawn into the movies. Angela's ambitions wane after she marries Lem and gives birth to twins, who also show up on the silver screen. Angela and her family meet a number of screen celebrities. *Actors. Grandfathers. Motion pictures. Hollywood.*

THE HOLLYWOOD REPORTER F2.2552

Hercules Film Productions. Jan **1926** [c20 Jan 1926; LP22276]. Si; b&w. 35mm. 5 reels, 4,755 ft.

Pres by Peter Kanellos. *Dir* Bruce Mitchell. *Story-Scen* Grover Jones.

Cast: Frank Merrill *(Billy Hudson)*, Charles K. French *(Basil Manning)*, Peggy Montgomery *(Lois Manning)*, William Hayes *(Dell Crossley)*, Jack Richardson *(Hymie Durning)*, Violet Schram *(Margaret Latham)*.

Action melodrama. When Basil Manning, the editor of the *Hollywood Morning Express*, refuses to support the election campaign of Hymie Durning, the degenerate city boss who wants to be mayor, Hymie threatens to expose the fact that Manning once served time in the state pen. Billy Hudson, known as the "Hollywood Reporter," wants to marry Manning's daughter, Lois, and the old man offers to give his consent to the match if Billy can come up with some dirt on Hymie. By chance, Billy learns that Hymie runs a gambling den in his house, and, with the aid of Dell Crossley, the paper's photographer, he gets a picture of the den which Manning headlines on the front page. Billy marries Lois, and Manning, having at last found the man who framed him years ealier, finally stands free of the stigma of a criminal reputation. *Reporters. Editors. Mayors. Political bosses. Photographers. Gambling. Elections. Injustice. Newspapers.*

THE HOLLYWOOD REVUE OF 1929 F2.2553

Metro-Goldwyn-Mayer Pictures. 20 Jun **1929** [Los Angeles premiere; released 23 Nov; c23 Sep 1929; LP800]. Sd (Movietone); b&w with color sequences (Technicolor). 35mm. 13 reels, 11,669 ft.

Prod Harry Rapf. *Dir* Charles Reisner. *Dial* Al Boasberg, Robert E. Hopkins. *Skit by* Joe Farnham. *Photog* John Arnold, Irving Ries,

Maximilian Fabian, John M. Nickolaus. *Art Dir* Cedric Gibbons, Richard Day. *Film Ed* William S. Gray, Cameron K. Wood. *Songs: "Singin' in the Rain," "You Were Meant for Me," "Tommy Atkins on Parade"* Arthur Freed, Nacio Herb Brown. *Song: "Low-Down Rhythm"* Raymond Klages, Jesse Greer. *Song: "For I'm the Queen"* Andy Rice, Martin Broones. *Song: "Gotta Feelin' for You"* Joe Trent, Louis Alter. *Songs: "Bones and Tambourines," "Strike Up the Band," "Tableaux of Jewels"* Fred Fisher. *Songs: "Lon Chaney Will Get You If You Don't Watch Out," "Strolling Through the Park One Day," "Your Mother and Mine," "Orange Blossom Time," "Minstrel Days,". "Nobody But You," "I Never Knew I Could Do a Thing Like That"* Joe Goodwin, Gus Edwards. *Score Arr* Arthur Lange, Ernest Klapholtz, Ray Heindorf. *Dance Ensembles* Sammy Lee, George Cunningham. *Rec Engr* Douglas Shearer. *Sd Asst* Russell Franks, William Clark, Wesley Miller, A. T. Taylor. *Asst Dir* Jack Cummings, Sandy Roth, Al Shenberg. *Prod Mgr* Joe Cohn. *Cost* David Cox, Henrietta Frazer, Joe Rapf. *Electrn* Louis Kolb.

Cast: Conrad Nagel, Jack Benny *(Masters of Ceremony)*, John Gilbert, Norma Shearer, Joan Crawford, Bessie Love, Lionel Barrymore, Cliff Edwards, Stan Laurel, Oliver Hardy, Anita Page, Nils Asther, The Brox Sisters, Natacha Natova and Co., Marion Davies, William Haines, Buster Keaton, Marie Dressler, Charles King, Polly Moran, Gus Edwards, Karl Dane, George K. Arthur, Ann Dvorak, Gwen Lee, Albertina Rasch Ballet, The Rounders, The Biltmore Quartet.

Musical revue. The show opens with a minstrel chorus and dance routine, and Jack Benny and Conrad Nagel are introduced as masters of ceremony; Joan Crawford sings "Gotta Feelin' for You," amidst a dance specialty, finishing with the Biltmore Quartet; Charles King does "Your Mother and Mine," before a minstrel chorus; and Conrad Nagel sings "You Were Meant for Me" to Anita Page; Cliff Edwards and his "uke" render "Nobody But You," and William Haines and Jack Benny do a comedy sketch; Bessie Love comes out of Benny's pocket in miniature and with a male chorus sings "I Could Never Do a Thing Like That," climaxed by a dance number; Marie Dressler and Polly Moran in a comedy number sing "For I'm the Queen," and Laurel and Hardy do a sketch as magicians; Marion Davies sings "Tommy Atkins on Parade" with a male chorus and does some tap dancing; concluding, the Brox Sisters introduce a song and dance ensemble. "The Tableau of Jewels" opens the second act, followed by "The Dance of the Sea," in which Keaton appears; Gus Edwards sings "Lon Chaney" and is followed by the Natova company in an adagio dance; Norma Shearer and John Gilbert appear in a Technicolor "Romeo and Juliet" balcony sequence with Lionel Barrymore, updated to flapper language; on a glass stage, Cliff Edwards and a dance ensemble appear in "Singin' in the Rain"; two comedy routines follow: "Charlie, Ike, and Gus" and "Marie, Polly, and Bess," climaxed by "Strolling Through the Park." The Technicolor finale features Charles King singing "Orange Blossom Time," followed by two dance numbers by the Albertina Rasch Ballet, then shifting abruptly to a replica of Noah's Ark and the principals in "Singin' in the Rain." *Actors. Dancers. Singers. Ballet. "Romeo and Juliet".*

THE HOLY SINNER **F2.2554**

Dist Worldart Film Co. 10 Jan **1929** [New York State license]. Si; b&w. 35mm. 6 reels.

Drama(?). No information about the nature of this film has been found.
Note: Country of origin undetermined.

HOME JAMES (Universal-Jewel) **F2.2555**

Universal Pictures. 2 Sep **1928** [c13 Apr 1928; LP25162]. Si; b&w. 35mm. 7 reels, 6,307 ft.

Dir William Beaudine. *Story Supv* Joseph Franklin Poland. *Scen* Morton Blumenstock. *Titl* Albert De Mond. *Story* Gladys E. Johnson. *Photog* John Stumar. *Film Ed* Robert Carlisle.

Cast: Laura La Plante *(Laura Elliot)*, Charles Delaney *(James Lacey, Jr.)*, Aileen Manning *(Mrs. Elliot)*, Joan Standing *(Iris Elliot)*, George Pearce *(James Lacey, Sr.)*, Arthur Hoyt *(William Waller, floorwalker)*, Sidney Bracy *(Haskins, the butler)*.

Comedy-drama. Laura Elliot, a department store clerk, meets James Lacey, son of the storeowner. Mistaking him for a chauffeur, she hires Lacey to help impress her visiting relatives. Lacey, amused by the situation, takes Laura and her relatives to his father's mansion and pretends that she is mistress of the household and he the servant. Lacey, Sr., arrives and is arrested for snooping around the house. The following morning finds affairs righted when Laura and James announce their engagement. *Salesclerks. Chauffeurs. Mistaken identity. Wealth. Department stores.*

HOME MADE **F2.2556**

B & H Enterprises. *Dist* First National Pictures. 20 Nov **1927** [c1 Nov 1927; LP24592]. Si; b&w. 35mm. 7 reels, 6,450 ft.

Pres by C. C. Burr. *Dir* Charles Hines. *Story-Scen* C. C. Carrington. *Titl* Paul Perez. *Photog* William J. Miller, Al Wilson.

Cast: Johnny Hines *(Johnny White)*, Margaret Seddon *(Mrs. White)*, De Witt Jennings *(Mr. White)*, Maude Turner Gordon *(Mrs. Fenton)*, Edmund Breese *(Mr. Tilford)*, Marjorie Daw *(The Girl)*, Charles Gerrard *(Robert Van Dorn)*.

Comedy. Johnny White, whose claim to fame is as hometown entertainer, leaves home after a disagreement with his stepfather and goes to New York to promote his mother's homemade jam. He takes a job as hotel waiter and in that capacity meets Dorothy Fenton, her aunt, and a Mr. Tilford, a jam manufacturer. Johnny takes Dorothy to a phonograph store, where they play records and dance; when he is invited to a party at which he is detailed to work as a waiter, he contrives to play both guest and waiter at once. Employing his talent of ventriloquism, he advertises Ulika Jam on a radio announcement, a ploy that results in financial success. He thus rescues Dorothy from her villainous suitor. *Entertainers. Waiters. Smalltown life. Salesmanship. Ventriloquism. Filial relations. Jam. New York City.*

THE HOME MAKER (Universal-Jewel) **F2.2557**

Universal Pictures. 22 Nov **1925** [c20 Jul 1925; LP21671]. Si; b&w. 35mm. 8 reels, 7,755 ft.

Dir King Baggot. *Scen* Mary O'Hara. *Photog* John Stumar.

Cast: Alice Joyce *(Eva Knapp)*, Clive Brook *(Lester Knapp)*, Billy Kent Schaeffer *(Stephen)*, George Fawcett *(Dr. Merritt)*, Virginia Boardman *(Mrs. Prouty)*, Maurice Murphy *(Henry)*, Jacqueline Wells *(Helen)*, Frank Newburg *(Harvey Bronson)*, Margaret Campbell *(Mattie Farnum)*, Martha Mattox *(Mrs. Anderson)*, Alfred Fisher *(John)*, Alice Flower *(Miss West)*, Elaine Ellis *(Molly Prouty)*.

Domestic drama. Source: Dorothy Canfield, *The Home-Maker* (New York, 1924). Lester Knapp is discharged from his position in the office of a department store and, in order for his wife to benefit from his insurance, attempts suicide. He succeeds only in crippling himself, and his wife, Eva, is forced to go to work. Eva becomes quite successful in her job, finding in it the rewards and fulfillment denied her by the drudgery of housework. Confined to a wheelchair, Lester takes care of the house and children, doing the housework both easily and well and making the three children happier than they have been in years. Lester regains the use of his limbs, but, realizing that his recovery means a return to the family's former unhappiness, he conspires with the family doctor to persuade Eva that the time has not yet arrived for him to walk. *Businesswomen. Cripples. Physicians. Family life. Department stores. Suicide.*

THE HOME STRETCH **F2.2558**

Thomas H. Ince Productions. *Dist* Paramount Pictures. 24 Apr **1921** [c23 Apr 1921; LP16417]. Si; b&w. 35mm. 5 reels, 4,512-4,602 ft.

Prod Thomas H. Ince. *Dir* Jack Nelson. *Scen* Louis Stevens. *Photog* Bert Cann.

Cast: Douglas MacLean *(Johnny Hardwick)*, Beatrice Burnham *(Margaret Warren)*, Walt Whitman *(Mr. Warren)*, Margaret Livingston *(Molly)*, Wade Boteler *(Mr. Duffy)*, Mary Jane Irving *(Gwen Duffy)*, Charles Mailes *(Mr. Wilson)*, Molly McConnell *(Mrs. Wilson)*, Jack Singleton *(Tommy Wilson)*, Joe Bennett *(Hi Simpkins)*, George Holmes *(Skeeter)*.

Melodrama. Source: Charles Belmont Davis, "When Johnny Comes Marching Home," in *Metropolitan Magazine* (40:27, Oct 1914). Johnny Hardwick inherits a thoroughbred, "Honeyblossom," and stakes his entire bankroll on her, but in rescuing Gwen Duffy from danger at the racetrack he causes his horse to lose. Later, in the city, Mr. Duffy hires Johnny as manager of his hotel, where he meets and falls in love with Margaret, the storekeeper's daughter. The appearance of his friend Molly results in a temporary rupture, and after winning money for Warren on Honeyblossom, Johnny goes away. A year later he returns and learns that Margaret is to marry Hi Simpkins. When Duffy brings Margaret to him, however, they are reunited. *Horseracing. Gambling. Hotel management.*

HOME STRUCK **F2.2559**

R-C Pictures. *Dist* Film Booking Offices of America. 9 Jan **1927** [c1 Jan 1927; LP23492]. Si; b&w. 35mm. 6 reels, 5,613 ft.

Pres by Joseph P. Kennedy. *Dir* Ralph Ince. *Cont* Ewart Adamson. *Story* Peter Milne. *Photog* Jules Cronjager. *Asst Dir* William Sheridan.

Cast: Viola Dana *(Barbara Page)*, Alan Brooks *(Lyn Holmes)*, Tom

Gallery *(Dick Cobb)*, Nigel Barrie *(Warren Townsend)*, George Irving *(President Wallace)*, Charles Howard *(Nick Cohen)*.

Domestic melodrama. Barbara Page, a chorus girl who yearns for a domestic life, is proposed to by Lyn Holmes, her theatrical agent, but instead she accepts Dick Cobb, a bank clerk. Her dreams are realized by their little flat, though Dick soon begins to insist on attending wild parties, to which she reluctantly agrees. Dick's fellow clerk, Warren Townsend, whose advances have been repelled by Barbara, advises Dick to "borrow" from the bank when he is short, then notifies the bank president. Dick escapes, and Townsend, pretending sympathy, offers to help if Barbara will yield to his demands, then Holmes offers Barbara a new chance in a comedy role. Later she scorns Holmes's suggestion that she sue for divorce and marry him, and the agent reunites the repentant husband with his wife. *Chorus girls. Theatrical agents. Bank clerks. Marriage. Embezzlement.*

HOME STUFF **F2.2560**

Metro Pictures. 16 Jun **1921** [c10 Jun 1921; LP16674]. Si; b&w. 35mm. 6 reels.

Dir Albert Kelley. *Story-Scen* Frank Dazey, Agnes Christine Johnston. *Photog* John Arnold. *Art Dir* A. F. Mantz.

Cast: Viola Dana *(Madge Joy)*, Tom Gallery *(Robert Deep)*, Josephine Crowell *("Ma" Deep)*, Nelson McDowell *("Pa" Deep)*, Priscilla Bonner *(Susan Deep)*, Robert Chandler *(Mr. "Pat")*, Aileen Manning *(Mrs. "Pat")*, Philip Sleeman *(Jim Sackett)*.

Rural comedy. When Madge Joy is replaced in a cheap roadshow by Susan Deep, a stagestruck girl who offers to pay the company expenses, she misses the night train out of Buckeye Junction and falls asleep in a haystack. In the morning Madge is discovered by young farmer Robert Deep, and explaining that she is a runaway orphan she is taken into the Deep family. Robert, who falls in love with her, learns that she is an actress and reveals his ambition to become a playwright. When Susan returns home, Madge calms the father's fury by threatening to leave with Robert unless he forgives his daughter. Later, Robert visits Madge in New York, where she is a Broadway star, and a happy reconciliation follows. *Farmers. Actors. Playwrights. Theater. New York City—Broadway.*

HOME TALENT **F2.2561**

Mack Sennett Productions. *Dist* Associated Producers. 22 May **1921** [c25 May 1921; LP16583]. Si; b&w. 35mm. 5 reels.

Prod-Dir Mack Sennett. *Adtl Dir* James E. Abbe. *Photog* Perry Evans, Fred Jackman. *Adtl Photog* James E. Abbe.

Cast: Charlie Murray *(The Landlord)*, Ben Turpin, James Finlayson, Eddie Gribbon, Kalla Pasha *(stranded actors)*, Phyllis Haver *(The Landlord's Daughter)*, Dot Farley, Kathryn McGuire, Harriet Hammond.

Comedy. A quartet of vaudeville performers, stranded in a country hotel, decides, after a furious quarrel, to pool their talents and put on a show to pay the rent. The rehearsals, in the presence of the landlord, provide the central episodes of a slave mart in Ancient Rome where beautiful captives are bid for by a tyrant and a heroic gladiator. During rehearsals, burglars enter and attempt a robbery after tying the landlord to a steam boiler, but the robbers are caught and he is rescued just as the boiler is about to explode. *Actors. Vaudeville. Robbery. Hotels. Rome—History—Empire.*

Note: The Roman sequences were directed and photographed by James E. Abbe.

THE HOME TOWNERS **F2.2562**

Warner Brothers Pictures. 3 Nov **1928** [c27 Oct 1928; LP25773]. Sd (Vitaphone); b&w. 35mm. 11 reels, 5,693 ft. [Also si, 15 Dec 1928; 4,841 ft.]

Dir Bryan Foy. *Scen-Dial* Addison Burkhart, Murray Roth. *Photog* Barney McGill, Willard Van Enger. *Asst Dir* Doc Salomon, Fred Fox.

Cast: Richard Bennett *(Vic Arnold)*, Doris Kenyon *(Beth Calhoun)*, Robert McWade *(H. P. Bancroft)*, Robert Edeson *(Mr. Calhoun)*, Gladys Brockwell *(Lottie Bancroft)*, John Miljan *(Joe Roberts)*, Vera Lewis *(Mrs. Calhoun)*, Stanley Taylor *(Wally Calhoun)*, James T. Mack *(Casey, the butler)*, Patricia Caron *(maid)*.

Comedy-drama. Source: George Michael Cohan, *The Home Towners* (New York opening: 23 Aug 1926). Vic Arnold, a middle-aged Manhattan millionaire, brings H. P. Bancroft, a childhood chum, all the way from South Bend in order for H. P. to be best man at his wedding to Beth Calhoun, a beautiful young woman half his age. Learning that Beth's father has received $200,000 from Vic and that Beth's brother is on Vic's payroll, H. P. quickly comes to the conclusion that Beth and her family are interested only in Vic's money; H. P. insults Beth in front of her parents, and she breaks off the engagement. H. P. later learns that he was wrong in his estimation of Beth's motives, and he reunites Beth and Vic, who again invite him to be best man. *Parasites. Millionaires. Weddings. New York City. South Bend.*

HOME-KEEPING HEARTS **F2.2563**

Cameo Classics. *Dist* Playgoers Pictures. 11 Sep **1921** [c30 Aug 1921; LU16907]. Si; b&w. 35mm. 5 reels.

Dir Carlyle Ellis. *Scen* Carlyle Ellis, Charles W. Barrell. *Story* Charles W. Barrell. *Photog* Walter Pritchard.

Cast: Thomas H. Swinton *(Robert Colton)*, Mary Ryan *(Mary Colton)*, Louella Carr *(Laurel Stewart)*, Edward Grace *(Squire Tead)*, Henry West *(Timothy Reece)*.

Rural melodrama. Diver Robert Colton is imprisoned for 10 years when found guilty, on circumstantial evidence, of causing the death of his employer; and his motherless daughter, Mary, is brought up by Squire Tead and his stern wife. When freed, Colton obtains work in Tead's creamery. There he discovers that Tead is bribing the cow inspector to condemn his best cattle so that a local plan for a cooperative creamery will be defeated. Colton discovers also that Tead is misappropriating school funds. In spite of Tead's threat to reveal his past, Colton defeats Tead in the local election by uncovering his dealings. When Colton saves Tead from drowning in a milk vat, the squire has a change of heart. Robert's name is cleared, and he is free to court and marry Laurel Stewart, the schoolmistress, thus giving a home to his daughter. *Divers. Schoolteachers. Creameries. Political corruption. Rural life. Cooperatives. Circumstantial evidence. Cows.*

HOMESICK **F2.2564**

Fox Film Corp. 16 Dec **1928** [c10 Dec 1928; LP25898]. Si; b&w. 35mm. 6 reels, 5,153 ft.

Pres by William Fox. *Dir* Henry Lehrman. *Story-Scen* John Stone. *Titl* William Kernell. *Photog* Charles Van Enger. *Film Ed* Ralph Dixon. *Asst Dir* Max Gold.

Cast: Sammy Cohen *(Sammy Schnable)*, Harry Sweet *(Ambrose)*, Marjorie Beebe *(Babe)*, Henry Armetta *(bicycle rider)*, Pat Harmon *(Polish bicycle rider)*.

Comedy. Babe, a lonely servant girl in California, puts a "husband wanted" ad in the newspaper, and two likely candidates answer it: Ambrose; and Sammy Schnable, a New Yorker who comes all the way west to see Babe. Ambrose and Sammy enter a transcontinental bicycle race, and Sammy finally wins Babe's love. *Domestics. New Yorkers. Bicycle racing. California.*

A HOMESPUN VAMP **F2.2565**

Realart Pictures. *Dist* Paramount Pictures. 12 Feb **1922** [c6 Dec 1921; LP17334]. Si; b&w. 35mm. 5 reels, 4,777 ft.

Dir Frank O'Connor. *Adapt* Harvey Thew. *Story* Hector Turnbull. *Photog* Hal Rosson.

Cast: May McAvoy *(Meg Mackenzie)*, Darrel Foss *(Stephen Ware)*, Lincoln Stedman *(Joe Dobbs)*, Josephine Crowell *(Mrs. Dobbs)*, Charles Ogle *(Donald Craig)*, Guy Oliver *(Duncan Craig)*, Helen Dunbar *(Mrs. Ware)*, Kathleen Kirkham *(Beatrice Carlisle)*.

Rural melodrama. Meg Mackenzie, an orphan, lives with her two stingy bachelor uncles, Donald and Duncan Craig, in a narrowminded rural community. They plan to marry her to Joe Dobbs, the blacksmith's son, but an author from the city, Stephen Ware, seeking a quiet place to work, arrives in the village and wins Meg's silent worship. The natives regard him with suspicion and accuse him of committing a robbery, and while the uncles are away, Meg saves him from an angry mob. Finding Meg with the injured man, the uncles consider her compromised and insist that he marry her; to save her from disgrace, he consents, telling her he will provide for her until he can have the marriage annulled. In the city, the unwanted bride determines to make herself desirable in the eyes of her husband, and he falls genuinely in love with her. *Orphans. Bachelors. Uncles. Blacksmiths. Authors. Marriage. Village life. Robbery.*

THE HOMESTEADER **F2.2566**

Micheaux Film Corp. 30 Sep **1922** [New York State license]. Si; b&w. 35mm. 7 reels.

Cast: Evelyn Preer.

Drama(?). No information about the nature of this film has been found.

HOMEWARD BOUND **F2.2567**

Famous Players–Lasky. *Dist* Paramount Pictures. 29 Jul **1923** [c8 Aug 1923; LP19279]. Si; b&w. 35mm. 7 reels, 7,000 ft.

Pres by Adolph Zukor. *Dir* Ralph Ince. *Scen* Jack Cunningham, Paul Sloane. *Story* Peter B. Kyne. *Photog* Ernest Haller.

Cast: Thomas Meighan *(Jim Bedford)*, Lila Lee *(Mary Brent)*, Charles Abbe *(Rufus Brent)*, William P. Carleton *(Rodney)*, Hugh Cameron *(Murphy)*, Gus Weinberg *(Captain Svenson)*, Maude Turner Gordon *(Mrs. Brannigan)*, Cyril Ring *(Rufus [Bill] Brent, Jr.)*, Katherine Spencer *(Clarissa Wynwood)*.

Melodrama. First Mate Jim Bedford replaces alcoholic Captain Svenson when shipowner Rufus Brent requests the captain to command a maiden voyage on a yacht recently purchased for his daughter, Mary. Bedford falls in love with Mary and marries her (in spite of Brent's objections) at the end of the cruise. Brent is won over, however, when Bedford rescues his disabled yacht during a storm at sea. *Ship crews. Alcoholism. Yachts. Storms.*

Note: Working title: *The Light to Leeward.*

THE HOMEWARD TRAIL *see* **THE WALLOP**

HONESTY—THE BEST POLICY **F2.2568**

Fox Film Corp. 8 Aug **1926** [c15 Aug 1926; LP23048]. Si; b&w. 35mm. 5 reels, 4,200 ft.

Pres by William Fox. *Dir* Chester Bennett. *Adtl Dir* Albert Ray. *Scen* L. G. Rigby. *Story* Howard Hawks. *Photog* Ernest G. Palmer. *Asst Dir* Daniel Keefe.

Cast—Original Film: Rockliffe Fellowes *(Nick Randall)*, Pauline Starke *(Mary Kay)*, Johnnie Walker *(Robert Dore)*, Grace Darmond *(Lily)*, Mickey Bennett *(freckled boy)*, Mack Swain *(Bendy Joe)*.

Cast—Added Sequence: Albert Gran *(publisher)*, Johnnie Walker *(author)*, Dot Farley *(author's wife)*, Heinie Conklin *(piano player)*.

Comedy-drama. An author's wife threatens to send him out to work unless he sells a story. Finding a publisher who will accept only true stories, the author proceeds to unravel his own past: *As a notorious criminal, with his wife as accomplice, he commits robberies, is pursued and captured, escapes, and eventually reforms.* Excited by the story, the publisher prepares to buy it. Overcome by his success, the author announces that his wife had been a much "dirtier crook" than himself, and he is about to reveal the details of her life when she overhears him and spoils the scene. *Authors. Publishers. Criminals—Rehabilitation. Robbery.*

Note: The added sequence directed by Albert Ray was completed on July 16, 1926.

HONEY **F2.2569**

Paramount Famous Lasky Corp. 29 Mar **1930** [c29 Mar 1930; LP1188]. Sd (Movietone); b&w. 35mm. 8 reels, 6,701 ft.

Dir Wesley Ruggles. *Adapt-Titl* Herman J. Mankiewicz. *Camera* Henry Gerrard. *Songs: "In My Little Hope Chest," "Sing You Sinners," "I Don't Need Atmosphere," "Let's Be Domestic" "What Is This Power I Have?"* W. Franke Harling, Sam Coslow. *Dance Dir* David Bennett. *Sd Rec* Harry M. Lindgren.

Cast: Nancy Carroll *(Olivia Dangerfield)*, Stanley Smith *(Burton Crane)*, Skeets Gallagher *(Charles Dangerfield)*, Lillian Roth *(Cora Falkner)*, Harry Green *(J. William Burnstein)*, Mitzi Green *(Doris)*, ZaSu Pitts *(Mayme)*, Jobyna Howland *(Mrs. Falkner)*, Charles Sellon *(Randolph Weeks)*.

Musical comedy. Source: Alice Duer Miller and A. E. Thomas, *Come Out of the Kitchen*! (novel: New York, 1916; play: New York, 1921). Olivia Dangerfield, daughter of a proud but impoverished Virginia family, is forced to lease the family mansion to a wealthy New York widow to pay off the mortgage. When the servants fail to arrive, with the exception of Doris, a maid, she has her brother Charles impersonate the butler while she herself assumes the position of cook. Mrs. Falkner arrives with her daughter, Cora, and Burton Crane, a prospective match, but Cora falls in love with Charles, the "butler"; through little Doris, Mrs. Falkner learns of the affair, which is confirmed when she sees Charles and Cora together at a Negro jubilee. Then Doris informs Mrs. Falkner that Olivia is the owner of the house, and the incensed widow prepares to leave; but Cora and Charles announce their engagement, leaving clear the path to romance for Olivia and Burton. *Widows. Domestics. Aristocrats. Impersonation. Courtship. Poverty. Virginia.*

THE HONEYMOON *see* **THE WEDDING MARCH**

HONEYMOON **F2.2570**

Metro-Goldwyn-Mayer Pictures. 29 Dec **1928** [c29 Dec 1928; LP25968]. Si; b&w. 35mm. 6 reels, 4,823 ft.

Dir Robert A. Golden. *Scen* George O'Hara. *Titl* Robert Hopkins. *Adapt* Richard Schayer. *Story* Lew Lipton. *Photog* Maximilian Fabian. *Art Dir* Cedric Gibbons. *Film Ed* Ben Lewis. *Wardrobe* Henrietta Frazer.

Cast: Polly Moran *(Polly)*, Harry Gribbon *(Harry)*, Bert Roach *(Bert)*, Flash *(The Dog)*.

Comedy. On their wedding day, Harry and Polly are presented with a police dog by Bert, a disappointed suitor with a keen sense of fun. The dog has been trained to prevent any man from so much as laying a hand on his mistress, and the frustrated bridegroom must spend his wedding night in vain contemplation of all that he is missing. The honeymoon is a disaster until the dog falls in love with a white cat, and everything straightens itself out. *Newlyweds. Honeymoons. Police dogs. Cats.*

THE HONEYMOON EXPRESS **F2.2571**

Warner Brothers Pictures. 2 Sep **1926** [New York premiere; released 9 Aug; c12 Aug 1926; LP23018]. Si; b&w. 35mm. 7 reels, 6,768 ft.

Dir James Flood. *Scen* Mary O'Hara. *Camera* David Abel. *Asst Camera* Willard Van Enger. *Asst Dir* William Cannon.

Cast: Willard Louis *(John Lambert)*, Irene Rich *(Mary Lambert)*, Holmes Herbert *(Jim Donaldson)*, Helene Costello *(Margaret Lambert)*, John Patrick *(Nathan Peck)*, Jane Winton *(Estelle)*, Virginia Lee Corbin *(Becky)*, Harold Goodwin *(Lance)*, Robert Brower *(Dick Donaldson)*.

Domestic drama. Source: Ethel Clifton and Brenda Fowler, *The Doormat* (a play; c2 Jan 1925). Wealth turns certain of the Lamberts to decadence and dissipation: John, the licentious father, gets entangled with an unscupulous gold digger named Estelle; his son Lance, an architect, loses ground in his profession through drinking; and Becky, the reckless flapper daughter, is infatuated with Nathan Peck, a vitiated millionaire. Margaret, the mother, who has lost her beauty through devotion to her household, realizes the futility of the sacrifice and leaves home with Jean (Mary?), her youngest and unspoiled daughter, whose aversion to men is expressed in her mannish attire. Margaret becomes an interior decorator in Jim Donaldson's office and soon regains her dignified womanly beauty. Meanwhile, Lance denounces his father for inviting disreputable people home and gets a job through his mother's influence. Margaret refuses John's pleas to return, and with Jim she saves Becky from suicide; Jean falls under the charms of Dick, Jim's brother; and the family is united again with Jim at its head. *Architects. Gold diggers. Millionaires. Interior decorators. Flappers. Wealth. Infidelity. Family life. Lechery. Alcoholism.*

HONEYMOON FLATS **F2.2572**

Universal Pictures. Apr or 30 Dec **1928** [c7 May 1928; LP25221]. Si; b&w. 35mm. 6 reels, 6,057 ft.

Dir Millard Webb. *Story Supv* Joseph Franklin Poland. *Scen* Morton Blumenstock. *Titl* Albert De Mond. *Photog* Ross Fisher. *Film Ed* Frank Hekinson.

Cast: George Lewis *(Jim Clayton)*, Dorothy Gulliver *(Lila Garland)*, Kathlyn Williams *(Mrs. Garland)*, Ward Crane *(Anthony Weir)*, Bryant Washburn *(Tom Twitchell)*, Phillips Smalley *(Mr. Garland)*, Jane Winton *(Jane Twitchell)*, Patricia Caron *(Mrs. French)*, Eddie Phillips *(Mr. French)*.

Comedy-drama. Source: Earl Derr Biggers, "Honeymoon Flats," in *Saturday Evening Post* (200:5–7, 2 Jul 1927). Lila Garland marries Jim Clayton against her parents' wishes. Disappointed that Lila did not marry wealth, Mrs. Garland tries to make her daughter discontented with her new home in Honeymoon Flats, a cheap suburban housing development. Mrs. Garland's interference and mysterious visits to Honeymoon Flats by Anthony Weir, Lila's former suitor, nearly cause the couple to separate. Peace is restored when both Weir and the Garlands leave for Europe. *Mothers-in-law. Marriage. Jealousy. Smalltown life. Housing.*

HONEYMOON HATE **F2.2573**

Paramount Famous Lasky Corp. 3 Dec **1927** [c3 Dec 1927; LP24721]. Si; b&w. 35mm. 6 reels, 5,415 ft.

Pres by Adolph Zukor, Jesse L. Lasky. *Dir* Luther Reed. *Screenplay* Ethel Doherty. *Titl* George Marion, Jr., Herman Mankiewicz. *Adapt* Doris Anderson. *Photog* Harry Fischbeck.

Cast: Florence Vidor *(Gail Grant)*, Tullio Carminati *(Prince Dantarini)*, William Austin *(Banning-Green)*, Corliss Palmer *(Mrs. Fremont Gage I)*, Shirley Dorman *(Mrs. Fremont Gage II)*, Effie Ellsler *(Miss Molosey)*, Genaro Spagnoli *(Bueno)*, Marcel Guillaume *(Pietro)*.

Romantic comedy. Source: Alice Muriel Williamson, "Honeymoon

Hate," in *Saturday Evening Post* (200:3–5, 24–25, 9–16 Jul 1927). Gail Grant, the impetuous daughter of a Pittsburgh steel magnate, arrives at a hotel in Venice and demands the Imperial Suite; in London, George Banning-Green, a persistent admirer, believes that she has gone to Berlin. Searching for "imperial" furnishings, the hotel manager goes to the palace of Prince Dantarini, who is selling the contents of his villa as an aftermath of the war. Dantarini agrees to be her guide in Venice, and when he proposes in his garden, Gail accepts. When their honeymoon trip is postponed because of a business appointment, they quarrel, and she locks herself in the bedroom while he calmly sits down to dinner. After announcing her plan to divorce him, Gail bumps into Banning-Green and introduces him to her husband, whereupon Dantarini becomes violently jealous; when he offers her her freedom, however, her will is broken, and a word from Banning-Green sends them into each other's arms. *Nobility. Wealth. Jealousy. Pittsburgh. London. Venice.*

HONKY TONK **F2.2574**

Warner Brothers Pictures. 4 Jun **1929** [New York premiere; released 31 Aug; c8 Jul 1929; LP521]. Sd (Vitaphone); b&w. 35mm. 7 reels, 6,412 ft. [Also si, 21 Sep 1929; 5,284 ft.]

Dir Lloyd Bacon. *Dial* Jack Yellen. *Titl* De Leon Anthony. *Adapt* C. Graham Baker. *Story* Leslie S. Barrows. *Photog* Ben Reynolds. *Songs: "I'm the Last of the Red-Hot Mammas," "I'm Doin' What I'm Doin' for Love," "He's a Good Man To Have Around," "I'm Feathering a Nest for a Little Bluebird," "I Don't Want To Get Thin"* Jack Yellen, Milton Ager. *Dance Dir* Larry Ceballos. *Asst Dir* Frank Shaw.

Cast: Sophie Tucker *(Sophie Leonard)*, Lila Lee *(Beth, her daughter)*, Audrey Ferris *(Jean Gilmore)*, George Duryea *(Freddie Gilmore)*, Mahlon Hamilton *(Jim)*, John T. Murray *(cafe manager)*.

Musical drama. Sophie Leonard, singer of "hot mamma" songs in a New York nightclub, gives notice that she is to retire when her daughter, Beth, returns from a European education unaware of her mother's true profession. She arrives ahead of schedule in a limousine with Jean Gilmore, a school companion and the sister of Freddie Gilmore, and is shocked at her mother's modest accommodation. Sophie is disappointed when she is unable to stay for dinner and reprimands her for going to wild parties with Freddie. Sophie confides to Jim that though she hates the cafe life, she will resume her job at the honky tonk; out of spite Freddie takes Beth to the club, and aghast, she renounces her mother and moves to a hotel. But as the result of Jim's intervention, Freddie is persuaded to ask Sophie's permission to marry Beth; and he convinces Beth of her unfair and cruel treatment of her mother. To Beth's surprise, Sophie realizes Freddie's worth and agrees to their plans; and a year later, Sophie is a grandmother. *Singers. Students. Motherhood. Courtship. Jazz life. Nightclubs. New York City.*

HONOR AMONG MEN **F2.2575**

Fox Film Corp. 8 Sep **1924** [c21 Sep 1924; LP20610]. Si; b&w. 35mm. 5 reels, 4,600 ft.

Pres by William Fox. *Dir-Scen* Denison Clift.

Cast: Edmund Lowe *(Prince Kaloney)*, Claire Adams *(Patricia Carson)*, Sheldon Lewis *(King Louis)*, Diana Miller *(Countess Zara De Winter)*, Frank Leigh *(Renauld)*, Fred Becker *(Colonel Erhaupt)*, Paul Weigel *(Baron Barrat)*, Hector Sarno *(Nichols)*, Fred Malatesta *(Count De Winter)*, Walter Wilkinson *(Little Crown Prince)*.

Romantic drama. Source: Richard Harding Davis, *The King's Jackal* (New York, 1898). "Prince Kaloney, while attempting to incite the people of Messina to reinstate their deposed king, is shot by the police. Patricia, an American heiress touring the world, nurses the prince. The king is not inclined to give up a life of secluded debauchery and he enlists a count's unfaithful wife and his mistress to betray the prince to the conspirators in office. When the king meets Patricia he forgets his mistress and seeks to wed her although she and the prince are in love. This enrages the discarded countess and she reveals the truth and the king's treachery when Renauld, of the conspirators, comes to inform the king that the republicans have been sold the plans of the trick expedition for the return of the monarch. The king is forced to abdicate and the prince sets out with aid of his American sweetheart to regain the throne for the little crown prince." (*Motion Picture News*, 18 Oct 1924, p625.) *Royalty. Infidelity. Monarchists. Imaginary kingdoms.*

HONOR BOUND **F2.2576**

Fox Film Corp. ca29 Apr **1928** [New York premiere; released 6 May; c30 Apr 1928; LP25196]. Si; b&w. 35mm. 7 reels, 6,188 ft.

Pres by William Fox. *Dir* Alfred E. Green. *Scen* C. Graham Baker. *Titl* William Kernell. *Adapt* Philip Klein. *Photog* Joseph August. *Film Ed* J. Edwin Robbins. *Asst Dir* Jack Boland.

Cast: George O'Brien *(John Ogletree)*, Estelle Taylor *(Evelyn Mortimer)*, Leila Hyams *(Selma Ritchie)*, Tom Santschi *(Mr. Mortimer)*, Frank Cooley *(Dr. Ritchie)*, Sam De Grasse *(Blood Keller)*, Al Hart *(Cid Ames)*, Harry Gripp *(Skip Collier)*, George Irving *(Governor)*.

Drama. Source: Jack Bethea, *Honor Bound* (Boston & New York, 1927). Evelyn accidentally kills her husband, whom she hated. A self-sacrificing youth (John Ogletree) takes the blame and goes to prison. Evelyn marries mineowner Mortimer and gets Ogletree, who is imprisoned nearby, bound over to be her chauffeur. Her husband discovers their affair, mistreats Ogletree, and sends him down into the mines. After Mortimer attempts to kill him, Ogletree escapes to the governor and is pardoned after revealing information about corruption in the prison. The guilty persons are apprehended. *Chauffeurs. State governors. Self-sacrifice. Manslaughter. Prisons. Coal mines.*

HONOR FIRST **F2.2577**

Fox Film Corp. 27 Aug **1922** [c22 Aug 1922; LP19034]. Si; b&w. 35mm. 5 reels, 5,075 ft.

Pres by William Fox. *Dir* Jerome Storm. *Scen* Joseph Franklin Poland. *Photog* Joseph August.

Cast: John Gilbert *(Jacques Dubois/Honoré Dubois)*, Renée Adorée *(Moira Serern)*, Hardee Kirkland *(Barry Serern)*, Shannon Day *(Piquette)*, Wilson Hummel *(Tricot, the Apache)*.

War melodrama. Source: George Gibbs, *The Splendid Outcast* (New York, 1920). Twin brothers are serving in the French army during the Great War. Jacques, a private, leads his brother's company to attack when Honoré, a lieutenant, panics and flees. Jacques, dressed in Honoré's coat, wins a vital victory, but he is mistaken for Honoré and decorated for gallantry in his brother's name. Jacques assumes Honoré's identity and goes to Paris where he meets Honoré. Honoré, after a serious disagreement, plots to have Jacques murdered but is himself killed by mistake. Jacques finds happiness with Moira, Honoré's wife from a loveless war marriage of convenience. *Brothers. Twins. Cowardice. Impersonation. World War I. France—Army.*

Note: Reissued in 1927.

THE HOODED MOB *see* AFTER DARK

HOODMAN BLIND **F2.2578**

Fox Film Corp. 16 or 20 Dec **1923** [c16 Nov 1923; LP19656]. Si; b&w. 35mm. 6 reels, 5,434 ft.

Pres by William Fox. *Dir* John Ford. *Scen* Charles Kenyon. *Photog* George Schneiderman.

Cast: David Butler *(Jack Yeulette)*, Gladys Hulette *(Nancy Yeulette/Jessie Walton)*, Regina Connelly *(Jessie Walton, the first)*, Frank Campeau *(Mark Lezzard)*, Marc MacDermott *(John Linden)*, Trilby Clark *(Mrs. John Linden)*, Jack Walters *(Bull Yeaman)*, Eddie Gribbon *(Battling Brown)*.

Melodrama. Source: Henry Arthur Jones and Wilson Barrett, *Hoodman Blind* (unpublished, uncopyrighted play). John Linden deserts his wife and daughter and goes west accompanied by another woman, Jessie Walton, whom he leaves after the birth of their daughter. He goes to South Africa and there finds wealth. Meanwhile, both mothers die, leaving the daughters, Nancy and Jessie, who closely resemble each other, to fend separately for themselves. Nancy grows up and marries a fisherman; Jessie becomes a streetwalker. Linden tries to send money to Nancy, but it is intercepted by his lawyer, Mark Lezzard. Linden returns to America and is reunited with his daughters after a heroic rescue of Jessie from a sinking boat by Nancy's husband. *Sisters. Lawyers. Fishermen. Prostitutes. Wanderlust. Fatherhood. Desertion. Mistaken identity. South Africa.*

HOODOO RANCH **F2.2579**

Action Pictures. *Dist* Weiss Brothers Artclass Pictures. 22 Jan **1926**. Si; b&w. 35mm. 5 reels, 4,414 ft.

Dir William Bertram.

Cast: Buddy Roosevelt.

Western melodrama. "... centering about hidden gold and a haunted ranch house which blows up. Hero defeats villain in various nefarious schemes, finds the gold and wins the girl." ("Motion Picture News Booking Guide," in *Motion Picture News*, 8 May 1926, p31.) *Ranches. Treasure. Haunted houses.*

HOOF MARKS **F2.2580**

Fred J. McConnell Productions. *Dist* Pathé Exchange. 13 Nov **1927** [c26 Oct 1927; LU24574]. Si; b&w. 35mm. 5 reels, 4,076 ft.

Dir Tenny Wright. *Story-Scen* Joseph Anthony Roach. *Photog* Edward Snyder, Roy Greiner.

Cast: Jack Donovan *(Cal Wagner)*, Edward Brady *(Rawhide Smith)*, Edward Cecil *(Harold Cole)*, William Steele *(Sam Trapp)*, Peggy Montgomery *(Alice Dixon)*, Peggy O'Day *(Henrietta Bowers)*, Peggy Shaw *(Marie Hudson)*.

Western melodrama. Cal Wagner is employed on Dixon's ranch with secret orders to prevent cattle rustling. He and Rawhide Smith see the rustlers in action but find that the hoofprints of their horses mysteriously disappear. The two are ambushed, and Cal, though outnumbered, puts his foes to flight, while Rawhide succeeds in capturing one of the gang. Alice Dixon, the owner's daughter, prevents the cowboys from lynching the rustler while foreman Sam Trapp and manager Harold Cole hold consultations to stall the sheriff. During a dance, Cole permits the rustler to escape, and when Cal questions him a fight ensues; Trapp shoots Cole, and Alice witnesses the murder; but she is kidnaped and taken to the gang's retreat. On circumstantial evidence, Cal is held for the crime, but Rawhide helps him escape, and they learn the secret of the rustlers' technique. They battle the gang until reinforcements arrive and Trapp's men are captured. *Cowboys. Rustlers. Ranch foremen. Ranchers. Murder. Lynching. Kidnaping.*

HOOFBEATS OF VENGEANCE **F2.2581**

Universal Pictures. 4 Jun **1929** [New York showing; released 16 Jun; c9 May 1928; LP25235]. Si; b&w. 35mm. 5 reels, 4,525 ft.

Dir Henry MacRae. *Scen* George H. Plympton. *Titl* Gardner Bradford. *Story* George H. Plympton, William Lord Wright. *Photog* George Robinson. *Film Ed* Thomas Malloy.

Cast: Rex *(himself, a horse)*, Jack Perrin *(Sgt. Jack Gordon)*, Helen Foster *(Mary Martin)*, Al Ferguson *(Jud Regan)*, Starlight *(herself, a horse)*, Markee *(himself, a horse)*.

Northwest melodrama. Rex, the Wonder Horse, vows vengeance on his master's murderer—Jud Regan, leader of a band of smugglers and foreman at a ranch owned by Mary Martin. Assigned to capture a group of smugglers, Sgt. Jack Gordon meets Mary and discovers that Regan, who is also her guardian, is a crook. Rex helps Gordon capture Regan and brings a troop of Mounties to aid Gordon when he gets into trouble. *Ranch foremen. Smugglers. Revenge. Murder. Northwest Mounted Police. Horses.*

HOOK AND LADDER **F2.2582**

Universal Pictures. 7 Jan **1924** [c28 Nov 1923; LP19661]. Si; b&w. 35mm. 6 reels, 5,568 ft.

Dir Edward Sedgwick. *Scen* E. Richard Schayer. *Story* Edward Sedgwick, Raymond L. Schrock. *Photog* Virgil Miller.

Cast: Hoot Gibson *(Ace Cooper)*, Mildred June *(Sally Drennan)*, Frank Beal *(Capt. "Smoky Joe" Drennan)*, Edwards Davis *("Big Tom" O'Rourke)*, Philo McCullough *(Gus Henshaw)*.

Western melodrama. Cowboy Ace Cooper, to avoid arrest, becomes a fireman, falls in love with the chief's daughter, Sally Drennan, and wins her in spite of the efforts of a crooked politician to separate them—efforts which climax in a fire from which Ace saves Sally. *Cowboys. Firemen. Political corruption.*

HOOK AND LADDER NO. 9 **F2.2583**

R-C Pictures. *Dist* FBO Pictures. 13 Nov **1927** [c1 Nov 1927; LP24613]. Si; b&w. 35mm. 6 reels, 5,240 ft.

Dir F. Harmon Weight. *Adapt-Cont* Peter Milne. *Photog* H. Lyman Broening.

Cast: Cornelius Keefe *(Johnny Graham)*, Edward Hearn *(Dan Duffy)*, Lucy Beaumont *(Mother Smith)*, Dione Ellis *(Mary Smith)*, Thomas Brower *(Chief Finnerby)*, Johnny Gough *(Joker)*.

Melodrama. Dan Duffy, a fireman too timid to make his love known to Mary Smith, watches from afar as she falls in love with his fellow fireman, Johnny. When Dan summons the courage to propose to Mary, he finds that Johnny has already won her. Feeling he has been doublecrossed, not only does Dan attack Johnny, but he cannot accept the situation after their marriage. When their house catches on fire, however, Dan helps Johnny in saving Mary and the baby and then realizes his own selfishness. *Firemen. Jealousy. Timidity. Fires.*

HOOK, LINE AND SINKER **F2.2584**

RKO Radio Pictures. 26 Dec **1930** [c15 Dec 1930; LP1806]. Sd (Photophone); b&w. 35mm. 8 reels, 6,570 ft.

Prod William Le Baron. *Assoc Prod* Myles Connolly. *Dir* Edward Cline. *Screenplay-Dial* Tim Whelan, Ralph Spence. *Story* Tim Whelan. *Photog* Nick Musuraca. *Art Dir* Max Ree. *Film Ed* Archie Marshek. *Rec Engr* Hugh McDowell. *Asst Dir* Frederick Fleck.

Cast: Bert Wheeler *(Wilbur Boswell)*, Robert Woolsey *(Addington Ganzy)*, Dorothy Lee *(Mary Marsh)*, Jobyna Howland *(Mrs. Marsh)*, Ralf Harolde *(John Blackwell)*, Bill Davidson *(The Duke of Winchester)*, Natalie Moorhead *(Duchess Bessie Vanessie)*, George Marion, Sr. *(bellboy)*, Hugh Herbert *(house detective)*, Stanley Fields *(McKay)*.

Comedy. About to be forced into marrying John Blackwell, Mary Marsh runs away from her mother and soon finds herself heir to a dilapidated hotel. She meets Wilbur Boswell and Addington Ganzy, insurance agents, and when she and Wilbur fall in love, the boys agree to help her operate the hotel. For a publicity stunt Ganzy fills the hotel with wealthy socialites; then Mrs. Marsh arrives with Blackwell in tow, and though she takes a violent dislike to Wilbur, she falls for Ganzy. Blackwell sends for his gang to slay the boys and clear the field for himself, but another gang, attracted by the jewelry of the dowagers, invades the scene. A pitched battle ensues when the rival gangs meet in the hotel lobby, and when the sheriff arrives, Wilbur and Ganzy modestly admit saving the jewels. Mrs. Marsh marries Ganzy, who in turn, being Mary's father, gives her to Wilbur. *Insurance agents. Socialites. Gangs. Courtship. Hotels. Publicity.*

THE HOOSIER SCHOOLMASTER **F2.2585**

Whitman Bennett Productions. *Dist* W. W. Hodkinson Corp. 14 Feb **1924** [c21 Jan 1924; LP19850]. Si; b&w. 35mm. 6 reels, 5,556 ft.

Pres by Whitman Bennett. *Dir* Oliver L. Sellers. *Scen* Eve Stuyvesant. *Photog* Edward Paul.

Cast: Henry Hull *(Ralph Hartsook)*, Jane Thomas *(Hannah Thompson)*, Frank Dane *(Dr. Small)*, Mary Foy *(Old Mis' Means)*, Walter Palm *(Old Jack Means)*, Nat Pendleton *(Bud Means)*, Dorothy Allen *(Mirandy Means)*, G. W. Hall *(Bill Means)*, George Pelzer *(Squire Hawkins)*, Arthur Ludwig *(Pete Jones)*, Frank Andrews *(John Pearson)*, Harold McArthur *(Walter Johnson)*, Tom Brown *(Shocky Thompson)*, Adolf Link *(Dutchy Snyder)*, Jerry Sinclair *(Prosecuting Attorney Bronson)*, Dorothy Walters *(Nancy Sawyer)*, Dick Lee *(Jeems Phillips)*.

Melodrama. Source: Edward Eggleston, *The Hoosier Schoolmaster; a Novel* (New York, c1871). Ralph Hartsook becomes a schoolmaster of the Indiana Flat Creek district. He stays at the home of Old Jack Means, a wealthy citizen who wants Ralph to marry his daughter Mirandy. Instead, Ralph falls in love with Hannah Thompson, a 20-year-old orphan who works at the Means home. Political boss Pete Jones and local physician Dr. Small, to divert suspicion from themselves, accuse war veteran John Pearson of looting the house of tolltaker Dutchy Snyder. Hannah's brother Shocky and Ralph save Pearson from being lynched by a mob. Then Ralph is accused of the crime because he was seen in the vicinity of Snyder's house the night of the robbery. In the ensuing trial, Ralph successfully defends himself, while Bud Means exposes Pete Jones and Dr. Small as leaders of a gang of robbers. Ralph and Hannah marry after she is released from her bondage at the Means home. *Schoolteachers. Physicians. Veterans. Tolltakers. Gangs. Orphans. Hoosiers. Robbery. Lynching. Bondage. Indiana.*

A HORSE ON BROADWAY **F2.2586**

Frank S. Mattison Productions. *Dist* Aywon Film Corp. 5 Oct **1926** [New York State license]. Si; b&w. 35mm. 6 reels.

Comedy(?). No information about the nature of this film has been found.

HORSE SENSE **F2.2587**

Ben Wilson Productions. *Dist* Arrow Film Corp. 8 Nov **1924** [c3 Oct 1924; LP20670]. Si; b&w. 35mm. 5 reels, 4,648 ft.

Dir Ward Hayes.

Cast: Richard Hatton *(Robert Mayfield, a wanderer and a drone)*, Marilyn Mills *(Molly McLane, proprietress of the Bar-X Ranch)*, Elias Bullock *(Nat Culver, foreman of the Bar-X Ranch)*, Leon Kent *(Sheriff Crawford)*, Ray Thompson *("Bluff" Harkins, bad man and bandit)*, Beverly *(herself, a horse)*, Star *(himself, a horse)*.

Western melodrama. En route to Inferno Flats, drifter Robert Mayfield encounters Bluff Harkins, who has robbed a bank and now forces Mayfield to exchange clothes. Mayfield narrowly escapes being lynched by Nat Culver—foreman of Molly McLane's Bar-X Ranch, Bluff's cohort, and the posse leader. Soon after Mayfield goes to work for Molly and sparks Culver's jealousy, the pair engage in an edge-of-a-cliff fight that leaves Mayfield seriously injured and determined to leave the Bar-X. In his absence, Culver lures Molly away from the ranch and abandons her in the wagon when the horses bolt. Mayfield prevents Molly from going over a cliff, and Culver's duplicity is exposed. Both Beverly and Star figure prominently in the action. *Wanderers. Ranch foremen. Posses. Bank robberies. Lynching. Horses.*

HORSE SHOES **F2.2588**

Monty Banks Enterprises. *Dist* Pathé Exchange. 17 Apr **1927** [c5 Mar 1927; LU23727]. Si; b&w. 35mm. 6 reels, 5,668 ft.

Pres by A. MacArthur. *Dir* Clyde Bruckman. *Story-Scen* Monty Banks, Charles Horan. *Photog* James Diamond.

Cast: Monty Banks *(Monty Milde)*, Ernie Wood *(Henry Baker, Jr.)*, Henry Barrows *(Henry Baker, Sr.)*, John Elliott *(William Baker)*, Jean Arthur *(his daughter)*, Arthur Thalasso *(conductor)*, George French *(mayor)*, Agostino Borgato *(judge)*, Bert Apling *(O'Toole)*.

Farce. Having just graduated from law school, Monty Milde takes the train for the city and meets the daughter of William Baker. They are mistaken for a newly-married couple, and the fact that Monty has the berth above the girl's makes their position all the more embarrassing. It develops that Monty has been hired as lawyer for the girl's father, who wants to prove that his brother has forged a will, depriving him and his daughter of their rightful fortune. A crucial letter is destroyed by his opponents when he is doublecrossed by a witness; however, Monty discovers that the watermark, a horseshoe, on the will is dated after the date appearing on the document. After much difficulty, he wins the case and actually marries the girl. *Lawyers. Brothers. Mistaken identity. Wills. Documentation.*

THE HORSE TRADER *see* **A TRICK OF HEARTS**

A HORSEMAN OF THE PLAINS **F2.2589**

Fox Film Corp. 11 Mar **1928** [c10 Feb 1928; LP25046]. Si; b&w. 35mm. 5 reels, 4,399 ft.

Pres by William Fox. *Dir* Benjamin Stoloff. *Scen* Fred Myton. *Story* Harry Sinclair Drago. *Photog* Dan Clark. *Asst Dir* Clay Crapnell.

Cast: Tom Mix *(Tom Swift)*, Sally Blane *(Dawn O'Day)*, Heinie Conklin *(Snowshoe)*, Charles Byer *(J. Rutherford Gates)*, Lew Harvey *(Flash Egan)*, Grace Marvin *(Esmeralda)*, William Ryno *(Michael O'Day)*, Tony the Wonder Horse *(himself)*.

Western melodrama. Tom, the sheriff of an adjoining town, is called upon to catch a band of swindlers who are fleecing visitors at the town fair, and en route he saves the life of Snowshoe, a Negro man who becomes his inseparable companion. Tom accosts Dawn O'Day, boss of a mortgaged ranch and the daughter of an invalid father. Gates, a leading citizen who is the crook leader, agrees to get her a driver in an obstacle race, and Tom offers his services but is waylaid by Gates's agents. At the last minute he escapes, takes the substitute driver's place, and wins a thrilling race. *Sheriffs. Confidence men. Fairs. Ranches. Mortgages. Horseracing. Horses.*

HORSESHOE LUCK **F2.2590**

Sunset Productions. 15 Aug **1924.** Si; b&w. 35mm. 5 reels, 4,760 or 4,999 ft.

Dir Joseph Franz.

Cast: J. B. Warner, Margaret Morris, Harry Todd.

Western melodrama. "Garrett Harper and 'Drywash' Hutton strike a rich claim, only to lose the map to it when the girl is deceived into turning it over to the leader of a band of crooks. There is a great race for the mine which is won by rightful owners when a dynamite cache is blown up completely annihilating the crooks." (*Motion Picture News Booking Guide*, 7:28, Oct 1924.) *Gangs. Mine claims. Documentation.*

THE HOSTAGE *see* **THREE JUMPS AHEAD**

HOT CURVES **F2.2591**

Tiffany Productions. 15 Jun **1930** [c18 Jun 1930; LP1380]. Sd (Photophone); b&w. 35mm. 9 reels, 7,893 ft.

Dir Norman Taurog. *Screenplay* Earle Snell. *Dial* Frank Mortimer, Benny Rubin. *Story* A. P. Younger, Frank Mortimer. *Photog* Max Dupont. *Film Ed* Clarence Kolster. *Mus & Lyr* Violinsky and Silverstein. *Rec Engr* Buddy Myers.

Cast: Benny Rubin *(Benny Goldberg)*, Rex Lease *(Jim Dolan)*, Alice Day *(Elaine McGrew)*, Pert Kelton *(Cookie)*, John Ince *(Manager McGrew)*, Mary Carr *(Grandma Dolan)*, Mike Donlin *(Scout)*, Natalie Moorhead *(Mazie)*, Paul Hurst *(Slug)*.

Comedy-drama. Baseball player Jim Dolan, en route to the spring training camp of the Pittsburgh Cougars, engages Benny, a soda vendor, to represent that he is a star player who signed with another team. Jim, who is disappointing, meets Elaine, the manager's daughter, and falls in love; but as he is about to leave the camp, his grandmother arrives, takes him in hand, and proves that he is a good pitcher. Benny becomes a star player and acquires a girl friend, Cookie, a practical joker, but Mazie, a gold digger, completely turns Jim's head with flattery; he begins to disregard McGrew's orders and incurs the disfavor of the whole team; and as a result, he is suspended. At the last minute, he is called into the World Series game, and Benny is reported killed in a plane crash attempting to retrieve him; but he suddenly appears on the field and insists on catching for Jim, who hits the winning home run. *Grandmothers. Gold diggers. Soda clerks. Baseball. Courtship. World Series. Pittsburgh Cougars.*

HOT FOR PARIS **F2.2592**

Fox Film Corp. 22 Dec **1929** [c18 Nov 1929; LP883]. Sd (Movietone); b&w. 35mm. 7 reels, 6,570 ft. [Also si; 5,613 ft.]

Pres by William Fox. *Dir-Story* Raoul Walsh. *Adapt-Cont* Charles J. McGuirk. *Dial* William K. Wells. *Photog* Charles Van Enger. *Sets* David Hall, Ben Carré. *Film Ed* Jack Dennis. *Songs: "I'm the Duke of Kakiyak," "Sweet Nothings of Love," "If You Want To See Paree," "Sing Your Little Folk Song"* Walter Donaldson, Edgar Leslie. *Sd* George Leverett. *Asst Dir* Archibald Buchanan. *Cost* Sophie Wachner.

Cast: Victor McLaglen *(John Patrick Duke)*, Fifi D'Orsay *(Fifi Dupré)*, El Brendel *(Axel Olson)*, Polly Moran *(Polly)*, Lennox Pawle *(Mr. Pratt)*, August Tollaire *(Papa Gouset)*, George Fawcett *(ship captain)*, Charles Judels *(Charlot Gouset)*, Eddie Dillon *(ship's cook)*, Rosita Marstini *(Fifi's mother)*, Agostino Borgato *(Fifi's father)*, Yola D'Avril *(Babette Dupré)*, Anita Murray *(Mimi)*, Dave Balles *(Monsieur Furrier)*.

Musical comedy–drama. John Patrick Duke, a rough sailor fond of women and liquor, is ignorant of the fact that he is the winner of the Grand Prix at Longchamp; and, having previously caused a riot in a French hotel, he misinterprets the efforts of the officials to inform him of his good fortune. After numerous humorous experiences, he and his pal, Axel Olson, are forced into accepting the money and as a result are able to entertain their French friends royally, especially, the seductive Fifi Dupré. *Sailors. Horseracing. Lotteries. Hotels. Paris. Longchamp.*

HOT HEELS **F2.2593**

Universal Pictures. 13 May **1928** [c20 Apr 1928; LP25180]. Si; b&w. 35mm. 6 reels, 5,864 ft.

Dir William James Craft. *Scen* Harry O. Hoyt. *Titl* Albert De Mond. *Story? (see note)* Jack Foley, Vin Moore. *Photog* Arthur Todd. *Film Ed* Charles Craft.

Cast: Glenn Tryon *(Glenn Seth Higgins)*, Patsy Ruth Miller *(Patsy Jones)*, Greta Yoltz *(Fannie)*, James Bradbury, Sr. *(Mr. Fitch)*, Tod Sloan *(himself, a jockey)*, Lloyd Whitlock *(Manager Carter)*.

Comedy. Glenn, owner of a smalltown hotel, is charmed by Patsy Jones, a dancer, and liquidates his assets to buy the stranded theatrical troupe to which she belongs. In answer to a telegram offering an engagement, Glenn takes the group to Cuba, only to find that the telegram was a trick. To recoup their losses, they enter "Hot Heels," their "treadmill trick" horse, in the races and win the prize. Glenn marries the dancing girl. *Dancers. Theatrical troupes. Horseracing. Hotels. Cuba. Horses—Mechanical.*

Note: Working titles: *Patents Pending; Painting the Town.* Jack Foley and Vin Moore are given screen credit for story but company records show that Harry O. Hoyt wrote both story and scenario.

HOT NEWS **F2.2594**

Paramount Famous Lasky Corp. 14 Jul **1928** [c14 Jul 1928; LP25446]. Si; b&w. 35mm. 7 reels, 6,528 ft.

Pres by Adolph Zukor, Jesse L. Lasky. *Dir* Clarence Badger. *Scen* Florence Ryerson. *Titl* George Marion, Jr. *Adapt* Lloyd Corrigan, Grover Jones. *Story* Harlan Thompson, Monte Brice. *Photog* William Marshall. *Film Ed* Tay Malarkey.

Cast: Bebe Daniels *(Pat Clancy)*, Neil Hamilton *(Scoop Morgan)*, Paul Lukas *(James Clayton)*, Alfred Allen *(Michael Clancy)*, Spec O'Donnell *(Spec)*, Ben Hall *(Benny)*, Mario Carillo *(Maharajah)*, Maude Turner Gordon *(Mrs. Van Vleck)*.

Comedy-drama. Pat Clancy, an aspiring newsreel camera girl, is hired by her father, a publisher, to work on *The Sun* and causes Scoop Morgan, the paper's best cameraman, to quit in protest of the hiring of a woman. *The Mercury* hires Scoop, and there begins a heated rivalry between him and Pat. Pat gets a few lucky breaks and manages to get a beat on Scoop during her brief career. After she exposes the theft of a jewel from the turban of a visiting maharajah, she and Scoop are kidnaped by Clayton, the thief, and taken aboard his yacht. Rescued, she and Scoop find love and happiness. *Publishers. Motion picture cameramen. Photographers. Royalty. Newsreels. Newspapers. Employment—Women.*

HOT STUFF F2.2595

First National Pictures. 5 May **1929** [c12 May 1930; LP401]. Talking sequences (Vitaphone); b&w. 35mm. 7 reels, 6,774 ft. [Also si; 7,466 ft.]

Pres by Richard A. Rowland. *Prod* Wid Gunning. *Dir* Mervyn LeRoy. *Scen* Louis Stevens. *Titl-Dial* Humphrey Pearson. *Story* Robert S. Carr. *Photog* Sidney Hickox. *Special Photog* Alvin Knechtel. *Art Dir* John J. Hughes. *Film Ed* Terry Morse. *Cost Dir* Max Ree.

Cast: Alice White *(Barbara Allen)*, Louise Fazenda *(Aunt Kate)*, William Bakewell *(Mack Moran)*, Doris Dawson *(Thelma)*, Ben Hall *(Sandy McNab)*, Charles Sellon *(Wiggam)*, Buddy Messinger *(Tuffy)*, Andy Devine *(Bob)*, Larry Banthim *(cop)*.

Comedy. Barbara Allen, who has been a gas station attendant in her hometown, is sent to college when her Aunt Kate receives a settlement in a lawsuit. Aunt Kate, who was so restrained by her parents that she never married, is determined to see that her niece does not suffer a like fate. Babs steps out and makes the flaming youth at the freshwater school think that she is really "hot stuff" by smoking and drinking, as well as by suggesting unlimited necking possibilities. But she is discovered to be a fraud by Mack Moran, who ultimately gives her his fraternity pin, informing her that it is still the nice girls who get the wedding rings. *Filling station attendants. Flappers. Aunts. Spinsters. College life. Reputation. Courtship.*

HOT WATER F2.2596

Harold Lloyd Corp. *Dist* Pathé Exchange. 2 Nov **1924** [c24 Sep 1924; LP20596, LP20638]. Si; b&w. 35mm. 5 reels, 4,899 ft.

Dir Sam Taylor, Fred Newmeyer. *Story* Sam Taylor, Tommy Gray, Tim Whelan, John Grey. *Photog* Walter Lundin.

Cast: Harold Lloyd *(Hubby)*, Jobyna Ralston *(Wifey)*, Josephine Crowell *(Her Mother)*, Charles Stevenson *(Her Big Brother)*, Mickey McBan *(Her Little Brother)*.

Comedy. After resolving to remain a bachelor, Harold falls in love and marries. However, he is burdened with his wife's family and is forced to take them to ride in his new automobile. Through the mother-in-law's constant interference they collide with a streetcar, and the automobile is wrecked. A drink gives him courage, and after some funny pranks he chases the mother from his house. *Mothers-in-law. Marriage. Family life. Automobile accidents.*

THE HOT-HEAD *see* **THE FLAMING HOUR**

HOTEL IMPERIAL F2.2597

Famous Players–Lasky. *Dist* Paramount Pictures. 1 Jan **1927** [New York premiere; released 26 Feb; c26 Feb 1927; LP23701]. Si; b&w. 35mm. 8 reels, 7,091 ft.

Pres by Adolph Zukor, Jesse L. Lasky. *Prod* Erich Pommer. *Dir* Mauritz Stiller. *Screenplay* Jules Furthman. *Photog* Bert Glennon.

Cast: Pola Negri *(Anna Sedlak)*, James Hall *(Paul Almasy)*, George Siegmann *(General Juschkiewitsch)*, Max Davidson *(Elias Butterman)*, Michael Vavitch *(Tabakowitsch)*, Otto Fries *(Anton Klinak)*, Nicholas Soussanin *(Baron Fredrikson)*, Golden Wadhams *(Major General Sultanov)*.

War drama. Source: Lajos Biró, *Színmü négy felvonásban* (Budapest, 1917). Six Hungarian Hussars, weary from fighting, ride into a frontier town and discover it occupied by Russians. Lieut. Paul Almasy orders them to fight, but his horse falls, and he drags himself to the porter's lodge of the Hotel Imperial, where he falls asleep. Anna, Elias, and Anton, the remaining servants, carry him to a bedroom; the next morning Anna persuades him to act as their waiter. Anna is courted by General Juschkiewitsch, whose advances she accepts in order to assure Paul's release. Tabakowitsch, a spy, returns from the front and orders Paul to prepare his bath; learning he has plans which may rout Hungarian forces, Paul kills him, and Anna makes the death appear to be by suicide. The general suspects foul play and has Paul investigated; but Anna comes to his defense, and the general tears off her finery. The Hungarians reclaim their town, and Anna and Paul are reunited. *Hussars. Russians. Waiters. Spies. Impersonation. Military occupation. World War I.*

THE HOTTENTOT F2.2598

Thomas H. Ince Productions. *Dist* Associated First National Pictures. 25 Dec **1922** [c5 Dec 1922; LP18460]. Si; b&w. 35mm. 6 reels, 5,953 ft.

Pres by Thomas H. Ince. *Supv* Thomas H. Ince. *Dir* James W. Horne. *Adtl Dir* Del Andrews. *Adapt* Del Andrews. *Photog* Henry Sharp.

Cast: Douglas MacLean *(Sam Harrington)*, Madge Bellamy *(Peggy Fairfax)*, Lila Leslie *(Mrs. Carol Chadwick)*, Martin Best *(Ollie Gilford)*, Truly Shattuck *(Mrs. May Gilford)*, Raymond Hatton *(Swift)*, Dwight Crittenden *(Maj. Reggie Townsend)*, Harry Booker *(Perkins)*, Bert Lindley *(McKesson)*, Stanhope Wheatcroft *(Larry Crawford)*.

Farce. Source: William Collier and Victor Mapes, *The Hottentot; a Comedy in Three Acts* (New York, 1923). Mistaking Sam Harrington, who greatly fears horses, for a famous steeplechase rider, Peggy Fairfax enthusiastically prevails upon him to ride the highspirited Hottentot. Dumped, he covers up gamely, then narrowly excapes having to ride Peggy's horse in a steeplechase. She is so disappointed, however, that Sam buys Hottentot as a gift for Peggy, overcomes his fear, and rides the horse to victory. *Phobias. Steeplechasing. Horses.*

Note: Horne and Andrews headed separate units, Horne being responsible for the body of the film and Andrews for the horseracing sequences. Remade in 1929 under the same title, q. v.

THE HOTTENTOT F2.2599

Warner Brothers Pictures. 10 Aug **1929** [c15 Jul 1929; LP524]. Sd (Vitaphone); b&w. 35mm. 8 reels, 7,241 ft. [Also si, 28 Sep 1929; 5,004 ft.]

Dir Roy Del Ruth. *Adapt-Dial* Harvey Thew. *Photog* Barney McGill. *Film Ed* Owen Marks.

Cast: Edward Everett Horton *(Sam Harrington)*, Patsy Ruth Miller *(Peggy Fairfax)*, Douglas Gerard *(Swift)*, Edward Earle *(Larry Crawford)*, Stanley Taylor *(Alec Fairfax)*, Gladys Brockwell *(Mrs. Chadwick)*, Maude Turner Gordon *(May Gilford)*, Otto Hoffman *(Perkins)*, Edmund Breese *(Ollie)*.

Comedy. Source: Victor Mapes and William Collier, *The Hottentot, A Comedy in Three Acts* (New York, 1923). The plot is similar to that of the 1923 version. *Phobias. Steeplechasing. Horses.*

THE HOUND OF SILVER CREEK F2.2600

Universal Pictures. 20 May **1928** [c20 Oct 1927; LP24564]. Si; b&w. 35mm. 5 reels, 4,095 ft.

Pres by Carl Laemmle. *Dir* Stuart Paton. *Story-Scen* Paul M. Bryan. *Titl* Gardner Bradford. *Photog* Jerry Ash. *Film Ed* Arthur Hilton.

Cast: Dynamite *(himself, the dog)*, Edmund Cobb *(Jack Brooks)*, Gloria Grey *(Molly White)*, Gladden James *(Marvin Henley)*, Billy "Red" Jones *(Spots Lawton)*, Frank Rice *(Slim Terwilliger)*, Frank Clark *(John Lawton)*.

Melodrama. Molly White, the new schoolmistress at Silver Creek, makes the acquaintance of Jack Brooks, a wealthy eastern sportsman, when his pedigreed police dog, Dynamite, saves her from serious injury, and they become fast friends. Henley, a neighbor of Brooks, is panic-stricken upon seeing his former enemy John Lawton while driving on a country road with his son Spots; Henley shoots Lawton, and Dynamite, who "witnesses" the shooting, saves Spots and runs off with some valuable papers that Henley tries to steal from Lawton. Jack, who takes in the boy, saves Molly from Henley's advances and leaves Dynamite to protect Molly. The dog, in retrieving the documents, is discovered by Henley but manages to subdue the villain until Jack arrives and places him in custody. Spots receives an inheritance, and Jack wins the love of Molly. *Schoolteachers. Sportsmen. Murder. Inheritance. Ozarks. Documentation. Police dogs.*

THE HOUR OF RECKONING F2.2601

John E. Ince. *Dist* George H. Davis. Sep **1927**. Si; b&w. 35mm. 6 reels, 5,900 ft.

Pres by George H. Davis. *Dir* John E. Ince. *Story* Frederic Chapin. *Photog* Bert Baldridge.

Cast: John E. Ince, Herbert Rawlinson, Grace Darmond, Harry von Meter, Virginia Castleman, John J. Darby, Edwin Middleton.

Drama. Accused of stealing company funds that actually the owner's son has pilfered, a clerk (played by Herbert Rawlinson) in a safe-manufacturing concern obtains from his employer's safe the papers that prove his sweetheart's father's claim to a lock patent. The hero is able to clear his name when he consents to rescue the owner's son from a locked safe—thus melting the iron heart of his employer. *Office clerks. Inventors. Embezzlement. Safes. Locks. Documentation.*

THE HOUSE BEHIND THE CEDARS **F2.2602**
Micheaux Film Corp. **1927.** Si; b&w. 35mm. 9 reels.
Writ Charles Chesnut.
Cast: Andrew S. Bishop, Shingzie Howard, William Crowell, Lawrence Chenault, Douglas Griffin.
Melodrama(?). No information about the precise nature of this film has been found. *Negro life.*

THE HOUSE OF DARKENED WINDOWS **F2.2603**
Eastern Film Corp. 4 Feb **1925** [New York State license]. Si; b&w. 35mm. 5 reels.
Cast: Lark Brownlee.
Melodrama(?). No information about the nature of this film has been found.
Note: May have been "manufactured" in Oct 1922.

THE HOUSE OF HORROR **F2.2604**
First National Pictures. 28 Apr **1929** [c27 Mar 1929; LP283]. Talking sequence, sd eff, & mus score (Vitaphone); b&w. 35mm. 7 reels, 5,919 ft. [Also si, 7 Apr 1929; 5,656 ft.]
Pres by Richard A. Rowland. *Dir* Benjamin Christensen. *Story-Scen* Richard Bee. *Dial* William Irish. *Titl* Tom Miranda. *Photog* Ernest Haller, Sol Polito. *Film Ed* Frank Ware. *Mus Score* Louis Silvers.
Cast: Louise Fazenda *(Louise)*, Chester Conklin *(Chester)*, James Ford *(Joe)*, Thelma Todd *(Thelma)*, William V. Mong *(mystery man)*, Emile Chautard *(old miser)*, William Orlamond *(Miller)*, Dale Fuller *(Gladys)*, Tenen Holtz *(Brown)*, Michael Visaroff *(chauffeur)*.
Mystery melodrama. Bachelor Chester and his spinster sister, Louise, are summoned from Ohio by a "mystery man" who instructs them to visit their Uncle Abner in New York City. A miserly recluse, Abner lives in an old house where he has gathered a strange collection of people: Brown and his wife Gladys; two untrustworthy servants; the mystery man; and Thelma and Joe, two young people on the track of a missing diamond owned by Abner. Chester and Louise arrive at the house and are frightened by weird happenings. After much fuss and confusion, the mystery of the diamond is solved, and Joe and Thelma are revealed to be newspaper reporters in search of a good story. *Bachelors. Spinsters. Uncles. Misers. Reporters. Brother-sister relationship. Domestics. New York City. Ohio.*

THE HOUSE OF SCANDAL **F2.2605**
Tiffany-Stahl Productions. 1 Apr **1928** [c16 Apr 1928; LP25154]. Si; b&w. 35mm. 6 reels, 5,297 ft.
Dir King Baggot. *Scen* Frances Hyland. *Titl* Viola Brothers Shore. *Story* E. Morton Hough. *Photog* Barney McGill. *Art Dir* Hervey Libbert. *Film Ed* Desmond O'Brien.
Cast: Pat O'Malley *(Pat Regan)*, Dorothy Sebastian *(Ann Rourke)*, Harry Murray *(Danny Regan)*, Gino Corrado *(Morgan)*, Lee Shumway *(The Butler)*, Jack Singleton *("A Man About Town")*, Ida Darling *(Mrs. Chatterton)*, Lydia Knott *(Mrs. Rourke)*.
Melodrama. While Danny Regan, an Irish immigrant, is trying on his brother's police uniform, an automobile accident causes him to rush out of the house and into the street where, naturally, he is mistaken for a police officer. He meets a young girl (Ann), who is actually one of a group of jewel thieves. Danny's failure to arrest the thieves—when instructed to do so by a visiting jeweler who has been flimflammed—causes trouble for his brother, Pat. Attempting to clear Pat, Danny is shot by one of the crooks. Danny's courage inspires Ann to give herself up. After serving her prison sentence, she and Danny, now a full-fledged officer of the law, marry. *Brothers. Irish. Immigrants. Police. Thieves. Jewelers. Mistaken identity. Automobile accidents.*

THE HOUSE OF SECRETS **F2.2606**
Chesterfield Motion Picture Corp. 1 Feb or 15 Jul **1929.** Sd (Photophone); b&w. 35mm. 7 reels, 6,400 ft.
Dir Edmund Lawrence. *Scen-Dial* Adeline Leitzbach. *Photog* George Webber, Irving Browning, George Peters, Lester Lang. *Film Ed* Selma Rosenbloom.
Cast: Joseph Striker *(Barry Wilding)*, Marcia Manning *(Margery Gordon)*, Elmer Grandin *(Dr. Gordon)*, Herbert Warren *(Detective Blake)*, Francis M. Verdi *(Sir Hubert Harcourt)*, Richard Stevenson *(Bill)*, Harry Southard *(Warton)*, Edward Roseman *(Wu Chang)*, Walter Ringham *(Home Secretary Forbes)*.
Mystery melodrama. Source: Sydney Horler, *The House of Secrets* (London, 1926). Arriving in London with an American detective friend, Joe Blake, to investigate a house he has inherited, Barry Wilding finds mystery, danger, and love. Because of Margery Gordon, Barry decides to investigate a strange note to Home Secretary Forbes, Margery's unexplained anxiety at his presence, and the curious lurkings of one Wu Chang. Flying knives, blackjacks out of nowhere, dungeons, and poisonous fumes add to the danger. The mystery is finally solved with the arrival of Forbes, who explains the strange presence of Sir Hubert Harcourt, a great scientist whose mind has snapped. Harcourt recovers his sanity, Margery is rescued from a dungeon, and the true source of the trouble turns out to be Warton and Bill—crooks in search of pirate treasure—who prove to be a bonus for Blake in his pursuit of the murderer of a manuscript collector. *Detectives. Scientists. Manuscript collectors. Chinese. Inheritance. Murder. Insanity. Treasure. Great Britain—Home Affairs Department. London.*

THE HOUSE OF SHAME **F2.2607**
Chesterfield Motion Picture Corp. 1 Oct **1928.** Si; b&w. 35mm. 6 reels, 5,300 ft.
Supv Lon Young. *Dir* Burton King. *Adapt-Cont* Arthur Hoerl. *Titl* De Leon Anthony, Lon Young. *Story* Lee Authmar. *Photog* M. A. Anderson. *Film Ed* De Leon Anthony.
Cast: Creighton Hale *(Harvey Baremore)*, Virginia Browne Faire *(Druid Baremore)*, Lloyd Whittock *(John Kimball)*, Florence Dudley *(Doris)*, Fred Walton *(M. Fanchon)*, Carlton King *(The Irate Husband)*.
Domestic drama. Harvey Baremore, who is cheating both his wife, Druid, and his employer, John Kimball, has Druid plead to his boss for him. The employer agrees to cover for the husband, apparently with a "friendship" with the wife as the price. This triangle is climaxed by the husband's discovery of his wife in his employer's apartment and his willingness to ignore the situation for a certain consideration. This whole affair is revealed, however, to have been staged by the employer, who loves the wife, to expose the husband for the rotter he is, and in consequence the wife acknowledges her love for the employer. The husband's entanglements with a gold-digging blonde come to light, and he is killed when hit by an automobile. *Gold diggers. Infidelity. Embezzlement. Automobile accidents.*

HOUSE OF SOLOMON *see* **SOLOMON IN SOCIETY**

THE HOUSE OF YOUTH **F2.2608**
Regal Pictures. *Dist* Producers Distributing Corp. 19 Oct **1924** [c17 Sep 1924; LP20618]. Si; b&w. 35mm. 7 reels, 6,669 ft.
Dir Ralph Ince. *Scen* C. Gardner Sullivan. *Photog* J. O. Taylor.
Cast: Jacqueline Logan *(Corinna Endicott)*, Malcolm McGregor *(Spike Blaine)*, Vernon Steele *(Rhodes Winston)*, Gloria Grey *(Amy Marsden)*, Richard Travers *(Mitch Hardy)*, Lucilla Mendez *(Linda Richards)*, Edwin Booth Tilton *(Cornelius Endicott)*, Aileen Manning *(Aunt Maggie Endicott)*, Hugh Metcalf *(butler)*, Barbara Tennant *(Mrs. Mitch Hardy)*.
Society drama. Source: Maude Radford Warren, *The House of Youth* (Indianapolis, 1923). Corinna Endicott attends a wild party with her pal Spike Blaine and there becomes reacquainted with Rhodes Winston, an English writer whom she nursed in Europe. They spend more and more time together, and eventually they become engaged. Then Mitch Hardy, a married cad, entices Corinna to a roadhouse, which is raided by police while he is forcing his attentions on her. The newspapers ruin Corinna's reputation, Rhodes breaks their engagement, and Corinna refuses Spike's offer of marriage, fearing that he feels only pity for her. Corinna resolves to make up for her mistakes, however, and with Spike she starts a fresh air farm for slum children. Although Rhodes eventually reappears and insists that he needs Corinna for his inspiration, she refuses him in favor of Spike. *Nurses. Cads. Authors. Jazz life. Prohibition. Reputation. Child welfare.*

THE HOUSE ON CEDAR HILL **F2.2609**
1926. Si; b&w. 35mm. [Feature length assumed.]
Prod-Dir-Writ Carlton Moss.
Biographical drama. This film is based on the life of Frederick Douglass. *Slavery. United States—History—Civil War. Frederick Douglass.*
Note: Indicated year is approximate.

THE HOUSE THAT JAZZ BUILT **F2.2610**
Realart Pictures. Apr **1921** [c4 Apr 1921; LP16354]. Si; b&w. 35mm. 6 reels, 5,225 ft.

Dir Penrhyn Stanlaws. *Scen* Douglas Bronston. *Photog* Paul Perry.

Cast: Wanda Hawley *(Cora Rodham)*, Forrest Stanley *(Frank Rodham)*, Gladys George *(Lila Drake)*, Helen Lynch *(Kitty Estabrook)*, Clarence Geldert *(Mr. Estabrook)*, Helen Dunbar *(Mrs. Drake)*, Robert Bolder *(Mr. Foster)*.

Domestic drama. Source: Sophie Kerr, "Sweetie Peach," in *Confetti; a Book of Short Stories* (New York, 1927). Frank and Cora Rodham begin married life in a modest suburban bungalow, where Cora is an efficient and happy housekeeper. When Frank acquires a position with a New York company and they take up city residence, Cora becomes fat, indolent, and carefree. Frank, tiring of Cora and finding relief in Lila Drake, plans to divorce Cora. But Cora regains her trim figure and after exposing Lila's heartlessness wins back her husband. *Marriage. Wealth. Infidelity. Jazz life.*

HOW BAXTER BUTTED IN **F2.2611**

Warner Brothers Pictures. 20 Jun **1925** [c19 May 1925; LP21484]. Si; b&w. 35mm. 7 reels, 6,302 ft.

Dir William Beaudine. *Scen* Owen Davis. *Adapt* Julien Josephson. *Photog* David Abel.

Cast: Dorothy Devore *(Beulah Dyer)*, Matt Moore *(Henry Baxter)*, Ward Crane *(Walter Higgins)*, Wilfred Lucas *(R. S. Falk)*, Adda Gleason *(Emmy Baxter)*, Turner Savage *(Jimmy Baxter)*, Virginia Marshall *(Mary Baxter)*, Otis Harlan *(Amos Nichols)*, Rags *(himself, a dog)*.

Comedy. Source: Harold Titus, "The Stuff of Heroes," in *American Magazine* (98:23–25, Aug 1924). Henry Baxter, a shy, backward clerk in the circulation department of a big city newspaper, constantly dreams of doing heroic things and falls in love with Beulah Dyer, a pretty stenographer. Henry saves up enough money to ask her to marry him, but when his brother dies unexpectedly, Henry finds himself responsible for his sister-in-law and her two children. Henry suggests to Walter Higgins, his superior on the paper, that a series of banquets-for-heroes be instituted under the auspices of the newspaper as a means of boosting circulation; the suggestion is accepted by the management, but Higgins takes all of the credit for it. Henry breaks down from overwork, and the managing editor of the paper learns from Beulah of Henry's devotion to his sister-in-law. Falk gives a hero's banquet for Henry, but during the proceedings Henry is informed that his house is on fire. He rushes there in time to save the two children from the flames, winning a promotion and Beulah's hand in marriage. *Office clerks. Stenographers. Timidity. In-laws. Newspapers. Fires. Dogs.*

HOW HUMAN LIFE BEGINS **F2.2612**

c28 Feb **1923** [MU2243]. Si; b&w. 35mm. 5 reels, 4,700 ft.

Copyright claimant Herman Jacob Brown.

Educational documentary. "The film shows the organs that secrete Ova and Spermatozoa and by means of animated chart describes the processes of Mitosis, Cell cleavage, and fertilization. It gives a life history of the gametes. It describes by means of animated charts the process of gland transplanting and shows the children resulting from such transplanting. It describes the action of glands. Shows goat herds and glands. It is wholly a film of scientific and topical interest." (Copyright records.) *Reproduction. Mitosis. Glands. Life.*

Note: Production and distributing companies have not been established.

HOW TO EDUCATE A WIFE **F2.2613**

Warner Brothers Pictures. 1 May **1924** [c21 May 1924; LP20226]. Si; b&w. 35mm. 7 reels, 6,800 ft.

Dir Monta Bell. *Scen* Douglas Z. Doty. *Adapt* Grant Carpenter. *Story* Elinor Glyn. *Photog* Charles Van Enger.

Cast: Marie Prevost *(Mabel Todd)*, Monte Blue *(Ernest Todd)*, Claude Gillingwater *(Henry Bancks)*, Vera Lewis *(Mrs. Bancks)*, Betty Francisco *(Betty Breese)*, Creighton Hale *(Billy Breese)*, Edward Earle *(Robert Benson)*, Nellie Bly Baker *(Katinka)*.

Comedy. Business failure Ernest Todd is advised by his friend, Billy Breese, to enlist his wife's charms as a means of winning customers. Although his wife is willing, he objects, and she leaves him when he protests her "stepping out" with a prospect. Later they meet, and pretending reconciliation they invite a friend to sign an important document. All goes amiss in a runaway auto, but he signs and the couple are reunited. *Businessmen. Insurance agents. Marriage. Business ethics.*

HOW TO HANDLE WOMEN (Universal-Jewel) **F2.2614**

Universal Pictures. 14 Oct **1928** [c12 Jun 1928; LP25372]. Si; b&w. 35mm. 6 reels, 5,591 ft.

Dir William J. Craft. *Scen-Cont* Carl Krusada. *Titl* Albert De Mond. *Adapt* Jack Foley. *Story* William J. Craft, Jack Foley. *Photog* Arthur Todd. *Film Ed* Charles Craft.

Cast: Glenn Tryon *(Leonard Higgins)*, Marian Nixon *(Beatrice Fairbanks)*, Raymond Keane *(Prince Hendryx)*, Mario Carillo *(Count Olaff)*, E. H. Harriman *(himself)*, Bull Montana *(The Turk)*, Cesare Gravina *(Tony)*, Robert T. Haines *(The Editor)*, Leo White *(The Secretary)*, Violet La Plante *(The Stenographer)*.

Farce. Len Higgins, a smalltown commercial artist, assists Prince Hendryx of Volgaria in floating a loan in the United States. As security, the prince has only his country's huge peanut crop. Higgins, a peanut-lover, induces the prince to change places with him; using clever salesmanship and cartoons, he sells the peanut crop and obtains the loan. Higgins gains recognition for his cleverness and wins the love of columnist Beatrice Fairbanks. *Commercial artists. Royalty. Columnists. Advertising. Peanuts. Imaginary kingdoms.*

Note: Copyrighted in May 1928 as *Fresh Every Hour*; reviewed in Apr 1928 as *The Prince of Peanuts*. Additional working titles: *Meet the Prince, Three Days*.

HOW WOMEN LOVE **F2.2615**

B. B. Productions. 15 Oct **1922** [c19 Aug 1922; LP18173]. Si; b&w. 35mm. 6 reels, 5,377 ft.

Prod Whitman Bennett. *Dir* Kenneth Webb. *Scen* George Farnum. *Adapt* Dorothy Farnum. *Photog* Edward Paul, Harry Stradling. *Art Dir* Elsa Lopez. *Tech Dir* Lyman Ketcham.

Cast: Betty Blythe *(Rosa Roma)*, Gladys Hulette *(Natalie Nevins)*, Julia Swayne Gordon *(Mrs. Nevins)*, Katherine Stewart *(Nana)*, Jane Thomas *(peasant sweetheart)*, Anna Ames *(Olga)*, Robert Frazer *(Griffith Ames)*, Charles Lane *(Ogden Ward)*, Henry Sedley *(Count Jurka)*, Signor N. Salerno *(Jacobelli)*, Harry Sothern *(Dmitri Kavec)*, Templar Saxe *(Casanova)*, Charles Beyer *(peasant lover)*, Giorgio Majeroni *(The Tenor)*.

Society melodrama. Source: Izola Forrester, *The Dangerous Inheritance; or, The Mystery of the Tittani Rubies* (Boston, 1920). Rosa Roma, an aspiring singer, is signed by backer Ogden Ward on condition that she not fall in love, appear in public, or use her own name. But she meets composer Griffith Ames, falls in love with him, and stars in his new opera. When Ward upbraids her, Rosa tries to satisfy her contract by means of a ruby necklace, which he has been secretly trying to obtain through devious means, but the rubies are stolen. Ames is accused of the theft, but the culprit finally confesses, and Rosa is reunited with Ames and her rubies. *Singers. Composers. Opera. Theft.*

HOWDY BROADWAY **F2.2616**

Dist Rayart Pictures. 16 Oct **1929** [New York State license]. Sd; b&w. 35mm. 7 reels, 6,317 ft.

Cast: Ellalee Ruby, Lucy Ennis, Jack J. Clark, Tommy Christian and His Band.

Musical comedy-drama. Fresh from his triumphant leadership in Burdette's crew victory over Clinton, Tommy is welcomed at his fraternity house and pins Betty that night at a dance. Later, Tommy reluctantly agrees to take his band to the Ramble Inn so that Lulu can dance for a Broadway producer. The speakeasy is raided, and Tommy stays behind to delay the police; he is consequently expelled from school, and he loses Betty's favor. Taking the band to New York, Tommy's happiness at getting a spot on Broadway is marred only by Betty's absence, but the band's success on opening night is made complete by Betty's arrival. Betty and Tommy make a hasty exit to get married. Songs include: "Sophomore Strut," "Atta Boy, Ole Kid," "I Want You To Know I Love You," "Gazoozalum Gazoo," "You're Gonna Be Blue," "Somebody's Sweetheart—Not Mine," "Howdy Broadway," "Gypsy Love." Specialty numbers during the Broadway show sequence include a song by Lucy Ennis and a tap dance by Jack Clark. *Musicians. Band leaders. Dancers. Athletes. College life. Boat racing. Speakeasies. Jazz life. Dance bands. New York City—Broadway.*

HULA **F2.2617**

Paramount Famous Lasky Corp. 27 Aug **1927** [c27 Aug 1927; LP24340]. Si; b&w. 35mm. 6 reels, 5,862 ft.

Pres by Adolph Zukor, Jesse L. Lasky. *Assoc Prod* B. P. Schulberg. *Dir* Victor Fleming. *Screenplay* Ethel Doherty. *Titl* George Marion, Jr. *Adapt* Doris Anderson. *Photog* William Marshall. *Film Ed* Eda Warren. *Asst Dir* Henry Hathaway.

Cast: Clara Bow *("Hula" Calhoun)*, Clive Brook *(Anthony Haldane)*,

Arlette Marchal *(Mrs. Bane)*, Arnold Kent *(Harry Dehan)*, Maude Truax *(Margaret Haldane)*, Albert Gran *(Old Bill Calhoun)*, Agostino Borgato *(Uncle Edwin)*.

Romantic drama. Source: Armine von Tempski, *Hula, a Romance of Hawaii* (New York, 1927). "Hula" Calhoun, the daughter of a Hawaiian planter, sidesteps the dissolute influence of her father through the guidance of her Uncle Edwin, who prefers a more natural existence to the society life of the family. Although Hula is adored by Harry Dehan, a boisterous rounder, she becomes infatuated with Anthony Haldane, a young English engineer who comes to supervise the construction of a dam on the estate. Haldane remains distant, however; and when saving her from a runaway horse, he informs her that he is married. At her birthday party, the broken-hearted girl turns to Dehan, and in a drunken frenzy she provokes Haldane by her dancing; he then promises to obtain a divorce, but Mrs. Haldane appears. Hula jealously bribes the foreman to dynamite a spot near the dam, convincing the wife that her husband is ruined. Haldane's wife agrees to the divorce, and he is free to marry Hula. *Planters. Uncles. English. Engineers—Civil. Filial relations. Divorce. Dams. Hula. Hawaii.*

HUMAN HEARTS (Universal-Jewel) **F2.2618**

Universal Film Manufacturing Co. ca5 Aug **1922** [New York premiere; released 2 Oct]. Si; b&w. 35mm. 7 reels, 6,350 ft.

Pres by Carl Laemmle. *Dir* King Baggot. *Scen* Lucien Hubbard, Marc Robbins. *Adapt* Marc Robbins, George C. Hull. *Photog* Victor Milner, Otto Dyar.

Cast: House Peters *(Tom Logan)*, Russell Simpson *(Paul Logan)*, Gertrude Claire *(Ma Logan)*, George Hackathorne *(Jimmy Logan)*, George West *(Old Mose)*, Lucretia Harris *(Carolina)*, Edith Hallor *(Barbara Kaye)*, Ramsey Wallace *(Benton)*, Mary Philbin *(Ruth)*, H. S. Karr *(Seth Bascom)*, Snitz Edwards *(Ran Schreiber)*, Gene Dawson *(Little Barbara)*, Emmett King *(governor)*, Wilton Taylor *(warden)*.

Rural melodrama. Source: Hal Reid, *Human Hearts* (a play; publication undetermined). City confidence woman Barbara Kaye visits the Logan farm in the Ozarks for the purpose of marrying Tom Logan for the fortune in coal beneath the Logan property. Paul, Tom's father, is suspicious of Barbara and disinherits Tom after his marriage. Angry with Logan and restless from the monotony of farm life, Barbara succumbs to the temptation of her former lover, Benton, and she returns to the city with the ex-convict and her daughter when Benton kills Paul Logan and Tom is imprisoned for the murder. Eventually, Barbara repents, confesses the truth, and is reconciled with Tom, who rescues his wife from the brutal Benton and takes his family back to the farm. *Confidence women. Farmers. Coal. Wealth. Farm life. Infidelity. Murder. Ozarks.*

THE HUMAN TERROR **F2.2619**

Dist Geneva Distributing Corp. 28 Feb **1924** [scheduled release]. Si; b&w. 35mm. 5 reels, 4,800 ft.

Cast: Alec B. Francis, Margaret Seddon.

Rural melodrama. No information about the precise nature of this film or its producer has been found.

THE HUMAN TORNADO **F2.2620**

R-C Pictures. *Dist* Film Booking Offices of America. 21 Jun **1925** [c21 Jun 1925; LP21596]. Si; b&w. 35mm. 5 reels, 4,472 ft.

Dir Ben Wilson. *Story-Cont* Cliff Hill. *Photog* Al Siegler, Lew Breslow.

Cast: Yakima Canutt *(Jim Marlow)*, Bert Sprotte *(Chet Marlow)*, Nancy Leeds *(Marion Daley)*, Lafe McKee *(Peter Daley)*, Joe Rickson *(Tom Crowley)*, Slim Allen *(Sheriff Cutter)*.

Western melodrama. Jim Marlow's brother, Chet, who has come west to manage the family mining properties, cheats Pete Daley out of his property. Pete enters Chet's office at night and robs the safe, being seen in the act by Tom Crowley. Pete hides the strongbox and sends a letter to his daughter, Marion, stating its location. Jim gets the letter and finds the strongbox, running afoul of Crowley, who shoots him. The sheriff arrests Jim for stealing the box, and Crowley attempts to take the box from the sheriff at gunpoint. The sheriff shoots Crowley, and Crowley, mortally wounded, tells the sheriff that Pete Daley was the man responsible for the original theft of the box. A lawyer who has been investigating Chet discovers that he has cheated Jim out of the substantial part of his rightful inheritance; Chet is sent to jail, and Jim settles down with Marion Daley. *Brothers. Sheriffs. Lawyers. Robbery. Inheritance. Documentation.*

HUMAN WRECKAGE **F2.2621**

Thomas H. Ince Corp. *Dist* Film Booking Offices of America. 17 Jun **1923** [c17 Jun 1923; LP19143]. Si; b&w. 35mm. 8 reels, 7,215 ft.

Dir John Griffith Wray. *Story* C. Gardner Sullivan. *Photog* Henry Sharp. *Coöp* Los Angeles Anti-Narcotic League.

Cast: Mrs. Wallace Reid *(Ethel MacFarland)*, James Kirkwood *(Alan MacFarland)*, Bessie Love *(Mary Finnegan)*, George Hackathorne *(Jimmy Brown)*, Claire McDowell *(Mrs. Brown)*, Robert McKim *(Dr. Hillman)*, Harry Northrup *(Steve Stone)*, Victory Bateman *(Mrs. Finnegan)*, Eric Mayne *(Dr. Blake)*, Otto Hoffman *(Harris)*, Philip Sleeman *(Dunn)*, George Clark *(The Baby)*, Lucille Ricksen *(Ginger Smith)*, George E. Cryer, Mayor of the City of Los Angeles *(a city official)*, Dr. R. B. von Kleinsmid, President of the University of Southern California *(an educator)*, Benjamin Bledsoe, U. S. Judge, 12th Federal District *(a jurist)*, Louis D. Oaks, Chief of Police, Los Angeles *(a police official)*, Martha Nelson McCan, Los Angeles Park Commissioner *(a civic leader)*, Mrs. Chester Ashley *(a civic leader)*, John P. Carter, former U. S. Internal Revenue Collector *(a civic leader)*, Mrs. Charles F. Gray, Parent-Teachers Assn. *(a civic leader)*, Dr. L. M. Powers, Health Commissioner, City of Los Angeles *(a health authority)*, Brig. C. R. Boyd, Salvation Army *(Salvation Army worker)*.

Sociological melodrama. "Treats of the evils of drugs, pointing out the disasters which visit several figures in general and the MacFarlands in particular. The husband is an attorney who suffers a nervous breakdown. Becomes addicted to morphine and his efforts to shake off the habit are fruitless until he realizes that his wife is encouraged to take up the habit because of his weakness and the futility of trying to cope with it." (*Motion Picture News*, 14 Jul 1923.) *Lawyers. Narcotics. Los Angeles. Salvation Army.*

THE HUMMING BIRD **F2.2622**

Famous Players–Lasky. *Dist* Paramount Pictures. 13 Jan **1924** [c23 Jan 1924; LP19848]. Si; b&w. 35mm. 8 reels, 7,490 or 7,577 ft.

Pres by Adolph Zukor, Jesse L. Lasky. *Dir* Sidney Olcott. *Adapt* Forrest Halsey. *Photog* Harry Fischbeck. *Film Ed* Patricia Rooney. *Tech Adv* Jacques D'Auray.

Cast: Gloria Swanson *(Toinette)*, Edward Burns *(Randall Carey)*, William Ricciardi *("Papa" Jacques)*, Cesare Gravina *(Charlot)*, Mario Majeroni *(La Roche)*, Adrienne D'Ambricourt *(The Owl)*, Helen Lindroth *(Henrietta Rutherford)*, Rafael Bongini *(Bouchet)*, Regina Quinn *(Beatrice)*, Aurelio Coccia *(Bosque)*, Jacques D'Auray *(Zi-Zi)*.

Underworld drama. Source: Maude Fulton, *The Humming Bird* (New York opening: 15 Jan 1923). Toinette, alias "The Humming Bird," is leader of a gang of apache thieves in the Montmartre section of Paris. American reporter Randall Carey falls in love with her. The Great War breaks out, Carey enlists, and Toinette inspires her gang to fight for France. Toinette, arrested as she is giving her spoils to the church, is imprisoned. When she hears that Carey has been badly wounded, she escapes and is reunited with him. Carey recovers, and Toinette receives the War Cross for her work in recruiting some heroic soldiers. *Reporters. Thieves. Apaches—Paris. Criminals—Rehabilitation. World War I. Paris—Montmartre.*

THE HUNCH **F2.2623**

S-L Productions. *Dist* Metro Pictures. 28 Nov **1921** [c8 Dec 1921; LP17331]. Si; b&w. 35mm. 6 reels. [Copyrighted as 5 reels.]

Dir George D. Baker. *Photog* Rudolph Bergquist. *Art Dir* E. J. Shulter.

Cast: Gareth Hughes *(J. Preston [Jimmy] Humphrey)*, Ethel Grandin *(Barbara Thorndyke)*, John Steppling *(John C. Thorndyke)*, Edward Flanagan *(George Taylor)*, Harry Lorraine *(Sheriff Henry Clay Greene)*, Gale Henry *(Minnie Stubbs)*, William H. Brown *(Hodges)*.

Comedy drama. Source: Percival Wilde, "The Hunch," in *Popular Magazine* (9:3–61, 20 Apr 1921). After a jovial evening, Jimmy Humphrey awakens in his bathtub to find "Buy Jerusalem Steel" written on his shirt; and playing a hunch, he borrows money from his future father-in-law, John Thorndyke, so as to buy 5,000 shares. When the stock falls, Thorndyke orders him to make good the loss; and to stall Thorndyke, Jimmy conspires with Barbara, his fiancée, and a friend, Taylor: a bloodstained knife and his hat are found, and a "murder mystery" is thus created. On the road, Jimmy is set upon by thieves, stripped of his clothing, and outfitted as a tramp. He is arrested as the murderer of Jimmy Humphrey, and before he is released, Barbara and Taylor are charged with being accessories. John Thorndyke arrives to release the prisoners, and it is discovered that Jerusalem Steel has reached a high mark on the market; Jimmy and

Barbara receive the parental blessing. *Courtship. Stock market. Steel industry. Hoaxes.*

THE HUNCHBACK OF NOTRE DAME (Universal Super-Jewel) **F2.2624**

Universal Pictures. 2 Sep **1923** [New York premiere; released 6 Sep; c6 Sep 1923; LP19381]. Si; b&w. 35mm. 12 reels, ca12,000 ft.

Pres by Carl Laemmle. *Dir* Wallace Worsley. *Scen* Edward T. Lowe, Jr. *Adapt* Perley Poore Sheehan. *Photog* Robert Newhard. *Adtl Photog* Tony Kornman. *Asst Dir* Jack Sullivan, William Wyler.

Cast: Lon Chaney *(Quasimodo)*, Ernest Torrence *(Clopin)*, Patsy Ruth Miller *(Esmeralda)*, Norman Kerry *(Phoebus)*, Kate Lester *(Madame de Gondelaurier)*, Brandon Hurst *(Jehan)*, Raymond Hatton *(Gringoire)*, Tully Marshall *(Louis XI)*, Nigel De Brulier *(Dom Claude)*, Harry Van Meter *(Monsieur Neufchatel)*, Gladys Brockwell *(Godule)*, Eulalie Jensen *(Marie)*, Winifred Bryson *(Fleur de Lys)*, Nick De Ruiz *(Monsieur le Torteru)*, Edwin Wallock *(King's Chamberlain)*, W. Ray Meyers *(Charmolou's assistant)*, William Parke, Sr. *(Josephus)*, John Cossar *(judge of court)*, Roy Laidlaw *(Charmolie)*, George MacQuarrie, Jay Hunt, Harry De Vere, Pearl Tupper, Eva Lewis, Jane Sherman, Helen Bruneau, Gladys Johnston, Cesare Gravina.

Drama. Source: Victor Hugo, *Notre-Dame de Paris* (1831). Quasimodo, an inarticulate, deformed human being, who is the bellringer of the Cathedral of Notre Dame, sacrifices his life to save Esmeralda, a Gypsy girl who once befriended him, from Jehan, the hunchback's evil master and brother to Dom Claude, chief priest of the cathedral. *Hunchbacks. Gypsies. Priests. Paris. Notre Dame de Paris. Cathedrals. Louis XI (France).*

THE HUNGER OF THE BLOOD (Franklyn Farnum Series) **F2.2625**

William N. Selig Productions. *Dist* Canyon Pictures. Mar **1921** [c2 Mar 1921; LU16210]. Si; b&w. 35mm. 5 reels.

Prod Col. William N. Selig. *Dir* Nate Watt. *Screenplay* William E. Wing. *Story* William C. Beale.

Cast: Franklyn Farnum *(Maslun)*, Ethel Ritchie *(Margaret Kenyon)*, Baby Jean O'Rourke *(Little Fawn)*.

Western melodrama. Maslun, a halfbreed, is entrusted with the tribal secret (that there is gold in Dead Man's Canyon on tribal land) just before his foster father, Chief Amek, dies. He finds and adopts a waif (a white girl), whom he names Little Fawn. She later goes into a trance in which the dead chief speaks through the child's lips and urges Maslun to find the gold for the tribe's sake. Maslun's attentions to Margaret Kenyon, a white girl who according to the white man's law owns the canyon, arouses the tribe's suspicions. Warriors kidnap Margaret, but she is rescued by Maslun. Little Fawn goes into another trance (which almost kills her) in which Amek informs Maslun of the gold's location. He goes to the canyon, is there attacked by his tribe, but is rescued by a band of cowboys. It is revealed that he is really a fullblooded white man, Margaret tells him of her love, and the gold is divided between the Indians and Margaret. *Halfcastes. Waifs. Indians of North America. Cowboys. Gold. Trances.*

HUNGRY HEARTS **F2.2626**

Goldwyn Pictures. 26 Nov **1922** [c1 Nov 1922; LP18529]. Si; b&w. 35mm. 7 reels, 6,540 ft.

Dir E. Mason Hopper. *Scen* Julien Josephson. *Titl* Montague Glass. *Photog* Robert Newhard.

Cast: Bryant Washburn *(David Kaplan)*, Helen Ferguson *(Sara Levin)*, E. A. Warren *(Abraham Levin)*, Rosa Rosanova *(Hannah Levin)*, George Siegmann *(Rosenblatt)*, Otto Lederer *(Gedalyah Mindel)*, Millie Schottland *(Mishel Mindel)*, Bert Sprotte *(Cossack)*, A. Budin *(Sopkin)*, Edwin B. Tilton *(The Judge)*.

Drama. Source: Anzia Yezierska, *Hungry Hearts* (Boston, 1920). The Levins come to the United States from Russia in hope of a better life but find it very difficult to make a living, even with everybody working. When Rosenblatt raises their rent, an enraged Hannah mutilates the walls, an act for which she must stand trial. Lawyer David Kaplan, who is Rosenblatt's nephew and Sara's sweetheart, successfully defends Hannah, marries Sara, and takes the Levin family out of the ghetto and into his suburban home. *Immigrants. Landlords. Lawyers. Jews. Russians. Finance—Personal.*

HUNTED MEN **F2.2627**

Big Productions Film Corp. *Dist* Syndicate Pictures. Apr **1930**. Si; b&w. 35mm. 5 reels, 4,853 ft.

Dir J. P. McGowan. *Story-Scen* Sally Winters. *Photog* Herbert Kirkpatrick.

Cast: Bob Steele, Jean Reno, Lew Meehan, Mac V. Wright, Thomas G. Lingham, Clark Comstock.

Western melodrama. "The plot is just a variation on the villain and his gang trying to steal the gal's ranch, with the hero calling the turn at the proper moment." (*Film Daily*, 25 May 1930, p17.) *Ranchers. Gangs.*

THE HUNTED WOMAN **F2.2628**

Fox Film Corp. 22 Mar **1925** [c22 Mar 1925; LP21328]. Si; b&w. 35mm. 5 reels, 4,954 ft.

Pres by William Fox. *Dir* Jack Conway. *Adapt-Scen* Robert N. Lee, Dorothy Yost. *Photog* Joe August.

Cast: Seena Owen *(Joanne Gray)*, Earl Schenck *(John Aldous)*, Diana Miller *(Marie)*, Cyril Chadwick *(Culver Rann)*, Francis McDonald *(Joe De Bar)*, Edward Piel *(Charlie)*, Victor McLaglen *(Quade)*.

Northwest melodrama. Source: James Oliver Curwood, *The Hunted Woman* (Garden City, New York, 1916). Author John Aldous goes to a lawless Alaskan settlement and there grubstakes two miners, De Bar and McDonald, who soon discover a rich gold mine. Joanne Gray, a refined woman who comes to the rough mining town, is insulted in her hotel room by Quade, the proprietor of the local dancehall. John comes to her assistance and learns that she is looking for her husband, who disappeared without a trace in the gold fields. John goes to investigate a grave marked with Gray's name, and De Bar, his tongue loosened by liquor, tells Joanne of his rich gold claim. Quade chances to hear De Bar's remark and tortures him until he discovers the mine's location. Quade starts for the mine after he dynamites the hillside above Aldous' cabin, trapping John and Joanne inside. Before they are rescued, they confess their mutual love. Once freed, John is told that Joanne's husband has been found dead, and the lovers are married. John then learns that Joanne's husband is, in fact, Rann, Quade's partner. Quade kidnaps Joanne and Rann claims her for his wife; Quade then kills Rann and is in turn killed by De Bar. John and Joanne look forward to a long and happy life together. *Authors. Miners. Gold mines. Torture. Murder. Bigamy. Mining towns. Dancehalls. Alaska.*

HUNTIN' TROUBLE **F2.2629**

Maloford Productions. *Dist* Photo Drama Co. 5 Mar **1924** [New York license application; c25 Jan 1924; LU19858]. Si; b&w. 35mm. 5 reels.

Dir Leo D. Maloney, Bob Williamson. *Writ for the screen by* Frances Beebe, Ford Beebe. *Photog* Jake Badaracco. *Ed* Fred Bain.

Cast: Leo Maloney *(Clay Rathbun)*, Bullet *(himself, a dog)*, Josephine Hill *(Eleanor Morgan)*.

Western melodrama. Clay Rathbun, a struggling young attorney, does not believe in violence. He is in love with Eleanor Morgan, daughter of Captain Morgan, an ex-ranger and brother of Ranger "Slim" Morgan, Clay's best friend. Gus Ogilbie, after serving 5 years in jail, comes out seeking revenge but fails to get the drop on Clay (whose father, now dead, helped to convict him). Eleanor, at her father's insistence, rejects Clay because he is not a ranger. When Slim is discovered near death, Clay puts on Slim's holster and for once in his life goes out "huntin' trouble"! Gus and his men show up, and Eleanor sends Bullet, Clay's dog, with her handkerchief to fetch Clay. Clay arrives in time to defeat the culprits in a fight, and Captain Morgan accepts Clay as his future son-in-law. *Lawyers. Rangers. Revenge. Dogs.*

Note: Story and character names have been taken from shooting script in the copyright files and may differ from the final film.

HUNTING BIG GAME IN AFRICA WITH GUN AND CAMERA **F2.2630**

African Expedition Corp. 6 Dec **1922** [c8 Feb 1923; MU2231]. Si; b&w. 35mm. 9 reels.

Story H. A. Snow. *Photog* Sydney Snow. *Mus Score* Gino Severi.

Personages: H. A. Snow, Sydney Snow.

Travelog. Professor Snow, his son Sydney, and crew sail for Cape Town, Africa, where they plan a safari north into the wilderness. En route to Cape Town, there are shots of a whale hunt and later the astonishing sight of millions of "Jackass Penguins" playing on the rocky shores. On the safari itself we share their adventures and misadventures: the diamond mines in Kimberley; the tsetse fly invasion killing their horses and oxen; the beauty of a herd of giraffe running across the plain; the deadly rhinoceros charging head on at the camera; the dancing of the village women and their warriors; and in the crater of an extinct volcano a herd of giant elephants, surrounded by the leaders of the safari and the natives. *Safaris. Diamond mines. Volcanoes. Cape Town. Kimberley. South Africa. Whales. Rhinoceros. Giraffe. Penguins. Elephants. Tsetse flies.*

HUNTING TIGERS IN INDIA **F2.2631**

Talking Picture Epics. *For* American Museum of Natural History. 9 Dec **1929** [New York premiere]. Sd (Photophone); b&w. 35mm. 8 reels, 7,886 ft.

Dir George M. Dyott, Leo Meehan. *Dial* George M. Dyott. *Photog* Dal Clawson. *Film Ed* J. Leo Meehan.

Travelog. A film record of the Vernay-Faunthrope expedition that was organized by Mrs. A. S. Vernay on behalf of the American Museum of Natural History in New York. As narrated by Comdr. George M. Dyott, the group travels all over India after paying its respects to Lord Reading, the Viceroy. Highlights include observing elephants in southern India, hunting rhinoceros with the Maharaja of Nepal, and a climaxing tiger hunt (also in Nepal). The life of the Indian people is depicted to some extent—for example, in scenes of bazaars and funerals in central India. *Hunting. Big game. Jungles. Bazaars. Funerals. India. Nepal. Mrs. A. S. Vernay. Rufus Daniel Isaacs. Elephants. Rhinoceros. Tigers.*

HUNTING TROUBLE *see* **HOLD THAT LION**

THE HUNTRESS **F2.2632**

Associated First National Pictures. 20 Aug **1923** [c22 Aug 1923; LP19330]. Si; b&w. 35mm. 6 reels, 6,236 ft.

Dir Lynn Reynolds. *Adapt* Percy Heath. *Photog* James C. Van Trees. *Art Dir* Milton Menasco. *Asst Dir* Harry Welfer.

Cast: Colleen Moore *(Bela)*, Lloyd Hughes *(Sam Gladding)*, Russell Simpson *(Big Jack Skinner)*, Walter Long *(Joe Hagland)*, Charles Anderson *(Black Shand Frazer)*, Snitz Edwards *(Musq'oosis)*, Wilfrid North *(John Gladding)*, Helen Raymond *(Mrs. John Gladding)*, William Marion *(William Gladding)*, Lila Leslie *(Mrs. William Gladding)*, Lawrence Steers *(Richard Gladding)*, Helen Walron *(Mrs. Richard Gladding)*, John Lince *(butler)*, Lalo Encinas *(Beavertail)*, Chief Big Tree *(Otebaya)*.

Melodrama. Source: Hulbert Footner, *The Huntress* (New York, 1922). Bela, reared by Indians, learns that she is a white orphan and runs away from the Indian village to avoid marrying a brave from the tribe. She determines to marry land prospector Sam Gladding, who resists her advances but later falls in love with Bela when an Indian sage gives him some advice. *Orphans. Prospectors. Indians of North America. Parentage.*

THE HURRICANE **F2.2633**

Dist Truart Film Corp. 26 Feb **1926** [New York State license]. Si; b&w. 35mm. 5 reels.

Cast: Alice Lake, Stuart Holmes, Jack Richardson.

Melodrama(?). No information about the nature of this film has been found.

HURRICANE **F2.2634**

Columbia Pictures. 30 Sep **1930** [c14 Oct 1929; LP764]. Sd (Movietone); b&w. 35mm. 7 reels, 5,735 ft. [Also si; 5,842 ft.]

Prod Harry Cohn. *Dir* Ralph Ince. *Cont* Enid Hibbard. *Dial* Norman Houston. *Titl* Weldon Melick. *Story* Evelyn Campbell, Norman Springer. *Photog* Teddy Tetzlaff. *Art Dir* Harrison Wiley. *Film Ed* David Berg. *Ch Sd Engr* John Livadary. *Asst Dir* C. C. Coleman.

Cast: Hobart Bosworth *(Hurricane Martin)*, Johnny Mack Brown *(Dan)*, Leila Hyams *(Mary Stevens)*, Allan Roscoe *(Captain Black)*, Tom O'Brien *(Dugan)*, Leila McIntyre *(Mrs. Stevens)*, Joe Bordeaux *(Pete)*, Eddie Chandler *(Bull)*.

Melodrama. Captain Black and his band of pirates are shipwrecked on a South Sea island, where they hold in custody several sailors they have shanghaied, among them, Dan, a youth of good breeding. When Black observes the vessel of the feared Hurricane Martin approaching, he plots to get his men aboard that vessel, incite a mutiny, and seize the cargo. Hurricane's former wife, who deserted him 20 years earlier, her daughter, and a sailor are rescued from a lifeboat; and thirsting for revenge, Hurricane plans to marry the girl, Mary, to the pirate Captain Black, though the mother avows her own innocence with her dying breath. Dan, who has fallen in love with Mary, protects her from Black, but Hurricane downs the leader and quells the mutiny. *Sea captains. Seafaring life. Shanghaiing. Ships. Piracy. Revenge. Mutiny. South Seas. Shipwrecks.*

HURRICANE HAL **F2.2635**

Ermine Productions. *Dist* Usla Co. ca13 Nov **1925** [c17, 20 Nov 1924; LU20803]. Si; b&w. 35mm. 4 reels, 3,872 ft.

Pers Supv Bernard D. Russell. *Scen* John P. McCarthy.

Cast: Jack Meehan.

Western melodrama. Buck Anderson, a young Texan, saves Bill Adams from Mexican bandits. In gratitude, Adams gives Buck a job on his ranch, where Buck antagonizes Lacey, the foreman, and falls in love with Virginia McFarland, the daughter of Adams' partner. McFarland and Adams decide to transport a large shipment of money in a buckboard driven by Lacey and accompanied by McFarland and Virginia. Lacey, who has been stealing cattle, arranges with his men to hold up the party. Buck sees the theft, follows the bandits to a cabin, and gets the drop on them; but he is tricked and forced to flee, taking Virginia with him. Buck is caught by the bandits but frees himself and goes after Lacey, who has taken both Virginia and the money with him. Lacey's horse is shot from under him, and he steals a railroad engine. Buck follows on his horse, boards the engine, and fights it out with Lacey. The train crashes through a burning bridge; Buck and Virginia escape; and Lacey is captured by the Federales. *Ranchers. Ranch foremen. Rustlers. Bandits. Federales. Locomotives. Texas. Mexican border. Train wrecks.*

HURRICANE HORSEMAN **F2.2636**

Action Pictures. *Dist* Weiss Brothers Artclass Pictures. 14 Oct **1925.** Si; b&w. 35mm. 5 reels, 4,440 ft.

Dir Robert Eddy. *Scen* A. E. Serrao, Katherine Fanning.

Cast: Wally Wales *(Wally Marden)*, Jean Arthur *(June Mathews)*, Vester Pegg *(Jim Marden)*, Charles Whitaker *(Mike Wesson)*, Kewpie King *(Kewpie Cook)*, Robert Chandler *(Parson Pettigrew)*, Bob Fleming *(sheriff)*.

Western melodrama. When a bank is robbed, the cashier is killed and suspicion for the murder unjustly falls on Jim Marden. He gives himself up, and his brother, Wally, promises to run down the killer. Wally, who suspects Mike Wesson, the foreman of the Flying X Ranch, of the crime, goes to the ranch and talks to him. While at the ranch Mike meets June Mathews, owner of the ranch, and he falls in love with her. When Wally and June are out riding, they are ambushed by Wesson, and Wally is wounded. One of Wesson's confederates later exposes Wesson's perfidy, and Wally brings the homicidal foreman to justice. Wally then weds June. *Brothers. Ranchers. Ranch foremen. Murder. Bank robberies.*

THE HURRICANE KID **F2.2637**

Universal Pictures. 25 Jan **1925** [c7 Nov 1924; LP20755]. Si; b&w. 35mm. 6 reels, 5,296 ft.

Pres by Carl Laemmle. *Dir* Edward Sedgwick. *Scen* E. Richard Schayer. *Adapt* Raymond L. Schrock. *Story* Will Lambert. *Photog* Virgil Miller. *Art Dir* Leo E. Kuter.

Cast: Hoot Gibson *(The Hurricane Kid)*, Marion Nixon *(Joan Langdon)*, William A. Steele *(Lafe Baxter)*, Arthur Machley *(Colonel Langdon)*, Violet La Plante *(Joan's friend)*, Harry Todd *(Hezekial Potts)*, Fred Humes *(Jed Hawks)*, Pal *(a horse)*.

Western melodrama. The Hurricane Kid runs afoul of Colonel Langdon's ranch foreman, Lafe Baxter, when Joan Langdon shows an obvious preference for The Kid, and The Kid responds by protecting Joan from Baxter. Out of gratitude The Kid tames a wild mare and rides it to victory in a race staged by Langdon and Hezekial Potts, with their ranches as stakes. *Cowboys. Ranch foremen. Horseracing. Wagers. Horses.*

HURRICANE'S GAL **F2.2638**

Allen Holubar Pictures. *Dist* Associated First National Pictures. ca2 Jul **1922** [Chicago premiere; released Jul 1922; c25 Jul 1922; LP18090]. Si; b&w. 35mm. 8 reels, 7,944 ft.

Pres by Allen Holubar. *Dir-Adapt* Allen Holubar. *Titl* Max Abramson. *Story* Harvey Gates. *Photog* Byron Haskin, William McGann. *Film Ed* Frank Lawrence. *Asst Dir* Harold S. Bucquet. *Naval Tech Adv* Lieut. Thomas Berrian, U. S. N.

Cast: Dorothy Phillips *(Lola)*, Robert Ellis *(Steele O'Connor)*, Wallace Beery *(Chris Borg)*, James O. Barrows *(Cap'n Danny)*, Gertrude Astor *(Phyllis Fairfield)*, William Fong *(Sing)*, Jack Donovan *(Lieutenant Grant)*, Frances Raymond *(Mrs. Fairfield)*.

Adventure melodrama. Lola ("Hurricane's Gal") has inherited her father's smuggling trade and fierce independence. She falls in love with Steele, a stowaway who is revealed to be a government agent. She takes revenge by kidnaping her rival for Steele's hand but realizes her error. Hydroplanes, destroyers, and schooners participate in a climax in which love conquers. *Smugglers. Government agents. Seafaring life.*

HUSBAND HUNTERS **F2.2639**

Tiffany Productions. 15 Jan **1927** [c17 Feb 1927; LP23673]. Si; b&w. 35mm. 6 reels, 5,600 ft.

Pres by M. H. Hoffman. *Dir* John G. Adolfi. *Cont* Esther Shulkin. *Story* Douglas Bronston. *Photog* Joseph A. Dubray, Steve Norton. *Art Dir* Edwin B. Willis. *Film Ed* Harold Young.

Cast: Mae Busch *(Marie Devere)*, Charles Delaney *(Bob Garrett)*, Jean Arthur *(Letty Crane)*, Walter Hiers *(Sylvester Jones)*, Duane Thompson *(Helen Gray)*, Mildred Harris *(Cynthia Kane)*, Robert Cain *(Bartley Mortimer)*, Jimmy Harrison *(Jimmy Wallace)*, Nigel Barrie *(Rex Holden)*, James Mack *(Mr. Casey)*, Marcin Asher *(Mr. Cohen)*, Fred Fisher *(Archibald Percival Springer)*.

Society comedy-drama. Marie and Helen, two sophisticated New York chorus girls who size up all their male acquaintances by the number of ciphers in their Bradstreet ratings, befriend Letty Crane, a poor girl from the country, when she fails to get work at the theater. Letty is befriended also by Bob Garrett, who lives in a nearby apartment. The girls purchase some clothes for Letty on credit, and their various attempts to avoid the collector provide comic moments. Letty, like Helen, is led down the primrose path by Bartley Mortimer, a wealthy married man. Cynthia, who also loves Bart, goes in Letty's place to elope with him, and they are killed at a railroad crossing. Heartbroken by the ruin of both her romance and career, Letty prepares to leave, but she is convinced of Bob's love and stays with him. *Chorus girls. Courtship. Wealth. Credit. Railroad accidents. New York City.*

HUSBANDS AND LOVERS **F2.2640**

Louis B. Mayer Productions. *Dist* First National Pictures. 2 Nov **1924** [c21 Oct 1924; LP20676]. Si; b&w. 35mm. 8 reels, 7,822 ft.

Pres by Louis B. Mayer. *Dir-Story* John M. Stahl. *Titl* Madge Tyrone. *Adapt* A. P. Younger. *Story* Frances Irene Reels. *Photog* Antonio Gaudio. *Art Dir* Jack Holden. *Film Ed* Robert Kern, Margaret Booth. *Asst Dir* Sidney Algier.

Cast: Lewis S. Stone *(James Livingston)*, Florence Vidor *(Grace Livingston)*, Dale Fuller *(Marie)*, Winter Hall *(Robert Stanton)*, Edithe Yorke *(Mrs. Stanton)*.

Domestic comedy-drama. Chided by her husband, James, for neglecting her appearance, Grace Livingston changes her style to that of a flapper. James disapproves of so great a change, while his debonair friend, Rex Phillips, is highly complimentary and attentive. In a darkened room Grace mistakes James for Rex and confesses her love for him, so James clears the way for a divorce. Grace and Rex are about to be married when James realizes he still loves Grace and must be emphatic about it, and he persuades Grace to elope with him—leaving Rex waiting at the altar. *Flappers. Marriage. Divorce.*

Note: Some sources credit Stahl with story. Given release dates vary from Jun to 28 Dec 1924.

HUSBANDS FOR RENT **F2.2641**

Warner Brothers Pictures. 31 Dec **1927** [c24 Dec 1927; LP24792]. Si; b&w. 35mm. 6 reels, 5,200 ft. [Later, ca19 Mar 1928, cut to 5 reels.]

Dir Henry Lehrman. *Adapt* C. Graham Baker. *Titl* Joseph Jackson, James A. Starr. *Story* Edwin Justus Mayer. *Photog* Barney McGill. *Film Ed* Clarence Kolster.

Cast: Owen Moore *(Herbert Willis)*, Helene Costello *(Molly Devoe)*, Kathryn Perry *(Doris Knight)*, John Miljan *(Hugh Frazer)*, Claude Gillingwater *(Sir Reginald Knight)*, Arthur Hoyt *(Waldo Squibbs)*, Helen Lynch *(maid)*, Hugh Herbert *(valet)*.

Romantic comedy. Herbert Willis, nephew of Sir Reginald Knight, and Doris, Knight's ward, plan to announce their engagement until Hugh Frazer, a dashing young cavalier, woos Doris and she falls for him. Meanwhile, Herbert has fallen in love with Molly Devoe, a striking beauty. Hugh and Doris announce their engagement, planning to have a double wedding with Herbert and Molly, although Hugh and Molly are strongly attracted to each other. On the eve of the double wedding, Hugh and Molly elope, and, Sir Reginald, seeing a way to save the situation, persuades Doris and Herbert to marry. After their doubts about each other are erased, Doris and Herbert settle into a happy marriage. *Uncles. Wards. Courtship. Weddings. Elopement. Mate swapping.*

HUSH **F2.2642**

Equity Pictures. *Dist* Jans Film Service. Feb **1921** [c24 Dec 1920; LP15956]. Si; b&w. 35mm. 6 reels.

Dir Harry Garson. *Story* Sada Cowan. *Photog* Arthur Edeson.

Cast: Clara Kimball Young *(Vera Stanford)*, J. Frank Glendon *(Jack Stanford)*, Kathlyn Williams *(Isabel Dane)*, Jack Pratt *(Hugh Graham)*, Bertram Grassby *(Herbert Brooks)*, Gerard Alexander *(Grace Brooks)*, Beatrice Le Plante *(maid)*, John Underhill *(butler)*.

Domestic melodrama. Vera Stanford, happily married, is tormented by a foolish moment in her past when she succumbed to the embraces of Herbert Brooks. Brooks marries into Vera's set of friends, and when they all meet at Bar Harbor, the sight of him preys so strongly on her conscience that she confesses the misdeed to her husband, who then suspects Hugh Graham, an artist, to be the man concerned. After Vera has been made miserable by her husband's obsession with vengeance, they finally decide to wipe the slate clean. *Artists. Marriage. Infidelity. Revenge. Bar Harbor.*

HUSH MONEY **F2.2643**

Realart Pictures. *Dist* Paramount Pictures. Nov **1921** [c10 Oct 1921; LP17064]. Si; b&w. 35mm. 5 reels, 4,819 ft.

Dir-Scen Charles Maigne. *Story* Samuel Merwin. *Photog* Gilbert Warrenton.

Cast: Alice Brady *(Evelyn Murray)*, George Fawcett *(Alexander Murray)*, Laurence Wheat *(Bert Van Vliet)*, Harry Benham *(Bishop Deems)*, Jerry Devine *(Terry McGuire)*.

Society drama. Evelyn Murray, only daughter of wealthy Wall Street banker Alexander Murray, while with her aristocratic fiancé, Bert Van Vliet, runs down and injures newsboy Terry McGuire. To avoid unpleasant consequences, Bert persuades her to flee the scene of the accident. Evelyn is conscience-stricken and informs her father; he is then forced to pay "hush money" to a garage attendant who has witnessed the accident. That evening Murray gives a dinner to honor John Deems, Bishop of New York, to whom he plans to contribute money for a youth foundation. Influenced by the bishop, Evelyn goes to the hospital, becomes acquainted with the injured boy, and arranges for his care. Opposed by her father and fiancé, Evelyn disappears and is reconciled to them only when they agree to adopt a less overbearing attitude toward their money and power. *Upper classes. Clergymen. Newsboys. Wealth. Blackmail. Social consciousness.*

HUTCH OF THE U. S. A. **F2.2644**

William Steiner Productions. *Dist* New-Cal Film Corp., Hurricane Film Corp. 15 Jun **1924** [c28 May 1924; LU20242]. Si; b&w. 35mm. 5 reels, 4,890 ft.

Dir James Chapin. *Story-Scen* J. F. Natteford. *Photog* Ernest Miller.

Cast: Charles Hutchison *(Capt. Juan de Barcelo/Hutch of the U. S. A.)*, Edith Thornton *(Marquita Flores)*, Frank Leigh *(General Moreno)*, Ernest Adams *("Saturday")*, Jack Mathis *(Benito Ruiz)*, Natalie Warfield *(duenna)*, Alphonse Martell *(President Bonilla)*, Frederick Vroom *(Grover Harrison)*.

Melodrama. "Hutch," a newspaper reporter, is sent to investigate conditions in the Republic of Guadala, where General Moreno is plotting to overthrow President Bonilla and establish a dictatorship. Hutch remains to aid the revolutionaries out of sympathy with their cause and because of his love for the general's ward, Marquita. Moreno's troops are defeated, but Hutch wins the girl. *Reporters. Dictators. Presidents. Revolutions. Imaginary republics. Latin America.*

Note: Copyright title: *Hutch—U. S. A.*

THE HYPNOTIST *see* **LONDON AFTER MIDNIGHT**

THE HYPOCRITE **F2.2645**

Micheaux Film Corp. Jun **1921.** Si; b&w. 35mm. 7 reels.

Melodrama(?). No information about the precise nature of this film has been found. *Hypocrisy. Negro life.*

I AM GUILTY **F2.2646**

J. Parker Read, Jr., Productions. *Dist* Associated Producers. May **1921** [c27 May 1921; LP16582]. Si; b&w. 35mm. 7 reels.

Dir Jack Nelson. *Story-Scen* Bradley King. *Photog* Charles J. Stumar.

Cast: Louise Glaum *(Connie MacNair)*, Mahlon Hamilton *(Robert MacNair)*, Claire Du Brey *(Trixie)*, Joseph Kilgour *(Teddy Garrick)*, Ruth Stonehouse *(London Hattie)*, May Hopkins *(Molly May)*, George Cooper *(Dillon)*, Mickey Moore *(The Child)*, Frederic De Kovert *(The Dancer)*.

Melodrama. Chorus girl Connie meets eminent lawyer Robert MacNair at a supper party, and after falling in love they are married. Four years later, though still in love, MacNair neglects her. While he is away on business, she attends a party with a friend, and in avoiding the host, Garrick, she is burned accidentally. A thief, hiding nearby, plants a revolver in her hand, and it thus appears that she has shot Garrick; but Dillon, the thief, is arrested. MacNair takes the case and through her burn discovers his wife's involvement. At the trial she confesses her part in the affair, but MacNair proves that Trixie, Garrick's mistress, is the murderer. *Chorus girls. Lawyers. Thieves. Mistresses. Murder.*

I AM THE LAW **F2.2647**
Edwin Carewe Productions. *Dist* Affiliated Distributors. 1 Jun **1922** [c24 May 1922, 1 Apr 1923; LP17941, LP18942]. Si; b&w. 35mm. 7 reels, 6,800 ft.

Pres by C. C. Burr. *Dir* Edwin Carewe. *Scen* Raymond L. Schrock. *Photog* Robert B. Kurrle.

Cast: Alice Lake *(Joan Cameron)*, Kenneth Harlan *(Robert Fitzgerald)*, Rosemary Theby *(Mrs. Georges Mardeaux)*, Gaston Glass *(Tom Fitzgerald)*, Noah Beery *(Sgt. Georges Mardeaux)*, Wallace Beery *(Fu Chang)*.

Northwest melodrama. Source: James Oliver Curwood, "The Poetic Justice of Uko San," in *Outing* (56:291–298, Jun 1910). Robert Fitzgerald, a Royal Mounted Policeman, rescues Joan Cameron from the evil clutches of dancehall owner Fu Chang, but she falls in love with Tom, Robert's brother, who is carrying on an affair with another officer's wife. Discovered by the husband, Tom apparently kills him; and Bob, believing himself to be dying and that Joan loves Tom, assumes responsibility for the crime and signs a confession. Although Bob recovers, his brother announces his death. When Bob reappears, Tom arrests him; and Bob is about to be lynched when Joan forces a confession from the widow of the slain officer. Tom commits suicide, and Joan realizes her love for Bob. *Northwest Mounted Police. Canadian Northwest. Brothers. Murder. Suicide.*

I AM THE MAN **F2.2648**
Chadwick Pictures. 15 Dec **1924** [c17 Mar 1925; LP21255]. Si; b&w. 35mm. 7 reels, 6,400 ft.

Dir Ivan Abramson. *Scen* Adeline Hendricks. *Photog* Marcel Le Picard. *Sets* Tec-Art Studios.

Cast: Lionel Barrymore *(James McQuade)*, Seena Owen *(Julia Calvert)*, Gaston Glass *(Daniel Harrington)*, Martin Faust *(Robert McQuade)*, Flora Le Breton *(Corrine Stanton)*, James Keane *(George Lawson)*, Joseph Striker *(Billy Gray)*.

Melodrama. James McQuade, the political boss of a metropolis, is in love with Julia Calvert, a beautiful young woman who, in turn, loves Daniel Harrington, the district attorney. In order to get Julia to the altar, McQuade resorts to blackmail, framing Julia's father for embezzlement and then offering to exchange her father's acquittal for her hand in marriage. Julie consents, and they become man and wife; he later becomes jealous of Harrington, and orders his brother, Robert, to keep an eye on the district attorney. McQuade then discovers that Robert himself is attempting to seduce Julia, and McQuade kills him, placing the blame on Corrine Stanton, an actress. Discovering that Corrine is his own daughter and striken with remorse, McQuade takes poison and confesses to the murder of his brother. Julia is thus free to wed Harrington. *Political bosses. District attorneys. Actors. Brothers. Frameup. Embezzlement. Blackmail. Murder.*

I AM THE WOMAN **F2.2649**
Victor Kremer Film Features. Oct **1921** [New York State]. Si; b&w. 35mm. 5 reels.

Dir Francis Ford.

Cast: Texas Guinan.

Western melodrama. No information about the precise nature of this film has been found.

I CAN EXPLAIN **F2.2650**
S-L Pictures. *Dist* Metro Pictures. 20 Mar **1922** [c30 Mar 1922; LP17697]. Si; b&w. 35mm. 5 reels, 5,164 ft.

Dir George D. Baker. *Adapt* Edgar Franklin. *Photog* Rudolph Berquist. *Art Dir* E. J. Shulter.

Cast: Gareth Hughes *(Jimmy Berry)*, Bartine Burkett *(Betty Carson)*, Grace Darmond *(Dorothy Dawson)*, Herbert Hayes *(Howard Dawson)*, Victor Potel *(Will Potter)*, Nelson McDowell *(Uncle Henry)*, Edwin Wallock *(Juan Pedro Vistuano Gardez)*, Albert Breig *(Miguel)*, Harry Lorraine *(General Huera)*, Tina Modotti *(Carmencita Gardez)*, Sidney D'Albrook *(Lôpez)*, Stanton Heck *(El Pavor)*, William H. Brown *(Reverend Mr. Clark)*.

Comedy-melodrama. Source: Edgar Franklin, "Stay Home," in *Argosy All-Story Weekly* (vols 138–139, Nov–Dec 1921). Jimmy Berry, junior partner in a flourishing business firm, is engaged to Betty Carson. He is taken into confidence by Dorothy Dawson, his partner's wife, who secretly plans to open a business branch in South America. Their secret meetings generate gossip, and Dawson, who is insanely jealous, threatens divorce, while Betty's uncle forbids her to see Berry. Dawson compels Berry to go to South America with him, and the appearance of Dorothy there leads to further complications. When Berry attempts to depart, he is captured and returned, with Dorothy, to the home of Gardez, an importer, who arranges a duel between Berry and Dawson. Dawson is wounded, and again Berry takes French leave, via motor car, but is kidnaped by an outlaw known as El Pavor. After numerous other complications, Berry escapes from South America and returns home in time to prevent Betty's marriage to another man. *Jealousy. Partnerships. Kidnaping. South America. Duels.*

Note: Also known as *Stay Home*.

I LOVE YOU (Reissue) **F2.2651**
Kay-Bee Pictures. *Dist* Tri-Stone Pictures. c18 Sep **1923** [LP19409]. Si; b&w. 35mm. 6 reels, 5,600 ft.

Note: A "re-edited and re-titled" Alma Rubens film originally released by Triangle Film Corp. on 13 Jan 1918.

I WANT MY MAN **F2.2652**
First National Pictures. 22 Mar **1925** [c9 Mar 1925; LP21224]. Si; b&w. 35mm. 7 reels, 6,172 ft.

Supv Earl Hudson. *Dir* Lambert Hillyer. *Scen* Joseph Poland, Earle Snell. *Adapt* Earl Hudson. *Photog* James Van Trees.

Cast: Doris Kenyon *(Vida)*, Milton Sills *(Gulian Eyre)*, Phyllis Haver *(Drusilla)*, May Allison *(Lael)*, Kate Bruce *(Mrs. Eyre)*, Paul Nicholson *(Philip)*, Louis Stern *(Mr. Eyre)*, Theresa Maxwell Conover *(Mrs. Sartori)*, Charles Lane *(French doctor)*, George Howard *(American doctor)*.

Melodrama. Source: Maxwell Struthers Burt, *The Interpreter's House* (New York, 1924). Gulian Eyre, an American soldier blinded in action during the World War, remains in France after the cessation of hostilities and marries his nurse, Vida. Gulian is later operated on by a skilled French surgeon and recovers his sight, only to find that Vida has left him and obtained a divorce. Gulian returns to his family in the United States and becomes engaged to Lael, a girl he had known before the war. During this time, Vida has also come to the United States and has become the companion of Gulian's mother. Gulian does not recognize Vida, whom he has never seen; in any event, she had told him that she was terribly disfigured in order to make him believe that she did not pity him. Gulian's wedding to Lael is halted when his brother-in-law kills himself after squandering the Eyre fortune. Lael soon breaks her engagement to the impoverished Gulian, who declares his love to Vida. Vida involuntarily reveals her identity, and Gulian's happiness is complete. *Veterans. Nurses. Surgeons. Blindness. Suicide. Bankruptcy. Divorce. World War I.*

IBÁÑEZ' TORRENT *see* **THE TORRENT**

THE ICE FLOOD (Universal-Jewel) **F2.2653**
Universal Pictures. 2 Oct **1926** [or 23 Jan 1927; c25 Aug 1926; LP23052]. Si; b&w. 35mm. 6 reels, 5,747 ft.

Pres by Carl Laemmle. *Dir* George B. Seitz. *Scen* George B. Seitz, Gladys Lehman. *Adapt* James O. Spearing. *Photog* Merritt Gerstad.

Cast: Kenneth Harlan *(Jack De Quincy)*, Viola Dana *(Marie O'Neill)*, Frank Hagney *(Dum-Dum Pete)*, Fred Kohler *("Cougar" Kid)*, De Witt Jennings *(James O'Neill)*, Kitty Barlow *(cook)*, James Gordon *(Thomas De Quincy)*.

Melodrama. Source: Johnston McCulley, "The Brute Breaker," in *All-Story Weekly* (87:231–281, 10 Aug 1918). Jack De Quincy, just out of Oxford, is dispatched by his father to clean up the tough lumber camps on his northwest property, and he proceeds undercover without any outside help. At one of the rougher camps, Marie O'Neill, daughter of the superintendent, and her crippled brother hear of a "wildcat" who has cleaned up another camp up the river; and they dream of his arrival at camp. On the night of his arrival, Jack offends Pete by dancing with Marie against the bully's orders, a fight ensues in which Pete is badly beaten, and Marie refuses to associate with Jack. Pete and Dan, who are the camp bootleggers, order Jack from the camp after their liquor has been stolen; overhearing their plotting, Marie and her father follow the villains; they are captured, and Marie is put on a launch in the river. By a double ruse, Jack manages to capture both Dan and Pete and rushes to the river to save Marie from the gathering ice floes. *Cripples. Bootleggers. Bullies. Brother-sister relationship. Lumber camps. Ice floes.*

ICEBOUND F2.2654

Famous Players–Lasky. *Dist* Paramount Pictures. 2 Mar **1924** [New York opening; released 10 Mar; c12 Mar 1924; LP19985]. Si; b&w. 35mm. 7 reels, 6,471 ft.

Pres by Adolph Zukor, Jesse L. Lasky. *Dir* William De Mille. *Scen* Clara Beranger. *Photog* L. Guy Wilky.

Cast: Richard Dix *(Ben Jordan)*, Lois Wilson *(Jane Crosby)*, Helen Du Bois *(Emma Jordan)*, Edna May Oliver *(Hannah)*, Vera Reynolds *(Nettie Moore)*, Mary Foy *(Sadie Fellowes)*, Joseph Depew *(Orin Fellowes)*, Ethel Wales *(Ella Jordan)*, Alice Chapin *(Mrs. Jordan)*, John Daly Murphy *(Henry Jordan)*, Frank Shannon *(Judge Bradford)*.

Rural melodrama. Source: Owen Davis, *Icebound* (Boston, 1923). Ben Jordan runs away after accidentally setting fire to a barn in his small New England community. He returns when his mother dies to find that she has left everything to her ward, Jane Crosby. Having fallen in love with Ben, Jane proposes to pay to keep him out of jail, and she offers him a job. Reluctantly, he accepts. Jane prepares to leave, transferring her inheritance to Ben, when he begins a flirtation with his cousin, Nettie; but Ben comes to his senses and declares his love for Jane. *Inheritance. Rural life. New England. Fires.*

IDAHO RED F2.2655

FBO Pictures. 21 Apr **1929** [c21 Apr 1929; LP474]. Si; b&w. 35mm. 6 reels, 4,769 ft.

Dir Robert De Lacey. *Story-Cont* Frank Howard Clark. *Titl* Helen Gregg. *Photog* Nick Musuraca. *Film Ed* Leona De Lacey. *Asst Dir* William Cody.

Cast: Tom Tyler *(Andy Thornton)*, Patricia Caron *(Mary Regan)*, Frankie Darro *(Tadpole)*, Barney Furey *(Dave Lucas)*, Lew Meehan *(George Wilkins, sheriff)*.

Western melodrama. An orphaned newspaper boy, Tadpole, eluding the authorities is aided by Andy Thorton, an ex-Marine, who acts as his guardian and takes him to his ranch in Idaho. A guest there, who introduces herself as Mary Regan, sister of Jim Regan, the half owner of the property who was killed in the war, manages the ranch along with Andy. Foreman Dave Lucas, who has been secretly manufacturing counterfeit money, tries unsucessfully to frame Andy, and to avoid suspicion, he and his men decide to leave town. Andy becomes suspicious, and Mary, discovering their secret workshop, sends word to the sheriff through Tad, but he is captured. Andy arrives before they are able to escape and is overcome by acid fumes; in an exciting chase, Andy follows the villains, leaping from his horse to their automobile, and captures them. *Newsboys. Orphans. Guardians. Ranchers. Counterfeiters. Inheritance. Idaho. United States Marines. Chases.*

IDLE HANDS F2.2656

Park-Whiteside Productions. *Dist* Pioneer Pictures. 10 Jun **1921** [trade review]. Si; b&w. 35mm. 6 reels, 5,400 ft.

Dir Frank Reicher. *Scen* J. Clarkson Miller. *Story* Willard King Bradley. *Photog* George Benoit.

Cast: Gail Kane *(Gloria Travers)*, Thurston Hall *(Henry Livingston)*, J. Herbert Frank *(Adolph Pym)*, William Bechtel *(Commissioner Deering)*, Nellie Burt *(Marjorie Travers)*, Paul Lane *(Robert Deering)*, Norbert Wicki *(Mock Lee)*.

Underworld melodrama. The Travers sisters move to New York in search of a stage career. Shortly after their arrival, Gloria's younger sister, Marjorie, disappears during a visit to Chinatown. Their mother dies of shock. Gloria appeals to the mayor for help, and he consults the commissioner on vice, who surreptitiously runs the underworld and works in opposition to all of the mayor's efforts to find the girl. After many misadventures involving the commissioner's son, who is an opium fiend, Marjorie is rescued unharmed. The mayor's interest in Marjorie has developed into love, and he asks her to be his wife. *Mayors. Sisters. Actors. Drug addicts. Abduction. Opium. Government—Local. New York City—Chinatown.*

THE IDLE RICH F2.2657

Metro Pictures. 26 Dec **1921** [c4 Jan 1922; LP17443]. Si; b&w. 35mm. 5 reels, 4,848 ft.

Dir Maxwell Karger. *Adapt* June Mathis. *Photog* Arthur Martinelli. *Art Dir* Julian Garnsey.

Cast: Bert Lytell *(Samuel Weatherbee)*, Virginia Valli *(Mattie Walling)*, John Davidson *(Dillingham Coolidge)*, Joseph Harrington *(Judge O'Reilly)*, Thomas Jefferson *(Uncle Coolidge)*, Victory Bateman *(Mrs. O'Reilly)*, Leigh Wyant *(Jane Coolidge)*, Max Davidson *(The Tailor)*.

Comedy. Source: Kenneth Harris, "Junk," in *Saturday Evening Post* (193:8–10, 25 Dec 1920). Young Sam Weatherbee, who leads a carefree existence on his inherited wealth, is staging an elaborate party in memory of his ancestors when he receives a wire notifying him that his fortune is lost, owing to the speculations of his executor. Down and out, Sam becomes heir to an old house in Los Angeles, formerly the residence of his father's sister and now presided over by O'Reilly and his wife. Finding the house filled with old junk, Sam conceives the idea of bartering it for food. Eventually he becomes prosperous as a junk dealer though ridiculed by his former society friends. His sweetheart, Mattie, who had previously considered him shiftless, defends him. His rival Dillingham tries to prevent Sam from obtaining a lease on his father's property, but Mattie, discovering his trickery, rejects Dillingham for Sam. *Idle rich. Junk dealers. Upper classes. Inheritance. Speculation. Los Angeles.*

THE IDLE RICH F2.2658

Metro-Goldwyn-Mayer Pictures. 15 Jun **1929** [c20 May 1929; LP385]. Sd (Movietone); b&w. 35mm. 9 reels, 7,351 ft.

Dir William C. De Mille. *Screenplay-Dial* Clara Beranger. *Photog* Leonard Smith. *Art Dir* Cedric Gibbons. *Film Ed* Conrad A. Nervig. *Rec Engr* Douglas Shearer. *Wardrobe* David Cox.

Cast: Conrad Nagel *(William Van Luyn)*, Bessie Love *(Helen Thayer)*, Leila Hyams *(Joan Thayer)*, Robert Ober *(Henry Thayer)*, James Neill *(Mr. Thayer)*, Edythe Chapman *(Mrs. Thayer)*, Paul Kruger *(Tom Gibney)*, Kenneth Gibson *(Frank Thayer)*.

Comedy. Source: Edith Ellis, *White Collars; a Comedy in Three Acts* (New York, 1926). Millionaire William Van Luyn marries Joan Thayer, a middle-class stenographer of little commonsense, and offers her family the benefits that his money can so easily provide. The family haughtily refuses, and Joan soon insists that he move in with her family and share the virtues and discomforts of her simple home life. William decides to give his fortune away to found a hospital and finds that his new relatives suffer a quick change of heart about accepting the benefits of his money. *Stenographers. Millionaires. Idle rich. Marriage. Middle classes.*

IDLE TONGUES F2.2659

Thomas H. Ince Corp. *Dist* First National Pictures. 21 Dec **1924** [c11 Nov 1924; LP20753]. Si; b&w. 35mm. 6 reels, 5,300 or 5,447 ft.

Pres by Thomas H. Ince. *Pers Supv* Thomas H. Ince. *Dir* Lambert Hillyer. *Adapt* C. Gardner Sullivan. *Photog* Karl Struss.

Cast: Percy Marmont *(Dr. Ephraim Nye)*, Doris Kenyon *(Katherine Minot)*, Claude Gillingwater *(Judge Daniel Webster Copeland)*, Lucille Ricksen *(Faith Copeland)*, David Torrence *(Cyrenus Stone)*, Malcolm McGregor *(Tom Stone)*, Vivia Ogden *(Althea Bemis)*, Marguerite Clayton *(Fanny Copeland)*, Ruby Lafayette *(Miss Pepper)*, Dan Mason *(Henry Ward Beecher Payson)*, Mark Hamilton *(Bluey Batcheldor)*.

Drama. Source: Joseph Crosby Lincoln, *Doctor Nye of North Ostable* (New York, 1923). After serving 5 years in prison for embezzling church funds, Dr. Ephraim Nye returns to Ostable and the scornful gossip of its residents, led by Althea Bemis. There is a typhoid epidemic, and Dr. Nye believes it to be caused by the water in a pond that Judge Copeland, the brother of Dr. Nye's dead wife, Fanny, wishes to use as the source of municipal water supply. Only Katherine Minot supports Dr. Nye, but biologists prove him correct; and Dr. Nye confronts Copeland with proof that he went to prison to protect Fanny, the actual criminal. Copeland finally consents to the marriage of his daughter, Faith, to Tom Stone, the son of his enemy; and Katherine spreads the news of her engagement to Dr. Nye through Althea. *Physicians. Judges. Biologists. Funds—Public. Embezzlement. Epidemics. Typhoid. Water pollution. Gossip.*

THE IDOL OF THE NORTH F2.2660

Famous Players–Lasky. *Dist* Paramount Pictures. 27 Mar **1921** [c11 May 1921; LP16497]. Si; b&w. 35mm. 6 reels, 5,802 ft.

Pres by Adolph Zukor. *Dir* R. William Neill. *Scen* Frank S. Beresford. *Titl* Tom McNamara. *Story* J. Clarkson Miller. *Photog* Lawrence E. Williams.

Cast: Dorothy Dalton *(Colette Brissac)*, Edwin August *(Martin Bates)*, E. J. Ratcliffe *(Lucky Folsom)*, Riley Hatch *(Ham Devlin)*, Jules Cowles *(One-Eye Wallace)*, Florence St. Leonard *(a soubrette)*, Jessie Arnold *(Big Blond)*, Marguerite Marsh *(Gloria Waldron)*, Joe King *(Sergeant McNair)*.

Melodrama. Colette Brissac, a dancehall girl brought up in the Canadian Northwest, refuses the protection of New Yorker Lucky Folsom, who later marries Gloria Waldron, an ambitious woman actually in love with Martin

Bates, an engineer. When Bates drifts into the mining town the miners force him, while drunk, to marry Colette. She nurses him back to health, and gradually they fall in love. The arrival of Folsom and Gloria threatens to break up their marriage, and Colette prevents a fight between the two men by wounding Folsom, causing the latter to come to his senses and teaching his wife a lesson. *Miners. Dancehall girls. Engineers. Canadian Northwest.*

IF I MARRY AGAIN **F2.2661**

First National Pictures. 15 Feb **1925** [c18 Dec 1924; LP20913]. Si; b&w. 35mm. 8 reels, 7,401 ft.

Supv Earl Hudson. *Dir* John Francis Dillon. *Ed Supv* Marion Fairfax. *Scen* Kenneth B. Clarke. *Photog* James C. Van Trees. *Art Dir* Milton Menasco. *Film Ed* LeRoy Stone.

Cast: Doris Kenyon *(Jocelyn Margot)*, Lloyd Hughes *(Charlie Jordan)*, Frank Mayo *(Jeffrey Wingate)*, Hobart Bosworth *(John Jordan)*, Anna Q. Nilsson *(Alicia Wingate)*, Myrtle Stedman *(Madame Margot)*, Dorothy Brock *(Sonny)*.

Society melodrama. Source: Gilbert Frankau, "If I Marry Again" (publication undetermined). Determined that his son, Charles, will not be ruined by love for Jocelyn Margot, the daughter of a notorious San Francisco madam, John Jordan, a stern and proud businessman, sends him to manage one of the family plantations in the Tropics. Before he goes, however, Charles marries Jocelyn and takes her with him. The elder Jordan does not forgive this insult to the family name and position, but Jocelyn proves to be an excellent wife and bears Charles a son. After 4 years, Jordan, unrelenting, sends his personal manager, Wingate, to the Tropics to buy off Jocelyn. As Wingate arrives, Charles dies of a fever; Jocelyn then becomes determined that her son, as the Jordan heir, will receive all the advantages of that family's name and fortune. Returning to San Francisco, she is ignored by Jordon and out of spite decides to reopen her mother's whorehouse under the Jordan name. After inviting the best of local society to the grand opening, she relents and abandons the scheme; Jordan, who finally realizes her basic worth, then recognizes her son as his heir, and Wingate, who has fallen in love with her, takes Jocelyn and the small boy into his home. *Planters. Filial relations. Inheritance. Whorehouses. Tropics. San Francisco.*

IF I WERE QUEEN **F2.2662**

R-C Pictures. *Dist* Film Booking Offices of America. 15 Oct **1922** [c15 Oct 1922; LP18383]. Si; b&w. 35mm. 6 reels, 5,955 or 6,092 ft.

Pres by P. A. Powers. *Dir* Wesley Ruggles. *Scen* Carol Warren. *Photog* Joseph A. Dubray.

Cast: Ethel Clayton *(Ruth Townley)*, Andrée Lejon *(Oluf)*, Warner Baxter *(Valdemir)*, Victory Bateman *(Aunt Ollie)*, Murdock MacQuarrie *(Duke of Wortz)*, Genevieve Blinn *(Sister Ursula)*.

Romantic drama. Source: Du Vernet Rabell, "The Three Cornered Kingdom" (publication undetermined). Ruth Townley, an American heiress, drops a locket received from her friend, Princess Oluf of Kosnia. It is retrieved by Prince Valdemir of Prebilof, who assumes its owner to be Oluf and falls in love with her. They are separated, but sometime later, after Oluf has announced her engagement to Prince Gregory of Masavania, they meet again. Valdemir will not believe she is Ruth Townley, and Ruth believes that Oluf wishes to marry Valdemir in order to ally their kingdoms. Finally, there are explanations, and Oluf unites with Gregory, while Ruth becomes Valdemir's princess. *Royalty. Mistaken identity. Imaginary kingdoms.*

IF I WERE SINGLE **F2.2663**

Warner Brothers Pictures. 17 Dec **1927** [c9 Dec 1927; LP24741]. Si; b&w. 35mm. 7 reels, 6,320 ft.

Dir Roy Del Ruth. *Story-Scen* Robert Lord. *Titl* Joseph Jackson. *Camera* Ed Du Par. *Film Ed* Ralph Dawson. *Asst Dir* Chauncy Pyle.

Cast: May McAvoy *(May Howard)*, Conrad Nagel *(Ted Howard)*, Myrna Loy *(Joan)*, André Beranger *(Claude)*.

Domestic comedy. Ted Howard, who still loves his wife after 2 years of marriage, nevertheless flirts with a young lady on the way to the golf course one morning, and he forgets to recover an expensive cigarette lighter that he lends her. That evening, his wife, May, introduces the strange lady as Joan, an old college friend; and when Joan returns the lighter, Ted and May have their first real quarrel. May decides to give him a lesson by flirting with her handsome music teacher, Claude, and by coincidence May and Claude are forced to hide in the tonneau of the car when Ted and Joan take a ride. When the car stalls, the party is waylaid; but Ted is so amazed to discover the hidden couple that he is little concerned about his own predicament. Finally, too cold and tired to quarrel, they are picked up by a milk truck and resolve to terminate their flirtations. *Music teachers. Friendship. Marriage. Flirtation. Robbery. Golf.*

IF MARRIAGE FAILS **F2.2664**

C. Gardner Sullivan Productions. *Dist* Film Booking Offices of America. 4 Aug **1925** [c4 Aug 1925; LP21699]. Si; b&w. 35mm. 7 reels, 6,006 ft.

Dir John Ince. *Scen-Story* C. Gardner Sullivan. *Photog* James Diamond. *Gowns* André-ani.

Cast: Jacqueline Logan *(Nadia)*, Belle Bennett *(Eleanor Woodbury)*, Clive Brook *(Joe Woodbury)*, Jean Hersholt *(Dr. Mallini)*, Donald MacDonald *(Gene Deering)*, Mathilde Comont *(Lisa)*, Cissy Fitzgerald *(Mrs. Loring)*.

Society drama. Joe and Eleanor Woodbury lead an unhappy married life: she is fond of the gay life, and he is not. Together, they visit Nadia, a lovely young woman who tells the future by gazing into a crystal ball, and Joe and Nadia fall in love at first sight. Although Eleanor is having an affair with Gene Deering, a lounge lizard, she wants to stay married to Joe and therefore tells Nadia that she is pregnant. The diminutive crystal-gazer promises to stop seeing Joe, and Eleanor resumes her illicit relationship with Deering. Following a raid on a roadhouse where they are carousing, Eleanor and Deering are involved in an automobile accident and she is slightly hurt. The doctor who attends her later informs Nadia that Eleanor is not expecting a child, and Nadia telephones Joe to tell him of his wife's double deception. Joe then tells Eleanor that he is going to divorce her and goes to Nadia. *Seers. Marriage. Divorce. Infidelity. Pregnancy. Automobile accidents. Roadhouses.*

"IF ONLY" JIM **F2.2665**

Universal Film Manufacturing Co. 28 Feb **1921** [c18 Feb 1921; P16167]. Si; b&w. 35mm. 5 reels, 4,635 ft.

Pres by Carl Laemmle. *Dir* Jacques Jaccard. *Scen* George C. Hull. *Photog* Harry Fowler.

Cast: Harry Carey *(Jim Golden)*, Carol Halloway *(Miss Dot Dennihan)*, Ruth Royce *(Miss Richards)*, Duke Lee *(Keno)*, Roy Coulson *(Henry)*, Charles Brinley *(Parky)*, George Bunny *(Uncle Johnny)*, Joseph Hazelton *(Bill Bones)*, Minnie Prevost *(squaw)*, Thomas Smith *(kid)*, Pal *(a dog)*.

Western melodrama. Source: Philip Verrill Mighels, *Bruvver Jim's Baby* (New York, 1904). Jim Golden, a gold miner in love with postmistress Miss Dot, has a reputation for being shiftless. He finds a baby abandoned by Indians, adopts it, and begins again to work his claim. Parky, a swindler, discovers that Jim has struck gold, and when the baby is taken ill and Jim is sent to fetch the doctor, Parky annexes the claim. Jim defeats the gang in a gunfight, rescues Miss Dot from Parky, and eventually marries her. *Waifs. Mine claims. Postmistresses. Swindlers. Dogs.*

IF WINTER COMES **F2.2666**

Fox Film Corp. 7 Mar **1923** [Springfield, Mass., showing; released 19 Aug; c20 Jul 1923; LP19448]. Si; b&w. 35mm. 12 reels, 12,000 ft. [Original length: 14 reels.]

Pres by William Fox. *Dir* Harry Millarde. *Scen* Paul Sloane. *Photog* Joseph Ruttenberg.

Cast: Percy Marmont *(Mark Sabre)*, Arthur Metcalfe *(Hapgood)*, Sidney Herbert *(Twyning)*, Wallace Kolb *(Harold Twyning)*, William Riley Hatch *(Rev. Sebastian Fortune)*, Raymond Bloomer *(Lord Tybar)*, Russell Sedgwick *(Young Perch)*, Leslie King *("Humpo")*, George Pelzer *(Old Bright)*, James Ten Brook *(The Coroner)*, Ann Forrest *(Nona, Lady Tybar)*, Margaret Fielding *(Mabel)*, Gladys Leslie *(Effie Bright)*, Dorothy Allen *(High Jinks)*, Eleanor Daniels *(Low Jinks)*, Virginia Lee *(Miss Winifred)*, Eugenie Woodward *(Mrs. Perch)*.

Melodrama. Source: Arthur Stuart-Menteth Hutchinson, *If Winter Comes* (Boston, 1921). Mark Sabre engages Effie Bright, a girl of Tidborough, to keep his coldblooded, snobbish wife, Mabel, company while he is at war. When Sabre comes home wounded, Effie, who has been dismissed, comes with her baby to ask for shelter. Mabel leaves Sabre when he takes Effie in, and he is subsequently ostracized. A scandal breaks when Effie kills her baby and commits suicide. Sabre has a nervous breakdown as a result of a coroner's examination conducted on the basis of untrue and incriminating evidence, but Sabre's former sweetheart, Nona, whose husband has died in the war, comes to his aid. *Veterans. Suicide. Frigidity. Snobbery. World War I. England.*

IF WOMEN ONLY KNEW F2.2667

J. N. Haulty–Gardner Hunting. *Dist* Robertson-Cole Distributing Corp. 24 Apr **1921** [c24 Apr 1921; LP16464]. Si; b&w. 35mm. 6 reels.

Dir E. H. Griffith. *Scen* Gardner Hunting. *Photog* William McCoy. *Art Dir* David G. Flynn. *Art Titl* Fred Waller, Jr.

Cast: Robert Gordon *(Maurice Travers)*, Blanche Davenport *(Mrs. Travers)*, Harold Vosburgh *(Professor Storey)*, Frederick Burton *(Donna's father)*, Charles Lane *(Dr. John Strong)*, Leon Gendron *(Billie Thorne)*, Madelyn Clare *(Madeline Marshall)*, Virginia Lee *(Donna Wayne)*, Lila Lee *(see note)*.

Drama. Source: Honoré de Balzac, *La Physiologie du mariage* (Paris, 1830). Remotely derived from Balzac, the plot centers on Maurice Travers, who, through the self-sacrificing efforts of his mother, is able to attend college, though his love for sports and consequent neglect of his studies prevent his graduation. Madeline Marshall, an orphan living with Maurice's mother, loves him, but Maurice marries Donna Wayne, daughter of a wealthy New Yorker; and in the city they lead a carefree life. Her father insists that he support her, but he cannot. Following the blindness and death of his mother, Donna elopes with a rich suitor, and after a divorce Maurice finds happiness with the faithful Madeline. *Motherhood. Education. Marriage. Divorce. Blindness. New York City.*

Note: Two sources list Lila Lee as a performer in the film.

IF YOU BELIEVE IT, IT'S SO F2.2668

Famous Players–Lasky. *Dist* Paramount Pictures. 2 Jul **1922** [New York premiere; released 14 Aug; c4 Jul 1922; LP18043]. Si; b&w. 35mm. 7 reels, 6,764 ft.

Pres by Adolph Zukor. *Dir* Tom Forman. *Adapt* Waldemar Young. *Story* Perley Poore Sheehan. *Photog* Harry Perry.

Cast: Thomas Meighan *(Chick Harris, a crook)*, Pauline Starke *(Alvah Morley, a country girl)*, Joseph Dowling *(Ezra Wood, a patriarch)*, Theodore Roberts *(Sky Blue, confidence man)*, Charles Ogle *(Colonel Williams)*, Laura Anson *(Tessie Wyngate)*, Charles French *(Frank Tine, realty agent)*, Tom Kennedy *(bartender)*, Ed Brady *(constable)*.

Crook drama. Intent on robbing an old man of his wallet, big city crook Chick Harris instead finds himself helping his victim and—impressed by his sincerity—resolving to begin life anew in the country. Chick becomes a respected real estate agent with the encouragement of Colonel Williams and his niece, Alvah Morley, frustrates the schemes of a former pal to cheat the townspeople, uses the pal's funds to build an orphanage, and exposes a corrupt sheriff. *Criminals—Rehabilitation. Sheriffs. Swindlers. Real estate business.*

IGNORANCE F2.2669

Dist Webster Pictures. 20 Jun **1922** [New York State license application]. Si; b&w. 35mm. 5 reels.

Cast: Earl Metcalfe.

Crook drama. "The subject matter of this film is a story of criminality. The majority of the scenes are laid in a low dance hall where a gang of criminals have their meeting place. There are two abductions shown; an attempt to kill the District Attorney; enticing a woman into a man's rooms and threatening her if she does not give up her jewels." Probably a story of a gang of white slavers made over into jewel thieves. (New York State license records.) *Robbery. White slave traffic. Kidnaping. Dancehalls.*

I'LL BE THERE *see* **OUT ALL NIGHT**

I'LL BE THERE F2.2670

Ward Lascelle Productions. *Dist* Sierra Pictures. Apr **1927**. Si; b&w. 35mm. 5 reels, 4,900 ft.

Dir Frank Yaconelli. *Photog* Harry Forbes.

Cast: Earle Douglas.

Melodrama(?). No information about the nature of this film has been found.

I'LL SHOW YOU THE TOWN (Universal-Jewel) F2.2671

Universal Pictures. 7 Jun **1925** [c22 May 1925; LP21498]. Si; b&w. 35mm. 8 reels, 7,440 ft.

Dir Harry A. Pollard. *Scen* Raymond L. Schrock, Harvey Thew. *Photog* Charles Stumar.

Cast: Reginald Denny *(Alec Dupree)*, Marion Nixon *(Hazel Deming)*, Edward Kimball *(Prof. Carlyle McCabe)*, Lilyan Tashman *(Fan Green)*, Hayden Stevenson *(Martin Green)*, Cissy Fitzgerald *(Agnes Clevenger)*, Neely Edwards *(Billie Bonner)*, William A. Carroll *(Professor Goodhue)*, Martha Mattox *(Aunt Sarah)*, Helen Greene *(Edith Torey)*, Lionel Braham *(Frank Pemberton)*.

Comedy. Source: Elmer Holmes Davis, *I'll Show You the Town* (New York, 1924). While at work on a book, a young college professor, Alec Dupree, is interrupted in succession by three well-meaning friends, who talk him into entertaining three women at dinner on the same evening. One of the women is a wealthy widow interested in saving the college, which is almost defunct; another is the wife of a friend; and the third is a beautiful young girl with whom Alec falls hopelessly in love. In trying to entertain all three, Alec involves himself in a net of scandal, misunderstanding, and disgrace, from which he finally extricates himself by fast-talking and high-stepping, ending up his evening with the beautiful young girl. *Authors. Professors. Widows. Scandal. College life.*

ILLUSION F2.2672

Paramount Famous Lasky Corp. 21 Sep **1929** [c21 Sep 1929; LP708]. Sd (Movietone); b&w. 35mm. 8 reels, 6,972 or 7,536 ft. [Also si; 6,141 ft.]

Prod B. P. Schulberg. *Dir* Lothar Mendes. *Titl* Richard H. Digges, Jr. *Adapt-Dial* E. Lloyd Sheldon. *Photog* Harry Fischbeck. *Film Ed* George Nichols, Jr. *Song: "When the Real Thing Comes Your Way"* Larry Spier. *Rec Engr* Harry M. Lindgren.

Cast: Charles (Buddy) Rogers *(Carlee Thorpe)*, Nancy Carroll *(Claire Jernigan)*, June Collyer *(Hilda Schmittlap)*, Regis Toomey *(Eric Schmittlap)*, Knute Erickson *(Mr. Jacob Schmittlap)*, Kay Francis *(Zelda Paxton)*, Eugenie Besserer *(Mrs. Jacob Schmittlap)*, Maude Turner Gordon *(Queen of Dalmatia)*, William Austin *(Mr. Z)*, Emilie Melville *(Mother Fay)*, Frances Raymond *(Mrs. Y)*, Catherine Wallace *(Mrs. Z)*, J. E. Nash *(Mr. X)*, William McLaughlin *(Mr. Y?)*, Eddie Kane *(Gus Bloomberg)*, Michael Visaroff *(Equerry)*, Paul Lucas *(Count Fortuny)*, Richard Cramer *(Magus)*, Bessie Lyle *(Consuelo)*, Col. G. L. McDonell *(Jarman [butler])*, Lillian Roth *(herself, a singer)*, Harriet Spiker *(midget)*, Anna Magruder *(fat lady)*, Albert Wolffe *(giant)*.

Society drama. Source: Arthur Chesney Train, *Illusion* (New York, 1929). A vaudeville magician team is broken up when Carlee, an ex-circus performer, becomes infatuated with socialite Hilda Schmittlap. Meanwhile his vaudeville partner, Claire, has chosen a new partner, but her "heart isn't in it" because she is disconsolate over Carlee. Curious about her new act, Carlee attends a performance and sees Claire nearly killed when she fails to substitute fake bullets for real ones. Rushing to her aid, Carlee realizes how much Claire means to him. *Magicians. Socialites. Vaudeville. Suicide.*

ILLUSION OF LOVE F2.2673

Al Leach. *Dist* Burton Young. 8 Feb **1929** [New York State license]. Si; b&w. 35mm. 5 reels.

Cast: John Ho, Florence Lee.

Drama(?). Although no information about the nature of this film has been found, New York State license records make a reference to the "Will of Dr. Sun Yat Sen." *Sun Yat-sen.*

IMPERFECT LADIES *see* **IT'S A GREAT LIFE**

THE IMPOSSIBLE MRS. BELLEW F2.2674

Famous Players–Lasky. *Dist* Paramount Pictures. 22 Oct **1922** [New York premiere; released 26 Nov; c28 Oct 1922; LP18363]. Si; b&w. 35mm. 8 reels, 7,155 ft.

Pres by Jesse L. Lasky. *Dir* Sam Wood. *Scen-Adapt* Percy Heath, Monte M. Katterjohn. *Photog* Alfred Gilks.

Cast: Gloria Swanson *(Betty Bellew)*, Robert Cain *(Lance Bellew)*, Conrad Nagel *(John Helstan)*, Richard Wayne *(Jerry Woodruff)*, Frank Elliott *(Count Radisloff)*, Gertrude Astor *(Alice Granville)*, June Elvidge *(Naomi Templeton)*, Herbert Standing *(Rev. Dr. Helstan)*, Mickey Moore *(Lance Bellew, Jr., age 4)*, Pat Moore *(Lance Bellew, Jr., age 6)*, Helen Dunbar *(Aunt Agatha)*, Arthur Hull *(Attorney Potter)*, Clarence Burton *(detective)*.

Society melodrama. Source: David Lisle, *The Impossible Mrs. Bellew* (New York, 1916). Lance Bellew ignores his wife, Betty, for his mistress, Naomi Templeton, but becomes so enraged when he finds Betty in the company of Jerry Woodruff that he shoots this family friend. For the good of her son, Betty does not contest Lance's plea of just cause and self-defense. A jury agrees with Lance, and Betty's reputation is ruined. After the court takes away her son she travels to France, becomes friends with author John Helstan, but agrees with his father that she should break off the relationship for John's own good. John believes Betty to be a good woman, but he changes his mind when he witnesses her behavior at a party given by Count Radisloff. Meanwhile, Lance and his Aunt Agatha have had a change of heart. Aunt Agatha takes Lance, Jr., to France, and John hears the truth in time to rescue Betty from the count. *Authors. Motherhood. Infidelity. Reputation. France.*

THE IMPOSTER **F2.2675**

Gothic Productions. *Dist* Film Booking Offices of America. 18 Apr **1926** [c16 Apr 1926; LP22704]. Si; b&w. 35mm. 6 reels, 5,457 ft.

Dir Chet Withey. *Scen* Ewart Adamson. *Story* Clifford Howard. *Photog* Roy Klaffki. *Asst Dir* Doran Cox.

Cast: Evelyn Brent *(Judith Gilbert [Canada Nell])*, Carroll Nye *(Dick Gilbert)*, James Morrison *(Gordon)*, Frank Leigh *(De Mornoff)*, Jimmy Quinn *(Lefty)*, Carlton Griffin *(Morris)*, Edna Griffin *(Ann Penn)*.

Crook melodrama. Dick Gilbert, the dissipated son of a wealthy family, is forced to raise money to pay off gambling debts and uses a valuable family jewel as security for a loan from Prince Borkoff, but it is stolen by Morris, a gambler. To save face for Dick, his sister Judith determines to recover the gem, and in the guise of Canada Nell, a girl of the streets, she meets Morris, who becomes infatuated with her. She learns that Mrs. Smith, a social climber, has purchased the jewel and (finding that it is stolen) plans to use it to further her position. Judith impersonates herself at a party and retrieves the jewel; through a series of maneuvers she evades capture by De Mornoff, a jewel thief, and returns the jewel to the family safe just before her brother pays off his debt. Bruce Gordon, a reporter, who wishes to reform her, arrives with the police on the tail of the gang; Judith reveals her true identity and accepts the proposal of Gordon. *Thieves. Brother-sister relationship. Prostitutes. Social climbers. Imposture. Jewels. Disguise.*

IMPULSE **F2.2676**

Berwilla Film Corp. *Dist* Arrow Film Corp. 15 Jul **1922** [c17 Sep 1922; LP18242]. Si; b&w. 35mm. 5 reels, 4,505 ft.

Prod Ben Wilson. *Dir* Norval MacGregor. *Scen* J. Grubb Alexander.

Cast: Neva Gerber *(Julia Merrifield)*, Jack Dougherty *(Robert Addis)*, Goldie Madden *(Virginia Howard)*, Douglas Gerrard *(David Usher)*, Ashton Dearholt *(Count Sansone)*, Helen Gilmore *(Mrs. Cameron)*, Miss Grey *(Felicia)*.

Society melodrama. Source: Maude Woodruff Newell, "Her Unknown Knight," in *People's Home Journal* (36:8–10, 36–40, Mar 1921; 14–24, Apr 1921). To enliven her impoverished, humdrum existence Julia Merrifield spends 2 weeks at a luxury resort under the guise of a society girl. She meets wealthy Robert Addis and falls in love with him, but they are separated in a train wreck. Back at her job, Julia finds life is as it was until she realizes that she is being sought by her villainous husband, David Usher, who deserted her more than a year earlier. To escape him she shoulders the blame for the embezzlement committed by a friend, then takes a job as a nurse to elderly Mrs. Cameron. Julia discovers that there is a plot by Usher against Mrs. Cameron, whose nephew is none other than Robert Addis. Though threatened by Usher, she reveals the evidence—thus saving Mrs. Cameron's life—and is united with Robert when Usher is killed by detectives. *Nurses. Desertion. Social classes. Resorts. Embezzlement.*

IN A MOMENT OF TEMPTATION **F2.2677**

R-C Pictures. *Dist* Film Booking Offices of America. 18 Sep **1927** [c18 Sep 1927; LP24556]. Si; b&w. 35mm. 6 reels, 5,665 ft.

Pres by Joseph P. Kennedy. *Dir* Philip Carle. *Adapt* Julia Crawford Ivers. *Story* Laura Jean Libbey. *Photog* Mack Stengler.

Cast: Charlotte Stevens *(Polly)*, Grant Withers *(Ed)*, Cornelius Keefe *(Martin Breen)*, Marie Walcamp *(Alice Gage)*, Kit Guard *(Blunty)*, Tom Ricketts *(Timothy Gage)*, John MacKinnon *(Leetch)*.

Melodrama. Polly, a shopgirl, discovers that Ed, her sweetheart, is a crook when he steals the purse of Alice Gage, a wealthy society girl. Martin Breen witnesses the crime, and because he tries to defend the girl, Alice's jealousy is aroused and she has Polly charged with being an accomplice in the crime. Timothy Gage, Alice's grandfather, is an invalid and is ruthlessly controlled by his grandchild; he suggests a trip to increase her affection for Martin and to rid himself of her tyranny. Meanwhile, Polly is released from prison on good behavior; and seeking revenge, she agrees to help Blunty rob the Gage residence; Gage catches them in the act but takes an interest in Polly and adopts her, while she also falls in love with Martin. Alice convinces Polly that she would ruin Martin. In attempting to protect Ed from a further robbery attempt, Polly tries to implicate herself, but Blunty convinces Martin and Gage that she is guiltless. Martin and Polly are reunited. *Shopgirls. Socialites. Grandfathers. Invalids. Jealousy. Theft. Robbery.*

IN BORROWED PLUMES **F2.2678**

Welcome Pictures. *Dist* Arrow Pictures. 10 Feb **1926** [c16 Feb 1926; LP22403]. Si; b&w. 35mm. 6 reels, 5,719 ft.

Dir Victor Hugo Halperin.

Cast: Marjorie Daw *(Mildred Grantley/Countess D'Autreval)*, Niles Welch *(Philip Dean)*, Arnold Daly *(Sam Wassup)*, Louise Carter *(Clara Raymond)*, Peggy Kelly *(Mrs. Harrison)*, Wheeler Oakman *(Jack Raymond)*, Dagmar Godowsky *(Clarice)*.

Society melodrama. Source: Leroy Scott, "In Borrowed Plumes," in *Smart Set.* Mildred Grantley, a penniless society girl who wants to be an actress, passes herself off as the Countess D'Autreval. Through a mutual friend, Mildred gets to know the wealthy Dean family, falling in love with Philip Dean, a handsome young bachelor. A woman claiming to be the real countess shows up and persuades Mildred to introduce her to the Deans. Mrs. Dean smells a rat, however, and hires a detective who exposes the woman as a famous international crook. The honest-to-goodness countess finally shows up, and Mildred and Philip enter that haven of happiness open only to true lovers. *Socialites. Bachelors. Detectives. Nobility. Imposture.*

IN BRONCHO LAND **F2.2679**

Ben Wilson Productions. *Dist* Rayart Pictures. Dec **1926.** Si; b&w. 35mm. 5 reels, 4,583 ft.

Dir Archie Ricks.

Cast: Dick Hatton.

Western comedy. "Handsome cowboy and plain featured one seek wives through matrimonial agency. Plain chap accompanies his application with pictures of handsome boy. Two girls arrive and handsome chap is in trouble until mystery is cleared with confession of the plain-featured boy." (*Motion Picture News Booking Guide,* 12:36, Apr 1927.) *Cowboys. Matrimonial agencies.*

IN EVERY WOMAN'S LIFE **F2.2680**

Associated First National Pictures. 28 Sep **1924** [c15 Sep 1924; LP20566]. Si; b&w. 35mm. 7 reels, 6,300 ft.

Pres by M. C. Levee. *Prod* M. C. Levee. *Dir* Irving Cummings. *Scen* Albert Shelby Le Vino. *Photog* Arthur L. Todd. *Art Dir* Jack Okey. *Film Ed* Charles J. Hunt. *Asst Dir* Charles Woolstenhulme. *Prod Mgr* Scott R. Beal.

Cast: Virginia Valli *(Sara Langford)*, Lloyd Hughes *(Julian Greer)*, Marc MacDermott *(Count Coti Desanges)*, George Fawcett *(Douglass Greer)*, Vera Lewis *(Diana Lansdale)*, Ralph Lewis *(captain)*, Stuart Holmes *(Charles Carleton)*, John Sainpolis *(Dr. Philip Logan)*.

Society drama. Source: Olive Wadsley, *Belonging* (New York, 1920). Sara Langford, an American girl in Paris, is courted by Count Desanges, who loves her but is considerably older; Thomas Carlton, who is married but is out for conquest; and Julian Greer, her true love. In rescuing Greer from the sea, the count is permanently paralyzed but manages to shoot Carlton when he attacks Sara. Ultimately, the true lovers are reunited. *Courtship. Paris. Sea rescue.*

IN FAST COMPANY **F2.2681**

Carlos Productions. *Dist* Truart Film Corp. 6 Jun **1924** [New York showing; released 15 Jul; c8 May 1024; LP20204]. Si; b&w. 35mm. 6 reels, 5,411 ft.

Dir James W. Horne. *Scen* Garrett Elsden Fort. *Story* Alfred A. Cohn. *Photog* William Marshall.

Cast: Richard Talmadge *(Perry Whitman, Jr.)*, Mildred Harris *(Barbara Belden)*, Sheldon Lewis *(Drexel Craig)*, Douglas Gerrard *(Reginald Chichester)*, Jack Herrick *(The "Bolivian Bull")*, Charles Clary *(Perry Whitman, Sr.)*, Snitz Edwards *(Mike Ricketts)*, Lydia Yeamans Titus *(maid)*.

Melodrama. Perry Whitman's wild escapades result in his being expelled from college, an event he celebrates by holding a wild party to which he invites the impoverished members of a theatrical troupe. He is disowned by his father and turned adrift with a $100 bill, which he loses. In trying to recover the money he saves a girl from becoming the victim of a matrimonial scheme; she eludes capture by kidnapers and marries him to save her fortune. Thus he wins his father's forgiveness. *Students. College life. Theatrical troupes. Filial relations.*

IN GAY MADRID F2.2682

Metro-Goldwyn-Mayer Pictures. 17 May **1930** [c12 May 1930; LP1286]. Sd (Movietone); b&w. 35mm. 9 reels, 7,654 ft.

Dir Robert Z. Leonard. *Cont-Dial* Bess Meredyth, Edward Field, Edwin Justus Mayer. *Photog* Oliver Marsh. *Art Dir* Cedric Gibbons. *Film Ed* William S. Gray. *Mus Score* Fred E. Ahlert, Xavier Cugat, Herbert Stothart. *Songs: "Santiago," "Dark Night," "Smile While We May," "Into My Heart"* Clifford Grey, Roy Turk. *Rec Dir* Douglas Shearer. *Rec Engr* Ralph Shugart. *Gowns* Adrian.

Cast: Ramon Novarro *(Ricardo)*, Dorothy Jordan *(Carmina)*, Lottice Howell *(La Goyita)*, Claude King *(Marquès de Castelar)*, Eugenie Besserer *(Doña Generosa)*, William V. Mong *(Rivas)*, Beryl Mercer *(Doña Concha)*, Nanci Price *(Jacinta)*, Herbert Clark *(Octavio)*, David Scott *(Ernesto)*, George Chandler *(Enrique)*, Bruce Coleman *(Corpulento)*, Nicholas Caruso *(Carlos)*.

Musical comedy-drama. Source: Alejandro Pérez Lugín, *La Casa de la Troya* (Madrid, 1915). Ricardo, the hero of many romantic escapades, is sent from Madrid by his irate father to continue his college studies. At school he meets and falls in love with Carmina, serenades her, and gradually wins her despite her feigned indifference. Then Octavio, a rejected suitor, reports to the Marques de Castelar that Ricardo is keeping La Goyita, a former "companion in arms," in his room; although he denies the charge, the engagement is broken. Ernesto, the girl's brother, challenges Ricardo to a duel in which he deliberately allows himself to be wounded, thus clearing the way for a reconciliation between the lovers. *Students. Brother-sister relationship. Filial relations. College life. Courtship. Duels. Spain. Madrid.*

IN HIGH GEAR F2.2683

Sunset Productions. *Dist* Aywon Film Corp. 1 Jul **1924.** Si; b&w. 35mm. 5 reels, 4,737 ft.

Dir Robert North Bradbury. *Story-Scen* Robert North Bradbury, Frank Howard Clark. *Photog* Bert Longenecker.

Cast: Kenneth McDonald, Helen Lynch.

Comedy-melodrama. "Jack Holloway and Alice Cromwell each wealthy and bored with the sham of the exclusive Mirimar resort assume disguises as poor people, eventually meet and fall in love. Alice is kidnapped and thrown into Chinatown den where Jack rescues her after a series of thrilling fights. Real identities are revealed and a happy marriage follows." (*Motion Picture News Booking Guide*, 7:29, Oct 1924.) *Chinese. Wealth. Disguise. Kidnaping. Resorts. Chinatown.*

Note: Reissued Jan 1930.

IN HOLLYWOOD WITH POTASH AND PERLMUTTER F2.2684

Goldwyn Pictures. *Dist* Associated First National Pictures. Sep **1924** [c16 Sept 1924; LP20572]. Si; b&w. 35mm. 7 reels, 6,685 ft.

Pres by Samuel Goldwyn. *Prod* Samuel Goldwyn. *Dir* Alfred Green. *Titl* Montague Glass. *Adapt* Frances Marion. *Photog* Arthur Miller, Harry Hallenberger. *Art Dir* Ben Carré. *Film Ed* Stuart Heisler.

Cast: Alexander Carr *(Morris Perlmutter)*, George Sidney *(Abe Potash)*, Vera Gordon *(Rosie Potash)*, Betty Blythe *(Rita Sismondi)*, Belle Bennett *(Mrs. Perlmutter)*, Anders Randolph *(Blanchard)*, Peggy Shaw *(Irma Potash)*, Charles Meredith *(Sam Pemberton)*, Lillian Hackett *(Miss O'Ryan)*, David Butler *(Crabbe)*, Sidney Franklin, Joseph W. Girard *(film buyers)*, Norma Talmadge, Constance Talmadge.

Comedy. Source: Montague Glass and Jules Eckert Goodman, *Business Before Pleasure* (New York opening: Aug 1917). Potash and Perlmutter give up their textile business to produce motion pictures. Though their initial effort is a failure, they interest a banker, Blanchard, in financing their productions, provided that they engage Rita Sismondi, an actress famous for vamp roles. She all but breaks up the homes of the partners. When they finally settle their differences, their new picture is a success and the vamp begins a romance with the director. *Actors. Jews. Vamps. Textile manufacture. Motion pictures. Hollywood.*

IN LOVE WITH LOVE F2.2685

Fox Film Corp. 28 Dec **1924** [c14 Dec 1924; LP20915]. Si; b&w. 35mm. 6 reels, 5,677 ft.

Pres by William Fox. *Dir* Rowland V. Lee. *Adapt-Scen* Robert N. Lee.

Cast: Marguerite De La Motte *(Ann Jordan)*, Allan Forrest *(Jack Gardner)*, Harold Goodwin *(Robert Metcalf)*, William Austin *(George Sears)*, Mary Warren *(Julia)*, Will Walling *(Mr. Jordan)*, Allan Sears *(Frank Oaks)*, Mabel Forrest *(Marion Sears)*.

Comedy. Source: Vincent Lawrence, *In Love With Love; a Play in Three Acts* (New York, c1927). Ann Jordan, the flirtatious and spoiled daughter of a wealthy contractor, is engaged to Robert Metcalf, a relaxed and boring young man. She then meets Frank Oaks, who aggressively sweeps her off her feet, and she is presently engaged to him also. Mr. Jordan, Ann's father, becomes interested in one of Robert's friends, Jack Gardner, an engineer who is preparing a design for a bridge competition. The elder Jordan invites Jack to the house and covertly copies Jack's plans for the bridge. Ann falls in love with Jack, who is eligible and seemingly indifferent; Jack is too modest to declare his love, so Ann is forced to propose to him, and Jack accepts. Jack's plan for the bridge wins the competition, but in Jordan's name rather than his own. Jack breaks off with Ann, believing that she has professed love for him only to help her father steal his plans. Jack and Ann are reconciled, however, when her father explains that he prevented Jack from winning the competition only to be sure that Jack was free to accept an extremely important position with the Jordan firm! *Contractors. Flirts. Engineers. Fatherhood. Bridges.*

IN OLD ARIZONA F2.2686

Fox Film Corp. 20 Jan **1929** [c4 Feb 1929; LP75]. Sd (Movietone); b&w. 35mm. 7 reels, 8,724 ft.

Dir Raoul Walsh, Irving Cummings. *Scen-Story-Dial* Tom Barry. *Camera* Arthur Edeson. *Film Ed* Louis Loeffler. *Song: "My Tonia"* Lew Brown, B. G. De Sylva, Ray Henderson. *Sd* Edmund H. Hansen. *Asst Dir* Archibald Buchanan, Charles Woolstenhulme.

Cast: Edmund Lowe *(Sgt. Mickey Dunn)*, Dorothy Burgess *(Tonia María)*, Warner Baxter *(The Cisco Kid)*, Farrell MacDonald *(Tad)*, Fred Warren *(piano player)*, Henry Armetta *(barber)*, Frank Campeau, Tom Santschi, Pat Hartigan *(cowpunchers)*, Roy Stewart *(commandant)*, James Bradbury, Jr. *(soldier)*, John Dillon *(second soldier)*, Frank Nelson, Duke Martin *(cowboys)*, James Marcus *(blacksmith)*, Joe Brown *(bartender)*, Alphonse Ethier *(sheriff)*, Solidad Jiminez *(cook)*, Helen Lynch, Ivan Linow.

Western melodrama. The Cisco Kid is a gay caballero whose flair for dramatic thievery and penchant for dangerous trysts keep him just one step ahead of Sgt. Mickey Dunn. The Kid's reputation has preceded him when he approaches the local stagecoach and needs to fire only two warning shots to wrest the Wells Fargo box from the driver. His infatuation with a Mexican girl named Tonia María exposes him to near capture because of the señorita's double-dealing association with Dunn. Eventually, a showdown becomes imminent, and the Kid exacts a final revenge by framing Tonia so that Dunn shoots her by accident while the Kid rides laughing off into the sunset. *Caballeros. Bandits. Robbery. Arizona. United States Army—Cavalry.*

IN OLD CALIFORNIA F2.2687

Audible Pictures. 1 Sep or 15 Oct **1929.** Sd (Photophone); b&w. 35mm. 6 reels, 5,400-5,500 ft. [Also si; 5,367 ft.]

Supv Lon Young. *Dir* Burton King. *Scen-Dial* Arthur Hoerl. *Story* Fred Hart. *Photog* Charles Boyle. *Film Ed* Earl Turner. *Rec Engr* Ernest Rovere. *Asst Dir* Bernard F. McEveety.

Cast: Henry B. Walthall *(Don Pedro DeLeón)*, Helen Ferguson *(Dolores Radanell)*, George Duryea *(Lieut. Tony Hopkins)*, Ray Hallor *(Pedro DeLeón)*, Orral Humphrey *(Ike Boone)*, Larry Steers *(Ollie Radanell)*, Richard Carlyle *(Arturo)*, Harry Allen *(Sergeant Washburn)*, Louis Stern *(Ramón De Hermosa)*, Paul Ellis *(José)*, Carlotta Monta *(Juanita)*, Gertrude Short, Gertrude Chorre *(see note)*.

Romantic drama. A flirtation begun in a California-bound stagecoach between Pedro DeLeón and Dolores Radanell is interrupted by bandits, and the runaway horses are halted by Lieut. Tony Hopkins, who also shows an interest in Dolores. Inviting Dolores and her gambler father, Ollie Radanell, to a fiesta at his wealthy father's ranch, Pedro spends much of his time drinking and brooding over the lieutenant's obvious success with Dolores and his father's bitterness because of Pedro's mother, Isabella. In the course of the evening Don Pedro loses his ranch to Radanell in a card game, and a showdown between the two men reveals that Radanell took Isabella and Dolores away from Don Pedro—making Dolores Pedro's sister. Pedro defends his father in a final shooting match with Hopkins. *Bandits. Ranchers. Gamblers. Brother-sister relationship. California.*

Note: Sources disagree as to which Gertrude is in the cast. Theme song: "Underneath a Spanish Moon."

IN OLD KENTUCKY F2.2688

Metro-Goldwyn-Mayer Pictures. 29 Oct **1927** [c29 Oct, 1 Nov 1927; LP25230, LP24610]. Si; b&w. 35mm. 7 reels, 6,646 ft.

Dir John M. Stahl. *Scen* A. P. Younger. *Titl* Marian Ainslee, Ruth Cummings. *Adapt* A. P. Younger, Lew Lipton. *Photog* Maximilian Fabian. *Set Dsgn* Cedric Gibbons, Ernest Fegte. *Film Ed* Basil Wrangell, Margaret Booth. *Asst Dir* David Friedman. *Wardrobe* Gilbert Clark.

Cast: James Murray *(Jimmy Brierly)*, Helene Costello *(Nancy Holden)*, Wesley Barry *("Skippy" Lowry)*, Dorothy Cumming *(Mrs. Brierly)*, Edward Martindel *(Mr. Brierly)*, Harvey Clark *(Dan Lowry)*, Stepin Fetchit *(Highpockets)*, Carolynne Snowden *(Lily May)*, Nick Cogley *(Uncle Bible)*.

Drama. Source: Charles T. Dazey, *In Old Kentucky; an American Play in Four Acts* (New York opening: 2 Jan 1922). Disillusioned by his experiences in the World War, Jimmy Brierly returns, a gambler and a drunk, to his family of Kentucky horsebreeders. He finds poverty threatening the estate, all the horses having been contributed to the war effort. Then a famous racehorse, once owned by Mr. Brierly, that Jimmy rode in the war is by coincidence repurchased. Entered in the Derby, it recoups the family fortune. *Veterans. Horsebreeders. Gamblers. Poverty. World War I. Kentucky. Kentucky Derby. Horses.*

IN QUEST OF THE GOLDEN PRINCE *see* **THE LOST EMPIRE**

IN SEARCH OF A HERO F2.2689

Paul Gerson Pictures. *Dist* Aywon Film Corp. 14 Sep **1926** [New York State license]. Si; b&w. 35mm. 5 reels.

Dir Duke Worne. *Writ* Arthur Hoerl.

Cast: Richard Holt *(Percy Browning)*, Jane Thomas *(Peggy Richmond)*, Jimmy Harrison *(Jack Strong)*, Gerry O'Dell *(Dinty)*, Al Kaufman *(Dugan)*, Claire Vinson *(Inez)*, Les Bates *(Big Dan)*.

No information about the nature of this film has been found.

IN SEARCH OF A THRILL F2.2690

Metro Pictures. 20 Nov **1923** [New York showing; released 10 Dec; c27 Nov 1923; LP19733]. Si; b&w. 35mm. 5 reels, 5,500 ft.

Dir Oscar Apfel. *Adapt-Cont* Basil Dickey, Winifred Dunn. *Photog* John Arnold.

Cast: Viola Dana *(Ann Clemance)*, Warner Baxter *(Adrian Torrens)*, Mabel Van Buren *(Lila Lavender)*, Templar Saxe *(Sir George Dumphy)*, Robert Schable *(Tommy Perkins)*, Walter Wills *(René de Farge)*, Rosemary Theby *(Jeanne)*, Billy Elmer *(Percy, the valet)*, Leo White *(dance professor)*.

Melodrama. Source: Kate Jordan, "The Spirit of the Road" (publication undetermined). Society girl Ann Clemance deepens her life during a trip abroad when Adrian Torrens, a social reformer, takes her on a tour through some impoverished areas of Paris. Made aware of her role in life—to help others—Ann adopts an orphan and marries Adrian. *Socialites. Poverty. Social reform. Adoption. Thrill-seeking. Paris.*

IN SEARCH OF WHITE RHINOCEROS *see* **THROUGH DARKEST AFRICA; IN SEARCH OF WHITE RHINOCEROS**

IN SOCIETY F2.2691

Pioneer Film Corp. 28 Jul **1921** [Port Washington, N. Y., showing]. Si; b&w. 35mm. 5 reels, 4,319 ft.

Cast: Edith Roberts.

Melodrama(?). No information about the precise nature of this film has been found. *Socialites.*

IN THE DAYS OF THE COVERED WAGON F2.2692

28 May **1924** [New York State license]. Si; b&w. 35mm. 5 reels.

Cast: Francis Ford.

Western melodrama. No information about the precise nature of this film has been found. *Frontier and pioneer life.*

Note: Production and distribution companies have not been determined.

IN THE DEVIL'S BOWL *see* **THE DEVIL'S BOWL**

IN THE FIRST DEGREE F2.2693

Sterling Pictures. 15 Apr **1927** [c21 Apr 1927; LP23889]. Si; b&w. 35mm. 6 reels, 5,428 ft.

Dir Phil Rosen. *Scen* Frances Guihan. *Story* Reginald Wright Kauffman. *Photog* Herbert Kirkpatrick.

Cast: Alice Calhoun *(Barbara Hurd)*, Bryant Washburn *(Philip Stanwood)*, Gayne Whitman *(John Pendleton)*, Trilby Clark *(Gladys Hutton)*, Gareth Hughes *(Jerry Pendleton)*, Joseph Girard *(James Hurd)*, Milton Fahrney *(warden)*, William De Vaull *(butler)*.

Melodrama. John Pendleton, secretary to wealthy stock speculator James Hurd, is in love with Barbara, Hurd's daughter, who is also admired by Philip Stanwood, a rich associate of her father. Stanwood is repelled and enlists Hurd's aid in winning the girl; he refuses until, faced with ruin, he has to accept Stanwood's financial aid. On the evening of Barbara's engagement to Stanwood, John is sent to get a necklace from Hurd, taking a gun for protection. Gladys, a former mistress of Stanwood's, interrupts with accusations and accidentally kills Hurd. John, however, is found over the body and is convicted of murder on circumstantial evidence. His brother, Jerry, follows Stanwood while John is being prepared for execution. In an automobile chase, Stanwood is killed, and Gladys, before dying, confesses the truth. Jerry manages to stay the execution, and Barbara and John find happiness together. *Secretaries. Courtship. Murder. Circumstantial evidence. Injustice. Capital punishment. Speculation.*

IN THE HEADLINES F2.2694

Warner Brothers Pictures. 31 Aug **1929** [c9 Aug 1929; LP584]. Sd (Vitaphone); b&w. 35mm. 8 reels, 6,427 ft. [Also si, 26 Oct; 5,212 ft.]

Dir John G. Adolfi. *Screenplay* Joseph Jackson. *Story* James A. Starr.

Cast: Grant Withers *(Nosey Norton)*, Marion Nixon *(Anna Lou Anderson)*, Clyde Cook *(Flashlight)*, Edmund Breese *(Eddy)*, Pauline Garon *(Blondie [Alice Adair])*, Frank Campeau *(Detective Robinson)*, Vivian Oakland *(Mrs. Kernell)*, Hallam Cooley *(Fancy Somerset)*, Robert Ober *(Parker)*, Ben Hall *(cub reporter)*, Spec O'Donnell *(Johnny)*, Jack Wise *(Levine)*.

Crime drama. A newspaper editor sends Anna Lou Anderson, a recent journalism graduate, to assist star reporter Nosey Norton when Norton, assigned to a double murder case, fails to come up with anything. Nosey has a hunch that the two brokers shot each other or were killed because of a woman, and he believes that office manager Parker is somehow implicated. Nosey's half sister, Alice Adair, offers to give him a large sum of money if he will take Anna Lou and get out of town. Nosey refuses the money, and Anna Lou is kidnaped. Believing that Alice and Parker kidnaped her to persuade Nosey to accept the money, Nosey visits Parker's apartment, arriving in time to prevent Anna from swallowing a drugged drink. Anna Lou tells him that after Kernell, one of the brokers, killed his partner, Randall, Parker killed Kernell. Parker and Alice get a prison term, while Nosey and Anna Lou get a paid honeymoon. *Reporters. Brokers. Office managers. Murder. Kidnaping.*

IN THE HOUR OF HIS NEED F2.2695

Mitchell Loeb. 15 Nov **1925.** Si; b&w. 35mm. 5 reels.

No information about the nature of this film has been found.

IN THE NAME OF LOVE F2.2696

Famous Players–Lasky. *Dist* Paramount Pictures. 10 Aug **1925** [c10 Aug 1925; LP21720]. Si; b&w. 35mm. 6 reels, 5,862 ft.

Pres by Adolph Zukor, Jesse L. Lasky. *Dir* Howard Higgin. *Scen* Sada Cowan. *Photog* C. Edgar Schoenbaum.

Cast: Ricardo Cortez *(Raoul Melnotte)*, Greta Nissen *(Marie Dufrayne)*, Wallace Beery *(M. Glavis)*, Raymond Hatton *(Marquis de Beausant)*, Lillian Leighton *(Mother Dufrayne)*, Edythe Chapman *(Mother Melnotte)*, Richard Arlen *(Dumas Dufrayne)*.

Romantic comedy. Source: Edward Bulwer-Lytton, *The Lady of Lyons; or, Love and Pride* (New York, 1838). Raoul Melnotte returns from Chicago to the French town of his birth in search of Marie Dufrayne, the sweetheart of his college days, finding that she has become a wealthy social climber in search of a titled husband. Raoul proposes to Marie, but she turns him down when she discovers that he is only a businessman. In league with her other two rejected suitors, Raoul then masquerades as a prince, revealing his true identity only after his wedding to Marie. Learning that she has married a common businessman, Marie is at first apoplectic, but true love wins out in the end, and she and Raoul settle down to married life. *Businessmen. Royalty. Social climbers. Imposture. Chicago. France.*

IN THE NAME OF THE LAW F2.2697

Emory Johnson Productions. *Dist* Film Booking Offices of America. 9 Jul **1922** [New York premiere; released 20 Aug; c6 Jul 1922; LP18034]. Si; b&w. 35mm. 7 reels, 6,126 ft.

Pres by P. A. Powers. *Dir* Emory Johnson. *Story-Scen* Emilie Johnson. *Titl* Carol Owen. *Camera* Ross Fisher. *Asst Dir* Dick Posson.

Cast—Prolog: Ben Alexander *(Harry O'Hara, aged 9)*, Josephine Adair *(Mary, aged 6)*, Johnny Thompson *(Johnnie O'Hara, aged 8)*, Jean Adair *(child)*.

Cast—The Story: Ralph Lewis *(Patrick O'Hara)*, Claire McDowell *(Mrs. O'Hara)*, Ella Hall *(Mary, aged 18)*, Emory Johnson *(Harry O'Hara, aged 22)*, Johnnie Walker *(Johnnie O'Hara, aged 20)*, Richard Morris *(Mr. Lucas)*.

Drama. A law student, the son of a respected San Francisco policeman, is falsely accused by his landlord of theft. In an attempt to repay the debt, the family is led through a set of occurrences culminating when the father unknowingly shoots his other son during a bank robbery. All is unraveled in a final courtroom scene. *Police. Lawyers. Debt. Family life. Theft. Robbery. San Francisco.*

Note: Copyright records give the policeman's family name as O'Hare.

IN THE NEXT ROOM **F2.2698**

First National Pictures. 26 Jan **1930** [c14 May 1930; LP1301]. Sd (Vitaphone); b&w. 35mm. 7 reels, 6,336 ft.

Dir Edward Cline. *Scen* Harvey Gates. *Dial* James A. Starr. *Photog* John Seitz. *Sd* Mel Le Mon.

Cast—Prolog: Jane Winton *(The Lady)*, Crauford Kent *(The Lover)*, Edward Earle *(The Husband)*.

Cast—The Story: Jack Mulhall *(James Godfrey)*, Alice Day *(Lorna)*, Robert E. O'Connor *(Tim Morel)*, John St. Polis *(Philip Vantine)*, Claude Allister *(Parks, the butler)*, Aggie Herring *(Mrs. O'Connor)*, De Witt Jennings *(Inspector Grady)*, Webster Campbell *(Snitzer)*, Lucien Prival *(French exporter)*.

Mystery melodrama. Source: Eleanor Robson Belmont and Harriet Ford, *In the Next Room* (New York opening: 27 Nov 1923). Burton Egbert Stevenson, *The Mystery of the Boule Cabinet; a Detective Story* (New York, 1911). Following a prolog set in 1889 in which an irate husband kills his wife's lover, New York in 1929 is revealed to be terrified by a series of knife murders. Police are mysteriously called to the house of Mr. Vantine, but he refuses to admit them; Jimmy Godfrey, a young reporter in love with Vantine's niece, Lorna, arrives and helps them unpack an antique cabinet in which they find a woman in a hypnotic trance. The son of the former owner of the cabinet arrives and goes for the police, but the girl disappears. Detective Morel is knocked unconscious, the son of the former owner falls dead, and Mr. Vantine gets bumped on the head. Lorna is abducted and taken to the wine cellar as Jimmy is calling the newspaper; but she is rescued by a one-legged butler. Meanwhile, the hypnotized girl revives and reveals that she and her partner had planned to smuggle diamonds into the house but that he was killed by poison. The detective discovers, however, that the cabinet was sent to the wrong address. ... *Reporters. Detectives. Smugglers. Murder. Hypnotism. Antiques. New York City.*

IN THE PALACE OF THE KING **F2.2699**

Goldwyn Pictures. *Dist* Goldwyn-Cosmopolitan Distributing Corp. 28 Oct **1923** [c10 Nov 1923; LP19708]. Si; b&w. 35mm. 9 reels, 8,657 ft.

Dir Emmett Flynn. *Adapt* June Mathis. *Photog* Lucien Andriot.

Cast: Blanche Sweet *(Dolores Mendoza)*, Edmund Lowe *(Don John)*, Hobart Bosworth *(Mendoza)*, Pauline Starke *(Inez Mendoza)*, Sam De Grasse *(King Philip II)*, William V. Mong *(Perez)*, Aileen Pringle *(Princess Eboli)*, Lucien Littlefield *(Adonis)*, Charles Clary *(Gomez)*, Harvey Clarke *(Alphonso)*, Tom Bates *(Eudaldo)*, D. N. Clugston *(chamberlain)*, Charles Gorham *(guard)*, Jack Pitcairn *(Captain of the Guard)*, David Kirby *(guard)*, Ena Gregory *(The Queen)*, Bruce Sterling *(Gaston)*, Charles Newton *(aide to Don John)*.

Spectacular romance. Source: Francis Marion Crawford, *In the Palace of the King; a Love Story of Old Madrid* (New York, 1900). King Philip of Spain, jealous of the popularity of his brother, Don John, sends him to fight the Moors, hoping he will not return. Don John is in love with Dolores, daughter of General Mendoza, but Mendoza discourages Dolores, knowing that if Don John does return, he is to marry the Queen of England's sister. Don John returns victorious. In a dispute over a secret letter, the king wounds Don John with his sword and leaves him for dead. When Mendoza takes the blame, Dolores, who was nearby and knows that the king is guilty, tells the court she had been dishonored by Don John—thus the reason for her father's wrath. Then Dolores threatens the king that she will tell the truth to his subjects unless her father is pardoned. Don John recovers, the king pardons Mendoza, and Dolores marries her sweetheart. *Brothers. Royalty. Moors. Jealousy. Spain. Madrid. Philip II (Spain). Don John of Austria.*

IN THE SOUTH SEAS WITH MR. AND MRS. PINCHOT *see* **SOUTH SEAS**

IN THE SPIDER'S WEB **F2.2700**

Dist Independent Pictures. Jan **1924.** Si; b&w. 35mm. 5 reels, 5,127 ft.

Dir Robert Bondrioz.

Cast: Howard Hampden *(Dr. Charles Maynard)*, Alice Dean *(Polly Powers)*, Charles Vanel *(Stephen Powers)*, Jean Paul Baer *(The Child)*.

Melodrama. Fainting at the news that she and her child have been deserted by her lover, Follies dancer Polly Powers receives medical attention from Dr. Maynard and eventually marries him, telling him that her husband is dead. Sometime later Powers reappears, becomes friendly with Maynard, and tricks Polly into going to his apartment. Learning the truth, Maynard follows them, but Powers slips out to kidnap his son, hoping thus to protect himself from the police. The net tightens, and Powers takes his own life. *Dancers. Physicians. Illegitimacy. Kidnaping. Desertion. Suicide. Follies.*

Note: Country of origin undetermined. May have been produced in 1917.

IN THE WATER **F2.2701**

Donald Mack Productions. 12 Jul **1923** [New York State license]. Si; b&w. 35mm. 5 reels, 4,500 ft.

Cast: Donald Mack, Elsie Hanneman.

Educational scenic. No information about the specific nature of this film has been found.

IN THE WEST **F2.2702**

Wild West Productions. *Dist* Arrow Film Corp. 20 Dec **1923** [c4 Dec 1923; LP19674]. Si; b&w. 35mm. 5 reels, 4,652 ft.

Story-Dir George Holt.

Cast: Neva Gerber *(Florence Jackson)*, Richard Hatton *(Bill Frazer)*, Arthur Morrison, Elias Bullock, Robert McKenzie *(see note)*.

Western melodrama. "A 'city chap' wins a girl [Florence Jackson] away from her cowboy sweetheart [Bill Frazer]. The mother, however, insists the chap go out west and make good. Hard work is not attractive to Jack Grimson and he wanders back to his city haunts, permitting the girl and her mother to believe he is still on the ranch. The cowboy stages a comeback and when he exposes the deception carried on by Grimson the girl is won back to him." (*Motion Picture News Booking Guide*, 6:38, Apr 1924.) *Cowboys. Gold mines.*

Note: Some sources indicate that the last three actors named are also in the cast.

INDISCRETION **F2.2703**

A. J. Bimberg. *Dist* Pioneer Film Corp. **1921** [c27 May 1921; LU16594]. Si; b&w. 35mm. 6 reels.

Dir William Davis.

Cast: Florence Reed *(Laura West)*, Lionel Atwill *(Howard Hollister)*, Gareth Hughes *(Stephen Rhodes)*.

Melodrama. While Laura West is engaged to marry Howard Hollister, she meets his friend Stephen Rhodes, who has just returned from India and has become converted to the worship of Gaia, the Eternal Mother. She visits Stephen's sanctuary, and his repeated attempts to convert her provoke a quarrel with Hollister after their marriage. *In a dream she goes again to the sanctuary and is initiated into Stephen's religion. She bears a child and realizing the baseness of his teachings she abandons it. Stephen threatens to kill the child if she does not return to him.* She awakens from her dream and becomes reconciled to her husband's point of view. *Marriage. Religion. India. Gaia. Dreams.*

Note: Some sources indicate that the roles of Lionel Atwill and Gareth Hughes should be reversed.

INEZ FROM HOLLYWOOD **F2.2704**

Sam E. Rork Productions. *Dist* First National Pictures. 30 Nov **1924** [c14 Nov 1924; LP20767]. Si; b&w. 35mm. 7 reels, 6,919 ft.

Dir Alfred E. Green. *Adapt* J. G. Hawks. *Photog* Arthur Edeson. *Sets* Jack Okey. *Film Ed* Dorothy Arzner. *Asst Dir* Jack Boland.

Cast: Anna Q. Nilsson *(Inez Laranetta)*, Lewis S. Stone *(Stewart Cuyler)*, Mary Astor *(Fay Bartholdi)*, Laurence Wheat *(Pat Summerfield)*, Rose Dione *(Marie d'Albrecht)*, Snitz Edwards *(The Old Sport)*, Harry Depp *(Scoop Smith)*, Ray Hallor *(Freddie)*, E. H. Calvert *(Gardner)*.

Drama. Source: Adela Rogers St. Johns, "The Worst Woman in Hollywood," in *Cosmopolitan* (76:53–58, Feb 1924). Thought to be "the worst woman in Hollywood" because of her vampire roles and lurid publicity, Inez Laranetta actually is more concerned with shielding her younger sister, Fay Bartholdi, from the life she knows—especially the devastating implulses of men. Stewart Cuyler, a wealthy and socially prominent New Yorker, is the only man Inez respects, but she refuses even his attentions. When Stewart searches for the man he believes to be his rival, he falls in love with Fay. Inez learns of their courtship, assumes Stewart's intentions to be dishonorable, and hastens to the scene intending to separate the couple. Stewart explains that he wishes to marry Fay but that Inez must give up her sister. For the sake of Fay's happiness, Inez sadly withdraws and finds some consolation in the love of her manager, Pat Summerfield. *Vamps. Actors. Sisters. Motion pictures. Hollywood.*

THE INFAMOUS MISS REVELL **F2.2705**

Metro Pictures. 17 Oct **1921** [c25 Aug 1921; LP17946]. Si; b&w. 35mm. 6 reels.

Dir Dallas M. Fitzgerald. *Adapt* Arthur J. Zellner. *Photog* Roy Klaffki. *Art Dir* Joseph Calder.

Cast: Alice Lake *(Julien Revell/Paula Revell)*, Cullen Landis *(Max Hildreth)*, Jackie Saunders *(Lillian Hildreth)*, Lydia Knott *(Mary Hildreth)*, Herbert Standing *(Samuel Pangborn)*, Alfred Hollingsworth *(Maxwell Putnam)*, Stanley Goethals, Francis Carpenter, May Giraci, Geraldine Condon *(The Revell Children)*.

Mystery melodrama. Source: William Carey Wonderly, "The Infamous Miss Revell" (publication undetermined). Twin sisters Julien and Paula Revell, compelled to support their younger brothers and sisters after the death of their father, are unable to get a booking for their musical act, and Julien accepts the "protection" of a man of wealth in return for a home for her family. When her protector dies, she inherits his fortune for her lifetime or until she marries. Max Hildreth, an underpaid teacher, and his sister Lillian, a clerk in a store, are hired to teach the Revell children. Lillian urges Max to marry the heiress so as to get possession of her fortune, but Max—though he has fallen in love with Julien—hesitates to declare himself. It appears that Julien's infamous past stands between them until it is revealed that Julien died shortly after her protector died and that the girl with whom Max is in love is actually Paula. *Twins. Sisters. Entertainers. Brother-sister relationship. Mistresses. Schoolteachers. Orphans. Inheritance.*

INFATUATION **F2.2706**

Corinne Griffith Productions. *Dist* First National Pictures. 27 Dec **1925** [c16 Dec 1925; LP22123]. Si; b&w. 35mm. 7 reels, 5,794 ft.

Dir Irving Cummings. *Photog* Hal Rosson.

Cast: Corinne Griffith *(Violet Bancroft)*, Percy Marmont *(Sir Arthur Little)*, Malcolm McGregor *(Ronald Perry)*, Warner Oland *(Osman Pasha)*, Clarissa Selwyn *(Lady Ethridge)*, Leota Lorraine *(Ronny's sister)*, Claire Du Brey *(Pasha's wife)*, Martha Mattox *(Mrs. Pritchard)*, Howard Davies *(Khedive)*.

Drama. Source: William Somerset Maugham, *Caesar's Wife, a Comedy in Three Acts* (London, 1922). A few days after his marriage to the beautiful Violet Bancroft, Sir Arthur Little is sent on a military mission to Cairo; he devotes himself to hard work and she turns to young Ronald Perry, her husband's secretary, for warmth and companionship. Violet and Ronald fall in love, and Violet, believing her position to be untenable, confesses her infatuation to Arthur and begs him to assign Ronald to another post. Arthur refuses, reminding Violet that "Caesar's wife must be above suspicion." Arthur is called away to dine with the khedive, and Violet learns that there is a plot against his life. She runs after him through the crowded streets and finds his carriage in time to prevent his assassination. Violet realizes then the depth of her love for Arthur and puts young Perry out of her mind. *English. Diplomats. Secretaries. Infidelity. Conspiracy. Cairo.*

THE INFIDEL **F2.2707**

Preferred Pictures. *Dist* Associated First National Pictures. ca2 Apr **1922** [Omaha premiere; c29 Mar 1922; LP17694]. Si; b&w. 35mm. 6 reels, 5,377 ft.

Pres by B. P. Schulberg. *Dir-Scen* James Young. *Story* Charles A. Logue. *Photog* Joseph Brotherton.

Cast: Katherine MacDonald *(Lola Daintry)*, Robert Ellis *(Cyrus Flint)*, Joseph Dowling *(Reverend Mead)*, Boris Karloff *(The Nabob)*, Melbourne MacDowell *("Bully" Haynes)*, Oleta Otis *(Miss Parliss)*, Charles Smiley *(Mr. Scudder)*, Loyola O'Connor *(Mrs. Scudder)*, Barbara Tennant *(Hope Scudder)*, Charles Force *(Chunky)*.

Melodrama. Lola Daintry, a beautiful young actress, and her companion, Chunky, pose as castaways and are taken to the island of Menang in the South Seas by Cyrus Flint, an idealist who owns large interests there, and the Reverend Mead. Lola accepts the hospitality of the missionary in preference to that of the nabob, although she dislikes preachers and does not believe in God. Flint, who is attracted to the girl, warns her against taking passage on a trading vessel in port captained by "Bully" Haynes; Lola, who has been persuaded by Haynes to trick Flint into leaving the island, later realizes that she cannot carry out the scheme and warns Flint of his danger. Scornfully, Flint decides to sell out and go to Australia, leaving the Christians at the mercy of the nabob. When the village is set afire, Lola implores Flint to call for aid; he fights the ship's crew; Haynes is mortally wounded; Lola, in desperation, prays for guidance; and Flint succeeds in communicating with marines, who quell the uprising. *Actors. Castaways. Missionaries. Atheism. South Sea Islands. United States Marines.*

THE INNER CHAMBER **F2.2708**

Vitagraph Co. of America. 11 Sep **1921** [c19 Jul 1921; LP16768]. Si; b&w. 35mm. 6 reels.

Dir Edward José. *Scen* C. Graham Baker.

Cast: Alice Joyce *(Claire Robson)*, Jane Jennings *(Mrs. Robson)*, Pedro De Cordoba *(Dr. George Danilo)*, Holmes E. Herbert *(Edward J. Wellman)*, John Webb Dillon *(Sawyer Flint)*, Grace Barton *(Mrs. Sawyer Flint)*, Ida Waterman *(Mrs. Finch-Brown)*, Josephine Whittell *(Nellie McGuire)*, Mrs. De Wolf Hopper *(Mrs. Candor)*.

Society melodrama. Source: Charles Caldwell Dobie, *The Blood Red Dawn* (New York, 1920). Claire Robson finds herself falling in love with Ned Wellman, a wealthy man who saves her from the unwelcome attentions of Flint, her former employer; but her romance is abruptly ended by Mrs. Candor, who has designs on Wellman and informs Claire that he is already married. Months later she consents to marry Dr. Danilo, out of respect and gratitude for his saving her mother's life, but she then discovers that Wellman's wife is dead and had been hopeless insane. At the wedding reception, Danilo learns of her connections with Wellman and Flint, and excited by jealousy he attempts to shoot Claire and then shoots himself. Dying, Danilo perceives Claire's innocence and accepts her love for Wellman. *Physicians. Filial relations. Reputation. Marriage. Suicide. Weddings.*

THE INNER MAN **F2.2709**

Syracuse Motion Picture Co. *Dist* Playgoers Pictures. 3 Dec **1922** [c11 Nov 1922; LU18393]. Si; b&w. 35mm. 5 reels, 4,914 ft.

Dir Hamilton Smith. *Story* Charles Mackay. *Photog* Arthur A. Cadwell.

Cast: Wyndham Standing *(Thurlow Michael Barclay, Jr.)*, J. Barney Sherry *(Thurlow Michael Barclay, Sr.)*, Louis Pierce *(Old Man Wolf)*, Leslie Hunt *(Bob)*, Dorothy Mackaill *(Sally)*, Gustav von Seyffertitz *(Jud Benson)*, Arthur Dewey *(Randall)*, Martin Kinney *(Ned Sawyer)*, Kathryn Kingsley *(Margaret Barclay)*, Nellie Parker Spaulding *(Mrs. Wolf)*, Arthur Caldwell, Jr. *(Ben Wolf)*.

Comedy-melodrama. Thurlow Michael Barclay, Jr., a mild-mannered, absentminded professor of mathematics, agrees to inspect his father's failing mine in Kentucky. He develops courage and discovers strength in his fist while foiling a plot by foreman Randall and Jud Bensen, thereby winning Sally's heart and earning the elder Barclay's respect. *Professors. Filial relations. Courage. Mining. Kentucky.*

INNOCENCE **F2.2710**

Columbia Pictures. *Dist* C. B. C. Film Sales. 1 Dec **1923** [c18 Jan 1924; LP19847]. Si; b&w. 35mm. 6 reels, 5,923 ft.

Prod Harry Cohn. *Dir* Edward J. Le Saint. *Scen* Jack Strumwasser.

Cast: Anna Q. Nilsson *(Fay Leslie)*, Freeman Wood *(Don Hampton)*, Earle Foxe *(Paul Atkins)*, Wilfred Lucas *(Collingwood)*, William Scott *(publicity agent)*, Marion Harlan *(chorus girl)*.

Society melodrama. Source: Lewis Allen Browne, "Circumstances Alter Divorce Cases" (unidentified magazine story). Broadway star Fay Leslie rejects the marriage proposal of Paul Atkins, a dancing partner from her vaudeville days, and marries wealthy Don Hampton, whose socially prominent parents object to having a "theater person" in the family. After the honeymoon, Hampton's jealousy of Atkins is kindled when Fay dances with Atkins at a nightclub party given for the newlyweds. Accused during the party of stealing a diamond necklace found in his pocket, Atkins is arrested, found guilty, and sent to prison. Because she believes he is innocent, Fay gives Atkins aid, thus arousing her husband's suspicions. Atkins escapes from prison and seeks refuge in Fay's bedroom, where her husband finds them (innocent enough). Hampton decides on divorce, but he still loves Fay, who, when given an opportunity to prove her innocence, clears both herself and Atkins. *Actors. Dancers. Vaudeville. Divorce. Prison escapes. Injustice.*

INNOCENT *see* **THE NIGHT MESSAGE**

THE INNOCENT CHEAT **F2.2711**

Ben Wilson Productions. *Dist* Arrow Film Corp. 26 Dec **1921** [c6 Jan 1922; LP17441]. Si; b&w. 35mm. 6 reels.

Prod-Dir Ben Wilson. *Adapt* J. Grubb Alexander. *Story* Peter B. Kyne. *Photog* Harry Gersted.

Cast: Roy Stewart *(John Murdock)*, Sidney De Gray *(Bruce Stanhope)*, George Hernandez *(Tim Reilly)*, Rhea Mitchell *(Peggy Adair)*, Kathleen Kirkham *(Mary Stanhope)*.

Melodrama. John Murdock, haunted by the memory of what he believes to have been an unrequited love, neglects his work, and through his miscalculation a disastrous train wreck occurs. He is discharged and wanders about in search of the woman responsible for his downfall. Meanwhile, in New York, Mary Stanhope, being sued for divorce by her husband, remains silent until the judge rules in favor of the husband, to whom is awarded custody of a child; she then unfolds a story of disloyalty, cruelty, and abuse, and the judge is so affected that he reverses the decision and awards her custody of the child. Later, in the Adirondacks, Mary meets John Murdock, now a tramp, and he recognizes her as the woman he loved. Attempting to kill the child, he learns from Mary that it is his own, and affected by the child's charm he decides to reform and is reconciled with Mary. *Tramps. Revenge. Divorce. Train wrecks. Adirondack Mountains. New York City.*

INNOCENT LOVE **F2.2712**

Republic Pictures. 10 Oct **1928** [New York State license]. Si; b&w. 35mm. 6 reels, 5,800 ft.

Cast: Gaston Glass, Claire Whitney.

Melodrama(?). No information about the nature of this film has been found.

INNOCENTS OF PARIS **F2.2713**

Paramount Famous Lasky Corp. 26 Apr **1929** [New York premiere; released 25 May; c24 May 1929; LP407]. Sd (Movietone); b&w. 35mm. 7 reels, 6,148 ft. [Also si; 7,816 ft.]

Dir Richard Wallace. *Screenplay* Ethel Doherty. *Adapt-Dial* Ernest Vajda. *Titl* George Marion, Jr. *Photog* Charles Lang. *Songs: "Louise," "It's a Habit of Mine," "On Top of the World Alone," "Wait Till You See My Chérie"* Leo Robin, Richard A. Whiting.

Cast: Maurice Chevalier *(Maurice Marny)*, Sylvia Beecher *(Louise Leval)*, Russell Simpson *(Émile Leval)*, George Fawcett *(Monsieur Marny)*, Mrs. George Fawcett *(Madame Marny)*, John Miljan *(Monsieur Renard)*, Margaret Livingston *(Madame Renard)*, David Durand *(Jo-Jo)*, Jack Luden *(Jules)*, Johnnie Morris *(musician)*.

Musical comedy. Source: Clarence Edward Andrews, *Innocents of Paris* (New York, 1928). Maurice Marny, a Paris junk dealer, jumps into the Seine to save little Jo-Jo, whose mother committed suicide, and takes the child to his grandfather, Émile Leval. Maurice falls in love with the boy's aunt, Louise, but Émile bitterly opposes the match. In the Flea Market, where he sings, Maurice attracts the attention of Monsieur Renard, a theater manager, and his wife, who offer him a part in their revue. Brokenhearted, Louise tries to persuade him to give up the stage, but to no avail. Émile, learning of their love, sets out for the theater with a pistol, but Louise has him arrested for attempted murder to protect Maurice and in desperation confesses her plot. Maurice returns to the theater and performs as a junkman rather than as the prince for which he is billed, and, triumphant, he renounces his career for the love of Louise. *Junk dealers. Aunts. Grandfathers. Singers. Theatrical managers. Musical revues. Paris.*

THE INSIDE OF THE CUP **F2.2714**

Cosmopolitan Productions. *Dist* Paramount Pictures. 16 Jan **1921** [c15 Jan 1921; LP16032]. Si; b&w. 35mm. 7 reels.

Dir Albert Capellani. *Scen* Albert Capellani, George Dubois Proctor. *Photog* Al Siegler.

Cast: William P. Carleton *(John Hodder)*, David Torrence *(Eldon Parr)*, Edith Hallor *(Alison Parr)*, John Bohn *(Preston Parr)*, Marguerite Clayton *(Kate Marcy)*, Richard Carlyle *(Richard Garvin)*, Margaret Seddon *(Mrs. Garvin)*, Albert Roccardi *(Wallis Plimpton)*, Frank A. Lyon *(Ferguson)*, Henry Morey *("Beatty")*, Irene Delroy *(Kate Marcy's friend)*, George Storey *(Garvin's child)*.

Drama. Source: Winston Churchill, *The Inside of the Cup* (New York, 1912). John Hodder becomes rector of St. John's, a fashionable church, situated near a slum neighborhood, in the town of Bremerton. Eldon Parr, a wealthy and prominent member of the parish, drives his daughter, Alison, and son, Preston, from home by his dishonest scheming. The girl becomes a settlement worker, and the son, forbidden to marry salesgirl Kate Marcy, is demoralized. Rector Hodder from the pulpit exposes the infamy of his congregation, pointing out the individuals and specifying their crimes, and refuses the elder Parr's demand that he resign, thus winning the heart of Parr's daughter. Garvin, a man ruined by Parr financially, shoots Parr, then kills himself. Kate and Preston are reclaimed, and the parish becomes popular with the poor as well as with the rich. *Clergymen. Churchmen. Settlement workers. Christianity. Social classes. Suicide. Slums. Social consciousness.*

INSIDE THE LINES **F2.2715**

RKO Productions. 5 Jul **1930** [New York opening; released 20 Jul; c20 Jul 1930; LP1448]. Sd (Photophone); b&w. 35mm. 8 reels, 6,652 ft.

Prod William Le Baron. *Dir* Roy J. Pomeroy. *Screenplay* Ewart Adamson. *Dial* John Farrow. *Photog* Nick Musuraca. *Art Dir* Max Ree. *Rec Engr* George Ellis.

Cast: Betty Compson *(Jane Gershon)*, Ralph Forbes *(Eric Woodhouse)*, Montagu Love *(Governor of Gibraltar)*, Mischa Auer *(Amahdi)*, Ivan Simpson *(Capper)*, Betty Carter *(Lady Crandall)*, Evan Thomas *(Major Bishop)*, Reginald Sharland *(Archie)*, William von Brincken *(Chief, Secret Service)*.

Spy melodrama. Source: Earl Derr Biggers, *Behind the Lines* (New York opening: Jan 1915). Jane Gershon and her fiancé, Eric Woodhouse, separate in Germany upon the outbreak of war. Later, they meet in the British fortress at Gibraltar as German spies, Jane posing as the daughter of a friend of the governor's family and Woodhouse as a British officer. Eric surprises Jane trying to obtain the key to the mine-control field in the harbor; she tries to dissuade him from destroying the British fleet; and noticing a gun covering her, he surrenders and feigns suicide. A trusted Hindu servant, Amahdi, denounces her for being a traitor to the Fatherland, threatens to kill her, and is shot by Eric before he can destroy the fleet. Jane discovers that her lover is a British agent, like herself, and they are united under one flag. *Spies. Germans. British. Hindus. Courtship. Mines (war explosives). World War I. Gibraltar.*

INSINUATION **F2.2716**

Margery Wilson Productions. *Dist* Russell Clark Syndicate. 10 Oct **1922** [New York State license]. Si; b&w. 35mm. 7 reels, 6,584 ft.

Dir-Story-Scen Margery Wilson.

Cast: Margery Wilson *(Mary Wright)*, Percy Holton *(Jimmie)*, Bradley Barker *(Dr. Crabtree)*, Agnes Neilsen *(Prudence Crabtree)*, Virginia Rumrill *(Baby Crabtree)*, A. K. Hall *("Spike" Henderson)*.

Domestic drama. "Mary Wright, specialty artist with a troup of barnstormers is made critically ill by the news that her brother has robbed the boxoffice. Dr. Crabtree a narrow-minded village physician takes care of her and falls in love with her. His maiden aunt, Prudence, fears that a marriage between the two would prove unwise. They marry anyway but Mary is unhappy except in the love for her baby girl. Dr. Crabtree receives $1,000 to keep in custody for an old miser, but Mary takes this money from the safe to pay for keeping her brother out of jail. Her husband discovers her guilt and divorces her. Finally Mary goes insane. Soon the news of her brother's innocence comes to her and this is followed by a reconciliation with her husband who brings the sick child to her mother." (*Moving Picture World*, 2 Sep 1922, p62.) *Barnstormers. Physicians. Brother-sister relationship. Theft. Divorce. Insanity.*

INSPIRATION **F2.2717**

Excellent Pictures. 10 May **1928** [c20 Mar 1928; LP25086]. Si; b&w. 35mm. 7 reels, 6,600-6,759 ft.

Pres by Samuel Zierler. *Dir* Bernard McEveety. *Story-Scen* Arthur Hoerl. *Titl* Harry Chandlee. *Photog* Marcel Le Picard. *Film Ed* Harry Chandlee.

Cast: George Walsh *(Gerald Erskine)*, Gladys Frazin *(Carlita)*, Marguerite Clayton *(Mary Keith)*, Earle Larrimore *(Jimmie)*, Bradley Barker *(George Gordon)*, Ali Yousoff *(Pietro)*, John Costello *(Captain Broady)*, Buddy Harris *(Bobby)*, Bernice Vert *(Anna Martin)*.

Romantic melodrama. Gerald Erskine, wrongly accused of being the father of an illegitimate child, is scorned by his sweetheart, Mary Keith, and disowned by his wealthy father. He seeks refuge in China and is persuaded by Carlita, a dancer, and Jimmy, a sailor, to return home and establish the truth. Jimmy and Carlita, who loves Gerald, accompany him to the States. There Carlita discovers and reveals to Miss Keith that a rival suitor of Gerald's has seduced the unfortunate girl and blamed Gerald. Miss Keith learns from the dying girl that Gerald is not the father, but nevertheless she and Gerald adopt the child when they marry. *Sailors. Dancers. Illegitimacy. Adoption. China.*

INTERFERENCE **F2.2718**

Paramount Famous Lasky Corp. 5 Jan **1929** [c10 Jan 1929; LP19]. Sd (Movietone); b&w. 35mm. 10 reels, 7,487 ft. [Also si; 7 reels, 6,643 ft.]

Dir Si Vers Lothar Mendes. *Dir Dial Scenes* Roy J. Pomeroy. *Cont* Louise Long. *Dial* Ernest Pascal. *Titl* Julian Johnson. *Adapt* Hope Loring. *Photog* Henry Gerrard. *Film Ed* George Nichols, Jr. *Ch Rec Engr* Franklin Hansen.

Cast: William Powell *(Philip Voaze)*, Evelyn Brent *(Deborah Kane)*, Clive Brook *(Sir John Marlay)*, Doris Kenyon *(Faith Marlay)*, Tom Ricketts *(Charles Smith)*, Brandon Hurst *(Inspector Haynes)*, Louis Payne *(Childers)*, Wilfred Noy *(Dr. Gray)*, Donald Stuart *(Freddie)*, Raymond Lawrence *(reporter)*.

Society melodrama. Source: Roland Pertwee and Harold Dearden, *Interference, a Play in Three Acts* (New York, 1929). Reported killed in action, Philip Voaze lives under an assumed name in London. Deborah Kane, a former love, discovers him and tries to blackmail his wife, Faith, who has since remarried. Learning of this attempt and that he has a fatal heart disease, he kills Deborah and turns himself in to the police. *Veterans. Blackmail. Bigamy. Heart disease. Murder. Personal identity.*

THE INTERFERIN' GENT **F2.2719**

Action Pictures. *Dist* Pathé Exchange. 21 Aug **1927** [c9 Jun 1927; LU24059]. Si; b&w. 35mm. 5 reels, 4,864 ft.

Pres by Lester F. Scott, Jr. *Dir* Richard Thorpe. *Scen* Betty Burbridge. *Story* Range Rider. *Photog* Ray Ries.

Cast: Buffalo Bill Jr. *(Bill Stannard)*, Olive Hasbrouck *(Ann Douglas)*, Al Taylor *(Ben Douglas)*, Harry Todd *(Buddy)*, Jack McDonald *(Joe Luke)*.

Western melodrama. Joe Luke, who is scheming to get the ranch of Ann Douglas for an irrigation project, hires an assassin to kill a man he believes to be Ben, her long-lost brother. The killing is witnessed by Bill Stannard, who returns some money intended for Ann, who then accepts him as her brother. Bill decides to keep up the deception and help her, while Ben Douglas, a sickly man who is actually the real brother, remains silent until forced to sign an insurance paper; but Ann remains ignorant of the fact. Ann's cattle are poisoned by Luke, but Bill forces him to pay their market price. Luke wounds Bill and tries to have him arrested as an imposter, but Ben exonerates Bill, who thereafter finds happiness with Ann. *Brother-sister relationship. Ranches. Irrigation. Impersonation. Murder.*

INTERNATIONAL EUCHARISTIC CONGRESS **F2.2720**

Fox Film Corp. *For* Catholic Church. 8 Nov **1926** [New York premiere]. Si; b&w. 35mm. [Feature length assumed.]

Documentary. Cardinal Bonzano is designated as the papal representative to the International Eucharistic Congress in Chicago in 1926 and then journeys to the United States. This film records the highlights of that designation, of Bonzano's subsequent trip to Chicago, and of the official and unofficial events of the congress itself. *Chicago. Cardinal Bonzano. Catholic Church.*

INTO HER KINGDOM **F2.2721**

Corinne Griffith Productions. *Dist* First National Pictures. 8 Aug **1926** [New York premiere; released 15 Aug; c30 Jul 1926; LP22990]. Si; b&w. 35mm. 7 reels, 6,447 ft.

Pres by Asher-Small-Rogers. *Dir* Svend Gade. *Titl* William Conselman. *Adapt* Carey Wilson. *Photog* Harold Wenstrom.

Cast: Corinne Griffith *(Grand Duchess Tatiana, at 12 and at 20)*, Einar Hanson *(Stepan, son of a peasant, at 14 and at 22)*, Claude Gillingwater *(Ivan, their tutor)*, Charles Crockett *(Senov, a carnival fakir)*, Evelyn Selbie *(Stepan's mother)*, Larry Fisher *(a farmhand)*, H. C. Simmons *(Czar Nicholas)*, Elinor Vanderveer *(Czarina)*, Byron Sage *(Czarevitch)*, Tom Murray *(Bolshevik guard)*, Marcelle Corday *(Tatiana's maid)*, Maj. Gen. Michael N. Pleschkoff *(court chamberlain)*, Max Davidson *(shoestring salesman)*, Allan Sears *(American customer)*, Mary Louise Miller *(daughter of Stepan and Tatiana)*, General Lodijensky, Maj. Gen. Ikanikoff, Maj. Gen. Bogomoletz, Lieut. George Blagoi, Lieut. Gene Walski, Feador Chalyapin, Jr., George Davis *(Russian officers and court leaders)*.

Romantic drama. Source: Ruth Comfort Mitchell, "Into Her Kingdom," in *Red Book Magazine* (44:71–75, Mar 1925). Stepan, a Russian peasant, is sent to Siberia for allegedly insulting the Grand Duchess Tatiana, and 7 years later, upon his release, he joins the Bolsheviks who are plotting to execute the imperial family. Ivan, his former tutor as well as that of the royal family, persuades him to flee to America with Tatiana, now a beautiful young lady, and though reluctant he is at last won over by her beauty. Although she does not love Stepan, because of his peasant birth, Tatiana follows; and they settle in New Jersey as husband and wife. Clerking in a store, she tells stories to neighborhood children of the experiences of a princess, matching her story with facts of her early life; Stepan, realizing his inequality, pledges to return her to Russia. There he finds diplomatic agents eager for information of the supposedly massacred royal family, but Tatiana, having become a mother, enters Russia with her child, disclaims her royal birth, and is happily reunited with Stepan. *Bolshevists. Political refugees. Russians. Immigrants. Royalty. Russia—History—1917–21 Revolution. New Jersey. Nicholas II (Russia). Alexandra Feodorovna. Romanov dynasty.*

INTO NO MAN'S LAND **F2.2722**

Excellent Pictures. 15 Jun **1928** [c29 Jul 1928; LP25426]. Si; b&w. 35mm. 7 reels, 6,700 ft.

Pres by Samuel Zierler. *Prod* Burton King. *Dir* Cliff Wheeler. *Dir of War Scenes* Arthur Guy Empey. *Cont* Elsie Werner. *Photog* Teddy Tetzlaff.

Cast: Tom Santschi *(Thomas Blaisdell/Western Evans)*, Josephine Norman *(Florence Blaisdell)*, Jack Daugherty *(Clayton Taggart)*, Betty Blythe *(The Countess)*, Crawford Kent *(The Duke)*, Mary McAllister *(Katherine Taggart)*, Syd Crossley *(Happy)*.

Melodrama. Source: Elsie Werner and Bennett Southard, "You're in the Army Now" (publication undetermined). Thomas Blaisdell, alias Western Evans, conceals his life as leader of a group of refined crooks from his daughter, Florence. Clayton Taggart, a young lawyer, falls in love with Florence while investigating a jewel robbery that he suspects Evans and his gang committed. Eventually greed overcomes the thieves, and Blaisdell shoots and kills "The Duke," one of his associates. Finding it necessary to flee the country, Blaisdell enlists to fight in France. Months later he meets Taggart in the trenches, and he intends to kill him until Taggart, badly wounded, breathes Florence's name. After the war Taggart and Florence marry, while Blaisdell, thought dead, becomes a drifter. One night he appears at his daughter's house, stating that he has news concerning her father. Florence does not recognize her father, who dies from the emotional strain, although a smile of recognition passes between Taggart and Blaisdell. *Thieves. Lawyers. Gangs. Fatherhood. Dual lives. Murder. World War I. France.*

INTO THE NIGHT **F2.2723**

Dist Raleigh Pictures. 14 Aug **1928** [New York State license]. Si; b&w. 35mm. 6 reels, 5,589 or 5,712 ft.

Dir Duke Worne. *Scen* James Bronis. *Titl* Joe Traub. *Story* George W. Pyper. *Photog* Jack Jellet.

Cast: Agnes Ayres *(Billie Mardon)*, Forrest Stanley *(Gavin Murdock)*, Robert Russell *(Walter Van Buren)*, Tom Lingham *(Howard K. Howard)*, Rhody Hathaway *(Jim Marden)*, Allan Sears *(John Harding)*, Corliss Palmer *(Mrs. Harding)*, Arthur Thalasso *(Pat Shannon)*.

Crime drama. "Based on girl's efforts to keep her dad out of clutches of the police and prove he is innocent of a crime for which he has been convicted. Steals confession from district attorney's home. Later a blackmailing detective compels her to help frame the husband of a woman who wants a divorce. She falls in love with the district attorney. The crooks who framed her papa appear and after a lot of excitement ... they clash with the district attorney, consequently get nabbed and confess that the little girl's daddy was not guilty." (*Film Daily*, 26 Aug 1928, p6.) *District attorneys. Detectives. Filial relations. Blackmail. Divorce. Frameup.*

INTRODUCE ME **F2.2724**

Douglas MacLean Productions. *Dist* Associated Exhibitors. 15 Mar **1925** [c5 Mar 1925; LU21202]. Si; b&w. 35mm. 7 reels, 6,710 ft.

Supv Al Santell. *Dir* George J. Crone. *Story* Wade Boteler, Raymond Cannon. *Photog* Jack MacKenzie, Paul Perry.

Cast: Douglas MacLean *(Jimmy Clark)*, Robert Ober *(Algy Baker)*, E. J. Ratcliffe *(John Perry)*, Anne Cornwall *(Betty Perry)*, Lee Shumway *(J.*

K. Roberts), Wade Boteler *(Bruno)*.

Farce. Jimmy Clark and Algy Baker, two Americans in Paris, see John Perry and his daughter, Betty, at the train station. Jimmy, falling in love with Betty at first sight, makes the Perrys' acquaintance, inadvertantly giving the elder Perry a loaded cigar and winning Betty's heart. A porter mistakes Jimmy for a famous mountain climber named Roberts and puts him on a trail with Roberts' gear. Arriving in the Alps, Jimmy is received as the noted climber, and, when the real Roberts appears, he laughingly backs up Jimmy's impersonation. Deathly afraid of heights, Jimmy is forced to climb a mountain, but, with some help from an unfriendly bear, he gets to the top. He lets himself partway down by a rope, which the bear then gnaws in two; Jimmy falls, gathering snow until he is a human snowball, bounding from crag to crag. He is then reunited with Betty, who tries to stop Jimmy's descent and becomes likewise entangled in the snowball. *Mistaken identity. Impersonation. Mountain climbing. Acrophobia. Paris. Switzerland. Alps. Bears.*

THE INVADERS **F2.2725**

Big Productions Film Corp. *Dist* Syndicate Pictures. Oct **1929.** Sd eff & mus score; b&w. 35mm. 7 reels, 6,200 ft. [Also si; 5 reels.]

Dir J. P. McGowan. *Scen* Walter Sterret. *Titl* William Stratton. *Story* Sally Winters. *Photog* Hap Depew.

Cast: Bob Steele, Edna Aslin, Thomas Lingham, J. P. McGowan, Celeste Rush, Tom Smith, Bud Osborne, Chief Yowlache.

Western melodrama. An Indian attack upon a wagon train leaves two children—sister and brother—as sole survivors, but they are soon separated when Major McLellan adopts the boy and the girl is taken to live with Indians as Black Fawn. Years later, after the boy has joined the cavalry and fallen in love with the major's daughter, he shows his bravery during an Indian attack on the fort (perpetrated by plotting among treacherous white men and Indian braves) and is reunited with his sister with the help of a squaw. *Indians of North America. Brother-sister relationship. Wagon trains. United States Army—Cavalry.*

THE INVISIBLE FEAR **F2.2726**

Anita Stewart Productions. *Dist* Associated First National Pictures. 10 Oct **1921** [c19 Oct 1921; LP17106]. Si; b&w. 35mm. 6 reels, 5,800 ft. [Later cut to 5 reels, 4,900 ft.]

Pres by Louis B. Mayer. *Dir* Edwin Carewe. *Scen* Madge Power. *Story* Hampton Del Ruth. *Photog* Robert B. Kurrle. *Art Dir* John D. Schulze. *Asst Dir* Clarence Bricker, Wallace Fox.

Cast: Anita Stewart *(Sylvia Langdon)*, Walter McGrail *(Arthur Comstock)*, Allan Forrest *(Bentley Arnold)*, Hamilton Morse *(Marshall Arnold)*, Estelle Evans *(Mrs. Marshall Arnold)*, George Kuwa *(Nagi)*, Edward Hunt *(butler)*, Ogden Crane *(John Randall)*.

Melodrama. Sylvia Langdon, living with the Arnolds, is engaged to their son, Bentley. Arthur Comstock, nephew of Arnold's partner, John Randall, is disinherited and steals his father's will. Sylvia and Arthur, while riding, are forced to seek refuge from a storm; in a struggle to repulse his advances, she knocks him unconscious with a candlestick; and, escaping, she sees the lodge in flames. Believing that she has killed Arthur, she keeps the incident secret. After the marriage of Sylvia and Bentley and the death of John Randall, she is overcome with fright at seeing Arthur at a party. Arthur is arrested for the murder of his uncle, and Sylvia is freed from her fear. *Murder. Fear. Documentation.*

THE INVISIBLE POWER **F2.2727**

Goldwyn Pictures. Oct **1921** [c15 Aug 1921; LP16872]. Si; b&w. 35mm. 7 reels, 6,613 ft.

Prod-Dir Frank Lloyd. *Story-Scen* Charles Kenyon. *Photog* Norbert Brodin. *Art Dir* Cedric Gibbons. *Asst Dir* Harry Weil.

Cast: House Peters *(Sid Chambers)*, Irene Rich *(Laura Chadwick)*, De Witt Jennings *(Mark Shadwell)*, Sydney Ainsworth *(Bob Drake)*, Jessie De Jainette *(Mrs. Shadwell)*, William Friend *(Mr. Miller)*, Gertrude Claire *(Mrs. Miller)*, Lydia Yeamans Titus *(The Giggling Neighbor)*.

Crook melodrama. Ex-convict Sid Chambers, while lodging with the Millers, meets schoolteacher Laura Chadwick, and in spite of his record she believes in him. They are married, move to the city, and are happy. Shadwell, the detective who sent Chambers to prison, tries to obtain information from him regarding a former friend and gang member, Bob Drake, who has committed a robbery; and refusing to cooperate, Chambers is sent to prison again on another charge. Meanwhile, Laura's child is born, and fearing that it will develop criminal instincts she gives it up for adoption. When Chambers is released, he vows to kill Shadwell, and Laura, in her effort to warn him, finds her child in Shadwell's home. Touched by her grief, Shadwell arranges to give Chambers his freedom, and the couple is reunited. *Criminals—Rehabilitation. Schoolteachers. Detectives. Adoption.*

THE INVISIBLE WEB **F2.2728**

Fidelity Pictures. 5 Aug **1921** [trade review]. Si; b&w. 35mm. [Feature length assumed.]

Dir-Writ Beverly C. Rule.

Mystery melodrama. A standard murder mystery in which the finger of suspicion points to four different people, then settles on a fifth person who does not enter the plot until the final reel. Characters include a wealthy banker; his young, vampirish wife; a police commissioner who pounds his desk while grilling his witnesses; a stock broker; a female detective; and a blackmailer. *Bankers. Stockbrokers. Detectives. Vamps. Police. Murder. Blackmail.*

IOWA UNDER FIRE **F2.2729**

Dist Pictorial Sales Bureau. c9 May **1924** [MU2542]. Si; b&w. 35mm. 8 reels.

Documentary. "The story of the Iowa troops in the World War ... opens with the training of these troops at Camps here in the United States, follows them aboard the transports, conducts them through the submarine area to the several landing ports in France and England. They are shown at work in the Service of Supplies and in the 10th Training Area. This is followed by battle action in the following sectors: Alsace, Chatteau Thierry, Junigny and the Meuse Argonne. Along with the battle scenes their activities in the rest areas and drilling sectors are also shown. Following the close of the Meuse Argonne battle and the Armistice, movements of the Iowa troops into Germany are depicted with the final review held in Germany and the sailing from France for the U. S. A." (Copyright records.) *United States Army. United States Army—Training. Submarines. World War I. England. France. Germany. Iowa.*

IRELAND IN REVOLT **F2.2730**

Chicago Tribune. *Dist* American Film Co. ca5 Feb **1921** [trade showing]. Si; b&w. 35mm. 5 or 6 reels.

Titl Mrs. Edwin F. Weigle. *Photog* Capt. Edwin F. Weigle.

Documentary. Captain Weigle, under assignment for the *Chicago Tribune*, presents what he regards as authentic scenes of the condition of Ireland in her period of revolt. He shows the ruins of factories, homes, and institutions; mobs; and barbed wire and machine gun squads in their armored cars. A prolog depicts the placidity and scenic beauty of the parts of Ireland not yet affected. *Ireland—History—Rebellion 1916–21.*

IRENE **F2.2731**

First National Pictures. 21 Feb **1926** [c10 Feb 1926; LP22387]. Si; b&w with col sequences (Technicolor). 35mm. 9 reels, 8,400 ft.

Pres by John McCormick. *Dir* Alfred E. Green. *Ed Dir-Cont* June Mathis. *Scen* Rex Taylor. *Titl* George Marion, Jr. *Photog* T. D. McCord. *Lighting Eff* Lawrence Kennedy. *Art Dir* John D. Schulze. *Film Ed* Edwin Robbins. *Mus* Harry Tierney, Joseph McCarthy. *Comedy Construc* Mervyn LeRoy.

Cast: Colleen Moore *(Irene O'Dare)*, Lloyd Hughes *(Donald Marshall)*, George K. Arthur *(Madame Lucy)*, Charles Murray *(Pa O'Dare)*, Kate Price *(Ma O'Dare)*, Ida Darling *(Mrs. Warren Marshall)*, Eva Novak *(Eleanor Hadley)*, Edward Earle *(Larry Hadley)*, Laurence Wheat *(Bob Harrison)*, Maryon Aye *(Helen Cheston)*, Bess Flowers *(Jane Gilmour)*, Lydia Yeamans Titus *(Mrs. Cheston)*, Cora Macey *(Mrs. Gilmour)*.

Romantic comedy. Source: James Montgomery, *Irene, a Musical Comedy* (New York opening: 1 Nov 1919). Irene O'Dare, a wistful Irish lass looking for a job in New York City, meets Donald Marshall, a wealthy aristocrat, who arranges for her to become a model in a new modiste's shop. But when the male proprietor, Madame Lucy, gives a fashion show, he leaves Irene behind to watch the shop. Donald finds her there and insists that she attire herself in a new French creation and accompany him to the fashion show. Irene is an immediate sensation with everyone there except Donald's mother, who hires a genealogist to report on the girl's ancestry. After being shown the report, Irene retreats to a fire escape, where Donald finds her lamenting her plight. Overhearing Irene profess love for him, Donald climbs through the window and embraces her. *Irish. Fashion models. Modistes. Aristocrats. Genealogists. Filial relations. Fashion shows. New York City.*

IRISH HEARTS F2.2732

Warner Brothers Pictures. 21 May **1927** [c14 May 1927; LP23958]. Si; b&w. 35mm. 6 reels, 5,597 ft.

Dir Byron Haskin. *Screenplay* Bess Meredyth, Graham Baker. *Story* Melville Crossman. *Camera* Virgil Miller. *Asst Dir* Gordon Hollingshead.

Cast: May McAvoy *(Sheila)*, Jason Robards *(Rory)*, Warner Richmond *(Emmett)*, Kathleen Key *(Clarice)*, Walter Perry *(Sheila's father)*, Walter Rodgers *(restaurant proprietor)*, Les Bates *(taxi driver)*.

Comedy-drama. Sheila, a happy and carefree colleen, loves Emmett, a shiftless Irish lad who goes to America to seek his fortune. While Sheila and her father are en route to join him, her father gives the steward her shamrock in payment for liquor, and she becomes wildly apprehensive. Learning Emmett has lost his job, Sheila is forced to work in a beanery, where she meets Rory, a poor American boy, who is attracted to her. Sheila is bitterly disappointed, however, when Emmett takes up with Clarice, a flashy flapper; she confides her troubles to Rory, who meanwhile is employed as a section hand in a shipyard. When she is jilted by Emmett, missiles of food and crockery send the wedding party flying into the street. Rory finds the lost shamrock and looks forward to happiness with the triumphant Sheila. *Immigrants. Irish. Flappers. Courtship. Weddings. Talismans. Shipyards.*

IRISH LUCK F2.2733

Famous Players–Lasky. *Dist* Paramount Pictures. 22 Nov **1925** [New York premiere; released 7 Dec; c8 Dec 1925; LP22093]. Si; b&w. 35mm. 7 reels, 7,008 ft.

Pres by Adolph Zukor, Jesse L. Lasky. *Dir* Victor Heerman. *Screenplay* Tom J. Geraghty. *Photog* Alvin Wyckoff. *Art Dir* Walter E. Keller.

Cast: Thomas Meighan *(Tom Donahue/Lord Fitzhugh)*, Lois Wilson *(Lady Gwendolyn)*, Cecil Humphreys *(Douglas)*, Claude King *(solicitor)*, Ernest Lawford *(Earl)*, Charles Hammond *(doctor)*, Louise Grafton *(Aunt)*, S. B. Carrickson *(Uncle)*, Charles McDonald *(Denis MacSwiney)*, Mary Foy *(Kate MacSwiney)*.

Melodrama. Source: Norman Venner, *The Imperfect Imposter* (New York, 1925). Tom Donahue, a New York traffic cop, wins a trip to Europe in a newspaper contest, and he decides to visit relatives in Ireland. Arriving in Dublin, he learns that he is an exact double for Lord Fitzhugh, a young Irish aristocrat with whom he becomes friends. The Earl of Killarney, Fitzhugh's uncle, who is on his deathbed, wishes to see his favorite nephew and wipe out past animosities. Fitzhugh, in the meantime, has disappeared, and his sister, Lady Gwendolyn, persuades Tom to take his place. Tom successfully impersonates Fitzhugh, thus assuring the latter's inheritance, and uncovers a conspiracy led by Douglas, another nephew, to kill Fitzhugh after the uncle's death and thus gain the estate. Fitzhugh is freed, and Tom wins the hand of Gwendolyn. *Police. Doubles. Aristocrats. Swindlers. Contests. Impersonation. Inheritance. Ireland. Dublin.*

Note: Most of the principal photography was done on location in Ireland.

IRON FIST F2.2734

Dist Rayart Pictures. Feb **1926.** Si; b&w. 35mm. 5 reels, 4,366 ft.

Dir J. P. McGowan.

Cast: Bob Reeves.

Western melodrama(?). No information about the nature of this film has been found.

THE IRON HORSE F2.2735

Fox Film Corp. 28 Aug **1924** [New York premiere; released 4 Oct 1925; c21 Nov 1924; LP20787]. Si; b&w. 35mm. 12 reels, 11,335 ft. [Cut for release to 11 reels, 10,424 ft.]

Pres by William Fox. *Dir* John Ford. *Scen* Charles Kenyon. *Titl* Charles Darnton. *Story* Charles Kenyon, John Russell. *Photog* George Schneiderman. *Adtl Photog* Burnett Guffey. *Mus Score* Erno Rapee. *Asst Dir* Edward O'Fearna.

Cast: George O'Brien *(Davy Brandon)*, Madge Bellamy *(Miriam Marsh)*, Cyril Chadwick *(Jesson)*, Fred Kohler *(Deroux)*, Gladys Hulette *(Ruby)*, James Marcus *(Judge Haller)*, J. Farrell MacDonald *(Corporal Casey)*, James Welch *(Private Schultz)*, Walter Rogers *(General Dodge)*, George Waggner *(Colonel Cody [Buffalo Bill])*, Jack Padjan *(Wild Bill Hickok)*, Charles O'Malley *(Major North)*, Charles Newton *(Collis P. Huntington)*, Charles Edward Bull *(Abraham Lincoln)*, Colin Chase *(Tony)*, Delbert Mann *(Charles Crocker)*, Chief Big Tree *(Cheyenne Chief)*, Chief White Spear *(Sioux Chief)*, Edward Piel *(Old Chinaman)*, James Gordon *(David Brandon, Sr.)*, Winston Miller *(Davy, as a child)*, Peggy Cartwright *(Miriam, as a child)*, Thomas Durant *(Jack Ganzhorn)*, Stanhope Wheatcroft *(John Hay)*, Frances Teague *(Polka Dot)*, Will Walling *(Thomas Marsh)*.

Western epic. During the Civil War, President Lincoln signs a bill (Pacific Railroad Act of 1 July 1862) that authorizes the construction of a transcontinental railroad. When the war ends, Davy Brandon joins the Union Pacific as a surveyor and meets Miriam, his childhood sweetheart, whose father is in charge of construction. Davy and Peter Jesson, a civil engineer, fight over Miriam; and subsequently, Miriam refuses Davy's offer of marriage. When a band of Indians, led by the renegade Deroux, attack a construction train, Davy recognizes Deroux as his father's murderer and kills him in a hand-to-hand fight. Davy then joins the Central Pacific, which is racing the Union Pacific to the center of the continent. The joining of the two railroads by the golden spike is accompanied by the union of Davy and Miriam. *Indians of North America. Surveyors. Engineers—Civil. Railroads. William Frederick Cody. Collis Potter Huntington. Abraham Lincoln. James Butler Hickok. John Milton Hay. Union Pacific Railroad. Central Pacific Railroad.*

Note: Cast also said to include "a regiment of U. S. troops and cavalry; 3,000 railway workmen; 1,000 Chinese laborers; 800 Pawnee, Sioux, and Cheyenne Indians; 2,800 horses; 1,300 buffalo; 10,000 Texas steers." Working titles: *The Trans-continental Railroad* and *The Iron Trail.* Fox records indicate that Charles Kenyon may have been completely responsible for both scenario and story.

THE IRON MAN F2.2736

Whitman Bennett Productions. *Dist* Chadwick Pictures. 28 Jun **1925** [trade review]. Si; b&w. 35mm. 5 reels.

Dir Whitman Bennett. *Scen* Lawrence Marsten. *Photog* Edward Paul.

Cast: Lionel Barrymore, Mildred Harris, Winifred Barry, Dorothy Kingdon, Alfred Mack, J. Moy Bennett, Isobel De Leon, Jean Del Val.

Society drama. "Callahan is a chocolate king and his daughter wants papa to buy her a prince so papa does and poor Claire Durban [played by Mildred Harris], whose mother was seeking a financial connection in her daughter's marriage to the prince, is jilted. Claire satisfies herself by marrying Philip Durban [played by Lionel Barrymore], steel magnate, and his millions. But it is one of those 'wife in name only' arrangements until Claire realizes Durban deserves her love. They patch it up while Miss Callahan discovers her prince isn't one at all and gets the worst of the bargain." (*Film Daily,* 28 Jun 1925, p9.) *Manufacturers. Social climbers. Royalty. Millionaires. Candy. Steel industry. Marriage of convenience.*

THE IRON MASK F2.2737

Elton Corp. *Dist* United Artists. 21 Feb **1929** [New York premiere; released 9 Mar; c2 Mar 1929; LP288]. Talking sequences, sd eff, & mus score (Movietone); b&w. 35mm. 11 reels, 8,855 ft. [Also si; 8,659 ft.]

Dir Allan Dwan. *Scen Ed* Lotta Woods. *Story* Elton Thomas. *Photog* Henry Sharp. *Adtl Photog* Warren Lynch. *Interior Decorator* Burgess Beall. *Prod Dsgn* Maurice Leloir. *Film Ed* William Nolan. *Song: "One for All, All for One"* Ray Klages, Louis Alter. *Mus Arr* Hugo Riesenfeld. *Asst Dir* Bruce Humberstone, Vinton Vernon, Sherry Shourds. *Prod Mgr* Robert Fairbanks. *Prod Asst* Charles Lewis. *Wardrobe* Maurice Leloir, Gilbert Clark. *Makeup* Fred C. Ryle. *Tech Eff* Walter Pallman. *Adv* Earle Browne, Arthur Woods, Jack Cunningham. *Ch Elec* J. W. Montgomery. *Prop Master* Paul Roberts. *Wardrobe Master* Paul Burns. *Asst Wardrobe Master* S. L. Chalif. *Tech Dir* Willard M. Reineck. *Artists* Ben Carré, H. W. Miles, David S. Hall, Edward M. Langley, William Buckland, Jack Holden.

Cast: Belle Bennett *(The Queen Mother)*, Marguerite De La Motte *(Constance)*, Dorothy Revier *(Milady de Winter)*, Vera Lewis *(Madame Peronne)*, Rolfe Sedan *(Louis XIII)*, William Bakewell *(Louis XIV/Louis XIV's twin)*, Gordon Thorpe *(The Young Prince/The Young Prince's twin)*, Nigel De Brulier *(Cardinal Richelieu)*, Ullrich Haupt *(Rochefort)*, Lon Poff *(Father Joseph)*, Charles Stevens *(Planchet, D'Artagnan's servant)*, Henry Otto *(The King's valet)*, Leon Bary *(Athos)*, Stanley J. Sandford *(Porthos)*, Gino Corrado *(Aramis)*, Douglas Fairbanks *(D'Artagnan)*.

Historical romance. Source: Alexandre Dumas, père, *Les Trois mousquetaires* (Paris, 1844). Alexandre Dumas, père, *Le Vicomte de Bragelonne, ou dix ans plus tard* (Paris, 1851). Anne of Austria, the wife of Louis XIII, gives birth to twins, and Cardinal Richelieu, learning of the double birth, smuggles the unwanted twin into Spain. Constance, a seamstress present at the birth, is kidnaped by Rochefort, and D'Artagnan, her lover, hastens to the rescue. Constance is killed, however, and D'Artagnan is ordered to guard the little prince. Rochefort kidnaps the second twin and rears him as the pretender to the throne. Years pass. Rochefort smuggles the pretender into the royal palace and imprisons

Louis XIV in a distant fortress. D'Artagnan rescues the king at the cost of not only his own life but the lives of his faithful comrades, Athos, Porthos, and Aramis. Louis XIV is reinstated and orders the pretender to spend the remainder of his life in an iron mask. *Twins. Seamstresses. Musketeers. Kidnaping. France—History—Bourbons. Spain. Louis XIII (France). Louis XIV (France). Cardinal Richelieu. Anne of Austria.*

IRON TO GOLD **F2.2738**

Fox Film Corp. 12 Mar **1922** [c12 Mar 1922; LP17683]. Si; b&w. 35mm. 5 reels, 4,513 ft.

Pres by William Fox. *Dir* Bernard J. Durning. *Scen* Jack Strumwasser. *Story* George Owen Baxter. *Photog* Don Short.

Cast: Dustin Farnum *(Tom Curtis)*, Marguerite Marsh *(Anne Kirby)*, William Conklin *(George Kirby)*, William Elmer *(Bat Piper)*, Lionel Belmore *(sheriff)*, Glen Cavender *(Sloan)*, Robert Perry *(Creel)*, Dan Mason *(Lem Baldwin, hotel keeper)*.

Western melodrama. After rescuing Anne Kirby from two highwaymen, Tom Curtis—himself an outlaw—learns that Anne's husband is the man who robbed him of his claim and decides to take vengeance on him through his wife. She convinces him that it is unjust for him to make her suffer for Kirby's evildoing, and when Curtis is wounded by one of the highwaymen, Anne returns with him to his home and cares for him. She diverts a posse in search of him and is reviled by her husband when she tells him of the event. Curtis surrenders but is free until his trial; Bat Piper is hired by Kirby to kill Curtis, and failing in his attempt, he is shot by Kirby, whom he tries to blackmail. Finding Anne in Curtis' room, Kirby begins a fight; but Piper, only wounded, arrives to clear Curtis of any crime and to kill Kirby. Anne leaves for the East, where Curtis soon follows. *Outlaws. Mine claims. Revenge.*

THE IRON TRAIL *see* **THE IRON HORSE**

THE IRON TRAIL **F2.2739**

Bennett Pictures. *Dist* United Artists. 30 Oct **1921** [c2 Nov 1921; LP17142]. Si; b&w. 35mm. 7 reels.

Dir R. William Neill. *Scen* Dorothy Farnum. *Photog* Ernest Haller.

Cast: Wyndham Standing *(Murray O'Neil)*, Thurston Hall *(Curtis Gordon)*, Reginald Denny *(Dan Appleton)*, Alma Tell *(Eliza Appleton)*, Harlan Knight *(Tom Slater)*, Betty Carpenter *(Natalie)*, Lee Beggs *(Dr. Cyrus Gray)*, Bert Starkey *(Denny)*, Danny Hayes *(Linn)*, Eulalie Jensen *(Mrs. Gordon)*.

Adventure melodrama. Source: Rex Beach, *The Iron Trail* (New York, 1913). Alaskan railroad magnate Curtis Gordon hires engineer Dan Appleton to design a railroad route up the Salmon River to the rich gold country. Gordon turns down the engineer's proposed route in favor of his own, and Appleton quits. Murray O'Neil, a rival builder, hires him and falls in love with his sister Eliza, while Appleton courts Natalie, Gordon's stepdaughter. Following Appleton's plan, O'Neil lays the trail with a bridge crossing the river in face of Gordon's opposition. When the bridge is near completion, the workmen leave in fear of ice floes. Working desperately, O'Neil and Appleton manage to complete the work just before the ice breaks on the bridge, which holds fast. The road is completed and the lovers are united. *Engineers—Civil. Railroads. Bridges. Alaska.*

THE IRRESISTIBLE LOVER (Universal-Jewel) **F2.2740**

Universal Pictures. 21 Oct **1927** [New York premiere; released 4 Dec; c15 Jul 1927; LP24201]. Si; b&w. 35mm. 7 reels, 6,958 ft.

Pres by Carl Laemmle. *Supv* Carl Laemmle, Jr. *Dir* William Beaudine. *Scen* Beatrice Van. *Titl* Albert De Mond. *Adapt* Edward Luddy, James J. Tynan. *Story? (see note)* Evelyn Campbell, Joseph Franklin Poland. *Photog? (see note)* George Robinson, John Stumar.

Cast: Norman Kerry *(J. Harrison Gray)*, Lois Moran *(Betty Kennedy)*, Gertrude Astor *(Dolly Carleton)*, Lee Moran *(lawyer)*, Myrtle Stedman *(Hortense Brown)*, Phillips Smalley *(Mr. Brown)*, Arthur Lake *(Jack Kennedy)*, Walter James *(Mr. Kennedy)*, George Pearce *(Smith)*.

Romantic comedy. J. Harrison Gray, a wealthy young Don Juan, finds himself entangled with five different women. After settling a suit through his attorney, Gray meets Dolly, a chorus girl with designs on him; she is knocked down by a passing car, but Gray, meanwhile, is attracted to Betty, a pretty passerby, and is himself struck by a vehicle. He awakes at the hospital beside his newly-found love, but a Mrs. Brown claims him and takes him to her home. In order to avoid the irate husband, Gray declares himself engaged to Dolly. Betty, his new love, invites him to her home for dinner, where her father reads of the engagement in the newspaper and declares his dislike for Gray (who does not reveal his identity). Complications ensue, and Betty's brother, along with the irate Mr. Brown, threaten Gray, finally forcing the couple to the altar. *Philanderers. Lawyers. Chorus girls. Brother-sister relationship. Mistaken identity. Automobile accidents.*

Note: Copyright records credit the story to Poland; other sources credit Campbell. Sources disagree in crediting photographer.

IS A MOTHER TO BLAME? **F2.2741**

M. R. M. Pictures. *Dist* Model Film Corp. 19 Oct **1922** [New York State license]. Si; b&w. 35mm. 5 reels, 4,900 ft.

Prod Al Gilbert. *Dir* Roy Sheldon. *Scen* Rob Wagner. *Story* Andre Van Remoortal. *Asst Dir* Walter Sheridan.

Drama(?). No information about the precise nature of this film has been found. *Motherhood.*

IS DIVORCE A FAILURE? **F2.2742**

Arthur Beck. *Dist* Associated Exhibitors. 16 Mar **1923** [c26 Feb 1923; LU18730]. Si; b&w. 35mm. 6 reels, 5,448 ft.

Pres by Arthur F. Beck. *Dir* Wallace Worsley. *Adapt-Scen* Leah Baird.

Cast: Leah Baird *(Carol Lockwood)*, Richard Tucker *(David Lockwood)*, Walter McGrail *(Kelcey Barton)*, Tom Santschi *(Smith)*, Alec B. Francis *(Philip Wilkinson)*, Pansy *(Pansy)*.

Drama. Source: Dorian Neve, *All Mine* (a play; publication undetermined). About to be divorced because of her infatuation with Kelcey Barton, Carol Lockwood is persuaded to take one last vacation cruise with her husband, David. They find that Kelcey is a fellow passenger. Their ship is wrecked; and Carol, David, Kelcey, and Smith, who is also in love with Carol, are cast up on a desert island. All vie for Carol's attention, but she shows no favoritism. After David swims through shark-infested waters to bring her protection, Carol realizes she still loves her husband. Kelcey and Smith unite against David, but their efforts are foiled by a volcanic eruption, a tornado, and the arrival of a rescue ship. *Divorce. Volcanoes. Tornadoes. Shipwrecks. Sharks.*

IS EVERYBODY HAPPY? **F2.2743**

Warner Brothers Pictures. 19 Oct **1929** [c6 Oct 1929; LP749]. Sd (Vitaphone); b&w. 35mm. 9 reels, 7,311 ft. [Also si.]

Dir Archie L. Mayo. *Story-Scen-Dial* Joseph Jackson, James A. Starr. *Titl* De Leon Anthony. *Photog* Ben Reynolds. *Film Ed* Desmond O'Brien. *Songs: "Wouldn't It Be Wonderful?" "I'm the Medicine Man for the Blues," "New Orleans," "Samoa"* Grant Clarke, Harry Akst. *Songs: "In the Land of Jazz," "Start the Band"* Ted Lewis. *Song: "St. Louis Blues"* W. C. Handy. *Song: "Tiger Rag"* The Original Dixieland Jazz Band. *Dance Dir* Larry Ceballos.

Cast: Ted Lewis *(Ted Todd)*, Alice Day *(Gail Wilson)*, Ann Pennington *(Lena Schmitt)*, Lawrence Grant *(Victor Molnár)*, Julia Swayne Gordon *(Mrs. Molnár)*, Otto Hoffman *(landlord)*, Purnell Pratt *(stage manager)*.

Domestic drama. Victor Molnár, an orchestra conductor in Budapest, retires and emigrates to the United States with his wife and young son, Ted, who takes with him a prized possession, a violin presented to him by Emperor Franz Joseph. In New York they rent an inexpensive apartment, and Ted looks up Lena, his former sweetheart, now a member of the Ziegfeld Follies; but ashamed of Ted's appearance, she greets him cooly. Ted is unable to find work with a symphony orchestra, and, faced with overdue rent, he borrows money on the precious violin, telling the family he has a job. Meanwhile, he practices on the saxophone in the park, where he meets Gail, who is employed by a theatrical manager; and when his parents discover him playing jazz in a Hungarian cafe, they are outraged and his father is heartbroken. Aided by Gail, Ted forms his own jazz band and becomes a star, and a reconciliation of the family takes place on Christmas Day. *Hungarians. Orchestra conductors. Saxophonists. Violinists. Family life. Jazz. Christmas. Budapest. New York City. Franz Josef. Ziegfeld Follies.*

IS LIFE WORTH LIVING? **F2.2744**

Selznick Pictures. *Dist* Select Pictures. Jun **1921** [c22 Jun 1921; LP16735]. Si; b&w. 35mm. 5 reels, 5,039 ft.

Pres by Lewis J. Selznick. *Dir* Alan Crosland. *Photog* Jules Cronjager.

Cast: Eugene O'Brien *(Melville Marley)*, Winifred Westover *(Lois Wilday)*, Arthur Housman *(Colton)*, George Lessey *(lawyer)*, Warren Cook *(Mr. Borden)*, Arthur Donaldson *(Isaac)*, Florida Kingsley *(Mrs. Grant)*.

Melodrama. Source: George Weston, "The Open Door," in *Saturday Evening Post* (193:5–7, 8 Jan 1921). Released on suspended sentence after being tried for a crime of which he is innocent, Melville Marley becomes a salesman for a typewriter-supply house. Unable to succeed in this venture, he buys a revolver in a pawnshop and goes to Central Park to kill himself. There he encounters Lois, a young girl who faints from despair and hunger on a park bench, and after taking her to his boardinghouse and securing her accommodation, he sets out with new determination and turns in a large order. Receiving a credit extension, he goes into business for himself; and with the aid of Lois, his new stenographer, a thriving business develops. Inevitably, love comes to them. *Salesmen. Hunger. Suicide. Injustice. Typewriters. New York City—Central Park.*

IS LOVE EVERYTHING? **F2.2745**

Garsson Enterprises. *Dist* Associated Exhibitors. 30 Nov **1924** [c9 Dec 1924; LU20872]. Si; b&w. 35mm. 6 reels, 5,221 ft.

Pres by Murray W. Garsson. *Dir* William Christy Cabanne. *Cont* Raymond S. Harris. *Titl* William B. Laub. *Story* William Christy Cabanne. *Photog* Walter Arthur, Philip Armand. *Film Ed* William B. Laub.

Cast: Alma Rubens *(Virginia Carter)*, Frank Mayo *(Robert Whitney)*, H. B. Warner *(Jordan Southwick)*, Walter McGrail *(Boyd Carter)*, Lilyan Tashman *(Edythe Stanley)*, Marie Schaefer *(Mrs. Carter)*, Irene Howley *(Mrs. Rowland)*.

Melodrama. At the prompting of her ambitious family, Virginia Carter marries wealthy Jordan Southwick, but she is haunted by regret and the memory of her true love, Robert Whitney. She remains loyal to Southwick, but he, nevertheless, prompted by her brother, Boyd, begins to suspect her of an affair with Robert. Troubled by doubt, Southwick decides to test Virginia's loyalties by arranging a yachting cruise, with Robert on board. The yacht is wrecked, and Virginia and Robert are rescued by a rumrunner, whose brutal crew he must fight to protect her from harm. When they finally return home safely, Virginia, believing Southwick to be lost at sea, consents to marry Robert; Southwick returns, however, and, finding his wife in the arms of his rival, signs on with the sea captain who rescued him, leaving the young lovers to find happiness with each other. *Brother-sister relationship. Rumrunners. Fidelity. Bigamy. Yachts. Shipwrecks.*

IS MATRIMONY A FAILURE? **F2.2746**

Famous Players–Lasky. *Dist* Paramount Pictures. ca2 Apr **1922** [Los Angeles premiere; released 30 Apr; c12 Apr 1922; LP17757]. Si; b&w. 35mm. 6 reels, 5,612 ft.

Pres by Jesse L. Lasky. *Dir* James Cruze. *Scen* Walter Woods. *Photog* Karl Brown.

Cast: T. Roy Barnes *(Arthur Haviland)*, Lila Lee *(Margaret Saxby)*, Lois Wilson *(Mabel Hoyt)*, Walter Hiers *(Jack Hoyt)*, ZaSu Pitts *(Mrs. Wilbur)*, Arthur Hoyt *(Mr. Wilbur)*, Lillian Leighton *(Martha Saxby)*, Tully Marshall *(Amos Saxby)*, Adolphe Menjou *(Dudley King)*, Sylvia Ashton *(Mrs. Pearson)*, Otis Harlan *(Mr. Pearson)*, Charles Ogle *(Pop Skinner)*, Ethel Wales *(Mrs. Skinner)*, Sidney Bracey *(bank president)*, William Gonder *(policeman)*, Lottie Williams *(maid)*, Dan Mason *(Silas Spencer)*, W. H. Brown *(chef)*, Robert Brower *(marriage license clerk)*.

Comedy. Source: Oscar Blumenthal and Gustav Kadelburg, *Die Thür ins Freie, Lustspiel en drei Akten* (Berlin, 1908; farce adapted by L. Ditrichstein as *Is Matrimony a Failure?* New York opening: 24 Aug 1909). The silver wedding anniversary of Mr. and Mrs. Amos Saxby is interrupted by the elopement of their daughter, Margaret, with Arthur Haviland, a bank clerk. Dudley King, a law student and rival suitor for Margaret, announces that the marriage license clerk is on vacation and that the license obtained by the elopers is invalid; he wires the proprietor of the lodge where the couple plan to spend their honeymoon, and Arthur and his wife return home, indignant. Demanding an explanation from the assistant clerk, Arthur learns that all marriages processed in November for the past 30 years are void because the clerk had not then been sworn in, and in consequence many households dissolve. But having gained their freedom, the husbands do not relish it, and when the license clerk returns, he declares all the marriages legal. Arthur rescues his bride just as King is about to carry her off, and the matrimonial routine begins. *Bank clerks. Marriage. Law. Elopement.*

IS MONEY EVERYTHING? **F2.2747**

D. M. Film Corp. *Dist* Lee-Bradford Corp. 1 Sep **1923.** Si; b&w. 35mm. 6 reels, 5,800 ft.

Dir-Writ Glen Lyons. *Photog* Alvin Knechtel.

Cast: Norman Kerry *(John Brand)*, Miriam Cooper *(his wife)*, Andrew Hicks *(Sam Slack)*, John Sylvester *(Rev. John Brooks)*, Martha Mansfield *(Mrs. Justine Pelham)*, William Bailey *(Roy Pelham)*, Lawrence Brooke *(Phil Graham)*.

Melodrama. "John Brand, deeply in love with his wife, becomes money mad with success and grows apart from her. He becomes involved with a married woman at the height of his career. His wife deliberately brings about his financial ruin to save him and they go back to the farm to find real happiness in their poverty." (*Motion Picture News Booking Guide*, 6: 38, Apr 1924.) *Farmers. Wealth. Marriage. Infidelity.*

IS THAT NICE? **F2.2748**

R-C Pictures. *Dist* Film Booking Offices of America. 7 Nov? **1926** [c7 Nov 1926; LP23729]. Si; b&w. 35mm. 5 reels, 4,501 ft.

Pres by Joseph P. Kennedy. *Dir* Del Andrews. *Adapt-Cont* Paul Gangelin. *Story* Walter A. Sinclair. *Camera* Jules Cronjager. *Asst Dir* Doran Cox. *Gag Man* Jack Collins.

Cast: George O'Hara *(Ralph Tanner)*, Doris Hill *(Doris Leslie)*, Stanton Heck *(John Gorman)*, Charles Thurston *(Sherman Dyke)*, Roy Laidlaw *(Horace Wildert)*, Babe London *(Winnie Nash)*, "Red" Kirby *(Bill Schultz)*, Ethan Laidlaw *(O'Brien)*.

Comedy-drama. Ralph Tanner, an enthusiastic cub reporter, writes a potentially libelous story on John Gorman, the city's political boss, and en route to show proofs to Wildert, the newspaper owner, he shows a copy to a girl in the outer office. Wildert and his managing editor, Dyke, are delighted until they learn Ralph has no evidence to back up his article and that an unknown girl has a copy of the piece. Ralph discovers that the girl has gone to Gorman with the article, and disguised as a window cleaner, he makes his way to Gorman's office. Following a complication involving Winnie (a husky stenographer), Ralph and the girl (Doris) obtain documents from Gorman that substantiate the article. *Stenographers. Reporters. Editors. Politicians. Libel. Documentation. Newspapers.*

IS YOUR DAUGHTER SAFE? **F2.2749**

Chadwick Pictures. 6 Jun **1927** [New York State license application]. Si; b&w. 35mm. 6 reels.

Pres by S. S. Millard. *Prod* S. S. Millard. *Dir* Louis King, Leon Lee. *Story* Max Abramson.

Cast: Vivian Winston *(The Girl)*, Jerome Young *(The Boy)*, Henry Roquemore *(The Beast)*, Georgia O'Dell *(The Madam)*, Slim Mahoney *(The White Slaver)*, William Dennis *(The Deceiver)*, Bernice Breacher *(The Victim)*, Palmer Morrison *(The Doctor)*, Winfield Jones *(The Governor)*, Joe Bonner *(The Rounder)*, Hugh Saxon *(The Gambler)*, Hazel Jones *(The Maid)*, Vera White, Hortense Petra, Virginia Hobbs, Alta Faulkner, Dorothy Jay, June D'Eon, Mildred Northmore, Ann Porter, Geraldine Johnson, Mildred McClune *(ladies of leisure)*, Mayor William Hale Thompson, Chicago Vice Commission.

Educational documentary(?). "It appears to be a composite picture, exhibiting parts of several different stories of white slave traffic, showing how Agents of the traffic lure unsuspecting girls to houses of ill repute and showing the treatment and life within these places. The last reel of the picture shows the effect of venereal disease on children born of parents afflicted with said disease. (New York State license records.) *White slave traffic. Prostitution. Venereal disease.*

IS ZAT SO? **F2.2750**

Fox Film Corp. 15 May **1927** [c15 May 1927; LP23997]. Si; b&w. 35mm. 7 reels, 6,950 ft.

Pres by William Fox. *Dir* Alfred E. Green. *Scen* Philip Klein. *Photog* George Schneiderman. *Asst Dir* Jack Boland.

Cast: George O'Brien *(Ed Chick Cowan)*, Edmund Lowe *(Hap Hurley)*, Kathryn Perry *(Marie Mestretti)*, Cyril Chadwick *(Robert Parker)*, Doris Lloyd *(Sue Parker)*, Dione Ellis *(Florence Hanley)*, Richard Maitland *(Maj. Fitz Stanley)*, Douglas Fairbanks, Jr. *(G. Clinton Blackburn)*, Philippe De Lacy *(Little Jimmy Parker)*, Jack Herrick *(Gas House Duffy)*.

Farce. Source: James Gleason and Richard Taber, *Is Zat So? a Comedy in Three Acts* (New York, 1928). "Hap, a fight manager, picks up Chick to make a fighter out of him. After losing out they are befriended by Blackburn, a young millionaire, and take the place of servants who have left. After a misunderstanding, Chick wins the championship and he and Hap win the girls of their choice. Chick also proves Blackburn's brother-in-law to be a crook." (*Moving Picture World*, 21 May 1927, p211.) *Boxers. Fight managers. Millionaires. Domestics. In-laws. Social classes.*

ISLAND WIVES **F2.2751**

Vitagraph Co. of America. ca4 Mar **1922** [Pittsburgh premiere; released 12 Mar; c6 Mar 1922; LP17607]. Si; b&w. 35mm. 5 reels, 4,994 ft.

Pres by Albert E. Smith. *Dir* Webster Campbell. *Scen* William B. Courtney. *Story* Bob Dexter. *Photog* Arthur Ross.

Cast: Corinne Griffith *(Elsa Melton)*, Charles Trowbridge *(Jimmy)*, Rockliffe Fellowes *(Hitchens)*, Ivan Christy *(McMasters)*, Edna Hibbard *(Piala)*, Norman Rankow *(Bibo)*, Peggy Parr *(McMasters' native wife)*, Barney Sherry *(yacht captain)*, John Galsworthy *(Lester)*, Mrs. Trowbridge *(Mrs. Lester)*.

Melodrama. Living on a desolate island in the South Seas, Elsa Melton is bitter and disillusioned with island life. She is coveted by McMasters, a lecherous derelict who is manager of the trading station. Jimmy, her husband, unaware of McMasters' desires, is unsympathetic with Elsa and embarks on a short sea trip; but he is caught in a sudden typhoon. McMasters attempts to attack Elsa, and she escapes in the storm to the beach, where she is found at dawn by Hitchens, a yachtsman, who understands her situation and takes her aboard his yacht. Hitchens causes her to believe that Jimmy has drowned at sea and at length persuades her to marry him, the ceremony being performed by the captain. In San Francisco she lives luxuriously with Hitchens but soon discovers him to be a rake and is again unhappy. When Hitchens tells her the marriage was invalid, Elsa returns to the island, where Jimmy's assistant recognizes Hitchens; and trying to escape, Hitchens is killed by a shark. Elsa and Jimmy are reunited, and he is promoted to a new job in Australia. *Traders. Rakes. Yachtsmen. Infidelity. South Sea Islands. San Francisco. Australia. Typhoons. Sharks.*

ISLE OF DOUBT **F2.2752**

Syracuse Motion Picture Co. *Dist* Playgoers Pictures. 10 Sep **1922** [c12 Aug 1922; LU18141]. Si; b&w. 35mm. 6 reels, 5,483 ft.

Dir Hamilton Smith. *Story-Scen* Derek Bram.

Cast: Wyndham Standing *(Dean Deland)*, Dorothy Mackaill *(Eleanor Warburton)*, George Fawcett *(Burton J. Warburton)*, Marie Burke *(Mrs. Warburton)*, Warner Richmond *(Gerry Patten)*, Arthur Dewey *(Bill Hardy)*.

Society drama. Eleanor Warburton, the daughter of a penniless father and a socially ambitious mother, is loved by wealthy Dean Deland but is interested only in Gerry Patten. A plan is conceived whereby Eleanor will marry Dean and, with Gerry's help, will make his life so miserable that he will divorce her and give her a considerable sum of money. But Dean discovers the plan and retaliates by taking Eleanor and Gerry to a South Sea island. Gerry is exposed as worthless, and the sullen Eleanor is forced to cook or starve. Not until Gerry tries to kill Dean, however, is Eleanor reconciled with her husband. *Social climbers. Marriage. Wealth. South Sea Islands.*

ISLE OF ESCAPE **F2.2753**

Warner Brothers Pictures. 1 Mar **1930** [c17 Feb 1930; LP1082]. Sd (Vitaphone); b&w. 35mm. 6 reels, 4,914 ft. [Also possibly si.]

Dir Howard Bretherton. *Screenplay* Lucien Hubbard, J. Grubb Alexander. *Song: "My Kalva Rose"* Al Bryan, Ed Ward. *Rec Engr* Cal Applegate.

Cast: Monte Blue *(Dave Wade)*, Myrna Loy *(Moira)*, Betty Compson *(Stella)*, Noah Beery *(Shane)*, Ivan Simpson *(Judge)*, Jack Ackroyd *(Hank)*, Nina Quartero *(Loru)*, Duke Kahanamoku *(Manua)*, Nick De Ruiz *(Dolobe)*, Rose Dione *(Ma Blackney)*, Adolph Milar *(Dutch planter)*.

Melodrama. Source: G. C. Dixon, *Isle of Escape* (a play). Jack McLaren, *Isle of Escape, a Story of the South Seas* (London, 1926). On a South Sea island, Stella operates a hotel for her mother, who is constantly drunk on liquor smuggled by Shane, the principal trader and virtual dictator of the island. Dave Wade, exhausted from the heat, lands on the shore near the hotel and reports having escaped from a nearby cannibal island. Stella has her servants, Manua and Loru, care for him, but Shane, to whom she is married but with whom she has never lived, orders him taken to his house, intent on stealing his gold. In a drunken orgy, Shane takes the gold, provoking a fight in which Stella aids Wade. When Ma Blackney dies and Stella recovers the gold, she suggests they go to another island and establish a trading business; but because of a misunderstanding, Stella is kidnaped by the natives and taken to the cannibal island. Disregarding their differences, Wade and Shane join forces and go to the island; Shane sacrifices himself to stall the cannibals while Stella and Wade flee to the sea. *Traders. Cannibals. Alcoholism. Robbery. Self-sacrifice. Hotels. South Sea Islands.*

ISLE OF FORGOTTEN WOMEN **F2.2754**

Columbia Pictures. 27 Sep **1927** [c20 Oct 1927; LP24544]. Si; b&w. 35mm. 6 reels, 5,645 ft.

Prod Harry Cohn. *Dir* George B. Seitz. *Adapt-Scen* Norman Springer. *Story* Louella Parsons. *Photog* Joseph Walker. *Makeup* Fred C. Ryle.

Cast: Conway Tearle *(Bruce Paine)*, Dorothy Sebastian *(Marua)*, Gibson Gowland *(John Stort)*, Alice Calhoun *(Alice Burroughs)*, Harry Semels, William Welch, Eddie Harris.

Melodrama. Bruce Paine, a fugitive from justice, comes to Paradise Island, having confessed to crimes committed by his father, though his fiancée, Alice Burroughs, retains her faith in him. Paine encounters John Stort, a dissolute trader, and Marua, a young native girl who is his "property." When Paine defends Marua from Stort's cruelty, a serious situation is averted only by Paine's refusal to fight, disappointing Marua, who wants him to be her master. Though Paine resists her advances, Stort becomes insanely jealous, and in a fierce battle Paine is victorious but badly hurt; a Captain Roper relays the state of affairs to Alice. Meanwhile, Stort determines to kill Paine, who has succumbed to island fever, but Marua throws herself across Paine's body to receive a fatal spear thrust, and, before dying, she shoots Stort. Alice arrives with the news that Paine's name has been cleared, and the lovers return home to be married while Marua is forgotten. *Fugitives. Traders. Jealousy. Self-sacrifice. South Sea Islands.*

THE ISLE OF HOPE **F2.2755**

Richard Talmadge Productions. *Dist* Film Booking Offices of America. 16 Aug **1925.** Si; b&w. 35mm. 6 reels, 5,800 ft.

Dir Jack Nelson. *Story-Scen* James Bell Smith. *Photog* William Marshall, Jack Stevens.

Cast: Richard Talmadge *(Robert Mackay)*, Helen Ferguson *(Dorothy Duffy)*, James Marcus *(Captain Duffy)*, Bert Strong *(first mate)*, Howard Bell *(second mate)*, Edward Gordon *(Chinese cook)*, George Reed *(Negro cook)*.

Action melodrama. Bob Mackay, a wealthy yachtsman, ships with Captain Duffy in search of buried treasure on the Isle of Hope. During a mutiny, the ship is set afire, and Bob is stranded on a desert isle in the company of Dorothy Duffy, the captain's daughter. They take refuge in a deserted castle and find the pirate gold. Dorothy is kidnaped by some sailors from her father's boat, and Bob rescues her. Bob and Dorothy are later rescued by some of Bob's friends and then are married at sea by a ship's captain. *Sea captains. Yachtsmen. Sailors. Mutiny. Treasure. Ship fires.*

ISLE OF LOST MEN (Imperial Photoplays) **F2.2756**

Trem Carr Productions. *Dist* Rayart Pictures. 2 Oct **1928.** Si; b&w. 35mm. 6 reels, 5,800 ft.

Pres by W. Ray Johnston. *Dir* Duke Worne. *Scen* George Pyper. *Titl* Dudley Early. *Story* Frederick Nebel. *Photog* Hap Depew. *Film Ed* John S. Harrington.

Cast: Tom Santschi *(Capt. Jan Jodahl)*, James Marcus *(Malay Pete)*, Allen Connor *(David Carlisle)*, Patsy O'Leary *(Alma Fairfax)*, Paul Weigel *(Preacher Jason)*, Jules Cowles *(ship's cook)*, Maude George *(Kealani)*, Sailor Sharkey.

Melodrama. "It seems that Malay Pete stole a baby gal [Alma Fairfax] from an Australian millionaire for re-ven-ge, and took her to the Isle of Lost Men where all the scum of the earth had been washed up, but still dirty. And the dirtiest of 'em all was this guy Water Wolf [Capt. Jan Jodahl] who ran a hell ship. But give him credit. He was willing to marry the kidnaped white gal who was so innocently dumb that she still thought Malay Pete her daddy. Meanwhile hero Dave had entered with a chart of an island that bore a bumper crop of rubies. Water Wolf steals the chart, then takes the gal for good measure but the hero recovers the chart and girl." (*Film Daily*, 9 Dec 1928, p10.) *Derelicts. Kidnaping. Parentage. Treasure. South Sea Islands. Documentation.*

THE ISLE OF LOST SHIPS **F2.2757**

Maurice Tourneur Productions. *Dist* Associated First National Pictures. 18 Mar **1923** [c13 Mar 1923; LP18766]. Si; b&w. 35mm. 8 reels, 7,425 ft.

Pres by M. C. Levee. *Prod* Ned Marin. *Dir* Maurice Tourneur. *Scen* Charles Maigne. *Photog* Arthur Todd. *Sets* Milton Menasco. *Film Ed* Frank Lawrence. *Asst Dir* Scott R. Beal.

Cast: Anna Q. Nilsson *(Dorothy Fairfax)*, Milton Sills *(Frank Howard)*, Frank Campeau *(Detective Jackson)*, Walter Long *(Peter Forbes)*, Bert Woodruff *(Patrick Joyce)*, Aggie Herring *(Mother Joyce)*, Herschel Mayall

(Captain Clark).

Melodrama. Source: Crittenden Marriott, *The Isle of Dead Ships* (Philadelphia, 1909). Detective Jackson is taking Frank Howard from South America to New York to face a murder charge when their ship is wrecked. All escape the wreck but Jackson, Howard, and wealthy Dorothy Fairfax. The wreck drifts into the Sargasso Sea, where a fleet of derelicts is inhabited by some 50 people headed by Peter Forbes. To save Dorothy from marriage to Forbes, Frank defeats the ex-sea captain in a fight, then marries her himself, though in name only. Frank calls on his past experience to equip a submarine and make an escape. He wins Dorothy's love and proves his innocence. *Sea captains. Detectives. Murder. Submarines. Sargasso Sea. Shipwrecks.*

Note: Remade in 1929.

THE ISLE OF LOST SHIPS **F2.2758**

First National Pictures. 29 Nov **1929** [c16 Oct 1929; LP785]. Sd (Vitaphone); b&w. 35mm. 9 reels, 7,576 ft. [Also si.]

Pres by Richard A. Rowland. *Dir* Irvin Willat. *Scen* Fred Myton. *Titl-Dial* Paul Perez, Fred Myton. *Photog* Sol Polito. *Film Ed* John Rawlins.

Cast: Jason Robards *(Frank Howard)*, Virginia Valli *(Dorothy Whitlock* [*or Renwick*]*)*, Clarissa Selwynne *(Aunt Emma* [*or Mrs. Renwick*]*)*, Noah Beery *(Captain* [*or Peter*] *Forbes)*, Robert E. O'Connor *(Jackson)*, Harry Cording *(Gallagher)*, Margaret Fielding *(Mrs. Gallagher)*, Katherine Ward *(Mother Joyce* [*or Burke*]*)*, Robert Homans *(Mr. Burke)*, Jack Ackroyd *(Harry)*, Sam Baker *(himself)*.

Melodrama. Source: Crittenden Marriott, *The Isle of Dead Ships* (Philadelphia & London, 1909). Aboard a ship sailing from Puerto Rico to New York is Frank Howard, the prisoner of Jackson, a detective. Howard and society girl Dorothy Whitlock, who with her aunt is also a passenger, become mutually attracted. The ship is swept into the Sargasso Sea, a wreckage-cluttered eddy in the central Atlantic, and is stranded amidst an "island" of ships, comprising a small colony dominated by Captain Forbes. Since any woman must be married immediately to prevent quarrels among the men, Forbes demands that Dorothy become his wife. But Dorothy chooses Howard; and when challenged by Forbes, Howard beats him. Burke, an Irish mechanic who operates the engines of a stranded submarine, leads Howard, Dorothy, and Jackson to the craft; and they escape Forbes and his gang. Jackson is resolved to help clear Howard, who finds happiness with Dorothy. *Detectives. Shipwrecks. Submarines. Derelicts. Sargasso Sea.*

Note: Remake of a 1923 film of the same title, q. v.

THE ISLE OF LOVE **F2.2759**

Dist Herald Productions. c12 Jun **1922** [LP18202]. Si; b&w. 35mm. 5 reels.

Pres by Fred J. Balshofer. *Dir-Writ* Fred J. Balshofer.

Cast: Julian Eltinge *(Clifford Townsend)*, Alma Francis *(Eunice)*, Lydia Knott *(Clifford Townsend's mother)*, Rodolph Valentino *(Jacques Rudanyi)*.

Romantic adventure melodrama. Clifford Townsend seeks and finds adventure in a revolution on the Isle of Love. He summons his friend Jacques Rudanyi to be the new king, and they, together with Vanette, an old acquaintance of Jacques', find themselves in opposition to an intriguing prince and duke. Townsend's plan to masquerade as a woman and vamp the prince fails, and the three are forced to flee—Townsend only barely escaping a firing squad. All reach the United States safely, Townsend is reunited with the girl he left behind, and Jacques and Vanette find happiness. *Royalty. Nobility. Vamps. Imaginary kingdoms. Revolutions.*

Note: According to its advertising and Balshofer's *One Reel a Week,* this film is a revision of *An Adventuress* (c1920), which Balshofer fashioned from a serious, anti-Kaiser film he made in 1918 and never released. In the original footage, Valentino had only a supporting part, but Balshofer padded his appearances with outtakes.

THE ISLE OF RETRIBUTION (Gold Bond Special) **F2.2760**

R-C Pictures. *Dist* Film Booking Offices of America. 25 Apr **1926** [c24 Apr 1926; LP22633]. Si; b&w. 35mm. 7 reels, 6,388 ft.

Dir James P. Hogan. *Adapt* Fred Kennedy Myton. *Photog* Jules Cronjager. *Asst Camera* Glen Gano. *Art Dir* Frank Ormston. *Asst Dir* Frank Geraghty.

Cast: Lillian Rich *(Bess Gilbert)*, Robert Frazer *(Ned Cornet)*, Victor McLaglen *(Doomsdorf)*, Mildred Harris *(Lenore Hardenworth)*, Kathleen Kirkham *(her mother)*, David Torrence *(Godfrey Cornet)*, Inez Gomez *(Sindy)*.

Melodrama. Source: Edison Marshall, *The Isle of Retribution* (Boston, 1923). Ned, son of Godfrey Cornet, a wealthy fur dealer, is a society wastrel and is sent by his father to oversee his properties in Alaska. In the group are Bess Gilbert (Cornet's secretary) and Mrs. Hardenworth and her daughter Lenore, who are after the Cornet fortune. During a ship's party, the captain gets drunk and wrecks his ship; the survivors reach a barren island off the coast of Alaska, belonging to Doomsdorf, a Russian who has fled from Siberia, and he makes captives of the castaways. Doomsdorf rules with an iron hand, beating Ned twice and threatening Lenore repeatedly, but he is unable to subdue Bess's spirit. Lenore and her mother betray Ned and Bess and escape; meanwhile, Ned, who has developed his strength, lures Doomsdorf into a beartrap, and Doomsdorf is buried by an avalanche of snow. Ned returns home with Bess as his wife. *Wastrels. Russians. Castaways. Manhood. Ships. Alaska. Avalanches.*

THE ISLE OF VANISHING MEN **F2.2761**

William F. Alder. 26 Feb **1924** [New York State license]. Si; b&w. 35mm. 6 reels, 5,400 ft.

Dir-Scen William F. Alder. *Photog* Paul Allen.

Travelog. This film is a record of the explorations of the Alder party in the interior of Dutch Guinea. It is concerned primarily with the Kia Kia (flesh eaters), a tribe of primitive headhunters, whose life and habits are presented in some detail. Among the aspects of Kia Kia life seen are the manner in which food is prepared, huts built, and bodies mutilated for decoration. *Headhunters. Cannibals. Kia Kia. Exploration. New Guinea.*

ISN'T LIFE WONDERFUL **F2.2762**

United Artists. 1 Dec **1924** [c1 Feb 1925; LP21265]. Si; b&w. 35mm. 9 reels, 8,600 ft.

Prod-Dir-Scen D. W. Griffith. *Photog* Hendrik Sartov, Hal Sintzenich. *Mus* Louis Silvers, Caesare Sudero.

Cast: Carol Dempster *(Inga)*, Neil Hamilton *(Paul)*, Erville Alderson *(The Professor)*, Helen Lowell *(The Grandmother)*, Marcia Harris *(The Aunt)*, Frank Puglia *(Theodor)*, Lupino Lane *(Rudolph)*, Hans von Schlettow *(leader of laborers)*, Paul Rehkopf, Robert Scholz *(laborers)*, Walter Plimmer, Jr. *(The American)*.

Romantic drama. Source: Geoffrey Moss, "Isn't Life Wonderful!" in *Defeat* (New York, 1924). Orphaned by the war, Inga, a Polish refugee, lives in Berlin with a professor and his family—an old grandmother, the professor's sister, and a son, Theodor. Another son, Paul, Inga's sweetheart, is still at the battlefront. Near starvation and living in cramped quarters, they show with weary faces the hardships they have endured. The professor takes a job correcting papers, and Theodor becomes a waiter. Paul returns, weakened from the war. He begins to work in a shipyard while Inga works in a shop, but he falls ill. During his convalescence, Paul and Inga decide to marry, although the family discourages them, pointing out the lack of money, inadequate housing, and the declining value of the mark. Paul procures a piece of land and secretly grows potatoes and builds a cottage, while Inga prepares her dowry by mending furniture in a secondhand shop. When the potatoes are ready to be harvested Paul brings some home, and with the liverwurst Theodor has brought, they have a feast. Grandmother brings out a wedding gown she has made for Inga. The next day Paul and Inga take a cart to harvest the potatoes. As they are returning, a group of hungry, desperate men attack them in the woods and take the crop. The couple are disconsolate, but they are comforted by the knowledge that they still have each other. In an appended ending "one year later" the couple are shown prospering in their new cottage. *Refugees. Professors. Poles. Orphans. Family life. Hunger. Potatoes. World War I. Berlin.*

IT **F2.2763**

Famous Players–Lasky. *Dist* Paramount Pictures. 5 Feb **1927** [New York premiere; released 19 Feb; c19 Feb 1927; LP23686]. Si; b&w. 35mm. 7 reels, 6,452 ft.

Pres by Adolph Zukor, Jesse L. Lasky. *Assoc Prod* B. P. Schulberg. *Dir* Clarence Badger. *Adtl Dir (see note)* Josef von Sternberg. *Scen* Hope Loring, Louis D. Lighton. *Titl* George Marion, Jr. *Adapt* Elinor Glyn. *Photog* H. Kinley Martin. *Ed in Ch* E. Lloyd Sheldon. *Asst Dir* Vernon Keays.

Cast: Clara Bow *(Betty Lou)*, Antonio Moreno *(Cyrus Waltham)*, William Austin *(Monty)*, Jacqueline Gadsdon *(Adela Van Norman)*, Gary Cooper *(newspaper reporter)*, Julia Swayne Gordon *(Mrs. Van Norman)*, Priscilla Bonner *(Molly)*, Eleanor Lawson *(first welfare worker)*, Rose Tapley *(second welfare worker)*, Elinor Glyn.

Comedy-drama. Source: Elinor Glyn, *"It"* (New York, c1927). Betty Lou and her friends at Waltham Department Store, after discussing Elinor

Glyn's story, *It*, decide that their boss, Cyrus Waltham, has IT. That evening Betty encounters Waltham and his friend, Monty; Monty asks her to dinner, and she chooses the Ritz. He tries to direct her to a secluded table, but she insists on fascinating Cyrus and accomplishes her purpose. When the authorities threaten to take away Molly's baby, Betty claims the child as hers and proves that she can support it. Misunderstanding, Monty tells Waltham of Betty's deceitfulness, and as a result Cyrus snubs her. Betty appears unexpectedly at Cyrus' yachting party and laughs in his face when he proposes to her. The yacht collides with another boat, and Adela, Cyrus' society fiancée, is thrown overboard. Betty swims to rescue her; Cyrus follows and they make up their differences. *Salesclerks. Children. Personality. Department stores. New York City.*

Note: Badger became ill during filming, and Sternberg directed some scenes during his absence.

IT CAN BE DONE **F2.2764**

Earle Williams Productions. *Dist* Vitagraph Co. of America. Mar **1921** [c4 Apr 1921; LP16353]. Si; b&w. 35mm. 5 reels, 4,600 ft.

Dir David Smith. *Story* Frederick J. Jackson. *Photog* Jack MacKenzie.

Cast: Earle Williams *(Austin Crane)*, Elinor Fair *(Eve Standish)*, Henry Barrows *(Webb Standish)*, Jack Mathies *(Jasper Braden)*, Jack Carlisle *(Bill Donahue)*, Alfred Aldridge *(Spike Dawson)*, William McCall *(Byron Tingley)*, Florence Hart *(Mrs. Standish)*, Mary Huntress *(Mrs. Faire)*.

Comedy-melodrama. At a dinner party given by Webb Standish, Austin Crane, an author of detective fiction, is accused of writing improbable stories. Eve, Webb's daughter, shares Crane's belief that his stories can be duplicated in reality. Accordingly, Crane fabricates a case to prove that Standish is a profiteer, discovers that he is really guilty, but for Eve's sake hesitates to expose him. His editor insists that he continue the game, however; and entering Standish's home with a former crook, Spike Dawson, Crane obtains incriminating evidence. *Authors. Editors. Profiteers.*

IT CAN BE DONE (Universal-Jewel) **F2.2765**

Universal Pictures. 24 Mar **1929** [c16 Mar 1929; LP220]. Talking sequences, sd eff, & mus score (Movietone); b&w. 35mm. 7 reels, 6,560 ft. [Also si; 6,090 ft.]

Dir Fred Newmeyer. *Dial Dir* A. B. Heath. *Scen* Joseph Poland. *Dial-Titl* Albert De Mond. *Adapt* Earle Snell, Nan Cochrane. *Story* Mann Page, Edward J. Montagne. *Photog* Ross Fisher. *Film Ed* Ted Kent. *Ed Dial Sequences* B. W. Burton.

Cast: Glenn Tryon *(Jerry Willard)*, Sue Carol *(Anne Rogers)*, Richard Carlyle *(Rogers)*, Richard Carle *(Watson)*, Jack Egan *(Ben Smith)*, Tom O'Brien *(detective)*.

Comedy. Jerry Willard, a clerk in a publishing house who is possessed of a massive inferiority complex, is fired from his job and, on the way out of the office, is mistaken for the boss, Watson, by Anne Rogers, the daughter of an author, who gives Jerry the manuscript of her father's latest book. Jerry reads this text—on how to succeed in business—and puts some of its ideas to work. He attempts to persuade Watson to publish the book and fails; undeterred, he then steals Watson's dress suit and addresses the Publishers' Convention, extolling the virtues of the Rogers book. The response is so enthusiastic that Watson not only decides to publish the book but takes Jerry into the firm as a junior partner. Jerry proposes to Anne and is accepted. *Office clerks. Authors. Publishers. Mistaken identity. Inferiority complex. Conventions.*

IT HAPPENED OUT WEST **F2.2766**

W. M. Smith Productions. Mar **1923** [scheduled release]. Si; b&w. 35mm. 5 reels, 4,560 ft.

Cast: Franklyn Farnum, Virginia Lee.

Western melodrama(?). No information about the nature of this film has been found.

IT IS THE LAW **F2.2767**

Fox Film Corp. 31 Aug **1924** [c30 Jun 1924; LP20369]. Si; b&w. 35mm. 7 reels, 6,895 ft.

Pres by William Fox. *Dir* J. Gordon Edwards. *Scen* Curtis Benton. *Photog* George W. Lane.

Cast: Arthur Hohl *(Albert Woodruff/"Sniffer")*, Herbert Heyes *(Justin Victor)*, Mimi Palmeri *(Ruth Allen)*, George Lessey *(Inspector Dolan)*, Robert Young *(Travers)*, Florence Dixon *(Lillian Allen)*, Byron Douglas *(Cummings)*, Olaf Hytten *(Bill Elliott)*, De Sacia Mooers *(Bernice)*, Guido Trento *(Manee)*, Byron Russell *(Harley)*.

Mystery melodrama. Source: Elmer Rice and Hayden Talbot, *It Is the Law* (New York opening: 29 Nov 1922). Unsuccessful suitor Albert Woodruff avenges himself by making it appear that he has been killed by his friend, Justin Victor, who won the hand of Ruth Allen. In fact, his double is murdered though Victor is sentenced for the crime. Years later, with the aid of his wife, Victor does kill Woodruff but is given his freedom on the grounds that he cannot be convicted twice for the same crime. *Revenge. Murder. Double jeopardy. Doubles.*

IT ISN'T BEING DONE THIS SEASON **F2.2768**

Vitagraph Co. of America. Jan **1921** [c9 Feb 1921; LP16125]. Si; b&w. 35mm. 5 reels.

Dir George L. Sargent. *Scen* C. Graham Baker, Harry Dittmar. *Photog* Arthur Ross.

Cast: Corinne Griffith *(Marcia Ventnor)*, Sally Crute *(Isabelle Ventnor)*, Webster Campbell *(Oliver Lawton)*, Charles Wellesley *(George Hunt)*, John Charles *(Afeif Bey)*.

Society melodrama. Source: Thomas Edgelow, "It Isn't Being Done This Season," in *Breezy Stories* (6:129–158, Aug 1918). Following her mother's advice to marry for wealth, model Marcia Ventnor turns down the proposal of Oliver Lawton, whom she loves, so as to accept wealthy George Hunt, an importer of oriental rugs. They go to Turkey on their honeymoon, and Hunt enlists her charms to secure a contract from rugmaker Afeif Bey, whose infatuation with Marcia provokes her husband's jealousy. The Hunts return home, and following Hunt's death she meets Lawton, who is sent to Turkey on the same mission, and she promises to marry him if he obtains the contract. He also is infuriated and tries to kill her, but with a trick knife. Realizing his seriousness, she is reunited with him, and they are married. *Fashion models. Importers. Wealth. Marriage. Rugs. Turkey.*

IT MUST BE LOVE **F2.2769**

John McCormick Productions. *Dist* First National Pictures. 22 Aug **1926** [c18 Aug 1926; LP23035]. Si; b&w. 35mm. 7 reels, 6,848 ft. [Copyrighted as 8 reels.]

Pres by John McCormick. *Dir* Alfred E. Green. *Adapt* Julian Josephson. *Photog* H. F. Koenekamp. *Comedy Construc* Mervyn LeRoy.

Cast: Colleen Moore *(Fernie Schmidt)*, Jean Hersholt *(Pop Schmidt)*, Malcolm McGregor *(Jack Dugan)*, Arthur Stone *(Peter Halitovsky)*, Bodil Rosing *(Mom Schmidt)*, Dorothy Seastrom *(Min)*, Cleve Moore *(Al)*, Mary O'Brien *(Lois)*, Ray Hallor *(Joe)*.

Comedy-drama. Source: Brooke Hanlon, "Delicatessen," in *Saturday Evening Post* (198:12–13, 24 Aug 1925). Fernie Schmidt, who lives with her parents in the rear of their delicatessen, finds the atmosphere and smells of the building repulsive. Pop Schmidt, who fails to understand his daughter's desire for a more pleasant home, has planned to marry her off to Peter Halitovsky, the sausage salesman. At a dance, Fernie meets Jack Dugan. He tells her he is in stocks, and she falls in love with him. When she returns home, Pop, incensed by her rejection of Peter, turns her away from the house. Fernie takes a job in a department store; and one Sunday, at a picnic, Jack proposes and she accepts. That evening, Fernie is invited home for dinner, and Pop announces his decision to buy a new home; Peter proposes, and she is about to reject him when Jack appears, announcing that he has purchased a delicatessen business. Fernie is happily resigned to her fate. *Filial relations. Family life. Delicatessens. Courtship. Ambition.*

ITCHING PALMS **F2.2770**

R-C Pictures. *Dist* Film Booking Offices of America. 22 Jul **1923** [c29 Apr 1923; LP20069]. Si; b&w. 35mm. 6 reels, 6,100 ft.

Dir James W. Horne. *Adapt-Scen* Wyndham Gittens, Helmer Bergman. *Photog* William Marshall. *Art Dir* W. L. Heywood. *Film Ed* J. Wilkinson.

Cast: Tom Gallery *(Jerry)*, Herschel Mayall *(Jerry's father)*, Virginia Fox *(Virgie)*, Tom Wilson *(Mac)*, Joseph Harrington *(Obadiah Simpkins)*, Victor Potel *(The Village Dumbbell)*, Gertrude Claire *(Grandma Gano)*, Robert Walker *(Dr. Peak)*, Tom Lingham *(Judge Barrett)*, Richard Cummings *(Constable Coman)*.

Crook farce-melodrama. Source: Roy Briant, *When Jerry Comes Home* (a play; publication undetermined). The son of Grandma Gano (Jerry's father) and Dr. Peak, a respected member of the community, commit a sizable robbery; Peak shoots his partner; and Grandma learns from her son's deathbed confession that the loot is hidden near a haunted house. Grandma and Jerry resolve to find the money while Peak tries to prevent their success with some farcical goings-on. The house goes up in flames, Jerry's sweetheart rescues Jerry, and the money is found in a well. Justice is served, however, when the loot proves to be counterfeit. *Physicians. Grandmothers. Counterfeiting. Robbery. Haunted houses.*

IT'S A GREAT LIFE **F2.2771**

Metro-Goldwyn-Mayer Pictures. 6 Dec **1929** [c9 Dec 1929; LP889]. Sd (Movietone); b&w with col sequences (Technicolor). 35mm. 11 reels, 8,575 ft. [Also si; 6,106 ft.]

Dir Sam Wood. *Treatment & Comedy Dial* Al Boasberg. *Dial* Willard Mack. *Story* Byron Morgan, Alfred Block. *Photog* Peverell Marley. *Art Dir* Cedric Gibbons. *Film Ed* Frank Sullivan. *Songs: "Smile, Smile, Smile," "Lady Love," "I'm the Son of a ——," "Following You," "It Must Be an Old Spanish Custom," "Hoosier Hop," "I'm Sailing on a Sunbeam"* Dave Dreyer, Ballard MacDonald. *Song: "Let a Smile Be Your Umbrella on a Rainy Day"* Irving Kahal, Francis Wheeler, Sammy Fain. *Dance Dir* Sammy Lee. *Rec Engr* Douglas Shearer. *Wardrobe* David Cox.

Cast: Rosetta Duncan *(Casey Hogan)*, Vivian Duncan *(Babe Hogan)*, Lawrence Gray *(Jimmy Dean)*, Jed Prouty *(Mr. Parker)*, Benny Rubin *(Benny Friedman)*.

Romantic musical comedy. Two sisters, Babe and Casey Hogan, employed in the sheet music section of a department store where they sing and dance, are fired and take smalltime vaudeville jobs. Babe falls in love with Jimmy Dean, their piano player, and the sisters split up when Babe and Jimmy get married. Ultimately, however, the two girls are reunited and resume their musical act. *Sisters. Salesclerks. Pianists. Dancers. Vaudeville. Department stores.*

Note: Reviewed also as *Imperfect Ladies.*

IT'S THE OLD ARMY GAME **F2.2772**

Famous Players–Lasky. *Dist* Paramount Pictures. 24 May **1926** [c25 May 1926; LP22763]. Si; b&w. 35mm. 7 reels, 6,889 ft.

Pres by Adolph Zukor, Jesse L. Lasky. *Dir* Edward Sutherland. *Scen* Tom J. Geraghty, J. Clarkson Miller. *Titl* Ralph Spence. *Photog* Alvin Wyckoff.

Cast: W. C. Fields *(Elmer Prettywillie)*, Louise Brooks *(Mildred Marshall)*, Blanche Ring *(Tessie Overholt)*, William Gaxton *(George Parker)*, Mary Foy *(Sarah Pancoast)*, Mickey Bennett *(Mickey)*, Josephine Dunn, Jack Luden *(society bathers)*, George Currie *(artist)*.

Farce. Source: Joseph Patrick McEvoy, "It's the Old Army Game" (publication undetermined). Elmer Prettywillie, the village druggist, is aroused by a woman who needs a 2-cent stamp in the middle of the night. Seeking again a state of somnolence, Prettywillie must contend with the clamorous collectors of garbage, and with those of his own castle who have caught forty winks and then some. The letter-carrying lady, in trying to post her missive, manages to summon the city's fire department to the pharmacy where, unable to find a fire, they sit and sip sodas while Prettywillie panders to their every want. When they leave, a bit of a blaze does erupt, but Prettywillie is forced to his own resources. Meanwhile, George Parker is smitten with Elmer's buxom assistant and uses the storefront to promote a bogus land deal. The Prettywillie fortune is thus inflated, enabling the purchase of a flivver, but Elmer ends up wrecking a Florida estate and finally the flivver, foiling the schemers and delighting the denizens of the town, whose jubilation Elmer takes for an acute case of distemper. He jails himself for safekeeping. *Pharmacists. Firemen. Family life. Smalltown life. Real estate business. Speculation. Fraud. Jails.*

JACK O' CLUBS **F2.2773**

Universal Pictures. 10 or 11 Feb **1924** [c5 Jan 1924; LP19797]. Si; b&w. 35mm. 5 reels, 4,717 ft.

Dir Robert F. Hill. *Scen* Rex Taylor. *Adapt (see note)* Raymond L. Schrock. *Story* Gerald Beaumont. *Photog* William Thornley.

Cast: Herbert Rawlinson *(John Francis Foley)*, Ruth Dwyer *(Tillie Miller)*, Eddie Gribbon *(Spike Kennedy)*, Esther Ralston *(Queenie Hatch)*, Joseph Girard *(Captain Dennis Malloy)*, Florence D. Lee *(Mrs. Miller)*, John Fox, Jr. *(Toto)*, Noel Stewart *(Otto)*.

Action melodrama. Source: Gerald Beaumont, "Jack o' Clubs," in *Red Book Magazine* (42:49–52, Dec 1923). Jack Foley, a tough policeman who patrols the city's worst beat, loses his nerve when he believes he has hurt Tillie Miller, the girl he loves, but he recovers his confidence after he finds that her injury was inflicted by Spike Kennedy, a gangster. He beats up Spike, thereby permanently cleaning up the neighborhood. *Police. Gangsters.*

Note: Company records make no mention of Raymond Schrock, but other sources credit him as adapter.

JACK OF HEARTS *see* **JACK O'HEARTS**

JACK O'HEARTS **F2.2774**

David Hartford Productions. *Dist* American Cinema Association. 1 Sep **1926** [c5 Jun 1926; LP22800]. Si; b&w. 35mm. 6 reels, 5,881 ft.

Prod-Dir David Hartford. *Screen Vers* Frances Nordstrom. *Photog* Walter Griffin.

Cast: Cullen Landis *(Jack Farber)*, Gladys Hulette, Bert Cummings, Antrim Short, John T. Dwyer, John Prince, Vester Pegg.

Inspirational melodrama. Source: Gordon Morris, *Jack in the Pulpit* (New York opening: 6 Jan 1925). Jack Farber, a young theological student who wants to get firsthand experiences of life before taking over his father's pulpit, goes to the big city against the wishes of his aunt. There he is the victim of circumstances and is sent to jail when a crook plants a purse in his pocket to avoid arrest. Upon release, Jack has difficulty in finding work because of his prison record and is unable to keep his conviction a secret because of the vigilance of Tim Corrigan, the detective who arrested him. Steve, whom Jack has befriended in prison, arranges for him to see an attorney, who advises him that if he serves his home pulpit for a year, he will inherit his aunt's fortune. He goes there with his crook friends, who agree to lead a clean and honest life; but Corrigan appears and warns him to leave town at the behest of Amos Pendleton, his uncle. Instead of delivering his prepared sermon, Jack tells the congregation the story of his misfortune; Steve confesses to framing him, and Corrigan declares Jack innocent. *Ministerial students. Clergymen. Uncles. Aunts. Detectives. Criminals—Rehabilitation. Circumstantial evidence. Redemption.*

Note: Copyright title: *Jack of Hearts.*

THE JACK RIDER **F2.2775**

Charles R. Seeling. *Dist* Aywon Film Corp. 15 Sep **1921** [New York State]. Si; b&w. 35mm. 5 reels, ca4,500 ft.

Dir Charles R. Seeling. *Story* Guinn Williams.

Cast: Big Boy Williams *(Frank Stevens)*, Thelma Worth *(Ruth Welsh)*, S. D. Wilcox *(John Welsh)*, J. Buckley Russell *(Howard Gribbon)*, Will Rogers, Jr. *(Little Buster)*.

Western comedy-melodrama. Frank Stevens comes west to claim the ranch he has inherited from his father on the condition that he first prove himself worthy. The hands make life difficult for Frank, who chooses a donkey for his transportation after being bucked off a horse; but he shows fine mettle while getting involved in rodeo stunts. Howard Gribbon frames Frank for a bank robbery and kidnaps Ruth Welsh, the banker's daughter; but Frank chances upon the real culprits and rescues Ruth just before the automobile goes over a cliff and kills the villain. *Cowboys. Inheritance. Kidnaping. Frameup. Bank robberies. Rodeos. Donkeys.*

JACKIE **F2.2776**

Fox Film Corp. 27 Nov **1921** [c27 Dec 1921; LP17409]. Si; b&w. 35mm. 5 reels, 4,943 ft.

Pres by William Fox. *Dir* Jack Ford. *Scen* Dorothy Yost. *Photog* George Schneiderman.

Cast: Shirley Mason *(Jackie)*, William Scott *(Mervyn Carter)*, Harry Carter *(Bill Bowman)*, George Stone *(Benny)*, John Cook *(Winter)*, Elsie Bambrick *(Millie)*.

Romantic drama. Source: Countess Hélène Barcynska, *Jackie* (New York, 1921). Jackie, a Russian waif in London who studies dancing, is noticed by Mervyn Carter, a wealthy young American who is struck by her talent and makes an appointment to see her. But Jackie's teacher apprentices her to Bowman, manager of a troupe of strolling players. Jackie becomes friends with Benny, a crippled boy, and when Bowman attempts to assault her, the two run away to London, where Benny plays an accordion and Jackie dances for a living. In the neighborhood of his sister, Carter finds them, sends Benny to the hospital for an operation, and arranges to have Jackie trained for a stage career. When she becomes successful, Bowman demands that she fulfill her contract with him and threatens to kill Carter, now her fiancé. She tries to buy off Bowman and is rescued from his clutches by Carter, who punishes Bowman and throws him out. Benny regains his health, and Jackie marries Carter. *Waifs. Dancers. Accordionists. Russians. Actors. Cripples. Theater. London.*

JACQUELINE, OR BLAZING BARRIERS (Pine Tree Special) **F2.2777**

Pine Tree Pictures. *Dist* Arrow Film Corp. 19 Mar **1923** [Patterson, N. J., premiere; released 1 Apr; c14 Apr 1923; LP18881]. Si; b&w. 35mm. 7 reels, 6,400 ft.

Dir Dell Henderson. *Adapt* Thomas F. Fallon, Dorothy Farnum. *Photog* George Peters, Charles Downs, Dan Maher.

Cast: Marguerite Courtot *(Jacqueline Roland)*, Helen Rowland

(Jacqueline, as child), Gus Weinberg *(her father)*, Effie Shannon *(her mother)*, Lew Cody *(Raoul Radon)*, Joseph Depew *(Raoul Radon, as a child)*, Russell Griffin *(Little Peter)*, J. Barney Sherry *(his father)*, Edmund Breese *(Edmund MacDonald)*, Edria Fisk *(his daughter)*, Sheldon Lewis *(Henri Dubois)*, Charles Fang *(Li Chang)*, Paul Panzer *(gambler)*, Taxie *(himself, a dog)*.

Melodrama. Source: James Oliver Curwood, "Jacqueline," in *Good Housekeeping Magazine* (67:39–42, Aug 1918). Jacqueline Roland, whom Raoul Radon has loved since childhood, meets Henri Dubois when she visits the city but is unresponsive to his attentions. Dubois later comes as the new boss to the lumber camp where Jacqueline lives. He is closely followed by his longtime blackmailer, Li Chang. Henri convinces Raoul that Jacqueline has transferred her affections to himself. Li Chang and Henri fight over Jacqueline and start a forest fire in the process. Raoul learns of Jacqueline's plight and searches for her unsuccessfully—she was rescued by her father—but he saves Henri for Jacqueline's sake. After thrilling efforts against the fire, Jacqueline and Raoul are reunited. *Lumbering. Quebec. Forest fires. Dogs.*

THE JADE CUP F2.2778

Gothic Productions. *Dist* Film Booking Offices of America. 30 May **1926** [c30 May 1926; LP22784]. Si; b&w. 35mm. 5 reels, 4,656 ft.

Dir Frank Hall Crane. *Cont* Ewart Adamson. *Story* Chet Withey. *Photog* Roy Klaffki. *Asst Dir* Gene Lowery.

Cast: Evelyn Brent *(Peggy Allen)*, Jack Luden *(Billy Crossan)*, Eugene Borden *(Milano the Wop)*, George Cowl *(Antoine Gerhardt)*, Charles Delaney *("Dice" Morey)*, Violet Palmer *(Poppy)*.

Mystery melodrama. Peggy Allen, a chorus girl engaged to Billy Crossan, a reformed gangster, agrees to pose for Antoine Gerhardt, a noted artist. Milano, spying on the studio, determines to steal Gerhardt's art treasures after conferring with Morey, the gang leader. In the absence of the artist, Morey robs the studio while Milano kidnaps Peggy and—to frame him—tells Billy she is at Gerhardt's; Peggy is captured after witnessing the murder of Gerhardt through an astronomical telescope. At Morey's retreat, the gang decides to do away with her; but Poppy, Morey's girl, believing her to be a rival for his affections, frees Peggy. In the ensuing chase, her car is wrecked; but the police capture the crooks, and she arrives at the studio to prove Billy's innocence. *Models. Chorus girls. Gangsters. Artists. Murder. Robbery. Telescopes. Kidnaping. Chases.*

JAKE THE PLUMBER F2.2779

R-C Pictures. *Dist* Film Booking Offices of America. 16 Oct **1927** [c16 Oct 1927; LP24637]. Si; b&w. 35mm. 6 reels, 5,186 ft.

Pres by Joseph P. Kennedy. *Dir-Story* Edward I. Luddy. *Cont* James J. Tynan. *Photog* Phillip Tannura. *Asst Dir* Bill Dagwell.

Cast: Jess Devorska *(Jake, the Plumber)*, Sharon Lynn *(Sarah Levine)*, Rosa Rosanova *(Mrs. Levine)*, Ann Brody *(Mrs. Schwartz)*, Bud Jamison *(Fogarty)*, Carol Halloway *(Mrs. Levis)*, William H. Tooker *(Mr. Levis)*, Dolores Brinkman *(Sadie Rosen)*, Eddie Harris *(Poppa Levine)*, Fanchon Frankel *(Rachael Rosenblatt)*.

Comedy-drama. Jake Schwartz, an apprentice for Fogarty, an Irish plumber, is forced to support his widowed mother on the miserly stipend of $12 a week but hopes eventually to be able to marry and support Sarah Levine, who supports *her* entire family by working in a garment factory. While on his way to work, Jake notices the careening automobile of Mrs. Sam Levis, wife of a retired manufacturer, who is subject to fainting spells; and mistaking her falling arm as an invitation to ride, he hops in the front seat; finding her unconscious, he takes the wheel and drives to his shop. Sarah, who has seen him from a streetcar, gives him the cold shoulder, plunging Jake into gloom; but Jake's mother and Mrs. Levis straighten out matters. All go as guests of Mr. Levis to the races, and when Levis' jockey is discovered drugged, Jake agrees to ride in the race, which he wins by default. Three years later, Jake is found to be happily married to Sarah and the father of two children. *Irish. Jews. Plumbers. Horseracing. Filial relations. Family life. Clothing manufacture.*

JAMESTOWN (Chronicles of America Series) F2.2780

Chronicles of America Pictures. *For* Yale University Press. *Dist* Pathé Exchange. 4 Nov **1923** [c14 May 1923; LP18970]. Si; b&w. 35mm. 4 reels.

Dir Edwin L. Hollywood. *Adapt* Roswell Dague.

Cast: Dolores Cassinelli *(Pocahontas)*, Robert Gaillard *(Sir Thomas Dale)*, Harry Kendall *(Capt. George Yeardley)*, Leslie Stowe *(The Reverend Richard Buck)*, Paul McAllister *(Don Diego de Molina)*, Leslie Austin *(John Rolfe)*.

Historical drama. Source: Mary Johnston, *Pioneers of the Old South; a Chronicle of English Colonial Beginnings* (New Haven, 1918). America's development at the time when England's control of Virginia was threatened by both the Indians and the Spanish is shown by describing Jamestown's Starving Time beginning in 1612. High Marshal Sir Thomas Dale holds Pocahontas as hostage in order to force Powhatan, her father, into joining the English colonists against the Spanish; but the marriage of John Rolfe to Pocahontas brings the groups together. *United States—History—Colonial period. Jamestown. Pocahontas. Powhatan. John Rolfe. Thomas Dale.*

JAN OF THE BIG SNOWS F2.2781

Charles M. Seay. *Dist* American Releasing Corp. 12 Mar **1922** [c17 Mar 1922; LP17654]. Si; b&w. 35mm. 5 reels, 4,531 ft.

Dir Charles M. Seay. *Copyright Author* Frederick Gage. *Photog* Eugene French, Charles E. Gilson.

Cast: Warner Richmond *(Jan Allaire)*, Louise Prussing *(Nancy Cummings)*, William Peavy *(Frederick Cummings)*, Baby Eastman Heywood *(Freddie)*, Frank Robbins *(Mukee)*, Richard Neill *(Blanding)*.

Northern melodrama. Source: James Oliver Curwood, *Honor of the Big Snows* (Indianapolis, 1911). Fred Cummings brings his young wife to an isolated northern trading post on the Hudson Bay, where she becomes the idol of the 17 inhabitants. She is particularly idolized by Jan Allaire, a young man inexperienced with women, who sees in Nancy the girl of his dreams. Blanding, a New York fur trader, arrives at the post, and his advances toward Nancy are noticed by Jan and his friends; according to their code of honor, they swear to protect her against Blanding. Nancy's husband disappears while on a trapping mission, and Jan discovers his frozen body but tells Nancy he is only injured. Blanding attempts an attack upon Nancy but is thrashed and sent from the post by Jan and his friends; forcing the truth from Jan, Nancy takes her child and returns to the United States, but Jan remains hopeful that someday she will return to him. *Trappers. Hudson Bay.*

JANE EYRE F2.2782

Hugo Ballin Productions. *Dist* W. W. Hodkinson Corp. 6 Nov **1921** [c6 Nov 1921; LP17553]. Si; b&w. 35mm. 7 reels, 6,550 ft.

Prod-Dir-Scen Hugo Ballin. *Photog* James Diamond.

Cast: Norman Trevor *(Mr. Rochester)*, Mabel Ballin *(Jane Eyre)*, Crauford Kent *(St. John Rivers)*, Emily Fitzroy *(Grace Poole, a servant)*, John Webb Dillon *(Mason, Mrs. Rochester's brother)*, Louis Grisel *(John Eyre, Jane's uncle)*, Stephen Carr *(John Reed)*, Vernie Atherton *(Miss Fairfax)*, Elizabeth Aeriens *(Mrs. Rochester)*, Harlan Knight *(Mr. Breckelhurst)*, Helen Miles *(Burns)*, Julia Hurley *(Rivers' maid)*, Sadie Mullen *(Miss Ingram)*, June Ellen Terry *(Adele, Mr. Rochester's ward)*, Florence Flagler *(Miss Mason)*, Bertha Kent *(Mr. Rochester's maid)*, Marie Shaffer *(Mrs. Reed)*.

Melodrama. Source: Charlotte Brontë, *Jane Eyre* (1847). Jane, an orphan living on the charity of her aunt, Mrs. Reed, is sent away to a school where she spends the next 10 years. To escape her depressing milieu, she obtains a position in the home of Fairfax Rochester as companion to Adele, Mr. Rochester's ward. When Rochester professes his love for Jane, she happily accepts his proposal of marriage. During the wedding ceremony, a man named Mason interrupts, declaring that Rochester has a wife who is insane and guarded in the house by Grace Poole, an alcoholic. Rochester declares that to all intents and purposes his wife has been dead for years, yet Jane leaves him and in her wanderings reaches the home of St. John Rivers, a young clergyman, who comes to love her and proposes. Meanwhile, Mrs. Rochester, escaping her keeper, sets fire to the house; in the conflagration she dies and Rochester is blinded. Jane returns to find Rochester praying for her return; a specialist restores his sight, and he is happily reunited with Jane. *Orphans. Clergymen. Wards. Alcoholism. Blindness. Bigamy. Insanity. England. Fires.*

JANGO F2.2783

Davenport Quigley Expeditions, Inc. c28 Feb **1929** [MP1039]. Si; b&w. 35mm. 9 reels.

Titl Nathan "Cy" Braunstein. *Film Ed* Nathan "Cy" Braunstein.

Personages: Dr. Daniel Davenport, Dr. Louis Neuman.

Travelog. Dr. Davenport leads an expedition in Africa. Action among the natives in West Africa, Cameroons, and the Congo are depicted through hunting episodes in which Dr. Louis Neuman of Brussels is shown killing different species for scientific purposes. Other scenes show dancing natives, the Ule and Uhangi Rivers, a medicine man casting a spell, and cannibal chiefs gathering for a hunt. When the group crossing the Sudan to

Abyssinia is caught in a sandstorm and finds the oasis dry, they must dig 22 feet to reach water. Eventually the natives and the hunter return to the river and board the boat to return to civilization. *Medicine men. Cannibals. Safaris. Ule River. Uhangi River. Sudan. Abyssinia. Cameroons. Congo. Flamingos.*

JANICE MEREDITH **F2.2784**

Cosmopolitan Pictures. *Dist* Metro-Goldwyn Distributing Corp. 8 Dec **1924** [c5 Jan 1925; LP20996]. Si; b&w. 35mm. 11 reels, 10,655 ft.

Dir E. Mason Hopper. *Adapt-Scen* Lillie Hayward. *Photog* Ira H. Morgan, George Barnes. *Sets* Joseph Urban. *Film Ed* Walter Futter. *Mus Score* Deems Taylor. *Asst Dir* E. J. Babille. *Cost* Gretl Urban Thurlow. *Wigs* Hepner. *Still Photog* Herman Zerenner.

Cast: Marion Davies *(Janice Meredith)*, Holbrook Blinn *(Lord Clowes)*, Harrison Ford *(Charles Fownes)*, Maclyn Arbuckle *(Squire Meredith)*, Hattie Delaro *(Mrs. Meredith)*, Joseph Kilgour *(George Washington)*, Mrs. Maclyn Arbuckle *(Martha Washington)*, George Nash *(Sir William Howe)*, [Frederick] Tyrone Power *(Lord Cornwallis)*, Robert Thorne *(Patrick Henry)*, Walter Law *(Gen. Charles Lee)*, Lionel Adams *(Thomas Jefferson)*, Nicolai Koesberg *(Lafayette)*, George Siegmann *(Colonel Rahl)*, W. C. Fields *(a British sergeant)*, Edwin Argus *(Louis XVI)*, Princess De Bourbon *(Marie Antoinette)*, Wilfred Noy *(Dr. Joseph Warren)*, Ken Maynard *(Paul Revere)*, Helen Lee Worthing *(Mrs. Loring)*, Spencer Charters *(Squire Hennion)*, Olin Howland *(Philemon Hennion)*, May Vokes *(Susie)*, Douglas Stevenson *(Charles Mowbray)*, Harlan Knight *(Theodore Larkin)*, Mildred Arden *(Tabitha Larkin)*, Lee Beggs *(Benjamin Franklin)*, Joe Raleigh *(Arthur Lee)*, Wilson Reynolds *(Parson McClave)*, Jerry Peterson *(Cato)*, Isadore Marcel *(inn-keeper)*, Keane Waters *(servant)*, Edgar Nelson *(tailor)*, Byron Russell *(Captain Parker)*, Colonel Patterson *(Major Pitcairn)*, George Cline *(Trooper Heirich Bruner)*, Burton McEvilly *(Alexander Hamilton)*.

Historical romance. Source: Paul Leicester Ford, *Janice Meredith, a Story of the American Revolution* (New York, c1899). Following a disappointment in love, Lord Brereton assumes the name of Charles Fownes, arranges passage to the American Colonies as a bondservant, and finds a place with Squire Meredith, a wealthy New Jersey landowner. When Charles falls in love with the squire's daughter, Janice, she is sent to live with an aunt in Boston. Janice learns of the planned British troop movement to the Lexington arsenal and gives the warning that results in Paul Revere's ride. Charles reveals his true station and becomes an aide to Washington. When he is captured by the British, Janice arranges his escape and later helps him learn the disposition of the British troops at Trenton. Janice returns to her home and agrees to marry Philemon Hennion, an aristocrat of her father's choosing. Charles and some Continental troops halt the wedding and confiscate the Meredith lands. Janice flees to Philadelphia, and Charles follows her. He is arrested but is freed when the British general, Howe, recognizes Charles as his old friend, Lord Brereton. Janice and her father retire with the British to Yorktown. During the bombardment by Washington's forces, Lord Clowes binds Janice and abducts her in his coach. Charles rescues her. With peace restored, Janice and Charles meet at Mount Vernon, where they are to be married in the presence of President Washington. *New Jersey. Boston. Mont Vernon. Philadelphia. United States—History—Revolution. George Washington. Thomas Jefferson. Benjamin Franklin. Louis XVI (France). William Howe. Charles Cornwallis. Patrick Henry. Alexander Hamilton. Charles Lee. Paul Revere. Marquis de Lafayette. Marie Antoinette.*

Note: The historical events depicted in the film include: Paul Revere's Ride; Washington Crossing the Delaware; The Boston Tea Party; Patrick Henry speaking before the Virginia House of Burgesses; The Winter at Valley Forge; The Battle of Yorktown and the Surrender of Cornwallis; The Battle of Lexington; The Battle of Trenton; The Farewell Ball for General Howe.

JASPER LANDRY'S WILL *see* **UNCLE JASPER'S WILL**

JAVA HEAD **F2.2785**

Famous Players–Lasky. *Dist* Paramount Pictures. ca28 Jan **1923** [Chicago premiere; released 25 Feb; c30 Jan 1923; LP18657]. Si; b&w. 35mm. 8 reels, 7,865 ft.

Pres by Jesse L. Lasky. *Dir* George Melford. *Adapt-Scen* Waldemar Young. *Photog* Bert Glennon.

Cast: Leatrice Joy *(Taou Yuen)*, Jacqueline Logan *(Nettie Vollar)*, Frederick Strong *(Jeremy Ammidon)*, Albert Roscoe *(Gerrit Ammidon)*, Arthur Stuart Hull *(William Ammidon)*, Rose Tapley *(Rhoda Ammidon)*, Violet Axzelle *(Laurel Ammidon)*, Audrey Berry *(Sidsall Ammidon)*, Polly Archer *(Camilla Ammidon)*, Betty Bronson *(Janet Ammidon)*, George Fawcett *(Barzil Dunsack)*, Raymond Hatton *(Edward Dunsack)*, Helen Lindroth *(Kate Vollar)*, Dan Pennell *(Broadrick)*, George Stevens, actor *(butler)*, Mimi Sherwood *(maid)*, Frances Hatton *(nurse)*.

Romantic melodrama. Source: Joseph Hergesheimer, *Java Head* (New York, 1919). Gerrit Ammidon sails for China believing that a feud between his father and Nettie Vollar's grandfather, Barzil Dunsack, has ruined any chance of his future happiness with Nettie. In Shanghai he rescues Manchu Princess Taou Yuen from a band of ruffians, then—given the choice of marriage or her death—makes her his wife. When they return to Java Head, the Ammidon family home in Salem, Massachusetts, Nettie falls ill at the news of his marriage. Gerrit is persuaded to visit Nettie, and he confesses his true love for her. Dope addict Edward Dunsack reveals this to Taou Yuen, whereupon she takes an overdose of opium and dies. Gerrit and Nettie marry and sail away. *Chinese. Feuds. Suicide. Opium. Shanghai. Salem (Massachusetts).*

JAWS OF STEEL **F2.2786**

Warner Brothers Pictures. 10 Sep **1927** [c30 Aug 1927; LP24343]. Si; b&w. 35mm. 6 reels, 5,569 ft.

Dir Ray Enright. *Scen* Charles R. Condon. *Story* Gregory Rogers. *Photog* Barney McGill. *Asst Dir* Joe Barry.

Cast: Rin-Tin-Tin *(Rinty)*, Jason Robards *(John Warren)*, Helen Ferguson *(Mary Warren)*, Mary Louise Miller *(Baby Warren)*, Jack Curtis *(Thomas Grant Taylor)*, Robert Perry *(The Sheriff)*, George Connors *(Alkali Joe)*.

Melodrama. John and Mary Warren invest their savings in a home and gold claim in a California desert town that turns out to be a "ghost town." Their puppy, Rinty, gets lost in the desert and grows up as a wild killer, hunted by the local citizens. While John is away, Taylor, the crooked promoter, tries to force his attentions on Mary, but she is saved by her husband; Taylor, hearing of John and Alkali Joe's new gold strike, goes to investigate the matter and kills Alkali Joe; and though attacked by Rinty, Taylor escapes. Rinty comforts Baby Warren when she is ill and convinces Mary that he is their lost dog, but he is injured in evading the posse. The child recovers with the return of the injured dog, who proves Taylor's guilt in the death of Joe and thus is spared from the hand of the law. *Children. Murder. Mine claims. Deserts. California. Dogs.*

THE JAZZ AGE **F2.2787**

FBO Pictures. 10 Feb **1929** [c16 Jan 1929; LP21]. Talking sequences & mus score (Photophone); b&w. 35mm. 7 reels, 6,246 ft. [Also si.]

Dir Lynn Shores. *Scen* Paul Gangelin. *Titl* Randolph Bartlett. *Camera* Ted Pahle. *Film Ed* Ann McKnight. *Asst Dir* Walter Daniels.

Cast: Douglas Fairbanks, Jr. *(Steve Maxwell)*, Marceline Day *(Sue Randall)*, H. B. Walthall *(Mr. Maxwell)*, Myrtle Stedman *(Mrs. Maxwell)*, Gertrude Messinger *(Marjorie)*, Joel McCrea *(Tod Sayles)*, William Bechtel *(Mr. Sayles)*, E. J. Ratcliffe *(Mr. Randall)*, Ione Holmes *(Ellen McBride)*, Edgar Dearing *(motor cop)*.

Melodrama. Steve Maxwell and Sue Randall, during an escapade, wreck one of her father's streetcars. Randall uses this incident to stop the elder Maxwell from opposing his illegal contract with the city. Steve tells all to the city council. When Randall threatens Steve with arrest, Sue admits her culpability and announces her intentions of marrying Steve. *Police. Jazz life. Government—Local. Fraud. Automobile accidents. Contracts. Streetcars.*

JAZZ CINDERELLA **F2.2788**

Chesterfield Motion Picture Corp. 14 Aug or 1 Sep **1930.** Sd (Photophone); b&w. 35mm. 7 reels, 6,181 ft.

Prod George R. Batcheller. *Dir* Scott Pembroke. *Dial? (see note)* Arthur Howell. *Adapt-Dial* Adrian Johnson, Scott Pembroke. *Story? (see note)* Edwin Johns, Oliver Jones. *Photog* M. A. Anderson. *Film Ed* Donn Hayes. *Songs: "You're Too Good To Be True," "Hot and Bothered Baby," "True Love"* Jesse Greer, Ray Klages.

Cast: Myrna Loy *(Mildred Vane)*, Jason Robards *(Herbert Carter)*, Nancy Welford *(Patricia Murray)*, Dorothy Phillips *(Mrs. Consuelo Carter)*, David Durand *(Danny Murray)*, Freddie Burke Frederick *(Junior Carter)*, Frank McGlynn *(Henry Murray)*, James Burtis *(Ollie)*, George Cowl *(Darrow)*, Murray Smith *(Epstein)*, William Strauss *(Fineman)*, Roland Ray *(Pierre)*, June Gittleson *(Sylvia de Sprout)*.

Society drama. Intending that her son, Herbert, marry debutante Mildred Vane, Mrs. Consuelo Carter is most dismayed when she learns that Herbert has fallen in love with Pat Murray, a model in Darrow's dress shop. Pat's emphatic refusal to take Mrs. Carter's "suggestion" that she give up Herbert leads to her being fired, and she reluctantly accepts

Herbert's invitation to weekend at the Carter country home. Finally realizing the hopelessness of the situation, Pat makes a spectacle of herself at a party; but Herbert is not fooled, and their love triumphs. *Socialites. Debutantes. Fashion models. Motherhood. Social classes. Courtship.*

Note: *Variety* varies from other sources in crediting Adrian Johnson and Arthur Howell with dialog, and Oliver Jones with story.

THE JAZZ GIRL **F2.2789**

Dist Motion Picture Guild. 15 Dec **1926.** Si; b&w. 35mm. 6 reels, 5,300 ft.

Pres by Louis T. Rogers. *Dir* Howard Mitchell. *Story* Bruce Truman. *Photog* Ernest Miller.

Cast: Gaston Glass *(Rodney Blake)*, Edith Roberts *(Janet Marsh)*, Howard Truesdale *(John Marsh)*, Murdock MacQuarrie *(Henry Wade)*, Coit Albertson *(Frank Arnold)*, Ernie Adams *(detective)*, Sabel Johnson *(Big Bertha)*, Dick Sutherland *(The Chef)*, Lea Delworth *(Sadie Soakum)*.

Society drama. The "tale of a girl tired of modern society turning amateur detective to catch rum runners, and meeting a reporter sent out for a story on the same thing, ... each believing the other to be in the liquor traffic. The boss runner himself stands between the two." (*Variety*, 15 Jun 1927, p25.) *Rumrunners. Reporters. Detectives.*

JAZZ HEAVEN **F2.2790**

RKO Productions. 3 Nov **1929** [c20 Oct 1929; LP865, LP901]. Sd (Photophone); b&w. 35mm. 7 reels, 6,372 ft. [Also si.]

Supv Myles Connolly. *Dir* Melville Brown. *Screenplay-Dial* Cyrus Wood, J. Walter Ruben. *Story* Pauline Forney, Dudley Murphy. *Photog* Jack MacKenzie. *Film Ed* Ann McKnight, George Marsh. *Song: "Someone"* Oscar Levant, Sidney Clare.

Cast: John Mack Brown *(Barry Holmes)*, Sally O'Neil *(Ruth Morgan)*, Clyde Cook *(Max Langley)*, Blanche Frederici *(Mrs. Langley)*, Joseph Cawthorn *(Herman Kemple)*, Albert Conti *(Walter Klucke)*, J. Barney Sherry *(John Parker)*, Adele Watson *(Miss Dunn)*, Ole M. Ness *(Professor Rowland)*, Henry Armetta *(Tony)*.

Comedy-drama. Barry Holmes, a song writer who lives in a New York boardinghouse, is struggling day and night to finish a new song, and his neighbor, Ruth Morgan, who works in a music publishing house, agrees to help him with it. Mr. Langley, their landlord, finding them together in Barry's room, orders them to vacate the premises, threatening to keep the piano as payment for back rent, though his son Max offers to help them rescue the instrument. Music publishers Kemple and Klucke agree to take the song if the lyrics are good, but Barry is in despair when the piano is accidentally wrecked. Max gives them entry to the piano factory at night, and unsuspectingly they broadcast the song and become an overnight success. Parker, the radio station owner, finally finds Ruth, who auctions off the song, with Klucke's firm closing the sale, and the lovers are happily united. *Composers. Publishers. Landlords. Pianos. Boardinghouses. Radio. New York City.*

THE JAZZ HOUNDS **F2.2791**

Reol Productions. **1922.** Si; b&w. 35mm. [Feature length assumed.]

Comedy(?). No information about the precise nature of this film has been found. *Jazz life. Negro life.*

Note: Indicated year is approximate.

JAZZ MAD (Universal-Jewel) **F2.2792**

Universal Pictures. 18 Nov **1928** [c25 Jan 1928; LP24918]. Si; b&w. 35mm. 7 reels, 6,032 ft.

Dir F. Harmon Weight. *Adapt-Cont* Charles Kenyon. *Titl* Walter Anthony. *Story* Svend Gade. *Photog* Gilbert Warrenton. *Film Ed* Edward Cahn.

Cast: Jean Hersholt *(Franz Hausmann)*, Marion Nixon *(Elsa Hausmann)*, George Lewis *(Leopold Ostberg)*, Roscoe Karns *(Sol Levy)*, Torben Meyer *(Kline)*, Andrew Arbuckle *(Schmidt)*, Charles Clary *(Mr. Ostberg)*, Clarissa Selwynne *(Mrs. Ostberg)*, Patricia Caron *(Miss Ostberg)*, Alfred Hertz *(conductor of symphony)*, Hollywood Bowl Symphony Orchestra.

Society drama. Elsa Hausmann would like to marry her suitor, Leo Ostberg, but she hesitates because her father, a European orchestra conductor, is unable to sell his music. Hoping to free his daughter to marry, Hausmann takes a job in vaudeville directing a "comedy symphony." Leo's father meets Hausmann at a social gathering shortly after seeing his act and insists that Leo break his engagement. Hausmann develops a nervous disorder under the strain of his misfortune, and his physicians decide that a severe shock will restore his mental balance. Elsa and Levy, a vaudeville booking agent, arrange for an orchestra to play his symphony in a great open-air theater. When Hausmann hears the strains of his own symphony, he staggers to his feet and rushes to the stage. He is introduced by the leader as the composer. Hausmann directs the orchestra through the remainder of the symphony, thus ensuring his own success and his daughter's happiness. *Composers. Orchestra conductors. Booking agents. Filial relations. Neurosis. Vaudeville. Jazz.*

Note: Released also as *The Symphony.*

THE JAZZ SINGER **F2.2793**

Warner Brothers Pictures. 6 Oct **1927** [New York premiere; released 4 Feb 1928; c6 Oct 1927; LP24505]. Talking sequences, mus score, & sd eff (Vitaphone); b&w. 35mm. 9 reels, 8,117 ft. [Also si.]

Dir Alan Crosland. *Scen* Al Cohn. *Titl* Jack Jarmuth. *Photog* Hal Mohr. *Film Ed* Harold McCord. *Song: "Mammy"* Sam Lewis, Joe Young, Walter Davidson. *Song: "Toot Toot Tootsie, Goodbye"* Gus Kahn, Ernie Erdman, Dan Russo. *Song: "Dirty Hands, Dirty Face"* Edgar Leslie, Grant Clarke, Al Jolson, Jimmy Monaco. *Song: "Blue Skies"* Irving Berlin. *Song: "Mother, I Still Have You"* Al Jolson, Louis Silvers. *Sd* George R. Groves. *Asst Dir* Gordon Hollingshead.

Cast: Al Jolson *(Jakie Rabinowitz/Jack Robin)*, May McAvoy *(Mary Dale)*, Warner Oland *(Cantor Rabinowitz)*, Eugenie Besserer *(Sara Rabinowitz)*, Bobby Gordon *(Jakie, 13 years old)*, Otto Lederer *(Moisha Yudelson)*, Cantor Josef Rosenblatt *(himself)*, Richard Tucker *(Harry Lee)*, Nat Carr *(Levi)*, William Demarest *(Buster Billings)*, Anders Randolf *(Dillings)*, Will Walling *(doctor)*, Roscoe Karns *(The Agent)*, Myrna Loy *(chorus girl)*.

Melodrama. Source: Samson Raphaelson, *The Jazz Singer* (New York, 1925). In the Jewish ghetto of New York City, Jakie Rabinowitz, son of an orthodox Jewish cantor, at 13 sings the Kol Nidre as appealingly as his father, and though his father's ambition is that his son succeed him, Jakie aspires to a theatrical career. When Jakie sings ragtime melodies at a beer garden on Yom Kippur, he is punished by his father, and as a result he runs away from home. Ten years later, as a mammy singer in San Francisco, Jack Robin makes an impression on Mary Dale, a theatrical dancer, whose sponsorship promotes his rise to fame. Returning to New York, Jack visits his mother and sings a jazzy song for her, bringing down the wrath of his father, who banishes him from the family. On the eve of his Broadway debut, which is also the eve of Yom Kippur, Jack learns his father is ill and cannot sing the Kol Nidre, and his Mama persuades him to cancel the show and come to the synagogue. He is forgiven, resumes his career on Broadway, and wins the love of Mary. *Jews. Cantors. Singers. Dancers. Family life. Motherhood. Jazz. Yom Kippur. New York City—Broadway. San Francisco.*

Note: Al Jolson also sings the Jewish chant "Kol Nidrei." Background music includes "The Sidewalks of New York," "My Gal Sal," "In the Good Old Summer Time," "Waiting for the Robert E. Lee," and "If a Girl Like You Loved a Boy Like Me."

JAZZLAND **F2.2794**

A. Carlos. *Dist* Quality Distributing Corp. 1 Dec **1928.** Si; b&w. 35mm. 6 reels, 5,700 ft.

Dir Dallas M. Fitzgerald. *Scen* Ada McQuillan. *Titl* Tom Miranda. *Story* Samuel Merwin. *Photog* Faxon Dean, Lauren A. Draper. *Film Ed* George McGuire.

Cast: Bryant Washburn *(Ernest Hallam)*, Vera Reynolds *(Stella Baggott)*, Carroll Nye *(Homer Pew)*, Forrest Stanley *(Hamilton Pew)*, Virginia Lee Corbin *(Martha Baggott)*, Violet Bird *(Kitty Pew)*, Carl Stockdale *(Joe Bitner)*, Edward Cecil *(Wilbraham)*, George Raph *(Nedick)*, Nicholas Caruso *(Jackson)*, Florence Turner *(Mrs. Baggott)*, Richard Belfield *(Mr. Baggott)*.

Drama. Fighting the invasion of their small New England town by a big city–type nightclub, the Jazzland, a young newspaperman and his brother endeavor to learn the identity of the club's owner—suspecting him to be the head of the town council. The heroine's younger sister gets involved with some nightclub ruffians, and the brother is murdered at the Jazzland, but the hero finally uncovers the criminal. *Reporters. Sisters. Brothers. Smalltown life. Nightclubs. Murder. Government—Local. Jazz life. New England.*

JAZZMANIA **F2.2795**

Tiffany Productions. *Dist* Metro Pictures. 12 Feb **1923** [c6 Mar 1923; LP18762]. Si; b&w. 35mm. 8 reels, 8,765 ft.

Pres by Robert Z. Leonard. *Dir* Robert Z. Leonard. *Titl* Alfred A.

Cohn. *Story-Adapt* Edmund Goulding. *Photog* Oliver T. Marsh. *Set Dsgn* Cedric Gibbons.

Cast: Mae Murray *(Ninon)*, Rod La Rocque *(Jerry Langdon)*, Robert Frazer *(Captain Valmar)*, Edward Burns *(Sonny Daimler)*, Jean Hersholt *(Prince Otto of Como)*, Lionel Belmore *(Baron Bolo)*, Herbert Standing *(Josephus Ranson)*, Mrs. J. Farrell MacDonald *(Marline)*, Wilfred Lucas *(Julius Furman, American capitalist)*, J. Herbert Frank *(Colonel Kerr)*, Carl Harbaugh *(Gavona)*, Harry Northrup *(American capitalist)*, Thomas Guise *(General Muroff)*, Henry Barrows *(August Daimler)*.

Melodrama. Queen Ninon of the Balkan country Jazzmania refuses to marry Prince Otto, who starts a revolution in retaliation. Persuaded by American newspaperman Sonny Daimler to abdicate and leave the country, she flies to Monte Carlo, where she meets Jerry Langdon, and then on to the United States. Ninon's love for jazz occupies her for a time, but she returns to her troubled country, quiets the revolution, establishes a republic, and marries Jerry Langdon. *Royalty. Reporters. Imaginary kingdoms. Jazz life. Airplanes. Monte Carlo. Balkans.*

JEALOUS HUSBANDS **F2.2796**

Maurice Tourneur Productions. *Dist* Associated First National Pictures. 12 Nov **1923** [c14 Nov 1923; LP19606]. Si; b&w. 35mm. 7 reels, 6,500 ft.

Pres by M. C. Levee. *Dir* Maurice Tourneur. *Story-Scen* Fred Kennedy Myton. *Photog* Scott R. Beal.

Cast: Earle Williams *(Ramón Martínez)*, Jane Novak *(Alice Martínez)*, Ben Alexander *(Bobbie, later called Spud)*, Don Marion *(Sliver)*, George Siegmann *("Red" Lynch)*, Emily Fitzroy *(Amaryllis)*, Bull Montana *("Portland Kid")*, J. Gunnis Davis *("Sniffer Charlie")*, Carl Miller *(Harvey Clegg)*, Wedgewood Nowell *(George Conrad)*, Carmelita Geraghty *(Carmen Inez)*.

Melodrama. Believing his wife, Alice, has been unfaithful, jealous husband Ramón Martínez condemns her and gives away their son, Bobbie, to some Gypsies. Alice is merely trying to protect Ramon's sister, Carmen, who is being blackmailed by a former lover, Harvey Clegg. Ramón and Alice separate; Carmen drowns in a shipwreck; but Bobbie, called Spud by the Gypsies, returns to prove his mother's innocence and thereby reunite his family. *Gypsies. Children. Fatherhood. Brother-sister relationship. Jealousy. Infidelity. Blackmail.*

JEALOUSY **F2.2797**

Paramount Famous Lasky Corp. 13 Sep **1929** [New York premiere; released 28 Sep; c27 Sep 1929; LP723]. Sd (Photophone); b&w. 35mm. 7 reels, 6,107 ft.

Dir Jean De Limur. *Screenplay* Eugene Walter. *Dial* John D. Williams. *Adapt* Garrett Fort. *Story* Louis Verneuil. *Photog* Alfred Gilks. *Art Dir* William N. Saulter. *Set Dsgn* Charles Kirk. *Wardrobe* H. M. K. Smith.

Cast: Jeanne Eagels *(Yvonne)*, Fredric March *(Pierre)*, Halliwell Hobbes *(Rigaud)*, Blanche Le Clair *(Renée)*, Henry Daniel *(Clément)*, Hilda Moore *(Charlotte)*, Carlotta Coerr *(Louise)*, Granville Bates *(lawyer)*, Virginia Chauvernet *(maid)*.

Domestic melodrama. Yvonne, proprietor of a Paris gown shop, marries Pierre, a poor artist, concealing from him an affair she had with Rigaud, an elderly boulevardier who bought the shop for her. Encountering financial difficulties, Yvonne goes to Rigaud for aid and finds him murdered. Pierre confesses to the murder, thereby exonerating Clément, an innocent man, suspected of killing Rigaud, whose sweetheart Rigaud wronged. Pierre submits to arrest, confident that he will get off with a light sentence. *Modistes. Artists. Mistresses. Men-about-town. Murder. Jealousy. Paris.*

JESSE JAMES **F2.2798**

Paramount Famous Lasky Corp. 15 Oct **1927** [c22 Oct 1927; LP24572]. Si; b&w. 35mm. 8 reels, 8,656 ft.

Pres by Adolph Zukor, Jesse L. Lasky. *Supv* Alfred L. Werker. *Dir* Lloyd Ingraham. *Story-Scen* Frank M. Clifton. *Photog* Allen Siegler. *Biographer–Tech Adv* Jesse James, Jr.

Cast: Fred Thomson *(Jesse James)*, Nora Lane *(Zerelda Mimms [Slade?])*, Montagu Love *(Frederick Mimms [Slade?])*, Mary Carr *(Mrs. Zerelda Samuels)*, James Pierce *(Frank James)*, Harry Woods *(Bob Ford)*, William Courtright *(Parson Bill)*, Silver King *(himself, a horse)*.

Biographical melodrama. Jesse James, a member of Quantrill's Partisan Rangers during the Civil War, meets Zerelda Mimms, a northern girl marooned on her uncle's southern plantation, and is saved from capture as a spy. After the war, Jesse is warned by his friend Parson Bill that his mother has been maimed by fanatic Union sympathizers and is threatened by Frederick Mimms with expulsion from the town. Jesse is about to wreak vengeance on Mimms when his daughter's screams bring help; he flees in a spectacular manner and becomes notorious as an outlaw bandit. Citzens attempt to trap him into surrender with the aid of Bob Ford, who betrays him for love of Zerelda, but Jesse escapes with Zerelda on his horse, Silver King, and forces Parson Bill to marry them in a stagecoach. *Outlaws. Revenge. United States—History—Civil War. Kansas. Missouri. Jesse Woodson James. Quantrill's Raiders. Horses.*

Note: Some sources substitute the name Slade for Mimms in the cast rendering.

JESSE JAMES AS THE OUTLAW **F2.2799**

Mesco Pictures. c2 Mar, 13 Apr **1921** [LP16405]. Si; b&w. 35mm. [Feature length assumed.]

Dir Franklin B. Coates. *Set Dsgn* Edgar Kellar.

Cast: Jesse James, Jr. *(himself/Jesse James)*, Diana Reed, Marguerite Hungerford.

Historical western melodrama. Robert Standing finishes Book I of Franklin B. Coates's life of Jesse James and assures Jesse James, Jr., that he still wishes to marry the latter's daughter, Lucille; and Mr. James persuades Robert to read Book II before he decides. ... *Returning home to Missouri after the war, determined to live a peaceful life, Jesse almost immediately finds it necessary to leave his friends in order to escape the Home Guards, who believe Jesse to be responsible for a bank robbery. And thus begins Jesse James's career as an outlaw; finding it impossible to live as a peaceful citizen with Zee, the woman he loves, he must dodge and battle the Home Guards and other posses, even to perform acts of kindness. Branded as an outlaw, he lives like one; and the maiming of members of his family by his pursuers forces Jesse to seek "a life for a life." Many of Jesse's exploits for good and evil are detailed, and it is revealed that some crimes attributed to him were actually committed by others. Finally, Jesse is assassinated by his friend Bob Ford.* Robert's devotion to Lucille is only increased by this story, and their future happiness receives the blessing of Jesse James, Jr. *Outlaws. Revenge. Murder. Robbery. Jesse Woodson James. Missouri. Texas. Minnesota.*

Note: A sequel to *Jesse James Under the Black Flag*, q.v.

JESSE JAMES UNDER THE BLACK FLAG **F2.2800**

Mesco Pictures. c2 Mar, 13 Apr **1921** [LU16406]. Si; b&w. 35mm. 8 reels, 7,521 ft.

Dir Franklin B. Coates. *Set Dsgn* Edgar Kellar.

Cast: Jesse James, Jr. *(himself/Jesse James)*, Diana Reed, Marguerite Hungerford, Franklin B. Coates *(himself)*.

Historical western melodrama. While Mr. Coates discusses his book with Jesse James, Jr., James's daughter, Lucille, briefly encounters young eastern millionaire Robert Standing, who has landed his airplane in a nearby field to get his bearings. It is love at first sight, and Robert tries for many months to learn the girl's name—despite his mother's objections. Finally succeeding, Robert visits Mr. James, who gives the young man Coates's book. Robert (and the audience) thus learns the story of Jesse James (Sr.), beginning in 1863, when he was a boy on the family farm near Kearney, Missouri. *Desiring revenge on the soldiers who mistreat his family, Jesse joins Quantrill's Missouri Guerillas and swears allegiance to their Black Flag. Because of a serious wound, Jesse is separated from the Guerillas and is thus prevented from surrendering with them after the war. But Jesse does receive the kind hospitality of Judge Bowman and the love of the woman he calls Zee, with whom he hopes to spend a peaceful future.* Robert now understands Lucille's reluctance to declare herself. *Outlaws. Jesse Woodson James. United States—History—Civil War. William Clarke Quantrill. Missouri. Kansas.*

Note: This story is continued in a sequel, *Jesse James as the Outlaw*, q. v.

JESUS OF NAZARETH **F2.2801**

Ideal Pictures. c15 Mar **1928** [LP25067]. Si; b&w. 35mm. 6 reels, 5,700 ft.

Ed-Titl Jean Conover.

Cast: Philip Van Loan *(The Christ)*, Anna Lehr *(Mary, His Mother)*, Charles McCaffrey *(Pontius Pilate)*.

Religious film. The life of the Christ is depicted with scenes of Mary and Joseph's arrival in Bethlehem; the birth of Jesus; the Wise Men coming from the East; Herod's order to his soldiers to kill all children under 3 years of age; the flight into Egypt; the return to Nazareth; Jesus at 12 instructing His elders in the Temple, later working as a carpenter, preaching His parables on the mountainside, giving sight to the blind, and praying for strength in the Garden of Gethsemane; the betrayal by Judas; Jesus before Pilate; Jesus scourged; the Crucifixion; the empty tomb; and the Ascension. *Judea. Jesus. Herod the Great. Pontius Pilate. Judas Iscariot.*

THE JEW *see* **HIS PEOPLE**

JEWELS OF DESIRE **F2.2802**

Metropolitan Pictures Corp. of California. *Dist* Producers Distributing Corp. 3 Jan **1927** [c20 Dec 1926; LP23451]. Si; b&w. 35mm. 6 reels, 5,427 ft.

Pres by John C. Flinn. *Dir* Paul Powell. *Adapt* Anthony Coldewey. *Photog* Georges Benoit. *Art Dir* Charles Cadwallader. *Asst Dir* Ed Bernoudy. *Prod Mgr* Bert Gilroy.

Cast: Priscilla Dean *(Margarita Solano)*, John Bowers *(Maclyn Mills)*, Walter Long *(Pedro)*, Luke Cosgrave *(Captain Blunt)*, Syd Crossley *(taxi driver)*, Ernie Adams *(The Rat)*, Raymond Wells *(Spanish Joe)*, Marie Percivale *(old Indian woman)*.

Romantic melodrama. Suggested by: Agnes Parsons, "Jewels of Desire" (publication undetermined). Margarita Solano inherits a large Spanish estate, which she finds in a state of disrepair. An old Indian servant gives her a casket in which she finds an ancient Spanish map, which Margarita and Captain Blunt examine. Maclyn Mills, an attorney, serves a summons on Margarita to foreclose a mortgage on the property, and with his help they embark on a search for a buried treasure indicated on the map. Pedro and his confederates, Spanish Joe and The Rat, steal the map, find the treasure, and kidnap Mills and Blunt; but Margarita rescues them and outwits Pedro. She is forced, however, to jump from a precipice, but is rescued from the sea by Mills. The bandits are brought to justice, and Margarita and Mills decide to share the treasure as husband and wife. *Lawyers. Inheritance. Treasure. Kidnaping. Mortgages. Documentation.*

JEWISH LIFE IN SOVIET RUSSIA *see* **FROM DEATH TO LIFE, JEWISH LIFE IN SOVIET RUSSIA**

THE JILT **F2.2803**

Universal Film Manufacturing Co. 13 Nov **1922** [New York premiere; released 26 Nov; c31 Oct 1922; LP18366]. Si; b&w. 35mm. 5 reels.

Pres by Carl Laemmle. *Dir* Irving Cummings. *Scen* Arthur Statter. *Story* R. Ramsey. *Photog* William Marshall.

Cast: Marguerite De La Motte *(Rose Trenton)*, Ralph Graves *(Sandy Sanderson)*, Matt Moore *(George Prothero)*, Ben Hewlett *(his secretary)*, Harry De Vere *(Rose's father)*, Eleanor Hancock *(her mother)*.

Drama. Mistaking pity for love, Rose Trenton agrees to marry George Prothero, who was blinded in the war. She breaks the engagement, however, when she realizes she loves Sandy Sanderson, and George goes to Europe. Upon his return George and Sandy go for a ride, and George returns alone with the explanation that Sandy was killed by an assailant and he (George) was unable to help. The next day Rose receives, in reply to her letter to a French eye specialist, a report that George was cured sometime ago. Sandy rushes in and describes George's attack on him; George confesses and leaves in disgrace. *Veterans. Blindness. Jealousy. Mendacity.*

Note: Working title: *Exiled.*

JIM THE CONQUEROR **F2.2804**

Metropolitan Pictures Corp. of California. *Dist* Producers Distributing Corp. 3 Jan **1927** [c27 Dec 1926; LP23510]. Si; b&w. 35mm. 6 reels, 5,324 ft.

Pres by John C. Flinn. *Dir* George B. Seitz. *Screenplay* Will M. Ritchey. *Photog* Hal Rosson. *Art Dir* Charles Cadwallader.

Cast: William Boyd *(Jim Burgess)*, Elinor Fair *(Polly Graydon)*, Walter Long *(Hank Milford)*, Tully Marshall *(Dave Mahler)*, Tom Santschi *(Sam Black)*, Marcelle Corday *(Judy)*.

Western melodrama. Source: Peter Bernard Kyne, *Jim the Conqueror* (New York, 1929). "After fleeting glimpses of the girl in Italy and New York, Jim is called home to take up the feud with the cattlemen and finds the girl owns one of the ranches. She turns on him but warns him of attempts against his life and he outwits a lynching party landing his enemies in jail. Thrilling western with exceptionally tense suspense." (*Moving Picture World,* 1 Jan 1927, p53.) *Ranchers. Cattlemen. Feuds. Courtship. Lynching. Italy. New York City.*

JIM THE PENMAN **F2.2805**

Whitman Bennett Productions. *Dist* Associated First National Pictures. Apr **1921** [c21 Mar, 5 Apr 1921; LP16298, LP16355]. Si; b&w. 35mm. 6 reels, 6,100 ft.

Prod Whitman Bennett. *Dir* Kenneth Webb. *Scen* Dorothy Farnum. *Photog* T. L. Griffith, Harry Stradling.

Cast: Lionel Barrymore *(James Ralston)*, Doris Rankin *(Nina Bronson)*, Anders Randolf *(Baron Hartfeld)*, Douglas MacPherson *(Louis Percival)*, Gladys Leslie *(Agnes Ralston)*, Charles Coghlan *(Captain Redwood)*, James Laffey *(E. J. Smith)*, Ned Burton *(Enoch Bronson)*, Arthur Rankin *(Lord Drelincourt)*.

Crook melodrama. Source: Charles Lawrence Young, *Jim the Penman; a Romance of Modern Society in Four Acts* (New York opening: 1 Nov 1886). In order to save Enoch Bronson, the father of the woman he loves, from financial ruin, bank cashier Jim Ralston forges a check in the name of Baron Hartfeld, who, on discovering the fraud, promises Jim immunity in return for aiding his gang of swindlers. Jim's love for Nina provokes forged letters breaking off her match with Percival and permits his marriage and subsequent rise to wealth. In a scheme to ruin Percival, Jim is exposed and accused by his wife. In remorse, he traps the baron and the gang in a yacht, sinks the boat, and dies with them. *Bank clerks. Swindlers. Forgery. Marriage.*

JIMMIE'S MILLIONS **F2.2806**

Carlos Productions. *Dist* Film Booking Offices of America. 1 Mar **1925** [c19 Feb 1925; LP21174]. Si; b&w. 35mm. 6 reels, 5,167 ft.

Pres by A. Carlos. *Dir* James P. Hogan. *Cont* Frank Howard Clark. *Story* John Moroso. *Photog* William Marshall. *Film Ed* Doane Harrison.

Cast: Richard Talmadge *(Jimmie Wicherly)*, Betty Francisco *(Susan Jane Montague)*, Charles Clary *(Luther Ball)*, Brinsley Shaw *(John Saunders)*, Dick Sutherland *(William Johnson)*, Ina Anson *(Patience Delavan)*, Lee Moran *(Speck Donnelly)*, Wade Boteler *(Mickey Flannagan)*.

Melodrama. Jimmie Wicherley, who is always late for everything, finds out that he will inherit his uncle's millions on the condition that, for a period of 3 months, he report to his uncle's lawyer promptly on time on a certain day each month. If Jimmie does not meet this condition, Saunders, another of his uncle's nephews, will inherit the fortune. Jimmie later has a fight with a truckdriver named Johnson and knocks him to the ground, where he remains, out cold. Saunders then bribes Johnson to disappear, and Jimmie is arrested for his "murder." A friend springs Jimmie from jail, and Jimmie captures Johnson and brings him before a judge. The case against Jimmie is dismissed, but he believes the fortune to be lost to him for not reporting to the lawyer while in jail. The lawyer, however, informs Jimmie that, being clearly the victim of circumstance, he will still inherit the fortune. Jimmie also wins the hand of the lawyer's ward, Susan. *Millionaires. Uncles. Truckdrivers. Lawyers. Inheritance. Punctuality. Bribery.*

Note: Known also as *Jimmy's Millions.*

JIMMY'S MILLIONS *see* **JIMMIE'S MILLIONS**

JOAN OF FLANDERS (Reissue) **F2.2807**

Dist Veterans Film Service. 1 Jan **1926.** Si; b&w. 35mm. 8 reels, 7,409 ft.

Note: Formerly titled *War Brides* and released by Selznick in 1916.

JOANNA **F2.2808**

Edwin Carewe Productions. *Dist* First National Pictures. ca6 Dec **1925** [New York premiere; released 13 or 27 Dec 1925; LP22084]. Si; b&w. 35mm. 8 reels, 7,762 ft.

Pres by Edwin Carewe. *Dir* Edwin Carewe. *Scen* Lois Leeson. *Photog* Robert B. Kurrle. *Adtl Photog* Al M. Greene. *Art Dir* John D. Schulze. *Film Ed* Edward McDermott. *Asst Dir* Wallace Fox.

Cast: Dorothy Mackaill *(Joanna Manners)*, Jack Mulhall *(John Wilmore)*, Paul Nicholson *(Frank Brandon)*, George Fawcett *(Anthony Eggleson)*, John T. Murray *(Lord Teddy Dorminster)*, Rita Carewe *(Georgie Leach)*, Dolores Del Rio *(Carlotta de Silva)*, Lillian Langdon *(Mrs. Roxanna Adams)*, Edwards Davis *(Grayson)*, Bob Hart *(The Chauffeur)*.

Society melodrama. Source: Henry Leyford Gates, *Joanna, of the Skirts Too Short and the Lips Too Red and the Tongue Too Pert* (New York, 1926). Joanna Manners, who works at James Grayson's exclusive woman's shop, comes into a mysterious legacy of $1 million. Her sudden wealth attracts the attentions of Frank Brandon, the bank president's nephew, and alienates the affections of her fiancé, architect John Wilmore. Through Brandon and Anthony Eggleson, who has charge of her financial affairs, she is introduced to Carlotta de Silva, a woman of the world in love with Brandon, and Carlotta helps Joanna lead a life of luxury and indulgence.

Joanna quarrels with John and goes abroad for 10 months, returning with a "heavy" reputation. In a fight to protect her honor she nearly kills Brandon. Later, after a vain attempt to get her old job back, she learns that she has been a pawn in a bet between Eggleson and Greyson of $1 million on her chastity. Eggleson adopts her, and she is reunited with John. *Architects. Wealth. Inheritance. Reputation. Wagers. Adoption.*

JOHN SMITH **F2.2809**

Selznick Pictures. *Dist* Select Pictures. 10 Jun **1922** [c30 May 1922; LP17947]. Si; b&w. 35mm. 6 reels, 6,000 ft.

Pres by Lewis J. Selznick. *Story-Dir* Victor Heerman. *Scen* Lewis Allen Browne. *Photog* Jules Cronjager.

Cast: Eugene O'Brien *(John Smith)*, Viva Ogden *(cook)*, W. J. Ferguson *(butler)*, Tammany Young *(chauffeur)*, Estar Banks *(Mrs. Lang)*, Frankie Mann *(maid)*, Mary Astor *(Irene Mason)*, George Fawcett *(Haynes)*, J. Barney Sherry *(Martin Lang)*, John Butler *(crook)*, Walter Greene *(district attorney)*, Warren Cook *(doctor)*, Henry Sedley *(lawyer)*, Daniel Haynes *(gangster)*.

Comedy-drama. John Smith, after unjustly serving a prison term, is discharged, and under the name of Hilliard he obtains a position with Martin Lang, who sends him to smooth out his domestic affairs. Smith is received coldly by Mrs. Lang and the servants, but his likable personality wins them over and peace is restored in the house. When he is made treasurer of a local charity organization, some of his former associates try to blackmail him into splitting the money; and when the funds are stolen and the chauffeur is murdered, he refuses to talk and is arrested. At the trial, Haynes, his probation officer, produces the real criminals, thus exonerating him without revealing his past. Haynes, realizing that Hilliard/Smith is in love with Mrs. Lang's secretary, destroys all records pertaining to John Smith and informs Hilliard that John Smith is dead. *Injustice. Blackmail. Theft. Trials. Charitable organizations. Documentation.*

JOHNNY BUFF–PANCHO VILLA BOXING EXHIBITION *see* **OFFICIAL MOTION PICTURES OF THE JOHNNY BUFF–PANCHO VILLA BOXING EXHIBITION HELD AT EBBET'S FIELD, BROOKLYN, N. Y., SEPTEMBER 14, 1922**

JOHNNY GET YOUR HAIR CUT **F2.2810**

Metro-Goldwyn-Mayer Pictures. 15 Jan **1927** [c21 Mar 1927; LP23770]. Si; b&w. 35mm. 7 reels, 6,781 ft.

Supv Jack Coogan, Sr. *Dir* B. Reeves Eason, Archie Mayo. *Scen* Florence Ryerson. *Titl* Ralph Spence. *Story* Gerald Beaumont. *Photog* Frank Good. *Film Ed* Sam S. Zimbalist.

Cast: Mattie Witting *(Mother Slap)*, Maurice Costello *(Baxter Ryan)*, Pat Hartigan *(Jiggs Bradley)*, James Corrigan *(Pop Slocum)*, Bobby Doyle *(Bobby Dolin)*, Knute Erickson *(Whip Evans)*, Jackie Coogan *(Johnny O'Day)*.

Comedy-drama. Johnny O'Day, an orphan practically reared with horses, saves the young daughter of horseowner Pop Ryan. As a result, he is allowed to ride under the owner's colors in a race, which he wins. *Orphans. Jockeys. Horseracing.*

JOHNNY RING AND THE CAPTAIN'S SWORD **F2.2811**

Temple Productions. 28 Aug **1921** [c13 Oct 1921; LU17088]. Si; b&w. 35mm. 5 reels.

Dir Norman L. Stevens. *Story* Russell H. Conwell. *Photog* Harry L. Keepers, Charles E. Gilson.

Cast: Ben Warren *(Russell H. Conwell)*, Frank Walker *(Johnny Ring)*.

Religious drama. The fellow townsmen of Russell Conwell, an infantry captain of the Union Army during the Civil War, present him with a handsome sword, which becomes an object of special care to Johnny Ring, an earnest, Christian youth who is the captain's orderly. In camp, Conwell, an atheist, refuses to allow the boy to read the Bible; nevertheless, Johnny prays for the captain's conversion. During a surprise attack, Johnny, saving the sword, is wounded and dies. Conwell is promoted to colonel, and later he is wounded and left for dead in the Battle of Kennesaw Mountain; in the pain and agony of recovery, he vows that if God spares his life he will accomplish the work of two men—for Johnny Ring, and for himself. (The story is said to be based on the true experiences of a Philadelphia minister.) *Orderlies. Atheism. Religious conversion. Christianity. Swords. United States—History—Civil War. Kennesaw Mountain.*

THE JOHNSTOWN FLOOD **F2.2812**

Fox Film Corp. 28 Feb **1926** [c28 Feb 1926; LP22511]. Si; b&w. 35mm. 6 reels, 6,357 ft.

Pres by William Fox. *Dir* Irving Cummings. *Story-Scen* Edfrid Bingham, Robert Lord. *Photog* George Schneiderman. *Asst Dir* Charles Woolstenhulme.

Cast: George O'Brien *(Tom O'Day)*, Florence Gilbert *(Gloria Hamilton)*, Janet Gaynor *(Ann Burger)*, Anders Randolf *(John Hamilton)*, Paul Nicholson *(Peyton Ward)*, Paul Panzer *(Joe Burger)*, George Harris *(Sidney Mandel)*, Max Davidson *(David Mandel)*, Walter Perry *(Pat O'Day)*, Sid Jordan *(Mullins)*.

Epic melodrama. Engineer Tom O'Day warns John Hamilton, a logging-camp owner, that the dam above the town of Johnstown is being weakened by the impounding of water for floating logs. Hamilton refuses, however, to heed the warning. Tom, who is in love with Gloria, Hamilton's daughter, plans to marry her while Hamilton is absent in Pittsburgh. When the dam bursts, the town is destroyed and countless lives are lost. Anna Burger, a workman's daughter, rides through the valley to warn the people; and although she is drowned, Tom and Gloria escape from the flooded church. *Engineers. Lumbering. Dams. Johnstown (Pennsylvania). Floods.*

THE JOLT **F2.2813**

Fox Film Corp. 20 Nov **1921** [c20 Nov 1921; LP17289]. Si; b&w. 35mm. 5 reels, 4,800 ft.

Pres by William Fox. *Dir* George E. Marshall. *Scen* Jack Strumwasser. *Story* George E. Marshall, Jack Strumwasser. *Photog* Jack MacKenzie.

Cast: Edna Murphy *(Georgette)*, Johnnie Walker *(Johnnie Stanton)*, Raymond McKee *(Terence Nolan)*, Albert Prisco *(Jerry Limur)*, Anderson Smith *(Colonel Anderson)*, Wilson Hummell *(Georgette's father)*, Lule Warrenton *(Georgette's mother)*.

Melodrama. While overseas with the A. E. F., Pvt. Johnnie Stanton marries Georgette, a French girl, and he takes her home to settle in a New York City flat. Johnnie is concerned lest his pal, Jerry Limur, member of a gang with which he was associated, reveal his past, but Jerry agrees to remain silent. Johnnie is unable to obtain employment, however, and collectors threaten his wife with foreclosure; but Jerry assures Georgette that he has a job for her husband. Discovering that Limur wants him to steal some papers from a returned officer, Johnnie at first refuses, then agrees to the proposition, remembering Georgette's distress. Caught in the act of extracting the papers by his buddy, Nolan, Johnnie is about to confess when his lookout enters. Nolan is wounded in a fight, but the thieves are captured and good fortune awaits Johnnie and Georgette. *Veterans. Criminals—Rehabilitation. Gangs. Poverty. World War I. New York City. Documentation.*

JOSSELYN'S WIFE **F2.2814**

Tiffany Productions. 15 Nov **1926** [c9 Nov 1926; LP23316]. Si; b&w. 35mm. 6 reels, 5,800 ft.

Dir Richard Thorpe. *Scen* Agnes Parsons. *Photog* Milton Moore, Mack Stengler. *Art Dir* Edwin B. Willis. *Film Ed* Harold Young.

Cast: Pauline Frederick *(Lillian Josselyn)*, Holmes Herbert *(Thomas Josselyn)*, Josephine Kaliz *(Pierre Marchand)*, Josephine Hill *(Ellen Marchand)*, Carmelita Geraghty *(Flo)*, Freeman Wood *(Mr. Arthur)*, Pat Harmon *(detective)*, Ivy Livingston *(maid)*, W. A. Carroll *(butler)*.

Domestic melodrama. Suggested by: Kathleen Norris, *Josselyn's Wife* (New York, 1918). After 6 months of marital bliss, Lillian Josselyn is filled with dread at the return of Pierre Marchand, her former lover, who left her to marry Ellen Latimer. When Pierre and Ellen visit the Josselyn home, Pierre tries to revive his former love; and Ellen, suspecting her husband of having an affair with Flo, a dancer, encourages the attentions of Arthur, a friend of Pierre's. Lillian reluctantly agrees to pose at Pierre's studio for a portrait but leaves when he attempts to force his attentions on her; to keep him from revealing her past, however, she returns to his studio, from which at length she is rescued by her husband. When Pierre is reported murdered, Lillian confesses, thinking she killed him; her husband confesses to the crime at the trial, but the judge discloses an admission of guilt made by Flo just before her death. *Dancers. Artists. Marriage. Infidelity. Murder.*

JOURNEY OF DEATH *see* **NORTH OF HUDSON BAY**

THE JOURNEY'S END **F2.2815**

Hugo Ballin Productions. *Dist* W. W. Hodkinson Corp. ca16 Jul **1921** [New York premiere; c24 Jul 1921; LP17971]. Si; b&w. 35mm. 8 reels, 7,500 ft. [Copyrighted as 7 reels.]

Prod-Dir-Adapt Hugo Ballin. *Photog* James Diamond.

Cast: Mabel Ballin *(The Girl)*, George Bancroft *(The Ironworker)*, Wyndham Standing *(The Mill Owner)*, Georgette Bancroft *(The Child)*, Jack Dillon *(The Uncle)*.

Melodrama. Source: Sister Eileen, "Ave Maria" (publication undetermined). The Girl, educated in a convent in Rome, writes to her uncle in America, expressing a desire to return home, and he offers her a place with his family. Arriving in the Pennsylvania foundry town, she finds the conditions under which she must live intolerable, and when The Ironworker proposes marriage she accepts. A few years pass, during which a child is born to them. When The Mill Owner comes to their home to discuss business, she falls in love with him, but rather than face temptation she leaves home with the child. Aware of his wife's love for The Mill Owner, the husband clears the way for their union by exchanging identities with a worker killed in an accident and goes abroad to seek forgetfulness in a Roman monastery. The Mill Owner and The Girl are married and take a honeymoon voyage to Rome. There they confront the former husband, who dies from the shock of the meeting. *Marriage. Infidelity. Convents. Foundries. Rome. Pennsylvania.*

Note: This film was produced without titles.

JOURNEY'S END (British-American) **F2.2816**

Tiffany-Gainsborough Productions. 8 Apr **1930** [New York premiere; released 15 Apr 1930; c12 Apr 1930; LP1231]. Sd (Photophone); b&w. 35mm. 13 reels, 11,455 ft. [Also si.]

Supv George Pearson. *Asst Supv* Gerald L. G. Samson. *Dir* James Whale. *Cont-Dial* Joseph Moncure March. *Photog* Benjamin Kline. *Art Dir* Hervey Libbert. *Film Ed* Claude Berkeley. *Sd Rec* Buddy Myers.

Cast: Colin Clive *(Captain Stanhope)*, Ian MacLaren *(Lieutenant Osborne)*, David Manners *(2d Lieutenant Raleigh)*, Anthony Bushell *(2d Lieutenant Hibbert)*, Billy Bevan *(2d Lieutenant Trotter)*, Charles Gerrard *(Private Mason)*, Robert A'Dair *(Captain Hardy)*, Thomas Whitely *(Sergeant Major)*, Jack Pitcairn *(Colonel)*, Warner Klinger *(German boy)*, Leslie Sketchley *(Corporal Ross)*.

War drama. Source: Robert Cedric Sheriff, *Journey's End* (London, 1929). The action unfolds in the confined area of a dugout on the Western Front. Stanhope, a British Army officer, shattered by the strain of 3 years' fighting, turns to liquor to bolster his courage. Osborne, his righthand man and a philosophical schoolmaster, tries to reassure young Raleigh, fresh from school, to the satisfaction of Stanhope, whom the boy optimistically worships as a college hero. Although Stanhope, who loves Raleigh's sister, resents the boy's presence, he is crushed by the boy's spirit and loyalty in battle. He confesses his own fears to Hibbert, a coward who feigns illness to avoid fighting; Osborne and Raleigh are selected to lead a raiding party on the German trenches, and Osborne calms the boy by quoting from *Alice in Wonderland* and talking of home. Many men, including Osborne, die in the raid, and Stanhope drowns his grief in drink; a rift develops between him and the boy until Raleigh is mortally wounded. Friendless and grief-stricken, he goes to face another furious attack. ... *Soldiers. Friendship. Courage. World War I. France. Great Britain—Army.*

THE JOY GIRL **F2.2817**

Fox Film Corp. 3 Sep **1927** [New York premiere; released 18 Sep; c14 Aug 1927; LP24368]. Si; b&w with col sequence (Technicolor). 35mm. 7 reels, 6,162 ft. [Also 6 reels, 5,877 ft.]

Pres by William Fox. *Dir* Allan Dwan. *Scen* Frances Agnew. *Titl* Malcolm Stuart Boylan. *Adapt* Adele Camondini. *Photog* George Webber, William Miller. *Asst Dir* Clarence Elmer, Edmund Grainger.

Cast: Olive Borden *(Jewel Courage)*, Neil Hamilton *(John Jeffrey Fleet)*, Marie Dressler *(Mrs. Heath)*, Mary Alden *(Mrs. Courage)*, William Norris *(Herbert Courage)*, Helen Chandler *(Flora)*, Jerry Miley *(Vicary)*, Frank Walsh *(Hugh Sandman)*, Clarence J. Elmer *(valet)*, Peggy Kelly *(Isolde)*, Jimmy Grainger, Jr. *(chauffeur)*.

Society comedy. Source: May Edginton, "The Joy Girl," in *Saturday Evening Post* (vol 199, 13 Nov–18 Dec 1926). Determined to marry into wealth, Jewel Courage rejects the love of John Fleet, supposedly a chauffeur but actually a millionaire, and instead she marries a real chauffeur who is posing as Fleet, the millionaire. Disillusioned, she nevertheless becomes a success in business, and realizing that she actually loves Fleet, she is delighted to learn he is in fact a wealthy man. *Businesswomen. Millionaires. Chauffeurs. Imposture. Wealth. Palm Beach.*

Note: Filmed on location in Palm Beach, Florida.

JOY STREET **F2.2818**

Fox Film Corp. 12 May **1929** [c16 May 1929; LP375]. Sd eff & mus score (Movietone); b&w. 35mm. 7 reels, 5,748 ft. [Also si; 5,754 ft.]

Pres by William Fox. *Dir-Story* Raymond Cannon. *Adapt-Scen* Charles Condon, Frank Gay. *Titl* Malcolm Stuart Boylan. *Photog* Ernest Miller. *Asst Dir* Ernest Murray.

Cast: Lois Moran *(Marie "Mimi" Colman)*, Nick Stuart *(Joe)*, Rex Bell *(Eddie)*, José Crespo *(Juan)*, Dorothy Ward *(Dot)*, Ada Williams *(Beverly)*, Maria Alba *(Agnes)*, Sally Phipps *(Mabel)*, Florence Allen *(Becky)*, Mabel Vail *(dean of girl's school)*, Carol Wines *(maid)*, John Breeden *(Tom)*, Marshall Ruth *(Dick)*, James Barnes *(Harry)*, Allen Dale *(Dizzy)*, Capt. Marco Elter *(skiing mailman)*, Destournelles De Constant *(teacher)*.

Society melodrama. Mimi, an unsophisticated American girl attending an exclusive Swiss boarding school, unexpectedly inherits a large fortune, returns to the United States, and quickly begins to live in a wild and reckless manner. Joe, a goodnatured, decent fellow, attempts to set her straight, but she keeps right on living riotously. Mimi is involved in a serious accident while joy-riding, however, and comes to her senses. She marries Joe and settles down to a life of domestic tranquility. *Flappers. Jazz life. Inheritance. Automobile accidents. Boarding schools. Switzerland.*

JUDGE HER NOT **F2.2819**

Harmony Film Co. *Dist* Sunnywest Films. 9 Jul **1921** [trade review; c13 May 1921; LU16501]. Si; b&w. 35mm. [Feature length assumed.]

Dir-Scen George Edward Hall.

Cast: Jack Livingston *(Ned Hayes)*, Pauline Curley *(May Harper)*.

Western melodrama. "May Harper, the lead in a small time burlesque company, takes the chorus girls to her ranch when the manager refuses them their salary. This is in charge of Jim Perris, an unscrupulous man, who has just found gold in an abandoned placer creek on the property. He plans to drive May away and secure possession of the land himself. Ned Hayes, a rough cowboy, becomes an obstacle in Perris's path when Ned 'falls for' May. Perris finds various ways of making life unpleasant for May and succeeds in having Hayes blamed for them. The girls are discredited in the eyes of the womenfolk and are about to be driven from town when Hayes, after a terrific battle with Perris and an accomplice, convinces the town that it is all Perris's work." (*Moving Picture World*, 9 Jul 1921, p235.) *Chorus girls. Cowboys. Burlesque. Reputation. Ranches.*

JUDGEMENT **F2.2820**

World Film Corp. 15 Feb **1922** [New York State license]. Si; b&w. 35mm. 6 reels.

Cast: Joe Moore, Eileen Sedgwick.

Drama. No information about the nature of this film has been found.

Note: Though information on this film is incomplete, there is no evidence that it is the same as the foreign production of the same title distributed by World at about the same time. In that film, based on Victor Hugo's *Marie Tudor*, Ellen Richter plays the title role.

JUDGMENT OF THE HILLS **F2.2821**

R-C Pictures. *Dist* Film Booking Offices of America. 1 Aug **1927** [New York premiere; released 6 Nov; c1 Aug 1927; LP24312]. Si; b&w. 35mm. 6 reels, 5,700 ft. [Copyrighted as 7 reels.]

Pres by Joseph P. Kennedy. *Dir* James Leo Meehan. *Adapt-Cont* Dorothy Yost. *Ch Camera* Allen Siegler. *Asst Dir* Charles Kerr.

Cast: Virginia Valli *(Margaret Dix)*, Frankie Darro *(Tad Dennison)*, Orville Caldwell *(Brant Dennison)*, Frank McGlynn, Jr. *(Jeb Marks)*, Johnny Gough *(Lige Turney)*.

Rural drama. Source: Larry Evans, "Judgment of the Hills," in *Cosmopolitan*. Tad, a wistful child of the Kentucky hills, worships his big brother, Brant, who is addicted to alcohol. At the persuasion of schoolteacher Margaret Dix, Brant allows Tad to attend school. When Brant does not evidence a desire to go to war, Margaret tells him he is unworthy to be called a man, and after receiving a draft summons, Brant meets Jeb, who has returned from the war badly maimed. Brant hides in the mountains until he is found by the sheriff and sent off to camp. He returns home as a decorated hero but hopelessly drunk. Stung by little Tad's reprovals, Brant resolves to reform, bringing happiness and understanding to the boy and Margaret. *Children. Brothers. Schoolteachers. War heroes. Mountain life. Cowardice. Alcoholism. World War I. Kentucky.*

JUDGMENT OF THE STORM F2.2822

Palmer Photoplay Corp. *Dist* Film Booking Offices of America. 6 Jan **1924** [c18 Dec 1923; LP19736]. Si; b&w. 35mm. 7 reels, 6,329 ft.

Dir Del Andrews. *Story* Ethel Styles Middleton. *Photog* Max Dupont, Henry Sharp.

Cast: Lloyd Hughes *(John Trevor)*, Lucille Ricksen *(Mary Heath)*, George Hackathorne *(Bob Heath)*, Myrtle Stedman *(Mrs. Trevor)*, Claire McDowell *(Mrs. Heath)*, Philo McCullough *(Martin Freeland)*, Bruce Gordon *(Dave Heath)*, Frankie Darro, Fay McKenzie *(The Heath Twins)*.

Melodrama. Dave, Mary Heath's brother, is accidentally killed in a gambling den. Her sweetheart, John Trevor, discovers that the den is secretly owned by his mother, whom he has considered to be independently wealthy. John denounces his mother, despite the fact that the money she earned supported him in college. As Dave was the head of the Heath household, John, feeling responsible for the boy's death, offers himself as a replacement. At first treated as a slave in the household, John later wins the family's love by risking his life during a snowstorm to save the Heath twins. *Businesswomen. Filial relations. Gambling. Family life. Storms.*

JUNE MADNESS F2.2823

Metro Pictures. 23 Oct **1922** [c26 Oct 1922; LP18375]. Si; b&w. 35mm. 6 reels, 5,600 ft.

Dir-Adapt-Scen Harry Beaumont. *Story* Crosby George. *Photog* John Arnold. *Art Dir* J. J. Hughes.

Cast: Viola Dana *(Clytie Whitmore)*, Bryant Washburn *(Ken Pauling)*, Gerald Pring *(Cadbury Todd, II)*, Leon Barry *(Hamilton Peeke)*, Eugenie Besserer *(Mrs. Whitmore)*, Snitz Edwards *(Pennetti)*, Anita Fraser *(Mamie O'Gallagher [Sonora])*.

Comedy. Clytie Whitmore finally consents to marry Cadbury Todd, but while walking down the aisle she runs out of the church and into the passing car of Ken Pauling, a well-known jazz musician. Shortly after returning home, Clytie escapes from her locked room and goes to Pennetti's roadhouse, where Ken is appearing, closely pursued by gossip columnist Hamilton Peeke. She dances in the show in place of Sonora, then escapes with Ken when the roadhouse is raided. They are married and receive the family blessing. *Musicians. Entertainers. Columnists. Jazz. Roadhouses.*

JUNGLE ADVENTURES F2.2824

Martin Johnson Film Co. *Dist* Exceptional Pictures. ca11 Sep **1921** [New York premiere; released Oct; c11 Sep 1921; MP2081]. Si; b&w. 35mm. 5 reels, 5,245 ft.

Titl Arthur Hoerl. *Film Ed* Arthur Hoerl.

Cast: Martin Johnson *(The Adventurer)*, Osa Johnson *(The Heroine of 1,000 Thrills)*.

Documentary travel film. On their travels in British North Borneo, Mr. and Mrs. Martin Johnson depart from Sandakan and proceed up the Kinibatangan River into the heart of unexplored country—mostly in native boats called *gobongs.* They hunt crocodiles, shoot rapids, visit with natives, examine the haunts of a gang of Malay pirates, and see many animals—water buffalo, elephants, monkeys, gibbons, apes, an orangutan, bears, and deer. The journey ends with the Johnsons' safe return to Sandakan. *Borneo. Kinibatangan River. Crocodiles. Water buffalo. Elephants. Monkeys. Apes. Bears. Deer. Herons. Cranes.*

Note: Cast also includes: an orangutan (The Elusive One), Cuss-Cuss (the Lazy One), Teddy (The One Who Laughs), a heron and a crane (The Flighty Ones), a crocodile (The Wicked One), and some "Giants of the Jungle." Known also as *Martin Johnson's Jungle Adventures.*

JUNGLE GODS F2.2825

Carl von Hoffman. ca1 Dec **1927** [New York State license]. Si; b&w. 35mm. 7 reels.

Melodrama(?). No information about the nature of this film has been found.

THE JUNGLE PRINCESS F2.2826

Adolph Kremnitzer. 6 Jun **1923** [New York State license]. Si; b&w. 35mm. 7 reels.

Cast: Juanita Hansen.

Animal drama. No information about the precise nature of this film has been found.

JUNGLE TRAIL OF THE SON OF TARZAN F2.2827

National Film Corp. *Dist* Howells Sales Co. 20 Oct **1923** [New York State license]. Si; b&w. 35mm. 6 reels, 6,345 ft.

Prod David P. Howells. *Dir* Harry Revier, Arthur Flaven. *Scen* Roy Somerville. *Cast Dir* Jean Temple.

Cast: Dempsey Tabler *(Tarzan/Lord Greystoke)*, Karla Schramm *(Jane/Lady Greystoke)*, Gordon Griffith *(Jack, Son of Tarzan)*, Kamuela C. Searle *(Jack, as a young man)*, Manilla Martans *(Meriem)*, Lucille Rubey, De Sacia Saville, Kathleen May, Frank Morrell *(The Sheik)*, Ray Thompson *(Malbihn)*, Eugene Burr *(Ivan Paulvitch)*, Frank Earle, May Giraci *(Meriem, as a child)*.

Action melodrama. Living in England once again, Tarzan and Jane are unaware of the presence of Ivan Paulvitch, Tarzan's jungle enemy. The Greystokes' son, Jack, has inherited Tarzan's love for the jungle, and he falls into Paulvitch's clutches through his interest in Akut, a performing ape. Via an ocean voyage, the scene of action switches to the jungle, where the Son of Tarzan performs many daring feats. *Africa. Jungles. Elephants. Apes.*

Note: This film is a reduced version of the 15-episode serial, *Son of Tarzan,* which was released by the National Film Corp., 1920–21.

JUST A MOTHER F2.2828

Norca Pictures. 6 Apr **1923** [New York State license]. Si; b&w. 35mm. 5 reels.

Cast: Burtram Gurleigh, Isabel Elson.

Melodrama. Source: William Babington Maxwell, *Mrs. Thompson; a Novel* (New York, 1911). No information about the precise nature of this film has been found. *Motherhood.*

JUST A SONG AT TWILIGHT F2.2829

Dixie Film Co. *Dist* Producers Security Corp. Dec **1922** [c6 Feb 1922; LP17528]. Si; b&w. 35mm. 5 reels.

Dir Carlton King. *Story* Henry Albert Phillips. *Photog* Harry L. Keepers.

Cast: Richard Barthelmess *(George Turner)*, Pedro De Cordoba *(Carlysle Turner)*, Evelyn Greeley *(Lucy Winter/Lucy Lee, her mother)*, Charles Wellesley *(Stephen Winter, Lucy's father)*, Nellie Grant *(Mrs. Lee)*, Frank A. Lyon *(a fake oil lands promoter)*.

Melodrama. Stephen Winter, an apparently wealthy widower living in luxury with his daughter Lucy, promises her in marriage to a count despite her love for George Turner, a gardener on his estate. Turner, with only a necklace bequeathed him by his aunt (which he gives to Lucy), is in search of his long-lost father; and when Winter recognizes the necklace from the past, he forbids his daughter to see him. In a vision of the past, Winter recalls that he and Carlysle Turner, a young banker, were in love with the same girl, and when she married Winter, his rival (Turner) presented her with a necklace as a remembrance. When the Winters are reduced to dire straits, the wife seeks aid from Turner, causing Winter to believe her unfaithful. Winter's vengeance is satisfied, for Turner is unwittingly found in his bank on the night of a robbery. George discovers an old letter from his father in the house, telling of his unjust imprisonment by Winter; and when confronted with the evidence, Winter confesses and obtains a pardon for young Turner's father. Lucy and George are then happily united. *Widowers. Gardeners. Bankers. Marriage. Poverty. Parentage. Revenge. Documentation.*

Note: This film appears to have been made in 1916 and advertised for release that year. It again appeared in 1922 as an "un-released" film.

JUST A WOMAN F2.2830

First National Pictures. 16 Jun **1925** [c18 May 1925; LP21468]. Si; b&w. 35mm. 7 reels, 6,363 ft.

Pres by M. C. Levee. *Dir* Irving Cummings. *Adapt* Jack Cunningham. *Photog* Arthur L. Todd. *Art Dir* Jack Okey. *Film Ed* Charles J. Hunt. *Asst Dir* Charles Woolstenhulme.

Cast: Claire Windsor *(June Holton)*, Conway Tearle *(Robert Holton)*, Dorothy Brock *(Bobby Holton)*, Percy Marmont *(George Rand)*, Dorothy Revier *(Clarice Clement)*, George Cooper, Edward Gribbon *(Oscar Dunn [see note])*.

Melodrama. Source: Eugene Walter, *Just a Woman* (a play; publication undetermined). Robert Holton, who works as a laborer for a large steel company, lives in contentment with his wife and child, sharing his house with George Rand, a good friend, who has invented a new process for refining steel. George insists that Robert receive half share of the proceeds of this process, and Robert, acting for George and himself, goes to the steel company, which makes him an attractive offer. Robert is willing to accept, but his wife, June, does not feel that the offer is high enough and undertakes herself to speak to the board of directors, which she forces to promote George to the company's presidency. With the sudden advent of riches and prestige, Robert loses his sense of values and becomes involved with Clarice Clement, an adventuress, who persuades him that his wife is involved with George in a romantic intrigue. Robert begins divorce proceedings, from which he is deterred only at the last minute, when he realizes that he loves his wife and child too much to part from them. Robert and June are reconciled, and he comes to realize that she has been faithful to him all along. *Business management. Inventors. Steel industry. Family life. Divorce. Marriage. Friendship.*

Note: Cooper and Gribbon are separately credited with the role of Oscar Dunn.

JUST ANOTHER BLONDE **F2.2831**

Al Rockett Productions. *Dist* First National Pictures. 19 Dec **1926** [c2 Dec 1926; LP23386]. Si; b&w. 35mm. 6 reels, 5,603 ft.

Dir Alfred Santell. *Scen* Paul Schofield. *Photog* Arthur Edeson. *Film Ed* Hugh Bennett. *Prod Mgr* Al Rockett.

Cast: Dorothy Mackaill *(Jeanne Cavanaugh)*, Jack Mulhall *(Jimmy O'Connor)*, Louise Brooks *(Diana O'Sullivan)*, William Collier, Jr. *(Kid Scotty)*.

Romantic drama. Source: Gerald Beaumont, "Even Stephen," in *Red Book*, (45:48–51, Oct 1925). Jimmy O'Connor, employed in a gambling establishment, is so honest that he is offered a banking job at any time; and for his sake, Scotty, his protegé and pal, decides to go straight. The boys go fifty-fifty in everything until Scotty falls in love with Diana, who operates a shooting booth at Coney Island. Jimmy declares that he disapproves of all women—except his mother—and Scotty despairs until he schemes to have Jimmy meet Jeanne, Diana's girl friend. It is only when they expect to be killed in an airplane crash that Jimmy tells Jeanne he loves her, but later he feigns indifference. Jeanne is heartbroken; Scotty explains that he can't marry Diana until Jimmy is safely engaged; and with that both boys are reconciled to their respective sweethearts. *Croupiers. Bank clerks. Misogynists. Concessionaires. Coney Island.*

Note: Also reviewed and released under the title: *The Girl From Coney Island*

JUST AROUND THE CORNER **F2.2832**

Cosmopolitan Productions. *Dist* Paramount Pictures. 11 Dec **1921** [c11 Dec 1921; LP17354]. Si; b&w. 35mm. 7 reels, 6,173 ft.

Dir-Adapt Frances Marion. *Photog* Henry Cronjager. *Set Dsgn* Joseph Urban.

Cast: Margaret Seddon *(Ma Birdsong)*, Lewis Sargent *(Jimmie Birdsong)*, Sigrid Holmquist *(Essie Birdsong)*, Edward Phillips *(Joe Ullman)*, Fred Thomson *(The Real Man)*, Peggy Parr *(Lulu Pope)*, Madame Rosa Rosanova *(Mrs. Finshreiber)*, William Nally *(Mr. Blatsky)*.

Melodrama. Source: Fannie Hurst, "Just Around the Corner," in *Just Around the Corner* (New York, 1914). Ma Birdsong, her son Jimmie (a messenger boy), and her daughter Essie live together in New York City's East Side. Essie is allured by the city's night life, theaters, and restaurants, and finally she becomes an usher in a cheap theater where she falls in love with Joe Ullman, a crooked ticket speculator. Her mother, in failing health, repeatedly begs to meet Essie's fiancé, but Ullman declines to pay visits. When Ma Birdsong is seized with a heart attack and pleads to see him, Essie finds him in a poolroom, but he sneers and refuses to accompany her. She then encounters a stranger and in despair tells him her story; he agrees to visit her mother and represent himself as her fiancé. Mrs. Birdsong dies, happy in the thought that Essie is to marry "a real man." Later, Essie and the stranger do get married. *Ushers. Messengers. Ticket agents. Filial relations. Family life. New York City—East Side.*

JUST IMAGINE **F2.2833**

Fox Film Corp. 23 Nov **1930** [c17 Oct 1930; LP1696]. Sd (Movietone); b&w. 35mm. 12 reels, 10,200 ft.

Assoc Prod B. G. De Sylva, Lew Brown, Ray Henderson. *Dir-Cont* David Butler. *Story-Dial* B. G. De Sylva, Lew Brown, Ray Henderson. *Photog* Ernest Palmer. *Art Dir* Stephen Goosson, Ralph Hammeras. *Film Ed* Irene Morra. *Songs: "The Drinking Song," "The Romance of Elmer Stremingway," "Never, Never Wed," "There's Something About an Old-Fashioned Girl," "Mothers Ought To Tell Their Daughters," "I Am the Words, You Are the Melody," "Dance of Victory," "Never Swat a Fly"* B. G. De Sylva, Lew Brown, Ray Henderson. *Mus Dir* Arthur Kay. *Dance Dir* Seymour Felix. *Rec Engr* Joseph E. Aiken. *Asst Dir* Ad Schaumer. *Cost Dsgn* Sophie Wachner, Dorothy Tree, Alice O'Neill.

Cast—Principals: El Brendel *(Single 0)*, Maureen O'Sullivan *(LN—18)*, John Garrick *(J—21)*, Marjorie White *(D—6)*, Frank Albertson *(RT—42)*, Hobart Bosworth *(Z—4)*, Kenneth Thomson *(MT—3)*, Wilfred Lucas *(X—10)*, Mischa Auer *(B—36)*, Joseph Girard *(Commander)*, Sidney De Gray *(AK—44)*, Joyzelle *(Loo Loo/Boo Boo)*, Ivan Linow *(Loko/Bobo)*

Cast—Young Ladies of the Ensemble: Bee Stephens, Kathryn Brown, Lucille Miller, Francis Hopkins, Raymonda Brown, Bonnie Winslow, Bernice Snell, Carol Miller, Peggy Beck, Adele Cutler, Mary Lansing, Theo De Voe, Rose Lee, Helen Mann, Mary Carr, Beverly Royde, Catherine NaVarre, Thelma Perriguey, Margaret La Marr, Bo Peep Karlin, Lorraine Bond, Joan NaVarre, Mildred Laube, Betty Halsey, Miriam Hellman, Paula Langlen, Peggy Cunningham, Mary Carlton, Edna Callahan, Jane Dunlap, Janet De Vine, Gloria Fayth, Adele Fergus, Betty Gordon, Kay Gordon, Dot Humphries, Lee Kenny, Betty Mitchell, Dot Palmer, Emily Renard, Elizabeth Turner, Marbeth Wright

Cast—Gentlemen of the Chorus: Charles Alexander, George Yeretzian, Murray Smith, Austin Grout, William Brandt, J. L. Riddick, Robert Keith, Fred Silver, Nate Barrager, Armond Jannssen, Gordon Orme, Louis Yaeckel, Roy Strohm, Clarence Simmons, Kenneth Allen, Jack Frost, Roy Tobin, Robert Lake, Ted Sharp, Ernest Smith, Ed Rockwell, Don Prosser, Arthur McCullock, Jack Barrett, Myron Sunde, Bob Knickerbocker, George Gramlich, Clarence Smith, Enrico Cucinelli, J. Harold Reeves.

Musical melodrama. Following a humoristic prolog recalling the customs and appearance of New York in 1880, the action flashes forward to 1980: At this time, if there are two or more suitors for a girl's hand, the matter is settled by a marriage tribunal. Thus, J—21, a young aviator, has been ruled against by the tribunal in favor of RT—42, a wealthier and more distinguished rival, but he is given a 4-month period during which he may strengthen his image. He is losing ground when offered the chance to pilot a rocketship to Mars, accompanied by RT—42. Single 0, who was killed by lightning in 1930 and revived by scientists 50 years later, unable to adjust to the many changes in the world during the interval, stows away on the ship. After many amusing incidents on Mars, J—21 returns to Earth just in time to present his appeal and reverse the verdict. *Courtship. Marriage tribunals. The Future. Reviviscence. Space travel. Mars. New York City.*

Note: According to the review in *Variety* (26 Nov 1930), the song "Never Swat a Fly" was eliminated, at least for the New York presentation.

JUST LIKE A WOMAN **F2.2834**

Grace S. Haskins. *Dist* W. W. Hodkinson Corp. 18 Mar **1923** [c15 Mar 1923; LP18965]. Si; b&w. 35mm. 5 reels, 4,900 ft.

Dir Scott R. Beal, Hugh McClung. *Adapt* Hal Conklin. *Story* Grace S. Haskins. *Photog* Chester Lyons, Reginald Lyons, John Leezer.

Cast: Marguerite De La Motte *(Peggy Dean)*, George Fawcett *(Judge Landon)*, Ralph Graves *(James Landon)*, Jane Keckley *(Abigail)*, Julia Calhoun *(Salina)*, J. Frank Glendon *(Peggy's brother)*.

Comedy-drama. After living in a boarding school for some years, Peggy Dean accepts the invitation of her Aunts Abigail and Salina to live with them. They warn her that she will be "on probation" because of the family's displeasure with Peggy's father for marrying an actress, so Peggy masquerades as an exceedingly prim and proper missionary. She must drop her disguise, however, to win James Landon. Disillusioned when he learns of her deceit, James leaves, but Peggy overtakes him in a racing car and brings about a reconciliation. *Missionaries. Spinsters. Aunts. Disguise. Boarding schools.*

JUST LIKE HEAVEN **F2.2835**

Tiffany Productions. 22 Oct **1930** [c17 Oct 1930; LP1650]. Sd (Photophone); b&w. 35mm. 7 reels, 5,850 ft.

Dir R. William Neill. *Story-Screenplay* Adele Buffington. *Photog* Max Dupont. *Sets* Ralph De Lacy. *Film Ed* Charles Hunt. *Rec Engr* Dean Daily. *Tech Dir* Andre Chotin.

Cast: Anita Louise *(Mimi)*, David Newell *(Tobey)*, Yola D'Avril *(Fifi)*, Gaston Glass *(Jean)*, Thomas Jefferson *(Michael)*, Mathilde Comont *(Madame Fogharde)*, Albert Roccardi *(Monsieur Fogharde)*, Torben Meyer *(Pierre)*, Emile Chautard *(Dulac)*.

Romantic drama. Tobey Mitchell, a young Parisian balloon vendor with ambitions to become a designer of pageants, jealously guards his stand in the Street of the Poor. One day Jean's Dog Circus takes his stand, and Tobey is defeated by the fierce indignation of Mimi, the show's dancer. Mimi's grandfather, Michael, has saved his money so that she may study with the great Dulac, but when he is robbed, Michael is killed by a fall down a staircase. Although he affects indifference, Tobey cares for the grief-stricken Mimi; but he is angered when she gives him ideas for the pageant. Nevertheless, he finances Mimi's dancing lessons, so that he has no money for the pageant contest. Fifi, a cafe entertainer who robbed Michael, offers to finance Tobey, but he refuses. Mimi, learning that he has paid for her lessons, deserts a dancing engagement; meanwhile Tobey agrees to Fifi's plan but tries to withdraw his pageant when he learns of her perfidy. To his surprise, Mimi is the star of the show, and he wins the contest as well as her love. *Balloon vendors. Dancers. Grandfathers. Pageants. Robbery. Courtship. Paris. Dog circus.*

JUST MARRIED **F2.2836**

Paramount Famous Lasky Corp. 18 Aug **1928** [c16 Aug 1928; LP25545]. Si; b&w. 35mm. 6 reels, 6,039 ft.

Pres by Adolph Zukor, Jesse L. Lasky. *Dir* Frank Strayer. *Adapt-Scen* Frank Butler, Gilbert Pratt. *Titl* George Marion. *Photog* Edward Cronjager. *Film Ed* B. F. Zeidman, William Shea.

Cast: James Hall *(Bob Adams)*, Ruth Taylor *(Roberta)*, Harrison Ford *(Jack Stanley)*, William Austin *(Percy Jones)*, Ivy Harris *(Mrs. Jack Stanley)*, Tom Ricketts *(Makepeace Witter)*, Maude Turner Gordon *(Mrs. Witter)*, Lila Lee *(Victoire)*, Arthur Hoyt *(steward)*, Wade Boteler *(purser)*, Mario Carillo *(Magnoir)*.

Farce. Source: Adelaide Matthews and Anne Nichols, *Just Married; a Comedy in Three Acts* (New York, c1929). Victoire, a model in a Paris dress shop, discovers that Percy Jones, who jilted her, is about to marry Roberta. Incensed and determined to break up the match, Victoire books passage on the ocean liner carrying Roberta and Percy back to the United States. Robert Adams, who sees Roberta as she is boarding the ship, becomes infatuated with her and likewise books passage. After many mistaken identities, cross-purposes, misunderstandings, and overheard conversations, Robert and Roberta become engaged, and a reluctant Percy agrees at last to marry Victoire. *Fashion models. Ocean liners. Paris.*

JUST OFF BROADWAY **F2.2837**

Fox Film Corp. 20 Jan **1924** [c20 Jan 1924; LP19882]. Si; b&w. 35mm. 6 reels, 5,544 ft.

Pres by William Fox. *Story-Scen* Frederic Hatton, Fanny Hatton. *Photog* G. O. Post.

Cast: John Gilbert *(Stephen Moore)*, Marian Nixon *(Jean Lawrence)*, Trilby Clark *(Nan Norton)*, Pierre Gendron *(Florelle)*, Ben Hendricks, Jr. *(Comfort)*.

Underworld melodrama. Jean Lawrence, unsuccessful as a musical comedy actress, is near starvation when she is rescued by Nan Norton, a gangland sweetheart, in a restaurant off Broadway. Jean becomes involved with a counterfeit ring, then falls in love with Stephen Moore, millionaire and amateur detective disguised as a counterfeiter. Moore rounds up the gang, removes his disguise, and marries Jean. *Millionaires. Detectives. Actors. Counterfeiters. Disguise. New York City—Broadway.*

JUST OFF BROADWAY **F2.2838**

Chesterfield Motion Picture Corp. 1 May **1929**. Si; b&w. 35mm. 7 reels, 6,300 ft.

Supv Lon Young. *Dir* Frank O'Connor. *Scen* Arthur Hoerl. *Titl* Arthur Hoerl, Lon Young. *Story* Fanny D'Morgal. *Photog* M. A. Anderson. *Film Ed* James Sweeney.

Cast: Donald Keith *(Tom Fowler)*, Ann Christy *(Nan Morgan)*, Larry Steers *(Marty Kirkland)*, De Sacia Mooers *(Rene)*, Jack Tanner *(William Grady)*, Sid Saylor *(Bennie Barnett)*, Beryl Roberts *(Bessie)*, Albert Dresden *(Ed Fowler)*.

Underworld melodrama. "His brother bumped off by a rival racketeer, Keith jumps from school into the night club circles of Broadway in quest of his man. He finds him and also a girl dancer for whom he promptly falls. The racketeer, on the pretense of sending the boy and girl off together to his apartment on a friendly party, rounds up his gunmen to plug the youngster. But the latter is not dumb and the racketeer falls into the clutches of the law when the night club hostess whom he has thrown over spills his activities to the detectives. So the school boy and dancer parade to the altar." (*Motion Picture News*, 26 Oct 1929, p30.) *Racketeers. Brothers. Dancers. Nightclub hostesses. Murder. Revenge. Nightclubs. New York City—Broadway.*

JUST OUT OF COLLEGE **F2.2839**

Goldwyn Pictures. 11 Feb **1921** [trade review; c2 Nov 1920; LP15764]. Si; b&w. 35mm. 5 reels.

Dir Alfred Green. *Scen* Arthur F. Statter. *Camera* George Webber.

Cast: Jack Pickford *(Ed Swinger)*, Molly Malone *(Caroline Pickering)*, George Hernandez *(Septimus Pickering)*, Edythe Chapman *(Mrs. Pickering)*, Otto Hoffman *(Professor Bliss)*, Irene Rich *(Miss Jones)*, Maxfield Stanley *(Herbert Poole)*, Maurice B. Flynn *(Paul Greer)*, Loretta Blake *(Genevieve)*.

Comedy. Source: George Ade, *Just Out of College, a Light Comedy in Three Acts* (New York, 1924). Mr. Pickering, wealthy businessman, wishes his daughter to marry his business associate, Herbert Poole, but Mrs. Pickering wants her to marry Professor Bliss. Naturally their daughter, Caroline, has yet another choice: Ed Swinger, a recent college graduate. Her father plots to get rid of Swinger by giving him $20,000 to invest and requesting that he double the amount in 60 days. Pickering then tells Poole to sell some valueless oil stock to Ed, who manages to retain $5,000 after the crooked deal. Ed meets college chum Paul Greer, who is trying to establish himself in advertising; both then meet Miss Jones, who convinces them she could make a fortune in pickles with $5,000. All efforts are combined, and Bingo Pickles are advertised everywhere. Pickering buys out the concern for $100,000. Ed then discloses himself as the financial backer and wins Caroline. *Professors. Businessmen. Courtship. Filial relations. Fraud. Pickles. Advertising.*

JUST OUTSIDE THE DOOR **F2.2840**

Weber Productions. *Dist* Select Pictures. 28 Jan **1921** [trade review; c24 Nov 1920; LP15838]. Si; b&w. 35mm. 5 reels.

Dir George Irving. *Scen* Harvey Thew.

Cast: Edith Hallor *(Madge Pickton)*, Betty Blythe *(Gloria Wheaton)*, Barney Sherry *(Edward Burleigh)*, Eddie Sutherland *(Ned Pickton)*, Arnold Gregg *(Dick Wheaton)*.

Melodrama. Source: Jules Eckert Goodman, *Just Outside the Door* (New York opening: 30 Aug 1915). Cold, calculating, and vain Gloria Wheaton persuades her fiancé, Edward Burleigh, to help her end her brother's infatuation for Madge Pickton, a welfare worker in the Burleigh Mills. They use the actions of Madge's weak-willed brother, Ned, to discredit Madge, but she resolutely defends her honor and continues to shield Ned. Finally, Ned admits his forgery and theft, and Madge is reunited with Dick. *Police. Brother-sister relationship. Social workers. Forgery. Theft. Textile manufacture.*

JUST PLAIN FOLKS **F2.2841**

Bud Barsky Corp. 18 Feb **1925** [New York State license]. Si; b&w. 35mm. 5 reels.

Dir Robert N. Bradbury.

Cast: Kenneth McDonald.

Melodrama(?). No information about the nature of this film has been found.

JUST SUPPOSE **F2.2842**

Inspiration Pictures. *Dist* First National Pictures. 10 Jan **1926** [c11 Jan 1926; LP22239]. Si; b&w. 35mm. 7 reels, 6,270 ft.

Dir Kenneth Webb. *Scen* C. Graham Baker. *Adapt* Violet E. Powell. *Photog* Stuart Kelson. *Sets* Tec-Art Studios. *Film Ed* William Hamilton. *Titl Eff* H. E. R. Studios.

Cast: Richard Barthelmess *(Prince Rupert)*, Lois Moran *(Linda Lee Stafford)*, Geoffrey Kerr *(Count Anton Teschy)*, Henry Vibart *(Baron Karnaby)*, George Spelvin *(King)*, Harry Short *(Crown Prince)*, Bijou Fernandez *(Mrs. Stafford)*, Prince Rokneddine *(private secretary)*.

Romantic drama. Source: A. E. Thomas, *Just Suppose, a Comedy in Three Acts* (New York, 1923). Prince Rupert of Koronia comes to the United States and, bored with pomp and circumstance, falls in love with Linda Lee Stafford. Called home when the crown prince dies unexpectedly, Rupert finds himself first in line for the throne, and a royal marriage is arranged for him. Before the wedding ceremony takes place, however, the widow of the late crown prince gives birth to twins, who become the heirs presumptive to the throne, a situation freeing Rupert to marry as he wishes. Linda Lee comes to Europe for a visit, and she and Rupert are married. *Royalty. Twins. Courtship. Imaginary kingdoms.*

JUST TONY **F2.2843**

Fox Film Corp. 20 Aug **1922** [c20 Aug 1922; LP19089]. Si; b&w. 35mm. 5 reels, 5,233 ft.

Pres by William Fox. *Dir-Writ* Lynn F. Reynolds. *Photog* Dan Clark.

Cast: Tony *(himself, a horse)*, Tom Mix *("Red" Ferris)*, Claire Adams *(Marianne Jordan)*, J. P. Lockney *(Oliver Jordan)*, Duke Lee *(Manuel Cordova)*, Frank Campeau *(Lew Hervey)*, Walt Robbins *("Shorty")*.

Western melodrama. Source: Max Brand, *Alcatraz* (New York, 1923). A wild mustang, leader of a desert herd of horses, seeks revenge against men who mistreated him. Cowboy "Red" Ferris saves him from being badly beaten, and the mustang shows his appreciation by rescuing Ferris and a rancher's daughter when they are in trouble. *Cowboys. Revenge. Horses.*

JUST TRAVELIN' **F2.2844**

Sierra Pictures. Jan **1927.** Si; b&w. 35mm. 5 reels.

Dir Horace B. Carpenter.

Cast: Bob Burns, Dorothy Donald.

Western melodrama(?). No information about the nature of this film has been found.

JUSTICE OF THE FAR NORTH **F2.2845**

Columbia Pictures. c3 Apr **1925** [LP21323]. Si; b&w. 35mm. 6 reels.

Dir-Story Norman Dawn. *Photog* Tony Mormann, George Madden.

Cast: Arthur Jasmine *(Umluk)*, Marcia Manon *(Wamba)*, Laska Winter *(Nootka)*, Chuck Reisner *(Mike Burke)*, Max Davidson *(Izzy Hawkins)*, George Fisher *(Dr. Wells)*, Katherine Dawn *(Lucy Parsons)*, Steve Murphy *(Broken Nose McGee)*, Ilak the Wolf Dog *(himself)*.

Northwest melodrama. Umluk, an Eskimo chief, falls into a crevice while hunting and is rescued by Dr. Wells, a distinguished Arctic explorer and scientist. Umluk returns to his igloo, where he finds Mike Burke, an ex-whaler who runs a trading post in partnership with Izzy Hawkins; Burke has been attempting to win the favor of Umluk's promised bride, a Russian halfbreed Eskimo named Wamba, by giving her trinkets and treating her like a white woman. Umluk forces Burke to leave, but the trader returns later and takes the willing Wamba away with him, forcing Wamba's sister, Nootka, to go with them as their cook and drudge. Umluk learns from Hawkins just what has happened and gives chase to the party in a light sled. Umluk soon catches sight of the three travelers, but an unlucky accident to his sled prevents him from catching them. Umluk eventually finds them in a rough settlement, and, after trials and tribulations, returns to his icy home with the faithful Nootka, leaving the degraded Wamba behind. *Scientists. Eskimos. Whalers. Cooks. Halfcastes. Exploration. Abduction. Trading posts. Arctic regions. Dogs.*

KATHLEEN MAVOURNEEN **F2.2846**

Tiffany Productions. 20 Jun **1930** [c5 Jun 1930; LP1344]. Sd (Photophone); b&w. 35mm. 6 reels, 5,196 ft.

Dir Albert Ray. *Adapt-Dial* Frances Hyland. *Photog* Harry Jackson.

Cast: Sally O'Neil *(Kathleen)*, Charles Delaney *(Terry)*, Robert Elliott *(Dan Moriarity)*, Aggie Herring *(Aunt Nora Shannon)*, Walter Perry *(Uncle Mike Shannon)*, Francis Ford *(butler)*.

Melodrama. Source: Dion Boucicault, "Kathleen Mavourneen" (a play; publication undetermined). Kathleen, an Irish lassie, comes to New York to marry Terry, a plumber. At a celebration in her Aunt Nora's flat, she meets Dan Moriarity, a political boss whom she regards as a "great gentleman." He invites her to his home on Long Island, and his attentions cause Terry to treat her with a jealous protectiveness. But Moriarity proposes marriage to her and informs Terry that they are to wed. At the wedding, however, a man accuses Moriarity's men of a gang killing; Moriarity shoots him in the back before Kathleen and tells the butler to dispose of the body. Terrified, and stopping only long enough to return her wedding ring, Kathleen rushes from the room and finds consolation in the arms of Terry. *Plumbers. Political bosses. Irish. Murder. Courtship. New York City.*

KATY DIDD *see* **DEAD GAME**

KAZAN **F2.2847**

Col. William N. Selig. *Dist* Export & Import Film Co. 28 Oct **1921** [trade review]. Si; b&w. 35mm. 6 reels, 6,900 ft.

Dir Bertram Bracken. *Photog* Eddie Beesley, Edwin Linden.

Cast: Jane Novak *(Joan Radisson)*, Ben Deeley *(Jim Thorpe)*, William Ryno *(Pierre Radisson)*, Benjamin Haggerty *(Frank Radisson)*, Edwin Wallock *("Black" McCready)*, Kazan *(The Dog)*.

Northwest melodrama. Source: James Oliver Curwood, *Kazan* (Indianapolis, 1914). Kazan, a dog who reverts to the life of the wild when his master is killed, becomes docile when he develops a loyalty to a girl in distress. Pierre Radisson is a trapper; his older son is a member of the Northwest Mounted Police. His younger son and daughter come north to see their father; the boy turns out to be a worthless sort, spending his time drinking and gambling. The girl is left to cope by herself. When she receives word that her older brother has been killed and that her father is dying in his cabin in the hills, she must trust a stranger, Deeley, to accompany her on the journey. While traveling they are about to be attacked by a pack of wolves led by Kazan, but the dog, recognizing the woman's voice, backs off. They arrive safely but find her father dead. The villain has preceded them on the trail and destroyed the evidence marking him as the slayer of the girl's brother and father. He then suggests to the Mounties that the man accompanying the girl is the killer. However, the father's watch falls open to reveal a note bearing the truth. The heavy, now fearing for his life, tries to attack the girl; but Kazan leaps in, throws him to the floor, and kills him. *Trappers. Brother-sister relationship. Murder. Northwest Mounted Police. Dogs. Wolves.*

KEEP GOING **F2.2848**

Dist Sierra Pictures. Dec **1926.** Si; b&w. 35mm. 5 reels, 4,900 ft.

Dir John Harvey. *Photog* Harry Forbes.

Cast: Earle Douglas.

Comedy-drama(?). No information about the nature of this film has been found.

KEEP SMILING **F2.2849**

Monty Banks Pictures. *Dist* Associated Exhibitors. 6 Sep **1925** [c28 Aug 1925; LU21781]. Si; b&w. 35mm. 6 reels, 5,400 ft.

Dir Gilbert W. Pratt, Albert Austin. *Story* Herman Raymaker, Clyde Bruckman, Monty Banks. *Photog* James Diamond, Lee Garmes, Barney McGill.

Cast: Monty Banks *(The Boy)*, Robert Edeson *(James P. Ryan)*, Anne Cornwall *(Rose Ryan)*, Stanhope Wheatcroft *(Gerald Deane)*, Glen Cavender *(doublecrosser)*, Donald Morelli *(Bordanni)*, Syd Crossley *(Ryan's butler)*, Ruth Holly *(Ryan's secretary)*, Martha Franklin *(The Mother)*, Jack Huff *(The Child)*.

Farce. The Boy, involved in a maritime disaster as a child, suffers from hydrophobia. He invents a life preserver that automatically inflates when it hits the water, using it to save the life of Rose Ryan, the daughter of a steamship magnate. The Boy takes his invention to Ryan and is mistaken by him for Bordanni, a speedboat racer. In order to present his invention properly, The Boy, totally unprepared and hysterical, is forced to drive Ryan's boat. He is accompanied by a crooked mechanic put on board by Gerald Deane, who is interested in wrecking the boat. More by luck than skill, the boy wins the race, convinces Ryan of the efficacy of the life preserver, and wins the love of Rose. *Inventors. Mechanics. Hydrophobia. Boat racing. Life preservers. Speedboats.*

THE KEEPER OF THE BEES (Gold Bond Special) **F2.2850**

Gene Stratton Porter Productions. *Dist* Film Booking Offices of America. ca19 Sep **1925** [Salt Lake City premiere; released 18 Oct; c18 Oct 1925; LP21966]. Si; b&w. 35mm. 7 reels, 6,712 ft.

Dir-Cont James Leo Meehan. *Camera* John Boyle. *Asst Dir* William Fisher.

Cast: Robert Frazer *(James Lewis MacFarlane)*, Josef Swickard *(Michael Worthington, The Bee Master)*, Martha Mattox *(Margaret Cameron)*, Clara Bow *(Alice Louise Cameron, "Lolly")*, Alyce Mills *(Molly Cameron)*, Gene Stratton *(Jean Meredith, the "Little Scout")*, Joe Coppa *("Angel Face")*, Ainse Charland *("Fat Ole Bill")*, Billy Osborne *("Nice Child")*.

Melodrama. Source: Gene Stratton Porter, *The Keeper of the Bees* (Garden City, New York, 1925). World War hero James Lewis MacFarlane, tired of being shunted from one government hospital to another for a wound that will not heal, runs away when he learns that he has but a year to live. He is befriended by The Bee Master, who is ill and soon dies. Jamie inherits half of the estate and apiary, with the other half going to "Little Scout," an 11-year-old girl who dresses as a boy. He marries a girl about to drown herself because she is to bear a child out of wedlock; his "wife" disappears immediately afterward, leaving a note signed "Alice Louise MacFarlane." With the aid of a neighbor, Margaret Cameron, Jamie soon recovers his health. He is notified that his "wife" has given birth to a son, but when he arrives at the hospital Jamie discovers another woman wearing his ring. She dies, and Molly Cameron (Mrs. Cameron's daughter), the girl he really married, appears and confesses that she married Jamie to get her sister Alice a wedding ring and a marriage certificate to protect her reputation. All ends well, and Jamie remarries Molly. *Tomboys. Veterans. Self-sacrifice. Marriage. Reputation. Bees.*

KEEPING UP WITH LIZZIE **F2.2851**

Rockett Film Corp. *Dist* W. W. Hodkinson Corp. ca28 May **1921** [Cleveland premiere; c21 Dec 1921; LP17384]. Si; b&w. 35mm. 6 reels.

Pres by Al Rockett, Ray Rockett. *Dir* Lloyd Ingraham. *Scen* Will M. Ritchey. *Photog* Ross Fisher.

Cast: Enid Bennett *(Lizzie Henshaw)*, Otis Harlan *(Sam Henshaw)*, Leo White *(Count Louis Roland)*, Victory Bateman *(Mrs. Henshaw)*, Landers Stevens *("Soc" Potter)*, Edward Hearn *(Dan Pettigrew)*, Harry Todd *(Mr. Pettigrew)*, Lila Leslie *(Mrs. Warburton)*.

Comedy-drama. Source: Irving Addison Bacheller, *Keeping Up With Lizzie* (New York, 1911). Determined that his daughter, Lizzie, will not marry the son of his business rival, Sam Henshaw sends her to finishing school, while Pettigrew, not to be outdone, sends his son, Dan, to Harvard. On returning to her small hometown, Lizzie, having toured Europe, sports the latest fashions and is accompanied by Count Louis Roland, who sees in her an opportunity to marry wealth, leaving Dan in the background. Lizzie's father, unable to keep up with her tastes, declares bankruptcy, and the count refuses to marry her until offered a large dowry, which Henshaw obtains from lender Socrates Potter. Dan discovers that the count is an impostor in time to prevent the wedding, and the count is caught trying to escape with the money. Dan wins Lizzie and settles down on his farm. *Grocers. Moneylenders. Farmers. Smalltown life. Wealth. Bankruptcy. Imposture. Boarding schools. Harvard University.*

KEMPY *see* **WISE GIRLS**

THE KENTUCKIANS **F2.2852**

Famous Players–Lasky. *Dist* Paramount Pictures. 20 Feb **1921** [c26 Jan 1921; LP16052]. Si; b&w. 35mm. 6 reels, 5,981 ft.

Pres by Adolph Zukor. *Dir* Charles Maigne. *Scen* Frank W. Tuttle. *Photog* André Barlatier.

Cast: Monte Blue *(Boone Stallard)*, Wilfred Lytell *(Randolph Marshall)*, Diana Allen *(Anne Bruce)*, Frank Joyner *(Mace Keaton)*, J. H. Gilmour *(Governor)*, John Miltern *(Colton, journalist)*, Thomas S. Brown *(Jake Stallard)*, J. W. Johnston *(Boone's brother)*, Russell Parker *(constable)*, John Carr *(Young Keaton)*, Albert Hewitt *(Young Stallard)*, Eugenie Woodward *(Ma Stallard)*, Wesley Jenkins *(Uncle Cadmus)*, Grace Reals *(Mrs. Marshall)*.

Rural melodrama. Source: John William Fox, *The Kentuckians* (New York, 1897). Boone Stallard, elected to the Kentucky Legislature by a mountain district, clashes with Randolph Marshall, a Blue Grass aristocrat who is engaged to Anne, the governor's daughter. When a feud breaks out in the mountains between the Keatons and the Stallards, Boone returns home and with the help of Marshall restores law and order; later, Marshall obtains a commutation of the sentence of Stallard's brother, who has been condemned to death. Boone, now realizing the differences between a rugged, simple mountaineer and an aristocrat, decides not to ask Anne to marry him. *Aristocrats. Mountaineers. Brothers. State governors. State legislatures. Politics. Social classes. Feuds. Kentucky.*

KENTUCKY COURAGE *see* **THE LITTLE SHEPHERD OF KINGDOM COME**

KENTUCKY DAYS **F2.2853**

Fox Film Corp. 2 Dec **1923** [c25 Nov 1923; LP19657]. Si; b&w. 35mm. 5 reels, 4,508 ft.

Pres by William Fox. *Dir* David Soloman. *Scen* Dorothy Yost. *Story* John Lynch.

Cast: Dustin Farnum *(Don Buckner)*, Margaret Fielding *(Elizabeth Clayborne)*, Miss Woodthrop *(Margarite Buckner)*, Bruce Gordon *(Gordon Carter)*, William De Vaull *(Scipio)*.

Romantic drama. In 1853, young southerner Don Buckner goes west in search of gold to recoup his dwindling fortune, spent mostly on his wife. During the years of his absence he fails to communicate with his wife or mother, even when he strikes gold, as he hopes to make this good fortune a surprise. His cousin, infatuated with Don's wife, tries to persuade her that Don is dead and forcibly kisses her. The mother, thinking her unfaithful, dies of a broken heart. Don returns, sees his mother's grave, and learns of his wife's "infidelity." He kills his cousin in a duel, orders his wife from his house, frees his slaves, sets fire to his house, and determines to return to California alone. His wife, however, persuades him to take her along. Don realizes he still loves her when she becomes lost in a sandstorm. He finds her; and reunited in their love, they continue on to California. *Filial relations. Cousins. Gold. Wealth. Fidelity. Manumission. Kentucky. California. Duels. Sandstorms.*

THE KENTUCKY DERBY (Universal-Jewel) **F2.2854**

Universal Film Manufacturing Co. ca29 Oct **1922** [Chicago premiere; released 4 Dec; c18 Oct 1922; LP18337]. Si; b&w. 35mm. 6 reels, 5,398 ft.

Pres by Carl Laemmle. *Dir* King Baggot. *Scen* George C. Hull. *Photog* Victor Milner.

Cast: Reginald Denny *(Donald Gordon)*, Lillian Rich *(Alice Brown)*, Emmett King *(Col. Moncrief Gordon)*, Walter McGrail *(Ralph Gordon)*, Gertrude Astor *(Helen Gordon)*, Lionel Belmore *(Col. Rome Woolrich)*, Kingsley Benedict *(Joe)*, Bert Woodruff *(Rance Newcombe)*, Bert Tracy *(Topper Tom)*, Harry Carter *(Bob Thurston)*, Wilfred Lucas *(Captain Wolff)*, Pat Harmon *(Jensen)*, Anna Hernandez *(Mrs. Clancy)*, Verne Winter *(Timmy Clancy)*.

Melodrama. Source: Charles T. Dazey, *The Suburban; a Melodrama in Four Acts* (c1902). Posing as relatives, Ralph and Helen Gordon visit Col. Moncrief Gordon's Kentucky mansion, hoping to marry Helen to the colonel's son, Donald. The colonel agrees, but Donald balks at the suggestion, then reveals his secret marriage to Alice Brown. The colonel turns them out, and Ralph conspires with Bob Thurston to frame Donald for theft of Colonel Gordon's wager money and to shanghai him. After 3 years Donald discovers the source of his misfortune, returns, finds his wife, hears of a plot against his father's best racehorse, wrings a complete confession from Thurston, and saves the Derby for his repentant father. *Kentucky colonels. Filial relations. Imposture. Marriage. Horseracing. Kentucky Derby.*

Note: Working titles: *They're Off; The Suburban Handicap.*

KENTUCKY HANDICAP **F2.2855**

Harry J. Brown Productions. *Dist* Rayart Pictures. 19 Nov **1926** [New York State license]. Si; b&w. 35mm. 6 reels, 5,420 ft.

Pres by W. Ray Johnston. *Dir* Harry J. Brown. *Scen* Henry Roberts Symonds.

Cast: Reed Howes, Alice Calhoun, Robert McKim, Lydia Knott, Josef Swickard, James Bradbury, Jr..

Action melodrama. "Villain causes hero's disbarment from race. Hero, broke, gets loan giving racing horse as security. Villain secures notes and tries to prevent hero from entering race but in fight he is forced to confess and hero's horse wins. There is a romance." (*Motion Picture News Booking Guide*, 12:37, Apr 1927.) *Horseracing. Debt. Kentucky.*

KENTUCKY PRIDE **F2.2856**

Fox Film Corp. 6 Sep **1925** [c14 Jun 1925; LP21626]. Si; b&w. 35mm. 7 reels, 6,597 ft.

Pres by William Fox. *Dir* John Ford. *Scen* Dorothy Yost. *Titl* Elizabeth Pickett. *Photog* George Schneiderman. *Asst Dir* Edward O'Fearna.

Cast: Henry B. Walthall *(Mr. Beaumont)*, J. Farrell MacDonald *(Donovan)*, Gertrude Astor *(Mrs. Beaumont)*, Malcolm Waite *(Carter)*, Belle Stoddard *(Mrs. Donovan)*, Winston Miller *(Danny Donovan)*, Peaches Jackson *(Virginia Beaumont)*, The Finn, Man o' War, Confederacy, Morvich, Virginia's Future, Fair Play, Negofol *(racehorses)*.

Melodrama. Mr. Beaumont, a Kentucky horseman of the old school, loses several of his horses at the card table and pins all his hopes on Virginia's Future, a colt entered in the Futurity. He bets heavily on the horse, which falls during the race and breaks a leg. Beaumont loses his fortune, and his wife deserts him for Greve Carter. Virginia's Future is nursed back to health by Mike Donovan, the trainer, and sold to another horseman. The mare gives birth to a colt, Confederacy, and is later sold to a foreign junk dealer, who mistreats her. Confederacy shows great promise and is entered in the Futurity, with Donovan's son, Danny, in the saddle. Beaumont and Donovan bet every cent they have on the horse, which wins. Beaumont uses part of his winnings to buy back Virginia's Future, putting her out to pasture. *Horsetrainers. Junk dealers. Horseracing. Kentucky Derby. Horses.*

KETTLE CREEK *see* **MOUNTAIN JUSTICE**

THE KIBITZER **F2.2857**

Paramount Famous Lasky Corp. 11 Jan **1930** [c8 Jan 1930; LP980]. Sd (Movietone); b&w. 35mm. 9 reels, 7,273 ft. [Also si; 6,569 ft.]

Dir Edward Sloman. *Scen* Marion Dix. *Adapt-Dial* Sam Mintz, Viola Brothers Shore. *Photog* Alfred Gilks. *Film Ed* Eda Warren. *Song: "Just Wait and See, Sweetheart"* Leo Robin, R. Whiting. *Rec Engr* Harry D.

Mills.

Cast: Harry Green *(Ike Lazarus)*, Mary Brian *(Josie Lazarus)*, Neil Hamilton *(Eddie Brown)*, Albert Gran *(James Livingston)*, David Newell *(Bert Livingston)*, Guy Oliver *(McGinty)*, Tenen Holtz *(Meyer)*, Henry Fink *(Kikapoupolos)*, Lee Kohlmar *(Yankel)*, E.H. Calvert *(Westcott)*, Thomas Curran *(Briggs)*, Eddie Kane *(Phillips)*, Henry A. Barrows *(Hanson)*, Paddy O'Flynn *(reporter)*, Dick Rush *(Mullins)*, Eugene Pallette *(Klaus)*.

Comedy-drama. Source: Joseph Swerling and Edward G. Robinson, *The Kibitzer, a Comedy* (New York & Los Angeles, 1929). Ike Lazarus, a Jewish tobacconist, does his kibitzing nightly when his friends gather at the store for pinochle. Josie, his daughter, who is engaged to Eddie Brown, goes with Bert, a financier's son, to a horserace, and they are followed by Ike and Eddie; Eddie loses his money on a "hot tip," given him by Ike, and when Josie threatens to elope with Bert, her father goes to Livingston, Bert's father, and thwarts the plot. As a reward, Livingston gives Ike some shares in American Steel. The market rises, then falls, but Harry's brother unwittingly sells the stock at its peak value. With the fortune he has acquired Ike finances a garage for Eddie, who is happily reunited with Josie. *Tobacconists. Jews. Speculation. Horseracing. Pinochle. Garages.*

THE KICK BACK **F2.2858**

R-C Pictures. *Dist* Film Booking Offices of America. ca29 Jul **1922** [New York premiere; released 3 Sep; c24 Jul 1922; LP18175]. Si; b&w. 35mm. 6 reels, 5,260 ft.

Prod P. A. Powers. *Dir* Val Paul. *Scen* George Edwardes-Hall. *Story* Harry Carey. *Photog* Robert Thornby, Robert De Grasse.

Cast: Harry Carey *(White Horse Harry)*, Henry B. Walthall *(Aaron Price)*, Charles J. Le Moyne *(Chalk Eye)*, Vester Pegg *(Ramon Pinellos)*, Mingenne *(Conchita Pinellos)*, Ethel Grey Terry *(Nellie)*.

Western melodrama. In order to get Harry's land and girl for himself, Aaron Price sends him to Mexico to bring back some horses with false papers. Harry is imprisoned in Mexico, escapes, and is imprisoned again at home. Just as he is about to be lynched a Mexican girl he has befriended brings the Texas Rangers to the rescue. *Texas Rangers. Lynching. Mexico. Documentation. Horses.*

KICK IN **F2.2859**

Famous Players–Lasky. *Dist* Paramount Pictures. ca3 Dec **1922** [Los Angeles premiere; released 1 Jan 1923; c13 Dec 1922; LP18660]. Si; b&w. 35mm. 7 reels, 7,074 ft.

Pres by Adolph Zukor. *Dir* George Fitzmaurice. *Adapt* Ouida Bergère. *Photog* Arthur Miller.

Cast: Betty Compson *(Molly Brandon)*, Bert Lytell *(Chick Hewes)*, May McAvoy *(Myrtle)*, Gareth Hughes *(Benny)*, Kathleen Clifford *("Frou Frou")*, Maym Kelso *(Mrs. Brandon)*, John Miltern *(District Attorney Brandon)*, Walter Long *(Whip Fogarty)*, Robert Agnew *(Jerry Brandon)*, Jed Prouty *(Jimmy Monahan)*, Carlton King *(Diggs Murphy)*, Charles Ogle *(John Stephens)*, Charles Stevenson *(Handsome, the Yegg)*.

Crook melodrama. Source: Willard Mack, *Kick In; a Play in Four Acts* (New York, 1925). Chick Hewes resolves to go straight when he is released from prison, but persecution by the police when he refuses to be a stool pigeon and the lack of concern with which Jerry Brandon kills a slum child with his automobile impel Chick to undertake one more job—at the home of District Attorney Brandon. There Chick discovers Jerry already stealing from his father's safe, but Molly Brandon prevents Chick from being arrested for Jerry's crime. Chick and Molly go west to begin anew. *Criminals—Rehabilitation. District attorneys. Informers. Brother-sister relationship.*

THE KICK-OFF **F2.2860**

Excellent Pictures. 15 Aug **1926** [c16 Aug 1926; LP23025]. Si; b&w. 35mm. 6 reels, 6,000 ft.

Dir Wesley Ruggles. *Titl* Jack Conway (of *Variety*). *Story* H. H. Van Loan. *Photog* Frank Zukor.

Cast: George Walsh *(Tom Stephens)*, Leila Hyams *(Marilyn Spencer)*, Bee Amann *(Ruth)*, Earle Larrimore *(Frank Preston)*, W. L. Thorne, Joseph Burke, Jane Jennings.

Melodrama. Tom Stephens, a well-known athlete at a smalltown college, transfers to Farnsworth University, where he becomes reacquainted with the landlady's daughter, Marilyn—a girl he earlier rescued from the manhandling of collegian Frank Preston. Frank assures his friends that the country "hick" will never make varsity quarterback, and at a school dance Frank makes fun of Tom's poor dancing, though this ridicule does not weaken Tom's popularity with Marilyn and her flirtatious friend Ruth. Soon Tom becomes first choice for varsity quarterback, and Frank inflicts an injury on Tom during practice, then plants liquor in Tom's locker, causing him to be disqualified; but he is reprieved in time to participate in the game. As the result of a trick instigated by Frank, Tom fails to appear initially, but he does arrive in time to tie the score. After recovery from a knockout, he leads the team to victory and is happily united with Mary and his mother. *Athletes. College life. Courtship. Football.*

Note: One source (*Variety*) indicates that the story was written by H. H. Van Loan; copyright records give credit to Wesley Ruggles.

THE KID **F2.2861**

Charles Chaplin Productions. *Dist* Associated First National Pictures. 6 Feb **1921** [c17 Jan 1921; LP16019]. Si; b&w. 35mm. 6 reels, 5,300 ft.

Prod-Dir-Writ Charles Chaplin. *Assoc Dir* Chuck Reisner. *Photog* Rollie Totheroh.

Cast: Jackie Coogan *(The Kid)*, Edna Purviance *(The Woman)*, Carl Miller *(The Man)*, Charles Chaplin *(The Tramp)*, Tom Wilson *(The Policeman)*, Chuck Reisner *(The Bully)*, Albert Austin *(a crook)*, Nellie Bly Baker *(slum woman)*, Henry Bergman *(proprietor of lodging house)*, Lita Grey *(The Flirting Angel)*.

Comedy-melodrama. A tenement tramp finds and raises The Kid, an abandoned baby, as his own. The baby's mother, The Woman, achieves fame as a singer and 5 years later is reconciled to the husband who has forsaken her. When the child is ordered removed to an orphan asylum, The Tramp rescues him and the parents find their long-lost son. Disconsolate over the loss of The Kid, The Tramp returns home, where he is found by a policeman who reunites him with The Woman and The Kid. *Tramps. Waifs. Singers. Police. Tenements.*

KID BOOTS **F2.2862**

Famous Players–Lasky. *Dist* Paramount Pictures. 4 Oct **1926** [c5 Oct 1926; LP23182]. Si; b&w. 35mm. 9 reels, 8,565 ft. [Also 6 reels, 5,650 ft.]

Pres by Adolph Zukor, Jesse L. Lasky. *Assoc Prod* B. P. Schulberg. *Dir* Frank Tuttle. *Screenplay* Tom Gibson. *Scen* Luther Reed. *Titl* George Marion, Jr. *Photog* Victor Milner.

Cast: Eddie Cantor *(Kid Boots)*, Clara Bow *(Jane Martin)*, Billie Dove *(Polly Pendleton)*, Lawrence Gray *(Tom Sterling)*, Natalie Kingston *(Carmen Mendoza)*, Malcolm Waite *(George Fitch)*, William Worthington *(Polly's father)*, Harry von Meter *(Carmen's lawyer)*, Fred Esmelton *(Tom's lawyer)*.

Comedy. Source: William Anthony McGuire, Otto Harbach, and J. P. McCarthy, *Kid Boots; a Musical Comedy* (New York opening: 31 Dec 1923). Following a football celebration, Tom Sterling is tricked into marrying Carmen Mendoza, a chorus girl; and while awaiting a divorce decree, he unexpectedly inherits $3 million. Tom rescues Kid Boots, a tailor's helper, from the irate clutches of a customer; and The Kid follows him to his apartment, where Carmen tries to prove that her marriage is a success so that she may share the fortune. Tom's lawyer, so as to deter Carmen from further demonstrations, advises him to keep The Kid nearby. Under an assumed name, Tom becomes a golf professional, and Kid Boots is made caddy-master. The Kid falls for Jane Martin, a swimming instructor, but she rejects him when he pretends to flirt with Carmen. Finally, Tom persuades Jane to help him; and with the aid of horses, mules, airplanes, and autos, she and The Kid arrive at the courthouse in time to clear Tom. *Chorus girls. Millionaires. Tailors. Divorce. Inheritance. Golf. Swimming.*

Note: The longer version reflects the information from the Paramount press book. The shortened version of the film apparently opened in New York on Oct 9.

THE KID BROTHER **F2.2863**

Harold Lloyd Corp. *Dist* Paramount Pictures. 17 Jan **1927** [c18 Jan 1927; LP23563]. Si; b&w. 35mm. 8 reels, 7,654 ft.

Pres by Adolph Zukor, Jesse L. Lasky. *Dir* Ted Wilde. *Story* John Grey, Tom Crizer, Ted Wilde. *Photog* Walter Lundin.

Cast: Harold Lloyd *(Harold Hickory)*, Jobyna Ralston *(Mary Powers)*, Walter James *(Jim Hickory)*, Leo Willis *(Leo Hickory)*, Olin Francis *(Olin Hickory)*, Constantine Romanoff *(Sandoni)*, Eddie Boland *("Flash" Farrell)*, Frank Lanning *(Sam Hooper)*, Ralph Yearsley *(Hank Hooper)*.

Comedy. Harold of Hickoryville, the bashful son of a country sheriff, is tricked into allowing a medicine show into town, headed by Mary Powers. His father instructs him to stop the show, but he only succeeds in becoming a butt for "Flash" Farrell's tricks, to the delight of Hank Hooper, the town bully, who accidentally sets the tent on fire. Harold's father orders them to leave town, then is himself accused of stealing public funds actually stolen by Flash. Convinced of his inferiority, Harold declines to join the search party, but unwittingly he finds himself confronted with Sandoni and Flash, who are dividing the swag. Harold's cleverness wins over Sandoni's strength when he discovers the brute's fear of water; he saves the Hickory name and wins the girl. *Sheriffs. Bullies. Strongmen. Rural life. Medicine shows. Inferiority complex. Fires.*

KID CANFIELD THE REFORM GAMBLER **F2.2864**

Kid Canfield. *Dist* E. R. Champion Distributing Co. 4 Feb **1922** [New York State license]. Si; b&w. 35mm. 5 reels, 4,800 ft.

Personages: Kid Canfield, C. Williams, Mrs. Sharkey.

Western drama. "Exposing the evil art of gambling by Kid Canfield and lectured on by Kid Canfield" (New York State license records). *Gambling.*

KID GLOVES **F2.2865**

Warner Brothers Pictures. 23 Mar **1929** [c19 Mar 1929; LP228]. Talking sequences, sd eff, & mus score (Vitaphone); b&w. 35mm. 7 reels, 6,235 ft. [Also si, 27 Apr 1929; 4,885 ft.]

Dir Ray Enright. *Scen-Titl-Dial* Robert Lord. *Story* Fred Myton. *Photog* Ben Reynolds. *Film Ed* George Marks.

Cast: Conrad Nagel *(Kid Gloves)*, Lois Wilson *(Ruth)*, Edward Earle *(Penny)*, Edna Murphy *(Lou)*, Maude Turner Gordon *(Aunt)*, Richard Cramer *(Butch)*, Tommy Dugan *(Duffy)*, John Davidson *(Stone)*.

Underworld melodrama. When a taxi carrying socialite Ruth Darrow drives into the middle of a gunbattle between hijacker Kid Gloves and a trio of bootleggers, Ruth is injured. She is taken to a nearby apartment, and The Kid helps to care for her. John Stone, Ruth's fiancé and a bootlegger with a respectable front, finds them together and blackmails The Kid into marrying the girl. The Kid and Ruth live together like brother and sister, and Stone, realizing that Ruth was not two-timing him, decides to bump off The Kid. To save her husband's life, Ruth agrees to leave The Kid and marry Stone. Stone is implicated in a killing, however, and forced to leave town. Ruth and The Kid decide to stay married, and The Kid determines to reform. *Socialites. Bootleggers. Hijackers. Criminals—Rehabilitation. Blackmail. Marriage.*

THE KID SISTER **F2.2866**

Columbia Pictures. 5 Jul **1927** [c11 Aug 1927; LP24284]. Si; b&w. 35mm. 6 reels, 5,477 ft.

Prod Harry Cohn. *Dir* Ralph Graves. *Cont* Harry O. Hoyt. *Photog* J. O. Taylor.

Cast: Marguerite De La Motte *(Helen Hall)*, Ann Christy *(Mary Hall)*, Malcolm McGregor *(Thomas Webster)*, Brooks Benedict *(Ted Hunter)*, Tom Dugan *(stage manager)*, Sally Long *(Ann Howe)*, Barrett Greenwood *(Ann's friend)*.

Romantic drama. Source: Dorothy Howell, "The Lost House" (publication undetermined). Mary Hall forsakes the quiet life of her village home to join her sister Helen, a New York chorus girl. During a stage performance, Thomas Webster, with his friend Ted Hunter, sees Helen and is attracted to her. Though Ted thinks her "too respectable," he accompanies Tom to the stage door, where Helen snubs him for his temerity, but Ted succeeds in impressing Mary. Soon, however, Tom contrives to meet Helen, who warns Mary not to encourage Ted, but to no avail. Ted induces Mary to go to a roadhouse, where he makes advances to her and is rendered unconscious in the struggle; she escapes in his car and emerges unharmed from an accident, though she is arrested. In return for bail money, Helen agrees to do anything Tom may ask of her—which turns out to be a proposal of marriage. Mary, disillusioned with the city, determines to go home to her waiting beau. *Sisters. Chorus girls. Courtship. Smalltown life. Roadhouses. Automobile accidents. New York City.*

THE KID'S CLEVER **F2.2867**

Universal Pictures. 17 Feb **1929** [c1 Oct 1928; LP25677]. Si; b&w. 35mm. 6 reels, 5,792 ft.

Supv Harry Decker. *Dir* William James Craft. *Scen* Jack Foley. *Scen? (see note)* Ernest S. Pagano. *Titl* Albert De Mond. *Story* Vin Moore. *Photog* Al Jones. *Art Dir* Charles D. Hall. *Film Ed* Charles Craft.

Cast: Glenn Tryon *(Bugs Raymond)*, Kathryn Crawford *(Ruth Decker)*, Russell Simpson *(John Decker)*, Lloyd Whitlock *(Ashton Steele)*, George Chandler *(Hank)*, Joan Standing *(a girl)*, Max Asher *(magician)*, Florence Turner *(matron)*, Virginia Sale *(secretary)*, Stepin Fetchit *(Negro man)*.

Comedy. Bugs Raymond, the inventor of a car with a fuelless motor, becomes acquainted with Ruth Decker, the daughter of a motor manufacturer who persuades her father to attend a demonstration of Bugs's car. A rival salesman bribes Bugs's mechanic to tamper with the engine, and the demonstration is a total failure. Bugs learns of this sabotage the following day, and he and Ruth forcibly persuade the elder Decker to take another ride in the car. The second demonstration is a success, and after Bugs retrieves a contract that Decker had signed with the rival salesman, Decker buys Bugs's invention. *Inventors. Automobile manufacturers. Salesmen.*

Note: Pagano is credited with scenario by some sources.

KIKI **F2.2868**

Norma Talmadge Productions. *Dist* First National Pictures. 4 Apr **1926** [c26 Mar 1926; LP22529]. Si; b&w. 35mm. 9 reels, 8,279 ft.

Pres by Joseph M. Schenck. *Dir* Clarence Brown. *Scen* Hans Kraly. *Photog* Oliver Marsh.

Cast: Norma Talmadge *(Kiki)*, Ronald Colman *(Renal)*, Gertrude Astor *(Paulette)*, Marc MacDermott *(Baron Rapp)*, George K. Arthur *(Adolphe)*, William Orlamond *(Brule)*, Erwin Connelly *(Joly)*, Frankie Darro *(Pierre)*, Mack Swain *(Pastryman)*.

Comedy-drama. Source: André Picard, *Kiki; pièce en trois actes* (Paris, 1920; as adapted by David Belasco). Kiki, a Parisian gamine who lives by her wits, graduates from newspaper seller to chorus girl, then is fired from the theater when she quarrels with Paulette, the star and sweetheart of Monsieur Renal, the manager. Renal relents when Kiki begs for help and takes her to dinner, to the discomfiture of Paulette, who intrudes on the party with Baron Rapp, who is secretly wooing Paulette. She tries to humiliate Kiki, but Renal out of sympathy takes her to his home and there becomes intrigued with her beauty. Kiki continues to feud with Paulette, who conspires with the baron to lure the girl away from Renal. Following a hair-pulling match with Paulette, Kiki feigns catalepsy. Renal's sympathy turns to love; and when she "wakes up," and kisses him, he proposes marriage. *Newsvendors. Chorus girls. Jealousy. Catalepsy. Theater. Paris.*

THE KILLER **F2.2869**

Benjamin B. Hampton Productions. *Dist* Pathé Exchange. 30 Jan **1921** [c28 Jan 1921; LU16055]. Si; b&w. 35mm. 6 reels.

Dir Howard Hickman. *Scen* E. Richard Schayer. *Photog* Harry Vallejo.

Cast: Claire Adams *(Ruth Emory)*, Jack Conway *(William Sanborn)*, Frankie Lee *(Bobby Emory)*, Frank Campeau *(Henry Hooper)*, Tod Sloan *(Artie Brower)*, Edward Peil *(Ramon)*, Frank Hayes *(Windy Smith)*, Will Walling *(John Emory)*, Milton Ross *(Buck Johnson)*, Tom Ricketts *(Tim Westmore)*, Zack Williams *(Aloysius Jackson)*.

Western melodrama. Source: Stewart Edward White, *The Killer* (Garden City, New York, 1920). Henry Hooper, suspected of murder, is living on the Arizona-Mexican border and persuades his partner, Emory, to visit him there with his children, Ruth and Bobby. He steals the written evidence of their partnership and has Emory killed by his Mexican henchman. A neighboring rancher, William Sanborn, perceives the peril of the children when he visits the ranch and returns to rescue them. Hooper is killed. *Children. Mexicans. Partnerships. Murder. Documentation. Arizona. Mexican border.*

KINDLED COURAGE **F2.2870**

Universal Pictures. 8 Jan **1923** [c22 Dec 1922; LP18532]. Si; b&w. 35mm. 5 reels, 4,418 ft.

Pres by Carl Laemmle. *Dir* William Worthington. *Scen* Raymond L. Schrock. *Story* Leete Renick Brown. *Photog* Virgil Miller.

Cast: Hoot Gibson *(Andy Walker)*, Beatrice Burnham *(Betty Paxton)*, Harold Goodwin *(Hugh Paxton)*, Harry Tenbrook *(Sid Garrett)*, James Gordon Russell *(sheriff)*, J. Russell Powell *(marshal)*, Albert Hart *(Overland Pete)*.

Western melodrama. "Andy Walker, bullied and taunted with being a coward, leaves town on a freight. The brakeman shoots two ruffians, but Andy is hailed as the hero and made a deputy sheriff. He is sent to capture Overland Pete and his gang. Scared, but game, he starts out and accidentally brought face to face with them, wins out and makes good. He also wins the love of the sister of one of the crooks, returns home with his bride, and whips the bully who taunted him as being yellow." (*Moving Picture World*, 10 Feb 1923, p576.) *Sheriffs. Railroad brakemen. Gangs. Brother-sister relationship. Cowardice. Courage.*

KINDRED OF THE DUST F2.2871

R. A. Walsh Co. *Dist* Associated First National Pictures. 27 Feb **1922** [c3 Aug 1922; LP18110]. Si; b&w. 35mm. 8 reels, 7,439 ft.

Pres by R. A. Walsh. *Dir* R. A. Walsh. *Scen* James T. O'Donohue. *Photog* Charles Van Enger, Lyman Broening. *Art Dir* William Cameron Menzies.

Cast: Miriam Cooper *(Nan of the Sawdust Pile)*, Ralph Graves *(Donald McKaye)*, Lionel Belmore *(The Laird of Tyee)*, Eugenie Besserer *(Mrs. McKaye)*, Maryland Morne *(Jane McKaye)*, Elizabeth Waters *(Elizabeth McKaye)*, W. J. Ferguson *(Mr. Daney)*, Caroline Rankin *(Mrs. Daney)*, Pat Rooney *("Dirty" Dan O'Leary)*, John Herdman *(Caleb Brent)*, Bruce Guerin *(Little Donald)*.

Romantic drama. Source: Peter Bernard Kyne, *Kindred of the Dust* (New York, 1920). Discovering that her husband is a bigamist, Nan returns with her child to her Puget Sound logging town. She is treated as an outcast by all save Donald, her childhood sweetheart, the son of a millionaire. Their romance is thwarted by his parents, but after she nurses him to recovery from an apparently fatal illness they are married. The subsequent arrival of a son prompts a family reconciliation. *Parenthood. Family life. Bigamy. Lumber industry. Puget Sound.*

KING COWBOY F2.2872

FBO Pictures. 26 Nov **1928** [c5 Nov 1928; LP25796]. Si; b&w. 35mm. 7 reels, 6,269 ft.

Dir Robert De Lacy. *Screenplay* Frank Howard Clark. *Titl* Helen Gregg, Randolph Bartlett. *Story* S. E. V. Taylor. *Photog* Norman Devol. *Film Ed* Henry Weher, Tod Cheesman. *Asst Dir* James Dugan.

Cast: Tom Mix *(Tex Rogers)*, Sally Blane *(Polly Randall)*, Lew Meehan *(Ralph Bennett)*, Barney Furey *("Shorty" Sims)*, Frank Leigh *(Abdul El Hassan)*, Wynn Mace *(Ben Suliman Ali)*, Robert Fleming *(Jim Randall)*.

Western melodrama. Tex Rogers, the foreman of the Randall ranch, arrives with a gang of tough cowpunchers in the small North African country of El Kubla looking for his boss, Jim Randall, who has been kidnaped by avaricious Riffs. Randall's daughter, Polly, is abducted by Abdul, the emir, and Tex rescues her at the price of his own freedom. But Polly is again carried off by Abdul; Tex escapes from jail and fights his way to Abdul's palace, again rescuing Polly. Abdul is killed in the confusion, and Tex is elected as the new Emir of El Kubla by the grateful populace, taking Polly as his wife. *Ranch foremen. Cowboys. Riffs. Royalty. Abduction. Jails. North Africa.*

THE KING OF JAZZ F2.2873

Universal Pictures. 7 May **1930** [New York premiere; released 17 Aug; c17 May 1930; LP1318]. Sd (Movietone); col (Technicolor). 35mm. 12 reels, 9,100 ft.

Pres by Carl Laemmle. *Prod* Carl Laemmle, Jr. *Devised and Dir by* John Murray Anderson. *Screenplay* Edward T. Lowe, Jr. *Comedy Sketches* Harry Ruskin. *Dial* Charles MacArthur. *Anim Cartoons* Walter Lantz, Bill Nolan. *Cinematog* Hal Mohr, Jerome Ash, Ray Rennahan. *Art Dir* Herman Rosse. *Asst Art Dir* Thomas F. O'Neill. *Supv Film Ed* Maurice Pivar. *Film Ed* Robert Carlisle. *Orch* Ferde Grofé. *Songs: "Happy Feet," "A Bench in the Park," "My Bridal Veil," "Song of the Dawn," "I Like To Do Things for You," "Music Has Charms," "My Lover"* Jack Yellen, Milton Ager. *Songs: "It Happened in Monterrey," "Ragamuffin Romeo"* Billy Rose, Mabel Wayne. *Song: "So the Bluebirds and the Blackbirds Got Together"* Billy Moll, Harry Barris. *Mus Comp: "Rhapsody in Blue"* George Gershwin. *Mus Arr* James Dietrich. *Dance Dir* Russell E. Markert. *Rec Supv* C. Roy Hunter. *Monitor* Harold I. Smith. *Asst Dir* Robert Ross. *Cost* Herman Rosse.

Cast: Paul Whiteman and His Orchestra, John Boles, Laura La Plante, Glenn Tryon, Jeanette Loff, Merna Kennedy, Stanley Smith, Slim Summerville, Otis Harlan, William Kent, Bing Crosby and the Rhythm Boys, The Sisters G, The Brox Sisters, George Chiles, Jacques Cartier, Frank Leslie, Charles Irwin, Al Norman, Grace Hayes, Paul Howard, Marion Stattler, Don Rose, Russell Markert Girls, Tommy Atkins Sextette, Nell O'Day, Wilbur Hall, John Fulton, Kathryn Crawford, Jeanie Lang, Beth Laemmle, Jack White, Walter Brennan, Churchill Ross, Johnson Arledge, Charlie Murray, George Sidney.

Musical revue. In an animated cartoon sequence, we see Paul Whiteman's huge scrapbook open to reveal how he was crowned the King of Jazz; Whiteman then introduces the members of the orchestra and the dancing chorus girls. At the *Daily Meow* operated by a female city editor, the Rhythm Boys are heard singing about the blackbirds and the bluebirds; in the "Bridal Veil" number, a young girl conjures up visions of bridal costumes through the ages. After hearing the grievances of a piccolo player, Whiteman and his boys play "A Bench in the Park." A series of blackout numbers involve a mixup in a business office, a lost motorcar, and the situation on the Eastern Front; John Boles relates the unrequited love of an artist for a Mexican girl in Monterrey and is joined by a chorus in "Song of the Dawn"; a number starring two goldfish is followed by a dance number, "Happy Times"; "Ragamuffin Romeo" depicts the story of a boy's ragdoll that suddenly comes to life, and Gershwin's *Rhapsody in Blue* features a huge piano and a bevy of dancing girls. The eternal triangle is presented in a new light in a comedy sketch called "Bogie Man"; and the finale, entitled "The Melting Pot," delineates how music of various nations is atmospherically transformed into jazz as it goes into the Melting Pot of the U. S. A. *Jazz.*

THE KING OF KINGS F2.2874

De Mille Pictures. *Dist* Producers Distributing Corp. 19 Apr **1927** [New York premiere; c14 Sep 1927; LP24454]. Si; b&w with col sequences (Technicolor). 35mm. 14 reels, 13,500 ft. [Copyrighted as 18 reels.]

Prod-Dir Cecil B. De Mille. *Story-Screenplay* Jeanie Macpherson. *Ch Photog* Peverell Marley. *Asst Photog* Fred Westerberg, Jacob A. Badaracco. *Art Dir* Mitchell Leisen, Anton Grot. *Film Ed* Anne Bauchens, Harold McLernon. *Assoc Ed* Clifford Howard. *Asst Dir* Frank Urson. *2d Asst Dir* William J. Cowen, Roy Burns. *Cost* Earl Luick, Gwen Wakeling. *Makeup* Fred C. Ryle. *Tech Engr* Paul Sprunck, Norman Osunn. *Res* Elizabeth McGaffee.

Cast—Principals and Others: H. B. Warner *(Jesus, the Christ)*, Dorothy Cumming *(Mary, the Mother)*, Ernest Torrence *(Peter)*, Joseph Schildkraut *(Judas)*, James Neill *(James)*, Joseph Striker *(John)*, Robert Edeson *(Matthew)*, Sidney D'Albrook *(Thomas)*, David Imboden *(Andrew)*, Charles Belcher *(Philip)*, Clayton Packard *(Bartholomew)*, Robert Ellsworth *(Simon)*, Charles Requa *(James, the Less)*, John T. Prince *(Thaddeus)*, Jacqueline Logan *(Mary Magdalene)*, Rudolph Schildkraut *(Caiaphas, High Priest of Israel)*, Sam De Grasse *(The Pharisee)*, Casson Ferguson *(The Scribe)*, Victor Varconi *(Pontius Pilate, Governor of Judea)*, Majel Coleman *(Proculla, wife of Pilate)*, Montagu Love *(The Roman Centurion)*, William Boyd *(Simon of Cyrene)*, M. Moore *(Mark)*, Theodore Kosloff *(Malchus, Captain of the High Priest's Guard)*, George Siegmann *(Barabbas)*, Julia Faye *(Martha)*, Josephine Norman *(Mary of Bethany)*, Kenneth Thomson *(Lazarus)*, Alan Brooks *(Satan)*, Viola Louie *(The Woman Taken in Adultery)*, Muriel McCormac *(The Blind Girl)*, Clarence Burton *(Dysmas, the Repentant Thief)*, James Mason *(Gestas, the Unrepentant Thief)*, May Robson *(The Mother of Gestas)*, Dot Farley *(Maid Servant of Caiaphas)*, Hector Sarno *(The Galilean Carpenter)*, Leon Holmes *(The Imbecile Boy)*, Jack Padgen *(Captain of the Roman Guard)*, Robert St. Angelo, Redman Finley, James Dime, Richard Alexander, Budd Fine, William De Boar, Robert McKee, Tom London, Edward Schaeffer, Peter Norris, Dick Richards *(soldiers of Rome)*, James Farley *(an executioner)*, Otto Lederer *(Eber, a Pharisee)*, Bryant Washburn *(a young Roman)*, Lionel Belmore *(a Roman noble)*, Monte Collins *(a rich Judean)*, Luca Flamma *(a gallant of Galilee)*, Sojin *(a prince of Persia)*, André Cheron *(a wealthy merchant)*, William Costello *(a Babylonian noble)*, Sally Rand *(slave to Mary Magdalene)*, Noble Johnson *(charioteer)*.

Additional Players—Male: Jere Austin, W. Azenberg, Fred Becker, Baldy Belmont, Ed Brady, Joe Bonomo, George Calliga, Fred Cavens, Colin Chase, Charles Clary, Denis D'Auburn, Victor De Linsky, Malcolm Denny, David Dunbar, Jack Fife, Sidney Franklin, Kurt Furberg, Bert Hadley, Edwin Hearn, Stanton Heck, Fred Huntley, Brandon Hurst, Otto Kottka, Edward Lackey, Theodore Lorch, Bertram Marburgh, James Marcus, George F. Marion, Earl Metcalf, Max Montor, Louis Natheaux, Richard Neill, Robert Ober, A. Palasthy, Louis Payne, Edward Piel, Albert Priscoe, Herbert Pryor, Warren Rodgers, Charles Sellon, Tom Shirley, Walter Shumway, Bernard Siegel, Phil Sleeman, Charles Stevens, Carl Stockdale, William Strauss, Mark Strong, Josef Swickard, Wilbert Wadleigh, Fred Walker, Will Walling, Paul Weigel, Charles West, Stanhope Wheatcroft.

Additional Players—Female: Emily Barrye, Elaine Bennett, Lucille Brown, Kathleen Chambers, Edna Mae Cooper, Josephine Crowell, Frances Dale, Milla Davenport, Anna De Linsky, Lillian Elliott, Anielka Elter, Evelyn Francisco, Margaret Francisco, Dale Fuller, Natalie Galitzen, Inez Gomez, Edna Gordon, Julia Swayne Gordon, Winifred Greenwood, Eulalie Jensen, Kadja, Jane Keckley, Isabelle Keith, Nora Kildare, Lydia Knott, Alice Knowland, Celia Lapan, Alla Moskova, Gertrude Norman, Patricia Palmer, Gertrude Quality, Rae Randall, Hedwig Reicher, Reeka Roberts, Peggy Schaffer, Evelyn Selbie, Semone Sergis, Anne Teeman, Barbara Tennant, Mabel Van Buren.

Religious spectacular. Beginning with the redemption of Mary Magdalene, the film presents selected dramatic episodes from the life of Jesus, the first part dealing with the events of His ministry—notably the casting out of the seven deadly sins from Mary Magdalene, the raising of Lazarus, the driving of the moneychangers from the temple, and instruction of the Lord's Prayer. The second half deals with the Passion: The Last Supper, the betrayal of Jesus by Judas, the trial before Pilate, the bearing of the Cross to Calvary, the Crucifixion, the Resurrection, and the Ascension. *Jews. Rome—History—Empire. Judea. Christianity. Jesus. Virgin Mary. Mary Magdalene. Joseph Caiaphas. Pontius Pilate. Judas Iscariot. Lazarus. Barabbas. The Twelve Disciples. Biblical characters.*

Note: Reissued in 1931 with a synchronized musical score.

KING OF THE HERD **F2.2875**

Frank S. Mattison Productions. *Dist* Aywon Film Corp. 1 Jul **1927** [New York State license; New York showing: 12 Sep 1929]. Si; b&w. 35mm. 6 reels, 5,600 ft.

Dir Frank S. Mattison. *Photog* Jack Fuqua.

Cast: Raymond McKee *(Paul Garrison)*, Nola Luxford *(Nancy Dorance?)*, Bud Osborne *(Barry Kahn)*, Laura Miskin, Billy Franey, Evelyn Francisco, Fred Shanley, Arthur Hotaling, Eddie Harris, Hugh Saxon, White Star *(King, a horse)*.

Western melodrama. Arizona cowboy Paul Garrison vows to capture King, the stallion leader of a herd of wild horses. The horse, meanwhile, ingeniously frees a stable of horses from the ranch of wealthy Clarence Dorance, whose polo pony Diana VII is the apple of King's eye. Paul saves the endangered Nancy Dorance from the stampede and recovers Diana VII, only to have her stolen by Scar Satilleo, an Indian, who paints the mare so as to disguise her. King sees through this ruse and frees his love, only to be finally captured by Garrison and his pal, Zip Jones. The cowboy then enters the Santa Barbara polo matches astride King, defeats a persistent rival, Barry Kahn, and wins both the Travor Cup and Nancy's hand in marriage. *Cowboys. Indians of North America. Disguise. Ranches. Polo. Santa Barbara. Horses. Stampedes.*

KING OF THE PACK **F2.2876**

Gotham Productions. *Dist* Lumas Film Corp. 1 Oct **1926** [c12 Oct 1926; LP23267]. Si; b&w. 35mm. 6 reels, 5,960 ft.

Pres by Sam Sax. *Supv* Renaud Hoffman. *Dir* Frank Richardson. *Story-Cont* James Bell Smith. *Titl* Delos Sutherland. *Photog* Ray June. *Asst Dir* Glenn Belt.

Cast: Peter the Great *(King, a dog)*, Charlotte Stevens *(Selah Blair)*, Robert Gordon *(Clint Sifton)*, Vera Lewis *("Widder" Gasper)*, Mary Cornwallis *(Kitty Carlyle)*, Danny Hoy *(Bud Gasper)*, Frank Brownlee *(Chuck Purdy)*, W. H. Davis *(Sam Blair)*, Frank Norcross *(Dr. Joe Stoddard)*.

Melodrama. Sam Blair, a poor mountain farmer of Tennessee, takes the "Widder" Gasper as his second wife, and she soon lives up to the vicious tradition of stepmothers. Selah, his daughter, has the firm friendship of her dog, King, who saves her from her stepmother's tyranny. Kitty Carlyle, a musical comedy star vacationing in the hills, is rescued from her runaway horse by Selah and King, and her gratitude takes the form of a $1,000 check to pay for Selah's education. After Sam dies, Clint Sifton, who loves Selah, advises her to hide the money from the "Widder" and her son, Bud. When King hides the money, the "Widder" and one of her moonshiners take Selah to a cave and threaten her; Bud gets into a fight over her and starts a fire in the cave, but King and Clint arrive to the rescue. The "Widder" tries to escape, but King forces her over a cliff to her death. *Farmers. Stepmothers. Actors. Moonshiners. Mountain life. Education. Tennessee. Dogs.*

KING OF THE RODEO **F2.2877**

Universal Pictures. 6 Jan **1929** [c19 Nov 1928; LP25852]. Si; b&w. 35mm. 6 reels, 5,509 ft.

Prod Hoot Gibson. *Dir* Henry MacRae. *Cont* George Morgan. *Titl* B. M. Bower, Harold Tarshis. *Story* B. M. Bower. *Photog* Harry Neumann. *Art Dir* David S. Garber. *Film Ed* Gilmore Walker.

Cast: Hoot Gibson *(Montana Kid)*, Kathryn Crawford *(Dulcie Harlan)*, Slim Summerville *(Slim)*, Charles K. French *(Chip, Sr.)*, Monty Montague *(Weasel)*, Joseph W. Girard *(Harlan)*, Jack Knapp *(Shorty)*, Harry Todd *(J. G.)*, Bodil Rosing *(Mother)*.

Western melodrama. The Montana Kid, son of Chip of the Flying U, takes his best relay horse and goes to Chicago for a rodeo, quickly falling in love with Dulcie Harlan, the daughter of a rodeo official. Weasel, a renegade cowboy, robs the cashier, and the Kid goes after him, capturing him after a frantic chase through traffic. *Cowboys. Rodeos. Chicago. Chases. Horses.*

KING OF THE SADDLE **F2.2878**

Dist Associated Exhibitors. c10 Sep **1926** [LU23087]. Si; b&w. 35mm. 5 reels.

Dir William J. Craft. *Story* Carl Krusada.

Cast: Bill Cody, Joan Meredith.

Comedy-drama. While at the stockyard in Kansas City, Billy and Nick are counting the last heads of steer for the Circle-Bar ranch. Bill receives a letter of payment from the ranchowner, John Blake, enclosing stock originally valued at $300,000 but now worth only $3, with the explanation that he is broke, his ranch is sealed tight by the sheriff, and this worthless stock is all he has left. Bill, disheartened, and Nick, who is as always hungry, go to a luncheonette, where Mary, the sympathetic waitress, gives them a free meal. It's love at first sight for Bill and Mary, but she is stunned and confused when she sees Bill's stock certificate bearing the name of John Blake, her father, whom she has not seen for many years. All ends well with the discovery of oil on the Blake ranch, with Mary united with her father and engaged to Bill, and with Nick hungry, as usual. *Ranchers. Waitresses. Oil lands. Cattle. Stockyards. Bankruptcy. Kansas City.*

THE KING OF THE TURF **F2.2879**

Film Booking Offices of America. 28 Feb **1926** [c28 Feb 1926; LP22428]. Si; b&w. 35mm. 7 reels, 6,210 ft.

Dir James P. Hogan. *Cont* J. Grubb Alexander. *Adapt* John C. Brownell, Louis Joseph Vance. *Photog* Jules Cronjager. *Asst Dir* Frank Geraghty.

Cast: George Irving *(Colonel Fairfax)*, Patsy Ruth Miller *(Kate Fairfax)*, Kenneth Harlan *(John Doe Smith)*, Al Roscoe *(Tom Selsby)*, Kathleen Kirkham *(Letitia Selsby)*, Mary Carr *(Martha Fairfax)*, David Torrence *(Martyn Selsby)*, Dave Kirby *(Red Kelly)*, William Franey *(Soup Conley)*, Eddie Phillips *(Dude Morlanti)*.

Melodrama. Col. Richard Fairfax, a courtly southern horsebreeder, is framed on the charge of embezzlement by Martyn Selsby, his business partner, and sentenced to jail. Selsby soon dies of apoplexy, first dictating a confession to exonerate Fairfax; Selsby's wife is afraid of scandal, however, and places the confession in a wall safe. Time passes. The colonel serves out his sentence and returns home in the company of four friends he has made in prison: John Doe Smith (a horsetrainer gone astray), Red Kelly, Soup Conley, and Dude Morlanti. Selsby's son, Tom, who is infatuated with the colonel's daughter, Kate, offers to give her his father's confession if she will marry him. Smith overhears this remark and with the help of his former cellmates recovers the confession. The colonel's name is cleared, and his horse, entered in an important race, wins a gold cup. Kate and John Doe hit it off just fine. *Kentucky colonels. Horsebreeders. Horsetrainers. Horseracing. Injustice. Frameup. Embezzlement. Documentation.*

THE KING OF WILD HORSES **F2.2880**

Hal Roach Studios. *Dist* Pathé Exchange. 6 Apr **1924** [New York premiere; released 13 Apr; c26 Mar 1924; LU20034]. Si; b&w. 35mm. 5 reels, 4,611 ft.

Prod Hal Roach. *Dir* Fred Jackman. *Scen* Carl Himm. *Story* Hal Roach. *Photog* Floyd Jackman.

Cast: Rex *(The Black)*, Edna Murphy *(Mary Fielding)*, Charles Parrott *(Boyd Fielding)*, Sidney De Gray *(John Fielding)*, Leon Bary *(Billy Blair)*, Pat Hartigan *(Wade Galvin)*, Frank Butler, Sidney D'Albrook.

Western melodrama. "The Black, by right of might, is undisputed leader of a band of wild horses. By his intelligence and agility he protects the herd and eludes various pursuers. The Fielding ranch is in [the] charge of a villainous foreman who has involved Fielding's weakling son in a cattle stealing escapade. Billy Blair, a cowpuncher, has two consuming passions. One is his love for Mary Fielding, the other his desire to capture The Black. His perseverance is rewarded, for he wins both girl and horse. All three co-operate in frustrating further villainy on the part of Galvin, the foreman, and in bringing him to justice." (*Exhibitors Trade Review*, 5 Apr 1924, p25.) Billy makes friends with The Black by rescuing him from a forest fire. *Cowboys. Rustling. Ranches. Forest fires. Horses.*

THE KING ON MAIN STREET **F2.2881**

Famous Players–Lasky. *Dist* Paramount Pictures. ca17 Oct **1925** [Washington premiere; released 9 Nov 1925; c12 Nov 1925; LP21990]. Si; b&w with col sequences (Technicolor). 35mm. 6 reels, 5,982 or 6,229 ft.

Pres by Adolph Zukor, Jesse L. Lasky. *Dir-Adapt* Monta Bell. *Screenplay* Douglas Z. Doty. *Photog* James Howe. *Art Dir* Sam Corso.

Cast: Adolphe Menjou *(Serge IV, King of Molvania)*, Bessie Love *(Gladys Humphreys)*, Greta Nissen *(Terese Manix)*, Oscar Shaw *(John Rockland)*, Joseph Kilgour *(Arthur Trent)*, Edgar Norton *(Jensen)*, Mario Majeroni *(Count Krenko)*, Carlotta Monterey *(Mrs. Nash)*, Marcia Harris *(Aunt Tabitha Humphreys)*, Edouard Durand *(Bourdier)*.

Romantic comedy-drama. Source: Gaston Arman de Caillavet, Robert de Flers, and Emmanuel Arène, *Le Roi; pièce en quatre actes* (Paris, ca1908). Serge IV, King of Molvania, is told that he must negotiate a large loan by either concluding an alliance with the House of Slavonia or through lease of oil lands to American capitalists. The king decides on the latter course and journeys to New York via Paris, where he meets Gladys Humphreys. In New York, tired of negotiations with oil representative Arthur Trent, he sneaks off to Coney Island where he has a wonderful time with a freckled boy named "Skinny" Smith. He meets Gladys again, and she introduces him to her fiancé, John Rockland, who (not knowing him to be a king) invites him to his home in Little Falls, New Jersey. There the king falls genuinely in love with Gladys but is caught in a delicate situation by Trent and is obliged to sign a lease lest her reputation be ruined. The king returns to Molvania, acquires a queen from the House of Slovania, and is told he can never leave his country again. *Royalty. Oilmen. Children. Imaginary kingdoms. Oil lands. Paris. New York City. Coney Island. Little Falls (New Jersey).*

Note: The opening and closing sequences with the king reviewing the cavalry, first alone and then with his queen, are in color.

KING, QUEEN, JOKER F2.2882

Famous Players–Lasky. *Dist* Paramount Pictures. 15 May **1921** [c29 Jan 1921; LP16091]. Si; b&w. 35mm. 5 reels, 5,137 ft.

Dir-Story-Scen Sydney Chaplin. *Photog* Murphy Darling.

Cast: Sydney Chaplin *(The King/The Joker)*, Lottie MacPherson *(The Queen/Chief Plotter)*.

Farce. Although the King of Coronia is threatened by revolution, he refuses to grant his people the trade charter they demand. The chief plotter kidnaps the king, substituting in his place a barber's assistant, the king's exact double. The barber has the time of his life until the king escapes and forces him to his heels. The king at last effects the reforms for which the plotters have schemed. *Royalty. Doubles. Barbers. Impersonation. Imaginary kingdoms. Trade agreements. France. England.*

Note: Photographed in England, France, and the United States.

KING TUT-ANKH-AMEN'S EIGHTH WIFE F2.2883

Max Cohen. 1 Jul **1923** [scheduled release]. Si; b&w. 35mm. 5 reels, 4,100 ft.

Dir-Story Andrew Remo. *Scen* George M. Merrick, Max Cohen. *Photog* John Bitzer.

Mystery melodrama. The theme concerns the tragedy that pursues those who violate the tombs of the Pharaohs. *Royalty. Tombs. Supernatural. Egypt. Tutankhamen.*

Note: Alternate Title: *The Mystery of Tut-Ankh-Amen's Eighth Wife.*

THE KINGDOM OF HUMAN HEARTS F2.2884

Wilbert Leroy Cosper. *For* Christian Philosophical Institute. 4 April **1921** [c11 Nov 1929; LU16177]. Si; b&w. 35mm. 10 reels.

Dir-Writ Wilbert Leroy Cosper.

Cast—Prolog: Hugh Metcalfe *(Knowledge)*, Lona Good *(Faith)*, Geoffrey Bell *(Love)*.

Cast—Story: Hugh Metcalfe *(The Philosopher)*, Sylvia Edney *(May Leslie)*, Jack Grey *(Jack Sheldon)*, Lana Good *(Ruth Leslie)*, Richard Lancester *(Monte Bruce)*, Jean Traig *(Mrs. Holden)*, Sheldy Roach *(Daniel Holden)*, Thora Lorraine *(Louise Holden)*, Ed Russell *(district attorney)*.

Melodrama. The film begins with a prolog depicting the Kingdom of Human Hearts, a land of plenty where Innocence rules and the Subjects are happy. But Innocence succumbs to Temptation—despite Knowledge's warning—with the result that Ignorance, Greed, and Fear live among the Subjects. Sin is born to Innocence and Temptation, and Knowledge apparently dies. Finally realizing the unhappy plight of her people, Innocence—with the help of Knowledge—finds Faith and Love. Later, Truth is born to Innocence and Love; they all eventually return to the Kingdom, Ignorance and Sin are overthrown, and all ends happily. ... Switching to a modern setting of a high school graduation, May Leslie is obviously the prettiest and most popular of her group—admired by boys, especially Jack Sheldon, and envied by the girls. But her head is quickly turned by Monte Bruce (a visitor from the city); May ignores The Philosopher's good advice and elopes with Monte. Only unhappiness befalls May: she gives birth to a sickly child, and Monte deserts her for Sylvia, a long-time companion. Monte and Sylvia become involved in a seance racket, which culminates in the murder of Monte by Daniel Holden, whose wife was wronged by Bruce. During all this time Jack has searched for May, and they are now reunited with the help of The Philosopher. *Philosophers. Spiritualism. Murder. Desertion. High school life. Personification.*

THE KINGDOM WITHIN F2.2885

Producers Security Corp. *Dist* W. W. Hodkinson Corp. 24 Dec **1922.** Si; b&w. 35mm. 7 reels, 6,036-6,800 ft.

Dir Victor Schertzinger. *Story* Kenneth B. Clarke. *Photog* John S. Stumar.

Cast: Russell Simpson *(Caleb Deming)*, Z. Wall Covington *(Danny West)*, Gaston Glass *(Amos)*, Pauline Starke *(Emily Preston)*, Hallam Cooley *(Will Preston)*, Ernest Torrence *(Krieg)*, Gordon Russell *(Dodd)*, Marion Feducha *(Connie)*.

Rural melodrama. Hated by his blacksmith father because of his crippled arm, Amos Deming grows up with a keen spiritual insight and a talent for making toys for children. Emily Preston, who lives next door to the Demings, is ostracized by the community because her brother is in jail, but Amos is able to break down her wall of bitterness. When Preston is freed, Krieg tries to implicate him in the murder of Dodd, a lumberman, and threatens Emily with dire consequences if she should talk. Answering Emily's calls for help, Amos struggles with Krieg and miraculously finds his arm cured. Stunned, Krieg stumbles outside into the waiting arms of the law, and Amos receives love and acceptance from his father and Emily. *Blacksmiths. Cripples. Toymakers. Brother-sister relationship. Miracles. Prejudice. Fatherhood. Murder.*

THE KINGFISHER'S ROOST F2.2886

Pinnacle Productions. 20 Feb **1922** [New York State]. Si; b&w. 35mm. 5 reels.

Dir-Story-Scen Louis Chaudet, Paul Hurst.

Cast: Neal Hart *(Barr Messenger)*, Yvette Mitchell *(Betty Brownlee)*, William Quinn *("Bull" Keeler)*, Ben Corbett *("Red" McGee)*, Chet Ryan *(Sheriff Breen)*, Jane Fosher *(Mrs. Brownlee)*, Floyd Anderson *(Dan McFee)*, W. S. Weatherwax *(Bill Jackson)*, John Judd *(Chief of the Rurales)*, Earl Simpson *(Pete, McGee's aide)*, Earl Dwyer *(Dave Butler, the grocer)*.

Western melodrama. "Barr Messenger, the victim of a frame-up, after which he is accused of being a cattle thief, escapes from the ranch and gets across the Mexican border. He had been in love with Betty Brownlee, who had disappeared from town shortly after the sum of $10,000 had been stolen from her firm. She gets a position as waitress in the headquarters of Red McGee, head of the 'Kingfisher' gang of outlaws. One night she innocently gives out some information about the gang and Red is ordered to seize her for the Kingfisher. Burr [*sic*] comes into the scene unexpectedly and fights Red as he is trying to kidnap Betty, and succeeds in running down the whole Kingfisher gang and discovering that they were responsible for framing him, at the same time learning that Betty's sister, not Betty, stole the $10,000." (*Moving Picture World,* 13 May 1922, p200.) *Waitresses. Sisters. Gangs. Rustling. Robbery. Frameup. Mexican border.*

KING'S CREEK LAW F2.2887

William Steiner Productions. *Dist* Photo Drama Co. ca6 Dec **1923** [New York showing; c16 Oct 1923; LU19497]. Si; b&w. 35mm. 5 reels.

Dir Leo Maloney, Bob Williamson. *Story-Adapt* Frances Beebe, Ford Beebe. *Photog* Ben Bail.

Cast in order of appearance: Leo Maloney *(Tom Hardy)*, Horace Carpenter *(The Sheriff)*, Frank Ellis *(James Lawton)*, Milton Brown *(Saul Jameson)*, Chet Ryan *(Kirk Jameson)*, Josephine Hill *(Milly Jameson)*, Bullet *(see note)*.

Western melodrama. Texas Ranger Tom Hardy is sent to the hardboiled town of King City to track down a murderer. The trail leads him into contact with Saul Jameson, an unreconstructed southerner who fancies himself to be the law in King's Creek and conducts his own trials without government interference. Kirk, Jameson's beloved son, becomes a suspect in the case, and Jameson decides to try him impartially despite his parental affection. Hardy, however, proves Kirk's innocence, exposes the real murderer, and thus reconciles Jameson to United States law. Hardy also wins the hand of Jameson's daughter, Milly. *Texas Rangers. Southerners.*

Vigilantes. Law. Murder. Dogs.

Note: The shooting script in the copyright files indicates that Bullet, the dog, may also be in the cast, portraying the murdered man's dog that is later adopted by Hardy, but this information cannot be confirmed.

KISMET **F2.2888**

First National Pictures. 30 Oct **1930** [New York premiere; released 18 Jan 1931; c28 Dec 1930; LP1877]. Sd (Vitaphone); b&w. 65mm (Vitascope). 10 reels, 8,253 ft.

Prod Robert North. *Dir* John Francis Dillon. *Screenplay* Howard Estabrook. *Photog* John Seitz. *Film Ed* Al Hall. *Rec Engr* Joseph Kane.

Cast: Otis Skinner *(Hajj)*, Loretta Young *(Marsinah)*, David Manners *(Caliph Abdallah)*, David Manners *(Caliph Adallah)*, Sidney Blackmer *(Wazir Mansur)*, Mary Duncan *(Zeleekha)*, Montagu Love *(The Jailer)*, Ford Sterling *(Amru)*, Theodore von Eltz *(The Guide Nazir)*, John St. Polis *(The Iman Mahmud)*, Edmund Breese *(Jawan)*, Blanche Frederici *(Narjis)*, Richard Carlyle *(The Muezzin)*, John Sheehan *(Kazim)*, Otto Hoffman *(Azaf)*, Charles Clary, Noble Johnson, Carol Wines, Sidney Jarvis, Lorris Baker, Olin Francis, Will Walling.

Costume melodrama. Source: Edward Knoblock, *Kismet; an "Arabian Night" in Three Acts* (New York, 1911). Hajj, beggar and thief, schemes with a guide to obtain gold from the famous bandit, the White Sheik, who is searching for his long-lost son; but Hajj recognizes the White Sheik as his enemy, Jawan, and refuses the guide his share; and the guide has Hajj arrested. Mansur, the Wazir of Police, offers Hajj the choice of losing his hand and his daughter, Marsinah, or assassinating the caliph. Saved from Hajj's dagger by his coat of mail, the caliph sends the beggar to prison, where he encounters Jawan, kills his enemy, exchanges clothing, and is released. Hajj is soon again in Mansur's clutches for trying to spirit his daughter from the wazir's harem, but Hajj kills Mansur (Jawan's son) just as the caliph enters. Rather than receiving further punishment, Hajj is released—for the caliph, who has disguised himself as his gardener's son, is about to marry Marsinah. *Beggars. Thieves. Royalty. Police. Disguise. Filial relations. Assassination. Revenge. Prisons. Harems.*

THE KISS **F2.2889**

Universal Film Manufacturing Co. 4 Jul **1921** [c22 Jun 1921; LP16706]. Si; b&w. 35mm. 5 reels, 4,488 ft.

Dir Jack Conway. *Scen* A. P. Younger. *Scen? (see note)* George Pyper. *Photog* Bert Glennon.

Cast: George Periolat *(Don Luis Baldarama)*, William E. Lawrence *(Audre Baldarama)*, J. P. Lockney *(Selistino Vargas)*, Carmel Myers *(Erolinda Vargas)*, J. J. Lanoe *(Carlos)*, Harvey Clarke *(Miguel Chavez)*, Jean Acker *(Isabella Chavez)*, Ed Brady *(Manuel Feliz)*.

Melodrama. Source: Johnston McCulley, "Little Erolinda," in *Adventure Magazine* (11:3–40, Feb 1916). At the harvest fiesta, Don Luis expects to announce the betrothal of his son, Audre, to Isabella, the daughter of a neighboring don, but Audre plans to elope with Erolinda, the daughter of the ranch superintendent. They are surprised by Vargas, who believes that his daughter has been dishonored and shoots Audre. The latter's vaqueros, believing him to be murdered, storm the house, but Erolinda holds them at bay. Audre pacifies his men, then kisses Erolinda in their sight, thus claiming her as his bride. *Ranch foremen. Honor. Ranches. California—Mexican period.*

Note: Some sources give George Pyper coauthorship credit for scenario; Universal records have been followed.

THE KISS **F2.2890**

Metro-Goldwyn-Mayer Pictures. 16 Nov **1929** [c26 Nov 1929; LP868]. Mus score (Movietone); b&w. 35mm. 7 reels. [Also si.]

Dir Jacques Feyder. *Scen* Hans Kraly. *Titl* Marian Ainslee. *Photog* William Daniels. *Art Dir* Cedric Gibbons. *Film Ed* Ben Lewis. *Mus Synchronization* William Axt. *Gowns* Adrian.

Cast: Greta Garbo *(Irene)*, Conrad Nagel *(André)*, Anders Randolf *(Guarry)*, Holmes Herbert *(Lassalle)*, Lew Ayres *(Pierre)*, George Davis *(Durant)*.

Romantic drama. Source: George M. Saville, "The Kiss" (publication undetermined). Irene, victim of a loveless marriage to wealthy Guarry, carries on a clandestine affair with André, a young lawyer whom she loves but forces herself to forget; and in desperation, he leaves and goes to Paris. Pierre, the youthful son of a Lyons financier, is fascinated by Irene, and when she gives him an innocent goodby kiss, Guarry, thinking she has been unfaithful to him, attacks the boy. The ensuing struggle results in Guarry's death. Irene recounts the events of the fateful evening to the police, but her story is full of contradictions and she keeps the boy's name out of the affair. Brought to trial, she is acquitted with André's help, but later she confesses that she killed her husband to save the boy's life. At last she finds happiness with André. *Lawyers. Infidelity. Marriage. Manslaughter. Trials. Lyons. Paris.*

THE KISS BARRIER **F2.2891**

Fox Film Corp. 31 May **1925** [c24 May 1925; LP21542]. Si; b&w. 35mm. 6 reels.

Pres by William Fox. *Dir* R. William Neill. *Scen* E. Magnus Ingleton. *Story* Frederick Hatton, Fanny Hatton.

Cast: Edmund Lowe *(Richard March)*, Claire Adams *(Marion Weston)*, Diana Miller *(Suzette)*, Marion Harlan *(Connie)*, Thomas Mills *(O'Hara)*, Charles Clary *(Colonel Hale)*, Grace Cunard *(widow)*.

Romantic melodrama. During the World War, Richard March, an aviator, is shot down over France. He is not badly hurt in the crash and steals a kiss from Marion Weston, the Red Cross nurse whose ambulance comes to his aid. After the war, Richard resumes his professional life as an actor and meets Marion by chance at a skating party. At first she snubs him, but he soon charms her, and they become constant companions. Marion later believes that Richard is having an affair with Suzette, his leading lady, and she again turns the cold shoulder toward him. Richard writes a play based on his own experiences, and Marion comes to see she misjudged him. Connie, who is jealous of Richard's love for Marion, attempts to compromise him. Connie herself later confesses her scheme to discredit Richard, and Richard and Marion are reunited. *Aviators. Nurses. Actors. Playwrights. Filial relations. World War I. France. Red Cross.*

A KISS FOR CINDERELLA **F2.2892**

Famous Players–Lasky. *Dist* Paramount Pictures. 22 Dec **1926** [c11 Jan 1926; LP22254]. Si; b&w. 35mm. 10 reels, 9,686 ft.

Pres by Adolph Zukor, Jesse L. Lasky. *Dir* Herbert Brenon. *Scen* Willis Goldbeck, Townsend Martin. *Photog* J. Roy Hunt. *Art Dir* Julian Boone Fleming.

Cast: Betty Bronson *(Cinderella)*, Tom Moore *(policeman)*, Esther Ralston *(fairy godmother)*, Henry Vibart *(Richard Bodie)*, Dorothy Cumming *(queen)*, Ivan Simpson *(Mr. Cutaway)*, Dorothy Walters *(Mrs. Maloney)*, Flora Finch *(second customer)*, Juliet Brenon *(third customer)*, Marilyn McLain *(Gladys)*, Pattie Coakley *(Marie-Thérèse)*, Mary Christian *(Sally)*, Edna Hagen *(Gretchen)*.

Fantasy-drama. Source: James Matthew Barrie, *A Kiss for Cinderella: a Comedy* (New York, 1920). Cinderella, a little slavey, works for a pittance cleaning up after a kindly artist during the World War. By inadvertently exposing a light during an air raid scare, she arouses the suspicion of a policeman, who follows her home and discovers that, in her spare time, she runs the Penny Friend Shop, devoting herself to the care and feeding of four war orphans. The policeman loses his heart to Cinderella and helps her to care for the little ones. Cinderella falls asleep in the snow one night and dreams of pumpkin coaches, fairy godmothers, and good fairies. She becomes ill from exposure, and the policeman proposes that they be married; Cinderella gratefully accepts. *Housemaids. Police. Drudges. Artists. Orphans. War victims. World War I. Dreams.*

A KISS IN A TAXI **F2.2893**

Famous Players–Lasky. *Dist* Paramount Pictures. 22 Feb **1927** [c26 Feb 1927; LP23711]. Si; b&w. 35mm. 7 reels, 6,439 ft.

Pres by Adolph Zukor, Jesse L. Lasky. *Dir* Clarence Badger. *Adapt-Screenplay* Doris Anderson. *Titl* Sam Hellman, George Marion, Jr. *Photog* H. Kinley Martin.

Cast: Bebe Daniels *(Ginette)*, Chester Conklin *(Maraval)*, Douglas Gilmore *(Lucien Cambolle)*, Henry Kolker *(Leon Lambert)*, Richard Tucker *(Henri Le Sage)*, Agostino Borgato *(Pierre)*, Eulalie Jensen *(Valentine Lambert)*, Rose Burdick *("Gay Lady")*, Jocelyn Lee *(secretary)*.

Farce. Source: Maurice Hennequin, Pierre Veber and Clifford Grey, *A Kiss in a Taxi*, adapted by Grey as *Sunny Days* (New York opening: 8 Feb 1928). Ginette, a waitress at the Café Pierre, loves Lucien, a poor artist, and objects to the attentions of others with whatever glassware is at hand, though Lucien's father forbids their marriage. While Leon Lambert and a "gay lady" are riding the boulevards, they stop at a florist's shop. At the same time, Ginette, pursued by her irate employer, runs down the boulevard and into the waiting taxi. Leon returns, offers a bouquet to the stranger, and forces a kiss; the chauffeur, losing control of the car, crashes through the cafe window. Leon buys the restaurant for Ginette, expecting her gratitude, but uses the card of Maraval, treasurer of the Artists'

Society. To escape an awkward situation, Leon poses as Ginette's father, then forces Maraval to assert himself as the girl's lover; with complications resolved, the lovers are united. *Waitresses. Artists. Imposture. Associations. Paris.*

A KISS IN THE DARK *see* **DO AND DARE**

A KISS IN THE DARK **F2.2894**

Famous Players–Lasky. *Dist* Paramount Pictures. 6 Apr **1925** [c10 Apr 1925; LP21346]. Si; b&w. 35mm. 6 reels, 5,767 ft.

Pres by Adolph Zukor, Jesse L. Lasky. *Dir* Frank Tuttle. *Scen* Townsend Martin. *Photog* Alvin Wyckoff. *Art Dir* Van Nest Polglase.

Cast: Adolphe Menjou *(Walter Grenham)*, Aileen Pringle *(Janet Livingstone)*, Lillian Rich *(Betty King)*, Kenneth MacKenna *(Johnny King)*, Ann Pennington *(dancer)*, Kitty Kelly *(chorus girl)*.

Comedy. Source: Frederick Lonsdale, *Aren't We All* (New York, c1924). Walter Grenham, who has a weakness for women, persuades an old friend, Janet Livingstone, to marry him, promising to remain faithful to her. They then prepare to embark for New York in the company of a young married couple, Betty and Johnny King, but, by misadventure, Betty and Walter are left behind in Havana. Walter takes a plane to Key West, where he overtakes Janet and explains everything to her satisfaction; Betty goes to New York and finds her husband in the arms of a chorus girl. With great difficulty and misunderstanding, Walter reunites the Kings and finally prepares to settle down to domestic bliss. *Chorus girls. Marriage. Havana. New York City. Key West.*

A KISS IN TIME **F2.2895**

Realart Pictures. Jul **1921** [c27 May 1921; LP16589]. Si; b&w. 35mm. 5 reels, 4,351 ft.

Dir Thomas N. Heffron. *Scen* Douglas Doty. *Photog* William E. Collins. *Asst Dir* Harold Schwartz.

Cast: Wanda Hawley *(Sheila Athlone)*, T. Roy Barnes *(Brian Moore)*, Bertram Johns *(Robert Codman Ames)*, Walter Hiers *(Bertie Ballast)*, Margaret Loomis *(nymph)*.

Comedy. Source: Royal Brown, "From Four to Eleven-Three," in *McClure's* (52:19, Oct 1920). Although she finds the stiff Bostonian manners of her fiancé, Robert Ames, unsuited to her temperament, artist-illustrator Sheila Athlone refuses to illustrate an author's story because of its "absurd" premise that a girl would kiss a man she met only 4 hours earlier. Author Brian Moore, setting out to prove his point, poses as a butcher boy and induces her to ride out to a country orchard. His advances are refused until he saves a child from an explosion, and 2 minutes before the time limit, in admiration of his bravery, she allows him to kiss her. *Illustrators. Authors. Bostonians.*

KISS ME AGAIN **F2.2896**

Warner Brothers Pictures. 1 Aug **1925** [23 Apr 1925; LP21387]. Si; b&w. 35mm. 7 reels, 6,722 ft.

Dir Ernst Lubitsch. *Scen* Hans Kraly. *Photog* Charles Van Enger.

Cast: Marie Prevost *(Loulou Fleury)*, Monte Blue *(Gaston Fleury)*, John Roche *(Maurice Ferrière)*, Clara Bow *(Grizette)*, Willard Louis *(Avocat Dubois)*.

Domestic comedy. Source: Victorien Sardou and Émile de Najac. *Cyprienne* or *Divorçons* (Paris, 1883). Gaston Fleury's wife, Loulou, takes a perfunctory interest in music but a deeper one in a musician named Maurice. Although Gaston has no intention of releasing his wife into the hands of Maurice, he feigns willingness to give Loulou a divorce. Loulou then becomes bored with Maurice, and clever maneuvering on the part of Gaston brings her to want desperately a reconciliation with him. He happily fulfills her wish. *Musicians. Divorce. Infidelity.*

KISSED (Universal Special) **F2.2897**

Universal Film Manufacturing Co. 22 May **1922** [c17 May 1922; LP17891]. Si; b&w. 35mm. 5 reels, 4,231 ft.

Dir King Baggot. *Scen* Doris Schroeder. *Photog* Ben Bail.

Cast: Marie Prevost *(Constance Keener)*, Lloyd Whitlock *(Dr. Sherman Moss)*, Lillian Langdon *(Mrs. Keener)*, J. Frank Glendon *(Merton Torrey)*, Arthur Hoyt *(Horace Peabody)*, Percy Challenger *(Editor Needham)*, Harold Miller *(Bob Rennesdale)*, Marie Crisp *(Miss Smith)*, Harold Goodwin *(Jim Kernochan)*.

Romantic comedy. Source: Arthur Somers Roche, "Kissed," in *Ainslee's Magazine* (41:1–39, Jul 1918). Constance Keener, who is betrothed to young millionaire Merton Torrey, confesses to him her desire for romance such as he does not give her. On the occasion of a masquerade ball, Torrey is unable to escort her; and while she is alone on the balcony, someone suddenly seizes and kisses her, then disappears. She attempts to discover her assailant's identity, but two other men are in identical costumes; later, she decides that he was Dr. Moss, and a few days later, she elopes with him. On the train, Connie realizes after being kissed that she has eloped with the wrong man. When the train comes to a stop, they are "held up" by a masked man who "kidnaps" and kisses her; realizing that he is the stranger, Connie unmasks Torrey, the man she had considered so unromantic. *Millionaires. Courtship. Disguise. Mistaken identity. Elopement.*

KISSES **F2.2898**

Metro Pictures. 3 Apr **1922** [c4 Apr 1922; LP17722]. Si; b&w. 35mm. 5 reels, 4,300 ft.

Dir Maxwell Karger. *Adapt-Scen* June Mathis. *Story* May Tully. *Photog* Allan Siegler. *Art Dir* Joseph Calder.

Cast: Alice Lake *(Betty Ellen Estabrook)*, Harry Myers *(Bill Bailey)*, Edward Connelly *(Thomas Estabrook)*, Edward Jobson *(John Maynard)*, Dana Todd *(Norman Maynard)*, Mignon Anderson *(Bessie Neldon)*, John MacKinnon *(Edward Neldon)*, Eugène Pouyet *(Gustave)*.

Romantic comedy. Betty Estabrook, daughter of a financier, meets Bill Bailey while returning home on a train and offers him one of her homemade candy kisses; Bill persuades her to dispense some candy at a charity bazaar, which she does with great success; but unhappily he discovers that Betty is engaged to Norman Maynard, son of a manufacturer of sweets. Betty's father dies as a result of financial complications, and determined to reimburse the creditors, she sells her house and all her possessions, causing Maynard to break off the engagement. Bill and Bessie Neldon join forces with Betty to manufacture candy, a venture that becomes so successful that Maynard begins to suffer from the competition and sows seeds of discontent among their workers. Bill thwarts the plan, but Betty sells the B-Kissed Candy Co. to Maynard for a sizable sum, which enables her and Bill to become engaged. *Businesswomen. Candy. Finance—Personal. Business management. Courtship.*

KIT CARSON **F2.2899**

Paramount Famous Lasky Corp. 23 Jun **1928** [c21 Aug 1928; LP25550]. Si; b&w. 35mm. 8 reels, 7,464 ft.

Dir Alfred L. Werker, Lloyd Ingraham. *Scen* Paul Powell. *Titl* Frederick Hatton. *Story* Frank M. Clifton. *Photog* Mack Stengler. *Film Ed* Duncan Mansfield.

Cast: Fred Thomson *(Kit Carson)*, Nora Lane *(Josefa)*, Dorothy Janis *(Sings-in-the-Clouds)*, Raoul Paoli *(Shuman)*, William Courtright *(Old Bill Williams)*, Nelson McDowell *(Jim Bridger)*, Raymond Turner *(Smokey)*.

Western melodrama. In a saloon in Taos, Kit Carson gets into a fight with Shuman over a Spanish dancer who has taken Kit's fancy; the following day, both men (who are part of a government peace-keeping mission ordered into the troubled Blackfeet country) ride north. On the way, Kit encounters Sings-in-the-Clouds, the daughter of the Blackfeet chief, rescuing her from an attacking bear. This single brave action establishes peaceful relations between the whites and the Indians. These relations are almost broken, however, when Shuman attacks the Indian girl with a knife; Kit shoots him in the hand and sends him packing. Shuman later attacks the girl in the desert and causes her death. Kit goes after him and throws him from a cliff into the Blackfeet circle of death. With the peace established, Kit returns to Taos. *Scouts—Frontier. Dancers. Blackfeet Indians. Taos. Kit Carson. Bears.*

KIT CARSON OVER THE GREAT DIVIDE **F2.2900**

Sunset Productions. *Dist* Aywon Film Corp. 3 Sep **1925** [New York State license]. Si; b&w. 35mm. 6 reels, 5,800 ft.

Dir-Writ Frank S. Mattison. *Titl* J. C. Hull. *Photog* Bert Longenecker. *Art Titl* Fowler Studios.

Cast: Roy Stewart *(Seaton Maurey)*, Henry B. Walthall *(Dr. Samuel Webb)*, Marguerite Snow *(Norma Webb, his wife)*, Sheldon Lewis *(Flint Bastille)*, Earl Metcalfe *(Basil Morgan)*, Charlotte Stevens *(Nancy Webb)*, Jack Mower *(Kit Carson)*, Arthur Hotaling *(Lt. John C. Frémont)*, Lew Meehan *(Josef La Rocque)*, Billy Franey *(Oswald Bliffing)*, Nelson McDowell *("Windy Bill" Sharp)*.

Western melodrama. No information about the precise nature of this film has been found. *Kit Carson. John Charles Frémont.*

Note: Also known as *With Kit Carson Over the Great Divide.*

KIVALINA OF THE ICE LANDS F2.2901

B. C. R. Productions. c25 Jun **1925** [LP21670]. Si; b&w. 35mm. 6 reels, 5,946 ft.

Dir Earl Rossman. *Titl* Katherine Hilliker. *Photog* Earl Rossman. *Film Ed* Katherine Hilliker.

Cast: Kivalina *(The Heroine)*, Aguvaluk *(The Hero)*, Nashulik *(witch doctor)*, Tokatoo *(Kivalina's brother)*, Nuwak *(The Master Hunter)*.

Drama. Aguvaluk, a great Eskimo hunter, plans to marry Kivalina and goes to the witch doctor for his consent. The witch doctor tells Aguvaluk that he may not marry until he has discharged all of his father's debts by bringing back the hides of 40 seals. The great hunter accomplishes this incredible feat and returns with the hides only to be told that, in order to pay off the interest on the debt, he must also bring in the hide of a silver fox. After great privation, Aguvaluk captures the fox, but before he can return to safety, he is caught in a fierce storm. He builds an ice shelter that protects him from the bitter cold and the following morning kills a small reindeer, satisfying his hunger with the meat and using the hide to make a small sled. Finally reaching home, Aguvaluk prepares to marry Kivalina, and there is a great feast. *Eskimos. Witch doctors. Storms. Seals. Fox.*

KNIGHT OF THE EUCHARIST F2.2902

Creston Feature Pictures. 7 Aug **1922** [New York State license application]. Si; b&w. 35mm. 7 reels, 6,500 ft.

Cast: James Flanagan.

Drama. "The picture has supposedly a religious theme, and in the carrying out of this theme, a religious organization, the Knights of Columbus, is shown severely criticising the Ku-Klux-Klan. Accusations are made against the characters of members of the Ku-Klux-Klan and their children .... The Ku-Klux-Klan are described as pursuing a Catholic lad, intent to do him bodily injury. Various scenes are depicted such as whipping the lad, beating his head with a torch holder ... . The Ku-Klux-Klan are pictured as planning to desecrate the altar and Eucharist of the Catholic Church, which the lad defends and is mortally injured." (New York State license records.) *Catholics. Eucharist. Religious persecution. Knights of Columbus. Ku Klux Klan.*

A KNIGHT OF THE WEST F2.2903

W. B. M. Photoplays. *Dist* C. O'D. Blanchfield. 5 Nov **1921** [trade review]. Si; b&w. 35mm. 5 reels, 4,600 ft.

Dir Robert McKenzie. *Titl* Reed Heustis. *Story* Eva B. Heazlit. *Photog* Len Powers.

Cast: Olin Francis *(Jack "Zip" Garvin)*, Estelle Harrison *(Dora McKittrick)*, Billy Franey *("Mana Palover")*, Otto Nelson *(Daniel McKittrick)*, May Foster *(Mother McKittrick)*, Claude Peyton *(Ralph Barton)*, Fay McKenzie *(Fray Murten)*.

Western comedy-drama. "Zip loves Dora, daughter of a neighboring ranch owner, but is very bashful. The ranch foreman also covets her and while a rustler himself seeks to throw suspicion upon Zip, but his plans miscarry. The arrival of his sister's little daughter precipitates Zip's love affair, but he still lacks courage. The girl's father, to help him, suggests that he use cave man stuff at a dance, but the villain beats him to it. Zip pursues the fleeing rustler and saves the girl, while the rustler gets his deserts and all ends happily." (*Moving Picture World,* 5 Nov 1921, p93.) *Cowboys. Ranch foremen. Rustlers. Brother-sister relationship.*

THE KNOCK ON THE DOOR F2.2904

Johnnie Walker. 10 Sep **1923** [New York showing]. Si; b&w. 35mm. 5 reels.

Dir William Hughes Curran.

Cast: Eddie Polo.

Comedy-drama(?). No information about the nature of this film has been found.

THE KNOCKER *see* **DOUBLE DEALING**

THE KNOCKOUT F2.2905

First National Pictures. 23 Aug **1925** [c25 Aug 1925; LP21772]. Si; b&w. 35mm. 8 reels, 7,450 ft.

Supv Earl Hudson. *Dir* Lambert Hillyer. *Ed Dir* Marion Fairfax. *Scen* Joseph Poland, Earle Snell. *Photog* Roy Carpenter. *Art Dir* Milton Menasco. *Film Ed* Arthur Tavares.

Cast: Milton Sills *(Sandy Donlin)*, Lorna Duveen *(Jean Farot)*, John Philip Kolb *(Black Jack Ducane)*, Edward Lawrence *(Mike Leary)*, Harry Cording *(Steve McKenna)*, Frankie Evans *(Brown)*, Harlan Knight *(Farot)*, Jed Prouty *(Mac)*, Claude King *(Parker)*.

Source: Morris De Camp Crawford, *The Come-Back* (New York, 1925). After winning the world's light heavyweight title, Sandy Donlin is told by a doctor that he will never fight again because of a torn ligament in his arm. Sandy quits the ring and accepts a position as the foreman of the northwoods lumber camp of J. Van Dyke Parker, a millionaire lumberman who is plotting to obtain the lands of Farot, his greatest business rival. Sandy meets Farot's daughter, Jean, and, despite her initial distrust of him, he falls in love with her. Parker's men dynamite the dam where Farot's logs are stored, jamming them in the river. Unable to get his logs to market, Farot is faced with bankruptcy. Sandy decides to return to the ring, hoping to raise enough money with his fists to meet Farot's notes. With Jean's ringside encouragement, Sandy wins the fight, saving Farot from his creditors and insuring a lifetime of happiness with Jean. *Lumber camp foremen. Prizefighters. Millionaires. Lumbermen. Business competition. Bankruptcy. Lumber camps. Land rights. Dams.*

THE KNOCKOUT KID F2.2906

Harry Webb Productions. *Dist* Rayart Pictures. 1 Sep **1925.** Si; b&w. 35mm. 5 reels, 4,901 ft.

Pres by W. Ray Johnston. *Dir* Albert Rogell. *Scen* Forrest Sheldon.

Cast: Jack Perrin *(Jack Lanning)*, Molly Malone *(Jenny Jenkins)*, Eva Thatcher *(Widow Jenkins)*, Bud Osborne *(Piute Sam)*, Martin Turner *(Snowball)*, Ed Burns *(ranch foreman)*, Jack Richardson *(assistant foreman)*, Starlight *(a horse)*.

Western comedy. Jack Lanning, the son of a millionaire, wins a prizefight and is disinherited by his father, who has a strong aversion to boxing. Jack then goes to Texas, accompanied by Snowball, his colored valet, and there he is suspected of rustling cattle and nearly lynched. He then meets the amorous Widow Jenkins, evades her advances, and falls in love with her niece, Jenny. Jack later saves the payroll of the widow's ranch from a band of mounted bandits and captures the leader of the gang. The widow marries the ranch foreman, and Jack and Jenny make plans to join them in matrimony. *Prizefighters. Millionaires. Ranch foremen. Widows. Rustlers. Valets. Lynching. Disinheritance. Texas.*

KNOCKOUT REILLY F2.2907

Famous Players–Lasky. *Dist* Paramount Pictures. 16 Apr **1927** [c2 Apr 1927; LP23887]. Si; b&w. 35mm. 7 reels, 7,080 ft.

Pres by Adolph Zukor, Jesse L. Lasky. *Assoc Prod* William Le Baron. *Dir* Malcolm St. Clair. *Screenplay* Pierre Collings, Kenneth Raisbeck. *Titl* John W. Conway. *Photog* Edward Cronjager.

Cast: Richard Dix *(Dundee Reilly)*, Mary Brian *(Mary Malone)*, Jack Renault *(Killer Agerra)*, Harry Gribbon *(Pat Malone)*, Osgood Perkins *(Spider Cross)*, Lucia Backus Seger *(Mrs. Reilly)*, Larry McGrath *(Kewpie Dugan)*, Myrtland La Varre *(Buck Lennard)*.

Melodrama. Source: Albert Payson Terhune, "The Hunch," in *Red Book Magazine* (35:33–37, Sep 1920). Dundee, a worker in a New Jersey steel mill, meets Mary Malone, sister of Pat Malone, a defeated boxer, at a cabaret and knocks out Killer Agerra when he tries to force himself on Mary. Dundee, under Pat's guidance, then trains for a scheduled bout with Agerra. But Dundee is framed for a shooting, and during his prison term he works on the rockpile developing his muscles. Following his release Dundee substitutes for another fighter against Agerra; Mary, on a hunch, tells him he was framed by his rival, spurring him on to win in the final round. *Boxers. Revenge. Frameup. Prisons. Steel industry. New Jersey.*

KNOW YOUR MEN F2.2908

Fox Film Corp. 13 Mar **1921** [c20 Mar 1921; LP16321]. Si; b&w. 35mm. 6 reels, 5,315 ft.

Pres by William Fox. *Dir* Charles Giblyn. *Scen* Paul H. Sloane. *Photog* Joseph Ruttenberg.

Cast: Pearl White *(Ellen Schuyler)*, Wilfred Lytell *(Roy Phelps)*, Downing Clarke *(Warren Schuyler)*, Harry C. Browne *(John Barrett)*, Estar Banks *(Mrs. Barrett)*, Byron Douglas *(Van Horn)*, William Eville *(Watson)*.

Society melodrama. Warren Schuyler, a wealthy widower in a small eastern town, is highly respected until the citizens are financially ruined by devaluation of the oil stock he has sold them. His daughter Ellen, engaged to New York socialite Roy Phelps, is deserted after her father dies, but fellow townsman John Barrett comes to her aid, and out of gratitude she marries him. After 3 years of irritation with her mother-in-law, she again meets Roy and is persuaded to leave her husband and child, but on perceiving Roy's fraudulence, and following a serious illness, she is reconciled with John. *Mothers-in-law. Speculation. Family life. Infidelity.*

KOSHER KITTY KELLY (Gold Bond Series) **F2.2909**

R-C Pictures. *Dist* Film Booking Offices of America. 5 Sep **1926** [c5 Sep 1926; LP23124]. Si; b&w. 35mm. 7 reels, 6,103 ft.

Pres by Joseph P. Kennedy. *Dir* James W. Horne. *Scen* Gerald C. Duffy. *Photog* Allan Siegler.

Cast: Viola Dana *(Kitty Kelly)*, Tom Forman *(Officer Pat Sullivan)*, Vera Gordon *(Mrs. Feinbaum)*, Kathleen Myers *(Rosie Feinbaum)*, Nat Carr *(Moses Ginsburg)*, Stanley Taylor *(Morris Rosen)*, Carroll Nye *(Barney Kelly)*, Aggie Herring *(Mrs. Kelly)*.

Comedy-drama. Source: Leon De Costa, *Kosher Kitty Kelly* (New York opening: 15 Jun 1925). Kitty Kelly, her brother Barney, and Mrs. Kelly are neighbors of Rosie Feinbaum and her mother, who live over the delicatessen of Moses Ginsburg, in New York's East Side. Rosie is in love with young Morris Rosen, a hospital intern; and Kitty, with Officer Pat Sullivan. With a gang, Barney attempts to hold up Ginsburg; and Officer Pat, pursuing the gang, wounds Barney in the shoulder. Although Kitty pleads with him, Pat places duty above love and takes Barney to a waiting ambulance. En route to the hospital, Kitty is comforted by Morris; and Pat and Rosie, believing the other two to be on intimate terms, team up together. Mrs. Kelly is infuriated, and a dispute with the Feinbaums develops into a neighborhood battle. Pat withdraws from the alderman race to assure Barney's parole; the boy sets out to get revenge, and Ginsburg's shop is set afire during a battle; Morris saves Rosie, and Pat saves Kitty. The original lovers are united, along with Ginsburg and Mrs. Feinbaum. *Hospital interns. Aldermen. Police. Irish. Jews. Gangs. Courtship. Delicatessens. New York City—East Side.*

K—THE UNKNOWN (Universal-Jewel) **F2.2910**

Universal Pictures. 23 Nov **1924** [c11 Aug 1924; LP20487]. Si; b&w. 35mm. 9 reels, 8,146 ft.

Pres by Carl Laemmle. *Dir* Harry Pollard. *Adapt* Hope Loring, Raymond L. Schrock, Louis D. Lighton. *Photog* Charles Stumar.

Cast: Virginia Valli *(Sidney Page)*, Percy Marmont *("K" Le Moyne)*, Margarita Fisher *(Charlotte Harrison)*, Francis Feeney *(George "Slim" Benson)*, John Roche *(Dr. Max Wilson)*, Maurice Ryan *(Joe Drummond)*, Myrtle Vane *(Aunt Harriett Kennedy)*, William A. Carroll *(Dr. Ed Wilson)*.

Melodrama. Source: Mary Roberts Rinehart, *K* (Boston & New York, 1915). While pursued by boyish admirers Joe and George, Sidney Page is attracted to a mysterious stranger, "K," who boards in her house, but she is much more interested in a surgeon, Max Wilson. When Joe shoots and injures Wilson, thinking he is with Sidney, the stranger operates, saves his life, and then reveals his identity as a famous surgeon and wins the girl. *Surgeons. Strangers. Courtship.*

Note: There is some doubt about the credit to Raymond L. Schrock.

THE LADDER JINX **F2.2911**

Vitagraph Co. of America. 20 Aug **1922** [c29 Jun 1922; LP18022]. Si; b&w. 35mm. 6 reels, 5,068 ft.

Pres by Albert E. Smith. *Dir* Jess Robbins. *Adapt* David Kirkland. *Story* Edgar Franklin. *Photog* Irving Ries.

Cast: Edward Horton *(Arthur Barnes, a bank teller)*, Margaret Landis *(Helen Wilbur, bank president's daughter)*, Wilbur Higby *(James Wilbur, bank president)*, Tully Marshall *(Peter Stalton, retiring cashier)*, Otis Harlan *(Thams Gridley, Barnes's uncle)*, Colin Kenny *(Richard Twing, another teller)*, Tom McGuire *(Judge Brown)*, Will R. Walling *(Officer Murphy)*, Tom Murray *(Detective Smith)*, Ernest Shields *(Cheyenne Harry, a crook)*, Max Asher *(Sam, bank porter)*.

Comedy. Peter Stalton, retiring as a bank cashier, is anxious that his nephew Richard Twing should succeed him. The directors, however, appoint Arthur Barnes, engaged to Helen Wilbur, the president's daughter. Being highly superstitious, Helen makes Arthur promise to cross back under a ladder under which he has walked earlier in the day. In doing so, he is accused of robbing a house and is pursued by the police. Passing the bank in which he works, he sees two robbers making a getaway just as the president and Helen arrive. Arthur pursues the bandits in their car, accompanied by Helen. They are arrested and accused of robbing Stalton's house and the bank, but Arthur is cleared by Sam, the Negro janitor, who exposes Richard Twing as the culprit. Arthur is freed and is happily reunited with his fiancée. *Bank clerks. Bankers. Janitors. Bank robberies. Courtship. Superstition.*

LADDIE **F2.2912**

Gene Stratton Porter Productions. *Dist* Film Booking Offices of America. 26 Sep **1926** [c15 Jul 1926; LP22917]. Si; b&w. 35mm. 7 reels, 6,931 ft.

Pres by Joseph P. Kennedy. *Dir* James Leo Meehan. *Adapt* Jeanette Porter Meehan. *Photog* Allen Siegler. *Asst Dir* Charles Kerr.

Cast: John Bowers *(Laddie)*, Bess Flowers *(Pamela Pryor)*, Theodore von Eltz *(Robert Paget)*, Eugenia Gilbert *(Shelley Stanton)*, David Torrence *(Paul Stanton)*, Eulalie Jensen *(Mrs. Stanton)*, Arthur Clayton *(Mahlon Pryor)*, Fanny Midgley *(Mrs. Pryor)*, Aggie Herring *(Candace)*, Gene Stratton *(Little Sister)*, John Fox, Jr. *(Leon)*.

Romantic drama. Source: Gene Stratton Porter, *Laddie; a True Blue Story* (Garden City, New York, 1913). Laddie, son of the Stantons, an Ohio pioneer family, falls in love with Pamela Pryor, daughter of a neighboring aristocratic English family, though the Pryors adopt a condescending attitude toward the Stanton family. Through the efforts of Little Sister, who knows of Laddie's love, the two secretly communicate, and Mr. Pryor takes a liking to Laddie when he tames a wild horse for him. Meanwhile, Shelley, a Stanton girl, falls in love with city lawyer Robert Paget; and when he leaves her under mysterious circumstances, she returns home heartbroken. The Pryors, disgraced because of a false accusation against their son in England, are at length forced to accept Laddie. It develops that Paget is actually the banished son of the Pryors; after a strained crisis Pryor forgives his son, and Laddie and Pamela, Robert and Shelley, and the Stantons and the Pryors are happily united. *Pioneers. English. Children. Family life. Courtship. Banishment. Ohio.*

LADDIE BE GOOD **F2.2913**

Bill Cody Productions. *Dist* Pathé Exchange. 1 Jan **1928** [c22 Dec 1927; LP24779]. Si; b&w. 35mm. 4 reels, 4,155 ft.

Prod-Story Bill Cody. *Dir* Bennett Cohn. *Cont* L. V. Jefferson. *Titl* Delos Sutherland. *Film Ed* Fred Burnworth.

Cast: Bill Cody *(himself)*, Rose Blossom *(Ruth Jones)*, George Bunny *(Pierpont Jones)*, Henry Herbert *(John Norton)*, Fred Gambold *(Henry Cody)*.

Comedy. Bill Cody leaves his western ranch to live in a big city. He would like to court Ruth Jones, who lives next door, but her father objects strongly and even hires an unscrupulous lawyer to seize Cody's land, which he covets. After several escapades with the police and the lawyer's gang of thugs, Cody convinces Ruth's father of his worth and obtains permission to marry her. *Ranchers. Lawyers. Gangs. Police. Courtship. Land rights.*

LADIES AT EASE **F2.2914**

Chadwick Pictures. *Dist* First Division Distributors. 15 Aug **1927.** Si; b&w. 35mm. 6 reels, 5,800 ft.

Pres by I. E. Chadwick. *Supv-Story* Leon Lee. *Dir* Jerome Storm. *Scen-Cont* Rob Wagner. *Titl* Jean La'Ple. *Photog* Ernest Miller. *Film Ed* Gene Milford.

Cast: Pauline Garon *(Polly)*, Gertrude Short *(Gert)*, Gardner James *(Bill Brewster)*, Raymond Glenn *(Buck Bevin)*, Lillian Hackett *(Mae Dotty)*, Jean Van Vliet *(June Dotty)*, William H. Strauss *(Abe Ginsburg)*, Charles Meakin *(John McMay)*, Henry Roquemore *(a producer)*.

Comedy. Lingerie models Polly and Gert steal the boyfriends of two sisters, who comprise a singing and dancing act. When the performers have the models fired, the models inadvertently take the sisters' place on stage. Their bumbling is enthusiastically welcomed by the audience and a follies producer; and the sisters take the models' former jobs. *Fashion models. Showgirls. Sisters. Theatrical producers. Mistaken identity.*

LADIES AT PLAY **F2.2915**

First National Pictures. 15 Nov **1926** [New York premiere; released 26 Dec; c21 Oct 1926; LP23240]. Si; b&w. 35mm. 7 reels, 6,119 ft.

Dir Alfred E. Green. *Scen* Carey Wilson. *Titl* George Marion, Jr. *Photog* George Folsey. *Prod Mgr* B. P. Fineman.

Cast: Doris Kenyon *(Ann Harper)*, Lloyd Hughes *(Gil Barry)*, Louise Fazenda *(Aunt Katherine)*, Ethel Wales *(Aunt Sarah)*, Hallam Cooley *(Terry)*, John Patrick *(Andy)*, Virginia Lee Corbin *(Dotty)*, Philo McCullough *(hotel clerk)*, Tom Ricketts *(Deacon Ezra Boody)*.

Bedroom farce. Source: Sam Janney, *Loose Ankles; a Comedy in Three Acts* (New York, 1928). Faced by the stipulation of a will that she be married within 3 days, Ann Harper plots with her cousin, Betty, to get herself "compromised" in order to force the consent of their disgruntled spinster aunts to a marriage—to be followed, as soon as possible, by a divorce. Gil Barry, a jobless and hungry country lad, is befriended by Terry and Andy, two unscrupulous cake-eaters who make the acquaintance of the spinsters (Katherine and Sarah) and take them on a spree. They promote Gil as a young man willing to be "compromised," and he is effectively vamped by Ann. The spinsters confront Ann and her unwilling lover and declare him to be ineligible; Ann declares she will nevertheless marry him, forfeiting the fortune; but Andy and Terry force them to relent and are amply rewarded by Ann. *Vamps. Spinsters. Aunts. Dandies. Inheritance. Marriage.*

LADIES BEWARE **F2.2916**
R-C Pictures. *Dist* Film Booking Offices of America. 26 Jun **1927** [c6 Jun 1927; LP24035]. Si; b&w. 35mm. 5 reels, 4,900 ft.
Pres by Joseph P. Kennedy. *Dir* Charles Giblyn. *Cont* Enid Hibbard. *Photog* Jules Cronjager. *Asst Dir* Ray McCarey.
Cast: George O'Hara *(Jack O'Diamonds)*, Nola Luxford *(Jeannie)*, Florence Wix *(Mrs. Ring)*, Kathleen Myers *(Georgette)*, Mario Carillo *(Count Bodevsky)*, Alan Brooks *(Renwick Clarke)*, Byron Douglas *(Deputy Commissioner Croswell)*, Bud Jamieson *(Tubbs)*, Jimmy Aubrey *(Handy)*.
Crook melodrama. Source: Fred Jackson, "Jack of Diamonds" (publication undetermined). Jack O'Diamonds, a jewel thief, being advised to leave the city by the police, hears about a house party being given by Georgette Ring, whom he has never met but knows to be the owner of a precious ruby. Proceeding there under the name of McFarland, he explains that an attempt will be made to steal the jewel and that he has been sent to capture the thief. Jeannie, a former cohort of his who has become Mrs. Ring's secretary, suspects his plan and begs him to desist. In a series of countermovements, Jeannie intercepts the jewel, but it is stolen by Count Bodevski, who then is captured by Jack. Jeannie reveals her love for Jack, and Georgette is happily united with Clarke. *Thieves. Secretaries. Impersonation.*

LADIES FIRST *see* **HOLD THAT LION**

LADIES IN LOVE **F2.2917**
Chesterfield Motion Picture Corp. 15 May **1930**. Sd (Photophone); b&w. 35mm. 7 reels, 6,200 ft.
Pres by George R. Batcheller. *Dir* Edgar Lewis. *Story-Sceenplay* Charles Beahan. *Photog* M. A. Anderson. *Film Ed* James Morley. *Sd* Lester E. Tope. *Asst Dir* Melville Shyer.
Cast: Alice Day *(Brenda Lascelle)*, Johnnie Walker *(Harry King)*, Freeman Wood *(Ward Hampton)*, Marjorie "Babe" Kane *(Marjorie)*, James Burtis *(Al Pine)*, Dorothy Gould *(Patsy Green)*, Elinor Flynn *(Mary Wood)*, Mary Carr *(Mrs. Wood)*, Mary Foy *(Mrs. Tibbs)*, Bernie Lamont *(Frank Jones)*.
Comedy-drama. Harry King, an attractive, unsophisticated young man living in a small Vermont town, bids farewell to his fiancée, Mary Wood, and his music students in hopes of selling his song to popular radio singer Brenda Lascelle, in New York. Having plenty of songs, Brenda refuses Harry's; but a sympathetic radio announcer, Al Pine, sneaks him into a party at Brenda's, where he makes a big hit. At the same party, Brenda has finally consented to marry Ward Hampton, the wealthy, vain, snobbish owner of the radio station, but Harry's confession of his love for her causes Brenda to waiver. To complicate matters, Mary arrives and explains the situation to Brenda, who nobly offers to step aside, but Harry finally learns of Mary's golddigging intentions, and he sends her back to Vermont. *Music teachers. Composers. Singers. Gold diggers. Radio announcers. Socialites. Vermont. New York City.*
Note: Songs: "Oh How I Love You" (theme), "Big Boy," "One Sweet Song."

LADIES LOVE BRUTES **F2.2918**
Paramount Famous Lasky Corp. 26 Apr **1930** [c25 Apr 1930; LP1256]. Sd (Movietone); b&w. 35mm. 10 reels, 7,171 ft.
Dir Rowland V. Lee. *Adapt-Dial* Waldemar Young, Herman J. Mankiewicz. *Photog* Harry Fischbeck. *Film Ed* Eda Warren. *Rec Engr* J. A. Goodrich.
Cast: George Bancroft *(Joe Froziati)*, Mary Astor *(Mimi Howell)*, Fredric March *(Dwight Howell)*, Margaret Quimby *(Lucille Gates)*, Stanley Fields *(Mike Mendino)*, Ben Hendricks, Jr. *(Slattery)*, Lawford Davidson *(George Wyndham)*, Ferike Boros *(Mrs. Forziati)*, David Durand *(Joey Forziati)*, Freddie Burke Frederick *(Jackie Howell)*, Paul Fix *(Slip)*, Claude Allister *(The Tailor)*, Crauford Kent, E. H. Calvert *(committeemen)*.
Society melodrama. Source: Zoë Akins, *Pardon My Glove* (a play). Joe Forziati, an Italian immigrant who has battled his way to success as a New York building contractor, decides to embark on a social career. Wyndham, his lawyer, arranges for him to be a guest at the home of socialite Mimi Howell, but his son Joey and his grandmother view his flashy new wardrobe dubiously. Mimi, who is on the verge of a divorce from her husband, Dwight, falls under the spell of Joe. Mike Mendino, a labor agitator whom Joe has defeated, plots revenge by arranging for Slip, one of his gang, to become Joe's chauffeur. Mimi breaks off their relationship because of their unequal social positions, but Joe has Slip kidnap her child so that he may return the boy himself; his own son is kidnaped by the gang, but after a battle with them, the child is retrieved. Mimi is reunited with her husband; and Joe, realizing the impossiblity of his aspirations, returns home with his son. *Contractors. Immigrants. Lawyers. Italians. Gangsters. Socialites. Children. Courtship. Kidnaping. New York City.*

LADIES MUST DRESS **F2.2919**
Fox Film Corp. 20 Nov **1927** [c14 Nov 1927; LP24651]. Si; b&w. 35mm. 6 reels, 5,599 ft.
Pres by William Fox. *Dir-Story* Victor Heerman. *Scen* Reginald Morris. *Titl* Malcolm Stuart Boylan. *Photog* Glen MacWilliams. *Asst Dir* Charles Woolstenhulme.
Cast: Virginia Valli *(Eve)*, Lawrence Gray *(Joe)*, Hallam Cooley *(Art)*, Nancy Carroll *(Mazie)*, Earle Foxe *(George Ward, Jr.)*, Wilson Hummell *(office manager)*, William Tooker *(Mr. Ward, Sr.)*.
Romantic comedy. "Eve and Joe are engaged, but Joe cannot help contrasting the drabness of her attire with the dressy clothes of their friends. She overhears him talking of this and breaks with him. Then, with the help of her friend, Mazie, she metamorphoses into a ravishing beauty. Joe is remorseful, but the situation is made more complex when he suspects Eve of questionable relations with her boss. In the end, he discovers she is innocent and that she still loves him." (*Moving Picture World*, 17 Dec 1927, p24.) *Women's wear. Fashion.*

LADIES MUST LIVE **F2.2920**
Mayflower Photoplay Corp. *Dist* Paramount Pictures. ca30 Oct **1921** [Los Angeles and Pittsburg premieres; released 6 Nov; c29 Oct 1921; LP17143]. Si; b&w. 35mm. 8 reels, 7,482 ft.
Dir-Adapt George Loane Tucker.
Cast: Robert Ellis *(Anthony Mulvain)*, Mahlon Hamilton *(Ralph Lincourt)*, Betty Compson *(Christine Bleeker)*, Leatrice Joy *(Barbara)*, Hardee Kirkland *(William Hollins)*, Gibson Gowland *(Michael Le Prim)*, Jack Gilbert *(The Gardener)*, Cleo Madison *(Mrs. Lincourt)*, Snitz Edwards *(Edward Barron)*, Lucille Hutton *(Nell Martin)*, Lule Warrenton *(Nora Flanagan)*, William V. Mong *(Max Bleeker)*, Jack McDonald *(The Butler)*, Marcia Manon *(Nancy)*, Arnold Gregg *(Ned Klegg)*.
Society melodrama. Source: Alice Duer Miller, *Ladies Must Live* (New York, 1917). Christine Bleeker, educated by her wealthy brother-in-law, William Hollins, plans to marry Ralph Lincourt when he is divorced. He, however, is equally pursued by Nancy Barron, whom Christine dislikes. Ned Klegg loves Barbara, a social secretary, and resents the attention paid her by Barron, Nancy's elderly husband. Nell Martin, a servant in the Hollins home, is in love with the gardener but is persecuted by the butler. Mulvain, an aviator, and his mechanic, Le Prim, arrive; and the latter absconds with Nancy in an auto, pursued by Mulvain and Christine, who force him to release her. Christine announces her engagement to Mulvain, who declares he is a poor man. In the resulting commotion, it transpires that Nell, threatened with exposure, has drowned herself. The shock brings a change of emotion: Barbara rejects Barron and accepts Klegg, and Christine accepts Mulvain, content to share his poverty. *Aviators. Secretaries. Housemaids. Butlers. Mechanics. Wealth. Social classes. Suicide. Courtship.*

LADIES MUST PLAY **F2.2921**
Columbia Pictures. 1 Aug **1930** [c6 Aug 1930; LP1478]. Sd (Movietone); b&w. 35mm. 7 reels, 5,978 ft.
Prod Harry Cohn. *Dir* Raymond Cannon. *Dial Dir* Lucile Gleason. *Scen* Dorothy Howell. *Dial* Jo Swerling. *Story* Paul Hervey Fox. *Camera* Joseph Walker. *Art Dir* Edward Jewell. *Film Ed* Gene Milford. *Ch Sd Engr* John Livadary. *Sd Engr* Edward Bernds. *Asst Dir* David Selman.
Cast: Dorothy Sebastian *(Norma)*, Neil Hamilton *(Anthony Gregg)*, Natalie Moorhead *(Connie)*, John Holland *(Geoffrey)*, Harry Stubbs *(Stormfield [Stormey] Button)*, Shirley Palmer *(Marie)*, Pauline Neff *(Mrs. Wheeler)*.
Society drama. Tony Gregg, a popular New York and Newport socialite, refuses to marry wealthy Connie Tremaine, though he has become bankrupt

through financial mismanagement. Instead, he arranges to send Norma Blake, his pretty stenographer, to Newport, where she is to meet and marry a millionaire on the condition that she pay Tony a 10 percent commission on whatever marriage settlement may materialize. Introduced as Tony's cousin, Norma makes a good impression at a party; and though she finds young Geoffrey West interesting, Tony directs her to Stormey Button, fat and wealthy. To precipitate the marriage proposal, Norma pretends to be drowning; her predicament becomes an actual one, however, and when Stormey cannot save her, Geoffrey comes to her rescue. Romance thus begins, and soon Norma and Geoffrey announce their engagement; on the eve of the wedding, however, Norma decides to marry Tony despite his poverty. *Fortune hunters. Stockbrokers. Socialites. Stenographers. Bankruptcy. Courtship. Newport (Rhode Island). New York City.*

LADIES' NIGHT IN A TURKISH BATH **F2.2922**

Asher-Small-Rogers. *Dist* First National Pictures. 1 Apr **1928** [c7 Feb 1928; LP24956]. Si; b&w. 35mm. 7 reels, 6,592 ft.

Dir Edward Cline. *Titl* Al Boasberg. *Adapt* Henry McCarty, Gene Towne. *Photog* Jack MacKenzie. *Film Ed* Edgar Adams.

Cast: Dorothy Mackaill *(Helen Slocum)*, Jack Mulhall *("Speed" Dawson)*, Sylvia Ashton *(Ma Slocum)*, James Finlayson *(Pa Slocum)*, Guinn Williams *(Sweeney)*, Harvey Clarke *(Mr. Spivens)*, Reed Howes *(Edwin Leroy)*, Ethel Wales *(Mrs. Spivers)*, Fred Kelsey.

Comedy-drama. Source: Charlton Andrews and Avery Hopwood, *Ladies' Night in a Turkish Bath* (a play; publication undetermined). Restaurateur Pa Slocum sells out and moves uptown just as "Speed" Dawson, a steelworker, is getting interested in his daughter, Helen, sidewalk salesgirl of Slocum's box lunches. Edwin Leroy, a physical instructor who has lived across the hall from the Slocums, is also wooing Helen. To Speed's disappointment, Helen, whom he liked because of her simple ways, begins to dress modishly—bare legs and short skirts. To Slocum's horror, his wife goes on a diet, causing her to be ill-tempered and unpredictable. Speed and Slocum decide to drown their sorrow at a dancehall when Helen and Mrs. Slocum go to a turkish bath with Edwin Leroy. Speed and Slocum flee to the bath when the dancehall is raided and discover that it is ladies' night. The humorous situation culminates in Speed's winning Helen. *Restaurateurs. Salesclerks. Steelworkers. Physical instructors. Nouveaux riches. Turkish baths.*

LADIES OF LEISURE **F2.2923**

Columbia Pictures. 1 Mar **1926** [c13 Feb 1926; LP22398]. Si; b&w. 35mm. 6 reels, 5,257 ft.

Dir Thomas Buckingham. *Story-Cont* Albert Lewin. *Photog* Dewey Wrigley.

Cast: Elaine Hammerstein *(Mamie Taylor)*, T. Roy Barnes *(Eric Van Norden)*, Robert Ellis *(Jack Forrest)*, Gertrude Short *(Marian Forrest)*, Thomas Ricketts *(Wadleigh)*, James Mason *(Eddie Lannigan)*, Joseph W. Girard *(detective)*.

Melodrama. Mamie Taylor, paid companion and good friend to Marian Forrest, is in love with Marian's brother, Jack, while Marian's affections are all directed toward Eric Van Norden, a bachelor who intends to remain that way. Eddie Lannigan, a blackmailer, threatens to expose Mamie's past, and she leaves the Forrest home, preparing to jump off a bridge. Van Norden chances by and, preventing the suicide, takes Mamie to his rooms. Jack Forrest follows them and accuses Van Norden of philandering. Mamie leaves by the back door, and Marian steps from the bedroom to tell her brother (falsely) that she and Van Norden were married that very afternoon. Jack returns to Mamie, and Van Norden realizes that he must at last marry Marian in order to protect her reputation. *Bachelors. Brother-sister relationship. Blackmail. Reputation. Suicide.*

LADIES OF LEISURE **F2.2924**

Columbia Pictures. 5 Apr **1930** [c1 May 1930; LP1295]. Sd (Movietone); b&w. 35mm. 10 reels, 9,118 ft. [Also si.]

Prod Harry Cohn. *Dir* Frank Capra. *Titl* Dudley Early. *Adapt-Dial* Jo Swerling. *Photog* Joe Walker. *Art Dir* Harrison Wiley. *Film Ed* Maurice Wright. *Ch Sd Engr* John P. Livadary. *Sd Mixing Engr* Harry Blanchard. *Asst Dir* David Selman.

Cast: Barbara Stanwyck *(Kay Arnold)*, Ralph Graves *(Jerry Strange)*, Lowell Sherman *(Bill Standish)*, Marie Prevost *(Dot Lamar)*, Nance O'Neil *(Mrs. Strange)*, George Fawcett *(Mr. Strange)*, Johnnie Walker *(Charlie)*, Juliette Compton *(Claire Collins)*.

Society melodrama. Source: Milton Herbert Gropper, *Ladies of the Evening* (New York opening: 23 Dec 1924). Jerry Strange, son of a well-known railroad contractor, has aspirations of becoming an artist and converts an expensive penthouse in New York to a studio. His girl friend, Claire Collins, borrows the studio for a party that turns into a drunken orgy; and when she refuses to leave with him, he takes a drive along the waterfront, where he meets Kay Arnold, ostensibly a gold digger. Perceiving her worth, he engages her as a model; his friend, Bill Standish, amused by Jerry's belief that Kay can be reformed, is discouraged by the girl and turns to Dot Lamar, her roommate. Although Jerry proposes to Kay, his parents forbid the marriage, and Mrs. Strange pleads with Kay to break the engagement. Kay embarks for Havana with Bill Standish, but, unable to continue, she jumps overboard. Jerry seeks her out at the hospital, and convinced of her love, he determines to stay by her. *Artists. Models. Gold diggers. Courtship. Social classes. New York City.*

LADIES OF THE MOB **F2.2925**

Paramount Famous Lasky Corp. 30 Jun **1928** [c30 Jun 1928; LP25428]. Si; b&w. 35mm. 7 reels, 6,792 ft.

Dir William Wellman. *Scen* John Farrow. *Titl* George Marion. *Adapt* Oliver H. P. Garrett. *Photog* Henry Gerrard. *Film Ed* Alyson Shaffer.

Cast: Clara Bow *(Yvonne)*, Richard Arlen *("Red")*, Helen Lynch *(Marie)*, Mary Alden *("Soft Annie")*, Carl Gerrard *(Joe)*, Bodil Rosing *(The Mother)*, Lorraine Rivero *(Little Yvonne)*, James Pierce *(The Officer)*.

Crook melodrama. Source: Ernest Booth, "Ladies of the Mob," in *American Mercury* (12:399–407, Dec 1927). Yvonne, a girl whose father was electrocuted when she was a child, is brought up by her mother to be a crook and to avenge her father's death by living outside the law. She falls in love with "Red," her partner in crime. Fearing that the electric chair will separate them, she tries to make him reform. Failing this, she shoots him in the shoulder when he tries to be included in a bank robbery. They give themselves up to pay the penalty and to start life anew without the constant fear of apprehension by the law. *Filial relations. Motherhood. Criminals—Rehabilitation. Bank robberies. Capital punishment.*

LADIES OF THE NIGHT CLUB **F2.2926**

Tiffany-Stahl Productions. 15 May **1928** [c26 May 1928; LP25300]. Mus score & sd eff (Photophone); b&w. 35mm. 7 reels, 6,533 ft.

Dir George Archainbaud. *Cont* Houston Branch, John Francis Natteford. *Titl* Paul Perez. *Story* Ben Grauman Kohn. *Photog* Harry Jackson. *Art Dir* Hervey Libbert. *Set Dressings* George Sawley. *Film Ed* L. R. Brown. *Asst Dir* Buck McGowan.

Cast: Ricardo Cortez *(George Merrill)*, Barbara Leonard *(Dimples Revere)*, Lee Moran *(Joe Raggs)*, Douglas Gerrard *(Cyril Bathstowe)*, Cissy Fitzgerald *(Bossy Hart)*, Charles Gerrard.

Comedy-drama. George Demonte, a millionaire patron of the "Bubble-Up" Nightclub, falls in love with Dimples Revere, half of a vaudeville team performing there. Joe Raggs, her partner, discovers he loves Dimples, buys an engagement ring, then learns that she has already promised to marry George. He tries to conceal his disappointment by telling her that "the wonderful news" he has to tell is that he has made a single booking engagement. *Singers. Dancers. Millionaires. Vaudeville. Nightclubs.*

LADIES TO BOARD **F2.2927**

Fox Film Corp. 3 Feb **1924** [c3 Feb 1924; LP19892]. Si; b&w. 35mm. 6 reels, ca6,100 ft.

Pres by William Fox. *Dir* J. G. Blystone. *Scen* Donald W. Lee. *Story* William Dudley Pelley. *Photog* Daniel Clark.

Cast: Tom Mix *(Tom Faxton)*, Gertrude Olmstead *(Edith Oliver)*, Philo McCullough *(Evan Carmichael)*, Pee Wee Holmes *(Bunk McGinnis)*, Gertrude Claire *(Mrs. Carmichael)*, Dolores Rousse *(model)*.

Comedy-drama. A little old lady dies, leaving her estate, consisting of a sanitarium for aging ladies, to Tom Faxton, a young man who rescued her when her automobile went out of control. At the rest home he meets Edith Oliver and woos her away from a neglectful boyfriend, Evan Carmichael, while Buck, Tom's sidekick, elopes with the establishment's housekeeper. *Housekeepers. Inheritance. Courtship. Sanitariums. Old age homes. Automobile accidents.*

THE LADY **F2.2928**

Norma Talmadge Productions. *Dist* First National Pictures. 8 Feb **1925** [c19 Jan 1925; LP21038]. Si; b&w. 35mm. 8 reels, 7,357 ft.

Pres by Joseph M. Schenck. *Dir* Frank Borzage. *Screenplay* Frances Marion. *Story* Martin Brown. *Photog* Tony Gaudio.

Cast: Norma Talmadge *(Polly Pearl)*, Wallace MacDonald *(Leonard St. Aubyns)*, Brandon Hurst *(St. Aubyns, Sr.)*, Alf Goulding *(Tom*

Robinson), Doris Lloyd *(Fannie St. Clair)*, Walter Long *(Blackie)*, George Hackathorne *(Leonard Cairns)*, Marc MacDermott *(Mr. Wendover)*, Paulette Duval *(Madame Adrienne Catellier)*, John Fox, Jr. *(Freckles)*, Emily Fitzroy *(Madame Blanche)*, John Herdman *(John Cairns)*, Margaret Seddon *(Mrs. Cairns)*, Edwin Hubbell *(London boy)*, Miles McCarthy *(Mr. Graves)*.

Melodrama. Source: Martin Brown, *The Lady* (New York opening: 4 Dec 1923). Polly Pearl, a singer in a second-rate English music hall, marries Leonard St. Aubyns, a feckless scion of nobility. Leonard's father immediately disinherits him, and Leonard soon squanders his small stake at Monte Carlo. Leonard later dies, and Polly is reduced to singing in a waterfront cafe in Marseilles in order to support herself and her young son. The elder St. Aubyns attempts to gain possession of the child, claiming that Polly is an unfit mother. Polly entrusts the boy to an English acquaintance, who returns with him to England. Soon after, Polly goes to London, but, after searching the streets for weeks, she can find no trace of her son. Years later, having become the owner of a cafe in Le Havre, Polly witnesses a young English soldier accidentally kill a drunken comrade in a fight. Polly discovers that the soldier is her son and attempts to assume the blame for the shooting, but her son, with the instincts of a gentleman, does not allow a woman to sacrifice herself for him. The boy escapes the authorities and embarks for America and a new life, leaving behind him a mother contented in the merits of her son. *Entertainers. Disinheritance. Motherhood. Marseilles. London. Monte Carlo. Le Havre.*

LADY BE GOOD **F2.2929**

First National Pictures. 6 May **1928** [c24 Apr 1928; LP25188]. Si; b&w. 35mm. 7 reels, ca6,600 ft.

Prod Charles R. Rogers. *Dir* Richard Wallace. *Scen* Adelaide Heilbron, Jack Wagner. *Titl* Gene Towne, Sidney Lazarus. *Photog* George Folsey. *Film Ed* Stuart Heisler.

Cast: Jack Mulhall *(Jack)*, Dorothy Mackaill *(Mary)*, John Miljan *(Murray)*, Nita Martan *(Madison)*, Dot Farley *(Texas West)*, James Finlayson *(Trelawney West)*, Aggie Herring *(landlady)*, Jay Eaton, Eddie Clayton *(dancers)*, Yola D'Avril *(assistant)*.

Romantic comedy. Source: Guy Bolton, Fred Thompson, and George Gershwin, *Lady Be Good* (New York opening: 1 Dec 1924). Jack and Mary, two vaudeville magicians engaged to marry, quarrel and separate. Mary becomes the temporary partner of a dancing artist, but she soon leaves him because of his improper advances. Stranded in a small western town near where Jack is playing, Mary goes to the theater and discovers that he is faring badly in her absence. Secretly she replaces Jack's assistant; he welcomes Mary with enthusiasm, and they happily reunite. *Magicians. Dancers. Vaudeville. Theater.*

THE LADY FROM HELL **F2.2930**

Stuart Paton Productions. *Dist* Associated Exhibitors. 7 Jan **1926** [c22 Jan 1926; LU22287]. Si; b&w. 35mm. 6 reels, 5,337 ft.

Dir Stuart Paton. *Adapt-Cont* J. Grubb Alexander. *Titl* John W. Krafft. *Film Ed* John W. Krafft.

Cast: Roy Stewart *(Sir Robin Carmichael)*, Blanche Sweet *(Lady Margaret Darnely)*, Ralph Lewis *(Earl of Kennet)*, Frank Elliott *(Sir Hugh Stafford)*, Edgar Norton *(Hon. Charles Darnely)*, Margaret Campbell *(Lady Darnely)*, Ruth King *(Lucy Wallace)*, Mickey Moore *(Billy Boy)*.

Western melodrama. Source: Norton S. Parker, "My Lord of the Double B" (publication undetermined). Sir Robin Carmichael, a Scotch officer, arrives in the United States and, under the name of Buck Evans, becomes the foreman of the Double B Ranch. Ross Wallace, the owner of the Double B, viciously attacks his wife; her son, Billy Boy, then kills Wallace with Robin's gun. Billy Boy runs off, and Robin returns to Scotland to prepare for his wedding to Lady Darnely. On the day he is married, Robin is extradited to the United States and forced to stand trial for Wallace's murder. He is convicted and sentenced to be hanged, but Billy Boy returns at the last minute and confesses to the murder, allowing Robin to begin his belated honeymoon. *Scotch. Ranch foremen. Nobility. Murder. Injustice. Extradition. Capital punishment. Trials. Scotland.*

THE LADY FROM LONGACRE **F2.2931**

Fox Film Corp. 2 Oct **1921** [c2 Oct 1921; LP17205]. Si; b&w. 35mm. 5 reels.

Pres by William Fox. *Dir* George E. Marshall. *Scen* Paul Schofield. *Photog* Ben Kline.

Cast: William Russell *(Lord Anthony Conway)*, Mary Thurman *(Princess Isabel/Molly Moncke)*, Mathilde Brundage *(Lady Jocelyn)*, Robert Klein *(Count de Se)*, Jean De Briac *(Ex-King Pedro)*, Francis Ford *(Count de Freitas)*, William Brunton *(Tiger Bugg)*, Douglas Gerard *(Sir Henry)*, Lillian Worth *(Lady Laura)*, Arthur Van Sickle *(Spaulding)*, Louis Dumar *(Count Cognasto)*.

Melodrama. Source: Victor Bridges, *The Lady From Longacre* (New York, 1919). Princess Isabel, in order to escape a loathsome marriage with the king of a neighboring principality, flees her kingdom for England, where she is rescued by Lord Anthony Conway. His friends are distressed by his gay escapades, and they rebel when he encourages them to entertain the princess, assuming her to be an actress whom she strongly resembles. Returning to her country with the Englishman, she realizes that she must marry the neighboring king to save her country, in spite of her love for Lord Anthony; but she finds that the king has been seduced by the charms of the actress, Molly Moncke, whom he marries, leaving the princess happily with Anthony. *Royalty. Actors. Doubles. Imaginary kingdoms. England.*

THE LADY IN ERMINE **F2.2932**

Corinne Griffith Productions. *Dist* First National Pictures. 1 Jan **1927** [New York premiere; released 9 Jan; c4 Jan 1927; LP23495]. Si; b&w. 35mm. 7 reels, 6,400 ft.

Pres by Asher-Small-Rogers. *Dir* James Flood. *Screenplay* Benjamin Glazer. *Photog* Harold Wenstrom. *Prod Mgr* E. M. Asher.

Cast: Corinne Griffith *(Mariana Beltrami)*, Einar Hansen *(Adrian Murillo)*, Ward Crane *(Archduke Stephan)*, Francis X. Bushman *(General Dostal)*, Jane Keckley *(Mariana's maid)*.

Romantic drama. Source: Rudolph Schanzer and Ernst Welisch, *Die Frau im Hermelin* (American adaptation and lyrics by Lorenz M. Hart and Jean Gilbert; New York, 1920). In 1810 as the Austrian army invades Italy, Countess Mariana Beltrami is married to Count Adrian Murillo before he leaves for the front. The imperious and handsome General Dostal makes his headquarters at the castle of Countess Beltrami and immediately vies for her favor with the Austrian Crown Prince, a member of his staff. Count Murillo breaks through the Austrian lines and returns to the castle; he is discovered and ordered shot as a spy. The countess tells of a similar invasion by the French when her grandmother saved her husband by appearing before a general wearing only an ermine coat. The drunken Austrian general dreams of a similar experience, and believing it to be real, he spares Count Murillo's life. *Spies. Nobility. Royalty. Disguise. Napoleonic Wars. Italy. Austria—Army.*

THE LADY LIES **F2.2933**

Paramount Famous Lasky Corp. 6 Sep or 21 Sep **1929** [c21 Sep 1929; LP706]. Sd (Movietone); b&w. 35mm. 8 reels, 7,004 ft.

Dir Hobart Henley. *Story-Dial* John Meehan. *Titl* Mort Blumenstock. *Adapt* Garrett Fort. *Photog* William Steiner. *Film Ed* Helene Turner.

Cast: Walter Huston *(Robert Rossiter)*, Claudette Colbert *(Joyce Roamer)*, Charles Ruggles *(Charlie Tyler)*, Patricia Deering *(Jo Rossiter)*, Tom Brown *(Bob Rossiter)*, Betty Garde *(Hilda Pearson)*, Jean Dixon *(Ann Gardner)*, Duncan Penwarden *(Henry Tuttle)*, Virginia True Boardman *(Amelia Tuttle)*, Verna Deane *(Bernice Tuttle)*.

Domestic drama. Source: John Meehan, *The Lady Lies* (New York opening: 26 Nov 1928). Jo and Bob Rossiter, the children of a widower who is having an affair with an attractive salesgirl, Joyce Roamer, attempt to intervene when their aunt and uncle, social snobs, indicate that the girl is beneath the family's social standing and therefore undesirable. The romance reaches a logical conclusion when Joyce so endears herself to the two children that they welcome her into their home. *Widowers. Salesclerks. Children. Uncles. Aunts. Filial relations. Snobbery. Courtship.*

Note: Also produced in a French-language version, *Une Femme a menti*.

LADY LUCK *see* **THE LUCKY LADY**

A LADY OF CHANCE **F2.2934**

Metro-Goldwyn-Mayer Pictures. 1 Dec **1928** [c28 Jan 1929; LP59]. Talking sequences (Movietone); b&w. 35mm. 8 reels, 7,126 ft. [Also si.]

Dir Robert Z. Leonard. *Scen* A. P. Younger. *Titl* Ralph Spence. *Adapt* Edmund Scott. *Photog* Peverell Marley, William Daniels. *Art Dir* Cedric Gibbons. *Film Ed* Margaret Booth. *Gowns* Adrian.

Cast: Norma Shearer *(Dolly)*, Lowell Sherman *(Bradley)*, Gwen Lee *(Gwen)*, John Mack Brown *(Steve Crandall)*, Eugenie Besserer *(Mrs. Crandall)*, Buddy Messinger *(Hank)*.

Comedy-drama. Source: Leroy Scott, "Little Angel" (publication undetermined). A crook known as "Angel Face" blackmails her victims, men whom she lures to her apartment and from whom she demands hush money when they are found by her supposed husband. When the gang leader cheats her by not dividing the last haul, Angel Face robs him and leaves the gang, only to be pursued by them even after she has married a presumably wealthy man whom she intended to fleece. But having fallen in love with him, she decides to go straight. *Criminals—Rehabilitation. Gangs. Blackmail.*

A LADY OF QUALITY (Universal-Jewel) **F2.2935**

Universal Pictures. 14 Jan **1924** [c13 Oct 1923; LP19500]. Si; b&w. 35mm. 8 reels, 8,640 ft.

Dir Hobart Henley. *Cont? (see note)* Marion Fairfax. *Adapt* Arthur Ripley, Marian Ainslee. *Photog* John Stumar.

Cast: Virginia Valli *(Clorinda Wildairs)*, Lionel Belmore *(Sir Geoffrey Wildairs,)*, Margaret Seddon *(Lady Daphne Wildairs)*, Peggy Cartwright *(Clorinda, age 6)*, Milton Sills *(Gerald Mertoun, Duke of Osmonde)*, Florence Gibson *(Dame Passett)*, Dorothea Wolbert *(Mistress Wimpole)*, Bert Roach *(Sir Christopher Crowell)*, Earle Foxe *(Sir John Ozen)*, Leo White *(Sir Humphrey Ware)*, George B. Williams *(Lord Porkfish)*, Willard Louis *(The Tavern Keeper)*, Patterson Dial *(Annie Wildairs)*, Yvonne Armstrong *(Annie, age 8)*, Bobby Mack *(The Groom)*.

Melodrama. Source: Frances Hodgson Burnett, *A Lady of Quality* (New York, 1896). Headstrong Clorinda Wildairs breaks off an affair with unprincipled Sir John Ozen to become engaged to a rich nobleman, Mertoun, the Duke of Osmonde. Clorinda accidently kills Sir John when he, piqued at her forthcoming marriage, threatens to blackmail her. She buries the body in the cellar and admits her act to the forgiving Osmonde before marrying him. *Nobility. Murder. Courtship. England.*

Note: Company records credit Marion Fairfax with continuity.

THE LADY OF SCANDAL **F2.2936**

Metro-Goldwyn-Mayer Pictures. 24 May **1930** [c26 May 1930; LP1321]. Sd (Movietone); b&w. 35mm. 8 reels, 6,858 ft.

Dir Sidney Franklin. *Scen* Hans Kraly. *Dial* Claudine West, Edwin Justus Mayer. *Photog* Oliver T. Marsh, Arthur Miller. *Art Dir* Cedric Gibbons. *Film Ed* Margaret Booth. *Rec Engr* Charles E. Wallace, Douglas Shearer. *Gowns* Adrian.

Cast: Ruth Chatterton *(Elsie)*, Basil Rathbone *(Edward)*, Ralph Forbes *(John)*, Nance O'Neil *(Lady Trench)*, Frederick Kerr *(Lord Trench)*, Herbert Bunston *(Lord Crayle)*, Cyril Chadwick *(Sir Reginald)*, Effie Ellsler *(Lady Minster)*, Robert Bolder *(Hilary)*, Moon Carroll *(Alice)*, Mackenzie Ward *(Ernest)*, Edgar Norton *(Morton)*.

Romantic society drama. Source: Frederick Lonsdale, *The High Road* (London opening: 7 Sep 1927). Elsie, a popular English actress, falls in love with John, a young nobleman, who takes her to visit the family estate where the relatives hope she will be sufficently bored to give him up; but her freshness soon invigorates the staid family members, and a secret affair develops between Elsie and Edward, the prospective bridegroom's cousin. When Elsie discovers that Edward is having an affair with a married woman, he declares he will give her up; however, when the woman's husband dies in Paris, Elsie, having been released from her betrothal to John, induces Edward to join the widow. She herself returns to the stage. *Actors. Nobility. Social classes. Courtship. England.*

THE LADY OF THE HAREM **F2.2937**

Famous Players–Lasky. *Dist* Paramount Pictures. 1 Nov **1926** [c1 Nov 1926; LP23278]. Si; b&w. 35mm. 6 reels, 5,717 ft.

Pres by Adolph Zukor, Jesse L. Lasky. *Dir* Raoul Walsh. *Screenplay* James T. O'Donohoe. *Photog* Victor Milner.

Cast: Ernest Torrence *(Hassan)*, William Collier, Jr. *(Rafi)*, Greta Nissen *(Pervaneh)*, Louise Fazenda *(Yasmin)*, André de Beranger *(Selim)*, Sojin *(Sultan)*, Frank Leigh *(Jafar)*, Noble Johnson *(tax collector)*, Daniel Makarenko *(chief of police)*, Christian Frank *(captain of military)*, Snitz Edwards *(Abdu)*, Chester Conklin *(Ali)*, Brandon Hurst, Leo White *(beggars)*.

Arabian Nights spectacular. Source: James Elroy Flecker, *Hassan; the Story of Hassan of Baghdad and How He Came To Make the Golden Journey to Samarkand* (a play; London, 1922). The glittering province of Khorasan groans under the heavy taxes and cruelties imposed by its tyrannical sultan; only Hassan, the kind-hearted confectioner, lives tranquilly. He joins Rafi, who arrives in the city in search of his beloved, Pervaneh, who has been taken by the sultan. In the slave market, Rafi gets enough money to buy her freedom, but she is abducted and taken to the palace by one of the sultan's men. Later, believing her dead, Rafi swears vengeance and organizes a band to terrorize the tyrant's officials. In disguise, the sultan attends a meeting of Rafi's cohorts and lures him to the palace by a message supposedly sent by Pervaneh; there the sultan stages a bacchanalian orgy to celebrate their death by torture. Hassan leads Rafi's men in a surprise attack on the palace in which the sultan is killed and his soldiers are routed. The lovers are united, and Hassan ascends the throne. *Confectioners. Royalty. Harems. Courtship. Disguise. Torture. Slavery. Khorasan.*

THE LADY OF THE LAKE **F2.2938**

FitzPatrick Pictures. 1 Nov **1930.** Si with synchronized mus score; b&w. 35mm. 5 reels, 4,749 ft.

Dir-Scen James A. FitzPatrick. *Photog* Bert Dawley. *Song: "Eileen, Sweet Eileen"* Nathaniel Shilkret.

Cast: Percy Marmont *(James FitzJames)*, Benita Hume *(The Lady of the Lake)*, Lawson Butt *(Roderick Dhu)*, James Carewe *(Lord Moray)*, Haddon Mason *(Malcolm Graeme)*, Hedda Bartlett *(Margaret)*, Leo Dryden *(Allan Bayne)*, Sara Francis *(Blanche of Devon)*, James Douglas *(Douglas)*.

Romantic melodrama. Source: Sir Walter Scott, *The Lady of the Lake.* Using lines from Scott's poem as titles, the story is told of Ellen Douglas (The Lady of the Lake), daughter of the outlawed Lord James ("the Douglas") and the three suitors for her hand—Roderick Dhu, James FitzJames, and Malcolm Graeme. She unwittingly comes to the aid of the King of Scotland and later is rewarded with the release of her imprisoned father and fiancé. *Royalty. Outlaws. Disguise. Gratitude. Scotland.*

LADY OF THE NIGHT **F2.2939**

Metro-Goldwyn Pictures. 23 Feb **1925** [c9 Mar 1925; LP21219]. Si; b&w. 35mm. 6 reels, 5,419 ft.

Pres by Louis B. Mayer. *Dir* Monta Bell. *Scen* Alice D. G. Miller. *Story* Adela Rogers St. Johns. *Photog* André Barlatier. *Art Dir* Cedric Gibbons. *Film Ed* Ralph Dawson.

Cast: Norma Shearer *(Molly/Florence)*, Malcolm McGregor *(David)*, George K. Arthur *(Chunky)*, Fred Esmelton *(Judge Banning)*, Dale Fuller *(Miss Carr)*, Lew Harvey *(Chris)*, Betty Morrisey *(Gertie)*.

Melodrama. Florence Banning graduates from finishing school on the same day that Molly is released from a reform school. Molly returns to the slums where she was born and takes up with her old friend, Chunky. Together they go to a dancehall, where Molly is saved from the advances of a fresh bystander by David, a young inventor with a workshop nearby. Molly and David become pals, and, at her suggestion, he sells his invention, an automatic safe-opening device, to a cartel of bankers and businessmen, instead of giving it to a gang of crooks on percentage. The cartel is headed by Judge Banning, and David soon meets his daughter, Florence, who greatly resembles Molly. David falls in love with her, but she will have nothing to do with him, believing that Molly has a prior claim to his affections. Molly discovers David's love for Florence and steps aside, enabling David and Florence to find happiness together. *Judges. Bankers. Businessmen. Doubles. Inventors. Safes. Cartels. Boarding schools. Reformatories. Dancehalls. Slums.*

LADY OF THE PAVEMENTS **F2.2940**

Art Cinema Corp. *Dist* United Artists. 22 Jan **1929** [Los Angeles premiere; released 16 Feb; c4 Feb 1929; LP79]. Talking & singing sequences (Movietone); b&w. 35mm. 9 reels, 8,329 ft. [Also si; 8 reels, 7,495 ft.]

Pres by Joseph M. Schenck. *Dir* D. W. Griffith. *Scen* Sam Taylor, Gerrit Lloyd. *Dial* George Scarborough. *Titl* Gerrit Lloyd. *Camera* Karl Struss. *Asst Camera* G. W. Bitzer. *Set Dsgn* William Cameron Menzies. *Film Ed* James Smith. *Theme song: "Where Is the Song of Songs for Me?"* Irving Berlin. *Mus Arr* Hugo Riesenfeld. *Cost* Alice O'Neill.

Cast: Lupe Velez *(Nanon del Rayon)*, William Boyd *([Count] Karl von Arnim)*, Jetta Goudal *(Countess Diane des Granges)*, Albert Conti *(Baron Finot)*, George Fawcett *(Baron Haussmann)*, Henry Armetta *(Papa Pierre)*, William Bakewell *(a pianist)*, Franklin Pangborn *(M'sieu Dubrey, dance master)*.

Romantic drama. Source: Karl Gustav Vollmoeller, "La Paiva" (publication undetermined). Karl von Arnim, military attaché with the Prussian legation at Paris, breaks his engagement to the beautiful French Countess Diane des Granges because she is unfaithful and in a fit of anger declares that he would rather marry a woman of the streets. Enraged, Diane conspires with Baron Finot, Napoleon III's chamberlain, to arrange for Karl to meet Nanon del Rayon, a singer at "The Smoking Dog" cabaret, in the guise of a real lady (La Paiva). The ruse is a success, and Karl and Nanon marry. Diane holds a wedding banquet for the newlyweds at "The Smoking Dog," where she reveals Nanon's real identity. Nanon flees, then returns to sing at the cabaret, where Karl comes to take her away. *Prostitutes. Singers. Nobility. Diplomats. Prussians. Paris. Antoine-Bernard (Baron) Finot. Napoleon III.*

Note: In addition to the theme song, Lupe Velez sings "Nena" and "At the Dance."

LADY RAFFLES **F2.2941**

Columbia Pictures. 25 Jan or 25 Feb **1928** [c24 Feb 1928; LP25006]. Si; b&w. 35mm. 6 reels, 5,471 ft.

Prod Harry Cohn. *Dir* R. William Neill. *Scen* Earl Hudson. *Story* Jack Jungmeyer, Fred Stanley. *Photog* Joe Walker. *Art Dir* Robert E. Lee. *Film Ed* Arthur Roberts. *Asst Dir* Max Cohn.

Cast: Estelle Taylor *(Lady Raffles)*, Roland Drew *(Warren Blake)*, Lilyan Tashman *(Lillian)*, Ernest Hilliard *(Dick)*, Winifred Landis *(Mrs. Blake)*.

Crook drama. Lady Raffles, a society crook, is surprised during a robbery and seeks cover at the back door of an adjoining mansion. There the butler mistakes her for a temporary maid hired to serve a party celebrating the homecoming of Warren Blake, the son of the mistress of the household. Warren has brought with him a priceless necklace as a birthday gift to his mother. Among the guests are Lillian and Dick, two shrewd jewel thieves. They recognize Lady Raffles and conclude that she is there on the same mission that brought them. The two crooks break the necklace while attempting to steal it, and it is sent out of reach for repairs. During the course of the evening Warren falls in love with Lady Raffles and eventually asks for her hand, in spite of assertions from Lillian and Dick that she is a thief. When Lillian and Dick try to sever the engagement by framing Lady Raffles, their plan fails, they are jailed, and Lady Raffles is cleared of all suspicion before her wedding. In the final reel she reveals herself as an agent of Scotland Yard. *Housemaids. Thieves. Disguise. Upper classes. Scotland Yard.*

LADY ROBINHOOD **F2.2942**

R-C Pictures. *Dist* Film Booking Offices of America. 26 Jul **1925** [c26 Jul 1925; LP21698]. Si; b&w. 35mm. 6 reels, 5,580 ft.

Dir Ralph Ince. *Cont* Frederick Myton. *Story* Clifford Howard, Burke Jenkins. *Photog* Silvano Balboni. *Asst Dir* Pandro S. Berman. *Prop Man* Gene Rossi.

Cast: Evelyn Brent *(Señorita Catalina/La Ortiga)*, Robert Ellis *(Hugh Winthrop)*, Boris Karloff *(Cabraza)*, William Humphrey *(governor)*, D'Arcy Corrigan *(padre)*, Robert Cauterio *(Raimundo)*.

Melodrama. Disguised as a masked bandit, Catalina, the ward of the governor of a Spanish province, avenges injustice, aids the poor, and plots a revolution. Hugh Winthrop, a young American who owns mines in the province, comes to inspect them and is kidnaped by Catalina, who suspects him of being an enemy of the people. He escapes but meets Catalina later at the governor's palace, where they are arrested for stealing state papers. Catalina escapes, and Hugh is sentenced to be executed. As he is standing before the firing squad, Catalina and her followers ride in and save him. The governor, who was responsible for many of the province's ills, is convicted; and Hugh and Catalina are united. *Revolutionaries. Bandits. Reformers. Disguise. Theft. Mines. Spain. Documentation.*

A LADY SURRENDERS **F2.2943**

Universal Pictures. 6 Oct **1930** [c22 Sep 1930; LP1587]. Sd (Movietone); b&w. 35mm. 10 reels, 8,485 ft.

Pres by Carl Laemmle. *Prod* Carl Laemmle, Jr. *Assoc Prod* E. M. Asher. *Dir* John M. Stahl. *Cont* Gladys Lehman. *Dial* Arthur Richman. *Photog* Jackson Rose. *Sets* Walter Kessler. *Film Ed* Maurice Pivar, William L. Cahn. *Rec Engr* Joseph R. Lapis, C. Roy Hunter.

Cast: Genevieve Tobin *(Mary)*, Rose Hobart *(Isabel)*, Conrad Nagel *(Winthrop)*, Basil Rathbone *(Carl Vaudry)*, Edgar Norton *(butler)*, Carmel Myers *(Sonia)*, Franklin Pangborn *(Lawton)*, Vivian Oakland *(Mrs. Lynchfield)*, Grace Cunard *(maid)*.

Domestic drama. Source: John Erskine, *Sincerity, a Story of Our Time* (Indianapolis, 1929). Manufacturer Winthrop Beauvel is married to Isabel, a successful novelist who is bored with her husband and is the pseudonymous author of a bitter tract on marriage. Winthrop reads the article, writes the author, and arranges to discuss it with her. Isabel asks her friend Mary to pose as the author and discuss the article with Winthrop. He is forced to spend the night in a hotel because of a rainstorm, and Isabel accuses him of unfaithfulness, using the incident as an excuse for a European divorce. En route, she meets Carl Vaudry, a flirt, and falls in love with him; on the day the divorce is to be granted, Vaudry jilts her, whereupon she drops the case and returns home. Meanwhile, Winthrop, thinking himself free, marries Mary. Following a violent encounter between the two women, Mary attempts suicide by throwing herself in front of a car; Isabel, realizing her seriousness, agrees to a bona fide divorce. *Manufacturers. Novelists. Flirts. Marriage. Infidelity. Divorce. Bigamy. Suicide. France.*

A LADY TO LOVE *see* **DIE SEHNSUCHT JEDER FRAU**

A LADY TO LOVE **F2.2944**

Metro-Goldwyn-Mayer Pictures. 28 Feb **1930** [New York premiere; released 8 Mar; c10 Mar 1930; LP1138]. Sd (Movietone); b&w. 35mm. 10 reels, 8,142 ft.

Dir Victor Seastrom. *Scen-Dial* Sidney Howard. *Photog* Merritt B. Gerstad. *Art Dir* Cedric Gibbons. *Film Ed* Conrad A. Nervig, Leslie F. Wilder. *Rec Engr* J. K. Brock, Douglas Shearer. *Gowns* Adrian.

Cast: Vilma Banky *(Lena)*, Edward G. Robinson *(Tony)*, Robert Ames *(Buck)*, Richard Carle *(postman)*, Lloyd Ingraham *(Father McKee)*, Anderson Lawler *(doctor)*, Gum Chin *(Ah Gee)*, Henry Armetta *(Angelo)*, George Davis *(Giorgio)*.

Romantic drama. Source: Sidney Howard, *They Knew What They Wanted, a Comedy in Three Acts* (Garden City, New York, 1925). Tony, a prosperous Neapolitan vineyardist in California, advertises for a young wife, passing off a photograph of his handsome hired man, Buck, as himself. Lena, a San Francisco waitress, takes up the offer, and though she is disillusioned upon discovering the truth, she goes through with the marriage because of her desire to have a home and partially because of her implied weakness for Buck, whose efforts to take her away from Tony confirm her love for her husband. *Vineyardists. Waitresses. Italians. Neapolitans. San Franciscans. Marriage. California.*

THE LADY WHO LIED **F2.2945**

First National Pictures. 12 Jul **1925** [c2 Jul 1925; LP21624]. Si; b&w. 35mm. 8 reels, 7,111 ft.

Pres by Edwin Carewe. *Dir* Edwin Carewe. *Scen* Lois Zellner, Madge Tyrone. *Adapt* Lois Leeson. *Photog* Robert B. Kurrle. *Adtl Photog* Al M. Green. *Art Dir* John D. Schulze. *Film Ed* LeRoy Stone. *Asst Dir* William Fox, of First National.

Cast: Lewis Stone *(Horace Pierpont)*, Virginia Valli *(Fay Kennion)*, Louis Payne *(Sir Henry Kennion)*, Nita Naldi *(Fifi)*, Edward Earle *(Alan Mortimer)*, Leo White *(valet)*, Purnell Pratt *(Ahmed)*, Sam Appel *(Saad Ben Youssof)*, Zalla Zarana *(Zetta)*, George Lewis *(Mahmud)*.

Melodrama. Source: Robert Smythe Hichens, "Snake-bite," in *Snake-bite, and Other Stories* (London, 1919). When Fay Kennion finds her fiancé, Horace Pierpont, in an innocent but apparently compromising situation with another woman, she breaks their engagement and marries instead Alan Mortimer, a weak and alcoholic physician practicing in Algeria. Pierpont later goes on a safari and persuades Fay and the doctor to accompany him as his guests. Despite genuine attempts to remain apart, Pierpont and Fay find themselves together more and more, and Mortimer eventually discovers them in a passionate embrace. Pierpont is later bitten by a snake, and Mortimer alone can save him. Mortimer at first refuses, but Fay, deeply in love with Pierpont, feigns love for her own husband and promises to return with him to Algeria if he will help Pierpont. Mortimer finally agrees and tends the other's wounds, saving Pierpont's life. On the trip back, the caravan is attacked by bandits; Mortimer is killed; and Fay and Pierpont are free to find happiness together. *Physicians. Bandits. Alcoholism. Safaris. Snakes. Algeria. Africa.*

LADY WINDERMERE'S FAN **F2.2946**

Warner Brothers Pictures. 26 Dec **1925** [c1 Dec 1925; LP22085]. Si; b&w. 35mm. 8 reels, 7,815 ft.

Dir Ernst Lubitsch. *Adapt* Julian Josephson. *Camera* Charles Van Enger. *Asst Camera* Willard Van Enger. *Asst Dir* George Hippard.

Cast: Ronald Colman *(Lord Darlington)*, Irene Rich *(Mrs. Erlynne)*, May McAvoy *(Lady Windermere)*, Bert Lytell *(Lord Windermere)*, Edward Martindel *(Lord Augustus)*, Helen Dunbar *(duchess)*, Carrie Daumery *(duchess)*, Billie Bennett *(duchess)*.

Comedy of manners. Source: Oscar Wilde, *Lady Windermere's Fan, a Play About a Good Woman, in Four Acts* (1892). The sensational and indiscreet Mrs. Erlynne returns to London and sends for Lord Windermere. She reveals that she is really his wife's mother, long thought dead by Lady

Windermere, and demands payment for her secrecy. She also asks for an invitation to his wife's birthday party. Windermere fails to persuade his wife to send the invitation, but Mrs. Erlynne mistakes the letter of refusal for the invitation. Her arrival at the party arouses the jealousy of Lady Windermere, who goes off to the apartment of Lord Darlington, an admirer. Mrs. Erlynne follows to persuade her daughter to return to her husband before it is too late. Darlington, Windermere, and some other men show up and find Lady Windermere's fan. Mrs. Erlynne comes out, and in front of her admirer, Lord Augustus, claims that she had taken the fan by mistake. Her audacity, however, wins Lord Augustus' heart. *Nobility. Infidelity. Motherhood. London.*

THE LADYBIRD **F2.2947**

Chadwick Pictures. *Dist* First Division Pictures. ca7 Mar **1927** [New York premiere; released 15 Jul 1927]. Si; b&w. 35mm. 7 reels, 6,568 ft.

Dir Walter Lang. *Scen* John F. Natteford. *Story* William Dudley Pelley. *Photog* Ernest Miller, Ted Tetzlaff. *Cost* Alice O'Neill.

Cast: Betty Compson *(Diana Whyman)*, Malcolm McGregor *(Duncan Spencer)*, Sheldon Lewis *(Spider)*, Hank Mann *(The Brother)*, Leo White *(Phillipe)*, John Miljan *(Jules Ranier)*, Ruth Stonehouse *(Lucille)*, Joseph Girard *(Jacob Gale)*, Jean De Briac *(Jacques)*, Mathew Matron *(The Proprietor)*.

Crook melodrama. Preferring to earn her own living, society girl Diana Whyman leaves her guardian's home, gets a dancing job in a New Orleans cabaret, and unwittingly falls in with a band of crooks—known as The Ladybirds—at carnival time. Diana goes through a maze of adventures, which involve the hero (Duncan Spencer), but it is Diana who overcomes the villain with jujitsu until the police arrive. *Dancers. Socialites. Guardians. Gangs. Jujitsu. Mardi Gras. New Orleans.*

LADYFINGERS *see* **ALIAS LADYFINGERS**

LADYFINGERS **F2.2948**

Metro Pictures. 31 Oct **1921.** Si; b&w. 35mm. 6 reels, 5,304 ft.

Dir Bayard Veiller. *Scen* Lenore J. Coffee. *Camera* Arthur Martinelli. *Art Dir* A. E. Freuderman.

Cast: Bert Lytell *(Herbert Ashe [Ladyfingers])*, Ora Carew *(Enid Camden)*, Frank Elliott *(Justin Haddon)*, Edythe Chapman *(Rachel Stetherill)*, De Witt Jennings *(Lieutenant Ambrose)*, Stanley Goethals *(Robert Ashe, at age of 4)*.

Comedy-drama. Source: Jackson Gregory, *Ladyfingers* (New York, 1920). Disapproving of her daughter's choice of husband, Rachel Stetherill disowns her and refuses to accept any responsibility for her grandson, Robert, when he is left an orphan. Instead, safecracker Herbert Ashe cares for the boy and teaches him the tricks of the trade. Years later, Stetherill lawyer Justin Haddon suspects that Robert, now a successful burglar, is the heir to the Stetherill estate and brings Rachel and her grandson together—hoping to discredit Robert and thus make Rachel's ward, Enid Camden, the rightful heir. Robert does not take the bait (Rachel's valuable pearls) but he does fall in love with Enid, realizes that he must pay a debt to society, surrenders to police, and serves 2 years in prison. Meanwhile, Rachel reveals that she recognizes Robert as her grandson. After his release, Robert takes up farming, marries Enid, and eventually is reunited with the indomitable Rachel. *Grandmothers. Burglars. Safecrackers. Criminals—Rehabilitation. Lawyers. Farmers. Inheritance.*

A LADY'S MORALS **F2.2949**

Metro-Goldwyn-Mayer Pictures. 8 Nov **1930** [c27 Oct 1930; LP1680]. Sd (Movietone); b&w. 35mm. 10 reels, 7,856 ft.

Dir Sidney Franklin. *Scen* Hans Kraly, Claudine West. *Dial* John Meehan, Arthur Richman. *Story* Dorothy Farnum. *Photog* George Barnes. *Art Dir* Cedric Gibbons. *Film Ed* Margaret Booth. *Songs: "Is It Destiny?" "Student's Song," "I Hear Your Voice"* Clifford Grey, Oskar Straus. *Song: "Oh, Why?"* Arthur Freed, Herbert Stothart, Harry M. Woods. *Song: "Lovely Hour"* Carrie Jacobs Bond. *Song: "Swedish Pastorale"* Howard Johnson, Herbert Stothart. *Dance Dir* Sammy Lee. *Rec Engr* J. K. Brock, Douglas Shearer. *Gowns* Adrian.

Cast: Grace Moore *(Jenny Lind)*, Reginald Denny *(Paul Brandt)*, Wallace Beery *(P. T. Barnum)*, Gus Shy *(Olaf)*, Jobyna Howland *(Josephine)*, Gilbert Emery *(Broughm)*, George F. Marion *(innkeeper)*, Paul Porcasi *(Maretti)*, Giovanni Martino *(Zerga)*, Bodil Rosing *(innkeeper's wife)*, Joan Standing *(Louise)*, Mavis Villiers *(Selma)*, Judith Vosselli *(Rosatti)*.

Musical drama. Paul Brandt, a young composer, falls hopelessly in love with the singer Jenny Lind, following her from city to city, hoping to impress her by his persistency. Jenny loses her voice while performing *Norma*, and in the chaos that ensues, Paul is struck on the head, gradually causing him to become blind. He is instrumental in bringing the songstress to a maestro who is able to restore her voice, thus proving his unselfish love. She returns with him to Sweden, still chaste and unstirred, but when it becomes evident that Paul is becoming blind, he leaves without explanation just as Jenny is beginning to respond to his love. She is about to make her American debut at the Castle Garden in New York under the direction of P. T. Barnum when she is happily reunited with Paul, now a wandering blind musician. *Singers. Composers. Opera. Courtship. Blindness. Sweden. Jenny Lind. Phineas Taylor Barnum. "Norma".*

Note: Miss Moore also sings the following arias in the film: "Casta Diva," from *Norma* by Bellini; and "Rataplan," from *The Daughter of the Regiment* by Donizetti. Originally reviewed as *The Soul Kiss*.

THE LAFFIN' FOOL **F2.2950**

Morris R. Schlank Productions. *Dist* Rayart Pictures. Feb **1927.** Si; b&w. 35mm. 5 reels, 5,127 ft.

Dir Bennett Cohn. *Photog* William Hyer.

Cast: Jack Perrin.

Western melodrama. "Beautiful girl's ranch is about to be sold because she cannot pay mortgage. A modern Shylock holds the deed and offers to give her time if she will marry him. She is helpless until hero arrives with buddies and he takes up the fight, paying off the mortgage and winning the girl." (*Motion Picture News Booking Guide*, 12:39, Apr 1927.) *Cowboys. Ranches. Mortgages.*

THE LAMPLIGHTER **F2.2951**

Fox Film Corp. 10 Apr **1921** [c10 Apr 1921; LP16428]. Si; b&w. 35mm. 6 reels, 6,050 ft.

Pres by William Fox. *Dir* Howard M. Mitchell. *Scen* Robert Dillon. *Photog* Glen MacWilliams.

Cast: Shirley Mason *(Gertie)*, Raymond McKee *(Willie Sullivan)*, Albert Knott *(The Lamplighter)*, Edwin Booth Tilton *(Malcolm Graham)*, Iris Ashton *(Emily Graham)*, Philo McCullough *(Philip Amory)*, Madge Hunt *(The Housekeeper)*.

Melodrama. Source: Marie Susanna Cummins, *The Lamplighter* (Boston, 1854). In the absence of wealthy Malcolm Graham, his daughter secretly marries Philip Amory. Her eyesight is destroyed inadvertently by her husband; and when a baby is born, her father, not convinced that she is married, gives the child to a sailor to deliver out of the country. The sailor, however, keeps the child in his family. Cruelly mistreated, the child runs away and is taken in by an old lamplighter. Fortune brings Gertie into her grandfather's house, where she becomes companion to her blind mother. Willie Sullivan, the lamplighter's assistant, finds her father, who has been in India, and they return to America. When mother and daughter arrive to meet their ship, Gertie is rescued from a fire by the sailor who had kept her, and following Amory's reunion with his wife she becomes engaged to Willie. *Sailors. Lamplighters. Grandfathers. Motherhood. Childhood. Illegitimacy. Blindness.*

THE LAND BEYOND THE LAW **F2.2952**

Charles R. Rogers Productions. *Dist* First National Pictures. 5 Jun **1927** [c12 May 1927; LP23954]. Si; b&w. 35mm. 7 reels, 6,157 ft.

Pres by Charles R. Rogers. *Dir* Harry J. Brown. *Story-Scen* Marion Jackson. *Photog* Sol Polito.

Cast: Ken Maynard *(Jerry Steele)*, Dorothy Dwan *(Ginger O'Hara)*, Tom Santschi *(Bob Crew)*, Noah Young *(Hanzup Harry)*, Gibson Gowland *(Silent "Oklahoma" Joe)*, Billy Butts *(Pat O'Hara)*, Tarzan *(himself, a horse)*.

Western melodrama. Jerry Steele is appointed special deputy by the governor to bring law and order to a troublesome region, infested by roustabouts in the employ of Bob Crew, whose respectability is a cloak for his rustling and killing. Steele comes to the aid of Ginger O'Hara, a young girl entrusted to Crew, when her guardian takes advantage of her; and the couple soon become romantically attached. "Hanzup" Harry, known as a bandit, is made one of his deputies, and following a series of encounters with the rustlers, the territory becomes a haven of security for pioneers from the East and Midwest. *Rustlers. Bandits. Territorial governors. Sheriffs. Courtship. Horses.*

THE LAND OF HOPE **F2.2953**

Realart Pictures. Jul **1921** [c23 May 1921; LP16574]. Si; b&w. 35mm. 5 reels, 4,964 ft.

Dir Edward H. Griffith. *Scen* Fred Myton, Robert Milton, Frederick Hatton, Fanny Hatton. *Story* Robert Milton, Frederick Hatton, Fanny Hatton. *Photog* Gilbert Warrenton.

Cast: Alice Brady *(Marya Nisko)*, Jason Robards *(Sascha Rabinoff)*, Ben Hendricks, Jr. *(Jan)*, Schuyler Ladd *(Serge Kosmanski)*, Laurence Wheat *(Stephen Ross)*, Martha McGraw *(Sophia)*, Betty Carsdale *(Mildred St. John)*, Fuller Mellish *(Josef Marinoff)*.

Melodrama. On her voyage to the United States Marya Nisko falls in love with another Polish immigrant, Sascha Rabinoff. Arriving and discovering her sister's poverty, she fails as a lady's maid and then arranges an introduction to a theatrical manager, though Sascha is opposed to her becoming a professional dancer. She obtains an engagement through Stephen Ross, who arranges for her training. Meanwhile, unable to pursue his education and reduced to the breadline, Sascha attracts the attention of a wealthy philanthropist, Josef Marinoff, who takes an interest in his idea for a home for immigrants, and through Marinoff's aid he and Marya are reunited. *Immigrants. Poles. Dancers. Philanthropists. Theater.*

THE LAND OF MISSING MEN **F2.2954**

Trem Carr Productions. *Dist* Tiffany Productions. 15 Oct **1930** [c3 Oct 1930; LP1625]. Sd (Photophone); b&w. 35mm. 6 reels, 5,179 ft.

Prod Trem Carr. *Dir-Story* J. P. McCarthy. *Screenplay* J. P. McCarthy, Bob Quigley. *Photog* Harry Neumann.

Cast: Bob Steele *(Steve O'Neil)*, Al St. John *(Buckshot)*, Edward Dunn *(Sheriff Bower)*, Caryl Lincoln *(Nita Madero)*, Al Jennings *(John Evans, ex-sheriff)*, Fern Emmett *(Martha Evans)*, Emilio Fernandez *(López)*, Noah Hendricks *(Texas)*, C. R. Dufau *(Señor Madero)*, S. S. Simon *(express agent)*.

Western melodrama. Steve O'Neil and his partner, Buckshot, are accused of holding up a stagecoach in cattle country. They stop at a saloon to ask the route to the border and find a number of dead men; a dying man tells them about a planned stage holdup and asks them to save his daughter, who is in the coach. Steve holds up the coach and kidnaps the girl, Nita Madero, but she escapes upon learning of her father's death. Meanwhile, Steve and Buckshot make their way to the outlaws' camp, where they are given shelter, though under suspicion. With a posse on the way, Bob and his pal engage in gunplay with the cattle thieves and bandits and expose the leader, who is Sheriff Bower. *Cowboys. Outlaws. Sheriffs. Posses. Stagecoach robberies. Texas.*

LAND OF THE LAWLESS **F2.2955**

Liberty Pictures. *Dist* Pathé Exchange. 25 Dec **1927** [c28 Nov 1927; LP24712]. Si; b&w. 35mm. 5 reels, 4,131 ft.

Dir Thomas Buckingham. *Scen* Paul Fejos. *Titl* Wyndham Gittens. *Story* Wallace Smith. *Photog* Leon Shamroy. *Asst Dir* Wynn Mace.

Cast: Jack Padjan *(Jim Catlin)*, Tom Santschi *(Kelter)*, Joseph Rickson *("Brush" Gallagher, his henchman)*, Charles Clary *(Steve Dorman, an old rancher)*, Vivian Winston *(Polly Dorman, his daughter)*, Frank Clark *(Simpson, a hired hand)*, Duke R. Lee *(bartender)*, Otto Fries *(deputy sheriff)*.

Western melodrama. Kelter, a killer, and his gang of desperadoes terrorize a wide district, and Jim Catlin, a Texas Ranger, is assigned to bring him in. Jim captures the interest of Kelter by demonstrating his riding and shooting ability and thus is accepted by the gang. He aids Polly Dorman in escaping the attentions of Kelter and informs her father of his identity. When Kelter finds Jim interfering with his plans, he takes him prisoner; but Jim tricks his guard and makes a getaway, returning with the sheriff in time to save Polly and her father from the drunken and brutal Kelter. *Texas Rangers. Gangs. Personal identity. Filial relations.*

LAND OF THE SILVER FOX **F2.2956**

Warner Brothers Pictures. 13 Oct **1928** [c9 Oct 1928; LP25704]. Sd (Vitaphone); b&w. 35mm. 7 reels, 5,179 ft. [Also si, 10 Nov 1928; 5,079 ft.]

Dir Ray Enright. *Scen-Dial* Howard Smith. *Titl* Joseph Jackson. *Story* Charles Condon. *Photog* Frank Kesson. *Film Ed* Owen Marks.

Cast: Rin-Tin-Tin *(Rinty)*, Leila Hyams *(Marie du Fronque)*, John Miljan *(James Crawford)*, Carroll Nye *(Carroll Blackton)*, Tom Santschi *(Butch Nelson)*, Princess Neola *(The Squaw)*.

Northwest melodrama. Smooth-faced, villainous James Crawford cruelly beats his handsome police dog, Rinty, and Carroll Blackton, a fur trader, buys the dog from him. Crawford later sends Carroll out with a sled-load of furs and hires Butch Nelson to kill him. Nelson robs Carroll and leaves him for dead, but Rinty saves his new master's life and cares for his wounds. When Carroll returns to civilization, he is accused of the robbery of the furs on circumstantial evidence and arrested by the Mounties. Rinty forces Nelson to confess, however, and Crawford and Nelson are arrested. *Fur traders. Circumstantial evidence. Robbery. Northwest Mounted Police. Police dogs.*

THE LANE THAT HAD NO TURNING **F2.2957**

Famous Players–Lasky. *Dist* Paramount Pictures. 15 Jan **1922** [c17 Jan 1922; LP17472]. Si; b&w. 35mm. 5 reels, 4,892 ft.

Pres by Adolph Zukor. *Dir* Victor Fleming. *Scen* Eugene Mullin. *Adapt* Gilbert Parker. *Photog* Gilbert Warrenton.

Cast: Agnes Ayres *(Madelinette)*, Theodore Kosloff *(Louis Racine)*, Mahlon Hamilton *(George Fournel)*, Wilton Taylor *(Joe Lajeunesse)*, Frank Campeau *(Tardiff)*, Lillian Leighton *(Marie)*, Charles West *(Havel)*, Robert Bolder *(Monsieur Poire)*, Fred Vroom *(Governor General)*.

Melodrama. Source: Gilbert Parker, *The Lane That Had No Turning and Other Tales Concerning the People of Pontiac* (New York, 1900). The Seigneur of Pontiac, estranged relative of Louis Racine, dies in Paris, leaving no will but a provision that 50,000 francs be paid Madelinette, Louis' wife, making possible her operatic career. Tardiff, former servant of the seigneur and an enemy of Louis, insinuates that there is a hidden will; however, Louis takes the title of his deceased relative and his estate. In a struggle with Tardiff, Louis' back is injured. As Madelinette prepares to make her operatic debut in Paris, George Fournel arrives from England with a letter from the seigneur indicating his rights to the estate. Meanwhile, following his wife's departure, Louis has an operation performed on his back, but it is unsuccessful. On returning, Madelinette is horrified by her husband's condition and decides to give up her career to care for him. She later discovers the hidden will, but it is stolen by Tardiff and taken to Fournel, who fulfills her request to burn it; in a jealous rage Louis kills Tardiff, then commits suicide. Madelinette finds happiness with Fournel and pursues her career. *Singers. Hunchbacks. Inheritance. Opera. Wills. Documentation. Canada. Paris.*

THE LARIAT KID (Universal-Jewel) **F2.2958**

Universal Pictures. 12 May **1929** [c29 Mar 1929; LP251]. Si; b&w. 35mm. 6 reels, 5,247 ft.

Dir Reaves Eason. *Cont* Jacques Jaccard, Sylvia Bernstein Seid. *Titl* Harold Tarshis. *Story* Buckleigh Fritz Oxford. *Photog* Harry Neumann. *Film Ed* Gilmore Walker.

Cast: Hoot Gibson *(Tom Richards)*, Ann Christy *(Mary Lou)*, Cap Anderson *(Scar Hagerty)*, Mary Foy *(Aunt Bella)*, Walter Brennan *(Pat O'Shea)*, Andy Waldron *(George Carson)*, Bud Osborne *(Trigger Finger)*, Joe Bennett *(Pecos Kid)*, Jim Corey *(Jackknife)*, Francis Ford *(Cal Gregg)*, Joe Rickson *(Tony)*.

Western melodrama. Deputy Sheriff Tom Richards rides into Hell's Gulch to bring order to that rowdy town and to avenge the murder of his father, who had been sheriff there. Tom falls in love with Mary Lou and rides to her rescue when she is kidnaped by Gregg. Tom arrests not only Gregg but also the rest of his gang, proving Gregg to have been his father's murderer. Tom and Mary Lou are married by the judge. *Sheriffs. Murder. Kidnaping. Revenge.*

THE LARIAT THROWER *see* **CROSS ROADS**

THE LASH **F2.2959**

First National Pictures. 14 Dec **1930** [c28 Dec 1930; LP1910]. Sd (Vitaphone); b&w. 65mm (Vitascope); 9 reels, 7,169 ft.

Dir Frank Lloyd. *Screenplay* Bradley King. *Photog* Ernest Haller. *Film Ed* Harold Young. *Rec Engr* Oliver S. Garretson.

Cast: Richard Barthelmess *(Francisco Delfino)*, Mary Astor *(Rosita García)*, Fred Kohler *(Peter Harkness)*, Marian Nixon *(Dolores Delfino)*, James Rennie *(David Howard)*, Robert Edeson *(Don Marino Delfino)*, Arthur Stone *(Juan)*, Barbara Bedford *(Lupe)*, Mathilde Comont *(Concha)*, Erville Alderson *(Judge Travers)*.

Romantic melodrama. Source: Lanier Bartlett and Virginia Stivers Bartlett, *Adoiós!* (New York, 1929). Returning from the university in Mexico to California (ca1850), Don Francisco Delfino finds his native land in the hands of unscrupulous Americans, his family estate in shambles, and his loved ones in fear. Anger drives Francisco to stampede a herd of cattle he is delivering to Peter Harkness. the crooked land commissioner, and still obtain his money—thus earning him the name "El Puma." Don Francisco and others start making Robin Hood–type bandit raids, one of which leads to Francisco's rescue by Sheriff David

Howard, their subsequent friendship, and David's love for Francisco's sister, Dolores. Finally avenging his father's murder by killing Harkness, Francisco must leave not only California but also his faithful love, Rosita, and his sometime sweetheart, Lupe; but David gives him a head start, and Rosita promises to meet him in Mexico. *Bandits. Sheriffs. Mexicans. Land commissioners. Revenge. Murder. Land grants. California. Stampedes.*
Note: Originally titled and reviewed as *Adiós.*

THE LASH OF PINTO PETE **F2.2960**
Ben Wilson Productions. *Dist* Arrow Film Corp. 15 Nov **1924** [c12 Nov 1924; LP20759]. Si; b&w. 35mm. 5 reels, 4,437 ft.
Dir Francis Ford.
Cast: Ashton Dearholt.
Melodrama. Driven from his throne by the scheming Targon, the King of Paloma is banished to the prison mines, where his son, Pietro, is bayoneted for protesting. A shipwreck allows the king to escape and find refuge with his followers on Paloma's rocky shore. Rosita cares for the blinded king and tells him of Pinto Pete, who defends the oppressed with his bullwhip. The paths of Rosita and Pinto Pete cross when both are captured by Targon's guards, the mystery man is revealed to be Pietro, and both escape to be reunited with the king. Swearing vengeance, Pinto Pete bravely and successfully undertakes the overthrow of Targon, and the throne is again occupied by the king, who abdicates in favor of Pinto Pete and Rosita. *Royalty. Blindness. Banishment. Abdication. Imaginary kingdoms. Whips. Shipwrecks.*

LASH OF THE LAW **F2.2961**
Goodwill Pictures. 2 Feb **1926** [New York State license]. Si; b&w. 35mm. 5 reels, 4,475 ft.
Cast: Bill Bailey.
Melodrama(?). No information about the nature of this film has been found.

LASH OF THE WHIP **F2.2962**
Ben Wilson Productions. *Dist* Arrow Film Corp. 1 May **1924** [c15 Aug 1924; LP20519]. Si; b&w. 35mm. 5 reels, 4,820 ft.
Prod Ben Wilson. *Dir-Writ* Francis Ford.
Cast: Ashton Dearholt *("Pinto Pete")*, Harry Dunkinson *(his servant)*, Florence Gilbert *(Florence)*, Francis Ford *("Hurricane" Smith)*, Frank Baker *(Frank Blake)*.
Western melodrama. "Hurricane" Smith, head of a steamship company, plots to keep the railroad from entering the city. The map of the proposed route becomes the instrument by which Blake and Florence are harrassed by Smith's gang and repeatedly are rescued by "Pinto Pete," who is adept with a whip. *Railroads. Ship lines. Whips. Documentation.*

THE LAST ALARM **F2.2963**
Paul Gerson Pictures. *Dist* Rayart Pictures. Jun **1926.** Si; b&w. 35mm. 6 reels, 5,274-5,800 ft.
Pres by W. Ray Johnston. *Dir* Oscar Apfel. *Story* John Francis Natteford.
Cast: Rex Lease, Wanda Hawley, Maurice Costello *(father of a fireman)*, Florence Turner *(wife of warehouse proprietor)*, Theodore von Eltz, Hazel Howell, Jimmy Aubrey.
Melodrama. Firemen Tom and Joe each loves the other's sister, although neither is able to support a wife. Tom's troubles are compounded by a rival for his sweetheart's hand. In a drawnout fight he bests the rival, who steals the revenue from the firemen's ball (of which Tom is treasurer) and hides the money in the storage warehouse in which Tom's sister works as a stenographer. While Tom, Joe, and their sweethearts search for the money, the villain also returns for his loot, and, in his haste, he sets the building afire—trapping the foursome behind a steel door. Their calls for help reach the street, an alarm is turned in, firemen come to the rescue, and the money is found in a blazing desk. *Firemen. Stenographers. Brother-sister relationship. Theft. Courtship. Fires.*
Note: Johnston presents this film "by arrangement with B. Berger."

THE LAST CARD **F2.2964**
Metro Pictures. 23 May **1921** [c22 Jun 1921; LP17931]. Si; b&w. 35mm. 6 reels, 5,817 ft.
Dir Bayard Veiller. *Scen* Molly Parro. *Adapt* Mary O'Hara. *Photog* Jackson Rose. *Art Dir* A. F. Mantz.
Cast: May Allison *(Elsie Kirkwood)*, Albert Roscoe *(Ralph Kirkwood)*, Stanley Goethals *(Freddie Kirkwood)*, Frank Elliott *(Tom Gannell)*, Irene Hunt *(Emma Gannell)*, Dana Todd *(Sorley)*, Wilton Taylor *(Chief of Police)*.
Crime melodrama. Source: Maxwell Smith, "Dated," in *Saturday Evening Post* (193:18–19, 3 Jul 1920). Tom Gannell, a criminal lawyer, detects an intrigue between his wife, Emma, and a college student, Sorley, who tends furnaces on their block. When Sorley goes to the cellar, his wife goes to the piano and plays "The End of a Perfect Day," and maddened by his wife's faithlessness, Gannell follows Sorley and kills him. The following day, the Kirkwoods leave on their annual trip to Florida; a coat belonging to Kirkwood and a pack of his cigarettes are found near the body; hearing of the murder, he returns home and is arrested for the crime. Kirkwood is defended by Gannell and found guilty. Mrs. Kirkwood, who suspects Gannell, induces the police to tap a telephone conversation between herself and Gannell: while talking she has her maid play "The End of a Perfect Day" on the piano. Finding his living room empty and hearing the sound of the furnace being raked, Gannell breaks and confesses his guilt but defies her to prove it. *Students. Lawyers. Infidelity. Murder. Florida.*

THE LAST CHANCE (Franklyn Farnum Series) **F2.2965**
William N. Selig Productions. *Dist* Canyon Pictures. Apr **1921** [c30 Mar 1921; LU16339]. Si; b&w. 35mm. 5 reels.
Prod Col. William N. Selig. *Dir* Webster Cullison. *Story* William E. Wing.
Cast: Franklyn Farnum *(Rance Sparr)*, Vester Pegg *(Black Sparr)*, Gertrude Hall *(Vivian Morrow)*, Churchill Scott *(Braden)*, David Mansfield *(Dynamite Dan)*.
Western melodrama. Black Sparr, a hard-fighting, hard-drinking rancher, puts his son, Rance, through rigorous experiences to learn the ways of men. Rance thinks himself in love with Vivian Morrow. Vivian, an ambitious girl, longs for a life of finery away from the ranch and succumbs to the proposal of Braden, who offers her luxury. Rance turns to drink and is revived by Kate, a town girl, who is kidnaped by gang leader Gregg but then is rescued in a showdown. Back on the ranch, Rance and Kate start a happy life, while Vivian and Braden are bitter and unhappy. *Ranchers. Gangs. Manhood. Fatherhood.*

THE LAST CHANCE **F2.2966**
Sierra Pictures. *Dist* Chesterfield Motion Pictures. 15 Jul **1926.** Si; b&w. 35mm. 5 reels, 4,450 ft.
Dir H. B. Carpenter. *Photog* Paul Allen.
Cast: Bill Patton.
Western melodrama. "Post-office inspector, detailed to capture mail sack thieves, tricks them into taking him in as a member of the gang and then causes their arrest. Romantic interest." (*Motion Picture News Booking Guide,* 11:34, Oct 1926.) *Postal inspectors. Gangs. Postal service. Mail theft.*

THE LAST COMMAND **F2.2967**
Paramount Famous Lasky Corp. 21 Jan **1928** [c21 Jan 1928; LP24895]. Si; b&w. 35mm. 9 reels, 8,154 ft.
Pres by Adolph Zukor, Jesse L. Lasky. *Supv* J. G. Bachmann. *Assoc Prod* B. P. Schulberg. *Dir* Josef von Sternberg. *Adapt-Screenplay* John F. Goodrich. *Titl* Herman J. Mankiewicz. *Story* Lajos Biró. *Photog* Bert Glennon. *Set Dsgn* Hans Dreier. *Film Ed* William Shea. *Makeup* Fred C. Ryle. *Tech Dir* Nicholas Kobyliansky.
Cast: Emil Jannings *(General Dolgorucki [Grand Duke Sergius Alexander])*, Evelyn Brent *(Natascha Dobrowa)*, William Powell *(Leo Andreiev)*, Nicholas Soussanin *(adjutant)*, Michael Visaroff *(Serge, the valet)*, Jack Raymond *(assistant director)*, Viacheslav Savitsky *(a private)*, Fritz Feld *(a revolutionist)*, Harry Semels *(soldier extra)*, Alexander Ikonnikov, Nicholas Kobyliansky *(drillmasters)*.
Romantic tragedy. Sergius Alexander, a former Russian general, now an extra in Hollywood, is discovered by Leo Andreiev, a onetime revolutionary leader now respectably established as a movie director, and is assigned to play the part of a Russian general. He is a decrepit old man, hardly able to withstand the wolfish competition of the other movie extras. A flashback to imperial Russia just before the Revolution shows the former general in his full glory as head of the Russian Army and the director as a revolutionary agitator. The general strikes Andreiev with his whip, falls in love with Natascha, a spy, but is beaten by the mob and rendered palsied and distraught as he watches the train carrying Natascha plunge into a river. Now Andreiev orders Sergius Alexander to reenact the scene of a Russian general facing his troops in revolt. For a few moments he tries to

hold them in line, but the emotional strain is fatal, and he collapses, dying. *Motion picture directors. Motion pictures. Russia—History—1917–21 Revolution. Hollywood.*

Note: Working title: *The General.* Sternberg claimed that he wrote the original scenario, basing it on an idea given him by Ernst Lubitsch.

THE LAST DANCE **F2.2968**

Audible Pictures. 8 Mar **1930.** Sd (Photophone); b&w. 35mm. 5,825-6,500 reels. [Also si.]

Supv Lon Young. *Dir* Scott Pembroke. *Story-Scen-Dial* Jack Townley. *Photog* M. A. Anderson. *Film Ed* Scott Himm. *Theme Song: "Sally, I'm Lovin' You, Sally"* Ray Canfield, Nell Moret. *Sd* Lester E. Tope.

Cast: Vera Reynolds *(Sally Kelly)*, Jason Robards *(Tom Malloy)*, George Chandler *(Sam Wise)*, Gertrude Short *(Sybil Kelly)*, Harry Todd *("Pa" Kelly)*, Lillian Leighton *("Ma" Kelly)*, Miami Alvarez *("Babe" LaMarr)*, Linton Brent *(Jones)*, James Hertz *(Edgar)*, Henry Roquemore *(Lucien Abbott)*, Fred Walton *(Weber)*.

Drama. Sally Kelly, taxi dancer at the Bon Ton Ballroom, dreams of escaping the Bronx, her Irish family, and Sammy, her conceited, saxophone-playing beau, and intends to marry a wealthy man and live on Park Avenue. Purchasing a large diamond ring on credit, Sally tells her family that she is engaged to Tom Malloy of the Malloy Tea Co., the word spreads to the newspapers, and Tom takes his friends to the Bon Ton to see Sally. Coincidence piles on complication before Sally realizes Tom's identity, but by then they have fallen in love, and Tom forgives Sally's pretensions. They have only to weather a phony breach-of-promise suit cooked up by Sammy before their happiness is complete. *Taxi dancers. Saxophonists. Irish. Social classes. Wealth. Mistaken identity. Breach of promise. Tea. New York City—Bronx.*

THE LAST DOOR **F2.2969**

Selznick Pictures. May **1921** [c1 May 1921; LP16490]. Si; b&w. 35mm. 5 reels, 4,453 ft.

Pres by Lewis J. Selznick. *Dir* William P. S. Earle. *Scen* Edward J. Montagne. *Story* Ralph Ince, W. Bert Foster. *Photog* Jules Cronjager.

Cast: Eugene O'Brien *("The Magnet")*, Charles Craig *(Freddie Tripp)*, Nita Naldi *(The Widow)*, Helen Pillsbury *(Mrs. Rogers)*, Martha Mansfield *(Helen Rogers)*, Katherine Perry *(guest)*, Warren Cook *(colonel)*.

Mystery melodrama. At a reception given at the Rogers mansion in his honor, Somerset Carroll surprises the guests by averring that he would give aid to a female convict reported to have escaped. Later, alone in the library, he is appealed to by a young girl who confesses to being pursued by the police, and he takes her to his own house. There she reveals herself to be Helen Rogers, playing a game with him on the advice of her guests. He then declares himself a crook, holding the real Carroll prisoner, with the intention of robbing the Rogers mansion. She follows and shields "The Magnet" from the police, the real Carroll having escaped and notified them, and through her interference he eludes his would-be captors. *Prison escapees. Imposture. Robbery.*

THE LAST EDITION **F2.2970**

Emory Johnson Productions. *Dist* Film Booking Offices of America. 8 Nov **1925** [c26 Oct 1925; LP21933]. Si; b&w. 35mm. 7 reels, 6,400 ft.

Dir Emory Johnson. *Story-Scen* Emilie Johnson. *1st Camera* Gilbert Warrenton. *Asst Camera* Frank Evans. *Asst Dir* Charles Watt, Jerry Callahan.

Cast: Ralph Lewis *(Tom McDonald)*, Lila Leslie *(Mary MacDonald)*, Ray Hallor *(Ray MacDonald)*, Frances Teague *(Polly MacDonald)*, Rex Lease *(Clarence Walker)*, Lou Payne *(George Hamilton)*, David Kirby *("Red" Moran)*, Wade Boteler *(Mike Fitzgerald)*, Cuyler Supplee *(Gerald Fuller)*, Leigh Willard *(Aaron Hoffman)*, Will Frank *(Sam Blotz [Blatz?])*, Ada Mae Vaughn *(stenographer)*, William Bakewell *("Ink" Donovan)*.

Melodrama. Tom MacDonald, assistant foreman of the San Francisco *Chronicle* pressroom, is passed over for the post of foreman in favor of a younger man. He gains satisfaction, though, when his son, Ray, obtains a good job in the district attorney's office. Reporter Clarence Walker, in love with MacDonald's daughter, Polly, is sent to obtain evidence against notorious bootlegger Sam Blotz, who is protected by Assistant District Attorney Gerald Fuller. Blotz and Fuller frame Ray to put Walker off their track. Although his conscience bothers him, Walker reports the story in time for the last edition. MacDonald attempts to stop the presses, and when Blotz's henchman, "Red" Moran, blows up the building, MacDonald is blamed and put in jail with his son. Walker eventually uncovers evidence exonerating the father and son, MacDonald is made foreman, and a new newspaper plant is built. *Newspapers. Journalists. Printers. District attorneys. Bootleggers. Political corruption.*

THE LAST FRONTIER **F2.2971**

Metropolitan Pictures Corp. of California. *Dist* Producers Distributing Corp. 16 Aug **1926** [c6 Aug 1926; LP23026]. Si; b&w. 35mm. 8 reels, 7,800 ft.

Pres by John C. Flinn. *Dir* George B. Seitz. *Adapt* Will M. Ritchey. *Photog* C. Edgar Schoenbaum.

Cast: William Boyd *(Tom Kirby)*, Marguerite De La Motte *(Beth)*, Jack Hoxie *(Buffalo Bill Cody)*, Junior Coghlan *(Buddy)*, Mitchell Lewis *(Lige)*, Gladys Brockwell *(Cynthia Jaggers)*, Frank Lackteen *(Pawnee Killer)*.

Western melodrama. Source: Courtney Ryley Cooper, *The Last Frontier* (Boston, 1923). Impoverished by the Civil War and eager to replenish his fortune in the West, Colonel Halliday, his wife, and his daughter, Beth, proceed toward Salina, Kansas, by wagon train, at the persuasion of Tom Kirby, a government scout and Beth's fiancé. Although Bill Hickok, Tom's friend, and a company of cavalry are in charge, Pawnee Killer, chief of the Sioux, attacks the wagon train; and Halliday and his wife are killed. Bill rides to Salina for help and to deliver the news to Buffalo Bill Cody. Beth, now hostile to Kirby, joins the household of Lige Morris, a trader in Salina, and at the suggestion of Bill, Kirby joins General Custer's scouting expedition. Lige tells Beth that Kirby is suspected of being in league with Pawnee Killer, but she learns from the post adjutant's daughter that he loves her. Beth seeks out Kirby just as the Sioux stampede a herd of buffalo through the town, and together they find refuge. Custer gives battle to the Indians, Pawnee Killer slays Lige, and the lovers are reconciled. *Scouts—Frontier. Traders. Sioux Indians. Wagon trains. Salina (Kansas). James Butler Hickok. William Frederick Cody. George Armstrong Custer. United States Army—Cavalry. Stampedes. Buffalo.*

Note: The initial project was conceived by Thomas H. Ince, then turned over to Hunt Stromberg, who later sold the rights to Metropolitan Pictures to complete the film.

THE LAST HOUR **F2.2972**

Mastodon Films. 1 Jan **1923** [c21 May 1923; LP18981]. Si; b&w. 35mm. 7 reels, 6,658 ft.

Pres by Edward Sloman. *Dir* Edward Sloman. *Photog* Max Dupont.

Cast: Milton Sills *(Steve Cline)*, Carmel Myers *(Saidee McCall)*, Pat O'Malley *(Philip Logan)*, Jack Mower *(Tom Cline)*, Alec Francis *(Reever McCall)*, Charles Clary *(William Mallory)*, Walter Long *(Red Brown)*, Eric Mayne *(Governor Logan)*, Wilson Hummell *(Quales)*.

Crook melodrama. Source: Frank R. Adams, "Blind Justice," in *Munsey's Magazine.* Forger Reever McCall and his daughter, Saidee, narrowly escape the police with the aid of reformed crook Steve Cline, whose brother has been killed by Detective William Mallory. Later, while serving as a war nurse, Saidee falls in love with Philip Logan, one of her patients and son of the governor. After the war everyone is again brought together by a banquet given for Governor Logan by Mallory, now a political boss. Mallory demands marriage of Saidee in return for silence about her past; Reever kills Mallory; and Steve takes the blame. Saidee attempts to save Steve from execution with a pardon she has forged but arrives too late. The gallows fails to function, however, and Reever confesses to the murder. (Reviews call attention to the fact that Detective Mallory kills Cline in cold blood in the presence of fellow officers and receives no official punishment for his crime.) *Nurses. Veterans. Political bosses. State governors. Murder. Capital punishment. Forgery. World War I.*

LAST LAP **F2.2973**

Dailey Productions. 1 May **1928.** Si; b&w. 35mm. 7 reels, 6,800 ft.

Dir Bruce Mitchell. *Scen* L. V. Jefferson. *Titl* R. Speers. *Photog* Nick Musuraca. *Film Ed* Horace Williams.

Cast: Rex Lease, Mildred Harris.

Drama(?). No information about the nature of this film has been found.

THE LAST MAN **F2.2974**

H. & B. Film Co. *Dist* Madoc Sales. Mar **1924.** Si; b&w. 35mm. 5 reels.

Dir Frederick Reel, Jr.

Cast: Bill Patton.

Western melodrama. "... concerning the adventures of a young easterner, Michael Halerin, who arrives in a small town where lawlessness is rampant. The sheriff of a neighboring town, a two-gun man, threatens that anyone who attempts to assume the role of sheriff of Flint will be 'the last man.' Halerin takes up the challenge, and fights the boasting sheriff. He saves from attack a beautiful girl and his ultimate triumph in restoring order in the town wins him the girl." (*Motion Picture News Booking Guide*, [7]:29, Oct 1924.) *Sheriffs. Jealousy.*

THE LAST MAN ON EARTH **F2.2975**

Fox Film Corp. 2 Nov **1924** [27 Oct 1924; LP20789]. Si; b&w. 35mm. 7 reels, 6,637 ft.

Pres by William Fox. *Dir* J. G. Blystone. *Scen* Donald W. Lee. *Photog* Allan Davey.

Cast—The Prolog: Jean Johnson *(Hattie, age 6)*, Buck Black *(Elmer, age 8)*, Maurice Murphy *(Elmer's pal)*, William Steele *(Hattie's father)*, Jean Dumas *(Hattie's mother)*, Harry Dunkinson *(Elmer's father)*, Fay Holderness *(Elmer's mother)*.

Cast—The Play: Earle Foxe *(Elmer Smith)*, Grace Cunard *(Gertie)*, Gladys Tennyson *(Frisco Kate)*, Derelys Perdue *(Hattie)*, Maryon Aye *(Red Sal)*, Clarissa Selwynne *(Dr. Prodwell)*, Pauline French *(Furlong)*, Marie Astaire *(Paula Prodwell)*.

Fantasy-farce. Source: John D. Swain, "Last Man on Earth," in *Munsey's Magazine* (80:193–208, 9 Nov 1923). When Elmer Smith's proposal of marriage is refused by Hattie, his childhood sweetheart, he seeks seclusion in the forest as a hermit. Sometime later (1954), an epidemic of "masculitis" kills all the males in the world over the age of 14 with the single exception of Elmer. When he is discovered by Gertie, a woman gangster on the run, he is taken to Washington and sold to the Government for $10 million. Two senators—the ladies from Virginia and California—then fight it out with boxing gloves in the U. S. Senate chamber to decide who will get Elmer as a husband. Hattie attends the fight, and Elmer—seeing her—rushes to her, claims her for his own, and marries her. A year later, twins are born to them, ensuring the continuation of the human race. *Hermits. Virginians. Californians. Twins. Human race. Reproduction. Women in politics. Boxing. United States Congress.*

THE LAST MOMENT **F2.2976**

J. Parker Read, Jr., Productions. *Dist* Goldwyn Distributing Corp. 7 Jun **1923** [c7 May 1923; LP18951]. Si; b&w. 35mm. 6 reels.

Pres by J. Parker Read, Jr. *Pers Supv* J. Parker Read, Jr. *Scen* J. Clarkson Miller. *Story* Jack Boyle. *Photog* J. O. Taylor. *Adv* Alex Hall.

Cast: Henry Hull *(Hercules Napoleon Cameron)*, Doris Kenyon *(Alice Winthrop)*, Louis Wolheim *("The Finn")*, Louis Calhern *(Harry Gaines)*, William Nally *("Big Mike")*, Mickey Bennett *(Danny)*, Harry Allen *(Pat Rooney)*, Donald Hall *(Mr. Winthrop)*, Danny Hayes *(bartender)*, Jerry Peterson *("The Thing")*, Robert Hazelton *(The Butler)*.

Melodrama. Hercules Napoleon Cameron, who finds his adventure in books, is searching the waterfront with Alice Winthrop for a friend's father when they are shanghaied and taken aboard "The Finn's" ship, bound for the South Seas. "The Finn" is a brutal captain who reinforces his authority with a caged, ape-like monster. "The Thing" escapes during a storm, destroys the captain and crew, then turns on Alice and Nap. Fearing that their last moment has arrived, they declare their love for each other, and Nap suddenly develops a heroic impulse. He holds off the monster for a time, Alice and Nap swim for shore closely followed by "The Thing," and Nap finally drowns the beast with the aid of a large abalone. *Monsters. Shanghaiing. Waterfront. Seafaring life. South Seas. Abalones.*

THE LAST MOMENT **F2.2977**

Samuel Freedman–Edward M. Spitz. *Dist* Zakoro Film Corp. 15 Feb **1928** [c2 Apr 1928; LP25120]. Si; b&w. 35mm. 6 reels, 5,600 ft.

Dir-Writ Paul Fejos. *Photog* Leon Shamroy. *Film Ed* Paul Fejos.

Cast: Otto Matiesen *(The Man)*, Julius Molnar, Jr. *(The Man as a Child)*, Lucille La Verne *(The Innkeeper)*, Anielka Elter *(A Woman)*, Georgia Hale *(His Second Wife)*, Isabelle Lamore *(His First Wife)*, Vivian Winston *(A Woman)*.

Experimental drama. The first title states that in the last moments of life a person visualizes the highlights of his lifetime. The opening shot shows a man struggling in water. A hand reaches up, indicating that the man is drowning. Then a series of quick shots: double and triple exposures of Pierrot's head, faces of women, flashing headlights, spinning wheels, a shower of stars, an explosion, and a child's book. The picture slows down to summarize the man's life: schooldays, a loving mother, a stern father, a religious confirmation, a birthday party, the circus, an adolescent affair with a circus performer, a quarrel with his father, leaving home, stowing away on a ship, wandering into a tavern in port, reciting for the drinkers, being run over by a car, an operation and recovery in the hospital, becoming an actor, marrying the nurse who took care of him, quarreling, a divorce, the death of his mother, the funeral, an affair with a married woman, a duel with her husband, the war, and his friend dying in his arms. He returns to civilian life, resumes acting, falls in love with his leading lady, marries; she dies. Dressed as Pierrot, he walks home, reaches the pond, looks at his reflection, and wades in until only his hand is visible. Then the hand disappears, and the film ends with a few bubbles rising to the surface. *Pierrot. Suicide. Life. Death.*

THE LAST OF MRS. CHEYNEY **F2.2978**

Metro-Goldwyn-Mayer Pictures. 6 Jul **1929** [c29 Jul 1929; LP554]. Sd (Movietone); b&w. 35mm. 7 reels, 8,651 ft. [Also si; 6,484 ft.]

Dir Sidney Franklin. *Scen* Hans Kraly, Claudine West. *Titl* Lucille Newmark. *Photog* William Daniels. *Art Dir* Cedric Gibbons. *Film Ed* Conrad A. Nervig. *Rec Engr* G. A. Burns, Douglas Shearer. *Wardrobe* Adrian.

Cast: Norma Shearer *(Mrs. Cheyney)*, Basil Rathbone *(Lord Arthur Dilling)*, George Barraud *(Charles)*, Herbert Bunston *(Lord Elton)*, Hedda Hopper *(Lady Maria)*, Moon Carroll *(Joan)*, Madeline Seymour *(Mrs. Wynton)*, Cyril Chadwick *(Willie Wynton)*, Maude Turner Gordon *(Mrs. Webley)*, George K. Arthur, Finch Smiles.

Comedy-drama. Source: Frederick Lonsdale, *The Last of Mrs. Cheyney, a Comedy in Three Acts* (London, 1926). Mrs. Fay Cheyney, an adventuress, poses as a wealthy Australian widow at a Monte Carlo hotel to fleece wealthy Mrs. Webley of a valuable pearl necklace. With her are Charles, the mastermind, and several other men who pretend to be her servants. Wavering between stealing the necklace and not, because she has fallen in love with Lord Arthur Dilling, Mrs. Webley's nephew, and has been accepted into "society," Mrs. Cheyney finally decides to take it during a houseparty at the Webleys'. Dilling discovers her with it and threatens to expose her unless she yields to his desires. Rather than yield to Dilling, Mrs. Cheyney, a principled woman, summons the guests to her room and confesses, leaving them to decide her fate. They plan to call in the police until Lord Elton, also in love with Mrs. Cheyney, recalls that she possesses a love letter he wrote her which could embarrass them all. The group decides to buy her off, but when she destroys both the letter and the check, they welcome her, as Lady Dilling, back into their society. *Adventuresses. Australians. Thieves. Socialites. Nobility. Imposture. Monte Carlo. Documentation.*

THE LAST OF THE DUANES **F2.2979**

Fox Film Corp. 24 Aug **1924** [c30 Jun 1924; LP20402]. Si; b&w. 35mm. 7 reels, 6,942 ft.

Pres by William Fox. *Dir* Lynn Reynolds. *Scen* Edward J. Montagne. *Photog* Dan Clark.

Cast: Tom Mix *(Buck Duane)*, Marian Nixon *(Jenny)*, Brinsley Shaw *(Cal Bain)*, Frank Nelson *(Euchre)*, Lucy Beaumont *(Mother)*, Harry Lonsdale *(Father)*.

Western melodrama. Source: Zane Grey, "The Last of the Duanes," in *Argosy* (Sep 1914). Compelled by continuing insults, Buck Duane is forced to fight and shoot Cal Bain. Escaping, he aids a dying cattle rustler and rescues Jenny from an outlaw band, then rounds up the members of the gang and delivers them to the Texas Rangers. *Texas Rangers. Rustlers. Gangs.*

Note: Remade in 1930 (see Entry F2.2980).

LAST OF THE DUANES **F2.2980**

Fox Film Corp. 31 Aug **1930** [c3 Aug 1930; LP1484]. Sd (Movietone); b&w. 35mm. 6 reels, 5,500 ft.

Pres by William Fox. *Assoc Prod* Edward Butcher, Harold B. Lipsitz. *Dir* Alfred L. Werker. *Screenplay-Dial* Ernest Pascal. *Photog* Daniel Clark. *Art Dir* William Darling. *Film Ed* Ralph Dietrich. *Songs: "Cowboy Dan," "The Outlaw Song"* Cliff Friend. *Rec Engr* Barney Fredericks. *Rec Engr, Spanish-language version* Eugene Grossman. *Asst Dir* William J. Scully. *Cost* Sophie Wachner.

Cast: George O'Brien *(Buck Duane)*, Lucille Brown *(Ruth Garrett)*, Myrna Loy *(Lola)*, Walter McGrail *(Bland)*, James Bradbury, Jr. *(Euchre)*, Nat Pendleton *(Bossamer)*, Blanche Frederici *(Mrs. Duane)*, Frank Campeau *(Luke Stevens)*, James Mason *(Morgan)*, Lloyd Ingraham *(Mr. Garrett)*, Willard Robertson *(Captain of the Rangers)*.

Western melodrama. Source: Zane Grey, "The Last of the Duanes," in *Argosy Magazine* (Sep 1914). The story is basically the same as that of the 1924 silent film, with the addition of songs. *Texas Rangers. Rustlers.*

Gangs. Courtship.

Note: Also produced in 1930 in a Spanish-language version.

THE LAST OF THE LONE WOLF **F2.2981**

Columbia Pictures. 26 Aug **1930** [c16 Sep 1930; LP1577]. Sd (Movietone); b&w. 35mm. 7 reels, 6,500 ft.

Prod Harry Cohn. *Dir* Richard Boleslavsky. *Dial Dir* Stuart Walker. *Scen* Dorothy Howell. *Dial* James Whittaker. *Adapt* John Thomas Neville. *Photog* Ben Kline. *Art Dir* Edward Jewell. *Tech Dir* Edward Shulter. *Film Ed* David Berg. *Ch Sd Engr* Russell Malmgren. *Asst Dir* C. C. Coleman.

Cast: Bert Lytell *(Michael Lanyard)*, Patsy Ruth Miller *(Stephanie)*, Lucien Prival *(Varril)*, Otto Matieson *(Prime Minister)*, Alfred Hickman *(King)*, Maryland Morne *(Queen)*, Haley Sullivan *(Camilla, Queen's maid)*, Pietro Sosso *(Master of Ceremonies)*, Henry Daniel *(Count von Rimpau)*, James Liddy *(Hoffman)*.

Adventure melodrama. Source: Louis Joseph Vance, "The Last of the Lone Wolf" (publication undetermined). When the King of Saxonia learns, through the prime minister, that his wife has given a ring he gave her to Count von Rimpau, he orders its retrieval. The prime minister commissions Michael Lanyard, an American being held under arrest, to get it, offering him his freedom in exchange. Simultaneously, the queen sends Stephanie, her lady-in-waiting, to retrieve the ring, which she wants to wear at the royal ball. Varril, a henchmen sent to watch Lanyard, follows on a train but is thrown off by Lanyard when he annoys Stephanie. With false credentials Lanyard gains admittance to the embassy and steals the ring from a safe, but, realizing he is suspected, he replaces it and escapes. At his hotel he finds Varril and overpowers him; learning of the queen's plight from Stephanie, he again steals the ring but is captured by Varril. He escapes, however, and slips the ring on the queen's finger at the ball, being thus rewarded with immunity and Stephanie's love. *Thieves. Royalty. Prime ministers. Imaginary kingdoms.*

THE LAST OUTLAW **F2.2982**

Paramount Famous Lasky Corp. 2 Jul **1927** [c29 Jun 1927; LP24140]. Si; b&w. 35mm. 6 reels, 6,032 ft.

Pres by Adolph Zukor, Jesse L. Lasky. *Dir* Arthur Rosson. *Screenplay* John Stone, J. Walter Ruben. *Adapt* J. Walter Ruben. *Story* Richard Allen Gates. *Photog* James Murray.

Cast: Gary Cooper *(Buddy Hale)*, Jack Luden *(Ward Lane)*, Betty Jewel *(Janet Lane)*, Herbert Prior *(Bert Wagner)*, Jim Corey *(Butch)*, Billy Butts *(Chick)*, Flash *(The Wonder Horse)*.

Western melodrama. Buddy Hale rescues Janet Lane from a runaway horse before arriving in Steer City, where, unknown to him, her brother, Ward, has just shot the sheriff. Ward, heading a crowd of indignant ranchers whose cattle are being systematically rustled, suspects the sheriff and Justice Bert Wagner of heading the thieves. Wagner makes Buddy sheriff and sends him to arrest his predecessor's murderer. One of Wagner's accomplices deliberately shoots Ward, and Buddy returns the dying man to his sister, thus incurring her enmity. The ranchers, led by Janet, steal back their cattle; and at Chick's insistence Janet discusses the situation with Buddy, who is convinced of Wagner's guilt. In a showdown, Butch and Wagner perish in a cattle stampede, while Janet is saved by Buddy, who then is made mayor. *Cowboys. Ranchers. Sheriffs. Rustlers. Judges. Mayors. Brother-sister relationship. Murder. Stampedes.*

THE LAST PERFORMANCE (Universal-Jewel) **F2.2983**

Universal Pictures. 2 Nov **1927** [New York premiere; released 13 Oct 1929; c5 Oct 1929; LP752]. Mus score, sd eff, & talking sequences (Movietone); b&w. 35mm. 7 reels, 6,171 ft. [Also si; 5,999 ft.]

Pres by Carl Laemmle. *Supv* Carl Laemmle, Jr. *Dir* Paul Fejos. *Story-Scen* James Ashmore Creelman. *Titl* Walter Anthony, Tom Reed. *Photog* Hal Mohr. *Film Ed* Edward Cahn, Robert Carlisle, Robert Jahns.

Cast: Conrad Veidt *(Erik the Great)*, Mary Philbin *(Julie)*, Leslie Fenton *(Buffo)*, Fred Mackaye *(Mark Royce)*, Gustav Partos *(theater manager)*, William H. Turner *(booking agent)*, Anders Randolf *(judge)*, Sam De Grasse *(district attorney)*, George Irving *(defense attorney)*.

Romantic melodrama. Erik, a foreign magician, loves Julie, his assistant, though he is more than 20 years her senior, and keeps Buffo, another assistant, under his hypnotic power. Mark Royce, a vagrant and starving youth caught stealing in Erik's apartment, is taken in at the suggestion of Julie, and he becomes Erik's protégé. Preparing at a New York hotel for a tour, Erik gives a birthday party for Julie, planning to announce their engagement. Julie conceals her love for Mark, and the wildly jealous Buffo shows Erik the two of them embracing in a garden. During the opening performance, in which Mark does a sword trick, Buffo is killed; Erik is charged with murder, and at his trial, because of his love for Julie, he confesses to the crime, then draws a dagger and kills himself. *Magicians. Thieves. Hypnotism. Jealousy. Murder. Suicide. New York City.*

Note: Working title: *Erik the Great*.

THE LAST ROUNDUP **F2.2984**

J. P. McGowan Productions. *Dist* Syndicate Pictures. Jul **1929.** Mus score; b&w. 35mm. 5 reels, 4,800 ft. [Also si.]

Dir J. P. McGowan. *Story-Titl* Sally Winters. *Photog* Hap Depew.

Cast: Bob Custer *(Denver Dixon)*, Hazel Mills *(Lucy Graves)*, Bud Osborne *([Heavy])*, Cliff Lyons, Hank Bell, J. P. McGowan, Adabelle Driver.

Western melodrama. "Denver Dixon, foreman of John Dunlap's Bar D Ranch, fights with 'Mile Ahead' Hardy, one of the hands, for being reckless while driving Lucy Graves, the new schoolmistress. For revenge Hardy quits, rustles Dunlap's cattle, and captures Lucy. Denver saves Lucy and wins her." ("Motion Picture News Booking Guide," in *Motion Picture News*, 15 Mar 1930, p89.) *Ranch foremen. Schoolteachers. Kidnaping. Rustling.*

THE LAST TRAIL **F2.2985**

Fox Film Corp. Nov **1921** [c18 Sep 1921; LP17117]. Si; b&w. 35mm. 7 reels, 6,355 ft.

Pres by William Fox. *Dir* Emmett J. Flynn. *Scen* Jules Furthman, Paul Schofield. *Photog* Lucien Andriot.

Cast: Maurice B. Flynn *(The Stranger)*, Eva Novak *(Winifred Samson)*, Wallace Beery *(William Kirk)*, Rosemary Theby *(Chiquita)*, Charles K. French *(Sheriff Nelson)*, Harry Springler *(Campbell)*, Harry Dunkinson *(Kenworth Samson)*.

Western melodrama. Source: Zane Grey, *The Last Trail, a Story of Early Days in the Ohio Valley* (New York, c1909). The successful operations of a lone bandit known as "The Night Hawk" terrorize a frontier town, and when a stranger arrives riding a fine horse, suspicions are aroused and he is mistaken for the criminal. Winifred, who is engaged to dam engineer William Kirk, shelters the stranger from the sheriff, but Kirk has him arrested. Kirk decides to steal the company payroll and dynamite the dam; he accomplishes these acts but is captured by the stranger, who is revealed to be a company agent detailed to investigate Kirk. *Strangers. Investigators. Bandits. Engineers—Civil. Dams. Theft. Ohio Valley.*

Note: Remade in 1927 under the same title, q. v.

THE LAST TRAIL **F2.2986**

Fox Film Corp. 23 Jan **1927** [c16 Jan 1927; LP23571]. Si; b&w. 35mm. 6 reels, 5,190 ft.

Pres by William Fox. *Dir* Lewis Seiler. *Scen* John Stone. *Photog* Dan Clark.

Cast: Tom Mix *(Tom Dane)*, Carmelita Geraghty *(Nita Carrol)*, William Davidson *(Morley)*, Frank Hagney *(Ben Ligget)*, Lee Shumway *(Joe Pascal)*, Robert Brower *(Pete)*, Jerry the Giant *(Tom Dane Pascal)*, Oliver Eckhardt *(Carrol)*, Tony *(The Wonder Horse)*.

Western melodrama. Source: Zane Grey, *The Last Trail, a Story of Early Days in the Ohio Valley* (New York, c1909). Tom Dane saves Joe Pascal and his wife from an Indian attack, and as a result the couple name their first son after Tom. Later, Pascal, now sheriff of Carson City, is plagued by persistent robberies of the stageline and is forced to provide a guard. The bandits are chasing the stage when Tom comes to help; Pascal is mortally wounded and places his son in the care of Tom. A U.S. Express agent arrives and suggests a stagecoach race to decide who shall get the contract; Kurt Morley, the bandit leader, lines up his men as contestants. But Jasper Carrol, the old contractor, with whose daughter Tom has fallen in love, is backed by Tom. In spite of attempts to thwart him, Tom wins the race, then rides down the bandits, who are trying to escape with the girl and the loot. *Sheriffs. Stagecoach robberies. Express service. Carson City.*

Note: Remake of a 1921 film of the same title, q. v.

THE LAST WARNING (Universal-Jewel) **F2.2987**

Universal Pictures. 6 Jan **1929** [c21 Dec 1928; LP25937]. Talking sequences, sd eff, & mus score (Movietone); b&w. 35mm. 8 reels, 7,980 ft. [Also si; 7,731 ft.]

Pres by Carl Laemmle. *Supv* Carl Laemmle, Jr. *Dir* Paul Leni. *Story Supv* Edward J. Montagne. *Scen* Alfred A. Cohn. *Dial-Titl* Tom Reed.

Adapt Alfred A. Cohn, Robert F. Hill, J. G. Hawks. *Photog* Hal Mohr. *Art Dir* Charles D. Hall. *Film Ed* Robert Carlisle. *Mus Score* Joseph Cherniavsky.

Cast: Laura La Plante *(Doris)*, Montague Love *(McHugh)*, Roy D'Arcy *(Carlton)*, Margaret Livingston *(Evalinda)*, John Boles *(Qualie)*, Burr McIntosh *(Josiah)*, Mack Swain *(Robert)*, Bert Roach *(Mike)*, Carrie Daumery *(Barbara)*, Slim Summerville *(Tommy)*, Torben Meyer *(Gene)*, D'Arcy Corrigan *(Woodford)*, Bud Phelps *(Sammy)*, Charles K. French *(doctor)*, Francisco Maran *(Jeffries)*, Ella McKenzie *(Ann)*, Fred Kelsey, Tom O'Brien *(inspectors)*, Harry Northrup *(coroner)*.

Mystery melodrama. Source: Thomas F. Fallon, *The Last Warning; a Melodrama in Three Acts* (New York, c1935). Wadsworth Camp, *House of Fear* (Garden City, New York, 1916). During a theatrical performance, Woodford, the play's leading man, is murdered. The theater is immediately closed, and suspicion is directed toward both the play's leading lady and the slain actor's understudy. After 5 years, a producer decides to reopen the closed theater by putting on a production of the fatal play, using what is available of the original cast. Rehearsals start, and with them strange happenings (falling scenery and weird voices) seemingly calculated to frighten off the company. Woodford's ghost appears and issues a last, unheeded warning to close the theater. On opening night the stage is suddenly plunged into darkness; when the lights come up, the leading man is nowhere to be found. Finally the guilty parties are disclosed, and the leading lady and the understudy are at last free to find happiness with each other. *Actors. Theatrical producers. Ghosts. Murder. Theater.*

THE LAST WHITE MAN F2.2988

Sanford Productions. 15 Feb **1924.** Si; b&w. 35mm. 5 reels, ca4,850 ft.

Dir Frank S. Mattison.

Cast: Matty Mattison.

Western melodrama. "... dealing with affairs of two men, drummed out of Army, who are in love with two daughters of Army captain. One becomes a campaigner for Lincoln's election, while other becomes a dishonest trader with the Indians. Affair culminates in an attack upon stockade by Indians, in which hero 'the last white man' left, and affairs are straightened out." (*Motion Picture News Booking Guide*, 6:40, Apr 1924.) *Traders. Indians of North America. Military life. Political campaigns. Abraham Lincoln.*

THE LATEST FROM PARIS F2.2989

Metro-Goldwyn-Mayer Pictures. 4 Feb **1928** [c4 Feb 1928; LP25375]. Si; b&w. 35mm. 8 reels, 7,743 ft.

Dir Sam Wood. *Story-Scen* A. P. Younger. *Titl* Joe Farnham. *Photog* William Daniels. *Sets* Cedric Gibbons, Arnold Gillespie. *Film Ed* Basil Wrangell.

Cast: Norma Shearer *(Ann Dolan)*, George Sidney *(Sol Blogg)*, Ralph Forbes *(Joe Adams)*, Tenen Holtz *(Abe Littauer)*, William Bakewell *(Bud Dolan)*, Margaret Landis *(Louise Martin)*, Bert Roach *(Bert Blevins)*.

Romantic comedy. Ann Dolan, a traveling saleswoman, falls in love with Joe Adams, a rival salesman for another cloak and suit firm. Their engagement is brief, however, because Ann, who is financing her brother's education, refuses to give up her peripatetic job. Joe takes up with a shopkeeper's daughter, but he returns to Ann when her brother marries. *Traveling saleswomen. Traveling salesmen. Brother-sister relationship. Education. Clothing business.*

Note: Copyright indication that the film has sound has not been confirmed.

LAUGH, CLOWN, LAUGH F2.2990

Metro-Goldwyn-Mayer Pictures. 14 Apr **1928** [c14 Apr 1928; LP25214]. Si; b&w. 35mm. 8 reels, 7,045 ft.

Dir Herbert Brenon. *Scen* Elizabeth Meehan. *Titl* Joe Farnham. *Photog* James Wong Howe. *Set Dsgn* Cedric Gibbons. *Film Ed* Marie Halvey. *Asst Dir* Ray Lissner. *Wardrobe* Gilbert Clark.

Cast: Lon Chaney *(Tito)*, Bernard Siegel *(Simon)*, Loretta Young *(Simonetta)*, Cissy Fitzgerald *(Giancinta)*, Nils Asther *(Luigi)*, Gwen Lee *(Lucretia)*.

Romantic drama. Source: David Belasco and Tom Cushing, *Laugh, Clown, Laugh!* (New York opening: 28 Nov 1923). Tito, a clown, adopts a girl whom he names Simonetta. The girl matures into an attractive woman, desired by Luigi, a wealthy nobleman. On the eve of her marriage, Simonetta learns that Tito loves her, and she responds, presumably, to avoid hurting him, by declaring that she returns his love. That night, disbelieving her, Tito falls while practicing a familiar trick—sliding down a tightwire—thus freeing Simonetta to marry the count. In an alternative (happy) ending, Tito survives his fall, Simonetta marries Luigi, and they all remain close friends. *Clowns. Tightrope walkers. Orphans. Circus. Adoption. Suicide.*

Note: Indication in copyright records that the film has sound has not been verified.

LAUGHING AT DANGER F2.2991

Carlos Productions. *Dist* Film Booking Offices of America. 23 Nov **1924** [c22 Dec 1924; LP20939]. Si; b&w. 35mm. 6 reels, 5,442 ft.

Pres by A. Carlos. *Dir* James W. Horne. *Story-Cont* Frank Howard Clark. *Photog* William Marshall. *Athletic stunts conceived and executed by* Richard Talmadge.

Cast: Richard Talmadge *(Alan Remington)*, Joe Girard *(Cyrus Remington)*, Joe Harrington *(Prof. Leo Hollister)*, Eva Novak *(Carolyn Hollister)*, Stanhope Wheatcroft *(Darwin Kershaw)*.

Comedy-melodrama. When he is jilted, Alan Remington, the son of a wealthy Washington politician, falls into a state of deep depression. On the advice of Professor Hollister, from whom he is purchasing a death ray, the elder Remington attempts to divert Alan by providing him with excitement. At this time, a gang of foreign agents, led by Darwin Kershaw, Remington's secretary, kidnap both the inventor and his daughter, Carolyn, and steal the death ray, but not before the resourceful girl has thrown the control key to the ray out of the window, where it lands in Alan's car. The conspirators attempt to regain the key, but they are mockingly foiled on several occasions by Alan, who thinks they are men hired by his father to jolt him out of his depression. Alan eventually realizes that the men are seriously trying to kill him, and he sets out to bring them to justice. Alan prevents the agents from destroying several naval gunboats, rescues the Hollisters, and rounds up the aliens, handing them over to the F. B. I. *Politicians. Inventors. Foreign agents. Secretaries. Death rays. Washington (District of Columbia). United States Navy. Federal Bureau of Investigation.*

LAUGHING AT DEATH F2.2992

FBO Pictures. 2 Jun **1929** [c2 Jun 1929; LP475]. Si; b&w. 35mm. 6 reels, 5,009 ft.

Dir Wallace W. Fox. *Scen* Frank Howard Clark. *Titl* Helen Gregg. *Photog* Virgil Miller. *Film Ed* Della King. *Asst Dir* Jack Smith.

Cast: Bob Steele *(Bob Thornton)*, Natalie Joyce *(Sonia Petrovich)*, Captain Vic *(Alexis)*, Kai Schmidt *(Emil Orloff)*, Ethan Laidlaw *(Karl Stronberg)*, Armand Trillor *(Boris, the valet)*, Hector V. Sarno *(Nikolai Petrovich)*, Golden Wadhams *(Libanian consul)*.

Adventure melodrama. Bob Thornton, an American athlete working his way through college, spends his summer vacation stoking on a trans-Atlantic liner, and on his last return voyage, he agrees to exchange identities with the Prince of Libania, who is sought by a group of conspirators from his country headed by Sonia Kerchoff, seeking revenge for her father's death. The plotters arrange to meet Bob in New York, but Sonia finds him so attractive that she is unable to poison him. Petrovitch, one of her cohorts, induces Bob to join them in a party, and he is attacked by thugs but is saved by Sonia. At a ball in his honor, Bob is forced into a duel with Alexis, whose brother was maimed by the prince, and in a swashbuckling encounter he subdues Alexis. They receive word of the prince's departure, and in an exciting climax, Bob saves him from a watery grave; with a reward from the prince, Bob and Sonia yield to their mutual love. *Athletes. Students. Stokers. Royalty. Revenge. Impersonation. Personal identity. Ocean liners. Duels.*

THE LAUGHING LADY F2.2993

Paramount Famous Lasky Corp. 28 Dec **1929** [c27 Dec 1929; LP949]. Sd (Movietone); b&w. 35mm. 8 reels, 7,200 ft. [Also si; 6,820 ft.]

Dir Victor Schertzinger. *Adapt* Bartlett Cormack, Arthur Richman. *Photog* George Folsey. *Song: "Another Kiss"* Victor Schertzinger.

Cast: Ruth Chatterton *(Marjorie Lee)*, Clive Brook *(Daniel Farr)*, Dan Healy *(Al Brown)*, Nat Pendleton *(James Dugan)*, Raymond Walburn *(Hector Lee)*, Dorothy Hall *(Flo)*, Hedda Harrigan *(Cynthia Bell)*, Lillian B. Tonge *(Parker)*, Marguerite St. John *(Mrs. Playgate)*, Hubert Druce *(Hamilton Playgate)*, Alice Hegeman *(Mrs. Collop)*, Joe King *(city editor)*, Helen Hawley *(Rose)*, Betty Bartley *(Barbara)*.

Society melodrama. Source: Alfred Sutro, *The Laughing Lady, a Comedy in Three Acts* (London, 1922). At a Southampton beach resort, Mrs. Hector Lee, known as Marjorie, is rescued from drowning by Dugan, the lifeguard; meanwhile, her husband, Hector, is attending a business meeting at a New York bank headed by Daniel Farr, a brilliant corporation attorney. That evening Dugan, buoyed by his friends' remarks and intoxicated, enters Marjorie's room, clad in pajamas, and is seen by the housekeeper trying to make love to her. Marjorie is dismissed from the hotel without any explanation, and a newspaper story spreads the attendant scandal. Hector, reading of the incident, decides on an immediate divorce, turning the case over to Farr. In the divorce court, Farr presents her as a depraved woman, unfit to care for her child. Marjorie refuses to defend herself, and subsequently she is dropped by all her society friends. Marjorie seeks revenge on Farr, but he becomes sympathetic after learning that Hector had been seeing another woman secretly, and ultimately they find happiness together. *Lawyers. Bankers. Lifeguards. Circumstantial evidence. Scandal. Divorce. Revenge. New York City.*

LAUGHTER **F2.2994**

Paramount-Publix Corp. 25 Sep **1930** [c24 Oct 1930; LP1686]. Sd (Movietone); b&w. 35mm. 8 reels, 7,134 ft.

Dir H. D'Abbadie D'Arrast. *Dial* Donald Ogden Stewart. *Story* H. D'Abbadie D'Arrast, Douglas Doty. *Photog* George Folsey. *Film Ed* Helene Turner. *Song: "Little Did I Know"* Irving Kahal, Pierre Norman, Sammy Fain. *Rec Engr* Ernest F. Zatorsky.

Cast: Nancy Carroll *(Peggy Gibson)*, Fredric March *(Paul Lockridge)*, Frank Morgan *(C. Mortimer Gibson)*, Glenn Anders *(Ralph Le Saint)*, Diane Ellis *(Marjorie Gibson)*, Leonard Carey *(Benham)*, Ollie Burgoyne *(Pearl)*.

Romantic comedy-drama. Peggy Gibson, a former Follies beauty, forsakes her life of carefree attachments to marry C. Mortimer Gibson, an elderly but very wealthy broker. A year later, three significant events occur almost simultaneously: Ralph Le Saint, a young sculptor, still in love with Peggy, plans his suicide in a mood of bitterness; Paul Lockridge, a pianist, also in love with her, returns from Paris and offers her his companionship as a diversion from her stuffy life; and Gibson's daughter, Marjorie, returns from schooling abroad. Marjorie is paired with Ralph, and their escapades result in considerable trouble for the old gentleman, while Paul implores Peggy to go to Paris with him, declaring "You are rich—dirty rich. You are dying. You need laughter to make you clean," but she refuses. When Marjorie plans to elope with Ralph, Peggy exposes the sculptor as a fortune hunter, and dejected, he commits suicide. As a result, Peggy confesses her unhappiness to Gibson, then joins Paul and laughter in Paris. *Sculptors. Pianists. Brokers. Fortune hunters. Marriage. Desertion. Suicide.*

LAVENDER AND OLD LACE **F2.2995**

Renco Film Co. *Dist* W. W. Hodkinson Corp. Jun **1921**. Si; b&w. 35mm. 6 reels, 5,770 ft.

Dir Lloyd Ingraham. *Camera* Ross Fisher.

Cast: Marguerite Snow *(Mary Ainslie)*, Seena Owen *(Ruth Thorne)*, Louis Bennison *(Capt. Charles Winfield/Carl Winfield)*, Victor Potel *(Joe Pendleton)*, Zella Ingraham *(Hepsey)*, Lillian Elliott *(Jane Hathaway)*, James Corrigan *(Jimmy Ball)*.

Melodrama. Source: Myrtle Reed, *Lavender and Old Lace* (New York, 1902). For 30 years Mary Ainslie has waited for Capt. Charles Winfield to return and make her his wife. A young man, a journalist on a Boston newspaper, is passing through the village and has trouble with his vision. He is taken to Miss Ainslie's by Ruth, the niece of a friend, Jane. The gray-haired woman is startled by his resemblance to the man for whom she promised to wait, and when she learns he is the son of Captain Winfield, now dead, she faints. From this moment, she slowly fades away, but before she dies she tells Carl that his father was once her sweetheart. Ruth and Carl, now in love, take this as a timely lesson in great devotion. *Spinsters. Reporters. Bostonians. Fidelity.*

THE LAVENDER BATH LADY **F2.2996**

Universal Film Manufacturing Co. 13 Nov **1922** [c26 Oct 1922; LP18341]. Si; b&w. 35mm. 5 reels, 4,113-4,500 ft.

Pres by Carl Laemmle. *Dir* King Baggot. *Scen* George Randolph Chester, Doris Schroeder. *Adapt* George Randolph Chester. *Story* Shannon Fife. *Photog* Victor Milner.

Cast: Gladys Walton *(Mamie Conroy)*, Charlotte Pierce *(Jeanette Gregory)*, Edward Burns *(David Bruce)*, Tom Ricketts *(Simon Gregory)*, Lydia Yeamans Titus *(Maggie)*, Mary Winston *(Susanne)*, Al MacQuarrie *(Dorgan)*, Harry Lorraine *(Drake)*, Earl Crain *(Hallet)*.

Comedy. Mamie Conroy, a shopgirl, and wealthy Jeanette Gregory become friends. When Mamie foils an attempted abduction of Jeanette, the latter's grandfather, Simon Gregory, brings Mamie into his home and treats her like a member of the family. But she is again involved in a kidnaping attempt and is herself accused of robbery. Explanations resolve everything, and Mamie falls in love with David Bruce, a detective passing as a crook. *Shopgirls. Grandfathers. Detectives. Family life. Kidnaping. Robbery. Friendship.*

LAW AGAINST LAW *see* **RENO**

LAW AND ORDER *see* **AFTER DARK**

THE LAW AND THE LADY **F2.2997**

Marlborough Productions. *Dist* Aywon Film Corp. 18 Dec **1924** [New York State license]. Si; b&w. 35mm. 6 reels, 5,700 ft.

Pres by Schuyler E. Grey. *Dir* John L. McCutcheon. *Scen* Lewis Allen Browne.

Cast: Len Leo *(Jack Langley)*, Alice Lake *(Marion Blake)*, Mary Thurman *(Minerva Blake)*, [Frederick] Tyrone Power *(John Langley, Sr.)*, Maurice Costello *(Cyrus Blake)*, Henry Sedley *(Don Hollins)*, Cornelius Keefe *(Stephen Clark)*, Joseph Depew *(office boy)*, Tom Blake *(Bill Sims)*, Joseph Burke *(butler)*, Jack McLean *(Hubert Townsend)*, Raphaella Ottiano *(Ma Sims)*.

Melodrama. When Cyrus Blake discovers that both his wife and her jewels are missing, he employs Jack Langley, a young lawyer, to go after them. Langley follows a trail of clues that leads him to a gang of yeggs headed by dapper Don Hollins, a personable thief. He also encounters and falls in love with Marion Folsom, whose real name later turns out to be Blake. Langley takes her for the wife of Cyrus Blake and, when he recovers the stolen jewels, he returns with her to the millionaire. While Cyrus is telling Langley that the beautiful girl is, in fact, his daughter, the real Mrs. Blake returns, having been kept prisoner by Hollins when she personally attempted to recover her jewelry. *Millionaires. Lawyers. Gangs. Mistaken identity. Kidnaping. Robbery.*

LAW AND THE MAN **F2.2998**

Trem Carr Productions. *Dist* Rayart Pictures. Jan **1928**. Si; b&w. 35mm. 6 reels, 5,916 ft.

Pres by W. Ray Johnston. *Dir* Scott Pembroke. *Scen-Adapt* Arthur Hoerl. *Photog* Ernest Depew. *Film Ed* Charles A. Post.

Cast: Tom Santschi *(Dan Creedon)*, Gladys Brockwell *(Margaret Grayson)*, Robert Ellis *(Ernest Vane)*, Tom Ricketts *(Quintus Newton)*, Florence Turner *(Miss Blair)*, James Cain *(Jimmy)*, Henry Roquemore *(Stanley Hudson)*.

Melodrama. Source: Octavus Roy Cohen, "False Fires" (publication undetermined). Dan Creedon, a corrupt political boss, reforms himself and his administration out of love for lawyer Margaret Grayson, whom he appoints district attorney. To his sorrow, Dan learns that Margaret is engaged to a crooked architect, Ernest Vane, and he goes so far as to assume Vane's guilt of forgery to be for Margaret's benefit. Margaret finally sees through Dan's ruse, appreciates his love for her, and realizes her fiancé's villainy. *Lawyers. District attorneys. Architects. Women in public office. Political bosses. Forgery.*

LAW AND THE OUTLAW **F2.2999**

Dist Exclusive Features. 26 May **1925** [New York State license]. Si; b&w. 35mm. 5 reels, 4,500 ft.

Cast: Tom Mix.

Note: Expansion of a 2-reeler, *The Law and the Outlaw,* released in 2 parts (Selig, 1913).

THE LAW AND THE WOMAN **F2.3000**

Famous Players–Lasky. *Dist* Paramount Pictures. ca15 Jan **1922** [New York premiere; released 5 Feb; c14 Dec 1921; LP17376]. Si; b&w. 35mm. 7 reels, 6,461 ft.

Pres by Adolph Zukor. *Dir* Penrhyn Stanlaws. *Scen* Albert S. Le Vino. *Photog* Karl Struss.

Cast: Betty Compson *(Margaret Rolfe)*, William P. Carleton *(Julian Rolfe)*, Cleo Ridgely *(Clara Foster)*, Casson Ferguson *(Phil Long)*, Henry Barrows *(Judge Thompson)*, Helen Dunbar *(Aunt Lucy)*, Clarence Burton *(Bates)*, J. S. Stembridge *(detective)*.

Melodrama. Source: Clyde Fitch, *The Woman in the Case, a Play in Four Acts* (Boston, 1915). When his bride, Margaret, questions him about his former loves, Julian Rolfe recalls his old flame Clara Foster, now living in Paris. At the same time, Clara meets Julian's ward, Phil Long, a millionaire soldier who tells her of Julian's marriage to Margaret, and they both sail for New York. Long calls on the Rolfes and tells Julian of his infatuation for Clara; Julian advises him to forget her and later tells Margaret about his past affair. Meanwhile, Phil informs Clara of the interview, and she threatens to show Margaret letters from Julian. Though he is unmoved by the threat, his wife advises him to inform Phil, whom he later meets in an angry confrontation; upon returning home, Julian discovers that his wife has burned the letters. Later, Phil is found murdered with evidence pointing to Julian, and he is tried and convicted on the day Margaret's child is born. Margaret disguises herself and playing on Clara's superstition elicits a confession of guilt from her just in time to avert Julian's execution. *Millionaires. Vamps. Marriage. Injustice. Superstition. Murder. Capital punishment. New York City. Paris.*

THE LAW DEMANDS **F2.3001**

Dist Weiss Brothers Clarion Photoplays. 15 Jun **1924.** Si; b&w. 35mm. 5 reels.

Dir Harry O. Hoyt.

Cast: Charles Hutchinson, Leah Baird.

Society melodrama. No information about the precise nature of this film has been found.

Note: This film was probably cut down from the 15-episode serial, *Wolves of Kultur,* produced by Western Photoplays and released by Pathé in 1918. The serial was written and directed by Joseph A. Golden, and it seems likely that Harry O. Hoyt supervised the reshaping of the original film. *The Radio Flyer* (1924) was also cut down from the same serial.

THE LAW FORBIDS (Universal-Jewel) **F2.3002**

Universal Pictures. 7 Apr **1924** [c21 Jan 1924; LP19844]. Si; b&w. 35mm. 6 reels, 6,203 ft.

Dir Jesse Robbins. *Scen* Lois Zellner, Ford I. Beebe. *Story* Bernard McConville. *Photog* Charles Kaufman, Jack Stevens.

Cast: Baby Peggy *(Peggy)*, Robert Ellis *(Paul Remsen)*, Elinor Fair *(Rhoda Remsen)*, Winifred Bryson *(Inez Lamont)*, James Corrigan *(John Martin)*, Anna Hernandez *(Martha Martin)*, Joseph Dowling *(Judge)*, Ned Sharks *(Clyde Vernon)*, Eva Thatcher *(Mrs. Grimes)*, Victor Potel *(Joel Andrews)*, William E. Lawrence *(Monte Hanley)*, Hayden Stevenson *(lawyer for defendant)*, William Welch *(lawyer for plaintiff)*, Bobby Bowes *(theatrical producer)*, Alexander *(himself)*.

Romantic drama. Paul and Rhoda Remsen, having marital difficulties, separate; and each is awarded their child Peggy for 6 months of the year. Rhoda and the child move to a farm town, while Paul remains in the big city to write a play for actress Inez Lamont, who is in love with him. Peggy knows that her mother still loves Paul, so she flees to the big city to explain the situation to her father. When Rhoda learns Peggy's whereabouts she comes to the city and views Paul's play, which is interrupted by a series of antics by Peggy's lunatic rooster. Inez, furious, stomps out after the performance and leaves Paul and Rhoda to reunite. *Playwrights. Actors. Divorce. Theater. Farm life. Roosters.*

THE LAW HUSTLERS *see* **THE LAW RUSTLERS**

LAW OF FEAR **F2.3003**

FBO Pictures. 8 Apr **1928** [c12 Mar 1928; LP25054]. Si; b&w. 35mm. 5 reels, 4,769 ft.

Dir Jerome Storm. *Screenplay* Ethel Hill. *Titl* Randolph Bartlett. *Story* William Francis Dugan. *Photog* Robert De Grasse. *Film Ed* Jack Kitchen.

Cast: Ranger *(himself, a dog)*, Jane Reid *(Marion)*, Sam Nelson *(Bud Hardy)*, Al Smith *(Steve Benton/The Hunchbacked Masked Bandit)*, Ida Lewis.

Melodrama. Ranger, the canine hero, avenges the murder of his mate, Lady Julie, by tracking the hunchbacked masked bandit to his death and revealing that the outlaw is actually the heroine's scheming brother-in-law. *Bandits. Brothers-in-law. Dogs.*

THE LAW OF THE LAWLESS **F2.3004**

Famous Players–Lasky. *Dist* Paramount Pictures. 22 Jul **1923** [c30 May 1923; LP19074]. Si; b&w. 35mm. 7 reels, 6,387 ft.

Pres by Jesse L. Lasky. *Dir* Victor Fleming. *Scen* E. Lloyd Sheldon, Edfrid Bingham. *Story* Konrad Bercovici. *Photog* George R. Meyer.

Cast: Dorothy Dalton *(Sahande)*, Theodore Kosloff *(Sender)*, Charles De Roche *(Costa)*, Tully Marshall *(Ali Mechmet)*, Fred Huntley *(Osman)*, Margaret Loomis *(Fanutza)*.

Melodrama. Source: Konrad Bercovici, "The Law of the Lawless," in *Ghitza, and Other Romances of Gypsy Blood* (New York, 1921). Sahande, a Tartar girl placed on the block to be sold, is bought by Costa, a Gypsy chief who outbids Sahande's fiancé, Sender. Costa marries the infuriated Sahande but agrees to give her 10 days in which either to return his love or have Sender fight him. Before the 10 days expire Sender and 30 of his men overtake Costa and imprison him in a tower. When a fire starts there, Sahande realizes she loves Costa and rescues him. *Tartars. Gypsies. Slavery. Fires.*

LAW OF THE MOUNTED **F2.3005**

El Dorado Productions. *Dist* Syndicate Pictures. Nov **1928.** Si; b&w. 35mm. 5 reels, 4,580 ft.

Dir J. P. McGowan. *Adapt* Philip Schuyler. *Story* Sally Winters. *Photog* Paul Allen.

Cast: Bob Custer, J. P. McGowan, Sally Winters, Frank Ellis, Cliff Lyons, Mary Mayberry, Lynn Sanderson, Mack V. Wright, Bud Osborne.

Northwest melodrama. In search of a band of fur thieves, a Northwest Mounted Policeman (played by Bob Custer) suffers many setbacks but uncovers the head of the gang (played by J. P. McGowan), who proves to be wanted for an old murder. *Gangs. Murder. Northwest Mounted Police.*

Note: *Film Year Book* also gives release dates of 1 Dec 1928 and 15 Jan 1929.

LAW OF THE PLAINS **F2.3006**

J. P. McGowan Productions. *Dist* Syndicate Pictures. 19 Aug **1929** [New York State license]. Si; b&w. 35mm. 5 reels, 4,800 ft.

Cast: Tom Tyler, Natalie Joyce.

Western melodrama. "O'Brien, negotiating sale of his rancho, is killed by Seagrue, who takes possession under the name of Serrano. Years later, O'Brien's son, Dan, avenges his dad's death." ("Motion Picture News Booking Guide," in *Motion Picture News*, 15 Mar 1930, p89.) *Ranches. Revenge. Filial relations.*

THE LAW OF THE RANGE **F2.3007**

Metro-Goldwyn-Mayer Pictures. 21 Jan **1928** [c21 Jan 1928; LP25183]. Si; b&w. 35mm. 6 reels, 5,393 ft.

Dir William Nigh. *Scen* Richard Schayer. *Titl* Robert Hopkins. *Story* Norman Houston. *Photog* Clyde De Vinna. *Film Ed* Dan Sharits. *Wardrobe* Lucia Coulter.

Cast: Tim McCoy *(Jim Lockheart)*, Joan Crawford *(Betty Dallas)*, Rex Lease *(The Solitaire Kid)*, Bodil Rosing *(Mother Lockheart)*, Tenen Holtz *(Cohen)*.

Western melodrama. Two brothers are separated in childhood by renegades who kidnap one of them during an attack on a wagon train. Jim Lockheart remains with his mother and becomes a Texas Ranger; Billy becomes the most desperate bandit in the Southwest—"The Solitaire Kid." Jim trails the Kid, and they discover (from similar tattoos) that they are brothers. The Kid is fatally wounded while protecting Jim from a bush fire, and he dies in Jim's arms with his mother nearby. Jim's sweetheart, Betty Dallas, misled at first by the tattoo into thinking that Jim is "The Solitaire Kid," later sees her mistake. *Brothers. Texas Rangers. Outlaws. Personal identity. Kidnaping. Wagon trains. Tattoos. Texas.*

LAW OF THE SNOW COUNTRY **F2.3008**

Bud Barsky Corp. 1 Apr **1926.** Si; b&w. 35mm. 5 reels.

Dir Paul Hurst.

Cast: Kenneth McDonald *(Sgt. Jimmy Burke)*, Jane Thomas *(Marie)*, Noble Johnson *(Martell)*, William Strauss *(Father Fajans)*, Hazel Howell *(The Blonde)*, Bud Osborne *(Pig Eye Perkins)*, Ben Corbett *(Jim Wolf)*, Billy Cinders *(Goofy Joe)*.

Northwest melodrama. "Story tells of obstacles Northwestern Mounted Policeman meets with in attempting to apprehend murderer. He miraculously escapes ambush and learns of dying murderer's name. After thrilling fight he secures confession from his man and saves girl from disaster." (*Motion Picture News Booking Guide,* 11:34, Oct 1926.) *Murder. Northwest Mounted Police.*

LAW OR LOYALTY **F2.3009**

Davis Distributing Division. c5 Jan **1926** [LP22226]. Si; b&w. 35mm. 5 reels, 4,800 ft.

Dir Lawson Harris. *Story* Robert S. Walker.

Northwest melodrama. David French, a stalwart member of the Northwest Mounted Police, is ordered to the coast and is therefore unable to keep an appointment to be married with his sweetheart, Jean Dupres. He writes to her, but she does not receive the letter. She arrives at the appointed meeting place, alone and broke, and must accept the hospitality of a despicable character known only as the "Timber Wolf." When Timber Wolf attacks Jean in her cabin, Pierre Santoi, a fine fellow who has fallen in love with her, kills him with a knife. Pierre takes to the woods and meets up with David, an old friend, who reluctantly arrests him. David takes Pierre back to stand trial and is instrumental in obtaining a verdict of justifiable homicide; David is reunited with Jean, and Pierre sets out for the white frontier. *Murder. Trials. Northwest Mounted Police.*

THE LAW RUSTLERS **F2.3010**

Ben Wilson Productions. *Dist* Arrow Film Corp. 30 Mar **1923** [c22Mar 1923; LP18802]. Si; b&w. 35mm. 5 reels, 4,849 ft.

Supv Ben Wilson. *Dir* Lewis King.

Cast: William Fairbanks *(Phil Stanley)*, Edmund Cobb *(Harry Hartley)*, Joseph Girard *(Sol Vane)*, Ena Gregory *(Glory Sillman)*, Ashton Dearholt *(Eph Sillman)*, Wilbur McGaugh *(John Cale)*, Claude Payton *(Doc Jordan)*.

Western melodrama. Source: W. C. Tuttle, "The Law Rustlers," in *Adventure Magazine* (30:162–179, 1 Sep 1921). Phil Stanley and Harry Hartley are wandering toward Alaska when they stop in a town controlled by a triumvirate of scoundrels and take the part of Glory Sillman, whose brother has been killed while trying to procure medicine for his dying wife. The council declares their banishment, but the pair refuse to leave, send Glory for the sheriff in a neighboring town, and round up the council and its confederates. Phil remains with Glory and her orphaned niece. *Wanderers. Sheriffs. Government—Local.*

Note: Known also as *The Law Hustlers.*

LAWFUL CHEATERS **F2.3011**

B. P. Schulberg Productions. 17 Jul **1925** [New York State license]. Si; b&w. 35mm. 5 reels, 4,898 ft.

Dir Frank O'Connor.

Cast: Clara Bow, David Kirby, Edward Hearn, Raymond McKee.

Melodrama. Dressed as a boy, a girl persuades a gang of crooks to reform. *Criminals—Rehabilitation. Male impersonation.*

LAWFUL LARCENY **F2.3012**

Famous Players–Lasky. *Dist* Paramount Pictures. 22 Jul **1923** [New York premiere; released 2 Sep; c18 Jul 1923; LP19247]. Si; b&w. 35mm. 6 reels, 5,503 ft.

Pres by Adolph Zukor. *Dir* Allan Dwan. *Adapt* John Lynch. *Photog* Hal Rosson. *Prod Mgr* John Lynch.

Cast: Hope Hampton *(Marion Dorsey)*, Conrad Nagel *(Andrew Dorsey)*, Nita Naldi *(Vivian Hepburn)*, Lew Cody *(Guy Tarlow)*, Russell Griffin *(Sonny Dorsey)*, Yvonne Hughes *(Billie Van de Vere)*, Dolores Costello *(Nora, a maid)*, Gilda Gray, Florence O'Denishawn, Alice Maison *(dancers at the Rendez-Vous)*.

Society melodrama. Source: Samuel Shipman, *Lawful Larceny* (New York opening: 2 Jan 1922). During his wife's absence, Andrew Dorsey is snared by Vivian Hepburn, owner of a crooked gambling house, and her silent partner, Guy Tarlow. Dorsey loses so much money that Vivian persuades him to give her one of his firm's checks for a large sum of money. Hearing her husband's confession, Marion Dorsey, returned from Europe, determines to retrieve the check. She disguises herself as a wealthy widow, vamps Tarlow, and persuades him to rob Vivian's safe and elope. Marion then steals the contents of the safe and later returns everything to the irate Vivian except the check and the money her husband lost. *Gambling. Disguise. Robbery.*

LAWFUL LARCENY **F2.3013**

RKO Productions. 17 Aug **1930** [c8 Aug 1930; LP1466]. Sd (Photophone); b&w. 35mm. 7 reels, 6,379 ft.

Prod William Le Baron. *Assoc Prod* Henry Hobart. *Dir* Lowell Sherman. *Screenplay* Jane Murfin. *Photog* Roy Hunt. *Film Ed* Marie Halvey. *Sd Rec* George Ellis.

Cast: Bebe Daniels *(Marion Corsey)*, Kenneth Thomson *(Andrew Dorsey)*, Lowell Sherman *(Guy Tarlow)*, Olive Tell *(Vivian Hepburn)*, Purnell B. Pratt *(Judge Perry)*, Lou Payne *(Davis)*, Bert Roach *(French)*, Maude Turner Gordon *(Mrs. Davis)*, Helene Millard *(Mrs. French)*, Charles Coleman *(butler)*.

Melodrama. Source: Samuel Shipman, *Lawful Larceny* (New York opening: 2 Jan 1922). Marion and Andrew Dorsey are happily married until Vivian Hepburn takes advantage of Marion's absence, vamps Andrew, and obtains his note for $25,000. Vivian threatens to ruin Andrew; he confesses all to Marion; and though she considers divorcing him, she later decides to seek employment as Vivian's secretary. Through Guy Tarlow, whom Vivian really loves and whom Marion vamps in revenge, Marion steals all her ill-gotten spoils. She is pursued by Tarlow, Vivian, and Judge Perry, who is in love with Vivian. Marion flays Vivian as a thief and a cheat and proves that she has been operating a crooked gambling establishment. With Vivian defeated, Tarlow departs, swearing eternal love and admitting reform; and Andrew persuades Marion to remain as a friend. *Vamps. Secretaries. Judges. Marriage. Blackmail. Gambling. Larceny.*

THE LAWLESS LEGION **F2.3014**

First National Pictures. 17 Feb **1929** [c14 Mar 1929; LP212]. Si; b&w. 35mm. 6 reels, 6,109 ft.

Pres by Charles R. Rogers. *Dir* Harry J. Brown. *Scen* Fred Allen, Bennett Cohn. *Titl* Lesley Mason. *Story* Bennett Cohn. *Photog* Frank Good. *Film Ed* Fred Allen.

Cast: Ken Maynard *(Cal Stanley)*, Nora Lane *(Mary Keiver)*, Paul Hurst *(Ramírez)*, J. P. McGowan *(Matson)*, Frank Rice *(Flapjack)*, Howard Truesdell *(Sheriff Keiver)*, Tarzan *(himself, a horse)*.

Western melodrama. Sheriff Keiver's daughter, Mary, promises to marry Cal Stanley if he will drive a large herd of cattle from drought-stricken East Texas across the bad lands controlled by Ramírez, a rustling renegade, to Grass Valley. Cal is drugged on the way, and Ramírez steals the herd. Cal is held responsible and goes after the herd himself, posing as a cattle buyer. He gets the cattle back and rounds up the rustlers, winning Mary's love for himself. *Sheriffs. Rustlers. Impersonation. Drought. Texas. Horses.*

LAWLESS MEN **F2.3015**

William Steiner. *Dist* New-Cal Film Corp. 15 Mar **1924** [c3 Mar 1924; LU19960]. Si; b&w. 35mm. 5 reels.

Pres by William Steiner. *Dir* Neal Hart. *Story-Scen* Neal Hart, Arthur Henry Gooden.

Cast: Neal Hart *(Steve McKay)*.

Western melodrama. "Steve McKay is unjustly sentenced for killing father of Ruth, the girl he loves. Released from prison he tracks down Black Bart, outlaw and the real murderer. Black Bart escapes and kidnaps Ruth, who is rescued by Steve as Bart falls to his death over a cliff. Steve's innocence is later proved and a happy marriage culminates the story." (*Motion Picture News Booking Guide,* [7]:30, Oct 1924.) *Murder. Injustice. Kidnaping.*

LAWLESS TRAILS **F2.3016**

B. A. Goodman Productions. *Dist* A. G. Steen. 26 Feb **1926** [New York State license]. Si; b&w. 35mm. 5 reels.

Dir-Scen Forrest Sheldon.

Cast: Bruce Gordon *(Bud Clews)*, Boris Bullock *(Frisco Mays)*, Josephine Hill *(Josephine Sturgess)*, Bob Williamson *(Shorty Hill)*, Milburn Morante *(Lafe Sturgess)*, Bud Osborne *(Slim Lamont)*, Victor Allen *(Mojave Kid)*.

Western melodrama. Josephine Sturgess returns from San Francisco to her father's ranch and is followed there by Frisco Mays, a crook with whom she has become innocently involved. Bud Clews discovers Mays in possession of a stolen necklace and takes it from him, allowing him to escape in order to protect Josephine's good name and reputation. The sheriff comes to the ranch looking for Mays, finds Bud with the necklace, and arrests him. Bud escapes from the sheriff's custody and trails Mays, forcing him to write a confession clearing both himself and Josephine. The sheriff accepts the confession, and Bud marries Josephine. *Cowboys. Ranchers. Sheriffs. Reputation. Theft. San Francisco.*

THE LAW'S LASH **F2.3017**

Fred J. McConnell Productions. *Dist* Pathé Exchange. 20 May **1928** [c9 May 1928; LP25258]. Si; b&w. 35mm. 5 reels, 4,683 or 4,902 ft.

Dir Noel Mason Smith. *Scen* Edward Meagher. *Story* George Pyper. *Photog* Harry Cooper.

Cast: Klondike *(Flame, a dog)*, Robert Ellis *(Ted Campbell)*, Mary Mayberry *(Margery Neame)*, Jack Marsh *(Mick Maloney)*, Richard R. Neill *(André La Rue)*, LeRoy Mason *(Pete Logan)*, William Walters *(Chippewa Jim)*.

Action melodrama. A gang leader kills a Royal Mounted policeman and beats Flame, a police dog. Corporal Campbell is assigned to capture the murderer. His sweetheart suspects that her foster father is the culprit. Campbell is trapped by the gang while he is following up his suspicions. Flame leads other Mounties to the hideout, searches out the hiding men, and reveals the name of the man who killed his master. *Foster fathers. Gangs. Murder. Northwest Mounted Police. Police dogs.*

LAZY LIGHTNING (Blue Streak Western) **F2.3018**
Universal Pictures. 12 Dec **1926** [c13 Sep 1926; LP23116]. Si; b&w. 35mm. 5 reels, 4,572 ft.
Pres by Carl Laemmle. *Dir* William Wyler. *Story-Scen* Harrison Jacobs. *Photog* Eddie Linden.
Cast: Art Acord *(Rance Lighton)*, Fay Wray *(Lila Rogers)*, Bobby Gordon *(Dickie Rogers)*, Vin Moore *(Sheriff Dan Boyd)*, Arthur Morrison *(Henry S. Rogers)*, George K. French *(Doctor Hull)*, Rex De Roselli *(William Harvey)*.
Western melodrama. Rance Lighton, a lazy wanderer, is arrested for vagrancy and taken to the Rogers Ranch, where Dickie Rogers, an invalid child who is confined to a wheelchair, takes a liking to the stranger. An old man mistakes the name "Lighton" for "Lightning," and the nickname sticks. Uncle Henry, heir to Dickie's share of the estate in the event of the boy's death, has been systematically cheated by Bill Harvey, who now threatens Uncle Henry and demands his money. When Uncle Henry sees Dickie sliding toward a cliff in his wheelchair, he makes no move to save him, but Lightning comes to his rescue. The boy becomes seriously ill as a result of the experience, and Uncle Henry sets out to get a serum needed by the doctor; mistrusting him, Lightning follows in a driving rainstorm, learns of Uncle Henry's conspiracy to withhold the serum, fights Harvey and Henry, returns with the serum to save the boy's life, and wins the love of Dickie's sister, Lila. *Wanderers. Children. Invalids. Uncles. Brother-sister relationship. Inheritance. Serums.*

LAZYBONES **F2.3019**
Fox Film Corp. 6 or 8 Nov **1925** [c30 Aug 1925; LP21997]. Si; b&w. 35mm. 8 reels, 7,234 ft.
Pres by William Fox. *Dir* Frank Borzage. *Scen* Frances Marion. *Photog* Glen MacWilliams, George Schneiderman. *Asst Dir* Orville O. Dull.
Cast: Charles "Buck" Jones *(Lazybones)*, Madge Bellamy *(Kit)*, Virginia Marshall *(Kit, as a child)*, Edythe Chapman *(Mrs. Tuttle)*, Leslie Fenton *(Dick Ritchie)*, Jane Novak *(Agnes Fanning)*, Emily Fitzroy *(Mrs. Fanning)*, ZaSu Pitts *(Ruth Fanning)*, William Norton Bailey *(Elmer Ballister)*.
Rural romantic drama. Source: Owen Davis, *Lazybones* (New York opening: 22 Sep 1924). In a small town about 1900, Agnes Fanning and Lazybones, a lovable but shiftless character, are sweethearts. Her sister, Ruth, returns home from school with a child (Kit) and a story of a marriage to a sailor who drowned. Lazybones saves Ruth from committing suicide and adopts Kit. Ruth marries Elmer Ballister. Agnes renounces Lazybones when he refuses to give up the child. Ruth dies after confessing to her mother. Years pass. Lazybones goes off to France during the World War. Returning, he plans to wed Kit, now a grown girl, but finds her in love with Dick Ritchie. Kit weds Dick, and it is intimated that Lazybones and Agnes may marry. *Illegitimacy. Suicide. Adoption. Smalltown life. World War I.*

LEAP YEAR **F2.3020**
Famous Players–Lasky. *Dist* Paramount Pictures. **1921** [scheduled release]. Si; b&w. 35mm. 5 reels.
Cast: Roscoe Arbuckle.
Comedy.
Note: Made but never released in the United States. Working title: *Skirt Shy.*

LEARNING TO LOVE (Talmadge Producing Corp.) **F2.3021**
Dist First National Pictures. 25 Jan **1925** [c7 Jan 1925; LP21000]. Si; b&w. 35mm. 7 reels, 6,181 ft.
Pres by Joseph M. Schenck. *Dir* Sidney A. Franklin. *Story-Scen* John Emerson, Anita Loos. *Photog* Victor Milner.
Cast: Constance Talmadge *(Patricia Stanhope)*, Antonio Moreno *(Scott Warner)*, Emily Fitzroy *(Aunt Virginia)*, Edythe Chapman *(Aunt Penelope)*, Johnny Harron *(Billy Carmichael)*, Ray Hallor *(Tom Morton)*, Wallace MacDonald *(Professor Bonnard)*, Alf Goulding *(John, the barber)*, Byron Munson *(Count Coo-Coo)*, Edgar Norton *(butler)*.
Comedy. Patricia Stanhope is a born flirt. After promising to marry one of her professors at finishing school, she becomes successively engaged to a college boy she meets on a train, to a young Chicago millionaire, and to a nutty French count. The only man who does not easily succumb to her charm and good looks is Scott Warner, the handsome lawyer who acts as her guardian. As the result of being engaged to four men at once, Patricia starts a public row that ends with three of the fiancés in jail. Scott saves her from scandal but tells her that he will personally force her to marry the next man with whom she becomes entangled. Having fallen in love with Scott, Patricia hides herself in his apartment for a night and then sends a hint of the escapade to a scandal sheet. To save her reputation, Scott gallantly marries the willing Patricia but refuses to live with her, and Patricia sadly sails to Paris to obtain a divorce. Discovering that he is truly in love with Patricia, Scott immediately follows her to France, where they finally spend their wedding night together in a hotel room filled with flowers. *Flirts. Lawyers. Divorce. Scandal sheets. Paris.*

THE LEATHERNECK **F2.3022**
Ralph Block Productions. *Dist* Pathé Exchange. 24 Feb **1929** [c26 Feb 1929; LP167]. Talking sequences (Photophone); b&w. 35mm. 8 reels, 6,965 ft. [Also si; 6,898 ft.]
Dir Howard Higgin. *Story-Cont* Elliott Clawson. *Titl* John Krafft. *Photog* John Mescall. *Prop* Allen Smiley. *Film Ed* Doane Harrison. *Song: "Only for You"* Josiah Zuro, Francis Gromon, Charles Weinberg. *Rec Engr* George Ellis. *Asst Dir* Leigh Smith. *Prod Mgr* Harry H. Poppe.
Cast: Alan Hale *(Otto Schmidt)*, William Boyd *(Joseph Hanlon)*, Robert Armstrong *(William Calhoun)*, Fred Kohler *(Heckla)*, Diane Ellis *(Tanya)*, James Aldine *(Tanya's brother)*, Paul Weigel *(Petrovitch)*, Jules Cowles *(cook)*, Wade Boteler *(top sergeant)*, Jack Richardson, Joseph Girard, Philo McCullough, Lee Shumway, Lloyd Whitlock, Mitchell Lewis *(officers of the court-martial)*.
Melodrama. At the headquarters of the 6th Marine Regiment in China, Privates Schmidt and Hanlon are placed on trial for desertion, and Hanlon tells the following story. *While his regiment was in Russia, he married Tanya, the daughter of an aristocrat. During the Revolution, he was separated from her, and she was reported dead. Time passed, and news was received of the whereabouts of the Russian (Heckla) responsible for the death of Tanya's family. Hanlon and Schmidt (joined by William Calhoun) deserted their posts in search of revenge. Heckla was killed; Calhoun was mortally wounded; and Schmidt was driven insane by water torture. Hanlon returned to his regiment with the crazed Schmidt.* Tanya unexpectedly appears at the court-martial and corroborates the details of her husband's story. Hanlon's reunion with Tanya is delayed by the 3 days he must serve in the guardhouse for desertion. *Aristocrats. Russians. Revenge. Torture. Insanity. Courts-martial. Russia—History—1917–21 Revolution. China. United States Marines.*

LEATHERNECKING **F2.3023**
RKO Productions. 12 Sep **1930** [New York opening; released 22 Sep; c19 Sep 1930; LP1603]. Sd (Photophone); b&w. 35mm. 9 reels, 7,150 ft.
Assoc Prod Louis Sarecky. *Dir* Edward Cline. *Cont* Jane Murfin. *Titl* John Krafft. *Adapt* Alfred Jackson. *Photog* J. Roy Hunt. *Art Dir* Max Ree. *Song: "All My Life"* Benny Davis, Harry Akst. *Adtl Mus* Oscar Levant. *Mus Dir* Victor Baravalle. *Dance Dir* Pearl Eaton. *Rec Engr* John Tribby. *Asst Dir* Frederick Fleck.
Cast: Irene Dunne *(Delphine)*, Ken Murray *(Frank)*, Louise Fazenda *(Hortense)*, Ned Sparks *(Sparks)*, Lilyan Tashman *(Edna)*, Eddie Foy, Jr. *(Chick)*, Benny Rubin *(Stein)*, Rita Le Roy *(fortune-teller)*, Fred Santley *(Douglas)*, William von Brinken *(Richter)*, Carl Gerrard *(colonel)*, Werther Weidler, Wolfgang Weidler *(Richter's sons)*.
Musical comedy-drama. Source: Herbert Fields, Richard Rogers, and Lorenz Hart, *Present Arms* (New York opening: 26 Apr 1928). Buck private Chick Evans, stationed with the U. S. Marines in Honolulu, conceives the idea of stealing his captain's uniform and Distinguished Service Medal so as to attract attention in high society. He succeeds in getting an invitation from Delphine Witherspoons to a party at her home; but his buddies decide to crash the party, and unwittingly they expose his rank. Realizing that Chick loves Delphine, Edna, a mutual friend, plans to bring them together aboard her yacht, but Delphine denounces him as an imposter. Chick arranges for the captain to fake a shipwreck; but a real storm arises, the boat goes under, and Chick and Delphine are marooned on a desert island. Upon returning to Honolulu, Chick is put in the brig, and Delphine begins to relent when a fortune-teller advises her that Chick is to be shot for desertion. Rushing to save him, she finds, instead, that he is being promoted to captain. *Imposture. Courtship. United States Marines. Honolulu. Shipwrecks.*

LEAVE IT TO GERRY **F2.3024**
Ben Wilson Productions. *Dist* Grand-Asher Distributing Corp. Jan **1924** [c30 Jan 1924; LP19877]. Si; b&w. 35mm. 6 reels, 5,863 ft.

Dir Arvid E. Gillstrom. *Story* Adam Hull Shirk.

Cast: Billie Rhodes *(Geraldine Brent)*, William Collier, Jr. *(Dan Forbes)*, Claire McDowell *(Mrs. Brent)*, Kate Lester *(Mrs. Masters)*, Kathleen Kirkham *(Mrs. Turner-Prescott)*, Joseph W. Girard *(Colonel Pettijohn)*, Allan Cavan *(Mr. Burton)*.

Comedy-drama. Geraldine Brent, a tomboyish girl, is separated from her mother and taken east by wealthy relatives. In her absence, her mother is dispossessed and sent to the poorhouse. "Gerry" learns of this action, unmasks the culprits—mortgage-holder Masters and oilman Colonel Pettijohn, who have discovered that the property is rich in oil—and puts matters aright. *Tomboys. Filial relations. Swindlers. Oil business. Poorhouses.*

LEAVE IT TO LESTER **F2.3025**

Paramount-Publix Corp. 11 Jun **1930** [New York State license]. Sd (Movietone); b&w. 35mm. 5 reels.

Dir Frank Cambria, Ray Cozine. *Song: "I'm Yours"* John W. Green. *Mus Arr* John W. Green. *Dance Ensemble* Maria Gambarelli.

Cast: Lester Allen, Evelyn Hoey, Hal Thompson.

Comedy. Persuading his newlywed friends, Jerry and Marian Townsend, to take him along on their European honeymoon as guide, Lester Aloysius Sebastian Brown launches the threesome on a series of comic adventures, beginning in a Paris nightclub, where Lester is roughed up by two husbands who mistake his companions for their wives. Then on to Switzerland and a forced landing near a wedding festival; to Cairo, where Jerry is abducted and found by Marian in a harem; and back to New York. *Newlyweds. Guides. Honeymoons. Nightclubs. Harems. Paris. Switzerland. Cairo.*

Note: There is no evidence that this film was ever released. It may have been cut into shorts later (for example, *Lester Allen in Paris,* 1 reel, 1931).

THE LEAVENWORTH CASE **F2.3026**

Whitman Bennett Productions. *Dist* Vitagraph Co. of America. Nov **1923** [c12 Oct 1923; LP19492]. Si; b&w. 35mm. 6 reels, 5,400 ft.

Dir Charles Giblyn. *Scen* Eve Stuyvesant. *Photog* Edward Paul.

Cast: Seena Owen *(Eleanor Leavenworth)*, Martha Mansfield *(Mary Leavenworth)*, Wilfred Lytell *(Anderson)*, Bradley Barker *(Raymond)*, Paul Doucet *(Harwell)*, William Walcott *(Leavenworth)*, Frances Miller Grant *(Dinah)*, Fred Miller *(Thomas)*.

Mystery melodrama. Source: Anna Katharine Green, *The Leavenworth Case* (New York, 1878). Eleanor Leavenworth is about to be arrested for the murder of her rich bachelor uncle, and suspicion is cast on each member of the Leavenworth household until Raymond, an attorney in love with Eleanor, solves the mystery and produces the culprit, who confesses and falls to his death while trying to escape. *Lawyers. Murder.*

THE LEECH **F2.3027**

Selected Pictures. *Dist* Pioneer Film Corp. 25 Jul **1921** [Port Washington, N. Y., showing]. Si; b&w. 35mm. 5 reels, 4,610 ft.

Dir Herbert Hancock. *Photog* Alvin Knechtel.

Cast: Ray Howard *(Teddy)*, Alex Hall *(Bill)*, Claire Whitney *(Dorothy)*, Katherine Leon *(Ruth)*, Ren Gennard *(Joe Turner)*.

Drama. Two popular, athletic brothers serve in the war and return to their hometown wounded. One has lost an arm but takes advantage of the vocational training offered by the government and obtains a position. The other, whose leg has been slightly wounded, decides resentfully that the world owes him a living. Dorothy tries to convince him otherwise, but he is adamant until a dream reveals to him his error. *Veterans. Amputees. Brothers. Parasites. Vocational rehabilitation. World War I. Dreams.*

Note: Reviewers suspected that this film was produced shortly after the end of the World War.

THE LEFT HAND BRAND **F2.3028**

William Steiner Productions. *Dist* New-Cal Film Corp. 7 Jun **1924** [c26 May 1924; LU20230]. Si; b&w. 35mm. 5 reels, 4,884 ft.

Pres by William Steiner. *Dir-Prepared for the screen by* Neal Hart. *Story* Jane Hurrle. *Photog* R. L. Lelander. *Film Ed* Fred Burnworth.

Cast: Neal Hart *(King Calhoun)*, Fred Burnworth *(Fred Randall)*.

Western melodrama. King Calhoun, a wandering cowpuncher, settles down on the Bar M Ranch after a vain attempt to save its owner from death at the hands of rustlers. Fred Randall, the owner's son, is then ambushed. Before he dies, Fred makes King promise to marry his girl, Maisee Lee, an orphan, but King vows to himself to get Fred's killer first. Ben Snaith, an influential and respected rancher, who is also after Maisee's hand, convinces the sheriff that King is Lefty, a wanted killer. King escapes from the sheriff's posse by using ventriloquism. Snaith, however, is finally exposed as Lefty and is captured with help of local Pueblo Indians. King, in the end, decides to keep his promise to Fred. *Cowboys. Rustlers. Posses. Revenge. Pueblo Indians. Ventriloquism.*

Note: Summary and character names are from shooting script in copyright records and may be different in the final film. The script is our source for credits for Fred Burnworth as both actor and film editor.

LEGALLY DEAD **F2.3029**

Universal Pictures. 30 Jul **1923** [New York premiere; released 20 Aug; c7 Jul 1923; LP19191]. Si; b&w. 35mm. 6 reels, 6,076 ft.

Pres by Carl Laemmle. *Dir* William Parke. *Scen* Harvey Gates. *Story* Charles Furthman. *Photog* Richard Fryer.

Cast: Milton Sills *(Will Campbell)*, Margaret Campbell *(Mrs. Campbell)*, Claire Adams *(Minnie O'Reilly)*, Edwin Sturgis *(Jake Dorr)*, Faye O'Neill *(Jake's sweetie)*, Charles A. Stevenson *(Malcolm Steel)*, Joseph Girard *(District Attorney)*, Albert Prisco *(The Anarchist)*, Herbert Fortier *(The Judge)*, Charles Wellesley *(The Governor)*, Robert Homans *(Detective Powell)*, Brandon Hurst *(Dr. Gelzer)*.

Melodrama. Newspaper reporter Will Campbell gets himself arrested and imprisoned so he can interview inmates and collect material for his theory that most victims of capital punishment are actually innocent and are wrongfully condemned to death. After Will is paroled he gets a job in a bank and thwarts an attempted robbery. A detective is shot, and Will, picking up the gun, pursues the murderer. Police arrest Will; he is tried, convicted, and sentenced to be hanged. Will's innocence is discovered too late. He is executed and declared legally dead, but a doctor using adrenaline restores his life. *Reporters. Capital punishment. Bank robberies. Resuscitation. Epinephrine.*

THE LEGEND OF HOLLYWOOD **F2.3030**

Charles R. Rogers Productions. *Dist* Producers Distributing Corp. 3 Aug **1924** [c3 Aug 1924; LP20576]. Si; b&w. 35mm. 6 reels, 5,414 ft.

Pres by Charles R. Rogers. *Dir* Renaud Hoffman. *Scen-Titl* Alfred A. Cohn. *Photog* Karl Struss. *Film Ed* Glenn Wheeler.

Cast: Percy Marmont *(John Smith)*, ZaSu Pitts *(Mary Brown)*, Alice Davenport *(Mrs. Rooney)*, Dorothy Dorr *("Blondie")*, Cameo *(himself)*.

Romantic drama. Source: Frank Condon, "The Legend of Hollywood," in *Photoplay* (25:34–36, Mar 1924). Idealistic scenario writer John Smith comes to Hollywood to gain recognition and takes up lodging in Mrs. Rooney's modest boardinghouse, where a movie-struck girl, Mary Brown, falls secretly in love with him. When his story is rejected by film companies, he fills seven glasses with wine, one of which is poisoned; moving them about and thus not knowing which is lethal, he drinks one a day. As the last is consumed, he receives a check in the mail, but by chance Mary has replaced the poisoned glass. All ends happily. *Authors. Motion picture scenarists. Motion pictures. Boardinghouses. Suicide. Hollywood.*

LEGION OF THE CONDEMNED **F2.3031**

Paramount Famous Lasky Corp. 10 Mar **1928** [c10 Mar 1928; LP25060]. Si; b&w. 35mm. 8 reels, 7,415 ft.

Pres by Adolph Zukor, Jesse L. Lasky. *Dir* William A. Wellman. *Scen* John Monk Saunders, Jean De Limur. *Titl* George Marion, Jr. *Photog* Henry Gerrard. *Film Ed* Alyson Shaffer.

Cast: Gary Cooper *(Gale Price)*, Fay Wray *(Christine Charteris)*, Barry Norton *(Byron Dashwood)*, Lane Chandler *(Charles Holabird)*, Francis McDonald *(Gonzolo Vasquez)*, Voya George *(Robert Montagnal)*, Freeman Wood *(Richard De Witt)*, E. H. Calvert *(commandant)*, Albert Conti *(Von Hohendorff)*, Charlot Bird *(Celeste)*, Toto Guette *(mechanic)*.

Melodrama. Finding his sweetheart, Christine, in the arms of a German officer, Price joins the French Air Legion. Christine is later revealed to be the spy whom Price has been ordered to drop behind enemy lines. They are reconciled, are captured by the Germans, and are rescued by his unit. *Aviators. Spies. World War I. France—Air Legion.*

Note: Uses much stock footage from *Wings.*

LEGIONNAIRES IN PARIS **F2.3032**

FBO Pictures. ca26 Dec **1927** [New York premiere; released 31 Jan 1928; c31 Dec 1927; LP24877]. Si; b&w. 35mm. 6 reels, 5,893 ft.

Pres by Joseph P. Kennedy. *Dir* Arvid E. Gillstrom. *Scen* Jefferson Moffitt. *Titl* Jack Conway (of *Variety*). *Story* Louis Sarecky. *Photog* Phil Tannura. *Film Ed* Archie F. Marshek. *Asst Dir* Ken Marr.

Cast: Al Cooke *(himself)*, Kit Guard *(himself)*, Louise Lorraine *(Annette)*, Virginia Sale *(Fifi)*, John Aasen *(Shorty, The Giant Gendarme)*.

Comedy. Representing their post at an A. E. F. convention in Paris, two buddies, Al and Kit, believe that the Paris police are seeking to arrest them. In reality, they are wanted so that they may be decorated for valor in battle. After a lengthy chase in which Al and Kit disguise themselves as waiters and fall into a den of counterfeiters, the police, led by Shorty, The Giant Gendarme, capture and award them their medals. *Veterans. Waiters. Counterfeiters. Police. World War I. Paris. American Expeditionary Force. American Legion.*

LENA RIVERS **F2.3033**
Chord Pictures. *Dist* Arrow Pictures. 31 May **1925** [c13 Mar 1925; LP21246]. Si; b&w. 35mm. 9 reels.
Dir Whitman Bennett. *Adapt* Dana Rush.
Cast: Earle Williams *(Henry Rivers Grahme)*, Johnny Walker *(Durward Belmont)*, Gladys Hulette *(Lena Rivers)*, Edna Murphy *(Carrie Nichols)*, Marcia Harris *(Granny Nichols)*, Doris Rankin *(Mathilde Nichols)*, Irma Harrison *(Anne Nichols)*, Frank Sheridan *(Henry Rivers Grahme, Jr.)*, Herman Lieb *(Captain Atherton)*, Harlan Knight *(The Old Sea Dog)*, William T. Hayes *(John Nichols)*, Frank Andrews *(Grandfather Nichols)*.
Melodrama. Source: Mary Jane Holmes, *Lena Rivers* (New York, 1856). John Nichols and his sister, Lena, separately leave the small yellow farmhouse in the New England hills where they grew up and go to the big city. John marries and becomes the father of two girls, Carrie and Anne; John's wife, Mathilde, is ashamed of his humble origins and forces him to break off contact with his family. Lena marries Henry Rivers Grahme, whom she knows only as Henry Rivers. When Henry's father learns of the marriage, he has Henry kidnaped and sent to sea for 6 months. Lena returns home destitute and dies in childbirth; her child, also known as Lena, is reared to young womanhood by Mrs. Nichols. When Lena's grandfather dies, her Uncle John takes her in, but she is not happy, for her aunt is cruel to her. Lena is later reunited with her father and marries Durwood Belmont, the stepson of her father. *Grandfathers. Aunts. Brother-sister relationship. Poverty. Family life. New England.*

LEND ME YOUR HUSBAND **F2.3034**
C. C. Burr Pictures. 15 Jun **1924** [c8 May 1924; LP20207]. Si; b&w. 35mm. 6 reels, 5,388 ft.
Dir William Christy Cabanne. *Scen* Raymond S. Harris. *Story* Marguerite Gove. *Photog* Jack Brown, Neil Sullivan.
Cast: Doris Kenyon *(Aline Stockton)*, David Powell *(Henry Seton)*, Dolores Cassinelli *(Mrs. Seton)*, J. Barney Sherry *(Burrows Stackton)*, Violet Mersereau *(Jenny MacDonald)*, Burr McIntosh *(Fergus MacDonald)*, Connie Keefe *(Robert Towers)*, Coit Albertson *(Count Ferrari)*, Helen D'Algy *(Countess Ferrari)*.
Society drama. Fast and wealthy society girl Aline Stockton is engaged to Robert Towers but becomes involved with Henry Seton, a married man of bad reputation. Seton makes love to the gardener's daughter, Jenny MacDonald, a friend of Aline's. Aline shields Jenny at the expense of her own reputation and saves her from suicide. Later, the true circumstances are revealed, and the lovers are reconciled. *Socialites. Infidelity. Reputation. Suicide.*

LEND ME YOUR WIFE *see* **THE CHICKEN IN THE CASE**

LEONARD-TENDLER BOXING EXHIBITION **F2.3035**
Leon D. Britton. *Dist* Penser's Productions. 24 Jul **1923** [scheduled release]. Si; b&w. 35mm. 4 reels.
Boxing film. Benny Leonard retains his lightweight championship title by defeating Lew Tendler in a 15-round battle at the Yankee Stadium, Monday evening, July 23, 1923. *Boxing. Benny Leonard. Lew Tendler. New York City—Yankee Stadium.*

THE LEOPARD LADY **F2.3036**
De Mille Pictures. *Dist* Pathé Exchange. 22 Jan **1928** [c12 Jan 1928; LP24852]. Si; b&w. 35mm. 7 reels, 6,650 ft.
Prod Bertram Millhauser. *Dir* Rupert Julian. *Adapt-Cont* Beulah Marie Dix. *Photog* John Mescall. *Film Ed* Claude Berkeley.
Cast: Jacqueline Logan *(Paula)*, Alan Hale *(Caesar)*, Robert Armstrong *(Chris)*, Hedwig Reicher *(Fran Holweg)*, James Bradbury, Sr. *(Herman Berlitz)*, Dick Alexander *(Hector, the lion tamer)*, William Burt *(Presner)*, Sylvia Ashton *(Mama Lolita)*, Kay Deslys, Willie May Carson *(Austrian maids)*.
Melodrama. Source: Edward Childs Carpenter, *The Leopard Lady: a Play in 5 Acts* (New York, 1928). Paula, a leopard trainer known as the Leopard Lady, is hired by police to join a circus and investigate a series of thefts and murders. She discovers that Caesar, a Cossack, owns an ape trained by him to be a vicious killer. At first the Leopard Lady hesitates to expose Caesar because he once saved her life. Later, when the ape almost kills her fiancé, she reveals the truth and sends for her chief to make the arrest. *Detectives. Cossacks. Murder. Theft. Circus. Leopards. Apes.*

THE LEOPARDESS **F2.3037**
Famous Players–Lasky. *Dist* Paramount Pictures. 26 Mar **1923** [c28 Feb 1923; LP18772]. Si; b&w. 35mm. 6 reels, 5,621 ft.
Pres by Adolph Zukor. *Dir* Henry Kolker. *Adapt* J. Clarkson Miller. *Photog* Gilbert Warrenton. *Film Ed* Tom Geraghty.
Cast: Alice Brady *(Tiare)*, Edward Langford *(Captain Croft)*, Montagu Love *(Scott Quaigg)*, Charles Kent *(Angus McKenzie)*, George André Beranger *(Pepe)*, Marguerite Forrest *(Evoa)*, Glorie Eller *(Mamoe)*.
Melodrama. Source: Katharine Newlin Burt, "The Leopardess" (publication undetermined). On a South Sea island, wealthy hunter Scott Quaigg finds Tiare, the daughter of a Scot and a native woman, and easily gains permission from her father to marry her. While returning to his home in New York, Quaigg treats Tiare roughly; and he throws Captain Croft overboard when he defends her. Boasting that he can tame Tiare with much the same methods he uses with his pet leopard, Quaigg instills fear in her with his whip and by preying on her superstition. Tiare mistakenly shoots Croft, and Quaigg releases the leopard to attack Tiare. The beast turns on its master but is killed by Croft, who returns to the South Seas with Tiare. *Hunters. Halfcastes. Scotch. Superstition. South Sea Islands. Leopards.*

LESSONS IN LOVE **F2.3038**
Constance Talmadge Productions. *Dist* Associated First National Pictures. May **1921** [c5 Apr 1921; LP16356]. Si; b&w. 35mm. 6 reels, 5,923 ft.
Pres by Joseph M. Schenck. *Dir* Chet Withey. *Scen* Grant Carpenter. *Photog* Oliver T. Marsh. *Tech Dir* Willard M. Reineck.
Cast: Constance Talmadge *(Leila Calthorpe)*, Flora Finch *(Agatha Calthorpe)*, James Harrison *(Robert Calthorpe)*, George Fawcett *(Hanover Priestley)*, Frank Webster *(Henry Winkley)*, Kenneth Harlan *(John Warren)*, Florence Short *(Ruth Warren)*.
Comedy. Source: Douglas Murray, *Perkins* (New York opening: 22 Oct 1918). Lawyer Hanover Priestley plots with his friend Henry Winkley to marry off young heiress Leila Calthorpe to Winkley's nephew, John Warren. When John refuses, preferring to select his own wife, they lure him east by a false report of Winkley's death. Indignant at his rebuff, Leila disguises herself as Perkins, a maid, and romances him, leading him to believe that Aunt Agatha is the heiress. Complications develop, and after saving her from a fire John discovers her identity and agrees to marry her. *Heiresses. Aunts. Housemaids. Lawyers. Disguise. Inheritance.*

LET 'ER BUCK **F2.3039**
Universal Pictures. 22 Mar **1925** [c8 Jan 1925; LP21022]. Si; b&w. 35mm. 6 reels, 5,500 ft.
Pres by Carl Laemmle. *Dir* Edward Sedgwick. *Story-Scen* Edward Sedgwick, Raymond L. Schrock. *Photog* Virgil Miller.
Cast: Hoot Gibson *(Bob Carson)*, Marion Nixon *(Jacqueline McCall)*, Charles K. French *(Col. Jeff McCall)*, G. Raymond Nye *(James Ralston)*, William A. Steele *(Kent Crosby)*, Josie Sedgwick *(Miss Mabel Thompson)*, Fred Humes *(sheriff)*.
Western melodrama. Bob Carson works on the the Texas ranch of Colonel McCall, with whose daughter, Jacqueline, he is in love. This romance evokes the anger of her cousin, Ralston, who challenges Bob to a gun duel. During the exchange of shots Ralston pretends to be shot, and Bob runs away, eventually drifting to Pendleton, Oregon, in time for the annual rodeo. There he gets into a fight with Kent Crosby, the foreman of Mabel Thompson's big ranch, and knocks him out, proceeding to ride a bucking broncho that has thrown all previous riders. The two McCalls and Ralston come north for the rodeo and meet Bob, who then learns of Ralston's ruse. Mabel realizes that Bob loves Jacqueline and, in desperation, proposes to him. Bob turns her down and is kidnaped by Ralston and Crosby, to keep him out of the chariot race, but he escapes from his bonds just in time to drive Mabel's team to a close victory. Ralston and Crosby are arrested by the sheriff, and Jacqueline and Bob renew their romance. *Cowboys. Ranch foremen. Rodeos. Kidnaping. Pendleton (Oregon). Texas. Duels.*
Note: Rodeo scenes were filmed at the 1924 Pendleton Round-Up.

LET 'ER GO GALLEGHER F2.3040

De Mille Pictures. *Dist* Pathé Exchange. 15 Jan **1928** [c27 Dec 1927; LP24801]. Si; b&w. 35mm. 6 reels, 5,888 ft.

Assoc Prod Ralph Block. *Dir* Elmer Clifton. *Adapt-Cont* Elliott Clawson. *Titl* John Krafft. *Photog* Lucien Andriot. *Art Dir* Stephen Goosson. *Film Ed* Harold McLernon. *Asst Dir* Gordon Cooper. *Cost* Adrian.

Cast: Junior Coghlan *(Gallegher)*, Harrison Ford *(Callahan)*, Elinor Fair *(Clarissa)*, Wade Boteler *(McGinty)*, E. H. Calvert *(the city editor)*, Ivan Lebedeff *(Four Fingers)*.

Crime melodrama. Source: Richard Harding Davis, "Gallegher: A Newspaper Story," in *Gallegher, and Other Stories* (New York, 1890). Witnessing a murder committed by Four Gingers, a notorious criminal, street urchin Gallegher relates the scene to his friend Callahan, a newspaper reporter. Callahan's scoop gives him a swelled head, which gets him fired and nearly causes him to lose his girl friend, Clarissa; but he answers a call from Gallegher, who has gamely followed Four Fingers and fallen into his hands; and the pair succeed in capturing the criminal. *Street urchins. Reporters. Newspapers. Murder.*

LET HIM BUCK F2.3041

William (Bill) Mix Productions. *Dist* Sanford Productions. 15 Oct **1924.** Si; b&w. 35mm. 5 reels.

Dir Frank Morrow.

Cast: Dick Carter, Gene Crosby.

Western melodrama. "Centers about cowboy whose father is charged with murder of banker. Circumstantial evidence is upset by confessions of villains whom hero tracks down. In locating the murderers, Bill rescues eastern girl visiting there and is rewarded by her acceptance of his proposal of marriage." (*Motion Picture News Booking Guide,* 8:51, Apr 1925.) *Cowboys. Bankers. Murder. Circumstantial evidence.*

LET IT RAIN F2.3042

Douglas MacLean Productions. *Dist* Paramount Pictures. 12 Feb **1927** [c19 Feb 1927; LP23687]. Si; b&w. 35mm. 7 reels, 6,052 ft.

Dir Eddie Cline. *Story-Scen* Wade Boteler, George J. Crone, Earle Snell. *Photog* Jack MacKenzie.

Cast: Douglas MacLean *("Let-It-Rain" Riley)*, Shirley Mason *(The Girl)*, Wade Boteler *(Kelly, a gob)*, Frank Campeau *(The Major of Marines)*, James Bradbury, Jr. *(Butch)*, Lincoln Stedman *(Bugs)*, Lee Shumway *(The Captain of Marines)*, James Mason, Edwin Sturgis, Ernest Hilliarp *(The Crooks)*.

Comedy-drama. "Riley, a marine sergeant and ringleader aboard ship in the traditional warfare between gobs and leathernecks, falls in love with a telephone girl and breaks arrest to go to her when his pet enemy is about to take shore leave. Together they unmask a mail robbery and Riley wins his commission and the girl. A rollicking farce with an adventure finish." (*Moving Picture World,* 12 Mar 1927, p133.) *Telephone operators. United States Navy. United States Marines. Mail theft.*

LET KATY DO IT (Reissue) F2.3043

Fine Arts Pictures. *Dist* Tri-Stone Pictures. **1923.** Si; b&w. 35mm. 5 reels.

Note: A "re-edited and re-titled" film starring Jane Grey and originally released by Triangle Film Corp. on 9 Jan 1916 (c3 Jan 1916; LP8009).

LET NOT MAN PUT ASUNDER F2.3044

Vitagraph Co. of America. Feb **1924** [c10 Jan 1924; LP19821]. Si; b&w. 35mm.

Prod-Dir J. Stuart Blackton. *Scen* Charles Gaskill.

Cast: Pauline Frederick *(Petrina Faneuil)*, Lou Tellegen *(Dick Lechmere)*, Leslie Austen *(Harry Vassall)*, Helena D'Algy *(Felicia De Proney)*, Pauline Neff *(Lady De Bohun)*, Violet De Barros *(Polly De Bohun)*, Maurice Costello *(Sir Humphrey)*, Martha Petelle *(Mrs. Vassall)*, Gladys Frazin *(Gentian Tyrell)*, Homer Lynn *(Chaillot)*.

Society drama. Source: Basil King, *Let Not Man Put Asunder; a Novel* (New York, 1901). Petrina Faneuil, a wealthy but lonely girl, marries a man of equal social status, Harry Vassall. Their friends Dick Lechmere and Felicia De Proney also marry, and thus begin a series of trials within the marriages and external social pressures that eventually cause both couples to divorce. After more misfortune and misery, Petrina and Harry are reunited; but Felicia dies, and Lechmere kills himself out of grief. *Social classes. Marriage. Divorce. Suicide.*

LET US BE GAY F2.3045

Metro-Goldwyn-Mayer Pictures. 11 Jul **1930** [New York premiere; released 9 Aug; c23 Jun 1930; LP1375]. Sd (Movietone); b&w. 35mm. 8 reels, 7,121 ft.

Dir Robert Z. Leonard. *Cont-Dial* Frances Marion. *Adtl Dial* Lucille Newmark. *Photog* Norbert Brodin. *Art Dir* Cedric Gibbons. *Film Ed* Basil Wrangell. *Rec Engr* Karl E. Zint, Douglas Shearer. *Gowns* Adrian.

Cast: Norma Shearer *(Kitty Brown)*, Rod La Rocque *(Bob Brown)*, Marie Dressler *(Mrs. Boucciault)*, Gilbert Emery *(Townley)*, Hedda Hopper *(Madge Livingston)*, Raymond Hackett *(Bruce)*, Sally Eilers *(Diane)*, Tyrrell Davis *(Wallace)*, Wilfred Noy *(Whitman)*, William O'Brien *(Struthers)*, Sybil Grove *(Perkins)*.

Comedy-drama. Source: Rachel Crothers, *Let Us Be Gay, a Comedy* (New York & Los Angeles, 1929). Kitty and Bob Brown part when he begins to take her for granted and engages in a flirtation with a vivacious blonde. Three years later, Mrs. Boucciault, a wealthy and scheming socialite, finds that her granddaughter, Madge, is infatuated with Bob, though she is engaged to Bruce. The society matron calls on Kitty, whom she has met in Paris, to enlist her help in breaking up the infatuation. After mistaking many other men for her prey, Kitty discovers him to be none other than her divorced husband. Difficulties ensue, however, as Kitty becomes the focus of attention for all the male guests, and Mrs. Boucciault spends most of her time chasing them away, finally sending for Kitty's children as a last resort. Consequently, Madge gives up her romance with Bob; and after some persuasion, he regains the affections of his former wife. *Grandmothers. Socialites. Children. Marriage. Divorce. Flirtation.*

LET WOMEN ALONE F2.3046

Peninsula Studios. *Dist* Producers Distributing Corp. 4 Jan **1925** [13 Jan 1925; LP21027]. Si; b&w. 35mm. 6 reels, 5,620 ft.

Prod Frank Woods. *Dir* Paul Powell. *Adapt* Frank Woods. *Photog* Joseph Walker. *Tech Dir* H. S. Wilcox.

Cast: Pat O'Malley *(Tom Benham)*, Wanda Hawley *(Beth Wylie)*, Wallace Beery *(Cap Bullwinkle)*, Ethel Wales *(Ma Benham)*, J. Farrell MacDonald *(Commodore John Gordon)*, Harris Gordon *(Jim Wylie)*, Betty Jane Snowdon *(Jean Wylie)*, Lee Willard *(Alec Morrison)*, Marjorie Morton *(Isabel Morrison)*.

Comedy-drama. Source: Viola Brothers Shore, "On the Shelf," in *Saturday Evening Post* (195:20–21, 22 Jul 1922). After her husband is reported lost at sea, Beth Wylie supports herself and her little daughter with the proceeds of a small interior decorating shop. Beth falls in love with Tom Benham, an insurance agent, and gives his bored mother a job as her assistant. Attempting to sell insurance to gruff Commodore Gordon, Beth's uncle, Tom announces his intention to marry her. The commodore disapproves and sets out to ruin Beth's business. Beth's husband turns out to be alive, engaged in smuggling Chinese into California on a schooner. Wylie kidnaps his wife and sets sail, but the commodore and Tom give chase in a tug. In a thrilling battle, Wylie is killed and Beth is rescued. Tom sells the commodore life insurance and obtains his blessing for a marriage to Beth. *Widows. Insurance agents. Chinese. Interior decorators. Smuggling.*

Note: Known also as *On the Shelf, On the Dotted Line,* and *The Dotted Line.*

LET'S FINISH THE JOB F2.3047

Better Films. *Dist* Phoenix Photoplay Exchange. 28 Apr **1928** [New York State license]. Si; b&w. 35mm. 5 reels.

Melodrama(?). No information about the nature of this film has been found.

LET'S GET MARRIED F2.3048

Famous Players–Lasky. *Dist* Paramount Pictures. ca1 Mar **1926** [New York premiere; released 29 Mar; c31 Mar 1926; LP22560]. Si; b&w. 35mm. 7 reels, 6,800 ft.

Pres by Adolph Zukor, Jesse L. Lasky. *Assoc Prod* William Le Baron. *Dir* Gregory La Cava. *Scen* J. Clarkson Miller. *Titl* John Bishop. *Adapt* Luther Reed. *Photog* Edward Cronjager.

Cast: Richard Dix *(Billy Dexter)*, Lois Wilson *(Mary Corbin, "the only girl")*, Nat Pendleton *(Jimmy, a friend)*, Douglas MacPherson *(Tommy, another)*, Gunboat Smith *(Slattery, an Arm of the Law)*, Joseph Kilgour *(Billy's father)*, Tom Findley *(Mary's father)*, Edna May Oliver *(J. W. Smith)*.

Farce. Source: Henry A. Du Souchet, *The Man From Mexico, a Farcical Comedy in 3 Acts* (New York, 1897). Billy Dexter, celebrating a football victory with his college chums, is arrested for roughhousing. He promises Mary, his girl, that he will reform; and his father presents him with an electric coupe and sends him to J. W. Smith, who proves to be an inebriated woman who sells hymnals. Instead of taking her to a recital, he goes with her to the cabaret from which he was evicted, and she incites a brawl that results in Billy's arrest and imprisonment on Blackwells Island for 30 days. He deceives Mary into believing he is on a missionary tour of the South Seas, then escapes and persuades her to marry him immediately. Their marriage ceremony is repeatedly interrupted by detectives trailing him, but he succeeds in evading them until the nuptial knot is tied. Subsequently, Billy is handed his prison discharge papers. *Students. Salesmen. College life. Prisons. Football. Courtship. Weddings. Blackwells Island.*

LET'S GO *see* **ACTION**

LET'S GO **F2.3049**

Richard Talmadge Productions. *Dist* Truart Film Corp. Nov? **1923** [c1 Nov 1923; LP19683]. Si; b&w. 35mm. 6 reels, 5,198 ft.

Dir William K. Howard. *Story-Scen* Keene Thompson. *Titl* Ralph Spence. *Photog* W. E. Shepherd.

Cast: Richard Talmadge *(Barry Macklin)*, Eileen Percy *(Lucy Frazer)*, George Nichols *(Jake Frazer)*, Tully Marshall *(Ezra Sprowl)*, Bruce Gordon *(Milo Sprowl)*, Al Fremont *(Ollie Banks)*, Matthew Betz *("Dip" McGurk)*, Louis King *(Luke Hazey)*, Aggie Herring *(Mrs. Hazey)*, John Steppling *(Andrew J. Macklin)*.

Action melodrama. Barry Macklin, the worthless son of the owner of a cement manufacturing company, is assigned to visit Hillsboro, a town scheduled for paving. Barry becomes involved in a plot to steal the paving funds from the bank; he suspects the mayor of embezzlement. Finally, when the real thieves turn up to rob the bank, Barry rounds them all up, including the mayor, and marries the new mayor's daughter, thus proving his worth to his father. *Mayors. Filial relations. Bank robberies. Road construction. Embezzlement. Cement.*

LET'S GO GALLAGHER **F2.3050**

R-C Pictures. *Dist* Film Booking Offices of America. 30 Aug **1925** [premiere?; released 20 Sep; c30 Aug 1925; LP21934]. Si; b&w. 35mm. 5 reels, 5,182 ft.

Dir Robert De Lacey, James Gruen. *Story-Cont* Percy Heath, James Gruen. *1st and 2d Camera* John Leezer, John Thompson. *Asst Camera* Buster Sorenson. *Asst Dir* Edward Sullivan. *Propertyman* Joe Thompson. *Utilityman* Louis Shapiro.

Cast: Tom Tyler *(Tom Gallagher)*, Barbara Starr *(Dorothy Manning)*, Olin Francis *(Black [Blackie?] Carter)*, Sam Peterson *(Thug Peters [Perkins?])*, Alfred Heuston *(Bendy Mulligan)*, Frankie Darro *(Little Joey)*.

Western melodrama. Cowboy Tom Gallagher, escaping from a saloon fight with Black Carter and Thug Peters, rescues Little Joey and his dog—who have been sent "parcel post" to Dorothy Manning's Bar M Ranch by her sister—from an approaching train. Tom completes the delivery and is hired by Dorothy as foreman. There he finds Carter and Peters, who have been rustling Dorothy's cattle and stealing right and left from the Bar M. Peters buys up the mortgage and then kidnaps Dorothy when Tom goes away to get the money to pay it off. Tom effects her rescue with the aid of Little Joey and Bendy Mulligan, a rheumatic old cowpuncher. The mortgage is paid off, and Bendy's accidental discovery of oil while taking a mud bath solves Dorothy's financial problems. Dorothy and Tom wed. *Ranchers. Ranch foremen. Cowboys. Rustlers. Kidnaping. Oil lands. Dogs.*

LET'S GO NATIVE **F2.3051**

Paramount-Publix Corp. 16 Aug **1930** [c15 Aug 1930; LP1487]. Sd (Movietone); b&w. 35mm. 9 reels, 6,787 ft.

Dir Leo McCarey. *Screenplay-Dial* George Marion, Jr., Percy Heath. *Photog* Victor Milner. *Songs: "Joe Jazz," "Let's Go Native," "It Seems To Be Spring," "I've Got a Yen for You," "My Mad Moment," "Don't I Do?" "Pampa Rose"* Richard A. Whiting, George Marion, Jr. *Dances & Ensembles* David Bennett. *Rec Engr* Harry D. Mills.

Cast: Jack Oakie *(Voltaire McGinnis)*, Jeanette MacDonald *(Joan Wood)*, Skeets Gallagher *(Jerry)*, James Hall *(Wally Wendell)*, William Austin *(Basil Pistol)*, Kay Francis *(Constance Cook)*, David Newell *(Chief Officer Williams)*, Charles Sellon *(Wallace Wendell)*, Eugene Pallette *(creditor's man)*.

Musical farce. Joan Wood, a modiste who has staked her fortune on a musical revue to be staged in Buenos Aires, finds herself unable to pay the rent of her apartment and fashion shop. Her sweetheart, Wally Wendell, is threatened with disinheritance unless he marries the daughter of a rival soap firm so as to effect a merger. Thus he joins Joan on a ship bound for South America, traveling as a stoker, along with his friend Basil and McGinnis, a cabdriver involved in a traffic accident. They are shipwrecked during a storm and make their way to a tropical island, rich in pearls and oil and lorded over by Jerry, who has educated the natives. Joan sells Jerry her costumes in exchange for the island, and when Wally's father arrives, he sanctions the marriage as a result of the transaction. Joan sells Mr. Wendell the island for $1 million, but a sudden earthquake causes the island to disappear into the ocean. *Modistes. Millionaires. Stokers. Taxi drivers. Real estate. Soap. Earthquakes. Tropics.*

LET'S GO PLACES **F2.3052**

Fox Film Corp. 2 Feb **1930** [c30 Dec 1929; LP1006]. Sd (Movietone); b&w. 35mm. 8 reels, 6,442 ft.

Pres by William Fox. *Dir* Frank Strayer. *Scen-Dial* William K. Wells. *Story* Andrew Bennison. *Photog* Conrad Wells. *Film Ed* Al De Gaetano. *Songs: "Parade of the Blues," "Hollywood Nights," "Reach for a Rainbow," "Out in the Cold," "Um, Um in the Moonlight"* Con Conrad, Sidney Mitchell, Archie Gottler. *Song: "Snowball Man"* James Hanley, James Brockman. *Song: "The Boop-Boop-a-Doopa-Doo Trot"* George A. Little, John Burke. *Song: "Fascinatin' Devil"* Joseph McCarthy, Jimmy Monaco. *Song: "Let's Go Places"* Cliff Friend, Jimmy Monaco. *Dance Dir* Danny Dare. *Sd* Frank MacKenzie. *Asst Dir* William Tummell.

Cast: Joseph Wagstaff *(Paul Adams)*, Lola Lane *(Marjorie Lorraine)*, Sharon Lynn *(Virginia Gordon)*, Frank Richardson *(J. Speed Quinn)*, Walter Catlett *(Rex Wardell)*, Dixie Lee *(Dixie)*, Charles Judels *(Du Bonnet)*, Ilka Chase *(Mrs. Du Bonnet)*, Larry Steers *(Ben King)*.

Romantic musical comedy. Paul Adams, a singer, assumes the name of operatic tenor Paul Du Bonnet and sets out for a career in Hollywood. En route to the coast, he meets Marjorie Lorraine, who falls in love with him, and in Hollywood he occupies the mansion of the famous singer. By the time Du Bonnet arrives, Paul has successfully launched a film career, though he has lost Marjorie because Du Bonnet's wife is claiming him, sight unseen. All is resolved, however, when Du Bonnet discovers Paul to be his long-lost nephew. *Singers. Actors. Uncles. Impersonation. Motion pictures. Hollywood.*

LET'S MAKE WHOOPEE *see* **RED WINE**

THE LETTER **F2.3053**

Paramount Famous Lasky Corp. 13 Apr **1929** [c13 Apr 1929; LP307]. Si; b&w. 35mm. 6 reels, 5,778 ft. [Also si; 5,490 ft.]

Supv Monta Bell. *Dir* Jean De Limur. *Adapt-Scen* Garrett Fort. *Dial* Jean De Limur, Monta Bell. *Titl* Mort Blumenstock. *Photog* George Folsey. *Film Ed* Jean De Limur, Monta Bell.

Cast: Jeanne Eagels *(Leslie Crosbie)*, O. P. Heggie *(Joyce)*, Reginald Owen *(Robert Crosbie)*, Herbert Marshall *(Geoffrey Hammond)*, Irene Brown *(Mrs. Joyce)*, Lady Tsen Mei *(Li-Ti)*, Tamaki Yoshiwara *(On Chi Seng)*, Irene Brown, Kenneth Thompson.

Drama. Source: William Somerset Maugham, *The Letter, a Play in Three Acts* (New York, 1925). Marooned on a rubber plantation in the East Indies, Leslie Crosbie turns to Geoffrey Hammond for the love and diversion that she does not find with her husband. Hammond falls in love with a Chinese woman, however, and Leslie shoots him dead. Placed on trial for her life, Leslie convinces both the jury and her husband that she killed Hammond in defense of her honor. The Chinese woman has an incriminating letter written by Leslie to Hammond, however, and Leslie must pay to recover it. Her husband foots the bill, and Leslie is faced with a bankrupt and loveless future. *Chinese. Planters. Marriage. Infidelity. Blackmail. Murder. Trials. Rubber. East Indies.*

Note: Also produced in a French-language version, *La Lettre*, q. v.

LA LETTRE **F2.3054**

Paramount-Publix Corp. Dec **1930** [New York showing]. Sd (Movietone); b&w. 35mm. 7 reels.

Dir Louis Mercanton. *French Dial Sequences* Roger Ferdinand.

Cast: Marcelle Romée *(Leslie Bennett)*, Gabriel Gabrio *(Philip Bennett)*, Paul Capellani *(Mr. Joyce)*, André Roanne *(George Nelson)*, Princess Hoang Thi The *(Li-Ti)*.

Melodrama. Source: William Somerset Maugham, *The Letter, a Play in Three Acts* (New York, 1925). A French-language version of the 1929 production, *The Letter*, q. v. Scenes from the English-language version were incorporated in the new version. *Chinese. Planters. Marriage. Infidelity. Blackmail. Murder. Trials. Rubber. East Indies.*

LEW TYLER'S WIVES **F2.3055**

Preferred Pictures. 15 Jun **1926** [c4 Aug 1926; LP23000]. Si; b&w. 35mm. 7 reels, 6,757 ft.

Pres by J. G. Bachmann. *Dir* Harley Knoles. *Adapt* Eugene Clifford, Arthur Hoerl. *Photog* William Miller.

Cast: Frank Mayo *(Lew Tyler)*, Ruth Clifford *(Jessie Winkler)*, Hedda Hopper *(Virginia Philips)*, Helen Lee Worthing *(Coleen Miles)*, Lew Brice *(Buzzy Mandelbush)*, Robert T. Haines *(Meech Garrick)*, Warren Cook *(Mr. Philips)*.

Domestic drama. Source: Wallace Irwin, *Lew Tyler's Wives; a Novel* (New York, 1923). Although in love with Virginia Philips, Lew Tyler refuses to be supported by his rich prospective father-in-law, causing her to break the engagement. Thus cast off by Virginia and insulted by her father, Tyler finds distraction in Jessie Winkler, an old friend; and through the efforts of Buzzy, a business partner, Lew and Jessie marry. Their marriage is unsuccessful, and Lew, haunted by the memory of Virginia, seeks forgetfulness in a liaison with Coleen Miles, a neighbor. On the night Jessie sees him with Coleen, their child dies, and Lew remorsefully dulls his sorrow by drinking. Jessie is granted a divorce, and Virginia's father, regretting his treatment of Lew, effects a reconciliation between him and Virginia, and they are married. On the night Virginia's child is born, Jessie comes to nurse her, and Lew humbly seeks a means of reparation for his failure; he agrees to finance a hospital for poor children and thereby ensures her happiness. *Nurses. Fathers-in-law. Drunkenness. Courtship. Marriage. Infidelity. Divorce.*

LIFE OF AN ACTRESS **F2.3056**

Chadwick Pictures. 15 Feb **1927**. Si; b&w. 35mm. 7 reels, 6,400 ft.

Pres by Jesse J. Goldburg. *Dir* Jack Nelson. *Scen* Harvey Gates. *Photog* Ernest Miller.

Cast: Barbara Bedford *(Nora Dowen)*, Bert Sprotte *(John Dowen)*, Lydia Knott *(Mother Dowen)*, John Patrick *(Bill Hawkes)*, Sheldon Lewis *(Hiram Judd)*, James Marcus *(Jacob Krause)*, John Hyams *(Mooch Kelly)*, Bobby Nelson *(Bobby Judd)*, Mary Foy.

Drama. Source: Langdon McCormick, *The Life of an Actress* (a play; c1907). Caught kissing an actor, Nora Dowen is hustled into marrying Hiram Judd, a harsh, miserly elder neighbor, but she soon runs away and joins a traveling group of actors. While trying to make good in her new profession, Nora has a child and sends him to live with her mother. Hiram gets his hands on the boy and tries to teach him to hate his mother. Nora does not progress beyond a "fifth rate" New York company, but she does find happiness as the wife of a former sweetheart when Hiram is killed by a train. *Actors. Marriage. Theatrical troupes. Motherhood. New York City.*

Note: Working title: *Romance of an Actress*.

THE LIFE OF GENEVIEVE **F2.3057**

Sirena Film Co. *Dist* Wanda Film Syndicate. 10 May **1922** [New York State license]. Si; b&w. 35mm. 6 reels, 5,600 ft.

Cast: Lydia Korwin.

Religious drama. No information about the precise nature of this film has been found.

Note: According to the New York State license records, the film was manufactured in 1920 and was intended to be shown in New York State in churches only.

THE LIFE OF RILEY **F2.3058**

First National Pictures. 3 Sep **1927** [New York premiere; released 18 Sep; c8 Sep 1927; LP24377]. Si; b&w. 35mm. 7 reels, 6,712 ft.

Prod E. M. Asher. *Dir* William Beaudine. *Scen* Curtis Benton. *Titl* Gene Towne, Sidney Lazarus. *Adapt* Howard J. Green. *Story* Mann Page. *Photog* Charles Van Enger.

Cast: Charlie Murray *(Timothy Riley, fire chief)*, George Sidney *(Otto Meyer, police chief)*, Stephen Carr *(Steve Meyer)*, June Marlowe *(Molly O'Rourke)*, Myrtle Stedman *(Penelope Jones)*, Sam Hardy *(Al Montague)*, Bert Woodruff *(Aaron Brown)*, Edwards Davis *(John King)*.

Comedy. Meyer, chief of police of Elmdale, and his friend Riley of the fire department are rivals for Penelope, a fascinating widow whom they both escort to the local circus and carnival. There, Molly, a girl who has eluded her guardians, meets Steve, Meyer's son, and the two fall in love. Meanwhile, Meyer and Riley are taken in by a sharper who operates a photo machine and a shell game and has an eye on the widow's wealth. Montague, perceiving that a successful demonstration of Riley's fire extinguisher would spoil his chances with the widow, fills it with gasoline; as a result Montague and the widow are trapped in a burning building. Molly, who has discovered the hoax, proves the worth of the invention and becomes engaged to Steve, while Riley wins the widow. Montague is arrested. *Widows. Firemen. Police. Inventors. Confidence men. Circus. Carnivals.*

THE LIFE OF THE PARTY **F2.3059**

Warner Brothers Pictures. 25 Oct **1930** [c2 Oct 1930; LP1602]. Sd (Vitaphone); col (Technicolor). 35mm. 8 reels, 7,152 ft.

Dir Roy Del Ruth. *Screenplay-Dial* Arthur Caesar. *Story* Melville Crossman. *Photog* Dev Jennings. *Film Ed* William Holmes. *Song: "Can It Be Possible?"* Sidney Mitchell, Archie Gottler, Joseph Meyer. *Songs: "One Robin Doesn't Make a Spring," "Somehow"* Frederick Loewe, Earle Crooker. *Rec Engr* Dolph Thomas.

Cast: Winnie Lightner *(Flo)*, Irene Delroy *(Dot)*, Jack Whiting *(A. J. Smith)*, Charles Butterworth *(Colonel Joy)*, Charles Judels *(Monsieur Le Maire)*, Arthur Edmund Carewe *(fake count)*, John Davidson *(bogus Mr. Smith)*, Arthur Hoyt *(secretary)*.

Musical comedy. Flo and Dot, song pluggers and clerks in a New York music shop, are exact opposites: the latter, beautiful and reserved, and the former, a typical gold digger. Foster, their employer, blames them for poor business and Le Maire, an excitable Frenchman courting their favor, wrecks the shop when asked to leave. Consequently, the girls are fired and take work in Le Maire's modiste shop. After being offered finery for a party, the girls take the clothes and depart for Havana—Dot having been sold on professional gold digging. There, Flo learns that Smith, a soft drink millionaire, is staying in their hotel but mistakes a Colonel Joy as their game; but as the wedding is set for Dot, she learns that Jerry Smith, with whom she is in love, is the actual millionaire. Le Maire arrives and exposes their plotting, but Jerry pays for their trouble and wins Dot as his wife. *Salesclerks. Gold diggers. Millionaires. Song promoters. Modistes. French. Mistaken identity. Music stores. Soft drinks. New York City. Havana.*

THE LIFE OF TIGER FLOWERS *see* **THE FIGHTING DEACON**

LIFE'S CROSSROADS **F2.3060**

Excellent Pictures. 20 Oct **1928** [c1 Nov 1928; LP25799]. Si; b&w. 35mm. 6 reels, 5,355 ft.

Pres by Samuel Zierler. *Dir* Edgar Lewis. *Story-Scen* Eloise Macie Lewis.

Cast: Gladys Hulette *(The Lady)*, Mahlon Hamilton *(The Man)*, William Conklin *(The Stranger)*, William Humphrey *(The Consul)*.

Melodrama. A man and a woman, each heartily disliking the other, are the sole survivors of a shipwreck off the African coast; washed ashore, they walk through the jungle toward civilization, quickly learning to help each other. After 18 days of fever, pain, hunger, and exhaustion, they come across the plantation of a demented scientist, who gives them food and shelter; the scientist takes a fancy to the woman and attempts to kill her disabled companion. The woman kills the scientist, and she and the man find their way to civilization. The woman discovers at the British Consulate that her husband has died, leaving her penniless, but she quickly finds consolation in the arms of the man. *Scientists. Insanity. Jungles. Africa. Great Britain—Diplomatic and consular service.*

LIFE'S DARN FUNNY **F2.3061**

Metro Pictures. 1 Aug **1921** [c25 Jul 1921; LP16807]. Si; b&w. 35mm. 6 reels.

Dir Dallas M. Fitzgerald. *Scen* Mary O'Hara, Arthur Ripley. *Photog* John Arnold. *Tech Dir* A. F. Mantz.

Cast: Viola Dana *(Zoe Robert)*, Gareth Hughes *(Clay Warwick)*, Eva Gordon *(Miss Dellaroc)*, Kathleen O'Connor *(Gwendolyn Miles)*, Mark Fenton *(Prince Karamazov)*.

Comedy. Source: Christine Jope Slade, "Caretakers Within," in *Saturday Evening Post* (193:12–13, 5 Feb 1921). When Zoe Robert, a young violinist, has nothing suitable to wear at a concert, her artist friend Clay Warwick improvises a gown from several yards of brocade to provide a sensation. Considering Clay a genius of design, Zoe takes advantage of the offer of a prima donna's apartment and goes into partnership with Clay to design clothes for wealthy customers. Their materials are charged to the account of the absent friend, but when their customers neglect to pay their bills, a collection agency strips the apartment of its furnishings. All looks bleak until celebrated art critic Prince Karamazov assures their future by ordering a new gown for his daughter. *Violinists. Artists. Couturiers. Critics.*

LIFE'S GREATEST GAME **F2.3062**

Emory Johnson Productions. *Dist* film Booking Offices of America. 28 Sep **1924** [c5 Oct 1924; LP20660]. Si; b&w. 35mm. 7 reels, 7,010 ft.

Dir Emory Johnson. *Story* Emilie Johnson. *Photog* Paul Perry. *Asst Dir* Charles Watt, Jerry Callahan.

Cast: Tom Santschi *(Jack Donovan, star pitcher, and later coach and manager for his town)*, Jane Thomas *(Mary Donovan, his wife)*, Dicky Brandon *(Jackie Donovan, Jr., age 3)*, Johnnie Walker *(Jackie Donovan, Jr., age 20)*, David Kirby *(Mike Moran, sportsman)*, Gertrude Olmstead *(Nora Malone, Jackie's sweetheart)*.

Melodrama. Chicago Cubs pitcher Jack Donovan refuses to throw a game for the benefit of gambler Mike Moran, and the latter gets his revenge by breaking up Donovan's home. Believing his wife and son to be dead in an ocean liner tragedy, Jack goes on in baseball and, 20 years later, is manager of the New York Giants. Jackie, Jr., leaves college, joins the Giants against his mother's wishes, and, recognizing his father, resolves to get even by deliberately losing a World Series game. His sportsmanship comes through, however, and he wins the deciding game against the Yankees and reunites his father with his ailing mother. *Filial relations. Baseball. Sportsmanship. Chicago Cubs. New York Giants. New York Yankees. World Series.*

Note: The cast includes also some 600 spectators in 1906 costume, a group of clever child actors, and other minor characters.

LIFE'S GREATEST QUESTION **F2.3063**

Quality Film Productions. *Dist* C. B. C. Film Sales. 10 Dec **1921** [or 12 Feb 1922?]. Si; b&w. 35mm. 5 reels.

Pres by George H. Davis. *Dir-Story-Scen* Harry Revier.

Cast: Roy Stewart *(Pvt. Dick Osborne)*, Louise Lovely *(Nan Cumberland)*, Harry von Meter *(Julio Cumberland)*, Dorothy Valegra *(Dorothy Cumberland)*, Eugene Burr *(John Carver)*.

Drama. "John Carver looked through the window of a little church in the North woods and saw the woman who had once been his own being made the wife of Julio Cumberland, the most prosperous citizen in the village. He is pursued by Private Dick Osborne, of the Royal Northwest Mounted Police, the lover of Nan's new stepdaughter, who recognizes the uninvited guest and knows Nan's story. Julio regards the conferences of his bride and Dick with jealous suspicion, and while spied upon by the criminal, attacks the officer, leaving him unconscious. Later the bride is found dead, and suspicion points to the officer as her murderer. John is captured and admits his guilt only when Dorothy prevails upon him to save the happiness of herself and the officer by confessing the crime." (*Moving Picture World,* 19 Aug 1922, p610.) *Fugitives. Murder. Northwest Mounted Police. San Francisco.*

Note: Some exteriors filmed in Golden Gate Park and San Francisco area.

LIFE'S MOCKERY **F2.3064**

Chadwick Pictures. 20 Jul **1928** [New York State license]. Si; b&w. 35mm. 7 reels, 5,430-5,700 ft.

Dir Robert F. Hill. *Story-Scen* Isadore Bernstein. *Titl* Leon Lee. *Photog* Ted Tetzlaff. *Film Ed* Gene Milford.

Cast: Betty Compson *(Kit Miller/Isabelle Fullerton)*, Alec B. Francis *(John Fullerton)*, Russell Simpson *(Wolf Miller)*, Theodore von Eltz *(Wade Fullerton)*, Dorothy Cumming *(Gladys Morrison)*.

Drama. "The former warden of the state prison has a theory that a criminal under proper environment can be completely cured. He gains the consent of the governor of the state to try his experiment on the daughter of a notorious gangster Lassen, the girl has been picked up unconscious in trying to escape from the police. When she recovers he leads her to believe that the memories of her past are part of her feverish imagination. Then his son falls in love with the girl, and it works out into a beautiful love story." (*Film Daily,* 29 Jul 1928, p4.) *State governors. Prison wardens. Criminals—Rehabilitation. Memory.*

Note: Also released as *Reform.*

LIGHT FINGERS **F2.3065**

Columbia Pictures. 29 Jul **1929** [c27 Aug 1929; LP648]. Sd (Movietone); b&w. 35mm. 7 reels, 5,700 ft. [Also si; 5,578 ft.]

Prod Harry Cohn. *Dir* Joseph Henabery. *Screenplay-Dial* John F. Natteford. *Story* Alfred Henry Lewis. *Photog* Ted Tetzlaff. *Art Dir* Harrison Wiley. *Asst Dir* David Selman.

Cast: Ian Keith *(Light Fingers)*, Dorothy Revier *(Dorothy Madison)*, Carroll Nye *(Donald Madison)*, Ralph Theodore *(Kerrigan)*, Tom Ricketts *(Edward Madison)*, Charles Gerrard *(London Tower)*, Pietro Sosso *(butler)*.

Crook melodrama. Light Fingers, a brilliant crook, manages to enter the house of the wealthy Madison family in the guise of a magazine writer, enabling him to steal their jewels. The young Donald Madison, who has just lost on the stock market, attempts to take his father's jewels but is prevented by his sister Dorothy. Light Fingers witnesses all this, but since Dorothy discovers that he too wishes to steal the jewels, they agree not to mention the whole incident. Light Fingers, having fallen in love with Dorothy, decides to go straight, but his gang steals the jewels anyway. Light Fingers retrieves them (intending to return them) but is caught by the police and accused of being the thief. Dorothy comes to his rescue, however, and explains the situation to the police, after which the two go out into the garden to attend to pleasant matters. *Criminals—Rehabilitation. Police. Robbery. Brother-sister relationship. Imposture.*

THE LIGHT IN THE CLEARING **F2.3066**

Dial Film Co. *Dist* W. W. Hodkinson Corp. 20 Nov **1921** [c5 Dec 1921; LP17284]. Si; b&w. 35mm. 7 reels.

Prod-Dir T. Hayes Hunter. *Scen* William R. Leighton. *Photog* Abe Scholtz.

Cast: Eugenie Besserer *(Roving Kate)*, Clara Horton *(Sally Dunkelberg)*, Edward Sutherland *(Barton Baynes)*, George Hackathorne *(Amos Grimshaw)*, Frank Leigh *(Ben Grimshaw)*, Andrew Arbuckle *(Horace Dunkelberg)*, Arthur Morrison *(Uncle Peabody)*, Alberta Lee *(Aunt Deel)*, Jack Roseleigh *(Joe Wright)*, Virginia Madison *(Mrs. Horace Dunkelberg)*, J. Edwin Brown *(Squire Fullerton)*.

Melodrama. Source: Irving Addison Bacheller, *The Light in the Clearing* (Indianapolis, 1917). When Barton Baynes's mother and father die, his Aunt Deel and Uncle Peabody provide a home for him. He grows up with Amos Grimshaw, son of a miserly moneylender who holds the farmers of the area in his power, and falls in love with Sally Dunkelberg. Bart becomes friendly with Joe Wright, who arranges for his education in town. There he meets Roving Kate, the Silent Woman, who sees death and the gallows in the palm of Amos and for Bart a future of fame and success. When Kate's fatherless son returns home to see his mother, he is killed by Amos Grimshaw; and Amos' father, Ben, who fights to save him, proves to have been the father of Kate's son. *Orphans. Misers. Moneylenders. Farmers. Parentage. Palmistry.*

THE LIGHT IN THE DARK **F2.3067**

Hope Hampton Productions. *Dist* Associated First National Pictures. Sep-Oct **1922** [c28 Aug 1922; LP18176]. Si; b&w with col sequence. 35mm. 6-8 reels, 5,600-7,500 ft.

Dir Clarence L. Brown. *Scen* William Dudley Pelley, Clarence L. Brown. *Photog* Alfred Ortlieb, Ben Carré.

Cast: Hope Hampton *(Bessie MacGregor)*, E. K. Lincoln *(J. Warburton Ashe)*, Lon Chaney *(Tony Pantelli)*, Theresa Maxwell Conover *(Mrs. Templeton Orrin)*, Dorothy Walters *(Mrs. Callerty)*, Charles Mussett *(Detective Braenders)*, Edgar Norton *(Peters)*, Dore Davidson *(Jerusalem Mike)*, Mr. McClune *(Socrates Stickles)*.

Romantic drama. Source: William Dudley Pelley, "The Light in the Dark" (publication undetermined). Poor Bessie MacGregor is struck by the automobile of wealthy Mrs. Templeton Orrin and is taken home to live with her. But Bessie leaves when Mrs. Orrin's brother, J. Warburton Ashe, trifles with her love. Thief Tony Pantelli befriends her, tries to obtain money for her care from Ashe, and, failing, steals a goblet that Ashe has brought home from Europe. The goblet, which gives off a glow and is reputed to have healing powers, is recovered, stolen again, again recovered and stolen, and finally lost in a river. Meanwhile, Ashe realizes he really loves Bessie, now cured, and they are united. *Thieves. Automobile accidents. Miracles. Holy Grail.*

A LIGHT IN THE WINDOW (Rayart Imperial Photoplay) **F2.3068**

Trem Carr Productions. *Dist* Rayart Pictures. 15 Oct **1927.** Si; b&w. 35mm. 6 reels, 5,960 ft.

Pres by W. Ray Johnston. *Dir* Scott Pembroke. *Scen* Leota Morgan. *Story* Arthur Hoerl. *Photog* Ernest Depew.

Cast: Henry B. Walthall *(Johann Graff)*, Patricia Avery *(Dorothy Graff)*, Erin La Bissoniere *(Maizie)*, Henry Sedley *(Peter Mayfield)*, Tom O'Grady *(Teddie Wales)*, Cornelius Keefe *(Bert Emmonds)*.

Drama. Dorothy Graff, the unsophisticated daughter of a stern, protective cobbler, dreams of wealth and a chance to lead a gay cabaret life, to which a chum introduces her. On one of her nights out she meets Bert Emmonds, they fall in love and elope, and Johann disowns his daughter. Unfortunate circumstances separate the Emmondses, and Dorothy must take a job as a cigarette girl. Bert finally finds her, Johann relents, and all are happily reunited. *Cobblers. Cigarette girls. Fatherhood. Wealth. Elopement. Cabarets.*

THE LIGHT OF WESTERN SKIES *see* **THE LIGHT OF WESTERN STARS** (Entry F2.3070)

THE LIGHT OF WESTERN STARS **F2.3069**

Famous Players–Lasky. *Dist* Paramount Pictures. 22 Jun **1925** [c24 Jun 1925; LP21589]. Si; b&w. 35mm. 7 reels, 6,859 ft.

Pres by Adolph Zukor, Jesse L. Lasky. *Dir* William K. Howard. *Screenplay* George C. Hull, Lucien Hubbard. *Photog* Lucien Andriot.

Cast: Jack Holt *(Gene Stewart)*, Billie Dove *(Madeline Hammond)*, Noah Beery *(Brand)*, Alma Bennett *(Bonita)*, William Scott *(Al Hammond)*, George Nichols *(Billy Stillwell)*, Mark Hamilton *(Monty Price)*, Robert Perry *(Nelse)*, Eugene Pallette *(Stub)*.

Western melodrama. Source: Zane Grey, *The Light of Western Stars, a Romance* (New York, 1914). During a poker game, Al Hammond kills one of Brand's men and flees across the Mexican border, fearing that Brand, a notorious bandit and killer, will attempt to revenge himself. Madeline Hammond, Al's sister, comes from the East and is accosted at the station by Gene Stewart, a drunken gunfighter who has vowed to marry the first white woman he sees. When he discovers who Madeline is, Gene summons decency enough to send for Al's foreman, who escorts her to her brother's ranch. Brand's men run off the Hammond cattle, and Madeline appeals to Gene for help. Sobering up, Gene organizes a posse and recovers the cattle, dispersing Brand's gang. Madeline and Gene fall in love; but when she sees him talking to Bonita, Al's sweetheart, she suspects him of philandering. Gene gets mad and rides over the border. Brand kidnaps Madeline and later captures Gene and Al. Brand sends Al back to his ranch to raise a $10,000 ransom, threatening to kill Gene if he does not return. Al returns with armed men instead of money, arriving just in time to save Gene from death and his sister from certain dishonor. Gene kills Brand, and the outlaw gang is broken up. *Bandits. Ranch foremen. Brother-sister relationship. Posses. Murder. Abduction. Drunkenness. Ransom. Mexico.*

Note: Remade in 1930 under the same title, q. v.

THE LIGHT OF WESTERN STARS **F2.3070**

Paramount Famous Lasky Corp. 19 Apr **1930** [c17 Apr 1930; LP1247]. Sd (Movietone); b&w. 35mm. 8 reels, 6,312 ft. [Also si; 5,035 ft.]

Dir Otto Brower, Edwin H. Knopf. *Adapt* Grover Jones, William Slavens McNutt. *Photog* Charles Lang. *Film Ed* Jane Loring. *Rec Engr* Earl Hayman.

Cast: Richard Arlen *(Dick Bailey)*, Mary Brian *(Ruth Hammond)*, Harry Green *(Pie Pan)*, Regis Toomey *(Bob Drexell)*, Fred Kohler *(Stack)*, William Le Maire *(Grif Meeker)*, George Chandler *(Slig)*, Sid Taylor *(Toe)*, Guy Oliver *(Sheriff)*, Gus Saville *(Pop)*.

Western melodrama. Source: Zane Grey, *The Light of Western Stars, a Romance* (New York, 1914). Dick Bailey's best friend, a young rancher, is killed by a mysterious assailant, whom Dick suspects to be Stack, who is in league with a crooked sheriff. On a spree Dick swears that he will marry the first woman he sees, who happens to be Ruth Hammond, his dead friend's sister, who arrives to take charge of the ranch. Revolted by his rough proposal, she proceeds to the ranch, accompanied by Pie Pan, a local peddler, who offers to hire cowhands for her. When Stack comes to inform Ruth that he has purchased the property for the past-due taxes, Dick intervenes, and she relents and agrees to hire him and his friends. Dick "steals" the gold taken from his friend by the sheriff so as to pay the taxes; he is disheartened, however, by the arrival of Bob Drexell, Ruth's prospective suitor, but their conflict is averted by the posse arriving to arrest Dick. The posse is dispersed by a stampede, and Dick forces a confession from Stack. He wins Drexell's respect and the love of the girl. *Cowboys. Ranchers. Sheriffs. Peddlers. Friendship. Posses. Courtship. Murder. Taxes. Stampedes.*

Note: Remake of the 1925 silent film of the same title. The title *The Light of Western Skies* as rendered in the *Catalog of Copyright Entries* appears to be incorrect.

THE LIGHT THAT FAILED **F2.3071**

Famous Players–Lasky. *Dist* Paramount Pictures. 25 Oct **1923** [New York showing; released 11 Nov; c13 Nov 1923; LP19603]. Si; b&w. 35mm. 7 reels, 7,013 ft.

Pres by Jesse L. Lasky. *Dir* George Melford. *Adapt* F. McGrew Willis, Jack Cunningham. *Photog* Charles Clarke.

Cast: Jacqueline Logan *(Bessie Broke)*, Percy Marmont *(Dick Heldar)*, David Torrence *(Torpenhow)*, Sigrid Holmquist *(Maisie Wells)*, Mabel Van Buren *(Madame Binat)*, Luke Cosgrave *(Binat)*, Peggy Schaffer *(Donna Lane)*, Winston Miller *(Young Dick)*, Mary Jane Irving *(Young Maisie)*.

Melodrama. Source: Rudyard Kipling, *The Light That Failed* (1891). Artist Dick Heldar becomes famous for his wartime sketches and returns to London, where he meets Maisie Wells, his childhood sweetheart, who encourages him to paint a masterpiece. Street urchin Bessie Broke becomes his model for the portrait and falls in love with Dick's friend Torpenhow. Bessie revenges herself on Dick for separating her from her lover by leading Maisie to believe that she is Dick's mistress. Dick finishes the protrait before his failing eyesight—caused by a sabre wound he received in the Sudan—completely deteriorates. Bessie, still angry, destroys the newly finished picture, but later she relents and reveals the truth about her relationship with Dick to the estranged Maisie, who hastens to Dick's studio and dedicates herself to caring for him. *Artists. Models. Blindness. Revenge. London.*

THE LIGHT TO LEEWARD *see* **HOMEWARD BOUND**

THE LIGHTHOUSE BY THE SEA **F2.3072**

Warner Brothers Pictures. 1 Dec **1924** [17 Nov 1924; LP20782]. Si; b&w. 35mm. 7 reels, 6,900 ft.

Dir Mal St. Clair. *Adapt* Darryl F. Zanuck. *Photog* Lyman Broening. *Art Dir* Lewis Geib, Esdras Hartley. *Film Ed* Howard Bretherton. *Asst Dir* Clarence Bricker, Clarence Kolster. *Elec Eff* F. N. Murphy. *Art Titl* Victor Vance.

Cast: William Collier, Jr. *(Albert Dorn)*, Louise Fazenda *(Flora Gale)*, Charles Hill Mailes *(Caleb Gale)*, Douglas Gerrard *(Edward Cavanna)*, Matthew Betz *(Joe Dagget)*, Rin-Tin-Tin *(himself, a dog)*.

Melodrama. Source: Owen Davis, *The Lighthouse by the Sea* (a play; c27 Jul 1920). On the rugged coast of Maine, Caleb Gale, the keeper of the Seville light, has gone blind with age, a fact that is carefully hidden from the authorities by his daughter, Flora, who has assumed his duties. During a storm, Albert Dorn and his dog, Rin-Tin-Tin, are shipwrecked off the coast and rescued by Flora, with whom Albert soon falls in love. One dark night, Joe Dagget, a notorious bootlegger, ties up Albert and knocks out the old man, in order to extinguish the light and run a load of contraband ashore, unseen. Rin-Tin-Tin chews through the ropes that bind Albert, but Albert is soon recaptured. Though bound in chains, Albert still manages to set fire to some waste, which Rin-Tin-Tin uses to ignite the kerosene that fuels the light. When he regains consciousness, the old man frees Albert to give chase to the criminals, who have taken Flora with them. Albert and Rin-Tin-Tin fight with the criminals until the revenue officers arrive, and Albert and Flora are then happily reunited. *Filial relations. Blindness. Bootlegging. Lighthouses. Maine. Shipwrecks. Dogs.*

LIGHTNIN' **F2.3073**

Fox Film Corp. 23 Aug **1925** [c26 Jul 1925; LP21685]. Si; b&w. 35mm. 8 reels, 8,050 ft.

Pres by William Fox. *Dir* John Ford. *Scen* Frances Marion. *Photog* Joseph August. *Asst Dir* Edward O'Fearna.

Cast: Jay Hunt *(Lightnin' Jones)*, Madge Bellamy *(Millie)*, Wallace MacDonald *(John Marvin)*, J. Farrell MacDonald *(Judge Townsend)*, Ethel Clayton *(Margaret Davis)*, James Marcus *(sheriff)*, Edythe Chapman *(Mrs. Bill Jones)*, Otis Harlan *(Zeb)*, Brandon Hurst *(Hammond)*, Richard Travers *(Raymond Thomas)*, Peter Mazutis *(Oscar)*.

Comedy-drama. Source: Winchell Smith and Frank Bacon, *Lightnin'; a Play in Prologue and Three Acts* (New York, 1918). Lightnin' Bill Jones, a man partial to the bottle, does chores and odd jobs around the Calivada Hotel, which is run by his wife and their adopted daughter, Millie. Real estate hucksters, learning that the hotel stands on a proposed railroad right of way, talk Mother Jones into selling the land, but, on the advice of John Marvin, a young lawyer in love with Millie, Bill refuses to sign the bill of sale. Mother Jones orders him from the house, and he goes to live in the Old Soldiers' Home. The schemers persuade Mother Jones to divorce Bill, and she takes him to court. Mother Jones has a change of heart, however, and is reconciled with Bill. The schemers are arrested, and John and Millie become engaged. *Swindlers. Lawyers. Divorce. Hotels. Railroads. Real estate. Soldiers' homes. Trials.*

Note: Remade in 1930 under the same title, q. v.

LIGHTNIN' **F2.3074**

Fox Film Corp. 28 Nov **1930** [New York premiere; released 7 Dec; c31 Oct 1930; LP1729]. Sd (Movietone); b&w. 35mm. 10 reels, 8,500 ft.

Dir Henry King. *Screen Adapt-Dial* S. N. Behrman, Sonya Levien. *Photog* Chester Lyons. *Art Dir* Harry Oliver. *Film Ed* Louis Loeffler. *Mus & Lyr* Joseph McCarthy, James F. Hanley. *Rec Engr* George P. Costello. *Asst Dir* Frank Dettman. *Cost* Sophie Wachner.

Cast: Will Rogers *("Lightnin" Bill Jones)*, Louise Dresser *(Mrs. Jones)*, Joel McCrea *(John Marvin)*, Helen Cohan *(Milly Jones)*, Jason Robards *(Thomas)*, Luke Cosgrave *(Zeb)*, J. M. Kerrigan *(Lem Townsend)*, Ruth Warren *(Margaret Davis)*, Sharon Lynn *(Mrs. Lower, the chiseler)*, Joyce Compton *(Diana)*, Rex Bell *(Ronald)*, Frank Campeau *(Mr. Brooks)*, Goodee Montgomery *(Mrs. Brooks)*, Philip Tead *(Monte Winslow)*, Walter Percival *(Everett Hammond)*, Charlotte Walker *(Mrs. Thatcher)*, Blanche Le Clair *(Mrs. Leonard)*, Bruce Warren *(Mr. Leonard)*, Antica Nast *(Mrs. Lord)*, Moon Carroll *(Mrs. Blue)*, Bess Flowers *(Mrs. Weeks)*, Gwendolyn Faye *(Mrs. Starr)*, Eva Dennison *(Mrs. George)*, Betty Alden *(Mrs. Graham)*, Lucille Young *(Mrs. Young)*, Betty Sinclair *(Mrs. Bigg)*, Roxanne Curtis *(flapper divorcée)*, Thomas Jefferson *(Walter Lannon)*.

Comedy-drama. Source: Winchell Smith and Frank Bacon, *Lightnin'; a Play in Prologue and Three Acts* (New York, 1918). A remake of the 1925 film of the same title, q. v. *Family life. Divorce. Hotels. Nevada. California.*

LIGHTNIN' JACK **F2.3075**

Anchor Film Distributors. 22 Dec **1924.** Si; b&w. 35mm. 5 reels.

Cast: Jack Perrin *(Lightnin' Jack Hardy)*, Josephine Hill *(Mildred Manning)*, Lew Meehan *(Spike Jordan)*, Jack Richardson, Jack Phipps *(The Knowles Brothers)*.

Western melodrama. No information about the precise nature of this film has been found.

LIGHTNIN' SHOT **F2.3076**

Trem Carr Productions. *Dist* Rayart Pictures. May **1928.** Si; b&w. 35mm. 5 reels, 4,797 ft.

Dir-Scen J. P. McGowan. *Story* Victor Rousseau. *Photog* Hap Depew. *Film Ed* Erma Horsley.

Cast: Buddy Roosevelt, J. P. McGowan, Frank Earle, Carol Lane, Jimmy Kane, Tommy Bay, Art Rowlands, Blanco.

Western melodrama. "Two elderly ranchers are engaged in a feud over possession of small strip of property, but this does not prevent their respective son and daughter from being very much in love. Another rancher schemes to obtain same land, indulging in incendiarism, kidnaping and other vicious acts before he is routed, and rival ranchers settle difference amicably." (*Motion Picture News Booking Guide*, [14]:264, 1929.) *Ranchers. Feuds. Incendiarism. Kidnaping. Property rights.*

LIGHTNING **F2.3077**

Tiffany Productions. 15 Jul **1927** [c8 Sep 1927; LP24378]. Si; b&w. 35mm. 7 reels, 6,049 ft.

Dir James C. McKay. *Adapt* John Francis Natteford. *Photog* George Stevens, Winney Wenstrom, Earl Walker. *Art Dir* George E. Sawley. *Film Ed* Leroy O. Lodwig.

Cast: Jobyna Ralston *(Mary Warren/Topsy)*, Margaret Livingston *(Dot Dean/Little Eva)*, Robert Frazier *(Lee Stewart)*, Guinn Williams *(Cuth Stewart)*, Pat Harmon *(Simon Legree)*, Lightning *(himself, a horse)*, Lady Bess *(herself, a horse)*.

Western drama. Source: Zane Grey, "Lightning," in *Hosses* (Charles Wright Gray, ed.; New York, 1927). In the Sevier Mountains of Utah, horsewranglers Lee and Cuth Stewart, famous for their skill, are unable after several encounters to capture the wild stallion Lightning. Later, in Chicago, where they are seeing the sights, the boys meet and flirt with Dot and Mary, two entertainers who are doing a Topsy and Eva act; by their third meeting the brothers are ready to propose, but the girls leave town unexpectedly with their money and no intentions of marriage. Back in Utah, Lightning, attracted to Lee's pet mare, Bess, invades their camp and takes her away. The boys' pursuit leads them into the desert, which the girls are crossing by airplane; after a forced landing, the boys take the girls "prisoner," putting them to work. The girls escape and almost die in a sandstorm, but Lee and Cuth rescue them and also subdue Lightning; all are happily reunited. *Wranglers. Showgirls. Airplanes. Utah. Sevier Mountains. Chicago. Deserts. Sandstorms. "Uncle Tom's Cabin". Horses.*

LIGHTNING BILL **F2.3078**

Goodwill Pictures. 29 Jun **1926** [New York State license]. Si; b&w. 35mm. 5 reels, 4,500 ft.

Dir Louis Chaudet.

Cast: Bill Bailey *(William W. Williams)*, Jean Arthur *(Marie Denton)*, Edward Heim *(John R. Denton)*, Jack Henderson *(Edward G. Hookem)*, Charles Meakin *(Daniel Carson)*, Tom Shirley *(Lionel Jay Murphy)*.

Western melodrama. Lightnin' Bill Williams, who owns a 50,000-acre spread near Cactusville, has lost his nerve after a fall from a cliff. Daniel Carson, an oil promoter, and Lionel Jay Murphy, a geologist, discover oil deposits under Bill's ranch and set out to swindle him. Ed Hookem, one of Bill's ranch hands, hypnotizes Bill, and he reverts to his former fighting self. Bill prevents a dynamite explosion in his well and inadvertently discovers that he has struck oil. Carson and Murphy are driven off, and Bill wins the love of Marie. *Geologists. Swindlers. Ranchers. Hypnotism. Oil wells. Explosions.*

LIGHTNING LARIATS **F2.3079**

R-C Pictures. *Dist* Film Booking Offices of America. 30 Jan **1927** [c3 Jan 1927; LP23504]. Si; b&w. 35mm. 5 reels, 4,536 ft.

Pres by Joseph P. Kennedy. *Dir* Robert De Lacey. *Scen* F. A. E. Pine. *Story* George Worthing. *Photog* Nicholas Musuraca. *Asst Dir* William Cody.

Cast: Tom Tyler *(Tom Potter)*, Dorothy Dunbar *(Janet Holbrooke)*, Frankie Darro *(Alexis, King of Roxenburg)*, Ruby Blaine *(Cynthia Storne)*, Fred Holmes *(Henry Storne)*, Ervin Renard *(First Officer)*, Carl Silvera *(Second Officer)*, Leroy Scott *(Gus)*.

Western melodrama. Following a political coup in the Balkan kingdom of Roxenburg, young King Alexis and his American governess Janet Holbrooke flee to America but are pursued by two Roxenburg officers. Out west, Tom Potter, a rancher, gives them shelter. A neighbor, Henry Storne, holds the mortgage on the ranch but is lenient because of his daughter Cynthia's interest in Tom. Resentful of Janet's presence, Cynthia informs the Roxenburg officers about Alexis, whom they kidnap, but Tom overtakes their car and rescues the boy. Cynthia then induces her father to foreclose on the ranch. During Tom's absence, the Roxenburgians again abscond with Alexis and Janet, but in a desperate ride Tom overcomes the officers. The elder Storne relents in his foreclosure proceedings, assuring the happiness of Janet and Tom. *Governesses. Royalty. Ranchers. Imaginary kingdoms. Mortgages. Kidnaping. Balkans.*

LIGHTNING REPORTER **F2.3080**

Ellbee Pictures. 10 Dec **1926** [New York State license]. Si; b&w. 35mm. 6 reels, 5,415 ft.

Dir-Scen Jack Noble. *Story* Tom Gibson. *Photog* Harry Davis.

Cast: Johnny Walker, Sylvia Breamer, Burr McIntosh, Lou Archer, Nelson McDowell, Joseph Girard, Mayme Kelso.

Melodrama. A young cub reporter helps a railroad president best a competitor in the stock market and falls in love with the president's daughter. *Reporters. Railroad magnates. Stock market. Business competition.*

THE LIGHTNING RIDER **F2.3081**

Stellar Productions. *Dist* W. W. Hodkinson Corp. 18 May **1924** [c18 May 1924; LP20431]. Si; b&w. 35mm. 6 reels, 5,771 ft.

Pres by Hunt Stromberg. *Pers Supv* Hunt Stromberg. *Dir* Lloyd Ingraham. *Titl* Walter Anthony. *Adapt* Doris Dorn. *Story* Shannon Fife. *Photog* Sol Polito. *Film Ed* Laurence Creutz. *Art Titl* Edward Withers.

Cast: Harry Carey *(Philip Morgan)*, Virginia Brown Faire *(Patricia Alvarez)*, Thomas G. Lingham *(Sheriff Alvarez)*, Frances Ross *(Claire Grayson)*, Leon Barry *(Ramon Gonzales)*, Bert Hadley *(Manuel)*, Madame Sul-Te-Wan *(Mammy)*.

Western melodrama. The border town of Caliboro appears to be menaced by a bandit known as The Black Mask. The real culprit, Gonzales, causes deputy sheriff Philip Morgan to lose his job, thus provoking Morgan to track down the bandit in his own disguise. *Sheriffs. Bandits. Disguise. Mexican border.*

LIGHTNING ROMANCE **F2.3082**

Harry J. Brown Productions. *Dist* Rayart Pictures. 15 Nov **1924.** Si; b&w. 35mm. 5 reels, 5,056 ft.

Dir Albert Rogell. *Story* Marion Jackson. *Photog* Ross Fisher.

Cast: Reed Howes *(Jack Wade)*, Ethel Shannon *(Lila Grandon)*, Wilfred Lucas *(Richard Wade)*, David Kirby *(Red Taylor)*, Cuyler Supplee *(Arnold Stewart)*, Frank Hagney *(Arizona Joe)*, H. C. Hallett *(butler)*, Rex *(a horse)*.

Melodrama. " ... concerning the adventures of a young chap who goes in for excitment. His wealthy father's menage is too tame, so he goes to Mexico and takes up with a band of desperadoes. In order to bring him home, his father cooks up an exciting situation in which the boy engages, believing he is facing all the perils and risks to save his father's fortunes. The event leads to a happy love romance with the father's secretary." (*Motion Picture News Booking Guide*, 8:52, Apr 1925.) *Secretaries. Gangs. Family life. Thrill-seeking. Mexico. Horses.*

LIGHTNING SPEED **F2.3083**

FBO Pictures. 26 Aug **1928** [c26 Aug 1928; LP25775]. Si; b&w. 35mm. 5 reels, 4,647 ft.

Story-Cont-Dir Robert North Bradbury. *Titl* Randolph Bartlett. *Photog* Robert De Grasse. *Film Ed* Della M. King. *Asst Dir* Sam Nelson.

Cast: Bob Steele *(Jack)*, Mary Mabery *(Betty)*, Perry Murdock *(Shorty)*, Barney Furey *(Velvet)*, William Welsh *(governor)*.

Action melodrama. Jack Pemberton, a newspaper reporter in love with Betty Standish, the governor's daughter, learns that Velvet, a notorious criminal, is planning to abduct Betty in order to force her father to sign a pardon freeing Velvet's brother, who is in the "big house" waiting to be hanged. Jack tries to warn Betty but to no avail, and she falls into Velvet's hands; Jack later gets on Velvet's trail, and the abductor tries to escape in a balloon. Jack rescues Betty, and Velvet falls to his death. *Brothers. Reporters. State governors. Kidnaping. Capital punishment. Balloons.*

THE LIGHTS OF NEW YORK **F2.3084**

Fox Film Corp. 12 Nov **1922** [c10 Dec 1922; LP18988]. Si; b&w with col sequences. 35mm. 6 reels, 5,581 ft.

Pres by William Fox. *Dir-Story-Scen* Charles J. Brabin. *Photog* George W. Lane.

Cast—First Episode: Clarence Nordstrom *(Robert Reid)*, Margaret Seddon *(Mrs. Reid)*, Frank Currier *(Daniel Reid)*, Florence Short *(Mary Miggs)*, Charles Gerard *(Jim Slade)*.

Cast—Second Episode: Marc MacDermott *(Charles Redding)*, Estelle Taylor *(Mrs. George Burton)*.

Melodrama. Two distinct stories of New York life are told in this film. In the first, Daniel, a foundling, is given a home by Robert Reid, an East Side pawnbroker. He is a good boy but is led astray by evil companions until a dream shocks him into the realization of what his life may become; Daniel then resolves to "go straight." In the second episode, wealthy Wall Street financier Charles Redding plunges into despair and dereliction after he learns of his fiancée's elopement with another man. Sometime later, a bachelor party of 13 brings him in from the street to alter their number. When the guests urge Redding to tell his life story, it is revealed that the host is the son of Redding's former fiancée. She and Redding are then reunited. *Foundlings. Pawnbrokers. Derelicts. Financiers. Bachelors. Dreams. New York City.*

LIGHTS OF NEW YORK **F2.3085**

Warner Brothers Pictures. 6 Jul **1928** [New York premiere; released 21 Jul; c21 Jun 1928; LP25394]. Sd (Vitaphone); b&w. 35mm. 7 reels, 5,267 ft.

Dir Bryan Foy. *Story-Scen-Dial* Hugh Herbert, Murray Roth. *Photog* Ed Du Par. *Film Ed* Jack Killifer.

Cast: Helene Costello *(Kitty Lewis)*, Cullen Landis *(Eddie Morgan)*, Gladys Brockwell *(Molly Thompson)*, Mary Carr *(Mrs. Morgan)*, Wheeler Oakman *(Hawk Miller)*, Eugene Pallette *(Gene)*, Robert Elliott *(Detective Crosby)*, Tom Dugan *(Sam)*, Tom McGuire *(Collins)*, Guy Dennery *(Tommy)*, Walter Percival *(Mr. Jackson)*, Jere Delaney *(Mr. Dickson)*.

Crime melodrama. Eddie Morgan and Gene leave their upstate homes to set up a barbershop in New York City. Two other men, underworld characters Jackson and Dickson, "assist" the young men in their business and secretly turn the shop into a front for bootleg operations. When nightclub owner Hawk Miller, who has framed Eddie with possession of bootleg liquor, is shot with a gun belonging to Kitty Lewis, Eddie's sweetheart, Detective Crosby nearly arrests the threesome, but the victim's discarded mistress, Molly Thompson, confesses to the crime. *Barbers. Mistresses. Prohibition. Bootlegging. New York City.*

LIGHTS OF OLD BROADWAY **F2.3086**

Cosmopolitan Productions. *Dist* Metro-Goldwyn Distributing Corp. 1 Nov **1925** [New York premiere; released 18 Oct or 8 Nov; c5 Nov 1925; LP22049]. Si; b&w. 35mm. 7 reels, 6,595 ft.

Dir Monta Bell. *Adapt-Scen* Carey Wilson. *Photog* Ira H. Morgan.

Cast: Marion Davies *(Fely/Anne)*, Conrad Nagel *(Dirk De Rhondo)*, Frank Currier *(Lambert De Rhondo, his father)*, George K. Arthur *(Andy)*, Charles McHugh *(Shamus O'Tandy)*, Eleanor Lawson *(Mrs. O'Tandy)*, Julia Swayne Gordon *(Mrs. De Rhondo)*, Mathew Betz *(Baby Blue)*, Wilbur Higby *(Fowler)*, Bodil Rosing *(Widow Gorman)*, George Bunny *(Tony Pastor)*, George Harris *(Joe Weber)*, Bernard Berger *(Lew Fields)*, Frank Glendon *(Thomas A. Edison)*, Buck Black *(Young Teddy Roosevelt)*, Karl Dane *(Roosevelt's father)*, William De Vaull *(De Rhondo's butler)*.

Romantic drama. Source: Laurence Eyre, *Merry Wives of Gotham; or, Two and Sixpence; a Comedy in Three Acts* (New York, 1930). Fely and Anne are twins orphaned when their mother dies en route from Ireland to America. Fely is adopted by the O'Tandys, who live in New York's shantytown, and Anne is adopted by the wealthy De Rhondos. Fely grows up without knowing her sister and becomes a dancer in Tony Pastor's theater. Dirk De Rhonde, Anne's stepbrother, is attracted to Fely, and after protecting her during the great Orangemen's riot falls in love with her. She consents to his proposal but later retracts when Dirk's father dispossesses her family. Fely's father, however, becomes wealthy when his investment in Edison's incandescent light pays off, but Dirk's father is ruined. Fely saves De Rhondo's bank from a run by making a large deposit, thus winning over Dirk's family and paving the way for their marriage. *Sisters. Twins. Orphans. Irish. Orangemen. Dancers. Adoption. Electricity. Wealth. New York City—Broadway. Tony Pastor. Joseph M. Weber. Lew Fields. Thomas Alva Edison. Theodore Roosevelt.*

Note: Working title: *Merry Wives of Gotham.*

LIGHTS OF THE DESERT **F2.3087**

Fox Film Corp. 11 Jun **1922** [c11 Jun 1922; LP19136]. Si; b&w. 35mm. 5 reels, 4,809 ft.

Pres by William Fox. *Dir* Harry Beaumont. *Scen* Paul Schofield. *Story* Gladys E. Johnson. *Photog* Frank Good.

Cast: Shirley Mason *(Yvonne Laraby)*, Allan Forrest *(Clay Truxall)*, Edward Burns *(Andrew Reed)*, James Mason *(Slim Saunders)*, Andrée Tourneur *(Marie Curtis)*, Josephine Crowell *(Ma Curtis)*, Lillian Langdon *(Susan Gallant)*.

Romantic western. When the other members of a stranded theatrical company pool their funds to return to San Francisco, Yvonne Laraby remains in Colt City, Nevada, at the request of Andrew Reed, an oil company foreman, to consider his marriage proposal. There she meets oil well owner Clay Truxall, a former acquaintance, who asks her to become his secretary. Yvonne falls in love with Truxall and persuades Reed to return to his sweetheart, Marie Curtis, whom he had deserted for Yvonne. *Actors. Oil magnates. Secretaries. Courtship. Nevada.*

LIGHTS OUT **F2.3088**

R-C Pictures. *Dist* Film Booking Offices of America. 11 Nov **1923** [c21 Aug 1923; LP19329]. Si; b&w. 35mm. 7 reels, 6,938 ft.

Dir Al Santell. *Adapt* Rex Taylor. *Photog* William Marshall.

Cast: Ruth Stonehouse *("Hairpin" Annie)*, Walter McGrail *(Sea Bass)*, Marie Astaire *(Barbara)*, Theodore von Eltz *("Eggs" [Egbert Winslow])*, Ben Deely *("High-Shine" Joe)*, Hank Mann *(Ben)*, Ben Hewlett *(Keith Forbes)*, Mabel Van Buren *(Mrs. Gallant)*, Fred Kelsey *(Decker)*, Harry Fenwick *(Peyton)*, Chester Bishop *(Bangs, a motion picture director)*, Max Ascher *(Wellabach, a film producer)*.

Crook melodrama. Source: Paul Dickey and Mann Page, *Lights Out* (New York opening: 16 Aug 1922). Notorious crooks "Hairpin" Annie and Sea Bass steal a suitcase on the train and discover that it is filled with scenarios. Its owner, Egbert Winslow, agrees to write a screenplay about the underworld with Sea Bass's help. Sea Bass, seeing a chance to expose a pal who has doublecrossed him, describes "High-Shine" Joe and some of his underworld activities. Joe sees the film in a South American theater and recognizes himself. He goes to the motion picture studio determined to kill Egbert Winslow, but bank president Peyton, who has been robbed by Joe, appears simultaneously with the police and saves Winslow. *Motion picture scenarists. Bankers. Robbery. Motion pictures.*

LILAC TIME **F2.3089**

First National Pictures. 18 Oct **1928** [c17 Sep 1928; LP25618]. Mus score & sd eff (Vitaphone); b&w. 35mm. 11 reels, 9,108 ft. [Also si; 8,817 ft.]

Pres by John McCormick. *Dir* George Fitzmaurice. *Scen* Carey Wilson. *Titl* George Marion. *Adapt* Willis Goldbeck. *Photog* Sidney Hickox. *Aerial Photog* Alvin Knechtel. *Art Dir* Horace Jackson. *Film Ed* Al Hall. *Mus* Nathaniel Shilkret. *Song: "Jeannine, I Dream of Lilac Time"* L. Wolfe Gilbert. *Asst Dir* Cullen Tate. *Res* Cullen Tate. *Tech Flight Commander* Dick Grace. *Tech Expert* Capt. L. J. S. Scott. *French Military Expert* Capt. Robert De Couedic. *Ordnance Expert* Harry Redmond.

Cast: Colleen Moore *(Jeannine [Jeannie] Berthelot)*, Gary Cooper *(Capt. Philip Blythe)*, Burr McIntosh *(General Blythe)*, George Cooper *(mechanic's helper)*, Cleve Moore *(Captain Russell)*, Kathryn McGuire *(Lady Iris Rankin)*, Eugenie Besserer *(Madame Berthelot)*, Emile Chautard *(mayor)*, Jack Stone *(The Infant)*, Edward Dillon *(Mike, a mechanic)*, Dick Grace, Stuart Knox, Harlan Hilton, Richard Jarvis, Jack Ponder, Dan Dowling *(aviators)*.

Drama. Source: Jane Cowl and Jane Murfin, *Lilac Time* (New York opening: 6 Feb 1917). Seven young English aviators are billeted at the Berthelot farm near the French front. One of the flyers, Philip Blythe, falls in love with farmer Berthelot's daughter, Jeannie, and on the morning before a dangerous mission declares his love for her. Philip is shot down, and Jeannie helps an ambulance crew to extricate his apparently lifeless body from the wrecked plane. In the following weeks, Jeannie searches in vain in all of the military army hospitals for Philip. She does encounter Philip's father, who, disapproving of her lowly origins, falsely informs her that Philip has died. In farewell, Jeannie sends a bouquet of lilacs to his room, and Philip, recognizing the flowers as her gift, painfully drags himself to his window in time to call her back to him. *Aviators. Farmers. Hospitals. World War I. France. Great Britain—Royal Flying Corps.*

LILIES OF THE FIELD **F2.3090**

Corinne Griffith Productions. *Dist* Associated First National Pictures. 29 Feb **1924** [c4 Mar 1924; LP19965]. Si; b&w. 35mm. 8-9 reels, 8,510 ft.

Supv Earl Hudson. *Dir* John Francis Dillon. *Screenplay* Marion Fairfax. *Scen* Adelaide Heilbron. *Photog* James C. Van Trees. *Architecture* Milton Menasco. *Film Ed* Arthur Tavares. *Song: "I'd Like To Be a Gypsy"* Ned Washington, Michael Cleary. *Fashions* Bates Gilbert.

Cast: Corinne Griffith *(Mildred Harker)*, Conway Tearle *(Louis Willing)*, Alma Bennett *(Doris)*, Sylvia Breamer *(Vera)*, Myrtle Stedman *(Mazie)*, Crauford Kent *(Walter Harker)*, Charlie Murray *(Charles Lee)*, Phyllis Haver *(Gertrude)*, Cissy Fitzgerald *(Florette)*, Edith Ransom *(Amy)*, Charles Gerrard *(Ted Conroy)*, Dorothy Brock *(Rose)*, Mammy Peters *(Mammy)*.

Drama. Source: William Hurlbut, *Lilies of the Field* (New York opening: 4 Oct 1921). Mildred Harker's husband, who loves another woman, finds an opportunity to divorce her. He remarries, taking custody of their child, Rose. Mildred works as a model, but she refuses to succumb to a life of easy virtue when Louis Willing, a wealthy admirer, decides to test her. She accepts his marriage proposal, however, when he convinces her of his love by helping her to regain custody of Rose. *Fashion models. Divorce. Infidelity. Virtue. Motherhood.*

Note: Remade in 1930 under the same title, q. v.

LILIES OF THE FIELD **F2.3091**

First National Pictures. 5 Jan **1930** [c26 Jan 1930; LP1033]. Sd (Vitaphone); b&w. 35mm. 7 reels, 5,979 ft. [Also si.]

Prod Walter Morosco. *Dir* Alexander Korda. *Scen-Dial* John F. Goodrich. *Photog* Lee Garmes. *Song: "I'd Like To Be a Gypsy"* Ned Washington, Herb Magidson, Michael H. Cleary. *Dance Dir* Roy Mack.

Cast: Corinne Griffith *(Mildred Harker)*, Ralph Forbes *(Ted Willing)*, John Loder *(Walter Harker)*, Eve Southern *(Pink)*, Jean Bary *(Gertie)*, Tyler Brooke *(Bert Miller)*, Freeman Wood *(Lewis Conroy)*, Ann Schaeffer *(first maid)*, Clarissa Selwynne *(second maid)*, Patsy Page *(baby)*, André Beranger *(barber)*, Douglas Gerrard *(headwaiter)*, Rita Le Roy *(Florette)*, Betty Boyd *(Joyce)*, May Boley *(Maizie)*, Virginia Bruce *(Doris)*, Charles Mailes *(judge)*, Ray Largay *(lawyer for Harker)*, Joe Bernard *(lawyer for Mildred)*, Tenen Holtz *(paymaster)*, Wilfred Noy *(butler)*, Alice Moe *(maid)*.

Society melodrama. Source: William Hurlbut, *Lilies of the Field* (1921). Innocent Mildred Harker is framed by her husband, Walter, in a divorce suit and loses custody of her child. Disillusioned and heartbroken, she takes up residence in a cheap hotel and becomes a showgirl at the New York Winter Palace Roof, where she meets a group of gold-digging "lilies." Ted Willing, a wealthy man-about-town, becomes her devoted admirer, but she is suspicious of accepting his financial help even when he mentions the whereabouts of her daughter. Later, she discovers that the child has forgotten her, and she accedes to Willing's proposal. During a party, she learns of her child's death, and, grief-striken, she rushes into the streets; she is fined for disorderly conduct, but Willing comes to the police station and she finds comfort in his arms. *Showgirls. Men-about-town. Children. Divorce. Motherhood. Frameup. New York City. Winter Palace.*

Note: Remake of the 1924 film of the same title, q. v.

LILIES OF THE STREETS **F2.3092**

Belban Productions. *Dist* Film Booking Offices of America. 3 May **1925** [c20 Apr 1925; LP21368]. Si; b&w. 35mm. 7 reels, 7,216 ft.

Dir Joseph Levering. *Scen* Harry Chandlee. *Story* Elizabeth J. Monroe. *Photog* Edward Paul, Murphy Darling, Charles Davis.

Cast: Virginia Lee Corbin *(Judith Lee)*, Wheeler Oakman *(Frank Delmore)*, Peggy Kelly *(Nita Moore)*, Johnnie Walker *(John Harding)*, Irma Harrison *(Margy Hopkins)*, Mary E. Hamilton *(Mrs. Hamilton)*, Elizabeth J. Monroe *(herself, Mrs. Hamilton's assistant)*.

Melodrama. Judith Lee, a wild young flapper, is injured in an automobile accident and accepts a ride home in a passing car driven by Frank Delmore, a smalltime hood whose specialty is blackmailing women. Delmore then takes her to an East Side dancehall where he gets into a fight. The police are called, and Judith ends up in jail. Margy Hopkins, Delmore's accomplice and mistress, is arrested along with Judith and persuades the unsuspecting girl to plead guilty to the charge against her. Judith takes the girl's advice, not realizing that she has been charged with prostitution; Delmore then uses Judith's criminal record to blackmail her mother. Delmore is mysteriously killed, and Judith, who believes her mother to be guilty of the murder, falsely confesses to the crime to protect her. Judith is sentenced to be executed, but Mrs. Hamilton, a police matron, persuades Margy, who shot Delmore out of jealousy, to confess to the crime. Judith is freed and, having learned her lesson, gives her heart to John Harding, a conservative young lawyer who worked with much diligence to secure her release. *Flappers. Police. Lawyers. Mistresses. Filial relations. Jazz life. Blackmail. Prostitution. Murder. Capital punishment.*

Note: The film was sponsored by Mrs. Hamilton, a New York policewoman involved in the rehabilitation of wayward girls.

LILIOM **F2.3093**

Fox Film Corp. 5 Oct **1930** [c2 Sep 1930; LP1581]. Sd (Movietone); b&w. 35mm. 11 reels, 8,472 ft.

Pres by William Fox. *Dir* Frank Borzage. *Screenplay-Dial* S. N. Behrman. *Cont* Sonya Levien. *Photog* Chester Lyons. *Art Dir* Harry Oliver. *Film Ed* Margaret V. Clancey. *Orig Mus Score* Richard Fall. *Songs: "Dream of Romance," "Thief Song"* Richard Fall, Marcella Gardner. *Sd Rec* George P. Costello. *Asst Dir* Lew Borzage. *Cost* Sophie Wachner.

Cast: Charles Farrell *(Liliom)*, Rose Hobart *(Julie)*, Estelle Taylor *(Madame Muskat)*, Lee Tracy *(Buzzard)*, James Marcus *(Linzman)*, Walter Abel *(carpenter)*, Mildred Van Dorn *(Marie)*, Guinn Williams *(Hollinger)*, Lillian Elliott *(Aunt Hulda)*, Bert Roach *(Wolf)*, H. B. Warner *(Chief Magistrate)*, Dawn O'Day *(Louise)*.

Romantic allegory. Source: Ferenc Molnár, *Liliom* (1909). Liliom, a merry-go-round barker at a Budapest amusement park, becomes enamored of Julie, a servant girl, and though under the influence of Madame Muskat, a sideshow entrepreneur, he marries the girl. Having not been a good provider, Liliom is spurred into action by the discovery that his wife is pregnant and eventually submits to the influence of Buzzard, who induces him to rob a bank cashier so that he can take Julie to America. But the plan goes afoul, and rather than be caught, Liliom kills himself and is carried by a celestial express to heaven. En route, he is accosted by the Chief Magistrate and is accorded another chance of 10 years on Earth. Julie does not know him, however, and resents his frantic attempts to enter her garden. Time demonstrates that promises of reform are useless, and he is returned to the heavenly train, where the Chief Magistrate convinces him that he can make his wife and daughter happy only by leaving them with cherished memories. *Barkers. Domestics. Courtship. Amusement parks. Merry-go-rounds. Suicide. Heaven. Penance. Budapest.*

Note: A silent version of *Liliom* was produced under the title *A Trip to Paradise* in 1921.

THE LILY **F2.3094**

Fox Film Corp. 3 Oct **1926** [c26 Sep 1926; LP23150]. Si; b&w. 35mm. 7 reels, 6,268 ft.

Pres by William Fox. *Dir* Victor Schertzinger. *Scen* Eve Unsell. *Photog* Glen MacWilliams. *Asst Dir* William Tummell.

Cast: Belle Bennett *(Odette)*, Ian Keith *(George Arnaud)*, Reata Hoyt *(Christiane)*, Barry Norton *(Max de Maigny)*, John St. Polis *(Comte de Maigny)*, Richard Tucker *(Huzar)*, Gertrude Short *(Lucie Plock)*, James Marcus *(Emile Plock)*, Lydia Yeamans Titus *(housekeeper)*, Thomas Ricketts *(Jean)*, Vera Lewis *(Mrs. Arnaud, Sr.)*, Betty Francisco *(Mrs. Arnaud, Jr.)*, Carmelita Geraghty *(old comte's mistress)*, Rosa Rudami.

Romantic drama. Source: Pierre Wolf and Gaston Leroux, *Le Lys*. The Comte de Maigny, father of Odette and Christiane, forces the former to give up her first love for his own selfish reasons; Odette reconciles herself to a loveless life but takes care that a similar fate does not befall her sister. Christiane's love for Arnaud, a married artist, has an unfavorable effect on the courtship of their brother, Max, with a wealthy heiress; furious with his younger daughter, the count is taken to task by Odette for pawning the house furnishings to support his mistress. The artist's wife finally agrees to a divorce, paving the way for Christiane's marriage and for the union of Odette with the family lawyer, who has loved her for years. De Maigny finds consolation with his mistress. *Sisters. Artists. Mistresses. Lawyers. Brother-sister relationship. Fatherhood. Courtship. Marriage. France.*

THE LILY AND THE ROSE (Reissue) **F2.3095**

Fine Arts Pictures. *Dist* Tri-Stone Pictures. **1923.** Si; b&w. 35mm. 5 reels.

Note: A "re-edited and re-titled" Lillian Gish film originally released by Triangle Film Corp. on 12 Dec 1915 (c6 Dec 1915; LP7979).

LILY OF THE DUST **F2.3096**

Famous Players–Lasky. *Dist* Paramount Pictures. 24 Aug **1924** [13 Aug 1924; LP20478]. Si; b&w. 35mm. 7 reels, 6,811 ft.

Pres by Adolph Zukor, Jesse L. Lasky. *Dir* Dimitri Buchowetski. *Scen* Paul Bern. *Photog* Alvin Wyckoff.

Cast: Pola Negri *(Lily Czepanek)*, Ben Lyon *(Richard von Prell)*, Noah Beery *(Colonel von Mertzbach)*, Raymond Griffith *(Karl Dehnecke)*, Jeanette Daudet *(Julia)*, William J. Kelly *(Walter von Prell)*.

Drama. Source: Hermann Sudermann, *Das hohe Lied* (Stuttgart & Berlin, 1908). Edward Brewster Sheldon, *The Song of Songs, a Play in 5 Acts* (c1914). While working in a bookstore Lily meets Prell, a young German officer, who falls in love with her; but the "old man," Mertzbach, hears about her and takes her for his own wife. Finding Lily in the arms of Prell, Mertzbach wounds him in a duel and turns her out. She then accepts the attentions of Dehnecke, and Prell overlooks her liaison; but his uncle refuses to accept her, and she returns to Dehnecke. *Marriage. Infidelity. Germany. Duels.*

THE LIMITED MAIL **F2.3097**

Warner Brothers Pictures. 5 Sep **1925** [c16 Jul 1925; LP21655]. Si; b&w. 35mm. 7 reels, 7,144 ft.

Dir George Hill. *Scen* Darryl F. Zanuck, Charles A. Logue. *Photog* Charles Van Enger, Allen Thompson. *Asst Dir* M. K. Wilson.

Cast: Monte Blue *(Bob Wilson/Bob Snobson)*, Vera Reynolds *(Caroline Dale)*, Willard Louis *(Joe Potts)*, Tom Gallery *(Jim Fowler)*, Master Jack Huff *(Bobby Fowler)*, Edward Gribbon *("Spike" Nelson)*, Otis Harlan *(Mr. Joffrey)*, Lydia Yeamans Titus *(Mrs. O'Leary)*.

Melodrama. Source: Elmer E. Vance, *The Limited Mail: A Realistic Picture of Life on the Rail. A Comedy-drama in Four Acts* (1889). Bob Wilson, who becomes a tramp after being jilted by his fiancée, prevents the Limited Mail from being wrecked during a mountain storm and becomes fast friends with Jim Fowler, a railway mail clerk. Jim gets Bob a job on the railroad, and Bob works himself up to the position of engineer on the Limited. Both of the men fall in love with Caroline Dale, but she prefers Bob. A runaway freight runs into the Limited, and Jim is killed. Bob becomes a tramp again, making pals with an ex-convict. When the sides of a tunnel give way, Bob again prevents a train wreck and is reunited with Caroline, who is a passenger on the train. Jim's son, Bobby, is saved from drowning in a mountain stream by the ex-con, and Bob and Caroline make plans to be married. *Railroad engineers. Railway mail clerks. Tramps. Postal service. Tunnels. Train wrecks.*

LINDA **F2.3098**

Mrs. Wallace Reid Productions. *Dist* Willis Kent Productions. 1 Apr **1929** [New York showing; c7 Dec 1928; LP25897]. Mus score & sd eff (Vitaphone); b&w. 35mm. 7 reels.

Pres by Willis Kent. *Dir* Mrs. Wallace Reid. *Screenplay* Wilfred Noy. *Titl* Ruth Todd. *Adapt* Maxine Alton, Frank O'Connor. *Photog* Henry Cronjager, Bert Baldridge, Ernest Laszlo. *Film Ed* Willis Kent. *Song: "Linda"* Al Sherman, Charles Tobias, Harry Tobias. *Asst Dir* Walter Sheridan. *Prod Mgr* Cliff Broughton.

Cast: Warner Baxter *(Dr. Paul Randall)*, Helen Foster *(Linda)*, Noah Beery *(Decker)*, Mitchell Lewis *(Stillwater)*, Kate Price *(Nan)*, Allan Connor *(Kenneth Whittmore)*, Bess Flowers *(Annette Whittmore)*.

Melodrama. Source: Margaret Prescott Montague, *Linda* (Boston & New York, 1912). Linda, a tender, romantic girl, is forced by her brutal father to marry Decker, an elderly lumberman who quickly realizes that Linda is not happy with him and does everything he can to make her life easier. Linda falls in love with Dr. Randall but remains with her husband until a scheming woman steps in and claims to be Decker's first and legal wife. Linda then goes to the city to live with her former schoolteacher and again meets Dr. Randall, but she must leave him to return north and care for Decker, who has been hurt in a lumbering accident. Learning that the woman claiming to be Decker's wife is a fraud, Linda gallantly sticks with her husband until he finally dies from his injuries. Linda and the good doctor are then free to find happiness with each other. *Physicians. Lumbermen. Schoolteachers. Marriage. Bigamy.*

LINGERIE **F2.3099**

Tiffany-Stahl Productions. 1 Jul **1928** [c3 Jul 1928; LP25427]. Si; b&w. 35mm. 6 reels, 5,676 ft.

Dir George Melford. *Story-Scen* John Francis Natteford. *Titl* Ben Grauman Kohn. *Photog* Jackson Rose. *Art Dir* Hervey Libbert. *Set Dsgn* George Sawley. *Film Ed* Byron Robinson.

Cast: Alice White *(Angele Ree ["Lingerie"])*, Malcolm McGregor *(Leroy Boyd)*, Mildred Harris *(Mary [or Rosemary])*, Armand Kaliz *(Jack Van Cleve)*, Cornelia Kellog *(Mary's mother)*, Kit Guard, Victor Potel *(Slim and Handsome, Leroy's buddies)*, Richard Carlyle *(Pembroke)*, Marcelle Corday *(modiste)*.

War drama. Leroy Boyd joins the Army when he discovers that Rosemary, his bride, is unfaithful and has married him for his money. In Paris, Boyd falls in love with a French girl whom he calls Lingerie. Sent home because he is seriously wounded, Boyd, paralyzed and unable to speak or hear, slowly recovers. While Rosemary is having an affair with her lover, Lingerie, now working in the Boyd household, helps to restore Boyd to health. When he is almost fully recovered, Boyd throws Rosemary and John, the lover, out of his house and marries Lingerie. *Soldiers. French. Infidelity. Paralysis. World War I. Paris.*

THE LION AND THE MOUSE **F2.3100**

Warner Brothers Pictures. 21 May **1928** [c21 May 1928; LP25280]. Sd (Vitaphone); b&w. 35mm. 7 reels, 6,352 ft.

Dir Lloyd Bacon. *Scen-Dial* Robert Lord. *Titl* James A. Starr. *Story* Charles Klein. *Photog* Norbert Brodin. *Film Ed* Harold McCord. *Rec Engr* George R. Groves. *Asst Dir* Frank Shaw.

Cast: May McAvoy *(Shirley Ross)*, Lionel Barrymore *("Ready Money" Ryder)*, Alec Francis *(Judge Ross)*, William Collier, Jr. *(Jeff Ryder)*, Emmett Corrigan *(Dr. Hays)*, Jack Ackroyd *(Smith, Jeff's valet)*.

Drama. John "Ready Money" Ryder, a financial genius, attempts to ruin a judge by alleging that the judge accepted a bribe of some oil stock. Actually, Judge Ross bought the stock at Ryder's recommendation. Ryder, the only person who can exonerate Judge Ross, withholds a letter proving purchase because he feels that Ross wrongly decided a case against him. Judge Ross is cleared through his daughter's efforts, and the two men are reconciled by the marriage of Ross's daughter to Ryder's son. *Judges. Financiers. Bribery. Oil business.*

LISTEN LESTER **F2.3101**

Sacramento Pictures. *Dist* Principal Pictures. 20 May **1924.** Si; b&w. 35mm. 6 reels, 6,242 ft.

Dir William A. Seiter. *Adapt* Louise Milestone, William A. Seiter. *Photog* John Stumar. *Film Ed* Owen Marks. *Asst Dir* Nate Watt.

Cast: Louise Fazenda *(Arbutus Quilty)*, Harry Myers *(Listen Lester)*, Eva Novak *(Mary Dodge)*, George O'Hara *(Jack Griffin)*, Lee Moran *(William Penn)*, Alec Francis *(Colonel Dodge)*, Dot Farley *(Miss Pink)*.

Comedy-drama. Source: Harry Linsley Cort, G. E. Stoddard and Harold Orlog, *Listen Lester* (a play; New York, 1918?). Colonel Dodge, a gay old widower, goes to Florida with his daughter, Mary, when Miss Arbutus Quilty, one of his former flames, threatens him with a breach-of-promise suit. He hires Miss Pink, a lady detective, to retrieve a packet of incriminating letters Miss Quilty plans to use as evidence, but Miss Quilty follows him to Florida. Listen Lester, a house detective at the resort where Dodge and Mary stay, becomes involved in the plan to recover the letters.

After a series of complications, Dodge decides to settle down with Miss Quilty and Mary weds Lester. *Widowers. Detectives. Filial relations. Breach of promise. Florida. Documentation.*

THE LITTLE ACCIDENT **F2.3102**

Universal Pictures. 1 Aug **1930** [New York premiere; released 1 Sep; c2 Aug 1930; LP1455]. Sd (Movietone); b&w. 35mm. 9 reels, 7,897 ft. [Also si; 7,289 ft.]

Pres by Carl Laemmle. *Assoc Prod* Albert De Mond. *Dir* William James Craft. *Screenplay* Gladys Lehman. *Dial* Anthony Brown. *Photog* Roy Overbaugh. *Film Ed* Harry Lieb. *Rec Engr* C. Roy Hunter.

Cast: Douglas Fairbanks, Jr. *(Norman)*, Anita Page *(Isabel)*, Sally Blane *(Madge)*, ZaSu Pitts *(Monica)*, Joan Marsh *(Doris)*, Roscoe Karns *(Gilbert)*, Slim Summerville *(Hicks)*, Henry Armetta *(Rudolpho Amendelara)*, Myrtle Stedman *(Mrs. Overbeck)*, Nora Cecil *(Dr. Zernecke)*, Bertha Mann *(Miss Hemingway)*, Gertrude Short *(Miss Clark)*, Dot Farley *(Mrs. Van Dine)*.

Comedy-drama. Source: Floyd Dell and Thomas Mitchell, *The Little Accident* (New York opening: 9 Oct 1928). Floyd Dell, *An Unmarried Father* (New York, 1927). On the day before his scheduled marriage to Madge, Norman Overbeck receives a letter from a maternity hospital in Chicago, and later he learns that he is the father of a 3-week-old boy. He suddenly leaves for Chicago, confiding in his friend Gilbert that a year ago he secretly married Isabel Drury in Boston and that she had the marriage annulled. Arriving at the hospital, Norman is subjected to a physical examination; in a reception room he meets Hicks, an expectant father, and Rudolpho, who is waiting to take home his wife and child. Norman denounces Isabel for letting the child out for adoption, and through a ruse, he kidnaps his own child and engages Monica, a wet nurse, to care for it. Monica offers to marry him, then Isabel changes her mind about adoption and demands her child. Matters are further complicated by the arrival of Madge; after much disputation, Norman and Isabel decide to start again. *Wet nurses. Infants. Fatherhood. Marriage—Annulment. Adoption. Hospitals.*

THE LITTLE ADVENTURESS **F2.3103**

De Mille Pictures. *Dist* Producers Distributing Corp. 11 Apr **1927** [c4 Apr 1927; LP23839]. Si; b&w. 35mm. 7 reels, 6,200 ft.

Pres by John C. Flinn. *Dir* William De Mille. *Adapt-Cont* Clara Beranger. *Photog* Charles Boyle. *Art Dir* Anton Grot. *Film Ed* Adelaide Cannon. *Asst Dir* Lidel Beck. *Prod Mgr* Morton S. Whitehill. *Cost* Adrian.

Cast: Vera Reynolds *(Helen Davis)*, Phyllis Haver *(Victoria Stoddard)*, Robert Ober *(Leonard Stoddard)*, Theodore Kosloff *(Antonio Russo)*, Victor Varconi *(George La Fuente)*, Fred Walton *(Dominick)*.

Domestic comedy. Source: Alan Alexander Milne, *The Dover Road, an Absurd Comedy in Three Acts* (New York, 1923). After 5 years of married life, Leonard Stoddard leaves his Victoria in tears and goes to the studio of Helen Davis, an artist, for sympathy. Believing that he loves her, Helen agrees to run away with him. Victoria, meanwhile, takes her troubles to Antonio Russo, an actor, and they also decide to run away. Helen and Leonard become stranded and are put up at the ranch of George La Fuente, a wealthy bachelor; and soon after, Victoria and Antonio arrive, lost and in quest of lodging. At dinner, Victoria and Leonard pretend to be strangers. Later, recriminations follow, but La Fuente intervenes and demands that they retire to their respective rooms. The following day, Victoria sympathizes with her husband, who has contracted a cold; but she is at last forced to accept La Fuente's declaration of love. *Adventuresses. Artists. Actors. Ranchers. Bachelors. Infidelity. Marriage.*

LITTLE ANNIE ROONEY **F2.3104**

Mary Pickford Co. *Dist* United Artists. 18 Oct **1925** [c8 Sep 1925; LP21807]. Si; b&w. 35mm. 9 reels, 8,850 ft.

Dir William Beaudine. *Titl* Tom McNamara. *Adapt* Hope Loring, Louis D. Lighton. *Story* Katherine Hennessey. *Photog* Charles Rosher, Hal Mohr. *Art Dir* John D. Schulze, Harry Oliver, Paul Youngblood. *Elec Eff* William S. Johnson.

Cast: Mary Pickford *(Little Annie Rooney)*, William Haines *(Joe Kelly)*, Walter James *(Officer Rooney)*, Gordon Griffith *(Tim Rooney)*, Carlo Schipa *(Tony)*, Spec O'Donnell *(Abie)*, Hugh Fay *(Spider)*, Vola Vale *(Mamie)*, Joe Butterworth *(Mickey)*, Eugene Jackson *(Humidor)*, Oscar Rudolph *(Athos)*.

Comedy-drama. Little Annie Rooney, the daughter of a policeman, divides her time between getting into mischief and caring for her father and her brother, Tim. Annie's father is killed in a gang brawl, and Annie and Tim become intent on revenge. When they learn that Joe Kelly, the apple of Annie's eye, has been blamed for the murder, Tim takes his father's gun and shoots him. Meanwhile, in the company of a band of neighborhood ruffians, Annie captures the real killer. Annie goes to the hospital where Joe lies fighting for his life and consents to a blood transfusion that saves him. Joe recovers and goes into the trucking business; Tim becomes a traffic cop. *Police. Filial relations. Brother-sister relationship. Murder. Revenge. Blood transfusion.*

LITTLE BIT OF HEAVEN *see* **A BIT OF HEAVEN**

THE LITTLE BOSS **F2.3105**

Ward Lascelle Productions. 21 Apr **1927** [New York State license]. Si; b&w. 35mm. 5 reels, 4,800 ft

Cast: Ruth Mix.

Western melodrama. No information about the precise nature of this film has been found.

THE LITTLE BUCKAROO **F2.3106**

FBO Pictures. 25 Feb **1928** [New York premiere; released 11 Mar; c1 Feb 1928; LP24934]. Si; b&w. 35mm. 5 reels, 4,801 ft.

Dir Louis King. *Story-Cont* Frank Howard Clark. *Photog* Roy Eslick. *Film Ed* Della M. King. *Asst Dir* Sam Nelson.

Cast: Buzz Barton *(David "Red" Hepner)*, Milburn Morante *(Toby Jones)*, Kenneth McDonald *(Jack Pemberton)*, Peggy Shaw *(Ann Crawford)*, Al Ferguson *(Luke Matthews)*, Walter Maly *(Sam Baxter)*, Robert Burns *(Al Durking, the sheriff)*, Florence D. Lee *(Mrs. Durking)*, James Welch *(Jim Crawford)*.

Western melodrama. In the desert, Red Hepner and his pal, Toby Jones, find by the body of a prospector a canteen on which a scratched message indicates that the dead man had been robbed and murdered and requests that the finder take care of a surviving daughter, Ann Crawford. Red and Toby, accompanied by Jack Pemberton, an old friend, proceed to Dugan's halfway house after rescuing Ann Crawford during a stage holdup. Pemberton marries Ann to prevent the ruffians at the halfway house from molesting her, but he promises to give her an annulment in the next town. At Ohi, Red and Toby overhear Luke Matthews, owner of the stageline (whom they suspect to be Jim Crawford's murderer), plan a fake holdup of the stage. Though their first attempt to prevent the holdup is unsuccessful, Red and Toby later capture the stagecoach driver (Baxter) and the bandits and bring them to Ohi. There Matthews, having accused Pemberton of murdering Crawford, has turned Pemberton over to a lynching party. Baxter and the bandits admit that Matthews is their leader; the authorities exchange Pemberton for Matthews; and Toby and Red ride off while Pemberton settles down with Ann. *Prospectors. Murder. Marriage of convenience. Stagecoach robberies. Lynching.*

A LITTLE CHILD SHALL LEAD THEM *see* **WHO ARE MY PARENTS?**

LITTLE CHURCH AROUND THE CORNER **F2.3107**

Warner Brothers Pictures. ca18 Mar **1923** [Omaha premiere; released 1 Apr; c15 Jan 1923; LP18673]. Si; b&w. 35mm. 6 reels, 6,300 ft.

Dir William A. Seiter. *Adapt* Olga Printzlau. *Photog* Homer Scott, E. B. Du Par. *Set Dsgn* Lewis Geib. *Film Ed* C. R. Wallace. *Elec Eff* F. N. Murphy.

Cast: Claire Windsor *(Leila Morton)*, Kenneth Harlan *(David Graham)*, Hobart Bosworth *(Morton)*, Walter Long *(Hex)*, Pauline Starke *(Hetty)*, Alec Francis *(Reverend Bradley)*, Margaret Seddon *(Mrs. Graham)*, George Cooper *(Jude)*, Winter Hall *(Doc Graham)*, Cyril Chadwick *(Mark Hanford)*, Fred Stanton, Winston Miller, Mary Jane Irving.

Drama. Source: Marion Russell, *Little Church Around the Corner; A Comedy-Drama in Four Acts* (c27 Oct 1902). Orphaned as a result of a mine explosion, David Graham educates himself for the ministry with the help of Morton, a mine-owner. David accepts a position in a wealthy church, of which Morton is a member, in hopes of persuading his parishioners to improve the conditions of the miners. When Morton refuses to repair a mine shaft, David returns to his people. There is an explosion in which Morton and his daughter are trapped. David saves them and brings peace between Morton and the angry miners. *Clergymen. Mining. Social consciousness. Mine disasters. Safety—Industrial.*

THE LITTLE CLOWN **F2.3108**

Realart Pictures. Mar **1921** [c3 Mar 1921; LP16227]. Si; b&w. 35mm. 5 reels, 5,031 ft.

Dir Thomas N. Heffron. *Scen* Eugene B. Lewis. *Photog* Faxon M. Dean.

Cast: Mary Miles Minter *(Pat)*, Jack Mullhall *(Dick Beverley)*, Winter Hall *(Colonel Beverley)*, Helen Dunbar *(Mrs. Beverley)*, Cameron Coffey *(Roddy Beverley)*, Neely Edwards *(Toto)*, Wilton Taylor *(Jim Anderson)*, Lucien Littlefield *(Connie Potts)*, Zelma Maja *(Liz)*, Laura Anson *(Nellie Johnson)*.

Comedy-melodrama. Source: Avery Hopwood, *The Little Clown; a Comedy in Three Acts* (New York, 1934). Pat, an orphan born and reared in the circus, is the protégée of Toto, the clown, who cherishes the hope of marrying her. In a southern town, Pat meets Dick Beverley, son of an aristocratic family, who joins the circus as a trick rider after a quarrel with his parents, and the two fall in love. Although finally accepted by the Beverleys, she is required to learn the social graces in their home. When her circus friends pay a visit, they are expelled for being intoxicated, but when Dick's younger brother confesses to spiking the punch all is forgiven and the couple are married. *Clowns. Equestrians. Circus. Class conflict. United States—South.*

LITTLE EVA ASCENDS **F2.3109**

S-L Pictures. *Dist* Metro Pictures. 8 Jan **1922** [c20 Jan 1922; LP17486]. Si; b&w. 35mm. 5 reels, 4,901 ft.

Dir George D. Baker. *Photog* Rudolph Berquist. *Art Dir* E. J. Shulter.

Cast: Gareth Hughes *(Roy St. George [Little Eva])*, Eleanor Fields *(Mattie Moore)*, May Collins *(Priscilla Price)*, Unice Vin Moore *(Blanche St. George [Eliza; Mrs. St. Clair])*, Benjamin Haggerty *(John St. George [Uncle Tom])*, Edward Martindel *(Mr. Wilson)*, Harry Lorraine *(Junius Brutus)*, Mark Fenton *(Mr. Moore)*, John Prince *(Mr. Price)*, Fred Warren *(Montgomery Murphy)*, W. H. Brown *(Richard Bansfield [Aunt Chloe])*.

Comedy-drama. Source: Thomas Beer, "Little Eva Ascends," in *Saturday Evening Post* (193:16–17, 9 Apr 1921). John, who plays Uncle Tom, and Roy, who plays Little Eva, are the sons of Blanche St. George, owner and leading lady of a repertory company that presents *Uncle Tom's Cabin* in tank towns; and both boys dislike their stage life. Roy is particularly sensitive about his role, since his girl lives in a nearby town. The troupe registers in a Connecticut village at the only hotel, where John notices his mother's agitation at meeting the proprietor, Mr. Wilson. John later learns that Wilson is their father, whom Blanche has left to pursue her career. John confesses his longing for a real life but is obligated to stay with Blanche until she can earn the money to buy the opera house. At the performance Roy acts Eva under protest, and all goes well until his ascent, which is jeered by the gallery; removing his wig, Roy escapes and heads for Wilson's farm. Wilson offers Blanche funds for her opera house in exchange for the boys, and the family is happily reunited. *Actors. Careerwomen. Family life. Theatrical troupes. Connecticut. "Uncle Tom's Cabin".*

THE LITTLE FIREBRAND **F2.3110**

Hurricane Film Corp. *Dist* Pathé Exchange. 3 Jul **1927** [c13 Aug 1925, 10 May 1927; LU21716, LU23951]. Si; b&w. 35mm. 5 reels, 4,615 ft.

Pres by William Steiner. *Dir* Charles Hutchison. *Story-Scen* Frederic Chapin.

Cast: Edith Thornton *(Dorothy Jackson)*, George Fawcett *(Godfrey Jackson)*, Lou Tellegen *(Harley Norcross)*, Eddie Phillips *(William)*, Joan Standing *(Miss Smyth)*, Lincoln Stedman *(Tubby)*, Gino Corrado *(Adonis Wenhoff)*, Helen Crawford *(maid)*, Ben Walker *(butler)*.

Comedy-drama. Multimillionaire Godfrey Jackson is unable to control his unruly, motherless daughter, Dorothy. He appoints Harley Norcross, a junior member of his law firm, as her guardian while he is away on business. Overhearing a disparaging remark Norcross makes about her, Dorothy vows that he will pay for it. Norcross lays down strict rules of conduct for the girl, forbidding her to drive, to attend dances, or to see her suitor, William. She proceeds to break all the rules, and as time passes, each begins to fall in love with the other. Dorothy inveigles Norcross into her car and gives him a hair-raising ride climaxed by a crash; she declares her love when she believes him unconscious; the couple are united. *Millionaires. Lawyers. Guardians. Adolescence. Filial relations. Courtship. Automobile accidents.*

Note: Some discrepancy in credits occurs because of the two widely-separated copyrights: Gino Corrado, for instance may not have appeared in the film's released version, and Harley may be Hartly.

THE LITTLE FRENCH GIRL **F2.3111**

Famous Players–Lasky. *Dist* Paramount Pictures. 18 May **1925** [c21 May 1925; LP21488]. Si; b&w. 35mm. 6 reels, 5,628 ft.

Pres by Adolph Zukor, Jesse L. Lasky. *Dir* Herbert Brenon. *Screenplay* John Russell. *Photog* Hal Rosson. *Art Dir* Frederick A. Foord.

Cast: Alice Joyce *(Madame Vervier)*, Mary Brian *(Alix Vervier)*, Neil Hamilton *(Giles Bradley)*, Esther Ralston *(Toppie Westmacott)*, Anthony Jowitt *(Owen Bradley)*, Jane Jennings *(Mother Bradley)*, Mildred Ryan *(Ruth Bradley)*, Eleanor Shelton *(Rosemary Bradley)*, Maurice Cannon *(Jerry Hamble)*, Maude Turner Gordon *(Lady Mary Hamble)*, Paul Doucet *(André Valenbois)*, Julia Hurley *(Madame Dumont)*, Mario Majeroni *(De Maubert)*.

Romantic drama. Source: Anne Douglas Sedgwick, *The Little French Girl* (New York, 1924). During the Great War, Owen Bradley neglects his fiancée, Toppie, in order to spend his leave with Madame Vervier, a mature and beautiful Frenchwoman. When Owen is killed, his brother, Giles, takes Alix Vervier, Madame Vervier's daughter, to England in order to introduce her to the Bradley family, thereby fulfilling a promise he once made to Owen. Alix is soon a favorite and becomes engaged to a viscount. Toppie later decides to enter a convent, and Giles, who has always been fond of her, declares his love; Toppie, however, cannot be dissuaded from a religious vocation by his pleas, so Alix, out of friendship for both Giles and Toppie, tells her the truth about Owen and Madame Vervier. Toppie denounces Madame Vervier and takes the veil. The viscount learns of the uncertain reputation of Alix' mother and breaks off the engagement. Alix returns to France, where she is soon joined by Giles, who declares his love for her and thus makes her a very happy little French girl. *Brothers. Nuns. Nobility. Parentage. World War I. France. England.*

THE LITTLE GIANT (Universal-Jewel) **F2.3112**

Universal Pictures. 3 Jan **1926** [c5 Oct 1925; LP21879]. Si; b&w. 35mm. 7 reels, 6,850 ft.

Dir-Adapt William Nigh. *Scen* Walter De Leon. *Photog* Sid Hickox.

Cast: Glenn Hunter *(Elmer Clinton)*, Edna Murphy *(Myra Clinton)*, David Higgins *(Uncle Clem)*, James Bradbury, Jr. *(Brad)*, Jean Jarvis *(Olga)*, Leonard Meeker *(Royce)*, Louise Mackintosh *(Mrs. Dansey)*, Thomas McGuire *(Mr. Dansey)*, Dodson Mitchell *(Mr. Enfield)*, Peter Raymond *(Dr. Porter)*.

Comedy-drama. Source: Hugh MacNair Kahler, "Once a Peddler," in *Saturday Evening Post*, (194: 6–7, 3 Sep 1921). Having been brought up by his Uncle Clem, an itinerant peddler, Elmer Clinton has no trouble becoming the sales manager for a company that manufactures washing machines. Royce Enfield, the son of the company's president, wants his father to sell the business and therefore undermines Elmer's sales campaign. In a real effort to help Elmer, Uncle Clem obtains numerous orders for washing machines, but these are intercepted by Royce before they can be filled. Elmer is fired and, finding out the reason why, whips Royce in a fight. The elder Enfield finds the orders his son purloined and rehires Elmer, finding a position for Uncle Clem also. *Peddlers. Uncles. Sales managers. Washing machines.*

A LITTLE GIRL IN A BIG CITY **F2.3113**

Lumas Film Corp. c20 Jul **1925** [LP21660]. Si; b&w. 35mm. 6 reels.

Supv Lon Young. *Dir* Burton King. *Scen* Victoria Moore. *Photog* Jack Young, C. J. Davis. *Asst Dir* Jack Hyland.

Cast: Gladys Walton *(Mary Barry)*, Niles Welch *(Jack McGuire)*, Mary Thurman *(Mrs. Howard Young)*, J. Barney Sherry *(Howard Young)*, Coit Albertson *(D. V. Cortelyou)*, Helen Shipman *(Rose McGuire)*, Sally Crute *(Mrs. Barry)*, Nellie Savage *(Dolly Griffith)*.

Melodrama. Source: James Kyrle MacCurdy, *A Little Girl in a Big City, a Play in Four Acts* (c1909). Mary Barry, a pretty and innocent smalltown girl, wins a beauty contest in *Gay Life* and goes to New York to meet D. V. Cortelyou, the magazine's publisher. Greatly taken with the young girl, Cortelyou arranges for her to live with Dolly Griffith, a woman of questionable reputation who often aids him in his nefarious schemes of blackmail and seduction. At a large party, ostensibly in Mary's honor, Cortelyou obtains some seemingly compromising evidence with which to blackmail Mrs. Young, the wife of a wealthy broker; Cortelyou then makes rough advances toward Mary, and one of his assistants, Jack McGuire, gives him a sound thrashing. Threatened with blackmail, Mrs. Young turns in desperation to Jack for help. Jack and Mary attempt to trap Cortelyou in a net of his own making, but the blackmailer is too smart, outwitting Jack and abducting Mary. Cortelyou also kidnaps Mrs. Young, keeping her and Mary in a deserted house. Jack learns of their whereabouts and arrives with a contingent of police. Cortelyou is arrested, Mrs. Young is saved from the consequences of scandal, and Jack proposes to Mary. *Police. Publishers. Beauty contests. Blackmail. Seduction. Abduction. New York City.*

THE LITTLE GIRL NEXT DOOR **F2.3114**

Blair Coan Productions. **1923** [c12 Apr 1923; LP18871]. Si; b&w. 35mm. 6 reels, 5,950 ft.

Dir W. S. Van Dyke. *Story* Louis Weadock. *Photog* André Barlatier.

Cast: Pauline Starke *(Mary Slocum)*, James Morrison *(Jim Manning)*, Carmel Myers *(Milly Amory)*, Mitchell Lewis *(Tug Wilson)*, Edward Kennedy *(Hank Hall)*.

Melodrama. James Manning comes to the city (Chicago) to seek his fortune. Tug Wilson offers him a job running errands, then frightens him into taking a steady position when James realizes he is involved in an opium ring. Milly Amory, with whom James entices men to Wilson's gambling den, falls in love with him and makes known his whereabouts to Mary Slocum in a seance when she comes to Chicago in search of James. He exposes the seance tricks to Mary, fights for his life with Wilson, who is killed by Milly, and returns to Harmony (Illinois) with Mary. *Spiritualism. Gambling. Seances. Opium. Illinois. Chicago.*

Note: According to the *Moving Picture World*, this film (which also is known as *You Are in Danger*) is an amplification of one incident in a film by the same title copyrighted in 1916 by Essanay. Copyright records for the 1916 film indicate that its story was based on an Illinois Vice Commission report.

THE LITTLE IRISH GIRL **F2.3115**

Warner Brothers Pictures. 6 Mar **1926** [c8 Mar 1926; LP22472]. Si; b&w. 35mm. 7 reels, 6,667 ft.

Dir Roy Del Ruth. *Adapt* Darryl Francis Zanuck. *Photog* Lyman Broening. *Adtl Photog* Willard Van Enger. *Film Ed* Clarence Kolster. *Asst Dir* Sandy Roth.

Cast: Dolores Costello *(Dot Walker)*, John Harron *(Johnny)*, Matthew Betz *(Jerry Crawford)*, Lee Moran *(Mr. Nelson)*, Gertrude Claire *(Granny)*, Joseph Dowling *(Captain Dugan)*, Dot Farley *(Gertie)*, Henry Barrows *(Bankroll Charlie)*.

Melodrama. Source: C. D. Lancaster, "The Grifters" (publication undetermined). Dot Walker, a come-on girl for grifters operating a crooked cardgame in San Francisco, uses her considerable charms on Johnny, a young fellow who has come to the city in an attempt to sell his grandmother's hotel. Johnny loses all his ready cash and then invites the fellows to return to his hometown to buy the hotel. They go with Johnny and attempt to swindle Granny out of $8,000. She is too smart for them, however, and instead swindles *them*. Dot reforms and wins Johnny's love. *Irish. Confidence men. Grandmothers. Criminals—Rehabilitation. Smalltown life. Hotels. San Francisco.*

LITTLE ITALY **F2.3116**

Realart Pictures. Jul **1921** [c16 Jul 1921; LP16767]. Si; b&w. 35mm. 5 reels, 4,875 ft.

Dir George Terwilliger. *Scen* Peter Milne. *Titl* Tom McNamara. *Story* Frederic Hatton, Fanny Hatton. *Photog* Gilbert Warrenton.

Cast: Alice Brady *(Rosa Mascani)*, Norman Kerry *(Antonio Tumullo)*, George Fawcett *(Marco Mascani)*, Jack Ridgway *(Father Kelly)*, Gertrude Norman *(Anna)*, Luis Alberni *(Ricci)*, Marguerite Forrest *(Bianca)*.

Domestic melodrama. Rosa Mascani disobeys her father's command that she marry Ricci, and she is banished from home. Later she makes a vow to marry the first man she meets, who happens to be Antonio Tumullo, a truck farmer, leader of a family with whom the Mascani have a deadly feud. Antonio's attempts to win the love of his wife are in vain, and she goes to live with her cousin in the Bronx, where her child is born. In an hour of distress when the baby is ill, Rosa realizes her love for Antonio and, seeking his forgiveness, returns to him. *Italians. Truck farmers. Feuds. Filial relations. New York City—Little Italy. New York City—Bronx.*

LITTLE JOHNNY JONES **F2.3117**

Warner Brothers Pictures. 19 Aug **1923** [c1 Aug 1923; LP19266]. Si; b&w. 35mm. 7 reels, 6,800 or 7,165 ft.

Dir Arthur Rosson, Johnny Hines. *Adapt* Raymond L. Schrock. *Photog* Charles E. Gilson. *Film Ed* Clarence Kolster. *Asst Dir* Charles Hines.

Cast: Johnny Hines *(Johnny Jones)*, Wyndham Standing *(The Earl of Bloomsburg)*, Margaret Seddon *(Mrs. Jones)*, Herbert Prior *(Sir James Smythe)*, Molly Malone *(Edith Smythe)*, George Webb *(Robert Anstead)*, Mervyn LeRoy *(George Nelson, jockey)*, Harry Myers *(The Chauffeur)*, Fatty Carr, Nat Carr *(see note)*, Pauline French *(Lady Jane Smythe)*, Brownie *(Johnny's dog)*.

Comedy-drama. Source: George M. Cohan, *Little Johnny Jones* (New York opening: 4 Nov 1904). Johnny Jones, an American jockey, is engaged by the Earl of Bloomsburg to ride Yankee Doodle in the English Derby. Robert Anstead, a crooked gentleman gambler, frames Johnny Jones as a thief, kidnaps Jones's sweetheart, Edith Smythe, and tries to sabotage the race. Jones vindicates himself, rescues Edith, and finishes the race first. *Jockeys. Gamblers. Horseracing. English Derby. Dogs.*

Note: Copyright records have been followed in listing Harry Myers in the part of the chauffeur; most sources, however, list "Fat" Carr in that part, and one source lists Nat Carr. Remade in 1929 by First National under the same title, q. v.

LITTLE JOHNNY JONES **F2.3118**

First National Pictures. 17 Nov **1929** [c1 Dec 1929;LP886]. Sd (Vitaphone); b&w. 35mm. 8 reels, 6,621 ft. [Also si; 5,020 ft.]

Dir Mervyn LeRoy. *Screen Vers* Adelaide Heilbron, Eddie Buzzell. *Dial-Titl* Adelaide Heilbron. *Photog* Faxon Dean. *Film Ed* Frank Ware. *Songs: "Yankee Doodle Boy," "Give My Regards to Broadway"* George M. Cohan. *Song: "Straight, Place, and Show"* Herman Ruby, M. K. Jerome. *Song: "Go Find Somebody To Love"* Herb Magidson, Michael Cleary. *Song: "My Paradise"* Herb Magidson, James Cavanaugh. *Song: "Painting the Clouds With Sunshine"* Al Dubin, Joe Burke.

Cast: Eddie Buzzell *(Johnny Jones)*, Alice Day *(Mary Baker)*, Edna Murphy *(Vivian Dale)*, Robert Edeson *(Ed Baker)*, Wheeler Oakman *(Wyman)*, Raymond Turner *(Carbon)*, Donald Reed *(Ramon)*.

Comedy-drama. Source: George M. Cohan, *Little Johnny Jones* (New York opening: 4 Nov 1904). Jockey Johnny Jones rides Yankee, Ed Baker's racehorse, to victory at the Meadowbrook race, thereby attracting the attention of Sam Johnson, a stable owner, who takes Johnny to New York to race. Mary, Johnny's sweetheart, fondly bids him farewell, but he soon consorts with Vivian Dale, a Broadway actress, with whom he falls in love. Johnny becomes noted for his rendition of "I'm a Yankee Doodle Dandy" at clubs, but he turns down an offer to go into show business. Mary and her father arrive to enter Yankee in a race, and Mary learns about Vivian, who tries to no avail to get Johnny to agree to throw the race. But when he is pocketed and his horse does lose, a telegram from Vivian causes him to be unjustly accused. Johnny goes to England, where he works in a Limehouse pub; and upon meeting Ed, he is given a chance to ride Yankee at Epsom Downs. He wins the race and Mary's love. *Jockeys. Actors. Horseracing. Pubs. New York City—Broadway. London—Limehouse. Epsom Downs.*

Note: Remake of the 1923 Warner Brothers film of the same title, q. v.

A LITTLE JOURNEY **F2.3119**

Metro-Goldwyn-Mayer Pictures. 1 Jan **1927** [c10 Jan 1927; LP23515]. Si; b&w. 35mm. 7 reels, 6,088 ft.

Dir Robert Z. Leonard. *Screenplay* Albert Lewin. *Titl* George Marion, Jr. *Photog* Ira Morgan. *Sets* Cedric Gibbons, Park French. *Film Ed* William Le Vanway. *Wardrobe* André-ani.

Cast: Claire Windsor *(Julia Rutherford)*, William Haines *(George Manning)*, Harry Carey *(Alexander Smith)*, Claire McDowell *(Aunt Louise)*, Lawford Davidson *(Alfred Demis)*.

Romantic comedy. Source: Rachel Crothers, *A Little Journey, a Comedy in Three Acts* (New York, 1923). Julia Rutherford, out of a sense of duty, sets out for San Francisco to marry millionaire Alexander Smith, an old family friend. On the train she encounters a fresh young bounder, George Manning, who comes to her rescue when she loses her ticket. They strike up a conversation, and soon a romance develops. Smith boards the train to surprise his fiancée, but upon discovering the situation, he leaves the sweethearts to their newfound happiness. *Millionaires. Courtship. Marriage. Trains. San Francisco.*

LITTLE LORD FAUNTLEROY **F2.3120**

Mary Pickford Co. *Dist* United Artists. ca11 Sep **1921** [New York premiere; released 13 Nov; c29 Nov 1921; LP17240]. Si; b&w. 35mm. 10 reels, 9,984 ft.

Dir Alfred E. Green, Jack Pickford. *Scen* Bernard McConville. *Photog* Charles Rosher. *Mus* Louis F. Gottschalk. *Lighting Eff* William S. Johnson.

Cast: Mary Pickford *(Cedric, Little Lord Fauntleroy/Dearest, Cedric's* *mother)*, Claude Gillingwater *(The Earl of Dorincourt)*, Joseph Dowling *(Haversham, the Earl's counsel)*, James Marcus *(Hobbs, the grocer)*, Kate Price *(Mrs. McGinty, the applewoman)*, Fred Malatesta *(Dick, the bootblack)*, Rose Dione *(Minna, the adventuress)*, Frances Marion *(her son, the pretender)*, Arthur Thalasso *(The Stranger, her husband)*, Colin Kenny *(Bevis, the Earl's son)*, Emmett King *(Reverend Mordaunt, the minister)*, Madame de Bodamere *(Mrs. Higgins, a tenant)*.

Comedy-drama. Source: Frances Hodgson Burnett, *Little Lord Fauntleroy* (1886). The widow of Captain Errol, youngest son of the Earl of Dorincourt, and her young son, Cedric, live in New York City in the early 1880's barely able to subsist. The earl, how heirless, commissions his solicitor, Haversham, to bring young Cedric from America to be trained for the title of Lord Fauntleroy. When they arrive at the castle, the mother (Dearest), wrongly accused of marrying for pecuniary reasons, is forced to live outside the castle while Cedric with his innocent and childish wit captivates the earl and wins the hearts of his royal guests. Haversham appears with a woman who claims that her son is the nearest relatives of Bevis, the eldest son, and she demands the title for him. When New York papers print the story with photographs, Cedric's friends—Dick, Hobbs, and Mrs. McGinty—journey to England to expose the conspiracy. The earl is overjoyed at the news, and there is a reconciliation between Dearest and the earl; all three live happily together in the castle. *Nobility. Heirs. Children. Bootblacks. Grocers. Costermongers. Newspapers. England. New York City.*

LITTLE MICKEY GROGAN **F2.3121**

FBO Pictures. 27 Dec **1927** [c27 Dec 1927; LP24834]. Si; b&w. 35mm. 6 reels, 5,815 ft.

Dir Leo Meehan. *Adapt-Scen* Dwight Cummins, Dorothy Yost. *Titl* Charles Kerr. *Story* Arthur Guy Empey. *Ch Camera* Al Siegler. *Film Ed* Dwight Cummins, Edward Schroeder. *Asst Dir* Charles Kerr.

Cast: Frankie Darrow *(Mickey Grogan)*, Lassie Lou Ahern *(Susan)*, Jobyna Ralston *(Winifred Davidson)*, Carroll Nye *(Jeffrey Shore)*, Billy Scott *(Al Nevers)*, Vadim Uraneff *(Crooked)*, Don Bailey *(truant officer)*, Crauford Kent *(Mr. Cabel)*.

Comedy. Street urchin Mickey Grogan is rescued by Susan, who works in a factory, and given a home. To show his appreciation Mickey introduces Susan to Jeffrey, an impoverished but attractive young architect whose career is impaired by his failing sight. Susan helps Jeffrey draw up plans for her employer's new factory; the plans are accepted; Jeffrey's eyesight is restored by surgery; and Jeffrey and Susan marry and adopt Mickey. *Street urchins. Factory workers. Architects. Contractors. Blindness.*

Note: Working title: *Mickey Grogan, Contractor.*

THE LITTLE MINISTER **F2.3122**

Famous Players–Lasky. *Dist* Paramount Pictures. 25 Dec **1921** [c21 Dec 1921; LP17404]. Si; b&w. 35mm. 6 reels, 6,031 ft.

Pres by Adolph Zukor. *Dir* Penrhyn Stanlaws. *Scen* Edfrid Bingham. *Photog* Paul Perry.

Cast: Betty Compson *(Babbie)*, George Hackathorne *(Gavin)*, Edwin Stevens *(Lord Rintoul)*, Nigel Barrie *(Captain Halliwell)*, Will R. Walling *(Dr. McQueen)*, Guy Oliver *(Thomas Whammond)*, Fred Huntly *(Peter Tosh)*, Robert Brower *(Hendry Munn)*, Joseph Hazelton *(John Spens)*, Mary Wilkinson *(Nanny Webster)*.

Melodrama. Source: James Matthew Barrie, *The Little Minister* (1891). James Matthew Barrie, *The Little Minister* (New York production: 26 Dec 1904). "When the weavers of Thrums, enraged by a reduction in prices for their products, rise against the manufacturers, Gavin, 'the little minister' intervenes with the constables in their behalf. Babbie, a supposed Gypsy girl, is suspected of having notified the rioters that the police were coming so they might be prepared to fight, and a price is placed on her capture. But when Gavin questions her, her beauty and appeal charms him and he aids her to escape. A romance between the pair impends, much to the dislike of the elders of the Scotch kirk and Gavin is about to be defrocked when the Gypsy girl is brought into the meeting and discloses that she is in reality Lady Barbara, daughter of Lord Rintoul, the baron-magistrate of the district. In aiding the girl to escape Gavin had told the constables she was his wife, which in Scotland constitutes legal marriage if admittance is made before witnesses." (*Moving Picture World*, 7 Jan 1922, p112.) *Weavers. Clergymen. Gypsies. Scotland.*

THE LITTLE MINISTER **F2.3123**

Vitagraph Co. of America. ca8 Jan **1922** [premiere; released 22 Jan; c21 Dec 1921; LP17381]. Si; b&w. 35mm. 6 reels, 5,800 ft.

Pres by Albert E. Smith. *Dir* David Smith. *Scen* C. Graham Baker, Harry Dittmar. *Photog* Stephen Smith, Jr.

Cast: Alice Calhoun *(Lady Babbie)*, James Morrison *(Gavin Dishart)*, Henry Hebert *(Lord Rintoul)*, Alberta Lee *(Margaret Dishart)*, William McCall *(Rob Dow)*, Dorothea Wolbert *(Nanny Webster)*, Maud Emery *(Jean)*, George Stanley *(Dr. McQueen)*, Richard Daniels *(Micah Dow)*, Charles Wheelock *(Captain Halliwell)*.

Melodrama. Source: James Matthew Barrie, *The Little Minister* (1891). Gavin Dishart, newly appointed minister to the village of Thrums in Scotland, arrives with his mother and makes a deep impression upon the residents, poverty-stricken weavers who frequently riot against the manufacturers. He does not, however, succeed in reforming Babbie, a Gypsy maid, who warns the townspeople of a raid by the soldiers; and although he eventually falls in love with her, she is warned against encouraging him because it will mean the loss of his position. Therefore, she promises to marry her guardian, Lord Rintoul. On her wedding night, Gavin learns of her situation and is injured in a quarrel. Babbie, followed by Rintoul, rushes to Gavin, who proposes marriage to her. Lord Rintoul is injured and carried down the river in a torrential storm, but The Little Minister rescues him; Rintoul relinquishes his claim and the couple are married in the little church. *Weavers. Clergymen. Gypsies. Scotland.*

LITTLE MISS HAWKSHAW **F2.3124**

Fox Film Corp. 23 Aug **1921** [c25 Sep 1921; LP17113]. Si; b&w. 35mm. 5 reels, 4,106 ft.

Pres by William Fox. *Dir-Story* Carl Harbaugh. *Photog* Otto Brautigan.

Cast—Prolog: Eileen Percy *(Patricia)*, Eric Mayne *(Sir Stephen O'Neill, her father)*, Leslie Casey *(her husband)*

Cast—New York Sequence: Eileen Percy *(Patsy)*, Francis Feeney *(Arthur Hawks)*, Frank Clark *(Mike Rorke)*, Vivian Ransome *(Miss Rorke)*, J. Farrell MacDonald *(Inspector Hahn)*, Fred L. Wilson *(J. Spencer Giles)*, Glen Cavender *(Sock Wolf)*.

Melodrama. Stephen O'Neill's daughter, Patricia, secretly marries a poor chap against her father's wishes and leaves for America when her husband is imprisoned on false charges. She dies en route, after giving birth to a daughter. Eighteen years later Patsy, the daughter, is living in the Bowery with the family of Mike Rorke and works at his newsstand. Meanwhile, Patsy's grandfather sends his nephew, Arthur Hawks, to America to find his daughter. Hawks acquires the services of J. Spencer Giles, a private detective who has incurred the enmity of Inspector Hahn. The inspector, hearing of the lost heiress, persuades Patsy to impersonate Sir Stephen's granddaughter; and Sir Stephen, struck by her resemblance to her mother, proves that she is actually the heiress. Hawks finds himself in love with the girl, and they are destined for a happy future. *Irish. Newsvendors. Heiresses. Detectives. Impersonation. New York City—East Side.*

LITTLE MISS SMILES **F2.3125**

Fox Film Corp. 15 Jan **1922** [c15 Jan 1922; LP17483]. Si; b&w. 35mm. 5 reels, 4,884 ft.

Pres by William Fox. *Dir* Jack Ford. *Scen* Jack Strumwasser, Dorothy Yost. *Photog* David Abel.

Cast: Shirley Mason *(Esther Aaronson)*, Gaston Glass *(Dr. Jack Washton)*, George Williams *(Papa Aaronson)*, Martha Franklin *(Mama Aaronson)*, Arthur Rankin *(Davie Aaronson)*, Alfred Testa *(Louis Aaronson)*, Richard Lapan *(Leon Aaronson)*, Sidney D'Albrook *("The Spider")*, Baby Blumfield *(Baby Aaronson)*.

Domestic melodrama. Source: Myra Kelly, *Little Aliens* (New York, 1910). The Aaronson family, who live in a New York tenement, suffer many hardships according to their station in life, but their worst sorrow occurs when Mama Aaronson is diagnosed as going blind. While Davie wishes to become a prizefighter, his parents strenuously object to his ambition. On the other hand, their cheerful young daughter Esther is beloved by a popular young doctor, Jack Washton. Davie falls into bad company and shoots a gangster who insults his sister; he is eventually cleared of the crime, however, and Esther marries Dr. Jack. *Prizefighters. Physicians. Gangsters. Brother-sister relationship. Family life. Blindness. Tenements. New York City.*

LITTLE OLD NEW YORK **F2.3126**

Cosmopolitan Pictures. *Dist* Goldwyn-Cosmopolitan Distributing Corp. 4 Nov **1923** [c21 Sep 1923; LP19451]. Si; b&w. 35mm. 11 reels, 10,366 ft.

Dir Sidney Olcott. *Adapt* Luther Reed. *Photog* Ira H. Morgan, Gilbert Warrenton. *Cost* Gretl Urban.

Cast: Marion Davies *(Patricia O'Day)*, Stephen Carr *(Patrick O'Day)*, J. M. Kerrigan *(John O'Day)*, Harrison Ford *(Larry Delavan)*, Courtenay Foote *(Robert Fulton)*, Mahlon Hamilton *(Washington Irving)*, Norval Keedwell *(Fitz-Greene Halleck)*, George Barraud *(Henry Brevoort)*, Sam Hardy *(Cornelius Vanderbilt)*, Andrew Dillon *(John Jacob Astor)*, Riley Hatch *(Mr. DePuyster)*, Charles Kennedy *(Reilly)*, Spencer Charters *(Bunny)*, Harry Watson *(Bully Boy Brewster)*, Louis Wolheim *(Hoboken Terror)*, Charles Judels *(Delmonico)*, Gypsy O'Brien *(Ariana DePuyster)*, Mary Kennedy *(Betty Schuyler)*, Elizabeth Murray *(Rachel Brewster)*, Thomas Findlay *(Chancellor Livingston)*, Marie Burke *(Mrs. Schuyler)*.

Historical romance. Source: Rida Johnson Young, *Little Old New York; a Comedy in Four Acts* (New York, 1928). Patricia O'Day comes to America to claim a fortune left to her brother, who has died en route. In that circumstance the fortune should revert to the stepson, Larry Delavan, but disguised as Patrick, her brother, Patricia gets the inheritance and wins the friendship of Larry Delavan when she assists him in financing Robert Fulton's steamship venture. During a riot Patricia reveals her true identity; she and Delavan marry and go to Ireland. *Immigrants. Irish. Inheritance. Impersonation. Steamboats. New York City. John Jacob Astor. Washington Irving. Cornelius Vanderbilt. Robert Fulton.*

THE LITTLE RED SCHOOLHOUSE **F2.3127**

Martin J. Heyl. *Dist* Arrow Film Corp. **1923** [c30 Apr 1923; LP18923]. Si; b&w. 35mm. 6 reels, 5,760 ft.

Dir John G. Adolfi. *Scen* James Shelley Hamilton. *Photog* George F. Webber.

Cast: Martha Mansfield *(Mercy Brent)*, Harlan Knight *(Jeb Russell)*, Sheldon Lewis *(Mr. Matt Russell)*, E. K. Lincoln *(John Hale)*, Edmund Breese *(Brent)*, Florida Kingsley *(hired girl)*, Paul Everton *(detective)*.

Melodrama. Source: Hal Reid, *The Little Red Schoolhouse* (a play; publication undetermined). Bootleggers secretly operate in the basement of the school where Mercy Brent teaches. Her sweetheart, John Hale, and his revenue agents succeed in breaking up the bootlegging activities and solving the murder of Jeb Russell with the aid of a strange phenomenon: a bolt of lightning causes the face of Matt Russell to be pictured on a schoolhouse window, thus proving Matt to be the murderer of his bootlegging partner—his father. *Schoolteachers. Revenue agents. Bootlegging. Patricide. Phenomena.*

LITTLE ROBINSON CRUSOE **F2.3128**

Jackie Coogan Productions. *Dist* Metro-Goldwyn Distributing Corp. 25 Aug **1924** [c9 Sep 1924; LP20591]. Si; b&w. 35mm. 7 reels, 6,216 ft.

Supv Jack Coogan, Sr. *Dir* Edward Cline. *Story-Scen* Willard Mack. *Photog* Frank B. Good, Robert Martin. *Art Dir* J. J. Hughes. *Film Ed* Irene Morra.

Cast: Jackie Coogan *(Mickey Hogan)*, Chief Daniel J. O'Brien *(Chief of Police)*, Will Walling *(Captain of Police)*, Tom Santschi *(Captain Dynes)*, C. H. Wilson *("Singapore" Scroggs)*, Eddie Boland *(wireless operator)*, Noble Johnson *(Marimba, cannibal chief)*, Tote Du Crow *(Ugandi, medicine man)*, Bert Sprotte *(Adolphe Schmidt)*, Gloria Grey *(Gretta Schmidt)*, Felix *("Friday")*.

Comedy-drama. Left an orphan by the death of his father, Mickey Hogan sails for Australia to live with relatives, but he is shipwrecked and stranded on an island inhabited by cannibals who worship him as a war god. He saves a white settlement on a neighboring island by sending an S. O. S. picked up by U. S. Marines. They rescue Mickey and return him to San Francisco, where he gets a reception by the local police force. *Orphans. Cannibals. South Sea Islands. San Francisco. United States Marines.*

THE LITTLE SAVAGE **F2.3129**

FBO Pictures. *Dist* RKO Productions. 19 May **1929** [c3 Jun 1929; LP426]. Si; b&w. 35mm. 6 reels, 4,781 ft.

Dir Louis King. *Story-Cont* Frank Howard Clark. *Titl* Randolph Bartlett. *Photog* Virgil Miller. *Film Ed* George Marsh. *Asst Dir* Jack Sullivan.

Cast: Buzz Barton *(Red)*, Milburn Morante *(Hank)*, Willard Boelner *(Baby)*, Patricia Palmer *(Kitty)*, Sam Nelson *(Norton)*, Ethan Laidlaw *(Blake)*.

Western melodrama. Hank Robbins, a scout, and Red, his pal, take into their care a baby found in the wreckage of a covered wagon ravaged by a bandit. Later, Blake, an outlaw, forces young Jim Norton to hold up a stage while Blake conceals himself, and the runaway horses are directed in the pathway of Kitty, who has just been discharged from a dancehall. Red pulls her to safety and takes her to a hotel where she cares for the baby. Wounded, Norton makes his way to town where he is found in the stable by Red and given aid by him; Kitty recognizes Norton as a former sweetheart, and Hank enters a poker game to win money for the lovers from Blake, the bandit. Trying to retrieve his money from Red, Blake is exposed as the bandit murderer of the child's parents, but he escapes with Hank's winnings. Red chases Blake and fells him with his slingshot, forcing him to the edge of a cliff; Blake's confession saves Norton from hanging, and the money is given to the bride and groom. *Scouts—Frontier. Infants. Outlaws. Gambling. Stagecoach robberies.*

THE LITTLE SHEPHERD OF KINGDOM COME **F2.3130**

First National Pictures. 8 Apr **1928** [c23 Mar 1928; LP25090]. Si; b&w. 35mm. 8 reels, 7,700 ft.

Pres by Richard A. Rowland. *Supv* Henry Hobart. *Prod-Dir* Alfred Santell. *Scen* Bess Meredyth. *Titl* Dwinelle Benthall, Rufus McCosh. *Camera* Lee Garmes. *Film Ed* Hugh Bennett.

Cast: Richard Barthelmess *(Chad Buford)*, Molly O'Day *(Melissa Turner)*, Nelson McDowell *(Old Joel Turner)*, Martha Mattox *(Maw Turner)*, Victor Potel *(Tom Turner, oldest son)*, Mark Hamilton *(Dolph Turner, youngest son)*, William Bertram *(Caleb Hazel, schoolmaster)*, Walter Lewis *(Old Tad Dillon)*, Gardner James *(Daws Dillon, his son)*, Ralph Yearsley *(Tad Dillon, another son)*, Gustav von Seyffertitz *(Nathan Cherry)*, Robert Milasch *(The Circuit Rider)*, Buck *(Jack, the dog)*, Claude Gillingwater *(Major Buford)*, David Torrence *(General Dean)*, Eulalie Jensen *(Mrs. Dean)*, Doris Dawson *(Margaret Dean, their daughter)*, Walter Rogers *(General Grant)*.

Romantic drama. Source: John William Fox, *The Little Shepherd of Kingdom Come* (New York, 1903). Chad, an orphan born in Kentucky, is adopted by Major Buford, who conceals his belief that the boy is his nephew. Chad is sent to school in Lexington, and when the Civil War breaks out he joins the Union Army, losing his foster father's affection along with that of Margaret Dean, his sweetheart back home. Chad, now a captain, finds that his duty takes him to the town of his birth. There he rediscovers Melissa Turner, his childhood sweetheart, and falls in love with her again. The war's end finds Major Buford dead. Offered the major's estate if he will return to the Bluegrass region, Chad declines, preferring to remain with Melissa. *Adoption. United States—History—Civil War. Kentucky. Ulysses Simpson Grant. Dogs.*

Note: First shown as *Kentucky Courage.*

THE LITTLE SNOB **F2.3131**

Warner Brothers Pictures. 11 Feb **1928** [c1 Feb 1928; LP24940]. Mus score & sd eff (Vitaphone); b&w. 35mm. 6 reels, 5,331 ft. [Also si.]

Dir John G. Adolfi. *Scen* Robert Lord. *Titl* Joe Jackson. *Story* Edward T. Lowe, Jr. *Photog* Norbert Brodin. *Asst Dir* John Daumery.

Cast: May McAvoy *(May Banks)*, Robert Frazier *(Jim Nolan)*, Alec Francis *(Colonel Banks)*, Virginia Lee Corbin *(Jane)*, Frances Lee *(Alice)*, John Miljan *(Walt Keene)*.

Comedy-drama. Colonel Banks, owner of the "Kentucky Derby," a Coney Island concession, sends his daughter, May, to a finishing school. She leaves her father and sweetheart Jim, laughingly remarking that she will "high hat" all her friends when she returns. At school she acquires the mannerisms and tastes of her worldly friends, Alice and Jane, and gets engaged to Walt Keene, who believes she is wealthy. Her association with them changes her into an insufferable snob. Her friends denounce her when, on a jaunt to Coney Island, they discover that her father is not a "Kentucky colonel." After a moment of panic, May decides to return to her former friends and life, and, jumping to the platform, she proceeds to "bark" to the crowd, proving to her father and Jim that she is not ashamed of them. Later, Keene returns to reclaim his diamond ring, saying, "I'll teach you to play with fire, you little carnival trollop." Jim comes to the rescue and gives Keene the thrashing of his life. *Concessionaires. Socialites. Kentucky colonels. Snobbery. Boarding schools. Coney Island.*

THE LITTLE WILD GIRL **F2.3132**

Hercules Film Productions. *Dist* Trinity Pictures. Oct **1928.** Si; b&w. 35mm. 6 reels, 5,100 or 5,300 ft.

Dir Frank S. Mattison. *Cont* Cecil Burtis Hill. *Titl* Gordon Kalem. *Story* Putnam Hoover. *Photog* Jules Cronjager. *Film Ed* Minnie Steppler.

Cast: Lila Lee *(Marie Cleste)*, Cullen Landis *(Jules Barbier)*, Frank Merrill *(Tavish McBride)*, Sheldon Lewis *(Wanakee)*, Boris Karloff *(Maurice Kent)*, Jimmy Aubrey *(Posty McKnuffle)*, Bud Shaw *(Oliver Hampton)*, Arthur Hotaling *(Duncan Cleste)*, Cyclone *(Momo, a dog)*.

Northwest melodrama. Vacationing in the Canadian Northwest, a playwright and a songwriter both fall in love with Marie Cleste and take her back with them to New York when her father and her sweetheart (Jules Barbier?) apparently die in a forest fire. (The father did perish; the sweetheart escaped, crippled, with his blinded Indian guide into the forest to hide his infirmities.) Marie becomes a Broadway star, only to find it necessary to leave New York hurriedly under suspicion of the murder of one of her "angels." (The real murderer escapes, but is later captured in the Northwest.) Returning to her hometown, Marie finds considerable local opposition to her presence; but she finally finds happiness in the arms of her sweetheart, who has returned also, inherited a fortune, and recovered the use of his legs. *Actors. Cripples. Playwrights. Composers. Indians of North America. Murder. Inheritance. Forest fires. Canadian Northwest. New York City—Broadway. Dogs.*

LITTLE WILDCAT **F2.3133**

Vitagraph Co. of America. 12 Nov **1922** [c10 Sep 1922; LP18210]. Si; b&w. 35mm. 5 reels, 5,000 ft.

Dir David Divad. *Scen* Bradley J. Smollen. *Story* Gene Wright. *Photog* Stephen Smith, Jr.

Cast: Alice Calhoun *(Mag o' the Alley)*, Ramsey Wallace *(Judge Arnold)*, Herbert Fortier *(Robert Ware)*, Oliver Hardy *("Bull" Mulligan)*, Adele Farrington *(Mrs. Wilding)*, Arthur Hoyt *(Mr. Wilding)*, Frank Crane *(Jack Wilding)*, James Farley *(Pete)*, Henry Hebert *(Capt. Carl Herman)*, Maud Emery *(Babette)*.

Romantic drama. Robert Ware obtains the release into his custody of Mag o' the Alley in order to turn her into a fine young lady and prove to his friend Judge Arnold that such a thing is possible. Years later, when Arnold is serving in the war, he meets and falls in love with a nurse. Though their acquaintance is brief, he remembers her when he comes home and relates the incident to Ware. Mag—now Margaret—overhears the conversation, reveals herself to be that nurse, and accepts Arnold, who admits that Ware was right. *Judges. Veterans. Criminals—Rehabilitation. Nurses. World War I.*

THE LITTLE WILDCAT **F2.3134**

Warner Brothers Pictures. 8 Dec **1928** [c21 Nov 1928; LP25870]. Talking sequences, sd eff, & mus score (Vitaphone); b&w. 35mm. 6 reels, 5,644 ft. [Also si, 5 Jan 1929; 6,161 ft.]

Dir Ray Enright. *Scen-Dial* E. T. Lowe, Jr. *Titl* James A. Starr. *Story* Gene Wright. *Photog* Ben Reynolds. *Film Ed* George Marks.

Cast: Audrey Ferris *(Audrey)*, James Murray *(Conrad Burton)*, Robert Edeson *(Joel Ketchum)*, George Fawcett *(Judge Holt)*, Hallam Cooley *(Victor Sargeant)*, Doris Dawson *(Sue)*.

Comedy. Conrad Burton, an American ace and airplane factory promoter, flies into a southern town, and southern belles Audrey and Sue Holt both announce their intentions of landing him. In an effort to force Conrad to marry her, Sue goes to his apartment to spend the night, thereby hoping to compromise her reputation; Audrey and her fiancé, Victor, follow closely after her. The girl's father, Judge Holt, arrives, and the ensuing battle must be broken up by the riot police. In a whirlwind comedy finish, the two couples elope in Conrad's airplane. *Aviators. Judges. Sisters. Reputation. Elopement. United States—South. Airplanes.*

THE LITTLE YELLOW HOUSE **F2.3135**

FBO Pictures. 18 Apr **1928** [New York showing; released 24 Apr; c24 Apr 1928; LP25239]. Si; b&w. 35mm.

Dir James Leo Meehan. *Cont* Charles Kerr. *Titl* Randolph Bartlett. *Adapt* Dorothy Yost. *Photog* Al Siegler. *Film Ed* Edward Schroeder.

Cast: Orville Caldwell *(Rob Hollis)*, Martha Sleeper *(Emmy Milburn)*, Lucy Beaumont *(Mrs. Milburn)*, William Orlamond *(Mr. Milburn)*, Edward Peil, Jr. *(Perry Milburn)*, Freeman Wood *(Wells Harbison)*, Edythe Chapman *(Grandmother Pentland)*.

Romantic melodrama. Source: Beatrice Burton Morgan, *The Little Yellow House* (Garden City, New York, 1928). Mrs. Rose Milburn, a devoted woman married to a drunkard, reluctantly gives up her bridal home to benefit her daughter's social standing and takes her family to live with her wealthy mother. Charlie Milburn's alcoholism causes his mother-in-law to turn him out of the house, and in the street he is killed by a passing truck. Rose and her son return to "the little yellow house," which has been bought and restored by Rob Hollis, an ex-sweetheart of Emmy Milburn, the daughter. Ensconced in an apartment in the city, Emmy is being led astray by Wells Harbison, an older married man. Wells is forcing his attentions on Emmy when Rob arrives in time to save her. They return together to the cherished house. *Mothers-in-law. Alcoholism. Motherhood. Family life. Housing.*

THE LITTLEST REBEL (Reissue) **F2.3136**

Photoplay Productions. *Dist* Jawitz Pictures. 23 Jan **1923** [New York State license]. Si; b&w. 35mm. 5 reels.

Note: Originally released in 1914, starring Elmo Lincoln.

LIVE AND LET LIVE **F2.3137**

Robertson-Cole Co. *Dist* R-C Pictures. 3 Jul **1921** [c3 Jul 1921; LP16875]. Si; b&w. 35mm. 6 reels, 5,900 ft.

Dir-Writ William Christy Cabanne. *Adapt* H. Tipton Steck. *Photog* George Benoit.

Cast: Harriet Hammond *(Mary Ryan)*, George Nichols *(Judge Loomis)*, Dulcie Cooper *(Jane Loomis)*, Harris Gordon *(Donald Loomis)*, Gerald Pring *(Albert Watson)*, Dave Winter *(Dr. Randall)*, Helen Lynch *(Lillian Boland)*, Josephine Crowell *(Mrs. Boland)*, Cora Drew *(Mrs. Randall)*, Helen Muir *(The Widow Jones)*.

Society melodrama. Mary Ryan, a reformed thief, encounters Jane Loomis, a friend, on a train; and Jane confides to Mary that although her uncle has invited her home with his family, she has decided to elope. Mary gets off at the town where the uncle lives, conceals her identity, and introduces herself as his niece. Judge Loomis, an upright man, has a son, Donald, who, Mary discovers, has ruined one of the village girls. She plans to expose him, but he locks her in a closet of his invalid sister's bedroom; the sister is then cured of her lameness in an attempt to stop him. Mary saves the village physician, Dr. Randall, from angry villagers and exposes Donald. After divulging her identity to Randall, whom she loves, she is forgiven and accepted by the uncle. *Criminals—Rehabilitation. Judges. Physicians. Uncles. Invalids. Fatherhood. Imposture.*

THE LIVE WIRE **F2.3138**

First National Pictures. 20 Set **1925** [c14 Sep 1925; LP21815]. Si; b&w. 35mm. 8 reels, 6,850 ft.

Pres by C. C. Burr. *Dir* Charles Hines. *Titl* John Krafft. *Photog* Charles E. Gilson, John Geisel, Paul Strand. *Film Ed* George Amy. *Asst Dir* Charlie Berner, Joe Bannon. *Prod Mgr* Benny Berk.

Cast: Johnny Hines *(The Great Maranelli)*, Edmund Breese *(Sawdust Sam)*, Mildred Ryan *(Dorothy Langdon)*, J. Barney Sherry *(Henry Langdon)*, Bradley Barker *(George Trent)*, Flora Finch *(Pansy Darwin)*.

Comedy. Source: Richard Washburn Child, "The Game of Light," in *Everybody's* (31:38, Jul 1914). The Great Maranelli is forced to quit the circus and, in the company of Sawdust Sam, takes to the open road. In his travels, he meets Dorothy Langdon, the daughter of the president of a power company, and goes to work for her father. The elder Langdon, engaged in opening an amusement park, is beset by troubles, all of them (unknown to him) caused by his partner, George Trent. On the park's opening night, the dynamo used to create power is wrecked by Trent, who also kidnaps Dorothy. The Great Maranelli rescues the girl and has the park's electrical circuits connected with the main city circuit. The park's opening is a success, and Maranelli becomes engaged to Dorothy. *Partnerships. Sabotage. Abduction. Amusement parks. Power companies. Electric power. Circus.*

LIVE WIRES **F2.3139**

Fox Film Corp. 17 Jul **1921** [c3 Jul 1921; LP16746]. Si; b&w. 35mm. 5 reels, 4,290 ft.

Pres by William Fox. *Dir* Edward Sedgwick. *Scen* Jack Strumwasser. *Story* Charles E. Cooke, Edward Sedgwick. *Photog* Victor Milner.

Cast: Johnnie Walker *(Bob Harding)*, Edna Murphy *(Rena Austin)*, Alberta Lee *(Mrs. Harding)*, Frank Clark *(James Harding)*, Bob Klein *(Slade)*, Hayward Mack *(James Flannery)*, Wilbur Higby *(Austin, known as Melody)*, Lefty James *(The Coach)*.

Melodrama. Bob Harding, a student in love with Rena Austin, his hometown sweetheart, is preparing to play an important football match when he receives word from home that his father has died. There he learns that his father has left nothing for college funds, and while he is trying to get a job his mother is tricked into signing an option on her property for a paltry sum. In an effort to stall off the crooks, Bob gets into a fight when they suggest he "throw" the game on which they have bet money. A tramp, who turns out to be Rena's long-lost father, steals the option from the crooks, and Rena obtains evidence that clears her father of a scheme in which he had innocently been involved. Freed by the police, Bob boards the train, is lifted from the roof of the speeding train by an airplane, and arrives at the field in time to save his team from defeat. *Students. Swindlers. College life. Football. Air stunts.*

LIVING LIES **F2.3140**

Mayflower Photoplay Corp. *Dist* Clark-Cornelius Corp. 1 May **1922.** Si; b&w. 35mm. 5 reels.

Dir Emile Chautard.

Cast: Edmund Lowe *(Dixon Grant)*, Mona Kingsley *(Miss Rowland)*, Kenneth Hill *(Eustace Bray)*.

Melodrama. Source: Arthur Somers Roche, "A Scrap of Paper," in *Saturday Evening Post.* Arthur Somers Roche, *Plunder* (Indianapolis, 1917). "Dixon Grant, a reporter, is instructed to run down a band of high financiers suspected by the editor of being involved in a number of illegitimate deals. Masterman, the head of the crooked syndicate, effects an alliance with two others in putting over a traction deal. The signed agreement is blown out of the window and ... falls into the hands of Grant. This fact is soon discovered by Masterman who offers to bribe the reporter and his sweetheart into surrendering the papers. They are tricked by Bray ... and tortured until Grant discloses the hiding place of the papers. Masterman sets out to locate the papers. Meanwhile, Grant and his sweetheart escape and manage to secure the necessary evidence to publish the traction scandal. Masterman ... has sought refuge in his house boat, [which] is caught in the stong current and its destruction follows." *(Moving Picture World,* 21 Jan 1922, p322.) *Reporters. Financiers. Traction. Newspapers. Fraud. Torture. Houseboats. Documentation.*

THE LOADED DOOR **F2.3141**

Universal Film Manufacturing Co. 4 Aug **1922** [New York premiere; released 14 Aug; c3 Aug 1922; LP18120]. Si; b&w. 35mm. 5 reels, 4,430 ft.

Dir Harry A. Pollard. *Scen* George Hively. *Photog* Sol Polito.

Cast: Hoot Gibson *(Bert Lyons)*, Gertrude Olmstead *(Molly Grainger)*, Bill Ryno *(Bud Grainger)*, Eddie Sutherland *(Joe Grainger)*, Noble Johnson *(Blackie Lopez)*, Joseph Harris *(Stan Calvert)*, Charles Newton *(Dad Stewart)*, Charles A. Smiley *(Purdy)*, Victor Potel *(Slim)*, C. L. Sherwood *(Fatty)*.

Western melodrama. Source: Ralph Cummins, "Cherub of Seven Bar," in *Short Stories Magazine* (97:114–140, 16 Dec 1921). Bert Lyons returns to the Grainger spread from the "outside world" to find his former employer dead and the ranch in the possession of Calvert, a narcotics smuggler, and Blackie Lopez, a rustler who has his eyes on Molly Grainger, Lyons' sweetheart. Bert tricks the outlaws as they are plotting his death and rescues Molly when she is kidnaped by Blackie. The gang is captured, and Lyons helps free Molly's brother Joe of a murder charge. *Cowboys. Smuggling. Narcotics.*

THE LOCKED DOOR **F2.3142**

Feature Productions. *Dist* United Artists. 16 Nov **1929** [c29 Oct 1929; LP801]. Sd (Movietone); b&w. 35mm. 8 reels, 6,844 ft.

Pres by Joseph P. Kennedy. *Dir* George Fitzmaurice. *Dir Dial Scenes* Earle Browne. *Scen* C. Gardner Sullivan. *Dial* George Scarborough. *Photog* Ray June. *Film Ed* Hal Kern.

Cast: Rod La Rocque *(Frank Devereaux)*, Barbara Stanwyck *(Ann Carter)*, William Boyd *(Lawrence Reagan)*, Betty Bronson *(Helen Reagan)*, Harry Stubbs *(The Waiter)*, Harry Mestayer *(district attorney)*, Mack Swain *(hotel proprietor)*, ZaSu Pitts *(telephone girl)*, George Bunny *(The Valet)*, Purnell Pratt *(police officer)*, Fred Warren *(photographers)*, Charles Sullivan *(guest)*, Edgar Dearing *(cop)*, Mary Ashcraft, Violet Bird, Eleanor Fredericks, Martha Stewart, Virginia McFadden, Lita Chevret, Leona Leigh, Greta von Rue, Dorothy Gowan, Kay English *(girls on rum boat)*, Edward Dillon.

Mystery melodrama. Source: Channing Pollock, *The Sign on the Door* (New York, 1924). Frank Devereaux, son of a wealthy businessman, takes Ann Carter, his father's secretary, to a floating cabaret under innocent circumstances and locks her in a private dining room; the club is raided, and their picture is taken by a news photographer. Anne leaves her job and gets another with Lawrence Reagan, whom she marries and with whom she lives happily until Devereaux begins to call on Helen, her sister-in-law. Reagan is informed by Dixon that Devereaux ruined his home; and during a confrontation between Reagan and Devereaux, the latter is accidentally shot. Ann, who is discovered locked in the room with the body, confesses to the crime; then Reagan admits his guilt; Devereaux, however, reveals on his deathbed the actual circumstances. *Secretaries. Marriage. Scandal. Murder. Seduction. Floating cabarets.*

Note: Remake of *The Sign on the Door,* 1921.

LOCKED DOORS **F2.3143**

Famous Players–Lasky. *Dist* Paramount Pictures. 5 Jan **1925** [c16 Dec 1924; LP20919]. Si; b&w. 35mm. 7 reels, 6,221 ft.

Pres by Adolph Zukor, Jesse L. Lasky. *Dir* William C. De Mille. *Story-Scen* Clara Beranger. *Photog* L. Guy Wilky.

Cast: Betty Compson *(Mary Reid Carter)*, Theodore Roberts *(Mr. Reid)*, Kathlyn Williams *(Laura Carter)*, Theodore von Eltz *(John Talbot)*, Robert Edeson *(Norman Carter)*, Elmo Billings *(Mickey)*.

Society melodrama. Mary Reid decides to marry wealthy Norman Carter, a successful architect much older than herself, in order to provide a home for her invalid father. After she is married, Mary visits friends who own a lodge in the mountains and falls in love with John Talbot, who, unknown to her, is an acquaintance and business associate of Carter. When John returns to the city, he confides to Carter his despair at being in love with a married woman. Carter then invites John to become a guest in the Carter home until he is able to forget his vacation romance. When John and Mary again meet, they manage to hide their shock and surprise from Carter, but Carter's sister soon suspects the guilty love and makes Carter suspicious. Deciding to renounce his love, John is bidding farewell to Mary in her bedroom at night when a fire breaks out downstairs. Seeking to save his wife, Carter finds John and Mary together. After everyone is rescued, Carter tells the illicit lovers that he has decided to step aside and that he will send John to Italy on business until he and Mary can obtain a divorce. *Architects. Filial relations. Marriage. Infidelity. Divorce. Fires.*

LOCKED OUT *see* **THE GIRL IN HIS ROOM**

LOCO LUCK (Blue Streak Western) **F2.3144**

Universal Pictures. 23 Jan **1927** [c14 Oct 1926; LP23238]. Si; b&w. 35mm. 5 reels, 4,827 ft.

Pres by Carl Laemmle. *Dir* Cliff Smith. *Scen* Doris Malloy. *Adapt* Isadore Bernstein. *Photog* Eddie Linden.

Cast: Art Acord *(Bud Harris)*, Fay Wray *(Molly Vernon)*, Aggie Herring *(Mrs. Vernon)*, William A. Steele *(Frank Lambert)*, Al Jennings *(Jesse Turner* [*Bush*]*)*, George F. Marion *("Dad" Perkins, postmaster)*, M. E. Stimson *(Mark Randell)*, George Grandee, George Kesterson.

Western melodrama. Source: Alvin J. Neitz, "The Eyes Win" (publication undetermined). Bud Harris, who is in love with Molly Vernon, leaves the Vernon ranch when there is an oil boom in the territory, then returns to find the property encumbered with debt. Bush, who holds the mortgage on the ranch, attempts to foreclose when he learns that there is oil on the land, and Bud enters a horserace to pay the debt. Bush conspires to kidnap Bud and takes him to a secluded cabin; his horse finds the cabin, however, and rescues him. Bud wins the race and administers a sound thrashing to the villain. Subsequently, oil seepage is found on the Vernon ranch, and Bud and Molly find happiness together. *Ranchers. Oil. Horseracing. Kidnaping. Mortgages.*

THE LODGE IN THE WILDERNESS **F2.3145**

Tiffany Productions. 11 Jul **1926** [c13 Jul 1926; LP22908]. Si; b&w. 35mm. 6 reels, 5,119 ft.

Dir Henry McCarthy. *Scen* Wyndham Gittens. *Photog* Jack MacKenzie.

Cast: Anita Stewart *(Virginia Coulson)*, Edmund Burns *(Jim Wallace)*, Duane Thompson *(Dot Marshall)*, Lawrence Steers *(John Hammond)*, Victor Potel *(Goofus, the halfwit)*, Eddie Lyons *(Buddy O'Brien)*, James Farley *(Bill Duncan)*.

Melodrama. Source: Gilbert Parker, "The Lodge in the Wilderness," in *Northern Lights* (New York, 1909). Jim Wallace, a young engineer, is engaged by Hammond, manager of an estate in the Northwest, to build flumes for a logging camp, but Donovan, the superintendent, dislikes him and places numerous obstacles in his way. Virginia Coulson, owner of the estate, and her maid Dot arrive, and when Hammond proposes to Virginia, she refuses his declaration in favor of Jim. Later, when Donovan is found murdered, suspicion points to Jim, who is convicted and sentenced to life imprisonment. Hammond gets evidence on the murderer, Goofus, a halfwit, and plans to use it to force Virginia to marry him; Goofus wounds Hammond and, seeing he has not killed him, starts a forest fire. Jim, who has escaped from prison with the aid of his friend, Buddy, rescues Virginia from the burning lodge; Goofus confesses to the murder, and Jim is freed.

Engineers. Halfwits. Lumber camps. Murder. Prison escapes. Injustice. Forest fires.

LONDON **F2.3146**
Burton Holmes Lectures. 6 Jan **1930** [New York State license]. Si(?); b&w. 35mm. 4 reels.
Travelog. No information about the precise nature of this film has been found. *London.*

LONDON AFTER MIDNIGHT **F2.3147**
Metro-Goldwyn-Mayer Pictures. 3 Dec **1927** [c3 Dec 1927; LP25289]. Si; b&w. 35mm. 7 reels, 5,687 ft.
Dir-Story Tod Browning. *Scen* Waldemar Young. *Titl* Joe Farnham. *Photog* Merritt B. Gerstad. *Sets* Cedric Gibbons, Arnold Gillespie. *Film Ed* Harry Reynolds. *Wardrobe* Lucia Coulter.
Cast: Lon Chaney *(Burke)*, Marceline Day *(Lucille Balfour)*, Henry B. Walthall *(Sir James Hamlin)*, Percy Williams *(Butler)*, Conrad Nagel *(Arthur Hibbs)*, Polly Moran *(Miss Smithson)*, Edna Tichenor *(Bat Girl)*, Claude King *(The Stranger)*.
Mystery drama. Five years after the "suicide" death of Roger Balfour in his London home, detective-inspector Burke is still investigating, unable to believe that Balfour committed suicide. Sir James Hamlin, Balfour's closest friend; Arthur Hibbs, Hamlin's nephew; Lucille, Balfour's daughter; and the butler: these are all still suspected. Inspector Burke, an accomplished hypnotist, solves the mystery by hypnotizing the primary suspects, Hibbs and Hamlin, placing them in the murder setting, and observing their reactions. Drawing a blank with Hibbs, who is in love with Lucille, Burke discovers that his man is Hamlin. *Detectives. Suicide. Murder. Hypnotism. London.*
Note: Working title: *The Hypnotist*

THE LONE CHANCE **F2.3148**
Fox Film Corp. 18 May **1924** [c18 May 1924; LP20212]. Si; b&w. 35mm. 5 reels, 4,385 ft.
Pres by William Fox. *Dir* Howard Mitchell. *Scen* Charles Kenyon. *Story* Frederick J. Jackson. *Photog* Bert Baldridge.
Cast: John Gilbert *(Jack Saunders)*, Evelyn Brent *(Margaret West)*, John Miljan *(Lew Brody)*, Edwin Booth Tilton *(governor)*, Harry Todd *(Burke)*, Frank Beal *(warden)*.
Melodrama. Jack Saunders, a penniless inventor in search of a girl he loves, assumes the guilt for a murder in return for $20,000 and promise of a pardon at the end of a year. When the agreement is not fulfilled, he breaks jail and appears, demanding justice, before the governor, whose daughter, Margaret, committed the crime in self-defense. Saunders prevents her forced marriage to politician Burke, and Margaret, recognizing her lost love, clears his name and is herself exonerated. *Inventors. State governors. Murder. Political corruption. Prison escapes.*
Note: Working title: *The Mark of Cain.*

THE LONE EAGLE *see* **THE EAGLE**

THE LONE EAGLE (Universal-Jewel) **F2.3149**
Universal Pictures. 18 Sep **1927** [c27 Aug 1927; LP24338]. Si; b&w. 35mm. 6 reels, 5,862 ft.
Pres by Carl Laemmle. *Dir* Emory Johnson. *Cont* John Clymer. *Scen* Emilie Johnson. *Titl* Tom Reed. *Story* Howard Blanchard. *Photog* Arthur Todd.
Cast: Raymond Keane *(Lieut. William Holmes)*, Barbara Kent *(Mimi)*, Nigel Barrie *(Captain Richardson)*, Jack Pennick *(Sven Linder)*, Donald Stuart *(Red McGibbons)*, Cuyler Supplee *(Lebrun)*, Frank Camphill *(lieutenant at desk)*, Marcella Daly *(Nannette)*, Eugène Pouyet *(innkeeper)*, Wilson Benge *(truckdriver)*, Brent Overstreet, Lieut. Egbert Cook *(aviators)*, Trixie *(herself, a dog)*.
Melodrama. Billy Holmes, an American aviator, is assigned to a unit of the Royal Flying Corps involved in constant action over the western front and during his initial encounter with the enemy is accused of cowardice. When he meets Mimi, a charming little French girl, Billy is inspired to boast of his bravery in action. During a skirmish between the unit and a squadron of German airplanes, Red McGibbons, an ace and close friend of Billy's, brings down the brother of Lebrun, leader of the Hun force, but is himself killed. Lebrun challenges the Allies to an air duel, and Billy accepts the challenge despite Mimi's objections. Although he is forced to the ground by the experienced Lebrun, as is his friend, Sven, Billy miraculously escapes injury, pursues the German in another plane, and downs him. After the Armistice Billy returns home with Mimi as his wife. *Aviators. Germans. French. Brothers. Cowardice. World War I. Great Britain—Royal Flying Corps. Dogs.*

LONE FIGHTER **F2.3150**
Sunset Productions. 1 Oct **1923.** Si; b&w. 35mm. 5 reels, 4,206 or 4,800 ft.
Dir Albert Russell.
Cast: Vester Pegg *(Harvey Bates)*, Josephine Hill *(Rose Trimball)*, Joe Ryan *(Macklyn Vance)*, Jim Gamble *(Patrick Trimball)*, J. B. Warner *(Certain Lee)*.
Western melodrama. Source: Keene Thompson, "Certain Lee" (publication undetermined). "Girl's sweetheart is railroaded to prison by cattle rustler, his rival. Texas Ranger [Certain Lee] arrives to clean up gang. Rescues girl. She is led to believe he sent her lover to jail. She aids gang to trap him. Her lover escapes jail and she learns of his guilt. She then aids ranger in capturing gang, and he wins her love." (*Motion Picture News Booking Guide*, 6:42, Apr 1924.) *Gangs. Rustlers. Texas Rangers.*

THE LONE HAND **F2.3151**
Universal Film Manufacturing Co. 16 Oct **1922** [c3 Oct 1922; LP18270]. Si; b&w. 35mm. 5 reels, 4,570 ft.
Dir Reeves Eason. *Dir? (see note)* Nat Ross. *Scen* A. P. Younger. *Photog* Virgil Miller.
Cast: Ed (Hoot) Gibson *(Laramie Lad)*, Marjorie Daw *(Jane Sheridan)*, Helen Holmes *(Margie Vanney)*, Hayden Stevenson *(Buck)*, Jack Pratt *(Jack Maltrain)*, William Welch *(Al Sheridan)*, Robert Kortman *(Curly)*.
Western comedy-melodrama. Source: Ralph Cummins, "Laramie Ladd" (publication undetermined). Laramie Lad interrupts his vacation to rescue Al Sheridan and his daughter, Jane, from attempts to swindle them out of their mining property, stays on to manage the mine, and finds happiness with Jane. *Swindlers. Mining. Wyoming.*
Note: Also advertised as *False Play*, directed by Nat Ross.

LONE HAND SAUNDERS **F2.3152**
R-C Pictures. *Dist* Film Booking Offices of America. 13 or 26 Sep **1926** [c23 Aug 1926; LP23093]. Si; b&w. 35mm. 6 reels, 5,453 ft.
Pres by Joseph P. Kennedy. *Dir* B. Reeves Eason. *Scen* Del Andrews. *Story* Frank M. Clifton. *Photog* Ross Fisher. *Asst Dir* Al Werker.
Cast: Fred Thomson *(Fred Saunders)*, Bess Flowers *(Alice Mills)*, Billy Butts *(Buddy)*, Frank Hagney *(Buck)*, Albert Priscoe *(Charlie)*, Bill Dyer *(sheriff)*, William Courtwright *(Dr. Bandy)*, Silver King *(himself, a horse)*.
Western melodrama. Buck and Charlie, two hardboiled cowboys, arrive at the Bar Nothing Ranch in Arizona and determine to take advantage of the peculiarity of the owner, Fred Saunders, known as "Lone Hand" because he never uses his right hand. Saunders rescues Buddy, a crippled boy, in the desert and places him in the town orphanage under the care of Alice Mills; but Saunders is accused of robbing the local stage. The sheriff, however, refuses to believe his friend is the culprit. Saunders reveals to Buddy that he is a surgeon, and that because his sister died before he could operate on her, he vowed never again to use his right hand. The stage is robbed again and the driver killed, infuriating the town against Saunders, who seems to fit the bandit's description; and Buck, the real culprit, leads a posse to him. Saunders persuades the posse to wait until he operates on Buddy, then tricks Buck into a confession, which Alice corroborates. *Ranchers. Bandits. Cowboys. Sheriffs. Orphans. Surgeons. Posses. Stagecoach robberies. Arizona. Horses.*

LONE HAND TEXAS **F2.3153**
Ward Lascelle Productions. 9 Sep **1924** [New York State license]. Si; b&w. 35mm. 5 reels.
Cast: Lester Cuneo.
Western melodrama. No information about the precise nature of this film has been found.

THE LONE HORSEMAN **F2.3154**
A. B. Maescher Productions. *Dist* Arrow Film Corp. 1 Jan **1923** [c26 Dec 1922; LP18539]. Si; b&w. 35mm. 5 reels, 4,471 ft.
Dir-Writ Fred Caldwell.
Cast: Jack Perrin, Josephine Hill.
Western melodrama. Prospector Abner Hall disappears and "Smoothe Joe" Holler warns Sheriff John Wallace to abandon his search for Hall. Meanwhile, Etta Smith comes to the Nevada town in search of her long-lost brother and is also kidnaped. John finds Hall and Etta in the hands of

Holler, who reveals an incriminating incident in John's past. But Harry Elliott exonerates the sheriff and reveals him to be the brother of Etta, who is happy in Harry's arms. *Prospectors. Sheriffs. Brother-sister relationship. Kidnaping. Nevada.*

THE LONE HORSEMAN **F2.3155**

J. P. McGowan Productions. *Dist* Syndicate Pictures. Nov **1929.** Si; b&w. 35mm. 5 reels.

Dir J. P. McGowan. *Story* Sally Winters. *Photog* Hap Depew.

Cast: Tom Tyler, J. P. McGowan, Black Jack, Mrs. B. Tanzey, Charlotte Winn, Tom Bay, Mack V. Wright.

Western melodrama. While Jack Gardiner is in the hospital, Slicker and Hawkes sell his ranch to Pat, a widow, and her niece, Peggy. Jack's efforts to establish his identity and recover his property are made more difficult by the discovery of gold on the ranch and the villains' attempts to obtain the gold for themselves, but he succeeds in trapping his enemies and winning Peggy. *Ranchers. Widows. Fraud. Personal identity. Gold.*

THE LONE PATROL **F2.3156**

Major Pictures. *Dist* Aywon Film Corp. 15 Dec **1928.** Si; b&w. 35mm. 5 reels, 4,880 ft.

Cast: William Bailey, Jean Dolores.

Northwest melodrama. No information about the precise nature of this film has been found. *Northwest Mounted Police.*

THE LONE RIDER **F2.3157**

D. M. Productions. *Dist* Rollo Sales Corp. Apr **1922** [New York State]. Si; b&w. 35mm. 5 reels.

Dir-Story Denver Dixon, Fred Caldwell. *Photog* Gordon MacLean. *Film Ed* Fred Allen.

Cast: Denver Dixon *(Lone Rider/Hobo)*, Alma Rayford *(Ruth Harrison)*, Edward Heim *(Jud Harrison)*, Charles Force *("Big" Greeves)*, Clyde McClary *("Bull" Davidson)*, Tommy Hines *("Slim")*.

Western melodrama. Ruth Harrison, daughter of cattle owner Jud Harrison, takes to a hobo who has attempted to stop foreman "Bull" Davidson from torturing a horse. She takes him home, and her father gives him a job, but soon cattle rustler "Big" Greeves tries to frame the innocent hobo, resulting in the poor boy's capture by Greeves and his gang. Ruth saves him, and after the hobo tells her of Greeves's nefarious deeds, they both go to her father, who confronts Greeves and his pawn, the sheriff. Soon the mysterious "Lone Rider," who appears sporadically throughout the film, is shown to be the hobo and in actuality a U. S. deputy marshal. All ends well, particularly for the U. S. deputy marshal and Ruth. *Cattlemen. Rustlers. Hoboes. United States marshals. Torture. Disguise.*

THE LONE RIDER **F2.3158**

Balshofer Productions. 3 Feb **1927** [New York State license]. Si; b&w. 35mm. 5 reels, 4,800 ft.

Cast: Fred Church.

Western melodrama(?). No information about the nature of this film has been found.

THE LONE RIDER **F2.3159**

Beverly Pictures. *Dist* Columbia Pictures. 9 Jun **1930** [c23 Jun 1930; LP1378]. Sd (Movietone); b&w. 35mm. 6 reels, 5,432 ft.

Dir Louis King. *Scen-Dial* Forrest Sheldon. *Story* Frank Howard Clark. *Photog* Ted McCord. *Film Ed* James Sweeney. *Sd Mix Engr* Lester E. Tope.

Cast: Buck Jones *(Jim Lanning)*, Vera Reynolds *(Mary)*, Harry Woods *(Farrell)*, George Pearce *(judge)*.

Western melodrama. Jim Lanning, known as the "Hell's River Kid," quits Ed Farell's notorious outlaw band to work on his own; he intercepts an attempt by Farrell's gang to rob a stagecoach and meets Mary, daughter of Judge Stevens of Gold City, who believes he has rescued her from the gang, and he reluctantly agrees to escort her. Impressed by his "bravery," the judge urges him to head the Vigilance Committee and protect the town from outlaws; and he accepts, thinking only of Mary, with whom he falls in love. Later, Jim is kidnaped by Farrell's men and is shot in an escape attempt. The vigilantes, learning his true identity, pursue him; but Jim confronts Farrell, and a great chase follows in which Farrell is drowned. Relinquishing his life of the past, Jim finds contentment with Mary. *Outlaws. Judges. Vigilantes. Criminals—Rehabilitation. Courtship. Stagecoach robberies. Chases.*

THE LONE STAR RANGER **F2.3160**

Fox Film Corp. 9 Sep **1923** [c15 Oct 1923; LP19496]. Si; b&w. 35mm. 6 reels, 5,259 ft.

Pres by William Fox. *Dir-Scen* Lambert Hillyer. *Photog* Daniel Clark.

Cast: Tom Mix *(Duane)*, Billie Dove *(Helen Longstreth)*, L. C. Shumway *(Lawson)*, Stanton Heck *(Poggin)*, Edward Peil *(Kane)*, Frank Clark *(Laramie)*, Minna Redman *(Mrs. Laramie)*, Francis Carpenter *(Laramie's son)*, William Conklin *(Major Longstreth/Cheseldine)*, Tom Lingham *(Captain McNally)*, Tony *(himself, a horse)*.

Western. Source: Zane Grey, *The Lone Star Ranger; a Romance of the Border* (New York, 1914). An outlaw named Duane, captured by the Texas Rangers, is promised a pardon if he rounds up a gang of cattle thieves. The man he suspects as the leader is revealed to be the father of Duane's sweetheart, Helen. Duane captures the gang, gets a pardon for Helen's father, and marries Helen. *Texas Rangers. Rustlers. Horses.*

THE LONE STAR RANGER **F2.3161**

Fox Film Corp. 5 Jan **1930** [c4 Dec 1929; LP911]. Sd (Movietone); b&w. 35mm. 7 reels, 5,736 ft. [Also si; 5,948 ft.]

Pres by William Fox. *Assoc Prod* James Kevin McGuinness. *Dir* A. F. Erickson. *Stgd by* A. H. Van Buren. *Scen* Seton I. Miller. *Dial* John Hunter Booth. *Photog* Daniel Clark. *Film Ed* Jack Murray. *Ch Rec* Barney Fredericks. *Asst Dir* Ewing Scott. *Cost* Sophie Wachner.

Cast: George O'Brien *(Buck Duane)*, Sue Carol *(Mary Aldridge)*, Walter McGrail *(Phil Lawson)*, Warren Hymer *(The Bowery Kid)*, Russell Simpson *(Colonel Aldridge)*, Roy Stewart *(Captain McNally)*, Lee Shumway *(Red Kane)*, Colin Chase *(Tom Laramie)*, Richard Alexander *(Jim Fletcher)*, Joel Franz *(Hank Jones)*, Joe Rickson *(Spike)*, Oliver Eckhardt *(Lem Parker)*, Caroline Rankin *(Mrs. Parker)*, Elizabeth Patterson *(Sarah Martin)*, Billy Butts *(Bud Jones)*, Delmar Watson *(Baby Jones)*, William Steele *(first deputy)*, Bob Fleming *(second deputy)*, Ralph Le Fevre *(stage driver)*.

Western melodrama. Source: Zane Grey, *The Lone Star Ranger; A Romance of the Border* (New York, 1914). Buck Duane, having shot a man in self-defense, is accused of many crimes that he did not commit. In order to prove his innocence, he joins the Texas Rangers, also hoping to win the approval of Mary Aldridge, a girl from the East. He is assigned to round up a gang of cattle rustlers who are supported by The Bowery Kid, a New Yorker, and led by the girl's father. *Texas Rangers. New Yorkers. Outlaws. Rustlers. Prejudice. Texas.*

THE LONE WAGON **F2.3162**

Sanford Productions. 15 Nov **1923** [New York showing: 4 Mar 1924]. Si; b&w. 35mm. 5 reels, 4,800-5,009 ft.

Dir-Writ Frank S. Mattison. *Photog* Elmer G. Dyer.

Cast: Matty Mattison, Vivian Rich, Lafayette McKee, Earl Metcalf, Gene Crosby.

Western melodrama. "... dealing with adventures of Southern family in going west. The hero, a Spaniard, is hired as guide. Daughter falls in love with him but family interferes. He saves the party from various Indian attacks, and finally the lovers are united." (*Motion Picture News Booking Guide,* 6:43, Apr 1924.) *Spanish. Guides. Indians of North America. Frontier and pioneer life.*

THE LONE WOLF **F2.3163**

John McKeown. *Dist* Associated Exhibitors. 27 Apr **1924.** Si; b&w. 35mm. 6 reels, 5,640 ft.

Dir-Writ S. E. V. Taylor. *Photog* Jack Brown, Albert Wilson, Dal Clawson.

Cast: Dorothy Dalton *(Lucy Shannon)*, Jack Holt *(Michael Lanyard)*, Wilton Lackaye *(William Burroughs)*, [Frederick] Tyrone Power *(Bannon)*, Charlotte Walker *(Clare Henshaw)*, Lucy Fox *(Annette Dupre)*, Edouard Durand *(Popinot)*, Robert T. Haines *(Solon)*, Gustav von Seyffertitz *(Wertheimer)*, Alphonse Ethier *(Eckstrom)*, William Tooker *(ambassador)*, Paul McAllister *(Count de Morbihan)*.

Mystery melodrama. Source: Louis Joseph Vance, "The Lone Wolf," in *Munsey's Magazine* (51:351, Mar 1914). International crook Michael Lanyard, alias "The Lone Wolf," offers to recover stolen plans for a defense apparatus in exchange for asylum in the United States. He meets Lucy Shannon, a member of the gang, called "The Pack," suspected of having the stolen plans. Lucy assists Lanyard in obtaining the plans and later helps him escape from the other members of the gang. Together, in a daring airplane ride, they deliver the plans. Lanyard learns that Lucy is a

Secret Service agent. *Secret service. Gangs. Disguise. Defense—National. Documentation.*

THE LONE WOLF RETURNS F2.3164

Columbia Pictures. 1 or 25 Aug **1926** [c10 Aug 1926; LP23012]. Si; b&w. 35mm. 6 reels, 5,750 ft.

Supv Harry Cohn. *Dir* Ralph Ince. *Scen* J. Grubb Alexander. *Photog* J. O. Taylor.

Cast: Bert Lytell *(The Lone Wolf/Michael Lanyard)*, Billie Dove *(Marcia Mayfair)*, Freeman Wood *(Mallison)*, Gustav von Seyffertitz *(Morphew)*, Gwen Lee *(Liane De Lorme)*, Alphonse Ethier *(Crane)*.

Crook melodrama. Source: Louis Joseph Vance, *The Lone Wolf Returns* (New York, 1923). The Lone Wolf, an international thief who is expert in dodging the police, is rifling a wall safe when he senses the approach of detectives. Secreting a necklace in a cigarette case, he makes a hasty retreat. In disguise, he climbs to the balcony of another house where a bal masque is in progress and conceals himself in Marcia Mayfair's boudoir. Later he mingles with the guests and dances with Marcia. Lanyard is disclosed as a stranger when detectives force the guests to unmask, but Marcia remains silent while Lanyard replaces the jewels lifted from her bedroom. Lanyard is warned by Detective Crane, who suspects him but has no evidence. A visit to a bohemian resort owned by Morphew, leader of a band of thieves, provokes a heated argument in which Lanyard is threatened; and Marcia and Lanyard barely escape being caught in a raid. Their romance is threatened when Marcia's jewels are again stolen, but Lanyard traps Morphew and his gang and brings them to justice. *Thieves. Detectives. Disguise. Courtship.*

Note: Also reviewed under the title *Return of the Lone Wolf.*

THE LONE WOLF'S DAUGHTER F2.3165

Columbia Pictures. 18 Feb **1929** [c11 Feb 1929; LP138]. Talking sequences (Movietone); b&w. 35mm. 7 reels, 7,134 ft. [Also si; 6,186 ft.]

Pres by Jack Cohn. *Dir* Albert Rogell. *Scen* Sig Herzig. *Dial* Harry Revier. *Story* Louis Joseph Vance. *Photog* James Van Trees. *Art Dir* Harrison Wiley. *Film Ed* William Hamilton. *Asst Dir* Tenny Wright.

Cast: Bert Lytell *(Michael Lanyard/The Lone Wolf)*, Gertrude Olmstead *(Helen Fairchild)*, Charles Gerard *(Count Polinac)*, Lilyan Tashman *(Velma)*, Donald Keith *(Bobby Crenshaw)*, Florence Allen *(Adrienne)*, Robert Elliott *(Ethier)*, Ruth Cherrington *(Mrs. Crenshaw)*.

Melodrama. Michael Lanyard, a reformed cracksman, adopts Adrienne, the daughter of an old friend, and goes to Southampton to attend a party celebrating her engagement to Bobby Crenshaw, the son of a wealthy society couple. The Count and Countess Polinac, international jewel thieves, also attend the party, and Count Polinac forces Lanyard to open the safe containing the jewelry of the guests by threatening to expose Lanyard's criminal past. Lanyard forestalls the count, however, and protects the valuables. The count and countess are arrested, and Michael's secret is kept safe. *Thieves. Safecrackers. Upper classes. Blackmail.*

LONELY HEART F2.3166

Joseph M. Shear. *Dist* Affiliated Distributors. Dec **1921** [New York State]. Si; b&w. 35mm. 5 reels, 5,054 ft.

Dir John B. O'Brien. *Photog* Lawrence E. Williams.

Cast: Robert Elliott, Kay Laurell.

Drama. Indian drama of the oil fields. *Indians of North America. Oil fields.*

THE LONELY ROAD F2.3167

Preferred Pictures. *Dist* Associated First National Pictures. 7 May **1923** [c18 Apr 1923; LP18874]. Si; b&w. 35mm. 6 reels, 5,102 ft.

Pres by B. P. Schulberg. *Dir* Victor Schertzinger. *Adapt* Lois Zellner. *Story* Charles Logue. *Photog* Joseph Brotherton. *Film Ed* Eve Unsell.

Cast: Katherine MacDonald *(Betty Austin)*, Orville Caldwell *(Warren Wade)*, Kathleen Kirkham *(Leila Mead)*, Eugenie Besserer *(Martha True)*, William Conklin *(Dr. Devereaux)*, James Neill *(Uncle Billy Austin)*, Frank Leigh *(Stewart Bartley)*, Charles French *(Hiram Wade)*, Stanley Goethals *(the Wades' son)*.

Domestic drama. Betty Austin gives up her dream of going to the city and marries Warren Wade, but she sadly finds him selfish and insistent on her acting like a "clinging vine." Disgusted, she joins her career-girl chum, Leila Mead, in the city, where she meets Dr. Devereaux. Shortly after returning home with Warren, their son is injured. Betty takes him to Dr. Devereaux, and Warren follows, accusing Betty of leaving him for the doctor. Their son is cured; Warren learns his mistake and gives Betty greater responsibility in managing family money matters. *Careerwomen. Physicians. Marriage. Parenthood. Finance—Personal.*

THE LONELY TRAIL F2.3168

Credit-Canada Productions. *Dist* Primex Pictures. 2 Jan **1922** [New York showing]. Si; b&w. 35mm. 5 reels.

Cast: Fred K. Beauvais *(Pierre Benoît)*, Christina McNulty *(Margaret Allen)*, W. L. Tremaine *(James K. Allen)*, Fred Bezerril *(George Travis)*, Rose McNulty *(Julie Benoît)*, Louis Curotto *(Fatty)*, Southard Browning *(Joe Merrick)*.

Melodrama. "The story ... is of a wealthy man and his daughter camping in the woods. Beauvais is their Indian guide, and saves the girl from the hands of the heavy. Finally, as the two part, the girl slips him a note telling him she loves him and that when he wants her she will return. Whether she ever did or not is still a mystery. However, the Indian guide had a good reason to want to square himself with the heavy, for years before the heavy ruined and deserted the Indian's sister." (*Variety*, 6 Jan 1922, p43.) *Guides. Indians of North America. Revenge. Canada.*

Note: Country of origin undetermined.

LONESOME F2.3169

Universal Pictures. 30 Sep **1928** [New York premiere; released 20 Jan 1929; c20 Jun 1928; LP25404]. Talking sequence & sd eff (Movietone); b&w. 35mm. 7 reels, 6,761 or 6,785 ft. [Also si, ca20 Jun 1928; 6,142 or 6,193 ft.]

Prod Supv Carl Laemmle, Jr. *Dir* Paul Fejos. *Adapt-Scen* Edward T. Lowe, Jr. *Dial-Titl* Tom Reed. *Story* Mann Page. *Photog* Gilbert Warrenton. *Film Ed* Frank Atkinson.

Cast: Barbara Kent *(Mary)*, Glenn Tryon *(John)*, Fay Holderness *(overdressed woman)*, Gustav Partos *(romantic gentleman)*, Eddie Phillips *(The Sport)*.

Romantic drama. Life in New York City is a humdrum affair for Mary, a switchboard operator, and John, a drill press operator, two lonely people who are unaware that they live in the same boardinghouse. Following a festive crowd to Coney Island, they meet on the beach and experience love at first sight. On a roller coaster they become separated, a fire breaks out, and Mary faints. In an effort to get to Mary, whose name he does not know, Joe is stopped by a policeman and taken to the station. By the time he is released, Mary has disappeared. Each wanders back to the boardinghouse, despondent. They gleefully discover they are neighbors. *Telephone operators. Drill press operators. Amusement parks. Boardinghouses. New York City. Coney Island.*

LONESOME CORNERS F2.3170

Playgoers Pictures. *Dist* Pathé Exchange. 23 Apr **1922** [c11 Apr 1922; LU17744]. Si; b&w. 35mm. 5-6 reels.

Prod-Dir-Writ Edgar Jones.

Cast: Edgar Jones *(Grant Hamilton)*, Henry Van Bousen *(Henry Warburton)*, Edna May Sperl *(Nola)*, Walter Lewis *(Jake Fowler)*, Lillian Lorraine *(Martha Forrest)*.

Romantic comedy-drama. Henry Warburton, who is compelled to wait 9 years before coming into a willed inheritance, retires to the backwoods and marries Nola, a girl with no refinement or social graces. At length, his friend Grant Hamilton visits him, sees in Nola possibilities to which Warburton is blind, and "kidnaps" her. Hiding in a cottage, Nola is educated by Hamilton and a governess while Warburton searches in vain for her, mystified by frequent notes advising him of her progress, the last of which tells him of a daughter's birth. A year later, Warburton returns to New York where he meets Hamilton and Nola; amazed at the transformation, he is happily reunited with his wife. *Inheritance. Marriage. Social classes. Education. Etiquette.*

LONESOME LADIES F2.3171

First National Pictures. 3 Jul **1927** [c29 Jun 1927; LP24131]. Si; b&w. 35mm. 6 reels, 5,718 ft.

Prod Ray Rockett. *Dir* Joseph Henabery. *Scen* Winifred Dunn. *Story* Lenore J. Coffee. *Photog* Sol Polito, Al M. Green.

Cast: Lewis Stone *(John Fosdick)*, Anna Q. Nilsson *(Polly Fosdick)*, Jane Winton *(Mrs. St. Clair)*, Doris Lloyd *(Helen Wayne)*, Edward Martindel *(Motley Hunter)*, Fritzi Ridgeway *(Dorothy)*, De Sacia Mooers *(Bee)*, Capt. E. H. Calvert *(Mr. Burton)*, Grace Carlisle *(Mrs. Burton)*, Fred Warren *(butler)*.

Domestic comedy-drama. Architect John Fosdick becomes complacent in his married life, preferring to read and smoke at night, while Polly, his wife, feels they should talk. Then Fosdick's former sweetheart, now Mrs. St. Clair, renews her acquaintance with him when she requires his professional services and tries unsuccessfully to vamp him. Fosdick tells his wife about his former intimacy with the widow but is relieved to find that Polly, being asleep, fails to hear him. Meanwhile, Fosdick's secretary, Helen Wayne, who wants him for herself, gives Mrs. Fosdick the impression that her husband is unfaithful, causing her to leave him and join some bachelor ladies in an apartment called "Liberty Hall." Fosdick's attempts at reconciliation are thwarted by Helen, but at a party given by roguish Motley Hunter, he is reunited with his wife. *Architects. Vamps. Secretaries. Widows. Marriage. Infidelity.*

THE LONESOME TRAIL **F2.3172**

G. A. Durlam Productions. *Dist* Syndicate Pictures. 7 Aug **1930** [New York showing; released 15 Sep]. Sd (Cinephone); b&w. 35mm. 6 reels, 5,786 ft.

Supv-Story-Dial G. A. Durlam. *Dir* Bruce Mitchell. *Film Ed* G. A. Durlam. *Sd* J. R. Balsley.

Cast: Charles Delaney *(Judd Rascomb)*, Ben Corbett *(Sweetheart)*, Jimmy Aubrey *(Tenderfoot)*, Monte Montague *(Gila Red)*, Virginia Brown Faire *(Martha)*, William McCall *(Rankin)*, George Berliner *(Crabb)*, George Hackathorne *(Oswald)*, William von Brincken *(man in white sombrero)*, George Rigas *(The Ring Tailored Roarer)*, Lafe McKee *(sheriff)*, Yakima Canutt *(Two Gun)*, Bob Reeves *(Alkali)*, Art Mix *(Slim)*.

Western melodrama. "There is a mysterious bandit who is holding up the express shipments from the ranches. The girl's father has a partner who is really the villain, and this develops in the climax, saving the hero who of course is suspected of being the bandit." (*Film Daily*, 17 Aug 1930, p14.) *Ranchers. Bandits. Stagecoach robberies.*

THE LONG CHANCE **F2.3173**

Universal Film Manufacturing Co. 2 Oct **1922** [c18 Sep 1922; LP18228]. Si; b&w. 35mm. 5 reels, 4,331 ft.

Dir Jack Conway. *Scen* Raymond Schrock. *Photog* Benjamin Reynolds.

Cast: Henry B. Walthall *(Harley P. Hennage)*, Marjorie Daw *(Kate Corbaly/Dana Corbaly)*, Ralph Graves *(Bob McGraw)*, Jack Curtis *("Borax" O'Rourke)*, Leonard Clapham *(John Corbaly)*, Boyd Irwin *("Boston" [T. Morgan Carey])*, William Bertram *(Sam Singer)*, Grace Marvin *(Soft Wind)*, George A. Williams *(Dr. Taylor)*.

Western melodrama. Source: Peter Bernard Kyne, *The Long Chance* (New York, 1914). Harley P. Hennage, town gambler, takes under his protection Dana Corbaly when her widowed mother dies. He becomes suspicious of the motives of Bob McGraw, a young engineer who has come to town to investigate the mining claim of Dana's father, John Corbaly. But events reveal that he is only the tool of Corbaly's former partner, capitalist T. Morgan Carey. The land is retained by Dana, but in the process Bob is injured and Hennage is killed. *Engineers. Gamblers. Capitalists. Mine claims.*

LONG LIVE THE KING **F2.3174**

Metro Pictures. 26 Nov **1923** [c7 Nov 1923; LP19596]. Si; b&w. 35mm. 10 reels, 9,364 ft.

Dir Victor Schertzinger. *Adapt* C. Gardner Sullivan, Eve Unsell. *Photog* Frank B. Good.

Cast: Jackie Coogan *(Crown Prince Otto)*, Rosemary Theby *(Countess Olga)*, Ruth Renick *(Princess Hedwig)*, Vera Lewis *(Archduchess Annunciata)*, Alan Hale *(King Karl)*, Allan Forrest *(Nikky)*, Walt Whitman *(The Chancellor)*, Robert Brower *(The King)*, Raymond Lee *(Bobby, the American boy)*, Monte Collins *(Adelbert)*, Sam Appel *(Black Humbert)*, Allan Sears *(Bobby's father)*, Ruth Handforth *(Mrs. Braithwaite, the governess)*, Larry Fisher *(Herman Spier)*, Eddie Boland *(chief guard)*, Loretta McDermott *(Countess Olga's maid)*, Henry Barrows *(The Bishop)*.

Juvenile melodrama. Source: Mary Roberts Rinehart, *Long Live the King* (Boston & New York, 1917). Crown Prince Otto of Livonia, wishing to be like an ordinary little boy, runs away with Bobby, an American playmate. The king dies, and when the prince does not appear, the people begin to rise in revolution. Finally Otto hears the death knell for the king. In his hasty return to the palace, Otto is intercepted by revolutionaries and held captive until his friend Lieutenant Nikky rescues him. He arrives at the palace in time to restore order. *Royalty. Children. Imaginary kingdoms. Revolutions.*

THE LONG, LONG TRAIL *see* **THE RAMBLIN' KID**

THE LONG LONG TRAIL **F2.3175**

Universal Pictures. 27 Oct **1929** [c14 Oct 1929; LP770]. Sd (Movietone); b&w. 35mm. 6 reels, 5,331 ft. [Also si; 5,948 ft.]

Pres by Carl Laemmle. *Dir* Arthur Rosson. *Cont-Dial* Howard Green. *Photog* Harry Neumann. *Film Ed* Gilmore Walker.

Cast: Hoot Gibson *(The Ramblin' Kid)*, Sally Eilers *(June)*, Kathryn McGuire *(Ophelia)*, James Mason *(Mike Wilson)*, Archie Ricks *(Jyp)*, Walter Brennan *("Skinny" Rawlins)*, Howard Truesdale *(Uncle Josh)*.

Western melodrama. Source: Earl Wayland Bowman, *The Ramblin' Kid* (Indianapolis, 1920). The Ramblin' Kid acquires an unjustified reputation by pretending drunkenness and playfully shooting up the town of Eagle Butte. While professing a scorn for women, he falls for June, who comes to visit his employer—her uncle, Colonel Josh, a rancher. His clumsiness in courtship is overcome when he saves June from quicksand after her horse falls over a cliff. The Kid corrals a wild mare and prepares to run her in the annual rodeo sweepstakes. Mike Wilson, owner of the favorite, has The Kid drugged before the race, but he rides and wins. When Wilson tries to abscond with the wager money, The Kid captures him and reveals the plot; reinstated in the esteem of his friends, he finds happiness with June. *Cowboys. Ranchers. Drunkenness. Reputation. Courtship. Rodeos. Quicksand.*

Note: Remake of the 1923 film, *The Ramblin' Kid*, q. v.

THE LONG LOOP *see* **THE LONG LOOP ON THE PECOS**

THE LONG LOOP ON THE PECOS **F2.3176**

Leo Maloney Productions. *Dist* Pathé Exchange. 9 Jan **1927** [c14 Jan 1927; LU23528]. Si; b&w. 35mm. 6 reels, 5,977 ft.

Dir Leo Maloney. *Scen* Ford I. Beebe. *Story* W. D. Hoffman. *Photog* Vernon Walker.

Cast: Leo Maloney *(Jim Rutledge)*, Eugenia Gilbert *(Rose Arnold)*, Frederick Dana *(Arnold)*, Albert Hart *(Vining)*, Tom London *(Laird)*, Bud Osborne, Chet Ryan, William Merrill McCormick, Robert Burns, Dick La Reno, Murdock MacQuarrie.

Western melodrama. Jim Rutledge, a newcomer to the Pecos country, is befriended by Clem Vining, who has been constantly persecuted by the Long Loop gang, which he believes to be led by "Bobcat" Arnold, owner of a neighboring ranch. When Vining's son is killed by the gang, Jim sets out to investigate and gets a job under another name on Arnold's ranch. By interfering when Laird, the foreman, is pressing unwelcome attention upon Rose Arnold, Rutledge comes into his disfavor; he soon discovers that men from both ranches are conspiring with Laird to rustle cattle on both ranches. Jim bluffs Laird into admitting his guilt and effects a reconciliation between Vining and Arnold. *Ranchers. Rustlers. Ranch foremen. Murder. Texas.*

Note: Also reviewed and released under the title: *The Long Loop.*

LONG PANTS **F2.3177**

Harry Langdon Corp. *Dist* First National Pictures. 26 Mar **1927** [New York premiere; released 10 Apr; c22 Mar 1927; LP23766]. Si; b&w. 35mm. 6 reels, 5,550 ft.

Dir Frank Capra. *Adapt* Robert Eddy. *Story* Arthur Ripley. *Photog* Elgin Lessley, Glenn Kershner. *Comedy Construc* Clarence Hennecke.

Cast: Harry Langdon *(The Boy)*, Gladys Brockwell *(his mother)*, Al Roscoe *(his father)*, Alma Bennett *(The Vamp)*, Frankie Darro *(Langdon as a small boy)*, Priscilla Bonner *(Priscilla)*.

Comedy-drama. The Boy, who pictures himself in daydreams as a Don Juan, feels that before he can gain recognition he must persuade his mother to let him graduate from knee breeches to long pants. When at last this battle is won, he cycles down the street to show himself to the neighbors. Romance comes to him in the form of a city vamp. Meanwhile, a neighbor and his wife are consulting with Harry's parents about the betrothal of Harry and their daughter, Priscilla. The Boy balks at the altar when he reads in a newspaper that his unknown sweetheart is in jail; and going to her rescue, he is himself jailed. Learning that The Vamp has killed her husband, he thinks of his mother and Priscilla and realizes that they are his real inspiration. *Vamps. Adolescence. Courtship. Clothes. Smalltown life. Don Juan.*

THE LOOK OUT GIRL **F2.3178**

Quality Pictures. 1 Nov **1928.** Si; b&w. 35mm. 7 reels, 6,600-7,300 ft.

Dir Dallas M. Fitzgerald. *Scen* Adrian Johnson. *Titl* Tom Miranda. *Story* Alice Ross Colver. *Photog* Faxon Dean, Chandler House. *Film Ed* M. McKay.

Cast: Jacqueline Logan *(Dixie Mowbray)*, Ian Keith *(Dean Richardson)*, William H. Tooker *(Dr. Tucker)*, Lee Moran *(Pete)*, Gladden James *(Conway)*, Henry Herbert *(sheriff)*, Jimmy Aubrey *(valet)*, Broderick O'Farrell *(Hargrave)*, Jean Huntley *(nurse)*, Geraldine Leslie *(modiste)*.

Mystery drama. A young doctor, Dean Richardson, rescues Dixie Mowbray, whose canoe has overturned in the lake near his home, and learns that she is fleeing from some mysterious pursuers. During her convalescence they fall in love, and the girl agrees to marry the doctor if he will ask no questions about her past. A Federal agent, a friend of the doctor's, is sent from Washington to find the gang responsible for a post office robbery. Suspense builds, and the agent discovers that his friend's wife acted as lookout for the gang. *Physicians. Detectives. Government agents. Gangs. Mail theft.*

LOOK YOUR BEST **F2.3179**

Goldwyn Pictures. 18 Feb **1923** [c25 Jan 1923; LP18641]. Si; b&w. 35mm. 6 reels, 5,304 ft.

Dir-Story-Cont Rupert Hughes. *Photog* Norbert Brodin. *Art Dir* Cedric Gibbons. *Dance Supv* Ruth St. Denis. *Asst Dir* James Flood.

Cast: Colleen Moore *(Perla Quaranta)*, Antonio Moreno *(Carlo Bruni)*, William Orlamond *(Pietro)*, Orpha Alba *(Nella)*, Earl Metcalfe *(Krug)*, Martha Mattox *(Mrs. Blitz)*, Francis McDonald *(Alberto Cabotto)*.

Comedy-drama. Perla Quaranta, a half-starved "daughter of Little Italy," is given the place in Carlo Bruni's "Butterfly Act" that is vacated by a chorus girl who has grown too fat. Although Perla becomes friendly with Krug, the wire-man, she rejects him as a suitor, and in revenge Krug causes Perla's wire to break, hoping she will be fired for gaining weight. Instead, Bruni thrashes Krug, a felony for which he spends 30 days in jail. When freed, Bruni produces a new and successful dance act with Perla as the star, and the couple marry, each encouraging the other in his struggle against food. *Dancers. Acrobats. Italians. Tightrope walkers. Obesity. Diet.*

Note: Working title: *The Bitterness of Sweets.*

LOOKING FOR TROUBLE (Blue Streak Western) **F2.3180**

Universal Pictures. 30 May **1926** [c19 Apr 1926; LP22625]. Si; b&w. 35mm. 5 reels, 4,362 ft.

Pres by Carl Laemmle. *Dir* Robert North Bradbury. *Scen* George C. Hively. *Story* Stephen Chalmers. *Photog* William Nobles, Harry Mason.

Cast: Jack Hoxie *(Jack William Pepper)*, Marceline Day *(Tulip Hellier)*, J. Gordon Russell *(Jasper Murchison)*, Clark Comstock *(Jim Hellier)*, Edmund Cobb *(Phil Curtis)*, Bud Osborne *(Lou Burkhold)*, Peggy Montgomery *(Laura Burkhold)*, William Dyer *(Sheriff Tom Plump)*, Harry Russell *(see note)*, Scout *(himself, a horse)*.

Western melodrama. Jasper Murchison operates a smalltown newspaper in Texas as a front for jewel smuggling. He publishes a scandalous notice about Tulip Hellier and Phil Curtis, a young easterner employed on the Hellier ranch. Jack Pepper, known as "Don Quickshot," forces Murchison to retract the story, and during their confrontation a gun is accidentally fired; Murchison tells the sheriff that Jack tried to kill him, and Jack becomes a hunted man. Hiding on the Hellier ranch, Jack discovers that Lou Burkhold, ostensibly bootlegging, is smuggling diamonds in league with Murchison; also that he is keeping Laura, his daughter, from her husband, Phil, so as to involve her in the conspiracy. Jack accuses Murchison of treachery and fraud, brings about the arrest of the gang, and wins the heart of Tulip. *Ranchers. Smugglers. Smalltown life. Newspapers. Texas. Horses.*

Note: *Moving Picture World* lists Harry Russell as playing the sheriff.

LOOPED FOR LIFE **F2.3181**

J. Joseph Sameth Productions. *Dist* Madoc Sales. 24 Jun **1924** [New York State license]. Si; b&w. 35mm. 5 reels.

Dir Park Frame. *Photog* Chuck Welty.

Cast: Art Acord *(Buck Dawn)*, Jack Richardson *(Jack Hawkesby)*, Marcella Pershing *(Mary Baker)*, Charles Adler *(sheriff)*.

Western melodrama. "For some reason, the heavy is first introduced as a lifelong friend of the hero, a most likable fellow, whose surprising descent to villainy is caused overnight by one pang of jealousy and one pint of Scotch. All the way through, one expects him either to reform or die penitent, but the film ends suddenly after the hero's last hair-breadth escape." (*Variety*, 8 Oct 1924, p31.) *Jealousy. Friendship. Drunkenness.*

LOOSE ANKLES **F2.3182**

First National Pictures. 2 Feb **1930** [c28 Jan 1930; LP1042]. Sd (Vitaphone); b&w. 35mm. 7 reels, 6,190 ft. [Also si.]

Dir Ted Wilde. *Scen-Dial* Gene Towne. *Photog* Arthur Todd. *Songs: "Loose Ankles," "Whoopin' It Up"* Jack Meskill, Pete Wendling. *Dance Dir* Roy Mack.

Cast: Loretta Young *(Ann Harper)*, Douglas Fairbanks, Jr. *(Gil Hayden)*, Louise Fazenda *(Aunt Sarah Harper)*, Ethel Wales *(Aunt Katherine Harper)*, Otis Harlan *(Major Rupert Harper)*, Daphne Pollard *(Agnes)*, Inez Courtney *(Betty)*, Norman Selby *(Terry)*, Eddie Nugent *(Andy)*, Raymond Keane *(Linton)*.

Farce. Source: Sam Janney, *Loose Ankles, a Comedy in Three Acts* (New York, 1928). Ann Harper is bequeathed $1 million provided that she marry a man who meets the approval of her Aunts Sarah and Katherine. Ann and her cousin Betty advertise for a man willing to undergo a temporary marriage for a cash consideration; Gil Hayden answers the advertisement, meets Ann, and falls in love with her in the process. Linton, a mercenary member of Gil's gigolo quartette, attempts to interest the girl; and she allows him to take her to a cafe. There she meets Gil along with her aunts—escorted by his gigolo friends who have come to spy on Ann. But the aunts become intoxicated on punch; and when the cafe is raided, they are saved by the gigolos. When Ann and Gil announce their marriage, Aunts Sarah and Katherine are forced to consent, to allay the exposure of their scandalous intrigue. *Aunts. Gigolos. Inheritance. Marriage.*

LORD BYRON OF BROADWAY **F2.3183**

Metro-Goldwyn-Mayer Pictures. 28 Feb **1930** [c24 Feb 1930; LP1088]. Sd (Movietone); b&w with col sequences (Technicolor). 35mm. 9 reels, 7,200 ft. [Also si.]

Dir William Nigh, Harry Beaumont. *Dial-Cont* Crane Wilbur, Willard Mack. *Photog* Henry Sharp. *Art Dir* Cedric Gibbons. *Film Ed* Anne Bauchens. *Ballet Music: "Blue Daughter of Heaven"* Dimitri Tiomkin, Raymond B. Eagan. *Songs: "Only Love Is Real," "A Bundle of Old Love Letters," "Should I?" "The Woman in the Shoe," "When I Met You," "You're the Bride and I'm the Groom"* Nacio Herb Brown, Arthur Freed. *Song: "Love Ain't Nothing But the Blues"* Joe Goodwin. *Ballet stgd by* Albertina Rasch. *Dance Dir* Sammy Lee. *Rec Engr* Douglas Shearer. *Wardrobe* David Cox.

Cast: Charles Kaley *(Roy)*, Ethelind Terry *(Ardia)*, Marion Shilling *(Nancy)*, Cliff Edwards *(Joe)*, Gwen Lee *(Bessie)*, Benny Rubin *(Phil)*, Drew Demarest *(Edwards)*, John Byron *(Mr. Millaire)*, Rita Flynn *(Redhead)*, Hazel Craven *(Blondie)*, Gino Corrado *(Riccardi)*, Paulette Paquet *(Marie)*.

Musical romance. Source: Nell Martin, *Lord Byron of Broadway* (New York, 1928). Roy, a cafe pianist and song writer, uses his various romantic attachments as sources for creative inspiration; and when a girl who is infatuated with him shows him a bundle of old love letters, he exploits this material so successfully that he goes on to repeat the process with number of other girls. He finally stages his own vaudeville act with Nancy, a girl he discovers in a piano store; his friend Joe tries to save Roy from his habit of breaking hearts but himself dies as a result of his efforts. Consequently, Roy agrees to marry Nancy and give up his posture of a Broadway Lord Byron. *Pianists. Composers. Dancers. Flirtation. Vaudeville. New York City—Broadway. Documentation.*

LORD JIM **F2.3184**

Famous Players–Lasky. *Dist* Paramount Pictures. 14 Dec **1925** [c14 Dec 1925; LP22118]. Si; b&w. 35mm. 7 reels, 6,702 ft.

Dir Victor Fleming. *Screenplay* George C. Hull. *Adapt* John Russell. *Photog* Faxon Dean.

Cast: Percy Marmont *(Lord Jim)*, Shirley Mason *(Jewel)*, Noah Beery *(Captain Brown)*, Raymond Hatton *(Cornelius)*, Joseph Dowling *(Stein)*, George Magrill *(Dain Waris)*, Nick De Ruiz *(sultan)*, J. Gunnis Davis *(Scoggins)*, Jules Cowles *(Yankee Joe)*, Duke Kahanamoku *(Tamb Itam)*.

Drama. Source: Joseph Conrad, *Lord Jim* (Edinburgh, 1900). Jim, the first mate on a ship carrying Moslem pilgrims, deserts his post when the craft strikes a derelict. He is brought before an admiralty court and loses his seaman's certificate. After several years of dissipation and vagabondage, Jim arrives in Patusan, where his past is unknown. He becomes a figure of respect, friend and advisor to the natives. Three of his former shipmates, who have turned to piracy, turn up, and Jim befriends them. They kill the rajah's son, and Jim's life is forfeit under the law. He is executed by the rajah, dying in the arms of Jewel, a girl with whom he has fallen in love. *Seamen. Vagabonds. Muslims. Pilgrims. Pirates. Murder. Admiralty courts. Capital punishment. Shipwrecks.*

LORNA DOONE **F2.3185**
Thomas H. Ince Corp. *Dist* Associated First National Pictures. ca1 Oct **1922** [Cleveland premiere; c12 May 1922; LP17967]. Si; b&w. 35mm. 7 reels, 6,200 ft.
Prod-Dir Maurice Tourneur. *Scen* Katherine Reed, Cecil G. Mumford, Wyndham Gittens, Maurice Tourneur. *Photog* Henry Sharp. *Set Dsgn* Milton Menasco. *Cost* Milton Menasco.
Cast: Madge Bellamy *(Lorna Doone)*, John Bowers *(John Ridd)*, Frank Keenan *(Sir Charles Ensor)*, Jack McDonald *("The Counsellor")*, Donald MacDonald *(Carver Doone)*, Norris Johnson *(Ruth)*, May Giraci *(Lorna, as a child)*, Charles Hatton *(John, as a child)*.
Romantic drama. Source: Richard Doddridge Blackmore, *Lorna Doone* (1869). Lorna, while traveling with her mother, the countess, on a lonely Devon road, is kidnaped by Sir Charles Ensor and his band of outlaws; and adored by Sir Charles, she is reared by them. While in search of evidence against the robbers, young John Ridd meets Lorna; they become friends, and John agrees to aid her should she ever need him. When Sir Charles dies, Carver Doone tries to force Lorna into marriage, but she is rescued by John. Later, Lorna's noble parentage is discovered, and she is taken to court. John comes to London, and when the king's heir is being baptized, he saves the child from an anarchists' plot and is acclaimed a hero. Lorna decides to surrender her station and returns to marry John. Just as the marriage ceremony is ending, a vengeful Doone shoots Lorna. John leads the peasants in a victorious attack on the Doones, and returning home, John finds Lorna on her way to recovery *Nobility. Outlaws. Parentage. Devonshire (England). London.*

LORRAINE OF THE LIONS (Universal-Jewel) **F2.3186**
Universal Pictures. 11 Oct **1925** [c24 Jul 1925; LP21682]. Si; b&w. 35mm. 7 reels, 6,700 ft.
Dir Edward Sedgwick. *Scen* Isadore Bernstein, Carl Krusada. *Story* Isadore Bernstein. *Photog* Virgil Miller.
Cast: Norman Kerry *(Don Mackay)*, Patsy Ruth Miller *(Lorraine)*, Fred Humes *(Bimi)*, Doreen Turner *(Lorraine, at 7)*, Harry Todd *(Colby)*, Philo McCullough *(Hartley)*, Joseph J. Dowling *(Livingston, Sr.)*, Frank Newburg *(Livingston, Jr.)*, Rosemary Cooper *(Mrs. Livingston)*.
Melodrama. John Livingston marries a circus performer. His wealthy father disowns him but later offers to care for his daughter, Lorraine. John agrees, and the girl is put on a boat bound for the United States. On the voyage, the ship strikes a derelict and sinks, leaving Lorraine stranded on a desert island. She is cared for by lions and a gorilla, growing to maturity with a wild and wholly natural grace. Don Mackay, a fortune-teller, is eventually consulted by Lorraine's wealthy grandfather, and he divines her whereabouts. Livingston mounts an expedition to the island and returns to civilization with the girl and her pet gorilla, Bimi. During a formal dinner Lorraine is ill at ease, and Bimi, who misbehaves in sympathy, is put in a cage. That night, there is a thunderstorm, and the frightened gorilla escapes from the cage, carrying off Lorraine. Don Mackay rescues her, and the gorilla attacks him. Bimi is shot and killed, leaving Lorraine alone to mourn for him. Don prepares to go, and Lorraine, who has fallen in love with him, announces that she intends to go along with him. *Grandfathers. Fortune-tellers. Circus. Naturalism. Shipwrecks. Apes. Lions.*

THE LOSER'S END **F2.3187**
William Steiner Productions. Nov **1924** [c24 Oct 1924; LU20708]. Si; b&w. 35mm. 5 reels.
Story Ford Beebe. *Photog* Jacob A. Badaracco.
Cast: Leo Maloney *(Bruce Mason)*, Roy Watson *(Captain Harris)*, Tom London *(Barney Morris)*, Whitehorse *(John Kincaid)*, Josephine Hill *(Lois Kincaid)*, Bud Osborne *(Lucky Harnish)*, Barney Furey *(Simmie Busch)*, Wong Ti Set *(cook)*, Bullet *(himself, a dog)*.
Western melodrama. While Bruce Mason, Barney Morris, and Lucky Harnish compete for the favor of Lois Kincaid, the ranchowner's daughter, Barney works to arrest Bruce for smuggling opium. After some action and confusion Harnish emerges as the real culprit, and Bruce wins Lois—both with the help of Bruce's dog, Bullet. *Ranch life. Narcotics. Smuggling. Dogs.*

LOST *see* **HIS FORGOTTEN WIFE**

LOST AND FOUND *see* **LOST AND FOUND ON A SOUTH SEA ISLAND**

LOST AND FOUND ON A SOUTH SEA ISLAND **F2.3188**
Goldwyn Pictures. ca25 Feb **1923** [Los Angeles premiere; released 11 Mar; c10 Mar 1923; LP18763]. Si; b&w. 35mm. 7 reels, 6,334 ft.
Dir R. A. Walsh. *Scen* Paul Bern. *Titl* Katherine Hilliker, H. H. Caldwell. *Story* Carey Wilson. *Photog* Clyde De Vinna, Paul Kerschner. *Film Ed* Katherine Hilliker, H. H. Caldwell.
Cast: House Peters *(Captain Blackbird)*, Pauline Starke *(Lorna)*, Antonio Moreno *(Lloyd Warren)*, Mary Jane Irving *(Baby Madge)*, Rosemary Theby *(Madge)*, George Siegmann *(Faulke)*, William V. Mong *(Skinner)*, Carl Harbaugh *(Waki)*, David Wing *(Kerito)*.
Melodrama. Faulke, a swindling white trader who persuaded Madge to leave Captain Blackbird, insists that her daughter, Lorna, marry Waki, a native leader, although Lorna loves Lloyd Warren. While in search of a doll for his other daughter, Baby Madge, Captain Blackbird comes to Pago Pago and gruffly refuses to aid Lloyd and Lorna, whom he does not recognize. A chance encounter with Faulke, however, reveals the trader's evil doings and Lorna's identity. The captain and his men rush to the island and rescue Lorna from the warring natives. *Traders. Personal identity. Dolls. South Sea Islands. Pago Pago.*
Note: Reviewed in most publications as *Lost and Found.* Working titles: *Captain Blackbird, Passions of the Sea.*

LOST AT SEA **F2.3189**
Tiffany Productions. 15 Aug or 1 Sep **1926** [c10 Aug 1926; LP23011]. Si; b&w. 35mm. 7 reels, 6,400 ft.
Prod Phil Goldstone. *Dir* Louis J. Gasnier. *Scen* Esther Shulkin. *Photog* Milton Moore, Mack Stengler. *Art Dir* Edwin B. Hills. *Film Ed* James C. McKay.
Cast: Huntly Gordon *(Richard Lane)*, Lowell Sherman *(Norman Travers)*, Jane Novak *(Natalie Travers)*, Natalie Kingston *(Nita Howard)*, Billy Kent Schaefer *(Bobby Travers)*, Joan Standing *(Olga)*, William Walling *(chief of detectives)*, Rev. Neal Dodd *(Reverend Atkinson)*, Buddy *(himself, a dog)*.
Melodrama. Suggested by: Louis Joseph Vance, "Mainstream" (publication undetermined). Richard Lane isolates himself in the African interior for 5 years after his sweetheart, Natalie, marries Norman Travers. Travers, who tires of family life and neglects his wife and son, drifts into an affair with Nita Howard, a cabaret dancer. When Travers' ship is reported lost inward from Europe, Lane hears the news and determines to return and win Natalie; soon Lane develops a fondness for Natalie and her child, Bobby, and she consents to marry him. Travers, however, is rescued from a desert island and refuses to grant Natalie a divorce. Lane finds Travers murdered; and thinking that Natalie is guilty, he surrenders himself to the police. She denies his guilt, but the chief of detectives discovers that Nita Howard is the murderess. Lane is happily united with Natalie. *Dancers. Marriage. Self-sacrifice. Murder. Infidelity. Africa. Shipwrecks. Dogs.*

LOST AT THE FRONT **F2.3190**
John McCormick Productions. *Dist* First National Pictures. 29 May **1927** [c12 May 1927; LP23955]. Si; b&w. 35mm. 6 reels, 5,254 or 5,559 ft.
Pres by John McCormick. *Prod-Writ* Frank Griffin. *Dir* Del Lord. *Scen* Hampton Del Ruth. *Titl* Ralph Spence. *Photog* James Van Trees. *Comedy Construc* Clarence Hennecke.
Cast: George Sidney *(August Krause)*, Charlie Murray *(Patrick Muldoon)*, Natalie Kingston *(Olga Pietroff)*, John Kolb *(Von Herfiz)*, Max Asher *(Adolph Meyerburg)*, Brooks Benedict *(The Inventor)*, Ed Brady *(Captain Kashluff)*, Harry Lipman *(Captain Levinsky)*, Nita Martan, Nina Romano *(two Russian girls)*.
Farce. Patrick, a New York Irish policeman, and August, a German barkeeper, are the best of friends, though both are rivals for Olga, a sculptress whose studio is nearby. When August is called to the front as a German reservist, he takes a wireless which he believes will help Germany in the war. Patrick and Olga decide they must confiscate the invention before it destroys the American Army, and Pat enlists in the Russian Army as he is too old to join that of the United States. They meet on the Russo-German front, where Pat takes August prisoner; they engage in a game of dodging both armies, disguising themselves as women, and get into a Russian Battalion of Death. In their subsequent attempt to escape, news of the Armistice arrives. Returning home, they find that Olga has married in their absence. *Irish. Germans. Sculptors. Police. Bartenders. Friendship. Radio. World War I. Russia.*

THE LOST BATTALION **F2.3191**
L. C. McCallum. *Dist* Producers Security Corp. **1921.** Si; b&w. 35mm. 6 reels.
Cast: Gaston Glass, Blanche Davenport.
Drama(?). No information about the nature of this film has been found.
Note: Reissued in 1926 by Aywon Film Corp.

THE LOST CHORD **F2.3192**
Chord Pictures. *Dist* Arrow Film Corp. 15 Jan **1925** [c2 Dec 1924; LP20922]. Si; b&w. 35mm. 7 reels, 6,300 ft.
Whitman Bennett Production. *Dir-Adapt* Wilfred Noy.
Cast: David Powell *(Arnold Grahme)*, Alice Lake *(Countess Zara)*, Dagmar Godowsky *(Pauline Zara)*, Henry Sedley *(Count Zara)*, Faire Binney *(Joan)*, Louise Carter *(Phyllis)*, Charles Mack *(Jack Brown)*, Dorothy Kingdon *(Helene Brown)*, Samuel Hines *(Arthur Ames)*, Signor N. Salerno *(Levina)*, Rita Maurice *(Baby Joan)*.
Romantic melodrama. Suggested by: Arthur Seymour Sullivan, "The Lost Chord." When Arnold Grahme, a celebrated organist, returns from an extended trip to Europe, he finds that Madelaine, with whom he is in love, has been forced by her family to marry the rich Count Zara, who treats her brutally, beating her with a riding crop and openly conducting an affair with his cousin, Pauline Zara. The count arranges with Pauline for the removal of Madelaine's child, Joan, who is taken to England and falsely reported dead of diphtheria. Arnold kills the count in a duel in Italy. Madelaine enters a convent to nurse her sorrow and a weak heart. Arnold finds her among the gentle sisters and asks her to marry him. After a long period of refusal, she consents—but dies moments later of a heart attack. After many years, Grahme meets Madelaine's daughter, who has become a musical comedy star; not knowing who she is, he proposes and they are about to be wed when he discovers that she is deeply in love with his nephew, Jack. Grahme gives her up, sacrificing his own happiness for that of the young people, and finding solace in his music. *Organists. Nobility. Singers. Cousins. Marriage. Flagellation. Diphtheria. Convents. Italy. Duels.*

THE LOST EMPIRE **F2.3193**
Edward A. Salisbury. *Dist* Frederick J. Burghard. 25 Mar **1924** [New York State license; New York showing ca20 Jan 1929]. Si; b&w. 35mm. 6 reels, 5,640 ft.
Pres by Edward A. Salisbury. *Titl* Merian Cooper. *Photog* Ernest B. Schoedsack. *Film Ed* Merian Cooper.
Travelog. One of a series of travelogs produced by Captain Salisbury, who in this film travels in the South Seas, Ceylon, and Arabia. *Pygmies. South Seas. Ceylon. Arabia. Abyssinia.*
Note: Originally titled but never exhibited (at least in New York) as *In Quest of the Golden Prince*, which was changed to *The Lost Empire* in 1929.

THE LOST EXPRESS **F2.3194**
Dist Rayart Pictures. 15 Aug **1926.** Si; b&w. 35mm. 5 reels.
Prod Morris R. Schlank. *Dir* J. P. McGowan.
Cast: Henry Barrows *(John Morgan)*, Eddie Barry *(Valentine Peabody)*, Martin Turner *(George Washington Jones)*, Helen Holmes *(Helen Martin)*, Olita Otis *(Mrs. Arthur Standish)*, Jack Mower *(Alvin Morgan)*, Lassie Lou Ahern *(Baby Alice Standish)*, Fred Church *(Arthur Standish)*, Al Hoxie *(see note)*.
Melodrama. Millionaire John Morgan rides his personal train to pick up his daughter, Mrs. Arthur Standish, and her child, Alice, to take them on a trip away from the son-in-law, Arthur. On the way Morgan and the train are kidnaped by order of Arthur so that he may attempt to reunite with his wife. After a complicated chase, Arthur meets his wife and they are reconciled. They then reach Morgan and explain the situation to him after which all are on good terms once more. *Railroads. Kidnaping. Filial relations.*
Note: Al Hoxie's inclusion in the cast cannot be confirmed.

LOST IN A BIG CITY **F2.3195**
Blazed Trail Productions. *Dist* Arrow Film Corp. 10 or 16 Jan **1923** [Gloversville, N. Y., premiere; released 6 Apr; c16 Mar 1923; LP18788]. Si; b&w. 35mm. 8 reels.
Dir George Irving. *Scen* L. Case Russell. *Photog* Joseph Settle.
Cast: John Lowell *(Harry Farley)*, Baby Ivy Ward *(Florence)*, Jane Thomas *(Helen)*, Charles Beyer *(Sidney Heaton/Richard Norman)*, Evangeline Russell *(Blanche Maberly)*, James Watkins *(Dick Watkins)*, Edgar Keller *(Salvatori)*, Whitney Haley *(Cuboni)*, Edward Phillips *(Trooper Ned Livingston)*, Ann Brody *(Mrs. Leary)*, Charles A. Robins *("Raisin" Jackson)*, Jimmie Phillips *(Dick Watkins)*, Charles Mackay *(Simeon Maberly)*, Jules Cowles *(Jasper)*, Leota Miller.
Melodrama. Source: N. S. Woods, *Lost in a Big City* (c9 Jun 1905). Prospector Harry Farley returns from Alaska to find that his sister, Helen, has gone to New York with Florence, her blind daughter, after being deserted by her husband, Richard Norman. Under the name of Sidney Heaton, Norman has married Blanche Maberly and fallen in with a bootlegging gang while succumbing to the blackmail of Dick Watkins. Helen dies, Heaton kidnaps Florence, but Harry tracks him to the Adirondacks. *Prospectors. Bootleggers. Brother-sister relationship. Blindness. Blackmail. Bigamy. Adirondack Mountains.*

LOST IN THE ARCTIC *see* **THE GREAT WHITE NORTH**

A LOST LADY **F2.3196**
Warner Brothers Pictures. 18 Dec **1924** [17 Dec 1924; LP20921]. Si; b&w. 35mm. 7 reels, 7,111 ft.
Dir Harry Beaumont. *Adapt* Dorothy Farnum. *Photog* David Abel.
Cast: Irene Rich *(Marian Forrester)*, Matt Moore *(Neil Herbert)*, June Marlowe *(Constance Ogden)*, John Roche *(Frank Ellinger)*, Victor Potel *(Ivy Peters)*, George Fawcett *(Captain Forrester)*, Eva Gordon *(Bohemian Mary)*, Nanette Valone *(Gypsy dancer)*.
Drama. Source: Willa Cather, *A Lost Lady* (New York, 1923). Married to Captain Forrester, a wealthy railroad tycoon considerably older than herself, beautiful and frustrated Marian Forrester runs off with Frank Ellinger, who promises to marry her after she obtains a divorce. Marian then discovers that the captain has bankrupted himself trying to save a workingman's bank, and she returns to him out of loyalty; but when she later hears that Ellinger, who she thought would wait for her, is about to be married to someone else, she attempts to go to him. Delayed by a storm, she misses her train and goes instead to the home of Neil Herbert, an old friend and admirer. She calls Ellinger from there and is bluntly rejected. Sometime later, when the captain succumbs to old age and sorrow, Neil takes her in permanently. Marian begins to drink too much and becomes slovenly, but Neil continues to help her until, finding her affectionate with a low country fellow, he disgustedly leaves her. Years later, Neil discovers that she is living in South America, apparently happy and still beautiful, the wife of an aged Latin millionaire. (Western locale.) *Railroad magnates. Infidelity. Divorce. Alcoholism. Bankruptcy. Banks. Denver.*

THE LOST LIMITED **F2.3197**
Harry J. Brown Productions. *Dist* Rayart Pictures. Apr **1927.** Si; b&w. 35mm. 6 reels, 5,264 ft.
Dir J. P. McGowan. *Story-Scen* Henry R. Symonds. *Photog* Walter Griffen.
Cast: Reed Howes *(Leonard Hathaway)*, Ruth Dwyer *(Nora Murphy)*, Henry Barrows *(Silas Brownley)*, Billy Franey *(Rambling Red)*, J. P. McGowan *(Thomas Webber)*, George French, Dot Farley.
Melodrama. Learning his father's railroad business from the ground up, ne'er-do-well Leonard Hathaway undertakes to win a large ore-hauling contract by making his the company with the fastest train. No trick is overlooked by the villain, Thomas Webber, but the hero thwarts his opponents and proves himself worthy. *Ne'er-do-wells. Filial relations. Business competition. Freightage. Railroads. South Dakota. Brighton Beach. Train wrecks.*
Note: According to *Variety*, the climactic train collision used "some library stuff, evidently of a stunt pulled some years ago at the South Dakota state fair or at the old Brighton Beach race track." (7 Sep 1927, p24.)

THE LOST ROMANCE **F2.3198**
Famous Players–Lasky. *Dist* Paramount Pictures. 31 Jul **1921** [c21 Jul 1921; LP16783]. Si; b&w. 35mm. 7 reels, 6,443 ft.
Pres by Jesse L. Lasky. *Dir* William C. De Mille. *Scen* Olga Printzlau. *Story* Edward Knoblock. *Photog* Guy Wilky.
Cast: Jack Holt *(Mark Sheridan)*, Lois Wilson *(Sylvia Hayes)*, Fontaine La Rue *(Elizabeth Erskine)*, Conrad Nagel *(Allen Erskine, M. D.)*, Mickey Moore *(Allen Erskine, Jr.)*, Mayme Kelso *(librarian)*, Robert Brower *(butler)*, Barbara Gurney *(nurse)*, Clarence Geldert *(police lieutenant)*, Clarence Burton *(detective)*, Lillian Leighton *(Matilda)*.
Domestic melodrama. Physician Allen Erskine and his friend Mark

Sheridan, an explorer, both become infatuated with Sylvia Hayes, who is visiting Allen's aunt, and she marries Erskine. The explorer leaves for Africa; and returning 6 years later, he finds that the Erskines' romance has faded and that only their child holds them together. Sheridan confides to Sylvia his continuing love for her, and she, convinced that her marriage was an error, confesses her love for him. Erskine agrees to a separation in the interest of her happiness. Realizing the situation, Aunt Elizabeth arranges for the child to be "kidnaped" for a day. Turning to each other for consolation, the Erskines are reunited, while Sheridan finds sympathy in the affections of the aunt. *Physicians. Explorers. Aunts. Marriage. Parenthood. Kidnaping.*

THE LOST TRAIL **F2.3199**

Anchor Film Distributors. *Dist* Rayart Pictures. May **1926**. Si; b&w. 35mm. 5 reels, 4,409 ft.

Dir J. P. McGowan. *Story* Charles Saxton.

Cast: Al Hoxie.

Western melodrama. "Story concerns young bandit buster who breaks up outlaw gang, which always made successful getaways by unknown trail. Does job singlehanded, saving girl and her father from bandit's clutches." (*Motion Picture News Booking Guide,* 11:36, Oct 1926.) *Outlaws.*

THE LOST TRIBE **F2.3200**

Sunset Productions. *Dist* Aywon Film Corp. 10 Oct **1924** [New York State license]. Si; b&w. 35mm. 5 reels, 4,800 ft.

Cast: Kenneth McDonald.

Melodrama(?). No information about the nature of this film has been found.

THE LOST WORLD **F2.3201**

First National Pictures. 2 Feb **1925** [world premiere; released 22 Jun 1925; c24 Jan 1925; LP21068]. Si; b&w. 35mm. 10 reels, 9,700 ft.

By arrangement with Watterson R. Rothacker. *Supv* Earl Hudson. *Dir* Harry O. Hoyt. *Adapt-Scen-Ed Dir* Marion Fairfax. *Photog* Arthur Edeson. *Ch Tech* Fred W. Jackman. *Architecture* Milton Menasco. *Tech Dir* Willis H. O'Brien. *Research* Willis H. O'Brien.

Cast: Bessie Love *(Paula White)*, Lloyd Hughes *(Ed Malone)*, Lewis Stone *(Sir John Roxton)*, Wallace Beery *(Professor Challenger)*, Arthur Hoyt *(Professor Summerlee)*, Margaret McWade *(Mrs. Challenger)*, Finch Smiles *(Austin, Challenger's butler)*, Jules Cowles *(Zambo)*, Bull Montana *(Apeman)*, George Bunny *(Colin McArdle)*, Charles Wellesley *(Major Hibbard)*, Alma Bennett *(Gladys Hungerford)*.

Adventure-fantasy. Source: Arthur Conan Doyle, *The Lost World; Being an Account of the Recent Amazing Adventures of Professor George E. Challenger, Lord John Roxton, Professor Summerlee, and Mr. E. D. Malone of the Daily Gazette* (London, 1912). During the presentation of a paper to a scientific society, Professor Challenger claims to have discovered a lost world in South America, a world filled with prehistoric animals and ape-men. Scorned by his peers, Challenger forms an expedition to return to South America with the dual purpose of validating his theory and rescuing Maple White, an explorer left behind on Challenger's last expedition. The Challenger party, leaving on its hard journey into the Amazon country, includes in its number: Paula White (Maple's daughter), Ed Malone (an intrepid Irish reporter), Sir John Roxton (one of Paula's suitors), an eminent expert on beetles, and Challenger's butler. The party reaches the high plateau where the lost world begins, finds the remains of Paula's father, and witnesses a fight between two prehistoric animals. They are later beset by ape-men and a brontosaurus. The party finally escapes from the lost world and returns to London, taking a brontosaurus with them. The beast breaks loose in London and creates havoc in the city until it falls through London Bridge and drifts down the Thames to freedom in the sea. Ed Malone and Paula White are married. *Scientists. Reporters. Butlers. Exploration. Ape-men. Prehistory. South America. Amazon River. London. Dinosauers.*

THE LOST ZEPPELIN **F2.3202**

Tiffany Productions. 20 Dec **1929** [c10 Dec 1929; LP909]. Sd (Photophone); b&w. 35mm. 8 reels, 6,882 ft. [Also si.]

Dir Edward Sloman. *Scen* Frances Hyland. *Dial* Charles Kenyon. *Story* Frances Hyland, John F. Natteford. *Photog* Jackson Rose. *Film Ed* Martin G. Cohn, Donn Hayes. *Rec Engr* Jerry Eisenberg. *Sd Tech* John Buddy Myers.

Cast: Conway Tearle *(Commander Hall)*, Virginia Valli *(Mrs. Hall)*, Ricardo Cortez *(Tom Armstrong)*, Duke Martin *(Lieutenant Wallace)*, Kathryn McGuire *(Nancy)*, Winter Hall *(Mr. Wilson)*.

Adventure melodrama. At a banquet preceding his flight to the South Pole, Hall, a zeppelin commander, learns that his wife, Miriam, whom he worships, is in love with Lieutenant Tom Armstrong, his best friend and partner in the flight. She requests a divorce, which he agrees to grant after the voyage. When the zeppelin reaches the pole, a gale causes it to crash and the men divide up into search parties; a plane with room for only one finds Hall and Tom, and Hall insists that Tom be rescued. Tom is welcomed in Washington as the only survivor but finds that Miriam still loves her husband. Later, news comes of Hall's rescue and miraculous recovery, and he is happily reunited with his wife. *Explorers. Friendship. Infidelity. Zeppelins. South Pole. Antarctic regions. Washington (District of Columbia).*

LOST—A WIFE **F2.3203**

Famous Players–Lasky. *Dist* Paramount Pictures. 13 Jul **1925** [c10 Jun 1925; LP21545]. Si; b&w. 35mm. 7 reels, 6,420 ft.

Pres by Adolph Zukor, Jesse L. Lasky. *Dir* William C. De Mille. *Screenplay* Clara Beranger. *Photog* L. Guy Wilky.

Cast: Adolphe Menjou *(Tony Hamilton)*, Greta Nissen *(Charlotte Randolph)*, Robert Agnew *(Dick)*, Edgar Norton *(Baron Deliguières)*, Mario Carillo *(George)*, Genaro Spagnoli *(Duke de Val)*, Eugenio Di Liguro *(Louis)*, Henrietta Floyd *(Mrs. Randolph)*, Toby Claude *(Baroness)*, Marcelle Corday *(Julie, Charlotte's maid)*.

Comedy. Source: Clare Kummer, *Banco! a Comedy in Three Acts* (1925). Alfred Savoir, *Banco! comèdie en trois actes et quatre tableaux* (Paris, 1920). Compulsive gambler Tony Hamilton bets his friend Dick $5,000 that he will marry Charlotte Randolph, despite the fact that she is a total stranger and is engaged to the Duke de Val. Tony wins his bet. During the honeymoon, Tony obtains Charlotte's permission to spend 10 minutes at roulette, and, after he has been gambling non-stop for 3 days, she returns to her mother and obtains a divorce. A year passes. Tony learns that Charlotte is about to marry a wealthy baron; he returns to France but is too late to prevent the marriage. Tony stages an automobile accident in front of Charlotte's mansion, and her servants carry him into the house. He hides in her room and gives her 5 minutes to decide whether to elope with him or face a public scandal. She insists that he prefers gambling to love, but he convinces her otherwise; and they take leave of the baronial mansion, once again to face the divorce court and the altar. *Gamblers. Nobility. Marriage. Divorce. Wagers. France.*

THE LOTTERY BRIDE **F2.3204**

United Artists. 22 Nov **1930** [c1 Oct 1930; LP1639]. Sd (Movietone); b&w with col sequence (Technicolor). 35mm. 10 reels, 7,472 ft.

Pres by Joseph M. Schenck. *Prod* Arthur Hammerstein. *Gen Supv* John W. Considine, Jr. *Dir* Paul L. Stein. *Cont-Dial* Howard Emmett Rogers. *Adapt* Horace Jackson. *Orig Story* Herbert Stothart. *Photog* Ray June. *Sets* William Cameron Menzies, Park French. *Film Ed* Robert J. Kern. *Mus Arr* Hugo Riesenfeld. *Songs: "You're an Angel," "I'll Follow the Trail," "My Northern Light"* J. Keirn Brennan, Rudolf Friml. *Song: "High and Low"* Desmond Carter, Howard Dietz, Arthur Schwartz. *Rec Engr* P. P. Reed, Frank Maher. *Cost* Alice O'Neill.

Cast: Jeanette MacDonald *(Jenny)*, John Garrick *(Chris)*, Joe E. Brown *(Hoke)*, ZaSu Pitts *(Hilda)*, Robert Chisholm *(Olaf)*, Joseph Macaulay *(Alberto)*, Harry Gribbon *(Boris)*, Carroll Nye *(Nels)*.

Musical drama. On a spring evening in Norway, cafe owner Hilda, attempting to revive her business, has booked an American jazz orchestra led by Hoke Curtis, who has arranged a marathon dance contest. Jennie, whose brother Nels is in trouble for gambling with bank funds, enters the contest with her brother so as to cover the shortage, though against the wishes of her sweetheart, Chris. After 84 hours, she is near hysteria and exhaustion when the police arrive in search of Nels, prompted by Alberto, an Italian aviator who seeks Jennie's favor; she helps him escape and is imprisoned for aiding him, and Chris, misunderstanding, leaves for a mining camp. After being released, Jennie offers herself as a lottery bride; her ticket is purchased by Chris, but he gives it to Olaf, his older brother. She takes up residence with them, pending marriage, and Chris goes with Alberto on a dirigible expedition to the Arctic Circle; the dirigible is wrecked by a storm, but Jennie organizes a rescue party, and, with the misunderstanding adjusted, Jennie and Chris are reunited. *Aviators. Musicians. Lotteries. Courtship. Dance marathons. Embezzlement. Dirigibles. Oslo. Norway. Arctic regions.*

LOTUS BLOSSOM **F2.3205**

Wah Ming Motion Picture Co. *Dist* National Exchanges. 1 Dec **1921** [c2 Nov 1921; LU17159]. Si; b&w. 35mm. 7 reels.

Dir Frank Grandon. *Scen* George Yohalem, Charles Furthman. *Story* James B. Leong. *Photog* Ross Fisher.

Cast: Lady Tsen Mei *(Moy Tai)*, Tully Marshall *(Quong Foo)*, Noah Beery *(Tartar Chief)*, Jack Abbe *(Quong Sung)*, Goro Kino *(The Emperor)*, James Wang *(Prof. Lowe Team)*, Chow Young *(Tsze Sin)*.

Drama. Chong, inventor of the first clock that would eliminate the use of the village's sacred bell, is sentenced to life imprisonment by the emperor. The philosopher-inventor is concealed by Quong Foo and his little daughter, Moy Tai, who gives him a lotus flower. Time passes, and Moy Tai is soon a beautiful girl loved by Quong Sung, whom her father adopted as a boy. He is sent away to complete his studies and falls under the spell of a light woman, Tzse Sin. When the sacred bell cracks, Foo is commisssioned by the emperor to cast a new one, but the metals refuse to mingle and he is threatened with death. In a Tartar attack, Quong Sung is killed; Moy Tai learns from Chong that the metals will fuse only with the addition of a human sacrifice. She sacrifices herself for her father's honor, and the new bell is cast. *Philosophers. Inventors. Clocks. Bells. Human sacrifice. China.*

THE LOTUS EATER **F2.3206**

Marshall Neilan Productions. *Dist* Associated First National Pictures. ca27 Nov **1921** [New York premiere; released Jan 1922; c12 Dec 1921; LP17467]. Si; b&w. 35mm. 7 reels, 6,960 ft.

Prod-Dir Marshall Neilan. *Scen* Marion Fairfax. *Story* Albert Payson Terhune. *Photog* David Kesson. *Art Dir* John D. Schulze. *Film Ed* Daniel J. Gray.

Cast: John Barrymore *(Jacques Lenoi)*, Colleen Moore *(Mavis)*, Anna Q. Nilsson *(Madge Vance)*, Ida Waterman *(Mrs. Hastings Vance)*, Frank Currier *(The Dean)*, J. Barney Sherry *(John Carson)*, Wesley Barry *(Jocko)*.

Romantic melodrama. Under the terms of the will of his father (an eccentric millionaire), Jacques Lenoi grows up at sea ignorant of the world and the wiles of the opposite sex. At 25, he falls in love with the first girl he meets, Madge Vance, and their marriage proves a failure when Jacques is unable to acquire his entire inheritance. While accompanying a naval aviator on a dirigible excursion, Jacques finds himself stranded on a small island where the shipwrecked denizens have banded together under the leadership of The Dean. Eventually Jacques finds himself in love with Mavis, an islander, but he dreams of his wife back home. Returning to New York, Jacques finds that his wife, believing him dead, has married a wealthy broker; and asked to choose between the two, she rejects them both and elopes with a count. Jacques returns to Mavis and finds happiness in the simple life of the island colony. *Seamen. Colonists. Marriage. Bigamy. Inheritance. Dirigibles. Wills. New York City.*

LOTUS LADY **F2.3207**

Audible Pictures. *Dist* Greiver Productions. 31 Oct **1930**. Sd; b&w. 35mm. 7 reels, 6,100 ft.

Supv Lon Young. *Dir* Phil Rosen. *Scen-Dial* Harry Sinclair Drago. *Photog* M. A. Anderson. *Film Ed* Carl Himm.

Cast: Fern Andra *(Tamarah)*, Ralph Emerson *(Larry Kelland)*, Betty Francisco *(Claire Winton)*, Lucien Prival *(Castro)*, Frank Leigh *(Brent)*, Edward Cecil *(George Kelland)*, Junior Pironne *(Laddie)*, Jimmy Leong *(Li)*, Joyzelle *(The Dancer)*.

Romantic drama. Determined to set aright some dishonest transactions perpetrated by his brother, Larry Kelland goes to Indochina where he is sold some worthless swampland for a tea plantation by Castro, a shady cafe owner. Kelland becomes acquainted with Tamarah, a native girl who works for Castro, and marries her—protecting her from Castro. After 5 years of struggle and hard work Kelland's old flame, Claire Winton, once a gold digger and now a wealthy widow, reappears and tries to ruin his marriage. She succeeds for a time, but Kelland sees her purpose and retrieves Tamarah from the cafe. Meanwhile, the discovery of oil on Kelland's plantation contributes to their future happiness. *Restaurateurs. Swindlers. Brothers. Miscegenation. Oil. Plantations. Swamps. Tea. Indochina.*

LOVE **F2.3208**

Metro-Goldwyn-Mayer Pictures. 29 Nov **1927** [New York premiere; released 2 Jan; c9 Jan 1928; LP24843]. Si; b&w. 35mm. 8 reels, 7,365 ft.

Prod-Dir Edmund Goulding. *Cont* Frances Marion. *Titl* Marian Ainslee, Ruth Cummings. *Adapt* Lorna Moon. *Photog* William Daniels. *Set Dsgn* Cedric Gibbons, Alexander Toluboff. *Film Ed* Hugh Wynn. *Mus Score* Ernst Luz. *Song: "That Melody of Love"* Howard Dietz, Walter Donaldson. *Wardrobe* Gilbert Clark.

Cast: Greta Garbo *(Anna Karenina)*, John Gilbert *(Vronsky)*, George Fawcett *(Grand Duke)*, Emily Fitzroy *(Grand Duchess)*, Brandon Hurst *(Karenin)*, Philippe De Lacy *(Serezha, the child)*.

Tragedy. Source: Leo Nikolaevich Tolstoy, *Anna Karenina* (1875–77). Anna Karenina, the wife of a Russian nobleman, falls in love with Vronsky, a young officer, forfeiting her right to her child. Realizing her tragic fate and the futility of her existence, she commits suicide by throwing herself in front of a moving train. *Nobility. Infidelity. Suicide. Russia.*

Note: In an alternative ending Anna and Vronsky are happily reunited 3 years later, after her husband's opportune death.

LOVE AMONG THE MILLIONAIRES **F2.3209**

Paramount-Publix Corp. ca5 Jul **1930** [New York premiere; released 19 Jul; c18 Jul 1930; LP1428]. Sd (Movietone); b&w. 35mm. 10 reels, 6,910 ft.

Dir Frank Tuttle. *Dial* Herman J. Mankiewicz. *Adapt* Grover Jones, William Conselman. *Story* Keene Thompson. *Photog* Allen Siegler. *Songs: "Believe It or Not, I've Found My Man," "That's Worth While Waiting For," "Love Among the Millionaires," "Rarin' To Go!" "Don't Be a Meanie"* L. Wolfe Gilbert, Abel Baer. *Rec Engr* M. M. Paggi.

Cast: Clara Bow *(Pepper Whipple)*, Stanley Smith *(Jerry Hamilton)*, Skeets Gallagher *(Boots McGee)*, Stuart Erwin *(Clicker Watson)*, Mitzi Green *(Penelope Whipple)*, Charles Sellon *(Pop Whipple)*, Theodore von Eltz *(Jordan)*, Claude King *(Mr. Hamilton)*, Barbara Bennett *(Virginia Hamilton)*.

Romantic musical-comedy. Near a railroad junction, Pepper and her sister, Penelope, work in their father's cafe. Boots McGee, a railroad detective, and Clicker Watson, a telegraph operator, are bitter rivals for Pepper's love; however, she falls in love with Jerry Hamilton, son of the railroad president masquerading as a brakeman; but Jordan, a junior executive, informs Mr. Hamilton, who wires his son to return home. Jerry does so, bringing his sweetheart. At the Hamilton mansion, Pepper finds that although his sister, Barbara, is sympathetic, Hamilton is bitterly opposed to the match; and fearful of jeopardizing the father's happiness, she agrees with Hamilton that she should disillusion the boy. Meanwhile, Pepper's father along with her former suitors arrive in time for a party; Pepper pretends drunkenness and breaks the engagement, but Mr. Whipple and Hamilton strike up a friendship, and Penelope, discovering the plot, announces that Pepper still loves Jerry. *Sisters. Waitresses. Detectives. Railroad magnates. Railroad brakemen. Telegraph operators. Millionaires. Social classes. Courtship.*

LOVE AND GLORY (Universal-Jewel) **F2.3210**

Universal Pictures. 7 Dec **1924** [31 Jul 1924; LP20451]. Si; b&w. 35mm. 7 reels, 7,094 ft.

Pres by Carl Laemmle. *Dir* Rupert Julian. *Scen* Elliott Clawson, Rupert Julian. *Photog* Gilbert Warrenton.

Cast: Charles De Roche *(Pierre Dupont)*, Wallace MacDonald *(Anatole Picard)*, Madge Bellamy *(Gabrielle)*, Ford Sterling *(Emile Pompaneau)*, Gibson Gowland *(Jules Malicorne)*, Priscilla Moran *(Little Marie)*, Charles De Ravenne *(The Imp)*, André Lancy *(Dissard)*, Madame De Bodamere *(The Imp's Mother)*.

Romantic drama. Source: Perley Poore Sheehan and Robert Hobart Davis, *We Are French!* (New York, 1914). During an uprising in Algeria in 1869, two Frenchmen—Anatole, the brother of Gabrielle, and Pierre, her sweetheart—join the colors and are later reported dead. Gabrielle is kidnaped and taken to Paris, and the soldiers return. Fifty years pass, and on the way to Paris to be decorated the brother dies, but the lover is reunited with his youthful sweetheart. *Brother-sister relationship. Kidnaping. France—Army—Foreign Legion. Algeria. Paris.*

LOVE AND LEARN **F2.3211**

Paramount Famous Lasky Corp. 14 Jan **1928** [c14 Jan 1928; LP24862]. Si; b&w. 35mm. 6 reels, 5,825 ft.

Pres by Adolph Zukor, Jesse L. Lasky. *Dir* Frank Tuttle. *Screenplay-Scen* Louise Long. *Titl* Herman J. Mankiewicz. *Adapt* Florence Ryerson. *Story* Doris Anderson. *Photog* Harry Fischbeck. *Film Ed* Verna Willis.

Cast: Esther Ralston *(Nancy Blair)*, Lane Chandler *(Anthony Cowles)*, Hedda Hopper *(Mrs. Ann Blair)*, Claude King *(Robert Blair)*, Jack J. Clark *(Hansen)*, Jack Trent *(Jim Riley)*, Hal Craig *(Sergeant Flynn)*, Helen

Lynch *(Rosie)*, Catherine Parrish *(jail matron)*, Martha Franklin *(Martha)*, Jerry Mandy *(gardener)*, Dorothea Wolbert *(maid)*, Johnny Morris *(bum)*, Guy Oliver *(detective)*.

Comedy. Determined to prevent her parents' divorce, Nancy Blair purposely causes trouble for herself, knowing that this ruse will reunite, at least temporarily, her warring mother and father. When they discover the trick they decide to stay together anyhow. *Divorce. Filial relations.*

LOVE AND THE DEVIL **F2.3212**

First National Pictures. 24 Mar **1929** [c26 Feb 1929; LP162]. Sd eff & mus score (Vitaphone); b&w. 35mm. 7 reels, 6,588 ft. [Also si, 24 Mar 1929; 6,370 ft.]

Pres by Richard A. Rowland. *Prod* Ned Marin. *Dir* Alexander Korda. *Titl* Paul Perez, Walter Anthony. *Story* Josef Laszlo, Leo Birinski. *Photog* Lee Garmes. *Film Ed* John Rawlins.

Cast: Milton Sills *(Lord Dryan)*, Maria Corda *(Giovanna)*, Ben Bard *(Barotti)*, Nellie Bly Baker *(Giovanna's maid)*, Amber Norman *(streetwalker)*.

Melodrama. Lord Dryan marries Giovanna, a beautiful and famous Italian opera singer, and takes her to live in England. Giovanna is deeply in love with Dryan, but the dank English climate soon depresses her, and she longs openly for the sunshine and plaudits of her former life, eventually persuading Dryan to return with her to Venice. Barotti, her former leading man, conspires with Giovanna's maid to gain access to Giovanna's room at night without her knowledge; Dryan finds them together and takes a shot at Barotti. Dryan believes Giovanna to have been unfaithful, and she disappears. Dryan is charged with her murder on circumstantial evidence, but he is acquitted. Dryan goes to kill Barotti, and the tenor falls to his death. Dryan and Giovanna are reunited. *Singers. Nobility. Italians. Opera. Injustice. Trials. Circumstantial evidence. England. Venice.*

LOVE AT FIRST SIGHT **F2.3213**

Chesterfield Motion Picture Corp. 28 Jan **1930** [New York showing; released 15 Feb 1930]. Sd (Photophone); b&w. 35mm. 7 reels, 6,160-6,500 ft.

Dir Edgar Lewis. *Story-Dial* Lester Lee, Charles Levison. *Photog* Dal Clawson. *Film Ed* Russell Shields. *Songs: "Sunshine," "Jig-a-Boo Jig," "What Is Living Without You?" "Love at First Sight"* Lester Lee, Charles Levison. *Sd* George Oschman.

Cast: Norman Foster *(Richard Norton)*, Suzanne Keener *(June Vernon)*, Doris Rankin *(Mrs. Vernon)*, Lester Cole *(Paul Russell)*, Abe Reynolds *(Abe Feinstein)*, Hooper L. Atchley *(Frank Belmont)*, Burt Mathews *(master of ceremonies)*, Dorothee Adam *("jig-a-boo" singer)*, Jim Harkins, Paul Specht and His Orchestra, Tracy and Elwood, Chester Hale Girls.

Musical comedy–drama. Finally landing a backer (Abe Feinstein) for their first full-length musical show, writers Paul Russell and Dick Norton spot their ideal leading lady in June Vernon—or, rather, Dick spots her and falls in love with her at first sight. Frank Belmont, owner of a popular nightclub, wants June to be in his new revue, and her ambitious mother is inclined to agree—even when Dick's show is a hit on opening night. Forced to choose between her mother and Dick, June joins Belmont's show, where she enjoys success, while Dick tears up June's contract and disappears. Sometime later a gay party from Belmont's, which includes June, stops at Kelly's "Honk A Tonk." Noticing that the pianist is especially good, the crowd persuades June to sing. The song she chooses results in her reunion with Dick, the pianist. Belmont walks out; and Paul, Dick, June, Abe, and Mrs. Vernon get together to work on a new show. *Singers. Playwrights. Theatrical backers. Pianists. Motherhood. Nightclubs.*

THE LOVE BANDIT **F2.3214**

Charles E. Blaney Productions. *Dist* Vitagraph Co. of America. 6 Jan **1924** [c7 Dec 1923; LP19704]. Si; b&w. 35mm. 6 reels, 5,800 ft.

Dir Dell Henderson. *Adapt* Lewis Allen Browne.

Cast: Doris Kenyon *(Amy Van Clayton)*, Victor Sutherland *(Jim Blazes)*, Jules Cowles *(Henri Baribeau)*, Christian Frank *(Buck Ramsdell)*, Mary Walters *(Maggie McGuire)*, Miss Valentine *("Frenchie" Annie)*, Cecil Spooner *(Madge Dempsey)*, Gardner James *(Frederick Van Clayton)*, Walter Jones *(John Lawson)*, Edward Bouldin *("Snapper" Rollins)*.

Western melodrama. Source: Charles E. Blaney and Norman Houston, *The Love Bandit* (a play, c11 May 1921). Jim Blazes falls in love with Amy Van Clayton when he meets her in a lumber camp. In New York, Amy discovers that her brother is in danger of being jailed for stealing from Jim, who is his boss. To protect her brother, Amy marries Jim, but he returns to the lumber camp alone because he feels that Amy does not love him. Amy follows; later, when Jim's life is in danger, she finds that she really does love him. *Brother-sister relationship. Marriage. Theft. Lumber camps. New York City.*

THE LOVE BRAND **F2.3215**

Universal Pictures. 13 Aug **1923** [c25 Jul 1923; LP19252]. Si; b&w. 35mm. 5 reels, 4,832 ft.

Pres by Carl Laemmle, Jr. *Dir* Stuart Paton. *Story-Scen* Adrian Johnson. *Story? (see note)* Raymond L. Schrock. *Photog* William Thornley.

Cast: Roy Stewart *(Don José O'Neil)*, Wilfrid North *(Peter Collier)*, Margaret Landis *(Frances Collier)*, Arthur Hull *(Charles Mortimer)*, Sidney De Grey *(Miguel Salvador)*, Marie Wells *(Teresa)*.

Western melodrama. Frances Collier sets a love trap for landowner Don José O'Neil to help her father acquire his potentially oil-rich land, then falls genuinely in love with her victim. A rejected suitor reveals her treachery, but when she willingly submits to being branded, O'Neil sees that she cares for him, and they are married. *Filial relations. Perfidy. Oil lands. Branding.*

Note: Universal records indicate that Adrian Johnson wrote both story and scenario but that there was no screen credit given for story and that studio publicity credited Raymond L. Schrock. Hence the error in most sources citing Schrock as author of the story.

THE LOVE CHARM **F2.3216**

Realart Pictures. *Dist* Paramount Pictures. ca27 Nov **1921** [Los Angeles premiere; released Dec; c9 Nov 1921; LP17178]. Si; b&w. 35mm. 5 reels, 4,540 ft.

Dir Thomas N. Heffron. *Scen* Percy Heath. *Story* Harvey J. O'Higgins. *Photog* William E. Collins. *Asst Dir* Maynard Laswell.

Cast: Wanda Hawley *(Ruth Sheldon)*, Mae Busch *(Hattie Nast)*, Sylvia Ashton *(Julia Nast)*, Warner Baxter *(Thomas Morgan)*, Carrie Clark Ward *(housekeeper)*, Molly McGowan *(Maybelle Mooney)*.

Comedy-drama. Ruth Sheldon, an orphan, goes to live with her Aunt Julia and Cousin Hattie Nast of Primpton. In the station she takes an interest in an article on "Love Charms." At the Nast home, she is obliged to serve as housekeeper, cook, and seamstress. Young banker Thomas Morgan is invited to dinner, and Hattie, noticing Morgan's attentions to Ruth, claims him as her own. Later, at a party, Ruth, in an effort to shock him, pretends to be a frivolous vamp but Harry Morgan informs Thomas of her plan. When Harry comes into money, Hattie decides that she cares for him rather than Thomas; this decision leaves Thomas free to marry Ruth. *Aunts. Cousins. Vamps. Bankers. Smalltown life. Drudgery.*

LOVE COMES ALONG **F2.3217**

RKO Productions. 5 Jan **1930** [c5 Jan 1930; LP1010]. Sd (Photophone); b&w. 35mm. 8 reels, 7,048 ft. [Also si.]

Dir Rupert Julian. *Screenplay* Wallace Smith. *Photog* J. Roy Hunt. *Art Dir* Max Ree. *Film Ed* Archie Marshek. *Mus Dir* Victor Baravalle. *Songs: "Night Winds," "Until Love Comes Along"* Oscar Levant, Sidney Clare. *Dance Dir* Pearl Eaton. *Rec Engr* John Tribby.

Cast: Bebe Daniels *(Peggy)*, Lloyd Hughes *(Johnny)*, Montagu Love *(Sangredo)*, Ned Sparks *(Happy)*, Lionel Belmore *(Brownie)*, Alma Tell *(Carlotta)*, Evelyn Selbie *(Bianca)*, Sam Appel *(Gómez)*.

Romantic melodrama. Source: Edward Knoblock, *Conchita, a Romantic Play in Three Acts* (c1924). Johnny Stark and the crew of a tramp steamer land on the island of Caparoja, where Colonel Sangredo, the local "potentate," tells them of the island's many pleasures. Johnny and his pal, Happy, encounter Peggy, a stranded American actress, singing in a tavern, while Sangredo discovers that his friend Carlotta has deserted him and obtains Peggy's services in singing at a fiesta. Johnny tells Peggy of his love and proposes an immediate marriage, but he is furious upon learning of the arrangement with Sangredo and she renounces him. When she sings to Johnny at the fiesta, Sangredo orders his arrest, but Peggy secures his freedom by agreeing to dine with the colonel; Johnny returns with his pal, however, and rescues her. *Singers. Sailors. Courtship. Caribbean.*

THE LOVE DOCTOR **F2.3218**

Paramount Famous Lasky Corp. 5 Oct **1929** [c4 Oct 1929; LP745]. Sd (Movietone); b&w. 35mm. 6 reels, 5,503 ft. [Also si, 19 Oct 1929; 5,378 ft.]

Dir Melville Brown. *Dial* Guy Bolton. *Titl* Herman Mankiewicz. *Adapt* Guy Bolton, J. Walter Ruben. *Photog* Edward Cronjager. *Film Ed* Otto Ludwig. *Rec Engr* Earl Hayman.

Cast: Richard Dix *(Dr. Gerald Sumner)*, June Collyer *(Virginia Moore)*,

Morgan Farley *(Bud Woodbridge)*, Miriam Seegar *(Grace Tyler)*, Winifred Harris *(Mrs. Woodbridge)*, Lawford Davidson *(Preston DeWitt)*, Gale Henry *(Lucy)*.

Farce. Source: Winchell Smith and Victor Mapes, *The Boomerang; Comedy in Three Acts* (New York, 1915). Gerald Sumner, a young physician and confirmed bachelor, opens his office and finds that he is without patients until a fond mother brings him her son, Bud Woodbridge, whose malady Sumner diagnoses as "love sickness." Woodbridge, in love with Grace Tyler, a fickle debutante who cannot take him seriously because of her infatuation for Sumner, follows Sumner's instructions to rest in the country and take quantities of distilled water administered by Virginia Moore, Sumner's nurse. Because Virginia is in love with Sumner she complies, hoping that his weekend visits will give *him* love sickness. Grace Tyler's arrival, and her insistence that Sumner marry her, complicate matters. The situation is resolved when Sumner admits that love cannot be cured; he marries Virginia and encourages Bud to marry Grace. *Physicians. Bachelors. Nurses. Socialites.*

LOVE 'EM AND LEAVE 'EM **F2.3219**

Famous Players–Lasky. *Dist* Paramount Pictures. 6 Dec **1926** [c3 Dec 1926; LP23404]. Si; b&w. 35mm.

Pres by Adolph Zukor, Jesse L. Lasky. *Assoc Prod* William Le Baron. *Dir* Frank Tuttle. *Adapt-Screenplay* Townsend Martin. *Photog* George Webber.

Cast: Evelyn Brent *(Mame Walsh)*, Lawrence Gray *(Bill Billingsley)*, Louise Brooks *(Janie Walsh)*, Osgood Perkins *(Lem Woodruff)*, Jack Egan *(Cartwright)*, Marcia Harris *(Miss Streeter)*, Edward Garvey *(Mr. Whinfer)*, Vera Sisson *(Mrs. Whinfer)*, Joseph McClunn *(August Whinfer)*, Arthur Donaldson *(Mr. McGonigle)*, Elise Cabanna *(Miss Gimple)*, Dorothy Mathews *(Minnie)*.

Comedy-drama. Source: John V. A. Weaver and George Abbott, *Love 'Em and Leave 'Em, a Comedy in Three Acts* (New York, 1926). While Mame Walsh is away on vacation, her younger sister, Janie, begins a flirtation with Mame's sweetheart, Bill Billingsley, who clerks in the same department store where they work. Mame stages a surprise party for Bill, at which she plans to accept his proposal, until she sees Janie secretly kissing him and announces she will adopt Janie's philosophy of "love 'em and leave 'em." She begins an obvious flirtation with Lem Woodruff, a petty crook and gambler. Janie, meanwhile, having dissipated the funds of the department store's welfare club in racetrack betting, tries to recover her losses with Lem's help. Miss Streeter, the club president, threatens to prosecute, and Janie places the blame on Mame. The store masquerade finds Janie dancing with doubt-torn Bill and flirting with Manager McGonigle, thereby winning promotions for all; and Mame, retrieving the club funds from Lem, is reunited with Bill. *Sisters. Flirts. Department stores. Boardinghouses. Gambling. Embezzlement. Clubs. New York City.*

THE LOVE GAMBLE **F2.3220**

Banner Productions. *Dist* Henry Ginsberg Distributing Corp. 11 Sep **1925** [New York showing; c11 Jul 1925; LP21648]. Si; b&w. 35mm. 6 reels.

Ben Verschleiser Production. *Dir* Edward Le Saint. *Cont* Harry O. Hoyt. *Titl* Frederick Hatton, Fanny Hatton. *Photog* King Gray, Orin Jackson.

Cast: Lillian Rich *(Peggy Mason)*, Robert Frazer *(Douglas Wyman)*, Pauline Garon *(Jennie Howard)*, Kathleen Clifford *(Fifi Gordon)*, Larry Steers *(Jim Gordon)*, Bonnie Hill *(Mrs. Wyman)*, Arthur Rankin *(Jack Mason)*, Brooks Benedict *(Joe Wheeler)*, James Marcus *(Dan Mason)*.

Melodrama. Source: Maysie Greig, *Peggy of Beacon Hill* (Boston, 1924). Peggy Mason, the part owner of a tearoom in Boston, falls in love with Douglas Wyman. On a walking trip, they stop at a lodge in the hills, and Peggy learns that Douglas is unhappily married. Peggy immediately leaves the lodge and is caught in a storm, from which she is rescued by an old suitor. Douglas' wife is found murdered, and when he will not establish an alibi for fear of ruining Peggy's reputation, Douglas is accused of and tried for the crime. Peggy learns of the trial at the last minute and hurries to the courtroom, arriving in time to clear Douglas of the charges against him. Douglas then declares his love for her, but Peggy, who has become engaged to her old suitor, must refuse him. The suitor, however, realizes that Peggy loves Douglas and releases her from the engagement; Peggy returns to Douglas and they are married. *Businesswomen. Murder. Marriage. Reputation. Trials. Teashops. Boston. Storms.*

THE LOVE GAMBLER **F2.3221**

Fox Film Corp. 12 Nov **1922** [c12 Nov 1922; LP19008]. Si; b&w. 35mm. 5 reels, 4,682 ft.

Pres by William Fox. *Dir* Joseph Franz. *Scen* Jules Furthman. *Photog* Joe August.

Cast: John Gilbert *(Dick Manners)*, Carmel Myers *(Jean McClelland)*, Bruce Gordon *(Joe McClelland)*, Cap Anderson *(Curt Evans)*, William Lawrence *(Tom Gould)*, James Gordon *(Col. Angus McClelland)*, Mrs. Cohen *(Mrs. McClelland)*, Barbara Tennant *(Kate)*, Edward Cecil *(Cameo Colby)*, Doreen Turner *(Ricardo [Kate's child])*.

Western melodrama. Source: Lillian Bennett-Thompson and George Hubbard, "Where the Heart Lies," in *Success Magazine* (Feb–Mar 1922). In a *Taming of the Shrew* theme, ranch hand Dick Manners wins his wager that he will tame a wild horse and "tame" and kiss Jean McClelland, the daughter of his employer—both by whistling a certain tune. Dick's romance with Jean, however, is interrupted when he marries a dying woman (Kate) to give her child a name. Kate recovers, but her subsequent suicide frees Dick; and Jean's love triumphs over her parents' objections. *Cowboys. Shrews. self-sacrifice. Illegitimacy. Suicide. Whistling. Wagers. Horses.*

LOVE, HATE AND A WOMAN **F2.3222**

J. G. Pictures. *Dist* Arrow Film Corp. Jul **1921** [c4 Aug 1921; LP16838]. Si; b&w. 35mm. 6 reels.

Dir-Writ Charles Horan.

Cast: Grace Davison *(The Girl [Daryl Sutherland])*, Ralph Kellard *(The Man [John Lockwood])*, Robert Frazer *(The Brother)*, Lila Peck *(The Sister)*, Charles McDonald *(Mr. Ramsey)*, Julia Swayne Gordon *(Mrs. Ramsey)*.

Society melodrama. Daryl Sutherland, in the guise of a society belle, makes the acquaintance of young artist John Lockwood at an exclusive mountain resort. Their friendship drifts into mutual attraction until Mrs. Ramsey, a devotee of the artist, determines to win his attentions and exposes Daryl as a cloak model. Daryl manages to protect Mrs. Ramsey from her irate husband by claiming that Lockwood is her husband. Later, Daryl suspects that he is the seducer of her dying sister; but following a series of dramatic incidents, Lockwood is exonerated and a happy reunion results. *Artists. Fashion models. Sisters. Seduction.*

THE LOVE HOUR **F2.3223**

Vitagraph Co. of America. ca30 Aug **1925** [c21 Aug 1925; LP21755]. Si; b&w. 35mm. 7 reels, 7,036 ft.

Dir Herman Raymaker. *Adapt-Scen* Bess Meredyth. *Photog* E. B. Du Par.

Cast: Huntley Gordon *(Rex Westmore)*, Louise Fazenda *(Jenny Tibbs)*, Willard Louis *(Gus Yerger)*, Ruth Clifford *(Betty Brown)*, John Roche *(Ward Ralston)*, Charles Farrell *(Kid Lewis)*, Gayne Whitman *(attorney)*.

Melodrama. Rex Westmore, idling at a seashore resort, protects Betty Brown from the unwanted advances of a sandy sheik, and mutual interest soon develops into love. They marry and after a honeymoon in Europe settle down to contented domesticity. Ward Ralston, Westmore's financial advisor and agent, falls in love with Betty and conspires with a dishonest physician to ruin Rex's health, thereby hoping to gain control of both Rex's wife and his money. The physician dopes Rex, telling Betty that only an operation in Europe, preformed by a noted Swiss surgeon, can save his life. Ralston then offers to finance the trip if Betty will divorce Rex and marry him. In her extremity, she consents, leading Rex to believe that she has fallen in love with Ralston, knowing that only by this deception will she be able to persuade her husband to go to Switzerland. Ralston's scheme is exposed, however, and he receives a sound thrashing. Betty and Rex are reunited. *Physicians. Surgeons. Marriage. Health. Resorts.*

LOVE HUNGRY **F2.3224**

Fox Film Corp. 8 Apr **1928** [c23 Mar 1928; LP25100]. Si; b&w. 35mm. 6 reels, 5,792 ft.

Pres by William Fox. *Dir* Victor Heerman. *Scen* Randall H. Faye. *Titl* Frances Agnew. *Story* Randall H. Faye, Victor Heerman. *Photog* Glen MacWilliams. *Film Ed* Alexander Troffey. *Asst Dir* Jasper Blystone.

Cast: Lois Moran *(Joan Robinson)*, Lawrence Gray *(Tom Harver)*, Marjorie Beebe *(Mamie Potts)*, Edythe Chapman *(Ma Robinson)*, James Neill *(Pa Robinson)*, John Patrick *(Lonnie Van Hook)*.

Romantic comedy. Joan Robinson, a discouraged chorus girl, returns home and finds boarder Tom Harver, an author who works in a publishing house, occupying one of the rooms. Tom encourages Joan to marry a wealthy man, but instead she chooses Tom, whom she loves in spite of his poverty. *Chorus girls. Authors. Publishers.*

Note: Some sources credit Glenn MacWilliams as titler.

LOVE IN THE DARK **F2.3225**

Metro Pictures. 20 Nov **1922** [New York premiere; released 11 Dec; c23 Nov 1922; LP18437]. Si; b&w. 35mm. 6 reels, 5,900 ft.

Prod-Dir Harry Beaumont. *Scen* J. G. Hawks. *Story* John Moroso. *Photog* John Arnold. *Art Dir* J. J. Hughes.

Cast: Viola Dana *(Mary Duffy)*, Cullen Landis *(Tim O'Brien)*, Arline Pretty *(Mrs. O'Brien)*, Bruce Guerin *("Red" O'Brien)*, Edward Connelly *(Dr. Horton)*, Margaret Mann *(Mrs. Horton)*, John Harron *(Robert Horton)*, Charles West *(Jimmy Watson)*.

Melodrama. Source: John Moroso, "Page Tim O'Brien," in *Munsey's Magazine* (77:172–192, Oct 1922). Mr. and Mrs. Tim O'Brien hire orphan Mary Duffy to care for their son, Red, then desert the two of them when eluding the police. Mrs. O'Brien abandons Tim, who can see only at night, and she is killed by an automobile. After finding a home with the Hortons, Mary discovers that Dr. Horton's son, Robert, is taking European Relief funds from Horton's safe to use for gambling, and she informs Tim of the theft. Tim agrees to recover the money from the gambler's safe, is nearly caught, and is reunited with Mary and Red. *Orphans. Thieves. Parenthood. Blindness. Desertion. Funds—Public.*

LOVE IN THE DESERT **F2.3226**

FBO Pictures. 17 Mar **1929** [c27 Jan 1929; LP103]. Talking sequences, sd eff, & mus score (Photophone); b&w. 35mm. 7 reels, 6,365 ft. [Also si, 27 Jan 1929; 5,365 ft.]

Dir George Melford. *Screenplay* Harvey Thew, Paul Percy. *Dial* Harvey Thew. *Titl* Randolph Bartlett. *Story* Louis Sarecky, Harvey Thew. *Photog* Paul Perry. *Film Ed* Mildred Richter. *Cost* Walter Pulunkett.

Cast: Olive Borden *(Zarah)*, Hugh Trevor *(Bob Winslow)*, Noah Beery *(Abdullah)*, Frank Leigh *(Harim)*, Pearl Varvell *(Fatima)*, William H. Tooker *(Mr. Winslow)*, Ida Darling *(Mrs. Winslow)*, Alan Roscoe *(Houdish)*, Fatty Carr *(Briggs)*.

Melodrama. En route to an irrigation project in North Africa, Bob Winslow is abducted by an outlaw band led by Abdullah and held for ransom. With the aid of Zarah, a beautiful Arabian, Bob escapes and makes his way to safety with her. Abdullah swears revenge and threatens a massacre if Zarah does not return to him as his bride. Zarah gives herself up, and Bob quickly rescues her. Abdullah's forces attack, and Bob kills the chieftan in a hand-to-hand fight. *Arabs. Abduction. Ransom. Irrigation. North Africa.*

LOVE IN THE ROUGH **F2.3227**

Metro-Goldwyn-Mayer Pictures. 6 Sep **1930** [c8 Oct 1930; LP1618]. Sd (Movietone); b&w. 35mm. 10 reels, 7,785 ft.

Dir Charles F. Reisner. *Dial* Joe Farnham, Robert E. Hopkins. *Adapt* Sarah Y. Mason. *Photog* Henry Sharp. *Art Dir* Cedric Gibbons. *Film Ed* Basil Wrangell. *Songs: "I'm Doing That Thing," "I'm Learning a Lot From You," "Go Home and Tell Your Mother," "Like Kelly Can," "One More Waltz"* Dorothy Fields, Jimmy McHugh. *Dance Dir* Sammy Lee. *Rec Engr* Ralph Shugart, Douglas Shearer. *Wardrobe* David Cox.

Cast: Robert Montgomery *(Kelly)*, Dorothy Jordan *(Marilyn)*, Benny Rubin *(Benny)*, J. C. Nugent *(Waters)*, Dorothy McNulty *(Virgie)*, Tyrrell Davis *(Tewksbury)*, Harry Burns *(gardener)*, Allan Lane *(Johnson)*, Catherine Moylan *(Martha)*, Edwards Davis *(Williams)*, Roscoe Ates *(proprietor)*, Clarence H. Wilson *(Brown)*.

Musical comedy. Source: Vincent Lawrence, *Spring Fever* (New York opening: 3 Aug 1925). A remake of the silent version, *Spring Fever* (1927), with musical interludes. *Salesclerks. Jews. Courtship. Golf. Country clubs.*

LOVE IS AN AWFUL THING **F2.3228**

Owen Moore Film Corp. *Dist* Selznick Distributing Corp. 30 Aug or 15 Sep **1922** [c5 Sep 1922; LP18198]. Si; b&w. 35mm. 7 reels, 6,853 ft.

Pres by Lewis J. Selznick. *Dir-Writ* Victor Heerman. *Photog* Jules Cronjager.

Cast: Owen Moore *(Anthony Churchill)*, Thomas Guise *(Judge Griggs)*, Marjorie Daw *(Helen Griggs)*, Kathryn Perry *(Ruth Allen)*, Arthur Hoyt *(Harold Wright)*, Douglas Carter *(Porter)*, Charlotte Mineau *(Marion)*, Snitz Edwards *(superintendent)*, Alice Howell *(superintendent's wife)*.

Farce. Shortly before Anthony Churchill is to marry Helen Griggs, an old flame shows up and insists he has promised to marry her. He then pretends that he and Helen are already married, but Helen, seeing him with his old flame, believes that he is deceiving her. All is explained, however, and the wedding proceeds. *Weddings. Courtship.*

THE LOVE KISS **F2.3229**

P. A. Powers. *Dist* Celebrity Pictures. 28 Dec **1930** [trade review; c1 Jun 1930; LU1359]. Sd; b&w. 35mm. 7 reels.

Dir-Story Robert R. Snody. *Scen-Dial* Harry G. Smith. *Photog* Dal Clawson, Walter Strenge.

Cast: Olive Shea *(Annabelle Lee)*, Forrest Stanley *(Roger Jackson)*, Joan Bourdelle *(Helen Foster)*, Alice Hegeman *(Miss Primm)*, Donald Meek *(William)*, Terry Carroll *(Ruth)*, Rita Crane *(Joan)*, Bertha Donn *(Mary)*, Sally Mack *(Sally)*.

Romantic drama. Roger Jackson, a professor and instructor of athletics at the Mount Eden School for Girls, is secretly loved by Annabelle Lee, arousing the jealousy of other girls, including Helen Foster. Annabelle wagers with Helen that she will be the first girl to be kissed by Jackson. She is saved from injury on a runaway horse by Jackson, but he resists her attentions and, instead, kisses Helen. Having lost the wager, Annabelle is forced to work in the kitchen; however, he wins a male doll in a basketball competition and gives it to her. At the school dance he mistakes Helen for Annabelle; and in an automobile pursuit, he is wrecked and injured. Annabelle is expelled, but she finds that Jackson loves her after all! *Professors. Athletic coaches. Students. Courtship. Jealousy. Boarding schools. Wagers. Automobile accidents.*

THE LOVE LETTER **F2.3230**

Universal Pictures. 9 Feb **1923** [New York premiere; released 12 Feb; c27 Jan 1923; LP18634]. Si; b&w. 35mm. 5 reels, 4,426 ft.

Pres by Carl Laemmle. *Dir* King Baggot. *Scen* Hugh Hoffman. *Story* Bradley King. *Photog* Victor Milner.

Cast: Gladys Walton *(Mary Ann McKee)*, Fontaine La Rue *(Kate Smith)*, George Cooper *(Red Mike)*, Edward Hearne *(Bill Carter)*, Walt Whitman *(Reverend Halloway)*, Alberta Lee *(Mrs. Halloway)*, Lucy Donohue *(Mrs. Carter)*.

Crook melodrama. While working in an overall factory Mary Ann McKee sends mash notes in the overalls prepared for shipment. She is involved in a robbery perpetrated by her boyfriend, Red Mike, but escapes and goes to the town from which she has received an answer to one of her notes. There Mary Ann marries blacksmith Bill Carter and is happy until Red Mike comes for her. The sight of Mary Ann saying farewell to her child causes Red Mike to relent, and he leaves the Carters in peace. *Blacksmiths. Robbery. Motherhood. Factories. Clothing manufacture.*

LOVE LETTERS **F2.3231**

Fox Film Corp. 10 Feb **1924** [c10 Feb 1924; LP19961]. Si; b&w. 35mm. 5 reels, 4,749 ft.

Pres by William Fox. *Dir* David Soloman. *Scen* Doty Hobart.

Cast: Shirley Mason *(Evelyn Jefferson)*, Gordon Edwards *(Jimmy Stanton)*, Alma Francis *(Julia Crossland)*, John Miljan *(Thomas Chadwick)*, William Irving *(Don Crossland)*.

Melodrama. Source: Fred Jackson, "Morocco Box," in *Argosy Magazine* (148:339–360, 6 Jan 1923). Two sisters, Evelyn Jefferson and Julia Crossland, meet rakish Thomas Chadwick, to whom, as young girls, they both wrote passionate love letters. Evelyn is unsuccessful in her attempts to retrieve the letters, which Chadwick keeps in a Morocco box. Finally Chadwick is killed by the brother of one of his discarded mistresses. The contents of the box, when opened, appear to have been destroyed, and both women are mollified. *Sisters. Rakes. Murder. Documentation.*

THE LOVE LIGHT **F2.3232**

Mary Pickford Productions. *Dist* United Artists. 9 Jan **1921** [c12 Jan 1921; LP16037]. Si; b&w. 35mm. 8 reels.

Dir-Writ Frances Marion. *Photog* Charles Rosher, Henry Cronjager. *Art Dir* Stephen Goosson.

Cast: Mary Pickford *(Angela)*, Evelyn Dumo *(Maria)*, Fred Thomson *(Joseph)*, Edward Phillips *(Mario)*, Albert Prisco *(Pietro)*, Raymond Bloomer *(Giovanni)*, George Rigas *(Tony)*, Jean De Briac *(Antonio)*.

Melodrama. Angela, who tends the lighthouse in an Italian fishing village while her two brothers, Antonio and Mario, are fighting at the front, finds a foreign sailor washed ashore who pretends to be an American. Angela cares for him, and they fall in love and are secretly married. In aiding his escape, she realizes she has helped a German spy and caused her brother's death, but the stranger falls to his death over a cliff. A child is born to Angela and, temporarily deranged when her sweetheart Giovanni returns blind from the war, she gives the baby to Maria, who has lost her own child. Maria is drowned in a storm, but Angela rescues her child and finds happiness with Giovanni. *Sailors. Spies. Germans. Blindness. Fishing villages. Lighthouses. World War I. Italy. Storms.*

LOVE, LIVE AND LAUGH **F2.3233**

Fox Film Corp. 3 Nov **1929** [c28 Oct 1929; LP795]. Sd (Movietone); b&w. 35mm. 10 reels, 8,090 ft.

Pres by William Fox. *Dir* William K. Howard. *Stgd by* Henry Kolker. *Scen* Dana Burnet. *Dial* Edwin Burke, George Jessel. *Camera* Lucien Andriot. *Asst Camera* Walter Scott. *Sets* William S. Darling. *Film Ed* Al De Gaetano. *Songs: "A Song of Margharita," "Two Little Baby Arms," "If You Believe in Me"* L. Wolfe Gilbert, Abel Baer. *Sd* Al Protzman. *Asst Dir* Phil Ford. *Cost* Sophie Wachner.

Cast: George Jessel *(Luigi)*, Lila Lee *(Margharita)*, David Rollins *(Pasquale Gallupi)*, Henry Kolker *(Enrico)*, John Loder *(Dr. Price)*, John Reinhardt *(Mario)*, Dick Winslow Johnson *(Mike)*, Henry Armetta *(Tony)*, Marcia Manon *(Sylvia)*, Jerry Mandy *(barber)*.

Drama. Source: Leroy Clemens and John B. Hymer, *The Hurdy-Gurdy Man, a Comedy-Drama in a Prologue and Three Acts* (c1922). Luigi, an Italian immigrant in the United States, settles down in Little Italy in New York City and falls in love with Margharita, whose uncle gives him a job in his music store. Luigi is recalled to Italy by his father's illness, and, becoming embroiled in the early stages of the war, goes to the Austro-Italian front. During the war, he is blinded and spends 3 years in a prison camp; returning to the United States, he finds that Margharita, thinking Luigi killed, has married her employer, Dr. Price. An operation by the doctor cures Luigi's blindness, and the girl plans to tell her husband of her love for Luigi. But Luigi, realizing that the revelation would destroy her happiness, goes to live with his friend Pasquale. *Immigrants. Italians. Prisoners of war. Hurdy-gurdies. Courtship. Blindness. Eye surgery. World War I. New York City—Little Italy. Italy—Army.*

LOVE MAKES 'EM WILD **F2.3234**

Fox Film Corp. 6 Mar **1927** [c13 Mar 1927; LP23833]. Si; b&w. 35mm. 6 reels, 5,508 ft.

Pres by William Fox. *Dir* Albert Ray. *Scen* Harold Shumate. *Photog* Chester Lyons. *Asst Dir* Horace Hough.

Cast: Johnny Harron *(Willie Angle)*, Sally Phipps *(Mary O'Shane)*, Ben Bard *(Blankenship)*, Arthur Housman *(Charlie Austin)*, J. Farrell MacDonald *(W. Barden)*, Natalie Kingston *(Mamie)*, Albert Gran *(Green)*, Florence Gilbert *(Lulu)*, Earle Mohan *(Sam)*, Coy Watson, Jr. *(Jimmy)*, Noah Young *(janitor)*, William B. Davidson *(Mamie's ex-husband)*.

Comedy-drama. Source: Florence Ryerson, "Willie the Worm," in *American Magazine* (102:52–55, Sep 1926). "Willie, a spineless office plodder, is told by quack doctors that he will die in six months, so he proceeds to even up scores with those who have bullied him. A real doctor tells him that the only thing the matter with his heart is love and he proceeds to marry the girl." (*Moving Picture World,* 19 Mar 1927, p213.) *Office clerks. Quacks. Death. Courtship.*

THE LOVE MART **F2.3235**

First National Pictures. 18 Dec **1927** [c12 Dec 1927; LP24753]. Si; b&w. 35mm. 8 reels, 7,388 ft.

Pres by Richard A. Rowland. *Dir* George Fitzmaurice. *Titl* Edwin Justus Mayer. *Adapt* Benjamin Glazer. *Camera* Lee Garmes. *Film Ed* Stuart Heisler. *Cost* Max Ree.

Cast: Billie Dove *(Antoinette Frobelle)*, Gilbert Roland *(Victor Jallot)*, Raymond Turner *(Poupet)*, Noah Beery *(Captain Remy)*, Armand Kaliz *(Jean Delicado)*, Emil Chautard *(Louis Frobelle)*, Boris Karloff *(Fleming)*, Mattie Peters *(Caresse)*.

Melodrama. Source: Edward Childs Carpenter, *The Code of Victor Jallot* (Philadelphia, 1907). Antoinette Frobelle, reigning belle of the South, is accused of having Negro ancestry and is sold as a slave to Victor Jallot, a young adventurer. He frees her, makes Captain Remy confess to his responsibility for the lie about her parentage, and then weds the girl. *Negroes. Slavery. Parentage. United States—South.*

THE LOVE MASTER **F2.3236**

Trimble-Murfin Productions. *Dist* Associated First National Pictures. Feb **1924** [c1 Feb 1924; LP19878]. Si; b&w. 35mm. 7 reels, 6,779 ft.

Pres by Laurence Trimble, Jane Murfin. *Dir-Writ* Laurence Trimble. *Cont* Donna Barrell, Joseph Barrell. *Story* Jane Murfin, Laurence Trimble. *Photog* Charles Dreyer, Glen Gano, John Leezer. *Film Ed* Cyril Gardner. *Asst Dir* Ray Connell.

Cast: Strongheart *(himself, a dog)*, Lady Julie *(herself, a dog [The Fawn])*, Lillian Rich *(Sally)*, Harold Austin *(David)*, Hal Wilson *(Alec McLeod)*, Walter Perry *(Andrew Thomas Francis Joseph Mulligan)*, Joseph Barrell *("The Ghost")*, Timber Wolves *("Sweet Adeline" Quartet)*.

Northwest melodrama. Believing he has killed Strongheart's legal master in a fight, David flees to northern Canada with the dog. There he finds employment and falls in love with Sally, the daughter of the trading post proprietor. Strongheart leaves the settlement to find a mate; and returning with "The Fawn," he finds David stricken with pneumonia. David recovers, wins money in a dograce, assisted by Strongheart and The Fawn, and marries Sally. A visit from David's father reveals that the man David believed he killed has recovered. *Factors. Dogracing. Pneumonia. Canada. Dogs.*

LOVE ME AND THE WORLD IS MINE (Universal-Jewel) **F2.3237**

Universal Pictures. 9 Feb **1928** [New York premiere; released 4 Mar; c18 Jan 1928; LP24892]. Si; b&w. 35mm. 6 reels, 6,813 ft.

Pres by Carl Laemmle. *Dir* E. A. Dupont. *Scen* Paul Kohner, E. A. Dupont. *Scen? (see note)* Edward Sloman, Edward J. Montagne. *Titl* Albert De Mond, Walter Anthony. *Adapt* Imre Fazekas. *Photog* Jackson J. Rose. *Film Ed* Edward Cahn, Daniel Mandell.

Cast: Mary Philbin *(Hannerl)*, Norman Kerry *(Von Vigilatti)*, Betty Compson *(Mitzel)*, Henry B. Walthall *(Van Denbosch)*, Mathilde Brundage *(Mrs. Van Denbosch)*, Charles Sellon *(Mr. Thule)*, Martha Mattox *(Mrs. Thule)*, George Siegmann *(porter)*, Robert Anderson *(orderly)*, Albert Conti *(Billie)*, Emily Fitzroy *(the porter's wife)*, Charles Puffy *(coachman)*.

Melodrama. Source: Rudolph Hans Bartsch, *Die Geschichte von der Hannerl und ihren Liebhabern* (Leipzig, 1913). Hannerl consents to marry a rich, elderly man because she is convinced that Von Vigilatti, her true love, is involved with one of her girl friends. Realizing her mistake on her wedding day, she casts aside her bridal veil and dashes to the station just as Von Vigilatti is leaving for the war. An unexpected 3-day leave allows him to hop off the train and marry her before he goes to the front. *Weddings. World War I. Vienna.*

Note: Universal records indicate that Edward Sloman and Edward J. Montagne worked on the scenario.

THE LOVE NEST **F2.3238**

Commercial Traders Cinema Corp. *Dist* Wid Gunning, Inc. 3 Jun **1922** [trade review; c5 Sep 1922; LP18212]. Si; b&w. 35mm.

Dir-Writ Wray Physioc.

Cast: Bernard Siegel *(Sim Corwin)*, Jean Scott *(Nan Corwin)*, Richard Travers *(Gordon Townley)*, Charles Graham *("Skipper" Weatherby)*, Robert Kenyon *(Ned Weatherby)*, Richard Lee *("Fiddler" Crabb)*, William Cavanaugh *(Jerry)*.

Drama. Gordon Townley comes from the city to a fishing village in Maine on secret business, and Nan Corwin finds him sufficiently attractive to rebuff her long-time sweetheart, Ned Weatherby. Ned goes to the city to make something of himself, fails, and returns to find Nan disillusioned with Townley. The latter is able to leave gracefully when he rescues Ned from a fight and learns that his wife has withdrawn her alimony suit. *Businessmen. Courtship. Alimony. Divorce. Fishing villages. Maine.*

LOVE NEVER DIES **F2.3239**

King W. Vidor Productions. *Dist* Associated Producers. 14 Nov **1921.** Si; b&w. 35mm. 7 reels, 6,751 ft.

Dir-Adapt King Vidor. *Photog* Max Dupont.

Cast: Lloyd Hughes *(John Trott)*, Madge Bellamy *(Tilly Whaley)*, Joe Bennett *(Joel Eperson)*, Lillian Leighton *(Mrs. Cavanaugh)*, Fred Gambold *(Sam Cavanaugh)*, Julia Brown *(Dora Boyles)*, Frank Brownlee *(Ezekiel Whaley)*, Winifred Greenwood *(Jane Holder)*, Claire McDowell *(Liz Trott)*.

Domestic melodrama. Source: William Nathaniel Harben, *The Cottage of Delight* (New York, 1919). The happy marriage of John Trott and Tilly Whaley is ended by Tilly's father when he learns of the notorious reputation of John's "mother." Because John assumes that Tilly, who was taken home by Mr. Whaley, left of her own accord, he leaves the small North Carolina town to work in the city. John becomes successful and wealthy, while Mr. Whaley prevails upon Tilly, who believes that John died in a train wreck, to marry Joel Eperson. While visiting Ridgeville John finds that Tilly's thoughts are still of him, but he decides to depart gracefully. Joel also perceives what his wife really wants, and he commits suicide. John and Tilly are reunited with everyone's blessings and with the new knowledge that Liz Trott is not related to John in any way. *Fatherhood. Parentage. Marriage. Reputation. Suicide. Smalltown life. North Carolina.*

THE LOVE OF PAQUITA **F2.3240**

Dist Hi-Mark Productions. 10 Sep **1927** [New York showing]. Si; b&w. 35mm. 6 reels.

Cast: Marilyn Mills, Floyd Ames, Walter Emerson, Wilbur Mack, Robert Fleming, Adar Bruno.

Melodrama. Apparently an action story in a Spanish locale featuring two horses and the riding skills of Marilyn Mills. *Horsemanship. Spain. Horses.*

THE LOVE OF SUNYA **F2.3241**

Swanson Producing Corp. *Dist* United Artists. 5 Mar **1927** [c12 Mar 1927; LP24030]. Si; b&w. 35mm. 8 reels, 7,311 ft.

Dir Albert Parker. *Screen Story* Earle Browne. *Photog* Robert Martin. *Art Dir* Hugo Ballin. *Asst Dir* Paul Madeux. *Prod Mgr* Robert Schable. *Consult on Crystal Sequence* Dudley Murphy.

Cast: Gloria Swanson *(Sunya)*, John Boles *(Paul Judson)*, Anders Randolf *(Goring)*, Andres De Segurola *(De Salvo)*, Hugh Miller *(Yogi)*, Ian Keith *(Anthony)*, Pauline Garon *(Anna Hagen)*, Flobelle Fairbanks *(Sunya's sister)*, Raymond Hackett *(Kenneth)*, Ivan Lebedeff *(Howard Morgan)*, Robert Schable *(Picquard)*, John Miltern *(Sunya's father)*, Forrest Huff.

Romantic drama. Source: Charles Guernon and Max Marcin, *Eyes of Youth* (New York opening: 22 Aug 1917). In the Mystic East, a young yogi learns of a sin he committed in his incarnation centuries ago and sets out to atone for it; after years of search he arrives in a small New York town where he recognizes Sunya and Paul Judson as reincarnations of the people he wronged. Sunya, having promised to marry Paul and go to South America on his first engineering assignment, is courted also by millionaire Robert Goring; by De Salvo, an opera impresario; and by Louis Anthony, a young bank cashier. She learns that her father is in financial straits, and the yogi reveals in a crystal that disaster and unhappiness will result regardless of whether she goes with De Salvo to become a singer or marries the millionaire to save her father. At length, Sunya decides to follow her heart and marry Paul. *Millionaires. Impresari. Bankers. Yogis. Seers. Ambition. Wealth. Reincarnation. Courtship. New York State.*

LOVE OF WOMEN **F2.3242**

Interlocutory Films. *Dist* Selznick Distributing Corp. 30 Jun **1924** [c26 Jun 1924; LP20376]. Si; b&w. 35mm. 6 reels, 5,802 ft.

Pres by H. Clay Miner. *Prod-Dir* Whitman Bennett. *Story* E. C. Holland. *Photog* Edward Paul. *Art Dir* Lawrence Hitt.

Cast: Helene Chadwick *(Cynthia Redfield)*, Montague Love *(Bronson Gibbs)*, Maurice Costello *(Mr. Redfield)*, Mary Thurman *(Veerah Vale)*, Lawford Davidson *(Ernest Herrick)*, Marie Shotwell *(Eugenie Redfield)*, Frankie Evans *(Frankie)*.

Society drama. Cynthia Redfield elopes with Ernest Herrick, against the wishes of her socially ambitious mother and an unscrupulous millionaire, Bronson Gibbs, who has courted Cynthia with his position. Four years later Gibbs plots with Veerah Vale, a Greenwich Village vamp, with whom Ernest becomes involved. Divorce proceedings follow with an interlocutory decree, but Cynthia and Ernest are reunited following a serious injury to their child. *Millionaires. Vamps. Elopement. Divorce. New York City—Greenwich Village.*

LOVE ON THE RIO GRANDE **F2.3243**

Independent Pictures. 25 Jul **1925**. Si; b&w. 35mm. 5 reels, 4,900 ft.

Scen Adele Buffington. *Story* Mona Marron.

Cast: Bill Cody.

Western melodrama(?). No information about the nature of this film has been found. *Rio Grande.*

LOVE OVER NIGHT **F2.3244**

Pathé Exchange. 25 Nov **1928** [c20 Aug 1928; LP25552]. Si; b&w. 35mm. 6 reels, 5,773 ft.

Prod Hector Turnbull. *Dir* Edward H. Griffith. *Scen* George Dromgold, Sanford Hewitt. *Titl* John Krafft. *Photog* John J. Mescall. *Art Dir* Mitchell Leisen. *Film Ed* Harold McLernon. *Asst Dir* E. J. Babille. *Prod Mgr* R. A. Blaydon.

Cast: Rod La Rocque *(Richard Hill, a ticket chopper)*, Jeanette Loff *(Jeanette Stewart)*, Richard Tucker *(Richard Thorne)*, Tom Kennedy *(detective)*, Mary Carr *(grandmother)*.

Comedy. Richard Hill, a changemaker on the subway, mistakenly believes that Jeanette Stewart, a beautiful young woman of moderate means, is an accomplice in a robbery and therefore follows her to the exclusive Long Island home of Richard Thorpe, a wealthy man-about-town whom Jeanette is to marry on the following day. Unknown to Richard, he is in turn followed by a detective who believes him to have been pilfering money from the Metropolitan Transit. Jeanette mistakes Richard for a burglar and knocks him cold; when he regains consciousness she takes pity on him, however, and helps him elude the detective. Richard asks Jeanette to marry him, but she refuses. The following day, Richard kidnaps Jeanette from church and forces her to marry him, letting her know that he is the son of a well-to-do hotel owner and not just a changemaker in a booth. *Detectives. Cashiers. Mistaken identity. Subways. Long Island. New York City.*

THE LOVE PARADE **F2.3245**

Paramount Famous Lasky Corp. 19 Nov **1929** [New York premiere; released 18 Jan 1930; c16 Jan 1930; LP1014]. Sd (Movietone); b&w. 35mm. 12 reels, 10,022 ft. [Also si; 7,094 ft.]

Dir Ernst Lubitsch. *Dial Dir* Perry Ivins. *Libretto* Guy Bolton. *Film Story* Ernest Vajda. *Photog* Victor Milner. *Art Dir* Hans Dreier. *Film Ed* Merrill White. *Songs: "Dream Lover," "My Love Parade," "Paris, Stay the Same," "Let's Be Common," "March of the Grenadiers," "Nobody's Using It Now," "Gossip," "Anything To Please the Queen," "Ooh, La La," "The Queen Is Always Right"* Victor Schertzinger, Clifford Grey. *Ch Rec Engr* Franklin Hansen.

Cast: Maurice Chevalier *(Count Alfred)*, Jeanette MacDonald *(Queen Louise)*, Lupino Lane *(Jacques)*, Lillian Roth *(Lulu)*, Edgar Norton *(Master of Ceremonies)*, Lionel Belmore *(Prime Minister)*, Albert Roccardi *(Foreign Minister)*, Carlton Stockdale *(Admiral)*, Eugene Pallette *(Minister of War)*, Russell Powell *(Afghan Ambassador)*, E. H. Calvert *(Ambassador)*, André Sheron *(Le Mari)*, Yola D'Avril *(Paulette)*, Winter Hall *(Priest)*, Ben Turpin *(Cross-Eyed Lackey)*, Anton Vaverka, Albert De Winton, William von Hardenburg *(Cabinet Minsters)*, Margaret Fealy, Virginia Bruce, Josephine Hall, Rosalind Charles, Helene Friend *(Ladies in Waiting)*.

Musical romance. Source: Leon Xanrof and Jules Chancel, *Le Prince Consort* (c1919). In the modern kingdom of Sylvania, the aged cabinet ministers worry over the fact that Queen Louise is unmarried. Then emissary Count Alfred returns in disgrace from Paris, where he has carried on numerous affairs with young ladies, and learning of his escapades, the queen invites him to demonstrate his romantic prowess. The cabinet is pleased by their blossoming romance as well as by that of Jacques, Alfred's valet, and Lulu, the queen's maid. Louise and Alfred marry, but he soon is irked at having to take orders from his royal wife, though he is forced to keep up appearances because of financial negotiations with a foreign power. When he is ordered to attend the opening of the royal opera, Alfred refuses and announces he is going to Paris to get a divorce and is cold to the queen's entreaties. But when she offers to make him king and therefore her equal, he relents and they find happiness together. *Royalty. Courtship. Marriage. Imaginary kingdoms. Paris.*

Note: Also made in a French-language version, *Parade d'amour*.

THE LOVE PIKER **F2.3246**

Cosmopolitan Corp. *Dist* Goldwyn-Cosmopolitan Distributing Corp. 22 Jul **1923** [c9 Jul 1923; LP19193]. Si; b&w. 35mm. 7 reels, 6,237 ft.

Dir E. Mason Hopper. *Scen* Frances Marion. *Story* Frank R. Adams. *Photog* George Barnes.

Cast: Anita Stewart *(Hope Warner)*, William Norris *(Peter Van Huisen)*, Robert Frazer *(Martin Van Huisen)*, Carl Gerrard *(Archie Pembroke)*, Arthur Hoyt *(Professor Click)*, Betty Francisco *(Edith Cloney)*, Winston Miller *(Willie Warner)*, Mayme Kelso *(Mrs. Warner)*, Frederick Truesdell *(Mr. Warner)*, Robert Bolder *(butler)*, Cordelia Callahan *(maid)*, James F. Fulton *(judge)*.

Society melodrama. Hope Warner, a young society girl, falls in love with a self-made engineer whose old-world father is still living in poverty. Hope fails to invite the eccentric old man to the wedding and feels so guilty about it that she interrupts the ceremony and personally brings him in. *Engineers. Filial relations. Poverty.*

THE LOVE PIRATE **F2.3247**

Richard Thomas Productions. *Dist* Film Booking Offices of America. 18 or 25 Nov **1923** [c6 Nov 1923; LP19566]. Si; b&w. 35mm. 5 reels, ca4,900 ft.

Dir Richard Thomas. *Adapt* William Lester. *Photog* Jack Fuqua.

Cast: Melbourne MacDowell *(Steve Carnan)*, Carmel Myers *(Ruby Le Mar)*, Charles Force *(Tim Gordan)*, Kathryn McGuire *(Ruth Revere)*, Clyde Fillmore *(Chief Deputy Hugh Waring)*, John Tonkey *(Cregg Winslow)*, Carol Halloway *(Mrs. Carnan)*, Edward W. Borman *(Joe Harris)*, Spottiswoode Aitken *(Cyrus Revere)*.

Melodrama. Steve Carnan, secret owner of a notorious cafe, while attempting to seduce budding musician Ruth Revere, is shot and killed in a struggle with Ruth's sweetheart, Chief Deputy Hugh Waring. An unexpected confession from Ruth's father, whom Carnan had doublecrossed, saves Waring. *Musicians. Seduction. Murder. Cafes.*

Note: Also reviewed as *The Silent Accuser.*

THE LOVE RACKET **F2.3248**

First National Pictures. 8 Dec **1929** [c21 Jan 1930; LP1020]. Sd (Vitaphone); b&w. 35mm. 7 reels, 6,118 ft. [Also si.]

Dir William A. Seiter. *Scen-Dial* John F. Goodrich. *Titl* Adele Commandini. *Photog* Sid Hickox. *Film Ed* John Rawlins.

Cast: Dorothy Mackaill *(Betty Brown)*, Sidney Blackmer *(Fred Masters)*, Edmund Burns *(George Wayne)*, Myrtle Stedman *(Marion Masters)*, Edwards Davis *(Judge Davis)*, Webster Campbell *(prosecuting attorney)*, Clarence Burton *(defense attorney)*, Alice Day *(Grace Pierce)*, Edith Yorke *(Mrs. Pierce)*, Martha Mattox *(Mrs. Slade)*, Tom Mahoney *(Detective McGuire)*, Jack Curtis *(John Gerrity)*.

Melodrama. Source: Bernard K. Burns, *The Woman on the Jury* (New York opening: 1923). Betty Brown, a decorator who loves George Wayne, goes with him to a mountain cabin on the promise that he will marry her in the future, but he soon leaves her. She goes to Europe to forget the affair and meets Masters. He falls in love with her, but she refuses to marry him because of her past; however, when Masters' married sister convinces her that she is foolish, Betty becomes his wife. Later, Betty and Masters are called for jury duty in the trial of a girl accused of killing a lover who had abandoned her and the child he had fathered. Betty is astounded to realize that Wayne was this man, and she alone votes not guilty; then, when she relates her own experiences with Wayne, the jury agrees on the acquittal. She is forgiven by her husband. *Interior decorators. Desertion. Trials. Juries.*

Note: Remake of a 1924 silent version entitled *The Woman on the Jury.*

THE LOVE SPECIAL **F2.3249**

Famous Players–Lasky. *Dist* Paramount Pictures. 17 Apr **1921** [c16 Apr 1921; LP16397]. Si; b&w. 35mm. 5 reels, 4,855 ft.

Dir Frank Urson. *Scen* Eugene B. Lewis. *Photog* Charles Edgar Schoenbaum.

Cast: Wallace Reid *(Jim Glover)*, Agnes Ayres *(Laura Gage)*, Theodore Roberts *(President Gage)*, Lloyd Whitlock *(Allen Harrison, a director)*, Sylvia Ashton *(Mrs. Whitney)*, William Gaden *(William Bucks)*, Clarence Burton *(Morris Blood)*, Snitz Edwards *(Zeka Logan)*, Ernest Butterworth *("Gloomy")*, Zelma Maja *(stenographer)*.

Melodrama. Source: Frank Hamilton Spearman, *The Daughter of a Magnate* (New York, 1903). Jim Glover, civil engineer for a western railroad, is ordered to act as guide to the company president, who is on an inspection trip with his sister, his daughter, and Harrison, one of the directors. Jim helps President Gage get an option on property of Zeka Logan, but Harrison intends to acquire the property himself for use as a bribe to win the hand of Laura. Laura overhears the plot and with Jim's help plunges through a blizzard to reach her father. She ends up in Jim's arms. *Engineers—Civil. Railroad magnates. Railroads. Land rights. Blizzards.*

THE LOVE THIEF (Universal-Jewel) **F2.3250**

Universal Pictures. 13 Jun **1926** [c22 May 1926; LP22762]. Si; b&w. 35mm. 7 reels, 6,822 ft.

Pres by Carl Laemmle. *Story-Scen-Dir* John McDermott. *Photog* John Stumar.

Cast: Norman Kerry *(Prince Boris Alexander Emanuel Augustus)*, Greta Nissen *(Princess Flavia Eugenia Marie)*, Marc MacDermott *(Prince Karl)*, Cissy Fitzgerald *(Countess Leopold Marjenka)*, Agostino Borgato *(King)*, Carrie Daumery *(Queen)*, Oscar Beregi *(Prime Minister)*, Nigel Barrie *(Captain Emanuel Menisurgo)*, Vladimir Glutz *(Napoleon Alexander Caesar)*, Charles Puffy *(Prince's guard)*, Clarence Thompson *(Prince Michael)*, Alphonse Martel *(Berzoff)*, Anton Vaverka *(Aide)*, Lido Manetti *(Captain)*.

Romantic melodrama. To avert war between their countries an official marriage is arranged between Crown Prince Boris of Moraine and Princess Flavia of Norvia. Prince Karl of Norvia sees in the alliance an opportunity to gain control of both kingdoms but upon visiting Boris finds him unyielding and independent. Flavia, shedding her stately dignity in the palace garden, is accosted by the flirtatious Boris, who believes her to be the princess' cousin; and falling in love, he realizes that he cannot go through with the planned marriage. Karl plots to have Boris abdicate, and at the pleas of the minister, Boris refuses to fight the regent and is disgraced. To assure his safety, Princess Flavia agrees to marry the imbecile prince, Michael; Boris is secretly substituted for Michael at the wedding, and though Karl protests, the ceremony proceeds. The regent's duplicity is exposed by Flavia, and all ends happily. *Royalty. Imaginary kingdoms. Courtship. Abdication. Weddings.*

THE LOVE THRILL (Universal-Jewel) **F2.3251**

Universal Pictures. 8 May **1927** [c15 Feb 1927; LP23676]. Si; b&w. 35mm. 6 reels, 6,038 ft.

Pres by Carl Laemmle. *Dir* Millard Webb. *Scen* James T. O'Donohoe. *Titl* Albert De Mond. *Adapt* Marion Orth. *Story* Millard Webb, Joseph Mitchell. *Photog* Gilbert Warrenton.

Cast: Laura La Plante *(Joyce Bragdon)*, Tom Moore *(Jack Sturdevant)*, Bryant Washburn *(J. Anthony Creelman)*, Jocelyn Lee *(Paula)*, Arthur Hoyt *(Bragdon)*, Nat Carr *(Solomon)*, Frank Finch Smiles, Charles F. Smiles *(Sharpe; see note)*.

Farce. Joyce Bragdon, of the insurance firm of Bragdon and Chadwick, in financial straits, attempts to enter the apartment of J. Anthony Creelman, a wealthy bachelor, to sell him an insurance policy. Failing to do so, she nevertheless manages to stave off angry creditors. Learning that Jack, a college chum of Creelman's, has died while engaged in exploration in Africa, she poses as his widow, and Creelman takes her to Jack's apartment. Meanwhile, Jack, who is not dead, arrives at his publisher's office, but because his reported death has increased sales of his book, he is advised to take an assumed name and shave off his beard. Joyce, playing the bereaved widow, is repulsed by Creelman's advances. Jack, perceiving the situation, pretends to be an old friend and becomes involved with Joyce. She attempts a getaway, but Jack follows and proposes to her. *Insurance agents. Explorers. Authors. Bachelors. Imposture.*

Note: Sources disagree about Smiles's given name.

THE LOVE TOY **F2.3252**

Warner Brothers Pictures. 13 Feb **1926** [c15 Feb 1926; LP22411]. Si; b&w. 35mm. 6 reels, 5,118 ft.

Dir Erle C. Kenton. *Story* Charles Logue. *Photog* John J. Mescall.

Cast: Lowell Sherman *(Peter Remsen)*, Jane Winton *(The Bride)*, Willard Louis *(King Lavoris)*, Gayne Whitman *(prime minister)*, Ethel Grey Terry *(Queen Zita)*, Helene Costello *(Princess Patricia)*, Maude George *(lady in waiting)*.

Comedy. Left standing at the altar by his fiancée, Peter Remsen goes to seek consolation in the small Kingdom of Luzania, where he becomes valet to the king in order to be near the Princess Patricia. The queen of neighboring Belgradia visits Luzania and falls in love with Peter, who repulses her advances and thereby precipitates a war. As the king is busy with a dancer, Peter takes charge of the army. The queen's men kidnap Patricia, but Peter rescues her in a tank and makes her his bride. *Valets. Royalty. Dancers. Kidnaping. Tanks (armored cars). Imaginary kingdoms.*

THE LOVE TRADER **F2.3253**

Pacific Pictures. *Dist* Tiffany Productions. 25 Sep or 9 Oct **1930.** Sd; b&w. 35mm. 6 reels, 5,700 ft.

Prod Joseph Henabery, Harold Shumate. *Dir* Joseph E. Henabery. *Story-Scen-Dial* Harold Shumate. *Photog* Ernest Miller, Pliny Goodfriend. *Sd* R. S. Clayton, Ted Murray.

Cast: Leatrice Joy *(Martha Adams)*, Roland Drew *(Tonia)*, Henry B. Walthall *(Captain Adams)*, Barbara Bedford *(Luane)*, Noah Beery *(Captain Morton)*, Chester Conklin *(Nelson)*, Clarence Burton *(John)*, William Welsh *(Benson)*, Tom Mahoney, Jack Curtis.

Romantic drama. Approaching the harbor of a South Sea island, hard, narrowminded Captain Adams expresses his disapproval of the "indecent" native people and their music, while his lovely young wife, Martha, is secretly drawn to the romantic atmosphere in general and to Tonia (the grandson of an American) in particular. While Tonia tricks Adams into crossing the island in search of pearls, Martha attends a Shark God festival and falls further under Tonia's spell. He asks her to stay, but she dutifully leaves with Adams, and—just before they reach New Bedford—she jumps overboard. *Sea captains. Halfcastes. Paganism. Pearls. Suicide. South Sea Islands. New Bedford (Massachusetts).*

THE LOVE TRAP **F2.3254**

Ben Wilson Productions. *Dist* Grand-Asher Distributing Corp. Sep **1923** [c30 Aug 1923; LP19353]. Si; b&w. 35mm. 6 reels, 5,719 ft.

Dir John Ince. *Scen* Nan Blair. *Story* Evelyn Campbell.

Cast: Bryant Washburn *(Martin Antrim)*, Mabel Forrest *(Joyce Lyndon)*, Wheeler Oakman *(Grant Garrison)*, Kate Lester *(Mrs. Lyndon)*, Mabel Trunnelle *(Rosalie)*, William J. Irving *(Freddie Rivers)*, Wilbur Higby *(Graves, the detective)*, Francis Powers *(Judge Lyndon)*, Billie Lord *(Beatrice)*, Laura La Varnie *(Mrs. Hawley)*, Sidney Franklin *(Mr. Hawley)*, Edith Stayart *(Miss Shepley, reporter)*, Betty Small *(The Maid)*.

Society melodrama. Society girl Joyce Lyndon is engaged to energetic Grant Garrison, who lures the judge's daughter to a roadhouse for the night and meets his death at the hands of an abandoned wife. Joyce escapes in fright and meets Martin Antrim, who shields her in exchange for an introduction to her circle of friends. Antrim elicits a confession from Garrison's widow, and Joyce recovers an incriminating handbag from the innkeepers when they attempt to blackmail her. *Socialites. Murder. Blackmail.*

THE LOVE TRAP **F2.3255**

Universal Pictures. 4 Aug **1929** [c27 Jul 1929; LP566]. Talking sequences & sd eff (Movietone); b&w. 35mm. 8 reels, 6,233 ft. [Also si; 6,349 ft.]

Dir William Wyler. *Scen* John B. Clymer, Clarence J. Marks. *Dial* Clarence Thompson. *Titl* Albert De Mond. *Story* Edward J. Montagne. *Photog* Gilbert Warrenton. *Film Ed* Maurice Pivar.

Cast: Laura La Plante *(Laura [Evelyn Todd])*, Neil Hamilton *(Peter Cadwallader [Paul Harrington])*, Robert Ellis *(Guy Emory)*, Jocelyn Lee *(Bunny)*, Norman Trevor *(Judge Cadwallader [Judge Harrington])*, Clarissa Selwynne *(Mrs. Cadwallader [Mrs. Harrington])*, Rita Le Roy *(Mary Cadwallader [Iris Harrington])*.

Bedroom comedy. Young taxi driver Peter Cadwallader marries Laura, a chorus girl, after she is fired from her job and evicted from her apartment. Cadwallader's uncle, a judge, tries to buy Laura off when he meets her becuase he associates her with a scandalous party he attended at the home of rakish Guy Emory. (Emory spilled a drink on Laura and tried to seduce her while her clothes were drying.) Eventually, the judge realizes his mistake and withdraws his offer. *Chorus girls. Taxi drivers. Judges. Uncles. Eviction. Bribery. Reputation.*

Note: Some sources show the indicated variation in role names.

THE LOVE WAGER **F2.3256**

Platinum Pictures. *Dist* Hollywood Pictures. 21 Feb **1927** [New York State license]. Si; b&w. 35mm. 6 reels, 5,900 ft.

Pierpont Milliken Production. *Dir-Writ* Clifford Slater Wheeler. *Photog* Earl Walker.

Cast: Gaston Glass, Lenore Bushman, Lucy Beaumont, Arthur Rankin, Sheldon Lewis, Jane Grey, W. W. Watson, Dorothea Raynor.

Society drama. A man (played by Arthur Rankin) receives a 20-year prison sentence for accidentally killing his mother (played by Lucy Beaumont). Rankin's cell-mate (played by Sheldon Lewis) kills himself and leaves a note introducing Rankin to a wealthy girl friend. The plot also touches upon a pearl necklace and a wealthy clubman (played by Gaston Glass), who makes a sizable wager that he can earn his own living for 6 months. *Manslaughter. Matricide. Suicide. Wagers. Prisons.*

LOVEBOUND **F2.3257**

Fox Film Corp. 15 Apr **1923** [c15 Apr 1923; LP19073]. Si; b&w. 35mm. 5 reels, 4,407 ft.

Pres by William Fox. *Dir* Henry Otto. *Scen* Josephine Quirk, Jules Furthman. *Story* George Scarborough. *Photog* David Abel.

Cast: Shirley Mason *(Bess Belwyn)*, Albert Roscoe *(John Mobley)*, Richard Tucker *(Paul Meredith)*, Joseph Girard *(David Belwyn)*, Edward Martindel *(Stephen Barker)*, Fred Kelsey *(Detective Hahn)*.

Crook melodrama. Bess Belwyn, daughter of a criminal who reforms in prison, becomes engaged to District Attorney John Mobley. To save her father from being denounced by his erstwhile accomplice, Bess, unaware of the consequences, becomes involved in a jewelry theft. She then tries in vain to confess and break the engagement. After she marries Mobley, the crook attempts to blackmail Bess, but she confesses everything to Mobley and in the subsequent fracas the crook is killed. *Criminals—Rehabilitation. District attorneys. Filial relations. Blackmail.*

Note: Working title: *The End of the Road.*

THE LOVELORN **F2.3258**

Cosmopolitan Productions. *Dist* Metro-Goldwyn-Mayer Distributing Corp. 17 Dec **1927** [c9 Jan 1928; LP24842]. Si; b&w. 35mm. 7 reels, 6,110 ft.

Dir John P. McCarthy. *Scen* Bradley King. *Titl* Frederic Hatton. *Story* Beatrice Fairfax. *Photog* Henry Sharp. *Set Dsgn* Cedric Gibbons, Alexander Toluboff. *Film Ed* John W. English. *Wardrobe* Gilbert Clark.

Cast: Sally O'Neil *(Georgie Hastings)*, Molly O'Day *(Ann Hastings)*, Larry Kent *(Bill Warren)*, James Murray *(Charlie)*, Charles Delaney *(Jimmy)*, George Cooper *(Joe Sprotte)*, Allan Forrest *(Ernest Brooks)*, Dorothy Cumming *(Beatrice Fairfax)*.

Romantic drama. Finding herself in love with Bill Warren, the sweetheart of her sister Georgie, shopgirl Ann Hastings seeks advice from Beatrice Fairfax, the author of a lovelorn column. Neither girl heeds Miss Fairfax's advice, and the coveted man retreats from both. Two standby lovers, Jimmy and Charlie, take his place to provide a happy ending. *Columnists. Sisters. Lovelorn. Beatrice Fairfax.*

THE LOVER OF CAMILLE **F2.3259**

Warner Brothers Pictures. 15 Sep **1924** [c10 Sep 1924; LP20564]. Si; b&w. 35mm. 8 reels, 7,300 ft.

Dir Harry Beaumont. *Adapt* Dorothy Farnum. *Photog* David Abel.

Cast: Monte Blue *(Jean Gaspard Deburau)*, Willard Louis *(Robillard)*, Pat Moore *(Charles Deburau, age 10)*, Pierre Gendron *(Charles Deburau, age 17)*, Carlton Miller *(Armand Duval)*, Rosa Rosanova *(Madame Rabouir)*, Marie Prevost *(Marie Duplessis)*, Winifred Bryson *("The Unknown")*, Brandon Hurst *(Bertrand)*, Rose Dione *(Madame Deburau)*, Trilby Clark *(Madame Rubard)*.

Romantic drama. Source: Sacha Guitry, *Deburau* (trans. by Granville Barker of *Deburau, comèdie en vers libres;* New York, 1920). Deburau, a Parisian Pierrot and idol of the populace, becomes involved with Marie Duplessis and is disillusioned when she casts him aside in favor of Armand. His wife, hearing of the affair, elopes with Robillard. Deburau takes comfort in his son's determination to follow in his stage role. Years later, Marie returns to him, delirious with fever, and marries him, thinking he is Armand. Unable to perform following her death, he finds happiness in seeing his son triumph in his former part. *Pierrot. Actors. Infidelity. Family life. Paris.*

LOVERS? **F2.3260**

Metro-Goldwyn-Mayer Pictures. 9 Apr **1927** [c2 May 1927; LP23918]. Si; b&w. 35mm. 6 reels, 5,291 ft.

Dir John M. Stahl. *Cont* Douglas Furber, Sylvia Thalberg. *Titl* Marian Ainslee, Ruth Cummings. *Photog* Max Fabian. *Art Dir* Cedric Gibbons, Merrill Pye. *Film Ed* Margaret Booth. *Asst Dir* Sidney Algier. *Wardrobe* André-ani.

Cast: Ramon Novarro *(José [or Ernesto])*, Alice Terry *(Felicia [or Teodora])*, Edward Martindel *(Don Julian)*, Edward Connelly *(Don Severo)*, George K. Arthur *(Pepito)*, Lillian Leighton *(Doña Mercedes)*, Holmes Herbert *(Milton)*, John Miljan *(Álvarez)*, Roy D'Arcy *(Señor Galdos)*.

Romantic drama. Source: José Echegaray y Eizaguirre, *El Gran Galeoto, drama en tres actos y en verso* (adapted as *The World and His Wife*, by Frederic Nordlinger; Madrid, 1881). Young José lives with his guardian, Don Julian, a middle-aged diplomat recently married to young Felicia. Society gossips in Madrid find the situation increasingly scandalous. Ernesto resents an overheard slur in a club and engages in a duel; Don Julian takes on the challenge and is mortally wounded. José, thereupon, kills his challenger. Later, José and Felicia are reunited on a ship bound for Argentina. *Diplomats. Guardians. Gossip. Spain. Duels.*

LOVERS IN QUARANTINE **F2.3261**

Famous Players–Lasky. *Dist* Paramount Pictures. 11 Oct **1925** [New York premiere; released 12 Oct; c13 Oct 1925; LP21904]. Si; b&w. 35mm. 7 reels, 6,570 ft.

Pres by Adolph Zukor, Jesse L. Lasky. *Dir* Frank Tuttle. *Screenplay* Townsend Martin, Luther Reed. *Photog* J. Roy Hunt. *Art Dir* Van Nest Polglase.

Cast: Bebe Daniels *(Diana)*, Harrison Ford *(Anthony Blunt)*, Alfred Lunt *(MackIntosh Josephs)*, Eden Gray *(Pamela Gordon)*, Edna May Oliver *(Amelia Pincent)*, Diana Kane *(Lola)*, Ivan Simpson *(The Silent Passenger)*, Marie Shotwell *(Mrs. Borroughs)*.

Romantic comedy. Source: F. Tennyson Jesse, *Quarantine* (New York opening: 16 Dec 1924). Engaged to African explorer Anthony Blunt, Pamela Gordon grows tired of waiting and becomes engaged to MackIntosh Josephs. Blunt returns, and he and Pamela decide to elope to Bermuda. To deceive MackIntosh, Pamela has Blunt pretend to make love to her hoydenish sister, Diana. The latter believes him and with the aid of Amelia Pincent, the girls' spinster chaperon, locks up Pamela in a closet and goes in her place aboard ship. The next day, Blunt discovers the substitution and is shocked. To get back at him, Diana, using her sister's trousseau, transforms herself into the ship's most popular female. Blunt becomes jealous. Complications arise when all the passengers are quarantined for a week on Quarantine Island, with the "honeymooners" put in a tiny cottage for privacy. When the quarantine is lifted, Diana marries Blunt, leaving Pamela to MackIntosh. *Sisters. Explorers. Chaperons. Courtship. Quarantine. Ships.*

LOVER'S ISLAND **F2.3262**

Encore Pictures. *Dist* Associated Exhibitors. c30 Dec **1925** [LU22204]. Si; b&w. 35mm. 5 reels, 4,624 ft.

Prod-Dir Henri Diamant-Berger. *Scen* Arthur Hoerl. *Photog* Alfred Ortlieb. *Film Ed* Marie St. Clair.

Cast: Hope Hampton *(Clemmy Dawson)*, James Kirkwood *(Jack Avery)*, Louis Wolheim *(Capt. Joshua Dawson)*, Ivan Linow *(Sam Johnson)*, Flora Finch *(Amanda Dawson)*, Flora Le Breton *(Julia Daw)*, Jack Raymond *(Randy Phelps)*.

Romantic melodrama. Source: T. Howard Kelly, "Lover's Island," in *Smart Set*. Clemmy Dawson, the daughter of a sea captain, lives in a small fishing village, where, in the summer season, she meets Jack Avery, who is visiting a nearby resort. When Clemmy is later attacked by Sam Johnson, her father (who does not know the identity of the man who sought to force his attentions on Clemmy) vows that he will force the responsible man to marry her. Clemmy names Avery, and her father proceeds to make plans for a wedding. In the meantime, Clemmy discovers that Avery already has a fiancée and, with a change of heart, she runs off, taking refuge on Lover's Island. She makes plans to marry the villainous Sam, but Avery, realizing that he has come to love her, goes to Lover's Island, stops the wedding, and marries Clemmy himself. *Sea captains. Courtship. Rape. Weddings. Fishing villages.*

LOVERS' LANE **F2.3263**

Warner Brothers Pictures. 10 Aug **1924** [c18 Aug 1924; LP20506]. Si; b&w. 35mm. 7 reels, 6,400 ft.

Dir Phil Rosen. *Dir? (see note)* William Beaudine. *Adapt* Dorothy Farnum. *Photog* Charles Van Enger.

Cast: Robert Ellis *(Dr. Tom Singleton)*, Gertrude Olmstead *(Mary Larkin)*, Crauford Kent *(Herbert Woodbridge)*, Kate Toncray *(Aunt Mattie)*, George Periolat *(Dr. Stone)*, Norval MacGregor *(Reverend Singleton)*, Frances Dale *(Mrs. Woodbridge)*, Bruce Guerin *(Dick Woodbridge)*, Ethel Wales *(Aunt Melissy)*, Maxine Elliott Hicks *(Simplicity)*, Charles A. Sellon *(Uncle Bill)*, Aileen Manning *(Miss Mealy)*, Dorothy Vernon *(Mrs. Stone)*.

Rural comedy-drama. Source: Clyde Fitch, *Lovers' Lane, a Play in Four Acts* (Boston, 1915). Unable to reconcile herself to being the wife of a country doctor, Mary Larkin forsakes Dr. Tom Singleton for Herbert Woodbridge, whom she is about to marry when he is revealed as having deserted a woman whose son the doctor cures. This situation brings about a reconciliation of the Woodbridges. *Physicians. Rural life. Infidelity.*

Note: Advertising in May 1924 names William Beaudine as director.

A LOVER'S OATH **F2.3264**

Ferdinand P. Earle. *Dist* Astor Pictures. 29 Sep **1925** [New York premiere]. Si; b&w. 35mm. 6 reels, 5,896 ft.

Dir Ferdinand P. Earle. *Photog* George Benoit. *Film Ed* Milton Sills.

Cast: Ramon Novarro *(Ben Ali)*, Kathleen Key *(Sherin)*, Edwin Stevens *(Hassen Ben Sabbath)*, Frederick Warde *(Omar Khayyam)*, Hedwig Reicher *(Hassan's wife)*, Snitz Edwards *(Omar's servant)*, Charles A. Post *(Commander of the Faithful)*, Arthur Edmund Carew *(Prince Yussuf)*, Paul Weigel *(Sheik Rustum)*, Philippe De Lacy *(his son)*, Warren Rodgers *(Haja)*.

Fantasy. Inspired by: Edward Fitzgerald, *The Rubáiyát of Omar Khayyám, the Astronomer-Poet of Persia, Rendered into English Verse* (London, 1899). "The plot introduces Omar as a leader of his people but deals rather with the love of his nephew, Ben Ali, for the fairest daughter of the tribe" (*Variety*, 7 Oct 1925, p44). *Persia. Omar Khayyám.*

LOVE'S BLINDNESS **F2.3265**

Metro-Goldwyn-Mayer Pictures. 4 Dec **1926** [c8 Nov 1926; LP23306]. Si; b&w. 35mm. 7 reels, 6,099 ft.

Pers Supv Elinor Glyn. *Dir* John Francis Dillon. *Adapt* Elinor Glyn. *Photog* John Arnold, Oliver Marsh. *Sets* Cedric Gibbons, James Basevi. *Film Ed* Frank Sullivan. *Wardrobe* Kathleen Kay, Maude Marsh, André-ani.

Cast: Pauline Starke *(Vanessa Levy)*, Antonio Moreno *(Hubert Culverdale, Eighth Earl of St. Austel)*, Lilyan Tashman *(Alice, Duchess of Lincolnwood)*, Sam De Grasse *(Benjamin Levy)*, Douglas Gilmore *(Charles Langley)*, Kate Price *(Marchioness of Hurlshire)*, Tom Ricketts *(Marquis of Hurlshire)*, Earl Metcalf *(Col. Ralph Dangerfield)*, George Waggner *(Oscar Issacson)*, Rose Dione *(Madame De Jainon)*, Ned Sparks *(valet)*.

Romantic drama. Source: Elinor Glyn, *Love's Blindness* (New York, 1925). Hubert Culverdale, Eighth Earl of St. Austel, helps finance a company to promote a friend's invention. When the company funds are stolen by a clerk, Hubert desperately seeks the aid of Benjamin Levy, a Jewish moneylender; Levy agrees to help on the condition that Hubert marry his daughter, Vanessa; and he finally consents. Though intelligent and beautiful, Vanessa has been reared in seclusion in Italy and is innocent of worldliness; she falls immediately in love with Hubert; but unresponsive to her, he studiously avoids her after their marriage. After weeks of unhappiness, Ralph Dangerfield, a cousin, calls Hubert's attention to her beauty, and when his jealousy is awakened at a dance, he begins to realize his love for her. Following the birth of her stillborn child, Vanessa's disillusionment turns to happiness when she learns of her father's bargain; and she accepts Hubert's genuine devotion. *Nobility. Jews. Inventors. Fatherhood. Theft. Marriage of convenience. Stillbirth. England.*

LOVE'S BOOMERANG **F2.3266**

Famous Players–Lasky. *Dist* Paramount Pictures. 19 Feb **1922** [c22 Feb 1922; LP17572]. Si; b&w. 35mm. 6 reels, 5,618 ft.

Pres by Adolph Zukor. *Dir* John S. Robertson. *Scen* Josephine Lovett. *Photog* Roy Overbaugh. *Asst Dir* Tom J. Geraghty.

Cast: Ann Forrest *(Perpetua)*, Bunty Fosse *(Perpetua, as a child)*, David Powell *(Brian McCree, an artist)*, John Miltern *(Russell Felton, a crook)*, Roy Byford *(Monsieur Lamballe)*, Florence Wood *(Madame Lamballe)*, Geoffrey Kerr *(Saville Mender)*, Lillian Walker *(Stella Daintry)*, Lionel D'Aragon *(Christian, a convict)*, Ollie Emery *(Madame Tourterelle)*, Amy Williard *(Jane Egg, a circus rider)*, Tom Volbecque *(Auguste, a clown)*, Frank Stanmore *(Corn Chandler)*, Ida Fane *(Mrs. Bugle)*, Sara Sample *(Perpetua's mother)*.

Melodrama. Source: Dion Clayton Calthrop, *Perpetua, or The Way to Treat a Woman* (New York, 1911). Artist Brian McCree adopts Perpetua, a 12-year-old orphan, and takes her to France, where for several years they lead a carefree life as members of a circus. Following her education in a convent, Russell Felton, a British swindler, recognizes Perpetua as the daughter of his abandoned wife; he introduces his friend Mender, a habitual drunkard who has willed him his fortune, and induces Brian to paint Mender's portrait. Although Perpetua loves Brian, Felton reveals her parentage and brings about her marriage to Mender. When the latter is poisoned, Perpetua is suspected of murder, having acquired the legal rights to his money. She is found guilty but later is exonerated by Felton's confession. Felton is killed by Christian, a former accomplice and ex-convict, and Perpetua admits her love for Brian. *Artists. Orphans. Swindlers. Circus. Murder. Parentage. England. France.*

Note: Filmed on location in England and France.

LOVE'S GREATEST MISTAKE **F2.3267**

Famous Players–Lasky. *Dist* Paramount Pictures. 13 Feb **1927** [c12 Feb 1927; LP23659]. Si; b&w. 35mm. 6 reels, 6,007 ft.

Pres by Adolph Zukor, Jesse L. Lasky. *Assoc Prod* William Le Baron. *Dir* Edward Sutherland. *Scen* Becky Gardiner. *Photog* Leo Tover.

Cast: Evelyn Brent *(Jane)*, William Powell *(Don Kendall)*, James Hall *(Harvey Gibbs)*, Josephine Dunn *(Honey McNeil)*, Frank Morgan *(William Ogden)*, Iris Gray *(Sara Foote)*, Betty Byrne *(Lovey Gibbs)*.

Society drama. Source: Frederic Arnold Kummer, *Love's Greatest Mistake* (New York, 1927). On a train bound for New York, where she hopes to find work, Honey McNeil captures the appreciative eye of William Ogden, a financier, who offers her a job. At the apartment of her married sister, Jane, Honey renews her acquaintance with Sara Foote, now a worldly New Yorker secretly jealous of Jane. Honey is disappointed when young architect Harvey Gibbs brings her home from an unspectacular evening, and she declines his numerous proposals. Ogden, already married, is also rejected by Honey, despite the luxury he offers her. Don Kendall, in conspiracy with Sara, tries to obtain love letters Ogden has written Honey, so as to blackmail him, and her refusal to give them up causes him to beat her brutally. Realizing that Ogden does not love her, Honey dismisses Gibbs, who doubts her. Jane leaves her husband and elopes with Don. Honey is ultimately united with Gibbs, who wins a prize for designing a church. *Sisters. Architects. Financiers. Infidelity. Blackmail. Jealousy. New York City.*

LOVE'S MASQUERADE **F2.3268**

Selznick Pictures. *Dist* Select Pictures. 20 Mar **1922** [c16 Mar 1922; LP17672]. Si; b&w. 35mm. 5 reels, 4,300 ft.

Pres by Lewis J. Selznick. *Dir* William P. S. Earle. *Story-Scen* Edward J. Montagne. *Photog* Jacob A. Badaracco.

Cast: Conway Tearle *(Russell Carrington)*, Winifred Westover *(Dorothy Wheeler)*, Florence Billings *(Rita Norwood)*, Robert Ellis *(Herbert Norwood)*, Danny Hayes *("Sly Sam")*, Arthur Houseman *(newspaper reporter)*, Robert Schable *(Ross Gunther)*.

Melodrama. Russell Carrington accepts the blame for a murder charge to protect Rita, the woman he loves, from being accused of killing her husband. He escapes the police, and in a fishing village he assumes the name of Carr and is about to marry Dorothy Wheeler, the town belle, when detectives hired by Rita break up the ceremony and arrest him. Refusing to defend himself, Carrington is sentenced to life imprisonment but is released a year later as the result of the statement of "Sly Sam," a burglar who saw Rita shoot her husband. Dorothy, who has been living with a wealthy aunt in New York, is about to marry wealthy Ross Gunther, but Carrington is released and visits her home on the night of her engagement party. He thrashes a newspaper reporter who threatens to expose her affair with him, and the lovers are happily reunited. *Burglars. Reporters. Murder. Injustice. Fishing villages. New York City.*

LOVES OF AN ACTRESS **F2.3269**

Paramount Famous Lasky Corp. 18 Aug **1928** [c16 Aug 1928; LP25544]. Mus score & sd eff (Vitaphone); b&w. 35mm. 8 reels, 7,434 ft. [Also si; 7,159 ft.]

Pres by Adolph Zukor, Jesse L. Lasky. *Dir-Screenplay* Rowland V. Lee. *Titl* Julian Johnson. *Story* Ernest Vajda. *Photog* Victor Milner. *Film Ed* E. Lloyd Sheldon, Robert Bassler. *Song: "Sunbeams Bring Dreams of You"* J. Keirn Brennan, Karl Hajos.

Cast: Pola Negri *(Rachel)*, Nils Asther *(Raoul Duval)*, Mary McAllister *(Lisette)*, Richard Tucker *(Baron Hartman)*, Philip Strange *(Count Vareski)*, Paul Lukas *(Dr. Durande)*, Nigel De Brulier *(Samson)*, Robert Fischer *(Count Morency)*, Helene Giere *(Marie)*.

Romantic drama. Born into a family of poor peasants, Rachel becomes the leading actress in the Comédie Française through the patronage of three influential men: Baron Hartman, the wealthiest man in France; Count Vareski, a relative of Napoleon; and Paul Lukas, the leading newspaper publisher in Europe. All three men are in love with her, but she throws them over when she falls in love with Raoul Duval, who is about to be appointed ambassador to Russia. Lukas threatens to publish Rachel's love letters to Raoul, but to protect Raoul's reputation Rachel pretends that she has only been toying with his emotions. Raoul goes to Russia, and Rachel, exhausted by life and love, dies peacefully. *Actors. Publishers. Diplomats. Blackmail. Paris. Russia. Comédie Française. Documentation.*

LOVES OF CARMEN **F2.3270**

Fox Film Corp. 4 Sep **1927** [c21 Aug 1927; LP24337]. Si; b&w. 35mm. 9 reels, 8,538 ft.

Pres by William Fox. *Dir* Raoul Walsh. *Scen* Gertrude Orr. *Titl* Katherine Hilliker, H. H. Caldwell. *Photog* Lucien Andriot, John Marta. *Film Ed* Katherine Hilliker, H. H. Caldwell. *Asst Dir* Archibald Buchanan.

Cast: Dolores Del Rio *(Carmen)*, Victor McLaglen *(Escamillo)*, Don Alvarado *(José)*, Nancy Nash *(Michaela)*, Rafael Valverda *(Miguel)*, Mathilde Comont *(Emilia)*, Jack Baston *(Morales)*, Carmen Costello *(Teresa)*, Fred Kohler *(Gypsy chief)*.

Romantic drama. Source: Prosper Mérimée, *Carmen* (1845). "Carmen, a gypsy, working in a Spanish cigar factory, is flaunted by Escamillo, the bullfighter, but infatuates José, a soldier, who aids her to escape from jail and follows her to the gypsy camp. Tiring of his love, Carmen finally fascinates Escamillo and the love-crazed José kills her at a bull fight just as Escamillo is being proclaimed by the audience." (*Moving Picture World*, 8 Oct 1927, p381.) *Gypsies. Bullfighters. Soldiers. Courtship. Cigars. Spain.*

Note: The entire film was originally tinted lavender.

THE LOVES OF RICARDO **F2.3271**

George Beban Productions. ca4 Sep **1926.** Si; b&w. 35mm. 8 reels, 7,477 ft.

Dir-Writ George Beban. *Photog* Allen Siegler.

Cast: George Beban *(Ricardo)*, Soliga Lee *(Annetta)*, Amille Milane *(Annetta [live sequence, see note])*, Jack Singleton *(Steve)*, Monte Collins, Jr. *(Steve [live sequence])*, Albano Valerio *(Marco)*, Mika Aldrich *(Flora)*, Signor Frondi *(Tony)*, Giulio Cortesi *(Mike Ferrera)*, E. E. MacLeod, Jr. *("Skeets")*, Norman Ives *("Hap")*, Helen Hunton *(Madge)*, Rosa Vega *(Rosetta)*, Estella De Barr, Jack Howard, Mrs. Giulio Cortesi, Maria Barbarita, Wenonah Forgay.

Melodrama. Grocer Ricardo loves his ward, Annetta, but allows her to marry Steve, an interloper. On the wedding night she realizes she loves Ricardo, not Steve. Meanwhile Ricardo has invested in some sub-marine real estate in Florida. While he is waiting for the tide to go out, he is kidnaped by some bootleggers. The outcome is happy: Ricardo is rescued, aided by his parrot; he wins Annetta; and Steve is claimed by another woman. *Grocers. Wards. Swindlers. Bootleggers. Real estate. Florida. Parrots.*

Note: George Beban, Amille Milane, and Monte Collins, Jr., appeared in a live, spoken sequence midway through the film. Re-edited in 1928 by FBO Pictures. See Entry F2.3272.

THE LOVES OF RICARDO **F2.3272**

George Beban Productions. *Dist* FBO Pictures. 17 Jun **1928** [c1 Feb 1928; LP24933]. Si; b&w. 35mm. 6 reels, 5,181 or 5,500 ft.

Prod-Dir-Writ George Beban. *Scen* G. Marion Burton. *Photog* Allen Siegler. *Adtl Photog* Lester Lang. *Film Ed* George Beban.

Cast: George Beban *(Ricardo Bitelli)*, Soliga Lee *(Annette)*, Albano Valerio *(Marco Martinelli)*, Mika Aldrich *(Mrs. Martinelli)*, Kenneth Gibson *(Cyril Duke)*, Jack Singleton *(Steve Randall)*, Jane Starr *(Belle)*.

Melodrama. Grocer Ricardo Bitelli—whose household consists of Mussolini, his horse; Toto, his parrot; and Annette, his 19-year-old charge—falls in love with Annette as her beauty blossoms into womanhood. His plans for marriage are shattered when Steve Randall, an unscrupulous dandy, enters their lives and proceeds to make love to Annette. Falling for Randall's youthful, dashing style, Annette marries him. Ricardo, broken-hearted but eager to assure Annette's happiness, turns his business over to her husband and goes to Florida. After the wedding, Annette discovers she prefers Ricardo; leaving Randall when he is revealed to be a bigamist, Annette goes to the Martinellis, wealthy friends of Ricardo's. Randall attempts to extort money from Martinelli, but Ricardo returns from Florida in time to stop him. Ricardo and Annette marry after Randall is killed in an auto accident. *Grocers. Wards. Dandies. Bigamy. Extortion. Florida. Horses. Parrots.*

Note: First released in 1926 with a live sequence; Amille Milane played Annette and Monte Collins, Jr., Steve Randall. It was cut from 8 reels to 6. See Entry F2.3271.

LOVE'S OLD SWEET SONG **F2.3273**

Norca Pictures. *Dist* Hopp Hadley. 1 Feb **1923** [c1 Nov 1922; LP18361]. Si; b&w. 35mm. 5 or 7 reels.

Dir Oscar Lund. *Scen* Jacques Byrne. *Story* Augustus Bertilla.

Cast: Louis Wolheim *(The Wanderer)*, Helen Weir *(Eunice)*, Donald Gallagher *(Charlie)*, Helen Lowell *(Mother)*, Baby Margaret Brown *(Babs)*, Ernest Hilliard *(Power)*.

Melodrama. Things look very bleak for Mrs. Marshall, an invalid whose ownership of a marble quarry depends on the delivery of a certain order to a cathedral. The shipment is ready and awaits only a confirmation of the order; but the awaited letter is being held by Power, a bank cashier who is determined to ruin both Mrs. Marshall and bank president Cooper by falsifying the bank's books. Cooper is jailed; his son, Charles, discovers Power's villainy and has several harrowing experiences in trying to get the marble shipment underway. In the end a tramp (The Wanderer) reveals himself to be a Secret Service agent and arrests Power. Her condition has kept Mrs. Marshall from accepting the love of Mr. Cooper, whose son loves Mrs. Marshall's daughter, Eunice; but now all are reunited, and Mrs. Marshall finds that she can walk. *Invalids. Wanderers. Bankers. Secret service. Motherhood. Quarries. Cathedrals. Railroads.*

Note: May have been produced by Lund Productions, which copyrighted the film, and released by Norca Pictures.

LOVE'S PENALTY **F2.3274**

Hope Hampton Productions. *Dist* Associated First National Pictures. Jun **1921** [cl Jan, 23 Jun 1921; P16292, P16698]. Si; b&w. 35mm. 5 reels, 4,685 ft.

Dir-Writ John Gilbert. *Photog* Alfred Ortlieb. *Tech Dir* Henry Mennesier. *Titl-Ed (see note)* Katherine Hilliker.

Cast: Hope Hampton *(Janis Clayton)*, Irma Harrison *(Sally Clayton)*, Mrs. Phillip Landau *(Martha Clayton)*, Percy Marmont *(Steven Saunders)*, Jack O'Brien *(Bud Gordon)*, Virginia Valli *(Mrs. Steven Saunders)*, Douglas Redmond *("Little Jack")*, Charles Lane *(Rev. John Kirchway)*, Mrs. L. Faure *(Madame Natalie)*.

Melodrama. Sally Clayton commits suicide when she is betrayed by Steven Saunders, and the tragedy kills her mother. Determined to revenge them, Janis Clayton becomes Saunders' personal secretary and encourages his attentions when he sends his wife to Europe aboard a ship directed by him to take a dangerous course. During a supper at his home, Janis reveals her plan to ruin him. He then attempts to kill her but is shot by a Bohemian artist whose wife and child have gone down with the ship. Janis becomes an outcast until she finds refuge in a clergyman's home and is reunited with her former lover, Bud. *Sisters. Filial relations. Revenge. Murder. Suicide.*

Note: A revised version, reviewed in *Motion Picture News* (30 Jul 1921), was retitled and edited by Katherine Hilliker and, according to this source, released by Paramount. "Miss Hilliker, in remoulding the picture, has supplied logical reasons for previously shallow spots ... and made the photoplay a most interesting drama."

LOVE'S REDEMPTION **F2.3275**

Norma Talmadge Film Co. *Dist* Associated First National Pictures. 19 Dec **1921** [c16 Dec 1921; LP17371]. Si; b&w. 35mm. 6 reels, 5,889 ft.

Pres by Joseph M. Schenck. *Dir* Albert Parker. *Adapt* Anthony Paul Kelly. *Photog* J. Roy Hunt.

Cast: Norma Talmadge *(Jennie Dobson, known as Ginger)*, Harrison Ford *(Clifford Standish)*, Montagu Love *(Frederick Kent)*, H. Cooper Cliffe *(John Standish)*, Ida Waterman *(Mrs. Standish)*, Michael M. Barnes *(Capt. Bill Hennessey)*, E. L. Fernandez *(overseer)*, Frazer Coulter *(club steward)*.

Melodrama. Source: Andrew Soutar, "On Principle," in *Snappy Stories* (34:1-29, 2 Apr 1918). Jennie Dobson, orphaned in Jamaica, grows to maturity under the guardianship of Capt. Bill Hennessey, a sea dog who tries to persuade Ginger to accompany him to England. She meets and falls in love with Clifford Standish, an Englishman in exile and an alcoholic. Establishing herself at his plantation, she saves him from being robbed and murdered, and he eventually proposes marriage. His brother comes from England to tell him he has inherited a fortune and is shocked when Clifford marries Ginger. In England she is coldly received by his relations; Clifford reverts to a life of dissipation; and when Ginger discovers a guest cheating at cards, a disturbance follows and Mrs. Standish insists that she return to Jamaica. Clifford, realizing the worth of her love, rejects his family and returns with her. *Planters. Guardians. Sea captains. Brothers. Orphans. Marriage. Alcoholism. Jamaica. England.*

Note: Working title: *Regeneration Isle*.

LOVE'S REDEMPTION **F2.3276**

Brewster Publication Co. *Dist* C. C. Pictures. 26 Nov **1921** [New York State; general release: 28 Sep 1922]. Si; b&w. 35mm. 5 reels, 4,210 ft.

Dir Eugene V. Brewster.

Cast: Dorian Romero, Blanche McGarity, Anetha Getwell, Edwin Markham, Hudson Maxim, Octavia Handworth.

Society drama. "Peggy Logan supports herself by playing violin on streets. Mike, her father, robs Worthington home and steals bracelet. Police pursue him home. Peggy throws bracelet out window. Ralph Boven, admirer of Lucille Worthington, banker's daughter, finds bracelet. Peggy befriended by Mrs. Worthington and Ralph. Peggy finds bracelet in Ralph's room, but on return it is gone, Ralph having pawned it to finance Lucille's bad stock debts. Mike Logan, fugitive in hills, is reformed by Edwin Markham's generosity in saving him from police. Ralph is arrested by police on suspicion of having stolen bracelet. Mike Logan arrives with Maxim Hudson, by whom he has been employed meanwhile, and whole matter is explained by Mike. Ralph happy in Peggy's friendship." *(Motion Picture News Booking Guide,* 4:67, Apr 1923.) *Violinists. Criminals—Rehabilitation. Robbery. Debt.*

LOVE'S WHIRLPOOL **F2.3277**

Regal Pictures. *Dist* W. W. Hodkinson Corp. 29 Feb or 2 Mar **1924** [cl Mar 1924; LP20040]. Si; b&w. 35mm. 6 reels, 6,177 ft.

Dir Bruce Mitchell. *Adapt* Elliott Clawson, Bruce Mitchell. *Story* Martha Lord. *Photog* Stephen Norton. *Film Ed* Jack Dennis.

Cast: James Kirkwood *(Jim Reagan)*, Lila Lee *(Molly)*, Robert Agnew *(Larry)*, Mathew Betz *("Pinky" Sellers)*, Edward Martindel *(Richard Milton)*, Margaret Livingston *(a maid)*, Madge Bellamy *(Nadine Milton)*, Clarence Geldert *(a lawyer)*, Joseph Mills *("Parson" Monks)*.

Crook melodrama. Hardened criminal Jim Reagan tries to persuade his brother, Larry, to go straight, but Larry attempts to rob a banker, Richard Milton, and is arrested. Milton refuses to be lenient, and when Larry is killed trying to escape from prison, Jim and his wife, Molly, resolve to have vengeance. Through spiritualism they dupe Milton into contributing large sums to charity, then kidnap Milton's daughter, Nadine, after rescuing her from a shipwreck. Molly softens, however, returns Nadine to her father and, although Jim is at first enraged, finally persuades him to reform. *Brothers. Bankers. Criminals—Rehabilitation. Robbery. Kidnaping. Spiritualism. Prisons.*

LOVE'S WILDERNESS **F2.3278**

Corinne Griffith Productions. *Dist* First National Pictures. 14 Dec **1924** [c2 Dec 1924; LP20818]. Si; b&w. 35mm. 7 reels, 7,037 ft.

Pres by Asher-Small-Rogers. *Dir* Robert Z. Leonard. *Cont* Eve Unsell. *Adapt* Helen Klumph. *Photog* Oliver Marsh. *Art Dir* Milton Menasco.

Cast: Corinne Griffith *(Linda Lou Heath)*, Holmes E. Herbert *(David Tennant)*, Ian Keith *(Paul L'Estrange)*, Maurice Cannon *(Pierre Bazin)*, Emily Fitzroy *(Matilda Heath)*, Anne Schaefer *(Prudence Heath)*, Bruce Covington *(Colonel Heath)*, David Torrence *(The Governor)*, Frank Elliott *(Van Arsdale)*, Adolph Millar *(Captain Moreau)*, Jim Blackwell *(Jubilo)*, W. H. Post *(Lamaire)*.

Melodrama. Source: Helen Campbell, "Wilderness" (publication undetermined). In a quiet Mississippi town, Linda Lou Heath, the orphaned daughter of an aristocratic family, is reared in seclusion by two strict aunts. She is in love with David Tennant, but when he leaves to do medical work in Africa, she marries Paul L'Estrange, a wanderer. She goes with Paul to an isolated farm in Canada, where he deserts her, feigning death in a river accident. Believing herself free to marry, Linda enters into wedlock with David and accompanies him to the penal colony on Devil's Island. During a violent storm, there is a prison break, and Linda discovers that one of the escaping prisoners is Paul. David finds them together and suspects that she still loves her first husband. David gallantly arranges a pardon for Paul, but, before the latter can be freed, he is killed by a fellow prisoner. Linda explains to David that Paul was nothing to her, and they are reconciled. *Orphans. Aunts. Physicians. Wanderers. Bigamy. Prison escapes. Penal colonies. Mississippi. Canada. Africa. Devil's Island.*

LOVETIME **F2.3279**

Fox Film Corp. 24 Jul **1921** [c24 Jul 1921; LP16849]. Si; b&w. 35mm. 5 reels, 4,533 ft.

Pres by William Fox. *Dir* Howard M. Mitchell. *Scen* Dorothy Yost. *Story* Hubert La Due. *Photog* Glen MacWilliams.

Cast: Shirley Mason *(Marie Gautier)*, Raymond McKee *(Arthur de Sivry, Marquis of Savoy/André Broque)*, Frances Hatton *(Margaret, Marie's mother)*, Edwin B. Tilton *(Lanstalot, her father)*, Mathilde Brundage *(Marchioness de Sivry)*, Wilson Hummell *(Count de Baudine)*, Harold Goodwin *(Pierre Lavone)*, Charles A. Smiley *(Father Lesurges)*, Correan Kirkham *(Yvonne de Fourgères)*.

Romantic melodrama. While painting in the French countryside, nobleman Arthur de Sivry falls in love with Marie, a peasant girl. His elderly uncle, Count de Baudine, a roué, presses an unwelcome suit for Marie until she is sent to Paris, where she joins a troop of entertainers. De Sivry, unable to paint without the inspiration of Marie, also goes to Paris and offers her the use of his apartment. The count, discovering their arrangement, spreads scandal reflecting on Marie and announces de Sivry's engagement to another woman. Marie's father comes to Paris and returns home to report his daughter's downfall. The marquis shows that he is anxious to make her his wife, however, and all ends happily. *Nobility. Peasants. Artists. Entertainers. Reputation. Courtship. Paris. France.*

LOVEY MARY **F2.3280**

Metro-Goldwyn-Mayer Pictures. 31 May **1926** [c20 Jun 1926; LP22936]. Si; b&w. 35mm. 7 reels, 6,167 ft.

Dir King Baggot. *Titl* George Marion, Jr. *Adapt* Agnes Christine Johnston, Charles Maigne. *Photog* Ira H. Morgan. *Settings* Cedric Gibbons, Arnold Gillespie. *Film Ed* Frank Davis. *Wardrobe* Lucia Coulter.

Cast: Bessie Love *(Lovey Mary)*, William Haines *(Billy Wiggs)*, Mary Alden *(Mrs. Wiggs)*, Vivia Ogden *(Miss Hazey)*, Martha Mattox *(Miss Bell)*, Jackie Coombs *(Tommy)*, Freddie Cox *(Baby Tommy)*, Gloria Holt *(Europena)*, Mary Jane Irving *(Asia)*, Annabelle Magnus *(Australia)*, Eileen Percy *(Kate)*, Russell Simpson *(Stubbins)*, Rosa Gore *(Miss Eichorn)*, Sunshine Hart *(Mrs. Chultz)*.

Comedy-drama. Source: Alice Hegan Rice, *Lovey Mary* (New York, 1903). Lovey Mary, an awkward but affectionate young orphan, grows up in an orphanage and comes to love young Tommy, the child of Kate, a disreputable woman. When Kate comes to take away her child, Lovey and Tommy run away from the orphanage and are given shelter by Miss Hazey, who is about to be married to a correspondent whom she has never seen; Lovey, however, recognizes him as Mr. Stubbins, the exterminator at the orphanage. Lovey becomes friendly with Billy Wiggs, who lives next door, and she works with the Wiggs girls—Asia, Australia, and Europena—in a tomato-canning factory. On the wedding day, Stubbins arrives drunk and exposes Lovey. Learning that Tommy's mother is dying, Lovey sends him back to her, thereby earning the right to keep him when she is happily married to Billy. *Orphans. Children. Exterminators. Courtship. Orphanages. Canneries.*

THE LOVIN' FOOL **F2.3281**

Sierra Pictures. Dec **1926.** Si; b&w. 35mm. 6 reels.

Dir H. B. Carpenter. *Photog* Paul Allen.

Comedy-drama(?). No information about the nature of this film has been found.

Note: May also have been known as *The Loving Fool.* Furthermore, *The Lovin' Fool,* released by Pizor in 1928, was probably a reissue of this film.

LOVIN' THE LADIES **F2.3282**

RKO Productions. 6 Apr **1930** [c6 Apr 1930; LP1239]. Sd (Photophone); b&w. 35mm. 7 reels, 6,139 ft.

Prod William Le Baron. *Dir* Melville Brown. *Dial-Adapt* J. Walter Ruben. *Photog* Edward Cronjager. *Art Dir* Max Ree. *Sd Rec* Lambert E. Day. *Asst Dir* Charles Kerr.

Cast: Richard Dix *(Peter)*, Lois Wilson *(Joan Bently)*, Allen Kearns *(Jimmy Farnsworth)*, Rita La Roy *(Louise Endicott)*, Renée Macready *(Betty Duncan)*, Virginia Sale *(Marie)*, Selmer Jackson *(George Van Horne)*, Anthony Bushell *(Brooks)*, Henry Armetta *(Sagatelli)*.

Romantic comedy. Source: William Le Baron, *I Love You* (New York opening: 28 Apr 1919). Jimmy Farnsworth bets his friend George Van Horne $5,000 that he can get any two people under the proper environment to fall in love and become engaged within a month. The two he chooses are young society girl Betty Duncan and Peter Darby, a dashing electrician who comes to her house and secretly agrees to pose as a society man at Jimmy's estate. The star-crossed Peter falls in love, however, with Joan Bently, Jimmy's fiancée; while at the same time, Marie, the maid, and vampish Louise Endicott become fascinated with Peter, to Jimmy's dismay. Disturbed by Louise's torrid advances, Peter threatens to resign his part of the agreement; and to complicate matters, Betty falls in love with the butler. Jimmy exposes Peter as an electrician, but Joan nevertheless accepts his proposal and all ends happily, at least for Joan and Peter. *Electricians. Socialites. Domestics. Wagers. Courtship.*

LOVING LIES **F2.3283**

Associated Authors. *Dist* Allied Producers and Distributors. 22 Jan **1924** [New York showing; released 15 Feb; c14 Jan 1924; LP19834]. Si; b&w. 35mm. 7 reels, 6,526 ft.

Pres by Frank Woods, Elmer Harris, Thompson Buchanan, Clark W. Thomas. *Dir* W. S. Van Dyke. *Story* Thompson Buchanan. *Mus Synopsis* James C. Bradford.

Cast: Evelyn Brent *(Ellen Craig)*, Monte Blue *(Capt. Dan Stover)*, Joan Lowell *(Madge Barlow)*, Charles Gerrard *(Tom Hayden)*, Ralph Faulkner *(Jack Ellis)*, Ethel Wales *(Penny Wise)*, Andrew Waldron *(Bill Keenan)*, Tom Kennedy *(Captain Lindstrom)*.

Melodrama. Source: Peter Bernard Kyne, "The Harbor Bar," in *Red Book* (22:1058-1075, Apr 1914). Dan Stover, captain of a harbor tug whose task is to keep ships away from a dangerous bar, lies to his wife Ellen about the nature of his work, saying that he remains in the harbor. One night, Stover is sent to rescue a ship on the harbor bar. He leaves without telling his wife; she awakens during a terrific storm and gives birth to a stillborn child. Stover's boss, a former sweetheart of Mrs. Stover's, encourages her to believe that Stover has been unfaithful, implicating Madge Barlow, the fiancée of Dan's mate, a boy who lost his life at sea. Believing the rumor, Ellen leaves on the next passenger ship just as Madge dies and Stover is bringing her baby home. The ship crashes on the harbor bar, Dan goes to the rescue, he admits the truth about his job, and they find happiness with the adopted baby. *Stillbirth. Tugboats. Seafaring life. Waterfront. Sea rescue. Illegitimacy. Adoption. Storms.*

LOWLAND CINDERELLA **F2.3284**

Dist Second National Pictures. 1 Nov **1922.** Si; b&w. 35mm. [Feature length assumed.]

Cast: John Morgan.

Melodrama(?). No information about the nature of this film has been found.

Note: Country of origin undetermined.

LOYAL LIVES **F2.3285**

Postman Pictures. *Dist* Vitagraph Co. of America. Jul **1923** [c26 Jul 1923; LP19241]. Si; b&w. 35mm. 6 reels, 5,950 ft.

Whitman Bennett Production. *Dir* Charles Giblyn. *Story* Charles G. Rich, Dorothy Farnum. *Photog* Edward Paul.

Cast: Brandon Tynan *(Dan O'Brien)*, Mary Carr *(Mary O'Brien)*, Faire Binney *(Peggy)*, William Collier, Jr. *(Terrence)*, Charles McDonald *(Michael O'Hara)*, Blanche Craig *(Lizzie O'Hara)*, Chester Morris *(Tom O'Hara)*, Tom Blake *(Brady)*, Blanche Davenport *(Mrs. Brady)*, John Hopkins *(Judkins)*, Mickey Bennett *(Terrence as a child)*.

Melodrama. Dan O'Brien, a postal employee, has a hard time making ends meet on his small salary, but he saves money to educate his son Terrence and adopts a little girl who is left on his doorstep. Seventeen years later Terrence, also a postal employee, is commended for bravery when he dives into a river with a mailbag he has retrieved from some crooks, and Dan O'Brien is personally congratulated by the postmaster general for preventing robbers from looting a safe. *Postal service. Adoption. Robbery. United States—Postmaster General.*

LUCK **F2.3286**

C. C. Burr. *Dist* Mastodon Films. Mar **1923** [c27 Mar 1923; LP18819]. Si; b&w. 35mm. 7 reels, 6,442 ft.

Pres by C. C. Burr. *Scen* Doty Hobart. *Titl* Ralph Spence. *Photog* Charles E. Gilson, Neil Sullivan.

Cast: Johnny Hines *(Robert Carter)*, Robert Edeson *(Judge Templeton)*, Edmund Breese *(Alan Crosby)*, Violet Mersereau *(Sylvia Templeton)*, Charles Murray *(The Plumber)*, Flora Finch *(his wife)*, Warner Richmond *(Pollard)*, Polly Moran *(fight enthusiast)*, Harry Fraser *(a lawyer)*, Matthew Betts *(fighting miner)*.

Burlesque. Source: Jackson Gregory, "Luck," in *People's Magazine.* Wagering $100,000 that he can start with nothing and earn $10,000 in a year, Robert Carter starts out in his track suit and proceeds through a series of adventures in pursuit of his goal. In a case of mistaken identity Bob gets involved in a prizefight, uses his winnings to start a new town, unsuccessfully holds a dance to earn more money, and finally wins Judge Templeton's confidence when he rescues Sylvia Templeton from a mine cave-in. The judge gives his blessing to the real estate development, thereby enabling Bob to sell his property and win his bet just as the year ends. *Judges. Real estate. Mine disasters. Mistaken identity. Prizefighting. Luck. Wagers.*

LUCK AND SAND **F2.3287**

Maloford Productions. *Dist* Weiss Brothers Clarion Photoplays. 24 Oct **1925.** Si; b&w. 35mm. 5 reels, 5,102 ft.

Dir Leo Maloney. *Scen* Ford Beebe.

Cast: Leo Maloney *(Jim Blake)*, Josephine Hill *(Lois Wetzel)*, Homer Watson *(Roy Wetzel)*, Florence Lee *(Roy's mother)*, Leonard Clapham *(Sanger)*, Roy Watson *(sheriff)*, Hal Gilbert *(Captain Harris)*.

Western melodrama. Captain Harris, a railroad civil engineer, is killed by Sanger and Foote after they have tried in vain to bribe him into telling them the location of the new right-of-way. They escape with Harris' map, and Jim Blake is unjustly suspected of the murder. The Harris map indicates that the new line will run through the ranch of Roy Wetzel, and Sanger offers to buy the land. Wetzel refuses, and Sanger has Wetzel framed for murder. Jim, who is in love with Lois Wetzel, Roy's sister, rescues Roy and proves Sanger to be the guilty party. Jim and Lois are married. *Engineers—Civil. Brother-sister relationship. Railroads. Murder. Bribery. Documentation.*

LUCKY BOY **F2.3288**

Tiffany-Stahl Productions. 2 Feb **1929** [c21 Sep 1928, 4 Feb 1929; LP25643, LP100]. Talking sequences and mus score (Photophone); b&w. 35mm. 10 reels, 8,708 ft.

Dir Norman Taurog, Charles C. Wilson. *Dir Sd Sequences* Rudolph Flothow. *Cont* Isadore Bernstein. *Dial* George Jessel. *Titl* Harry Braxton, George Jessel. *Story* Viola Brothers Shore. *Photog* Harry Jackson. *Adtl Photog* Frank Zucker. *Art Dir* Hervey Libbert. *Set Dressings* George Sawley. *Film Ed* Desmond O'Brien, Russell Shields. *Mus Score* Hugo Riesenfeld. *Songs: "Lucky Boy," "My Mother's Eyes"* L. Wolfe Gilbert, Abel Baer. *Songs: "Old Man Sunshine," "My Real Sweetheart," "Bouquet of Memories"* Lewis Young, William Axt. *Song: "My Blackbirds Are Bluebirds Now"* Irving Caesar, Cliff Friend. *Song: "California Here I Come"* Al Jolson, B. G. De Sylva, Joseph Meyer. *Mus Cond* Sacha Bunchuk.

Cast: George Jessel *(Georgie Jessel)*, Gwen Lee *(Mrs. Ellis)*, Richard Tucker *(Mr. Ellis)*, Gayne Whitman *(Mr. Trent)*, Margaret Quimby *(Eleanor)*, Rosa Rosanova *("Momma" Jessel)*, William Strauss *(Jacob Jessel)*, Mary Doran *(Becky)*.

Comedy-drama. Georgie Jessel, a Jewish jeweler's son from the Bronx, wants to break into show business and, after being turned down by several theatrical managers, makes plans to put on a show of his own by renting a neighborhood theater for one night. Georgie sells tickets to friends and neighbors, but there is not enough money to pay the full rent and he must call off the show. Humiliated, Georgie goes to San Francisco, where he becomes a success singing in a nightclub and falls in love with Eleanor Ellis. When his mother becomes ill, Georgie returns to the East and becomes a star in a Broadway musical comedy. Because of a special kindness to Eleanor's mother, Georgie receives her long-withheld permission to marry Eleanor, thereby making his happiness complete. *Jewelers. Singers. Jews. Theatrical managers. Filial relations. Theater. Nightclubs. New York City—Bronx. New York City—Broadway. San Francisco.*

LUCKY CARSON **F2.3289**

Vitagraph Co. of America. 18 Dec **1921** [c1 Dec 1921; LP17260]. Si; b&w. 35mm. 5 reels.

Dir Wilfrid North. *Scen* Bradley J. Smollen.

Cast: Earle Williams *(David [Lucky] Carson)*, Earl Schenck *(Rudolph Kluck)*, Betty Ross Clarke *(Doris Bancroft)*, Gertrude Astor *(Madame Marinoff)*, Colette Forbes *(Edith Bancroft)*, James Butler *(Tommy Delmaer)*, Loyal Underwood *("Runt" Sloan)*.

Melodrama. Source: Aquila Kempster, *Salvage* (New York, 1906). Having lost all his funds betting on the races in London, John Peters contemplates suicide; then, overhearing the conversation of two men, he considers a new course of action. He stuns one of them—Kluck—and after changing clothes with him, he makes his way to the United States, where he wins at the races, speculates successfully on Wall Street, and amasses a fortune under the sobriquet "Lucky" Carson. Kluck arrives in America, makes Carson's acquaintance, and begs for his help, which is freely given. Carson manages to retrieve some incriminating correspondence between Kluck and an adventuress, Madame Marinoff, who is threatening him. Kluck accuses him of a conspiracy, and a quarrel ensues when Carson reveals his true identity; but Doris Bancroft, Kluck's sister-in-law, discovers that he is innocent. *Gamblers. Horseracing. Impersonation. London. New York City—Wall Street. Documentation.*

LUCKY DAN **F2.3290**

Phil Goldstone Productions. 27 Nov **1922** [New York State license]. Si; b&w. 35mm. 5 reels, 4,700 ft.

Dir William K. Howard.

Cast: Richard Talmadge *("Lucky Dan")*, George A. Williams *(Father of The Girl)*, Dorothy Woods *(The Girl)*, S. E. Jennings *(Slim Connors)*.

Action melodrama. "'Lucky Dan' is a reckless, carefree, daring young cowboy in love with a pretty lass. The latter returns that 'on-to-the-altar' admiration, but her daddy is one of those gentlemen with Missourian leanings, namely, he must be shown. And at the outset daddy doesn't think much of Dan as a business man. But then inheritances always do come in handy and in this particular instance, an unexpected inheritance not only made popper see things different, but incidentally earned a wife for our hero—thus leaving no doubt that between the two the much-welcomed inheritance would be well taken care of. And so it ends." (*Moving Picture World*, 23 Dec 1922, p777.) Slim Connors plays a villain who tries to prevent Dan from acquiring his inheritance. *Cowboys. Inheritance. Fatherhood. Courtship.*

LUCKY DEVIL **F2.3291**

Famous Players–Lasky. *Dist* Paramount Pictures. 13 Jul **1925** [c10 Aug 1925; LP21721]. Si; b&w. 35mm. 6 reels, 5,935 ft.

Pres by Adolph Zukor, Jesse L. Lasky. *Dir* Frank Tuttle. *Scen* Townsend Martin. *Story* Byron Morgan. *Photog* Alvin Wyckoff. *Art Dir* Julian Boone Fleming.

Cast: Richard Dix *(Randy Farman)*, Esther Ralston *(Doris McDee)*, Edna May Oliver *(Mrs. McDee)*, Tom Findley *(Franklyne, Sr.)*, Anthony Jowitt *(Rudolph Franklyne)*, Joseph Burke *(The Professor)*, Mary Foy *(Mrs. Hunt)*, "Gunboat" Smith *(Sailor Sheldon)*, Charles Sellon *(Sheriff)*, Charles Hammond *(Tobias Sedgmore)*, Charles McDonald *(Tom Barrity)*, George Webb *("Frenchy" Roget)*, Eddie James *("Dutch" Oldham)*.

Comedy-drama. Randy Farman, who demonstrates camping outfits in a department store, wins a racing car in a raffle and sets out for the West. He runs out of gas, loses all his money, and falls in love with a girl called Doris, who, accompanied by her aunt, is on her way to Nampa City to claim an inheritance. Arriving at their destination, Doris and her aunt discover that the uncle, who sent for them, is locked up in the crazy house, having invented the entire story of the bequest. Randy enters an exhibition fight with the champion boxer and stays long enough to win the entrance fee for an automobile race at the county fair. The sheriff has attached Randy's car for nonpayment of a hotel bill, and Randy must drive the entire race with the sheriff in the seat beside him. Randy wins the race, a substantial prize, and Doris' love. *Demonstrators—Commercial products. Sheriffs. Prizefighters. Automobile racing. Fairs. Department stores. Insane asylums. Hotels.*

LUCKY FOOL **F2.3292**

Dist Rayart Pictures. 18 Apr **1927** [New York State license]. Si; b&w. 35mm. 5 reels.

Cast: Billy West, Kathleen Myers, Virginia Myers.

Comedy(?). No information on the nature of this film has been found.

THE LUCKY HORSESHOE **F2.3293**

Fox Film Corp. 30 Aug **1925** [c23 Aug 1925; LP21784]. Si; b&w. 35mm. 5 reels.

Pres by William Fox. *Dir* J. G. Blystone. *Scen* John Stone. *Story* Robert Lord. *Photog* Dan Clark. *Asst Dir* Jasper Blystone.

Cast: Tom Mix *(Tom Foster)*, Billie Dove *(Eleanor Hunt)*, Malcolm Waite *(Denman)*, J. Farrell MacDonald *(Mack)*, Clarissa Selwynne *(Aunt Ruth)*, Ann Pennington *(dancer)*, J. Gunnis Davis *(valet to Denman)*.

Western melodrama. Tom Foster, the foreman of the Hunt ranch, assumes charge of the property upon the death of its owner, taking also into his care Eleanor Hunt, a beautiful young girl. Though in love with the girl, Tom is too diffident to propose, and she is taken to Europe by her aunt. Eleanor returns 2 years later with European airs and accompanied by Denman, her European fiancé. Tom has much improved the ranch in the interim, but Eleanor seems to be intent on marrying Denman. Tom's pal, Mack, tells Tom about the rakish exploits of Don Juan, hoping thereby to instill in him a bit of romance. Tom is kidnaped by Denman's hirelings and, knocked on the head, dreams that he is the fabled Juan, fighting like a lion for love. He awakens, frees himself from his bonds, and rides like a madman to the ranch. He arrives in time to prevent the wedding, and he marries Eleanor himself. *Ranch foremen. Abduction. Weddings. Dreams. Don Juan.*

LUCKY IN LOVE **F2.3294**

Pathé Exchange. 17 Aug **1929** [c4 Sep 1929; LP678]. Sd (Photophone); b&w. 35mm. 8 reels, 6,870 ft.

Supv Robert Kane. *Dir* Kenneth Webb. *Dial Supv* James Seymour. *Story-Dial* Gene Markey. *Photog* Philip Tannura, Harry Stradling. *Set Dsgn* Clark Robinson. *Film Ed* Edward Pfitzenmeier. *Songs: "Love Is a Dreamer," "For the Likes o' You and Me," "When They Sing the 'Wearing of the Green' in Syncopated Time"* Sammy Stept, Bud Green. *Mus Dir* Sacha Bunchuk. *Sd* V. S. Ashdown, J. A. Delaney.

Cast: Morton Downey *(Michael O'More)*, Betty Lawford *(Lady Mary Cardigan)*, Colin Keith-Johnston *(Capt. Brian Fitzroy)*, Halliwell Hobbes *(Earl of Balkerry)*, J. M. Kerrigan *(Connors)*, Edward McNamara *(Tim O'More)*, Richard Taber *(Paddy)*, Edward O'Connor *(Rafferty)*, Mary Murray *(Kate)*, Mackenzie Ward *(Cyril)*, Louis Sorin *(Abe Feinberg)*,

Sonia Karlov *(Lulu Bellew)*, Tyrrell Davis *(Potts)*, Elizabeth Murray *(landlady)*.

Comedy-drama. Michael O'More, an American who lives in Ireland with his uncle, a horsetrainer for the Earl of Balkerry, loves Lady Mary Cardigan, granddaughter of the Earl. He finds a rival in Capt. Brian Fitzroy, a rake who intends to buy the impoverished earl's castle and marry Lady Mary. After nearly killing Fitzroy in a brawl over Lady Mary, Michael flees to the United States. There he becomes financially secure when department store magnate Abe Feinberg offers him a job. Feinberg commissions Michael to establish a linen mill on the earl's estate. He and Mary, who is in the United States evading Fitzroy, return to Ireland and marry. *Horsetrainers. Irish. Nobility. Rakes. Department stores. Linen mills.*

THE LUCKY LADY **F2.3295**

Famous Players–Lasky. *Dist* Paramount Pictures. 26 Apr **1926** [c27 Apr 1926; LP22642]. Si; b&w. 35mm. 6 reels, 5,942 ft.

Pres by Adolph Zukor, Jesse L. Lasky. *Dir* Raoul Walsh. *Scen* James T. O'Donohoe, Robert Emmet Sherwood. *Story* Bertram Bloch. *Photog* Victor Milner.

Cast: Greta Nissen *(Antoinette)*, Lionel Barrymore *(Count Ferranzo)*, William Collier, Jr. *(Clarke)*, Marc MacDermott *(Franz Garletz)*, Madame Daumery *(Duchess)*, Sojin *(secretary to Garletz)*.

Romantic comedy-drama. Immediately following the death of San Guido's prince, Prime Minister Franz Garletz determines that Princess Antoinette shall marry Count Ferranzo, a roué. Antoinette, a convent student who secretly goes to the local inn to watch the stage show, begins a flirtation with Clarke, a young American tourist, but leaves quickly at the toll of vespers. To avoid the abbé, she hides in the trunk of Clarke's car, and when he drives past the convent, she makes known her presence. When told of the impending marriage, Antoinette determines to make herself as ugly as possible; at the same time, however, she disguises herself as a coquette and attracts Ferranzo. Hearing of the betrothal, Clarke gains entrance to her apartment; she assures him of her love, but he is taken prisoner. Garletz, determined to put an end to the coquette and Clarke, sends them across the border; there, Antoinette discloses her identity, and the lovers are married. *Students. Royalty. Coquetry. Disguise. Imaginary kingdoms. Convents.*

Note: Working title: *Lady Luck.*

LUCKY LARKIN **F2.3296**

Ken Maynard Productions. *Dist* Universal Pictures. 2 Mar **1930** [c11 Nov 1929; LP854]. Mus score & sd eff (Movietone); b&w. 35mm. 8 reels, 5,875 ft. [Also si; 5,779 ft.]

Pres by Carl Laemmle. *Dir* Harry J. Brown. *Story-Scen* Marion Jackson. *Titl* Leslie Mason. *Camera* Ted McCord. *Film Ed* Fred Allen.

Cast: Ken Maynard *(Lucky Larkin)*, Nora Lane *(Emmy Lou Parkinson)*, James Farley *(Martin Brierson)*, Harry Todd *(Bill Parkinson)*, Paul Hurst *(Pete Brierson)*, Charles Clary *(Colonel Lee)*, Blue Washington *(Hambone)*, Tarzan *(himself, a horse)*.

Western melodrama. Colonel Lee, a homesteader, is the object of terrorists who want to drive him off the range so that his horses cannot be entered in the county races, and he refuses an offer of Martin Brierson to buy him out. Pete, Brierson's brother, in hiding because of his criminal record, burns the colonel's barn and injures his horses. Convinced of Brierson's responsibility for the terror tactics, "Lucky" Larkin plans to ride Tarzan, the colonel's pet colt. Brierson does his best to disqualify the horse, but Larkin tricks him and wins the race. Larkin captures Pete and forces him to confess. The Brierson brothers are brought to justice, and Larkin wins Emmy Lou, a homesteader's daughter. *Homesteaders. Terrorists. Brothers. Horseracing. Horses.*

LUCKY SPURS **F2.3297**

H. B. Carpenter Productions. *Dist* Chesterfield Motion Picture Corp. 1 Feb **1926**. Si; b&w. 35mm. 5 reels, 4,366 ft.

Dir? (see note) H. B. Carpenter, V. V. Clegg. *Photog* J. P. Whalen.

Cast: Bill Patton.

Western melodrama. "Foundling is brought up in ignorance of parents. Later youth falls in love with a ranch owner's daughter and it develops that he is son of rancher's former partner and rightfully half-owner of wealthy establishment." ("Motion Picture News Booking Guide," in *Motion Picture News*, 8 May 1926, p35.) *Foundlings. Ranchers. Parentage. Inheritance.*

Note: Sources disagree in crediting direction.

LUCKY STAR **F2.3298**

Fox Film Corp. 18 Aug **1929** [c5 Aug 1929; LP569]. Mus score, talking sequences, & sd eff (Movietone); b&w. 35mm. 10 reels, 8,784 ft. [Also si; 8,725 ft.]

Pres by William Fox. *Dir* Frank Borzage. *Scen* Sonya Levien. *Dial* John Hunter Booth. *Titl* Katherine Hilliker, H. H. Caldwell. *Photog* Chester Lyons, William Cooper Smith. *Art Dir* Harry Oliver. *Film Ed* Katherine Hilliker, H. H. Caldwell. *Rec Engr* Joseph Aiken. *Asst Dir* Lew Borzage.

Cast: Charles Farrell *(Timothy Osborn)*, Janet Gaynor *(Mary Tucker)*, Guinn "Big Boy" Williams *(Martin Wrenn)*, Paul Fix *(Joe)*, Hedwig Reicher *(Mrs. Tucker)*, Gloria Grey *(Milly)*, Hector V. Sarno *(Pop Fry)*.

Melodrama. Source: Tristram Tupper, "Three Episodes in the Life of Timothy Osborn," in *Saturday Evening Post* (199:5–7, 9 Apr 1927). Mary Tucker is a drudge on the impoverished farm of her widowed mother, a woman who actually wants to give her children a better life than she has had. When after the war the local men return from overseas, Ma Tucker wants Mary to wed Martin Wrenn, an ex-sergeant who enters the town, as two gossips point out, "still wearing his uniform." Wrenn gets back his old job as electrical lineman while ex-lineman Timothy Osborn, the man Mary loves, takes odd mending jobs because he is paralyzed from a war injury. As Ma Tucker is about to give Mary to Wrenn, Osborn regains his former strength, gives Wrenn a thrashing, and weds Mary. *Drudges. Veterans. Linemen. Paralysis. Marriage—Arranged. World War I.*

LUCRETIA LOMBARD **F2.3299**

Warner Brothers Pictures. 18 Nov or 8 Dec **1923** [c13 Nov 1923; LP19605]. Si; b&w. 35mm. 7 reels, 7,500 ft.

Harry Rapf Production. *Dir* Jack Conway. *Scen* Bertram Millhauser, Sada Cowan. *Story* Kathleen Norris.

Cast: Irene Rich *(Lucretia Lombard)*, Monte Blue *(Stephen Winship)*, Marc MacDermott *(Sir Allen Lombard)*, Norma Shearer *(Mimi)*, Alec B. Francis *(Judge Winship)*, John Roche *(Fred Winship)*, Lucy Beaumont *(Mrs. Winship)*, Otto Hoffman *(Sandy, Lombard's servant)*.

Melodrama. Source: Kathleen Norris, *Lucretia Lombard* (New York, 1922). Lucretia Morgan marries elderly Sir Allen Lombard, who becomes a dissolute, chair-ridden drug addict and dies after a few years from an overdose of narcotics. She falls in love with District Attorney Stephen Winship, who reciprocates but, at his father's request, marries Mimi, ward of the Winships. Fate brings the two (Stephen and Lucretia) together after a "series of stirring sequences" culminating in Mimi's death when a dam bursts during a forest fire. *District attorneys. Narcotics. Marriage. Dams. Forest fires.*

Note: Film was copyrighted as *Lucretia Lombard* but released as both *Lucretia Lombard* and *Flaming Passion.*

THE LULLABY **F2.3300**

R-C Pictures. *Dist* Film Booking Offices of America. 20 Jan **1924** [c20 Jan 1924; LP20346]. Si; b&w. 35mm. 7 reels, 6,951 ft.

Dir Chester Bennett. *Scen* Hope Loring, Louis D. Lighton. *Story* Lillian Ducey. *Photog* Jack MacKenzie.

Cast: Jane Novak *(Felipa/Antoinette)*, Robert Anderson *(Tony)*, Fred Malatesta *(Pietro)*, Dorothy Brock *(Baby Antoinette)*, Cleo Madison *(Mrs. Marvin)*, Otis Harlan *(Thomas Elliott)*, Peter Burke *(Thomas, Jr.)*, Lydia Yeamans Titus *(Mary)*.

Melodrama. Tony is sentenced to be hanged for the murder of his friend, Pietro, whom he found seducing his bride, Felipa, and she is sentenced to 20 years' imprisonment as an accessory. Born in prison, her child is taken from her at the age of 3 and is adopted by the judge, now governor, who sentenced the parents. Years later, upon the mother's release, she relinquishes her legal claim to the child and is given refuge by its guardians. *State governors. Judges. Seduction. Murder. Prisons. Adoption. Capital punishment.*

LUMMOX **F2.3301**

Feature Productions. *Dist* United Artists. 18 Jan **1930** [c18 Jan 1930; LP1038]. Sd (Movietone); b&w. 35mm. 9 reels, 7,533 ft.

Pres by Joseph M. Schenck. *Dir* Herbert Brenon. *Dial* Fannie Hurst. *Adapt* Elizabeth Meehan. *Photog* Karl Struss. *Art Dir* William Cameron Menzies, Park French. *Film Ed* Marie Halvey. *Mus Score* Hugo Riesenfeld, Jack Danielson. *Rec Engr* David Forrest. *Asst Dir* Ray Lissner. *Wardrobe* Alice O'Neill.

Cast: Winifred Westover *(Bertha Oberg)*, Dorothy Janis *(Chita)*, Lydia Yeamans Titus *(Annie Wennerberg)*, Ida Darling *(Mrs. Farley)*, Ben Lyon *(Rollo Farley)*, Myrta Bonillas *(Veronica Neidringhouse)*, Cosmo Kyrle

Bellew *(John Bixby)*, Anita Bellew *(Mrs. John Bixby)*, Robert Ullman *(Paul Bixby, age 5)*, Clara Langsner *(Mrs. Wallenstein, Sr.)*, William Collier, Jr. *(Wally Wallenstein)*, Edna Murphy *(May Wallenstein)*, Torben Meyer *(Silly Willie)*, Fan Bourke *(Mrs. McMurtry)*, Myrtle Stedman *(Mrs. Ossetrich)*, Danny O'Shea *(Barney)*, William Bakewell *(Paul Charvet)*, Sidney Franklin *(Mr. Meyerbogen)*.

Society melodrama. Source: Fannie Hurst, *Lummox* (New York, 1923). Bertha, a ponderous, inarticulate servant ("Lummox") is dismissed from a boardinghouse for interfering to save Chita, a fellow worker, from the advances of sailor, and she finds work as a cook in the home of wealthy Mrs. Farley, whose son, Rollo, a poet, seduces her; learning he is engaged to a society girl, Bertha leaves, disguising her condition. After the birth of her son, she consents to his adoption by a wealthy family who promise to give him every advantage. Bertha nurses Mrs. Wallenstein, an aged woman despised by her daughter-in-law, May; rather than see her taken away to an institution, Bertha allows her to die but is accused of murder and driven from the house; she then strikes up a friendship with Willie, a slow-witted servant who works for the Bixbys, who are keeping her child. Bertha serves for many years in the home of Mrs. Ossetrich but is dismissed because of a theft committed by Chita, whom she has helped. One evening she is drawn to a piano recital, and she is at last fulfilled by the music of her son, whom she never meets. *Housemaids. Domestics. Pianists. Poets. Seduction. Illegitimacy. Motherhood. Adoption. Old age.*

THE LUNATIC AT LARGE **F2.3302**

First National Pictures. 2 Jan **1927** [c28 Dec 1926; LP23478]. Si; b&w. 35mm. 6 reels, 5,521 ft.

Supv Earl Hudson. *Dir* Fred Newmeyer. *Titl* Ralph Spence. *Photog* L. William O'Connell.

Cast: Leon Errol *(Sam Smith)*, Dorothy Mackaill *(Beatrix Staynes)*, Jack Raymond *(Mandell Essington)*, Warren Cook *(Dr. Wilkins)*, Kenneth MacKenna *(William Carroll/Henry Carroll)*, Tom Blake *(Maxwell)*, Charles Slattery *(Lunt)*, Theresa Maxwell Conover *(Aunt Teddy)*.

Farce. Source: J. Storer Clouston, unidentified stories. Sam Smith, an exponent of the easy life, is tricked into a private sanitarium for the wealthy, where he is believed to be a patient who is expected there. He meets Bill Carroll, who has been railroaded to the asylum by Henry Carroll, his insane twin brother who wants to marry Beatrix Staynes, already betrothed to Bill. Bill enlists the aid of Sam, who escapes and makes his way to the Staynes home. There a party is in progress to celebrate the wedding, to take place in a dirigible. Sam reaches the aviation field in time to grab a ladder dangling from the dirigible, and he succeeds in stopping the wedding. The dirigible is wrecked and lands in the yard of the sanitarium where Bill is waiting for Beatrix; Henry is cured by the crash, and Bill and Beatrix are happily married. *Brothers. Twins. Mistaken identity. Insanity. Weddings. Sanitariums. Dirigibles.*

THE LURE OF A WOMAN **F2.3303**

Progress Picture Association. **1921.** Si; b&w. 35mm. 5 reels.

Dir J. M. Simms. *Photog* Howard Curtis. *Asst Dir* Mrs. Osborne.

Cast: Regina Cohee, Dr. A. Porter Davis, Charles Allen, Mrs. J. D. Brown, Roberto Taylor, Lenore Jones, John Cobb, Alonzo Nixon, Susie Dudley, Veronica Miller, Emily Gates, Alice Johnson.

Melodrama(?). No information about the precise nature of this film has been found. *Negro life.*

THE LURE OF EGYPT **F2.3304**

Federal Photoplays of California. *Dist* Pathé Exchange. 15 May **1921** [c4 May 1921; LU16476]. Si; b&w. 35mm. 6 reels.

Dir Howard Hickman. *Scen* Elliott Clawson, E. Richard Schayer. *Photog* Harry Vallejo.

Cast: Robert McKim *(Prince Dagmar)*, Claire Adams *(Margaret Lampton)*, Joseph J. Dowling *(Professor Lampton)*, Carl Gantvoort *(Michael Amory)*, Maude Wayne *(Millicent Mervill)*, William Lion West *(Nishi)*, Frank Hayes *(Abdul)*, Zack Williams *(Theodore)*, Aggie Herring *(Mrs. Botts)*, George Hernandez *(Mr. Botts)*, Harry Lorraine *(Gondo Koro)*.

Melodrama. Source: Norma Lorimer, *There Was a King in Egypt* (New York, 1918). Professor Lampton's work of excavating the tomb of Akhnaton (Ikhnaton) is held up by lack of funds, and Prince Dagmar, scion of a Balkan royal family, finances him with the ulterior motive of robbing the tomb of its treasures. Michael Amory, an artist assisting Lampton, loves Margaret, but believing her to be in love with the prince he departs with Gondo Koro, a Bedouin prophet who knows the location of the tomb. Dagmar sends Millicent, an adventuress, to obtain the information from Michael, and when Dagmar enters the tomb at night Michael surprises him. The thieves wound Michael, but they are captured and he and Margaret are reconciled. *Royalty. Artists. Bedouins. Archeology. Treasure. Egypt. Ikhnaton.*

LURE OF GOLD (William Steiner Productions) **F2.3305**

Mar **1922** [c6 Mar 1922; LU17610]. Si; b&w. 35mm. 5 reels, 4,891 ft.

Dir–Story–Screen Adapt Neal Hart. *Photog* Jake Badaracco.

Cast: Neal Hart *(Jack Austin)*, William Quinn *(Chuck Wallace)*, Ben Corbett *(Latigo Bob)*.

Western melodrama. After striking gold, prospector Jack Austin arrives in a small western town to settle. He saves Jane Hampton from death when she is attacked by a wild steer and earns her gratitude. Learning that she is a concert singer, he becomes her friend. Jack enters a local rodeo and captures the main prize by riding a steer. Buck Kelly and his henchman, Latigo Bob, learn of the hero's wealth and determine to rob him; but Jane hears about the plot and frustrates it. Jack and Jane's happiness is assured. *Prospectors. Singers. Rodeos. Gold.*

Note: Character names are from shooting script in copyright files and may differ from those in the final film.

THE LURE OF JADE **F2.3306**

Robertson-Cole Co. *Dist* R-C Pictures. 13 Nov **1921** [c13 Nov 1921; LP17283]. Si; b&w. 35mm. 6 reels, 5,935 ft.

Dir Colin Campbell. *Scen* Marion Orth. *Photog* Dev Jennings. *Art Dir* W. L. Heywood.

Cast: Pauline Frederick *(Sara Vincent)*, Thomas Holding *(Capt. Louis Corey)*, Arthur Rankin *(Allan Corey)*, Leon Bary *(Stuart Beresford)*, Hardee Kirkland *(Rear Admiral Vincent)*, L. C. Shumway *(Captain Willing)*, Clarissa Selwynne *(Alida Corey)*, Togo Yamamoto *(Sara's servant)*, Goro Kino *(Willing's servant)*.

Melodrama. Source: George M. Cohan and Max Marcin, *House of Glass; a Drama in Four Acts* (New York, 1916). Sara, daughter of Rear Admiral Vincent, who has a passion for collecting jade, has previously been in love with Captain Corey, but she insisted that he marry his fiancée, Alida, who remains intensely jealous of Sara. At a party Captain Willing jokingly boasts of the superiority of his jade collection and invites Sara to see it; they are locked in a room by his servant, and Sara, forced to exit by the bedroom window, is seen by Alida, whose gossip causes Sara to be ostracized. As a result, Vincent suffers a stroke and dies, and Sara swears vengeance on Alida. Fifteen years later, she is a hotel owner on a South Sea island where fate sends Captain Corey, Alida, and their young son, Allan. Sara plots with Beresford to compromise Alida, but Allan, in a drunken frenzy, kills Beresford. Sara takes the blame to save him, leaving the Coreys' happiness untouched. *Reputation. Revenge. Jealousy. Jade. South Sea Islands. United States Navy.*

THE LURE OF LOVE **F2.3307**

Pictures in Motion. *Dist* Ace-High Productions. 28 Apr **1924.** Si; b&w. 35mm. 5 reels, 4,600 ft.

Dir Leon E. Dadmun.

Cast: Zena Keefe, Edward Earle.

Melodrama. "Concerns young Russian exiled from homeland by officer who desires hero's sister. In America he works in a steel mill and makes his way up the ladder, defeating a plot to undermine his prestige with the workmen. He also wins the love of the daughter of steel mill owner and eventually locates his sister and brings her from Russia." (*Motion Picture News Booking Guide*, 8:53, Apr 1925.) *Immigrants. Russians. Brother-sister relationship. Exile. Steel industry.*

LURE OF THE MINE **F2.3308**

26 Sep **1929** [New York State license]. Si; b&w. 35mm. 5 reels, 4,500 ft.

Cast: Montana Bill *(Alan Roscoe)*.

Western melodrama(?). No information about the nature of this film has been found.

THE LURE OF THE NIGHT CLUB **F2.3309**

R-C Pictures. *Dist* Film Booking Offices of America. 29 May **1927** [c8 Jun 1927; LP24056]. Si; b&w. 35mm. 6 reels, 5,770 ft.

Pres by Joseph P. Kennedy. *Dir* Thomas Buckingham. *Cont* Buckleigh Fritz Oxford. *Story* Burke Jenkins. *Ch Camera* Robert Newhard. *Asst Dir* Jimmy Dugan.

Cast: Viola Dana *(Mary Murdock)*, Robert Ellis *(John Stone)*, Jack Daugherty *(Tom Loring)*, Bert Woodruff *(Pop Graves)*, Lydia Yeamans

Titus *(Aunt Susan)*, Robert Dudley *(hired man)*.

Romantic drama. Mary Murdock, a country girl who has achieved success as a Broadway entertainer, gets a day off to revisit the scenes of her childhood. Tom Loring, her former sweetheart, renews his attempts to win her, and John Stone, the club manager, allows her to break her contract and return to the country to marry Loring. Loring goes to town to market an invention, and a storm virtually demolishes the farm and most of the stock. Mary tells Stone of the misfortune when he arrives on her birthday, and he agrees to hire her for a short time at the cabaret. Mary is grateful for Stone's help, but Loring suspects an affair and goes to New York to vindicate his honor; indignant at his behavior, Mary decides to stay on Broadway. Stone tries to reconcile the couple, but Mary finds the manager is the worthier man. *Dancers. Inventors. Farmers. Rural life. Courtship. Nightclubs. New York City—Broadway. Storms.*

LURE OF THE TRACK **F2.3310**

Charles Makranzy Productions. *Dist* Lee-Bradford Corp. Dec **1925.** Si; b&w. 35mm. 5 reels, 4,800 ft.

Cast: Sheldon Lewis, Maclyn Arbuckle, Dot Farley.

Melodrama. " ... with climax enacted during running of the Derby, on which hero, a jockey, has staked all. Though object of plots, he pilots mount to victory, his winnings enabling him to save sweetheart and her father from ruin." ("Motion Picture News Booking Guide," in *Motion Picture News*, 8 May 1926, p35.) *Jockeys. Horseracing.*

LURE OF THE WEST **F2.3311**

Chesterfield Motion Picture Corp. Nov **1926.** Si; b&w. 35mm. 5 reels, 4,344-4,500 ft.

Prod H. T. Henderson. *Dir-Story* Alvin J. Neitz.

Cast: Eileen Sedgwick, Les Bates, Ray Childs, D. Maley, Alfred Hewston, Elsie Bower, Carlos Silvera.

Western melodrama. "Story is woven around a quack selling bottled cures in a small western town. The saloon owner buys the services of the quack's daughter as an entertainer and, soon after sending the old boy and the sick daughter away to the city, sets to work pawing the gal and emoting vile thoughts. The hero has no particular status, remaining the mysterious stranger to the bitter end." (*Variety*, 22 Aug 1928, p34.) *Strangers. Quacks. Entertainers. Patent medicines. Saloons.*

Note: May have been produced some years earlier than release.

THE LURE OF THE WILD **F2.3312**

Columbia Pictures. 12 Dec **1925** [c28 Dec 1925; LP22172]. Si; b&w. 35mm. 6 reels, 5,570 ft.

Prod Harry Cohn. *Dir* Frank R. Strayer. *Story-Cont* Tom J. Hopkins. *Photog* George Meehan. *Film Ed* Charles J. Hunt.

Cast: Jane Novak *(Agnes Belmont)*, Alan Roscoe *(James Belmont)*, Billie Jean *(Baby Cuddles)*, Richard Tucker *(Gordon Daniels)*, Mario Carillo *(Poleon Dufresne)*, Pat Harmon *(Mike Murdock)*, Lightning *(Shep)*.

Melodrama. Jim Belmont, believing that his wife has committed adultery with Gordon Daniels, takes his small daughter, Cuddles, and heads for the Canadian wilderness. Daniels then pays Murdock to murder Jim; after Jim's death, Shep, Jim's faithful dog, assumes responsibility for the child, going to Poleon Dufresne, a trapper, for help. Poleon takes in the dog and the little girl and sends for Agnes Belmont, who quickly hurries to her child's side. Daniels follows Agnes (who, in fact, has been faithful to both the person and the memory of her husband) and attempts to kill her. Shep saves her life and drives Daniels off a cliff to his death. Agnes and Dufresne wed, providing a happy home for Shep and Cuddles. *Trappers. Children. Motherhood. Murder. Canada. Dogs.*

LURE OF THE YUKON **F2.3313**

Norman Dawn Alaskan Co. *Dist* Lee-Bradford Corp. 1 Aug **1924.** Si; b&w. 35mm. 6 reels, 5,170 ft.

Dir-Writ Norman Dawn. *Photog* George Madden.

Cast: Eva Novak *(Sue McGraig)*, Spottiswoode Aitken *(Sourdough McCraig)*, Kent Sanderson *(Bob Force)*, Arthur Jasmine *(Kuyak)*, Howard Webster *(Dan Baird)*, Katherine Dawn *(Ruth Baird)*, Eagle Eye *(Black Otter)*.

Northwest melodrama. Sourdough McCraig and his daughter, Sue, set off for the Alaskan gold fields pursued by Dan Baird, who keeps his wife hidden away. Fortunately, they also meet up with Bob Force, who comes to Sue's aid when her father dies and again to her rescue when Baird captures her and starts an avalanche. Thrills abound before the hero balks the villain and wins the girl. *Prospectors. Filial relations. Infidelity. Alaska. Avalanches.*

THE LURE OF YOUTH **F2.3314**

Metro Pictures. 10 Jan **1921** [c15 Jan 1921; LP16203]. Si; b&w. 35mm. 6 reels.

Prod Bayard Veiller. *Dir* Philip E. Rosen. *Story-Scen* Luther Reed. *Photog* Robert Kurrle. *Art Interiors* Sidney Ullman.

Cast: Cleo Madison *(Florentine Fair)*, William Conklin *(Morton Mortimer)*, Gareth Hughes *(Roger Dent)*, Lydia Knott *("Ma" Dent)*, William Courtwright *("Pa" Dent)*, Helen Weir *(Marjorie Farnol)*.

Romantic drama. Famous actress Florentine Fair, who is satiated with theatrical life, falls in love with Roger Dent, an unsophisticated youth with a passion for writing plays. Taking him to New York as her protégé, she encourages him to write. Although her lover, Mortimer, is at first insanely jealous, he finds merit in Dent's new play and finances him on Broadway. The young dramatist offers his hand in marriage to the actress, but she refuses and accepts Mortimer. *Playwrights. Actors. Theater. New York City—Broadway.*

Note: Working title: *White Ashes*.

LURING LIPS **F2.3315**

Universal Film Manufacturing Co. 25 Jul **1921** [c16 Jul 1921; LP16771]. Si; b&w. 35mm. 5 reels, 4,263 ft.

Pres by Carl Laemmle. *Dir* King Baggot. *Scen* George Hively. *Photog* Virgil Miller.

Cast: Darrel Foss *(Dave Martin)*, Ramsey Wallace *(Frederick Vibart)*, William Welsh *(James Tierney)*, Carlton King *(Mark Fuller)*, Edith Roberts *(Adele Martin)*, M. E. Stimson *(detective)*.

Melodrama. Source: John A. Moroso, "The Gossamer Web" (publication undetermined). Dave Martin, receiving teller in a Wall Street bank, marries Adele, secretary to the office manager, Frederick Vibart, who visits their home and shows continued interest in her. When a loss of $50,000 is discovered at the bank, Dave comes under suspicion and is arrested and convicted. Just before his release from prison, he sees Adele and Vibart together in a newsreel and becomes bitterly jealous. When released, he rushes to confront them as they are leaving for South America. Adele, however, has evidence that Vibart actually stole the money, and as Vibart is arrested she confesses to Dave that she lured Vibart so as to prove her suspicions. *Bank clerks. Secretaries. Injustice. Newsreels.*

LUXURY **F2.3316**

Lyric Productions. *Dist* Arrow Film Corp. Jan **1921** [c9 Dec 1920; LU15887]. Si; b&w. 35mm. 6 reels. [Copyrighted as 5 reels.]

Dir Marcel Perez.

Cast: Rubye De Remer *(Blanche Young)*, Walter Miller *(Harry Morton)*, Frederick Kalgren *(Joseph Burns)*, Henry Pemberton *(John Morton, Harry's stepbrother)*, Grace Parker *(John Morton's wife)*, Rose Mintz *(Olga Pompom)*, Thomas Megraine *(Detective Healy)*.

Society melodrama. Harry Morton gives a wild bachelor party before his marriage to Blanche Young. Joseph Burns, a rejected suitor of Blanche's, tells her about the party and begs her to marry him, but in vain. On the wedding night, Harry disappears; and Burns is suspected of kidnaping him but is exonerated. Blanche also is kidnaped, but both she and Harry escape. The real culprit turns out to be the wife of Harry's brother John, who was trying to prevent Harry's marriage before his 30th birthday so that John, and not Harry, would inherit their father's fortune. Blanche and Harry do marry before then and come into their fortune. *Inheritance. Kidnaping. Wealth.*

Note: Working title: *The Unmarried Bride*.

LYING LIPS **F2.3317**

Thomas H. Ince Productions. *Dist* Associated Producers. 30 Jan **1921** [c4 Feb 1921; LP16126]. Si; b&w. 35mm. 7 reels.

Supv Thomas H. Ince. *Dir* John Griffith Wray. *Scen* Bradley King. *Story* May Edginton. *Photog* Charles Stumar, Henry Sharp.

Cast: House Peters *(Blair Cornwall)*, Florence Vidor *(Nancy Abbott)*, Joseph Kilgour *(William Chase)*, Margaret Livingston *(Lelia Dodson)*, Margaret Campbell *(Mrs. Abbott)*, Edith Yorke *(Mrs. Prospect)*, Calvert Carter *(Horace Prospect)*, Emmett C. King *(John Warren)*.

Society melodrama. Pending her engagement to William Chase, a wealthy Londoner, English aristocrat Nancy Abbott visits Canada and there meets Blair Cornwall, a rancher whom she comes to love but for whom she will not accept a life of hardship. On her return voyage, her ship, on which he also sails, is sunk by a mine, and the two save themselves on a piece of wreckage. In a moment of terror she swears her love, but when a ship is sighted she requests that she be rescued alone, and Blair conceals himself. Before her marriage to Chase, Nancy reencounters Blair, who is using an assumed name, and at her wedding she collapses at the altar, declaring that she loves another man. Just before his departure for Australia, she and Blair are reunited. *Ranchers. Wealth. Weddings. Mines (explosives). Canada. London. Shipwrecks.*

Note: Working title: *The Magic Life.*

THE LYING TRUTH **F2.3318**

Eagle Producing Co. *Dist* American Releasing Corp. 26 Mar **1922** [c26 Mar 1922; LP17915]. Si; b&w. 35mm. 5-6 reels, 5,338 ft.

Dir-Story-Scen Marion Fairfax. *Photog* René Guissart. *Tech Dir* Charles D. Hall.

Cast: Noah Beery *(Lawrence De Muidde)*, Marjorie Daw *(Sue De Muidde)*, Tully Marshall *(Horace Todd)*, Pat O'Malley *(Bill O'Hara)*, Charles Mailes *(Sam Clairborne, Sr.)*, Claire McDowell *(Mrs. Sam Clairborne)*, Adele Watson *(Ellie Clairborne)*, George Dromgold *(Sam Clairborne, Jr.)*, Robert Brauer *(Mose)*, Wade Boteler *(Bill O'Hara, Sr.)*.

Melodrama. Following the death of his parents, Bill O'Hara is reared by the Clairbornes, owners of the local newspaper. They have a son of their own—Sam. Just before the death of Mr. Clairborne, Bill becomes heir to the estate, and Sam is disowned because of his dope addiction. Because the newspaper is losing money, Bill plots a bogus "murder" to create news, and the town is soon in an uproar. When Sam's body is found in the swamps, evidence points to Bill, his foster brother; and De Muidde, the backer of the narcotics gang, seeks to avenge himself for the exposé by having Bill lynched. Mrs. Clairborne arrives just in time, however, with Sam's suicide note, which clears Bill. *Inheritance. Narcotics. Newspapers. Hoaxes. Suicide. Lynching.*

LYING WIVES (Emerald Productions) **F2.3319**

Ivan Players. 13 Jun **1925** [New York premiere; c23, 31 Mar 1925; LU21290]. Si; b&w. 35mm. 7 reels.

Pres by Ivan Abramson. *Dir-Story* Ivan Abramson. *Photog* Frank Zucker.

Cast: Clara Kimball Young *(Patricia Chase)*, Richard Bennett *(Ted Stanhope)*, Madge Kennedy *(Margery Burkley)*, Edna Murphy *(Elsie Chase)*, Niles Welch *(Wallace Graham)*, J. Barney Sherry *(Alvin Chase)*, Buddy Harris *(Wallace Graham, Jr.)*, Bee Jackson *(Betty Lee)*.

Melodrama. Ted Stanhope, a middle-aged millionaire, represents himself to Margery Burkley, a beautiful young stenographer, as a friend of her father, who vanished when she was just an infant. When Wallace Graham marries Margery, Patricia Chase, who is in love with Wallace despite the fact that she is married, tries to break up the marriage by making Wallace suspicious of Stanhope's intentions. When a baby is born to Margery, Patricia leads Wallace to believe that Stanhope is the child's father. To further worsen matters between the Grahams, Patricia arranges for Wallace to be arrested for embezzlement. After he is released from jail, Wallace learns that Margery has visited Stanhope during the time of his incarceration and, overcome with jealous spite, he arranges to go away with the eager Patricia, who calmly packs and informs her husband that she is leaving him. Graham has a change of heart when he learns that Stanhope is, in reality, Margery's father, and that she visited him only to arrange for bail money. Margery and Graham are happily reunited; Patricia returns to her husband, but he orders her from the house. *Stenographers. Millionaires. Marriage. Jealousy. Injustice. Embezzlement. Middle age. Parentage.*

THE MAD DANCER **F2.3320**

Jans Productions. 15 Feb **1925** [c19 Feb 1925; LP21175]. Si; b&w. 35mm. 7 reels, 5,500 ft.

Dir Burton King. *Cont* William B. Laub. *Photog* Charles Davis. *Sets* Tec-Art Studios. *Film Ed* William B. Laub.

Cast: Ann Pennington *(Mimi)*, Johnny Walker *(Keith Arundel)*, Coit Albertson *(Serge Verlaine)*, John Woodford *(Robert Halleck)*, Frank Montgomery *(Jean Gaboule)*, Rica Allen *(Ada Halleck)*, William F. Haddock *(Elmer Halleck)*, John Costello *(John Arundel)*, Nellie Savage *(Princess Gibesco)*, Echlin Gayer *(Prince Carl)*, Clarence Sunshine *(Cupid Karsleed)*.

Society melodrama. Source: Louise Winter, "The Mad Dancer," in *Young's Magazine* (48:3–32, Dec 1924). Mimi, known in the Latin Quarter as "The Mad Dancer," poses in the nude for sculptor Verlaine. When her father later commits suicide, she goes to the United States to live with his family, but she is insulted by them for having posed for Verlaine. Mimi soon walks out and goes to live in Washington, where she becomes engaged to Keith Arundel, the son of a United States senator. Verlaine appears in Washington for the official unveiling of the statue for which Mimi posed, meets Mimi again, and unsuccessfully attempts to force her to marry him by threatening to reveal that she was the model for this statue of "the mad dancer." Mimi later enters Verlaine's room and smashes the head of the statue beyond recognition. When the mutilated work is unveiled, the sculptor in his fury relates Mimi's history to the assembled guests. Keith knocks him down. Senator Arundel later bribes Verlaine into publicly retracting his statement, and Keith and Mimi are married. *Sculptors. Dancers. Reputation. Bribery. Paris—Quartier Latin. Washington (District of Columbia). United States Congress.*

MAD HOUR **F2.3321**

First National Pictures. 4 Mar **1928** [c27 Feb 1928; LP25013]. Si; b&w. 35mm. 7 reels, 6,625 ft.

Pres by Robert Kane. Allan Dwan Production. *Dir* Joseph C. Boyle. *Titl* Casey Robinson, Tom Geraghty. *Adapt* Tom Geraghty. *Photog* Ernest Haller. *Film Ed* Terrell Morse.

Cast: Sally O'Neill *(Cuddles)*, Alice White *(Aimee)*, Donald Reed *(Jack Hemingway, Jr.)*, Larry Kent *(Elmer Grubb)*, Lowell Sherman *(Joe Mack)*, Norman Trevor *(Hemingway, Sr.)*, Eddie Clayton *(Red)*, James Farley *(inspector)*, Rose Dione *(modiste)*, Tully Marshall *(lawyer)*, Margaret Livingston *(maid)*, Jack Egan *(chauffeur)*, Kate Price *(jail matron)*, Mary Foy *(police matron)*, Ione Holmes *(bride)*.

Melodrama. Source: Elinor Glyn, *The Man and the Moment* (New York, 1914). Cuddles Magrue, daughter of a cabdriver, has a taste for luxury that worries her father. After a gin party Cuddles marries Jack Hemingway, a wealthy lounge lizard, and they move into the Ritz. In the morning Jack's father disinherits him. Jack becomes involved with some jewel thieves, and he accepts the hospitality of Joe Mack, a known crook. Cuddles is unwittingly implicated in a theft and is sent to jail. There she gives birth to a son, which is taken from her; and the marriage is annulled. Released, she returns home on the night of her former husband's second marriage; distraught, she commits suicide. *Taxi drivers. Thieves. Upper classes. Wealth. Injustice. Marriage—Annulment.*

THE MAD MARRIAGE **F2.3322**

Universal Film Manufacturing Co. 31 Jan **1921** [c20 Jan 1921; LP16044]. Si; b&w. 35mm. 5 reels, 4,531 ft.

Pres by Carl Laemmle. *Dir* Rollin Sturgeon. *Scen* Marion Fairfax. *Photog* Alfred Gosden.

Cast: Carmel Myers *(Jane Judd)*, Truman Van Dyke *(Jerry Paxton)*, William Brunton *(Willie)*, Virginia Ware *(Mrs. Brendon)*, Margaret Cullington *(Harmonia)*, Jane Starr *(Althea)*, Arthur Carewe *(Christiansen)*, Nola Luxford *(Bob)*, Lydia Yeamans Titus *(Mrs. Boggs)*.

Melodrama. Source: Marjorie Benton Cooke, *Cinderella Jane* (Garden City, New York, 1917). Jerry, a struggling young artist in Greenwich Village, marries a studio helper, Jane Judd, an aspiring playwright, knowing that she will not interfere with his work. She takes part in a pageant for which Jerry designs the costumes and attracts the attention of Christiansen, a young playwright with whom she works secretly on a play. After the birth of their child, Jerry and Jane become closer, but he is violently jealous of her accompanying Christiansen to the successful opening of his play and offers her a divorce. However, their child's illness brings them back together. *Artists. Playwrights. Children. Theater. New York City—Greenwich Village.*

THE MAD MARRIAGE **F2.3323**

Rosemary Films. c7 Feb **1925** [LU21111]. Si; b&w. 35mm. 5 reels, 5,000 ft.

Pres by Myles Connolly. *Dir* Frank P. Donovan. *Photog* Lester Lang, Frank Zukor.

Cast: Rosemary Davies, Harrison Ford, Maurice Costello, Richard Carle, Paul Panzer, Florence Turner, Gaston Glass, Montague Love, Walter McGrail, Mary Thurman.

Melodrama. Alice Darvil, an innocent and simple girl of 16, lives with her harsh father in a sequestered country cottage. Walter Butler, an author, is caught in a storm while on a walking tour and seeks shelter for the night in the Darvil home. He is attracted to Alice, and, when he meets her later in a neighboring village (after she has been thrown out of her house), he takes her to live with him. He soon marries her, but, when he is forced to leave for a business trip, she runs away. A child, Mary Jane, is born to her, and she becomes a domestic in the house of Mrs. Leslie, a charitable woman of wealth. There she meets Colonel Anderson, a wealthy old man whom she also marries. Alice and the colonel drift apart and, when he dies, he leaves his considerable fortune to Mary Jane. Walter Butler, who has become a recluse, writing books of spiritual consolation under the name of Malvern, tires of the solitary life and decides to open his home to visitors. Mary Jane, not knowing that he is her father, comes to visit Butler's home, and Butler falls in love with her. They are about to be married, when Butler discovers that Mary Jane is his daughter. Butler is then reconciled with Alice, and Mary Jane marries her young sweetheart. *Authors. Bigamy. Incest. Village life.*

THE MAD WHIRL (Universal-Jewel) **F2.3324**
Universal Pictures. 1 Mar **1925** [22 Nov 1924; LP20808]. Si; b&w. 35mm. 7 reels, 6,184 ft.

Pres by Carl Laemmle. *Dir* William A. Seiter. *Scen* Edward T. Lowe, Jr. *Titl* Harvey Thew. *Adapt* Frederic Hatton, Fanny Hatton. *Screen Treatment* Lewis Milestone. *Photog* Merritt B. Gerstad. *Art Dir* Leo E. Kuter. *Asst Dir* Nate Watt.

Cast: May McAvoy *(Cathleen Gillis)*, Jack Mulhall *(Jack Herrington)*, Myrtle Stedman *(Gladys Herrington)*, Barbara Bedford *(Margie Taylor)*, Alec B. Francis *(John Herrington)*, Ward Crane *(Benny Kingsley)*, George Fawcett *(Martin Gillis)*, Marie Astaire *(Julia Carling)*, Joe Singleton *(Spivens)*.

Society melodrama. Source: Richard Washburn Child, "Here's How," in *Fresh Waters and Other Stories* (New York, 1924). Though they are old enough to know better, John and Myrtle Herrington keep pace with their son, Jack, on his endless round of drinking bouts and jazz parties. When Jack encounters Cathleen Gillis, a childhood chum who has just returned from boarding school, he begins to follow her around. Cathleen's father, Martin Gillis, objects to Jack's attentions to his daughter and warns the girl against him. Despite this advice, Cathleen is attracted to Jack and tries to reform him; he promises to give up his way of life but soon relapses. Cathleen forgives him; and, in need of, and filled with love for, each other, the young couple elope. Martin Gillis, angered by his daughter's sudden marriage, pays a visit to the elder Herringtons and bitterly condemns the quality of their lives. John and Myrtle at first resent the attack; but, when Gillis leaves, they slowly become convinced of the error of their ways and decide to act their age. *Jazz life. Middle age. Parenthood.*

MADAM SATAN **F2.3325**
Metro-Goldwyn-Mayer Pictures. 20 Sep **1930** [c1 Oct 1930; LP1622]. Sd (Movietone); b&w. 35mm. 13 reels, 10,320 ft.

Prod-Dir Cecil B. De Mille. *Screenplay* Jeanie Macpherson. *Dial* Gladys Unger, Elsie Janis. *Photog* Harold Rosson. *Art Dir* Cedric Gibbons, Mitchell Leisen. *Film Ed* Anne Bauchens. *Songs: "Meet Madam," "We're Going Somewhere," "The Cat Walk"* Clifford Grey, Herbert Stothart. *Song: "This Is Love"* Clifford Grey, Herbert Stothart. *Ballet Mécanique* Herbert Stothart. *Songs: "All I Know Is You Are in My Arms," "Low Down," "Auction Number" "Satan's Song," "Live and Love Today"* Elsie Janis, Jack King. *Dance Dir* Le Roy Prinz. *Rec Engr* J. K. Brock, Douglas Shearer. *Asst Dir* Mitchell Leisen, Cullen Tate. *Gowns* Adrian.

Cast: Kay Johnson *(Angela Brooks)*, Reginald Denny *(Bob Brooks)*, Lillian Roth *(Trixie)*, Roland Young *(Jimmy Wade)*, Elsa Peterson *(Martha)*, Irwin Boyd *(captain)*, Wallace MacDonald *(first mate)*, Wilfred Lucas *(Roman senator)*, Tyler Brooke *(Romeo)*, Lotus Thompson *(Eve)*, Vera Marsh *(Call of the Wild)*, Martha Sleeper *(fish girl)*, Doris McMahon *(Water)*, Marie Valli *(Confusion)*, Julanne Johnston *(Miss Conning Tower)*, Albert Conti *(empire officer)*, Earl Askam *(pirate)*, Betty Francisco *(Little Rolls Riding Hood)*, Ynez Seabury *(Babo)*, Countess De Liguoro *(Spain)*, Katherine Irving *(Spider Girl)*, Aileen Ransom *(Victory)*, Theodore Kosloff *(Electricity)*, Jack King *(Herman)*, Edward Prinz *(Biff)*, Maine Geary, Allan Lane, Kenneth Gibson, Youcca Troubetzkoy, Henry Stockbridge, June Nash, Mary Carlisle, Mary McAllister, Dorothy Dehn, Louis Natheaux, Ella Hall, Edwards Davis, Kasha Haroldi, Katherine De Mille, Vera Gordon, Natalie Storm, Elvira Lucianti, Marguerita Swope, Dorothy Vernon, Lorimer Johnson, John Byron, Abe Lyman and His Band.

Spectacular. Wealthy socialite Angela Brooks finds she is losing the love of her husband, Bob, to a wild young showgirl named Trixie; advised by her maid, she sets out to recapture her husband by taking on the personality of the mysterious "Madam Satan." At a costume party given aboard a giant dirigible, Angela entrances her husband by her modish vamping, amidst a spectacular electrical ballet in which characters simulate everything from sparkplugs to lightning bolts. After she has successfully ensnared him, the dirigible is struck by lightning, and the guests are forced to parachute from the ship, Angela giving hers to the distraught Trixie. Realizing his love for Angela, Bob gives her his parachute and dives from the ship, suffering only minor injuries by landing in the Central Park reservoir. Husband and wife are blissfully reunited. *Socialites. Vamps. Marriage. Infidelity. Ballet. Parachuting. Dirigibles. Reservoirs. New York City.*

MADAME BEHAVE **F2.3326**
Christie Film Co. *Dist* Producers Distributing Corp. ca21 Nov **1925** [Boston premiere; released 6 Dec; c31 Oct 1925; LP21956]. Si; b&w. 35mm. 6 reels, 5,417 ft.

Prod Al Christie. *Dir* Scott Sidney. *Adapt* F. McGrew Willis. *Photog* Gus Peterson, Alec Phillips.

Cast: Julian Eltinge *(Jack Mitchell/"Madame Behave")*, Ann Pennington *(Gwen Townley)*, Lionel Belmore *(Seth Corwin)*, David James *(Dick Corwin)*, Tom Wilson *(Creosote)*, Jack Duffy *(M. T. House)*, Stanhope Wheatcroft *(Percy Fairweather)*, Evelyn Francisco *(Laura [or Evelyn?] Barnes)*.

Farce. Source: Jean Arlette, unidentified play. M. T. House threatens to dispossess Dick Corwin and Jack Mitchell if they do not pay their rent by noon. The boys decide to "touch" Dick's uncle, Seth Corwin, who is suing M. T. House in court. (Dick loves Gwen Townley, Corwin's ward, while Jack is in love with Gwen's chum, Laura.) The case is postponed for 2 weeks so that an unknown woman, the principal witness, can be found. Corwin's lawyer urges him to marry the mystery woman, since a wife cannot testify against her husband; and Dick is assigned the task of finding her. M. T. House overhears the scheme and decides to marry her himself. Jack is mistaken for a burglar and evades capture by disguising himself as a woman. The deception is so successful that Dick urges Jack to pose as the unknown woman, "Madame Behave." After various complications, Corwin and M. T. House are reconciled, while the young folks participate in a double wedding. *Uncles. Landlords. Lawsuits. Female impersonation. Dispossession.*

Note: Title also rendered: *Al Christie's "Madame Behave."* Working title: *Madame Lucy*.

MADAME LUCY *see* **MADAME BEHAVE**

MADAME SANS-GÊNE **F2.3327**
Famous Players–Lasky. *Dist* Paramount Pictures. 20 Apr **1925** [c23 Apr 1925; LP21388]. Si; b&w. 35mm. 10 reels, 9,994 ft.

Pres by Adolph Zukor, Jesse L. Lasky. *Dir* Léonce Perret. *Screenplay* Forrest Halsey. *Photog* George Webber.

Cast: Gloria Swanson *(Catherine Hubscher)*, Emile Drain *(Napoléon)*, Charles De Roche *(Lefebvre)*, Madelaine Guitty *(La Rousotte)*, Warwick Ward *(Neipperg)*, Henry Favieres *(Fouché, Minister of Police)*, Renée Heribelle *(Eliza, a princess)*, Suzanne Bianchetti *(Empress Marie Louise)*, Denise Lorys *(Madame De Bulow)*, Jacques Marney *(Savary)*.

Historical comedy. Source: Victorien Sardou and Émile Moreau, *Madame Sans-Gêne; comédie en trois actes, précédée d'un prologue* (Paris, 1907). Catherine Hubscher, the proprietress of a laundry in Paris, is known as Madame Sans-Gêne. Among the clients of this carefree woman are Napoléon, a young artillery lieutenant, and Lefebvre, a handsome soldier. After the French Revolution, Napoléon becomes emperor and Lefebvre is appointed a field marshal with the title of Duke of Danzig. Catherine becomes the Duchess of Danzig and alienates Napoléon's sisters by her rough manners at court. Napoléon orders Lefebvre to divorce her but relents when she reminds him of his unpaid laundry bills and of her faithful service to the army during the Revolution. *Laundresses. France—History—Revolution. Paris. Napoleon I. Marie Louise. François Joseph Lefebvre. Catherine Hubscher. Joseph Fouché.*

MADAME X **F2.3328**
Metro-Goldwyn-Mayer Pictures. 17 Aug **1929** [c29 Jul 1929; LP557]. Sd (Movietone); b&w. 35mm. 10 reels, 8,806 ft.

Dir Lionel Barrymore. *Scen-Dial* Willard Mack. *Photog* Arthur Reed. *Art Dir* Cedric Gibbons. *Film Ed* William S. Gray. *Rec Engr* Russell Franks, Douglas Shearer. *Wardrobe* David Cox.

Cast: Lewis Stone *(Floriot)*, Ruth Chatterton *(Jacqueline)*, Raymond Hackett *(Raymond)*, Holmes Herbert *(Noel)*, Eugenie Besserer *(Rose)*, John P. Edington *(doctor)*, Mitchell Lewis *(Colonel Hanby)*, Ullrich Haupt *(Laroque)*, Sidney Toler *(Merivel)*, Richard Carle *(Perissard)*, Carroll Nye

(Darrell), Claude King *(Valmerin)*, Chappell Dossett *(judge)*.

Drama. Source: Alexandre Bisson, *Madame X* (New York opening: 2 Feb 1910). Jacqueline leaves her husband for another man, and when she returns to take care of her sick son, her husband flatly rejects her. She leaves without seeing the boy; and beginning her path on the downgrade, she meets and helps a cardsharp named Laroque. When they return to France, her home, Laroque decides that because of her name he can squeeze out a goodly sum from her. At the threat of blackmail, Jacqueline, in a rage, shoots him and is subsequently defended in court by her son, who does not know her true identity. In the final court scene, Jacqueline confesses, without using names, that she shot Laroque so as not to allow her son to discover her degrading life. *Cardsharps. Public defenders. Desertion. Motherhood. Murder. Blackmail. Degeneracy. Trials. France.*

Note: Remake of *Madame X*, 1920.

MADE FOR LOVE **F2.3329**

Cinema Corp. of America. *Dist* Producers Distributing Corp. ca9 Jan **1926** [Los Angeles premiere; released 14 Feb 1926; c8 Dec 1925; LP22095]. Si; b&w. 35mm. 7 reels, 6,703 ft.

Pres by Cecil B. De Mille. *Dir* Paul Sloane. *Prod Ed* Elmer Harris. *Story-Adapt* Garrett Fort. *Photog* Arthur Miller. *Art Dir* Max Parker. *Asst Dir* William J. Scully.

Cast: Leatrice Joy *(Joan Ainsworth)*, Edmund Burns *(Nicholas Ainsworth)*, Ethel Wales *(Lady Diana Trent)*, Bertram Grassby *(Mahmoud Bey)*, Brandon Hurst *(Pharaoh)*, Frank Butler *(Freddie Waddams)*, Lincoln Stedman *(The Cherub)*, Neely Edwards *(Pierre, the pet of the boulevards)*.

Romantic drama. Nicholas Ainsworth, a young American archeologist, discovers in Egypt the lost tomb of two lovers, Princess Herath and Aziru. He is so engrossed in his work that he neglects his wife, Joan, who carries on flirtations with an Englishman, an American, and a Frenchman. An Egyptian prince, a tomb robber, gives Nicky a book recounting the story of the two lovers and warns him of the curse laid upon the tomb by a pharaoh in 2000 B. C. Joan is captured by Bedouins but is rescued by the prince. Nicky misinterprets the situation and angrily accuses Joan of running off with the prince, whereupon she leaves Nicky and accepts the attentions of the prince. Joan learns that Nicky has returned to the tomb and rides to warn him of the curse. Both are trapped when the tomb is sealed by an explosion. The prince is killed by a falling rock at the moment he clears a passage for them. Nicky realizes his love for Joan, and they are reunited. *Archeologists. Royalty. Bedouins. Grave robbers. Curses. Infidelity. Egypt.*

MADE IN HEAVEN **F2.3330**

Goldwyn Pictures. May **1921** [c17 Apr 1921; LP16546]. Si; b&w. 35mm. 5 reels, 4,684 ft.

Dir Victor Schertzinger. *Scen* Arthur F. Statter. *Story* William Hurlbut. *Photog* Ernest Miller. *Art Dir* Cedric Gibbons.

Cast: Tom Moore *(William Lowry)*, Helene Chadwick *(Claudia Royce)*, Molly Malone *(Elizabeth Royce)*, Kate Lester *(Mrs. Royce)*, Al Filson *(Mr. Royce)*, Freeman Wood *(Davidge)*, Charles Eldridge *(Lowry, Sr.)*, Renée Adorée *(Miss Lowry)*, Herbert Prior *(Leland)*, Fronzie Gunn *(Ethel Hadden)*, John Cossar *(Mr. Hadden)*.

Romantic comedy. William Lowry, an Irish immigrant, rescues Claudia Royce from a burning building, and upon hearing that her parents are trying to force her to accept millionaire Leland, whom she does not love, he proposes a marriage of convenience to himself. She accepts, and Bill arranges a fake ceremony; but when she falls in love with Davidge, Bill refuses her a "divorce." Later, Bill gets rich in the manufacture of a patented fireman's pole, and when he buys a house for Claudia she realizes her love for him and they are legally married. *Irish. Immigrants. Millionaires. Marriage of convenience. Marriage—Fake. Fire departments.*

A MADE-TO-ORDER HERO (Ranch Rider Western) **F2.3331**

Universal Pictures. 3 Jun **1928** [c20 Oct 1927; LP24569]. Si; b&w. 35mm. 5 reels, 4,120 ft.

Pres by Carl Laemmle. *Dir* Edgar Lewis. *Story-Cont* William Lester. *Titl* Gardner Bradford. *Photog* Al Jones. *Film Ed* Harry Marker.

Cast: Ted Wells *(Bert Lane)*, Marjorie Bonner *(Margery Murray)*, Pearl Sindelar *(Aunt Saphrona)*, Jack Pratt *(Fred Van Ratt)*, Ben Corbett *(Babbling Ben)*, Pee Wee Holmes *(Bill Purtwee)*, Scotty Mattraw *(Scotty)*, Dick L'Estrange *(Lazy [Ichabod])*.

Western melodrama. Bert Lane, owner of the 3X Ranch, learns that his sweetheart, Margery Murray, is coming to visit him, accompanied by her Aunt Saphrona, who insists that her niece marry a society man or at least a hero. Bert and his men impersonate the Borden gang and hold up the stage in which the women are traveling so as then to come to their "rescue," but they are driven off by Van Ralt, a passenger, who becomes Aunt Saphrona's hero. Bert later rescues Margery from a runaway; and in a staged raid, his men abduct Margery and Saphrona. Meanwhile, Bert learns that Van Ralt is actually Borden, a notorious killer; he absconds with Margery and her aunt's jewels, but Bert frees himself and routs the gang. Saphrona pronounces her blessings on the new hero. *Ranchers. Aunts. Bandits. Impersonation. Abduction.*

MADELON *see* **MELODY OF LOVE**

MADEMOISELLE MIDNIGHT **F2.3332**

Tiffany Productions. *Dist* Metro-Goldwyn Distributing Corp. 14 Apr **1924** [c23 Jun 1924; LP20327]. Si; b&w. 35mm. 7 reels, 6,778 ft.

Pres by Robert Z. Leonard. *Dir* Robert Z. Leonard. *Story-Scen* John Russell, Carl Harbaugh. *Photog* Oliver T. Marsh.

Cast—The Prolog: Mae Murray *(Renée de Gontran)*, John Sainpolis *(Colonel de Gontran)*, Paul Weigel *(Napoleon III)*, Clarissa Selwynne *(Eugénie)*, Earl Schenck *(Maximilian)*, J. Farrell MacDonald *(Duc de Moing)*.

Cast—The Story: Mae Murray *(Renée de Quiros)*, Monte Blue *(Owen Burke)*, Robert McKim *(João)*, Robert Edeson *(Don Pedro de Quiros)*, Nick De Ruiz *(Don José de Quiros)*, Nigel De Brulier *(Dr. Sanchez)*, Johnny Arthur *(Carlos de Quiros)*, Otis Harlan *(Padre Francisco)*, Evelyn Selbie *(Chiquita, a maid)*, Mathilde Comont *(duenna)*.

Melodrama. Inheriting from her French grandmother a taste for midnight adventure, Renée de Quiros sets out to win a young American diplomat visiting Mexico. An outlaw, João, raids her home, killing her father, and later obtains her uncle's consent to marry her, but she escapes her enemies and is united with the American for a midnight wedding. *Diplomats. Mexico. Mexico—History—European intervention. Napoleon III. Eugénie. Maximilian Emperor of Mexico.*

MADEMOISELLE MODISTE **F2.3333**

Corinne Griffith Productions. *Dist* First National Pictures. 21 Mar **1926** [c26 Apr 1926; LP22634]. Si; b&w. 35mm. 7 reels, 6,230 ft.

Pres by Asher-Small-Rogers. *Dir* Robert Z. Leonard. *Titl* Ralph Spence. *Adapt* Adelaide Heilbron. *Photog* George Barnes. *Art Dir* J. J. Hughes. *Film Ed* Cyril Gardner. *Prod Mgr* Scott R. Beal.

Cast: Corinne Griffith *(Fifi)*, Norman Kerry *(Étienne)*, Willard Louis *(Hiram Bent)*, Dorothy Cumming *(Marianne)*, Rose Dione *(Madame Claire)*.

Romantic comedy-drama. Source: Henry Martyn Blossom and Victor Herbert, *Mademoiselle Modiste, a Comic Opera* (New York, 1905). Hiram Bent, a St. Louis hat dealer, goes to Paris with his conservative, prudish wife. At a fashion show, Madame Claire fails to interest them and sends for Fifi, a particularly successful model and saleswoman who makes a large sale and wins Hiram's admiration. While delivering a hat to the fiancée of Étienne Du Beauvray, Fifi complains to an officer (actually Étienne) about his horse destroying the hat; so Fifi is forced to improvise a hat for Marianne. Later, Étienne meets Fifi at the salon, and a romance develops. Impressed by her sales ability, Bent buys out Madame Claire and establishes Fifi as "Mademoiselle Modiste." Étienne, suspicious of Bent's activities, challenges him to a duel, but the misunderstanding is soon cleared up and Fifi is happily united with Étienne. *Milliners. Salesclerks. Courtship. Fashion shows. Paris. Saint Louis (Missouri).*

THE MADNESS OF LOVE (Entertainment Series) **F2.3334**

Wray Physioc Co. *Dist* Wid Gunning, Inc. Apr **1922** [c25 Mar 1922; LP18309]. Si; b&w. 35mm. 5 reels, 4,817 ft.

Dir-Writ Wray Physioc.

Cast: Jean Scott *(Mary Anne Strong)*, Charles Craig *(Capt. James Strong)*, Bernard Siegel *(Sim Calloway)*, Willard Cooley *(David Calloway)*, Ivan Christy *(Ben Tompkins)*, Richard Lee *(Dr. Abel Hanks)*.

Melodrama. Sim Calloway has been unscrupulously acquiring Capt. James Strong's fleet of ships. Therefore, Strong is horrified to learn that his daughter, Mary Anne, is in love with artist David Calloway, Sim's nephew; forbids her to see him; and locks her in her room. Furious, Calloway causes David to be taken on a long sea voyage, intercepts his letters to Mary Anne, and finally tells her that David has died, thus causing her mind to become unbalanced. Strong is eager for revenge, but Calloway is trapped in a cellar, where he gloats madly over the purloined love letters.

David returns, recognition slowly returns to Mary Anne, and they are united. *Artists. Fatherhood. Ships. Insanity. Documentation.*

MADNESS OF YOUTH **F2.3335**

Fox Film Corp. 8 Apr **1923** [c8 Apr 1923; LP18989]. Si; b&w with col sequences. 35mm. 5 reels, 4,719 ft.

Pres by William Fox. *Dir* Jerome Storm. *Scen* Joseph Franklin Poland. *Story* George Frank Worts. *Photog* Joseph August.

Cast: John Gilbert *(Jaca Javalie)*, Billie Dove *(Nanette Banning)*, Donald Hatswell *(Peter Reynolds)*, George K. Arthur *(Ted Banning)*, Wilton Taylor *(Theodore P. Banning)*, Ruth Boyd *(Madame Jeanne Banning)*, Luke Lucas *(Mason, butler)*, Julanne Johnston *(The Dancer)*.

Drama. Source: George Frank Worts, "Red Darkness," in *Argosy All-Story Weekly* (147:161–182, 363–385, 540–567, 759–782, 18 Nov–9 Dec 1922). "Describes the final adventure of a youthful crook of good blood, whose weakness is a desire to rob the rich. He protects himself from suspicion by assuming the role of an evangelist, known as 'the holy man,' going about preaching, making converts of others and then when the psychological moment offers, makes his 'haul' and 'getaway.' His carefully laid plans, however, do not provide for such an obstacle arising as his falling in love with the daughter of the man he plans to rob. She unconsciously awakens the better man and when the way is prepared the mad youth finds himself a convert of his own preachments, and that what he desires more is to live aright and become eligible for the hand of the girl who brings about the change of heart and desire." (*Motion Picture News*, 28 Apr 1923, p2058.) *Evangelists. Criminals—Rehabilitation. Imposture.*

THE MADONNA OF AVENUE A **F2.3336**

Warner Brothers Pictures. 22 Jun **1929** [c3 Jun 1929; LP440]. Sd (Vitaphone); b&w. 35mm. 8 reels, 6,461 ft. [Also si; 5,249 ft.]

Dir Michael Curtiz. *Scen-Titl* Ray Doyle. *Dial* Francis Powers. *Story* Mark Canfield. *Photog* Byron Haskin. *Film Ed* Ray Doyle. *Song: "My Madonna"* Fred Fisher, Louis Silvers.

Cast: Dolores Costello *(Maria Morton)*, Grant Withers *(Slim Shayne)*, Douglas Gerrard *(Arch Duke)*, Louise Dresser *(Georgia Morton)*, Otto Hoffman *(Monk)*, Lee Moran *(Gus)*.

Melodrama. Maria Morton, who attends a young women's boarding school, leads a carefree and innocent life, unaware that her mother is a hostess in an East Side nightclub. While walking on the beach, she is attracted to Slim Shayne, an adventurer, who persuades her to spend the evening on his boat (actually a rumrunner); and in an encounter with revenue officials, he escapes and Maria is expelled from school. Going to Avenue A in New York, the girl is appalled to discover her mother's secret, and she marries Slim, hoping thus to reform him. Mrs. Morton, unaware that he is her son-in-law, has Slim framed by her underworld friends for a murder; but learning of their marriage and that her daughter is pregnant, she insures herself for $10,000 to pay a lawyer to free Slim, then takes poison. Slim is saved and finds happiness with Maria. *Nightclub hostesses. Lawyers. Rumrunners. Revenue agents. Motherhood. Scandal. Suicide. Boarding schools. New York City—Lower East Side.*

MADONNA OF THE STREETS **F2.3337**

Edwin Carewe Productions. *Dist* First National Pictures. 19 Oct **1924** [c7 Oct 1924; LP20639]. Si; b&w. 35mm. 8 reels, 7,507 ft.

Pres by Edwin Carewe. *Dir* Edwin Carewe. *Titl* Frederic Hatton, Fanny Hatton. *Adapt* Frank Griffin. *Photog* Robert Kurrle. *Art Dir* John D. Schulze. *Asst Dir* Wallace Fox.

Cast: Nazimova *(Mary Carlson/Mary Ainsleigh)*, Milton Sills *(Rev. John Morton)*, Claude Gillingwater *(Lord Patrington)*, Courtenay Foote *(Dr. Colbeck)*, Wallace Beery *(Bill Smythe)*, Anders Randolf *("Bull" Morgan)*, Tom Kennedy *(see note)*, John T. Murray *("Slippery" Eddie Foster)*, Vivian Oakland *(Lady Sarah Joyce)*, Harold Goodwin *(Walter Bowman)*, Rosa Gore *(Mrs. Elyard)*, Maybeth Carr *(Judy Smythe)*, Herbert Prior *(Nathan Norris)*.

Drama. Source: William Babington Maxwell, *The Ragged Messenger* (London, 1904). Rev. John Morton, who is determined to follow as closely as possible the teachings of Jesus, inherits a considerable fortune when his uncle dies. Shortly thereafter he succumbs to the wiles of Mary Carlson and marries her. To Mary's dismay, John uses his money for charitable work. When John learns that not only has Mary been unfaithful to him but she was also his uncle's mistress and became Mrs. Morton in order to share the inheritance she believed to be rightfully hers, he sends her away with his secretary. Years later, John regrets his harshness; and he is reunited with Mary when she appears at a home for fallen women, which he is dedicating. *Clergymen. Mistresses. Inheritance. Charity. London—Limehouse.*

Note: Some sources credit Tom Kennedy in the role of "Bull" Morgan.

MADONNA OF THE STREETS **F2.3338**

Columbia Pictures. 25 Nov **1930** [c10 Dec 1930; LP1810]. Sd (Movietone); b&w. 35mm. 8 reels, 6,932 ft.

Prod Harry Cohn. *Dir* John S. Robertson. *Adapt-Cont-Dial* Jo Swerling. *Photog* Sol Polito. *Art Dir* Edward Jewell. *Tech Dir* Edward Shulter. *Film Ed* Gene Havlick. *Sd Engr* Ben Harper. *Asst Dir* C. C. Coleman.

Cast: Evelyn Brent *(May)*, Robert Ames *(Morton)*, Ivan Linow *(Slumguillion)*, Josephine Dunn *(Marion)*, Edwards Davis *(Clark)*, Zack Williams *(Blink)*, Ed Brody *(Ramsey)*, Richard Tucker *(Kingsley)*.

Melodrama. Source: William Babington Maxwell, *The Ragged Messenger* (London, 1904). Following the death of her millionaire companion, May Fisher is disheartened upon learning that the entire estate is willed to Peter Morton, his nephew, who operates a mission on San Francisco's Barbary Coast. To get into his good graces, she takes the post as his assistant and for months works at his side, arousing the jealousy of Marion, Peter's fiancée; but she falls in love with him and refuses to claim the money when he advertises for May Fisher; and when her life is threatened, he realizes their mutual love and they are married. Her true identity, however, is revealed by Kingsley, the uncle's lawyer, and she confesses the truth to Peter, who—feeling betrayed—leaves her. But all is forgiven when she saves his life. *Mission workers. Lawyers. Inheritance. Personal identity. Missions. San Francisco—Barbary Coast.*

THE MAGIC CUP **F2.3339**

Realart Pictures. Apr **1921** [c11 Apr 1921; LP16385]. Si; b&w. 35mm. 5 reels, 4,587 ft.

Dir John S. Robertson. *Story-Scen* E. Lloyd Sheldon. *Photog* Roy Overbaugh. *Asst Dir* J. Malcolm Dunn.

Cast: Constance Binney *(Mary Malloy)*, Vincent Coleman *(Bob Norton)*, Blanche Craig *(Mrs. Nolan)*, William H. Strauss *(Abe Timberg)*, Charles Mussett *(Peter Venner)*, J. H. Gilmour *(The Patrician)*, Malcolm Bradley *("Paste" Parsons)*, Cecil Owen *(The Derelict)*.

Melodrama. Mary Malloy, a scullery maid in a hotel, becomes acquainted with cub reporter Bob Norton, and he falls in love with her. When Mary sees a neighbor evicted, she helps by pawning an old silver goblet bearing her family crest. Two pawnbrokers plot to use Mary as a decoy when they substitute paste gems for real pearls, one posing as Lord Fitzroy, the owner of the goblet. Bob becomes suspicious and finds the real Lord Fitzroy, who is able to prove that Mary is his granddaughter. The couple live happily ever after. *Scullions. Reporters. Pawnbrokers. Grandfathers. Hotels.*

THE MAGIC FLAME **F2.3340**

Samuel Goldwyn, Inc. *Dist* United Artists. 14 Aug **1927** [c16 Aug 1927; LP24275]. Si; b&w. 35mm. 9 reels, 8,308 ft. [Also 7,850 ft.]

Pres by Samuel Goldwyn. *Dir* Henry King. *Cont* June Mathis. *Titl* George Marion, Jr., Nellie Revell. *Adapt* Bess Meredyth. *Photog* George Barnes. *Art Dir* Carl Oscar Borg. *Theme Song* Sigmund Spaeth. *Asst Dir* Robert Florey. *Adv* Captain Marco.

Cast: Ronald Colman *(The Clown [Tito]/The Count)*, Vilma Banky *(The Aerial Artist [Bianca])*, Augustino Borgato *(The Ringmaster)*, Gustav von Seyffertitz *(The Chancellor)*, Harvey Clarke *(The Aide)*, Shirley Palmer *(The Wife)*, Cosmo Kyrle Bellew *(The Husband)*, George Davis *(The Utility Man)*, André Cheron *(The Manager)*, Vadim Uraneff *(The Visitor)*.

Romantic melodrama. Source: Rudolph Lothar, *König Harlekin, ein Maskenspiel in vier Aufzügen* (Munich, 1904). Bianca, the aerial star of Baretti's circus, loves Tito, the clown, and resents the advances of the handsome Crown Prince of Illyria, who poses as Count Cassati. The prince pursues the wife of a neighboring squire and kills her husband when he discovers them together. Maddened by Bianca's refusals, the prince lures her to his hotel with a forged letter, but she drops from the window, using her gymnastic skill to escape. Tito comes to her aid and in a struggle with the prince casts him from the window into the sea. Bearing a striking resemblance to the prince, Tito assumes his identity and thus evades prosecution. Believing Tito to have been killed by the prince, Bianca leaves the circus to seek vengeance. During the coronation, she is about to assassinate the "prince" when he reveals his identity, and together they escape to the circus. *Clowns. Aerialists. Doubles. Courtship. Murder. Revenge. Impersonation. Circus. Imaginary kingdoms.*

THE MAGIC GARDEN **F2.3341**

Gene Stratton Porter Productions. *Dist* Film Booking Offices of America. 30 Jan **1927** [c13 Jan 1927; LP23594]. Si; b&w. 35mm. 7 reels, 6,807 ft.

Pres by Joseph P. Kennedy. *Dir-Adapt* J. Leo Meehan. *Cont* Charles Kerr. *Photog* Allen Siegler. *Art Dir* Carroll Clark. *Asst Dir* Charles Kerr.

Cast: Joyce Coad *(Amaryllis Minton, as a child)*, Margaret Morris *(Amaryllis Minton, grown)*, Philippe De Lacy *(John Guido Forrester, as a child)*, Raymond Keane *(John Guido, grown)*, Charles Clary *(Paul Minton)*, William V. Mong *(John Forrester)*, Cesare Gravina *(Maestro)*, Paulette Duval *(Countess di Varesi)*, Walter Wilkinson *(Peter Minton, as a child)*, Earl McCarthy *(Peter Minton, grown)*, Alfred Allen *(chief Clare)*, Katherine Clare Ward *(Mrs. O'Rourke)*, Ruth Cherrington *(duenna)*.

Romantic drama. Source: Gene Stratton Porter, *The Magic Garden* (Garden City, New York, 1927). Amaryllis Minton, left to her own resources following her parents' divorce, visits her brother, Peter, and in the country she meets young John Guido Forrester, an aspiring violinist, with whom in her childish way she falls in love. John saves her from an attempted suicide and takes her home to the "magic garden," where they vow eternal love before John's father takes him to Italy to study. Ten years later, Amaryllis goes to Venice and there meets John on the night of his debut. Though under the influence of the Countess di Varesi, he reaffirms his love for her. Upon their return, Amaryllis' father rents the Forrester home, and they await the return of John; Peter invites him on a yachting cruise, and the yacht is reported sunk. Amaryllis weeps in the arms of John's father, but in the moonlight John returns to her, playing "Amaryllis" on his violin. *Violinists. Suicide. Yachts. Gardens. Venice.*

THE MAGIC LIFE *see* **LYING LIPS**

THE MAGIC SKIN *see* **SLAVE OF DESIRE**

THE MAGICIAN **F2.3342**

Metro-Goldwyn-Mayer Pictures. 24 Oct **1926** [c19 Oct 1926; LP23232]. Si; b&w. 35mm. 7 reels, 6,960 ft. [Copyrighted as 8 reels.]

Dir-Adapt Rex Ingram. *Photog* John F. Seitz. *Film Ed* Grant Whytock.

Cast: Alice Terry *(Margaret Dauncey)*, Paul Wegener *(Oliver Haddo)*, Ivan Petrovich *(Dr. Arthur Burdon)*, Firmin Gemier *(Dr. Porhoet)*, Gladys Hamer *(Susie Boud)*.

Fantasy-melodrama. Source: William Somerset Maugham, *The Magician* (London, 1908). Oliver Haddo, a student of the occult, demonstrates on numerous occasions his powers of magic and after years of search finds a formula in a Paris library for the creation of human life. Margaret Dauncey, the niece of Dr. Porhoet, is a sculpture student and is injured while working on a huge faun. Dr. Arthur Burdon, a noted American surgeon, performs a delicate operation on her spine before many famous doctors, including Haddo; and during her convalescence, Margaret and Dr. Burdon become romantically involved. By trickery Haddo gains entrance to Margaret's apartment and puts her under a hypnotic spell. Burdon follows them to Monte Carlo, but she is irretrievably under Haddo's power. In the Sorcerer's Tower, Haddo is about to extract her virgin blood for his secret formula, when Burdon and Dr. Porhoet arrive and overcome him; Haddo falls into a fiery furnace, and the tower is destroyed, freeing Margaret from the spell. *Sculptors. Surgeons. Magicians. Hypnotism. Occult. Libraries. Paris. Monte Carlo.*

Note: Filmed in actual locales in France.

THE MAGNIFICENT BRUTE **F2.3343**

Universal Film Manufacturing Co. Mar **1921** [c12 Mar 1921; LP16283]. Si; b&w. 35mm. 5 reels, 4,606 ft.

Dir Robert Thornby. *Scen* Lucien Hubbard. *Story* Malcolm Stuart Boylan. *Photog* William Fildew.

Cast: Frank Mayo *(Victor Raoul)*, Dorothy Devore *(Yvonne)*, Percy Challenger *(Fontaine)*, Alberta Lee *(Mrs. Fontaine)*, J. J. Lance *(Marquis Courtière)*, William Eagle Eye *(Indian)*, Charles Edler *(Kendrick)*, Dick Sutherland *(Randall)*, Eli Stanton, Buck Moulton *(woodsmen)*, Lillian Ortez *(maid)*.

Northwest melodrama. French Canadian trapper Victor Raoul returns to the trading post at St. Ignace to find a rival for the affections of Yvonne, his business partner's daughter, in the Marquis Courtière, Parisian representative of the fur company. Raoul quarrels with Fontaine over the visitor's business dealings and his attentions to Yvonne. When Fontaine is later attacked and robbed, Victor is framed by the agent and almost lynched, but he is saved by a statement from Yvonne and the arrival of the Mounted Police. *Trappers. Fur industry. Canadian Northwest. Northwest Mounted Police.*

THE MAGNIFICENT FLIRT **F2.3344**

Paramount Famous Lasky Corp. 2 Jun **1928** [c2 Jun 1928; LP25334]. Si; b&w. 35mm. 7 reels. [Copyrighted as 4,998 ft.]

Pres by Adolph Zukor, Jesse L. Lasky. *Dir* Harry D'Abbadie D'Arrast. *Scen* Jean De Limur, Harry D'Abbadie D'Arrast. *Titl* Herman J. Mankiewicz. *Photog* Henry Gerrard. *Film Ed* Frances Marsh.

Cast: Florence Vidor *(Madame Florence Laverne)*, Albert Conti *(Count D'Estrange)*, Loretta Young *(Denise Laverne, the daughter)*, Matty Kemp *(Hubert, the count's nephew)*, Marietta Millner *(Fifi, a perfect lady)*, Ned Sparks *(Tim, an American in Paris)*.

Farce. Source: José Germain Drouilly, *Maman, comèdie en trois actes* (Paris, 1924). D'Estrange, a sophisticated count trying to save his nephew, Hubert, from the daughter of Madame Laverne, whom he believes to be a heartless flirt, succumbs to the mother in spite of efforts to fight off fascination. To discourage Hubert, he tries to compromise Madame Laverne, but she tricks him into marrying her, and all ends happily with the couples on their way to a double honeymoon in Venice. *Nobility. Flirts. Uncles. Courtship. Venice. Paris.*

MAID OF THE WEST **F2.3345**

Fox Film Corp. 3 Jul **1921** [c17 Jul 1921; LP16848]. Si; b&w. 35mm. 5 reels, 4,193 ft.

Pres by William Fox. *Dir* Philo McCullough, C. R. Wallace. *Scen* John Montague. *Story* W. E. Spencer. *Photog* Otto Brautigan.

Cast: Eileen Percy *(Betty)*, William Scott *(Bert Cragnair)*, Hattie Buskirk *(Mrs. Sedgwick)*, Charles Meakin *(Bruce)*, June La Vere *(maid)*, Jack Brammall *(butler)*, Frank Clark *(Amos Jansen)*.

Society melodrama. Betty, an orphan heiress living in Texas with her aunt and uncle, attempts to elope with Bert, an aviator from Waco, but is prevented by her uncle. On her 20th birthday she is sent to New York to be properly introduced in society, and there she finds Bert masquerading as her aunt's chauffeur. Mrs. Sedgwick presents Betty with a valuable pearl necklace one evening, and when the lights are extinguished the pearls are stolen by two servants in league with a gang of crooks. After a series of skirmishes with Bert, the thieves are cornered by Betty, and following their arrest she and Bert depart for a honeymoon in his plane. *Heiresses. Aviators. Chauffeurs. Aunts. Uncles. Thieves. Domestics. Texas. New York City.*

THE MAILMAN **F2.3346**

Emory Johnson. *Dist* Film Booking Offices of America. 9 Dec **1923** [c3 Nov 1923; LP19561]. Si; b&w. 35mm. 7 reels, 7,160 ft.

Dir Emory Johnson. *Story-Adapt* Emilie Johnson. *Photog* Ross Fisher.

Cast: Ralph Lewis *(Bob Morley)*, Johnnie Walker *(Johnnie)*, Martha Sleeper *(Betty)*, Virginia True Boardman *(Mrs. Morley)*, Dave Kirby *(Jack Morgan)*, Josephine Adair *(Virginia)*, Taylor Graves *(Harry)*, Hardee Kirkland *(Captain Franz)*, Richard Morris *(Admiral Fleming)*, Rosemary Cooper *(Mrs. Thompson)*.

Melodrama. Veteran postman Bob Morley and his son Johnnie are commended for their service to the U. S. Mail Service. Johnnie takes a position on the *Enterprise*, a ship carrying registered mail. He is convicted of theft and murder when the cargo is stolen and the ship's officer is shot. A confession from the real culprit saves Johnnie from being executed. *Mail carriers. Theft. Murder. Mail ships. Postal service.*

THE MAIN EVENT **F2.3347**

De Mille Pictures. *Dist* Pathé Exchange. 18 Nov **1927** [c5 Nov 1927; LP24640]. Si; b&w. 35mm. 7 reels, 6,472 ft.

Dir William K. Howard. *Adapt-Cont* Rochus Gliese. *Photog* Lucien Andriot. *Art Dir* Rochus Gliese. *Film Ed* Claude Berkeley. *Asst Dir* J. Gordon Cooper. *Cost* Adrian.

Cast: Vera Reynolds *(Glory Frayne)*, Rudolph Schildkraut *(Regan, Sr.)*, Julia Faye *(Margie)*, Charles Delaney *(Johnnie Regan)*, Robert Armstrong *(Red Lucas)*, Ernie Adams *(slug-nutty fighter)*.

Romantic melodrama. Source: Paul Allison, "That Makes Us Even" (publication undetermined). Glory Frayne, a cabaret dancer, is in love with Red Lucas, a prizefighter whose opponent, Johnnie Regan, she meets accidentally when he comes to her cabaret performance. When Johnnie is attracted to her, Glory sees in the situation an opportunity of clinching the forthcoming fight for Lucas, and she deliberately keeps Johnnie away from training. Reprimanded by his father for his poor condition, Johnnie insists that his love for Glory means more to him than the fight. Glory, realizing her love for Johnnie, regrets her plotting and admits her feelings to Lucas, who takes up with Margie, Glory's girl friend. Glory tries to persuade Johnnie to stay out of the ring, but learning of her scheming, he goes to his defeat. Afterwards, she assures him of her love, and they are married. *Dancers. Prizefighters. Filial relations. Cabarets.*

MAIN STREET **F2.3348**

Warner Brothers Pictures. 25 Apr **1923** [Los Angeles premiere; released 17 Jun; c28 May 1923; LP19003]. Si; b&w. 35mm. 9 reels, 8,943 ft.

Dir Harry Beaumont. *Adapt* Julien Josephson. *Photog* Homer Scott, E. B. Du Par. *Film Ed* Harry Beaumont. *Asst Film Ed* Lewis Milestone. *Asst Dir* Nate Watt, Frank Strayer.

Cast: Florence Vidor *(Carol Milford)*, Monte Blue *(Dr. Will Kennicott)*, Harry Myers *(Dave Dyer)*, Robert Gordon *(Erik Valborg)*, Noah Beery *(Adolph Valborg)*, Alan Hale *(Miles Bjornstam)*, Louise Fazenda *(Bea Sorenson)*, Anne Schaefer *(Mrs. Valborg)*, Josephine Crowell *(Widow Bogart)*, Otis Harlan *(Ezra Stowbody)*, Gordon Griffith *(Cy Bogart)*, Lon Poff *(Chet Dashaway)*, J. P. Lockney *(Luke Dawson)*, Gilbert Clayton *(Sam Clark)*, Jack McDonald *(Nat Hicks)*, Michael Dark *(Guy Pollock)*, Estelle Short *(Mrs. Dashaway)*, Glen Cavender *(Harry Haydock)*, Kathryn Perry *(Mrs. Dave Dyer)*, Aileen Manning *(Mrs. Stowbody)*, Mrs. Hayward Mack *(Mrs. Haydock)*, Louis King *(Mr. Volstead)*, Josephine Kirkwood *(Mrs. Sam Clark)*, Louise Carver *(Mrs. Donovan)*, Hal Wilson *(Del Snaflin)*.

Rural drama. Source: Sinclair Lewis, *Main Street* (New York, 1920). Carol Milford, an intelligent, artistic girl from the city, moves to Gopher Prairie when she marries one of its esteemed citizens, Dr. Will Kennicott. She is disappointed in the small, unsightly, and unprogressive town and decides to uplift it, but the townspeople do not respond and think she is putting on airs. Bored by her neighbors and misunderstood by her husband, Carol becomes friends with Erik Valborg, who shares her views; but she refuses his offer of love and escape. When Erik leaves town, Carol is denounced as the cause of his "waywardness," but Will defends Carol and shames the townspeople for their suspicions. Carol learns to appreciate her husband's love and accept the life of Gopher Prairie. *Uplifters. Physicians. Smalltown life. United States—Midwest.*

MAKERS OF MEN **F2.3349**

Bud Barsky Corp. 8 May **1925** [New York State license]. Si; b&w. 35mm. 6 reels, 5,500 ft.

Dir Forrest Sheldon. *Scen* William E. Wing.

Cast: Kenneth McDonald *(Jimmy Jones)*, Clara Horton *(Lillian Gilman)*, J. P. McGowan *(Sergeant Banks)*, William Burton *(Hiram Renfrew)*, William Lowery *(Steppling)*, Ethan Laidlaw *(Shiftless Poole)*.

Melodrama. Jimmy Jones is afflicted with a nervous disorder that causes him to start and tremble at any unexpected noise. Despite many manful attempts to cure himself, Jimmy is looked upon as a coward by the people of his town; even Lillian Gilman, the girl he admires, shares in the popular contempt for him. When the World War breaks out, Jimmy goes to France, where he comes under the influence of Sergeant Banks, a canny veteran who doesn't know what fear is. Banks teaches Jimmy the ropes and hardens his moral and physical fibre. Jimmy returns home a new man, whips his rival, and wins Lillian for his wife. *Cowardice. World War I. United States Army—Training.*

MAKING A MAN **F2.3350**

Famous Players–Lasky. *Dist* Paramount Pictures. 17 Dec **1922** [New York premiere; released 22 Jan 1923; c26 Dec 1922; LP18564]. Si; b&w. 35mm. 6 reels, 5,594 ft.

Pres by Jesse L. Lasky. *Dir* Joseph Henabery. *Scen* Albert Shelby Le Vino. *Photog* Faxon Dean.

Cast: Jack Holt *(Horace Winsby)*, J. P. Lockney *(Jim Owens)*, Eva Novak *(Patricia Owens)*, Bert Woodruff *(Henry Cattermole)*, Frank Nelson *(Shorty)*, Robert Dudley *(Bailey)*.

Drama. Source: Peter Bernard Kyne, "Humanizing Mr. Winsby," in *Red Book* (24:1137–1147, 25:151–165, Apr–May 1915). Wealthy, snobbish, patronizing Horace Winsby is refused by Patricia Owens, then must leave his California valley because of restiveness by farmers whose mortgages he is foreclosing. In New York Horace runs up large bills, cannot pay them when his wallet is stolen, is put out of his hotel, and finally is helped by Shorty, a park bum. Patricia and her father come to New York and find a changed Horace washing dishes, and everything is resolved. *Tramps. Self-reliance. Wealth. Snobbery. Mortgages. California. New York City.*

MAKING GOOD *see* **THE RIGHT WAY**

MAKING GOOD **F2.3351**

Sanford Productions. 12 Feb **1923** [scheduled release]. Si; b&w. 35mm. 5 reels.

Cast: Pete Morrison, Eileen Sedgwick.

Western melodrama(?). No information about the nature of this film has been found.

THE MAKING OF O'MALLEY **F2.3352**

First National Pictures. 28 Jun **1925** [c23 Jun 1925; LP21576]. Si; b&w. 35mm. 8 reels, 7,496 ft.

Supv Earl Hudson. *Dir* Lambert Hillyer. *Ed Dir* Marion Fairfax. *Scen* Eugene Clifford. *Photog* Roy Carpenter. *Art Dir* Milton Menasco. *Film Ed* Arthur Tavares.

Cast: Milton Sills *(O'Malley)*, Dorothy Mackaill *(Lucille Thayer)*, Helen Rowland *(Margie)*, Warner Richmond *(Danny the Dude)*, Thomas Carrigan *(Herbert Browne)*, Julia Hurley *(Margie's grandmother)*, Claude King *(Captain Collins)*, Allen Brander *(doctor)*, Charles Graham *(Sergeant Patterson)*, Jack De Lacey *(clerk)*, Blanche Craig *(stout dowager)*, Thomas Wigney Percyval *(lawyer)*, Charles Craig *(Englishman)*.

Melodrama. Source: Gerald Beaumont, "The Making of O'Malley," in *Red Book* (43:38–42, Oct 1924). Jim O'Malley, a patrolman who is a stickler for the letter of the law, is assigned to duty as a traffic cop near a grade school, where he meets Lucille Thayer, a beautiful teacher. Jim becomes a favorite with the children and arranges for Margie, a little lame girl, to be in the care of a surgeon. Jim discovers the hideout of a gang of bootleggers and sets up a raid that nets all but Herbert Browne, the gang's leader. Jim later recognizes Browne during a party at Lucille's house and place him under arrest, only to discover that he is her fiancé. In a spirit of self-sacrifice, Jim lets Browne go and allows himself to be dismissed from the force. Danny the Dude, Margie's father, whom Jim sent to prison, is released and, learning of Jim's kindness to Margie, exposes Browne as the leader of the bootleggers. Jim's sacrifice then becomes known, and he is reinstated to the force with honors, winning Lucille's love for his many kindnesses towards her. *Police. Schoolteachers. Children. Cripples. Surgeons. Bootleggers. Self-sacrifice. Elementary school life.*

MAKING THE GRADE **F2.3353**

David Butler Productions. *Dist* Western Pictures Exploitation Co. 1 Sep **1921** [New York State license]. Si; b&w. 35mm. 5 reels, 4,735 ft.

Pres by Irving M. Lesser. *Dir* Fred J. Butler. *Titl* A. P. Younger. *Adapt* A. P. Younger. *Photog* Robert Newhard, Robert Martin.

Cast: David Butler *(Eddie Ramson)*, Helen Ferguson *(Sophie Semenoff)*, William Walling *(Mr. Ramson)*, Lillian Lawrence *(Mrs. Ramson)*, Jack Cosgrove *(Captain Carleton)*, Alice Wilson *(Mrs. Garnie Crest)*, Otto Lederer, Jack Rollins.

Comedy-drama. Source: Wallace Irwin, "Sophie Semenoff," in *Saturday Evening Post* (193:10–11, 27 Nov 1920). At the behest of his father, fun-loving Eddie Ramson joins an expedition to Russia under the command of Captain Carleton. He is rarely sober but does find time to win the heart of peasant schoolmarm Sophie Semenoff. Sophie is under considerable pressure from the Bolsheviki to marry, and there are merry chases which result in Eddie's taking Sophie for his wife. Back in the U. S. A., Eddie and Sophie meet his mother's disapproval, and Sophie is again pursued and kidnaped by American agents of Russian anarchists. Mrs. Ramson gets the upper hand over the abductors, Sophie reveals that they really sought her family jewels, and the family is happily reconciled—knowing Sophie is a princess. *Russians. Bolshevists. Schoolteachers. Royalty. Drunkenness. Russia.*

Note: Working title: *Sophie Semenoff.*

MAKING THE GRADE **F2.3354**

Fox Film Corp. 17 Feb **1929** [c25 Feb 1929; LP151]. Talking sequences & mus score (Movietone); b&w. 35mm. 6 reels, 5,903 ft. [Also si; 5,024 ft.]

Pres by William Fox. *Dir* Alfred E. Green. *Scen* Harry Brand, Edward Kaufman. *Dial-Titl* Malcolm Stuart Boylan. *Photog* L. W. O'Connell, Norman Devol. *Film Ed* J. Edwin Robbins. *Mus Score* Erno Rapee. *Rec Engr* Barney Fredericks. *Asst Dir* Jack Boland.

Cast: Edmund Lowe *(Herbert Littell Dodsworth)*, Lois Moran *(Lettie Ewing)*, Lucien Littlefield *(Silas Cooper)*, Albert Hart *(lawyer)*, James Ford *(Bud Davison)*, Rolfe Sedan *(valet)*, John Alden *(Egbert Williamson)*, Sherman Ross *(Arthur Burdette)*, Gino Conti *(Frank Dinwiddie)*, Mary

Ashley *(Lettie's friend)*, Lia Tora *(another girl friend)*.

Society comedy-drama. Source: George Ade, "Making the Grade," in *Hearst's International Cosmopolitan* (84:38–41, Mar 1928). Wealthy Herbert Dodsworth, the son of a small town's leading family, returns home and attempts to prove his manhood. At first he fails at everything: an address to the Royal Order of Woodchucks ends in comic disaster, and he falls overboard while fishing for tuna. Herbert falls in love with Lettie Ewing, a waitress in a tearoom, however, and finally proves himself to be as good a man as any of his successful ancestors. *Waitresses. Manhood. Social classes. Smalltown life. Fraternities. Teashops.*

MAKING THE VARSITY **F2.3355**

Excellent Pictures. 15 Jul **1928** [c21 Jul 1928; LP25479]. Si; b&w. 35mm. 7 reels, 6,400 ft.

Pres by Samuel Zierler. *Dir* Cliff Wheeler. *Titl* Lee Anthony. *Story* Elsie Werner, Bennett Southard. *Photog* Edward Kull. *Film Ed* Lee Anthony. *Football Supv* Jeff Cravath.

Cast: Rex Lease *(Ed Ellsworth)*, Arthur Rankin *(Wally Ellsworth)*, Gladys Hulette *(Estelle Carter)*, Edith Yorke *(Mrs. Ellsworth)*, Florence Dudley *(Gladys Fogarty)*, Carl Miller *(Jerry Fogarty)*, James Latta *(Gridley)*.

Melodrama. Ed, the more serious of two brothers, is fulfilling a deathbed promise to his grandmother by acting as guardian to his undisciplined brother, Wally. At a college they attend, Wally is nearly suspended when he becomes involved with a girl whose brother runs a disreputable country house. Ed, an honor student, uses his influence to persuade the dean to let Wally remain. Wally begins to gamble; he loses money and forges his brother's name to pay his debts. Confronted by Ed, Wally apparently reforms. But before the big game (both boys are on the football team), Ed learns that Wally intends to throw the game. On the second play Ed punches Wally, knocking him unconscious: his team wins the game; Wally realizes his mistake; and they forgive each other. *Students. Brothers. College life. Football. Dissipation.*

MALCOLM STRAUSS' SALOME *see* **SALOME**

MALE WANTED **F2.3356**

Housman Comedies. *Dist* Lee-Bradford Corp., Freedom Film Co. 26 Nov **1923** [New York State license]. Si; b&w. 35mm. 5 reels, 4,771 ft.

Cast: Huntley Gordon, Arthur Housman, Diana Allen.

Comedy-drama. No information about the nature of this film has been found.

MAMA'S AFFAIR **F2.3357**

Constance Talmadge Film Co. *Dist* Associated First National Pictures. Jan **1921** [c23 Feb 1921; LP16173]. Si; b&w. 35mm. 6 reels, 5,950 ft.

Prod Joseph M. Schenck. *Dir* Victor Fleming. *Scen* John Emerson, Anita Loos. *Photog* Oliver Marsh.

Cast: Constance Talmadge *(Eve)*, Effie Shannon *(Mrs. Orrin)*, Katherine Kaelred *(Mrs. Marchant)*, George Le Guere *(Henry Marchant)*, Kenneth Harlan *(Dr. Harmon)*, Gertrude Le Brandt *(Bundy)*.

Domestic drama. Source: Rachel Barton Butler, *Mamma's Affair: a Comedy in Three Acts* (New York, 1925). Following a burlesque prolog showing Eve in the Garden of Eden eating the forbidden fruit, Mrs. Orrin, a wealthy, selfish, impulsive widow, contrives to keep her self-sacrificing daughter in her service by marrying her off to Henry, the son of Mrs. Orrin's best friend. The mother's doctor falls in love with Eve, however, and in face of all opposition he marries her. *Widows. Physicians. Motherhood. Biblical characters.*

MAMBA **F2.3358**

Tiffany Productions. 10 Mar **1930** [c26 Mar 1930; LP1197]. Sd (Photophone); col (Technicolor). 35mm. 9 reels, 7,014 ft. [Also si.]

Dir Albert Rogell. *Cont-Dial* Tom Miranda, Winifred Dunn. *Story* F. Schumann-Heink, John Reinhardt. *Photog* Charles Boyle. *Art Dir* André Chautin. *Sd Rec* Louis J. Myers.

Cast: Jean Hersholt *(August Bolte [Mamba])*, Eleanor Boardman *(Helen von Linden)*, Ralph Forbes *(Karl von Reiden)*, Claude Fleming *(Major Cromwell)*, Will Stanton *(Cockney servant)*, William von Brincken *(Major von Shultz)*, Hazel Jones *(Hassim's daughter)*, Arthur Stone *(British soldier)*, Torben Meyer *(German soldier)*, André De Segurola *(Guido)*, Edward Martindel *(Fullerton)*, Noble Johnson *(Hassim)*, Josef Swickard *(Count von Linden)*.

Melodrama. August Bolte, a wealthy planter in New Posen, a German possession in East Africa, is hated by the settlers and the natives, who call him Mamba (the name of a poisonous snake) because of his extreme cruelty. On a visit to Germany, Bolte marries Helen, the beautiful daughter of Count von Linden, who sacrifices herself in a distasteful marriage to save her father from disgrace and prison. Revolted by Bolte's coarseness, she finds consolation in Karl von Reiden, a young officer returning on their boat. At a reception given by Bolte, he flaunts his bride before the guests, including Karl and Major Cromwell, his close friend; when a native declares Bolte responsible for the death of his daughter, Helen is terrified by her husband's wrath, but news arrives of war between England and Germany. Bolte escapes arrest for evading conscription but is killed by the natives; Karl goes to rescue Helen, and they are saved from a native onslaught by a British detachment. *Planters. Germans. British. Marriage. World War I. German East Africa.*

MAMMY **F2.3359**

Warner Brothers Pictures. 26 Mar **1930** [c1 Apr 1930; LP1192]. Sd (Vitaphone); b&w with col sequences (Technicolor). 35mm. 8 reels, 7,750 ft. [Also si.]

Dir Michael Curtiz. *Story-Scen-Dial* Gordon Rigby, Joseph Jackson. *Photog* Barney McGill. *Songs: "To My Mammy," "Across the Breakfast Table Looking at You," "Let Me Sing and I'm Happy," "Knights of the Road"* Irving Berlin. *Rec Engr* George R. Groves.

Cast: Al Jolson *(Al Fuller)*, Lois Moran *(Nora Meadows)*, Louise Dresser *(Mrs. Fuller)*, Lowell Sherman *(Westy)*, Noah Beery *(Tonopaw Red)*, Hobart Bosworth *(Meadows)*, Tully Marshall *(Slats)*, Mitchell Lewis *(Tambo)*, Lee Moran *(Flat Feet)*, Jack Curtis *(Sheriff)*, Stanley Fields *(Pig Eyes)*, Ray Cooke *(Props)*.

Musical drama. Source: Irving Berlin and James Gleason, *Mr. Bones, a Musical Comedy of Minstrel Days in Two Acts* (c1928). Al Fuller joins up with a group of hoboes—Slats, Flat Feet, and Pig Eyes—entertaining them with his songs and good humor. As they go to sleep around an open fire, he recalls the circumstances that led him to his present plight: As the end man in the Meadow Merry Minstrels, he is in love with Nora, the owner's daughter, who has a weakness for Westy, also in the act. The show is constantly in desperate straits, and when Al tries hard to amuse the local sheriff, they are surprised to learn he wants to invest in and join the act. They become prosperous and Al is able to go home to see his mother. Hoping to help Nora, he avows his love for her, provoking Westy's jealousy. Tambo, who has been exposed cheating at cards, causes Westy to be wounded in the act by Al. He is arrested but escapes on a freight bound for home; eventually Tambo confesses to the deed, and Al is thus proven innocent. *Tramps. Sheriffs. Filial relations. Minstrel shows. Courtship. Jealousy.*

THE MAN ALONE **F2.3360**

Motion Picture Utility Co. *Dist* Anchor Film Distributors. 1 Feb **1923.** Si; b&w. 35mm. 5 reels, 5,000 or 6,000 ft.

Pres by Morris R. Schlank. *Dir* William H. Clifford. *Scen* Clarence Badger. *Photog* J. O. Taylor. *Sets* Valentine. *Film Ed* Mack Stengler.

Cast: Hobart Bosworth *(Ben Dixon)*, Jamie Gray *(Ellen Hill)*, William Conklin *(Charles Temple)*, George Barnum *(Martin Hill)*, Pauline French *(Aunt Matilda)*, James Hall *(Caspar Dent)*, Ina Burns *(waif)*, Freeman Wood *(George Perry)*, Lou Morrison *(Captain Peter)*.

Melodrama. Ellen Hill, a nervous but very rich young lady, goes to the hills for a rest, and there she meets kindly Ben Dixon, owner of the Dixon gold mine. They fall in love and decide to marry, but Ellen changes her mind when Ben comes to visit her and her father and demonstrates manners that are hardly acceptable in high society. Ben then gets shanghaied to a rough ship; in the meantime, the people back home assume he has committed suicide. Following this line, Charles Temple, an avaricious stockbroker, bids for Dixon's property but is thwarted when Dixon is released and returns to the city. Ellen has since fallen in love with young George Perry, who was previously employed by Dixon to teach him some manners. Dixon gives them his blessing and sadly goes off to his mines, reconciled to a bachelor fate. *Social classes. Stockbrokers. Bachelors. Mines. Shanghaiing. Manners.*

MAN AND MAID **F2.3361**

Metro-Goldwyn Pictures. 20 Apr **1925** [c22 Apr 1925; LP21490]. Si; b&w. 35mm. 6 reels, 5,307 ft.

Pres by Louis B. Mayer. *Dir* Victor Schertzinger. *Scen* Elinor Glyn. *Photog* Chet Lyons. *Art Dir* Cedric Gibbons. *Asst Dir* T. J. McDermott.

Cast: Lew Cody *(Sir Nicholas Thormonde)*, Harriet Hammond *(Alathea*

Bulteel), Renée Adorée *(Suzette)*, Paulette Duval *(Coralie)*, Alec Francis *(Burton)*, Crauford Kent *(Col. George Harcourt)*, David Mir *(Maurice)*, Gerald Grove *(The Honorable Bobby Bulteel)*, Jacqueline Gadsden *(Lady Hilda Bulteel)*, Winston Miller *(little Bobby)*, Jane Mercer *(little Hilda)*, Irving Hartley *(Alwood Chester)*, Dagmar Desmond *(Odette)*, Leonie Lester *(Alice)*.

Romantic drama. Source: Elinor Glyn, *Man and Maid* (Philadelphia, 1922). During the World War, Alathea Bulteel, a Red Cross nurse, discovers the prostrate form of an English officer among the ruins of a bombed building in Paris. She cares for him until help arrives, leaving before he regains consciousness. After the war Alathea is forced to find work and, by chance, obtains a position as the private secretary of the same man, who is revealed to be Sir Nicholas Thormonde. Convalescing from injuries received during the fighting, he passes the time in dalliance with Suzette, a pretty demimondaine. Alathea performs her duties so well that Nicholas falls in love with her, despite her plain clothes and dark glasses. One day, Nicholas kisses her, and she leaves his house, believing that he intends to take advantage of her. Nicholas follows her, however, and asks for her hand in marriage; she refuses his offer, believing him to be insincere. Alathea's father then contracts a gambling debt of 5,000 francs, which Nicholas secretly pays. Not knowing of this kindness, Alathea goes to him and offers to marry him for the sum. Nicholas accepts, and they are happy until Suzette reappears. Believing that Nicholas is still interested in the girl, Alathea leaves. She and Nicholas are reunited, however, when she comes to realize the depth of his love for her. *Nurses. Secretaries. Prostitutes. Marriage. Gambling. World War I. Paris. Red Cross.*

THE MAN AND THE MOMENT **F2.3362**

First National Pictures. 7 Jul **1929** [c27 Jul 1929; LP547]. Sd (Vitaphone); b&w. 35mm. 7 reels, 7,086 ft. [Also si; 6,539 ft.]

Pres by Richard A. Rowland. *Dir* George Fitzmaurice. *Screen Vers* Agnes Christine Johnston. *Dial* Paul Perez. *Story* Elinor Glyn. *Photog* Sol Polito. *Cost* Max Ree.

Cast: Billie Dove *(Joan)*, Rod La Rocque *(Michel)*, Gwen Lee *(Viola)*, Robert Schable *(Skippy)*, Charles Sellon *(Joan's guardian)*, George Bunny *(butler)*.

Romantic comedy-drama. Young ingenue Joan, only a short time removed from her sequestered Nebraska upbringing, has trouble with her airplane motor, force-landing into the midst of bachelor Michel Towne's weekend yachting party. Michel rescues and returns her home to her stern and unsympathetic guardian, thereby incurring the wrath of the persistent Viola Hatfield, who has herself vowed to marry Michel as soon as her divorce is final. Michel, seeing a way out of his dilemma, proposes to Joan so that they may marry and immediatly separate, thereby thwarting the impositions of both Viola and Joan's guardian. She reluctantly agrees to a secret ceremony, and having been persuaded by the now much-adoring Michel to stay aboard the yacht for a celebration dinner, she is forced into a compromising position. She escapes the following morning but is spurned by her guardian after her confession and takes up forlornly with Viola's wastrel brother, Skippy Hatfield. The repentant Michel finally convinces Joan of his reform but is compromised by the untimely appearance of perservering Viola through a private entrance to his mansion, and Joan disgustedly leaves. She roars off in her plane, but not before Michel manages to get on board, and when the motor again fails, the apparently doomed lovers are reconciled before the crash. Michel's yacht rescues them the following morning, and Viola, at last finally untied from her previous matrimonial bonds, is informed of the marriage. *Bachelors. Guardians. Nebraskans. Divorce. Marriage. Airplanes. Yachts.*

MAN AND WIFE **F2.3363**

Effanem Productions. *Dist* Arrow Film Corp. 25 Mar **1923** [c22 Mar 1923; LP18803]. Si; b&w. 35mm. 5 reels, 5,500 ft.

Dir John L McCutcheon. *Story-Adapt* Leota Morgan.

Cast: Maurice Costello *(Caleb Perkins)*, Gladys Leslie *(Dolly Perkins)*, Norma Shearer *(Dora Perkins)*, Edna May Spooner *(Mrs. Perkins)*, Robert Elliott *(Dr. Howard Fleming)*, Ernest Hilliard *(Walter Powell)*.

Domestic drama. After he is told of the death of his wife, Dora, in a hotel fire, Dr. Howard Fleming goes to the country hoping to ease his sorrow. While visiting a farm, he falls in love with and marries Dolly Perkins, who—unbeknownst to Howard—is Dora's sister. Howard is later told that Dora is actually alive, though hopelessly insane. He restores her sanity with surgery, but when Dora learns of Howard's bigamy, she has a relapse. A second operation kills her; Howard returns to Dolly, their child, and a happy future. *Surgeons. Sisters. Bigamy. Rural life. Insanity.*

MAN AND WOMAN **F2.3364**

A. H. Fischer, Inc. *Dist* Jans Film Service. 1 Sep **1921**. Si; b&w. 35mm. 6 reels.

Dir-Story-Scen Charles Logue. *Photog* A. Fried.

Cast: Diana Allen *(Diana Murdock)*, Joe King *(Joe)*, Edwin Sturgis *(The Flash)*, John L. Shine *(Greasy)*, Tatjana Irrah *(The Duchess)*, Eleanor Cozzat *(The Waif)*, G. H. Carlyle *(The Beast)*, A. C. Milar *(Murdock)*, Gordon Standing *(Bradley)*, James Alling *(Bishop Graham)*, Herbert Standing *(Governor-General)*, Pat Jennings *(The First Mate)*, Pat Fischer *(Perkins)*.

Melodrama. Bradley, an engineer, becomes a Tahiti beachcomber after the collapse of a bridge he built. Murdock, a former employer of Bradley, arrives on the island with his lovely daughter, Diana, who wagers with a guest of the governor-general that she could dress the lowest outcast in good clothing and pass him off as a gentleman. She chooses Bradley, who finds out about the hoax and, determined to teach her a lesson, takes her to Leper Island where she is treated like an outcast. Murdock recognizes Bradley and offers him a chance to redeem himself by overseeing the repairs made on a lighthouse. Diana, having now understood Bradley, remains on Tahiti with him. *Engineers. Beachcombers. Leprosy. Lighthouses. Tahiti.*

MAN BAIT **F2.3365**

Metropolitan Pictures Corp. of California. *Dist* Producers Distributing Corp. 27 Dec **1926** [c29 Nov 1926; LP23382]. Si; b&w. 35mm. 6 reels, 5,947 ft.

Pres by John C. Flinn. *Dir* Donald Crisp. *Adapt* Douglas Z. Doty. *Photog* Hal Rosson. *Art Dir* Charles Cadwallader. *Asst Dir* Emile De Ruelle.

Cast: Marie Prevost *(Madge Dreyer)*, Kenneth Thomson *(Gerald Sanford)*, Douglas Fairbanks, Jr. *(Jeff Sanford)*, Louis Natheaux *(Delancy Hasbrouck)*, Eddie Gribbon *(Red Welch)*, Betty Francisco *(Betty Gerber)*, Adda Gleason *(Florence Hasbrouck)*, Sally Rand *(Nancy)*, Fritzi Ridgeway *(Gloria)*.

Romantic comedy-drama. Source: Norman Houston, "Man Bait" (publication undetermined). Madge Dreyer, a salesgirl in a department store, is fired when she strikes one of the owners for making an impertinent proposition. At dinner with a girl friend, Betty Gerber, Madge decides to work as a "taxi-dancer" where Betty works in the evenings and where Betty's beau, Red Welch, is the bouncer. Jeff Sanford, a spirited society youth, leads an expedition to Roseman's and becomes involved in a free-for-all, following which Sanford strikes up a breezy courtship with Madge and they are soon engaged. The Sanford family, however, are bitterly opposed to an alliance that will bring a dancehall girl into their circle. Arriving at the Sanford residence, Madge is greeted by Mrs. Hasbrouck, the Sanford sister, with icy politeness; then Delancy is shocked to find that she is his ex-employee. Jeff returns from a business trip, discovers that his brother, Gerald, has fallen in love with Madge, and he himself is happily united with a former sweetheart. *Salesclerks. Bouncers. Taxi dancers. Brothers. Social classes. Courtship.*

THE MAN BETWEEN **F2.3366**

Finis Fox Productions. *Dist* Associated Exhibitors. 15 Jul **1923** [c7 Jun 1923; LU19061]. Si; b&w. 35mm. 6 reels, 5,176 ft.

Dir-Writ Finis Fox. *Scen* Lois Zellner.

Cast: Allan Forrest *(Jules Lamont/Pierre Lebec)*, Edna Murphy *(Zephne Lamont)*, Fred Malatesta *(Joe Cateau)*, Vola Vale *(Joe Cateau's bride, Rosie)*, Kitty Bradbury *(Madame Lamont)*, Philo McCullough *(Dick Lyman)*, Doreen Turner *(Julie Lamont)*.

Crime melodrama. Canadian woodsman Jules Lamont leaves his wife, Zephne, after a misunderstanding and becomes infatuated with Joe Cateau's bride, a showgirl. Joe is killed when the two men fight, and Jules goes to prison, where he meets Pierre Lebec, an inmate who closely resembles Jules. When Jules learns that Pierre is about to be released, he persuades him to go to his own home and pose as Jules himself. Pierre does so and falls in love with Zephne, who believes him to be Jules. Pierre remains in disguise, "the man between," until the real Lamont returns and is killed. Then Zephne learns the truth about Pierre, and they marry. *Woodsmen. Showgirls. Doubles. Impersonation. Prisons. Canada.*

MAN CRAZY F2.3367

Charles R. Rogers Productions. *Dist* First National Pictures. 27 Nov **1927** [c14 Nov 1927; LP24649]. Si; b&w. 35mm. 6 reels, 5,542 ft.

Prod Charles R. Rogers. *Dir* John Francis Dillon. *Adapt-Cont* Perry Nathan. *Titl* Dwinelle Benthall, Rufus McCosh. *Photog* James Van Trees.

Cast: Dorothy Mackaill *(Clarissa Janeway)*, Jack Mulhall *(Jeffery Pell)*, Edythe Chapman *(Grandmother Janeway)*, Phillips Smalley *(James Janeway)*, Walter McGrail *(Van Breamer)*, Ray Hallor *(Danny)*.

Society comedy-drama. Source: Grace Sartwell Mason, "Clarissa and the Post Road," in *Saturday Evening Post* (196:5–7, 14 Jul 1923). Clarissa Janeway, the carefree daughter of an aristocratic New England family, irritates her sedate grandmother with her droves of suitors and by opening a hot dog stand along the old Boston Post Road to help Danny, crippled in the war. Her grandmother finds this situation a reflection on the family name and wants to marry Clarissa off to Van Breamer, from another pioneer family of Cape Cod, but she is interested in Jeff, a handsome truckdriver. Clarissa is about to accept Van Breamer at a party when she hears the horn of Jeff's truck and goes to greet him; overhearing two bootleggers plotting to hijack Jeff's truck, she follows in her roadster and finds him bound and gagged by the road; then, through a ruse, the two stop the truck and capture the bootleggers. At the Janeway home, Jeff is recognized as the son of another prominent family, and Grandmother is pacified by their happy romance. *Veterans. Grandmothers. Truckdrivers. Bootleggers. Cripples. Hijackers. Aristocrats. Social classes. Food stands. New England.*

A MAN FOUR-SQUARE F2.3368

Fox Film Corp. 9 May **1926** [c2 May 1926; LP22705]. Si; b&w. 35mm. 5 reels, 4,744 ft.

Pres by William Fox. *Dir* R. William Neill. *Scen* Charles Darnton, John Stone. *Photog* Reginald Lyons. *Asst Dir* Mike Miggins.

Cast: Buck Jones *(Craig Norton)*, Marion Harlan *(Polly)*, Harry Woods *(Ben Taylor)*, William Lawrence *(Jim Clanton)*, Jay Hunt *(Polly's father)*, Sidney Bracey *(Homer Webb)*, Florence Gilbert *(Bertie Roberts)*, Frank Beal *(Wallace Roberts)*.

Western melodrama. Source: William MacLeod Raine, *A Man Four-Square* (Boston, 1919). Craig Norton, a young well-to-do rancher, returns from a holiday in the city to clear his foreman and friend of the charge of cattle rustling and is himself implicated and pursued by the sheriff's posse. His friend also suspects Craig of doublecrossing him with Polly, his sweetheart. A heroic rescue of the friend and Polly by Craig gains him the love of the girl and the forgiveness of the friend, who now realizes his own shortcomings. *Ranch foremen. Posses. Rustlers. Friendship. Courtship.*

Note: Copyright title: *The Man Four-Square.*

THE MAN FROM BEYOND F2.3369

Houdini Picture Corp. 2 Apr **1922** [New York premiere; released 20 Aug; c27 Jul 1921; LP16833]. Si; b&w. 35mm. 7 reels, 6,500 ft.

Dir Burton King. *Adapt* Coolidge Streeter. *Story* Harry Houdini. *Photog* Frank Zucker, Irving B. Ruby, Harry A. Fischbeck, A. G. Penrod, Louis Dunmyre, L. D. Littlefield.

Cast: Harry Houdini *(The Man From Beyond)*, Arthur Maude *(Dr. Gilbert Trent)*, Albert Tavernier *(Dr. Crawford Strange)*, Erwin Connelly *(Dr. Gregory Sinclair)*, Frank Montgomery *(François Duval)*, Luis Alberni *(Captain of the Barkentine)*, Yale Benner *(Milt Norcross)*, Jane Connelly *(Felice Strange/Felice Norcross)*, Nita Naldi *(Marie Le Grande)*.

Mystery melodrama. On an Arctic expedition Dr. Gregory Sinclair and François Duval find a man (Houdini) frozen in a block of ice, revive him, and take him home for further study. They interrupt the wedding of Felice Strange to Dr. Gilbert Trent, but when the revived Houdini insists that she is his sweetheart, Felice Norcross, the ceremony is postponed and he is hustled off to an asylum. Houdini escapes, realizes that 100 years have elapsed, and resolves to help Felice Strange (descended from Felice Norcross) to find her missing father. In doing so he fights Trent, Dr. Strange's captor, to the edge of a cliff and prevents Felice from going over Niagara Falls. *Suspended animation. Reincarnation. Arctic regions. Weddings. Niagara Falls.*

THE MAN FROM BLANKLEY'S F2.3370

Warner Brothers Pictures. 28 Mar **1930** [New York premiere; released 24 May; c15 Apr 1930; LP1228]. Sd (Vitaphone); b&w. 35mm. 8 reels, 6,167 ft. [Also si.]

Dir Alfred E. Green. *Screenplay* Harvey Thew. *Dial-Titl* Joseph Jackson. *Photog* James Van Trees. *Rec Engr* Hal Bumbaugh.

Cast: John Barrymore *(Lord Strathpeffer)*, Loretta Young *(Margery Seaton)*, William Austin *(Mr. Poffley)*, Albert Gran *(Uncle Gabriel Gilwattle)*, Emily Fitzroy *(Mrs. Tidmarsh)*, Dick Henderson *(Mr. Tidmarsh)*, Edgar Norton *(Dawes)*, Yorke Sherwood *(Mr. Bodfish)*, Dale Fuller *(Miss Flinders)*, D'Arcy Corrigan *(Mr. Ditchwater)*, Louise Carver *(Mrs. Gilwattle)*, May Milloy *(Mrs. Ditchwater)*, Diana Hope *(Mrs. Bodfish)*, Tiny Jones *(Miss Bule)*, Gwendolen Logan *(maid)*, Angella Mawby *(Gwennie)*, Sybil Grove *(maid)*.

Comedy. Source: F. Anstey, *The Man From Blankley's, and Other Sketches* (London, 1893). Mr. and Mrs. Tidmarsh, a middle-class English couple, give a dinner party in honor of their wealthy uncle, Gabriel Gilwattle, hoping to receive his financial aid in their struggle to keep up appearances. Regrets reduce their table to 13; and because Gabriel is superstitious, they hire a guest from Blankley's, sight unseen; further cancellations obviate this necessity, and Margery Seaton, their governess, is invited; but the "hired guest" arrives anyhow and is announced as Lord Strathpeffer. Margery recognizes the tipsy man as a former lover, and he is assumed to be an imposter. Sobering, Strathpeffer realizes he has come to the wrong party and asserts his right to his title; but Gwennie hides her father's watch in Strathpeffer's pocket as he is renewing his romance with Margery. A police inspector arrives hunting for the missing lord, establishing his authenticity and the fact that he is not, after all, the hired guest. *English. Uncles. Nobility. Hired guests. Governesses. Middle classes. Superstition. Drunkenness. Mistaken identity.*

MAN FROM BROADWAY F2.3371

Sunset Productions. Oct **1924** [scheduled release]. Si; b&w. 35mm. 5 reels, 4,790 ft.

Western melodrama(?). No information about the nature of this film has been found.

THE MAN FROM BRODNEY'S F2.3372

Vitagraph Co. of America. 16 Dec **1923** [New York showing; released Dec; c22 Nov 1923; LP19638]. Si; b&w. 35mm. 8 reels, 7,100 ft.

Pres by Albert E. Smith. *Dir* David Smith. *Adapt* C. Graham Baker.

Cast: J. Warren Kerrigan *(Hollingsworth Chase)*, Alice Calhoun *(Princess Genevra)*, Wanda Hawley *(Lady Agnes Deppingham)*, Miss Du Pont *(Mrs. Browne)*, Pat O'Malley *(Robert Browne)*, Kathleen Key *(Neenah)*, Bertram Grassby *(Rasnea)*.

Melodrama. Source: George Barr McCutcheon, *The Man From Brodney's* (New York, 1908). According to the wills of two men who owned it, the East African island of Japat is to go to their grandchildren, Robert Browne and Agnes Deppingham, provided that they live there 6 months and marry each other. Should the stipulation be ignored, the island reverts to the natives. Browne, an American, is married but comes to Japat to comply with half of the provision. Lady Agnes Deppingham arrives on Japat and proceeds to lure Browne away from his wife. The natives, led by Rasnea, intend to take possession of the island, by force if necessary. Hollingsworth Chase, an American attorney representing the interests of his British firm, meets Princess Genevra, a guest of Lady Deppingham, and falls in love with her. Together they become involved in the native uprisings on the island, which finally goes to the heirs. Princess Genevra gives up her throne and title to marry Chase; and Browne, realizing his mistake in flirting with Lady Deppingham, asks his wife's forgiveness. *Lawyers. Royalty. English. Inheritance. Wills. Revolts. East Africa.*

THE MAN FROM DOWNING STREET F2.3373

Vitagraph Co. of America. 2 Apr **1922** [c13 Mar 1922; LP17634]. Si; b&w. 35mm. 5 reels, 4,950 ft.

Pres by Albert E. Smith. *Dir* Edward José. *Scen* Bradley J. Smollen. *Story* Clyde C. Westover, Lottie Horner, Florine Williams. *Photog* Ernest Smith.

Cast: Earle Williams *(Capt. Robert Kent)*, Charles Hill Mailes *(Colonel Wentworth)*, Boris Karloff *(Maharajah Jehan)*, Betty Ross Clarke *(Doris Burnham)*, Kathryn Adams *(Norma Graves)*, Herbert Prior *(Captain Graves)*, Eugenia Gilbert *(Sarissa)*, James Butler *(Lieutenant Wyndham)*, George Stanley *(Sir Edward Craig)*.

Adventure melodrama. Capt. Robert Kent is assigned by British Secret Service in India to discover the identity of a traitor responsible for a leakage in British code messages. Disguising himself as a rajah, he penetrates the most exclusive circles of Indian society; suspicion at first falls upon Wyndham, a man of weak character, but he is mysteriously killed at the home of Colonel Wentworth, and in turn Maharajah Jehan and Captain Graves are involved. Pursuing his investigations, Kent meets

Sarissa, a beautiful dancing girl—also a Secret Service agent—with whom he falls in love and whose assistance is largely responsible for his success. Following many complications, he proves the traitor to be Colonel Wentworth. *Dancers. Royalty. Secret service. Traitors. Disguise. Cryptography. India.*

THE MAN FROM GLENGARRY **F2.3374**

Ernest Shipman. *Dist* W. W. Hodkinson Corp. 15 Mar **1923** [Trade showing: released 6 May 1923]. Si; b&w. 35mm. 6 reels, 5,200 ft.

Dir Henry MacRae. *Scen* Kenneth O'Hara. *Adapt* Faith Green. *Photog* Jacques Bizeul. *Film Ed* Elmer J. McGovern.

Cast: Anders Randolph *(Big MacDonald)*, Warner P. Richmond *(Ranald MacDonald)*, Harlan Knight *(Rev. Alexander Murray)*, Marian Swayne *(Kate Murray, his daughter)*, E. L. Fernandez *(Louis Lenoir)*, Jack Newton *(Eugene St. Clair)*, Pauline Garon *(Mamie St. Clair)*, Frank Badgley *(Frank De Lacey)*, William Colvin *(Colonel Thorpe)*, Marion Lloyd *(Kerstin McLeod)*.

Melodrama. Source: Ralph Connor, *Man From Glengarry; a Tale of the Ottawa* (Chicago, 1901). Heads of rival lumber camps meet in a fight. Louis Lenoir, a renegade French Canadian, causes the death of "Big" MacDonald, a hard-fighting Scotsman whose life is guided by his dogmatic religious beliefs. His son, Ranald, is left to settle the blood feud. In spite of the pleas of his sweetheart, the daughter of a minister, he participates in a gang fight on the logs in mid-river just as a log drive to Ottawa begins. Attempting to stop the fight, the girl becomes involved, falls into danger, and is carried toward a whirlpool; but MacDonald, having abandoned his attack on Lenoir, rescues her. At the finish Lenoir, grateful because his life has been spared, experiences a reformation. *French Canadians. Scotch. Traitors. Lumbering. Canada. Ottawa. Whirlpools.*

MAN FROM GOD'S COUNTRY **F2.3375**

Phil Goldstone Productions. 17 Oct **1924** [New York premiere]. Si; b&w. 35mm. 5 reels.

Dir Alvin J. Neitz. *Scen* George C. Hill. *Photog* Roland Price.

Cast: William Fairbanks *(Bill Holliday)*, Dorothy Revier *(Carmencita)*, Lew Meehan *(Pete Hurly)*, Milton Ross *(Don Manuel)*, Carl Silvera *(Romero)*, Andrew Waldron *(Judge Packard)*.

Western melodrama. An American adventurer and a Mexican vaquero, who are the best of friends, are rivals for the hand of Carmencita, a beautiful Mexican. She is wounded by a brutal American foreman, and the adventurer, who is unjustly blamed for the deed, is almost lynched. Matters are resolved when the adventurer wins the Spanish charmer, and the Mexican gracefully makes his exit. *Cowboys. Mexicans. Ranch foremen. Friendship. Lynching.*

THE MAN FROM HARDPAN **F2.3376**

Leo Maloney Productions. *Dist* Pathé Exchange. 6 Mar **1927** [c17 Jan 1927; LU23550]. Si; b&w. 35mm. 6 reels, 5,814 ft.

Dir Leo D. Maloney. *Story-Scen* Ford I. Beebe. *Photog* Vernon Walker.

Cast: Leo Maloney *(Robert Alan)*, Eugenia Gilbert *(Elizabeth Warner)*, Rosa Gore *(Sarah Lackey)*, Murdock MacQuarrie *(Henry Hardy)*, Paul Hurst *(Larry Lackey)*, Ben Corbett *(Jack Burton)*, Albert Hart *(sheriff)*.

Western melodrama. Elizabeth Warner falls heir to half of her father's ranch, the remaining half being left to Robert Alan, son of her father's lifelong friend. Alan is robbed on the way to the ranch. His papers stolen, he is impersonated by Larry Lackey, an escaped convict, at the instigation of the housekeeper, Sarah Lackey, who feels she has been forgotten. She convinces the sheriff that Alan is the escaped convict and has him jailed, then persuades Elizabeth to buy "Larry's part" of the ranch. As the deal is about to be consummated, Alan escapes and by a ruse forces Larry to reveal his true identity. Alan becomes manager of the ranch and the prospective husband of Elizabeth. *Prison escapees. Ranch managers. Sheriffs. Housekeepers. Inheritance. Ranches. Impersonation. Documentation.*

MAN FROM HEADQUARTERS (Famous Authors) **F2.3377**

Trem Carr Productions. *Dist* Rayart Pictures. Aug **1928**. Si; b&w. 35mm. 6 reels, 5,946 ft.

Dir Duke Worne. *Scen* Arthur Hoerl. *Photog* Hap Depew. *Film Ed* J. S. Harrington.

Cast: Cornelius Keefe *(Yorke Norray)*, Edith Roberts *(Countess Jalna)*, Charles West *(No. 1)*, Lloyd Whitlock *(No. 2)*, Ludwig Lowry *(No. 3)*, Wilbert Emile *(No. 4)*, Dave Harlow *(No. 5)*, Fred Huston *(Duke Albert)*, Joseph Mack.

Mystery melodrama. Source: George Bronson Howard, *The Black Book* (New York, 1920). Finding himself fighting a gang of international crooks for the possession of secret documents and a gold shipment, Yorke Norray, an American Secret Service agent, has even rougher going when he falls for one of his opponents, Countess Jalna, who seeks to help the starving people of her country. Complications include the murder (on a train) of a duke, the American's contact, and the dividing of the documents between the opposing sides. The agent successfully rounds up the conspirators. *Secret service. Nobility. Starvation. Conspiracy. Murder. Documentation.*

THE MAN FROM HELL'S RIVER **F2.3378**

Irving Cummings Productions. *Dist* Western Pictures Exploitation Co. May **1922** [c16 Mar 1922; LU17647]. Si; b&w. 35mm. 5 reels.

Prod-Dir-Writ Irving Cummings. *Photog* Abe Fried.

Cast: Irving Cummings *(Pierre de Barre)*, Eva Novak *(Mabella)*, Wallace Beery *(Gaspard, The Wolf)*, Frank Whitson *(Sergeant McKenna)*, Robert Klein *(Lopente)*, William Herford *(The Padre)*, Rin-Tin-Tin *(himself)*.

Northwest melodrama. Source: James Oliver Curwood, "God of Her People" (publication undetermined). Mabella, a girl living at a Canadian fur-trading post, though engaged to Pierre, a member of the Royal Mounted Police, is forced to marry Gaspard, a vicious halfbreed who has incriminating evidence about her father, Lopente. Pierre is distressed; and Mabella, brutally mistreated and neglected by Gaspard, goes to the police station for protection. Gaspard, however, abducts her and forces her to go away with him on a dogsled. Pierre, discovering that Gaspard is wanted for a crime, pursues them; Rin-Tin-Tin, his dog, kills Gaspard, effecting the rescue of Mabella. Father La Croi reveals that Mabella, an orphan discovered during a snowstorm, is not of Indian parentage, and she is happily united with Pierre. *Traders. Halfcastes. Canadian Northwest. Northwest Mounted Police. Dogs.*

Note: Reviewed also under the title *Hell's River.*

THE MAN FROM HOME **F2.3379**

Famous Players–Lasky. *Dist* Paramount Pictures. ca6 May **1922** [New York premiere; released 21 May; c9 May 1922; LP17872] Si; b&w. 35mm. 7 reels, 6,895 ft.

Pres by Adolph Zukor. *Dir* George Fitzmaurice. *Scen* Ouida Bergère. *Photog* Roy Overbaugh.

Cast: James Kirkwood *(Daniel Forbes Pike)*, Anna Q. Nilsson *(Genevieve Granger-Simpson)*, Geoffrey Kerr *(Horace Granger-Simpson)*, Norman Kerry *(Prince Kinsillo)*, Dorothy Cumming *(Princess Sabina)*, José Ruben *(Ribière)*, Annette Benson *(Faustina Ribière)*, John Miltern *(The King)*, Clifford Grey *(Secretary to the King)*.

Melodrama. Source: Booth Tarkington and Harry Leon Wilson, *The Man From Home, a Play in Four Acts* (New York, 1908). Prince Kinsillo of Italy wishes to repair his dwindling fortunes by marrying Genevieve Granger-Simpson, a wealthy American girl, whose guardian, Daniel Forbes Pike of Kokomo, Indiana, comes to Italy to interview the prospective husband. En route through Italy, Pike meets the king traveling incognito and is unaware of his identity. Later, the king's mistress, Faustina, wife of Ribière, is murdered by the prince, and in making his escape he leaves a blood-stained handkerchief in the king's possession. Ribière, accused of murdering his wife, is sheltered by Pike, whom Kinsillo's father tries to blackmail for protecting a criminal. Pike ultimately denounces the blackmailer and exposes the prince as the assassin. Genevieve, who has been impressed by the passionate advances of the prince, eagerly accepts the attentions of her worthy guardian, and together they return to Kokomo. *Tourists. Nobility. Fortune hunters. Murder. Blackmail. Italy. Indiana.*

Note: Filmed on location in Italy.

THE MAN FROM LONE MOUNTAIN **F2.3380**

Arrow Pictures. Jun **1925** [c5 Jun 1925; LP21534]. Si; b&w. 35mm. 5 reels, 4,530 ft.

Dir Ben Wilson. *Story-Scen* George W. Pyper.

Cast: Ben Wilson.

Western melodrama. A girl arrives in a remote western cowtown looking for John Milton, an innocent escaped convict who was jailed for a crime her brother committed. She goes into a saloon, where she meets Black Bart, the leader of an outlaw gang, who soon steals her money and forces her to work for him. Bart and the girl go to the cabin of "the man from lone mountain," a mysterious hermit who keeps a hoard of gold hidden near his cabin. Using her feminine wiles, the girl quickly finds the cache of gold, which Bart steals. The man comes after Bart and the girl, captures them, and ties them to their horses. He later realizes that the girl has been innocent of deliberate wrongdoing and unties her. He also frees Bart, the two men fight, and he is overpowered by Bart. Bart then rides into town with the girl, and the man follows, again fighting Bart, whom he badly beats and hands over to the sheriff. The man turns out to be the sought-for John Milton, and he and the girl decide to share life together on Lone Mountain. *Fugitives. Prison escapees. Outlaws. Hermits. Brother-sister relationship. Theft.*

THE MAN FROM LOST RIVER **F2.3381**
Goldwyn Pictures. Nov **1921** [c29 Sep 1921; LP17030]. Si; b&w. 35mm. 6 reels, 5,694 ft.
Dir Frank Lloyd. *Scen* Lambert Hillyer, Arthur Statter. *Story* Katharine Newlin Burt. *Photog* Norbert Brodin.
Cast: House Peters *(Barnes)*, Fritzi Brunette *(Marcia)*, Allan Forrest *(Fosdick)*, James Gordon *(Rossiter)*, Monte Collins *(Mr. Carson)*, Milla Davenport *(Mrs. Carson)*.
Melodrama. Fosdick, a New York society man of weak character, joins a band of lumberjacks in the North Woods, where he is disliked by his mates and the foreman, Jim Barnes. Marcia Judd, though admired by Barnes, falls in love with Fosdick, and they are married. Fosdick soon becomes discontented and abandons her, however, but returns when oil is discovered on her land. A plague strikes the Lost River locality following his return, and Fosdick runs away when Marcia is taken ill; but he falls victim to the plague and dies. Marcia recovers and finds happiness with Barnes. *Lumbering. Cowardice. Plague. Lost River.*

THE MAN FROM MEDICINE HAT (Reissue) **F2.3382**
Dist American Film Co. c12 Jan **1921** [LP16011]. Si; b&w. 35mm. 5 reels.
Note: A Leo Maloney–Helen Holmes feature originally released under the title *The Manager of the B & A* (Signal-Mutual, ca 1916).

THE MAN FROM NEVADA **F2.3383**
J. P. McGowan Productions. *Dist* Syndicate Pictures. Aug **1929.** Si; b&w. 35mm. 5 reels, 4,758 ft.
Dir J. P. McGowan. *Story* Sally Winters. *Photog* Hap Depew.
Cast: Tom Tyler *(Jack Carter)*, Natalie Joyce *(Virginia Watkins)*, Al Ferguson *(Luke Baldridge)*, Alfred Hewston *(Jim Watkins)*, Kip Cooper *("Wart" Watkins)*, Godfrey Craig *("Wiggles" Watkins)*, Frank Crane *("Wobbles" Watkins)*, Bill Nolte *("Bowery" Walker)*.
Western melodrama. "J. P. [McGowan] plays to the kid angle this time, showing a flock of them and a timid papa who finally keeps his land after learning from Tom that a jilt on the chin is better than good penmanship in sticking to a land claim. There's a girl, Natalie Joyce, in the motherless big sister role. Not much love stuff. J. P. is all for the men. Plenty of hard riding." (*Variety,* 18 Sep 1929, p55.) *Children. Widowers. Brother-sister relationship. Land rights.*

THE MAN FROM NEW YORK **F2.3384**
Great Western Pictures. *Dist* E. R. Champion Distributing Co. 17 Dec **1923** [New York State license application]. Si; b&w. 35mm.
Cast: Fred Church *(Bob Tarrant)*, Marie Wells *(Ruth Crawford)*, Morgan Jones *(Dad Crawford)*, W. W. Jones *(Red Dawson)*, Rita Pickering *(Trini)*.
Western melodrama(?). No information about the nature of this film has been found.

THE MAN FROM NOWHERE **F2.3385**
Big Productions Film Corp. *Dist* Syndicate Pictures. 4 Apr **1930** [New York showing]. Si; b&w. 35mm. 5 reels, 4,900 ft.
Dir J. P. McGowan. *Story-Scen* Sally Winters. *Photog* Hap Depew.
Cast: Bob Steele *(Terry Norton)*, Ione Reed *(Grace McCloud)*, Clark Comstock *(Pat McCloud)*, Bill Nestel *(Dan McCloud)*, Perry Murdock *("Smiley" McCloud)*, Tom Forman *(Hank Jordan)*, Clark Coffey *(Sheriff Blake)*.
Western melodrama. "About a tramp cowboy budding [sic] in on a western family fray where a step-brother is trying to wrestle estate away from a sick man and falls for the blonde niece. A couple of acrobatic fights, slow motion horsemanship and everything ends okay after one killing." (*Variety,* 9 Apr 1930, p42.) *Tramps. Cowboys. Stepbrothers. Land rights.*
Note: May also be known as *Western Honor.*

THE MAN FROM OKLAHOMA **F2.3386**
Harry Webb Productions. *Dist* Rayart Pictures. 4 Aug **1926** [New York State license]. Si; b&w. 35mm. 5 reels, 4,807 ft.
Dir? (see note) Harry Webb, Forrest Sheldon.
Cast: Jack Perrin.
Western melodrama. "Young stranger appears on scene of intrigue and through aid of clever dog clears up mysterious shooting and unravels maze of deceit in which ranch foreman and unwelcome suitor of ranch mistress figure. He marries girl." (*Motion Picture News Booking Guide,* 11:37, Oct 1926.) *Strangers. Ranchers. Ranch foremen. Oklahomans. Dogs.*
Note: Sources disagree in crediting direction.

THE MAN FROM RED GULCH **F2.3387**
Hunt Stromberg Productions. *Dist* Producers Distributing Corp. 13 Dec **1925** [c9 Nov 1925; LP22009]. Si; b&w. 35mm. 6 reels, 5,437 ft.
Pres by Hunt Stromberg. *Dir* Edmund Mortimer. *Adapt* Elliott J. Clawson. *Photog* Georges Benoit.
Cast: Harry Carey *(Sandy)*, Harriet Hammond *(Betsey)*, Frank Campeau *(Falloner)*, Mark Hamilton *(Frisbee)*, Lee Shumway *(Lasham)*, Doris Lloyd *(Madame Le Blanc)*, Frank Norcross *(Colonel Starbottle)*, Virginia Davis *(Cissy)*, Mickey Moore *(Jimmy)*.
Western melodrama. Source: Bret Harte, "The Idyll of Red Gulch." In the days of the California Gold Rush of '49, Sandy is at odds with his partner, Falloner, over the latter's heavy drinking. Falloner is killed by Lasham, who many years before ran off with Falloner's wife. Sandy brings Falloner's children, Cissy and Jimmy, and their Aunt Betsey to Sacramento from Missouri. He then sets out to find the mother and to avenge his partner's death. Lasham induces Betsey to take the night boat for Sandy Bar with him, under the pretense of finding the children's mother. Sandy rides after them and swims to the steamer, arriving in time to save a frightened Betsey from Lasham. In a fight, Lasham is knocked overboard and drowns. The mother, who under the name Madame Le Blanc has been living with Lasham, helping him with his gambling and other nefarious schemes, becomes a novice in a convent. Sandy and Betsey are wed. *Children. Novices. Family life. Infidelity. Murder. Gold rushes. Missouri. Sacramento. California.*

THE MAN FROM TEXAS **F2.3388**
Ben Roy Productions. **1921.** Si; b&w. 35mm. 5 reels.
Dir Ben F. Wilson.
Western melodrama(?). No information about the precise nature of this film has been found. *Texans. Negro life.*

THE MAN FROM THE RIO GRANDE **F2.3389**
Denver Dixon Productions. *Dist* Aywon Film Corp. 16 Apr **1926** [New York State license]. Si; b&w. 35mm. 5 reels.
Cast: George Kesterson, Dorothy Lee.
Western melodrama(?). No information about the nature of this film has been found.

THE MAN FROM THE WEST (Blue Streak Western) **F2.3390**
Universal Pictures. 31 Oct **1926** [c9 Aug 1926; LP23022]. Si; b&w. 35mm. 5 reels, 4,474 ft.
Pres by Carl Laemmle. *Dir* Albert Rogell. *Adapt-Scen* Harrison Jacobs. *Story* Josephine Dodge. *Photog* Eddie Linden.
Cast: Art Acord *(Art Louden)*, Eugenia Gilbert *(Iris Millard)*, Irvin Renard *(Carter Blake)*, William Welsh *(Bill Hayes)*, Vin Moore *(Lloyd Millard)*, Dick Gilbert *(Hanna)*, Georgie Grandee, Eunice Vin Moore.
Western melodrama. Art Louden, foreman of the Bar H Ranch, is contemptuous of the masculine city flappers and effeminate city sheiks who are vacationing on the ranch, and when reproached by the owner, Bill Hayes, for discourtesy to a guest, Art complains that there are no "she-women" left. Seeing a newspaper photo of Iris Millard, he is attracted by her apparent innocence; then she arrives with her father, and Art is disillusioned to find her as snobbish and as jazzily dressed as the others. His disdain, however, causes Iris to play up to his ideas. Carter Blake, who is conspiring to steal some jewels, blames Art for the theft; Blake's partner (Battling Burke) and Slip Hanna doublecross him and abscond with the jewels. After numerous complications, Art overcomes the crooks and rescues Iris. *Ranch foremen. Thieves. Flappers. Mannishness. Effeminacy. Robbery. Dude ranches.*

THE MAN FROM WYOMING F2.3391

Universal Pictures. 28 Jan **1924** [c14 Dec 1923; LP19728]. Si; b&w. 35mm. 5 reels, 4,717 ft.

Dir Robert North Bradbury. *Adapt-Cont* Isadore Bernstein. *Photog* Merritt Gerstad.

Cast: Jack Hoxie *(Ned Bannister)*, Lillian Rich *(Helen Messiter)*, William Welsh *(David Messiter)*, Claude Payton *(Jack Halloway)*, Ben Corbett *(Red)*, Lon Poff *(Jim McWilliams)*, George Kuwa *(Sing Lee Wah)*, James Corrigan *(The Governor of Wyoming)*.

Western melodrama. Source: William MacLeod Raine, *Wyoming, a Story of the Outdoor West* (New York, 1908). Ned Bannister, manager of a sheep ranch, is accused of the murder of David Messiter, a neighboring cattle rancher. Bannister's employer, Halloway, would like to own the cattle rancher's spread. When Helen Messiter, niece of the deceased, arrives to investigate the murder, Halloway, the real culprit, tries to seduce her. Bannister saves Helen, and he marries her after his innocence is established. *Ranchers. Ranch managers. State governors. Seduction. Murder. Wyoming.*

A MAN FROM WYOMING F2.3392

Paramount-Publix Corp. 12 Jul **1930** [c12 Jul 1930; LP1416]. Sd (Movietone); b&w. 35mm. 8 reels, 5,989 ft.

Dir Rowland V. Lee. *Screenplay* John V. A. Weaver, Albert Shelby Le Vino. *Story* Joseph Moncure March, Lew Lipton. *Photog* Harry Fischbeck. *Film Ed* Robert Bassler. *Rec Engr* Eugene Merritt.

Cast: Gary Cooper *(Jim Baker)*, June Collyer *(Patricia Hunter)*, Regis Toomey *(Jersey)*, Morgan Farley *(Lieutenant Lee)*, E. H. Calvert *(Major-General Hunter)*, Mary Foy *(inspector)*, Emil Chautard *(French mayor)*, Ed Deering *(sergeant)*, William B. Davidson *(major)*, Ben Hall *(orderly)*, Parker McConnell *(captain in dugout)*.

War melodrama. With the declaration of war, Jim Baker and Jersey, his coworker, who are working on a bridge construction job in Wyoming, join the Army and are sent to France with the Engineer Corps. Patricia Hunter, an American society girl in the Ambulance Corps, impatient with the routine of her job, goes A. W. O. L. and wanders into the territory held by Jim's company; he rescues her from enemy shellfire and reprimands her. At a rest camp they see much of each other, fall in love, and are secretly married. Later, when Jim is recalled to the front and she is about to be court-martialed for her absence, she reads of his death; and to drown her misery, she opens the family chateau to entertain servicemen. Jim, only wounded, is sent to the hospital and miscontrues her gaiety; he tries to persuade her to return with him to Wyoming, and when she refuses, he returns to the front. On the day of the Armistice, however, he finds her waiting for him in the town where they were married. *Soldiers. Socialites. Engineers—Civil. Ambulance drivers. Courts-martial. World War I. Wyoming. France. United States Army—Engineer Corps. United States Army—Ambulance Corps.*

THE MAN GETTER *see* **TRAIL'S END**

THE MAN GETTER F2.3393

W. M. Smith Productions. caFeb **1923** [scheduled release]. Si; b&w. 35mm. 5 reels, 4,440 ft.

Cast: Franklyn Farnum, Peggy O'Day.

Western melodrama(?). No information about the nature of this film has been found.

Note: Possibly the same film as *The Trail's End* (W. M. Smith Productions, 1922).

THE MAN HUNTER (Reissue) F2.3394

Fox Film Corp. 7 Dec **1924.** Si; b&w. 35mm. 5 reels.

Note: A William Farnum feature originally released by Fox (23 Feb 1919; c23 Feb 1919; LP13439) in 6 reels.

THE MAN HUNTER F2.3395

Warner Brothers Pictures. 3 May **1930** [c23 Apr 1930; LP1249]. Sd (Vitaphone); b&w. 35mm. 6 reels, 4,383 ft.

Dir Ross Lederman. *Scen-Dial* James A. Starr. *Story* Lillie Hayward. *Photog* James Van Trees. *Sd Engr* Cal Applegate.

Cast: Rin-Tin-Tin *(Rinty)*, Charles Delaney *(Jim Clayton)*, Nora Lane *(Lady Jane Winston)*, John Loder *(George Castle)*, Pat Hartigan *(Crosby)*, Christiane Yves *(maid)*, Floyd Shackleford *(Simba)*, Billy Bletcher *(Buggs)*, John Kelly *(Charlie)*, Joe Bordeaux *(Dennis)*.

Adventure melodrama. Lady Jane Winston, seeking to further her interests in the West Africa Ivory and Rubber Co., which George Castle has been managing to suit his own interests, becomes involved with a beachcomber, Jim Clayton, once in her company's employ, and a dog that adopts Jim as his master. The two save Jane's life, and she deputizes Jim to help her trap Castle; he discovers a cache of ivory that Castle has hidden but is surprised by Castle's men and imprisoned. Rinty takes a message to Lady Jane and then helps effect Jim's escape. Castle kidnaps Jane and inspires a native uprising against the whites. While Jim and his friends are defending her, Rinty goes to a British outpost for help and thus saves the day. *Beachcombers. Businesswomen. British. Ivory. Rubber. Ivory Coast. Dogs.*

MAN HUNTERS F2.3396

Rialto Productions. 18 Oct **1923** [New York State license application]. Si; b&w. 35mm. 6 reels.

Melodrama(?). No information about the nature of this film has been found.

THE MAN I LOVE F2.3397

Paramount Famous Lasky Corp. 25 May **1929** [c24 May 1929; LP406]. Sd (Movietone); b&w. 35mm. 7 reels, 6,669 ft. [Also si; 6,453 ft.]

Assoc Prod David Selznick. *Dir* William Wellman. *Story-Screenplay-Dial* Herman J. Mankiewicz. *Photog* Henry Gerrard. *Film Ed* Allyson Shaffer. *Song: "Celia"* Leo Robin, Richard Whiting.

Cast: Richard Arlen *(Dum-Dum Brooks)*, Mary Brian *(Celia Fields)*, Baclanova *(Sonia Barondoff)*, Harry Green *(Curly Bloom)*, Jack Oakie *(Lew Layton)*, Pat O'Malley *(D. J. McCarthy)*, Leslie Fenton *(Carlo Vesper)*, Charles Sullivan *(Champ Mahoney)*, Sailor Vincent *(K. O. O'Hearn)*, Robert Perry *(gateman)*.

Comedy-drama. Dum-Dum Brooks, a palooka fighter around Los Angeles, falls in love with Celia Fields, and they decide to marry in spite of the protests of his manager, Curly Bloom, and leave for New York. There Brooks wins a contract with promoter D. J. McCarthy and the admiration of Sonia Barondoff, an exotic socialite who is jealously guarded by her lover, Carlo Vesper. Over a period of 6 months Brooks wins 15 fights and is touted for a bout with the champion. Before the fight, Vester induces Brooks to drink heavily and precipitates a brawl in Sonia's apartment; the next morning, Brooks learns that Celia has left him and that he has been signed for the fight. But Brooks fights badly until Celia rises in the audience and roots for him, causing him to win. Celia leaves for California, but Brooks is reunited with her on the train, and together they renounce fame. *Prizefighters. Socialites. Fight managers. Fight promoters. Jealousy. Los Angeles. New York City.*

THE MAN IN BLUE (Universal-Jewel) F2.3398

Universal Pictures. 21 Jun **1925** [c25 Feb 1925; LP21189]. Si; b&w. 35mm. 6 reels, 5,634 ft.

Dir Edward Laemmle. *Scen* E. Richard Schayer. *Photog* Clyde De Vinna.

Cast: Herbert Rawlinson *(Tom Conlin)*, Madge Bellamy *(Tita Sartori)*, Nick De Ruiz *(Gregoria Vitti)*, André de Beranger *(Carlo Guido)*, Cesare Gravina *(Tony Sartori)*, Jackie Morgan *(Pat Malone)*, Dorothy Brock *(Morna Malone)*, D. J. Mitsoras *(Cesare Martinelli)*, Carrie Clark Ward *(Mrs. Shaughnessy)*, C. F. Roark *(Mr. Shaughnessy)*, Martha Mattox *(Bendetta)*.

Melodrama. Source: Gerald Beaumont, "The Flower of Napoli," in *Red Book* (42:47–51, Mar 1924). Tom Conlin, an Irish cop walking a beat in an Italian neighborhood, falls in love with Tita Sartori, the daughter of a florist. Tita returns Tom's affection but keeps him at a distance, believing him to be married; Tita is also wooed by an unscrupulous politician of considerable wealth. This politician is responsible for the death of an Italian youth, who was also in love with Tita. He later kidnaps Tita, confining her to his apartment. She is rescued by Tom, who captures the murderer after a brutal battle in a restaurant. Tita learns that Tom is single, and she admits her love for him. *Police. Politicians. Florists. Italians. Irish. Kidnaping. Murder.*

THE MAN IN HOBBLES F2.3399

Tiffany-Stahl Productions. 20 Feb **1928** [c7 Dec 1928; LP25895]. Si; b&w. 35mm. 6 reels, 5,967 ft.

Dir George Archainbaud. *Titl* Frederick Hatton, Fanny Hatton. *Adapt* J. F. Natteford. *Photog* Harry Jackson. *Art Dir* Hervey Libbert. *Set Dressings* George Sawley. *Film Ed* Desmond O'Brien.

Cast: John Harron *(The Boy)*, Lila Lee *(The Girl)*, Lucien Littlefield,

Sunshine Hart, Betty Egan, Eddie Nugent, William Anderson *(The Girl's Family)*, Vivian Oakland *(The Other Woman)*.

Comedy-drama. Source: Peter Bernard Kyne, "The Man in Hobbles," in *Saturday Evening Post* (185:13, 29 Mar 1913). "A young photographer marries the daughter of a shiftless family and finds he has them all on his hands. He leaves for New York, makes good and sends for his wife. His wife goes to him—so does her family until hubby puts his foot down." ("Motion Picture New Booking Guide," in *Motion Picture News*, 15 Mar 1930, p92.) *Photographers. Marriage. In-laws. New York City.*

MAN IN THE ROUGH **F2.3400**

FBO Pictures. 20 May **1928** [c19 Mar 1928; LP25119]. Si; b&w. 35mm. 5 reels, 4,785 ft.

Dir Wallace Fox. *Screenplay-Cont* Frank Howard Clark. *Titl* Randolph Bartlett. *Story* W. C. Tuttle. *Photog* Phil Tannura. *Film Ed* Della M. King. *Asst Dir* Jack Smith.

Cast: Bob Steele *(Bruce Sherwood)*, Marjorie King *(Tess Winters)*, Tom Lingham *(Cale Winters)*, William Norton Bailey *(Jim Kane)*, Jay Morley *(Buck Helm)*.

Western melodrama. Bruce Sherwood, a carefree cowboy, learns from gunman Buck Helm that Buck has been hired to kill Cale Winters, an old prospector living with his daughter, Tess. When Bruce, masquerading as Buck, goes to warn the old man, he is mistaken for the killer by Tess and is nearly shot. Then Bruce is overpowered and imprisoned by Buck and Jim Kane, a crooked real estate agent who is trying to force Cale to sell his mine. Just as Jim is about to kill the old man and disfigure Tess's face because she refuses to marry him, Bruce shows up and drives the two outlaws away. *Prospectors. Hired killers. Cowboys. Real estate agents.*

THE MAN IN THE SADDLE (Universal-Jewel) **F2.3401**

Universal Pictures. 11 Jul **1926** [c22 Jun 1926; LP22856]. Si; b&w. 35mm. 6 reels, 5,492 ft.

Pres by Carl Laemmle. *Dir* Lynn Reynolds. *Dir? (see note)* Clifford S. Smith. *Story-Scen* Charles A. Logue. *Photog* Edwin Linden.

Cast: Hoot Gibson *(Jeff Morgan, Jr.)*, Charles Mailes *(Jeff Morgan, Sr.)*, Clark Comstock *(Pete)*, Fay Wray *(Pauline Stewart)*, Sally Long *(Laura Mayhew)*, Emmett King *(Tom Stewart)*, Lloyd Whitlock *(Lawrence)*, Duke R. Lee *(Snell)*, Yorke Sherwood *(banker)*, William Dyer *(sheriff)*.

Western melodrama. A party of campers return to Tom Stewart's ranch resort to report they have been held up by bandits. Lawrence, their guide, explains that it is a staged stunt for their benefit; Stewart confirms this and refunds the losses but writes to his old pal Jeff Morgan, a former gunfighter, telling him of his predicament. Morgan sends his son, Jeff, Jr., a superb rider and dead shot but otherwise an awkward lout; at the insistence of Pauline, Stewart places Jeff in charge of a camping party. Laura Mayhew, a city girl in league with Lawrence, sends up a flare signal at night, and while Jeff chases some bears into the woods, Lawrence and his men hold up the camp. Jeff is overpowered in a fight but pursues the men to their hideout and by a clever ruse gets the drop on them. Later, he forces a confession of guilt from Lawrence, and Laura is arrested. Jeff and Pauline are united. *Guides. Bandits. Campers. Dude ranches. Bears.*

Note: Copyright records credit Clifford S. Smith as director.

THE MAN IN THE SHADOW **F2.3402**

David Hartford Productions. *Dist* American Cinema Association. 15 Oct **1926** [c24 Dec 1926; LP23481]. Si; b&w. 35mm. 6 reels, 5,632 ft.

Dir-Supv David Hartford. *Adapt* Frances Nordstrom. *Story* Anne Francis. *Photog* Walter Griffin. *Film Ed* Walter Griffin.

Cast: David Torrence *(Robert Rodman)*, Mary McAllister *(Lucy Rodman)*, Arthur Rankin *(Bob Rodman)*, Joseph Bennett *(Dallis Alvoid)*, Myrtle Stedman *(Mary Alvoid)*, John T. Dwyer *(Thomas Walsh)*, Margaret Fielding *(Kate Jackson)*, Edward Coxen *(Harry Jackson)*.

Crime melodrama. After the election of Robert Rodman as governor, Dallis Alvoid, son of Rodman's companion Mary Alvoid, becomes a trusted employee in a bank. Dallis is discouraged when Lucy Rodman, his sweetheart, is courted by the wealthy Ralph Hadley. Thomas Walsh, a gambler and blackmailer, leads Dallis to gamble with bank funds and permits him to win; later, when the boy falls in debt to him, Walsh offers to cancel the debt if he gives him a plan of the bank. Harry Jackson, who is being blackmailed also by Walsh, shoots him, and when Dallis discovers the body, circumstantial evidence points to him as the murderer. Dallis is sentenced to death, but Lucy brings word of Jackson's dying confession and he is saved. *State governors. Bank clerks. Political corruption. Gambling. Circumstantial evidence. Capital punishment.*

THE MAN LIFE PASSED BY **F2.3403**

Metro Pictures. 24 Dec **1923** [c26 Dec 1923; LP19738]. Si; b&w. 35mm. 7 reels, 6,200 ft.

Dir-Writ Victor Schertzinger. *Scen* Winifred Dunn. *Photog* Chester A. Lyons.

Cast: Jane Novak *(Hope Moore)*, Percy Marmont *(John Turbin)*, Eva Novak *(Joy Moore)*, Cullen Landis *(Harold Trevis)*, Lydia Knott *(John's mother)*, Hobart Bosworth *("Iron Man" Moore)*, Gertrude Short *(Paula)*, Ralph Bushman *(Jerry)*, Lincoln Stedman *(Muggsy)*, George Siegmann *(Crogan)*, André de Beranger *(Leo Friend)*, Larry Fisher *(Peters)*, William Humphrey *(The Lawyer)*.

Melodrama. Inventor John Turbin vows vengeance when "Iron Man" Moore, a wealthy iron industrialist, steals his plans. Poverty and disappointment make him a derelict, but he forgives his enemy after Moore's daughters, Hope and Joy, befriend him. *Inventors. Derelicts. Industrialists. Iron.*

A MAN MUST LIVE **F2.3404**

Famous Players–Lasky. *Dist* Paramount Pictures. 19 Jan **1925** [c24 Dec 1924; LP20966]. Si; b&w. 35mm. 7 reels, 6,116 ft.

Pres by Adolph Zukor, Jesse L. Lasky. *Dir* Paul Sloane. *Scen* James Ashmore Creelman. *Photog* Hal Rosson.

Cast: Richard Dix *(Geoffrey Farnell)*, Jacqueline Logan *("Mops" Collins)*, George Nash *(Job Hardcastle)*, Edna Murphy *(Eleanor Ross-Fayne)*, Charles Beyer *(Clive Ross-Fayne)*, Dorothy Walters *(Mrs. Jaynes)*, William Ricciardi *(cabaret owner)*, Arthur Houseman *(Tod Cragge)*, Lucius Henderson *(Ross-Fayne)*, Jane Jennings *(Mrs. Ross-Fayne)*.

Romantic melodrama. Source: Ida Alexa Ross Wylie, "Jungle Law," in *Good Housekeeping*. Jeff Farnell is forced by circumstances to take a job on a New York scandal sheet while he awaits the settlement of his claim against a steel company. Job Hardcastle, the hardened city editor of the paper, sends Jeff to get a story on "Mops" Collins, a society divorcée who has been reduced to dancing in a cabaret. Jeff takes pity on Mops, who is dying of consumption, and takes her into his apartment, telling Hardcastle that he could not find her. Afraid of losing his job, Jeff hunts for a big story, finding it when he discovers that Clive Ross-Fayne, a friend he thought lost in the war, has been arraigned on charges of narcotics peddling. To get a picture of Clive to go with his story, Jeff goes to the Ross-Fayne residence, where he discovers that Clive's sister, Eleanor, is the girl with whom he fell in love at a dance before the war, whose name he never knew. Jeff then tries to kill the story, but Hardcastle nevertheless publishes it. Mops dies. Jeff is fired after he assaults Hardcastle, but he is reconciled with the Ross-Fayne family when Clive is freed. Jeff gets a $100,000 settlement from the steel company and asks Eleanor to marry him. *Reporters. Dancers. Editors. Cabarets. Narcotics. Tuberculosis. Scandal sheets. Lawsuits. Steel industry.*

THE MAN NEXT DOOR **F2.3405**

Vitagraph Co. of America. ca27 May **1923** [New York premiere; c21 May 1923; LP18983]. Si; b&w. 35mm. 7 reels, 6,945 ft.

Pres by Albert E. Smith. *Dir* Victor Schertzinger. *Dir? (see note)* David Smith. *Scen* C. Graham Baker. *Photog* Stephen Smith, Jr.

Cast: David Torrence *(Colonel Wright)*, Frank Sheridan *(Curley)*, James Morrison *(Jimmy)*, Alice Calhoun *(Bonnie Bell)*, John Steppling *(David Wisner)*, Adele Farrington *(Mrs. Wisner)*, Mary Culver *(Catherine Kimberly)*, Bruce Boteler *(Tom Kimberly)*, Peanuts *(a dog)*.

Society comedy-drama. Source: Emerson Hough, *The Man Next Door* (New York, 1917). Wealthy cattleman Colonel Wright moves east with his foreman, Curley, and his daughter, Bonnie Bell, to give her the benefits of education and city living. They take up residence next to the Wisners, a prominent society family; and Bonnie Bell falls in love with Jimmy Wisner, whom she believes to be the gardener. Colonel Wright not only opposes Bonnie Bell's match with a gardener—he also carries on a feud with Mr. Wisner. Jimmy and Bonnie Bell elope, Jimmy reveals his identity, and the couple is warmly received by both fathers. *Ranchers. Ranch foremen. Gardeners. Social classes. Family life. Elopement. Dogs.*

Note: At least one source credits David Smith as director.

THE MAN NOBODY KNOWS **F2.3406**

Pictorial Clubs. c22 Nov **1925** [MP3456]. Si; b&w. 35mm. 6 reels.

Dir Errett LeRoy Kenepp. *Titl* Bruce Barton. *Photog* Errett LeRoy Kenepp. *Mus Setting* Alexander Savine.

Historical drama. Source: Bruce Barton, *The Man Nobody Knows; A Discovery of Jesus* (Indianapolis, 1925). With the use of actors, the life of

Jesus is presented by means of titles telling the simple and moving story of His life combined with documentary footage showing the very places in the Holy Land where Jesus once lived and preached. The musical setting is an arrangement of the themes of familiar hymns and great oratorios. *Jesus. Palestine.*

Note: Produced on location in Palestine.

A MAN OF ACTION **F2.3407**

Thomas H. Ince Corp. *Dist* Associated First National Pictures. ca3 Jun **1923** [New York premiere; released 10 Jun; c9 May 1923; LP18937]. Si; b&w. 35mm. 6 reels, 5,599 ft.

Pres by Thomas H. Ince. *Dir* James W. Horne. *Story* Bradley King. *Photog* Max Dupont.

Cast: Douglas MacLean *(Bruce MacAllister)*, Marguerite De La Motte *(Helen Sumner)*, Raymond Hatton *(Harry Hopwood)*, Wade Boteler *(Spike McNab)*, Arthur Millett *(Dr. Sumner)*, Kingsley Benedict *(Andy)*, Arthur Stuart Hull *(Eugene Preston)*, William Courtright *(The "Deacon")*, Katherine Lewis *("Frisk-O" Rose)*.

Crook farce. Goaded by his fiancée, Helen Sumner, into proving that he is a man of action, Bruce MacAllister tells Eugene Preston, his estate administrator, that he is going east for a meeting; but actually he mixes in the San Francisco underground incognito. When Bruce is mistaken for the well-known "Chicago Kid," he makes no objection and ends up leading the gang in a robbery of his own fortune in diamonds. He discovers Preston's intention to steal the jewels for himself, the loot changes hands many times, Helen calls the police, and the timely arrival of Helen's father straightens out matters. *Gangs. Impersonation. Robbery. San Francisco.*

MAN OF COURAGE **F2.3408**

Dist Aywon Film Corp. 21 Apr **1922** [trade review]. Si; b&w. 35mm. [Feature length assumed.]

Pres by Nathan Hirsh.

Cast: E. K. Lincoln *(William Gregory)*, Spottiswoode Aitken *(Stephen Gregory, his father)*, Fred Bloom *(Morgan Deane)*, Millicent Fisher *(Dorothy Deane)*, Helen Dunbar *(Mrs. Deane)*, John Eberts *(Johnny Rivers)*, James Youngdeer *(Aquila, a bandit)*, George Gebhart *(El Cholo)*.

Western melodrama. "Lincoln has the role of a molly-coddle son of wealthy parents whose regeneration is brought about through being hit on the head and shipped off in a freight car in dress clothes. In this attire he hits a border town just at the time that his former sweetheart has been carried off a transcontinental train by a band of Mexican bandits, and he goes to her rescue, establishing his manhood when he manages to rescue her from the hands of the hold-up men." (*Variety,* 21 Apr 1922, p41.) *Mollycoddles. Bandits. Mexicans. Manhood. Abduction. Mexican border.*

A MAN OF IRON **F2.3409**

Chadwick Pictures. ca18 Jun **1925** [c29 Jun 1925; LP21613]. Si; b&w. 35mm. 6 reels, 6,200 ft.

Dir Whitman Bennett. *Adapt* Lawrence Marsten.

Cast: Lionel Barrymore *(Philip Durban)*, Mildred Harris *(Claire Bowdoin)*, Winifred Barry *(Martha Durban)*, Dorothy Kingdon *(Edith Bowdoin)*, Alfred Mack *(Hugh Bowdoin)*, J. Moy Bennett *(Denis Callahan)*, Isobel De Leon *(Maybelle Callahan)*, Jean Del Val *(Prince Novakian)*.

Melodrama. Philip Durban, a wealthy iron manufacturer, marries Claire Bowdoin, the young daughter of a family of impoverished bluebloods. Claire, who enters into matrimony only to provide for her mother's welfare, remains at first coldly indifferent to Philip, and he, in turn, remains aloof. Claire eventually comes to love Philip, but he fails to respond to any of her advances. She eventually goes abroad, where she encounters Prince Novakian, an Italian, who becomes infatuated with her. Philip learns of Novakian's amorous advances and goes to Italy, where he is challenged to a duel for taking a punch at the prince. Philip is wounded in the duel, and Novakian is slain. Under the stress and excitement of the moment, Claire casts aside her pose of indifference and rushes to her husband, tending his wounds and at long last convincing him of her love. *Iron manufacturers. Royalty. Poverty. Marriage. Italy. Duels.*

A MAN OF NERVE **F2.3410**

R-C Pictures. *Dist* Film Booking Offices of America. 20 Sep **1925** [c1 Oct 1925; LP21863]. Si; b&w. 35mm. 5 reels, 4,452 ft.

Dir Louis Chaudet. *Scen* George Hively. *Story* John Harold Hamlin. *Photog* Allen Davey.

Cast: Bob Custer *(Hackamore Henderson)*, Jean Arthur *(Loria Gatlin)*, Leon Holmes *(Buddy Simms)*, David Dunbar *(Rangey Greer)*, Buck Moulton *(bandit)*, Ralph McCullough *(Art Gatlin)*.

Western melodrama. Hackamore Henderson, a tough trail hand, is sent to look for strays and falls in love with Loria Gatlin, who runs a millinery store in a small town. Old Joe Simms, Hackamore's boss, is murdered, and Hackamore is jailed on suspicion of having committed the crime. A lynch mob gathers, and Hackamore escapes with the help of Loria and young Buddy Simms. Hackamore later captures the real killer, establishes his own innocence, and weds Loria. *Cowboys. Milliners. Murder. Lynching.*

A MAN OF QUALITY **F2.3411**

Excellent Pictures. 1 Oct **1926** [c14 Oct 1926; LP23268]. Si; b&w. 35mm. 6 reels, 5,640 ft.

Pres by Samuel Zierler. *Dir* Wesley Ruggles. *Story* H. H. Van Loan. *Photog* Frank Zucker.

Cast: George Walsh *(Jack Banning)*, Ruth Dwyer *(Marion Marcy)*, Brian Donlevy *(Richard Courtney)*, Lucien Prival *(Spanish Joe)*, Laura De Cardi *(Dorina)*.

Crook melodrama. Jack Banning, a Secret Service operative, is assigned to thwart the activities of a gang of silk smugglers. Disguised as a motorcycle officer, Banning patrols their rendezvous by day, and at night he poses as a crook, "Strongarm Samson." He soon is attracted to Marion Macy, a banker's daughter, also sought after by Courtney, who heads the smugglers; but she recognizes him and informs Courtney that he is a policeman. Banning is captured by Courtney's henchman, Spanish Joe, but escapes; Marion is lured to the hideout, and Dorina, also an undercover agent, awaits the officers while Banning returns to rescue Marion from Courtney's clutches after a desperate battle. The smugglers are captured, and Banning is united with Marion. *Smugglers. Secret service. Disguise. Courtship. Silk.*

THE MAN OF STONE **F2.3412**

Selznick Pictures. *Dist* Select Pictures. 10 Nov **1921** [c2 Nov 1921; LP17135]. Si; b&w. 35mm. 5 reels, 4,676 ft.

Pres by Lewis J. Selznick. *Dir* George Archainbaud. *Scen* Lewis Allen Browne. *Story* John Lynch, Edmund Goulding. *Photog* Jules Cronjager.

Cast: Conway Tearle *(Captain Deering)*, Betty Howe *(Laila)*, Martha Mansfield *(Lady Fortescue)*, Colin Campbell *(Lieutenant Waite)*, Warren Cook *(Lord Branton)*, Charles D. Brown *(Lord Reggie)*.

Melodrama. Captain Deering, a British officer whose gallant career has earned him the sobriquet "The Man of Stone," returns to London and finds that he has been jilted by his fiancée, Lady Mary Fortescue. Returning to duty in Arabia, he drinks heavily; and when he becomes seriously ill, he is cared for by Laila, a desert maiden who falls in love with him, accompanies him into the interior, and saves him from death at the hands of a robber. Lady Mary, who falls out with her suitor, arrives with the hope of winning back Deering. Representing herself as Deering's wife, she sends Laila from the camp; Deering follows Laila and rescues her from bandits; and in his absence the camp is attacked and Lady Mary is slain. Deering then resolves to devote his future to Arabian problems with Laila as his wife. *Alcoholism. Deserts. Arabia. London. Great Britain—Army.*

THE MAN OF THE FOREST **F2.3413**

Zane Grey Pictures. *Dist* W. W. Hodkinson Corp. Jun **1921.** Si; b&w. 35mm. 7 reels, 6,800 ft.

Prod Benjamin B. Hampton. *Scen* Howard Hickman, Richard Schayer, W. H. Clifford. *Photog* Joseph A. Dubray.

Cast: Carl Gantvoort *(Milt Dale)*, Claire Adams *(Helen Raynor)*, Robert McKim *(Harvey Riggs)*, Jean Hersholt *(Lem Beasley)*, Harry Lorraine *(Al Auchincloss)*, Eugenia Gilbert *(Bessie Beasley)*, Frank Hayes *(Los Vegas)*, Charlotte Pierce *(Bo Raynor)*, Charles B. Murphy *(Snake Anson)*, Frederick Starr *(Jim Wilson)*, Tote Du Crow *(Lone Wolf)*.

Western melodrama. Source: Zane Grey, *The Man of the Forest* (New York, 1920). In poor health, Al Auchincloss sends for his two nieces, Helen and Bo, and Milt Dale, who lives alone in the forest, to help round up the cattle. Helen's attraction to Milt annoys Harvey Riggs, who was sent to the ranch to be reformed but who has gotten involved with Beasley, a bootlegger, in a plot to secure control. Harvey gets rid of Milt by framing him and has the girls kidnaped; but when Harvey tries to poison Auchincloss, he is shot by a Los Vegas cowboy. Milt rescues the girls, and the forgery charge is proven false, thus leaving the path clear for Milt and Helen's romance. Animals serve for comic relief in several scenes. *Bootleggers. Ranchers. Uncles. Cowboys. Forgery. Frameup. Kidnaping. Bears. Monkeys. Lions.*

MAN OF THE FOREST F2.3414

Famous Players–Lasky. *Dist* Paramount Pictures. 27 Dec **1926** [c24 Dec 1926; LP23484]. Si; b&w. 35mm. 6 reels, 5,187 ft.

Pres by Adolph Zukor, Jesse L. Lasky. *Assoc Prod* B. P. Schulberg. *Dir* John Waters. *Screenplay* Fred Myton. *Adapt* Max Marcin. *Photog* C. Edgar Schoenbaum.

Cast: Jack Holt *(Milt Dale)*, Georgia Hale *(Nancy Raynor)*, El Brendel *(Horace Pipp)*, Warner Oland *(Clint Beasley)*, Tom Kennedy *(sheriff)*, George Fawcett *(Nancy's uncle)*, Ivan Christie *(Snake Anson)*, Bruce Gordon *(Jim Wilson)*, Vester Pegg *(Moses)*, Willard Cooley *(deputy sheriff)*, Guy Oliver *(first deputy)*, Walter Ackerman *(second deputy)*, Duke R. Lee *(Martin Mulvery)*.

Western melodrama. Source: Zane Grey, *Man of the Forest* (New York, 1920). Milt Dale discovers that Clint Beasley is scheming to kidnap Nancy Raynor, who is to inherit a ranch from her dying uncle. Dale outwits the gang by kidnaping the girl himself and taking her to his cabin. Nancy seizes his gun and has him jailed. Distressed over her uncle's death, she is easy prey for the amorous attentions of Beasley; but when she begins to mistrust him, Beasley takes her to his ranch. With the aid of his pet cougar, Dale escapes jail; at Beasley's ranch a struggle ensues, and Beasley is killed. Nancy, realizing Dale's innocence, admits her love for him, and they are united. *Uncles. Swindlers. Kidnaping. Inheritance. Cougars.*

THE MAN ON THE BOX F2.3415

Warner Brothers Pictures. 17 Oct **1925** [c12 Sep 1925; LP21819]. Si; b&w. 35mm. 8 reels, 7,481 ft.

Dir Charles Reisner. *Scen* Charles A. Logue. *Photog* Nick Barrows. *Asst Dir* Leslie Charlesworth.

Cast: Sydney Chaplin *(Bob Warburton)*, David Butler *(Bob's brother-in-law)*, Alice Calhoun *(Betty Annesly)*, Kathleen Calhoun *(Mrs. Lampton)*, Theodore Lorch *(Mr. Lampton)*, Helene Costello *(Bob's sister)*, E. J. Ratcliffe *(Colonel Annesly)*, Charles F. Reisner *(Badkoff)*, Charles Gerrard *(Count Karaloff)*, Henry Barrows *(Warburton, Sr.)*.

Comedy. Source: Harold MacGrath, *The Man on the Box* (New York, 1904). Bob Warburton, a wealthy young bachelor, falls in love with Betty Annesly and, in order to be near her, talks himself into a job as her father's gardener. Betty learns of his deception and, to teach him a lesson, insists that he serve at table for an important luncheon. Bob refuses, and Count Karaloff offers the loan of his butler. Bob learns that Badkoff, the butler, is an enemy agent assigned to steal the plans for a helicopter from Betty's father, Colonel Annesly. Disguising himself, Bob poses as a maid from an employment agency and protects the plans. Bob and Betty are later married. *Bachelors. Gardeners. Butlers. Foreign agents. Imposture. Female impersonation. Espionage. Helicopters.*

MAN POWER F2.3416

Paramount Famous Lasky Corp. 9 Jul **1927** [c9 Jul 1927; LP24172]. Si; b&w. 35mm. 6 reels, 5,617 ft.

Pres by Adolph Zukor, Jesse L. Lasky. *Assoc Prod* B. P. Schulberg. *Dir* Clarence Badger. *Screenplay* Louise Long. *Titl* George Marion, Jr. *Adapt* Ray Harris, Sam Mintz. *Photog* Edward Cronjager.

Cast: Richard Dix *(Tom Roberts)*, Mary Brian *(Alice Stoddard)*, Philip Strange *(Randall Lewis)*, Charles Hill Mailes *(Judson Stoddard)*, Oscar Smith *(Ptomaine)*, George Irving *(James Martin)*, Charles Clary *(Albert Rollins)*, Charles Schaeffer *(Reverend Guthrie)*.

Comedy melodrama. Source: Byron Morgan, "Man Power" (publication undetermined). Tom Roberts, an ex-officer of the Tank Corps, has become a drifter. He finds work, however, at the Stoddard Machinery Co., after rescuing Alice Stoddard at a train crossing, and becomes reacquainted with Ptomaine, formerly a cook in Tom's regiment. While pursuing a courtship with Alice, Tom discovers that the tractors manufactured by the company are malfunctioning as a result of the plotting of the manager, Randall Lewis, thereby threatening Stoddard with bankruptcy. Tom's knowledge of tanks enables him to perfect the tractor, and during a flood that threatens the village dam, he and Ptomaine use the tractor to save the town from disaster; Tom wins the girl. *Veterans. Wanderers. Cooks. Courtship. Bankruptcy. Tanks (armored cars). Tractors. Dams. Floods.*

MAN RUSTLIN' F2.3417

Independent Pictures. *Dist* Film Booking Offices of America. 10 Jan **1926** [c8 Jan 1926; LP22235]. Si; b&w. 35mm. 5 reels, 4,666 ft.

Dir Del Andrews. *Cont* Burl R. Tuttle, Jay Chapman. *Story* William Branch. *Photog* Art Reeves.

Cast: Bob Custer *(Buck Hayden)*, Florence Lee *(Mary Wilson)*, Jules Cowles *(Jim Tucker)*, Sam Allen *(Pop Geers)*, James Kelly *(Angus MacGregor)*, Pat Beggs *(Smudge Perkins)*, Howard Fay *(Weary)*, Skeeter Bill Robbins *(Slim)*.

Western comedy. At the urging of Mary Wilson, his schoolteacher sweetheart, Buck Hayden becomes a reporter for the local newspaper. In his quest for news, Bob goes after some bandits, gets caught in the crossfire of a feud, and recovers the loot from a Wells Fargo stagecoach robbery. Bob is so successful writing up his adventures that he becomes a syndicated columnist for an eastern newspaper, getting hitched to Mary to celebrate his new job. *Reporters. Schoolteachers. Columnists. Stagecoach robberies. Wells Fargo & Co.. Feuds.*

THE MAN SHE BROUGHT BACK F2.3418

Charles Miller Productions. *Dist* Playgoers Pictures. 24 Sep **1922** [c12 Aug 1922; LU18140]. Si; b&w. 35mm. 5 reels, 4,792 ft.

Dir Charles Miller. *Story-Scen* Col. Jasper Ewing Brady. *Photog* Lawrence E. Williams.

Cast: Earle Foxe *(John Ramsey)*, Doris Miller *(Margo)*, Frank Losee *(Fenton)*, Charles Mackay *(Major Shanley)*, Donald Russ *(Songatawa)*, Harry Lee *(Sergeant Hawkins)*, Frederick Burton *(Bruce Webster)*.

Northwest melodrama. Despite his cowardly streak, John joins the Royal Northwest Mounted Police. His courage fails him on his first assignment, and he is discharged in disgrace. He overcomes his fears, gets his man, and pursues a romance with Margo, his commander's daughter. *Cowardice. Northwest Mounted Police.*

THE MAN TAMER F2.3419

Universal Film Manufacturing Co. 30 May **1921** [c18 May 1921; LP16569]. Si; b&w. 35mm. 5 reels, 4,516 ft.

Dir Harry B. Harris. *Scen* A. P. Younger. *Photog* Earl M. Ellis.

Cast: Gladys Walton *(Kitty Horrigan)*, Rex De Roselli *(Jim Horrigan)*, William Welsh *(Hayden Delmar)*, C. B. Murphy *(Tim Murphy)*, J. Parker McConnell *(Charlie Parrish)*, Roscoe Karns *(Bradley P. Caldwell, Jr.)*, C. Norman Hammond *(Bradley P. Caldwell, Sr.)*.

Melodrama. Source: John Barton Oxford, "The Man-Tamer," in *Red Book* (30:96–102, Apr 1918). Kitty Horrigan's father, a lion tamer in Delmar's Circus, is maimed by one of his cats. Kitty continues the act alone but must resist the advances of both Delmar, the circus manager, and Bradley Caldwell, Sr., a profligate millionaire. When she leaves the circus, Caldwell engages her to "tame" his son, Bradley, Jr., and in the process she falls in love with the young man. When he resumes his drinking, she returns to the circus but is rescued from Delmar by the repentant young millionaire. *Millionaires. Lion tamers. Circus. Alcoholism.*

Note: A. P. Younger is also given screen credit for story; Universal records have been followed.

THE MAN THOU GAVEST ME *see* **THE ETERNAL STRUGGLE**

MAN TO MAN (Universal-Jewel) F2.3420

Universal Film Manufacturing Co. 20 Mar **1922** [c2 Mar 1922; LP17603]. Si; b&w. 35mm. 6 reels, 5,629 ft.

Pres by Carl Laemmle. *Dir* Stuart Paton. *Scen* George C. Hull. *Photog* William Thornley. *Art Dir* E. E. Sheeley.

Cast: Harry Carey *(Steve Packard)*, Lillian Rich *(Terry Temple)*, Charles Le Moyne *(Joe Blenham)*, Harold Goodwin *(Slim Barbee)*, Willis Robards *(Bill Royce)*.

Western melodrama. Source: Jackson Gregory, *Man to Man* (New York, 1920). Steven Packard, son of a wealthy Arizona rancher but a derelict of the South Seas, rescues an island woman from the brutal attentions of a Russian, and when the woman dies she leaves her young daughter in his care. Hearing that his father has died and left him his ranch and an inheritance, Steve returns home with the child, then goes to Arizona to claim his inheritance, endangered by his grandfather because of a family feud. The ranch foreman, Blenham, an agent of the grandfather, undermines his position on the ranch, discovers the hiding place of the inheritance, and involves Steve in a mortgage that threatens the ranch. He seeks to stampede Steve's cattle, but Steve exposes his villainy and wins over the grouchy grandfather and the heart of Terry Temple, a neighboring rancher. *Grandfathers. Ranch foremen. Inheritance. Ranches. South Sea Islands. Arizona.*

MAN TO MAN F2.3421

Warner Brothers Pictures. 6 Dec **1930** [c23 Nov 1930; LP1763]. Sd (Vitaphone); b&w. 35mm. 8 reels, 6,281 ft.

Dir Allan Dwan. *Screenplay-Dial* Joseph Jackson. *Photog* Ira Morgan. *Film Ed* George Marks. *Rec Engr* Clare A. Riggs.

Cast: Phillips Holmes *(Michael Bolton)*, Grant Mitchell *(Barber John Bolton)*, Lucille Powers *(Emily)*, Barbara Weeks *(Alice)*, Charles Sellon *(judge)*, Dwight Frye *(Vint Glade)*, Russell Simpson *(Uncle Cal)*, Paul Nicholson *(Ryan)*, Robert Emmett O'Connor *(sheriff)*, George Marion, Sr. *(Jim McCord)*, Otis Harlan *(Rip Henry)*, James Neill *(B. B. Beecham)*, Johnny Larkins *(Bildad)*.

Drama. Source: Ben Ames Williams, "Barber John's Boy" (publication undetermined). Michael Bolton, a handsome and popular college athlete, is compelled to leave school when it is discovered that his father, Barber John Bolton, is serving a prison term for murder. Returning to his hometown in Kentucky, Michael gets a job in Jim McCord's bank through the influence of his Uncle Cal after other businessmen have refused to hire him. He falls in love with Emily, the banker's secretary, greatly displeasing Vint, who tries to conceal his feelings. Soon Barber John is paroled on good conduct and is greeted by his old cronies, but Michael, feeling his father has placed a stigma on him, does not go to the station to meet him. When Barber John reopens his shop, he goes to the bank to change a large bill; the same day $2,000 is stolen from the bank. Thinking his father is guilty of the theft, Michael writes a confession to save him, then attempts to escape; but he is brought back in time to hear his father admit to the crime. Emily, however, exposes Vint, who confesses to the theft, thus exonerating both father and son and restoring the latter's faith in his father. *Students. Athletes. Barbers. Bankers. Bank clerks. Uncles. Secretaries. Smalltown life. Filial relations. Murder. Bank robberies. Parole. Kentucky.*

Note: Initially reviewed as *Barber John's Boy*.

THE MAN TRACKERS F2.3422

Universal Film Manufacturing Co. Jul **1921** [c8 Jul 1921; LP16753]. Si; b&w. 35mm. 5 reels, 4,329 ft.

Dir Edward Kull. *Scen* George Plympton. *Story* Edward Kull, George Plympton. *Photog* Jacob Kull.

Cast: George Larkin *(Jimmy Hearn)*, Josephine Hill *(Molly Killbride)*, Al Smith *(Hanley)*, Barney Furey *(Jules)*, Ruth Royce *(Lizette)*, Harold Holland *(Inspector)*, Ralph Fee McCullough *(Morgan)*.

Northwest melodrama. Molly Killbride, daughter of the inspector in the Royal Mounties, is in love with trooper Jimmy Hearn, but her father prefers that she marry Harry Morgan, a wealthy young civilian. Morgan, however, is allied with a gang of outlaws headed by Hanley, and when Morgan taunts Jimmy into a fist fight the gang causes him to be railroaded to prison for felonious assault. Meanwhile, Morgan gradually gains Molly's esteem, and she is turned against Jimmy. When Jimmy is released, he tracks Hanley to the mountains and overpowers him. Jimmy is reinstated by Jules, a halfwitted Indian who convinces the inspector of his innocence, and he regains Molly's love. *Gangs. Halfwits. Indians of North America. Northwest Mounted Police.*

MAN TROUBLE F2.3423

Fox Film Corp. 24 Aug **1930** [c7 Jun 1930; LP1373]. Sd (Movietone); b&w. 35mm. 8 reels, 7,800 ft.

Pres by William Fox. *Dir* Berthold Viertel. *Dial* George Manker Watters, Edwin Burke. *Adapt* George Manker Watters, Marion Orth. *Camera* Joseph August. *Sets* William S. Darling. *Film Ed* J. Edwin Robbins. *Songs: "Now I Ask You," "You Got Nobody To Love," "Pick Yourself Up—Brush Yourself Off," "You Do, Don't You?" "What's the Use of Living Without Love?"* James Hanley, Joseph McCarthy. *Rec Engr* Donald Flick. *Asst Dir* J. Edmund Grainger. *Cost* Sophie Wachner.

Cast: Milton Sills *(Mac)*, Dorothy Mackaill *(Joan)*, Kenneth MacKenna *(Graham)*, Sharon Lynn *(Trixie)*, Roscoe Karns *(Scott)*, Oscar Apfel *(Eddie)*, James Bradbury, Jr. *(Goofy)*, Harvey Clark *(Uncle Joe)*, Edythe Chapman *(Aunt Maggie)*, Lew Harvey *(Chris)*.

Melodrama. Source: Ben Ames Williams, "A Very Practical Joke," in *Saturday Evening Post* (198:36–37, 5 Dec 1925). Mac, a New York gunman and bootlegger, saves the life of a down-and-out singer named Joan; and taking a liking to her, he gives her a job in his cabaret. Meanwhile, attracted by the folksy Christmas column of newspaperman George Graham, Joan is persuaded to join him in visiting his Aunt Maggie and Uncle Joe, who mistake them for a married couple. But Mac learns of the incident and takes her away from the country retreat. Later, Graham expresses his faith in Joan and confronts Mac at the cabaret, demanding that he be allowed to see her. Learning of a plot by a rival bootleg faction to kill him, Mac goes to shoot it out with the gang and dies, giving the young couple his blessing. *Bootleggers. Singers. Columnists. Courtship. Cabarets. Christmas. New York City.*

THE MAN UNCONQUERABLE F2.3424

Famous Players–Lasky. *Dist* Paramount Pictures. 2 Jul **1922** [c12 Jul 1922; LP18049]. Si; b&w. 35mm. 6 reels, 5,795 ft.

Pres by Jesse L. Lasky. *Dir* Joseph Henabery. *Scen* Julien Josephson. *Story* Hamilton Smith. *Photog* Faxon M. Dean.

Cast: Jack Holt *(Robert Kendall)*, Sylvia Breamer *(Rita Durand)*, Clarence Burton *(Nilsson)*, Ann Schaeffer *(duenna)*, Jean De Briac *(Perrier)*, Edwin Stevens *(Michaels)*, Willard Louis *(Governor of Papeete)*.

Melodrama. New Yorker Robert Kendall visits a pearl fishery he has inherited on Papeete in the South Seas to investigate rumors of mismanagement and pearl theft, and there he meets Rita Durand, a French girl, her father, and Perrier, a suave Frenchman. Perrier and Nilsson, an employee of the fishery, find a valuable pearl and attempt to hide it from Durand, but he forces them to turn it over to him. Nilsson stabs Durand, steals the pearl, and tries to blame Kendall for Durand's death. Nilsson and Perrier shoot Kendall, leaving him for dead, but he follows them to Rita's house, shoots Nilsson, and, rescuing Rita, kills Perrier in a fistic struggle. *New Yorkers. Theft. Murder. Pearl fisheries. South Seas. Papeete.*

THE MAN UNDER COVER F2.3425

Universal Film Manufacturing Co. 10 Apr **1922** [c4 Apr 1922; LP17728]. Si; b&w. 35mm. 5 reels, 4,566 ft.

Pres by Carl Laemmle. *Dir* Tod Browning. *Scen* Harvey Gates. *Story* Louis Victor Eytinge. *Photog* Virgil Miller.

Cast: Herbert Rawlinson *(Paul Porter)*, George Hernandez *(Daddy Moffat)*, William Courtwright *(Mayor Harper)*, George Webb *(Jones Wiley)*, Edwin Booth Tilton *("Coal Oil" Chase)*, Gerald Pring *(Holt Langdon)*, Barbara Bedford *(Margaret Langdon)*, Willis Marks *(Colonel Culpepper)*, Betty Eliason, Betty Stone *(The Kiddies)*.

Crook melodrama. Paul Porter and his swindler friend Daddy Moffat visit Paul's hometown and find an old friend, Holt Langdon, local bank cashier, in trouble over oil investments. Because of his friendship and love for Langdon's sister, Margaret, Paul resolves to help him by robbing the bank. Finding Holt a victim of suicide inside the bank, he makes it appear that Holt died defending the premises. Paul determines to reform, and he aids Margaret by buying a local newspaper. When two confidence men induce the populace to invest in a fake oil well scheme, Paul and Daddy Moffat, with the help of lawyer Colonel Culpepper, start another phony oil well and force the confidence men to buy it out at a high price. Paul returns the townspeople's money and tells Margaret the story; she then agrees to marry him. *Bank clerks. Confidence men. Oil wells. Smalltown life. Suicide. Bank robberies. Newspapers.*

THE MAN UPSTAIRS F2.3426

Warner Brothers Pictures. 22 Jan **1926** [c21 Jan 1926; LP22285]. Si; b&w. 35mm. 7 reels.

Dir Roy Del Ruth. *Screenplay* E. T. Lowe, Jr. *Photog* Allan Thompson.

Cast: Monte Blue *(Geoffrey West)*, Dorothy Devore *(Marion Larnard)*, Helen Dunbar *(Aunt Hattie)*, John Roche *(Captain Fraser-Freer)*, Stanley Taylor *(Norman Fraser-Freer)*, Carl Stockdale *(Enright)*, Charles Conklin *(Mose)*.

Comedy-drama. Source: Earl Derr Biggers, "The Man Upstairs" (publication undetermined). Geoffrey West, a traveler and adventurer, sees a girl in a London hotel and uses the personals column of a newspaper to get in touch with her. The girl, Marion Larnard, then sets a test for Geoffrey: he is to write her a letter each day for 5 days and, if he proves himself to be an interesting fellow, she will have dinner with him. As a joke, Geoffrey convinces Marion that he has done away with a certain Captain Fraser-Freer; Marion is, at first, quite concerned, but when she realizes that Geoffrey is jesting, she decides to teach him a lesson. She arranges with Fraser-Freer to disappear and has Geoffrey arrested for his murder. Letting Geoffrey fret for a while, Marion eventually arranges for his release and assures him that he has indeed proved himself to be an interesting fellow. *Adventurers. Murder. Agony column. Hoaxes. Injustice. Murder. Newspapers.*

MAN WANTED F2.3427

Herbert L. Steiner. *Dist* Clark-Cornelius Corp. 13 Oct **1922.** Si; b&w. 35mm. 4,956 ft.

Prod Herbert L. Steiner. *Dir* John Francis Dillon.

Cast: Arthur Housman, Frank Losee, Flora Finch, Huntley Gordon,

Diana Allen.

Comedy-drama. "Helen Westmore's dad resolves that his daughter's future husband must be a worker. This starts Helen's admirer, Edgar Little, whose dad has oodles of money, in search of a job. He lands first as a soda dispenser and later as a handy man about an Old Maids' Retreat. While attending a performance Edgar is hypnotized by a Prof. Kosoff. Edgar believes himself to be King Solomon. The count, who has kidnapped Helen, believes Edgar insane. Edgar finds Helen missing, locates her, and by feigning insanity rescues her from the count and returns her to her father. All ends well for Edgar and Helen." (*Motion Picture News Booking Guide*, 4:70, Apr 1923.) *Soda clerks. Spinsters. Filial relations. Hypnotism. Insanity. Kidnaping.*

THE MAN WHO **F2.3428**

Metro Pictures. 4 Jul **1921** [c5 Jul 1921; LP16738]. Si; b&w. 35mm. 6 reels.

Dir Maxwell Karger. *Scen* June Mathis. *Adapt* Arthur J. Zellner. *Photog* Arthur Martinelli. *Tech Dir* M. P. Staulcup.

Cast: Bert Lytell *(Bedford Mills)*, Lucy Cotton *(Helen Jessop)*, Virginia Valli *(Mary Turner)*, Frank Currier *(St. John Jessop)*, Tammany Young *("Shorty" Mulligan)*, Fred Warren *("Bud" Carter)*, Clarence Elmer *(Radford Haynes)*, William Roselle *("Bing" Horton)*, Mary Louise Beaton *(Sarah Butler)*, Frank Strayer *(Jack Hyde)*.

Comedy. Source: Lloyd Osbourne, "The Man Who," in *Saturday Evening Post* (193:3–5, 1 Jan 1921). Bedford Mills, wounded in France, meets aristocratic Helen Jessop at a party given by her father for returning war heroes in his Fifth Avenue home. Bedford falls violently in love with Helen, but discovering that he is only a poor bank clerk she insists that he must first become a man of importance. He decides that, in view of the soaring prices of shoes, he will refuse to wear shoes on the street. Causing a sensation, he is arrested and then released, but all New York reads of his exploits. Although scorned by Miss Jessop, he is accompanied on his barefoot strolls by Mary Turner, a neighboring artist who believes in his campaign and loves him despite the fact that her father is president of the Shoe Trust. *Bank clerks. Veterans. Artists. Shoes. Trusts. Social conformity. Price control. New York City.*

THE MAN WHO CAME BACK **F2.3429**

Fox Film Corp. 17 Aug **1924** [c30 Jun 1924; LP20419]. Si; b&w. 35mm. 9 reels, 8,293 ft.

Pres by William Fox. *Dir* Emmett Flynn. *Scen* Edmund Goulding. *Photog* Lucien Andriot.

Cast: George O'Brien *(Henry Potter)*, Dorothy Mackaill *(Marcelle)*, Cyril Chadwick *(Captain Trevelan)*, Ralph Lewis *(Thomas Potter)*, Emily Fitzroy *(Aunt Isabel)*, Harvey Clark *(Charles Reisling)*, Edward Piel *(Sam Shu Sin)*, David Kirby *(Gibson)*, James Gordon *(Captain Gallon)*, Walter Wilkinson *(Henry Potter, age 4)*, Brother Miller *(Henry Potter, age 12)*.

Melodrama. Source: John Fleming Wilson, *The Man Who Came Back* (New York, 1912). Jules Eckert Goodman, *The Man Who Came Back* (a play; 1916). Henry Potter is banished from his home because of his unregenerate character. Marcelle, a girl who loves him, also leaves home, and they meet again in Shanghai, where she has become addicted to morphine. They awaken each other's self-respect, and her love brings about his redemption and reconciliation with his father. *Degeneracy. Filial relations. Narcotics. Morphine. Shanghai.*

THE MAN WHO FIGHTS ALONE **F2.3430**

Famous Players–Lasky. *Dist* Paramount Pictures. 15 Sep **1924** [c15 Aug 1924; LP20494]. Si; b&w. 35mm. 7 reels, 6,337 ft.

Pres by Adolph Zukor, Jesse L. Lasky. *Dir* Wallace Worsley. *Scen* Jack Cunningham. *Photog* L. Guy Wilky.

Cast: William Farnum *(John Marble)*, Lois Wilson *(Marion)*, Edward Horton *(Bob Alten)*, Lionel Belmore *(Meggs)*, Barlowe Borland *(Mike O'Hara)*, George Irving *(Dr. Raymond)*, Dawn O'Day *(Dorothy)*, Rose Tapley *(Aunt Louise)*, Frank Farrington *(Struthers)*.

Melodrama. Source: William Blacke and James Shelley Hamilton, "The Miracle of Hate" (publication undetermined). Construction engineer John Marble is stricken by paralysis and imagines the growth of love between his wife and his best friend, Bob Alten. Although bent on suicide, the shock of seeing his wife and child endangered on a broken bridge causes him to recover from his illness and discover that his suspicions are unfounded. *Engineers. Marriage. Paralysis. Jealousy. Suicide.*

THE MAN WHO FOUND HIMSELF **F2.3431**

Famous Players–Lasky. *Dist* Paramount Pictures. 23 Aug **1925** [New York premiere; released 28 Sep; c19 Oct 1925; LP21914]. Si; b&w. 35mm. 7 reels, 7,354 ft.

Pres by Adolph Zukor, Jesse L. Lasky. *Dir* Alfred E. Green. *Screenplay* Tom J. Geraghty. *Story* Booth Tarkington. *Photog* Alvin Wyckoff. *Art Dir* Walter E. Keller.

Cast: Thomas Meighan *(Tom Macauley)*, Virginia Valli *(Nora Brooks)*, Frank Morgan *(Lon Morris)*, Ralph Morgan *(Edwin Macauley, Jr.)*, Charles Stevenson *(Edwin Macauley, Sr.)*, Julia Hoyt *(Evelyn Corning)*, Lynne Fontanne *(Mrs. Macauley, Jr.)*, Mildred Ryan *(Polly Brooks)*, Hugh Cameron *(Hoboken Williams, The Optimist)*, Victor Moore *(Humpty Dumpty Smith, The Pessimist)*, Russell Griffin *(Tom Macauley, Jr.)*, Norman Trevor *(Commodore Branding)*, John Harrington *(warden of Sing Sing)*.

Melodrama. Tom Macauley and his younger brother, Edwin, are directors in their father's bank. Edwin speculates with the bank's funds, but banker Lon Morris, a supposed friend, plots successfully to have Tom shoulder the blame. In prison, Tom becomes a trusty, but he breaks out when he learns that Morris is to marry Nora Brooks, his fiancée. He confronts Morris and Nora with the truth, beats up Morris for good luck, and returns to prison. His father dies heartbroken, and Tom is scorned by Edwin's wife when he is released. With the aid of two prison buddies (The Optimist and The Pessimist), Tom breaks into the Macauley bank (now controlled by Morris), steals funds, plants them in Morris' house, and notifies the bank examiners. Morris, who actually has been embezzling funds, goes to the bank to obtain more money before making a getaway. He is shot by a watchman; Tom learns that Nora has been a wife in name only; and he marries her. *Bankers. Bank directors. Scapegoats. Trusties. Speculation. Embezzlement. Prison escapes. Sing Sing.*

Note: Working title: *Up the River.*

THE MAN WHO LAUGHS **F2.3432**

Universal Pictures. 27 Apr **1927** [New York premiere; released 4 Nov 1928; c7 May 1928; LP25227]. Mus score and sd eff (Movietone); b&w. 35mm. 10 reels, 10,195 ft. [Also si.]

Pres by Carl Laemmle. *Prod Supv* Paul Kohner. *Dir* Paul Leni. *Story Supv* Dr. Bela Sekely. *Scen* J. Grubb Alexander. *Titl* Walter Anthony. *Adapt (see note)* Charles E. Whittaker, Marion Ward, May McLean. *Photog* Gilbert Warrenton. *Tech & Art Dir* Charles D. Hall, Joseph Wright, Thomas F. O'Neill. *Film Ed* Maurice Pivar, Edward Cahn. *Song: "When Love Comes Stealing"* Walter Hirsch, Lew Pollack, Erno Rapee. *Cost* David Cox, Vera West. *Prod Staff* John M. Voshell, Jay Marchant, Louis Frielander. *Tech Research* Professor R. H. Newlands.

Cast: Conrad Veidt *(Gwynplaine)*, Mary Philbin *(Dea)*, Olga Baclanova *(Duchess Josiana)*, Josephine Crowell *(Queen Anne)*, George Siegmann *(Dr. Hardquannone)*, Brandon Hurst *(Barkilphedro, the Jester)*, Sam De Grasse *(King James)*, Stuart Holmes *(Lord Dirry-Noir)*, Cesare Gravina *(Ursus)*, Nick De Ruiz *(Wapentake)*, Edgar Norton *(Lord High Chancellor)*, Torben Meyer *(The Spy)*, Julius Molnar, Jr. *(Gwynplaine, as a child)*, Charles Puffy *(innkeeper)*, Frank Puglia, Jack Goodrich *(clowns)*, Carmen Costello *(Dea's mother)*, Zimbo *(Homo, the Wolf)*.

Melodrama. Source: Victor Hugo, *L'Homme qui rit* (1869). Gwynplaine, a small boy, his features distorted into a permanent wide grin by order of James II because his father is a political enemy, becomes a famous clown. He and Dea, a blind girl, travel with the van of Ursus, a mountebank. Romance develops until Gwynplaine discovers he is heir to a peerage. Barkilphedro, attached to Queen Anne's court, discovers Gwynplaine's claim to the title. The queen, seeing an opportunity to discipline her half sister, Duchess Josiana, has Gwynplaine restored to his wealth and decrees that he shall marry Josiana. Gwynplaine renounces his title, defies Josiana, and follows Dea and Ursus, who have been banished from England. In his flight Gwynplaine is pursued by soldiers of the queen and Barkilphedro. Escaping unharmed, he finds Dea just as the boat she and Ursus are taking is about to leave. *Clowns. Charlatans. Nobility. Blindness. Ugliness. James II (England). Anne (England). Wolves. Dogs.*

Note: Company records indicate that, although uncredited, Charles Whittaker, Marion Ward, and May McLean worked on the adaptation.

THE MAN WHO MARRIED HIS OWN WIFE **F2.3433**

Universal Film Manufacturing Co. 1 May **1922** [c28 Apr 1922; LP17810]. Si; b&w. 35mm. 5 reels, 4,313 ft.

Dir Stuart Paton. *Scen* George Hively. *Photog* Arthur Reeves.

Cast: Frank Mayo *(Jasper Marsden [John Morton])*, Sylvia Breamer

(Elsie Haynes), Marie Crisp *(Miss Muriel Blythe)*, Howard Crampton *(Judge Lawrence)*, Francis McDonald *(Freddie Needham)*, Joe Girard *(John Marsden)*.

Melodrama. Source: John Fleming Wilson and Mary Ashe Miller, "The Man Who Married His Own Wife," in *Hearst's International* (72:33–37, Apr 1922). John Morton, a sea captain, saves the life of heiress Elsie Haynes when she is shipwrecked. When the two reach port, they are married despite Morton's disfigured face, injured in rescuing the girl. Morton grows wealthy, but believing that his wife shuns him because of his ugliness and uncouth manners, he disappears and is believed to be dead. During his absence, he has plastic surgery performed on his face, returning it to a natural contour, and is educated in social graces. Then, returning to his wife, he discovers that she has always loved him and that to regain her love he must struggle against her memory of him as he was. *Sea captains. Plastic surgery. Marriage. Ugliness. Shipwrecks.*

THE MAN WHO PAID **F2.3434**

Dist Producers Security Corp. Mar **1922.** Si; b&w. 35mm. 5 reels.

Dir Oscar Apfel. *Story-Scen* Marion Brooks.

Cast: Wilfred Lytell *(Oliver Thornton)*, Norma Shearer *(Jeanne, his wife)*, Florence Rogan *(Little Jeanne, their child)*, Fred C. Jones *(Louis Duclos, a trapper)*, Bernard Siegel *(Anton Barbier, his partner)*, David Hennessy *(McNeill, Oliver's storekeeper)*, Charles Beyer *(Guy Thornton, Oliver's brother)*, Erminie Gagnon *(Lizette, nurse girl at Thornton's)*, Frank Montgomery *(Songo, an Indian guide)*.

Northwest melodrama. "In the desolated wilds is a Trading Post, to which Oliver Thornton went to seek obscurity after being falsely convicted of a crime in the States. Fate brought him a wife, a girl from the wilds, and soon a child, and all was happy until his prison record became known to a villainous trapper who used this information to turn Thorton's wife against him. Failing in this, Duclos, the trapper, and his Indian aides, kidnap the wife. Thornton's brother arrives at the Post with news of Oliver's name being cleared of the crime for which he was innocently convicted. The two brothers rescue Oliver's wife and Duclos, the trapper, is killed by one of the Indians whom he had double-crossed." (*Moving Picture World*, 25 Mar 1922, p404.) *Trappers. Brothers. Indians of North America. Reputation. Kidnaping. Injustice. Trading posts. Canada.*

THE MAN WHO PLAYED GOD **F2.3435**

Distinctive Productions. *Dist* United Artists. ca24 Sep **1922** [Cleveland premiere; released 1 Oct; c1 Sep 1922; LP18468]. Si; b&w. 35mm. 6 reels, 5,855 ft.

Dir Harmon Weight. *Scen* Forrest Halsey. *Photog* Harry A. Fischbeck. *Art Dir* Clark Robinson.

Cast: George Arliss *(John Arden)*, Ann Forrest *(Marjory Blaine)*, Ivan Simpson *(Carter)*, Edward Earle *(Philip Stevens)*, Effie Shannon *(Mildred Arden)*, Miriam Battista *(a little girl)*, Mickey Bennett *(a little boy)*, Mary Astor *(a young woman)*, Pierre Gendron *(a young man)*, Margaret Seddon *(an old woman)*, J. D. Walsh *(an old man)*.

Drama. Source: Jules Eckert Goodman, *The Silent Voice* (New York opening: 29 Dec 1914). At the height of his success musician John Arden loses his hearing as the result of an explosion. His young wife's devotion is sorely tested by his melancholy and cynicism, but her sense of duty prevents Marjorie from leaving him for Philip Stevens. At the point of suicide, John discovers that other people have greater problems, and he turns to philanthropy. His hearing is restored after a fall, and John realizes his wife's loyalty. *Musicians. Deafness. Philanthropy.*

THE MAN WHO PLAYED SQUARE **F2.3436**

Fox Film Corp. 23 Nov **1924** [c23 Nov 1924; LP20820]. Si; b&w. 35mm. 7 reels, 6,500 ft.

Pres by William Fox. *Dir* Al Santell. *Scen* John Stone. *Story* William Wallace Cook.

Cast: Buck Jones *(Matt Black)*, Ben Hendricks, Jr. *(Spangler)*, David Kirby *(Piggy)*, Hank Mann *(The Cook)*, Howard Foster *(Spoffard)*, William Scott *(Steve)*, Wanda Hawley *(Bertie)*.

Western melodrama. Fighting over the rich Red Eagle gold mine, Steve and Spoffard, its coowners, mortally wound each other. In his final moments, Steve signs over his half-interest claim in the mine to his friend Matt Black; the other half of the mine is inherited by Spoffard's daughter, Bertie. Matt goes to the mine and asks for work, concealing his identity in order to protect himself. During a fire in the mine, Bertie is trapped below ground, and Matt rescues her. When the miners are later incited to riot by the dishonest foreman, Spangler, Matt helps to put it down and then protects Bertie from a villainous attack by Spangler, killing him in a fight. Matt then realizes that he loves Bertie and tears up his claim to the mine; but Bertie, who has come to love Matt in return, offers to marry him, giving him a whole interest in the mine. *Gold mines. Inheritance. Mine disasters.*

THE MAN WHO SAW TOMORROW **F2.3437**

Famous Players–Lasky. *Dist* Paramount Pictures. ca29 Oct **1922** [New York premiere; released 5 Nov; c1 Nov 1922; LP18360]. Si; b&w. 35mm. 7 reels, 6,993 ft.

Pres by Adolph Zukor. *Dir* Alfred E. Green. *Adapt* Will M. Ritchey, Frank Condon. *Story* Perley Poore Sheehan, Frank Condon. *Photog* Alvin Wyckoff.

Cast: Thomas Meighan *(Burke Hammond)*, Theodore Roberts *(Capt. Morgan Pring)*, Leatrice Joy *(Rita Pring)*, Albert Roscoe *(Jim McLeod)*, Alec Francis *(Sir William De Vry)*, June Elvidge *(Lady Helen Deene)*, Eva Novak *(Vonia)*, Laurance Wheat *(Larry Camden)*, John Miltern *(Professor Jansen)*, Robert Brower *(Bishop)*, Edward Patrick *(Botsu)*, Jacqueline Dyris *(Maya)*.

Romantic drama. In trying to decide whom to marry—Rita Pring, the daughter of a South Seas ship captain, or Lady Helen Deene, an Englishwoman with wealth and influence—Burke Hammond consults Professor Jansen, a psychologist. Jansen induces in Burke a hypnotic trance in which he sees his future with each of the women. If he marries Helen, he will have fame, material comforts, and political power, but no love from his wife. If he marries Rita, his life will be humble but happy until Captain Pring's first mate, Jim McLeod, stirs up trouble and a shot is fired at Burke. Jansen cannot tell if the shot means death to Burke; nevertheless, Burke unhesitatingly chooses life with Rita. *Psychologists. Hypnotism. Divination. Marriage.*

THE MAN WHO WAITED **F2.3438**

Jacob Wilk. *Dist* Playgoers Pictures. 19 Nov **1922** [c11 Nov 1922; LU18391]. Si; b&w. 35mm. 5 reels, 4,064 ft.

Dir-Story Edward I. Luddy.

Cast: Frank Braidwood *(Frank Magee)*, Inez MacDonald *(June Rance)*, Jay Morley *(Joe Rance)*, Jack Pierce *(Black Pete)*, Vonda Phelps *(June, as a baby)*, Dan Maines *(Sandy)*, Joe Bonner *(Manuel Sánchez)*, Milla Davenport *(Madre Sánchez)*.

Western melodrama. Frank Magee teams up with Sandy, his father's ex-partner, and falls in love with June Rance, daughter of his father's murderer. Sánchez and Black Pete learn from Sandy the whereabouts of his mine, kill Rance, and attempt to file a claim on the mine. When Frank tries to overtake them, he is too late but finds that June has filed ahead of the Mexicans. *Miners. Mexicans. Mine claims. Murder.*

THE MAN WHO WON **F2.3439**

Fox Film Corp. 26 Aug **1923** [c23 Aug 1923; LP19334]. Si; b&w. 35mm. 5 reels, 5,050 ft.

Pres by William Fox. *Dir* William A. Wellman. *Scen* Ewart Adamson. *Photog* Joseph August. *Asst Dir* Ed Bernoudy.

Cast: Dustin Farnum *(Wild Bill)*, Jacqueline Gadsden *(Jessie)*, Lloyd Whitlock *("Lord" James)*, Ralph Cloninger *(Scipio, known as "Zip")*, Mary Warren *(Birdie)*, Pee Wee Holmes *(Toby Jenks)*, Harvey Clark *(Sunny Oaks)*, Lon Poff *(Sandy Joyce)*, Andy Waldron *(Minkie)*, Ken Maynard *(Conroy)*, Muriel McCormac, Mickey McBan *(The Twins)*, Bob Marks *(The Drunkard)*.

Western melodrama. Source: Ridgwell Cullum, *Twins of Suffering Creek* (Philadelphia, 1912). Wild Bill, a gambler, promises to protect the children of Scipio, an unlucky miner who sets out to find "Lord" James, a bandit who stole Jessie, his wife. Toby, Sunny, and Sandy—three gambler friends of Bill's—help him take care of the children. To give Scipio a chance to get Jessie away from James, Bill drives the stage filled with gold to the bank in town, counting upon James and his gang to follow him. James's gang holds up the stage, and Bill shoots them all. Scipio returns home with his repentant wife, but Bill is shot and dies when he reaches the bank. Scipio finds oil on his land, and he and Jessie look forward to a happy future. *Gamblers. Bandits. Miners. Marriage. Oil lands.*

THE MAN WITH TWO MOTHERS **F2.3440**

Goldwyn Pictures. Feb **1922** [c11 Feb 1922; LP17543]. Si; b&w. 35mm. 5 reels, 4,423 ft.

Dir Paul Bern. *Scen* Julien Josephson. *Story* Alice Duer Miller. *Photog* Percy Hilburn.

Cast: Cullen Landis *(Dennis O'Neill)*, Sylvia Breamer *(Claire Mordaunt)*, Mary Alden *(Widow O'Neill)*, Hallam Cooley *(Richey)*, Fred Huntly *(Butler)*, Laura La Varnie *(Mrs. Bryan)*, Monte Collins *(Tim Donohue)*, William Elmer *(Clancy)*.

Comedy-drama. Dennis O'Neill comes to America from Ireland at the request of his wealthy aunt, who intends to make him heir to the family fortune accrued from a junk business, but Mrs. Bryan objects to the presence of his widowed mother, who reminds her of their humble origins. Claire, niece of Mrs. Bryan, supports Dennis in his determination not to abandon his mother, and he installs Mrs. O'Neill in a nearby apartment of Tim Donohue, a friend from the old country, from whose window she can signal to Dennis. Dennis discovers that Hansen, manager of the junk firm, and his assistant, Richey, a suitor of Claire's, are padding the payroll. He finds that his affections for Claire are reciprocated, but Richey informs her that he is keeping another girl in the Donohue apartment. Dennis produces his mother, takes vengeance on Richey, and wins Claire—all to the satisfaction of Mrs. Bryan. *Irish. Junk dealers. Filial relations. Inheritance.*

THE MAN WITHOUT A CONSCIENCE **F2.3441**

Warner Brothers Pictures. 7 Jun **1925** [c21 Feb 1925; LP21176]. Si; b&w. 35mm. 7 reels, 7,182 ft.

Dir James Flood. *Adapt* Hope Loring, Louis Duryea Lighton. *Story* Max Kretzer.

Cast: Willard Louis *(Amos Mason)*, Irene Rich *(Shirley Graves)*, June Marlowe *(Ann Sherman)*, John Patrick *(Douglas White)*, Robert Agnew *(James Warren)*, Helen Dunbar *(Mrs. Graves)*, Kate Price *(Mrs. McBride)*.

Melodrama. Ruthlessly determined to succeed at any cost, Amos Mason comes to New York with his fiancée, Ann Sherman. By unscrupulous dealings and with the use of Ann's savings, Amos meets with considerable success and casts aside Ann, who is forced to take a job as maid in the Graves mansion. Amos begins to court Shirley Graves and causes Ann's dismissal. Mrs. Graves persuades Shirley to marry Amos, despite her love for the penniless Douglas White. Ann marries James Warren, an architect, whom Amos hires to build a mansion, and Ann tells Shirley of Amos' previous perfidy. Shirley has an affair with Douglas White but becomes disgusted with illicit sex when she believes him to be unfaithful to her. Amos' schemes fall flat, and he is arrested for swindling. In prison he repents, Shirley's attitude toward him softens, and they are reconciled when he is freed. *Housemaids. Swindlers. Architects. Infidelity. New York City.*

THE MAN WITHOUT A COUNTRY **F2.3442**

Fox Film Corp. c18 Jan **1925** [LP21146]. Si; b&w. 35mm. 10 reels, 10,000 ft.

Dir Rowland V. Lee. *Adapt-Scen* Robert N. Lee. *Photog* G. O. Post.

Cast: Edward Hearn *(Lieutenant Nolan)*, Pauline Starke *(Anne Bissell)*, Lucy Beaumont *(Mrs. Nolan)*, Richard Tucker *(Aaron Burr)*, Earl Metcalf *(Lieutenant Riddle)*, Edward Coxen *(Lieutenant Harper)*, Wilfred Lucas *(Major Bissell)*, Francis Powers *(Colonel Morgan)*, Harvey Clark *(Peter)*, William Walling *(Captain Shaw)*, William Conklin *(Captain Danforth)*, Edward Peil *(Captain Kearney)*, Albert Hart *(President Jefferson)*, Emmett King *(President Monroe)*, George Billings *(President Lincoln)*.

Historical drama. Source: Edward Everett Hale, *The Man Without a Country* (Boston, 1865). Early in the 19th century, Lieutenant Nolan becomes involved in the Burr conspiracy. When Burr is tried for treason, Nolan refuses to reaffirm his allegiance to the United States and declares openly that he hopes never again to see or hear anything of the United States. He is court-martialed and sentenced to be placed on an American warship, never again to see his native land, or to hear mention of it. Years pass: Nolan is transfered from ship to ship in the Navy and sees action with Decatur at Algiers and later in an encounter with a pirate ship. Nolan's sweetheart, Anne Bissell, appeals in vain to a succession of Presidents to have him pardoned. When the Civil War begins, Nolan is a broken old man, passionate in his love for his country. He is finally pardoned by President Lincoln, but he dies on receipt of the news. *Treason. Courts-martial. United States Navy. Aaron Burr. Thomas Jefferson. James Monroe. Abraham Lincoln.*

THE MAN WITHOUT A HEART **F2.3443**

Banner Productions. 1 or 17 Sep **1924** [c10 Sep 1924; LP20579]. Si; b&w. 35mm. 6 reels, 6,000 ft.

Dir Burton King. *Adapt* Harry Chandlee. *Photog* Edward Paul.

Cast: Kenneth Harlan *(Rufus Asher)*, Jane Novak *(Barbara Wier)*, David Powell *(Edmund Hyde)*, Faire Binney *(Linda Hyde)*, Bradley Barker *(Hugh Langley)*, Tommy Tremaine *(Margo Hume)*, Mary McCall *(Fanny Van Dyke)*, Muriel Ruddell *(Jane Wilkins)*, Tom Blake *(Pat O'Toole)*.

Romantic drama. Source: Ruby Mildred Ayres, *The Man Without a Heart* (New York, 1924). When Rufus Asher suspects that Barbara Wier is plotting with his sister's husband, Edmund Hyde, he abducts Barbara and takes her to a lonely mountain retreat. Mistaking Rufus for a vagabond, Barbara shoots him, then nurses him back to health, explaining that she and Edmund were trying to stop an elopement of Edmund's wife with another man, Hugh Langley. *Brother-sister relationship. Abduction. Infidelity.*

MAN, WOMAN, AND SIN **F2.3444**

Metro-Goldwyn-Mayer Pictures. 19 Nov **1927** [c29 Nov 1927; LP24744]. Si; b&w. 35mm. 7 reels, 6,280 ft.

Dir-Story Monta Bell. *Scen* Alice D. G. Miller. *Titl* John Colton. *Photog* Percy Hilburn. *Sets* Cedric Gibbons, Merrill Pye. *Film Ed* Blanche Sewell. *Wardrobe* Gilbert Clark.

Cast: John Gilbert *(Al Whitcomb)*, Jeanne Eagels *(Vera Worth)*, Gladys Brockwell *(Mrs. Whitcomb)*, Marc MacDermott *(Bancroft)*, Philip Anderson *(Al Whitcomb, as a child)*, Hayden Stevenson *(The Star Reporter)*, Charles K. French *(The City Editor)*, Aileen Manning.

Drama. Al Whitcomb, a poor boy who grew up in the slums, began his career folding newspapers. When he is a reporter, he falls in love with Vera Worth, the society editor, unaware that the rent on her apartment is being paid by the newspaper's owner. While visiting her, Al kills the owner in self-defense, but Vera perjures herself at the trial to protect her reputation. However, she later tells the court the truth, thereby freeing Al. *Reporters. Newspapers. Slums. Negro life. Manslaughter. Perjury.*

MAN, WOMAN, AND WIFE **F2.3445**

Universal Pictures. 13 Jan **1929** [c28 May 1928; LP25311]. Mus score & sd eff (Movietone); b&w. 35mm. 7 reels, 6,589 ft. [Also si; 6,674 ft.]

Dir Edward Laemmle. *Story Supv* J. G. Hawks. *Story-Scen* Charles Logue. *Titl* Walter Anthony. *Photog* Ben Reynolds. *Film Ed* Daniel Mandell. *Song: "Love Can Never Die"* Herman Ruby, Joseph Cherniavsky.

Cast—First Version: Norman Kerry *(Rance Rogers)*, Pauline Starke *(Julia)*, Marion Nixon *(Bella Rogers)*, Byron Douglas *(Senator Blake)*, Kenneth Harlan *(Bill)*, Crauford Kent *(Wade)*.

Cast—Final Version: Norman Kerry *(Ralph Brandon)*, Pauline Starke *(Rita)*, Marion Nixon *(Helen Brandon)*, Byron Douglas *(Senator Blake)*, Kenneth Harlan *(Jack Mason)*, Crauford Kent *(Ward Rogers)*.

Society melodrama. Suggested by: Arthur Somers Roche, "Fallen Angels," in *Red Book* (vol 49, May–Sep 1927). Helen Brandon, an unhappily married woman, marries former suitor Jack Mason when her husband, Ralph, is killed in action. The report of Ralph's death is false; he returns to the States, a deserter, under an assumed name and becomes a derelict. Rita, a former sweetheart, rescues him, and he is nearly rehabilitated when he kills Rita's ex-boyfriend, gangster Ward Rogers, to preserve his wife's reputation. Ralph tries to escape prison, aided by Rita, but he is killed when he deliberately walks into machine gun fire to protect Helen from possible future blackmail attempts. *Derelicts. Gangsters. Bigamy. Blackmail. Murder. Self-sacrifice. World War I. United States Army—Desertion.*

Note: Also reviewed as *Fallen Angels.*

THE MAN WORTH WHILE **F2.3446**

Romaine Fielding Productions. 9 Sep **1921** [trade review]. Si; b&w. 35mm. 5 reels, 5,000 ft.

Dir Romaine Fielding.

Cast: Joan Arliss *(Mary Alden)*, Lawrence Johnson *(The Child)*, Eugene Acker *(Herbert Loring)*, Margaret Seddon *(Mrs. Ward)*, Frederick Eckhart *(André)*, Peggy Parr *(Cecile)*, Herbert Standing *(Mrs. Forbes-Grey [see note])*, Vanda Tierendelli *(Miss Flo)*, Barney Gilmore *(The Judge)*, Natalie O'Brien *(The Dancer)*, "Tex" Cooper *(The Parson)*, Kid Broad *(A Lifer)*, Emile Le Croix *(The Doctor)*, Frank De Vernon *(Eddie Loring)*, Burt Hodkins *(Percy)*, Clarence Heritage *(The Sheriff)*, Ruth Buchanan *(The Operator)*, Tammany Young *("Useless")*, Billy Quirk *(Napoleon)*, Romaine Fielding *(Don Ward)*.

Northwest melodrama. Source: Ella Wheeler Wilcox, unidentified poem. Don "Smiler" Ward, a ranger, is about to marry Mary Alden when Eddie Loring, son of a wealthy lumber king, tricks her into marrying him, then deserts her. Smiler trails Loring to his office, then is arrested for attempted murder and sent to prison. Mary has a child that, upon reaching a knowing age, asks about his father. Mary goes to Loring's home, seeking to be recognized as his wife. That same night, Loring is killed—but by a French Canadian whose girl Loring had wronged. Smiler, now out of prison, with his sweetheart cleared of Loring's murder, at long last has reason to smile. *French Canadians. Rangers. Injustice. Murder. Desertion. Lumber industry.*

Note: Source for Herbert Standing's role may be in error.

MAN-MADE WOMEN F2.3447

De Mille Pictures. *Dist* Pathé Exchange. 9 Sep **1928** [c16 Jul 1928; LP25474]. Si; b&w. 35mm. 6 reels, 5,762 ft.

Prod Ralph Block. *Dir* Paul L. Stein. *Screenplay* Alice D. G. Miller. *Titl* Edwin Justus Mayer. *Story-Adapt* Ernest Pascal. *Photog* John Mescall. *Art Dir* Stephen Goosson. *Film Ed* Doane Harrison. *Asst Dir* Gordon Cooper. *Prod Mgr* Harry Poppe.

Cast: Leatrice Joy *(Nan Payson)*, H. B. Warner *(Jules Moret)*, John Boles *(John Payson)*, Seena Owen *(Georgette)*, Jay Eaton *(Garth)*, Jeanette Loff *(Marjorie)*, Sidney Bracy *(Owens)*.

Romantic comedy-drama. John Payson reprimands his bride, Nan, when she is accidentally trapped in a bachelor friend's wine cellar and comes home late for her dinner party. When Payson requests that she drop her free-wheeling friends, Nan maintains that his friends are boring; and she leaves him to take a position as companion to Georgette, a woman whose rent is being paid by Nan's bachelor friend, Jules Moret. Believing that Jules is transferring his affection to Nan, Georgette leaves in a huff. Moret proposes a similar arrangement with Nan, but, preferring marriage, Nan returns to her husband. *Bachelors. Newlyweds. Mistresses. Infidelity. Marriage.*

MANHANDLED F2.3448

Famous Players–Lasky. *Dist* Paramount Pictures. 4 Aug **1924** [c22 Jul 1924; LP20414]. Si; b&w. 35mm. 7 reels, 6,998 ft.

Pres by Adolph Zukor, Jesse L. Lasky. *Dir* Allan Dwan. *Supv Ed* William Le Baron. *Scen* Frank W. Tuttle. *Titl* Julian Johnson. *Photog* Hal Rosson. *Film Ed* Julian Johnson.

Cast: Gloria Swanson *(Tessie McGuire)*, Tom Moore *(Jimmy Hogan)*, Lilyan Tashman *(Pinkie Doran)*, Ian Keith *(Robert Brandt)*, Arthur Housman *(Chip Thorndyke)*, Paul McAllister *(Paul Garretson)*, Frank Morgan *(Arno Riccardi)*, M. Collosse *(Bippo)*, Marie Shelton *(a model)*, Carrie Scott *(landlady)*, Ann Pennington *(herself)*, Brooke Johns *(himself)*, Frank Allworth.

Society drama. Source: Arthur Stringer, "Manhandled," in *Saturday Evening Post* (196:5–7, 22–23; 22, 29 Mar 1924). When her boyfriend, Jimmy, forgets a date, Tessie McGuire, a department store clerk, attends a party at the studio of Robert Brandt where she makes a hit with impersonations. There Riccardi offers her a job impersonating a Russian countess in his style emporium. While she is fighting off suitors, Jimmy becomes successful with his automobile invention; but when he returns to find Tessie wealthy in gowns he accuses her of being "manhandled." Repenting her mistake, she is forgiven when he realizes her true feelings. *Salesclerks. Couturiers. Inventors. Courtship. Impersonation. Automobiles.*

MANHATTAN F2.3449

Famous Players–Lasky. *Dist* Paramount Pictures. ca26 Oct **1924** [New York premiere; released 10 Nov; c7 Nov 1924; LP20777]. Si; b&w. 35mm. 7 reels, 6,415 ft.

Pres by Adolph Zukor, Jesse L. Lasky. *Dir* R. H. Burnside. *Screenplay* Paul Sloane, Frank W. Tuttle. *Photog* Hal Rosson.

Cast: Richard Dix *(Peter Minuit)*, Jacqueline Logan *(Mary Malone)*, Gregory Kelly *(Spike, her brother)*, George Siegmann *(Bud McGinnis)*, Gunboat Smith *(Joe Madden)*, Oscar Brimberton Figman, Edna May Oliver *(Mrs. Trapes)*, Alice Chapin *(housekeeper)*, James Bradbury *(trainer)*.

Crook comedy-melodrama. Source: Jeffery Farnol, *The Definite Object, a Romance of New York* (Boston, 1917). Peter Minuit, a member of the "400" and a descendant of New York City's first citizens, is tired of having nothing to do but spend money and seeks adventure in Hell's kitchen. Posing as "Gentleman George," a safecracker, he accompanies Spike Malone to that notorious district, where he makes the acquaintance of crooks and falls in love with Spike's sister, Mary. Gang leader Bud McGinnis also seeks Mary's favor, and his power keeps Mary's admirers at a distance. Peter takes boxing lessons; and, though Mary has consented to marry Bud to save Peter and Spike, the pseudocrook administers a beating to Bud and takes Mary to his Fifth Avenue home to be his bride. *Gentlemen crooks. Safecrackers. Brother-sister relationship. Robbery. Impersonation. New York City—Hell's Kitchen.*

MANHATTAN COCKTAIL F2.3450

Paramount Famous Lasky Corp. 24 Nov **1928** [c23 Nov 1928; LP25858]. Si; b&w. 35mm. 8 reels, 6,051 ft.

Dir Dorothy Arzner. *Scen* Ethel Doherty. *Titl* George Marion. *Story* Ernest Vajda. *Photog* Harry Fischbeck. *Film Ed* Doris Drought. *Song: "Gotta Be Good"* Victor Schertzinger.

Cast: Nancy Carroll *(Babs)*, Richard Arlen *(Fred)*, Danny O'Shea *(Bob)*, Paul Lukas *(Renov)*, Lilyan Tashman *(Mrs. Renov)*.

Melodrama. Upon graduation from college, Babs and Bob leave their peaceful, smalltown life and go to New York in an effort to make the Broadway big time. Mrs. Renov, the wife of a theatrical producer, takes a fancy to Bob and gets him a part in one of her husband's shows; Renov discovers his wife's infidelity and quickly fires Bob. Renov meets Babs and gives her a part in his show. Fred, Babs's college sweetheart, comes to New York to look for her, and Mrs. Renov turns her attentions to him, feigning interest in one of his plays. Renov hires Fred as his assistant and, suspecting him of philandering, frames him on a forgery charge. Babs goes to Renov to plead for Fred's release, and he attacks her. Bob clubs Renov with an iron bar and, attempting to escape, falls to his death. Unnerved by city life, Babs returns to the small college town where Fred is a professor. *Professors. Theatrical producers. Playwrights. Murder. Infidelity. Theater. Smalltown life. Forgery. Frameup. New York City—Broadway.*

MANHATTAN COWBOY F2.3451

El Dorado Productions. *Dist* Syndicate Pictures. Oct or 1 Nov **1928.** Si; b&w. 35mm. 5 reels, 4,694 ft.

Dir J. P. McGowan. *Scen* Sally Winters, Ernest Vajda. *Story* Sally Winters. *Photog* Paul Stern.

Cast: Bob Custer, Lafe McKee, Mary Mayberry, Charles Whittaker, John Lowell Russell, Lynn Sanderson, Mack V. Wright, Cliff Lyons, Dorothy Vernon.

Western melodrama. Sent west to learn about work, the playboy son (played by Bob Custer) of a wealthy father attracts the foreman's daughter (played by Mary Mayberry) and the consequent enmity of a fellow ranchhand. The bad guys are set straight after an abduction of the girl and her rescue by the hero. *Idlers. Cowboys. Ranch foremen. Abduction.*

MANHATTAN KNIGHTS F2.3452

Excellent Pictures. 27 Aug **1928** [c7 Sep 1928; LP25601]. Si; b&w. 35mm. 7 reels.

Dir Burton King. *Story-Cont* Adeline Leitzbach. *Photog* Edward Kull, Walter Haas. *Film Ed* De Leon Anthony.

Cast: Barbara Bedford *(Margaret)*, Walter Miller *(Robert Ferris)*, Betty Worth *(Julia)*, Ray Hallor *(James Barton)*, Crauford Kent *(Henry Ryder)*, Eddie Boland *(Chick Watson)*, Noble Johnson *(Doc Mellis)*, Joseph Burke *(Barry)*, Leo White *(Giuseppi)*, Maude Truax.

Melodrama. When well-born James Barton loses $50,000 at cards to three sharpers (Doc Mellis, Henry Ryder, and Chick Watson), his sister, Margaret, sets out to recover the post-dated check he was forced to give them. Bob Ferris, a wealthy bachelor, falls in love with Margaret and assists in her effort to help James. Doc Mellis is murdered by Ryder, who then holds Jimmy as a hostage; Margaret and Bob find Jimmy, only to be captured as well. The three captives are shut up in a burning warehouse, but they manage to escape and take Ryder into the courts of law to stand trial for murder, kidnaping, and arson. *Gamblers. Hostages. Brother-sister relationship. Murder. Kidnaping. Arson.*

MANHATTAN MADNESS (Reissue) F2.3453

Fine Arts Pictures. *Dist* Tri-Stone Pictures. **1924.** Si; b&w. 35mm. 5 reels.

Note: A "re-edited and re-titled" Douglas Fairbanks film originally released by Triangle Film Corp. on 1 Oct 1916.

MANHATTAN MADNESS F2.3454

Fine Arts Pictures. *Dist* Associated Exhibitors. 20 Sep **1925** [c20 Jul 1925; LU21633]. Si; b&w. 35mm. 6 reels, 5,580 ft.

Dir John McDermott. *Scen* E. V. Durling. *Story* Frank Dazey, Charles T. Dazey. *Photog* Jules Cronjager.

Cast: Jack Dempsey *(Steve O'Dare)*, Estelle Taylor *(The Girl)*, George Siegmann *(Dr. Harlan)*, Frank Campeau *(The Butler)*, Bull Montana *(The Chauffeur)*, Nelson McDowell *(Hank)*, Bill Franey *(Zeke)*, Theodore Lorch *(Count Von Eckmann)*, Jane Starr *(The Maid)*, Robert Graves *(Jack Russell)*, Tom Wilson *(porter)*, Christian Frank *("Dutch" Herman)*, Glen Cavender *("Broken Nose" Murphy)*, Harry Tenbrook *("Lefty" Lewis)*.

Melodrama. Steve O'Dare, a western rancher with little use for the effete East, is forced to go to New York on business and wires his club begging the crowd to provide him with a little action. On the train to Manhattan, Steve is attracted to a beautiful and mysterious woman, whom he later sees at a nightclub. In order to close an important deal, Steve goes to the house of Count von Eckmann, where he once again encounters the girl, who is screaming for help. Steve is forced to fight off a gang of criminals, knocking some out and shooting at others. After a series of fistic encounters and strange disappearances, Steve fights his way to the dining room of Eckmann's house, where he finds the entire company of "criminals" at a formal dinner. Realizing that he has been on the receiving end of a practical joke, Steve grabs the girl and takes her off to visit a preacher. *Ranchers. Abduction. Hoaxes. Clubs. New York City.*

Note: This film is a remake of a Triangle film of the same name that stars Douglas Fairbanks.

THE MANICURE GIRL **F2.3455**

Famous Players–Lasky. *Dist* Paramount Pictures. 6 Jul **1925** [c11 Jul 1925; LP21646]. Si; b&w. 35mm. 6 reels, 5,959 ft.

Pres by Adolph Zukor, Jesse L. Lasky. *Dir* Frank Tuttle. *Screenplay* Townsend Martin. *Story* Frederick Hatton, Fanny Hatton. *Photog* J. Roy Hunt. *Art Dir* Julian Boone Fleming.

Cast: Bebe Daniels *(Maria Maretti)*, Edmund Burns *(Antonio Luca)*, Dorothy Cumming *(Flora)*, Hale Hamilton *(James Morgan)*, Charlotte Walker *(Mrs. Morgan)*, Ann Brody *(Mother Luca)*, Marie Shotwell *(Mrs. Wainright)*, Mary Foy *(Mrs. Root-Chiveley)*.

Romantic drama. Maria Maretti, a manicurist in the beauty shop of a large metropolitan hotel, is engaged to Antonio Luca, an electrician who operates a small radio repair business. At the hotel, Maria meets James Morgan, a wealthy guest who, when Maria will not go out with him, sends her $10 for theater tickets. Over Antonio's objections, Maria does not return the money; instead she and Antonio go to a play. After the performance, Antonio is too niggardly to hire a taxi; and while he is chasing his hat down a windy street, Maria accepts a ride with Morgan. Later, she and Antonio fight, and she goes to Morgan for consolation, belatedly discovering that he is married. Maria reunites Morgan with his wife, then gladly returns to the penitent Antonio. *Manicurists. Electricians. Radio repairmen. Italians. Marriage. Beauty shops. Hotels.*

MANNEQUIN **F2.3456**

Famous Players–Lasky. *Dist* Paramount Pictures. 11 Jan **1926** [c11 Jan 1926; LP22252]. Si; b&w. 35mm. 7 reels, 6,981 ft.

Pres by Adolph Zukor, Jesse L. Lasky. *Dir* James Cruze. *Screenplay* Frances Agnew. *Adapt* Walter Woods. *Photog* Karl Brown.

Cast: Alice Joyce *(Selene Herrick)*, Warner Baxter *(John Herrick)*, Dolores Costello *(Joan Herrick [Orchid])*, ZaSu Pitts *(Annie Pogani)*, Walter Pidgeon *(Martin Innesbrook)*, Freeman Wood *(Terry Allen)*, Charlot Bird *(Toto)*.

Drama. Source: Fannie Hurst, *Mannequin* (New York, 1926). Annie Pogani, a dull-witted nursemaid who loves children, steals a baby girl from Selene Herrick, a wealthy woman who cares more for auctions than for family life. The girl, known as Orchid, is reared by Annie in an East Side tenement; when Annie dies, Orchid finds work as a model in a fashionable shop, where she meets Martin Innesbrook, a reporter who is making his reputation by writing editorials against the practice of acquitting female criminals just because they are women. During a fight with Terry Allen, a low fellow more used to taking than to asking, Terry is inadvertently impaled on Orchid's brooch. She is brought to trial for murder and, after a difficult trial, found innocent. Her true identity is finally discovered, and she is reunited with her father, who was the judge at her trial. She and Martin look forward to walking the road of life together. *Nursemaids. Children. Fashion models. Judges. Reporters. Abduction. Injustice. Murder. Trials. New York City.*

A MAN'S FIGHT **F2.3457**

Dist Independent Pictures. 12 Apr **1927** [New York State license]. Si; b&w. 35mm. 5 reels.

Drama(?). No information about the nature of this film has been found.

Note: May be the same as a 1919 film by the same title, distributed by United Picture Theatres and starring Dustin Farnum.

A MAN'S HOME **F2.3458**

Selznick Pictures. *Dist* Select Pictures. Dec **1921** [c5 Oct 1921; LP17037]. Si; b&w. 35mm. 7 reels, 6,235 ft. [Later, ca10 Jan 1922, cut to 6 reels, 5,985 ft.]

Pres by Lewis J. Selznick. *Dir* Ralph Ince. *Scen* Edward J. Montagne. *Photog* William J. Black.

Cast: Harry T. Morey *(Frederick Osborn)*, Kathlyn Williams *(Frances Osborn)*, Faire Binney *(Lucy Osborn)*, Margaret Seddon *(Amanda Green)*, Grace Valentine *(Cordelia Wilson)*, Roland Bottomley *(Jack Wilson)*, Matt Moore *(Arthur Lynn)*.

Domestic melodrama. Source: Anna Steese Richardson and Edmund Breese, *A Man's Home* (Albany, N. Y., opening: Jun 1917). Frederick Osborn, a self-made man who suddenly becomes rich, finds that his wife is exclusively concerned with travel and "fast company," and he indulges her while pursuing his business activities. His daughter, Lucy, falls in love with Arthur Lynn, a wealthy neighbor's son, while Mrs. Osborn becomes involved with blackmailers Jack and Cordelia Wilson. Fearing his wife's social reputation will endanger Lucy's future, Frederick calls her home, but en route she is induced to bribe a bogus prohibition officer in league with Wilson. The Wilsons are dismissed, owing to Cordelia's past affair with Lynn, then attempt to rob Mrs. Osborn. Osborn arrives in time to thrash Wilson; Cordelia confesses that Lucy's innocence has touched her and refuses Osborn's offer of money. *Businessmen. Nouveaux riches. Family life. Wealth. Blackmail. Prohibition.*

MAN'S LAW AND GOD'S **F2.3459**

Finis Fox Productions. *Dist* American Releasing Corp. 16 Apr **1922** [c16 Apr 1922; LP18107]. Si; b&w. 35mm. 5 reels, 4,791 ft.

Dir-Writ Finis Fox.

Cast: Jack Livingston *(Bruce MacDonald)*, Ethel Shannon *(Kitty Roshay)*, Kate Anderson *(Mrs. MacDonald, Bruce's mother)*, Bobby Mack *("Uncle Jimmie")*, Joy Winthrop *(Aunt Jenny)*, George Cummings *("Cameo" Brooks)*, Rosa Melville *(Helen DeBrose)*.

Melodrama. "Uncle Jimmie" advertises in a matrimonial paper on behalf of his friend Bruce, a "Mountie," without Bruce's knowledge. Kitty, the daughter of a copper king, answers the advertisement in fun. Bruce's mother is killed by a gambler, who later forces his attentions on Kitty; and when she escapes she is mistaken by Bruce for a dancehall girl wanted by the police. The gambler is killed, Bruce realizes his love for Kitty, and "Uncle Jimmie" finds his lost sweetheart—Kitty's aunt. *Dancehall girls. Gamblers. Matrimonial agencies. Copper. Northwest Mounted Police.*

A MAN'S MAN **F2.3460**

Dist Film Booking Offices of America. cl Jul **1923** [LP20289]. Si; b&w. 35mm. 5 reels.

Dir Oscar Apfel. *Scen* Thomas J. Geraghty. *Photog* L. Guy Wilky.

Cast: J. Warren Kerrigan *(John Stuart Webster)*, Lois Wilson *(Dolores Ruey)*, Kenneth Harlan *(Billy Geary)*, Edward Coxen *(John Cafferty)*, Ida Lewis *(Mother Jenks)*, Harry von Meter *(Ricardo Ruey)*, Eugene Pallette *(Captain Benevido)*, Ernst Pasque *(Captain Arredondo)*, Arthur Allardt *(Dr. Pacheo)*, Joseph J. Dowling *(President Sarros)*, John Steppling *(Neddy Jerome)*, Wallace Worsley *(Henry Jenks)*.

Romantic melodrama. Source: Peter Bernard Kyne, "A Man's Man," in *Red Book* (27:Aug–Oct 1916; 28:Nov 1916–Feb 1917). Returning to his native Denver from a fruitless hunt for adventure, John Stuart Webster makes the acquaintance of beautiful Dolores Ruey when she cries for help in defending herself from a masher. As their close friendship develops into romance, John receives word that his old pal, Billy Geary, needs assistance in fighting off natives who covet his South American property. John hastens to Buenaventura, meeting en route the gallant and hunted son (Ricardo Ruey) of the former president of the republic, and finds Dolores in the same town. Billy falls in love with Dolores; John graciously tries to back out of the love triangle; Ricardo successfully carries out a revolution with John's help, thereby regaining his rightful position; and John is reunited with Dolores, who is revealed to be Ricardo's sister. *Adventurers. Brother-sister relationship. Revolutions. Courtship. Property rights. South America. Denver.*

Note: Probably a reediting of the 1917 *A Man's Man*, which is 7 reels in length and has at least the same cast, director, scenarist, and source, though not entirely the same story line.

A MAN'S MAN **F2.3461**

Metro-Goldwyn-Mayer Pictures. 25 May **1929** [c20 May 1929; LP383]. Sd eff & mus score (Movietone); b&w. 35mm. 8 reels, 6,683 ft.

Dir James Cruze. *Scen* Forrest Halsey. *Titl* Joe Farnham. *Photog* Merritt B. Gerstad. *Art Dir* Cedric Gibbons. *Film Ed* George Hively. *Song: "My Heart Is Bluer Than Your Eyes, Cherie"* Al Bryan, Monte

Wilhitt. *Wardrobe* David Cox.

Cast: William Haines *(Mel)*, Josephine Dunn *(Peggy)*, Sam Hardy *(Charlie)*, Mae Busch *(Violet)*, John Gilbert *(himself)*, Greta Garbo *(herself)*, Gloria Davenport.

Comedy-drama. Source: Patrick Kearney, *A Man's Man; a Comedy of Life Under the "L"* (New York, 1925). Going to Hollywood in an attempt to break into the movies, Peggy marries Mel, a personable but gullible soda jerk. Mel later buys some worthless oil stock from Charlie, a discredited sometime assistant director who makes a play for Peggy, persuading her that he will make her a star. Mel and Peggy eventually learn the truth about Charlie, and Mel thrashes him in a fight. *Soda clerks. Actors. Motion picture directors. Hollywood.*

A MAN'S MATE **F2.3462**

Fox Film Corp. 16 Mar **1924** [c16 Mar 1924; LP20019]. Si; b&w. 35mm. 6 reels, 5,041 ft.

Pres by William Fox. *Dir* Edmund Mortimer. *Story-Scen* Charles Kenyon. *Photog* G. O. Post.

Cast: John Gilbert *(Paul)*, Renée Adorée *(Wildcat)*, Noble Johnson *(Lion)*, Wilfrid North *(Monsieur Bonard)*, Thomas Mills *(Father Pierre)*, James Neill *(Veraign)*, Jack Giddings *(Lynx)*, Patterson Dial *(Sybil)*.

Romantic drama. Artist Paul Bonard loses his memory when he receives a blow on the head from one of two apaches fighting over Wildcat, a sultry stepper in a cafe. He becomes an apache himself, falls in love with Wildcat and paints her portrait—his masterpiece. Wildcat learns Paul's identity and restores him to his family, though realizing that she will lose him. Surgery restores Paul's memory, but some subconscious force guides him back to the cafe and Wildcat's love. *Apaches—Paris. Artists. Amnesia. Paris.*

Note: Working title: *The Apache.*

A MAN'S PAST (Universal-Jewel) **F2.3463**

Universal Pictures. 1 Oct **1927** [New York premiere; released 25 Dec; c3 Sep 1927; LP24381]. Si; b&w. 35mm. 6 reels, 5,916 ft. [Also 6,135 ft.]

Pres by Carl Laemmle. *Dir* George Melford. *Cont* Emil Forst. *Titl* Tom Reed. *Adapt* Paul Kohner. *Photog* Gilbert Warrenton.

Cast: Conrad Veidt *(Paul La Roche)*, Barbara Bedford *(Yvonne Fontaine)*, Ian Keith *(Dr. Fontaine)*, Arthur Edmund Carew *(Lieutenant Destin)*, Charles Puffy *(prison doctor)*, Corliss Palmer *(Sylvia Cabot)*, Edward Reinach *(Dr. Renaud)*.

Melodrama. Source: Emerich Foeldes, *Diploma* (a play; publication undetermined). Imprisoned at the French garrison on the Isle of St. Noir for putting to death a patient suffering from an incurable illness, Dr. Paul La Roche escapes to the mainland, where he meets Dr. Henry Fontaine, his boyhood friend, and Fontaine's beautiful sister, Yvonne. As Fontaine is going blind, La Roche performs several operations for him, attracting the attention of Dr. Renaud, in Algiers, who offers him a position. La Roche, practicing as Fontaine, reveals his love for Yvonne during an excursion to a Bedouin camp. Then, Lieutenant Destin, from the prison, arrives and threatens La Roche with exposure unless he surrenders the hand of Yvonne; during a chess game with Dr. Fontaine, the doctor calls Destin's hand and shoots him. La Roche saves him with an operation and as a result is granted a full pardon. *Surgeons. Physicians. Bedouins. Mercy killing. Blindness. Prisons. Chess. France. Algiers.*

MAN'S SIZE **F2.3464**

Fox Film Corp. 21 Jan **1923** [c21 Jan 1923; LP19208]. Si; b&w. 35mm. 5 reels, 4,316 ft.

Pres by William Fox. *Dir* Howard M. Mitchell. *Scen* Joseph Franklin Poland. *Photog* George Schneiderman, Ernest Miller.

Cast: William Russell *(Tom Morse)*, Alma Bennett *(Jessie McRae)*, Stanton Heck *(Bully West)*, Charles K. French *(Angus McRae)*, James Gordon *(Carl Morse)*, Carl Stockdale *(Whaley)*.

Melodrama. Source: William MacLeod Raine, *Man Size* (New York, 1922). While on business in Canada Tom Morse meets and falls in love with Jessie McRae, a headstrong girl who has been badly treated by her father. McRae, because of an old feud with Tom's uncle, forbids Tom to see Jessie and "sells" her to Bully West, a bootlegger. Tom and his uncle visit McRae to settle the argument and learn that Jessie has been sold. Tom rescues Jessie and returns her to her repentant father. *Businessmen. Bootleggers. Fatherhood. Feuds. Canada.*

THE MANSION OF ACHING HEARTS **F2.3465**

B. P. Schulberg Productions. 27 Feb **1925**. Si; b&w. 35mm. 6 reels, 6,147 ft.

Dir James P. Hogan. *Adapt* Frederick Stowers. *Photog* Harry Perry.

Cast: Ethel Clayton *(Pauline Craig)*, Barbara Bedford *(Martha)*, Priscilla Bonner *(a city girl)*, Philo McCullough *(John Dawson)*, Edward Delaney *(a city boy)*, Cullen Landis *(Bill Smith)*, Sam De Grasse *(Martin Craig)*, Eddie Phillips *(a "sheik")*, Edward Gribbon *(Fritz Dahlgren)*, Helen Hogo *(Bill, as a child)*.

Domestic drama. Suggested by: Harry von Tilzer and Arthur J. Lamb, "The Mansion of Aching Hearts" (a song; c1902). Believing his wife, Pauline, to have been unfaithful, Martin Craig, a hard-hearted banker, drives her and her small son from home. Sometime later, Pauline becomes separated from the child during a storm and believes him to be drowned. Martin finds the boy and, not knowing that he is his own son, raises him as a foundling. Years pass. Pauline becomes a matron in a home for friendless girls and meets Martha, a young girl whom Martin has persecuted as a fallen woman. Pauline becomes enraged and goes with Martha to confront Martin. She meets her son, known as Bill Smith, and becomes friends with him, eventually telling him that she is his mother. Bill then, with the help of a mob, attempts to drive his mother away, as his vengeance on her for having deserted him as an infant. Martin comes forward, however, and tells the villagers of the unfounded suspicions that resulted in Pauline's separation from Bill. Pauline and Martin are then reconciled. *Bankers. Foundlings. Infidelity. Village life. Girls' homes.*

MANSLAUGHTER **F2.3466**

Famous Players–Lasky. *Dist* Paramount Pictures. 24 Sep **1922** [c25 Sep 1922; LP18327]. Si; b&w. 35mm. 10 reels, 9,061 ft.

Pres by Jesse L. Lasky. *Dir* Cecil B. De Mille. *Adapt-Scen* Jeanie Macpherson. *Photog* Alvin Wyckoff, Guy Wilky. *Art Dir* Paul Iribe. *Choreog* Theodore Kosloff. *Cost* Paul Iribe.

Cast: Thomas Meighan *(Daniel O'Bannon)*, Leatrice Joy *(Lydia Thorne)*, Lois Wilson *(Evans, her maid)*, John Miltern *(Gov. Stephen Albee)*, George Fawcett *(Judge Homans)*, Julia Faye *(Mrs. Drummond)*, Edythe Chapman *(Adeline Bennett)*, Jack Mower *(Drummond, a policeman)*, Dorothy Cumming *(Eleanor Bellington)*, Casson Ferguson *(Bobby Dorset)*, Mickey Moore *(Dicky Evans)*, James Neill *(butler)*, Sylvia Ashton *(prison matron)*, Raymond Hatton *(Brown)*, "Teddy" *("Gloomy Gus")*, Mabel Van Buren, Ethel Wales, Dale Fuller *(prisoners)*, Edward Martindel *(Wiley)*, Charles Ogle *(doctor)*, Guy Oliver *(musician)*, Shannon Day *(Miss Santa Claus)*, Lucien Littlefield *(witness)*, Clarence Burton, William Boyd, J. Farrell MacDonald, Theodore von Eltz, Nora Cecil, Madame Sul-Te-Wan, Charles West, Emmett King, Sidney Bracy, Fred Kelsey, Spottiswoode Aitken.

Society drama. Source: Alice Duer Miller, *Manslaughter* (New York, 1921). Lydia Thorne, a wealthy girl who loves speed and thrills, is unsympathetic when Evans, her maid, is jailed for stealing her jewels. District Attorney Daniel O'Bannon visits Lydia to make her see the error of her own ways, but instead he views a scene of Lydia and her friends that reminds him of a Roman orgy. O'Bannon feels it is his duty, therefore, to send Lydia to jail for her own good when her automobile driving causes the death of a motorcycle policeman. Lydia is resentful, and her rebuff of O'Bannon, who has come to love her, causes him such remorse that he turns to drink and dissipation. Meanwhile, Lydia reforms, realizes she loves O'Bannon, and resolves to do charitable work. She and Evans open a soup kitchen after their release, and a chance meeting with O'Bannon starts him on the road to recovery. With Lydia's encouragement he becomes himself again, runs for governor, but withdraws his candidacy to marry Lydia when he sees that her record would be a liability to him in politics. *Lawyers. District attorneys. Socialities. Automobile driving. Thrill-seeking. Jazz life. Charity. Politics. Drunkenness. Theft. Manslaughter.*

Note: Remade in 1930 under the same title, q. v.

MANSLAUGHTER **F2.3467**

Paramount-Publix Corp. 23 Jul **1930** [New York premiere; released 9 Aug; c9 Aug 1930; LP1479]. Sd (Movietone); b&w. 35mm. 10 reels, 7,954 ft.

Dir-Adapt George Abbott. *Photog* Archie J. Stout. *Film Ed* Otto Levering. *Rec Engr* Earl Hayman.

Cast: Claudette Colbert *(Lydia Thorne)*, Fredric March *(Dan O'Bannon)*, Emma Dunn *(Miss Bennett)*, Natalie Moorhead *(Eleanor)*, Richard Tucker *(Albee)*, Hilda Vaughn *(Evans)*, G. Pat Collins *(Drummond)*, Gaylord Pendleton *(Bobby)*, Stanley Fields *(Peters)*, Arnold Lucy *(Piers)*, Ivan

Simpson *(Morson)*, Irving Mitchell *(Foster)*.

Romantic drama. Source: Alice Duer Miller, *Manslaughter* (New York, 1921). Lydia Thorne, a spoiled and selfish girl of wealth and position, meets Dan O'Bannon, a serious-minded district attorney, but their growing affection is disturbed by her thoughtlessness in speeding on the road and by a petty theft involving her maid, Evans. While being chased by a policeman for speeding, she causes the officer to be killed, and despite the efforts of an able defense lawyer, she is convicted of manslaughter and vows vengeance against O'Bannon. Prison discipline awakens her dormant kindness and generosity; meanwhile, O'Bannon resigns his position and leads an aimless, wild life, but eventually he manages to pull himself together. Released from prison, Lydia demands that O'Bannon's new employer discharge him. O'Bannon protests, claiming that he still loves her; and though she sends him away, later she finds happiness in his arms. *Lawyers. District attorneys. Socialites. Courtship. Manslaughter. Automobile driving. Prisons.*

Note: Remake of the 1922 film of the same title, q. v.

MANTRAP **F2.3468**

Famous Players–Lasky. *Dist* Paramount Pictures. 18 **1926** [New York premiere; released 24 Jul; c30 Aug 1926; LP23057]. Si; b&w. 35mm. 7 reels, 6,077 ft.

Pres by Adolph Zukor, Jesse L. Lasky. *Assoc Prod* B. P. Schulberg, Hector Turnbull. *Dir* Victor Fleming. *Screenplay* Adelaide Heilbron, Ethel Doherty. *Titl* George Marion, Jr. *Photog* James Howe.

Cast: Ernest Torrence *(Joe Easter)*, Clara Bow *(Alverna)*, Percy Marmont *(Ralph Prescott)*, Eugene Pallette *(E. Wesson Woodbury)*, Tom Kennedy *(Curly Evans)*, Josephine Crowell *(Mrs. McGavity)*, William Orlamond *(Mr. McGavity)*, Charles Stevens *(Lawrence Jackfish)*, Miss Du Pont *(Mrs. Barker)*, Charlot Bird *(stenographer)*.

Domestic comedy-drama. Source: Sinclair Lewis, *Mantrap* (New York, 1926). Ralph Prescott, a New York bachelor lawyer, throughly despises women, having to listen constantly to their excuses for seeking a divorce. To escape them he agrees to go on a camping trip with Mr. Woodbury to Mantrap Landing in the Canadian woods. Woodbury soon tires of Ralph's pampered condition, and they part ways after woodsman Joe Easter separates them in a fight. Joe takes Ralph to his trading post and there introduces him to Alverna, his wife, a former manicurist, who immediately begins to flirt with him; she pleads to be taken back to civilization when he leaves, and she joins him against his wishes. Ralph swears he will ask Joe to divorce her; then they are stranded when his canoe is stolen and are rescued by an aviator who is en route to a forest fire. Alverna tries to vamp the aviator; Joe arrives; and when Ralph admits his agreement to her plan, Alverna rejects both of them. Later, she promises to be faithful to Joe, but he realizes she will always be a coquette. *Lawyers. Woodsmen. Traders. Bachelors. New Yorkers. Manicurists. Flirts. Misogynists. Canada.*

MAN—WOMAN—MARRIAGE **F2.3469**

Allen Holubar. *Dist* Associated First National Pictures. Mar **1921** [c29 Jun 1921; LP16717]. Si; b&w. 35mm. 9 reels.

Pres by Albert A. Kaufman. *Dir-Story* Allen Holubar. *Scen* Olga Scholl. *Photog* Lyman Broening. *Choreog* Marion Morgan.

Cast: Dorothy Phillips *(Victoria)*, Ralph Lewis *(The Father)*, Margaret Mann *(The Mother)*, James Kirkwood *(David Courtney)*, Robert Cain *(Bruce Schuyler)*, J. Barney Sherry *(Henshaw)*, Shannon Day *(Bobo)*, Frances Parks *(Milly)*, Emily Chichester *(Jerry)*.

Spectacular drama. Rebelling against a forced engagement to Schuyler, Victoria falls in love with young attorney David Courtney and marries him. At first they are happy, but when David is drawn into political corruption and accepts the attentions of other women, she tries to compete with them, then denounces him. When he runs for U. S. Senator, she is nominated as a darkhorse candidate against him and wins. He is indicted for bribery during the campaign and while in prison is redeemed through her visits. In each crisis Victoria dreams of the women of corresponding ages: the stone age, the age of chivalry, Amazons and their supremacy over men, the life of debauchery in the Roman era, and the dawn of Christianity in her dream of David as Constantine and herself as a Christian slave who converts the pagan world. *Lawyers. Women in politics. Criminals—Rehabilitation. Women's rights. Politics. Bribery. Political corruption. Christianity. Stone Age. Middle Ages. United States Congress. Rome—History—Empire. Constantine I. Amazons. Dreams.*

Note: Copyright title: *Man, Woman, Marriage.*

THE MARCH HARE **F2.3470**

Realart Pictures. Jun **1921** [c27 Jun 1921; LP16709]. Si; b&w. 35mm. 5 reels, 4,431 ft.

Dir Maurice Campbell. *Scen* Percy Heath. *Story* Elmer Harris. *Photog* H. Kinley Martin.

Cast: Bebe Daniels *(Lizbeth Ann Palmer)*, Grace Morse *(Clara Belle Palmer)*, Herbert Sherwood *(Lucius Palmer)*, Mayme Kelso *(Mrs. Curtis Palmer)*, Helen Jerome Eddy *(Susie)*, Sidney Bracey *(Meadows)*, Frances Raymond *(Mrs. Rollins)*, Melbourne MacDowell *(Senator Rollins)*, Harry Myers *(Tod Rollins)*.

Comedy. Known as "The March Hare" among her friends, Lizbeth Palmer, daughter of a Los Angeles millionaire, comes to New York with a chaperon to visit her aunt. After betting the chaperon that she can live on 75c for an entire week, she assumes the part of a flower girl in a restaurant and there makes a hit with young millionaire Tod Rollins, who invites her to his home. While visiting her aunt, Mrs. Curtis Palmer, Lizbeth discovers that the butler's accomplice has taken her name in an attempt to swindle her aunt. Under an assumed name, Lizbeth exposes them as they are about to steal the aunt's jewels, wins her original bet, and captures Tod for a husband. *Flower girls. Aunts. Chaperons. Thieves. Millionaires. Wagers. Imposture. New York City.*

MARCUS GARLAND **F2.3471**

Micheaux Film Corp. **1925.** Si; b&w. 35mm. [Feature length assumed.]

Cast: Salem Tutt Whitney, Amy Birdsong.

Melodrama(?). No information about the precise nature of this film has been found. *Negro life.*

Note: Indicated year is approximate.

MARE NOSTRUM **F2.3472**

Metro-Goldwyn-Mayer Pictures. 15 Feb **1926** [New York premiere; released 29 Aug; c30 Aug 1926; LP23075]. Si; b&w. 35mm. 11 reels, 11,000 ft. [Cut to 10 reels, 9,894 ft. for release.]

Prod-Dir Rex Ingram. *Adapt* Willis Goldbeck. *Photog* John F. Seitz. *Art Dir* Ben Carré. *Film Ed* Grant Whytock. *Prod Mgr* Joseph C. Boyle.

Cast: Uni Apollon *(The Triton)*, Alex Nova *(Don Esteban Ferragut)*, Kada-Abd-el-Kader *(his son, Ulysses)*, Hughie Mack *(Caragol)*, Alice Terry *(Freya Talberg)*, Antonio Moreno *(Ulysses Ferragut)*, Mademoiselle Kithnou *(his wife, Doña Cinta)*, Michael Brantford *(their son, Esteban)*, Rosita Ramirez *(their niece, Pepita)*, Frederick Mariotti *(Toni, the mate)*, Madame Paquerette *(Dr. Fedelmann)*, Fernand Mailly *(Count Kaledine)*, André von Engelman *(submarine commander)*.

War drama. Source: Vicente Blasco-Ibáñez, *Mare Nostrum* (1918). Captain Ulysses Ferragut, the last of a famous Spanish family of seafaring fame, meets Freya Talberg, a beautiful and ruthless German spy, in Pompeii and falls in love with her. Freya's superiors plan to use Ulysses' knowledge of the Mediterranean to assist them in supplying their submarines with fuel, using Freya as bait. Later, Ulysses returns to Naples to find Freya and her spy ring departed, and he learns that his son Esteban, whom he idolizes, has been killed on a torpedoed liner. Seeking revenge for the death of his son and his own mistakes, he turns his ship, the *Mare Nostrum*, over to the French and volunteers as commander. Freya, disheartened by the results of her work, sends for Ulysses, but the memory of Esteban causes him to cast her off, and she is executed by the French for espionage. Ulysses' ship is torpedoed; and though he sinks, his attacker is itself swallowed up by the sea. *Spanish. Germans. Spies. Seafaring life. Submarines. World War I. Mediterranean Sea. Pompeii. Naples.*

Note: Filmed on location in Spain and Italy and on the Mediterranean Sea.

MARIANNE **F2.3473**

Cosmopolitan Productions. *Dist* Metro-Goldwyn-Mayer Distributing Corp. 24 Aug **1929** [c3 Sep 1929; LP653]. Si; b&w. 35mm. 7 reels, 10,124 ft. [Also si; 6,563 ft.]

Dir Robert Z. Leonard. *Screenplay* Dale Van Every. *Titl* Joe Farnham. *Photog* Oliver Marsh. *Art Dir* Cedric Gibbons. *Film Ed* Basil Wrangell. *Songs: "When I See My Sugar," "Marianna," "Oo-La-La"* Roy Turk, Fred Albert. *Songs: "Hang On to Me," "Just You, Just Me"* Ray Klages, Jesse Greer. *Song: "Blondy"* Arthur Freed, Nacio Herb Brown. *Rec Engr* Ralph Shugart. *Wardrobe* Adrian.

Cast—Sound Version: Marion Davies *(Marianne)*, George Baxter *(André)*, Lawrence Gray *(Stagg)*, Cliff Edwards *(Soapy)*, Benny Rubin *(Sam)*, Scott Kolk *(Lieutenant Frane)*, Robert Edeson *(general)*, Emil Chautard *(Père Joseph)*.

Cast—Silent Version: Marion Davies *(Marianne)*, Oscar Shaw *(Stagg)*, Robert Castle *(André)*, Robert Ames *(Soapy)*, Scott Kolk *(Lieutenant Frane)*, Emil Chautard *(Père Joseph)*, Mack Swain *(general)*, Oscar Apfel *(major)*.

War drama. Marianne, a fresh and bubbly French heroine, runs an inn and also a nursery in a small French town during the World War. Separated from her childhood sweetheart, André, she promises to wait for him. Her town is partially destroyed, and a company of American soldiers is quartered there, awaiting orders to return home. Fond of a pig about to be slaughtered, Marianne claims it as a pet and goes through much to save it from becoming bacon, in the process captivating Private Stagg, who is put in the stockade for trying to rescue the porcine object of her affections from a ravenous lieutenant. Marianne and Stagg fall in love but are reconciled to parting when André returns home blinded, and Stagg ships off for home. She soon perceives that André is in love with his nurse and, gathering up her quartet of war orphans, leaves for America and her man. *Innkeepers. Orphans. Blindness. Nurseries. World War I. France. United States Army. Pigs.*

THE MARK OF CAIN *see* **THE LONE CHANCE**

MARK OF THE BEAST **F2.3474**

Thomas Dixon. *Dist* W. W. Hodkinson Corp. 24 Jun **1923**. Si; b&w. 35mm. 6 reels, 5,988 ft.

Dir-Writ Thomas Dixon. *Photog* Harry Fischbeck.

Cast: Robert Ellis *(Dr. David Hale)*, Madelyn Clare *(Ann Page)*, Warner Richmond *(Donald Duncan)*, Gustav von Seyffertitz *(John Hunter)*, Helen Ware *(Jane Hunter)*.

Melodrama. Ann Page, affianced to psychologist David Hale, is subconsciously influenced to marry Donald Duncan instead because he apparently resembles her dead father. But she learns that Duncan is a brute and a crook when he takes her to a cabin in the woods and attacks her. Hale, having followed the pair to the cabin (out of professional curiosity), rescues Ann. They are free to marry when Duncan's mother, who hasn't seen him in 10 years, kills her son for his stolen jewelry. *Psychologists. Burglars. Murder. Electra complex.*

MARKED MONEY **F2.3475**

Pathé Exchange. 11 Nov **1928** [c29 Oct 1928; LP25781]. Si; b&w. 35mm. 6 reels, 5,490 ft.

Hector Turnbull Production. *Dir* Spencer Gordon Bennett. *Titl* John Krafft. *Adapt* George Dromgold, Sanford Hewitt. *Story* Howard J. Green. *Photog* Edward Snyder. *Art Dir* Edward Jewell. *Film Ed* Harold McLernon. *Film Ed? (see note)* Fred D. Maguire. *Mus Dir* Josiah Zuro. *Asst Dir* E. J. Babille. *Prod Mgr* R. A. Blaydon.

Cast: Junior Coghlan *(Boy)*, George Duryea *(Clyde)*, Tom Kennedy *(Bill Clemons)*, Bert Woodruff *(Captain Fairchild)*, Virginia Bradford *(Grace Fairchild)*, Maurice Black *(Donovan)*, Jack Richardson *(Scudder)*.

Melodrama. An orphaned boy and a tin box containing $25,000 in cash are entrusted to Captain Fairchild, a close friend of the boy's late father. In an effort to steal the money, Donovan and Scudder, a couple of crooks, kidnap Grace, the captain's daughter, and hold her for ransom. The boy and Clyde, a Navy flier and Grace's fiancé, rescue Grace and reunite her with her father. *Aviators. Sea captains. Orphans. Kidnaping. Ransom.*

Note: Maguire is also credited by some sources with the editing of this film.

MARLIE THE KILLER **F2.3476**

Fred J. McConnell Productions. *Dist* Pathé Exchange. 4 Mar **1928** [c8 Feb 1928; LP24968]. Si; b&w. 35mm. 5 reels, 4,600 ft.

Dir Noel Mason Smith. *Scen* George W. Pyper. *Story* Hazel Christie MacDonald. *Photog* Harry Cooper.

Cast: Klondike *(Marlie, a dog)*, Francis X. Bushman, Jr. *(Bob Cleveland)*, Joseph W. Girard *(John Cleveland)*, Blanche Mehaffey *(Marion Nichols)*, Richard Alexander *(Sam McKee)*, Sheldon Lewis *(Tom Arnold)*.

Action melodrama. John Cleveland sends his son Bob to hasten the construction of a dam he is financing and to fire the foreman, Sam Arnold, whom Cleveland believes to be responsible for the delay. Forewarned, Arnold and his cohorts waylay Bob, force his car over a cliff, and leave him for dead. Passersby rescue Bob and take him to the construction camp. There Bob pretends he has lost his memory to gain enough evidence to jail the villains. Marion Nichols, Arnold's secretary, helps Bob and his dog, Marlie, to thwart Arnold's plans to blow up the dam. Marlie finishes off Arnold by chasing him to the edge of a steep cliff. *Construction foremen. Filial relations. Amnesia. Dams. Construction camps. Dogs.*

MARRIAGE **F2.3477**

Fox Film Corp. 13 Feb **1927** [c13 Feb 1927; LP23666]. Si; b&w. 35mm. 6 reels, 5,458 ft.

Pres by William Fox. *Dir* R. William Neill. *Adapt-Scen* Gertrude Orr. *Titl* Elizabeth Pickett. *Photog* Rudolph Bergquist. *Asst Dir* R. Lee Hough.

Cast: Virginia Valli *(Marjorie Pope)*, Allan Durant *(Professor Trafford)*, Gladys McConnell *(Daphne Pope)*, Lawford Davidson *(Sir Roderick Dover)*, Donald Stuart *(MacDurgan)*, Frank Dunn *(Magnet)*, Edwards Davis *(Pope)*, James Marcus *(Solomson)*, Billie Bennett *(Mrs. Pope)*.

Society drama. Source: Herbert George Wells, *Marriage* (London, 1912). Marjorie Pope, who is engaged to Magnet, a wealthy suitor whom she does not love, elopes with Trafford, an inventor, after his airplane crashes on the grounds of her parents' rural home. Soon, however, Marjorie, irked by his dedication and idealism, persuades Trafford to market his wonderful invention, but her extravagance leads her into an affair with Sir Roderick. Trafford turns her out of their African home, but she returns to nurse him back to health when he is injured by a lion. *Inventors. Marriage. Aviation. Infidelity. Airplane accidents. Africa. Lions.*

MARRIAGE BY CONTRACT **F2.3478**

Tiffany-Stahl Productions. 9 Nov **1928** [New York premiere; released 1 Dec; c21 Nov 1928; LP25855]. Mus score (Photophone); b&w. 35mm. 8 reels, 7,182 ft. [Also si; 7,786 ft.]

Prod John M. Stahl. *Dir* James Flood. *Cont* Frances Hyland. *Titl* Paul Perez. *Story* Edward Clark. *Photog* Ernest Miller. *Film Ed* L. R. Brown. *Mus Score* Manny Baer. *Song: "When the Right One Comes Along"* L. Wolfe Gilbert, Mabel Wayne. *Song: "Come Back to Me"* Dave Goldberg, A. E. Joffe. *Sd* Emmanuel Baer.

Cast: Patsy Ruth Miller *(Margaret)*, Lawrence Gray *(Don)*, Robert Edeson *(Winters)*, Ralph Emerson *(Arthur)*, Shirley Palmer *(Molly)*, John St. Polis *(father)*, Claire McDowell *(mother)*, Ruby Lafayette *(grandma)*, Duke Martin *(Dirke)*, Raymond Keane *(Drury)*.

Drama. *Margaret and Don—an average American girl and boy—enter into a companionate marriage; Don goes philandering the first night after their honeymoon, and Margaret leaves him. She finds that no decent man of her own class will marry her and finally enters into another companionate marriage with Dirke, a self-made man much beneath her social station. Margaret has children and is content, but Dirke leaves her at the end of the marriage contract. She then marries a rich old man, quickly divorcing him to marry Drury, a suave young fellow who soon runs through all her alimony. Margaret kills Drury and is dragged away by the police.* It all turns out to be a dream, however, and Margaret marries Don the next day in a church ceremony. *Philanderers. Police. Marriage—Companionate. Divorce. Murder. Dreams.*

THE MARRIAGE CHANCE **F2.3479**

Hampton Del Ruth Productions. *Dist* American Releasing Corp. 10 Dec **1922.** Si; b&w. 35mm. 6 reels, 5,840 ft.

Dir-Writ Hampton Del Ruth. *Photog* Dal Clawson.

Cast: Alta Allen *(Eleanor Douglas)*, Milton Sills *(William Bradley)*, Henry B. Walthall *(Dr. Paul Graydon)*, Tully Marshall *(Timothy Lamb)*, Irene Rich *(Mary Douglas)*, Mitchell Lewis *(The Mute)*, Laura La Varnie *(Martha Douglas)*, Nick Cogley *(Uncle Remus)*.

Comedy-melodrama. The film begins in a comic vein—bordering on farce—and continues so up to the point where Eleanor Douglas is about to marry young district attorney William Bradley. She drinks the glass of water offered to her by Dr. Paul Graydon and loses consciousness. *Pronounced dead by Dr. Graydon, Eleanor is buried; but a cat, which also drinks from the glass, apparently dies, is about to be buried, but suddenly regains consciousness. Bradley hastens to exhume Eleanor's body, finds the coffin empty, and finally discovers Eleanor at Dr. Graydon's—lying on an operating table, still in her wedding dress, the doctor on the floor dead. Eleanor is suspected of shooting Graydon, but her sister confesses.* The scene then fades back to the wedding, where Eleanor awakens from a fainting spell and realizes she has been dreaming. *Physicians. District attorneys. Vivisection. Weddings. Dreams. Cats.*

THE MARRIAGE CHEAT **F2.3480**

Thomas H. Ince Corp. *Dist* Associated First National Pictures. 5 Apr **1924** [c7 May 1924; LP20158]. Si; b&w. 35mm. 7 reels, 6,426 ft.

Pres by Thomas H. Ince. *Pers Supv* Thomas H. Ince. *Dir* John Griffith

Wray. *Adapt* C. Gardner Sullivan. *Story* Frank R. Adams. *Photog* Henry Sharp.

Cast: Leatrice Joy *(Helen Canfield)*, Adolphe Menjou *(Bob Canfield)*, Percy Marmont *(Paul Mayne)*, Laska Winter *(Rosie)*, Henry Barrows *(captain of yacht)*, J. P. Lockney *(captain of supply ship)*.

Melodrama. Helen Canfield leaps from the pleasure yacht of her philandering husband and is picked up by natives of a South Seas island. There she falls in love with missionary Paul Mayne and gives birth to her husband's baby. When Canfield returns for her, Paul reluctantly gives her up. During a storm, however, the husband is drowned, and the lovers are then reunited. *Missionaries. South Sea Islands. Infidelity.*

THE MARRIAGE CIRCLE **F2.3481**

Warner Brothers Pictures. 3 Feb **1924** [New York premiere; released 16 Feb 1924; c12 Dec 1923; LP19705]. Si; b&w. 35mm. 8 reels, 8,200 ft.

Dir Ernst Lubitsch. *Adapt-Scen* Paul Bern. *Photog* Charles Van Enger. *Asst Dir* James Flood, Henry Blanke.

Cast: Florence Vidor *(Charlotte Braun)*, Monte Blue *(Dr. Franz Braun)*, Marie Prevost *(Mizzi Stock)*, Creighton Hale *(Dr. Gustav Mueller)*, Adolphe Menjou *(Prof. Josef Stock)*, Harry Myers *(detective)*, Dale Fuller *(neurotic patient)*, Esther Ralston.

Comedy of manners. Source: Lothar Goldschmidt, *Nur ein Traum, Lustspiel in 3 Akten* (München, 1909). Professor Stock sees his long-awaited chance to divorce his wife Mizzi when she begins a flirtation with Braun, the husband of her best friend, Charlotte. Charlotte is in turn admired by Dr. Mueller, Braun's business partner. Neither Braun nor Charlotte takes his admirer seriously, and in the end Mizzi and Dr. Mueller turn their attention to each other. *Physicians. Flirts. Professors. Marriage. Vienna.*

THE MARRIAGE CLAUSE (Universal-Jewel) **F2.3482**

Universal Pictures. 12 Sep **1926** [c12 Jun 1926; LP22821]. Si; b&w. 35mm. 8 reels, 7,680 ft.

Pres by Carl Laemmle. *Dir-Adapt* Lois Weber. *Photog* Hal Mohr.

Cast: Francis X. Bushman *(Barry Townsend)*, Billie Dove *(Sylvia Jordan)*, Warner Oland *(Max Ravenal)*, Henri La Garde *(doctor)*, Grace Darmond *(Mildred Le Blanc)*, Caroline Snowden *(Pansy)*, Oscar Smith *(Sam)*, André Cheron *(critic)*, Robert Dudley *(secretary)*, Charles Meakin *(stage manager)*.

Romantic drama. Source: Dana Burnet, "Technic," in *Saturday Evening Post* (197:14–15, 16 May 1925). Sylvia Jordan, a pretty but timid girl, applies for a part in a play being produced in a New York theater, and director Barry Townsend accuses her of stealing a pocketbook. Her display of emotion convinces him of her acting potential, and under his guidance she becomes a highly praised star on Broadway. They fall in love, and Sylvia accepts Barry's proposal; but when Ravenal, the producer, presents her with a 3-year contract, he inserts a clause forbidding her to marry. When Ravenal declines to renew Barry's contract, Sylvia demands his reinstatement; but Barry, misunderstanding because of the insinuations of Mildred Le Blanc, leaves the theater. On her opening night, Sylvia becomes ill; but learning that Barry is in the audience, she performs brilliantly though at length breaks down. Hearing of her collapse, Barry visits her in the hospital, and his love helps her recovery. *Actors. Theatrical directors. Theatrical producers. Marriage. Contracts. New York City—Broadway.*

MARRIAGE IN TRANSIT **F2.3483**

Fox Film Corp. 29 Mar **1925** [c5 Apr 1925; LP21363]. Si; b&w. 35mm. 5 reels, 4,800 ft.

Pres by William Fox. *Dir* R. William Neill. *Scen* Dorothy Yost. *Story* Grace Livingston Hill Lutz. *Photog* G. O. Post.

Cast: Edmund Lowe *(Holden/Cyril Gordon)*, Carol Lombard *(Celia Hathaway)*, Adolph Milar *(Haynes)*, Frank Beal *(Burnham)*, Harvey Clark *(aide)*, Fred Walton *(valet)*, Wade Boteler, Fred Butler, Byron Douglas, Fred Becker, Edward Chandler.

Comedy-melodrama. A gang of crooks led by Holden steals a government code, and Cyril Gordon, a Secret Service agent who bears a strong resemblance to the gang leader, is assigned to recover the stolen documents. Cyril successfully impersonates Holden and recovers the papers. He also gets himself a bride when, in the name of Holden, he marries Celia, a beautiful young woman who was about to sacrifice herself in matrimony to the gangster. Cyril discloses his identity to the girl, and they journey together to Washington, where Cyril reports to his superiors. Holden catches up with the newlyweds and traps them in a hotel room, but Cyril outfights Holden and escapes with his new wife. The gang is broken up, and Celia announces to Cyril that she would be honored to continue as his wife. *Secret service. Marriage. Impersonation. Cryptography. Washington (District of Columbia). Documentation.*

"MARRIAGE LICENSE?" **F2.3484**

Fox Film Corp. 5 Sep **1926** [c22 Aug 1926; LP23133]. Si; b&w. 35mm. 8 reels, 7,168 ft.

Pres by William Fox. *Dir* Frank Borzage. *Scen* Bradley King. *Titl* Elizabeth Pickett. *Photog* Ernest Palmer.

Cast: Alma Rubens *(Wanda Heriot)*, Walter McGrail *(Marcus Heriot)*, Richard Walling *(Robin)*, Walter Pidgeon *(Paul)*, Charles Lane *(Sir John)*, Emily Fitzroy *(Lady Heriot)*, Langhorne Burton *(Cheriton)*, Edgar Norton *(Beadon)*, George Cowl *(Amercrombie)*, Lon Poff *(footman)*.

Domestic drama. Source: F. Tennyson Jesse and Harold Marsh Harwood, *The Pelican* (New York opening: 21 Sep 1925). Wanda Heriot, a Canadian girl, is married to Marcus, an English nobleman whose family, dominated by ancestral traditions, rejects her as an outsider. Through the scheming of Lady Heriot, the girl's friendship with an elderly man is misrepresented; and following a divorce, her child is declared illegitimate. After years of self-sacrifice, Wanda has met and fallen in love with Paul. Her ex-husband, Marcus, discovers that his son, Robin, has grown to manhood in France and wants to become a soldier. To give an honorable name to her son, she sacrifices her happiness with Paul and agrees to remarry her repentant ex-husband. *Canadians. English. Nobility. Marriage. Social classes. Self-sacrifice. Illegitimacy. Motherhood.*

Note: Working title: *The Pelican*.

THE MARRIAGE MAKER **F2.3485**

Famous Players–Lasky. *Dist* Paramount Pictures. 17 Sep **1923** [New York premiere; released 14 Oct; c26 Sep 1923; LP19454]. Si; b&w. 35mm. 7 reels, 6,295 ft.

Pres by Adolph Zukor. *Dir* William De Mille. *Scen* Clara Beranger. *Photog* L. Guy Wilky.

Cast: Agnes Ayres *(Alexandra Vancy)*, Jack Holt *(Lord Stonbury)*, Charles De Roche *(Sylvani)*, Robert Agnew *(Cyril Overton)*, Mary Astor *(Vivian Hope-Clarke)*, Ethel Wales *(Mrs. Hope-Clarke)*, Bertram Johns *(Fish)*.

Romantic fantasy. Source: Edward Knoblock, *The Faun; or, Thereby Hangs a Tale* (New York opening: 16 Jan 1911). Sylvani plays matchmaker by arranging a marriage between moneyed Vivian Hope-Clarke and Cyril Overton, the boy she loves. He then convinces penniless nobleman Lord Stonbury to follow his instincts and marry Alexandra Vancy, the girl *he* loves. *Nobility. Marriage. Wealth. Poverty.*

THE MARRIAGE MARKET **F2.3486**

Columbia Pictures. *Dist* C. B. C. Film Sales. 25 Oct **1923** [c8 Feb 1924; LP19898]. Si; b&w. 35mm. 6 reels, 6,297 ft.

Prod Harry Cohn. *Dir* Edward J. Le Saint. *Story* Evelyn Campbell.

Cast: Kate Lester *(Miss Whitcomb)*, Mayme Kelso *(Miss Blodgett)*, Pauline Garon *(Theodora Bland)*, Marc Robbins *(Mr. Piggott)*, Vera Lewis *(Mrs. Piggott)*, Alice Lake *(Lillian Piggott)*, Jack Mulhall *(Wilton Carruthers)*, Willard Louis *(Seibert Peckham)*, Shannon Day *(reform school girl)*, Jean De Briac *(Count Demitri)*.

Comedy-drama. Theodora Bland, a wealthy young flapper, is expelled from her fashionable boarding school and sent home accompanied by the assistant headmistress, Miss Blodgett. They are accidentally separated on the train, and Theodora befriends a girl who has escaped from reform school. Theodora meets author Wilton Carruthers when she gets off the train at the wrong stop, and, finally arriving home, she learns that Carruthers is the fiancé of her snobbish stepsister, Lillian. After unsuccessful attempts by her mother and Lillian to marry Theodora to oil magnate Seibert Peckham, Theodora steals Carruthers from Lillian (more attracted to a dance teacher) and installs the reform school girl in her house as a maid. *Flappers. Authors. Stepsisters. Oilmen. Boarding schools. Reformatories.*

MARRIAGE MORALS **F2.3487**

Weber & North Productions. 15 Aug **1923** [c26 Jul 1923; LP19244]. Si; b&w. 35mm. 7 reels, 6,400 ft.

Prod Bobby North. *Dir-Writ* William Nigh. *Asst Dir* Ben Behrens. *Photog* Jack Brown, Sidney Hickox, Jo Moran. *Art Dir* John D. Schulze.

Cast: Tom Moore *(Young Harry Ryan)*, Ann Forrest *(Mary Gardner)*, Russell Griffin *(Harry, Jr.)*, John Goldsworthy *(J. C. Black)*, Harry T. Morey *(Marvin)*, Edmund Breese *(Harry's father)*, Florence Billings *(Molly Mahoney)*, Ben Hendricks, Jr. *(John Brink)*, Shannon Day *(his* *wife)*, Mickey Bennett *(Mary's brother)*, Charles Craig, Tom Lewis *(Harry's pals)*.

Romantic drama. *Harry Ryan, a wealthy spendthrift, falls in love with Mary Gardner, a beauty shop employee, and marries her. Mary, discouraged because she is unable to cure Ryan of his dissolute ways, leaves him. She returns after a change of heart to find her husband bedridden and despondent.* At the moment of reconciliation it is revealed that in reality Mary, unattached, was only dreaming, as the result of reading a book entitled *Marriage Morals*, by J. C. Black. *Cosmetologists. Spendthrifts. Marriage. Reading. Dreams.*

THE MARRIAGE OF WILLIAM ASHE **F2.3488**

Metro Pictures. 17 Jan **1921** [c15 Jan 1921; LP16025]. Si; b&w. 35mm. 6 reels.

Supv Bayard Veiller. *Dir* Edward Sloman. *Scen* Ruth Ann Baldwin. *Photog* Jackson Rose. *Art Interiors* John Holden.

Cast: May Allison *(Kitty Bristol)*, Wyndham Standing *(William Ashe)*, Zeffie Tillbury *(Lady Tranmore)*, Frank Elliott *(Geoffrey Cliffe)*, Robert Bolder *(Lord Parham)*, Lydia Yeamans Titus *(Lady Parham)*, Clarissa Selwynne *(Lady Mary Lyster)*.

Society melodrama. Source: Mary Augusta (Arnold) Ward, *The Marriage of William Ashe* (New York, 1905). Margaret Mayo and Mary Augusta (Arnold) Ward, *The Marriage of William Ashe; a Play in Five Acts* (publication undetermined). Lady Kitty Bristol leaves a French convent school after reading *Freedom*, a radical work by Geoffrey Cliffe. In London she meets both Cliffe and William Ashe, Secretary of Home Affairs, and she marries Ashe. Kitty makes numerous sketches, which amuse her husband, of British Cabinet members, and at Cliffe's advice when she is snubbed by Lady Parham she publishes them. She then creates a scandal by appearing seminude at a charity entertainment. Ashe is forced to resign, and upon discovering his wife gone he chastizes Cliffe for his influence. Later he finds her at the convent, where they are reconciled. *Artists. Nonconformists. Marriage. Radicalism. Great Britain—Home Affairs Department. London.*

THE MARRIAGE PLAYGROUND **F2.3489**

Paramount Famous Lasky Corp. 21 Dec **1929** [c21 Dec 1929; LP932]. Sd (Movietone); b&w. 35mm. 9 reels, 7,182 ft. [Also si; 6,610 ft.]

Dir Lothar Mendes. *Screenplay* J. Walter Ruben. *Adapt-Dial* Doris Anderson. *Photog* Victor Milner. *Rec Engr* M. M. Paggi.

Cast: Mary Brian *(Judith Wheater)*, Fredric March *(Martin Boyne)*, Lilyan Tashman *(Joyce Wheater)*, Huntley Gordon *(Cliffe Wheater)*, Kay Francis *(Zinnia La Crosse)*, William Austin *(Lord Wrench)*, Seena Owen *(Rose Sellers)*, Philippe De Lacy *(Terry)*, Anita Louise *(Blanca)*, Little Mitzi *(Zinnie)*, Billy Seay *(Astorre [Bun])*, Ruby Parsley *(Beatrice [Beechy])*, Donald Smith *(Chipstone [Chip])*, Jocelyn Lee *(Sybil Lullmer)*, Maude Turner Gordon *(Aunt Julia Langley)*, David Newell *(Gerald Omerod)*, Armand Kaliz *(Prince Matriano)*, Joan Standing *(Miss Scopy)*, Gordon De Main *(Mr. Delafield)*.

Society drama. Source: Edith Wharton, *The Children* (New York, 1928). Joyce and Cliffe Wheater, a much-divorced American couple, leave their seven children to fend for themselves as they tour the smart resorts of Europe. Judith, the eldest, takes care of the group. Martin Boyne, an American tourist, meets Judith and the children at the Lido and remembers that he knew their father in America; attracted to Judith, he is quick to sympathize with the problems of the children. Although he is the way to Switzerland to meet Rose Sellers, his fiancée, Martin delays the trip to help the children through a crisis that threatens to separate them. When he leaves, Judith despairs, feeling that he regards her as only a child, and she decides to take the children to Switzerland; there Martin realizes he loves her, and when Wheater, repenting of his neglect, telephones him to bring the children back, Martin declares that he is marrying Judith and will himself care for the children. *Children. Marriage. Divorce. Parenthood. Switzerland. Venice.*

THE MARRIAGE WHIRL **F2.3490**

Corinne Griffith Productions. *Dist* First National Pictures. 19 Jul **1925** [c21 Jul 1925; LP21666]. Si; b&w. 35mm. 8 reels, 7,672 ft.

Dir Alfred Santell. *Ed Dir* June Mathis. *Scen* Bradley King. *Photog* T. D. McCord. *Art Dir* John Hughes. *Film Ed* Cyril Gardner.

Cast: Corinne Griffith *(Marian Hale)*, Kenneth Harlan *(Arthur Carleton)*, Harrison Ford *(Tom Carrol)*, E. J. Ratcliffe *(John J. Carleton)*, Charles Lane *(Reuben Hale)*, Edgar Norton *(Dick Mayne)*, Nita Naldi *(Toinette)*.

Melodrama. Source: J. Hartley Manners, *The National Anthem, a Drama in Four Acts* (New York, 1922). Marian Hale meets Arthur Carleton, a wild youth with a love of jazz and gin, who takes her to a series of intemperate parties. Marian falls in love with Arthur, and when he promises to reform, she becomes his wife. Arthur plays the married part for a while; but he becomes increasingly bored, and soon their home is filled with booze and boisterousness. Marian's father sees her drunk and dies from the shock. Arthur and Marian go to Paris, and he neglects her, conducting a romance with Toinette, a cabaret dancer. Marian renews her acquaintance with Tom Carrol, a quiet and refined man who was once her suitor. Arthur returns home with Toinette, and Marian finds him making love to her. She orders them out and, in a distraught state, accidentally takes poison. Realizing her danger, she telepones Bob, who speeds to her in time to prevent an agonizing death. Arthur and Toinette are killed in an automobile accident, and Marian recovers and finds happiness at last with Bob. *Dancers. Jazz life. Marriage. Drunkenness. Automobile accidents. Paris.*

MARRIED? **F2.3491**

Jans Productions. 17 Feb **1926** [New York premiere]. Si; b&w. 35mm. 6 reels.

Dir George Terwilliger. *Story* Marjorie Benton Cooke. *Photog* Walter Blakely. *Adtl Photog* Louis Dunmyre.

Cast: Owen Moore *(Dennis Shawn)*, Constance Bennett *(Marcia Livingston)*, Evangeline Russell *(Kate Pinto)*, Julia Hurley *(Madame Du Pont)*, Nick Thomas *(Joe Pinto)*, Antrim Short *(Chuck English)*.

Melodrama. Dennis Shawn is the foreman of the timber holdings of an estate, the sole surviving heir of which is Marcia Livingston, a flapper who lives for jazz and gin. A lumber trust wants both the Livingston timber and the neighboring estate of an old lady. The woman refuses to sell her land, and she demands from Marcia, in return for this refusal, the right to choose Marcia's husband. Marcia agrees, and she and Dennis are married by telephone. Marcia refuses to live with Dennis, so the rugged lumberman kidnaps her from her Park Avenue roost and takes her to the North Country. She and Dennis eventually learn to love each other, preserving the Livingston timber holdings intact. *Heiresses. Flappers. Jazz life. Lumber industry. Trusts. Marriage of convenience. New York City—Park Avenue.*

MARRIED ALIVE **F2.3492**

Fox Film Corp. 17 Jul **1927** [c12 Jun 1927; LP24116]. Si; b&w. 35mm. 5 reels, 4,557 ft.

Pres by William Fox. *Dir* Emmett Flynn. *Scen* Gertrude Orr. *Photog* Ernest Palmer. *Asst Dir* Ray Flynn.

Cast: Lou Tellegen *(James Duxbury)*, Margaret Livingston *(Amy Duxbury)*, Matt Moore *(Charles Orme)*, Claire Adams *(Viola Helmesley Duxbury)*, Gertrude Claire *(Lady Rockett)*, Marcella Daly *(Blanche Fountain Duxbury)*, Henry Sedley *(Max Ferbur)*, Eric Mayne *(Dr. McMaster)*, Charles Lane *(Mr. Fountain)*, Emily Fitzroy *(Mrs. Maggs Duxbury)*.

Domestic comedy-drama. Source: Ralph Strauss, *Married Alive* (New York, 1925). A college professor who approves of polygamy among the lower forms of animal life goes to the seashore for rest, meets a man (Duxbury) who reveals himself to be married to four women. The professor proceeds to inform the wives of this infamy: one, an actress, doesn't care; the preacher's daughter is duly heartbroken. An old battle-ax proves to be actually married to the scoundrel, thus enabling the professor to marry the fourth, a lady of royalty. *Professors. Actors. Royalty. Marriage. Polygamy. Resorts.*

THE MARRIED FLAPPER **F2.3493**

Universal Film Manufacturing Co. 31 Jul **1922** [c22 Jul 1922; LP18088]. Si; b&w. 35mm. 5 reels, 4,662 ft.

Dir Stuart Paton. *Scen* Doris Schroeder. *Story* Bernard Hyman. *Photog* Jackson J. Rose.

Cast: Marie Prevost *(Pamela Billings)*, Kenneth Harlan *(Bill Billings)*, Philo McCullough *(Glenn Kingdon)*, Frank Kingsley *(Oliver Holbrook)*, Lucille Rickson *(Carolyn Carter)*, Kathleen O'Connor *(Gwen Barker)*, Hazel Keener *(Muriel Vane)*, Tom McGuire *(John Holbrook)*, Burton Wilson *(Robert Mills)*, William Quinn *("Wild Ben" Clark)*, Lydia Titus *(Mrs. Brewer)*, Martha Mattox *(Aunt Libby)*.

Comedy. A decline in family fortunes forces Bill to become a racing car driver. His wife, Pam, has been carrying on a bold flirtation with a wily philanderer, who, tiring of her, turns his attention to a younger girl. When Pam tries to defend her reputation, Bill breaks in; and a fight ensues in which he is injured. In a reconciliation, Pam takes his place as driver and

wins the race. *Philanderers. Marriage. Reputation. Automobile racing.*
Note: Working titles: *They're Off; Never Mind Tomorrow.*

MARRIED FLIRTS **F2.3494**
Metro-Goldwyn-Mayer Corp. *Dist* Metro-Goldwyn Distributing Corp. 27 Oct **1924** [c14 Oct 1924; LP20654]. Si; b&w. 35mm. 7 reels, 6,765 ft.
Pres by Louis B. Mayer. *Dir* Robert G. Vignola. *Scen* Julia Crawford Ivers. *Titl* Frederic Hatton, Fanny Hatton. *Photog* Oliver Marsh. *Settings* Charles L. Cadwallader. *Film Ed* Frank E. Hull. *Cost* Sophie Wachner.
Cast—Story: Pauline Frederick *(Nellie Wayne)*, Conrad Nagel *(Perley Rex)*, Mae Busch *(Jill Wetherell)*, Huntly Gordon *(Pendleton Wayne)*, Paul Nicholson *(Peter Granville)*, Patterson Dial *(Evelyn Draycup)*, Alice Hollister *(Mrs. Callender)*.
Cast—Celebrities: John Gilbert, Hobart Henley, Robert Z. Leonard, May McAvoy, Mae Murray, Aileen Pringle, Norma Shearer.
Society drama. Source: Louis Joseph Vance, *Mrs. Paramor* (New York, 1924). Nellie Wayne loses her husband, Pendleton, to Jill Wetherell by neglecting him and her appearance to pursue her literary ambitions. Nellie goes to Europe, where she becomes fashionable and a famous novelist under the name of Mrs. Paramor. She encounters Jill with Perley Rex, whom the vamp has married after jilting Pendleton. Intending to teach Jill a lesson, Nellie applies her charms to Perley until he offers to divorce Jill, but Nellie refuses and sends for Pendleton, whom she still loves. (Toward the end some of the Metro-Goldwyn-Mayer stars are shown at a banquet and Mah-Jong party at which Mrs. Paramor entertains the screen stars who are to work in the picturization of one of her novels.) *Novelists. Vamps. Mah-Jong. Motion pictures. Hollywood.*

MARRIED IN HOLLYWOOD **F2.3495**
Fox Film Corp. ca23 Sep **1929** [New York premiere; released 27 Oct; c26 Sep 1929; LP713]. Sd (Movietone); b&w with col sequences. 35mm. 9,700 ft.
Pres by William Fox. *Dir* Marcel Silver. *Dir Mus Numbers* Edward Royce. *Adapt-Dial* Harlan Thompson. *Photog* Charles Van Enger, Sol Halperin. *Film Ed* Dorothy Spencer. *Songs: "Dance Away the Night," "Peasant Love Song"* Harlan Thompson, Dave Stamper. *Songs: "A Man, a Maid," "Deep in Love"* Harlan Thompson, Oskar Straus. *Songs: "Bridal Chorus," "National Anthem"* Harlan Thompson, Arthur Kay. *Sd* George Leverett. *Asst Dir* Virgil Hart, Sid Bower. *Wardrobe* Sophie Wachner, Alice O'Neill.
Cast: J. Harold Murray *(Prince Nicholai)*, Norma Terris *(Mary Lou Hopkins/Mitzi Hofman)*, Walter Catlett *(Joe Glitner)*, Irene Palasty *(Annushka)*, Lennox Pawle *(King Alexander)*, Tom Patricola *(Mahai)*, Evelyn Hall *(Queen Louise)*, John Garrick *(stage prince)*, Douglas Gilmore *(Adjutant Octavian)*, Gloria Grey *(Charlotte)*, Jack Stambaugh *(Captain Jacobi)*, Bert Sprotte *(Herr von Herzen)*, Lelia Karnelly *(Frau von Herzen)*, Herman Bing *(German director)*, Paul Ralli *(Namari)*, Carey Harrison, Roy Seegar *(detectives)*, Donald Gallaher *(movie director)*.
Musical romance. Source: Leopold Jacobson and Bruno Hardt-Warden, *Married in Hollywood* (Vienna, 1928). Oskar Straus, *Ein Waltzertraum; Operette* (Wien, 1907). Heir to a Balkan throne, Prince Nicholai falls in love with an American vocalist who is touring with an operetta company in Europe. When he makes known his intention to renounce his heritage and marry Mary Lou, his mother has him locked up and orders Mary Lou back to the United States. En route she is "discovered" by a motion picture producer, and she becomes a star. Forced by a revolution to flee their fatherland, the royal family makes its way to America. There Nicholai and Mary Lou are happily reunited when he is selected from a group of extras to play the part of a prince in one of her films. *Royalty. Singers. Motion picture extras. Imaginary kingdoms. Motion pictures. Revolutions. Opera. Balkans.*

MARRIED PEOPLE **F2.3496**
Hugo Ballin Productions. *Dist* W. W. Hodkinson Corp. 17 Sep **1922.** Si; b&w. 35mm. 6 reels, 5,733 ft.
Dir Hugo Ballin. *Scen* Hugo Ballin, George S. Hellman. *Photog* James R. Diamond.
Cast: Mabel Ballin *(Dorothy Cluer)*, Percy Marmont *(Robert Cluer)*, Ernest Hilliard *(Lord Cranston)*, Bobby Clarke *(Timmy)*, Dick Lee *(Mike)*, Bertha Kent *(Mary)*, John Webb Dillon *(Bleauvelt)*, Louis Dean *(The Doctor)*, Charles Fang *(The Chinese)*, Baby Peggy Rice *(Betty)*.
Domestic drama. Unused to the luxury her husband is able to provide, Dorothy Cluer indulges in great extravagance, which is permitted by Robert yet results in considerable discord between the couple. The marriage disintegrates, and Dorothy is about to run off with a disreputable English lord when she shoots a boy (Timmy), mistaking him for a burglar. Grief-stricken, Dorothy suddenly realizes the error of her ways, takes care of Timmy, and adopts both him and a little girl in whom Robert has been interested. Thus the Cluers are reconciled, with the children acting as a firm bond between them. *Children. Wealth. Nobility. Marriage. Adoption.*

MARRY IN HASTE **F2.3497**
Phil Goldstone Productions. 1 Feb **1924** [New York showing]. Si; b&w. 35mm. 5 reels.
Dir Duke Worne. *Story* Jean Duvane.
Cast: William Fairbanks *(Wayne Sturgis)*, Dorothy Revier *(Joan Prescott)*, Alfred Hollingsworth *(manager)*, Gladden James *(Monte Brett)*, William Dyer *(champion)*, Al Kaufman *(Jack Dugan)*.
Comedy-drama. A wealthy Wyomingite disowns his son, Wayne Sturgis, for marrying art student Joan Prescott. After several years on a small farm, Joan suffers from disillusion, unhappiness, and poor health. The marriage is nearly ruined by the attentions that Brett, a neighbor, pays Joan. Wayne struggles to make good and is eventually rewarded when his father forgives him and welcomes the young couple home. *Artists. Students. Filial relations. Bohemianism. Farm life. Marriage. Disinheritance. Wyoming.*

MARRY ME **F2.3498**
Famous Players–Lasky. *Dist* Paramount Pictures. 29 Jun **1925** [c30 Jun 1925; LP21627]. Si; b&w. 35mm. 6 reels, 5,526 ft.
Pres by Adolph Zukor, Jesse L. Lasky. *Dir* James Cruze. *Screenplay* Anthony Coldeway. *Adapt* Walter Woods. *Photog* Karl Brown.
Cast: Florence Vidor *(Hetty Gandy)*, Edward Everett Horton *(John Smith, #2)*, John Roche *(John Smith, #1)*, Helen Jerome Eddy *(Sarah Hume)*, Fanny Midgley *(Granny)*, Ed Brady *(Norman Frisbie)*, Z. Wall Covington *(Jenkins)*, Anne Schaefer *(Mrs. Hume)*, Erwin Connelly *(Jackson)*.
Comedy. Source: Anne Caldwell, *The Nest Egg* (New York opening: 22 Nov 1910). Hetty Gandy, an attractive schoolteacher, visits a chicken farm and falls in love with John Smith, who soon proposes marriage to her. Before she can give her consent, she is called away, leaving behind an egg inscribed with the date on which she will marry John. The egg is to be given to John for his breakfast, but it goes into cold storage instead. Five years pass, and Hetty waits in vain for John to come and claim her as his bride, meanwhile turning away the proposals of Norman Frisbie, a real estate salesman. One day a wire arrives from "John Smith" telling her to be ready to go to an adjoining town with him. The entire town knows of John's coming, and a reception is arranged. When he arrives, Hetty is appalled to find that the John Smith who wired her is not her beloved, but rather a hypochondriac, who, believing himself to have become sick from the cold-storage egg on which Hetty had written years earlier, is suing the dealer from whom he purchased it. To avoid embarrassment, Hetty goes with John to a nearby town and, through a series of unlucky circumstances, is forced to spend the night with him in a hotel room. In order to protect Hetty from scandal, John marries her. They soon come to love each other, and Hetty's love cures John of his hypochondria. *Schoolteachers. Real estate agents. Hypochondriacs. Reputation. Eggs. Chickens.*

MARRY THE GIRL **F2.3499**
Sterling Pictures. 1 Mar **1928** [c3 Mar 1928; LP25035]. Si; b&w. 35mm. 6 reels, 5,300 ft.
Pers Supv Joe Rock. *Dir* Philip Rosen. *Cont-Titl* Frances Guihan. *Story* Wyndham Gittens. *Photog* Herbert Kirkpatrick. *Film Ed* Leotta Whytock. *Mus Cues* Michael Hoffman.
Cast: Barbara Bedford *(Elinor, the girl)*, Robert Ellis *(Harry Wayland, the boy)*, De Witt Jennings *(Martin Wayland, the father)*, Freddie Frederick *(Sonny, the child)*, Florence Turner *(Miss Lawson, the housekeeper)*, Paul Weigel *(The Butler)*, Allan Roscoe *(Cliff Lawson, the secretary)*.
Melodrama. Cliff Lawson and his sister, servants in the home of Martin Wayland, an elderly millionaire, cause Wayland to evict his son Harry by forging a check and blaming Harry. Having convinced Wayland that his son, who has disappeared, is dead, the Lawsons present Elinor and Sonny, Harry's alleged widow and child, hoping to claim Harry's inheritance and, eventually, the old man's fortune. Elinor is a poor widow who has been duped by Lawson into believing that Wayland is dying of loneliness and that her presence would be a comfort to him because the real widow cannot be found. Wayland becomes fond of Elinor and her son, and he makes out his will in her favor. Harry returns, exposes Lawson's scheme to his father, fires both the servants, and marries Elinor. *Swindlers. Domestics. Millionaires. Widows. Forgery. Inheritance. Wills.*

MARRY THE POOR GIRL **F2.3500**

Carter De Haven Productions. *Dist* Associated Exhibitors. 11 Dec **1921** [c6 Dec 1921; LU17299]. Si; b&w. 35mm. 5 reels, 5,500 ft.

Dir Lloyd Ingraham. *Scen* Rex Taylor.

Cast: Mrs. Carter De Haven *(Julia)*, Carter De Haven *(Jack Tanner)*.

Domestic comedy. Source: Owen Davis, *Marry the Poor Girl* (New York production: 23 Sep 1920). At a houseparty, Jack Tanner, one of the guests, accidentally falls into a fountain, and to ward off a cold he gets drunk. While in this condition, he mistakes his room and enters the bathroom next to Julia Paddington's boudoir and goes to sleep in the bathtub. The next morning Mrs. Paddington insists that he has compromised her daughter's reputation beyond repair unless he marries her. Julia accepts though engaged to Bradley. Rebuffed by their former sweethearts, Julia and Jack begin to find solace in each other. A chorus girl is hired to compromise Jack, but Julia grows jealous and decides to remain Mrs. Tanner. *Marriage. Reputation. Drunkenness.*

Note: " ... every member of an excellent supporting cast can be said to contribute heavily to the picture's success. The names of the latter are not shown on the screen, possibly because it was intended to keep only the two principals in the limelight; if so, a rank injustice has been inflicted on the other players ... ." (*Exhibitor's Trade Review,* 29 Apr 1922.)

MARS *see* **RADIO-MANIA**

LA MARSEILLAISE *see* **CAPTAIN OF THE GUARD**

THE MARSHAL OF MONEYMINT **F2.3501**

Ben Wilson Productions. *Dist* Arrow Film Corp. 14 Jun **1922** [c25 Apr 1922; LP17784]. Si; b&w. 35mm. 5 reels, 4,726 ft.

Prod Ben Wilson. *Story-Dir* Roy Clements.

Cast: Jack Hoxie *(Jack Logan)*, Jim Welch *(Jimsy MacTavish)*, James Rock *(Buck Lanning)*, William Lester *(Slick Boyle)*, Andrée Tourneur *(Mollie Benton)*, Claude Payton *(Velvet Joe Sellers)*, Goldie Madden *(Mandie St. Claire)*.

Western melodrama. Velvet Joe, a sinister influence in the town of Moneymint, attempts to frighten mineowners and thus take over their claims; Jack Logan and his partner seek the sheriff's aid, but he refuses to give it, making Jack a marshal and leaving him to fight his own battle. A nearby claim mined by Mollie Benton is also threatened, and when she finds Logan in a compromising situation, she believes him to be her persecutor. Unaware of his design, Mollie solicits the aid of Joe in the town, but Jack rides into the saloon and speeds away with her to the mine, where they are followed by Joe and his henchman. Jack convinces her of Joe's perfidy; and with her aid, he wins a battle against the men. *United States marshals. Sheriffs. Mine claims.*

MARTIN JOHNSON'S JUNGLE ADVENTURES *see* **JUNGLE ADVENTURES**

MARTIN LUTHER, HIS LIFE AND TIME **F2.3502**

Lutheran Film Division. c17 Nov **1924** [LP20769]. Si; b&w. 35mm. 6 or 8 reels.

Titl Rev. M. G. G. Scherer. *Adapt* Rev. M. G. G. Scherer, Ernest Maas.

Biographical drama. Source: P. Kurz, "Martin Luther, His Life and Time" (publication undetermined). A portrayal of the life of Martin Luther in the context of "a need for someone to return the church to God." The story begins with the birth of Luther and follows his boyhood, student days at Magdeburg, and life as a monk. There are scenes of Johann Tetzel selling indulgences, Luther nailing his 95 theses on the door of the Wittenberg church, various defenses of his doctrines, and his confinement at Warburg. Luther returns to Wittenberg, and later Magdelana (*i.e.*, Katharina von Bora) leaves the convent to marry him. The picture closes with a Christmas scene of Luther, his wife and children, and "a mass of people leaning towards him with outstretched arms." (Copyright records.) *Christmas. The Reformation. The Church. Religion. Wittenberg. Magdeburg. Warburg. Martin Luther. Johann Tetzel. Katharina von Bora.*

THE MARTYR SEX **F2.3503**

Phil Goldstone Productions. 8 Apr **1924** [New York showing; released caMar 1924]. Si; b&w. 35mm. 5 reels, 5,000 ft.

Dir Duke Worne. *Scen* Jefferson Moffitt. *Story* Leete Renick Brown. *Photog* Roland Price.

Cast: William Dyer *(Horseshoe Sam)*, William Fairbanks *(Dr. Ross Wayne)*, Les Bates *(Branch Paxton)*, Billie Bennett *(his wife)*, Dorothy Revier *(Beulah Paxton)*, Pat Harmon *(Lem Paxton)*, Frank Hagney *(Ed Carter)*.

Rural melodrama. Summoned to a cabin in the southern woods, Dr. Ross Wayne treats Branch Paxton, wounded in a feud, by amputating an arm. At the same time he warns Paxton that his daughter, Beulah, who has been mistreated, must be given rest and quiet. Paxton recovers and swears vengeance on Wayne, believing that the doctor amputated out of malice. Paxton, his son Lem, and a renegade friend named Ed Carter decide to kill Wayne when he makes a housecall. Wayne escapes with Beulah, now weak and dying, to a shack in the woods. The three men follow in pursuit. Wayne tricks Lem into entering the cabin and forcibly transfers blood from him to Beulah, thus saving her life. The situation is resolved, and all ends happily. *Physicians. Fatherhood. Rural life. Amputation. Blood transfusion. Feuds.*

MARY OF THE MOVIES **F2.3504**

Columbia Productions. *For* R-C Pictures. *Dist* Film Booking Offices of America. 27 May **1923** [c27 May 1923; LP20122]. Si; b&w. 35mm. 7 reels, 6,500 ft.

Conceived & supv by Louis Lewyn, Jack Cohn. *Dir* John McDermott. *Scen* Louis Lewyn. *Titl* Joseph W. Farnham. *Photog* George Meehan, Vernon Walker.

Cast—The Principals: Marion Mack *(Mary)*, Florence Lee *(her mother)*, Mary Kane *(her sister)*, Harry Cornelli *("Lait" Mayle, the postman)*, John Geough *(Reel S. Tate, the squire)*, Raymond Cannon *(Oswald Tate, his son)*, Rosemary Cooper *(Jane, the extra girl)*, Creighton Hale *(himself* [*the boy*]*)*, Francis McDonald *(James Seiler, a salesman)*, Henry Burrows *(the producer)*, John McDermott *(himself, the director)*, Jack Perrin *(Jack, Mary's brother)*, Ray Harford *(The Old Man)*.

Cast—Celebrities: Barbara La Marr, Douglas MacLean, Bryant Washburn, Johnnie Walker, J. Warren Kerrigan, Herbert Rawlinson, Alec Francis, Richard Travers, David Butler, Louise Fazenda, Anita Stewart, Estelle Taylor, Rosemary Theby, Bessie Love, Marjorie Daw, Tom Moore, Elliott Dexter, ZaSu Pitts, Carmel Myers, Rex Ingram, Maurice Tourneur, Edward J. Le Saint, Wanda Hawley.

Drama. To earn money needed by her family, Mary goes to Hollywood to break into the movies. Although she meets many celebrities, she has no luck. After being frightened by a "boulevard sheik," she takes a job as a waitress in a studio restaurant. Finally, through her resemblance to a star who is taken ill, she gets the lead in a picture. *Actors. Waitresses. Motion pictures. Hollywood.*

THE MASK **F2.3505**

Col. William N. Selig. *Dist* export & Import Film Co. 17 Jun **1921** [trade review]. Si; b&w. 35mm. 7 reels.

Pres by George H. Hamilton. *Dir* Bertram Bracken. *Scen* Arthur Lavon. *Photog* Edwin Linden.

Cast: Jack Holt *(Kenneth Traynor/Handsome Jack)*, Hedda Nova *(Helen Traynor)*, Mickey Moore *(Mickey, their son)*, Fred Malatesta *(Señor Enrico Keralio)*, Harry Lonsdale *(Winthrop Parker)*, Byron Munson *(Arthur Steele)*, Janice Wilson *(Rae Madison)*, William Clifford *(François)*.

Mystery drama. Source: Arthur Hornblow, *The Mask, a Story of Love and Adventure* (New York, 1913). "Devoted couple destined to part, the husband starting on long trip, bound to Africa. Sent to look after American interests in one of the world's largest diamond mines. Man's business associate is secretly in love with his wife and is in league with husband's valet to keep him in Africa. There is a twin brother, formerly a scapegrace, who is redeemed by rescuing the diamond engineer. They return to America in time to block villain's plan." (*Motion Picture News Booking Guide,* 1:72, Dec 1921.) *Engineers—Mining. Brothers. Twins. Valets. Ocean liners. Diamond mines. South Africa.*

THE MASK OF LOPEZ **F2.3506**

Monogram Pictures. *Dist* Film Booking Offices of America. 27 Jan **1924** [c27 Jan 1924; LP19876]. Si; b&w. 35mm. 5 reels, 4,900 ft.

Prod Harry J. Brown. *Dir* Albert Rogell. *Story-Scen* Marion Jackson. *Photog* Ross Fisher.

Cast: Fred Thomson *(Jack O'Neil)*, Wilfred Lucas *(Richard O'Neil)*, David Kirby *("Angel Face" Harry)*, Hazel Keener *(Doris Hampton)*, Frank Hagney *(Steve Gore/Lopez)*, George Magrill *(Pancho)*, Pee Wee Holmes *(Shorty)*, Bob Reeves *(Dick)*, Dick Sutherland *(Mexican)*, Silver King *(himself, a horse)*.

Western melodrama. Attracted to ranchowner Doris Hampton, Jack O'Neil impersonates convict "Angel Face" Harry, who is to be released from prison (a reform measure) to work on Doris' ranch. Jack discovers that Doris' cattle are being stolen by her foreman, Steve Gore, finds Gore's hiding place, and keeps him at bay until Doris rides up at the critical moment with help. *Ranchers. Ranch foremen. Criminals—Rehabilitation. Impersonation.*

THE MASK OF LOVE *see* **SUCH MEN ARE DANGEROUS**

THE MASK OF THE KU KLUX KLAN **F2.3507**

Frank B. Coigne. *Dist* Jawitz Pictures. Dec **1923** [scheduled release]. Si; b&w. 35mm. 6 reels, 5,800 ft.

Film Ed? (see note) Hopp Hadley.

Drama(?). No information about the nature of this film has been found except that "it shows meetings of a masked organization which committed deeds of violence—one of whose supposed members announced his intention of desecrating the altar of a Roman Catholic church. It shows the whipping of a young boy and an attack upon him before the altar of the church." (New York State license records.) *Sacrilege. Ku Klux Klan. Catholic Church.*

Note: Reedited by Hopp Hadley of Producers Service.

MASKED ANGEL **F2.3508**

Chadwick Pictures. *Dist* First Division Distributors. 29 Jun **1928.** Si; b&w. 35mm. 6 reels, 5,632 ft.

Prod I. E. Chadwick. *Dir* Frank O'Connor. *Scen* Maxine Alton. *Titl? (see note)* Isadore Bernstein, Leon Lee. *Photog* Ted Tetzlaff. *Film Ed* Gene Milford.

Cast: Betty Compson *(Betty Carlisle)*, Erick Arnold *(Jimmy Pruett)*, Wheeler Oakman *(Luther Spence)*, Jocelyn Lee *(Lola Dugan)*, Grace Cunard *(Cactus Kate)*, Lincoln Plummer *(Wilbur Ridell)*, Robert Homans *(Detective Bives)*, Jane Keckley *(The Nurse)*.

Romantic drama. Source: Evelyn Campbell, "Remorse" or "Rescue," in *Red Book*. Unjustly accused of theft, cabaret hostess Betty Carlisle ducks into a hospital to escape capture and pretends to visit a blinded, crippled soldier. They become interested in each other, fall in love, and marry. Through Betty's encouragement, the soldier recovers his health; he, in turn, forgives Betty for her past, which is revealed to him by a malicious former acquaintance of hers. *Cabaret hostesses. Soldiers. Cripples. Theft. Reputation. Blindness. Hospitals.*

Note: Bernstein appears to have been responsible for titles, but at least one source credits Lee.

THE MASKED AVENGER **F2.3509**

Doubleday Productions. *Dist* Western Pictures Exploitation Co. 6 Feb **1922** [New York State license]. Si; b&w. 35mm. 5 reels, ca4,750 ft.

Supv Charles W. Mack. *Dir* Frank Fanning. *Story-Scen* Henry McCarthy, Leo Meehan.

Cast: Lester Cuneo *(Austin Patterson)*, Mrs. Wallace Reid *(Valerie Putnam)*, Billy Reid *(The School Boy)*, Claude Payton *(Bruno Douglas)*, William Donovan *(Sheriff Dan Dustin)*, Phil Gastrock *(Ebenezer Jones)*, Tempe Pigott *("Aunt Phoebe Dyer")*, Burt Maddock *("Lariat Bill Williams")*, Ah Wing *(Quong Lee)*.

Western melodrama. "'Pat of Paradise' owns a ranch in a neighborhood which has been continually raided by a band of mysterious masked riders. The ranch owners of the district hold a series of conferences in an effort to get rid of the thieves. Patterson ignores the plans of his neighbors until the masked riders appropriate some of his own cattle. Then he determines to be avenged and discover the identity of the thieves. Masking, he haunts his ranch at night and finally discovers the robbers, but neighbors, seeing him, think he is one of them. He proves his innocence in a thrilling wind-up." (*Moving Picture World*, 8 Apr 1922, p664.) *Ranchers. Rustling.*

THE MASKED BRIDE **F2.3510**

Metro-Goldwyn-Mayer Pictures. 13 Dec **1925** [c7 Dec 1925; LP22123]. Si; b&w. 35mm. 6 reels, 5,699 ft.

Dir Christy Cabanne. *Adtl Dir (see note)* Josef von Sternberg. *Scen* Carey Wilson. *Titl (see note)* Marian Ainslee, Katherine Hilliker, H.H. Caldwell. *Story* Leon Abrams. *Photog* Oliver Marsh. *Art Dir* Cedric Gibbons, Ben Carré. *Film Ed* Frank E. Hull. *Asst Dir* Robert Florey.

Cast: Mae Murray *(Gaby)*, Francis X. Bushman *(Grover)*, Roy D'Arcy *(prefect of police)*, Basil Rathbone *(Antoine)*, Pauline Neff *(Grover's sister)*, Chester Conklin *(wine waiter)*, Fred Warren *(Vibout)*, Leo White *(floor manager)*.

Romantic drama. Gaby, a dancer and sometime thief working in a Montmartre cafe, meets Grover, an American millionaire who is doing research on French crime. He arranges to interview Gaby for his study, and, after several discussions, they fall in love. A wedding date is set, but Antoine, Gaby's former partner in both dancing and crime, forces her to steal a valuable necklace from Grover by threatening to kill him if she doesn't. Antoine is arrested by the prefect of police, and Grover, realizing that Gaby stole the necklace to protect his life, continues with the preparations for the wedding. *Millionaires. Thieves. Police. Criminology. Paris—Montmartre.*

Note: The film was begun by Sternberg, who was replaced by Cabanne. Sources disagree in crediting titles, citing either Ainslee or the team of Hilliker and Caldwell.

THE MASKED DANCER **F2.3511**

Eastern Productions. *Dist* Principal Pictures. 15 Feb **1924.** Si; b&w. 35mm. 5 reels, 4,720-4,987 ft.

Dir Burton King. *Adapt-Scen* John Lynch. *Photog* Charles Davis, Neil Sullivan.

Cast: Lowell Sherman *(Madhe Azhar, an East Indian prince)*, Helene Chadwick *(Betty Powell, The Masked Dancer)*, Leslie Austin *(Robert Powell)*, Joe King *(Fred Sinclair)*.

Melodrama. Source: Rudolph Lothar, *Die Frau mit der Maske* (Berlin, c1922). Azhar, an East Indian prince, and Robert Powell both become infatuated with a masked cabaret dancer, who is Betty Powell, trying to regain the love of her estranged husband—none other than Robert Powell. She allows Robert to court her, demanding that he elope with her, but he refuses to desert his wife. She unmasks and declares her intention of divorcing him. But they are reunited. *Royalty. Dancers. Disguise. Marriage. East Indians.*

MASKED EMOTIONS **F2.3512**

Fox Film Corp. 23 Jun **1929** [c18 Jun 1929; LP483]. Mus score & sd eff (Movietone); b&w. 35mm. 7 reels, 5,419 ft. [Also si; 5,389 ft.]

Pres by William Fox. *Dir* David Butler, Kenneth Hawks. *Scen* Harry Brand, Benjamin Markson. *Titl* Douglas Z. Doty. *Photog* Sidney Wagner. *Asst Dir* Ad Schaumer.

Cast: George O'Brien *(Bramdlet Dickery)*, Nora Lane *(Emily Goodell)*, J. Farrell MacDonald *(Will Whitten)*, David Sharpe *(Thad Dickery)*, James Gordon *(Captain Goodell)*, Edward Peil, Sr. *(Lee Wing)*, Frank Hagney *(Lagune)*.

Melodrama. Source: Ben Ames Williams, "A Son of Anak," in *Saturday Evening Post* (vol 201, 13 Oct–10 Nov 1928). Thad Dickery, the younger brother of Bram Dickery, falls into the clutches of Lee Wing when he is discovered aboard a ship that harbors smuggled Chinese. The ship is owned by Captain Goodell, the father of Bram's sweetheart, Emily, and when Bram discovers that the brother has been stabbed by the smugglers, he vengefully attacks Lee Wing and his confederate, causing the drowning of the former. Relieved that Emily is not involved in the conspiracy, he rushes his brother to the mainland, where he is treated for his wounds. Bram is subsequently reunited with his sweetheart. *Brothers. Smugglers. Chinese. Kidnaping.*

THE MASKED LOVER **F2.3513**

Golden Stars Film Productions. **1928.** Si; b&w. 35mm. [Feature length assumed.]

Cast: Jack Hollyday, Muriel Kingston, Lee Timmons.

Melodrama(?). No information about the nature of this film has been found.

THE MASKED WOMAN **F2.3514**

First National Pictures. 16 Jan **1927** [c12 Jan 1927; LP23523]. Si; b&w. 35mm. 6 reels, 5,434 ft.

Dir Silvano Balboni. *Scen* June Mathis. *Titl* Gerald C. Duffy. *Photog* John Boyle.

Cast: Anna Q. Nilsson *(Diane Delatour)*, Holbrook Blinn *(Baron Tolento)*, Einar Hansen *(Dr. René Delatour)*, Charlie Murray *(André O'Donohue)*, Gertrude Short *(Mimi)*, Ruth Roland *(Dolly Green)*, Richard Pennell *(Monsieur Lapoule)*, Cora Macey *(matron)*, Paulette Day *(baby)*.

Society melodrama. Source: Charles Méré, *La Femme masquée, pièce en quatres actes* (Paris, 1923). Baron Tolento desires Diane Delatour, his physician's wife, and donates money to their favorite charity, a children's home, in hope of gaining her favor. When Delatour is called away, Tolento inveigles Diane into attending a party at his house. There he threatens to ruin her husband if she does not submit to his demands within 3 months.

Diane retaliates by showing him a letter proving that Tolento has only 3 months to live, according to a specialist. Delatour learns of his wife's presence at the party from one of the baron's women, and when Tolento makes Diane heir to his fortune, he becomes convinced of her infidelity. But the statement of Mimi, the baron's mistress, proves the innocence of Diane, and she is reconciled with her husband. *Nobility. Physicians. Mistresses. Marriage. Lechery. Children's homes. Paris.*

THE MASKS OF THE DEVIL **F2.3515**

Metro-Goldwyn-Mayer Pictures. 17 Nov **1928** [c17 Nov 1928; LP25843]. Sd eff & mus score (Movietone); b&w. 35mm. 8 reels, 5,575 ft. [Also si.]

Dir Victor Seastrom. *Cont* Frances Marion. *Titl* Marian Ainslee, Ruth Cummings. *Adapt* Svend Gade. *Photog* Oliver Marsh. *Sets* Cedric Gibbons. *Film Ed* Conrad A. Nervig. *Song: "Live and Love"* William Axt, David Mendoza. *Asst Dir* Harold S. Bucquet. *Gowns* Adrian.

Cast: John Gilbert *(Baron Reiner)*, Alma Rubens *(Countess Zellner)*, Theodore Roberts *(Count Palester)*, Frank Reicher *(Count Zellner)*, Eva von Berne *(Virginia)*, Ralph Forbes *(Manfred)*, Ethel Wales *(Virginia's aunt)*, Polly Ann Young *(dancer)*.

Drama. Source: Jakob Wassermann, *Die Masken Erwin Reiners* (Berlin, 1910). Baron Reiner, a charming though unscrupulous Viennese aristocrat, becomes infatuated with Virginia, an innocent schoolgirl who is engaged to his best friend, Manfred. In order to seduce the girl, Reiner finances an oceanographic expedition for Manfred that takes him away for months. Reiner intercepts all of Manfred's letters and eventually bends Virginia to his satanic will. Manfred returns and wounds Reiner in a duel. Reiner recovers and takes the young girl for his own. *Aristocrats. Scientists. Students. Seduction. Oceanography. Vienna. Duels.*

MASQUERADE **F2.3516**

Fox Film Corp. 14 Jul **1929** [c24 Jul 1929; LP539]. Sd (Movietone); b&w. 35mm. 7 reels, 5,674 ft.

Pres by William Fox. *Dir* Russell J. Birdwell. *Stgd by* Lumsden Hare. *Dial-Scen* Frederick Hazlitt Brennan, Malcolm Stuart Boylan. *Photog* Charles Clarke, Don Anderson. *Film Ed* Ralph Dietrich. *Sd* Frank MacKenzie. *Asst Dir* William A. O'Connor.

Cast: Alan Birmingham *(Dan Anisty/Dan Maitland)*, Leila Hyams *(Sylvia Graeme)*, Arnold Lucy *(Bannerman)*, Clyde Cook *(Blodgett)*, Farrell MacDonald *(Joe Hickey)*, George Pierce *(Andrew Graeme)*, Rita Le Roy *(girl)*, Frank Richardson *(singer)*, John Breeden *(1st reporter)*, Jack Pierce *(2d reporter)*, Pat Moriarity *(3d reporter)*, Jack Carlisle *(4th reporter)*.

Melodrama. Source: Louis Joseph Vance, *The Brass Bowl* (Indianapolis, 1907). Sylvia Graeme is a young, ingenuous girl whose father, Andrew, is in jail where he likely will remain owing to some incriminating papers being secured, she believes, in the apartment secretary of world traveler Dan Maitland. She is nearly surprised by Maitland and his companion Blodgett after she has broken in, and her escape is marred by leaving behind her gloves and purse. Crook Dan Anisty, also after the same papers, hovers about these events waiting for an opportunity to purloin the files. At one point he blackjacks Maitland and takes his place, trying to induce Sylvia to surrender the files by masquerading as Maitland. Maitland in turn impersonates Anisty, much to the dismay and confusion of both Miss Graeme and Blodgett. The climax is an encounter between the two look-alikes on the roof of the apartment building, with Maitland besting his double and winning Miss Graeme in the bargain. *Doubles. Filial relations. Robbery. Impersonation. Documentation.*

THE MASQUERADE BANDIT **F2.3517**

R-C Pictures. *Dist* Film Booking Offices of America. 30 May **1926** [c26 May 1926; LP22766]. Si; b&w. 35mm. 5 reels, 4,919 ft.

Dir Robert De Lacey. *Scen* William E. Wing. *Story* Enid Hibbard, Ethel Hill. *Photog* John Leezer. *Asst Dir* John Burch.

Cast: Tom Tyler *(Jeff Morton)*, Dorothy Dunbar *(Molly Marble)*, Ethan Laidlaw *(Duncan)*, Alfred Heuston *(Pat)*, Ray Childs *(Spike)*, Raye Hamilton *(Kate Mahoney)*, Earl Haley *(Tony)*, Frankie Darro *(Tim [Hank?] Marble)*.

Western melodrama. Cowboy adventurer Jeff Morton's former friend Larry Evans is wounded holding up a train. Before he dies, Evans wills his ranch to Jeff, telling him that the loot is concealed in a cache to which a horse can lead him. The ranch hands—Pat, Tony, and Spike—are in sympathy with Jeff, but Duncan, the foreman, is suspicious of his story about the cache. Hank Marble, a cabaret owner, sides with Duncan, but his daughter Molly, who is set on his trail, falls in love with him. Jeff discovers the money and mailbags under a waterfall, informs the others, and all agree to return the money and thus achieve exoneration; Duncan, however, steals the cache, and Jeff is accused of treachery. Jeff pursues and fights Duncan, who falls off a cliff to his death. Jim and Molly are united. *Bandits. Ranchers. Cowboys. Ranch foremen. Inheritance. Train robberies.*

THE MASQUERADER **F2.3518**

Richard Walton Tully Productions. *Dist* Associated First National Pictures. ca29 Jul **1922** [St. Paul premiere; released 14 Aug; c12 Jul 1922; LP18056]. Si; b&w. 35mm. 8 reels, 7,835 ft.

Pres by Richard Walton Tully. *Dir* James Young. *Scen* Richard Walton Tully. *Art Dir* Wilfred Buckland. *Film Ed* A. Carle Palm.

Cast: Guy Bates Post *(John Chilcote, M. P./John Loder)*, Ruth Sinclair *(Eve Chilcote, his wife)*, Edward M. Kimball *(Brock, Chilcote's valet)*, Herbert Standing *(Herbert Fraide, his father-in-law)*, Lawson Butt *(Mr. Lakely)*, Marcia Manon *(Lady Lillian Astrupp)*, Barbara Tennant *(Bobby Blessington, Chilcote's secretary)*.

Drama. Source: John Hunter Booth, *The Masquerader; a Play Founded on Katherine Cecil Thurston's Novel* (New York opening: 3 Sep 1917). A distinguished British statesman, through excessive indulgence, has nearly ruined his political career and his homelife. He persuades a struggling journalist, who is his cousin and his exact double, to change places with him and thus redeem his political career. The moral dilemma posed by the wife's love for the double is solved by the statesman's death. *Politicians. Journalists. Doubles. Impersonation. Dissipation. Great Britain—Parliament.*

THE MASTER OF BEASTS (Jungle Series) **F2.3519**

Hagenbeck Film Corp. *Dist* Aywon Film Corp. 1 Jan **1922.** Si; b&w. 35mm. 5 reels.

Pres by Nathan Hirsh. *Wild Animals* Hagenbeck Menagerie.

Cast: Charles Vogt, Claire Lotto.

Adventure melodrama. "Story deals with a shipwrecked party in the African Jungle, and their adventures in protecting themselves from the savages and wild beasts. Man and woman survive the perils of the wild places and are brought back to civilization. They join a circus, the woman as a trapeze performer and the man as an animal tamer. The man is cleared of the murder charge from which he was trying to escape when shipwrecked." (*Motion Picture News Booking Guide,* Apr 1922.) *Trapezists. Animal tamers. Jungles. Animals. Circus. Africa. Shipwrecks.*

MASTER OF THE RANGE **F2.3520**

Dist Anchor Film Distributors. 17 Sep **1928** [New York State license]. Si; b&w. 35mm. 5 reels, 4,500 ft.

Cast: Cliff (Tex) Lyons.

Western melodrama(?). No information about the nature of this film has been found.

MASTERS OF MEN **F2.3521**

Vitagraph Co. of America. ca13 May **1923** [New York premiere; c2 Apr 1923; LP18847]. Si; b&w. 35mm. 7 reels, 6,740 ft.

Pres by Albert E. Smith. *Dir* David Smith. *Scen* C. Graham Baker. *Photog* Stephen Smith, Jr.

Cast: Earle Williams *(Lieutenant Breen)*, Alice Calhoun *(Mabel Arthur)*, Cullen Landis *(Dick Halpin)*, Wanda Hawley *(Bessie Fleming)*, Dick Sutherland *("Pig" Jones)*, Charles Mason *(Sawyer)*, Bert Apling *(Mr. Thorpe)*, Jack Curtis *(Captain Bilker)*, Martin Turner *("Nigger")*.

Melodrama. Source: Morgan Robertson, *Masters of Men; a Romance of the New Navy* (New York, 1901). Accused of theft by Mabel Arthur's brother, Dick Halpin accepts the blame and runs away to join the Navy to save Mabel from humiliation. Later he is shanghaied with Lieutenant Breen by Captain Bilker and his henchmen. They endure cruel treatment until they finally escape and rejoin their ships in Santiago Harbor just as war is breaking with Spain. Dick is commissioned for his courage in the battle with Spanish warships; Mabel's brother confesses his guilt of the theft; and the misunderstanding between Dick and Breen over Mabel and Bessie Fleming is cleared up to everyone's satisfaction. *Brother-sister relationship. Shanghaiing. United States Navy. Cuba—History. United States—History—War of 1898.*

THE MATCH-BREAKER **F2.3522**

Metro Pictures. ca11 Sep **1921** [Chicago and Atlanta premieres; released 19 Sep; c7 Dec 1921; LP17330]. Si; b&w. 35mm. 5 reels, 4,860 ft.

Dir Dallas M. Fitzgerald. *Scen* Arthur J. Zellner. *Photog* John Arnold.

Art Dir A. F. Mantz.

Cast: Viola Dana *(Jane Morgan)*, Jack Perrin *(Thomas Butler, Jr.)*, Edward Jobson *(Thomas Butler, Sr.)*, Julia Calhoun *(Mrs. Murray)*, Wedgewood Nowell *(Jack De Long)*, Kate Toncray *(Aunt Martha)*, Lenore Lynard *(Madge Lariane)*, Fred Kelsey *(detective)*, Arthur Millett *(Richard Van Loytor)*.

Romantic comedy. Source: Meta White, "The Match Breaker" (publication undetermined). Jane Morgan, to avoid marrying family lawyer Richard Van Loytor, takes her maid, Murray, and leaves home to make her own career. Finding it difficult to get work, she decides she is most accomplished as a "match-breaker" and offers her services in that capacity. Young broker Thomas Butler, Jr., who is concerned lest his father be snared by widow Madge Lariane, meets Jane at lunch and hires her to go to Coronado where his father is in Madge's coils, but they are seen by a detective in the employ of Butler, Sr. Thinking his son is the victim of a vamp, Mr. Butler hires Jane to break up the affair, but learning that she is the woman in the case he denounces her before young Tom. Madge traps Mr. Butler on his yacht with the aid of a confederate and tries to blackmail him. Jane follows them but is set adrift in a boat; she is rescued by Tom, and they return to foil the plotters and to get married themselves. *Vamps. Brokers. Widows. Filial relations. Blackmail. Yachts.*

THE MATINEE IDOL **F2.3523**

Columbia Pictures. 14 Mar **1928** [c5 Apr 1928; LP25136]. Si; b&w. 35mm. 6 reels, 5,925 ft.

Prod Harry Cohn. *Dir* Frank R. Capra. *Cont* Peter Milne. *Adapt* Elmer Harris. *Photog* Phillip Tannura. *Art Dir* Robert E. Lee. *Film Ed* Arthur Roberts. *Asst Dir* Eugene De Rue.

Cast: Bessie Love *(Ginger Bolivar)*, Johnnie Walker *(Don Wilson/Harry Mann)*, Lionel Belmore *(Col. Jaspar Bolivar)*, Ernest Hilliard *(Wingate)*, Sidney D'Albrook *(J. Madison Wilberforce)*, David Mir *(Eric Barrymaine)*.

Comedy-drama. Source: Robert Lord, "Come Back to Aaron" (publication undetermined). Members of a vacationing New York theater company become temporarily stranded in an upstate town and there to pass time they attend the Great Bolivar Stock Company's Civil War melodrama. Don Wilson, one of the sophisticated actors, is accidently hired to play a part in the melodrama when Ginger Bolivar, star of the production and daughter of the director-writer-producer, chooses him from a line of applicants to play a Confederate soldier who dies in her arms. Don's friends are so convulsed over the performance that they make arrangements to bring the group to New York. There Ginger mistakes the audience's laughter for ridicule. Thinking she has failed as a dramatic actress, she returns home. A few days later, Don, having fallen in love with her, arrives to claim Ginger. *Actors. Theatrical troupes. New York State. New York City.*

MATINEE LADIES **F2.3524**

Warner Brothers Pictures. 9 Apr **1927** [c2 Apr 1927; LP23831]. Si; b&w. 35mm. 7 reels, 6,352 ft.

Dir Byron Haskin. *Scen* Graham Baker. *Story* Albert S. Howson, Sidney R. Buchman. *Camera* Frank Kesson. *Asst Dir* Henry Blanke.

Cast: May McAvoy *(Sallie Smith)*, Malcolm McGregor *(Bob Ward)*, Hedda Hopper *(Mrs. Aldrich)*, Margaret Seddon *(Mrs. Smith)*, Richard Tucker *(Tom Mannion)*, Jean Lefferty *(Maizie Blossom)*, Cissy Fitzgerald *(Madame Leonine)*, William Demarest *(man-about-town)*.

Society melodrama. Bob Ward, a law student in financial straits, accepts work as a paid dancing companion at a roadhouse, where he spends afternoons with women tired of the bonds of matrimony. He meets Sallie Smith, a cigarette girl, and their mutual bond of sympathy grows into love. Tom Mannion, a wealthy idler who has made advances to Sallie, persuades her to attend a yacht party, while Bob consents to a financial agreement with a Mrs. Aldrich, causing a quarrel between himself and Sallie. After uncovering Mrs. Aldrich's true motives, Bob rescues Sallie from the advances of Mannion aboard the yacht during a severe storm. They are picked up by a rescue party and are happily united. *Students. Cigarette girls. Gigolos. Bootleggers. Finance—Personal. Jazz life. Roadhouses. Yachts.*

THE MATING CALL **F2.3525**

Caddo Co. *Dist* Paramount Pictures. 21 Jul **1928** [c4 Sep 1928; LP25596]. Si; b&w. 35mm. 7 reels, 6,352 ft.

Pres by Howard Hughes. *Prod* Howard Hughes. *Dir* James Cruze. *Titl* Herman J. Mankiewicz. *Adapt* Walter Woods. *Photog* Joseph Morgan. *Film Ed* Walter Woods. *Song: "The Mating Call"* William Axt, David Mendoza.

Cast: Thomas Meighan *(Leslie Hatton)*, Evelyn Brent *(Rose Henderson)*, Renée Adorée *(Catherine)*, Alan Roscoe *(Lon Henderson)*, Gardner James *(Marvin Swallow)*, Helen Foster *(Jessie)*, Luke Cosgrave *(Judge Peebles)*, Cyril Chadwick *(Anderson)*, Will R. Walling.

Drama. Source: Rex Beach, *The Mating Call* (New York, 1927). After the Armistice, Leslie Hatton, a Florida farmer, returns home to discover that his wife, Rose, has had their marriage annulled in order to marry wealthy Lon Henderson. Leslie returns to farming for solace, and Rose, quickly disillusioned by Henderson's infidelity, again offers herself to Leslie. He wants no part of her, however, and goes instead to Ellis Island, where he persuades Catherine, an aristocratic Russian immigrant, to marry him in return for a home in the United States. Jessie Peebles, a young girl disillusioned by an affair with Henderson, drowns herself in a pond on Leslie's farm, and Henderson, head of the local Ku Klux Klan, orders Leslie tried before a Klan tribunal. Leslie is found not guilty when letters are produced that link Henderson with the dead girl. Leslie's ordeal has had a good side, however, for he and Catherine have realized that what was to have been a marriage of convenience has become a marriage of love. *Veterans. Farmers. Aristocrats. Immigrants. Russians. Marriage—Annulment. Marriage of convenience. Suicide. Florida. Ellis Island. Ku Klux Klan.*

MATRIMONIAC (Reissue) **F2.3526**

Fine Arts Pictures. *Dist* Film Distributors League. **1921.** Si; b&w. 35mm. 5 reels.

Note: A Douglas Fairbanks–Constance Talmadge film originally released by Triangle Film Corp. on 16 Dec 1916.

THE MATRIMONIAL BED **F2.3527**

Warner Brothers Pictures. 2 Aug **1930** [c21 Jul 1930; LP1431]. Sd (Vitaphone); b&w. 35mm. 8 reels, 6,242 ft.

Dir Michael Curtiz. *Screenplay* Harvey Thew, Seymour Hicks. *Dial* Harvey Thew. *Photog* Dev Jennings. *Song: "Fleur d'Amour"* Sidney Mitchell, George W. Meyer. *Rec Engr* Earl Sitar.

Cast: Frank Fay *(Adolphe Noblet/Leopold)*, Lilyan Tashman *(Sylvaine)*, James Gleason *(Gustave Corton)*, Beryl Mercer *(Corinne)*, Marion Byron *(Marianne)*, Vivian Oakland *(Suzanne Trebel)*, Arthur Edmund Carew *(Dr. Friedland)*, James Bradbury, Sr. *(Chabonnais)*, Florence Eldridge *(Juliette)*.

Domestic comedy-drama. Source: Yves Mirande and André Mouëzy-Éon, *The Matrimonial Bed* (adapted from the French by Edward Seymour Hicks; New York opening: 12 Oct 1927). On the fifth anniversary of the death of Adolphe Noblet in a railway accident, Juliette, his widow, visits his grave. Now remarried, she is the wife of Gustave, a former friend of the family, and has borne his child. The maid, Corinne, cherishes the memory of her former master through a portrait, and Marianne, a new servant, sees in him the likeness of a hairdresser, Leopold Trebel, with whom Sylvaine, Juliette's friend, is in love. When Leopold is invited to dinner, all are astonished at the likeness, and he concludes they must be mad. Innumerable complications follow when Dr. Friedland hypnotizes him, restoring his former memory as Adolphe, as he does not recognize Sylvaine or Marianne; then his other wife appears with his four children! He finally agrees to a scheme to regain his former self, and he leaves with Suzanne, his "new" wife, learning the names of his children. ... *Hairdressers. Children. Marriage. Amnesia. Bigamy. Family life. Paris.*

Note: Studio publicists credit the story as an "original" by Harvey Thew.

THE MATRIMONIAL WEB **F2.3528**

Vitagraph Co. of America. 2 Oct **1921** [c9 Sep 1921; LP16947]. Si; b&w. 35mm. 5 reels, 4,970 ft.

Dir Edward José. *Story-Scen* C. Graham Baker.

Cast: Alice Calhoun *(Helen Anderson)*, Joseph Striker *(Harvey Blake)*, William Riley Hatch *(Revenue Officer Anderson)*, Armand Cortez *(Gregory)*, Charles Mackay *(Cyrus Blake)*, Elsie Fuller *(Miriam Blake)*, Ernest Hilliard *(Irving Sneed)*, Marion Barney *(Mrs. Sanborn)*, Edith Stockton *(Dorothy Sanborn)*, G. C. Frye *(Judge Cameron)*, Richard Lee *(smuggler)*.

Melodrama. Revenue Officer Anderson is informed that opium smugglers are operating in his district. He and his assistant, Gregory, are unable to locate a wireless used by the criminals, but his daughter, Helen, offers her aid. Meanwhile, at Cyrus Blake's summer residence, Blake remarks that if a woman is betrayed by a man, he is duty-bound to protect her with his name. His son, Harvey, arrives home from college but escapes the houseparty by retiring to a nearby island. Helen, finding him suspicious, follows to investigate. At the party, Mrs. Sanborn, in desperate circumstances, plots to have her daughter, Dorothy, spend the night with Harvey on the island, thus forcing a marriage. Thinking Harvey is the smuggler, Helen conceals herself in his cabin and there finds the wireless; she prevents the forced marriage and helps capture the real smuggler. *Revenue agents. Smugglers. Reputation. Opium. Radio.*

MAYBE IT'S LOVE **F2.3529**

Warner Brothers Pictures. 4 Oct **1930** [c12 Sep 1930; LP1559]. Sd (Vitaphone); b&w. 35mm. 8 reels, 6,568 ft.

Dir William Wellman. *Screenplay-Dial* Joseph Jackson. *Story* Mark Canfield. *Photog* Robert Kurrle. *Film Ed* Edward McDermott. *Songs: "Maybe It's Love," "All-American"* Sidney Mitchell, Archie Gottler, George W. Meyer.

Cast: Joan Bennett *(Nan Sheffield)*, Joe E. Brown *(Speed Hanson)*, James Hall *(Tommy Nelson)*, Laura Lee *(Betty)*, Anders Randolf *(Mr. Nelson)*, Sumner Getchell *(Whiskers)*, George Irving *(President Sheffield)*, George Bickel *(Professor)*, Howard Jones *(Coach Bob Brown)*, Bill Banker *(Bill)*, Russell Saunders *("Racehorse" Russell)*, Tim Moynihan *(Tim)*, W. K. Schoonover *(Schoony)*, E. N. Sleight *(Elmer)*, George Gibson *(George)*, Ray Montgomery *(Ray)*, Otto Pommerening *(Otto)*, Kenneth Haycraft *(Ken)*, Howard Harpster *(Howard)*, Paul Scull *(Paul)*, Stuart Erwin *(Brown of Harvard)*.

Comedy. Because Upton College has failed to defeat the Parsons football team in 12 years, the trustees of Upton insist that President Sheffield must resign if Upton does not beat Parsons in the coming season. Overhearing this threat, Nan, the president's daughter, and Speed Hanson, football star, develop a plan: Nan changes her studious appearance and with her ravishing charms recruits a choice football team for Upton; but the coach wants Tommy Nelson, the spoiled son of a wealthy father, whom Sheffield will not admit because of his poor credentials. Tommy registers under an assumed name and discovers Nan's plot; he informs the team of her methods, and they scheme to get even by pretending drunkenness before the game. After sufficient punishment, she is forgiven and they win the game for her; and Tommy, forgiven by his father, wins the love of Nan. *Football. Courtship. College life.*

Note: The cast includes some members of the 1928 and 1929 All-American football teams.

THE MAYOR OF FILBERT (Reissue) **F2.3530**

Dist Tri-Stone Pictures. **1923**. Si; b&w. 35mm. 5 reels.

Note: A "re-edited and re-titled" William Christy Cabanne production originally released by Triangle Film Corp.

MAYTIME **F2.3531**

B. P. Schulberg Productions. *Dist* Preferred Pictures. 16 Nov **1923** [Newark, N. J., showing; released 11 Dec; c21 Nov 1923; LP19631]. Si; b&w. 35mm. 8 reels, 7,500 ft.

Pres by B. P. Schulberg. *Dir* Louis Gasnier. *Adapt* Olga Printzlau. *Photog* Karl Struss.

Cast: Ethel Shannon *(Ottilie Van Zandt/Ottilie, the granddaughter)*, Harrison Ford *(Richard Wayne/Richard, the grandson)*, William Norris *(Matthew)*, Clara Bow *(Alice Tremaine)*, Wallace MacDonald *(Claude Van Zandt)*, Josef Swickard *(Colonel Van Zandt)*, Martha Mattox *(Mathilda)*, Betty Francisco *(Ermintrude)*, Robert McKim *(Monte Mitchell)*.

Romantic drama. Source: Rida Johnson Young and Cyrus Wood, *Maytime* (New York, 1917). Rida Johnson Young and Sigmund Romberg, *Maytime* (New York opening: 16 Aug 1917). Ottilie Van Zandt, the beautiful daughter of a wealthy colonel, loves the gardener's son, Richard Wayne, but is forced by her family to marry her cousin, Claude. Richard leaves before the wedding, vowing to return wealthy and to marry Ottilie, but, since she is already married when he does return, Richard marries Alice Tremaine on impulse. Years later, to save Ottilie, a lonely widow, from being evicted, Richard purchases her house at auction and gives it to her. Two generations later, Ottilie, the granddaughter of the first Ottilie, lives in the old house and teaches dancing. Richard Wayne, grandson of the first Richard, is a wealthy young man of the jazz set, who thinks of Ottilie as a little old-fashioned but has affection for her. Their friendship culminates in a romance and marriage that began years before with their grandparents. *Dance teachers. Social classes. Wealth. Poverty. Marriage. Jazz life.*

MAZEL TOV **F2.3532**

Listo-Picon Films. *Dist* Kerman Films. 27 Feb **1924** [New York State license; New York showing caAug]. Si; b&w. 35mm. 8 reels, 7,700 ft.

Cast: Molly Picon, Jacob Kalich.

Comedy. "... of genuine Jewish life" (*Variety*, 3 Sep 1924, p22). *Jews.*

Note: Subtitles in Yiddish.

McFADDEN'S FLATS **F2.3533**

Asher-Small-Rogers. *Dist* First National Pictures. 6 Feb **1927** [c26 Jan 1927; LP23593]. Si; b&w. 35mm. 8 reels, 7,846 ft.

Pres by Asher-Small-Rogers. *Prod* Edward Small. *Dir* Richard Wallace. *Scen* Charles Logue. *Adapt* Jack Wagner, Jack Jevne, Rex Taylor. *Photog* Arthur Edeson.

Cast: Charlie Murray *(Dan McFadden)*, Chester Conklin *(Jock McTavish)*, Edna Murphy *(Mary Ellen McFadden)*, Larry Kent *(Sandy McTavish)*, Aggie Herring *(Mrs. McFadden)*, De Witt Jennings *(Patrick Halloran)*, Cissy Fitzgerald *(Mrs. Halloran)*, Dorothy Dwan *(Edith Halloran)*, Freeman Wood *(Desmond Halloran)*, Dot Farley *(Bridget Maloney)*, Leo White *(hat salesman)*, Harvey Clark *(interior decorator)*.

Comedy-drama. Source: Gus Hill, *McFadden's Row of Flats* (c1896). McFadden, an Irish contractor, and McTavish, a Scotch barber, become fast friends, and McTavish's son, Jock, meets and falls in love with Mary Ellen, McFadden's daughter. McFadden, having increased his store of worldly goods, sends his daughter to a finishing school, to the dismay of young Jock, and Dan provokes frequent outbursts from McTavish, whose outlook on life is the antithesis of his own. McFadden's ambition to complete a flat building is well underway when he suddenly finds himself in financial straits, and when McTavish secretly helps him out, all eventually works out well for the friends and the young lovers. *Irish. Scotch. Barbers. Contractors. Wealth. Boarding schools.*

McGUIRE OF THE BIG SNOWS *see* **McGUIRE OF THE MOUNTED**

McGUIRE OF THE MOUNTED **F2.3534**

Universal Pictures. 9 Jul **1923** [c19 Jun 1923; LP19138]. Si; b&w. 35mm. 5 reels, 5,020 ft.

Dir Richard Stanton. *Scen* George Hively. *Story* Raymond L. Schrock, George Hively. *Photog* Ben Kline.

Cast: William Desmond *(Bob McGuire)*, Louise Lorraine *(Julie Montreau)*, Willard Louis *(Bill Lusk)*, Vera James *(Katie Peck)*, J. P. Lockney *(André Montreau)*, William A. Lowery *(Major Cordwell)*, Peggy Browne *(Mrs. Cordwell)*, Frank Johnson *(Henri)*, Jack Walters *(Sergeant Murphy)*.

Melodrama. Bob McGuire, Royal Northwest Mounted officer trailing a ring of opium smugglers, suspects gambling house proprietor Big Bill Lusk. Lusk's plan is to frame McGuire by drugging him and marrying him to Katie Peck, a dancehall girl who knows the plot. McGuire's superior officer is killed, and McGuire is accused of the murder; but Katie, who has fallen in love with McGuire, discloses that Lusk is the murderer and exposes the smugglers' plot. *Dancehall girls. Gambling. Smuggling. Murder. Opium. Northwest Mounted Police.*

Note: Working title: *McGuire of the Big Snows.*

ME, GANGSTER **F2.3535**

Fox Film Corp. 14 Oct **1928** [c14 Oct 1928; LP25717]. Mus score (Movietone); b&w. 35mm. 7 reels, 6,042 ft.

Pres by William Fox. *Dir* Raoul Walsh. *Scen* Charles Francis Coe, Raoul Walsh. *Titl* William Kernell. *Photog* Arthur Edeson. *Film Ed* Louis Loeffler. *Asst Dir* Archibald Buchanan.

Cast: June Collyer *(Mary Regan)*, Don Terry *(Jimmy Williams)*, Anders Randolf *(Russ Williams)*, Stella Adams *(Lizzie Williams)*, Burr McIntosh *(Bill Lane)*, Walter James *(Captain Dodds)*, Gustav von Seyffertitz *(factory owner)*, Al Hill *(Danny)*, Herbert Ashton *(sucker)*, Bob Perry *(Tuxedo George)*, Harry Castle *(Philly Kid)*, Carol Lombard *(Blonde Rosie)*, Joe Brown *(Joe Brown)*, Nigel De Brulier *(Danish Looie)*, Arthur Stone *(Dan the Dude)*.

Crime melodrama. Source: Charles Francis Coe, *Me—Gangster* (New York, 1927). Jimmy Williams, a slum youth who has slowly drifted from petty theft to armed robbery, knocks over a joint on his own and comes up with $50,000. He hides the money but has no chance to spend it, for he is picked up by the police, tried, and sentenced to jail. During his 2 years on the rock pile, Jimmy has a change of heart: his mother dies tragically, and he comes under the beneficent influence of Mary Regan. Paroled for good behavior before the end of his term, Jimmy decides to go straight, planning to return the $50,000 to its rightful owner. His old gang learns of the plan, however, and attempts to steal the money from him before he can turn it over to the police; but with Mary's help, Jimmy outwits the gangsters and returns the cash. Jimmy then sets out with Mary on the road to a new life. *Criminals—Rehabilitation. Gangsters. Robbery. Prisons. Parole.*

THE MEANEST MAN IN THE WORLD **F2.3536**

Principal Pictures. *Dist* Associated First National Pictures. 22 Oct **1923** [c22 Oct 1923; LP19519]. Si; b&w. 35mm. 6 reels, 5,600 ft.

Dir Edward F. Cline. *Scen* Austin McHugh. *Photog* Arthur Martinelli.

Cast: Bert Lytell *(Richard Clark)*, Blanche Sweet *(Jane Hudson)*, Bryant Washburn *(Ned Stevens)*, Maryon Aye *(Nellie Clarke)*, Lincoln Stedman *(Bart Nash, the office boy)*, Helen Lynch *(Kitty Crockett, the stenographer)*, Ward Crane *(Carleton Childs)*, Frances Raymond *(Mrs. Clarke)*, Carl Stockdale *(Hiram Leeds)*, Tom Murray *(Andy Oatman)*, Forrest Robinson *(Michael O'Brien)*, Robert Dunbar *(Franklin Fielding)*, Victor Potel *(Lute Boon)*, William Conklin *(Frederick Leggett)*.

Melodrama. Source: George M. Cohan, *The Meanest Man in the World; Play in Three Acts* (c1920). Everett S. Ruskay, *The Meanest Man in the World; Play in One Act* (c21 Aug 1915). Soft-hearted lawyer Richard Clarke determines to get tough and collect the debts owed him. He begins with "J. Hudson," who happens to be *Miss* Jane Hudson, a very attractive damsel in distress. As her property is in danger of appropriation by dishonest oil speculators, Jane joins forces with Clarke; and together they raise enough money to finance oil-drilling operations. Incidentally, they fall in love. *Lawyers. Swindlers. Oil wells.*

THE MEASURE OF A MAN **F2.3537**

Universal Pictures. 14 Oct **1924** [New York premiere; released 28 Dec; c23 Sep 1924; LP20602]. Si; b&w. 35mm. 5 reels, 4,979 ft.

Dir Arthur Rosson. *Screenplay* Wyndham Gittens. *Scen* Isadore Bernstein. *Photog* Jackson Rose.

Cast: William Desmond *(John Fairmeadow)*, Albert J. Smith *(Jack Flack)*, Francis Ford *("Pale" Peter)*, Marin Sais *(Clare, his wife)*, William J. Dyer *(Billy the Beast)*, Bobby Gordon *(Donald, son of "Pale" Peter)*, Harry Tenbrook *(Charley, the bartender)*, Zala Davis *(Jenny Hitch)*, William Turner *(Tom Hitch)*, Mary McAllister *(Pattie Batch)*.

Melodrama. Source: Norman Duncan, *The Measure of a Man; a Tale of the Big Woods* (New York, 1911). Overcoming his addiction to drink, John Fairmeadow leaves the Bowery for a western logging camp posing as a minister. His fistic ability and his gentle manner reform the town drinkers and put the saloon out of business. Meanwhile, John also protects pretty orphan Pattie Batch from the attentions of Jack Flack; Flack is killed by saloon keeper Pale Peter after the body of his wife, Clare, who was betrayed by Flack, is discovered in the river; and John is united to Pattie. *Clergymen. Reformers. Saloon keepers. Orphans. Alcoholism. Temperance. Imposture. Lumber camps. New York City—Bowery.*

MEDALS *see* **SEVEN DAYS LEAVE**

THE MEDDLER **F2.3538**

Universal Pictures. 28 Jun **1925** [c28 Mar 1925; LP21316]. Si; b&w. 35mm. 5 reels, 4,890 ft.

Dir Arthur Rosson. *Scen? (see note)* Isadore Bernstein, W. Scott Darling. *Story* Miles Overholt. *Photog* Gilbert Warrenton.

Cast: William Desmond *(Richard Gilmore)*, Dolores Rousse *(Gloria Canfield)*, Claire Anderson *(Dorothy Parkhurst)*, Albert J. Smith *(Bud Meyers)*, Jack Daugherty *(Jesse Canfield)*, C. L. Sherwood *(sheriff)*, Kate Lester *(Mrs. Gilmore)*, Georgie Grandee *(secretary)*, Donald Hatswell *(Captain Forsythe)*.

Western melodrama. Richard Gilmore, a staid Wall Street broker, is jilted by Dot Parkhurst when he fails to provide her with the romance and adventure that she wants out of life. Richard then goes west in an effort to prove himself a man and becomes a highwayman known as "The Meddler," robbing people only to return to them all that he stole, keeping only a valueless memento for himself. He meets and falls in love with Gloria Canfield when he robs the stage on which she is riding, and later he rescues her from bandits, winning her love and the forgiveness of her brother, Jesse. Dot marries a retired Army officer, and Richard, having proved himself an honest man, makes plans to stay in the West with Gloria. *Brokers. Highwaymen. Brother-sister relationship. Manhood. Stagecoach robberies. New York City—Wall Street.*

Note: Sources disagree on actual scenario credit.

THE MEDDLIN' STRANGER **F2.3539**

Action Pictures. *Dist* Pathé Exchange. 12 Jun **1927** [c7 Apr 1927; LU23835]. Si; b&w. 35mm. 5 reels, 4,575 ft.

Pres by Lester F. Scott, Jr. *Dir* Richard Thorpe. *Story-Scen* Christopher B. Booth. *Photog* Ray Ries.

Cast: Wally Wales *(Wally Fraser)*, Nola Luxford *(Mildred Crawford)*, Charles K. French *(Her Father)*, Mabel Van Buren *(Her Mother)*, James Marcus *("Big Bill" Dawson)*, Boris Karloff *(Al Meggs)*.

Western melodrama. Wally Fraser comes to Juniper City to take revenge on the murderer of his father, whom he believes to be Dawson, a local banker. After rescuing the daughter of rancher Crawford from a runaway team, Wally warns Crawford that Al Meggs is cheating in a poker game; in a fight Meggs kills a man and seeks shelter with Dawson. Crawford hires Wally to help drive to the railroad a shipment of cattle, the funds from which are to pay off notes to Dawson. Wally forces Dawson to accept the money and give them a receipt, but they are robbed by Meggs; Wally finds Meggs dying, and before Dawson can shoot him, Meggs finishes off the villain. Wally wins the rancher's daughter, Mildred. *Cowboys. Bankers. Murder. Revenge. Gambling.*

MEDDLING WOMEN **F2.3540**

Chadwick Pictures. 15 Nov **1924** [c1 Aug 1924, 31 Mar 1925; LP20492, LU21288]. Si; b&w. 35mm. 7 reels, 6,600 ft.

Story-Dir Ivan Abramson. *Photog* Frank Zucker.

Cast: Lionel Barrymore *(Edwin Ainsworth/John Wells)*, Sigrid Holmquist *(Grace Ainsworth)*, Dagmar Godowsky *(Madeline)*, Hugh Thompson *(Harold Chase)*, Ida Darling *(Mrs. Ainsworth)*, Alice Hegeman *(Claudia Browne)*, Antonio D'Algy *(Vincente)*, William Bechtel *(Dr. Giani)*.

Melodrama. *Edwin Ainsworth, a successful playwright, marries Grace Carruthers, and Edwin's mother does everything in her power to make life miserable for the newlywed couple, insinuating that Grace is in love with Harold Chase, an opera impresario. Eventually the mother's meddling causes the couple to separate, and Edwin becomes infatuated with Madeline, a cabaret dancer who works in a bootleg joint. Edwin is later knocked unconscious in a fight with Madeline's dancing partner and loses his memory, being led by Madeline to believe that he is John Wells, a notorious bootlegger. Grace believes John to be dead and marries Harold Chase. Edwin later regains his memory and returns to Grace; Madeline follows and shoot him dead on his front doorstep.* It all turns out to have been a dream, however. *Playwrights. Dancers. Mothers-in-law. Impresari. Bootleggers. Marriage. Murder. Cabarets. Amnesia. Dreams.*

THE MEDICINE MAN **F2.3541**

Tiffany Productions. 15 Jun **1930** [c11 Jun 1930; LP1358]. Sd (Photophone); b&w. 35mm. 7 reels, 6,211 or 7,839 ft. [Also si.]

Dir Scott Pembroke. *Scen* Ladye Horton. *Adapt* Eve Unsell. *Photog* Art Reeves, Max Dupont. *Film Ed* Russell Schoengarth. *Rec Engr* Dean Daily.

Cast: Jack Benny *(Dr. John Harvey)*, Betty Bronson *(Mamie Goltz)*, E. Alyn Warren *(Goltz)*, Eva Novak *(Hulda)*, Billy Butts *(Buddy)*, Adolph Milar *(Peter)*, Georgie Stone *(Steve)*, Tommy Dugan *(Charley)*, Vadim Uraneff *(Gus)*, Caroline Rankin *(Hattie)*, Dorothea Wolbert *(Sister Wilson)*.

Romantic drama. Source: Elliott Lester, *The Medicine Man* (a play; publication undetermined). Mamie Goltz, a country girl who is forced to work for her tyrannical father in his general store, finds romance in the person of Dr. John Harvey, a medicine man with a traveling troupe, though her father has planned to marry her to Peter, an unwholesome young widower. When Harvey invites Mamie to demonstrate his cosmetics, her father gives her a beating. Despite the punishment, Mamie eludes her father to keep a tryst with Harvey; and he, realizing she loves him, does not take advantage of her. Harvey is obliged to leave town when his assistants win a poker game, but he manages to marry Mamie before Goltz can get a marriage license for Peter. Gus, a hired man, tries to dissuade the furious Goltz from pursuing them; and in the struggle, Goltz is killed. *Medicine men. Merchants. Widowers. Filial relations. Smalltown life. General stores. Courtship.*

MEDITERRANEAN CRUISE **F2.3543**

Burton Holmes Lectures. 6 Jan **1930** [New York State license]. Si(?); b&w. 35mm. 4 reels.

Travelog. No information about the precise nature of this film has been found. *Mediterranean Sea.*

MEET THE PRINCE *see* **HOW TO HANDLE WOMEN**

MEET THE PRINCE **F2.3544**

Metropolitan Pictures Corp. of California. *Dist* Producers Distributing Corp. 9 Aug **1926** [c16 Jun 1926; LP22819]. Si; b&w. 35mm. 6 reels, 5,929 ft. [Copyrighted as 7 reels.]

Dir Joseph Henabery. *Adapt* Jane Murfin, Harold Shumate. *Photog* Karl Struss.

Cast: Joseph Schildkraut *(Prince Nicholas Alexnov)*, Marguerite De La Motte *(Annabelle Ford)*, Vera Steadman *(Cynthia Stevens)*, Julia Faye *(Princess Sophia Alexnov)*, David Butler *(Peter Paget)*, Helen Dunbar *(Mrs. Gordon McCullan)*, Bryant Washburn, Bessie Love.

Comedy-melodrama. Source: Frank R. Adams, "The American Sex," in *Munsey's Magazine* (35:30–38, Jun 1925). Prince Nicholas Alexnov falls asleep on the fire escape of an East Side tenement in New York and dreams of his elegant palace in Russia: *An old servant tries to rouse him, but he will not wake up even though a revolution is imminent; at a conference held in the drawing room, the Princess Sophia, among others, is excited over the threatening labor strikes; a wounded footman staggers in shouting "Revolution"; and after killing a ruffian who pursues his sister, Nicholas escapes with her.* Wakened by a broken milk bottle, the prince finds himself in the shabby milieu of his sister and his faithful friends. Nicholas goes to pawn a plaque but instead buys a painting from Annabelle Ford, in his pride pretending to be a collector. At a party given by wealthy Cynthia Stevens, Nicholas ignores the hostess in favor of Annabelle, who is courted also by Peter Paget; and he poses as a butler at Paget's country home to be near her. Ultimately, Paget is united with Sophia, and Nicholas carries off the rebellious Annabelle. *Royalty. Immigrants. Russians. Butlers. Impersonation. Russia—History—1917–21 Revolution. New York City—East Side. Dreams.*

MELODIES **F2.3545**

Goodwill Pictures. 10 Nov **1926** [New York State license]. Si; b&w. 35mm. 5 reels, 4,200 ft.

Dir Francis Ford. *Photog* Alfred Gosden.

Cast: Jack Mower, Florence Ulrich.

Melodrama(?). No information about the nature of this film has been found.

MELODY LANE **F2.3546**

Universal Pictures. 21 or 28 Jul **1929** [c17 Jul 1929; LP545]. Sd (Movietone); b&w. 35mm. 8 reels, 6,760 ft. [Also si; 5,609 ft.]

Dir Robert F. Hill. *Adapt* J. G. Hawks, Robert F. Hill. *Photog* Joseph Brotherton. *Song: "Roly Boly Eyes"* Eddie Leonard. *Songs: "Here I Am," "There's Sugar Cane 'Round My Door," "The Boogy Man is Here"* Eddie Leonard, Grace Stern, Jack Stern. *Song: "The Song of the Islands"* Charles E. King.

Cast: Eddie Leonard *(Des Dupree)*, Josephine Dunn *(Dolores Dupree)*, Rose Coe *(Constance Dupree)*, George E. Stone *(Danny Kay)*, Huntley Gordon *(Juan Rinaldi)*, Jane La Verne *(Constance Dupree)*, Blanche Carter *(nurse)*, Jake Kern *(orchestra leader)*, Monte Carter *(stage manager)*.

Musical melodrama. Source: Joseph Swerling, *The Understander, a Play* (publication undetermined). Des Dupree, a hoofer, and his wife, Dolores, are partners in vaudeville until Dolores takes their daughter and leaves Des for a bigger part in a stock company. Three years later, they meet again in a New York theater, but their roles have changed: Des is now a down-and-out prop man while Dolores is a dramatic star, having achieved a major role in a play at the theater in which Des works. Des soon maneuvers a meeting with his daughter, and the two take to each other after only a few lullabies. During one of their visits the child falls and injures herself, whereupon Dolores becomes very upset and refuses to leave the child for her opening night. After much persuasion from Des, she finally consents to go, and when she returns, she finds that the child has pulled through as a result of her father's soothing songs. This crisis prompts Dolores to beg her husband's forgiveness—which he promptly gives—and they are reunited. *Actors. Prop men. Dancers. Parenthood. Desertion. Vaudeville. Theater.*

THE MELODY MAN **F2.3547**

Columbia Pictures. 15 Jan **1930** [c18 Feb 1930; LP1090]. Sd (Movietone); b&w. 35mm. 7 reels, 6,386 ft. [Also si.]

Prod Harry Cohn. *Dir* R. William Neill. *Dial Dir* James Seymour. *Cont-Dial* Howard J. Green. *Camera* Ted Tetzlaff. *Asst Camera* Henry Freulich. *Art Dir* Harrison Wiley. *Film Ed* Leonard Wheeler. *Song: "Broken Dreams"* Ballard MacDonald, Arthur Johnston, Dave Dreyer. *Sd Engr* John P. Livadary. *Sd Mix Engr* G. R. Cooper. *Asst Dir* Sam Nelson.

Cast: William Collier, Jr. *(Al Tyler)*, Alice Day *(Elsa)*, John St. Polis *(Von Kemper)*, Johnny Walker *(Joe Yates)*, Mildred Harris *(Martha)*, Albert Conti *(Prince Friedrich)*, Tenen Holtz *(Gustav)*, Lee Kohlmar *(Adolph)*, Bertram Marburgh *(Van Bader)*, Anton Vaverka *(Franz Josef)*, Major Nichols *(Bachman)*.

Drama. Source: Herbert Fields, Richard Rogers, and Lorenz Hart, *The Melody Man* (New York opening: 13 May 1924). Earl von Kemper, a famous Viennese composer, has scored a great success with his *Dream Rhapsody* at a concert for the emperor and empress, but when he finds the woman he loves entertaining Crown Prince Friedrich in her boudoir, he shoots and kills him and escapes to the United States with his daughter. Fifteen years later, in New York, the musician is earning his living by playing his violin, with Gustav and Adolph, at a small restaurant. Elsa, his talented daughter, becomes acquainted with Al Tyler, a young jazz musician, and secretly arranges scores for his band; when they replace Kemper's trio at the cafe, he refuses to let his daughter associate with the jazz artists. Al happens to hear *Dream Rhapsody*, and Elsa arranges a jazz version that Al makes famous; but Baden, the Austrian Minister of Police, hears and recognizes it. Kemper, about to be apprehended, leaves the young lovers on the pretext of returning for a European engagement. *Composers. Musicians. Fugitives. Royalty. Filial relations. Murder. Jazz. Courtship. Vienna. New York City. Franz Josef.*

MELODY OF LOVE (Universal-Jewel) **F2.3548**

Universal Pictures. 10 Oct **1928** [San Francisco showing; released 2 Dec; c16 Oct 1928; LP25744]. Sd (Movietone); b&w. 35mm. 9 reels, 6,733 ft. [Also si; 6,733 ft.]

Dir A. B. Heath. *Story-Scen-Titl* Robert Arch. *Dial* Robert Welsh. *Photog* Walter Scott. *Film Ed* B. W. Burton. *Rec Engr* C. Roy Hunter.

Cast: Walter Pidgeon *(Jack Clark)*, Mildred Harris *(Madelon)*, Jane Winton *(Flo Thompson)*, Tommy Dugan *(Lefty)*, Jack Richardson *(music publisher)*, Victor Potel *(The Gawk)*, Flynn O'Malley *(see note)*.

Romantic drama. During the Great War, Jack Clark, a songwriter in love with chorus girl Flo Thompson, enlists in the Army and is sent to France where he meets Madelon, a little French singer who falls madly in love with him. Jack is wounded in combat and loses the use of his right arm; returning to the United States, he is jilted by Flo and becomes a derelict. Madelon, meantime, crosses the ocean and finds work singing in a cabaret; Jack finds her by chance and, in his excitement at seeing her once again, recovers the use of the arm. As he sits down at the piano to play for Madelon, Jack knows that he has at last found the woman of his dreams. *Composers. Singers. Chorus girls. Derelicts. Cabarets. Paralysis. World War I.*

Note: Reviewed in *Photoplay* as *Madelon*, with Miss Winton as *Grace Darling* and O'Malley as *The Sergeant*.

MEMORY LANE **F2.3549**

John M. Stahl Productions. *Dist* First National Pictures. 17 Jan **1926** [c11 Jan 1926; LP22240, LP22349]. Si; b&w. 35mm. 8 reels, 6,825 ft.

Pres by Louis B. Mayer. *Dir* John M. Stahl. *Story* John M. Stahl,

Benjamin Glazer. *Photog* Percy Hilburn. *Set Dsgn* Cedric Gibbons, Arnold Gillespie. *Film Ed* Margaret Booth. *Asst Dir* Sidney Algier.

Cast: Eleanor Boardman *(Mary)*, Conrad Nagel *(Jimmy Holt)*, William Haines *(Joe Field)*, John Steppling *(Mary's father)*, Eugenie Ford *(Mary's mother)*, Frankie Darrow *(urchin)*, Dot Farley, Joan Standing *(maids)*, Kate Price *(woman in telephone booth)*, Florence Midgley, Dale Fuller, Billie Bennett.

Romantic drama. Joe Field and Mary are sweethearts, but when Joe leaves town to find his fortune, Mary becomes engaged to Jimmy Holt, a fine fellow with both money and social standing. Joe returns shortly before the wedding and, when he cannot persuade Mary to return to him, abducts her. He quickly repents of this rash action and starts back to town, but a mechanical breakdown in his car prevents him from returning before morning with Mary. Jim never doubts Mary's chastity and they are married, settling down to a life of children and laughter. Joe returns once again, and Jim invites him to dinner. Joe seems to have become an overdressed, vulgar fellow, and Mary delights in her choice of a husband. Jim, however, knows that Joe's vulgarity has been put on, a final kindness on his part to insure Mary's happiness. *Courtship. Marriage. Abduction. Self-sacrifice.*

MEN **F2.3550**

Famous Players–Lasky. *Dist* Paramount Pictures. 4 May **1924** [New York premiere; released 26 May; c28 May 1924; LP20256]. Si; b&w. 35mm. 7 reels, 6,634 ft.

Pres by Adolph Zukor, Jesse L. Lasky. *Dir-Writ* Dimitri Buchowetzki. *Adapt* Paul Bern. *Photog* Alvin Wyckoff.

Cast: Pola Negri *(Cleo)*, Robert Frazer *(Georges Kleber)*, Robert Edeson *(Henri Duval)*, Joseph Swickard *(Cleo's father)*, Monte Collins *(François)*, Gino Corrado *(The Stranger)*, Edgar Norton *(The Baron)*.

Drama. Cleo, a waitress in a Marseilles waterfront cafe, is lured to Paris by a baron who betrays her. Disillusioned, she resolves to use men as stepping stones to a life of luxury. After becoming a stage favorite on the boulevards and satiated with an easy life, she meets Georges, a poor youth whose honest love restores her faith in men. *Waitresses. Actors. Nobility. Marseilles. Paris.*

MEN AND WOMEN **F2.3551**

Famous Players–Lasky. *Dist* Paramount Pictures. 23 Mar **1925** [c27 Mar 1925; LP21277]. Si; b&w. 35mm. 6 reels, 6,223 ft.

Pres by Adolph Zukor, Jesse L. Lasky. *Dir* William De Mille. *Scen* Clara Beranger. *Photog* L. Guy Wilky.

Cast: Richard Dix *(Will Prescott)*, Claire Adams *(Agnes Prescott)*, Neil Hamilton *(Ned Seabury)*, Henry Stephenson *(Arnold Kirke)*, Robert Edeson *(Israel Cohen)*, Flora Finch *(Kate)*.

Melodrama. Source: David Belasco and Henry C. De Mille, *Men and Women; a Drama of Our Times in Four Acts* (New York, 1890?). Will Prescott and Ned Seabury work as cashiers in the bank of Israel Cohen. Ned speculates in the stock market and lives well on his investments, spending a substantial part of his money on Will's wife, Agnes, who longs for the luxuries that Will cannot provide her on his salary. Will eventually succumbs to temptation and places $30,000 of the bank's money with Arnold Kirke, Ned's broker. A sudden change in market conditions wipes out Kirke, and the distraught broker commits suicide; the theft is discovered, and Israel Cohen places the responsibility for the crime on Ned rather than Will. Will at first allows Ned to take the blame, but his better nature prevails and he confesses. Will is jailed, and a repentant Agnes goes to Cohen and pleads for his freedom. Cohen is impressed with the woman's sincerity and arranges for Will's release from jail, sending him to South America to manage a coffee plantation. *Bankers. Brokers. Speculation. Suicide. Embezzlement. Stock market.*

MEN ARE LIKE THAT **F2.3552**

Paramount Famous Lasky Corp. 22 Mar **1930** [c22 Mar 1930; LP1168]. Sd (Movietone); b&w. 35mm. 7 reels, 5,467 ft.

Dir Frank Tuttle. *Scen* Marion Dix. *Adapt-Dial* Herman J. Mankiewicz. *Photog* A. J. Stout. *Film Ed* Verna Willis.

Cast: Hal Skelly *(Aubrey Piper)*, Doris Hill *(Amy Fisher)*, Charles Sellon *(Pa Fisher)*, Clara Blandick *(Ma Fisher)*, Morgan Farley *(Joe Fisher)*, Helene Chadwick *(Clara Hyland)*, William B. Davidson *(Frank Hyland)*, Eugene Pallette *(traffic cop)*, George Fawcett *(judge)*, Gordon De Main *(Rogers)*, E. H. Calvert *(superintendent)*.

Comedy-drama. Source: George Edward Kelly, *The Show-Off, a Transcript of Life in Three Acts* (Boston, 1924). A sound version of the play, previously produced by Famous Players–Lasky in 1926 under the title *The Show-Off*, q. v. *Inventors. Clerks. Egotists. Marriage. Pennsylvania Railroad Co.. Philadelphia.*

MEN IN MASKS *see* **AFTER DARK**

MEN IN THE RAW **F2.3553**

Universal Pictures. 16 Oct **1923** [New York premiere; released 4 Nov; c20 Oct 1923; LP19465]. Si; b&w. 35mm. 5 reels, 4,313 ft.

Dir George E. Marshall. *Scen* George Hively. *Photog* Harry Fowler, Ray Ramsey.

Cast: Jack Hoxie *(Windy Watkins)*, Marguerite Clayton *(Eunice Hollis)*, Sid Jordan *(Bill Spray)*, J. Morris Foster *(Phil Hollis)*, Tom Kerrick *(Les Elder)*, William A. Lowery *(Marshal Flynn)*, Art Manning *(Tom Morley)*.

Western. Source: W. Bert Foster, "Men in the Raw," in *Ace High Magazine*. Notorious liar Windy Watkins is pursued by Marshal Flynn when he tells a story about mining in Northwest Canada and the murder of his partner. Watkins escapes, and Flynn, who has been trailing Watkins from Canada, finds him in a canyon full of stolen cattle. It is revealed that the man who rustled the cattle also killed Watkins' partner. Watkins wins his freedom after he helps Flynn catch the culprit. *United States marshals. Liars. Rustling. Murder. Montana.*

MEN OF DARING **F2.3554**

Universal Pictures. 5 Jun **1927** [c22 Mar 1927; LP23786]. Si; b&w. 35mm. 7 reels, 6,155 ft.

Pres by Carl Laemmle. *Dir* Albert Rogell. *Story-Scen* Marion Jackson. *Photog* William Nobles. *Art Dir* David S. Garber.

Cast: Jack Hoxie *(Jack Benton)*, Ena Gregory *(Nancy Owen)*, Marin Sais *(Mother Owen)*, Francis Ford *(Black Roger)*, James Kelly *(Piney)*, Ernie Adams *(Ace)*, Robert Milash *(King)*, Bert Lindley *(Colonel Murphy)*, Bert Apling *(Lone Wolf)*, William Malan *(Jasper Morton)*, John Hall, Joseph Bennett *(David Owen)*, Scout *(himself, a horse)*.

Western melodrama. Jack, falsely accused of a crime committed by Black Roger, a bandit leader, joins his pals—Ace and King. They throw in their lot with the Mortonites, a small religious sect whose wagon train is set upon by Black Roger's men. Among the travelers is Nancy Owen, coveted by Black Roger, but with whom Jack is smitten; the bandit incites the Indians against the train, and old Morton is slain. Jack promises to lead the train and captures David, Nancy's brother, who is sent to kidnap her by Roger. When the Indians attack again, Jack sends his horse to the nearest Army post and thereby saves the train. Black Roger is killed, and Jack is united with Nancy. *Bandits. Indians of North America. Courtship. Brother-sister relationship. Wagon trains. Religious sects. Horses.*

MEN OF PURPOSE **F2.3555**

R. B. Chester. *Dist* Veterans Film Service. c21 Dec **1925** [LP22164]. Si; b&w. 35mm. 10 reels.

Documentary. Using the official war films of all of the countries that participated in the World War, this film is a composite military history of that conflict. *World War I.*

MEN OF STEEL **F2.3556**

First National Pictures. 11 Jul **1926** [New York premiere; released 24 Jul; c6 Jul 1926; LP22868]. Si; b&w. 35mm. 10 reels, 9,143 ft.

Pres by Richard A. Rowland. *Supv* Earl Hudson. *Dir* George Archainbaud. *Story-Scen* Milton Sills. *Photog* Roy Carpenter. *Art Dir* Milton Menasco. *Film Ed* Arthur Tavares. *Cost* June Rand.

Cast: Milton Sills *(Jan Bokak)*, Doris Kenyon *(Mary Berwick)*, May Allison *(Clare Pitt)*, Victor McLaglen *(Pete Masarick)*, Frank Currier *(Cinder Pitt)*, George Fawcett *(Hooker Grimes)*, John Kolb *(Anton Berwick)*, Harry Lee *(Frazer)*, Henry West *(Wolfe)*, Taylor Graves *(Alex)*.

Melodrama. Suggested by: Ralph G. Kirk, "United States Flavor," in *Saturday Evening Post* (196:18–19, 14 Jun 1924). Jan Bokak, an ignorant mine laborer engaged to Mary Berwick, is accused of the murder of her brother, Anton, on the night of his betrothal and accepts the blame to save her other brother, Alex. He escapes and makes his way to the steel mills owned by Cinder Pitt, where he becomes a leader among the workers and wins the admiration of Pitt, who has long tried to become his friend. Labor agitators try to wreck the mill, and Jan is seriously injured as he saves the life of Clare, Pitt's daughter; Pitt takes Jan to his home to recuperate, and Jan and Clare become engaged. In the mining town, Mary's mother reveals on her deathbed that she is the runaway wife of Pitt, the millowner. When Mary finds her way to the Pitt home and sees Jan with Clare, she accuses him of the murder; at the mill, in dramatic fashion, Jan proves his innocence and forces a confession from Masarick. On the day of the wedding, Mary is hurt in an automobile accident, and Jan decides to marry her instead, incurring the wrath of the workers. Pitt learns of Mary's parentage and quells the mob, assuring them that Jan will get half interest in the mill. *Miners. Brother-sister relationship. Parentage. Steel industry. Murder. Ambition. Labor. Courtship. Self-sacrifice. Weddings.*

MEN OF THE NIGHT **F2.3557**

Sterling Pictures. 15 or 24 Jul **1926** [c28 Jul 1926; LP22987]. Si; b&w. 35mm. 6 reels, 5,700 ft.

Dir Albert Rogell. *Adapt* Lucille De Nevers. *Story* Florence Wagner.

Cast: Herbert Rawlinson *(J. Rupert Dodds)*, Gareth Hughes *(Dick Foster)*, Wanda Hawley *(Trixie Moran)*, Lucy Beaumont *(Mrs. Abbott)*, Jay Hunt *(Thomas Bogen)*, Mathilda Brundage *(Lady Broderick)*.

Crook melodrama. Mrs. Abbott, an elderly newspaper vendor in dire straits, is taken in by Rupert Dodds, an art dealer, and Dick Foster, his young companion, who see in her transparent honesty an excellent shield for illegal activities in their art shop, where they remold gold and silver articles. Mrs. Abbott soon grows fond of Dick, who calls her "Mother," and she promotes his love for Trixie, the bookkeeper; but she becomes suspicious of Dodds and Dick when she overhears them congratulating themselves over their recent success. Mrs. Abbott discovers that they are planning to rob the home of Lady Broderick, a wealthy customer, and she follows them to prevent the crime, but she is captured and held accountable for robbing the safe. She is tried and convicted just as Dick confesses and clears her of the crime; and in the belief that Dick will reform, the judge sets him free. It develops that Mrs. Abbott is the long-lost sister of Lady Broderick and is the heiress to an English estate. Dick and Trixie are married and spend their honeymoon in England. *Newsvendors. Art dealers. Bookkeepers. Criminals—Rehabilitation. Robbery. Inheritance. Motherhood. Circumstantial evidence. England.*

MEN OF THE NORTH **F2.3558**

Metro-Goldwyn-Mayer Pictures. 27 Sep **1930** [c1 Oct 1930; LP1621]. Sd (Movietone); b&w. 35mm. 7 reels, 7,200 ft.

Dir Hal Roach. *Cont-Dial* Richard Schayer. *Story* Willard Mack. *Photog* Ray Binger. *Art Dir* Cedric Gibbons. *Film Ed* Thomas Held. *Dances Stgd by* Sammy Lee. *Rec Engr* Douglas Shearer.

Cast: Gilbert Roland *(Louis)*, Barbara Leonard *(Nedra)*, Arnold Korff *(John Ruskin)*, Robert Elliott *(Sergeant Mooney)*, George Davis *(Corporal Smith)*, Nina Quartaro *(Woolie-Woolie)*, Robert Graves, Jr. *(priest)*.

Northwest melodrama. Louis, a happy-go-lucky French Canadian, is accused of stealing gold from a mine in the Canadian Northwest, but he evades the law. He falls in love with Nedra, the mine owner's daughter, and rescues her and her father from a snowslide. Later, Louis is pursued by Sergeant Mooney of the Mounted Police on a dogsled, but when Louis saves the Mountie's life, he is vindicated of the crime and wins the lasting devotion of the girl. *Miners. French Canadians. Thieves. Gold. Courtship. Canadian Northwest. Northwest Mounted Police. Avalanches.*

Note: Working title: *Monsieur le Fox.*

THE MEN OF ZANZIBAR **F2.3559**

Fox Film Corp. 21 May **1922** [c21 May 1922; LP18014]. Si; b&w. 35mm. 5 reels, 4,999 ft.

Pres by William Fox. *Dir* Rowland V. Lee. *Adapt-Scen* Edward J. Le Saint. *Photog* David Abel.

Cast: William Russell *(Hugh Hemingway)*, Ruth Renick *(Polly Adair)*, Claude Peyton *(George Sheyer)*, Harvey Clarke *(Wilbur Harris)*, Arthur Morrison *(Arthur Fearing)*, Michael Dark *(Sir George Firth)*, Lila Leslie *(Lady Firth)*.

Mystery melodrama. Source: Richard Harding Davis, "The Men of Zanzibar," in *The Lost Road* (New York, 1913). Wilbur Harris, the American Consul in Zanzibar, receives notice from an American detective agency that a fugitive is believed to be heading for the African coast; at the same time Bostonian Hugh Hemingway arrives and arouses suspicion by the removal of his beard. Harris believes him to be the defaulter but is equally suspicious of George Sheyer, who also fits the description. Hemingway is attracted to Polly, the consul's secretary, but does not press his hand because of her friendship with Fearing, whom he believes Polly loves. Hemingway finds evidence against Sheyer, but Hemingway confesses to the theft as a subterfuge to protect Fearing; Fearing then admits his guilt, but part of the money, which he is willing to return, is stolen. Sheyer is determined to be the thief; and learning that Polly is only Fearing's sister, Hemingway tells her of his love. *Bostonians. Detectives. Mistaken identity. Brother-sister relationship. United States—Diplomatic and consular service. Zanzibar.*

MEN WHO FORGET **F2.3560**

Geneva Distributing Corp. 25 Nov **1923** [scheduled release]. Si; b&w. 35mm. 5 reels, 4,800 ft.

Dir Reuben Gillmer. *Auth-Scen* F. Martin Thornton.

Cast: James Knight, Marjorie Villers, Bernard Dudley, Evelyn Boucher, James Barker.

Melodrama. Two sailors, Seth and John, fight a wrestling match, the winner to marry Eileen, whom they both love. Seth wins, but in his absence John lies about the match and marries Eileen. Learning the truth, Eileen leaves him, then marries Seth when she hears that John has died at sea. John returns, takes stock of the situation, and commits suicide. *Sailors. Suicide. Bigamy. Wrestling.*

MEN WITHOUT LAW **F2.3561**

Columbia Pictures. 15 Oct **1930** [c4 Nov 1930; LP1702]. Sd (Movietone); b&w. 35mm. 7 reels, 6,090 ft.

Prod Harry Cohn. *Dir* Louis King. *Cont-Dial* Dorothy Howell. *Story* Lewis Seiler. *Photog* Ted McCord. *Art Dir* Edward Jewell. *Asst Art Dir* Edward Shulter. *Film Ed* Ray Snyder. *Ch Sd Engr* John Livadary. *Sd Rec Engr* Ben Harper. *Asst Dir* Mac V. Wright.

Cast: Buck Jones *(Buck Healy)*, Tom Carr *(Tom Healy)*, Harry Woods *(Murdock)*, Fred Burns *(Sheriff Jim)*, Fred Kelsey *(Deputy Sheriff)*, Sid Saylor *(Hank)*, Carmelita Geraghty *(Juanita)*, Lydia Knott *(Mrs. Healy)*, Victor Sarno *(Señor Del Rey)*.

Western melodrama. During the war, Buck Healy saves Manuel Del Rey from a barrage, thus winning the favor of his father, a Mexican rancher, but the boy later dies. After the war, Buck returns home to Gunsight, Arizona, a border town. He finds that his brother, Tom, has become an outlaw, who is arrested following a bank robbery. Buck prevails on the sheriff to release Tom into his custody, but the boy is captured by his outlaw friends as is Buck himself when he attempts to rescue his brother. Murdock, the outlaw leader, finds a letter from Señor Del Rey on Buck, and he impersonates the latter in order to rob the Mexican rancher. He kidnaps Del Rey's daughter, Juanita, whom Buck met earlier, but Buck manages a sensational escape and saves Juanita, who thereafter sees him in a better light. *Cowboys. Brothers. Veterans. Ranchers. Outlaws. Bank robberies. Friendship. Impersonation. Courtship. Arizona. Mexico.*

MEN WITHOUT WOMEN **F2.3562**

Fox Film Corp. 31 Jan **1930** [New York premiere; released 9 Feb; c19 Dec 1929; LP1016]. Sd (Movietone); b&w. 35mm. 9 reels, 7,774 ft.

Pres by William Fox. *Assoc Prod* James Kevin McGuinness. *Dir* John Ford. *Stage Dir* Andrew Bennison. *Screenplay-Dial* Dudley Nichols. *Story* John Ford, James Kevin McGuinness. *Photog* Joseph August. *Art Dir* William S. Darling. *Film Ed* Paul Weatherwax. *Mus Score* Peter Brunelli, Glen Knight. *Sd* W. W. Lindsay, Donald Flick. *Asst Dir* Edward O'Fearna. *Tech Adv* Schuyler E. Grey.

Cast: Kenneth MacKenna *(Chief Torpedoman Burke)*, Frank Albertson *(Ensign Price)*, Paul Page *(Handsome)*, Walter McGrail *(Cobb)*, Warren Hymer *(Kaufman)*, Farrell MacDonald *(Costello)*, Stuart Erwin *(Jenkins)*, George Le Guere *(Pollosk)*, Ben Hendricks, Jr. *(Murphy)*, Harry Tenbrook *(Winkler)*, Warner Richmond *(Lieutenant Commander Bridewell)*, Roy Stewart *(Captain Carson)*, Charles Gerard *(Commander Weymouth, R. N.)*, Pat Somerset *(Lieutenant Digby, R. N.)*, Robert Parrish, John Wayne.

Action melodrama. After a period of drinking and flirting in Shanghai dives, some American sailors are called back to their submarine, which is under the command of Bridewell. Their craft is hit by a freighter and sinks to the bottom of the China Sea, provoking various emotional reactions from the crew. Burke, a British naval officer, brings a ship to their aid, is recognized as a disgraced officer by one of the crew, Weymouth, but remains behind to rescue the last American through a torpedo tube, thus protecting the woman he loves and establishing his bravery. *Sailors. Courage. Submarines. United States Navy. Great Britain—Royal Navy. Shanghai. China Sea.*

MEN, WOMEN AND MONEY **F2.3563**

Lester Park. 15 Aug **1924**. Si; b&w. 35mm. 5 reels.

Cast: Walter Miller, Marguerite Courtot.

Melodrama(?). No information about the nature of this film has been found.

MEN WOMEN LOVE **F2.3564**

Macfadden True Story Pictures. c29 Aug **1926** [LU22666]. Si; b&w. 35mm. [Feature length assumed.]

Romantic drama. The paths of disparate lives cross through the advertising of a matrimonial bureau: Nora Lang, who no longer can afford singing lessons and finds work as a dishwasher in a Greek restaurant, places the advertisement, while architect Keith Hall faces a dilemma posed by his grandfather's will—he must marry within 48 hours or lose his inheritance to his hated cousin, Wilton Clark. Accepting Keith's offer of marriage and quick divorce, Nora goes to Europe to study with her newly acquired wealth, but she deliberately neglects to sever her matrimonial ties to Keith. Two years later she returns transformed into Mademoiselle Nola, a lovely woman with a golden voice. Keith witnesses her operatic performance, goes backstage, and falls in love with the diva. Seeking a divorce from Nora, Keith asks his friend and lawyer, Edward Ralston, to find his wife, and his agents produce Nola. Still unrecognized, Nora finally reveals her identity, and the couple is happily reconciled. *Architects. Singers. Lawyers. Cousins. Inheritance. Personal identity. Marriage of convenience. Wills. Matrimonial agencies. Opera.*

THE MENACING PAST **F2.3565**

Milburn Morante. *Dist* Rollo Sales Corp. 15 Apr **1922** [scheduled release]. Si; b&w. 35mm. 5 reels.

Cast: George Chesebro, Fritzi Ridgeway.

Western melodrama(?). No information about the nature of this film has been found.

Note: The New York State license application for this film was "abandoned." The film may be the same as *The Hate Trail,* q.v.

MENSCHEN HINTER GETTERN **F2.3566**

Cosmopolitan Productions. *Dist* Metro-Goldwyn-Mayer Distributing Corp. **1930.** Sd (Movietone); b&w. 35mm. [Length undetermined.]

Dir Paul Fejos. *Dial* Walter Hasenclever, Ernst Toller.

Cast: Gustav Diessl *(Fred Morris)*, Heinrich George *(Butch)*, Egon von Jordan *(Kent)*, Dita Parlo *(Ann Marlowe)*, Anton Pontner, Paul Morgan, Hans Heinrich von Twardowski, Karl Ettinger, Peter Erkelenz, Adolf Edgar Licho, Herman Bing.

Melodrama. German-language version of *The Big House,* q. v. *Convicts. Brother-sister relationship. Manslaughter. Courtship. Prison revolts. Prison escapes. Bookshops.*

Note: Other production credits are probably the same as for *The Big House.*

THE MERRY CAVALIER **F2.3567**

Richard Talmadge Productions. *For* Carlos Productions. *Dist* Film Booking Offices of America. 29 Aug **1926** [c29 Aug 1926; LP23095]. Si; b&w. 35mm. 5 reels.

Pres by A. Carlos. *Dir* Noel Mason. *Story-Cont* Grover Jones. *Photog* Jack Stevens.

Cast: Richard Talmadge *(Dick Hemper)*, Charlotte Stevens *(Nan Cosgrove)*, William H. Tooker *(Dave Hemper)*, Joseph Harrington *(Luke Cosgrove)*, B. O'Farrell *(physician)*, Jack Richardson *(Mel Bronson)*.

Melodrama. Dick Hemper, son of a millionaire lumberman, becomes listless because of enforced idleness in attending his sick father. The family doctor suggests that an actress friend impersonate a lady in distress, thus awakening Dick's interest. Dick overhears the plot, and when Nan Cosgrove, whose father owns property on Hemper land, tells him that Bronson, the foreman, is trying to cheat her father, Dick dismisses her as an imposter; but nevertheless he goes to the lumber country with her. Bronson, who wants Cosgrove to sign over the deed on his property, has Dick, then also Cosgrove, kidnaped. After a series of thrilling stunts, Dick finds Cosgrove bound and gagged in a boat, and he rescues Nan from Bronson's advances. Dick and Nan get married. *Idlers. Physicians. Mistaken identity. Courtship. Kidnaping. Lumber camps. Stunts.*

THE MERRY WIDOW **F2.3568**

Metro-Goldwyn-Mayer Pictures. 26 Aug **1925** [New York premiere; c14 Sep 1925; LP21826]. Si; b&w. 35mm. 10 reels, 10,027 ft.

Dir Erich von Stroheim. *Adapt-Scen* Erich von Stroheim, Benjamin Glazer. *Titl* Marian Ainslee. *Photog* Oliver T. Marsh, Ben Reynolds, William Daniels. *Sets* Cedric Gibbons, Richard Day. *Film Ed* Frank E. Hull. *Mus Score* William Axt, David Mendoza. *Asst Dir* Eddy Sowders, Louis Germonprez. *Cost* Richard Day, Erich von Stroheim.

Cast: Mae Murray *(Sally)*, John Gilbert *(Prince Danilo)*, Roy D'Arcy *(Crown Prince Mirko)*, Josephine Crowell *(Queen Milena)*, George Fawcett *(King Nikita)*, Tully Marshall *(Baron Sadoja)*, Albert Conti *(Danilo's adjutant)*, Sidney Bracy *(Danilo's footman)*, Don Ryan *(Mirko's adjutant)*, Hughie Mack *(innkeeper)*, Ida Moore *(innkeeper's wife)*, Lucille von Lent *(innkeeper's daughter)*, Dale Fuller *(Sadoja's chambermaid)*, Charles Magelis *(Flo Epstein)*, Harvey Karels *(Jimmy Watson)*, Edna Tichenor *(Dopey Marie)*, Gertrude Bennett *(Hard-boiled Virginia)*, Zala Zorana *(Frenchie Christine)*, Jacquelin Gadsdon *(Madonna)*, Estelle Clark *(French barber)*, D'Arcy Corrigan *(Horatio)*, Clara Wallacks, Frances Primm *(Hansen sisters)*, Zack Williams *(George Washington White)*, Edward Connelly *(ambassador)*, Merewyn Thayer *(ambassador's wife)*, Lon Poff *(Sadoja's lackey)*.

Romantic comedy. Source: Leo Stein and Victor Léon, *Die lustige Witwe; Operette in drei Akten* (Wien, 1906). Prince Danilo and Crown Prince Mirko of the Kingdom of Monteblanco meet Sally O'Hara, a follies girl on tour, and both seek to win her favor. Favoring Danilo, Sally accepts his proposal to dinner, and he does his charming best to seduce her. Mirko finds them in a compromising situation, and Danilo, overcome by genuine love for Sally, announces his intention of making her his wife. The king and queen prevent the marriage, and Sally, believing that Danilo has jilted her, spitefully marries Baron Sadoja, the richest man in the kingdom. The Baron dies of excitement on their wedding night, and Sally goes to Paris, where she becomes known as "The Merry Widow." Mirko later follows her there with the intention of seeking her hand and fortune in marriage. Danilo goes also, and Sally agrees to marry Mirko to further torment him. Danilo strikes Mirko, and a duel is arranged. Believing that Sally loves Mirko, Danilo allows the crown prince to shoot him. Danilo is only wounded, however, and discovers then that Sally loves him still. The king dies, the crown prince is assassinated, and Danilo becomes king, taking Sally as his queen. *Royalty. Chorus girls. Widows. Imaginary kingdoms. Marriage. Reputation. Assassination. Paris. Duels.*

MERRY WIVES OF GOTHAM *see* **LIGHTS OF OLD BROADWAY**

MERRY-GO-ROUND (Universal Super-Jewel) **F2.3569**

Universal Pictures. 1 Jul **1923** [New York premiere; released 3 Sep; c16 Jun 1923; LP19121]. Si; b&w. 35mm. 10 reels, 9,178 ft.

Pres by Carl Laemmle. *Prod* Irving Thalberg. *Dir* Rupert Julian. *Adtl Dir* Erich von Stroheim. *Treatment-Adapt (see note)* Finis Fox. *Titl* Mary O'Hara. *Story* Harvey Gates. *Photog* Charles Kaufman, William Daniels. *Art Dir* E. E. Sheeley. *Set Dsgn* Richard Day. *Film Ed* Maurice Pivar, James McKay. *Mus* Ben Reynolds. *Asst Dir* Eddy Sowders, Louis Germonprez. *Cost* Erich von Stroheim, Richard Day. *Art Titl* Harry B. Johnson.

Cast: Norman Kerry *(Count Franz Maxmillian von Hohenegg)*, Mary Philbin *(Agnes Urban)*, Cesare Gravina *(Sylvester Urban)*, Edith Yorke *(Ursula Urban)*, George Hackathorne *(Bartholomew Gruber)*, George Siegmann *(Shani Huber)*, Dale Fuller *(Mariana Huber)*, Lillian Sylvester *(Mrs. Aurora Rossreiter)*, Spottiswoode Aitken *(Minister of War [Gisella's father])*, Dorothy Wallace *(Komtasse Gisella von Steinbrueck)*, Al Edmundsen *(Nepomuck Navrital)*, Albert Conti *(Rudi [Baron von Leightsinn])*, Charles L. King *(Nicki [Baron von Nubenmuth])*, Fenwick Oliver *(Eitel [Prince Eitel Hogemut])*, Sidney Bracey *(Gisella's groom)*, Anton Vaverka *(Emperor Franz Josef)*, Maude George *(Madame Elvira)*, Helen Broneau *(Jane)*, Jane Sherman *(Marie)*.

Romantic drama. Count Franz Maxmillian von Hohenegg, young and dashing personal aide to Franz Josef in prewar Vienna, though engaged to the stately Countess Gisella (daughter of the war minister), encounters pretty ingenue Agnes Urban, organ-grinder for a merry-go-round and employee (along with Sylvester, her father, a puppeteer), of Shani Huber, a brutal concessionaire. The count, posing as a necktie salesman, courts the comely lass, his infatuation deepening; realizing his love, he tries unsuccessfully to break off his engagement, and the wedding takes place as planned. Agnes and her father denounce the count when they discover his imposture, but Agnes continues to care for him. During the war Agnes bands together with some of the circus people, including Bartholomew, a hunchback and fellow circus worker in love with her, whose pet orangutan kills the evil Huber. The count meets Sylvester Urban dying on the battlefield and is stunned at the old man's hateful denunciation, delivered with his dying breath. Franz returns from the war a widower, stripped of his rank. He is rejected by Agnes, who, believing him dead, has promised to marry Bartholomew, but Franz and Agnes are united when Bartholomew steps aside. *Hurdy-gurdies. Puppeteers. Concessionaires. Hunchbacks. Royalty. Nobility. Amusement parks. Merry-go-rounds. Imposture. World*

War I. Vienna. Franz Josef. Apes.

Note: Credits on the film have been followed. Irving Thalberg replaced Stroheim, the film's original director, with Rupert Julian halfway through the production. In a telegram to the *New York Times*, published 22 Jul 1923, Julian states that with the exception of about 600 ft., the entire production was directed by him. That Finis Fox wrote the treatment is unconfirmed. No screen credit was given for writers. Fox's name appears in company records.

MERTON OF THE MOVIES **F2.3570**

Famous Players–Lasky. *Dist* Paramount Pictures. 3 Nov **1924** [10 Sep 1924; LP20550]. Si; b&w. 35mm. 8 reels, 7,655 ft.

Pres by Adolph Zukor, Jesse L. Lasky. *Prod-Dir* James Cruze. *Scen* Walter Woods. *Photog* Karl Brown.

Cast—The Story: Glenn Hunter *(Merton Gill)*, Charles Sellon *(Pete Gashwiler)*, Sadie Gordon *(Mrs. Gashwiler)*, Gale Henry *(Tessie Kearns)*, Luke Cosgrave *(Lowell Hardy)*.

Cast "In Movieland": Viola Dana *(Sally Montague, "Flips")*, De Witt Jennings *(Jeff Baird)*, Elliott Roth *(Harold Parmalee)*, Charles Ogle *(Mr. Montague)*, Ethel Wales *(Mrs. Montague)*, Frank Jonasson *(Henshaw)*, Eleanor Lawson *(Mrs. Patterson)*.

Comedy-drama. Source: Harry Leon Wilson, *Merton of the Movies* (Garden City, New York, 1922). George S. Kaufman and Marc Connelly, *Merton of the Movies, a Play in Four Acts* (New York, 1925). When he is fired from the village general store, Merton Gill comes to Hollywood in hopes of becoming a movie actor. He is unable to find work until slapstick comedy star "Flips" gets him on the lot. After setbacks and complications, he gets a part in a burlesque of his idol, Harold Parmalee, which he mistakes as a serious drama. Believing himself a failure, he is surprised to get a contract for comedy parts and finds that "Flips" will be his sweetheart. *Actors. Motion pictures. Hollywood.*

A MESSAGE FROM MARS **F2.3571**

Metro Pictures. 11 Apr **1921** [c24 Mar 1921; LP16310]. Si; b&w. 35mm. 6 reels, 5,187 ft.

Dir Maxwell Karger. *Scen* Arthur J. Zellner, Arthur Maude. *Photog* Arthur Martinelli.

Cast: Bert Lytell *(Horace Parker)*, Raye Dean *(Minnie Talbot)*, Maude Milton *(Martha Parker)*, Alphonz Ethier *(The Messenger)*, Gordon Ash *(Arthur Dicey)*, Leonard Mudie *(Fred Jones)*, Mary Louise Beaton *(Mrs. Jones)*, Frank Currier *(Sir Edwards)*, George Spink *(The Butler)*.

Comedy-fantasy. Source: Richard Ganthoney, *A Message From Mars; a Fantasy-Comedy in Three Acts* (New York, 1923). Horace Parker, a wealthy young egotist who agrees to finance a device for communicating with Mars provided that he is credited with its invention, remains home to study his plans rather than accompany Minnie, his fiancée, to a party. When he falls asleep, a figure appears, announcing itself as a messenger from Mars, whose mission is to convert the earth's most selfish man. Out in the streets the messenger shows him poverty and suffering, and he overhears Minnie's reproval of him at the party. On being taken to the home of a soldier whose wife he has refused to help, he awakens to find their house afire, rescues the woman, and invites other unfortunates to his own home, thus regaining the esteem of his fiancée. *Egotists. Inventors. Telecommunication. Social consciousness. Dreams. Mars.*

THE MESSAGE OF HOPE **F2.3572**

Genevieve M. Murphy. c15 Jul **1923** [LP19226]. Si; b&w. 35mm. 4 reels.

Story Genevieve M. Murphy.

Sociological drama. Ethel Lee, a young social worker for the Charity Organization Society, brings hope to those living in poverty and suffering from tuberculosis. The unsanitary conditions under which these people live and work are shown. Ethel is determined to help the society raise the necessary funds to construct a tuberculosis hospital. Dr. Blank, a physician who also works with the poor, proposes marriage, but Ethel refuses to consider his offer until the money is raised. Ethel persuades Joy, Blank's sister, to emulate her brother and herself in helping the poor become useful citizens, and Joy obtains from her mother and Mr. Weber, a banker to whom she is secretly engaged, the funds necessary for the hospital. Ethel is then free to accept Blank's proposal. *Physicians. Social workers. Charitable organizations. Tuberculosis. Poverty.*

MESSENGER OF THE BLESSED VIRGIN **F2.3573**

Mission Film Society. c22 Apr **1930** [LU1243]. Si; b&w. 35mm. 9 reels.

Religious drama. Dorothy Vernon, who has had a happy life in a peaceful village with her parents and her Uncle John, a happy-go-lucky artist, is paralyzed as the result of a fall incurred during a storm; and in consequence grief and unhappiness come to the family. Uncle John, traveling abroad, hears of the miracles of the Blessed Virgin at Lourdes; an old woman recounts the story of Bernadette, a peasant girl of the Pyrenees, who is inspired by a vision of the Immaculate Conception; the villagers, under the direction of Abbé Peyromal of Lourdes, build a chapel at the grotto where Bernadette intercedes with the Virgin for the accomplishment of miraculous cures. The uncle cables Dorothy's parents, and they bring her to Lourdes, where through faith and prayer she is cured. *Paralytics. Artists. Uncles. Religion. Miracles. Bernadette of Lourdes. Virgin Mary. Lourdes.*

LE METTEUR EN SCÈNE *see* **FREE AND EASY**

MEXICALI ROSE **F2.3574**

Columbia Pictures. 26 Dec **1929** [c21 Jan 1930; LP1018]. Sd (Movietone); b&w. 35mm. 7 reels, 5,735 ft. [Also si; 5,126 ft.]

Prod Harry Cohn. *Dir* Erle C. Kenton. *Dial Dir* James Seymour. *Cont* Norman Houston. *Dial* Gladys Lehman, Norman Houston. *Story* Gladys Lehman. *Photog* Ted Tetzlaff. *Film Ed* Leon Barsha. *Asst Dir* Sam Nelson.

Cast: Barbara Stanwyck *(Mexicali Rose)*, Sam Hardy *(Happy Manning)*, William Janney *(Bob Manning)*, Louis Natheaux *(Joe, the Croupier)*, Arthur Rankin *(Loco, the Halfwit)*, Harry Vejar *(Ortiz)*, Louis King *(Dad, the Drunk)*, Julia Beharano *(Manuela)*.

Romantic drama. Happy Manning, an unrefined but likable owner of a saloon on the Mexican border, who loves Rose, a scheming and ruthless woman, spends most of his savings on the education of his younger brother, Bob, who believes he owns a gold mine. At a football game between Oregon and California, Bob introduces Happy to his young fiancée, with whom he plans to spend a honeymoon at Happy's "mine." Meanwhile, Happy suspects a secret liaison between Rose and Joe, the croupier, and when his suspicions are confirmed, he orders her out of town. She vows revenge. When, to his surprise, Bob turns up married to Rose, Happy pretends not to know her and deceives his brother into believing he is a miner. When Rose begins to scatter her affections, she is suddenly found dead, killed by Loco, a halfwit. *Students. Saloon keepers. Dancehall girls. Croupiers. Halfwits. Brothers. Revenge. Mexican border.*

MIAMI **F2.3575**

Tilford Cinema Corp. *Dist* W. W. Hodkinson Corp. 27 Apr **1924** [c27 Apr 1924; LP20298]. Si; b&w. 35mm. 7 reels, 6,317 ft.

Prod-Dir Alan Crosland. *Story* John Lynch. *Photog* Dal Clawson.

Cast: Betty Compson *(Joan Bruce)*, Lawford Davidson *(Ranson Tate)*, Hedda Hopper *(Mary Tate)*, J. Barney Sherry *(David Forbes)*, Lucy Fox *(Veronica Forbes)*, Benjamin F. Finney, Jr. *(Grant North)*.

Society melodrama. Joan Bruce, leader of the jazz set at Miami, is courted by two men—Ranson Tate, an unscrupulous villain who deserted his wife on becoming wealthy, and Grant North, a young man who ignores her advances until he saves her from drowning. She is compromised by Tate but ultimately is rescued by North. *Jazz life. Desertion. Miami.*

MICHAEL O'HALLORAN **F2.3576**

Gene Stratton Porter Productions. *Dist* W. W. Hodkinson Corp. 10 Jun **1923** [c16 May 1923; LP18974]. Si; b&w. 35mm. 7 reels, 7,600 ft.

Supv Gene Stratton Porter. *Dir-Adapt* James Leo Meehan. *Photog* Floyd Jackson.

Cast: Virginia True Boardman *(Michael O'Halloran)*, Ethelyn Irving *(Peaches)*, Irene Rich *(Nellie Minturn)*, Charles Clary *(James Minturn)*, Claire McDowell *(Nancy Harding)*, Charles Hill Mailes *(Peter Harding)*, Josie Sedgwick *(Leslie Winton)*, William Boyd *(Douglas Bruce)*.

Melodrama. Source: Gene Stratton Porter, *Michael O'Halloran* (Garden City, New York, 1915). "Two stories are interwoven in this plot, the marital troubles of the wealthy Minturns and the adventures of Mickey O'Halloran and his little crippled girl pal being utilized as contrasting examples of life amid riches and poverty" (*Exhibitors Trade Review*, 7 Jul 1923). Orphan newsboy Michael O'Halloran "adopts" Peaches, a little crippled girl, when her grandmother's death leaves her alone in the world. A chance acquaintance with lawyer Douglas Bruce draws Michael into contact with the Hardings, a farm couple, who bring Michael and Peaches to the country. Wholesome food and good fresh air give Peaches the strength to walk. Also friends of Douglas Bruce are the James Minturns, a wealthy young couple whose marriage breaks up over Nellie Minturn's neglect of their children for a society life. Nellie eventually realizes her error, devotes herself to hospital work, and is reunited with James while bird-calling in the woods. *Orphans. Cripples. Lawyers. Wealth. Poverty. Rural life. Birds.*

THE MICHIGAN KID (Universal-Jewel) **F2.3577**

Universal Pictures. ca30 Jun **1928** [New York premiere; released 21 Oct; c13 Jun 1928; LP25366]. Si; b&w. 35mm. 6 reels, 6,030 ft.

Dir Irvin Willat. *Scen* Peter Milne. *Titl* Walter Anthony. *Adapt* J. Grubb Alexander. *Adapt-Scen (see note)* J. G. Hawks, Charles Logue, Irvin Willat. *Photog* Charles Stumar. *Film Ed* Harry Marker.

Cast: Renée Adorée *(Rose Morris)*, Fred Esmelton *(Hiram Morris)*, Virginia Grey *(Rose, as a child)*, Conrad Nagel *(Jimmy Cowan, the Michigan Kid)*, Maurice Murphy *(Jimmy Cowan, as a child)*, Adolph Milar *(Shorty)*, Lloyd Whitlock *(Frank Hayward)*, Donald House *(Frank Hayward, as a child)*.

Northwest melodrama. Source: Rex Beach, "The Michigan Kid," in *The Goose Woman, and Other Stories* (New York, 1925). Jimmy Cowan leaves home as a young boy to seek his fortune in Alaska so that he may marry his childhood sweetheart, Rose Morris. He becomes known as the Michigan Kid, a notoriously lucky gambler and proprietor of a gambling hall. Hayward, Cowan's boyhood rival for Rose, also resides in Alaska. He has sent for Rose, intending to marry her, but when he loses at gambling some money belonging to his company and shoots the dealer, he is forced to escape to a hiding place, leaving Cowan to meet Rose's train. Cowan and Rose renew their acquaintance, and when Rose decides that Hayward is unworthy of her love, she marries Cowan. *Gamblers. Embezzlement. Alaska.*

Note: The following persons worked on the treatment and adaptation but were not given screen credit: J. G. Hawks, Charles Logue, and Irvin Willat.

MICKEY (Reissue) **F2.3578**

Dist R-C Pictures. 7 Nov **1923** [New York State license]. Si; b&w. 35mm. 6 reels.

Note: A Mack Sennett film starring Mabel Normand and released in 1918 (c25 Feb 1918; LP12164).

MICKEY GROGAN, CONTRACTOR *see* **LITTLE MICKEY GROGAN**

MIDNIGHT **F2.3579**

Realart Pictures. *Dist* Paramount Pictures. 19 Feb **1922** [c21 Feb 1922; LP17571]. Si; b&w. 35mm. 5 reels, 4,653 ft.

Dir Maurice Campbell. *Story-Scen* Harvey Thew. *Photog* H. Kinley Martin.

Cast: Constance Binney *(Edna Morris)*, William Courtleigh *(William Morris)*, Sidney Bracey *(Dodd)*, Arthur S. Hull *(George Potter)*, Herbert Fortier *(Bishop Astor)*, Helen Lynch *(Grace Astor)*, Edward Martindel *(Senator Dart)*, Jack Mulhall *(Jack Dart)*.

Mystery melodrama. Edna Morris, daughter of the American Ambassador to a South American republic, weds Potter, an embassy attaché; on the same day, Potter is threatened with arrest for embezzlement, and to escape he leaps into the bay. Believing him to be drowned, Edna's father retires to the United States. Edna soon falls in love with Jack Dart, and their engagement is announced; then Potter reappears and reveals himself to Morris, demanding payment for his silence; and Morris, fearful of scandal, forbids Edna to marry Jack. Edna nevertheless elopes with Jack, and on returning from her midnight wedding she finds Potter dead in her father's library. She is horrified at the thought that she may have married Jack before Potter's death, but it is later proved that he died 10 minutes before the marriage took place. *Embezzlement. Bigamy. Blackmail. Marriage. United States—Diplomatic and consular service. South America.*

THE MIDNIGHT ACE **F2.3580**

Dunbar Film Corp. 5 May **1928** [New York State license]. Si; b&w. 35mm. 7 reels, 6,500 ft.

Cast: A. B. De Comatheire, Mabel Kelly, Oscar Roy Dugas, Walter Cornick, Susie Sutton, William Edmonson, Roberta Brown, Bessie Givens, Anthony Gayztera, Pete Smith, Edward Day, Clarence Penalver.

Melodrama. A young black girl falls in love with a master criminal, believing him to be a good and decent man. A detective, in love with the girl, informs her that the man she loves is in reality a crook and a philanderer who beats his wife. The girl learns of the master criminal's plan for a robbery and informs the detective of it. The master criminal is captured and brought to trial, later escaping from the courtroom and making a break for freedom. The car in which he flees goes over a cliff, however, and carries him to a rocky death. The detective and the girl find love and happiness with each other. *Philanderers. Detectives. Robbery. Infidelity. Negro life. Trials.*

A MIDNIGHT ADVENTURE (Imperial Photoplays) **F2.3581**

Duke Worne Productions. *Dist* Rayart Pictures. May **1928.** Si; b&w. 35mm. 6 reels, 5,138 or 5,262 ft.

Dir Duke Worne. *Story-Scen* Arthur Hoerl. *Photog* Walter Griffin. *Film Ed* Malcolm Sweeney.

Cast: Cullen Landis *(Fred Nicholson)*, Edna Murphy *(Jeanne Wentworth)*, Ernest Hilliard *(Randolph Sargent)*, Jack Richardson *(Anthony Munroe)*, Allan Sears *(Bart Gainsborough)*, Virginia Kirkley *(Alicia Gainsborough)*, Maude Truax *(Patricia Royles)*, Ben Hall *(Bertram Wellington Coy)*, Betty Caldwell *(Josephine Franklin)*, Tom O'Grady *(Mr. Caldwell)*, Fred Kelsey *(Cassidy)*, Edward Cecil *(Wilkins)*, Amber Norman *(Mrs. Caldwell)*.

Mystery comedy-drama. A houseful of guests in a country mansion becomes involved in a net of crime when one of them is murdered at midnight. Suspicion falls on several women, each of whom was known intimately by the victim before her marriage and subsequently was blackmailed by him, and narrows to one girl, who is loved by a district attorney and another man. The former doubts her, but the latter proves her innocence and discovers the real murderer. *District attorneys. Murder. Blackmail.*

THE MIDNIGHT ALARM **F2.3582**

Vitagraph Co. of America. 19 Aug **1923** [New York premiere; released Dec; c30 Jul 1923; LP19257]. Si; b&w. 35mm. 7 reels, 7,100 ft.

Dir David Smith. *Adapt* C. Graham Baker. *Photog* Stephen Smith, Jr.

Cast: Alice Calhoun *(Sparkle/Mrs. Thornton)*, Percy Marmont *(Capt. Harry Westmore)*, Cullen Landis *(Chaser)*, Joseph Kilgour *(Silas Carrington)*, Maxine Elliott Hicks *(Aggie)*, George Pearce *(Mr. Tilwell)*, Kitty Bradbury *(Mrs. Tilwell)*, J. Gunnis Davis *(Springer)*, Jean Carpenter *(Susan)*, May Foster *(Mrs. Berg)*, Fred Behrle *(Bill)*.

Melodrama. Source: James W. Harkins, Jr., *The Midnight Alarm; a Drama in Five Acts* (c1889). Mrs. Thornton, a widow whose husband was slain by Carrington, his business partner who was also executor of Thornton's estate, is killed in an automobile accident while attempting to flee from the villainous Carrington. Her daughter, Sparkle, survives and is found years later by Carrington. He is determined to disinherit her by destroying the documents that establish her identity. Carrington is thwarted by Mr. Tilwell, Sparkle's long-lost grandfather, and finally dies in a fire. Sparkle gets her inheritance, is reunited with her grandparents, and marries her sweetheart. *Grandparents. Personal identity. Inheritance. Automobile accidents. Fires. Documentation.*

A MIDNIGHT BELL **F2.3583**

Charles Ray Productions. *Dist* Associated First National Pictures. Aug **1921** [c8 Sep 1921; LP16946]. Si; b&w. 35mm. 6 reels, 6,140 ft.

Pres by Arthur S. Kane. *Dir* Charles Ray. *Adapt* Richard Andres. *Photog* George Rizard. *2d Camera* Ellsworth H. Rumer. *Tech Dir* Robert Bennett. *Film Ed* Harry Decker. *Asst Dir* Albert Ray. *Art Titles* Edward Withers.

Cast: Charles Ray *(Martin Tripp)*, Donald MacDonald *(Stephen Labaree)*, Van Dyke Brooke *(Abner Grey)*, Doris Pawn *(Annie Grey)*, Clyde McCoy *(Mac)*, Jess Herring *(Spike)*, S. J. Bingham *("Bull" Barton)*, Bert Offord *("Slick" Sweeney)*.

Comedy-melodrama. Source: Charles Hale Hoyt, *A Midnight Bell*, in Douglas L. Hunt, ed., *Five Plays* (Princeton, 1941). Martin Tripp, a rubber heel salesman, is fired for stopping off in a small country town. He gets a job with storekeeper Abner Grey and becomes enamored of Grey's daughter, Annie, while boarding at the Grey home. Another boarder, Stephen Labaree, bets Martin that he will not spend the night in a nearby church, said to be haunted; there, though badly frightened by several ghosts, he stays the night. He discovers later an underground passage, built by some thieves, leading from the church to the bank. Both he and Annie are held prisoner by the crooks, but Martin brings the villagers to the rescue by ringing the church bell. He delivers the crooks to the sheriff and wins the heart of Annie. *Salesmen. Ghosts. Thieves. Churches. Boardinghouses.*

MIDNIGHT DADDIES **F2.3584**

Mack Sennett Productions. *Dist* Sono Art–World Wide Pictures. 3 Oct

1930 [c27 Dec 1930; LP1856]. Sd (Photophone); b&w. 35mm. 6 reels, 5,644 ft.

Prod-Dir Mack Sennett. *Story-Dial* John A. Waldron, Earle Rodney, Hampton Del Ruth, Harry McCoy. *Photog* John W. Boyle. *Film Ed* William Hornbeck.

Cast: Andy Clyde *(Wilbur Louder)*, Harry Gribbon *(Charlie Mason)*, Rosemary Theby *(Wilbur's wife)*, Addie McPhail *(Charlie's sweetheart)*, Alma Bennett *(a vamp)*, Jack Cooper *(modiste shop owner)*, Katherine Ward *(Wilbur's mother-in-law)*, Vernon Dent, Natalie Joyce.

Comedy. Charlie Mason, proprietor of a nearly bankrupt modiste shop, takes his models to the beach to divert their minds from unpaid salaries. There he becomes reacquainted with Wilbur Louder, his cousin from Iowa, who with his wife and mother-in-law has come to the city to celebrate his silver anniversary. Taking advantage of Wilbur's weakness for pretty girls, Charlie plots to have the girls separate him from some of his money. He is particularly flattered by one girl named Camille; and when Charlie asks him out that night, their destination proves to be the Cafe Royal, where Wilbur is pleased to see the girls awaiting his arrival. Learning of the party, his wife decides to teach him a lesson and invites Camille to a surprise dinner party, seating her next to Charlie. He becomes inebriated and unwittingly exposes his plotting; Wilbur threatens to kill himself, but all is resolved when his wife forgives him. *Modistes. Fashion models. Cousins. Iowans. Vamps. Dance contests. Bankruptcy. Wedding anniversaries.*

THE MIDNIGHT EXPRESS **F2.3585**

Columbia Pictures. *Dist* C. B. C. Film Sales. 1 Jun **1924** [c30 Oct 1924; LP20720]. Si; b&w. 35mm. 6 reels, 5,967 ft.

Dir-Adapt George W. Hill.

Cast: Elaine Hammerstein *(Mary Travers)*, William Haines *(Jack Oakes)*, George Nichols *(John Oakes)*, Lloyd Whitlock *(Joseph Davies)*, Edwin Booth Tilton *(James Travers)*, Pat Harmon *(Silent Bill Brachely)*, Bertram Grassby *(Arthur Bleydon)*, Phyllis Haver *(Jessie Sybil)*, Roscoe Karns *(Switch Hogan)*, Jack Richardson *(Detective Collins)*, Noble Johnson *(deputy sheriff)*, Dan Crimmins, George Meadows *(railroad operators)*.

Melodrama. Disowned by his railroad president father for leading a dissolute life, Jack Oakes resolves to turn over a new leaf and takes a job in the railroad yards. He does well and is promoted to engineer while falling in love with Mary Travers, the daughter of the engineer of the Midnight Express. When Jack accidentally causes the death of a friend, he requests transfer to a small station in the mountains. Escaped convict Silent Bill Brachely shows up one night to repay Jack for sending him to prison, and a fight ensues during which Jack realizes that a runaway freight train is heading for collision with the Midnight Express. Jack knocks out Bill just in time to derail the freight train, thus redeeming himself in the eyes of Mary and his father. *Railroad engineers. Railroad magnates. Filial relations. Railroads. Regeneration.*

Note: Based on an oldtime melodrama of the same title.

MIDNIGHT FACES **F2.3586**

Otto K. Schreier Productions. *Dist* Goodwill Pictures. 25 Mar **1926** [New York State license application]. Si; b&w. 35mm. 5 reels, 4,926 ft.

Dir-Writ Bennett Cohn. *Titl* Forrest K. Sheldon. *Photog* King Grey. *Elec Eff* Edward Bush. *Film Ed* Fred Bain. *Tech Eff* Clyde Whittaker.

Cast: Francis X. Bushman, Jr. *(Lynn Claymore)*, Jack Perrin *(Richard Mason)*, Kathryn McGuire *(Mary Bronson)*, Edward Peil, Sr. *(Suie Chang)*, Charles Belcher *(Samuel Lund)*, Nora Cecil *(Mrs. Hart)*, Martin Turner *(Trohelius Snapp)*, Eddie Dennis *(Useless McGurk)*, Al Hallett *(Otis)*, Andy Waldron *(Peter Marlin)*, Larry Fisher *(Red O'Connor)*.

Melodrama. Eight people gather in a deserted house in the Florida Everglades: Richard Mason, an attorney; Trohelius, his Negro valet; Mary Bronson; a Chinaman; Samuel Lund, who is paralyzed; Otis, the butler; Mrs. Hart, the housekeeper; and Lynn Claymore, who has just inherited the house from an uncle he claims to know nothing about. Mary is kidnaped. Lynn's uncle is found to be alive, and Mason (in league with the butler and the maid) turns out to be a swindler. Lund is discovered to be the leader of the gang of swindlers; for his own ends, he has been pretending to be a cripple. The Chinaman, who is an undercover agent, arrests the crooks; and Lynn and Mary seem destined for better things. *Swindlers. Lawyers. Valets. Butlers. Housekeepers. Chinese. Cripples. Uncles. Florida Everglades.*

Note: This film may also have been released as *Midnight Fires.*

MIDNIGHT FIRES *see* **MIDNIGHT FACES**

THE MIDNIGHT FLOWER **F2.3587**

N. Nelson. *Dist* Aywon Film Corp. 9 Oct **1923** [New York premiere]. Si; b&w. 35mm. 5 reels, 4,700 ft.

Pres by Nathan Hirsh. *Dir* Capt. Leslie T. Peacock.

Cast: Gaston Glass *(The Minister)*, Vola Vale *(Myra)*.

Romantic drama. Myra is called the "Midnight Flower" because each evening at midnight she does a wild dance atop a gaming table in a local gambling den. A young Spaniard in love with Myra, who would rescue her, stages a holdup at the most profitable table and passes the money on to her. In attempting to escape, she is caught, arrested, and jailed. While she is in prison, she meets a young evangelist who runs a mission in the slums. They fall in love, and on her release Myra joins him in the missionary work. This sets the local tongues wagging and complicates the affair until it is revealed that Myra is the daughter of a wealthy family—lost to a kidnaper when she was an infant. *Evangelists. Dancers. Gambling. Robbery. Kidnaping. Parentage. Prisons.*

Note: *Film Daily* gives 1926 as year of release.

THE MIDNIGHT FLYER **F2.3588**

R-C Pictures. *Dist* Film Booking Offices of America. 6 Dec **1925** [c6 Dec 1925; LP22087]. Si; b&w. 35mm. 7 reels, 6,030 ft.

Dir Tom Forman. *Story-Cont* J. Grubb Alexander, Arthur Guy Empey. *Camera* Harry Perry. *Asst Dir* Sam Nelson.

Cast: Cullen Landis *(David Henderson)*, Dorothy Devore *(Mary Baxter)*, Buddy Post *(Mel Slater)*, Charles Mailes *(Silas Henderson)*, Frankie Darro *(Young Davey)*, Claire McDowell *(Liza Slater)*, Barbara Tennant *(Mother Henderson)*, Elmo Billings *(Young Mel Slater)*, Alphonz Ethier *(Jeb Slater)*.

Melodrama. Si Henderson is the only mountaineer to get a job with the railroad when it starts coming through the West Virginia mountains. This development incurs the wrath of Jeb Slater, who keeps alive the century-old feud between the Slaters and the Hendersons. He tries to kill Si but shoots Mrs. Henderson instead. Dying, she makes Si and her son, David, promise to let the feud die with her. Years pass; David and Jeb's son, Mel, work together; but David lives in constant fear of Mel, who is a drunken bully. Both love Mary Baxter, but she cares only for David. Jeb is released from prison and wrecks the Midnight Flyer, crippling Si and thus forcing him to retire. David, on his first run as engineer, is tormented by Mel to the point of jumping off the train just before it hits a wagon. Both David and Mel are fired. Two detectives come to arrest Jeb; Mel kills one of them; and in a drunken rampage, Mel imprisons Mary and the superintendent, Kellogg, in a train and heads it on a collision course toward the Midnight Flyer. David, overcoming his fears, boards the train, defeats Mel in a fight, and stops the train. *Railroad engineers. Railroads. Feuds. Mountain life. Cowardice. West Virginia. Train wrecks.*

THE MIDNIGHT GIRL **F2.3589**

Chadwick Pictures. 15 Feb **1925** [c17 Mar 1925; LP21256]. Si; b&w. 35mm. 7 reels, 6,300 ft.

Dir Wilfred Noy. *Adapt* Wilfred Noy, Jean Conover. *Story* Garrett Fort. *Photog* G. W. Bitzer, Frank Zukor.

Cast: Lila Lee *(Anna)*, Gareth Hughes *(Don Harmon)*, Dolores Cassinelli *(Nina)*, Charlotte Walker *(Mrs. Schuyler)*, Bela Lugosi *(Nicholas Schuyler)*, Ruby Blaine *(Natalie Schuyler)*, John D. Walsh *(Victor)*, William Harvey *(Nifty Louis)*, Sidney Paxton *(Joe)*, Signor N. Salerno *(manager)*.

Melodrama. Anna, a Russian with a beautiful voice, comes to the United States and experiences great difficulty in becoming established as a singer. She meets and falls in love with Don Harmon, orchestra leader and the son of an opera impresario. The elder Harmon's leading singer, a temperamental diva named Nina, is losing her voice, and Harmon dismisses her. Don then gives Anna a job dancing in a production number, "The Midnight Girl," that is part of the floor show at the cafe where he works. A theatrical agent working for Don's father discovers Anna and arranges for the girl to see him. The elder Harmon makes a pass at her, and she takes a shot at him, inadvertently wounding Nina, who is hiding behind the curtain in Harmon's study. The accident brings him to his senses, and he is reconciled to his former star. Don marries Anna, and the happy bride becomes a star in the Harmon opera. *Singers. Dancers. Impresari. Russians. Orchestra conductors. Opera.*

THE MIDNIGHT GUEST **F2.3590**

Universal Pictures. 17 Mar **1923** [New York premiere; released 19 Mar; c20 Feb 1923; LP18711]. Si; b&w. 35mm. 5 reels, 4,795 ft.

Dir George Archainbaud. *Story-Scen* Rupert Julian. *Adapt* A. P.

Younger. *Photog* Charles Stumar.

Cast: Grace Darmond *(Gabrielle)*, Mahlon Hamilton *(John Dryden)*, Clyde Fillmore *(William Chatfield)*, Pat Harmon *(Monk)*, Mathilde Brundage *(Aunt Sally)*.

Society drama. Gabrielle is caught while attempting to rob the home of philanthropist William Chatfield, but, rather than turn her over to the police, Chatfield offers her a home and rehabilitation. His cynical friend John Dryden scoffs at the idea and later proposes to Gabrielle that she be his mistress. Although Gabrielle is attracted to Dryden, she scorns his offer and undergoes a transformation while he hunts in the Congo. There is a rather vague ending in which Dryden returns, gives a wild party, is shot, changes his attitude, and declares his love for Gabrielle. "... The spectator is left slightly in doubt as to whether the heroine married the kindly philanthropist ... or the super-cynic ... ." (*Exhibitors Trade Review*, 31 Mar 1923.) It is suggested, however, that Dryden won the bride. *Criminals—Rehabilitation. Philanthropists. Robbery. Congo.*

Note: Working titles: *One Dark Night; Flesh.*

THE MIDNIGHT KISS **F2.3591**

Fox Film Corp. 10 Oct **1926** [c21 Jul 1926; LP22939]. Si; b&w. 35mm. 5 reels, 5,025 ft.

Pres by William Fox. *Dir* Irving Cummings. *Adapt-Scen* Alfred A. Cohn. *Photog* Abe Fried.

Cast: Richard Walling *(Thomas H. Atkins, Jr.)*, Janet Gaynor *(Mildred Hastings)*, George Irving *(Thomas H. Atkins, Sr.)*, Doris Lloyd *(Ellen Atkins)*, Tempe Piggot *(Grandma)*, Gladys McConnell *(Lenore Hastings)*, Herbert Prior *(Smith Hastings)*, Gene Cameron *(Spencer Hastings)*, Arthur Housman *(Uncle Hector)*, Bodil Rosing *(Swedish maid)*.

Comedy-drama. Source: Anne Morrison and Patterson McNutt, *Pigs, Comedy in Three Acts* (New York, c1924). Although Thomas and Ellen Atkins are good and sincere parents, they must tolerate an irascible grandmother, a lazy uncle who feigns sickness, and a brother who believes himself to be a poet. They also tolerate the concern of little Thomas for all the sick animals in the village. When Atkins, Sr., needs money to meet a note, young Thomas, with the aid of his sweetheart, Mildred Hastings, secures money by threatening to expose an older sister's love affair. He buys 250 pigs, works with them overnight, and sells them for $10 a head; after eloping with Mildred, he returns home to his proud and happy family. *Grandmothers. Uncles. Poets. Children. Family life. Parenthood. Animal care. Village life. Pigs.*

MIDNIGHT LIFE **F2.3592**

Gotham Productions. *Dist* Lumas Film Corp. 28 Aug **1928** [c17 Aug 1928; LP25542]. Si; b&w. 35mm. 5 reels, 4,863 ft.

Pres by Sam Sax. *Supv* Harold Shumate. *Dir* Scott R. Dunlap. *Scen* Adele Buffington. *Titl* Delos Sutherland. *Adapt* Arthur Statter. *Photog* Ray June. *Film Ed* Scott R. Dunlap, Ray Snyder.

Cast: Francis X. Bushman *(Jim Logan)*, Gertrude Olmstead *(Betty Brown)*, Eddie Buzzell *(Eddie Delaney)*, Monte Carter *(Steve Saros)*, Cosmo Kyrle Bellew *(Harlan Phillips)*, Carlton King.

Crime melodrama. Source: Reginald Wright Kauffman, *The Spider's Web* (New York, 1913). When a close friend is murdered by the underworld, Jim Logan, a lieutenant in New York's Finest, sets out to find the men responsible. He follows a bloody trail of clues until at last he finds the finger man, Harlan Phillips, the leader of a gang of warehouse thieves who is also an eminent Gothamite. Learning that Logan is onto him, Phillips and his gunmen set a trap for him; Logan learns of the trap and, by a smart stratagem, lures Phillips into his own trap, where he is brutally shot. The case closed, Logan helps two young dancers in Phillips' underworld cafe find a new life together. *Detectives. Police. Dancers. Gangs. Murder. New York City.*

MIDNIGHT LIMITED **F2.3593**

Paul Gerson Pictures. *Dist* Rayart Pictures. 1 Feb **1926.** Si; b&w. 35mm. 6 reels, 5,800 ft.

Pres by B. Berger. *Dir* Oscar Apfel. *Scen* J. F. Natteford. *Photog* Ernest Smith.

Cast: Gaston Glass *(Alan Morse)*, Wanda Hawley *(Mary Foster)*, Sam Allen *(Sam Foster)*, William Humphrey *(John Reynolds)*, Mathilda Brundage *(Mrs. Reynolds)*, Richard Holt *(Hal Reynolds)*, L. J. O'Connor *(John O'Connor)*, Eric Mayne *(Dr. Harrington)*, Fred Holmes *(Dr. Jones)*, Hayford Hobbs *(dispatcher)*.

Melodrama. Alan Morse, vagrant and sometime crook, stops off at a lonely wayside railroad station and attempts to rob the safe. He is caught in the act by the stationmaster, Sam Foster, who suffers a paralytic stroke brought on by the excitement. Alan then meets Mary Foster, Sam's daughter, and is overcome by both love and pity for her. Alan, who was once a telegraph operator, stays at the station to help the Fosters, and assumes Sam's duties and responsibilities. Some of Alan's old bandit friends show up, but Alan foils their attempts to rob a gold shipment. The bandits then release the brakes on a line of freight cars left on a steep incline, and Alan is forced to blow up a bridge to prevent the cars from running into the Midnight Limited. Alan is forgiven his previous trespasses, and he and Mary make plans to be married with her father's consent. *Tramps. Telegraph operators. Bandits. Stationmasters. Robbery. Railroads. Strokes.*

MIDNIGHT LOVERS **F2.3594**

John McCormick Productions. *Dist* First National Pictures. 25 Oct **1926** [New York premiere; released 7 Nov; c29 Oct 1926; LP23253]. Si; b&w. 35mm. 7 reels, 6,100 ft.

Dir John Francis Dillon. *Scen* Carey Wilson. *Titl* George Marion, Jr. *Photog* James C. Van Trees. *Prod Mgr* John McCormick.

Cast: Lewis Stone *(Maj. William Ridgewell, R. F. C.)*, Anna Q. Nilsson *(Diana Fothergill)*, John Roche *(Owen Ffolliott)*, Chester Conklin *(Moriarity)*, Dale Fuller *(Heatley)*, Purnell Pratt *(Wibley)*, Harvey Clark *(Archer)*.

Romantic comedy. Source: J. E. Harold Terry, *Collusion* (a play; publication undetermined). Married during his furlough from the Royal Flying Corps, Maj. William Ridgewell jeopardizes his marital happiness by taking his bride on an aerial honeymoon; and his leaving her with an awkward male servant in a ridiculously masculine apartment serves to turn Diana to an affair with Owen Ffolliott, a ne'er-do-well and hopeless fop. On the day of Armistice, Ridgewell receives a letter from Diana suggesting that they get a divorce; and Archer, her lawyer, arranges for collusion between Diana and Ridgewell, whereby his absence constitutes desertion. Because he loves her, Ridgewell agrees, but before the legal time elapses he returns home and sleeps in Diana's bed, wearing her nightgown; she tries to sleep on the couch but is driven by the cold to sleep with her husband. Ridgewell throws out Owen and Archer the following morning and is reconciled with his wife. *Aviators. Lawyers. Ne'er-do-wells. Infidelity. Divorce. World War I. Great Britain—Royal Flying Corps.*

MIDNIGHT MADNESS **F2.3595**

De Mille Pictures. *Dist* Pathé Exchange. 25 Mar **1928** [c3 Mar 1928; LP25042]. Si; b&w. 35mm. 6 reels, 5,659 ft.

Hector Turnbull Production. *Dir* F. Harmon Weight. *Adapt-Cont* Robert N. Lee. *Photog* David Abel. *Art Dir* Stephen Goosson. *Film Ed* Harold McLernon. *Asst Dir* George Webster. *Cost* Adrian.

Cast: Jacqueline Logan *(Norma Forbes)*, Clive Brook *(Michael Bream)*, Walter McGrail *(Childers)*, James Bradbury *(John Forbes)*, Oscar Smith *(Manubo)*, Vadim Uraneff *(Joe)*, Louis Natheaux *(masher)*, Clarence Burton *(a sailor)*, Virginia Sale *(The Gargoyle)*, Frank Hagney *(Harris)*, Emmett King *(Robert Strong)*.

Melodrama. Source: Daniel Nathan Rubin, *The Lion Trap, a Comedy in Four Acts* (c1924). Norma Forbes, who operates a shooting gallery with her father, accepts the marriage proposal of Bream, a millionaire diamond miner. Just before the wedding he discovers that she is a gold digger. Despite his affection for her, he decides to teach her a lesson by deliberately subjecting her to a rough life in the African jungle. She eventually realizes her affections and shows her love for him. *Gold diggers. Millionaires. Diamond mines. Africa.*

THE MIDNIGHT MESSAGE **F2.3596**

Goodwill Pictures. 8 Sep **1926** [New York State license]. Si; b&w. 35mm. 5 reels.

Dir Paul Hurst. *Story-Scen* H. H. Van Loan.

Cast: Wanda Hawley *(Mary Macy)*, Mary Carr *(Widow Malone)*, John Fox, Jr. *(The Boy)*, Stuart Holmes *("Red Fagan)*, Creighton Hale *(Billy Dodd)*, Mathilda Brundage *(Mrs. Richard Macy)*, Otis Harlan *(Richard Macy)*, Earl Metcalf *("Burl")*, Karl Silvera *("Thin")*, Wilson Benge *(butler)*.

Melodrama. A Western Union messenger, whose mother makes a precarious living with an old sewing machine, interrupts a burglary, scares off the thieves, and rescues a beautiful young girl. He later captures the thieves, and with the $1,000 given him by the girl's father he buys his mother a new sewing machine. *Seamstresses. Messengers. Filial relations. Burglary. Western Union. Sewing machines.*

MIDNIGHT MOLLY **F2.3597**

Gothic Pictures. *Dist* Film Booking Offices of America. 11 Jan **1925** [c11 Jan 1925; LP21118]. Si; b&w. 35mm. 6 reels, 5,400 ft.

Dir Lloyd Ingraham. *Story-Scen* Fred Kennedy Myton. *Photog* Silvano Balboni. *Asst Dir* Pan Berman.

Cast: Evelyn Brent *(Margaret Warren/Midnight Molly)*, John Dillon *(Daley)*, Bruce Gordon *(John Warren)*, Leon Bary *(George Calvin)*, John Gough *(Fogarty)*.

Melodrama. Midnight Molly is trapped by police as she attempts to steal a painting. She escapes the detectives, but, while still on the lam, she is hit by a car, taken to a hospital, and erroneously identified as Mrs. John Warren, the wife of a prominent mayoralty candidate. Since the real Mrs. Warren, who is the exact image of Molly, has just run off with George Calvin, Warren is glad to identify Molly as his wife and take her home with him. Molly recovers and continues to impersonate Warren's wife, protecting him from the political consequences of a divorce scandal. Calvin learns of the deception, returns to the city, and attempts to blackmail Warren. He is not successful, but Detective Daley, who also suspects Molly's alias, requests her fingerprints. Forcing the real Mrs. Warren to return for fingerprinting, Molly is cleared of suspicion, and Daley closes the case. Mrs. Warren and Calvin are killed in an automobile accident, and Molly and Warren are free to marry. *Thieves. Detectives. Doubles. Politics. Impersonation. Marriage. Automobile accidents.*

MIDNIGHT MYSTERY **F2.3598**

RKO Productions. 1 Jun **1930** [c1 Jun 1930; LP1396]. Sd (Photophone); b&w. 35mm. 7 reels, 6,463 ft.

Prod William Le Baron. *Assoc Prod* Bertram Millhauser. *Dir* George B. Seitz. *Adapt-Dial* Beulah Marie Dix. *Photog* Joseph Walker. *Sd Engr* Clem Portman.

Cast: Betty Compson *(Sally Wayne)*, Hugh Trevor *(Gregory Sloane)*, Lowell Sherman *(Tom Austen)*, Rita La Roy *(Madeline Austen)*, Ivan Lebedeff *(Mischa Kawelin)*, Raymond Hatton *(Paul Cooper)*, Marcelle Corday *(Harriet Cooper)*, June Clyde *(Louise Hollister)*, Sidney D'Albrook *(Barker)*, William P. Burt *(Rogers)*.

Mystery melodrama. Source: Howard Irving Young, *Hawk Island* (New York opening: 16 Sep 1929). Wealthy young bachelor Gregory Sloane is host at a house party given at his island castle off the Maine coast on a stormy night. The guests include: Sally Wayne, his fiancée and a mystery writer; Madeline, who is carrying on a flirtation with Mischa Kawelin, a Russian pianist; Paul Cooper and his wife, Harriet; and Louise Hollister. While Tom overhears Madeline declaring her love to Mischa, Gregory and Sally argue over her refusal to marry him. Gregory and Mischa feign a quarrel in which they are separated by Paul and Tom; Gregory stages a fake murder of Mischa on the balcony, then confesses the hoax to Sally; but Tom, confronting Mischa, kills him, laying the crime to Gregory's confession. Sally, however, discovers a button from Tom's coat in Mischa's hand, and by making him believe he has taken strychnine, she forces him to confess the murder. *Bachelors. Authors. Lawyers. Pianists. Murder. Hoaxes. Maine.*

MIDNIGHT ON THE BARBARY COAST **F2.3599**

Associated Independent Producers. 15 May **1929.** Si; b&w. 35mm. 5 reels, 4,250 ft.

Dir-Scen Robert J. Horner. *Titl* Jack Harrison. *Photog* Jack Draper. *Film Ed* William Austin.

Cast: William Barrymore, Kalla Pasha, Jack Richardson.

Melodrama(?). No information about the precise nature of this film has been found. *San Francisco—Barbary Coast.*

THE MIDNIGHT PATROL (Reissue) **F2.3600**

23 Jul **1921** [trade review]. Si; b&w. 35mm. 5 reels.

Note: A Thomas H. Ince production originally released by Select Pictures in 1918.

MIDNIGHT ROSE (Universal-Jewel) **F2.3601**

Universal Pictures. 26 Feb **1928** [c11 Nov 1927; LP24654]. Si; b&w. 35mm. 6 reels, 5,689 ft.

Pres by Carl Laemmle. *Dir* James Young. *Story-Cont* J. Grubb Alexander. *Titl* Tom Reed. *Photog* Joseph Brotherton. *Film Ed* Byron Robinson.

Cast: Lya De Putti *(Midnight Rose)*, Kenneth Harlan *(Tim Regan)*, Henry Kolker *(Corbin)*, Lorimer Johnston *(English Edwards)*, George Larkin *(Joe, the Wop)*, "Gunboat" Smith *(Casey)*, Wendell Phillips Franklin *(Sonny)*, Frank Brownlee *(Grogan)*.

Crime melodrama. Midnight Rose, a dancer in the Gold Coast Cabaret, loves Tim Regan, an underworld gang leader who decides to go straight in spite of entreaties from other gang members. A dying gangster requests that Tim adopt his 4-year-old son, Sonny; and realizing that the boy needs a mother, Tim induces Rose to marry him. She soon tires of housework, grows jealous of Tim's fondness for Sonny, and consequently returns to the cabaret, where Corbin, her former suitor, rehires her. When Tim, disillusioned, participates in a gang robbery, Corbin informs the police, whereupon Tim is caught and sent to prison. Rose experiences a nervous collapse as a result, culminating in childbirth, and on the verge of hysteria she attempts to drown herself; her child is taken from her, and Corbin, having a change of heart, arranges for Tim's pardon and reunites her with her baby and Sonny. Tim accuses Rose of infidelity and is about to shoot her when the children remind him of her sacrifice, and they are reconciled. *Gangsters. Dancers. Criminals—Rehabilitation. Children. Marriage. Robbery. Suicide.*

MIDNIGHT SECRETS **F2.3602**

Robert J. Horner Productions. *Dist* Rayart Pictures. 1 Oct **1924.** Si; b&w. 35mm. 5 reels, 4,313 ft.

Dir Jack Nelson. *Photog* Jack Wilson.

Cast: George Larkin, Ollie Kirby, Pauline Curley, Jack Richardson.

Melodrama. "Crooked politicians abduct sweetheart of newspaper reporter who has evidence of their crimes. They take her aboard boat but before harm can come to her, the hero fights off the henchmen of the political boss and rescues her." (*Motion Picture News Booking Guide,* 8: 57, Apr 1925.) *Reporters. Political bosses. Newspapers. Abduction.*

MIDNIGHT SHADOWS **F2.3603**

Dearholt Productions. *Dist* Arrow Film Corp. 15 Jun **1924** [c19 Jun 1924; LP20321]. Si; b&w. 35mm. 5 reels, 4,087 ft.

Dir-Writ Francis Ford.

Cast: Edmund Cobb.

Western mystery-melodrama. An abandoned hotel, near a gold mine which has been the scene of a series of robberies, is reopened by two strangers. Among the first guests are mine owner "J. B. Smith," detective "Harry Smith," who turns out to be the ringleader, and "Bill Smith" and a woman, real detectives who eventually capture the culprits. " ... features fast action and thrill stunts" (*Motion Picture News Booking Guide,* [7]:35, Oct 1924). *Detectives. Robbery. Hotels. Gold mines. Stunts.*

THE MIDNIGHT SPECIAL **F2.3604**

Chesterfield Motion Picture Corp. 15 Dec **1930** [or 1 Jan 1931]. Si; b&w. 35mm. 6 reels, 5,850 ft.

Dir Duke Worne. *Story-Scen-Dial* Arthur Hoerl. *Photog* M. A. Anderson. *Film Ed* Tom Persons.

Cast: Glenn Tryon *(Gerald Boone)*, Merna Kennedy *(Ellen Harboard)*, Mary Carr *(Mrs. Boone)*, Phillips Smalley *(Mr. Harboard)*, Jimmy Aubrey *(Joe)*, Tom O'Brien *(Dan Padden)*, Norman Phillips, Jr. *(Billy)*.

Melodrama. Through the machinations of the division superintendent (George Walton?), railroad dispatcher Gerald Boone, although tied to a chair at the time, is held responsible for both the crash and robbery of a midnight special in which socialite Ellen Harboard's father is injured, and Walton's henchmen get off with the loot. Gerald's little brother, Billy, is instrumental in discovering Walton's schemes, and the Boone brothers see a lot of action before the robbers are rounded up and turned over to the police. Gerald becomes the new division superintendent and marries Ellen. *Railroad superintendents. Railroad dispatchers. Brothers. Socialites. Train robberies. Frameup. Train wrecks.*

THE MIDNIGHT SUN (Universal-Jewel) **F2.3605**

Universal Pictures. 23 Apr **1926** [New York premiere; released 14 Nov; c27 Mar 1926; LP22558]. Si; b&w. 35mm. 9 reels, 8,767 ft.

Pres by Carl Laemmle. *Dir* Dimitri Buchowetski. *Scen* A. P. Younger. *Photog* Jackson Rose, Ernest Smith.

Cast: Laura La Plante *(Olga Balashova)*, Pat O'Malley *(Grand Duke Sergius)*, Raymond Keane *(Alexei Oroloff)*, George Siegmann *(Ivan Kusmin)*, Arthur Hoyt *(Yessky)*, Earl Metcalf *(Nickoli Orloff)*, Mikhael Vavitch *(duke's adjutant)*, Nicholas Soussanin *(duke's aide)*, Cesare Gravina *(opera director)*, Nina Romano *(Barbara)*, Medea Radzina *(Anisya)*, Albert Prisco *(messenger [or radical])*, George B. Williams *(ruined banker)*.

Melodrama. Source: Lauridas Brunn, "The Midnight Sun" (publication undetermined). Through the influence of Ivan Kusmin, a powerful Russian banker, an American girl, under the name of Olga Balashova, advances from the ranks of the Imperial Russian Ballet to prima ballerina. Olga meets young Alexei, officer of the grand duke's personal guard, and they fall in love. Alexei is grief-stricken to learn that his brother, leader of a group of nihilists, has been sentenced to Siberia for insulting Sergius, the grand duke; and Olga secretly promises Sergius an evening alone with her if he will pardon the brother. Alexei finds her with the duke and, believing the worst, strikes him, then is later sentenced to death when captured with some revolutionaries. Olga, who is tricked by Kusmin into believing that Alexei is awaiting her, accompanies him aboard a yacht, but Sergius pursues in a fast destroyer and saves her from his clutches. Olga yields herself to Sergius to save Alexei, who faints before a firing squad; realizing their true love, Sergius leaves Olga and Alexei to their happiness. *Dancers. Nobility. Brothers. Revolutionaries. Nihilists. Capital punishment. Ballet. Russia.*

THE MIDNIGHT TAXI **F2.3606**

Warner Brothers Pictures. 1 Sep **1928** [c1 Sep 1928; LP25587]. Sd (Vitaphone); b&w. 35mm. 6 reels, 5,729 ft. [Also si, 3 Oct 1928; 5,057 ft.]

Dir John Adolfi. *Scen* Freddie Foy. *Titl* Joseph Jackson. *Adapt-Dial* Harvey Gates. *Story* Gregory Rogers. *Photog* Frank Kesson. *Film Ed* Owen Marks. *Asst Dir* Fred Fox. Lewis Geib, Esdras Hartley, Victor Vance. *Tech* F. N. Murphy.

Cast: Antonio Moreno *(Tony Driscoll)*, Helene Costello *(Nan Parker)*, Myrna Loy *(Gertie Fairfax)*, William Russell *(Joseph Brant)*, Tommy Dugan *(Al Corvini)*, Bobby Agnew *(Jack Madison)*, Pat Hartigan *(Detective Blake)*, Jack Santoro *(Lefty)*, William Hauber *(Squint)*, Paul Kreuger *(Dutch)*, Spencer Bell *(Rastus)*.

Melodrama. Tony Driscoll and Joseph Brant pool $200,000 to finance a bootlegging venture and take a ride together on a train. Tony meets Nan Parker on the train and conceals the money in her coat. Brant hires two gunmen to stick up Tony and himself but the holdup is a failure, for it is interrupted by detectives looking for stolen jewelry. The jewelry is found on Tony (planted there by Al Corvini, one of Brant's henchmen), and Tony is arrested and taken off the train. Released on bail later, Tony charters an airplane and returns to the speeding train. There is a gunbattle, and the police arrest Brant and his men. Tony is cleared of the charges against him and decides to go straight, having fallen in love with Nan. *Bootleggers. Detectives. Thieves. Frameup. Trains. Airplanes.*

MIDNIGHT THIEVES **F2.3607**

Kerman Films. *Dist* A. G. Steen. 26 Feb **1926** [New York State license]. Si; b&w. 35mm. 5 reels.

Cast: Herbert Rawlinson, Grace Darmond.

Society melodrama(?). No information about the nature of this film has been found.

THE MIDNIGHT WATCH **F2.3608**

Trem Carr Productions. *Dist* Rayart Pictures. Feb **1927.** Si; b&w. 35mm. 6 reels, 5,780 ft.

Pres by W. Ray Johnston. *Dir* Charles Hunt. *Story* Trem Carr. *Photog* Harold Wenstrom.

Cast: Roy Stewart *(Bob Breemer)*, Mary McAllister *(Rose Denton)*, David Torrence *(Chief Callahan)*, Ernest Hilliard, Marcella Daly.

Society mystery. College boy–detective Bob Breemer takes on the job of clearing his sweetheart, social secretary Rose Denton, of charges of stealing a pearl necklace from her wealthy employers. Displeased with Bob's self-assurance, Chief Callahan punishes him with the midnight watch, but Bob uncovers the thief—an underworld leader, friend of Callahan, and member of the necklace owner's social set. *Students. Detectives. Secretaries. Police. Theft.*

THE MIDSHIPMAN **F2.3609**

Metro-Goldwyn-Mayer Pictures. 4 Oct **1925** [c5 Nov 1925; LP22136]. Si; b&w. 35mm. 8 reels, 7,498 ft.

Dir Christy Cabanne. *Scen* F. McGrew Willis. *Story* Carey Wilson. *Photog* Oliver Marsh.

Cast: Ramon Novarro *(James Randall)*, Harriet Hammond *(Patricia Lawrence)*, Wesley Barry *(Ted Lawrence)*, Margaret Seddon *(Mrs. Randall)*, Crauford Kent *(Basil Courtney)*, Pauline Key *(Rita)*, Maurice Ryan *("Fat")*, Harold Goodwin *("Tex")*, William Boyd *("Spud")*.

Romantic drama. James Randall, an upperclassman at the Naval Academy, falls in love with Patricia Lawrence, the sister of a plebe. She is engaged to Basil Courtney, a wealthy reprobate who arranges with Rita to discredit James. On the night of the big dance, Rita goes to the guardhouse where James is supposed to be on duty and arranges to be found with him. Ted Lawrence has taken his place, however, and James sees Ted with Rita in the guardhouse. Honorbound to report Ted for violation of academy rules, James decides to resign instead. Courtney abducts Patricia, and James rescues her. James discovers Rita's complicity in Courtney's schemes and decides to stay in the academy, marrying Patricia upon his graduation. *Midshipmen. Abduction. Brother-sister relationship. United States Naval Academy.*

MIDSTREAM **F2.3610**

Tiffany-Stahl Productions. 1 Jun or 29 Jul **1929** [c9 Sep 1929; LP687]. Talking & singing sequences (Photophone); b&w. 35mm. 8 reels, 6,337 ft. [Also si; 7,472 ft.]

Dir James Flood. *Scen* Frances Guihan. *Dial-Titl* Frederick Hatton, Fanny Hatton. *Story* Bernice Boone. *Photog* Jackson Rose. *Film Ed* Desmond O'Brien. *Mus* Hugo Riesenfeld. *Theme Song: "Midstream"* L. Wolfe Gilbert, Abel Baer.

Cast—The Story: Ricardo Cortez *(James Stanwood)*, Claire Windsor *(Helene Craig)*, Montagu Love *(Dr. Nelson)*, Larry Kent *(Martin Baker)*, Helen Jerome Eddy *(Mary Mason)*.

Cast—"Faust" Singers: Leslie Brigham *(Mephistopheles)*, Louis Alvarez *(Faust)*, Genevieve Schrader *(Marguerite)*, Florence Foyer *(Marthe)*.

Drama. Aging Wall Street financier Jim Stanwood falls in love with his young and beautiful neighbor, Helene Craig. To win her, he goes abroad and gets a rejuvenation operation, telegraphs his office of his death, and returns as a "nephew" who has inherited everything. Shortly before Stanwood is to marry Helene, he collapses during a performance of *Faust* and returns to his former appearance. Mary, his devoted secretary, comes to his side when Helene shrinks from him in horror. *Financiers. Secretaries. Rejuvenation. Impersonation. New York City. "Faust".*

THE MIGHTY **F2.3611**

Paramount Famous Lasky Corp. 16 Nov **1929** [c15 Nov 1929; LP863]. Sd (Movietone); b&w. 35mm. 9 reels, 6,802 ft. [Also si; 6,097 ft.]

Dir John Cromwell. *Treatment* Nellie Revell. *Titl* Herman Mankiewicz. *Adapt-Dial* William Slavens McNutt, Grover Jones. *Story* Robert N. Lee. *Camera* J. Roy Hunt. *Film Ed* George Nichols, Jr., Otto Levering. *Rec Engr* M. M. Paggi. *Asst Dir* Archie Hill.

Cast: George Bancroft *(Blake Greeson)*, Esther Ralston *(Louise Patterson)*, Warner Oland *(Sterky)*, Raymond Hatton *(Dogey Franks)*, Dorothy Revier *(Mayme)*, Morgan Farley *(Jerry Patterson)*, O. P. Heggie *(J. K. Patterson)*, Charles Sellon *(The Mayor)*, E. H. Calvert *(Major General)*, John Cromwell *(Mr. Jameison)*.

Action melodrama. Blake Greeson, a fearless gunman for mobster Sterky, is drafted into the military service and goes to war. Greeson glories in his battle victories and is admired by Jerry Patterson, who is afraid to fight. In proving himself to Greeson, Jerry is mortally wounded, but before dying he has Greeson promise to tell his family about his bravery. Greeson returns home a major and a war hero, but when he accepts the position of chief of police, Louise, Jerry's sister, disapproves. Nevertheless, when a rival gang plans a bank robbery, Greeson sends his force to confront them, thus upholding the law and winning Louise. *Gangsters. Police. Criminals—Rehabilitation. Veterans. Cowardice. Bank robberies. World War I.*

THE MIGHTY DEBRAU **F2.3612**

Delman Film Corp. 28 Mar **1923** [New York State license application]. Si; b&w. 35mm. 8 reels, 7,500 ft.

Melodrama(?). No information about the nature of this film has been found.

MIGHTY LAK' A ROSE **F2.3613**

Edwin Carewe Productions. *Dist* Associated First National Pictures. 12 Feb **1923** [c23 Jan 1923; LP18605]. Si; b&w. 35mm. 8 reels, 8,153 ft.

Pres by Edwin Carewe. *Pers Supv–Dir* Edwin Carewe. *Story-Scen* Curtis Benton. *Titl* George V. Hobart. *Adapt* Adelaide Heilbron. *Photog* Sol Polito. *Tech Dir* John D. Schulze. *Film Ed* Robert De Lacy. *Asst Dir* Phillip W. Masi.

Cast: James Rennie *(Jimmy Harrison)*, Sam Hardy *(Jerome Trevor)*, Anders Randolf *("Bull" Morgan)*, Harry Short *("Slippery Eddie" Foster)*, Dorothy Mackaill *(Rose Duncan)*, Helene Montrose *("Hard-boiled" Molly Malone)*, Paul Panzer *(Humpty Logan)*, Dora Mills Adams *(Mrs. Trevor)*, Jean Bronte *(Jean, the dog)*.

Melodrama. Blind violinist Rose Duncan unknowingly falls in with a gang of crooks who use her as a decoy. Under her influence they all—especially Jimmy Harrison—resolve to go straight but decide to pull one more job so that Rose may have surgery. Jimmy is caught and goes to prison while Rose, now cured, successfully pursues her musical career. On the night of her debut Jimmy is released and reunited with Rose. *Violinists. Criminals—Rehabilitation. Blindness. Dogs.*

MIKE **F2.3614**
Metro-Goldwyn-Mayer Pictures. Apr **1926** [c11 Jan 1926; LP22405]. Si; b&w. 35mm. 7 reels, 6,755 ft.
Pres by Louis B. Mayer. *Dir-Story* Marshall Neilan. *Scen* Marion Jackson. *Photog* David Kesson.
Cast: Sally O'Neill *(Mike)*, William Haines *(Harlan)*, Charlie Murray *(Father)*, Ned Sparks *(Slinky)*, Ford Sterling *(Tad)*, Frankie Darro *(boy)*, Junior Coughlan *(boy)*, Muriel Frances Dana *(girl)*, Sam De Grasse *(Brush)*.
Melodrama. Mike, the daughter of a railroad section boss, lives with her father and three other children in a remodeled boxcar attached to a railroad work train. Harlan, a sectionhand, saves the life of one of the children and invites Mike to a village dance, first telling her that he once was a telegrapher but was discharged for allowing the Transcontinental Limited to go through an open switch. Slinky and his gang plot to hold up the mail train, and Mike learns of their plans. They lock her in a boxcar and set it in motion. Harlan rescues her and then wires the nearest government station for help. With the aid of precision bombing by Marine aviators, Mike and Harlan bring Slinky and his gang to justice. Harlan is reinstated in his former job and marries Mike. *Aviators. Telegraph operators. Gangs. Railroads. Aerial bombardment. United States Marines.*

MILE A MINUTE MORGAN **F2.3615**
Sanford Productions. *Dist* Aywon Film Corp. 1 Jan **1924.** Si; b&w. 35mm. 5 reels, 4,700-5,089 ft.
Dir Frank S. Mattison. *Dir? (see note)* Horace Carpenter. *Photog* Elmer G. Dyer.
Cast: Matty Mattison *(Paul Bunyon, Jr.)*, Vivian Rich *(Patricia Jennings)*, Billy Franey *(Philo Brown)*, Lafayette McKee *(Chester Jennings)*, Gene Crosby *(Cissy Green)*, Leonard Clapham *(Kenneth Winster)*.
Comedy-drama. Paul Bunyon, disowned son of a millionaire, and his pal, Philo Brown, get jobs (under assumed names) in a lumber yard owned by Bunyon, Sr. Paul falls in love with Patricia Jennings, the manager's daughter. Philo's boasts that Paul is a fighter, known as "Mile a Minute Morgan," get him a match with a professional. Paul intends to skip out, but Patricia persuades him to stay. When Kenneth Winster steals the purse money and abducts Patricia, Paul knocks out his opponent, chases Winster, recovers the money, saves Patricia, and wins his father's respect. *Boxers. Millionaires. Filial relations. Disinheritance. Lumber industry.*
Note: Some sources credit Horace Carpenter as director.

THE MILE-A-MINUTE MAN **F2.3616**
Camera Pictures. *Dist* Lumas Film Corp. Dec **1926** [c30 Apr 1926; LP22665]. Si; b&w. 35mm. 5 reels, 5,000 ft.
Dir Jack Nelson. *Story-Cont* Edward J. Meagher. *Photog* Arthur Reeves. *Asst Dir* Rudolph Bylek.
Cast: William Fairbanks *(Sp. P. [Speedy] Rockett)*, Virginia Brown Faire *(Paula Greydon)*, George Periolat *(C. O. [Old Ironsides] Rockett)*, Jane Keckley *(Mrs. J. P. Greydon)*, George Cheeseboro *(James Brett)*, Barney Furey *(Joe Weeks)*, Paul Dennis *(Bob)*, Hazel Howell *(Eleanor Hoyt)*.
Melodrama. Old Ironsides, an automobile manufacturer, is infuriated to learn that his competitor, Greydon, has improved the motor on his racing "Greyhound," which is superior to his own "Skyrocket." His son Speedy, the factory superintendent, who is in love with Paula Greydon, informs his father that a new highspeed carburetor will restore supremacy to the Rockett car. At a social affair, Mr. Rockett and his son become involved with fortune hunters Eleanor Hoyt and Mrs. Pennywaite, aided and abetted by Brett, who is an avid suitor of Paula's and has a financial investment in the Greydon car. Later he attempts to waylay Speedy, and in desperation he kidnaps him the night before the race; after many difficulties, Speedy escapes, reaches the track via airplane, and wins the race, in spite of Brett's attempts at sabotage. Paula and Speedy's marriage consolidates the business firms. *Automobile manufacture. Fortune hunters. Business competition. Courtship.*

MILE-A-MINUTE ROMEO **F2.3617**
Fox Film Corp. 28 Oct or 18 Nov **1923** [c18 Nov 1923; LP19651]. Si; b&w. 35mm. 6 reels, 5,306 ft.
Pres by William Fox. *Dir* Lambert Hillyer. *Scen* Robert N. Lee.
Cast: Tom Mix *(Lucky Bill)*, Betty Jewel *(Molly)*, J. Gordon Russell *(Landry)*, James Mason *(Morgan)*, Duke Lee *(sheriff)*, James Quinn *(coroner)*, Tony *(himself, a horse)*.
Western melodrama. Source: Max Brand, *Gun Gentlemen; a Western Story* (New York, 1927). Three men—Lucky Bill, Landry, and Morgan—are in love with Molly. Lucky Bill wins her by skillful horsemanship and dogged determination. *Horsemanship. Courtship. Horses.*

THE MILKY WAY **F2.3618**
Western Pictures Exploitation Co. 15 Feb **1922** [New York State license]. Si; b&w. 35mm. 5 reels, 4,850 ft.
Cast: David Butler.
Western melodrama(?). No information about the nature of this film has been found.

A MILLION BID **F2.3619**
Warner Brothers Pictures. 28 May **1927** [c19 May 1927; LP23986]. Si; b&w. 35mm. 7 reels, 6,310 ft.
Dir Michael Curtiz. *Scen* Robert Dillon. *Camera* Hal Mohr. *Asst Dir* Henry Blanke.
Cast: Dolores Costello *(Dorothy Gordon)*, Warner Oland *(Geoffrey Marsh)*, Malcolm McGregor *(Dr. Robert Brent)*, Betty Blythe *(Mrs. Gordon)*, William Demarest *(George Lamont)*, Douglas Gerrard *(Lord Bobby Vane)*, Grace Gordon *(The Gordon Maid)*.
Society melodrama. Source: George Cameron, *A Million Bid* (New York opening: 5 Oct 1908). To please her selfish and calculating mother, Dorothy Gordon is induced to marry wealthy Geoffrey Marsh, though she loves Robert Brent, a young brain surgeon. Aboard his yacht, Marsh attempts to force himself on the girl during a storm; he is repulsed, and Dorothy is rescued from the sinking boat, while Marsh is assumed to be dead. Dr. Brent restores her health, and in time they are married and are expecting a child when Brent announces he is to perform an operation on an aphasia victim whom Dorothy recognizes as Marsh. Though their marriage and happiness are at stake, Brent refuses to neglect his professional duty, and the operation is a success. Marsh, however, realizing the consequences, feigns continued loss of memory and leaves them to their happiness. *Surgeons. Aphasia. Filial relations. Marriage. Wealth. Brain surgery. Shipwrecks.*

THE MILLION DOLLAR COLLAR **F2.3620**
Warner Brothers Pictures. 12 Jan **1929** [c10 Jan 1929; LP1]. Talking sequences, sd eff, & mus score (Vitaphone); b&w. 35mm. 6 reels, 5,561 ft. [Also si, 9 Feb 1929; 4,878 ft.]
Dir D. Ross Lederman. *Story-Scen-Dial* Robert Lord. *Titl* James A. Starr. *Photog* Nelson Laraby. *Film Ed* William Holmes.
Cast: Rin-Tin-Tin *(Rinty, a dog)*, Matty Kemp *(Bill Holmes)*, Evelyn Pierce *(Mary French)*, Philo McCullough *(Joe French)*, Tommy Dugan *(Ed Mack)*, Allan Cavan *(The Chief)*, Grover Liggon *(Scar)*.
Crime melodrama. Bill rescues Rinty from a car wreck not realizing that there is a stolen $50,000 diamond necklace hidden in the dog's collar. He discovers this fact when he falls into the hands of a criminal gang. Mary, a member of the gang but sick of it all, and Rinty help him escape, and with the reward money the young lovers begin their honeymoon. *Gangs. Theft. Dogs.*

THE MILLION DOLLAR HANDICAP **F2.3621**
Metropolitan Pictures. *Dist* Producers Distributing Corp. 7 Feb **1925** [c20 Jan 1926; LP22281]. Si; b&w. 35mm. 6 reels, 6,117 ft.
Pres by John C. Flinn. *Dir* Scott Sidney. *Adapt* F. McGrew Willis. *Photog* J. Devereaux Jennings. *Adtl Photog* Dewey Wrigley. *Art Dir* Charles Cadwallader. *Asst Dir* Douglas Dawson. *Prod Mgr* George Bertholon. *Prod Asst* Robert Ross.
Cast: Vera Reynolds *(Alis Porter)*, Edmund Burns *(George Mortimer)*, Ralph Lewis *(John Porter)*, Ward Crane *(Phillip Crane)*, Tom Wilson *(Tom)*, Clarence Burton *(Langdon)*, Danny Hoy *(jockey)*, Rosa Gore *(Marilda Porter)*, Walter Emerson *(Alan Porter)*, Lon Poff *(milkman)*.
Melodrama. Source: William Alexander Fraser, *Thoroughbreds* (New York, 1902). John Porter, a southern horsebreeder, buys a filly named Dixie after she puts up a strong showing in a race, discovering later that the animal had been doped for the contest. Porter is paralyzed later from

a fall from a horse, and his son, Alan, embezzles a sum of money from the bank in order to straighten out the family finances. George Mortimer, who is in love with Alan's sister, Alis, takes the blame for the crime and is discharged from his job. Alis enters Dixie in a race and, disguised as a boy, rides the horse to victory. Alis' father is cured by the excitement, Alan's accounts are balanced, and George looks forward to a life with Alis. *Horsebreeders. Bank clerks. Embezzlement. Paralysis. Disguise. Banks. Horseracing. Horses.*

MILLION DOLLAR MYSTERY **F2.3622**

Trem Carr Productions. *Dist* Rayart Pictures. Aug **1927.** Si; b&w. 35mm. 6 reels, 5,800-6,022 ft.

Dir Charles J. Hunt. *Scen* Arthur Hoerl. *Story* Harold MacGrath. *Photog* Ernest Depew.

Cast: James Kirkwood *(James Norton)*, Lila Lee *(Florence Grey)*, Henry Sedley *(Leo Braine)*, Erin La Bissoniere *(Olga Perigoff)*, Elmer Dewey *(Boris Orloff)*, Edward Gordon *(Alec Felton)*, John Elliott *(Stanley Hargreaves/Inspector Jedson)*, Ralph Whiting.

Mystery drama. "Notorious band of crooks pursue former member, now a man of wealth. One of their number [James Norton] falls in love with the man's daughter [Florence Grey]. It develops that this man is a member of the Secret Service and he succeeds in bringing the band to justice." (*Motion Picture News Booking Guide,* 13:34, Oct 1927.) *Secret service. Gangs. Wealth.*

A MILLION FOR LOVE **F2.3623**

Sterling Pictures. 15 Apr **1928** [c28 Apr 1928; LP25194]. Si; b&w. 35mm. 6 reels, ca5,400 ft.

Dir Robert F. Hill. *Scen-Titl* Frances Guihan. *Story* Peggy Gaddis. *Photog* Herbert Kirkpatrick. *Film Ed* Leotta Whytock.

Cast: Reed Howes *(Danny Eagan)*, Josephine Dunn *(Mary Norfleet)*, Lee Shumway *(D. A. Norfleet)*, Mary Carr *(Mrs. Eagan)*, Lewis Sargent *(Jimmy Eagan)*, Jack Rich *(Slim)*, Frank Baker *(Pete)*, Alfred Fisher *(Judge)*.

Crook melodrama. Charged with killing Pete, a gang leader, Danny Eagan, so as to protect the reputation of the girl he loves, refuses to defend himself. Mary Norfleet, daughter of the district attorney, comes forward at last in his defense, explaining that she was with Danny the evening Pete was murdered. Danny is freed when prosecution witness "Slim" Morton, a crony of the murdered man, confesses. *Gangs. District attorneys. Murder. Reputation. Trials.*

A MILLION TO BURN **F2.3624**

Universal Pictures. 26 Oct **1923** [New York premiere; released 12 Nov; c8 Oct 1923; LP19480]. Si; b&w. 35mm. 5 reels, 4,556 ft.

Dir William Parke. *Scen* Raymond Schrock. *Story* Tom Whitside. *Photog* John Stumar.

Cast: Herbert Rawlinson *(Thomas Gwynne)*, Kalla Pasha *(Nickoli Rubnov)*, Beatrice Burnham *(Daisy Jones)*, Tom McGuire *(P. D. Riley)*, Melbourne MacDowell *(Mark Mills)*, Margaret Landis *(Sybil Mills)*, George F. Marion *(Old Ben Marlowe)*, Frederick Stanton *(Langden)*, Frederick Bertrand *(The Auditor)*.

Comedy. The owner of a resort hotel promotes Tom Gwynne, a college boy working as a waiter, to manager. As a result of his mismanagement the hotel loses several thousand dollars. Tom inherits a million and buys the hotel to continue his experimental management, which is to give the employees time and opportunity for self-expression—to do what they like best to do. With the grounds full of acrobats, musicians, and dancers, the hotel goes bankrupt. The old manager returns, buys the hotel, but retains Tom—now that he has learned his lesson—as manager. *Waiters. Acrobats. Musicians. Dancers. Millionaires. Resorts. Hotel management.*

THE MILLIONAIRE **F2.3625**

Universal Film Manufacturing Co. 14 Nov **1921** [c5 Nov 1921; LP17167]. Si; b&w. 35mm. 5 reels, 4,730 ft.

Dir Jack Conway. *Scen* Wallace Clifton. *Story* Hulbert Footner. *Photog* E. J. Vallejo.

Cast: Herbert Rawlinson *(Jack Norman)*, Bert Roach *(Bobo Harmsworth)*, William Courtwright *(Simon Fisher)*, Verne Winter *(Jimmy)*, Lillian Rich *(Kate Blair)*, Margaret Mann *(Grandmother)*, Fred Vroom *(Delmar)*, Mary Huntress *(Mrs. Clever)*, Doris Pawn *(Marion Culbreth)*, E. A. Warren *(Evers)*.

Melodrama. On the morning that Simon Fisher discharges him, Jack Norman, who has fallen in love with Kate Blair, the bookkeeper, is notified that he has fallen heir to $80 million, the estate of murdered financier Silas Gyde, who once loved Norman's mother. Kate decides that she will not marry Jack until she can see what effect sudden wealth will have upon him. After many adventures, Jack discovers that the gang that murdered Silas is after him, and he persuades an actor friend to pose as the heir, while he acts as secretary. His friend Bobo is vamped by Marion, a female gang member, who marries, then tries to rob, Bobo; but Jack arrives with the police and captures the entire gang. *Millionaires. Bookkeepers. Actors. Gangs. Inheritance. Impersonation.*

THE MILLIONAIRE **F2.3626**

Micheaux Film Corp. ca10 Dec **1927** [New York showing; c15 Feb 1928; LU24983]. Si; b&w. 35mm. 7 reels.

Prod-Dir-Writ Oscar Micheaux.

Cast: Grace Smith, J. Lawrence Criner, Cleo Desmond, Lionel Monagas, William Edmonson, Vera Bracker, S. T. Jacks, E. G. Tatum.

Melodrama. Pelham Guitry, a Negro soldier of fortune, goes to South America where, after 15 years of hard work, he makes his fortune. Returning to New York, he meets Elia Wellington, a woman controlled by the underworld, and she tries to trap him into marriage. Pelham defeats the forces of crime and reforms the girl, who learns to take pleasure in her beauty and especially in her talents. *Soldiers of fortune. Millionaires. Criminals—Rehabilitation. Negro life. New York City. South America.*

THE MILLIONAIRE COWBOY **F2.3627**

Harry Garson Productions. *Dist* Film Booking Offices of America. 5 Oct **1924** [c5 Oct 1924; LP20740]. Si; b&w. 35mm. 5 reels, 4,841 ft.

Dir Harry Garson. *Scen* Frank S. Beresford. *Story* Darryl Francis Zanuck. *Photog* Louis W. Physioc.

Cast: Lefty Flynn *(Charles Christopher Meredyth, Jr., known as "Gallop")*, Gloria Grey *(Pauline Truce)*, Charles Crockett *(Granville Truce, her father)*, Frederic Peters *(Grafter Torso, a border bandit)*, Daddy Hoosier *(Buffalo Jones, a desert bandit)*.

Western melodrama. Following a night of particularly wild dissipation, Charles Meredyth decides to cure his son, Gallop, of his convivial habits, tells him that he has killed a taxi driver, and offers to help him escape. Gallop lands in a small southwestern town whose only inhabitants are its founder, Granville Truce; his daughter, Pauline; and a gang of Mexican bandits. Gallop discovers that Truce has developed a rust remover from cactus oil and markets the product. While routing the bandits, Gallop puts the town on the map and a ring on Pauline's finger. *Millionaires. Inventors. Cowboys. Bandits. Mexicans. Fatherhood. Business management. Cactus.*

A MILLIONAIRE FOR A DAY **F2.3628**

Guy Empey Productions. *Dist* Pioneer Film Corp. 18 Jul **1921** [Port Washington, New York, showing]. Si; b&w. 35mm. 6 reels, 5,620 ft.

Dir Wilfred North. *Scen* William Addison Lathrop. *Story* Arthur Guy Empey.

Cast: Arthur Guy Empey *(Bobbie Walters)*, Harry Burkhardt *(Jim Warner)*, Florence Martin *(Dorothy Wright)*, Templar Saxe *(Gamble Mason)*, Williams Eville *(Surething Silvers)*.

Comedy-melodrama. "Bobbie Walters succeeds in amassing a large bank roll in spite of his adversaries and then sets out to celebrate his good fortune. But it is short lived. The Wall Street sharks get to him good and proper with the result [that] Bobbie climbs down from his perch, a sadder but wiser man. But Bobbie is adamant. Besides, he has a girl waiting for him to get rich, and so he starts all over again. This time, however, the villains are bested, even though they dynamite his costly oil derricks and Bobbie emerges with a million and a wife." (*Moving Picture World,* 1 Jul 1922, p54.) *Millionaires. Wealth. Speculation. Oil business. New York City—Wall Street.*

THE MILLIONAIRE ORPHAN **F2.3629**

Fred Balshofer Productions. 26 May **1926** [New York State license]. Si; b&w. 35mm. 5 reels.

Dir-Writ Robert J. Horner.

Cast: William Barrymore *(Jack Randall)*, Jack Richardson *(William Hampton)*, Hal Ferner *(Norman Davies)*, Pauline Curley *(Fay Moreland)*, Rex McIlvaine *(Henry Moreland)*.

Melodrama(?). No information about the precise nature of this film has been found. *Millionaires. Orphans.*

THE MILLIONAIRE POLICEMAN (Royal) F2.3630

Banner Productions. *Dist* Ginsberg-Kann Distributing Corp. 10 Jun **1926** [c8 May 1926; LP22719]. Si; b&w. 35mm. 5 reels, 5,189 ft.

Dir Edward J. Le Saint. *Adapt-Scen* Dorothy Yost.

Cast: Herbert Rawlinson *(Steven Wallace)*, Eva Novak *(Mary Gray)*, Eugenie Besserer *(Mrs. Gray)*, Arthur Rankin *(Jimmy Gray)*, Lillian Langdon *(Mrs. Wallace)*.

Melodrama. Source: Samuel J. Briskin, "The Millionaire Policeman" (publication undetermined). Steven Wallace, a millionaire's son, demonstrates a failure of courage in hesitating to rescue his female riding companion while a mounted policeman comes to her aid. Stung by the realization of his cowardice, he leaves town and later applies for a position on the police force. He finds lodging with the Gray family and falls for Mary, the cheerful young daughter. Steve warns young Jimmy, whom he finds fighting, to avoid bad company, and the boy resents his interference. On the day of Steve and Mary's engagement the hardware store is robbed, and although Mary tries to clear her brother, Steve suspects Jimmy's participation in the crime and arrests him. In an escape attempt Jimmy starts a fire and is killed in a fall; Steve rescues Mrs. Gray, is awarded a medal for heroism, and, before returning home, marries Mary. *Millionaires. Police. Brother-sister relationship. Robbery. Cowardice. Courtship. Fires.*

MILLIONAIRES F2.3631

Warner Brothers Pictures. 13 Nov **1926** [c3 Nov 1926; LP23289]. Si; b&w. 35mm. 7 reels, 6,903 ft.

Dir Herman C. Raymaker. *Screenplay* Raymond L. Schrock. *Adapt* Edward Clark, Graham Baker. *Camera* Byron Haskins. *Asst Camera* Frank Kesson. *Asst Dir* Ted Stevens.

Cast: George Sidney *(Meyer Rubens)*, Louise Fazenda *(Reba)*, Vera Gordon *(Esther Rubens)*, Nat Carr *(Maurice)*, Helene Costello *(Ida)*, Arthur Lubin *(Lew)*, Jane Winton *(Lottie)*, Otto Hoffman *(detective)*, William Strauss *(helper in Meyer's tailor shop)*.

Comedy-drama. Source: Edward Phillips Oppenheim, *The Inevitable Millionaires* (Boston, 1925). Meyer Rubens, a poor Jewish tailor on New York's East Side, is constantly reproached by his wife, Esther, whose sister, Reba, has made a wealthy marriage. Reba's unscrupulous husband, Maurice, persuades Meyer to buy some apparently worthless oil stock that reaps a fortune. With great wealth at their command, Meyer and Esther move to Fifth Avenue and live in luxury. Meyer finds himself in constant difficulty because of his ignorance of social graces; and at Reba's suggestion, Esther decides to get a divorce. Maurice employs Lottie to flirt with Meyer and create a case against him, but his plan fails. Ida, who is in love with Meyer's son, Lew, informs Esther that Meyer is actually adored by the society set, while she herself is merely tolerated. As a result she returns to Meyer, and Lew and Ida are happily married. *Millionaires. Jews. Tailors. Social classes. Nouveaux riches. Family life. Wealth. New York City—East Side. New York City—Fifth Avenue.*

MIN AND BILL F2.3632

Metro-Goldwyn-Mayer Pictures. 21 Nov **1930** [New York premiere; released 29 Nov; c2 Dec 1930; LP1770]. Sd (Movietone); b&w. 35mm. 7 reels, 6,200 ft.

Dir George Hill. *Scen-Dial* Frances Marion, Marion Jackson. *Photog* Harold Wenstrom. *Art Dir* Cedric Gibbons. *Film Ed* Basil Wrangell. *Rec Engr* Douglas Shearer. *Wardrobe* René Hubert.

Cast: Marie Dressler *(Min)*, Wallace Beery *(Bill)*, Dorothy Jordan *(Nancy)*, Marjorie Rambeau *(Bella)*, Donald Dillaway *(Dick)*, De Witt Jennings *(Groot)*, Russell Hopton *(Alec)*, Frank McGlynn *(Mrs. Southard)*, Gretta Gould *(Mrs. Southard)*.

Drama. Source: Lorna Moon, *Dark Star* (Indianapolis, c1929). Min, a hard-boiled proprietress of a waterfront hotel, who has as her sweetheart Bill, a fisherman, brings up Nancy, a girl who was deserted by her own mother in infancy. Local authorities try to persuade Min that she is not a fit mother and that Nancy should be sent to school. Between the truant officer and prohibition officials, Min is forced to send her to live with the school principal's family, though Nancy insists that she would rather stay with Min. Meanwhile, Bella, Nancy's actual mother—now a down-and-out floozie—turns up, but Min sends her back to San Francisco. Min sacrifices to send Nancy to a proper boarding school, where she falls in love with Dick, a wealthy boy who loves her in spite of her background and plans to marry her. Bella, finding out about her daughter's good fortune, returns and tells Min she will reveal her identity so as to benefit from Dick's money. In a struggle, Min's face is burned, and she is forced to shoot Bella to stop her. Min is informed on by a jealous sailor; and as her daughter sails on her honeymoon, Min is led away by the police. *Hotelkeepers. Fishermen. Guardians. Courtship. Waterfront. Motherhood. Manslaughter.*

MIND OVER MOTOR F2.3633

Ward Lascelle Productions. *Dist* Principal Pictures. 15 Jan **1923** [c1 Jan 1923; LP18613]. Si; b&w. 35mm. 5 reels.

Prod-Dir Ward Lascelle. *Scen* H. Landers Jackson. *Titl* Bennet Copen, H. Landers Jackson.

Cast: Trixie Friganza *(Tish)*, Ralph Graves *(Jasper McCutcheon)*, Clara Horton *(Bettina Bailey)*, Lucy Handforth *(Lizzie)*, Caroline Rankin *(Aggie)*, Grace Gordon *(Marie)*, Pietro Sosso *(officer)*, George Guyton *(Gardiner)*, Mrs. Lee *(mother)*, Larry Steers *(Ellis)*, Edward Hearne *(starter)*.

Comedy-melodrama. Source: Mary Roberts Rinehart, "Mind Over Motor," in *Saturday Evening Post* (185:8, 5 Oct 1912). A race promoter (Ellis) induces Tish, an "automaniac," to finance innocently a motor race. Jasper McCutcheon, Tish's friend, is about to win the race when Ellis' paid cohorts force him out. Informed by the sheriff that she will be jailed for conspiracy unless an outsider wins the race, Tish jumps in a car and drives to victory. *Automobile racing. Conspiracy.*

MINE TO KEEP F2.3634

Bryant Washburn Productions. *Dist* Grand-Asher Distributing Corp. 20 Aug **1923** [New York premiere; c23 Aug 1923; LP19340]. Si; b&w. 35mm. 6 reels, 5,761 ft.

Pres by Samuel V. Grand. *Prod-Dir* Ben Wilson. *Scen* Arthur Statter. *Story* Evelyn Campbell. *Photog* Edwin Linden, Jack Stevens.

Cast: Bryant Washburn *(Victor Olney)*, Mabel Forrest *(Constance Rives)*, Wheeler Oakman *(Clint Mowbray)*, Charlotte Stevens *(Carmen Joy)*, Laura La Varnie *(Mrs. Joy)*, Peaches Jackson, Mickey Moore, Pat Moore *(Joy children)*, Francis Ford *(Jack Deering)*, Harry Dunkinson *(Sewell)*, Charles Mason *(Pelton)*, Edith Stayart *(Mrs. Deering)*.

Romantic drama. Former playboy Victor Olney becomes jealous of his wife's love soon after he and Constance are married. He is especially hostile toward Clint Mowbray, a former suitor. When Mowbray implies that there was an affair between Olney and a dancer who was injured at Olney's bachelor party, Constance leaves her husband to nurse the girl back to health. Olney's mother-in-law convinces him that Constance was not unfaithful. They are reconciled when Olney goes to Constance and it is ascertained that there was nothing between him and the dancer. *Mothers-in-law. Dancers. Marriage. Jealousy.*

THE MINE WITH THE IRON DOOR F2.3635

Sol Lesser Productions. *Dist* Principal Pictures. 2 Oct **1924**. Si; b&w. 35mm. 8 reels, 6,180 ft.

Dir Sam Wood. *Scen* Arthur Statter, Mary Alice Scully. *Adapt* Hope Loring, Louis D. Lighton. *Photog* Glen MacWilliams.

Cast: Pat O'Malley *(Hugh Edwards)*, Dorothy Mackaill *(Marta)*, Raymond Hatton *(Bill Jansen)*, Charlie Murray *(Thad Grove)*, Bert Woodruff *(Bob Hill)*, Mitchell Lewis *(Sonora Jack)*, Creighton Hale *(Dr. James Burton)*, Mary Carr *(Mother Burton)*, William Collier, Jr. *(Chico)*, Robert Frazer *(Natachee)*, Clarence Burton *(sheriff)*.

Western melodrama. Source: Harold Bell Wright, *The Mine With the Iron Door* (New York, 1923). Bob Hill and Thad Grove, two prospectors, find a small child in the desert cabin of bandit Sonora Jack. The little girl, Marta, who has been kidnaped by Jack, is taken by the men, who vainly attempt to find her parents. Marta grows to womanhood and falls in love with Hugh Edwards, a young fugitive from justice. Edwards saves Natachee, an educated Indian, from the depredations of a bandit gang, and in return the grateful Indian shows Edwards the location of the "mine with the iron door," a hidden and extremely rich gold mine. Sonora Jack returns and kidnaps Marta, offering to exchange her for knowledge of the location of the "mine with the iron door." Edwards and Natachee go after the bandit and kill him while saving Marta. Edwards is proved to be innocent of the charge of embezzlement placed against him, and he and Marta are married. *Fugitives. Indians of North America. Prospectors. Bandits. Injustice. Kidnaping. Gold mines.*

MINNIE F2.3636

Marshall Neilan Productions. *Dist* Associated First National Pictures. Dec **1922** [c14 Nov 1922; LP18404]. Si; b&w. 35mm. 7 reels, 6,696 ft.

Pres by Marshall Neilan. *Co-Dir* Marshall Neilan, Frank Urson. *Scen* Marshall Neilan. *Titl* Frances Marion. *Story* George Patullo. *Photog*

David Kesson, Karl Struss. *Film Ed* Daniel J. Gray. *Asst Dir* Thomas Held.

Cast: Leatrice Joy *(Minnie)*, Matt Moore *(newspaperman)*, George Barnum *(Minnie's father)*, Josephine Crowell *(stepmother)*, Helen Lynch *(stepsister)*, Raymond Griffith *(chewing gum salesman)*, Richard Wayne *(young doctor)*, Tom Wilson *(boardinghouse janitor)*, George Dromgold *(local "cut-up")*.

Comedy-drama. Minnie, the ugliest girl in town, pretends to have a lover—complete with letters and gifts. Threatened with exposure by her suspicious stepsister, Minnie tells a newspaperman that an unclaimed body is her dead lover. He perceives her inner beauty, and they fall in love. When the town gathers to celebrate Minnie's father's successful attempts to perfect a wireless-powered machine, excitement is aroused by a handsome young couple—none other than Minnie, transformed by plastic surgery, and her young man. *Reporters. Inventors. Stepsisters. Ugliness. Plastic surgery.*

THE MIRACLE BABY **F2.3637**

R-C Pictures. *Dist* Film Booking Offices of America. 9 Aug **1923** [New York premiere; released 19 Aug; c6 Aug 1923; LP19281]. Si; b&w. 35mm. 6 reels, 6,336 ft.

Dir Val Paul. *Adapt* Isadore Bernstein. *Adapt? (see note)* Jacques Jaccard. *Photog* William Thornley.

Cast: Harry Carey *(Neil Allison)*, Margaret Landis *(Judy Stanton)*, Charles J. L. Mayne *("Hopeful" Mason)*, Edward Hearn *(Hal Norton)*, Hedda Nova *(Violet)*, Edmund Cobb *(Jim Starke)*, Alfred Allen *(Dr. Amos Stanton)*, Bert Sprotte *(Sam Brodford)*.

Western melodrama. Source: Frank Richardson Pierce, "The Miracle Baby," in *American Magazine* (94:21–23, Nov 1921). Metalurgist Neil Allison is tricked into assaying some false samples from a young crook's mine. When Neil sees that he has been duped, a quarrel ensues, and Starke, the youth, is stabbed by an unknown assassin. Neil runs away thinking he has committed murder and becomes the unwitting partner of the victim's father. They adopt a baby, and events take them to town, where Allison is cleared of the murder charge. *Metalurgists. Mining. Murder. Adoption.*

Note: *Variety* (30 Aug 1923) gives credit for adaptation to Bernstein-Jaccard (Jacques Jaccard?).

THE MIRACLE CHILD (HE GIVETH AND TAKETH) *see* **MOONSHINE VALLEY**

THE MIRACLE MAKERS **F2.3638**

Leah Baird Productions. *Dist* Associated Exhibitors. 14 Oct **1923** [c9 Nov 1923; LU19582]. Si; b&w. 35mm. 6 reels, 5,834 ft.

Arthur Beck Production. *Dir* W. S. Van Dyke. *Story* Leah Baird. *Photog* André Barlatier.

Cast: Leah Baird *(Doris Mansfield)*, George Walsh *(Fred Norton)*, Edith Yorke *(Mrs. Emma Norton)*, George Nichols *(Capt. Joe Mansfield)*, Edythe Chapman *(Mrs. Martha Mansfield)*, Richard Headrick *(The Boy)*, Mitchell Lewis *(Bill Bruce)*.

Melodrama. Bill Bruce, smuggler of Chinese laborers into the country, captures Doris Mansfield and forces her to marry him. Later, he is apprehended and sent to prison, but Doris, who was engaged to air coast patrolman Fred Norton before her marriage, does not explain her situation to her fiancé. He, thinking she no longer loves him, signs up for duty in France. Years later, Bruce, released from prison, seeks out his wife, who has had a child, and tries to make amends, but he falls into a well and suffers a fatal injury. Fred Norton, who has returned from France, marries Doris. *Smugglers. Chinese. Coast patrol. Marriage. Immigration. World War I.*

THE MIRACLE OF LIFE **F2.3639**

S. E. V. Taylor. *Dist* Associated Exhibitors. 28 Feb **1926** [c23 Jan 1926; LU22296]. Si; b&w. 35mm. 5 reels, 4,757 ft.

Dir S. E. V. Taylor. *Scen* Elizabeth Musgrave. *Story* Olga Printzlau. *Photog* A. G. Penrod.

Cast: Percy Marmont *(Blair Howell)*, Mae Busch *(Janet Howell)*, Nita Naldi *(Helen)*.

Domestic drama. Blissful newlyweds Blair and Janet Howell disagree on only one thing: he loves children; she prefers her freedom. When Janet learns that her husband's wishes are to be fulfilled, she calls upon her friend Helen, who once suggested that she could help in such a situation. She makes an appointment with Helen's physician friend but has a change of heart and happily accepts her fate. (According to a synopsis in the copyright files, Janet has a dream in which she has an abortion; Blair divorces her, remarries, and has a brood of children; and she pursues a life of pleasure which leaves her an ugly, dissipated old woman. A *Film Daily* review, however, ascribes Janet's decision to her exposure to the butler's lovable baby.) *Physicians. Marriage. Motherhood. Abortion. Divorce. Dreams.*

Note: Reissued with synchronized music score in 1929 by Public Welfare Pictures.

THE MIRACLE OF MANHATTAN **F2.3640**

Selznick Pictures. *Dist* Select Pictures. 10 Apr **1921** [c9 Apr 1921; LP16369]. Si; b&w. 35mm. 5 reels, 4,174 ft.

Pres by Lewis J. Selznick. *Dir* George Archainbaud. *Scen* Edward J. Montagne. *Story* Bradley King. *Photog* William Wagner.

Cast: Elaine Hammerstein *(Mary Malone/Evelyn Whitney)*, Matt Moore *(Larry Marshall)*, Ellen Cassity *(Stella Warren)*, Nora Reed *(an intruder)*, Walter Greene *(Tony the Dude)*, Leonora Ottinger *(Mrs. Peabody)*, Jack Raymond *(Robert Van Cleek)*.

Melodrama. New York society girl Evelyn Whitney, engaged to a man of her set, determines to prove that she can make her own living in the Lower East Side. After failing as a factory worker and waitress, she makes good as Mary Malone, a cafe singer, and falls in love with ex-gangleader Larry Marshall. When Stella, a jealous rival, attacks her, Larry shoots the girl, and Evelyn flees to her home where she has a lengthy illness. Learning of his trial, she reaches the courtroom in time to give evidence that frees him, and they are married. *Entertainers. Gangsters. Trials. New York City—Lower East Side.*

THE MIRAGE **F2.3641**

Regal Pictures. *Dist* Producers Distributing Corp. 28 Dec **1924** [c29 Dec 1924, 10 Jan 1925; LP20970, LP21134]. Si; b&w. 35mm. 6 reels, 5,770 ft.

Dir George Archainbaud. *Adapt* C. Gardner Sullivan. *Photog* Henry Sharp.

Cast: Florence Vidor *(Irene Martin)*, Clive Brook *(Henry Galt)*, Alan Roscoe *(Al Manning)*, Vola Vale *(Betty Bond)*, Myrtle Vane *(Mrs. Martin)*, Charlotte Stevens *(Irene's sister)*.

Comedy. Source: Edgar Selwyn, *The Mirage* (New York opening: 30 Sep 1920). Leaving her family and sweetheart behind, Irene Martin departs from her small hometown and goes to New York, hoping for a career as an opera singer. She finds a part in the show on the Knickerbocker Roof and meets Henry Galt, a wealthy businessman, who asks her to a party. The next day she receives a box of roses and $50 from Galt, sent to her as payment for entertaining his guests. Deeply insulted, Irene goes to Galt to demand an apology and to return the money, but he explains that he often hires chorus girls to entertain prospective customers and then makes an agreement with Irene for her professional services. Entertaining at Galt's parties, Irene remains aloof, and Galt, who recognizes her worth, falls in love with her. Al Manning, Irene's sweetheart, is sent to New York to do business with Galt, and, finding Irene in Galt's company, he suspects the worst, "propositions" her, and informs her mother that Irene is a fallen woman. Galt realizes that he has compromised Irene's reputation and asks her to marry him. Irene at first refuses, mistaking his love for gallantry, but when she finally realizes that his love is genuine, she gladly accepts his proposal. *Entertainers. Businessmen. Reputation. New York City.*

MISFIT BECOMES CHAPERON *see* **THE GALLOPING KID**

MISMATES **F2.3642**

First National Pictures. 26 Jul **1926** [New York premiere; released 10 Oct; c29 Jul 1926; LP22988]. Si; b&w. 35mm. 7 reels, 6,905 ft. [Copyrighted as 8 reels.]

Supv Earl Hudson. *Dir* Charles Brabin. *Scen* Sada Cowan.

Cast: Doris Kenyon *(Judy Winslow)*, Warner Baxter *(Ted Carroll)*, May Allison *(Belle)*, Philo McCullough *(Jim Winslow)*, Charles Murray *(Black)*, Maude Turner Gordon *(Mrs. Winslow)*, John Kolb *(Watson)*, Cyril Ring *(Helwig)*, Nancy Kelly *(Jimsy)*.

Domestic melodrama. Source: Myron C. Fagan, *Mismates* (New York opening: 13 Apr 1925). Wealthy Jim Winslow marries Judy O'Grady, a manicurist, and is disinherited by his family. He soon tires of the struggle to earn a living and appeals to his parents, who demand that he divorce Judy. Judy, determined not to give up her child, Jimsy, or to allow a divorce, takes a position at an establishment used as a front by criminals; and when she is innocently involved in a crime and is arrested, she is convicted by the false testimony of her husband. Jim informs her that

Jimsy is dead, and she swears that upon her release she will seek revenge, though she is comforted by Ted Carroll, her lawyer and former beau. Judy escapes and confronts Jim with a revolver during a masked ball at his home, but she is diverted by the appearance of Jimsy. Carroll obtains proof of her innocence, assures her of a pardon, and is happily united with Judy, now free of Jim. *Manicurists. Lawyers. Prison escapees. Children. Social classes. Marriage. Divorce. Injustice.*

MISS BLUEBEARD **F2.3643**

Famous Players–Lasky. *Dist* Paramount Pictures. 26 Jan **1925** [c6 Jan 1925; LP21011]. Si; b&w. 35mm. 7 reels, 6,453 ft.

Pres by Adolph Zukor, Jesse L. Lasky. *Dir* Frank Tuttle. *Scen* Townsend Martin. *Photog* J. Roy Hunt.

Cast: Bebe Daniels *(Colette Girard)*, Robert Frazer *(Larry Charters)*, Kenneth MacKenna *(Bob Hawley)*, Raymond Griffith *(The Honorable Bertie Bird)*, Martha Madison *(Lulu)*, Diana Kane *(Gloria Harding)*, Lawrence D'Orsay *(Colonel Harding)*, Florence Billings *(Eva)*, Ivan Simpson *(Bounds)*.

Bedroom farce. Source: Avery Hopwood, *Little Miss Bluebeard; a Comedy in Three Acts* (New York, 1923). Gábor Drégely, *Der Gatte des Fräuleins; Lustspiel in drei Aufzügen* (Wien, 1916). In order to escape the demands on his time and energy by female admirers, Larry Charters, a popular writer of popular songs, arranges to have his friend Bob Hawley impersonate him. Traveling on the Continent, Bob meets a French actress, Colette, on a train. In France, Bob and Colette are accidentally left behind at a village station, and they go to the mayor to find rooms for the night. Believing that they want to get married, the intoxicated mayor marries Bob to Colette in Larry's name. Bob and Colette later take the train for Paris, where Larry is introduced to his new and unexpected wife. Larry immediately falls in love with Colette and arranges for her to stay with him, but she remains his wife in name only. Bob becomes engaged to Gloria, one of Colette's friends. At a houseparty, Collette disguises herself as one of Larry's old girl friends in an attempt to test his love and loyalty. After considerable confusion and misadventure, Colette and Larry perceive their mutual love and make plans actually to be married. *Composers. Actors. Mayors. Impersonation. Trains. France. Paris.*

MISS BREWSTER'S MILLIONS **F2.3644**

Famous Players–Lasky. *Dist* Paramount Pictures. 7 Mar **1926** [New York premiere; released 22 Mar; c22 Mar 1926; LP22507]. Si; b&w. 35mm. 7 reels, 6,200 or 6,457 ft.

Pres by Adolph Zukor, Jesse L. Lasky. *Dir* Clarence Badger. *Scen* Lloyd Corrigan, Harold Shumate. *Adapt* Monty Brice. *Photog* H. Kinley Martin.

Cast: Bebe Daniels *(Polly Brewster)*, Warner Baxter *(Thomas B. Hancock, Jr.)*, Ford Sterling *(Ned Brewster)*, André de Beranger *(Mr. Brent)*, Miss Beresford *(landlady)*.

Comedy. Suggested by: George Barr McCutcheon, *Brewster's Millions* (New York, 1905). Winchell Smith and Byron Ongley, *Brewster's Millions; a Comedy in Four Acts* (New York, 1925). Polly Brewster, a penniless Hollywood extra, inherits a million dollars; young lawyer Tom Hancock informs her, however, that she cannot spend the money but must invest it. Her Uncle Ned Brewster arrives; and in revenge for indignities his brother made him suffer, he offers Polly $5 million on the condition that she spend the inherited million within 30 days. Polly gleefully sets about investing, gives a great ball and fashion show, and runs down a man with her car and has him sue for a large sum. Uncle Ned proves to be penniless, but Polly finds that her investment in a motion picure company has yielded a handsome return, and she finds happiness with Tom. *Actors. Uncles. Lawyers. Inheritance. Motion pictures. Fashion shows. Hollywood.*

MISS LULU BETT **F2.3645**

Famous Players–Lasky. *Dist* Paramount Pictures. ca13 Nov **1921** [Los Angeles premiere; released 1 Jan 1922; c7 Dec 1921; LP17328]. Si; b&w. 35mm. 7 reels, 5,904 ft.

Pres by Adolph Zukor. *Dir* William C. De Mille. *Adapt* Clara Beranger. *Photog* L. Guy Wilky.

Cast: Lois Wilson *(Lulu Bett)*, Milton Sills *(Neil Cornish)*, Theodore Roberts *(Dwight Deacon)*, Helen Ferguson *(Diana Deacon)*, Mabel Van Buren *(Mrs. Dwight Deacon)*, May Giraci *(Manona Deacon)*, Clarence Burton *(Ninian Deacon)*, Ethel Wales *(Grandma Bett)*, Taylor Graves *(Bobby Larkin)*, Charles Ogle *(station agent)*.

Melodrama. Source: Zona Gale, *Miss Lulu Bett* (New York, 1920). Spinster Lulu Bett is a drudge in the home of her married sister, Mrs. Dwight Deacon, whose husband is justice of the peace and dentist in the small town where they live. The monotony of Lulu's life is broken by the arrival of Dwight's brother, Ninian, who takes pity on her. He arranges a supper party in her honor and jokingly recites the marriage ceremony with Lulu; Dwight, in his official capacity, realizes the ceremony is binding, and Lulu remains with Ninian until she learns that he has another wife, who is missing. Returning home, Lulu is treated by Dwight as a deserted wife to avoid exposing his brother as a bigamist; and she is the object of unrelenting gossip. Finally, Lulu refuses to be a servant and accepts the attentions of Neil Cornish, the village schoolteacher; and after being notified that Ninian's wife is alive, she is happily married to Neil. *Spinsters. Drudges. Dentists. Brothers. Justices of the peace. Schoolteachers. Bigamy. Smalltown life. Reputation.*

MISS NOBODY **F2.3646**

First National Pictures. 27 Jun **1926** [c27 May 1926; LP22778]. Si; b&w. 35mm. 7 reels, 6,859 ft.

Dir Lambert Hillyer. *Editorial Dir* Wid Gunning. *Titl* George Marion, Jr. *Photog* John Boyle. *Art Dir* E. J. Shulter. *Film Ed* Al Hall. *Prod Mgr* John McCormick.

Cast: Anna Q. Nilsson *(Barbara Brown)*, Walter Pidgeon *(Bravo)*, Louise Fazenda *(Mazie Raleigh)*, Mitchell Lewis *(Harmony)*, Clyde Cook *(Bertie)*, Arthur Stone *(Happy)*, Anders Randolf *(J. B. Hardiman)*, Claire Du Brey *(Ann Adams)*, Jed Prouty *(The Farmer)*, Caroline Rankin *(his wife)*, George Nichols *(The Sheriff)*, Oleta Otis *(Miriam Arnold)*, James Gordon *(police sergeant)*, Fred Warren *(sideshow spieler)*.

Society drama. Source: Tiffany Wells, "Shebo" (publication undetermined). While returning from France, Barbara Brown, the madcap daughter of an American millionaire, receives news that her father has died in New York and that she is penniless. Disillusioned and broke in San Francisco, she accepts a last-minute invitation to a New Year's Eve party where she avoids the direct attentions of Hardiman, a roué, by disguising herself as a boy. She is picked up by a gang of hoboes and accepted by them, although their leader, Bravo, sees through her disguise. When her life is endangered by a brakeman's cunning, she and Bravo leave their pals Shorty and Dinky and stay at a smalltown hotel. Bravo buys Barbara some feminine attire, indicating both his awareness of her pretense and his romantic interest, and she consequently suspects him of a robbery; but it is explained that he is actually an author hoboing to grasp local color. They decide to tramp through life together. *Hoboes. Authors. Railroad brakemen. Bankruptcy. Disguise. New Year's Eve. San Francisco.*

MISS PAUL REVERE **F2.36**

Dist Russell Clark Syndicate. caMar **1922.** Si; b&w. 35mm. [Feature length assumed.]

Melodrama(?). No information about the nature of this film has been found.

MISSING DAUGHTERS **F2.3648**

Choice Productions. *Dist* Selznick Distributing Corp. 25 May **1924** [c20 May 1924; LP20224]. Si; b&w. 35mm. 7 reels, 6,676 ft.

Dir-Story William H. Clifford. *Photog* Ray June.

Cast: Eileen Percy *(Eileen Allen)*, Pauline Starke *(Pauline Hinton)*, Claire Adams *(Claire Mathers)*, Eva Novak *(Eva Rivers)*, Walter Long *(Guy Benson)*, Robert Edeson *(chief, secret service)*, Rockliffe Fellowes *(John Rogers)*, Sheldon Lewis *(Tony Hawks)*, Walt Whitman *(The Beachcomber)*, Frank Ridge *(Frank Linke)*, Chester Bishop *(Anthony Roche)*.

Melodrama. Eva Rivers, in love with her employer, John Rogers, lives with two friends, Eileen and Pauline. Rogers, secretly a member of the U.S. Secret Service, is trailing Anthony Roche, owner of the Golden Calf Restaurant, whom he believes to be engaged in illegal activities. Eileen, who has become Roche's secretary, meets Rogers at the Golden Calf and casts suspicion on Eva's character. Eileen, Pauline, and Eva, accompanied by some of Roche's henchmen, visit Claire Mathers at her beach cottage. Discovering that Claire is a government agent, the men gag and bind her and kidnap the three girls, flying them to a coastal cafe. Claire escapes to notify the police, and Rogers, posing as Roche's partner, rescues the girls after Benson, owner of the cafe, accidentally shoots Roche. *Secretaries. Secret service. Kidnaping. Airplanes.*

THE MISSING LINK **F2.3649**

Warner Brothers Pictures. 6 May **1927** [New York premiere; released 1 Sep; c20 Apr 1927; LP23882]. Si; b&w. 35mm. 7 reels, 6,485 ft.

Dir Charles F. Reisner. *Story-Scen* Darryl Francis Zanuck. *Camera* Dev

Jennings. *Asst Camera* Fred West. *Asst Dir* Sandy Roth.

Cast: Syd Chaplin *(Arthur Wells)*, Ruth Hiatt *(Beatrice Braden)*, Tom McGuire *(Colonel Braden)*, Crauford Kent *(Lord Dryden)*, Nick Cogley *(Captain)*, Sam Baker *("The Missing Link")*, Akka *(chimpanzee)*, Otto Fries, Kewpie Morgan.

Farce. Lord Dryden, a famous hunter bound for Africa to join his friend Colonel Braden in a hunt for "The Missing Link," hires young poet Arthur Wells to carry his baggage. Dryden, a confirmed woman-hater, receives notice that Beatrice Braden, the colonel's daughter, has fallen in love with Dryden. Seeing in Wells an opportunity to avoid the girl, Dryden persuades the timid Arthur to take his place. In Africa, Arthur and Beatrice lose no time in falling in love, but when a hunt is suggested, Arthur retires, feigning illness, and mistakenly believes that Akka, a pet chimp, is the "Missing Link." With the aid of Akka, the hero manages to subdue the real "Missing Link" and wins the love of Beatrice. *Misogynists. Hunters. Poets. Evolution. Impersonation. Africa. Chimpanzees.*

MISSING MILLIONS **F2.3650**

Famous Players–Lasky. *Dist* Paramount Pictures. 17 Sep **1922** [New York premiere; released 22 Jan 1923; c9 Dec 1922; LP18879]. Si; b&w. 35mm. 6 reels, 5,870 ft.

Pres by Adolph Zukor. *Dir* Joseph Henabery. *Scen* Albert Shelby Le Vino. *Photog* Gilbert Warrenton.

Cast: Alice Brady *(Mary Dawson, a crook de luxe)*, David Powell *(Boston Blackie, a gentleman crook)*, Frank Losee *(Jim Franklin, a financier)*, Riley Hatch *(John Webb, a detective)*, John B. Cooke *(Handsome Harry Hawks, a crook-servant)*, William B. Mack *(Thomas Dawson, Mary's father)*, George Le Guere *(Daniel Regan, a ship purser)*, Alice May *(Mrs. Regan, his mother)*, H. Cooper Cliffe *(Sir Arthur Cumberland, a thief)*, Sydney Deane *(Donald Gordon, a secretary)*, Beverly Travers *(Claire Dupont, a passenger)*, Sidney Herbert *(Frank Garber, a criminal lawyer)*.

Crook drama. Source: Jack Boyle, "A Problem in Grand Larceny" and "An Answer in Grand Larceny," in *Red Book* (32:36–40, 71–76, Dec 1918–Jan 1919). Mary Dawson is determined to repay Jim Franklin for sending her father to Sing Sing in violation of a promise to drop his charges of theft. She and fellow crook Boston Blackie steal some gold being shipped to Franklin to satisfy his creditors. However, Daniel Regan, the ship's purser who unwittingly aided Mary in her theft, is arrested and accused of the crime. Mary and Boston Blackie return the gold in order to clear Regan, while Franklin commits suicide when the gold is delayed. *Gentlemen crooks. Financiers. Pursers. Theft. Perfidy. Suicide. Sing Sing.*

THE MISSISSIPPI GAMBLER **F2.3651**

Universal Pictures. 3 Nov **1929** [c17 Oct 1929; LP778]. Sd (Movietone); b&w. 35mm. 7 reels, 5,432 ft. [Also si; 5,025 ft.]

Pres by Carl Laemmle. *Dir* Reginald Barker. *Scen* Edward T. Lowe, Jr. *Dial* Winifred Reeve, H. H. Van Loan. *Titl* Dudley Early. *Story* Karl Brown, Leonard Fields. *Photog* Gilbert Warrenton. *Film Ed* R. B. Wilcox. *Song: "Father Mississippi"* L. Wolfe Gilbert, Harry Akst. *Rec Engr* Joseph R. Lapis.

Cast: Joseph Schildkraut *(Jack Morgan)*, Joan Bennett *(Lucy Blackburn)*, Carmelita Geraghty *(Suzette Richards)*, Alec B. Francis *(Junius Blackburn)*, Otis Harlan *(Tiny Beardsley)*, William Welsh *(Captain Weathers)*.

Romantic drama. Morgan, a handsome gentleman who works the Mississippi riverboats, wins a large sum of money, entrusted to Junius Blackburn, in a poker game; and while Blackburn retires to his cabin, his daughter, Lucy, shows Morgan a locket that she will give only to the man she loves. Suzette, consumed with jealousy, denounces Morgan to Lucy, saying he took her father's money; and after preventing her father's suicide, Lucy demands that Morgan return the winnings, but he refuses. Morgan gives her the chance, however, to win back the money in a card game or lose herself to him, and in desperation she agrees. He pretends to lose, but Lucy, finding that he held the winning hand, sends the locket to him via a Negro servant. *Gamblers. Suicide. Filial relations. Riverboats. Mississippi River.*

MISTAKEN ORDERS **F2.3652**

Larry Wheeler Productions. *Dist* Rayart Pictures. 5 May **1926.** Si; b&w. 35mm. 5 reels.

Prod? (see note) Morris R. Schlank. *Dir* J. P. McGowan.

Cast: Helen Holmes *(Helen Barton)*, Jack Perrin *(Tom Lawson)*, Henry Barrows *(General Barton)*, Hal Walters *(Vince Barton)*, Harry Tenbrook *(Tony Sharkey)*, Cecil Kellog *(The Night Operator)*, Mack V. Wright *(The Day Agent)*, Arthur Millett *(Tom Lawson's father)*, Alice Belcher *(Jane Moriarity)*.

Melodrama(?). No information about the nature of this film has been found.

Note: This film may originally have been produced by Schlank for Anchor Productions.

MISTER AND MISERABLE JONES *see* **DANGEROUS CURVE AHEAD**

MISTER ANTONIO **F2.3653**

Tiffany-Stahl Productions. 1 or 15 Oct **1929** [c23 Sep 1929; LP742]. Sd (Photophone); b&w. 35mm. 8 reels, 6,978 ft. [Also si; 5,362 ft.]

Dir James Flood, Frank Reicher. *Scen-Dial-Titl* Frederick Hatton, Fanny Hatton. *Photog* Ernest Miller. *Film Ed* Arthur Roberts.

Cast: Leo Carrillo *(Antonio Camaradino)*, Virginia Valli *(June Ramsey)*, Gareth Hughes *(Joe)*, Frank Reicher *(Milton Jorny)*, Eugenie Besserer *(Mrs. Jorny)*, Franklin Lewis *(Earl Jorny)*.

Comedy-drama. Source: Booth Tarkington, *Mister Antonio; a Play In Four Acts* (New York, 1935). Antonio Camaradino, florist and street musician, befriends a man robbed of his overcoat and money in a disreputable bar. Tony recognizes the man as Jorny, mayor of Avalonia, a straitlaced town where Tony was once arrested for playing his hurdy-gurdy. Tony's travels take him again to Avalonia. Camped on the outskirts of town, he meets June Ramsey, a cousin of the mayor's wife, ejected from town by the mayor because his reelection campaign is jeopardized by her having been seen in a roadhouse. Under considerable pressure because he wishes to conceal his previous encounter with Tony from the opposition, Jorny returns Tony's favor by asking June's forgiveness and inviting her to return to Avalonia. June accepts his apologies; she then follows Tony, with whom she has fallen in love. *Italians. Florists. Street musicians. Mayors. Reputation. Political campaigns. Hurdy-gurdies.*

MR. BARNES OF NEW YORK *see* Entry F2.3726

MR. BILLINGS SPENDS HIS DIME **F2.3654**

Famous Players–Lasky. *Dist* Paramount Pictures. ca4 Mar **1923** [New York premiere; released 19 Mar; c7 Mar 1923; LP18771]. Si; b&w. 35mm. 6 reels, 5,585 ft.

Pres by Jesse L. Lasky. *Dir* Wesley Ruggles. *Scen* Albert Shelby Le Vino. *Photog* Charles E. Schoenbaum.

Cast: Walter Hiers *(John Percival Billings)*, Jacqueline Logan *(Suzanna Juárez)*, George Fawcett *(Gen. Pablo Blanco)*, Robert McKim *(Captain Gómez)*, Patricia Palmer *(Priscilla Parker)*, Joseph Swickard *(Estaban Juárez)*, Guy Oliver *(John D. Starbock)*, Edward Patrick *(White)*, Clarence Burton *(Diego)*, George Field *(Manuel)*, Lucien Littlefield *(Martin Green)*.

Comedy. Source: Dana Burnet, "Mr. Billings Spends His Dime," in *Redbook Magazine* (35:27–32, 52–56, 77–81, Jun–Aug 1920). Department store clerk John Percival Billings, an avid reader of romance, falls in love with Suzanna Juárez when he sees her picture on a cigar band. With the lucky dime he receives from a customer he buys a cigar and thereby obtains information that he sells to some conspirators. With the money thus received, John travels to Santo Dinero and meets Suzanna, whose father, President Estaban Juárez, is struggling to avert a revolution. Eventually, John is the means of saving the government and wins Suzanna. *Salesclerks. Revolutions. Cigars. Latin America.*

MR. BINGLE *see* Entry F2.3727

MR. POTTER OF TEXAS **F2.3655**

San Antonio Pictures. *Dist* Producers Security Corp. 15 Jun **1922.** Si; b&w. 35mm. 5 reels, 4,400 ft.

Dir Leopold Wharton. *Scen* George Rader.

Cast: Maclyn Arbuckle *(Mr. Potter of Texas)*, Louiszita Valentine *(Ida Potter)*, Corinne Uzzell *(Lady Annerly)*, Robert Frazier *(Charles Errol)*, Raymond Hodge *(Ralph Errol)*, Gloria Smythe *(Amy Lincoln)*, Robert Allen *(Sergeant Bracket)*, Gerard Witherby *(Lieutenant Dean)*, Harry Carr *(The Levantine)*.

Comedy-drama. Source: Archibald Clavering Gunter, *Mr. Potter of Texas* (London, 1888). Arriving in Texas with only a few dollars, Sam Potter puts his youth and determination to good use, works hard, and eventually becomes an oil millionaire. Potter accepts an invitation from boyhood friends to visit England, whence he continues his journey to Egypt in the company of his daughter. There a deathbed confession by Lord Annerly clears Potter of a crime for which he has been sought, and Lady Annerly ends Potter's life as a widower. (Reviews mention a revolution in Egypt, but they are too vague to determine Potter's relation to it.) *Millionaires. Widowers. Oil. Revolutions. Texas. Egypt. England.*

MR. WU F2.3656

Metro-Goldwyn-Mayer Pictures. 26 Mar **1927** [c9 May 1927; LP23953]. Si; b&w. 35mm. 8 reels, 7,603 ft.

Dir William Nigh. *Adapt-Cont* Lorna Moon. *Titl* Lotta Woods. *Photog* John Arnold. *Sets* Cedric Gibbons, Richard Day. *Film Ed* Ben Lewis. *Wardrobe* Lucia Coulter.

Cast: Lon Chaney *(Mr. Wu/Mr. Wu's grandfather)*, Louise Dresser *(Mrs. Gregory)*, Renée Adorée *(Nang Ping)*, Holmes Herbert *(Mr. Gregory)*, Ralph Forbes *(Basil Gregory)*, Gertrude Olmstead *(Hilda Gregory)*, Mrs. Wong Wing *(Ah Wong)*, Claude King *(Mr. Muir)*, Sonny Loy *(Little Wu)*, Anna May Wong *(Loo Song)*.

Melodrama. Source: Maurice Vernon and Harold Owen, *Mr. Wu* (New York opening: 14 Oct 1914). In the prolog, Grandfather Wu is seen as a boy, then as a young man whose marriage to a mandarin's daughter yields a child. As Mr. Wu's daughter emerges into womanhood, a marriage is arranged for Nang Ping with a mandarin. Despite the seclusion of her father's palace, she meets and falls in love with Basil Gregory, a young Englishman, and reveals her secret when he asks her to marry him. Wu learns of the situation, and despite his great love for her, he takes her life—according to custom—in atonement, then determines to wreak vengeance on Basil's family. Inviting Mrs. Gregory and her daughter to his home, Wu threatens to have Basil killed and the daughter betrayed; the mother offers her own life, but failing, she stabs Wu, thus freeing her children. *Chinese. English. Fatherhood. Seduction. Revenge. Murder.*

THE MISTRESS OF SHENSTONE F2.3657

Robertson-Cole Pictures. 27 Feb **1921** [c27 Feb 1921; LP16343]. Si; b&w. 35mm. 6 reels, 5,900 ft.

Dir Henry King. *Story* Florence L. Barclay. *Photog* J. D. Jennings.

Cast: Pauline Frederick *(Lady Myra Ingleby)*, Roy Stewart *(Jim Airth)*, Emmett C. King *(Sir Deryck Brand)*, Arthur Clayton *(Ronald Ingram)*, John Willink *(Billy Cathcart)*, Helen Wright *(Margaret O'Mara)*, Rosa Gore *(Amelia Murgatroyd)*, Helen Muir *(Eliza Murgatroyd)*, Lydia Yeamans Titus *(Susannah Murgatroyd)*.

Romantic melodrama. Source: Florence L. Barclay, *The Mistress of Shenstone* (New York, 1910). Lady Ingleby, lonely while her husband is at the front, receives news of his death owing to an inadvertent order of one of his comrades, and she retires in mourning to the Cornish coast. There she meets young Jim Airth, who saves her life on the beach. A romance develops, but when she learns that he is the man who gave the fatal order, they part. Later, she returns to the coast and decides she cannot live without him. *Widows. World War I. Cornwall (England).*

MIXED FACES F2.3658

Fox Film Corp. 22 Oct **1922** [c22 Oct 1922; LP19052]. Si; b&w. 35mm. 5 reels, 4,400 or 4,505 ft.

Pres by William Fox. *Dir* Rowland V. Lee. *Scen* Paul Schofield. *Photog* David Abel.

Cast: William Russell *(Judge J. Woodworth Granger/Jimmy Gallop)*, Renée Adorée *(Mary Allen Sayre)*, De Witt Jennings *(Murray McGuire)*, Elizabeth Garrison *(Mrs. Sayre)*, Charles French *(Mr. Sayre)*, Aileen Manning *(Mrs. Molly Crutcher)*, Harvey Clarke *(William Haskins)*.

Comedy-melodrama. Source: Roy Norton, *Mixed Faces* (New York, 1921). Judge Granger, a candidate for mayor, attempts to persuade Mary Allen Sayre to marry him. She meets his double, Jimmy Gallop, a young traveling salesman, and mistakes him for the judge. Gallop accepts her friendship and soon afterward discovers the reason for her cordiality. He is bribed by Granger's opponents to impersonate the judge in making a speech while they themselves kidnap the judge. This act almost wrecks the judge's chances of election and ends in Gallop's being nearly murdered. Gallop saves himself, helps out in the judge's campaign, and finds that Mary is in love with him. The judge transfers his affections to his devoted secretary. *Judges. Politicians. Traveling salesmen. Doubles. Impersonation.*

MOANA F2.3659

Famous Players–Lasky. *Dist* Paramount Pictures. 7 Jan **1926** [New York premiere; c24 Feb 1926; MP3348]. Si; b&w. 35mm. 7 reels, 6,133 ft.

Dir-Scen-Photog Robert Flaherty. *Titl* Robert Flaherty, Julian Johnson. *Asst Dir* Frances Flaherty. *Tech Asst* Lancelot H. Clark. *Prod Asst* David Flaherty.

Cast: Ta'avale, Fa'amgase, Tu'ugaita, Moana, Pe'a.

Travelog. The rites, customs, and daily lives of the Samoans are depicted. *Samoa.*

MOBY DICK F2.3660

Warner Brothers Pictures. 14 Aug **1930** [New York premiere; released 20 Sep; c26 Aug 1930; LP1519]. Sd (Vitaphone); b&w. 35mm. 9 reels, 7,200 ft.

Dir Lloyd Bacon. *Screenplay-Dial* J. Grubb Alexander. *Photog* Robert Kurrle. *Rec Engr* David Forrest.

Cast: John Barrymore *(Ahab)*, Joan Bennett *(Faith)*, Lloyd Hughes *(Derek)*, May Boley *(Whale Oil Rosie)*, Walter Long *(Stubbs)*, Tom O'Brien *(Starbuck)*, Nigel De Brulier *(Elijah)*, Noble Johnson *(Queequeg)*, William Walling *(blacksmith)*, Virginia Sale *(old maid)*, Jack Curtis *(first mate)*, John Ince *(Reverend Mapple)*.

Drama. Source: Herman Melville, *Moby Dick, or The Whale* (1851). The plot is similar to that of the 1926 silent film *The Sea Beast*, q. v. *Sea captains. Clergymen. Whaling. Courtship. New Bedford (Massachusetts).*

Note: Also produced in a German-language version.

MOCCASINS F2.3661

Independent Pictures. c29 May **1925** [LP21512]. Si; b&w. 35mm. 5 reels.

Pres by Jesse J. Goldburg. *Supv* Jesse J. Goldburg. *Dir* Robert North Bradbury. *Story-Cont* George W. Pyper.

Cast: Bill Cody *(Tom Williams)*, Peggy O'Dare *(Wright, Avery)*, Mack V. Wright *(Robert Barlow)*, Frank Austin *(John Avery)*, Frank Rice *("Hard Tack" Avery, sheriff)*.

Western melodrama. " ... dealing with the plot against a young rancher who inherits land from his uncle. An enemy of the dead man aids the scheme, while his daughter takes young Williams' part. The hero stands his ground and wins his fight against the villains and the hand of the girl as well." (*Motion Picture News Booking Guide*, 8:58, Mar 1925.) *Ranchers. Inheritance.*

MOCKERY F2.3662

Metro-Goldwyn-Mayer Pictures. 13 Aug **1927** [c12 Oct 1927; LP24747]. Si; b&w. 35mm. 7 reels, 5,957 ft.

Dir-Story Benjamin Christensen. *Cont* Bradley King. *Titl* Joe Farnham. *Photog* Merritt B. Gerstad. *Sets* Cedric Gibbons, Alexander Toluboff. *Film Ed* John W. English. *Wardrobe* Gilbert Clark.

Cast: Lon Chaney *(Sergei)*, Ricardo Cortez *(Dimitri)*, Barbara Bedford *(Tatiana)*, Mack Swain *(Mr. Gaidaroff)*, Emily Fitzroy *(Mrs. Gaidaroff)*, Charles Puffy *(Ivan)*, Kai Schmidt *(butler)*.

Melodrama. Source: Stig Esbern, unidentified story. In Siberia at the time of the revolution, the Countess Tatiana promises Sergei, a hungry peasant, food, a job, and her friendship, if he will guide her safely to Novokursk. Sergei, although forced to undergo torture at the hands of the Bolsheviks, accomplishes his task and is awarded a menial job in the kitchen as compensation. He falls under revolutionary influences and comes to hate the countess and all her class. He runs amok when there is an uprising in the village and attacks the countess. Dimitri, an army officer in love with Tatiana, arrives with his soldiers, but she tells him that Sergei has protected her. In a second uprising, Sergei does prove his loyalty by giving his very life to defend her. *Scullions. Bolshevists. Russia—History—1917–21 Revolution. Siberia.*

Note: Working title: *Terror.* According to early publicity on the film, the script was taken from an original story by Stig Esbern.

A MODERN CAIN F2.3663

J. W. Fife Productions. **1925.** Si; b&w. 35mm. [Feature length assumed.]

Cast: Norman Ward *(William Moore)*, Ted Williams *(Paul Moore)*, Fred Williams *(Everett Moore)*, Z. V. Young *(James Hagan)*, Vivian Carrols *(Leonore Blackwell)*, Harriett Harris *(Mrs. Blackwell)*, Youth Mason *(Samuel Egan)*, Munzell Everett *(Mrs. Egan)*.

Melodrama. John and Paul, Negro twin brothers, are orphaned at an early age and left in the care of an uncle. Grown to manhood, they go into business together and fall in love with the same girl. Paul, avaricious and inflamed with jealousy, pushes John off a cliff and reports him as missing. John, who is not killed, becomes a halfwit and wanders around in an amnesic fog until he is cured by a doctor. John returns home and finds that Paul has died from dope addiction. He marries his sweetheart, and thus all ends well. *Orphans. Twins. Physicians. Drug addicts. Halfwits. Negro life. Fratricide. Narcotics. Amnesia.*

Note: Indicated year is approximate.

MODERN DAUGHTERS F2.3664

Trem Carr Productions. *Dist* Rayart Pictures. May **1927.** Si; b&w. 35mm. 6 reels, 5,401 or 5,451 ft.

Pres by W. Ray Johnston. *Dir* Charles J. Hunt. *Story-Scen* J. Stuart Woodhouse. *Photog* Ernest Depew.

Cast: Edna Murphy, Bryant Washburn, Ernest Hilliard, Virginia Lyons, Jack Fowler, Hazel Flint.

Drama. An indulgent father, a hair-brained flapper (played by Edna Murphy), a villainous owner of the local dive, and a newspaper editor (played by Bryant Washburn) enact this story of the younger generation. Suspecting something worthwhile beneath her blonde curls, the newspaperman falls in love with the girl and gets involved in some wild parties. The couple is lured into a roadhouse on the night of a long-expected raid, her father is killed, and the editor is convicted and sentenced to death in the electric chair. Through the girl's efforts, the governor grants a stay of execution, and all ends happily. *Flappers. Editors. State governors. Jazz life. Roadhouses. Capital punishment.*

A MODERN JEAN VAL JEAN; OR A FRAME UP **F2.3665**

Al Hagan. 11 Jun **1930** [New York State license]. Si; b&w. 35mm. 5 reels, 4,500 ft.

Cast: Al Hagan.

Biographical drama. According to its advertising, this film purports to be "a true story in 6 [*sic*] reels of Convict 6661, who served 15 years in Fulsom Prison. A modern Jean Val Jean ... his story of great human interest: 'A frame up' ... conviction ... escape ... final capture." (New York State license records.) *Convicts. Frameup. Prisons. Prison escapes. Fulsom Prison.*

MODERN LOVE (Universal-Jewel) **F2.3666**

Universal Pictures. 21 Jul **1929** [c22 Jun 1929; LP496]. Talking sequences (Movietone); b&w. 35mm. 6 reels, 6,501 ft. [Also si; 5,730 ft.]

Pres by Carl Laemmle. *Dir* Arch Heath. *Story-Cont* Beatrice Van. *Dial-Titl* Albert De Mond. *Photog* Jerry Ash.

Cast: Charley Chase *(John Jones)*, Kathryn Crawford *(Patricia Brown)*, Jean Hersholt *(Renault)*, Edward Martindel *(Weston)*, Anita Garvin *(a brunette)*.

Comedy-drama. Patricia Brown, a designer for an exclusive dressmaking concern, wants to marry John Jones and at the same time keep her well-paying position. Although John has set ideas about woman's place being in the home and is against secret weddings, his code of ethics is forgotten when Patricia persuades him to marry and keep separate homes. All goes well until Patricia meets Renault, the owner of the firm, who has come to the United States for the first time; finding her ideas and personality to his liking, he offers her a trip to Europe to further her design techniques. When John is forced to act as butler at a dinner party given for Renault, Patricia decides to give up her job; but when the factory experiences a crisis, she changes her mind. After bidding her farewell, John comes across her sketches of women's fashions, shows them to the officials, and as a result wins a vacation; Patricia meanwhile has decided to return to him. *Couturiers. Businessmen. Marriage. Women's wear. Women's rights.*

MODERN MARRIAGE *see* **MODERN MATRIMONY**

MODERN MARRIAGE **F2.3667**

F. X. B. Pictures. *Dist* American Releasing Corp. 7 Apr **1923** [c1 Jun 1923; LP19098]. Si; b&w. 35mm. 7 reels, 6,331 ft.

Supv Whitman Bennett. *Dir* Lawrence C. Windom. *Adapt* Dorothy Farnum. *Photog* Edward Paul. *Art Dir* Elsa Lopez. *Tech Dir* Jack Stricker. *Art Titl* Fred Waller, Jr.

Cast: Francis X. Bushman *(Hugh Varley)*, Beverly Bayne *(Denise Varley)*, Roland Bottomley *(Frank Despard)*, Ernest Hilliard *(Cort Maitland)*, Zita Moulton *(Nita Blake)*, Frankie Evans *(Hugh, Jr.)*, Arnold Lucy *(Elihu Simpson)*, Pauline Dempsey *(Mammy)*, Blanche Craig *(Blossom Young)*.

Mystery melodrama. Source: Derek Vane, "Lady Varley" (publication undetermined). Varley, neglectful of his wife, learns that she is infatuated with philanderer Despard. When she goes to his apartment to recover certain incriminating letters, she makes a quick exit and does not know that the man is subsequently murdered. She seeks refuge in another apartment, the occupant of which, Maitland, is aware of her affair with Despard. When Maitland attempts burglary and assault, he accidently shoots himself, and, dying, he confesses to the murder of Despard and thus exonerates the wife. *Philanderers. Murder. Burglary. Marriage. Documentation.*

MODERN MATRIMONY **F2.3668**

Selznick Pictures. 8 or 15 Sep **1923** [c8 Sep 1923; LP19438]. Si; b&w. 35mm. 5 reels, 4,960 ft.

Supv Myron Selznick. *Dir-Writ* Victor Heerman. *Scen* Sarah Y. Mason. *Photog* Jules Cronjager.

Cast: Owen Moore *(Chester Waddington)*, Alice Lake *(Patricia Waddington)*, Mayme Kelso *(Mrs. Flynn)*, Frank Campeau *(Mr. Flynn)*, Kate Lester *(Mrs. Rutherford)*, Victor Potel *(Junior Rutherford)*, Snitz Edwards *(Mr. Baltman)*, Douglas Carter *(Rastus)*.

Comedy-drama. Chester Waddington secretly marries society girl Patricia Flynn. Their marriage is disclosed at a party planned to announce the engagement of Patricia to another suitor. Waddington buys a mansion in the suburbs on the instalment plan, then loses his job for taking an option on some land that his employer does not want. The land becomes valuable, and Waddington realizes his investment. *Socialites. Marriage. Land speculation. Instalment buying.*

Note: Working title: *Modern Marriage.*

A MODERN MONTE CRISTO *see* **STEPPING FAST**

MODERN MOTHERS **F2.3669**

Columbia Pictures. 13 May **1928** [c15 Jun 1928; LP25393]. Si; b&w. 35mm. 6 reels, 5,540 ft.

Prod Harry Cohn. *Dir* Philip Rosen. *Story-Scen* Peter Milne. *Photog* Joe Walker. *Art Dir* Joseph Wright. *Film Ed* Ben Pivar. *Asst Dir* Joe Cook.

Cast: Helene Chadwick *(Adele Dayton)*, Douglas Fairbanks, Jr. *(David Starke)*, Ethel Grey Terry *(Mazie)*, Barbara Kent *(Mildred)*, Alan Roscoe *(John)*, Gene Stone *(Gilbert)*, George Irving *(theater manager)*.

Drama. Famous actress Adele Dayton visits her daughter, Mildred, whom she left with relatives as an infant. The guardians, Mazie and John, permit the visit provided Adele conceals her relationship from Mildred. While Adele is there, she unwittingly attracts the admiration of Mildred's sweetheart, aspiring playwright David Starke, when she helps him sell one of his plays to a Broadway producer. David goes to New York city to launch the play, neglecting Mildred. On opening night Mildred visits Adele and finds her in an embrace with David; she upbraids Adele for stealing David's affection from her and returns to her home in Massachusetts. Realizing she has hurt her own daughter, Adele sacrifices her love for David and spurns him by affecting a cold, indifferent attitude. He returns to Mildred and marries her. *Actors. Playwrights. Motherhood. Guardians. New York City—Broadway. Massachusetts.*

MODERN YOUTH **F2.3670**

Sam Efrus Productions. *Dist* Sun Pictures. 10 Apr **1926** [New York State license]. Si; b&w. 35mm. 5 reels.

Dir Jack Nelson.

Cast: Geno Corrado, Olive Kirby, Rhea Mitchell, Charles Clary, Milburn Morante, Lorimer Johnston, Joseph Girard, Alma Rayford, Roy Laidlaw, Charles Belcher.

Melodrama(?). No information about the nature of this film has been found.

THE MOHICAN'S DAUGHTER **F2.3671**

P. T. B., Inc. *Dist* American Releasing Corp. 7 May **1922** [c7 May 1922; LP18109]. Si; b&w. 35mm. 5 reels, 4,697 ft.

Dir-Scen S. E. V. Taylor. *Photog* Oliver Marsh, Lester Lang. *Art Dir* Charles Cadwallader.

Cast: Nancy Deaver *(Jees Uck)*, Hazel Washburn *(Kitty Shannon)*, Sazon Kling *(Neil Bonner)*, William Thompson *(Amos Pentley)*, Jack Newton *(Jack Hollis)*, Paul Panzer *(Father La Claire)*, Nick Thompson *(Chatanna)*, Mortimer Snow *(Nashinta)*, John Webb Dillon *(a halfbreed)*, Myrtle Morse *(Inigo, his wife)*, Rita Abrams *(their child)*.

Romantic drama. Source: Jack London, "The Story of Jees Uck," in *Faith of Men and Other Stories* (New York, 1904). Jees Uck, a halfbreed maiden desired by Chatanna, chief of the tribe with which she lives, defies tribal law by getting medicine from the trading post for the sick child of her friend, Inigo. Nashinta, the medicine man, defends her against the chief. Chatanna kills Nashinta and puts the blame on Jees Uck, who flees into the arms of Neil Bonner, trading post manager, who loves her. The post is attacked, but Jees Uck surrenders to save her white friends. Neil finds evidence against the chief, delivers him to the authorities, and marries Jees Uck. *Halfcastes. Medicine men. Mahican Indians. Medicines. Trading posts.*

THE MOJAVE KID **F2.3672**

R-C Pictures. *Dist* Film Booking Offices of America. 25 Sep **1927** [c15 Jul 1927; LP24240]. Si; b&w. 35mm. 5 reels, 4,924 ft.

Pres by Joseph P. Kennedy. *Dir* Robert North Bradbury. *Story-Cont* Oliver Drake. *Photog* E. T. McManigal. *Asst Dir* Wallace Fox.

Cast: Bob Steele *(Bob Saunders)*, Lillian Gilmore *(Thelma Vaddez)*, Buck Connors *(Silent)*, Bob Fleming *(Big Olaf)*, Jay Morley *(Bull Dugan)*, Theodore Henderson *(Panamint Pete)*, Nat Mills *(Zeke Hatch)*.

Western melodrama. Bob Saunders, whose father has mysteriously disappeared, follows into the desert three outlaws whom he believes to have knowledge of his father's fate. At their headquarters, located at an old Indian ruin, Bob is captured, but he meets Thelma, granddaughter of Big Olaf, and "Silent" Jim, a captive. After Silent is told that Bob is his son, Bob is tortured so that Silent may be forced to tell the secret of a hidden treasure, but Bob slips his bonds and holds the gang at gunpoint. Bob bargains with Olaf to win their freedom by fighting one of the gang, and he wins. The gang turn on Olaf, who destroys them in an explosion while Bob rescues the girl from Bull, a gang member. *Cowboys. Bandits. Treasure. Fatherhood. Torture. Deserts.*

MOLLY AND ME **F2.3673**

Tiffany-Stahl Productions. 1 Mar **1929** [c27 Feb 1929; LP191]. Talking sequences & mus score (Photophone); b&w. 35mm. 8 reels, 8,250 ft. [Also si; 7,476 ft.]

Dir Albert Ray. *Scen* Lois Leeson. *Dial-Titl* Frederick Hatton, Fanny Hatton. *Story* Harold Riggs Durant. *Story? (see note)* Lois Leeson. *Photog* Frank Zucker, Ernest Miller. *Film Ed* Russell Shields. *Mus Score* Hugo Riesenfeld. *Song: "In the Land of Make Believe"* L. Wolfe Gilbert, Abel Baer. *Mus Cond* Joseph Littau. *Sd Supv* Rudolph Flothow.

Cast: Belle Bennett *(Molly Wilson)*, Joe E. Brown *(Jim Wilson)*, Alberta Vaughn *(Peggy Lanier)*, Charles Byer *(Dan Kingsley)*.

Comedy-drama. Vaudeville headliners Molly and Jim Wilson have been waiting for 10 years for their chance on Broadway, but when it comes, it comes for Jim alone, headlining the Frolics at $1,000 a week. Molly stays in New York with Jim for a while, but eventually she returns to her former vaudeville troupe. Jim falls in love with his co-star, Peggy Lanier, and writes to Molly, asking for his freedom. He then discovers that Peggy is engaged and, coming to his senses, goes to find Molly. They do their old act together, and Molly pretends that she has not had time to read the letter. Jim tears it up, and he and Molly are reconciled. *Singers. Vaudeville. Marriage. New York City—Broadway.*

Note: Lois Leeson is also credited with the story in some sources.

MOLLY O' **F2.3674**

Mack Sennett–Mabel Normand Productions. *For* Associated Producers. *Dist* Associated First National Pictures. ca20 Nov **1921** [New York premiere; released Dec; c24 Oct 1921; LP17222]. Si; b&w. 35mm. 8 reels, 7,588 ft.

Supv-Story Mack Sennett. *Dir* F. Richard Jones. *Scen* Mary Hunt, Fred Stowers. *Titl* John Grey. *Photog* Fred Jackman. *Electrical Eff* Paul Guerin. *Art Dir* Sanford D. Barnes. *Film Ed* Allen McNeil. *Asst Dir* Ray Grey. *Cost* Violet Schofield.

Cast: Mabel Normand *(Molly O')*, George Nichols *(Tim O'Dair)*, Anna Hernandez *(Mrs. Tim O'Dair)*, Albert Hackett *(Billy O'Dair)*, Eddie Gribbon *(Jim Smith)*, Jack Mulhall *(Dr. John S. Bryant)*, Lowell Sherman *(Fred Manchester)*, Jacqueline Logan *(Miriam Manchester)*, Ben Deely *(Albert Faulkner)*, Gloria Davenport *(Mrs. James W. Robbins)*, Carl Stockdale *(The Silhouette Man)*, Eugenie Besserer *(Antonia Bacigalupi)*.

Comedy. Molly O'Dair, whose mother is a washerwoman and whose father is a ditch-digger, sees the picture of Dr. John Bryant, an eligible young bachelor millionaire, in the newspaper and falls in love with him. Later she meets him at the country club where she goes to deliver washing, and attracted by her charms, he gives her a ride in his car. Bryant's fiancée, Miriam, understands, and at a masked ball, when he mistakes Molly for her, she returns his ring. Molly is thrown into a compromising situation with the doctor owing to the interference of Jim Smith, Mr. O'Dair's choice for her, and consequently she is turned into the street. Finding her in Bryant's bedroom the following morning, O'Dair is about to shoot him, but he learns that they are married. Later, Molly is abducted by a society crook in a dirigible, but she is rescued and reunited with her husband. *Laundresses. Physicians. Millionaires. Abduction. Dirigibles.*

MONEY MAD *see* **PAYING THE PIPER**

THE MONEY MANIAC **F2.3675**

Léonce Perret. *Dist* Pathé Exchange. Jul **1921** [c2 Jul 1921; LU16722]. Si; b&w. 35mm. 5 reels, 5,000 ft.

Dir-Writ Léonce Perret. *Photog* Jacques Monteran.

Cast: Robert Elliott *(Didier Bouchard)*, Henry G. Sell *(Milo d'Espail)*, Marcya Capri *(Roland Garros)*, Lucy Fox *(Thérèse Garros)*, Ivo Dawson *(Joe Hoggart)*, Eugene Breon *(Bill Shopps)*.

Melodrama. Source: Louis Letang, *La Divine* (Paris, 1914). Louis Letang, *Rolande Immolée* (Paris, 1914). En route to America, Joe Hoggart persuades several other immigrants to pool their money to buy a tract of land, which years later proves to be rich in oil. Hoggart, with the assistance of Shopps, seeks to control the other members' certificates. In Spain, he finds that Garros has died, and he kidnaps Garros' daughter Rolande and announces her death. Bouchard, another member of the group, who has become wealthy, gathers all its members and the heirs together. Hoggart lures them into a building where, ostensibly, the sale is to take place, and imprisons them, but they escape in time to be present at the sale. Bouchard marries Thérèse, another Garros daughter, and d'Espail, learning that Rolande is still alive, rescues her from Hoggart. *Immigrants. Speculation. Kidnaping. Oil lands. Spain. France. England.*

Note: Filmed on location in the United States, Spain, France, and England.

MONEY! MONEY! MONEY! **F2.3676**

Preferred Pictures. *Dist* Associated First National Pictures. Jan **1923** [c18 Dec 1922; LP18558]. Si; b&w. 35mm. 6 reels, 5,995 ft.

Pres by B. P. Schulberg. *Dir* Tom Forman. *Adapt* Hope Loring. *Story* Larry Evans. *Photog* Joseph Brotherton.

Cast: Katherine MacDonald *(Priscilla Hobbs)*, Carl Stockdale *(George C. Hobbs)*, Frances Raymond *(Mrs. Hobbs)*, Paul Willis *(Lennie Hobbs)*, Herschel Mayall *(Mr. Carter)*, Brenda Fowler *(Mrs. Carter)*, Margaret Loomis *(Caroline Carter)*, Charles Clary *(J. J. Grey)*, Jack Dougherty *(Reggie Grey)*.

Society drama. Socially ambitious Priscilla Hobbs and her mother persuade Priscilla's father, George Hobbs, to borrow a large sum of money from snobbish Mr. Carter until they receive the inheritance promised to Mrs. Hobbs. Reggie Grey, who has fallen in love with Priscilla, recognizes this as a scheme on Carter's part to get his hands on Hobbs's factory and has his banker father buy a partnership with Hobbs when Mrs. Hobbs's inheritance proves to be much smaller than anticipated. *Social climbers. Swindlers. Partnerships. Inheritance.*

MONEY TALKS **F2.3677**

Metro-Goldwyn-Mayer Pictures. 26 Apr **1926** [c19 May 1926; LP22816]. Si; b&w. 35mm. 6 reels, 5,139 ft.

Dir Archie Mayo. *Titl* Joe Farnham. *Adapt* Jessie Burns, Bernard Vorhaus. *Story* Rupert Hughes. *Photog* William Daniels. *Art Dir* Cedric Gibbons, Merrill Pye. *Film Ed* Ben Lewis. *Wardrobe* Kathleen Kay, Maude Marsh, André-ani.

Cast: Claire Windsor *(Phoebe Starling)*, Owen Moore *(Sam Starling)*, Bert Roach *(Oscar Waters)*, Ned Sparks *(Lucius Fenton)*, Phillips Smalley *(J. B. Perkins)*, Dot Farley *(Mrs. Chatterton)*, Kathleen Key *(vamp)*, George Kuwa *(Ah Foo)*.

Comedy. Sam Starling, an easygoing spendthrift, is left by his wife, Phoebe, owing to the constant annoyance of creditors, and he sets out to prove himself. He visits a money-losing island hotel, and without consent of Perkins, the proprietor, he begins an extensive advertising campaign promoting the hotel as a health resort. Phoebe's mother and Sam contrive to have Phoebe visit the resort. Sam enlists the aid of a female doctor, but just as his boat is about to depart with his invalids aboard, he discovers that the doctor is not present. In consequence, he himself impersonates her, advising Phoebe to make up with her husband and extolling Sam's virtues. It is revealed that the boat is actually a rumrunner, and Sam is forced to "vamp" the bootlegger captain to save Phoebe; he signals for help and has the villains arrested. Sam's resort scheme is successful, and he is happily reunited with his wife. *Spendthrifts. Mothers-in-law. Health resorts. Hotels. Female impersonation. Advertising. Rumrunners.*

MONEY TO BURN **F2.3678**

Fox Film Corp. 2 Apr **1922** [c2 Apr 1922; LP17822]. Si; b&w. 35mm. 5 reels, 4,850 ft.

Pres by William Fox. *Dir* Rowland V. Lee. *Photog* David Abel. *Scen* Jack Strumwasser.

Cast: William Russell *(Lucky Garrity)*, Sylvia Breamer *(Countess*

Vecchi), Hallam Cooley *(Ted Powell)*, Harvey Clark *(Eppings, the butler)*, Otto Matieson *(Count Vecchi)*.

Romantic comedy. Source: Sewell Ford, *Cherub Divine* (New York, 1909). "Lucky" Garrity, who has amassed a large fortune on Wall Street, buys unseen a country estate on Long Island, hoping to retire there. Although the servants declare the house to be haunted, Lucky is determined to remain and invites several friends, including Ted Powell, who is acquainted with the former owners of the estate. When Lucky finds that Adele Stratford (Countess Vecchi) is still living in the house owing to her husband's illness, he offers her a place as permanent guest. When his position on the market becomes endangered by rival investors, Adele urges Lucky to return and fight them, and he does so. Following the death of the count, Lucky and Adele are happily united. *Wealth. Speculation. Courtship. Haunted houses. Long Island.*

MONEY TO BURN **F2.3679**

Gotham Productions. *Dist* Lumas Film Corp. 6 Dec **1926** [c4 Nov 1926; LP23347]. Si; b&w. 35mm. 6 reels, 5,900 ft.

Pres by Sam Sax. *Supv* Renaud Hoffman. *Dir* Walter Lang. *Adapt-Cont* James Bell Smith. *Photog* Ray June.

Cast: Malcolm McGregor *(Dan Stone)*, Dorothy Devore *(Dolores Valdez)*, Eric Mayne *(Don Diego Valdez)*, Nina Romano *(María González)*, George Chesebro *(Manuel Ortego)*, Orfa Casanova *(Señora Sanguinetti)*, Jules Cowles *(The Giant)*, John Prince *(Bascom)*, Arnold Melvin *(The Mysterious Native)*, Josephine *(Caramba, the monkey)*.

Melodrama. Source: Reginald Wright Kauffman, *Money To Burn; an Adventure Story* (New York, 1924). Returning to her South American home from a college in the United States, Dolores Valdez falls in love with Dan Stone, the ship's doctor, who believes he has accidentally killed a man protecting Dolores. Dolores' uncle, Don Diego, tries to persuade her to marry Manuel Ortego, with whom he is engaged in a mysterious business. Dan is given sanctuary by Ortego on the condition that he cure a certain Bascom, who is ill; Dan and Dolores uncover the counterfeiting operation of her uncle, but they are observed by a giant Negro who captures Dan and then, becoming his friend, helps him escape. Dan is aided by the U. S. Marines and routs the counterfeiters. Dolores learns she is the true heir to the Valdez estate; she and Dan go on a honeymoon with the giant Negro as their valet. *Physicians. Uncles. Counterfeiters. Valets. South America. United States Marines. Monkeys.*

THE MONKEY TALKS **F2.3680**

Fox Film Corp. 20 Feb **1927** [c27 Feb 1927; LP23470]. Si; b&w. 35mm. 6 reels, 5,500 ft.

Pres by William Fox. *Dir* Raoul Walsh. *Scen* L. G. Rigby. *Photog* L. William O'Connell. *Asst Dir* R. Lee Hough.

Cast: Olive Borden *(Olivette)*, Jacques Lerner *(Jocko Lerner* [*or Fano*]*)*, Don Alvarado *(Sam Wick* [*or Pierre*]*)*, Malcolm Waite *(Bergerin)*, Raymond Hitchcock *(Lorenzo)*, Ted McNamara *(Firmin)*, Jane Winton *(Maisie)*, August Tollaire *(Mata)*.

Melodrama. Source: René Fauchois, *Le Singe qui parle* (Paris, 1925). Three members of a traveling French circus—including Fano, the handyman—are stranded and decide to recoup their fortunes by disguising Fano as a talking monkey. Fano soon becomes a sensation, but his old war friend Pierre falls in love with Olivette, a wire walker, whom he also loves; he remains silent to preserve his identity. Bergerin, a lion tamer, steals the talking monkey and replaces him with a real chimpanzee, but Fano is mortally wounded in saving Olivette from an attack by the chimpanzee. Thus Olivette and Pierre find happiness together. *Handymen. Tightrope walkers. Lion tamers. Circus. Disguise. France. Monkeys. Chimpanzees.*

MONSIEUR BEAUCAIRE **F2.3681**

Famous Players–Lasky. *Dist* Paramount Pictures. 18 Aug **1924** [c29 Jul 1924; LP20433]. Si; b&w. 35mm. 10 reels, 9,932 ft.

Pres by Adolph Zukor, Jesse L. Lasky. *Prod* Sidney Olcott. *Screenplay* Forrest Halsey. *Photog* Harry Fischbeck. *Art Dir* Natacha Rambova. *Film Ed* Patricia Rooney. *Cost* George Barbier.

Cast: Rudolph Valentino *(Duke de Chartres/Beaucaire)*, Bebe Daniels *(Princess Henriette)*, Lois Wilson *(Queen Marie of France)*, Doris Kenyon *(Lady Mary)*, Lowell Sherman *(King Louis XV)*, Paulette Duval *(Madame Pompadour)*, John Davidson *(Richelieu)*, Oswald Yorke *(Miropoix)*, Flora Finch *(Duchesse de Montmorency)*, Louis Waller *(François)*, Ian MacLaren *(Duke of Winterset)*, Frank Shannon *(Badger)*, Templar Powell *(Molyneux)*, H. Cooper Cliffe *(Beau Nash)*, Downing Clarke *(Lord Chesterfield)*, Yvonne Hughes *(Duchesse de Flauhault)*, Harry Lee *(Voltaire)*, Florence O'Denishawn *(Colombine)*.

Romantic drama. Source: Booth Tarkington, *Monsieur Beaucaire* (New York, 1900). Booth Tarkington and Evelyn Greenleaf Sutherland, *Monsieur Beaucaire, a Play,* in *Dramas by Present-day Writers* (New York, 1927). The Duke of Chartres, stung by the taunts of Princess Henriette, refuses the king's command to marry the princess and escapes to England, posing as the French Ambassador's barber. Fascinated by Lady Mary, he forces Lord Winterset to introduce him as Monsieur Beaucaire, but he is exposed as the barber. After being pardoned by King Louis, he returns to his true love, the Princess Henriette. *Barbers. France—History—Bourbons. Louis XV (France). Marie Leczinska. Jeanne Antoinette Poisson. Duc de Richelieu, Louis François Armand de Vignerot du Plessis. Richard Nash. Voltaire. Lord Chesterfield.*

MONSIEUR LE FOX *see* **MEN OF THE NORTH**

THE MONSTER **F2.3682**

Metro-Goldwyn Pictures. 16 Mar **1925** [c9 Mar 1925; LP21216]. Si; b&w. 35mm. 7 reels, 6,425 ft.

Dir Roland West. *Scen* Willard Mack, Albert Kenyon. *Titl* C. Gardner Sullivan. *Photog* Hal Mohr. *Film Ed* A. Carle Palm. *Prod Mgr* W. L. Heywood.

Cast: Lon Chaney *(Dr. Ziska)*, Gertrude Olmsted *(Betty Watson)*, Hallam Cooley *(Watson's Head Clerk)*, Johnny Arthur *(The Under Clerk)*, Charles A. Sellon *(The Constable)*, Walter James *(Caliban)*, Knute Erickson *(Daffy Dan)*, George Austin *(Rigo)*, Edward McWade *(Luke Watson)*, Ethel Wales *(Mrs. Watson)*.

Horror film. Source: Crane Wilbur, *The Monster* (New York opening: 9 Aug 1922). Dr. Ziska, an insane surgeon who believes that he can bring the dead back to life, presides over a sanitarium where he conducts bizarre experiments. He selects his human subjects from passing motorists, whom he abducts and confines in a dark dungeon. When the evil doctor kidnaps Luke Watson, Johnny, Watson's clerk, who has just received a diploma as a detective from a correspondence school, sets out to find him. He penetrates the sanitarium and is captured by Ziska, who intends to use him in an experiment. Ziska also captures Betty, Watson's daughter, and Hal, the senior Watson clerk. Johnny escapes from the sanitarium and returns with help, arriving just in time to save Betty from a horrible death under the mad doctor's knife. *Surgeons. Detectives. Office clerks. Insanity. Kidnaping. Correspondence courses. Sanitariums.*

MONTANA BILL **F2.3683**

Western Star Productions. *Dist* Pioneer Film Corp. 24 Jul **1921** [Brooklyn showing]. Si; b&w. 35mm. 5 reels, 4,447 ft.

Dir Phil Goldstone. *Scen* A. M. Levey. *Photog* Edgar Lyons.

Cast: William Fairbanks, Maryon Aye, Robert Kortman, Jack Waltemeyer, Ernest Van Pelt, Hazel Hart.

Western melodrama. "Montana Bill gets a job at a ranch where he falls foul of the ranch foreman who resents the interest which Bill arouses in Ruth, the ranch-owner's daughter. The foreman plots to have Bill suspected of his own cattle thefts, and later, of the murder of one of his accomplices. After several incidents Bill's enemies are defeated and his integrity is established." (*National Film Archive Catalogue, Part III, Silent Fiction Films, 1895-1930;* The British Film Institute, London, 1966, p248.) *Cowboys. Ranch foremen. Rustling. Murder.*

MONTANA MOON **F2.3684**

Metro-Goldwyn-Mayer Pictures. 20 Mar **1930** [c17 Mar 1930; LP1147]. Sd (Movietone); b&w. 35mm. 10 reels, 7,917 ft. [Also si.]

Dir Malcolm St. Clair. *Story-Cont* Sylvia Thalberg, Frank Butler. *Dial* Joe Farnham. *Photog* William Daniels. *Art Dir* Cedric Gibbons. *Film Ed* Carl L. Pierson, Leslie F. Wilder. *Songs: "The Moon Is Low," "Happy Cowboy"* Nacio Herb Brown, Arthur Freed. *Songs: "Montana Call," "Let Me Give You Love," "Trailin' in Old Montana"* Herbert Stothart, Clifford Grey. *Rec Engr* Paul Neal, Douglas Shearer. *Gowns* Adrian.

Cast: Joan Crawford *(Joan)*, John Mack Brown *(Larry)*, Dorothy Sebastian *(Elizabeth)*, Ricardo Cortez *(Jeff)*, Benny Rubin *("The Doctor")*, Cliff Edwards *(Froggy)*, Karl Dane *(Hank)*, Lloyd Ingraham *(Mr. Prescott)*.

Western musical-comedy. Joan, a sophisticated society girl from the East, escapes from her father's train en route to his ranch and meets Larry, a typical western cowpoke, on the open range. Larry's stern yet gentle nature soon subdues her fiery manner, and they are married. Soon they discover themselves unable to adjust to Joan's ideas of eastern propriety;

Jeff, a city slicker, arrives to threaten their relationship; but Larry disguises himself as a bandit and regains her affections. *Socialites. Cowboys. Courtship. Marriage. Disguise. Montana.*

MONTE CARLO **F2.3685**

Metro-Goldwyn-Mayer Pictures. 1 Mar **1926** [c5 Apr 1926; LP22563]. Si; b&w. 35mm. 7 reels, 6,129 ft.

Dir Christy Cabanne. *Adapt-Scen* Alice D. G. Miller. *Titl* Joe Farnham. *Story* Carey Wilson. *Photog* William Daniels. *Art Dir* Cedric Gibbons, Merrill Pye. *Film Ed* William Le Vanway. *Wardrobe* Kathleen Kay, Maude Marsh, André-ani.

Cast: Lew Cody *(Tony Townsend)*, Gertrude Olmsted *(Sally Roxford)*, Roy D'Arcy *(Prince Boris)*, Karl Dane *(The Doorman)*, ZaSu Pitts *(Hope Durant)*, Trixie Friganza *(Flossie Payne)*, Margaret Campbell *(Grand Duchess Marie)*, André Lanoy *(Ludvig)*, Max Barwyn *(Sarleff)*, Barbara Shears *(Princess Ilene)*, Harry Myers *(Greves)*, Cesare Gravina *(Count Davigny)*, Antonio D'Algy *(Varo)*, Arthur Hoyt *(Bancroft)*.

Romantic comedy. Three smalltown girls—Flossie, a giantess; Hope Durant, a seamstress, and Sally Roxford, a schoolteacher—win a trip to Monte Carlo, sponsored by their local newspaper, with Bancroft, the star reporter, as their guide. Tony Townsend, an American who has been evicted from numerous hotels in Monte Carlo for failure to pay bills, registers at the same hotel as Sally and accidentally meets her while evading detectives on a balcony. Tony borrows the uniform of a Prince Boris, which he finds in an adjoining suite, and is mistaken for the prince. At a fashion show that night, Sally models for Pierre, a great designer, and Tony becomes enamored of her, while Flossie mistakes the doorman for a duke and Hope takes a waiter for a count. Following his escape from anarchists, Tony declares his love for Sally, is jailed as an imposter, but is released through the intervention of the real prince and leaves for America with Sally. *Reporters. Amazons. Schoolteachers. Seamstresses. Royalty. Anarchists. Mistaken identity. Fashion shows. Monte Carlo.*

MONTE CARLO **F2.3686**

Paramount-Publix Corp. 27 Aug **1930** [New York premiere; released 4 Sep; c11 Oct 1930; LP1634]. Sd (Movietone); b&w. 35mm. 10 reels, 8,077 ft. [Also si.]

Dir Ernst Lubitsch. *Screenplay* Ernest Vajda. *Adtl Dial* Vincent Lawrence. *Photog* Victor Milner. *Art Dir* Hans Dreier. *Songs: "Always in All Ways," "Give Me a Moment Please," "Beyond the Blue Horizon," "Whatever It Is, It's Grand," "Trimmin' the Women," "She'll Love Me and Like It" "I'm a Simple-Hearted Man," "Day of Days"* Leo Robin, Richard Whiting, W. Franke Harling. *Rec Engr* Harry D. Mills.

Cast: Jack Buchanan *(Count Rudloph Fallière)*, Jeanette MacDonald *(Countess Vera von Conti)*, ZaSu Pitts *(Maria)*, Tyler Brooke *(Armand)*, Claud Allister *(Prince Otto von Seibenheim)*, Lionel Belmore *(Duke Gustave von Seibenheim)*, John Roche *(Paul)*, Albert Conti *(master of ceremonies)*, Helen Garden *(Lady Mary)*, Donald Novis *(Monsieur Beaucaire)*, Erik Bey *(Lord Winterset)*, David Percy *(herald)*, Sidney Bracy *(hunchback at casino)*, Edgar Norton, Geraldine Dvorak.

Musical comedy. Source: Hans Müller, *The Blue Coast* (publication undetermined). Rudolph Fallière, a wealthy and handsome count visiting Monte Carlo, sees the impoverished Countess Vera lose heavily at roulette, tries to meet her, but somehow always is prevented from doing so. By accident he meets her hairdresser, Paul, and the next day passes himself off as the new hairdresser, hoping to reveal his love for her. Learning she is to discharge him for lack of funds, Rudolph induces her to let him play her last 1,000*f* note at the casino; although he does not play, he returns with 100,000*f* and, overjoyed, she kisses him; but the next day she reverts to her usual deferential attitude. Rudolph kisses her fiercely and departs, refusing her offers to return. She finally accepts the proposal of Prince Liebenheim out of financial distress; but Rudolph arranges for her to attend a performance of *Monsieur Beaucaire* in which a prince poses as a hairdresser to win his lady, and realizing the similarity with her own relationship to Rudolph, the countess leaves Liebenheim for her true love. *Hairdressers. Nobility. Courtship. Gambling. Opera. Monte Carlo. "Monsieur Beaucaire".*

MONTE CRISTO **F2.3687**

Fox Film Corp. ca1 Apr **1922** [Boston premiere; released 3 Sep; c3 Sep 1922; LP18994]. Si; b&w. 35mm. 10 reels, 9,828 ft.

Pres by William Fox. *Dir* Emmett J. Flynn. *Scen* Bernard McConville. *Story* Alexander Salvini. *Adtl Story* Charles Fechter. *Photog* Lucien Andriot.

Cast: John Gilbert *(Edmond Dantes, Count of Monte Cristo)*, Estelle Taylor *(Mercedes, Countess de Morcerf)*, Robert McKim *(De Villefort, king's attorney)*, William V. Mong *(Caderousse, the innkeeper)*, Virginia Brown Faire *(Haidee, an Arabian princess)*, George Siegmann *(Luigi Vampa, an ex-pirate)*, Spottiswoode Aitken *(Abbé Faria)*, Ralph Cloninger *(Fernand, Count de Morcerf)*, Albert Prisco *(Baron Danglars)*, Gaston Glass *(Albert de Morcerf)*, Al Filson *(Morrel, shipowner)*, Harry Lonsdale *(Dantes, father of Edmund)*, Francis McDonald *(Benedetto, son of De Villefort)*, Jack Cosgrove *(Governor of Chateau d'If)*, Maude George *(Baroness Danglars)*, Renée Adorée *(Eugénie Danglars, her daughter)*, George Campbell *(Napoleon)*, Willard Koch *(tailor at Chateau d'If)*, Howard Kendall *(surgeon)*.

Romantic drama. Source: Alexandre Dumas, père, *Le Comte de Monte Cristo* (1844). Dantes, a young French sailor, is snatched from the arms of his bride, Mercedes, and placed in a dungeon on charges of treason trumped up by Danglars, Fernand, and De Villefort. Dantes tunnels into the cell of the Abbé Faria, spends the next 20 years receiving the benefits of the Abbé's great fund of knowledge, then escapes by substituting himself for Faria's dead body. After finding a treasure on the island of Monte Cristo with a map given to him by the Abbé, Dantes returns to France, eventually gets revenge on all of his enemies, and is reunited with Mercedes. *Nobility. Treason. Treasure. France. Prisons. Napoleon I.*

Note: Reissued in 1927 (New York showing: Apr 1927).

MONTMARTRE ROSE **F2.3688**

Excellent Pictures. 1 Apr **1929** [c20 Mar 1929; LP290]. Si; b&w. 35mm. 6 reels, 5,862 ft.

Dir (see note) Bernard F. McEveety, Frederick Hiatt. *Screenplay* Jacques Jaccard, Sylvia Bernstein. *Adapt* Isadore Bernstein. *Photog* William Miller, Walter Haas. *Film Ed* Betty Davis.

Cast: Marguerite De La Motte, Rosemary Theby, Harry Myers, Paul Ralli, Frank Leigh, Martha Mattox.

Melodrama. Source: Adeline Hendricks, "Montmartre Rose" (publication undetermined). Henri Duschene, a Paris jeweler, becomes engaged to Rose, the queen of the Montmartre cafes. Henri's respectable country uncle is horrified by the proposed match and arranges with the heartless, man-hating Jeanne to make Henri think that Rose has been unfaithful to him. Henri is disillusioned and turns to drink. Henri's mother comes to town and discovers Jeanne's perfidy. She tells Rose everything and moves in with her. Henri gets into a drunken rage and goes to Rose's apartment to revenge himself on her. Finding his mother there, he falls into a dead faint. Rose and his mother nurse him back to health, and he and Jeanne are soon married. *Jewelers. Man-haters. Motherhood. Alcoholism Paris—Montmartre.*

Note: Sources disagree in crediting direction.

MOONLIGHT AND HONEYSUCKLE **F2.3689**

Realart Pictures. Jul **1921** [c8 Jun 1921; LP16655]. Si; b&w. 35mm. 5 reels, 4,294 ft.

Dir Joseph Henabery. *Scen* Barbara Kent. *Photog* Faxon M. Dean.

Cast: Mary Miles Minter *(Judith Baldwin)*, Monte Blue *(Ted Musgrove)*, Willard Louis *(Senator Baldwin)*, Grace Goodall *(Hallie Baldwin)*, Guy Oliver *(Congressman Hamil)*, William Boyd *(Robert V. Courtney)*, Mabel Van Buren *(Mrs. Langley)*.

Comedy. Source: George Scarborough, *Moonlight and Honeysuckle* (New York production: 29 Sep 1919). U. S. Senator Baldwin of Arizona succumbs to the charms of a widow who refuses to marry him as long as his daughter is single. His daughter, Judith, would prefer a trial marriage properly chaperoned at the Baldwins' country lodge. She finds Congressman Hamil a bore, but the liveryman notifies the Washington press that they have eloped. Courtney, her other suitor, arrives early at the lodge, and the news brings Ted Musgrove, Baldwin's ranch manager who has always loved Judith. Meanwhile, Baldwin, who has secretly married the widow, arrives at the lodge; and after the turmoil Judith decides that Ted is her man. *Widows. Marriage. Marriage—Trial. Politics. United States Congress. Arizona.*

MOONLIGHT FOLLIES **F2.3690**

Universal Film Manufacturing Co. 26 Sep **1921** [c13 Sep 1921; LP16962]. Si; b&w. 35mm. 5 reels, 4,468 ft.

Dir King Baggot. *Scen* A. P. Younger. *Story* Percival Wilde. *Photog* Bert Glennon.

Cast: Marie Prevost *(Nan Rutledge)*, Lionel Belmore *(James Rutledge)*, Marie Crisp *(Cissie Hallock)*, George Fisher *(Rene Smythe)*, George

Fillmore *(Tony Griswold)*.

Comedy. Vivacious Nan Rutledge spends most of her time staging moonlight dances at her father's country home and provoking men into falling in love with her. When her father orders her to pick a husband and settle down, she selects at random wealthy woman-hater Anthony Griswold. When he finally proposes, she accepts, then changes her mind in front of guests. But he abducts her, takes her to his mountain cabin, and sends for the parson. *Flirts. Misogynists. Fatherhood.*

Note: Working title: *The Butterfly.*

THE MOONSHINE MENACE F2.3691

American Film Co. c7 Apr **1921** [LP16366]. Si; b&w. 35mm. 5 reels.

Dir J. P. McGowan.

Melodrama. Source: Alice McGowan, *Judith of the Cumberlands* (New York, 1908). Judith, who has just returned after several years' absence "fer learnin," falls in love with newly elected Justice of the Peace Creed Bonbright, even though their families have just gotten over a feud. Her young brother, Pony, and her Cousins Andy and Jeff are arrested for selling moonshine from Blatch Turrentine's still. Bonbright's offer of help is spurned by the boys. Pony escapes, and with Uncle Jep's aid, Jeff and Andy also escape. Blatch becomes jealous of Judith's new suitor, and one night, with several of the boys, he jumps Bonbright. In defending himself, Bonbright knocks Blatch over the cliff; Bonbright is also knocked off the cliff but lands safely in the still. Blatch convinces the others to report him murdered by Bonbright, and the latter is arrested. Blatch comes out of hiding to persuade Judith to elope with him; seeing him drunk with moonshine, she tricks him into going into Turkey Tracks, where Bonbright is being held, to get married. Blatch's sudden appearance in public causes Bonbright to be freed. The boys make another attempt to get Bonbright, but in an ensuing fight Blatch is killed. Bonbright then leads Judith away. *Moonshiners. Justices of the peace. Feuds. Mountain life. Cumberland Mountains.*

MOONSHINE VALLEY F2.3692

Fox Film Corp. 27 Aug **1922** [c27 Aug 1922; LP19009]. Si; b&w. 35mm. 6 reels, 5,679 ft.

Pres by William Fox. *Dir* Herbert Brenon. *Scen* Mary Murillo, Herbert Brenon. *Story* Mary Murillo, Lenora Asereth. *Photog* Tom Malloy.

Cast: William Farnum *(Ned Connors)*, Sadie Mullen *(his wife)*, Holmes Herbert *(Dr. Martin)*, Dawn O'Day *(Nancy, a child)*, Jean Bronte *(Jeane, the dog)*.

Western melodrama. Ned Connors becomes a drunkard after his wife leaves him to marry Dr. Martin. One day, while wandering in the woods, Ned finds a child (Nancy), takes her home, and finds that she brings new happiness into his life. When Nancy becomes ill, Ned goes for Dr. Martin, who recognizes Nancy as his own wife's child. Ned kills Martin when the latter attempts to abduct Nancy; the child effects a reconciliation between Ned and his ex-wife. *Children. Physicians. Alcoholism. Infidelity. Parenthood. Dogs.*

Note: Working title: *The Miracle Child (He Giveth and Taketh).*

MORAL FIBRE F2.3693

Vitagraph Co. of America. 18 Sep **1921** [c2 Aug 1921; LP16825]. Si; b&w. 35mm. 6 reels.

Dir Webster Campbell. *Scen* William B. Courtney. *Story* William Harrison Goadby.

Cast: Corinne Griffith *(Marion Wolcott)*, Catherine Calvert *(Grace Elmore)*, William Parke, Jr. *(Jared Wolcott)*, Harry C. Browne *(George Elmore)*, Joe King *(John Corliss)*, Alice Concord *(Nancy Bartley)*.

Melodrama. Jared Wolcott, storekeeper in a small country town, lives with his young sister, Marion. He succumbs to the flirtations of a Mrs. Elmore from a wealthy summer resort, and when he proposes and learns she is married he commits suicide. Marion vows to avenge her brother, and years later, as a successful illustrator in New York, she is engaged to illustrate George Elmore's latest novel. At the Elmore country home she leads Mrs. Elmore to believe she has won her husband's love, although she is actually romantically involved with John Corliss. The revelation that Corliss is Mrs. Elmore's brother leads her to forego her revenge, and disclosing her identity to the family, she leaves. Corliss follows, and they are united. *Flirts. Illustrators. Novelists. Brother-sister relationship. Suicide. Revenge. New York City.*

THE MORAL SINNER F2.3694

Famous Players–Lasky. *Dist* Paramount Pictures. 19 May **1924** [c7 May 1924; LP20217]. Si; b&w. 35mm. 6 reels, 5,437 ft.

Pres by Adolph Zukor, Jesse L Lasky. *Dir* Ralph Ince. *Adapt* J. Clarkson Miller. *Photog* William Miller.

Cast: Dorothy Dalton *(Leah Kleschna)*, James Rennie *(Paul Sylvain)*, Alphonse Ethier *(Anton Kleschna, alias Garnie)*, Frederick Lewis *(Schram, his confederate)*, Walter Percival *(Raoul Berton)*, Paul McAllister *(General Berton)*, Florence Fair *(Claire Berton)*.

Crime melodrama. Source: Charles Morton Stewart McLellan, *Leah Kleschna, a Play in Five Acts* (London, 1920). Leah Kleschna, the daughter of a Paris thief, is forced into a life of crime through fear of her father's rough associates. Paul Sylvain, a wealthy young criminologist, rescues Leah from a burning building, and she falls in love with him. Leah's father later sends her to Paul's study to steal the legendary Sylvain diamonds, but Paul detects her, taking her into his gentle custody. Raoul Berton, a French general's son who is also in Kleschna's power, then breaks into Paul's study; Paul and Leah hide, and Raoul steals the jewels. Made strong by Paul's love, Leah recovers the stolen diamonds and then, as penance, goes to work in the fields side by side with the peasants. Paul later finds Leah and persuades her to become his wife. *Criminologists. Thieves. Criminals—Rehabilitation. Paris.*

MORALS F2.3695

Realart Pictures. *Dist* Paramount Pictures. Nov **1921** [c8 Nov 1921; LP17177]. Si; b&w. 35mm. 5 reels, 5,152 ft.

Dir William D. Taylor. *Adapt* Julia Crawford Ivers. *Photog* James C. Van Trees.

Cast: May McAvoy *(Carlotta)*, William P. Carleton *(Sir Marcus Ordeyne)*, Marian Skinner *(Mrs. McMurray)*, Nicholas De Ruiz *(Hamdi)*, Starke Patterson *(Harry)*, William Lawrence *(Sebastian Pasquale)*, Kathlyn Williams *(Judith Mainwaring)*, Bridgetta Clark *(Antoinette)*, Sidney Bracey *(Stinson)*.

Society melodrama. Source: William John Locke, *The Morals of Marcus Ordeyne, a Play in Four Acts* (New York, 1906). William John Locke, *The Morals of Marcus Ordeyne* (London, 1905). Reared in a Turkish harem and threatened with marriage to a man she does not love, Carlotta escapes to London with an English adventurer. When he is killed, she is left destitute and attaches herself to Sir Marcus Ordeyne and begs his protection. He takes her home out of pity, and her charm and innocence cause him to fall in love with her. When he plans to marry her, Judith Mainwaring, who looks upon Carlotta as a rival, tells her he merely pities her and is marrying her to avoid a scandal. Carlotta runs away with Pasquale, a friend of Sir Marcus, though she loves her guardian. Later, Mrs. Mainwaring meets Carlotta in Paris and tells the girl the truth—that Sir Marcus is searching for her. Realizing his love for her, Carlotta is reunited with her benefactor. *Guardians. Marriage. Harems. Turkey. London. Paris.*

MORALS FOR MEN F2.3696

Tiffany Productions. 16 Nov **1925** [New York premiere; released Dec; c23 Nov 1925; LP22045]. Si; b&w. 35mm. 8 reels, 7,443 ft.

Supv-Adapt A. P. Younger. *Dir* Bernard Hyman. *Titl* Philbin Stoneman. *Photog* Roland Price. *Lighting Eff* Raymond Simbro. *Art Dir* Edwin B. Willis. *Tech Dir* Charles Leonard. *Film Ed* James C. McKay. *Still Photog* Mack Stengler.

Cast: Conway Tearle *(Joe Strickland)*, Agnes Ayres *(Bessie Hayes)*, Alyce Mills *(Marion Winslow)*, Otto Matieson *(Frank Bowman)*, Robert Ober *(Harvey Larkin)*, John Miljan *(Leonard Wallace)*, Mary Beth Milford *(Mary)*, Eve Southern *(Mrs. Strickland)*, Marjery O'Neill.

Melodrama. Suggested by: Gouverneur Morris, "The Lucky Serum" (publication undetermined). Joe Strickland, a civil engineer, has fallen to the level of living off Bessie Hayes, a bootlegger. Bessie believes Joe is trying to steal their savings, and they decide to part. She opens a manicuring establishment and marries wealthy Harvey Larkin; shortly after their marriage, Harvey begins to neglect Bessie for the company of others. Joe saves society girl Marion Winslow from drowning, reforms himself, and marries Marion. Bessie is blackmailed by Frank Bowman, a former confederate, and goes to Joe for help. Marion becomes jealous and threatens divorce. Harvey casts Bessie out when she confesses her past. She straightens matters out between Joe and Marion, but realizing that she, a woman, will never be forgiven for her past sins, she commits suicide. *Engineers—Civil. Bootleggers. Manicurists. Marriage. Blackmail. Double standard. Suicide.*

MORAN OF THE LADY LETTY **F2.3697**

Famous Players–Lasky. *Dist* Paramount Pictures. 12 Feb **1922** [c15 Feb 1922; LP17563]. Si; b&w. 35mm. 7 reels, 6,360 ft.

Pres by Jesse L. Lasky. *Dir* George Melford. *Adapt* Monte M. Katterjohn. *Photog* William Marshall.

Cast: Dorothy Dalton *(Moran [Letty Sternersen])*, Rodolph Valentino *(Ramon Laredo)*, Charles Brinley *(Captain Sternersen)*, Walter Long *(Captain Kitchell)*, Emil Jorgenson *(Nels)*, Maude Wayne *(Josephine Herrick)*, Cecil Holland *(Bill Trim)*, George Kuwa *("Chopstick" Charlie)*, Charles K. French *(tavern owner)*.

Adventure melodrama. Source: Frank Norris, *Moran of the Lady Letty; a Story of Adventure Off the California Coast* (New York, 1898). In San Francisco, Ramon Laredo, a wealthy young socialite, meets Moran, a strong and unconventional girl, on his way to a yachting party. Later, Ramon is drugged, shanghaied, and taken aboard a smuggling schooner bound for Mexico. On board, he suffers from the brutality of Captain Kitchell. Moran's ship, the *Lady Letty*, catches fire and is boarded by Kitchell's men; Ramon discovers the girl dressed as a man, the only survivor of the crew, and keeps her identity a secret from the captain. Arriving in Mexico, Ramon and Kitchell find a treasure on the beach, and Kitchell plots to gain possession of both the money and Moran, whom he perceives to be a girl. A fight on the schooner between Ramon and the crew and Kitchell and his smugglers results in the captain's subjugation; Ramon takes command, and the ship returns to San Francisco. There, Kitchell escapes and attacks Moran, who is saved by Ramon while Kitchell is drowned. Ramon embraces Moran and announces his plans to marry her. *Socialites. Smugglers. Ships. Impersonation. Treasure. Shanghaiing. Mexico. San Francisco. Ship fires.*

MORAN OF THE MARINES **F2.3698**

Paramount Famous Lasky Corp. 13 Oct **1928** [c15 Oct 1928; LP25715]. Si; b&w. 35mm. 7 reels, 5,444 ft.

Dir Frank Strayer. *Screenplay* Agnes Brand Leahy. *Scen* Sam Mintz, Ray Harris. *Titl* George Marion. *Story* Linton Wells. *Photog* Edward Cronjager. *Film Ed* Otto Lovering.

Cast: Richard Dix *(Michael Moran)*, Ruth Elder *(Vivian Marshall)*, Roscoe Karns *("Swatty")*, Brooks Benedict *(Basil Worth)*, Capt. E. H. Calvert *(General Marshall)*, Duke Martin *(The Sergeant)*, Tetsu Komai *(Sun Yat)*.

Comedy-drama. After getting into a fight with a drunkard, Mike Moran spends 10 days on the rock pile and is disinherited by his wealthy uncle; out of luck and work, Mike joins the Marines and is soon court-martialed for kissing Vivian Marshall, a general's daughter. Mike's unit is ordered to China, and Mike goes along under guard. Vivian accompanies her father and is captured by a Chinese bandit; Mike rescues her and is himself taken prisoner. Vivian leads a Marine detachment to his rescue, and Mike is quickly pardoned, reinstated by his uncle, and firmly established in Vivian's affections. *Uncles. Chinese. Kidnaping. Disinheritance. Courts-martial. United States Marines. China.*

MORAN OF THE MOUNTED **F2.3699**

Harry J. Brown Productions. *Dist* Rayart Pictures. 3 Aug **1926** [New York State license]. Si; b&w. 35mm. 5 reels, 5,403 ft.

Dir Harry J. Brown. *Story-Scen* J. F. Natteford. *Titl* Arthur Q. Hagerman. *Photog* William Tuers.

Cast: Reed Howes *(Moran)*, Sheldon Lewis *(Lamont)*, J. P. McGowan *(Sergeant Churchill)*, Bruce Gordon *(Carlson)*, Virginia Warwick *(Fleurette)*, Billy Franey *("Mooch" Mullens)*, Harry Semels *(Dubuc)*, Chief Yowlache *(Biting Wolf)*.

Northwest melodrama. Suspected of having killed the father of the girl he loves, Trooper Moran of the Northwest Mounted Police is given a week to find the culprit or else do away with himself. Aware of a quarrel between the man and an Indian trader, Moran trails and finds the Indian and places him under arrest. The Indian declares himself to be innocent but admits to having been present when the man was shot. The evidence finally points to a French trapper, who is forced to confess. Moran clears himself and marries the girl. *Indians of North America. Trappers. Traders. Murder. Northwest Mounted Police.*

MORE PAY—LESS WORK **F2.3700**

Fox Film Corp. 4 Jul **1926** [c27 Jun 1926; LP22860]. Si; b&w. 35mm. 6 reels, 6,027 ft.

Pres by William Fox. *Supv* Kenneth Hawks. *Dir* Albert Ray. *Scen* Rex Taylor. *Photog* Sidney Wagner. *Asst Dir* Horace Hough.

Cast: Albert Gran *(Cappy Ricks)*, Mary Brian *(Betty Ricks)*, E. J. Ratcliffe *(Dad Hinchfield)*, Charles Rogers *(Willie Hinchfield)*, Otto Hoffman *(Henry Tweedle)*, Charles Conklin *(janitor)*.

Comedy-drama. Source: Peter Bernard Kyne, "No Shenanigans" (publication undetermined). Betty, the daughter of shipowner Cappy Ricks, falls in love with Willie Hinchfield, the son of Cappy's hated business rival. When the son and daughter start to work for their respective parents, business difficulties increase, and many comic situations result from their efforts to conduct a secret romance. Willie steals one of the best customers of the Ricks line, and one of Cappy's tugs goes to the rescue of a steamer near the Golden Gate Bridge. The steamer makes port on schedule for the delivery of cargo, and Willie explains his actions to Betty, who agrees to accept his marriage proposal. Ricks and Hinchfield decide they will have to become business partners in order to avoid conflicting business interests. *Businessmen. Filial relations. Business competition. Partnerships. Ship lines. San Francisco.*

Note: Some sources give varying renderings of character names.

MORE TO BE PITIED THAN SCORNED **F2.3701**

Waldorf Productions. *Dist* C. B. C. Film Sales. 20 Aug **1922** [c15 Aug 1922; LP18237]. Si; b&w. 35mm. 6 reels, 5,800 ft.

Prod Harry Cohn. *Dir* Edward Le Saint. *Photog* King Gray, Gilbert Warrenton.

Cast: J. Frank Glendon *(Julian Lorraine)*, Rosemary Theby *(Josephine Clifford)*, Philo McCullough *(Vincent Grant)*, Gordon Griffith *("Troubles")*, Alice Lake *(Viola Lorraine)*, Josephine Adair *(Ruth Lorraine)*.

Melodrama. Source: Charles E. Blaney, *More To Be Pitied Than Scorned; or, Her Death Before Dishonor* (c1903). Actor Julian Lorraine comes home one day to find his wife, Viola, in the company of Vincent Grant. Assuming the worst, he takes their daughter, Ruth, to stay with Josephine Clifford, his leading lady. Viola tries to follow him and explain, but she is injured by an automobile and loses her memory. Years pass, Julian marries Josephine, and Viola recovers both her memory and her child. When Vincent threatens harm to the girl unless Viola marries him, she takes Ruth back to Julian. In the performance of a play Vincent accidentally shoots Josephine and is himself killed, thus clearing the way for the reunion of Julian and Viola. *Actors. Amnesia. Motherhood. Theater. Automobile accidents.*

MORGAN'S LAST RAID **F2.3702**

Metro-Goldwyn-Mayer Pictures. 5 Jan **1929** [c5 Jan 1929; LP25969]. Si; b&w. 35mm. 6 reels, 5,264 ft.

Dir Nick Grinde. *Cont* Bradley King. *Titl* Harry Braxton. *Story* Madeleine Ruthven, Ross B. Wills. *Photog* Arthur Reed. *Film Ed* William Le Vanway. *Wardrobe* Lucia Coulter.

Cast: Tim McCoy *(Capt. Daniel Clairbourne)*, Dorothy Sebastian *(Judith Rogers)*, Wheeler Oakman *(John Bland)*, Allan Garcia *(Morgan)*, Hank Mann *(Tex)*, Montague Shaw *(General Rogers)*.

Historical drama. "Dan Claibourne refuses to fight against his state when Tennessee secedes during the Civil War preliminaries. His sweetheart brands him a traitor. Dan joins Morgan's raiders of the Confederate Army and gets opportunity to rescue the girl during a raid." ("Motion Picture News Booking Guide," in *Motion Picture News*, 15 Apr 1930, p93.) *United States—History—Civil War. Morgan's Raid. John Morgan. Tennessee.*

MORGANSON'S FINISH **F2.3703**

Tiffany Productions. May **1926** [c15 May 1926; LP22737]. Si; b&w. 35mm. 7 reels, 6,500 ft.

Dir Fred Windemere.

Cast: Anita Stewart *(Barbara Wesley)*, Johnnie Walker *(Dick Gilbert)*, Mahlon Hamilton *(Dan Morganson)*, Victor Potel *(Ole Jensen)*, Crauford Kent *(G. T. Williams, Gen. Mgr.)*, Rose Tapley *(doctor's wife)*.

Northwest melodrama. Source: Jack London, "Morganson's Finish" (publication undetermined). When Dick Gilbert, who is in love with Barbara Wesley, receives a factory promotion, the two become engaged. Morganson, a jealous rival, convinces the general manager that Dick should not receive the promotion, and in despair Dick resigns his position. At a party given by Morganson, Dick hears a discussion of the recent gold strike in Alaska and decides to go there; Morganson accompanies him to the gold country, and after they make a strike, Morganson causes a snowslide to bury Dick. Escaping, Dick uncovers an even larger gold deposit; and Ole, their hired man, tells him of Morganson's treachery. Barbara arrives, and following a confrontation between the two rivals, Morganson is knocked over a cliff, is injured, and dies from exposure. Dick succeeds in uncovering the mine and marries Barbara. *Factory management. Courtship. Gold rushes. Alaska. Avalanches.*

MORIARTY *see* **SHERLOCK HOLMES**

MOROCCO **F2.3704**

Paramount-Publix Corp. 14 Nov **1930** [New York opening; released 6 Dec; c5 Dec 1930; LP1793]. Sd (Movietone); b&w. 35mm. 12 reels, 8,237 ft.

Dir Josef von Sternberg. *Screenplay-Dial* Jules Furthman. *Photog* Lee Garmes. *Adtl Photog* Lucien Ballard. *Art Dir* Hans Dreier. *Film Ed* Sam Winston. *Songs: "Give Me the Man Who Does Things," "What Am I Bid for My Apples?"* Leo Robin, Karl Hajos. *Rec Engr* Harry D. Mills.

Cast: Gary Cooper *(Tom Brown)*, Marlene Dietrich *(Amy Jolly)*, Adolphe Menjou *(Kennington)*, Ullrich Haupt *(Adjutant Caesar)*, Juliette Compton *(Anna Dolores)*, Francis McDonald *(Corporal Tatoche)*, Albert Conti *(Colonel Quinnovieres)*, Eve Southern *(Madame Caesar)*, Michael Visaroff *(Barratire)*, Paul Porcasi *(LoTinto)*, Emil Chautard *(French general)*.

Romantic drama. Source: Benno Vigny, *Amy Jolly, die Frau aus Marrakesch* (Berlin-Friedenau, 1927). Tom Brown, a devil-may-care American Legionnaire and ruthless in his treatment of women, is singled out for attention by cabaret singer Amy Jolly despite the clamor of other suitors, among them debonair man-of-the-world Kennington. Surreptitiously she arranges a rendezvous with Tom in her apartment, where he finds her embittered with life and scornful of men, though hypnotically attractive. He leaves abruptly and goes into the street to meet an officer's wife, but Amy, intrigued by him, follows and interrupts their interview; the woman urges the street beggars to attack Amy, but Tom defends her, and he is arrested and assigned to a dangerous mission. Learning that Kennington has offered her wealth and happiness, Tom elects to remain at a desert outpost after accomplishing his mission. Amy hears that he is wounded and goes to the post, accompanied by Kennington; realizing their love, Kennington offers to aid Tom in deserting the Legion. Tom, however, tells Amy that if she loves him, she must be prepared to be a good soldier; as he marches with his column into the desert, Amy joins the ragged wives and sweethearts who follow in the trail of the departing soldiers. *Singers. France—Army—Foreign Legion. Morocco.*

Note: Miss Dietrich also sings "Quand l'amour meurt" by Millandy and Crémieux.

A MOST IMMORAL LADY **F2.3705**

First National Pictures. 22 Sep **1929** [c20 Oct 1929; LP786]. Sd (Vitaphone); b&w. 35mm. 8 reels, 7,145 ft. [Also si.]

Dir John Griffith Wray. *Scen-Dial-Titl* Forrest Halsey. *Photog* John Seitz. *Film Ed* Peter Fritch.

Cast: Leatrice Joy *(Laura Sargeant)*, Walter Pidgeon *(Tony Williams)*, Sidney Blackmer *(Humphrey Sargeant)*, Montagu Love *(John Williams)*, Josephine Dunn *(Joan Porter)*, Robert Edeson *(Bradford-Fish)*, Donald Reed *(Pedro the Gigolo)*, Florence Oakley *(Natalie Davis)*, Wilson Benge *(Hoskins the Butler)*.

Society drama. Source: Townsend Martin, *A Most Immoral Lady* (New York opening: 8 Oct 1928). Laura Sargeant takes a tip in the stock market from a financier so as to help her husband, Humphrey, repay Bradford-Fish his loans, and Humphrey crashes. Out of contrition she agrees to join her husband in blackmailing John Williams; then Laura meets and falls in love with Tony, Williams' nephew. When she tries to save Tony from a similar blackmail situation, but fails, he is disillusioned by her trickery and hurriedly marries Joan Porter. Laura leaves Humphrey and goes to Paris for a divorce. There she becomes a cafe singer and again meets Tony and Joan with Pedro, a gigolo with whom Joan is wildly infatuated. Realizing that Tony is seeking a divorce from Joan, Laura finds happiness with him. *Singers. Gigolos. Speculation. Blackmail. Divorce. Paris.*

MOTHER **F2.3706**

R-C Pictures. *Dist* Film Booking Offices of America. 1 May **1927** [c7 Mar 1927; LP23732]. Si; b&w. 35mm. 7 reels, 6,885 ft.

Pres by Joseph P. Kennedy. *Dir* J. Leo Meehan. *Adapt-Cont* Dorothy Yost. *Photog* Allen Siegler. *Asst Dir* Charles Kerr.

Cast: Belle Bennett *(Mary Ellis)*, Crauford Kent *(Lee Ellis)*, William Bakewell *(Jerry Ellis)*, Joyce Coad *(Betty Ellis)*, Mabel Julienne Scott *(Mrs. Wayne)*, Sam Allen *(Corporal Cotter)*, Charlotte Stevens *(Edna Larkin)*.

Society melodrama. Source: Kathleen Norris, *Mother* (New York, 1911). The Ellis family constitutes a typical American middleclass home. Lee Ellis is an architect, though in a subordinate position in a large firm; Mary, his wife, intensely sympathetic and broadminded, is devoted to her husband, son, and daughter. Ellis is discharged, and he vainly tries to obtain a position with another firm. As Jerry prepares to leave school and go to work, Mary receives a small legacy, which she invests in business for her husband. Soon they become prosperous; Jerry gets his longed-for car, and Betty, the daughter, is sent to private school. Jerry, indulging in jazz parties, falls under the influence of Mrs. Wayne, a wealthy widow, who persuades Ellis to accompany her on a weekend excursion. Jerry, rebelling against his mother's influence, decides to elope with Edna Larkin, gold-digging flapper. Mary manages to intercept their train, which is wrecked; Jerry sustains a broken leg, and the family is once again happily united. *Architects. Flappers. Middle classes. Family life. Motherhood. Jazz life. Train wrecks.*

MOTHER ETERNAL **F2.3707**

Ivan Abramson. *Dist* Graphic Film Corp. 17 Apr **1921** [New York premiere; c26 Mar 1921; LU16395]. Si; b&w. 35mm. 9 reels.

Prod-Dir-Writ Ivan Abramson. *Photog* John Stumar.

Cast: Vivian Martin *(Alice Baldwin)*, Thurston Hall *(Edward Stevens, Sr.)*, Earl Metcalfe *(Dr. Emerson)*, Jack Sherrill *(Edward Stevens, Jr.)*, Vivienne Osborne *(Julia Brennon)*, J. W. Johnston *(William Brennon)*, Baby Ruth Sullivan *(Mary Baldwin)*, Pearl Shepard *(Mary Baldwin, 25 years later)*, Clyde Hunnewell *(Charles Baldwin)*.

Domestic melodrama. Unable to support her second child, a boy, Alice Baldwin gives up the baby to the wife of Edward Stevens, a wealthy manufacturer. Her other child, a daughter, grows up, marries, and selfishly neglects her mother. Twenty years pass, and Alice's son, Edward, Jr., wins a place in the Stevens piano factory and falls in love with Julia Brennon, the owner's daughter. Meanwhile, the mother leaves home when her son-in-law objects to her presence, and she is rescued from a suicide attempt by Edward and Julia. At his foster father's home he realizes her identity, and at last they find happiness together. *Motherhood. Adoption. Suicide. Personal identity. Pianos.*

THE MOTHER HEART **F2.3708**

Fox Film Corp. 29 May **1921** [c29 May 1921; LP16644]. Si; b&w. 35mm. 5 reels, 4,806 ft.

Pres by William Fox. *Dir-Story* Howard M. Mitchell. *Scen* Frank Howard Clark. *Photog* Glen MacWilliams.

Cast: Shirley Mason *(May Howard)*, Raymond McKee *(Billy Bender)*, Edwin Booth Tilton *(George Stuart)*, Cecil Van Auker *(John Howard)*, William Buckley *(Clifford Hamilton)*, Peggy Eleanor *(Ella Howard)*, Mrs. Raymond Hatton *(Mrs. Howard)*, Lillian Langdon *(Mrs. Lincoln)*.

Melodrama. Forced to theft when in dire straits, family man John Howard is arrested for stealing food from a grocery store and is put in jail. The shock kills his wife, and his children are sent to an orphanage. Ella is adopted by a wealthy widow, and May finds a place on the farm of George Stuart, where she attracts the attentions of farmhand Billy Bender. Clifford Hamilton, manager of Stuart's grocery stores, calls at the farm with some papers and comes to know May and later her sister, who has been named heir to the widow. After firing the manager for dishonesty, Stuart finds that Hamilton is responsible for May's father's being jailed, and he reunites Howard with his children. *Orphans. Sisters. Widows. Poverty. Farm life. Family life. Theft. Adoption.*

MOTHER KNOWS BEST **F2.3709**

Fox Film Corp. 28 Oct **1928** [c28 Sep 1928; LP25647]. Talking sequences, mus score, & sd eff (Movietone); b&w. 35mm. 9 reels, 10,116 ft.

Pres by William Fox. *Dir* John Blystone. *Dial Supv* Charles Judels, Dave Stamper. *Scen* Marion Orth. *Dial* Eugene Walter. *Titl* William Kernell, Edith Bristol. *Photog* Gilbert Warrenton. *Film Ed* Margaret V. Clancey. *Mus* Erno Rapee, S. L. Rothafel. *Song: "Sally of My Dreams"* William Kernell. *Rec Engr* Joseph Aiken. *Asst Dir* Jasper Blystone.

Cast: Madge Bellamy *(Sally Quail)*, Louise Dresser *(Ma Quail)*, Barry Norton *(The Boy)*, Albert Gran *(Sam Kingston)*, Joy Auburn *(Bessie)*, Annette De Kirby *(Bessie, as a child)*, Stuart Erwin *(Ben)*, Ivor De Kirby *(Ben, as a child)*, Lucien Littlefield *(Pa Quail)*, Dawn O'Day *(Sally, as a child)*.

Drama. Source: Edna Ferber, "Mother Knows Best," in *Mother Knows Best, a Fiction Book* (Garden City, New York, 1927). Ma Quail robs the till in her husband's drugstore in order to finance singing and dancing lessons for her daughter, Sally, who, even as a kidlet of 8, is a clever impersonator. Years pass, and domineering, ambitious Ma Quail drives her daughter into a career in show business, guiding her from amateur nights to vaudeville to A. E. F. shows and finally to the Broadway big time. Although Sally becomes a fine dramatic actress, her mother never allows her to develop a personality of her own and strictly forbids her any romantic life; whenever Sally falls in love with a young fellow, Ma drives him away. Sally eventually has a nervous breakdown, and a doctor makes Ma realize that she is ruining her daughter's life. Ma then reunites Sally with the boy she loves, and Sally returns to her former prominence as an actress. *Stage mothers. Actors. Physicians. Motherhood. Drugstores. Vaudeville. Amateur nights. World War I. New York City—Broadway.*

MOTHER MACHREE **F2.3710**

Cardinal Films. *Dist* Creston Feature Pictures. 9 Apr **1922** [New York State showing]. Si; b&w. 35mm. ca7 reels.

Cast: Amanda Trinkle *(Mother Machree)*, James La Para *(Prince Yellow Dwarf)*, Jack Hopkins *(Spirit of Bad Council)*.

Allegory. This film appears to have dealt allegorically with certain aspects of the history of Ireland. *Ireland—History.*

MOTHER MACHREE **F2.3711**

Fox Film Corp. 22 Jan **1928** [premiere; released Mar 1928; c12 Jun 1927; LP24071]. Si; b&w. 35mm. 7 reels, 6,807 ft. [Also mus score & sd eff (Movietone); released 21 Oct 1928.]

Pres by William Fox. *Dir* John Ford. *Scen* Gertrude Orr. *Titl* Katherine Hilliker, H. H. Caldwell. *Photog* Chester Lyons. *Film Ed* Katherine Hilliker, H. H. Caldwell. *Asst Dir* Edward O'Fearna.

Cast: Belle Bennett *(Ellen McHugh)*, Neil Hamilton *(Brian McHugh)*, Philippe De Lacy *(Brian, as a child)*, Pat Somerset *(Robert De Puyster)*, Victor McLaglen *(Terrence O'Dowd)*, Ted McNamara *(Harpist of Wexford)*, John MacSweeney *(Irish priest)*, Eulalie Jensen *(Rachel Van Studdiford)*, Constance Howard *(Edith Cutting)*, Ethel Clayton *(Mrs. Cutting)*, William Platt *(Pips)*, Jacques Rollens *(Signor Bellini)*, Rodney Hildebrand *(Brian McHugh, Sr.)*, Joyce Wirard *(Edith Cutting, as a child)*, Robert Parrish *(child)*.

Society melodrama. Source: Rida Johnson Young, "The Story of Mother Machree," in *Munsey's Magazine* (81:1–32, Feb 1924). In an Irish village in 1899, Ellen McHugh's husband is killed in a storm. Convinced that in America lies the best future for her son, Brian, she arrives only to face discouragement until Terrence O'Dowd induces her to join a sideshow, posing as a "half-woman." Brian is placed in a fashionable school, but when his mother's profession is discovered, the principal forces Ellen to surrender the boy legally into his care. She becomes a housekeeper in the Fifth Avenue home of the Cuttings and rears her employer's daughter, Edith. Years later, Edith and Brian meet and fall in love on the eve of war; eventually the boy and his mother are reunited, and all ends happily. *Immigrants. Irish. Widows. Housekeepers. Motherhood. Boarding schools. Sideshows. Ireland. New York City—Fifth Avenue.*

MOTHER O' MINE **F2.3712**

Thomas H. Ince Productions. *Dist* Associated Producers. 5 Jun **1921** [cJun 1921; LP16605]. Si; b&w. 35mm. 7 reels, 6,004 ft.

Supv Thomas H. Ince. *Dir* Fred Niblo. *Adapt* C. Gardner Sullivan. *Photog* Henry Sharp.

Cast: Lloyd Hughes *(Robert Sheldon)*, Betty Ross Clark *(Dolly Wilson)*, Betty Blythe *(Fan Baxter)*, Joseph Kilgour *(Willard Thatcher)*, Claire McDowell *(Mrs. Sheldon)*, Andrew Robson *(district attorney)*, Andrew Arbuckle *(Henry Godfrey)*.

Melodrama. Source: Charles Belmont Davis, "The Octopus," in *Her Own Sort, and Others* (New York, 1917). With a letter of introduction from his mother, smalltown bank clerk Robert Sheldon gets a position with financier Willard Thatcher, in reality his father who earlier deserted his mother, disclaiming the child. The boy's honest face and straightforward ways are used by Thatcher to victimize another banker, but when Bob denounces him a struggle ensues and Thatcher is accidentally killed. Bob is tried for the crime; the only witness is Fan Baxter, the banker's mistress, who accuses Sheldon of murder; and he is sentenced to die. His sweetheart, Dolly, with the aid of Mrs. Sheldon, forces Fan to admit to perjury, and a last-minute ride through a storm saves Robert from electrocution. *Bank clerks. Bankers. Mistresses. Desertion. Parentage. Murder. Perjury. Capital punishment.*

MOTHER O' MINE (Reissue) **F2.3713**

Dist Universal Pictures. 23 Sep **1929** [New York State license]. Si; b&w. 35mm. 6 reels.

Note: Originally released 3 Sep 1917 by Bluebird Photoplays in 5 reels.

MOTHERHOOD; LIFE'S GREATEST MIRACLE **F2.3714**

Blue Ray Productions. *Dist* States Cinema Corp. **1928** [c18 Aug 1925; MU3238]. Si; b&w. 35mm. 6 reels, 5,800 ft.

Screen Adapt Lita Lawrence.

Cast: George E. Patton, Adelaide M. Chase.

Domestic drama. Following scenes of the Christ Child in the manger, the story is told of two couples—the wealthy Robert Marsh Sinclairs and the poor Fred Martins—and their contrasting lives. Both wives learn of their approaching motherhood at the same time, both fathers are pleased, but the women react very differently. Florence Sinclair fears any interference with her social life and begs her doctor for an abortion. The doctor refuses and assures Florence that she will feel different in time. Mae Martin, on the other hand, joyfully accepts her burden and carefully follows her physician's directions. Apparently, preparation and actual delivery of Florence and Mae are shown in considerable detail. Happily, Florence later realizes her error and regrets that she ever considered destroying her beloved daughter. *Physicians. Motherhood. Obstetrics. Childbirth. Abortion. Wealth. Jesus.*

MOTHER'S BOY **F2.3715**

Pathé Exchange. 12 May **1929** [c19 May 1929; LP395]. Sd (Photophone); b&w. 35mm. 8 reels, 7,423 ft.

Prod Robert T. Kane. *Dir* Bradley Barker. *Dial Supv* James Seymour. *Story-Dial-Scen* Gene Markey. *Photog Supv* Philip Tannura. *Photog* Harry Stradling, Walter Strenge. *Set Dsgn* Clark Robinson. *Film Ed* Edward Pfitzenmeier. *Songs: "There'll Be You and Me," "Come to Me," "I'll Always Be Mother's Boy," "The World Is Yours and Mine"* Bud Green, Sam H. Stept. *Rec Engr* V. S. Ashdown, J. A. Delaney.

Cast: Morton Downey *(Tommy O'Day)*, Beryl Mercer *(Mrs. O'Day)*, John T. Doyle *(Mr. O'Day)*, Brian Donlevy *(Harry O'Day)*, Helen Chandler *(Rose Lyndon)*, Osgood Perkins *(Jake Sturmberg)*, Lorin Raker *(Joe Bush)*, Barbara Bennett *(Beatrix Townleigh)*, Jennie Moskowitz *(Mrs. Apfelbaum)*, Jacob Frank *(Mr. Apfelbaum)*, Louis Sorin *(Mr. Bumble)*, Robert Gleckler *(Gus Le Grand)*, Tyrrell Davis *(Duke of Pomplum)*, Allan Vincent *(Dinslow)*, Leslie Stowe *(evangelist)*.

Musical drama. Tommy O'Day, an Irish lad with a golden voice who lives on the Lower East Side of New York, is unjustly accused by his father of stealing the family savings. Tommy leaves home and meets up with Joe Bush, a press agent who gets him a place singing in a cabaret. Tommy is a success and soon obtains a leading part in a Broadway revue. As the curtain is about to go up on opening night, however, Tommy receives word from his sweetheart, Rose Lyndon, that his mother, whom he has not seen since leaving home, is apparently dying. Tommy deserts the show and goes to her bedside, bringing her back to life and health with a beautiful song. Tommy's mother completely recovers, and he is excused by the revue manager. Tommy becomes a star. *Singers. Press agents. Irish. Filial relations. Theft. Family life. Musical revues. Cabarets. New York City—Lower East Side. New York City—Broadway.*

MOTHER'S CRY **F2.3716**

First National Pictures. ca4 Dec **1930** [New York premiere; released 7 Dec 1930 or 4 Jan 1931; c28 Dec 1930; LP1879]. Sd (Vitaphone); b&w. 35mm. 8 reels, 6,860 ft.

Prod Robert North. *Dir* Hobart Henley. *Adapt–Adtl Dial* Lenore J. Coffee. *Photog* Gilbert Warrenton. *Film Ed* Frank Ware.

Cast: Dorothy Peterson *(Mary Williams)*, David Manners *(Artie)*, Helen Chandler *(Beatty)*, Edward Woods *(Danny)*, Sidney Blackmer *(Gerald Hart)*, Evelyn Knapp *(Jenny)*, Pat O'Malley *(Frank Williams)*, Jean Bary *(Sadye)*, Claire McDowell *(Mary's mother)*, Charles Hill Mailes *(Mary's father)*, Reginald Pasch *(Karl Muller)*, Medyth Burel.

Domestic drama. Source: Helen Grace Carlisle, *Mother's Cry* (New York, 1930). Seamstress Mary Williams, the widowed mother of four children, spends her life in devotion to them although heartache is her chief reward. Jenny is a hard-working image of her mother, and Artie becomes a promising architect; but Danny falls in with gangsters and trouble with the police, and Beatty, a "romantic dreamer" and member of the intelligentsia, has an affair with wealthy and married Gerald Hart. Following his release from prison, Danny plans to blackmail Artie, who has changed his name, but he finds a readier opportunity in Hart's love letters to Beatty. Unfortunately, the confrontation between Beatty and Danny results in Beatty's death and, ultimately, Danny's execution in the electric chair. Artie leaves home in order to sever all connection with the incident, but Mary finds solace in his success. *Seamstresses. Widows. Architects. Gangsters. Intelligentsia. Motherhood. Blackmail. Family life. Murder. Capital punishment.*

MOTHERS OF MEN *see* **THE BROADWAY MADONNA**

MOTHERS-IN-LAW **F2.3717**

B. P. Schulberg Productions. *Dist* Preferred Pictures. 9 Sep **1923** [c1 Nov 1923; LP19557]. Si; b&w. 35mm. 7 reels, 6,725 ft.

Pres by B. P. Schulberg. *Dir* Louis Gasnier. *Adapt* Olga Printzlau. *Story* Frank Dazey, Agnes Christine Johnston. *Photog* Karl Struss.

Cast: Ruth Clifford *(Vianna Courtleigh)*, Gaston Glass *(David Wingate)*, Vola Vale *(Ina Phillips)*, Crauford Kent *(Alden Van Buren)*, Josef Swickard *(Newton Wingate)*, Edith Yorke *("Mom" Wingate)*, Doris Stone *(Tessie Clark)*.

Domestic melodrama. Farmer's son David Wingate marries city girl Vianna Courtleigh over his parents' objections. Her father gives him a job with the company; a baby is born to the young couple; but their happiness is marred by David's desire for a quiet domestic life in opposition to Vianna's love of excitement. David's mother comes to live with them when her husband dies. She observes their unhappiness and, after deciding that Vianna is at fault, determines to teach her a lesson. She kidnaps the baby, threatening to keep him until Vianna reforms. Eventually Vianna sees the folly of her ways and seeks forgiveness from David. *Mothers-in-law. Family life. Marriage.*

A MOTION TO ADJOURN **F2.3718**

Ben Wilson Productions. *Dist* Arrow Film Corp. 2 Nov **1921** [c7 Nov 1921; LP17163]. Si; b&w. 35mm. 6 reels.

Prod Ben Wilson. *Dir-Scen* Roy Clements.

Cast: Harry Rattenberry *(Silas Warner)*, Roy Stewart *(Silas Warner, Jr.)*, Sidney D'Albrook *(Archie Warner)*, Evelyn Nelson *(Louise Warner)*, Norval MacGregor *(Doc Bleeker)*, Marjorie Daw *(Sally Bleeker)*, Peggy Blackwood *(Valentine)*, William Carroll *(Joe Selinsky)*, Charles L. King *(The Bartender)*, Bill White *(Faro Dan)*, Jim Welsh *(Butterfly Kid)*.

Comedy-melodrama. Source: Peter Bernard Kyne, "A Motion To Adjourn," in *Saturday Evening Post* (187:5, 5 Sep 1914). Silas Warner, Jr., playboy son of a wealthy New York broker, is disinherited and sent from home by his father when he assumes the blame for a near-theft committed by his brother, Archie. In a western mining community, he is inducted into the "Ornery and Worthless Men of the World," a fraternity of fortune seekers, and a compromising situation forces him to marry Sally Bleeker. Sally is sent away to finishing school when her father dies; there she meets Louise, Silas' sister; and the girls become pals. While visiting the Warner home, Sally recognizes Silas, Jr.'s, picture, and when her miner-guardians come to New York to bring her home, there is a final meeting of the order and a happy reconciliation of Silas with his family. *Miners. Fortune hunters. Brothers. Guardians. Fraternities. Disinheritance. New York City.*

MOTORING THRU SPAIN **F2.3719**

Burton Holmes Lectures. 27 Jan **1929.** Si; b&w. 35mm. 4 reels.

Travelog. No information about the precise nature of this film has been found. *Spain.*

MOULDERS OF MEN **F2.3720**

R-C Pictures. *Dist* Film Booking Offices of America. 27 Feb **1927** [c27 Feb 1927; LP23804]. Si; b&w. 35mm. 7 reels, 6,413 ft.

Pres by Joseph P. Kennedy. *Dir* Ralph Ince. *Cont* Dorothy Yost. *Adapt* J. G. Hawks. *Story* John Chapman Hilder. *Photog* Allen Siegler. *Asst Dir* James Dugan.

Cast: Conway Tearle *(Dr. William Matthews)*, Margaret Morris *(Anne Grey)*, Frankie Darro *(Sandy Barry)*, Rex Lease *(Jim Barry)*, Eugene Pallette *(Barney Mulholland)*, Jola Mendez *(Betty, a schoolgirl)*, William Knight *(Detective Mailey)*.

Crime melodrama. In order to raise money for surgery for his crippled brother, Jim Barry accepts a job with Warner, leader of a gang of narcotics smugglers. Chased by Federal authorities, Warner escapes, but Jim is captured and then is questioned by Dr. Matthews, a noted physician and prominent member of the Elks who is specially assigned to the narcotics squad. Jim refuses to talk, but Matthews, discovering the condition of his brother, Sandy, takes him to an Elks' hospital where a successful operation is performed on his leg. Warner, meanwhile, informs Jim that Matthews is mistreating Sandy and that he has died. Jim tries to take revenge on Matthews, but, learning he has been duped by the gangster, gives evidence leading to Warner's conviction. Matthews is united with his sweetheart, Anne Grey, a newspaper reporter. *Brothers. Physicians. Cripples. Smugglers. Reporters. Narcotics. Tenements. Benevolent and Protective Order of Elks.*

MOUNTAIN JUSTICE **F2.3721**

Ken Maynard Productions. *Dist* Universal Pictures. 4 May **1930** [c14 Apr 1930; LP1232]. Sd (Movietone); b&w. 35mm. 6 reels, 6,797 ft. [Also si; 5,804 ft.]

Pres by Carl Laemmle. *Dir* Harry J. Brown. *Story-Scen* Bennett Cohen. *Dial-Titl* Leslie Mason. *Photog* Ted McCord. *Film Ed* Fred Allen. *Rec Engr* C. Roy Hunter.

Cast: Ken Maynard *(Ken McTavish)*, Kathryn Crawford *(Coral Harland)*, Otis Harlan *(Jud McTavish)*, Paul Hurst *(Lem Harland)*, Richard Carlyle *(Judge Keets)*, Les Bates *(Abner Harland)*, Pee Wee Holmes *("Rusty")*, Blue Washington *(Sam)*, Fred Burns *(Sandy McTavish)*.

Western melodrama. Sandy McTavish is shot from ambush on his Oklahoma ranch and dies in the arms of his son, Ken, after showing him a letter of warning and muttering the words "Kettle Creek—Kentucky." Ken goes there in search of the murderer, posing as deaf in the hope that handwriting will disclose the author of the letter. He becomes involved in a feud between the McTavishes and the Harlands and incidentally meets Coral Harland. His pose is detected; but a note from Coral discloses that she wrote the letter to his father. After fighting against terrific odds, Ken brings the murderer to justice and wins Coral for his bride. *Ranchers. Filial relations. Murder. Feuds. Deafness. Oklahoma. Kentucky. Documentation.*

Note: Initially reviewed as *Kettle Creek.*

THE MOUNTAIN WOMAN **F2.3722**

Fox Film Corp. 23 Jan **1921** [c23 Jan 1921; LP16065]. Si; b&w. 35mm. 6 reels.

Pres by William Fox. *Dir* Charles Giblyn. *Scen* Ashley T. Locke. *Photog* Joseph Ruttenberg.

Cast: Pearl White *(Alexander McGiverns)*, Corliss Giles *(Jerry O'Keefe)*, Richard C. Travers *(Jack Halloway)*, George Barnum *(Aaron McGiverns)*, Warner Richmond *(Bud Sellers)*, John Webb Dillon *(Will Brent)*, J. Thornton Baston *(Jase Mallows)*, Charles Graham *(Lute Brown)*.

Rural melodrama. Source: Charles Neville Buck, *A Pagan of the Hills* (New York, 1919). In the hills of Kentucky, Alexander McGivens, known as "the girl in pants," is reared by her father as if she were a boy. When her father, Aaron, is wounded in a fight with Bud Sellers, the girl undertakes to get her father's logs to market with the help of a crew from the lumber camp. Her numerous suitors include a young Irishman, Jerry O'Keefe, roughneck Jase Mallows, and a wealthy young easterner, Jack Halloway. After delivering the logs, she entrusts her money to the repentant Bud Sellers, and on her return trip she is captured by Mallows and his followers. She finally reaches home, where she offers her hand to O'Keefe, the soft-spoken mountaineer. *Tomboys. Irish. Fatherhood. Mountain life. Lumbering. Kentucky.*

MOUNTAINS OF MANHATTAN **F2.3723**

Gotham Productions. *Dist* Lumas Film Corp. 3 Jun **1927** [c6 May 1927; LP23935]. Si; b&w. 35mm. 6 reels, 5,785 ft.

Pres by Sam Sax. *Dir* James P. Hogan. *Scen* Alyce Garrick. *Titl* Delos Sutherland. *Story* Herbert C. Clark. *Photog* Ray June. *Film Ed* Edith Wakeling. *Prod Mgr* Glenn Belt.

Cast: Dorothy Devore *(Marion Wright)*, Charles Delaney *(Jerry Nolan)*, Kate Price *("Ma" Nolan)*, Bobby Gordon *(Isadore Ginsberg)*, George Chesebro *(Hoyt Norcross)*, James P. Hogan *("Bull" Kerry)*, Clarence H. Wilson *(Jim Tully)*, Robert E. Homans *("Big Bill" Wright)*.

Society drama. Jerry Nolan, a boxing champion, gives up the ring to work as an iron "rigger" by day and to study engineering at night. Jerry complains to "Bull" Kerry, his foreman on a skyscraper job, that many of the steel beams have been drilled incorrectly, and Kerry's disinterest provokes suspicion. Marion Wright, daughter of the contractor, is attracted to Jerry, who saves little Isadore Ginsberg from a beating at the hands of Kerry and takes him home to his Irish mother. Jerry saves Marion from injury in an accident at the construction site, winning the gratitude of Mr. Wright, who fires Kerry and gives his job to Jerry. The foreman retaliates by calling a strike, climaxing with Jerry and "Bull" Kerry in a clash on the steel girders; Kerry confesses his and Norcross' complicity, and the lovers are united in marriage. *Boxers. Irish. Jews. Children. Construction. Skyscrapers. Strikes.*

THE MOUNTED STRANGER **F2.3724**

Universal Pictures. 8 Feb **1930** [c28 Jan 1930; LP1034]. Sd (Movietone); b&w. 35mm. 6 reels, 5,896 ft. [Also si; 5,554 ft.]

Pres by Carl Laemmle. *Dir-Adapt-Dial* Arthur Rosson. *Photog* Harry Neumann. *Film Ed* Gilmore Walker. *Rec Engr* C. Roy Hunter.

Cast: Hoot Gibson *(Pete Ainslee)*, Buddy Hunter *(Pete, as a boy)*, Milton Brown *("Pop" Ainslee)*, Fred Burns *(Steve Gary)*, James Corey *("White-Eye")*, Francis Ford *("Spider" Coy)*, Walter Patterson *(his lookout)*, Francelia Billington *(Mrs. Coy)*, Louise Lorraine *(Bonita Coy)*.

Western melodrama. Source: Henry Herbert Knibbs, "Ridin' Kid From Powder River" (publication undetermined). Pete Ainslee, as a boy, witnesses his father's murder by Steve Gary, and years later, known as The Ridin' Kid, he wounds Gary, then rides to Cactus Bar, where he and "Spider" trap Gary's gang and force them to depart. Taking cover in an abandoned mine, Pete meets Bonita and saves her life. They become friends, though she is jealously guarded by another man who betrays Pete into the hands of the gang. By a ruse, Bonita saves Pete; but during their escape, she is wounded and Pete rides into town for a doctor. The gang follows and attempts to capture Steve, but he stampedes their horses. Disgruntled, the gang turns on Gary, and he is killed; Pete returns to find Bonita out of danger and happily awaiting him. *Cowboys. Gangs. Murder. Revenge. Stampedes.*

THE MOVING GUEST **F2.3725**

Morris R. Schlank Productions. 2 Feb **1927** [trade review]. Si; b&w. 35mm. [Feature length assumed.]

Pres by W. Ray Johnston.

Cast: Al Alt.

Comedy. Expecting her husband to receive a bonus, a wife so obligates them both by credit purchases that they cannot meet even their first payments. Movers arrive just as they are having a housewarming. *Instalment buying.*

MR. BARNES OF NEW YORK **F2.3726**

Goldwyn Pictures. May **1922** [c16 Apr 1922; LP17762]. Si; b&w. 35mm. 5 reels, 4,804 ft.

Dir Victor Schertzinger. *Scen* Gerald Duffy, J. E. Nash. *Photog* George Brewster.

Cast: Tom Moore *(Mr. Barnes, of New York)*, Anna Lehr *(Marina Paoli)*, Naomi Childers *(Enid Anstruther)*, Lewis Willoughby *(Gerard Anstruther)*, Ramon Samaniegos *(Antonio)*, Otto Hoffman *(Tomasso)*, Sydney Ainsworth *(Danella)*.

Melodrama. Source: Archibald Clavering Gunter, *Mr. Barnes of New York* (Leipzig, Tauchnitz, 1888). While vacationing in Corsica, Mr. Barnes of New York witnesses a duel between Paoli and a British naval officer, in which the Coriscan is killed. Marina, Paoli's sister, vows a vendetta against the slayer, but the only clue to his identity is the name "Gerard Anstruther" engraved on his pistol. In an art gallery in Paris, Mr. Barnes sees a picture, painted by Marina, of the duel scene, and his interest brings him under suspicion. Barnes later meets Enid Anstruther, an English girl who admires the painting, and he follows her to Nice. There he discovers that Gerard, who is Paoli's murderer, wishes to marry Marina. Her guardian, Count Danella, plots to have Marina wed Gerard, then reveals to her that he is the killer of her brother; Barnes, however, proves that Gerard lent his pistol to a fellow officer who later confessed to the slaying. The count, defeated in his scheme, is killed by Tomasso, who mistakes him for Gerard; and the lovers are happily united. *New Yorkers. English. Revenge. Paintings. Corsica. Nice. Duels.*

MR. BILLINGS SPENDS HIS DIME *see* Entry F2.3654

MR. BINGLE **F2.3727**

San Antonio Pictures. *Dist* Producers Security Corp. 20 Aug **1922.** Si; b&w. 35mm. 5 reels.

Dir Leopold Wharton.

Cast: Maclyn Arbuckle.

Comedy drama. " ... centering about faithful bookkeeper, who has difficulty in supporting his family. His cousin's children have every luxury, but are greedy and unscrupulous. Their father returns, apparently penniless, and they turn him out. Bookkeeper takes him in, and when he dies, he leaves millions to him. Bookkeeper establishes orphanage and takes in children. Court ruling strips fortune from him and he loses orphans but child of his own arrives, and he again finds complete happiness." (*Motion Picture News Booking Guide*, 3:49, Oct 1922.) *Bookkeepers. Family life. Greed. Orphanages. Inheritance.*

MR. POTTER OF TEXAS *see* Entry F2.3655

MR. WU *see* Entry F2.3656

MULHALL'S GREAT CATCH **F2.3728**

Harry Garson Productions. *Dist* Film Booking Offices of America. 4 Jul **1926** [c28 Jun 1926; LP22846]. Si; b&w. 35mm. 5 reels, 5,430 ft.

Dir Harry Garson. *Cont* Jefferson Moffitt. *Adapt* Rex Taylor. *Story* Gerald Beaumont. *Photog* Harry J. Brown. *Asst Dir* Joe O'Brien.

Cast: Lefty Flynn *(Joe Mulhall)*, Kathleen Myers *(Nora McCarron)*, Henry Victor *(Otto Nelson)*, Harry Dunkinson *(Con McCarren)*, Harry Arros *(Captain Collins)*.

Melodrama. Joe Mulhall, a city fireman, and Otto Nelson, pride of the police force, vie for the hand of Nora McCarron. Joe and Rizzoli ring in a fire alarm in the industrial district, and Joe makes a daring rescue of two women, delivering them to Rizzoli. Officer Nelson, attracted to the scene, falls onto Joe from the roof, knocks him out, and makes a rescue; the newspapers give Nelson all the credit, and his stock rises with Nora. Joe asks Nora to the Fire and Police Ball, but he is delayed and she goes with Nelson; furthermore he disgraces himself by spilling refreshments on the mayor and the commissioner. That night Nora feels sorry for him and signals him from her window. In her father's office she is captured by two burglars; Nelson investigates and is knocked unconscious. Joe arrives, overcomes the burglars as they dynamite the safe, and wins the favor of Nora. *Firemen. Police. Burglars. Safecrackers. Courtship.*

MURDER ON THE ROOF **F2.3729**

Columbia Pictures. 19 Jan **1930** [c6 Feb 1930; LP1056]. Sd (Movietone); b&w. 35mm. 6 reels, 5,400 ft. [Also si.]

Prod Harry Cohn. *Dir* George B. Seitz. *Adapt-Cont-Dial* F. Hugh Herbert. *Story* Edward Doherty. *Photog* Joe Walker. *Art Dir* Harrison Wiley. *Film Ed* Robert Jahns. *Ch Sd Engr* John P. Livadary. *Asst Dir* David Selman.

Cast: Dorothy Revier *(Molly)*, Raymond Hatton *(Drinkwater)*, Margaret Livingston *(Marcia)*, David Newell *(Ted Palmer)*, Paul Porcasi *(Joe Carozzo)*, Virginia Brown Faire *(Monica)*, William V. Mong *(Anthony Sommers)*, Louis Natheaux *(Victor)*, Fred Kelsey *(Ryan)*, Richard Cramer *(Joe Larkin)*, Pietro Sosso *(Emile)*, Hazel Howell *(Lucille)*.

Mystery melodrama. Joe Carozzo, the proprietor of the Corsair Nightclub, uses his establishment as a cover for secret dealings with the New York underworld. He commissions lawyer Anthony Sommers to acquire a stolen diamond from Larkin, an underworld figure; and during the course of a conference among the three men, Larkin is stabbed to death. Sommers, found in a drunken stupor, is arrested and convicted of manslaughter. Molly, a charming singer, is hired and soon takes the place of Marcia, a dancer, in Joe's eyes, though she is loved by Ted Palmer, son of a wealthy family. Molly, actually Sommers' daughter, encourages Joe's attentions to gain evidence against him. Marcia accuses her of murdering Carozzo, but Drinkwater, an undercover reporter who has witnessed the shooting, clears her, and she is reunited with Ted. *Singers. Dancers. Gamblers. Gangsters. Reporters. Cigarette girls. Filial relations. Murder. Nightclubs. New York City.*

MURDER WILL OUT **F2.3730**

First National Pictures. 6 Apr **1930** [c10 May 1930; LP1343]. Sd (Vitaphone); b&w. 35mm. 7 reels, 6,200 ft.

Dir Clarence Badger. *Adapt-Dial* J. Grubb Alexander. *Photog* John Seitz. *Rec Engr* Alex Hurdley.

Cast: Jack Mulhall *(Leonard Staunton)*, Lila Lee *(Jeanne Baldwin)*, Noah Beery *(Lieutenant Condon)*, Malcolm McGregor *(Jack Baldwin)*, Tully Marshall *(Dr. Mansfield)*, Alec B. Francis *(Senator Baldwin)*, Hedda Hopper *(Aunt Pat)*, Claude Allister *(Alan Fitzhugh)*.

Mystery melodrama. Source: Will F. Jenkins, "The Purple Hieroglyph," in *Snappy Stories* (59:3–28, 1 Mar 1920). Leonard Staunton, engaged to Jeanne Baldwin, daughter of a U.S. Senator, is preparing to spend a weekend at the Baldwin estate when Alan Fitzhugh, a club-member, arrives with a note, imprinted with a purple hieroglyph, in which he (Fitzhugh) is threatened. Staunton, telling Jeanne of the plot, stays with Fitzhugh until after midnight, but the next day Fitzhugh's mutilated body is found. Following the funeral, Dr. Mansfield, one of the pallbearers, accidentally smokes a poisoned cigarette; and Staunton, Jeanne, and Detective Condon take him to his home for an antidote; his body disappears, and footprints lead to a slipper with a purple hieroglyph.

Numerous other blackmail threats follow, and Jeanne is kidnaped. En route to the ransom rendezvous, Staunton is captured in a speedboat, but a U. S. submarine saves the day and the criminals prove to be none other than Fitzhugh, Mansfield, and Lieutenant Condon. *Physicians. Hieroglyphics. Blackmail. Kidnaping. Murder. United States Congress.*

THE MUSIC MASTER **F2.3731**

Fox Film Corp. 23 Jan **1927** [c23 Jan 1927; LP23582]. Si; b&w. 35mm. 8 reels, 7,754 ft.

Pres by William Fox. *Dir* Allan Dwan. *Adapt* Philip Klein. *Photog* George Webber, William Miller. *Art Dir* Sam Corso. *Scenic Dir* Al Panci. *Interior Decorator* Miss S. Baxter. *Asst Dir* Clarence Elmer. *Cost* Emery J. Herrett. *Draperies* J. G. Horton.

Cast: Alec B. Francis *(Anton von Barwig)*, Lois Moran *(Helene Stanton)*, Neil Hamilton *(Beverly Cruger)*, Norman Trevor *(Andrew Cruger)*, Charles Lane *(Richard Stanton)*, William T. Tilden *(Joles)*, Helen Chandler *(Jenny)*, Marcia Harris *(Miss Husted)*, Kathleen Kerrigan *(Mrs. Andrew Cruger)*, Howard Cull *(August Poons)*, Armand Cortez *(Pinac)*, Leo Feodoroff *(Fico)*, Carrie Scott *(Mrs. Mangenborn)*, Dore Davidson *(pawnbroker)*, Walter Catlett *(medicine show barker)*.

Drama. Source: Charles Klein, *The Music Master* (New York, 1935). Anton von Barwig, formerly an orchestra leader in Vienna, searches for his daughter who was taken from him by his wife many years before. Out of pride, he refuses help and is gradually forced to sell all his belongings. After being fleeced for years by a detective, he meets Helene Stanton, who is his long-lost daughter. She comes into his life as a charming young society girl seeking music lessons for her fiancé, Beverly Cruger, a boy of promising musical talents; sensing his kinship with her, Barwig finally confronts her foster father, who had run away with his wife in Vienna. Though her father is persuaded to make the sacrifice of effacing himself so as not to ruin her chance for social success, she discovers the relationship and brushes social considerations aside to be reunited with him. *Music teachers. Orchestra conductors. Parentage. Vienna.*

MUST WE MARRY? **F2.3732**

Trinity Pictures. 1 Dec **1928** [New York State license]. Si; b&w. 35mm. 6 reels, 5,100-5,400 ft.

Dir Frank S. Mattison. *Scen* Cecil Burtis Hill. *Story-Titl* Rachel Barton Butler. *Photog* Jules Cronjager. *Film Ed* Minnie Steppler.

Cast: Pauline Garon *(Betty Jefferson)*, Lorraine Eason *(Thelma Duncan)*, Bud Shaw *(Kenneth Parson)*, Vivian Rich *(Luella Jefferson)*, Edward Brownell *(Jimmy Kelton)*, Louise Carver *(Mrs. Skittons)*, Charles Hall, Thomas A. Curran.

Comedy-drama. "The young hero [Kenneth Parson] with a fortune is the object of a scheming gal [Thelma Duncan] who tries to win him away from his sweetie [Betty Jefferson] by getting him in a compromising situation in a lonely cabin. He promises to marry her, but his sweetie steps in and pulls a trick herself and wins him back again." (*Film Daily,* 3 Mar 1929, p7.) *Gold diggers. Wealth. Reputation.*

THE MUZZLE *see* **FREEDOM OF THE PRESS**

MY AMERICAN WIFE **F2.3733**

Famous Players–Lasky. *Dist* Paramount Pictures. 31 Dec **1922** [New York premiere; released 11 Feb 1923; c2 Jan 1923; LP18599]. Si; b&w. 35mm. 6 reels, 6,091 ft.

Pres by Jesse L. Lasky. *Dir* Sam Wood. *Scen* Monte M. Katterjohn. *Photog* Alfred Gilks.

Cast: Gloria Swanson *(Natalie Chester)*, Antonio Moreno *(Manuel La Tassa)*, Josef Swickard *(Don Fernando De Contas)*, Eric Mayne *(Carlos De Grossa)*, Gino Corrado *(Pedro De Grossa)*, Edythe Chapman *(Donna Isabella La Tassa)*, Aileen Pringle *(Hortensia De Varela)*, Walter Long *(Gomez)*, F. R. Butler *(Horace Beresford)*, Jacques D'Auray *(Gaston Navarre)*, Loyal Underwood *(Danny O'Hara)*, Mary Land *(maid)*.

Melodrama. Source: Hector Turnbull, *My American Wife* (publication undetermined). A horserace brings together Kentuckian Natalie Chester and Argentinean Manuel La Tassa. At a party Pedro De Grossa insults Natalie, and consequently Manuel challenges him to a duel. To assure his son's success Carlos De Grossa hires Gomez to ambush Manuel. While Manuel is recuperating Natalie discovers the perfidy. She bribes Gomez to expose the De Grossas, Pedro leaves the country, and Manuel finally accepts his duty to participate in his government with the help of Natalie, his new wife. *Kentuckians. Horseracing. Argentina. Duels.*

MY BEST GIRL **F2.3734**

Mary Pickford Corp. *Dist* United Artists. 31 Oct **1927** [c22 Dec 1927; LP24780]. Si; b&w. 35mm. 9 reels, 7,460 ft.

Dir Sam Taylor. *Scen* Hope Loring. *Adapt* Allen McNeil, Tim Whelan. *Photog* Charles Rosher. *2d Camera* David Kesson. *Art Dir* Jack Schulze. *Asst Dir* Bruce Humberstone. *Comedy Construc* Clarence Hennecke.

Cast: Mary Pickford *(Maggie Johnson)*, Charles Rogers *(Joe Grant)*, Sunshine Hart *(Ma Johnson)*, Lucien Littlefield *(Pa Johnson)*, Carmelita Geraghty *(Liz Johnson)*, Hobart Bosworth *(Mr. Merrill)*, Evelyn Hall *(Mrs. Merrill)*, Avonne Taylor *(Millicent Rogers)*, Mack Swain *(judge)*, Frank Finch Smiles *(butler)*, William Courtwright *(stock clerk)*, John Junior *(Nick Powell)*, Harry Walker *(floorwalker)*.

Romantic comedy. Source: Kathleen Norris, *My Best Girl* (New York, 1927). Maggie, a shopgirl in a five-and-ten-cent store, falls in love with the owner's son, who gives up his society sweetheart for her. Learning of their affair, the boy's father unsuccessfully tries to buy Maggie off. When she also indicates her willingness to give his son up, the father becomes convinced of her worth and agrees to the marriage. *Shopgirls. Courtship. Wealth. Fatherhood. Five-and-ten-cent stores.*

MY BOY **F2.3735**

Jackie Coogan Productions. *Dist* Associated First National Pictures. ca25 Dec **1921** [New York, Los Angeles, and Washington premieres; released 2 Jan 1922; c27 Dec 1921; LP17446]. Si; b&w. 35mm. 5 reels, 4,967 ft.

Pres by Sol Lesser. *Supv* Jack Coogan, Sr. *Dir* Victor Heerman, Albert Austin. *Titl* Shirley Vance Martin, Max Abramson. *Photog* Glen MacWilliams, Robert Martin. *Film Ed* Irene Morra.

Cast: Jackie Coogan *(Jackie Blair)*, Claude Gillingwater *(Captain Bill)*, Mathilde Brundage *(Mrs. Blair)*, Patsy Marks *(Little Girl)*.

Comedy-drama. Jackie Blair arrives in the United States as a steerage passenger and faces deportation because his mother has died during the voyage. Captain Bill, a retired skipper, tries his best to amuse Jackie while arrangements are being made for his return trip, but Jackie escapes and follows the captain to his shanty home. Although the captain loves the boy, his poverty and age preclude his keeping him. Meanwhile, a wealthy matron who is Jackie's grandmother, missing Jackie at Ellis Island, begins a search for him. When the captain is taken ill, Jackie earns money by dancing in the streets and buys medicine for his patron, and at the settlement house where he attends a party given by the rich matron Jackie steals some grapes. Tracked by the police to the captain's shanty, Jackie is taken into custody and learns that he is Mrs. Blair's grandson; he and the captain then find a happy home with his wealthy relative. *Orphans. Immigrants. Sea captains. Grandmothers. Ellis Island.*

MY DAD **F2.3736**

R-C Pictures. *Dist* Film Booking Offices of America. 23 Jul **1922** [c13 Jul 1922; LP18054]. Si; b&w. 35mm. 6 reels, 5,600 ft.

Prod-Dir Cliff Smith. *Scen* E. Richard Schayer. *Story* Walter Richard Hall. *Photog* John Thompson.

Cast: Johnnie Walker *(Tom O'Day)*, Wilbur Higby *(Barry O'Day)*, Mary Redmond *(Mrs. O'Day)*, Ruth Clifford *(Dawn)*, Les Bates *(La Due)*, Harry von Meter *(The Factor)*, Rin-Tin-Tin *(himself, a dog)*.

Northwest melodrama. Tom is in love with the stepdaughter of the trading post factor, who mysteriously dominates Tom's father. Jealous of Tom, the factor exposes the father as a murderer, but Tom proves otherwise, thus clearing his father, convicting the factor, and winning the girl. *Factors. Murder. Filial relations. Dogs.*

MY FRIEND FROM INDIA **F2.3737**

De Mille Pictures. *Dist* Pathé Exchange. 19 Dec **1927** [c18 Dec 1927; LP24764]. Si; b&w. 35mm. 6 reels, 5,750 ft.

Supv F. McGrew Willis. *Dir* E. Mason Hopper. *Adapt-Cont* Rex Taylor. *Photog* Dewey Wrigley. *Art Dir* Charles Cadwallader. *Film Ed* James Morley. *Asst Dir* E. J. Babille. *Cost* Adrian.

Cast: Franklin Pangborn *(William Valentine)*, Elinor Fair *(Bernice)*, Ben Hendricks, Jr. *(Charles)*, Ethel Wales *(Arabella Mott)*, Jeanette Loff *(Marion)*, Tom Ricketts *(Judge Belmore)*, Louis Natheaux *(R. Austin Webb)*, Tom Dugan *(bogus Hindu Prince)*, George Ovey *(Hindu Prince's valet)*, Edgar Norton.

Farce. Source: Henry A. Du Souchet, *My Friend From India, a Farcical Comedy in Three Acts* (New York, 1912). Valentine, a wealthy young globe-trotter, falls in love with a girl during a brief encounter before being separated from her. Later, in a lottery scrape, he seeks refuge in a friend's house, disguising himself as a Hindu prince, and discovers that the girl he encountered the previous day is Bernice, his friend's sister. *Hindus. Disguise. Lotteries.*

MY FRIEND, THE DEVIL **F2.3738**

Fox Film Corp. 19 Nov **1922** [c19 Nov 1922; LP19113]. Si; b&w. 35mm. 8 reels, 9,555 ft.

Pres by William Fox. *Dir* Harry Millarde. *Scen* Paul H. Sloane. *Photog* Joseph Ruttenberg.

Cast: Charles Richman *(George Dryden)*, Ben Grauer *(George Dryden as a boy)*, William Tooker *(Dr. Brewster)*, Adolph Milar *(Dryden's stepfather)*, John Tavernier *(The Old Doctor)*, Myrtle Stewart *(George Dryden's mother)*, Barbara Castleton *(Anna Ryder)*, Alice May *(Mrs. Ryder)*, Peggy Shaw *(Beatrice Dryden)*, Robert Frazer *(The Artist)*, Mabel Wright *(The Governess)*.

Melodrama. Source: Georges Ohnet, *Le Docteur Rameau* (Paris, ca1889). George Dryden, an atheist since (as a boy) he saw his mother killed by lightning, becomes a prominent surgeon and marries a woman who soon dies of heart disease. Years later, on his daughter's wedding day, he discovers that his wife had a serious love affair with an artist. Infuriated, he drives his daughter away. She becomes ill, suffering an emotional collapse. The doctor exhausts his knowledge trying to save her and finally, in desperation, he calls upon God. The girl is miraculously cured and George Dryden's faith is restored. *Surgeons. Fatherhood. Religious conversion. Atheism. Neurasthenia. Infidelity. Weddings.*

MY HOME TOWN **F2.3739**

Atlas Educational Film Co. 15 Jun **1925** [New York State license]. Si; b&w. 35mm. 6 reels, 5,346 ft.

Cast: Wesley Barry, Adelaide Rendelle.

Melodrama(?). No information about the nature of this film has been found.

MY HOME TOWN **F2.3740**

Trem Carr Productions. *Dist* Rayart Pictures. Mar **1928.** Si; b&w. 35mm. 6 reels, 5,424-5,608 ft.

Pres by W. Ray Johnston. *Dir* Scott Pembroke. *Story-Scen* Arthur Hoerl. *Photog* Hap Depew. *Film Ed* Charles A. Post.

Cast: Gladys Brockwell *(Mae Andrews)*, Gaston Glass *(David Warren)*, Violet La Plante *(Priscilla)*, Carl Stockdale *(The Evangelist)*, Henry Sedley *(Denver Eddy)*, William Quinn *(Joey)*, Ruth Cherrington *(The Mother)*, Frank Clark *(The Father)*.

Drama. Jailed when he accidentally causes the death of a police officer, smalltown boy David Warren escapes to the big city with the help of some hoboes. Later he learns that his benefactors are crooks; they try to extort money from his mother; and he falls in love with Mae Andrews, the sister of a gang member. Out of a genuine love for the boy the girl stages a phony love scene so that he will return home. He does leave, believing them all crooked, but he later learns of the girl's honesty and sincerity and is reunited with her. *Hoboes. Brother-sister relationship. Manslaughter. Extortion. Smalltown life.*

MY HUSBAND'S FRIEND **F2.3741**

Dist Webster Pictures. 20 Jun **1922** [New York State license application]. Si; b&w. 35mm. 5 reels.

Cast: Frank Mills.

Drama. "The story tells of a busy husband who asks his friend to take his wife about. One night the friend escorts the wife home, pretends to leave the house but does not. The husband discovers his wife in the friend's arms in her room. She declares her innocence, claiming she mistook the friend for her husband. The husband enraged, takes his son and leaves her and their daughter. Years pass. The wife opens a questionable gambling place. Here, her son whom she does not recognize, comes to gamble and falls in love with his own sister. The girl, however, is busy making love to the son of her mother's former lover. She boldly tries to seduce him but without success. Meanwhile the father, looking for the son, discovers his wife. She reiterates her innocence so the father goes to his one time 'friend' for proof. The friend satisfies the husband with his story, and faith in his wife is once more restored." (New York State license records.) *Infidelity. Gambling. Incest. Friendship.*

MY HUSBAND'S WIVES **F2.3742**

Fox Film Corp. 16 Nov **1924** [c15 Oct 1924; LP20656]. Si; b&w. 35mm. 5 reels, 4,609 ft.

Pres by William Fox. *Dir* Maurice Elvey. *Scen* Dorothy Yost. *Story* Barbara La Marr. *Photog* Joseph Valentine.

Cast: Shirley Mason *(Vale Harvey)*, Bryant Washburn *(William Harvey)*, Evelyn Brent *(Marie Wynn)*, Paulette Duval *(Madame Corregio)*.

Domestic drama. Vale Harvey invites Marie Wynn, an old schoolchum, to visit her, not knowing that Marie was once married to her husband, William Harvey. Marie loses no time in trying to regain William's affection and to make Vale uncomfortable. Vale is so upset that she dreams of a flirtation between William and Italian actress Madame Corregio—but William orders Marie out of the house when he realizes her purpose. The Harveys are happily reconciled. *Flirts. Actors. Italians. Marriage. Divorce.*

MY LADY FRIENDS **F2.3743**

Carter De Haven Productions. *Dist* Associated First National Pictures. 31 Oct **1921** [c25 Oct 1921; LP17130]. Si; b&w. 35mm. 6 reels, 5,650 ft.

Pres by Carter De Haven. *Dir* Lloyd Ingraham. *Adapt* Rex Taylor. *Photog* Barney McGill.

Cast: Carter De Haven *(James Smith)*, Mrs. Carter De Haven *(Catherine Smith)*, Thomas G. Lingham *(Edward Early)*, Helen Raymond *(Lucille Early)*, Helen Lynch *(Eva Johns)*, Lincoln Stedman *(Tom Trainer)*, May Wallace *(Hilda)*, Hazel Howell, Clara Morris, Ruth Ashby *(Nora, Gwen, Julia, Three Lady Friends)*.

Comedy. Source: Emil Nyitray and Frank Mandel, *My Lady Friends* (New York opening: 3 Dec 1919). James Smith, millionaire Bible publisher, is concerned with spending the fortune he has acquired, while his wife, remembering their thrifty days, strives to make every penny count, despite the extravagant example set by Lucille, the wife of lawyer Edward Early. Smith receives a letter from two lady friends, both planning to visit him at his Atlantic City bungalow, and seeks the aid of Early, a neighbor. Both wives become suspicious and have a detective investigate the situation. In a series of fast maneuvers, James manages to separate the ladies from the wives; the latter are reconciled with their husbands after a general explanation, and Mrs. Smith determines to outspend the lady friends. *Millionaires. Publishers. Detectives. Thrift. The Bible. Atlantic City.*

MY LADY OF WHIMS **F2.3744**

Dallas M. Fitzgerald Productions. *Dist* Arrow Pictures. c25 Dec **1925** [LP22173]. Si; b&w. 35mm. 7 reels.

Dir Dallas M. Fitzgerald. *Scen* Doris Schroeder. *Photog* Jack Young.

Cast: Clara Bow *(Prudence Severn)*, Donald Keith *(Bartley Greer)*, Carmelita Geraghty *(Wayne Leigh)*, Francis McDonald *(Rolf)*, Lee Moran *(Dick Flynn)*.

Society melodrama. Source: Edgar Franklin, "Protecting Prue," in *Argosy Allstory Weekly* (vol 162, 16 Aug–13 Sep 1924). Bartley Greer, a young man with no prospects in particular, is hired by wealthy Mr. Severn to keep an eye on his wayward daughter, Prudence, who has become a Greenwich Village bohemian. Bartley obtains a room in the house where Prudence is living, and the two become the best of friends, spending much of their time together. When Prudence finds out that Bartley has been hired by her father, she shows him the door and becomes engaged to Rolf, an artist with women as well as with watercolor. Bartley learns that Prudence and Rolf are to be married on a yacht and halts the wedding, carrying off the not-too-unwilling Prudence for his own. *Artists. Bohemianism. Courtship. Fatherhood. Weddings. Yachts. New York City—Greenwich Village.*

MY LADY'S LATCHKEY **F2.3745**

Katherine MacDonald Pictures. *Dist* Associated First National Pictures. Jan **1921** [c9 Mar 1921; LP16238]. Si; b&w. 35mm. 6 reels, 5,500 ft.

Dir Edwin Carewe. *Scen* Finis Fox. *Photog* Joseph Brotherton.

Cast: Katherine MacDonald *(Annesley Grayle, the girl in quest of romantic adventure)*, Edmund Lowe *(Nelson Smith, a victim of evil companions)*, Claire Du Brey *(Countess Santiago, a victim of unrequited love)*, Howard Gaye *(Lord Annesley-Seton, cousin by marriage to Annesley Grayle)*, Lenore Lynard *(Lady Annesley-Seton, formerly poor but now wedded to riches)*, Thomas Jefferson *(Ruthven Smith, whose jewel belt disappears at midnight)*, Helena Phillips *(Mrs. Ellsworth, who presides over the House of Gloom)*.

Mystery melodrama. Source: Charles Norris Williamson and Alice Muriel Williamson, *The Second Latchkey* (Garden City, New York, 1920). Young Annesley Grayle, weary of a gloomy, uneventful existence with her aunt, accepts the proposal of a young American that she pose as his wife. Later, they are actually married. When, at a ball, she hears her husband accused of stealing a valuable diamond and realizes that he is indeed a thief, she hides the jewel to save him. She plans to report him to the police, but, seeing that he intends to reform, she remains with him and saves him from being shot by a jealous countess. *Criminals—Rehabilitation. Marriage. Theft.*

MY LADY'S LIPS **F2.3746**

B. P. Schulberg Productions. 1 Jul **1925.** Si; b&w. 35mm. 7 reels, 6,609 ft.

Dir James P. Hogan. *Story-Cont* John Goodrich. *Photog* Allen Siegler.

Cast: Alyce Mills *(Dora Blake)*, William Powell *(Scott Seddon)*, Clara Bow *(Lola Lombard)*, Frank Keenan *(Forbes Lombard)*, Ford Sterling *(Smike)*, John Sainpolis *(inspector)*, Gertrude Short *(crook girl)*, Matthew Betz *(Eddie Gault)*, Sojin.

Melodrama. Newspaper editor Forbes Lombard discovers that his daughter, Lola, has been consorting with gamblers, and star reporter Scott Seddon sees a chance for an exclusive story by getting the goods on the gang himself. Posing as an ex-con, Scott gains acceptance by the gang and falls in love with Dora Blake, the beautiful gang leader. There is a police raid, and Scott attempts to help Dora to escape. They are both captured, however, and are subjected to a brutal third degree, each signing a false confession in order to end this ordeal by interrogation. Released from prison, Scott finds that, despite Dora's promise to the contrary, she has returned to gambling. Scott declares his love for her, and they decide to get married and begin a new life together. *Editors. Reporters. Gamblers. Police. Criminals—Rehabilitation. Injustice. Imposture. Third degree.*

MY LADY'S PAST **F2.3747**

Tiffany-Stahl Productions. 1 Apr **1929** [c30 May 1929; LP434]. Talking sequences, mus score, & sd eff (Photophone); b&w. 35mm. 9 reels, 8,077 ft. [Also si; 5,668 ft.]

Dir Albert Ray. *Story-Cont* Frances Hyland. *Dial-Titl* Frederic Hatton, Fanny Hatton. *Photog* Harry Jackson. *Film Ed* George Merrick. *Mus Score* Hugo Riesenfeld. *Song: "A Kiss To Remember"* Hugo Riesenfeld.

Cast: Belle Bennett *(Mamie Reynolds)*, Joe E. Brown *(Sam Young)*, Alma Bennett *(typist)*, Russell Simpson *(John Parker)*, Joan Standing *(maid)*, Billie Bennett *(gossip)*, Raymond Keane.

Society drama. Sam Young, who has ambitions as a novelist, has been engaged to Mamie Reynolds for 10 years; after finally getting a work accepted, he falls for the blandishments of the girl who types his manuscript. Mamie gives a dinner party to celebrate Sam's success and to announce their marriage, but he fails to appear and she is disgraced by the local gossip. She is about to leave town when a young man, disappointed in love, shoots himself on her doorstep, and it is thought he has had a secret affair with Mamie; as a result, Mamie becomes a notorious character and Sam begins to feel himself the injured party in their romance. An elderly banker courting Mamie is challenged by Sam, but Sam receives a sound licking and is arrested for hurling rocks through Mamie's windows. Released from jail, Sam learns of Mamie's impending wedding and, after renewing his suit, rescues her from the wedding guests and the bridegroom. *Novelists. Typists. Bankers. Courtship. Reputation. Weddings. Suicide.*

MY MAN **F2.3748**

Vitagraph Co. of America. 10 Feb **1924** [New York premiere; released Feb; c7 Feb 1924; LP19899]. Si; b&w. 35mm. 7 reels, 6,800 ft.

Pres by Albert E. Smith. *Dir* David Smith. *Scen* Donald Buchanan. *Photog* Stephen Smith, Jr.

Cast: Patsy Ruth Miller *(Molly Marley)*, Dustin Farnum *(Sledge)*, Niles Welch *(Dicky Reynolds)*, Margaret Landis *(Fern Burbank)*, George Webb *(Bert Glider)*, William Norris *(Henry Peters)*, Edith Yorke *(Mrs. Peters)*, Violet Palmer *(Jessie Peters)*, Sidney De Grey *(Christopher Marley)*.

Melodrama. Source: George Randolph Chester, *A Tale of Red Roses* (Indianapolis, c1914). A political boss named Sledge meets a wealthy opponent's daughter, Molly Marley. Sledge determines to win Molly although she is engaged to Bert Glider, a lounge lizard intending to exploit Molly for her money. Unable to convince Molly of Glider's nefarious motives, Sledge kidnaps her on her wedding day and contrives to make it appear that Mr. Marley has lost all of his investments. Glider cancels his marriage plans; Sledge returns Marley's money to him and marries Molly. *Political bosses. Wealth. Courtship.*

MY MAN **F2.3749**

Warner Brothers Pictures. 15 Dec **1928** [c18 Dec 1928; LP25926]. Mus score, sd eff, & talking sequences (Vitaphone); b&w. 35mm. 12 reels, 9,247 ft. [Also si, 12 Jan 1929; 6,136 ft.]

Dir Archie Mayo. *Scen* Robert Lord. *Dial* Joe Jackson. *Titl* Joe Jackson, James A. Starr. *Story* Mark Canfield. *Photog* Frank Kesson. *Film Ed* Owen Marks. *Song: "Second-Hand Rose"* Grant Clarke, James Hanley. *Song: "My Man"* Channing Pollock, Maurice Yvain. *Song: "If You Want a Rainbow, You Must Have the Rain"* Billy Rose, Mort Dixon, Oscar Levant. *Song: "I'm an Indian"* Blanche Merrill, Leo Edwards. *Song: "I Was a Florodora Baby"* Ballard MacDonald, Harry Carroll. *Song: "I'd Rather Be Blue With You Than Happy With Somebody Else"* Billy Rose, Fred Fisher.

Cast: Fanny Brice *(Fannie Brand)*, Guinn Williams *(Joe Halsey)*, Edna Murphy *(Edna Brand)*, André De Segurola *(Landau)*, Richard Tucker *(Waldo)*, Billy Seay *(Sammy)*, Arthur Hoyt *(Thorne)*, Ann Brody *(Mrs. Schultz)*, Clarissa Selwynne *(forelady)*.

Musical drama. Fannie Brand, an industrious girl who supports her brother and sister by working in a theatrical costume house, falls in love with Joe Halsey, a young fellow who earns a precarious living demonstrating an elastic exerciser in a drugstore window. Fannie and Joe set a date to be married, but the wedding is called off when Fannie finds Joe making love to her unprincipled sister, Edna. Fannie auditions for Landau, a theatrical producer, and goes on the Broadway stage. Fannie is a great success, and she and Joe soon find their way back into each other's arms. *Theatrical producers. Costumers. Demonstrators—Commercial products. Sisters. Actors. Theater. Drugstores. New York City—Broadway.*

MY NEIGHBOR'S WIFE **F2.3750**

Clifford S. Elfelt Productions. *Dist* Davis Distributing Division. 21 May **1925** [New York showing; c5 Jan 1926; LP22225]. Si; b&w. 35mm. 6 reels.

Dir Clarence Geldert. *Photog* Joseph Walker.

Cast: E. K. Lincoln *(Jack Newberry)*, Helen Ferguson *(Florence Keaton)*, Edwards Davis *(Mr. Keaton)*, Herbert Rawlinson *(Allen Allwright)*, William Russell *(Eric von Greed)*, William Bailey *(Greed's assistant)*, Chester Conklin *(cameraman)*, Tom Santschi *(inventor)*, Mildred Harris *(inventor's wife)*, Douglas Gerard *(Bertie)*, Margaret Loomis *(Kathlyn Jordan)*, Ralph Faulkner *(William Jordan)*, Philippe De Lacy *(William Jordan, Jr.)*.

Comedy. Source: James Oliver Curwood, "The Other Man's Wife," in *Back to God's Country and Other Stories* (New York, 1920). Jack Newberry, the son of a millionaire trying to make it on his own in the motion picture business, spends his last dime on a property and then borrows $40,000 from his sweetheart's father in order to finance the film. He hires a foreign director, Eric von Greed, to shoot the film, which, to everyone's surprise, is a great success. Having proven himself in the business world, Jack marries his girl. *Millionaires. Motion picture directors. Motion pictures. Hollywood.*

MY OFFICIAL WIFE **F2.3751**

Warner Brothers Pictures. 16 Oct **1926** [c22 Sep 1926; LP23142]. Si; b&w. 35mm. 8 reels, 7,846 ft.

Dir Paul L. Stein. *Adapt* C. Graham Baker. *Camera* David Abel. *Asst Camera* Willard Van Enger. *Asst Dir* Henry Blanke.

Cast: Irene Rich *(Hélène, Countess Orloff)*, Conway Tearle *(Alexander [Sascha])*, Jane Winton *(demimondaine)*, Gustav von Seyffertitz *(grand duke)*, Stuart Holmes *(Ivan)*, John Miljan *(Nicholas)*, Emile Chautard *(Count Orloff, Hélène's father)*, Sidney Bracey *(valet to Sascha)*, Michael Vavitch *(commandant)*, Tom Ford, Russell Ritchie, Tom Costello, Igor Presnikoff *(Sascha's four companions)*.

Romantic melodrama. Source: Archibald Clavering Gunter, *My Official Wife* (a play: publication undetermined). Countess Hélène, who is engaged to Ivan, a dissolute scion of the nobility, attends a masquerade alone and is accosted by six young men of Ivan's set who take her by force to an inn and cast lots for her. Sascha, son of a grand duke, assaults her; and to forestall trouble, his father accuses Hélène of being in league with Nihilists. Following a hearing, she is exiled to Siberia; but the remorseful Sascha arranges to have her rescued and sent to Vienna. There Hélène becomes a cafe dancer, and Sascha, under the name of Alexander, falls in love with her. Her desire for revenge leads her to return to Russia as his "official wife," and he leads her to believe that his friend Nicholas is the guilty party. Before leaving for the war, Sascha discloses his identity; following the Revolution, Sascha flees to Vienna, destitute, and there meets Hélène, who forgives him and finds happiness in his love. *Nobility. Dancers. Nihilists. Revenge. Rape. Personal identity. World War I. Russia. Siberia. Russia—History—1917-21 Revolution. Vienna.*

MY OLD DUTCH (Universal-Jewel) **F2.3752**

Universal Pictures. 23 May **1926** [c10 Apr 1926; LP22593]. Si; b&w. 35mm. 8 reels, 7,750 ft.

Pres by Carl Laemmle. *Dir-Adapt* Lawrence Trimble. *Photog* Edward Gheller.

Cast: May McAvoy *(Sal Gratton)*, Pat O'Malley *(Joe Brown)*, Cullen Landis *(Herbert Brown)*, Jean Hersholt *('Erb 'Uggins)*, Agnes Steele *(Mrs. Shudd)*, Patsy O'Byrne *(Mrs. Smiff)*, Edgar Kennedy *(Bill Sproat)*, Frank Crane *(James Vrayford)*, Rolfe Sedan *(Al)*, Violet Kane *(Mary Avenell, age 3)*, Kathleen O'Malley *(Herbert Brown, infant)*, Sheila O'Malley *(Herbert Brown, age 3)*, Newton Hall *(Herbert Brown, age 12)*, Zama Zameria *(Mrs. Avenell)*, Jane Winton *(Lady Diana Crowes)*, George Siegmann *(workhouse superintendent)*.

Melodrama. Source: Arthur Shirley and Albert Chevalier, *My Old Dutch* (London opening: 1920). Sal Gratton, a London "coster" girl, rejects Bill Sproat, a bully, for Joe Brown, another costermonger with whom she has fallen in love, and they are married. Following the birth of their son, Sal suddenly falls heir to a fortune, and they resolve to spend it all to educate their boy in ignorance of his parentage so that he may become a gentleman. Herbert, after his graduation, becomes a notorious turfman and loses his money; his snobbish fiancée, Lady Diana Crowes, dismisses him; and learning of his parentage, he returns to Sal and Joe penniless. The Great War brings him to his senses, and he is reunited with Diana in a war hospital, softened by the tragedy. Returning to London, Herbert finds that his parents have been evicted and sent to the poorhouse; they are reunited and live happily with their son and Diana. *Costermongers. Turfmen. Marriage. Parentage. Family life. Poorhouses. Social classes. World War I. London.*

MY OLD KENTUCKY HOME **F2.3753**

Pyramid Pictures. *Dist* American Releasing Corp. 9 Apr **1922** [c9 Apr 1922; LP18106]. Si; b&w. 35mm. 7 reels, 7,382 ft.

Ray C. Smallwood Production. *Dir* Ray C. Smallwood. *Story* Anthony Paul Kelly. *Photog* Michael Joyce, Ollie Leach.

Cast: Monte Blue *(Richard Goodloe)*, Julia Swayne Gordon *(Mrs. Goodloe)*, Frank Currier *(Colonel Sanders)*, Sigrid Holmquist *(Virginia Sanders)*, Arthur Carew *("Con" Arnold)*, Lucy Fox *(Calamity Jane)*, Matthew Betz *(Steven McKenna)*, Billy Quirk *(Loney Smith)*, Pat Hartigan *(Detective Monahan)*, Tom Blake *(Nitro Jim)*, Dixie, Corsair, Lightning *(themselves, horses)*.

Melodrama. Released from Sing Sing, to which he was unjustly sentenced, and encouraged by two "sharpers," Richard Goodloe returns to the home of his wealthy southern mother in dread fear that she and Virginia Sanders should learn of his prison record—a fear which is constantly nurtured by his rival, Con Arnold. Richard enlists the aid of his two friends to help Dixie, his mother's horse, win the Kentucky Derby. Realizing Dixie's inability to do so, they substitute Calamity Jane's Lightnin', which does win the race. Arnold exposes the substitution and Richard's past, but his triumph is interrupted by a detective, who arrests Arnold for past crimes. *Swindlers. Southerners. Criminals—Rehabilitation. Horseracing. Kentucky Derby. Horses.*

MY OWN PAL **F2.3754**

Fox Film Corp. 28 Feb **1926** [c14 Feb 1926; LP22399]. Si; b&w. 35mm.

Pres by William Fox. *Dir* J. G. Blystone. *Scen* Lillie Hayward. *Photog* Daniel Clark. *Asst Dir* Jasper Blystone.

Cast: Tom Mix *(Tom O'Hara)*, Olive Borden *(Alice Deering)*, Tom Santschi *(August Deering)*, Virginia Marshall *(Jill)*, Bardson Bard *(Baxter Barton)*, William Colvin *(Jud McIntire)*, Virginia Warwick *(Molly)*, Jay Hunt *(clown)*, Hedda Nova *(Mrs. Jud McIntire)*, Tom McGuire *(Pat McQuire)*, Helen Lynch *(Trixie Tremaine)*, Jacques Rollens *(Slippery Sam)*.

Western melodrama. Source: Gerald Beaumont, "My Own Pal" (publication undetermined). Tom O'Hara, a cowboy, tires of the wide-open spaces and starts out for the city; on the way, he befriends a little girl named Jill, taking her away from her father, the brutal manager of a circus. Once in the city, Tom rescues Alice Deering from a runaway horse and is given a job on the police force by her grateful uncle. Tom arrests a member of a gang of jewel thieves but is later outwitted by the gang, which makes a big killing. Baxter Barton, the leader of the gang, kidnaps Alice, and Tom rides to her rescue, bringing the gang to justice and winning Alice's undying love. *Cowboys. Gangs. Thieves. Police. Robbery. Circus.*

MY PAL **F2.3755**

Arrow Pictures. 30 Aug **1925** [c24 Jun 1925; LP21592]. Si; b&w. 35mm. 5 reels.

Dir Ward Hayes. *Story* Robert Walker, Ward Hayes.

Cast: Dick Hatton, Marilyn Mills, Star *(a horse)*, Beauty *(a horse)*.

Western melodrama. Red Barrett, a brutal cowhand, shoots at Star, a beautiful wild stallion, and wounds him in the thigh. Dick Hammond, who chances upon the horse, gives him water and cares for his wounds; Star, who has known no human kindness for years, becomes devoted to the gentle cowpoke. After a few weeks, Star's wound has healed, and Dick rides him proudly to the Miller ranch, where the newly-tamed stallion is greeted with wonder. Jim Bledso, Miller's foreman, who has been embezzling money from his boss, asks Miller for the hand of his daughter, Marion. Miller consents, but the willful girl, who is in love with Dick, turns him down. The following day, Miller receives notice that his bank account, which should have held $40,000, is overdrawn. He immediately suspects Bledso and is confiding his fears to Dick when Jim walks in and gets the drop on the men, tying them up. Star unties Dick's bonds, and Dick goes after Jim and the other cowhands, finding them in the act of dividing Miller's money. Dick and the cowhands fight, and he is about to be beaten when Miller arrives with the sheriff's men. Jim is arrested, Miller makes Dick the new foreman, and Dick makes Marion his wife. *Cowboys. Ranch foremen. Sheriffs. Embezzlement. Ranches. Horses.*

MY SON **F2.3756**

First National Pictures. 19 Apr **1925** [c1 Apr 1925; LP21291]. Si; b&w. 35mm. 7 reels, 6,552 ft.

Pres by Edwin Carewe. *Dir* Edwin Carewe. *Scen* Finis Fox. *Photog* L. W. O'Connell. *Art Dir* John D. Schulze. *Film Ed* Laurence Croutz. *Asst Dir* Wallace Fox.

Cast: Nazimova *(Ana Silva)*, Jack Pickford *(Tony, her son)*, Hobart Bosworth *(Ellery Parker, the sheriff)*, Ian Keith *(Felipe Vargas, a fisherman)*, Mary Akin *(Rosa Pina)*, Charles Murray *(Capt. Joe Bamby)*, Constance Bennett *(Betty Smith)*, Dot Farley *(Hattie Smith)*.

Domestic drama. Source: Martha M. Stanley, *My Son, a Play in Three Acts* (New York, 1929). In a small New England fishing village populated largely by Portuguese, Ana Silva keeps the general store in order to provide for her adored son, Tony. When a wealthy woman named Hattie Smith arrives in the village for a summer vacation, her daughter, Betty, flirts with Tony and upsets his relationship with his sweetheart, Rosa Pina. Tony falls in love with the irresponsible flapper and steals Mrs. Smith's diamond bracelet in order to finance a tip to New York with Betty. Ana discovers the theft and confronts Tony with the evidence; he attempts to run away, and his mother hits him over the head with a shovel, knocking him unconscious. She then arranges with Captain Bamby for Tony to be taken away on a boat in order to save him from arrest by Sheriff Parker, who has discovered Tony's misdeed. Rosa sails away with Tony on Bamby's boat, and Ana gives her heart to Felipe. *Flappers. Portuguese. Motherhood. Theft. General stores. Fishing villages. New England.*

MY WIFE AND I **F2.3757**

Warner Brothers Pictures. 16 May **1925** [c14 Mar 1925; LP21247]. Si; b&w. 35mm. 7 reels, 7,134 ft.

Dir Millard Webb. *Adapt* Millard Webb, Julien Josephson.

Cast: Irene Rich *(Mrs. James Borden)*, Huntly Gordon *(Mr. James Borden)*, John Harron *(Stuart Borden)*, John Roche *(Spencer Hobart)*, Constance Bennett *(Aileen Alton)*, Tom Ricketts *(valet)*.

Society melodrama. Stuart Borden is infatuated with Aileen Alton, a notorious coquette who is interested only in men and money. When Stuart's debts become too high, his millionaire father cuts him off without a cent, and Aileen dumps him. Aileen later meets Stuart's father and soon has him in her coils. The elder Borden begins to neglect his family, and his wife gradually comes to know of his infidelity. Stuart does not know that his rival for Aileen's affections is his father, and, driven to despair, he goes to Aileen with the intention of killing whatever man he finds with her. Mrs. Borden learns of her son's plans and arrives at Aileen's house just in time to prevent patricide. The Bordens are considerably chastened by this experience and begin life anew, hoping to find peace again within the family circle. *Flirts. Millionaires. Family life. Infidelity. Patricide. Debt.*

MY WILD IRISH ROSE **F2.3758**

Vitagraph Co. of America. ca11 Jun **1922** [New York premiere; released 30 Aug 1922; c25 May 1922; LP17915]. Si; b&w. 35mm. 7 reels, 7,650? ft.

Pres by Albert E. Smith. *Dir* David Smith. *Scen* C. Graham Baker, Harry Dittmar. *Photog* Stephen Smith, Jr.

Cast: Pat O'Malley *(Conn, the Shaughraun)*, Helen Howard *(Arte [Rose?] O'Neale)*, Maud Emery *(Claire Ffolliott)*, Pauline Starke *(Moya)*, Edward Cecil *(Robert Ffolliott)*, Henry Hebert *(Captain Molineaux)*, James Farley *(Corry Kinchella)*, Bobby Mack *(Harvey Duff)*, Frank Clark *(Father Dolan)*, Richard Daniels *(Barry)*.

Melodrama. Source: Dion Boucicault, *The Shaughraun* (1874). Robert Ffolliott, a prominent Fenian of the village of Ballyraggett, is in love with Arte (Rose) O'Neale, who lives with his sister, Claire; but through the trickery of Magistrate Kinchella, he is arrested and sentenced to penal servitude in Australia. Kinchella, who poses as his friend, actually holds the mortgage on the Ffolliot home. Conn, the beloved shaughraun of the district, disguises himself as a sailor, boards the prisoner's vessel, rescues Robert, and returns secretly to Ireland with him. Captain Molineaux learns of his presence, and Robert surrenders under duress. Meanwhile Kinchella receives notification of clemency to be extended to all Fenians surrendering themselves but does not inform Robert. He plots to have him shot while escaping jail, but Conn intervenes and saves him. On the seaside cliffs, Kinchella attacks Arte (Rose), but Robert hurls him to his death. Harvey Duff turns evidence against his patron, and Robert is released; he is united with Arte (Rose), and Conn with Moya. *Fenians. Penal colonies. Ireland.*

MY YIDDISHE MAMA **F2.3759**

Judea Films. 29 May **1930** [New York State license; c4 Oct 1930; LU1641]. Sd (in Yiddish); b&w. 35mm. 5 reels, 4,400 ft. [Also 6 reels, 5,250 ft.]

Dir Sidney M. Goldin.

Cast: Mae Simon.

Domestic drama. Referring to Abraham and Isaac, a prolog stresses the desirability of honoring one's parents, especially mothers, who sacrifice their lives for their children. The story opens with a surprise birthday party for Eddie Rabinowitz given by his parents (David and Mae, played by Mae Simon), his brother (Seymour), and his sister (Helen), all of whom obviously are fond of one other. When David is killed, however, Mae must go to work, and the children cause her no end of anguish: Eddie Stein leads Helen astray, and Seymour spends his mother's money. Years later, Seymour, now a prominent lawyer, hears of a woman abandoned by her children, agrees to force them to support her, and is introduced to his own mother. Mae forgives him, and the family is reunited. *Jews. Lawyers. Widows. Filial relations. Motherhood. Isaac. Abraham.*

Note: May also have been known as *The Yiddish Mama.*

THE MYSTERIOUS DR. FU MANCHU **F2.3760**

Paramount Famous Lasky Corp. 10 Aug **1929** [c9 Aug 1929; LP595]. Sd (Movietone); b&w. 35mm. 8-9 reels, 7,663 ft. [Also si; 7,695 ft.]

Dir Rowland V. Lee. *Screenplay-Dial* Florence Ryerson, Lloyd Corrigan. *Comedy Dial* George Marion, Jr. *Photog* Harry Fischbeck. *Ed Sd Vers* George Nichols, Jr. *Ed Si Vers* Bronson Howard. *Rec Engr* Eugene Merritt.

Cast: Warner Oland *(Dr. Fu Manchu)*, Jean Arthur *(Lia Eltham)*, Neil Hamilton *(Dr. Jack Petrie)*, O. P. Heggie *(Nayland Smith)*, William Austin *(Sylvester Wadsworth)*, Claude King *(Sir John Petrie)*, Charles Stevenson *(General Petrie)*, Noble Johnson *(Li Po)*, Evelyn Selbie *(Fai Lu)*, Charles Giblyn *(Weymouth)*, Donald MacKenzie *(Trent)*, Lawford Davidson *(Clarkson)*, Laska Winter *(Fu Mela)*, Charles Stevens *(Singh)*, Chappell Dossett *(Reverend Mr. Eltham)*, Tully Marshall *(ambassador)*.

Suspense drama. Source: Sax Rohmer, "The Mysterious Dr. Fu Manchu" (publication undetermined). During the Boxer Rebellion, benevolent scientist Dr. Fu Manchu saves the life of little Lia Eltham; but soon after, his own wife and child are killed by the allied troops. Still in shock, he vows to kill an allied officer for each bloodstain on the sacred tapestry-dragon and proceeds in his plan by hypnotizing the now grown Lia to do his bidding. Under Fu's spell, Lia meets and falls in love with Jack Petrie, grandson of an officer whom Fu is determined to kill. The grandfather is mysteriously murdered, and Jack and his father go to their country home, where Fu finds them and kills the elder Petrie. In the meantime, Jack has warned Lia of Fu's nefarious deeds, and both are saved from the doctor's treacherous hands by Lia's kindly Chinese servant. *Scientists. Soldiers. Revenge. Murder. Hypnotism. China—History—Boxer Rebellion.*

MYSTERIOUS GOODS **F2.3761**

Charles R. Seeling Productions. *Dist* Aywon Film Corp. Oct **1923.** Si; b&w. 35mm. 5 reels, ca4,800 ft.

Dir Charles R. Seeling.

Cast: George Larkin, Ollie Kirby.

Melodrama. "... the adventures of a detective on the trail of the stolen plans for a valuable invention. The climax is reached in a scene where the detective meets the crooks in a hand-to-hand encounter in a wagon. The horses run wild and the hero narrowly escapes death as they gallop along a railroad track toward an approaching express train." (*Motion Picture News Booking Guide,* 6:49, Apr 1924.) *Detectives. Inventions. Railroads. Documentation.*

THE MYSTERIOUS ISLAND **F2.3762**

Metro-Goldwyn-Mayer Pictures. 5 Oct **1929** [c28 Oct 1929; LP799]. Talking sequence, mus score, & sd eff (Movietone); col (Technicolor) with b&w sequences. 35mm. 10 reels, 8,569 ft. [Also si.]

Dir-Screenplay Lucien Hubbard. *Adtl Dir (see note)* Maurice Tourneur, Benjamin Christensen. *Photog* Percy Hilburn. *Art Dir* Cedric Gibbons. *Film Ed* Carl L. Pierson. *Mus Score* Martin Broones, Arthur Lange. *Rec Engr* Douglas Shearer. *Tec Eff* James Basevi, Louis H. Tolhurst, Irving Ries.

Cast: Lionel Barrymore *(Dakkar)*, Jane Daly *(Sonia)*, Lloyd Hughes *(Nikolai)*, Montagu Love *(Falon)*, Harry Gribbon *(Mikhail)*, Snitz Edwards *(Anton)*, Gibson Gowland *(Dmitry)*, Dolores Brinkman *(Teresa)*.

Adventure melodrama. Source: Jules Verne, *L'Isle mysterieuse* (Paris, 1874). In the Kingdom of Hetvia, in 1850, Count Dakkar devotes his life and fortune to probing the mysteries of the ocean depths by constructing two submarines on his island off the mainland. Falon, a nobleman, is anxious to overthrow the throne by revolution and seeks the inventor's aid; failing, he captures Dakkar and his crew while his assistant, Nikolai, is testing one of the sea craft; but Dakkar's men rescue him from torture. Falon's men damage the submarine, which descends to the ocean floor, where Dakkar's party observe an underground city populated by strange creatures whose gratitude they win by slaying a dragon with torpedoes. Sonia, Dakkar's sister, wrecks the other submarine in a battle with Falon's men, and Falon's blood incites the underwater creatures to divert an octopus that mortally wounds Dakkar. After the island is recaptured, Dakkar willingly chooses burial in his submarine. *Nobility. Scientists. Oceanography. Submarines. Revolutions. Imaginary kingdoms. Octopi.*

Note: Some footage shot by Maurice Tourneur, then by Benjamin Christiansen, in 1927, was incorporated in the final production.

THE MYSTERIOUS LADY **F2.3763**

Metro-Goldwyn-Mayer Pictures. 4 Aug **1928** [c11 Aug 1928; LP25530]. Si; b&w. 35mm. 9 reels, 7,652 ft.

Dir Fred Niblo. *Adapt-Cont* Bess Meredyth. *Titl* Marian Ainslee, Ruth Cummings. *Photog* William Daniels. *Sets* Cedric Gibbons. *Film Ed* Margaret Booth. *Asst Dir* Harold S. Bucquet. *Wardrobe* Gilbert Clark.

Cast: Greta Garbo *(Tania)*, Conrad Nagel *(Karl von Heinersdorff)*, Gustav von Seyffertitz *(General Alexandroff)*, Albert Pollet *(Max)*, Edward Connelly *(Colonel von Raden)*, Richard Alexander *(aide to the general)*.

Romantic drama. Source: Ludwig Wolff, *Der Krieg im Dunkel* (Berlin, 1915). Tania, an exotic St. Petersburg spy, falls in love with an Austrian captain, Karl von Heinersdorff, while taking some important documents from him. Karl is imprisoned for the loss of the papers but escapes to find Tania, to whom he affirms his love. Tania then turns traitor and delivers to Heinersdorff some papers formerly in the possession of her superior, General Alexandroff. The general discovers the theft, and Tania shoots him, after which she and Karl escape to Austria. *Spies. Traitors. Saint Petersburg. Austria. Russia. Documentation.*

MYSTERIOUS RIDER **F2.3764**

Zane Grey Pictures. *Dist* W. W. Hodkinson Corp. 23 Oct **1921.** Si; b&w. 35mm. 6 reels, 5,500 ft.

Dir Benjamin B. Hampton. *Photog* Gus Peterson, F. H. Sturges.

Cast: Robert McKim *(Hell Bent Wade)*, Claire Adams *(Columbine)*, Carl Gantvoort *(Wilson Moore)*, James Mason *(Jack Bellounds)*, Walt Whitman *(Bellounds)*, Frederick Starr *(Ed Smith)*, Maude Wayne *(Madge Smith)*, Frank Hayes *("Smokey Joe" Lem Billings)*, Aggie Herring *(Maria, the cook)*.

Drama. Source: Zane Grey, *The Mysterious Rider* (New York, 1921). Columbine, though in love with foreman Wilson Moore, agrees—out of gratitude to her foster father, Bellounds—to marry the ranchowner's ne'er-do-well son, Jack Bellounds. While Wilson becomes friends with the ever-present Mysterious Rider (Hell Bent Wade), Jack is ensnared by Madge and Ed Smith into a scheme to rustle cattle from his father. The blame for the stolen stock falls on Wilson, and in the ensuing events Wade recognizes Ed Smith to be the murderer of his wife and discovers Columbine to be his long-lost daughter. Wade kills Smith in a fight, Wilson is cleared, Jack is exposed, and Columbine is united with her true love. *Orphans. Ranchers. Ranch foremen. Ne'er-do-wells. Rustling. Gambling. Parentage.*

THE MYSTERIOUS RIDER **F2.3765**

Famous Players–Lasky. *Dist* Paramount Pictures. 5 Mar **1927** [c5 Mar 1927; LP23736]. Si; b&w. 35mm. 6 reels, 5,957 ft.

Pres by Adolph Zukor, Jesse L. Lasky. *Assoc Prod* B. P. Schulberg. *Dir* John Waters. *Screenplay* Fred Myton, Paul Gangelin. *Titl* Alfred Hustwick. *Photog* C. Edgar Schoenbaum.

Cast: Jack Holt *(Bent Wade)*, Betty Jewel *(Dorothy King)*, Charles Sellon *(Cliff Harkness)*, David Torrence *(Mark King)*, Tom Kennedy *(Lem Spooner)*, Guy Oliver *(Jack Wilson)*, Albert Hart *(sheriff)*, Ivan Christie *(Tom Saunders)*, Arthur Hoyt *(King's secretary)*.

Western melodrama. Source: Zane Grey, *The Mysterious Rider* (New York, 1921). In the California desert, homesteaders who are struggling for an existence find their land titles are jeopardized when Cliff Harkness obtains a Spanish land grant superseding their claims. He offers to sell them his title for $25,000; Bent Wade advises them to buy off Harkness, and after desperate efforts the money is turned over to Wade. Meanwhile, Mark King, a city capitalist representing a power company, offers Harkness a much larger sum; Harkness doublecrosses Wade by signing his receipt with disappearing ink and resells the land to King. Faced with eviction, the homesteaders try to lynch Wade, but his friend Lem intervenes and he is jailed. Wade escapes and goes from ranch to ranch, warning the ranchers not to give up their homes without a legal fight; he threatens Harkness with torture, forces him to confess his treachery, and proves the original receipt is legal. He finds happiness with King's daughter, Dorothy. *Homesteaders. Capitalists. Power companies. Land grants. Deserts. California. Documentation.*

THE MYSTERIOUS STRANGER **F2.3766**

Carlos Productions. *Dist* Film Booking Offices of America. 5 Jul **1925.** Si; b&w. 35mm. 6 reels, 5,270 ft.

Dir Jack Nelson. *Scen* James Bell Smith.

Cast: Richard Talmadge *(Paul Lesage)*, Joseph Swickard *(Raoul Lesage)*, Carmelita Geraghty *(April Lesage)*, Sheldon Lewis *(Herman Bennett)*, Duane Thompson *(Helen Dresden)*, Bert Bradley *(Arnold)*, Robert Carleton *(chauffeur)*.

Action melodrama. Raoul Lesage suspects his wife, April, of infidelity with Herman Bennett, an artist, and forsakes her, living for the next 20 years in a hermitage surrounded by high walls. He is accompanied in this solitary life only by his young son, Paul, who, at the age of 21, has not seen anything of women or the world. One night, Paul walks in his sleep and wanders from his home. He falls into the company of his mother (whom he does not recognize), Bennett, and Bennett's beautiful ward, Helen, with whom Paul soon falls in love. After a series of thrilling adventures, Paul foils Bennett and reunites his parents; he and Helen hear wedding bells. *Artists. Hermits. Wards. Filial relations. Infidelity. Somnambulism.*

THE MYSTERIOUS WITNESS **F2.3767**

R-C Pictures. *Dist* Film Booking Offices of America. 24 Jun **1923** [c24 Jun 1923; LP19192]. Si; b&w. 35mm. 5 reels, 4,850 ft.

Dir Seymour Zeliff.

Cast: Robert Gordon *(Johnny Brant)*, Elinor Fair *(Ruth Garland)*, Nanine Wright *(Mrs. John Brant)*, Jack Connolly *(Ed Carney)*, J. Wharton James *(Jim Garland)*.

Western melodrama. Source: Eugene Manlove Rhodes, *The Stepsons of Light* (Boston, 1921). Young cowpuncher Johnny Brant is sending money home to his mother but is thought to be a miser by the ranch foreman, who abuses Brant, giving him all the worst jobs. Brant is in love with the rancher's daughter, Ruth, who is being courted by the foreman. When Brant is framed for the rancher's murder, the foreman sends for Brant's mother and forces her to give up her money to save Brant, but Brant discovers that the foreman is the real culprit. *Cowboys. Ranch foremen. Frameup. Murder. Filial relations.*

THE MYSTERY BRAND **F2.3768**

Ben Wilson Productions. *Dist* Rayart Pictures. Jan **1927.** Si; b&w. 35mm. 5 reels, 4,763-4,800 ft.

Dir Ben Wilson.

Cast: Ben Wilson, Neva Gerber.

Western melodrama. "Hero and villain love same girl. Hero is made sheriff and starts out on trail of cattle rusters. Discovers them but is overcome; girl rescues him and he resumes chase. Tries to capture them, is beaten again, but girl brings up posse and tables are turned. Villain is chief rustler." (*Motion Picture News Booking Guide*, 12:45, Apr 1927.) *Sheriffs. Rustlers. Posses.*

THE MYSTERY CLUB (Universal-Jewel) **F2.3769**

Universal Pictures. 12 Sep **1926** [c24 Jun 1926; LP22855]. Si; b&w. 35mm. 7 reels, 6,969 ft.

Pres by Carl Laemmle. *Dir* Herbert Blache. *Scen* Helen Broderick, Edward J. Montagne. *Photog* Jackson Rose.

Cast: Matt Moore *(Dick Bernard)*, Edith Roberts *(Nancy Darrell)*, Mildred Harris *(Mrs. Kate Vanderveer)*, Charles Lane *(John Cranahan)*, Warner Oland *(Eli Sinsabaugh)*, Henry Herbert *(Scott Glendenning)*, Charles Puffy *(Alonzo)*, Alphonse Martell *(Sengh)*, Finch Smiles *(Wilkins)*, Earl Metcalf *(Red)*, Nat Carr *(Eric Hudson)*, Jed Prouty *(Amos Herriman)*, Alfred Allen *(Inspector Burke)*, Sidney Bracey *(detective)*, Monte Montague *(Snaky)*.

Mystery melodrama. Source: Arthur Somers Roche, "The Crimes of the Armchair Club," in *Hearst's* (vols 35-37, Apr 1919-Mar 1920). The Mystery Club, an organization of millionaires, draws up an agreement at the instigation of Cranahan, wagering that crimes can be committed without detection by the police; Inspector Burke serves as arbiter. A forfeiture of $25,000 is set, and the members draw secret lots to decide who is to be the criminal. When Burke himself is reported murdered, the members agree to cancel the agreement but cannot find the document. The jewels of Mrs. Vanderveer are also missing, and in their place she finds a note implicating the club and causing the members to suspect one another. Nancy telephones club member Dick Bernard, her sweetheart, that the jewels will be returned for a fee, which Dick delivers to her in a low dive; subsequently, a kidnaping and forgery charge is laid at the club's door. Cranahan finally explains that he has schemed to get the club members interested in criminology, and thus relieved of their "crimes" they gladly contribute to an institute for criminal reform. *Millionaires. Wagers. Forgery. Robbery. Kidnaping. Hoaxes. Criminology. Clubs. Documentation.*

THE MYSTERY OF LOST RANCH **F2.3770**

Vitagraph Co. of America. c13 Jun **1925** [LP21550]. Si; b&w. 35mm. 5 reels.

Dir Harry S. Webb, Tom Gibson. *Cont* George Hull. *Story* Barr Cross.

Cast: Pete Morrison.

Western melodrama. Two men claiming to be scientists arrive in Colorado looking for Blair, a fellow scientist who disappeared while developing a death ray. The men hire Pete, who finds Blair living with his daughter on a ranch in an inaccessible valley near the Grand Canyon, where the scientist is testing his ray on birds and wild animals. Pete then discovers that the two men from the East are, in reality, agents of a foreign government, who hope to steal Blair's invention. Pete quickly sides with Blair, defeating the foreign agents with the help of Blair's daughter, whom he comes to love. Pete hands the agents over to law officers and returns to the ranch in Lost Valley. *Scientists. Foreign agents. Inventions. Death rays. Colorado. Grand Canyon.*

THE MYSTERY OF TUT-ANKH-AMEN'S EIGHTH WIFE *see* **KING TUT-ANKH-AMEN'S EIGHTH WIFE**

MYSTERY RIDER **F2.3771**

Dist Associated Independent Producers. 28 Jun **1928** [New York State license]. Si; b&w. 35mm. 5 reels, 4,500 ft.

Dir-Scen Robert J. Horner. *Titl* Bert Ames. *Photog* Paul Allen. *Film Ed* Frank Penrock.

Cast: Pawnee Bill Jr., Bruce Gordon, Bud Osborne.

Western melodrama(?). No information about the nature of this film has been found.

THE MYSTERY ROAD (United States/Great Britain) **F2.3772**

Famous Players–Lasky British Producers. *Dist* Paramount Pictures. 10 Jul **1921** [c14 Jul 1921; LP16761]. Si; b&w. 35mm. 5 reels, 4,965 ft.

Dir Paul Powell. *Scen* Margaret Turnbull. *Adapt* Mary Hamilton O'Connor. *Photog* Hal Young.

Cast: David Powell *(Gerald Dombey)*, Nadja Ostrovska *(Myrtile Sargot)*, Pardoe Woodman *(Christopher Went)*, Mary Glynne *(Lady Susan Farrington)*, Ruby Miller *(Vera Lypasht)*, Percy Standing *(Luigi)*, Lewis

Gilbert *(Jean Sargot)*, Irene Tripod *(Widow Dumesnel)*, Lionel D'Aragon *(Pierre Naval)*, Arthur Cullen *(Earl of Farrington)*, R. Judd Green *(The Vagabond)*, Ralph Forster *(The Priest)*.

Society melodrama. Source: Edward Phillips Oppenheim, *The Mystery Road* (Boston, 1923). Gerald Dombey confesses to his fiancée, Lady Susan Farrington, that while in southern England he has had an affair with a peasant girl, Vera Lypasht. Later, while motoring to Nice accompanied by his friend Christopher Went, he encounters Myrtile Sargot, a girl who has left home to escape parental abuse; eventually he persuades Lady Susan to give her refuge, though Susan is mistrustful of the arrangement. One night in a cafe, Gerald again meets Vera with her "brother" Luigi, and thereafter he continues to see her. When Gerald discovers that Luigi is her lover and that Christopher has fallen in love with Susan, he attempts suicide; but he is deterred when he realizes that he is in love with Myrtile. *Infidelity. Parenthood. Suicide. Nice.*

MYSTERY VALLEY **F2.3773**

Trem Carr Productions. *Dist* Rayart Pictures. Jul **1928.** Si; b&w. 35mm. 5 reels, 4,538 ft.

Dir-Scen J. P. McGowan. *Titl* Erma Horsley. *Photog* Hap Depew. *Film Ed* Erma Horsley.

Cast: Buddy Roosevelt, Carol Lane, Tommy Bay, Jimmy Kane, Art Rowlands.

Western melodrama. Source: Howard E. Morgan, "Snow Dust" (publication undetermined). "Owner of San Cristobal ranch is shot while writing his son that the only proof to the ranch title is grant hidden in house. The son returns to find that local gambler has taken over property. After gold has been discovered on his father's land, the boy and girl he has met wage a pitched battle with gang, and unearth proof that gambler killed father." *(Motion Picture News Booking Guide,* [14]:268, 1929.) *Gamblers. Ranches. Land grants. Documentation. Gold.*

THE MYSTIC **F2.3774**

Metro-Goldwyn-Mayer Pictures. 27 Sep **1925** [c11 Sep 1925; LP21824]. Si; b&w. 35mm. 7 reels, 6,147 ft.

Story-Dir Tod Browning. *Scen* Waldemar Young. *Photog* Ira Morgan. *Sets* Cedric Gibbons, Hervey Libbert. *Film Ed* Frank Sullivan.

Cast: Aileen Pringle *(Zara)*, Conway Tearle *(Michael Nash)*, Mitchell Lewis *(Zazarack)*, Robert Ober *(Anton)*, Stanton Heck *(Carlo)*, David Torrence *(Bradshaw)*, Gladys Hulette *(Doris Merrick)*, De Witt Jennings *(inspector of police)*.

Drama. Michael Nash, an American crook, arranges for three Hungarian Gypsies to come to the United States, having them then stage a seance that enables him to gain control over the wealth of Doris Merrick, a beautiful and unsuspecting heiress. They raise the spirit of her late father and thereby expose the crooked dealings of Bradshaw, Doris' guardian. Overcome by a fit of conscience, Michael later returns Doris' money. The police deport the Gypsies, and Michael follows them to their native country, declaring his love for one of their number, Zara, who fully returns his affection. *Guardians. Gypsies. Heiresses. Swindlers. Police. Deportation. Spiritualism. Hungary.*

THE NAKED TRUTH *see* **T. N. T. (THE NAKED TRUTH)**

NAME THE MAN **F2.3775**

Goldwyn Pictures. *Dist* Goldwyn-Cosmopolitan Distributing Corp. 15 Jan **1924** [Trade screening; released 27 Jan; c15 Jan 1924; LP19824]. Si; b&w. 35mm. 8 reels, 7,771 ft.

Dir Victor Seastrom. *Ed Dir* June Mathis. *Scen* Paul Bern. *Photog* Charles Van Enger.

Cast: Mae Busch *(Bessie Collister)*, Conrad Nagel *(Victor Stowell)*, Hobart Bosworth *(Christian Stowell)*, Creighton Hale *(Alick Gell)*, Patsy Ruth Miller *(Fenella Stanley)*, Winter Hall *(Governor Stanley)*, Aileen Pringle *(Isabelle)*, De Witt Jennings *(Dan Collister)*, Evelyn Selbie *(Lisa Collister)*, Mark Fenton *(Constable Cain)*, Anna Hernandez *(Mrs. Quayle)*, Mrs. Charles Craig *(Mrs. Brown)*, Cecil Holland *(coroner)*, Lucien Littlefield *(Sharf)*, William Orlamond *(Taubman)*, Charles Mailes *(attorney general)*, Andrew Arbuckle *(Vondy)*.

Melodrama. Source: Hall Caine, *The Master of Man; the Story of a Sin* (New York & Philadelphia, 1921). Victor Stowell, son of the deemster of the Isle of Man, is engaged to Fenella Stanley. He becomes involved in an intrigue with local girl Bessie Collister, becomes the deemster on his father's death, and is forced to try Bessie for killing her illegitimate child. When Bessie refuses to name the father of the baby, Fenella and Alick Gell, who loves Bessie, guess that it is Victor. Bessie is condemned to die, but Victor helps her escape to meet and marry Alick. He then confesses all, serves a jail sentence, and marries Fenella at the expiration of the term. *Judges. Infanticide. Parentage. Illegitimacy. Isle of Man.*

NAME THE WOMAN **F2.3776**

Columbia Pictures. 25 May **1928** [c29 Jun 1928; LP25477]. Si; b&w. 35mm. 6 reels, 5,544 ft.

Prod Harry Cohn. *Dir-Writ* Erle C. Kenton. *Cont* Peter Milne. *Adapt* Elmer Harris. *Photog* Ben Reynolds. *Art Dir* Joseph Wright. *Film Ed* Ben Pivar. *Asst Dir* Charles C. Coleman.

Cast: Anita Stewart *(Florence)*, Huntly Gordon *(Marshall)*, Gaston Glass *(Joe Arnold)*, Chappell Dossett *(judge)*, Julanne Johnston *(Nina Palmer)*, Jed Prouty *(Sam Palmer)*.

Drama. Source: Erle C. Kenton, "Bridge" (publication undetermined). On trial for murder, Joe Arnold is acquitted when a masked lady, the wife of Prosecuting Attorney Marshall, who was with him the night the murder occurred (during Mardi Gras festivities), risks her reputation and her husband's position by testifying in Arnold's behalf. Arnold is freed, and Marshall resigns his office, realizing that his wife's misconduct is a reflection of his own neglect. *District attorneys. Murder. Infidelity. Trials. Mardi Gras.*

NAMELESS MEN **F2.3777**

Tiffany-Stahl Productions. 15 Feb **1928** [c24 Feb 1928; LP25004]. Si; b&w. 35mm. 6 reels, 5,708 ft.

Dir Christy Cabanne. *Scen* John Francis Natteford. *Titl* Viola Brothers Shore, Harry Braxton. *Story* E. Morton Hough. *Photog* Chester Lyons. *Set Dsgn* Burgess Beal. *Film Ed* Martin G. Cohn.

Cast: Claire Windsor *(Mary)*, Antonio Moreno *(Bob)*, Eddie Gribbon *(Blackie)*, Ray Hallor *(Hughie)*, Charles Clary *(Mac)*, Carolynne Snowden *(maid)*, Sally Rand, Stepin Fetchit.

Underworld drama. Detective Robert Strong serves a 6-month "prison term" so as to gain the confidence of Hugh Cameron, a youth who participated in a robbery, and thus find out where the money is hidden. Serving the last few months of his 2-year term, Hugh confides to Strong the name of his partner, Blackie, who was not caught, and arranges to meet Strong at a certain hotel on his release. Something in his manner causes Blackie and Hugh to suspect Strong, who has fallen in love with Hugh's sister, Mary. The two crooks bind Strong and Mary and go to claim the money, hidden in the floor of a bank building. Blackie returns to kidnap Mary, having been doublecrossed by Hugh; but Strong escapes, shoots it out with Blackie on his getaway boat, and recovers Mary. Hughie gets off lightly, and all ends happily. *Detectives. Brother-sister relationship. Robbery. Prisons. Banks.*

NANCY FROM NOWHERE **F2.3778**

Realart Pictures. *Dist* Paramount Pictures. 22 Jan **1922** [c7 Feb 1922; LP17546]. Si; b&w. 35mm. 5 reels, 5,167 ft.

Dir Chester M. Franklin. *Adapt* Douglas Doty. *Photog* George Folsey.

Cast: Bebe Daniels *(Nancy)*, Edward Sutherland *(Jack Halliday)*, Vera Lewis *(Mrs. Kelly)*, James Gordon *(Mr. Kelly)*, Myrtle Stedman *(Mrs. Halliday)*, Alberta Lee *(Martha)*, Helen Holly *(Elizabeth Doane)*, Dorothy Hagan *(Mrs. Doane)*.

Comedy-melodrama. Source: Grace Drew Brown and Katherine Pinkerton, "Spring Fever" (publication undetermined). Nancy, who is adopted from an orphanage by the Kellys, is reared in sordid surroundings and mistreated as the household drudge. She accidentally makes the acquaintance of Jack Halliday, son of a wealthy city family who is fishing near her home. When Mrs. Kelly beats Nancy for accepting the attentions of her husband, the girl escapes into the woods and conceals herself in the rear of Jack's car as he drives into the city. Arriving home, Jack discovers her and orders a beautiful new wardrobe for her. Jack's fiancée, Elizabeth, infuriated, recalls his parents from their trip; and while he is out buying flowers for Nancy, they persuade her that she can bring only unhappiness to their son. In her old garments she returns to the Kelly shack, where Jim Kelly tries to attack her; but Jack arrives to rescue her, and they are happily united. *Drudges. Orphans. Social classes. Adoption. Courtship.*

NANOOK OF THE NORTH **F2.3779**

Revillon Frères. *Dist* Pathé Exchange. 11 Jun **1922** [c17 May 1922; LU17888]. Si; b&w. 35mm. 6 reels.

Dir-Scen-Photog Robert Flaherty. *Titl* Carl Stearns Clancy, Robert Flaherty. *Asst Film Ed* Charles Gelb.

Personages: Nanook, Nyla, Allee, Cunayou, Comock.

Educational documentary. Nanook and his family typify Eskimo life in the Arctic. Their continuous search for food necessitates their nomadic life. In the summer they journey to the river to fish for salmon and hunt walrus. In the winter they often approach starvation before any food is found. At night the entire family assists in building an igloo, then crawl under fur robes to sleep, using their clothes for pillows. In the morning the quest continues. *Eskimos. Nomads. Fishing. Arctic regions.*

THE NARROW STREET **F2.3780**

Warner Brothers Pictures. Oct **1924** [or 11 Jan 1925; c14 Oct 1924; LP20667]. Si; b&w. 35mm. 7 reels, 6,700 ft.

Dir William Beaudine. *Scen* Julien Josephson. *Photog* Ray June.

Cast: Matt Moore *(Simon Haldane)*, Dorothy Devore *(Doris)*, David Butler *(Ray Wyeth)*, George Pearce *(Edgar Deems)*, Russell Simpson *(Garvey)*, Gertrude Short *(Nell Mangan)*, Joe Butterworth *(office boy)*, Kate Toncray *(Aunt Albina)*, Tempe Pigott *(Aunt Agnes)*, Madame Sul-Te-Wan *(Easter)*.

Light comedy. Source: Edwin Bateman Morris, *The Narrow Street* (Philadelphia, 1924). Carefully sheltered by his maiden aunts and afraid of his own shadow, Simon Haldane is stunned to find a strange girl in his bedroom one morning, but he chivalrously summons a doctor to administer to her chill. The word leaks out that Simon is married, and the whole office staff of the Faulkner Iron Works visit Simon to have a look at Doris. Breezy salesman Ray Wyeth turns Doris' head for a while, but Simon—with newfound courage—not only wins her back but also emerges as manager in an office shakeup. Learning that Doris is the daughter of his employer, Simon falters briefly, but Doris saves the situation. *Aunts. Timidity. Ironworks. Factory management.*

Note: Remade by Warner Brothers in 1930 as *Wide Open* with Edward Everett Horton and Patsy Ruth Miller.

NAUGHTY **F2.3781**

Chadwick Pictures. *Dist* First Division Distributors. 15 Aug **1927.** Si; b&w. 35mm. 6 reels, 4,667 ft.

Pres by I. E. Chadwick. *Dir-Story-Scen* Hampton Del Ruth. *Titl* Jean La'Ple. *Photog* Ernest Miller.

Cast: Pauline Garon, Johnny Harron, Walter Hiers.

Farce. "A girl is told by a fortune-teller that she will go on a vacation, meet a doctor, fall in love with him and so on. She does. They are married by a burglar in a minister's garb. They go home and the husband is called away by the very same burglar and a fat boy friend spends the night there, as hubby is out in a driving rain in his car. He and the wifey are shown together in several scenes, each in sleeping attire, pajamas to be explicit and a lead up to where the wife taps on the wall for the fat boy to come to her room. He does and even edges close to her bed at her request, only to be told there's a man under the bed. Hubby returns. Friend is holding wifey who has fainted. The mistaken situation gag with the captured burglar helping straighten things." (*Variety,* 12 Oct 1927, p21.) *Physicians. Fortune-tellers. Burglars. Marriage. Imposture.*

NAUGHTY BABY **F2.3782**

First National Pictures. 19 Jan **1929** [c10 Dec 1928; LP25900]. Sd eff & mus score (Vitaphone); b&w. 35mm. 7 reels, 6,360 ft. [Also si, 16 Dec 1928; 6,406 ft.]

Pres by Richard A. Rowland. *Dir* Mervyn LeRoy. *Scen* Tom Geraghty. *Titl* Tom Geraghty, Gerald Geraghty. *Story* Charles Beahan, Garrett Fort. *Photog* Ernest Haller. *Film Ed* LeRoy Stone.

Cast: Alice White *(Rosalind McGill)*, Jack Mulhall *(Terry Vandeveer)*, Thelma Todd *(Bonnie Le Vonne)*, Doris Dawson *(Polly)*, James Ford *(Terry's pal)*, Natalie Joyce *(Goldie Torres)*, Frances Hamilton *(Bonnie's pal)*, Fred Kelsey *(Dugan)*, Rose Dione *(Madame Fleurette)*, Fanny Midgley *(Mary Ellen Toolen)*, Larry Banthim *(Toolen)*, Georgie Stone *(Tony Caponi)*, Benny Rubin *(Benny Cohen)*, Andy Devine *(Joe Cassidy)*.

Comedy-drama. Rosie McGill, a hat snatcher at a posh hotel, sets her cap for wealthy Terry Vandeveer and goes to Long Beach, where she masquerades as a society girl; as expected, she meets Terry there, and he is greatly attracted to her. Back in the city, Rosie quits her job and then is quickly exposed as a fraud at a fancy party. As she is telling Terry the truth about herself, it appears from a large check that bounces that Terry is also a fraud. Rosie sticks by him, however, and wins his love. His uncle then appears and explains that Terry's check bounced only because his substantial allowance had been temporarily cut off. Terry and Rosie look forward to a long and prosperous life together. *Checkgirls. Uncles. Imposture. Wealth. Hotels. Long Beach.*

NAUGHTY BUT NICE **F2.3783**

John McCormick Productions. *Dist* First National Pictures. 26 Jun **1927** [c11 Jun 1927; LP24067]. Si; b&w. 35mm. 7 reels, 6,520 ft.

Pres by John McCormick. *Dir* Millard Webb. *Scen* Carey Wilson. *Photog* George Folsey.

Cast: Colleen Moore *(Berenice Summers)*, Donald Reed *(Paul Carroll)*, Claude Gillingwater *(Judge John R. Altwold)*, Kathryn McGuire *(Alice Altwold)*, Hallam Cooley *(Ralph Ames)*, Edythe Chapman *(Mrs. Altwold)*, Clarissa Selwynne *(Miss Perkins)*, Burr McIntosh *(Uncle Seth Summers)*.

Romantic comedy. Source: Lewis Allen Browne, "The Bigamists" (publication undetermined). Berenice Summers, a plain, bespectacled girl, gains freedom from her uncle's Texas ranch when oil is discovered on his property, and she invades an eastern finishing school, there blossoming from an unnoticed wallflower into a stunning beauty. Berenice and her friend encounter the school principal in the lobby of a hotel where they are to meet Paul Carroll for a theater date and invent a story about visiting Alice's parents, Judge and Mrs. Altwold. To make their bluff good, they enter the room of Ralph Ames of the Secret Service; Berenice introduces the stranger as her husband, and the girls leave with the judge and his wife. Through a series of coincidences, Berenice and Ames meet at the judge's house, with resulting entanglements. Berenice sleeps on the roof, is chased by a policeman, and is ultimately united with Paul Carroll in marriage. *Judges. Secret service. Mistaken identity. Personality. Boarding schools.*

THE NAUGHTY DUCHESS **F2.3784**

Tiffany-Stahl Productions. 10 Oct **1928** [c3 Oct 1928; LP25690]. Si; b&w. 35mm. 6 reels, 5,271 ft.

Dir-Adapt-Cont Tom Terriss. *Titl* Frederick Hatton, Fanny Hatton. *Photog (see note)* Ernest Miller, Chester Lyons. *Film Ed* Leete Renick.

Cast: Eve Southern *(Hortense)*, H. B. Warner *(Duke de St. Maclou)*, Duncan Renaldo *(Armand)*, Maude Turner Gordon *(Comtesse)*, Gertrude Astor *(Ninon)*, Martha Mattox *(housekeeper)*, Herbert Evans *(Berensac)*.

Romantic melodrama. Source: Anthony Hope Hawkins, *The Indiscretion of the Duchess; Being a Story Concerning Two Ladies, a Nobleman, and a Necklace* (New York, 1894). As the train carrying the Duke de St. Maclou is leaving the Gare du Nord, a beautiful, veiled woman enters his compartment, informs him that she has just murdered a man to protect her honor, and begs him for help. A detective arrives moments later, and the duke pretends that the veiled lady is his wife. The detective stays on the train, and the duke and his "duchess," Hortense, are forced to continue the deception. Arriving at his chateau, they are greeted as man and wife, and the duke must invent an argument with his "bride" to provide an excuse for not sharing the bridal suite with her. The detective arrives the next day and, identifying Hortense, informs the worried duke that she is wanted only as a witness in a case pending in civil court. Hortense is allowed to remain in the duke's custody, and he decides to make her his duchess in fact. *Nobility. Detectives. Murder. Imposture. Trains.*

Note: Chester Lyons is credited by *Variety* with the photography; Ernest Miller is credited by other sources.

NAUGHTY NANETTE **F2.3785**

R-C Pictures. *Dist* Film Booking Offices of America. 15 Apr **1927** [c15 Apr 1927; LP23888]. Si; b&w. 35mm. 5 reels, 5,051 ft.

Pres by Joseph P. Kennedy. *Dir* James Leo Meehan. *Cont* Doris Schroeder. *Story* Charles H. Smith. *Photog* Allen Siegler. *Asst Dir* Charles Kerr.

Cast: Viola Dana *(Nanette Pearson)*, Patricia Palmer *(Lola Leeds)*, Edward Brownell *(Bob Dennison)*, Helen Foster *(Lucy Dennison)*, Joe Young *(Bill Simmons)*, Sidney De Gray *(Grandfather Dennison)*, Alphonse Martel *(Carlton)*, Mary Gordon *(Mrs. Rooney)*, Florence Wix *(Mrs. Trainor)*, Barbara Clayton *(Dorothy Trainor)*.

Comedy-drama. Nanette, an extra in a Hollywood studio, finds a poor girl, Lucy Dennison, on the set. Lucy's wealthy grandfather has broken up her parents and left her homeless because her mother was once a chorus girl. Lucy becomes ill, and Nanette loses her job at the studio; Nanette, who has previously met Bob Dennison, decides to impersonate Lucy and get into the good graces of the grandfather, but Lola Leeds, a jealous actress who comes to Santa Barbara on location, exposes her as an imposter. Nanette confesses to the grandfather, who agrees to take in Lucy but refuses to consent to the marriage of Bob and Nanette. Bob and Bill—a former sweetheart of Nanette—chase her train in a flivver, and the lovers are happily united. *Actors. Motion picture extras. Grandfathers. Chorus girls. Impersonation. Wealth. Motion pictures. Courtship. Hollywood. Santa Barbara. Chases.*

THE NAVIGATOR **F2.3786**

Metro-Goldwyn Pictures. 13 Oct **1924** [c14 Oct 1924; LP20689]. Si; b&w. 35mm. 6 reels, 5,600 ft.

Pres by Joseph M. Schenck. *Dir* Donald Crisp, Buster Keaton. *Story-Titl* Clyde Bruckman, Joseph Mitchell, Jean Havez. *Photog* Elgin Lessley, Byron Houck. *Electrn* Denver Harmon. *Tech Dir* Fred Gabourie.

Cast: Buster Keaton *(Buster [The Sap])*, Kathryn McGuire *(Betsy [The Girl])*, Frederick Vroom *(her father)*, Noble Johnson, Clarence Burton, H. M. Clugston *(gangsters, cannibals, spies, etc.)*.

Comedy. "The sight of a colored couple in an affectionate embrace leads the Sap to decide on marriage. Betsy O'Brien declines the honor, so he engages single passage on a steamship for Australia. Circumstances bring both the Sap and the girl on board a deserted steamship that is cast adrift. Both the children of wealthy parents, they have a hard time making both ends meet. They finally drift to a tropical isle and are threatened by cannibals. He rescues her by appearing, like a strange ocean monster, in a diving suit. A submarine takes them away." (*Moving Picture World*, 13 Sep 1924, p159.) *Marriage. Navigation. Diving. Submarines.*

NAVY BLUES **F2.3787**

Metro-Goldwyn-Mayer Pictures. 20 Dec **1929** [c2 Jan 1930; LP959]. Sd (Movietone); b&w. 35mm. 9 reels, 6,936 ft. [Also si; 6,195 ft.]

Dir Clarence Brown. *Dial* J. C. Nugent, Elliott Nugent, W. L. River. *Adapt* Dale Van Every. *Story* Raymond L. Schrock. *Photog* Merritt B. Gerstad. *Art Dir* Cedric Gibbons. *Film Ed* Hugh Wynn. *Song: "Navy Blues"* Roy Turk, Fred E. Ahlert. *Rec Engr* G. A. Burns, Douglas Shearer. *Wardrobe* David Cox.

Cast: William Haines *(Kelly)*, Anita Page *(Alice)*, Karl Dane *(Swede)*, J. C. Nugent *(Mr. Brown)*, Edythe Chapman *(Mrs. Brown)*, Gertrude Sutton *(Hilda)*, Wade Boteler *(chief petty officer)*.

Comedy. Kelly, a sailor on shore leave, meets Alice at a dancehall, and she takes his flirtatious behavior seriously. When her parents object to the relationship, Alice leaves home to join Kelly, causing him to reconsider his position; and he sees to it that she is properly installed in a hotel just as his liberty expires. After a cruise, Kelly returns and is happily united with the girl. *Sailors. Flirtation. Dancehalls.*

THE NEAR LADY **F2.3788**

Universal Pictures. 3 Dec **1923** [c7 Nov 1923; LP19598]. Si; b&w. 35mm. 5 reels, 4,812 ft.

Dir Herbert Blache. *Scen* Hugh Hoffman. *Story* Frank R. Adams. *Photog* William Thornley.

Cast: Gladys Walton *(Nora Schultz)*, Jerry Gendron *(Basil Van Bibber)*, Hank Mann *(lodger)*, Kate Price *(Bridget Schultz)*, Otis Harlan *(Herman Schultz)*, Florence Drew *(Aunt Maggie Mahaffey)*, Emmett King *(Stuyvesant Van Bibber)*, Henrietta Floyd *(Mrs. S. Van Bibber)*.

Comedy. Basil Van Bibber, son of a prominent family, and Nora Schultz, daughter of a butcher who invented a sausage machine that made the Van Bibbers rich, pretend to be in love to please their parents; but when Nora tries to protect the young Van Bibber from a charge of reckless driving, they find they really are in love. *Butchers. Social classes. Filial relations. Automobile driving.*

NEAR THE RAINBOW'S END **F2.3789**

Tiffany Productions. 10 Jun **1930.** Sd (Photophone); b&w. 35mm. 6 reels, 5,178 ft.

Prod Trem Carr. *Dir* J. P. McGowan. *Story-Scen* Sally Winters. *Dial* Charles A. Post. *Photog* Hap Depew, T. E. Jackson. *Sets* E. R. Hickson. *Film Ed* Charles J. Hunt. *Song: "Ro-Ro-Rolling' Along"* Murray Mencher, Billy Moll, Harry Richman. *Rec Engr* Neil Jackson, C. F. Franklin.

Cast: Bob Steele *(Jim Bledsoe)*, Louise Lorraine *(Ruth Wilson)*, Lafe McKee *(Tom Bledsoe)*, Al Ferguson *(Buck Rankin)*, Alfred Hewston *(Tug Wilson)*.

Western melodrama. Despite past friendliness, cattle ranchers Tom and Jim Bledsoe (father and son) fence off their range to prevent its use by neighboring sheep ranchers Tug Wilson and Buck Rankin, suggesting that they hope to end their recent loss of cattle. Buck shoots Tug in an argument over where to take the sheep, and Jim is accused of murder and of stampeding the sheep. Believing Jim guilty, Tug's daughter, Ruth, aids Buck in capturing him; but Jim escapes, Ruth gets help from the sheriff, and a sheepherder reveals Buck's responsibility for both the rustling of the Bledsoe's cattle and Tug's murder. (Incidental songs.) *Ranchers. Rustlers. Sheepherders. Filial relations. Cattle. Sheep. Murder.*

'NEATH WESTERN SKIES **F2.3790**

J. P. McGowan Productions. *Dist* Syndicate Pictures. 18 Oct **1929.** Si; b&w. 35mm. 5 reels, 4,924 ft.

Dir J. P. McGowan. *Story-Scen-Titl* Sally Winters. *Photog* Frank Cotner. *Photog? (see note)* Hap Depew.

Cast: Tom Tyler *(Tex McCloud)*, Hank Bell *("Wildcat" Riley)*, Harry Woods *(Jim Canfield)*, J. P. McGowan *(Dugan)*, Bobby Dunn *(Percival Givens)*, Lotus Thompson *(Ann Givens)*, Alfred Heuston *(James Garfield)*, Barney Furey *(Lem Johnson)*.

Western melodrama. "Tom Tyler is the owner of oil property and of course the gang is out to spoil his chances of getting the drilling under way. So they steal his drills, and through a mixup the drills get into possession of the gal. Along comes Tom, and the girl and himself work out the plot to the point where they have the game properly licked and recover the drills eventually." (*Film Daily*, 15 Dec 1929, p8.) *Gangs. Oil.*

Note: *Film Year Book* (1931) credits Hap Depew with photography.

NEBRASKA UNDER FIRE **F2.3791**

Dist Pictorial Sales Bureau. c17 Oct **1924** [MU2734]. Si; b&w. 35mm. 8 reels.

Documentary. "The story of Nebraska troops in the World War ... opens with the training of these troops at Camp Cody and at Camp Funston. It follows them aboard the transports, to their landing in France and England. They are shown at work in the Service of Supply and in the Rolampant training area. Following this, participation of these troops in battles around Chatteau Thierry, St. Mihiel, the Meuse Argonne are given. Following the close of the Meuse Argonne battle and the Armistice Day, movements of the Nebraska troops into Germany with the Army of Occupation are depicted. Also the final review held in Germany, and their embarkation for the U. S. A." (Copyright records.) *United States Army. United States Army—Training. World War I. England. France. Germany. Camp Cody. Camp Funston. Nebraska.*

THE NECESSARY EVIL **F2.3792**

First National Pictures. 17 May **1925** [c7 May 1925; LP21419]. Si; b&w. 35mm. 7 reels, 6,307 ft.

Pers Supv Earl Hudson. *Dir* George Archainbaud. *Scen* Eve Unsell. *Photog* George Folsey. *Art Dir* Milton Menasco. *Film Ed* Arthur Tavares.

Cast: Ben Lyon *(Frank Jerome)*, Viola Dana *(Shirley Holmes)*, Frank Mayo *(Dick Jerome)*, Thomas Holding *(David Devanant)*, Gladys Brockwell *(Frances Jerome)*, Mary Thurman *(Hattie)*, Betty Jewel *(Belle)*, Martha Madison *(Esther)*, Arthur Housman *(Pug)*, Beach Cooke *(Reggie)*.

Melodrama. Source: Stephen Vincent Benét, "Uriah's Son," in *Red Book* (43:81–85, May 1924). On her deathbed, Frances Jerome secures David Devanant's promise to care for her young son, Frank. Frank grows to manhood a wild and reckless fellow, seemingly having inherited his father's proclivity for drink and women; he is eventually expelled from college for marrying a gold digger during a drunken episode. The girl, Hattie, demands from Devanant a large sum of money in return for a divorce from Frank; Devanant refuses, and Hattie and her brother steal some bonds from the wealthy man. Devanant pretends to believe that Frank stole the bonds and sends him to the tropics, where Frank learns that Devanant had likewise sent his father to the tropics. He becomes homicidal and returns to the United States in time to prevent a wedding between Devanant and Shirley, Devenant's ward, with whom Frank also is in love. Devanant explains to Frank that he had known that Frank did not steal the bonds but that he thought a few months out of the country would do much to develop his manhood. The kindly Devanant then dies of a heart attack, leaving Frank and Shirley to find consolation in each other. *Gold diggers. Wards. Theft. Drunkenness. Divorce. Manhood. Tropics.*

NED McCOBB'S DAUGHTER **F2.3793**

Pathé Exchange. 12 Jan **1929** [c18 Nov 1928; LP25853]. Sd (Photophone); b&w. 35mm. 7 reels, 6,015 ft. [Also si, 2 Dec 1928; 6,070 ft.]

Dir William J. Cowen. *Adapt-Screenplay* Beulah Marie Dix. *Titl* Edwin Justus Mayer. *Camera* David Abel. *Art Dir* Edward Jewell. *Film Ed* Anne Bauchens. *Asst Dir* Roy Burns. *Prod Mgr* John Rohlfs.

Cast: Irene Rich *(Carrie)*, Theodore Roberts *(Ned McCobb)*, Robert Armstrong *(Babe Callahan)*, George Barraud *(George Callahan)*, Edward

Hearn *(Butterworth)*, Carol Lombard *(Jennie)*, Louis Natheaux *(Kelly)*.

Melodrama. Source: Sidney Howard, *Ned McCobb's Daughter* (a play, publication undetermined). Rumrunner Babe Callahan uses the home of his married brother, George, as a front for his operations. Carrie, George's wife, unaware of the arrangement, runs a restaurant in part of the large house, owned by her father, who is captain of the local ferry for which George collects the fares. George proves to be more the scoundrel than his bootlegging brother when he steals money from the fares to buy jewelry to purchase the affections of Jennie, a waitress. When a government official, Kelly, investigates the cellar of the house, George kills him, hiding the body in an apple bin. Prohibition officers arrive searching for Kelly but find instead trucks with false bottoms. The officials leave, staking-out nearby. Babe's first instinct is to flee, but he remains to protect Carrie and the children. George loads the trucks with the body and liquor, and he takes two of the children to avert suspicion. Carrie frantically enlists Babe's aid. A wild chase culminates with George plunging over a cliff to his death but not before Babe, racing alongside, rescues the children. Babe is arrested but promises Carrie he will return to her. *Rumrunners. Bootleggers. Waitresses. Prohibition. Restaurants. Murder. Infidelity. Ferryboats. Chases.*

THE NE'ER-DO-WELL (Reissue) **F2.3794**

Selig Polyscope Co. *Dist* Film Market. **1921.** Si; b&w. 35mm. 7 reels.

Note: Originally released 20 Mar 1916 in 10 reels.

THE NE'ER-DO-WELL **F2.3795**

Famous Players–Lasky. *Dist* Paramount Pictures. 29 Apr **1923** [New York premiere; released 6 May; c2 May 1923; LP18935]. Si; b&w. 35mm. 8 reels, 7,414 ft.

Pres by Adolph Zukor. *Dir* Alfred E. Green. *Scen* Louis Stevens. *Photog* Ernest Hallor. *Adtl Photog* William Miller.

Cast: Thomas Meighan *(Kirk Anthony)*, Lila Lee *(Chiquita)*, Gertrude Astor *(Edith Cortlandt)*, John Miltern *(Stephen Cortlandt)*, Gus Weinberg *(Andres Garavel)*, Sid Smith *(Ramón Alfarez)*, George O'Brien *(Clifford)*, Jules Cowles *(Allen Allan)*, Laurance Wheat *(Runnels)*, Cyril Ring.

Comedy-drama. Source: Rex Beach, *The Ne'er Do Well* (New York, 1911). Disgusted with his spendthrift son, Kirk Anthony's father has Kirk shanghaied and taken to Panama, where he (Kirk) attracts the attention of Mrs. Edith Cortlandt; falls in love with Chiquita, the daughter of a Panamanian general; gets a railroad job through Stephen Cortlandt (Edith's husband); and decides to make something of himself when he meets Allen Allan, a Negro soldier of fortune. Stephen Cortlandt's death is blamed on Kirk until Edith produces a suicide note; he succeeds in his railroad position and returns to the United States with Chiquita to ask his father's forgiveness. *Soldiers of fortune. Spendthrifts. Ne'er-do-wells. Filial relations. Shanghaiing. Railroads. Suicide. Panama.*

THE NEGRO OF TODAY **F2.3796**

C. B. Campbell Studio. **1921.** Si; b&w. 35mm. [Feature length assumed.]

Documentary(?). No information about the precise nature of this film has been found. *Negro life.*

NELLIE, THE BEAUTIFUL CLOAK MODEL **F2.3797**

Goldwyn Pictures. *Dist* Goldwyn-Cosmopolitan Distributing Corp. 24 Feb or 2 Mar **1924** [c2 Mar 1924; LP19979]. Si; b&w. 35mm. 7 reels, 6,098 or 6,533 ft.

Dir Emmett Flynn. *Adapt* H. H. Van Loan. *Photog* Lucien Andriot.

Cast: Claire Windsor *(Nellie)*, Betsy Ann Hisle *(Nellie, at 5 years old)*, Edmund Lowe *(Jack Carroll)*, Mae Busch *(Polly Joy)*, Raymond Griffith *(Shorty Burchell)*, Lew Cody *(Walter Peck)*, Hobart Bosworth *(Thomas Lipton/Robert Horton)*, Lilyan Tashman *(Nita)*, Dorothy Cumming *(Mrs. Horton)*, Will Walling *(Blizzard Dugan)*, Mayme Kelso *(Miss Drake)*, William Orlamond *(Mosely)*, Arthur Houseman, David Kirby *(gangsters)*.

Melodrama. Source: Owen Davis, *Nellie the Beautiful Cloak Model; a Modern Panoramic Melodrama in 4 Acts and 15 Scenes* (publication undetermined). Nellie Horton, when mistreated by her father, is taken in charge by Thomas Lipton. She grows up in poverty not knowing her true identity as the heiress to her mother's millions. Upon the death of her benefactor, she becomes a model in a fashionable shop. There she falls into the hands of her mother's unscrupulous nephew, who contrives to do away with her in order to obtain her fortune. His final plan to destroy her is foiled when her lover, Jack Carroll, rescues her from the tracks of a speeding train. Finally, Nellie (Allyn Horton) is reunited with her mother and finds happiness. *Heiresses. Fashion models. Adoption. Parentage.*

Note: Style show displaying high fashion of this time.

NERO (United States/Italy) **F2.3798**

Fox Film Corp. 22 May **1922** [New York premiere; released 17 Sep; c17 Sep 1922; LP19072]. Si; b&w. 35mm. 12 reels, ca11,500 ft.

Pres by William Fox. *Dir* J. Gordon Edwards. *Story-Scen* Virginia Tracy, Charles Sarver. *Ch Camera* Harry Plimpton. *Art Dir* John D. Braddon. *Film Ed* Hettie Grey Baker.

Cast: Jacques Gretillat *(Nero)*, Alexander Salvini *(Horatius)*, Guido Trento *(Tulius)*, Enzo De Felice *(Otho)*, Nero Bernardi *(The Apostle)*, Adolfo Trouche *(Hercules)*, Nello Carolenuto *(Galba)*, Americo De Giorgio *(Gracchus)*, Alfredo Galaor *(Garth)*, Ernando Cecilia *(a Roman general)*, Enrico Kant *(a Roman captain)*, Paulette Duval *(Poppaea)*, Edy Darclea *(Acte)*, Violet Mersereau *(Marcia)*, Lina Talba *(Julia)*, Lydia Yaguinto *(first handmaiden)*, Maria Marchiali *(second handmaiden)*.

Spectacle. This is a spectacle based on the history of the Roman Empire in the reign of Nero. The story deals with the tyrant's rise to power; his infatuation with Princess Marcia, a young Christian girl; her romance with Horatius, a young Roman soldier who saves her from Nero; and Nero's downfall and death through the plottings of his consort, the Empress Poppaea. The spectacular scenes include portrayal of the Circus Maximus, chariot races, martyrdom of the Christians, the burning of Rome, and the charge of the Roman legionnaires, who rescue Rome and eliminate Nero. *Christianity. Rome—History—Empire. Nero. Poppaea Sabina.*

THE NERVOUS WRECK **F2.3799**

Christie Film Co. *Dist* Producers Distributing Corp. 10 Oct **1926** [New York premiere; released 1 Nov; c8 Oct 1926; LP23194]. Si; b&w. 35mm. 7 reels, 6,730 ft.

Pres by Al Christie. *Dir* Scott Sidney. *Adapt* F. McGrew Willis. *Photog* Alec Phillips.

Cast: Harrison Ford *(Henry Williams)*, Phyllis Haver *(Sally Morgan)*, Chester Conklin *(Mort)*, Mack Swain *(Jerome Underwood)*, Hobart Bosworth *(Jud Morgan)*, Paul Nicholson *(Bob Wells)*, Vera Steadman *(Harriet Underwood)*, Charles Gerrard *(Reggie De Vere)*, Clarence Burton *(Andy McNab)*.

Farce. Source: Owen Davis, *The Nervous Wreck; a Comedy in Three Acts* (New York, 1926). E. J. Rath, *The Nervous Wreck* (New York, 1923). Believing himself to be the victim of a fatal illness, Henry Williams of Pittsburgh strikes out for Arizona, stops at a ranch for a meal, and decides to stay on with Jud Morgan and his daughter, Sally. Henry volunteers to take Sally, who is betrothed to Sheriff Bob Wells, across the desert to the train station, and they run out of gasoline. Henry elopes against his will, holds up a car with a monkey wrench to get gasoline, is forced to act as a waiter at the ranch of Jerome Underwood (the man he holds up), is chased by the sheriff and Sally's father, escapes in an automobile equipped with a wagon wheel, and in the climactic chase—after tumbling down a mountainside with Sally—decides that he is cured. He then is happily married to the girl. *Hypochondriacs. Sheriffs. Ranches. Arizona. Pittsburgh.*

THE NEST **F2.3800**

Excellent Pictures. 1 Aug or 1 Sep **1927** [c16 Aug 1926; LP23024]. Si; b&w. 35mm. 8 reels, 7,393 ft.

Pres by Samuel Zierler. *Dir* William Nigh. *Scen* Charles E. Whittaker. *Photog* Jack Brown, Harry Stradling.

Cast: Holmes Herbert *(Richard Elliott)*, Thomas Holding *(Archer Hamilton)*, Pauline Frederick *(Mrs. Hamilton)*, Ruth Dwyer *(Susan Hamilton)*, Reginald Sheffield *(Martin Hamilton)*, Rolland Flander *(Monroe)*, Jean Acker *(Belle Madison)*, Wilfred Lucas *(Howard Hardy)*.

Domestic drama. Source: Paul Géraldy, *Les Noces d'argent, comédie en quatre actes* (Paris, 1917). Following the death of Archer Hamilton, Richard Elliott, his best friend and executor of the estate, resumes his boyhood courtship of Mrs. Hamilton, who finds her daughter, Susan, and son, Martin, increasingly unmanageable. When Susan elopes with her sweetheart, Mrs. Hamilton reconciles herself to the situation, but she realizes her daughter's selfishness when she finds herself unwanted in the newlyweds' apartment. Mrs. Hamilton goes to Paris and returns transformed into a vivacious flapper; she pretends to take an interest in night life and appears to such an advantage that she excites the jealousy of Martin's girl, Belle, who has been luring him into a gambling establishment where he has lost a large sum of borrowed and illegally obtained money. Mrs. Hamilton tries to come to terms with Belle's friends; Elliott then comes to her rescue, and taking matters into his hands, he offers Martin a job to pay off his debts and puts Susan in her place. He and Mrs. Hamilton are happily married. *Widows. Flappers. Courtship. Motherhood. Family life. Rejuvenation. Gambling. Paris.*

THE NET **F2.3801**

Fox Film Corp. 2 Dec **1923** [c8 Oct 1923; LP19555]. Si; b&w. 35mm. 7 reels, 6,135 ft.

Pres by William Fox. *Dir* J. Gordon Edwards. *Scen* Olga Linek Schnoll, Virginia Tracy. *Photog* Bennie Miggins.

Cast: Barbara Castleton *(Allayne Norman)*, Raymond Bloomer *(Bruce Norman)*, Albert Roscoe *(The Man)*, Peggy Davis *(The Model)*, William H. Tooker *(Mr. Royce)*, Helen Tracy *(The Nurse)*, Eliah Nadel *(The Boy)*, Claire De Lorez *(The Vamp)*, Arthur Gordini *(The Artist)*, Alexander Gaden *(The Inspector)*, Byron Douglas *(The Doctor)*.

Melodrama. Source: Maravene Thompson, *The Woman's Law* (New York, 1914). Maravene Thompson, *The Net* (unpublished play). Allayne Norman's husband, Bruce, a gambler and a drinker, quarrels with her cousin, an artist, and kills him. Burce flees, having exchanged identities with a stranger who, suffering from amnesia, wanders into the studio and falls unconscious. He persuades Allayne to tell the police that the senseless man is her husband, the murderer. She does, to protect her son. Bruce dies, the man regains his memory, his innocence is proven, and he marries Allayne. *Artists. Murder. Amnesia.*

NEVADA **F2.3802**

Paramount Famous Lasky Corp. 8 Aug **1927** [New York showing; released 10 Sep; c10 Sep 1927; LP24393]. Si; b&w. 35mm. 7 reels, 6,258 ft. *Pres by* Adolph Zukor, Jesse L. Lasky. *Dir* John Waters. *Screenplay* John Stone, L. G. Rigby. *Titl* Jack Conway (of *Variety*). *Photog* C. Edgar Schoenbaum.

Cast: Gary Cooper *(Nevada)*, Thelma Todd *(Hettie Ide)*, William Powell *(Clan Dillon)*, Philip Strange *(Ben Ide)*, Ernie S. Adams *(Cash Burridge)*, Christian J. Frank *(Sheriff of Winthrop)*, Ivan Christy *(Cawthorne)*, Guy Oliver *(Sheriff of Lineville)*.

Western melodrama. Source: Zane Grey, *Nevada, a Romance of the West* (New York, 1928). Nevada, a feared gunfighter, springs his pal, Cash Burridge, from the jail in Lineville. Reaching Winthrop, they decide to take respectable jobs on the ranch of Ben Ide, an Englishman whom they rescue from Cawthorne's men. Ide, who fears the activity of cattle rustlers, dispatches Nevada to protect his daughter, Hettie, arousing the enmity of Clan Dillon, the ranch foreman and a suitor for Hettie's hand. To escape the law, Nevada and Cash join up with Cawthorne, who is under orders from Dillon, leader of the rustlers. During a raid, Dillon shoots both Cash and Cawthorne, but Nevada learns of his treachery from his dying pal; in a confrontation, Nevada is wounded by Dillon but is saved by the arrival of the posse and the evidence given by the wounded Cawthorne against the leader. *English. Desperadoes. Rustlers. Ranchers. Ranch foremen. Posses. Criminals—Rehabilitation. Jailbreaks.*

NEVER MIND TOMORROW *see* **THE MARRIED FLAPPER**

NEVER SAY DIE **F2.3803**

Douglas MacLean Productions. *Dist* Associated Exhibitors. 31 Aug **1924** [c5 Jul, 31 Aug 1924; LU20371, LP22445]. Si; b&w. 35mm. 6 reels, 5,891 ft.

Dir George J. Crone. *Scen* Raymond Cannon. *Story* Raymond Griffith, Wade Boteler. *Photog* Jack MacKenzie.

Cast: Douglas MacLean *(Jack Woodbury)*, Lillian Rich *(Violet Stevenson)*, Helen Ferguson *(La Cigale)*, Hallam Cooley *(Hector Walters)*, Lucien Littlefield *(Griggs)*, Tom O'Brien *(Gun Murray)*, André Lanoy *(Verchesi)*, Wade Boteler *(Dr. Fraser)*, Eric Mayne *(Dr. Galesby)*, William Conklin *(Dr. Gerhardt)*, George Cooper *(Gaston Gibbs)*.

Comedy. Source: William H. Post and William Collier, *Never Say Die* (New York opening: Nov 1912). A corps of noted physicians mistakes the buzzing of a bee for heart tremors and erroneously gives Jack Woodbury 3 months to live. Jack's avaricious friend, Hector, persuades his sweetheart, Violet, to marry Jack, intending to pick up an easy inheritance by marrying the Widow Woodbury. Jack fails to die at the appointed time, and Violet finds she has fallen in love with him. *Physicians. Greed. Inheritance. Bees.*

NEVER THE TWAIN SHALL MEET **F2.3804**

Cosmopolitan Corp. *Dist* Metro-Goldwyn Distributing Corp. 13 Sep **1925** [c14 Sep 1925; LP21876]. Si; b&w. 35mm. 8 reels, 8,143 ft.

Dir Maurice Tourneur. *Ed Dir–Titl* Peter B. Kyne. *Scen* Eugene Mullin. *Photog* Ira H. Morgan, J. B. Shackelford. *Sets* Joseph Urban. *Film Ed* Donn Hayes. *Cost* Dhetl Urban.

Cast: Anita Stewart *(Tamea)*, Bert Lytell *(Dan Prichard)*, Huntley Gordon *(Mark Mellenger)*, Justine Johnstone *(Maisie Morrison)*, George Siegmann *(James Muggridge)*, Lionel Belmore *(Gaston Larrieau)*, William Norris *(Squibbs)*, Emily Fitzroy *(Mrs. Pippy)*, Princess Marie de Bourbon *(Miss Smith)*, Florence Turner *(Julia)*, James Wang *(Sooey Wan)*, Ben Deeley *(doctor)*, Roy Coulson *(assistant doctor)*, Thomas Ricketts *(Andrew J. Casson)*, Ernest Butterworth *(Captain Hackett)*.

Melodrama. Source: Peter Bernard Kyne, *Never the Twain Shall Meet* (New York, 1923). Tamea, the beautiful offspring of a French sea captain and the queen of a South Sea island, accompanies her father on a voyage to San Francisco. Arriving in port, her father is told that he has leprosy; and putting Tamea in the care of his friend, Dan Pritchard, he kills himself. With the help of Mellenger, a reporter, Dan cares for the girl, becoming increasingly fond of her, much to the dismay of his fiancée, Maisie. Dan's business fails, and Tamea returns to her island paradise. Dan soon follows, and they are wed in a native ceremony. Heat and inactivity weigh heavily on Dan, and he soon goes into a moral decline. Mellenger arrives on the island, accompanied by Maisie; Dan later returns to the United States with her, and Mellenger stays on the island, offering Tamea his comfort and love. *Sea captains. Reporters. Leprosy. Suicide. Bankruptcy. South Sea Islands. San Francisco.*

NEVER TOO LATE **F2.3805**

Goodwill Pictures. 12 Nov **1925** [New York State license application]. Si; b&w. 35mm. 5 reels, 4,620 ft.

Dir Forrest Sheldon. *Story* Samuel M. Pyke. *Photog* Frank Cotner. *Film Ed* M. P. Schreck.

Cast: Francis X. Bushman, Jr. *(Johnny Adams)*, Harriet Loweree *(Helen Bentley)*, Gino Corrado *(Count Gaston La Rue)*, Ollie Kirby *(Mabel Greystone)*, Charles Belcher *(Arthur Greystone)*, Roy Laidlaw *(Robert Leland)*, Lorimer Johnson *(John Kemp, "The Boss")*.

Melodrama. La Rue, a notorious smuggler, kidnaps Helen Bentley, whom Jim Adams saves from a "torture den" until the arrival of customs authorities. *Smugglers. Customs officers. Kidnaping. Torture.*

NEW BROOMS **F2.3806**

Famous Players–Lasky. *Dist* Paramount Pictures. 12 Oct **1925** [c12 Oct 1925; LP23080]. Si; b&w. 35mm. 6 reels, 5,443 ft.

Pres by Adolph Zukor, Jesse L. Lasky. *Dir* William De Mille. *Screenplay* Clara Beranger. *Photog* L. Guy Wilky.

Cast: Neil Hamilton *(Thomas Bates, Jr.)*, Bessie Love *(Geraldine Marsh)*, Phyllis Haver *(Florence Levering)*, Robert McWade *(Thomas Bates, Sr.)*, Fred Walton *(Williams)*, Josephine Crowell *(Margaret)*, Larry Steers *(George Morrow)*, James Neill *(Kneeland)*.

Comedy. Source: Frank Craven, *New Brooms; a Comedy in Three Acts* (New York, 1925). Thomas Bates, Jr., "a bird who brings his father a long bill at the first of every month," calls his father a grouch and criticizes his old-fashioned business methods. The father lets his son take over the management of his broom factory and the household for a year in an attempt to make a man of him. Geraldine Marsh, an old friend of the family whose father has just died, is taken into the family as a housekeeper. Tom falls in love with her and breaks his engagement with the mercenary Florence Levering, his father's ward. Convinced, however, that Geraldine loves his father, he sees to it that both Geraldine and his father leave the household. After a year, Tom admits his failure and asks his father's help. Geraldine also returns, and Tom happily discovers that she has not married his father. *Housekeepers. Filial relations. Family life. Factory management. Brooms.*

NEW CHAMPION **F2.3807**

Perfection Pictures. *Dist* Columbia Pictures. 1 Sep **1925** [c15 Sep 1925; LP21819]. Si; b&w. 35mm. 5 reels, 4,470 ft.

Dir Reeves Eason. *Story* Dorothy Howell. *Photog* George Meehan.

Cast: William Fairbanks *(Bob Nichols)*, Edith Roberts *(Polly Rand)*, Lotus Thompson *(Lucy Nichols)*, Lloyd Whitlock *(Jack Melville)*, Frank Hagney *(Knockout Riley)*, Al Kaufman *(fight promoter)*, Marion Court *(Mrs. Nichols)*, Bert Apling *(blacksmith)*.

Action melodrama. While in training for a championship fight, Knockout Riley stays at the home of Bob Nichols, who works for the village blacksmith. Riley injures his hand in an automobile accident shortly before the bout, and Bob takes his place, fighting under Riley's name. At first,

Bob takes a beating in the match, but he keeps his nerve and wins by a knockout. Bob marries Polly Rand, and Riley marries Lucy Nichols, Bob's sister. *Prizefighters. Blacksmiths. Brother-sister relationship. Smalltown life. Automobile accidents.*

THE NEW COMMANDMENT **F2.3808**

Dist First National Pictures. 1 Nov **1925** [c15 Oct 1925; LP21910]. Si; b&w. 35mm. 7 reels, 6,428 or 6,980 ft.

Pres by Robert T. Kane. *Dir* Howard Higgin. *Screen Adapt* Sada Cowan, Howard Higgin. *Photog* Ernest Haller. *Adtl Photog* Ernest G. Palmer. *Art Dir* Robert M. Haas. *Film Ed* Paul F. Maschke.

Cast: Blanche Sweet *(Renée Darcourt)*, Ben Lyon *(Billy Morrow)*, Holbrook Blinn *(William Morrow)*, Clare Eames *(Mrs. Parr)*, Effie Shannon *(Marquise de la Salle)*, Dorothy Cumming *(Countess Stoll)*, Pedro De Cordoba *(Picard)*, George Cooper *(Red)*, Diana Kane *(Ethel)*, Lucius Henderson *(Henri Darcourt)*, Betty Jewel.

Romantic drama. Source: Frederick Palmer, *Invisible Wounds* (New York, 1925). Mrs. Ormsby Parr, a scheming society woman who has buried three husbands, hopes to arrange a marriage between her stepdaughter and Billy Morrow. She arranges for Billy's father to take them on a cruise to Europe. Off the coast of France, Billy learns of the scheme and makes for shore with his newfound friend, Red, an ex–taxi driver. In Paris they encounter artist Gaston Picard, who is bethrothed to the Countess Stoll but nevertheless is in love with his American model, Renée Darcourt. Billy and Renée fall in love, but he comes to doubt her intentions because of her profession and his suspicion of Picard. War breaks out, and he joins the Foreign Legion. He is wounded and taken to a hospital where Renée is a nurse. Their doubts and jealousies vanish and all ends happily. *Stepmothers. Nurses. Artists. Models. World War I. Paris. France—Army—Foreign Legion.*

THE NEW DISCIPLE **F2.3809**

Dist Federation Film Corp. 18 Dec **1921** [New York premiere; released Apr 1922]. Si; b&w. 35mm. 6-7 reels.

Dir Ollie Sellers. *Scen* William Pigott. *Story* John Arthur Nelson.

Cast: Pell Trenton *(John McPherson)*, Alfred Allen *(Peter Fanning)*, Norris Johnson *(Mary Fanning)*, Margaret Mann *(Marion Fanning)*, Walt Whitman *(Sandy McPherson)*, Alice H. Smith *(Mother McPherson)*, Arthur Stuart Hull *(Frederick Wharton)*, Walter Perkins *(Daddy Whipple)*, Charles Prindley *(Jennings)*.

Drama. Industrialist Peter Fanning, who amassed his wealth during the World War, continues to expand his fortune through exploitation of his factory employees. When labor troubles finally result in a strike, John McPherson, who believes that both sides are wrong, is caught in the middle; and he endeavors to persuade the capitalists and the laborers to reduce their demands. The strike prevents Fanning from meeting contract deadlines, and his competitors take advantage of his financial embarrassment and press him to sell, but the workers finally agree to accept the American Plan and to join with the farmers to purchase and operate the mill on a cooperative basis—leaving McPherson free to pursue romance with Mary Fanning. (Apparently, author Nelson took his inspiration from Woodrow Wilson's *The New Freedom*, and passages from it are used in the film.) *Industrialists. Capitalists. Farmers. Labor. Strikes. Factory management. Cooperatives. Thomas Woodrow Wilson. American Plan.*

THE NEW KLONDIKE **F2.3810**

Famous Players–Lasky. *Dist* Paramount Pictures. 15 Mar **1926** [c15 Mar 1926; LP22497]. Si; b&w. 35mm. 8 reels, 7,445 ft.

Pres by Adolph Zukor, Jesse L. Lasky. *Dir* Lewis Milestone. *Scen* Thomas J. Geraghty. *Orig Story* Ring Lardner. *Photog* Alvin Wyckoff. *Art Dir* Walter E. Keller.

Cast: Thomas Meighan *(Tom Kelly)*, Lila Lee *(Evelyn Lane)*, Paul Kelly *(Bing Allen)*, Hallie Manning *(Flamingo Applegate)*, Robert Craig *(Morgan West)*, George De Carlton *(Owen)*, J. W. Johnston *(Joe Cooley)*, Brenda Lane *(Bird Dog)*, Tefft Johnson *(Colonel Dwyer)*, Danny Hayes *(The Spieler)*.

Comedy-drama. On a boat to Florida, ballplayer Tom Kelly falls in love with Evelyn Dale. Arriving at spring training camp, Tom learns that he has been dropped from the team by Joe Cooley, who is afraid that his position as manager of the team will be jeopardized by Tom's superior knowledge of baseball. Not knowing what to do, Tom allows a real estate developer to use his name in advertising, and he begins to make a lot of money. Tom's success impresses his former teammates, and they invest all their money with him. Morgan West, a crooked real estate dealer in league with Cooley, then sells Tom a worthless swamp. Tom gets the money back, however, and, when Cooley is fired by the team's owner, Tom is appointed in his place, soon finding Evelyn loyally at his side. *Swindlers. Real estate agents. Baseball. Swamps. Florida.*

Note: Filmed on locations in Florida.

NEW LIVES FOR OLD **F2.3811**

Famous Players–Lasky. *Dist* Paramount Pictures. 22 Feb **1925** [New York premiere; c2 Mar 1925; LP21207]. Si; b&w. 35mm. 7 reels, 6,796 ft.

Pres by Adolph Zukor, Jesse L. Lasky. *Dir* Clarence Badger. *Adapt* Adelaide Heilbron. *Photog* Guy Wilky.

Cast: Betty Compson *(Olympe)*, Wallace MacDonald *(Hugh Warren)*, Theodore Kosloff *(De Montinbard)*, Sheldon Lewis *(Pugin)*, Jack Joyce *(Jean Bertaut)*, Margaret Seddon *(Widow Turrene)*, Joseph Dowling *(Senator Warren)*, Helen Dunbar *(Mrs. Warren)*, Gale Henry *(Berthe)*, Marvel Quivey *(Nancy)*, Ed Faust *(cafe manager)*.

War drama. In 1918, Olympe, a Parisian cabaret dancer, goes on holiday to her aunt's Normandy farm, where, disguised as a peasant girl, she becomes engaged to Capt. Hugh Warren of the American Expeditionary Force. Hugh goes to the front, and Olympe returns to Paris, where she is persuaded to join the French Secret Service and spy on De Montinbard, who is suspected of working for Germany. Using her charms, Olympe obtains proof of De Montinbard's guilt, but he escapes. Olympe is despised by the Parisians, who believe her to have been a traitor, and a fictitious death is arranged for her by the war ministry. Olympe, who is now known as Betty, marries Hugh in her aunt's home, and they come to the United States, where Hugh's aristocratic mother does not approve of his peasant bride. De Montinbard turns up under an alias and recognizes Olympe. She denounces him as a spy, and he denounces her as a notorious cabaret dancer. De Montinbard is arrested by French agents, Olympe is presented with the Legion of Honor, and she is finally accepted without reservation by Hugh and his proud family. *Spies. Secret service. Peasants. Dancers. Traitors. Aunts. Espionage. Reputation. World War I. Paris. Normandy.*

NEW MINISTER **F2.3812**

Dist East Coast Productions. 15 Sep **1922** [New York State]. Si; b&w. 35mm. 5 reels, 4,500 ft.

Cast: Muriel Kingston.

Comedy-drama(?). No information about the nature of this film has been found. *Clergymen.*

NEW ORLEANS **F2.3813**

Tiffany-Stahl Productions. 2 Jun **1929** [c9 Sep 1929; LP686]. Talking & singing sequences (Photophone); b&w. 35mm. 8 reels, 6,799 ft. [Also si; 6,689 ft.]

Dir Reginald Barker. *Story-Cont* John Francis Natteford. *Dial-Titl* Frederick Hatton, Fanny Hatton. *Photog* Harry Jackson. *Mus* Hugo Riesenfeld. *Theme Song: "Pals Forever"* Hugo Riesenfeld, Ted Shapiro, John Raphael. *Mus Score* Irvin Talbot.

Cast: Ricardo Cortez *(Jim Morley)*, William Collier, Jr. *(Billy Slade)*, Alma Bennett *(Marie Cartier)*.

Melodrama. Billy, a jockey, and Jim, an assistant manager of a New Orleans racetrack, are close friends. They become bitter enemies because of Marie, an unprincipled young woman who marries Jim after betraying her first fiancé, Billy, on their wedding day. Marie's extravagance causes Jim to steal money from the office safe and to bet on Billy. Billy wins, but Jim is arrested and sent to jail when Marie neglects to replace the stolen money. Jim serves his term and is reunited with Billy after Marie and her lover are turned out of the house. *Jockeys. Infidelity. Gambling. Theft. Racetracks. New Orleans.*

THE NEW SCHOOL TEACHER **F2.3814**

C. C. Burr Pictures. 1 Jun **1924** [c4 Dec 1923; LP19671]. Si; b&w. 35mm. 6 reels, 5,284 ft.

Pres by C. C. Burr. *Dir* Gregory La Cava.

Cast: Doris Kenyon *(Diana Pope?)*, Charles "Chic" Sale *(Professor Fibble)*, Mickey Bennett *(Philander Pope?)*, Russell Griffin, Freddy Strange, Kent Raymond, Henry O'Connor, Edward Weisman, Edward Quinn, Jack Jacobs, Billy Quinn, Buddy Raynor, Paul Jachia, Fred Gorman, Bert Gorman, Warren Gorman *(his pupils)*, Polly Archer, Robert Bentley, May Kitson, Harlan Knight, Helen Gerould, Leslie King.

Comedy-drama. Source: Irvin Shrewsbury Cobb, "The Young Nuts of America," in *Irvin Cobb at His Best* (Garden City, New York, 1923). A country schoolteacher's pupils play boyish tricks on him until he wins their admiration by rescuing Philander Pope, one of their colleagues, from the burning schoolhouse. In addition, Fibble wins Diana Pope from Cory, her fiancé. *Schoolteachers. Fires.*

THE NEW TEACHER **F2.3815**

Fox Film Corp. 20 Aug **1922** [c20 Aug 1922; LP19151]. Si; b&w. 35mm. 5 reels, 4,453 ft.

Pres by William Fox. *Dir* Joseph Franz. *Adapt* Dorothy Yost. *Photog* Frank B. Good.

Cast: Shirley Mason *(Constance Bailey)*, Allan Forrest *(Bruce Van Griff)*, Earl Metcalf *(Edward Hurley)*, Otto Hoffman *(Joseph Hurley)*, Ola Norman *(Mrs. Brissell)*, Pat Moore *(George Brissell)*, Kate Price *(Mrs. Brennan)*.

Romantic drama. Source: Margaret Elizabeth Sangster, *The Island of Faith* (New York, 1921). Society girl Constance Bailey becomes a schoolteacher in New York's Lower East Side, telling her fiancé, Bruce Van Griff, that she is sailing to Europe. Seeing that he has been tricked, Van Griff joins the police force, getting a post on the corner where the school is located. Van Griff rescues Constance from one difficulty after another and convinces her that she needs a husband and protector. *Schoolteachers. Police. Courtship. New York City—Lower East Side.*

NEW TOYS **F2.3816**

Inspiration Pictures. *Dist* First National Pictures. 1 Mar **1925** [c3 Feb 1925; LP21085]. Si; b&w. 35mm. 8 reels, 7,250 ft.

Dir John S. Robertson. *Scen* Josephine Lovett. *Titl* Agnes Smith. *Photog* Roy Overbaugh. *Sets* Tec-Art Studios. *Film Ed* William Hamilton. *Art Titles* H. E. R. Studios.

Cast: Richard Barthelmess *(Will Webb)*, Mary Hay *(Mary Lane)*, Katherine Wilson *(Natalie Woods)*, Clifton Webb *(Tom Lawrence)*, Francis Conlon *(Sam Clark)*, Bijou Fernandez *(Mrs. Lane)*, Tammany Young *(doorman)*, Pat O'Connor *(Will Webb, Jr.)*, Jules Jordon *(Blumberg)*, Jacob Kingsbury *(Blutz)*.

Domestic comedy. Source: Arthur Hammerstein and Milton Herbert Gropper, *New Toys; a Comedy in Three Acts* (New York opening: 18 Feb 1924). Will Webb marries Mary Lane, an actress in amateur theatricals, and settles down to domestic life. Natalie Woods, an old girl friend of Will's about whom Mary has previously known nothing, returns from Europe and sets out to recapture Will's affections. Mary is extremely discomfited and jealous. When an old friend of hers, Tom Lawrence, offers her the leading part in one of his plays, she gladly accepts it. Will vows to miss the opening but finally attends at the urging of Natalie, his companion for the evening. During the performance Mary's putty nose comes loose and she falls down a staircase onstage, closing the play on opening night. After this shortened "run," Lawrence attempts to force his attentions on Mary, but she rejects him. Mary and Will are reconciled and renew their domestic life together. *Actors. Playwrights. Marriage. Theater. Theater—Amateur.*

NEW YEAR'S EVE **F2.3817**

Fox Film Corp. 24 Feb **1929** [c26 Feb 1929; LP165]. Sd eff & mus score (Movietone); b&w. 35mm. 7 reels, 5,984 ft. [Also si; 5,959 ft.]

Pres by William Fox. *Supv* Kenneth Hawks. *Dir* Henry Lehrman. *Scen* Dwight Cummins. *Titl* William Kernell. *Photog* Conrad Wells. *Mus Score* S. L. Rothafel. *Asst Dir* Max Gold.

Cast: Mary Astor *(Marjorie Ware)*, Charles Morton *(Edward Warren)*, Earle Foxe *(Barry Harmon)*, Florence Lake *(Pearl)*, Arthur Stone *(Steve)*, Helen Ware *(landlady)*, Freddie Frederick *(little brother)*, Jane La Verne *(little girl)*, Sumner Getchell *(Edward's friend)*, Stuart Erwin *(landlady's son)*, Virginia Vance *(little girl's mother)*.

Melodrama. Source: Richard Connell, "$100.00," in *Hearst's International Cosmopolitan* (85:98–101, Aug 1928). Saddled with the care of a younger brother and unable to find work, Marjorie Ware puts aside her scruples and goes to see a gambler who has long cast a lustful eye on her. A pickpocket kills the gambler, and the police find Marjorie at the scene of the crime, charging her with the murder. The pickpocket later falls to his death, however, and evidence is uncovered that sets Mary free, cleared of all suspicion of guilt in the gambler's death. Mary is then reunited with Edward Warren, a man who once did her a great kindness. *Gamblers. Pickpockets. Brother-sister relationship. Murder. Injustice. New Year's Eve.*

NEW YORK **F2.3818**

Famous Players–Lasky. *Dist* Paramount Pictures. 5 Feb **1927** [c5 Feb 1927; LP23660]. Si; b&w. 35mm. 7 reels, 6,877 ft.

Pres by Adolph Zukor, Jesse L. Lasky. *Assoc Prod* William Le Baron. *Dir* Luther Reed. *Screenplay* Forrest Halsey. *Story* Becky Gardiner, Barbara Chambers. *Photog* J. Roy Hunt.

Cast: Ricardo Cortez *(Michael Angelo Cassidy)*, Lois Wilson *(Marjorie Church)*, Estelle Taylor *(Angie Miller)*, William Powell *(Trent Regan)*, Norman Trevor *(Randolph Church)*, Richard "Skeets" Gallagher *(Buck)*, Margaret Quimby *(Helena Matthews)*, Lester Scharif *(Izzy Blumenstein)*, Charles Byer *(Jimmie Wharton)*.

Society melodrama. The Ritz Social Club, a Bowery cabaret, is the rendezvous of four old friends: Michael Angelo Cassidy, a trap drummer and composer; Buck, his arranger; Izzy, who breaks into politics; and Trent, who has become a gun-carrying gangster. Angie Miller admires Mike but surrenders to the proposals of Trent. Mike meets Marjorie Church, a society heiress, and 5 years later, having become a successful song writer, falls madly in love with her. Angie goes to Mike's apartment to congratulate him, and when Trent thinks she is unfaithful, he accidentally shoots her and hides the body. When the body is discovered, Mike is held for murder. Buck discovers evidence of Trent's guilt at the time Mike is convicted, and when Buck forces a confession from Trent, the judge reverses the verdict. *Politicians. Drummers. Composers. Gangsters. Friendship. Manslaughter. Trials. New York City—Bowery.*

Note: Filmed on locations in Manhattan.

NEW YORK NIGHTS **F2.3819**

United Artists. 28 Dec **1929** [c28 Dec 1929; LP950]. Sd (Movietone); b&w. 35mm. 9 reels, 7,447 ft.

Pres by Joseph M. Schenck. *Supv* John W. Considine, Jr. *Dir* Lewis Milestone. *Adapt* Jules Furthman. *Photog* Ray June. *Film Ed* Hal Kern. *Song: "A Year From Today"* Al Jolson, Ballard MacDonald, Dave Dreyer. *Rec Engr* Oscar Lagerstrom.

Cast: Norma Talmadge *(Jill Deverne)*, Gilbert Roland *(Fred Deverne)*, John Wray *(Joe Prividi)*, Lilyan Tashman *(Peggy)*, Mary Doran *(Ruthie Day)*, Roscoe Karns *(Johnny Dolan)*.

Domestic melodrama. Source: Hugh Stanislaus Stange, *Tin Pan Alley* (New York opening: 1 Nov 1928). Chorus girl Jill Deverne supports her song-writer husband, Fred, who has a strong bent for alcohol. When he finishes a new song, she consents to show it to racketeer Joe Prividi, the producer of her musical show, but Fred objects to favors from him; nevertheless Prividi, who covets Jill, agrees to use the song. Fred and his partner, Johnny Dolan, arrive drunk at a nightclub appointment; and in a raid, the police discover Fred with Ruthie, a chorus girl. Disgusted and angered by Fred's behavior, Jill becomes Prividi's girl. Later, at a private party, Prividi shoots a drunken gambler who tries to force himself on her; and when she goes to him at the jail, Jill finds Fred down and out and plans for a new future. Prividi hires gunmen to shoot Fred upon his release, but Prividi is taken prisoner aboard a train, and Jill and Fred begin life anew. *Chorus girls. Composers. Gangsters. Infidelity. Alcoholism. Manslaughter.*

NEW YORK TROOPS IN THE WORLD WAR *see* **GOLD CHEVRONS**

THE NEWS PARADE **F2.3820**

Fox Film Corp. 27 May **1928** [c23 May 1928; LP25284]. Si; b&w. 35mm. 7 reels, 6,679 ft.

Pres by William Fox. *Dir* David Butler. *Scen* Burnett Hershey. *Titl* Malcolm Stuart Boylan. *Story* David Butler, William M. Conselman. *Photog* Sidney Wagner, Joseph A. Valentine. *Film Ed* Irene Morra. *Asst Dir* Ad Schaumer. *Tech Ed* Russell Muth.

Cast: Nick Stuart *("Newsreel Nick" Naylor)*, Sally Phipps *(Sally Wellington)*, Brandon Hurst *(A. K. Wellington)*, Cyril Ring *(Prince Oscar)*, Earle Foxe *(Mysterious Stranger, Ivan Vodkoff)*, Franklin Underwood *(Bill Walpole)*, Truman Talley *(Director-in-Chief Talley)*.

Comedy. Photographer "Newsreel Nick" pulls an assignment to get some footage of A. K. Wellington, a camera-shy millionaire. Following the man and his daughter to Lake Placid, Palm Beach, and Havana, Nick saves both of them from a kidnaping plot in Havana and gets his footage as well. *Cameramen. Millionaires. Kidnaping. Motion pictures. Newsreels. Lake Placid. Palm Beach. Havana.*

Note: Truman Talley was head of Fox News Service in 1928.

THE NEXT CORNER **F2.3821**

Famous Players–Lasky. *Dist* Paramount Pictures. 18 Feb **1924** [c4 Mar 1924; LP19970]. Si; b&w. 35mm. 7 reels, 7,081 ft.

Pres by Adolph Zukor, Jesse L. Lasky. *Dir* Sam Wood. *Scen* Monte Katterjohn. *Photog* Alfred Gilks.

Cast: Conway Tearle *(Robert Maury)*, Lon Chaney *(Juan Serafin)*, Dorothy Mackaill *(Elsie Maury)*, Ricardo Cortez *(Don Arturo)*, Louise Dresser *(Nina Race, Elsie's mother)*, Remea Radzina *(Countess Longueval)*, Dorothy Cumming *(Paula Vrain)*, Mrs. Bertha Feducha *(Julie, Elsie's maid)*, Bernard Seigel *(The Stranger)*.

Romantic melodrama. Source: Kate Jordan, *The Next Corner* (Boston, 1921). Neglected by her busy husband, Elsie Maury falls in love with Don Arturo, a Spanish nobleman, and allows herself to be taken to his home outside Paris. A guilty conscience forces her to write a letter to her husband, but Arturo reads it and attempts to prevent its being mailed. Elsie is about to yield to him when a peasant, whose daughter Don Arturo has betrayed, kills him. Elsie flees, returns to her husband, and awaits the arrival of the letter. When it finally comes, the envelope contains blank paper. Elsie confesses everything to her husband and is forgiven. *Spanish. Nobility. Infidelity. Murder. Paris.*

NICE PEOPLE **F2.3822**

Famous Players–Lasky. *Dist* Paramount Pictures. ca2 Jul **1922** [Los Angeles premiere; released 4 Sep 1922; c25 Jul 1922; LP18094]. Si; b&w. 35mm. 7 reels, 6,244 ft.

Pres by Adolph Zukor. *Dir* William De Mille. *Adapt* Clara Beranger. *Photog* Guy Wilky.

Cast: Wallace Reid *(Billy Wade)*, Bebe Daniels *(Theodora [Teddy] Gloucester)*, Conrad Nagel *(Scotty Wilbur)*, Julia Faye *(Hallie Livingston)*, Claire McDowell *(Margaret Rainsford)*, Edward Martindel *(Hubert Gloucester)*, Eve Southern *(Eileen Baxter-Jones)*, Bertram Jones *(Trever Leeds)*, William Boyd *(Oliver Comstock)*, Ethel Wales *(Mrs. Heyfer)*.

Society drama. Source: Rachel Crothers, "Nice People," in A. H. Quinn, *Contemporary American Plays* (New York, c1923). Teddy Gloucester, one of the group of jazz age "nice people," is caught in a farmhouse during a storm with her intoxicated companion, Scotty. A stranger (Billy Wade) also seeking shelter saves her from Scotty's unwelcome attentions but not from the scandal which results from her father's discovery of her and Scotty—alone—the next morning. Hurt by the snubbing she receives from her friends, Teddy settles down and agrees to become an old-fashioned wife to Billy. *Jazz life. Drunkenness. Scandal. Reputation.*

THE NIGHT BIRD **F2.3823**

Universal Pictures. 16 Sep **1928** [c15 Aug 1928; LP25539]. Si; b&w. 35mm. 7 reels, 6,702 ft.

Dir Fred Newmeyer. *Scen* Earle Snell. *Titl* Albert De Mond. *Adapt* Nick Barrows, Earle Snell. *Story* Frederick Hatton, Fanny Hatton. *Photog* Arthur Todd. *Film Ed* Maurice Pivar.

Cast: Reginald Denny *(Kid Davis)*, Betsy Lee *(Madelena)*, Sam Hardy *(Gleason)*, Harvey Clark *(Silsburg)*, Corliss Palmer *(blonde)*, Jocelyn Lee *(redhead)*, Alphonse Martel *(Pete)*, George Bookasta *(Joe)*, Michael Visaroff *(Mario)*.

Comedy. Kid Davis, girlshy contender for the light heavyweight championship, bolts a party and starts home across Central Park, meeting on the way Madelena, a young Italian girl who has run away from home rather than marry a man she does not love. She insists on going home with The Kid and spends the night chastely in his apartment. The two fall in love, but Gleason, The Kid's manager, convinces Madelena that a match with The Kid is impossible. She sadly returns home, and The Kid goes into the ring, disheartened and unprepared. He is taking a bad beating when Madelena's brother comes to ringside and tells him that he must come and save Madelena from marriage to another man. The Kid then knocks out his opponent in nothing flat, goes to Madelena's home, stops the ceremony, and insists that it cannot continue unless he is the groom. It does, and he is. *Prizefighters. Fight managers. Italians. Brother-sister relationship.*

THE NIGHT BRIDE **F2.3824**

Metropolitan Pictures. *Dist* Producers Distributing Corp. 28 Mar **1927** [c29 Mar 1927; LP23793]. Si; b&w. 35mm. 6 reels, 5,736 ft.

Pres by John C. Flinn. *Supv* F. McGrew Willis. *Dir* E. Mason Hopper. *Scen* Fred Stanley. *Adapt* Zelda Sears. *Story* Frederic Chapin. *Photog* Dewey Wrigley.

Cast: Marie Prevost *(Cynthia Stockton)*, Harrison Ford *(Stanley Warrington)*, Franklin Pangborn *(John Stockton)*, Robert Edeson *(Adolphe Biggles)*, Constance Howard *(Renée Stockton)*, Richard Crawford *(Addison Walsh)*, George Kuwa *(Japanese gardener)*.

Bedroom farce. Cynthia Stockton's roadster collides with that of Stanley Warrington, an author and woman-hater, on a one-way road, but he refuses to yield to her impetuous demands; appropriating a milkman's truck, she finally makes her way home. Cynthia, engaged to Addison Walsh, finds him in the arms of her sister, Renée, just before the wedding, and, disillusioned, she wanders to Warrington's home and sleeps in a vacant room. Horrified, Warrington begs her to return home, but she refuses. When they are interrupted by Cynthia's father, she insists that she and Warrington have just been married. Complications ensue as Stockton proposes to send the couple on a wedding tour; when their steamship leaves the harbor, the couple reach an understanding and are married by the captain. *Authors. Sisters. Misogynists. Weddings. Automobile accidents. Chases.*

THE NIGHT CAP *see* **SECRETS OF THE NIGHT**

THE NIGHT CLUB **F2.3825**

Famous Players–Lasky. *Dist* Paramount Pictures. 27 Apr **1925** [c28 Apr 1925; LP21413]. Si; b&w. 35mm. 6 reels, 5,732 ft.

Pres by Adolph Zukor, Jesse L. Lasky. *Dir* Frank Urson, Paul Iribe. *Screenplay* Keene Thompson. *Adapt* Walter Woods. *Photog* Peverell Marley.

Cast: Raymond Griffith *(Robert White)*, Vera Reynolds *(Grace Henderson)*, Wallace Beery *(Diablo)*, Louise Fazenda *(Carmen)*.

Farce. Source: William Churchill De Mille and Cecil B. De Mille, *After Five; a Farce Comedy in Three Acts* (New York, c1913). Bob White, a charter member of "The Night Club," a loose organization of avowed bachelors, finally decides to marry, only to be left standing at the altar. Bob then learns that he will inherit $1 million if he marries Grace Henderson, but he has become a misogynist and goes into seclusion. Bob later meets Grace by chance, and, not knowing who she is, he falls in love with her. When Grace learns his identity, she believes that he has professed his love with the intention of marrying her for the money, and she spurns him. Learning that Grace will inherit the million if he dies, Bob attempts to kill himself. He eventually proves his love to Grace, and, after an encounter with a bandit, she consents to marry him. *Misogynists. Bachelors. Bandits. Marriage. Inheritance. Suicide.*

THE NIGHT CRY **F2.3826**

Warner Brothers Pictures. 27 Feb **1926** [c4 Mar 1926; LP22446]. Si; b&w. 35mm. 7 reels, 6,100 ft.

Dir Herman C. Raymaker. *Adapt* Ewart Adamson. *Story* Paul Klein, Edward Meagher. *Photog* Ed Du Par. *Adtl Photog* Walter Robinson. *Film Ed* Clarence Kolster. *Asst Dir* William McGann, Al Zeidman.

Cast: Rin-Tin-Tin *(himself, a dog)*, John Harron *(John Martin)*, June Marlowe *(Mrs. John Martin)*, Gayne Whitman *(Miguel Hernández)*, Heinie Conklin *(Tony)*, Don Alvarado *(Pedro)*, Mary Louise Miller *(The Martin Baby)*.

Melodrama. A giant condor decimates a herd of sheep, and Rin-Tin-Tin is unjustly accused of having turned killer. Under the law of the range, the sheepmen order the dog killed; but John Martin, his owner, relents and hides the dog instead. The condor takes Martin's baby, and Rin-Tin-Tin rescues her, killing the bird in a brutal fight. *Sheepmen. Dogs. Condors. Sheep.*

THE NIGHT FLYER **F2.3827**

James Cruze, Inc. *Dist* Pathé Exchange. 5 Feb **1928** [c17 Jan 1928; LP24873]. Si; b&w. 35mm. 7 reels, 5,954 ft.

Pres by James Cruze. *Dir* Walter Lang. *Adapt-Cont-Titl* Walter Woods. *Photog* Ernest Miller. *Art Dir* Charles Cadwallader. *Film Ed* Mildred Johnson. *Asst Dir* Arthur Kemp.

Cast: William Boyd *(Jimmy Bradley)*, Jobyna Ralston *(Kate Murphy)*, Philo McCullough *(Bat Mullins)*, Ann Schaeffer *(Mrs. Murphy)*, De Witt Jennings *(Bucks)*, John Milerta *(Tony)*, Robert Dudley *(Freddy)*.

Action melodrama. Source: Frank Hamilton Spearman, *Held for Orders: Being Stories of Railroad Life* (New York, 1901). Jimmy Bradley, a fireman on the old locomotive No. 99, loves Kate Murphy, daughter of the proprietress of the local lunch counter. His rival, Bat Mullins, is engineer of the new mail train scheduled to make a competition run. When Mullins overturns the new train, Bradley completes the run and earns the contract for his company by delivering the mail in record time on No. 99.

A promotion to engineer helps him win Kate. *Railroad firemen. Railroad engineers. Railroads. Postal service.*

THE NIGHT HAWK F2.3828

Stellar Productions. *Dist* W. W. Hodkinson Corp. 17 Feb **1924.** Si; b&w. 35mm. 6 reels, 5,100-5,200 ft.

Pres by Hunt Stromberg. *Dir* Stuart Paton. *Adapt* Joseph Poland. *Story* Carlysle Graham Raht.

Cast: Harry Carey *("The Hawk")*, Claire Adams *(Clia Milton)*, Joseph Girard *(Sheriff Milton)*, Fred Malatesta *(José Valdez)*, Nicholas De Ruiz *(Manuel Valdez)*.

Western melodrama. New York City police are chasing "Night Hawk," a crook, when José Valdez, a Mexican, helps him escape in exchange for Night Hawk's promise to kill a certain sheriff. Night Hawk agrees to do the job, but, arriving in the West, he falls in love with the sheriff's daughter and is unable to complete his mission. He joins the sheriff's posse when José's father illegally makes himself sheriff; then, singlehanded, Night Hawk rescues the girl from José's brigands. *Criminals—Rehabilitation. Sheriffs. Gangs. Mexicans. New York City.*

THE NIGHT HORSEMEN F2.3829

Fox Film Corp. ca4 Sep **1921** [Cleveland premiere; released Sep; c18 Sep 1921; LP17118]. Si; b&w. 35mm. 5 reels, 4,970 ft.

Pres by William Fox. *Dir-Scen* Lynn F. Reynolds. *Photog* Ben Kline.

Cast: Tom Mix *(Whistling Dan)*, May Hopkins *(Kate Cumberland)*, Harry Lonsdale *(Old Joe Cumberland)*, Joseph Bennett *(Dr. Byrne)*, Sid Jordan *(Buck Daniels)*, Bert Sprotte *(Mac Strann)*, Cap Anderson *(Jerry Strann)*, Lon Poff *(Haw Haw)*, Charles K. French *(Marshal)*.

Western melodrama. Source: Max Brand, *The Night Horseman* (New York, 1920). The day before he is to marry Kate Cumberland, Whistling Dan disappears, following the wild geese. His trail brings him to a saloon where Jerry Strann forces him into a fight, and the latter is shot; though warned that Jerry's brother, Mac, will soon be on his trail, Dan stays to nurse the boy back to health. Buck Daniels, foreman of the Cumberland Ranch, is sent by Kate, whose father is dying and wishes to see Dan; Mac Strann follows and sets fire to the Cumberland barn and kills Dan's dog. Dan tracks down Mac, but is dissuaded from shooting him by Kate, whose love for him overcomes the call of the wild geese. *Brothers. Incendiarism. Nature. Geese. Dogs.*

NIGHT LIFE F2.3830

Tiffany Productions. 1 Nov **1927** [c16 Nov 1927; LP24668]. Si; b&w. 35mm. 7 reels, 6,235 ft.

Dir George Archainbaud. *Cont* Gertrude Orr. *Titl* Viola Brothers Shore, Harry Braxton. *Story* Albert S. Le Vino. *Photog* Chester Lyons. *Sets* Burgess Beall. *Film Ed* Desmond O'Brien.

Cast: Alice Day *(Anna, a waif)*, Johnny Harron *(Max)*, Eddie Gribbon *(Nick, his coadjutor)*, Walter Hiers *(manager)*, Lionel Braham *(war profiteer)*, Kitty Barlow *(his wife)*, Dawn O'Day, Mary Jane Irving, Audrey Sewell *(his daughters)*, Earl Metcalf *(amorous swain)*, Patricia Avery *(amorous maid)*, Leopold Archduke of Austria *(Chief of Detectives)*, Snitz Edwards *(merry-go-round manager)*, Violet Palmer *(beer garden waitress)*, Lydia Yeamans Titus *(landlady)*.

Drama. Max, a sleight-of-hand artist, and his partner Nick, impoverished by the war, return to Vienna, the scene of earlier, happy days. Like many people driven to desperation, Max becomes a professional thief rather than starve; and Nick, in spite of scruples, also succumbs. Soon they are again prosperous, and Max is accosted by Anna, a poor girl reduced to picking pockets; he takes her to a restaurant and then to an amusement park, and they are soon caught up in a blissful romance, spending the night on the Ferris wheel. Anna takes a job as waitress in a beer garden, witnesses Max stealing a diamond brooch from a customer, and compels him to return it; Nick, convinced that her intrusion is destroying his friendship, causes her arrest. Ultimately, however, Nick takes the blame for the crime, leaving the lovers to start a new life. *Magicians. Thieves. Pickpockets. Waitresses. War victims. Friendship. Beer gardens. Ferris wheels. Vienna.*

NIGHT LIFE IN HOLLYWOOD F2.3831

A. B. Maescher Productions. *Dist* Arrow Film Corp. 15 Nov **1922** [c2 Aug 1922; LP18104]. Si; b&w. 35mm. 6 reels, 6,059 ft.

Pres by Mrs. A. B. Maescher. *Dir-Story* Fred Caldwell. *Co-Dir? (see note)* Jack Pratt.

Cast: J. Frank Glendon *(Joe)*, Josephine Hill *(Leonore Baxter, a motion picture star)*, Gale Henry *(Carrie)*, J. L. McComas *(Pa Powell)*, Elizabeth Rhodes *(Ma Powell)*, Jack Connolly *(Elkins, a motion picture actor)*, Delores Hall *(Amy, Joe's boyhood sweetheart)*, Wallace Reid, and family *(themselves)*, Theodore Roberts *(himself)*, Sessue Hayakawa, and wife *(themselves)*, Tsuru Aoki *(himself)*, William Desmond *(himself)*, Bryant Washburn, and family *(themselves)*, Bessie Love *(herself)*, J. Warren Kerrigan, and mother *(themselves)*, Johnny Jones *(himself)*, Denishawn Dancers.

Melodrama. Joe and his sister, Carrie, set out from Arkansas for the modern Babylon they believe Hollywood to be. Their attempts to lead a wild life backfire, they soon realize that Hollywood people are no different from the folks back home, and even their parents, Ma and Pa Powell, approve of Joe's love for Leonore Baxter when they understand the situation. The several scenes of Hollywood and its stars include Will Rogers' home and an Easter service at the Hollywood Bowl. *Actors. Motion pictures. Hollywood. Arkansas.*

Note: One source gives Jack Pratt as codirector.

NIGHT LIFE OF NEW YORK F2.3832

Famous Players–Lasky. *Dist* Paramount Pictures. 3 Aug **1925** [c4 Aug 1925; LP21695]. Si; b&w. 35mm. 8 reels, 6,998 ft.

Pres by Adolph Zukor, Jesse L. Lasky. *Dir* Allan Dwan. *Scen* Paul Schofield. *Story* Edgar Selwyn. *Photog* George Webber.

Cast: Rod La Rocque *(Ronald Bentley)*, Ernest Torrence *(John Bentley)*, Dorothy Gish *(Meg)*, Helen Lee Worthing *(Carrie Reed)*, George Hackathorne *(Jimmy)*, Arthur Housman *(Jerry)*, Riley Hatch *(William Workman)*.

Romantic comedy. Because of an unhappy romance as a young man, John Bentley hates New York City, but his son, Ronald, tired of living in Iowa, is determined to take up residence in Manhattan. The elder Bentley therefore conspires with his New York manager, William Workman, to involve Ronald in so much trouble that he will gladly return to the sedate life of an Iowa burgher. Arriving in Manhattan, Ronald strikes up an acquaintance with Meg, a telephone operator, whose brother, Jimmy, has come under the evil influence of Jerry. Jerry and Jimmy rob a wealthy woman, and Ronald is charged with the crime on circumstantial evidence, keeping quiet in order to protect Jimmy. Meg comes forward with evidence to clear him, however, and they are married, going to live in town. Ronald's father, who has come to New York, decides to remain in the city and make up for lost time! *Telephone operators. Business management. Brother-sister relationship. Robbery. Circumstantial evidence. New York City. Iowa.*

THE NIGHT MESSAGE F2.3833

Universal Pictures. 17 Mar **1924** [c21 Feb 1924; LP19945]. Si; b&w. 35mm. 5 reels, 4,591 ft.

Dir-Writ Perley Poore Sheehan. *Scen* Raymond L. Schrock. *Photog* Jackson Rose.

Cast: Howard Truesdell *("Old Man" Lefferts)*, Gladys Hulette *(Elsie Lefferts)*, Charles Cruz *(Lee Longstreet)*, Margaret Seddon *(Mrs. Longstreet)*, Norman Rankow *(Harney Lefferts)*, Robert Gordon *(Hank Lefferts)*, Edgar Kennedy *(Lem Beeman)*, Joseph W. Girard *(Governor Pringle)*.

Rural melodrama. The Lefferts-Longstreet feud is renewed when young Harney Lefferts is shot accidentally by Lem Beeman, telegraph operator and suitor of Elsie Lefferts. Evidence points to Lee Longstreet, Elsie's true love, and Beeman does not confess until Lee is tried, convicted, and sentenced to die. Then, in a heroic act, Beeman telegraphs his confession to the prison, thereby halting the execution. He saves Lee but loses his own life when he goes out in a storm to repair damaged lines. The feud is ended, and Lee marries Elsie. *Telegraph operators. Feuds. Capital punishment.*

Note: Working title: *Innocent.*

THE NIGHT OF LOVE F2.3834

Samuel Goldwyn, Inc. *Dist* United Artists. 22 Jan **1927** [New York premiere; released Jan; c10 Jan 1927; LP23580]. Si; b&w. 35mm. 8 reels, 7,600 ft.

Pres by Samuel Goldwyn. *Dir* George Fitzmaurice. *Adapt-Scen* Lenore J. Coffee. *Photog* George Barnes, Thomas Brannigan. *Art Dir* Karl Oscar Borg.

Cast: Ronald Colman *(Montero)*, Vilma Banky *(Princess Marie)*, Montagu Love *(Duke de la Garda)*, Natalie Kingston *(Donna Beatriz)*, John George *(jester)*, B. Hyman, Gibson Gowland *(bandits)*, Laska Winters *(a Gypsy bride)*, Sally Rand *(a Gypsy dancer)*.

Romantic drama. Source: Pedro Calderón de la Barca, unidentified work. In feudal Spain, Montero, son of a Gypsy leader, is about to take a bride according to primitive ritual, when the Duke de la Garda demands his right as feudal lord—to take the bride to his castle for a night. Rather than accede to the duke's advances, the girl chooses death by her own hand. Montero swears vengeance on the duke and turns outlaw and bandit. When the duke takes the king's niece, Princess Marie, for his bride, following a spectacular wedding feast, Montero and his outlaws kidnap Marie and the duke, taking them to an abandoned castle overlooking the sea; the duke is branded and returned, while Marie, in spite of herself, falls in love with Montero but returns to the duke. Disguised as a priest, the duke overhears her confession of love and imprisons her; Montero is captured and is to be burned at the stake, but he inspires the mob to riot and kill the duke. *Nobility. Gypsies. Bandits. Droit du seigneur. Revenge. Abduction. Suicide. Middle Ages. Spain.*

A NIGHT OF MYSTERY **F2.3835**

Paramount Famous Lasky Corp. 7 Apr **1928** [c7 Apr 1928; LP25133]. Si; b&w. 35mm. 6 reels, 5,741 ft.

Pres by Adolph Zukor, Jesse L. Lasky. *Dir* Lothar Mendes. *Adapt-Scen* Ernest Vajda. *Titl* Herman J. Mankiewicz. *Photog* Harry Fischbeck. *Film Ed* Frances Marsh.

Cast: Adolphe Menjou *(Captain Ferréol)*, Evelyn Brent *(Gilberte Boismartel)*, Nora Lane *(Thérèse D'Egremont)*, William Collier, Jr. *(Jérôme D'Egremont)*, Raoul Paoli *(Marcasse)*, Claude King *(Marquis Boismartel)*, Frank Leigh *(Rochemore)*, Margaret Burt *(Rochemore's secretary)*.

Melodrama. Source: Victorien Sardou, *Ferréol* (Paris, 1875). Bound for Africa the next day, Captain Ferréol visits the private rooms of Gilberte Boismartel, his former sweetheart who is married to a French magistrate, to return her love letters. As he leaves, he sees Marcasse, a watchman, kill Rochemore, the man who stole his wife. Marcasse defies Ferréol to report the murder because he has seen Ferréol visit Gilberte. In Africa Ferréol hears that Jérôme, the wayward brother of his sweetheart, Thérèse, has been accused of murdering Rochemore; he rushes back and confesses to the murder to save Jérôme, but a flaw in his statement proves his innocence. *Murder. Brother-sister relationship. France—Army.*

THE NIGHT OWL **F2.3836**

Harry J. Brown Productions. *Dist* Rayart Pictures. 30 Dec **1926** [New York State license]. Si; b&w. 35mm. 5 reels, 5,080 ft.

Dir Harry J. Brown. *Story-Scen* Henry Roberts Symonds. *Photog* William Tuers.

Cast: Reed Howes *(Larry Armitage)*, Gladys Hulette *(Mary Jackson)*, Harold Austin *(Jimmy Jackson)*, Joseph W. Girard *(William Armitage)*, Dave Kirby *(Harlem Red)*, James Mason *(Gentleman Joe)*.

Action melodrama. "Night club devotee is abducted by orders of wealthy father. Abductors betray themselves and boy discovers plot to rob his father and kidnap him. Cigarette girl is member of gang but, through love for boy, switches her loyalty, and he is enabled to prevent attempted robbery." *(Motion Picture News Booking Guide*, 12:46, Apr 1927.) *Cigarette girls. Abduction. Robbery. Nightclubs.*

NIGHT PARADE **F2.3837**

RKO Productions. 27 Oct **1929** [c27 Oct 1929; LP900]. Sd (Photophone); b&w. 35mm. 8 reels, 6,665 ft. [Also si; 6,503 ft.]

Prod William Le Baron. *Assoc Prod* Louis Sarecky. *Dir* Malcolm St. Clair. *Scen-Dial* James Gruen, George O'Hara. *Photog* William Marshall. *Art Dir* Max Ree. *Film Ed* Jack Kitchen. *Sd* Lambert Gay.

Cast: Hugh Trevor *(Bobby Murray)*, Lloyd Ingraham *(Tom Murray)*, Dorothy Gulliver *(Doris)*, Aileen Pringle *(Paula Vernoff)*, Robert Ellis *(John Zelli)*, Lee Shumway *(Sid Durham)*, Ann Pennington *(dancer)*, Charles Sullivan *(Huffy)*, Walter Kane *(Jake)*, Barney Furey *(Bennie)*, James Dugan *(Artie)*, Nate Slott *(Phil)*, Marie Astaire *(Ethel)*.

Melodrama. Source: George Abbott, Edward Paramore and Hyatt Daab, "Ringside" (publication undetermined). Middleweight champion Bobby Murray is expected to be defeated in a forthcoming bout with McCabe, an opinion shared by sportswriter Sid Durham, who nevertheless respects Tom Murray, the boy's father and manager. John Zelli, a gambling racketeer, induces Paula Vernoff to lure Bobby into secret meetings; and befuddled by drink and Paula's urging, he agrees to throw the fight. Durham learns of the sellout and informs Tom; Bobby confesses and at the same time learns that Doris, a childhood friend, loves him. Tom takes out revenge on Zelli, and just as Bobby seems sure to be defeated in the ring, the arrival of his father and Doris spurs him on to win. *Prizefighters. Sportswriters. Fight managers. Racketeers. Filial relations. Bribery. Drunkenness.*

THE NIGHT PATROL **F2.3838**

Richard Talmadge Productions–Carlos Productions. *Dist* Film Booking Offices of America. 14 Mar **1926** [c14 Mar 1926; LP22512]. Si; b&w. 35mm. 6 reels, 5,085 ft.

Prod Richard Talmadge. *Dir* Noel Mason Smith. *Story-Scen* Frank Howard Clark. *Photog* Jack Stevens, Charles Lang. *Film Ed* Doane Harrison.

Cast: Richard Talmadge *(Tom Collins)*, Rose Blossom *(Louise Hollister)*, Mary Carr *(Mrs. Hollister)*, Gardner James *(The Boy [Roy Hollister])*, Josef Swickard *(John Pendleton)*, Grace Darmond *(Goldie Ferguson)*, Victor Dillingham *(Chuck Wolcott)*, Arthur Conrad *(Terry the Rat)*.

Crook melodrama. Policeman Tom Collins, in love with Louise Hollister, is compelled to arrest her brother, Roy, who is framed for the murder of another policeman by a gang of robbers. Collins, who believes the boy innocent, disguises himself as a notorious criminal, becomes a member of the gang, and learns that Wolcott, the leader, is the actual killer. He frustrates an attempt to rob banker Pendleton's house, gathers evidence to free Roy, and on the night of Roy's execution, owing to a breakdown in telegraph communications, is forced to race against time through a storm to save the boy. He regains the girl's love and wins a promotion. *Police. Brother-sister relationship. Murder. Disguise. Robbery. Frameup. Capital punishment.*

NIGHT RIDE **F2.3839**

Universal Pictures. 12 Jan **1930** [c4 Jan 1930; LP979]. Sd (Movietone); b&w. 35mm. 6 reels, 5,418 ft. [Also si.]

Pres by Carl Laemmle. *Dir* John S. Robertson. *Dial* Tom Reed, Edward T. Lowe, Jr. *Titl* Charles Logue. *Adapt* Edward T. Lowe, Jr. *Photog* Alvin Wyckoff. *Film Ed* Milton Carruth, A. Ross. *Rec Engr* C. Roy Hunter. *Sd Syst* Smith, Harold I. Monitor.

Cast: Joseph Schildkraut *(Joe Rooker)*, Barbara Kent *(Ruth Kearns)*, Edward G. Robinson *(Tony Garotta)*, Harry Stubbs *(Bob O'Leary)*, De Witt Jennings *(police captain)*, Ralph Welles *(Blondie)*, Hal Price *(Mac)*, George Ovey *(Ed)*.

Crime melodrama. Source: Henry La Cossitt, unidentified story in *Adventure Magazine*. Star reporter Joe Rooker links gunman Tony Garotta to a double murder and payroll robbery through the discovery of one of Garotta's cigarettes at the scene of the crime; meanwhile, Joe is married to Ruth Kearns. Garotta confronts Joe at the police reporters' room and threatens revenge through his wife. Garotta escapes, word arrives that Joe's house has been bombed, and Joe starts out for Garotta; but he and Bob are captured by Garotta and put aboard a speedboat. Joe manages to take Garotta prisoner and learns that Ruth is safe. *Reporters. Gangsters. Murder. Robbery. Revenge.*

THE NIGHT ROSE **F2.3840**

Goldwyn Pictures. Dec **1921** [c5 Oct 1921; LP17040]. Si; b&w. 35mm. 6 reels, 5,630 ft.

Dir Wallace Worsley. *Scen* Arthur F. Statter. *Story* Leroy Scott.

Cast: Leatrice Joy *(Georgia Rodman)*, Lon Chaney *(O'Rourke)*, John Bowers *(Graham)*, Cullen Landis *(Jimmy)*, Richard Tucker *(Clancy)*, Mary Warren *(Mrs. Rodman)*, Edythe Chapman *(Mrs. Rodman)*, Betty Schade *(Sally)*, Maurice B. Flynn *(Pierson)*, H. Milton Ross *(Courey)*, John Cossar *(Garrison)*.

Underworld melodrama. When taken to a San Francisco cafe by her sweetheart, Jimmy, Georgia Rodman witnesses the shooting of a policeman by an underworld gang: O'Rourke, whom Jimmy believes to be his friend, sends one of his men to their table to inquire about Georgia, and when he shoots the policeman Georgia and Jimmy are held for questioning. As a result, Georgia is turned out of her home, and O'Rourke gives the couple a room in his hotel. Assistant District Attorney Steven Graham links the missing couple with O'Rourke's activities and collects evidence against him. O'Rourke plans to bribe Graham and have Jimmy shot on the night of his annual ball, and Sally, O'Rourke's ex-mistress, learning of the plan, turns against him and informs Georgia; finding Jimmy wounded, she seeks revenge at the ball, but Sally shoots O'Rourke. Georgia is reunited with her family and Jimmy, while Graham finds happiness with her sister, Mary. *Police. Gangs. Family life. San Francisco.*

Note: Working title: *Flower of Darkness*. "This picture was produced by Goldwyn . . . under the title of *The Night Rose*. It came under the ban of the New York censors for some reason, and only recently, with certain eliminations, was pronounced fit for exhibition in the Empire State." (*Exhibitors Trade Review*, 19 Aug 1922, p823.) Though the plot apparently underwent no real alterations, the title was changed to *Voices of the City* and O'Rourke became Duke McGee.

THE NIGHT SHIP **F2.3841**

Gotham Productions. *Dist* Lumas Film Corp. 1 Feb **1925** [c7 Feb 1925; LP21105]. Si; b&w. 35mm. 6 reels, 5,620 ft.

Pres by Samuel Sax. *Dir-Story-Scen* Henry McCarthy. *Photog* Jack MacKenzie.

Cast: Mary Carr *(Martha Randall)*, Tom Santschi *(Capt. Jed Hobbs)*, Robert Gordon *(Bob Randall)*, Margaret Fielding *(Elizabeth Hobbs)*, Charles A. Sellon *(Jimson Weed)*, Willis Marks *(David Brooks)*, Charles W. Mack *(Eli Stubbs)*, Mary McLane *(Janet Hobbs)*, L. J. O'Connor *(Cassidy)*, Julian Rivero *(Pedro Lopez)*.

Melodrama. After being marooned in the South Seas for 6 years, Bob Randall returns to his home in Faith Harbor, Maine. He discovers that his sweetheart has married Jed Hobbs, a villainous sea captain, and that his mother, dispossessed of her home by Hobbs, has met an early death. Bob vows revenge, finds Hobbs at the village inn, and floors him in a fight. In the company of Jimson Weed, a new-found friend, Bob boards Hobbs's boat, hoping to prove him guilty of smuggling contraband. Bob and Jimson discover a load of guns and gunpowder bound for Central America and capture the members of the crew one by one. Hobbs at first eludes capture, but when he is cornered by Bob, he drops a lighted match into the powder hold. The ship is destroyed in the resulting explosion, but Hobbs alone is killed. Bob is then reunited with his former sweetheart, who is now free to marry him. *Smuggling. Maine. South Seas. Ship explosions.*

THE NIGHT WATCH **F2.3842**

Dist Truart Film Corp. 2 Mar **1926** [New York State license]. Si; b&w. 35mm. 5 reels.

Dir Fred Caldwell.

Cast: Mary Carr *(Mrs. Blackwell)*, Charles Delaney *(George Blackwell)*, Gloria Grey *(Nellie Powell)*, Jack Richardson *(Mr. Powell)*, Muriel Reynolds, Raymond Rousenville, Ethel Schram, Charles W. Mack, Fred Caldwell.

Melodrama. A feud between the Powell and Blackwell families frustrates young lovers George and Nellie, but U. S. revenue agents end the dispute when the Powell clan has to escape arrest for moonshining. *Revenue agents. Moonshiners. Mountain life. Feuds.*

THE NIGHT WATCH **F2.3843**

First National Pictures. 9 Sep **1928** [c29 Aug 1928; LP25578]. Sd eff & mus score (Vitaphone); b&w. 35mm. 7 reels, 6,676 ft.

Pres by Richard A. Rowland. *Supv* Ned Marin. *Dir* Alexander Korda. *Cont* Lajos Biró. *Titl* Dwinelle Benthall, Rufus McCosh. *Photog* Karl Struss. *Film Ed* George McGuire.

Cast: Billie Dove *(Yvonne)*, Paul Lukas *(Captain Corlaix)*, Donald Reed *(D'Artelle)*, Nicholas Soussanin *(Brambourg)*, Nicholas Bela *(Leduc)*, George Periolat *(Fargasson)*, William Tooker *(Mobrayne)*, Gus Partos *(Dagorne)*, Anita Garvin *(Ann)*.

Drama. Source: Michael Morton, *In the Night Watch* (New York opening: 29 Jan 1921). On the night of 1 August 1914, Commander Corlaix of the French Navy and his wife, Yvonne, arrange a shipboard dinner for the officers of his cruiser. Afterward, Lieutenant D'Artelle asks Yvonne to stay on board with him, and when Corlaix (learning by classified wireless that war has been declared) abruptly orders her from the ship, she goes instead with D'Artelle to his cabin. The ship is sunk by a torpedo, and Corlaix is brought up before the Admiralty Court on charges of incompetence. Yvonne comes forward to testify and, by compromising herself, proves her husband's adherence to duty. Corlaix, realizing Yvonne's great love for him, forgives her for her indiscretions, and they are reunited. *Admiralty courts. Cruisers. World War I. France—Navy.*

NIGHT WORK **F2.3844**

Pathé Exchange. 3 Aug **1930** [c6 Jun 1930; LP1362]. Sd (Photophone); b&w. 35mm. 9 reels, 8,394 ft.

Prod E. B. Derr. *Dir* Russell Mack. *Story-Screenplay-Dial* Walter De Leon. *Photog* John Mescall. *Art Dir* Edward Jewell. *Film Ed* Joseph Kane. *Mus Dir* Josiah Zuro. *Songs:* "Deep in Your Heart," "I'm Tired of My Tired Man" Mort Harris, Ted Snyder. *Rec Engr* Charles O'Loughlin, Homer Ackerman. *Asst Dir* Ray McCarey.

Cast: Eddie Quillan *(Willie)*, Sally Starr *(Mary)*, Frances Upton *(Aggie)*, John T. Murray *(Calloway)*, George Duryea *(Harvey Vanderman)*, Ben Bard *(Pinkie)*, Robert McWade *(Phil Reisman)*, Douglas Scott *(Oscar)*, Addie McPhail *(Trixie)*, Kit Guard *(Squint)*, Georgia Caine *(Mrs. Ten Eyck)*, George Billings *(Buster)*, Charles Clary *(Mr. Vanderman)*, Tom Dugan *(Johnny Harris)*, Arthur Hoyt *(George Twining)*, Billie Bennett *(Miss Brown)*, Tempe Pigott *(Flora)*, Ruth Lyons *(Miss Allenby)*, Nora Lane *(Arlene Ogalthorpe)*, Marjorie "Babe" Kane *(cabaret singer)*, Jack Mack *(Biff Miller)*, Arthur Lovejoy *(effeminate man)*, Marion Ballou *(Mrs. Morgan)*, Martha Mattox *(Mrs. McEvoy)*, James Donlan *(Mr. McEvoy)*, Harry Bowen *(cabdriver)*, Violet Harris *(Ruth Hiatt)*, Vincent Barnett *(headwaiter)*.

Comedy-drama. Willie Musher, assistant window-trimmer and jack-of-all-trades at Tracy's Department Store, consistently shoulders the blame for patrons who deem themselves aggrieved and one day is awarded a $10 bill. On his way to the bank, he stops to examine a car that is campaigning for funds for an orphans' home; he holds his bank book in such a way that Mary, a nurse, takes the bill and leaves him a receipt. Later, he is alarmed to learn he has obligated himself to support a baby, but taking an interest in Mary and little Oscar, he gets a job as waiter in a nightclub to support the child. To Willie's chagrin, he learns that Vanderman, Sr., wants to adopt Oscar, apparently the offspring of his son, Harvey. Willie dreams of hair-raising stunts to kidnap Oscar; finding that he has been promoted, he proves that Oscar is not Vanderman's grandson, adopts the boy, and asks Mary to marry him. *Window trimmers. Waiters. Nurses. Orphans. Adoption. Department stores. Finance—personal.*

NINE AND THREE-FIFTHS SECONDS **F2.3845**

A. G. Steen. 5 Aug **1925** [New York State license]. Si; b&w. 35mm. 6 reels, 5,386 ft.

Dir Lloyd B. Carleton. *Scen* Roy Clements. *Photog* Edward Henderson, Gordon Pollock.

Cast: Charles Paddock *(Charles Raymond)*, Helen Ferguson *(Mary Bowser)*, George Fawcett *(Jasper Raymond)*, Jack Giddings *(Walter Raymond)*, Peggy Schaffer *(Lucille Pringle)*, G. Raymond Nye *(Link Edwards)*, Otis Harlan *(Motherbund)*.

Action melodrama. Charles Raymond, a college athlete who is disowned by his father, becomes a hobo and begins riding the rails. He is thrown off a train in the West and meets Mary Bowser, the daughter of a rancher. Charles later wins a race against a horse. Mary is kidnaped by a jealous suitor, who abducts her on horseback. Charles pursues them on foot and rescues Mary. He later establishes a new sprinting record at the Olympics and takes Mary for his wife. *Tramps. Sprinters. Ranchers. Kidnaping. Olympic Games.*

NINE POINTS OF THE LAW **F2.3846**

Rainbow Film Co. *Dist* Joan Film Sales. 1 Mar **1922** [c25 Feb 1922; LP17629]. Si; b&w. 35mm. 6 reels, 5,500 ft.

Dir Wayne Mack. *Scen* Ford Beebe. *Story* L. V. Jefferson. *Film Ed* Lloyd Lonergan.

Cast: Helen Gibson *(Cherie Du Bois)*, Edward Coxen *(Bruce McLeod)*, Leo Maloney *(Fred Cullum)*, Aggie Herring *(Mrs. Prouty)*.

Western melodrama. Bruce McLeod returns from the goldfields to find that his wife has left home with another man, taking their child. After the death of the mother, the child is adopted by Cherie, a local dancehall girl ostracized by the community. Cullum, a gambler who earlier seduced Mrs. McLeod, drifts into the town, and failing to win Cherie, he swears vengeance. McLeod, seeking the man who wrecked his home, falls in love with Cherie but scorns her when he discovers that she is a dancer. Ultimately, the child identifies Cullum as the gambler who lured Mrs. McLeod from her home. In the ensuing fight, Cullum is shot by a halfbreed, and Bruce is happily united with Cherie. *Dancehall girls. Gamblers. Halfcastes. Desertion. Adoption.*

Note: Original title: *A Girl's Decision.*

THE NINETY AND NINE **F2.3847**

Vitagraph Co. of America. 17 Dec **1922** [c12 Dec 1922; LP18503]. Si; b&w. 35mm. 7 reels, 6,800 ft.

Pres by Albert E. Smith. *Dir* David Smith. *Scen* C. Graham Baker. *Story* Ramsay Morris. *Photog* Steve Smith, Jr.

Cast: Warner Baxter *(Tom Silverton [Phil Bradbury])*, Colleen Moore *(Ruth Blake)*, Lloyd Whitlock *(Mark Leveridge)*, Gertrude Astor *(Kate Van Dyke)*, Robert Dudley *(Abner Blake)*, Mary Young *(Rachel)*, Arthur Jasmine *(Bud Bryson)*, Ernest Butterworth *(Reddy)*, Aggie Herring *(Mrs. Dougherty)*, Dorothea Wolbert *(Mrs. Markham)*, Rex Hammel *(Eric Van*

Dyke), Charles Moore *(Sam Grant).*

Melodrama. Source: Ramsay Morris, *The Ninety and Nine* (New York opening: 7 Oct 1902). "The production has everything to recommend it to those who like sensational drama of the old school. A falsely accused hero, recurring emphasis on the strain of the lost sheep, a faithful sweetheart, a mustached villain, the fantastic character of a half-wit and a stupendous climax ... " (*Moving Picture World,* 23 Dec 1922). A mysterious murder forces Phil Bradbury to flee to a small town, where he assumes the name of Tom Silverton and falls in love with Ruth Blake. Phil's former sweetheart, Kate Van Dyke, and her new fiancé, Mark Leveridge, come to the town; Mark tries to frame Phil for the murder; and Phil is about to leave town when a forest fire threatens the next town. He runs a locomotive through the blazing timber to save the inhabitants, receives proof of his innocence, and marries Ruth. *Fugitives. Halfwits. Murder. Disguise. Forest fires.*

NIX ON DAMES **F2.3848**

Fox Film Corp. 24 Nov **1929** [c31 Oct 1929; LP858]. Sd (Movietone); b&w. 35mm. 7 reels, 5,998 ft.

Pres by William Fox. *Assoc Prod* George Middleton. *Dir* Donald Gallaher. *Screenplay-Dial* Maude Fulton, Frank Gay. *Story* Maude Fulton. *Photog* Charles G. Clarke. *Sets* Duncan Cramer. *Film Ed* Dorothy Spencer. *Songs: "Two Pals," "Say the Word," "The Song of My Heart," "Oh, Lord, Pour Down Your Waters and Baptize Me," "Fading Away"* L. Wolfe Gilbert, Abel Baer. *Red Engr* Harold Hobson. *Asst Dir* Horace Hough. *Cost* Sophie Wachner.

Cast: Mae Clarke *(Jackie Lee),* Robert Ames *(Bert Wills),* William Harrigan *(Johnny Brown),* Maude Fulton *(Stella Foster),* George MacFarlane *(Ed Foster),* Frederick Graham *(Baring),* Camille Rovelle *(Miss Woods),* Grace Wallace *(Bonnie Tucker),* Hugh McCormack *(Jim Tucker),* Ben Hall *(Cliff),* Marshall Ruth *(Billy),* Billy Colvin *(Hoffman),* Louise Beavers *(Magnolia).*

Romantic comedy-drama. Bert Wills and Johnny Brown, two acrobats who are both avowed woman-haters, return to a theatrical boardinghouse in New York City so that one of them, who has been injured, may recuperate. There they both fall in love with Jackie Lee, a girl who aspires to their own profession, and soon they become rivals for her favor. When they go back to work, a fight between the partners causes a final separation, but happiness does come to all concerned. *Acrobats. Actors. Misogynists. Boardinghouses. New York City.*

NO BABIES WANTED **F2.3849**

Plaza Pictures. 7 Jun **1928** [New York showing]. Si; b&w. 35mm. 6 reels, 5,215 ft.

Dir John Harvey. *Scen* Harriet Hinsdale, H. T. Crist. *Titl* Harry Chandlee. *Photog* L. William O'Connell. *Film Ed* Harry Chandlee.

Cast: Priscilla Moran *(Patsy O'Day),* William V. Mong *(Michael O'Day),* Dorothy Devore *(Martha Whitney),* Emily Fitzroy *("Old Ironsides," the landlady),* Cissy Fitzgerald *(The Orphanage Woman),* John Richard Becker *(The Baby),* Dinty *(himself).*

Domestic drama. Michael O'Day and his 8-year-old granddaughter, Patsy, adopt a deserted baby, who is left in the little girl's care when the old man is injured and sent to the hospital. The girl's efforts to keep the baby out of the hands of a hard-boiled landlady and the orphanage constitute the remaining action. *Children. Grandfathers. Foundlings. Landladies.*

Note: May also be known as *The Baby Mother.*

NO CONTROL **F2.3850**

Metropolitan Pictures Corp. of California. *Dist* Producers Distributing Corp. 7 Apr **1927** [c16 Apr 1927; LP23869]. Si; b&w. 35mm. 6 reels, 5,573 ft.

Pres by John C. Flinn. *Dir* Scott Sidney, E. J. Babille. *Scen* Zelda Sears, Tay Garnett. *Photog* Georges Benoit. *Art Dir* Charles Cadwallader.

Cast: Harrison Ford *(John Douglas, Jr.),* Phyllis Haver *(Nancy Flood),* Jack Duffy *(Noah Flood),* Tom Wilson *(Asthma),* Toby Claude *(Mrs. Douglas),* E. J. Ratcliffe *(John Douglas),* Larry Steers *(Kid Dugan).*

Farce. Source: Frank Condon, "Speed But No Control," in *Saturday Evening Post* (196:14–15, 21 Jun 1924). Nancy Flood, whose father operates a one-ring circus, decides to take a business job to earn extra money. John Douglas, a tired businessman ignored by his family, departs on a business trip and leaves John, Jr., in charge of the office. Young Douglas starts a flirtation with Nancy, who applies at a realty office, actually a cover for a poolroom operated by Kid Dugan; John saves her from Dugan's advances and gives her a job. When Douglas returns, he discharges Nancy for incompetency, and John, Jr., accepts Flood's offer to manage the circus. Desperate for money, they enter a dancing horse in a race. Knowing the animal to be particularly frightened by the circus lion, John manages to prod the horse into the home stretch by the sound of the lion's roar. The circus is thus rescued, and John is united with Nancy. *Businessmen. Courtship. Circus. Horseracing. Billiard parlors. Horses. Lions.*

NO DEFENSE **F2.3851**

Vitagraph Co. of America. 25 Dec **1921** [c21 Dec 1921; LP17380]. Si; b&w. 35mm. 6 reels, 5,700 ft.

Pres by Albert E. Smith. *Dir* William Duncan. *Scen* C. Graham Baker. *Photog* George Robinson.

Cast: William Duncan *(John Manning),* Edith Johnson *(Ethel Austin),* Jack Richardson *(Frederick Apthorpe),* Henry Hebert *(Milton Hulst),* Mathilde Brundage *(Mrs. Austin),* Charles Dudley *(MacRoberts).*

Melodrama. Source: J. Raleigh Davies, "The Comeback" (publication undetermined). Mrs. Austin is a penniless society matron whose only hope is in a wealthy marriage for her daughter, Ethel, who favors engineer John Manning while the mother prefers wealthy lawyer Frederick Apthorpe. Manning, determining to secure his position, leaves with Milton Hulst, a crooked lawyer, in search of gold in the North, secretly marrying Ethel before departing. Manning, Hulst, and a third partner, MacRoberts, strike it rich, but Hulst steals the gold and murders MacRoberts with Manning's revolver. Manning is arrested but escapes the police and is cared for by an Indian. Meanwhile Ethel marries Apthorpe, who has become district attorney; when Hulst tries to blackmail her with evidence of her previous marriage, Manning intervenes and Hulst is killed by Ethel. Manning confesses to the crime, is prosecuted by Apthorpe, and is sentenced to be hanged. When Apthorpe is elected governor, he refuses to keep his promise to pardon Manning until Ethel threatens to expose Apthorpe and kill herself. When Manning is freed, Ethel and Apthorpe separate and she is reunited with Manning. *Engineers. Lawyers. District attorneys. State governors. Wealth. Bigamy. Injustice. Blackmail.*

NO DEFENSE **F2.3852**

Warner Brothers Pictures. 6 Apr **1929** [c1 Apr 1929; LP267]. Talking sequences, sd eff, & mus score (Vitaphone); b&w. 35mm. 7 reels, 5,558 ft. [Also si, 11 May 1929; 4,712 ft.]

Dir Lloyd Bacon. *Scen* Robert Lord. *Titl* Joe Jackson. *Story* J. Raleigh Davies. *Photog* Frank Kesson. *Film Ed* Tommy Pratt.

Cast: Monte Blue *(Monte Collins),* May McAvoy *(Ruth Harper),* Lee Moran *(Snitz),* Kathryn Carver *(Lois Harper),* William H. Tooker *(Harper, Sr.),* William Desmond *(John Harper),* Bud Marshall *(construction laborer).*

Melodrama. Monte Collins, the foreman of a western railroad construction crew, is greatly attracted to Ruth Harper, the daughter of the railroad's owner, and goes to visit her in Boston. There he cuts a sorry figure in ill-fitting evening clothes. Monte quickly returns west in the company of Ruth's brother, John, who has been placed in charge of purchasing new materials for a bridge under construction. In order to provide luxuries for his avaricious wife, John orders substandard steel, and the bridge collapses. Monte assumes the blame for the accident in order to shield John's father, who is in bad health, from the possibly fatal shock of learning of his son's negligence. Ruth learns of Monte's sacrifice and goes away with him, willing to share whatever fate brings. *Construction foremen. Railroad magnates. Socialites. Social classes. Self-sacrifice. Railroads. Bridges. Boston.*

NO MAN'S GOLD **F2.3853**

Fox Film Corp. 29 Aug **1926** [c8 Aug 1926; LP23030]. Si; b&w. 35mm. 6 reels, 5,745 ft.

Pres by William Fox. *Dir* Lewis Seiler. *Adapt-Scen* John Stone. *Photog* Dan Clark. *Asst Dir* Wynn Mace.

Cast: Tom Mix *(Tom Stone),* Eva Novak *(Jane Rogers),* Frank Campeau *(Frank Healy),* Forrest Taylor *(Wat Lyman),* Harry Grippe *(Lefty Logan),* Malcolm Waite *(Pete Krell),* Mickey Moore *(Jimmy),* Tom Santschi, Tony *(himself, a horse).*

Western melodrama. Source: J. Allen Dunn, *Dead Man's Gold* (New York, 1920). On the orders of Krell, a miner en route to restake a lost mine is killed by Healy. Tom and his sidekick, Lefty, discover the dying man, who divides a map of the mine into three parts and leaves his small son in their care. They attend a rodeo, and there Tom comes to the aid of Jane Rogers, one of the contestants, and licks Krell when he interferes. Krell is joined by Healy, and they set out for the mine; Jane, learning of

Healy's plotting with Krell, rides to warn Tom and is captured by Krell. With the aid of his horse, Tony, Tom rescues Jane, then demolishes the shack in which the gang is hiding. With the demise of the villains, Tom and Jane are united. *Children. Claim jumpers. Mine claims. Rodeos. Documentation. Horses.*

NO MAN'S LAND *see* **NO MAN'S LAW** (Entry F2.3855)

NO MAN'S LAW **F2.3854**

Independent Pictures. *Dist* Film Booking Offices of America. 18 Oct **1925** [premiere?; released 1 Nov; c18 Oct 1925; LP22014]. Si; b&w. 35mm. 5 reels, 4,042 ft.

Prod Jesse J. Goldburg. *Dir* Del Andrews. *Cont* William E. Wing. *Story* Walter J. Coburn.

Cast: Bob Custer *(Dave Carson)*, Adalyn Mayer *(Marion Moore)*, Ralph McCullough *(Donald Moore)*, Bruce Gordon *(Monte Mallory)*, Ethan Laidlaw *(Nick Alby)*.

Western melodrama. Gambler Monte Mallory cheats John Carson out of his ranch near the Mexican border and turns it into a notorious gambling resort known as The White Owl. Carson, appalled at his loss, kills himself. Mallory's latest victim is Donald Moore, whose sister, Marion, he covets. Mallory entices her into his office and offers to forget the $10,000 Donald owes him if she will be nice to him. She is rescued by a stranger (Carson's son, Dave). That night, Dave recovers Donald's I.O.U.'s and joins forces with famed bandit Quantrell, who also has a score to settle with Mallory. Marion is kidnaped by Alby, Mallory's henchman, but Dave and Quantrell follow in pursuit. There ensues a long battle, which culminates in Dave's rescuing Marion from a fire after beating Mallory to within an inch of his life. *Gamblers. Bandits. Brother-sister relationship. Revenge. Kidnaping. Mexican border.*

NO MAN'S LAW **F2.3855**

Hal Roach. *Dist* Pathé Exchange. 1 May **1927** [c7 Apr 1927; LU23836]. Si; b&w. 35mm. 7 reels, 6,903 ft.

Pres by Hal Roach. *Dir* Fred Jackman. *Scen* Frank Butler. *Story* F. Richard Jones. *Photog* Floyd Jackman, George Stevens.

Cast: Rex *(himself, a horse)*, Barbara Kent *(Toby Belcher)*, Jimmy Finlayson *(Jack Belcher)*, Theodore von Eltz *(Spider O'Day)*, Oliver Hardy *(Sharkey Nye)*.

Western melodrama. Spider O'Day and Sharkey Nye, two bad men, flee the sheriff and his posse into Death Valley and soon grow mistrustful of each other. They stumble onto Jack Belcher's little cabin and mine, watched over by Rex, a wild horse whose special mission is to protect Toby, Jake's foster daughter. They plot to jump Belcher's claim, but O'Day has a change of heart when he falls for Toby. The enraged killer, Nye, suggests a game of checkers to settle the dispute; although O'Day wins, Nye shoots him and proceeds to do away with Belcher and attack Toby, but Rex comes to the rescue and kills the villain. O'Day recovers and is happily united with the girl. *Foster fathers. Desperadoes. Mine claims. Checkers. Horses.*

Note: Also reviewed under the title *No Man's Land*.

NO MAN'S WOMAN **F2.3856**

Helen Gibson Productions. *Dist* Associated Photoplays. 5 Feb **1921** [trade review]. Si; b&w. 35mm. 5 reels.

Dir Wayne Mack, Leo Maloney. *Adapt* Ford I. Beebe. *Story* L. V. Jefferson.

Cast: Helen Gibson *(The Girl)*, Edwin Coxen *(The Man)*, Leo Maloney *(Cullen)*.

Western melodrama. "On his return from an adventure in the gold fields, a young Westerner returns to his home only to learn that his wife and child had been taken away by a gambler named Cullen. He vows to seek revenge and starts out in search for them. In his search he meets a dance hall belle, touted 'no man's woman.' Meanwhile Cullen has deserted the girl and child. The dance hall belle, while trying to save another neighbor's child, finds herself nursing the wronged woman. The wanderer reaches the home, but the wronged woman recognizing him, tells the dancer her story and then dies. The dancer takes the child to her home, ... [and] she loses the respect of her friends. The wanderer arrives at the saloon just in time to save her from Cullen, but ridicules her on learning that she is a dance hall performer. Cullen is persistent in his wooing and [his] appeals to the wanderer with whom she has fallen in love fail. In a final effort the girl brings the child to the saloon so that she might win him. The child on seeing Cullen rushes to him and calls him 'Daddy Cullen.' The wanderer realizing he has finally met his man proceeds to punish him. A bystander who had a grudge against Cullen shoots him. Realizing that the dance hall girl had been a good mother to his child, the wanderer decides to settle down and all ends happily." (*Exhibitor's Trade Review*, 5 Feb 1921, p979.) *Gold miners. Gamblers. Dancehall girls. Wanderers. Children. Desertion. Revenge.*

NO MORE WOMEN **F2.3857**

Associated Authors. *Dist* Allied Producers and Distributors. 18 Jan **1924** [New York premiere; released 15 Feb; c15 Jan 1924; LP19828]. Si; b&w. 35mm. 6 reels, 6,186 ft.

Pres by Frank Woods, Thompson Buchanan, Elmer Harris, Clark W. Thomas. *Prod-Writ* Elmer Harris. *Dir* Lloyd Ingraham. *Mus Synop* James C. Bradford. *Casting Dir* Horace Williams.

Cast: Matt Moore *(Peter Maddox)*, Madge Bellamy *(Peggy Van Dyke)*, Kathleen Clifford *(Daisy Crenshaw)*, Clarence Burton *("Beef" Hogan)*, George Cooper *(Tex)*, H. Reeves-Smith *(Howard Van Dyke)*, Stanhope Wheatcroft *(Randolph Parker)*, Don *(herself, a dog)*.

Romantic comedy-drama. Peggy Van Dyke, daughter of an oil millionaire, meets geologist Paul Maddox, a confirmed bachelor since he found out that his fiancée, Daisy Crenshaw, is fickle. Peggy and her dog follow Maddox to his mountain retreat, and there she wins him. *Geologists. Bachelors. Mountain life. Dogs.*

NO MOTHER TO GUIDE HER **F2.3858**

Fox Film Corp. 14 Oct **1923** [c18 Dec 1923; LP19734]. Si; b&w. 35mm. 7 reels, 6,650 ft.

Pres by William Fox. *Dir* Charles Horan. *Scen* Michael O'Connor. *Photog* Thomas Malloy.

Cast: Genevieve Tobin *(Mary Boyd, grown up)*, John Webb Dillon *(Charles Pearson)*, Lolita Robertson *(his wife)*, Katherine Downer *(Kathleen, their daughter)*, Dolores Rousse *(Kathleen, grown up)*, Frank Wunderlee *(Jim Boyd)*, Maude Hill *(his wife)*, Ruth Sullivan *(Mary, his daughter)*, J. D. Walsh *(The Grandfather)*, Jack Richardson *(James Walling)*, George Dewey *(Donald, his son)*, Jack McLean *(Donald, grown up)*, Lillian Lee *(Walling's sister)*, Marion Stevenson *(Widow Mills)*, William Quinn *(Billy, her son)*, Irving Hartley *(Billy, grown up)*.

Melodrama. Source: Lillian Mortimer, "No Mother To Guide Her, a Melodrama in Four Acts," in Garrett H. Leverton, ed., *The Great Diamond Robbery and Other Recent Melodramas* (Princeton, 1940). Kathleen Pearson secretly marries Donald Walling and then discovers that the marriage was fraudulent and that the clergyman was fake. She goes abroad with her friend Mary Boyd. Returning, Mary shields Kathleen by claiming to be the mother of the apparently illegitimate child who accompanies them. After Walling dies in an automobile accident, the marriage is proved to be legal. Mary's name is cleared, and she weds the man she loves. *Self-sacrifice. Marriage—Fake. Illegitimacy. Automobile accidents.*

NO, NO, NANETTE **F2.3859**

First National Pictures. 3 Jan **1930** [New York premiere; released 16 Feb; c26 Feb 1930; LP1166]. Sd (Vitaphone); b&w with col sequences (Technicolor). 35mm. 10 reels, 9,100 ft. [Also si.]

Prod Ned Marin. *Dir* Clarence Badger. *Dial* Beatrice Van. *Adapt* Howard Emmett Rogers. *Photog* Sol Polito. *Film Ed* Frank Mandel. *Songs: "King of the Air," "No, No, Nanette," "Dancing to Heaven"* Al Bryan, Ed Ward. *Song: "As Long As I'm With You,"* Grant Clarke, Harry Akst. *Song: "Dance of the Wooden Shoes"* Ned Washington, Herb Magidson, Michael Cleary. *Dance Numbers* Larry Ceballos. *Rec Engr* Hal Bumbaugh.

Cast: Bernice Claire *(Nanette)*, Alexander Gray *(Tom Trainor)*, Lucien Littlefield *(Jim Smith)*, Louise Fazenda *(Sue Smith)*, Lilyan Tashman *(Lucille)*, Bert Roach *(Bill Early)*, ZaSu Pitts *(Pauline)*, Mildred Harris *(Betty)*, Henry Stockbridge *(Brady)*, Jocelyn Lee *(Flora)*.

Musical comedy. Source: Frank Mandel, Otto Harbach, Vincent Youmans, Emil Nyitray and Irving Caesar, *No, No, Nanette* (New York opening: 16 Sep 1925). Tom, who has written a musical show for his sweetheart, Nanette, is unable to find a producer who will star Nanette. After weeks of searching, she persuades James Smith, a millionaire Bible publisher and former friend of her father's, to back the show, though without the consent of Smith's stingy, old-fashioned spouse. In his desire to help, Smith pays the bills of two chorus girls; but Early, their manager, fails to give them the money; his suspicious wife, Lucille, notifies Mrs. Smith, who hires detectives to watch him. Smith goes to Atlantic City for the show, followed by Early and the wives, who take a liking to Nanette.

Complications ensue when they meet the chorus girls, but the men claim to be amateur talent scouts and are forgiven when the receipts come in. *Composers. Chorus girls. Theatrical backers. Publishers. Millionaires. The Bible. Musical revues. Atlantic City.*

NO OTHER WOMAN **F2.3860**

Fox Film Corp. 10 Jun **1928** [c1 Jun 1928; LP25320]. Si; b&w. 35mm. 6 reels, 5,071 ft.

Pres by William Fox. *Dir* Lou Tellegen. *Scen* Jessie Burns, Bernard Vorhaus. *Titl* Katherine Hilliker, H. H. Caldwell. *Story* Polan Banks. *Photog* Ernest Palmer, Paul Ivano. *Film Ed* J. Edwin Robbins. *Asst Dir* A. F. Erickson.

Cast: Dolores Del Rio *(Carmelita Desano)*, Don Alvarado *(Maurice)*, Ben Bard *(Albert)*, Paulette Duval *(Mafalda)*, Rosita Marstini *(Carmelita's aunt)*, André Lanoy *(Grand Duke Sergey)*.

Melodrama. "Frenchman is engaged to marry South American heiress but a fortune-hunting friend disrupts the romance and marries the girl himself. She later realizes her mistake after her no-good husband has frittered away most of her fortune and she turns back to her first love, which has always been paramount." *(Motion Picture News Booking Guide,* [14]:271, 1929.) *Fortune hunters. French. Marriage.*

NO PLACE TO GO **F2.3861**

Henry Hobart Productions. *Dist* First National Pictures. 30 Oct **1927** [c24 Oct 1927; LP24547]. Si; b&w. 35mm. 7 reels, 6,431 ft.

Prod Henry Hobart. *Dir* Mervyn LeRoy. *Adapt-Scen* Adelaide Heilbron. *Titl* Dwinelle Benthall, Rufus McCosh. *Photog* George Folsey.

Cast: Mary Astor *(Sally Montgomery)*, Lloyd Hughes *(Hayden Eaton)*, Hallam Cooley *(Ambrose Munn)*, Myrtle Stedman *(Mrs. Montgomery)*, Virginia Lee Corbin *(Virginia Dare)*, Jed Prouty *(Uncle Edgar)*, Russ Powell *(cannibal chief)*.

Romantic comedy. Source: Richard Connell, "Isles of Romance," in *Saturday Evening Post* (196:14–15, 12 Apr 1924). Sally Montgomery, daughter of a banker, is in love with Hayden Eaton, a sensible bank clerk, though Sally is uncertain because of her longing for "romance" and wants to be wooed in an exotic setting. A yachting trip with their friends Ambrose and Virginia is planned to the South Seas. Under the Southern Cross, Sally's romantic instincts are gratified by the beauty of the scene, and she induces Eaton to accompany her to a nearby island, which to their dismay is inhabited by cannibals. The disillusioned lovers are rescued by the party. Mrs. Montgomery then arranges a wedding at home (as Sally has been "compromised"), but their honeymoon apartment is divided by a line that neither will cross. In the end, frightened by an electric sign depicting a cannibal, Sally finds comfort in her husband's arms. *Bank clerks. Cannibals. Reputation. Yachts. South Sea Islands.*

NO QUESTIONS ASKED *see* **HIS MYSTERY GIRL**

NO TRESPASSING **F2.3862**

Holtre Productions. *Dist* W. W. Hodkinson Corp. 11 Jun **1922.** Si; b&w. 35mm. 7 reels, 6,900 ft.

Dir Edwin L. Hollywood. *Scen* Howard Irving Young. *Photog* Robert A. Stuart. *Art Dir* E. Douglas Bingham.

Cast: Irene Castle *(Mabel Colton)*, Howard Truesdale *(James Colton)*, Emily Fitzroy *(Mrs. James Colton)*, Ward Crane *(Roscoe Paine)*, Eleanor Barry *(Mrs. Paine)*, Blanche Frederici *(Dorinda)*, Charles Eldridge *(Lute)*, Leslie Stowe *(Captain Dean)*, Betty Bouton *(Nellie Dean)*, Al Roscoe *(Victor Carver)*, Harry Fisher *(Simeon Eldridge)*, George Pauncefort *(George Davis)*.

Rural melodrama. Source: Joseph Crosby Lincoln, *The Rise of Roscoe Paine* (New York, 1912). Roscoe Paine owns the lane that runs through the Cape Cod fishing village in which he lives, but he allows anyone to use it out of gratitude for the many kindnesses shown to him and his invalid mother. Therefore, Roscoe refuses James Colton's offer to buy the property until he desperately needs the money. Roscoe and Colton go out on a launch to close the deal; and Victor Carver, who is in the village to get information for Colton's Wall Street rival, causes the boat to explode. Mabel Colton rows to their rescue; Roscoe makes the financial decisions needed to save Colton's stock market investments while the financier is unconscious; Carver confesses his villainy; Colton bestows his new property on the town and offers Roscoe a fine position; Mrs. Paine is suddenly cured; and romance blooms between Roscoe and Mabel. *Financiers. Fishermen. Filial relations. Gratitude. Stock market. Cape Cod. Ship explosions.*

Note: Working title: *The Rise of Roscoe Payne.*

NO WOMAN KNOWS (Universal-Jewel) **F2.3863**

Universal Film Manufacturing Co. 19 Sep **1921** [c17 Sep 1921; LP16969]. Si; b&w. 35mm. 7 reels, 7,031 ft.

Pres by Carl Laemmle. *Dir* Tod Browning. *Scen* Tod Browning, George Yohalem. *Photog* William Fildew.

Cast in order of appearance: Max Davidson *(Ferdinand Brandeis)*, Snitz Edwards *(Herr Bauer)*, Grace Marvin *(Molly Brandeis)*, Bernice Radom *(Little Fanny Brandeis)*, Danny Hoy *(Aloysius)*, E. A. Warren *(Rabbi Thalman)*, Raymond Lee *(Little Theodore Brandeis)*, Joseph Swickard *(The Great Schabelitz)*, Richard Cummings *(Father Fitzpatrick)*, Joseph Sterns *(Little Clarence Hyle)*, Mabel Julienne Scott *(Fanny Brandeis)*, John Davidson *(Theodore Brandeis)*, Earl Schenck *(Clarence Hyle)*, Stuart Holmes *(Michael Fenger)*.

Drama. Source: Edna Ferber, *Fanny Herself* (New York, 1917). Fanny Brandeis, a midwestern smalltown girl, is forced to sacrifice much of her early youth so that her brother, Theodore, may study violin in Europe. When he marries a chorus girl in Dresden and causes his mother's death from a broken heart, Fanny decides to live her own life. In Chicago, she becomes a highly efficient businesswoman in a department store, spurred on by her admirer, Michael Fenger, while Hyle, her childhood sweetheart, tries to revive her spiritual nature. Theodore, who is deserted by his wife, returns from Europe with his baby daughter and is aided by Fanny, but when he again disappears she submerges herself in the business world. She is about to accept Fenger's offer to sail for Honolulu when Hyle makes her realize that her true happiness lies in his security and love. *Businesswomen. Violinists. Chorus girls. Smalltown life. Department stores. Dresden. Chicago.*

THE NO-GUN MAN **F2.3864**

Harry Garson Productions. *Dist* Film Booking Offices of America. 27 Dec **1924** [16 Nov 24; LP20891]. Si; b&w. 35mm. 5 reels, 4,522 ft.

Dir Harry Garson. *Story-Cont* Dorothy Arzner, Paul Gangelin. *Photog* Louis W. Physioc.

Cast: Lefty Flynn *(Robert Gerome Vincent)*, William Jack Quinn *(Bill Kilgore)*, Gloria Grey *(Carmen Harroway)*, Raymond Turner *(Obediah Abraham Lincoln Brown)*, Bob Reeves *(Oklahoma George)*, Harry McCabe *(Snooper)*, James Gordon Russell *(Tom West)*.

Western melodrama. After robbing a small suburban bank, a gang of outlaws led by Bill Kilgore hides out in the neighboring town of Red Rock. Failing to interest Carmen Harroway by his rough romantic attentions, Kilgore forbids the terrorized townspeople to patronize her small confectionery store. A stranger, Bob Vincent, appears in town and, after becoming friendly with Carmen, inexplicably joins Kilgore's gang, passing himself off as a forger. Kilgore and Vincent plan to rob a mail train, but, just before the appointed time, Kilgore kidnaps Carmen, and Vincent, who tries to help her, is knocked out in a fight. Kilgore ties him to a handcar and sends it down the line toward an oncoming train, but Vincent frees himself and stops the train, thus averting the robbery. Kilgore and his gang are captured with the help of Vincent, who turns out to be the president of the robbed bank. He retrieves the stolen bonds and asks Carmen if she would like to become a banker's wife. *Bankers. Confectioners. Outlaws. Bank robberies. Train robberies.*

NOAH'S ARK **F2.3865**

Warner Brothers Pictures. 1 Nov **1928** [Hollywood premiere; released 15 Jun 1929; c28 May 1929; LP417]. Talking sequences & mus score (Vitaphone); b&w. 35mm. 11 reels, 9,507 ft. [Also si; 27 Jul 1929; 9,058 ft.]

Dir Michael Curtiz. *Screenplay-Dial* Anthony Coldeway. *Titl* De Leon Anthony. *Story* Darryl Francis Zanuck. *Photog* Hal Mohr, Barney McGill. *Miniature Eff* Fred Jackman. *Film Ed* Harold McCord. *Mus Score & Synchronization* Louis Silvers. *Song: "Heart o' Mine"* Billy Rose, Louis Silvers.

Cast: Dolores Costello *(Mary/Miriam)*, George O'Brien *(Travis/Japheth)*, Noah Beery *(Nickoloff/King Nephilim)*, Louise Fazenda *(Hilda/tavern maid)*, Guinn "Big Boy" Williams *(Al/Ham)*, Paul McAllister *(minister/Noah)*, Nigel De Brulier *(soldier/high priest)*, Anders Randolf *(The German/leader of soldiers)*, Armand Kaliz *(The Frenchman/leader of king's guards)*, Myrna Loy *(dancer/slave girl)*, William V. Mong *(The Innkeeper/guard)*, Malcolm Waite *(The Balkan/Shem)*, Noble Johnson *(broker)*, Otto Hoffman *(trader)*, Joe Bonomo *(aide to leader of soldiers)*.

Biblical drama. On a train from Constantinople to Paris in 1914, Mary (an Alsatian girl with a theatrical troupe), two American youths (Bill and Al), a German, a Frenchman, a Russian, and a minister become involved in an argument over Christianity which is abruptly terminated by a collision. All find shelter in a nearby inn where a fight ensues; and Hilda, the innkeeper, contrives the escape of Travis, Mary, and Al as a cavalry troop arrives with the news that war has been declared. ... In Paris, Travis and Mary fall in love, and soon Al enlists, as does Travis; meanwhile, Mary becomes a canteen dancer searching for Travis. When Mary repulses a Russian's advances, he causes her to be incriminated as a German spy; but on the day set for her execution, Travis recognizes her at the last minute. Comparison is made at this point between the World War situation and the Biblical account of the Flood: *At the Festival of Jaghut, the revelries are to climax with a human sacrifice, while Noah and his small following reside in primitive simplicity on the outskirts of the city. A group of carousing soldiers see Miriam, betrothed of Japheth, the youngest of Noah's three sons, and carry her away for the king, who, struck by her beauty, orders that she be prepared for the sacrifice; meanwhile, Noah receives a message from God directing him to build and provision the Ark. Noah interrupts the festival, warning of the consequences; and as the high priest prepares to kill Miriam, a bolt of lightning strikes him and a second bolt topples the idol. As water floods the temple, Japheth's sight is miraculously restored and he rescues Miriam; and borne on the waters, they reach the Ark and are received by Noah.* Reverting to the modern story, Red Cross workers are busy administering to the war injured when a messenger arrives, bringing news of the Armistice; and Mary and Travis, though tattered and dirty, join in the celebration of a new era of peace. *French. Germans. Russians. Spies. Dancers. Religion. Christianity. Oriental Express. World War I. Biblical characters. Constantinople. Paris. Noah. Japheth. Floods.*

NOBODY **F2.3866**

Roland West Productions. *Dist* Associated First National Pictures. Jul **1921** [c23 Jun 1921; LP16699]. Si; b&w. 35mm. 7 reels, 6,396 ft.

Prod-Dir-Story Roland West. *Scen* Charles H. Smith, Roland West. *Photog* Harry Fischbeck. *Asst Dir* Joseph Rothman.

Cast: Jewel Carmen *(Little Mrs. Smith)*, William Davidson *(John Rossmore)*, Kenneth Harlan *(Tom Smith)*, Florence Billings *(Mrs. Fallon)*, J. Herbert Frank *(Hedges)*, Grace Studiford *(Mrs. Rossmore)*, George Fawcett *(Hiram Swanzey)*, Lionel Pape *(Noron Ailsworth)*, Henry Sedley *(Rossmore's secretary)*, Ida Darling *(Mrs. Van Cleek)*, Charles Wellesley *(Clyde Durand)*, William De Grasse *(Rossmore's skipper)*, Riley Hatch *(The "Grouch" Juror)*.

Mystery melodrama. When financier John Rossmore is found murdered in his library, suspicion points to Hedges, his butler, who was instrumental in obtaining his divorce. At the trial, when the jury retires, Tom Smith, a young businessman who has sworn he does not know Rossmore, holds out for acquittal and tells his story to the jurors: *While he and his wife are vacationing in Palm Beach, Rossmore is attracted to Little Mrs. Smith, and the Smiths are invited on a yachting trip. After Tom is recalled to New York on business, Rossmore drugs Mrs. Smith and seduces her, offering blackmail for her silence. Terror-stricken, she goes to Rossmore's home, enters with a key given her, and shoots him.* The jurors agree never to divulge the story, and they acquit the butler. *Businessmen. Butlers. Juries. Murder. Seduction. Palm Beach.*

NOBODY'S BRIDE **F2.3867**

Universal Pictures. ca18 Mar **1923** [Cleveland premiere; released 2 Apr; c6 Mar 1923; LP18760]. Si; b&w. 35mm. 5 reels, 4,861 ft.

Dir Herbert Blache. *Scen* Albert Kenyon. *Story* Evelyn Campbell. *Photog* Virgil Miller.

Cast: Herbert Rawlinson *(Jimmy Nevins)*, Edna Murphy *(Doris Standish)*, Alice Lake *(Mary Butler)*, Harry Van Meter *(Morgan)*, Frank Brownlee *(Vesher Charley)*, Sidney Bracey *(Smithy, the dip)*, Phillips Smalley *(Cyrus W. Hopkins)*, Robert Dudley *(Uncle Peter Standish)*, Lillian Langdon *(Mrs. Myrtle Standish)*.

Crook melodrama. Jimmy Nevins—once wealthy and now engaged to Doris Standish—is reduced to poverty and jilted by her when he is befriended by Mary Butler, the leader of a gang of crooks. The gang dupes him into driving the getaway car for a robbery of the Standish home during Doris' wedding to a wealthy man. Doris balks, runs away from the ceremony, and demands that Jimmy take her away. They go to Mary's apartment, where the furious gang finds them and decides to hold Doris for ransom. Mary sacrifices herself so that Jimmy and Doris can go free. *Gangs. Robbery. Abduction. Weddings.*

NOBODY'S FOOL **F2.3868**

Universal Film Manufacturing Co. 31 Oct **1921** [c14 Oct 1921; LP17099]. Si; b&w. 35mm. 5 reels, 4,640 ft.

Dir King Baggot. *Scen* Doris Schroeder. *Story* Roy Clements. *Photog* Bert Glennon.

Cast: Marie Prevost *(Polly Gordon)*, Helen Harris *(Mary Hardy)*, Vernon Snively *(Vincent DePuyster)*, R. Henry Guy *(Dr. Hardy)*, Percy Challenger *(Joshua Alger)*, Harry Myers *(Artemis Alger)*, George Kuwa *(Ah Gone)*, Lucretia Harris *(Melinda)*, Lydia Titus *(housekeeper)*.

Comedy. Polly Gordon, a poor and unattractive girl, is taken to the college dance by eligible Vincent DePuyster only as part of a fraternity initiation. Suitors flock to her, however, when she inherits half a million dollars from her aunt, but she grows cynical and dismisses them. Her friend Mary, now married to Dr. Hardy, suggests a retreat to the mountains; there she meets author Artemis Alger, who is seeking to escape from women. After an initial clash, Alger comes to love her but finds a rival in young DePuyster. After further complications, Hardy and Mary arrive in a storm, and matters are cleared up. *Authors. Wealth. Courtship. College life. Fraternities.*

NOBODY'S KID **F2.3869**

Robertson-Cole Pictures. 17 Apr **1921** [c17 Apr 1921; LP16463]. Si; b&w. 35mm. 5 reels.

Dir Howard Hickman. *Scen* Howard Hickman, Catherine Carr. *Photog* Robert Newhard.

Cast: Mae Marsh *(Mary Cary)*, Kathleen Kirkham *(Katherine Trent)*, Anne Schaefer *(Miss Bray)*, Maxine Elliott Hicks *(Pinky Moore)*, John Steppling *(Dr. Rudd)*, Paul Willis *(John Maxwell)*.

Comedy-drama. Source: Kate Langley Bosher, *Mary Cary, "Frequently Martha"* (New York, 1910). Following the death of her parents, Mary, refused recognition by her grandfather because of the circumstances of her parents' marriage, is placed in an orphanage. There she is mistreated, humiliated, and, when caught by a matron outside the grounds playing ball with a youthful admirer, flogged. Later, she learns that her grandfather is a well-known judge and that her father was a British aristocrat. A letter to her uncle brings prompt aid, and rescued from her surroundings she remains faithful to a young admirer. *Orphans. Judges. Grandfathers. Orphanages. Adolescence. Parentage.*

NOBODY'S MONEY **F2.3870**

Famous Players–Lasky. *Dist* Paramount Pictures. 28 Jan **1923** [New York premiere; released 18 Feb; c23 Jan 1923; LP18651]. Si; b&w. 35mm. 6 reels, 5,584 ft.

Pres by Jesse L. Lasky. *Dir* Wallace Worsley. *Adapt* Beulah Marie Dix. *Photog* Charles E. Schoenbaum.

Cast: Jack Holt *(John Webster)*, Wanda Hawley *(Grace Kendall)*, Harry Depp *(Eddie Maloney)*, Robert Schable *(Carl Russell)*, Walter McGrail *(Frank Carey)*, Josephine Crowell *(Mrs. Judson)*, Julia Faye *(Annette)*, Charles Clary *(Governor Kendall)*, Will R. Walling *(Briscoe)*, Clarence Burton *(Kelly)*, Aileen Manning *(Prue Kimball)*, James Neill *(Miller)*.

Comedy-drama. Source: William Le Baron, *Nobody's Money* (New York opening: 17 Aug 1921). John Webster, lumbermill owner in the guise of a book agent, agrees to pose as Douglas Roberts, the pseudonym of Carl Russell and Frank Carey, to shield them from income tax agents. He falls in love with Governor Kendall's daughter, Grace, and successfully manages the governor's reelection campaign. Meanwhile, Webster's friend, Eddie Maloney, foils Briscoe's efforts to plant a bribe in the governor's safe by stealing the money, which nobody will claim. Webster discloses his identity and marries Grace. *Book agents. Authors. State governors. Politics. Income tax. Impersonation.*

NOBODY'S WIDOW **F2.3871**

De Mille Pictures. *Dist* Producers Distributing Corp. 10 Jan **1927** [New York premiere; released 24 Jan; c15 Jan 1927; LP23545]. Si; b&w. 35mm. 7 reels, 6,421 ft.

Dir Donald Crisp. *Adapt* Clara Beranger, Douglas Doty. *Photog* Arthur Miller.

Cast: Leatrice Joy *(Roxanna Smith)*, Charles Ray *(Hon. John Clayton)*, Phyllis Haver *(Betty Jackson)*, David Butler *(Ned Stevens)*, Dot Farley *(Roxanna's maid)*, Fritzi Ridgeway *(Mademoiselle Renée)*, Charles West *(valet)*.

Domestic farce. Source: Avery Hopwood, *Nobody's Widow* (New York opening: 15 Nov 1910). While traveling in Europe, Roxanna Smith hurriedly marries the Duke of Moreland (John Clayton), a rather flirtatious

Englishman; on their wedding night she finds him kissing another woman and as a result returns to the United States, announcing that her husband suddenly died. At the home of her friend Betty Jackson, who is also accommodating the duke as a guest, Roxanna finds him still in love with her but rejects his pleas. Betty arranges a private party for herself and the duke, hoping for some "excitement," but their discovery by Roxanna proves the latter's jealousy. Finally the duke convinces Roxanna of his true repentance. *Nobility. Widows. Philanderers. English.*

A NOISE IN NEWBORO **F2.3872**

Metro Pictures. 12 Mar **1923** [c23 Mar 1923; LP18797]. Si; b&w. 35mm. 6 reels, 5,188 ft.

Dir Harry Beaumont. *Adapt* Rex Taylor. *Story* Edgar Franklin. *Photog* John Arnold.

Cast: Viola Dana *(Martha Mason)*, David Butler *(Ben Colwell)*, Eva Novak *(Anne Paisley)*, Allan Forrest *(Buddy Wayne)*, Betty Francisco *(Leila Wayne)*, Alfred Allen *(Eben Paisley)*, Malcolm McGregor *(Harry Dixon)*, Joan Standing *(Dorothy Mason)*, Bert Woodruff *("Dad" Mason)*, Hank Mann.

Comedy-drama. Not especially attractive and ignored by her townspeople, Martha Mason goes to New York to make a name for herself. Seven years later and now a famous artist, Martha returns to her hometown to find that Ben Colwell, to whom she still considers herself engaged, has transferred his interests to Anne Paisley and become involved in unscrupulous politics. When Ben hears that Martha is worth a considerable sum of money and wishes to donate to a civic cause, he gives her increased attention, and Martha encourages him in order to expose his true nature to the town. Having done so, she returns to New York and Buddy Wayne, happy that she has finally caused some noise in Newboro. *Artists. Politics. Smalltown life. New York City.*

NOISY NEIGHBORS **F2.3873**

Paul Bern. *Dist* Pathé Exchange. 27 Jan **1929** [c21 Jan 1929; LP42]. Talking sequences (Photophone); b&w. 35mm. 6 reels, 5,735 ft. [Also si; 6 reels, 5,735 ft.]

Dir Charles Reisner. *Adapt-Cont* Scott Darling. *Titl-Dial* John Krafft. *Orig Story* F. Hugh Herbert. *1st Camera* David Abel. *Film Ed* Anne Bauchens. *Asst Dir* Lonnie D'Orsa. *Prod Mgr* Richard Blaydon.

Cast: Eddie Quillan *(Eddie)*, Alberta Vaughn *(Mary)*, Quillan Family *(family)*, Theodore Roberts *(Colonel Carstairs)*, Ray Hallor *(David)*, Russell Simpson *(Ebenezer)*, Robert Perry, Mike Donlin, Billy Gilbert *(three sons)*.

Comedy-melodrama. A family of down-and-out vaudevillians find out they are the last of the Van Revels and therefore heirs to a southern estate and a blood feud with the Carstairs that started 60 years before over a game of croquet. Eddie falls in love with the daughter of the family next door. A mountaineer branch of the Carstairs starts the feud all over again and comes to the house to shoot up Eddie and his family. *Vaudevillians. Inheritance. Feuds. Mountain life.*

THE NON-STOP FLIGHT **F2.3874**

Emory Johnson Productions. *Dist* Film Booking Offices of America. 28 Mar **1926** [c12 Apr 1926; LP22702]. Si; b&w. 35mm. 6 reels, 6,000 ft.

Dir Emory Johnson. *Story-Scen* Emilie Johnson. *Photog* Gilbert Warrenton. *Asst Dir* Jerry Callahan.

Cast: Knute Erickson *(Lars Larson)*, Marcella Daly *(Anna Larson)*, Virginia Fry *(Marie Larson)*, C. Ogden *(Jack Nevers)*, Frank Hemphill *(Jan Johnson)*, David Dunbar *(Captain Holm)*, Peggy O'Neil *(Olga Nelson)*, Bob Anderson *(Eric Swanson)*, Otis Stantz, Skiles Ralph Pope *(pilots)*.

Adventure melodrama. Lars Larson, a Swedish sea captain, returns home after a long voyage and finds that his wife, Anna, and their child have been kidnaped by Carl Holm; bitter against the world, he becomes a smuggler. Twenty years later, the United States Navy is preparing for its epochal nonstop airplane flight from San Francisco to Hawaii. Owing to a fuel shortage the plane is forced to alight on the sea, where the commander and Jack Nevers, second officer, keep up the crew's spirits; and while they are being sought by a battle fleet, the PN9 drifts to an uncharted desert island, where they find Jan Johnson, an old sailor, and Marie Larson, who survived shipwreck. Nevers falls in love with Marie, Larson's lost daughter. Aboard Larson's ship, Ah Wing, leader of some Chinese coolies, spies Marie on the island and determines to possess her; a battle ensues between the Chinese and the aviators and ship's crew. A Navy submarine arrives, and its crew aids in subduing the Chinese; Larson discovers that Marie is his daughter; and she is united with Jack. *Sea captains. Smugglers. Sailors. Chinese. Swedes. Aviation. Kidnaping. Seaplanes. Submarines. San Francisco. Hawaii. Pacific Ocean. United States Navy.*

NONE BUT THE BRAVE **F2.3875**

Fox Film Corp. 5 Aug **1928** [c31 Jul 1928; LP25494]. Si; b&w with col sequence (Technicolor). 35mm. 6 reels, 5,034 ft.

Pres by William Fox. *Dir* Albert Ray. *Scen* Dwight Cummins, Frances Agnew. *Titl* Norman McLeod. *Story* Fred Stanley, James Gruen. *Photog* Charles Van Enger, Edward Estabrook. *Film Ed* Alex Troffey. *Asst Dir* Horace Hough.

Cast: Charles Morton *(Charles Stanton)*, Sally Phipps *(Mary)*, Sharon Lynn *(Paula)*, J. Farrell MacDonald *(John Craig)*, Tom Kennedy *(Noah)*, Billy Butts *(Freckles)*, Alice Adair *(Mary's cook)*, Tyler Brooke *(hotel clerk)*, Earle Foxe, Gertrude Short, Dorothy Knapp *(see note)*.

Romantic comedy. Charles Stanton, a college hero, fails at business. He becomes a lifeguard, falling in love with a concessionaire. When he throws an obstacle race to aid an injured fellow contestant, he is substantially rewarded and wins the girl. *Lifeguards. Concessionaires. Beauty contests. Resorts.*

Note: Unconfirmed sources indicate that Earl Foxe, Gertrude Short, and Dorothy Knapp are in cast. A beauty pageant sequence is in color.

NONE SO BLIND **F2.3876**

State Pictures. *Dist* Arrow Film Corp. 19 Feb **1923** [New Jersey premiere; released 1 May; c12 Feb 1923; LP18662]. Si; b&w. 35mm. 6 reels.

Dir Burton King. *Story* Leota Morgan, Kathleen Kerrigan. *Photog* Alfred Ortlieb.

Cast: Dore Davidson *(Aaron Abrams)*, Zena Keefe *(Rachel Abrams Mortimer/Ruth)*, Anders Randolf *(Roger Mortimer)*, Edward Earle *(Sheldon Sherman)*, Sonia Nodell *(Rebecca)*, Bernard Siegel *(Saul Cohen)*, Robert Bentley *(Louis Cohen)*, Maurice Costello *(Russell Mortimer)*, Gene Burnell *(Hazel Mortimer)*.

Drama. Rachel Abrams, daughter of struggling ghetto pawnbroker Aaron Abrams, elopes with Russell Mortimer, a wealthy young member of society. Russell's father quickly offers $10,000 to terminate the match. Aaron accepts over Rachel's objections, hoping to use the money for revenge. Rachel dies in giving birth to a daughter, Ruth; Aaron becomes a ruthless moneylender on Wall Street; and love develops between Ruth and Sheldon Sherman, protégé of Russell Mortimer, and between Hazel Mortimer, Russell's daughter, and Saul Cohen, son of an old friend of Aaron Abrams. Under a pseudonym Aaron does put the squeeze on Russell and insists that Ruth marry Saul. There are complications of love and finance; Abrams sends Ruth away for giving her love to a gentile; but the old man finally relents, and all are reconciled. *Jews. Pawnbrokers. Moneylenders. Grandfathers. New York City—Wall Street.*

Note: Working title: *Shylock of Wall Street.*

THE NOOSE **F2.3877**

First National Pictures. 29 Jan **1928** [c4 Jan 1928; LP24832]. Si; b&w. 35mm. 8 reels, 7,331 ft.

Pres by Richard A. Rowland. *Prod* Henry Hobart. *Dir* John Francis Dillon. *Screenplay* H. H. Van Loan, Willard Mack. *Adapt-Cont* James T. O'Donohoe. *Titl* Garrett Graham. *Photog* James C. Van Trees. *Film Ed* Jack Dennis.

Cast: Richard Barthelmess *(Nickie Elkins)*, Montagu Love *(Buck Gordon)*, Robert E. O'Connor *(Jim Conley)*, Jay Eaton *(Tommy)*, Lina Basquette *(Dot)*, Thelma Todd *(Phyllis)*, Ed Brady *(Seth McMillan)*, Fred Warren *(Dave)*, Charles Giblyn *(Bill Chase)*, Alice Joyce *(Mrs. Bancroft)*, William Walling *(warden)*, Robert T. Haines *(governor)*, Ernest Hilliard *(Craig)*, Emile Chautard *(priest)*, Romaine Fielding *(judge)*, Yola D'Avril, Corliss Palmer, Kay English, Cecil Brunner, Janice Peters, Ruth Lord, May Atwood *(cabaret girls)*.

Melodrama. Source: Willard Mack, *The Noose, A Drama in Three Acts* (New York opening: 20 Oct 1926). H. H. Van Loan, *The Noose* (New York, 1926). A hijacker is told by a gangster, whom he believes to be his father, that his mother is the governor's wife. In an angry protest against crime, the boy kills the gangster/father. He is arrested, tried, and sentenced to die. The governor's wife expresses interest in the case and saves her son's life on the execution day by begging her husband to pardon him. *Hijackers. State governors. Patricide. Capital punishment.*

NORTH OF ALASKA F2.3878

Sanford Productions. 15 Apr **1924.** Si; b&w. 35mm. 5 reels, 4,700 ft.

Dir Frank S. Mattison.

Cast: Matty Mattison, Lorraine Eason, Jack Richardson, Gene Crosby, Bill Franey, Marcella Daly.

Melodrama. No information about the nature of this film has been found.

NORTH OF HUDSON BAY F2.3879

Fox Film Corp. 18 Nov **1923** [c10 Sep 1923; LP19470]. Si; b&w. 35mm. 5 reels, 4,973 ft.

Pres by William Fox. *Dir* Jack Ford. *Story-Scen* Jules Furthman. *Photog* Don Clark.

Cast: Tom Mix *(Michael Dane)*, Kathleen Key *(Estelle McDonald)*, Jennie Lee *(Dane's mother)*, Frank Campeau *(Cameron McDonald)*, Eugene Pallette *(Peter Dane)*, Will Walling *(Angus McKenzie)*, Frank Leigh *(Jeffrey Clough)*, Fred Kohler *(Armand LeMoir)*.

Melodrama. Rancher Michael Dane goes to northern Canada to join his brother, Peter, who has struck gold with his partner, Angus McKenzie. En route, Dane meets and falls in love with Estelle McDonald. Arriving at the trading post, Dane discovers that Peter has been murdered. Local authorities accuse McKenzie and summarily sentence him to walk the "death trail," a kind of torture involving starvation and exposure in which the prisoner is made to walk, accompanied by guards, until he dies. Dane becomes an object of the same torture when he tries to help the wrongfully accused man. They both escape, and Dane gets into a terrific fight with a pack of wolves. Estelle follows the group in a canoe, pursued by Cameron McDonald, her uncle, who is the real murderer of Peter Dane. McDonald dies after a thrilling chase over a waterfall, and Dane and Estelle escape to civilization. *Ranchers. Brothers. Murder. Injustice. Torture. Hudson Bay. Canada. Waterfalls. Wolves.*

Note: Working title: *Journey of Death*.

NORTH OF NEVADA F2.3880

Monogram Pictures. *Dist* Film Booking Offices of America. 24 Feb **1924** [c7 Feb 1924; LP19907]. Si; b&w. 35mm. 5 reels, 4,929 ft.

Prod Harry J. Brown. *Dir* Albert Rogell. *Story-Scen* Marion Jackson. *Photog* Ross Fisher.

Cast: Fred Thomson *(Tom Taylor)*, Hazel Keener *(Marion Ridgeway)*, Josef Swickard *(Mark Ridgeway)*, Joe Butterworth *(Red O'Shay)*, Chester Conklin *(Lem Williams)*, Taylor Graves *(Reginald Ridgeway)*, George Magrill *(Joe Deerfoot)*, Wilfred Lucas *(C. Hanaford)*, Silver King *(himself, a horse)*.

Western melodrama. Mark Ridgeway, the owner of a large ranch in Nevada, intends to leave the property to his foreman, Tom Taylor, but when he dies intestate the ranch goes to his niece and nephew, Marion and Reggie Ridgeway. These two easterners arrive at the ranch, and Tom falls in love with Marion. Joe Deerfoot, an evil, college-educated Indian, offers Reggie $10,000 for the ranch, aware that the water rights on the property are worth a fortune. Reggie, a stupid, effeminate boy, agrees to the deal and signs the contract. Joe kidnaps Marion to force her also to sign it, but Tom, having overheard the plans, rides Silver King to Joe's lair in the mountains. There, with the horse's help, he overcomes Joe and rescues Marion. *Ranch foremen. Indians of North America. Ranches. Water rights. Inheritance. Effeminacy. Nevada.*

NORTH OF NOME F2.3881

Arrow Pictures. 30 Aug **1925** [c5 Jun 1925; LP21536]. Si; b&w. 35mm. 6 reels.

Dir Raymond K. Johnston. *Story* Harvey Gates. *Theme suggested by* George Edward Lewis.

Cast: Robert McKim *(Henri Cocteau)*, Gladys Johnston *(Zelma Killaly)*, Robert N. Bradbury *(Bruce McLaren)*, Howard Webster *(Quig Lanigan)*, William Dills *(Tate Killaly)*.

Melodrama. When Tate Killaly and his daughter, Zelma, cross the river to the trading post of Henri Cocteau, located in a little Alaska town, Zelma is attacked by Quig Lanigan, Cocteau's tool and a man of evil impulses. A stranger steps in and saves her from harm. Zelma later finds the stranger suffering from snow blindness on the trail and takes him home to her cabin, where she nurses him back to health. Zelma and the stranger fall in love, and he tells her that he is a fugitive from justice and victim of injustice. Chitna, Zelma's Indian servant, goes into town for supplies and tells Tate and Cocteau of the stranger's presence. The men, who know there is a $5,000 reward for the stranger, go to the cabin and capture him. Zelma helps him escape, but when she is led to believe that the stranger has killed her father, she turns against him and is instrumental in his recapture. When she finds out that her father is alive, Zelma realizes her mistake and gets her father to help the stranger. Cocteau is killed in a snowslide, and the stranger, Bruce McLaren, is informed that the real criminal has confessed, making Bruce a free man again. *Traders. Fugitives. Filial relations. Injustice. Snow blindness. Alaska. Avalanches.*

NORTH OF THE RIO GRANDE F2.3882

Famous Players–Lasky. *Dist* Paramount Pictures. 14 May **1922** [c23 May 1922; LP17916]. Si; b&w. 35mm. 5 reels, 4,770 ft.

Pres by Jesse L. Lasky. *Dir* Rollin Sturgeon. *Dir? (see note)* Joseph Henabery. *Scen* Will M. Ritchie. *Photog* Faxon M. Dean.

Cast: Jack Holt *(Bob Haddington, a rancher)*, Bebe Daniels *(Val Hannon, his sweetheart)*, Charles Ogle *(Colonel Haddington, Bob's father)*, Alec B. Francis *(Father Hillaire)*, Will R. Walling *(John Hannon, Val's father)*, Jack Carlyle *(Brideman, a gambler)*, Fred Huntley *(Briston)*, Shannon Day *(Lola Sanchez)*, Edythe Chapman *(Belle Hannon)*, George Field *(Paul Perez)*, W. B. Clarke *(Clendenning)*.

Western melodrama. Source: Vingie E. Roe, *Val of Paradise* (New York, 1921). Bob Haddington, son of Colonel Haddington, leads a posse against marauders in a settlement. During his absence, one of the prize horses is stolen and his father is killed. Bob swears revenge and becomes known as Velantrie, leader of a band of semi-outlaws, and befriends a priest, Father Hillaire. At a mission, he meets Val, daughter of John Hannon, a wealthy ranchowner. Later, Bob is suspected of being the feared "Black Rustler," but he learns that Hannon is indeed the guilty party and the man who killed his father. Bob decides to leave; but he meets Hannon, who has been wounded, and exchanges places with him. Hannon confesses to Val and dies in her arms; she rides to rescue Bob just as he is about to be hanged. *Ranchers. Clergymen. Outlaws. Revenge. Arizona. Horses.*

Note: Photographed on location in Arizona. Initial publicity credits Joseph Henabery as director.

NORTH OF 36 F2.3883

Famous Players–Lasky. *Dist* Paramount Pictures. 22 Dec **1924** [10 Dec 1924; LP20843]. Si; b&w. 35mm. 8 reels, 7,908 ft.

Pres by Adolph Zukor, Jesse L. Lasky. *Dir* Irvin Willat. *Screenplay* James Shelley Hamilton. *Photog* Alfred Gilks.

Cast: Jack Holt *(Dan McMasters)*, Ernest Torrence *(Jim Nabours)*, Lois Wilson *(Taisie Lockheart)*, Noah Beery *(Sim Rudabaugh)*, David Dunbar *(Dell Williams)*, Stephen Carr *(Cinquo Centavos)*, Guy Oliver *(Major McCoyne)*, William Carroll *(Sánchez)*, Clarence Geldert *(Colonel Griswold)*, George Irving *(Pattison)*, Ella Miller *(Milly)*.

Western melodrama. Source: Emerson Hough, *North of 36* (New York, 1923). In order to find a market for her cattle, Taisie Lockheart, owner of a large Texas ranch, decides to drive a herd across the thousand miles of Indian territory between the Lone Star State and the new railhead at Abilene. Sim Rudabaugh, the State Treasurer, who is amassing a fortune by the accumulation of land scrip, plots to steal the scrip for Taisie's ranch but is foiled by Dan McMasters, who is in love with her. When suspicion unjustly falls on Dan, he is fired by Taisie; he then joins up with Rudabaugh so as to discover Rudabaugh's plans and forestall them. On the trail, Rudabaugh's men stampede Taisie's herd at night, and only the skill of her ranchhands prevents the loss of the cattle. Rudabaugh then kills two Comanche squaws, and the Indians go on the warpath but are fought off by the Lockheart men, led by the foreman, Jim Nabours. After a gala arrival in Abilene, Taisie sells her cattle at $20 a head and Dan overpowers Rudabaugh in a fight, handing him over to the Comanche chief. Taisie and Dan are reconciled and soon get married. *Ranchers. Ranch foremen. State treasurers. Comanche Indians. Land scrip. Cattle. Texas. Abilene (Kansas). Documentation.*

NORTH STAR F2.3884

Howard Estabrook Productions. *Dist* Associated Exhibitors. 27 Dec **1925** [c30 Dec 1925; LU22202]. Si; b&w. 35mm. 5 reels, 4,715 ft.

Dir Paul Powell. *Scen* Charles Horan. *Photog* Joseph Walker.

Cast: Virginia Lee Corbin *(Marcia Gale)*, Stuart Holmes *(Dick Robbins)*, Ken Maynard *(Noel Blake)*, Harold Austin *(Wilbur Gale)*, Clark Gable *(Archie West)*, William Riley *(Wayne Connor)*, Syd Crossley, Jerry Mandy *(tramps)*, Marte Faust *(Indian)*, Jack Fowler *(Dr. Jim Craig)*.

Melodrama. Source: Rufus King, *North Star: a Dog Story of the Canadian Northwest* (New York, 1925). During a wild party, Wilbur Gale hits another man and, incorrectly believing that he has killed him, flees to the Northwoods. Wilbur's dog, North Star, runs away and is taken in by Noel Blake, a newspaper reporter. Receiving a letter from her brother, Marcia Gale sets out to find him, taking with her Dick Robbins, a false friend who sees an opportunity for blackmail; arriving in Canada, Robbins hires an Indian guide and sets off alone to find Wilbur. Marcia does not know where to turn, but Noel Blake offers his services, and they go after Robbins. When Noel and Marcia arrive at Wilbur's cabin, they find the two men fighting. Noel rescues Wilbur, and North Star drives Robbins off a cliff to his death. Learning that he is not wanted for murder, Wilbur returns to the United States to be best man at the wedding of his sister and Noel. *Brother-sister relationship. Reporters. Guides. Indians of North America. Blackmail. Weddings. Canada. Dogs.*

NORTHERN CODE **F2.3885**

Gotham Productions. *Dist* Lumas Film Corp. 13 Oct **1925** [New York State license]. Si; b&w. 35mm. 6 reels, 5,900 ft.

Dir Leon De La Mothe. *Scen* Everett C. Maxwell. *Photog* Donald Parker.

Cast: Robert Ellis *(Louis Le Blanc)*, Eva Novak *(Marie La Fane)*, Francis McDonald *(Raoul La Fane)*, Josef Swickard *(Père Le Blanc)*, Jack Kenney *(Pierre De Val)*, Claire De Lorez *(Señorita Méndez)*, Raye Hampton *(Mama Le Blanc)*.

Northwest melodrama. When Raoul La Fane, a drunken Canadian trapper, attacks his young wife, Marie, she takes a shot at him. La Fane falls, and Marie, who thinks that she has killed him, flees into the white wilderness. Louis Le Blanc aids her, and later they are married. Raoul then shows up, and Marie tells Louis her guilty secret. Louis then sets out on Raoul's trail; he finds him, and the two men get into a brutal fight. Raoul falls over a cliff and dies, and Louis returns to a grateful Marie. *Bigamy. Manslaughter. Drunkenness. Canadian Northwest.*

NOT A DRUM WAS HEARD **F2.3886**

Fox Film Corp. 27 Jan **1924** [c27 Jan 1924; LP19880]. Si; b&w. 35mm. 5 reels, 4,823 ft.

Pres by William Fox. *Dir* William A. Wellman. *Scen* Doty Hobart. *Story* Ben Ames Williams. *Photog* Joseph August.

Cast: Charles Jones *(Jack Mills)*, Betty Bouton *(Jean Ross)*, Frank Campeau *(Banker Rand)*, Rhody Hathaway *(James Ross)*, Al Fremont *(The Sheriff)*, William Scott *(Bud Loupel)*, Mickey McBan *(Jack Loupel, Jr.)*.

Melodrama. Jack Mills loses his sweetheart, Jean Ross, to his friend, Bud Loupel. Behind in his payments on a house, Bud steals money from the bank where he works. The owner finds out, but Jack takes the blame by holding up the bank and pretending to rob it of the money Bud has already taken. Bud shoots the owner and is severely wounded himself. Jack takes the rap at the trial, but Bud admits he is guilty before dying from his wounds. Jack promises to care for Jean and the baby. *Bank clerks. Courtship. Theft. Friendship. Self-sacrifice. Bank robberies.*

Note: The title refers to the "silent sacrifice which one man made in facing punishment by hanging, so that the other man could go back to his wife and child, undisgraced" (*Moving Picture World,* 9 Feb 1924).

NOT BUILT FOR RUNNIN' **F2.3887**

William Steiner Productions. *Dist* Ambassador Pictures. 17 Sep **1924** [New York State license application; c15 Sep 1924; LU20565]. Si; b&w. 35mm. 5 reels, 4,700 ft.

Dir Leo Maloney. *Story-Scen* Ford Beebe. *Photog* Jake Badaracco.

Cast: Leo Maloney *("Sonny Jack" Parr)*, Josephine Hill *(Lou Coberly)*, Whitehorse *("Grizzly" Dobbs)*, Milton Fahrney *(Tod Randall)*, Bud Osborne *(Jess Raglan)*, Leonard Clapham *(Lem Dodge)*, Evelyn Thatcher *(Martha Coberly)*, Won Lefong *(Chink)*, Bullet *(himself, a dog)*.

Western comedy-melodrama. "Sonny Jack" and his stuttering pal, "Griz," get work on Lou Coberly's ranch, although she is unable to pay them. Sonny's courage wins the enmity of a neighboring rancher who kidnaps Lou, but the scheme is spoiled by Sonny, who discovers that the rancher is her father. They are reunited, and Sonny wins the hand of his employer. *Ranchers. Kidnaping. Dogs.*

NOT DAMAGED **F2.3888**

Fox Film Corp. 25 May **1930** [c1 May 1930; LP1298]. Sd (Movietone); b&w. 35mm. 7 reels, 6,500 ft.

Pres by William Fox. *Dir* Chandler Sprague. *Stgd by* Melville Burke. *Adapt-Cont* Frank Gay. *Dial* Harold Atteridge. *Photog* Chester Lyons. *Film Ed* Alexander Troffey. *Songs: "Nothing's Gonna Hold Us Down," "Whisper You Love Me"* Cliff Friend, Jimmy Monaco. *Mus Numbers* Danny Dare. *Sd Rec* Pat Costello. *Asst Dir* Horace Hough. *Cost* Sophie Wachner.

Cast: Lois Moran *(Gwen Stewart)*, Walter Byron *(Kirk Randolph)*, Robert Ames *(Charlie Jones)*, Inez Courtney *(Maude Graham)*, George Corcoran *(Elmer)*, Rhoda Cross *(Jennie)*, Ernest Wood *(Peebles)*.

Romantic comedy–drama. Source: Richard Connell, "The Solid Gold Article," in *Collier's Weekly* (83:5–48, 11 May 1929). Gwen Stewart, a salesclerk in the men's furnishings section of a department store, falls in love with wealthy young Kirk Randolph. In spite of the fact that she is engaged to the floorwalker, Elmer, and is warned by her roommate, Maude, the adventuresome Gwen goes to Kirk's apartment, where she is soon convinced of his less than honorable intentions. But when she is making plans with Elmer for their future and he makes advances, she returns to Kirk for a "wild time" and is treated to the delights of a Greenwich Village studio. The next morning she is surprised to find herself in Kirk's bed, but he contents her by the assurance that he spent the night in another room. *Salesclerks. Floorwalkers. Socialites. Courtship. Department stores. New York City—Greenwich Village.*

NOT FOR PUBLICATION **F2.3889**

Ralph Ince Productions. *Dist* Film Booking Offices of America. 31 Aug **1927** [c10 Jun 1927; LP24185]. Si; b&w. 35mm. 7 reels, 6,140 ft.

Pres by Joseph P. Kennedy. *Prod-Dir* Ralph Ince. *Scen* Ewart Adamson. *Photog* Allen Siegler. *Asst Dir* Charles Gillette.

Cast: Ralph Ince *("Big Dick" Wellman)*, Roy Laidlaw *(Commissioner Brownell)*, Rex Lease *(Philip Hale)*, Jola Mendez *(Beryl Wellman)*, Eugene Strong *(Eli Barker)*, Thomas Brower *(Pike, the editor)*.

Melodrama. Source: Robert Wells Ritchie, "The Temple of the Giants" (publication undetermined). As a reward for political support, "Big Dick" Wellman is awarded a contract for construction of a dam by Water Commissioner Brownell, an action opposed by Pike, editor of the *Sentinel,* who thinks Wellman is dishonest. Seeking to establish the unreliability of Wellman, Pike directs reporter Philip Hale to burglarize Wellman's safe to secure evidence against him. Wellman and Pike reach an agreement, and the former ceases his support of Brownell, who threatens him and in a struggle is accidentally killed. Hale schemes to be hired by Wellman and becomes romantically involved with Wellman's sister, Beryl, thus antagonizing Barker, whom Hale suspects as the blackmailer. Wellman dynamites the dam, carrying himself and Barker to their deaths but assuring the happiness of Hale and Beryl. *Editors. Reporters. Brother-sister relationship. Courtship. Political corruption. Blackmail. Water power. Dams.*

NOT FOR SALE **F2.3890**

E. K. Fox. *Dist* Reputable Pictures. 24 Mar **1924** [New York State license]. Si; b&w. 35mm. 5 reels, 4,250 ft.

Cast: William Parke, Jr., Dixie Lee, Clayton Fry.

Drama(?). No information about the nature of this film has been found.

Note: E. K. Fox is listed as "manufacturer" on New York State license application.

NOT GUILTY **F2.3891**

Whitman Bennett Productions. *Dist* Associated First National Pictures. Jan **1921** [c23 Feb 1921; LP16174]. Si; b&w. 35mm. 7 reels, 6,170 ft.

Pres by Albert A. Kaufman. *Dir* Sidney A. Franklin. *Scen* J. Grubb Alexander, Edwin Bower Hesser.

Cast: Sylvia Breamer *(Elsa Chetwood)*, Richard Dix *(Paul Ellison/ Arthur Ellison)*, Molly Malone *(Margy Ellison)*, Elinor Hancock *(Mrs. Ellison)*, Herbert Prior *(Newell Craig)*, Lloyd Whitlock *(Frank Mallow)*, Alberta Lee *(Martha, the chaperon)*, Charles West *(Herbert Welch)*, Alice Forbes *(Virginia Caldwell)*.

Mystery melodrama. Source: Harold MacGrath, *Parrot and Company* (Indianapolis, 1913). Paul Ellison, who falls in love with Elsa, exchanges identities with his twin, Arthur, because he feels himself responsible for his brother's downfall, and assumes guilt for a murder. Five years later Elsa meets Arthur, whom she believes to be Paul, and they become engaged. In Rangoon, Paul is recognized by Elsa and Craig, a gambler. Though Paul confesses to the crime, Craig, in his dying moments, admits he is the real murderer. Elsa and the two brothers are then reconciled. *Twins. Brothers. Gamblers. Murder. Impersonation. Rangoon.*

NOT ONE TO SPARE *see* **WHICH SHALL IT BE?**

NOT QUITE DECENT **F2.3892**

Fox Film Corp. 7 Apr **1929** [c3 Apr 1929; LP251]. Talking sequences, sd eff, & mus score (Movietone); b&w. 35mm. 5 reels, 4,965 ft. [Also si; 4,653 ft.]

Pres by William Fox. *Prod* James K. McGuinness. *Dir* Irving Cummings. *Scen* Marion Orth. *Dial* Edwin Burke. *Titl* Malcolm Stuart Boylan. *Photog* Charles Clarke. *Film Ed* Paul Weatherwax. *Mus Score* S. L. Rothafel. *Song: "Empty Arms"* Con Conrad, Sidney Mitchell, Archie Gottler. *Sd* Arthur L. von Kirbach. *Asst Dir* Charles Woolstenhulme.

Cast: Louise Dresser *(Mame Jarrow)*, June Collyer *(Linda Cunningham)*, Allan Lane *(Jerry Connor)*, Oscar Apfel *(Canfield)*, Paul Nicholson *(Al Gergon)*, Marjorie Beebe *(Margie)*, Ben Hewlett *(a crook)*, Jack Kenney *(another crook)*.

Melodrama. Source: Wallace Smith, "The Grouch Bag," in *Hearst's International Cosmopolitan.* On her way to New York for her first stage appearance, Linda Cunningham meets Mame Jarrow, a nightclub singer; Linda later drops by to hear Mame sing, accompanied by their angel, Paul Nicholson, a wealthy roué. Mame gradually comes to realize that Linda is her own daughter, from whom she was separated years before by pious relatives. Using all her wiles, Mame attempts to keep Linda from falling prey to Nicholson, and when all else fails, she sends for Jerry Connor, Linda's smalltown sweetheart. Linda returns home with Jerry, and Mame sings her heart out in smoky rooms, never disclosing to Linda that she is her mother. *Singers. Theatrical backers. Rakes. Motherhood. Nightclubs.*

NOT SO DUMB **F2.3893**

Metro-Goldwyn-Mayer Pictures. 17 Jan **1930** [c17 Feb 1930; LP1076]. Sd (Movietone); b&w. 35mm. 9 reels, 7,650 or 6,875 ft. [Also si.]

Dir King Vidor. *Cont* Wanda Tuchock. *Dial* Edwin Justus Mayer. *Titl* Lucille Newmark. *Photog* Oliver Marsh. *Art Dir* Cedric Gibbons. *Film Ed* Blanche Sewell. *Rec Engr* Fred R. Morgan, Douglas Shearer. *Gowns* Adrian.

Cast: Marion Davies *(Dulcy)*, Elliott Nugent *(Gordon)*, Raymond Hackett *(Bill)*, Franklin Pangborn *(Leach)*, Julia Faye *(Mrs. Forbes)*, William Holden *(Mr. Forbes)*, Donald Ogden Stewart *(Van Dyke)*, Sally Starr *(Angela)*, George Davis *(Perkins)*, Ruby Lafayette *(Grandma)*.

Comedy. Source: George S. Kaufman and Marc Connelly, *Dulcy, a Comedy in Three Acts* (New York, 1921). Dulcy, the slightly wacky but well-meaning fiancée of Gordon, an anxiously up-and-coming business buff, is bent on hostessing a party to bring her future hubby's potential partners into line. The crusty Mr. Forbes is the object of their fawning flattery, which backfires at every turn; and the obstreperous Van Dyke is a mad financier whose favor is finally surrendered so as not to interfere with his lechery. But it is the scatterbrained Dulcy who in the end does all the wrong things for the right reasons and secures her fiancé's financial future and her own "world-without-end" bargain. *Businessmen. Financiers. Lechery.*

Note: Initially reviewed as *Dulcy.* This film is a remake of the 1923 film of that name made by the Constance Talmadge Film Co.

NOT SO LONG AGO **F2.3894**

Famous Players–Lasky. *Dist* Paramount Pictures. 7 Sep **1925** [c9 Sep 1925; LP21802]. Si; b&w. 35mm. 7 reels, 6,943 ft.

Pres by Adolph Zukor, Jesse L. Lasky. *Dir* Sidney Olcott. *Screenplay* Violet Clark. *Photog* James Wong Howe.

Cast: Betty Bronson *(Betty Dover)*, Ricardo Cortez *(Billy Ballard)*, Edwards Davis *(Jerry Flint)*, Julia Swayne Gordon *(Mrs. Ballard)*, Laurence Wheat *(Sam Robinson)*, Jacquelin Gadsdon *(Ursula Kent)*, Dan Crimmins *(Michael Dover)*.

Comedy-drama. Source: Arthur Richman, *Not So Long Ago, a Comedy in Prologue, Three Acts, and Epilogue* (New York, 1924). Betty, the romantic daughter of inventor Michael Dover, obtains work as a seamstress at the fashionable home of Mrs. Ballard, one of the Four Hundred. Betty falls in love with handsome Billy Ballard, falsely telling one of her suitors that Billy has been courting her. Her father learns of this "romance" and announces that he will ask Billy his intentions. In desperation, Betty goes to Billy and confesses her deception; he goodnaturedly agrees to go along with her story and asks her father for permission to call on her. Billy quickly falls in love with the dreamy girl, but his mother strongly disapproves and fires Betty. One of Michael's inventions, a horseless carriage, is given a public test and explodes. Billy breaks off his engagement to Ursula Kent (engineered by his mother), pays off Michael's debt to Jerry Flint, a moneylender, and marries Betty. *Inventors. Seamstresses. Filial relations. Courtship. Horseless carriages.*

NOTCH NUMBER ONE **F2.3895**

Ben Wilson Productions. *Dist* Arrow Film Corp. 13 Sep **1924** [c14 Apr 1924; LP20076]. Si; b&w. 35mm. 5 reels, 4,746 ft.

Story Daniel F. Whitcomb.

Cast: Ben Wilson, Marjorie Daw.

Western melodrama. Tom Watson, foreman of the Moore Ranch, is silently in love with Dorothy, the owner's daughter, who is engaged to Dave Leonard. One night Dave becomes violent after smoking some marihuana (loco weed) given him by Pete, a ranch hand recently fired by Tom. Moore tries to restrain Dave. Pete, seeking revenge, shoots Moore. Tom, believing Dave guilty, takes the blame and becomes a fugitive. He is captured after rescuing 6-year-old Dickie Moore, who had become lost on the desert. Pete is found dead, but with a confession that frees Tom. *Ranch foremen. Fugitives. Murder. Deserts. Marihuana.*

Note: Working title: *The First Notch.*

NOTHING BUT THE TRUTH **F2.3896**

Paramount Famous Lasky Corp. 20 Apr **1929** [c19 Apr 1929; LP328]. Sd (Movietone); b&w. 35mm. 8 reels, 7,256 ft.

Dir Victor Schertzinger. *Dial Dir* William Collier, Sr. *Screenplay* John McGowan. *Dial* William Collier, Sr. *Photog* Edward Cronjager. *Film Ed* Morton Blumenstock, Robert Bassler. *Song: "Do Something"* Bud Green, Sammy Stept.

Cast: Richard Dix *(Robert Bennett)*, Berton Churchill *(E. M. Burke)*, Louis John Bartels *(Frank Connelly)*, Ned Sparks *(Clarence Van Dyke)*, Wynne Gibson *(Sabel Jackson)*, Helen Kane *(Mabel Jackson)*, Dorothy Hall *(Gwen Burke)*, Madeline Grey *(Mrs. E. M. Burke)*, Nancy Ryan *(Ethel Clark)*.

Farce. Source: James Montgomery, *Nothing But the Truth, a Comedy in Three Acts* (New York, 1920). Robert Bennett, the junior partner in a brokerage firm, bets $10,000 of his sweetheart's money that he will tell nothing but the truth for 24 hours, quickly getting himself, his friends, and his employer into a number of difficult situations. He does not tell a lie, however, and wins the bet. He then tells a whole string of lies to straighten out the troubles into which he has gotten himself. *Brokers. Liars. Wagers.*

NOTHING TO WEAR **F2.3897**

Columbia Pictures. 5 Nov **1928** [c14 Jan 1929; LP30]. Si; b&w. 35mm. 6 reels, 5,701 ft.

Prod Jack Cohn. *Dir* Erle C. Kenton. *Story-Cont* Peter Milne. *Photog* Joseph Walker. *Art Dir* Harrison Wiley. *Film Ed* Ben Pivar. *Asst Dir* Tenny Wright.

Cast: Jacqueline Logan *(Jackie Standish)*, Theodore von Eltz *(Phil Standish)*, Bryant Washburn *(Tommy Butler)*, Jane Winton *(Irene Hawley)*, William Irving *(detective)*, Edythe Flynn *(maid)*.

Comedy. Peeved that her husband will not buy her a fur coat, Jackie Standish visits her former sweetheart, Tommy Butler. Tommy assures her that she will get the coat. The following day Phil buys the coat to soothe his wife and includes a note which leads her to believe that it is a gift from Tommy. To conceal it from her husband, Jackie gives the coat to Tommy, whose sweetheart, Irene, thinks it is a gift for her. Eventually the mistake is corrected; Tommy marries Irene, and Jackie is reunited with her husband. *Women's wear. Marriage.*

NOTORIETY *see* **THE WILD PARTY**

NOTORIETY **F2.3898**

L. Lawrence Weber–Bobby North. *Dist* Apollo Trading Corp. 3 Oct **1922** [Boston premiere; released Nov; c26 Oct 1922; LP18353]. Si; b&w. 35mm. 8 reels, 7,800 ft.

Dir-Writ William Nigh. *Photog* James Diamond.

Cast: Maurine Powers *("Pigeon" Deering)*, Mary Alden *(Ann Boland)*, Rod La Rocque *(Arthur Beal)*, George Hackathorne *("Batty")*, Richard Travers *(Tom Robbins)*, J. Barney Sherry *(Horace Wedderburn)*, Mona Lisa *(Dorothy Wedderburn)*, Anders Randolf *(The Theatrical Agent)*, John Goldsworthy *(Van Dyke Gibson)*, Ida Waterman *(Mrs. Beal)*, William Gudgeon *(The Hired Man)*.

Melodrama. Pigeon Deering, a girl of the tenements, while watching a society ball through a window, witnesses a murder and is arrested. Because she craves notoriety, Pigeon confesses to the crime. During her trial, attorney Arthur Beal exposes the murderer and urges her not to accept any offer from theatrical producers hoping to cash in on her "fame." When Pigeon rejects his advice, Arthur fakes an offer, which she accepts, and has her brought to his country farm for "rehearsals." An attack by a hired man, who assumes from her publicity that she is susceptible, finally convinces Pigeon of her mistake, and she accepts Arthur's proposal of marriage. *Lawyers. Reputation. Murder. Theater.*

A NOTORIOUS AFFAIR **F2.3899**

First National Pictures. 4 May **1930** [c26 Apr 1930; LP1262]. Sd (Vitaphone); b&w. 35mm. 7 reels, 6,218 ft.

Prod Robert North. *Dir* Lloyd Bacon. *Adapt-Dial* J. Grubb Alexander. *Photog* Ernest Haller. *Set Dsgn* Anton Grot. *Film Ed* Frank Ware. *Sd Rec* Oliver S. Garretson. *Asst Dir* John Daumery, Irving Asher. *Cost* Edward Stevenson.

Cast: Billie Dove *(Patricia Hanley Gherardi)*, Basil Rathbone *(Paul Gherardi)*, Kay Francis *(Countess Balakireff)*, Montagu Love *(Sir Thomas Hanley)*, Kenneth Thompson *(Dr. Allen Pomroy)*, Philip Strange, Gino Corrado, Elinor Vandivere.

Romantic drama. Source: Audrey Carter and Waverly Carter, *Fame* (London opening: Mar 1929). Patricia Hanley disturbs a dinner planned for her engagement to an aristocrat by announcing her marriage to violinist Paul Gherardi. Through the help of Patricia and Countess Balakireff, Paul achieves fame; but he soon collapses from overwork. The doctor called to treat him is Allen Pomroy, an old lover of Patricia's and formerly an African game hunter. Paul goes to a seaside resort with the countess, but she is annoyed by his increasing nervousness and irritability, and he suffers a paralytic attack. Patricia and Pomroy take him to a famous surgeon for an operation and accompany him to the coast for a rest; he accuses her of wanting to desert him for the doctor, but when she proves that she does not love Pomroy, he recovers. *Violinists. Paralytics. Physicians. Hunters. Aristocrats. Marriage. London.*

THE NOTORIOUS LADY **F2.3900**

Sam E. Rork Productions. *Dist* First National Pictures. 27 Mar **1927** [c14 Mar 1927; LP23755]. Si; b&w. 35mm. 7 reels, 6,040 ft.

Pres by Sam E. Rork. *Dir* King Baggot. *Adapt* Jane Murfin. *Photog* Tony Gaudio.

Cast: Lewis Stone *(Patrick Marlowe/John Carew)*, Barbara Bedford *(Mary Marlowe/Mary Brownlee)*, Ann Rork *(Kameela)*, Earl Metcalfe *(Anthony Walford)*, Francis McDonald *(Manuela Silvera)*, Grace Carlyle *(Marcia Rivers)*, E. J. Ratcliffe *(Dr. Digby Grant)*, J. Gunnis Davis *(William)*.

Melodrama. Source: Patrick Hastings, *The River* (a play; publication undetermined). Patrick Marlowe, a British Army officer who adores his wife, kills another man when he finds her in his room; though innocent, Mary claims to be guilty to save her husband's life. Patrick takes the name of John Carew and goes to South Africa near the diamond fields; later, Mary goes with Mrs. Rivers to Africa and en route meets Anthony Walford, who falls in love with her. Patrick, who hopes to get some diamonds for Mary, is joined by Anthony on a hazardous expedition down the Munghana(?) River; and though they find diamonds, they are attacked by natives and Anthony's leg is broken. At Anthony's request Patrick returns, but thinking Mary loves the other man, he avoids her. Following their reconciliation, an expedition finds Anthony in time to save him. *English. Marriage. Murder. Perjury. Diamonds. South Africa. Great Britain—Army.*

NOW WE'RE IN THE AIR **F2.3901**

Paramount Famous Lasky Corp. 22 Oct **1927** [c22 Oct 1927; LP24571]. Si; b&w. 35mm. 6 reels, 5,798 ft.

Pres by Adolph Zukor, Jesse L. Lasky. *Dir* Frank Strayer. *Scen* Tom J. Geraghty. *Titl* George Marion, Jr. *Story* Monte Brice, Keene Thompson. *Camera* Harry Perry.

Cast: Wallace Beery *(Wally)*, Raymond Hatton *(Ray)*, Russell Simpson *(Lord Abercrombie McTavish)*, Louise Brooks *(Grisette Chelaine)*, Emile Chautard *(Monsieur Chelaine)*, Malcolm Waite *(Professor Saenger)*, Duke Martin *(top sergeant)*.

Comedy. "Wally and Ray are cousins intent upon getting the fortune of their Scotch grandad, an aviation nut. They become mixed-up with the U. S. flying corps and are wafted over the enemy lines in a runaway balloon. Through misunderstanding they are honored as heroes of the enemy forces, and sent back to the U. S. lines to spy. Here they are captured and almost shot, but everything ends happily." (*Moving Picture World*, 17 Dec 1927, p24.) *Cousins. Scotch. Spies. Balloons. United States Army—Air Corps.*

THE NTH COMMANDMENT **F2.3902**

Cosmopolitan Productions. *Dist* Paramount Pictures. 18 Mar **1923** [c3 Apr 1923; LP18845]. Si; b&w. 35mm. 8 reels, 7,339 ft.

Supv Frances Marion. *Dir* Frank Borzage. *Scen* Frances Marion. *Photog* Chester Lyons.

Cast: Colleen Moore *(Sarah Juke)*, James Morrison *(Harry Smith)*, Eddie Phillips *(Jimmie Fitzgibbons)*, Charlotte Merriam *(Angine Sprunt)*, George Cooper *(Max Plute)*.

Drama. Source: Fannie Hurst, "The Nth Commandment," in *Every Soul Hath Its Song* (New York, 1916). Flattered by the attentions of dapper Jimmie Fitzgibbons, department store clerk Sarah Juke breaks off with her less glamorous sweetheart, Harry Smith, but returns to him when she learns that Harry has consumption. (Besides, Jimmie is fearful of any contact with Sarah.) Harry and Sarah marry, and the passing months see the couple happy but struggling to make ends meet. Harry's failing health demands that he move to a milder climate, but Sarah's appeals to an aid society bring no solution. Jimmie, now a successful song writer, reappears and hopes to lure Sarah away from Harry, but instead he loses $300 to her in wagers and is repulsed when he tries to make love to her. Sarah takes the money to Harry with the explanation that she received it for dancing. (Copyright synopsis says that the aid society does provide assistance.) *Salesclerks. Composers. Tuberculosis. Medical aid. Charitable organizations.*

NUMBER PLEASE *see* **WHAT A NIGHT!**

NUMBERED MEN **F2.3903**

First National Pictures. 7 Jun **1930** [New York opening; released 3 Aug; c3 Aug 1930; LP1464]. Sd (Vitaphone); b&w. 35mm. 8 reels, 6,480 ft.

Dir Mervyn LeRoy. *Screenplay-Dial* Al Cohn, Henry McCarthy. *Photog* Sol Polito. *Film Ed* Terrell Morse. *Rec Engr* Earl Sitar.

Cast: Conrad Nagel *(Bertie Gray)*, Bernice Claire *(Mary Dane)*, Raymond Hackett *(Bud Leonard)*, Ralph Ince *(King Callahan)*, Tully Marshall *(Lemuel Barnes)*, Maurice Black *(Lou Rinaldo)*, William Holden *(Warden Lansing)*, George Cooper *(Happy Howard)*, Blanche Frederici *(Mrs. Miller)*, Ivan Linow *(Pollack)*, Frederick Howard *(Jimmy Martin)*.

Melodrama. Source: Dwight Taylor, "Jailbreak" (publication undetermined). Bud Leonard, serving a 10-year prison term for counterfeiting, tells Bertie Gray, a fellow prisoner, that his sweetheart, Mary Dane, has promised to wait for him; meanwhile, Lou Rinaldo, who framed Bud, makes a play for Mary. According to the prison honor system, some men are permitted to work on the road gang; and Mary gets work at a farmhouse where convicts often eat, hoping thus to see Bud. Rinaldo traces her there and plans to have Bud and Callahan, another prisoner framed by Rinaldo, caught while attempting to escape. Mary thwarts Bud's escape, and Callahan shoots Rinaldo and is himself killed. Though it means an extra prison sentence for him, Bertie informs on Rinaldo to save Bud, happy in the knowledge that Mary will soon have her young lover. *Convicts. Prisons. Courtship. Self-sacrifice. Frameup.*

THE NUT **F2.3904**

Douglas Fairbanks Pictures. *Dist* United Artists. 6 Mar **1921** [c3 Mar 1921; LP16229]. Si; b&w. 35mm. 6 reels.

Prod Douglas Fairbanks. *Dir* Theodore Reed. *Scen* William Parker, Lotta Woods. *Story* Kenneth Davenport. *Photog* William McGann, Harry Thorpe.

Cast: Douglas Fairbanks *(Charlie Jackson)*, Marguerite De La Motte *(Estrell Wynn)*, William Lowery *(Philip Feeney)*, Gerald Pring *(Gentleman George)*, Morris Hughes *(Pernelius Vanderbrook, Jr.)*, Barbara La Marr *(Claudine Dupree)*.

Society farce. Charlie Jackson, a Greenwich Village bachelor, is in love with his neighbor, Estrell Wynn, who has a theory that poor children can be made into proper citizens by being exposed periodically to homes of the wealthy. To aid her theory, he entertains rich patrons, but they leave in indignation at a premature fireworks explosion. After a number of wild adventures, Charlie rescues Estrell from rival Feeney, and with the aid of millionaire cub reporter Vanderbrook they are married. *Bachelors. Reporters. Millionaires. Social service. Poverty. New York City—Greenwich Village.*

THE NUT-CRACKER **F2.3905**

Samuel S. Hutchinson Productions. *Dist* Associated Exhibitors. 28 Mar **1926** [c12 Mar 1926; LU22474]. Si; b&w. 35mm. 6 reels, 5,782 ft.

Dir Lloyd Ingraham. *Scen* Madge Myton. *Photog* Jack MacKenzie.

Cast: Edward Everett Horton *(Horatio Slipaway)*, Mae Busch *(Martha*

Slipaway), Harry Myers *(Oscar Briggs)*, Thomas Ricketts *(Isaac Totten)*, Martha Mattox *(Julia Trotten)*, George Kuwa *(Saki)*, Katherine Lewis *(Hortense)*, Albert Priscoe *(Señor Gonzales)*, George Periolat *(Señor Gómez)*.

Comedy. Source: Frederic Stewart Isham, *The Nut-Cracker* (Indianapolis, c1920). Henpecked Horatio Slipaway is hit by a streetcar and, regaining consciousness in a hospital, feigns amnesia. Playing the market with a $500 insurance settlement, Horatio makes a fortune and conveniently assumes the identity of a Peruvian millionaire. His wife, Martha, eventually learns of this "rich South American" who so closely resembles her husband and, dressing herself in finery, goes to see if it is her Horatio. Horatio finally "regains" his memory, and he and Martha are reunited. *Millionaires. Peruvians. Amnesia. Insurance. Speculation. Streetcar accidents.*

O. U. WEST F2.3906

Harry Garson Productions. 29 Mar **1925** [c29 Mary 1925; LP21662]. Si; b&w. 35mm. 5 reels.

Dir Harry Garson. *Story-Cont* Helen Broneau. *Photog* Billy Ivers.

Cast: Lefty Flynn *(O. U. West)*, Ann May *(Tina Jones)*, Milton Ross *(Cass Jones)*, Evelyn Francisco *(Sally Walker)*, Bill Donovan *(ranch foreman)*, Raymond Turner *(porter)*, Ed Burns *(Luke Crawley)*, Fred Burns *(Jazebel Crawley)*, Jim Burns *(Sep Crawley)*.

Western melodrama. Oliver U. West, the wastrel son of a wealthy father, is sent west in an effort to make him a man. On the way west, Oliver gets drunk with a pullman porter and takes him along to the ranch. Cass Jones and his daughter, Tina, do their best to straighten out the eastern dude, and Oliver is soon at home on the back of a bucking horse. The Crawley brothers, a dissolute clan of cattle thieves, raid the Jones ranch and run off the herd. Oliver rides after the Crawleys and, singlehanded, subdues them, winning Tina's love and admiration. *Wastrels. Porters. Rustlers. Drunkenness. Manhood. Horses.*

THE OATH F2.3907

Mayflower Photoplay Corp. *Dist* Associated First National Pictures. Apr **1921** [c7 Apr 1921; LP16367]. Si; b&w. 35mm. 8 reels, 7,806 ft.

Dir R. A. Walsh. *Scen-Titl* Ralph Spence. *Photog* Dal Clawson.

Cast: Miriam Cooper *(Minna Hart)*, Robert Fischer *(Israel Hart)*, Conway Tearle *(Hugh Coleman)*, Henry Clive *(Gerard Merriam)*, Ricca Allen *(Anna Cassaba)*, Anna Q. Nilsson *(Irene Lansing)*.

Melodrama. Source: William John Locke, *Idols* (London, 1899). When Hugh Coleman loses Irene Lansing to his best friend, Gerard Merriam, he consoles himself by secretly marrying Minna Hart, the daughter of a wealthy Jewish banker who has lent him money on a personal note. Learning that Hart would not consent to his daughter's marrying a gentile, Coleman swears an oath that they will part and will never reveal their marriage. When Hart is slain and robbed, Hugh is tried for the crime, but Irene's testimony that she was with him at the time brings an acquittal. After explanations the two couples are reunited. *Jews. Marriage—Mixed. Murder.*

OATH-BOUND F2.3908

Fox Film Corp. 13 Aug **1922** [c13 Aug 1922; LP19032]. Si; b&w. 35mm. 5 reels, 4,468 ft.

Pres by William Fox. *Dir* Bernard J. Durning. *Scen* Jack Strumwasser. *Story-Scen* Edward J. Le Saint. *Photog* Don Short.

Cast: Dustin Farnum *(Lawrence Bradbury)*, Ethel Grey Terry *(Constance Hastings)*, Fred Thomson *(Jim Bradbury)*, Maurice B. Flynn *(Ned Hastings)*, Norman Selby *(Hicks)*, Aileen Pringle *(Alice)*, Bob Perry *(The Gang Leader)*, Herschel Mayall *(Captain Steele)*.

Melodrama. Wealthy shipowner Lawrence Bradbury is determined to catch silk thieves who operate by means of his ships. His brother Jim, the ringleader, hoodwinks Lawrence into thinking he is a revenue officer. The skipper and a friend are suspected, but the friend proves to be the revenue man and the crooked brother is caught. *Shipowners. Revenue agents. Brothers. Thieves. Silk.*

OBEY THE LAW F2.3909

Columbia Pictures. 5 Nov **1926** [c3 Dec 1926; LP23402]. Si; b&w. 35mm. 6 reels, 5,626 ft.

Supv Harry Cohn. *Dir* Alfred Raboch. *Photog* J. O. Taylor.

Cast: Bert Lytell *(Phil Schuyler)*, Edna Murphy, Hedda Hopper, Larry Kent, Sarah Padden, Eugenia Gilbert, William Welsh.

Crook-society drama. Source: Max Marcin, *Obey the Law* (a play). Following her schooling in Paris, Norma Andrews returns home with the wealthy Schuylers, unaware that Frank, her father, is in prison on a grand larceny charge. She is accompanied by Harry Lyle, her father's underworld confederate, to the Schuyler residence in Long Island, where he soon learns the location and combination of the safe. On the day of his release, Andrews meets Phil Schuyler and Norma, who have become engaged. Lyle brings Andrews a jeweled pendant for Norma's wedding present; later, when two detectives arrive in search of the thieves, Lyle allows himself to be arrested to avoid disgracing Andrews. Phil and Norma are happily united. *Thieves. Filial relations. Long Island. Paris.*

OBEY YOUR HUSBAND F2.3910

Morris R. Schlank Productions. *Dist* Anchor Film Distributors. 15 May **1928.** Si; b&w. 35mm. 6 reels, 5,600 ft.

Dir Charles J. Hunt. *Story-Scen* Arthur Hoerl. *Photog* Robert E. Cline. *Film Ed* William Holmes.

Cast: Gaston Glass *(Arthur Reade)*, Dorothy Dwan *(Joyce Kennedy)*, Alice Lake *(Belle)*, Henry Sedley *(Leland Houghton)*, Robert Homans *(Stephens)*, Robert Elliott *(Mr. Kennedy)*, Jack Johnston *(district attorney)*, Joseph Burke *(Jim)*.

Domestic drama. Story "based on the wife who takes matrimony lightly ... but who really doesn't have many weaknesses except for cards. ... Husband and wife all innocent of the murder of the card sharp, who is rightfully bumped off by his discarded paramour." (*Variety*, 15 Aug 1928, p17.) *Gamblers. Mistresses. Marriage. Murder.*

OBJECT—ALIMONY F2.3911

Columbia Pictures. 22 Dec **1928** [c23 Mar 1929; LP239]. Si; b&w. 35mm. 7 reels, 6,141 ft.

Prod Jack Cohn. *Dir* Scott R. Dunlap. *Scen* Peter Milne. *Adapt* Sig Herzig. *Story* Elmer Harris. *Photog* Joseph Walker. *Art Dir* Harrison Wiley. *Tech Dir* Edward Shulter. *Film Ed* Ben Pivar.

Cast: Lois Wilson *(Ruth Rutledge)*, Hugh Allan *(Jimmy Rutledge)*, Ethel Grey Terry *(Mrs. Carrie Rutledge)*, Douglas Gilmore *(Renaud Graham)*, Roscoe Karns *(Al Bryant)*, Carmelita Geraghty *(Mabel)*, Dickey Moore *(Jimmy Rutledge, Jr.)*, Jane Keckley *(boardinghouse owner)*, Thomas Curran *(Philip Stone)*.

Drama. Ruth Butler, a clerk in an emporium, marries Jimmy Rutledge and thereby greatly displeases his mother, the owner of the emporium, because of Ruth's lowly origins. Renaud Graham, one of Mrs. Rutledge's friends, becomes interested in Ruth, forces his way into her apartment, and attempts to make violent love to her. Jimmy walks in on their embrace and, suspecting the worst, leaves Ruth. In the family way, Ruth finds refuge in a boardinghouse where she meets Al Bryant, an aspiring writer. Ruth tells Al her life story, and he makes it into a bestselling novel and then into a play. Jimmy sees the play and comes to his senses, winning Ruth's forgiveness. *Salesclerks. Novelists. Playwrights. Social classes. Marriage. Alimony. Boardinghouses.*

Note: Reviewed in *Variety* under the title *Object—Matrimony.*

OBJECT—MATRIMONY *see* **OBJECT—ALIMONY**

THE OBLIGIN' BUCKAROO F2.3912

Action Pictures. *Dist* Pathé Exchange. 16 Oct **1927** [c19 Jul 1927; LU24189]. Si; b&w. 35mm. 5 reels, 4,575 ft.

Pres by Lester F. Scott, Jr. *Dir* Richard Thorpe. *Scen* Frank L. Inghram. *Story* Bert B. Perkins. *Photog* Ray Ries.

Cast: Buffalo Bill Jr. *(Bill Murray)*, Olive Hasbrouck *(Tess Cole)*, Sherry Tansey *(Steve Cole)*, Harry Todd *(Bozo Muldoon)*, Raye Hampton *(Fifi)*, Charles Whitaker *(Blackie)*.

Western melodrama. Bill Murray, induced by a sharper to pay the mortgage on a western hotel he has inherited, finds the structure fallen into ruin. Muldoon's Merry Maids theatrical troupe is stranded when the theater burns, and they are offered a job in the local dancehall. Bill rescues them from a bully and offers the use of his hotel. They put the hotel in order and incidentally discover that Bill is half owner in a mining claim grubstaked by one George Cole. The present owners, Steve and Tess, are being forced to sell out to Blackie and Joe when Bill arrives; and in the struggle, the partnership paper is destroyed. Blackie convinces the sheriff that Bill has killed Texas, but Bill proves his innocence and establishes his partnership in the mine. *Swindlers. Theatrical troupes. Chorus girls. Sheriffs. Bullies. Hotels. Mortgages. Mine claims. Documentation.*

OFF THE HIGHWAY F2.3913

Hunt Stromberg Corp. *Dist* Producers Distributing Corp. 15 Aug **1925** [c20 Aug 1925; LP22119]. Si; b&w. 35mm. 8 reels, 7,641 ft.

Supv Hunt Stromberg. *Dir* Tom Forman. *Adapt* Dorothy Farnum.

Cast: William V. Mong *(Caleb Fry/Tatterly)*, Marguerite De La Motte *(Ella Tarrant)*, John Bowers *(Donald Brett)*, Charles Gerard *(Hector Kindon)*, Geno Corrado *(Rabbitt)*, Buddy Post *(Grizzly Bear)*, Joseph Swickard *(master)*, Smoke Turner *(student)*.

Drama. Source: Thomas Gallon, *Tatterly, the Story of a Dead Man* (New York, 1897). Miserly Caleb Fry, who lives all alone with his servant, Tatterly (whom he closely resembles), disinherits his nephew, Donald Brett, when Donald becomes an artist rather than a businessman. Caleb wills his entire fortune instead to Hector Kindon, a cousin. Tatterly dies, and Caleb, moved by some strange whim, assumes Tatterly's identity, leading the world to believe that Caleb Fry has died. Kindon turns out to be a worthless, drunken scoundrel, and Caleb is forced to live with Donald, who, thinking him to be Tatterly, willingly takes him in. Caleb gets his hands on several thousand dollars, ruins Kindom in the market, and gives his new fortune to Donald, who immediately marries Ella Tarrant. Caleb goes to live with them in the country. *Misers. Uncles. Domestics. Artists. Doubles. Disinheritance. Impersonation. Speculation. Stock market.*

THE OFF-SHORE PIRATE (Metro Special) F2.3914

Metro Pictures. 31 Jan **1921** [c7 Feb 1921; LP16128]. Si; b&w. 35mm. 6 reels.

Dir of Prod Bayard Veiller. *Dir* Dallas M. Fitzgerald. *Adapt* Waldemar Young. *Photog* John Arnold. *Adtl Photog* Lieut. Joseph Waddell. *Art Interiors & Eff* A. F. Mantz. *Asst Dir* Al Kelley.

Cast: Viola Dana *(Ardita Farnam)*, Jack Mulhall *(Toby Moreland)*, Edward Jobson *(Uncle John Farnam)*, Edward Cecil *(Ivan Nevkova)*.

Romantic comedy. Source: F. Scott Fitzgerald, "Offshore Pirate," in *Saturday Evening Post* (192:10–11, 29 May 1920). Wealthy society girl Ardita Farnam is held up in her roadster by two thugs and is rescued by Nevkova, a Russian in search of a rich wife, with whom she falls in love against her uncle's wishes. When Uncle John proposes a yachting trip to visit Colonel Moreland and his son, Toby, she refuses to go; and when a stranger and six Negroes take possession of the yacht, she is furious and bargains with the crew to overpower their leader and return to town. Following the injured man ashore, she discovers that it is all a plot by her uncle to save her from the Russian; and as Toby Moreland, the stranger, is more to her taste, she is more than satisfied. *Socialites. Uncles. Fortune hunters. Ship crews. Russians. Strangers. Negroes.*

THE OFFENDERS F2.3915

Independent Pictures. 14 Jun **1924** [New York State license]. Si; b&w. 35mm. 5 reels, 4,130 ft.

Dir Fenwicke L. Holmes. *Story* Katherine Holmes.

Cast: Margery Wilson, Percy Helton.

Melodrama. "Girl is held at mercy of gang of crooks, her only friend being a half-wit. A murder is committed and blame shifted to the girl. The half-wit has seen it but cannot remember. When he is cured, his testimony frees the girl." *(Motion Picture News Booking Guide,* 6:52, Apr 1924.) *Gangs. Murder. Halfwits. Vermont.*

Note: Filmed at Randolph, Vermont.

THE OFFICE SCANDAL F2.3916

Pathé Exchange. 3 Mar **1929** [c30 Jan 1929; LP69]. Talking sequences (Photophone); b&w. 35mm. 7 reels, 6,291 ft. [Also si; 6,511 ft.]

Ralph Block Production. *Dir* Paul L. Stein. *Titl* John Krafft. *Orig Story–Adapt* Paul Gangelin, Jack Jungmeyer. *1st Camera* Jake Badaracco. *Film Ed* Doane Harrison. *Asst Dir* E. J. Babille. *Prod Mgr* Harry Poppe. *Prop Man* Walter Broadfoot.

Cast: Phyllis Haver *(Jerry Cullen)*, Leslie Fenton *(Andy Corbin)*, Raymond Hatton *(Pearson)*, Margaret Livingston *(Lillian Tracy)*, Jimmie Adams *(Delaney)*, Jimmy Aldine *(Freddie)*, Dan Wolheim.

Melodrama. Jerry, a sob sister, befriends a down-and-out reporter and gets a job for him on the newspaper. A murder mystery breaks but is dropped after all clues run into a blank wall. Then the widow of the murdered man drops a hint that implicates the reporter, but the girl he loves finally forces a confession from the actual murderer. *Columnists. Reporters. Newspapers. Murder.*

THE OFFICE WIFE F2.3917

Warner Brothers Pictures. 23 Aug **1930** [c12 Aug 1930; LP1483]. Sd (Vitaphone); b&w. 35mm. 8 reels, 5,390 ft.

Dir Lloyd Bacon. *Screenplay-Dial* Charles Kenyon. *Photog* William Rees. *Film Ed* George Marsh.

Cast: Dorothy Mackaill *(Anne Murdock)*, Lewis Stone *(Lawrence Fellows)*, Hobart Bosworth *(Mr. McGowan)*, Blanche Frederici *(Kate Halsey)*, Joan Blondell *(Catherine Murdock)*, Natalie Moorhead *(Linda Fellows)*, Brooks Benedict *(Mr. Jameson)*, Dale Fuller *(Miss Andrews)*, Walter Merrill *(Ted O'Hara)*.

Romantic drama. Source: Faith Baldwin, *The Office Wife* (New York, 1930). Lawrence Fellows is a whirling dervish as the head of his own advertising agency, provoking the secret admiration of his 40-year-old secretary, Miss Andrews. The lady begins to suffer from an emotional strain, and Fellows gives her a leave of absence, replacing her with Anne Murdock, a comely young lass who formerly had been merely temporary help. Anne proves to be such a package of charm and wit that Fellows falls for her in a big way, thereby neglecting Linda, his wife. Mrs. Fellows, too, has been involved in an affair, and soon goes to Paris to break the tie that binds. The boss and Anne then merge into a permanent partnership, with the latter retaining all hiring responsibilities for any future girl Friday. *Secretaries. Marriage. Infidelity. Divorce. Advertising.*

OFFICER JIM F2.3918

Mrs. Frank J. Hart. *Dist* Lee-Bradford Corp. 7 Aug **1926.** Si; b&w. 35mm. 5 reels, 5,141 ft.

Dir Wilbur McGaugh.

Cast: Joseph Swickard, Gloria Grey, Roy Hughes.

Melodrama. "Policeman prevents bank hold-up and chases thieves but is worsted temporarily. Recovered he takes up chase and finally collars the entire gang. Meets a daughter of president of bank and mutual love is in evidence with marriage resulting." *(Motion Picture News Booking Guide,* 12:47, Apr 1927.) *Police. Bankers. Bank robberies. Chases.*

OFFICER O'BRIEN F2.3919

Pathé Exchange. 15 Feb **1930** [c27 Jan 1930; LP1041]. Sd (Photophone); b&w. 35mm. 8 reels, 6,740 ft. [Also si; 6,511 ft.]

Assoc Prod Ralph Block. *Dir* Tay Garnett. *Story-Adapt-Dial* Thomas Buckingham. *Photog* Arthur Miller. *Art Dir* Edward Jewell. *Set Dresser* Theodore Dickson. *Film Ed* Jack Ogilvie. *Rec Engr* Earl A. Wolcott, Harold Stine. *Asst Dir* Robert Fellows. *Cost Dsgn* Gwen Wakeling. *Script Clerk* Robert Grey. *Prop Man* Robert McCrellis.

Cast: William Boyd *(Bill O'Brien)*, Ernest Torrence *(John P. O'Brien)*, Dorothy Sebastian *(Ruth Dale)*, Russell Gleason *(Johnny Dale)*, Clyde Cook *(Limo Lewis)*, Ralf Harolde *(Mike Patello)*, Arthur Housman *(Tony Zurick)*, Paul Hurst *(Captain Antrim)*, Tom Maloney *(detective)*, Toyo Fujita *(Kono)*.

Crime melodrama. Bill O'Brien is promoted to lieutenant in the police department for his arrest of Mike Patello, gang leader and racketeer, for murder. Ruth Dale, who loves Bill, is concerned when her brother, Johnny, who witnessed the murder, proposes to testify against the racketeer. Meanwhile, Captain Antrim informs Bill that his father has just been released from prison and does not know his son is a policeman. On the way from prison, O'Brien (J. P.) meets Limo, a former cockney pal who recognizes Bill and keeps J. P. from seeing his son; later, J. P. arrives intoxicated and is enraged, forcing Bill to knock him unconscious. J. P. is arrested for robbery but returns the loot to save his son from disgrace; Johnny is killed before testifying against Patello, who is released but confronted by J. P., who proves his guilt and, when he struggles with the police, kills him. Bill plans to resign, but confident of Ruth's love, he decides to remain on the force. *Police. Gangsters. Brother-sister relationship. Filial relations. Murder.*

OFFICIAL MOTION PICTURES OF THE JOHNNY BUFF–PANCHO VILLA BOXING EXHIBITION HELD AT EBBET'S FIELD, BROOKLYN, N. Y., SEPTEMBER 14, 1922 F2.3920

Leon D. Britton. *Dist* Arista Film Corp. 25 Sep **1922.** Si; b&w. 35mm. 5 reels.

Boxing film. Filipino Pancho Villa wrests the American flyweight championship from veteran Johnny Buff with an 11th-round knockout. *Boxing. Johnny Buff. Pancho* [boxer] *Villa. New York City—Brooklyn. Ebbet's Field.*

OH, BABY! **F2.3921**
Al Lichtman. *Dist* Universal Pictures. 7 Aug **1926** [New York premiere; released 16 Jan 1927; c21 Jul 1926; LP22945]. Si; b&w. 35mm. 7 reels, 7,152 ft.

Pres by Carl Laemmle. *Dir-Story* Harley Knoles. *Scen* Arthur Hoerl. *Photog* Marcel Le Picard, Stuart Kelson.

Cast: Little Billy *(Billy Fitzgerald)*, David Butler *(Jim Stone)*, Madge Kennedy *(Dorothy Brennan)*, Creighton Hale *(Arthur Graham or Charley Burns)*, Ethel Shannon *(Mary Bond)*, Flora Finch *(Aunt Phoebe)*, Joe Humphreys, "Bugs" Baer, Graham McNamee, Fred Veats, S. Jay Kaufman, Damon Runyon, Ripley, Frank O'Neil, Sid Mercer *(at the ringside)*.

Comedy. Billy, a diminutive manager of prizefighters, is priming Jim Stone for the heavyweight championship, when Charley Burns (Arthur Graham?) discloses that for the past 8 years he has invented a mythical wife and daughter for the benefit of his Aunt Phoebe, who now requests a visit from them. He finally persuades Billy to pose as his daughter, Evangeline, while Miss Brennan, a magazine writer, consents to take the role of his wife. Billy narrowly escapes the ordeal of being put to bed by Miss Bond, Aunt Phoebe's young companion; later, he dons his pink dress and orders his chauffeur to race to New York. At Madison Square Garden, Jim is panic-stricken as Billy fails to show up, but after many humorous incidents, Billy, in a party dress and blonde wig, manages to crash the gate and call instructions to Jim in the ring. Jim wins the bout, and Billy's identity is discovered. Meanwhile, Aunt Phoebe learns from Charley's butler that he has no family; she tracks him to the Garden, and then to a nightclub, where all are happily united. *Fight managers. Aunts. Authors. Prizefighters. Midgets. Female impersonation. Madison Square Garden.*

OH BILLY, BEHAVE **F2.3922**
Dist Rayart Pictures. 27 Oct **1926** [New York State license]. Si; b&w. 35mm. 5 reels.

Comedy(?). No information about the nature of this film has been found.

OH, DOCTOR! (Universal-Jewel) **F2.3923**
Universal Pictures. 1 Feb **1925** [c12 Nov 1924; LP20773]. Si; b&w. 35mm. 7 reels, 6,587 ft.

Pres by Carl Laemmle. *Dir* Harry A. Pollard. *Adapt-Cont* Harvey Thew. *Photog* Gilbert Warrenton.

Cast: Reginald Denny *(Rufus Billups, Jr.)*, Mary Astor *(Dolores Hicks)*, Otis Harlan *(Mr. Clinch)*, William V. Mong *(Mr. McIntosh)*, Tom Ricketts *(Mr. Peck)*, Lucille Ward *(Aunt Beulah Rush)*, Mike Donlin *(Buzz Titus)*, Clarence Geldert *(Doctor Seaver)*, Blanche Payson *(osteopath)*, George Kuwa *(Chang)*, Martha Mattox *("Death Watch" Mary Schulta)*, Helen Lynch *(maid)*.

Comedy. Source: Harry Leon Wilson, *Oh, Doctor! A Novel* (New York, 1923). Frail hypochondriac Rufus Billups, Jr., borrows money from Messrs. Clinch, McIntosh, and Peck and promises to repay them with the entire fortune he is to inherit in 3 years. To be certain that Rufus stays alive the loan sharks hire a pretty nurse, Dolores Hicks, to take care of him. When Rufus learns that Dolores prefers strong, courageous men, he throws himself into a series of dangerous stunts to the consternation of his creditors. Finally, Dolores maneuvers a scheme by which Rufus will repay only the principal of his loan if he lives until the end of his contract, and Rufus descends from his flagpole perch to declare his love for Dolores. *Hypochondriacs. Nurses. Moneylenders. Osteopaths. Inheritance.*

OH, FOR A MAN! **F2.3924**
Fox Film Corp. 14 Dec **1930** [c5 Nov 1930; LP1720]. Sd (Movietone); b&w. 35mm. 9 reels, 7,800 ft.

Dir Hamilton MacFadden. *Screenplay-Dial* Philip Klein, Lynn Starling. *Photog* Charles Clarke. *Art Dir* Stephen Goosson. *Film Ed* Al De Gaetano. *Mus Dir* Arthur Kay. *Song: "I'm Just Nuts About You"* William Kernell. *Sd Rec* E. Clayton Ward. *Cost* Sophie Wachner.

Cast: Jeanette MacDonald *(Carlotta Manson)*, Reginald Denny *(Barney McGann)*, Warren Hymer *("Pug" Morini)*, Marjorie White *("Totsy" Franklin)*, Alison Skipworth *(Laura)*, Albert Conti *(Peck)*, Bela Lugosi *(Frescatti)*, André Cheron *(Costello)*, William Davidson *(Kerry Stokes)*, Donald Hall, Evelyn Hall, Bodil Rosing, Althea Henly.

Comedy-drama. Source: Mary T. Watkins, "Stolen Thunder," in *Saturday Evening Post* (202:18–19, 7 Jun 1930). Opera singer Carlotta Manson catches Barney McGann burglarizing her apartment one evening, and thinking he has possibilities as a singer, she decides to give him a chance. With her wiles and prestige she arranges singing lessons for him through her impresario, but Barney decidedly has little aptitude as a professional singer. He is about to give up the entire project when Carlotta confesses that she is in love with him. They marry and go to Italy, where she presents him with a villa in the mountains overlooking a lake; but he longs for his friends in New York and eventually deserts her. Heartbroken, Carlotta returns to opera; and when she sings poorly at her New York opening, Barney reproves her for a poor showing and with a little persuasion decides to stay with her. *Singers. Burglars. Opera. Courtship. New York City. Italy.*

OH, JO! **F2.3925**
Dist Paramount Pictures. 15 May **1921** [scheduled release]. Si; b&w. 35mm. 5 reels, 4,956 ft.

Dir F. Richard Jones.

Cast: Dorothy Gish.

No information about the nature of this film has been found.

Note: Also listed in trade magazine release charts as *Old Jo*. Probably these are working titles for either *The Ghost in the Garret*, q. v., or *The Country Flapper*, q. v.

OH, KAY! **F2.3926**
First National Pictures. 26 Aug **1928** [c17 Aug 1928; LP25536]. Si; b&w. 35mm. 6 reels, 6,100 ft. [Copyrighted as 7 reels.]

Pres by John McCormick. *Dir* Mervyn LeRoy. *Scen* Carey Wilson. *Titl* Pelham Grenville Wodehouse. *Adapt* Elsie Janis. *Photog* Sid Hickox. *Film Ed* Paul Weatherwax.

Cast: Colleen Moore *(Lady Kay Rutfield)*, Lawrence Gray *(Jimmy Winter)*, Alan Hale *(Jansen)*, Ford Sterling *(Shorty McGee)*, Claude Gillingwater *(Judge Appleton)*, Julanne Johnston *(Constance Appleton)*, Claude King *(The Earl of Rutfield)*, Edgar Norton *(Lord Braggot)*, Percy Williams *(The Butler)*, Fred O'Beck *(Captain Hornsby)*.

Romantic comedy. Source: Guy Bolton and Pelham Grenville Wodehouse, *Oh, Kay!* (New York opening: 8 Nov 1926). On the eve of her wedding to the insipid Lord Braggot, Lady Kay Rutfield seeks solace in a solitary sail on her sloop. A storm blows up, and Kay is rescued by a passing rumrunner bound for the United States. The ship anchors in Long Island Sound, and Kay makes her escape, taking refuge in the deserted mansion of wealthy Jimmy Winter. That evening, Jimmy, who is to be wed on the following day, returns home unexpectedly, and Kay (in order to elude a detective named Jansen, who has mistaken her for a bootlegger) persuades him to let her pose for a night as his wife. Shorty, a bootlegger, has hidden some hooch in the basement and, to protect it, passes himself off as the new butler. The night of the following day finds Jimmy and Kay engaged, and Shorty long gone with his illegal swill. *English. Bootleggers. Detectives. Butlers. Rumrunners. Imposture. Sea rescue. Long Island.*

OH, MABEL BEHAVE **F2.3927**
Triangle Film Corp. *Dist* Photocraft Productions. 20 Jan **1922.** Si; b&w. 35mm. 5 reels.

Dir Mack Sennett, Ford Sterling. *Titl* Joseph Farnham.

Cast: Mack Sennett *(Blaa Blaa)*, Ford Sterling *(Squire Peachem)*, Owen Moore *(Randolph Roanoke)*, Mabel Normand *(innkeeper's daughter)*.

Burlesque. "Squire Peachem used the mortgage he holds on the innkeeper's property as a lever to win his daughter, but the daughter cannot see it that way as she loves a young swell, Randolph Roanoke. The squire, with the aid of his trusty but ignorant henchman, Blaa Blaa, seeks to sidetrack Roanoke which leads to complications, but how poorly he succeeds and how the daughter brings things around so that she has her own way furnishes the action for the burlesque which contains fights, a comedy duel, stunts and thrills." (*Moving Picture World*, 17 Dec 1921, p855.) *Innkeepers. Mortgages. Duels. Stunts.*

Note: According to its New York State license application, this film was produced ca1917.

OH MARY BE CAREFUL **F2.3928**
Goldwyn Pictures. *Dist* Pioneer Film Corp. 1 Sep **1921** [New York State]. Si; b&w. 35mm. 5 reels.

Dir Arthur Ashley. *Story* George Weston. *Photog* William Fildew.

Cast: Madge Kennedy *(Mary Meacham)*, George Forth *(Morgan Smith)*, George Stevens, actor *(Judge Adams)*, Bernard Thornton *(Dick Lester)*, A. Drehle *(Dr. Chase)*, Marguerite Marsh *(Susie)*, Harry Fraser *(Professor Putnam)*, Dixie Thompson *(Luke)*, Mae Rogers *(Nellie Burns)*, Kathleen McEchran *(Kate Lester)*, Harry Myers *(Bobby Burns)*, Marcia Harris *(Myra Meacham)*.

Comedy. "Mary Meacham, the most popular girl in college, goes to live with her maiden aunt, Miss Myra. Auntie is a man-hater who has various theories for testing the desirable qualities of the male sex. Mary sees a dreary man-less time before her and sends an S. O. S. to various sisters and their brothers to visit her while Auntie is away. Then a tree surgeon comes on business and proves to be a most attractive young man. Mary tries Auntie's theories plus some of her own. Complications ensue. When Auntie returns, Mary finds the surgeon is the man she wants." (*Moving Picture World,* 17 Sep 1921, p321.) *Flirts. Man-haters. Tree surgeons. Spinsters. Aunts.*

Note: According to an advertisement (*Motion Picture News,* 10 Sep 1921), "this picture was made by the Goldwyn Pictures Corp. in 1917, but release of the picture was withheld."

OH! SAILOR, BEHAVE! **F2.3929**

Warner Brothers Pictures. 16 Aug **1930** [c23 Jul 1930; LP1437]. Sd (Vitaphone); b&w. 35mm. 9 reels, 6,223 ft.

Dir Archie Mayo. *Screenplay-Dial* Joseph Jackson. *Adtl Dial* Sid Silvers. *Photog* Dev Jennings. *Songs: "Love Comes in the Moonlight," "Leave a Little Smile," "Tell Us Which One Do You Love," "Highway to Heaven"* Al Dubin, Joe Burke. *Rec Engr* Clare A. Riggs.

Cast: Irene Delroy *(Nanette Dodge)*, Charles King *(Charlie Carroll)*, Lowell Sherman *(Prince Kosloff)*, Vivian Oakland *(Kunegundi)*, Noah Beery *(Romanian general)*, Ole Olsen *(Simon)*, Chick Johnson *(Peter)*, Lotti Loder *(Louisa)*, Charles Judels *(De Medici)*, Elsie Bartlett *(Mitzi)*, Lawrence Grant *(Von Klaus)*, Gino Corrado *(Stephan)*.

Musical comedy-drama. Source: Elmer Rice, *See Naples and Die, a Comedy in Three Acts* (New York, 1930). Social climber Nanette Dodge and Charlie Carroll, a reporter for the *Paris Herald* sent to interview a Romanian general, meet in Venice and fall in love. At the same time, Simon and Peter, American sailors, are searching for a peg-legged robber and become embroiled in trouble with Louisa, a local siren who leads them on. Charlie, thwarted in his interview, is aided by Kuni, the general's favorite. In London, Nanette's sister, Mitzi, receives a blackmail threat from Kosloff, a Russian prince with whom she has had an affair; Nanette determines to vamp the prince so as to obtain the incriminating letters, but he tricks her and she is forced to marry him to save her sister. Learning of her marriage, Charlie decides to marry Kuni. But Nanette arrives with an explanation. The prince kidnaps Nanette but is shot when he appears disguised as the general, leaving Charlie and Nanette free to marry. *Sailors. Reporters. Social climbers. Vamps. Romanians. Russians. Royalty. Courtship. Marriage. Venice. London. "Paris Herald."*

OH, WHAT A NIGHT! **F2.3930**

Sterling Pictures. 5 Nov **1926** [c29 Nov 1926; LP23381]. Si; b&w. 35mm. 5 reels, 4,909 ft. [Copyrighted as 6 reels.]

Dir Lloyd Ingraham. *Adapt* Colin Clements. *Story* Florence Ryerson. *Photog* Herbert Kirkpatrick.

Cast: Raymond McKee *(Bob Brady)*, Edna Murphy *(June Craig)*, Charles K. French *(John Craig)*, Ned Sparks *("Slicky")*, Jackie Coombs *(baby)*, Hilliard Karr *(fat man)*, Frank Alexander *(second fat man)*.

Farce. The night before the premiere of Bob Brady's play, he is asked to rewrite the last act. On his way to the producer's apartment, Bob is accused of having stolen a fat man's watch and hides from the pursuing mob in the entrance to a jeweler's store, where he becomes acquainted with June Craig. Bob reaches the producer's apartment and is typing away when Slicky, the burglar, jimmies open the producer's liquor stock and drinks generous samples. From her apartment, June sees him; and believing that Bob is the burglar, she forces him into her own apartment, while awaiting the police. Numerous complications ensue: Slicky steals June's necklace, but when he takes refuge in a room with a baby, the pearls disappear. Bob convinces June of his innocence and decides to incorporate his experience into his play. *Playwrights. Burglars. Infants. Mistaken identity.*

OH, WHAT A NURSE! **F2.3931**

Warner Brothers Pictures. 20 Mar **1926** [c20 Feb 1926; LP22416]. Si; b&w. 35mm. 7 reels, 6,930 ft.

Dir Charles Reisner. *Adapt* Darryl Francis Zanuck. *Photog* John Mescall. *Adtl Photog* Nelson Larabee. *Asst Dir* Sandy Roth.

Cast: Sydney Chaplin *(Jerry Clark)*, Patsy Ruth Miller *(June Harrison)*, Gayne Whitman *(Clive Hunt)*, Matthew Betz *(Capt. Ladye Kirby)*, Edith Yorke *(Mrs. Clark)*, David Torrence *(Big Tim Harrison)*, Ed Kennedy *(Eric Johnson)*, Raymond Wells *(mate)*, Henry Barrows *(editor of the "Gazette")*.

Farce. Source: Robert Emmet Sherwood and Bertram Bloch, "Oh, What a Nurse!" (publication undetermined). Cub reporter Jerry Clark substitutes for Dolly Wimple, the editor of a newspaper advice-to-the-lovelorn column, and advises wealthy June Harrison not to marry Clive Hunt, a man whom she does not love. This advice maddens June's penniless uncle, political boss Tim Harrison, who is in league with Hunt to get his hands on June's fortune. After a series of mad adventures involving rumrunners and female impersonators, Jerry saves June from a forced marriage with Hunt and marries her himself. *Reporters. Columnists. Rumrunners. Female impersonation. Political bosses. Lovelorn. Newspapers.*

OH, YEAH! **F2.3932**

Pathé Exchange. 19 Oct **1929** [c9 Nov 1929; LP842]. Sd (Photophone); b&w. 35mm. 8 reels, 6,890 ft. [Also si; 5,657 ft.]

Dir-Adapt Tay Garnett. *Dial Dir* James Gleason. *Photog* Arthur Miller. *Song: "Love Found Me"* Tay Garnett, George Waggner, George Green. *Sd* Earl A. Wolcott, Harold Stine. *Asst Dir* Robert Fellows.

Cast: Robert Armstrong *(Dude)*, James Gleason *(Dusty)*, Patricia Caron *(Pinkie)*, ZaSu Pitts *(The Elk)*, Bud Fine *(Pop Eye)*, Frank Hagney *(Hot Foot)*, Harry Tyler *(Splinters)*, Paul Hurst *(Superintendent)*.

Comedy-melodrama. Source: Andrew W. Somerville, "No Brakes," in *Saturday Evening Post* (201: 20–21, 8 Dec 1928). Dude and Dusty, two drifters, blow into Linda, a railroad town, on the brakebeams of a freight train, preceded by crooks Hot Foot and Pop Eye. Dude meets Pinkie, who runs the camp commissary; and to make an impression on her, he washes twice a day and grooms his hair with axle grease, to the disgust of Dusty. Then Dusty meets The Elk, a waitress who favors him with admiring stares. When Dude rescues the superintendent's child from the wheels of a train, his romance begins to prosper, but both Dude and Dusty lose their earnings in a crap game to Splinters, who is himself robbed. Dude is suspected, though Hot Foot and Pop Eye are guilty, and he skips town with Dusty. They battle with the villains on a moving flatcar that barely avoids collision with a passenger train and crashes; the injured boys are reunited with their girls, and the villains are placed under arrest. *Vagabonds. Waitresses. Commissaries. Railroads. Train wrecks.*

OH, YOU TONY! **F2.3933**

Fox Film Corp. 21 Sep **1924** [c5 Sep 1924; LP20543]. Si; b&w. 35mm. 7 reels, 6,302 ft.

Pres by William Fox. *Dir* J. G. Blystone. *Story-Scen* Donald W. Lee. *Photog* Daniel Clark.

Cast: Tom Mix *(Tom Masters)*, Claire Adams *(Betty Faine)*, Dick La Reno *(Mark Langdon)*, Earle Foxe *(Jim Overton)*, Dolores Rousse *(The Countess)*, Charles K. French *(Blakely)*, Pat Chrisman *(The Chief)*, Miles McCarthy *(Senator from Arizona)*, Mathilda Brundage *(Senator's wife)*, May Wallace *(etiquette instructor)*.

Western comedy-melodrama. Tom Masters goes to Washington to represent ranchers on a legislative matter. He is easily deceived by crooked lobbyists, headed by Jim Overton, who gain control of his ranch and savings. With the aid of his partner, Betty Faine, he discovers the plot and saves his property by staking it on Tony, a racehorse. *Ranchers. Lobbyists. Horseracing. Washington (District of Columbia). United States Congress. Horses.*

OIL AND ROMANCE **F2.3934**

Bear Productions. *Dist* Aywon Film Corp. 3 Sep **1925** [New York State license]. Si; b&w. 35mm. 5 reels, 4,850 ft.

Dir Harry L. Fraser.

Cast: Gordon Clifford, Charlotte Pierce.

Western melodrama(?). No information about the nature of this film has been found.

AN OKLAHOMA COWBOY **F2.3935**

J. Charles Davis Productions. 20 May **1929.** Si; b&w. 35mm. 5 reels, 4,814 ft.

Cast: Art Acord, Ione Reed.

Western melodrama(?). No information about the precise nature of this film has been found. *Cowboys. Oklahomans.*

OKLAHOMA CYCLONE **F2.3936**

Tiffany Productions. 8 Aug **1930.** Sd (Photophone); b&w. 35mm. 6 reels, 5,916 ft.

Prod Trem Carr. *Dir-Story-Scen* J. P. McCarthy. *Adapt* Ford Beebe.

Cast: Bob Steele *(Oklahoma Cyclone)*, Nita Rey *(Carmelita)*, Al St.

John *(Slim)*, Charles L. King *(McKim)*, Hector Sarno *(The Don)*, Slim Whittaker *(Rawhide)*, Shorty Hendrix *(Shorty)*, Emilio Fernandez *(Pânchez Gómez)*.

Western melodrama. Feigning flight from the law, Jim Smith (the "Oklahoma Cyclone") maneuvers his way into McKim's gang and is immediately attracted to Carmelita, though he temporarily heeds McKim's warning to avoid her. The gang robs a bank and goes across the border, where McKim is keeping prisoner a dying sheriff—Jim's father, the discovery of whose whereabouts was Jim's object in joining the gang. McKim perceives Jim's ruse and sets out to teach him a lesson; Jim is getting the worst of the ensuing fight when Slim pulls his gun to keep the other gang members at bay. Jim rallies, and Carmelita brings a posse. *Sheriffs. Gangs. Robbery. Filial relations. Mexican border.*

Note: Songs: "Song of the Range," "Let Me Live Out on the Prairie."

THE OKLAHOMA KID F2.3937

J. P. McGowan Productions. *Dist* Syndicate Pictures. Nov **1929.** Si; b&w. 35mm. 5 reels, 4,883 ft.

Dir J. P. McGowan. *Scen* Walter Sterret. *Titl* William Stratton. *Story* Sally Winters. *Photog* Hap Depew.

Cast: Bob Custer, Henry Roquemore, Vivian Ray, Tommy Bay, J. P. McGowan, Walter Patterson.

Western melodrama. Sent from Oklahoma to New Mexico to buy and deliver Mr. Stading's T Bar S cattle, The Oklahoma Kid finds himself in the midst of trouble caused by the swindling Petty gang. He is beaten and impersonated by Pete Gibbs, but a map of Oklahoma tatooed on The Kid's arm leads to exposure of the impersonator and a roundup of the gang. Meanwhile, The Kid successfully woos Grace Standing. *Oklahomans. Cattlemen. Gangs. Impersonation. Tattoos. New Mexico. Documentation.*

THE OKLAHOMA SHERIFF F2.3938

Big Productions Film Corp. *Dist* Syndicate Pictures. 10 Jul **1930** [New York showing]. Si; b&w. 35mm. 5 reels, 4,890 ft.

Dir J. P. McGowan. *Story* Sally Winters. *Photog* Herbert Kirkpatrick.

Cast: Bob Steele, Jean Reno, Perry Murdock, Cliff Lyons, Mac V. Wright, Thomas G. Lingham, Clark Comstock.

Western melodrama. "Yarn of a sheriff in familiar surroundings who has a crooked deputy. Sheriff also objects to his daughter's b.f. who is a hero. Crooked deputy kills the sheriff in a robbery. B.f. saves the dough and captures the murderer and a couple of henchmen. Finis—the girl and boy clinch." (*Variety*, 16 Jul 1930, p29.) *Sheriffs. Robbery. Murder. Fatherhood. Oklahoma.*

OLD AGE HANDICAP F2.3939

Trinity Pictures. 18 May **1928** [New York showing; released Sep]. Si; b&w. 35mm. 6 reels, 5,573 ft.

Dir Frank S. Mattison. *Scen* Charles A. Taylor. *Titl* Putnam Hoover. *Adapt* Cecil Burtis Hill. *Story* Tod Underwood. *Photog* Jules Cronjager. *Film Ed* Minnie Steppler.

Cast: Alberta Vaughn, Gareth Hughes, Vivian Rich, Olaf Hytten, Mavis Villiers, Bud Shaw, Jimmy Humes, Carolyn Wethall, Robert Rodman, Frank Mattison, Jr., Ford Jessen, Hall Cline, Edna Hearn, Arthur Hotaling, White Star.

Melodrama. A youth (played by Gareth Hughes) from a large, poor family prefers a shantytown girl (played by Alberta Vaughn), who becomes a popular cabaret dancer, to the daughter of the banker. The dancer saves the youth's sister from being molested by the town bad boy—at some danger to her own reputation—and rides the family's horse to victory and a $5,000 purse in a handicap rigged by the banker. *Dancers. Brother-sister relationship. Poverty. Wealth. Shantytowns. Horseracing. Reputation. Cabarets. Horses.*

OLD CLOTHES F2.3940

Jackie Coogan Productions. *Dist* Metro-Goldwyn Distributing Corp. 8 Nov **1925** [New York premiere; released 22 Nov; c1 Dec 1925; LP22057]. Si; b&w. 35mm. 6 reels, 5,915 ft.

Prod under pers supv of Jack Coogan, Sr. *Dir* Edward Cline. *Writ* Willard Mack. *Titl* Robert Hopkins. *Photog* Frank B. Good, Harry Davis.

Cast: Max Davidson *(Max Ginsberg)*, Joan Crawford *(Mary Riley)*, Allan Forrest *(Nathan Burke)*, Lillian Elliott *(Mrs. Burke)*, James Mason *(Dapper Dan)*, Stanton Heck *(The Adjuster)*, Dynamite *(himself, a horse)*, Jackie Coogan *(Tim Kelly)*.

Comedy. Max Ginsberg, an elderly Jew, and his little Irish partner, Tim Kelly, have made their fortune in rags but lose it by investing in Vista Copper and return to the junk business. They take in Mary Riley, an impoverished young girl, as a boarder and later as a partner. Mary falls in love with Nathan Burke, the son of wealthy parents. Nathan's mother, however, disapproves of Mary. The Burke family fortune suffers a setback, but Tim saves the day with the Vista Copper stock, and all ends well for Mary and Nathan. *Junk dealers. Jews. Irish. Social classes. Speculation. Wealth. Horses.*

THE OLD CODE F2.3941

Morris R. Schlank Productions. *Dist* Anchor Film Distributors. 14 Nov **1928** [New York showing]. Si; b&w. 35mm. 6 reels, 5,900 ft.

Pres by Morris R. Schlank. *Dir* Benjamin Franklin Wilson. *Scen* E. C. Maxwell. *Story* James Oliver Curwood. *Photog* Frank Cotner, Jack Jackson. *Film Ed* Earl C. Turner.

Cast: Walter McGrail *(Pierre Belleu)*, Lillian Rich *(Marie d'Arcy)*, Cliff Lyons *(Jacques de Long)*, Melbourne MacDowell *(Steve MacGregor)*, J. P. McGowan *(Raoul de Valle)*, Neva Gerber *(Lola)*, Ervin Renard *(Henri Langlois)*, Mary Gordon *(Mary MacGregor)*, Rhody Hathaway *(Father Le Fane)*, John Rainbow.

Northwest melodrama. An Indian girl loves French trapper Pierre Belleu, but he has eyes only for an orphan, Marie d'Arcy, who also lives in the far north settlement. The villain is a menace to both girls, and the hero finally effects justice in a duel with the villain on a deserted island. *Trappers. Orphans. French Canadians. Indians of North America.*

OLD ENGLISH F2.3942

Warner Brothers Pictures. 21 Aug **1930** [New York premiere; released 27 Sep; c13 Sep 1930; LP1567]. Sd (Vitaphone); b&w. 35mm. 11 reels, 7,926 ft.

Dir Alfred E. Green. *Screenplay* Walter Anthony, Maude Howell. *Photog* James Van Trees. *Film Ed* Owen Marks. *Mus Dir* Erno Rapee. *Mus Cond* Louis Silvers. *Rec Engr* Clare A. Riggs. *Cost* Earl Luick.

Cast: George Arliss *(Sylvanus Heythorp)*, Leon Janney *(Jock)*, Doris Lloyd *(Mrs. Larne)*, Betty Lawford *(Phyllis Larne)*, Ivan Simpson *(Joe Phillin)*, Harrington Reynolds *(Farney)*, Reginald Sheffield *(Bob Phillin)*, Murray Kinnell *(Charles Ventnor)*, Ethel Griffies *(Adela Heythorp)*, Henrietta Goodwin *(Letty)*.

Drama. Source: John Galsworthy, *Old English* (London, 1924). Sylvanus Heythorp, past 80, and known about Liverpool as "Old English," is unable to pay his debts although he is the director of numerous companies and chairman of a shipbuilding firm. He tries to persuade his creditors to accept an allotment from his salary and not to force him into disgrace—all but Charles Ventnor agree. Rosamund Larne, widow of Heythorp's illegitimate son, and her two children, Phyllis and Jock, arrive requesting funds above her regular allowance; Heythorp refuses but decides to establish a fund for Phyllis, whom he loves devotedly. Joe Phillin, whose son Bob loves Phyllis, is induced to sell his ships to Heythorp for £60,000 and turn over a 10 percent commission to Heythorp's grandchildren. Ventnor, learning Heythorp's secret, demands an audience and threatens to expose him. Old English orders a great dinner of his favorite dishes and wines and against the wishes of his servants gorges himself with abandon. When Phyllis and Bob return from the theater they find he has died in his easy chair by the fire. *Bankruptcy. Fatherhood. Old age. Shipbuilding. Liverpool.*

OLD FOLKS AT HOME (Reissue) F2.3943

Fine Arts Pictures. *Dist* Film Distributors League. **1921.** Si; b&w. 35mm. 5 reels.

Note: A Sir Beerbohm Tree–Mildred Harris film originally released by Triangle Film Corp. on 15 Oct 1916.

THE OLD FOOL F2.3944

Outlook Photoplays. *Dist* W. W. Hodkinson Corp. 31 Dec **1923.** Si; b&w. 35mm. 6 reels, ca6,140 ft.

Dir Edward Venturini. *Story-Scen* J. C. Fabrini. *Photog* Ned Van Buren.

Cast: James Barrows *(Grandad Steele)*, Henry Hunt *(Peter Steele)*, Jimmy Mason *(Henry Steele)*, Lloyd Hughes *(John Steele)*, Barbara Tennant *(Dora Steele)*, Betty Francisco *(Mary Manners)*, Ben Hendricks, Jr. *(Pete Harkins)*, Louise Fazenda *(Dolores Murphy)*, O. V. Harrison *(Larry Bellows)*, Monte Collins *(Pop Hardy)*, Tom Mean *(Rogers)*.

Western melodrama. Finding life difficult with a son who feels that the old man is a burden, Civil War veteran Grandad Steele goes to Texas to find a happy refuge with his grandson John. The local sheriff is accused of smuggling rifles and ammunition across the Mexican border. John pursues the sheriff, who has kidnaped his sweetheart, Mary, and arrives in time to rescue her. The sheriff escapes but is later downed by Grandad with his Civil War sword. *Grandfathers. Veterans. Sheriffs. Family life. Texas. Mexican border.*

OLD HOME WEEK **F2.3945**

Famous Players–Lasky. *Dist* Paramount Pictures. 25 May **1925** [c26 May 1925; LP21502]. Si; b&w. 35mm. 7 reels, 6,780 ft.

Pres by Adolph Zukor, Jesse L. Lasky. *Dir* Victor Heerman. *Screenplay* Thomas J. Geraghty. *Story* George Ade. *Photog* Alvin Wyckoff. *Art Dir* Walter E. Keller.

Cast: Thomas Meighan *(Tom Clark)*, Lila Lee *(Ethel Harmon)*, Charles Dow Clark *(Marshall Coleman)*, Max Figman *(Townsend Barton)*, Charles Sellon *(Uncle Henry)*, Zelma Tiden *(Mary Clark)*, Sidney Paxton *(Judge Harmon)*, Joseph Smiley *(Jim Ferguson)*, Jack Terry *(Frikkle)*, Leslie Hunt *(Otey Jinks)*, Isabel West *(Mrs. Clark)*, Clayton Frye *(Congressman Brady)*.

Comedy. Tom Clark, the part owner of a luckless gas station in New York, returns to his place of birth for Old Home Week, posing as the millionaire president of the Amalgamated Oil Co. He is chosen as the orator for the homecoming banquet and given complete financial control over an oil well drilled in the town by Coleman and Barton, a pair of oily swindlers. Tom discovers that the well is a fake and has it connected secretly with the local reservoir. A wire from Tom's partner is intercepted, and Tom is exposed as a fraud. Coleman and Barton are about to leave town when Tom fakes a gusher and quickly sells the well back to the swindlers at a profit. The swindlers realize that they have been outsmarted, and their anger convinces the townspeople that Tom has acted in the best interests of the community. Tom is again the toast of the town, feted by its inhabitants and rewarded with the kisses of his sweetheart. *Swindlers. Smalltown life. Imposture. Oil wells. Filling stations.*

THE OLD HOMESTEAD **F2.3946**

Famous Players–Lasky. *Dist* Paramount Pictures. 8 Oct **1922** [c7 Oct 1922; LP18326]. Si; b&w. 35mm. 8 reels, 7,696 ft.

Pres by Jesse L. Lasky. *Dir* James Cruze. *Scen* Julian Josephson. *Adapt* Perley Poore Sheehan, Frank E. Woods. *Photog* Karl Brown.

Cast: Theodore Roberts *(Uncle Joshua Whitcomb)*, George Fawcett *(Eph Holbrook)*, T. Roy Barnes *(Happy Jack)*, Fritzi Ridgeway *(Ann)*, Harrison Ford *(Reuben Whitcomb)*, James Mason *(Lem Holbrook)*, Kathleen O'Connor *(Rose Blaine)*, Ethel Wales *(Aunt Matilda)*, Edwin J. Brady *(Ike Goodsell)*, Frank Hayes *(Si Prime)*, Z. Wall Covington *(Seth Perkins)*, Charles Williams *(Gabe Waters)*.

Rural melodrama. Source: Denman Thompson, *The Old Homestead* (Boston production: 1886). When Lem Holbrook steals some money from his father, Eph Holbrook, to give to Rose, Reuben Whitcomb is accused and jailed. There he meets Happy Jack, and they escape; but Reuben's father, Uncle Josh, is forced to mortgage his farm to Eph to cover the loss. Reuben's sweetheart, Ann, is disturbed by reports that he has gone to meet Rose, but Uncle Josh hears from Happy Jack that he has actually gone to China. Happy Jack goes to search for Reuben while Uncle Josh finds it harder and harder to meet his payments. Just as he is about to sell out, a violent storm levels all of the town except Uncle Josh's farm, prompting Lem to confess to the robbery. Reuben returns, and all are reconciled. *Fugitives. Chinese. Portuguese. Hawaiians. Siamese. Filial relations. Theft. Finance—Personal. Family life. New Hampshire.*

Note: There is an elaborate supporting cast of Chinese, Portuguese, Hawaiians, Siamese, and others.

OLD IRONSIDES **F2.3947**

Paramount Famous Lasky Corp. 6 Dec **1926** [world premiere; c3 Mar 1928; LP25029]. Si; b&w. 35mm. 12 reels, 10,089 ft. [Released 3 Mar 1928. 8 reels, 7,910 ft.]

Pres by Adolph Zukor, Jesse L. Lasky. *Supv* B. P. Schulberg. *Dir* James Cruze. *Scen* Dorothy Arzner, Walter Woods, Harry Carr. *Titl* Rupert Hughes. *Suggested & Adapt* Harry Carr, Walter Woods. *Story* Laurence Stallings. *Photog* Alfred Gilks. *Adtl Photog* Charles Boyle. *Asst Dir* Harold Schwartz. *Sp Eff* Roy Pomeroy.

Cast: Esther Ralston *(Esther)*, Wallace Beery *(Bos'n)*, George Bancroft *(Gunner)*, Charles Farrell *(The Commodore)*, Johnny Walker *(Lt. Stephen Decatur)*, George Godfrey *(cook)*, Guy Oliver *(first mate)*, Eddie Fetherston *(Lieutenant Somers)*, Effie Ellsler *(Esther's mother)*, William Conklin *(Esther's father)*, Fred Kohler *(second mate)*, Charles Hill Mailes *(Commodore Preble)*, Nick De Ruiz *(The Bashaw)*, Mitchell Lewis *(pirate chief)*, Frank Jonasson, Frank Bonner, Duke Kahanamoku *(pirate captains)*, Arthur Ludwig *(second mate)*, Spec O'Donnell *(cabin boy)*, Boris Karloff *(a Saracen guard)*, Tetsu Komai.

Historical drama. Following a fiery patriotic speech by Pinckney in Philadelphia before a gathering of young boys, the scene shifts to Boston and the launching of the frigate *Constitution*, where the same boys are midshipmen now lined up for inspection by Commodore Preble. At the docks in Salem, the merchant ship *Esther*, under Bos'n, recruits a country boy in search of adventure. The commodore vies for the hand of Esther, the captain's daughter, but is involved in a fight with a boatswain when the ship is taken by pirates; the crew is sold into slavery and the captain held for ransom. The *Philadelphia* is captured, and Stephen Decatur proposes to recapture or destroy it. In the melee, Bos'n, Gunner, and Commodore escape and are picked up by the *Constitution*, where Gunner is lashed for desertion. They all participate in the battle at Tripoli in which "Old Ironsides" is damaged; Esther is reunited with her father and the commodore, and they proceed to Singapore. *Piracy. United States—History—Naval. Salem (Massachusetts). Tripoli. Stephen Decatur. Edward Preble. Charles Cotesworth Pinckney. U. S. S. "Constitution".*

Note: Two sequences were shown in "Magnascope."

OLD LOVES AND NEW **F2.3948**

Sam E. Rork Productions. *Dist* First National Pictures. 11 Apr **1926** [c20 Apr 1926; LP22616]. Si; b&w. 35mm. 8 reels, 7,423 ft. [Also 6,500 ft.]

Pres by Sam E. Rork. *Dir* Maurice Tourneur. *Adapt* Marion Fairfax. *Photog* Henry Cronjager. *Art Dir* Jack Okey. *Film Ed* Patricia Rooney. *Asst Dir* Ben Silvey.

Cast: Lewis Stone *(Gervas Carew)*, Barbara Bedford *(Marny)*, Walter Pidgeon *(Clyde Lord Geradine)*, Katherine MacDonald *(Lady Elinor Carew)*, Tully Marshall *(Hosein)*, Ann Rork *(Kitty)*, Arthur Rankin *(Denny O'Meara)*, Albert Conti *(Dr. Chalmers)*.

Romantic drama. Source: Edith Maude Hull, *The Desert Healer* (Boston, 1923). Gervas Lord Carew returns from the war to find that his wife, Elinor, has deserted him for Lord Geradine, leaving their infant son dying. Embittered and disillusioned, he goes to Algeria and devotes himself to healing the desert tribesmen, who revere him. Meanwhile, Lord Geradine casts aside the faithless Elinor and marries Marny O'Meara; later he travels to Algeria for his health; and Marny, captured by desert brigands, is rescued by Carew, known as El Hakim, and is attracted to him. Elinor traces Geradine and scores him for his cruelty; she meets her husband again but refuses to return to him when he pretends to be a poor man. Carew rescues Marny from a beating by her husband, carrying her into the desert. Geradine determines to avenge himself but is killed by his hunting elephant, which he has cruelly mistreated; thus Lord Carew and Marny find themselves joined in a new love. *Nobility. Desertion. Revenge. Sahara. Algeria. Elephants.*

THE OLD NEST **F2.3949**

Goldwyn Pictures. Oct **1921** [c27 Jul 1921; LP16789]. Si; b&w. 35mm. 8 reels, 8,021 ft.

Dir Reginald Barker. *Scen* Rupert Hughes. *Photog* Percy Hilburn, Philip Hatkin. *Asst Dir* Charles Stallings.

Cast: Dwight Crittenden *(Dr. Horace Anthon)*, Mary Alden *(Mrs. Anthon)*, Nick Cogley *(Uncle Ned)*, Fanny Stockbridge *(Hannah)*, Laura La Varnie *(Mrs. Guthrie)*, Johnny Jones *(Tom, age 13)*, Richard Tucker *(Tom, age 36)*, Marshall Ricksen *(Arthur, age 14)*, Buddy Messenger *(Jim, age 10)*, Cullen Landis *(Jim, age 22–32)*, Lucille Ricksen *(Kate, age 9)*, Louise Lovely *(Kate, age 21–31)*, Robert De Vilbiss *(Frank, age 6)*, J. Parks Jones *(Frank, age 18–28)*, Marie Moorehouse *(Emily, The Baby)*, Billie Cotton *(Emily, age 12)*, Helene Chadwick *(Emily, age 22)*, Theodore von Eltz *(Stephen McLeod)*, Molly Malone *(Molly McLeod)*, Maurice B. Flynn *(Harry Andrews)*, Roland Rushton *(Mr. Atkinson)*.

Domestic drama. Source: Rupert Hughes, "The Old Nest," in *Saturday Evening Post* (186:6, 3 Jun 1911). Dr. and Mrs. Anthon, who live in a small town, have a large family. Arthur, the oldest child, is killed in a railroad wreck; Tom grows up to be a successful lawyer; Kate marries and lives in New York; Frank becomes a gifted artist in Paris; Jim is sent away from home by his father for stealing; Emily, the youngest, goes to New York to visit Kate and gets married. With home ties severed, the children become forgetful of their parents until one day Jim returns for money. The mother dreams that the train on which her son is returning is imperiled by a wrecked bridge, and when she awakens, terrified, Tom arrives with his brothers and sisters to announce that he has been appointed Attorney

General of the United States. *Physicians. Lawyers. Artists. Thieves. Family life. Parenthood. United States—Attorney General. Dreams.*

THE OLD OAKEN BUCKET **F2.3950**

May Tully. *Dist* F. B. Warren Corp. Nov **1921** [c12 Dec 1921; LP17356]. Si; b&w. 35mm. 5 reels, 5,089 ft.

Prod-Dir May Tully. *Scen* May Tully, E. S. Harrison. *Photog* John La Mond.

Cast: Joseph Smiley *(The Man)*, Bobby Connelly *(The Boy)*, Paul Kelly *(The Youth)*, Violet Axzelle *(The Little Girl)*, Mary Beth Barnelle *(The Maiden)*, Kate Blancke *(The Woman)*.

Pastoral. A Wall Street financier, oppressed with care and worry, sees some children playing near a great hotel and becomes desirous of reliving the scenes of his childhood; he hurries to his car, is driven to the old country homestead where he was born, and begins to tramp through the orchard. *A bite of fruit brings back memories of his sweetheart days, afternoon ballgames, the daily hike to the old swimming hole, and the days of his youth through the stages of maturity until he leaves for the city to make his fortune.* He joins in a game with some youngsters, and he notices an attractive middle-aged woman on the road whom he recognizes as his boyhood sweetheart. They exchange greetings and walk down the rustic lane, happily. *Financiers. Childhood. Rural life. New York City—Wall Street.*

OLD SAN FRANCISCO **F2.3951**

Warner Brothers Pictures. 21 Jun **1927** [New York premiere; released 4 Sep; c10 May 1927; LP23957]. Si; b&w. 35mm. 8 reels, 7,961 ft.

Dir Alan Crosland. *Scen* Anthony Coldewey. *Titl* Jack Jarmuth. *Story* Darryl Francis Zanuck. *Photog* Hal Mohr. *Vitaphone Score* Hugo Riesenfeld.

Cast: Dolores Costello *(Dolores Vásquez)*, Warner Oland *(Chris Buckwell)*, Charles Emmett Mack *(Terrence O'Shaughnessy)*, Josef Swickard *(Don Hernández Vásquez)*, John Miljan *(Don Luis)*, Anders Randolf *(Michael Brandon)*, Sojin *(Lu Fong)*, Angelo Rossitto *(dwarf)*, Anna May Wong *(Chinese girl)*.

Melodrama. Chris Buckwell, cruel and greedy czar of San Francisco's tenderloin, is heartless in his persecution of the Chinese, though he himself is secretly a halfcaste. Buckwell, eager to possess the land of Don Hernández Vásquez, sends Michael Brandon, an unscrupulous attorney, to make an offer. Brandon's nephew, Terrence, meets the grandee's beautiful daughter, Dolores, while Vásquez refuses the offer. Terry tries to save the Vásquez land grants, but when Chris causes the grandee's death, Dolores takes an oath to avenge her father. Learning that Chris is halfcaste, Dolores induces his idiot dwarf brother to denounce him; he captures her and Terry, but they are saved from torture and death by the great earthquake of 1906 that kills the villain. *Halfcastes. Chinese. Spanish. Politicians. Lawyers. Dwarfs. Idiots. Brothers. Land rights. Revenge. San Francisco—Earthquake 1906. San Francisco.*

OLD SHOES **F2.3952**

Peerless Productions. *Dist* Hollywood Pictures. ca28 Mar **1925** [Los Angeles premiere; released 1927]. Si; b&w. 35mm. 7 reels.

Dir-Story Frederick Stowers.

Cast: Noah Beery, Johnny Harron, Viora Daniels, Ethel Grey Terry, ZaSu Pitts, Russell Simpson, Snitz Edwards.

Domestic drama. Widowed and left with a young son (played by Johnny Harron), Mary consents to marry her dead husband's brother (played by Noah Beery), a harsh man whom she once rejected. She soon discovers that she still loves her dead husband—a fact that prompts her present husband to inflict pain on his wife and stepson at every opportunity. The youth finally triumphs in a fight with his stepfather; the latter regains consciousness, starts off to wreak revenge with a sabre, and angers a horse, which tramples him to death. *Brothers. Widows. Stepfathers. Revenge. Horses.*

THE OLD SOAK (Universal-Jewel) **F2.3953**

Universal Pictures. 11 Oct **1926** [New York showing; released 24 Oct 1926; c26 Jun 1926; LP22850]. Si; b&w. 35mm. 8 reels, 7,445 ft.

Pres by Carl Laemmle. *Dir* Edward Sloman. *Adapt-Scen* Charles Kenyon. *Photog* Jackson Rose.

Cast: Jean Hersholt *(Clement Hawley, Sr.)*, George Lewis *(Clemmy Hawley)*, June Marlowe *(Ina Heath)*, William V. Mong *(Cousin Webster)*, Gertrude Astor *(Sylvia De Costa)*, Louise Fazenda *(Annie)*, Lucy Beaumont *(Mrs. Hawley)*, Adda Gleason *(Lucy)*, Tom Ricketts *(roué)*, George Siegmann *(Al)*, Arnold Gregg *(Shelly Hawley)*.

Domestic melodrama. Source: Don Marquis, *The Old Soak, a Comedy in Three Acts* (New York, 1926). To the distress of his family, Clem Hawley, retired from his garage business, spends his time and money in the company of Al, the local bootlegger. Clemmy, his son, is employed at a bank owned by his cousin Webster and makes nightly trips to New York to see Ina Heath, a showgirl, whom he impresses as being the son of a wealthy family. Traveling with some friends, Ina stops by their town on Long Island and is dismayed to learn of Clemmy's humble background; but when she is stranded, she decides to stay for dinner. Mrs. Hawley is informed of the disappearance of some valuable stock certificates. Clemmy confesses to the theft and to having given Webster the stock as a loan, but Old Clem takes the blame. Ina and Clem then force the hand of Webster, who is in cahoots with the bootleggers; Clem saves his son from admitting his wrong to Mrs. Hawley; and Clemmy and Ina are happily reconciled. *Bank clerks. Bootleggers. Showgirls. Family life. Alcoholism. Long Island.*

AN OLD SWEETHEART OF MINE **F2.3954**

Harry Garson Productions. *Dist* Metro Pictures. 16 Apr **1923** [c9 May 1923; LP19119]. Si; b&w. 35mm. 6 reels, 5,400 ft.

Dir Harry Garson. *Adapt* Louis Duryea Lighton. *Photog* L. William O'Connell. *Lighting Eff* Harry Collins. *Art Dir* Joseph Wright. *Film Ed* Violet Blair.

Cast: Pat Moore *(John Craig as a boy)*, Elliott Dexter *(John Craig as a man)*, Mary Jane Irving *(Mary Ellen Anderson as a girl)*, Helen Jerome Eddy *(Mary Ellen Anderson as a woman)*, Turner Savage *(Stuffy Shade as a boy)*, Lloyd Whitlock *(Stuffy Shade as a man)*, Barbara Worth *(Irene Ryan)*, Arthur Hoyt *(Frederick McCann)*, Gene Cameron *(William Norton)*.

Romantic drama. Source: James Whitcomb Riley, "An Old Sweetheart of Mine." John Craig, while rummaging through an old trunk, is reminded of his first sweetheart, Mary Ellen Anderson. In a flashback, one sees their childhood together, their association in business, and her assistance in preventing some oil swindlers from cheating the townspeople out of profits from an oil well on their property. His dream ends when Mary Ellen, his wife, enters the attic with their two children. *Childhood. Nostalgia. Family life. Courtship. Oil wells.*

THE OLD SWIMMIN' HOLE **F2.3955**

Charles Ray Productions. *Dist* Associated First National Pictures. Feb **1921** [c9 Mar 1921; LP16239]. Si; b&w. 35mm. 5 reels.

Pres by Arthur S. Kane. *Dir* Joseph De Grasse. *Adapt* Bernard McConville. *Photog* George Rizard. *Asst Camera* Ellsworth H. Rumer. *Film Ed* Harry L. Decker. *Asst Dir* Robert Bennett, Clarence De Witt.

Cast: Charles Ray *(Ezra)*, James Gordon *(His Pa)*, Laura La Plante *(His Ma)*, Blanche Rose *(Myrtle)*, Marjorie Prevost *(Esther)*, Lincoln Stedman *(Skinny)*, Lon Poff *(Schoolmaster)*.

Rural comedy. Source: James Whitcomb Riley, *The Old Swimmin' Hole and 'Leven More Poems* (Indianapolis, 1883). Ezra, a carefree country boy who spends idle time fishing or at the swimming hole, greatly admires Myrtle, a girl who turns his life into misery. He does daring stunts for her edification and risks censure by passing her notes and sugarhearts in school, but when he takes her boatriding his rival, Skinny, takes her away from him. Then he discovers Esther, a longtime admirer, whose love is revealed when she shares her lunch with him on the riverbank. *Childhood. Rural life. Swimming.*

OLIMPIA **F2.3956**

Metro-Goldwyn-Mayer Pictures. 11 Oct **1930** [Los Angeles premiere]. Sd (Movietone); b&w. 35mm. 9 reels.

Dir-Adapt Miguel De Zarraga.

Cast: José Crespo *(Kovacs)*, Maria Alba *(Princess Olimpia)*, Elvira Moria *(Princess Ettingen)*, Carmen Rodríguez *(Condesa Lina)*, Juan De Homs *(Conde Alberto)*, Luis Llaneza *(Colonel Krehl)*, Juan Eulate Aristi *(Gral. Principe Ettingen)*, Gabriel Rivas *(burgomeastre)*, Mario Dominici *(Embajador de Francia)*.

Romantic drama. Source: Ferenc Molnár, *Olympia* (Budapest, 1928). A Spanish-language version of *His Glorious Night*, q. v. *Royalty. Social classes. Courtship. Imaginary kingdoms.*

OLIVER TWIST **F2.3957**

Jackie Coogan Productions. *Dist* Associated First National Pictures. 30 Oct **1922** [New York premiere; released Nov; c10 Nov 1922; LP18385]. Si; b&w. 35mm. 8 reels, 7,761 ft. [Copyrighted as 7,600 ft.]

Pres by Sol Lesser. *Supv* Jack Coogan, Sr. *Dir* Frank Lloyd. *Titl* Walter Anthony. *Adapt* Frank Lloyd, Harry Weil. *Photog* Glen MacWilliams,

Robert Martin. *Lighting Eff* Louis Johnson. *Art Dir* Stephen Goosson. *Film Ed* Irene Morra. *Cost* Walter J. Israel.

Cast: Jackie Coogan *(Oliver Twist)*, Lon Chaney *(Fagin)*, Gladys Brockwell *(Nancy Sikes)*, George Siegmann *(Bill Sikes)*, Edouard Trebaol *(Artful Dodger)*, Lionel Belmore *(Mr. Brownlow)*, Carl Stockdale *(Monks)*, Eddie Boland *(Toby Crackit)*, Taylor Graves *(Charlie Bates)*, Lewis Sargent *(Noah Claypool)*, James Marcus *(Bumble the Beadle)*, Aggie Herring *(Mrs. Corney)*, Joan Standing *(Charlotte)*, Esther Ralston *(Rose Maylie)*, Florence Hale *(Mrs. Bedwin)*, Nelson McDowell *(Sowerberry)*, Joseph Hazelton *(Mr. Grimwig)*, Gertrude Claire *(Mrs. Maylie)*.

Costume melodrama. Source: Charles Dickens, *Oliver Twist*. Dramatization of that part of the Dickens novel in which Oliver is orphaned, apprenticed to an undertaker, taught pickpocketing by Fagin, rescued by Mr. Brownlow, kidnaped and plotted against by Monks and the Sikeses, and recovered by Mr. Brownlow—happy and secure in the knowledge that he will receive the inheritance due him. *Orphans. Thieves. Undertakers. London.*

OLIVER TWIST, JR. **F2.3958**

Fox Film Corp. 13 Mar **1921** [c13 Mar 1921; LP16322]. Si; b&w. 35mm. 5 reels.

Pres by William Fox. *Dir* Millard Webb. *Story* F. McGrew Willis. *Photog* William C. Foster.

Cast: Harold Goodwin *(Oliver Twist, Jr.)*, Lillian Hall *(Ruth Norris)*, George Nichols *(schoolmaster)*, Harold Esboldt *(Dick)*, Scott McKee *(Artful Dodger)*, Wilson Hummell *(Fagin)*, G. Raymond Nye *(Bill Sykes)*, Hayward Mack *(Monks)*, Pearl Lowe *(Mrs. Morris)*, George Clair *(James Harrison)*, Fred Kirby *(Judson)*, Irene Hunt *(Nancy)*.

Melodrama. Source: Charles Dickens, *Oliver Twist*. In this "modernized" version of the familiar story, Oliver's mother, cast off by her family for marrying against their wishes, dies in childbirth, leaving only a locket as a clue to his identity, and the child is brought up in a New York orphanage. Aged 17, Oliver is persuaded to run away by Monks, who promises him a good home, but he falls in with a gang of thieves headed by Fagin. They discover the whereabouts of the boy's wealthy grandfather, James Harrison, but during a robbery attempt Oliver is shot and found on the grounds by Ruth Norris, who befriends him. After learning his identity, he finds happiness with Ruth. *Orphans. Thieves. Personal identity. New York City.*

OLYMPIA **F2.3959**

Metro-Goldwyn-Mayer Pictures. 14 Nov **1930** [Berlin premiere]. Sd (Movietone); b&w. 35mm. 9 reels, 7,173 ft.

Dir Jacques Feyder. *Screenplay* Yves Mirande, Leo Birinski, Heinrich Fraenkel. *Photog* William Daniels. *Art Dir* Cedric Gibbons. *Rec Engr* Douglas Shearer.

Cast: Nora Gregor *(Olympia)*, Theo Shall *(Captain Kovacs)*, Julia Serda *(Princess Plata-Ettingen)*, Karl Ettinger *(Police Commander Krehl)*, Arnold Korff *(General Prince Plata-Ettingen)*, Hans Junkermann *(Albert)*, Annemarie Frey *(Lina)*.

Romantic drama. Source: Ferenc Molnár, *Olympia* (Budapest, 1928). A German-language version of *His Glorious Night*, q. v. *Royalty. Social classes. Courtship. Imaginary kingdoms.*

THE OLYMPIC HERO **F2.3960**

James P. Lyons. *Dist* Zakoro Film Corp., Supreme Pictures. 15 Jun **1928.** Si; b&w. 35mm. 5 reels.

Dir R. William Neill. *Story-Scen* Ronald De Gastro. *Titl* Walter Weems. *Photog* Faxon Dean. *Film Ed* Henry Weber.

Cast: Charles Paddock *(Charlie Patterson)*, Julanne Johnston *(Mary Brown)*, Donald Stuart *(assistant coach)*, Harvey Clark *(Coach Regan)*, Crauford Kent *(man-about-town)*, Jack Selwyn *(Harold Fellows)*, Emile Chautard *(Grandpa Brown)*, Richard Pennell *(professor)*, Aileen Manning *(physical instructress)*, Bob Maxwell *(Balfor Champ)*, Raoul Paoli *(French Champ)*.

Comedy-drama(?). A story with a college background revolves around sprinter Charles Paddock, utilizing newsreel footage of the 1924 Olympic Games. *Sprinters. College life. Olympic Games.*

Note: This film was reissued by Supreme Pictures in Feb 1929 as *The All American*.

O'MALLEY OF THE MOUNTED **F2.3961**

William S. Hart Co. *Dist* Paramount Pictures. 6 Feb **1921** [New York premiere; released Feb; c20 Dec 1920; LP15959]. Si; b&w. 35mm. 6 reels, 5,626 ft.

Dir-Picturized by Lambert Hillyer. *Story* William S. Hart. *Photog* Joe August. *Art Dir* J. C. Hoffner. *Paintings* Harry Barndollar.

Cast: William S. Hart *(O'Malley)*, Eva Novak *(Rose Lanier)*, Leo Willis *(Red Jaeger)*, Antrim Short *(Bud Lanier)*, Alfred Allen *(Big Judson)*, Bert Sprotte *(The Sheriff)*.

Western melodrama. Sergeant O'Malley of the Royal Northwest Mounted Police is sent into the United States in search of the killer of La Grange, a hardened saloon keeper. He tracks his man (Bud Lanier) to the Baldy Mountain. Bud is a member of a bandit gang, and to gain the gang's confidence, O'Malley robs a bank in broad daylight. He meets and falls in love with Bud's sister, Rose, who helps him escape when he is suspected of being a traitor to the gang. Discovering that Bud killed La Grange to protect a dead sister's honor, he frees Bud at the border, then clears his action with the commanding officer and returns to the woman he loves. *Gangs. Brother-sister relationship. Northwest Mounted Police.*

O'MALLEY RIDES ALONE **F2.3962**

Dist Syndicate Pictures. 1 Jan **1930.** Si; b&w. 35mm. 5 reels, 4,700 ft.

Dir J. P. McGowan. *Scen* Jacques Jaccard. *Story* Sally Winters. *Photog* Hap Depew.

Cast: Bob Custer *(Sergeant O'Malley)*, Phyllis Bainbridge *(Joyce McGregor)*, Martin Cichy, Bud Osborne, Cliff Lyons, Perry Murdock, J. P. McGowan *(McGregor)*.

Northwest melodrama. "McGowan [McGregor] had made a cleanup prospecting for gold. He takes the wrong road home. His granddaughter [Joyce] gives away the secret to the villain [Sled]. So the old man is held up and shot. The gold, however, is confiscated by a Royal mounty [Sergeant O'Malley] fortuitously assigned to that district but a short time previously. A second mounty is in on the deal, and between these two, the old man and the gal, they nab the real crooks and the red-coated cop wins the blonde." (*Variety*, 5 Feb 1930, p31.) *Grandfathers. Prospectors. Gold. Robbery. Northwest Mounted Police.*

OMAR THE TENTMAKER **F2.3963**

Richard Walton Tully Productions. *Dist* Associated First National Pictures. Dec **1922** [c9 Nov 1922; LP18376]. Si; b&w. 35mm. 8 reels, 8,090 ft.

Pres by Richard Walton Tully. *Dir* James Young. *Adapt* Richard Walton Tully. *Photog* George Benoit. *Art Dir* Wilfred Buckland.

Cast: Guy Bates Post *(Omar the Tentmaker)*, Virginia Brown Faire *(Shireen)*, Nigel De Brulier *(Nizam ul Mulk)*, Noah Beery *(The Shah of Shahs)*, Rose Dione *(Shah's mother)*, Patsy Ruth Miller *(Little Shireen)*, Douglas Gerrard *(Hassan)*, Will Jim Hatton *(Little Mahruss)*, Boris Karloff *(Imam Mowaffak)*, Maurice B. Flynn *(The Christian Crusader)*, Edward M. Kimball *(Omar's father)*, Walter Long *(The Executioner)*, Evelyn Selbie *(Zarah)*, John Gribner *(Mahruss)*, Gordon Mullen, George Rigas *(Emissaries to the Shah)*.

Romantic melodrama. Source: Richard Walton Tully, *Omar the Tentmaker* (New York opening: 13 Jan 1914). The student Omar loves and secretly marries Shireen, but she is taken away by the Shah of Shahs to join his household. For spurning the shah, Shireen is thrown into a dungeon, then sold into slavery when her child is born. Years pass: Omar's boyhood friends, Nizam and Hassan, have become grand vizier and governor, respectively, and Omar has brought up Little Shireen, whom he believes to be the daughter of the shah. When Omar is arrested and tortured for sheltering a Christain crusader, Nizam frees Omar, punishes Hassan for ordering the torture, and reunites Shireen with Omar and their daughter. *Tentmakers. Parenthood. Slavery. The Crusades. Persia.*

ON HER HONOR (Reissue) **F2.3964**

Powell Producing Co. *Dist* Tri-Art Distributing Corp. 18 Jan **1922** [New York State license]. Si; b&w. 35mm. 5 reels, 4,750 ft.

Note: Apparently a re-release of *The Dazzling Miss Davison*, starring Marjorie Rambeau and originally released by Mutual 18 Jun 1917.

ON PAROLE *see* **THE WESTERN WALLOP**

ON PROBATION **F2.3965**

William Steiner Productions. 1 Dec **1924** [c18 Dec 1924; LU20926]. Si; b&w. 35mm. 5 reels.

Dir Charles Hutchinson. *Scen* J. F. Natteford. *Photog* Ernest Miller.

Cast: Edith Thornton *(Mary Forrest)*, Robert Ellis *(Bruce Winter)*, Joseph Kilgour *(Judge Winter)*, Wilfred Lucas *(Detective Reilly)*, Helen Lynch *(Nan Miller)*, Eddie Phillips *(Phil Coleman)*, Betty Francisco

(Dolores Coleman), Lincoln Stedman *(Ralph Norton)*.

Melodrama. Mary Forrest, a wealthy society girl who leads a life of unrestrained revelry, is arrested for speeding by Detective Reilly. She is arraigned before Judge Walker, whose son, Bruce, is in love with her; the judge levies a heavy fine and warns her that another offense will result in jail. During a subsequent raid on a roadhouse, Mary tries to escape arrest but wrecks her car in the attempt. She is tried, convicted of reckless driving, and sentenced to a year in jail. Judge Walker offers to put her on probation if anyone will accept responsibility for her conduct. None of her society friends is willing to risk having to serve her term if she breaks probation, but when Mary shows a genuine sense of contrition, the judge himself accepts the responsibility. He later gives his son permission to marry Mary and makes him personally accountable for her actions. *Socialites. Judges. Probation. Reckless driving. Roadhouses.*

ON THE BANKS OF THE WABASH **F2.3966**

Vitagraph Co. of America. Oct **1923** [c19 Oct 1923; LP19521]. Si; b&w. 35mm. 7 reels, 7,156 ft.

Dir J. Stuart Blackton. *Scen* Elaine Sterne. *Photog* Nicholas Musuraca. *Art Dir* Joseph Clement.

Cast: Mary Carr *(Anne Bixler)*, Burr McIntosh *("Cap" Hammond)*, James Morrison *(David)*, Lumsden Hare *(Paul Bixler)*, Mary MacLaren *(Yvonne)*, Madge Evans *(Lisbeth)*, George Neville *(Sash Brown)*, Marcia Harris *(Tilda Spiffen)*, Ed Roseman *(Westerley Spiffen)*.

Rural melodrama. Source: Paul Dresser, "On the Banks of the Wabash Far Away" (a song; c1897). David Hammond, an inventor, is the son of a ship's captain. He leaves his sweetheart, Lisbeth Bixler, and goes to the city to promote his invention. Lisbeth's father, an unsuccessful artist, deserts his family, secretly intending to commit suicide. When he fails to return, "Cap" Hammond protects Bixler's wife and children. David forgets Lisbeth until he returns to perfect his invention and finds that she still loves him. During a fire caused by a flooding of a nearby river, Lisbeth rescues David; and both are picked up by "Cap" Hammond, who has saved the whole village. Bixler returns, his courage renewed, and all are happily reunited. *Artists. Inventors. Suicide. Wabash River. Floods.*

ON THE BORDER **F2.3967**

Warner Brothers Pictures. 15 Mar **1930** [c18 Feb 1930; LP1085]. Sd (Vitaphone); b&w. 35mm. 5 reels, 4,452 ft. [Also possibly si.]

Dir William McGann. *Story-Scen-Dial* Lillie Hayward. *Photog* William Rees. *Rec Engr* Dolph Thomas.

Cast: Rin-Tin-Tin *(Rinty)*, Armida *(Pepita)*, John B. Litel *(Dave)*, Philo McCullough *(Farrell)*, Bruce Covington *(Don Josè)*, Walter Miller *(Border Patrol Commander)*, William Irving *(Dusty)*.

Action melodrama. At the impoverished hacienda of Don José, near the Mexican border, five men, headed by Farrell, stop with truckloads of vegetables, but the rancher's dog, Rinty, detects the presence of the Chinese the men are smuggling. Farrell, who covets Pepita, the rancher's daughter, plans to buy the ranch for smuggling operations; meanwhile, Dave and Dusty, two apparent tramps who are border agents, discover the smugglers' ruse, and Pepita and Rinty take an interest in Dave. Don José innocently falls in with the plans of Farrell's men. Following a series of complications, Dave is captured by the smugglers but is saved in a last-minute rescue by Rinty. The border patrol subdues the gang at the ranch, and Rinty overpowers Farrell as he flees in an automobile. *Ranchers. Smugglers. Border patrol. Tramps. Chinese. Mexican border. Dogs.*

ON THE DIVIDE **F2.3968**

El Dorado Productions. *Dist* Syndicate Pictures. 1 Sep **1928.** Si; b&w. 35mm. 5 reels, 4,360 ft.

Supv J. Charles Davis, 2d. *Dir* J. P. McGowan. *Scen* Sally Winters. *Photog* Paul Allen.

Cast: Bob Custer *(Jim Carson)*, Peggy Montgomery *(Sally Martin)*, Lafe McKee, Bud Osborne, J. P. McGowan.

Western melodrama. Jim Carson arrives in Lariat County in time to avert the foreclosure of the mortgaged Martin ranch by a gang of range-grabbers. A special interest in Sally Martin quickly develops, but it takes a little while longer for Jim to recover the stolen mortgage, battle his way through a dozen bad guys, and identify the chief villain by his broken watchcase. Peace being restored to the area, Jim and Sally are free to settle on the Martin ranch. *Gangs. Mortgages. Ranches.*

ON THE DOTTED LINE *see* **LET WOMEN ALONE**

ON THE GO **F2.3969**

Action Pictures. *Dist* Weiss Brothers Artclass Pictures. 4 Apr **1925** [c3 Apr 1925; LU21313]. Si; b&w. 35mm. 5 reels, 4,825 ft.

Pres by Lester F. Scott, Jr. *Dir* Richard Thorpe. *Story* Frank L. Inghram. *Photog* Ray Ries.

Cast: Buffalo Bill Jr. *(Bill Drake)*, Helen Foster *(Nell Hall)*, Lafe McKee *(Mr. Hall)*, Nelson McDowell *(Philip Graves)*, Raye Hampton *(Matilda Graves)*, Charles Whitaker *(Tom Evans)*, Louis Fitzroy *(Mr. Evans)*, George F. Marion *(Eb Moots)*, Alfred Hewston *(Snoopy O'Sullivan)*, Morgan Davis *(Sheriff)*, Pietro Sosso *(city specialist)*.

Western melodrama. Bill Drake finds a girl who has fainted in the middle of the road and takes her back to the ranch where he works. The owner of the ranch, Evans, refuses the girl shelter, and Bill places her in the care of Graves, the local undertaker. To be near the girl, Bill takes a job in the general store. Tom Evans, the son of the ranchowner, loses his father's payroll at cards and robs the store in order to replace the money. Bill is accused of the crime and taken into custody, but he escapes and finds Tom, bringing him in for the sheriff. In the meantime, a detective hired by the girl's father has found her, and the father has arrived to take her home by train. Bill rides after the train, leaps through a window, and proposes to the startled girl. *Undertakers. Detectives. Ranchers. General stores. Theft. Gambling. Fatherhood.*

ON THE HIGH CARD **F2.3970**

Dist Arrow Film Corp. 21 May **1921** [trade review]. Si; b&w. 35mm. 5 reels.

Story Tex O'Reilly. *Photog* Arthur Boegar.

Cast: Harry Myers *(Harry Holt)*, Tex O'Reilly *(Hank Saunders)*, Ben Hill *(Ben Stiles)*, Gene Baker *(Conchita)*, Charles Graham *(Pecos Bill/Don Antonio)*, Alice Ray *(Polly Updike)*.

Western melodrama. Polly Updike learns of her father's death on the day of her arrival in Rim Rock, where Ben Stiles, Pecos Bill, and Conchita run a saloon and the law is represented by Harry Holt and Hank Saunders. Deciding that Polly must be married for protection, Harry and Hank arrange for the men in the saloon to draw lots. Harry wins, and Polly indignantly refuses to marry him; but Harry continues to protect her though Pecos Bill tells Polly that Harry killed her father. Harry and Hank rescue Polly from Mexicans and again, later, from Pecos Bill. Learning that Bill is actually the murderer, Polly rewards Harry's exploits with her hand in marriage. *Saloon keepers. Filial relations. Mexicans. Murder. Gambling.*

ON THE HIGH SEAS **F2.3971**

Famous Players–Lasky. *Dist* Paramount Pictures. 17 Sep **1922** [Los Angeles premiere; released 5 Nov; c11 Oct 1922; LP18331]. Si; b&w. 35mm. 6 reels, 5,171 ft.

Pres by Adolph Zukor. *Dir* Irvin Willat. *Adapt-Scen* E. Magnus Ingleton. *Story* Edward Brewster Sheldon. *Photog* Charles Edgar Schoenbaum.

Cast: Dorothy Dalton *(Leone Deveraux)*, Jack Holt *(Jim Dorn, a stoker)*, Mitchell Lewis *(Joe Polack, a ruffian)*, Winter Hall *(John Deveraux)*, Michael Dark *(Harold Van Allen)*, Otto Brower *(Lieutenant Gray, U. S. N.)*, William Boyd *(Dick Deveraux)*, James Gordon *(Captain of S. S. Andren)*, Alice Knowland *(Aunt Emily)*, Vernon Tremaine *(maid)*.

Melodrama. Forced to abandon a burning ship, Leone Deveraux, Jim Dorn, and Joe Polack drift for 3 days before finding and boarding a plague-ravaged derelict. When Joe attacks Leone, Jim comes to her aid; and she declares her love for him. They are rescued by a battleship, and Leone abandons Jim for her wealthy family and fiancé, Harold Van Allen. Just as Leone and Harold are about to be married Jim abducts her and reveals himself to be a wealthy son of a prominent family. *Stokers. Shipwrecks. Plague. Sea rescue. Abduction.*

ON THE LEVEL **F2.3972**

Fox Film Corp. 18 May **1930** [c26 Apr 1930; LP1299]. Sd (Movietone); b&w. 35mm. 6 reels, 5,815 ft. [Also si; 6,350 ft.]

Pres by William Fox. *Assoc Prod* James K. McGuinness. *Dir* Irving Cummings. *Story-Scen-Dial* William K. Wells, Andrew Bennison. *Adapt* Dudley Nichols. *Photog* L. William O'Connell, Dave Ragin. *Sets* William Moll. *Film Ed* Al De Gaetano. *Song: "Good Intentions"* Cliff Friend, Jimmy Monaco. *Song: "Good for Nothing But Love"* William Kernell. *Ch Sd Rec* George Leverett. *Asst Dir* Charles Woolstenhulme. *Cost* Sophie Wachner.

Cast: Victor McLaglen *(Biff Williams)*, William Harrigan *(Danny Madden)*, Lilyan Tashman *(Lynn Crawford)*, Fifi D'Orsay *(Mimi)*, Arthur

Stone *(Don Bradley)*, Leila McIntyre *(Mom Whalen)*, Mary McAllister *(Mary Whalen)*, Ben Hewlett *(Buck)*, Harry Tenbrook *(Dawson)*, R. O. Pennell *(professor)*.

Melodrama. Biff Williams, an iron riveter with a weakness for women, falls for the blandishments of glamorous Lynn Crawford, a decoy for racketeers who have an option on property they intend to sell before the option expires. She induces Biff to help sell lots to workingmen at cost, and he involves his pal Danny Madden, who lives with him in Mom Whalen's rooming house. But Biff overtakes the racketeers before their train leaves, returns the money to his fellow workers, and finds romance with Mimi, whom he previously bypassed for the blonde. *Riveters. Racketeers. Courtship. Fraud. Real estate. Boardinghouses.*

ON THE MAKE *see* **A DEVIL WITH WOMEN**

ON THE NIGHT STAGE (Reissue) **F2.3973**

Dist Tri-Stone Pictures. c4 Dec **1923** [LP19670]. Si; b&w. 35mm. 5 reels.

Note: A William S. Hart film originally released by Mutual Film Corp. on 15 Apr 1915.

ON THE SHELF *see* **LET WOMEN ALONE**

ON THE STROKE OF THREE **F2.3974**

Associated Arts Corp. *Dist* Film Booking Offices of America. 30 Nov **1924** [9 Nov 1924; LP20830]. Si; b&w. 35mm. 7 reels, 6,767 ft.

Dir F. Harmon Weight. *Scen* O. E. Goebel, Philip Lonergan. *Photog* Victor Milner, Paul Perry. *Asst Dir* Thornton Freeland.

Cast: Kenneth Harlan *(Judson Forrest)*, Madge Bellamy *(Mary Jordon)*, Mary Carr *("Ma" Forrest)*, John Miljan *(Henry Mogridge)*, Robert Dudley *(Jasper Saddler)*, Leonore Matre *(Lillian Haskins)*, Edwards Davis *(Lafayette Jordon)*, Edward Phillips *(Austin Dudley)*, Dorothy Dahm *(Emily Jordon)*.

Melodrama. Source: Henry Payson Dowst, *The Man From Ashaluna* (Boston, c1920). A financier, Lafayette Jordon, attempts to buy property in the Ashaluna Valley, in order to build a reservoir as part of a power development project. The chief obstacle to his plan is a young inventor, Judson Forrest, who refuses to part with the family homestead, which blocks a proposed sluiceway. Seeking money to finance the development of his invention of a new kind of stove, Judson mortgages the family home and goes to New York, where he falls in love with Mary Jordon, the daughter of the financier. While he is away, the village banker sells the mortgage on the Judson homestead to Henry Mogridge, Judson's lawyer, who begins foreclosure procedures. When Judson hears of this transaction, he breaks off with Mary, believing that she has been "using" him. With the help of some friends, Judson raises the necessary money to prevent the loss of his home and pays off the mortgage in the nick of time. When he learns that neither of the Jordons knew of Mogridge's action, he is reconciled to Mary and obtains her father's permission to marry her. *Financiers. Bankers. Lawyers. Inventors. Water power. Stoves. Mortgages. New York City.*

Note: Working title: *Sold for Cash.*

ON THE STROKE OF TWELVE **F2.3975**

Trem Carr Productions. *Dist* Rayart Pictures. Nov **1927**. Si; b&w. 35mm. 6 reels, 5,842 or 5,970 ft.

Pres by W. Ray Johnston. *Dir* Charles J. Hunt. *Scen* Arthur Hoerl. *Photog* Hap Depew.

Cast: David Torrence *(Henry Rutledge)*, June Marlowe *(Doris Bainbridge)*, Danny O'Shea *(Jack Rutledge)*, Lloyd Whitlock *(James Horton)*, Lillian Worth *(Marie Conyers)*, Charles West *(Charles Wright)*, Martin Turner *(George)*.

Society drama. Source: Joseph Le Brandt, *On the Stroke of Twelve* (a play; c1898). "Secretary [James Horton?] and nurse [Marie Conyers?] of wealthy capitalist [Henry Rutledge] combine to have latter throw son [Jack Rutledge] out, despite the pleas of his ward [Doris Bainbridge], who loves boy. Later the capitalist is shot by secretary, and crime is pinned on son, who is sent to prison. In a jail break, boy saves warden's daughter and is pardoned. He returns home to expose secretary and nurse." (*Motion Picture News Booking Guide,* [14]:272, 1929.) *Secretaries. Nurses. Wards. Filial relations. Murder. Injustice. Prison escapes.*

ON THE THRESHOLD **F2.3976**

Renaud Hoffman Productions. *Dist* Producers Distributing Corp. 23 Feb **1925** [c23 Feb 1925; LP21263]. Si; b&w. 35mm. 6 reels.

Pres by Charles R. Rogers. *Dir* Renaud Hoffman. *Adapt* Alfred A. Cohn. *Photog* Jack MacKenzie. *Film Ed* Leonard Wheeler. *Prod Asst* Glenn Belt. *Titl Illus* Niel McGuire.

Cast: Gladys Hulette *(Rosemary Masters)*, Henry B. Walthall *(Andrew Masters)*, Robert Gordon *(Rod Yates)*, Willis Marks *(Bible Bo)*, Sam De Grasse *(Daniel Masters)*, Charles Sellon *(Judge Stivers)*, Margaret Seddon *(Martha McKay)*.

Melodrama. Source: Wilbur Hall, "On the Threshold," in *Saturday Evening Post.* When the wife of Andrew Masters dies in childbirth, he denies the existence of God and vows that he will save his daughter, Rosemary, from a similar fate by forbidding her to marry. Eighteen years pass; Rosemary grows into beautiful young maidenhood, still deeply in love with her childhood sweetheart, Rod Yates. When Masters realizes that the love between his daughter and Rod is serious, he forbids them to meet. The lovers respect this prohibition until Rod is appointed manager of a large ranch and finds the courage to visit Rosemary. Rod is alone with the girl long enough to ask her to marry him, but they are interrupted by her father. The sight of Rosemary in Rod's arms brings on a paralytic stroke, and the old man falls senseless to the floor. Dan Masters, Andrew's worthless brother, plots with Judge Stivers to draw up a will, disinheriting Rosemary, to be presented to Andrew if he should regain consciousness before dying. When the old man finally awakens, he refuses to sign his brother's proposed will and instead makes one out leaving all his money to Rosemary; Masters dies just as he is giving Rod and Rosemary his blessing to be married. *Ranch managers. Judges. Brothers. Fatherhood. Atheism. Childbirth. Wills. Strokes. Disinheritance.*

ON THIN ICE **F2.3977**

Warner Brothers Pictures. 30 Jan **1925** [c24 Jan 1925; LP21064]. Si; b&w. 35mm. 7 reels, 6,675 ft.

Dir Mal St. Clair. *Adapt* Darryl Francis Zanuck. *Photog* Byron Haskins. *Film Ed* Clarence Kolster.

Cast: Tom Moore *(Charles White)*, Edith Roberts *(Rose Lore)*, William Russell *(Dapper Crawford)*, Theodore von Eltz *(Dr. Paul Jackson)*, Wilfred North *(Harrison Breen)*, Gertrude Robinson *(forger)*, Texas Kid, Jimmy Quinn *(gangsters)*.

Crook melodrama. Source: Alice Ross Colver, *The Dear Pretender* (Philadelphia, 1924). After a bank is held up, Rose Lore returns to the bank officers a satchel she has found which she believes contains the loot. When the satchel is opened, it contains only washers, and Rose is convicted of complicity in the holdup. Released on parole, Rose is followed by detectives who expect her to lead them to the missing money. Dapper Crawford, who engineered the heist, also believes that she has hidden the money and arranges for another of the thieves, Charles White, to impersonate Rose's long-lost brother. Charles finds no trace of the loot but falls in love with Rose and decides to go straight. Dapper attempts to use force on Rose to get her to talk, and Charles comes to her rescue. While Charles and Dapper are fighting, the police raid the thieves' den, and Dapper is inadvertently shot by one of his own men. Before he dies, Dapper clears Rose of all guilt in the robbery. One of the officers of the bank is discovered to be the thief. Charles and Rose are married, and Charles becomes a traffic cop. *Police. Bankers. Criminals—Rehabilitation. Impersonation. Robbery.*

ON TIME **F2.3978**

Carlos Productions. *Dist* Truart Film Corp. 1 Mar **1924** [c1 Mar 1924; LP20000]. Si; b&w. 35mm. 6 reels, 6,030 ft.

Dir Henry Lehrman. *Scen* Garrett Fort. *Titl* Ralph Spence. *Story* Al Cohn. *Photog* William Marshall. *Film Ed* Ralph Spence.

Cast: Richard Talmadge *(Harry Willis)*, Billie Dove *(Helen Hendon)*, Stuart Holmes *(Richard Drake)*, George Siegmann *(Wang Wu)*, Tom Wilson *(Casanova Clay)*, Charles Clary *(Horace Hendon)*, Douglas Gerard *(Mr. Black)*, Fred Kirby *(Dr. Spinks)*, Frankie Mann *(Mrs. Spinks)*.

Action melodrama. Harry Willis returns to Helen Hendon discouraged by his failure to make a fortune in 6 months as he promised. Accepting a job that will pay him $10,000 for following instructions for a day, Harry soon finds himself in a series of adventures that include an imbroglio at a costume ball, a doctor's attempts to transplant a gorilla's brains into his head, and a brawl in a temple with some Chinese who want a small idol belonging to him. When he applies for a marriage license, Harry discovers that these incidents were created to test his capacity to become a movie star. He wins both Helen and a movie contract. *Actors. Chinese. Motion pictures. Hoaxes.*

ON TO RENO **F2.3979**

James Cruze, Inc. *Dist* Pathé Exchange. 1 Jan **1928** [c12 Dec 1927; LP24750]. Si; b&w. 35mm. 6 reels, 5,494 ft.

Dir James Cruze. *Screenplay* Walter Woods. *Titl* John Krafft, Walter Woods. *Story* Joseph Jackson. *Photog* Ernest Miller. *Art Dir* Charles Cadwallader. *Film Ed* Mildred Johnson. *Asst Dir* Vernon Keays.

Cast: Marie Prevost *(Vera)*, Cullen Landis *(Bud)*, Ethel Wales *(Mrs. Holmes)*, Ned Sparks *(Herbert Holmes)*, Jane Keckley *(The Housekeeper)*.

Comedy-drama. When Vera and Bud, a young married couple, become financially hardpressed, Vera accepts an offer from Mrs. Holmes, a rich matron who wishes Vera to impersonate her in Reno to fulfill the residence requirements for her divorce. When Bud finds she has gone to Reno, he immediately suspects that she plans to divorce him. Mr. Holmes goes to Reno, hoping to effect a last-minute reconciliation, discovers Vera's impersonation, and threatens to have her arrested for fraud if she leaves before the 3-month period is up. He unpacks and prepares to remain with her. Mrs. Holmes and Bud arrive, and both couples are happily reconciled after Bud discovers that Holmes is the very man with whom he wishes to renew a contract that will improve his and Vera's finances. *Businessmen. Finance—Personal. Divorce. Impersonation. Reno.*

ON TRIAL **F2.3980**

Warner Brothers Pictures. 1 Dec **1928** [21 Nov 1928; LP25861]. Sd (Vitaphone); b&w. 35mm. 9 reels, 9,290 ft. [Also si, 29 Dec 1928; 5,455 ft.]

Dir Archie Mayo. *Scen* Robert Lord, Max Pollock. *Titl-Dial* Robert Lord. *Photog* Byron Haskins. *Film Ed* Tommy Pratt. *Cost* Earl Luick.

Cast: Pauline Frederick *(Joan Trask)*, Bert Lytell *(Robert Strickland)*, Lois Wilson *(May Strickland)*, Holmes Herbert *(Gerald Trask)*, Richard Tucker *(prosecuting attorney)*, Jason Robards *(defense attorney)*, Franklin Pangborn *(Turnbull)*, Fred Kelsey *(clerk)*, Johnny Arthur *(Stanley Grover)*, Vondell Darr *(Doris Strickland)*, Edmund Breese *(judge)*, Edward Martindel *(Dr. Morgan)*.

Mystery melodrama. Source: Elmer Rice, *On Trial; a Dramatic Composition in Four Acts* (New York, 1919). Robert Strickland is placed on trial for the murder of his business associate, Gerald Trask, and for the robbery of $20,000 from Trask's safe. Put on the stand, Strickland confesses his guilt and requests that the trial be terminated. The request is denied, and Mrs. Trask takes the stand, relating the events of the night of the murder: Strickland shot her husband and was immediately captured by Glover, her husband's secretary; a shadowy accomplice, however, escaped. The following day, Strickland's small daughter, Doris, is placed on the stand and informs the jury that on the day of the murder her father had discovered that her mother had spent the day with Trask. On the third day of the trial, Mrs. Strickland takes the stand and exposes Trask as a blackmailer and lecher. Glover is later discovered to have stolen the money, and Strickland, found innocent of the charge of premeditated murder, is released to find comfort with his loving family. *Businessmen. Murder. Blackmail. Robbery. Lechery. Trials.*

ON WITH THE SHOW **F2.3981**

Warner Brothers Pictures. 28 May **1929** [New York premiere; released 13 Jul; c19 Jun 1929; LP479]. Sd (Vitaphone); col (Technicolor). 35mm. 12 reels, 9,592 ft.

Dir Alan Crosland. *Ensemble Dir* Larry Ceballos. *Scen-Dial* Robert Lord. *Photog* Tony Gaudio. *Film Ed* Jack Killifer. *Songs: "On With the Show," "Birmingham Bertha," "Let Me Have My Dreams," "Am I Blue?" "Welcome Home," "In the Land of Let's Pretend," "Don't It Mean a Thing to You?" "Lift the Juleps to Your Two Lips"* Harry Akst, Grant Clarke.

Cast: Betty Compson *(Nita)*, Louise Fazenda *(Sarah)*, Sally O'Neil *(Kitty)*, Joe E. Brown *(Ike)*, Purnell B. Pratt *(Sam Bloom)*, William Bakewell *(Jimmy)*, Fairbanks Twins *(Twins)*, Wheeler Oakman *(Durant)*, Sam Hardy *(Jerry)*, Thomas Jefferson *(Dad)*, Lee Moran *(Pete)*, Harry Gribbon *(Joe)*, Arthur Lake *(Harold)*, Josephine Houston *(Harold's fiancée)*, Henry Fink *(Father)*, Otto Hoffman *(Bert)*, Ethel Waters *(herself)*, Harmony Four Quartette *(themselves)*, Four Covans *(themselves)*, Angelus Babe *(herself)*.

Musical comedy-drama. Source: Humphrey Pearson, *On With the Show* (a play; publication undetermined). Jerry, the manager of a Broadway musical revue trying out in Milbank, New Jersey, is plagued by staggering expenses and the complaints of unpaid workers: Harold, the juvenile, insists that his mother needs money; Bert complains that he hasn't had a square meal in a week; and Nita, the star, becomes temperamental over a matter of $400 back salary. As Willie Durant, the show's backer, has ceased to be a guarantor of capital, Jerry is only able to carry on with the help of Dad, the elderly stage doorman, who gives him his life savings. After the show opens, Sam Bloom threatens to have his men remove the scenery unless he is paid in 5 minutes, but he is distracted by Sarah, the soubrette of the revue. During the second act, the backstage is roused by the news that the boxoffice has been robbed. Kitty, who is loved by Jimmy, succeeds in bringing Durant to terms, but her effort causes a break with her sweetheart. Meanwhile, when Nita refuses to go onstage without her money, Kitty goes on in her place and greatly pleases the audience, assuring the play a successful run. It is later discovered that Dad has taken the receipts, and when the financial problems are cleared to the satisfaction of all, Kitty finds that she still has a future with Jimmy. *Actors. Theatrical managers. Stage doormen. Courtship. Musical revues. New Jersey.*

ON YOUR BACK **F2.3982**

Fox Film Corp. 14 Sep **1930** [c20 Jun 1930; LP1422]. Sd (Movietone); b&w. 35mm. 8 reels, 6,600 ft.

Pres by William Fox. *Assoc Prod* George Middleton. *Dir* Guthrie McClintic. *Screenplay-Dial* Howard J. Green. *Photog* Joseph August. *Art Dir* Jack Schulze. *Film Ed* Frank Hull. *Rec Engr* Arthur L. von Kirbach. *Asst Dir* Horace Hough. *Cost* Sophie Wachner.

Cast: Irene Rich *(Julianne)*, Raymond Hackett *(Harvey, her son)*, H. B. Warner *(Raymond Pryer)*, Wheeler Oakman *("Lucky" Jim Seymour)*, Marion Shilling *(Jeanne Burke)*, Ilka Chase *(Dixie Mason)*, Charlotte Henry *(Belle)*, Rose Dione *(Mrs. Dupinnet)*, Arthur Hoyt *(Victor)*.

Society drama. Source: Rita Weiman, "On Your Back," in *Liberty Magazine* (7:9–17, 22 Feb 1930.). Julianne rises from the rank of a Broadway modiste to owner of a fashionable Fifth Avenue salon, guided by a worn deck of cards and her faith in the future of her only son, Harvey, whom she sends to college. "Lucky" Jim Seymour suggests a plan by which she can benefit financially—extending credit to struggling showgirls under the egis of broker Raymond Pryer. Jeanne Burke, who is having an affair with Pryer, meets Harvey in a college town and becomes engaged to him; following graduation, Harvey takes a job in Pryer's office but leaves when he learns of her affair. Julianne, who disapproves of the girl, presses for payment of her account under threat of exposure, but Jeanne counters with the threat of revealing the particulars of Julianne's sideline activities. Ultimately, the mother relents. *Modistes. Couturiers. Showgirls. Students. Brokers. Motherhood. Credit. New York City.*

ON YOUR TOES (Universal-Jewel) **F2.3983**

Universal Pictures. 27 Nov **1927** [c21 Nov 1927; LP24682]. Si; b&w. 35mm. 6 reels, 5,918 ft.

Pres by Carl Laemmle. *Dir* Fred Newmeyer. *Scen* Earl Snell, Gladys Lehman. *Titl* Albert De Mond. *Adapt* Pierre Couderc, James Davis. *Story* Earl Snell. *Photog* Ross Fisher.

Cast: Reginald Denny *(Elliott Beresford)*, Barbara Worth *(Mary Sullivan)*, Hayden Stevenson *(Jack Sullivan)*, Frank Hagney *(Mello)*, Mary Carr *(Grandmother)*, Gertrude Howard *(Mammy)*, George West *(Mose)*.

Comedy-drama. When fight manager Jack Sullivan is insulted by heavyweight champion "Punch" Mello, he vows to bring in an opponent to take away his title and goes to Virginia with his daughter, Mary, to look up Elliott Beresford, son of the former champion, Kid Roberts. Elliott's grandmother, however, tells him Elliott is a dance teacher, which Jack considers "sissified." Mary and Elliott are attracted to each other, and when he opens a dance school in New York, Mary shames him into getting a "man's job"; as a taxi driver, he gets in a jam and knocks out Jack's new protégé, then, at Mary's urging, decides to become a fighter. He is defeated in his first fight but is finally matched with the champion; when he learns from his grandmother that his father was Kid Roberts, he is inspired to win, then takes Mary in his arms. *Prizefighters. Fight managers. Dance teachers. Taxi drivers. Grandmothers. Manhood. New York City. Virginia.*

ON ZE BOULEVARD **F2.3984**

Metro-Goldwyn-Mayer Pictures. 25 Jun **1927** [c11 Jul 1927; LP24162]. Si; b&w. 35mm. 6 reels, 5,671 ft.

Dir Harry Millarde. *Screenplay* Richard Schayer, Scott Darling. *Titl* Joe Farnham, Earl Baldwin. *Story* F. Hugh Herbert, Florence Ryerson. *Photog* André Barlatier, William Daniels. *Art Dir* Cedric Gibbons, Frederic Hope. *Film Ed* George Hively. *Wardrobe* René Hubert.

Cast: Lew Cody *(Gaston Pasqual)*, Renée Adorée *(Musette)*, Anton Vaverka *(Ribot)*, Dorothy Sebastian *(Gaby de Sylva)*, Roy D'Arcy *(Count* *de Guissac).*

Farce. Gaston, a French waiter, wins a large sum of money in a gambling pool and embarks on a wild spending spree while his sweetheart, Musette, who has always been practical and thrifty, remains level-headed and makes fun of his irresponsible actions. Gaston is beset by two society crooks who almost succeed in swindling him of his winnings, but the clever resourcefulness of Musette brings him to his senses. *Waiters. Swindlers. Wealth. Gambling. Thrift. France.*

ONCE A GENTLEMAN **F2.3985**

James Cruze Productions. *Dist* Sono Art–World Wide Pictures. 1 Sep **1930** [c17 Jul 1930; LP1474]. Sd; b&w. 35mm. 9 reels.

Prod-Dir James Cruze. *Screenplay* Walter Woods. *Dial* Maude Fulton. *Story* George Frank Worts. *Photog* Jackson Rose. *Rec Engr* W. C. Smith, Fred J. Lau.

Cast: Edward Everett Horton *(Oliver)*, Lois Wilson *(Mrs. Mallin)*, Francis X. Bushman *(Bannister)*, King Baggot *(Van Warner)*, Emerson Treacy *(Junior)*, George Fawcett *(Colonel Breen)*, Frederick Sullivan *(Wadsworth)*, Gertrude Short *(Dolly)*, Estelle Bradley *(Gwen)*, William J. Holmes *(Ogelthorpe)*, Cyril Chadwick *(Jarvis)*, Evelyn Pierce *(Natalie)*, Drew Demarest *(Timson)*, William O'Brien *(Reeves)*, Charles Coleman *(Wuggins)*.

Society comedy. As a reward for his perfection as a valet, Oliver receives from Mr. Van Warner, his employer, a month's paid vacation, a complete wardrobe, and an admonition to enjoy himself as a gentleman. Before Oliver leaves, however, Warner asks him to call on his friend Colonel Breen at the Gotham Club. The colonel is away, but Oliver is assumed to be a close friend and is introduced as just having arrived from India, a fact strengthened by his knowledge of the recipe of the colonel's favorite drink, Bombay Bombshell. Mr. Bannister insists that Oliver be his guest, and another member presents him with 5,000 shares of American Tin. At the Bannister home he falls in love with Mrs. Mallin, the housekeeper, and is helpful with Junior, the wayward son. When, to his dismay, he loses his money in a market crash, Oliver is branded an imposter by Colonel Breen; but he is reinstated by Van Warner and wins the love of Mrs. Mallin. *Valets. Housekeepers. Mistaken identity. Clubs. New York City.*

ONCE AND FOREVER **F2.3986**

Tiffany Productions. 15 Oct **1927** [c14 Oct 1927; LP24514]. Si; b&w. 35mm. 6 reels, 5,629 ft.

Supv L. L. Ostrow. *Dir* Phil Stone. *Story-Scen* Houston Branch. *Photog* Max Dupont, Earl Walker. *Art Dir* George E. Sawley. *Film Ed* Martin G. Cohn.

Cast: Patsy Ruth Miller *(Antoinette)*, John Harron *(Georges)*, Burr McIntosh *(Governor)*, Emily Fitzroy *(Katherine)*, Adele Watson *(Henriette)*, Vadim Uraneff *(Axel)*.

Romantic melodrama. On the French island of Royale, Antoinette, a young and hoydenish girl, soon falls in love with Georges, the governor's son. He is called off to war, and Antoinette's life is made miserable by Katherine, the village gossip; when her son, Axel, a vicious lout, accosts Antoinette, the girl is banished from the island by the governor, who believes her a moral menace. Georges returns home blinded, and a famous surgeon is summoned to perform an operation to restore his eyesight; agitated by the girl's absence, Georges persuades the governor to find her. His search uncovers her in a Paris jail unjustly accused of a crime and therefore embittered. She returns and is happily reunited with her lover when he regains his sight. *French. Surgeons. Colonial administration. Injustice. Gossip. Blindness. Reputation. Prisons. Paris.*

ONCE IN A LIFETIME **F2.3987**

Paul Gerson Pictures. 22 Oct **1925** [New York State license]. Si; b&w. 35mm. 5 reels.

Dir Duke Worne. *Scen* Grover Jones. *Photog* Ernest Smith. *Set Dsgn* Thomas Walthaw. *Film Ed* J. Logan Pearson. *Asst Dir* Walter Bell.

Cast: Richard Holt *(Glenn Horton)*, Mary Beth Milford *(Edna Perry)*, Wilbur Higgins *(Martin Perry)*, Theodore Lorch *(Tommy)*, Les Bates *(Hobo)*, Jack O'Brien *(Marty Taylor)*.

Melodrama. Glenn Horton, a youth addicted to golf, arouses the wrath of passers-by when he practices his swing on his front lawn. He drives golf balls so recklessly that he is finally chased into the freight yards by an irate crowd. There he rescues the mayor's daughter from a thug who is kidnaping her, and he and the girl are carried off in a boxcar. After a series of adventures, Glenn saves the mayor from assassination by the very thug who attempted to kidnap the girl. Glenn and the mayor's daughter are married. *Mayors. Golf. Kidnaping. Assassination. Railroads.*

ONCE UPON A TIME **F2.3988**

Dist Henry Bollman. 14 Jan **1922** [trade review]. Si; b&w. 35mm. 5 reels, 4,800 ft.

Dir-Story Ruth Bryan Owen. *Photog* Dudley Read.

Cast: Ruth Bryan Owen, Community Players of Cocoanut Grove (Florida).

Melodrama. "The Shah of an Eastern [Indian] province is dethroned by a jealous subordinate whose favorite pastime is sending young girls to their death, who fail to amuse him. The most beautiful one of all is not discovered by him until the end and the timely return of the Shah who had survived, despite all belief to the contrary, saves her. ... It is legendary in style, is a story of an indefinite period ... the subtitles are written in Biblical phrase." *(Moving Picture World,* 14 Jan 1922, p207.) *Royalty. Capital punishment. India.*

Note: One source spells Bollman as Ballmar.

ONE A MINUTE **F2.3989**

Thomas H. Ince Productions. *Dist* Paramount Pictures. 19 Jun **1921** [c20 Jun 1921; LP16685]. Si; b&w. 35mm. 5 reels, 4,510 ft.

Supv Thomas H. Ince. *Dir* Jack Nelson. *Scen* Joseph Franklin Poland. *Photog* Bert Cann.

Cast: Douglas MacLean *(Jimmy Knight)*, Marian De Beck *(Miriam Rogers)*, Victor Potel *(Jingo Pitts)*, Frances Raymond *(Grandma Knight)*, Andrew Robson *(Silas P. Rogers)*, Graham Pettie *(Martin Duffey)*.

Farce. Source: Fred Jackson, *One a Minute; a Farce in Three Acts* (c1918). When Jimmy Knight undertakes to operate a drugstore left him by his father, he finds the store's methods old-fashioned, and a syndicate, headed by Silas Rogers, offers to buy him out. But in order to impress Miriam, Rogers' daughter, he determines to become a success by selling a cure-all patented medicine of his father's invention, and he begins by making several extraordinary cures. The syndicate members obtain a restraining warrant from pure food and drug inspectors, and Jimmy is tried; but when the judge has a sudden attack of gastritis the medicine relieves him and Jimmy is declared innocent. Afterwards, Jimmy is elected mayor and wins Miriam. *Pharmacists. Mayors. Judges. Patent medicines. Business management. Pure Food and Drug Administration.*

ONE CHANCE IN A MILLION **F2.3990**

Gotham Productions. *Dist* Lumas Film Corp. 1 Apr **1927** [c21 Mar 1927; LP23824]. Si; b&w. 35mm. 5 reels.

Pres by Sam Sax. *Dir* Noel Mason Smith. *Story-Cont* L. V. Jefferson. *Photog* James Brown.

Cast: William Fairbanks *(Jerry Blaine)*, Viora Daniels *(Ruth Torrence)*, Charles K. French *(Richard Torrence)*, Henry Herbert *(Robert Weston)*, Eddie Borden *(Horace Featherby)*, Duke Martin *(Pat Drogan)*.

Crook melodrama. Ruth Torrence, daughter of Richard Torrence, a retired capitalist, is rescued from a runaway horse by Jerry Blaine. Jerry then causes her to break her engagement to Robert Weston, who is visiting the Torrence estate, and he warns Ruth's father to guard Ruth's diamonds. Jerry learns that Weston is a thief, and he works himself into the confidence of the gang when he himself is accused of stealing the necklace. Weston and his friend Featherby are exposed as the crooks by Jerry, who reveals himself as a secret agent on their track; Jerry is thus reinstated in the good opinion of Ruth. *Thieves. Secret agents. Capitalists.*

ONE CLEAR CALL **F2.3991**

Louis B. Mayer Productions. *Dist* Associated First National Pictures. ca20 May **1922** [Chicago premiere; released May; c21 Jun 1922; LP17983]. Si; b&w. 35mm. 8 reels, 7,450 ft. [Copyrighted as 7 reels.]

Pres by Louis B. Mayer. *Dir* John M. Stahl. *Scen* Bess Meredyth. *Photog* Ernest G. Palmer. *Film Ed* Madge Tyrone.

Cast: Milton Sills *(Dr. Alan Hamilton)*, Claire Windsor *(Faith)*, Henry B. Walthall *(Henry Garnett)*, Irene Rich *(Maggie Thornton)*, Stanley Goethals *(Sonny Thornton)*, William Marion *(Tom Thornton)*, Joseph Dowling *(Colonel Garnett)*, Edith Yorke *(Mother Garnett)*, Doris Pawn *(Phyllis Howard)*, Donald MacDonald *(Dr. Bailey)*, Shannon Day *(Jim Ware's daughter)*, Annette De Foe *(Yetta)*, Fred Kelsey *(Starnes)*, Albert MacQuarrie *(Jim Holbrook)*, Nick Cogley *(Toby)*.

Melodrama. Source: Frances Nimmo Greene, *One Clear Call* (New York, 1914). In a small town in Alabama, Henry Garnett operates a disreputable cafe and gambling establishment, unbeknownst to his blind mother who thinks him dead; yet his childhood friend, Dr. Alan Hamilton, continues to befriend the outcast. Hamilton is attracted to Faith, a young mother he attends at the hospital who decides to settle in the town; but she refuses his attentions because of her past. When the Ku Klux Klan raids the Owl with the intention of lynching Garnett, who is fatally ill, Hamilton induces the raiders to desist; and he explains to Faith that he must find Garnett's wife before Garnett dies. Learning that Faith is the missing wife, Hamilton, drunk, becomes remorseful over the betrayal of his friend. When called upon to operate on a child, however, he is sobered by the crisis and delivers Faith to her husband, who exhorts Hamilton to care for her and later takes poison. Hamilton and Faith are united, and Mother Garnett retains her belief in the nobility of her dead son. *Physicians. Filial relations. Blindness. Gambling. Suicide. Cafes. Regeneration. Alabama. Ku Klux Klan.*

ONE DARK NIGHT *see* **THE MIDNIGHT GUEST**

ONE EIGHTH APACHE **F2.3992**

Berwilla Film Corp. *Dist* Arrow Film Corp. 15 Jul **1922** [c8 Aug 1922; LP18122]. Si; b&w. 35mm. 6 reels, 5,634 ft.

Dir Ben Wilson. *Scen* J. Grubb Alexander.

Cast: Roy Stewart *(Brant Murdock)*, Kathleen Kirkham *(Norma Biddle)*, Wilbur McGaugh *(Charlie Longdeer)*, George M. Daniel *(Tyler Burgess)*, Dick La Reno *(Joseph Murdock)*.

Western drama. Source: Peter Bernard Kyne, unidentified story in *Red Book Magazine.* When Tyler Burgess goes west to make his fortune, a marriage is arranged between Norma, his society sweetheart, and Brant, the son of a cattle and oil baron. With the aid of a renegade Indian, Burgess breaks up their wedding by casting aspersions on Brant's birth and killing Brant's father. Burgess then marries Norma, but they are unhappy. Brant exposes the frameup, the Indian kills Burgess, and Brant and Norma are reunited. *Socialites. Ranchers. Apache Indians. Murder. Marriage.*

ONE EXCITING NIGHT **F2.3993**

D. W. Griffith, Inc. *Dist* United Artists. 10 Oct **1922** [Boston premiere; released 24 Dec 1922; c14 Dec 1922; LP18507]. Si; b&w. 35mm. 11 reels, 11,500 ft.

Dir D. W. Griffith. *Story* Irene Sinclair. *Photog* Hendrik Sartov. *Adtl Photog* Irving B. Ruby. *Mus Score Arr and Synchronized by* Albert Pesce.

Cast: Carol Dempster *(Agnes Harrington)*, Henry Hull *(John Fairfax)*, Porter Strong *(Romeo Washington)*, Morgan Wallace *(J. Wilson Rockmaine)*, C. H. Crocker-King *(The Neighbor)*, Margaret Dale *(Mrs. Harrington)*, Frank Sheridan *(The Detective)*, Frank Wunderlee *(Samuel Jones)*, Grace Griswold *(Auntie Fairfax)*, Irma Harrison *(The Maid)*, Herbert Sutch *(Clary Johnson)*, Percy Carr *(The Butler)*, Charles E. Mack *(a guest)*.

Mystery comedy-melodrama. Traveling through Africa on safari, a group of white hunters and their wives suffer under the tropical hardships; one of their number dies in childbirth. The little baby girl is adopted by the overbearing Mrs. Harrington and brought to the United States, where the treatment she receives in the home of her "mother" is none too kindly. Years later, the unsuspecting Agnes is a guest at the home of John Fairfax, where two schemes are being pursued: Mrs. Harrington is trying to ensnare the wealthy J. Wilson Rockmaine into a marriage trap with the lovely but unwilling Agnes, and a gang of bootleggers is trying to uncover a large sum of money hidden in the house. There are two murders; everyone is suspected; and Agnes, Fairfax, Romeo (the colored servant), and the maid are all locked in the house while detectives seek the slayers. At the height of a violent storm Agnes discovers Rockmaine to be guilty, then is informed of her real father's wealth. Agnes and John marry. *Bootleggers. Detectives. Treasure. Murder. Childbirth. Safaris. Africa.*

ONE GLORIOUS DAY **F2.3994**

Famous Players–Lasky. *Dist* Paramount Pictures. 5 Feb **1922** [c31 Jan 1922; LP17509]. Si; b&w. 35mm. 5 reels, 5,100 ft.

Pres by Jesse L. Lasky. *Dir* James Cruze. *Adapt* Walter Woods. *Story* Walter Woods, A. B. Barringer. *Photog* Karl Brown.

Cast: Will Rogers *(Ezra Botts)*, Lila Lee *(Molly McIntyre)*, Alan Hale *(Ben Wadley)*, John Fox *("Ek")*, George Nichols *(Pat Curran)*, Emily Rait *(Mrs. McIntyre)*, Clarence Burton *(Bert Snead)*.

Comedy. Professor Botts, a meek psychology professor, who is secretly in love with Molly McIntyre, his housekeeper's daughter, tells the spiritualist society of which he is chairman that he will leave his body, go into a trance, and reappear in a spiritual form. When "Ek"—a spirit with aggressive tendencies—enters his body, the professor surprises the entire town by thrashing some scheming politicians who have threatened him, and then, slightly intoxicated, he whips Ben Wadley, a scoundrel who has designs on Molly. When the spirit "Ek" leaves his body and the spirit of the professor again enters its fleshly form, Ezra learns that Molly loves him—although he cannot remember any of the events that occurred during his trance—and he is nominated for mayor. *Professors. Politicians. Spiritualism. Psychology.*

Note: Working title: *Ek.*

ONE GLORIOUS NIGHT **F2.3995**

Columbia Pictures. 1 Dec **1924** [c10 Dec 1924; LP20902]. Si; b&w. 35mm. 6 reels, 5,846 ft.

Dir Scott Dunlap. *Story* Harvey Gates, J. Grubb Alexander.

Cast: Elaine Hammerstein *(Mary Stevens)*, Al Roscoe *(Kenneth McLane)*, Phyllis Haver *(Sarah Graham)*, Freeman Wood *(Chester James)*, Lillian Elliott *(Mrs. Clark)*, Mathilda Brundage *(Mrs. Graham)*, Clarissa Selwynne *(Mrs. James)*, Baby Vondell Darr *(Mary)*, Edwin Coxen *(club secretary)*.

Society melodrama. Although she is in love with Kenneth McLane, a poor draftsman, Mary Stevens decides to marry Chester James, a young lawyer whose practice pays for his cigarettes while his mother pays for his yacht. When she tells Ken, he reproaches her for selling out and goes off to the oil fields alone. After Chester and Mary are married, his mother, upon whom they are financially dependent, dictates their every action, going so far as to forbid them to have children. Mary insists that they try to make it on their own, and they move out, but Chester soon returns to his mother, leaving Mary with an unborn child and unpaid bills. When the baby is born, it is put up for adoption and, unknown to Mary, is given a home with Ken, who has returned a millionaire from the oil fields. Mary disappears and is missing for 5 years. Ken finally finds her in a driving snowstorm on Christmas Eve, and he unites her with the little girl she has never seen. *Draftsmen. Lawyers. Mothers-in-law. Millionaires. Adoption. Motherhood. Oedipus complex. Oil fields. Christmas.*

ONE GLORIOUS SCRAP **F2.3996**

Universal Pictures. 20 Nov **1927** [c14 Oct 1927; LP24517]. Si; b&w. 35mm. 5 reels, 4,172 ft.

Pres by Carl Laemmle. *Dir* Edgar Lewis. *Titl* Gardner Bradford. *Adapt* George H. Plympton, George Morgan. *Story* Leigh Jacobson. *Photog* Eddie Linden. *Art Dir* David S. Garber.

Cast: Fred Humes *(Larry Day)*, Dorothy Gulliver *(Joan Curtis)*, Robert McKenzie *(Professor Parkinson)*, Francis Ford *(Ralph Curtis)*, George French *(Ezra Kramer)*, Cuyler Supplee *(Carl Kramer)*, Benny Corbett *(Benny)*, Gilbert "Pee Wee" Holmes *(Pee Wee)*, Dick L'Estrange *(Lazy)*, Scotty Mattraw *(Scotty)*.

Western melodrama. During a protracted drought, Larry Day and his riders from the Bar None find and rescue Professor Parkinson, an alleged rainmaker. Ralph Curtis, the ranchowner, is being sought by Ezra Kramer, who owns the only water-bearing ranch and wants to buy out Curtis and at the same time marry his son to Joan Curtis. Curtis is forced to discharge all his men except Larry, who remains because of his affection for Joan. Kramer gets a message that rain is due in another day, and he and Parkinson plan to benefit by cashing in on the rain-machine or by bringing the ranchers to terms. Larry learns of the plot and is held captive in Kramer's cabin; rescued in time by his men, he exposes the swindle, and the promised rain begins to fall. *Ranchers. Swindlers. Rainmakers. Water rights. Drought.*

ONE HOUR OF LOVE **F2.3997**

Tiffany Productions. 15 Jan **1927** [c6 Jan 1927; LP23509]. Si; b&w. 35mm. 7 reels, 6,500 ft.

Dir Robert Florey. *Scen* Sarah Y. Mason. *Photog* Milton Moore, Mack Stengler. *Art Dir* Edwin B. Willis. *Film Ed* James McKay.

Cast: Jacqueline Logan *("Jerry" McKay)*, Robert Frazer *(James Warren)*, Montagu Love *(J. W. McKay)*, Taylor Holmes *(Joe Monahan)*, Duane Thompson *(Neely)*, Mildred Harris *(Gwen)*, Hazel Keener *(Vi)*, William Austin *(Louis Carruthers)*, Henry Sedley *(Tom Webb)*, Billy Bletcher *("Half Pint" Walker)*.

Romantic drama. Source: Emerson Hough, *The Broken Gate* (New York, 1917). Jerry McKay, a spoiled and willful society girl, on the eve of a flighty engagement, decides to accompany her father to inspect some property he owns, managed by a handsome young engineer, James Warren. Jerry demonstrates her prowess as a marksman, though Warren has forbidden the use of firearms; and Tom Webb, an unscrupulous rancher, accuses Warren of inciting his men against him. Warren's stern reproval infuriates Jerry, and she bets her friends that she can get him to propose within a week. She succeeds in winning his approval and then falls in love with him, but they are temporarily parted when he learns of the wager. She returns, however, to seek his forgiveness. *Socialites. Ranchers. Engineers. Courtship. Flirtation. Wagers.*

ONE HOUR PAST MIDNIGHT **F2.3998**

Jupiter Film Corp. 20 Jun **1924** [New York State license application; c28 Nov 1923; LP19673]. Si; b&w. 35mm. 5 reels, 4,724 ft.

Dir-Story B. C. Rule.

Mystery thriller. Well-known inventor Joffrey Brent hears an intruder in his house soon after the village clock strikes 1 a.m. Investigating, he gets into a struggle; and a body is seen falling to the floor. In the morning, his daughter, Dorothy, discovers him missing. Instead of calling the police she summons her aunt to stay the night. Dorothy falls asleep in the library and awakens when the clock again strikes once. She goes upstairs, and the grim intruder reappears. The next morning, the maids discover the corpse of a retired businessman from a distant city who has no apparent connection with Brent. Dorothy decides to spend the next night at her aunt's but returns with Niles Whitney, her sweetheart, in search of some wanted object. Finding a detective on guard, Niles goes off alone to a cigar store, not realizing that the detective is really the intruder in disguise. Upon his return, Niles discovers her unconscious. The police commissioner shows up with the father, and the intruder is revealed to be Stephen Ellis, an old "friend" who came to rob Brent, kidnaped him, and concealed him in an old country house. Ellis had returned to look for the combination to Brent's safe. Later Ellis is arrested and confesses everything. *Burglars. Inventors. Kidnaping.*

ONE HYSTERICAL NIGHT **F2.3999**

Universal Pictures. 6 Oct **1929** [c24 Sep 1929; LP722]. Sd (Movietone); b&w. 35mm. 6 reels, 5,279 ft. [Also si; 5,268 ft.]

Dir William J. Craft. *Scen* Earl Snell. *Story-Dial* Reginald Denny. *Photog* Arthur Todd. *Film Ed* Reginald Denny.

Cast: Reginald Denny *(William Judd [Napoleon])*, Nora Lane *(Nurse [Josephine])*, E. J. Ratcliffe *(Wellington)*, Fritz Feld *(Paganini)*, Slim Summerville *(Robin Hood)*, Joyzelle *(Salome)*, Jules Cowles *(William Tell)*, Walter Brennan *(Paul Revere)*, Henry Otto *(Dr. Hayden)*, Margaret Campbell *(Mrs. Bixby)*, Peter Cawthorne *(Mr. Bixby)*, D. R. O. Hatswell *(Claude Bixby)*, Rolfe Sedan *(Arthur Bixby)*, Lloyd Whitlock *(Attorney Thurston)*.

Farce. Thinking he is going to a costume ball, William Judd, heir to a fortune, accompanies his scheming aunt and uncle to an insane asylum dressed as Napoleon Bonaparte. Inside, the doctors refuse to release Judd, because the relatives have told them about Judd's "delusion of grandeur." Among the inmates Judd finds a girl dressed as the Empress Josephine (actually a nurse sent to humor him), and they escape from the institution with the entire group of inmates following in their wake. Judd arrives home in time to expose his relatives' avarice to his lawyer. Assured of the nurse's sanity, Judd offers her his heart and his fortune. *Nouveaux riches. Nurses. Uncles. Aunts. Delusion of grandeur. Greed. Insane asylums.*

ONE INCREASING PURPOSE **F2.4000**

Fox Film Corp. 2 Jan **1927** [c2 Jan 1927; LP23500]. Si; b&w. 35mm. 8 reels, 7,677 ft.

Pres by William Fox. *Dir* Harry Beaumont. *Scen* Bradley King. *Photog* Rudolph Bergquist. *Asst Dir* James Dunne.

Cast: Edmund Lowe *(Sim Paris)*, Lila Lee *(Elizabeth Glade)*, Holmes Herbert *(Charles Paris)*, May Allison *(Linda Travers Paris)*, Lawford Davidson *(Dr. Byrne)*, Emily Fitzroy *(Mrs. Andiron)*, George Irving *(Mr. Glade)*, Huntley Gordon *(Andrew Paris)*, Josef Swickard *(Old Gand)*, Jane Novak *(Alice Paris)*, Nicholas Soussanin *(Jule)*, Tom Maguire *(Blinky)*, Gwynneth Bristowe *(Mrs. Yeoman)*, Fisher White *(Mr. Yeoman)*, Pat Somerset, Frank Elliott.

Drama. Source: Arthur Stuart-Menteth Hutchinson, *One Increasing Purpose* (Boston, 1925). Sim Paris, having survived the war unscathed, returns home to England and finds that his elder brother, Charles, is so engrossed in making money that he is losing the love of his wife; another brother, who is caring for an invalided relative in expectation of a remembrance in the will, is also losing his wife to the doctor who has been in attendance. The male nurse discovers her secret and blackmails the wife. Paris thus returns to this state of affairs; and after visiting the home of a former comrade and noting the happiness that prevails there, he believes that his mission in life is to straighten out the lives of other people. With this purpose, he and his wife go throughout England preaching the doctrine of unselfishness. *Brothers. Invalids. Nurses. Family life. Blackmail. World War I. England.*

ONE LAW FOR THE WOMAN **F2.4001**

Charles E. Blaney Pictures. *Dist* Vitagraph Co. of America. 25 May **1924** [c5 May 1924; LP20173]. Si; b&w. 35mm. 6 reels, 5,800 ft.

Prod-Story Charles E. Blaney. *Dir* Del Henderson. *Scen* Harry Chandlee.

Cast: Cullen Landis *(Ben Martin)*, Mildred Harris *(Polly Barnes)*, Cecil Spooner *(Phillis Dair)*, Stanton Heck *(Brennan)*, Otis Harlan *(Judge Blake)*, Bertram Grassby *(Bartlett)*, Charlotte Stevens *(Nellie)*.

Western melodrama. After having a fraudulent mine lease foisted upon him, mining engineer Ben Martin discovers gold. When agents expose the fraud, Ben, with the help of his girl Polly, gains possession of the genuine lease, and after being saved from a flooded mine they are married. *Engineers. Swindlers. Mining.*

ONE MAD KISS **F2.4002**

Fox Film Corp. 13 Jul **1930** [c17 Jun 1930; LP1381]. Sd (Movietone); b&w. 35mm. 7 reels, 5,786 ft.

Pres by William Fox. *Dir* Marcel Silver, James Tinling. *Stage Dir* Frank Merlin. *Adapt-Dial* Dudley Nichols. *Story* Adolf Paul. *Photog* Charles Van Enger, Ross Fisher. *Film Ed* Louis Loeffler. *Songs: "Oh, Where Are You?" "One Mad Kiss"* José Mojica, Troy Saunders. *Songs: "Behind the Mask," "Monkey on a String," "Oh! Have I a Way With the Girls!"* James Hanley, Joseph McCarthy. *Song: "Only One," "The Gay Heart"* Dave Stamper, Clare Kummer. *Song: "Once in a While"* Dave Stamper, Clare Kummer, Cecil Arnold. *Songs: "In My Arms," "I Am Free"* William Kernell. *Song: "Lament"* Dudley Nichols, José Mojica. *Addtl Songs for Spanish Version: "Gitana," "Florero Españole," "Fiesta"* Jarge Del Moral, José Mojica, Troy Saunders. *Dance Dir* Juan Duval. *Sd Rec* George Leverett. *Asst Dir* Virgil Hart.

Cast: José Mojica *(José Savedra)*, Mona Maris *(Rosario)*, Antonio Moreno *(Don Estrada)*, Tom Patricola *(Paco)*.

Romantic musical. José Savedra, an outlaw-hero in Spain, fights the corrupt governmental authorities in the interest of the oppressed, coming into conflict with Paco, an official who has dishonorable designs on Rosario, a dancehall girl. After numerous manipulations, he is captured by the authorities, but Rosario, by pretending love for the governor, is able to smuggle him a gun. Eventually, he manages to escape and is reunited with Rosario, who has come to love him. *Outlaws. Dancehall girls. Political corruption. Spain.*

Note: It has not been determined from existing sources who directed the final version; one source credits James Tinling as redirecting the film, while all others credit Marcel Silver. A similar discrepancy exists regarding camera crediting. Also produced in a Spanish-language version.

THE ONE MAN *see* **CRASHIN' THRU**

THE ONE MAN DOG **F2.4003**

FBO Pictures. *Dist* RKO Productions. 11 Feb **1929** [New York showing: c2 Feb 1925; LP148]. Si; b&w. 35mm. 6 reels, 4,481 ft.

Dir Leon D'Usseau. *Story-Cont* Frank Howard Clark. *Titl* Helen Gregg. *Photog* Robert De Grasse. *Film Ed* Tod Chessman. *Asst Dir* William Cody.

Cast: Ranger *(Grit, a dog)*, Sam Nelson *(Larry)*, Edward Hearne *(Pierre)*, Virginia Bradford *(Babette)*, William Patton *(Gadsky)*, Art Robbins *(trapper)*.

Northwest melodrama. Tim O'Brien, the factor of a trading post in Canada, is murdered by Gadsky, and Larry Sherman is unjustly accused of the crime. Larry's dog, Grit, goes after Gadsky and is instrumental in his capture. Gadsky escapes, however, and Grit drives him off a cliff to his death. Larry is cleared of all suspicion in O'Brien's death. *Factors. Injustice. Murder. Trading posts. Canada. Dogs.*

A ONE MAN GAME **F2.4004**

Universal Pictures. 30 Jan **1927** [c18 Oct 1926; LP23248]. Si; b&w. 35mm. 5 reels, 4,689 ft.

Pres by Carl Laemmle. *Dir* Ernst Laemmle. *Story-Scen* William Lester. *Photog* Harry Mason, Al Jones. *Art Dir* David S. Garber.

Cast: Fred Humes *(Fred Hunter)*, Fay Wray *(Roberts)*, Harry Todd *(Sam Baker)*, Clarence Geldert *(Jake Robbins)*, Norbert Myles *(Stephen Laban)*, Lotus Thompson *(Millicent Delacey)*, William Malan *(John Starke)*, Julia Griffith *(Mrs. Delacey)*, Bud Osborne.

Western melodrama. The efforts of crooked rancher Stephen Laban to force his local bank into an unsecured loan are foiled by Fred Hunter and Jake Robbins, and Laban vows vengeance on the pair; but he is temporarily thwarted by the arrival from the East of society girl Millicent Delacey. Knowing her weakness for social prestige, Hunter arranges to masquerade as the Duke of Black Butte, a visiting nobleman on a hunting expedition; Millicent and her social-climbing mother completely succumb to the duke's charm. Laban arranges a scheme to lure the posse in search of the duke's kidnapers while he and his men rob the bank. Hunter escapes with the aid of Roberts, the tomboy daughter of his friend; and after the robbers are apprehended, he realizes his love for Roberts. *Social climbers. Tomboys. Ranchers. Bank robberies. Imposture. Kidnaping.*

ONE MAN IN A MILLION **F2.4005**

Sol Lesser. *Dist* Robertson-Cole Distributing Corp. 13 Feb **1921** [c13 Feb 1921; LP16201]. Si; b&w. 35mm. 6 reels.

Dir-Story George Beban. *Scen* Dorothy Yost. *Photog* Ross Fisher.

Cast: George Beban *(Lupino Delchini)*, Helen Jerome Eddy *(Flora Valenzi)*, Irene Rich *(Madame Maureveau)*, Lloyd Whitlock *(Clyde Hartley)*, George B. Williams *(Gustave Koppel)*, Jennie Lee *(Mrs. Koppel)*, Wade Boteler *(immigration inspector)*, George Beban, Jr. *(The Belgian Waif)*, Bo-Bo *(himself, a parrot)*, Toddles *(himself, a dog)*.

Drama. Lupino Delchini, a waiter in a little restaurant, is discharged for giving food to a penniless beggar; and Hartley, a detective, rewards the Italian by getting him an appointment as poundmaster. Flora is attracted to Lupino by his kindness, but when he adopts a small Belgian boy he falls in love with Madame Maureveau, whom he believes to be the boy's mother. Madame Maureveau accepts his marriage offer only to avoid being deported; actually, she is in love with Hartley, who traces her real son to another family. Renouncing his engagement, Delchini finds happiness with the boy and Flora. *Immigrants. Waifs. Adoption. Animal care. Pounds. Dogs. Parrots.*

ONE MAN TRAIL **F2.4006**

Hollywood Producers Finance Association. 24 Dec **1926.** Si; b&w. 35mm. 5 reels.

Cast: Monty Montague, Ena Gregory.

Western melodrama. No information about the precise nature of this film has been found.

Note: There is some evidence that this film is a revision of the 1921 Fox film of similar title starring Buck Jones, using long shots from the earlier film to augment this "quickie." See Entry F2.4027.

ONE MILLION IN JEWELS **F2.4007**

William B. Brush. *Dist* American Releasing Corp. 4 Feb **1923.** Si; b&w. 35mm. 5 or 7 reels, 5,326 ft.

Dir-Writ J. P. McGowan. *Photog* William Tuers.

Cast: Helen Holmes *(Helen Morgan)*, J. P. McGowan *(Burke)*, Elinor Fair *(Sylvia Ellis)*, Nellie Parker Spaulding *(Jane Angle)*, Charles Craig *(George Beresford)*, Leslie Casey *(William Abbott)*, Herbert Pattee *(Morgan)*.

Crime melodrama. U. S. Secret Serviceman Burke is assigned to capture a gang of thieves attempting to smuggle some valuable jewels from Cuba into the United States. Helen Morgan, leader of the gang, secretly loves Burke. Sylvia, whom Burke had befriended, is unwittingly used by Helen in her scheme. In an effort to save Burke's life, Helen is shot; and she dies. Burke marries Sylvia after she helps him fulfill his mission. *Smugglers. Secret service. Cuba.*

ONE MINUTE TO PLAY **F2.4008**

R-C Pictures. *Dist* Film Booking Offices of America. 28 Aug or 12 Sep **1926** [c28 Aug 1926; LP23062]. Si; b&w. 35mm. 8 reels, 7,732 ft.

Pres by Joseph P. Kennedy. *Dir* Sam Wood. *Story-Cont* Byron Morgan. *Camera* Charles Clarke. *Asst Dir* Jack McKeown.

Cast: Red Grange *(Red Wade)*, Mary McAllister *(Sally Rogers)*, Charles Ogle *(John Wade)*, George Wilson *(Player "33")*, Ben Hendricks, Jr. *("Biff" Wheeler)*, Lee Shumway *(Tex Rogers)*, Al Cooke *(brakeman)*, Kit Guard *(trainman)*, King Tut *(himself, a dog)*, Lincoln Stedman *(Toodles)*, Jay Hunt *(President Todd)*, Edythe Chapman *(Mrs. Wade)*.

Sports drama. Red Wade, a high school football celebrity, wants to attend Claxton College because of its gridiron ratings but meets with opposition from his father, who insists that he attend his own alma mater—Barlow; Red wins but at the cost of giving up football. On the train he meets Sally Rogers from Barlow and her admirer, Biff Wheeler of the Claxton football team; in an impromptu intercollegiate scrap, Red leads the outnumbered Barlow students to victory and misses the Claxton train stop, but he decides to go on to Barlow because of Sally. Eventually he is persuaded to play football against his father's orders, and he proves to be a valuable player on the team. The elder Wade, having become wealthy, offers an endowment to the school; but learning that Red has disregarded his orders, he threatens to withdraw the offer if Red plays. Though the president advises Red to play, he feigns drunkenness and is disqualified. Mr. Wade, attending the game, is won over to the boy's attitude and advises him to "go in and win." *College life. Filial relations. Football.*

ONE MOMENT'S TEMPTATION **F2.4009**

Dist Second National Pictures. 1 Sep **1922.** Si; b&w. 35mm. 5 reels, 4,800 ft.

Dir A. J. Rooke.

Cast: James Knight, Marjorie Villers.

Melodrama(?). No information about the nature of this film has been found.

ONE NIGHT AT SUSIE'S **F2.4010**

First National Pictures. 19 Oct **1930** [c14 Oct 1930; LP1646]. Sd (Vitaphone); b&w. 35mm. 8 reels, 5,760 ft.

Dir John Francis Dillon. *Screenplay-Dial* Forrest Halsey, Kathryn Scola. *Photog* Ernest Haller. *Rec Engr* Dolph Thomas.

Cast: Billie Dove *(Mary)*, Douglas Fairbanks, Jr. *(Dick)*, Helen Ware *(Susie)*, Tully Marshall *(Buckeye Bill)*, James Crane *(Houlihan)*, John Loder *(Hayes)*, Claude Fleming *(Drake)*.

Crook melodrama. Source: Frederick Hazlitt Brennan, "One Night at Susie's" (publication undetermined). Susie, a friend to gangsters and ex-convicts, rears Dick Rollins, son of a dead convict, making certain that he steers clear of underworld elements, and gets him a job as a press agent. When he brings home Mary, a chorus girl, and announces their engagement, Susie is infuriated. Hayes, the producer of Mary's show, gives them an engagement party, but at the last minute Dick has to work; later, he discovers that Mary killed Hayes to escape from his advances and assumes the blame himself. Despite Mary's protests, Dick is convicted of manslaughter. Although Susie regrets the turn of events, she places hope in Mary's future with Dick. While in prison, Dick writes a play for Mary; unable to obtain a producer for it, Mary accepts the offer of Drake to stage the play if she is included in the deal. Houlihan, who has unsuccessfully pursued Mary, learns of her relations with Drake and informs Susie. After denial, Mary confesses the truth to Susie; Susie promises not to tell Dick, and the lovers are reunited upon his release. *Chorus girls. Playwrights. Gangsters. Convicts. Press agents. Theatrical producers. Manslaughter.*

ONE NIGHT IN ROME **F2.4011**

Metro-Goldwyn-Mayer Corp. *Dist* Metro-Goldwyn Distributing Corp. 29 Sep **1924** [c23 Oct 1924; LP20744]. Si; b&w. 35mm. 7 reels, 5,883 ft.

Dir Clarence G. Badger. *Scen* J. Hartley Manners. *Photog* Rudolph Bergquist.

Cast: Laurette Taylor *(Duchess Mareno/Madame L'Enigme)*, Tom Moore *(Richard Oak)*, Alan Hale *(Duke Mareno)*, William Humphrey *(George Milburne)*, Joseph Dowling *(Prince Danieli)*, Miss Du Pont *(Zephyer Redlynch)*, Warner Oland *(Mario Dorando)*, Brandon Hurst *(Count Beetholde)*, Edna Tichenor *(Italian maid)*, Ralph Yearsley *(gardener)*.

Drama. Source: J. Hartley Manners, *One Night in Rome, a Drama* (New York opening: 2 Dec 1919). Guilty of wartime treachery, Duke Mareno leaves a suicide note accusing his wife of infidelity. The duke's father, Prince Danieli, thereupon denounces the duchess, who flees to London and becomes a popular fortune-teller, known as Madame L'Enigme. When Richard Oak, whom the duchess knew in Italy, invites her to perform for a charity ball, he finally recognizes her and confesses his undying love. But the duchess does not respond and tries to keep her identity secret. Singer Mario Dorando also recognizes her and informs Prince Danieli. Duchess Mareno's anxiety mounts until her father-in-law finally appears with the news that the duke was actually killed by his gardener in revenge for a woman he had wronged. Her position in society restored, the Duchess Mareno accepts Richard. *Nobility. Fortune-tellers. Traitors. Murder. Suicide. Infidelity. London. Rome.*

ONE OF THE BRAVEST **F2.4012**

Gotham Productions. *Dist* Lumas Film Corp. Oct **1925** [c19 Oct 1925; LP21923]. Si; b&w. 35mm. 6 reels, 5,679 ft.

Pres by Samuel Sax. *Supv* Renaud Hoffman. *Dir* Frank O'Connor. *Cont*

Henry McCarty. *Story* James J. Tynan. *Photog* Ray June. *Film Ed* Irene Morra. *Asst Dir* Glenn Belt.

Cast: Ralph Lewis *(John Kelly)*, Edward Hearn *(Dan Kelly)*, Sidney Franklin *(Morris Levin)*, Pat Somerset *("Satin" Sanderson)*, Claire McDowell *(Mrs. Kelly)*, Marion Mack *(Sarah Levin)*.

Melodrama. Though Dan Kelly is brave enough to save tailor Morris Levin and his daughter Sarah from three thugs, he has a deadly fear of fires. After receiving his assignment as fireman, Dan disgraces himself in the eyes of his father—John Kelly, captain of Engine 95 and one of the bravest firefighters in the department. Mrs. Kelly is persuaded by conman "Satin" Sanderson to invest the money entrusted to her husband for the fireman's ball in a phony stock. John finds the money missing and blames Dan. Sarah gets her father to give Dan enough money to replace the missing funds. When a three-alarm fire breaks out, Dan sees a chance to redeem himself and rushes to the scene. He spots Sanderson in the burning building, mounts a scaling ladder, beats up the swindler, saves his father, and with Sanderson jumps to safety into a net. The Irish and Jewish families become reconciled, and Dan and Sarah are betrothed. *Firemen. Tailors. Confidence men. Irish. Jews. Pyrophobia.*

ONE PUNCH O'DAY **F2.4013**

Harry J. Brown Productions. *Dist* Rayart Pictures. 28 Jul **1926** [New York State license]. Si; b&w. 35mm. 5 reels, 5,064 ft.

Dir Harry J. Brown. *Scen* Henry R. Symonds.

Cast: Billy Sullivan *(Jimmy O'Day)*, Charlotte Merriam *(Alice Felton)*, Jack Herrick *(Joe Hemingway)*, William Malan *(Elwood Felton)*, J. C. Fowler *(Charles Hargreaves)*, Eddie Diggins *(Kid Martin)*.

Action melodrama. "Boxing champ by staging impromptu fight obtains money needed to pay for lease on land where there is oil, foiling deceitful option holder. He wins girl and aids her father, in whom was entrusted confidence of people whose savings were invested in oil well." (*Motion Picture News Booking Guide*, 11:41, Oct 1926.) *Prizefighters. Property rights. Oil wells.*

ONE ROMANTIC NIGHT **F2.4014**

United Artists. 3 May **1930** [c5 May 1930; LP1275]. Sd (Movietone); b&w. 35mm. 8 reels, 6,592 ft.

Pres by Joseph M. Schenck. *Assoc Prod* John W. Considine, Jr. *Dir* Paul L. Stein. *Adapt-Dial* Melville Baker. *Photog* Karl Struss. *Sets* William Cameron Menzies, Park French. *Film Ed* James Smith. *Mus Arr* Hugo Riesenfeld. *Sd Engr* Frank Maher. *Asst Dir* Herbert Sutch.

Cast: Lillian Gish *(Alexandra)*, Rod La Rocque *(Prince Albert)*, Conrad Nagel *(Dr. Nicholas Haller)*, Marie Dressler *(Princess Beatrice)*, O. P. Heggie *(Father Benedict)*, Albert Conti *(Count Lutzen)*, Edgar Norton *(Colonel Wunderlich)*, Billie Bennett *(Symphorosa)*, Philippe De Lacy *(George)*, Byron Sage *(Arsene)*, Barbara Leonard *(Mitzi)*.

Romantic drama. Source: Ferenc Molnár, *The Swan, a Romantic Comedy in Three Acts* (trans. by Melville Baker; New York, 1929). Because of political exigencies and his father's royal command, the fun-loving Prince Albert is persuaded to court the favor of Alexandra, daughter of the dowager Princess Beatrice. At her country home, Alexandra makes it clear to the prince that a forced marriage would be distasteful to her; and as a result, he tries to win her. Beatrice, piqued by her daughter's coolness, compels her to make a last effort to accept the prince by inviting Dr. Haller, an astronomer, to a ball planned in Albert's honor. Albert declares his love, believing Alexandra is in love with the astronomer, and realizing her love for the prince, she dismisses Haller. Albert announces he must wed a Princess Marie, but at Alexandra's suggestion he agrees to elope with her to South America. *Royalty. Astronomers. Elopement. Courtship.*

ONE SHOT RANGER **F2.4015**

Lariat Productions. 14 Oct **1925** [New York State license application; c24 Oct 1925; LP21948]. Si; b&w. 35mm. 5 reels, 4,850 ft.

Cast: Pete Morrison, Betty Goodwin, Lightning *(himself, a horse)*.

Western melodrama. The hero (played by Pete Morrison) has an unscrupulous rival for the heroine (played by Betty Goodwin). When the rival is spurned by Betty, he gets even by persuading her to ride one of the wildest horses on the range. The horse runs away with her, and Pete knocks down the rival and races to her rescue. Pete later saves Betty from the insults of a crowd of bullies. In the climax, Pete saves a cowboy from being lynched by severing the rope with a single shot, while the posse rides to the rescue. He then saves Betty by leaping from a high bluff into a lake while on Lightning's back. *Rangers. Cowboys. Posses. Lynching. Horses.*

ONE SHOT ROSS (Reissue) **F2.4016**

Triangle Film Corp. *Dist* Tri-Stone Pictures. 12 Nov **1925** [New York State license]. Si; b&w. 35mm. 5 reels.

Note: A Roy Stewart film originally released by Triangle Film Corp. on 14 Oct 1917.

ONE SPLENDID HOUR **F2.4017**

Excellent Pictures. 1 May **1929** [c26 Apr 1929; LP348]. Si; b&w. 35mm. 6 reels, 6,129 ft.

Pres by Samuel Zierler. *Dir* Burton King. *Screenplay* Sylvia Bernstein, Jacques Jaccard. *Adapt* Isadore Bernstein. *Story* Adeline Leitzbach. *Photog* William Miller, Walter Haas. *Film Ed* Betty Davis.

Cast: Viola Dana *(Bobbie Walsh)*, George Periolat *(Senator Walsh)*, Allan Simpson *(Dr. Thornton)*, Lewis Sargent *(Jimmy O'Shea)*, Jack Richardson *(Peter Hoag)*, Lucy Beaumont *(Mother Kelly)*, Florice Cooper *(Rose Kelly)*, Ernie S. Adams *(Solly)*, Hugh Saxon *(The Roué)*, Charles Hickman *(police captain)*.

Society melodrama. In search of thrills, socialite Bobbie Walsh visits a lurid downtown cafe and there meets Dr. Thornton, a neighborhood settlement worker in search of a wayward girl. Bobbie is attracted to Thornton and returns to the cafe on the following day, first disguising herself "as a wayward girl." Bobbid is assaulted by one of the customers, and Thornton comes to her rescue, besting two men in a fight. Thornton and Bobbie are arrested and taken to night court. Bobbie reveals her true identity, and she and Thornton become fast friends. *Socialites. Physicians. Settlement workers. Thrill-seeking. Disguise. Cafes.*

ONE STOLEN NIGHT **F2.4018**

Vitagraph Co. of America. 29 Jan **1923** [New York premiere; released Jan 1923; c18 Jan 1923; LP18597]. Si; b&w. 35mm. 5 reels, 4,900 ft.

Dir Robert Ensminger. *Scen* Bradley J. Smollen. *Photog* Steve Smith, Jr.

Cast: Alice Calhoun *(Diantha Ebberly)*, Herbert Heyes *(Herbert Medford)*, Otto Hoffman *(Horace Ebberly)*, Adele Farrington *(Mrs. Ebberly)*, Russ Powell *(Sheik Amud)*, Oliver Hardy *(see note)*.

Melodrama. Source: D. D. Calhoun, "The Arab" (publication undetermined). Diantha Ebberly travels with her parents to the edge of the Sahara to meet her longtime betrothed, Herbert Medford, whom she has never seen. She is rescued from a swarm of beggars by an "Arab," then meets him again when she slips out at night in native dress. They fall in love, but Diantha is abducted by Sheik Amud, then returned safely home by the "Arab." The next morning Diantha discovers her fiancé and lover to be one and the same. *Arabs. Sheiks. Disguise. Abduction. Sahara.*

Note: *Moving Picture World* (10 Feb 1923) credits Oliver Hardy as Sheik Amud. Remade by Warner Brothers under the same title in 1929.

ONE STOLEN NIGHT **F2.4019**

Warner Brothers Pictures. 16 Mar **1929** [c7 Mar 1929; LP196]. Talking sequences (Vitaphone); b&w. 35mm. 6 reels, 5,243 ft. [Also si, 20 Apr; 4,797 ft.]

Dir Scott R. Dunlap. *Scen-Dial-Titl* Edward T. Lowe, Jr. *Photog* Frank Kesson.

Cast: Betty Bronson *(Jeanne)*, William Collier, Jr. *(Bob)*, Mitchell Lewis *(Blossom)*, Harry Todd *(Blazer)*, Charles Hill Mailes *(Doad)*, Nina Quartaro *(Chyra)*, Rose Dione *(Madame Blossom)*, Otto Lederer *(Abou-Ibu-Adam)*, Angelo Rossitto *(The Dwarf)*, Jack Santoro *(Brandon)*, Harry Schultz *(The Sheik)*.

Melodrama. Source: D. D. Calhoun, "The Arab" (publication undetermined). Bob and his brother, Stanton, are members of a British cavalry regiment in the Sudan. Stanton steals the commissary funds, and Bob assumes the blame, deserting his post and joining up with a cheap vaudeville troupe. Bob falls in love with Jeanne, the stooge in a whip act. Sheik Achmed takes a fancy to Jeanne and kidnaps her with the help of Madame Blossom, the whip expert. Jeanne turns out to be too white for the sheik, however, and he throws her out. Bob and Jeanne then find a happy future together. *Brothers. Sheiks. Actors. Theft. Kidnaping. Vaudeville. Whips. Sudan. Great Britain—Army.*

Note: Song: "My Cairo Love."

ONE WAY STREET **F2.4020**

First National Pictures. 12 Apr **1925** [c20 Mar 1925; LP21251]. Si; b&w. 35mm. 6 reels, 5,600 ft.

Supv-Adapt Earl Hudson. *Dir* John Francis Dillon. *Scen* Arthur Statter, Mary Alice Scully. *Photog* Arthur Edeson.

Cast: Ben Lyon *(Bobby Austin)*, Anna Q. Nilsson *(Lady Sylvia Hutton)*, Marjorie Daw *(Elizabeth Stuart)*, Dorothy Cumming *(Lady Frances Thompson)*, Lumsden Hare *(Sir Edward Hutton)*, Mona Kingsley *(Kathleen Lawrence)*, Thomas Holding *(John Stuart)*.

Society melodrama. Source: Beale Davis, *One Way Street* (New York, c1924). Bobby Austin becomes infatuated with Lady Sylvia Hutton, a leading member of British society, and asks that she divorce her husband and marry him instead. Lady Sylvia refuses, and Bobby terminates their relationship. To escape the humiliation of being put aside, the irate noblewoman then makes it appear that Bobby has cheated at cards and orders him from her house. Elizabeth Stuart, a beautiful young woman in love with Bobby, finds proof of Lady Hutton's duplicity and confronts her with it. Lady Sylvia becomes enraged and then suddenly loses her beauty, becoming in seconds a withered old hag. She subsequently reveals that she was once an operatic favorite, had been cast aside when her voice gave out, and had lately been restored to the appearance of youth by a surgeon so that she might return to society and again bask in its acclaim. Bobby tells Elizabeth of his love, while Lady Sylvia finds solace in the arms of her husband. *Singers. Upper classes. Rejuvenation. Infidelity. Plastic surgery.*

ONE WEEK OF LOVE **F2.4021**

Selznick Pictures. ca5 Nov **1922** [Los Angeles and San Francisco premieres; released Nov; c30 Oct 1922; LP18415]. Si; b&w. 35mm. 7 reels, 6,960 ft.

Pres by Lewis J. Selznick. *Prod* Myron Selznick. *Dir* George Archainbaud. *Story* Edward J. Montagne, George Archainbaud. *Ch Cinematog* Jules Cronjager. *Film Ed* H. P. Bretherton, Harold McCord. *Asst Dir* Edward Sturgis.

Cast: Elaine Hammerstein *(Beth Wynn)*, Conway Tearle *(Buck Fearnley)*, Kate Lester *(Mrs. Wynn, Beth's aunt)*, Hallam Cooley *(Francis Fraser)*.

Melodrama. Spoiled society girl Beth Wynn agrees to stake her marriage to Francis Fraser on the outcome of an airplane race with him. Fraser wins, but Beth crashes into a Mexican mountainside and is found by bandits. Buck Fearnley, an uncouth American renegade, takes her to his shack. Then begins a weeklong conflict the end of which finds Beth triumphant, Buck regenerated, and the two in love. Buck reunites Beth with Fraser, but a flood wrecks their train, Fraser is drowned, and Buck rescues Beth. *Socialites. Traitors. Bandits. Airplane racing. Mexico. Train wrecks. Floods.*

Note: McCord is credited as editor by *Variety*.

ONE WILD WEEK **F2.4022**

Realart Pictures. Aug **1921** [c4 Aug 1921; LP16839]. Si; b&w. 35mm. 5 reels, 4,244 ft.

Dir Maurice Campbell. *Scen* Percy Heath. *Story* Frances Harmer. *Photog* H. Kinley Martin.

Cast: Bebe Daniels *(Pauline Hathaway)*, Frank Kingsley *(Bruce Reynolds)*, Mayme Kelso *(Emma Jessop)*, Frances Raymond *(Mrs. Brewster)*, Herbert Standing *(Judge Bancroft)*, Edwin Stevens *(Oliver Tobin)*, Edythe Chapman *(Mrs. Dorn)*, Carrie Clark Ward *(Cook)*, Bull Montana *(Red Mike)*.

Comedy-melodrama. On her 18th birthday Pauline Hathaway is informed by the family lawyer that she will inherit half a million dollars, provided that her behavior meets with his approval; otherwise, the money will revert to her aunt. With new clothes Pauline sets out to visit her mother's friend, Mrs. Brewster. Framed en route by a pickpocket, she is sentenced to a reformatory for 30 days. In court, however, she has been seen by Bruce Reynolds, an amateur investigator and nephew of Mrs. Brewster who is convinced of her innocence. Meanwhile, Mrs. Brewster's anxiety prompts a search, and Aunt Emma and Lawyer Tobin are confident that Pauline has forfeited her fortune. But Pauline escapes, and after proving her innocence she keeps her fortune and wins a husband. *Aunts. Investigators. Inheritance. Frameup. Reformatories.*

THE ONE WOMAN IDEA **F2.4023**

Fox Film Corp. 2 Jun **1929** [c6 Jun 1929; LP442]. Mus score (Movietone); b&w. 35mm. 7 reels, 6,111 ft. [Also si; 6,106 ft.]

Pres by William Fox. *Supv* Philip Klein. *Dir* Berthold Viertel. *Scen* Marion Orth. *Photog* L. William O'Connell. *Mus Score* Arthur Kay. *Asst Dir* Horace Hough.

Cast: Rod La Rocque *(Prince Ahmed)*, Marceline Day *(Lady Alicia Douglas/Alizar, halfcaste dancing girl)*, Shirley Dorman, Sharon Lynn, Sally Phipps *(lady passengers on the boat)*, Ivan Lebedeff *(Hosain [Dheyyid Mizra])*, Douglas Gilmore *(Lord Douglas)*, Gino Corrado *(Bordinas, agent of Douglas)*, Joseph W. Girard *(captain of steamship)*, Arnold Lucy *(Ali)*, Frances Rosay *(Zuleide, mother of Alizar)*, Jamiel Hassen *(bodyguard)*, Tom Tamarez *(bodyguard)*, Coy Watson *(Buttons)*.

Romantic melodrama. Source: Alan Williams, "The One-Woman Idea," in *Young's Magazine* (54:123–143, Oct 1927). On an ocean liner bound for Persia, Prince Ahmed is attracted to Lady Alicia, the English wife of Lord Douglas, because she wears a ring that is a duplicate of his own, presented to her father by the father of the prince. Returning to his palace, the prince is confronted by Alizar, a dancing girl who is a double for his love, but he is unable to feel a similar affection for her. Meanwhile, Lord Douglas and Lady Alicia visit Persia; his lordship enters the women's quarters of the palace and is discovered struggling with Alizar, but he flees in time to save his life, while the girl kills herself. Lord Douglas is later captured, and while his wife pleads for his life, he is slain by the mother of Alizar. *Royalty. Nobility. Dancers. Doubles. English. Suicide. Ocean liners. Persia.*

ONE WOMAN TO ANOTHER **F2.4024**

Paramount Famous Lasky Corp. 17 Sep **1927** [c24 Sep 1927; LP24449]. Si; b&w. 35mm. 5 reels, 4,022 ft.

Pres by Adolph Zukor, Jesse L. Lasky. *Dir* Frank Tuttle. *Screenplay* J. L. Campbell. *Titl* George Marion, Jr. *Photog* L. Guy Wilky.

Cast: Florence Vidor *(Rita Farrell)*, Theodore von Eltz *(John Bruce)*, Marie Shotwell *(Mrs. Gray)*, Hedda Hopper *(Olive Gresham)*, Roy Stewart *(Rev. Robert Farrell)*, Joyce Coad *(The Niece)*, Jimsy Boudwin *(The Nephew)*.

Farce. Source: Frances Nordstrom, *The Ruined Lady* (New York opening: 19 Jan 1920). John Bruce and Rita Farrell are constantly frustrated in their attempts to get married. They agree on a date, but unexpectedly her brother, the Reverend Robert Farrell, arrives along with his niece and nephew, both of whom he places in her care for 6 months while he travels to the Orient. John continues his suit until the niece is stricken with scarlet fever and a quarantine keeps John away. Meanwhile, John is vamped by a Miss Chapin; and Rita, with the aid of her friend Olive Gresham, schemes to compromise John into immediate marriage. Although Miss Chapin is forced to stay overnight with John in his car, Rita manages to faint, attired in a negligee, into his arms. To save him from a trouncing at the hands of Farrell, Rita claims that they are married. After a mad chase through a traffic jam, the lovers are united. *Children. Vamps. Clergymen. Scarlet fever. Quarantine. Chases.*

ONE WONDERFUL NIGHT **F2.4025**

Universal Film Manufacturing Co. ca26 Nov **1922** [Chicago premiere; released 17 Dec; c18 Nov 1922; LP18426]. Si; b&w. 35mm. 5 reels, 4,473 ft.

Pres by Carl Laemmle. *Dir* Stuart Paton. *Scen* George C. Hull. *Photog* G. W. Warren.

Cast: Herbert Rawlinson *(John D. Curtis)*, Lillian Rich *(Hermione Fane)*, Dale Fuller *(maid)*, Sidney De Grey *(A. F. Fane)*, Joseph W. Girard *(Chief of Detectives)*, Jean De Briac *(Jean de Curtois)*, Amelio Mendez *(Anatole)*, Sidney Bracey *(Juggins)*, Spottiswoode Aitken *(minister)*.

Mystery melodrama. Source: Louis Tracy, *One Wonderful Night; a Romance of New York* (New York, 1912). John Curtis discovers that Jean de Curtois, whose assault he has witnessed, was married a few hours earlier to Hermione Fane so that she might escape marriage to Count de Mauriat and retain her fortune. John obligingly marries Hermione himself, then mollifies her wrathful father by exposing the count as not only a phony but also the instigator of a plot against de Curtois. *Filial relations. Marriage. Imposture.*

ONE YEAR TO LIVE **F2.4026**

First National Pictures. 15 Mar **1925** [c12 Feb 1925; LP21127]. Si; b&w. 35mm. 7 reels, 6,064 ft.

Pres by M. C. Levee. *Dir* Irving Cummings. *Screenplay* J. G. Hawks. *Titl* Robert Hopkins. *Photog* Arthur L. Todd. *Art Dir* Jack Okey. *Film Ed* Charles J. Hunt. *Asst Dir* Charles Woolstenhulme.

Cast: Aileen Pringle *(Elsie Duchanier)*, Dorothy Mackaill *(Marthe)*, Sam De Grasse *(Dr. Lucien La Pierre)*, Rosemary Theby *(Lolette)*, Leo White *(The Stage Manager)*, Joseph Kilgour *(Maurice Brunel)*, Antonio Moreno *(Capt. Tom Kendrick)*, Rose Dione *(Nanette)*, Chester Conklin *(Froquin)*.

Melodrama. Source: John Hunter, newspaper series (see note). Elsie Duchanier, the maid of the star dancer in Brunel's Follies, falls in love with Capt. Tom Kendrick, an American soldier stationed in France. Kendrick is reassigned to the United States, and Dr. La Pierre, who is also in love with Elsie, tells her that she has only one year to live. Elsie then accepts Maurice Brunel's offer to make her the main attraction of his new follies. Elsie soon becomes famous and is showered with gifts and attention, but she does not submit to Brunel's advances, the price he demands for making her a star. Tom returns to France and meets La Pierre, who confesses that his "one year to live" warning to Elsie was an unsuccessful attempt at seduction. La Pierre also tells Tom of Brunel's desire for Elsie, and Tom finds her just in time to prevent Brunel's unwelcome advances. Elsie and Tom are happily reunited. *Dancers. Theatrical producers. Physicians. Actors. Life expectancy. Follies. France. United States Army.*

Note: The film is based on a newpaper series by John Hunter in which a number of celebrities were asked what they would do with their lives if they had only one year to live.

THE ONE-MAN TRAIL F2.4027

Fox Film Corp. 27 Mar **1921** [c27 Mar 1921; LP16392]. Si; b&w. 35mm. 5 reels, 5,000 ft.

Pres by William Fox. *Dir* Bernard J. Durning. *Scen* William K. Howard. *Story* Jack Strumwasser, Clyde C. Westover. *Photog* Frank B. Good.

Cast: Buck Jones *(Tom Merrill)*, Beatrice Burnham *(Cressy)*, Helene Rosson *(Grace Merrill)*, James Farley *(Jim Crenshaw)*.

Western melodrama. Tom Merrill returns home to find that his father has been murdered by Crenshaw, a gambler whom the father tried to prevent from eloping with his daughter, and embarks on a trail of vengeance. Crenshaw, having taken another name as a saloon owner, tires of Grace and has an eye on Cressy, whose sister Tom saves from drowning. Crenshaw has the sister kidnaped, but Tom pursues them on horseback and squares accounts with the gambler, then wins Cressy. *Gamblers. Revenge. Brother-sister relationship. Murder. Kidnaping.*

ONE-ROUND HOGAN F2.4028

Warner Brothers Pictures. 17 Sep **1927** [c10 Sep 1927; LP24386]. Si; b&w. 35mm. 7 reels, 6,357 ft.

Dir Howard Bretherton. *Scen* Charles R. Condon. *Story* F. L. Giffen, George Godfrey. *Photog* Norbert Brodin. *Asst Dir* Eddie Sowders.

Cast: Monte Blue *(Robert Emmet Hogan)*, Leila Hyams *(Helen Davis)*, James J. Jeffries *(Tim Hogan)*, Frank Hagney *("Big Joe" Morgan)*, Tom Gallery *(Ed Davis)*, Texas Kid *(Texas Kid)*, Abdul the Turk *(Sniffy)*.

Melodrama. Robert Emmet Hogan, son of Tim Hogan, a great pugilist, battles his way to light heavyweight championship of the world. Ed Davis, his closest friend, who worships Hogan and aspires to a career of his own, introduces the fighter to Helen, his sister, who despises the ring and its followers. Hogan, at the insistence of his ambitious manager, "Big Joe" Morgan, is matched to fight a leading contender, but at the last minute Ed is persuaded to substitute for the contender; Hogan agrees to fight Ed if he will abandon his plans for a career; Hogan scores a knockout, and Morgan strikes Ed in a fury, killing him. Hogan, though found innocent of manslaughter, swears to quit the ring. Taunted by Morgan's accusation of cowardice, Hogan challenges him in the ring. The Texas Kid divulges the secret of Davis' murder to Helen; learning the truth from Helen, Hogan wins the fight and Helen's confidence. *Prizefighters. Fight managers. Brother-sister relationship. Manslaughter. Cowardice. Courtship. Friendship.*

$1,000 REWARD F2.4029

Charles R. Seeling Productions. *Dist* Aywon Film Corp. Dec **1923.** Si; b&w. 35mm. 5 reels, ca4,800 ft.

Dir Charles R. Seeling.

Cast: Big Boy Williams.

Western melodrama. "... a cowboy who is falsely accused of a murder ... escapes and in another town becomes a deputy sheriff. In line of duty he captures a thief who turns out to be the man who accused him. The hero forces a confession from the captured thief, who admits he is the guilty man." *(Motion Picture News Booking Guide,* 6:66, Apr 1924.) *Sheriffs. Cowboys. Thieves. Murder.*

ONLY A SHOP GIRL F2.4030

C. B. C. Film Sales. 5 Dec **1922** [Newark premiere; released Dec; c12 Dec 1922; LP18504]. Si; b&w. 35mm. 7 reels, 6,400 ft.

Prod Harry Cohn. *Dir-Scen* Edward J. Le Saint.

Cast: Estelle Taylor *(Mame Mulvey)*, Mae Busch *(Josie Jerome)*, Wallace Beery *(Jim Brennan)*, William Scott *(Danny Mulvey)*, James Morrison *(Charles Black)*, Josephine Adair *(Angelina Jerome)*, Willard Louis *(James Watkins)*, Claire Du Brey *(Mrs. Watkins)*, Tully Marshall *(manager of Watkins' store)*.

Melodrama. Source: Charles E. Blaney, *Only a Shopgirl; a Play in Four Acts* (c1922). Just released from prison, Danny Mulvey visits his sweetheart, Josie, and finds his sister, Mame, involved with department store owner James Watkins. Watkins is murdered while making advances to Josie, and Danny takes the blame from Josie upon himself. Mame, who was caught in a tenement fire on the night of the murder, makes a deathbed confession that clears Danny. *Shopgirls. Brother-sister relationship. Murder. Department stores.*

ONLY SAPS WORK F2.4031

Paramount-Publix Corp. 6 Dec **1930** [c5 Dec 1930; LP1794]. Sd (Movietone); b&w. 35mm. 9 reels, 6,644 ft.

Dir Cyril Gardner, Edwin H. Knopf. *Screenplay* Sam Mintz, Percy Heath, Joseph L. Mankiewicz. *Photog* Rex Wimpy. *Film Ed* Edward Dmytryk. *Rec Engr* Earl Hayman.

Cast: Leon Errol *(James Wilson)*, Richard Arlen *(Lawrence Payne)*, Mary Brian *(Barbara Tanner)*, Stuart Erwin *(Oscar)*, Anderson Lawler *(Horace Baldwin)*, Charles Grapewin *(Simeon Tanner)*, George Irving *(Dr. White)*, Nora Cecil *(Mrs. Partridge)*, Charles Giblyn *(Dr. Jasper)*, Fred Kelsey *(Murphy)*, G. Pat Collins *(Rafferty)*, George Chandler *(elevator boy)*, Jack Richardson *(chef)*, Clarence Burton *(Sergeant Burns)*, Clifford Dempsey *(Detective Smith)*.

Comedy. Source: Owen Davis, *Easy Come, Easy Go; a Farce in Three Acts* (New York, 1926). Lawrence Payne becomes innocently and unknowingly involved in a bank robbery when he offers to drive his boardinghouse mate, James Wilson—a quick-fingered, glib-tongued crook—to the train station. Both board the train and make their way to a health resort where Larry has obtained a job as pantry boy; en route, Larry meets Barbara Tanner, who is taking her father to the resort, and Horace Baldwin, her languid boyfriend. At the resort, Jim convinces the doctors he is a detective working on the crime he has himself committed; and Oscar, a bellboy ambitious to become a detective, volunteers to help him by shadowing Barbara's father and Baldwin. Meanwhile, Jim, who has represented himself as the resort owner, goes through numerous subterfuges in hiding from Barbara. Learning that Jim has robbed a bank, Lawrence insists on his returning the money, but at this juncture two detectives enter and there is a wild chase. Two bonafide officials expose the sleuths as crooks, and they in turn expose Jim. Larry is absolved of his escapades and finds happiness with Barbara. *Pantry boys. Bellboys. Robbers. Detectives. Resorts. Bank robberies.*

ONLY THE BRAVE F2.4032

Paramount Famous Lasky Corp. 8 Mar **1930** [c7 Mar 1930; LP1128]. Sd (Movietone); b&w. 35mm. 8 reels, 6,024 ft. [Also si.]

Dir Frank Tuttle. *Dial* Edward E. Paramore, Jr. *Titl* Richard H. Digges, Jr. *Adapt* Agnes Brand Leahy. *Story* Keene Thompson. *Photog* Harry Fischbeck. *Film Ed* Doris Drought. *Rec Engr* J. A. Goodrich.

Cast: Gary Cooper *(Capt. James Braydon)*, Mary Brian *(Barbara Calhoun)*, Phillips Holmes *(Capt. Robert Darrington)*, James Neill *(Vance Calhoun)*, Morgan Farley *(Tom Wendell)*, Guy Oliver *(Gen. U. S. Grant)*, John Elliott *(Gen. Robert E. Lee)*, E. H. Calvert *(The Colonel)*, Virginia Bruce *(Elizabeth)*, Elda Voelkel *(Lucy Cameron)*, William Le Maire *(The Sentry)*, Freeman Wood *(Elizabeth's lover)*, Lalo Encinas *(General Grant's secretary)*.

Romantic adventure drama. Cavalry Capt. James Braydon leaves Union Army Headquarters to visit his sweetheart, Elizabeth; and finding her in the arms of a civilian, he returns embittered and volunteers for spy duty. He is detailed to carry false dispatches behind Southern lines where they will mislead the Confederate Army. At a ball given for Confederate officers by Barbara Calhoun, Braydon flirts with the hostess to pique the jealousy of Darrington, who loves her, and to subject himself to arrest; but Barbara defends him even when she discovers him to be a spy, and they fall in love. Ultimately he is forced to leap from a window to assure his capture. The Confederates act on the fraudulent dispatches, though upon discovering his deception they order him executed. The Union attack comes in time to save him, but he is wounded in the battle. After the surrender at Appomattox Courthouse, Braydon and Barbara are the principals in a military wedding. *Spies. Appomattox Courthouse. United States—History—Civil War. Ulysses Simpson Grant. Robert Edward Lee.*

THE ONLY THING F2.4033

Metro-Goldwyn-Mayer Pictures. *Dist* Metro-Goldwyn Distributing Corp. 22 Nov **1925** [c1 Dec 1925; LP22059]. Si; b&w. 35mm. 6 reels, 5,736 ft.

Pers Supv–Story–Adapt Elinor Glyn. *Dir* Jack Conway. *Photog* Chester Lyons. *Sets* Cedric Gibbons, Richard Day. *Film Ed* Aubrey Scott. *Cost* David Mir.

Cast: Eleanor Boardman *(Princess Thyra)*, Conrad Nagel *(Duke of Chevenix)*, Edward Connelly *(The King)*, Louis Payne *(Lord Charles Vane)*, Arthur Edmund Carewe *(Gigberto)*, Vera Lewis *(Princess Erek)*, Carrie Clark Ward *(Princess Anne)*, Constance Wylie *(Countess Arline)*, Dale Fuller *(governess)*, Ned Sparks *(Gibson)*, Mario Carillo *(prime minister)*, David Mir *(Kaylkur)*, Mary Hawes *(Thyra's maid)*, Michael Pleschkoff *(Captain of the Guards)*, Buddy Smith *(Young Arnold)*, Joan Crawford *(Young Lady Catherine)*, Frank Braidwood *(Young Porteous)*, Derek Glynne *(Young Cheney)*.

Romantic drama. For reasons of state, Princess Thyra of Swendbord is betrothed to the King of Chekia, a small but politically important kingdom on the shores of the Mediterranean. Harry Vane, the Duke of Chevenix, envoy of the King of England, arrives in Chekia and falls in love with Thyra. On the wedding day, a revolution occurs followed by a red reign of terror. The king is killed, and Thyra is carried off by Gigberto, the rebel leader. Gigberto and Thyra are captured and imprisoned by the rebels and sentenced to die together. Harry substitutes himself for Gigberto, and he and Thyra are tied together and thrown into the bay. Harry frees their bonds and, supporting Thyra, swims to his nearby yacht, where Thyra declares her love. *Royalty. Diplomats. Imaginary kingdoms. Revolutions. Mediterranean Sea.*

ONLY 38 **F2.4034**

Famous Players–Lasky. *Dist* Paramount Pictures. 17 Jun **1923** [c19 Jun 1923; LP19125]. Si; b&w. 35mm. 7 reels, 6,175 ft.

Pres by Adolph Zukor. *Dir* William C. De Mille. *Scen* Clara Beranger. *Photog* Guy Wilky.

Cast: May McAvoy *(Lucy Stanley)*, Lois Wilson *(Mrs. Stanley)*, Elliott Dexter *(Prof. Charles Giddings)*, George Fawcett *(Hiram Sanborn)*, Robert Agnew *(Bob Stanley)*, Jane Keckley *(Mrs. Newcomb)*, Lillian Leighton *(Mrs. Peters)*, Taylor Graves *(Sydney Johnson)*, Anne Cornwall *(Mary Hedley)*.

Romantic comedy-drama. Source: A. E. Thomas, *Only 38; a Comedy in Three Acts* (New York, 1922). The death of her clergyman husband causes Mrs. Stanley, young mother of teenage twins, to change her style of life. She sends her children to a college where she accepts a position as a librarian, discards her old-fashioned clothes, and, to her straitlaced children's chagrin, dances with an admirer at a college hop. Mrs. Stanley sacrifices her own happiness and gives up her admirer for the sake of the children, but later the youngsters are shown that their selfish attitude threatens to ruin their mother's life. *Widows. Librarians. Twins. Motherhood. College life.*

Note: Press book states source as a story by Walter Pritchard Eaton.

THE ONLY WOMAN **F2.4035**

Norma Talmadge Productions. *Dist* First National Pictures. 26 Oct **1924** [c21 Oct 1924; LP20677]. Si; b&w. 35mm. 7 reels, 6,770 ft.

Pres by Joseph M. Schenck. *Dir* Sidney Olcott. *Story* C. Gardner Sullivan. *Photog* Tony Gaudio.

Cast: Norma Talmadge *(Helen Brinsley)*, Eugene O'Brien *(Rex Herrington)*, Edwards Davis *("Fighting Jerry" Herrington, Rex's father)*, Winter Hall *(William Brinsley)*, Matthew Betz *(Ole Hanson)*, E. H. Calvert *(Rodney Blake)*, Stella Di Lanti *(Bingo)*, Murdock MacQuarrie *(yacht captain)*, Rev. Neal Dodd *(minister)*, Brooks Benedict *(first officer)*, Charles O'Malley *(steward)*.

Drama. "Fighting Jerry" Herrington persuades Helen Brinsley to marry his wastrel son, Rex, by threatening financial and social disgrace for her father. Helen's married life is unhappy, but she sticks to her bargain. Promised a divorce by Mr. Herrington if she can make a man of Rex, Helen takes him on a sailing cruise away from liquor. They are shipwrecked, and Rex develops character. Helen declines freedom from Rex, realizing she has fallen in love with her husband. *Fatherhood. Marriage. Alcoholism. Manhood.*

Note: The Reverend Dodd was the minister of Hollywood's Little Church Around the Corner.

OPEN ALL NIGHT **F2.4036**

Famous Players–Lasky. *Dist* Paramount Pictures. 13 Oct **1924** [c19 Aug 1924; LP20504]. Si; b&w. 35mm. 6 reels, 5,671 ft.

Pres by Adolph Zukor, Jesse L. Lasky. *Dir* Paul Bern. *Scen* Willis Goldbeck. *Photog* Bert Glennon.

Cast: Viola Dana *(Thérèse Duverne)*, Jetta Goudal *(Lea)*, Adolphe Menjou *(Edmond Duverne)*, Raymond Griffith *(Igor)*, Maurice B. Flynn *(Petit Mathieu)*, Gale Henry *(Isabelle Fevre)*, Jack Giddings *(Von De Hoven)*, Charles Puffy *(Bibendum)*.

Farce. Source: Paul Morand, unidentified stories. Provoked by her mild-mannered husband and desiring a taste of dominance and discipline, Thérèse is presented to Petit Mathieu, a famous bicyclist at the Cirque d'Hiver in Paris, by her friend Isabelle. Meanwhile, her husband, Edmond, is charmed by Lea, but upon discovering his wife with the handsome cyclist, he develops a temper and is soon reconciled to her. *Bicyclists. Circus. Paris. Cirque d'Hiver.*

OPEN RANGE **F2.4037**

Paramount Famous Lasky Corp. 5 Nov **1927** [c5 Nov 1927; LP24630]. Si; b&w. 35mm. 6 reels, 5,599 ft.

Pres by Adolph Zukor, Jesse L. Lasky. *Dir* Clifford S. Smith. *Screenplay* John Stone, J. Walter Ruben. *Titl* Roy Briant. *Photog* Hal Rosson.

Cast: Betty Bronson *(Lucy Blake)*, Lane Chandler *(Tex Smith)*, Fred Kohler *(Sam Hardman)*, Bernard Siegel *(Brave Bear)*, Guy Oliver *(Jim Blake)*, Jim Corey *(Red)*, George Connors *(Sheriff Daley)*, Flash *(The Wonder Horse)*.

Western melodrama. Source: Zane Grey, "Open Range" (publication undetermined). Cowpuncher Tex Smith is intrigued by a poster portrait of Lucy Blake, who lives in the cattle settlement of Marco. At the same time, Brave Bear, an Indian chief, bitter at the encroachments of whites, conspires with Sam Hardman to steal the town's cattle during a rodeo, and Tex is mistakenly identified as one of the rustlers. At the rodeo he tries to impress Lucy by riding a bronco; and when she loses control of her team in the buggy race he rescues her, but he evades the sheriff's men. Red and Hardman plan to get Tex before the sheriff gets him; but Lucy, convinced of his innocence, hides him at her ranch. Tex discovers the gang's hideout and forces a confession from Hardman, who warns Brave Bear. When the Indians attack the town, Tex and his men stampede the cattle ahead of them, and Tex saves Lucy and her father from their burning shelter; Hardman falls on his own knife and dies. *Cowboys. Rustlers. Indians of North America. Rodeos. Buggy racing. Stampedes.*

THE OPEN SWITCH **F2.4038**

Larry Wheeler Productions. *Dist* Rayart Pictures. 30 Jun **1926.** Si; b&w. 35mm. 5 reels.

Dir J. P. McGowan.

Cast: Helen Holmes.

Melodrama(?). No information about the precise nature of this film has been found. *Railroads.*

THE OPEN TRAIL *see* **THE RED RIDER**

OPENED SHUTTERS **F2.4039**

Universal Film Manufacturing Co. Aug **1921** [c12 Aug 1921; LP16854]. Si; b&w. 35mm. 5 reels, 4,534 ft.

Dir William Worthington. *Scen* Doris Schroeder. *Story* Clara Louise Burnham. *Photog* George Barnes.

Cast: Joseph Swickard *(Sam Lacey)*, Edith Roberts *(Sylvia Lacey)*, Joe Singleton *(Nat Morris)*, Mai Wells *(Martha Lacey)*, Clark Comstock *(Judge Calvin Trent)*, Edward Burns *(John Dunham)*, Charles Clary *(Jacob Johnson)*, Floye Brown *(Mrs. Lem Foster)*, Nola Luxford *(Edna Derwent)*, Andrew Waldron *(Capt. Lem Foster)*, Lorraine Wieler *(Minty)*.

Light melodrama. When her father, an indigent artist, dies, Sylvia Lacey goes to live with her Aunt Martha and her uncle, Judge Trent, in New England, where she is unwanted and humiliated. Though she and John Dunham, her uncle's young law partner, fall in love, she believes he intends to marry the daughter of a wealthy neighbor. Gradually Sylvia's charm and patience change the attitudes of her relatives, and through her efforts several conflicting branches of the family are reconciled. After John rescues Sylvia during a storm, she realizes his love for her. *Uncles. Aunts. Judges. Lawyers. Family life. New England. Storms.*

THE OPENING NIGHT **F2.4040**

Columbia Pictures. 14 Nov **1927** [c13 Dec 1927; LP24754]. Si; b&w. 35mm. 6 reels, 5,524 ft.

Prod Harry Cohn. *Dir-Adapt-Cont* Edward H. Griffith. *Story* Albert Payson Terhune. *Photog* Ray June. *Art Dir* Robert E. Lee. *Asst Dir* Max Cohn.

Cast: Claire Windsor *(Carol Chandler)*, John Bowers *(Jimmy Keane)*, E. Alyn Warren *(Robert Chandler)*, Grace Goodall *(Gertrude Ames)*, Bobby Mack *(Aaron Hinkle)*, William Welsh *(fisherman)*.

Drama. When a theatrical producer, believed to be drowned during a storm at sea, turns up as a lonely, broken amnesiac 3 months later, he arrives just in time to see his wife marrying her leading man. Rather than mar their happiness, he keeps his identity secret and takes a job washing automobiles. When he sees his own Rolls-Royce pull up for service, as a final dramatic gesture he climbs into the car and, picking up the speaking aparatus, murmurs to the absent chauffeur, "Home." He then drops dead. *Actors. Theatrical producers. Theater. Amnesia. Automobile servicing. Rolls-Royce automobiles.*

ORCHIDS AND ERMINE **F2.4041**

John McCormick Productions. *Dist* First National Pictures. 6 Mar **1927** [c23 Feb 1927; LP23692]. Si; b&w. 35mm. 7 reels, 6,734 ft.

Pres by John McCormick. *Dir* Alfred Santell. *Story-Scen* Carey Wilson. *Titl* Ralph Spence. *Photog* George Folsey. *Comedy Construc* Mervyn LeRoy.

Cast: Colleen Moore *("Pink" Watson)*, Jack Mulhall *(Richard Tabor)*, Sam Hardy *(Hank)*, Gwen Lee *(Ermintrude)*, Alma Bennett *(The Vamp)*, Hedda Hopper *(The Modiste)*, Kate Price *(Mrs. McGinnis)*, Jed Prouty *(Leander Blom)*, Emily Fitzroy *(Mrs. Blom)*, Caroline Snowden *(Hattie)*, Yola D'Avril *(a telephone operator)*, Brooks Benedict *(The Chauffeur)*.

Romantic comedy. "Pink" Watson, a telephone operator at the Ritz Hotel, after disconcerting experiences with genuine and pseudo Midases, gives up her dreams of one day sporting honest orchids and ermine when Richard Tabor, an unassuming but wealthy young oilman, arrives. Disliking notoriety, Tabor compels Hank, his valet, to exchange identities with him, and Tabor proceeds to fall in love with Pink and she with him, while Hank succeeds in winning the heart of Ermintrude, the flower girl, who believes him to be the millionaire. After a series of amusing misadventures, each lands in jail. When all is resolved, Pink finds herself married to a real millionaire. *Telephone operators. Millionaires. Oilmen. Valets. Flower girls. Hotels. Millionaires. Mistaken identity.*

THE ORDEAL **F2.4042**

Famous Players–Lasky. *Dist* Paramount Pictures. 21 May **1922** [c2 May 1922; LP17817]. Si; b&w. 35mm. 5 reels, 4,592 ft.

Pres by Adolph Zukor. *Dir* Paul Powell. *Scen* Beulah Marie Dix. *Story* William Somerset Maugham. *Photog* Harry Perry.

Cast: Clarence Burton *(George Bruce)*, Agnes Ayres *(Sybil Bruce)*, Conrad Nagel *(Dr. Robert Acton)*, Edna Murphy *(Helen Crayshaw)*, Anne Schaefer *(Minnie)*, Eugene Corey *(Gene)*, Adele Farrington *(Madame St. Levis)*, Edward Martindel *(Sir Francis Maynard)*, Shannon Day *(Kitty)*, Claire Du Brey *(Elise)*.

Domestic melodrama. In order to provide for her crippled sister, Helen, and her brother, Geoffrey, Sybil marries George Bruce, a drunkard 20 years her senior. Bruce becomes jealous of Sybil's attentions to young physician Robert Acton, and when Bruce suffers a heart attack and calls for digitalis, Sybil allows the vial to break and he dies. She inherits her husband's fortune, which she retains on the condition that she does not remarry, and has Helen cured by an operation. Although Sybil and Acton fall in love, he refuses to commit himself without a legal marriage. Meanwhile, Helen, who has drifted into a dissolute life, is abducted and is about to be forced into a marriage when she is rescued from a fire by Sybil and Acton. Minnie, a family nurse, confesses in her dying moments that she poisoned Bruce. Realizing that her money has yielded more grief than happiness, Sybil consents to give up the fortune and marry Acton. *Physicians. Brother-sister relationship. Marriage. Wealth. Alcoholism. Inheritance. Murder.*

ORPHAN OF THE SAGE **F2.4043**

FBO Pictures. 23 Dec **1928** [c23 Dec 1928; LP25972]. Si; b&w. 35mm. 6 reels, 4,923 ft.

Dir Louis King. *Story-Cont* Oliver Drake. *Titl* Helen Gregg. *Photog* Nick Musuraca. *Film Ed* Jack Kitchen, Della King. *Asst Dir* Ken Marr.

Cast: Buzz Barton *(David [Red] Hepner)*, Frank Rice *(Hank Robbins)*, Tom Lingham *(Jeff Perkins)*, Annabelle Magnus *(Mary Jane Perkins)*, Bill Patton *(Nevada Naldene)*.

Western melodrama. When Red Hepner and his pal, Hank, an old Army scout, join a wagon train headed for Oregon, Nevada Naldene, another old fighter, quickly comes to resent their presence. Hank beats Naldene in a fight, and Naldene frames him for a robbery; Red and Hank are asked then to leave the wagon train. Red discovers Naldene talking to a band of hostile Indians and rides to warn the wagon train. There is a bitter fight between the settlers and the Indians, and Red must ride to Fort Hall for aid. The soldiers rout the Indians, and Red and Hank drift along. *Scouts—Frontier. Indians of North America. Settlers. Frameup. Wagon trains. Oregon. United States Army—Cavalry.*

ORPHAN SALLY **F2.4044**

New Superior Productions. *Dist* Lee-Bradford Corp. Dec **1922.** Si; b&w. 35mm. 5 reels, 4,703 ft.

Dir Edward L. Hemmer.

Cast: Sidney Mason, Flora Finch, Margaret Beecher, Maud Sylvester.

Comedy-drama. "Tells of the experience of an orphan who became tired of life on a farm and visited the Great White Way. Her money gives out and in desperation she sells her pets, three puppies, to a young man. By a curious twist of fate she gets a position as a servant in the young man's home. They eventually fall in love. An unprincipled bounder tries to take advantage of her. He learns that she is really the daughter of a great financier and tries to blackmail him. When things look blackest for Sally, her father comes forth and acknowledges her." *(Motion Picture News Booking Guide,* 4:81, Apr 1923.) *Orphans. Domestics. Financiers. Parentage. Blackmail. New York City. Dogs.*

ORPHANS OF THE GHETTO **F2.4045**

Dist Arista Film Corp. 22 Jun **1922** [New York State license]. Si; b&w. 35mm. 6 reels, 5,700 ft.

Cast: Arthur Donaldson *(pawnbroker)*.

Melodrama(?). No information about the precise nature of this film has been found. *Pawnbrokers. Ghettos.*

Note: May have been produced in 1914 by the Hanover Film Co.

ORPHANS OF THE STORM **F2.4046**

D. W. Griffith, Inc. *Dist* United Artists. 28 Dec **1921** [Boston premiere; c12 Dec 1921; LP18035]. Si; b&w. 35mm. 14 reels, 13,500 ft. [Released 30 Apr 1922. 12 reels, 12,000 ft.]

Pres by D. W. Griffith. *Prod-Dir* D. W. Griffith. *Scen* Marquis de Trolignac. *Photog* Hendrik Sartov, Paul Allen, G. W. Bitzer. *Asst Photog* Herbert Sutch. *Art Dir* Charles M. Kirk. *Set Dsgn* Edward Scholl. *Assembly* James Smith, Rose Smith. *Mus Arr* Louis F. Gottschalk, William Frederick Peters. *Tech Dir* Frank Wortman.

Cast: Lillian Gish *(Henriette Girard)*, Dorothy Gish *(Louise)*, Joseph Schildkraut *(Chevalier de Vaudrey)*, Frank Losee *(Count de Linières)*, Katherine Emmett *(Countess de Linières)*, Morgan Wallace *(Marquis de Praille)*, Lucille La Verne *(Mother Frochard)*, Sheldon Lewis *(Jacques Frochard)*, Frank Puglia *(Pierre Frochard)*, Creighton Hale *(Picard)*, Leslie King *(Jacques-Forget-Not)*, Monte Blue *(Danton)*, Sidney Herbert *(Robespierre)*, Lee Kohlmar *(King Louis XVI)*, Adolphe Lestina *(doctor)*, Kate Bruce *(Sister Geneviève)*, Flora Finch *(starving peasant)*, Louis Wolheim *(executioner)*, Kenny Delmar *(The Chevalier, as a boy)*, Herbert Sutch *(meat-carver at fête)*, James Smith, Rose Smith *(dancers)*.

Historical melodrama. Source: Adolphe Philippe Dennery and Eugène Cormon, *The Two Orphans* (adapted by N. Hart Jackson and Albert Marshman Palmer; New York, 1874). Louise is taken to Paris by her adopted sister, Henriette, to cure her blindness. Henriette is abducted by a marquis but is rescued by another aristocrat. Louise falls into the clutches of a beggar woman; Henriette and her lover are sentenced to the guillotine, but fortunately Danton comes to their rescue. *Sisters. Blindness. France—History—Revolution. Louis XVI (France). Maximilien Robespierre. Georges Jacques Danton.*

Note: Additional material for this film was apparently drawn from Charles Dickens' *A Tale of Two Cities* and Thomas Carlyle's *The French Revolution.* Working title: *The Two Orphans.*

THE OTHER KIND OF LOVE **F2.4047**

Phil Goldstone Productions. 28 Jun **1924** [New York State license]. Si; b&w. 35mm. 5 reels, 4,800 ft.

Dir Duke Worne. *Adapt-Scen* Jefferson Moffitt. *Photog* Roland Price.

Cast: William Fairbanks *(Adam Benton)*, Dorothy Revier *(Elsie Brent)*, Edith Yorke *(Mary Benton)*, Robert Keith *(George Benton)*, Rhea Mitchell *(The Chorus Girl)*.

Melodrama. Source: Buckleigh Fritz Oxford, "Thicker Than Water" (publication undetermined). George Benton returns home from college after having forged a check, and his older brother, Adam, sacrifices his life savings to save George from jail. George soon weds Elsie, an orphan who lives on the Benton farm; but shortly after the newlywed couple leaves the farm on their honeymoon a girl arrives on the farm and identifies herself as George's first wife. Adam rushes to the cabin where George and Elsie are staying, and the brothers fight. Adam is knocked senseless, and George, who thinks that he has killed his brother, rushes horrified from the cabin and falls over a cliff. Adam regains consciousness and rescues George. George reforms and makes good with his first wife; Adam marries Elsie. *Brothers. Orphans. Chorus girls. Forgery. Bigamy. Rural life.*

OTHER MEN'S DAUGHTERS **F2.4048**

Bryant Washburn Productions. *Dist* Grand-Asher Distributing Corp. Oct **1923** [c12 Oct 1923; LP19491]. Si; b&w. 35mm. 6 reels, 5,936 ft.

Prod-Dir Ben Wilson. *Scen* Frank Sullivan. *Story* Evelyn Campbell. *Photog* Edwin Linden, Jack Stevens.

Cast: Bryant Washburn *(Alaska Kid)*, Mabel Forrest *(Dorothy Kane)*, Kathleen Kirkham *(Lottie Bird)*, Wheeler Oakman *("Winnie")*, Sidney De Grey *(Mr. Kane)*, Martha Franklin *(Mrs. Kane)*, Roscoe Karns *(Hubert)*, William Turner *(President of the Board)*, Ben Wilson, Jr. *(page)*.

Melodrama. Dorothy Kane leaves home when she is censured by her father, a businessman, who is despotic with his family but very generous with his female companions in the city. Dorothy unwittingly becomes involved with his nightclub friends—Lottie, Trixie, and Alaska. At a dinner party attended by elderly men and young girls, Dorothy meets her father and decides to denounce him to Mrs. Kane, but later feels that it would grieve her already neglected mother too much. *Businessmen. Filial relations. Infidelity. Family life.*

THE OTHER SIDE **F2.4049**

Dist American Releasing Corp. Nov **1922.** Si; b&w. 35mm. 6 reels.

Dir Hugh Dierker.

Cast: Helen Lynch, Fritzi Brunette.

Melodrama(?). No information about the nature of this film has been found.

THE OTHER TOMORROW **F2.4050**

First National Pictures. 9 or 19 Feb **1930** [c15 Mar 1930; LP1157]. Sd (Vitaphone); b&w. 35mm. 7 reels, 5,800 ft. [Also si.]

Dir Lloyd Bacon. *Scen* Fred Myton. *Dial-Titl* James A. Starr. *Story* Octavus Roy Cohen. *Photog* Lee Garmes.

Cast: Billie Dove *(Edith Larrison)*, Kenneth Thompson *(Nort Larrison)*, Grant Withers *(Jim Carter)*, Frank Sheridan *(Dave Weaver)*, William Granger *(Drum Edge)*, Otto Hoffman *(Ted Journet)*, Scott Seaton *(Ed Conover)*.

Romantic drama. After a European honeymoon, Edith returns to her rural Georgia home and meets Jim Carter, her childhood sweetheart who still loves her, at a church social. When Nort, her husband, overhears Dave Weaver and Drum Edge discussing Edith's relationship with Jim, his vanity is hurt; but nevertheless she invites Jim to her birthday party against Nort's wishes. A quarrel ensues when Nort orders Jim not to attend. Chagrined by Nort's accusations, she leaves him and goes to her father; but she loses her way in a storm and accidentally stumbles onto Jim's house. Ted Journet, town gossip, comes upon Edith's car, and Nort learns through him that she spent the night in Jim's house. Nort draws up a divorce claim against his wife and vows to kill his rival, but Sheriff Weaver shoots him before he is able to kill Jim, who is reunited with Edith. *Rural life. Marriage. Gossip. Divorce. Infidelity. Revenge. Georgia.*

THE OTHER WOMAN **F2.4051**

J. L. Frothingham Productions. *Dist* W. W. Hodkinson Corp. Apr **1921.** Si; b&w. 35mm. 5 reels, 5,000 ft.

Dir Edward Sloman. *Photog* Tony Gaudio.

Cast: Jerome Patrick *(Langdon Kirven/John Gorham)*, Jane Novak *(Naomi Joyce)*, Helen Jerome Eddy *(Avery Kirven)*, William Conklin *(Spencer Ellis)*, Joseph J. Dowling *(Colonel Joyce)*, Frankie Lee *(Bobbie Kirven)*, Lincoln Palmer *(Charles Beattle)*, Kate Price *(housekeeper)*.

Melodrama. Source: Norah Davis, *The Other Woman* (New York, 1920). Langdon Kirven suffers from amnesia and has no recollection of his wife, children, or former business, having taken on another identity, that of John Gorham. After 5 years Spencer Ellis, Kirven's best friend, recognizes Kirven in the park; but when he approaches, he notices the difference in personality and assumes that it is a matter of close resemblance. Nevertheless, Ellis offers the man a job in another city. After 2 years Kirven reaches a prominent position, but when he becomes engaged to Ellis' cousin, Ellis returns to expose him as a former convict and as a married man. The shock jars his memory, and he returns to his family—but only temporarily, for he again becomes John Gorham and returns to Ellis' cousin, whom he marries. When his second wife has a child, Kirven's first wife, now aware of his sickness and his position, tells him it is best to give the other woman the protection of his name. *Businessmen. Dual personality. Amnesia. Bigamy.*

THE OTHER WOMAN'S STORY **F2.4052**

B. P. Schulberg Productions. 15 Nov **1925.** Si; b&w. 35mm. 6 reels, 6,080 ft.

Dir B. F. Stanley. *Scen* John Goodrich. *Story* Peggy Gaddis. *Photog* Gilbert Warrenton, Allen Siegler.

Cast: Alice Calhoun *(Mrs. Colby)*, Robert Frazer *(Colman Colby)*, Helen Lee Worthing *(Jean Prentiss)*, David Torrence *(judge)*, Riza Royce *(maid)*, Mahlon Hamilton *(Robert Marshall)*, Gertrude Short *(Gertie Van)*.

Melodrama. "Robert Marshall is found dead. Colman Colby is arrested for the murder. At the trial it develops that Mrs. Colby was divorcing her husband to marry Marshall, of whom he had always been jealous. It also comes out that Jean Prentiss, named as corespondent in the Colby case, was deeply in love with Colby, although totally innocent. All witnesses seeing the dead man at his home the night of the murder testify that he 'looked at the door behind him.' The jury goes out and brings in a verdict of guilty. Meantime Jean remembers a girl's face through the window at the Marshall funeral. Searching in the Rogues' Gallery she locates the girl. This underworld denizen, Gertie Van, offers evidence that convicts Mrs. Colby of the crime committed in a jealous rage. Colby and Jean are united." (*Exhibitor's Trade Review,* 31 Oct 1925, p34.) *Divorce. Murder. Infidelity. Trials. Funerals.*

OTHER WOMEN'S CLOTHES **F2.4053**

Hugo Ballin Productions. *Dist* W. W. Hodkinson Corp. 19 Feb **1922** [c24 Apr 1922; LP17786]. Si; b&w. 35mm. 6 reels, 5,600 ft.

Prod-Dir-Writ Hugo Ballin. *Photog* James R. Diamond.

Cast: Mabel Ballin *(Jacqueline Lee)*, Raymond Bloomer *(Barker Garrison,)*, Crauford Kent *(Rupert Lewis)*, May Kitson *(Mrs. Roger Montayne)*, William H. Strauss *(Joe Feinberg)*, Aggie La Field *(Bessie Horowitz)*, Rose Burdick *(Ellen Downe)*.

Society drama. Source: Ethel Donoher, "The Luxury Tax" (publication undetermined). Model Jacqueline Lee meets Barker Garrison, a wealthy bachelor. Scheming to give her a life of luxury, he invents an old lady who leaves her fortune to Jacqueline. At a party given by Jacqueline, Garrison's intoxicated friend Rupert Lewis—who knows of the scheme—confesses his love for Jacqueline; rejected, he proposes a toast to "the old lady in Rio de Janeiro ... Barker Garrison"; and discovering the truth, Jacqueline disappears. Meanwhile, Garrison travels over Europe in search of her, and later, in New York, while motoring, he sees a girl fall beneath the wheels of a car and finds her to be Jacqueline. When she recovers, he learns that she has become a famous actress under an assumed name. Perceiving that he loves her, she promises never to leave him. *Bachelors. Millionaires. Models. Actors. Luxury. Hoaxes. New York City.*

OTHER WOMEN'S HUSBANDS **F2.4054**

Warner Brothers Pictures. 17 Mar **1926** [c17 Mar 1926; LP22504]. Si; b&w. 35mm. 7 reels, 6,721 ft.

Dir Erle C. Kenton. *Adapt* Edward T. Lowe, Jr., Jack Wagner. *Story* Edward T. Lowe, Jr. *Photog* Charles Van Enger.

Cast: Monte Blue *(Dick Lambert)*, Marie Prevost *(Kay, his wife)*, Huntly Gordon *(Jack Harding, his friend and attorney)*, Phyllis Haver *(Roxana)*, Marjorie Gay *(Roxana's friend)*, John Patrick *(Dick's chum)*.

Comedy-drama. When his wife, Kay, goes out of town on a visit, Dick Lambert attends a party arranged by an old college friend, Jack Harding, with whom Kay has flirted on a previous dinner engagement; there he finds solace in the charms of Roxana, and he soon is making excuses to his wife for his frequent absences from home. Kay finally accepts an invitation from a handsome attorney—none other than Jack. Learning that Dick is attending a masked ball with Roxana, Kay attends in an identical costume; there Dick makes love to her, thinking she is his paramour. While Kay determines to obtain a divorce, Dick, weary of Roxana's vulgarity, longs for Kay. In the divorce court, Kay declares her love for Dick and cannot carry out the separation; Dick fights it out with Jack; the attorney decides to drop the case; and husband and wife are reunited. *Mistresses. Lawyers. Jealousy. Infidelity. Mistaken identity. Divorce.*

OUR BLUSHING BRIDES F2.4055

Metro-Goldwyn-Mayer Pictures. 19 Jul **1930** [c7 Jul 1930; LP1439]. Sd (Movietone); b&w. 35mm. 11 reels, 9,138 ft.

Dir Harry Beaumont. *Cont-Dial* Bess Meredyth, John Howard Lawson. *Titl* Helen Mainardi. *Story* Bess Meredyth. *Photog* Merritt B. Gerstad. *Art Dir* Cedric Gibbons. *Film Ed* George Hively, Harold Palmer. *Ballet Stgd by* Albertina Rasch. *Rec Engr* Russell Franks, Douglas Shearer. *Gowns* Adrian.

Cast: Joan Crawford *(Jerry)*, Anita Page *(Connie)*, Dorothy Sebastian *(Franky)*, Robert Montgomery *(Tony)*, Raymond Hackett *(David)*, John Miljan *(Martin)*, Hedda Hopper *(Mrs. Weaver)*, Albert Conti *(Monsieur Pantoise)*, Edward Brophy *(Joe Munsey)*, Robert E. O'Connor *(The Detective)*, Martha Sleeper *(Evelyn Woodforth)*, Mary Doran, Norma Drew, Wilda Mansfield, Gwen Lee, Catherine Moylan, Claire Dodd *(mannequins)*.

Society drama. Jerry, a model, Connie, a perfume salesclerk, and Francine, in linen sales, all work in a metropolitan department store. They also occupy the same dingy living quarters and have the same desire to replace them with luxury. Francine's opportunity comes in the person of Martin, a wealthy young man who frequents her department; Connie gets an apartment through David Jardine, son of the store owner; and Jerry reluctantly accepts the attentions of Tony, David's older brother, but when he fails to mention matrimony after taking her to his bachelor retreat, she drops him. Later, Martin is arrested as a thief and Francine is taken into custody with him, while Jerry learns that David plans to marry Evelyn, a society girl. On the eve of his wedding, Connie takes poison, though Jerry goes to the reception and brings back David, who sees her die happy. ... Jerry is rewarded, however, with a promise of marriage from Tony. *Salesclerks. Fashion models. Thieves. Department stores. Courtship. Luxury. Suicide.*

OUR DAILY BREAD *see* **CITY GIRL**

OUR DANCING DAUGHTERS F2.4056

Cosmopolitan Productions. *Dist* Metro-Goldwyn-Mayer Distributing Corp. 1 Sep **1928** [c1 Sep 1928; LP25605]. Sd eff & mus score (Movietone); b&w. 35mm. 9 reels, 7,652 ft.

Dir Harry Beaumont. *Story-Cont* Josephine Lovett. *Titl* Marian Ainslee, Ruth Cummings. *Photog* George Barnes. *Sets* Cedric Gibbons. *Film Ed* William Hamilton. *Song: "I Loved You Then As I Love You Now"* Ballard MacDonald, William Axt, David Mendoza. *Asst Dir* Harold S. Bucquet. *Wardrobe* David Cox.

Cast: Joan Crawford *(Diana Medford)*, John Mack Brown *(Ben Blaine)*, Nils Asther *(Norman)*, Dorothy Sebastian *(Beatrice)*, Anita Page *(Ann)*, Kathlyn Williams *(Ann's mother)*, Edward Nugent *(Freddie)*, Dorothy Cumming *(Diana's mother)*, Huntly Gordon *(Diana's father)*, Evelyn Hall *(Freddie's mother)*, Sam De Grasse *(Freddie's father)*.

Drama. Diana Medford, a vivacious, wide-eyed young girl devoted to Terpsichore and hip flasks, falls in love with Ben Blaine, the son of a millionaire. She is soon badly disappointed, however, for Ben marries Ann, a hard-drinking blonde pushed into marriage by an avaricious mother. Ann falls downstairs and kills herself, however, and Ben, free of his tempestuous bride, turns to Diana for love and consolation. *Flappers. Millionaires. Alcoholism. Courtship. Jazz life.*

OUR HOSPITALITY F2.4057

Joseph M. Schenck Productions. *Dist* Metro Pictures. 3 Nov **1923** [world premiere; released 19 Nov; c20 Nov 1923; LP19675]. Si; b&w. 35mm. 7 reels, 6,220 ft.

Dir Buster Keaton, John Blystone. *Story-Scen-Titl* Jean Havez, Joseph Mitchell, Clyde Bruckman. *Photog* Elgin Lessley, Gordon Jennings. *Art Dir* Fred Gabourie.

Cast: Buster Keaton *(William McKay)*, Natalie Talmadge *(Virginia Canfield)*, Buster Keaton, Jr. *(The Baby)*, Joseph Keaton *(Lem Doolittle)*, Kitty Bradbury *(Aunt Mary)*, Joe Roberts *(Joseph Canfield)*, Leonard Clapham *(James Canfield)*, Craig Ward *(Lee Canfield)*, Ralph Bushman *(Clayton Canfield)*, Edward Coxen *(John McKay)*, Jean Dumas *(Mrs. McKay)*, Monte Collins *(Rev. Benjamin Dorsey)*, James Duffy *(Sam Gardner)*.

Burlesque melodrama. Sole surviving son William McKay settles a family feud by marrying the rival feudist's daughter, Virginia Canfield. Before the wedding, city boy McKay attempts to escape the little Kentucky hamlet unobserved. When the Canfield men give chase, he hitches a ride on a pioneer railroad train, then is swept over a high falls. A floating log saves McKay, and he rescues Virginia when she follows the chase and falls in the water. *Feuds. Village life. Railroads. Kentucky.*

OUR LEADING CITIZEN F2.4058

Famous Players–Lasky. *Dist* Paramount Pictures. 14 Jun **1922** [c14 Jun 1922; LP17980]. Si; b&w. 35mm. 7 reels, 6,634 ft.

Pres by Adolph Zukor. *Dir* Alfred E. Green. *Scen* Waldemar Young. *Story-Adapt* George Ade. *Photog* L. Guy Wilky, William Marshall.

Cast: Thomas Meighan *(Daniel Bentley, a lawyer)*, Lois Wilson *(Katherine Fendle, his fiancée)*, William P. Carleton *(Oglesby Fendle, a capitalist)*, Theodore Roberts *(Col. Sam De Mott, a politician)*, Guy Oliver *(Cale Higginson, Dan's friend)*, Laurence Wheat *(J. Sylvester Dubley, a law student)*, James Neill *(Hon. Cyrus Blagdon, a Congressman)*, Lucien Littlefield *(The Editor)*, Charles Ogle *(The Judge)*, Tom Kennedy *(Boots)*, Sylvia Ashton *(Mrs. Brazey)*, Ethel Wales *(Eudora Mawdle)*.

Comedy-drama. At the outbreak of war, Dan Bentley, smalltown lawyer and celebrated fisherman, enlists and goes to France. There he meets Katherine Fendle, who is in Red Cross work. She is the sister of a wealthy citizen of his hometown. Dan distinguishes himself and is given a reception upon returning home. Katherine persuades him to run for Congress against Blagdon, the regular nominee and machine man; and Oglesby Fendle and Colonel De Mott offer to finance him if he agrees to protect their interests. Dan refuses, believing that Katherine has used him to further her brother's ends, and disappears from town. Blagdon sides with the schemers, but Katherine gets Dan back in the race; when he is elected, Dan goes to Washington with his new bride. *Lawyers. Brother-sister relationship. Smalltown life. Fishing. Politics. World War I. France. Red Cross. United States Congress.*

OUR MEXICAN NEIGHBORS F2.4059

Arthur P. Church–Margaret G. Church. c27 Dec **1922** [MP2226]. Si; b&w. 35mm. 5 reels.

Travelog. Although the first and last parts of this film include scenes of historical interest in various parts of Mexico, most of it depicts the life and customs of Mexico City. *Mexico. Mexico City.*

OUR MODERN MAIDENS F2.4060

Metro-Goldwyn-Mayer Pictures. 24 Aug **1929** [c12 Aug 1929; LP591]. Mus score & sd eff (Movietone); b&w. 35mm. 8 reels, 6,976 ft. [Also si.]

Dir Jack Conway. *Story-Cont* Josephine Lovett. *Titl* Marian Ainslee, Ruth Cummings. *Photog* Oliver Marsh. *Art Dir* Cedric Gibbons. *Film Ed* Sam S. Zimbalist. *Mus Score* William Axt. *Dance Dir* George Cunningham. *Gowns* Adrian.

Cast: Joan Crawford *(Billie)*, Rod La Rocque *(Abbott)*, Douglas Fairbanks, Jr. *(Gil)*, Anita Page *(Kentucky)*, Edward Nugent *(Reg)*, Josephine Dunn *(Ginger)*, Albert Gran *(B. Bickering Brown)*.

Drama. Billie Brown and Gil Jordan are two jazz age youngsters who get married. After Billie persuades a reluctant friend, Glenn Abbott, to get Gil a diplomatic post in Paris, she and Gil wed in elaborate style. All is well until Billie discovers Gil's affair with a girl named Kentucky. Giving them good wishes, she leaves her husband. Sometime later in France, she and Abbott meet again, are drawn to each other, and end the film hand in hand. *Jazz life. Infidelity. France. United States—Diplomatic and consular service.*

OUT ALL NIGHT (Universal-Jewel) F2.4061

Universal Pictures. 4 Sep **1927** [c22 Aug 1927; LP24333]. Si; b&w. 35mm. 6 reels, 6,170 ft.

Pres by Carl Laemmle. *Dir* William A. Seiter. *Cont* Harvey Thew. *Titl* Tom Reed. *Adapt* Marcel Perez, Charles Diltz. *Story* Gladys Lehman. *Photog* Arthur Todd.

Cast: Reginald Denny *(John Graham)*, Marian Nixon *(Molly O'Day)*, Wheeler Oakman *(Kerrigan)*, Dorothy Earle *(Rose)*, Dan Mason *(uncle)*, Alfred Allen *(captain)*, Robert Seiter *(purser)*, Ben Hendricks, Jr. *(Dr. Allen)*, Billy Franey *(taxi driver)*, Harry Tracey *(valet)*, Lionel Braham *(officer)*.

Farce. Wealthy young bachelor John Graham falls in love with Molly O'Day, a musical comedy star. They meet in the elevator of his apartment house and are forced to remain in it overnight because of a mechanical failure; when it is repaired the next morning, they head for the marriage license bureau. After the wedding, Molly discovers that her contract calls for a salary cut in case of marriage, so they decide to keep the marriage secret. When Molly sails for London, John boards the ship, posing as the ship surgeon; their attempts to see each other are constantly frustrated by the chief officer, who falls for Molly, and by her roommate, Rose Lundy. John is involved in numerous complications because of his ignorance of medicine. Meanwhile, Kerrigan, the show manager, proposes to Molly, and upon being told of her contract, he tears it to bits, while John, pursued by an irate crew, falls happily into her arms. *Actors. Physicians. Ship crews. Imposture. Mistaken identity. Contracts. Elevators. Ocean liners.*

Note: Working titles: *Completely at Sea* and *I'll Be There.*

OUT OF LUCK **F2.4062**

Universal Pictures. 23 Jul **1923** [New York premiere; released 5 Aug; c9 Jul 1923; LP19198]. Si; b&w. 35mm. 6 reels, 5,518 ft.

Pres by Carl Laemmle. *Dir-Story* Edward Sedgwick. *Scen* George C. Hull, Raymond L. Schrock. *Photog* Virgil Miller.

Cast: Hoot Gibson *(Sam Pertune)*, Laura La Plante *(Mae Day)*, Howard Truesdell *(Ezra Day)*, Elinor Hancock *(Aunt Edith Bristol)*, De Witt Jennings *(Captain Bristol)*, Freeman Wood *(Cyril La Mount)*, Jay Morley *(Boggs)*, Kansas Moehring *("Kid" Hogan)*, John Judd *("Pig" Hurley)*.

Comedy-drama. Believing he has committed murder, Sam Pertune, a simple westerner, enlists in the Navy, then cannot get released when he learns that his "victim" is alive. He becomes the butt of jokes—and then a hero when he saves the captain from a maniac. Invited to the captain's house, Pertune rescues him again and wins a promotion and a sweetheart, who turns out to be the captain's niece. *Sailors. Lunatics. Murder. United States Navy.*

Note: Working title *Superstition.*

OUT OF THE CHORUS **F2.4063**

Realart Pictures. Feb **1921** [c10 Feb 1921; LP16145]. Si; b&w. 35mm. 5 reels, 4,888 ft.

Dir Herbert Blache. *Scen* Coolidge Streeter. *Story* Harry Chandlee, William B. Laub. *Photog* Jacob A. Badaracco. *Asst Dir* Joseph Nadel.

Cast: Alice Brady *(Florence Maddis)*, Vernon Steel *(Ross Van Beekman)*, Charles Gerard *(Ned Ormsby)*, Emily Fitzroy *(Mrs. Van Beekman)*, Constance Berry *(Margaret Van Beekman)*, Edith Stockton *(Fola)*, Ben Probst *(Feinstein)*, Richard Carlyle *(Maddox)*.

Society melodrama. When dancer Florence Maddis marries Ross Van Beekman, son of an aristocratic New York family, her friends predict that the union will not be successful, but she manages to fit into the family circle and has no desire to return to Broadway. Her mother-in-law disapproves of her, however, and persuaded by Ned Ormsby, one of Flo's admirers, she arranges for Flo to appear flirtatious. When Ross suspects Flo of harboring Ormsby, he fires a pistol at her closet; and since Ormsby is found shot in his house, Ross confesses, believing himself guilty, while Flo returns to the Winter Palace. Ross is freed, however, when Maddox, an enemy of Ormsby's, confesses to the crime, and Flo is happily reunited with the family and Ross. *Dancers. Jealousy. Marriage. Winter Palace. New York City—Broadway.*

OUT OF THE CLOUDS **F2.4064**

Westart Pictures. 15 Jun **1921** [Brooklyn showing]. Si; b&w. 35mm. 5 reels.

Dir Leonard Franchon. *Writ* W. M. Smith. *Photog* A. H. Vallet.

Cast: Al Hart, Jack Mower, Robert Conville.

Western melodrama. No information about the precise nature of this film has been found.

OUT OF THE DEPTHS **F2.4065**

Art-O-Graph Productions. *Dist* Pioneer Film Corp. 16 Sep **1921** [trade review]. Si; b&w. 35mm. [Feature length assumed.]

Dir? (see note) Otis B. Thayer, Frank Reicher.

Cast: Violet Mersereau, Edmund Cobb.

Western melodrama. Two young engineers, developing irrigation for desert land, are attracted to the same girl. One of the men makes an unsuccessful attempt to do away with his coworker, who, as it turns out, is the girl's long-lost brother. *Engineers. Brother-sister relationship. Irrigation. Deserts.*

Note: Sources disagree in crediting direction.

OUT OF THE PAST **F2.4066**

Dallas M. Fitzgerald Productions. *Dist* Peerless Pictures. 26 Sep **1927.** Si; b&w. 35mm. 6 reels, 5,700 ft.

Dir Dallas M. Fitzgerald. *Cont* H. Tipton Steck. *Story* John S. Lopez. *Photog* Milton Moore.

Cast: Robert Frazer *(Beverley Carpenter)*, Mildred Harris *(Dora Prentiss)*, Ernest Wood *(Harold Nesbitt)*, Rose Tapley *(Mrs. Prentiss)*, Mario Marano *(Juan Sorrano)*, Joyzelle Joyner *(Saida)*, Harold Miller *(Capt. John Barrister)*, Byron Sage *(Beverly Carpenter, Jr.)*, William Clifford.

Melodrama. Grief-stricken at the death of her soldier lover, Dora Prentiss is persuaded to marry a financier whom she does not love. The marriage is not successful, and the husband departs for the South Seas, leaving a suicide note. While he enjoys something akin to an orgy amid dark-skinned dancers, the soldier reappears and brings happiness to the girl. The husband also returns, but he cannot bring himself to destroy his wife's obvious bliss and disappears. *Soldiers. Financiers. Marriage. Desertion. South Seas.*

OUT OF THE RUINS **F2.4067**

First National Pictures. 19 Aug **1928** [c17 Aug 1928; LP25538]. Si; b&w. 35mm. 7 reels, 6,100 ft.

Pres by Richard A. Rowland. *Prod* Henry Hobart. *Dir* John Francis Dillon. *Scen* Gerald C. Duffy. *Titl* Casey Robinson. *Photog* Ernest Haller. *Film Ed* Cyril Gardner.

Cast: Richard Barthelmess *(Lieut. Pierre Dumont)*, Robert Frazer *(Paul Gilbert)*, Marian Nixon *(Yvonne Gilbert)*, Emile Chautard *(Père Gilbert)*, Bodil Rosing *(Mère Gilbert)*, Eugene Pallette *(Volange)*, Rose Dione *(Mère Gourdain)*.

Drama. Source: Philip Hamilton Gibbs, *Out of the Ruins, and Other Little Novels* (London, 1927). While on leave in Paris during the World War, Pierre Dumont, an intrepid soldier, falls in love with Yvonne, the sister of Paul Gilbert, his comrade-in-arms. Forced to return to the lines, Pierre is tormented with desire for the girl, and during a lull in the fighting, he returns to Paris, where he and Yvonne are married. Pierre is later stricken by conscience and returns to his regiment; court-martialed as a deserter, he is placed before a firing squad. After the war, Yvonne is forced by her parents into a betrothal with a man she does not love; Pierre (whose comrades did not have the heart to kill him) returns to Paris and is reunited with Yvonne, whose father goes to Army Headquarters to report Pierre. His commandant, however, swayed by Paul's tender recital of the love between Pierre and Yvonne, declares Pierre to be officially dead, clearing the way for the couple's happiness. *Soldiers. Deserters—Military. Courts-martial. Brother-sister relationship. Friendship. World War I. Paris. France—Army.*

OUT OF THE SILENT NORTH **F2.4068**

Universal Film Manufacturing Co. 19 Jun **1922** [c12 Jun 1922; LP17952]. Si; b&w. 35mm. 5 reels, 4,211 ft.

Pres by Carl Laemmle. *Dir* William Worthington. *Scen* Wallace Clifton, George Hull. *Story* Harry Sinclair Drago, Joseph Noel. *Photog* Art Reeves.

Cast: Frank Mayo *(Pierre Baptiste)*, Barbara Bedford *(Marcette Vallois)*, Frank Leigh *(Ashleigh Nefferton)*, Harris Gordon *(Reginald Stannard)*, Christian J. Frank *(Pete Bellew)*, Frank Lanning *(Jean Cour)*, Louis Rivera *(Mattigami)*, Dick La Reno *("Lazy" Lester)*.

Northwest melodrama. At a remote Canadian trading post, Pierre Baptiste, a simple French Canadian, loves Marcette, the storekeeper's daughter. In midwinter, Stannard, a stranger from England, arrives in search of a gold claim and infatuates Marcette. Urged on by Nefferton, a supposed friend who plots to steal his claim, Stannard sets out on the eve of a storm; and Marcette, fearing for his safety, sends Pierre after him. He finds Stannard unconscious in the snow and saves him; Stannard then induces Pierre to work his claim with him, and during the summer they strike a rich gold vein. While Stannard is recuperating from an injury, Nefferton seeks to jump the claim, but Pierre discovers that Nefferton has incorrectly filed the location notice. In a race to the recorders's office, Pierre wins and also learns that he is still loved by Marcette. *French Canadians. English. Traders. Mine claims. Canadian Northwest. Documentation.*

OUT OF THE STORM **F2.4069**

Tiffany Productions. 10 Apr **1926** [c3 Apr 1926; LP22567]. Si; b&w. 35mm. 7 reels, 6,500 ft. [Copyrighted as 6 reels.]

Dir Louis J. Gasnier. *Scen* Lois Hutchinson, Leete Renick Brown. *Photog* George Meehan, Mack Stengler. *Film Ed* James C. McKay.

Cast: Jacqueline Logan *(Mary [Madge?] Lawrence)*, [Frederick] Tyrone Power *(Mr. Lawrence)*, Edmund Burns *(James Morton)*, Montagu Love *(Timothy Keith)*, Eddie Phillips *(Leonard Keith)*, George Fawcett *(Judge Meeman)*, Crawford Kent *(attorney for the defense)*, Jay Hunt *(justice of* *the peace)*, Joseph W. Girard *(The Warden)*, Leon Holmes *(Spec, office boy)*, Frona Hale *(aunt)*.

Melodrama. Source: Arthur Stringer, "The Travis Coup" (publication undetermined). When Leonard Keith, son of a famous publisher, is implicated in a chorus girl's suicide, he is protected by James Morton, assistant editor of his father's newspaper, although he and Leonard are rivals for the love of Mary Lawrence. Mary, who is in love with Jim, rejects her father's wish that she marry Leonard; and on the night that Morton plans to elope with Mary, Leonard entices her to a restaurant and forces a scene in which she slightly wounds him with a pistol. The pair elope as planned, but Leonard dies from blood poisoning, and Jim is arrested for his murder and convicted. Mary, who becomes ill from wandering in a storm, learns of Jim's predicament only on the day set for his execution; as he is being led to the death chamber, Mary, with the aid of Spec, an office boy, convinces the governor of Jim's innocence, and he is freed. *Editors. Publishers. Office boys. Chorus girls. Elopement. Murder. Capital punishment. Newspapers. Storms.*

OUT OF THE WEST **F2.4070**

R-C Pictures. *Dist* Film Booking Offices of America. 26 Sep or 10 Oct **1926** [c23 Aug 1926; LP23038]. Si; b&w. 35mm. 5 reels, 4,609 ft.

Pres by Joseph P. Kennedy. *Dir* Robert De Lacy. *Cont* Wyndham Gittens. *Story* Frederick Arthur Mindlin. *Photog* John Leezer. *Asst Dir* John Burch.

Cast: Tom Tyler *(Tom Hanley)*, Bernice Welch *(Bernice O'Connor)*, L. J. O'Connor *(Jim Rollins)*, Ethan Laidlaw *(Bide Goodrich)*, Alfred Hewston *(John O'Connor)*, Frankie Darro *(Frankie)*, Gertrude Claire *("Grannie" Hanley)*, Barney Furey *(a scout)*.

Western melodrama. John O'Connor and Jim Rollins, rival ranchmen, each has a baseball team, though Rollins' usually wins because O'Connor's foreman and pitcher, Bide Goodrich, is paid by Rollins to throw the game. When Tom Hanley and his grandmother settle on O'Connor's ranch, the boss discovers that he is a good pitcher; and Rollins, who has bet heavily on the Fourth of July game, plots to eliminate Tom. While riding with O'Connor's daughter, Bernice, Tom is roped and captured but overcomes his attacker; he makes friends with Frankie, the O'Connor mascot, and his pup, Sitting Bull. On the night of a dance Tom is kidnaped and taken to a cave, but through Frankie's vigilance he is freed and races to the game in time to win it with a homerun. Goodrich kidnaps Bernice from the ranch, but Tom pursues and overcomes the kidnaper; later, he refuses an offer to play in big league and is happily united with Bernice. *Ranchers. Ranch foremen. Grandmothers. Baseball. Courtship. Kidnaping. Fourth of July. Dogs.*

OUT WITH THE TIDE **F2.4071**

Peerless Pictures. 1 or 22 Jun **1928.** Si; b&w. 35mm. 6 reels, 5,700 ft.

Dir Charles Hutchison. *Scen* Elaine Towne. *Titl* Paul Perez. *Story* John C. Brownell, G. Marion Burton. *Photog* Leon Shamroy. *Film Ed* Paul Perez.

Cast: Dorothy Dwan *(Joan Renshaw)*, Cullen Landis *(John Templeton)*, Crauford Kent *(Ralph Kennedy)*, Mitchell Lewis *(Captain Lund)*, Ernest Hilliard *(Snake Doyle)*, Sojin *(Chee Chee)*, James Aubrey *(Jimmy)*, Arthur Thalasso *(Clancey)*, Etta Lee, Harry Semels, Charles Alexandra.

Melodrama. Newspaper reporter John Templeton is suspected of being "The Snake," the murderer of a banker who is the father of the reporter's sweetheart, Joan Renshaw. The reporter escapes from the police and—with the girl—trails "The Snake" to Shanghai, where they lure him into confessing that he was hired by the banker's partner. *Reporters. Bankers. Hired killers. Murder. Shanghai.*

OUTCAST **F2.4072**

Famous Players–Lasky. *Dist* Paramount Pictures. ca3 Dec **1922** [New York premiere; released 11 Dec; c12 Dec 1922; LP18502]. Si; b&w. 35mm. 7 reels, 7,309 ft.

Dir Chet Withey. *Scen* Josephine Lovett.

Cast: Elsie Ferguson *(Miriam)*, David Powell *(Geoffrey Sherwood)*, William David *(Tony Hewlitt)*, Mary MacLaren *(Valentine Moreland)*, Charles Wellesley *(John Moreland)*, Teddy Sampson *(Nellie Essex)*, William Powell *(De Valle)*.

Melodrama. Source: Hubert Henry Davies, *Outcast* (New York opening: 2 Nov 1914). Miriam is homeless, half-starved, and desperate when she meets Geoffrey Sherwood, who is disconsolate over the loss of his sweetheart, Valentine, to another man. He helps Miriam, they fall in love, and Miriam saves Valentine (who has decided to return to Geoffrey) from the wrath of her husband. But Valentine rejoins her husband, while Miriam, thinking herself to be second in Geoffrey's affections, departs for South America but is pursued and prevented from suicide by Geoffrey. *Infidelity. Suicide.*

OUTCAST **F2.4073**

First National Pictures. 11 Nov **1928** [c7 Nov 1928; LP25806]. Mus score & sd eff (Vitaphone); b&w. 35mm. 8 reels, 6,854 ft. [Also si; 6,622 ft.]

Pres by Richard A. Rowland. *Dir* William A. Seiter. *Scen* Agnes Christine Johnston. *Titl* Forrest Halsey, Gene Towne. *Photog* John Seitz. *Film Ed* Hugh Bennett.

Cast: Corinne Griffith *(Miriam)*, James Ford *(Tony)*, Edmund Lowe *(Geoffrey)*, Huntley Gordon *(Hugh)*, Kathryn Carver *(Valentine)*, Louise Fazenda *(Mable)*, Claude King *(Moreland)*, Sam Hardy *(Jack)*, Patsy O'Byrne *(Mrs. O'Brien)*, Lee Moran *(Fred)*.

Drama. Source: Hubert Henry Davies, *Outcast* (New York opening: 2 Nov 1914). Miriam, a streetwalker, is evicted from her San Francisco boardinghouse and, down to her last $3, meets Geoffrey, an intoxicated society fellow trying to forget a broken heart. Geoffrey likes Miriam and, on a whim, takes her to the church where his lost love, Valentine, is being married to wealthy Moreland. Geoffrey becomes greatly attached to Miriam and rents her an apartment. Miriam falls deeply in love with him and becomes desperate when the heartless Valentine vamps her way back into his life. Miriam attempts to return to the streets only to discover that, deeply in love with someone for the first time in her life, she cannot give herself to another man. Miriam then contrives to show Geoffrey that Valentine is a schemer who loves only money, and Geoffrey, come at last to his senses, takes Miriam in his arms. *Prostitutes. Socialites. Vamps. Boardinghouses. San Francisco.*

OUTCAST SOULS **F2.4074**

Sterling Pictures. 24 Jan **1928** [New York premiere; c22 Dec 1927; LP24790]. Si; b&w. 35mm. 6 reels, 4,866 ft.

Supv Joe Rock. *Dir* Louis Chaudet. *Scen* Jean Plannette. *Titl* H. Tipton Steck. *Adapt-Story* Norman Houston. *Photog* Herbert Kirkpatrick. *Film Ed* H. Tipton Steck. *Mus Cues* Michael Hoffman.

Cast: Priscilla Bonner *(Alice Davis)*, Charles Delaney *(Charles Turner)*, Ralph Lewis *(John Turner)*, Lucy Beaumont *(Mrs. Mary Davis)*, Tom O'Brien *(Officer)*.

Melodrama. Source: John Peter Toohey, "On the Back Seat," in *Collier's* (76:13–14, 12 Sep 1925). Alice Davis and Charles Turner are arrested for petting in an automobile and marry on impulse. When Alice's mother comes to live with them, she quickly sees that she is not wanted, and she finds a job soliciting for a bus touring company. In the meantime Charles's father, having sold all his property, arrives in town to live with his son and daughter-in-law. He also finds living with his children disagreeable, leaves the house, and accidentally meets Mrs. Davis. They fall in love and decide to announce their engagement, but Charles is arrested for embezzling company funds. At first reluctant to help his son, Mr. Turner is persuaded by Mrs. Davis to give up his life's savings to save Charles, and both couples are happily reunited. *Mothers-in-law. Fathers-in-law. Marriage. Embezzlement. Tourist agencies.*

THE OUTLAW DOG **F2.4075**

R-C Pictures. *Dist* Film Booking Offices of America. 22 May **1927** [c16 Apr 1927; LP23874]. Si; b&w. 35mm. 5 reels, 4,727 ft.

Pres by Joseph P. Kennedy. *Dir* J. P. McGowan. *Cont* F. A. E. Pine. *Story* Ewart Adamson. *Photog* Joe Walker. *Asst Dir* Mack V. Wright.

Cast: Ranger *(himself, a dog)*, Helen Foster *(Helen Meadows)*, Rex Lease *(Bill Brady)*, Alfred Allen *(Henry Jordan)*, Harry Tenbrook *(Mike)*, Bruce Gordon *(Ed)*, Spencer Bell *("Snowball" Black)*, Vic Allen *(sheriff)*.

Melodrama. Ranger, a police dog belonging to Henry Jordan, is accused of attacking his owner, who has been rendered speechless. Ranger takes refuge with Bill Brady, a lonely telegraph operator at Swift Bend, and helps ward off two hoboes who try to steal the payroll. Helen Meadows, Bill's sweetheart, discovers the dog's identity, but Bill refuses to surrender him. Brady and Ranger rescue Helen from the hoboes, who dynamite a nearby bridge, and Ranger succeeds in stopping the train at the crucial moment. Cleared by a statement from Jordan, Ranger is given to Helen and Bill as a wedding present. *Telegraph operators. Hoboes. Thieves. Mutes. Railroads. Dogs.*

THE OUTLAW EXPRESS **F2.4076**

Leo Maloney Productions. *Dist* Pathé Exchange. 14 Nov **1926** [c22 Oct 1926; LU23251]. Si; b&w. 35mm. 6 reels, 5,479 ft.

Dir Leo D. Maloney. *Story-Scen* Ford I. Beebe. *Photog* Harry Cooper.

Cast: Leo Maloney *(Miles Wayburn)*, Joan Renee *(Ann Townsend)*, Melbourne MacDowell *(sheriff)*, Albert Hart *(Carl Larson)*, Henry Otto *(John Mills)*, Paul Hurst *(secretary)*, Bud Osborne *("Blackie" Lewis)*, Evelyn Thatcher *(Ma Hemstetter)*, Nelson McDowell *("Chaw" Egan)*, Fred Burns *("Borax" Jones)*, Frank Ellis *(Scott)*.

Western melodrama. When one of its prize operators is killed by stagecoach robbers, Wells Fargo & Co. details Miles Wayburn to Cougar Pass to investigate. En route, he meets Ann Townsend on the coach and learns that she is the daughter of a sheriff who is suspected of being the bandit leader. Wayburn also learns that many of the local citizens share his suspicions of the sheriff, but when he receives a warning to leave town he deduces that the note was written by Larson, the express company agent. Wayburn finds himself accused and pursued by vigilantes, but he captures the robbers and proves the agent's guilt. *Sheriffs. Vigilantes. Bandits. Stagecoach robberies. Express service. Wells Fargo & Co.*.

OUTLAWED **F2.4077**

Sylvanite Productions. *Dist* Pioneer Pictures. 21 May **1921** [trade review]. Si; b&w. 35mm. 5 reels.

Dir-Writ Alvin J. Neitz.

Cast: Carlyn Wagner *(Barbara Benton)*, Bill Patton *(Bob Fleming)*, Buck Connors *(Bud Knowles)*, Joseph Rickson *(Tom Benton)*, Lee Pate *(John Cortwright)*, Pop Kennard *(Howard Gordon)*, Steve Clemento *(Frank Kayner)*, George Sewards *(Dick May)*, Edward Burns *("Sophy" Robbin)*.

Western melodrama. Bob Fleming, cowboy and U. S. marshal, is racing a train on horseback. From the train pretty Barbara Benton attempts to take a photograph of him, but as she leans forward her hat blows out the window. Bob catches the hat and leaps onto the train, but he is stopped by a porter. Bob pulls his gun in order to make the man step aside. The passengers, seeing this action, assume it to be a holdup and deposit their valuables in the hat. Arriving at the ranch, Barbara learns that Bob works there as a hand. The sheriff, who is also attracted to Barbara, arrests Bob as a cattle thief. Barbara, learning that the sheriff and her father are the leaders of a group of thieves, is forced to testify falsely that Bob is a train robber, and he is sentenced to be hanged. She herself is taken by the sheriff as hostage. But Bob escapes, forms a posse, kills the sheriff, and frees Barbara. *United States marshals. Sheriffs. Cowboys. Ranchers. Posses. Train robberies. Capital punishment.*

OUTLAWED **F2.4078**

Dist Krelbar Pictures, Collwyn Pictures. 17 Apr **1928** [New York State license]. Si; b&w. 35mm. 5 reels.

Cast: Al Hoxie.

Western melodrama(?). No information about the nature of this film has been found.

Note: May have been produced in 1926 by Anchor Film Distributors.

OUTLAWED **F2.4079**

FBO Pictures. 21 Jan **1929** [c7 Jan 1929; LP25975]. Si; b&w. 35mm. 7 reels, 6,057 ft.

Dir Eugene Forde. *Story-Cont* George W. Pyper. *Titl* Helen Gregg. *Photog* Norman Devol. *Film Ed* Henry Webber. *Asst Dir* James Dugan.

Cast: Tom Mix *(Tom Manning)*, Sally Blane *(Anne)*, Frank M. Clark *(Seth)*, Al Smith *(Dervish)*, Ethan Laidlaw *(McCasky)*, Barney Furey *(Sagebrush)*, Al Ferguson *(sheriff)*.

Western melodrama. Tom Manning, unjustly arrested for murder and robbery, escapes from the sheriff and rides to the camp of his friend, Sagebrush, who shoots the manacles from his wrists. The next day, Tom saves Seth Jenkins and his daughter, Anne, from a stampeding herd of wild horses. Tom later captures Wolf Dervish, the leader of the outlaw gang, and proves himself to be innocent of the unjust charges against him. Tom and Anne fall in love. *Sheriffs. Outlaws. Murder. Robbery. Injustice. Stampedes.*

THE OUTLAW'S DAUGHTER (Blue Streak Western) **F2.4080**

Universal Pictures. 20 Sep **1925** [c15 Aug 1925; LP21730]. Si; b&w. 35mm. 5 reels, 4,423 ft.

Dir John B. O'Brien. *Story-Cont* Harold Shumate. *Photog* Ben Kline.

Cast: Josie Sedgwick *(Flora Dale)*, Edward Hearne *(Jim King)*, Robert Walker *(Slim Cole)*, Jack Gavin *(Steven Dale)*, Harry Todd *(bookkeeper)*, Ben Corbett *(Bill)*, Bob Burns *(sheriff)*.

Western melodrama. Slim Cole, a notorious outlaw, shoots at Jim King, missing him but wounding Flora Dale in the arm. Jim takes care of the injured girl, who, when she recovers, goes to work in his office. During a fight between miners and bandits at the King mine, Flora saves Jim's life, toppling Cole to his death from an aerial ore bucket. *Outlaws. Miners. Mines.*

OUTLAWS OF RED RIVER **F2.4081**

Fox Film Corp. 8 May **1927** [c17 Aug 1927; LP23892]. Si; b&w. 35mm. 6 reels, 5,327 ft.

Pres by William Fox. *Dir* Lewis Seiler. *Scen* Harold Shumate. *Titl* Malcolm Stuart Boylan. *Story* Gerald Beaumont. *Photog* Dan Clark. *Asst Dir* Wynn Mace.

Cast—Prolog: Lee Shumway *(Mr. Torrence)*, Ellen Woonston *(Mrs. Torrence)*, Jimmy Downs *(Tom Morley)*, Virginia Marshall *(Mary, as a child)*.

Cast—Main Story: Tom Mix *(Tom Morley)*, Marjorie Daw *(Mary Torrence)*, Arthur Clayton *(Sam Hardwick)*, William Conklin *(Captain Dunning)*, Duke Lee *(Dick Williams)*, Francis McDonald *(Ben Tanner)*.

Western melodrama. Tom, a fighting ace of the Texas Rangers, continually searches for the bandit leader who killed his parents during his childhood. In trailing a notorious gang of stagecoach robbers, Tom poses as one of the bandits; and though recognized by the leader, he gains access to the bandits' lair and learns that a girl, Mary Torrence, identified as the leader's daughter, is an orphan by the same circumstances that deprived him of his parents. Together they fight a doublecrossing bandit, and with the help of other rangers the gang's stockade is destroyed by an armored coach and the girl is rescued. *Texas Rangers. Bandits. Orphans. Stagecoach robberies. Murder.*

Note: Some sources render the heroine's character name as Lola Torrence.

OUTLAWS OF THE SEA **F2.4082**

John Brunton. *Dist* American Releasing Corp. ca30 Mar **1923**. Si; b&w. 35mm. 5 reels, 5,355 ft.

Dir-Writ Jack Okey. *Titl* William B. Laub. *Photog* Paul Allen.

Cast: Pierre Gendron *(Robert Graham)*, Marguerite Courtot *(Polly Grimshaw)*, Gordon Standing *(Leonard Craven)*, Herbert Pattee *(Capt. Abel Grimshaw)*.

Melodrama. Polly Grimshaw and her father, Capt. Abel Grimshaw, unwittingly become involved in a liquor-smuggling operation led by Leonard Craven, owner of the boat Grimshaw pilots around the coast of Florida. Polly's sweetheart, Robert Graham, commander of a revenue cutter, discovers their involvement when they subject themselves to his prosecution. A trial ensues and the captain is cleared. *Revenue agents. Filial relations. Prohibition. Smuggling. Florida.*

OUTLAW'S PARADISE **F2.4083**

Bud Barsky Productions. *Dist* Wild West Pictures. Mar **1927**. Si; b&w. 35mm. 5 reels, 4,800 ft.

Cast: Al Hoxie.

Western melodrama(?). No information about the nature of this film has been found.

OUTSIDE THE LAW (Universal-Jewel) **F2.4084**

Universal Film Manufacturing Co. Jan **1921** [c25 Jan 1921; LP16049]. Si; b&w. 35mm. 8 reels, 8,000 ft.

Pres by Carl Laemmle. *Dir-Story* Tod Browning. *Scen* Lucien Hubbard, Tod Browning. *Photog* William Fildew.

Cast: Priscilla Dean *(Molly Madden [Silky Moll])*, Ralph Lewis *("Silent" Madden)*, Lon Chaney *("Black Mike" Sylva/Ah Wing)*, Wheeler Oakman *("Dapper Bill" Ballard)*, E. A. Warren *(Chang Lo)*, Stanley Goethals *("That Kid")*, Melbourne MacDowell *(Morgan Spencer)*, Wilton Taylor *(inspector)*.

Crook melodrama. "Silent" Madden, a crook, and his daughter, Molly, are persuaded to reform by Chang Lo, a Confucian, but a frameup by gang leader "Black Mike" sends Madden to prison. Molly joins Sylva's gang, agreeing to aid in a jewel robbery, but learning that she likewise is to be framed, she and "Dapper Bill" abscond with the jewels. In a battle with the gang, Black Mike is killed and Molly and Bill are captured by the police; Chang Lo gains their release, however, by returning the stolen jewels. *Criminals—Rehabilitation. Confucians. Chinese. Gangs. Frameup. San Francisco—Chinatown.*

Note: Reissued caMay 1926. A review indicated the film was "re-cut and re-edited," but there is no apparent difference in length or story line.

OUTSIDE THE LAW (Universal Special) **F2.4085**

Universal Pictures. 18 Sep **1930** [c2 Aug 1930; LP1517]. Sd (Movietone); b&w. 35mm. 9 reels, 7,116 ft.

Pres by Carl Laemmle. *Assoc Prod* E. M. Asher. *Dir* Tod Browning. *Screenplay* Tod Browning, Garrett Fort. *Photog* Roy Overbaugh. *Art Dir* William R. Schmidt. *Film Ed* Milton Carruth. *Synchronization & Score* David Broekman. *Rec Engr* C. Roy Hunter. *Sd Tech* William W. Hedgecock.

Cast: Mary Nolan *(Connie)*, Edward G. Robinson *(Cobra)*, Owen Moore *("Fingers" O'Dell)*, Edwin Sturgis *(Jake)*, John George *(Humpy)*, Delmar Watson *(The Kid)*, De Witt Jennings *(police captain)*, Rockliffe Fellowes *(Officer O'Reilly)*, Frank Burke *(district attorney)*, Sidney Bracy *(assistant)*.

Crime melodrama. Cobra Collins, a gang leader, demands a 50-50 cut in the return from a bank robbery planned by "Fingers" O'Dell. Connie, in league with Fingers, makes the acquaintance of Cobra to throw him off the trail, but Fingers carries out the robbery and, with Connie, hides in an apartment. They make friends with a 4-year-old child only to learn that his father is a police captain living next door. Cobra discovers the location of their hideout and makes a call just before the police captain arrives; and in an exchange of gunfire, the policeman and both Cobra and Fingers are wounded critically. While Connie calls a doctor, Cobra searches frantically for his share of the money and dies trying to escape. When Connie and Fingers are brought to trial, they are given light sentences for having saved the life of the wounded officer. *Gangs. Children. Police. Bank robberies.*

THE OUTSIDE WOMAN **F2.4086**

Realart Pictures. Feb **1921** [c8 Feb 1921; LP16127]. Si; b&w. 35mm. 5 reels, 4,225 ft.

Scen Douglas Bronston. *Photog* Paul Perry. *Art Dir? (see note)* Una Hopkins.

Cast: Wanda Hawley *(Dorothy Ralston)*, Clyde Fillmore *(Dr. Frederick Ralston)*, Sidney Bracey *(Mr. Cambridge)*, Rosita Marstini *(Mrs. Cambridge)*, Misao Seki *(Togo)*, Thena Jasper *(Gussie)*, Mary Winston *(Mrs. Trent)*, Jacob Abrams *(Curator)*.

Comedy. Source: Philip Bartholomae and Paul B. Sipe, *All Night Long* (a play; production undetermined). Newlywed Dorothy Ralston exchanges an Aztec idol belonging to her husband for a peddler's silk shawl, and Cambridge, an artist and her neighbor, realizes the idol's value and buys it from the peddler. When her husband informs her that the statue is a rare objet d'art and she learns of its new owner, Dorothy slips up the fire escape to retrieve it and hides from the artist, who happens to be knocked unconscious by a jujitsu throw of his Japanese servant. She revives him and buys back the idol for a kiss. The arrival of Dr. Ralston, the irate wife of the artist, and the police provides a general mixup, which is followed by a happy denouement. *Brides. Artists. Japanese. Art. Jujitsu.*

Note: No definite credit for direction has been established for this film. *Variety* notes that Miss Hopkins was involved in the production.

THE OUTSIDER **F2.4087**

Fox Film Corp. 17 Jan **1926** [c17 Jan 1926; LP22334]. Si; b&w. 35mm. 6 reels, 5,424 ft.

Pres by William Fox. *Dir* Rowland V. Lee. *Adapt* Robert N. Lee. *Photog* G. O. Post. *Asst Dir* Daniel Keefe.

Cast: Jacqueline Logan *(Leontine Sturdee)*, Lou Tellegen *(Anton Ragatzy)*, Walter Pidgeon *(Basil Owen)*, Roy Atwell *(Jerry Sidon)*, Charles Lane *(Sir Jasper Sturdee)*, Joan Standing *(Pritchard)*, Gibson Gowland *(Shadow)*, Bertram Marburgh *(Dr. Talley)*, Crauford Kent *(Dr. Ladd)*, Louis Payne *(Dr. Helmore)*.

Drama. Source: Dorothy Brandon, *The Outsider; a Play in Three Acts* (London, 1926). Leontine Sturdee, an aristocratic English dancer, goes to a Gypsy camp in Hungary to learn some native dances and there meets Ragatzy, a mystic who has effected many impressive cures. Leontine sustains an injury so serious that she is unable to walk, but she refuses the help of Ragatzy, whom she considers a fraud. Leontine returns to England, and leading British surgeons pronounce her a hopeless cripple. Ragatzy comes to England and begs Leontine (whom he has come to love) for a chance to cure her. She consents, but at first he can do nothing for her. As he is about to leave her, however, Leontine realizes that she loves Ragatzy and walks to him. *Dancers. Mystics. Surgeons. Gypsies. Faith cure. England. Hungary.*

OUTWARD BOUND **F2.4088**

Warner Brothers Pictures. 29 Nov **1930** [c31 Oct 1930; LP1695]. Sd (Vitaphone); b&w. 35mm. 10 reels, 7,568 ft.

Dir Robert Milton. *Adapt* J. Grubb Alexander. *Photog* Hal Mohr. *Film Ed* Ralph Dawson. *Sd* Glenn E. Rominger.

Cast: Leslie Howard *(Tom Prior)*, Douglas Fairbanks, Jr. *(Henry)*, Helen Chandler *(Ann)*, Beryl Mercer *(Mrs. Midget)*, Alec B. Francis *(Scrubby)*, Alison Skipworth *(Mrs. Cliveden-Banks)*, Lionel Watts *(Rev. William Duke)*, Montagu Love *(Mr. Lingley)*, Dudley Digges *(Thompson, the Examiner)*.

Allegorical drama. Source: Sutton Vane, *Outward Bound* (New York opening: 7 Jan 1924). Ann and Henry, a young English couple, facing an impossible love affair, find they cannot live without each other. They board an ocean liner through a dense fog, where they encounter Tom Prior, a prodigal son; his mother, Mrs. Midget, whose identity the son does not know; Mrs. Cliveden-Banks, an affected socialite; a clergyman who is keen about his missionary work in the London slums; Mr. Lingley, a captain of industry; and the steward, Scrubby. Gradually, Tom realizes that the passengers are unaware of their destinations with the exception of the lovers, and that they are all "half-way" persons who have committed suicide. Arriving at their destination, they are all judged by the Examiner. On the return voyage, Henry is saved from asphyxiation by his dog breaking a window pane; he returns to the phantom ship long enough to retrieve Ann, and together they are rescued by an ambulance. *Socialites. Clergymen. Charwomen. Immortality. Suicide. Ocean liners. England. Dreams. Dogs.*

OUTWITTED **F2.4089**

Independent Pictures. ca21 Jan **1925** [New York showing; c1 Jul 1925; LP21631]. Si; b&w. 35mm. 5 reels.

Pres by Jesse J. Goldburg. *Dir-Writ* J. P. McGowan. *Photog* Walter Griffin. *Film Ed* Betty Davis.

Cast: Helen Holmes *(Helen Kinney)*, William Desmond *(Jack Blaisdel)*, J. P. McGowan *(Tiger McGuire)*, Grace Cunard *(Lucy Carlisle)*, Alec Francis *(John Kinney)*, Emily Fitzroy *(Meg)*.

Society melodrama. Tiger McGuire, the head of a gang of counterfeiters, is captured by Jack Blaisdel, a Treasury agent, and sentenced to 20 years in jail. On the way to prison, Tiger escapes and rejoins his old gang, vowing to get even with Jack. John Kinney, the Assistant Secretary of the Treasury, suspends Jack from the department for being away from his normal duties but on the plea of his daughter, Helen (who is in love with Jack), gives him 48 hours to bring Tiger in. During a dance at her home, Helen is kidnaped by Tiger, who takes her aboard the yacht he uses as a hideout. Jack discovers the whereabouts of the craft and outwits the gang, rescuing Helen and recapturing Tiger. *Counterfeiters. T-Men. United States—Treasury Department.*

OVER THE BORDER **F2.4090**

Famous Players–Lasky. 4 Jun **1922** [c6 Jun 1922; LP17964]. Si; b&w. 35mm. 7 reels, 6,837 ft.

Pres by Adolph Zukor. *Dir* Penrhyn Stanlaws. *Adapt* Albert Shelby Le Vino. *Photog* Paul Perry.

Cast: Betty Compson *(Jen Galbraith)*, Tom Moore *(Sergeant Flaherty)*, J. Farrell MacDonald *(Peter Galbraith)*, Casson Ferguson *(Val Galbraith)*, Sidney D'Albrook *(Snow Devil)*, L. C. Shumway *(Corporal Byng)*, Jean De Briac *(Pretty Pierre)*, Edward J. Brady *(Inspector Jules)*, Joe Ray *(Borden)*.

Northwest melodrama. Source: Gilbert Parker, "She of the Triple Chevron," in *Pierre and His People: Tales of the Far North* (New York, 1893). Jen Galbraith is in love with Sgt. Tom Flaherty of the Royal Mounted. She is the daughter of Peter Galbraith, who is engaged in smuggling moonshine whiskey across the Canadian border. When she tries to warn her father and brother of the approaching police, she is arrested with the entire gang. Released on bail, her brother Val in an altercation shoots Snow Devil, a police spy; and trying to cross the border, he is caught in a blizzard. Flaherty is sent to intercept him but is drugged by the girl's father; Jen, however, braves the storm and delivers his dispatch. Flaherty later arrests Val on the murder charge, but the dying confession of his friend, Pierre, clears Val; and the lovers are happily united. *Smugglers. Bootleggers. Filial relations. Brother-sister relationship. Murder. Canadian Northwest. Northwest Mounted Police. Blizzards.*

OVER THE WIRE F2.4091

Metro Pictures. 18 Jul **1921** [cl Jul 1921; LP16739]. Si; b&w. 35mm. 6 reels.

Dir Wesley Ruggles. *Scen* Edward T. Lowe, Jr. *Story* Arthur Somers Roche. *Photog* Allan Siegler. *Art Interiors* J. J. Hughes.

Cast: Alice Lake *(Kathleen Dexter)*, Al Roscoe *(John Grannan)*, George Stewart *(Terry Dexter)*, Alan Hale *(James Twyford)*.

Melodrama. Terry Dexter embezzles a large sum of money from his employer, John Grannan, and loses it in speculation, then tries to recover the money by gambling. His devoted sister Kathleen gives him securities to cover the loss, but Grannan refuses to accept them, hoping to teach Terry a lesson. The terror-stricken boy commits suicide, and Kathleen vows revenge on the employer. With the aid of James Twyford she becomes Grannan's secretary and persuades him to marry her, and after revealing her motive she elopes with Twyford, but Grannan defeats their plans. When Twyford tries to kill Grannan, he is foiled by Kathleen, who realizes her wrong and admits that she now loves her husband. *Brother-sister relationship. Secretaries. Revenge. Speculation. Gambling. Embezzlement. Suicide.*

OVER THE WORLD WITH ROOSEVELT F2.4092

Alex B. Ebin. 3 Jan **1924** [scheduled release]. Si; b&w. 35mm. 4 reels.

Educational film(?). No information about the nature of this film has been found, and the identification with T. R. is assumed. *Theodore Roosevelt.*

OVER THERE F2.4093

Super Film Attractions. 23 May **1928** [trade review]. Si; b&w. 35mm. 6 reels.

Film Ed Sidney Lust.

Documentary. A compilation of United States and allied governments' war films. According to the *Variety* review (23 May 1928, p39), the titles avoid mention of specific dates and places of military actions. *World War I.*

OVERLAND BOUND F2.4094

Presidio Productions. *Dist* Raytone Talking Pictures. 15 Apr **1930.** Sd (Telefilm); b&w. 35mm. 6 reels, 5,200-5,509 ft.

Dir Leo Maloney. *Scen-Dial* Ford I. Beebe. *Story* Ford I. Beebe, Joseph Kane. *Photog* William Nobles. *Film Ed* Fred Bain.

Cast: Leo Maloney *(Lucky Lorimer)*, Allene Ray *(Mary Winters)*, Jack Perrin *(Larry Withers/Jimmy Winters)*, Lydia Knott *(Ma Winters)*, Wally Wales *(Buck Hawkins)*, Charles K. French *(Underwood)*, R. J. Smith *(Keno Creager)*, William J. Dyer *(Boss Wheeler)*, Bullet *(a dog)*.

Western melodrama. To trick Ma and Mary Winters into selling their rundown ranch, which will be in the path of a future railroad, Underwood engages Keno Creager to impersonate Jimmy Winters, who ran away from his mother and sister many years earlier. Lucky Lorimer, a horsetrading drifter, and Larry Withers, a waiter in Boss Wheeler's saloon, discover the plot, Larry reveals that he is Jimmy, and they both head for the Winters place. They find Creager already there doing his dirty work, and they cannot prevent the signing of the deed, but Lucky (by means of a fake murder charge) tricks Creager into denying that he is Jimmy Winters. Happily reunited, the Winters add Lucky to their number. *Horsetraders. Vagabonds. Fraud. Impersonation. Railroads. Ranches. Land rights. Dogs.*

THE OVERLAND LIMITED F2.4095

Gotham Productions. *Dist* Lumas Film Corp. 14 Jul **1925** [New York showing; c7 Jul 1925; LP21635]. Si; b&w. 35mm. 6 reels, 6,389 ft.

Pres by Sam Sax. *Supv* Renaud Hoffman. *Dir* Frank O'Neill. *Story* James J. Tynan. *Photog* Jack MacKenzie.

Cast: Malcolm McGregor *(David Barton)*, Olive Borden *(Ruth Dent)*, Alice Lake *(Violet Colton)*, Ethel Wales *(Mrs. Barton)*, Ralph Lewis *(Ed Barton)*, John Miljan *(Brice Miller)*, Roscoe Karns *(Pat Madden)*, Emmett King *(Carson North)*, Charles Hill Mailes *(Schuyler Dent)*, Charles West *(Bitterroot Jackson)*, Charles "Buddy" Post *("One Round" Farrell)*, Evelyn Jennings *(Agnes Jennings)*.

Melodrama. David Barton, consulting engineer for a railroad, designs and oversees the construction of a bridge over a mountain gorge, despite the opposition of Brice Miller, David's rival for the hand of Ruth Dent. Big Ed, David's father, is the railroad engineer selected to take the first train over the new bridge. Miller sabotages the bridge, and the train derails, killing Miller's mother. David is blamed for the collapse until a contrite Miller comes forward and confesses. David's father, who has survived the derailment, later takes the Overland Limited over the rebuilt span. *Engineers—Civil. Railroad engineers. Filial relations. Bridges. Railroads. Sabotage. Train wrecks.*

THE OVERLAND STAGE F2.4096

Charles R. Rogers Productions. *Dist* First National Pictures. 31 Jan **1927** [c14 Dec 1926; LP23435]. Si; b&w. 35mm. 7 reels, 6,392 ft.

Pres by Charles R. Rogers. *Dir* Albert Rogell. *Story-Scen* Marion Jackson. *Photog* Sol Polito. *Prod Mgr* Harry J. Brown.

Cast: Ken Maynard *(Jack Jessup)*, Kathleen Collins *(Barbara Marshall)*, Tom Santschi *(Hawk Lespard)*, Sheldon Lewis *(Jules)*, Dot Farley *(Aunt Viney)*, Florence Turner *(Alice Gregg)*, Jay Hunt *(John Gregg)*, William Malan *(John Marshall)*, Paul Hurst *(Hell A-Poppin' Casey)*, Fred Burns *(Butterfield)*.

Western melodrama. At a trading post in the Northern Dakotas, Hawk Lespard, an unscrupulous trader, is opposed by Jack Jessup, posing as a gambler but actually a scout for the Overland Stage Co., and Kunga-Sunga, a wizard with the lariat. John Gregg comes to town as storekeeper with his niece, Barbara Marshall, and Jessup falls in love with her. Meanwhile, Lespard's gang disguise themselves as Indians and give the post a bad name for whites and incites the Sioux chiefs against the white man. In a fight Jessup is disclosed as Kunga-Sunga, and the superstitious Indians, aroused by Lespard, force him into hiding. Lespard leads a renegade band against a wagon train of new settlers, but Jack, in disguise, informs the chief of the trader's treachery, and the settlers defeat their attackers. The Indians are reconciled when Lespard reveals his true intentions and Barbara and Jack are married. *Gamblers. Traders. Scouts—Frontier. Sioux Indians. Settlers. Disguise. Wagon trains. Dakota Territory. Overland Stage Co..*

THE OVERLAND TELEGRAPH F2.4097

Metro-Goldwyn-Mayer Pictures. 2 Mar **1929** [c12 Mar 1929; LP204]. Si; b&w. 35mm. 6 reels, 4,815 ft.

Dir John Waters. *Scen* George C. Hull. *Titl* Harry Sinclair Drago. *Adapt* Edward Meagher. *Story* Ward Wing. *Photog* Arthur Reed. *Film Ed* William Le Vanway. *Wardrobe* Lucia Coulter.

Cast: Tim McCoy *(Captain Allen)*, Dorothy Janis *(Dorothy)*, Frank Rice *(Easy)*, Lawford Davidson *(Briggs)*, Clarence Geldert *(Major Hammond)*, Chief Big Tree *(medicine man)*.

Historical drama. "Young army captain tries his luck against marauding Indians, and incidentally wins the hand of the prettiest girl at the post. Action takes place at outbreak of Civil War." ("Motion Picture News Booking Guide," in *Motion Picture News,* 15 Apr 1920, p97.) *Indians of North America. Telegraph. United States—History—Civil War. Glacier National Park.*

Note: Filmed on location in Glacier National Park.

THE PACE THAT KILLS F2.4098

Willis Kent Productions. c7 Dec **1928** [LP25896]. Si; b&w. 35mm. 7 reels.

Pres by Willis Kent. *Dir* Norton S. Parker, William A. O'Connor. *Titl* Ruth Todd. *Photog* Ernest Laszlo. *Film Ed* Edith Wakeling.

Cast: Owen Gorin *(Eddie)*, Thelma Daniels *(Eddie's sweetheart)*, Florence Turner *(Eddie's mother)*, Florence Dudley *(Grace)*, Harry Todd *(Uncle Caleb)*, Arnold Dallas *(King of the Underworld)*, Virginia Roye *(Fanny)*.

Melodrama. When Grace drops out of sight in a metropolis, her brother, Eddie, a simple country boy, goes to the city to look for her. He finds work in a department store and meets Fanny O'Rell, a city girl who introduces him to narcotics; Eddie soon becomes an addict and loses his job. Turning into a tormented derelict, Eddie wanders the city streets and meets up with Grace, who, an addict also, has become a prostitute. Grace is jailed, and Eddie enters a hospital, where, after months of agony, he is cured of his habit and allowed to return home to the welcoming arms of his family and his childhood sweetheart. *Drug addicts. Prostitutes. Derelicts. Brother-sister relationship. Narcotics. Department stores. Hospitals.*

THE PACE THAT THRILLS F2.4099

First National Pictures. 4 Oct **1925** [c25 Sep 1925; LP21849]. Si; b&w. 35mm. 7 reels, 6,911 ft.

Pers Supv Earl Hudson. *Dir* Webster Campbell. *Titl* John Krafft. *Story* Byron Morgan. *Photog* T. D. McCord. *Film Ed* John Krafft.

Cast: Ben Lyon *(Danny Wade)*, Mary Astor *(Doris)*, Charles Beyer *(Duke)*, Tully Marshall *(Hezekiah Sims)*, Wheeler Oakman *(director)*, Thomas Holding *(John Van Loren)*, Evelyn Walsh Hall *(Mrs. Van Loren)*,

Warner Richmond *(Jack Van Loren)*, Fritzi Brunette *(Paula)*, Paul Ellis *(toreador)*.

Melodrama. Paula, a chorus girl married to an aristocratic dipsomaniac, tries to protect her infant son from a drunken prank and inadvertently causes the death of her husband. She is accused of murder and sentenced to life in prison on circumstantial evidence; her son, Danny, is put in an orphanage. Years later Danny becomes a movie star and spends every cent he earns in an effort to prove his mother's innocence, refusing, therefore, to take any chances with his own life. He is accused of cowardice by the newspapers and finally agrees to enter an automobile race. Danny loses the race but proves himself to be a man; his mother is released from jail. *Chorus girls. Actors. Alcoholism. Injustice. Cowardice. Murder. Manhood. Circumstantial evidence. Orphanages. Automobile racing. Motion pictures. Prisons.*

PADLOCKED **F2.4100**

Famous Players–Lasky. *Dist* Paramount Pictures. 4 or 9 Aug **1926** [c9 Aug 1926; LP23006]. Si; b&w. 35mm. 7 reels, 6,700 ft.

Pres by Adolph Zukor, Jesse L. Lasky. *Dir* Allan Dwan. *Scen* James Shelley Hamilton. *Adapt* Becky Gardiner. *Photog* James Howe.

Cast: Lois Moran *(Edith Gilbert)*, Noah Beery *(Henry Gilbert)*, Louise Dresser *(Mrs. Alcott)*, Helen Jerome Eddy *(Belle Galloway)*, Allan Simpson *(Norman Van Pelt)*, Florence Turner *(Mrs. Gilbert)*, Richard Arlen *("Tubby" Clark)*, Charles Lane *(Monte Hermann)*, Douglas Fairbanks, Jr. *("Sonny" Galloway)*, Charlot Bird *(Blanche Galloway)*, Josephine Crowell *(Mrs. Galloway)*, André Lanoy *(Lorelli)*, Irma Kornelia *(Pearl Gates)*.

Society melodrama. Source: Rex Beach, *Padlocked* (New York, 1926). Edith Gilbert, the daughter of Henry Gilbert—a wealthy but bigoted and puritanical reformer—leaves home following her mother's death to seek her fortune on Broadway. Through her boardinghouse roommate, Edith gets work as a cafe dancer. At the cafe, she attracts man-about-town Monte Hermann and also Norman Van Pelt, a youth who falls in love with her. At Hermann's suggestion, Mrs. Alcott, an unsavory society woman, takes Edith under her protective wing; and despite Edith's denials of his base suspicions, Norman leaves for Europe to forget her. Meanwhile, Gilbert, who has married Belle Galloway, a designing spinster, is shocked to learn that Edith is a cabaret dancer and has her committed to a reformatory, where she is crushed mentally and physically. Discovering that Belle is only a scheming hypocrite, however, Gilbert pays her to leave him, and he seeks out Edith to atone for the past. They go abroad, and Edith is happily reunited with Norman. *Dancers. Reformers. Fatherhood. Bigotry. Courtship. Reformatories. New York City.*

THE PAGAN **F2.4101**

Metro-Goldwyn-Mayer Pictures. 27 Apr **1929** [c1 Apr 1929; LP262]. Singing sequences & mus score (Movietone); b&w. 35mm. 9 reels, 7,459 ft. [Also si; 7,359 ft.]

Dir W. S. Van Dyke. *Scen* Dorothy Farnum. *Titl* John Howard Lawson. *Story* John Russell. *Photog* Clyde De Vinna. *Song: "Pagan Love Song"* Nacio Herb Brown. *Art Dir* Cedric Gibbons. *Film Ed* Ben Lewis. *Mus & Lyr* Arthur Freed. *Asst Dir* Harold S. Bucquet.

Cast: Ramon Novarro *(Henry Shoesmith, Jr.)*, Renée Adorée *(Madge)*, Donald Crisp *(Henry Slater)*, Dorothy Janis *(Tito)*.

Melodrama. Henry Shoesmith, Jr., a handsome islander, devotes his days to singing and his nights to romance. He falls in love with Tito, a native girl who has been adopted by Slater, a trader, and when Slater and Tito leave the island, Henry gives up his idle ways and turns to storekeeping. Tito and Slater later return to the island, and the rough trader attempts to force her to marry him. Henry learns of this and abducts the willing girl, taking her to his mountain home. Slater later takes her back; Henry again rescues her. All ends well. *Storekeepers. Traders. Marriage. South Sea Islands. Tuamotu Archipelago.*

Note: Produced and photographed on location in the Tuamotu Archipelago.

PAGAN PASSIONS **F2.4102**

Rellimeo Film Syndicate. *Dist* Selznick Distributing Corp. 29 Feb or 8 Mar **1924** [c8 Mar 1924; LP19991]. Si; b&w. 35mm. 6 reels, 5,600 ft.

Dir Colin Campbell. *Photog* Joseph Brotherton.

Cast: Wyndham Standing *(John Dangerfield)*, June Elvidge *(Mrs. Dangerfield)*, Barbara Bedford *(Shirley Dangerfield)*, Raymond McKee *(Billy Dangerfield)*, Sam De Grasse *(Frank Langley)*, Rosemary Theby *(Dreka Langley)*, Tully Marshall *(Dr. Trask)*.

Melodrama. Source: Grace Sanderson Michie, "Pagan Passions" (publication undetermined). Dreka Langley leaves her Malay Peninsula home after her alcoholic husband shoots himself. On the way to join her brother in China, she stops, gives birth to a baby, and leaves him with a Chinese family. Dreka meets John Dangerfield and persuades him to leave his wife and daughter. They sink into the depths of the Chinese underworld until Dangerfield, deserted by Dreka, regains his health and former position. He unwittingly adopts Dreka's child, Frank, and sends him to school in California. There Frank meets and falls in love with Dangerfield's daughter, Shirley, but, believing he is Chinese, he returns to China. He finds his mother, who tells him he is Caucasian before she dies from a bullet wound intended for him. Dangerfield returns to his forgiving wife, and Frank marries Shirley. *Dissipation. Race relations. Suicide. Malaya. China. California.*

PAID **F2.4103**

Metro-Goldwyn-Mayer Pictures. 30 Dec **1930** [c15 Dec 1930; LP1807]. Sd (Movietone); b&w. 35mm. 10 reels, 7,946 ft.

Dir Sam Wood. *Dial* Charles MacArthur. *Adapt* Lucien Hubbard, Charles MacArthur. *Photog* Charles Rosher. *Art Dir* Cedric Gibbons. *Film Ed* Hugh Wynn. *Rec Engr* Douglas Shearer. *Gowns* Adrian.

Cast: Joan Crawford *(Mary Turner)*, Robert Armstrong *(Joe Garson)*, Marie Prevost *(Agnes Lynch)*, Kent Douglass *(Bob Gilder)*, John Miljan *(Inspector Burke)*, Purnell B. Pratt *(Edward Gilder)*, Hale Hamilton *(District Attorney Demarest)*, Polly Moran *(Polly)*, Robert Emmett O'Connor *(Cassidy)*, Tyrrell Davis *(Eddie Griggs)*, William Bakewell *(Carney)*, George Cooper *(Red)*, Gwen Lee *(Bertha)*, Isabel Withers *(Helen Morris)*.

Drama. Source: Bayard Veiller, *Within the Law* (New York opening: 11 Sep 1912). Mary Turner, a shopgirl, is sentenced to a 3-year prison term for a crime she did not commit, and she declares in the courtroom that she will someday even the score for the way in which she has been treated by the law. After serving her term, she becomes associated with three criminals: Joe Garson, Agnes Lynch, and Red, with whom she instigates numerous activities bordering on embezzlement, blackmail, and larceny, but which are always within the law. To gain revenge on her former employer, she marries his son, Bob, who loves her and for whom she comes to care. His father, Edward Gilder, attempts to have the marriage annulled, and failing in this, he persuades Eddie Griggs to act as informer and aid Joe and Red in robbing Bob's home. But Mary learns of the scheme and exposes Eddie, causing Joe to kill him. The police do not believe her claim of self-defense, but Joe is ultimately captured and through third degree methods is forced to confess, thus freeing Mary to be happily reunited with Bob. *Shopgirls. Informers. Filial relations. Blackmail. Embezzlement. Larceny. Injustice. Revenge. Courtship. Prisons.*

Note: Initially reviewed as *Within the Law*.

PAID BACK **F2.4104**

Universal Film Manufacturing Co. 28 Aug **1922** [c10 Aug 1922; LP18145]. Si; b&w. 35mm. 5 reels, 4,920 ft.

Pres by Carl Laemmle. *Dir* Irving Cummings. *Scen* Hope Loring. *Story* Louis Duryea Lighton. *Photog* William Fildew, Jackson Rose.

Cast: Gladys Brockwell *(Carol Gordon)*, Mahlon Hamilton *(David Hardy)*, Stuart Holmes *(Jack Gregory)*, Lillian West *(Dorothy Britton)*, Kate Price *(Carol's servant)*, Edna Murphy *(Eloise Hardy)*, Arthur Stuart Hull *(Jason Lockhart)*, Wilfred Lucas *(ship captain)*.

Melodrama. Wealthy orphan Carol Gordon marries the executor of her estate, though she does not love him. Soon afterward, trying to help a friend who is being blackmailed, she is misunderstood by her husband to be herself compromised. The blackmailer then turns his attentions to her, and Carol lures him to a South Sea island. There she meets the island's superintendent, and she marries him when her husband dies. *Orphans. Blackmail. South Sea Islands.*

PAID TO LOVE **F2.4105**

Fox Film Corp. 23 Jul **1927** [New York premiere; released 14 Aug; c15 May 1927; LP24014]. Si; b&w. 35mm. 7 reels, 6,888 ft.

Pres by William Fox. *Dir* Howard Hawks. *Scen* William M. Conselman, Seton I. Miller. *Adapt* Benjamin Glazer. *Story* Harry Carr. *Photog* L. William O'Connell. *Asst Dir* James Tinling.

Cast: George O'Brien *(Crown Prince Michael)*, Virginia Valli *(Gaby)*, J. Farrell MacDonald *(Peter Roberts)*, Thomas Jefferson *(King)*, William Powell *(Prince Eric)*, Merta Sterling *(maid)*, Hank Mann *(servant)*.

Romantic comedy-drama. American banker Peter Roberts travels to a Balkan kingdom in order to establish more firmly its financial status, and in the process he befriends the crown prince, who, he feels, should be getting married. Roberts attempts to facilitate a match by taking the prince to an apache cafe, and there they find the perfect girl, Gaby. The prince becomes enamored of her, and after some maneuvering, the girl is made a duchess so that she may be in the proper class for marrying a crown prince. *Bankers. Royalty. Courtship. Imaginary kingdoms. Balkans.*

PAINT AND POWDER **F2.4106**

Chadwick Pictures. 16 Sep **1925** [New York license application; c31 Oct 1925; LP21959]. Si; b&w. 35mm. 7 reels, 7,000 ft.

Pres by I. E. Chadwick. *Pers Dir* Hunt Stromberg. *Story-Adapt* Harvey Gates. *Titl* Frederick Hatton, Fanny Hatton. *Photog* Sol Polito. *Art Dir* Edward Withers. *Ed* Ralph Dixon.

Cast: Elaine Hammerstein *(Mary Dolan)*, Theodore von Eltz *(Jimmy Evarts)*, Mrs. Charles Craig *(Mrs. Evarts)*, John Sainpolis *(Mark Kelsey)*, Stuart Holmes *(Phillip Andrews)*, Derelys Perdue *(Mazie Hull)*, Pat Hartigan *(Tim McCardle)*, Russell Simpson *(Riley)*, Charles Murray *(The Cabman)*.

Melodrama. Singing waiter Jimmy Evarts and dancer Mary Dolan, who both work in a Lower East Side cabaret owned by Riley, are in love. Riley is controlled by Tim McCardle, Boss of the Bowery. Theatrical producer Mark Kelsey visits the cabaret, and his wallet is stolen by McCardle. In turn, Jimmy steals the wallet from McCardle and uses the money to dress up Mary. She tries out for a Broadway show and fails; Jimmy is arrested and sent to jail; and Kelsey offers Mary a job in a show. She becomes a star; and when Jimmy is released, Kelsey reunites the two lovers. Jimmy finds Mary scantily clad in the apartment of one of the show's backers, Phillip Andrews, and jumps to conclusions. Repenting, Jimmy returns to find Mary wed to Kelsey. Heartbroken, he leaves her to the producer. *Waiters. Dancers. Theatrical producers. Theatrical backers. Theft. Theater. Cabarets. New York City—East Side. New York City—Broadway.*

THE PAINTED ANGEL **F2.4107**

First National Pictures. 1 Dec **1929** [c6 Dec 1929; LP888]. Sd (Vitaphone); b&w. 35mm. 7 reels, 6,470 ft. [Also si.]

Dir Millard Webb. *Scen-Dial-Titl* Forrest Halsey. *Photog* John Seitz. *Film Ed* Harold Young. *Songs: "Help Yourself to Love," "A Bride Without a Groom"* Herman Ruby, M. K. Jerome.

Cast: Billie Dove *(Mamie Hudler/Rodeo West)*, Edmund Lowe *(Brood)*, George MacFarlane *(Oldfield)*, Cissy Fitzgerald *(Ma Hudler)*, J. Farrell MacDonald *(Pa Hudler)*, Norman Selby *(Jule)*, Nellie Bly Baker *(Sippie)*.

Melodrama. Source: Fannie Hurst, "Give the Little Girl a Hand," in *Procession* (New York, 1929). Mamie Hudler, a San Francisco nightclub entertainer, is nearly killed when she refuses the attentions of Oldfield but is saved by Brood, a violinist, who is disabled by a bullet intended for her. Changing her name to Rodeo West, Mamie goes to New York where she becomes "queen of the nightclubs," with Brood, her manager, protecting her from her grafting family and especially her brother Jule. After a row with the family, Brood threatens to leave. Then Oldfield, who has struck oil, appears at the club; Rodeo plays up to him; and he later proposes marriage. Brood congratulates her, but his attitude enrages her. Brood then confesses his love for her and is about to leave when Rodeo unexpectedly dresses in a bridal costume and announces her engagement to him; all ends happily. *Entertainers. Violinists. Family life. Nightclubs. San Francisco. New York City.*

PAINTED FACES **F2.4108**

Tiffany-Stahl Productions. 20 Nov **1929** [c16 Nov 1929; LP861]. Sd (Photophone); b&w. 35mm. 8 reels, 6,665 ft. [Also si.]

Dir Albert Rogell. *Adapt-Dial-Titl* Frederic Hatton, Fanny Hatton. *Story* Frances Hyland. *Photog* Ben Kline, Jackson Rose. *Film Ed* Richard Cahoon. *Song: "Somebody Just Like You"* Abner Silver.

Cast: Joe E. Brown *(Hermann [or Beppo])*, Helen Foster *(Nancy, his adopted daughter)*, Richard Tucker *(district attorney)*, William B. Davidson *(ringmaster)*, Barton Hepburn *(Buddy Barton, ballyhoo man)*, Dorothy Gulliver *(Babe Barnes)*, Lester Cole *(Roderick)*, Sojin *(cafe proprietor)*, Jack Richardson *(stage manager)*, Howard Truesdell, Baldy Belmont, Jerry Drew, Walter Jerry, Russ Dudley, Purnell Pratt, Clinton Lyle *(jurymen)*, Alma Bennett, Mabel Julienne Scott, Florence Midgley, May Wallace *(jurywomen)*.

Melodrama. On a vaudeville backstage, between acts, a man is murdered; all evidence points to the guilt of Buddy, a young performer, and he is brought to trial for murder. When the jury ballot is counted, 11 are for conviction, but one juryman, Beppo (or Hermann), a clown, is in opposition and keeps the jury "hung" for 5 days; at length, the clown reveals that the murdered man (Roderick) had betrayed his adopted daughter, Nancy, and as a result he had taken revenge. The clown is about to confess, when the jurors agree to a verdict of "not guilty," and all ends happily. *Clowns. Juries. Vaudeville. Murder. Fatherhood. Trials.*

THE PAINTED FLAPPER **F2.4109**

Chadwick Pictures. 15 Oct **1924** [c1 Aug 1924; LP20491]. Si; b&w. 35mm. 6 reels, 6,000 ft.

Dir John Gorman. *Photog* André Barlatier.

Cast: James Kirkwood *(Richard Whitney)*, Pauline Garon *(Arline Whitney)*, Crauford Kent *(Egbert Van Alyn)*, Kathlyn Williams *(Isabel Whitney)*, Claire Adams *(Eunice Whitney)*, Hal Cooley *(Danny Lawrence)*, John Harron *(Jimmy Arnold)*, Maine Geary *(Lester Howe)*, Anita Simons *(Lucy May)*, Al Roscoe *(Lord Raynesford)*, Carlton Griffin *(Lord Coventry)*, Pauline French *(Leita Stokes)*.

Romantic drama. Source: Alan Pearl, *The Painted Flapper* (c1922). Flapper Arline Whitney saves her sister Eunice from marrying Van Alyn, a socialite whom she and her boyfriend, Richard, expose as an international crook, and effects the reunion of her mother and father. *Flappers. Sisters. Family life. Filial relations.*

THE PAINTED LADY **F2.4110**

Fox Film Corp. 28 Sep **1924** [c7 Sep 1924; LP20574]. Si; b&w. 35mm. 7 reels, 6,938 ft.

Pres by William Fox. *Dir* Chester Bennett. *Scen* Thomas Dixon, Jr. *Photog* Alfred Gosden.

Cast: George O'Brien *(Luther Smith)*, Dorothy Mackaill *(Violet)*, Harry T. Morey *(Captain Sutton)*, Lucille Hutton *(Pearl Thompson)*, Lucille Ricksen *(Alice Smith)*, Margaret McWade *(Mrs. Smith)*, John Miljan *(Carter)*, Frank Elliott *(Roger Lewis)*, Lucien Littlefield *(Matt Logan)*.

Melodrama. Source: Larry Evans, "The Painted Lady," in *Saturday Evening Post* (185:7, 30 Nov 1912). After being released from imprisonment for a crime committed by her sister, Violet is forced to become a woman of easy virtue, and on an excursion to a South Sea isle she meets Luther Smith, a sailor seeking vengeance for the death of *his* sister. She feels unworthy of his love, but their paths cross again when he rescues her from Captain Sutton, the man responsible for the other girl's tragedy. *Sisters. Brother-sister relationship. Revenge. Prostitution. South Sea Islands.*

PAINTED PEOPLE **F2.4111**

Associated First National Pictures. Jan **1924** [c21 Jan 1924; LP19840]. Si; b&w. 35mm. 7 reels, 6,820 [Also 6,897 ft.]

Dir Clarence Badger. *Ed Dir* Marion Fairfax. *Scen* Edward J. Montagne. *Photog* Rudolph Berquist. *Art Dir* Milton Menasco. *Film Ed* George McQuire.

Cast: Colleen Moore *(Ellie Byrne)*, Ben Lyon *(Don Lane)*, Charlotte Merriam *(Stephanie Parrish)*, Joseph Striker *(Preston Dutton)*, Charles Murray *(Tom Byrne)*, Russell Simpson *(Fred Lane)*, Mary Alden *(Mrs. Byrne)*, Mary Carr *(Mrs. Lane)*, Sam De Grasse *(Henry Parrish)*, June Elvidge *(Mrs. Dutton)*, Anna Q. Nilsson *(Leslie Carter)*, Bull Montana *(Ed Decker)*.

Comedy-drama. Source: Richard Connell, "The Swamp Angel," in *Collier's* (71:3–4, 10 Feb 1923; 13–14, 17 Feb; 11–12, 24 Feb; 13–14, 3 Mar; 11–12, 10 Mar). Ellie Byrne and Don Lane grow up together, friends and neighbors, in the shabby section of a factory town. Don worships Stephanie Parrish, the wealthiest girl in town, while Ellie admires Preston Dutton, the most sought-after young man. Don goes to the city, determined to get an education, make money, and eventually win Stephanie. Ellie becomes a maid to a prominent actress; 5 years later she herself has become famous on the stage. Ellie writes a play about her early life of poverty. Don rewrites the play, which, opening in their hometown, is a great success. Stephanie agrees to marry Don, and Ellie gets engaged to Preston Dutton; but before the weddings Ellie and Don realize how hard they worked for each other. *Actors. Playwrights. Housemaids. Social classes. Poverty. Smalltown life.*

PAINTED PONIES (Universal-Gibson Special) **F2.4112**

Universal Pictures. 25 Sep **1927** [c20 Jul 1927; LP24228]. Si; b&w. 35mm. 6 reels, 5,416 ft.

Pres by Carl Laemmle. *Dir* Reeves Eason. *Scen* Arthur Statter. *Titl* Tom Reed. *Adapt* Frank Beresford. *Photog* Harry Neumann. *Art Dir* David S. Garber.

Cast: Hoot Gibson *(Bucky Simms)*, William Dunn *(Pinto Pete)*, Charles Sellon *(Mr. Blenning)*, Otto Hoffman *(Jim)*, Ethlyne Clair *(Pony Blenning)*, Slim Summerville *(Beanpole)*, Chief White Spear, Black Hawk, Chief Big

Tree, Mary Lopez.

Western melodrama. Source: John Harold Hamlin, "Painted Ponies," in *Western Story Magazine*. Buck Sims, a riding champion, drops into Toptown to participate in the annual rodeo and meets Mary Blenning, who with her crippled father operates a merry-go-round in a small park. Pete, the town bully and Mary's suitor, informs Buck he is not wanted, and in the fight that ensues Pete is badly beaten. Buck plays a trick on his friends by speeding up the merry-go-round; then, himself riding the painted ponies, he playfully fires his gun in the air. Pete shoots Mary's father and has Buck arrested for the shooting, but Mary refuses to prosecute. At the rodeo, Buck wins the honors from Pete, who kidnaps the girl and kills Jim, his confederate. Buck grapples with Pete in a canoe and takes him prisoner as Mary swims to shore. *Bullies. Courtship. Rodeos. Merry-go-rounds. Amusement parks.*

PAINTED POST **F2.4113**

Fox Film Corp. 1 Jul **1928** [c1 Jun 1928; LP25359]. Si; b&w. 35mm. 5 reels, 4,952 ft.

Pres by William Fox. *Dir* Eugene Forde. *Scen* Buckleigh F. Oxford. *Titl* Delos Sutherland. *Story* Harry Sinclair Drago. *Photog* Dan Clark. *Film Ed* Robert W. Bischoff. *Asst Dir* Clay Crapnell.

Cast: Tom Mix *(Tom Blake)*, Natalie Kingston *(Barbara Lane)*, Philo McCullough *(Ben Tuttle)*, Al St. John *(Joe Nimble)*, Fred Gamble *(theatrical manager)*, Tony *(himself, a horse)*.

Western melodrama. "... the sheriff, with the assistance of the girl, outwits the desperado band and the loot is recovered and the girl saved" (*Motion Picture News Booking Guide*, [14]:273, 1929). *Sheriffs. Desperadoes. Theatrical managers. Horses.*

PAINTED TRAIL **F2.4114**

Trem Carr Productions. *Dist* Rayart Pictures. Feb **1928.** Si; b&w. 35mm. 5 reels, 4,444-4,571 ft.

Dir J. P. McGowan. *Story-Scen* Tom Roan. *Photog* Bob Cline. *Film Ed* Mac V. Wright.

Cast: Buddy Roosevelt *(Blaze Marshall)*, Betty Baker *(Betty Winters)*, Leon De La Mothe *(Bluff Gunter)*, Lafe McKee *(Dan Winters)*, Tommy Bay *(Badger James)*.

Western melodrama. "Federal agent sets out to ferret out a bunch of smugglers working on the border. Chief of gang has forced himself as guest in a ranch house against the owner and his daughter's wishes. Agent, posing as crook, gains gang's confidence, and in the showdown is successful in bringing gang to justice." (*Motion Picture News Booking Guide*, [14]: 273, 1929.) *Smugglers. Ranchers. Government agents.*

Note: At least one source credits J. P. McGowan for the scenario.

PAINTING THE TOWN *see* **HOT HEELS**

PAINTING THE TOWN (Universal-Jewel) **F2.4115**

Universal Pictures. 30 Jul **1927** [New York showing; released 7 Aug; c5 Jul 1927; LP24170]. Si; b&w. 35mm. 6 reels, 5,909 ft.

Pres by Carl Laemmle. *Dir* William James Craft. *Adapt-Cont* Harry O. Hoyt, Vin Moore. *Titl* Albert De Mond. *Story* Harry O. Hoyt. *Photog* Al Jones.

Cast: Glenn Tryon *(Hector Whitmore)*, Patsy Ruth Miller *(Patsy Deveau)*, Charles Gerrard *(Raymond Tyson)*, George Fawcett *(fire commissioner)*, Sidney Bracey *(secretary)*, Max Ascher *(Wilson)*, Monte Collins *(justice of the peace)*.

Comedy. Patsy Deveau, a Follies girl, accompanied by Raymond Tyson, a city millionaire, is stopped by a policeman for speeding; while Tyson is paying the fine, Hector Whitmore, a smalltown inventor, imagines he is making a hit with Patsy displaying his inventions, including a car capable of traveling 150 miles an hour and stopping in two car lengths. She pretends to be flattered and casually suggests he see her in New York; he faithfully follows. Tyson persuades her to play along, hoping to sell Hector's car to the fire department; his initial attempt at a demonstration is sabotaged; Patsy, however, disgusted with Tyson, pleads Hector's cause. Hector takes the official on a perilous drive, refusing to stop until the contract is signed. Having thus proved the worth of his wonder car, he wins the contract and Patsy as well. *Inventors. Millionaires. Reckless driving. Follies. Automobiles. Fire departments. New York City.*

A PAIR OF HELLIONS **F2.4116**

Max O. Miller Productions. *Dist* Lee-Bradford Corp. 1 Mar **1924.** Si; b&w. 35mm. 6 reels, 5,698 ft.

Dir Walter Willis. *Story* Peter Clark MacFarlane.

Cast: Ranger Bill Miller, Patricia Palmer, Luther Jones, Mable Turner.

Melodrama. A cattle rustler is caught branding stolen calves and is run out of town. He goes to New York, where he meets a girl at a dancehall who leads him into the clutches of a notorious gang. The gang is lifting his fat bankroll when the police raid the hideout and arrest the gang. The rustler pleads for clemency for the girl, and she is left to nurse him back to health. He marries her, and they return together to the West, where he is seized by a band of angry ranchers who threaten to lynch him. The ranchers are deterred by an irate Irish lady with a rolling pin, and the rustler is forgiven when he promises to discontinue all lawlessness. *Rustlers. Ranchers. Gangs. Police. Irish. Lynching. Dancehalls. New York City.*

PAJAMAS **F2.4117**

Fox Film Corp. 23 Oct **1927** [c17 Oct 1927; LP24510]. Si; b&w. 35mm. 6 reels, 5,876 ft.

Pres by William Fox. *Dir* J. G. Blystone. *Story-Scen* William Conselman. *Titl* Malcolm Stuart Boylan. *Photog* Glen MacWilliams. *Asst Dir* Jasper Blystone.

Cast: Olive Borden *(Angela Wade)*, John J. Clark *(Daniel Wade)*, Lawrence Gray *(John Weston)*, Jerry Miley *(Russell Forrest)*.

Romantic comedy. "Taking a dislike to John Weston, a breezy young Canadian who has come to close a business deal with her father, Angela Wades [*sic*] replaces her father's pilot in his private airplane and manages to crash in the Canadian wilds. Propinquity brings love, and when assistance comes they deliberately avoid rescue to continue their idyl. An amusing outworking of a familiar plot." (*Moving Picture World*, 10 Dec 1927, p40.) *Canadians. Businessmen. Air pilots. Airplanes. Canadian Rockies.*

Note: Exteriors filmed on locations near Lake Louise and Lake O'Hare in the Canadian Rockies.

PAL O' MINE **F2.4118**

Columbia Pictures. *Dist* C. B. C. Film Sales. 15 Mar **1924** [c1 May 1924; LP20145]. Si; b&w. 35mm. 6 reels, 6,000 ft.

Dir Edward J. Le Saint. *Story* Edith Kennedy.

Cast: Irene Rich *(Julia Montfort)*, Josef Swickard *(Verdugo)*, Willard Louis *(Sam Hermann)*, Albert Roscoe *(Frank Travers)*, Pauline Garon *(Babette)*, Jean De Briac *(George Mendoza)*.

Drama. Opera singer Julia Montfort returns to the stage when her husband loses his job and subsequently gives him work secretly paid for by herself. He becomes disillusioned when a temperamental artist threatens to reveal the secret, but ultimately his faith in her is restored. *Singers. Opera. Marriage. Unemployment. Finance—Personal.*

THE PALACE OF PLEASURE **F2.4119**

Fox Film Corp. 10 Jan **1926** [c3 Jan 1926; LP22269]. Si; b&w. 35mm. 6 reels, 5,467 ft.

Pres by William Fox. *Dir* Emmett Flynn. *Scen* Bradley King. *Adapt* Benjamin Glazer. *Photog* Ernest Palmer. *Asst Dir* Ray Flynn.

Cast: Edmund Lowe *(Ricardo Madons)*, Betty Compson *(Lola Montez)*, Henry Kolker *(premier)*, Harvey Clark *(police chief)*, Nina Romano *(maid)*, Francis McDonald *(Captain Fernandez)*, George Siegmann *(Caesar)*.

Romantic melodrama. Source: Adolf Paul, "Lola Montez" (publication undetermined). Don Sebastian, the premier of Portugal, puts a price on the head of Ricardo Madons, a royalist who is accused of treason. Madons is violently in love with Lola Montez, a singer and actress, and kidnaps her when she will not come with him of her own free will. He forces her to marry him but does not hold her to her wedding vows. Don Sebastian, who is also in love with Lola, persuades her to lead Madons into a trap. As the royalist is about to be captured by the soldiers, however, Lola realizes her love for Madons and, at the cost of being wounded, saves his life. They flee together over the border to Spain, where Madons nurses Lola back to health and happiness. *Singers. Actors. Prime ministers. Royalists. Abduction. Treason. Spain. Portugal.*

THE PALM BEACH GIRL **F2.4120**

Famous Players–Lasky. *Dist* Paramount Pictures. 17 May **1926** [c18 May 1926; LP22744]. Si; b&w. 35mm. 7 reels, 6,918 ft.

Pres by Adolph Zukor, Jesse L. Lasky. *Dir* Erle Kenton. *Scen* Forrest Halsey. *Story* Byron Morgan. *Photog* Lee Garmes.

Cast: Bebe Daniels *(Emily Bennett)*, Lawrence Gray *(Jack Trotter)*, Josephine Drake *(Aunt Jerry)*, Marguerite Clayton *(Julia)*, John G. Patrick *(Herbert Moxon)*, Armand Cortez *(Tug Wilson)*, Roy Byron *(sheriff)*,

Maude Turner Gordon *(Aunt Beatrice)*.

Society comedy. Source: Harold Marsh Harwood, *Please Help Emily* (London, 1926). Emily Bennett arrives in Palm Beach from a midwestern farm. Covered with soot from a tugboat, she is hustled into a jim crow bus by a bellboy who refuses her tip but slips her a card suggesting that they meet later. Her Aunts Jerry and Beatrice, accompanied by society millionaire Jack Trotter and Julia, his companion, fail to recognize her until she wipes her nose with a handkerchief. Following several hours of hectic activity, the aunts struggle to transform Emily into a society debutante. When she is invited to christen Jack's motorboat, she nearly falls overboard, and later she discovers some bootleggers loading their wares into the boat. After a hair-raising ride, she is set adrift and is forced to operate the boat alone; eventually she succeeds in returning the craft to the racecourse, and through sheer luck she wins the race and Jack as well. *Aunts. Bootleggers. Social classes. Disguise. Racial segregation. Boat racing. Palm Beach.*

Note: Photographed on location in Palm Beach, Florida.

PALS F2.4121

Truart Film Corp. Nov **1925** [c3 Dec 1925; LP22070]. Si; b&w. 35mm. 5 reels, 4,613 ft.

Dir John P. McCarthy. *Story* George Hively. *Photog* William Thompson.

Cast: Louise Lorraine *(Molly Markham)*, Art Acord *(Bruce Taylor)*, Rex *(The Dog)*, Black Beauty *(The Horse)*, Leon Kent *(Obediah Dillwater)*, Andrew Waldron *(Molly's grandpa)*.

Western comedy-drama. Source: Perry O'Neill, unidentified story. Bruce Taylor arrives in the mountain town of Caliente with his dog (Rex), horse (Blackie), and an abandoned baby found by Rex in an automobile in the desert. The town has no foundling home, and Bruce is forced to care for the infant himself. Molly Markham offers to help and arouses the jealousy of her "suitor," Obediah Dillwater, who has Molly's grandfather under financial obligation. Obediah conspires to have Bruce arrested for kidnaping the baby, but Bruce escapes from jail with the aid of Rex and Blackie. He brings back the sheriff to prove his innocence and rescues Molly from a forced marriage to Obediah. Molly, Bruce, the baby, and Blackie and Rex, the "pals," all look forward to a happy life together. *Foundlings. Mountain life. Dogs. Horses.*

PALS FIRST F2.4122

Edwin Carewe Productions. *Dist* First National Pictures. 8 Aug **1926** [c21 Jul 1926; LP22931]. Si; b&w. 35mm. 7 reels, 6,843 ft.

Pres by Edwin Carewe. *Dir* Edwin Carewe. *Scen* Lois Leeson. *Titl* Ralph Spence. *Adapt* Olga Printzlau. *Photog* Robert B. Kurrle.

Cast: Lloyd Hughes *(Richard Castleman/Danny Rowland)*, Dolores Del Rio *(Jeanne Lamont)*, Alec Francis *(Dominie)*, George Cooper *(The Squirrel)*, Edward Earle *(Dr. Harry Chilton)*, Hamilton Morse *(Judge Lamont)*, George Reed *(Uncle Alex)*, Alice Nichols *(Aunt Caroline)*, Alice Belcher *(Charley Anderson)*.

Crook melodrama. Source: Francis Perry Elliott, *Pals First; a Romance of Love and Comradery* (New York, 1915). Lee Wilson Dodd, *Pals First; a Comedy in a Prologue and Three Acts* (New York, 1925). Richard Castleman, master of Winnecrest Hall in Louisiana, goes on a sea voyage recommended by his cousin and physician, Harry Chilton, who thereupon begins romancing Castleman's fiancée, Jeanne Lamont. When word arrives of Castleman's death, Chilton prepares to usurp the fortune and property of the dead man. Danny Rowland, who is found wounded by two wandering crooks, Dominie and The Squirrel, opportunely arrives at the estate seeking food and rest; and because of his resemblance to Castleman, he is welcomed as the master. Dominie is introduced as an English cleric and The Squirrel as an Italian count, while Danny falls in love with Jeanne, who believes him to be her fiancé. Chilton, however, suspects the trio and finally unmasks them. It then develops that Danny actually is Castleman, who had decided to reform the two men who befriended him and to expose the dishonesty of his cousin. *Cousins. Physicians. Criminals—Rehabilitation. Impersonation. Mistaken identity. Louisiana.*

PALS IN BLUE (Reissue) F2.4123

William N. Selig. *Dist* Exclusive Features. 15 Apr **1924** [New York State license]. Si; b&w. 35mm. 5 reels, 4,900 ft.

Note: Originally released by Selig Polyscope Co. in 1915, in 3 reels, starring Tom Mix.

PALS IN PARADISE F2.4124

Metropolitan Pictures Corp. of California. *Dist* Producers Distributing Corp. 22 Nov **1926** [c1 Nov 1926; LP23281]. Si; b&w. 35mm. 7 reels, 6,696 ft.

Pres by John C. Flinn. *Supv* Will M. Ritchey. *Dir* George B. Seitz. *Adapt* Albert Kenyon, Will M. Ritchey. *Photog* Georges Benoit. *Art Dir* Charles Cadwallader. *Asst Dir* Ed Bernoudy. *Prod Mgr* Bert Gilroy.

Cast: Marguerite De La Motte *(Geraldine Howard)*, John Bowers *(Bill Harvey)*, Rudolph Schildkraut *(Abraham Lezinsky)*, May Robson *(Esther Lezinsky)*, Alan Brooks *(John Kenton)*, Ernie Adams *(Butterfly Kid)*, Bruce Gordon *(Gentleman Phil)*.

Melodrama. Source: Peter Bernard Kyne, "Pals in Paradise" (publication undetermined). Bill Harvey, a young prospector who has taken over a mining claim belonging to one John Howard (now deceased), strikes gold and precipitates a rush to the California site. With Esther and Abraham Lezinsky, he establishes a town known as Paradise. Geraldine, Howard's daughter, arrives with a claim to her father's mine. Kenton, who has a police record, convinces Jerry that she should fight him and speaks disparagingly of Bill. Jerry accuses Bill of stealing her claim papers, then discovers that he is innocent; but when he tells her Kenton is a crook, she indignantly declares herself engaged to him. Kenton and his henchmen stage a raid on the express office, and Bill arrests him—winning the confidence and finally the love of Jerry. *Prospectors. Mine claims. Courtship. California.*

PALS IN PERIL F2.4125

Action Pictures. *Dist* Pathé Exchange. 26 Jun **1927** [c6 May 1927; LU23931]. Si; b&w. 35mm. 5 reels, 4,710 ft.

Pres by Lester F. Scott, Jr. *Dir* Richard Thorpe. *Cont* Frank L. Inghram. *Story* Walter J. Coburn. *Photog* Ray Ries.

Cast: Buffalo Bill Jr. *(Bill Gordon)*, George Ovey *(Shorty Gilmore)*, Edward Hearn *(Blackie Burns)*, Robert Homans *(Sheriff Kipp)*, Bert Lindley *(Luther Fox)*, Olive Hasbrouck *(Mary Bassett)*, Harry Belmore *(Hank Bassett)*, Raye Hampton *(Mrs. Bassett)*.

Western melodrama. Bill and Shorty, two cowhands, are jailed for fighting with Blackie, who works for Luther Fox. The sheriff agrees to release them if they will work for Fox, and they consent. When they are dispatched to collect an overdue payment from the Bassett ranch, they learn that Bassett's son, Pete, has been railroaded to prison by Blackie and Fox and that the Bassett cattle were mortgaged to raise money to fight the case. Peter returns home and, accompanied by Shorty, sets out to find the stolen cattle. Bill, who suspects the sheriff, tracks the rustlers to their lair, frees their captives, and makes them prisoners. Bill finds happiness with Mary. *Sheriffs. Cowboys. Rustlers. Injustice.*

PALS OF THE PRAIRIE F2.4126

FBO Pictures. 7 or 9 Jul **1929** [c7 Jul 1929; LP574]. Mus score & sd eff (Photophone); b&w. 35mm. 6 reels, 4,776 ft. [Also si.]

Dir Louis King. *Screenplay* Frank Howard Clark. *Titl* Helen Gregg. *Story* Oliver Drake. *Photog* Virgil Miller. *Film Ed* George Marsh. *Asst Dir* John Burch.

Cast: Buzz Barton *(Red Hepner)*, Frank Rice *(Hank Robbins)*, Tom Lingham *(Don José Valencia)*, Duncan Renaldo *(Francisco)*, Milburn Morante *(Pedro Terrazzes)*, Natalie Joyce *(Dolores)*, Bill Patton *(Pete Sangor)*.

Western melodrama. Red Hepner and his comrade, Hank Robbins, ride into the little Mexican village of Cajón to find the townsfolk under a reign of terror imposed by the mysterious badman, El Lobo, and the mayor critical of a budding romance between his son Francisco and fiery Dolores. The mayor favors a match between Dolores and Peter Sangor, a resident American in Cajón, who provokes Red's immediate disdain and soon has him locked up after Red bombards him with tomatoes. Sangor kidnaps Francisco despite Red and Hank's efforts; the two pals try to free him but are captured by the bandits and soon escape with the news that Sangor is El Lobo. Red goes to town for help while Hank remains to cut Francisco loose from his bonds just as he is about to be forced to watch Sangor ravage his heart's desire. Their showdown is suddenly joined by the rest of El Lobo's band, followed closely by Don José and the *rurales*, summoned by Red. The bandits are done in, and the mayor has the two heroes name their reward; they ask him to permit the marriage of Francisco and Dolores. *Mayors. Bandits. Rurales. Disguise. Kidnaping. Mexico.*

PALS OF THE WEST **F2.4127**

Film Art Productions. *Dist* Clark-Cornelius Corp. 3 Oct **1922.** Si; b&w. 35mm. 5 reels, 4,021-4,083 ft.

Cast: R. Lee Hill *(Paul Preston)*, William A. Lowery *(Dan Hallet)*, M. McWade *(Lee Wong)*, Esther Ralston *(Nina)*, Jack Patterson *("Black Bill")*.

Western melodrama. "Dan Hallet and Paul Preston, inseparable pals, rescue Nina, white girl, from bondage of Lee Wong. Nina, later, still under Wong's influence, contrives to get him job as cook wih Hallet and Preston at their mining camp. Wong, with help of Black Bill, tries to make bad feeling between the pals, trying to make it seem that Paul is about to rob Dan and take the girl. The Oriental's scheme fails and events prove that Nina is really the daughter of Dan. Romantic finish between Paul and Nina." (*Motion Picture News Booking Guide,* 4:82, Apr 1923.) According to *Variety,* the halfcaste Wong's grudge against Dan stems from the fact that long ago he deserted Wong's half sister, who was white and the mother of Nina, upon learning of the Oriental blood in the family. *Halfcastes. Chinese. Prejudice. Desertion. Friendship. Mining.*

Note: Also known as *Her Half Brother.*

PAMPERED YOUTH **F2.4128**

Vitagraph Co. of America. 1 Feb **1925** [c24 Jan 1925; LP21072]. Si; b&w. 35mm. 7 reels, 6,640 ft.

Pres by Albert E. Smith. *Dir* David Smith. *Scen* Jay Pilcher. *Photog* David Smith, Stephen Smith, Jr.

Cast: Cullen Landis *(George Minafer, as a man)*, Ben Alexander *(George Minafer, as a boy)*, Allan Forrest *(Eugene Moran)*, Alice Calhoun *(Isabel Minafer)*, Emmett King *(Major Amberson)*, Wallace MacDonald *(Wilbur Minafer)*, Charlotte Merriam *(Lucy Morgan)*, Kathryn Adams *(Fanny Minafer)*, Aggie Herring *(Mrs. Foster)*, William J. Irving *(George Amberson)*.

Drama. Source: Booth Tarkington, *The Magnificent Ambersons* (Garden City, New York, 1918). At the turn of the 20th century, the Ambersons are the leading family in a small Indiana town: their home is the local showplace, and their views are news. Major Amberson's daughter, Isabel, is unable to decide between two suitors until one of them, Eugene Moran, disgraces himself by a drunken serenade. Isabel then marries the other, Wilbur Minafer, whom she does not love, and Eugene leaves town. When Wilbur dies, she centers all her affection on her son, George, who develops from a spoiled child into a shallow, self-centered man. After a number of years, Eugene, now a widower, returns to the town, having made a fortune in the manufacture of automobiles. George falls in love with Eugene's daughter but resents Eugene's obvious attachment to Mrs. Minafer. When Major Amberson dies, George, who has dissipated the family fortune, is forced to go to work. Matured by his job, George is reconciled to Eugene when Eugene rescues Mrs. Minafer from a fire in the Amberson mansion. *Automobile manufacturers. Motherhood. Filial relations. Family life. Courtship. Indiana. Fires.*

PARADE D'AMOUR *see* **THE LOVE PARADE**

PARADE OF THE WEST **F2.4129**

Ken Maynard Productions. *Dist* Universal Pictures. 19 Jan **1930** [c19 Dec 1929; LP928]. Sd (Movietone); b&w. 35mm. 6 reels, 5,900 ft. [Also si; 5,582 ft.]

Dir Harry J. Brown. *Story-Scen* Bennett Cohen. *Titl-Dial* Lesley Mason. *Photog* Ted McCord. *Film Ed* Fred Allen. *Rec Engr* C. Roy Hunter.

Cast: Ken Maynard *(Bud Rand)*, Gladys McConnell *(Mary Owens)*, Otis Harlan *(Professor Clayton)*, Frank Rice *(Stuffy)*, Bobby Dunn *(Shorty)*, Jackie Hanlon *(Billy Rand)*, Fred Burns *(Copeland)*, Frank Yaconelli *(Sicily Joe)*, Stanley Blystone *(Dude)*, Blue Washington *(Sambo)*, Tarzan *(himself, a horse)*, Rex *(Mankiller)*.

Western melodrama. Bud Rand, a cowboy who is charged with the care of Little Billy Rand, accepts an offer to appear with Copeland's Wild West Show to ride a horse called "Mankiller." Dude, Copeland's righthand man, resents Bud's attentions to Mary, one of the performers, and when they fight it out, Bud is the victor. In revenge Dude loosens the cinch on the horse, causing Bud to be trampled. Bud is forced to stay behind when the show moves on; Dude intercepts letters from Bud and tells Mary and Billy that he is a coward. When Billy is taken ill, Bud goes to see him and is told of the situation; he rides Mankiller and breaks him, regaining the boy's confidence and Mary's love, while the culprits are routed. *Cowboys. Children. Wild West shows. Cowardice. Horsemanship. Horses.*

PARADISE **F2.4130**

Ray Rockett Productions. *Dist* First National Pictures. 26 Sep **1926** [c25 Aug 1926; LP23045]. Si; b&w. 35mm. 8 reels, 7,090 ft.

Dir Irvin Willat. *Scen* Paul Schofield. *Titl* Frances Agnew, Morton Barnard. *Photog* Charles Van Enger. *Prod Mgr* Ray Rockett.

Cast: Milton Sills *(Tony)*, Betty Bronson *(Chrissie)*, Noah Beery *(Quex)*, Lloyd Whitlock *(Teddy)*, Kate Price *(Lady George)*, Charlie Murray *(Lord Lumley)*, Claude King *(Pollock)*, Charles Brook *(Perkins)*, Ashley Cooper *(McCoustie)*.

Romantic melodrama. Source: Cosmo Hamilton and John Russell, *Paradise* (Boston, 1925). After a daredevil demonstration of aviator stunts, Anthony Fortescue-Stirling, more familiarly known as Tony, is cast adrift by his father. He meets Chrissie, of vaudeville fame, at a fancy-dress ball and falls in love with her. Teddy Sherwood, his best friend, is also taken with her, but she marries Tony. After Tony is cited for service in the war, his father gives him the deed to "Paradise," a South Sea island. Teddy offers to provide transportation, intending to eliminate his rival en route, but fails in that intention. On the island, caretaker Bill Quex—determined to keep the property for himself—provokes the resentment of Tony and his bride by his punishment of the natives; and in a final showdown, he is knocked out by Tony, while the natives take out their vengeance on him. Teddy confesses his actions, sends the crew to rescue the husband and wife, and commits suicide, leaving Tony and Chrissie to their happiness. *Veterans. Aviators. Friendship. Vaudeville. Revenge. Suicide. South Sea Islands.*

PARADISE FOR TWO **F2.4131**

Famous Players–Lasky. *Dist* Paramount Pictures. 23 Jan **1927** [c3 Feb 1927; LP23631]. Si; b&w. 35mm. 7 reels, 6,187 ft.

Pres by Adolph Zukor, Jesse L. Lasky. *Assoc Prod* William Le Baron. *Dir* Gregory La Cava. *Screenplay* J. Clarkson Miller. *Adapt* Ray Harris, Thomas J. Crizer. *Story* Howard Emmett Rogers. *Photog* Edward Cronjager.

Cast: Richard Dix *(Steve Porter)*, Edmund Breese *(Uncle Howard)*, Betty Bronson *(Sally Lane)*, André Beranger *(Maurice)*, Peggy Shaw.

Domestic comedy. Bachelor Steve Porter, who is the center of a hectic night life, is fascinated by the silhouette of a girl across the courtyard. His guardian-trustee, Uncle Howard, hearing of Steve's parties, refuses to give him more money until he is married. Steve's friend, Maurice, a theatrical producer, proposes that they hire a girl to pose as Porter's wife, and Sally Lane is signed to play this part. The three men soon discover Sally's delightful personality, and Steve's interest grows stronger; Uncle Howard's suspicions are aroused, however, and he moves in with them. Sally soon grows tired of the charade and does not believe Steve's pleas of love. Howard, infuriated by the situation, goes for a policeman, but Steve, realizing Sally is the same girl he has seen in the window, convinces her of his love. *Bachelors. Uncles. Guardians. Theatrical producers. Impersonation. Inheritance.*

PARADISE ISLAND **F2.4132**

Tiffany Productions. 15 Jul **1930** [c6 Jul 1930; LP1407]. Sd (Photophone); b&w. 35mm. 8 reels.

Dir Bert Glennon. *Screenplay* Monte Katterjohn. *Story* M. B. Deering. *Photog* Max Dupont. *Film Ed* Byron Robinson. *Songs: "I've Got a Girl in Every Port," "Drinking Song," "Lazy Breezes," "Just Another Dream"* Val Burton. *Mus & Lyr* Will Jason. *Rec Engr* Dean Daily.

Cast: Kenneth Harlan *(Thorne)*, Marceline Day *(Ellen)*, Tom Santschi *(Lutze)*, Paul Hurst *(Beauty)*, Betty Boyd *(Poppi)*, Victor Potel *(Swede)*, Gladden James *(Armstrong)*, Will Stanton *(Limey)*.

Romantic musical drama. Ellen Bradford arrives on a South Sea island to marry Roy Armstrong but finds that he has gone heavily into debt through gambling with Lutze, owner of the local saloon and gambling hall. Realizing her predicament, Lutze helps her, hoping she will eventually fall in love with him; but Thorne and Beauty, two carefree sailors, make an appearance and win back Armstrong's notes from Lutze. Thorne captures the affections of Ellen. *Sailors. Saloon keepers. Gambling. Debt. Courtship. South Sea Islands.*

PARAMOUNT ON PARADE **F2.4133**

Paramount Famous Lasky Corp. 19 Apr **1930** [c29 May 1930; LP1336]. Sd (Movietone); b&w with col sequences (Technicolor). 35mm. 13 reels, 9,125 ft.

Supv Elsie Janis. *Dir* Dorothy Arzner, Otto Brower, Edmund Goulding, Victor Heerman, Edwin H. Knopf, Rowland V. Lee, Ernst Lubitsch,

Lothar Mendes, Victor Schertzinger, Edward Sutherland, Frank Tuttle. *Photog* Harry Fischbeck, Victor Milner. *Set Dsgn* John Wenger. *Songs: "Paramount on Parade Theme Song," "Any Time's the Time To Fall in Love," "What Did Cleopatra Say?" "I'm True to the Navy Now"* Elsie Janis, Jack King. *Song: "We're the Masters of Ceremony"* Ballard MacDonald, Dave Dreyer. *Song: "Torna a Sorrento"* Leo Robin, Ernesto De Curtis. *Songs: "I'm in Training for You," "Dancing To Save Your Sole," "Let Us Drink to the Girl of My Dreams"* L. Wolfe Gilbert, Abel Baer. *Song: "My Marine"* Richard A. Whiting, Raymond B. Eagan. *Song: "All I Want Is Just One Girl"* Richard A. Whiting, Leo Robin. *Song: "I'm Isadore, the Toreador"* David Franklin. *Song: "Sweepin' the Clouds Away"* Sam Coslow. *Dance & Ensemble Dir* David Bennett.

Cast: Iris Adrian, Richard Arlen, Jean Arthur, Mischa Auer, William Austin, George Bancroft, Clara Bow, Evelyn Brent, Mary Brian, Clive Brook, Virginia Bruce, Nancy Carroll, Ruth Chatterton, Maurice Chevalier, Gary Cooper, Cecil Cunningham, Leon Errol, Stuart Erwin, Henry Fink, Kay Francis, Skeets Gallagher, Edmund Goulding, Harry Green, Mitzi Green, Robert Greig, James Hall, Phillips Holmes, Helen Kane, Dennis King, Abe Lyman and His Band, Fredric March, Nino Martini, Mitzi Mayfair, Marion Morgan Dancers, David Newell, Jack Oakie, Warner Oland, Zelma O'Neal, Eugene Pallette, Joan Peers, Jack Pennick, William Powell, Charles (Buddy) Rogers, Lillian Roth, Rolfe Sedan, Stanley Smith, Fay Wray.

Musical revue. SHOWGIRLS ON PARADE: a Technicolor spectacle of chorus girls and ushers to the tune of the theme song. TITLES: Dissolves including studio scenes and toe-dancing by Mitzi Mayfair. INTRODUCTION: Jack Oakie, Skeets Gallagher, and Leon Errol open with "We're the Masters of Ceremony." LOVE TIME: Charles Rogers and Lillian Roth with a boy-girl chorus on a cuckoo-clock set sing "Any Time's the Time To Fall in Love." MURDER WILL OUT: a travesty on detective mysteries with William Powell as Philo Vance, Clive Brook as Sherlock Holmes, Eugene Pallette as Sergeant Heath, Warner Baxter as Dr. Fu Manchu, and Jack Oakie as the victim. ORIGIN OF THE APACHE: a slapstick sketch with Maurice Chevalier and Evelyn Brent dancing in a bedroom, directed by Lubitsch. SONG OF THE GONDOLIER: Italian tenor Nino Martini appears in a Technicolor sketch singing "Torna a Sorrento." IN A HOSPITAL: a comedy sketch with Leon Errol, Helen Kane, and David Newell. IN A GIRL'S GYM: Jack Oakie as the instructor and Zelma O'Neal as the jealous sweetheart, including the song "I'm in Training for You." THE TOREADOR: Harry Green as the Toreador and Kay Francis as Carmen in a comic sketch with the Marion Morgan dancers, with Green singing "I'm Isadore, the Toreador." THE MONTMARTRE GIRL: Ruth Chatterton in a Paris cafe sings "My Marine" to a quartette including Stuart Erwin, Stanley Smith, and Fredric March. PARK IN PARIS: Chevalier as a Paris gendarme patrols a park singing "All I Want Is Just One Girl." MITZI HERSELF: Mitzi Green sings the Chevalier song as Charlie Mack of Moran and Mack would sing it, then as Chevalier sings it. THE SCHOOLROOM: Helen Kane is the teacher in a modernistic schoolroom singing "What Did Cleopatra Say?" to the children, who answer "Boop Boopa Doop." THE GALLOWS SONG: Skeets Gallagher demands that Dennis King sing, before he is hanged, Mana-Zucca's "Nichavo," a Russian love song—all in Technicolor. DANCE MAD: Nancy Carroll, with chorus support and Abe Lyman's band, does "Dancing To Save Your Sole." DREAM GIRL: a sentimental interlude in Technicolor with Richard Arlen, Jean Arthur, Mary Brian, Gary Cooper, James Hall, Fay Wray, among others, featuring "Let Us Drink to the Girl of My Dreams." THE REDHEAD: Clara Bow appears with Jack Oakie, Skeets Gallagher, and a chorus of 42 sailors in "I'm True to the Navy Now." IMPULSES: George Bancroft, at a social function with Kay Francis, William Austin, and others, demonstrates contrasts in social behavior. THE RAINBOW REVELS: Chevalier and a girls' chorus appear as Paris chimney sweeps in the Technicolor finale, singing "Sweeping the Clouds Away." *Actors. Theater. Vaudeville.*

THE PARASITE **F2.4134**

B. P. Schulberg Productions. 20 Jan **1925**. Si; b&w. 35mm. 6 reels, 5,140 ft.

Dir Louis Gasnier. *Scen* Eve Unsell. *Photog* Joseph Goodrich.

Cast: Owen Moore *(Arthur Randall)*, Madge Bellamy *(Joan Laird)*, Bryant Washburn *(Dr. Brooks)*, Mary Carr *(Mrs. Laird)*, Lilyan Tashman *(Laura Randall)*, Bruce Guerin *(Bertie)*.

Society melodrama. Source: Helen Reimensnyder Martin, *The Parasite* (Philadelphia, 1913). After divorcing his wife, Laura, Arthur Randall becomes prosperous, and Laura attempts unsuccessfully to win him back. Randall's son becomes ill, and he engages Joan Laird and her mother to care for the boy. Society misunderstands, and Joan is branded as a parasite. Laura kidnaps the boy, Bertie, and Joan gives chase. Laura's car goes over a cliff, and she is killed. Bertie survives the crash, however, and he and Joan attempt to find their way to a refuge. They become lost in the hills; and to keep Bertie from dying of hunger and thirst, Joan cuts her arm and forces the boy to drink her blood. Rescue comes, and Joan marries Randall. *Divorce. Marriage. Reputation. Fatherhood. Thirst. Automobile accidents.*

PARDON MY FRENCH **F2.4135**

Goldwyn Pictures. Nov **1921** [c22 Sep 1921; LP16981]. Si; b&w. 35mm. 6 reels, 5,500 ft.

Prod Messmore Kendall. *Dir* Sidney Olcott. *Scen* Harry O. Hoyt. *Titl* Irvin S. Cobb. *Story* Edward Childs Carpenter. *Photog* John Stumar.

Cast: Vivian Martin *(Polly)*, George Spink *(Bunny)*, Thomas Meegan *(J. Hawker)*, Nadine Beresford *(Mrs. Hawker)*, Ralph Yearsley *(Zeke Hawker)*, Grace Studiford *(Countess Carstairs)*, Walter McEwen *(Marquis de Void)*, Wallace Ray *(MacGillicuddy)*.

Comedy. Source: Edward Childs Carpenter, "Polly in the Pantry" (publication undetermined). Polly, ingenue of a show troupe that is stranded in a small town, returns to New York broke. She and Bunny obtain jobs as French maid and butler with a *nouveau riche* Kansas family, the Hawkers. Polly meets the neighbor, MacGillicuddy, a famous actor; and the Hawker son, Zeke, unsuccessfully attempts to attract her attentions. At a party given by Mrs. Hawker, Zeke denounces her to the guests as the maid; and when Mrs. Hawker's jewels are stolen, Polly is suspected and arrested. But Polly recognizes the Countess Carstairs and the Marquis de Void, "patrons" of the Hawkers, in the rogues' gallery. Polly and the police arrive in time to prevent the marriage of Zeke and the phony countess. The crooks are arrested, and Mac and Polly are united. *Domestics. Actors. Kansans. Nouveaux riches. Imposture. Theft.*

PARDON MY GUN **F2.4136**

Pathé Exchange. 5 or 29 Jun **1930** [c29 Jun 1930; LP1817]. Mus score & sd eff (Photophone); b&w. 35mm. 7 reels, 5,654 ft.

Prod E. B. Derr. *Dir* Robert De Lacy. *Ed in Ch* Eugene Walter. *Scen-Dial* Hugh Cummings. *Story* Betty Scott. *Photog* Edward Snyder. *Film Ed* Fred Allen. *Song: "Deep Down South"* George Green. *Sd Engr* Ben Winkler, Homer Ackerman.

Cast: Sally Starr *(Mary)*, George Duryea *(Ted)*, Mona Ray *(Peggy)*, Lee Moran *(Jeff)*, Robert Edeson *(Pa Martin)*, Frank MacFarlane *(Hank)*, Tom MacFarlane *(Tom)*, Harry Woods *(Copper)*, Stompie *("Lightnin")*, Lew Meehan *(Denver)*, Ethan Laidlaw *(Tex)*, Harry Watson, Al Norman, Ida May Chadwick, Abe Lyman and His Band.

Western comedy. Ted Duncan is in love with the boss's daughter, Mary. But Copper, who runs the adjoining ranch, also loves Mary and seeks to separate the two. At the annual relay race, Mary's father puts his money on his own horse, jockeyed by Duncan; Copper does all he can to prevent Duncan's winning the race and hopefully the girl. Later, a barn dance serves as the setting for a variety of performances: yodeling youths, dancing, a song by Mona Ray (playing Peggy), drum acrobatics by Abe Lyman, and a one-handed clarinet duet by one of the boys in the band. *Ranchers. Jockeys. Horseracing. Jealousy.*

PARDON MY NERVE! **F2.4137**

Fox Film Corp. 5 Mar **1922** [c5 Mar 1922; LP17681]. Si; b&w. 35mm. 5 reels, 4,093 ft.

Pres by William Fox. *Dir* Reaves Eason. *Scen* Jack Strumwasser. *Photog* George Schneiderman. *Asst Dir* Michael Eason.

Cast: Charles Jones *(Racey Dawson)*, Eileen Percy *(Molly Dale)*, Mae Busch *(Marie)*, G. Raymond Nye *(Bill McFluke)*, Joe Harris *(Jack Harpe)*, Otto Hoffman *(Luke Tweezy)*, William Steele *(Nebraska Jones)*, Robert Daly *(Henry Dale)*.

Western melodrama. Source: William Patterson White, *The Heart of the Range* (Garden City, New York, 1921). Although his skill as a gunman makes numerous enemies, Racey Dawson becomes friends with Molly Dale, daughter of a rancher, Marie, a dancehall girl, and Marie's dog. Henry Dale, influenced by a band of gamblers, is persuaded while intoxicated to sign a bill of sale for his ranch; a quarrel follows, he is murdered, and Racey puts a bullet through the signature, thereby invalidating the paper. Pursuing the villain to an upstairs room, Racey gives McFluke a beating, then is accused of having murdered him. The dog, however, brings in a knife and lays it at the feet of the accuser. After being vindicated, Racey returns to the ranch with Molly, who accepts his marriage offer. *Ranchers. Dancehall girls. Gamblers. Murder. Documentation. Dogs.*

PARIS **F2.4138**

Metro-Goldwyn-Mayer Pictures. 24 May **1926** [c26 May 1926; LP22780]. Si; b&w. 35mm. 6 reels, 5,580 ft.

Dir-Writ Edmund Goulding. *Titl* Joe Farnham. *Photog* John Arnold. *Settings* Cedric Gibbons, Merrill Pye. *Film Ed* Arthur Johns. *Wardrobe* Kathleen Kay, Maude Marsh, André-ani.

Cast: Charles Ray *(Jerry)*, Joan Crawford *(The Girl)*, Douglas Gilmore *(The Cat)*, Michael Visaroff *(Rocco)*, Rose Dione *(Marcelle)*, Jean Galeron *(Pianist)*.

Romantic melodrama. Jerry, a wealthy and carefree American youth, encounters a beautiful girl in the notorious Birdcage Cafe in Paris and incurs the jealousy of her sweetheart, a ferocious apache. The apache knifes Jerry, and The Girl accompanies Jerry to his palatial villa, then nurses him back to health; Jerry tactfully pays her to dance with the apache when again threatened, but The Girl is brutally hurt by her lover and imprisoned as a consequence—yet she loves him. Jerry, in gratitude, showers her with money and jewels, and her sweetheart abuses and threatens her on a visit to the prison. While at the races with Jerry, The Girl receives word that the apache is free and swears to kill her; she confesses her love for him, and Jerry leaves her. She returns to the cafe and dances with her lover, who tries to strangle her in a moment of fury, but Jerry intervenes; The Girl begs him to desist, and understanding that she truly loves the apache, Jerry does so. *Dancers. Apaches—Paris. Jealousy. Paris.*

PARIS **F2.4139**

First National Pictures. 7 Nov **1929** [c4 Dec 1929; LP887]. Sd (Vitaphone); b&w with col sequences (Technicolor). 35mm. 10 reels, 9,007 ft. [Also si.]

Supv Bobby North. *Dir* Clarence Badger. *Danc Dir* Larry Ceballos. *Scen-Dial-Titl* Hope Loring. *Photog* Sol Polito. *Film Ed* Edward Schroeder. *Songs: "My Lover," "Crystal Girl," "Miss Wonderful," "I Wonder What Is Really on His Mind," "I'm a Little Negative," "Somebody Mighty Like You"* Al Bryan, Eddie Ward. *Song: "Among My Souvenirs"* Edgar Leslie, Horatio Nicholls.

Cast: Irene Bordini *(Vivienne Rolland)*, Jack Buchanan *(Guy Pennell)*, Louise Closser Hale *(Cora Sabbot)*, Jason Robards *(Andrew Sabbot)*, ZaSu Pitts *(Harriet)*, Margaret Fielding *(Brenda Kaley)*.

Romantic musical comedy. Source: Martin Brown, *Paris* (New York opening: 8 Oct 1928). Andrew, an American art student in Paris, meets and falls in love with Vivienne Rolland, an actress, and she agrees to marry him with his mother's consent. Cora Sabbot, Andrew's mother, arrives in Paris with Brenda Kaley, intent upon breaking up the match, and bluntly refuses to receive Vivienne. Guy Pennell, a handsome English revue artist who is in love with Vivienne, also determines to break up the couple and gives Cora some brandy after she faints, causing her to lose her puritanical notions and to begin a scandalous flirtation with him. Vivienne tries unsuccessfully to find out if Guy really loves Cora, and in spite of Andrew's protests, Cora and Guy announce their engagement. Vivienne and Andrew come to a parting of ways, and, learning of Guy's conspiracy with Cora, she sends him away but at length is reconciled to him. *Students. Actors. Social classes. Motherhood. Flirtation. Paris.*

PARIS AT MIDNIGHT **F2.4140**

Metropolitan Pictures. *Dist* Producers Distributing Corp. 18 Apr **1926** [c15 Mar 1926; LP22499]. Si; b&w. 35mm. 7 reels, 6,995 ft.

Dir E. Mason Hopper. *Adapt* Frances Marion. *Photog* Norbert Brodin. *Adtl Photog* Dewey Wrigley. *Art Dir* Charles Cadwallader. *Prod Mgr* George Bertholon. *Prod Asst* E. J. Babille.

Cast: Jetta Goudal *(Delphine)*, Lionel Barrymore *(Vautrin)*, Mary Brian *(Victorine Tallefer)*, Edmund Burns *(Eugène de Rastagnic)*, Emile Chautard *(Papa Goriot)*, Brandon Hurst *(Count Tallefer)*, Jocelyn Lee *(Anastasie)*, Mathilde Comont *(Madame Vauquer)*, Carrie Daumery *(Mademoiselle Miche)*, Fannie Yantis *(Julie)*, Jean De Briac *(Frederick Tallefer)*, Charles Requa *(Maxine de Trailers)*.

Drama. Source: Honoré de Balzac, *Le Père Goriot* (Paris, 1896). Vautrin, an escaped convict who has taken refuge in a cheap boardinghouse in Paris, sets about righting the wrongs suffered by the other lodgers. He kills a man in a duel in order to reunite Victorine Tallefer with her estranged father; he brings selfish Delphine Goriot back to the bedside of her dying father, who has sacrificed everything to provide for her and her sister, Anastasie; and he then reunites Victorine with Eugène de Rastagnic, an artist with whom she has fallen in love. Disguised as Papa Goriot, Vautrin then eludes the police. *Prison escapees. Police. Artists. Boardinghouses. Paris.*

PARIS BOUND **F2.4141**

Pathé Exchange. 3 Aug **1929** [c6 Oct 1929; LP753]. Sd (Photophone); b&w. 35mm. 8 reels, 6,687 ft.

Supv Maurice Revnes. *Prod* Arthur Hopkins. *Dir* Edward H. Griffith. *Dial Dir–Dial* Frank Reicher. *Adapt* Horace Jackson. *Photog* Norbert Brodin, Norbert Scully. *Film Ed* Helen Warne. *Rec Engr* George Ellis, Charles O'Loughlin. *Asst Dir* William Scully. *Prod Mgr* George Webster. *Cost* Gwen Wakeling.

Cast: Ann Harding *(Mary Hutton)*, Fredric March *(Jim Hutton)*, George Irving *(James Hutton, Sr.)*, Leslie Fenton *(Richard Parrish)*, Hallam Cooley *(Peter)*, Juliette Crosby *(Nora Cope)*, Charlotte Walker *(Helen White)*, Carmelita Geraghty *(Noel Farley)*, Ilka Chase *(Fanny Shipman)*.

Romantic drama. Source: Philip Barry, *Paris Bound, a Comedy* (New York, 1929). Mary Archer weds Jim Hutton with all the ritual of a church wedding, the bride believing that each should be allowed perfect freedom in personal contacts. Among the wedding guests is the young composer Richard Parrish, hardly disguising his admiration for the bride, and Noel Farley, whose passion is exceeded only by the pain of losing Jim to another woman. When a child is born to them, Mary declines to accompany Jim on a European business trip, and Noel, who owns a villa at Antibes, lures him into a rendezvous. Meanwhile, Mary sees much of Richard, her composer friend; later, learning of the rendezvous, she considers a Paris divorce so as to marry Richard, but when Jim unexpectedly returns, their mutual love is confirmed. *Businessmen. Composers. Marriage. Infidelity. Jealousy. Weddings. Paris. Antibes.*

THE PARISH PRIEST **F2.4142**

Herman J. Garfield. 5 Feb **1921** [trade review]. Si; b&w. 35mm. 6 reels, 5,500 ft.

Dir Joseph Franz. *Photog* Harry Gersted.

Cast: William Desmond *(Rev. John Whalen)*, Thomas Ricketts *(Dr. Thomas Cassidy)*, Carl Miller *(Dr. Edward Welsh)*, J. Morris Foster *(James Welsh)*, Walter Perry *(Michael Sullivan)*, Margaret Livingston *(Agnes Cassidy)*, Ruth Renick *(Helen Durkin)*, Billie Bennett *(Katherine Carrigan)*.

Melodrama. Source: Daniel L. Hart, *The Parish Priest* (New York opening: 30 Aug 1900). "John Whalen has just been ordained into the priesthood, and, incidentally, injected the last ray of sunshine into the heart of his dying mother. The fine old lady's last wish, while attending the ordination of her son, is that Ned Welsh, a young physician, and his lifelong sweetheart, Nellie Durkin, become married. From this time on the young priest's greatest efforts are in carrying out this wish. He also ... prevents Agnes, Ned's [*sic*] sweetheart, from leaving the peaceful little village when she thinks that her lover is switching his affections by recounting the tale of another girl who left the town and her swain to marry a city chap in all its sordid details. Agnes capitulates and shortly afterward Father Whalen is able to bring the couple together, with a wedding day set." (*Moving Picture World*, 5 Feb 1921, p728.) *Priests. Physicians. Motherhood. Village life.*

PARISIAN LOVE **F2.4143**

B. P. Schulberg Productions. 1 Aug **1925.** Si; b&w. 35mm. 7 reels, 6,324 ft.

Dir Louis Gasnier. *Adapt* Lois Hutchinson. *Story* F. Oakley Crawford. *Photog* Allen Siegler.

Cast: Clara Bow *(Marie)*, Donald Keith *(Armand)*, Lillian Leighton *(La Frouchard)*, James Gordon Russell *(D'Avril)*, Hazel Keener *(Margot)*, Lou Tellegen *(Pierre Marcel)*, Jean De Briac *(The Knifer)*, Otto Matiesen *(apache leader)*, Alyce Mills *(Jean D'Arcy)*.

Melodrama. Marie and Armand, dancers in a Paris nightclub, set out to rob the home of Pierre Marcel, a wealthy scientist, taking The Knifer along with them. Marcel walks in on them unexpectedly, and Armand is wounded, with the result that The Knifer is restrained from killing the scientist. The grateful Marcel nurses Armand back to health and introduces him to the beautiful Jean. Marie becomes jealous and lures Marcel into marriage, immediately afterward telling him of her cruel deception. Armand returns from abroad, and Marie flies into his arms. Marie's apache friends, who helped her deceive Marcel, attempt to kill Armand and instead accidentally shoot her. Armand nurses her back to health, and

Marcel leaves to get a divorce that will free Marie to find happiness with Armand. *Dancers. Apaches—Paris. Scientists. Imposture. Marriage. Divorce. Paris.*

PARISIAN NIGHTS **F2.4144**

Gothic Pictures. *Dist* Film Booking Offices of America. 27 Sep **1925** [c30 Dec 1924; LP21458]. Si; b&w. 35mm. 7 reels, 6,278 ft.

Dir Al Santell. *Scen* Frederick Myton, Doty Hobart. *Story* Emil Forst. *Photog* Ernest Hallor. *Asst Dir* Robert Florey, Roland Asher.

Cast: Elaine Hammerstein *(Adele)*, Gaston Glass *(Jacques)*, Lou Tellegen *(Jean)*, William J. Kelly *(Fontane)*, Boris Karloff *(Pierre)*, Renée Adorée *(Marie)*.

Melodrama. Adele La Rue, an American sculptress working in Paris, lacks the inspiration to create a masterpiece, until Jean Ballard, a wild apache leader, takes refuge from the police in her apartment. Adele saves him from capture on the condition that he pose as the model for one of her works. Adele and Jean fall in love, finding happiness with each other until Marie, Jean's former love, insults him by telling him he is no better than a rich woman's lap dog. Jean returns to the underworld and becomes involved in a gang war with a rival gang, the Wolves. Looking for Jean, Adele goes to a cafe he is known to frequent, where she is captured by the Wolves. When Jean comes to rescue her, he is also captured. The Wolves heat knives with which to torture the reunited lovers, but before they can be used, the police arrive and open fire on the Wolves' hideout. During the excitement, Marie, who has joined the Wolves, repents of her hate and releases Adele and Jean. They jump from an open window just as the hideout is destroyed by artillery fire. Jean decides to repent, and the lovers look forward to a romantic future together. *Sculptors. Police. Apaches—Paris. Gangs. Torture. Paris.*

A PARISIAN SCANDAL **F2.4145**

Universal Film Manufacturing Co. 5 Dec **1921** [c29 Nov 1921; LP17259]. Si; b&w. 35mm. 5 reels, 4,739 ft.

Pres by Carl Laemmle. *Dir* George L. Cox. *Scen* Doris Schroeder. *Story* Louise Winter. *Photog* William Fildew.

Cast: George Periolat *(Count Louis Oudoff)*, Lillian Lawrence *(Countess Oudoff)*, Marie Prevost *(Liane-Demarest)*, Bertram Grassby *(Baron Stransky)*, George Fisher *(Emile Carret)*, Lillian Rambeau *(Sophie Demarest)*, Tom Gallery *(Basil Hammond)*, Mae Busch *(Mamselle Sari)*, Rose Dione *(Princess)*.

Comedy-drama. Basil Hammond, a young man without social or romantic interests, goes to Paris to study paleontology and to bring back a report to his guardian on the manners and moral character of her granddaughter, Liane. At first he is repulsed by her attempts to vamp him, but eventually he falls in love with her. Basil discovers that Liane is engaged to Count Oudoff, and when the count insults him at a party, a duel is arranged. Liane intervenes to save Basil, and in despair he returns to America; on the steamer he finds Liane, and she promises to marry him. *Guardians. Grandmothers. Students. Vamps. Paleontology. Paris. Duels.*

THE PART TIME WIFE **F2.4146**

Gotham Productions. *Dist* Lumas Film Corp. Sep **1925** [c12 Nov 1925; LP21989]. Si; b&w. 35mm. 6 reels, 6,100 ft.

Pres by Sam Sax. *Prod* Sam Sax. *Dir* Henry McCarty. *Scen* Victoria Moore, Henry McCarty. *Adapt* James J. Tynan. *Photog* Jack MacKenzie. *Asst Dir* Glenn Belt.

Cast: Alice Calhoun *(Doris Fuller)*, Robert Ellis *(Kenneth Scott)*, Freeman Wood *(DeWitt Courtney)*, Edwards Davis *(Ben Ellis)*, Janice Peters *(Nita Northrup)*, Patricia Palmer *("Toddles" Thornton)*, Charles West *(Allen Keane)*.

Melodrama. Source: Peggy Gaddis, "The Part-Time Wife," in *Snappy Stories Magazine* (Aug 1925). Doris Fuller, noted screen star, marries poor newspaperman Kenneth Scott. His pride is hurt when he is called "Mr. Doris Fuller" and by the disparity between their earnings. She quits to become his "full time" wife but returns to the screen when she sees him becoming a nervous wreck trying to write a play to boost their earnings. Kenneth erroneously believes her to be having an affair with her leading man, DeWitt Courtney, and begins to pay ardent attention to Nita Northrup, a rising young actress. His actions cause a real breach, and they separate. Kenneth's play is a success, but he is not happy. They are reconciled after Doris is injured in the studio, and she once more becomes his "full time" wife. *Actors. Reporters. Playwrights. Marriage. Infidelity. Motion pictures.*

Note: The cast includes also "The Studio Crew," playing themselves.

PART TIME WIFE **F2.4147**

Fox Film Corp. 28 Dec **1930** [c18 Nov 1930; LP1788]. Sd (Movietone); b&w. 35mm. 6,500 ft.

Dir Leo McCarey. *Screenplay-Dial* Raymond L. Schrock, Leo McCarey, Howard Green. *Photog* George Schneiderman. *Film Ed* Jack Murray. *Rec Engr* Al Bruzlin.

Cast: Edmund Lowe *(Jim Murdock)*, Leila Hyams *(Mrs. Murdock [Betty Rogers])*, Tom Clifford *(Tommy Milligan)*, Walter McGrail *(Johnny Spence)*, Louis Payne *(butler)*, Sam Lufkin *(caddie master)*, Bodil Rosing *(maid)*, George "Red" Corcoran *(chauffeur)*.

Comedy. Source: Stewart Edward White, "The Shepper-Newfounder," in *Saturday Evening Post* (202:10–11, 29 Mar 1930). Jim Murdock, a gas and oil man immersed in his business activities, neglects his wife, who is crazy about golf and finds that Johnny Spence is a willing partner in her favorite sport. She and Jim separate, and she turns to modeling as a source of income. Jim takes up golf on the advice of his physician, and on the links he meets Tommy Milligan, an Irish caddie whose philosophizing eventually brings about a change in Jim, who realizes the reasons for the failure of his marriage. When he is accidentally matched with his wife in a game, she discovers the new side of his personality, and their new friendship leads to a reconciliation as man and wife. *Businessmen. Irish. Caddies. Fashion models. Oil business. Marriage. Golf. Divorce.*

PARTED CURTAINS **F2.4148**

Warner Brothers Pictures. ca5 Oct **1921** [New York premiere; released 5 Nov 1921; c26 Sep 1922; LP18257]. Si; b&w. 35mm. 6 reels, 5,739 ft.

Dir? (see note) John Bracken. *Story* Tom J. Hopkins. *Auth? (see note)* James C. Bradford.

Cast: Henry Walthall *(Joe Jenkins)*, Mary Alden *(Mrs. Masters)*, Edward Cecil *(Wheeler Masters)*, Margaret Landis *(Helen)*, Mickey Moore *(Bobby Masters)*, William Clifford *("The Weasel")*.

Crook melodrama. Joe Jenkins is released from prison and determines to go straight, but his friend Tom Vaughn ("The Weasel") tries to change his mind. Joe fails to find work, however, and attempts to rob wealthy artist Wheeler Masters, who takes Joe in, discovers his artistic ability, and encourages him. To keep "The Weasel" from revealing Mrs. Masters as his former sweetheart, Joe, now a famous artist, takes the blame for a theft "The Weasel" commits in Masters' house, thus wrecking his chances for happiness with Mrs. Masters' sister, Helen. Joe exonerates himself by preventing "The Weasel" from abducting the Masters' child and is united with Helen. *Artists. Criminals—Rehabilitation. Theft. Abduction.*

Note: *Motion Picture News* gives director as John Bracken. *Moving Picture World* gives author as James C. Bradford.

THE PARTING OF THE TRAILS **F2.4149**

J. P. McGowan Productions. *Dist* Syndicate Pictures. 1 Mar **1930.** Mus score; b&w. 35mm. 5 reels. [Also si; Oct 1929.]

Dir J. P. McGowan. *Story-Scen* Sally Winters. *Photog* Hap Depew.

Cast: Bob Custer *(Rambler Raymond)*, Bobby Dunn *(Restless Roberts)*, Henry Roquemore *(J. Addington Fiske)*, George A. Miller *(King Slocum)*, Tommy Bay *("Lucky" Hardy)*, Vivian Ray *(Corliss Fiske)*.

Western melodrama. Drifters Rambler Raymond and Restless Roberts meet up with J. Addington Fiske, an eastern millionaire seeking diversion. Worried by his absence, Fiske's daughter, Corliss, offers a reward for information of his whereabouts, and rustler Lucky Hardy kidnaps Fiske for ransom. With the help of the girl, Rambler rescues Fiske and wins the reward and Corliss. *Wanderers. Millionaires. Rustlers. Kidnaping. Ransom.*

PARTNERS *see* **THE FOX**

PARTNERS AGAIN **F2.4150**

Samuel Goldwyn, Inc. *Dist* United Artists. 15 Feb **1926** [c13 Feb 1926; LP22397]. Si; b&w. 35mm. 6 reels, 5,562 ft.

Pres by Samuel Goldwyn. *Dir* Henry King. *Titl* Montague Glass. *Adapt* Frances Marion. *Photog* Arthur Edeson.

Cast: George Sidney *(Abe Potash)*, Alexander Carr *(Mawruss Perlmutter)*, Betty Jewel *(Hattie Potash)*, Allan Forrest *(Dan)*, Robert Schable *(Schenckmann)*, Lillian Elliott *(Rosie Potash)*, Earl Metcalf *(aviator)*, Lew Brice *(Pazinsky)*, Gilbert Clayton *(Sammett)*, Anna Gilbert *(Mrs. Sammett)*.

Comedy. Source: Montague Glass and Jules Eckert Goodman, *Partners Again* (New York opening: 1 May 1922). Abe Potash and Mawruss Perlmutter become partners in the automobile business, taking over a franchise for the Schenckmann Six. Abe becomes involved in merchandising a new engine with his nephew, and Abe and Mawruss split up. Abe's venture comes a cropper, and he must flee from both angry stockholders and the police. Mawruss does not forsake his old friend, however, and arranges air passage across the Canadian border for Abe. The stock manipulators are later caught and Abe returns to the United States with a clear conscience, renewing his friendship with Mawruss. *Automobile manufacturers. Salesmen. Police. Aviators. Fraud. Partnerships.*

PARTNERS IN CRIME **F2.4151**

Paramount Famous Lasky Corp. 17 Mar **1928** [c17 Mar 1928; LP25085]. Si; b&w. 35mm. 7 reels, 6,600 ft.

Pres by Adolph Zukor, Jesse L. Lasky. *Dir* Frank Strayer. *Story-Screenplay* Grover Jones, Gilbert Pratt. *Titl* George Marion, Jr. *Photog* William Marshall. *Film Ed* William Shea.

Cast: Wallace Beery *(Mike Doolan, The Detective)*, Raymond Hatton *("Scoop" McGee, The Reporter)*, Raymond Hatton *("Knife" Reagan, Terror of the Underworld)*, Mary Brian *(Marie Burke, The Cigarette Girl)*, William Powell *(Smith)*, Jack Luden *(Richard Deming, Assistant District Attorney)*, Arthur Housman *(Barton)*, Albert Roccardi *(Kanelli, The Restaurant Owner)*, Joseph W. Girard *(Chief of Police)*, George Irving *(B. R. Cornwall)*, Bruce Gordon *(Dodo)*, Jack Richardson *(Jake)*.

Crook comedy-drama. After being dismissed for imitating his boss's voice on radio, former Assistant District Attorney Richard Deming witnesses a store robbery and is taken captive by the criminals. Suspected of the crime, he is sought by the police, but his sweetheart, Marie, convinced of his innocence, enlists the help of two friends, a newspaper reporter and a half-witted detective. Hoping to win the girl's favor, the two go to the gangsters' hideout, encounter a violent gang war, and accidently set off a case of police tear bombs. The police, summoned by Marie, arrive just in time to save the kidnaped attorney. *Gangs. Reporters. Detectives. District attorneys. Robbery.*

PARTNERS OF FATE **F2.4152**

Fox Film Corp. Jan **1921** [c2 Jan 1921; LP15998]. Si; b&w. 35mm. 5 reels.

Pres by William Fox. *Dir* Bernard Durning. *Scen* Robert Dillon. *Story* Stephen Chalmers. *Photog* Glen MacWilliams, Otto Brautigan.

Cast: Louise Lovely *(Helen Meriless)*, William Scott *(John Fraser)*, Rosemary Theby *(Frances Lloyd)*, Philo McCullough *(Byron Millard)*, George Siegmann *(purser)*, Richard Cummings *(Bill Ricketts)*, Eileen O'Malley *(baby)*.

Melodrama. Helen Meriless, a serious young girl, marries a shallow man, while Frances Lloyd, a butterfly type, marries a level-headed engineer. Both start their honeymoon on the same ship. A shipwreck causes a mixup of the married persons; Helen and her husband remain faithful to each other, but Frances and her husband separately engage in adulterous activities. A rescue ship carries away the faithless couple, leaving the others to their fate; but the latter survive and eventually triumph. *Engineers. Marriage. Infidelity. Tropics. Shipwrecks.*

PARTNERS OF THE SUNSET **F2.4153**

Western Pictures. Feb **1922** [New York State]. Si; b&w. 35mm. 5 reels, 4,950 ft.

Pres by Bert Lubin. *Dir* Robert H. Townley. *Story* Walter Richard Hall. *Photog* John K. Holbrook.

Cast: Allene Ray *(Patricia Moreland)*, Robert Frazer *(David Brooks)*, Mildred Bright *(Violet Moreland)*, J. W. Johnston *(Jim Worth)*.

Western melodrama. Supposedly wealthy, Patricia and Vi Moreland find themselves penniless and dependent upon relatives when their father dies. They accept an uncle's offer to live on his Texas ranch, which is desired by an unscrupulous neighbor, Jim Worth. Young geologist David Brooks (who sells windmills) happens along and persuades the girls to refuse Worth's offer to buy the ranch. Worth has Vi kidnaped, and he gets the upper hand when Brooks rescues her. The geologist turns the tables, however, and Worth does not live to see either Brooks's windmill strike oil or happiness come to Brooks and Patricia. *Uncles. Geologists. Sisters. Wealth. Ranch life. Windmills. Oil. Texas.*

PARTNERS OF THE TIDE **F2.4154**

Irvin V. Willat Productions. *Dist* W. W. Hodkinson Corp. Mar **1921** [c20 Mar 1921; LP16484]. Si; b&w. 35mm. 7 reels, 6,500 ft.

Prod-Writ Irvin V. Willat. *Dir* L. V. Jefferson. *Photog* Paul Eagler.

Cast: Jack Perrin *(Bradley Nickerson)*, Marion Faducha *(Bradley as a boy)*, Gordon Mullen *(Sam Hammond)*, Daisy Robinson *(Augusta Baker)*, Gertrude Norman *(Grandma Baker)*, J. P. Lockney *(Capt. Ezra Titcomb)*, Joe Miller *(Carl Swenson)*, Bert Hadley *(James Williams)*, Fred Kohler *(first mate)*, Florence Midgley *(Temperance Allen)*, Ashley Cooper *(Seth Rogers)*.

Melodrama. Source: Joseph Crosby Lincoln, *Partners of the Tide* (New York, 1905). The Allen spinsters adopt Bradley Nickerson, who grows up with Gussie Baker, the little girl next door. Fifteen years later he is first mate of the *Thomas Doane,* owned by Granny Baker. A plot to sink the ship is averted by Bradley and a sailor, but ultimately the ship is sabotaged. The insurance company hires Bradley to investigate the wreck, but Sam Hammond, a deepsea diver, also in love with Gussie, is tampering with Bradley's diving gear at the moment a fire breaks out. Rowing to the burning ship, Bradley rescues Hammond, who then leaves him stranded, but Gussie rows out to save him, realizing at last the depth of her love. *Spinsters. Ship crews. Insurance—Marine. Shipwrecks. Ship fires. Diving.*

PARTY GIRL **F2.4155**

Victory Pictures. *Dist* Tiffany Productions. 1 Jan **1930** [New York premiere; released 25 Jan; c17 Jan 1930; LP1001]. Sd (Photophone?); b&w. 35mm. 9 reels, 7,401 ft. [Also si; 6,750 ft.]

Dir Victor Halperin. *Scen-Dial* Monte Katterjohn, George Draney, Victor Halperin. *Photog* Henry Cronjager, Robert Newhard. *Film Ed* Russell Schoengarth. *Songs: "Farewell," "Oh, How I Adore You"* Harry Stoddard, Marcy Klauber. *Rec Engrs* R. S. Clayton, William R. Fox, Alfred M. Granich, Ben Harper.

Cast: Douglas Fairbanks, Jr. *(Jay Rountree)*, Jeanette Loff *(Ellen Powell)*, Judith Barrie *(Leeda Cather)*, Marie Prevost *(Diana Hoster)*, John St. Polis *(John Rountree)*, Sammy Blum *(Sam Metten)*, Harry Northrup *(Robert Lowry)*, Almeda Fowler *(Maude Lindsay)*, Hal Price *(Lew Albans)*, Charles Giblyn *(Lawrence Doyle)*, Sidney D'Albrook *(investigator)*, Lucien Prival *(Paul Newcast)*, Florence Dudley *(Miss Manning)*.

Society drama. Source: Edwin Balmer, *Dangerous Business* (New York, 1927). John Rountree, a wealthy manufacturer, refuses to avail himself of "party girls" to sell his products, condemning the method as immoral and unfair. Jay, his collegiate son, is engaged to marry Ellen Powell, his father's secretary. While attending a fraternity banquet, Jay and his friends crash a typical business party in the same hotel, and there he meets Leeda Cather, a wild party girl who is in trouble and wants to get married. After getting Jay intoxicated, Leeda takes him to her apartment, and the next morning she claims he has ruined her; as a result, he marries her. Ellen, herself a secretly reformed party girl, is heartbroken and returns to her former life. A police investigation uncovers Leeda's guilt, and in evading arrest, she falls from an apartment window and is killed. Jay, now free, is reconciled with Ellen. *Manufacturers. Party girls. Students. Business ethics. Jazz life.*

Note: Initially reviewed under the title *Dangerous Business.*

THE PASSAIC TEXTILE STRIKE **F2.4156**

S. B. Russack. *Dist* International Workers Aid. 14 Oct **1926** [New York State license]. Si; b&w. 35mm. 7 reels, 6,263 ft.

Documentary. According to the licensing records of the New York State Motion Picture Commission, this film contains references to the exploitation of the millworkers and to the attitude of the millowners. *Factory workers. Strikes. Labor. Textile manufacture. Mills. Passaic (New Jersey).*

THE PASSING OF WOLF MACLEAN **F2.4157**

Ermine Productions. *Dist* Usla Co. 29 Nov **1924** [trade review; c17 Nov, 20 Nov 1924; LU20802]. Si; b&w. 35mm. 5 reels, 4,712 ft.

Dir Paul Hurst. *Orig Story* George Hively.

Cast: Jack Meehan *(The Stranger)*, Mark Fenton *(Bert Granger)*, Alma Rayford *(Alice Granger)*, Al Hallett *(Parson Dan Williams)*, John Fox, Jr. *(Benny Granger)*.

Western melodrama. Bert Granger, addicted to strong drink and heavy gambling, owns a saloon in which his children, Benny and the winsome Alice, entertain the habitués. At the bar one night, The Stranger interferes in a drunken quarrel and becomes involved in a bitter fight, from which he emerges victorious. He is strongly attracted to Alice, and he strikes up a conversation while, at the gambling table, her father is being cheated in a crooked card game and loses the deed to the saloon. When a reward is posted for Wolf Maclean, The Stranger, who resembles the description given of the notorious bandit, is arrested. The gamblers arrange for a quick hanging, but Parson Dan Williams saves The Stranger by announcing that he himself is Wolf Maclean and that the gamblers are his confederates in crime. Before the astonished populace can arrest the gamblers, the parson is killed by one of their vengeful number. The Stranger is cleared and wins Alice; Bert Granger reforms and opens a general store, with Benny as his partner. *Strangers. Bandits. Clergymen. Gambling. Mistaken identity. Saloons.*

PASSING THRU **F2.4158**

Thomas H. Ince Productions. *Dist* Paramount Pictures. 14 Aug **1921** [c5 Oct 1921; LP17038]. Si; b&w. 35mm. 5 reels, 5,108 ft.

Pres by Thomas H. Ince. *Supv* Thomas H. Ince. *Dir* William A. Seiter. *Scen* Joseph Franklin Poland. *Story* Agnes Christine Johnston. *Photog* Bert Cann.

Cast: Douglas MacLean *(Billy Barton)*, Madge Bellamy *(Mary Spivins)*, Otto Hoffman *(James Spivins)*, Cameron Coffey *(Willie Spivins)*, Willard Robards *(Silas Harkins)*, Edithe Yorke *(Mother Harkins)*, Fred Gambold *(Hezikiah Briggs)*, Margaret Livingston *(Louise Kingston)*, Louis Natheaux *(Fred Kingston)*, Bert Hadley *(Henry Kingston)*.

Rural comedy. Bank teller Billy Barton shoulders the blame for a cash shortage for which Fred Kingston, a fellow employee, is responsible and is sentenced to prison. On his way there, the train is wrecked and he escapes. In the town of Culterton, he meets and falls in love with Mary Spivins, the bank president's daughter, and charms the populace by playing the mouth organ. He obtains work as a farmhand with Silas Harkins, taking the farm mule as wages. When Spivins orders Harkins arrested for assault, Billy learns it was a kick from the mule that laid out Spivins. At the bank he finds Spivins bound while Fred and the clerk are robbing the safe; Billy is locked in the safe, and all efforts to save him prove futile until the wall is kicked out by the mule. Through the efforts of Willie Spivins, the bank is dynamited, but all ends happily. *Fugitives. Bank clerks. Robbers. Harmonica players. Mules.*

Note: Copyright title: *Passin' Through.*

THE PASSION FLOWER **F2.4159**

Norma Talmadge Film Co. *Dist* Associated First National Pictures. Apr **1921** [c5 May 1921; LP16467]. Si; b&w. 35mm. 7 reels, 6,755 ft.

Pres by Joseph M. Schenck. *Dir* Herbert Brenon. *Adapt* Herbert Brenon, Mary Murillo. *Photog* J. Roy Hunt.

Cast: Norma Talmadge *(Acacia, The Passion Flower)*, Courtenay Foote *(Esteban, her stepfather)*, Eulalie Jensen *(Raimunda, her mother)*, Harrison Ford *(Norbert, The Poet)*, Charles Stevenson *(Tio Eusebio, a grand old man)*, Alice May *(Julia, his blind wife)*, H. D. McClellan, Austin Harrison, Herbert Vance *(their sons)*, Robert Agnew *(Faustino, their youngest son)*, Harold Stern *(Little Carlos)*, Natalie Talmadge *(Milagros, a flirt)*, Mrs. Jacques Martin *(Old Juliana, servant of Raimunda)*, Elsa Fredericks *(Francesca, servant of Raimunda)*, Robert Payton Gibb *(Norbert's father, the old potter)*, Augustus Balfour *(The Padre)*, Walter Wilson *(Rubio, The "Hound" of Esteban)*, Mildred Adams *(Doña Isabel, a friend of Raimunda)*, Julian Greer *(Acacia's father)*, Edward Boring *(Bernabe)*.

Tragedy. Source: Jacinto Benevente y Martínez, *La Malquerida* (1913; New York opening, as *The Passion Flower*, trans. by J. G. Underhill: 13 Jan 1920). Acacia despises her stepfather, Esteban, and consents to marry her cousin, Norbert. Secretly infatuated with her, Esteban has his servant falsely inform her fiancé that she is betrothed to Faustino, and Norbert breaks the engagement. When Acacia accepts Faustino, he is murdered and Norbert is arrested, but after being found not guilty Norbert is pursued by Faustino's vengeful brothers; and he informs on the plotters, Esteban and Rubio. Acacia is forced into the arms of her father, and Raimunda, seeing her husband's passion for Acacia, calls for aid and is shot by him. In her dying moments, as Esteban is arrested, she admits her failure as a mother. One source describes a different conclusion in which the mother kills the stepfather after discovering his passion. *Stepfathers. Poets. Motherhood. Infidelity. Revenge.*

PASSION FLOWER **F2.4160**

Metro-Goldwyn-Mayer Pictures. 6 Dec **1930** [c8 Dec 1930; LP1791]. Sd (Movietone); b&w. 35mm. 9 reels, 7,171 ft.

Dir William De Mille. *Adtl Dial* Laurence G. Johnson, Edith Fitzgerald. *Adapt-Dial* Martin Flavin. *Photog* Hal Rosson. *Art Dir* Cedric Gibbons. *Film Ed* Conrad A. Nervig. *Rec Engr* J. K. Brock, Douglas Shearer. *Gowns* Adrian.

Cast: Kay Francis *(Dulce Morado)*, Kay Johnson *(Katherine Pringle Wallace)*, Charles Bickford *(Dan Wallace)*, Winter Hall *(Leroy Pringle)*, Lewis Stone *(Antonio Morado)*, ZaSu Pitts *(Mrs. Harney)*, Dickey Moore *(Tommy)*.

Drama. Source: Kathleen Norris, "Passion Flower," in *Delineator* (114: 9–11, 16–17, 17–18, 18–19, Mar–Jun; 115:17–18, 19–20, 26–27, Jul–Sep 1929). Two cousins, Dulce and Cassy (Katherine), marry into differing stations in life: Dulce weds Morado, a wealthy Spanish aristocrat, and Cassy falls in love with Dan Wallace, the family chauffeur. Cassy's father orders them to leave his home, and they are married at Don Morado's estate. Dan refuses Morado's offer of a farm as a wedding gift, preferring to make his own way, but after 5 years he fails to rise further than a stevedore, while Cassy bears him two children and is ever faithful and loving. Finally, he accepts Morado's offer, and they take along with them their former landlady and nurse, Mrs. Harney. Against his better judgment, Dan falls in love with Dulce; and when Morado dies, the two of them go to Paris. As Dan is about to divorce his wife, he is conscience-striken by memories of his family and returns to them. *Nurses. Children. Stevedores. Chauffeurs. Aristocrats. Marriage. Spanish. Wealth. Ambition. Family life. Paris.*

PASSION FRUIT **F2.4161**

Metro Pictures. ca8 Jan **1921** [New York premiere; released 7 Feb; c23 Feb 1921; LP16176]. Si; b&w. 35mm. 6 reels.

Dir John E. Ince. *Scen* Edward T. Lowe, Jr. *Story* Carey Wilson. *Photog* Rudolph Bergquist. *Art Dir* John Hughes.

Cast: Doraldina *(Regina Dominant)*, Edward Earle *(Pierce Lamont)*, Stuart Holmes *(Anders Rance)*, Sidney Bracey *("The Ancient")*, Florence Turner *(Nuanua)*, W. H. Bainbridge *(Peter Dominant)*.

Romantic melodrama. Regina Dominant lives with her father on a small South Sea island and is jealously regarded by the overseer, Rance, who wants to possess Regina and her estate. Rance poisons Dominant as a means of gaining control of the girl, but her confidence is won by Pierce Lamont, to whom she entrusts the management of the estate. Rance excites the natives to revolt against Regina, claiming she is halfcaste; however, Regina's maid reveals Rance's guilt and kills him. With peace restored, Pierce and Regina are happily united. *Halfcastes. Revolts. South Sea Islands.*

THE PASSION SONG **F2.4162**

Excellent Pictures. *Dist* Interstate Pictures. 15 Oct **1928** [c1 Nov 1928; LP25800]. Si; b&w. 35mm. 6 reels, 5,080 ft.

Pres by Samuel Zierler. *Dir* Harry O. Hoyt. *Scen* Elizabeth Hayter. *Titl* Camille Collins. *Photog* André Barlatier. *Film Ed* Leonard Wheeler.

Cast: Gertrude Olmsted *(Elaine Van Ryn)*, Noah Beery *(John Van Ryn)*, Gordon Elliott *(Keith Brooke)*, Edgar Washington Blue *(Ulambo)*.

Melodrama. Source: Francis Fenton, "Paid With Tears" (publication undetermined). Having made a fortune in South Africa and retired to the English countryside, John Van Ryn is visited by Keith Brooke, a close friend from the veld. Keith and John's wife, Elaine, are in love, but neither betrays the passion. Keith soon returns to Africa and becomes a derelict; Van Ryn also returns to the dark continent in an effort to help put down a native rebellion led by Ulambo, his sworn enemy. Van Ryn is killed by Ulambo, and Keith and Elaine are at last free to find happiness with each other. *English. Boers. Derelicts. South Africa. England.*

THE PASSIONATE PILGRIM **F2.4163**

Cosmopolitan Productions. *Dist* Paramount Pictures. ca1 Jan **1921** [New York premiere; released Jan; c31 Dec 1920; LP15990]. Si; b&w. 35mm. 7 reels, ca6,550 ft.

Dir Robert G. Vignola. *Scen? (see note)* Donnah Darrell, George Dubois Proctor. *Photog* Al Ligouri. *Asst Dir* Phil Carle.

Cast: Matt Moore *(Henry Calverly)*, Mary Newcomb *(Cecily)*, Julia Swayne Gordon *(Madame Watt)*, Tom Guise *(Senator Watt)*, Frankie Mann *(Marjorie Daw)*, Rubye De Remer *(Miriam)*, Claire Whitney *(Esther)*, Van Dyke Brooke *(Hitt)*, Charles Gerard *(Qualters)*, Sam J. Ryan *(Mayor McIntyre)*, Arthur Donaldson *(O'Rell)*, Albert Roccardi *(Amme)*, Bernard A. Reinold *(Listerly)*, Charles Brook *(Trent)*, Helen Lindroth *(Nurse Russell)*.

Society melodrama. Source: Samuel Merwin, *The Passionate Pilgrim, Being the Narrative of an Oddly Dramatic Year in the Life of Henry Calverly, 3rd* (Indianapolis, 1919). Author Henry Calverly serves a 3-year sentence to protect Madame Watt, his mother-in-law, who killed her husband. During this time, his wife Cecily dies. Upon his release, he obtains a job as a reporter, under the name of Stafford, with a newspaper owned by the Cantey estate. He writes an exposé of Mayor Tim McIntyre, who through his alliance with Qualters, a trustee of the estate, has Calverly fired. Majorie Daw, a "sob-writer" for the newspapers, arranges for him to assist Miriam Cantey, invalid daughter of the testator, in writing a biography of her father. Calverly and Miriam fall in love, and her intense attachment hastens her recovery. Together they expose Qualters and McIntyre, who have been conspiring against her; and Miriam announces Calverly as her future husband. *Authors. Reporters. Filial relations. Newspapers. Political corruption.*

Note: George Dubois Proctor is given credit in most sources for the scenario, but the copyright records credit Donnah Darrell instead.

THE PASSIONATE QUEST **F2.4164**

Warner Brothers Pictures. 10 or 17 Jul **1926** [c19 Jul 1926; LP22935]. Si; b&w. 35mm. 7 reels, 6,671 ft.

Dir J. Stuart Blackton. *Adapt* Marian Constance Blackton. *Camera* Nick Musuraca. *Asst Camera* William Adams. *Asst Dir* George Webster.

Cast: May McAvoy *(Rosina Vonet)*, Willard Louis *(Matthew Garner)*, Louise Fazenda *(Madame Mathilde)*, Gardner James *(Philip Garth)*, Jane Winton *(The Leading Lady)*, Holmes Herbert *(Erwen)*, De Witt Jennings *(Benjamin Stone)*, Vera Lewis *(Mrs. Gardner)*, Nora Cecil *(Mrs. Flint)*, Frank Butler *(Lord "Reggie" Towers)*, Charles Stevenson *(Rossil)*, William Herford *(Bone)*.

Society melodrama. Source: Edward Phillips Oppenheim, *The Passionate Quest* (Boston, 1924). Rosina Vonet, Philip Garth, and Matthew Garner, chafing against the narrow prejudices of Benjamin Stone, their guardian, determine to fulfill their ambitions in London: Rosina, a stage career; Philip, a career as a poet; and Matthew, a financial wizard. Philip, who loves Rosina, becomes despondent and alcoholic over his failure. Rosina obtains a role in a musical comedy; though also unsuccessful, she is charmed by Erwen, an author, who excites Philip's jealousy. Meanwhile, Matthew marries a wealthy widow and vindictively ruins his guardian's business while posing as a philanthropist. Intent on circumventing Rosina, Matthew persuades her to accept a job as a model with Madame Mathilde and schemes to seduce her. Erwen, Philip, and Matthew's irate wife denounce him, and his fortune is lost on the market. Philip wins a contract with a London editor and is happily reconciled with Rosina. *Guardians. Authors. Actors. Financiers. Fashion models. Poets. Prejudice. Alcoholism. Ambition. London.*

PASSIONATE YOUTH **F2.4165**

Truart Film Corp. ca28 Jun **1925.** Si; b&w. 35mm. 6 reels, 6,751 ft.

Dir Dallas M. Fitzgerald. *Scen* J. Grubb Alexander. *Titl* Ben Allah. *Photog* Milton Moore. *Film Ed* Jean Spencer Ware. *Asst Dir* Al Kelley.

Cast: Beverly Bayne *(Mary Rand)*, Frank Mayo *(John Rand)*, Pauline Garon *(Henrietta Rand)*, Bryant Washburn *(Corbin)*, Carmelita Geraghty *(Peggy)*, Ralph McCullough *(Matt Rutherford)*, Ernest Wood *(Jimmy Wellington)*, Lawrence Underwood *(prosecuting attorney)*, Jack Fowler *(district attorney)*, Walter Deming *(Harry Perrin)*, James McElhern *(Deacon Collins)*, William McIllwain *(Judge Ford)*.

Melodrama. Mary Rand, who wants the best both for herself and for her daughter, Henrietta, divorces her husband, a poor minister, and returns to her lucrative law practice. She soon falls in love with her law partner, Corbin, who in turn falls in love with Henrietta and romances both mother and daughter. Mary is elected district attorney; Corbin is found murdered, and Henrietta is blamed for the crime. John Rand, who was a lawyer before he became a minister, defends his daughter in court and proves that the gun found on her person was not the gun used to shoot Corbin. Henrietta is freed, and John and Mary are reconciled. *Clergymen. Lawyers. District attorneys. Women in public office. Divorce. Motherhood. Fatherhood. Trials.*

PASSIONS OF THE SEA *see* **LOST AND FOUND ON A SOUTH SEA ISLAND**

PASSION'S PATHWAY **F2.4166**

Jean Perry & Edward Small Co. *Dist* Lee-Bradford Corp. 1 Aug **1924.** Si; b&w. 35mm. 6 reels, 6,090 ft.

Dir Bertram Bracken. *Photog* Ross Fisher.

Cast: Estelle Taylor *(Dora Kenyon)*, Jean Perry *(Hugh Kenyon)*, Wilfred Lucas *(Richard Stanton)*, Tully Marshall *(butler)*, Snitz Edwards *(Simpson, the bookkeeper)*, Margaret Landis, Kate Price *(The Landlady)*, Edward Kimball *(John Deering)*, Fred De Silva *(General "Scorpio")*, Kenneth Gibson *(Atherton's son)*, Ben Deely *(Howard Atherton)*.

Melodrama. Hugh Kenyon defends a mine in Mexico against the attack of a gang of gringo outlaws. When he returns to the United States, wounded in the arm, he is discharged by his employer, who has been persuaded by a rejected suitor of Hugh's wife that he has been dishonest in his dealings. Hugh cannot find work and is completely unable to support his wife and young child. He is driven to desperation by his situation, and he goes to the palatial home of his former employer, forcing his way in with a gun in his hand. He confronts the man and demands enough money to help his starving family. The mine owner takes pity on Hugh and finally comes to believe in his innate honesty and sincerity. The man who falsely accused Hugh is, in turn, discharged, and Hugh gets his job back. *Gangs. Unemployment. Revenge. Mines. Mexico.*

A PASTEBOARD CROWN **F2.4167**

Nathan and Semerad. *Dist* Playgoers Pictures. 16 Apr **1922** [c25 Mar 1922; LU17680]. Si; b&w. 35mm. 5 reels, 4,468 ft.

Dir Travers Vale. *Scen* Thomas F. Fallon. *Story* Clara Morris. *Photog* Jacques Bizeul.

Cast: Evelyn Greeley *(Sybil Lawton)*, Robert Elliott *(Stewart Thrall)*, Gladys Valerie *(Edna Thrall)*, Eleanor Woodruff *(Cora Manice)*, Jane Jennings *(Mrs. Lawton)*, Dora Mills Adams *(Claire Morrell)*, Albert Roccardi *(William Buckley)*.

Society melodrama. Sybil Lawton, a society girl, is left penniless by the death of her father, and though her mother wishes her to marry into wealth, her sole ambition is to achieve fame in the theater. Her youthful charm and talent interest Stewart Thrall, a producer, who finds her a position with an Omaha stock company. Under Sybil's encouragement, fellow actor Jim Roberts, disillusioned by an unhappy marriage, improves and becomes her self-appointed guardian. Sybil returns to New York and begins rehearsals for *Romeo and Juliet* with Thrall as her costar and Roberts as stage manager. Meanwhile, Thrall's unhappy wife obtains a divorce, and Roberts, recognizing her as the woman who ruined his life, blames Thrall and shoots him at a performance as he bends over Juliet on her bier. Thrall recovers, however, and having declared his love for Sybil, he looks forward to happiness with her. *Actors. Socialites. Theatrical producers. Stage managers. Theater. Marriage. Omaha. New York City. "Romeo and Juliet".*

THE PASTEBOARD LOVER *see* **FAITHLESS LOVER**

THE PATENT LEATHER KID **F2.4168**

First National Pictures. 1 Sep **1927** [c29 Dec 1927; LP24816]. Si; b&w. 35mm. 12 reels, 11,955 ft.

Pres by Richard A. Rowland. *Prod-Dir* Alfred Santell. *Scen* Winifred Dunn. *Titl* Gerald C. Duffy. *Adapt* Adela Rogers St. Johns. *Photog* Arthur Edeson, Ralph Hammeras, Alvin Knechtel. *Prod Mgr* Al Rockett. *Makeup* Fred C. Ryle.

Cast: Richard Barthelmess *(The Patent Leather Kid)*, Molly O'Day *(Curley Boyle, the Golden Dancer)*, Lawford Davidson *(Lieut. Hugo Breen)*, Matthew Betz *(Jake Stuke)*, Arthur Stone *(Jimmy Kinch)*, Raymond Turner *(Mobile Molasses)*, Hank Mann *(sergeant)*, Walter James *(Officer Riley)*, Lucien Prival *(The German Officer)*, Nigel De Brulier *(The French Doctor)*, Fred O'Beck, Cliff Salm, Henry Murdock, Charles Sullivan, John Kolb, Al Alborn *(tank crew)*.

Drama. Source: Rupert Hughes, "Patent Leather Kid," in *Patent Leather Kid and Several Others* (New York, 1927). The Patent Leather Kid, a boxer from New York's Lower East Side, has little affection for his country, now at war with Germany. His contempt deepens when his girl leaves him to entertain the troops in France. The Kid and his trainer are drafted, and the trainer is shot in a military action. This loss spurs on the Kid to acts of heroism, but he is badly injured and becomes partially paralyzed. With his girl friend (who has become an Army nurse) the Kid sees a military parade; and as the colors unfurl, his previously paralyzed hand slowly rises in salute. *Boxers. Nurses. Paralysis. Miracles. World War I. New York City—Lower East Side.*

THE PATENT LEATHER PUG **F2.4169**

Harry J. Brown Productions. *Dist* Rayart Pictures. 21 Jan **1926** [New York State license]. Si; b&w. 35mm. 5 reels, 4,800 ft.

Dir Albert Rogell. *Story* Grover Jones.

Cast: Billy Sullivan *(Billy Griffin)*, Ruth Dwyer *(Catherine Curtis)*, J. P. McGowan *(James Curtis)*.

Melodrama. Persuaded by Catherine's father, Billy enters the boxing ring and defeats the champion to win Catherine. *Prizefighting.*

PATENTS PENDING *see* **HOT HEELS**

PATHS OF FLAME **F2.4170**

Denver Dixon Productions. *Dist* Aywon Film Corp. 16 Apr **1926** [New York State license]. Si; b&w. 35mm. 5 reels, 4,750 ft.

Cast: George Kesterson, Dorothy Lee.

Western melodrama(?). No information about the nature of this film has been found.

PATHS TO PARADISE **F2.4171**

Famous Players–Lasky. *Dist* Paramount Pictures. 29 Jun **1925** [c24 Jun 1925; LP21596]. Si; b&w. 35mm. 7 reels, 6,741 ft.

Pres by Adolph Zukor, Jesse L. Lasky. *Dir* Clarence Badger. *Screenplay* Keene Thompson. *Photog* H. Kinley Martin.

Cast: Betty Compson *(Molly)*, Raymond Griffith *(The Dude From Duluth)*, Tom Santschi *(Callahan)*, Bert Woodruff *(bride's father)*, Fred Kelsey *(confederate)*.

Comedy. Source: Paul Armstrong, *The Heart of a Thief* (New York opening: 5 Oct 1914). A confidence man, posing as a dude from Duluth, goes to a den in Chinatown, where Molly, the queen of crooks, separates tourists from their bankrolls. After the dude has let himself be had, he flashes a badge and claims to be a detective, quickly hinting that he can be bought off. Molly gives him every cent she has, and he takes off, having fleeced the fleecers. Molly and the dude meet later at a wealthy home, where he is posing as a detective and she as a maid, both planning to steal a valuable necklace. Constantly running afoul of each other, they decide to become partners. They steal the necklace with the greatest of ease, start for Mexico by car, and are chased by every motorcycle cop between San Francisco and the border. As they cross to safety, Molly decides that she wants to go straight and convinces the dude to return the necklace to its rightful owner. Having accomplished this restoration, Molly and the dude prepare to settle down to an honest life together. *Police. Detectives. Housemaids. Confidence men. Imposture. San Francisco—Chinatown. California. Mexican border. Chases.*

THE PATRIOT **F2.4172**

Paramount Famous Lasky Corp. 1 Sep **1928** [c4 Sep 1928; LP25593]. Talking sequences, sd eff, & mus score (Movietone); b&w. 35mm. 12 reels, 10,172 ft. [Also si; 9,819 ft.]

Pres by Adolph Zukor, Jesse L. Lasky. *Dir* Ernst Lubitsch. *Titl* Julian Johnson. *Adapt* Hans Kraly. *Photog* Bert Glennon. *Set Dsgn* Hans Dreier. *Film Ed* Ernst Lubitsch. *Mus* Domenico Savino, Gerard Carbonaro. *Cost* Ali Hubert.

Cast: Emil Jannings *(Czar Paul, the first)*, Florence Vidor *(Countess Ostermann)*, Lewis Stone *(Count Pahlen)*, Vera Voronina *(Mademoiselle Lapoukhine)*, Neil Hamilton *(Crown Prince Alexander)*, Harry Cording *(Stefan)*.

Historical drama. Source: Alfred Neumann, *Der Patriot; Drama in 5 Akten* (Stuttgart, 1927). In 18th-Century Russia, the Czar, Paul, is surrounded by murderous plots and trusts only Count Pahlen. Pahlen wishes to protect his friend, the mad king, but because of the horror of the king's acts, he feels that he must remove him from the throne. Stefan, whipped by the czar for not having the correct number of buttons on his gaiters, joins with the count in the plot. The crown prince is horrified by their plans and warns his father, who, having no love for his son, places him under arrest for his foolish accusations. Pahlen uses his mistress, the Countess Ostermann, to lure the czar into the bedroom, where she tells the czar of the plot. The czar summons Pahlen, who reassures him of his loyalty. Later that night the count and Stefan enter his bedroom, and presently the czar is dead. But moments later Stefan turns a pistol on Pahlen. As the count lies dying on the floor, the countess appears and embraces Pahlen as he says, "I have been a bad friend and lover—but I have been a Patriot." *Royalty. Mistresses. Patriotism. Insanity. Conspiracy. Assassination. Russia. Paul I (Russia).*

PATSY **F2.4173**

Fred Swanton. *Dist* Truart Film Corp. 1 Feb **1921.** Si; b&w. 35mm. 5 reels, 5,300 ft.

Dir-Scen John McDermott.

Cast: ZaSu Pitts *(Patsy)*, John MacFarlane *(Pops)*, Tom Gallery *(Bob Brooks)*, Marjorie Daw *(Margaret Vincent)*, Fannie Midgley *(Mrs. Vincent)*, Wallace Beery *(Gustave Ludermann)*, Harry Todd *(tramp)*, Milla Davenport *(matron)*, Henry Fortson *(Bones)*.

Comedy-drama. Source: Er Lawshe, *Patsy; Comedy Melodrama in Four Acts* (c1914). Patsy, an orphan and a tomboy, runs away from the woman who has adopted her to do most of the work on her farm. She wends her way cross-country to California, has many adventures and mishaps, and meets a kindly scientist, who, believing her to be a boy, takes her home with him. Theirs is a tough neighborhood, and Patsy must fight her way into the local gang, but she earns the urchins' respect and is elected their leader. Finally, Patsy foils the plot by several crooks to involve her benefactor in a swindling scheme and reunites the scientist with his daughter. *Orphans. Tomboys. Scientists. Street urchins. Adoption. Fatherhood. California.*

THE PATSY **F2.4174**

Metro-Goldwyn-Mayer Pictures. 10 Mar **1928** [c10 Mar 1928; LP25189]. Si; b&w. 35mm. 8 reels, 7,289 ft.

Dir King Vidor. *Scen* Agnes Christine Johnston. *Titl* Ralph Spence. *Photog* John Seitz. *Set Dsgn* Cedric Gibbons. *Film Ed* Hugh Wynn. *Wardrobe* Gilbert Clark.

Cast: Marion Davies *(Patricia Harrington)*, Orville Caldwell *(Tony Anderson)*, Marie Dressler *(Ma Harrington)*, Dell Henderson *(Pa Harrington)*, Lawrence Gray *(Billy)*, Jane Winton *(Grace Harrington)*.

Comedy-drama. Source: Barry Connors, *The Patsy* (New York opening: 23 Dec 1925). Patsy Harrington, younger of two daughters, is browbeaten by her mother and sister, Grace. Her father, something of a "patsy" himself, consoles her. Patsy's attempts to attract the attention of one of Grace's beaux, Tony Anderson, a young real estate agent, make up the plot. Heeding her father's advice on how to ensnare Tony, Patsy reads a book on personality development. The book inspires her to do several imitations of Pola Negri, Mae Murray, and Lillian Gish to show Tony how much "personality" she has. Failing to impress Tony, she stages a fake escapade with a young man to make Tony jealous. Instead, she arouses the fury of the whole family. In the end, Pa asserts himself as the real boss of the Harrington household, Patsy gets her man, and sister Grace focuses her attention on someone else. *Sisters. Real estate agents. Family life. Fatherhood. Personality. Pola Negri. Mae Murray. Lillian Gish.*

Note: Indication in copyright records that the film has sound has not been verified.

PAWN TICKET 210 **F2.4175**

Fox Film Corp. 24 Dec **1922** [c31 Dec 1922; LP19086]. Si; b&w. 35mm. 5 reels, 4,871 ft.

Pres by William Fox. *Dir* Scott Dunlap. *Scen* Jules Furthman. *Photog* George Schneiderman.

Cast: Shirley Mason *(Meg)*, Robert Agnew *(Chick Saxe)*, Irene Hunt *(Ruth Sternhold)*, Jacob Abrams *(Abe Levi)*, Dorothy Manners *(Mrs. Levi)*, Fred Warren *(Harris Levi)*.

Melodrama. Source: David Belasco and Clay M. Greene, "Pawn Ticket No. 210" (unpublished play). Harris Levi brings up Meg, who was left in his father's pawnshop by her mother, Ruth Sternhold. Anxious that she have a good environment, Harris takes her to live with his friend Robert Strong. When Ruth returns to claim Meg, Strong is revealed to be both Meg's father and the man with whom Harris' wife eloped. Meg is happily reunited with her parents and her sweetheart, Chick Saxe. *Jews. Waifs. Pawnbrokers. Parentage.*

PAWNED **F2.4176**

Select Pictures. *Dist* Selznick Distributing Corp. 13 Nov **1922** [c30 Oct 1922; LP18352]. Si; b&w. 35mm. 5 reels, 4,973 ft.

Pres by J. Parker Read, Jr. *Prod* J. Parker Read, Jr. *Dir* Irvin V. Willat. *Adapt (see note)* Frank L. Packard.

Cast: Tom Moore *(John Bruce)*, Edith Roberts *(Claire Veniza)*, Charles Gerard *(Dr. Crang)*, Josef Swickard *(Paul Veniza)*, Mabel Van Buren *(Mrs. Veniza)*, James Barrows *(Old Hawkins)*, Eric Mayne *(Gilbert Larmond)*, Billy Elmer *(Joe Burke)*.

Melodrama. Source: Frank L. Packard, *Pawned* (New York, 1921). Broke and stranded, John Bruce agrees to return to New York to investigate the operation of a nightclub for its owner, Gilbert Larmond. There he meets Claire Veniza, who operates a mobile pawnshop with her father in cooperation with the club, follows her home, becomes involved in a street fight, and stumbles into Claire's room seriously injured. Claire is forced to agree to marry drug-addicted Dr. Crang in return for medical aid to John. Claire and John fall in love, however; John saves Larmond from Crang's plots; and Old Hawkins, Claire's real father, keeps Claire from the doctor's clutches by driving his cab (which he believes to carry only Crang but actually includes Claire) off a ferryboat. Old Hawkins and Crang drown, but John rescues Claire. *Pawnbrokers. Physicians.*

Fatherhood. Nightclubs. Narcotics. New York City.

Note: Advertising suggests Packard may have adapted his novel for the screen.

PAY AS YOU ENTER F2.4177

Warner Brothers Pictures. 12 May **1928** [c3 May 1928; LP25208]. Mus score and sd eff (Vitaphone); b&w. 35mm. 5 reels, 4,975 ft. [Also si.]

Dir Lloyd Bacon. *Scen* Fred Stanley. *Titl* Joe Jackson. *Story* Gregory Rogers. *Photog* Norbert Brodin. *Asst Dir* Frank Shaw.

Cast: Louise Fazenda *(Mary Smith)*, Clyde Cook *(Clyde Jones)*, William Demarest *("Terrible Bill" McGovern)*, Myrna Loy *(Yvonne de Russo)*.

Comedy. Mary Smith, waitress on a lunch wagon concession, loves "Terrible Bill," the conductor, who courts Yvonne, a notorious gold digger. Clyde Jones, the motorman on the lunch wagon, loves Mary but is too shy to approach her. Bill becomes interested in Mary when she is awarded $1,000 damages from an automobile accident. Hoping to take the money and run, Bill tries to elope with Mary on a streetcar. He is prevented from accomplishing his end by Clyde, who overtakes Bill and brings the wildly careening streetcar under control. *Waitresses. Costermongers. Automobile accidents. Lunch wagons. Streetcars.*

THE PAY OFF F2.4178

W. T. Lackey Productions. *Dist* Ellbee Pictures. 15 Jan **1926.** Si; b&w. 35mm. 5 reels, 4,864 ft.

Dir Dell Henderson. *Photog* William Tuers.

Cast: Dorothy Drew, Robert McKim.

Melodrama(?). No information about the nature of this film has been found.

THE PAY OFF F2.4179

RKO Radio Pictures. 15 Oct **1930** [c15 Oct 1930; LP1677]. Sd (Photophone); b&w. 35mm. 8 reels, 6,930 ft.

Dir Lowell Sherman. *Adapt-Dial* Jane Murfin. *Story* Samuel Shipman. *Photog* J. Roy Hunt. *Art Dir* Max Ree. *Film Ed* Rose Smith. *Rec Engr* Bailey Sesler.

Cast: Lowell Sherman *(Gene Fenmore)*, Marion Nixon *(Annabelle)*, Hugh Trevor *(Rocky)*, William Janney *(Tommy)*, Helene Millard *(Dot)*, George F. Marion *(Mouse)*, Walter McGrail *(Emory)*, Robert McWade *(Frank)*, Alan Roscoe *(district attorney)*, Lita Chevret *(Margy)*, Bert Moorehouse *(Spat)*.

Crook melodrama. Annabelle and Tommy, engaged to be married, are robbed by a gang of thieves headed by Gene Fenmore. Tommy recognizes Rocky, a younger member of the gang, and with Annabelle attempts to rob Rocky and some of his cohorts; however, they are foiled, and Fenmore decides to give them jobs working for him. Against Fenmore's orders, Rocky induces Tommy and Annabelle to join them in a holdup; Rocky kills a shopowner, and the young couple are caught and arrested for the crime. In order to clear them, Fenmore confesses to having planned the robbery, then brings Rocky to task for his ruse; in the ensuing melee, Rocky is killed and Fenmore's gang turns against him. *Thieves. Gangs. Robbery. Murder.*

PAYABLE ON DEMAND F2.4180

William Steiner Productions. *Dist* Photo Drama Co. 1 Apr **1924** [c24 Mar 1924; LU20024]. Si; b&w. 35mm. 5 reels, 4,500 ft.

Dir Leo Maloney. *37 Beebe, Ford* Frances Beebe.

Cast: Leo Maloney *(Buck McDavid)*, Josephine Hill *(Mona Selby)*, Chet Ryan *(Alf)*, Jim Corey *(Slim Miller)*, Eva Thatcher *(Mrs. Martin Selby)*, Harry Belmour *(Martin Selby)*, Bullet *(himself, a dog)*.

Western comedy-melodrama. Buck McDavid, a poor homesteader, and his neighbor Alf contend for the hand of Mona Selby. She prefers Buck, but Alf enlists the aid of Mona's mother to acquire Buck's note from Mona's father and foreclose on his property. The disappearance of the note and the efforts to recover it result in Alf's defeat and Mrs. Selby's consent to the marriage of Buck and Mona. *Homesteaders. Mortgages. Documentation. Dogs.*

PAYDAY *see* **HELL'S HOLE**

PAYING THE LIMIT F2.4181

Paul Gerson Pictures. 10 Feb **1924** [scheduled release]. Si; b&w. 35mm. 5 reels.

Dir-Writ Tom Gibson. *Photog* George Crocker.

Cast: Ora Carew *(The Girl [Raffles])*, Helen Nowell *(Joan Lowden)*, Eddie O'Brien *(Thunder Lowden)*, Arthur Wellington *(Jerry Davis)*, Jay Morley *(Tom Dover)*, Stanley J. Sanford *(Ole)*, Dick Stevens *(Baptiste Tudor)*.

Melodrama. In an effort to reform, Raffles obtains a job as maid in a wealthy household after her release from jail. There she learns that a former accomplice is luring her employer's daughter into marriage for her money. Raffles is accused when the daughter steals from her father at the lover's bidding. Raffles clears herself, wins the respect of her employer, and marries the foreman. *Housemaids. Criminals—Rehabilitation. Theft.*

PAYING THE PIPER F2.4182

Famous Players–Lasky. *Dist* Paramount Pictures. Jan **1921** [c12 Jan 1921; LP16015]. Si; b&w. 35mm. 6 reels, 5,332 ft.

Pres by Adolph Zukor. *Prod-Dir* George Fitzmaurice. *Scen* Ouida Bergère. *Photog* Arthur Miller.

Cast: Dorothy Dickson *(Barbara Wyndham)*, Alma Tell *(Marcia Marillo)*, George Fawcett *(John Grahame)*, Rod La Rocque *(Larry Grahame)*, Robert Schable *(Charles R. Wyndham)*, Katherine Emmett *(Mrs. Wyndham)*, Reginald Denny *(Keith Larne)*.

Society drama. Larry and Barbara, both the products of rich but broken homes, plan a marriage of convenience. He really loves Marcia, a dancer, and Barbara vamps Keith, an architect. Keith's good sense prevails, and he marries Marcia and helps Larry make a man of himself. Barbara, after an unsuccessful attempt at an acting career, returns and asks forgiveness. *Actors. Dancers. Architects. Marriage of convenience.*

Note: Working title: *Money Mad.*

PAYING THE PRICE F2.4183

Lee-Bradford Corp. 1 Dec **1924.** Si; b&w. 35mm. 5 reels, 4,400 ft.

Cast: Owen Lynch, Jean Leslie.

Melodrama. No information about the nature of this film has been found.

PAYING THE PRICE F2.4184

Columbia Pictures. 5 Apr **1927** [c2 Apr 1927; LP23823]. Si; b&w. 35mm. 6 reels, 5,558 ft.

Prod Harry Cohn. *Dir* David Selman. *Scen* Dorothy Howell. *Photog* George Meehan.

Cast: Marjorie Bonner, Priscilla Bonner, John Miljan, George Hackathorne, Mary Carr, Eddie Phillips, William Welsh, William Eugene.

Melodrama. Basil Payson, a heavy loser at a fashionable gambling club owned by Michael Donovan, confronts Donovan with evidence of cheating and finds himself accused, on circumstantial evidence, of the owner's murder. As Payson is about to be found guilty by the jury, a dissenting juror, Thomas Gordon, admits to being guilty of the crime and in a flashback reveals his story: *Following a church service, in which the minister condemns a nearby town for its evil conditions, Gordon is coaxed by his daughters into visiting the town. Al and Donovan have the family drugged in a cafe and carry off the unconscious girls. Mrs. Gordon, with the aid of the minister, finds the villains and the abducted girls. Gordon, learning of the story, goes to Donovan's home and kills him.* The jury, however, convinced he has rid them of a public menace, free Payson and pledge not to reveal Gordon's story. *Clergymen. Sisters. Juries. Gambling. Murder. Cheating. Abduction. Trials.*

PAYMENT GUARANTEED F2.4185

American Film Co. *Dist* Pathé Exchange. c7 Mar **1921** [LP16234]. Si; b&w. 35mm. 5 reels.

Dir George L. Cox. *Story-Scen* Lois Zellner. *Photog* George Rizard.

Cast: Margarita Fisher *(Emily Heath)*, Cecil Van Auker *(Stephen Strange)*, Hayward Mack *(Harry Fenton)*, Harry Lonsdale *(Jim Barton)*, Harvey Clark *(reporter)*, Marjorie Manners *(Myrtle)*, Alice Wilson *(Gertie)*.

Melodrama. Harry Fenton, a Wall Street broker on the verge of bankruptcy, uses his fiancée, Emily Heath, to obtain a loan from wealthy young businessman Stephen Strange. Gaining Stephen's confidence, Emily is offered a check if she will break her engagement to Fenton. Following an automobile accident in which Stephen is rendered unconscious, she appropriates the check, but repudiating Fenton and his scheming she discovers a true affection for Stephen. *Businessmen. Brokers. Bankruptcy. Finance—Personal. Automobile accidents. New York City—Wall Street.*

PEACEFUL PETERS F2.4186

Ben Wilson Productions. *Dist* Arrow Film Corp. 15 Oct **1922** [c12 Oct 1922; LP18315]. Si; b&w. 35mm. 5 reels, 4,696 ft.

Dir Lewis King. *Scen* Daniel Whitcomb. *Photog* Jack Fuqua. *Film Ed* Earl C. Turner.

Cast: William Fairbanks *("Peaceful Peters")*, Harry La Mont *(Jim Blalock)*, W. L. Lynch *(Peter Hunter)*, Evelyn Nelson *(Mary Langdon)*, Wilbur McGaugh *("Sad" Simpson)*, Monte Montague *("Cactus" Collins)*.

Western melodrama. Source: Wilbur C. Tuttle, "Peaceful," in *Short Stories Magazine*. A dying prospector tells "Peaceful Peters" of a mine he has discovered for "Buddy's Gal" and of his ambush by claim jumpers, and he gives Peters the location of the mine. In town Peters discovers the crooked dealings of dancehall-owner Jim Blalock and assayer Peter Hunter. Meanwhile, he has narrowly escaped efforts to frame him for a robbery and a murder, and he rescues Mary Langdon—who has come to the dancehall to answer an advertisement for a dance teacher—from Blalock. Peters wins the love of Mary, who turns out to be the dead prospector's niece—"Buddy's Gal." *Prospectors. Dance teachers. Mine claims. Frameup. Dancehalls. Assayers.*

PEACOCK ALLEY **F2.4187**

Tiffany Productions. *Dist* Metro Pictures. 23 Jan **1922** [c3 Dec 1921, 9 Jan 1922; LP17279, LP17468]. Si; b&w. 35mm. 8 reels, 7,500 ft.

Supv-Dir Robert Z. Leonard. *Scen* Edmund Goulding. *Titl* Frederic Hatton, Fanny Hatton. *Story* Ouida Bergère. *Photog* Oliver Marsh. *Art Sets* Charles Cadwallader.

Cast: Mae Murray *(Cleo of Paris)*, Monte Blue *(Elmer Harmon)*, Edmund Lowe *(Phil Garrison)*, W. J. Ferguson *(Alex Smith)*, Anders Randolph *(Hugo Fenton)*, William Tooker *(Joseph Carleton)*, Howard Lang *(Abner Harmon)*, William Frederic *(Mayor of Harmontown)*, M. Durant *(Monsieur Dubois)*, Jeffrys Lewis *(Toto)*, Napoleon *(himself, a dog)*.

Drama. When Elmer Harmon goes to Paris to sign a contract with the French Government, he meets Cleo, a dancer with whom he falls in love and who is instrumental in acquiring the contract for him. They are married, and Elmer takes his bride back to his hometown in Pennsylvania where the natives are shocked by Cleo's manners and her Parisian attire. In New York, Elmer exhausts his finances, forges his uncle's name to a check, and is arrested. Cleo, in an effort to raise money for her husband's bail, accepts a theatrical engagement, but Elmer misunderstands her association with an old friend and denounces her, returning to Harmontown. Later, he learns the truth and returns to ask her forgiveness. *Dancers. Xenophobia. Marriage. Forgery. Pennsylvania. Paris. New York City. Dogs.*

PEACOCK ALLEY **F2.4188**

Tiffany Productions. 10 Jan **1930** [c25 Nov 1929; LP990]. Sd (Photophone); b&w with col sequences (Technicolor). 35mm. 7 reels, 6,060 ft.

Dir Marcel De Sano. *Screenplay* Frances Hyland. *Dial* Wells Root, Carey Wilson. *Story* Carey Wilson. *Photog* Benjamin Kline, Harry Zech. *Art Dir* Hervey Libbert. *Film Ed* Clarence Kolster. *Rec Engr* Buddy Myers.

Cast: Mae Murray *(Claire Tree)*, George Barraud *(Stoddard Clayton)*, Jason Robards *(Jim Bradbury)*, Richard Tucker *(Martin Saunders)*, W. L. Thorne *(Dugan)*, Phillips Smalley *(Bonner)*, E. H. Calvert *(Paul)*, Arthur Hoyt *(Crosby)*, Billy Bevan *(Walter)*.

Romantic drama. Chorus girl Claire Tree, who has long been in love with Clayton, local millionaire, meets him at the Peacock Alley Hotel in New York. When he again refuses to marry her, she announces that she is marrying Jim Bradbury, her girlhood sweetheart from Texas. Jim, an ambitious young attorney, arrives and they are married; but when he forgets to sign her into the hotel, Dugan, the house detective, orders them from Jim's room, insisting that Claire spent the previous night there with another man. Jim insists on confronting Clayton; but Claire is indignant that he has so little faith in her, and he finally leaves her. Disillusioned, Claire plunges into a new show, but on her opening night Clayton affirms that he now believes in marriage, and Claire accepts him. *Chorus girls. Millionaires. Lawyers. Texans. Marriage. Hotels. New York City.*

THE PEACOCK FAN **F2.4189**

Chesterfield Motion Picture Corp. 1 Aug **1929**. Si; b&w. 35mm. 6 reels, 5,387 ft.

Pres by George R. Batcheller. *Prod* Lon Young. *Dir* Phil Rosen. *Scen* Arthur Hoerl. *Titl* Lee Authmar. *Story* Adeline Leitzbach. *Photog* M. A. Anderson. *Film Ed* James Sweeney.

Cast—Prolog: Lotus Long *(Feliti)*, Fujii Kishii *(Okuri)*, Wong Foo *(Men Ching)*.

Cast—Story: Lucien Prival *(Dr. Chang Dorfman)*, Dorothy Dwan *(Peggy Kendall)*, Tom O'Brien *(Sergeant O'Brien)*, Rosemary Theby *(Mrs. Rossmore)*, Carlton King *(Mr. Rossmore)*, Gladden James *(Bertram Leslie)*, David Findlay *(Jerry Carlyle)*, James Wilcox *(Bob Kendall)*, Fred Malatesta *(Thomas Elton)*, Alice True *(Lily)*, Spencer Bell *(Arthur)*, John Fowler *(Dr. Whalen)*.

Mystery melodrama. A prolog shows the tragic history of a peacock fan, which figured in a jealous Chinese husband's murder of his wife and her lover. In the story the fan comes into the possession of a wealthy American curio collector, who is mysteriously murdered. Dr. Chang Dorfman enters the scene to unravel the mystery, implicates a dozen people, and finally fastens the guilt on the collector's wife and her lover. *Collectors. Chinese. Murder. Infidelity. Occult.*

PEACOCK FEATHERS (Universal-Jewel) **F2.4190**

Universal Pictures. 18 Oct **1925** [c5 Sep 1925; LP21797]. Si; b&w. 35mm. 7 reels, 6,747 ft.

Dir Svend Gade. *Adapt* James O. Spearing, Svend Gade. *Photog* Charles Stumar.

Cast: Jacqueline Logan *(Mimi Le Brun)*, Cullen Landis *(Jerry Chandler)*, Ward Crane *(Andrew Fuller)*, George Fawcett *(Uncle George)*, Emmett King *(Reverend Chandler)*, Youcca Troubetzkoy *(Lionel Clark)*, Aggie Herring *(Mrs. Hayes)*, Dunbar Raymond *(Mrs. Le Brun)*.

Drama. Source: Temple Bailey, *Peacock Feathers* (New York, 1926). Mimi Le Brun, the luxury-loving daughter of an impoverished upperclass family, falls in love with Jerry Chandler, a poor Yale man with the ambition to be a writer. Jerry proposes, but Mimi turns him down in favor of Andy Fuller, an oil millionaire. When Jerry inherits a ranch from his uncle, he and Mimi decide to be married, anticipating that Jerry's windfall will make them rich. Arriving at his ranch on their honeymoon, they discover, to their shock and disappointment, that the place is neither comfortable nor profitable. Despite her feelings, Mimi stays on, and she and Jerry try to make a go of it. As their first Christmas together approaches, Jerry goes into the hills for a tree. While he is gone, Andy shows up and persuades Mimi to go away with him. As she is leaving, she sees a signal fire on the mountain and, realizing that Jerry is in trouble, rounds up a rescue party. She saves Jerry's life and, overcome with the sudden intensity of her love for him, gladly nurses his hurt leg back to health, anticipating a long and happy life together with him. *Authors. Millionaires. Uncles. Courtship. Marriage. Honeymoons. Ranches. Christmas. Yale University.*

THE PEARL OF LOVE **F2.4191**

Paul W. Whitcomb Productions. *Dist* Lee-Bradford Corp. caDec **1925**. Si; b&w. 35mm. 6 reels, 5,800 ft.

Dir Leon E. Dadmun.

Cast: Betty Balfour, Gladys Leslie *(Mara)*, Burr McIntosh *(Captain Kittridge)*, Russell Griffin *(Sea Waif)*, Effie Shannon *(Mrs. Kittridge)*, Raymond Lowney *(Moses)*, Charles Lane *(Captain Pinnel)*, Alice Chapin *(Mrs. Pinnel)*, Walter Gilbert *(Ned Train)*, Paul Winchell *(Atkinson)*, Aleta Dore *(Sally Kittridge)*, Joseph Selman *(Mr. Adams)*, Dorothy Allen.

Melodrama. Source: Harriet Beecher Stowe, *The Pearl of Orr's Island, a Story of the Coast of Maine* (Boston, 1862). "Adventures of a youth saved from a shipwreck. He is adopted and grows to love foster sister. A band of smugglers take foul means to connect him with their nefarious enterprises, but the exposure of the leader of the smugglers by another saved from the ship from which Moses was rescued brings a happy conclusion to the romance." (*Motion Picture News Booking Guide*, 8:63, Apr 1925.) *Smugglers. Adoption. Maine. Shipwrecks.*

PECK'S BAD BOY **F2.4192**

Irving M. Lesser. *Dist* Associated First National Pictures. Jun **1921** [c8 Jun 1921; LP16659]. Si; b&w. 35mm. 5 reels, 5,000 ft.

Pres by Irving M. Lesser. *Dir-Adapt* Sam Wood. *Titl* Irvin S. Cobb. *Photog* Alfred Gilks, Harry Hallenberger.

Cast: Jackie Coogan *(Peck's Bad Boy)*, Wheeler Oakman *(The Man in the Case)*, Doris May *(The Girl in the Case)*, Raymond Hatton *(The Village Grocer)*, James Corrigan *(Pa Peck)*, Lillian Leighton *(Ma Peck)*, Charles Hatton *(Jackie's pal)*, Gloria Wood *(Jackie's girl)*, Queenie *(herself, a dog)*.

Comedy. Source: George Wilbur Peck, *Peck's Bad Boy and His Pa* and other titles (1883 and later). When a circus comes to town, Jackie, his pal, and his dog cause a commotion by releasing a lion from its cage, and consequently Jackie's father refuses him circus money. So Jackie disguises his pal as a girl, contrives to have Mr. Peck keep a date with "her," and collects "blackmail" just before his father and mother discover the "girl's" true identity. In other escapades, he puts ants in his father's pleurisy pad while the family is in church; rescues his dog from the dogcatcher; and conceals some important papers in the pocket of young Dr. Martin, his sister's beau, causing the doctor's arrest. Jackie admits to the last offense, and the doctor saves the boy and the dog from an oncoming train. *Physicians. Childhood. Parenthood. Circus. Family life. Dogs.*

PEG O' MY HEART **F2.4193**

Metro Pictures. 18 Dec **1922** [c10 Jan 1923; LP18736]. Si; b&w. 35mm. 8 reels, 7,900 ft.

Made under supv of J. Hartley Manners. *Dir* King Vidor. *Scen* Mary O'Hara. *Photog* George Barnes.

Cast: Laurette Taylor *(Margaret O'Connell [Peg])*, Mahlon Hamilton *(Sir Gerald Adair [Jerry])*, Russell Simpson *(Jim O'Connell)*, Ethel Grey Terry *(Ethel Chichester)*, Nigel Barrie *(Christian Brent)*, Lionel Belmore *(Hawks)*, Vera Lewis *(Mrs. Chichester)*, Sidna Beth Ivins *(Mrs. Jim O'Connell)*, D. R. O. Hatswell *(Alaric Chichester)*, Aileen O'Malley *(Margaret O'Connell, as a child)*, Fred Huntly *(butler)*, Michael *(a dog)*.

Comedy-drama. Source: J. Hartley Manners, *Peg o' My Heart* (New York, 1918). Peg, the daughter of a poor Irish farmer and an upper class Englishwoman whose family has disowned her, is sent to England to live with the Chichesters. Their snobbish ways alienate her, and her only friend is Jerry, who lives on a neighboring estate. When Peg learns that the Chichesters' only interest in her is the money paid to them by her uncle and that Jerry is really Sir Gerald Adair, she returns, disillusioned, to Ireland. Jerry follows and persuades Peg to marry him. *Irish. Upper classes. Snobbery. England. Dogs.*

PEGGY OF THE SECRET SERVICE **F2.4194**

Dist Davis Distributing Division. 16 Nov **1925** [New York license application; c4 Dec 1925; LP22078]. Si; b&w. 35mm. 5 reels, 4,950 ft.

Prod Mrs. S. Cole. *Dir* J. P. McGowan. *Scen* William Lester. *Story* Finis Fox. *Photog* Bob Cline.

Cast: Peggy O'Day *(Peggy)*, Eddie Phillips *(Hal Tracey)*, William H. Ryno *(Frank Jordan)*, Clarence L. Sherwood *(Spike Hennessy)*, Dan Peterson *(Buck Brice)*, Richard Neill *(Mahmoud el Akem)*, V. L. Barnes *(Abdullah)*, Ethel Childers *(Abdullah's favorite wife)*.

Comedy-melodrama. The Algerian consul solicits the aid of the Chief of the Secret Service in the apprehension of the sultan's brother, Abdullah, who has fled with the royal harem and the royal jewels to the United States. The chief assigns Peggy, his most reliable feminine operative, to the case. Newspaperman Hal Tracy, Peggy's sweetheart, is on the scene when Peggy attempts to arrest Abdullah. In the ensuing fight, Hal is thrown overboard, and Peggy—for the first time in her life forgetting her duty—dives in after him. She follows Abdullah to his mountain hideout and later gains entrance to his harem in the guise of an Algerian woman. Her position becomes more perilous each night, and she finds herself struggling with Abdullah just as Hal arrives with help. Abdullah is arrested, and the jewels are recovered. Peggy and Hal are denied permission to marry, since the chief has another assignment for Peggy. *Royalty. Algerians. Reporters. Secret service. Disguise. Harems.*

PEGGY PUTS IT OVER **F2.4195**

Vitagraph Co. of America. Aug **1921** [c28 Jun 1921; LP16712]. Si; b&w. 35mm. 5 reels.

Dir G. V. Seyffertitz. *Scen* C. Graham Baker, Harry Dittmar. *Story* G. Burr-Lynner. *Photog* King Gray, Vincent Scully.

Cast: Alice Calhoun *(Peggy Conrow)*, Edward Langford *(Dr. David Ransome)*, Leslie Stowe *(Silas Tucker)*, Charles Mackay *(Maxfield Conrow)*, Helen Lindroth *(Aunt Agatha)*, Cornelius MacSunday *(Constable)*, Dick Lee *(Rusty)*.

Rural comedy-drama. After receiving her degree in civil engineering, Peggy Conrow returns to her father's estate near the village of Oldtown, which has fallen into a state of disrepair. Her father, who has offered to supervise and finance local improvements, is called away, and Peggy resolves to take up his work. Opposed by stingy taxpayers, she proposes to establish a new town on her own land but meets with opposition from Dr. Ransome, who conceives her to be a headstrong upstart. She kidnaps the doctor, and when busybody Silas Tucker sees David kissing her in her studio there is a scandal. Peggy clears her honor, however, by stating that she is party to an elopement; and when her father's plans are adopted by the town council, she decides actually to marry David. *Engineers—Civil. Town planning. Village life.*

THE PELICAN *see* **"MARRIAGE LICENSE?"**

THE PELL STREET MYSTERY **F2.4196**

Robert J. Horner Productions. *Dist* Rayart Pictures. 1 Nov **1924.** Si; b&w. 35mm. 5 reels, 4,776 ft.

Dir Joseph Franz.

Cast: George Larkin, Carl Silvera.

Melodrama. "... centering about a newspaper reporter who is running down clews to murderer of wealthy man in Chinatown. He takes up with a notorious gang and when they learn who he is they set upon him. The timely interference of the police saves him, and he wins a girl and a scoop for his paper as well." (*Motion Picture News Booking Guide*, 8:63, Apr 1925.) *Reporters. Chinese. Police. Murder. Chinatown.*

PENNY OF TOP HILL TRAIL **F2.4197**

Andrew J. Callaghan. *Dist* Federated Film Exchange. 17 Jun **1921** [trade review]. Si; b&w. 35mm. 5 reels, 5,000 ft.

Dir Arthur Berthelet. *Scen* Finis Fox, Beatrice Van.

Cast: Sam Lauder, Bessie Love *(Penny)*, Wheeler Oakman *(Kurt Walters)*, Raymond Cannon *(Jo Gary)*, Harry De Vere *(Louis Kingdon)*, Lizette Thorne *(Mrs. Kingdon)*, Gloria Hunt *(Betty Kingdon)*, George Stone *(Francis Kingdon)*, Herbert Hertier *(Hebler)*.

Western comedy-drama. Source: Belle Kanaris Maniates, *Penny of Top Hill Trail* (Toronto, c1919). Penny arrives by airplane in the neighborhood of the Kingdon ranch. Her behavior is thought suspicious, and she is put in jail, where Kurt Walters, foreman of the ranch and deputy sheriff, recognizes her as a girl his friend Jo met in Chicago who confessed to being a thief. When he enters the cell to talk with Penny, he finds a visitor and orders her to leave, taking Penny, who has promised to go straight, to Mrs. Kingdon. Penny begins to tantalize him and complicates his life with her pranks. But he continues to fall more and more in love with her. A crisis develops when a mysterious stranger and the other girl who was in Penny's cell arrive. It is then revealed that Penny is not a thief but a motion picture star hiding from a manager who wants her to renew her contract. She prefers the golden sand to the silver screen and remains on the ranch with Kurt. *Thieves. Actors. Ranchers. Sheriffs. Airplanes. Motion pictures.*

PENNY PHILANTHROPIST **F2.4198**

5 Jan **1923** [New York State license]. Si; b&w. 35mm. 5 reels, 4,178 ft.

Cast: Ralph Morgan, Peggy O'Neil.

Drama(?). No information about the nature of this film has been found.

Note: Country of origin and production and distribution companies not determined; released in New York State by Webster Pictures.

PENROD **F2.4199**

Marshall Neilan Productions. *Dist* Associated First National Pictures. ca29 Jan **1922** [Chicago premiere; released 20 Feb; c30 Jan 1922; LP17530]. Si; b&w. 35mm. 8 reels, 8,037 ft.

Pres by Marshall Neilan. *Supv-Dir* Marshall Neilan. *Scen* Lucita Squier. *Photog* David Kesson, Ray June. *Film Ed* Daniel J. Gray. *Asst Dir* Frank O'Connor, Thomas Held.

Cast: Wesley Barry *(Penrod)*, Tully Marshall *(Mr. Schofield)*, Claire McDowell *(Mrs. Schofield)*, John Harron *(Robert Williams)*, Gordon Griffith *(Sam Williams)*, Newton Hall *(George Bassett)*, Harry Griffith *(Foster)*, Cecil Holland *(John Barrett)*, Sunshine Morrison *(Herman)*, Florence Morrison *(Verman)*, Marjorie Daw *(Margaret)*, Clara Horton *(Marjorie Jones)*, Peggy Jane *(Baby Rennsdale)*, Wheeler Dryden, Mayme Kelso, Grace Green, Earl Crain, Fred Thomson, Theodore Chapin, Junior Alden, Winston Radom, Adelaide Baxter, Francis Plottner, Charles Meakin, Harry Todd, Lina Basquette, Julian Lenne, Bernice Radom, George Dromgold, Virginia True Boardman, Charles Arling, Noah Beery, Jr., Bennie Billings, Jack Condon, Peggy Cartwright, Bradford Ralston, Stephen Welz, Billie Bennett, May Baxter, Kenneth Green, Carrie Clark Ward, R. D. Saunders, Blanche Light, Eugenie Besserer.

Comedy-drama. Source: Booth Tarkington, *Penrod* (New York, 1914). Booth Tarkington, *Penrod, a Comedy in Four Acts* (New York, 1921). Penrod Schofield, who has a reputation as a troublemaker, is the president of the American Boys' Protective Association, which meets each week to report the wrongs inflicted by parents, unkind neighbors, and thoughtless policemen. During a hectic summer Penrod breaks up an amateur theatrical production and scandalizes a dancing class by his antics during a cotillion.

Rupe Collins, the town tough boy, bullies the gang until he runs afoul of Herman and Verman, two colored children who get rid of Rupe with the use of scythes and lawnmowers in a hair-raising manner. The ire of leading citizens is aroused by the gang's mischief, but when the boys capture two notorious bandits, the threats turn into praise and Penrod becomes the hero of his adored Marjorie Jones. *Childhood. Gangs. Bandits. Protective associations. Theater—Amateur. Smalltown life.*

PENROD AND SAM **F2.4200**

J. K. McDonald. *Dist* Associated First National Pictures. 18 Jun **1923** [c18 Jun 1923; LP19118]. Si; b&w. 35mm. 7 reels, 6,275 ft.

Pres by J. K. McDonald. *Dir* William Beaudine. *Scen* Hope Loring, Louis D. Lighton. *Titl suggested by* Booth Tarkington. *Photog* Ray June, Edward Ulman. *Film Ed* Edward McDermott.

Cast: Ben Alexander *(Penrod Schofield)*, Joe Butterworth *(Sam Williams)*, Buddy Messinger *(Rodney Bitts)*, Newton Hall *(Georgie Bassett)*, Gertrude Messinger *(Marjorie Jones, Penrod's sweetheart)*, Joe McGray *(Herman)*, Eugene Jackson *(Verman)*, Rockliffe Fellowes *(Mr. Schofield)*, Gladys Brockwell *(Mrs. Schofield)*, Mary Philbin *(Margaret Schofield)*, Gareth Hughes *(Robert Williams, Margaret's sweetheart)*, William V. Mong *(Deacon Bitts)*, Martha Mattox *(Miss Spence, schoolteacher)*, Vic Potel *(town drunkard)*, Bobby Gordon *(Maurice Levy)*, Cameo *(Duke, Penrod's dog)*.

Comedy-drama. Source: Booth Tarkington, *Penrod and Sam* (1916). Penrod and Sam, two inseparable boys, organize a secret society and exclude Georgie Bassett and Rodney Bitts from the fraternity. When the lot on which the boys play is sold by Penrod's father to Mr. Bitts, Rodney refuses to allow Penrod to play there. Penrod is griefstricken because his pet dog, which recently died, is buried on the lot. Penrod's father sees his son's distress, buys back the lot, and gives it to Penrod. *Childhood. Family life. Fatherhood. Smalltown life. Dogs.*

THE PEOPLE VS. NANCY PRESTON **F2.4201**

Hunt Stromberg Productions. *Dist* Producers Distributing Corp. 1 Nov **1925** [c26 Oct 1925; LP21945]. Si; b&w. 35mm. 7 reels, 6,638? ft.

Pres by Hunt Stromberg. *Dir* Tom Forman. *Adapt* Marion Orth. *Photog* Sol Polito. *Art Dir* Edward Withers. *Ed* Ralph Dixon. *Surgical Adv* Bertrand Wolfran, M. D.

Cast: Marguerite De La Motte *(Nancy Preston)*, John Bowers *(Mike Horgan)*, Frankie Darro *(Bubsy)*, David Butler *(Bill Preston)*, William V. Mong *(Pasquale)*, Alphonz Ethier *(Tierney)*, Ed Kennedy *(Gloomy Gus)*, Gertrude Short *(Agnes)*, Ray Gallagher *(Texas Darcy)*, Jackie Saunders *(Hazy Mazie)*, Mary Gordon *(Mrs. Tifft)*.

Underworld melodrama. Source: John A. Moroso, *The People Against Nancy Preston* (New York, 1921). After his release from Sing Sing, Bill Preston is unable to go straight as he is constantly hounded by "Gloomy Gus," an operative of the Tierney Detective Agency. Bill is killed during a bank robbery, and his wife Nancy and son Bubsy are taken into the protection of Mike Horgan, Bill's friend from Sing Sing who had studied medicine part-time. Eluding "Gloomy Gus," Mike obtains a job in a factory but is arrested and sent to jail for robbery; Nancy, a former underworld character known as "Straw Nancy," is also arrested but is freed. Falsely accused of the murder of Pasquale, a fence for cheap crooks who tried to abuse her, she escapes. She is joined by Mike when he breaks out of prison. They go to a small town, and there Mike begins to practice medicine under his real name, Stafford. Tierney discovers the pair but falls ill and is nursed back to health by Mike and Nancy. When "Gloomy Gus" arrives with a warrant, he experiences a change of heart and proves Nancy's innocence. Mike and Nancy then marry. *Criminals—Rehabilitation. Detectives. Physicians. Detective agencies. Robbery. Sing Sing.*

PERCH OF THE DEVIL (Universal-Jewel) **F2.4202**

Universal Pictures. 6 Mar **1927** [c13 Sep 1926; LP23106]. Si; b&w. 35mm. 7 reels, 6,807 ft.

Pres by Carl Laemmle. *Dir* King Baggot. *Adapt* Mary O'Hara. *Photog* Charles Stumar.

Cast: Mae Busch *(Ida Hook)*, Pat O'Malley *(Gregory Compton)*, Jane Winton *(Ora Blake)*, Theodore von Eltz *(Lord Mobray)*, Mario Carillo *(Marchese Valdonia)*, Lincoln Stedman *(Freddy Dipper)*, George Kuwa *(Charley Lee)*, Gertrude Oakman *(Ruby Miller)*, Martha Franklin *(Mrs. Stout)*.

Society melodrama. Source: Gertrude Franklin Atherton, *Perch of the Devil* (New York, 1914). Ida, a mining-camp girl, marries young engineer Gregory Compton, and they move to his ranch in Butte, where he is prospecting for gold. She complains bitterly of the lonely life, and when Ora Blake, a wealthy young widow, stops at the ranch she sympathizes with Ida and at the same time captivates Gregory. With Gregory's consent Ora takes Ida to Europe. There Ida's horizon expands, and she wins the love of Lord Mobray. She soon tires of European society, however, and yearns to return to Gregory. News arrives of Gregory's discovery of gold, but the perfidious Ora changes the wording of Ida's cabled reply so as to make her appear mercenary. Returning to Butte with Ora—crestfallen to learn of Greg's bitterness concerning their estrangement—Ida learns from Lord Mobray of her companion's perfidy, and she attacks her at the mine. Greg is forced to dynamite a mine shaft, thus flooding the tunnel in which Ida and Ora are struggling; Ida saves Ora, and Greg comes to the rescue. Greg repents and is reunited with his wife. *Engineers. Prospectors. Widows. Vamps. Infidelity. Jealousy. Ranches. Mines. Butte (Montana).*

PERCY **F2.4203**

Thomas H. Ince Corp. *Dist* Pathé Exchange. 5 Apr **1925** [c12 Feb 1925; LP21124]. Si; b&w. 35mm. 6 reels, 5,980 ft.

Dir R. William Neill. *Adapt* Eve Unsell, J. G. Hawks. *Photog* James Diamond.

Cast: Charles Ray *(Percival Rogeen)*, Louise Dresser *(Mrs. Rogeen)*, Joseph Kilgour *(Jasper Rogeen)*, Clyde McAtee *(James)*, Dave Winter *(Breezy Barnes)*, Charles Murray *(Holy Joe)*, Victor McLaglen *(Reedy Jenkins)*, Betty Blythe *(Lolita)*, Barbara Bedford *(Imogene Chandler)*, Don Marion *(Percival Rogeen, as a boy)*.

Comedy-melodrama. Source: William Henry Hamby, *The Desert Fiddler* (Garden City, New York, 1921). Much to the disgust of his father, Percival Rogeen, whose only accomplishment is playing the violin, has been brought up by his doting mother as a mollycoddle. When the elder Rogeen runs for the Senate, his campaign manager, Breezy Barnes, offers to make a man of Percival. Barnes takes Percival to a cabaret and gets him drunk. Intoxicated for the first time in his life, Percival engineers a campaign stunt that ends in a street riot. He jumps on a freight train to avoid an enraged mob and ends up on the Mexican border, where he is saved by Holy Joe from a band of tramps who mistake him for a railroad detective. Joe, who makes a living by gambling at cards and selling Bibles, takes Percival to a local dancehall, where Percival makes a hit with his fiddling. Percival and Joe later go to work for Imogene Chandler, picking cotton on her ranch. Reedy Jenkins, the political boss of the district, shuts off the water at the local dam with the intention of driving out the cotton farmers. Percival goes to the dam, beats Jenkins in a fight, and dynamites the floodgates. Percival later marries Imogene and returns with her to the East. *Violinists. Political bosses. Politics. Motherhood. Manhood. Drunkenness. Cabarets. Dancehalls. Dams. Mexican border.*

THE PERFECT ALIBI **F2.4204**

William Steiner Productions. *Dist* Photo Drama Co. 10 Jul **1924** [c3 Jun 1924; LU20264]. Si; b&w. 35mm. 5 reels, 5,108 ft.

Copyright Auth Frances Beebe, Ford Beebe. *Photog* Ben Bail.

Cast: Leo Maloney *(Mack McGregor)*, Bullet *(himself, a dog)*, Leonard Clapham *(Ollie Summers)*, Jim Corey *(Lon Elwell)*.

Western melodrama. Mack McGregor, a ranger, is engaged to Marion, daughter of Captain Atwood, the company commander. Mack and Marion find evidence implicating her brother, Rodney, in a robbery. On her pleas, Mack refuses to pursue the criminal and is dismissed from the service. Ollie Summers and Lon Elwell, the real culprits, blackmail Rodney, who, in desperation, plans to rob his father's safe. He does not follow through, and the crime is committed by Ollie and Lon. Captain Atwood arrives with Ollie and Lon to arrest his son, but Bullet, Mack's dog, uncovers evidence proving him innocent and then helps capture the two desperadoes. *Rangers. Fatherhood. Brother-sister relationship. Blackmail. Robbery. Dogs.*

Note: Story, cast (except for Leo Maloney), and character names are based on shooting script in the copyright records and may differ from the final film.

THE PERFECT CLOWN **F2.4205**

Chadwick Pictures. 15 Dec **1925** [c16 Nov 1925; LP22003]. Si; b&w. 35mm. 6 reels, 5,700 ft.

Dir Fred Newmeyer. *Story* Thomas J. Crizer.

Cast: Larry Semon *(Bert Larry)*, Kate Price *(Mrs. Sally Mulligan)*, Dorothy Dwan *(The Girl)*, Joan Meredith *(her chum)*, Otis Harlan *(The Boss)*, G. Howe Black *(The Porter)*.

Slapstick comedy. Bert Larry, a broker's clerk in love with the office manager's secretary, is given a bag containing $10,000 to deliver to the bank. Larry finds the bank closed and attempts to get to the president's home with the aid of "Snowball," the office porter. Together they spend a hectic night: Snowball's car has a flat tire in a cemetery, they are forced to change clothes with a pair of escaped convicts, and they are chased by the police. In the morning, there is great excitement at the office when it is learned that the money did not reach the bank. Everything is straightened out in the end, and Larry gets a reward and the girl. *Brokers. Clerks. Secretaries. Prison escapees. Disguise. Cemeteries. Banks.*

A PERFECT CRIME **F2.4206**

Allan Dwan Productions. *Dist* Associated Producers. 27 Mar **1921** [c21 Feb 1921; LP16171]. Si; b&w. 35mm. 5 reels.

Dir Allan Dwan. *Photog* Lyman Broening. *Asst Dir* Wilfred Buckland.

Cast: Monte Blue *(Wally Griggs)*, Jacqueline Logan *(Mary Oliver)*, Stanton Heck *("Big Bill" Thaine)*, Hardee Kirkland *(Halliday)*.

Drama. Source: Carl Clausen, "A Perfect Crime," in *Saturday Evening Post* (193:18–19, 25 Sep 1920). Wally Griggs, a timid bank messenger, lives another life as a dashing young sport whose tales of wild adventure interest bank president Halliday and romantically fascinate Mary, who has been swindled out of a fortune by Thaine, now district attorney. When Wally decides to hide some bank bonds and is arrested by Thaine, he sues for false imprisonment and wins back Mary's money. He then returns the bank funds, pretending aphasia, and decides to become an author. *Messengers. District attorneys. Authors. Banks. Personality. Aphasia.*

THE PERFECT CRIME **F2.4207**

FBO Pictures. 4 Aug **1928** [New York showing; c2 Aug 1928; LP22503]. Talking sequences, sd eff, & mus score (Photophone); b&w. 35mm. 7 reels, 6,331 ft. [Also si.]

Dir Bert Glennon. *Screenplay* Ewart Adamson. *Dial* Victor Currier. *Titl* Randolph Bartlett. *Adapt* William Le Baron. *Photog* James Howe. *Film Ed* Archie F. Marshek. *Asst Dir* Charles Kerr.

Cast: Clive Brook *(Benson)*, Irene Rich *(Stella)*, Ethel Wales *(Mrs. Frisbie)*, Carroll Nye *(Trevor)*, Gladys McConnell *(Mrs. Trevor)*, Edmund Breese *(Wilmot)*, James Farley *(Jones)*, Phil Gastrock *(butler)*, Tully Marshall *(Frisbie)*, Jane La Verne *(Trevor baby)*.

Melodrama. Source: Israel Zangwill, *The Big Bow Mystery* (New York, 1895). *Benson, the world's leading criminologist, is disappointed in love and becomes a recluse, obsessed with the idea of the "perfect crime." He finally gives in to his unholy impulses and murders Frisbie, leaving behind no clues. Stella, the woman who jilted Benson, then comes back to him, and he at last sees the chance to find happiness and fulfillment. Something arises to upset his plans, however: Trevor, a young married man who once lived with Frisbie, is accused of the murder on circumstantial evidence and sentenced to die. Stricken by conscience, Benson confesses to the crime, freeing Trevor and sealing his own doom.* It all turns out to be a dream, however, and Benson awakens a wiser man. *Criminologists. Murder. Injustice. Circumstantial evidence. Dreams.*

THE PERFECT DREAMER **F2.4208**

Young Producers Filming Co. **1922.** Si; b&w. 35mm. [Feature length assumed.]

Melodrama(?). No information about the precise nature of this film has been found. *Negro life.*

THE PERFECT FLAPPER **F2.4209**

Associated First National Pictures. 25 May **1924** [c21 May 1924; LP20227]. Si; b&w. 35mm. 7 reels, 7,000 ft.

Pers Supv Earl Hudson. *Dir* John Francis Dillon. *Ed Dir* Marion Fairfax. *Scen* Joseph Poland. *Photog* James C. Van Trees. *Architecture* Milton Menasco. *Film Ed* Arthur Tavares.

Cast: Colleen Moore *(Tommie Lou Pember)*, Sydney Chaplin *(Dick Trayle)*, Phyllis Haver *(Gertrude Trayle)*, Lydia Knott *(Aunt Sarah)*, Frank Mayo *(Reed Andrews)*, Charles Wellesley *(Joshua Pember)*.

Romantic comedy. Source: Jessie Henderson, "The Mouth of the Dragon," in *Ainslee's* (51:138–141, Mar–Apr 1923). Because she is modest and relatively old-fashioned, young debutante Tommie Lou finds herself unpopular at her coming-out party. Resorting to unconventional jazz attitudes, she becomes a great success at the cost of provoking a quarrel and a divorce suit between a married couple. When she falls in love with the wife's lawyer, however, the divorce case is forgotten, and she reforms. *Lawyers. Debutantes. Flappers. Jazz life.*

A PERFECT GENTLEMAN **F2.4210**

Monty Banks Enterprises. *Dist* Pathé Exchange. 15 Jan **1928** [c19 Jul 1927; LU24193]. Si; b&w. 35mm. 6 reels, 5,626 ft.

Pres by A. MacArthur. *Dir* Clyde Bruckman. *Story-Scen* Charles Horan. *Photog* James Diamond. *Film Ed* William Holmes.

Cast: Monty Banks *(Monty Brooks)*, Ernest Wood *(George Cooper)*, Henry Barrows *(John Wayne)*, Ruth Dwyer *(his daughter)*, Arthur Thalasso *(ship's officer)*, Hazel Howell *(his wife)*, Agostino Borgato *(Barco)*, Mary Foy *(The Aunt)*, Syd Crossley *(The Valet)*, Jackie Coombs *(The Baby)*.

Farce. Monty, a trusted bank employee, is about to be married to Helen Wayne, the president's daughter. En route to the wedding he has a flat tire and is accidentally knocked unconscious; his valet, attempting to revive him, gets him hopelessly intoxicated. At the bride's house, Monty's dislike for the aunt combined with his drunken behavior result in his expulsion, and George Cooper, a rival for the hand of Helen, exaggerates Monty's actions to the Waynes. Some South Americans persuade Cooper to finance a revolution with bank funds; and after stealing the money, he sends Monty to South America with the funds. Aboard ship Monty encounters Helen and her father, as well as the crooks, and after a series of whirlwind battles he saves the money and is exonerated by his sweetheart's father. *Bankers. Bank clerks. Valets. Theft. Drunkenness. Marriage. Revolutions.*

THE PERFECT SAP **F2.4211**

Ray Rockett Productions. *Dist* First National Pictures. 16 or 23 Jan **1927** [c4 Jan 1927; LP23496]. Si; b&w. 35mm. 6 reels, 5,981 ft.

Dir Howard Higgin. *Photog* John Boyle. *Prod Mgr* Ray Rockett.

Cast: Ben Lyon *(Herbert Alden)*, Virginia Lee Corbin *(Ruth Webster)*, Lloyd Whitlock *(Tracy Sutton)*, Diana Kane *(Roberta Alden)*, Byron Douglas *(Stephen Alden)*, Christine Compton *(Mrs. Stephen Alden)*, Charles Craig *(Fletcher)*, Sam Hardy *(Nick Fanshaw)*, Tammany Young *(George Barrow)*, Helen Rowland *(Cissie Alden)*.

Comedy-mystery. Source: Howard Irving Young, *Not Herbert, a Comedy of the Night in Four Acts* (New York, 1926). Wealthy young Herbert Alden, a would-be detective, is practicing housebreaking with his valet, an ex-convict, when he meets George and Polly, two real thieves; they are discovered, and, following a chase, they go to Herbert's city apartment. George arranges with one of them, Tony-the-Lizard, to rob the guests at a ball given by Herbert's father at his country home. Herbert discovers that Tony is Tracy Sutton, a social lion engaged to Herbert's sister, Roberta; and believing Herbert to be a famous criminal, Tony seeks his advice. At the last minute Herbert sounds the alarm and reveals his identity. Polly, who is at the ball in disguise, is accused by Ruth Webster of participation in the robbery, but Polly unmasks Ruth as a notorious thief. After revealing her own identity as a newspaper writer, Polly is united with Herbert. *Detectives. Thieves. Reporters. Valets. Impersonation. Courtship.*

PERIL OF THE RAIL **F2.4212**

Morris R. Schlank Productions. *Dist* Anchor Film Distributors. 30 Oct **1926** [New York State license]. Si; b&w. 35mm. 5 reels.

Pres by Morris R. Schlank. *Prod-Dir* J. P. McGowan. *Story* William E. Wing. *Photog* Walter Griffin. *Film Ed* Betty Davis.

Cast: Helen Holmes *(Helen Martin)*, Edward Hearn *(Jack Hathaway)*, Wilfred North *(Pepper Martin)*, Lloyd Whitlock *(Barker)*, Dick Rush *(The Manager)*, Dan Crimmins *("Slippery" McGee)*, Norma Wills *(Slippery's wife)*, Rex *(a dog)*.

Melodrama. No information about the precise nature of this film has been found. *Railroads. Dogs.*

PERILS OF THE COAST GUARD **F2.4213**

Gerson Pictures. *Dist* Rayart Pictures. Mar **1926.** Si; b&w. 35mm. 6 reels, 5,375 ft.

Dir Oscar Apfel.

Cast: Cullen Landis *(Capt. Tom Norris)*, Dorothy Dwan *(Natalie)*.

Melodrama. "Frustrating social ambitions millionaire uncle has for her, Natalie Aldrich marries Tom Norris of the Coast Guard, who saved her from drowning. Oyster pirates who infest coast are arrested through Tom's efforts and uncle is also saved from a watery grave through his heroism." (*Motion Picture News Booking Guide,* 11:42, Oct 1926.) *Uncles. Millionaires. Oysters. United States Coast Guard.*

PERILS OF THE WEST **F2.4214**

Dist Primrose Film Co. Sep **1922** [New York State]. Si; b&w. 35mm. 5 reels, 4,500 ft.

Cast: William Hackett.

Western melodrama(?). No information about the nature of this film has been found.

PERJURY (Fox Special) **F2.4215**

Fox Film Corp. 14 Aug **1921** [New York premiere; released 30 Oct; c4 Sep 1921; LP17115]. Si; b&w. 35mm. 9 reels, 8,372 ft.

Pres by William Fox. *Dir* Harry Millarde. *Scen* Mary Murillo. *Adapt* Ruth Comfort Mitchell. *Photog* Edward Wynard.

Cast: William Farnum *(Robert Moore)*, Sally Crute *(Martha Moore)*, Wallace Erskine *(John Gibson)*, Alice Mann *(Helen Moore)*, Gilbert Rooney *(Jimmy Moore)*, Grace La Vell *(Mira)*, Jack Crane *(Ralph Mills)*, Frank Joyner *(Edward Williams)*, Frank Shannon *(Phil Rourke)*, John Webb Dillon *(District Attorney Choate)*.

Melodrama. Source: Julius Steger, *Guilty, a Modern Drama in Four Acts* (adapted from Richard Voss, *Schuldig*; c21 Oct 1920). Robert Moore, general manager for wealthy John Gibson, is frequently visited by his employer, who is fond of Robert's children. A scandal is invented relating Gibson and Moore's wife, and hearing of it at a club, Robert attempts to thrash the instigator of the gossip and hurries to tell Gibson, who, he discovers, has been killed. Although he protests his innocence, Robert is tried and convicted of murder. His wife remarries but finds herself tied to a brute who causes constant dissension. Twenty years later, the real murderer confesses and Moore is set free, but he is reluctant to leave prison. He is persuaded to visit his former wife and defends her against an attack by her husband, whom he shoots in self-defense. Robert is vindicated and reunited with his family. *Gossip. Murder. Perjury. Injustice.*

PERSONALITY **F2.4216**

Columbia Pictures. 14 Feb **1930** [c18 Feb 1930; LP1091]. Sd (Movietone); b&w. 35mm. 7 reels, 6,304 ft. [Also si.]

Prod Harry Cohn. *Dir* Victor Heerman. *Cont-Dial* Gladys Lehman. *Camera* Ted Tetzlaff. *Art Dir* Harrison Wiley. *Film Ed* David Berg. *Ch Sd Engr* John P. Livadary. *Asst Dir* Sam Nelson.

Cast: Sally Starr *(Lil Morse)*, Johnny Arthur *(Sandy Jenkins)*, Blanche Frederici *(Ma)*, Frank Hammond *(Pa)*, Buck Black *(Junior)*, Lee Kohlmar *(Mr. Himmelschlosser)*, John T. Murray *(Mr. Keller)*, Vivian Oakland *(Mrs. Keller)*, George Pearce *(Mr. Abbott)*.

Romantic comedy. Sandy Jenkins, a $40-a-week draftsman, marries Lil Morse, though her mother disapproves of the match, preferring Mr. Himmelschlosser, Sandy's employer. After their honeymoon, the couple take an apartment in the same building with Lil's family, and she takes up domestic duties with enthusiasm. Lil plans a surprise birthday dinner for Sandy, but he and his friends inadvertently discover the food beforehand and eat it; Sandy pacifies Lil by promising to take the party to the theater, but he becomes jealous at Mr. Himmelschlosser's boasting and self-esteem; as a result he schemes to get work with a rival advertising agency and on credit takes an expensive apartment. But during a business deal, his deception is discovered and he is fired; as a result he is estranged from Lil. He is reinstated in his job and is reunited with his wife, however, when his employer, Mr. Abbott, reaps the results of a property sale arranged by Sandy. *Draftsmen. Family life. Marriage. Personality. Credit. Advertising.*

PETER IBBETSON *see* **FOREVER**

PETER PAN **F2.4217**

Famous Players–Lasky. *Dist* Paramount Pictures. 29 Dec **1924** [c23 Dec 1924; LP20980]. Si; b&w. 35mm. 10 reels, 9,593 ft.

Pres by Adolph Zukor, Jesse L. Lasky. *Dir* Herbert Brenon. *Adapt-Screenplay* Willis Goldbeck. *Photog* James Howe. *Sp Eff* Roy Pomeroy.

Cast: Betty Bronson *(Peter Pan)*, Ernest Torrence *(Captain Hook)*, Cyril Chadwick *(Mr. Darling)*, Virginia Brown Faire *(Tinker Bell)*, Anna May Wong *(Tiger Lily)*, Esther Ralston *(Mrs. Darling)*, George Ali *(Nana, the dog)*, Mary Brian *(Wendy)*, Philippe De Lacey *(Michael)*, Jack Murphy *(John)*.

Fantasy. Source: James Matthew Barrie, *Peter Pan, or the Boy Who Wouldn't Grow Up* (1904). Peter Pan, the boy who never grew up, is looking for his shadow in the Darling nursery when he awakens the Darling children—Wendy, John, and Michael. Peter tells the children of never-never land, teaches them to fly, and guides them to his forest home, where he is the king of the Little Lost Boys. Tinker Bell, a fairy, becomes jealous of Wendy and persuades one of the boys to shoot her with an arrow. Wendy recovers and is adopted by the boys as their mother. Captain Hook, a notorious pirate whose hand Peter once cut off, kidnaps the children after a fierce fight with Indians who are the children's friends and guardians. Peter, discovering that the children are missing, goes to the pirate ship and frees them. The children fight the pirates and subdue them. Captain Hook is forced to walk the plank. Peter then returns with the Darling children to their nursery. Wendy asks him to stay, but Peter refuses and returns to his home in the woods. *Pirates. Indians of North America. Childhood. Jealousy. Kidnaping. Family life.*

LE PETIT CAFÉ **F2.4218**

Paramount-Publix Corp. **1930** [New York premiere 20 Jan 1931]. Sd (Movietone); b&w. 35mm. [Feature length assumed.]

Dir Ludwig Berger. *Dial* Bataille-Henri. *Adapt* Vincent Lawrence, Bataille-Henri. *Mus* Richard Whiting, Newell Chase.

Cast: Maurice Chevalier *(Albert Lorifian)*, Yvonne Valle *(Yvonne Philibert)*, Tania Fedor *(Mademoiselle Berengère)*, André Berley *(Pierre Bourdin)*, Emile Chautard *(Philibert)*, Françoise Rosay *(Mademoiselle Edwige)*, George Davis *(Paul Michel)*, Jacques Jou-Jerville *(M. Cadeaux)*.

Musical comedy. Source: Tristan Bernard, *Le petit café, comèdie en trois actes* (Paris, 1912). French-language version of *Playboy of Paris*, q. v. *Waiters. Courtship. Inheritance. Restaurateurs. Paris. Duels.*

THE PHANTOM BULLET (Universal-Jewel) **F2.4219**

Universal Pictures. 9 May **1926** [c30 Apr 1926; LP22742]. Si; b&w. 35mm. 6 reels, 6,148 or 5,820 ft.

Pres by Carl Laemmle. *Dir* Clifford S. Smith. *Adapt-Cont* Curtis Benton. *Photog* Harry Neumann.

Cast: Hoot Gibson *(Tom Farlane)*, Eileen Percy *(Jane Terrill)*, Allan Forrest *(Don Barton)*, Pat Harmon *(Bill Haynes)*, Nelson McDowell *(Zack Peters)*, William H. Turner *(Judge Terrill)*, John T. Prince *(Tom Farlane, Sr.)*, Pee Wee Holmes *(Short)*, Rosemary Cooper *(Dolores)*.

Western melodrama. Source: Oscar J. Friend, *Click of the Triangle T* (Chicago, 1925). Tom Farlane, a cowpuncher on a ranch in Wyoming and an ardent amateur photographer, receives word from his father's Texas ranch that his father has been murdered, with no clue except the fatal bullet fired from an automatic. Determined to find the killer, Tom goes to Texas under the guise of a soft city slicker and is greeted with derision by his father's men. Tom poses himself and Jane, his sweetheart, in the seat of a buckboard, fastening his camera to the corral fence; as he snaps the shutter, a shot is fired behind them. Don Barton, the guilty foreman, tries to convince Jane that Tom has a dancehall girl on the side, but when Tom sees the figure of Barton in the developed print, he tracks down Barton and Jane, rescuing her as Barton's car swerves over a cliff into the river. *Ranchers. Cowboys. Ranch foremen. Photographers. Murder. Disguise. Wyoming. Texas.*

THE PHANTOM BUSTER **F2.4220**

Action Pictures. *Dist* Pathé Exchange. 14 Aug **1927** [c20 Jun 1927; LU24105]. Si; b&w. 35mm. 5 reels, 4,497 ft.

Pres by Lester F. Scott, Jr. *Dir* William Bertram. *Scen* Betty Burbridge. *Story* Walter J. Coburn.

Cast: Buddy Roosevelt *(Jeff McCloud/Bill Turner)*, Alma Rayford *(Babs)*, Charles Whitaker *(Cassidy)*, Boris Karloff *(Ramon)*, John Junior *(Jim)*, Walter Maly *(Jack)*, Lawrence Underwood *(sheriff)*.

Action melodrama. Bull Turner, trusted employee of a construction company, is also the "Phantom" who has twice stolen the payroll. Jeff McCloud, a stranger, realizes that without his beard he would strongly resemble Turner; and the latter throws suspicion on him, though Jeff escapes from the sheriff. Jim Breed kills and robs Turner in an argument over their spoils; Jeff takes Turner's place and keeps a rendezvous with the gang, learning of a plan to smuggle arms over the border. Jeff is ambushed by Breed but is cared for by Babs, whose grandfather is planning to marry her to Turner; he is denounced by Breed as an imposter and attacked by Cassidy, but help arrives from the rangers, and the gang is routed. *Rangers. Smugglers. Bandits. Construction. Mistaken identity. Robbery. Mexican border.*

THE PHANTOM CITY **F2.4221**

Charles R. Rogers Productions. *Dist* First National Pictures. 23 Dec **1928** [c26 Sep 1928; LP25655]. Si; b&w. 35mm. 6 reels, 5,887 ft.

Pres by Charles R. Rogers. *Supv* Harry J. Brown. *Dir* Albert Rogell. *Titl* Fred Allen. *Story* Adele S. Buffington. *Photog* Ted McCord.

Cast: Ken Maynard *(Tim Kelly)*, Eugenia Gilbert *(Sally Ann Drew)*, James Mason *(Joe Bridges)*, Charles Mailes *(Benedict)*, Jack McDonald *(Simon)*, Blue Washington *(himself)*, Tarzan *(himself, a horse)*.

Western melodrama. Three people are mysteriously summoned to the deserted mining town of Gold City: Tim Kelly; Sally Ann Drew, Tim's beautiful ward; and Joe Bridges, part owner with Sally Ann of the abandoned and seemingly worthless Sally Ann mine. Bridges' men try to force their way into the mine, and two of them are shot by a mysterious phantom, who then warns Tim to keep away from the mine. Tim tries to force Bridges to sign over to him that share of the Sally Ann mine which had been appropriated from Tim's father by Bridges' father years before. Tim is tied up by Bridges, only to be freed by the phantom, who turns out to be Tim's father in disguise. Bridges steals the elder Kelly's gold, and Tim goes after him. Bridges is killed when his car goes off a cliff, and Tim returns to Sally Ann and his father with the stolen gold. *Wards. Phantoms. Disguise. Filial relations. Gold mines.*

THE PHANTOM EXPRESS **F2.4222**

Banner Productions. *Dist* Henry Ginsberg Distributing Corp. Nov **1925** [c11 Dec 1925; LP22102]. Si; b&w. 35mm. 5 reels, 4,614 ft.

Dir John Adolfi. *Story-Cont* Tom J. Hopkins. *Photog* A. Fried, Charles Davis.

Cast: Ethel Shannon *(Nora Lane)*, George Periolat *(John Lane)*, David Butler *(Jack Warren)*, Frankie Darro *(Daddles)*, George Siegmann *(Rufus Hardy)*, William Tooker *(George Mott)*, John Webb Dillon *(Herny Muncy)*.

Melodrama. Jack Warren, the substitute engineer on a small railroad, falls in love with Nora Lane, the daughter of the engineer of the Phantom Express. The elder Lane takes the express for a trial run, and Rufus Hardy, one of Nora's rejected suitors, deliberately throws the wrong switch, wrecking the train. Nora's father temporarily loses both his mind and his job. Jack takes over as engineer on the express, and Nora's father, recovered from his mental illness, prevents Hardy from again wrecking the train. The elder Lane gets his job back, Hardy is subjected to legal action, and Jack is promoted. Jack and Nora are married. *Railroad engineers. Filial relations. Mental illness. Railroads. Train wrecks.*

THE PHANTOM FLYER (Air Thriller) **F2.4223**

Universal Pictures. 26 Feb **1928** [c20 Oct 1927; LP24565]. Si; b&w. 35mm. 5 reels, 4,253 ft.

Pres by Carl Laemmle. *Dir-Story-Adapt* Bruce Mitchell. *Titl* Gardner Bradford. *Photog* William Adams. *Film Ed* Lee Anthony.

Cast: Al Wilson *(Dick Stanton)*, Lillian Gilmore *(Mary Crandall)*, Buck Connors *(John Crandall)*, Billy "Red" Jones *(Nick Crandall)*, Don Fuller *(Slim Decker)*, Myrtis Crinley *(Isabella Pipp)*, Mary Cornwallis *(Julia Hart)*, Larry Steers *(Joe Calvert)*.

Western melodrama. John Crandall, who is homesteading a western tract with the aid of his daughter, Mary, his son, Nick, and Isabella, an orphan girl, is opposed by Julia Hart, a cattle owner, over the water rights of the ranch. Mary catches Julia's men running brands on their cattle and after a chase is rescued by Dick Stanton, a border patrol aviator, who agrees to help her. Joe Calvert shoots Nick in an attempted raid and sabotages her airplane wheel, but Dick repairs it in the air; together they get the doctor for Nick. When Crandall discovers that his "first entry" papers have been stolen, Dick goes to the Hart ranch to investigate. Crandall is forced to sign a quit-claim deed, and Dick arrives just as Calvert abducts Mary in a plane; Slim and Dick follow, and Calvert falls to his death in a fight. Julia relinquishes the deed, and all ends happily. *Homesteaders. Ranchers. Border patrol. Property rights. Water rights. Aviation. Abduction. Documentation.*

Note: Also reviewed as *The Phantom Ranger.*

THE PHANTOM HORSEMAN **F2.4224**

Universal Pictures. 3 Mar **1924** [c4 Feb 1924; LP19883]. Si; b&w. 35mm. 5 reels, 4,399 ft.

Dir Robert North Bradbury. *Story-Scen* Isadore Bernstein. *Photog* Merritt B. Gerstad.

Cast: Jack Hoxie *(Bob Winton)*, Lillian Rich *(Dorothy Mason)*, Neil McKinnon *(Fred Mason)*, Wade Boteler *(Jefferson Williams)*, William McCall *(deputy sheriff)*, Ben Corbett *(Benny)*, George A. Williams *(judge)*, Ruby Lafayette *(Maxwell's mother)*.

Western melodrama. Sheriff Bob Winton sets out to capture a mysterious bandit named "The Hawk," a phantom rider who is admired by the townspeople because he steals from the Williams Lumber Co., a ruthless outfit determined to own all the land in the vicinity. Bob discovers that his sweetheart Dorothy's brother, Fred, is "The Hawk." Noting that the Williams Lumber Co. has a mortgage on Dorothy's ranch, Bob decides to shield Fred. Bob is accused of killing a guard at the lumber company, but Fred confesses and commits suicide, naming himself as "The Hawk." The ranch is saved from the lumber company. *Sheriffs. Ranches. Mortgages. Lumbering. Land rights. Disguise. Suicide.*

Note: Working title: *The Phantom Rider.*

THE PHANTOM IN THE HOUSE **F2.4225**

Trem Carr Productions. *Dist* Continental Talking Pictures. 1 Nov **1929** [c1 Nov 1929; LP966]. Sd (Photophone); b&w. 35mm. 6 reels, 5,725 ft. [Also si, 1 Dec; 5,803 ft.]

Dir Phil Rosen. *Adapt-Cont-Dial* Arthur Hoerl. *Photog* Herbert Kirkpatrick. *Song: "You'll Never Be Forgotten"* Abner Silver, Maceo Pinkard. *Sd* Neil Jack.

Cast: Ricardo Cortez *(Paul Wallis)*, Nancy Welford *(Dorothy Milburn)*, Henry B. Walthall *(Boyd Milburn)*, Grace Valentine *(Peggy Milburn)*, Thomas A. Curran *(Judge Thompson)*, Jack Curtis *("Biffer" Bill)*, John Elliott *(Police Captain)*.

Society melodrama. Source: Andrew Soutar, *The Phantom in the House* (London, 1928). Peggy Milburn, eager to help her husband, Boyd, a struggling inventor, goes to the apartment of Roger Stanwick, a wealthy bachelor, to seek his aid; when he realizes she is offering only her friendship and tries to overpower her, she kills him; and for their child's sake, Boyd takes the blame for the crime, being discovered near the body, and is sentenced to life imprisonment. Meanwhile, his inventions bring wealth to Peggy; and having changed her name and achieved a place in society, she aspires to marry Dorothy to a title, though the girl loves Paul Wallis. Boyd returns after 15 years, is introduced as a family friend, and backs Dorothy in her decision to marry for love, though his wife threatens to expose him. Judge Thompson tells Paul about the girl's father; an argument ensues; and Bill, a prisonmate of Boyd's, kills the judge. Paul is accused of the crime, but Dorothy learns the truth from Boyd, and Bill is caught. Peggy repents and vows to begin again with her husband and daughter. *Inventors. Socialites. Manslaughter. Self-sacrifice. Circumstantial evidence. Murder. Prisons.*

PHANTOM JUSTICE **F2.4226**

Richard Thomas Productions. *Dist* Film Booking Offices of America. 27 Jan or 17 Feb **1924** [c13 Jan 1924; LP19875]. Si; b&w. 35mm. 7 reels, 6,238 ft.

Dir Richard Thomas. *Adapt* Burnell Manley. *Story* Daniel Whitcomb. *Photog* Jack Fuqua.

Cast: Rod La Rocque *(Kingsley)*, Garry O'Dell *("Spike" Lorel)*, Kathryn McGuire *(Beatrice Brooks)*, Frederick Vroom *(Dr. Wills)*, Lillian Leighton *(Mother Meg)*, Frederick Moore *("Gyp" Doyle)*, Gordon Dumont *("Can" Weasel)*, Estelle Taylor *("Goldie" Harper)*, Rex Ballard *("Duke" Ruggles)*, Norval MacGregor *(Wolfe)*.

Crime drama. *On a visit to the dentist, Kingsley, an attorney, is confronted by a well-known criminal, who asks him to defend "Goldie" Harper, a girl accused of killing a man whose body has not been found. The attorney agrees to take the case, and Goldie is released. Eventually, police detectives discover the dead man's body in Kingsley's back yard.* This eventuality causes the attorney to awaken: he finds himself in the dentist's office—and realizes it was all a dream! *Lawyers. Dentists. Murder. Dreams.*

PHANTOM OF THE DESERT **F2.4227**

Webb-Douglas Productions. *Dist* Syndicate Pictures. 1 Nov **1930.** Sd (Cinephone); b&w. 35mm. 6 reels, 5,700 ft.

Dir Harry S. Webb. *Story-Cont-Dial* Carl Krusada. *Photog* William Nobles. *Film Ed* Fred Bain. *Sd Engr* Ralph M. Like.

Cast: Jack Perrin *(Jack Saunders)*, Eva Novak *(Mary Van Horn)*, Josef Swickard *(Colonel Van Horn)*, Lila Eccles *(Nora)*, Ben Corbett *(Benny Mack)*, Edward Earle *(Dan Denton)*, Robert Walker *(Steve)*, Pete Morrison *(Jim)*, Starlight *(Phantom, a horse)*.

Western melodrama. While Dan, Jim, and Steve rustle brood mares from Colonel Van Horn, they blame the loss on a phantom stallion, and the colonel offers a large reward for the horse—dead or alive. Jack Saunders, a new hand, persuades Van Horn through his daughter, Mary, to reward only the capture of the live horse, and he later finds evidence that the source of the trouble is two-legged. Using Mary's horse as bait, Jack captures the phantom horse, finds the stolen herd, and effects Steve's confession. *Rustling. Deserts. Phantoms. Horses.*

THE PHANTOM OF THE FOREST **F2.4228**

Gotham Productions. *Dist* Lumas Film Corp. Jan **1926** [c25 Jan 1926; LP22323]. Si; b&w. 35mm. 6 reels, 5,800 ft.

Supv Renaud Hoffman. *Dir* Henry McCarthy. *Adapt* James J. Tynan.

Photog Ray June. *Film Ed* Irene Morra. *Prod Mgr* Glenn Belt.
Cast: Betty Francisco *(Helen Taylor)*, Eddie Phillips *(Frank Wallace)*, James Mason *(Walt Mingin)*, Frank Foster Davis *(Joe Deering)*, Irene Hunt *(Mrs. Deering)*, Rhody Hathaway *(John Wallace)*, White Fawn *(a dog)*, Thunder *(a dog)*.
Melodrama. Source: Frank Foster Davis, "The Phantom of the Forest" (publication undetermined). As a puppy, Thunder runs wild in the forest, but grown into a strong, smart dog, he becomes attached to Helen Taylor, a young woman who owns land under which, unknown to her, there are valuable oil deposits. Certain land speculators attempt to gain control of the land by foreclosing on Helen's mortgage, but Frank Wallace steps in and pays off the necessary interest himself. The speculators set fire to the forest, and Helen and Frank narrowly escape. Thunder fights his way through the flames and rescues a sick child. Frank and Helen are united. *Land speculation. Oil lands. Mortgages. Incendiarism. Forest fires. Dogs.*

THE PHANTOM OF THE NORTH **F2.4229**
All-Star Productions. *Dist* Biltmore Pictures. 28 May **1929** [New York showing]. Si; b&w. 35mm. 5 reels, 4,600 ft.
Dir Harry Webb. *Scen* George Hull, Carl Krusada. *Story* Flora E. Douglas. *Photog* Arthur Reeves, William Thornley. *Film Ed* Fred Bain.
Cast: Edith Roberts *(Doris Rayburn)*, Donald Keith *(Bob Donald)*, Kathleen Key *(Colette)*, Boris Karloff *(Jules Gregg)*, Joe Bonomo *(Pierre Blanc)*, Josef Swickard *(Colonel Rayburn)*, Muro *(himself)*, Arab *(himself)*.
Northwest melodrama. A young trapper's furs are stolen by a man who then kills another trapper, and the trapper is suspected of the murder. Fleeing, the trapper is almost drowned in the rapids, but he manages to save himself, though the villain is destroyed. There are scenes showing "wild wolves" (actually well-fed police dogs) chasing well-groomed "wild horses." *Trappers. Thieves. Murder. Rapids. Wolves. Police dogs. Horses.*

THE PHANTOM OF THE OPERA (Universal-Jewel) **F2.4230**
Universal Pictures. 6 Sep **1925** [New York premiere; released 15 Nov; c1 Aug 1925; LP21689]. Si; b&w with col sequences (Technicolor). 35mm. 10 reels, 8,464 ft.
Pres by Carl Laemmle. *Dir* Rupert Julian. *Adtl Dir* Edward Sedgwick. *Titl* Tom Reed. *Adapt* Raymond Schrock, Elliott J. Clawson. *Photog* Virgil Miller. *Adtl Photog* Milton Bridenbecker, Charles J. Van Enger. *Art Dir* Charles D. Hall. *Film Ed* Maurice Pivar.
Cast: Lon Chaney *(The Phantom)*, Mary Philbin *(Christine Daae)*, Norman Kerry *(Raoul de Chagny)*, Snitz Edwards *(Florine Papillon)*, Gibson Gowland *(Simon)*, John Sainpolis *(Philippe de Chagny)*, Virginia Pearson *(Carlotta)*, Arthur Edmund Carewe *(Ledoux)*, Edith Yorke *(Mama Valerius)*, Anton Vaverka *(prompter)*, Bernard Siegel *(Joseph Buguet)*, Olive Ann Alcorn *(La Sorelli)*, Cesare Gravina *(manager)*, George B. Williams *(M. Ricard)*, Bruce Covington *(M. Moncharmin)*, Edward Cecil *(Faust)*, John Miljan *(Valentin)*, Alexander Bevani *(Mephistopheles)*, Grace Marvin *(Martha)*, Ward Crane *(Count Ruboff)*, Chester Conklin *(orderly)*, William Tryoler *(director of opera orchestra)*.
Melodrama. Source: Gaston Leroux, *Le Fantôme de l'Opéra* (Paris, 1910). Christine Daae, an understudy at the Paris Opéra, is guided to stardom by a mysterious and compelling voice that emanates from behind the walls of her dressing room. The voice eventually summons her to a meeting, and she discovers a sinister man whose face is covered by a mask. He demands that she give up her fiancé, Raoul, and devote herself to her music and her mentor. She agrees, and he allows her to sing again. Realizing that she is going back on her word, The Phantom kidnaps Christine, takes her to his underground chambers, and is revealed, when his mask is removed, to be hideous beyond description. Raoul and Ledoux (of the secret police) follow The Phantom, and he traps them in an infernal device. A mob follows, and The Phantom flees. Raoul and Ledoux escape, rescuing Christine. The mob forces The Phantom into the Seine, where he drowns, grotesquely defiant to the last. *Singers. Monsters. Detectives. Kidnaping. Opera. Paris. "Faust".*

THE PHANTOM OF THE OPERA (Reissue) **F2.4231**
Universal Pictures. 15 Dec **1929.** Talking sequences, mus score, & sd eff (Movietone); b&w with col sequences (Technicolor). 35mm. 8,382 ft.
Dir of Sd Sequences Ernst Laemmle. *Dial* Frank McCormack. *Rec Engr* C. Roy Hunter.
Cast: Edward Martindel *(Philippe de Chagny* [*see note*]*)*.
Note: This reissue changed in some respects the original film. Talking sequences were added, featuring Mary Philbin and Norman Kerry. Scenes featuring John Sainpolis were deleted and others filmed with Edward Martindel in the part of Philippe de Chagny. Scenes from the original in which part of the opera *Faust* is performed were dubbed in with arias from that work. The part of John Miljan was deleted altogether.

PHANTOM OF THE RANGE **F2.4232**
FBO Pictures. 22 Apr **1928** [c12 Mar 1928; LP25055]. Si; b&w. 35mm. 5 reels, 4,781 ft.
Dir James Dugan. *Cont* Frank Howard Clark. *Titl* Randolph Bartlett. *Story* Oliver Drake. *Camera* Nick Musuraca. *Film Ed* Pandro S. Berman. *Asst Dir* William Cody.
Cast: Tom Tyler *(Duke Carlton)*, Charles McHugh *(Tim O'Brien)*, Duane Thompson *(Patsy O'Brien)*, Frankie Darro *(Spuds O'Brien)*, James Pierce *("Flash" Corbin)*, Marjorie Zier *(Vera Van Swank)*, Beans *(himself, a dog)*.
Western drama. Duke Carlton, an actor stranded in a small western town, gets a job as a cowboy on Tim O'Brien's ranch as a reward for beating up "Flash" Corbin, a real estate agent who has been trying to swindle the rancher. A romance develops between the actor and Patsy O'Brien, the rancher's daughter, but it is interrupted by the appearance of his former stage partner, Vera Van Swank, who claims him as her husband. He clears himself of the bigamy charge, foils a plot to cheat the rancher out of a $90,000 land property, and wins the daughter's hand. *Cowboys. Ranchers. Actors. Swindlers. Real estate business. Bigamy. Dogs.*

PHANTOM OF THE TURF **F2.4233**
Duke Worne Productions. *Dist* Rayart Pictures. Mar **1928.** Si; b&w. 35mm. 6 reels, 5,905 ft.
Dir Duke Worne. *Scen* Arthur Hoerl. *Story* Leota Morgan. *Photog* Walter Griffin. *Film Ed* Malcolm Sweeney.
Cast: Helene Costello *(Joan)*, Rex Lease *(John Nichols)*, Forrest Stanley *(Dunbarton)*, Danny Hoy *(Billy)*, Clarence H. Wilson *(The Lawyer)*, Major *(Phantom, a horse)*.
Melodrama. When the owner of the famous thoroughbred Phantom is found dead, Dunbarton steps in and declares himself to be the guardian of the two missing heirs and has Joan impersonate the daughter. The real son, John Nichols, returns, falls in love with his "sister," and begins to unravel the mystery of his father's death. Phantom wins the thrilling horserace at the climax—to the consternation of the villain, who had tried to substitute another horse. *Heirs. Guardians. Horseracing. Impersonation. Fraud. Horses.*

THE PHANTOM RANGER *see* **THE PHANTOM FLYER**

THE PHANTOM RIDER *see* **THE PHANTOM HORSEMAN**

THE PHANTOM RIDER **F2.4234**
Dist Syndicate Pictures. 24 Sep **1929** [New York showing; released Sep 1929]. Si; b&w. 35mm. 5 reels, 4,800 ft.
Dir J. P. McGowan. *Photog* Frank Cotner.
Cast: Tom Tyler, J. P. McGowan, Harry Woods, Lotus Thompson.
Western melodrama. "Dick Cartwright loves Grace Darling despite Cartwright-Darling feud. Cal Hardy, jealous of Dick, shoots Grace's brother Bob and tries to shoot Dick later, but misses. Attempting to again shoot Bob, he is seen by Dick and in the struggle, is himself killed. Hardy was the 'Phantom Rider.' Dick wins reward and Grace." ("Motion Picture News Booking Guide" in *Motion Picture News*, 15 Mar 1930, p97.) *Ranchers. Farmers. Feuds. Murder. Phantoms.*

PHANTOM SHADOWS **F2.4235**
J. J. Fleming Productions. *Dist* Davis Distributing Division. 15 Jan **1925.** Si; b&w. 35mm. 5 reels, 4,875 ft.
Dir Al Ferguson.
Cast: Al Ferguson, Lucille Du Bois.
Melodrama(?). No information about the nature of this film has been found.

PHANTOM SHADOWS **F2.4236**
J. J. Fleming Productions. *Dist* Davis Distributing Division. 15 Jan **1925** [c14 Jan 1926; LP22265]. Si; b&w. 35mm. 5 reels.
Dir Frank Grandon.
Cast: Al Ferguson, Lucille Du Bois.
Melodrama. "... in which hero, after serving sentence for another's crime, seeks to go away with heroine. He must first obtain papers which gang leader holds concerning her father, and in getting them again falls in

leader's power. He beats him up and escapes. Leader again seeks to frame him, and kidnaps girl. Hero overtakes them, beats up villain and clears girl's father." (*Motion Picture News Booking Guide*, 8:64, Apr 1925.) *Filial relations. Gangs. Kidnaping. Frameup.*

Note: Al Ferguson is also credited with the direction.

PHYLLIS OF THE FOLLIES F2.4237

Universal Pictures. Jun **1928** [first showing; released 25 Nov; c9 May 1928; LP25234]. Si; b&w. 35mm. 6 reels, 5,907 ft.

Dir Ernst Laemmle. *Scen* John B. Clymer. *Titl* Albert De Mond. *Story* Arthur Gregor. *Photog* George Robinson.

Cast: Alice Day *(Phyllis Sherwood)*, Matt Moore *(Howard Decker)*, Edmund Burns *(Clyde Thompson)*, Lilyan Tashman *(Mrs. Decker)*, Duane Thompson *(Mabel Lancing)*.

Comedy. Phyllis Sherwood, a follies girl, and Mrs. Decker, an ex–follies girl, decide to trick one of lawyer Decker's clients, who has sworn off follies girls and is attracted only to married women. Client Thompson falls in love with Phyllis, believing her to be Mrs. Decker. After several complications, the deception is revealed. Thompson is overjoyed to find that Phyllis is single, and the Deckers take a second honeymoon. *Chorus girls. Lawyers. Impersonation. Follies.*

PIECES OF CHINA F2.4238

Isaac O. Upham. *Dist* Pathé Exchange. 25 Jun **1926** [San Francisco premiere]. Si; b&w. 35mm. 6-8 reels.

Travelog. Subtitled "Adventures with picture camera in land of dragon. Travel de luxe, giving moving record of Mr. Upham's 10,000-mile journey covering one year in China." Highlights include visits to Shanghai, Hong Kong, the Imperial Palace in Peking, and the gorges of the Yangtze River. *China. Shanghai. Hong Kong. Peking. Yangtze River.*

PIED PIPER MALONE F2.4239

Famous Players–Lasky. *Dist* Paramount Pictures. 4 Feb **1924** [c6 Feb 1924; LP19886]. Si; b&w. 35mm. 8 reels, 7,264 ft.

Pres by Adolph Zukor, Jesse L. Lasky. *Dir* Alfred E. Green. *Scen* Tom Geraghty. *Titl* Booth Tarkington, Tom Geraghty. *Story* Booth Tarkington. *Photog* Ernest Hallor.

Cast: Thomas Meighan *(Jack Malone)*, Lois Wilson *(Patty Thomas)*, Emma Dunn *(Mother Malone)*, Charles Stevenson *(James P. Malone)*, George Fawcett *(Captain Clarke)*, Cyril Ring *(Charles Crosby, Jr.)*, Claude Brook *(Charles Crosby, Sr.)*, Joseph Burke *(Mr. Thomas)*, Peaches Jackson *(Betty Malone)*, Charles Winninger *(Louie, the barber)*, Hugh Cameron *(photographer)*, Dorothy Walters *(housekeeper)*, Pearl Sindelar, Marie Schaefer, Elizabeth Henry, Jean Armour, Blanch Standing, Mollie Ring *(The Malone Sisters)*, Charles Mussett, Walter Downing, Henry Mayo, Lawrence Barnes, David Wall, Ed Williams *(The Malone Brothers)*, Helen Macks, Marilyn McLain, Florence Rogan, Rita Rogan, Louise Jones, Marie Louise Bobb, Louise Sirkin, Billy Lauder, Charles Walters, Edwin Mills, Leonard Connelly, Bobby Jackson, Dorothy McCann, Billy Baker, Marshall Green *(children)*.

Comedy-drama. Jack Malone, mate of the *Langland*, is accused of drunkenness by Crosby, a rival suitor of his sweetheart, Patty Thomas. He and the captain, who really was drunk, are both fired. He is finally vindicated by the children of the town, and Patty agrees to wait for him when he goes to sea in a ship his brothers have purchased for him and the captain. *Ship crews. Children. Sea captains. Drunkenness. South Carolina.*

Note: All exterior scenes were made in Georgetown, South Carolina, making use of the Revolutionary War home of General Lafayette. Working title: *Uncle Jack.*

THE PILGRIM F2.4240

Charlie Chaplin Film Co. *Dist* Associated First National Pictures. 25 Feb **1923** [New York premiere; c24 Jan 1923; LP18607]. Si; b&w. 35mm. 4 reels, 4,300 ft.

Dir-Writ Charles Chaplin. *Assoc Dir* Chuck Reisner. *Photog* Rollie Totheroh.

Cast: Charles Chaplin *(The Pilgrim)*, Edna Purviance *(The Girl)*, Kitty Bradbury *(her mother)*, Mack Swain *(The Deacon)*, Loyal Underwood *(The Elder)*, Dinky Dean *(The Boy)*, Mai Wells *(his mother)*, Sydney Chaplin *(her husband)*, Chuck Reisner *(The Crook)*, Tom Murray *(The Sheriff)*, Monta Bell *(policeman)*, Henry Bergman *(The Traveler)*, Raymond Lee *(The Real Pastor)*, Edith Bostwick, Florence Latimer *(ladies of the parish)*.

Comedy. "The Pilgrim," an escaped convict, steals a minister's clothes and accepts a position in a Texas church. A pantomimed sermon on David and Goliath is one of the amusing situations that ensue. The Pilgrim's true identity is revealed when he tries to recover from a crook friend some money stolen from The Pilgrim's landlady, but the sheriff turns him loose at the Mexican border. *Criminals—Rehabilitation. Clergymen. Impersonation. Texas. Mexican border. Biblical characters.*

PILGRIMS OF THE NIGHT F2.4241

J. L. Frothingham. *Dist* Associated Producers. 26 Sep **1921** [c15 Aug, 5 Nov 1921; LP16874, LP17387]. Si; b&w. 35mm. 6 reels, 5,772 ft.

Pres by J. L. Frothingham. *Dir-Scen* Edward Sloman. *Photog* Tony Gaudio.

Cast: Lewis S. Stone *(Philip Champion/Lord Ellingham)*, Rubye De Remer *(Christine)*, William V. Mong *(Ambrose)*, Kathleen Kirkham *(Lady Ellingham)*, Raymond Hatton *(Le Blun)*, Walter McGrail *(Gilbert Hannaway)*, Frank Leigh *(Marcel)*.

Underworld melodrama. Source: Edward Phillips Oppenheim, *Passers-By* (Boston, 1910). Philip Champion, the son of a British earl, is exiled to Paris after having served a prison term to shield his wife and there forms an alliance with his brother-in-law, Marcel, who conducts a fashionable gambling establishment as the head of a band of criminals. Marcel is arrested and sent to prison, and Champion escapes. Ambrose, a hunchbacked street musician, escapes with Christine, Champion's daughter, and frames Champion for robbery. While visiting Marcel, whom she believes to be her father, Christine swears to kill Champion. Gilbert Hannaway, an amateur criminologist, informs her in London that the man she seeks is now Lord Ellingham; however, in an attempt on his life, she discovers that he is her true father. Marcel escapes but is killed by Ambrose, who also dies, and the money is recovered from his street organ by a monkey. Hannaway and Christine become engaged. *Criminologists. Street musicians. Hunchbacks. Gangs. Robbery. Frameup. Parentage. Gambling. Paris. London. Monkeys.*

THE PINCH HITTER (Reissue) F2.4242

Kay-Bee Pictures. *Dist* Tri-Stone Pictures. **1923.** Si; b&w. 35mm. 5 reels.

Note: A "re-edited and re-titled" Charles Ray film originally released by Triangle Film Corp. on 29 Apr 1917.

THE PINCH HITTER F2.4243

Dist Associated Exhibitors. 13 Dec **1925** [c30 Dec 1925; LU22201]. Si; b&w. 35mm. 7 reels, 6,259 ft.

Dir Joseph Henabery. *Story* C. Gardner Sullivan. *Photog* Jules Cronjager.

Cast: Glenn Hunter *(Joel Martin)*, Constance Bennett *(Abby Nettleton)*, Jack Drumier *(Obadiah Parker)*, Reginald Sheffield *(Alexis Thompson)*, Antrim Short *(Jimmy Slater)*, George Cline *(Coach Nolan)*, Mary Foy *(Aunt Martha)*, James E. Sullivan *(college dean)*, Joseph Burke *(Charlie)*.

Comedy. Joel Martin, a shy and diffident New Englander, goes to college, where he becomes the victim of rough hazing and practical jokes by the upperclassmen. Joel is allowed no spending money by his uncle and becomes known as a tightwad. He falls in love with Abby Nettleton, a waitress in the college beanery, and she encourages him to try out for the college baseball team. Joel makes the team, but he does not realize that he has been given a number and a uniform only because the coach thinks that he will make a good team mascot. During a crucial game, no other players are available, and Joel is put in as a pinch hitter. He hits a homerun, wins the game for his team, and becomes the campus hero. *New Englanders. Waitresses. Athletic coaches. Uncles. Baseball. College life.*

PINK GODS F2.4244

Famous Players–Lasky. *Dist* Paramount Pictures. ca24 Sep **1922** [New York premiere; released 1 Oct; c4 Oct 1922; LP18314]. Si; b&w. 35mm. 8 reels, 7,180 ft. [Copyrighted as 7 reels.]

Pres by Jesse L. Lasky. *Dir* Penrhyn Stanlaws. *Scen* Ewart Adamson. *Adapt* J. E. Nash, Sonya Levien. *Photog* Paul Perry.

Cast: Bebe Daniels *(Lorraine Temple)*, James Kirkwood *(John Quelch)*, Anna Q. Nilsson *(Lady Margot Cork)*, Raymond Hatton *(Jim Wingate)*, Adolphe Menjou *(Louis Barney)*, Guy Oliver *(Mark Escher)*, George Cowl *(Col. Pat Temple)*, Arthur Trimble *(Dick Cork)*.

Melodrama. Source: Cynthia Stockley, "Pink Gods and Blue Demons" (publication undetermined). Because John Quelch, owner of vast diamond mines, is constantly fearful of theft and convinced that any woman will "sell her soul" for diamonds, he deals harshly with any employee caught stealing and has Lady Margot Cork watched while she is visiting Lorraine Temple. John and Margot fall in love, but she cancels their engagement when she learns of the "brutal" punishment of Jim Wingate for swallowing a diamond. John sees Lorraine's weakness and tempts her with a fortune in gems. She makes advances, but John repulses her with the explanation that he had intended only to show her the error of her ways. Wingate dynamites the mine and the mansion; Margot and Lorraine's husband arrive in time to hear Lorraine thank John for the lesson before she dies; Margot and John are reconciled. Conflicting synopses create doubt that Lorraine actually dies in the explosion. *Greed. Diamond mines. South Africa.*

THE PINTO KID F2.4245

FBO Pictures. 29 Apr **1928** [c19 Mar 1928; LP25074]. Si; b&w. 35mm. 5 reels, 4,884 ft.

Dir Louis King. *Scen* Oliver Drake. *Titl* Frank T. Daugherty. *Story* Jean Dupont, John Twist. *Photog* Roy Eslick. *Film Ed* Della M. King.

Cast: Buzz Barton *(David "Red" Hepner)*, Frank Rice *(Hank Robbins)*, James Welsh *(Andy Bruce)*, Gloria Lee *(Janet Bruce)*, Milburn Morante *(Pat Logan)*, Hugh Trevor *(Dan Logan)*, William Patton *(Rufe Sykes)*, Walter Shumway *(Bert Lowery)*.

Western melodrama. Red Hepner and his sidekick Hank Robbins are rewarded with jobs on Janet Bruce's ranch when they pull her from a pool of quicksand. They show their appreciation by rescuing her from Lowery, a city shark, and preventing him from gaining possession of her ranch. *Cowboys. Swindlers. Ranches. Quicksand.*

THE PIONEER SCOUT F2.4246

Paramount Famous Lasky Corp. 21 Jan **1928** [c21 Jan 1928; LP24896]. Si; b&w. 35mm. 7 reels, 6,118 ft.

Dir Lloyd Ingraham, Alfred L. Werker. *Story-Scen* Frank M. Clifton. *Titl* Garrett Graham. *Photog* Mack Stengler. *Film Ed* Duncan Mansfield.

Cast: Fred Thomson *(Fred)*, Nora Lane *(Mary Baxter)*, William Courtwright *(Old Bill)*, Tom Wilson *(Handy Anderson)*.

Western melodrama. A typical western story of " . . . old wagon train days, gangs of thieves who dress as Indians, the menace with a hook for a hand, horses beating up the dust and men beating up each other" (*Variety*, 11 Apr 1928). Fred Thomson as Fred, a frontier scout, falls in love with Mary Baxter, who is making her way across the plains in her father's covered wagon. Handy Anderson, the hooked menace, tries to win the girl but is repulsed. He takes Fred prisoner and tries to kidnap the girl. Fred's horse diverts Anderson's attention, and his master, freed, organizes a posse to rescue the girl. *Scouts—Frontier. Frontier and pioneer life. Horses.*

PIONEER TRAILS F2.4247

Vitagraph Co. of America. Nov **1923** [c13 Sep 1923; LP19389]. Si; b&w. 35mm. 7 reels, 6,920 ft.

Dir David Smith. *Story-Scen* C. Graham Baker. *Photog* Stephen Smith, Jr.

Cast: Cullen Landis *(Jack Dale/Jack Plains)*, Alice Calhoun *(Rose Miller)*, Bertram Grassby *(Philip Blaney)*, Otis Harlan *("Easy Aaron" Cropsey)*, Dwight Crittenden *(Rodney Miller)*, Virginia True Boardman *(Mrs. Salter)*, Aggie Herring *("Laundry Lou")*, Nelson McDowell *(Parson)*, Joe Rickson *(The Sheriff)*.

Melodrama. In a prolog, 4-year-old Jack Dale is his family's sole survivor after an Indian raid on their wagon party and is reared by Mrs. Salter, another traveler. Twenty years later Jack Dale, known as Jack "Plains," rescues some passengers in a runaway crash and meets Rose Miller, her father, and his associate in business, Philip Blaney, who desires Rose. Jealousy causes Blaney to accuse Dale of a murder that is committed, but he is vindicated, his family history is revealed, and he marries Rose. *Pioneers. Indians of North America. Wagon trains. Murder. Parentage.*

PIONEER'S GOLD F2.4248

Sanford Productions. 1 Apr **1924** [New York State license]. Si; b&w. 35mm. 5 reels, 4,700 ft.

Cast: Pete Morrison.

Western melodrama(?). No information about the nature of this film has been found.

PIONEERS OF THE WEST F2.4249

William (Bill) Mix Productions. 1 Jun **1927** [New York State license]. Si; b&w. 35mm. 5 reels.

Cast: Dick Carter, Dorothy Earle.

Western melodrama(?). No information about the nature of this film has been found.

PIONEERS OF THE WEST F2.4250

J. P. McGowan Productions. *Dist* Syndicate Pictures. Nov **1929**. Si; b&w. 35mm. 5 reels, 4,262 ft.

Dir-Scen J. P. McGowan. *Story* Sally Winters. *Photog* Hap Depew.

Cast: Tom Tyler *(Phil Sampson)*, J. P. McGowan *(Tom Dorgan)*, George Brownhill *(superintendent)*, Mack V. Wright *("Spike" Harkness)*, Tommy Bay *("Bull' Bradley)*, Charlotte Winn *(Dorothy McClure)*.

Western melodrama. Tom Dorgan takes the rap for a train holdup and a murder, goes to prison, and escapes during a fire. Meanwhile, the express company has hired agent Phil Sampson to recover the stolen loot. The agent links Dorgan to Dorothy McClure, the daughter of the murdered man, and arrives at her ranch simultaneously with two rough characters delegated by Dorgan to watch over the girl—Bull Bradley and Spike Harkness, who claims to be her cousin. Dorgan arrives, he produces the missing package, and several scuffles break out. Bradley is bumped off by the cousin, and Dorgan explains that Bradley was his son and guilty of the crimes for which he went to prison. Thus, all ends well for the agent and the girl. *Investigators. Train robberies. Murder. Prison escapes. Express service.*

PIRATES OF THE SKY F2.4251

Hurricane Film Corp. *Dist* Pathé Exchange. 22 May **1927** [c15 Feb 1926; LU22412; c6 May 1927; LU23932]. Si; b&w. 35mm. 5 reels, 4,828 ft.

Dir Charles Andrews. *Story-Scen* Elaine Wilmont. *Photog* Leon Shamroy.

Cast: Charles Hutchison *(Bob Manning)*, Wanda Hawley *(Doris Reed)*, Crauford Kent *(Bruce Mitchell)*, Jimmy Aubrey *(Jeff Oldring)*, Ben Walker *(Stone)*.

Action melodrama. Baffled by the mysterious disappearance of a mail plane, the United States Secret Service solicits the aid of Bob Manning, an amateur criminologist. Among the reporters covering the story is Doris Reed, who has previously been engaged to Manning. Doris pickets Manning's house, as do Joe Parker and "Slim," two of Bruce Mitchell's gang, which is responsible for the plane's disappearance. Manning goes to her rescue, and both he and she are captured and taken to a deserted warehouse. Doris convinces Mitchell she is in league with the crooks. Manning escapes, however, and in some daring aerial stunts thwarts the bandits with the help of Doris. The couple are happily reunited. *Criminologists. Reporters. Secret service. Postal service. Airplanes.*

PITFALLS OF PASSION F2.4252

S. S. Millard. 16 Nov **1927** [trade review]. Si; b&w. 35mm. 5 reels.

Dir-Story Leonard Livingstone. *Photog* Ted Tetzlaff.

Cast: Prudence Sutton, Larry O'Dell.

Melodrama. "There is Jimmy, fresh from the farm. He has eloped with, but not married, his country sweetie. After Jimmy's passion and money have gone he listens to the sinister suggestion of Louie, poolroom bum. This results in the young girl being bartered to Madame Francine, proprietress of a high hat establishment. Louis takes most of the dough with the near-husband getting a cut. Jimmy is not again seen until, trying to escape from dicks, he runs into the hospital ward where May is being treated for the diseases she acquired in her crimson life. He has been plugged by the cops after having—in a subtitle—murdered the woman he was living with. May rises in her cot to gloat that he has gotten his for his perfidy and weakness." (*Variety*, 16 Nov 1927, p25.) *Prostitution. Murder. Venereal disease. Perfidy. Whorehouses.*

Note: Country of origin undetermined.

PLASTERED IN PARIS F2.4253

Fox Film Corp. 23 Sep **1928** [c11 Sep 1928; LP25614]. Sd eff (Movietone); b&w. 35mm. 6 reels, 5,641 ft.

Pres by William Fox. *Dir* Benjamin Stoloff. *Scen* Harry Brand, Andrew Rice. *Dial* Edwin Burke. *Titl* Malcolm Stuart Boylan. *Story* Harry Sweet, Lou Breslow. *Photog* Charles Clarke.

Cast: Sammy Cohen *(Sammy Nosenblum)*, Jack Pennick *(Bud Swenson)*, Lola Salvi *(Marcelle)*, Ivan Linow *(Sergeant Cou Cou)*, Hugh Allan *(Hugh)*, Marion Byron *(Mimi)*, Michael Visaroff *(French general)*, Albert Conti *(Abou Ben Abed)*, August Tollaire *(doctor)*.

Comedy. Sammy Nosenblum and Bud Swenson, who went to France to fight for democracy in 1918, return to Paris for an American Legion convention 10 years later. Sammy believes a war wound has caused him to become a kleptomaniac, and Bud makes him go to a famous specialist, who does him no good. Sammy and Bud are later drafted by mistake into the French Foreign Legion and, arriving in North Africa, rescue the commandant's daughter from a harem. *Kleptomania. Veterans. Psychiatrists. Harems. Paris. North Africa. France—Army—Foreign Legion. American Legion.*

THE PLASTIC AGE *see* **RED LIPS**

THE PLASTIC AGE **F2.4254**

B. P. Schulberg Productions. 15 Dec **1925**. Si; b&w. 35mm. 7 reels, 6,488 ft.

Dir Wesley Ruggles. *Adapt* Eve Unsell, Frederica Sagor. *Photog* Gilbert Warrenton, Allen Siegler.

Cast: Donald Keith *(Hugh Carver)*, Clara Bow *(Cynthia Day)*, Mary Alden *(Mrs. Carver)*, Henry B. Walthall *(Henry Carver)*, Gilbert Roland *(Carl Peters)*, J. Gordon Edwards, Jr. *(Norrie Parks)*, Felix Valle *(Merton Billings)*, David Butler *(Coach Henry)*.

Melodrama. Source: Percy Marks, *The Plastic Age* (New York, 1924). Impressionable Hugh Carver, once a championship runner in prep school, falls in love with Cynthia Day at college and goes to the dogs. He begins to lose races and incurs the wrath of his parents. Cynthia eventually realizes that she has done Hugh a great disservice in encouraging his infatuation and refuses to see him any longer. Hugh then regains his athletic prowess and wins the big football game for his school. Upon his graduation, a changed Cynthia returns to him, and it looks like wedding bills for old man Carver. *Flappers. Filial relations. College life. Track. Football. Track.*

THE PLAY GIRL **F2.4255**

Fox Film Corp. 22 Apr **1928** [c29 Mar 1928; LP25110]. Si; b&w. 35mm. 6 reels, 5,200 ft.

Pres by William Fox. *Dir* Arthur Rosson. *Story-Scen* John Stone. *Titl* Norman Z. McLeod. *Photog* Rudolph Berquist. *Film Ed* Ralph Dietrich. *Asst Dir* William Tummel.

Cast: Madge Bellamy *(Madge Norton [Logan?])*, John Mack Brown *(Bradley Lane)*, Walter McGrail *(David Courtney)*, Lionel Belmore *(The Greek Florist)*, Anita Garvin *(Millie)*, Thelma Hill *(The Salesgirl)*, Harry Tenbrook *(The Chauffeur)*.

Romantic comedy. When Madge, a clerk in a flower shop, is sent to a bachelor's apartment to deliver and arrange a bouquet, she discovers a guest, young and handsome Bradley Lane, taking a bath. She loses her job and becomes a playgirl until Bradley, her true love, asks her to marry him. *Florists. Bachelors.*

PLAY SAFE **F2.4256**

Monty Banks Enterprises. *Dist* Pathé Exchange. 30 Jan **1927** [c17 Jan 1927; LU23549]. Si; b&w. 35mm. 5 reels, 4,915 ft.

Supv Howard Estabrook. *Dir* Joseph Henabery. *Scen* Charles Horan, Harry Sweet. *Story* Monty Banks. *Photog* Blake Wagner.

Cast: Monty Banks *(The Boy)*, Virginia Lee Corbin *(Virginia Craig, heiress)*, Charles Mailes *(Silas Scott, crooked trustee)*, Charles Gerard *(his son)*, Bud Jamieson *(Big Bill)*, Rosa Gore, Syd Crossley, Max Ascher, Fatty Alexander.

Comedy-melodrama. Virginia Craig, sole heiress to the Craig estate, leaves home when Silas Scott, the dishonest trustee of the estate, tries to force her to marry his worthless son. Monty, The Boy, an employee in Virginia's factory, rescues her from a ruffian's insult when she takes refuge from a storm. Monty persuades Virginia to occupy his room for the night while he seeks lodging elsewhere; later he rents an automobile and takes the girl on a calamitous ride. Meanwhile, the trustee, alarmed at Virginia's interest in Monty, takes her back to the mansion and discharges the boy. It is arranged for Monty to appear to be the leader of a gang that lures Virginia into a trap; but she and Monty are pursued by the villains through a railroad yard and a freight train. Through Monty's wits and courage, they elude the pursuers and halt the train. *Heiresses. Factories. Chases.*

PLAY SQUARE **F2.4257**

Fox Film Corp. 14 Aug **1921** [c14 Aug 1921; LP16876]. Si; b&w. 35mm. 5 reels, 4,163 ft.

Pres by William Fox. *Dir* William K. Howard. *Story-Scen* Jack Strumwasser. *Photog* Victor Milner.

Cast: Johnie Walker *(Johnny Carroll)*, Edna Murphy *(Betty Bedford)*, Hayward Mack *(Bill Homer)*, Laura La Plante *(May Laverne)*, Jack Brammall *(Reddy)*, Wilbur Higby *(Judge Kerrigan)*, Nanine Wright *(Johnny's mother)*, Harry Todd *(Betty's father)*, Al Fremont *(Detective McQuade)*.

Crook melodrama. Johnny Carroll falls among thieves in the city and when arrested by Detective McQuade for picking Judge Kerrigan's pocket is released by the judge, who remembers the boy from his hometown and persuades him to reform. He returns home, takes a job in a grocery store, and revives his romance with Betty Bedford. All goes well until his confederates track him down and induce him to crack the safe in Mr. Bedford's store, threatening to reveal his criminal career if he refuses. He opens the safe but refuses to be a party to the crime and fights the gang. Betty returns with help, the thieves are captured, and Johnny and Betty are married. *Grocers. Thieves. Judges. Criminals—Rehabilitation.*

PLAYBOY OF PARIS **F2.4258**

Paramount-Publix Corp. 18 Sep or Oct **1930** [c17 Oct 1930; LP1654]. Sd (Movietone); b&w. 35mm. 9 reels, 6,512 ft.

Dir Ludwig Berger. *Screenplay* Vincent Lawrence. *Adapt* Percy Heath. *Photog* Henry Gerrard. *Film Ed* Merrill White. *Songs: "My Ideal," "It's a Great Life If You Don't Weaken," "In the Heart of Old Paree," "Yvonne's Song"* Leo Robin, Richard Whiting, Newell Chase. *Rec Engr* M. M. Paggi.

Cast: Maurice Chevalier *(Albert)*, Frances Dee *(Yvonne)*, O. P. Heggie *(Philibert)*, Stuart Erwin *(Paul)*, Eugene Pallette *(Pierre)*, Dorothy Christy *(Berengère)*, Cecil Cunningham *(Hedwige)*, Tyler Brooke *(Cadeaux)*, Frank Elliott *(Mr. Jabert)*, William B. Davidson *(Mr. Bannock)*, Erin La Bissoniere *(Jacqueline)*, Charles Giblyn *(Gastonet)*, Frederick Lee *(Plouvier)*, Edmund Breese *(general)*, Olaf Hytten *(doctor)*, Edward Lynch *(manager)*, Guy Oliver *(street cleaner)*, William O'Brien *(waiter)*.

Musical comedy. Source: Tristan Bernard, *Le Petit Cafe, comédie en trois actes* (Paris, 1912). Yvonne, daughter of Philibert, a Paris cafe owner, is in love with dreamy, blundering Albert, a waiter, though he pays little attention to her. Philibert plans to marry his daughter to a wealthy Parisian, but upon learning that Albert is to come into a large inheritance, he conspires to place him under a longterm contract, confident that he willingly will pay a forfeit to break it. Albert, however, elects to remain a waiter by day and devote his nights to a gay social life with Berengère, a gold digger; he drops dishes and insults patrons, but Philibert will not discharge him. Angrily, Yvonne follows him to a rendezvous with Berengère at a restaurant and denounces him as a waiter, precipitating a fight between the two girls. Albert defends Yvonne against another gentleman and is challenged to a duel—but the man refuses to fight a waiter. Insulted, Albert slaps him, but Yvonne faints from fright, and all ends happily as Albert realizes his love for her. *Waiters. Courtship. Inheritance. Gold diggers. Restaurateurs. Paris. Duels.*

Note: Also produced in a French-language version, *Le Petit Café*, q. v.

PLAYING AROUND **F2.4259**

First National Pictures. 19 Jan **1930** [c28 Jan 1930; LP1043]. Sd (Vitaphone); b&w. 35mm. 7 reels, 5,972 ft. [Also si.]

Dir Mervyn LeRoy. *Scen* Adele Commandini, Frances Nordstrom. *Dial-Titl* Humphrey Pearson. *Photog* Sol Polito. *Songs: "You're My Captain Kidd," "That's the Lowdown on the Lowdown," "We Learn About Love Every Day," "Playing Around"* Sam H. Stept, Bud Green. *Rec Engr* Earl Sitar.

Cast: Alice White *(Sheba Miller)*, Chester Morris *(Nickey Solomon)*, William Bakewell *(Jack)*, Richard Carlyle *(Pa Miller)*, Marion Byron *(Maude)*, Maurice Black *(Joe)*, Lionel Belmore *(Morgan)*, Shep Camp *(master of ceremonies)*, Ann Brody *(Mrs. Fenerbeck)*, Nellie V. Nichols *(Mrs. Lippincott)*.

Society melodrama. Source: Viña Delmar, "Sheba" (publication undetermined). Sheba Miller, a stenographer with a desire for luxuries, lives with her elderly father, who operates a cigar counter. Though adored by Jack, a soda jerker, she will not consider marrying him unless he receives a long-anticipated raise. Jack takes her out to the Pirate's Den, an exclusive nightclub, where Sheba defiantly enters a leg contest and is awarded the prize by Nickey Solomon, a gangster, who is the judge. Impressed by Nickey's flashy car and grooming, she accepts his attentions and finally his marriage proposal, though Jack and Pa Miller are both dubious about him. Finding himself without money for their honeymoon, Nickey robs Miller's cigar counter and shoots him; but Jack's identification of Nickey leads to his arrest. Pa Miller recovers; and Sheba, chastened by her experience, agrees to marry Jack, who gets his raise. *Stenographers. Soda clerks. Gangsters. Filial relations. Robbery. Nightclubs. Cigarstores.*

PLAYING DOUBLE **F2.4260**

Western Pictures Exploitation Co. 15 Jan **1923** [New York State license]. Si; b&w. 35mm. 5 reels.

Cast: Dick Hatton.

Western melodrama(?). No information about the nature of this film has been found.

PLAYING IT WILD **F2.4261**

Vitagraph Co. of America. 19 Apr **1923** [New York license application; c24 Apr 1923; LP18893]. Si; b&w. 35mm. 6 reels, 5,400 ft.

Pres by Albert E. Smith. *Dir* William Duncan. *Story-Scen* C. Graham Baker. *Photog* George Robinson.

Cast: William Duncan *(Jerry Hoskins)*, Edith Johnson *(Beth Webb)*, Francis Powers *(Old Man Webb)*, Dick La Reno *(Sheriff Gideon)*, Edmund Cobb *(Chris Gideon, his son)*, Frank Beal *(Wetherby, a painter)*, Frank Weed *(Bill Rucker)*.

Western melodrama. Roaming cowboy Jerry Hoskins wins Old Man Webb's newspaper in a poker game and resolves to help rid the town of crooked Sheriff Gideon. In the guise of "Terrible Terry" Jerry robs stagecoaches, ridicules Gideon as a coward, and proclaims his fear of Bill Rucker. Rucker is elected sheriff; Jerry discloses his ruse and wins Beth Webb. *Sheriffs. Cowboys. Politics. Newspapers. Poker. Stagecoach robberies.*

PLAYING WITH FIRE **F2.4262**

Universal Film Manufacturing Co. 19 Dec **1921** [c10 Dec 1921; LP17347]. Si; b&w. 35mm. 5 reels, 4,994 ft.

Pres by Carl Laemmle. *Dir* Dallas M. Fitzgerald. *Scen* Doris Schroeder. *Clayton, William M.* J. U. Giesy. *Photog* Milton Moore.

Cast: Gladys Walton *(Enid Gregory)*, Kathryn McGuire *(Janet Fenwick)*, Eddie Gribbon *(Bill Butler)*, Hayward Mack *(Bruce Tilford)*, Harold Miller *(Jack Taylor)*, Hallam Cooley *(Kent Lloyd)*, Sidney Franklin *(Pat Isaacs)*, Lydia Knott *(Miss Seraphina)*, Harriet Laurel *(Maggie Turner)*, Elinor Hancock *(Mrs. Taylor)*, Danny Hoy *(Rats)*.

Romantic comedy. Enid Gregory, a pianist at the Melody Shop, a music store on Broadway, is content with her snappy, routine existence until Janet Fenwick, a society girl whose father committed suicide under a cloud of financial disgrace, comes to Enid's boardinghouse. Enid gets Janet a job, and Janet teaches Enid society manners, awakening her ambition; and Enid's interest turns from Billy to Kent Lloyd, whom she meets on a beach outing. Jack Taylor, Janet's fiancé, informs Janet of an affidavit held by her father's partner, Bruce Tilford, that would clear his name. Enid tries to obtain the paper from Tilford but is trapped in his apartment. There Jack and Bruce engage in a fight, and when a fire breaks out, Enid rescues Bruce. Later, Bruce promises to surrender the paper, and Lloyd proposes to Enid and promises to work his way to a partnership in his father's plumbing company. *Pianists. Upper classes. Plumbers. Music stores. Documentation. New York City.*

PLAYING WITH SOULS **F2.4263**

Thomas H. Ince Corp. *Dist* First National Pictures. 3 May **1925** [c3 Mar 1925; LP21196]. Si; b&w. 35mm. 7 reels, 5,831 ft.

Dir Ralph Ince. *Adapt* C. Gardner Sullivan. *Photog* Hal Mohr.

Cast: Jacqueline Logan *(Bricotte)*, Mary Astor *(Margo)*, Belle Bennett *(Amy Dale)*, Clive Brook *(Matthew Dale, Sr.)*, William (Buster) Collier, Jr. *(Matthew Dale, Jr.)*, Jessie Arnold *(Louise, the French maid)*, Don Marion *(Matthew Dale, Jr., age 12)*, Helen Hoge *(Matthew Dale, Jr., age 4)*, Josef Swickard *(Monsieur Jomier)*.

Melodrama. Source: Clara (Longworth) Comtesse de Chambrun, *Playing With Souls* (New York, 1922). When Matt and Amy Dale separate, their son, Matthew, is put in an English school and kept in ignorance of his parents' identities. As he grows to manhood, reflections on his paternity increasingly obsess Matthew, and he finally goes to Paris in search of information about his family. There he meets Bricotte, a girl of Montmartre of questionable morals. News of Matthew's late hours and his heavy drinking reaches his father, who comes to Paris and introduces himself to Matthew as a friend. The elder Dale arranges to have Bricotte in his own apartment when Matthew arrives, causing Matthew to suspect her of cheating on him. Matthew's mother is also in Paris, changed by the passing years. Matthew meets her, and she uses her feminine arts to vamp him. They are discovered by the elder Dale, who reveals to Matthew both his own and his mother's true identities. Matthew attempts to commit suicide but is saved by his father. He returns to England and marries Margo, his fiancée. Matt and Amy Dale are reunited for their twilight years. *Parenthood. Incest. Suicide. England. Paris.*

THE PLAYTHING OF BROADWAY **F2.4264**

Realart Pictures. Feb **1921** [c4 Feb 1921; LP16088]. Si; b&w. 35mm. 5 reels, 5,360 ft.

Dir Jack Dillon. *Scen* E. Lloyd Sheldon. *Photog* Gilbert Warrenton.

Cast: Justine Johnstone *(Lola)*, Crauford Kent *(Dr. Jennings)*, Macey Harlam *(Pell)*, Edwards Davis *(Whitney)*, George Cowl *(Dr. Dexter)*, Lucy Parker *(Mrs. O'Connor)*, Claude Cooper *(The Patriarch)*, Garry McGarry *(Dr. Hastings)*, Gertrude Hillman *(Mrs. Ford)*, Mrs. Charles Willard *(Mrs. Slattery)*.

Society melodrama. Source: Sidney Morgan, "Emergency House" (publication undetermined). Lola, a dancer who is the favorite of the wealthy members of the Thirty Club, helps to win a bet by attempting to gain the affections of Dr. Jennings, who works in the lower East Side slums. To be near him she becomes a children's nurse and is so devoted to the work that Jennings is won over, but when she tries to obtain money for his "Emergency House" by dancing at the club, he discovers her past and abandons his welfare work. Lola is called to a dying child and set upon by a mob, but she is rescued through Jennings and they are reconciled. *Dancers. Nurses. Physicians. Social service. Clubs. Wagers. Slums. New York City—Broadway. New York City—Lower East Side.*

PLAYTHINGS OF DESIRE **F2.4265**

Jans Productions. 15 Dec **1924** [c2 Oct 1924; LP20924]. Si; b&w. 35mm. 7 reels, 5,500 ft.

Herman F. Jans Production. *Dir* Burton King. *Adapt* William B. Laub.

Cast: Estelle Taylor *(Gloria Dawn)*, Mahlon Hamilton *(Pierre du Charme)*, Dagmar Godowsky *(Renée Grant)*, Mary Thurman *(Anne Cabbot)*, Lawrence Davidson *(James Malvern)*, Walter Miller *(Brom Jones)*, Edmund Breese *(Governor Cabbot)*, Bradley Barker *(Wheeler Johnson)*, Ida Pardee *(Gloria's mother)*, Lee Beggs *(caretaker)*.

Society melodrama. Source: Wesley J. Putnam, "Playthings of Desire" (publication undetermined). After James Malvern, a rich playboy and philanderer, marries Gloria Dawn, a successful stage actress, the newlywed couple entrain for Malverncroft, the family lodge in the Canadian wilderness, where they spend their honeymoon. When Gloria's boat is caught in the swift current above a steep waterfall, she is rescued from certain death by Pierre du Charme, a guide and also caretaker of the Malvern estate. Gloria soon discovers that Malvern is unfaithful to her, and she allows herself to fall in love with Pierre. When Malvern is found murdered, Pierre, who has followed the Malverns to New York, is charged with the crime. After a sensational trial, the innocent guide is sentenced to death, but he is saved from the electric chair when Gloria discovers the real culprit—Wheeler Johnson, a theatrical agent who had a grudge against Malvern. Pierre and Gloria make plans to be married and to return together to the Canadian woods. *Philanderers. Actors. Guides. Theatrical agents. Murder. Injustice. Trials. Capital punishment. New York City. Canada.*

PLAYTHINGS OF DESTINY **F2.4266**

Anita Stewart Productions. *Dist* Associated First National Pictures. May **1921** [c15 Jun 1921; LP16676]. Si; b&w. 35mm. 7 reels, 6,200 ft.

Pres by Louis B. Mayer. *Dir* Edwin Carewe. *Adapt* Anthony Paul Kelly. *Photog* Robert Kurrle.

Cast: Anita Stewart *(Julie Leneau)*, Herbert Rawlinson *(Geoffrey Arnold)*, Walter McGrail *(Hubert Randolph)*, Grace Morse *(Claire)*, William V. Mong *(Conklin)*, Richard Headrick *(Julie's child)*.

Society melodrama. Source: Jane Murfin, *Playthings of Destiny* (a play; production undetermined). Julie Leneau, a country schoolteacher in Canada, becomes the bride of Geoffrey Arnold, but her happiness is shattered by a woman named Claire who convinces Julie that she is Arnold's lawful wife. Julie flees and nearly perishes in a blizzard before she is found by government official Hubert Randolph, with whom she is snowbound and whom she later accepts in marriage so as to give an honorable name to her child. In Jamaica he rises in a government post, and Julie's baby is accepted as his own. When Geoffrey visits Randolph, her former love is rekindled, and during a tropical storm in which Geoffrey is injured she discovers that he has not been unfaithful. Learning the truth, Randolph surrenders his wife and her child to Geoffrey. *Schoolteachers. Infidelity. Canada. Jamaica. Blizzards. Storms.*

PLEASURE BEFORE BUSINESS **F2.4267**

Columbia Pictures. 20 Apr **1927** [c30 Apr 1927; LP23896]. Si; b&w. 35mm. 6 reels, 5,569 ft.

Prod Harry Cohn. *Dir* Frank Strayer. *Screenplay* William Branch. *Photog* J. O. Taylor.

Cast: Pat O'Malley *(Dr. Burke)*, Virginia Brown Faire *(Ruth Weinberg)*, Max Davidson *(Sam Weinberg)*, Rosa Rosanova *(Sarah Weinberg)*, Lester Bernard *(Morris Fishbein)*, Tom McGuire *(Scotchman)*, Jack Raymond *(Louie)*, Henri Menjou *(Captain)*.

Comedy. Sam Weinberg, an industrious cigar manufacturer, falls into bad health, and his daughter, Ruth, an assistant to Dr. Burke, uses her dowry to promote his leisure, pretending that it is a legacy from her Uncle Max. Sam embarks on an orgy of spending and betting on golf games and horseraces. Then, Max unexpectedly arrives from Australia; and Morris, who has been promised Ruth, retrieves his engagement ring. Realizing he has spent the dowry money, Sam regrets having bet a large sum on a racehorse, Sarah. The horse refuses to budge until the jockey speaks to her in Yiddish; she then wins the prize money for Sam. Morris tries to repair the engagement, but Ruth is happily united with the Irish doctor. *Physicians. Irish. Jews. Invalids. Dowries. Wealth. Wagers. Cigars. Golf. Horseracing. Horses.*

THE PLEASURE BUYERS **F2.4268**

Warner Brothers Pictures. 19 Dec **1925** [c8 Sep 1925; LP21808]. Si; b&w. 35mm. 7 reels.

Dir Chet Withey. *Adapt* Hope Loring, Louis D. Lighton. *Photog* Joseph Walker. *Asst Dir* William McGann.

Cast: Irene Rich *(Joan Wiswell)*, Clive Brook *(Tad Workman)*, Gayne Whitman *(Gene Cassenas)*, June Marlowe *(Helen Ripley)*, Chester Conklin *(Burke)*, Don Alvarado *(Tommy Wiswell)*, Edward Peil *(Kildare)*, Frank Campeau *(Quintard)*, Winter Hall *(General Ripley)*, Frank Leigh *(Terry)*.

Melodrama. Source: Arthur Somers Roche, *The Pleasure Buyers* (New York, 1925). Sitting in his own livingroom, Gene Cassenas is fatally shot by an unknown assailant. Tad Workman, the former police commissioner, is called in on the case, and six persons are placed under suspicion: Joan Wiswell, a beautiful socialite; Tommy Wiswell, her brother; Terry, a former business associate of the murdered man; Helen Ripley, the fiancée of the murdered man; her father, General Ripley; and a valet. With precise deduction, Tad finally proves that the valet killed Cassenas by rigging up a clock to fire a gun at a given time. *Police. Socialites. Valets. Businessmen. Brother-sister relationship. Murder.*

PLEASURE CRAZED **F2.4269**

Fox Film Corp. 7 Jul **1929** [c5 Aug 1929; LP570]. Sd (Movietone); b&w. 35mm. 7 reels, 5,460 ft.

Pres by William Fox. *Supv* Philip Klein. *Dir* Donald Gallaher. *Pictorial Dir* Charles Klein. *Scen* Douglas Z. Doty. *Dial* Clare Kummer. *Photog* Ernest Palmer, Glen MacWilliams. *Film Ed* J. Edwin Robbins. *Sd* Donald Flick. *Asst Dir* Edmund Grainger. *Cost* Sophie Wachner.

Cast: Marguerite Churchill *(Nora Westby)*, Kenneth MacKenna *(Capt. Anthony Dean)*, Dorothy Burgess *(Alma Dean)*, Campbell Gullan *(Gilbert Ferguson)*, Douglas Gilmore *(Nigel Blain)*, Henry Kolker *(Colonel Farquar)*, Frederick Graham *(Holland)*, Rex Bell *(chauffeur)*, Charlotte Merriam *(maid)*.

Melodrama. Source: Monckton Hoffe, *The Scent of Sweet Almonds* (a play; publication undetermined). Alma Dean and her husband, Anthony, rent a house from a trio of crooks who have the intention of stealing the wife's jewels. The female member of the group remains in the guise of a housekeeper, and gradually she and Anthony become very fond of each other. In the meantime, Alma is playing around with a poor writer, and Anthony, miserable, leaves her, accidentally carrying away a flask containing poison. Previously, the writer dared Alma to commit suicide, but when she sees her husband take this very flask, she says nothing. The "housekeeper," learning of the state of affairs, chases after Anthony and wrecks her car at the garage where he is buying gasoline. The situation is satisfactorily resolved. *Authors. Housekeepers. Thieves. Infidelity. Suicide. Automobile accidents.*

PLEASURE MAD **F2.4270**

Louis B. Mayer Productions. *Dist* Metro Pictures. 5 Nov **1923** [c14 Nov 1923; LP19688]. Si; b&w. 35mm. 8 reels, 7,547 ft.

Dir Reginald Barker. *Scen* A. P. Younger. *Photog* Norbert Brodin, Alvin Wyckoff.

Cast: Huntley Gordon *(Hugh Benton)*, Mary Alden *(Marjorie Benton)*, Norma Shearer *(Elinor Benton)*, William Collier, Jr. *(Howard Benton)*, Winifred Bryson *(Geraldine de Lacy)*, Ward Crane *(David Templeton)*, Frederick Truesdell *(John Hammond)*, Joan Standing *(Hulda)*.

Domestic drama. Source: Blanche Upright, *The Valley of Content* (New York, 1922). Hugh Benton makes money, moves his family to the city, and finds companionship with a younger woman. He divorces his wife and encourages his children to leave home. Finally, when he becomes involved in a shooting, he realizes his wife's loyalty and returns to her. *Marriage. Divorce. Urban life. Family life.*

PLEASURES OF THE RICH **F2.4271**

Tiffany Productions. *Dist* Renown Pictures. Feb **1926** [c26 Feb 1926; LP22427]. Si; b&w. 35mm. 7 reels, 6,471 ft.

Dir Louis Gasnier.

Cast: Helene Chadwick *(Mary Wilson)*, Mary Carr *(Kate Wilson)*, Marcin Asher *(Henry [Pushcart] Wilson)*, Jack Mulhall *(Frank Clayton)*, Lillian Langdon *(Mrs. Clayton)*, Dorothea Wolbert *(Maggie, the maid)*, Hedda Hopper *(Mona Vincent)*, Julanne Johnston *(Phyliss Worthing)*, Katherine Scott *(Mrs. Worthing)*.

Comedy-drama. Source: Harold MacGrath, "The Wrong Coat" (publication undetermined). Henry Wilson, a wealthy grocer who started with a pushcart and worked his way up to 40 trucks, although married becomes interested in Mona Vincent, a divorcee. Mona also is trying to win Frank Clayton, wealthy scion with whom Wilson's daughter, Mary, is in love. Mona promises Mary to give up Mr. Wilson if Mary will give her Clayton. Mary agrees, but distressed by the loss she then tries to drown herself. Wilson learns that Mona has made a fool of him and returns to his wife. Mary is rescued and marries Clayton. *Nouveaux riches. Grocers. Infidelity. Divorce. Suicide.*

THE PLUNDERER **F2.4272**

Fox Film Corp. 30 Mar **1924** [c24 May 1924; LP20023]. Si; b&w. 35mm. 6 reels, 5,812 ft.

Pres by William Fox. *Dir* George Archainbaud. *Scen* Doty Hobart. *Story* Roy Norton. *Photog* Jules Cronjager.

Cast: Frank Mayo *(Bill Matthews)*, Evelyn Brent *(The Lily)*, Tom Santschi *(Bill Presbey)*, James Mason *(The Wolf)*, Peggy Shaw *(Joan Presbey)*, Edward Phillips *(Richard Townsend)*, Dan Mason *(Bells Parks)*.

Western melodrama. Source: Roy Norton, *The Plunderer* (New York, 1912). After graduating from mining school, engineer Richard Townsend goes west with his friend Bill Matthews to develop his father's abandoned gold mine. Bill discovers from The Lily, owner of the mining town saloon, that the mine is being plundered through secret tunnels by Bill Presbey, father of Joan, Richard's sweetheart. After fights, a strike, the dynamiting of a dam, a fire, and a mine cave-in, Presbey yields to Joan's pleas and Bill's fists and returns the gold. The Lily reforms, and everything points to happiness for her and Bill, as well as for Richard and Joan. *Engineers—Mining. Saloons. Gold mines.*

PLUNGING HOOFS **F2.4273**

Universal Pictures. 10 Apr **1929** [New York premiere; released 14 Apr; c15 Jun 1928; LP25380]. Si; b&w. 35mm. 5 reels, 4,344 ft.

Dir Henry MacRae. *Scen* George Morgan. *Titl* Gardner Bradford. *Story* Basil Dickey, William Lord Wright. *Photog* George Robinson. *Film Ed* Thomas Malloy.

Cast: Starlight, Rex *(themselves, horses)*, Jack Perrin *(Parson Jed Campbell)*, Barbara Worth *(Nanette)*, J. P. McGowan *(Jim Wales)*, David Dunbar *("Squint" Jones)*.

Western melodrama. Jed Campbell, a "skypilot," and Nanette, a dancehall girl, meet when each goes to rescue Rex, "King of the Wild Horses," from a trap set by "Squint" Jones, an employee of saloonkeeper Jim Wales. Wales, an evil man, has designs on Nanette and wants to capture Rex. Because Nanette is ashamed of her occupation she refuses Campbell's marriage proposal. Eventually they settle their differences; Rex and Starlight eliminate Wales, and Nanette marries Jed. *Clergymen. Dancehall girls. Horsethieves. Saloons. Horses.*

POINTED HEELS **F2.4274**

Paramount Famous Lasky Corp. 21 Dec **1929** [c27 Dec 1929; LP948]. Sd (Movietone); b&w with col sequences (Technicolor). 35mm. 7 reels, 5,689 ft. [Also si.]

Dir A. Edward Sutherland. *Dial Dir* Perry Ivins. *Adapt-Dial* Florence Ryerson, John V. A. Weaver. *Photog* Rex Wimpy. *Film Ed* Jane Loring. *Song: "I Have To Have You"* Richard A. Whiting, Leo Robin. *Song: "Ain't-Cha?"* Mack Gordon, Max Rich. *Rec Engr* Harry M. Lindgren.

Cast: William Powell *(Robert Courtland)*, Fay Wray *(Lora Nixon)*, Helen Kane *(Dot Nixon)*, Richard "Skeets" Gallagher *(Dash Nixon)*, Phillips Holmes *(Donald Ogden)*, Adrienne Dore *(Kay Wilcox)*, Eugene Pallette *(Joe Clark)*.

Society drama. Source: Charles William Brackett, "Pointed Heels," in *College Humor* (Dec 1928–Jan 1929). Robert Courtland, a wealthy theatrical producer, and Joe Clark, his dance director, are rehearsing a new musical comedy when Lora Nixon, in whom Courtland is interested, quits the production to marry young Donald Ogden, a composer. Ogden's wealthy family, however, stop his allowance, and the couple are forced to occupy a modest flat. He tries to continue work on a symphony, and Lora takes back her chorus job. Lora's brother, Dash, and his wife, Dot, scornful of his serious endeavors, taunt Donald into writing a popular song and induce Courtland to back another revue in which they have parts. Courtland persuades Donald that he is hampering Lora's chances for a career; and after a visit to Courtland's apartment, Lora decides to leave her husband. But when his song proves the hit of the show, Lora is reunited with Donald. *Chorus girls. Theatrical producers. Composers. Marriage. Social classes. Musical revues.*

POINTS WEST (Universal-Jewel) **F2.4275**

Universal Pictures. 25 Aug **1929** [c15 Jun 1929; LP484]. Si; b&w. 35mm. 6 reels, 5,491 ft.

Pres by Carl Laemmle. *Dir* Arthur Rosson. *Titl* Harold Tarshis. *Adapt* Rowland Brown. *Photog* Harry Neumann.

Cast: Hoot Gibson *(Cole Lawson, Jr.)*, Alberta Vaughn *(Dorothy)*, Frank Campeau *(McQuade)*, Jack Raymond *(His Nibs)*, Martha Franklin *(The Mother)*, Milt Brown *(Parsons)*, Jim Corey *(Steve)*.

Western melodrama. Source: B. M. Bower, *Points West* (Boston, 1928). Cole Lawson, son of a rancher who is murdered by McQuade (an outlaw his father previously sent to prison), sets out to revenge his father's death. Cole finds McQuade's mountain retreat and gains entrance by posing as a horsethief. He meets Dorothy, the landlady's daughter, whom McQuade plans to marry; a romance develops between them, and he tells her about his mission. She aids him in identifying McQuade, but Cole is overheard revealing his plans, and McQuade gives him 3 minutes to live. Cole outwits him and escapes, taking refuge in the girl's house. McQuade prepares for his wedding, but at the last moment Cole overcomes McQuade, prevents the marriage, and thus wins the girl for himself. *Ranchers. Outlaws. Murder. Imposture. Courtship. Revenge.*

POISON **F2.4276**

William Steiner Productions. *Dist* New-Cal Film Corp. 1 Aug **1924** [c16 Jun 1924; LU20312]. Si; b&w. 35mm. 5 reels, 5,000 ft.

Prod William Steiner. *Dir* James Chapin. *Story-Scen* Charles Hutchison. *Photog* Ernest Miller.

Cast: Charles Hutchison *(Bob Marston)*, Edith Thornton *(Doris Townsend)*, Otto Lederer *(Gale Preston)*, John Henry *(Rog Harvey)*, Ethel Stairt *(Grace Elliston)*, Frank Hagney *(Joe Tracey)*, John O'Brien *(himself)*, Jack Mathis *(Gordon)*.

Crook melodrama. Assigned to apprehend a gang of bootleggers, San Francisco detective Bob Marston, also a society man, stages a raid on the gang's cave. After a series of daredevil stunts and adventures, he rescues his girl and rounds up the crooks. *Bootleggers. Detectives. San Francisco.*

POISONED PARADISE: THE FORBIDDEN STORY OF MONTE CARLO **F2.4277**

Preferred Pictures. *Dist* Al Lichtman Corp. 29 Feb **1924** [c28 Feb 1924; LP19944]. Si; b&w. 35mm. 7 reels, 6,800 ft.

Pres by B. P. Schulberg. *Dir* Louis Gasnier. *Scen* Waldemar Young. *Photog* Karl Struss.

Cast: Kenneth Harlan *(Hugh Kildair/Gilbert Kildair)*, Clara Bow *(Margot Le Blanc)*, Barbara Tennant *(Mrs. G. Kildair)*, André de Beranger *(Krantz)*, Carmel Myers *(Mrs. Belmire)*, Raymond Griffith *(Martel)*, Josef Swickard *(Professor Durand)*, Evelyn Selbie *(Madame Tranquille)*, Michael Varconi *(Dr. Bergius)*, Frankie Lee *(Hugh Kildair, as child)*, Peaches Jackson *(Margot Le Blanc, as child)*.

Melodrama. Source: Robert William Service, *Poisoned Paradise; a Romance of Monte Carlo* (New York, 1922). Margot Le Blanc loses her small fortune at Monte Carlo and makes the acquaintance of Hugh Kildair, an artist, who hires her as a housekeeper. A gang of thieves set a trap for Kildair when they find that he knows a mathematical system guaranteed to win at the gambling table. The gang is foiled by the arrival of the police; and Kildair, realizing he has fallen in love with Margot, marries her. *Artists. Housekeepers. Thieves. Gambling. Monte Carlo.*

POKER FACES (Universal-Jewel) **F2.4278**

Universal Pictures. 5 Sep **1926** [c22 May 1926; LP22756]. Si; b&w. 35mm. 8 reels, 7,808 ft.

Pres by Carl Laemmle. *Dir* Harry A. Pollard. *Adapt-Cont* Melville W. Brown. *Photog* Charles Stumar.

Cast: Edward Everett Horton *(Jimmy Whitmore)*, Laura La Plante *(Betty Whitmore)*, George Siegmann *(George Dixon)*, Tom Ricketts *(Henry Curlew)*, Tom O'Brien *(Pug)*, Dorothy Revier *(Pug's wife)*, Leon Holmes *(office boy)*.

Domestic comedy. Source: Edgar Franklin, "Poker Faces," in *Argosy All-Story Weekly* (153:641–661, 842–861, 18 Aug–25 Aug 1923; 154:68–87, 270–288, 444–461, 1–15 Sep 1923). Jimmy Whitmore, a struggling office worker, is constantly harassed by his wife's incessant reminders that they need a new rug and by the insinuating remarks of Henry Curlew, his employer. Having been found satisfactory by Curlew, however, he is given an important assignment—that of getting a contract with George Dixon, a tough customer. When Jimmy finds that his wife has gone to work to earn extra money, he is forced to engage a prizefighter's wife as a stand-in for the evening; at the arranged dinner he meets Dixon and Curlew's new secretary, who turns out to be Betty, Jimmy's wife. Curlew offers Dixon the use of his secretary to dictate some letters at his hotel and forces Jimmy and his "wife" into a nearby room. Complications ensue as the fighter attempts to retrieve his wife; and Curlew arrests Dixon, who is a crook. Jimmy is rewarded for his astuteness and promoted to junior partner. *Businessmen. Secretaries. Prizefighters. Marriage. Impersonation.*

THE POLICE PATROL **F2.4279**

Gotham Productions. *Dist* Lumas Film Corp. 28 Aug **1925** [c20 Jul 1925; LP21659]. Si; b&w. 35mm. 6 reels.

Pres by Sam Sax. *Supv* Lon Young. *Dir* Burton King. *Scen* Victoria Moore. *Photog* C. J. Davis, Jack Brown. *Asst Dir* Jack Hyland.

Cast: James Kirkwood *(Officer Jim Ryan)*, Edna Murphy *(Alice Bennett/Dorothy Stone)*, Edmund Breese *(Tony Rocco)*, Bradley Barker *(Maurice Ramon)*, Frankie Evans *(Buddy Bennett)*, Joseph Smiley *(Lieutenant Burke)*, Robert McKim *(see note)*, Blanche Craig *(Nora Mullen)*, Edward Roseman *("Chicago" Charley)*, Tammany Young *("The Crasher")*, Charles Craig *(Perkins)*, James Laffey *(Inspector Regan)*, Monya Andrée *(Mademoiselle Semonoff)*.

Melodrama. Source: A. Y. Pearson, "The Police Patrol" (publication undetermined). Patrolman Jim Ryan falls in love with Alice Bennett, a dressmaker, only to realize later that she is a dead ringer for Dorothy Stone, a noted thief. When Jim is ordered to arrest Alice for Dorothy's crimes, he tells the captain that it would be a grave injustice, but the captain will not believe him. Jim is suspended from the force and sets out to bring Dorothy Stone before the law. Using Alice to impersonate Dorothy, Jim gets in touch with her gang. Dorothy is killed in a fight, and Alice is kidnaped. Jim goes after the abductor in a police launch and rescues Alice. Jim is reinstated to the force, and he and Alice are wed. *Police. Dressmakers. Doubles. Impersonation. Abduction.*

Note: Robert McKim also is credited with the role of Lieutenant Burke.

POLLY OF THE FOLLIES **F2.4280**

Constance Talmadge Film Co. *Dist* Associated First National Pictures. 30 Jan **1922** [c16 Jan 1922; LP17499]. Si; b&w. 35mm. 7 reels, 6,137 ft.

Pres by Joseph M. Schenck. *Dir* John Emerson. *Story-Scen* John Emerson, Anita Loos. *Photog* J. Roy Hunt. *Tech Dir* Willard M. Reineck, Lawrence Hitt.

Cast: Constance Talmadge *(Polly Meacham)*, Horace Knight *(Silas Meacham)*, Thomas Carr *(Jimmy Meacham)*, Harry Fisher *(Pop Cummings)*, Frank Lalor *(Daddy Hood)*, George Fawcett *(Mr. Jones)*, Ina Rorke *(Mrs. Jones)*, Mildred Arden *(Hattie Jones)*, Kenneth Harlan *(Bob Jones)*, Paul Doucet *(Clarence Hope)*, Theresa Maxwell Conover *(Mrs. Potter)*, Billie Dove *(Alysia Potter)*, James Gleason *(Paul Gordon)*, Bernard Randall *(Flo Ziegfeld)*, John Daly Murphy *(Julius Caesar)*.

Comedy-drama. Mrs. Jones of Long Island, in her struggle for social recognition, is anxious for her son Bob to marry Alysia Potter. At a party, Bob and Alysia, under the influence of alcohol, decide to elope and go to Bowling Green, Connecticut, where Silas Meacham has begun a campaign against motion pictures. While waiting for the justice of the peace, Bob and Alysia see Polly Meacham staging "The Way to a Man's Heart." Mr. and Mrs. Jones, their daughter Hattie, and Mr. Potter arrive on the trail of the elopers and persuade them to wait 6 months before marriage. On Bob's advice Polly comes to New York and gets a place with the Ziegfeld Follies, but her debut is spoiled by stage fright. Alysia replaces her and is a success, and while Bob is trying to console Polly, Alysia announces that she is breaking the engagement so as to leave Bob and Polly free to wed. *Actors. Social classes. Elopement. Motion pictures. Long Island. Connecticut. Ziegfeld Follies. Florenz Ziegfeld.*

Note: Working title: *Good for Nothing.*

POLLY OF THE MOVIES **F2.4281**

James Ormont Productions. *Dist* First Division Distributors. 15 Oct **1927.** Si; b&w. 35mm. 7 reels, 6,612-6,900 ft.

Dir Scott Pembroke. *Scen* George Dromgold, Jean Plannette. *Titl* Jean Plannette. *Story* Arthur Hoerl. *Photog* Ted Tetzlaff. *Sp Eff* Robert Stevens.

Cast: Jason Robards *(Angus Whitcomb)*, Gertrude Short *(Polly Primrose)*, Mary Foy *(Mrs. Beardsley)*, Corliss Palmer *(Liza Smith)*, Stuart Holmes *(Benjamin Wellington Fairmount)*, Jack Richardson *(Rolland Harrison)*, Rose Dione *(Lulu Fairmount)*.

Comedy-drama. "Plain little girl from Hohokus aspires to be a movie actress, so her small town lover, who has inherited $25,000, goes to Hollywood with her and puts his money into featuring her in a picture. Intended for a melodrama, their picture is a comedy scream and a film magnate pays them well for its purchase and they decide to wed." (*Motion Picture News Booking Guide,* [14]:274–275, 1929.) *Actors. Motion pictures. Smalltown life. Inheritance.*

PONJOLA **F2.4282**

Sam E. Rork Productions. *Dist* Associated First National Pictures. 29 Oct **1923** [c1 Nov 1923; LP19556]. Si; b&w. 35mm. 7 reels, 6,960 ft.

Pres by Sam E. Rork. *Dir* Donald Crisp. *Dir? (see note)* James Young. *Scen* Charles Logue. *Photog* Paul Perry.

Cast: Anna Q. Nilsson *(Lady Flavia Desmond [Countess Tyrecastle])*, James Kirkwood *(Lundi Druro)*, Tully Marshall *(Count Blauhimel)*, Joseph Kilgour *(Conrad Lypiatt)*, Bernard Randall *(Eric Luff)*, Ruth Clifford *(Gay Lypiatt)*, Claire Du Brey *(Luchia Luff)*, Claire McDowell *(Mrs. Hope)*, Charles Ray, Edwin Sturgis.

Melodrama. Source: Cynthia Stockley, *Ponjola* (London, 1923). Disguised as a man, Countess Tyrecastle follows Lundi Druro to Africa after he saves her from suicide, although she knows he is engaged. His fiancée proves to be unfaithful, however, and she rehabilitates Druro when he becomes despondent. Together they discover a valuable gold mine, and she reveals her identity following the death of Conrad Lypiatt, a treacherous partner. *Disguise. Suicide. Gold mining. Africa.*

Note: Some sources credit James Young as director.

THE PONY EXPRESS **F2.4283**

Famous Players–Lasky. *Dist* Paramount Pictures. 4 Sep **1925** [San Francisco premiere; c13 Oct 1925; LP21902]. Si; b&w. 35mm. 10 reels, 9,949 ft. [Released 12 Oct; 9,801 ft.]

Pres by Adolph Zukor, Jesse L. Lasky. *Dir* James Cruze. *Screenplay* Walter Woods. *Story* Henry James Forman, Walter Woods. *Photog* Karl Brown. *Music score arr by* Hugo Riesenfeld. *Asst Dir* Harold Schwartz.

Cast: Betty Compson *(Molly Jones)*, Ricardo Cortez *(Jack Weston)*, Ernest Torrence *("Ascension" Jones)*, Wallace Beery *("Rhode Island" Red)*, George Bancroft *(Jack Slade)*, Frank Lackteen *(Charlie Bent)*, John Fox, Jr. *(Billy Cody)*, William Turner *(William Russell)*, Al Hart *(Senator Glen)*, Charles Gerson *(Sam Clemens)*, Rose Tapley *(Aunt)*, Vondell Darr *(baby)*, Hank Bell, Ernie Adams.

Western epic. Source: Henry James Forman and Walter Woods, *The Pony Express; a Romance* (New York, 1925). In the 1860's Senator Glen of California heads a secret society called the "Knights of the Golden Circle" in a conspiracy to have California secede from the Union, annex part of Mexico, and establish a new empire. He sends his men to Sacramento to eliminate debonair gambler "Frisco Jack" Weston, who has spoken against him, but Weston escapes to Julesburg, Colorado. There he becomes a Pony Express rider and a rival of Glen's agent, Jack Slade, superintendent of the Overland Stage Co., for the hand of Molly Jones. Weston succeeds in foiling Glen's plans to prevent news of Lincoln's election from reaching California by carrying the message himself. Among other intrigues, a halfbreed Indian, Charlie Bent, in league with Glen, leads a band of Sioux in an attack on Julesburg. Weston marries Molly before marching off to war. *Secret societies. Conspiracy. California. Colorado. United States—History—Civil War. William Frederick Cody. Samuel Langhorne Clemens. Abraham Lincoln. Brigham Young. Knights of the Golden Circle. Pony Express. Overland Stage Co.*

Note: The novel by Forman and Woods was written for the film and published simultaneously with its release. Brigham Young is also said to be among the historical personages depicted.

PONY EXPRESS RIDER **F2.4284**

Robert J. Horner Productions. *Dist* Aywon Film Corp. 27 Mar **1926** [New York State license]. Si; b&w. 35mm. 5 reels, 4,750 ft.

Dir Robert J. Horner. *Photog* Lauren A. Draper.

Cast: Kit Carson, Pauline Curley.

Western melodrama. "Bill Miller, youngest member of the notorious Range Riders, gets job as pony express rider. Indians become dangerous on war path. Bill forestalls plan of bandit chief to rob mails, wins the love of a girl and the respect of Uncle Sam." ("Motion Picture News Booking Guide," in *Motion Picture News,* 15 Mar 1930, p98.) *Indians of North America. Bandits. Pony Express.*

POOR, DEAR MARGARET KIRBY **F2.4285**

Selznick Pictures. Feb **1921** [c3 Mar 1921; LP16230]. Si; b&w. 35mm. 5 reels, 4,581 ft.

Pres by Lewis J. Selznick. *Dir* William P. S. Earle. *Scen* Lewis Allen Browne. *Photog* William Wagner.

Cast: Elaine Hammerstein *(Margaret Kirby)*, William B. Donaldson *(John Kirby)*, Ellen Cassidy *(Lucille Yardsley)*, Helen Lindroth *(Mrs. Dunning)*, Warburton Gamble *(Gordon Pell)*.

Society melodrama. Source: Kathleen Norris, *Poor, Dear Margaret Kirby & Other Stories* (New York, 1913). Margaret Kirby refuses her husband's request to help him obtain a loan from her guest, Gordon Pell. The husband, John, in financial difficulties, then attempts suicide and becomes seriously ill. Margaret takes in boarders and is compelled to mix with people outside her social set. Lucille, John's former admirer, creates a misunderstanding by means of forged telegrams, but the discernment of Gordon Pell clarifies the situation and Margaret and John are reunited. *Debt. Marriage. Suicide. Documentation.*

POOR GIRLS **F2.4286**

Columbia Pictures. 5 May **1927** [c22 Apr 1927; LP23891]. Si; b&w. 35mm. 6 reels, 5,428 ft.

Prod Harry Cohn. *Dir* William James Craft. *Screenplay* William Branch. *Story* Sophie Bogen. *Photog* Norbert Brodin.

Cast: Dorothy Revier *(Peggy Warren)*, Edmund Burns *(Richard Deane)*, Ruth Stonehouse *(Katherine Warren/Texas Kate)*, Lloyd Whitlock *(Eugene Ward)*, Marjorie Bonner *(Vivian Stewart)*.

Society drama. Peggy Warren, who is in love with schoolmate Richard Deane, is unaware that her mother, Katherine, leads a dual life as Texas Kate, owner of a notorious nightclub, though her jazzy roommate, Vivian Stewart, recognizes the mother on a visit. Jealous of Richard's attentions to Peggy, Vivian insists that they all go to Texas Kate's on the night of the commencement dance; stunned by the revelation, Peggy leaves home and moves to a dingy tenement, but Richard learns that Katherine has been forced to be a club hostess to secure Peggy's position in society. Vivian, learning of Peggy's whereabouts, informs her she is engaged to Richard, and Peggy replies that she is to marry Eugene Ward, a rounder. Richard and Mrs. Warren devise a plan to save Peggy from Ward, and all are happily reconciled. *Students. Nightclub hostesses. Motherhood. Dual lives. Courtship. Nightclubs.*

A POOR GIRL'S ROMANCE **F2.4287**

R-C Pictures. *Dist* Film Booking Offices of America. 23 May **1926** [c23 May 1926; LP22755]. Si; b&w. 35mm. 6 reels.

Dir F. Harmon Weight. *Screenplay* Enid Hibbard, Betty Roberts. *Story* Laura Jean Libbey. *Photog* Jules Cronjager. *Asst Dir* John Kerr.

Cast: Creighton Hale *(Wellington Kingston)*, Gertrude Short *(Anne Beaudeau)*, Rosa Rudami *(Madeline Sheivers)*, Clarissa Selwyn *(Rebecca Morgan)*, Charles Requa *(Theodore Chappell)*, Johnny Gough *(Johnny Mahoney)*, Mrs. M. Cecil *(Mrs. Finney)*, Forrest Taylor *(tramp)*.

Society melodrama. Anne, a boardinghouse worker in New York's tenement district and an inveterate daydreamer, is rescued from the abuse of neighborhood hoodlums by Wellington Kingston, a society man who returns her to Mrs. Finney's boardinghouse in his Rolls-Royce. When she is goaded by a drunken guest into attending a society ball, Kingston relieves her embarrassment by introducing her as Princess Anne, visiting incognita; but Madeline Sheivers, angling for Kingston, maliciously exposes Anne. Mrs. Finney, enraged by her associating with the rich, turns her out; she accepts a cafe job, leaves it when a customer makes unwelcome advances, and becomes a model at the Fifth Avenue establishment of

Theodore Chappell, who is tiring of the attentions of Madeline. Anne stays over at Rebecca Morgan's apartment and invites Kingston to dinner; making his departure, he sees Madeline shoot Chappell. Anne tries to assume the guilt, but Johnny, a cabdriver friend, convinces the police of Madeline's guilt. Kingston and Anne are happily united. *Fashion models. Social classes. Murder. Boardinghouses. Tenements. Rolls-Royce automobiles. New York City.*

POOR MEN'S WIVES **F2.4288**

Preferred Pictures. *Dist* Al Lichtman Corp. ca28 Jan **1923** [New York premiere; released 15 Feb; c20 Mar 1923; LP18865]. Si; b&w. 35mm. 7 reels, ca6,900 ft.

Pres by B. P. Schulberg. *Dir* Louis J. Gasnier. *Writ-Adapt* Agnes Christine Johnston, Frank Dazey. *Titl* Eve Unsell. *Photog* Karl Struss.

Cast: Barbara La Marr *(Laura Bedford; afterward Laura Maberne)*, David Butler *(Jim Maberne)*, Betty Francisco *(Claribel)*, Richard Tucker *(Richard Smith-Blanton)*, ZaSu Pitts *(Apple Annie)*, Muriel McCormac, Mickey McBan *(The Twins)*.

Domestic drama. Laura Bedford marries poor taxi driver Jim Maberne, and her chum Claribel marries wealthy Richard Smith-Blanton. When the two women accidentally meet sometime later, Laura eagerly accepts Claribel's invitation to an artists' ball. Because of her poverty, Laura is obliged to obtain a ball gown on approval. At the ball she repulses the advances of Smith-Blanton. When her children ruin the dress the next day, Laura takes her husband's savings to pay for it. Jim discovers the loss and orders Laura out. When, later, he comes upon her struggling against Smith-Blanton, Claribel tells him the whole story. Jim gives Smith-Blanton a beating and takes his wife home. *Taxi drivers. Wealth. Poverty. Marriage.*

THE POOR MILLIONAIRE **F2.4289**

Richard Talmadge Productions. *Dist* Biltmore Pictures. 7 Apr **1930.** Si; b&w. 35mm. 5 reels, 5,200 ft.

Dir George Melford. *Story-Scen* Henry Lehrman, Rex Taylor.

Cast: Richard Talmadge *(Sidney Thomas/Putt Magee)*, Constance Howard *(Babs Long)*, George Irving *(Calvin Long)*, Frederick Vroom *(Attorney Wallace)*, John Hennings *(Peter Cline)*, Fannie Midgley *(Mrs. Mansford)*, Jay Hunt *(butler)*.

Society melodrama. "Richard Talmadge plays the double role of hero and villain, he being twins, as it were. His brother is the villain who is an escaped convict, while the hero has inherited a dead uncle's fortune. The villain steps in, impersonates the hero, and raises the devil before the hero finally straightens everything out." Includes society scenes and acrobatic stunts. (*Film Daily,* 22 Jun 1930, p14.) *Millionaires. Twins. Brothers. Prison escapees. Inheritance. Impersonation. Stunts.*

THE POOR NUT **F2.4290**

Jess Smith Productions. *Dist* First National Pictures. 7 Aug **1927** [c11 Jun 1927; LP24069]. Si; b&w. 35mm. 7 reels, 6,897 ft.

Dir Richard Wallace. *Screenplay-Cont* Paul Schofield. *Photog* David Kesson. *Prod Mgmt* Henry Hobart.

Cast: Jack Mulhall *(John Miller)*, Charlie Murray *("Doc")*, Jean Arthur *(Margie)*, Jane Winton *(Julia)*, Glenn Tryon *("Magpie" Welch)*, Cornelius Keefe *(Wallie Pierce)*, Maurice Ryan *("Hub" Smith)*, Henry Vibart *(Professor Demming)*, Bruce Gordon *(Coach Jackson)*, William Courtwright *(Colonel Small)*.

Comedy-drama. Source: J. C. Nugent and Elliott Nugent, *The Poor Nut* (New York, 1925). John Miller, a student at Harmon College, suffers from an inferiority complex, and though a prize scholar he longs to belong to the track team or a social fraternity. In his letters to Julia, a student at Beldon College, however, he boasts of his athletic prowess, incurring the jealousy of Welch, his rival. Inspired by Julia, John goes out for the track team and runs against Welch in a relay race. Deciding that he must be inferior to Welch, John loses the race; but Margie, who has taken a liking to him, convinces John that he should win. In the final relay he wins the meet and the acclaim of his fellow classmates, as well as the love of Margie. *Students. College life. Inferiority complex. Jealousy. Track. Fraternities.*

A POOR RELATION **F2.4291**

Goldwyn Pictures. Dec **1921** [c29 Nov 1921; LP17243]. Si; b&w. 35mm. 5 reels, 4,609 ft.

Dir Clarence Badger. *Scen* Bernard McConville. *Photog* Marcel Le Picard.

Cast: Will Rogers *(Noah Vale)*, Sylvia Breamer *(Miss Fay)*, Wallace MacDonald *(Johnny Smith)*, Sydney Ainsworth *(Sterrett)*, George B. Williams *(Mr. Fay)*, Molly Malone *(Scallops)*, Robert De Vilbiss *(Rip)*, Jeanette Trebaol *(Patch)*, Walter Perry *(O'Halley)*.

Comedy. Source: Edward E. Kidder, *A Poor Relation, Comedy Drama in Three Acts* (c7 Mar 1911). Slaving to perfect an invention, Noah Vale tries to keep two orphans—Rip and Patch—and himself by peddling books and is helped by Scallops, a girl who occasionally brings them food. He appeals to Fay, a wealthy relative, for help in marketing his invention and arouses the interest of Fay's pretty daughter. Sterrett, Fay's partner, steals the model but returns it when he discovers it to be worthless. Johnny Smith, Fay's secretary, is fired when he proposes to the boss's daughter; and visiting Vale's attic, he is comforted by his epigrams. Johnny takes them to a newspaper editor, and they are so successful that both Smith and Vale are hired. Vale decides to give up inventing for writing, and Johnny marries Miss Fay despite her father's opposition. *Peddlers. Orphans. Inventors. Authors.*

THE POOR WORM *see* **DOUBLE DEALING**

THE POPULAR SIN **F2.4292**

Famous Players–Lasky. *Dist* Paramount Pictures. 22 Nov **1926** [c22 Nov 1926; LP23367]. Si; b&w. 35mm. 7 reels, 6,244 ft.

Pres by Adolph Zukor, Jesse L. Lasky. *Assoc Prod* William Le Baron. *Dir* Malcolm St. Clair. *Screenplay* James Ashmore Creelman. *Story* Monta Bell. *Photog* Lee Garmes.

Cast: Florence Vidor *(Yvonne Montfort)*, Clive Brook *(Jean Corot)*, Greta Nissen *(La Belle Toulaise)*, Philip Strange *(George Montfort)*, André Beranger *(Alphonse Martin)*, Iris Gray *(Lulu)*.

Domestic comedy. George Montfort, involved in an extra-marital affair with Lulu, an actress, plans a trip to Biarritz with her, but when his wife, Yvonne, finds the tickets, he swears he bought them for her. George gives the second ticket to Jean Corot, a playwright, and upon their return he learns that his wife is madly in love with Jean. George gives them his blessing, and they are married. One day, Alphonse Martin brings La Belle Toulaise to their home, and she insists that Jean write a play for her. At the premiere of *The Popular Sin,* Yvonne applauds her husband's triumph but finds him backstage in the arms of the siren. A divorce is arranged, and Jean soon finds himself married to La Belle Toulaise but is soon disillusioned to discover that she is having an affair with George Montfort. Realizing his love for Yvonne, Jean decides to divorce La Belle Toulaise. *Actors. Playwrights. Infidelity. Jealousy. Divorce. Paris. Biarritz.*

THE PORCELAIN LAMP **F2.4293**

Harry Levey Service Corp. 29 Jan **1921** [trade review]. Si; b&w. 35mm. 5 reels.

Supv Herb Hyman. *Dir* Ben Blake. *Scen* Don Carlos Ellis. *Photog* Flanders, Van Derveer. *Res* Don Carlos Ellis.

Cast: Eugene Borden *(Anton Daimier)*, Doris Sheerin *(his wife)*, Harry Bannister *(Grayson Whitney)*, Herbert Fields *(his friend)*, Walter Brown *(Mercury)*.

Educational drama. When Grayson Whitney, an engineer whose hobby is antiques, is asked the history of an old porcelain lamp, he relates the story of Anton Daimier and his search to find a satisfactory liquid fuel: *Destitute, Daimier plans to pawn his porcelain lamp for funds to continue his experiments. He falls asleep at his table and dreams that Mercury, god of travel, shows him the evolution of travel from ancient days. When he awakes, it is dark; he takes a bottle from the shelf to fill the lamp; but when he lights it, there is an explosion. He has taken the wrong bottle from the shelf, one containing gasoline. Daimier realizes that this is the liquid fuel for which he has been searching and with the assistance of his employer invents a gasoline engine.* Grayson finishes the story by revealing he obtained the lamp from Anton Daimier's granddaughter in France. *Engineers. Antiques. Automobiles. Gasoline. Combustion. France. Mercury (god). Mythological characters.*

PORT OF DREAMS *see* **GIRL OVERBOARD**

THE PORT OF MISSING GIRLS **F2.4294**

Brenda Pictures. Mar **1928** [c4 Feb 1928; LP24954]. Si; b&w. 35mm. 8 reels, ca7,250 ft.

Dir Irving Cummings. *Story-Scen* Howard Estabrook. *Titl* Viola Brothers Shore. *Photog* Charles Van Enger. *Film Ed* George Nichols, Jr.

Cast: Barbara Bedford *(Ruth King)*, Malcolm McGregor *(Buddie Larkins)*, Natalie Kingston *(Catherine King)*, Hedda Hopper *(Mrs. C. King)*,

George Irving *(Cyrus King)*, Wyndham Standing *(Mayor McKibben)*, Charles Gerard *(DeLeon)*, Paul Nicholson *(George Hamilton)*, Edith Yorke *(Mrs. Blane)*, Bodil Rosing *(Elsa)*, Rosemary Theby *(school matron)*, Lotus Thompson *(Anne)*, Amber Norman *(Marjorie)*.

Society melodrama. Neglected by her moneyed parents and disillusioned with her boyfriend (Buddie Larkins, a bootlegger and philanderer), aspiring vocalist Ruth King joins a school for stage and fancy dancing, thus playing into the hand of DeLeon, its owner, who encourages students to live on the premises hoping to lure them into compromising situations. Buddie delivers a liquor order to the school hotel and discovers Ruth there. King, a lawyer, learns that DeLeon is responsible for the suicide of the daughter of one of his clients, Mrs. Blane. He and Buddie effect DeLeon's arrest and bring Ruth back home. *Singers. Dancers. Bootleggers. Philanderers. Lawyers. Seduction. Family life. Adolescence. Suicide. Dance schools.*

PORTS OF CALL **F2.4295**

Fox Film Corp. 4 Jan **1925** [c28 Dec 1924; LP20981]. Si; b&w. 35mm. 6 reels, 5,500 ft.

Pres by William Fox. *Dir* Denison Clift. *Scen* Edfrid Bingham. *Story* Garrett Elsden Fort.

Cast: Edmund Lowe *(Kirk Rainsford)*, Hazel Keener *(Marjorie Vail)*, William Davidson *(Randolph Sherman)*, William Conklin *(Archer Rainsford)*, Bobby Mack *(Sly)*, Lilyan Tashman *(Lillie)*, Alice Ward *(Mrs. Rainsford)*, Mary McLean *(Peggy)*.

Melodrama. Kirk Rainsford, a wealthy young clubman, attends a charity bazaar at the home of Marjorie Vail, the society girl he hopes to marry. A fire breaks out among the booths and everyone is pulled to safety except little Peggy, Marjorie's kid sister. Marjorie pleads with Kirk to save the child, but he lacks the courage, and Randolph Sherman, Kirk's rival for Marjorie's affections, plays the hero part. For Kirk's public display of cowardice, he is disowned by his father and rejected by Marjorie, who soon marries Sherman. Kirk drifts to the South Seas, eventually landing in Manila, where he becomes a derelict. When Lillie, a fellow drifter, is roughly handled in a bar, Kirk goes to her assistance; she expresses appreciation for his bravery and soon effects his regeneration through her faith in him. Kirk and Lillie journey to the interior, and they obtain work on a plantation recently purchased by Randolph Sherman. During a native uprising, Sherman is killed, and Kirk saves Marjorie from certain death. Marjorie still loves him and asks him to stay, but Kirk decides to go off with Lillie, whose love for him has finally made him a man. *Socialites. Wanderers. Cowardice. Regeneration. Uprisings. Plantations. South Seas. Manila. Fires.*

POT LUCK PARDS **F2.4296**

William Steiner Productions. c26 Jul **1924** [LU20421]. Si; b&w. 35mm. 5 reels, 4,927 ft.

Copyright Auth Forrest Sheldon.

Cast: Pete Morrison *("Chick" Andrews)*.

Western comedy-drama. "Chick" Andrews and his three companions, after losing their jobs at the Holman ranch, get Mary Haynes, Uncle Billy Gray, and Mother Gray, ex-members of a traveling theater company, out of jail on Chick's I. O. U. To celebrate the Grays' 50th wedding anniversary, Chick takes them to the Holman ranch. There he ties up Amos Holman and his irresponsible son Gil to get them out of the way, and he tells his guests that the ranch is his. "Flush" Dyer and his henchman free Gil and, by threatening to expose him to his father as a check forger, persuade him to rob his father's safe and blame it on Chick. Amos, however, overhears the plot, Chick recovers the check, and Flush is arrested. In the end all are reconciled, Mary and the Grays come to live on the ranch, and a love affair develops between Chick and Mary. *Cowboys. Actors. Theatrical troupes. Ranches. Blackmail. Forgery.*

Note: Copyright title: *Pot-Luck Pards*. Summary and character names are taken from shooting script in copyright records and may be different from the plot and names used in the finished film.

POTASH AND PERLMUTTER **F2.4297**

Goldwyn Pictures. *Dist* Associated First National Pictures. 10 Sep **1923** [premiere; released 16 Sep; c19 Sep 1923; LP19413]. Si; b&w. 35mm. 8 reels, 7,636 ft.

Pres by Samuel Goldwyn. *Dir* Clarence Badger. *Scen* Frances Marion. *Photog* Rudolph Berquist. *Art Dir* William B. Ihnen. *Prod Mgr* Charles J. Hunt. *Cost* Madame Frances, Madame Stein, Madame Blaine, Evelyn McHorter. *Art Titl* Oscar C. Buchheister.

Cast: Alexander Carr *(Morris Perlmutter)*, Barney Bernard *(Abe Potash)*, Vera Gordon *(Rosie Potash)*, Martha Mansfield *(The Head Model)*, Ben Lyon *(Boris Andrieff)*, Edward Durand *(Feldman)*, Hope Sutherland *(Irma Potash)*, De Sacia Mooers *(Ruth Goldman)*, Jerry Devine *(The Office Boy)*, Lee Kohlmar *(Pasinsky)*, Leo Donnelly *(The Wide-Awake Salesman)*, Tiller Girls *(cabaret dancers)*.

Comedy. Source: Montague Glass and Charles Klein, *Potash and Perlmutter, a Play in Three Acts* (New York, 1935). Two Jewish Americans, Abe Potash and Morris Perlmutter, become partners in the clothing business. They hire Andrieff, a poor Russian violinist, as a fitter. Andrieff falls in love with Irma Potash, to the disappointment of Abe, who had hoped to have his daughter marry Feldman, a wealthy lawyer. Andrieff is arrested following the shooting on the premises of a labor agitator, but the man recovers and Andrieff is vindicated. He marries Irma with parental blessing. *Jews. Labor agitators. Violinists. Lawyers. Partnerships. Clothing business.*

THE POTTERS **F2.4298**

Famous Players–Lasky. *Dist* Paramount Pictures. 15 Jan **1927** [New York premiere; released 31 Jan; c31 Jan 1927; LP23606]. Si; b&w. 35mm. 7 reels, 6,680 ft.

Pres by Adolph Zukor, Jesse L. Lasky. *Dir* Fred Newmeyer. *Screenplay* J. Clarkson Miller. *Adapt* Sam Mintz, Ray Harris. *Photog* Paul Vogel. *Asst Dir* Ray Lissner.

Cast: W. C. Fields *(Pa Potter)*, Mary Alden *(Ma Potter)*, Ivy Harris *(Minnie)*, Jack Egan *(Bill)*, Richard "Skeets" Gallagher *(Red Miller)*, Joseph Smiley *(Rankin)*, Bradley Barker *(Eagle)*.

Domestic comedy. Source: Joseph Patrick McEvoy, *The Potters; an American Comedy* (Chicago, 1923). Pa Potter works as a lowly office stenographer but fancies himself a financial wizard. Pa robs the family piggy bank behind the back of his muzzling mate, Ma Potter, and sinks the family's savings cache of $4,000 into some oil stock on the say of "entrepreneurs" Rankin and Eagle, who throw in a fifth share as a bonus. Pa passes the gift on to daughter Minnie for her birthday and settles down to some extraordinary computation, anticipating an income of $20,000 a day from his shrewd investment. Ma gets wind of her spouse's wiggling and orders him to the oil fields to regain the loot. Pa's pullman is uncoupled from the locomotive, however, and he awakes the next morning to find himself still in New York. Rankin receives a wire indicating a strike, and Pa sells back the stock, netting himself a thousand extra in the bargain, but Ma and Bill, having heard of the gusher, are crestfallen. The two camps soon switch their moods, however, when it is discovered that the oil is on Minnie's land after all. *Financiers. Stenographers. Family life. Speculation. Fraud. Filial relations. Oil wells. New York City.*

THE POVERTY OF RICHES **F2.4299**

Goldwyn Pictures. Nov **1921** [c29 Sep 1921; LP17029]. Si; b&w. 35mm. 6 reels, 5,641 ft.

Dir Reginald Barker. *Scen* Arthur F. Statter. *Photog* Percy Hilburn.

Cast: Richard Dix *(John Colby)*, Leatrice Joy *(Katherine Colby)*, John Bowers *(Tom Donaldson)*, Louise Lovely *(Grace Donaldson)*, Irene Rich *(Mrs. Holt)*, De Witt Jennings *(Lyons)*, Dave Winter *(Stephen Phillips)*, Roy Laidlaw *(Hendron)*, John Cossar *(Edward Phillips, Sr.)*, Frankie Lee *(John, in prolog)*, Dorothy Hughes *(Katherine, in prolog)*.

Domestic drama. Source: Leroy Scott, "The Mother," in *Cosmopolitan* (56:350, Feb 1914). Katherine Holt marries John Colby and is desirous of having children, but her husband wishes to wait until he has attained further financial and social success; thus Katherine lavishes her affections on the children of Grace and Tom Donaldson. John is successful and enters wider social spheres, but he still refuses her request for children and neglects the home for business. Nevertheless, she refuses a former suitor, Phillips, when he proposes that she divorce John. Colby finally apologizes for his indifference and promises to fulfill her wishes when he is appointed manager. That evening, in an automobile accident, she sustains injuries that prevent her from bearing children. She reproaches her husband, who realizes he has sacrificed his life in the pursuit of wealth. *Marriage. Wealth. Family life. Children. Childlessness.*

POWDER MY BACK **F2.4300**

Warner Brothers Pictures. 10 Mar **1928** [c1 Mar 1928; LP25028]. Si; b&w. 35mm. 7 reels, 6,185 ft.

Dir Roy Del Ruth. *Scen* Robert Lord. *Titl* Jack Jarmuth. *Adapt* Joseph Jackson. *Story* Jerome Kingston. *Photog* Frank Kesson. *Film Ed* Owen Marks. *Asst Dir* Joe Barry.

Cast: Irene Rich *(Fritzi Foy)*, Audrey Ferris *(Ruth Stevens)*, André

Beranger *(Claude)*, Anders Randolf *(Rex Hale)*, Carroll Nye *(Jack Hale)*.

Drama. Rex Hale, a reform mayor, closes the musical comedy "Powder My Back" because he feels that it is immoral. Indignant, Fritzi Foy, star of the comedy, determines to revenge herself on Hale. Gaining entrance to his home by pretending to be injured in an automobile accident, Fritzi has Claude, her press agent, masquerade as a doctor and advise that she should not be disturbed until she has completely recovered. Hale is enraged, but his son, Jack, falls in love with Fritzi though he is already engaged to Ruth Stevens, an attractive flapper. When she sees that her plan has caused unhappiness for an innocent person, Fritzi dissuades Jack, who returns to his old sweetheart; she ends up with the mayor! *Actors. Mayors. Flappers. Press agents. Musical revues.*

POWER **F2.4301**

Dist Pathé Exchange. 23 Sep **1928** [c17 1928; LP25625]. Si; b&w. 35mm. 7 reels, 6,092 ft.

Ralph Block Production. *Dir* Howard Higgin. *Story-Cont* Tay Garnett. *Titl* John Krafft. *Photog* Peverell Marley. *Art Dir* Mitchell Leisen. *Film Ed* Doane Harrison. *Asst Dir* Robert Fellows. *Prod Mgr* Harry Poppe.

Cast: William Boyd *(Husky)*, Alan Hale *(Handsome)*, Jacqueline Logan *(Lorraine La Rue)*, Jerry Drew *(menace)*, Joan Bennett *(a dame)*, Carol Lombard *(another dame)*, Pauline Curley *(still another dame)*.

Comedy-melodrama. Husky and Handsome, two tough dam builders who spend most of their time stealing each other's women, make a pact stipulating that henceforth each is to lay off the other's dame. The agreement is no sooner sealed than they spy Lorraine La Rue, a demure little thing struggling with a heavy suitcase. The boys go after her, and she soon promises separately to marry each of them, after first borrowing all their savings for "an operation on my sick mother." The boys discover her duplicity too late and arrive at the train station in time to see Lorraine disappearing around the bend with all their money—and the town dude! *Construction crews. Gold diggers. Dudes. Dams.*

THE POWER DIVINE **F2.4302**

Premium Picture Productions. *Dist* Independent Pictures. 1 Apr **1923.** Si; b&w. 35mm. 5 reels.

Dir? (see note) H. G. Moody, William J. Craft.

Cast: Mary Wynn *(Sally Slocum)*, Jack Livingston *(Bob Harvey)*, Caroline Brunson *(Mrs. Slocum)*, Ralph Parker *(Doc Singletree)*, Al Ferguson *(Luke Weston)*.

Rural melodrama. "Youth educated in the east returns home unaware of feud existing between his and another family. Falls in love with girl of the other family. His rival turns the townspeople and the girl against him. But in time love conquers all." *(Motion Picture News Booking Guide,* 5:42, Oct 1923.) *Feuds. Kentucky.*

Note: Some sources credit William J. Craft as director.

THE POWER OF A LIE **F2.4303**

Universal Pictures. ca24 Dec **1922** [Chicago premiere; released 7 Jan 1923; c29 Dec 1922; LP18545]. Si; b&w. 35mm. 5 reels, 4,910 ft.

Pres by Carl Laemmle. *Dir* George Archainbaud. *Scen* Charles Kenyon. *Photog* Charles Stumar.

Cast: Mabel Julienne Scott *(Betty Hammond)*, David Torrence *(John Hammond)*, Maude George *(Joan Hammond)*, Ruby Lafayette *(Mrs. Hammond)*, Earl Metcalfe *(Richard Burton)*, June Elvidge *(Lily Cardington)*, Phillips Smalley *(Jeremiah Smith)*, Stanton Heck *(Mr. Lawrence)*, Winston Miller *(Julian Hammond)*.

Drama. Source: Johan Bojer, *The Power of a Lie* (London, 1908). At a wild surprise party John Hammond signs a note for his struggling friend, architect Richard Burton, but later denies his presence at the affair in order to preserve his reputation. Richard consequently is tried for forgery and deserted by all save Betty Hammond, his sweetheart and John's sister. John confesses to his lie just as the jury is about to deliberate, thus exonerating Richard. *Architects. Brother-sister relationship. Mendacity. Forgery. Reputation.*

THE POWER OF LOVE **F2.4304**

Perfect Pictures. 27 Sep **1922** [Los Angeles premiere]. Si; b&w. 35mm. 5 reels, 4,600 ft.

Dir Nat Deverich. *Photog* Harry Fairall.

Cast: Elliott Sparling *(Terry O'Neil)*, Barbara Bedford *(Maria Almeda)*, Noah Beery *(Don Almeda)*, Aileen Manning *(Ysabel Almeda)*, Albert Prisco *(Don Alvarez)*, John Herdman *(The Old Padre)*.

Melodrama. "Because of financial reverses Don Almeda offers his daughter, Maria, to Don Alvarez, though she does not love him. Terry O'Neill arrives at the Southern California settlement in which the Almedas live, and is slightly wounded when Alvarez's henchmen seek to rob him. He is found by Maria, to whom he loses his heart. Just before the wedding, O'Neill waylays Alvarez ... and takes his place at a fiesta. Alvarez appears and denounces him. Later, Alvarez ... slays the padre with O'Neill's knife. Denouncing O'Neill as the murderer, Alvarez tries to shoot him, but wounds Maria, who throws herself in front of him. Later, she succeeds in proving that Alvarez is the thief and murderer, and everything ends happily for Maria and O'Neill." *(Moving Picture World,* 21 Oct 1922, p704.) *Clergymen. Finance—Personal. Robbery. Murder. California.*

Note: Employs the Fairall process of producing stereoscopic effects.

THE POWER OF SILENCE **F2.4305**

Tiffany-Stahl Productions. 20 Oct **1928** [c27 Sep 1928; LP25689]. Si; b&w. 35mm. 6 reels, 5,554 ft.

Dir Wallace Worsley. *Story-Cont* Frances Hyland. *Titl* Frederick Hatton, Fanny Hatton. *Photog* L. Guy Wilky. *Film Ed* Byron Robinson.

Cast: Belle Bennett *(Mamie Stone)*, John Westwood *(Donald Stone)*, Marian Douglas *(Gloria Wright)*, Anders Randolf *(district attorney)*, John St. Polis *(defense attorney)*, Virginia Pearson *(Mrs. Wright)*, Raymond Keane *(Jim Wright)*, Jack Singleton *(hotel clerk)*.

Mystery drama. Although Mamie Stone has been accused of the murder of Jim Wright on circumstantial evidence, she refuses to testify in her own defense at her trial. Her lawyer, however, discloses that Wright, a philanderer, was the common-law father of Mamie's son, Donald, and the jury acquits her. Jim's wife, Gloria, who hates Mamie, persuades Donald to leave his mother's house and strike out on his own; when Mamie learns of this, she bitterly denounces Gloria and reveals that she has known all along that Gloria killed Wright to protect her own honor and reputation. Overcome by love and gratitude for Mamie's sacrificial silence, Gloria vows that together they will do everything to make Donald's life a happy one. *Philanderers. Lawyers. Motherhood. Self-sacrifice. Murder. Trials.*

POWER OF THE PRESS *see* **FREEDOM OF THE PRESS**

THE POWER OF THE PRESS **F2.4306**

Columbia Pictures. 31 Oct **1928** [c20 Dec 1928; LP25940]. Si; b&w. 35mm. 7 reels, 6,465 ft.

Prod Jack Cohn. *Dir* Frank Capra. *Adapt-Cont* Frederick A. Thompson, Sonya Levien. *Story* Frederick A. Thompson. *Photog* Chet Lyons, Ted Tetzlaff. *Art Dir* Harrison Wiley. *Film Ed* Frank Atkinson. *Asst Dir* Buddy Coleman.

Cast: Douglas Fairbanks, Jr. *(Clem Rogers)*, Jobyna Ralston *(Jane Atwill)*, Mildred Harris *(Marie)*, Philo McCullough *(Blake)*, Wheeler Oakman *(Van)*, Robert Edeson *(city editor)*, Edwards Davis *(Mr. Atwill)*, Del Henderson *(Johnson)*, Charles Clary *(district attorney)*.

Melodrama. Clem Rogers, a hustling cub reporter, discovers that Jane Atwill, the daughter of a mayoral candidate, was with the district attorney when he was murdered. The story makes page one, and Jane is arrested, insisting that she has no idea who fired the fatal shot. With her father's political chances ruined, Jane is released on bail. She angrily goes to the paper and convinces Clem of her innocence. Working together, Clem and Jane eventually prove that Blake, her father's political opponent, was responsible for the murder. Clem again has a story on the front page, and he and Jane are married. *Reporters. Political bosses. Murder. Injustice. Newspapers. Political campaigns.*

THE POWER OF THE WEAK **F2.4307**

Chadwick Pictures. *Dist* Independent Pictures. 24 May **1926** [New York State license]. Si; b&w. 35mm. 7 reels, 6,609 ft.

Dir William J. Craft. *Story-Scen* William J. Craft, Wyndham Gittens. *Photog* Arthur Reeves.

Cast: Arnold Gregg, Alice Calhoun *(Myra)*, Carl Miller *(Raymond)*, Spottiswoode Aitken *(The Father)*, Marguerite Clayton, Jack Fowler.

Melodrama. A woman inherits a lumber camp and goes there to take a hand in its management. A man with an interest in the tall timber is attracted to her and asks for her hand in marriage. She refuses, and the man, out of wounded vanity, attempts to ruin her business. A young fellow, who has been disinherited by his father for falling in love with a chorus girl, comes to the Northland to forget the girl, who, learning of the disinheritance, has thrown him over. The youth falls in love with the boss of the lumber camp, protects her from the unwanted advances of her rejected suitor, and helps her to set her business straight. *Businesswomen. Disinheritance. Lumber camps. Business management.*

THE POWER WITHIN **F2.4308**

Achievement Films. *Dist* Pathé Exchange. 18 Dec **1921** [c6 Dec 1921; LU17313]. Si; b&w. 35mm. 6 reels.

Dir-Adapt Lem F. Kennedy. *Story* Robert Norwood. *Photog* George Peters.

Cast: William H. Tooker *(Job Armstrong)*, Nellie P. Spaulding *(Mrs. Armstrong)*, Robert Kenyon *(Bob Armstrong)*, Dorothy Allen *(Dorothy Armstrong)*, Robert Bentley *(Count Bazaine)*, Pauline Garon *(Pauline)*, William Zohlmen *(Little Bobby)*.

Religious melodrama. Job Armstrong, a self-made millionaire shipowner, believes his own powers are sufficient to promote him to even greater heights, and although he hears the biblical story of Job, he does not recognize the analogy to his own case. Circumstances, initiated by the treachery of his son-in-law, Count Bazaine, who plots to get the shipyards for a foreign concern, cause him to lose successively his son and daughter. Pauline, the French widow of his son, and her small son bring a glimmer of happiness, however, into his life. Then, when his home burns and it appears that fate has taken away Pauline's son, Armstrong comes to realize the value of Divine power and love that meet every human need. Pauline exposes Bazaine as her husband's murderer, Job's business is restored, and he wins back health and happiness. *Shipowners. Millionaires. Widows. French. Shipbuilding. Faith. Religion. Job.*

THE PRAIRIE KING (Universal-Jewel) **F2.4309**

Universal Pictures. 15 May **1927** [c5 May 1927; LP23943]. Si; b&w. 35mm. 6 reels, 5,689 ft.

Pres by Carl Laemmle. *Dir* Reeves Eason. *Adapt-Cont* Frank Howard Clark. *Story* William Wallace Cook. *Photog* Harry Neumann. *Art Dir* David S. Garber.

Cast: Hoot Gibson *(Andy Barden)*, Barbara Worth *(Edna Jordan)*, Albert Prisco *(Dan Murdock)*, Charles Sellon *(Pop Wygant)*, Rosa Gore *(Aunt Hattie)*, Sidney Jarvis *(Jim Gardner)*, George Periolat *(Don Fernández)*.

Western melodrama. A prospector leaves his mine to three people, unknown to one another, who have befriended him. Murdock, determined to possess the mine at any cost, orders his men to keep the others from the mine. Edna Jordan is advised by her lawyer to take immediate possession on the premise that the final owner will have to meet certain conditions. Barden, a cowpuncher and the third beneficiary, protects Edna from Murdock's henchmen and takes a job at the mine. Murdock turns the girl against him, but at a fiesta Barden exposes Murdock in a duel; the latter proposes marriage to Edna and captures Barden and his pal. Barden withdraws in the girl's favor and wins the claim, since he has fulfilled the condition of generosity; but he and Edna race to the claim office and record the mine in both their names. *Prospectors. Cowboys. Lawyers. Inheritance. Wills. Mine claims.*

THE PRAIRIE MYSTERY **F2.4310**

Bud Osborne Feature Films. *Dist* Truart Film Corp. 15 Aug **1922** [New York license application; released 1923?; c23 May 1922; LU17949]. Si; b&w. 35mm. 5 reels.

Dir-Writ George Edward Hall.

Cast: Bud Osborne, Pauline Curley.

Western melodrama. Copyright synopsis: "Jim Holmes saves a boy and girl from an Indian massacre. Adopts them. 17 years later he means to marry the girl but when Jim finds she loves the boy, he sacrifices himself and dresses in the boy's cowl and leads the Vigalantes [*sic*] a chase. They do not suspect the boy. Jim escapes the Vigalantes and is captured by the masked riders. He escapes bringing the Vigalantes to the masked riders and captures them. The leader of the masked riders turns out to be a society woman of the neighborhood. Jim gives the girl to the boy and rides away." *Orphans. Indians of North America. Vigilantes. Adoption. Massacres.*

THE PRAIRIE PIRATE **F2.4311**

Hunt Stromberg Corp. *Dist* Producers Distributing Corp. 11 Oct **1925** [c23 Sep 1925; LP21841]. Si; b&w. 35mm. 5 reels, 4,603 ft.

Dir Edmund Mortimer. *Adapt* Anthony Dillon. *Photog* George Benoit. *Art Dir* Edward Withers. *Film Ed* Harry L. Decker.

Cast: Harry Carey *(Brian Delaney)*, Jean Dumas *(Ruth Delaney)*, Lloyd Whitlock *(Howard Steele)*, Trilby Clark *(Teresa Esteban)*, Robert Edeson *(Don Esteban)*, Tote Du Crow *(José)*, Evelyn Selbie *(Madre)*, Fred Kohler *(Agullar)*.

Western melodrama. Source: W. C. Tuttle, "The Yellow Seal," in *Liberty* (10 Jan 1925). Ruth Delaney is murdered by an unknown assailant, and her brother, Brian, becomes a bandit in order to track down the killer. He befriends Don Esteban and his daughter, Teresa, thereby incurring the enmity of Howard Steele, a gambler. Brian and Teresa are to be wed, but Steele kidnaps the girl and rides into the hills. Brian follows. The men fight, and Brian forces the gambler to exchange clothes with him. The posse pursuing Brian kills Steele, mistaking him for Brian. Brian and Teresa are married, and evidence comes to light that proves Steele to have been the killer of Brian's sister. *Bandits. Gamblers. Posses. Brother-sister relationship. Mistaken identity. Murder. Kidnaping.*

THE PRAIRIE WIFE **F2.4312**

Eastern Productions. *Dist* Metro-Goldwyn Distributing Corp. 23 Feb **1925** [c9 Mar 1925; LP21217]. Si; b&w. 35mm. 7 reels, 6,487 ft.

Dir-Cont Hugo Ballin. *Titl* Katherine Hilliker, H. H. Caldwell. *Story* Arthur Stringer. *Photog* James Diamond. *Film Ed* Katherine Hilliker, H. H. Caldwell. *Asst Dir* James Chapin.

Cast: Dorothy Devore *(Chaddie Green)*, Herbert Rawlinson *(Duncan MacKail)*, Gibson Gowland *(Ollie)*, Leslie Stuart *(Percy)*, Frances Prim *(Olga)*, Boris Karloff *(Diego)*, Erich von Ritzau *(doctor)*, Rupert Franklin *(Rufus Green)*.

Western melodrama. While in Europe, Chaddie Green, a society girl, discovers that she has been left penniless. She returns to the United States and meets Duncan MacKail, who is equally broke though he owns grainland in the West. Duncan and Chaddie are married and go west to homestead. Duncan hires Ollie, a Swedish caretaker, who frightens Chaddie. When business takes Duncan away, Chaddie goes to take care of Percy Woodhouse, an Englishman who has become ill at his place 15 miles away. Her horse runs away, and she is forced to spend the night there. She sleeps under a wagon, but Duncan is nevertheless angry and jealous. Chaddie moves Percy to her house in order both to nurse him back to health and to use his presence to restrain the violent Ollie. Duncan leaves in a fit of jealousy, but he soon returns with Olga, a servant, as a peace offering. Percy and Olga fall in love. Ollie hangs himself, leaving a note confessing to murderous instincts. Chaddie has a baby, and she and Duncan find happiness and prosperity in their prairie home. *Caretakers. Swedes. English. Homesteaders. Suicide. Jealousy.*

PREJUDICE **F2.4313**

Dist Arista Film Corp. Jan **1922** [c18 Oct 1921; LU17105]. Si; b&w. 35mm. 9 reels.

Dir Joseph Belmont. *Writ* Rita Barre.

Cast: Zena Keefe.

Drama. Job Abramonoff, the leader of a Jewish community in Russia, is arrested for the ritual murder of Sonja Mulnikow, the little sister of Sascha, a gentile and the childhood friend of Job's daughter, Manya. Sascha, who is sympathetic to the plight of the Jews, is led to point the accusing finger at Job against his better judgment. He reads a book, *The Philosophy of Race Prejudice,* which tells how Maneth, the Egyptian high priest, tried to dupe Alexander the Great into believing that his young friend Cassander was the victim of such a sacrifice by the Jews. Convinced of his error, Sascha tries to save the Abramonoff family and stop the pogrom that began when Job was arrested. Sonja is revealed to be alive and well, but it is too late: the mob has broken into the prison and stoned Job to death. Sascha, horror-stricken, confesses to Manya that he was prejudiced and asks forgiveness. *Jews. Pogroms. Prejudice. Ritual murder. Russia. Egypt. Alexander the Great.*

Note: Working titles: *The Ritual Murder* and *The Proscribed.* There is some doubt about the nationality of the film. From the evidence available, it is not clear whether, in the story, Manya survives her father or dies with him.

PREP AND PEP **F2.4314**

Fox Film Corp. 18 Nov **1928** [c16 Nov 1928; LP25832]. Mus score & sd eff (Movietone); b&w. 35mm. 6 reels, 6,806 ft.

Pres by William Fox. *Dir* David Butler. *Story-Scen* John Stone. *Titl* Malcolm Boylan. *Photog* Sidney Wagner, Joseph Valentine. *Film Ed* Irene Morra. *Asst Dir* Ad Schaumer.

Cast: David Rollins *(Cyril Reade)*, Nancy Drexel *(Dorothy Marsh)*, John Darrow *(Flash Wells)*, E. H. Calvert *(Colonel Marsh)*, Frank Albertson *(Bunk Hill)*, Robert Peck *(Coach)*.

Comedy-drama. Cyril Reade, the son of Culver Military Academy's greatest athlete, enters the school and proves to be a complete washout at sports and games. Cyril at first feels like quitting, but he begins to make a name for himself when he breaks a horse and qualifies for the crack Black Horse Troop; Cyril later rescues the commandant's daughter from a fire, winning her gratitude and his father's nickname of "Tiger." *Cadets. Athletes. Military schools. Culver Military Academy. Horses.*

PREPARED TO DIE **F2.4315**

Cliff Reid. Dec **1923** [scheduled release]. Si; b&w. 35mm. 5 reels.

Dir William Hughes Curran. *Scen* Keene Thompson.

Cast: Eddie Polo *(John Pendleton Smythe)*, Ena Gregory *(Vivienne Van de Vere)*, James McElhern *(storekeeper)*.

Society melodrama. Smythe, a "society snob," decides to commit suicide by injecting himself into a Kentucky feud. His efforts are interpreted as heroics. He wins a girl and returns home. *Socialites. Snobbery. Suicide. Kentucky. Feuds.*

PRETTY CLOTHES **F2.4316**

Sterling Pictures. 15 Oct **1927** [c20 Oct 1927; LP24543]. Si; b&w. 35mm. 6 reels, 5,652 ft.

Supv Joe Rock. *Dir* Phil Rosen. *Scen* Frances Guihan. *Titl* Wyndham Gittens. *Adapt* Edwin Myers. *Story* Peggy Gaddis. *Photog* Herbert Kirkpatrick.

Cast: Jobyna Ralston *(Marion Dunbar)*, Gertrude Astor *(Rose Dunbar)*, Johnny Walker *(Russell Thorpe)*, Lloyd Whitlock *(Philip Bennett)*, Charles Clary *(Thorpe, Sr.)*, Jack Mower *(Albert Moore)*, Lydia Knott *(Mrs. Dunbar)*.

Society drama. Marion Dunbar, a poor girl interested in pretty clothes, attends a fashion show with her hard-working sister Rose and there meets Russell Thorpe, a wealthy young man, and Philip Bennett, whom Russell's father has secretly appointed to see that he does not become romantically entangled. Russell pursues Marion, who is infatuated, but Thorpe, Sr., arranges for Bennett to compromise the girl by having her accept an expensive gown as a gift. When Russell and Marion decide to marry, he takes her to meet his father, who receives her in a fury; and Russell is led to believe that Marion took the dress from Bennett for reprehensible reasons. After a quarrel, she leaves him; but they meet again at the bedside of her dying mother when Russell is persuaded to pose as Marion's husband, and the lovers are reconciled. *Sisters. Filial relations. Social classes. Fashion shows. Courtship. Wealth. Clothes.*

PRETTY LADIES **F2.4317**

Metro-Goldwyn Pictures. 6 Sep **1925** [c10 Aug 1925; LP21723]. Si; b&w. 35mm. 6 reels, 5,828 ft.

Dir Monta Bell. *Adapt* Alice D. G. Miller. *Photog* Ira H. Morgan.

Cast: ZaSu Pitts *(Maggie Keenan)*, Tom Moore *(Al Cassidy)*, Ann Pennington *(herself)*, Lilyan Tashman *(Selma Larson)*, Bernard Randall *(Aaron Savage)*, Helena D'Algy *(Adrienne)*, Conrad Nagel *(Maggie's dream lover)*, Norma Shearer *(Frances White)*, George K. Arthur *(Roger Van Horn)*, Lucille Le Sueur *(Bobby)*, Paul Ellis *(Warren Hadley)*, Roy D'Arcy *(Paul Thompson)*, Gwen Lee *(Fay)*, Dorothy Seastrom *(Diamond Tights)*, Lew Harvey *(Will Rogers)*, Chad Huber *(Frisco)*, Walter Shumway *(Mr. Gallagher)*, Dan Crimmins *(Mr. Shean)*, Jimmie Quinn *(Eddie Cantor)*.

Comedy-drama. Source: Adela Rogers St. Johns, "Pretty Ladies," in *Cosmopolitan Magazine*. Maggie Keenan, the star comedienne in the Follies, accidentally falls into the orchestra pit and breaks Al Cassidy's drum. They fall in love, and Al writes a production number for her that makes him famous. They are married and settle happily into domesticity: Al writes songs and Maggie bears children. Al is called to Atlantic City to write a production number for Selma Larson, a beautiful star in the Follies, and he succumbs to her charms. Maggie learns of Al's infidelity, but, when he returns home repentant, she refuses to hear his contrite confession. They resume life together, and Al's indiscretion is never mentioned. *Drummers. Composers. Actors. Family life. Infidelity. Follies. Vaudeville. New York City. Atlantic City. Will Rogers. Eddie Cantor. Ed Gallagher. Al Shean.*

THE PRICE OF A PARTY **F2.4318**

Howard Estabrook Productions. *Dist* Associated Exhibitors. 19 Oct **1924.** Si; b&w. 35mm. 6 reels, 5,456 ft.

Dir Charles Giblyn. *Scen* Charles F. Roebuck. *Photog* John Seitz.

Cast: Hope Hampton *(Grace Barrows)*, Harrison Ford *(Robert Casson)*, Arthur Carew *(Kenneth Bellwood)*, Mary Astor *(Alice Barrows)*, Dagmar Godowsky *(Evelyn Dolores)*, Fred Hadley *(Stephen Darrell)*, Edna Richmond *(Evelyn's maid)*, Donald Lashey *(hall boy)*, Florence Richardson *(jazz queen)*.

Society melodrama. Source: William Briggs MacHarg, "The Price of a Party," in *Cosmopolitan* (70:74–80). Kenneth Bellwood, an unscrupulous broker, discovers that hated business rival Robert Casson has secured a valuable option in Brazil and quickly determines to keep Robert in New York until it expires, arranging with Grace Barrows (a cabaret dancer who needs money to help her sick mother) to use her wiles to keep Robert at home. Robert quickly falls under her spell, and Grace increasingly regrets her duplicity. Grace's innocent young sister, Alice, comes to New York and falls under Bellwood's influence. Learning that Alice is going to visit Bellwood's apartment, Grace goes there herself, accompanied by Evelyn Dolores, Bellwood's former mistress. Grace leaves, Evelyn kills Bellwood, and Alice is accused of the crime. Evelyn commits suicide, leaving a note confessing to the crime. Robert forgives Grace, and Alice is sent home. *Brokers. Dancers. Mistresses. Sisters. Suicide. Murder.*

THE PRICE OF FEAR **F2.4319**

Universal Pictures. 28 Oct **1928** [c3 Aug 1928; LP25512]. Si; b&w. 35mm. 5 reels, 4,230 ft.

Supv William Lord Wright. *Dir* Leigh Jason. *Story-Scen* William Lester. *Titl* Val Cleveland. *Photog* Charles Stumar. *Film Ed* Harry Marker.

Cast: Bill Cody *(Grant Somers)*, Duane Thompson *(Mary Franklin)*, Tom London *("Flash" Hardy)*, Grace Cunard *(Satin Sadie)*, Monty Montague *(Monte)*, Ole M. Ness *(Michael Shane)*, Jack Raymond *(Toad Magee)*.

Western melodrama. Grant Somers, a wealthy clubman and amateur detective, signs on as a waiter in the Red Rooster Cafe in an attempt to track down The Professor, a notorious gang leader. Toad Magee, a stool pigeon, is murdered by Hardy, one of The Professor's gang, and Grant is blamed for the crime. Grant later meets Mary Franklin, a detective who is working as a maid in The Professor's home; she learns of a plot against Grant's life and warns him in time for him to make his escape. When The Professor finds out that Mary is a detective, he orders her death, but Grant arrives in time to rescue her. The police arrest The Professor and his gang, and Mary and Grant seem set on becoming partners for life. *Detectives. Waiters. Housemaids. Gangs. Informers. Murder.*

THE PRICE OF HONOR **F2.4320**

Columbia Pictures. 5 Mar **1927** [c23 Feb 1927; LP23700]. Si; b&w. 35mm. 6 reels, 5,936 ft.

Prod Harry Cohn. *Dir* E. H. Griffith. *Story-Scen* Dorothy Howell. *Photog* J. O. Taylor.

Cast: Dorothy Revier *(Carolyn McLane)*, Malcolm McGregor *(Anthony Fielding)*, William V. Mong *(Daniel B. Hoyt)*, Gustav von Seyffertitz *(Peter Fielding)*, Erville Alderson *(Ogden Bennett)*, Dan Mason *(Roberts)*.

Melodrama. Daniel B. Hoyt, an innocent man sentenced to life imprisonment through circumstantial evidence, is paroled after 15 years because he is not expected to live. He plans to visit his niece, Carolyn McLane, who believes him dead, and remain unseen. Anthony Fielding, son of the judge who sentenced Hoyt, proposes to Carolyn; she mistakes her uncle for a burglar, but Bennett, the family lawyer, is forced to tell her the story of her uncle's past. Learning of his son's relationship with Carolyn, Judge Fielding refuses to consent to their marriage. Hoyt commits suicide, leaving a letter to the judge stating that he is making his son, Tony, victim of a plot that will cause his arrest. Tony is arrested for Hoyt's murder, and the letter is mistakenly destroyed before reaching the judge, but Carolyn discovers a duplicate, thus saving her lover and assuring their happiness. *Lawyers. Judges. Uncles. Parole. Injustice. Circumstantial evidence. Revenge. Suicide. Documentation.*

THE PRICE OF PLEASURE (Universal-Jewel) **F2.4321**

Universal Pictures. 15 Mar **1925** [2 Dec 1924; LP20833]. Si; b&w. 35mm. 7 reels, 6,618 ft.

Dir Edward Sloman. *Scen* J. G. Hawks. *Adapt* Raymond L. Schrock. *Story* Elizabeth Holding, Marion Orth. *Photog* John Stumar.

Cast: Virginia Valli *(Linnie Randall)*, Norman Kerry *(Garry Schuyler)*, Louise Fazenda *(Stella Kelly)*, Kate Lester *(Mrs. Schuyler)*, George Fawcett *(John Osborne)*, T. Roy Barnes *(Bi'll McGuffy)*, James O. Barrows *(Jenkins)*, Marie Astaire *(Grace Schuyler)*.

Society melodrama. While at work in the hardware section of a large New York department store, Linnie Randall longs aloud for just one week of real pleasure. She is overheard by Garry Schuyler, the scion of an aristocratic family, who, as a lark, decides to grant her wish. They have a wonderful week together. When they are to part on the seventh day, they realize they are in love, and they immediately get married. Linnie then meets Garry's mother and sister, who disapprove of her and make her life miserable. When she overhears Garry's mother say that Garry's life has been ruined by marriage to a shopgirl, Linnie runs from the house. Garry chases her in a car and accidentally runs over her. Believing that she is dead, he becomes mentally ill and is taken to Europe for a cure by his family. Linnie recovers and supports herself by dancing in a cabaret. When Garry returns, he discovers that not only is Linnie alive but that she is also the mother of a child. Finding her, he saves her from the legal chicanery of his family and the unwanted advances of her dancing partner. Linnie and Garry are happily reunited. *Shopgirls. Dancers. In-laws. Mental illness. Social classes. Marriage. Automobile accidents.*

THE PRICE OF POSSESSION **F2.4322**

Famous Players–Lasky British Producers. *Dist* Paramount Pictures. 27 Feb **1921** [c27 Feb 1921; LP16200]. Si; b&w. 35mm. 5 reels, 4,933 ft.

Pres by Jesse L. Lasky. *Dir* Hugh Ford. *Scen* Eve Unsell. *Story* Winifred Boggs. *Photog* George Folsey.

Cast: Ethel Clayton *(Helen Carston)*, Rockliffe Fellowes *(Jim Barston, a bushrider/Jim Barston, heir to Barston Manor)*, Maude Turner Gordon *(Lady Dawnay)*, Reginald Denny *(Robert Dawnay)*, Clarence Heritage *(Lord Dawnay)*, George Backus *(Samuel Poore)*, Isabel West *(Mrs. Poore)*, Pearl Shepard *(Eva Poore)*.

Romantic drama. When Jim Barston is mysteriously shot and killed in Australia, his wife, Helen, lays claim to the estate of Gerald Mortimer Barston in England on grounds that Jim was the missing son and heir. Although unable to prove her husband's birth by legal means, she convinces the trustees and is installed as mistress of the manor. The real heir appears and produces his birth certificate. Though Helen believes him at first to be an imposter, she finally accepts him as the true heir and relinquishes the estate, but he persuades her to stay and marry him. *Inheritance. Imposture. Australia. England. Documentation.*

THE PRICE OF SILENCE **F2.4323**

Sunrise Pictures. 1 Jan **1921** [trade review]. Si; b&w. 35mm. 6 reels.

Dir Fred Leroy Granville. *Photog* Leland Lancaster.

Cast: Peggy Hyland *(Beryl Brentano)*, Campbell Gullan *(Col. Luke Darrington)*, Tom Chatterton *(Lennox Dunbar)*, Daisy Robinson *(Leo Gordon)*, Dorothy Gordon *(Mrs. Brentano)*, Van Dycke *(Frank Darrington)*.

Mystery melodrama. Source: Augusta Jane Evans Wilson, *At the Mercy of Tiberius* (New York, 1887). Beryl Brentano's mother is in need of an operation but is unable to pay for it. Beryl goes for the needed cash to her grandfather, who has disowned her mother for marrying against his will. She obtains it and leaves, unseen by any of the servants; later that night, her grandfather is found dead, presumably murdered. Beryl, thinking her brother is the killer, offers no self-defense and is arrested, tried, and convicted of the murder. A year passes, and the butler tells the prosecuting attorney that the ghost of his master is fighting with his murderer. Upon investigation, it is discovered that lightning had sketched on the window a picture of the death of the grandfather, who met his end by no violence. Beryl, freed from prison, finds that her mother has died and that there is no trace of her brother. Through advertising she communicates with her brother, now a priest, and learns the truth: while he was quarreling with his grandfather, a bolt of lightning struck him dead. *Priests. Grandfathers. Butlers. Ghosts. Brother-sister relationship. Phenomena. Self-sacrifice.*

THE PRICE OF SUCCESS **F2.4324**

Waldorf Pictures. *Dist* Columbia Pictures. 15 Aug **1925** [c1 Sep 1925; LP21787]. Si; b&w. 35mm. 6 reels.

Dir Tony Gaudio. *Story* Tom J. Hopkins.

Cast: Alice Lake *(Ellen Harden)*, Lee Shumway *(George Harden)*, Gaston Glass *(Wally)*, Florence Turner *(Mrs. Moran)*, Spec O'Donnell *(Jimmy Moran)*, Edward Kipling *(butler)*, Alma Bennett *(Ardath Courtney)*.

Melodrama. Born and reared in a Maine village, Ellen Harden has lived in New York for 5 years, finding contentment in the love of her successful husband, George. All this changes, however, when she discovers that he is having an affair with Ardath Courtney, a social butterfly who is struggling to maintain the appearance of wealth. Ellen, determined to win George back by arousing his jealousy, vigorously flirts with Wally Van Tine, the wealthy son of the millowner for whom George works; Ellen also lets George know that she knows that he has been unfaithful. George repents of his philandering, and he and Ellen discover new depths of contentment together. *Mainers. Socialites. Flirts. Marriage. Infidelity. Mills. New York City.*

THE PRICE OF YOUTH **F2.4325**

Berwilla Film Corp. *Dist* Arrow Film Corp. 15 Mar **1922** [c17 Mar 1922; LP17650]. Si; b&w. 35mm. 5 reels, 4,995 ft.

Prod-Dir Ben Wilson. *Scen* Hope Loring. *Story* Wyndham Martin.

Cast: Neva Gerber *(Adela Monmouth)*, Spottiswoode Aitken *(Gregory Monmouth)*, Ashton Dearholt *(Owen Barwell)*, Charles L. King *(Hugh Monmouth)*, Joseph Girard *(Dr. Holt)*, Jack Pratt *(Spencer Trayes)*, Pietro Sosso *(Kerenski)*.

Society melodrama. Adela Monmouth, who lives with her father (Gregory) and brother (Hugh) in a Virginia country home, is encouraged by her sweetheart, Owen Barwell, to pursue her musical career. Her musical aspiration moves her father at last to tell her of her mother's past: having also been a musician, she had been induced by another man to go to the city, deserting Gregory and the two children. Later, the shock of Hugh's death proves fatal to his father, and Adela goes to New York, hoping to achieve success as a singer. There she is aided by a wealthy manipulator, Spencer Trayes, whom she permits to invest her remaining money with remarkable results. Later, she discovers that Trayes has been supporting her with his own money, and she schemes to bring about his downfall on the exchange. Owen then reveals that Trayes is in fact the promoter who years before had eloped with her mother. Trayes is defeated on the market, and Adela accepts Owen's proposal of marriage. *Singers. Filial relations. Desertion. Stock market. New York City. Virginia.*

THE PRICE SHE PAID **F2.4326**

Columbia Pictures. *Dist* C. B. C. Film Sales. 1 Apr or 15 Sep **1924** [c13 Sep 1924; LP20600]. Si; b&w. 35mm. 6 reels, 5,957 ft.

Dir Henry MacRae.

Cast: Alma Rubens *(Mildred Gower)*, Frank Mayo *(Dr. Donald Keith)*, Eugenie Besserer *(Mrs. Elton Gower)*, William Welsh *(Gen. Lemuel Sidall)*, Lloyd Whitlock *(Jack Prescott)*, Otto Hoffman *(Seth Kehr)*, Edwards Davis *(Attorney Ellison)*, Wilfred Lucas *(James Presbury)*, Ed Brady *(deputy sheriff)*, Freeman Wood *(Stanley Baird)*.

Society drama. Source: David Graham Phillips, *The Price She Paid* (New York, 1912). Young society girl Mildred Gower is forced to accept the proposal of General Sidall to save her extravagant mother from bankruptcy, but she has a strong affection for young Dr. Keith. Disgusted with her marriage, she leaves Sidall but falls victim to a plot to trap her aboard his yacht. In an ensuing fire she is rescued by Keith, who has fallen in love with her. *Bankruptcy. Marriage. Infidelity. Ship fires.*

THE PRIDE OF PALOMAR **F2.4327**

Cosmopolitan Corp. *Dist* Paramount Pictures. 26 Nov **1922** [c15 Nov 1922; LP18459]. Si; b&w. 35mm. 8 reels, 7,494 ft.

Dir Frank Borzage. *Scen* Grant Carpenter, John Lynch. *Photog* Chester A. Lyons.

Cast: Forrest Stanley *(Don Mike Farrell)*, Marjorie Daw *(Kay Parker)*, Tote Du Crow *(Pablo)*, James Barrows *(Father Dominic)*, Joseph Dowling *(Don Miguel)*, Alfred Allen *(John Parker)*, George Nichols *(Conway)*, Warner Oland *(Okada)*, Mrs. Jessie Hebbard *(Mrs. Parker)*, Percy Williams *(butler)*, Mrs. George Hernandez *(Caroline)*, Edward Brady *(Lostolet)*, Carmen Arselle *(Mrs. Supaldio)*, Eagle Eye *(Nogi)*, Most Mattoe *(Alexandria)*.

Melodrama. Source: Peter Bernard Kyne, *The Pride of Palomar* (New York, 1921). Mike Farrell, the son of a Spanish don, comes home from his army service to discover that his father is dead and his ranch, Palomar, is in the hands of John Parker. While Parker is maneuvering to turn Palomar over to Okada (a Japanese potato baron who desires the land for a colonization scheme), Mike falls in love with Kay Parker and by a clever ruse and with a good horse regains the ranch. *Veterans. Japanese. Colonization. Potatoes. California.*

THE PRIDE OF PAWNEE **F2.4328**

FBO Pictures. 9 Jun **1929** [c9 Jul 1929; LP573]. Si; b&w. 35mm. 6 reels, 4,750 ft.

Dir Robert De Lacy. *Screenplay* Frank Howard Clark. *Titl* Helen Gregg. *Story* Joseph Kane. *Photog* Nick Musuraca. *Film Ed* Jack Kitchen. *Asst Dir* John Burch.

Cast: Tom Tyler *(Kirk Stockton)*, Ethlyne Clair *(Madge Wilson)*, Barney Furey *(Scotty Wilson)*, Frankie Darrow *(Jerry Wilson)*, Jack Hilliard *(George La Forte)*, Lew Meehan *(André Jeel)*, Jimmy Casey

(Jeel's henchman).

Western melodrama. "The Wolves" are a renegade band posing as Indians and are led by George La Forte unbeknownst to the members of the miner organization of which he is the head. The gang, on one of its raids, holds up a stagecoach carrying Madge Wilson and her little brothers, the children of miner Scotty Wilson. Although a Wells Fargo man named Kirk Stockwood manages temporarily to halt the gang in its nefarious pursits, he is unable to prevent La Forte from developing an unwanted affection for Madge, who is not at all averse to Stockwood's attentions. Stockwood is held for ransom, which La Forte will pay if Madge marries him. Kirk manages to arrive in time to block Madge's forthcoming marriage to La Forte, allowing them to develop their mutal affection. *Miners. Gangs. Ransom. Marriage. Stagecoach robberies. Wells Fargo & Co..*

PRIDE OF SUNSHINE ALLEY **F2.4329**

Bud Barsky Corp. *Dist* Sunset Productions. 2 Sep **1924** [New York State license]. Si; b&w. 35mm. 5 reels.

Supv Bud Barsky. *Dir* William James Craft. *Story* Samuel M. Pyke. *Photog* Arthur Reeves.

Cast: Kenneth McDonald *(Tim)*, Monte Collins *(Pat)*, Violet Schram *(Mary O'Neill)*, Eddie O'Brien, William Gould, Phil Ford, Edith Yorke, Charles K. French.

Comedy-melodrama. Tim, a rookie policeman, becomes engaged to Mary O'Neill, whose brother is mixed up with a gang of car thieves. One of the gang, Red Mike, makes himself obnoxious to Mary (who had once rejected his marriage proposal), and Tim beats him in a fight. To gain revenge, Mike frames Tim's father, Pat, for murder, and Tim takes the blame. Tim is released on bail and through Mary's brother learns that Mike was behind the frameup. He brings the gang to justice, is reinstated on the force, and marries Mary. *Police. Gangs. Brother-sister relationship. Frameup.*

THE PRIDE OF THE FORCE **F2.4330**

Dist Rayart Pictures. 11 Sep **1925** [New York State license]. Si; b&w. 35mm. 5 reels, 5,164 ft.

Dir Duke Worne. *Scen* Arthur Hoerl.

Cast: Tom Santschi *(Officer Moore)*, Edythe Chapman *(Mother Moore)*, Gladys Hulette *(Mary Moore)*, James Morrison *(Jimmy Moore)*, Francis X. Bushman, Jr. *(Jack Griffen)*, Crauford Kent *(Charley Weldon)*, Joseph Girard *(police captain)*.

Melodrama. Popular patrolman Danny Moore fails of promotion when he stops to aid an injured child and lets several thugs escape. When Danny is later informed of the plans of a criminal gang to rob Jack Griffen's bank, he gets departmental permission to set a trap and rounds up the robbers, gaining himself his promotion at last. It is a hollow honor, however, for, along with the thieves, he had to arrest his own daughter, Mary, who seemed to be an accomplice of the thieves. Jack Griffen, who is in love with Mary, comes forward, however, and proves the girl's innocence. Danny gets his sergeant's stripes, and Mary and Jack make plans to get married. *Police. Bankers. Gangs. Fatherhood. Bank robberies.*

THE PRIMAL LAW **F2.4331**

Fox Film Corp. 11 Sep **1921** [c11 Sep 1921; LP17000]. Si; b&w. 35mm. 6 reels, 5,320 ft.

Pres by William Fox. *Dir* Bernard J. Durning. *Scen* Paul Schofield. *Story* E. Lloyd Sheldon. *Photog* Lucien Andriot.

Cast: Dustin Farnum *(Brian Wayne)*, Mary Thurman *(Janice Webb)*, Harry Dunkinson *(Carson)*, Philo McCullough *(Travers)*, William Lowery *(Meacham)*, Charles Gorman *(Norton)*, Glen Cavender *(Ruis)*, Frankie Lee *(Bobbie Carson)*, Rosita Marstini *(La Belle)*, Allan Cavan *(Mat Lane)*, Edwin Booth Tilton *(Peter Webb)*.

Western melodrama. Janice Webb comes from the East with her father and Walter Travers to the western ranch of Brian Wayne and Carson. Travers, who plans to marry Janice, plots to depreciate the land value of the property by stealing cattle and having the ranch raided by a band of villains headed by Ruis. Carson is killed, but in his dying moments he has Brian promise to keep his young son Bobbie from his notorious mother, La Belle, who deserted him as an infant. At last Brian agrees to sell the ranch to Travers, but Bobbie reveals that the men have discovered oil on the ranch. Realizing that he has been tricked, Brian destroys the deed. Travers tries to fight the case in court, but justice prevails and Brian also wins Janice. *Ranches. Oil. Fatherhood. Land rights. Documentation.*

THE PRIMAL LURE (Reissue) **F2.4332**

Kay-Bee Pictures. *Dist* Film Distributors League. 3 Sep **1921** [trade review]. Si; b&w. 35mm. 5 reels.

Note: A William S. Hart film originally released by Triangle Film Corp. on 21 May 1916.

PRIMITIVE LOVE **F2.4333**

Frank E. Kleinschmidt. ca28 May **1927** [New York showing]. Si; b&w. 35mm. 6 reels, 5,400 ft.

Dir Frank E. Kleinschmidt. *Photog* Frank E. Kleinschmidt.

Cast: Ok-Ba-Ok *(Modern Caveman)*, Sloca Bruna *(His Wife)*, Wenga *(Flapper Daughter)*.

Documentary. A portrayal of the Eskimo way of life, which focuses on a family consisting of father, mother, and two grown daughters and on several small boys and two young trappers. There is an effort to give some continuity to the sequences with the courtship of a daughter by rival trappers, but the emphasis is on the daily struggle for existence in the Arctic wastes—including scenes of hunting a polar bear on ice floes, 'hand-to-hand' combat with the bear, and a walrus hunt. *Trappers. Eskimos. Arctic regions. Alaska. Polar bears. Walruses.*

THE PRIMITIVE LOVER **F2.4334**

Constance Talmadge Film Co. *Dist* Associated First National Pictures. ca20 May **1922** [Cincinnati premiere; c5 May 1922: LP17826]. Si; b&w. 35mm. 7 reels, 6,172 ft.

Pres by Joseph M. Schenck. *Dir* Sidney Franklin. *Scen* Frances Marion. *Photog* David Abel. *Art Dir* Stephen Goosson.

Cast: Constance Talmadge *(Phyllis Tomley)*, Harrison Ford *(Hector Tomley)*, Kenneth Harlan *(Donald Wales)*, Joe Roberts *("Roaring" Bill Rivers)*, Charles Pino *(Indian herder)*, Chief Big Tree *(Indian chief)*, Mathilda Brundage *(Mrs. Graham)*, George Pierce *(Judge Henseed)*, Clyde Benson *(attorney)*.

Romantic comedy. Source: Edgar Selwyn, *The Divorcée* (a play; publication undetermined). Phyllis Tomley, a romance-stricken woman, is married to the prosaic Hector, who fears the memory of Wales, a former rival who has supposedly died while exploring in South America. Wales returns and impresses Phyllis with wondrous stories of his adventures; Hector, however, informs her that his "death" was a publicity hoax to promote his new novel; and Wales accuses Hector of robbing him of Phyllis. When she is about to begin divorce proceedings in Reno, Hector is inspired by an Indian chief's unruly treatment of his squaw to kidnap both Phyllis and Wales, taking them to a mountain cabin. Frantic with hunger, Phyllis visits Hector's cabin, insults him, and is promptly spanked. While Wales escapes and goes for help, Hector rescues Phyllis from a Mexican herder and is consequently reconciled to her. *Novelists. Indians of North America. Divorce. Hoaxes. Reno.*

THE PRIMROSE PATH **F2.4335**

Arrow Pictures. 15 Sep **1925** [c5 Sep 1925; LP21793]. Si; b&w. 35mm. 6 reels.

Dir Harry O. Hoyt. *Screenplay* Leah Baird. *Photog* André Barlatier.

Cast: Wallace MacDonald *(Bruce Armstrong)*, Clara Bow *(Marilyn Merrill)*, Arline Pretty *(Helen)*, Stuart Holmes *(Tom Canfield)*, Pat Moore *(Jimmy Armstrong)*, Tom Santschi *(Big Jim Snead)*, Lydia Knott *(Mrs. Armstrong)*, Templar Saxe *(Dude Talbot)*.

Melodrama. Source: E. Lanning Masters, "The Primrose Path" (publication undetermined). Bruce Armstrong, the weak-willed son of a wealthy family, gambles with Tom Canfield and writes bad checks to cover his losses. To save himself from jail, Bruce agrees to help Canfield in his smuggling operations. During a fight over jewels, Big Jim Snead kills Canfield and attacks Bruce, who kills Snead in self-defense. The only witness to the shooting seems to be Jimmy Armstrong, Bruce's little brother, whom he has crippled in a drunken fit. Rather than subject the child to the rigors of a murder trial, Bruce confesses to Snead's murder. Dude Talbot, another of Canfield's gang, who also witnessed the killing, puts his own freedom in jeopardy and returns to testify at Bruce's trial, demonstrating by his testimony that Bruce killed Snead in self-defense. Bruce is pardoned and marries Marilyn Merrill, a beautiful dancer who stood by him through thick and thin. *Gamblers. Smugglers. Brothers. Cripples. Dancers. Murder. Trials.*

A PRINCE OF A KING **F2.4336**

Z. A. Stegmuller. *Dist* Selznick Distributing Corp. 13 Oct **1923** [c13 Oct 1923; LP19542]. Si; b&w. 35mm. 6 reels, 5,217 ft.

Dir Albert Austin. *Adapt* Douglas Doty.

Cast: Dinky Dean *(Gigi, the Prince)*, Virginia Pearson *(Queen Claudia)*, Eric Mayne *(King Lorenzo)*, John Sainpolis *(Mario)*, Joseph Swickard *(Urbano)*, Mitchell Lewis *(Andrea, the giant)*, Sam De Grasse *(Duke Roberto)*, Brutus *(himself, a dog)*.

Juvenile melodrama. Source: Alice Farwell Brown, "John of the Woods" (publication undetermined). Duke Roberto, who poisons King Lorenzo to seize the throne, seeks to kill the heir, Prince Gigi. A troupe of Gypsy acrobats finds the prince, and their leader, Andrea, adopts him. Finally the old court physician discovers Gigi; he is restored to the throne and punishes his enemies. *Acrobats. Gypsies. Royalty. Imaginary kingdoms. Dogs.*

THE PRINCE OF BROADWAY **F2.4337**

Chadwick Pictures. 1 Jan **1926** [c3 Dec 1925; LP22072]. Si; b&w. 35mm. 6 reels, 5,800 ft.

Supv Hampton Del Ruth. *Dir* John Gorman. *Adapt* Frederic Chapin.

Cast: George Walsh *(George Burke)*, Alyce Mills *(Nancy Lee)*, Freeman Wood *(Wade Turner)*, Capt. Robert Roper *(The Champion)*, Tommy Ryan *(Jack Root, matchmaker)*, Charles McHugh *(Tim McCane)*, G. Howe Black *("Snowball")*, Frankie Genaro, Ad Wolgast, Billy Papke, Leach Cross, Gene Delmont *(The Fighters)*.

Melodrama. Source: John Gorman, unidentified play. George Burke, heavyweight boxing champion of the world, is called "The Prince of Broadway" because he trains by drinking and dancing all night. After he is knocked out, his manager tears up his contract and tells him he is through. Actress Nancy Lee, his childhood sweetheart, rescues him from the gutter and sends him to the ranch owned by her admirer, Wade Turner. Wade, jealous of George, tells his foreman, Buck Marshall, to hinder George's comeback. Former champion and neighbor Jim Jeffries offers to help George get back into condition. Wade tells Nancy that George is not training, but she does not believe him. She goes out to the ranch and uncovers the conspiracy. George regains the championship and wins Nancy's hand. *Prizefighters. Ranch foremen. Actors. James J. Jeffries.*

PRINCE OF DIAMONDS **F2.4338**

Columbia Pictures. 26 Mar **1930** [c12 Apr 1930; LP1230]. Sd (Movietone); b&w. 35mm. 7 reels, 6,383 or 6,418 ft. [Also si.]

Prod Harry Cohn. *Dir* Karl Brown, A. H. Van Buren. *Adapt* Paul Hervey Fox. *Story* Gene Markey. *Photog* Ted Tetzlaff. *Art Dir* Harrison Wiley. *Film Ed* David Berg. *Ch Sd Engr* John P. Livadary. *Sd Mix Engr* E. L. Bernds. *Asst Dir* Buddy Coleman.

Cast: Aileen Pringle *(Eve Marley)*, Ian Keith *(Rupert Endon)*, Fritzi Ridgeway *(Lolah)*, Tyrrell Davis *(Lord Adrian)*, Claude King *(Gilbert Crayle)*, Tom Ricketts *(Williams)*, E. Alyn Warren *(Li Fang)*, Gilbert Emery *(Smith, the Cockney)*, Frederick Sullivan *(Ormsley)*, Sybil Grove *(Miss Wren)*, Col. G. L. McDonell *(Betterton)*, Joyzelle *(dancing girl)*.

Adventure melodrama. Gilbert Crayle, a wealthy diamond merchant, purchases the ancestral castle of Rupert Endon, a bankrupt English aristocrat who has won the love of Eve Marley, once engaged to Crayle. Eve's brother, Lord Adrian, schemes with Crayle to have Endon falsely accused of stealing a diamond; and to save Endon from prison, Eve agrees to marry Crayle. Endon escapes and by cargo steamer goes to China, where he acquires the reputation of a fearless adventurer. Through the auspices of Li Fang and a gang of cutthroats, he discovers a diamond mine in the jungle and with his fortune returns to London to seek revenge. He creates a furore in the financial world and brings Crayle to the brink of ruin; in a confrontation, Crayle is shot; but Lolah, a native girl who loves Endon, admits to the crime and kills herself to escape capture. *Diamond merchants. Aristocrats. Adventurers. Courtship. Diamond mines. Jungles. England. London. China.*

THE PRINCE OF HEADWAITERS **F2.4339**

Sam E. Rork Productions. *Dist* First National Pictures. 9 Jul **1927** [New York opening; released 17 Jul; c6 Jun 1927; LP24039]. Si; b&w. 35mm. 7 reels, 6,400 ft.

Pres by Sam E. Rork. *Dir* John Francis Dillon. *Adapt* Jane Murfin. *Photog* James Van Trees.

Cast: Lewis Stone *(Pierre)*, Priscilla Bonner *(Faith Cable)*, E. J. Ratcliffe *(John Cable)*, Lilyan Tashman *(Mae Morin)*, John Patrick *(Barry Frost)*, Robert Agnew *(Elliott Cable)*, Ann Rork *(Beth)*, Cleve Moore, Dick Folkens, Lincoln Stedman *(college boys)*, Cecille Evans *(Susanne)*, Marion McDonald *(Judy)*, Nita Cavalier *(Elsie)*.

Society drama. Source: Viola Brothers Shore and Garrett Fort, "The Prince of Headwaiters," in *Liberty Magazine* (3:41–44, 9 Apr 1927). Pierre, a Paris art student, marries Faith Cable, daughter of an aristocratic New England family, against the wishes of her father, who forces her to abandon her husband. Faith dies, and Pierre remains ignorant of the fact that before her death she gave birth to a son. Years later, as headwaiter of the Ritz Hotel, Pierre meets three college boys and their girls during a New Year's celebration. In his efforts to save one of them from a notorious gold digger, he discovers that the boy is his son. John Cable warns Pierre that he will ruin the boy's life if he reveals the truth to him; but Pierre is determined to save his son, though he is insulted for interfering. Enlisting the aid of his son's sweetheart, Beth, he manages to save the boy from disgrace and reunite him with Beth without divulging his own identity. *Waiters. Students. New Englanders. Marriage. Social classes. Fatherhood. New Year's Eve. Paris. Ritz Hotel (Paris).*

THE PRINCE OF HEARTS **F2.4340**

Imperial Pictures. *Dist* Classplay Pictures. 19 Dec **1929** [New York State license]. Si? b&w. 35mm. 6 reels.

Dir Cliff Wheeler. *Story* John Reinhardt.

Cast: Norman Kerry *(Prince Casimir)*, Barbara Worth *(Nancy Hamilton)*, John Reinhardt *(Prince Milan)*, George Fawcett *(King Alexander)*, Julia Griffith *(Queen Marie)*, Hans Joby *(Prime Minister)*, Sam Blum *(innkeeper)*.

Melodrama(?). No information about the precise nature of this film has been found.

A PRINCE OF HIS RACE **F2.4341**

Colored Players Film Corp. 2 Jul **1926** [New York State license]. Si; b&w. 35mm. 8 reels.

Dir Roy Calnek.

Cast: Harry Henderson *(Tom Beuford)*, William A. Clayton, Jr. *(Jim Stillman)*, Lawrence Chenault *(Mr. Arnold)*, Arline Mickey *(The Arnolds' maid)*, Ethel Smith *(Miss Arnold)*, Shingzie Howard.

Melodrama. "Tom Beuford, a member of good family, has fallen into disgrace through unscrupulous associates and is found in jail serving the last 6 months of a 5 year term for manslaughter. His sweetheart's appeal to the Governor results in a 24 hour leave of absence so that he can solace his dying mother. A nerve-wracking, death-defying drive over the State highway brings him to her bedside in time to see her breathe her last. En route home, the auto in which Tom is riding is seen by the man whose testimony sent Tom to jail. After Tom's release from jail, he is thwarted in his attempt to see his sweetheart by the same man who sent him to jail. This rival advises Tom to leave town and, during Tom's absence, succeeds in gaining the consent of the young woman through her father, and everything is arranged for the wedding. Just as the wedding is about to be performed, Tom returns and there is an unexpected climax." (*New York Age*, 4 Dec 1926.) *Filial relations. Negro life. Jails. Manslaughter. Weddings.*

Note: This film was manufactured during April and May of 1926.

THE PRINCE OF PEANUTS *see* **HOW TO HANDLE WOMEN**

THE PRINCE OF PEP **F2.4342**

Carlos Productions. *Dist* Film Booking Offices of America. 20 Dec **1925** [c5 Nov 1925; LP21973]. Si; b&w. 35mm. 5 reels, 4,911 ft.

Pres by A. Carlos. *Dir* Jack Nelson. *Athletic stunts conceived and executed by* Richard Talmadge. *Story-Cont* James Bell Smith. *Photog* William Marshall, Jack Stevens. *Tech Dir* Eugene McMurtrie. *Ed* Doane Harrison.

Cast: Richard Talmadge *(Dr. James Leland)*, Nola Luxford *(Marion Nord)*, Carol Wines *(Ruth Wheeler)*, Marcella Daly *(see note)*, Brinsley Shaw *(Hugh Powell)*, Victor Dillingham *(Buck Sanders)*, Arthur Conrad *("Eddie-the-Sniff" [Ed])*.

Melodrama. Dr. James Leland, a wealthy and philanthropic young physician who has inherited his wealth from his father, spends most of his time entertaining children in the city hospitals. His secretary and business manager, Hugh Powell (also inherited from his father), is secretly allied with dope-peddler Buck Sanders. Powell is assisted by Ruth Wheeler, a pretty girl in love with him but engaged to Dr. Jim. When Dr. Jim catches Powell stealing drugs, Powell knocks him unconscious and—thinking him dead—dumps him in the river. Though Dr. Jim regains consciousness, he has lost his memory and develops a dual personality: first as "Jimmy," who is cared for by Marion Nord, who helps her doctor father run a clinic on MacDougal Street; then as "Black Flash," a mysterious bandit—loved by Marion—who robs wealthy gamblers for the benefit of Dr. Nord's clinic. Powell bribes Sanders and his men to kidnap Marion, but Jimmy becomes aware of the plot. The police arrive to apprehend the culprits, though not before Jimmy is knocked out. Dr. Jim recovers his memory and returns to his rightful place in society with Marion by his side. *Physicians. Secretaries. Children. Narcotics. Philanthropy. Dual personality. Amnesia. Clinics. Hospitals.*

Note: Most sources give Marcella Daly in the part of *Eleanor* Wheeler, accomplice, but the title continuity in the copyright files gives Carol Wines in the part, with, however, the character name *Ruth* Wheeler.

THE PRINCE OF PILSEN **F2.4343**

Belasco Productions. *Dist* Producers Distributing Corp. 2 May **1926** [c19 Apr 1926; LP22700]. Si; b&w. 35mm. 7 reels, 6,600 ft.

Pres by John C. Flinn. *Dir* Paul Powell. *Screen Vers* Anthony Coldewey. *Photog* James C. Van Trees. *Art Dir* Charles L. Cadwallader. *Asst Dir* William von Brincken.

Cast: George Sidney *(Hans Wagner)*, Anita Stewart *(Nellie, his daughter)*, Allan Forrest *(Frederick, Prince of Pilsen)*, Myrtle Stedman *(Princess Bertha of Thorwald)*, Otis Harlan *(bandit chief)*, Rose Tapley *(lady in waiting)*, William von Brincken *(captain of the guard)*, William von Hardenburg *(court physician)*.

Comedy-drama. Source: Frank Pixley and Gustav Luders, *The Prince of Pilsen, a Musical Comedy in Two Acts* (New York, c1902). Hans Wagner, a Cincinnati brewer who is Grand Imperial Chief of the Loyal Order of Squirrels, goes to his old Central European home, Altheim, accompanied by his daughter, Nellie, and is accorded a flattering reception. The Prince of Pilsen, who is unhappy about his impending marriage to Princess Bertha of a neighboring principality, arrives as Hans is inviting the villagers to a banquet; seeing that the prince is interested in his daughter, Hans introduces him as the son of a friend. At the banquet, Hans, in his lodge uniform, is mistaken for the prince and is driven to the castle of Thorwald; assuming that he is being "initiated," he allows himself to be taken to Princess Bertha. Meanwhile Nellie and the prince, in pursuit, are waylaid by bandits and spend the night in a cave, but they arrive at the castle in time to prevent Hans from being executed for imposture. The princess, who has fallen in love with Hans, relinquishes the prince to Nellie, and all ends happily. *Brewers. Bandits. Royalty. Jousting. Secret societies. Imaginary kingdoms. Cincinnati.*

THE PRINCE OF TEMPTERS **F2.4344**

Robert Kane Productions. *Dist* First National Pictures. 17 Oct **1926** [c6 Oct 1926; LP23192]. Si; b&w. 35mm. 8 reels, 7,780 ft.

Pres by Robert T. Kane. *Dir* Lothar Mendes. *Scen* Paul Bern. *Photog* Ernest Haller.

Cast: Lois Moran *(Monica)*, Ben Lyon *(Francis)*, Lya De Putti *(Dolores)*, Ian Keith *(Mario Ambrosio, later Baron Humberto Giordano)*, Mary Brian *(Mary)*, Olive Tell *(Duchess of Chatsfield)*, Sam Hardy *(Apollo Beneventa)*, Henry Vibart *(Duke of Chatsfield)*, Judith Vosselli *(Signora Wembley)*, Frazer Coulter *(lawyer)*, J. Barney Sherry *(Papal Secretary)*.

Romantic drama. Source: Edward Phillips Oppenheim, *The Ex-Duke* (London, 1927). While in Italy, the Duke of Chatsfield secretly marries a peasant girl, and they have a child, Francis. The boy's parents die after having separated, and he is reared in a monastery. When he is 20, Francis takes his final vows, while his uncle, a duke, learns that Francis is the true heir to the dukedom; a dispensation is granted by the Pope, and the boy assumes the title. In London, Mario, a penniless novice, masquerading as Baron Giordano, hopes to marry Monica, Francis' beautiful cousin; and to eliminate his rival he engages Dolores, his ex-mistress, to ensnare Francis. He succumbs to her wiles but on a visit to his relatives falls in love with Monica, and they become engaged; Monica, however, breaks off the betrothal after finding that Dolores loves him. Francis returns, embittered, to London and embarks on a series of flirtations; but learning of Monica's acceptance of Mario's offer, he returns to the monastery. Dolores tells Monica of the Baron's scheming, kills herself, and the lovers are reconciled. *Nobility. Courtship. Primogeniture. Suicide. Monasteries. Italy. London. Papacy.*

PRINCE OF THE PLAINS **F2.4345**

Trem Carr Productions. *Dist* Rayart Pictures. Sep **1927**. Si; b&w. 35mm. 5 reels, 4,036 or 4,134 ft.

Dir Robin Williamson. *Scen* Arthur Hoerl. *Story* Victor Rousseau. *Photog* Ernest Depew.

Cast: Tex Maynard, Betty Caldwell, Walter Shumway.

Western melodrama. "Girl, beset by scheming uncle, meets her prince of the plains. They fall in love but a rival for her hand kills her uncle and blames her prince. Jailed, he escapes to capture real culprit, forces a confession and wins his girl." (*Motion Picture News Booking Guide*, [14]: 275, 1929.) *Uncles. Murder. Courtship.*

PRINCE OF THE SADDLE **F2.4346**

Fred Balshofer Productions. 11 Nov **1926** [New York State license]. Si; b&w. 35mm. 5 reels, 4,500 ft.

Cast: Fred Church, Boris Bullock.

Western melodrama(?). No information about the nature of this film has been found.

A PRINCE THERE WAS **F2.4347**

Famous Players–Lasky. *Dist* Paramount Pictures. ca13 Nov **1921** [New York premiere; released 15 Jan 1922; c26 Nov 1921; LP17247]. Si; b&w. 35mm. 6 reels, 5,553 ft.

Pres by Adolph Zukor. *Supv* Frank E. Woods. *Dir* Tom Forman. *Adapt* Waldemar Young. *Photog* Harry Perry.

Cast: Thomas Meighan *(Charles Edward Martin)*, Mildred Harris *(Katherine Woods)*, Charlotte Jackson *(Comfort Brown)*, Nigel Barrie *(Jack Carruthers)*, Guy Oliver *(Bland)*, Arthur Hull *(J. J. Stratton)*, Sylvia Ashton *(Mrs. Prouty)*, Fred Huntley *(Mr. Cricket)*.

Society melodrama. Source: George M. Cohan, *A Prince There Was, a Comedy in Three Acts* (New York, 1927). Darragh Aldrich, *Enchanted Hearts* (Garden City, New York, 1917). Charles Edward Martin, a wealthy society idler, meets Katherine Woods, whose father was ruined financially by J. J. Stratton, Martin's broker, although Martin is unaware of his scheming. Katherine is unsuccessfully trying to gain an income by writing magazine stories; but Comfort Brown, who works in her boardinghouse, seeks a magazine editor to plead Katherine's case and encounters Martin, a friend of the editor, whom she likens to a prince she has read about in fairy tales. Under the name of Prince, Martin takes up residence in the boardinghouse, posing as assistant editor of the magazine; when he falls in love with Katherine, he buys out the magazine so as to publish her stories. Katherine is happy until Stratton reveals Martin's true identity and makes Katherine believe he ruined her father, but Stratton is eventually exposed and the lovers are reunited. *Authors. Editors. Brokers. Boardinghouses.*

THE PRINCESS AND THE PLUMBER **F2.4348**

Fox Film Corp. 21 Dec **1930** [c5 Nov 1930; LP1772]. Sd (Movietone); b&w. 35mm. 7 reels, 6,480 ft.

Assoc Prod Al Rockett. *Dir* Alexander Korda. *Screenplay-Dial* Howard J. Green. *Photog* L. William O'Connell, Dave Ragin. *Art Dir* Stephen Goosson. *Film Ed* Margaret V. Clancey. *Mus Dir* Arthur Kay. *Rec Engr* Arthur L. von Kirbach. *Asst Dir* Ewing Scott. *Cost* Sophie Wachner.

Cast: Charles Farrell *(Charlie Peters)*, Maureen O'Sullivan *(Princess Louise)*, H. B. Warner *(Prince Conrad of Daritzia)*, Joseph Cawthorn *(Merkl)*, Bert Roach *(Albert Bowers)*, Lucien Prival *(Baron von Kemper)*, Murray Kinnell *(Worthing)*, Louise Closser Hale *(Miss Eden)*, Arnold Lucy.

Romantic comedy. Source: Alice Duer Miller, "The Princess and the Plumber," in *Saturday Evening Post* (202:3–5, 18–19, 18–19, 14–28 Dec 1929). Louise, the unsophisticated Princess of Daritzia, goes vacationing in the mountains of Switzerland with Albert Bowers, a rich young American bachelor, and the Baron von Kemper. At a mountain cabin, the baron tries to force his attentions on the young princess but is thwarted by the intervention of Albert. Seeking revenge, the baron spreads the rumor that the princess has been compromised by Albert, supported by the fact that Albert sprains his ankle and keeps Louise out overnight. Her father demands an immediate marriage, to which the couple consent, having fallen in love. *Royalty. Nobility. Bachelors. Imaginary kingdoms. Switzerland.*

THE PRINCESS FROM HOBOKEN **F2.4349**

Tiffany Productions. 1 Mar **1927** [c16 Apr 1927; LP23870]. Si; b&w. 35mm. 6 reels, 5,419 ft.

Dir Allan Dale. *Story-Scen* Sonya Levien. *Photog* Robert Martin, Joseph Dubray. *Art Dir* Edwin B. Willis. *Film Ed* James C. McKay.

Cast: Edmund Burns *(Terence O'Brien)*, Blanche Mehaffey *(Sheila O'Toole)*, Ethel Clayton *(Mrs. O'Brien)*, Lou Tellegen *(Prince Anton Balakrieff)*, Babe London *(Princess Sonia Alexandernova Karpoff)*, Will R. Walling *(Mr. O'Brien)*, Charles McHugh *(Pa O'Toole)*, Aggie Herring *(Ma O'Toole)*, Charles Crockett *(Whiskers)*, Robert Homans *(McCoy)*, Harry Bailey *(Cohen)*, Sidney D'Albrook *(Tony)*, Broderick O'Farrell *(immigration officer)*, Boris Karloff *(Pavel)*.

Farce. To enliven their business, the O'Tooles, restaurant owners in Hoboken, New Jersey, transform their restaurant into the Russian Inn when they hear that a famous Russian princess is stranded in Chicago. Sheila, the daughter, is persuaded to impersonate the princess, who unfortunately arrives at the restaurant on opening night. Among the patrons are Terry O'Brien, who begs an introduction, and Prince Anton, an unscrupulous Russian who has been living in luxury on funds for Russian refugees. In a series of amusing complications, the prince is unmasked after he threatens to reveal Sheila's imposture. Sheila at last finds happiness with O'Brien. *Restaurateurs. Russians. Royalty. Impersonation. Hoboken.*

PRINCESS JONES **F2.4350**

Vitagraph Co. of America. Jan **1921** [c8 Jan 1921; LP16002]. Si; b&w. 35mm. 5 reels.

Dir G. V. Seyffertitz. *Scen* Sam Taylor, A. Van Buren Powell. *Story* Joseph Franklin Poland. *Photog* Vincent Scully.

Cast: Alice Calhoun *(Princess Jones)*, Vincent Coleman *(Arthur Forbes)*, Helen Du Bois *(Matilda Cotton)*, Robert Lee Keeling *(Roger Arlington)*, Robert Gaillard *(Detective Carey)*, Joseph Burke *(Jed Bramson)*, Sadie Mullen *(Tessa)*.

Light comedy. Princess Jones, a country storekeeper's niece who dreams of wealth and position, takes a vacation at a nearby fashionable resort—without realizing its cost—and meets wealthy Arthur Forbes, whose uncle sent him to the country to become an artist. Arthur's love for Princess leads him to buy her an expensive gown (Princess has given him a small amount of money for the purchase of a gown), which causes her to be mistaken for a Balkan princess by both the other guests and kidnapers; but Arthur rescues Princess and receives his uncle's approval of their marriage; and Princess becomes friends with the real princess. *Storekeepers. Uncles. Royalty. Wealth. Mistaken identity. Resorts.*

THE PRINCESS OF NEW YORK (United States/Great Britain) **F2.4351**

Famous Players–Lasky. *Dist* Paramount Pictures. 7 Aug **1921** [c8 Aug 1921; LP16845]. Si; b&w. 35mm. 5 reels, 4,984 ft.

Dir Donald Crisp. *Scen* Margaret Turnbull. *Photog* Hal Young.

Cast: David Powell *(Geoffrey Kingsward)*, Mary Glynne *(Helen Stanton)*, Saba Raleigh *(Mrs. Raffan)*, George Bellamy *(Sir George Meretham)*, Dorothy Fane *(Violet Meretham)*, Ivo Dawson *(Allan Meretham)*, Philip Hewland *(Colonel Kingsward)*, R. Heaton Grey *(Mr. Greet)*, Windham Guise *(Eardley Smith)*, Jane West *(Mrs. Eardley Smith)*, H. Lloyd *(moneylender)*, Lionel Yorke *(Reddish)*, William Parry *(magistrate)*.

Society melodrama. Source: Cosmo Hamilton, *The Princess of New York* (New York, 1911). American heiress Helen Stanton, while visiting London, is introduced to the Merethams, people of title but of bad repute. She meets Geoffrey Kingsward, who falls in love with Helen and tries to warn her but is unable to gain her confidence. Sir George induces his son, Allan, to woo Helen and thereby recoup the family fortune; when Sir George hears of her father's bankruptcy, he persuades her to pawn some jewels and lend him the money, with which he absconds. Helen is about to be arrested when Geoffrey comes to her aid; meanwhile, a letter arrives contradicting the report of her father's bankruptcy and advising her to marry Geoffrey. *Heiresses. Swindlers. Upper classes. Bankruptcy. London.*

PRINCESS OF THE DARK (Reissue) **F2.4352**

Dist Biltmore Pictures. 15 Feb **1928** [New York State license]. Si; b&w. 35mm.

Note: Originally released by Triangle Film Corp. in 1917.

THE PRINCESS ON BROADWAY **F2.4353**

Dallas M. Fitzgerald Productions. *Dist* Pathé Exchange. 13 Mar **1927** [c31 Jan 1927; LU23609]. Si; b&w. 35mm. 6 reels, 5,705 ft.

Pres by J. C. Barnstyn. *Dir* Dallas M. Fitzgerald. *Scen* Doris Schroeder. *Photog* Jack Young.

Cast: Pauline Garon *(Mary Ryan)*, Dorothy Dwan *(Rose Ryan)*, Johnny Walker *(Leon O'Day)*, Harold Miller *(Seymour)*, Ethel Clayton *(Mrs. Seymour)*, Neely Edwards *(Bill Blevins)*, Ernest Wood, George Walsh.

Comedy-drama. Source: Ethel Donoher, "Silver Lanterns" (publication undetermined). Waitress Mary Ryan loses her job, and Leon O'Day, a theatrical agent, obtains work for her in the chorus of a traveling show. Leon and his partner, Turner, induce Seymour, a young society man, to finance a new show, and they tell Seymour that Mary is a Russian princess though incognita; her impersonation completely fools Seymour, and she gets the contract. Seymour's mother invites Mary to tea, and she becomes a society sensation. Mrs. Seymour, interested in social reform, accompanies her son and Mary to the night court where Mary's missing sister, Rose, is brought in under arrest. Mary claims her sister and is denounced by Mrs. Seymour as a designing hussy. Seymour is later apologetic, but Mary realizes that she has actually loved Leon all the while. *Waitresses. Theatrical agents. Chorus girls. Sisters. Imposture. Social reform.*

THE PRINTER'S DEVIL **F2.4354**

Warner Brothers Pictures. 21 Aug **1923** [c21 Aug 1923; LP19323]. Si; b&w. 35mm. 6 reels, 5,500 ft.

Dir William Beaudine. *Story-Scen* Julien Josephson. *Film Ed* Clarence Kolster.

Cast: Wesley Barry *(Brick Hubbard)*, Harry Myers *(Sidney Fletcher)*, Kathryn McGuire *(Vivian Gates)*, Louis King *(Lem Kirk)*, George Pearce *(Ira Gates)*, Raymond Cannon *(Alec Sperry)*, Mary Halter *(Dora Kirk)*, Harry Rattenberry *(Chet Quimby)*.

Comedy-drama. Printer's devil Brick Hubbard induces Sidney Fletcher to invest in *The Gazette,* a local newspaper. Sidney writes an editorial that arouses the anger of banker Ira Gates, whose daughter, Vivian, Sidney is courting. Gates's bank is robbed, and Sidney is suspected until Brick finds the real criminals. Sidney marries Vivian after he is cleared. *Printers. Bankers. Newspapers. Courtship. Robbery.*

THE PRISONER **F2.4355**

Universal Pictures. ca18 Feb **1923** [Cleveland premiere; released 18 Mar; c7 Feb 1923; LP18665]. Si; b&w. 35mm. 5 reels, 4,795 ft.

Dir Jack Conway. *Scen* Edward T. Lowe, Jr. *Photog* Benjamin Reynolds.

Cast: Herbert Rawlinson *(Philip Quentin)*, Eileen Percy *(Dorothy Garrison)*, George Cowl *(Lord Bob)*, June Elvidge *(Lady Francis)*, Lincoln Stedman *(Dickey Savage)*, Gertrude Short *(Lady Jane)*, Bertram Grassby *(Prince Ugo Ravorelli)*, Mario Carillo *(Count Sallonica)*, Hayford Hobbs *(Duke Laselli)*, Lillian Langdon *(Mrs. Garrison)*, Bert Sprotte *(Courant)*, Boris Karloff *(Prince Kapolski)*, Esther Ralston *(Marie)*, J. P. Lockney *(Father Bivot)*.

Melodrama. Source: George Barr McCutcheon, *Castle Craneycrow* (Chicago, 1902). While traveling in Europe Philip Quentin encounters his former sweetheart, Dorothy Garrison, and finds that she is now engaged to Prince Ugo Ravorelli, whom Philip recognizes as the man wanted for a murder in Brazil. Philip avoids being trapped by Prince Ugo into a fatal duel, then kidnaps Dorothy at her wedding. She is at first adamant, but after Philip saves her from Courant, the prince's henchman, Dorothy realizes she loves Philip. *Nobility. Murder. Imaginary kingdoms. Duels.*

THE PRISONER OF ZENDA **F2.4356**

Metro Pictures. 31 Jul **1922** [New York premiere; released 11 Sep; c29 Jul 1922; LP18096]. Si; b&w. 35mm. 10 reels, 10,467 ft.

Prod-Dir Rex Ingram. *Scen* Mary O'Hara. *Photog* John F. Seitz. *Prod Mgr* Starret Ford.

Cast: Lewis Stone *(Rudolf Rassendyll/King Rudolf)*, Alice Terry *(Princess Flavia)*, Robert Edeson *(Colonel Sapt)*, Stuart Holmes *(Duke [Black] Michael)*, Ramon Samaniegos *(Rupert of Hentzau)*, Barbara La Marr *(Antoinette de Mauban)*, Malcolm McGregor *(Count von Tarlenheim)*, Edward Connelly *(Marshall von Strakencz)*, Lois Lee *(Countess Helga)*.

Romantic adventure. Source: Edward E. Rose, *The Prisoner of Zenda; a Romantic Play and a Prologue in Four Acts* (c1897). Anthony Hope, *The Prisoner of Zenda; Being the History of Three Months in the Life of an English Gentleman* (New York, 1896). While the weak and drunken King Rudolph of Ruritania awaits his coronation, he is drugged by his brother, Black Michael, who is preparing a coup d'état. Michael's plans are thwarted by the substitution at Rudolph's coronation of Rassendyll, an Englishman who is the king's exact double. Michael, discovering the ruse, kidnaps the real king and holds him captive in the castle at Zenda. Rassendyll aids in the king's rescue and renounces the love of the Princess Flavia, the king's bethrothed, to return to England. *Royalty. Brothers. English. Doubles. Imaginary kingdoms.*

PRISONERS **F2.4357**

Walter Morosco Productions. *Dist* First National Pictures. 19 May **1929** [c21 May 1929; LP399]. Talking sequences (Vitaphone); b&w. 35mm. 8 reels, 7,857 ft. [Also si; 7,383 ft.]

Pres by Richard A. Rowland. *Dir* William A. Seiter. *Screenplay-Dial* Forrest Halsey. *Titl* Paul Perez. *Photog* Lee Garmes. *Film Ed* LeRoy

Stone.

Cast: Corinne Griffith *(Riza)*, Ian Keith *(Nicholas)*, Otto Matiesen *(Sebfi)*, Baron von Hesse *(Kore)*, Julanne Johnston *(Lenke)*, Ann Schaeffer *(Aunt Maria)*, Bela Lugosi *(The Man)*, Charles Clary *(Warden Rimmer)*, Jean Laverty, James Ford, Harry Northrup.

Drama. Source: Ferenc Molnár, *Prisoners* (Joseph Szebeyei, trans.; Indianapolis, c1925). Riza steals 300 florins from a cafe owner, and Nicholas, a young lawyer, is assigned to defend her in court. Riza has seen Nicholas before and declares her love for him. Nicholas disbelieves her but listens to her story, learning that she stole the money in order to buy finery with which she hoped to attract his attention. Nicholas' fiancée, Lenke, begins to suspect that he is infatuated with Riza and secretly offers to repay the 300 florins to the cafe owner if Riza will leave town. Riza refuses and is sentenced to 8 months in jail. Nicholas recognizes her deep love for him in this sacrificial act and, discovering an equal love in his own heart, determines to marry Riza when she is released from jail. *Restaurateurs. Lawyers. Theft. Trials. Jails.*

PRISONERS OF LOVE **F2.4358**

Betty Compson Productions. *Dist* Goldwyn Distributing Corp. Jan **1921** [c8 Jan 1921; LP16147]. Si; b&w. 35mm. 6 reels, 5,884 ft.

Dir Arthur Rosson. *Story* Catherine Henry. *Photog* Ernest G. Palmer, Ross Fisher.

Cast: Betty Compson *(Blanche Davis)*, Ralph Lewis *(her father)*, Claire McDowell *(her mother)*, Clara Horton *(her sister)*, Emory Johnson *(James Randolph)*, Kate Toncray *(his mother)*, Roy Stewart *(Martin Blair)*.

Melodrama. Indignant over the sudden discovery of her father's double life, Blanche Davis leaves home and under an assumed name obtains employment in San Francisco with lawyers Blair and Randolph. She becomes involved with Randolph, and though not married they live as man and wife. When her father comes to San Francisco with her younger sister, Randolph falls in love with the latter and Blair, loving Blanche, determines to see her righted and takes her east. Her father gives Randolph a check to settle matters with his former mistress; seeing her father's signature, Blanche decides, for her sister's sake, not to interfere with their marriage. *Sisters. Mistresses. Lawyers. Fatherhood. Marriage—Common law. Infidelity. San Francisco.*

PRISONERS OF THE STORM (Universal-Jewel) **F2.4359**

Universal Pictures. 24 Nov **1926** [trade review; released 19 Dec; c2 Aug 1926; LP23001]. Si; b&w. 35mm. 6 reels, 6,102 ft.

Pres by Carl Laemmle. *Dir* Lynn Reynolds. *Adapt-Scen* Charles A. Logue. *Photog* Gilbert Warrenton.

Cast: House Peters *("Bucky" Malone)*, Peggy Montgomery *(Joan Le Grande)*, Walter McGrail *(Sergeant McClellan)*, Harry Todd *(Pete Le Grande)*, Fred De Silva *(Dr. Chambers)*, Clark Comstock *(Angus McLynn)*, Evelyn Selbie *(Lillian Nicholson)*.

Northwest melodrama. Source: James Oliver Curwood, "The Quest of Joan" (publication undetermined). Miners Bucky Malone and Pierre Le Grande are closing their northern mine for the winter when Sergeant McClellan of the Mounted Police overhears their trivial quarrel; later, he sees Le Grande's dogsled arrive at its destination without Le Grande. McClellan finds evidence that Le Grande has been murdered and suspects Malone; attempting to make an arrest, the sergeant is wounded, then carried to a cabin by Malone, who goes to the settlement for a doctor. There he meets Le Grande's daughter, Joan, and Dr. Chambers, a disbarred physician, but a blizzard keeps the doctor from making the trip; ultimately, however, Joan and the doctor follow Malone to the cabin. Chambers tries to turn Joan against Malone, accusing him of killing her father; the cabin is buried by a snowslide; and in their efforts to escape, Chambers is killed by an explosion and exposed as the murderer. *Miners. Physicians. Murder. Canadian Northwest. Northwest Mounted Police. Blizzards. Avalanches.*

PRIVATE AFFAIRS **F2.4360**

Renaud Hoffman Productions. *Dist* Producers Distributing Corp. 20 Apr **1925** [c28 Apr 1925; LP21443]. Si; b&w. 35mm. 6 reels, 6,132 ft.

Pres by Gilbert Heyfron. *Dir* Renaud Hoffman. *Adapt-Scen-Titl* Alfred A. Cohn. *Photog* Jack MacKenzie.

Cast: Gladys Hulette *(Agnes Bomar)*, Robert Agnew *(Fred Henley)*, Mildred Harris *(Amy Lufkin)*, David Butler *(Lee Cross)*, Arthur Hoyt *(Alf Stacy)*, Betty Francisco *(Irma Stacy)*, Willis Marks *(Howard Bomar)*, Charles Sellon *(Joe Hines)*, Hardee Kirkland *(Andy Gillespie)*, J. Frank Glendon *(John Maddox)*, Frank Coffyn *(Ben Morse)*, Charles W. Mack.

Drama. Source: George Patullo, "The Ledger of Life," in *Saturday Evening Post* (194:10–11, 4 Mar 1922). After the death of the postmaster in the small town of Twin Forks, a package of letters is found in his desk, dated 5 years previously and never delivered. The delayed letters are put in the mail, causing numerous complications in the lives of the local residents. Amy Lufkin, complacently married to a fine man, receives a proposal from Lee Cross, a former sweetheart who in the interim has made a fortune in oil. Andy Gillespie, the town drunkard, discovers that he has inherited a fortune. Irma Stacy, the druggist's wife, opens a letter from her husband's old sweetheart just as he opens one from her old sweetheart, causing a good deal of anger in both of them. Amy becomes dissatisfied with her lot until Lee Cross returns to town and proves to have become a vain, vulgar dandy; she then returns gratefully to domestic life. Irma Stacy and her husband make up. Fred Henley's dog-raising scheme fails, and Andy, more sober than usual, appoints him the superintendent of his new factories, enabling Fred to marry his sweetheart, Agnes. *Pharmacists. Postmasters. Oilmen. Dandies. Smalltown life. Marriage. Alcoholism. Postal service. Dogs.*

PRIVATE IZZY MURPHY **F2.4361**

Warner Brothers Pictures. 30 Oct **1926** [c20 Oct 1926; LP23177]. Si; b&w. 35mm. 8 reels, 7,889 ft.

Dir Lloyd Bacon. *Adapt* Philip Lonergan. *Story* Raymond L. Schrock, Edward Clark. *Camera* Virgil Miller. *Asst Camera* Walter Robinson. *Asst Dir* Sandy Roth.

Cast: George Jessel *(Izzy Murphy)*, Patsy Ruth Miller *(Eileen Cohannigan)*, Vera Gordon *(Sara Goldberg)*, Nat Carr *(The Shadchen, Moe Ginsburg)*, William Strauss *(Jacob Goldberg)*, Spec O'Donnell *(The Monohan Kid)*, Gustav von Seyffertitz *(Cohannigan)*, Douglas Gerrard *(Robert O'Malley)*, Tom Murray *(The Attorney)*.

Comedy-drama. Isadore Goldberg, an enterprising Russian Jew, comes to the United States and establishes himself in the delicatessen business so that he can one day send for his parents. Forced to vacate his store, Izzy relocates in an Irish neighborhood; there, after he changes his surname to "Murphy," his business prospers. While waiting for a subway train, Izzy recovers a girl's handkerchief; later, he meets her in his store and learns that she is Eileen Cohannigan, from whose father he buys foodstuffs. After the arrival of Izzy's parents, he embarks for France with an all-Irish regiment and inspires his comrades to deeds of valor. He is welcomed home by Cohannigan, but when Cohannigan learns that he is Jewish, he denounces his daughter for loving him. With the aid of his service buddies, however, Izzy and Eileen head for City Hall to be married. *Immigrants. Jews. Irish. Russians. Prejudice. Courtship. Delicatessens. World War I. New York City.*

THE PRIVATE LIFE OF HELEN OF TROY **F2.4362**

First National Pictures. 9 Dec **1927** [New York premiere; released 8 Jan 1928; c23 Dec 1927; LP24793]. Si; b&w. 35mm. 8 reels, 7,694 ft.

Pres by Richard A. Rowland. *Prod-Adapt-Scen* Carey Wilson. *Dir* Alexander Korda. *Titl* Ralph Spence, Gerald Duffy, Casey Robinson. *Photog* Lee Garmes, Sid Hickox. *Film Ed* Harold Young. *Mus Settings* Carl Edouarde. *Cost* Max Ree.

Cast: Maria Corda *(Helen)*, Lewis Stone *(Menelaus)*, Ricardo Cortez *(Paris)*, George Fawcett *(Eteoneus)*, Alice White *(Adraste)*, Gordon Elliott *(Telemachus)*, Tom O'Brien *(Ulysses)*, Bert Sprotte *(Achilles)*, Mario Carillo *(Ajax)*, Charles Puffy *(Malapokitoratoreadetos)*, George Kotsonaros *(Hector)*, Constantine Romanoff *(Aeneas)*, Emilio Borgato *(Sarpedon)*, Alice Adair *(Aphrodite)*, Helen Fairweather *(Athena)*, Virginia Thomas *(Hera)*, Gus Partos.

Satiric comedy. Source: John Erskine, *The Private Life of Helen of Troy* (Indianapolis, 1925). Robert Emmet Sherwood, *The Road to Rome, a Play* (New York, 1927). "Queen Helen of Troy, piqued by her husband's lack of interest in her, elopes with Paris to Sparta. Menelaus, her husband, egged on by his henchman, starts a war with Paris, finally effecting the return of Helen. The time-honored custom demands that he have the pleasure of killing her, but her seductive loveliness restrains him. And so at the end of the story, we find Helen engaging in a new flirtation with the Prince of Ithaca." *(Moving Picture World, 17 Dec 1927, p23.) Troy. Sparta. Helen of Troy. Paris Prince of Troy. Achilles. Ajax. Hector. Aeneas. Sarpedon. Ulysses. Telemachus. Menelaus. Mythological characters.*

Note: Also known as *Helen of Troy*.

A PRIVATE SCANDAL **F2.4363**

Realart Pictures. Jun **1921** [c14 Jun 1921; LP16671]. Si; b&w. 35mm. 5 reels, 4,363 ft.

Dir Chester M. Franklin. *Scen* Eve Unsell. *Story* Hector Turnbull. *Photog* J. O. Taylor.

Cast: May McAvoy *(Jeanne Millett)*, Bruce Gordon *(Jerry Hayes)*, Ralph Lewis *(Phillip Lawton)*, Kathlyn Williams *(Carol Lawton)*, Lloyd Whitlock *(Alec Crosby)*, Gladys Fox *(Betty Lawton)*.

Domestic melodrama. French orphan Jeanne Millett is adopted by Philip Lawton and his wife, Betty, and lives with them on their California estate, where she captures the heart of horsetrainer Jerry Hayes. When Betty fancies herself neglected and becomes involved with Alec Crosby, Lawton returns from a business trip, his suspicion and jealousy awakened by gossip. To shield Betty, Jeanne claims that Crosby is her lover, and Jerry injures Crosby in a fight; but Betty confesses that the innocent girl lied to save her. Jerry is convinced of Jeanne's loyalty, and the Lawtons come to a better understanding. *Orphans. Horsetrainers. Infidelity. Jealousy. California.*

PRODIGAL DAUGHTERS **F2.4364**

Famous Players–Lasky. *Dist* Paramount Pictures. 15 Apr **1923** [c11 Apr 1923; LP18864]. Si; b&w. 35mm. 6 reels, 6,216 ft.

Pres by Jesse L. Lasky. *Dir* Sam Wood. *Scen* Monte M. Katterjohn. *Photog* Alfred Gilks.

Cast: Gloria Swanson *(Elinor ["Swiftie"] Forbes)*, Ralph Graves *(Roger Corbin)*, Vera Reynolds *(Marjory Forbes)*, Theodore Roberts *(J. D. Forbes)*, Louise Dresser *(Mrs. Forbes)*, Charles Clary *(Stanley Garside)*, Robert Agnew *(Lester Hodges)*, Maude Wayne *(Connie)*, Jiquel Lanoe *(Juda Botanya)*, Eric Mayne *(Dr. Marco Strong)*, Antonio Corsi.

Society drama. Source: Joseph Hocking, *Prodigal Daughters* (New York, 1921). "Swiftie" and Marjory Forbes—the daughters of J. D. Forbes, wealthy owner of a locomotive works, and Mrs. Forbes, a clubwoman who exercises no restraint over them—are attracted to the jazz life and eventually leave home in order to live the lives they please in Greenwich Village. Marjory marries songwriter Lester Hodges, who later deserts her. Swiftie attracts the interest of aviator Roger Corbin, employed by her father, and gambler Stanley Garside. She loses a considerable sum to Garside, then promises to marry him in 60 days when she wagers her losses against marriage. In a Christmas Eve raid by prohibition agents, however, Swiftie escapes with Roger's help and follows Marjory's example by returning home. Both girls repent; Swiftie finds happiness with Roger. *Clubwomen. Sisters. Flappers. Gamblers. Composers. Aviators. Jazz life. Parenthood. Locomotives. Christmas. New York City—Greenwich Village.*

THE PRODIGAL JUDGE **F2.4365**

Vitagraph Co. of America. 10 Feb **1922** [trade review; released 19 Feb; c18 Feb 1922; LP17561]. Si; b&w. 35mm. 8 reels, 7,803 ft.

Pres by Albert E. Smith. *Dir* Edward José. *Scen* John Lynch, Edward José. *Photog* Joe Shelderfer, Charles Davis.

Cast: Jean Paige *(Betty Malroy)*, Maclyn Arbuckle *(Judge Slocum Price)*, Ernest Torrence *(Solomon Mahaffy)*, Earle Foxe *(Bruce Carrington)*, Arthur Carew *(Colonel Fentress)*, Horace Braham *(Charles Norton)*, Charles Kent *(General Quintard)*, Charles Eaton *(Hannibal)*, Robert Milasch *(Bob Yancy)*, George Bancroft *(Cavendish)*, Peggy Shanor *(Bess Hicks)*, Lillian Van Arsdale *(Mrs. Cavendish)*, Mary Curren *(Mrs. Hicks)*, Curren Children *(Cavendish Children)*.

Romantic drama. Source: Vaughan Kester, *The Prodigal Judge* (Indianapolis, 1911). Returning to his estate in North Carolina, Judge Slocum Price, a member of Congress in 1830, finds that his wife has taken their child and eloped with David Gatewood; and the domestic tragedy causes him to become a vagabond. Five years later, the judge and his companion (Solomon Mahaffy) on a Mississippi River boat meet a child known as Hannibal, accompanied by Bob Yancy. The judge suspects Hannibal to be his missing son. Colonel Fentress, an outlaw leader, has the boy kidnaped from Yancy, but Hannibal escapes and takes refuge on a skiff; meanwhile, the judge, who has been arrested for innocently passing counterfeit money, escapes, finds Hannibal on the river, and discovers that actually Fentress was the abductor of his wife. Betty Malroy, a friend of Hannibal's, marries Charley Norton, her childhood sweetheart; but Fentress has him shot on their wedding day. Following the rescue of Betty and Hannibal from Fentress, the judge challenges him to a duel. Solomon schemes to go in the judge's place and is mortally wounded; but the judge arrives and shoots Fentress. The judge regains his fortune, and Betty is won over to the affections of Bruce Carrington, who is trapped with her in the rapids. *Judges. Vagabonds. Inheritance. Desertion. Fatherhood. North Carolina. United States Congress. Rapids.*

THE PROMISED LAND **F2.4366**

Cosray. *Dist* Elvin Film Corp. 30 Oct **1925** [New York State license]. Si; b&w. 35mm. 5 reels, ca4,500 ft.

No information about the nature of this film has been found.

THE PROPHET'S PARADISE **F2.4367**

Selznick Pictures. *Dist* Select Pictures. 28 Feb **1922** [c28 Feb 1922; LP17608]. Si; b&w. 35mm. 5 reels, 3,845 ft.

Pres by Lewis J. Selznick. *Dir* Alan Crosland. *Scen* Lewis Allen Browne. *Story* C. S. Montayne. *Photog* Jules Cronjager.

Cast: Eugene O'Brien *(Howard Anderson)*, Sigrid Holmquist *(Mary Talbot)*, Bigelow Cooper *(Hassard)*, Arthur Housman *(Kadir)*, Nora Booth *(Nelda)*, Joseph Burke *(John Talbot)*, John Hopkins *(Kranda)*.

Melodrama. Howard Anderson, a young American tourist who finds himself somewhat bored in Constantinople, meets Hassard, a clever crook, who determines to get his money. Hassard, meanwhile, kidnaps Mary, the daughter of wealthy American John Talbot, who is studying Byzantine ruins, and holds her for ransom. Hassard detains Anderson to show him the local slave market, where Anderson sees Mary Talbot (who has been told that her father will die if she fails to play her part). To prevent her sale to a lecherous Turk, Anderson buys her; and following his discovery of the frameup, there is a fight and he escapes with Mary. Anderson, however, is knocked senseless by one of Talbot's employees who mistake him for one of the kidnapers. Later, meeting Mary in a Fifth Avenue traffic jam, Anderson claims her as his own. *Slavery. Kidnaping. Archeology. Constantinople. New York City.*

THE PROSCRIBED *see* **PREJUDICE**

PROTECTION **F2.4368**

Fox Film Corp. 5 May **1929** [c3 May 1929; LP347]. Si; b&w. 35mm. 7 reels, 5,536 ft. [Also si; 5,511 ft.]

Pres by William Fox. *Dir* Benjamin Stoloff. *Scen* Frederick Hazlitt Brennan. *Story* J. Clarkson Miller. *Photog* Joseph Valentine. *Asst Dir* Sam Wurtzel.

Cast: Robert Elliott *(Wallace Crockett)*, Paul Page *(Chick Slater)*, Dorothy Burgess *(Myrtle Hines)*, Ben Hewlett *(James Rollans)*, Dorothy Ward *(Judy Revis)*, Joe Brown *(Joe Brown)*, Roy Stewart *(Ollie Bogardt)*, William H. Tooker *(Harry Lamson)*, Arthur Hoyt *(society editor)*.

Melodrama. Chick Slater, a newspaper reporter, is assigned to write a feature article about a bootlegger who has applied modern business methods to rumrunning, and during his investigations he discovers that several high city officials have been providing the bootlegger with protection for his illegal activities. Chick writes up the facts, but the bootlegger uses his influence to have the story killed. Chick then quits his job and goes to work for a crusading independent daily. The story is printed, and the paper plays a major part in breaking up the bootlegging ring. *Reporters. Bootleggers. Newspapers. Business management.*

PROUD FLESH **F2.4369**

Metro-Goldwyn Pictures. 27 Apr **1925** [22 Apr 1925; LP21377]. Si; b&w. 35mm. 7 reels, 5,770 ft.

Pres by Louis B. Mayer. *Dir* King Vidor. *Scen* Harry Behn, Agnes Christine Johnston. *Photog* John Arnold. *Asst Dir* David Howard.

Cast: Eleanor Boardman *(Fernanda)*, Pat O'Malley *(Pat O'Malley)*, Harrison Ford *(Don Jaime)*, Trixie Friganza *(Mrs. McKee)*, William J. Kelly *(Mr. McKee)*, Rosita Marstini *(Vicente)*, Sojin *(Wong)*, Evelyn Sherman *(Spanish aunt)*, George Nichols *(Spanish uncle)*, Margaret Seddon *(Mrs. O'Malley)*, Lillian Elliott *(Mrs. Casey)*, Priscilla Bonner *(San Francisco girl)*.

Romantic comedy. Source: Lawrence Rising, *Proud Flesh* (New York, 1924). Fernanda, the orphaned daughter of a victim of the San Francisco earthquake, is cared for by relatives in Spain until she reaches the age of 18, when her most ardent admirer, Don Jaime, asks her to marry him. Fernanda perversely refuses him and goes to San Francisco, where she meets Pat O'Malley, a plumbing contractor. They are attracted to each other; Pat takes Fernanda to visit his home; but she is repulsed by the rough manners of Mrs. O'Malley and by the inelegance of the O'Malley house. Fernanda breaks off her flirtation with Pat, and he kidnaps her, taking her to his mountain cabin. They are followed by Don Jaime, who amiably takes Fernanda off with him. Pat returns home and is berated by his mother for falling in love with a girl of a different class. Fernanda then arrives and informs Pat that she can no longer live without his love. *Orphans. Plumbers. Kidnaping. Social classes. Motherhood. San Francisco—Earthquake 1906. San Francisco. Spain.*

PROUD HEART *see* **HIS PEOPLE**

PROWLERS OF THE NIGHT (Blue Streak Western) **F2.4370**

Universal Pictures. 21 Nov **1926** [c30 Aug 1926; LP23078]. Si; b&w. 35mm. 5 reels, 4,390 ft.

Pres by Carl Laemmle. *Dir-Story* Ernst Laemmle. *Scen* Emil Forst. *Photog* Edward Ulman.

Cast: Fred Humes *(Jack Morton)*, Barbara Kent *(Anita Parsons)*, Slim Cole *(Al Parsons)*, John T. Prince *(George Moulton)*, Joseph Belmont *(Sheriff Brandon)*, Walter Maly *(Bell)*.

Western melodrama. Sheriff Jack Norton is badly wounded in a gun battle with bandits and is helped by Anita Parsons, the daughter, as he later learns, of the bandit leader. Torn between his love for the girl and his devotion to duty, Jack decides the latter is too strong to resist. He pursues the bandits and gives chase when they rob the town bank. Through clever maneuvering he is able to capture the gang, but Anita's father is slain. Anita, finding that her father was unworthy and that Jack was faithful to his duty, forgives him and becomes his wife. *Sheriffs. Bandits. Filial relations. Bank robberies. Courtship.*

PROWLERS OF THE SEA **F2.4371**

Tiffany-Stahl Productions. 20 Jun **1928** [c19 Jun 1928; LP25386]. Si; b&w. 35mm. 6 reels, 5,160 ft.

Supv Roy Fitzroy. *Dir* John G. Adolfi. *Scen* John Francis Natteford. *Titl* Leslie Mason. *Photog* Ernest Miller. *Art Dir* Hervey Libbert. *Sets* George Sawley. *Film Ed* Desmond O'Brien. *Asst Dir* M. K. Wilson.

Cast: Carmel Myers *(Mercedes)*, Ricardo Cortez *(Carlos De Neve)*, George Fawcett *(General Hernândez)*, Gino Corrado *(The Skipper)*, Frank Lackteen *(Ramón Sánchez)*, Frank Leigh *(Felipe)*, Shirley Palmer *(Cuban maid)*.

Drama. Source: Jack London, "The Siege of the Lancashire Queen," in *Tales of the Fish Patrol* (New York, 1905). Cuban authorities, having difficulties preventing revolutionaries from smuggling guns, appoint Carlos De Neve, a man known for his honesty, to captain the coast guard. Since Carlos will not accept bribes, Ramón Sánchez, one of the rebels, asks his beautiful friend, Mercedes, to utilize her charms and keep the captain occupied on the night of a prospective haul. She does her duty, but in the process she and the captain fall in love. The revolutionaries are caught, and the general promises to punish Carlos severly until Mercedes arrives and pleads for his freedom. The general relents on the condition that Mercedes join his forces, and the two are exiled for the duration of their honeymoon. *Revolutionaries. Smuggling. Coast patrol. Cuba.*

Note: Licensed in New York State as *Sea Prowlers*.

PROXIES **F2.4372**

Cosmopolitan Productions. *For* Famous Players–Lasky. *Dist* Paramount Pictures. 1 May **1921** [c7 May 1921; LP16485]. Si; b&w. 35mm. 7 reels, 6,283 ft.

Dir-Scen George D. Baker. *Photog* Harold Wenstrom, Charles J. Hunt. *Set Dsgn* Joseph Urban.

Cast: Norman Kerry *(Peter Mendoza)*, Zena Keefe *(Clare Conway)*, Raye Dean *(Carlotta Darley)*, Jack Crosby *(Homer Carleton)*, Paul Everton *(John Stover)*, William H. Tooker *(Christopher Darley)*, Mrs. Schaffer *(Mrs. Darley)*, Robert Broderick *(Detective Linton)*.

Crook melodrama. Source: Frank R. Adams, "Proxies," in *Cosmopolitan* (69:53–57, 112–113, Aug 1920). Peter Mendoza and Clare Conway, ex-criminals, are butler and maid in the home of wealthy Christopher Darley and are engaged. John Stover, who recognizes Peter as a former convict, informs Darley and tries to embroil him in a fraudulent stock scheme, but he refuses. When Stover obtains a proxy empowering him to outvote Darley, Peter contrives a general holdup of guests at a party, steals the proxy, and burns it. After escaping from the house, the couple disclose their motive to Darley; he then presents them with a country house as a wedding present. *Criminals—Rehabilitation. Butlers. Housemaids. Fraud. Documentation.*

THE PRUDE *see* **THE DANGEROUS FLIRT**

PUBLIC OPINION *see* **A WOMAN OF PARIS**

PUBLIC OPINION *see* **THRU DIFFERENT EYES**

PUBLICITY MADNESS **F2.4373**

Fox Film Corp. 2 Oct **1927** [c2 Oct 1927; LP24463]. Si; b&w. 35mm. 6 reels, 5,893 ft.

Pres by William Fox. *Dir* Albert Ray. *Scen* Andrew Bennison. *Titl* Malcolm Stuart Boylan. *Story* Anita Loos. *Photog* Sidney Wagner. *Asst Dir* Horace Hough.

Cast: Lois Moran *(Violet Henly)*, Edmund Lowe *(Pete Clark)*, E. J. Ratcliffe *(Uncle Elmer Henly)*, James Gordon *(Brutus Banning)*, Arthur Housman *(Oscar Hawks)*, Byron Munson *(Henry Banning)*, Norman Peck *(Wilbur)*.

Comedy. Considering a nonstop flight from the Pacific Coast to Hawaii to be impossible, Pete Clark, advertising and publicity manager for the Henly soap manufacturing company, puts up $100,000 of the company's money for a promotional contest. When Lindbergh makes headlines crossing the Atlantic, Pete realizes the flight is possible and decides to enter the race himself so as to collect the prize money and save himself from disgrace. After a series of amusing stunts, he does reach Hawaii and thereby wins the admiration of Violet, the boss's daughter. *Advertising. Publicity. Airplanes. Airplane racing. Soap. Hawaii. Charles Augustus Lindbergh.*

PUPPETS **F2.4374**

Al Rockett Productions. *Dist* First National Pictures. 20 Jun **1926** [New York premiere; released 11 Jul; c21 Jun 1926; LP22831]. Si; b&w. 35mm. 8 reels, 7,468 or 7,486 ft.

Dir George Archainbaud. *Scen* John F. Goodrich. *Photog* Charles Van Enger. *Art Dir* Milton Menasco. *Film Ed* Arthur Tavares. *Asst Dir* Al Lena. *Prod Mgmt* Al Rockett.

Cast: Milton Sills *(Nicki)*, Gertrude Olmstead *(Angela)*, Francis McDonald *(Bruno)*, Mathilde Comont *(Rosa)*, Lucien Prival *(Frank)*, William Ricciardi *(Sandro)*, Nick Thompson *(Joe)*.

Melodrama. Source: Frances Lightner, *Puppets* (a play; publication undetermined). Nicola Riccobini, a puppet master in New York's Italian quarter, is an energetic and domineering man in the family, in contrast to his dreamy, poetic cousin Bruno. Rosa (the wardrobe mistress), Sandro (the veteran handyman who worships Nicki), and Frank (a sinister betrayer of girls who plays the piano for puppet performances) constitute the group. Nicki falls in love with Angela, a wistful runaway, but is summoned to war before they can be married and instructs Bruno to protect her from Frank. When Nicki is reported dead, Bruno and Angela fall in love, though she is desired also by Frank; then Nicki returns unexpectedly, deaf from shell shock; and the lovers plot in his presence to run away. Frank conspires to have Angela abducted, but Nicki intervenes. The shock cures his deafness; and when Bruno struggles with Nicki, the theater catches on fire. Bruno's cowardice is revealed, and Angela is reunited with Nicki. *Italians. Veterans. Puppets. Shell shock. Theater. World War I. New York City—Little Italy. Fires.*

PUPPETS OF FATE **F2.4375**

Metro Pictures. 28 Mar **1921** [c29 Mar 1921; LP16340]. Si; b&w. 35mm. 6 reels.

Dir Dallas M. Fitzgerald. *Scen* Ruth Ann Baldwin, Molly Parro. *Story* Brian Oswald Donn-Byrne. *Photog* John Arnold. *Art Dir* Sidney Ullman.

Cast: Viola Dana *(Sorrentina Palombra)*, Francis McDonald *(Gabriel Palombra)*, Jackie Saunders *("Babe" Reynolds)*, Fred Kelsey *(Bobs)*, Thomas Ricketts *(Father Francesco)*, Edward Kennedy *(Mike Reynolds)*.

Melodrama. Gabriel Palombra, who operates a Punchinello street show in Venice, decides to fulfill his ambition of going to America. He leaves behind his wife, Sorrentina, promising to send for her. In the United States, disillusioned, he takes a job as porter in a barbershop, but when he is rewarded for returning a lost pocketbook, manicurist "Babe" Reynolds persuades him to bet on a winning horse. Under her influence he rises to wealth. Meanwhile, Sorrentina arrives in New York and takes work as a flower girl. Having married Gabriel, "Babe" brings charges of bigamy against him, but the judge, perceiving her game, sentences Gabriel, then paroles him to Sorrentina for life. *Italians. Immigrants. Porters. Flower girls. Manicurists. Bigamy. Barbershops. Puppets. Venice.*

PURE GRIT **F2.4376**

Universal Pictures. 31 Dec **1923** [c17 Nov 1923; LP19621]. Si; b&w. 35mm. 5 reels, 4,571 ft.

Dir Nat Ross. *Scen* Isadore Bernstein. *Photog* Ben Kline.

Cast: Roy Stewart *(Bob Evans)*, Esther Ralston *(Stella Bolling)*, Jere Austin *(Jim Kemp)*, Jack Mower *(Frank Bolling)*, Verne Winter *(Buddy Clark)*.

Melodrama. Source: William MacLeod Raine, *A Texas Ranger* (New York, 1911). Posing as Stella Bolling's brother, whom he has killed, escaped convict Jim Kemp persuades Stella to help him escape to the Mexican border. Bob Evans, a Texas Ranger, chases them, routs a band of rustlers, captures Kemp, and rescues Stella from a burning cabin. *Fugitives. Rustlers. Texas Rangers. Impersonation. Mexican border.*

Note: Working title: *A Texas Ranger.*

PURITAN PASSIONS **F2.4377**

Film Guild. *Dist* W. W. Hodkinson Corp. 2 Sep **1923.** Si; b&w. 35mm. 7 reels, 6,600 or 6,859 ft.

Dir Frank Tuttle. *Scen* James Ashmore Creelman, Frank Tuttle. *Photog* Fred Waller, Jr.

Cast: Glenn Hunter *(Lord Ravensbane/The Scarecrow)*, Mary Astor *(Rachel)*, Osgood Perkins *(Dr. Nicholas)*, Maude Hill *(Goody Rickby)*, Frank Tweed *(Gillead Wingate)*, Dwight Wiman *(Bugby)*, Thomas Chalmers *(The Minister)*.

Drama. Source: Percy Mackaye, *The Scarecrow; or The Glass of Truth, a Tragedy of the Ludicrous* (New York, 1908). Goody Rickby conspires with Satan to avenge herself when Gillead Wingate refuses to acknowledge their illegitimate child. Years pass, and Wingate becomes a powerful figure in his Salem, Massachusetts, community. Satan appears, ready to effect Goody's revenge. He makes a scarecrow come to life and plans to marry him to Rachel, Wingate's ward, thereby causing her and Wingate to be hanged for having been associated with witchcraft. Their plan is partially foiled when the scarecrow falls in love, acquires a soul, and sacrifices himself to save Rachel. *Witchcraft. Demonology. Scarecrows. The Devil. Salem (Massachusetts).*

PURPLE DAWN **F2.4378**

Charles R. Seeling. *Dist* Aywon Film Corp. ca10 May **1923** [New York showing]. Si; b&w. 35mm. 5 reels, 4,850 ft.

Pres by Nathan Hirsh. *Dir-Story-Script* Charles R. Seeling. *Photog* Raymond Walker, Vernon Walker.

Cast: Bert Sprotte *(Red Carson, sea captain)*, William E. Aldrich *(Bob)*, James B. Leong *(Quan Foo)*, Edward Piel *(Wong Chang, Tong leader)*, Bessie Love *(Mui Far)*, William Horne *(Mr. Ketchell)*, Priscilla Bonner *(Ruth Ketchell, Bob's sweetheart)*.

Melodrama. Bob, a young sailor, unwittingly becomes involved in drug smuggling activities in San Francisco when he is sent to deliver a package of opium to Wong Chang, a Tong leader. A rival gang waylays him, steals the drugs, and drops him off in the country. In his wandering, he gets a job in a country store and falls in love with local girl Ruth Ketchell, forgetting the Chinese girl, left behind in the city, who loves him. Wong Chang finds him and returns him to the ship's captain, who beats Bob for allegedly stealing the drugs. The Tong kidnap Ruth and threaten to kill Bob, but the Chinese girl, who happens to be Wong Chang's daughter, saves the two. The last hundred feet of the film are tinted a light purple (hence the film's title), showing the Chinese girl, aware of the futility of her love, walking off in the early morning light after having united the loving couple. It is not clear whether she commits suicide or returns to her Chinese fiancé. *Sea captains. Sailors. Gangs. Chinese. Tongs. Smuggling. Narcotics. San Francisco.*

Note: There is some doubt about the credit to Vernon Walker for photography.

THE PURPLE HIGHWAY **F2.4379**

Kenma Corp. *Dist* Paramount Pictures. 5 Aug **1923** [c3 Jul 1923; LP19185]. Si; b&w. 35mm. 7 reels, 6,574 ft.

Dir Henry Kolker. *Adapt* Rufus Steele. *Photog* George Webber, Henry Cronjager.

Cast: Madge Kennedy *(April Blair)*, Monte Blue *(Edgar Prentice, known as Edgar Craig)*, Vincent Coleman *(Dudley Quail)*, Pedro De Cordoba *(Joe Renard)*, Dore Davidson *(Manny Bean)*, Emily Fitzroy *(Mrs. Carney)*, William H. Tooker *(Mr. Quail)*, Winifred Harris *(Mrs. Quail)*, John W. Jenkins *(Shakespeare Jones)*, Charles Kent *(Mr. Olgivie)*.

Comedy-drama. Source: Luther Reed and Hamilton Hale, *Dear Me, or April Changes; an Optimistic Comedy in Three Acts* (New York opening: Jan 1921). Two inmates and a cleaning girl at a home for struggling artists achieve success and fame when they pool their talents and produce a smash hit Broadway musical. Edgar, the playwright, is in love with April, the exchargirl leading lady, but she doesn't discover that she loves him until it's almost too late. *Artists. Charwomen. Actors. Playwrights. Theater. Musical revues. New York City—Broadway.*

PURSUED **F2.4380**

W. T. Lackey Productions. *Dist* Ellbee Pictures. 30 Aug **1925.** Si; b&w. 35mm. 5 reels, 4,869 ft.

Dir Dell Henderson. *Story* J. Benson Stafford.

Cast: Gaston Glass *(Dick Manning)*, Dorothy Drew *(Helen Grant)*, George Siegmann *(John Grant)*, Arthur Rankin *(Larry, the Kid)*, Gertrude Astor *(Madame La Grande)*, Stuart Holmes *(Robert Killifer)*, Lafe McKee *(district attorney)*.

Melodrama. Dick Manning, an assistant district attorney, who is on the track of a gang of murderers, is abducted while visiting his sweetheart, Helen Grant. Helen's police dog tracks down the abductors, and Helen goes to their den, passing herself off as Chicago Ann, a notorious female gangster who dresses in men's clothing. The leader of the gang is attracted to Helen, but his jealous sweetheart exposes her as a fraud. Helen is made prisoner, but she manages to escape with the help of a friendly gangster. Helen alerts the police, and the den is raided in time to save Dick's life. *District attorneys. Male impersonation. Gangs. Abduction. Police dogs.*

PUT 'EM UP **F2.4381**

Universal Pictures. 11 Mar **1928** [c2 Nov 1927; LP24624]. Si; b&w. 35mm. 5 reels, 4,200 ft.

Pres by Carl Laemmle. *Dir* Edgar Lewis. *Scen* William Lester. *Titl* Gardner Bradford. *Story* George H. Plympton. *Photog* Wilbur Kline. *Art Dir* David S. Garber. *Film Ed* Harry Marker.

Cast: Fred Humes *(Tom Evans)*, Gloria Grey *(Helen Turner)*, Pee Wee Holmes *(Shorty Mullins)*, Tom London *(Jake Lannister)*, Harry Semels *(Lloyd Turner)*, Ben Corbett *(Tradin' Sam)*, Charles Colby *(Dobby Flinn)*, Bert Starkey *(Slim Hansom)*.

Western melodrama. Tom Evans and his cronies see the local stage intercepted by Lannister's men, one of whom, Mullins, tries to force his attentions on a passenger, Helen Turner, who is returning from school; but she is rescued by Tom. Lannister tries to persuade Helen's father to join forces with him and to consent to his marriage to Helen, but when she arrives, her experience turns her against him. Later, Lannister's men subdue Tom while the villain holds Helen prisoner. When Lannister threatens the death of her father, Helen consents to marriage; but the return of Tom's riderless horse signals his pals, who then rescue Tom from a cliff and ride to the Turner homestead to save Helen for him. *Cowboys. Bandits. Abduction.*

PUTTIN' ON THE RITZ **F2.4382**

United Artists. 14 Feb **1930** [New York premiere; released 1 Mar; c1 Mar 1930; LP1175]. Sd (Movietone); b&w with col sequence (Technicolor). 35mm. 10 reels, 8,225 ft.

Pres by Joseph M. Schenck. *Prod-Writ* John W. Considine, Jr. *Dir* Edward Sloman. *Dial* William K. Wells. *Photog* Ray June. *Art Dir* William Cameron Menzies, Park French. *Film Ed* Hal Kern. *Songs: "With You," "Alice in Wonderland," "Puttin' On the Ritz"* Irving Berlin. *Mus Arr* Hugo Riesenfeld. *Song: "There's Danger in Your Eyes, Cherie"* Harry Richman, Jack Meskill, Pete Wendling. *Dance Dir* Maurice L. Kusell. *Rec Engr* Oscar Lagerstrom. *Asst Dir* Jack Mintz. *Cost* Alice O'Neill.

Cast: Harry Richman *(Harry Raymond)*, Joan Bennett *(Dolores Fenton)*, James Gleason *(James Tierney)*, Aileen Pringle *(Mrs. Teddy Van Renssler)*, Lilyan Tashman *(Goldie DeVere)*, Purnell Pratt *(George Barnes)*, Richard Tucker *(Fenway Brooks)*, Eddie Kane *(Bob Wagner)*, George Irving *(Dr. Blair)*, Sidney Franklin *(Schmidt)*.

Musical melodrama. Harry Raymond, a washed-up vaudevillian, takes a job as song promoter for the Wagner music publishers. He is unable, however, to convince them his song ideas are worthwhile, and his conceit over a song submitted by showgirl Dolores Fenton gets him fired. His friend Jim, Dolores, and her friend Goldie work up an act that gets playing time until Harry riles the audience into a free-for-all; then they split into duo teams and Harry and Dolores become a Broadway sensation with their number "With You." They become engaged, but prosperity goes to Harry's head, and he takes up with Mrs. Van Renssler, a thrill-mad socialite, and scorns his former friends at a Christmas Eve party; in a drunken frenzy, he is temporarily blinded by bad liquor but conceals his condition from Dolores. Jim takes him to the opening night of her show, and when the audience insists that she sing "With You," Harry joins her in the song from the balcony; later, she forgives him, and they are happily reunited. *Singers. Song promoters. Showgirls. Socialites. Vaudeville. Courtship. Drunkenness. Blindness. Thrill-seeking.*

PUTTING IT OVER **F2.4383**

Phil Goldstone Productions. 1 Jun **1922.** Si; b&w. 35mm. 5 reels.

Pres by Phil Goldstone. *Dir-Story-Scen* Grover Jones.

Cast: Richard Talmadge *(Bob Merritt)*, Doris Pawn *(Barbara Norton)*, Thomas Ricketts *(Arnold Norton)*, Harry Van Meter *(Mark Durkham)*, Henry Barrows *(James Merritt)*, Victor Metzetti *(Tate Busby)*, William Horne *(George Norton)*, Earl Schaeffer *("Porky" Donovan)*, Andrew Waldron *(Lem Kendall)*.

Comedy-drama. State political power James Merritt gives his wayward son, Bob, a 13th chance to make good by defeating Arnold Norton in the coming Carterville mayoral election. Bob tries his mightiest until he meets Norton's daughter, Barbara, and learns of the underhanded efforts being made against Norton by Mark Durkham, the elder Merritt's political henchman. Switching to the other side, Bob successfully works for Norton's victory and Barbara's favor—thereby getting involved in a prizefight and other exciting events. *Politicians. Mayors. Reformers. Elections. Prizefighting.*

QUALITY STREET **F2.4384**

Cosmopolitan Productions. *Dist* Metro-Goldwyn-Mayer Distributing Corp. 2 Nov **1927** [New York premiere; released 31 Dec; c17 Oct 1927; LP24506]. Si; b&w. 35mm. 8 reels, 7,193 ft.

Dir Sidney Franklin. *Adapt-Scen* Hans Kraly, Albert Lewin. *Titl* Marian Ainslee, Ruth Cummings. *Photog* Hendrik Sartov. *Sets* Cedric Gibbons, Allen Ruoff. *Film Ed* Ben Lewis. *Wardrobe* René Hubert.

Cast: Marion Davies *(Phoebe Throssel)*, Conrad Nagel *(Dr. Valentine Brown)*, Helen Jerome Eddy *(Susan Throssel)*, Flora Finch *(Mary Willoughby)*, Margaret Seddon *(Nancy Willoughby)*, Marcelle Corday *(Henrietta Turnbull)*, Kate Price *(Patty)*.

Romantic comedy-drama. Source: James Matthew Barrie, *Quality Street* (1904). The prolonged courtship of Phoebe Throssel with Dr. Valentine Brown is abruptly interrupted by the doctor's decision to join the English forces in the Napoleonic Wars. Meanwhile, Phoebe languishes in Green Willow Village, comforted by her sister, Susan; but with the passing of years, she develops into spinsterhood. When Dr. Brown returns after 10 years, Phoebe believes he will be disappointed at her aged appearance and transforms herself into a mythical niece and starts a flirtation with the doctor; finding herself in a number of embarrassing situations, she reverts to her former person to find that he loves her in spite of the changes wrought by time. *Physicians. Spinsters. Courtship. Impersonation. Napoleonic Wars. England.*

QUARANTINED RIVALS **F2.4385**

Gotham Productions. *Dist* Lumas Film Corp. 28 Feb **1927** [c15 Mar 1927; LP23838]. Si; b&w. 35mm. 7 reels, 6,806 ft.

Pres by Sam Sax. *Dir* Archie Mayo. *Cont* Jack Jevne. *Titl* Al Boasberg. *Cinematog* Ray June. *Film Ed* Edith Wakeling. *Prod Mgr* Glenn Belt. *Prod Asst* H. C. Clark.

Cast: Robert Agnew *(Bruce Farney)*, Kathleen Collins *(Elsie Peyton)*, John Miljan *(Ed, The Barber)*, Ray Hallor *(Robert Howard)*, Viora Daniels *(Minette, The Manicurist)*, Big Boy Williams *(Joe, The Plumber)*, Clarissa Selwynne *(Mrs. Peyton)*, George Pierce *(Mr. Peyton)*, William A. O'Connor *(Mort)*, Josephine Borio *(The Maid)*.

Romantic comedy. Source: George Randolph Chester, "Quarantined Rivals," in *McClure's Magazine* (26:261, Jan 1906). Elsie Peyton is ardently admired by Bruce Farney, whom she and her father favor, and Bob Howard, her mother's preference. The domineering Mrs. Peyton sees to it that Bruce, who is on the football team, is discouraged from taking Elsie to the game. Bruce stops in a barbershop and is subjected to the flirtations of Minette, the manicurist, who wants to make Ed, the barber, jealous. Bruce is disillusioned to see Elsie with Howard at the game and follows them in his car; Mrs. Peyton calls Minette to the house for a manicure. When Bruce arrives, he is ordered out, but the house is placed under a 2-week quarantine for smallpox. Hilarious complications ensue as Bruce is obliged to room with his rival, but by a clever trick Bruce marries Elsie in spite of the quarantine, which proves to have been unnecessary. *Manicurists. Barbers. Courtship. Motherhood. Football. Quarantine. Smallpox.*

THE QUARTERBACK **F2.4386**

Famous Players–Lasky. *Dist* Paramount Pictures. 11 Oct **1926** [c13 Oct 1926; LP23221]. Si; b&w. 35mm. 8 reels, 7,114 ft.

Pres by Adolph Zukor, Jesse L. Lasky. *Dir* Fred Newmeyer. *Football Supv* Fielding H. ("Hurry Up") Yost. *Adapt* Ray Harris. *Story* William Slavens McNutt, William O. McGeehan. *Photog* Edward Cronjager.

Cast: Richard Dix *(Jack Stone)*, Esther Ralston *(Louise Mason)*, Harry Beresford *(Elmer Stone)*, David Butler *("Lumpy" Goggins)*, Robert Craig *(Denny Walters)*, Mona Palma *(Nellie Webster)*.

Romantic comedy. Elmer Stone, quarterback of the 1899 Colton College football squad, marries Nellie Webster, pledging himself to stay at school until his team defeats State University; 1926 finds Elmer still studying, and though his wife has died, Jack, their son, is now a schoolmate. While being hazed, young Stone is blindfolded and told to kiss the first girl he meets, who turns out to be Louise Mason. Trying out for the team, Jack becomes friendly with "Lumpy" Goggins, and they develop a unique system for milk delivery, based on forward passing. At the county fair, Louise persuades Jack to race against Streak Hodkins; Jack wins but refuses the prize money. As a consequence, Jack is disqualified from playing on the team and blames this action on Louise. He is reinstated by the dean, however, and, spurred on by Louise, he leads the team to victory. *Milkmen. Filial relations. College life. Football. Courtship. Fairs.*

QUEEN HIGH **F2.4387**

Paramount-Publix Corp. 23 Aug **1930** [c22 Aug 1930; LP1510]. Sd (Movietone); b&w. 35mm. 9 reels, 7,905 ft.

Prod Frank Mandel, Laurence Schwab. *Dir* Fred Newmeyer. *Screenplay* Frank Mandel. *Photog* William Steiner. *Film Ed* Barney Rogan. *Song: "I Love the Girls in My Own Peculiar Way"* E. Y. Harburg, Henry Souvain. *Songs: "It Seems to Me," "I'm Afraid of You"* Dick Howard, Ralph Rainger. *Song: "Brother Just Laugh It Off"* Arthur Schwartz, Ralph Rainger. *Song: "Everything Will Happen for the Best"* B. G. De Sylva, Lewis Gensler. *Mus Arr* John W. Green. *Rec Engr* C. A. Tuthill.

Cast: Stanley Smith *(Dick Johns)*, Ginger Rogers *(Polly Rockwell)*, Charles Ruggles *(T. Boggs Johns)*, Frank Morgan *(George Nettleton)*, Helen Carrington *(Mrs. Nettleton)*, Theresa Maxwell Conover *(Mrs. Rockwell)*, Betty Garde *(Florence Cole)*, Nina Olivette *(Coddles)*, Rudy Cameron *(Cyrus Vanderholt)*, Tom Brown *(Jimmy)*.

Musical comedy. Source: Laurence Schwab, B.G. De Sylva, and Lewis Gensler, *Queen High* (New York opening: 8 Sep 1926). Edward Henry Peple, *A Pair of Sixes; a Farce in Three Acts* (New York, 1917). Business partners T. Boggs Johns and George Nettleton, who operate a garter-manufacturing business, are so constantly at odds that their lawyer, Cyrus Vanderholt, proposes that they settle their differences by a hand of draw poker; the winner is to take over the business for a year and the loser to become a butler in the household of the other. Meanwhile, Nettleton gives his niece, Polly Rockwell, a stenographic position, as Johns has previously hired his nephew, Dick. Johns loses the game; and when Florence, his fiancée, shows up as a guest at Nettleton's home, complications ensue as he is pursued by Coddles, the maid. Meanwhile Dick and Polly fall in love, and Polly suggests that Johns pretend to be happy under his new "master" and flirt with his wife. Nettleton becomes extremely jealous. When the partners find that the agreement is not legally binding, they unite in chasing out the rascally lawyer. *Lawyers. Stenographers. Butlers. Housemaids. Partnerships. Garters. Courtship. Poker.*

QUEEN KELLY **F2.4388**

Joseph P. Kennedy. *Dist* United Artists. **1928.** Si; b&w. 35mm. 8 reels. [Original length: ca11 reels.]

Prod Joseph P. Kennedy. *Dir-Story-Scen* Erich von Stroheim. *Photog* Ben Reynolds, Gordon Pollock, Paul Ivano. *Art Dir* Harold Miles, Richard Day. *Film Ed* Viola Lawrence. *Mus* Adolf Tandler. *Asst Dir* Eddy Sowders, Louis Germonprez. *Cost* Max Ree.

Cast: Gloria Swanson *(Patricia Kelly, an orphan)*, Walter Byron *(Prince "Wild" Wolfram von Hohenberg Falsenstein)*, Seena Owen *(Queen Regina V, his cousin and fiancée)*, Sidney Bracey *(Prince Wolfram's valet)*, William von Brinken *(adjutant to Wolfram)*, Sylvia Ashton *(Kelly's aunt)*, Tully Marshall *(Jan Vooyheid)*.

Romantic melodrama. In Kronberg, capital of Ruritania, the queen prepares to marry her cousin, Prince Wolfram, but during exercises with his squadron the prince sees Patricia Kelly, among some girls from an orphanage. Determined to meet her again, he has the convent set afire, kidnaps her, and takes her to his chateau. Queen Regina emerges in a fury and chases Patricia from the chateau with a lash. Her victim throws herself in the river and drowns, and the prince commits suicide by her coffin. (The foregoing description reflects the European release version; in Stroheim's version, Kelly's suicide fails, and she returns to the convent. A telegram arrives from her guardian aunt, who operates a brothel in German East Africa, and the aunt forces Patricia to marry Jan Vooyheid, a degenerate, drunken cripple, the wedding taking place with the aunt lying on her deathbed. In the unfinished scenario, Wolfram is transferred to Africa and meets Patricia following the death of her husband. The queen having been assassinated, Wolfram ascends the throne, and Patricia becomes Queen Kelly.) *Royalty. Orphans. Abduction. Suicide. Flagellation. Incendiarism. Whorehouses. Imaginary kingdoms. German East Africa.*

Note: Stroheim was removed from the film before the production was completed, and his 11-reel version was reduced to 8 by Miss Swanson. Although the film was distributed in Europe, it was not released commercially in the United States.

QUEEN O' DIAMONDS **F2.4389**

R-C Pictures. *Dist* Film Booking Offices of America. 24 Jan **1926** [c24 Jan 1926; LP22342]. Si; b&w. 35mm. 6 reels, 5,129 ft.

Dir Chet Withey. *Story-Cont* Fred Myton. *Photog* Roy Klaffki.

Cast: Evelyn Brent *(Jeanette Durant/Jerry Lyon)*, Elsa Lorimer *(Mrs. Ramsey)*, Phillips Smalley *(Mr. Ramsey)*, William N. Bailey *(LeRoy Phillips)*, Theodore von Eltz *(Daniel Hammon)*.

Melodrama. Jerry Lyon, chorus girl, is persuaded to pose as her look-alike, Jeanette Durant, a Broadway star whose husband, LeRoy Phillips, is a diamond thief. The impersonation results in Jerry's becoming innocently involved in a theft ring, and consequently she is suspected of murder. After a series of misadventures, Jerry proves her innocence. *Thieves. Doubles. Chorus girls. Impersonation. Murder. Theft. New York City—Broadway.*

THE QUEEN OF SHEBA **F2.4390**

Fox Film Corp. 4 Sep **1921** [premiere; released 11 Dec; c17 Apr 1921; LP16470]. Si; b&w. 35mm. 9 reels, 8,279 ft.

Pres by William Fox. *Dir* J. Gordon Edwards. *Supv chariot race* Tom Mix. *Story* Virginia Tracy. *Photog* John W. Boyle.

Cast: Betty Blythe *(The Queen of Sheba)*, Fritz Leiber *(King Solomon)*, Claire De Lorez *(Queen Amrath, wife of Solomon)*, George Siegmann *(King Armud of Sheba)*, Herbert Heyes *(Tamaran, courtier of Sheba)*, Herschel Mayall *(Menton, Sheba's Minister of State)*, G. Raymond Nye *(Adonijah, brother of Solomon)*, George Nichols *(King David)*, Genevieve Blinn *(Beth-Sheba)*, Pat Moore *(Sheba's son, aged 4)*, Joan Gordon *(Nomis, Sheba's sister)*, William Hardy *(Olos, Sheba's giant slave)*, Paul Cazeneuve *(The Envoy of the Pharaoh)*, John Cosgrove *(King of Tyre)*, Nell Craig *(The Princess Vashti)*, Al Fremont *(A Captain of Adonijah's Army)*, Earl Crain *(Joab, a soldier)*.

Spectacular. Solomon is crowned King of Israel, and his brother Adonijah becomes his bitter enemy. When the country of Sheba is captured by King Armud and he gathers the maidens of the land, the sister of one of the captured maidens, seeking vengeance, goes to Armud's court and there entices and marries the king, then kills him on their wedding day. As the Queen of Sheba, she visits Solomon; and they fall in love, provoking the wrath of his wife, Amrath, whose horses theirs outrun in a chariot race. The pharaoh, Amrath's father, threatens war if they marry, and the Queen of Sheba returns with her newborn son to her own country. When he is 4 years old she sends him to Solomon, but the boy is abducted by the jealous Adonijah, who marches on Solomon but is repulsed by the queen's armies. After a tender parting with Solomon, she returns home with her son. *Royalty. Revenge. Israel. Solomon. Sheba. Israel. Egypt. Biblical characters.*

QUEEN OF SPADES **F2.4391**

Bear Productions. *Dist* Aywon Film Corp. 16 Sep **1925** [New York State license]. Si; b&w. 35mm. 5 reels, 4,800 ft.

Dir Harry L. Fraser.

Cast: Gordon Clifford, Charlotte Pierce.

Western melodrama(?). No information about the nature of this film has been found.

QUEEN OF THE CHORUS **F2.4392**

Morris R. Schlank Productions. *Dist* Anchor Film Distributors. 5 Mar **1928.** Si; b&w. 35mm. 6 reels, 5,916 ft.

Dir Charles J. Hunt. *Story-Scen* Adele Buffington. *Photog* Robert E. Cline.

Cast: Virginia Browne Faire *("Queenie" Dale)*, Rex Lease *(Billy Cooke)*, Lloyd Whitlock *(Gordon Trent)*, Betty Francisco *(Flossie De Vere)*, Harriet Hammond *(Mrs. Gordon Trent)*, Charles Hill Mailes *(Rufus Van Der Layden)*, Crauford Kent *(Spencer Steele)*.

Romantic drama. "The pure little chorus gal [Queenie Dale] falls in love with the youth [Billy Cooke] posing as his millionaire boss. The latter [Gordon Trent] returns from Europe to find the gal he has been trying to play engaged to his secretary." (*Film Daily*, 10 Jun 1928, p7.) "Regular screen type of battle when boy finds his employer tried to gyp him of his girl by showing her bills and getting her to compromise herself as sacrifice to save youth from bars" (*Variety*, 6 Jun 1928, p25). *Chorus girls. Millionaires. Secretaries. Impersonation.*

QUEEN OF THE MOULIN ROUGE **F2.4393**

Pyramid Pictures. *Dist* American Releasing Corp. ca2 Sep **1922** [Los Angeles premiere; released 10 Sep 1922; c12 Sep 1922; LP18872]. Si; b&w. 35mm. 7 reels, 6,704 ft.

Dir Ray C. Smallwood. *Scen* Garfield Thompson, Peter Milne. *Photog* Michael Joyce. *Art Dir-Set Dsgn* Ben Carré. *Mus Arr* Joseph E. Zivelli. *Asst Dir* George McGuire.

Cast: Martha Mansfield *(Rosalie Anjou)*, Joseph Striker *(Tom Richards)*, Henry Harmon *(Louis Rousseau)*, Fred T. Jones *(Jules Riboux)*, Jane Thomas *(Gigolette)*, Tom Blake *(Moozay)*, Mario Carillo *(Albert Lenoir)*.

Drama. Source: Paul M. Potter and John T. Hall, *The Queen of the Moulin Rouge* (New York opening: 7 Dec 1908). Louis Rousseau believes that the technically perfect music of his violin student, Tom Richards, lacks a soul because Tom has not suffered. Therefore, he convinces Rosalie Anjou, whom Tom saved from apaches and now loves, that she must dance at the notorious Moulin Rouge to earn the money Tom needs for his lessons. While keeping Tom ignorant of her activities, Rosalie becomes a great success and is selected Queen of the Moulin Rouge. Rousseau takes Tom to the coronation and, as he hoped, Tom denounces Rosalie and pours his pain and rage into his music. Rousseau confesses his scheme and Tom rushes to the banks of the Seine just in time to save Rosalie from a watery grave. *Violinists. Dancers. Apaches—Paris. Paris. Moulin Rouge.*

QUEEN OF THE NIGHT CLUBS **F2.4394**

Warner Brothers Pictures. 16 Mar **1929** [c19 Feb 1929; LP137]. Sd (Vitaphone); b&w. 35mm. 6 reels, 5,424 ft. [Also si, 13 Apr 1929; 5,236 ft.]

Dir Bryan Foy. *Story-Screenplay-Dial* Murray Roth, Addison Burkhart. *Photog* Ed Du Par. *Asst Dir* Freddie Foy.

Cast: Texas Guinan *(Tex Malone)*, John Davidson *(Don Holland)*, Lila Lee *(Bee Walters)*, Arthur Housman *(Andy Quinland)*, Eddie Foy, Jr. *(Eddie Parr)*, Jack Norworth *(Phil Parr)*, George Raft *(Gigola)*, Jimmie Phillips *(Nick)*, William Davidson *(assistant district attorney)*, John Miljan *(Lawyer Grant)*, Lee Shumway *(Crandall)*, Joe Depera *(Roy)*, Agnes Franey *(flapper)*, Charlotte Merriam *(girl)*.

Drama. After working as a hostess for Nick and Andy, Tex Malone leaves their employ and opens a club of her own. Looking for talent to book for the floor show, Tex hires Bee Walters and thereby breaks up Bee's act with Eddie Parr. Andy spitefully kills Tex's friend, Holland, and young Eddie is arrested for the crime on circumstantial evidence. Tex then learns from Eddie's father, Phil, that Eddie is her long-lost son. At the trial, Tex comes to Eddie's defense and persuades one member of the jury that there is reasonable doubt of Eddie's guilt. The jury repairs to Tex's club, where Tex discovers a piece of evidence that conclusively links Andy with the murder. Eddie is freed, and Tex and Phil get together for a second honeymoon. *Nightclub hostesses. Entertainers. Murder. Motherhood. Circumstantial evidence. Juries. Trials. Nightclubs.*

Note: Song: "It's Tough To Be a Hostess on Broadway."

QUEENIE **F2.4395**

Fox Film Corp. 9 Oct **1921** [c9 Oct 1921; LP17200]. Si; b&w. 35mm. 6 reels, 5,174 ft.

Pres by William Fox. *Dir* Howard M. Mitchell. *Scen* Dorothy Yost. *Photog* George Schneiderman.

Cast: Shirley Mason *(Queenie Gurkin)*, George O'Hara *(Vivian Van Winkle)*, Wilson Hummell *(Simon Pepper/Abner Quigley)*, Aggie Herring *(Pansy Pooley)*, Lydia Titus *(Mrs. Mulliken)*, Adolphe Menjou *(Count Michael)*, Clarissa Selwynne *(Mrs. Torrence)*, Pal *(himself, a dog)*.

Comedy. Source: Wilbur Finley Fauley, *Queenie, the Adventures of a Nice Young Lady* (New York, 1921). Simon Pepper, a miserly recluse since the death of his young wife 30 years earlier, is attended by housekeeper Pansy Pooley and his secretary and valet, Abner Quigley. Pansy obtains Pepper's consent to employ her niece, Queenie, as her assistant. Queenie, who has done odd jobs at a girls' school, is disillusioned by her new life until her hat is retrieved by Vivian Van Winkle, son of a noodle king who has poetic aspirations under the name of Cocobola. Though forbidden to visit Pepper, she meets him and he takes a liking to her, but one evening he disappears. Quigley decides to impersonate Pepper, and he marries Pansy to launch a career. Queenie is about to marry Count Michael, but during the ceremony Pepper returns to expose the imposter, and Queenie is then happily married to Van Winkle. *Misers. Housekeepers. Secretaries. Poets. Imposture. Dogs.*

A QUESTION OF HONOR **F2.4396**

Anita Stewart Productions. *Dist* Associated First National Pictures. ca11 Mar **1922** [Chicago premiere; c9 Mar 1922; LP17617]. Si; b&w. 35mm. 7 reels, 6,500 ft.

Pres by Louis B. Mayer. *Dir* Edwin Carewe. *Scen* Josephine Quirk. *Photog* Robert B. Kurrle. *Set Dsgn* William Darling. *Art Titl* Frank F. Greene.

Cast: Anita Stewart *(Anne Wilmot)*, Edward Hearn *(Bill Shannon)*, Arthur Stuart Hull *(Leon Morse)*, Walt Whitman *(Sheb)*, Bert Sprotte *(Charles Burkthaler)*, Frank Beal *(Stephen Douglas)*, Adele Farrington *(Mrs. Katherine Wilmot)*, Mary Land *(Mrs. Elton, Morse's sister)*, Ed Brady *(John Bretton)*, Doc Bytell *(Parsons)*.

Melodrama. Source: Ruth Cross, "A Question of Honor," in *People's Home Journal* (35:10–11, 12–13, Apr–Jun 1920). Bill Shannon, an engineer in charge of a dam project in the Sierras, is offered a bribe to sell out to Morse, a Wall Street promoter who wants the damsite for his new railroad. Unable to succeed, Morse arrives at the site with his fiancée, Anne Wilmot, and his sister. There Shannon rescues Anne from a swift mountain stream, and she ultimately wins his affection and adopts his position on the dam controversy. Failing to buy off Shannon, Morse conspires with Charles Burkthaler, a rancher, to dynamite the dam. Overhearing the plot, Anne goes to warn Shannon; but he leaves when he hears her cajoling Morse, who has become jealous of his attentions. Anne discovers the men wiring the explosives, but in severing the wire leading to the dam she is buried beneath rubble from the explosion; following a fight, Shannon settles accounts with Burkthaler and Morse, and Anne is rescued by his men. *Engineers—Civil. Bribery. Dams. Railroads. Explosives. Sierras.*

QUICK ACTION **F2.4397**

American Film Co. c7 Feb **1921** [LP16110]. Si; b&w. 35mm. 5 reels.

Dir Edward Sloman.

Cast: William Russell.

Action comedy-drama. Monty—breezy, athletic, and brave—risks his life to win a beautiful debutante. At the same time he discovers a buried treasure and finds a husband for his aunt, who makes good her offer of $50,000 to establish him in marriage. *Socialites. Debutantes. Spinsters. Aunts. Treasure.*

Note: Probably produced before 1921; release date undetermined.

QUICK CHANGE **F2.4398**

Dell Henderson Productions. *Dist* Rayart Pictures. 6 Jul **1925** [New York State license]. Si; b&w. 35mm. 5 reels, 4,800 ft.

Pres by W. Ray Johnston. *Dir* Dell Henderson.

Cast: George Larkin.

Melodrama(?). Source: A. E. Ullman, "Quick Change," in *Short Stories Magazine*. No information about the nature of this film has been found.

QUICK TRIGGERS (Ranch Rider Western) **F2.4399**

Universal Pictures. 15 Jul **1928** [c20 Oct 1927; LP24563]. Si; b&w. 35mm. 5 reels, 4,472 ft.

Pres by Carl Laemmle. *Dir* Ray Taylor. *Story-Scen* Basil Dickey. *Titl* Gardner Bradford. *Photog* Al Jones. *Art Dir* David S. Garber. *Film Ed* Ben Pivar.

Cast: Fred Humes *(Larry Day)*, Derelys Perdue *(Jeanne Landis)*, Wilbur Mack *(Jeff Thorne)*, Robert Chandler *(Jake Landis)*, Gilbert "Pee Wee" Holmes *(Pee Wee)*, Scotty Mattraw *(Scotty)*, Dick L'Estrange *(Lazy)*, Ben Corbett *(Benny)*.

Western melodrama. Larry Day, foreman of the 3X Ranch, and his men are pursuing a gang of rustlers when Jake Landis, who is being forced into rustling by Thorne, the bandit chief, is saved by his daughter Jeanne, who gives him her horse and then confronts Larry. They soon fall in love. Meanwhile, a wandering horse leads the men to Landis, who is then arrested and locked up at the ranch. Jeanne attends a dance at the ranch, and Jeff Thorne threatens to accuse her father of the commission of all their crimes unless she agrees to marry him. Larry overhears, and the rustlers meet head on with the ranch men and are captured. Larry and Jeanne are united. *Ranchers. Ranch foremen. Rustlers. Filial relations. Horses.*

QUICKER'N LIGHTNIN' **F2.4400**

Action Pictures. *Dist* Weiss Brothers Artclass Pictures. 21 Aug **1925** [New York State license]. Si; b&w. 35mm. 5 reels, 4,222 ft.

Pres by Lester F. Scott, Jr. *Dir* Richard Thorpe. *Scen* Betty Burbridge. *Story* Reginald C. Barker.

Cast: Buffalo Bill Jr. *(Quicker'n Lightnin')*, B. F. Blinn *(John Harlow)*, Dorothy Dorr *(Helen Harlow)*, Harry Todd *(Al McNutt)*, J. Gordon Russell *(Mowii)*, Raye Hampton *(squaw)*, Lucille Young *(Morella)*, Charles Roberts *(Truxillo)*.

Western melodrama. Indians murder John Harlow and abduct his daughter, Helen. Quicker'n Lightnin' rescues Helen before Mowii's squaw can sacrifice her to the sun god. *Indians of North America. Abduction. Murder. Human sacrifice. Religion.*

QUICKSANDS **F2.4401**

Agfar Corp. *Dist* American Releasing Corp., Paramount Famous Lasky Corp. 28 Feb **1923** [c21 May 1927; LP24011]. Si; b&w. 35mm. 6-7 reels.

Prod-Story Howard Hawks. *Dir* Jack Conway. *Photog* Harold Rosson, Glen MacWilliams.

Cast: Helene Chadwick *(The Girl)*, Richard Dix *(1st Lieutenant)*, Alan Hale *(Ferrago)*, Noah Beery *("Silent" Krupz)*, J. Farrell MacDonald *(Colonel Patterson)*, George Cooper *(Matt Patterson)*, Tom Wilson *(Sergeant Johnson)*, Dick Sutherland *(Cupid)*, Hardee Kirkland *(Farrell)*, Louis King *(Bar-fly)*, Jean Hersholt, Walter Long, Jack Curtis, William Dyer, Frank Campeau, Edwin Stevens, James Marcus, Lionel Belmore *(members of the ring)*.

Melodrama. A young lieutenant stationed at the Mexican border, whose job is to capture a ring of narcotics smugglers, spies his sweetheart, the daughter of a U. S. Customs official, in a cantina suspected of being the headquarters of the dope ring. Believing that she is part of the ring, he decides to resign his job. Word arrives that the girl and her father are being held prisoners by the gang. The lieutenant goes to aid them and is captured. Finally, the U. S. Army rescues the trio and the girl is revealed to be a secret agent. *Secret agents. Smugglers. Narcotics. Customs (tariff). Mexican border. United States Army.*

Note: This film was originally produced in 1923 by Agfar Corp. and released by the American Releasing Corp. It shows but one copyright number, obtained in 1927, when it was re-released by Paramount Famous Lasky Corp. with a length of 5 reels and 4,593 ft. There is an indication that the working title for the re-release was *Boots and Saddles*.

QUINCY ADAMS SAWYER **F2.4402**

Sawyer-Lubin Productions. *Dist* Metro Pictures. ca27 Nov **1922** [Baltimore and Washington premieres; released 4 Dec; c29 Dec 1922; LP18554]. Si; b&w. 35mm. 8 reels, 7,895 ft.

Dir Clarence G. Badger. *Adapt-Scen* Bernard McConville. *Photog* Rudolph Bergquist.

Cast: John Bowers *(Quincy Adams Sawyer)*, Blanche Sweet *(Alice Pettengill)*, Lon Chaney *(Obadiah Strout)*, Barbara La Marr *(Lindy Putnam)*, Elmo Lincoln *(Abner Stiles)*, Louise Fazenda *(Mandy Skinner)*, Joseph Dowling *(Nathaniel Sawyer)*, Claire McDowell *(Mrs. Putnam)*, Edward Connelly *(Deacon Pettengill)*, June Elvidge *(Betsy Ann Ross)*, Victor Potel *(Hiram Maxwell)*, Gale Henry *(Samanthey)*, Hank Mann *(Ben Bates)*, Kate Lester *(Mrs. Sawyer)*, Billy Franey *(Bob Wood)*, Taylor Graves, Harry Depp *(Cobb twins)*, Andrew Arbuckle.

Rural comedy-melodrama. Source: Charles Felton Pidgin, *Quincy Adams Sawyer and Mason's Corner Folks* (Boston, 1900). Boston lawyer Quincy Adams Sawyer comes to Mason's Corner to aid Mrs. Putnam in settling her husband's estate. Lindy Putnam tries to vamp him, but Quincy and blind Alice Pettingill strike up a romance. Obadiah Strout, Mrs. Putnam's lawyer, stirs up trouble between blacksmith Nathaniel Sawyer and Quincy that puts Alice in danger. Quincy reveals Strout's efforts to swindle Mrs. Putnam and rescues Alice, whose sight is restored in the excitement. *Lawyers. Bostonians. Blacksmiths. Swindlers. Blindness.*

THE QUITTER **F2.4403**

Columbia Pictures. 1 Apr **1929** [c14 Jun 1929; LP469]. Si; b&w. 35mm. 6 reels, 5,671 ft.

Prod Harry Cohn. *Dir* Joseph Henabery. *Screenplay* Dorothy Howell.

Titl Harry Corn. *Photog* Joseph Walker. *Art Dir* Harrison Wiley. *Film Ed* Arthur Roberts. *Asst Dir* Charles C. Coleman.

Cast: Ben Lyon *(Neal Abbott)*, Dorothy Revier *(Patricia)*, Fred Kohler *(Duffy Thompson)*, Charles McHugh *(Shorty)*, Sherry Hall *(Nick)*, Jane Daly *(Doris)*, Henry Otto *(Dr. Abbott)*, Claire McDowell *(Mrs. Abbott)*.

Melodrama. Source: Dorothy Howell, "The Spice of Life" (publication undetermined). Neal Abbott, a drifter, saves the day by prescribing a treatment for cafe owner Duffy Thompson's prize racehorse, and later at the cafe he meets Patricia, an entertainer. He explains to her the story of his downfall—his training as a surgeon, his first operation, then the automobile collision that occurs on a motor trip with his mother. When his mother requires emergency surgery, he falters, and she dies as a result. Later, Duffy is jealously enraged and starts a fight with Neal, throwing him down the stairs. When Neal is leaving with Patricia, Duffy is about to shoot him, and Patricia—in turn—shoots Duffy; she tells Neal that she actually loved Duffy and had used Neal only to make him jealous. Neal, however, operates on Duffy and saves his life, at which point Patricia confesses her true love for Neal. *Surgeons. Restaurateurs. Wanderers. Entertainers. Filial relations. Horses.*

R. S. V. P. **F2.4404**

Charles Ray Productions. *Dist* Associated First National Pictures. 5 Dec **1921** [c10 Dec 1921; LP17498]. Si; b&w. 35mm. 6 reels, 5,630 ft.

Pres by Arthur S. Kane. *Dir* Charles Ray. *Titl* Withers. Edward. *Story* Rob Wagner. *Photog* George Rizard. *Asst Camera* Ellsworth H. Rumer. *Tech Dir* Richard Bennett. *Film Ed* Harry L. Decker. *Asst Dir* Albert Ray, Charles Van Deroef.

Cast: Charles Ray *(Richard Morgan)*, Florence Oberle *(Mrs. Morgan, his aunt)*, Harry Myers *(Benny Fielding)*, Tom McGuire *(Augustus Jonathan Plimpton)*, Jean Calhoun *(Betty, his daughter)*, Robert Grey *(private detective)*, William Courtright *(butler)*, Ida Schumaker *(Minnie Meadows)*.

Comedy. Richard Morgan, a struggling young artist who refuses loans from his wealthy aunt, shares his luck with neighboring cartoonist Benny Fielding but has no money for models. Betty Plimpton, an old playmate of Richard's, pays him a visit, and mistaking her for a model he uses her for a portrait. When the picture is finished, Betty persuades her father to invite Richard to a dance at their residence. Richard and Benny lack presentable clothes, but both contrive to attend the affair and to dance and talk with the elusive model, whom neither realizes to be the daughter of the host. A suspicious butler sets the house detective onto them, and the chase ends in Richard's studio, where Betty's portrait clears up matters and brings about her marriage to him. *Artists. Cartoonists. Models. Butlers. Detectives. Mistaken identity.*

A RACE FOR LIFE **F2.4405**

Warner Brothers Pictures. 28 Jan **1928** [c18 Jan 1928; LP24891]. Mus score (Vitaphone); b&w. 35mm. 5 reels, 4,777 ft. [Also si.]

Dir D. Ross Lederman. *Story-Scen* Charles R. Condon. *Titl* James A. Starr. *Photog* Ed Du Par. *Film Ed* Charles Henkel, Jr. *Asst Dir* Chauncy Pyle.

Cast: Rin-Tin-Tin *(Rinty, a dog)*, Virginia Brown Faire *(Virginia Calhoun)*, Carroll Nye *(Robert Hammond)*, Bobby Gordon *(Danny O'Shea)*, James Mason *(Bruce Morgan)*, Pat Hartigan *(tramp)*.

Melodrama. The boy, Danny, and his dog, Rinty, leave home and wander onto a racetrack looking for work. The boy, having considerable riding skill, is assigned to ride the star horse, Black Raider, in the big sweepstakes. The owner of a rival stable, determined to win the race, tries to prevent Black Raider from running. With Rinty's help, however, Danny takes the big prize. *Children. Horseracing. Dogs. Horses.*

RACE WILD **F2.4406**

Ellbee Pictures. 14 Jul **1926** [New York State license]. Si; b&w. 35mm. 6 reels, 5,240 ft.

Dir Oscar Apfel. *Photog* William Tuers.

Cast: Rex Lease, Eileen Percy, David Torrence, John Miljan.

Melodrama. A Kentucky colonel will lose the family homestead unless his prize racehorse, Race Wild, wins the Kentucky Derby. A schemer who covets the homestead contrives to keep the horse out of the race, uncoupling the railroad car in which it is being shipped to Churchill Downs. The colonel's daughter and the jockey get the horse to the track, however, and the schemer drugs the jockey. The girl disguises herself in his colors and rides Race Wild to victory. *Kentucky colonels. Jockeys. Mortgages. Horseracing. Kentucky Derby. Horses.*

RACING BLOOD **F2.4407**

Gotham Productions. *Dist* Lumas Film Corp. Jun or 15 Aug **1926** [c23 Jul 1926; LP22950]. Si; b&w. 35mm. 6 reels, 5,500 ft.

Pres by Sam Sax. *Supv* Renaud Hoffman. *Dir* Frank Richardson. *Story-Scen* James Bell Smith. *Photog* Ray June. *Asst Dir* Bert Clark. *Prod Mgr* Glenn Belt.

Cast: Robert Agnew *(James Fleming)*, Anne Cornwall *(Muriel Sterling)*, John Elliott *(John Sterling)*, Clarence Geldert *(Harris Fleming)*, Charles A. Sellon *("Doc" Morton)*, Robert Hale *(Jackey Joe Brooks)*.

Melodrama. Harris Fleming, after losing the estate of his nephew to John Sterling—whose rival horse, "The Devil," wins a race—wires his nephew at college and then kills himself. When Jimmy Fleming receives the wire, he is about to attend a dance with Muriel Sterling and puts it aside; Muriel happily informs him of her father's recent good fortune, and opening the telegram, Jimmy is stunned to learn of the tragic turn of events. He leaves and obtains a job with a small California newspaper as a reporter, and Muriel loses contact with him. At a circus auction, Jimmy buys a handsome horse, in reality Muriel's racer—stolen from her uncle. Later, when Muriel meets Jimmy riding the horse, she does not disclose the horse's identity. Unable to hire a jockey, Jimmy decides to ride the horse in a steeplechase; but when his weight prohibits the entry, Muriel rides it herself and wins not only the race but also Jimmy's love. *Reporters. Horseracing. Suicide. Auctions. Horses.*

THE RACING FOOL **F2.4408**

Harry J. Brown Productions. *Dist* Rayart Pictures. Aug **1927.** Si; b&w. 35mm. 5 reels, 4,956 ft.

Pres by W. Ray Johnston. *Dir* Harry J. Brown. *Scen* George W. Pyper. *Photog* Ben White.

Cast: Reed Howes *(Jack Harlowe)*, Ruth Dwyer *(Helen Drake)*, Ernest Hilliard *(Colwyn Kane)*, William Franey *(Henry Briggs)*, James Bradbury, Sr. *(Tom Harlowe)*, Myles McCarthy *(Cornelius Drake)*.

Action melodrama. Racing driver Jack Harlowe falls in love with Helen Drake, the daughter of his father's rival automobile manufacturer. Having promised his father to drive in the big race, Howes must refuse the girl's request that he drive for her father, but when he learns that another man (who has his eye on the girl) plans to drive for her father and throw the race, Howes receives parental permission to win the race for the rival. *Automobile manufacturers. Automobile racing. Filial relations.*

RACING FOR LIFE **F2.4409**

Columbia Productions. *Dist* C. B. C. Film Sales. 8 Aug **1924** [New York showing; released 1 May or 1 Sep; c31 Jun 1924; P20454]. Si; b&w. 35mm. 5 reels, 4,954 ft.

Dir Henry MacRae. *Story-Scen* Wilfred Lucas. *Photog* Allan Thompson.

Cast: Eva Novak *(Grace Danton)*, William Fairbanks *(Jack Grant)*, Philo McCullough *(Carl Grant)*, Wilfred Lucas *(Hudford)*, Ralph De Palma *(The Champion)*, Lydia Knott *(Mrs. Grant)*, Frankie Darro *(Jimmy Danton)*, Edwin Booth Tilton *(David Danton)*, Frank Whitson *(Hudford's partner)*, Harley Moore *(Murray)*, Harry La Verne *(Diggett)*, George Atkinson *(Jackson Heath)*, Paul J. Derkum *(race starter)*, Ed Kennedy *(Tom Grady)*.

Action melodrama. Grace Danton's father loses his best driver and is in danger of losing money he needs to erase debts. Grace's sweetheart, Jack Grant, agrees to drive in the race if Danton does not prosecute his brother, who has stolen money from Danton. Jack is abducted by his brother, but he escapes in time to win the race and the hand of Grace. *Brothers. Debt. Theft. Automobile racing. Abduction.*

RACING HEARTS **F2.4410**

Famous Players–Lasky. *Dist* Paramount Pictures. 15 Jul **1923** [New York and Detroit premieres; released 11 Mar; c6 Feb 1923; LP18769]. Si; b&w. 35mm. 6 reels, 5,691 ft.

Pres by Adolph Zukor. *Dir* Paul Powell. *Scen* Will M. Ritchey. *Story* Byron Morgan. *Photog* Bert Baldridge.

Cast: Agnes Ayres *(Virginia Kent)*, Richard Dix *(Roddy Smith)*, Theodore Roberts *(John Kent)*, Robert Cain *(Fred Claxton)*, Warren Rogers *(Jimmy Britt)*, J. Farrell MacDonald *(Silas Martin)*, Edwin J. Brady *(Pete Delaney)*, Fred J. Butler *(Burton Smith)*, Robert Brower *(Horatio Whipple)*, Kalla Pasha *(mechanic)*, James A. Murphy, Johnny Wonderlich, Eddie Hefferman *(racing drivers)*.

Comedy-melodrama. Because he refuses to advertise the automobiles he manufactures, John Kent's business is failing. In an effort to gain some publicity, his daughter, Virginia, has a racing car built while Kent is away.

Kent's rival sends his son, Roddy Smith, to spy on the operations and bribes another worker to drive the car and throw the race. Virginia discovers the plot, cannot persuade Roddy to break his promise to drive his father's car, and enters the race herself. She drives to a thrilling victory and marries Roddy. *Automobile manufacture. Automobile racing. Advertising. Bribery. Business management.*

RACING LUCK **F2.4411**

Grand-Asher Distributing Corp. *Dist* Associated Exhibitors. 11 May **1924** [c18 Apr 1924; LU20088]. Si; b&w. 35mm. 6 reels, 5,516 ft.

Dir Herman C. Raymaker. *Story* Jean Havez, Lex Neal. *Photog* Ray June.

Cast: Monty Banks *(The Boy [Mario])*, Helen Ferguson *(The Girl [Rosina])*, Martha Franklin *(The Mother [Mrs. Bianchi])*, D. J. Mitsoras *(The Father [Bianchi])*, Lionel Belmore *(The Uncle)*, Francis McDonald *(Tony Mora)*, William Blaisdell *(cafe proprietor)*, Al Martin, Al Thompson, Ed Carlie, Scaduto *(members of Tony's gang)*.

Comedy. Mario Bianchi comes to the United States and moves in with his uncle, who runs a restaurant in New York City. Mario falls in love with his uncle's adopted daughter, Rosina, and gets into trouble with gangster Tony Mora, knocking Tony down for forcing his attentions on the girl. Tony forces Mario's uncle to fire him and sees to it that Mario cannot keep a job. Mario, mistaken for a famous racing driver, signs with a car manufacturer to drive in an important race. Tony sabotages the car, but Mario wins anyway, receiving a substantial amount of prize money. Mario and Rosina are married. *Italians. Uncles. Restaurateurs. Gangsters. Mistaken identity. Automobile racing. New York City.*

RACING ROMANCE **F2.4412**

Harry J. Brown Productions. *Dist* Rayart Pictures. 26 Feb **1926** [New York State license]. Si; b&w. 35mm. 5 reels, 5,352 ft.

Pres by W. Ray Johnston. *Dir* Harry J. Brown. *Story-Scen* Henry Roberts Symonds. *Photog* William Tuers.

Cast: Reed Howes, Virginia Brown Faire, Harry S. Northrup, Mathilda Brundage, Victor Potel, Ethan Laidlaw.

Melodrama. A young man and girl in Kentucky, who were childhood sweethearts, are separated by a family feud until the young man saves the girl's racehorse from a burning stable. The girl is planning to enter the horse in a big race in a last, desperate attempt to pay off the mortgage on her family's ancestral homestead, and the boy offers to ride it for her. The mortgage-holder attempts to prevent him from riding in the race and has him framed on a trumped-up charge. The sheriff and his men station themselves at the gates of the racetrack, and the young man must hitch the racehorse to a peanut wagon in order to gain access to the track. The young man wins the race, lifts the girl's mortgage, and wins her love. *Sheriffs. Feuds. Horseracing. Mortgages. Kentucky. Fires. Horses.*

RACING ROMANCE **F2.4413**

Balshofer Productions. 4 Aug **1927** [New York State license]. Si; b&w. 35mm. 5 reels, 4,900 ft.

Cast: William Barrymore.

Action melodrama(?). No information about the nature of this film has been found.

A RACING ROMEO **F2.4414**

R-C Pictures. *Dist* Film Booking Offices of America. 1 Sep **1927** [c1 Sep 1927; LP24690]. Si; b&w. 35mm. 7 reels, 5,992 ft.

Pres by Joseph P. Kennedy. *Dir* Sam Wood. *Story-Cont* Byron Morgan. *Camera* Charles G. Clarke. *Asst Dir* Jack McKeown.

Cast: Harold "Red" Grange *(Red Walden)*, Jobyna Ralston *(Sally)*, Trixie Friganza *(Aunt Hattie)*, Walter Hiers *(Sparks)*, Ben Hendricks, Jr. *(Rube Oldham)*, Warren Rogers *(Silas, the chauffeur)*, Ashton Dearholt *(motion picture director)*, Jerry Zier *(leading lady)*.

Romantic comedy-drama. When Red Walden loses out in the annual town motor race, Aunt Hattie Wayne and her niece Sally advise him to pay more attention to his garage. Six months later, as he is preparing for marriage to Sally, she breaks a mirror and fears that bad luck will follow. Then Red, driving Aunt Hattie down a country road, crashes into a tree and is sent walking for help; a wild chase follows when Red is given a ride by Sally's maid. Asserting himself, Red prepares to enter the motor sweepstakes against Rube Oldham, a champion driver. Red arouses Sally's jealousy by flirting with Lorraine Blair, the leading lady of a motion picture company, but he wins Sally back when he wins the race. *Aunts. Mechanics. Actors. Automobile racing. Smalltown life. Superstition. Motion pictures.*

THE RACKET **F2.4415**

Caddo Co. *Dist* Paramount Famous Lasky Corp. 30 Jun **1928** [c30 Jun 1928; LP25429]. Si; b&w. 35mm. 8 reels, 7,646 ft.

Pres by Howard Hughes. *Dir* Lewis Milestone. *Scen* Harry Behn, Del Andrews. *Titl* Eddie Adams. *Adapt* Bartlett Cormack. *Photog* Tony Gaudio. *Film Ed* Tom Miranda.

Cast: Thomas Meighan *(Captain McQuigg)*, Marie Prevost *(Helen Hayes, an entertainer)*, Louis Wolheim *(Nick Scarsi, bootleg king)*, George Stone *(Joe Scarsi, Nick's brother)*, John Darrow *(Ames, a cub reporter)*, Skeets Gallagher *(Miller, a reporter)*, Lee Moran *(Pratt, a reporter)*, Lucien Prival *(Chick, a gangster)*, Tony Marlo *(Chick's chauffeur)*, Henry Sedley *(Corcan, a bootlegger)*, Sam De Grasse *(district attorney)*, Burr McIntosh *("The Old Man")*, G. Pat Collins *(Johnson, a patrolman)*.

Underworld melodrama. Source: Bartlett Cormack, *The Racket, a Play* (New York, 1928). In defiance of a warning, a bootleg gang transports liquor and is stopped by the police. Through the intervention of a powerful politician who wants the votes controlled by the gang, Nick Scarsi, the leader, is freed. Later, Scarsi is caught murdering a patrolman. McQuigg, a police captain with a long-standing grudge against Scarsi, captures him and kills him when he tries to escape. *Police. Gangs. Bootleggers. Politicians. Murder. Revenge.*

THE RACKETEER **F2.4416**

Pathé Exchange. 9 Nov **1929** [c9 Nov 1929; LP843]. Sd (Photophone); b&w. 35mm. 7 reels, 6,119 ft. [Also si; 6,035 ft.]

Assoc Prod Ralph Block. *Dir* Howard Higgin. *Dial Dir* Rollo Lloyd. *Story-Scen* Paul Gangelin. *Dial* A. A. Kline. *Photog* David Abel. *Art Dir* Edward Jewell. *Set Dresser* T. E. Dickson. *Film Ed* Doane Harrison. *Rec Engr* D.A. Cutler, Clarence M. Wickes. *Asst Dir* George Webster. *Prod Mgr* Harry Poppe. *Cost* Gwen Wakeling.

Cast: Robert Armstrong *(Keene)*, Carol Lombard *(Rhoda)*, Roland Drew *(Tony)*, Jeanette Loff *(Millie)*, John Loder *(Jack)*, Paul Hurst *(Mehaffy)*, Winter Hall *(Mr. Simpson)*, Winifred Harris *(Mrs. Simpson)*, Kit Guard *(Gus)*, Al Hill *(Squid)*, Bobby Dunn *(The Rat)*, Hedda Hopper *(Mrs. Lee)*, Bud Fine *(Weber)*.

Romantic melodrama. Mahlon Keene, a suave racketeer, notices Mehaffy, a policeman, arrest a shabby, drunken violinist for vagrancy and bribes him to forget the charge; after Keene and his henchman depart, Rhoda Philbrook appears in a taxi, addresses the musician as "Tony," and has him driven away. Meanwhile, Keene arranges for a planned robbery to be delayed. At a charity function, Keene takes an interest in Rhoda when he detects her cheating at cards; she reveals that she has left her husband for the violinist, whom she hopes to regenerate; and for Rhoda's sake Keene arranges for Tony's appearance at a concert. When threatened by Weber, a rival, Keene shoots him and, after the concert, bids farewell to Rhoda. The rival gang take revenge on Keene, leaving Tony and Rhoda to a new life together. *Racketeers. Violinists. Gambling. Murder.*

THE RADIO FLYER **F2.4417**

Dist Weiss Brothers Artclass Pictures. 24 Dec **1924** [New York State license]. Si; b&w. 35mm. 5 reels.

Dir Harry O. Hoyt.

Cast: Charles Hutchison, Leah Baird.

Society melodrama. No information about the specific nature of this film has been found.

Note: This film was probably cut down from the 15-episode serial, *Wolves of Kultur*, produced by Western Photoplays and released by Pathé in 1918. The serial was written and directed by Joseph A. Golden, and it seems likely that Harry O. Hoyt supervised the reshaping of the original film for this version. *The Law Demands* (1924) was also cut down from the same serial.

RADIO-MANIA **F2.4418**

Herman Holland. *Dist* Teleview Corp., W. W. Hodkinson Corp. 15 Jul **1923.** Si; b&w. 35mm. 6 reels, 5,100-5,700 ft.

Pres by Herman Holland. *Dir* R. William Neill. *Scen* Lewis Allen Browne. *Titl* Joseph W. Farnham. *Photog* George Folsey. *Asst Dir* Charles Van Arsdale.

Cast: Grant Mitchell *(Arthur Wyman)*, Margaret Irving *(Mary Langdon)*, Gertrude Hillman *(Mrs. Langdon)*, W. H. Burton *(Mr. Sterling)*, Isabelle Vernon *(a landlady)*, J. D. Walsh *(Buz Buz)*, J. Burke *(Gin Gin)*, Peggy

Smith *(Pux Pux)*, Betty Borders *(Tuz Tuz)*, Alice Effinger, Peggy Williams *(Martian flappers)*.

Drama. With the prize money he receives for an article on Einstein, inventor Arthur Wyman works on a radio with which he hopes to communicate with Mars. *He does see Martians—grotesque individuals with large heads for their oversize brains—who prove their existence by telling him how to turn coal into diamonds and clay into gold.* Arthur awakens, realizes that he has been dreaming, and becomes very bitter at what he considers his failure, but Mary Langdon encourages him, and Arthur perfects a tickless alarm clock. *Inventors. Telecommunication. Radio. Alchemy. Mars. Albert Einstein.*

Note: "Originally shown [27 Dec 1922] under the title 'Mars' ... as a demonstration of the Teleview. The film has been retitled, cut and reissued." (*Exhibitors Trade Review,* 4 Aug 1923, p432.) The Teleview "is a device which resembles the old-fashioned stereoscope. ... It is explained that the glass used in the 'Teleview' is ordinary window glass, the effect being obtained by a revolving shutter arrangement operated by a small motor concealed in the equipment. ... The 'Teleview' pictures are taken with a camera with two lenses. When viewed by the naked eye they are blurred and vague. Through the machine they are remarkably clear but seem restricted to small projection space." (*Variety,* 5 Jan 1923, p42.)

RAFFLES **F2.4419**

Samuel Goldwyn, Inc. *Dist* United Artists. 26 Jul **1930** [c26 Jul 1930; LP1469]. Sd (Movietone); b&w. 35mm. 8 reels, 6,509 ft. [Also si.]

Prod Samuel Goldwyn. *Dir* Harry D'Abbadie D'Arrast, George Fitzmaurice. *Screenplay* Sidney Howard. *Photog* George Barnes, Gregg Toland. *Art Dir* William Cameron Menzies, Park French. *Film Ed* Stuart Heisler. *Sd Rec* Oscar Lagerstrom. *Asst Dir* H. B. Humberstone. *Tech Dir* Gerald Grove, John Howell.

Cast: Ronald Colman *(Raffles)*, Kay Francis *(Gwen)*, Bramwell Fletcher *(Bunny)*, Frances Dade *(Ethel)*, David Torrence *(McKenzie)*, Alison Skipworth *(Lady Melrose)*, Frederick Kerr *(Lord Melrose)*, John Rogers *(Crawshaw)*, Wilson Benge *(Barraclough)*.

Crime melodrama. Source: Ernest William Hornung, *The Amateur Cracksman* (New York, 1899). Ernest William Hornung and Eugene Wiley Presbrey, *Raffles, the Amateur Cracksman* (New York opening: 27 Oct 1903). Raffles, a clever, suave safecracker who successfully eludes Scotland Yard, falls hopelessly in love with Lady Gwen and decides to go straight. Then his close friend Bunny attempts suicide in desperation over a debt, and he decides to go through with a final robbery to save him. Lady Melrose, who is fascinated by the handsome Raffles, possesses a fabulous diamond necklace, and he seeks to get into her good graces; but Inspector McKenzie learns that burglars are planning to rob Lady Melrose. Using this information to his advantage, Raffles takes the necklace from Crawshaw for safekeeping and returns to London; he is followed by the inspector but manages to win the confidence of Lady Gwen. Cornered, he admits to being an amateur cracksman and escapes through a secret opening in a grandfather's clock, with plans to meet Gwen later in Paris. *Safecrackers. Thieves. Socialites. Criminals—Rehabilitation. Courtship. Scotland Yard. London.*

RAFFLES, THE AMATEUR CRACKSMAN (Universal-Jewel) **F2.4420**

Universal Pictures. 24 May **1925** [c10 Apr 1925; LP21350]. Si; b&w. 35mm. 6 reels, 5,557 ft.

Dir King Baggot. *Scen* Harvey Thew. *Photog* Charles Stumar.

Cast: House Peters *(Raffles)*, Miss Du Pont *(Gwendolyn Amersteth)*, Hedda Hopper *(Mrs. Clarice Vidal)*, Frederick Esmelton *(Captain Bedford)*, Walter Long *(Crawshay)*, Winter Hall *(Lord Amersteth)*, Kate Lester *(Lady Amersteth)*, Freeman Wood *(Bunny Manners)*, Roland Bottomley *(Lord Crowley)*, Lillian Langdon *(Mrs. Tilliston)*, Robert Bolder *(Mr. Tilliston)*.

Melodrama. Source: Ernest William Hornung, *Raffles; Further Adventures of the Amateur Cracksman* (New York, 1901). Eugene Wiley Presbrey, *Raffles, the Amateur Cracksman; a Drama in Four Acts* (New York opening: 27 Oct 1903). On board a ship from India bound for England, Raffles, a mysterious cracksman who once astounded all Britain with his daring thefts, warns one of the passengers to take special care of her necklace lest it be stolen. Soon after, the pearls disappear without a trace. They are, however, returned to the lady in a box of cigarettes when the boat reaches port. Raffles later attends a house party that is also attended by Captain Bedford, a noted criminologist who guarantees that a famous string of pearls can't be stolen. Raffles steals the pearls, and Bedford lays a trap for him with the help of a paroled thief. Lady Gwendolyn, with whom Raffles has fallen in love, learns of the trap and comes to his rooms to warn him. Raffles packs and makes his escape, taking Gwen along. Raffles and Gwen are married, and he returns the pearls and promises to reform. All is forgiven. *Safecrackers. Criminologists. Criminals—Rehabilitation. Nobility. Theft. India. London.*

THE RAG MAN **F2.4421**

Metro-Goldwyn Pictures. 16 Feb **1925** [c9 Mar 1925; LP21215]. Si; b&w. 35mm. 6 reels, 5,968 ft.

Supv Jack Coogan, Sr. *Dir* Eddie Cline. *Story-Scen* Willard Mack. *Photog* Frank Good, Robert Martin. *Film Ed* Irene Morra.

Cast: Jackie Coogan *(Tim Kelly)*, Max Davidson *(Max Ginsberg)*, Lydia Yeamans Titus *(Mrs. Mallory)*, Robert Edeson *(Mr. Bernard)*, William Conklin *(Mr. Kemper)*, Dynamite *(The Horse)*.

Comedy. When a fire breaks out in an orphanage on the East Side of New York, little Tim Kelly runs away in his night clothes. Chased by a cop, Tim takes refuge in the junk wagon of Max Ginsberg. The lonely old man takes pity on Tim, and the two become fast friends; Tim soon becomes a partner in Max's rag and bottle business. Max is also an inventor who has been cheated by a lawyer out of a fortune he had expected through the patenting of a new sort of shuttle. Tim goes to the lawyer and forces him to make full restitution to Max. The partners thereby receive a large sum of money and proceed to live like gentlemen, playing golf and becoming well known as the city's largest antique dealers. *Ragmen. Orphans. Lawyers. Inventors. Shuttles. Golf. New York City—East Side. Horses.*

THE RAGE OF PARIS **F2.4422**

Universal Film Manufacturing Co. 3 Oct **1921** [c24 Sep 1921; LP17011]. Si; b&w. 35mm. 5 reels, 4,968 ft.

Dir Jack Conway. *Scen* Lucien Hubbard, Douglas Doty. *Photog* Harry Vallejo.

Cast: Miss Du Pont *(Joan Coolidge)*, Elinor Hancock *(Mrs. Coolidge)*, Jack Perrin *(Gordon Talbut)*, Leo White *(Jean Marot)*, Ramsey Wallace *(Mortimer Handley)*, Freeman Wood *(Jimmy Allen)*, Eve Southern *(Mignonne Le Place)*, Mathilde Brundage *(Madame Courtigny)*, J. J. Lanoe *(Monsieur Dubet)*.

Melodrama. Source: Du Vernet Rabell, "The White Peacock Feathers" (publication undetermined). "Forced into a loveless marriage by her mother, Joan Coolidge, a beautiful American girl, finds her husband a brute. She runs away to Paris and studies dancing and becomes The Rage of Paris. Her portrait is hung in the art gallery. Her former sweetheart, a civil engineer fresh from conquests in Arabia, sees the portrait and finds her. When he goes to Arabia she follows. Her husband trails her across the ocean into the desert, but is killed by a half-crazed native during a sandstorm. Joan and her old lover are finally reunited." (*Exhibitor's Trade Review,* 1 Oct 1921.) *Dancers. Engineers—Civil. Deserts. Arabia. Paris. Sandstorms.*

Note: Douglas Doty did not receive screen credit for coauthoring the scenario.

THE RAGGED EDGE **F2.4423**

Distinctive Pictures. *Dist* Goldwyn-Cosmopolitan Distributing Corp. 3 or 14 May **1923** [c21 Jun 1923; LP19145]. Si; b&w. 35mm. 7 reels, 6,800 ft.

Dir Harmon Weight. *Adapt* Forrest Halsey.

Cast: Alfred Lunt *(Howard Spurlock)*, Mimi Palmeri *(Ruth Endicott)*, Charles Fang *(Ah Cum)*, Wallace Erskine *(The Doctor)*, George MacQuarrie *(McClintock)*, Charles Slattery *(O'Higgins)*, Christian Frank *(The Wastrel)*, Grace Griswold *(Prudence Jedson)*, Alice May *(Angelina Jedson)*, Percy Carr *(hotel manager)*, Marie Day *(The Aunt)*, Charles Kent *(Rev. Luther Enschede)*, Sidney Drew *(Reverend Dalby)*, Hattie Delaro *(Mrs. Dalby)*.

Romantic drama. Source: Harold MacGrath, *The Ragged Edge* (New York, 1922). Howard Spurlock, wrongfully accused of theft, believes police are seeking his arrest. On "the ragged edge," he takes refuge in China, where he meets and is nursed back to health by Ruth Endicott, daughter of a missionary. They marry and go to an island in the South Seas where, later, his innocence is proved. *Fugitives. Missionaries. Injustice. South Sea Islands. China.*

THE RAGGED HEIRESS **F2.4424**

Fox Film Corp. 19 Mar **1922** [c19 Mar 1922; LP17738]. Si; b&w. 35mm. 5 reels, 4,888 ft.

Pres by William Fox. *Dir* Harry Beaumont. *Story-Scen* Jules Furthman. *Photog* Lucien Andriot.

Cast: Shirley Mason *(Lucia Moreton)*, John Harron *(Glen Wharton)*, Edwin Stevens *(Sam Moreton)*, Cecil Van Auker *(James Moreton)*, Claire McDowell *(Sylvia Moreton)*, Aggie Herring *(Nora Burke)*, Eileen O'Malley *(Lucia, age 3)*.

Society melodrama. Facing a prison term, James Moreton makes provision for the care of his motherless daughter, Lucia, by his brother and sister-in-law; she is cruelly treated by them and runs away with her nurse, Nora Burke. As a young woman, she takes the name Lucia Burke, and after Nora's death she gets a domestic position in the home of her uncle—each unaware of the other's identity. The uncle receives word that the girl's father is to pay them a visit, and in desperation he persuades Lucy to pose as their missing ward. Moreton, sensing that his daughter is in love with young Glen Wharton, tries to bring about their marriage; but Lucy confesses that she is being forced to act the part of his daughter. Sam and his wife then confess to the girl's disappearance, and Lucy is astonished to discover that she is actually Moreton's daughter. Reunited with her father, she receives her rightful inheritance and is united with young Wharton. *Uncles. Domestics. Fatherhood. Inheritance. Impersonation. Personal identity.*

RAGGED ROBIN **F2.4425**

Sanford Productions. 15 Aug **1924.** Si; b&w. 35mm. 5 reels, 4,850 ft.

Dir Frank S. Mattison.

Cast: Matty Mattison.

Melodrama. No information about the nature of this film has been found.

RAGS AND SILKS (Reissue) **F2.4426**

12 Sep **1922** [New York State license]. Si; b&w. 35mm.

Note: A retitling, at least, of *Restless Souls* (Triangle Film Corp., 1919) and not to be confused with Vitagraph's *Restless Souls* (1922). Released by the Alexander Film Corp. in 1922, *Rags and Silks* may have had the alternate title *Restless Souls.*

RAGS TO RICHES **F2.4427**

Warner Brothers Pictures. 24 Sep **1922** [New York premiere; released 7 Oct; c16 Sep 1922; LP18226]. Si; b&w. 35mm. 7 reels, 7,209 ft.

Prod Harry Rapf. *Dir* Wallace Worsley. *Scen* Walter De Leon, William Nigh. *Story* Grace Miller White. *Film Ed* Clarence Kolster.

Cast: Wesley Barry *(Marmaduke Clarke)*, Niles Welch *(Dumbbell [Ralph Connor])*, Ruth Renick *(Mary Warde, an orphan)*, Russell Simpson *(The Sheriff)*, Minna Redman *(The Sheriff's Wife)*, Richard Tucker *(Blackwell Clarke)*, Eulalie Jensen *(Mrs. Blackwell Clarke)*, Jane Keckley *(Marmaduke's governess)*, Sam Kaufman *(Tony, the "Wop")*, Dick Sutherland *(Bull)*, Jimmy Quinn *(Louis, the Dope)*, Snitz Edwards, Aileen Manning *(Purist's League members)*.

Drama. Marmaduke Clarke, a wealthy boy in search of adventure, leaves home to join a gang of crooks. He and Dumbbell strike out by themselves and find work on a farm. Dumbbell falls in love with Mary Warde, but they incur the wrath of the Purist's League when they go to a dance. When a Purist's League delegation, the sheriff, the Clarkes, detectives hired by Mr. Clarke, and the gang of crooks intent on kidnaping Marmaduke, Dumbbell, and Mary all meet up together, Dumbbell reveals himself to be Ralph Connor, Secret Service agent, and turns the gang over to the sheriff. *Gangs. Reformers. Secret service.*

Note: Copyright title: *From Rags to Riches.*

RAGTIME **F2.4428**

James Ormont Productions. *Dist* First Division Distributors. 1 Sep **1927.** Si; b&w. 35mm. 7 reels, 6,441-6,700 ft.

Pres by James Ormont. *Dir* Scott Pembroke. *Scen-Titl* George Dromgold, Jean Plannette. *Story* Joseph Mitchell. *Photog* Ted Tetzlaff, Ernest Miller.

Cast: John Bowers *(Ted Mason)*, Marguerite De La Motte *(Beth Barton)*, Robert Ellis *(Steve [Slick] Martin)*, Rose Dione *(Yvonne [Goldie] Martin)*, William H. Strauss *(Max Ginsberg)*, Kate Bruce *(Mrs. Mason)*, Bernard Siegel.

Society drama. Love comes to Tin Pan Alley pianist Ted Mason and society girl Beth Barton, and Ted writes a song inspired by her charms. Goldie Martin steals the song for her dancer husband, Steve, who publishes it as his own and benefits from its success. Beth, however, is ostracized by her peers and dismissed by her music teacher for her connection with a popular song. Ted writes another, loftier, song, which pleases everyone; he exposes Martin and wins Beth. *Pianists. Socialites. Composers. Dancers. Publishers. Plagiarism. Ragtime. New York City—Tin-pan Alley.*

THE RAIDERS **F2.4429**

William N. Selig Productions. *Dist* Canyon Pictures. May-Jun **1921** [c14 May 1921; LU16500]. Si; b&w. 35mm. 5 reels, 4,850 ft.

Dir Nate Watt. *Scen* William E. Wing.

Cast: Franklyn Farnum *(Private Fitzgerald of the Royal Mounted)*, Bud Osborne *(Private Herrick)*, Vester Pegg *(Bob Thiele)*, Claire Windsor *("Honey" Moore)*, Frederick Soult *("Big" Moore)*, H. Abbott *(Oscar Nelson)*, J. K. Van Buren *(Dave Moore)*, John Hatfield *(Hank Nelson)*.

Northwest melodrama. Source: Bertrand W. Sinclair, "The Whiskey Runners" (publication undetermined). Northwest Mounted Policemen Fitzgerald and Herrick, who are later joined by Indian guide Uncas, have been detailed to track down a gang of whisky-runners. They stop at a farm operated by "Big" Moore; and there Fitzgerald attracts Moore's daughter, "Honey," who has grown distrustful of her childhood sweetheart, Bob Thiele. The Mounties track the smugglers to their lair and rout them; but afterwards, Herrick is killed by a mysterious shot aimed at Fitzgerald. Uncas investigates and finds a clue pointing to Honey's brother Dave. Thiele, however, is revealed as the true murderer and the leader of the smugglers. Thiele defeats Fitzgerald in a fight and is about to shoot him when he is struck dead by lightning. Fitzgerald reports back to headquarters but returns to claim Honey as his bride. *Rumrunners. Indians of North America. Brother-sister relationship. Murder. Lightning. Northwest Mounted Police.*

RAILROADED **F2.4430**

Universal Pictures. 11 Jun **1923** [c4 Jun 1923; LP19057]. Si; b&w. 35mm. 5 reels, 5,390 ft.

Dir Edmund Mortimer. *Scen* Charles Kenyon. *Photog* Allen Davey.

Cast: Herbert Rawlinson *(Richard Ragland)*, Esther Ralston *(Joan Dunster)*, Alfred Fisher *(Hugh Dunster)*, David Torrence *(Judge Garbin)*, Lionel Belmore *(Foster)*, Mike Donlin *(Corton)*, Herbert Fortier *(Bishop Selby)*.

Melodrama. Source: Marguerite Bryant, *Richard* (New York, 1922). Richard Garbin, willful son of Judge Garbin, one of England's most prominent jurists, is railroaded into prison. He escapes, vowing vengeance against Corton, the man who framed him and caused the death of one of his friends. Changing his name to Ragland, he meets his father at a dinner party. Judge Garbin proposes that Richard finish his prison sentence on the estate of his friend, Hugh Dunster. There Richard meets and falls in love with Dunster's daughter, Joan. Joan discovers why Richard is there and prevents him from carrying out his plan of revenge against Corton; they obtain Judge Garbin's blessing and sail for Africa. *Judges. Filial relations. Disguise. Revenge. England.*

Note: Working title: *Thicker Than Water.*

RAIN OR SHINE **F2.4431**

Columbia Pictures. 15 Aug **1930** [c14 Aug 1930; LP1487]. Sd (Movietone); b&w. 35mm. 9 reels, 8,228 ft.

Prod Harry Cohn. *Dir* Frank Capra. *Dial-Cont* Dorothy Howell, Jo Swerling. *Photog* Joseph Walker. *Art Dir* Harrison Wiley. *Film Ed* Maurice Wright. *Songs: "Happy Days Are Here Again," "Rain or Shine"* Jack Yellen, Milton Ager. *Song: "Sitting on a Rainbow"* Jack Yellen, Dan Dougherty. *Ch Sd Engr* John P. Livadary. *Sd Mix Engr* Edward L. Bernds. *Asst Dir* Sam Nelson.

Cast: Joe Cook *(Smiley)*, Louise Fazenda *(Frankie)*, Joan Peers *(Mary)*, William Collier, Jr. *(Bud)*, Tom Howard *(Amos)*, David Chasen *(Dave)*, Alan Roscoe *(Dalton)*, Adolph Milar *(Foltz)*, Clarence Muse *(Nero)*, Edward Martindel *(Mr. Conway)*, Nora Lane *(Grace Conway)*, Tyrrell Davis *(Lord Gwynne)*.

Melodrama. Source: James Gleason, *Rain or Shine* (New York opening: 9 Feb 1928). Smiley Johnson, who acts as Mary Rainey's business and personal manager, falls in love with her and tries, against all odds, to make a success of her father's circus. But Mary becomes infatuated with Bud Conway, a college boy who joins the circus for a lark; and in every town, their business in killed by rain. Bob plans to have his father give the circus financial backing, but Smiley's ridiculous behavior at a dinner spoils the project, causing Mary to fire him and make Dalton, the ringmaster, manager. He and Foltz, the lion tamer, conspire to stir up dissension and make a profit. But Smiley returns and dismisses all the performers, putting on a one-man show with the assistance of Bud and his friends. The audience, however, protests until a riot call is sounded, resulting in a tent fire from which Bob rescues Mary. Convinced of the sincerity of the young lovers, Smiley makes a graceful exit. *Students. Ringmasters. Lion tamers. Business management. Circus. Courtship. Fires.*

RAINBOW **F2.4432**

Vitagraph Co. of America. 20 Nov **1921** [c14 Oct 1921; LP17090]. Si; b&w. 35mm. 5 reels.

Dir Edward José. *Scen* C. Graham Baker. *Story* Harry Dittmar.

Cast: Alice Calhoun *(Rainbow Halliday)*, Jack Roach *(George Standish)*, William Gross *(Shang Jordan)*, Charles Kent *(Andy MacTavish)*, Tom O'Malley *(Denny Farrell)*, George Lessey *(Rufus Halliday)*, Cecil Kern *(Estelle Jackson)*, Tammany Young *(Kid Short)*, Ivan Christie *(Joe Sheady)*.

Society drama. Rainbow Halliday, an orphan, is reared by three self-appointed guardians who work the Rainbow Copper Mine, willed her by her father. She is rescued from the advances of Joe Sheady by young easterner George Standish, who claims ownership of the mine but does not force his rights and instead returns to Chicago to marry a former sweetheart. Rainbow's uncle, Rufus, who is taken ill in Chicago, invites her to visit him; there she discovers that Standish's father did not record the sale of the mine, knowing that Rufus had sold the mine to Rainbow's father. Insulted by George's fiancée, Rainbow decides to surrender the mine and returns home; Standish arrives and is held captive by her guardians, but he is rescued by Rainbow when Sheady sets fire to the cabin. He finds love with Rainbow, and the mine becomes their joint property. *Orphans. Guardians. Mine claims. Copper. Chicago. Documentation.*

THE RAINBOW **F2.4433**

Tiffany-Stahl Productions. 1 Feb **1929** [c11 Jan 1929; LP11]. Sd eff (Photophone); b&w. 35mm. 7 reels, 6,114 ft, 68 min. [Also si.]

Dir Reginald Barker. *Story-Cont* L. G. Rigby. *Titl* Frederic Hatton, Fanny Hatton. *Photog* Ernest Miller. *Art Dir* Hervey Libbert. *Set Dressings* George Sawley. *Film Ed* Robert J. Kern. *Mus Score* Joseph Littau.

Cast: Dorothy Sebastian *(Lola)*, Lawrence Gray *(Jim Forbes)*, Sam Hardy *(Derby Scanlon)*, Harvey Clarke *(Baldy)*, Paul Hurst *(Pat)*, Gino Corrado *(Slug)*, King Zany *(Dummy)*.

Western melodrama. A crook plants a gold-strike story and starts a stampede for the deserted mining town on the edge of Death Valley. One of the suckers who comes seeking gold falls for the girl who is walking with the racketeer. In the climax a mob tracks the escaping gang of crooks to their doom in a sandstorm. *Prospectors. Gold rushes. Hoaxes. Sandstorms.*

RAINBOW CHASERS *see* **CONFIDENCE**

THE RAINBOW MAN **F2.4434**

Sono-Art Productions. *Dist* Paramount Pictures. 18 May **1929** [c17 May 1929; LP390]. Sd; b&w. 35mm. 10 reels, 8,630 ft.

Supv George W. Weeks, O. E. Goebel. *Dir* Fred Newmeyer. *Screenplay* George J. Crone. *Adapt-Cont* Frances Agnew. *Dial* Frances Agnew, Eddie Dowling. *Story* Eddie Dowling. *Photog* Jack MacKenzie. *Film Ed* J. R. Crone. *Songs: "Little Pal," "Rainbow Man"* Eddie Dowling, James F. Hanley. *Song: "Sleepy Valley"* Andrew B. Sterling. *Prod Mgr* J. R. Crone.

Cast: Eddie Dowling *(Rainbow Ryan)*, Frankie Darrow *(Billy Ryan)*, Sam Hardy *(Doc Hardy)*, Lloyd Ingraham *(Colonel Lane)*, Marian Nixon *(Mary Lane)*, George Hayes *(Bill)*.

Comedy-drama. Rainbow Ryan, a minstrel performer, adopts Billy Ryan, the son of an acrobat friend who is killed while performing on stage. Playing in a small town, Rainbow falls in love with Mary Land, the daughter of a strict hotelkeeper who disapproves of all theatrical people. Rainbow moves on with the show, and Mary belatedly discovers that Billy is the child of her dead sister. Mary goes after Rainbow, and he sends Billy back home with her, renouncing his love for her for fear of going against her father's command that she have nothing to do with entertainers. The minstrel show is booked into a small town near Mary's, however, and Billy runs away to see Rainbow. Mary follows, and she and Rainbow are reunited. *Acrobats. Singers. Hotelkeepers. Filial relations. Smalltown life. Minstrel shows. Adoption.*

RAINBOW RANGE **F2.4435**

Dist Anchor Film Distributors. 3 Dec **1929** [New York State license]. Si; b&w. 35mm. 5 reels, 4,300 ft.

Cast: Cheyenne Bill.

Western melodrama(?). No information about the nature of this film has been found.

RAINBOW RANGERS **F2.4436**

William Steiner Productions. *Dist* New-Cal Film Corp. 1 Jul **1924** [c12 Jun 1924; LU20301]. Si; b&w. 35mm. 5 reels, 4,982 ft.

Dir-Writ Forrest Sheldon. *Photog* Ross Fisher.

Cast: Pete Morrison *(Buck Adams)*, Peggy Montgomery *(Rose Warner)*, Lew Meehan *(Manual Lopez)*, Eddie Dennis *(Anteater Jake)*, Nelson McDowell *(Deacon Slim)*, Milburn Morante *(English Charlie)*, Martin Turner *(Barbecue Sam)*, Lafe McKee *(Luke Warner)*, Victor Allen *(Frank Owens)*, Raye Hampton *(Tilly)*.

Western comedy-melodrama. Rose Warner and her father, Luke, are attacked by a band of desperadoes and are rescued by wandering rangers, including an ex-parson, English Charlie, and Barbecue Sam, a Negro cook. "The rescuing rangers are comic types .... They always appear in the nick of time when the girl is about to be left at the mercy of the bandits and put them to rout. The love interest is taken care of toward the finish between 'Buck,' head of the comic heroes, and the girl." (*Film Daily*, 24 Aug 1924.) *Rangers. Bandits. Clergymen. Cooks.*

RAINBOW RILEY **F2.4437**

Burr and Hines Enterprises. *Dist* First National Pictures. 7 Feb **1926** [c2 Feb 1926; LP22350]. Si; b&w. 35mm. 7 reels, 7,057 ft.

Pres by C. C. Burr. *Dir* Charles Hines. *Titl* John W. Krafft. *Photog* Charles E. Gilson, Albert Wetzel, William Wallace. *Film Ed* George Amy, John W. Krafft. *Asst Dir* Charlie Berner. *Prod Mgr* Benny Berk.

Cast: Johnny Hines *(Steve Riley)*, Brenda Bond *(Alice Ripper)*, Bradley Barker *(Tilden McFields)*, Dan Mason *(Dr. Lem Perkins)*, John Hamilton *(halfwit)*, Harlan Knight *(Zeb White)*, Herbert Standing *(newspaper editor)*, Ben Wilson *(Captain Jones)*, Lillian Ardell *(Becky)*.

Comedy. Source: Thompson Buchanan, *The Cub* (New York opening: 1 Nov 1910). Steve Riley, a cub reporter on the *Louisville Ledger*, is assigned to cover a feud in the Kentucky mountains between the Ripper and White clans; Steve falls in love with Alice Ripper, greatly offending the Ripper clan; he ignores Betty White (who loves him) and greatly offends the White clan. Both sides set out to eliminate Steve, and he is forced to go into hiding, taking Alice with him. They are captured by Tilden McFields, one of Alice's suitors, who lets Steve go when Alice promises to renounce his love. Steve later rescues Alice, and both feuding clans are soon in pursuit. Steve holds them off until he is rescued by the state militia. He then returns to Louisville, taking with him a great story and a new wife. *Reporters. Feuds. Newspapers. Mountain life. Louisville (Kentucky). Kentucky.*

THE RAINBOW TRAIL **F2.4438**

Fox Film Corp. 24 May **1925** [c19 Apr 1925; LP21417]. Si; b&w. 35mm. 6 reels, 5,251 ft.

Pres by William Fox. *Dir-Adapt* Lynn Reynolds. *Photog* Daniel Clark.

Cast: Tom Mix *(John Shefford)*, Anne Cornwall *(Fay Larkin)*, George Bancroft *(Jake Willets)*, Lucien Littlefield *(Joe Lake)*, Mark Hamilton *(Beasley Willets)*, Vivian Oakland *(Bessie Erne)*, Thomas Delmar *(Venters)*, Fred De Silva *(Shadd)*, Steve Clements *(Nas Ta Bega)*, Doc Roberts *(Lassiter)*, Carol Halloway *(Jane)*, Diana Miller *(Anne)*.

Western melodrama. Source: Zane Grey, *The Rainbow Trail; a Romance* (New York, 1915). John Shefford discovers from a settler that his missing uncle, Lassiter, has trapped himself and a young woman in Paradise Valley by hurling a boulder from a cliff into the only means of egress from the valley. The way toward Paradise Valley lies through a rough frontier settlement, and John joins a wagon train to avoid arousing suspicion. Once in town, he rescues Fay Larkin, the adopted daughter of the woman trapped with his uncle, just as Fay is about to be forced into marriage uith Willets, the leader of the outlaw gang that chased his uncle into the valley. John goes to the valley with Fay and rescues his uncle and Fay's guardian. Shadd kidnaps Fay, and John rescues her, killing Shadd. *Uncles. Settlers. Outlaws. Wagon trains.*

Note: This production is a sequel to *The Riders of the Purple Sage*, a 1925 Fox film in which Mix plays the part of Lassiter.

THE RAINMAKER **F2.4439**

Famous Players–Lasky. *Dist* Paramount Pictures. 10 May **1926** [c10 May 1926; LP22699]. Si; b&w. 35mm. 7 reels, 6,055 ft.

Pres by Adolph Zukor, Jesse L. Lasky. *Dir* Clarence Badger. *Scen* Hope Loring, Louis Duryea Lighton. *Photog* H. Kinley Martin.

Cast: William Collier, Jr. *(Bobby Robertson)*, Georgia Hale *(Nell*

Wendell), Ernest Torrence *(Mike)*, Brandon Hurst *(Doyle)*, Joseph Dowling *(Father Murphy)*, Tom Wilson *(Chocolate)*, Martha Mattox *(head nurse)*, Charles K. French *(hospital doctor)*, Jack Richardson *(western doctor)*, Melbourne MacDowell *(Benson)*.

Melodrama. Source: Gerald Beaumont. ("Heavenbent," in *Redbook Magazine)*. Bobby Robertson, a popular jockey known familiarly as "The Rainmaker" because of his seeming ability to call forth rain by prayer, collects from both "mud horse" promoters and those who want clear weather; actually, a war wound tells him when his prayers are likely to be efficacious. Thrown in a race, Bobby comes under the ministrations of nurse Nell Wendell, formerly a honky-tonk girl, and falls in love with her. Mike, a bartender friend of Nell's, asks her to work in a new establishment he is opening; she rejects his offer, but when she is discharged, she returns to the old life. When Bobby leaves the hospital, he finds her in a border saloon. Through lack of rain and water, a plague breaks out in the town; and Doyle, a competitor of Mike's, prevents aid from coming. Bobby, in desperation, prays for rain, and the town is saved by a torrential downpour. Mike dies, however, leaving his money to Nell and Bobby, who marry and settle down on a farm. *Veterans. Jockeys. Dancehall girls. Rainmakers. Bartenders. Plague. Hospitals. Saloons.*

THE RAMBLIN' GALOOT **F2.4440**

Action Pictures. *Dist* Associated Exhibitors. 21 Nov **1926** [c10 Nov 1926; LU23319]. Si; b&w. 35mm. 5 reels, 4,438 ft.

Pres by Lester F. Scott, Jr. *Dir* Fred Bain. *Story* Barr Cross. *Photog* Ray Ries.

Cast: Buddy Roosevelt *(Buddy Royle)*, Violet La Plante *(Pansy Price)*, Frederick Lee *(Roger Farnley?)*.

Western melodrama. Cowpuncher Buddy Royle, who is a golf enthusiast, teaches the game to Colonel Price and his daughter, Pansy, on the banker's ranch. Roger Farnley, a bank cashier, belongs to a gang of counterfeiters, and he schemes to frame Buddy by planting fake bills in the bank payroll and having his gang rob the colonel. Buddy is kidnaped by the counterfeiters, but Pansy is alerted and frees him. Buddy exposes the cashier, reveals his identity as an agent of the Bankers' Association, and finds romance with Pansy. *Cowboys. Bank examiners. Bankers. Ranchers. Counterfeiters. Golf.*

THE RAMBLIN' KID **F2.4441**

Universal Pictures. 3 Sep **1923** [New York premiere; released 14 Oct; c17 Sep 1923; LP19423]. Si; b&w. 35mm. 6 reels, 6,395 ft.

Dir Edward Sedgwick. *Scen* E. Richard Schayer. *Photog* Virgil Miller.

Cast: Hoot Gibson *(The Ramblin' Kid)*, Laura La Plante *(Carolyn June)*, Harold Goodwin *(Skinny Rawlins)*, William Welsh *(Lafe Dorsey)*, W. T. McCulley *(Sheriff Tom Poole)*, Charles K. French *(Joshua Heck)*, G. Raymond Nye *(Mike Sabota)*, Carol Holloway *(Mrs. Ophelia Cobb)*, Goober Glenn *(Parker)*, George King *(Sing Pete)*, Gyp Streeter *(John Judd)*.

Western melodrama. Source: Earl Wayland Bowman, *The Ramblin' Kid* (Indianapolis, 1920). The Ramblin' Kid, a cowboy, falls in love with Carolyn June, a beautiful easterner, and wins her after he triumphs in a rodeo in spite of having been doped by his enemy, Sabota the Greek, a crafty racetrack tout. *Cowboys. Touts. Rodeos.*

Note: Working title: *The Long, Long Trail,* the title under which it was remade in 1929.

THE RAMBLING RANGER (Blue Streak Western) **F2.4442**

Universal Pictures. 10 Apr **1927** [c28 Feb 1927; LP23708]. Si; b&w. 35mm. 5 reels, 4,439 ft.

Pres by Carl Laemmle. *Dir* Del Henderson. *Story-Scen* George C. Hively. *Photog* William Nobles. *Art Dir* David S. Garber.

Cast: Jack Hoxie *(Hank Kinney)*, Dorothy Gulliver *(Ruth Buxley)*, C. E. Anderson *(Sam Bruce)*, Monte Montague, Jr. *("Royal Highness")*, Charles Avery *(Seth Buxley)*, Monte Montague *(Sheriff Boy)*, Scout *(Hank's horse)*, Bunk *(Hank's dog)*.

Western melodrama. Hank Kinney, a ranger, witnesses the accidental death of a man and the survival of a motherless infant. Kinney asks the county sheriff to process adoption papers and goes with the child to take up the mining claim left him by his father. Sam Bruce, the richest and most hated man in Copperville, tries to jump the claim and swears vengeance when Kinney kicks him off the property. Kinney strikes up a friendship with Ruth Buxley, daughter of the general store proprietor; and Bruce, who covets the girl, instigates a rumor that Hank is unfit to rear a child and sends the sheriff's posse to get the the baby. Hank escapes with the child, however, and sets out to verify the legality of the adoption. Bruce cows the girl into marrying him, but Hank stops the wedding and claims her for himself. *Rangers. Infants. Courtship. Weddings. Adoption. Mine claims. Documentation. Horses. Dogs.*

RAMONA **F2.4443**

Inspiration Pictures. *Dist* United Artists. May **1928** [c6 Mar 1928; LP25048]. Si; b&w. 35mm. 8 reels, 7,650 ft.

Dir Edwin Carewe. *Scen-Titl* Finis Fox. *Cinematog* Robert B. Kurrle. *Asst Cinematog* Al M. Greene. *Art Dir* Al D'Agostino. *Sets* Tec-Art Studios. *Film Ed* Jeanne Spencer. *Theme Song* Mabel Wayne. *Lyr* L. Wolfe Gilbert. *Asst Dir* Leander De Cordova, Richard Easton.

Cast: Dolores Del Rio *(Ramona)*, Warner Baxter *(Alessandro)*, Roland Drew *(Felipe)*, Vera Lewis *(Señora Moreno)*, Michael Visaroff *(Juan Canito)*, John T. Prince *(Father Salvierderra)*, Mathilde Comont *(Marda)*, Carlos Amor *(sheepherder)*, Jess Cavin *(bandit leader)*, Jean *(himself, a dog)*, Rita Carewe *(baby)*.

Historical melodrama. Source: Helen Hunt Jackson, *Ramona* (Boston, 1884). Ramona, a halfbreed, is adopted by Señora Moreno, a wealthy Spanish sheep rancher, and reared under cruel restraints, her only consolation being in Felipe, the woman's son. At sheep-shearing time, Ramona discovers her ancestry and defies her guardian by eloping with Alessandro, a young Indian chieftain. Their pastoral happiness is marred by the death of their daughter after an outlaw attack; they retreat to the mountains, where Alessandro, accused of horsethievery, is murdered by a settler. Ramona suffers a nervous collapse and becomes a wandering outcast; Felipe finds her and tries to restore her memory. His efforts are fruitless until a childhood song reminds Ramona of her youthful abandon and returns her to the present. *Indians of North America. Spanish. Halfcastes. Race relations. Amnesia. Murder. Dogs.*

THE RAMPANT AGE **F2.4444**

Continental Talking Pictures. 15 Jan **1930** [c30 Dec 1929; LP 11146]. Sd (Photophone); b&w. 35mm. 6 reels, 5,743 ft.

Prod Trem Carr. *Dir* Phil Rosen. *Scen* Harry O. Hoyt. *Dial* John Elliott. *Story* Robert S. Carr. *Photog* Herbert Kirkpatrick. *Rec Engr* Neil Jack, C. F. Franklin.

Cast: James Murray *(Sandy Benton)*, Merna Kennedy *(Doris Lawrence)*, Eddie Borden *(Eddie Mason)*, Margaret Quimby *(Estelle)*, Florence Turner *(Mrs. Lawrence)*, Patrick Cunning *(De Witt)*, Gertrude Messinger *(Julie)*, John Elliott *(Mr. Benton)*.

Society melodrama. While the youthful society set is partying at the Long Island estate of the Bentons, Sandy, their son, is visiting Doris Lawrence and her grandmother nearby. Doris, a sweet and conservative type, declines to join the party, and Sandy returns to his guests. During a football game, Estelle is "tackled" by Sandy—an incident she uses as an excuse to engage in romance. The next day, Sandy takes Estelle for a ride in his airplane, and she insists that they land in a field and spend the night with friends. Doris learns of this incident and decides to be "modern"; and escorted to a party by Eddie Mason, she flirts with De Witt to make Sandy jealous. She enters a slave auction at a charity bazaar and stays out late at a beach party with De Witt. Infuriated, Sandy berates her, causing her to take off capriciously in his airplane; he goes to her rescue, but she crashes into a hangar. In the hospital, they affirm their love for each other and promise fidelity. *Socialites. Aviators. Jazz life. Courtship. Bazaars. Airplane accidents. Long Island.*

RAMSHACKLE HOUSE **F2.4445**

Tilford Cinema Corp. *Dist* Producers Distributing Corp. 31 Aug **1924** [c1 Sep 1924; LP20701]. Si; b&w. 35mm. 6 reels, 6,257 ft.

Dir Harmon Weight. *Scen* Coolidge Streeter. *Photog* Larry Williams, Bert Wilson.

Cast: Betty Compson *(Pen Broome)*, Robert Lowing *(Don Counsell)*, John Davidson *(Ernest Riever)*, Henry James *(Pendleton Broome)*, William Black *(Keesing)*, Duke Pelzer *(Spike Talley)*, Josephine Norman *(Blanche Paglar)*, Joey Joey *(alligator wrestler)*.

Melodrama. Source: Hulbert Footner, *Ramshackle House* (New York, 1922). Pen Broome, who lives with her father on their rundown estate in southern Florida, helps Don Counsell hide from detectives who seek him for the murder of his business partner. Don is being framed by Ernest Riever, who holds the real murderer, Spike Talley, captive aboard his yacht; and Don is finally captured by Riever and placed in a ballast bulkhead into which water is allowed to flow. Pen finds the yacht with the aid of a Seminole Indian and offers Riever marriage in return for Don's life just as Spike breaks in and, fearing a doublecross, denounces Riever for the murder. Detectives enter and rescue Don, while Riever shoots himself. *Seminole Indians. Murder. Suicide. Florida.*

THE RANCHERS **F2.4446**
Phil Goldstone Productions. *Dist* Advance Pictures. 20 Sep **1923** [New York State license]. Si; b&w. 35mm. 5 reels.
Cast: George Elliot.
Western melodrama(?). No information about the nature of this film has been found. *Ranchers.*

RANCHERS AND RASCALS **F2.4447**
William Steiner Productions. 19 Sep **1925** [New York State license]. Si; b&w. 35mm. 5 reels, 4,600 ft.
Cast: Leo Maloney, Josephine Hill, Whitehorse, Evelyn Thatcher, Barney Furey, Patricia Darling, Tom London, Bud Osborne, Bullet *(himself, a dog).*
Western melodrama(?). No information about the precise nature of this film has been found. *Ranchers. Dogs.*

RANGE BLOOD **F2.4448**
Ashton Dearholt Productions. *Dist* Arrow Film Corp. 15 May **1924** [c10 Apr 1924; LP20064]. Si; b&w. 35mm. 5 reels, 4,650 ft.
Dir-Writ Francis Ford.
Cast: Edmund Cobb.
Western melodrama. "... dealing with the intrigue of an unscrupulous woman to acquire ownership of a ranch which she believes will be bought for a handsome price by a railroad. The foreman instructed to drive out the owners of the ranch, falls in love with the girl who lives there with her mother. He then decides to protect her and several fights ensue. Eventually the invaders are driven off and the young foreman wins the girl." (*Motion Picture News Booking Guide,* [7]:40, Oct 1924.) *Ranch foremen. Property rights. Ranches. Railroads.*

RANGE BUZZARDS **F2.4449**
Lariat Productions. *Dist* Vitagraph Co. of America. c12 Sep **1925** [LP21816]. Si; b&w. 35mm. 5 reels.
Dir Tom Gibson. *Story-Cont* Victor Roberts.
Cast: Pete Morrison *(Dave Weston).*
Western melodrama. A representative of a firm that deals in phosphate discovers a valuable deposit of that mineral on a ranch owned by Grandma Daniels. He hires a thug named Jim Bascomb to force the old lady, who does not know of her good fortune, to sell him the ranch. Dave Weston, a cowboy, gets the deed to the ranch back for Grandma and protects her granddaughter from the smooth advances of the phosphate dealer. Dave brings the criminals to justice and wins the hand of the young girl. *Cowboys. Grandmothers. Phosphate. Land rights. Ranches.*

RANGE COURAGE (Blue Streak Western) **F2.4450**
Universal Pictures. 24 Jul **1927** [c9 Jun 1927; LP24089]. Si; b&w. 35mm. 5 reels, 4,388 ft.
Pres by Carl Laemmle. *Dir* Ernst Laemmle. *Adapt* Robert F. Hill. *Photog* Al Jones. *Art Dir* David S. Garber.
Cast: Fred Humes *(Lem Gallagher)*, Gloria Grey *(Betty Martin)*, Dick Winslow *(Jimmy Blake)*, William A. Steele *(Tex Lucas)*, Robert Homans *(Pop Gallagher)*, Arthur Millett *(John Martin)*, Monte Montague *(Bart Allan)*, Charles L. King *(Red Murphy)*, Morgan Brown *(sheriff).*
Western melodrama. Source: Gene Markey, "Blinky," in *Blue Book* (36: 140–149, Jan 1923). Lem Gallagher returns west after a 5-year period of European cultivation and finds that his sweetheart, Betty Martin, spurns his sophistication; she dares him to ride an outlaw horse, and he refuses, thus earning the reputation of a mollycoddle. Tex Lucas, a hotel owner, attacks and kills Jed Wilson for admiring Betty; Lem, who witnesses the shooting, is suspected of the killing. Lem tames the outlaw horse and rides him to the scene of the murder, where he finds an empty shell from a peculiar gun. Evading Tex's henchmen, he goes to the villain's hideout; Tex escapes and forces Betty to cross the border with him. Lem overcomes his captors, pursues and overcomes Tex, and regains the admiration of Betty. *Ranchers. Manhood. Murder. Mexican border. Horses.*

RANGE JUSTICE **F2.4451**
Arrow Pictures. 8 Aug **1925** [c24 Jun 1925; LP21591]. Si; b&w. 35mm. 5 reels.
Dir Ward Hayes. *Story* George W. Pyper.
Cast: Dick Hatton, Star *(a horse).*
Western melodrama. Dick Williams, who has just inherited the Bar M Ranch, saves Joan Avery, the sheriff's daughter, when her horse bolts after it is frightened by a timber wolf. Robert Barlow, the town moneylender, steals a substantial sum of money from Keller and arranges for Dick to be framed for the theft. When Keller meets up with Dick, the men get into a fight, during which Barlow shoots and kills Keller. Dick is blamed for the murder and is arrested by the sheriff, who, believing in Dick's innocence, allows him to escape. The deputy sheriff proves Barlow to have been Keller's murderer, but the hangman is cheated, for John Martin, who has been looking for Barlow during the past 18 years, finds him and, in an attempt to strangle him, knocks him off a cliff. *Ranchers. Sheriffs. Moneylenders. Inheritance. Frameup. Murder. Theft. Wolves. Horses.*

THE RANGE PATROL **F2.4452**
Premium Picture Productions. *Dist* Independent Pictures. Aug **1923.** Si; b&w. 35mm. 5 reels, 4,800 ft.
Dir H. G. Moody. *Photog* H. C. Cook.
Cast: Jack Livingston, Mary Wynn, Al Ferguson.
Western melodrama. "Tells of the efforts and adventures of a sergeant in the Range Patrol of Arizona to track down a band of cattle rustlers and rescue his sweetheart from their clutches" (*Motion Picture News Booking Guide,* 5:44, Oct 1923.) *Rangers. Rustlers. Arizona.*

THE RANGE PIRATE **F2.4453**
Westart Pictures. 22 Jun **1921** [Woodhaven, N. Y., showing]. Si; b&w. 35mm.
Dir Leonard Franchon. *Writ* W. M. Smith. *Photog* A. H. Vallet.
Cast: Al Hart, Jack Mower, Robert Conville.
Western melodrama. No information about the precise nature of this film has been found.

THE RANGE RAIDERS **F2.4454**
Bud Barsky Productions. *Dist* Wild West Pictures. Feb **1927.** Si; b&w. 35mm. 5 reels, 4,500 ft.
Dir Paul Hurst.
Cast: Al Hoxie.
Western melodrama. "Hero prevents theft of ranch property by man who also desires possession of girl with whom hero is in love. He succeeds in driving villain over border and claims girl." (*Motion Picture News Booking Guide,* 12:51, Apr 1927.) *Ranches. Property rights.*

RANGE RIDERS *see* **STRAIGHT SHOOTIN'**

THE RANGE RIDERS **F2.4455**
Ben Wilson Productions. *Dist* Rayart Pictures. Apr **1927.** Si; b&w. 35mm. 5 reels, 4,231 ft.
Dir Ben Wilson. *Scen* Robert Dillon. *Titl* Earl C. Turner. *Photog* Eddie Linden. *Film Ed* Earl C. Turner.
Cast: Ben Wilson *(Senora Shannon)*, Neva Gerber *(Betty Grannan)*, Al Ferguson *("Sundown" Sykes)*, Ed La Niece *(Henry Fellows)*, Earl C. Turner *(Captain Lane)*, Fang *(Pard, the dog).*
Western melodrama. "Range rider is sent out to run down a band of thieves. He falls in love with a sister of one of the gang. When a boy is killed by the leader, he starts out in earnest and brings back his man." (*Motion Picture News Booking Guide,* 13:38, Oct 1927.) *Cowboys. Gangs. Thieves. Brother-sister relationship. Dogs.*

THE RANGE TERROR **F2.4456**
Independent Pictures. *Dist* Film Booking Offices of America. 25 Jan **1925** [c25 Jan 1925; LP21082]. Si; b&w. 35mm. 5 reels, 4,753 ft.
Dir William James Craft. *Cont* George Plympton. *Story* James Ormont. *Photog* Art Reeves.
Cast: Bob Custer *(Speed Meredith)*, Thais Valdemar *(Virginia Allen)*, Claire De Lorez *(Teresa)*, Boris Bullock *(Bud Allen)*, H. J. Herbert *(Reagan)*, Bobby Mack *(Sims)*, Tom Sharkey *(Burke)*, Milburn Morante *(Sam Lee)*, Alaska *(a dog).*
Western melodrama. Having been robbed and mortally wounded, Bud Allen lives long enough to give a description of his assailant to Texas Ranger Speed Meredith. Sometime later, when Speed prevents a holdup of the Goldville stage, he meets Bud's sister, Virginia, for whom he feels both sympathy and love. When Speed begins to suspect a professional gambler named Reagan of Bud's murder, he arranges for Virginia to pose as a saloon entertainer in order to help him produce evidence of the gambler's

guilt. Virginia discovers Bud's money belt among Reagan's possessions, and Speed then positively identifies Reagan by stripping off the gambler's glove and disclosing the absence of a finger as described by Bud. Speed and Reagan fight, setting fire to the saloon. Reagan escapes and is torn to pieces by Bud's dog. Speed decorates the dog with a ranger badge and asks Virginia to enter into partnership with him on a permanent basis. *Gamblers. Texas Rangers. Murder. Robbery. Stagecoach robberies. Saloons. Dogs.*

RANGE VULTURES **F2.4457**

Ward Lascelle Productions. 17 Jun **1925** [New York State license]. Si; b&w. 35mm. 5 reels, 4,800 ft.

Cast: Lester Cuneo.

Western melodrama. "The Range Vultures are a band of outlaws who kill, kidnap, rob and blackmail. Cuneo, the Ranger pretends to be a thief and joins the vultures. He finds a girl in the camp kidnapped and held for $5000 ransom. He is sent to collect the ransom and tells the sheriff where the gang is hiding and how they work. The Vultures learn of this and they all attempt to kill him. He escapes wounded. In trying to rescue the girl, the Ranger and Vultures engage in continuous fighting and shooting. The picture is made up entirely of crime and outlawry." (New York State license records.) *Gangs. Sheriffs. Texas Rangers. Kidnaping. Ransom.*

RANGELAND **F2.4458**

William Steiner Productions. 26 Jan **1922** [New York license application; c28 Jan 1922; LU17504]. Si; b&w. 35mm. 5 reels, 4,500 ft.

Dir-Scen Neal Hart. *Scen* Paul Hurst. *Photog* Jacob A. Badaracco.

Cast: Ben Corbett *(Chuck Quigley)*, Patrick Megehee *(Sheriff John Hampton)*, Neal Hart *(Ned Williams)*, Max Wesell *(Bud Spaugh)*, William Quinn *(Buck Kelley)*, Blanche McGarity *(Betty Howard)*.

Western melodrama. Ex-cowboy Ned Williams, now a deputy sheriff feared by outlaws, captures a pair of men who are tampering with their neighbors' cattle and thus incurs the wrath of Bud Spaugh, their leader. Ned is ordered to arrest a cattle thief in the area: the "rustler" turns out to be a forlorn little girl who steals to keep her brothers and sisters from starving, and Ned becomes attached to her. Spaugh frames Ned with a holdup, then kidnaps the girl. Ned escapes, rescues the girl, and in a struggle in the lava pits succeeds in making a prisoner of Spaugh. *Sheriffs. Rustlers. Kidnaping. Texas.*

THE RANGER AND THE LAW **F2.4459**

Dist Capital Film Co. 22 Jan **1921** [trade review]. Si; b&w. 35mm. 5 reels.

Dir Robert Kelly. *Story* Henry McCarty, Leo Meehan.

Cast: Lester Cuneo *(Dick Dawson)*, Walter I. McCloud *(Matthew Dawson)*, Francelia Billington *(Ann Hobbs)*, Clark Comstock *(Red Hobbs)*, Roy Watson *(Slim Dixon)*, Phil Gastrock *(Apache Joe, "The Weasel")*, Maxwell Morgan *(Daniel Ferguson)*, Fernando Galvez, David Kirby, Lester Howley *(bootleggers)*.

Western melodrama. Dick Dawson decides against going into business with his father and goes west to become a forest ranger. He is thought to be a mollycoddle until he levels Slim Dixon, a whisky runner disguised as a ranger. Dixon seeks revenge and informs the leader of the gang, Red Hobbs, of Dick's potential danger. Dick meets Red's daughter, Ann, who is prohibited from seeing Dick again. When she is caught signaling him from the mountain peak, her father binds her hands and feet and places her in a mine. Dick rushes to save her but is first confronted with Hobbs; a fist fight ensues, and Hobbs rolls into the river and drowns. Dick reaches Ann just as Dixon is about to carry her off on horseback; undaunted, Dick disposes of Dixon and proposes marriage to Ann. *Forest rangers. Gangs. Rumrunners. Mollycoddles. Filial relations.*

RANGER BILL **F2.4460**

William (Bill) Mix Productions. 15 Jan **1925.** Si; b&w. 35mm. 5 reels.

Cast: Dick Carter, Dorothy Wood.

Western melodrama. "Concerns search for valuables alleged by sheriff's son to have been stolen in stage coach robbery. Hero is under suspicion, but he turns the tables and exposes the sheriff and his son, who has wronged the sister of hero's sweetheart. The love romance reaches a happy conclusion." (*Motion Picture News Booking Guide*, 8:66, Apr 1925.) *Sheriffs. Brother-sister relationship. Stagecoach robberies.*

RANGER OF THE BIG PINES **F2.4461**

Vitagraph Co. of America. 26 Jul **1925** [c22 Aug 1925; LP21771]. Si; b&w. 35mm. 7 reels, 7,032 ft.

Dir William S. Van Dyke. *Adapt-Scen* Hope Loring, Louis D. Lighton. *Photog* Allan Thompson.

Cast: Kenneth Harlan *(Ross Cavanagh)*, Helene Costello *(Virginia Weatherford)*, Eulalie Jensen *(Lize Weatherford)*, Will Walling *(Sam Gregg)*, Lew Harvey *(Joe Gregg)*, Robert Graves *(Redfield)*.

Western melodrama. Source: Hamlin Garland, *Cavanagh, Forest Ranger; a Romance of the Mountain West* (New York & London, 1910). After being away from Sulfur Springs for 10 years, Virginia Weatherford returns home from college. She is shocked to discover that her mother, running a hotel with a rough clientele, has become as hardened and tough as her roomers. Virginia falls in love with Ross Cavanagh, a forest ranger who reconciles her to her new life. Cavanagh runs afoul of Sam Gregg, a cattle baron, who resents the new government tax on all cattle grazed on public land. Gregg sends his men to persuade Cavanagh, by whatever means necessary, to ignore the new tax. There is a pitched battle, and Virginia helps Cavanagh fight off Gregg's men. After enforcing the tax, Cavanagh returns to the East, taking Virginia and her mother with him. *Forest rangers. Cattlemen. Hotels. Taxes.*

RANGER OF THE NORTH **F2.4462**

FBO Pictures. 9 Oct **1927** [c9 Oct 1927; LP24724]. Si; b&w. 35mm. 5 reels, 4,977 ft.

Pres by Joseph P. Kennedy. *Dir* Jerome Storm. *Adapt* Leon D'Usseau. *Story* Ewart Adamson. *Ch Camera* Charles Boyle. *Asst Dir* Ray McCarey.

Cast: Ranger *(himself, a dog)*, Hugh Trevor *(Bob Fleming)*, Lina Basquette *(Felice MacLean)*, Bernard Siegel *(Bruce MacLean/Eagle Claw)*, Jules Rancourt *(Louis Dubois)*, William Van Vleck *(Haggerty)*.

Adventure melodrama. Bob Fleming, a city-bred youth, goes deep into the northern woods, and at the cabin of Bruce MacLean he meets and falls in love with Felice, MacLean's granddaughter, also loved by Dubois, a trapper. Dubois insults Bob, and when he refuses to fight, Felice turns to Dubois in pique. Bob removes a porcupine quill from Ranger, a wild dog, who then attacks Dubois when he tries to kill Bob. MacLean persuades Bob to investigate a mountain, reputed to hold a treasure; while climbing he falls into a pit in which he discovers a skeleton and a map showing the location of the gold. He and Ranger find the treasure but are trapped in a cave by Eagle Claw. Ranger is able to escape, and, though detained, he leads Felice to the cave and kills Eagle Claw and his dog. In a thrilling canoe chase, Dubois and his accomplice plunge to their deaths in the falls. *Trappers. Indians of North America. Treasure. Canadian Northwest. Chases. Dogs.*

RANGER'S OATH **F2.4463**

William M. Pizor Productions. **1928.** Si; b&w. 35mm. 5 reels, 4,300 ft.

Dir Robert J. Horner. *Scen* L. V. Jefferson. *Titl* Jack Kelly. *Photog* Lauren A. Draper. *Film Ed* William Austin.

Cast: Al Hoxie.

Western melodrama(?). No information about the nature of this film has been found.

RANSOM **F2.4464**

Columbia Pictures. 30 Jun **1928** [c21 Jul 1928; LP25516]. Si; b&w. 35mm. 6 reels, 5,484 ft.

Prod Harry Cohn. *Story-Dir* George B. Seitz. *Cont* Dorothy Howell. *Titl* Mort Blumenstock. *Adapt* Elmer Harris. *Photog* Joseph Walker. *Art Dir* Joseph Wright. *Asst Dir* Joe Nadel.

Cast: Lois Wilson *(Lois Brewster)*, Edmund Burns *(Burton Meredith)*, William V. Mong *(Wu Fang)*, Blue Washington *(Oliver)*, James B. Leong *(Scarface)*, Jackie Coombs *(Bobby)*.

Melodrama. Burton Meredith, a chemist working for the government, discovers the formula for a highly deadly gas, and Wu Fang, the leader of the Chinese underworld, sets out to rob him of the discovery. He kidnaps Bobby Brewster, the son of Burton's fiancée, Lois, and promises to return the boy unharmed if Lois can obtain the poison gas for him. Lois goes to Burton's laboratory and begs him for the formula; he refuses, and, in a frenzy, she steals a vial of gas and, before Burton can stop her, takes it to Wu Fang. The bottle does not contain the nerve gas, however, and Wu Fang prepares to torture her. Burton discovers the location of the Chinese hideout and rescues Bobby and Lois from death. The police arrive and arrest the gang, and Lois and Burton decide to get hitched. *Chinese. Chemists. Widows. Gangs. Lethal gas. Kidnaping. Torture.*

RANSON'S FOLLY F2.4465

Inspiration Pictures. *Dist* First National Pictures. 30 May **1926** [c4 May 1926; LP22672]. Si; b&w. 35mm. 8 reels, 7,322 ft.

Dir Sidney Olcott. *Adapt* Lillie Hayward. *Photog* David W. Gobbett.

Cast: Richard Barthelmess *(Lieutenant Ranson)*, Dorothy Mackaill *(Mary Cahill)*, Anders Randolf *(The Post Trader)*, Pat Hartigan *(Sergeant Clancy)*, William Norton Bailey *(Lieutenant Crosby)*, Brooks Benedict *(Lieutenant Curtis)*, Col. C. C. Smith, U. S. A. *(Colonel Bolland)*, Pauline Neff *(Mrs. Bolland)*, Billie Bennett *(Mrs. Truesdale)*, Frank Coffyn *(Post Adjutant)*, Capt. John S. Peters, U. S. A. *(Judge Advocate)*, Taylor Duncan *(Captain Car)*, Jack Fowler *(Colonel Patten)*, E. W. Corman *(Pop Henderson)*, Bud Pope *(Abe Fisher)*, Forrest Seabury *(drummer)*, Chief Eagle Wing *(Indian Pete)*, Chief Big Tree *(Chief Standing Bear)*.

Romantic drama. Source: Richard Harding Davis, *Ranson's Folly* (New York, 1902). Lieutenant Ranson, an adventuresome United States Army officer, finds life dreary at his outpost on the western frontier, though he is in love with Mary Cahill. Ranson decides to hold up the stagecoach as a harmless prank, disguised as the "Red Rider," a notorious bandit; in the stage are a Miss Post and her aunt, coming to visit Colonel Bolland. Ranson doubles back to the post, dons his dress uniform, and claims a dance with Miss Post. Word arrives that the paymaster, following the stage, has been shot by the "Red Rider" after the stage holdup; and concluding that Ranson is guilty, military police arrest him and confine him to his quarters, where he is visited by Mary, who alone believes him innocent. At the court-martial Mary's father gives evidence against Ranson; and realizing that he might be freed at Cahill's expense, Ranson pleads guilty. When Cahill discovers his daughter's love for Ranson, he confesses, but word is received of the guilty party's capture elsewhere. The course of true love is cleared. *Stagecoach robberies. Military life. Frontier and pioneer life. Courts-martial. United States Army.*

RAPID FIRE ROMANCE F2.4466

Harry J. Brown Productions. *Dist* Rayart Pictures. 6 Oct **1926** [New York State license]. Si; b&w. 35mm. 5 reels, 5,178 ft.

Dir Harry J. Brown.

Cast: Billy Sullivan *(Tommy Oliver)*, Marjorie Bonner *(Dixie Denman)*, Harry Buckley *("Satin Fingers")*, Johnny Sinclair *("Breezy" Denman)*.

Action melodrama. "Falling in with crooks, Tommy Oliver plays role of willing disciple with hope of inducing girl member of gang to forsake pathway of crime. Girl reforms and they both succeed in saving small town bank from thieves. They face future happiness." *(Motion Picture News Booking Guide,* 11:43, Oct 1926.) *Gangs. Criminals—Rehabilitation. Imposture. Banks.*

RARIN' TO GO F2.4467

Action Pictures. 15 Aug **1924** [c22 Jul 1924; LU20417]. Si; b&w. 35mm. 5 reels, 4,641 ft.

Prod Lester F. Scott, Jr. *Dir* Richard Thorpe.

Cast: Buffalo Bill Jr. *(Bill Dillon)*, Olin Francis *(Hawk Morton)*, L. J. O'Connor *(John Taylor)*, James Kelly *(Mr. Harper)*, Dorothy Wood *(Miss Harper)*, Karleen Day *(Miss Williams)*.

Western melodrama. Source: Ralph Cummins, "Rattler Rock," in *Ace High Magazine* (12:241–280, 18 Aug 1923). Bill Dillon is denied employment at the Harper ranch but gets a job with the Taylors, whose difficulties with an irrigation project are then resolved through Bill's friendship with Dorothy Harper. Discovering a plot to steal the payroll, Dillon is harassed by foreman Hawk Morton, but he escapes to rescue Dorothy and her father. *Ranch foremen. Theft. Ranches. Irrigation.*

THE RATTLER F2.4468

Ermine Productions. 4 Jan **1925** [c17, 19 Jan 1925; LU21074]. Si; b&w. 35mm. 5 reels.

Dir Paul Hurst. *Scen* George Hively. *Photog* Frank Cotner.

Cast: Jack Mower *(Chick McGuire)*, George Williams *(Pop Warner)*, Alma Rayford *(Arline Warner)*, William Buckley *(Cecil Aubrey)*, Vester Pegg *(Blink Dudley)*.

Western melodrama. Chick McGuire and Arline Warner are in love, but Arline's father, who owns the large cattle ranch on which Chick works as a ramrod, opposes the marriage and demands instead that Arline marry Cecil Aubrey, the son of an old friend in the East. When Chick and Arline make plans to elope, they are overheard by Cecil, who plots to kidnap the lovers with the help of Blink Dudley, a fence-cutting sheepman whom Chick once overcame in a fight. By treachery and violence, Blink and Cecil kidnap Chick and Arline and take them to a cabin in the mountains. Chick is tied up and forced to watch a mock marriage between Cecil and Arline, presided over by Blink. Chick frees himself and knocks out Cecil, but Blink escapes. Chick sends Arline back to the ranch with Cecil and follows Blink into the desert. Blink gets the drop on Chick at a poisoned waterhole, but Chick distracts his attention by imitating a rattler and shoots him in the arm. Chick takes Blink back to the Warner ranch, Cecil is sent home in disgrace, and Pop Warner gives his permission for Chick and Arline to marry. *Cowboys. Sheepmen. Elopement. Kidnaping. Marriage—Fake. Snakes.*

RAWHIDE F2.4469

Action Pictures. *Dist* Associated Exhibitors. 23 May **1926** [c5 May 1926; LU22675]. Si; b&w. 35mm. 5 reels, 4,460 ft.

Pres by Lester F. Scott, Jr. *Dir* Richard Thorpe. *Scen* Frank L. Inghram. *Story* Ralph Cummins.

Cast: Buffalo Bill Jr. *(Rawhide Rawlins)*, Al Taylor *(Jim Reep)*, Molly Malone *(Nan)*, Joe Rickson *(Strobel)*, Charles Whitaker *(Blackie Croont)*, Harry Todd *(Two Gun)*, Ruth Royce *(Queenie)*, Lafe McKee *(The Law)*.

Western melodrama. Rawhide Rawlins returns to Paradise Hole after having spent 5 years evading the law for his supposed killing of Charlie Reep, who with Strobel and himself operated a mine. He forces Croont, Strobel's henchman, to apologize to blind Nan, the saloon pianist, for his insults and witnesses a deal between Jim Reep and Strobel. Still keeping his identity secret, Rawhide visits Charlie's grave with Two Gun, an eccentric character, and suggests that he was framed; he incurs the enmity of Nan, who believes that he was involved in a plot that resulted in the death of her father and sister. Nan is revealed to be cured of her blindness and to be aware of Strobel's perfidy; Rawhide forces Strobel to sign over the mine claim and rescues Nan from kidnapers. *Fugitives. Pianists. Mine claims. Blindness. Personal identity. Kidnaping. Saloons.*

THE RAWHIDE KID (Universal-Jewel) F2.4470

Universal Pictures. 29 Jan **1928** [c28 Oct 1927; LP24595]. Si; b&w. 35mm. 6 reels, 5,383 ft.

Pres by Carl Laemmle. *Dir* Del Andrews. *Cont* Arthur Statter. *Titl* Tom Reed. *Adapt* Isadore Bernstein. *Story* Peter B. Kyne. *Photog* Harry Neumann. *Art Dir* David S. Garber. *Film Ed* Rodney Hickok.

Cast: Hoot Gibson *(Dennis O'Hara)*, Georgia Hale *(Jessica Silverberg)*, Frank Hagney *(J. Francis Jackson)*, William H. Strauss *(Simon Silverberg)*, Harry Todd *(comic)*, Tom Lingham *(deputy)*.

Western melodrama. Dennis O'Hara, a spirited young Irishman who is a constant source of annoyance to J. Francis Jackson, the town's leading citizen, beats Jackson each year in the annual horserace until Jackson acquires the winning horse in a gambling game. Simon Silverberg and his daughter, Jessica, arrive in town and try to sell clothing, but the men, led by Jackson, drive them from town. Dennis intervenes on their behalf and takes them to his cabin. When Dennis earns the money to buy back his horse and Jackson refuses to sell it, Dennis steals the horse; later, Dennis returns to find Jackson virtually in control of the town and wagering his fortune against Simon that he will win the annual race. Jackson conspires to prevent Dennis from winning, and after much difficulty with the other riders, Dennis does beat Jackson's rider, then whips Jackson. Dennis and Jessica are united. *Irish. Jews. Peddlers. Gambling. Horseracing. Smalltown life.*

THE RE-CREATION OF BRIAN KENT F2.4471

Principal Pictures. 15 Feb **1925.** Si; b&w. 35mm. 7 reels, 6,878 ft.

Prod Sol Lesser. *Dir* Sam Wood. *Scen* Arthur Statter, Mary Alice Scully. *Photog* Glen MacWilliams.

Cast: Kenneth Harlan *(Brian Kent)*, Helene Chadwick *(Betty Joe)*, Mary Carr *(Auntie Sue)*, ZaSu Pitts *(Judy)*, Rosemary Theby *(Mrs. Kent)*, T. Roy Barnes *(Harry Green)*, Ralph Lewis *(Homer Ward)*, Russell Simpson *(Jap Taylor)*, De Witt Jennings *(Detective Ross)*, Russell Powell *(Sheriff Knox)*.

Melodrama. Source: Harold Bell Wright, *The Re-creation of Brian Kent* (Chicago, 1919). To support a demanding wife, bank clerk Brian Kent embezzles a large sum of money and, overcome with remorse, attempts to commit suicide by casting himself adrift in a small boat on a rough river. The boat is caught in willows, however, and Brian meets Judy, a little slavey who introduces him to her mistress, Auntie Sue, a schoolteacher. Under Auntie Sue's benign influence, Brian reforms and writes a book. Falling in love with Betty Jo, Brian incurs the enmity of Judy, who tells her father of Brian's unsavory past. Judy's father starts out for the bank, but Auntie Sue gets there first and persuades the bank president (a former pupil of hers) not to prosecute Brian. Brian's wife attempts to visit him and is drowned. Brian finds happiness with Betty Jo. *Bankers. Bank clerks. Drudges. Schoolteachers. Authors. Criminals—Rehabilitation. Embezzlement. Suicide.*

READIN' 'RITIN' 'RITHMETIC **F2.4472**

Leland Stanford Ramsdale Productions. *Dist* Artlee Pictures. 30 Dec **1926**. Si; b&w. 35mm. 5 reels, 4,983 ft.

Dir Robert Eddy.

Cast: Edna Marion, Gordon White.

Action melodrama. "College athletic hero loves professor's daughter but her father frowns upon such a match because of hero's poor ability as a scholar. He wins her in the end, but only after entangling engagements, rebuffs and near arrest for murder." (*Motion Picture News Booking Guide*, 12:51, Apr 1927.) *Students. Professors. Athletes. College life. Murder.*

THE REAL ADVENTURE **F2.4473**

Florence Vidor Productions–Cameo Pictures. *Dist* Associated Exhibitors. 28 May **1922** [c17 May 1922; LU17950]. Si; b&w. 35mm. 5 reels, 4,932 ft.

Prod Arthur S. Kane. *Dir* King Vidor. *Scen* Mildred Considine. *Photog* George Barnes.

Cast: Florence Vidor *(Rose Stanton)*, Clyde Fillmore *(Rodney Aldrich)*, Nellie Peck Saunders *(Mrs. Stanton)*, Lilyan McCarthy *(Portia)*, Philip Ryder *(John Walbraith)*.

Domestic melodrama. Source: Henry Kitchell Webster, *The Real Adventure* (New York, 1915). Rose Stanton, following her marriage to wealthy Rodney Aldrich, realizes that he is uninterested in her intellect. She takes up law studies to help him in his work; and when he scoffs at the idea, she leaves him, determined to prove herself an equally intelligent marriage partner. In New York, Rose becomes a chorus girl, then seizes the opportunity to design costumes for Broadway shows. Soon she opens a salon and is very successful; she realizes, however, that whatever a man's interest in a woman's work, his deepest concern will be with her as a woman. As she is about to sign a Broadway contract, Rodney confesses his admiration and respect for her, and she agrees to return to the career of wife and mother. *Lawyers. Businesswomen. Couturiers. Marriage. New York City—Broadway.*

RECAPTURED LOVE **F2.4474**

Warner Brothers Pictures. 8 Jul **1930** [c20 Jun 1930; LP1370]. Sd (Vitaphone); b&w. 35mm. 8 reels, 6,120 ft.

Dir John G. Adolfi. *Screenplay-Dial* Charles Kenyon. *Camera* John Stumar. *Film Ed* Jimmy Gibbons. *Rec Engr* Cal Applegate.

Cast: Belle Bennett *(Helen Parr)*, John Halliday *(Brentwood Parr)*, Dorothy Burgess *(Peggy Price)*, Richard Tucker *(Rawlings)*, Junior Durkin *(Henry Parr)*, George Bickel *(Crofts)*, Brooks Benedict *(Pat)*, The Sisters G *(themselves)*, Bernard Durkin, Earle Wallace *(dancers)*.

Comedy-drama. Source: Basil Dillon Woon, *Misdeal* (a play; publication undetermined). After 18 years of happily married life with Helen, eminent Detroit businessman Brentwood Parr "steps out" and is vamped by Peggy Price, a nightclub entertainer introduced to him by Crofts, an older business friend. Although his friend Rawlings disapproves of the relationship, Parr continues to see Peggy during feigned "business trips"; but Helen learns of his affair and gets a Paris divorce. Parr marries Peggy. Helen returns from abroad and embarks on a lively social life. Soon tiring of his young wife's hectic existence, Parr seeks rest and seclusion at the country home of his former wife. After much coaxing by Parr and his son, Henry, Helen decides to start over again, buying off the young entertainer, then making her husband pay her for his folly. *Businessmen. Entertainers. Vamps. Marriage. Infidelity. Divorce. Paris. Detroit.*

RECEIVED PAYMENT **F2.4475**

Vitagraph Co. of America. 8 Jan **1922** [c3 Jan 1922; LP17425]. Si; b&w. 35mm. 5 reels, 4,800 ft.

Pres by Albert E. Smith. *Dir* Charles Maigne. *Scen* William B. Courtney. *Story* John Lynch. *Photog* Arthur Ross.

Cast: Corinne Griffith *(Celia Hughes)*, Kenneth Harlan *(Cary Grant)*, David Torrence *(Daniel Milton)*, William David *(Dunbar)*, Charles Hammond *(Andrew Ferris)*, Henry Sedley *(Roger Dayne)*, Regina Quinn *(Felice Huxley)*, Dorothy Walters *(Mrs. Starr)*, Dan Duffy *(Starr)*.

Society melodrama. Daniel Milton, who has disowned his only daughter for marrying against his will, is told by Ferris, his butler, that she is dead; Milton refuses to believe him, however, and when Ferris' daughter, Celia, a dancer, returns to the city, Ferris sends her to him, informing her that she is Milton's granddaughter. Ferris tries to burn letters proving the death of Milton's granddaughter, but Celia discovers the deception and resolves to return to the stage and break her engagement to Cary Grant. On the night of her premiere, Milton, Ferris, and Felice Huxley, Milton's ward, are in a box to greet her; Milton's former secretary, Dayne, jealous of Celia's inheritance rights, tries to shoot her; but Ferris protects her and is himself struck down. Before he dies, Ferris tells Milton the truth and is forgiven; Celia is reunited with Cary. *Dancers. Butlers. Fatherhood. Theater. Parentage. New York City. Documentation.*

THE RECKLESS AGE (Universal-Jewel) **F2.4476**

Universal Pictures. ca8 Jun **1924** [New York premiere; released 17 Aug; c17 May 1924; LP20213]. Si; b&w. 35mm. 7 reels, 6,954 ft.

Dir Harry Pollard. *Scen* Rex Taylor. *Photog* William Fildew.

Cast: Reginald Denny *(Dick Minot)*, Ruth Dwyer *(Cynthia Meyrick)*, John Steppling *(Spencer Meyrick)*, May Wallace *(Auntie Meyrick)*, William Austin *(Lord Harrowby)*, Tom McGuire *(Martin Wall)*, Fred Malatesta *(Manuel Gonzales)*, Henry A. Barrows *(John Thacker)*, Frederick Vroom *(Owen Jephson)*, William E. Lawrence *(John Paddock)*, Hayden Stevenson *(Henry Trimmer)*, Frank Leigh *(George Jenkins)*.

Comedy-drama. Source: Earl Derr Biggers, *Love Insurance* (Indianapolis, 1914). Lord Harrowby, about to marry Cynthia Meyrick, takes out an insurance policy against the loss of his wealthy bride. Sent to usher at the proceedings, the company's confidential agent, Dick Minot, falls for Cynthia, and through a series of comic situations he wins her and fulfills his obligation. *Insurance agents. Weddings.*

RECKLESS CHANCES **F2.4477**

Herald Productions. *Dist* Playgoers Pictures. 15 Jan **1922** [c31 Dec 1921; LU17414]. Si; b&w. 35mm. 5 reels.

Dir J. P. McGowan. *Story* Anthony Coldewey. *Photog* Chuck Welty.

Cast: J. P. McGowan *(Terry Nolan)*, Dorothy Wood *(Nora Murphy)*, Andrew Waldron *(Dan Murphy)*, Robert Walker *(Harry Allen)*.

Action melodrama. Terry Nolan, stationmaster of a railway station that is robbed of metal ore, is suspected and arrested, but he escapes from the sheriff. While making his getaway he meets Nora, daughter of railroad superintendent Dan Murphy, whose car has collided with a wagon; and she drives him back to town. Assuming the name of "Tim McCloskey," he obtains a position as yard foreman and risks being jailed to be near her, though Dan objects to his daughter's marrying a trainman. Terry marries her aboard a flat car, however, in the presence of her father and Harry Allen, a disappointed suitor, who pursue them on the fender of a locomotive. It is revealed that "Tim" is actually an escaped thief, but Nora accidentally learns that Allen is behind the thefts. Nora is captured by the gang, but Terry follows to their hideout, rounds up the bandits, and rescues Nora. *Stationmasters. Gangs. Railroads. Robbery. Courtship.*

RECKLESS COURAGE **F2.4478**

Action Pictures. *Dist* Weiss Brothers Artclass Pictures. c8 May **1925** [LU21444]. Si; b&w. 35mm. 5 reels, 4,851 ft.

Pres by Lester F. Scott, Jr. *Dir* Tom Gibson. *Scen* Betty Burbridge. *Story* Victor Roberts. *Photog* Ray Ries.

Cast: Buddy Roosevelt *(Bud Keenan)*, J. C. Fowler *(Jasper Bayne)*, Helen Foster *(Doris Bayne)*, William McIllwain *(butler)*, Jay Morley *(Jim Allen)*, Jack O'Brien *(Scar Degan)*, N. E. Hendrix *(Shorty Baker)*, Merrill McCormick *(Chuck Carson)*, Eddie Barry *(Slim Parker)*, Princess Neola *(Winona)*, Robert Burns *(The Law)*.

Western melodrama. Doris Bayne is instructed by her wealthy father to deliver a valuable diamond necklace by air. The plane she hires is robbed in flight, and Doris is forced to throw the necklace from the craft's open cockpit. It lands at the feet of Bud Keenan, an honest ranch foreman. Bud picks it up and soon finds himself looking down the barrel of a pistol held by Doris, who has parachuted from the plane. Doris ties up Bud, but he soon escapes and follows her, rescuing her after she falls down an embankment. Bud takes Doris to his ranch and goes for a doctor. The leader of the crooks, Scar Degan, appears and demands the necklace, which Doris has thoughtfully given to a squaw for safekeeping; Degan then takes Doris to the gang's hideout. Bud gets the necklace from the squaw and goes to the hideout, trading the jewels for the girl. Bud later gets into a fight with the thugs that ends with the thieves dead and Bud in possession of the necklace, which he returns to Doris. *Ranch foremen. Gangs. Indians of North America. Robbery. Abduction. Airplanes. Parachuting.*

THE RECKLESS LADY F2.4479

First National Pictures. 24 Jan **1926** [c27 Jan 1926; LP22331]. Si; b&w. 35mm. 8 reels, 7,336 ft.

Pres by Robert Kane. *Dir* Howard Higgin. *Scen* Sada Cowan. *Photog* Ernest Haller. *Art Dir* Robert M. Haas. *Film Ed* Paul F. Maschke. *Prod Mgr* Joseph C. Boyle.

Cast: Belle Bennett *(Mrs. Fleming)*, James Kirkwood *(Colonel Fleming)*, Lois Moran *(Sylvia Fleming)*, Lowell Sherman *(Feodor)*, Ben Lyon *(Ralph Hillier)*, Marcia Harris *(Sophie)*, Charlie Murray *(gendarme)*.

Melodrama. Source: Philip Hamilton Gibbs, *The Reckless Lady* (London, 1924). Mrs. Fleming, a young wife and mother, has an affair with Feodor, a Russian scoundrel who has paid off her gambling debts. Her husband discovers the liaison and divorces her. Mrs. Fleming then goes to Monte Carlo with her daughter, Sylvia, and supports herself by careful gambling. Several years pass. Feodor comes to Monaco and meets Sylvia, who arouses his lustful nature. Mrs. Fleming learns of his interest in her daughter, but Feodor threatens to reveal her past if she stands in his way. Mrs. Fleming tries to win enough at the gambling tables to get Sylvia out of the country, but she loses everything. She is about to kill herself when her former husband fortuitously arrives and prevents her from doing so. Mrs. Fleming finally tells Sylvia of the past, and the girl becomes immediately disgusted with Feodor. The elder Flemings are reunited, and Sylvia settles her affections on a fine young fellow named Ralph. *Russians. Infidelity. Motherhood. Gambling. Debt. Divorce. Suicide. Monte Carlo.*

THE RECKLESS MOLLYCODDLE F2.4480

Paul Gerson Pictures. *Dist* Aywon Film Corp. 18 Jan **1927** [New York State license; New York showing 24 Sep 1927]. Si; b&w. 35mm. 5 reels.

Cast: Richard Holt.

Comedy-drama(?). No information about the nature of this film has been found.

RECKLESS MONEY F2.4481

Sherman H. Dudley, Jr. **1926.** Si; b&w. 35mm. [Feature length assumed.]

Photog Watkins.

Cast: Sherman H. Dudley, Jr., John La Rue.

Melodrama(?). No information about the precise nature of this film has been found. *Negro life.*

RECKLESS RIDING BILL F2.4482

William (Bill) Mix Productions. *Dist* Sanford Productions. 1 Sep **1924.** Si; b&w. 35mm. 5 reels.

Dir Frank Morrow.

Cast: Dick Carter, Alys Morrell.

Western melodrama. "Hero runs a gambling house but is on the level. Heroine, a schoolteacher, arrives and is rescued from runaway stage coach by hero. Local postmaster frames up hero to discredit him. Hero gives away gambling house and reforms. Postmaster robs safe and turns suspicion on hero, but in the end hero vindicates himself and wins the girl." (*Motion Picture News Booking Guide,* 8:66, Apr 1925.) *Schoolteachers. Postmasters. Frameup. Gambling. Robbery.*

RECKLESS ROMANCE F2.4483

Christie Film Co. *Dist* Producers Distributing Corp. 9 Nov **1924** [c15 Nov 1924; LP20968]. Si; b&w. 35mm. 6 reels, 5,530 ft.

Dir Scott Sidney. *Titl* Joseph W. Farnham. *Adapt* Walter Woods, F. McGrew Willis. *Photog* Gus Peterson, Paul Garnett.

Cast: T. Roy Barnes *(Jerry Warner)*, Harry Myers *(Christopher Skinner)*, Wanda Hawley *(Beatrice Skinner)*, Sylvia Breamer *(Edith Somers)*, Tully Marshall *(Judge Somers)*, Jack Duffy *(Grandpa)*, Lincoln Plumer *(Uncle Bellamy)*, Morgan Wallace *(Harold Shrewsbury, an oil stock salesman)*, George French *(Lyman Webster)*.

Farce. Source: Herbert Hall Winslow and Emil Nyitray, *What's Your Wife Doing?* (New York opening: 1 Oct 1923). Jerry Warner falls in love with Edith Somers but cannot obtain her father's permission to marry her. Jerry is given $10,000 by his uncle, however, and makes a proposition to Edith's father: if Jerry can retain the money for 30 days, Edith's father will withdraw his objections to the marriage. Edith's father agrees. Jerry immediately invests half of the money in an apparently worthless stock and lends the other half to a friend. Desperate for money, Jerry then accepts the offer made by his friends, Beatrice and Christopher Skinner, that he act as the corespondent in a temporary divorce they must obtain in order to prevent Christopher's disinheritance. After numerous complications, the Skinners manage to stay married, and the value of Jerry's stock doubles, enabling him to claim Edith for his own. *Fatherhood. Disinheritance. Marriage. Divorce. Courtship. Speculation.*

THE RECKLESS SEX F2.4484

Phil Goldstone Productions. *Dist* Truart Film Corp. 5 Feb **1925** [New York State license]. Si; b&w. 35mm. 6 reels, 5,961 ft.

Dir Alvin J. Neitz. *Story* Travers Wells. *Photog* Bert Baldridge. *Adtl Photog* Edgar Lyons.

Cast: Madge Bellamy *(Mary Hamilton)*, William Collier, Jr. *(Juan)*, Wyndham Standing *(Carter Trevor)*, Claire McDowell *(Concha)*, Johnnie Walker *(Robert Lanning, Jr.)*, Gertrude Astor *(Lucile Duprê)*, Alec B. Francis *(Emanuel García)*, Gladys Brockwell *(Mrs. García)*, David Torrence *(Robert Lanning)*, Helen Dunbar, Walter Long.

Melodrama. Robert Lanning, a proper Bostonian who owns an estate in New Mexico near the Mexican border, suspects that one of his employees is smuggling arms into Mexico and therefore sends his son and namesake, Robert, to investigate. On the way, Robert meets Mary Hamilton, a stranded actress from a roadshow company of *Uncle Tom's Cabin;* Mary, who played Little Eva in the production, is still dressed in her costume, and he mistakes her for a child and takes her with him to the ranch. Robert finally uncovers the smugglers and, with the help of the Mexican Rurales, brings the gang to justice. Robert then discovers that Mary is not a child and wins her for his wife. *Actors. Bostonians. Rurales. Smuggling. Firearms. New Mexico. Mexican border. "Uncle Tom's Cabin".*

RECKLESS SPEED F2.4485

Hercules Film Productions. *Dist* Bud Barsky Corp. 9 Oct **1924.** Si; b&w. 35mm. 5 reels, 4,800 ft.

Pres by Peter Kanellos. *Dir* William James Craft. *Story* William E. Wing.

Cast: Frank Merrill *(Speed Creswell)*, Virginia Warwick *(Vera Wray)*, Joseph Girard *(Dad Creswell)*, Gino Corrado *(David Brierly)*, Eddie O'Brien *(Creswell's valet)*, Slim Cole *(Mr. Jackson)*.

Melodrama(?). No information about the nature of this film has been found.

RECKLESS WIVES F2.4486

Literary Art Films. *Dist* Independent Films. 5 Feb **1921** [trade review]. Si; b&w. 35mm. [Feature length assumed.]

Cast: Myra Murray *(Babette Corbin)*, Leslie Austen *(George Cameron)*, Jane Thomas *(Florence Corbin)*, Helen McDonald *(Joy Ayres)*, Gerald C. Kaehn *(Horace Black)*, Richard Baker *(Father Cameron)*.

Melodrama. Wealthy Babette Corbin has everything but her husband's love. When by chance she sees in a magazine a picture of a handsome artist, George Cameron, she is determined to win his love. Babette and Florence, her husband's niece, then spend their summer at a hotel near Cameron's country home; and Babette, with flattery and wealth, soon wins his affection. Complications arise when both Florence and Joy, a young girl pursued by the village pastor, are also captivated by Cameron. Babette's husband finds out about the affair and is annoyed by the thought of the notoriety it may bring him. When Florence is rejected by Cameron, she drowns herself. Babette realizes the baneful effect her behavior has on others, and Cameron—also affected by the tragedy—settles down with Joy. *Artists. Clergymen. Marriage. Infidelity. Suicide.*

RECKLESS YOUTH F2.4487

Selznick Pictures. *Dist* Select Pictures. 30 Mar **1922** [c30 Mar 1922; LP17733]. Si; b&w. 35mm. 6 reels, 5,700 ft.

Pres by Lewis J. Selznick. *Dir* Ralph Ince. *Scen* Edward J. Montagne. *Photog* Jules Cronjager, Jack Brown.

Cast: Elaine Hammerstein *(Alice Schuyler)*, Niles Welch *(John Carmen)*, Myrtle Stedman *(Mrs. Schuyler-Foster)*, Robert Lee Keeling *(Mr. Schuyler-Foster)*, Huntley Gordon *(Harrison Thornby)*, Louise Prussing *(Mrs. Dahlgren)*, Frank Currier *(Cumberland Whipple)*, Kate Cherry *(Martha Whipple)*, Constance Bennett *(chorus girl)*.

Society drama. Source: Cosmo Hamilton, "Reckless Youth" (publication undetermined). Alice Schuyler, who suffers from the dullness and discipline of convent life, is expelled for breaking a regulation and sent to her grandparents, while her mother embarks on a second honeymoon. There she is kept under equally unpleasant conditions, and desperate to free herself, she runs away with lodge-keeper John Carmen to the city and agrees to marry him. As Mrs. John Carmen, Alice becomes a society sensation; and Carmen, who loves her, disapproves of her uninhibited social life but does not intervene. Alice accepts the attentions of young

Harrison Thornby, but when John discovers her at a dance with him, he orders her home. In defiance, Alice leaves in Thornby's car, which is wrecked; and while unconscious, Alice dreams that she has been abducted by Thornby aboard his yacht and that there is a collision with a steamer. Awakening, she is remorseful and returns to her grandmother; but John follows, declaring that his feeling are unchanged, and they agree to begin again. *Grandparents. Marriage. Convents. Dreams.*

THE RECOIL **F2.4488**

Milburn Morante. 10 Dec **1921** [New York State]. Si; b&w. 35mm. 5 reels.

Cast: George Chesebro, Evelyn Nelson, Virginia Morante.

Melodrama. No information about the precise nature of this film has been found. *Northwest Mounted Police.*

THE RECOIL **F2.4489**

Goldwyn Pictures. *Dist* Metro-Goldwyn Distributing Corp. 27 Apr **1924** [c25 May 1924; LP20237]. Si; b&w. 35mm. 7 reels, 7,089 ft.

Pres by J. Parker Read, Jr. *Dir* T. Hayes Hunter. *Screen Dramatization* Gerald C. Duffy. *Photog* René Guissart. *Art Dir* Henri Menessier. *Film Ed* Alex Troffey. *Gowns* Drecol.

Cast: Mahlon Hamilton *(Gordon Kent)*, Betty Blythe *(Norma Selbee)*, Clive Brook *(Marchmont)*, Fred Paul *(William Southern)*, Ernest Hilliard *(Jim Selbee)*.

Romantic melodrama. Source: Rex Beach, "The Recoil," in *Big Brother and Other Stories* (New York, 1923). After selling his South American mines in Paris, Gordon Kent falls in love with penniless Norma Selbee and marries her. When she elopes with an admirer (Marchmont), Kent and a detective pursue them, revealing Marchmont's criminal past and the existence of Norma's first husband, Jim Selbee. Initially condemning the couple to their mutual misery, Kent later relents when his wife saves him from a blackmail plot instigated by Selbee and returns to her. *Mines. Infidelity. Blackmail. Paris.*

Note: Also known as *Recoil.*

RECOMPENSE **F2.4490**

Warner Brothers Pictures. 26 Apr **1925** [26 Feb 1925; LP21190]. Si; b&w. 35mm. 7 reels, 7,379 ft.

Dir Harry Beaumont. *Scen* Dorothy Farnum. *Photog* David Abel.

Cast: Marie Prevost *(Julie Gamelyn)*, Monte Blue *(Peter Graham)*, John Roche *(Dr. Sampson)*, George Siegmann *(Stenhouse)*, Charles Stevens *(Mosheshoe)*, Virginia Brown Faire *(Angelica)*, William B. Davidson *(Colonel Donovan)*, Katherine Lewis *(Mrs. Donovan)*.

Melodrama. Source: Robert Keable, *Recompense; a Sequel to "Simon Called Peter"* (London, 1924). Following an unconventional romance in London, Peter Graham, a clergyman, returns to France as a chaplain. He soon abandons his calling and becomes a doctor, serving with the same unit as Julie, a nurse with whom he fell in love in London. The unit is later transfered to the South African front. When the war ends, Julie resumes her profession at a Cape Town hospital, and Peter finds work in the interior, working for Stenhouse, a dishonest trader. Stenhouse shoots Peter in a drunken rage, and Julie nurses him back to health. Peter returns to London and starts a mission. He meets a former love, Angelica, whom he finds pregnant and abandoned in the streets. Peter takes her in and asks her to marry him. Julie returns to London to assist Dr. Sampson at his hospital, and she helps deliver Angelica's baby. Angelica dies, and Peter and Julie decide that their happiness lies with each other. *Clergymen. Chaplains. Physicians. Missions. World War I. London. Cape Town. South Africa. France.*

RED BLOOD **F2.4491**

Morris R. Schlank Productions. *Dist* Rayart Pictures. 25 Aug **1926** [New York State license]. Si; b&w. 35mm. 5 reels.

Dir J. P. McGowan. *Story* G. A. Durlam. *Photog* Robert Cline. *Film Ed* Thelma Smith. *Asst Dir* Mack V. Wright.

Cast: Al Hoxie *(Buck Marsden)*, Nayone Warfield *(Edith Custer)*, Lew Meehan *(Dick Willis)*, Eddie Barry *(Donald Custer)*, J. P. McGowan *(Eagle Custer)*, Frances Kellogg *(Carlotta)*, Walter Patterson *("Sodapop")*, Len Sewards *("Broom")*.

Western melodrama. No information about the precise nature of this film has been found.

RED BLOOD AND BLUE **F2.4492**

Roberts & Cole. *Dist* Aywon Film Corp. 25 Feb **1925**. Si; b&w. 35mm. 5 reels, 4,900 ft.

Dir James C. Hutchinson. *Story* Guinn Williams. *Photog* James C. Hutchinson. *Adtl Photog* J. P. Whalen.

Cast: Big Boy Williams *(Tom Butler)*, Peggy O'Day *(Leona Lane)*, John Barley *(Dave Butler)*, Fred Butler *(Jim Lane)*, Frank Baker *(Bill Gronn)*, Irvin Woffard *(Pete Smith)*, Oliver Drake *("Slim")*.

Western melodrama(?). No information about the nature of this film has been found.

RED CLAY (Blue Streak Western) **F2.4493**

Universal Pictures. 17 Apr **1927** [c28 Apr 1925; LP21418]. Si; b&w. 35mm. 5 reels, 4,626 ft.

Pres by Carl Laemmle. *Dir* Ernst Laemmle. *Scen* Charles Logue, Frank L. Inghram. *Titl* Ruth Todd. *Story* Sarah Saddoris. *Photog* Ben Kline. *Art Dir* David S. Garber.

Cast: William Desmond *(Chief John Nisheto)*, Marceline Day *(Agnes Burr)*, Albert J. Smith *(Jack Burr)*, Byron Douglas *(Senator Burr)*, Billy Sullivan *(Bob Lee)*, Lola Todd *(Betty Morgan)*, Noble Johnson *(Chief Bear Paw)*, Felix Whitefeather *(Indian chief)*, Ynez Seabury *(Minnie Bear Paw)*.

Melodrama. During the World War, Chief John Nisheto is drafted and, while fighting in France, saves the life of Jack Burr, the son of a congressman favorable to the Indians. After the war, John returns home and begins to go out with Jack's sister, Agnes. Although John is both scholar and star football player, Jack objects, not knowing that John is the man who once saved his life. John is later mortally wounded and dies in Jack's arms, revealing at last his own heroism in the trenches. Jack repents of his prejudice and does his best to bring comfort to his sister. *War heroes. Indians of North America. Racial prejudice. Football. World War I. France. United States Congress.*

RED COURAGE **F2.4494**

Universal Film Manufacturing Co. 10 Oct **1921** [c27 Sep 1921; LP17026]. Si; b&w. 35mm. 5 reels, 4,481 ft.

Dir Reaves Eason. *Scen* Harvey Gates. *Photog* Virgil Miller.

Cast: Hoot Gibson *(Pinto Peters)*, Joel Day *(Chuckwalla Bill)*, Molly Malone *(Jane Reedly)*, Joe Girard *(Joe Reedly)*, William Merrill McCormick *(Percy Gibbons)*, Charles Newton *(Tom Caldwell)*, Arthur Hoyt *(Nathan Hitch)*, Joe Harris *(Blackie Holloway)*, Dick Cummings *(Judge Fay)*, Mary Philbin *(Eliza Fay)*, Jim Corey *(Steve Carrol)*, Mac V. Wright *(Sam Waters)*.

Western melodrama. Source: Peter Bernard Kyne, "The Sheriff of Cinnabar" (publication undetermined). Pinto Peters and his pal Chuckwalla Bill acquire a newspaper in the town of Cinnabar, which is run by the mayor and boss Joe Reedly, guardian of Jane with whom Pinto is in love. They decide to wage a reform campaign and are elected sheriff and mayor, respectively, through the efforts of Judge Fay, who speaks in their behalf. Jane, however, is won over by Blackie, owner of a gambling house. Pinto thrashes Reedly for bothering Eliza, the judge's daughter, and orders him from town. When Reedly is mysteriously killed, Eliza's fiancé, Nathan, is blamed, but Pinto suspects Blackie and catches him trying to abscond with Jane and her fortune. He is jailed, and Jane is reunited with Pinto. *Sheriffs. Mayors. Judges. Gamblers. Newspapers. Political corruption.*

THE RED DANCE **F2.4495**

Fox Film Corp. 25 Jun **1928** [New York premiere; released 2 Dec; c25 Jun 1928; LP25395]. Mus score (Movietone); b&w. 35mm. 10 reels, 9,250 ft. [Also si.]

Pres by William Fox. *Dir* Raoul Walsh. *Scen* James Ashmore Creelman. *Titl* Malcolm Stuart Boylan. *Adapt* Pierre Collings, Philip Klein. *Story* Eleanor Browne. *Photog* Charles Clarke, John Marta. *Film Ed* Louis Loeffler. *Mus Score* S. L. Rothafel, Erno Rapee. *Song: "Someday, Somewhere, We'll Meet Again"* Lew Pollack, Erno Rapee. *Asst Dir* Archibald Buchanan.

Cast: Charles Farrell *(The Grand Duke Eugen)*, Dolores Del Rio *(Tasia)*, Ivan Linow *(Ivan Petroff)*, Boris Charsky *(an agitator)*, Dorothy Revier *(Princess Varvara)*, Andres De Segurola *(General Tanaroff)*, Demetrius Alexis *(Rasputin)*.

Romantic drama. Source: Henry Leyford Gates, *The Red Dancer of Moscow* (New York, 1928). "The Grand Duke Eugen is considered a menace by the reactionary court group which is undermining the morale of the Czar's army. Tasia, a peasant girl, is persuaded to shoot him on the eve of his marriage to Princess Varvara. She misses and is glad because she loves him. Comes the Revolution, making her the Red Dancer of Moscow, while Ivan, her peasant admirer, rises to be a general. Eugen is again in danger but is saved from firing squad and restored to Tasia by the magnanimous Ivan." (*National Board of Review Magazine*, vol.3, no. 7, Jul 1928, p11.) *Royalty. Peasants. Dancers. Russia—History—1917–21 Revolution. Grigori Efimovich Rasputin.*

RED DICE **F2.4496**

De Mille Pictures. *Dist* Producers Distributing Corp. 14 Mar **1926** [c7 Mar 1926; LP22641]. Si; b&w. 35mm. 7 reels, 7,257 ft.

Pres by Cecil B. De Mille. *Dir* William K. Howard. *Prod Ed* Jeanie Macpherson. *Adapt* Jeanie Macpherson, Douglas Doty. *Photog* Lucien Andriot. *Art Dir* Max Parker. *Asst Dir* Richard Donaldson.

Cast: Rod La Rocque *(Alan Beckwith)*, Marguerite De La Motte *(Beverly Vane)*, Ray Hallor *(Johnny Vane)*, Gustav von Seyffertitz *(Andrew North)*, George Cooper *(Squint Scoggins)*, Walter Long *(Nick Webb)*, Edithe Yorke *(Mrs. Garrison)*, Clarence Burton *(butler)*, Charles Clary *(district attorney)*, Alan Brooks *(Conroy)*.

Crook melodrama. Source: Octavus Roy Cohen, *The Iron Chalice* (Boston, 1925). Alan Beckwith, down and out and behind in his rent, goes to the home of North, a notorious bootlegger and underworld figure, and proposes that for $300 he will insure his life in North's favor for $100,000; he tosses two red dice, one showing two and the other four, and they agree that on December 24 Alan must die, and to allay suspicion, he must marry a woman of North's choosing. Vane and Conroy, two of North's subordinates who have doublecrossed him, are marked to die; Vane's sister Beverly begs North to relent; and he consents on the condition that she marry Alan. After their marriage, under the guard of Squint, their distrust develops into love and Alan tries to buy off North. Alan and Vane attempt to hijack North's rum cargo, but Beverly arrives with revenue agents, Squint proves to be an undercover man, and the gang is overcome. *Bootleggers. Revenue agents. Gangs. Insurance. Debt.*

RED GOLD **F2.4497**

Anchor Productions. 30 Jun **1930.** Si; b&w. 35mm. 5 reels, 4,500 ft.

Cast: Cliff (Tex) Lyons.

Western melodrama(?). No information about the nature of this film has been found.

RED HAIR **F2.4498**

Paramount Famous Lasky Corp. 10 Mar **1928** [c10 Mar 1928; LP25061]. Si; b&w with col sequence (Technicolor). 35mm. 7 reels, 6,331 ft.

Pres by Adolph Zukor, Jesse L. Lasky. *Assoc Prod* B. P. Schulberg. *Dir* Clarence Badger. *Screenplay* Agnes Brand Leahy. *Titl* George Marion, Jr. *Adapt* Percy Heath, Lloyd Corrigan. *Photog* Alfred Gilks. *Film Ed* Doris Drought. *Asst Dir* Archie Hill.

Cast: Clara Bow *("Bubbles" McCoy)*, Lane Chandler *(Robert Lennon)*, William Austin *(Dr. Eustace Gill)*, Jacqueline Gadsdon *(Minnie Luther)*, Lawrence Grant *(Judge Rufus Lennon)*, Claude King *(Thomas L. Burke)*, William Irving *("Demmy")*.

Comedy. Source: Elinor Glyn, *The Vicissitudes of Evangeline* (New York, 1905). Gold digger "Bubbles" McCoy, a manicurist, finds that Robert Lennon, the man she has chosen to marry, is under the guardianship of three bachelor friends, all of whom have courted her and given her many expensive gifts. Against the guardians' advice, Lennon announces the engagement. At the engagement party, "Bubbles", angry and irritated because of criticism against her, removes all the sartorial gifts she wears, leaps half nude into the swimming pool, and is pulled out by her sympathetic, forgiving fiancé. *Bachelors. Manicurists. Gold diggers.*

RED HOT HOOFS **F2.4499**

R-C Pictures. *Dist* Film Booking Offices of America. 19 Dec **1926** [c29 Oct 1926; LP23275]. Si; b&w. 35mm. 5 reels, 4,681 ft.

Pres by Joseph P. Kennedy. *Dir* Robert De Lacey. *Adapt-Cont* F. A. E. Pine. *Story* George Worthington Yates, Jr. *Photog* John Leezer. *Asst Dir* Sam Nelson.

Cast: Tom Tyler *(Tom Buckley)*, Frankie Darro *(Frankie Buckley)*, Dorothy Dunbar *(Frances Morris)*, Stanley Taylor *(Gerald Morris)*, Harry O'Connor *(Jim Morris)*, Al Kaufman *(Battling Jack Riley)*, Barney Furey *(Al Skelly)*.

Western melodrama. When Battling Jack Riley, a heavyweight contender, selects the Bar X Ranch for his training quarters, foreman Tom Buckely becomes concerned over Riley's attentions to Frances Morris, the owner's daughter, whom Tom loves. Gerald, Frances' twin brother, confesses to a theft of money from the bank in which he works, and to retrieve the money Tom agrees to fight Riley for three rounds, to the disgust of Frances. Riley sees Tom give Gerald the money and has the boy kidnaped on the way to the bank, then uses him as a decoy to lure Frances to a cabin. Frankie, unseen by Riley, returns to the ranch for his brother, Tom, who arrives in time to defeat Riley after a terrific struggle and to rescue Frances. *Ranch foremen. Ranchers. Boxers. Twins. Brothers. Brother-sister relationship. Kidnaping.*

RED HOT LEATHER (Blue Streak Western) **F2.4500**

Universal Pictures. 17 Oct **1926** [c3 Aug 1926; LP22998]. Si; b&w. 35mm. 5 reels, 4,555 ft.

Pres by Carl Laemmle. *Dir-Story* Albert Rogell. *Adapt-Scen* Harrison Jacobs. *Photog* William Nobles.

Cast: Jack Hoxie *(Jack Lane)*, Ena Gregory *(Ellen Rand)*, William Malan *(Daniel Lane)*, Tom Shirley *(Ross Kane)*, William H. Turner *(Morton Kane)*, George K. French *(Dr. Robert Marsh)*, Billy Engle *("Dinkey" Hook)*, Jim Corey *("Red" Hussey)*, Leo Sailor *("Noisy" Bates)*.

Western melodrama. Jack Lane is returning from the East after an unsuccessful attempt to obtain a loan to pay off the mortgage on his father's ranch. On the train, he meets Ellen Rand, who is smitten at the sight of her first real cowboy. Later he learns that she is the nurse who is to care for his paralytic father, growing weaker at the prospect of losing his ranch. Jack plans to enter the local rodeo to earn the money, though Morton Kane, who holds the mortgage and has secretly discovered oil on the ranch, plots with his son Ross to keep him from the events. He is waylaid by Kane's men but escapes and races for the rodeo in Kane's car; and with Ellen's help he arrives in time to win the relay and bucking events. The ranch is thus saved, Jack's father recovers, and Jack is united with Ellen. *Ranchers. Paralytics. Nurses. Cowboys. Mortgages. Rodeos. Oil lands.*

RED HOT RHYTHM **F2.4501**

Pathé Exchange. 23 Nov **1929** [c27 Dec 1929; LP993]. Sd (Photophone); b&w with col sequences (Technicolor). 35mm. 9 reels, 6,175 ft. [Also si; 6,981 ft.]

Supv William Conselman. *Dir* Leo McCarey. *Scen-Dial* Earl Baldwin, Walter De Leon. *Story* William Conselman, Leo McCarey. *Photog* John J. Mescall. *Art Dir* Edward Jewell. *Set Dresser* Ted Dickson. *Rec Engr* Charles O'Loughlin, Ben Winkler. *Prod Mgr* Richard Blaydon. *Cost* Gwen Wakeling.

Cast: Alan Hale *(Walter)*, Kathryn Crawford *(Mary)*, Walter O'Keefe *(Sam)*, Josephine Dunn *(Claire)*, Anita Garvin *(Mable)*, Ilka Chase *(Mrs. Fioretta)*, Ernest Hilliard *(Eddie Graham)*, Harry Bowen *(Whiffle)*, James Clemmons *(Singe)*.

Musical comedy. Walter, a songwriter who is in love with Mary, a nightclub singer, prefers to make a living by fleecing crackpot songwriters and promoting their creations. When Walter writes "At Last I'm in Love" for Mary, she promises to plug the song at the Frivolity Club, but he leaves in a huff when she flirts with Sam, a legitimate song publisher. On the street, he gives refuge to Claire, a girl accused of a theft, and hires her as his secretary. Mrs. Fioretta gives Walter a large sum to publish her song, "The Night Elmer Died," but Sam induces Mary to get Walter to stop the deal. When Walter discovers that Claire is having an affair with Sam, he returns to Mary at the club; they are reunited as she sings his song. *Singers. Composers. Secretaries. Publishers. Theft. Nightclubs. New York City.*

RED HOT ROMANCE **F2.4502**

John Emerson and Anita Loos Productions. *Dist* Associated First National Pictures. ca22 Jan **1922** [New York premiere; released 13 Feb; c8 Feb 1922; LP17532]. Si; b&w. 35mm. 6 reels, 6,051 ft.

Dir Victor Fleming. *Story-Scen* John Emerson, Anita Loos. *Photog* Ernest G. Palmer, Oliver T. Marsh.

Cast: Basil Sydney *(Rowland Stone)*, Henry Warwick *(Lord Howe-Greene)*, Frank Lalor *(King Caramba XIII)*, Carl Stockdale *(General de Castanet)*, Olive Valerie *(Madame Puloff de Plotz)*, Edward Connelly *(Col. Cassius Byrd)*, May Collins *(Anna Mae Byrd)*, Roy Atwell *(Jim Conwell)*, Tom Wilson *(Thomas Snow)*, Lillian Leighton *(Mammy)*, Snitz Edwards *(Signor Frijole)*.

Satire. Washingtonian Rowland Stone, who is in love with Anna Mae Byrd, lives in the family mansion awaiting his 25th birthday when he is to inherit his father's fortune. His Negro friend Thomas Snow hocks furniture to pay the bills and help him keep up appearances. Enrico de Castanet arrives from the country of Bunkonia in the "Pyranees," accompanied by the international vamp and spy Countess de Plotz, in hopes of attracting a pliable American consul who will not interfere with their revolutionary plot; Colonel Byrd is appointed. Rowland discovers that his inheritance is merely a job with his father's insurance company and that he is obligated not to lose any of the company's money. Arriving in Bunkonia, he is persuaded by the conspirators to insure the lives of the drunken king and council, whom they plan to assassinate. Rowland finds himself in the position of protector to royalty, and after many exciting adventures he saves the country and wins Anna Mae and his inheritance. *Insurance agents. Negroes. Royalty. Insurance. Imaginary kingdoms. Revolutions.*

RED HOT SPEED (Universal-Jewel) **F2.4503**

Universal Pictures. 27 Jan **1929** [c1 Dec 1928; LP25891]. Talking sequences, sd eff, & mus score (Movietone); b&w. 35mm. 7 reels, 6,621 ft. [Also si; 6,288 ft.]

Dir Joseph E. Henabery. *Scen* Gladys Lehman, Matt Taylor. *Titl* Albert De Mond. *Adapt* Faith Thomas. *Story* Gladys Lehman. *Photog* Arthur Todd. *Film Ed* Ray Curtiss, Jack English.

Cast: Reginald Denny *(Darrow)*, Alice Day *(Buddy Long)*, Charles Byer *(George)*, Thomas Ricketts *(Colonel Long)*, De Witt Jennings *(Judge O'Brien)*, Fritzi Ridgeway *(Slavey)*, Hector V. Sarno *(Italian father)*.

Comedy. Buddy Long, the beautiful daughter of a newspaper publisher who is conducting an antispeeding campaign, is arrested for speeding and, giving the assumed name of Mary Jones, is paroled into the custody of Assistant District Attorney Darrow. The county *vs.* "Mary Jones" becomes a test case, and Colonel Long, Buddy's father, goes to Darrow's apartment unexpectedly one evening to meet the girl. Buddy and Darrow learn he is coming, and Buddy escapes by a window; Darrow persuades a dimwitted slavey to impersonate "Mary Jones," and Colonel Long, none the wiser, decides that the girl is a mental case. Buddy and Darrow fall in love and receive her father's permission to be married, never letting on that "Mary Jones" and Buddy are one and the same. *Publishers. District attorneys. Newspapers. Drudges. Halfwits. Reckless driving. Impersonation.*

RED HOT TIRES **F2.4504**

Warner Brothers Pictures. 31 Oct **1925** [c12 Aug 1925; LP21729]. Si; b&w. 35mm. 7 reels, 6,600 ft.

Dir Erle C. Kenton. *Scen* Edward T. Lowe, Jr. *Story* Gregory Rogers. *Photog* Charles J. Van Enger.

Cast: Monte Blue *(Al Jones)*, Patsy Ruth Miller *(Elizabeth Lowden)*, Fred Esmelton *(Hon. R. C. Lowden)*, Lincoln Stedman *(George Taylor)*, Charles Conklin *(coachman)*, Jimmy Quinn *(Al Martin)*, Tom McGuire, William Lowery, Malcolm Waite *(crooks)*.

Farce. The first time Al Jones sees Elizabeth Lowden, he becomes so distracted that he runs his car into a steamroller. The second time he sees her, Elizabeth's car frightens his horse, causing him to fall. She rushes him to a hospital, and her father, who is the local chief of police, throws her in jail for speeding. Al becomes argumentative at this injustice and soon joins Elizabeth behind bars. He is released, and in an effort to get back in, he arouses the enmity of a gang of crooks. The crooks later kidnap Elizabeth, and Al rescues her. Overcoming his fear of automobiles, they elope in a speedster. *Police. Gangs. Automobile accidents. Abduction. Jails. Horses.*

RED KIMONO **F2.4505**

Mrs. Wallace Reid Productions. *Dist* Vital Exchanges. 16 Nov **1925** [New York State license]. Si; b&w. 35mm. 7 reels.

Dir Walter Lang. *Adapt* Dorothy Arzner. *Story* Adela Rogers St. Johns. *Photog* James Diamond.

Cast: Priscilla Bonner *(Gabrielle Darley)*, Theodore von Eltz, [Frederick] Tyrone Power, Mary Carr, Virginia Pearson, Mrs. Wallace Reid.

Melodrama. Gabrielle Darley is lured into prostitution by a village sport, who uses her earnings to support both himself and her. Gabrielle later discovers that her lover is planning to marry another woman, and she shoots him dead as he is buying a wedding ring in a jewelry store. Gabrielle is tried and acquitted. With no visible means of support, Gabrielle is at first taken up by a publicity-hungry socialite, but this woman soon tires of Gabrielle and turns her out into the street. Gabrielle is prepared to return to her old whorehouse in New Orleans when she is redeemed by the love of the chauffeur of her sometime benefactress. The chauffeur is inducted and goes overseas, leaving a penitent Gabrielle to await his return from France. *Prostitutes. Chauffeurs. Socialites. Murder. Trials. Whorehouses. World War I. New Orleans.*

RED LIGHTS **F2.4506**

Goldwyn Pictures. *Dist* Goldwyn-Cosmopolitan Distributing Corp. 9 Sep **1923** [New York premiere; released 30 Sep; c23 Aug 1923; LP19342]. Si; b&w. 35mm. 7 reels, 6,841 ft.

Dir Clarence G. Badger. *Adapt* Carey Wilson, Alice D. G. Miller. *Photog* Rudolph Berquist.

Cast: Marie Prevost *(Ruth Carson)*, Raymond Griffith *(Sheridan Scott)*, Johnnie Walker *(John Blake)*, Alice Lake *(Norah O'Neill)*, Dagmar Godowsky *(Roxy)*, William Worthington *(Luke Carson)*, Frank Elliott *(Kirk Allen)*, Lionel Belmore *(Alden Murray)*, Jean Hersholt *(Ezra Carson)*, George Reed *(porter)*, Charles B. Murphy *(The Henchman)*, Charles West *(The Conductor)*.

Mystery melodrama. Source: Edward E. Rose, *The Rear Car; a Mystery Play* ... (New York, 1926). Railroad president Luke Carson is informed that his daughter, Ruth, who as a child was kidnaped from his home, has been found in Los Angeles. Mr. Carson takes the train west to meet her. On the West Coast, Ruth's life is in jeopardy—mysterious figures shrouded in dark robes skulk through a maze of scenes amidst flashing red lights. Ruth's fiancé, John Blake, enlists the services of Sheridan Scott, a "crime deflector" who theoretically eliminates the criminal before he can begin his operations. However, the "crime deflector" does succeed in solving the mystery, and all ends happily. *Detectives. Railroad magnates. Kidnaping. Crime control.*

THE RED LILY **F2.4507**

Metro-Goldwyn Pictures. 8 Sep **1924** [c2 Sep 1924; LP20538]. Si; b&w. 35mm. 7 reels, 6,975 ft.

Dir-Story Fred Niblo. *Scen* Bess Meredyth. *Photog* Victor Milner. *Art Dir* Ben Carré. *Film Ed* Lloyd Nosler. *Asst Dir* Doran Cox.

Cast: Enid Bennett *(Marise La Noue)*, Ramon Novarro *(Jean Leonnec)*, Wallace Beery *(Bobo)*, Frank Currier *(Hugo Leonnec)*, Rosemary Theby *(Nana)*, Mitchell Lewis *(D'Agut)*, Emily Fitzroy *(Mama Bouchard)*, George Periolat *(Papa Bouchard)*, Milla Davenport *(Madame Poussot)*, Dick Sutherland *(The Toad)*, Gibson Gowland *(Le Turc)*, George Nichols *(concierge)*.

Drama. Finding herself destitute and homeless, Marise La Noue runs away to Paris with the mayor's son, Jean Leonnec, to be married. They are separated, and in time he becomes a thief and she, a woman of the streets. Years later they meet again. He is arrested and after serving a prison term returns to find her a changed woman. *Thieves. Prostitutes. Paris.*

RED LIPS **F2.4508**

Universal Pictures. 2 Dec **1928** [c22 May 1928; LP25293]. Si; b&w. 35mm. 7 reels, 6,947 ft.

Prod Supv Arthur E. Shadur. *Dir-Adapt* Melville Brown. *Story Supv* Edward J. Montagne. *Scen* James T. O'Donohue. *Titl* Tom Reed. *Photog* John Stumar. *Film Ed* Ray Curtiss.

Cast: Marion Nixon *(Cynthia Day)*, Charles Buddy Rogers *(Hugh Carver [or Buddy])*, Stanley Taylor *(Stewart Freeman [or Carl Peters])*, Hayden Stevenson *("Pop" Moultin)*, Andy Devine *(a sophomore [or Professor Fountain])*, Robert Seiter *(Roache)*, Hugh Trevor *("Spike" Blair [or Norris Parker])*, Earl McCarthy *(an upper classmate)*.

Drama. Source: Percy Marks, *The Plastic Age* (New York & London, 1924). At college Hugh Carver is thrown off the track team when his date, Cynthia Day, is found in his dormitory room. She leaves the campus, and he begins to lead a reckless life until Cynthia returns and her presence reforms Hugh. Reinstated to the team, he sets a world's record and makes plans to marry Cynthia. *Students. College life. Track.*

Note: Originally released in May 1928 as *Cream of the Earth*. Working title: *The Plastic Age*.

RED LOVE **F2.4509**

Lowell Film Productions. *Dist* Davis Distributing Division. May **1925** [c4 Dec 1925; LP22076]. Si; b&w. 35mm. 6 reels, 6,300 ft.

Dir Edgar Lewis. *Story* L. Case Russell.

Cast: John Lowell *(Thunder Cloud)*, Evangeline Russell *(Starlight)*, F. Serrano Keating *(James Logan, Little Antelope)*, William Calhoun *(Sheriff La Verne)*, Ann Brody *(Mrs. La Verne)*, William Cavanaugh *(Dr. George Lester)*, Wallace Jones *(Bill Mosher)*, Charles W. Kinney *(Sam Gibbons)*, Frank Montgomery *(Two Crows)*, Dexter McReynolds *(Scar-Face)*, "Chick" Chandler *(Tom Livingston)*.

Western melodrama. Thunder Cloud, a Sioux and a graduate of Carlisle, becomes an outcast when he believes he has slain the villainous Bill

Mosher, a white man. He steals horses and cattle but always leaves money or a promissory note for what he takes. He falls in love with Starlight, the halfbreed daughter of Sheriff La Verne, and eventually abducts her during the Indian Fair and takes her to his hideout. They are followed by Little Antelope, also in love with Starlight. The adopted son of white parents, he is now a member of the Indian Police. Thunder Cloud recognizes Little Antelope as his younger brother, but nevertheless he is arrested. At the trial, it is revealed that Mosher was not slain and that the allegation was only a plot against Thunder Cloud. Starlight gives up her job as teacher to marry Thunder Cloud. *Sioux Indians. Brothers. Schoolteachers. Halfcastes. Fairs. Indian Police. Carlisle Indian School.*

RED MAJESTY **F2.4510**

Harold Noice. *Dist* Od Films. 4 May **1929** [New York premiere]. Si; b&w. 35mm. 6 reels, 5,300 ft.

Dir-Titl-Photog-Film Ed Harold Noice.

Documentary. Starting from Para, Brazil, Mr. Noice proceeds up the Amazon River to Manáos, then continues up the Río Negro and the Río Vaupes to the interior of Brazil, where dwell the primitive Tariano Indians. A simple folk who live in a communal style surrounded by tropical scenery, the Tarianos share their tasks, possessions, and dwellings. Mr. Noice portrays both the events of everyday life and the more exotic customs. *Indians of South America. Tariano Indians. Brazil. Manáos. Amazon River. Río Vaupes. Río Negro.*

THE RED MARK **F2.4511**

James Cruze, Inc. *Dist* Pathé Exchange. 26 Aug **1928** [c9 Aug 1928; LP25518]. Si; b&w. 35mm. 8 reels, 7,937 ft.

Dir James Cruze. *Adapt-Cont* Julien Josephson. *Story* John Russell. *Photog* Ira Morgan. *Art Dir* Charles Cadwallader. *Film Ed* Mildred Johnson. *Asst Dir* Vernon Keays.

Cast: Nina Quartaro *(Zelie)*, Gaston Glass *(Bibi-Ri)*, Gustav von Seyffertitz *(De Nou)*, Rose Dione *(Mother Caron)*, Luke Cosgrave *(Papa Caron)*, Eugene Pallette *(Sergeo)*, Jack Roper *(Bombiste)*, Charles Dervis *(lame priest)*.

Melodrama. De Nou, the executioner on the penal island of Nouméa, lusts after Zelie, a beautiful young girl who is in love with Bibi-Ri, a young pickpocket recently released from prison. When Bibi-Ri learns the identity of his new rival, he is overcome by cowardice, suggesting that Zelie enter a convent in order to save both their lives. She refuses. Bibi-Ri kills one of De Nou's aides, Bombiste, in a fight and is sentenced to be beheaded. Faced with certain death, the boy becomes brave and arranges for Zelie's safe passage to the mainland. As De Nou is about to execute Bibi-Ri, he discovers by a red birthmark on the boy's neck that Bibi-Ri is his long-lost son. De Nou collapses, and Bibi-Ri is set free to find happiness at last with Zelie. *Pickpockets. Executioners. Convicts. Birthmarks. Capital punishment. Penal colonies. New Caledonia.*

THE RED MILL **F2.4512**

Cosmopolitan Productions. *Dist* Metro-Goldwyn-Mayer Distributing Corp. 29 Jan **1927** [c2 Mar 1927; LP23721]. Si; b&w. 35mm. 7 reels, 6,337 ft.

Dir William Goodrich. *Adapt-Scen* Frances Marion. *Titl* Joe Farnham. *Photog* Hendrik Sartov. *Sets* Cedric Gibbons, Merrill Pye. *Film Ed* Daniel J. Gray. *Wardrobe* André-ani.

Cast: Marion Davies *(Tina)*, Owen Moore *(Dennis)*, Louise Fazenda *(Gretchen)*, George Siegmann *(Willem)*, Karl Dane *(Captain Edam)*, J. Russell Powell *(burgomaster)*, Snitz Edwards *(Caesar)*, William Orlamond *(governor)*, Fred Gambold *(innkeeper)*, Ignatz *(himself, a mouse)*.

Comedy-melodrama. Source: Victor Herbert and Henry Martyn Blossom, *The Red Mill; a Musical Comedy* (New York, 1906). Tina, a general slavey at the Red Mill Inn who suffers from the extreme temper of her employer, Willem, falls in love with Dennis, a visitor to the Netherlands. Gretchen, the burgomaster's daughter, is betrothed to the elderly governor, though she is actually in love with Captain Edam. Tina masquerades as Gretchen in order to prevent the forced marriage, and when she is locked in a haunted mill, she is rescued by Dennis. *Drudges. Courtship. Haunted houses. Inns. Mills. Netherlands. Mice.*

THE RED MIRAGE *see* **THE FOREIGN LEGION**

THE RED RAIDERS **F2.4513**

Charles R. Rogers Productions. *Dist* First National Pictures. 4 Sep **1927** [c6 Sep 1927; LP24349]. Si; b&w. 35mm. 7 reels, 6,214 or 7,050 ft.

Pres by Charles R. Rogers. *Supv* Harry J. Brown. *Dir* Albert Rogell. *Story-Scen* Marion Jackson. *Titl* Don Ryan. *Photog* Ross Fisher.

Cast: Ken Maynard *(Lieut. John Scott)*, Ann Drew *(Jane Logan)*, Paul Hurst *(Sergeant Murphy)*, J. P. McGowan *(Captain Ortwell)*, Chief Yowlache *(Scar Face Charlie)*, Harry Shutan *(Private Izzy)*, Tom Day *(Earl Logan)*, Hal Salter *(Spike Dargan)*.

Western melodrama. Lieut. John Scott, an adventurous young United States Army officer, is assigned to a frontier military post in the heart of Sioux territory. Encountering a band of Indians attacking a stagecoach, John thwarts the raid and wins the admiration of Jane Logan, en route to join her brother at a nearby ranch. He establishes himself with his men by subduing an outlaw horse turned over to him as a prank, but he is rebuked by Captain Ortwell when he objects to engaging the services of Scar Face Charlie, a treacherous Indian who is spying at the post. In spite of attempts to declare peace, Charlie incites the Sioux to war; and though Scott arouses their superstitious dread by appearing in disguise as a medicine man, the troops are still induced to leave the fort by a message from Charlie. Lieutenant Scott, however, leads the men back to the fort, and the Sioux attack is repulsed. *Sioux Indians. Frontier and pioneer life. United States Army—Cavalry.*

THE RED RIDER (Blue Streak Western) **F2.4514**

Universal Pictures. 2 Aug **1925** [c3 Jul 1925; LP21633]. Si; b&w. 35mm. 5 reels.

Dir Clifford S. Smith. *Story* Isadore Bernstein. *Photog* Harry Neumann. *Adtl Photog* Robert Kurrle.

Cast: Jack Hoxie *(White Elk)*, Mary McAllister *(Lucille Cavanagh)*, Jack Pratt *(Black Panther)*, Natalie Warfield *(Natauka)*, Marin Sais *(Silver Waters)*, William McCall *(John Cavanagh)*, Francis Ford *(Brown Bear)*, George Connors *(Tom Fleming)*, Frank Lanning *(Medicine Man)*, Clark Comstock, Duke R. Lee, Chief Big Tree *(Indian chiefs)*, William Welsh *(Ben Hanfer)*, Virginia True Boardman *(Polly Fleming)*.

Western melodrama. White Elk, a light-skinned Indian chief, incurs the enmity of Chief Black Panther when he prevents him from looting a westbound wagon train. White Elk, who is betrothed to an Indian princess, is torn from her by his love for a white girl from the East. When he is tricked into signing away the lands of his tribe, White Elk is condemned to be burned alive by Black Panther. He is saved from certain death by a cloudburst and makes his escape. He is later told that he is really a white man, who as a child was saved from death and brought up as an Indian. The white girl with whom he has fallen in love is captured by the Indians and strapped in a canoe that is set adrift above a waterfall. White Elk saves the girl, and the Indian princess takes her place in the canoe, offering herself as a sacrifice. White Elk discovers that his father is the old scout who leads the wagon train, and he and the white girl make plans to be united. *Indians of North America. Scouts—Frontier. Human sacrifice. Property rights. Wagon trains. Waterfalls. Treaties.*

Note: Known also as *The Open Trail.*

RED RIDERS OF CANADA **F2.4515**

FBO Pictures. 4 Apr **1928** [c10 Feb 1928; LP24977]. Si; b&w. 35mm. 7 reels, 6,419 ft.

Dir Robert De Lacy. *Adapt-Cont* Oliver Drake. *Titl* Randolph Bartlett. *Story* William Byron Mowery. *Photog* Nick Musuraca. *Film Ed* Jay Joiner.

Cast: Patsy Ruth Miller *(Joan Duval)*, Charles Byer *(Sgt. Brian Scott)*, Harry Woods *(Monsieur Le Busard)*, Rex Lease *(Pierre Duval)*, Barney Furey *(Nicholas)*.

Northwest melodrama. Canadian Mountie Sgt. Brian Scott captures Le Busard, leader of a gang of fur pirates who murdered Joan Duval's father, and takes him to Joan's cabin to spend the night. Le Busard escapes by tricking Joan into accompanying him to his hideout, where Joan's brother, Pierre, is held prisoner. The treacherous "pirate" detains Joan and orders Pierre's death, but Scott arrives in time to save them. After a terrific fight, Pierre dies in his sister's arms from wounds inflicted by Le Busard, whom he has killed. Scott and Joan return to headquarters and marry after turning over Le Busard's henchmen to the authorities. *French Canadians. Fur pirates. Brother-sister relationship. Murder. Northwest Mounted Police.*

RED SIGNALS **F2.4516**

Sterling Pictures. 1 Mar **1927** [c5 Mar 1927; LP23752]. Si; b&w. 35mm.

Dir J. P. McGowan. *Cont* Burl Armstrong. *Story* William Wallace Cook. *Photog* Herbert Kirkpatrick.

Cast: Wallace MacDonald *(Lee Bryson)*, Earle Williams *(Mark Bryson)*,

Eva Novak *(Mary Callahan)*, J. P. McGowan *(Jim Twyler)*, Sylvia Ashton *(Opal Summers)*, William Moran *(Lafe Reeves)*, Robert McKenzie *(Tim Callahan)*, Billy Franey *(One-Round Hogan)*, Frank Rice *(The Professor)*.

Melodrama. When Mark Bryson arrives to become superintendent of a railroad, Twyler, the freight conductor and secretly the leader of a gang of train robbers, throws three tramps off a train, one of whom he recognizes as a wanted man. He captures the kid, intending to collect the reward, but Mark claims him as Lee, his wayward brother, and gives him a job and a chance to reform. Twyler and Lee are both fired as the result of a train wreck, and Lee is induced to join the gang of robbers but is soon discovered to be a traitor. In a thrilling chase between an automobile and a runaway train, Twyler is brought to justice and Lee is revealed as a secret agent for the railroad. He is happily united with Mary Callahan, a telegraph operator. *Secret agents. Telegraph operators. Brothers. Railroads. Train robberies. Chases.*

THE RED SWORD **F2.4517**

FBO Pictures. *Dist* RKO Productions. 17 Feb **1929** [c17 Feb 1929; LP147]. Si; b&w. 35mm. 7 reels, 6,243 ft.

Dir Robert G. Vignola. *Scen* Wyndham Gittens. *Titl* Randolph Bartlett. *Story* S. E. V. Taylor. *Photog* Nick Musuraca. *Film Ed* Ann McKnight. *Asst Dir* Phil Carle.

Cast: William Collier, Jr. *(Paul)*, Marian Nixon *(Vera)*, Carmel Myers *(Katherine/Russian actress)*, Demetrius Alexis *(Veronoff)*, Allan Roscoe *(Litovski)*, Charles Darvas *(Fideleff)*, Barbara Bozoky *(cook)*.

Melodrama. Litovski, a Cossack general, stops at an inn and, inflamed by wine, attempts to rape the innkeeper's wife, Katherine, causing her to fall to her death. The innkeeper rushes at Litovski with a knife, and Litovski blinds him with a knout. Six years pass. The innkeeper's daughter, Vera, grows to womanhood and falls in love with violinist Paul Shilkiv, Litovski's illegitimate son. Vera attempts to kill Litovski, but Paul forestalls her. Litovski falls to his death, and Paul and Vera prepare to be wed. *Cossacks. Innkeepers. Violinists. Rape. Illegitimacy. Blindness. Whips. Russia.*

RED TRAIL **F2.4518**

Norca Pictures. 28 Mar **1923** [New York State license]. Si; b&w. 35mm. 6 reels, 5,300 ft.

Cast: Nora Swinburne.

Melodrama(?). No information about the nature of this film has been found.

THE RED WARNING **F2.4519**

Universal Pictures. 17 Dec **1923** [c7 Nov 1923; LP19597]. Si; b&w. 35mm. 5 reels, 4,759 ft.

Dir Robert North Bradbury. *Story-Scen-Titl* Isadore Bernstein. *Photog* William Nobles.

Cast: Jack Hoxie *(Phillip Haver)*, Elinor Field *(Louise Ainslee)*, Fred Kohler *(Tom Jeffries)*, Frank Rice *(Toby Jones)*, Jim Welsh *(David Ainslee)*, William Welsh *(George Ainslee)*, Ben Corbett *(Bud Osman)*, Ralph Fee McCullough *(Harry Williams)*.

Western melodrama. David Ainslee tries to find a lost gold mine to pay off a note on his ranch and save his daughter, Louise, from ruffian Tom Jeffries. Dying, he entrusts the map to two strangers. Phillip Haver sees that the girl pays off her note, while Toby Jones finds the mine. The two fight off Jeffries, reveal him as a cattle thief, and rescue Louise. *Prospectors. Rustlers. Gold mines. Mortgages. Documentation.*

RED WINE **F2.4520**

Fox Film Corp. 23 Dec **1928** [c17 Dec 1928; LP25917]. Sd eff (Movietone); b&w. 35mm. 7 reels, 6,194 ft.

Pres by William Fox. *Dir-Story* Raymond Cannon. *Ed Supv* Malcolm Stuart Boylan. *Titl* Garrett Graham. *Adapt* Andrew Bennison, Charles Condon. *Photog* Daniel Clark. *Asst Dir* Ad Schaumer. *Cost* Sophie Wachner.

Cast: June Collyer *(Alice Cook)*, Conrad Nagel *(Charles H. Cook)*, Arthur Stone *(Jack Brown)*, Sharon Lynn *(Miss Scott)*, E. Alyn Warren *(Jack's 1st friend)*, Ernest Hilliard *(Jack's 2d friend)*, Ernest Wood *(Jack's 3d friend)*, Marshall Ruth *(Jack's 4th friend)*, Dixie Gay *(stenographer)*, Margaret La Marr *(Spanish cigarette girl)*, Bo Ling *(Chinese dancer)*, Dolores Johnson *(Mrs. Brown)*, Michael Tellegen *(headwaiter)*, Betty Lorraine *(Slinky)*, Lialani Deas *(Hawaiian dancer)*.

Domestic comedy. Charles H. Cook, a young married man of rigid, habitually good conduct, is persuaded by some friends to go out on the town for a night and gets involved in a wild party at a restaurant. Charles passes out, and, as a practical joke, his friends arrange things so that, when he comes to, he thinks he has been unfaithful to his wife, Alice. The following night is the Cooks' wedding anniversary, and Alice makes Charles take her to the restaurant where he had disgraced himself only the night before. Charles is ribbed by waiters and habitués, and it takes a good bit of explaining before Alice forgives him and they dance the anniversary waltz together. *Waiters. Marriage. Wedding anniversaries. Restaurants. Hoaxes.*

Note: This film was released in Los Angeles under the title *Let's Make Whoopee.*

THE REDEEMING SIN **F2.4521**

Vitagraph Co. of America. 25 Jan **1925** [c10 Jan 1925; LP21013]. Si; b&w. 35mm. 7 reels, 6,227 ft.

Pres by Albert E. Smith. *Dir* J. Stuart Blackton. *Cont* Marian Constance. *Adapt* Marian Constance. *Photog* L. W. O'Connell.

Cast: Nazimova *(Joan)*, Lou Tellegen *(Lupin)*, Carl Miller *(Paul Dubois)*, Otis Harlan *(Papa Chuchu)*, Rosita Marstini *(Mère Michi)*, William Dunn *(Gaston)*, Rose Tapley *(Marquise)*.

Melodrama. Source: L. V. Jefferson, "The Redeeming Sin" (publication undetermined). Joan, an apache dancer in a Paris nightclub, falls in love with Paul Dubois, an aristocratic sculptor, and asks him to help her become a good girl. She becomes a lady, and Paul falls in love with her. When Joan later sees him with another woman, her affection turns to rage, and she encourages Lupin, the leader of a gang of thieves, to steal a string of pearls from Paul's mother and to murder Paul. Paul is stabbed by one of Lupin's gang, and the pearls are stolen; but Joan's triumph is hollow, for she discovers that the woman she saw with Paul is his sister. Joan repents and arranges for Lupin to return the pearls; Joan sees Paul in church, and they are thus reunited. *Dancers. Apaches—Paris. Sculptors. Brother-sister relationship. Jealousy. Theft. Paris.*

THE REDEEMING SIN **F2.4522**

Warner Brothers Pictures. 16 Feb **1929** [c4 Feb 1929; LP81]. Talking sequences, mus score, & sd eff (Vitaphone); b&w. 35mm. 8 reels, 6,921 ft. [Also si; 6,145 ft.]

Titl-Dial Joe Jackson. *Adapt* Harvey Gates. *Film Ed* Tommy Pratt.

Cast: Dolores Costello *(Joan Billaire)*, Conrad Nagel *(Dr. Raoul de Boise)*, Georgie Stone *(a sewer rat)*, Philippe De Lacy *(Petit)*, Lionel Belmore *(Father Colomb)*, Warner Richmond *(Lupine)*, Nina Quartero *(Mitzi)*.

Romantic melodrama. At the Café du Chat Noir, Joan Billaire, a dancer, attacks Mitzi for schooling her brother, Petit, in picking pockets and is saved from a knifing by Lupine, a thief. Later, Lupine enlists Petit's aid in a robbery, and the boy is accidentally wounded by him. Joan calls on Dr. Raoul de Boise, who informs the police; and when the boy dies, she is prevented from shooting Raoul by the intervention of Father Colomb. As Joan becomes romantically involved with the doctor, the jealous Lupine wounds Raoul. Joan confesses her part in robbing the church but is forced to marry Lupine as the price. Learning Raoul is alive, Lupine in a jealous rage confesses to killing Petit and is himself killed by the gendarmes. *Dancers. Pickpockets. Thieves. Clergymen. Physicians. Police. Brother-sister relationship. Jealousy. Robbery. Paris.*

REDEMPTION **F2.4523**

Metro-Goldwyn-Mayer Pictures. 5 Apr **1930** [c17 Mar 1930; LP1148]. Sd (Movietone); b&w. 35mm. 7 reels, 6,019 ft. [Also si; 6,819 ft.]

Prod Arthur Hopkins. *Dir* Fred Niblo. *Screenplay* Dorothy Farnum. *Dial* Edwin Justus Mayer. *Titl* Ruth Cummings. *Photog* Percy Hilburn. *Art Dir* Cedric Gibbons. *Film Ed* Margaret Booth. *Rec Engr* Douglas Shearer. *Gowns* Adrian.

Cast: John Gilbert *(Feyda)*, Renée Adorée *(Masha)*, Conrad Nagel *(Victor)*, Eleanor Boardman *(Lisa)*, Claire McDowell *(Ann Pavlovna)*, Nigel De Brulier *(Petushkov)*, Tully Marshall *(Artimiev)*, Mack Swain *(magistrate)*, Erville Alderson *(see note)*, George Spelvin *(Magistrate)*, Sidney Bracy *(waiter)*, Dick Alexander *(policeman)*, Charles Quartermaine *(see note)*, Agostino Borgato *(see note)*.

Melodrama. Source: Leo Nikolaevich Tolstoy, *The Living Corpse* (1911). Feyda, a Russian wastrel, wins the love of Lisa from his friend Victor, and their marriage produces a child; but Feyda, tiring of the routine of domestic bliss, returns to his old haunts for gambling and drinking. He becomes estranged from his wife and takes up with his former Gypsy sweetheart, Masha. Thinking her husband has been drowned,

Lisa marries Victor; but later, investigations ensue from a bigamy charge against her; realizing he is destroying the lives of his wife and his best friend, Feyda remorsefully shoots himself. *Wastrels. Gypsies. Marriage. Alcoholism. Gambling. Bigamy. Suicide. Russia.*

Note: Studio press release data credit Quartermaine with the role of Artimiev and also both Borgato and Alderson with that of Petushkov.

REDHEADS PREFERRED **F2.4524**

Tiffany Productions. 1 Dec **1926** [c24 Dec 1926; LP23477]. Si; b&w. 35mm. 6 reels, 5,300 ft.

Dir Allan Dale. *Story-Scen* Douglas Bronston. *Photog* Milton Moore, Joseph A. Dubray. *Art Dir* Edwin B. Willis. *Film Ed* Malcolm Knight.

Cast: Raymond Hitchcock *(Henry Carter)*, Marjorie Daw *(Angela Morgan)*, Theodore von Eltz *(John Morgan)*, Cissy Fitzgerald *(Mrs. Henry Carter)*, Vivian Oakland *(Mrs. Bill Williams)*, Charles A. Post *(Bill Williams)*, Leon Holmes *(office boy)*, Geraldine Leslie *(Miss Crisp)*.

Farce. John Morgan, a model husband, in order to promote a business contract with Henry Carter, drinks heavily and goes to an artists' ball with a redheaded girl, hoping to conceal the escapade from his wife, Angela. Through an acquaintance with Mrs. Williams, the "lady-friend" of Henry, Angela learns of her husband's scheme; and donning a red wig, she goes as his escort to the ball. The arrival of Carter's jealous wife leads to numerous amusing complications. When Angela learns the purpose of his deceit, she manages affairs so that Morgan succeeds in getting the contract but keeps her identity secret. *Salesmen. Redheads. Philanderers. Personal identity.*

REDSKIN **F2.4525**

Paramount Famous Lasky Corp. 23 Feb **1929** [c23 Feb 1929; LP161]. Mus score & sd eff (Movietone); b&w with col sequences (Technicolor). 35mm. 9 reels, 7,643 ft. [Also si; 7,402 ft.]

Dir Victor Schertzinger. *Story-Scen* Elizabeth Pickett. *Titl* Julian Johnson. *Photog* Edward Cronjager. *Technicolor Sequences* Ray Rennahan, Edward Estabrook. *Film Ed* Otto Lovering. *Mus Score* J. S. Zamecnik. *Song: "Redskin"* Harry D. Kerr, J. S. Zamecnik.

Cast: Richard Dix *(Wing Foot)*, Gladys Belmont *(Corn Blossom)*, Jane Novak *(Judy)*, Larry Steers *(John Walton)*, Tully Marshall *(Navajo Jim)*, Bernard Siegel *(Chahi)*, George Rigas *(Chief Notani)*, Augustina Lopez *(Yina)*, Noble Johnson *(Peublo Jim)*, Joseph W. Girard *(commissioner)*, Jack Duane *(Barrett)*, Andrew J. Callaghan *(Anderson)*, Myra Kinch *(Laughing Singer)*, Philip Anderson *(Wing Foot, age 9)*, Lorraine Rivero *(Corn Blossom, age 6)*, George Walker *(Pueblo Jim, age 15)*, Paul Panzer.

Western drama. After attending preparatory school and college in the East, Wing Foot returns to his Navajo tribe and denies their customs and beliefs, becoming an outcast among his own people. Wing Foot later secretly visits the village of a rival tribe in order to see Corn Blossom, his sweetheart, who has also been to school in the East. Her people discover his presence, and he is forced to flee into the desert, where he discovers oil. White prospectors also find the oil, and Wing Foot races them to the claim office, filing his claim first. Faced with marriage to a man she does not love, Cotton Blossom takes refuge in the Navajo village. Her people come to take her back, and a pitched battle between the tribes is averted only when Wing Foot arrives and tells both tribes of the new good fortune of all the Indian nations. He then claims Corn Blossom as his own. *Navajo Indians. Prospectors. Deserts. Oil lands. Canyon de Chelly (Arizona).*

Note: The final 6 minutes of this film were projected in Magnascope. Filmed on location in Canyon de Chelly.

THE REFEREE **F2.4526**

Selznick Pictures. *Dist* Select Pictures. 10 May **1922** [c10 May 1922; LP17869]. Si; b&w. 35mm. 5 reels, 4,665 ft.

Pres by Lewis J. Selznick. *Dir* Ralph Ince. *Scen* Lewis Allen Browne. *Photog* William Wagner.

Cast: Conway Tearle *(John McArdle)*, Anders Randolf *(Steve Roberts)*, Gladys Hulette *(Janie Roberts)*, Gus Platz, Frank Ryan *(fighters)*, Joe Humphries *(announcer)*, Patsy Haley *(referee)*.

Melodrama. Source: Gerald Beaumont, "John McArdle, Referee," in *Redbook Magazine* (37:50, Jul 1921). The career of middleweight champion John McArdle is short-lived when he sustains injuries in a motor accident that prevent him from fighting, and he becomes known as Honest John McArdle, owner of a billiard parlor. Although John is in love with Janie Roberts, Steve, her father, opposes her marrying a man in the fighting profession. John is offered a referee job in a big fight; and in the course of the fight, he realizes that it is "fixed" and orders both fighters from the ring. Consequently, Steve changes his mind about McArdle's character and consents to his marriage with Janie. *Referees. Prizefighting. Bribery. Billiard parlors.*

REFORM *see* **LIFE'S MOCKERY**

REFUGE **F2.4527**

Preferred Pictures. *Dist* Associated First National Pictures. 12 Mar **1923** [c7 Mar 1923; LP18751]. Si; b&w. 35mm. 6 reels, 5,932 ft.

Pres by B. P. Schulberg. *Dir* Victor Schertzinger. *Scen* Florence Hein. *Story* Lois Zellner. *Photog* Joseph Brotherton, Ernest Miller. *Film Ed* Eve Unsell.

Cast: Katherine MacDonald *(Nadia)*, Hugh Thompson *(Gene)*, J. Gunnis Davis *(Dick)*, J. Gordon Russell *(Louis)*, Eric Mayne *(General De Rannier)*, Arthur Edmund Carew *(Prince Ferdinand)*, Mathilde Brundage *(Madame De Rannier)*, Fred Malatesta *(Gustav Kenski)*, Grace Morse *(Marie)*, Victor Potel *(Alphonse)*, Olita Otis *(The Princess)*.

Melodrama. Prince Ferdinand intends to marry Countess Nadia in order to gain favor with the people of Moravia and destroy evidence of the rightful prince's claim to the throne. Nadia will have none of it, however, and runs away with Gustav Kenski; but when he is knocked unconscious, she marries Gene, a soldier whom she meets on the road. Nadia is abducted by Ferdinand, then rescued by Gene, who proves to be the real prince. *Royalty. Soldiers. Imaginary kingdoms. Disguise. Abduction.*

REGENERATION **F2.4528**

Norman Film Manufacturing Co. 25 Dec **1923.** Si; b&w. 35mm. 5 reels, 4,820 ft.

Cast: M. Maxwell, Stella Mayo.

Melodrama. No information about the precise nature of this film has been found. *Negro life.*

REGENERATION ISLE *see* **LOVE'S REDEMPTION**

A REGULAR FELLOW **F2.4529**

Famous Players–Lasky. *Dist* Paramount Pictures. 5 Oct **1925** [c6 Oct 1925; LP21881]. Si; b&w. 35mm. 5 reels, 5,027 ft.

Pres by Adolph Zukor, Jesse L. Lasky. *Dir* Edward Sutherland. *Screenplay* Keene Thompson. *Story* Reginald Morris, Joseph Mitchell. *Photog* Charles Boyle.

Cast: Raymond Griffith *(prince)*, Mary Brian *(girl)*, [Frederick] Tyrone Power *(king)*, Edgar Norton *(valet)*, Nigel De Brulier *(revolutionary)*, Gustav von Seyffertitz *(prime minister)*, Kathleen Kirkham *(girl's companion)*, Carl Stockdale, Michael Dark *(royal aides)*, Lincoln Plummer *(tourist guide)*, Jacqueline Gadsden *(princess)*, Jerry Austin *(lover)*.

Comedy. The prince of a mythical Balkan kingdom, appointed to oversee his country's public relations, officiates at ship launchings, cornerstone layings, and parades. He falls in love with a tourist, but his family insists that he marry a princess from a neighboring country. The prince manages to get away temporarily from his duties and family pressure to have an Elysian episode with his sweetheart. His father dies, however, and the prince reluctantly returns to the capital for his own coronation. After he becomes king, he arranges with a friendly anarchist for a revolution to take place; the revolution is a success, and the ex-king is immediately elected the president of the new republic. Now free to marry anyone of his own choosing, he makes the tourist his first lady. *Royalty. Presidents. Tourists. Anarchists. Revolutions. Imaginary kingdoms. Balkans.*

Note: This film was copyrighted under the title *He's a Prince.*

A REGULAR SCOUT **F2.4530**

R-C Pictures. *Dist* Film Booking Offices of America. 15 Nov or 26 Dec **1926** [c15 Nov 1926; LP23332]. Si; b&w. 35mm. 6 reels, 5,564 or 5,601 ft.

Pres by Joseph P. Kennedy. *Dir-Scen* David Kirkland. *Story* Buckleigh F. Oxford. *Photog* Ross Fisher. *Asst Dir* Douglas Dawson.

Cast: Fred Thomson *(Fred Blake)*, Olive Hasbrouck *(Olive Monroe)*, William Courtright *(Luke Baxter)*, T. Roy Barnes *(Steve Baxter)*, Margaret Seddon *(Mrs. Monroe)*, Buck Black *(Buddy Monroe)*, Robert McKim *(Ed Powell)*, Harry Woods *(Scar Stevens)*, Silver *(Silver King)*.

Western melodrama. Fred Blake avenges the death of his mother, who expires after a bandit's raid, and discovers letters in the dead man's possession revealing him to be the long-lost son of the wealthy Monroe family. Fred impersonates the son and is accepted by Mrs. Monroe and Olive, her daughter, though he is followed by a mysterious stranger who has witnessed his struggle with the real son. His arrival defeats the plans of lawyer Luke Baxter and his son Steve, who want to fleece Mrs. Monroe.

Fred's bitterness fades, and he becomes interested in a Boy Scout troop as well as in Olive; but when honored for rescuing a boy, he confesses his deception and is arrested. Maurauders raid the Monroe home and kidnap Olive; but with the help of the Scouts and Silver King, Fred escapes, rescues Olive, and is cleared by the stranger. *Bandits. Strangers. Lawyers. Revenge. Impersonation. Kidnaping. Courtship. Boy Scouts. Documentation. Horses.*

REILLY OF THE RAINBOW DIVISION *see* **RILEY OF THE RAINBOW DIVISION**

THE REJECTED WOMAN **F2.4532**

Distinctive Pictures. *Dist* Goldwyn-Cosmopolitan Distributing Corp. 4 May **1924** [c3 May 1924; LP20175]. Si; b&w. 35mm. 8 reels, 7,761 ft.

Dir Albert Parker. *Story-Adapt* John Lynch. *Photog* Roy Hunt. *Art Dir* Clark Robinson.

Cast: Alma Rubens *(Diane Du Prez)*, Bela Lugosi *(Jean Gagnon)*, George MacQuarrie *(Samuel Du Prez)*, Conrad Nagel *(John Leslie)*, Frederick Burton *(Leyton Carter)*, Antonio D'Algy *(Craig Burnett)*, Aubrey Smith *(Peter Leslie)*, Wyndham Standing *(James Dunbar)*, Juliette La Violette *(Aunt Rose)*, Leonora Hughes *(Lucille Van Tuyl)*.

Society melodrama. Aviator John Leslie meets Diane Du Prez in Canada when he seeks shelter from a storm, but he returns home at the news of his father's death. Sent by her father to New York, she goes out socially with John; but her rough dress and manners are unacceptable to his friends, and she accepts the offer of Dunbar, his business manager, to give her financial aid. Her father's interference causes John to marry Diane; and though at first he rejects her when he learns of her arrangement with Dunbar, a reconciliation is effected. *Aviators. Canadians. Marriage. Class conflict. Filial relations. New York City.*

THE REJUVENATION OF AUNT MARY **F2.4533**

Metropolitan Pictures Corp. of California. *Dist* Producers Distributing Corp. 8 Aug **1927** [c20 Jun 1927; LP24104]. Si; b&w. 35mm. 6 reels, 5,844 ft.

Pres by John C. Flinn. *Dir* Erle C. Kenton. *Cont* Raymond Cannon. *Photog* Barney McGill. *Art Dir* Charles Cadwallader. *Asst Dir* Ed Bernoudy.

Cast: May Robson *(Aunt Mary Watkins)*, Harrison Ford *(Jack Watkins)*, Phyllis Haver *(Martha Rankin)*, Franklin Pangborn *(Melville)*, Robert Edeson *(Judge Hopper)*, Arthur Hoyt *(Gus Watkins)*, Betty Brown *(Alma)*.

Farce. Source: Anne Warner, *The Rejuvenation of Aunt Mary* (New York, 1916). Aunt Mary Watkins, who is being taken advantage of by her nephew Gus, believes that her other nephew, Jack, is studying to become a successful physician, though in fact he spends all his time and money perfecting a racing car motor. When Aunt Mary decides to visit him, he converts his domicile into a "sanitarium" in which his friends pretend to be patients. Jack and his chum, Mel, accidentally crash into the car of Judge Hopper, Aunt Mary's former sweetheart, and they are reunited at the "sanitarium"; on a trial run, the boys are arrested for speeding, while Martha, Aunt Mary, and Gus are arrested in a cafe raid. Jack is dismissed in time to enter the race with the help of Aunt Mary, who substitutes as his mechanic. Finding a new lease on life, Aunt Mary marries the judge, and Jack wins Martha, the pretty nurse. *Aunts. Judges. Mechanics. Nurses. Automobile racing. Rejuvenation. Sanitariums.*

RELATIVITY *see* **YOUNG IDEAS**

EL RELICARIO **F2.4534**

Miguel C. Torres Productions. 15 Nov **1926** [New York State license]. Si; b&w. 35mm. 7 reels.

Cast: Miguel C. Torres, Sally Rand, Judy King.

Comedy(?). No information about the nature of this film has been found.

Note: This film is probably a Spanish-language film of American origin designed for Spanish-speaking audiences, in the United States and elsewhere.

REMEMBER **F2.4535**

Columbia Pictures. 20 Dec **1926** [c6 Jan 1927; LP23508]. Si; b&w. 35mm. 6 reels, 5,494 ft.

Supv Harry Cohn. *Dir* David Selman. *Adapt* J. Grubb Alexander. *Story* Dorothy Howell. *Photog* J. O. Taylor. *Art Dir* Charles O. Seessel.

Cast: Dorothy Phillips *(Ruth Pomeroy)*, Earl Metcalfe *(Jimmy Cardigan)*, Lola Todd *(Constance Pomeroy)*, Lincoln Stedman *(Slim Dugan)*, Eddie Featherstone *(Billy)*.

Romantic drama. Nurse Ruth Pomeroy secretly falls in love with mechanician Jimmy Cardigan when he is injured at a racetrack. On his recovery Jimmy accepts a dinner invitation at the Pomeroy home and there falls in love with Constance, Ruth's self-centered sister. When Jimmy leaves for the war, Connie accepts his signet ring and vows fidelity, but on the battlefield he waits in vain for letters while Connie amuses herself with Billy, an old flame. Ruth, learning of Jimmy's anxiety over Connie, writes to him, signing Connie's name. Returning blinded from the war, Jimmy does not know that Connie has deserted him, and Ruth assumes her place. With his sight restored, Jimmy realizes that the self-sacrificing Ruth is the girl he loves. *Mechanics. Sisters. Veterans. Blindness. Courtship. World War I.*

REMEMBRANCE **F2.4536**

Goldwyn Pictures. 8 Oct **1922** [c31 Aug 1922; LP18241]. Si; b&w. 35mm. 6 reels, 5,650 ft.

Dir-Writ Rupert Hughes. *Photog* Norbert Brodin. *Art Dir* Cedric Gibbons.

Cast: Claude Gillingwater *(John P. Grout)*, Kate Lester *(Mrs. Grout)*, Patsy Ruth Miller *(Mab)*, Cullen Landis *(Seth Smith)*, Max Davidson *(Georges Cartier)*, Richard Tucker *(J. P. Grout, Jr.)*, Dana Todd *(Ethelwolf Grout)*, Nell Craig *(Julia)*, Esther Ralston *(Beatrice)*, Helen Hayward *(Mrs. Frish)*, Lucille Ricksen, Arthur Trimble *(children)*, William Carroll *(MacClune)*.

Domestic drama. John P. Grout collapses under the strain of making enough money to keep his family happy. Only his favorite daughter, Mab, remains unimpressed by possessions and social status, and she falls in love with Seth Smith, a clerk in his department store. While Grout hovers near death the family changes its attitude. He recovers to save himself from financial ruin, the family reduces its demands on him, and Seth becomes a successful businessman. *Fatherhood. Family life. Social classes. Department stores. Wealth.*

THE REMITTANCE WOMAN **F2.4537**

R-C Pictures. *Dist* Film Booking Offices of America. 13 Apr or 13 May **1923** [c21 May 1923; LP18978]. Si; b&w. 35mm. 6 reels, 6,500 ft.

Dir Wesley Ruggles. *Scen* Carol Warren. *Photog* Joseph A. Dubray.

Cast: Ethel Clayton *(Marie Campbell)*, Rockliffe Fellowes *(George Holt)*, Mario Carillo *(Moses d'Acosta)*, Frank Lanning *(Tsang Tse)*, Tom Wilson *(Higginson)*, Etta Lee *(Liu Po-Yat)*, James B. Leong *(Chuen To Yan)*, Edward Kimball *(Anthony Campbell)*, Toyo Fujita *(Sun Yu-Wen)*.

Melodrama. Source: Achmed Abdullah, *The Remittance Woman* (Garden City, New York, 1924). *Anthony Campbell's threat to send his daughter, Marie, to China as punishment for her continued extravagance is welcomed by her, since her sweetheart, George Holt, also intends a business trip to the Orient. When they arrive, however, the vase given to Marie by her Chinese maid, Liu, plunges them into danger, and they are sentenced to death for its possession. Marie and George are being led to their execution* when Marie awakens, realizes she has had a nightmare, and makes George promise that they will honeymoon anywhere except China. *Spendthrifts. Businessmen. China. Dreams.*

REMORSELESS LOVE **F2.4538**

Selznick Pictures. *Dist* Select Pictures. Aug **1921** [c30 Jul 1921; LP16866]. Si; b&w. 35mm. 5 reels, 4,186 ft.

Pres by Lewis J. Selznick. *Dir* Ralph Ince. *Scen* Edward J. Montagne. *Story* Mary Lanier Magruder. *Photog* William Wagner.

Cast: Elaine Hammerstein *(Ruth Baird)*, Niles Welch *(Enoch Morrison)*, Jerry Devine *(Dave Hatfield)*, Ray Allen *(Hester Morrison)*, James Seeley *(Cosmo Hatfield)*; Effingham Pinto *(Cameron Hatfield)*.

Melodrama. Ruth Baird, related to both the Hatfields and Morrisons—two feuding Tennessee families—is in love with Enoch Morrison, who is opposed by her Uncle Cosmo and Cousin Cameron. The lovers go by boat to an island to have their fortunes told by a Negress, and Enoch leaves his gun behind in the woods. Their boat is lost in a storm, and they are forced to spend the night on the island. The next day Enoch is arrested for the murder of Cameron, who is found shot near his abandoned gun; but at his trial he remains silent, fearing to compromise Ruth. The girl determines to defy his accusers, but she is saved from exposure by the announcement that little Dave shot Cameron accidentally with Enoch's gun. Enoch is acquitted, and his marriage to Ruth brings a reconciliation between the families. *Fortune-tellers. Feuds. Murder. Trials. Reputation. Tennessee.*

REMOTE CONTROL **F2.4539**

Metro-Goldwyn-Mayer Pictures. 15 Nov **1930** [c12 Nov 1930; LP1725]. Sd (Movietone); b&w. 35mm. 7 reels, 5,958 ft.

Dir Malcolm St. Clair, Nick Grinde. *Adtl Dir (see note)* Edward Sedgwick. *Screenplay* Sylvia Thalberg, Frank Butler. *Dial* F. Hugh Herbert, Robert E. Hopkins. *Photog* Merritt B. Gerstad. *Art Dir* Cedric Gibbons. *Film Ed* Harry Reynolds. *Song: "Just a Little Closer"* Howard Johnson, Joseph Meyer. *Rec Engr* Douglas Shearer. *Wardrobe* Vivian Baer.

Cast: William Haines *(William J. Brennan)*, Charles King *(Sam Ferguson)*, Mary Doran *(Marion Ferguson)*, John Miljan *(Dr. Kruger)*, Polly Moran *(Polly)*, J. C. Nugent *(Smedley)*, Edward Nugent *(radio engineer)*, Wilbur Mack *(chief of police)*, James Donlan *(Blodgett)*, Edward Brophy *(Al)*, Warner P. Richmond *(Max)*, Russell Hopton *(Frank)*.

Comedy-drama. Source: Clyde North, Albert C. Fuller, and Jack T. Nelson, *Remote Control* (New York opening: 10 Sep 1929). William J. Brennan, who works in a music shop, aspires to become a radio announcer, but when Smedley, his employer, finds him practicing with a dummy microphone during working hours, he hurries William out to wait on Marion Ferguson, a customer with whom William flirts and whom he pursues into the street. After being fired, he follows Marion to a radio broadcasting studio, where he meets Sam Ferguson, his old friend and Marion's brother, and volunteers to help him revive the waning life of the station. In addition to attracting many performers, an advertisement brings Dr. Kruger, leader of the Ghost Gang, who plans to direct the activities of his gangsters by broadcasting instructions under the guise of a clairvoyant mystic. William interferes in his plans, and Kruger orders him kidnaped and plots to have him eliminated during a bank robbery; but William contrives a scheme for tipping off the police and his friends by using newspaper headlines, and he is rescued in a final hectic chase. *Radio announcers. Gangsters. Clairvoyants. Kidnaping. Bank robberies. Radio. Chases.*

Note: According to *Motion Picture News* (Oct 1930) Edward Sedgwick was the last of four directors to work on this film. Later reviews, however, indicate that Malcolm St. Clair and Nick Grinde received final credit for the direction.

THE RENDEZVOUS **F2.4540**

Goldwyn Pictures. *Dist* Goldwyn-Cosmopolitan Distributing Corp. 11 Nov **1923** [2 Dec 1923; LP19825]. Si; b&w. 35mm. 8 reels, 7,415 ft.

Dir Marshall Neilan. *Adapt* Josephine Lovett. *Story* Madeleine Ruthven. *Photog* David Kesson.

Cast: Conrad Nagel *(Walter Stanford)*, Lucille Ricksen *(Vera)*, Richard Travers *(Prince Sergei)*, Kathleen Key *(Varvara)*, Emmett Corrigan *(Vassily)*, Elmo Lincoln *(Godunoff)*, Sydney Chaplin *(Winkie)*, Kate Lester *(Mrs. Stanford)*, Cecil Holland *(Nichi)*, Lucien Littlefield, Max Davidson *(commissars)*, Eugenie Besserer *(Nini)*, R. O. Pennell *(Czar)*.

Romantic melodrama. The czar banishes Prince Sergei to Siberia for marrying without his consent. The wife, Varvara, dies leaving a baby girl named Vera. Forced to flee, the prince leaves the girl in the care of Vassilly, a friend. Years later, the countryside is raided by Cossacks. Walter Stanford, an American soldier, saves Vera, now 18 years old, from being attacked by a Cossack chief. The Cossack forces Vera to marry him, then brutally beats her. The soldier returns, claims the girl, and marries her after the Cossack's accidental burial alive. *Soldiers. Royalty. Cossacks. Banishment. World War I. Russia. Siberia.*

RENEGADE HOLMES, M. D. **F2.4541**

Arrow Pictures. 15 Mar **1925** [c22 Apr 1925; LP21391]. Si; b&w. 35mm. 5 reels.

Dir Ben Wilson. *Story* Arthur Statter.

Cast: Ben Wilson, Marceline Day.

Western melodrama. Dr. Holmes meets an old college friend, Albert Darnton, and invites him home for dinner, introducing him to his wife, Marie. Holmes is soon called out to visit a sick patient, and Darnton, who knew her when she was a cabaret singer in Chicago, frightens Marie, who rushes to her room, followed closely by Darnton. Holmes returns home, finds Darnton in his bedroom, and throws him out. Disillusioned, Holmes then leaves his wife and seeks solace in nature, living on the ranch of Egan, who, Holmes later learns, is rustling cattle. Marie becomes sick, and Mary Galbraith rides out to get Holmes, the only doctor within 40 miles. Holmes returns to Marie and is reconciled with her. Holmes tells the sheriff of Egan's secret life of crime, Egan is arrested, and Holmes whips Darnton in a fight. *Singers. Physicians. Marriage. Rustling. Friendship.*

RENEGADES **F2.4542**

Fox Film Corp. 26 Oct **1930** [c3 Oct 1930; LP1648]. Sd (Movietone); b&w. 35mm. 11 reels, 8,400 ft.

Pres by William Fox. *Dir* Victor Fleming. *Adapt-Cont-Dial* Jules Furthman. *Photog* L. William O'Connell. *Sets* William Darling. *Film Ed* Harold Schuster. *Song: "I Got What I Wanted"* Cliff Friend, Jimmy Monaco. *Sd Engr* Arthur L. von Kirbach. *Asst Dir* William Tummel. *Cost* Sophie Wachner. *Tech Adv* Louis Van Den Ecker.

Cast: Warner Baxter *(Deucalion)*, Myrna Loy *(Eleanore)*, Noah Beery *(Machwurth)*, Gregory Gaye *(Vologuine)*, George Cooper *(Biloxi)*, C. Henry Gordon *(Captain Mordiconi)*, Colin Chase *(Sergeant-Major Olson)*, Bela Lugosi *(The Marabout)*.

Adventure melodrama. Source: André Armandy, *Le Renêgat* (Paris, 1929). At Fort Amalfa, outpost of the Foreign Legion in Morocco, four rebellious legionnaires are jailed: Deucalion, a French officer betrayed by Eleanore, a spy; Machwurth, a German; Biloxi, an American; and Vologuine, a Russian. They escape and join the defense of a nearby post, where their bravery wins them military honors. To avenge himself, Deucalion attempts to strangle Eleanore, but native police interfere; thinking they have caused the death of a policeman, all but Biloxi desert. Deucalion becomes military leader of an Arab tribe, kidnaps Eleanore, and has her treated as a servant. Eleanore plans revenge by winning the favor of the Arab ruler; meanwhile, Machwurth and Biloxi, on a gunrunning expedition, are attacked by legionnaires, but they are saved by the Arabs. Deucalion enters the fort under a truce, but his former captain refuses to surrender; realizing he is a despised renegade, Deucalion gives his life to save the legionnaires when his own band attacks the fort. *Traitors. Spies. Friendship. Arabs. Russians. France—Army—Foreign Legion. Morocco.*

RENO **F2.4543**

Goldwyn Pictures. *Dist* Goldwyn-Cosmopolitan Distributing Corp. 1 Dec **1923** [San Francisco premiere; released 9 Dec; c9 Dec 1923; LP19709]. Si; b&w. 35mm. 7 reels, 6,612 ft.

Dir-Writ Rupert Hughes. *Photog* John J. Mescall.

Cast: Helene Chadwick *(Mrs. Emily Dysart Tappan)*, Lew Cody *(Roy Tappan)*, George Walsh *(Walter Heath)*, Carmel Myers *(Mrs. Dora Carson Tappan)*, Dale Fuller *(Aunt Alida Kane)*, Hedda Hopper *(Mrs. Kate Norton Tappan)*, Kathleen Key *(Yvette, the governess)*, Rush Hughes *(Jerry Dysart, Emily's brother)*, Marjorie Bonner *(Marjory Towne)*, Robert De Vilbiss *(Paul Tappan, Emily's son)*, Virginia Loomis *(Ivy Tappan, Emily's daughter)*, Richard Wayne *(Arthur Clayton)*, Hughie Mack *(The Justice of Peace)*, Boyce Combe *(Hal Carson)*, Victor Potel *(McRae, The Detective)*, Percy Hemus *(Lemile Hake)*, Maxine Elliott Hicks *(Mattie Hake)*, Billy Eugene *(Tod Hake)*, Adele Watson *(Mrs. Tod Hake)*, Evelyn Sherman *(Mrs. Towne)*, Jack Curtis *(Hod Stoat)*, Patterson Dial *(Mrs. Hod Stoat)*.

Domestic melodrama. Roy Tappan obtains a divorce from Emily, his second wife, and marries Dora Carson, who has just divorced her husband. Emily, left penniless with two children, marries Walter Heath, a former suitor. She then discovers that she cannot live with her new husband because the divorce is not legal in her home state. Tappan and his new wife soon run out of money, each having thought the other was wealthy. His aunt promises to support him in exchange for his two children. He kidnaps the children and hides them from Emily in his aunt's home. After Emily and Walter find them, they go to Yellowstone Park, where they are considered legally married. Tappan follows and is killed after a fight with Walter when a boiling geyser throws him into the air and drops him onto the rocks below. *Divorce. Geysers. Reno. Yellowstone National Park.*

Note: Working title: *Law Against Law.*

RENO **F2.4544**

Sono-Art Productions. 1 Oct **1930** [c16 Oct 1930; LP1661]. Sd; b&w. 35mm. 8 reels, 7,200 ft.

Pres by George W. Weeks. *Dir* George J. Crone. *Adapt-Dial* Harry Chandlee, Douglas W. Churchill. *Song: "As Long As We're Together"*

Ben Bard, Leslie Barton. *Rec Engr* Jack Gregor.

Cast: Ruth Roland *(Felicia Brett)*, Montagu Love *(Alexander W. Brett)*, Kenneth Thomson *(Richard Belden)*, Sam Hardy *(J. B. Berkley)*, Alyce McCormick *(Ann Hodge)*, Edward Hearn *(Tom Hodge)*, Doris Lloyd *(Lola Fealey)*, Judith Vosselli *(Rita Rogers)*, Virginia Ainsworth *(Marie)*, Beulah Monroe *(Mrs. Martin)*, Douglas Scott *(Bobby Brett)*, Emmett King *(Judge Cooper)*, Henry Hall *(prosecuting attorney)*, Gayne Whitman *(defending attorney)*.

Domestic drama. Source: Cornelius Vanderbilt, Jr., *Reno* (New York, 1929). On the eve of their wedding anniversary celebration, Felicia and Alexander Brett quarrel bitterly over his insistence that a certain Rita Rogers be invited; despite her refusal, Rita appears among the quests and Felicia pointedly ignores her presence. When her husband's tyranny becomes intolerable, Felicia takes her 4-year-old son, Bobby, and leaves for Reno to obtain a divorce. En route, she meets Dick Belden, a former sweetheart. In Reno they are met by Tom and Ann Hodge, with whom she is to live, and J. B. Berkley. During a luncheon given for Lola Fealey, Lola excuses herself to call Brett, with whom she is conspiring to frame Felicia. By a ruse involving young Bobby, Felicia is placed in a compromising situation, and Brett brings suit to obtain custody of the child. To regain custody of Bobby, Felicia agrees to visit Brett, but Rita exposes the conspiracy in a moment of anger. Brett attempts to kidnap Bobby but is killed in an automobile chase. *Children. Marriage. Divorce. Frameup. Wedding anniversaries. Reno. Chases.*

A RENO DIVORCE F2.4545

Warner Brothers Pictures. 22 Oct **1927** [c14 Oct 1927; LP24504]. Si; b&w. 35mm. 6 reels, 5,492 ft.

Dir-Story Ralph Graves. *Scen* Robert Lord. *Photog* Norbert Brodin. *Asst Dir* John Daumery.

Cast: May McAvoy *(Carla)*, Ralph Graves *(David)*, Hedda Hopper *(Hedda Frane)*, Robert Ober *(Eric Frane)*, William Demarest *(James, the chauffeur)*, Anders Randolf *(David's father)*, Edwards Davis *(judge)*.

Romantic drama. Carla, a society debutante, motoring to her country estate, strikes a careless pedestrian and insists on taking the young man to her home to receive medical attention; he tells her his name is David and that he is a struggling artist down on his luck though he is actually the disinherited son of a steel magnate, rejected because of his art career. A mutual attraction develops; he tries to prolong his stay, and she agrees to let him paint a picture of her dog. Carla's intimate friends Hedda and Eric Frane, recently divorced, are invited to a house party, and Hedda determines to win David. Eric openly woos Carla, and playing on her weakness for gambling, he plans to win her in a fixed roulette game; David, torn with jealousy, denounces Carla as a heartless flirt, and she is deeply hurt. David and Carla are reconciled, then separated by a false accusation; Hedda's plan to lure him away ultimately fails, and he is reunited with the girl. *Artists. Socialites. Disinheritance. Gambling. Divorce. Jealousy. Reno. Dogs.*

RENT FREE F2.4546

Famous Players–Lasky. *Dist* Paramount Pictures. 1 Jan **1922** [c27 Dec 1921; LP17403]. Si; b&w. 35mm. 5 reels, 4,661 ft.

Pres by Jesse L. Lasky. *Dir* Howard Higgin. *Adapt* Elmer Rice. *Story* Izola Forrester, Mann Page. *Photog* Charles E. Schoenbaum.

Cast: Wallace Reid *(Buell Arnister, Jr.)*, Lila Lee *(Barbara Teller)*, Henry Barrows *(Buell Arnister, Sr.)*, Gertrude Short *(Justine Tate)*, Lillian Leighton *(Maria Tebbs)*, Clarence Geldert *(Count de Mourney)*, Claire McDowell *(Countess de Mourney)*, Lucien Littlefield *("Batty" Briggs)*.

Romantic comedy. Buell Arnister, Jr., prefers poverty as an artist to the lawyer's career planned for him by his father. Dispossessed of his studio, he camps on the rooftop of a nearby mansion, where he meets Barbara Teller, who has been cheated out of her inheritance by her stepmother and is likewise forced to tent on the roof with her friend Justine Tate. During a storm, he invites the girls to take shelter in an unoccupied bedroom. Buell finds in the pocket of a dressing gown a note addressed to his father and signed by James Teller, stating that his last will gives Barbara her rights. During the absence of Mrs. Teller, Buell and Barbara fall in love, and Buell begins doing newspaper sketches—among them, one of the Count de Mourney, Mrs. Teller's new husband, whom he invites to dinner. Mrs. Teller has Buell and the girls arrested, but Buell produces the note, which leads to the discovery of a second will by which Barbara regains her property. *Artists. Filial relations. Dispossession. Inheritance. Wills. Documentation.*

REPORTED MISSING F2.4547

Owen Moore Pictures. *For* Selznick Pictures. *Dist* Select Pictures. 5 Apr **1922** [c15 Apr 1922; LP17803]. Si; b&w. 35mm. 7 reels, 6,750 ft.

Pres by Lewis J. Selznick. *Supv* Myron Selznick. *Dir* Henry Lehrman. *Scen* Lewis Allen Browne. *Titl* H. I. Phillips, John Medbury, Will B. Johnson, E. V. Durling, Tom Bret. *Story* Owen Moore, Henry Lehrman. *Photog* Jules Cronjager. *Film Ed* George M. Arthur.

Cast: Owen Moore *(Richard Boyd)*, Pauline Garon *(Pauline Blake)*, Tom Wilson *(Sam)*, Togo Yamamoto *(J. Young)*, Frank Wunderlee *(Captain Ferguson)*, Robert Cain *(Andrew Dunn)*, Nita Naldi *(Nita)*, Mickey Bennett *(a boy)*.

Comedy-melodrama. Richard Boyd, a wealthy idler who has inherited the Boyd Shipping Company, decides to prove himself to his fiancée, Pauline. A fleet of ships on which the company has an option is coveted by Oriental merchant-tycoon J. Young. Aided by Andrew Dunn, general manager of the Boyd concern, Young has Boyd and Pauline shanghaied; and Sam, his Negro valet, follows. Following a spectacular shipwreck, the couple are rescued; there is a race between a hydroplane and a motorboat; but after a series of exploits in Young's stronghold, Richard, aided by Sam, gets the ships and the girl. *Idlers. Orientals. Shipping companies. Motorboats. Hydroplanes. Shanghaiing. Shipwrecks.*

Note: Title writers Phillips, Medbury, and Johnson were writers respectively for the *New York Globe*, the *New York Journal*, and the *New York Evening World*.

REPUTATION (Universal-Jewel) F2.4548

Universal Film Manufacturing Co. May **1921** [c3 May 1921; LP16554]. Si; b&w. 35mm. 7 reels, 7,153 ft.

Dir Stuart Paton. *Scen* Doris Schroeder. *Scen? (see note)* Lucien Hubbard. *Photog* Harold Janes. *Mus Score* Hugo Riesenfeld.

Cast—The Story: Priscilla Dean *(Fay McMillan, later Laura Figlan/ Pauline Stevens)*, May Giraci *(Pauline Stevens, as a child)*, Harry Van Meter *(Monty Edwards)*, Harry Carter *(Dan Frawley)*, Niles Welch *(Jimmie Dorn)*, William Welsh *(Max Gossman)*, Spottiswoode Aitken *(Karl)*, Rex De Roselli *(theater owner)*, William Archibald *(photographer)*, Harry Webb *(photographer's assistant)*, Madge Hunt *(matron)*.

Cast—Stage Sequence: Allan Garcia *(leading man)*, James McLaughlin *(heavy man)*, Kathleen Myers, Joey McCreery *(ingenues)*, Alice H. Smith *(char-woman)*, François Dumas *(char-man)*, Joe Ray *(stage manager)*.

Melodrama. Source: Edwina Levin, "False Colors" (publication undetermined). Actress Fay McMillan finds her child, Pauline, whom she deserted years ago, in an orphanage, but Monty, her financer, objects to her taking it back. In Paris she becomes a sensation as Laura Figlan; while intoxicated, however, she cancels her American engagement. Meanwhile, her daughter, having left the orphanage and "inherited" her mother's talent, tries to substitute for Laura and carries out the impersonation successfully. The mother, now a dope addict, hears of the imposture and comes to the theater and shoots Frawley, leaving Pauline to take the blame. As Pauline is about to be sentenced, Laura discovers that she is aiding in the prosecution of her own child, and after writing a confession she kills herself. *Actors. Impersonation. Suicide. Motherhood. Theater. Narcotics. Paris.*

Note: Several sources also credit Lucien Hubbard as coauthor of scenario; Universal records have been followed.

THE RESCUE F2.4549

Samuel Goldwyn, Inc. *Dist* United Artists. 12 Jan **1929** [c12 Jan 1929; LP80]. Mus score & sd eff (Movietone); b&w. 35mm. 9 reels, 7,980 ft. [Also si; 7,910 ft.]

Pres by Samuel Goldwyn. *Dir* Herbert Brenon. *Scen* Elizabeth Meehan. *Titl* Katherine Hilliker, H. H. Caldwell. *Photog* George Barnes. *Art Dir* William Cameron Menzies. *Film Ed* Marie Halvey, Katherine Hilliker, H. H. Caldwell. *Mus* Hugo Riesenfeld. *Asst Dir* Ray Lissner.

Cast: Ronald Colman *(Tom Lingard)*, Lily Damita *(Lady Edith Travers)*, Alfred Hickman *(Mr. Travers)*, Theodore von Eltz *(Carter)*, John Davidson *(Hassim)*, Philip Strange *(D'Alacer)*, Bernard Siegel *(Jorgensen)*, Sojin *(Daman)*, Harry Cording *(Belarab)*, Laska Winters *(Immada)*, Duke Kahanamoku *(Jaffir)*, Louis Morrison *(Shaw)*, George Rigas *(Wasub)*, Christopher Martin *(Tenga)*.

Romantic adventure drama. Source: Joseph Conrad, *The Rescue* (London, 1920). Englishman Tom Lingard, owner of the trading brig *Lightning*, works the waters of the Java Sea. Hassim, rajah of Wajo, rescues Lingard from the natives of his village and consequently is driven from his throne; thus he and his sister, Immada, take refuge with Lingard, who determines to restore the rajah to power. Just as preparations are nearing completion, the yacht of Travers, a wealthy Englishman, goes aground nearby. Though Travers resents Lingard's attempts to help, his wife is drawn to the adventurer. Lingard effects the release of Travers and D'Alacer from Daman's men, but the natives revolt and seize Travers' ship; Mrs. Travers goes to summon Lingard, but in their mutual passion, all is forgotten. The ship is dynamited, killing all, and Lingard remorsefully sends the girl away. *Traders. Hindus. English. Royalty. Brother-sister relationship. Ship grounding. Yachts. Java Sea.*

THE RESPONDENT *see* **THE SPENDERS**

RESTLESS SOULS **F2.4550**

Vitagraph Co. of America. 28 May **1922** [c2 May 1922; LP17814]. Si; b&w. 35mm. 5 reels, 4,080 ft.

Pres by Albert E. Smith. *Dir* Robert Ensminger. *Scen* Fred Schaefer, Calder Johnstone. *Photog* George Robinson.

Cast: Earle Williams *(James Parkington)*, Francelia Billington *(Lida Parkington)*, Arthur Hoyt *(Edgar Swetson)*, Martha Mattox *(Mrs. Fortescue)*, Nick Cogley *(Uncle Ben)*.

Melodrama. Source: Richard Harding Davis, "Playing Dead," in *Metropolitan Magazine* (41:7, Mar 1915). James Parkington, finding that Lida, his wife, is more absorbed in Swetson, a neosymbolist lecturer, than she is in him, resolves to feign a suicide to secure her happiness. Although Parkington has willed his estate to Lida, Maria Fortescue, his aunt, lays claim to the estate upon his "death." Learning that Maria has inherited the estate, Swetson turns his attentions to her. Parkington, eager to know the results of his scheme, comes out of seclusion in disguise and visits the home, where he is recognized by his dog. He overhears a discussion of a second will, restores the original will, and, when discovered by Maria and Swetson, orders them from the house. Swetson reveals that he is married to Maria, and Parkington and Lida are reconciled. *Aunts. Occult. Symbolism. Infidelity. Personal identity. Suicide. Wills. Dogs.*

RESTLESS WIVES **F2.4551**

C. C. Burr Pictures. 1 Jan **1924** [c10 Dec 1923; LP19686]. Si; b&w. 35mm. 7 reels, 6,317 ft.

Dir Gregory La Cava. *Titl* Raymond S. Harris. *Adapt* Mann Page. *Story* Izola Forrester. *Photog* Jack Brown. *Film Ed* Raymond S. Harris.

Cast: Doris Kenyon *(Polly Benson)*, James Rennie *(James Benson)*, Montague Love *(Hugo Cady)*, Edmund Breese *(Hobart Richards)*, Burr McIntosh *(Pelham Morrison)*, Coit Albertson *(Curtis Wilbur)*, Naomi Childers *(Mrs. Drake)*, Maud Sinclair *(Mrs. Cady)*, Edna May Oliver *(Benson's secretary)*, Richard Thorpe *(a lawyer)*, Fern Oakley *(a maid)*, Donald Bruce *(butler)*, Tom Blake *(Dorgan)*, De Sacia Mooers.

Domestic melodrama. Source: Izola Forrester, "Restless Wives," in *Ainslee's Magazine*. When Polly Benson's husband forgets their wedding anniversary, she accepts the invitation of Curtis Wilbur, an admirer. Her infatuation with Wilbur leads to divorce from Benson. Still in love with Polly, Benson abducts her, taking her to his cabin in the woods. There he is accidentally shot by one of his servants, and in a fire that follows, Polly realizes she still loves him. *Marriage. Divorce. Abduction. Fires.*

RESTLESS YOUTH **F2.4552**

Columbia Pictures. 30 Nov **1928** [c21 Feb 1929; LP156]. Si; b&w. 35mm. 7 reels, 5,963 ft.

Prod Jack Cohn. *Dir* Christy Cabanne. *Adapt* Howard Green. *Photog* Joe Walker. *Art Dir* Harrison Wiley. *Film Ed* Ben Pivar. *Asst Dir* Buddy Coleman.

Cast: Marceline Day *(Dixie Calhoun)*, Ralph Forbes *(Bruce Neil)*, Norman Trevor *(John Neil)*, Robert Ellis *(Robert Haines)*, Mary Mabery *(Susan)*, Gordon Elliott *(George Baxter)*, Roy Watson.

Society melodrama. Source: Cosmo Hamilton, "Restless Youth" (publication undetermined). Expelled from college for staying out after hours, Dixie Calhoun takes a job as secretary to Bruce Neil, a young lawyer to whom she soon becomes engaged. Bruce takes Dixie home to meet his father, John Neil (the district attorney *and* the board chairman of Dixie's former college), and John persuades her to give up Bruce to avoid ruining his son's career. Dixie goes to an employment agency, and one of the clerks attempts to have his way with her. Dixie hits him with a brass urn, killing him. She is placed on trial for murder, and John Neil makes a vitriolic attack on her character. Bruce comes to her defense, however, and convinces the jury of her essential goodness. Dixie is found not guilty, and she and Bruce are reconciled. *Secretaries. Lawyers. Office clerks. Fatherhood. Murder. Trials. Employment agencies.*

RESURRECTION **F2.4553**

Inspiration Pictures–Edwin Carewe Productions. *Dist* United Artists. 19 Mar **1927** [c10 Mar 1927; LP23778]. Si; b&w. 35mm. 10 reels, 9,120 ft.

Prod-Dir Edwin Carewe. *Scen* Finis Fox. *Titl* Tom Miranda. *Adapt* Edwin Carewe, Count Ilya Tolstoy. *Camera* Robert Kurrle. *2d Camera* Al M. Green. *Film Ed* Jeanne Spencer. *Asst Dir* Wallace Fox. *Spec Eff Photog* Frank H. Booth. *Literary Adv* Count Ilya Tolstoy. *Military Adv* Maj. Gen. Michael N. Pleschkoff.

Cast: Rod La Rocque *(Prince Dimitri Nekhludof)*, Dolores Del Rio *(Katusha Maslova)*, Marc MacDermott *(Major Schoenboch)*, Lucy Beaumont *(Aunt Sophya)*, Vera Lewis *(Aunt Marya)*, Clarissa Selwynne *(Princess Olga Ivanovitch Nekhludof)*, Eve Southern *(Princess Sonia Korchagin)*, Count Ilya Tolstoy *(old philosopher)*.

Romantic drama. Source: Leo Nikolaevich Tolstoy, *Resurrection* (1899). Prince Dimitri comes from St. Petersburg to spend the summer in a rural district and falls in love with Katusha, an orphaned peasant girl who works for his relatives. Later, en route to the Turkish-Russian front, Dimitri's regiment bivouacs near the village, and Katusha secretly yields to his passion; her condition soon arouses the suspicions of her aunt, and she is sent from the home in disgrace. Bereft by the death of her child, Katusha is eventually reduced to prostitution as a livelihood, and she finds herself imprisoned on a charge of poisoning and robbing a merchant. Dimitri, summoned to the jury at her trial, feels his responsibility and agrees to marry her. Though innocent of the crime, she is banished to Siberia; their old love is rekindled, but she refuses to become his wife and bears exile alone. *Royalty. Peasants. Injustice. Desertion. Illegitimacy. Prostitution. Russia. Siberia.*

RETRIBUTION *see* **THE CHILD THOU GAVEST ME**

THE RETURN OF BOSTON BLACKIE **F2.4554**

Chadwick Pictures. *Dist* First Division Distributors. 1 Aug **1927.** Si; b&w. 35mm. 6 reels, 5,865 ft.

Supv Arthur Beck. *Dir* Harry O. Hoyt. *Scen-Adapt* Leah Baird.

Cast: Corliss Palmer, Raymond Glenn, Rosemary Cooper, Coit Albertson, William Worthington, Florence Wix, J. P. Lockney, Violet Palmer, Strongheart.

Crook melodrama. Source: Jack Boyle, a story, title unknown, in *Cosmopolitan Magazine*. Just out of jail and vowing to go straight, gentleman crook Boston Blackie (played by Raymond Glenn) undertakes the reformation of a pretty blonde (played by Corliss Palmer), who has stolen a necklace from a cabaret dancer (played by Rosemary Cooper). When he learns that the jewels belong to the girl's mother and were presented to the vamp by the girl's philandering father, Boston Blackie saves the day by performing one last job: replacing the necklace in its owner's safe. *Criminals—Rehabilitation. Gentlemen crooks. Dancers. Vamps. Theft. Dogs.*

THE RETURN OF DR. FU MANCHU **F2.4555**

Paramount-Publix Corp. 2 May **1930** [New York premiere; released 17 May; c16 May 1930; LP1308]. Si; b&w. 35mm. 8 reels, 6,586 ft.

Dir Rowland V. Lee. *Scen-Dial* Florence Ryerson, Lloyd Corrigan. *Photog* Archie J. Stout. *Rec Engr* Eugene Merritt.

Cast: Warner Oland *(Dr. Fu Manchu)*, Neil Hamilton *(Dr. Jack Petrie)*, Jean Arthur *(Lia Eltham)*, O. P. Heggie *(Nayland Smith)*, William Austin *(Sylvester Wadsworth)*, Evelyn Hall *(Lady Agatha Bartley)*, Margaret Fealy *(Lady Helen Bartley)*, Evelyn Selbie *(Fai Lu)*, Shayle Gardner *(Inspector Harding)*, David Dunbar *(Lawrence)*, Tetsu Komai *(Chang)*, Toyo Fujita *(Ah Ling)*, Ambrose Barker *(reporter)*.

Mystery melodrama. Source: Sax Rohmer, *The Return of Dr. Fu Manchu* (New York, 1916). Having apparently committed suicide from ingesting poison in *The Mysterious Dr. Fu Manchu*, though merely in a state of cataleptic suspension induced by a secret potion, the nefarious Chinese physician is declared dead by Inspector Nayland Smith. Having sworn vengeance on the English families responsible for the death of his wife and son in the Boxer Rebellion, Fu goes to an English estate of the Bartleys, where their nephew, Jack Petrie, is about to marry Lia Eltham: Fai Lu, Lia's Chinese servant, dies mysteriously, and Lia and Lady Agatha are abducted. Fu requests that Jack appear on the moors to save Lia, and Smith, disguised as Jack, attempts the mission and is taken to a deserted dyeworks via airplane. Fu escapes the police, though paralyzed by a bullet wound, and forces Jack to operate on him while Lia is put into a trance. Fu bargains with Smith and his detectives for his freedom but is killed in his attempt to escape. *Physicians. Chinese. Detectives. Murder. Revenge. China—History—Boxer Rebellion. England. Scotland Yard.*

Note: Also produced in a German-language version.

THE RETURN OF DRAW EGAN (Reissue) **F2.4556**

Kay-Bee Pictures. *Dist* Tri-Stone Pictures. c25 May **1924** [LP20238]. Si; b&w. 35mm. 5 reels.

Note: A William S. Hart film originally released by Triangle Film Corp. on 15 Oct 1916.

THE RETURN OF PETER GRIMM **F2.4557**

Fox Film Corp. 7 Nov **1926** [c7 Nov 1926; LP23336]. Si; b&w. 35mm. 7 reels, 6,961 ft. [Copyrighted as 8 reels.]

Pres by William Fox. *Dir* Victor Schertzinger. *Adapt* Bradley King. *Photog* Glen MacWilliams. *Asst Dir* William Tummell.

Cast: Alec B. Francis *(Peter Grimm)*, John Roche *(Frederick Grimm)*, Janet Gaynor *(Catherine)*, Richard Walling *(James Hartman)*, John St. Polis *(Andrew MacPherson)*, Lionel Belmore *(Reverend Bartholomey)*, Elizabeth Patterson *(Mrs. Bartholomey)*, Bodil Rosing *(Marta)*, Mickey McBan *(William)*, Florence Gilbert *(Annamarie)*, Sammy Cohen *(The Clown)*.

Melodrama. Source: David Belasco, *The Return of Peter Grimm; a Play in Three Acts* (1911). "Old Peter Grimm makes his ward Katie promise to marry his nephew Frederik [*sic*] and then dies. Frederik proves to be a scapegrace and Peter's spirit returns to right matters and finally succeeds in doing so by communicating with Jimmie who is in a delirium." (*Moving Picture World,* 20 Nov 1926, p164.) Peter thus thwarts selfishness and greed and rewards virtue. *Uncles. Wards. Marriage. Supernatural. Ghosts.*

RETURN OF THE LONE WOLF *see* **THE LONE WOLF RETURNS**

REVELATION **F2.4558**

Metro-Goldwyn Pictures. 22 Jun **1924** [New York premiere; released 28 Jul; c2 Jul 1924; LP20368]. Si; b&w. 35mm. 9 reels, 8,752 ft.

Dir-Writ George D. Baker. *Photog* John Arnold. *Art Dir* John J. Hughes. *Film Ed* Grant Whytock, Lew Ostrow. *Art Titl* Jack W. Robson.

Cast: Viola Dana *(Joline Hofer)*, Monte Blue *(Paul Granville)*, Marjorie Daw *(Mademoiselle Brevoort)*, Lew Cody *(Count de Roche)*, Frank Currier *(Prior)*, Edward Connelly *(Augustin)*, Kathleen Key *(Madonna)*, Ethel Wales *(Madame Hofer)*, George Siegmann *(Hofer)*, Otto Matiesen *(Du Clos)*, Bruce Guerin *(Jean Hofer)*.

Drama. Source: Mabel Wagnalls, *The Rosebush of a Thousand Years* (New York, 1918). Scorned by her father for her sinful ways, Joline Hofer leaves her child in a convent and becomes the sensation of a Paris cabaret. She poses for Paul Granville, a poor American artist, who hence becomes famous. Despite his reluctance to use her as a model for a painting of the Madonna, she obtains the assignment, undergoes a spiritual transformation, is reunited with her child, and finds happiness with the artist. *Artists. Models. Regeneration. Convents. Paris.*

REVENGE **F2.4559**

Edwin Carewe Productions. *Dist* United Artists. Oct **1928** [c17 Oct 1928; LP25735]. Mus score & sd eff (Movietone); b&w. 35mm. 7 reels, 6,541 ft.

Dir Edwin Carewe. *Screenplay-Titl* Finis Fox. *Photog* Robert Kurrle, Al M. Greene. *Film Ed* Jeanne Spencer. *Mus Score* Hugo Riesenfeld.

Cast: Dolores Del Rio *(Rascha)*, James Marcus *(Costa)*, Sophia Ortiga *(Binka)*, LeRoy Mason *(Jorga)*, Rita Carewe *(Tina)*, José Crespo *(Stefan)*, Sam Appel *(Jancu)*, Marta Golden *(Leana)*, Jess Cavin *(Lieutenant De Jorga)*.

Melodrama. Source: Konrad Bercovici, "The Bear Tamer's Daughter," in *Ghitza and Other Romances of Gypsy Blood* (New York, 1921). Rascha, the wild daughter of Costa, the Gypsy bear tamer, swears revenge on Jorga, her father's enemy, when he cuts off her braids (a sign of disgrace among the Gypsies). Jorga later repents of his cruel act and cuts off the braids of all the other Gypsy women, returning Rascha's braids to her while she is sleeping. Rascha awakens and beats Jorga with a whip, exciting him to stifle her cries with his hot, passionate lips. Jorga later kidnaps Rascha and takes her to a mountain cave, where he sets out to tame her. Rascha comes to love Jorga and later helps him to elude the vengeance of her irate father. *Gypsies. Bear tamers. Flagellation. Kidnaping.*

RICH BUT HONEST **F2.4560**

Fox Film Corp. 22 May **1927** [c15 May 1927; LP23984]. Si; b&w. 35mm. 6 reels, 5,480 ft.

Pres by William Fox. *Dir* Albert Ray. *Scen* Randall H. Faye. *Photog* Sidney Wagner. *Asst Dir* Horace Hough.

Cast: Nancy Nash *(Florine Candless)*, Clifford Holland *(Bob Hendricks)*, Charles Morton *(Dick Carter)*, J. Farrell MacDonald *(Diamond Jim O'Grady)*, Tyler Brooke *(Barney Zoom)*, Ted McNamara *(Heinie)*, Marjorie Beebe *(Maybelle)*, Ernie Shields *(Archie)*, Doris Lloyd *(Mrs. O'Grady)*.

Comedy-drama. Source: Arthur Somers Roche, "Rich But Honest," in *Hearst's International Cosmopolitan* (81:78–81, Nov 1926). Florine and Maybelle, two department store workers, attend a dance; Florine wins a Charleston contest and forces Diamond Jim, who flirts with her, to get her a job in the theater. Maybelle proves a success with her clowning; but when Florine appears on the stage in the pose of Lady Godiva, Bob, her steady sweetheart, misunderstands and insults her. Dick, a wealthy idler, proves his mettle by whipping the former suitor and thus wins Flo for his wife. *Dancers. Salesclerks. Department stores. Theater. Charleston (dance). Godiva.*

RICH GIRL, POOR GIRL **F2.4561**

Universal Film Manufacturing Co. 24 Jan **1921** [c14 Jan 1921; LP16029]. Si; b&w. 35mm. 5 reels, 4,675 ft.

Pres by Carl Laemmle. *Dir* Harry B. Harris. *Scen* A. P. Younger. *Story* J. G. Hawks. *Photog* Earl M. Ellis.

Cast: Gladys Walton *(Nora McShane/Beatrice Vanderfleet)*, Gordon McGregor *(Terry McShane)*, Harold Austin *(Reginald)*, Antrim Short *(Muggsy)*, Joe Neary *(Spider)*, Wadsworth Harris *(Vanderfleet)*, Charles W. Herzinger *(Boggs)*.

Society melodrama. Nora McShane, resident of a tenement quarter known as Fish Alley, enters the grounds of the nearby home of the wealthy Vanderfleets and there meets Beatrice, the daughter of the house. Discovering that they look very much alike, Beatrice suggests that they exchange identities for a short while. Beatrice is later taken captive and held for ransom by Nora's drunken father. Meanwhile, Nora meets Reginald, Beatrice's admirer, and tells him the story; then Reggie and Mr. Vanderfleet go to the rescue of Beatrice, McShane is jailed, and Nora is adopted by the family. *Doubles. Social classes. Impersonation. Kidnaping. Slums.*

RICH MEN'S SONS **F2.4562**

Columbia Pictures. 20 May **1927** [c1 Jun 1927; LP24022]. Si; b&w. 35mm. 6 reels, 5,854 ft.

Prod Harry Cohn. *Dir* Ralph Graves. *Scen* Dorothy Howell. *Photog* Norbert Brodin.

Cast: Ralph Graves *(Arnold Treadway)*, Shirley Mason *(Carla Gordon)*, Robert Cain *(Niles McCray)*, Frances Raymond *(Mrs. Treadway)*, George Fawcett *(Samuel Treadway)*, Johnny Fox *(The Office Boy)*, Scott Seaton *(John Gordon)*.

Society drama. Source: Dorothy Howell, "The Lightning Express" (publication undetermined). Arnold Treadway, son of a railroad magnate, promises to end his idle leisure. At a cafe he meets Carla Gordon, whose father owns the Gordon Iron Works, and Niles McCray, business adviser to the firm. When Arnold and McCray become embroiled in a dispute over a champagne bottle, Carla leaves, forgetting an expensive vanity case, which then is taken by another girl in the party. Carla's father has a heart attack, and she determines to operate the business herself. Arnold, who has been disinherited, is arrested for stealing the vanity, but Carla puts him to work. He saves her by obtaining his father's signature to a contract, which she had sought in vain to execute, thus winning the hand of his employer. *Idlers. Railroad magnates. Businesswomen. Courtship. Disinheritance. Business management. Ironworks. Heart disease.*

RICH MEN'S WIVES **F2.4563**

Preferred Pictures. *Dist* Al Lichtman Corp. ca19 Aug **1922** [San Francisco premiere; released 15 Sep; c2 Sep 1922; LP18348]. Si; b&w. 35mm. 7 reels, 6,500-7,040 ft.

Pres by B. P. Schulberg. *Supv* B. P. Schulberg. *Dir* Louis J. Gasnier. *Scen* Lois Zellner. *Story* Frank Dazey, Agnes Christine Johnston. *Photog* Karl Struss.

Cast: House Peters *(John Masters)*, Claire Windsor *(Gay Davenport)*, Rosemary Theby *(Mrs. Lindley-Blair)*, Gaston Glass *(Juan Camillo)*, Myrtle Stedman *(Mrs. Davenport)*, Richard Headrick *(Jackie)*, Mildred June *(Estelle Davenport)*, Charles Clary *(Mr. Davenport)*, Carol Holloway *(maid)*, Martha Mattox *(nurse)*, William Austin *(Reggie)*.

Society drama. Wealthy John and Gay Masters lead a busy social life to the neglect of their son, Jackie. Also feeling herself slighted, Gay innocently flirts with Juan Camillo but is caught in a compromising situation and is sent away by John. Gay, forbidden to see her son, is penniless and miserable, while John also is unhappy and takes to drink. Gay slips into Master's house during a night of revelry to see Jackie, whom she rescues from playing the role of a cupid for the entertainment of the guests. Gay then upbraids John, who repents and asks forgiveness, thus reuniting the family. *Dissipation. Wealth. Parenthood.*

RICH PEOPLE **F2.4564**

Pathé Exchange. 7 Dec **1929** [c26 Dec 1929; LP960]. Sd (Photophone); b&w. 35mm. 8 reels, 7,074 ft. [Also si; 6,306 ft.]

Assoc Prod Ralph Block. *Dir* Edward H. Griffith. *Stgd by* Anthony Brown. *Scen-Dial* A. A. Kline. *Camera* Norbert Brodin. *Art Dir* Edward Jewell. *Sets* Ted Dickson. *Film Ed* Charles Craft. *Rec Engr* George Ellis, Cliff Stein. *Asst Dir* E. J. Babille. *Prod Mgr* Harry Poppe. *Cost* Gwen Wakeling.

Cast: Constance Bennett *(Connie Hayden)*, Regis Toomey *(Jeff MacLean)*, Robert Ames *(Noel Nevins)*, Mahlon Hamilton *(Beverly Hayden)*, Ilka Chase *(Margery Mears)*, John Loder *(Captain Danforth)*, Polly Ann Young *(Sally Vanderwater)*.

Society melodrama. Source: Jay Gelzer, "Rich People," in *Good Housekeeping* (86:16–20, 87:96–99, Mar–Jul 1928). Connie Hayden, the pampered daughter of a multimillionaire, is startled when her mother demands a divorce and blames their family's wealth as the cause of the marital rift. Connie is engaged to, but does not love, wealthy society man Noel Nevins; she meets Jeff MacLean, an insurance salesman, who saves her from two men who accost her on a deserted road during a storm, and his interest in efficiency methods interests her. Soon she begins to find the thought of marrying Noel intolerable, but Jeff resists marrying into wealth; while she is entertaining aboard her father's yacht, Eric Danforth, a former beau, advises her to go after her man; returning to Jeff's cabin, she cooks breakfast for him, and their affection is renewed. Connie tries unsuccessfully to break her previous engagement; but on her wedding day, Jeff's dog arrives with a note announcing his departure. Arrayed in her bridal gown, she drives to his cabin and assures him of her love. *Millionaires. Insurance agents. Social classes. Wealth. Courtship. Divorce. Efficiency.*

THE RICH SLAVE **F2.4565**

Dist Jaxon Film Corp. 18 Jun **1921** [trade review]. Si; b&w. 35mm. 6 reels, 5,500 ft.

Dir Romaine Fielding.

Cast: Joseph Smiley *(Harrison Frayne)*, Arthur Elton *(Sneed)*, Martha Forrest *(Nurse)*, Mabel Taliaferro *(Gladys Claypool)*, Romaine Fielding *(Whitney Gage)*, June Day *(Claire Gage)*.

Melodrama. No. 17 is the only name of orphan Gladys Claypool in the unhappy charge, with others, of a brutal superintendent. Her freedom is sought, however, by financiers eager for the possession of some valuables to which she is entitled. A nurse agrees to help them in exchange for a sum of money, and the superintendent intervenes, hoping for a cut of the nurse's profit. The girl suffers greatly, and her life is severely threatened; but she meets a young man who helps her. He goes west, and the plotters try to remove him in a train wreck, but he survives to find the girl's grandfather and proof of her clear title to the disputed property. *Orphans. Financiers. Nurses. Grandfathers. Property rights. Orphanages. Train wrecks.*

RICHARD, THE LION-HEARTED **F2.4566**

Associated Authors. *Dist* Allied Producers and Distributors. 15 Oct **1923** [c3 Oct 1923; LP19468]. Si; b&w. 35mm. 8 reels, 7,298 ft.

Prod Frank E. Woods, Thompson Buchanan, Elmer Harris, Clark W. Thomas. *Dir* Chet Withey. *Scen* Frank E. Woods. *Photog* Joseph Walker. *Mus Synopsis* James C. Bradford. *Historical Research* Arthur Woods.

Cast: Wallace Beery *(King Richard, the Lion-Hearted)*, Charles Gerrard *(Sultan Saladin)*, Kathleen Clifford *(Queen Berangaria)*, Marguerite De La Motte *(Lady Edith Plantagenet)*, John Bowers *(Sir Kenneth, Knight of the Leopard)*, Clarence Geldert *(Sir Conrade de Montserrat)*, Wilbur Higby *(Sir Thomas Devaux)*, Tully Marshall *(The Bishop of Tyre)*.

Spectacular drama. Source: Sir Walter Scott, *The Talisman* (1825). Adventures of King Richard when he travels with Queen Berangaria, the knights and ladies of his court, and his army of crusaders to Palestine to fight Sultan Saladin and the Saracen hordes for possession of the Holy Land. *Saracens. The Crusades. Great Britain—History—Plantagenets. Richard the Lion-Hearted. The Holy Land.*

THE RICHEST MAN IN THE WORLD *see* **SINS OF THE CHILDREN**

THE RIDDLE TRAIL **F2.4567**

Morris R. Schlank Productions. 27 Nov **1928** [New York State license]. Si; b&w. 35mm. 5 reels, 4,500 ft.

Cast: Cliff (Tex) Lyons.

Western melodrama(?). No information about the nature of this film has been found.

RIDE 'EM HIGH **F2.4568**

Action Pictures. *Dist* Pathé Exchange. 9 Oct **1927** [c16 Aug 1927; LU24319]. Si; b&w. 35mm. 5 reels, 4,542 ft.

Pres by Lester F. Scott, Jr. *Dir* Richard Thorpe. *Scen* Frank L. Inghram. *Story* Christopher B. Booth. *Photog* Ray Ries.

Cast: Buddy Roosevelt *(Jim Demming)*, Charles K. French *(Bill Demming)*, Olive Hasbrouck *(Betty Allen)*, Robert Homans *(Rufus Allen)*, George Magrill *(Paul Demming)*.

Western melodrama. When his father is killed resisting arrest on a murder charge, Jim Demming, ignoring his father's warning, rides to Happy Valley to learn the truth. There he meets Betty Allen and defends her against Paul Demming, whose family is involved in a feud with the Allens. Jim offers to help the Allens pay off their debts by riding in the local rodeo. Paul learns that Jim is his cousin and causes him to lose the contest. Paul tries to bribe a lawyer to destroy his father's will, which bequeaths property to Jim, but the lawyer refuses and tells Jim the truth. Jim seeks out his cousin to revenge himself, but Paul is ultimately killed by his own men by mistake. The family feud ends with the marriage of Betty and Jim. *Cowboys. Cousins. Revenge. Feuds. Rodeos. Ranches. Wills.*

RIDE FOR YOUR LIFE **F2.4569**

Universal Pictures. 25 Feb **1924** [c8 Feb 1924; LP19893]. Si; b&w. 35mm. 6 reels, 5,310 ft.

Dir Edward Sedgwick. *Adapt* Raymond L. Schrock, E. Richard Schayer. *Story* Johnston McCulley. *Photog* Virgil Miller.

Cast: Hoot Gibson *(Bud Watkins)*, Laura La Plante *(Betsy Burke)*, Harry Todd *("Plug" Hanks)*, Robert McKim *("Gentleman Jim" Slade)*, Howard Truesdell *(Dan Burke)*, Fred Humes *(The Cocopah Kid)*, Clark Comstock *(Tim Murphy)*, Mrs. George Hernandez *(Mrs. Donnegan)*, William Robert Daly *(Dan Donnegan)*.

Western melodrama. Bud Watkins loses his ranch and savings to gambling house proprietor "Gentlemen Jim" Slade. The Cocopah Kid, a notorious bandit, lures away Betsy Burke, Bud's sweetheart and the daughter of the local sheriff. The Cocopah Kid, mortally wounded, dies in Bud's house; and by impersonating the dead man, Bud regains his lost ranch and saves Betsy from Slade's clutches. Bud's disguise is exposed when a posse catches him, and he gets a reward for capturing The Cocopah Kid. Betsy perceives that she has fallen in love with Bud, not the bandit. *Bandits. Ranchers. Posses. Impersonation. Gambling.*

RIDER OF MYSTERY RANCH **F2.4570**

Bennett Productions. *Dist* Aywon Film Corp. 14 May **1924** [New York State license]. Si; b&w. 35mm. 5 reels, 4,600 ft.

Cast: Art Mix.

Western melodrama. No information about the precise nature of this film has been found.

THE RIDER OF THE KING LOG **F2.4571**

Associated Exhibitors. *Dist* Pathé Exchange. c4 May **1921** [LU16479]. Si; b&w. 35mm. 7 reels.

Dir Harry O. Hoyt. *Scen* Holman Francis Day. *Photog* Eugene French.

Cast: Frank Sheridan *(John Xavier Kavanagh)*, Irene Boyle *(Clare Kavanagh)*, Richard Travers *(Kenneth Marthorn)*, Emily Chichester *(Cora Marthorn)*, Arthur Donaldson *(Stephen Marthorn)*, Charles Slattery *(Tim Mulkern)*, Carleton Brickett *(Donald Kezar)*, John Woodford *(Abner Kezar)*, William Black *(Warren Britt)*, Albert Roccardi *(Father Laflamme)*.

Melodrama. Source: Holman Francis Day, *The Rider of the King Log; a Romance of the Northeast Border* (New York, 1919). John Kavanagh, a Maine lumberman, clashes with Stephen Marthorn, owner of a spruce-logging company, when Marthorn orders his men to make their drive before Cavanagh can get his logs down the river. His daughter, Clare, is disliked by Cora Marthorn, but Cora's brother, Kenneth, refuses to join the fight against the lumberman. Marthorn finds aid in Donald Kezar, a former friend of Kavanagh's who turned against him when refused his daughter's hand. Kavanagh has a heart attack and prepares for his death, instructing his daughter to make the drive. Clare, dressed in white, and the townsfolk accompany his body to the church. Learning that Kenneth is on her side, she succeeds in getting the logs to the mill with his aid, and they are happily married. *Fatherhood. Brother-sister relationship. Lumbering. Funerals. Maine.*

RIDER OF THE LAW **F2.4572**

Bud Barsky Productions. 15 Jan **1927.** Si; b&w. 35mm. 5 reels, 4,500 ft.
Dir Paul Hurst.
Cast: Al Hoxie.
Western melodrama. "Bashful hero lets Eastern party headed by his aunt run his ranch until girl with whom he is in love is in danger. He then asserts his rights and prevents kidnapping of girl by bandits." (*Motion Picture News Booking Guide*, 12:52, Apr 1927.) *Outlaws. Kidnaping.*

RIDERS AT NIGHT **F2.4573**

Charles R. Seeling Productions. *Dist* Aywon Film Corp. 1 Oct **1923.** Si; b&w. 35mm. 5 reels, 4,800 ft.
Cast: Big Boy Williams.
Western melodrama. "A gang of bad men terrorizes the country. Their revenge is directed against the daughter of a rancher who defies the leader. The attempt to abduct the girl is foiled by Jim Bart." (*Motion Picture News Booking Guide,* 6:58, Apr 1924.) *Ranchers. Gangs. Abduction.*

RIDERS OF BORDER BAY **F2.4574**

Art Mix Productions. *Dist* Aywon Film Corp. 15 Oct **1925.** Si; b&w. 35mm. 5 reels, 4,900 ft.
Cast: George Kesterson.
Western melodrama(?). No information about the nature of this film has been found.

RIDERS OF MYSTERY **F2.4575**

Independent Pictures. c29 May **1925** [LP21511]. Si; b&w. 35mm. 5 reels.
Pres by Jesse J. Goldburg. *Supv* Jesse J. Goldburg. *Dir* Robert North Bradbury. *Story-Cont* George W. Pyper. *Photog* Bert Longenecker.
Cast: Bill Cody *(Bob Merriwell)*, Frank Rice *(Jerry Jones)*, Tom Lingham *(John Arliss)*, Peggy O'Dare *(Helen Arliss)*, Mack V. Wright *(Dan Blair)*.
Western melodrama. Dan Blair, stagecoach driver, reports that he has been held up by the Phantom Bandits, and John Arliss, the sheriff, rides after them. He is ambushed and left for dead, but Bob Merriwell and Jerry Jones, honest prospectors, find him and save his life. Arliss sends the two men into town with a message for his daughter, Helen, but before it can be delivered, Blair, the leader of the Phantoms, incites the townspeople against Bob, framing him for the supposed murder of the sheriff. Jerry helps Bob to escape, and he and Bob and Helen go to aid her father. With Helen's help, Bob later learns that Blair is planning to rob the mining company of the payroll. Bob substitues dirt for the gold, sets a trap for the Phantoms, rounds up the gang, and saves Helen, who has been kidnaped by Blair. *Outlaws. Prospectors. Sheriffs. Stagecoach drivers. Kidnaping. Frameup. Stagecoach robberies.*

RIDERS OF THE DARK **F2.4576**

Metro-Goldwyn-Mayer Pictures. 21 Apr **1928** [c21 Apr 1928; LP25224]. Si; b&w. 35mm. 6 reels, 5,014 ft.
Dir Nick Grinde. *Story-Cont* W. S. Van Dyke. *Titl* Madeleine Ruthven. *Photog* George Nagle. *Film Ed* Dan Sharits. *Wardrobe* Lucia Coulter.
Cast: Tim McCoy *(Lieutenant Crane)*, Dorothy Dwan *(Molly Graham)*, Rex Lease *(Jim Graham)*, Roy D'Arcy *(Eagan)*, Frank Currier *(Old Man Redding)*, Bert Roach *(Sheriff Snodgrass)*, Dick Sutherland *(Rogers)*.
Western melodrama. A newspaper editor in favor of law and order is killed, and his facilities are destroyed. His son and daughter, Jim and Molly Graham, carry on, aided by Texas Ranger Lieutenant Crane. Crane arrests Molly to protect her when she accidentally shoots one of the men who killed her father. The bandits attack the jail to get Molly, but they are warded off by the timely arrival of the cavalry. *Editors. Newspapers. Texas Rangers. Manslaughter. United States Army—Cavalry.*

RIDERS OF THE LAW **F2.4577**

Sunset Productions. 15 Dec **1922.** Si; b&w. 35mm. 5 reels, 4,721 ft.
Pres by Anthony J. Xydias. *Dir-Writ* Robert North Bradbury.
Cast: Jack Hoxie, Marin Sais.
Northwest melodrama. "The story deals, as its name implies, with the rigid law of the Northwest and with Jack Meadows' efforts to set free the girl's father, who is the sheriff. The man has been wounded by outlaws and found in a dying state by Jack and his pal. The two set out to bring the criminals to justice. The girl at first misjudges Jack and believes him responsible for her father's disappearance. When he proves the respected deputy is in reality the leader of a band of liquor smugglers and captures the culprits, she changes her mind. Jack's identity as a government ranger is established." (*Motion Picture News Booking Guide,* 4:88, Apr 1923.) *Sheriffs. Smugglers. Secret agents.*
Note: Reissued Dec 1929.

RIDERS OF THE PURPLE SAGE **F2.4578**

Fox Film Corp. 15 Mar **1925** [c8 Mar 1925; LP21236]. Si; b&w. 35mm. 6 reels, 5,578 ft.
Dir Lynn Reynolds. *Scen* Edfrid Bingham. *Photog* Dan Clark.
Cast: Tom Mix *(Jim Lassiter)*, Beatrice Burnham *(Millie Erne)*, Arthur Morrison *(Frank Erne)*, Seesel Ann Johnson *(Bess Erne, as a child)*, Warner Oland *(Lew Walters/Judge Dyer)*, Fred Kohler *(Metzger)*, Charles Newton *(Herd)*, Joe Rickson *(Slack)*, Mabel Ballin *(Jane Withersteen)*, Charles Le Moyne *(Richard Tull)*, Harold Goodwin *(Bern Venters)*, Marion Nixon *(Bess Erne)*, Dawn O'Day *(Fay Larkin)*, Wilfred Lucas *(Oldring)*.
Western melodrama. Source: Zane Grey, *Riders of the Purple Sage* (New York, 1911). When a lawyer named Lew Walters is run out of town, he abducts Millie Erne and her daughter and forces them to accompany him. Millie's brother, Jim Lassiter, is a Texas Ranger who then dedicates his life to tracking down Walters. During his search for the lawyer, Lassiter becomes ramrod on Jane Withersteen's big spread, where he befriends a young cowboy, Venters. Venters later goes after an outlaw gang and captures its leader, who turns out to be a beautiful young woman with whom he falls in love. Finally Jane tells Lassiter that the man he is hunting is now a local judge known as Dyer. Lassiter walks into Dyer's courtroom and picks him off with deadly precision. A posse is formed, and Lassiter and Jane are forced to flee, finally taking refuge on a plateau. The only approach to their hiding place is by a set of stairs cut into the side of the cliff; and when Lassiter rolls down a boulder from the heights to block the pursuer's path, he and Jane are trapped there for life, a prospect neither finds displeasing. *Lawyers. Bandits. Cowboys. Texas Rangers. Brother-sister relationship. Kidnaping.*

RIDERS OF THE RANGE **F2.4579**

Art-O-Graph Film Co. *Dist* Truart Film Corp. 15 Feb **1923.** Si; b&w. 35mm. 5 reels.
Dir-Scen Otis B. Thayer.
Cast: Edmund Cobb *(Martin Lethbridge)*, Frank Gallagher *(Blunt Vanier)*, Clare Hatton *(Gregg Randall)*, Roy Langdon *(Bob Randall)*, Harry Ascher *(Red Morriss)*, E. Glendower *(Soapweed Harris)*, B. Bonaventure *(Roddy, the sheriff)*, Levi Simpson *(Wagner)*, Dolly Dale *(Dolly)*, Helen Hayes *(Inez)*, Mae Dean *(Neil Barclay)*, Ann Drew *(Mary Smithson)*.
Western melodrama. Source: Courtney Ryley Cooper, "Riders of the Range" (publication undetermined). Martin Lethbridge, president of the cattlemen's association, is called upon to investigate reports of a growing number of cattle raids. The sheep ranchers, led by Gregg Randall, are suspected, and they also ascribe to the cattlemen the increased casualties among their herds. Complications set in when Lethbridge falls in love with Randall's daughter, Dolly, but he prevails against a secret society of dishonest cattlemen, exposes Blunt Vanier as the cause of conflict, and leads Dolly to the altar. *Ranchers. Protective associations. Secret societies. Sheep. Cattle.*

RIDERS OF THE RIO GRANDE **F2.4580**

J. P. McGowan Productions. *Dist* Syndicate Pictures. 27 Sep **1929** [New York showing; released Sep 1929]. Mus score b&w. 35mm. 5 reels, 4,900-5,277 ft. [Also si.]
Dir J. P. McGowan. *Story-Titl* Sally Winters. *Photog* Hap Depew.
Cast: Bob Custer *(Jack Beresford)*, Edna Aslin *(Barbara Steelman)*, H. B. Carpenter *(Dan Steelman)*, Kip Cooper *(John Steelman)*, Bob Erickson *(Pinto Quantrell)*, Martin Cichy *("Snakey" Smiley,)*, Merrill McCormick *("Tough" Hawkins)*.

Western melodrama. "Quantrell and his gang hold Snowden, an engraver, forcing him to make counterfeit plates. Snakely, one of the gang, kidnaps Barbara, a rancher's daughter, but Jack Beresford outwits the gang and wins Barbara." ("Motion Picture News Booking Guide," in *Motion Picture News*, 15 Mar 1930, p100.) *Engravers. Gangs. Kidnaping. Counterfeiting.*

RIDERS OF THE SAND STORM **F2.4581**

Roberts & Cole. *Dist* Aywon Film Corp. 9 Sep **1925** [New York State license]. Si; b&w. 35mm. 5 reels, 4,800 ft.

Cast: Big Boy Williams, Peggy O'Day.

Western melodrama(?). No information about the nature of this film has been found.

RIDERS OF THE STORM **F2.4582**

J. Charles Davis Productions. 20 Jun **1929.** Si; b&w. 35mm. 5 reels.

Dir-Story J. P. McGowan. *Photog* Paul Allen.

Cast: Yakima Canutt, Ione Reed, Dorothy Vernon, Bobby Dunn, Charles Whittaker.

Western melodrama. No information about the precise nature of this film has been found.

RIDERS OF THE WEST **F2.4583**

Ben Wilson Productions. *Dist* Rayart Pictures. Mar **1927.** Si; b&w. 35mm. 5 reels, 4,834 ft.

Dir Ben Wilson. *Scen* Robert Dillon. *Photog* Eddie Linden.

Cast: Ben Wilson, Neva Gerber, Ed La Niece, Bud Osborne, Fang *(himself, a dog)*.

Western melodrama. "Reformed bandit becomes sheriff and cleans up a lawless town. He saves a silver mine from bandits and wins a beautiful girl." (*Motion Picture News Booking Guide,* 13:38, Oct 1927.) *Bandits. Criminals—Rehabilitation. Sheriffs. Silver mines.*

RIDERS OF VENGEANCE **F2.4584**

William M. Pizor Productions. 10 Sep **1928** [New York State license]. Si; b&w. 35mm. 5 reels, 4,200-4,800 ft.

Dir-Scen Robert J. Horner. *Titl* Jack D. Trop. *Photog* Lauren A. Draper. *Film Ed* Robert J. Horner.

Cast: Montana Bill.

Western melodrama(?). No information about the nature of this film has been found.

RIDERS UP **F2.4585**

Universal Pictures. 5 May **1924** [c14 Apr 1924; LP20072]. Si; b&w. 35mm. 5 reels, 4,904 ft.

Dir Irving Cummings. *Scen* Monte Brice. *Photog* Ben Reynolds.

Cast: Creighton Hale *(Johnny [Information Kid])*, George Cooper *(Henry, the Rat)*, Kate Price *(Mrs. Ryan)*, Robert Brower *(General Jeff)*, Ethel Shannon *(Norah Ryan, The Fiddlin' Doll)*, Edith Yorke *(Johnny's mother)*, Charlotte Stevens *(Johnny's sister)*, Harry Tracey *(Cross-eyed Negro)*, Hank Mann *(a boarder)*.

Drama. Source: Gerald Beaumont, *Riders Up* (New York, 1922). Johnny, a racetrack tout in Tijuana, is unsuccessful in his gambling but leads his New England family to believe he is engaged in legitimate business. He finally wins on a long shot and intends to return home, though he dislikes leaving his sweetheart, Norah Ryan. As a parting gesture Johnny takes his blind, elderly friend Jeff to the track, tells him his favorite horse has won, then gives Jeff his own winnings when he learns that the old man has staked all of his savings. The kindly intervention of Norah's mother enables Johnny to go home with Norah as his wife. *Touts. Horseracing. Gambling. Blindness. Tijuana (Mexico).*

Note: Working title: *When Johnny Comes Marching Home.*

RIDGEWAY OF MONTANA **F2.4586**

Universal Pictures. 12 May **1924** [c14 Apr 1924; LP20073]. Si; b&w. 35mm. 5 reels, 4,843 ft.

Dir Clifford S. Smith. *Scen? (see note)* E. Richard Schayer, Isadore Bernstein. *Adapt? (see note)* Raymond L. Schrock. *Photog* Harry Neumann.

Cast: Jack Hoxie *(Buck Ridgeway)*, Olive Hasbrouck *(Aline Hanley)*, Herbert Fortier *(Simon Hanley)*, Lew Meehan *(Steve Pelton)*, Charles Thurston *(Reverend McNabb)*, Pat Harmon *(Pete Shagmire)*, Lyndon Hobart *(Pierre Gendron)*.

Western melodrama. Source: William MacLeod Raine, *A Sacrifice to Mammon* (New York, 1906). Cattle owner Buck Ridgeway captures a rustler band, but the leader, Pelton, escapes. Buck is accompanied to the city to market his cattle by Aline, his neighbor's daughter, who is determined to make him fall for her. Resisting her advances, he pursues Pelton, but when he and Aline are trapped overnight by a blizzard he is compelled to marry her. She realizes her love for him after being rescued from Pelton. *Rustlers. Montana. Blizzards.*

Note: R. L. Schrock was given screen credit for the adaptation and Isadore Bernstein for coauthoring the scenario; Universal records list only Schayer.

RIDIN' COMET **F2.4587**

Ben Wilson Productions. *Dist* Film Booking Offices of America. 29 Apr **1925** [c26 Apr 1925; LP21552]. Si; b&w. 35mm. 5 reels, 4,354 ft.

Dir Ben Wilson. *Scen* George W. Pyper. *Story* William David Ball. *Photog* Eddie Linden, Don Cunliff. *Asst Dir* Art Parks.

Cast: Yakima Canutt *(Slim Ranthers)*, Dorothy Woods *(Bess Livingston)*, Bob Walker *(Austin Livingston)*, Bill Donovan *(Max Underly)*, Archie Ricks *(sheriff)*, William Hackett *(doctor)*, Meadowlark *(The Wonder Horse)*.

Western melodrama. Slim Ranthers objects to the development of an irrigation project on his ranch and incurs the enmity of those involved in it. Max Underly, Slim's rival for the affections of Bess Livingston, has Slim unjustly accused of cattle rustling. Since the accusation does not deter Slim, Max and his men ambush him at night, wounding him in the arm. Slim eventually defeats Max and wins the affections of Bess. *Ranchers. Injustice. Irrigation. Rustling. Horses.*

THE RIDIN' DEMON **F2.4588**

Universal Pictures. 18 Aug **1929** [c15 Aug 1928; LP25541]. Si; b&w. 35mm. 5 reels, 4,380 ft.

Supv William Lord Wright. *Dir* Ray Taylor. *Story-Cont* Basil Dickey. *Titl* Val Cleveland. *Photog* Joseph Brotherton. *Film Ed* Gene Havlick.

Cast: Ted Wells *(Dan Riordan/Pat Riordan)*, Kathleen Collins *(Marie)*, Lucy Beaumont *(Mrs. Riordan)*, Otto Bibber *(sheriff)*.

Western melodrama. Pat Riordan is caught cheating at cards and is shot; only slightly wounded, he escapes and, while bathing his wounds in a stream, meets Marie Devon, who takes pity on him and helps him out. Meanwhile, Dan Riordan, Pat's brother and Marie's fiancé, comes across the pair, and they all ride to the Riordan ranch, where the boys' mother is awaiting a visit from Pat, whom she has not seen for a long time. The sheriff comes looking for Pat, and Dan, wanting to give his brother time to visit with his unsuspecting mother, dresses in Pat's clothes and leads the sheriff on a merry chase across hill and dale. Dan and Marie later get Pat across the Mexican border, having kept Mother Riordan from learning that her sons were cut from different cloth. *Sheriffs. Brothers. Twins. Filial relations. Mexican border.*

RIDIN' EASY **F2.4589**

Arrow Pictures. 7 Jun **1925** [c2 Jun 1925; LP21524]. Si; b&w. 35mm. 5 reels, 4,483 ft.

Dir Ward Hayes. *Story* Gerry O'Dell.

Cast: Dick Hatton.

Western melodrama. A stranger (played by Dick Hatton) arrives in the town of Big Horn and quickly runs afoul of Red Hawks's gang, some of whose members nearly beat him to death. Mary Lyons and her father come to the stranger's aid and take him to their ranch to tend his wounds. The town moneylender, who holds the mortgage on the Lyons ranch, persuades Hawks to rustle the cattle that Lyons is driving to market in order to pay off the mortgage. Dick learns of this plan and rides to warn Lyons. On the trail, he is waylaid by Hawks and several of his men. Dick eludes them and arrives in time to save Lyons. Red kidnaps Mary, taking her to the justice of the peace. Hawks is forcing the justice to marry them when the stranger arrives and knocks Hawks senseless. The stranger and Mary then make good use of the justice. *Strangers. Moneylenders. Gangs. Justices of the peace. Rustling. Mortgages. Ranches.*

RIDIN' FOOL **F2.4590**

Ward Lascelle Productions. 3 Jul **1924** [New York State license]. Si; b&w. 35mm. 5 reels, 4,800 ft.

Cast: Lester Cuneo.

Western melodrama. No information about the precise nature of this film has been found.

A RIDIN' GENT F2.4591
Ben Wilson Productions. *Dist* Rayart Pictures. Dec **1926**. Si; b&w. 35mm. 5 reels, 5,027 ft.
Dir Bennett Cohn.
Cast: Jack Perrin, Starlight *(a horse)*.
Western melodrama. "Ranch owner wills property to foster-daughter and is killed by cousin who wants property. He steals the will but daughter arrives at ranch, and befriended by the ridin' gent, who discovers will, they turn tables on cousin. He escapes but is captured and beaten. Gent marries girl." (*Motion Picture News Booking Guide,* 12:52, Apr 1927.) *Ranchers. Wards. Cousins. Inheritance. Wills.*

THE RIDIN' KID FROM POWDER RIVER F2.4592
Universal Pictures. 30 Nov **1924** [c20 Oct 1924; LP20678]. Si; b&w. 35mm. 6 reels, 5,727 ft.
Dir Edward Sedgwick. *Scen* E. Richard Schayer. *Adapt* Raymond L. Schrock, LeRoy Armstrong. *Scen? (see note)* Raymond L. Schrock, Rex Taylor. *Photog* virgil Miller.
Cast: Hoot Gibson *(Bud Watkins)*, Gladys Hulette *("Miss")*, Gertrude Astor *("Kansas" Lou)*, Tully Marshall *(The Spider)*, Walter Long *(Steve Lanning)*, Sidney Jordan *("Buzzard" Davis)*, William A. Steele *("Lightnin" Bill Smith)*, Howard Truesdell *("Pop" Watkins)*, Frank Rice *(Cal Huxley)*, Nelson McDowell *(Luke Meggary)*, Fred Humes *(The Scorpion)*, Bowditch Turner *(Manuel)*, Newton House *(Bud, at 10)*.
Western melodrama. Source: Henry Herbert Knibbs, "The Ridin' Kid From Powder River" or "The Saddle Hawk" (publication undetermined). After 15 years of searching, Bud Watkins finally has his revenge on the cattlemen's gunman who killed his homesteader foster father, Pop Watkins. Bud finds refuge from the sheriff at the ranch of The Spider, falls in love with the bandit's daughter, "Miss," and is betrayed to the sheriff by his rival, Steve Lanning. In an attempt to escape, Miss is shot and Bud risks discovery to get a doctor from town. Miss recovers and is kidnaped by Steve when she and Bud again attempt to leave, but Bud rescues her after a thrilling ride. *Ranchers. Homesteaders. Sheriffs. Murder. Revenge.*
Note: Working title: *The Saddle Hawk*. Writing credits are in accordance with Universal Story Department records. Reviews also variously credit Armstrong and Schrock with story, Schrock with scenario; copyright records credit Schrock and Rex Taylor with scenario.

RIDIN' LAW F2.4593
Biltmore Productions. *Dist* Big 4 Film Corp. 24 May **1930**. Sd (Cinephone); b&w. 35mm. 6 reels, 5,600 ft.
Pres by John R. Freuler. *Dir* Harry Webb. *Story-Scen* Carl Krusada. *Photog* William Nobles. *Film Ed* Fred Bain. *Sd* William Garrity.
Cast: Jack Perrin *(Jack Rowland)*, Rene Borden *(Carmencita)*, Yakima Canutt *(Buck Lambert)*, Jack Mower *(Ricardo)*, Ben Corbett, Robert Walker, Fern Emmett, Pete Morrison, Olive Young, Starlight *(a horse)*.
Western melodrama. Seeking his father's murderer in Mexico, young cowboy Jack Rowland falls into the clutches of Buck Lambert's band of smugglers, who suspect Jack of being a Federal agent. Ricardo helps Carmencita, a dancer, to extricate Jack, keeping Buck ignorant of their disloyalty to him, and they reveal that they are working for the Mexican Government to apprehend the gang. With Jack's help, their mission is accomplished, Jack discovers Buck to be the man he seeks, and he happily learns that Ricardo is not Carmencita's sweetheart, but her brother. (Incidental Songs.) *Cowboys. Smugglers. Dancers. Government agents. Brother-sister relationship. Mexico. Horses.*

RIDIN' LUCK F2.4594
Trem Carr Productions. *Dist* Rayart Pictures. Oct **1927**. Si; b&w. 35mm. 5 reels, 4,137 ft.
Dir Edward R. Gordon. *Scen* Arthur Hoerl. *Story* Francis James. *Photog* Ernest Depew.
Cast: Tex Maynard, Ruby Blaine, Jack Anthony, Charles O'Malley, Charles Schaeffer, Art Wilting, Marshall Ruth.
Western melodrama. "Rancher's son returns from college in time to help father wage war on gang of rustlers. Boy saves pretty girl from attack by hoodlum, who later kills the boy's father and blames girl's brother for crime. The posse is about to hang the brother, when boy and girl ride in with real murderer." (*Motion Picture News Booking Guide,* [14]:277, 1929.) *Ranchers. Rustlers. Gangs. Posses. Brother-sister relationship. Murder. Lynching.*

RIDIN' MAD F2.4595
Ben Wilson Productions. *Dist* Arrow Film Corp. 11 Oct **1924** [c5 Sep 1924; LP20584]. Si; b&w. 35mm. 5 reels, 5,778 ft.
Dir-Writ Jacques Jaccard.
Cast: Yakima Canutt *(Steve Carlson)*, Lorraine Eason *(Marion Putman, his fiancée)*, Wilbur McGaugh *(Allen Walker)*, Helen Rosson *(Ruth Carlson)*, Annabelle Lee *(Beth Carlson)*, Dick La Reno *(Thornton Hawks)*.
Western melodrama. Steve Carlson is forced to kill a man in self-defense and leaves town. His sister, Ruth, falls in love with Walker, a scheming oil promoter who plans to leave her, and in an attempt to force his hand Steve is beaten in a fight and jailed. When Marion, Steve's sweetheart, proves Walker's part in her father's death, Steve escapes and forces a confession, thus freeing himself from the charge of manslaughter. *Brother-sister relationship. Manslaughter. Oil business.*

RIDIN' PRETTY F2.4596
Universal Pictures. 22 Feb **1925** [c8 Dec 1924; LP20894]. Si; b&w. 35mm. 5 reels, 4,812 ft.
Dir Arthur Rosson. *Cont* Raymond L. Schrock, George Hively. *Adapt* Isadore Bernstein. *Story* Raymond L. Schrock, George Hively . *Photog* Jackson Rose.
Cast: William Desmond *(Sky Parker)*, Ann Forrest *(Maize)*, Stanhope Wheatcroft *(Miller)*, Billy Sullivan *(Stringbean)*, Slim Cole *(Big Bill)*, Tex Young *(Shorty)*, Bill Gillis *(Gloom)*, Frank Rice *(Barb Wire)*.
Western comedy. Sky Parker, an Arizona cowboy, inherits a fortune from his eccentric uncle in San Francisco; under the terms of the will, however, he must live in his uncle's mansion for a year before claiming the bequest. Sky arrives in San Francisco accompanied by five cowboys, who immediately begin to raise western hell, stealing two Clydesdale horses from a brewery and shooting the gargoyles from the mansion roof. Sky's cousin, Miller, persuades a beautiful young girl, Maize, to help him prevent Sky from obtaining the inheritance, but she soon falls in love with the rugged ramrod and refuses to continue with their attempted fraud. Sky, not knowing of her duplicity, asks Maize to marry him; filled with shame, she runs away instead and boards a fast train. Trying to stop her, Sky chases the train in a car, which crashes; he then steals a cop's motorcycle, boarding the speeding train from that precarious perch. On the train, Maize confesses her guilt, Sky forgives her, and they declare their love for each other. When they return to his mansion, Sky punches Miller and throws him out of the house. *Cowboys. Inheritance. Arizona. San Francisco. Stunts. Chases. Horses.*

THE RIDIN' RASCAL (Blue Streak Western) F2.4597
Universal Pictures. 19 Sep **1926** [c8 Jul 1926; LP22898]. Si; b&w. 35mm. 5 reels, 4,510 ft.
Pres by Carl Laemmle. *Dir* Clifford S. Smith. *Scen* Harrison Jacobs. *Photog* Eddie Linden.
Cast: Art Acord *(Larrabie Keller)*, Olive Hasbrouck *(Phyllis Sanderson)*, Al Jennings.
Western melodrama. Source: William MacLeod Raine, *Mavericks* (New York, c1912). Larrabie Keller, a homesteader, is accused of being a cattle rustler, and when Keller refuses to fight Phil Sanderson, whose sister, Phyllis, has struck his fancy, he is insulted by Bill Healy, to whom he administers a severe drubbing. Phyllis, finding Keller beside a branding fire, believes him guilty; and when he is wounded by Healy, she takes Keller to Yeager, another homesteader, who cares for him and to whom he reveals that he is a Texas Ranger. In town, there is an attempt to frame Keller, but he is freed from jail by Phyllis. The rustlers lead a posse after him; and in a fight with Keller, Healy plunges to his death over a cliff. With the aid of Phil, he rounds up the rustlers and is forgiven. *Homesteaders. Cattlemen. Rustlers. Brother-sister relationship. Texas Rangers.*

A RIDIN' ROMEO F2.4598
Fox Film Corp. 22 May **1921** [c22 May 1921; LP16597]. Si; b&w. 35mm. 5 reels, 4,700 ft.
Pres by William Fox. *Dir-Scen* George E. Marshall. *Titl* Ralph Spence. *Story* Tom Mix. *Photog* Ben Kline. *Film Ed* Ralph Spence.
Cast: Tom Mix *(Jim Rose)*, Rhea Mitchell *(Mabel Brentwood)*, Pat Chrisman *(Highlow, the Indian)*, Sid Jordan *(Jack Walters)*, Harry Dunkinson *(King Brentwood)*, Eugenie Ford *(Queenie Farrell)*, Minnie *(squaw)*.
Western burlesque. King Brentwood, who is accused of breach of promise by a local widow, is opposed to Jim Rose as a suitor for his daughter, Mabel, and bans him from the ranch. Learning the widow is to

pay him a visit, Brentwood orders his men to hold up the stage and scare the woman away, but Jim rescues her, hoping to gain his approval, and is roughed up for his trouble. Later, Jim finds a baby he supposes to have been deserted and is arrested for abduction, but the widow wins over Brentwood and helps Jim get Brentwood's consent to marry his daughter. *Widows. Courtship. Breach of promise.*

THE RIDIN' ROWDY **F2.4599**

Action Pictures. *Dist* Pathé Exchange. 24 Apr **1927** [c5 Mar 1927; LU23728]. Si; b&w. 35mm. 5 reels, 4,794 ft.

Pres by Lester F. Scott, Jr. *Dir* Richard Thorpe. *Scen* Frank L. Inghram. *Story* Walter J. Coburn. *Photog* Ray Ries.

Cast: Buffalo Bill Jr. *(Bill Gibson)*, Olive Hasbrouck *(Patricia Farris)*, Al Hart *(Mose Gibson)*, Harry Todd *(Deefy)*, Lafe McKee *(Doc)*, Jack McCready *(Shuler)*, Charles Whitaker *(Miller)*, Walter Brennan, Raye Hampton.

Western melodrama. Billy Gibson, the irresponsible son of Mose Gibson, a cattle rancher, plays a joke on his father and is banished to a remote outpost for the winter. There he is accompanied by Deefy, an eccentric who affects loss of hearing. When Bill finds a herd of sheep grazing on their land, he rides a chuckwagon to issue a warning and meets Patricia Farris, whose estate has been swindled from her; she rejects him when he forces a kiss. Bill returns to his father's ranch to find he has been charged with illegal land registration and fencing; he finds papers implicating Miller and Schuler in framing his father. A confrontation follows between sheepmen and cattlemen, and Bill finds happiness with Patricia. *Ranchers. Sheepmen. Cattlemen. Filial relations. Deafness. Land rights. Documentation.*

RIDIN' STRAIGHT **F2.4600**

Dist Rayart Pictures. 27 Oct **1926** [New York State license]. Si; b&w. 35mm. 5 reels.

Cast: Bob Reeves.

Western melodrama(?). No information about the nature of this film has been found.

THE RIDIN' STREAK (Bob Custer Westerns) **F2.4601**

Independent Pictures. *Dist* Film Booking Offices of America. 29 Nov **1925** [c29 Nov 1925; LP22083]. Si; b&w. 35mm. 5 reels, 4,540 ft.

Prod Jesse J. Goldburg. *Dir* Del Andrews. *Cont* James Ormont. *Story* William Elwell Oliver. *Photog* Tony Kornman.

Cast: Bob Custer *(Bill Pendleton)*, Peggy Udell *(Ruth Howells)*, Roy Laidlaw *(Judge Howells)*, Frank Brownlee *(J. S. Dokes)*, Newton Barbar *(Gus Dokes)*, Billy Lord *(Tim)*, Paul Walters *(Leete Gleed)*, Claude Payton *(sheriff)*.

Western melodrama. Bill Pendleton, former rodeo champion and newly elected sheriff, is scheduled to hold an auction of the goods and chattels of Ruth Howells. J. S. Dokes, who holds her notes, is determined that his "no-account" son, Gus, will marry Ruth, but she refuses him. Dokes stages a pony express race on the day of the auction to distract potential bidders, hoping that he can buy the property at a cheaper price. Bill decides to resign his post temporarily and to enter the race. He overcomes the interference of Dokes's men, wins the race, and arrives in time to buy Ruth's pet horse, "The White Duchess." Meanwhile, Gus has abducted Ruth. Bill leaps on White Duchess and rides to the rescue. *Sheriffs. Auctions. Horseracing. Abduction.*

RIDIN' THE WIND **F2.4602**

Monogram Pictures. *Dist* Film Booking Offices of America. 9 Aug **1925** [premiere?; released 27 Sep; c9 Aug 1925; LP22015]. Si; b&w. 35mm. 6 reels, 5,800 ft.

Dir Del Andrews. *Co-Dir* Al Werker. *Story-Cont (see note)* Marion Jackson. *Story* Frank M. Clifton. *Camera* Ross Fisher.

Cast: Fred Thomson *(Jim Harkness)*, Jacqueline Gadsdon *(May Lacy)*, Lewis Sargent *(Dick Harkness)*, David Dunbar *(leader of the Black Hat Gang)*, Betty Scott *(Dolly Dutton)*, David Kirby *(Sheriff Lacy)*, Silver King *(himself, a horse)*.

Western melodrama. Jim Harkness has made every sacrifice to give his younger brother, Dick, an education and welcomes him home from college. Dick, however, did not go to college but became a member of the notorious Black Hat Gang, which has been ravaging the countryside. Jim prevents a train robbery by the gang and captures one of the masked bandits, who turns out to be Dick. He returns the goods his brother stole, Dick repents, and Jim marries May Lacy, the sheriff's "school m'arm" daughter. *Brothers. Schoolteachers. Gangs. Train robberies. Horses.*

Note: Most sources give writing credit to Marion Jackson, but copyright records list Frank M. Clifton.

RIDIN' THROUGH *see* **STRAIGHT THROUGH**

RIDIN' THRU **F2.4603**

Prairie Productions. 30 Mar **1923** [New York State license]. Si; b&w. 35mm. 5 reels.

Cast: Dick Hatton.

Western melodrama(?). No information about the nature of this film has been found.

RIDIN' THUNDER (Blue Streak Western) **F2.4604**

Universal Pictures. 14 Jun **1925** [c28 Mar 1925; LP21317]. Si; b&w. 35mm. 5 reels, 4,358 ft.

Dir Clifford S. Smith. *Cont* Carl Krusada. *Adapt* Isadore Bernstein. *Photog* Harry Neumann.

Cast: Jack Hoxie *(Jack Douglas)*, Katherine Grant *(Jean Croft)*, Jack Pratt *(Cal Watson)*, Francis Ford *(Frank Douglas)*, George Connors *(Bill Croft)*, Bert De Marc *(Art Osgood)*, William McCall *(sheriff)*, Broderick O'Farrell *(governor)*.

Western melodrama. Source: B. M. Bower, *Jean of the Lazy A* (Boston, 1915). When Bill Croft, a notorious gunfighter, is bushwhacked, innocent rancher Frank Douglas is accused of the crime on circumstantial evidence and sentenced to be hanged. Jack Douglas, Frank's son, sets out to prove his father's innocence with the help of Jean, the murdered man's daughter; Jack eventually apprehends the killer and forces him to confess, but the sheriff is unable to stop the execution without an official pardon. Jack rides to find the governor, and after a wild cross-country race with a train, he gets the pardon and returns home in time to save his father's life. *Ranchers. State governors. Murder. Injustice.*

Note: Copyrighted as *Riding Thunder.*

RIDIN' WEST **F2.4605**

Harry Webb Productions. *Dist* Aywon Film Corp. 17 Nov **1924** [New York State license]. Si; b&w. 35mm. 5 reels, 4,760 ft.

Dir Harry Webb.

Cast: Jack Perrin.

Western melodrama. "... concerning an intrigue to rob a sum of money in the possession of a ranch owner. Since the hero has endeavored to borrow a large sum to pay off a mortgage on his father's property, suspicion falls upon him. In a shooting affray a man is killed, and the hero is blamed for that also. But a little boy, who has seen the robbery take place, clears the suspected man." (*Motion Picture News Booking Guide*, 8: 68, Apr 1925.) *Ranchers. Robbery. Mortgages. Murder.*

RIDIN' WILD *see* **THE SAGEBRUSH TRAIL**

RIDIN' WILD **F2.4606**

Universal Film Manufacturing Co. 19 Nov **1922** [c13 Nov 1922; LP18413]. Si; b&w. 35mm. 5 reels, 4,166 ft.

Dir Nat Ross. *Cont* Roy Myers, Edward T. Lowe, Jr. *Story* Roy Myers. *Photog* Virgil Miller.

Cast: Ed (Hoot) Gibson *(Cyril Henderson)*, Edna Murphy *(Grace Nolan)*, Wade Boteler *(Art Jordan)*, Jack Walker *(George Berge)*, Otto Hoffman *(Andrew McBride)*, Wilton Taylor *(Sheriff Nolan)*, Bert Wilson *(Alfred Clark)*, Gertrude Claire *(Mrs. Henderson)*, William Welsh *(John Henderson)*.

Western melodrama. Trained by his Quaker mother to be gentle, Cyril Henderson receives only laughter from the townspeople when he tries to act tough to impress Grace Nolan, who is allowing Art Jordan, the town bully, to occupy her time so as to pique Cyril. The murder of Andrew McBride, who holds the mortgage on the Henderson's property, is blamed on the elder Henderson, and Cyril unsuccessfully tries to take the blame. Finally stirred to real action, Cyril kidnaps Grace, releases her, fights with Jordan when the latter captures the girl, and forces a confession to McBride's murder from the villain. Cyril and Grace find bliss, and justice gets a firm grip on Jordan. *Bullies. Murder. Mortgages. Society of Friends.*

RIDIN' WILD **F2.4607**

Robert J. Horner Productions. *Dist* Aywon Film Corp. 16 Sep **1925** [New York State license]. Si; b&w. 35mm. 5 reels, 4,800 ft.

Pres by Nathan Hirsh. *Dir* Leon De La Mothe. *Story-Cont* Robert J.

Horner, Matilda Smith. *Photog* Virgil Miller, Lauren A. Draper.

Cast: Kit Carson *(Jim Warren)*, Pauline Curley *(Betty Blake)*, Jack Richardson *(Scarface Jordan)*, Walter Maly *(Fred Blake)*, C. L. James *(Red Hanson)*.

Western melodrama. No information about the precise nature of this film has been found. *Tucson (Arizona).*

Note: Produced on location in Tucson, Arizona. *Ridin' Wild* is also the working title for *Sagebrush Trail*, released in 1922.

RIDING DOUBLE **F2.4608**

William Steiner Productions. *Dist* Photo Drama Co. 1 Jun **1924** [c22 Apr 1924; LU20106]. Si; b&w. 35mm. 5 reels, 4,500 ft.

Prod William Steiner. *Dir* Leo Maloney. *Story-Scen* Frances Beebe, Ford Beebe.

Cast: Leo Maloney *("Hoss" Martin)*, Josephine Hill *(Elizabeth Walters)*, James Carey, Leonard Clapham, Barney Furey, Bullet *(himself, a dog)*.

Western melodrama. "Hoss" Martin befriends "Chuck" Willis, a war veteran long separated from his mother. They arrive at the old home to find Gabe Lawrence posing as the son. Gabe is scheming with Luke Steele to deprive the mother of the ranch, but Hoss shows them up, installs his friend in his proper place, and wins the love of sister Elizabeth. *Veterans. Swindlers. Filial relations. Imposture. Dogs.*

Note: Copyright title: *Ridin' Double*. Character names have been taken from shooting script and may have been changed in final film.

RIDING FOOL **F2.4609**

H. Jane Raum Productions. *Dist* Sierra Pictures. 29 Dec u*l924*. Si; b&w. 35mm. 5 reels, 4,352 ft.

Dir Horace B. Carpenter.

Cast: Bob Burns, Dorothy Donald.

Western melodrama. No information about the precise nature of this film has been found.

RIDING FOR FAME **F2.4610**

Universal Pictures. 19 Aug **1928** [c16 Feb 1928; LP24995]. Si; b&w. 35mm. 6 reels, 5,424 ft.

Dir-Writ Reaves Eason. *Cont* Reaves Eason, Slim Summerville. *Titl* Harold Tarshis. *Story (see note)* Arthur Statter. *Photog* Harry Neumann. *Art Dir* David S. Garber. *Film Ed* Gilmore Walker.

Cast: Hoot Gibson *(Scratch 'Em Hank Scott)*, Ethlyne Clair *(Kitty Barton)*, Charles K. French *(Dad Barton)*, George Summerville *(High-Pockets)*, Allan Forrest *(Donald Morgan)*, Ruth Cherrington *(Miss Hemingway)*, Chet Ryan, Robert Burns.

Western melodrama. Hank, a champion broncobuster, arrives at the Barton ranch to break some horses being sold to Morgan, an unprincipled man who pays for the horses and then has his accomplices steal the money from Barton. Suspicion is cast on Hank as the thief, but his quick wits, fast riding, and courage pull him out of his difficulty. With Morgan and his men in jail and the money returned to Barton, Hank begins to make plans for the future with Kitty, Barton's daughter. *Broncobusters. Theft. Horses.*

Note: Company records indicate that Arthur Statter wrote the original story, which was rewritten by Eason.

RIDING FOR LIFE **F2.4611**

Anchor Film Distributors. *Dist* Rayart Pictures. Apr **1926**. Si; b&w. 35mm. 5 reels, 4,357 ft.

Pres by W. Ray Johnston. *Dir* J. P. McGowan. *Story* Joseph Kane. *Photog* Ray Cline.

Cast: Bob Reeves, Aline Goodwin, Hal Walters, Bob Fleming.

Western melodrama. "Hero wrongfully accused of depot robbery. To clear himself he trails bandits who would force his brother to sign confession of robbery. Succeeds in handing over villain to sheriff and saving girl from runaway." *(Motion Picture News Booking Guide*, 11:44, Oct 1926.) *Brothers. Bandits. Robbery.*

THE RIDING RENEGADE **F2.4612**

FBO Pictures. 19 Feb **1928** [c4 Feb 1928; LP24948]. Si; b&w. 35mm. 5 reels, 4,729 ft.

Dir Wallace W. Fox. *Story-Cont* Frank Howard Clark. *Titl* Randolph Bartlett. *Photog* Charles Boyle. *Film Ed* Della M. King. *Asst Dir* Frederick Fleck.

Cast: Bob Steele *(Bob Taylor)*, Dorothy Kitchen *(Janet Reynolds)*, Lafe McKee *(Sheriff Jim Taylor)*, Bob Fleming *(Ed Stacey)*, Ethan Laidlaw *(Pete Hobart)*, Nick Thompson *(White Cloud, Indian Chief)*, Pedro Riga *(Little Wolf)*.

Western melodrama. Bob Taylor, son of a sheriff, becomes a wanderer and is adopted by an Indian tribe when he saves the life of Little Wolf, son of Chief White Cloud. He and Little Wolf prevent Pete Hobart and Ed Stacey from robbing the stagecoach by riding away with the strongbox and Janet Reynolds, a passenger; but Bob's father arrests him for robbery, and Pete Hobart escapes with the box after wounding Little Wolf. Eventually Sheriff Taylor perceives that his son has behaved properly, and he forgives him before pursuing Stacey and Hobart. The two bandits overpower Sheriff Taylor, but Bob and the Indians rescue him. *Wanderers. Sheriffs. Indians of North America. Bandits. Filial relations. Stagecoach robberies.*

RIDING RIVALS **F2.4613**

Action Pictures. *Dist* Weiss Brothers Artclass Pictures. 2 May **1926**. Si; b&w. 35mm. 5 reels, 4,402 ft.

Dir Richard Thorpe. *Scen* Betty Burbridge.

Cast: Wally Wales.

Western melodrama. "Cowboy with disreputable father, discontinues love affair because of family stain, but is instrumental in clearing father of murder charge. Girl disregards 'bar sinister' and romance blooms again." *(Motion Picture News Booking Guide*, 11:44, Oct 1926.) *Cowboys. Murder. Filial relations.*

RIDING ROMANCE **F2.4614**

Morris R. Schlank Productions *Dist* Anchor Film Distributors. 15 Aug **1926**. Si; b&w. 35mm. 5 reels, 4,800 ft.

Dir J. P. McGowan. *Story* William Lester. *Photog* Walter Griffin.

Cast: Al Hoxie, Marjorie Bonner, Arthur Morrison, Steve Clements.

Western melodrama. "For a start he [Al Hoxie] saves the ranch belonging to the heroine, prevents villain from forcing her into a marriage with him and also proves that villain framed the girl's brother into jail by planting stolen cattle in his possession. For all of which hero receives the just reward—the girl." *(Film Daily*, 15 Aug 1926, p9.) *Brother-sister relationship. Frameup. Rustling. Ranches.*

RIDING TO FAME **F2.4615**

Ellbee Pictures. 1 Jul **1927** [New York showing]. Si; b&w. 35mm. 6 reels, 5,367 ft.

Pres by W. T. Lackey. *Dir-Story-Scen* A. B. Barringer. *Photog* Kenneth Gordon MacLean, Robert Cline.

Cast: George Fawcett *(Old Man Randolph)*, Rosemary Theby *(Marge)*, Gladys McConnell *(Rose Randolph)*, Arthur Rankin *(Jackie)*, Bert Tansey *(Spec)*, Henry Sedley *(Joe Riordan)*, Lafe McKee *(Dr. Lorentz)*, Dora Baker, Raymond Turner.

Melodrama. "There is the owner [Old Man Randolph] out to clean up on the big race, the difficulty in entering the horse, a riding jockey for a hero [Jackie] and a crook out to see that the old man's horse doesn't win. Added to this one there is the owner's crippled little daughter [Rose Randolph] whose operation depends upon the success of the race. Obstacles galore, suspense to the last minute and then the grand and glorious finish with hero dashing on to the track a second late, catching up with the riders, passing them and then on to a finish first." *(Film Daily*, 10 Jul 1927, p6.) *Jockeys. Cripples. Children. Horseracing. Fatherhood.*

RIDING WITH DEATH **F2.4616**

Fox Film Corp. 13 Nov **1921** [c13 Nov 1921; LP17288]. Si; b&w. 35mm. 5 reels, 4,110 ft.

Pres by William Fox. *Dir-Story* Jacques Jaccard. *Scen* Agnes Parsons. *Photog* Frank B. Good.

Cast: Charles Jones *(Dynamite Steve Dorsey)*, Betty Francisco *(Anita Calhoun)*, Jack Mower *(Val Nelson)*, J. Farrell MacDonald *(Sheriff Pat Garrity)*, H. von Sickle *(Col. Lee Calhoun)*, William Steele *(Chick Dillon)*, William Gettinger *(Garrity's pal)*, Bill Gillis *(Capt. Jack Hughes)*, Artie Ortega *(Tony Carilla)*, Tina Medotti *(Rosa Carilla)*.

Western melodrama. Dynamite Steve Dorsey of the Texas Rangers finds his pal Val Nelson murdered by a member of Sheriff Pat Garrity's gang and vows vengeance. At the ranch of Col. Lee Calhoun, Steve relates the news to Anita, his sweetheart. Garrity, who covets Anita and has plotted to steal the colonel's payment of the mortgage on his ranch, arrives to foreclose but finds Steve there. Steve is captured by Garrity's men and jailed, but he manages to notify the Rangers, and Captain Hughes arrives at the town just in time to rout Garrity's gunmen and prevent Steve's death. Steve obtains evidence on which to convict the sheriff of Val's murder, and following the showdown Anita admits her love for Steve. *Texas Rangers. Sheriffs. Murder. Mortgages. Political corruption.*

THE RIGHT MAN F2.4617

Dist Rayart Pictures. 27 Mar **1925** [New York State license]. Si; b&w. 35mm. 5 reels, 4,800 ft.

Dir John Harvey. *Story* W. P. Grist. *Photog* Jack Young.

Cast: George Larkin.

Melodrama(?). No information about the nature of this film has been found.

THE RIGHT OF THE STRONGEST F2.4618

Zenith Pictures. *Dist* Selznick Distributing Corp. Apr **1924** [c23 Oct 1923; LP19526]. Si; b&w. 35mm. 7 reels, 6,240 ft.

Dir Edgar Lewis. *Titl* Katherine Hilliker, H. H. Caldwell. *Adapt* Doty Hobart. *Story* Frances Nimmo Greene. *Photog* Vernon Walker.

Cast: E. K. Lincoln *(John Marshall)*, Helen Ferguson *(Mary Elizabeth Dale)*, George Siegmann *("Trav" Williams)*, Tom Santschi *("Babe" Davis)*, Robert Milasch *("Bud" Davis)*, F. B. Phillips *("Uncle Beck" Logan)*, Tully Marshall *("Mister" Sykes)*, James Gibson *("Shan" Thaggin)*, Coy Watson *(Tony Thaggin)*, Gertrude Norman *(Aunt Millie Davis)*, Milla Davenport *(Melissa Thaggin)*, June Elvidge *(Anna Bell Lee)*, Winter Hall *(Austin Lee, Sr.)*, Niles Welch *(Austin, Jr.)*, Beth Kosick *(Sue Thaggin)*, Leonard Clapham *(Fred Dearing)*.

Rural melodrama. To a valley held by squatters since their ancestors took it from the Indians come two strangers who are regarded with hostility by the natives. Engineer John Marshall's mission is mysterious and he chooses to live in a cabin long believed to be haunted. The cabin's history is connected with district schoolteacher Mary Elizabeth Dale. She comes to the valley unaware that her father, Welchel Dale, original owner of the cabin, was lynched by some angry bootleggers who suspected that he was a revenue agent. The squatters learn that Marshall's mission is to take over their land, enabling Marshall's company to dam the valley, thus providing power for a nearby industrial town. After convincing Marshall that the company should pay the squatters for the land, Mary Elizabeth helps him when an angry mob arrives to lynch him. During the melee two villainous men and one innocent boy are killed; when peace finally comes to the valley, the folk, sobered by the deaths, accept Marshall's generous compensation and consent to move. John weds Mary. *Squatters. Engineers. Bootleggers. Schoolteachers. Land rights. Lynching. Power companies.*

THE RIGHT THAT FAILED F2.4619

Metro Pictures. 20 Feb **1922** [c27 Feb 1922; LP17688]. Si; b&w. 35mm. 5 reels.

Dir Bayard Veiller. *Adapt* Lenore Coffee. *Photog* Arthur Martinelli. *Tech Dir* A. F. Mantz. *Prod Mgr* Joseph Strauss.

Cast: Bert Lytell *(Johnny Duffey)*, Virginia Valli *(Constance Talbot)*, De Witt Jennings *(Mr. Talbot)*, Philo McCullough *(Roy Van Twiller)*, Otis Harlan *(Mr. Duffey)*, Max Davidson *(Michael Callahan)*.

Society melodrama. Source: John Phillips Marquand, "The Right That Failed," in *Four of a Kind* (New York, 1923). John Duffey, lightweight champion of New York, knocks out Kid Reagan in a sensational bout but sustains a broken wrist and is ordered to rest for several months. Johnny visits Craigmoor, a fashionable summer resort, so as to pursue there a society girl, Constance Talbot, whom he has met by accident and who is unaware of his vocation. Mr. Talbot likes Johnny and has little use for Roy Van Twiller, his daughter's fiancé; Roy, however, recognizes Johnny and wires for his father, manager, and challenger to come establish his identity. But the trio are informed of the situation by Mr. Talbot and swear they have never seen Johnny. Johnny, to get even, knocks out Roy, breaking the injured hand; he then informs Constance that he is a roughneck, but she and her family happily accept him. *Prizefighters. Social classes. Resorts. Personal identity.*

THE RIGHT TO LOVE F2.4620

Paramount-Publix Corp. 27 Dec **1930** [c26 Dec 1930; LP1840]. Sd (Movietone); b&w. 35mm. 9 reels, 7,120 ft.

Dir Richard Wallace. *Screenplay* Zoë Akins. *Photog* Charles Lang. *Film Ed* Eda Warren. *Rec Engr* M. M. Paggi.

Cast: Ruth Chatterton *(Naomi Kellogg, the girl/Naomi Kellogg, the mother/Brook Evans)*, Paul Lukas *(Eric Helge)*, David Manners *(Joe Copeland)*, Irving Pichel *(Caleb Evans)*, Louise Mackintosh *(Mrs. Copeland)*, Oscar Apfel *(Mr. Kellogg)*, Veda Buckland *(Mrs. Kellogg)*, Robert Parrish *(Willie)*, Lillian West *(Martha)*, Edna West *(Mrs. Waite)*, Ruth Lyons *(Alice)*, George Baxter *(Tony)*, William Stack *(Dr. Fowler)*, George Pearce *(Dr. Scudder)*.

Drama. Source: Susan Glaspell, *Brook Evans* (London, 1928). In the farming regions of the Midwest, Naomi Kellogg falls in love with Joe Copeland, the son of a neighboring family, though they must meet secretly at a brook between their farms because of a disagreement between their families. Joe, however, loses his life in a harvesting machine accident, and when Naomi's parents learn of their secret love, they are outraged at the violation of their strict moral code and insist that she accept the marriage offer of Caleb Evans, a man of righteousness. After the marriage, a child is born to Naomi on their western ranch, and she devotes her life to young Brook. When Brook falls in love with Tony, Naomi encourages her to elope with him though Caleb indignantly opposes the match. When Naomi reveals that Caleb is not actually the girl's natural father, Brook rejects her mother's affections and turns to her father, who convinces her that she should go to China as a missionary. In the East she becomes fascinated with impulsive Eric Helge, freely accepting his love. Later she is repentant, but upon receiving a stirring message from her mother, who in the interim has died, Brook decides to defy convention and duty and hastens after Eric to embark on a new life. *Farmers. Missionaries. Filial relations. Motherhood. Ranches. China. United States—Midwest.*

THE RIGHT WAY F2.4621

Thomas Mott Osborne. *Dist* Producers Security Corp., Standard Productions. 28 Feb **1921** [Syracuse, New York, showing; released Apr]. Si; b&w. 35mm. 7 reels.

Pres by Thomas Mott Osborne. *Pers Supv* Edward A. MacManus. *Dir* Sidney Olcott. *Scen* Basil Dickey.

Cast: Edwards Davis *(The Father)*, Helen Lindroth *(The Mother)*, Joseph Marquis *(The Rich Boy)*, Vivienne Osborne *(The Sweetheart)*, Sidney D'Albrook *(The Poor Boy)*, Annie Ecleston *(His Mother)*, Helen Ferguson *(His Sweetheart)*, Elsie McLeod *(His Sister)*, Tammany Young *(The Smiler)*, Thomas Brooks *(The New Warden)*.

Drama. With the intention of contrasting older, harsh methods of treatment of prisoners with the reforms advocated by the Mutual Welfare League (a prisoners' organization based on the honor system), the story is told of two boys—one poor and one rich—and their prison experiences. The Poor Boy, a victim of his slum environment, goes to a reformatory for a minor offense and there learns to become a perfect crook. Thanks to a stool pigeon, he is eventually sent to a prison, which is conducted under traditional methods of lockstep, prison labor, silence, contract labor, brutal punishment, and torture. Meanwhile, The Rich Boy is sentenced to the same prison—now under a newer, more humane regime—for forging his father's signature. He becomes friends with The Poor Boy, who has been released and returned to prison for assaulting the stool pigeon. The Smiler, another member of The Poor Boy's gang, is unjustly condemned to electrocution for the murder of the stool pigeon. Although they are trusted members of the Mutual Welfare League, the boys escape and find evidence that clears The Smiler; but they are too late, and an innocent man is executed. For their efforts, however, the boys are paroled, to the joy of their waiting sweethearts. *Informers. Social classes. Injustice. Penology. Prisons. Prison reform. Capital punishment. Wealth. Poverty. Forgery. Honor system.*

Note: Osborne was a warden of Sing Sing Prison and of the U. S. Naval Prison at Portsmouth, New Hampshire, before producing this film. Reissued by Standard Productions in 1927 as *Within Prison Walls* (New York State license applications for *The Right Way*: 14 Jan & 26 Oct 1927; "revised" print with changed title reviewed by Commission: 14 Jan 1928; *Within Prison Walls*, New York showing: 13 Sep 1928). Also reviewed as *Making Good.*

RILEY OF THE RAINBOW DIVISION F2.4622

Morris R. Schlank Productions. *Dist* Anchor Film Distributors. 15 Jul **1928.** Si; b&w. 35mm. 6 reels, 6,040 ft.

Dir Robert Ray. *Story-Scen* Arthur Hoerl. *Titl* Al Martin. *Photog* Harry Forbes. *Film Ed* Dave Rothschild.

Cast: Creighton Hale *(Riley)*, Al Alt *(Henry Graham)*, Pauline Garon *(Gertie Bowers)*, Joan Standing *(Mabel)*, Jack Carlyle *(Sergeant McMullen)*, Lafayette McKee, Rolfe Sedan, Jack Raymond.

Comedy. "This is a film of the training camps before the boys went overseas. ... The two buddies in the training camp [are] scheduled to marry their sweeties, but are placed in the guard house on their wedding day. The gals disguise themselves as doughboys, and circulate among the soldiers without being detected. ... The climax shoots a fair thrill with capture of spies in a balloon." (*Film Daily*, 27 Jan 1929, p5.) *Spies. Disguise. Balloons. World War I. United States Army—Training. United States Army—Rainbow (42d) Division.*

Note: Also reviewed as *Reilly of the Rainbow Division*.

RILEY THE COP **F2.4623**

Fox Film Corp. 25 Nov **1928** [c19 Dec 1928; LP25842]. Sd eff & mus score (Movietone); b&w. 35mm. 6 reels, 6,132 ft. [Also si; 5,993 ft.]

Pres by William Fox. *Dir* John Ford. *Story-Cont* Fred Stanley, James Gruen. *Photog* Charles Clarke. *Film Ed* Alex Troffey. *Asst Dir* Phil Ford. **Cast:** Farrell MacDonald *(James Riley)*, Louise Fazenda *(Lena Krausmeyer)*, Nancy Drexel *(Mary Coronelli)*, David Rollins *(Joe Smith)*, Harry Schultz *(Hans Krausmeyer)*, Mildred Boyd *(Caroline)*, Ferdinand Schumann-Heink *(Julius Kuchendorf)*, Del Henderson *(Judge Coronelli)*, Mike Donlin *(crook)*, Russell Powell *(Mr. Kuchendorf)*, Tom Wilson *(sergeant)*, Billy Bevan *(Paris cabman)*, Otto Fries *(Munich cabman)*.

Comedy-drama. Joe Smith, an ordinary lad who works at the town bakery, becomes engaged to wealthy Mary Coronelli, and her snobbish aunt takes her to Europe to break up the affair. Using his own hard-earned savings, Joe goes after her and is unjustly accused of embezzlement when the bakery funds are discovered missing. Riley the cop, a lifelong flatfoot well liked by all, is detailed to bring Joe back to the United States and follows him to Europe; Riley falls in love with a German flapper in a beer garden only to discover that she is the sister of Krausmeyer, the adjoining beat cop and Riley's nemesis. Riley brings Joe back to the United States, and he is proven innocent. All ends well. *Police. Flappers. Germans. Irish. Aunts. Embezzlement. Injustice. Snobbery. Bakeries. Germany. Paris.*

RINTY OF THE DESERT **F2.4624**

Warner Brothers Pictures. 21 Apr **1928** [c10 Apr 1928; LP25148]. Sd eff (Vitaphone); b&w. 35mm. 5 reels, 4,820 ft. [Copyrighted as 6 reels.]

Dir D. Ross Lederman. *Scen* Harvey Gates. *Titl* James A. Starr. *Story* Frank Steele. *Photog* Frank Kesson. *Asst Dir* Henry Blanke.

Cast: Rin-Tin-Tin *(Rinty)*, Audrey Ferris *(June)*, Carroll Nye *(Pat)*, Paul Panzer *(Mike Doyle)*, Otto Hoffman *(Pop Marlow)*.

Melodrama. Rinty, a dog of the desert, finds his way to the city, and there he is given a home by June, granddaughter of Pop Marlow, dime museum proprietor. Pop fires Mike Doyle, an animal trainer, when he finds Doyle forcing his attentions on June. Later, Pop mysteriously disappears. June asks her sweetheart, Pat, a police detective, to take Rinty and find him. Rinty leads Pat to an underworld haunt where Pop is held prisoner by Doyle's gang. Pat is attacked by the gangsters' bulldog, and in the darkened room he mistakes him for Rinty. Pop Marlow saves Rinty from unjust death; and reunited with June and Pat, they look forward to a happy future. *Animal trainers. Detectives. Grandfathers. Gangs. Museums. Dogs.*

RIO RITA **F2.4625**

RKO Productions. 6 Oct **1929** [New York premiere; released 15 Sep; c15 Sep 1929; LP211, LP899]. Sd (Photophone); b&w with col sequences (Technicolor). 35mm. 15 reels, 11,506 ft.

Prod William Le Baron. *Dir-Scen* Luther Reed. *Dial* Russell Mack. *Photog* Robert Kurrle, Lloyd Knechtel. *Art Dir* Max Ree. *Film Ed* William Hamilton. *Mus Dir* Victor Baravalle. *Songs: "You're Always in My Arms (But Only in My Dreams)," "Sweetheart We Need Each Other," "Following the Sun Around," "Rio Rita," "If You're in Love You'll Waltz," "The Kinkajou," "The Rangers' Song,"* Harry Tierney, Joseph McCarthy. *Song: "Long Before You Came Along"* E. Y. Harburg, Harold Arlen. *Dance Dir* Pearl Eaton. *Rec Engr* Hugh McDowell. *Cost* Max Ree. *Chorus Master* Pietro Cimini.

Cast: Bebe Daniels *(Rita Ferguson)*, John Boles *(Capt. Jim Stewart)*, Don Alvarado *(Roberto Ferguson)*, Dorothy Lee *(Dolly)*, Bert Wheeler *(Chick)*, Robert Woolsey *(Lovett)*, Georges Renevant *(Ravinoff)*, Helen Kaiser *(Mrs. Bean)*, Tiny Sanford *(Davalos)*, Nick De Ruiz *(Parone)*, Sam Nelson *(McGinn)*, Fred Burns *(Wilkins)*, Eva Rosita *(Carmen)*, Sam Blum *(cafe proprietor)*.

Musical revue. Source: Guy Bolton and Fred Thompson, *Rio Rita* (as produced by Florenz Ziegfeld; New York opening: 2 Feb 1927). In a Mexican border town, reward signs are posted for a mysterious bandit known as the Kinkajou. Also in the town is a mysterious Gringo, Jim, who wins the affections of Rita and the hatred of General Ravinoff. Rita refuses to believe the lies of the rascally Ravinoff about Jim until, at a party given at his villa, he offers proof that Jim is a Texas Ranger assigned to arrest her brother (rumored to be the Kinkajou). Broken-hearted, Rita dismisses Jim, but later she saves his life from assassins who lie in wait for him. Ravinoff constructs, on the Mexican side of the Rio Grande, a palatial barge, in which he operates a gambling resort, and one evening he stages a party, hoping to impress Rita. Jim appears in disguise, and his explanations bring renewed faith and love; Rita diverts Ravinoff while Jim frees the barge, permitting it to float to the American side; there Jim unmasks Ravinoff as the Kinkajou, clearing Rita's brother, and a wedding follows with the Texas Rangers officiating. *Bandits. Texas Rangers. Brother-sister relationship. Courtship. Gambling. Mexican border. Rio Grande.*

RIP ROARIN' ROBERTS **F2.4626**

Approved Pictures. *Dist* Weiss Brothers Artclass Pictures. 15 Nov **1924** [c6 Dec 1924; LU20851]. Si; b&w. 35mm. 5 reels, 4,660 ft.

Pres by Lester F. Scott, Jr. *Dir* Richard Thorpe. *Story* Robert J. Horton.

Cast: Buddy Roosevelt *(Buddy Roberts)*, Brenda Lane *(Estelle Morgan)*, Joe Rickson *("Hawk" Andrews)*, Al Richmond *("Red" Turner)*, John Webb Dillon *(Sam Morgan)*, Bert Lindley *(Poker Dick)*, Lew Bennett *(sheriff)*.

Western melodrama. Source: Robert J. Horton, "A Man of Action," in *Western Story Annual*. Looking for adventure and a $1,000 reward, Buddy Roberts has himself appointed a deputy sheriff in the town of Sleepy Hollow, in order to bring to justice a notorious bandit, The Hawk. Buddy beats Red Turner, The Hawk's righthand man, in a fight, after Turner makes a drunken attack on Estelle Morgan, Buddy's girl. When Red rides to The Hawk's camp, Buddy follows him and is then captured by The Hawk's men. Making his escape, Buddy returns to town, where he is hidden by Estelle. The Hawk and his men ride into town, and the bandit is killed in a gunfight with Buddy. Buddy and Estelle make plans to be married. *Sheriffs. Bandits.*

RIP ROARING LOGAN **F2.4627**

William M. Pizor Productions. **1928.** Si; b&w. 35mm. 5 reels, 4,160 ft. *Dir* Robert J. Horner. *Scen* L. V. Jefferson. *Titl* Jack Kelly. *Photog* Lauren A. Draper. *Film Ed* William Austin.

Cast: Al Hoxie.

Western melodrama(?). No information about the nature of this film has been found.

THE RIP SNORTER **F2.4628**

Ben Wilson Productions. *Dist* Arrow Pictures. 14 Feb **1925** [c18 Feb 1925; LP21232]. Si; b&w. 35mm. 5 reels, 4,998 ft.

Dir Ward Hayes. *Story* Mark Goldaine.

Cast: Dick Hatton *(Dick Meadows)*, Archie Ricks *(Harry Vogelsang)*, William Rhine *(Philip Saunders)*, Robert Walker *(Robert Willis)*, Milburn Morante *(Tom Moffit)*, Robert McGowan *("Cole Slaw" Randall)*, Marilyn Mills *(Betty Saunders)*, Emma Gertes *(Aunt Betty, who loves romance)*.

Western melodrama. Willis, the foreman of the Saunders ranch, derisively bets Dick Meadows that he cannot ride the wild horse, Killer. Dick succeeds in staying on the bronc and wins a considerable sum from Willis, in whose company he sets out for the town bank. Randall, a bandit hired by Willis, waylays them, but Dick routs him. Willis later lures Betty to Randall's home, holds her there against her will, and sends the bandit for a minister. Betty sends a message to Dick by means of her trained horse, and Dick rescues her, thrashing Willis while she clouts Randall with a chair. The minister arrives, and Dick whispers to him that he will probably need his services in the near future. *Cowboys. Ranch foremen. Bandits. Wagers. Horses.*

RIP VAN WINKLE **F2.4629**

Ward Lascelle Productions. *Dist* W. W. Hodkinson Corp. 2 Oct **1921** [c23 Sep 1921; LP16985]. Si; b&w. 35mm. 7 reels, 6,700 ft.

Prod-Dir Ward Lascelle. *Scen* Agnes Parsons. *Photog* David Abel, George Larson.

Cast: Thomas Jefferson *(Rip Van Winkle)*, Milla Davenport *(Gretchen Van Winkle)*, Daisy Robinson *(Meenie Van Winkle)*, Gertrude Messinger *(Meenie Van Winkle, 20 years later)*, Pietro Sosso *(Derrick Van Beekman)*, Max Asher *(Nick Vedder)*, Francis Carpenter *(Hendrick Vedder)*.

Folk drama. Source: Joseph Jefferson and Dion Boucicault, *Rip Van Winkle, a Play* (New York, 1895). Washington Irving, "Rip Van Winkle." Convivial idler Rip Van Winkle, disappointed in life because of domestic unhappiness, roams the Catskill Mountains where some strange little folk give him a drink that brings on a deep sleep. Twenty years later he awakens, unaware that he is an old man; discovers that times and surroundings have changed; and eventually is reunited with his wife, who has been tamed by an ill-tempered second husband. *Idlers. Shrews. Marriage. Catskill Mountains.*

RIP VAN WINKLE (Reissue) **F2.4630**

Sunbeam Feature Film Co. **1921** [c1 Jun 1921; LP16601]. Si; b&w. 35mm. 5 reels.

Note: Reissue of the 1914 version starring Thomas Jefferson "in the role Rip Van Winkle as made famous on the stage by his father Joseph Jefferson."

THE RIP-TIDE **F2.4631**

A. B. Maescher. *Dist* Arrow Film Corp. 15 May **1923** [c11 May 1923; LP18943]. Si; b&w. 35mm. 6 reels, 6,270 ft.

Dir Jack Pratt. *Story* J. Grubb Alexander. *Photog* Harry L. Keepers.

Cast: Dick Sutherland *(The First Man)*, George Rigas *(The Philosopher)*, J. Frank Glendon *(Prince Tagor)*, Stuart Holmes *(Count Boris Voronsky)*, Russell Simpson *(The Maharajah)*, Rosemary Theby *(Countess Dagmar)*, Diana Alden *(Princess Indora)*.

Melodrama. While his father, the maharajah, is serving as India's envoy to Great Britain, Prince Tagor learns British ways and even becomes a Church of England minister—to the maharajah's displeasure. Tagor goes to India as a missionary and asks his betrothed, Princess Indora, to wait for him. Indora succumbs to the attentions of Count Boris Voronsky, however, and, when Tagor suddenly returns, he marries them at Indora's request. Indora and Boris are still honeymooning when Countess Dagmar reveals that Boris is her husband, and Tagor accedes to his father's desire for vengeance. Believing that Indora loves Boris, he spares the count's life in a duel, but Indora afterward spurns Boris and accidentally causes his death. Tagor and Indora declare their love for each other. *Diplomats. Clergymen. Missionaries. Revenge. India. Church of England. Duels.*

THE RISE OF ROSCOE PAYNE *see* **NO TRESPASSING**

RISKY BUSINESS **F2.4632**

De Mille Pictures. *Dist* Producers Distributing Corp. 4 Oct **1926** [c23 Aug 1926; LP23041]. Si; b&w. 35mm. 7 reels, 6,594 ft.

Pres by John C. Flinn. *Dir* Alan Hale. *Adapt* Beulah Marie Dix. *Photog* James Diamond. *Art Dir* Max Parker. *Film Ed* Claude Berkeley. *Asst Dir* Harry Haskins. *Prod Mgr* Gordon Cooper.

Cast: Vera Reynolds *(Cecily Stoughton)*, Ethel Clayton *(Mrs. Stoughton)*, Kenneth Thomson *(Ted Pyncheon)*, Ward Crane *(Coults-Browne)*, Louis Natheaux *(Lawrence Wheaton)*, ZaSu Pitts *(Agnes Wheaton)*, George Irving *(Schubal Peabody)*, Louise Cabo *(Rosalie)*.

Society drama. Source: Charles William Brackett, "Pearls Before Cecily," in *Saturday Evening Post* (195:8–9, 17 Feb 1923). Cecily Stoughton, a pampered rich girl, loves Ted Pyncheon, a struggling country physician, but her mother plans to marry her off to Coults-Browne, a wealthy man, and conspires with him to prove to Cecily that riches are essential to happiness. Ted invites Cecily and her mother to a weekend at the home of his sister, Agnes Wheaton, in the town where he practices; through Mrs. Stoughton's machinations all goes wrong, and when the maid becomes ill, Cecily and her mother are forced to do the housework; thus, Ted has little time for his sweetheart. The engagement is broken, and Coults-Browne invites Cecily to a party at his palatial home; but she is unimpressed by the tinsel glamor and drunken gaiety and is forced to leave on foot. Stopping to rest, she discovers Ted, battling to save the life of a boy struck down by Coults-Browne's automobile; realizing her love for him, he is reconciled with and marries her. *Physicians. Motherhood. Smalltown life. Courtship. Wealth.*

THE RITUAL MURDER *see* **PREJUDICE**

RITZY **F2.4633**

Famous Players–Lasky. *Dist* Paramount Pictures. 9 Apr **1927** [c9 Apr 1927; LP23861]. Si; b&w. 35mm. 6 reels, 5,306 ft.

Pres by Adolph Zukor, Jesse L. Lasky. *Assoc Prod* B. P. Schulberg. *Dir* Richard Rosson. *Screenplay* Percy Heath, Robert N. Lee. *Titl* George Marion, Jr. *Story* Elinor Glyn. *Photog* Charles Lang.

Cast: Betty Bronson *(Ritzy Brown)*, James Hall *(Harrington Smith, Duke of Westborough)*, William Austin *(Algy)*, Joan Standing *(Mary)*, George Nichols *(Nathan Brown)*, Roscoe Karns *(Smith's valet)*.

Comedy-drama. Touring America as Harrington Smith, the Duke of Westborough visits the Brown Iron Works at Ivor City, and there he is entertained by Nathan Brown and his daughter, Ritzy, who poses as a blasé sophisticate. She confides in Harrington that she feels herself destined to become a duchess, and when the news reaches the local paper, Ritzy determines to make good her ambition and insists on going to Europe. Brown induces Harrington to cure Ritzy, and the latter tells him about a friend, Algy, who can play the part of a nobleman. During the voyage, she continually throws herself in Algy's path, while she stifles her affection for Harrington. In London, Ritzy is finally made to realize the fallacy of her infatuation with titles and finds happiness with Harrington—the Duke. *Nobility. English. Ironworks. Fatherhood. London.*

THE RIVER **F2.4634**

Fox Film Corp. 22 Dec **1928** [New York premiere; released 6 Oct 1929; c23 Jan 1929; LP47]. Talking sequences & mus score (Movietone); b&w. 35mm. 7 reels, 6,536 ft. [Also si; 8 reels, 7,704 ft.]

Pres by William Fox. *Dir* Frank Borzage. *Dial staged by* A. H. Van Buren, A. F. Erickson. *Scen* Philip Klein, Dwight Cummins. *Dial* John Hunter Booth. *Photog* Ernest Palmer. *Set* Harry Oliver. *Film Ed* Barney Wolf. *Mus* Maurice Baron. *Mus Cond* Erno Rapee. *Asst Dir* Lew Borzage.

Cast: Charles Farrell *(Allen John Spender)*, Mary Duncan *(Rosalee)*, Ivan Linow *(Sam Thompson)*, Margaret Mann *(Widow Thompson)*, Alfred Sabato *(Marsdon)*, Bert Woodruff *(The Miller)*.

Romantic drama. Source: Tristram Tupper, *The River* (Philadelphia, 1928). Allen John Spender, a young and credulous lad, is traveling down the river on his barge when he meets and is captivated by Rosalee, worldly-wise and beautiful. Rosalee, having been the mistress of a man just sent to jail for murder, is stirred by his fresh and ingenuous character, though she has sworn eternal faithfulness to her former lover. Though himself enchanted, Spender plans to continue his wandering ways until the former lover returns and forces the issue. Spender disposes of him, Rosalee recaptures her innocence, and the two find happiness as they resume his journey down the river. *Wanderers. Mistresses. Murder. Barges.*

THE RIVER INN *see* **ROADHOUSE NIGHTS**

RIVER OF ROMANCE **F2.4635**

Paramount Famous Lasky Corp. 29 Jun **1929** [c19 Jul 1929; LP538]. Sd (Movietone); b&w. 35mm. 8 reels, 7,009 ft. [Also si; 7,082 ft.]

Dir Richard Wallace. *Screenplay* Ethel Doherty. *Titl* Joseph Mankiewicz. *Adapt* Dan Totheroh, John V. A. Weaver. *Photog* Victor Milner. *Film Ed* Allyson Shaffer. *Song: "My Lady Love"* Leo Robin, Sam Coslow. *Rec Engr* Harry M. Lindgren.

Cast: Charles "Buddy" Rogers *(Tom Rumford/Colonel Blake)*, Mary Brian *(Lucy Jeffers)*, June Collyer *(Elvira Jeffers)*, Henry B. Walthall *(Gen. Jeff Rumford)*, Wallace Beery *(Gen. Orlando Jackson)*, Fred Kohler *(Captain Blackie)*, Natalie Kingston *(Mexico)*, Walter McGrail *(Major Patterson)*, Anderson Lawler *(Joe Patterson)*, Mrs. George Fawcett *(Madame Rumford)*, George Reed *(Rumbo)*.

Romantic drama. Source: Booth Tarkington, *Magnolia* (New York opening: 27 Aug 1923). Tom Rumford, just turned 21 and the son of a grand and traditional plantation-owner and southern general, returns to the South of the 1840's from Philadelphia, where he was brought up by Quaker relatives. Infatuated with his father's coquettish ward, Elvira Jeffers, he becomes engaged and thereby invites the wrath of her former lover, Major Patterson. Patterson, just released from jail, challenges Tom to a duel, and when Tom merely laughs off the crude insult, he is himself disgraced under the Old Southern Code and banished from his father's home. He wanders forlornly into a Natchez saloon, is befriended by notorious rogue Gen. Orlando Jackson, and there proves his mettle by trouncing a feared killer when insulted. Tom's feat earns him praise. Disguised as the "Notorious Colonel Blake," Tom returns home for the masquerade ball-debut of Elvira's younger sister, Lucy, whose affection for Tom remained steadfast throughout his earlier trials. Tom exposes Patterson, reveals his own identity, regains his father's good graces, and marries Lucy. *Wards. Cowardice. Plantations. Saloons. United States—South. Natchez. Society of Friends. Duels.*

THE RIVER PIRATE **F2.4636**

Fox Film Corp. 26 Aug **1928** [c27 Aug 1928; LP25575]. Talking sequences, mus score, & sd eff (Movietone); b&w. 35mm. 7 reels, 6,937 ft.

Pres by William Fox. *Dir* William K. Howard. *Scen* John Reinhardt, Benjamin Markson. *Titl* Malcolm Stuart Boylan. *Photog* Lucien Andriot. *Film Ed* Jack Dennis. *Asst Dir* Gordon Cooper.

Cast: Victor McLaglen *(Sailor Fritz)*, Lois Moran *(Marjorie Cullen)*,

Nick Stuart *(Sandy)*, Earle Foxe *(Shark)*, Donald Crisp *(Caxton)*, Robert Perry *(Gerber)*.

Melodrama. Source: Charles Francis Coe, *The River Pirate* (New York, 1928). Sandy is a Manhattan waterfront urchin who, through no fault of his own, is sentenced to reform school; there he meets Sailor Fritz, a convict who has been assigned to the school to teach the art of sailmaking. Fritz is later paroled and helps Sandy to escape from the reformatory, apprenticing him to another trade: warehouse pilfering. On the docks, Sandy meets Marjorie Cullen, a detective's daughter who tries to get him to go straight, but he remains loyal to Fritz. Fritz eventually is captured by the police in a loft robbery, and Sandy escapes, finally free to quit the life of crime and marry Marjorie. *Convicts. Street urchins. Detectives. Sailors. Sailmaking. Robbery. Reformatories. Waterfront. New York City.*

THE RIVER WOMAN **F2.4637**

Gotham Productions. *Dist* Lumas Film Corp. 1 Dec **1928** [c11 Sep 1928; LP25615]. Talking sequences & sd eff (Sonora-Bristolphone); b&w. 35mm. 7 reels, 6,565 ft.

Pres by Sam Sax. *Supv* Harold Shumate. *Dir* Joseph E. Henabery. *Adapt-Cont* Adele Buffington. *Titl* Casey Robinson. *Story-Dial* Harold Shumate. *Photog* Ray June. *Film Ed* Donn Hayes. *Asst Dir* William A. O'Connor. *Prod Mgr* Donn Diggins.

Cast: Lionel Barrymore *(Bill Lefty)*, Jacqueline Logan *(The Duchess)*, Charles Delaney *(Jim Henderson)*, Sheldon Lewis *(Mulatto Mike)*, Harry Todd *(The Scrub)*, Mary Doran *(Sally)*.

Melodrama. Bill Lefty, the two-fisted owner of a saloon on the turgid Mississippi, proposes to The Duchess, a beautiful barroom hostess; she can't get her mind off stoker Jim Henderson, however, and puts Bill off. Jim comes to Bill's saloon and delights the crowd with his piano playing. There is a brawl, and Jim and Bill fight side by side, cleaning up Mulatto Mike's gang. The river floods, and Bill finds that The Duchess is in love with Jim and relinquishes his claim on her. The Duchess and Jim escape from the rising waters in a small boat, and Bill dies in his saloon. *Stokers. Pianists. Barroom hostesses. Saloons. Mississippi River. Floods.*

RIVER'S END **F2.4638**

Warner Brothers Pictures. 8 Nov **1930** [c25 Oct 1930; LP1682]. Si; b&w. 35mm. 8 reels, 6,774 ft.

Dir Michael Curtiz. *Scen-Dial* Charles Kenyon. *Story* James Oliver Curwood. *Photog* Robert Kurrle. *Set Dsgn* Ben Carré. *Film Ed* Ralph Holt.

Cast: Charles Bickford *(Keith/Conniston)*, Evelyn Knapp *(Miriam)*, J. Farrell MacDonald *(O'Toole)*, ZaSu Pitts *(Louise)*, Walter McGrail *(Martin)*, David Torrence *(McDowell)*, Junior Coughlan *(Mickey)*, Tom Santschi *(Shotwell)*.

Northwest melodrama. Conniston goes into the Far North in search of Keith, who is wanted for murder; he gets his man, but on their return trip Conniston dies. MacDonald, Conniston's guide, takes a liking to Keith and suggests that since Keith resembles Conniston, he should pretend to be Conniston. Keith agrees, but when he arrives, he finds that the fraud is unnecessary since he has been cleared of guilt. He meets Conniston's girl, Miriam, who, taken in by the deception, loves him more than the real Conniston; but when she is informed by a jealous suitor, Martin, of Conniston's previous and still valid marriage, Keith is forced to tell Evelyn the truth. He does not reveal the true story to the Mounties and consequently is flogged. But when he leaves town, he finds Evelyn on the boat waiting for him. *Doubles. Guides. Murder. Impersonation. Northwest Mounted Police.*

ROAD AGENT **F2.4639**

Anchor Film Distributors. *Dist* Rayart Pictures. May **1926.** Si; b&w. 35mm. 5 reels, 4,472 ft.

Dir J. P. McGowan. *Story* Charles Saxton.

Cast: Al Hoxie.

Western melodrama. "Hero, fugitive from justice, strongly resembles inheritor of ranch and enters employ of rogue who plans possession of ranch and girl. Turns over a new leaf and outwits rogue saving double from sheriff. Goes to finish term with promise to come back to girl." (*Motion Picture News Booking Guide,* 11:44, Oct 1926.) *Fugitives. Ranchers. Criminals—Rehabilitation. Doubles. Impersonation. Regeneration.*

THE ROAD DEMON **F2.4640**

Fox Film Corp. 20 Feb **1921** [c20 Feb 1921; LP16269]. Si; b&w. 35mm. 5 reels.

Pres by William Fox. *Dir-Story-Scen* Lynn Reynolds. *Photog* Frank Good, Ben Kline.

Cast: Tom Mix *(Hap Higgins)*, Claire Anderson *(Patricia O'Malley)*, Charles K. French *(Dad Higgins)*, George Hernandez *(John O'Malley)*, Lloyd Bacon *(Luther McCabe, auto driver)*, Sid Jordan *(Lone Weatherby)*, Charles Arling *(Wade Waters)*, Harold Goodwin *(Johnny Brooks, mechanic)*, Billy Elmer *(Wilson)*, Frank Tokawaja *(Japanese businessman)*, Lee Phelps *(Ryan)*.

Action melodrama. Hap Higgins, a desert cowhand, swaps his horse for a broken-down automobile and soon transforms it into the fastest racer on the west coast. On the way to Los Angeles he indulges in racing with Luther McCabe, a champion driver, and arouses the interest of his friend, Patricia O'Malley, whose father represents a large automobile concern. In the final race, Hap wins a foreign contract for O'Malley and the hand of his daughter. *Cowboys. Automobile racing.*

ROAD HOUSE **F2.4641**

Fox Film Corp. 15 Jul **1928** [c15 Jul 1928; LP25466]. Si; b&w. 35mm. 5 reels, 4,991 ft.

Pres by William Fox. *Dir (see note)* Richard Rosson, James Kevin McGuinness. *Scen* John Stone. *Story* Philip Hurn. *Photog* George Schneiderman. *Asst Dir* Park Frame.

Cast: Maria Alba *(Spanish Marla)*, Warren Burke *(Larry Grayson)*, Lionel Barrymore *(Henry Grayson)*, Julia Swayne Gordon *(Mrs. Henry Grayson)*, Tempe Piggott *(Grandma Grayson)*, Florence Allen *(Helen Grayson)*, Eddie Clayton *(Jim, Larry Grayson's pal)*, Jack Oakie *(Sam)*, Jane Keckley *(maid)*, Joe Brown *(himself)*, Kay Bryant *(Mary, Larry's girl friend)*.

Melodrama. Larry Grayson, jazz age son of permissive parents, drifts from wild parties with his classmates to more heady, roadhouse entertainment. There he becomes involved with an underworld gang and falls in love with Spanish Marla, one of their vamps. Larry leaves home after an argument with his father, throws in with the gang (who are using him for their own purposes), and is blamed for a murder. Tried and convicted, Larry is given a light sentence when the judge places most of the blame on his overindulgent parents. *Vamps. Gangs. Parenthood. Filial relations. Jazz life. Murder. Trials. Roadhouses.*

Note: Sources disagree in crediting direction.

THE ROAD SHOW *see* **CHASING RAINBOWS**

THE ROAD TO ARCADY **F2.4642**

J. W. Film Corp. Jan **1922** [c8 Oct, 21 Oct, 16 Nov 1921; LU17210]. Si; b&w. 35mm. 5 reels.

Dir Burton King. *Story* Edith Sessions Tupper. *Photog* Ernest Haller.

Cast: Virginia Lee *(Antoinette Gerard)*, Harry Benham *(John T. Hamilton)*, Roger Lytton *(Benson Churchill)*, Stephen Gratton *(Oliver Gerard)*, Julia Swayne Gordon *(Helen Girard)*, Mildred Wayne *(Sue Dennison)*, Hugh Huntley *(Bob Gerard)*.

Society melodrama. In order to promote a marriage between her daughter Antoinette and multimillionaire Benson Churchill, Helen Gerard tells Antoinette that her father has stolen funds and that the marriage will save the family. Though in love with John Hamilton, Antoinette agrees to marry Churchill. When she visits Hamilton's office with Churchill to look over plans for their home, Churchill learns that the young couple are in love; later Antoinette revolts and reveals the reason for her being forced into the marriage, and Churchill, having many years before loved Hamilton's mother, releases her. As a wedding present Churchill releases to Gerard the financial assets he has purchased as a lever to force the marriage. *Millionaires. Wealth. Marriage. Motherhood.*

THE ROAD TO BROADWAY **F2.4643**

Motion Picture Guild. 28 Sep **1926** [New York State license; New York showing: 25 May 1927]. Si; b&w. 35mm. 6 reels.

Pres by Louis T. Rogers. *Dir* Howard Mitchell.

Cast: Edith Roberts *(Mary Santley)*, Gaston Glass *(John Worthington)*, Ervin Renard *(Nobert Richter)*.

Comedy. Contrary to the wishes of her father, who wants her to marry a young man whom she has never seen, Mary Santley comes to New York in search of film fame. At the urging of a publicity man, she goes into a New York hospital, carrying only a pocketbook full of French money, and pretends to have lost her memory. Several "Frenchmen" from central casting appear and threaten to murder her because she is a Russian traitor. John Worthington, the Louisville lad she was to have married, arrives on the scene and proceeds to duel with the phony Frenchmen. New York reporters get the story, resulting in good publicity for the film company. John Worthington, having earned Mary's love, discloses to her that he is the very man she was to have wed. *Publicists. Reporters. French. Motion pictures. Imposture. Amnesia. Hospitals. New York City. Duels.*

THE ROAD TO GLORY **F2.4644**

Fox Film Corp. 7 Feb **1926** [c7 Feb 1926: LP22413]. Si; b&w. 35mm. 6 reels, 6,038 ft.

Pres by William Fox. *Dir-Story* Howard Hawks. *Scen* L. G. Rigby. *Photog* Joseph August. *Asst Dir* James Tinling.

Cast: May McAvoy *(Judith Allen)*, Leslie Fenton *(David Hale)*, Ford Sterling *(James Allen)*, Rockliffe Fellowes *(Del Cole)*, Milla Davenport *(Aunt Selma)*, John MacSweeney *(butler)*, Hank *(a dog)*.

Drama. As the result of the automobile accident that kills her father, Judith Allen gradually loses her sight. Bitter and depressed, she breaks off with her fiancé, David Hale, and retires to a lodge in the mountains, renouncing God. David learns of her whereabouts and, attempting to reach her during a storm, is badly injured by a falling tree. Judith is at his bedside and, moved by her great love for him, prays for his recovery. David's condition immediately begins to improve, and Judith, her faith in God fully restored, recovers her sight. *Atheists. Blindness. Faith cure. Automobile accidents. Dogs.*

THE ROAD TO LONDON **F2.4645**

Screenplays Productions. *Dist* Associated Exhibitors. Jun **1921** [c3 Jun 1921; LP16660]. Si; b&w. 35mm. 5 reels, 4,713 ft.

Pres by Lee Ochs. *Dir* Eugene Mullin. *Photog* Charles Davis.

Cast: Bryant Washburn *(Rex Rowland)*, Saba Raleigh *(The Duchess)*, Gibb McLaughlin *(The Count)*, Joan Morgan *(The Lady Emily)*, George Folsey *(Rex's father)*, Rev. Dr. Batchelor *(The Vicar)*, Sir Bertran Hays *(Captain of H. M. S. Olympic)*.

Melodrama. Source: David Skaats Foster, *The Road to London* (New York, 1914). Rex Rowland, son of an American millionaire, visiting London, encounters The Duchess, The Count, and The Lady Emily, niece of The Duchess, and arranges to steal The Lady Emily from The Count, who plans to marry her. In hot pursuit through London and its environs, the couple appropriate a physician's car, drive to the suburbs, and escape in a powered canoe. Masquerading as another couple, they are received overnight as guests at a country estate. Later, the pursuers, both on water and land, are eluded; and after the couple are married in a quiet village, they end up in the bridal suite of a United States–bound liner. *Tourists. Aristocrats. Millionaires. London. Chases.*

Note: Produced on location in London.

THE ROAD TO MANDALAY **F2.4646**

Metro-Goldwyn-Mayer Pictures. 28 Jun **1926** [c12 Jul 1926; LP22907]. Si; b&w. 35mm. 7 reels, 6,562 ft.

Dir Tod Browning. *Scen* Elliott Clawson. *Titl* Joe Farnham. *Story* Tod Browning, Herman Mankiewicz. *Photog* Merritt Gerstad. *Art Dir* Cedric Gibbons, Arnold Gillespie. *Film Ed* Errol Taggart.

Cast: Lon Chaney *(Singapore Joe)*, Lois Moran *(Joe's daughter)*, Owen Moore *(The Admiral)*, Henry B. Walthall *(Father James)*, Kamiyama Sojin *(English Charlie Wing)*, Rose Langdon *(Pansy)*, John George *(servant)*.

Melodrama. Joe, a former sea captain whose wife died during the birth of their child at sea, is now a pockmarked, disreputable divekeeper in Singapore where he indulges in shady operations with Herrick, known as The Admiral. They ship for Mandalay, where Joe's daughter lives with a priest, Father James, and tends a curio shop, unaware that her father regularly sends money to Father James for her support. Although his daughter clearly finds him abhorrent, Joe determines to take her away until he learns that The Admiral has fallen in love with her and plans to marry her. He persuades Father James (actually his brother) not to perform the ceremony, and The Admiral is shanghaied by Joe's men. The girl, suspecting Joe, goes to his brothel in Singapore and is about to be assaulted by Charlie, a lecherous Chinaman, when Joe intervenes and is stabbed. The Admiral comes to her rescue and escapes with her on a boat. *Sea captains. Brothers. Clergymen. Chinese. Parentage. Curio shops. Whorehouses. Mandalay. Singapore.*

ROAD TO PARADISE **F2.4647**

First National Pictures. 20 Jul **1930** [c28 Jul 1930; LP1450]. Sd (Vitaphone); b&w. 35mm. 9 reels, 6,935 ft. [Also si.]

Dir William Beaudine. *Adapt-Dial* F. Hugh Herbert. *Photog* John Seitz. *Film Ed* Edward Schroeder. *Rec Engr* Robert B. Lee.

Cast: Loretta Young *(Margaret Waring/Mary Brennan)*, Jack Mulhall *(George Wells)*, George Barraud *(Jerry, the Gent)*, Raymond Hatton *(Nick, Jerry's pal)*, Purnell Pratt *(Updike)*, Kathlyn Williams *(Mrs. Wells)*, Dot Farley *(Lola)*, Winter Hall *(Brewster)*, Ben Hendricks, Jr. *(Flanagan)*, Georgette Rhodes *(Yvonne)*, Fred Kelsey *(Casey)*.

Melodrama. Source: Dodson Mitchell and Zelda Sears, *Cornered* (New York opening: Dec 1920). Mary Brennan, an orphan reared by Nick and Jerry the Gent, two thieves, bears a strong resemblance to Margaret Waring, an heiress. Against her will, Mary is persuaded to go with her guardians to the Waring mansion and impersonate Margaret in the latter's absence. Mrs. Wells's son, George, though at first deceived by the disguise, senses that Mary is not Margaret and falls in love with her. Later, as Mary, Nick, and Jerry are entering the safe, Margaret returns and Jerry wounds her; Mary tricks the police into believing that Margaret is the thief; George sees through the ruse, but protects her out of love. Through a pair of lockets, Margaret discovers that Mary is a long-lost twin sister; thus, the prosecution is dropped and George's proposal is accepted by Mary. *Orphans. Thieves. Twins. Sisters. Heiresses. Impersonation. Courtship.*

Note: A silent version, made in 1924 and entitled *Cornered*, was also directed by William Beaudine.

THE ROAD TO ROMANCE **F2.4648**

Metro-Goldwyn-Mayer Pictures. 24 Sep **1927** [c26 Sep 1927; LP24438]. Si; b&w. 35mm. 7 reels, 6,544 ft.

Dir John S. Robertson. *Cont* Josephine Lovett. *Titl* Joe Farnham. *Photog* Oliver Marsh. *Sets* Cedric Gibbons, Richard Day. *Film Ed* William Hamilton. *Wardrobe* Gilbert Clark.

Cast: Ramon Novarro *(José Armando)*, Marceline Day *(Serafina)*, Marc MacDermott *(Pópolo)*, Roy D'Arcy *(Don Balthasar)*, Cesare Gravina *(Castro)*, Bobby Mack *(drunkard)*, Otto Matiesen *(Don Carlos)*, Jules Cowles *(Smoky Beard)*.

Romantic melodrama. Source: Joseph Conrad and Ford Maddox Ford, *Romance* (1903). On the Cuban island of Riego, Don Balthasar, executor of the Riego estate and governor of the island, keeps the invalid Don Carlos and his sister Serafina prisoners in a castle, plotting to seize their inheritance and marry Serafina. A monk sends to Spain for aid, and José Armando, a vagabond adventurer, arrives. He escapes a pirate band, headed by Smoky Beard, that attacks his ship, and later, encountering Serafina, identifies himself as a Captain of the Dragoons and makes passionate love to her. Called before Balthasar, he poses as a pirate, but when his identity is revealed he falls into the clutches of the governor, who plans to marry Serafina upon the death of Don Carlos. José escapes with her to a sea cave, where they are trapped by Balthasar's men; the lovers pretend to surrender, and José is about to be hanged when Spanish troops arrive to save them. *Spanish. Pirates. Adventurers. Invalids. Brother-sister relationship. Inheritance. Colonial administration. Cuba. Caribbean.*

THE ROAD TO RUIN **F2.4649**

Cliff Broughton Productions. *Dist* True Life Photoplays. c23 Mar **1928** [LP25123]. Si; b&w. 35mm. 6 reels, 5,187 ft.

Pres by Willis Kent. *Dir* Norton S. Parker. *Story* Willis Kent. *Photog* Henry Cronjager. *Film Ed* Edith Wakeling. *Asst Dir* David Hampton.

Cast: Helen Foster *(Sally Canfield)*, Grant Withers *(Don Hughes)*, Florence Turner *(Mrs. Canfield)*, Charles Miller *(Mr. Canfield)*, Virginia Roye *(Eve Terrell)*, Tom Carr *(Jimmy)*, Don Rader *(Al)*.

Drama. Lack of parental guidance leads Sally Canfield down the ruinous road. Exposed to liquor and cigarettes, she succumbs to their effects and drifts through a series of love affairs with older, worldlier men. Apprehended by the police one evening during a strip poker game, Sally is reprimanded and sent home. She discovers several weeks later that she is pregnant, submits to an illegal abortion, and dies of shock the next evening after unwittingly being paired off with her father in a bawdy house. *Parenthood. Adolescence. Abortion. Alcoholism. Incest. Smoking. Whorehouses.*

THE ROAD TO YESTERDAY **F2.4650**

De Mille Pictures. *Dist* Producers Distributing Corp. 15 Nov **1925** [c26 Oct 1925; LP21944]. Si; b&w. 35mm. 10 reels, 9,980 ft.

Pers Dir Cecil B. De Mille. *Adapt* Jeanie Macpherson, Beulah Marie Dix. *Photog* Peverell Marley. *Art Dir* Paul Iribe, Max Parker, Anton Grot, Mitchell Leisen. *Film Ed* Anne Bauchens. *Mus Score* Rudolph Berliner. *Asst Dir* Frank Urson.

Cast: Joseph Schildkraut *(Kenneth Paulton)*, Jetta Goudal *(Malena*

Paulton), Vera Reynolds *(Beth Tyrell)*, William Boyd *(Jack Moreland)*, Julia Faye *(Dolly Foules)*, Casson Ferguson *(Adrian Tompkyns)*, Trixie Friganza *(Harriett Tyrell [Aunt])*, Clarence Burton *(Hugh Armstrong)*, Josephine Norman *(Anne Vener)*, Charles West *(Watt Earnshaw)*, Junior Coghlan *(Boy Scout)*, Iron Eyes Cody *(Indian)*, Walter Long *(extra, egging on the crowd in the burning-at-the-stake)*, Dick Sutherland *(torturer)*, Chester Morris *(extra at party)*, Sally Rand.

Romantic drama. Source: Beulah Marie Dix and Evelyn Greenleaf Sutherland, *The Road to Yesterday* (New York opening: 31 Dec 1906). Kenneth and Malena Paulton are honeymooning at a Grand Canyon hotel, but despite her love for Ken, Malena cannot stand his caresses. Ken attributes her attitude to his infirm arm, which he keeps in a sling. He goes to Jack Moreland, a young minister who is spending his summer in charge of a nearby boys' camp, for advice; he tells Ken to pray to God for help. Staying at the same hotel are Beth Tyrell and her Aunt Harriett, who is a believer in the occult and in reincarnation. Beth falls in love with Jack but turns down his proposal when she learns he is a minister. A specialist examines Ken's arm and tells him it must be operated on at once. Ken denounces Jack. By coincidence all four are on the same train to Chicago when it is involved in a wreck. Malena is trapped, and Beth, in a delirium, is transported back in time to the England of the 17th century where the characters reenact their past lives: Ken is a knight; Malena, a Gypsy girl; and Jack, her lover of old. Awakening from her dream, Beth finds herself in Jack's arms. Ken rescues Malena, who has lost all fear of him. Happiness comes to both couples. *Clergymen. Reincarnation. Marriage. Frigidity. Occult. Religion. Grand Canyon. Boy Scouts. Train wrecks.*

ROADHOUSE NIGHTS **F2.4651**

Paramount Famous Lasky Corp. 23 Feb **1930** [c13 Feb 1930; LP1073]. Sd (Movietone); b&w. 35mm. 8 reels, 7,207 ft.

Dir Hobart Henley. *Scen-Dial* Garrett Fort. *Story* Ben Hecht. *Photog* William Steiner. *Film Ed* Helene Turner. *Song: "It Can't Go On Like This"* E. Y. Harburg, Jay Gorney. *Songs: "Everything Is On the Up and Up," "Hello, Everybody, Folks," "Everybody Wants My Girl"* Eddie Jackson, Lou Clayton, Jimmy Durante. *Sd* Edwin Schabbehar.

Cast: Helen Morgan *(Lola Fagan)*, Charles Ruggles *(Willie Bindbugel)*, Fred Kohler *(Sam Horner)*, Jimmy Durante *(Daffy)*, Fuller Mellish, Jr. *(Hogan)*, Leo Donnelly *(City Editor)*, Tammany Young *(Jerry)*, Joe King *(Hanson)*, Lou Clayton *(Joe)*, Eddie Jackson *(Moe)*.

Comedy-melodrama. Hanson, a reporter with a reputation for drinking on the job, is sent to get a story on the town of Moran, where Sam Horner, a bootlegger, has control; when he fails, the editor sends Willie Bindbugel, who discovers the gang's headquarters to be a roadhouse where Lola Fagan, his own childhood sweetheart, sings. Unaware of Hanson's demise, Willie remains, and in an effort to save him, Lola causes him to think he has been fired and suggests they elope, but they are overtaken by Horner. Pretending to be drunk, Willie informs the paper of his distress by telegraphic code, via the telephone; Horner discovers Lola's duplicity and tries to shoot Willie, but with the aid of Daffy, a singer-comedian, the plot is averted and the Coast Guard arrives to save the day for the lovers. *Reporters. Singers. Bootleggers. Gangsters. Roadhouses. United States Coast Guard.*

Note: Initially reviewed as *The River Inn*.

ROADS OF DESTINY **F2.4652**

Goldwyn Pictures. 3 Apr **1921** [trade review; c26 Jan 1921; LP16050]. Si; b&w. 35mm. 5-6 reels, 4,955 ft.

Dir Frank Lloyd. *Scen* J. E. Nash. *Photog* J. D. Jennings.

Cast: Pauline Frederick *(Rose Merritt)*, John Bowers *(David Marsh)*, Richard Tucker *(Lewis Marsh)*, Jane Novak *(Ann Hardy)*, Hardee Kirkland *(Mr. Hardy)*, Willard Louis *(McPherson)*, Maude George *(Fate)*, Maurice B. Flynn *(Colby)*.

Melodrama. Source: Channing Pollack, *Roads of Destiny* (New York opening: Nov 1918). O. Henry, *Roads of Destiny*. Lewis Marsh, who betrays Rose Merritt and refuses to marry her, is in love with Ann Hardy, who is loved also by his brother David. Lewis pleads with David not to take Ann from him, and while asleep David has three different dreams in which the characters in his own tragedy act out the same conclusion to each episode: *In Alaska, the mistress of a gambling hall owner is killed by him when she falls in love with a young inventor who loves another woman. In the second episode a similar incident involves a number of Long Island society people. The third episode introduces a Mexican girl as the betrayed woman.* Awakening, David decides to marry Ann, and Rose and Lewis are reconciled. (Pauline Frederick plays the principal roles in the dream sequences.) *Brothers. Mistresses. Mexicans. Waifs. Gambling. Alaska. Dreams.*

ROARIN' BRONCS **F2.4653**

Action Pictures. *Dist* Pathé Exchange. 27 Nov **1927** [c18 Nov 1927; LU24677]. Si; b&w. 35mm. 5 reels, 4,375 ft.

Pres by Lester F. Scott, Jr. *Dir* Richard Thorpe. *Scen* Frank L. Inghram. *Story* Norton S. Parker. *Photog* Ray Ries.

Cast: Buffalo Bill Jr. *(Bill Morris)*, Ann McKay *(Rose Tracy)*, Harry Todd, Lafe McKee, George Magrill *(Henry Ball)*.

Western melodrama. Bill Morris, a member of the U. S. Border Patrol assigned to investigate the smuggling of Chinese across the border, gets work at the Tracy and Ball Ranch, suspected to be the smugglers' headquarters. Unable to operate a motorcycle with sidecar, two ranch hands are helped by Bill, who chases Rose Tracy's frightened horse. Henry Ball, the ranch partner's son and leader of the smugglers, fancies Rose, but Bill fails to obtain evidence against him until he overhears his plans at a party given for Rose. Bill gives chase on the motorcycle but is overwhelmed by the smugglers, who take cover in an abandoned shack. Although bound, Bill manages to operate a tractor to rout the gang and take them prisoner. *Border patrol. Cowboys. Smugglers. Chinese. Motorcycles. Mexican border.*

A ROARING ADVENTURE (Blue Streak Western) **F2.4654**

Universal Pictures. 8 Feb **1925** [c14 Feb 1925; LP21158]. Si; b&w. 35mm. 5 reels, 4,800 ft.

Dir Clifford S. Smith. *Cont* Percy Heath. *Adapt* Isadore Bernstein. *Photog* Harry Neumann.

Cast: Jack Hoxie *(Duffy Burns)*, Mary McAllister *(Gloria Carpenter)*, Marin Sais *(Katherine Dodd)*, J. Gordon Russell *(Robert Carpenter)*, Jack Pratt *(Brute Kilroy)*, Francis Ford *(Colonel Burns/Bennett Hardy)*, Margaret Smith *(Kitty Dodd, aged 5)*.

Western melodrama. Source: Jack Rollens, "The Tenderfoot" (publication undetermined). Duffy Burns returns from college in the East and discovers that his father's cattle are being systematically stolen by a band of unknown outlaws. Duffy resolves to catch the culprits, conceals his identity, and goes to work on his father's ranch. There he meets Gloria Carpenter, daughter of one of the outlaws, and falls in love with her. Gloria returns the affection, but she is puzzled by Duffy's constant attentions to the Widow Dodd. Duffy and a sheriff's posse round up the bandits, Gloria's father reforms, and Duffy wins Gloria's love when he explains that his friendship with the widow has been strictly in the interest of capturing the cattle rustlers. *Ranchers. Widows. Rustling. Disguise.*

ROARING BILL ATWOOD **F2.4655**

Ben Wilson Productions. *Dist* Rayart Pictures. Oct or Nov **1926**. Si; b&w. 35mm. 5 reels, 4,405 or 4,500 ft.

Dir Bennett Cohn.

Cast: Dick Hatton.

Western melodrama. "Bully seeks downfall of sheriff and has him captured and held. Forces half-wit to assume role and then bullies him in front of girl. Arrival of real sheriff's wife upsets plans and then half-wit outwits bully, becoming his natural self, a noted man hunter. Girl changes her mind about him." (*Motion Picture News Booking Guide*, 12:52, Apr 1927.) *Sheriffs. Halfwits. Abduction.*

ROARING FIRES **F2.4656**

Ellbee Pictures. 29 Jul **1927** [New York showing]. Si; b&w. 35mm. 6 reels, 5,009 or 5,700 ft.

Dir W. T. Lackey. *Story-Scen* A. B. Barringer. *Titl* David Walker. *Photog* Fred Stevens. *Film Ed* W. T. Lackey.

Cast: Roy Stewart *(David Walker)*, Alice Lake *(Sylvia Summers)*, Lionel Belmore *(John D. Summers)*, Bert Berkeley *(Paddy Flynn)*, Raymond Turner *(Dennison De Puyster)*, Spottiswoode Aitken *(Calvert Carter)*, Robert Walker, Culvert Curtis.

Melodrama. "Story is of a wealthy girl reforming the slums with speeches. The old man refuses to make the fire traps safe. A heroic fireman is thrown in, [and] there is a story of the old fireman, with the last three horses, dreaming of by-gone glory." (*Variety*, 3 Aug 1927, p18.) *Reformers. Firemen. Slums. Fire protection. Horses.*

Note: There is some confusion about the direction credit; Barringer also may have directed.

THE ROARING FORTIES *see* **ROBES OF SIN**

ROARING GUNS **F2.4657**
7 Mar **1930** [New York State license]. Si; b&w. 35mm. 5 reels, 4,500 ft.
Cast: Al Hoxie.
Western melodrama(?). No information about the nature of this film has been found.
Note: May have been produced by Anchor Film Distributors in 1926. Distribution company not determined; New York State license issued to Industrial Film Co.

ROARING RAILS **F2.4658**
Stellar Productions. *Dist* Producers Distributing Corp. 21 Sep **1924.** Si; b&w. 35mm. 6 reels, 5,753 ft.
Supv Hunt Stromberg. *Dir* Tom Forman. *Story* Doris Dorn, Hunt Stromberg. *Photog* Sol Polito.
Cast: Harry Carey *(Big Bill Benson)*, Frankie Darro *(Little Bill)*, Edith Roberts *(Nora Burke)*, Wallace MacDonald *(Malcolm Gregory)*, Frank Hagney *(Red Burley)*.
Melodrama. While serving in a Marine brigade at Chateau-Thierry, Bill Benson adopts a war orphan and returns with him to the United States. Bill is discharged from his job as a railroad engineer when his neglect causes a wreck. Bill's ward, Little Bill, is blinded in an explosion at a bridge. Bill has no money for an operation for Little Bill, but when Gregory, the son of the railroad president, kills a man, Bill agrees to help him if he will pay for an operation for Little Bill. Gregory escapes with Bill's assistance, but he goes back on his word and does not help the child. Bill gets a job laying track for another railroad and falls in love with the foreman's daughter. During a raging forest fire, Bill drives an engine through the blazing woods, saving both Little Bill and the railroad company. Little Bill's sight is restored, Bill becomes an engineer again, and he marries the foreman's daughter. *Veterans. Railroad engineers. Orphans. Blindness. Railroads. World War I. Château-Thierry. Klamath Falls (Oregon). United States Marines. Explosions. Train wrecks. Forest fires.*
Note: Filmed on location at Klamath Falls, Oregon.

ROARING RANCH **F2.4659**
Hoot Gibson Productions. *Dist* Universal Pictures. 27 Apr **1930** [c19 Apr 1930; LP1245]. Sd (Movietone); b&w. 35mm. 7 reels, 6,094 ft. [Also si; 5,242 ft.]
Pres by Carl Laemmle. *Dir-Story-Dial* Reaves Eason. *Photog* Harry Neumann. *Film Ed* Gilmore Walker. *Sd Engr* C. Roy Hunter.
Cast: Hoot Gibson *(Jim Dailey)*, Sally Eilers *(June Marlin)*, Wheeler Oakman *(Ramsey Kane)*, Bobby Nelson *(Teddie)*, Frank Clark *(Tom Marlin)*, Leo White *(Reginald Sobieski)*.
Western melodrama. Jim, the owner of a dilapidated ranch, loves June Marlin, who is also courted by Ramsey Kane, a geologist. Ramsey discovers oil on Jim's ranch and schemes to buy the property at a low rate. When Jim resists, Ramsey enlists the aid of a confederate who poses as a count but also fails to persuade Jim to sell. In revenge, Ramsey has Jim's ranchhouse burned; and in saving two children for whom he is caring, Jim captures the culprits and turns them over to the sheriff. Discouraged, Jim accepts the "count's" offer, but when he learns that oil has been found on his land, he destroys the unrecorded contract of sale and turns the culprits over to the law. *Ranchers. Geologists. Children. Oil. Imposture. Arson. Courtship. Documentation.*

ROARING RIDER **F2.4660**
Action Pictures. *Dist* Weiss Brothers Artclass Pictures. 2 Jan **1926.** Si; b&w. 35mm. 5 reels, 4,387 ft.
Dir Richard Thorpe.
Cast: Wally Wales.
Western melodrama. "... in which hero enters community where ranchers are terrorized by gang of cattle thieves. Hero falls in love with girl, and takes up pursuit of gang, ultimately ending the menace which hangs over the community." ("Motion Picture News Booking Guide," in *Motion Picture News*, 8 May 1926, p41.) *Ranchers. Rustling.*

ROARING ROAD **F2.4661**
Bud Barsky Productions. 1 May **1926.** Si; b&w. 35mm. 5 reels.
Dir Paul Hurst.
Cast: Kenneth McDonald, Jane Thomas.
Action melodrama. "An across-the-continent automobile race is principal theme of plot. Young racing driver combines best features of two rival cars, thus producing automobile which is best entry in race. He triumphs over other contestants, incidentally winning girl of his heart." (*Motion Picture News Booking Guide*, 11:44, Oct 1926.) *Automobiles. Automobile racing.*

ROBES OF SIN **F2.4662**
William Russell Productions. *Dist* Jans Productions. **1924** [c20 Apr 1926; LP22636]. Si; b&w. 35mm. 6 reels.
Pres by Herman F. Jans. *Dir* Russell Allen. *Titl* William B. Laub. *Adapt* George Hinley. *Story* Louis Waldeck. *Photog* Ross Fisher.
Cast: Sylvia Breamer *(Ruth Rogens)*, Jack Mower *(John Rogens)*, Lassie Lou Ahern *(their baby)*, Bruce Gordon *(Cyler Bryson)*, Gertrude Astor *(Adelaide Thomas)*, Helene Sullivan *(Mrs. Bryson)*, William Buckley *(The Banjo Kid)*.
Society melodrama. In his attempts to break up a gang of bootleggers, John Rogens, a trusted U. S. Government agent who lives and works in "the roaring forties," New York's Times Square district, is neglectful of his wife, Ruth. When Adelaide, a smartly dressed woman, moves into a neighboring apartment, Ruth strikes up a friendship, and through her friend she meets Cyler Bryson, a wealthy man who develops a liking for Ruth. Unaware of Bryson's association with the bootleggers, Ruth accepts an invitation from him but conceals this association from her husband. Adelaide becomes jealous, however, and informs Bryson's wife of the relationship. Meanwhile, John, who has secured evidence against the gang but not against Bryson, agrees to help Adelaide's sweetheart if she leads him to the mastermind. After arresting Bryson, whom he finds at a nightclub with his wife, John, realizing his neglect, is reconciled with Ruth. *Government agents. Bootleggers. Prohibition. Marriage. New York City.*
Note: Reissued and copyrighted by Jans Productions as *The Roaring Forties* (c20 Apr 1926; LP22636).

ROBIN HOOD **F2.4663**
Douglas Fairbanks Pictures. *Dist* United Artists. 18 Oct **1922** [Chicago premiere; released 28 Jan 1923; c1 Nov 1922; LP18416]. Si; b&w. 35mm. 11 reels, 10,680 ft.
Dir Allan Dwan. *Scen Ed* Lotta Woods. *Story* Elton Thomas. *Photog* Arthur Edeson. *Trick Photog* Paul Eagler. *Supv Art Dir* Wilfred Buckland. *Art Dir* Irvin J. Martin, Edward M. Langley. *Tech Dir* Robert Fairbanks. *Film Assembly* William Nolan. *Cost* Mitchell Leisen. *Research Dir* Arthur Woods. *Literary Consultant* Edward Knoblock.
Cast: Douglas Fairbanks *(The Earl of Huntingdon/Robin Hood)*, Wallace Beery *(Richard the Lion-Hearted)*, Sam De Grasse *(Prince John)*, Enid Bennett *(Lady Marian Fitzwalter)*, Paul Dickey *(Sir Guy of Gisbourne)*, William Lowery *(The High Sheriff of Nottingham)*, Roy Coulson *(The King's Jester)*, Billie Bennett *(Lady Marian's serving woman)*, Merrill McCormick, Wilson Benge *(henchmen to Prince John)*, Willard Louis *(Friar Tuck)*, Alan Hale *(Little John)*, Maine Geary *(Will Scarlett)*, Lloyd Talman *(Alan-a-Dale)*.
Romantic drama. The Earl of Huntingdon accompanies King Richard on a crusade but returns to England when he learns of Prince John's efforts to secure the throne for himself. Under the name of Robin Hood he leads a group of men who "take from the rich; give to the poor." He rescues Lady Marian from Prince John's prison but is himself captured. The timely reappearance of King Richard returns Robin Hood to Lady Marian and foils the efforts of Prince John. *Outlaws. The Crusades. Robin Hood. Richard the Lion-Hearted. Great Britain—History—Plantagenets.*
Note: Known also as *Douglas Fairbanks in Robin Hood.*

ROBIN HOOD, JR. **F2.4664**
Dist Export & Import Film Co., East Coast Productions. 3 Apr **1923** [New York State license application; c25 Jun 1923; LP19168]. Si; b&w. 35mm. 4 reels.
Pres by Franklyn E. Backer. *Dir* Clarence Bricker. *Dial* Carol Owen. *Photog* Vernon Walker. *Lighting Eff* Harry Ludlum. *Art Dir* Paul Cosgrove. *Tech Dir* Walter Hansen.
Cast: Frankie Lee *(The Boy, afterward Robin Hood)*, Peggy Cartwright *(The Girl, afterward Maid Marian)*, Stanley Bingham *(The Father, afterward King Richard)*, Ashley Cooper *(The Doctor, afterward Prince John)*, Harry La Mont *(Sir Guy of Gisbourne)*, Phillip Dunham *(High Sheriff of Nottingham)*.
Juvenile adventure. Dedicated "to Mr. Douglas Fairbanks and his immortal classic 'Robin Hood'," the story deals with two youngsters and their creation of an imaginary kingdom in which they and others in their environment are cast as the fabled characters. *Childhood. Robin Hood. England.*

ROCKING MOON **F2.4665**

Metropolitan Pictures. *Dist* Producers Distributing Corp. 10 Jan **1926** [c11 Jan 1926; LP22259]. Si; b&w. 35mm. 7 reels, 6,013 ft.

Dir George Melford. *Adapt* Jack Cunningham, Elliott J. Clawson. *Photog* Charles G. Clarke, Joe La Shelle. *Art Dir* Charles Cadwallader. *Asst Dir* Edward Bernoudy. *Prod Mgr* George Bertholon.

Cast: Lilyan Tashman *(Sasha Larianoff)*, John Bowers *(Gary Tynan)*, Rockliffe Fellowes *(Nick Nash)*, Laska Winters *(Soya)*, Luke Cosgrave *(Colonel Jeff)*, Eugene Pallette *(Side Money)*.

Northwest melodrama. Source: Barrett Willoughby, *Rocking Moon; a Romance of Alaska* (New York & London, 1925). Sasha Larianoff, who runs a fox ranch on Rocking Moon Island off the coast of Alaska, hires Gary Tynan, an American soldier of fortune, to help her when her brother is injured. Nick Nash, who holds the mortgage on the fox ranch, feigns love for Sasha while conspiring with his band of poachers to steal Sasha's pelts during a celebration. Nash finally makes his move, overpowers Gary, and takes the swag to a cave. Gary regains his wits and leads a party of traders to the cave, catching Nash and his men redhanded. Gary decides to stay on and become an equal partner with Sasha on her fox ranch. *Soldiers of fortune. Brother-sister relationship. Poachers. Mortgages. Alaska. Fox.*

Note: Filmed on location in Alaska.

A RODEO MIXUP **F2.4666**

Ashton Dearholt. *Dist* Arrow Film Corp. 1 Apr **1924** [c27 Feb 1924; LP19947]. Si; b&w. 35mm. 5 reels, 4,528 ft.

Dir-Writ Francis Ford.

Cast: Florence Gilbert *(Edith Cummins)*, Francis Ford *(her uncle)*, Helen Hayes *(her maid)*, Edmund Cobb *(William Saunders)*, Ashton Dearholt *(The Bum)*, Burt Maddock *(Arizona Dick)*.

Western melodrama. A thrill-seeking easterner, Edith Cummins, is delighted when the foreman of her uncle's ranch assumes the disguise of a captured bandit and attempts to kidnap her. The real bandit escapes, however, and does the kidnaping. The posse captures the foreman, sees its mistake, then captures the real kidnaper. *Ranch foremen. Posses. Thrill-seeking. Ranch life. Disguise. Kidnaping.*

ROGUE OF THE RIO GRANDE **F2.4667**

Cliff Broughton Productions. *Dist* Sono Art–World Wide Pictures. 15 Oct **1930** [c7 Nov 1930; LP1712]. Sd; b&w. 35mm. 7 reels, 7,000 ft.

Pres by George W. Weeks. *Supv* Cliff Broughton. *Dir* Spencer Gordon Bennett. *Screenplay-Dial* Oliver Drake. *Songs: "Argentine Moon," "Carmita," "Corazon," "Song of the Bandoleros"* Herbert Meyers, Oliver Drake. *Rec Engr* Alfred M. Granich, Jack Gregor.

Cast: José Bohr *(El Malo)*, Raymond Hatton *(Pedro)*, Myrna Loy *(Carmita)*, Carmelita Geraghty *(Dolores)*, Walter Miller *(Sheriff Rankin)*, Gene Morgan *(Seth, the mayor)*, William P. Burt *(tango dancer)*, Florence Dudley *(Big Bertha)*.

Western musical comedy. El Malo, a notorious Mexican bandit, pays a surprise visit to the office of Seth Landport, mayor of Sierra Blanca, robs the safe, and departs with his men. The mayor reports the theft to Sheriff Rankin, who posts a reward for the bandit's capture. Later, El Malo and his aide, Pedro, visit the local cantina, where the bandit resumes his acquaintance with Carmita, a dancer, and Pedro renews his friendship with Dolores. As the mayor's description of him is inaccurate, El Malo discusses the bandit's arrest with the sheriff, who has never seen him previously, and incurs the enmity of Carmita's dance partner, who learns his true identity. El Malo witnesses a stage robbery instigated by Seth, the mayor, and declares him to be the bandit (El Malo) in the presence of the sheriff. Then, El Malo reveals his identity and is about to be taken into custody when the lights are extinguished while the dance partner seeks revenge; but El Malo, Pedro, and Carmita ride for the border. *Bandits. Dancers. Sheriffs. Mayors. Personal identity. Mexico.*

THE ROGUE SONG **F2.4668**

Metro-Goldwyn-Mayer Pictures. 28 Jan **1930** [New York premiere; released 10 May; c26 Mar 1930; LP1176]. Sd (Movietone); col (Technicolor). 35mm. 12 reels, 9,723 ft.

Dir Lionel Barrymore. *Screenplay* Frances Marion, John Colton. *Suggested by* Wells Root. *Photog* Percy Hilburn, C. Edgar Schoenbaum. *Art Dir* Cedric Gibbons. *Film Ed* Margaret Booth. *Ballet Mus* Dimitri Tiomkin. *Songs: "When I'm Looking at You," "Song of the Shirt," "Rogue Song"* Herbert Stothart, Clifford Grey. *Song: "The White Dove"* Franz Lehár, Clifford Grey. *Ballet* Madame Albertina Rasch. *Rec Engr* Paul Neal, Douglas Shearer. *Asst Dir* Charles Dorian. *Gowns* Adrian.

Cast: Lawrence Tibbett *(Yegor)*, Catherine Dale Owen *(Princess Vera)*, Nance O'Neil *(Princess Alexandra)*, Judith Vosselli *(Countess Tatiana)*, Ullrich Haupt *(Prince Serge)*, Elsa Alsen *(Yegor's mother)*, Florence Lake *(Nadja)*, Lionel Belmore *(Ossman)*, Wallace MacDonald *(Hassan)*, Kate Price *(Petrovna)*, H. A. Morgan *(Frolov)*, Burr McIntosh *(Count Peter)*, James Bradbury, Jr. *(Azamat)*, Stan Laurel *(Ali-Bek)*, Oliver Hardy *(Murza-Bek)*.

Musical romance. Source: Franz Lehár, A. M. Willner and Robert Bodansky, *Gipsy Love, a New Musical Play in Three Acts* (London, 1912). Yegor, tribal chieftain of a band of mountain bandits in southern Russia, meets and falls in love with Princess Vera, who is attracted by his singing. He learns, however, that his sister, Nadja, has been betrayed by Prince Serge, Vera's brother, and, kidnaping her, he takes her to his mountain fortress for revenge. She causes him to be captured; but when he sings to her as he is being flogged, she realizes the sincerity of his love and orders him released. Though the lovers part, it is with the hope that in the future their happiness will be realized. *Bandits. Singers. Gypsies. Royalty. Courtship. Russia.*

ROLLED STOCKINGS **F2.4669**

Paramount Famous Lasky Corp. 18 Jun **1927** [c18 Jun 1927; LP24103]. Si; b&w. 35mm. 7 reels, 6,249 ft.

Pres by Adolph Zukor, Jesse L. Lasky. *Assoc Prod* B. P. Schulberg. *Dir* Richard Rosson. *Screenplay* Percy Heath. *Titl* Julian Johnson. *Story* Frederica Sagor. *Photog* Victor Milner. *Film Ed* Julian Johnson.

Cast: James Hall *(Jim Treadway)*, Louise Brooks *(Carol Fleming)*, Richard Arlen *(Ralph Treadway)*, Nancy Phillips *(The Vamp)*, El Brendel *(Rudolph)*, David Torrence *(Mr. Treadway)*, Chance Ward *(coach)*.

Romantic drama. Jim Treadway disappoints his father in not making the boat crew at college while his freshman brother, Ralph, makes the team and upholds the family tradition. Both boys are smitten, however, by the charms of Carol Fleming, but Ralph is handicapped by hazing and strict training rules. On the eve of the big college race, Jim takes Carol to a dance and leaves Ralph burning with jealousy; deciding to brave official disapproval, Ralph goes to the dance and takes a jazzy young blonde to a roadhouse. Jim follows and ejects his brother after a fight and is himself found with the girl. After being acclaimed a hero, Ralph confesses that he is to blame for Jim's disgrace, and Carol finds happiness with the older brother. *Brothers. College life. Courtship. Jealousy. Rowing. Roadhouses.*

ROLLING HOME (Universal-Jewel) **F2.4670**

Universal Pictures. 6 Jun **1926** [New York premiere; released 27 Jun; c7 May 1926; LP22695]. Si; b&w. 35mm. 7 reels, 6,993 ft.

Pres by Carl Laemmle. *Dir* William A. Seiter. *Scen* Rex Taylor, John McDermott. *Photog* Arthur Todd.

Cast: Reginald Denny *(Nat Alden)*, Marian Nixon *(Phyllis)*, E. J. Ratcliffe *(Mr. Grubbell)*, Ben Hendricks, Jr. *(Dan Mason)*, Margaret Seddon *(Mrs. Alden)*, George Nichols *(Colonel Lowe)*, Alfred Allen *(General Wade)*, C. E. Thurston *(sheriff)*, George F. Marion, Alfred Knott *(selectmen)*, Anton Vaverka *(Pemberton)*, Howard Enstedt *(office boy)*, Adele Watson *(aunt)*.

Comedy. Source: John Hunter Booth, *Rolling Home, a Play in Three Acts* (New York, 1935). Nat Alden, an enthusiastic but unlucky promoter, fails in a venture and is evicted from the office of Mr. Grubbell, a capitalist involved in the deal; outside he meets Dan Mason, an old Army buddy, who is now Grubbell's chauffeur. Nat induces Mason to take leave and drive him to his home in a Rolls-Royce, for the townspeople have been led to believe he is a millionaire. Nat is met by a brass band and cheers, and the leading citizens press him for charity contributions. He convinces the people that the local waterfall will bring wealth, and with a fake check he buys the power franchise. A capitalist offers to buy him out; he accepts the offer to cover his check; but Grubbell appears and denounces Nat and Mason as crooks. Then Grubbell learns that the franchise is genuine and makes a better offer; Nat accepts and settles down with Phyllis, who had rejected him as a millionaire. *Veterans. Millionaires. Capitalists. Chauffeurs. Fraud. Water power. Smalltown life. Rolls-Royce automobiles.*

ROMANCE **F2.4671**

Metro-Goldwyn-Mayer Pictures. 26 Aug **1930** [c28 Jul 1930; LP1438]. Sd (Movietone); b&w. 35mm. 10 reels, 6,977 ft. [Also si.]

Dir Clarence Brown. *Cont-Dial* Bess Meredyth, Edwin Justus Mayer. *Photog* William Daniels. *Art Dir* Cedric Gibbons. *Film Ed* Hugh Wynn. *Rec Engr* Ralph Shugart, Douglas Shearer. *Gowns* Adrian.

Cast: Greta Garbo *(Rita Cavallini)*, Lewis Stone *(Cornelius Van Tuyl)*,

Gavin Gordon *(Tom Armstrong)*, Elliott Nugent *(Harry)*, Florence Lake *(Susan Van Tuyl)*, Clara Blandick *(Miss Armstrong)*, Henry Armetta *(Beppo)*, Mathilde Comont *(Vannucci)*, Countess De Liguoro *(Nina)*.

Romantic drama. Source: Edward Brewster Sheldon, *Romance, a Play in Three Acts with a Prologue and an Epilogue* (New York, 1913). On New Year's Eve, an aging bishop tells his grandson, Harry, of the great love affair of his youth: *At an evening party given by Cornelius Van Tuyl, Tom Armstrong, the son of an aristocratic family and the rector of St. Giles, meets the famous opera singer Rita Cavallini and falls in love with her, in spite of rumors that she is Van Tuyl's mistress. Tom persists although his family disapproves of Rita, but at length their romance is ended on another New Year's Eve by mutual agreement because of their differing stations in life.* The bishop tells how he later married another woman and counsels Harry to marry the woman he loves regardless of the consequences. *Singers. Clergymen. Social classes. Courtship. Reputation. Opera. New Year's Eve.*

ROMANCE AND BRIGHT LIGHTS *see* **ROMANCE OF THE UNDERWORLD**

ROMANCE AND RUSTLERS **F2.4672**

Arrow Pictures. 1 Mar **1925** [c7 Apr 1925; LP21339]. Si; b&w. 35mm. 5 reels, 4,939 ft.

Dir Ben Wilson. *Story-Scen* George Morgan.

Cast: Yakima Canutt *(Bud Kane)*, Dorothy Woods *(Ruth Larrabee)*, Harris Gordon *(George Wallace)*, Joe Girard *(John Larrabee)*.

Western melodrama. Lonesome Bud Kane rides into town, gets drunk, and staggers home only to find an unknown goldenhaired girl sleeping in his bunk. He does not awaken her and discovers the following day that she is Ruth Larrabee, the daughter of the rancher for whom he works. He later saves Ruth's life when her horse bolts, and the two fall in love. The Larrabee ranch is hit by rustlers, and Bud goes after them, accidentally losing his hatband. The band is found by George Wallace, who is both Larrabee's foreman and the leader of the rustlers. Larrabee uses the hatband to substantiate his accusation that Bud is the real cattle thief. Bud is ordered off the property by the elder Larrabee and immediately sets out to bring the rustlers in once and for all. He is captured by Wallace, however, and taken back to the Larrabee ranch, where he is held for the sheriff. Discovering the true identity of the rustlers, Ruth confronts Wallace, who makes a run for it. Bud follows and, besting him in a rough fight, hands Wallace over to the sheriff. Bud is forgiven by Larrabee, who gives his consent for Bud to romance Ruth. *Cowboys. Ranchers. Ranch foremen. Rustlers. Circumstantial evidence.*

ROMANCE LAND **F2.4673**

Fox Film Corp. 11 Feb **1923** [c3 Feb 1923; LP19050]. Si; b&w. 35mm. 5 reels, 3,975 or 4,500 ft.

Pres by William Fox. *Dir* Edward Sedgwick. *Scen* Joseph Franklin Poland. *Photog* Dan Clark.

Cast: Tom Mix *("Pep" Hawkins)*, Barbara Bedford *(Nan Harvess)*, Frank Brownlee *("Scrub" Hazen)*, George Webb *(Counterfeit Bill)*, Pat Chrisman *(White Eagle)*, Wynn Mace *(sheriff)*.

Western melodrama. Source: Kenneth Perkins, *The Gun Fanner* (New York, 1922). "This is one of Tom Mix's typical acrobatic romances. It has the usual spectacular feats, and the story of a hero who wins the girl because he excels in daring and accomplishing." (*Moving Picture World*, 24 Feb 1923.) "Pep" Hawkins, enthralled by stories of knighthood, travels around in a suit of steel armor and rescues Nan Harvess, a similarly romantic daughter of a rancher, by stopping her runaway horses. Nan falls in love with Pep but is already promised to her father's foreman. Her uncle, however, consents to hold a tournament consisting of a chariot race and other acrobatic stunts. To the victor would be given Nan's hand in marriage. Pep wins the tournament in spite of Nan's uncle's attempts to thwart him, and after rescuing Nan when she is kidnaped Pep carries his bride away heroically. *Cowboys. Ranch foremen. Uncles. Tournaments. Kidnaping. Courtship. Knighthood.*

THE ROMANCE OF A MILLION DOLLARS **F2.4674**

J. G. Bachmann. *Dist* Preferred Pictures. 15 Jul **1926** [c4 Aug 1926; LP22999]. Si; b&w. 35mm. 6 reels, 5,300 ft.

Pres by J. G. Bachmann. *Dir* Tom Terriss. *Adapt* Arthur Hoerl. *Photog* William Miller, Stuart Kelson.

Cast: Glenn Hunter *(Breck Dunbarton)*, Alyce Mills *(Marie Moore)*, Gaston Glass *(West MacDonald)*, Jane Jennings *(Mrs. Dunbarton)*, Bobby Watson *(The Detective)*, Lea Penman *(Mrs. Olwin)*, Thomas Brooks *(Ezra Dunbarton)*.

Melodrama. Source: Elizabeth Dejeans, *Romance of a Million Dollars* (Indianapolis, 1922). At 17, Breck Dunbarton is paroled from a reformatory and placed in the custody of his kindly Uncle Ezra, who assures him of his implicit trust and makes him equal heir with his other nephew, West. At college Breck is falsely accused of a theft, and following his expulsion he joins the Army and goes to France. At the front he meets Marie Moore, an ambulance driver; and learning of his uncle's death, he returns home after the Armistice. When Marie is sent to be Mrs. Dunbarton's companion, both Breck and West fall in love with her. Following the disappearance of some money and the robbery of a guest, suspicion falls on Breck, who is aware of West's connection with the affair but unable to find proof. Marie discovers that West, in disguise as Madame Volnova, is the thief; she is rescued by Breck and Mrs. Dunbarton; and West confesses, redeeming Breck's honor and giving him not only the fortune but also the girl. *Uncles. Ambulance drivers. Thieves. Juvenile delinquents. Disguise. Parole. Female impersonation. Reformatories. World War I. France.*

ROMANCE OF A ROGUE **F2.4675**

A. Carlos. *Dist* Quality Distributing Corp. ca27 Aug **1928** [New York premiere; released 1 Oct]. Si; b&w. 35mm. 6 reels, 5,900-6,100 ft.

Dir King Baggot. *Scen* Adrian Johnson. *Titl* Tom Miranda. *Photog* Faxon Dean, Chandler House. *Film Ed* William Holmes.

Cast: H. B. Warner *(Bruce Lowry)*, Anita Stewart *(Charmain)*, Alfred Fisher *(John Cristopher)*, Charles Gerrard *(Leonard Hardingham)*, Fred Esmelton, Billy Franey.

Melodrama. Source: Ruby Mildred Ayres, *The Romance of a Rogue* (New York, 1923). Story concerns a man's desire for vengeance on the man whose lies sent him to prison on the eve of his wedding. Apparently, the villain is paralyzed and confined to a wheelchair. *Prisons. Revenge. Perjury. Paralysis. Paraplegia.*

ROMANCE OF AN ACTRESS *see* **LIFE OF AN ACTRESS**

ROMANCE OF THE NILE **F2.4676**

Dist Kerman Films. 28 May **1924** [New York State license]. Si; b&w. 35mm. 5 reels.

Melodrama(?). No information about the nature of this film has been found. *Nile River.*

ROMANCE OF THE RIO GRANDE **F2.4677**

Fox Film Corp. 8 Nov **1929** [New York premiere; released 17 Nov; c11 Nov 1929; LP845]. Sd (Movietone); b&w. 35mm. 10 reels, 8,460 ft. [Also si; 7,757 ft.]

Pres by William Fox. *Dir* Alfred Santell. *Scen* Marion Orth. *Photog* Arthur Edeson. *Sets* Joseph Wright. *Film Ed* Paul Weatherwax. *Songs: "You'll Find Your Answer in My Eyes," "Ride On Vaquero," "My Toreador Starts To Snore"* L. Wolfe Gilbert, Abel Baer. *Sd* Frank Pierce. *Asst Dir* Marty Santell. *Cost* Sophie Wachner.

Cast: Warner Baxter *(Pablo Wharton Cameron)*, Mona Maris *(Manuelita)*, Mary Duncan *(Carlotta)*, Antonio Moreno *(Juan)*, Robert Edeson *(Don Fernando)*, Agostino Borgato *(Vincente)*, Albert Roccardi *(Padre Miguel)*, Solidad Jiminez *(Catalina)*, Majel Coleman *(Dorry Wayne)*, Charles Byer *(Dick Rivers)*, Merrill McCormick *(Luca)*.

Western drama. Source: Katharine Fullerton Gerould, *Conquistador* (New York, 1923). Pablo, the son of a Mexican mother and an American father, hates his grandfather, Don Fernando, for disowning his mother. As the supervisor of a railroad construction gang, he is injured in an attack by bandits and brought to the ranch of his grandfather. Following his recovery, Pablo plans to leave, though he has fallen in love with Manuelita; but a clash develops between Pablo and Juan, who has designs on becoming the family heir; and touched by Don Fernando's remorse at his treatment of his daughter, Pablo is reconciled to him and finds happiness with the girl. *Ranchers. Grandfathers. Filial relations. Railroads. Mexico.*

ROMANCE OF THE UNDERWORLD **F2.4678**

Fox Film Corp. 11 Nov **1928** [c26 Oct 1928; LP25757]. Sd eff & mus score (Movietone); b&w. 35mm. 7 reels, 6,162 ft.

Pres by William Fox. *Dir* Irving Cummings. *Scen* Douglas Doty. *Titl* Garrett Graham. *Story* Sidney Lanfield, Douglas Doty. *Photog* Conrad Wells. *Film Ed* Frank Hull. *Song: "Judy"* Irving Kahal, Pierre Norman, Sammy Fain. *Asst Dir* Charles Woolstenhulme.

Cast: Mary Astor *(Judith Andrews)*, Ben Bard *(Derby Dan Manning)*,

Robert Elliott *(Edwin Burke)*, John Boles *(Stephen Ransome)*, Oscar Apfel *(Champagne Joe)*, Helen Lynch *(Blondie Nell)*, William H. Tooker *(Asa Jenks)*.

Underworld melodrama. Source: Paul Armstrong, *A Romance of the Underworld* (New York opening: Mar 1911). Judith Andrews, once a sweet country girl, falls upon hard times in the city and is reduced to soliciting in a dancehall. She meets Stephen Ransome, a young man of good family and excellent character, who knows nothing of her past, and marries him, insisting only that he ask nothing about her former life. Derby Dan Manning, Judith's former pimp, learns of the marriage and blackmails her until Edwin Burke, a phlegmatic, undemonstrative detective, puts him away. Stephen learns of Judith's past but forgives her, his love for her having quickly overcome his initial disappointment. *Prostitutes. Pimps. Detectives. Blackmail.*

Note: Also known as *Romance and Bright Lights*.

ROMANCE OF THE WASTELAND **F2.4679**

Art Mix Productions. *Dist* Aywon Film Corp. 10 Oct **1924** [New York State license]. Si; b&w. 35mm. 5 reels, 4,860 ft.

Cast: Art Mix.

Western melodrama(?). No information about the nature of this film has been found.

ROMANCE OF THE WEST **F2.4680**

Arthur Hammond. *Dist* Jack D. Trop. 15 Jun **1930.** Si; b&w. 35mm. 6 reels, 5,494 ft.

Dir-Story-Scen-Dial Robert Tansey, John Tansey. *Film Ed* Robert Tansey, John Tansey.

Cast: Jack Perrin *(Jack Walsh)*, Edna Marion *(Mary Winter)*, Tom London *(K. O. Mooney)*, Henry Roquemore *("Slick" Graham)*, Ben Corbett *(Buck)*, Fern Emmett *(landlady)*, Dick Hatton *(parson)*, Edwin August *(Chuck Anderson)*, Starlight *(a horse)*.

Western melodrama. Rescuing Mary Winter from the unwelcome attentions of a drunk, Jack Walsh learns that she has been lured into Mexico by the false promises of an ex-prizefighter, K. O. Mooney. Jack upbraids Mooney, the scoundrel kidnaps Mary, and there is a wild chase, which ends in the cabin of a Mexican with a grudge against Mooney. Jack wins the showdown fight with Mooney and the heart of Mary. *Prizefighters. Kidnaping. Mexico. Chases. Horses.*

ROMANCE RANCH **F2.4681**

Fox Film Corp. 29 Jun **1924** [c23 Jun 1924; LP20330]. Si; b&w. 35mm. 5 reels, 4,471 ft.

Pres by William Fox. *Dir* Howard M. Mitchell. *Scen* Dorothy Yost. *Story* Jessie Maude Wybro. *Photog* Bert Baldridge.

Cast: John Gilbert *(Carlos Brent)*, Virginia Brown Faire *(Carmen Hendley)*, John Miljan *(Clifton Venable)*, Bernard Seigel *(Felipe Varillo)*, Evelyn Selbie *(Tessa)*.

Romantic melodrama. Carlos Brent's grandfather informs him that he is rightful owner of a ranch in the possession of the Hendley family. A belated letter establishes his claim, but Carlos is reluctant to evict the usurpers because he loves Carmen, Hendley's daughter. He solves his problem by abducting and marrying Carmen, thus becoming the ranch's legal owner. *Grandfathers. Inheritance. Ranches. Documentation.*

ROMANCE ROAD **F2.4682**

Granada Productions. *Dist* Truart Film Corp. 15 Jul **1925** [New York State license]. Si; b&w. 35mm. 5 reels, 4,300 ft.

Dir Fred Windemere. *Photog* Lenwood Abbott.

Cast: Raymond McKee *(Patrick O'Brien)*, Billy Bletcher *(Buddy)*, Marjorie Meadows *(Mary Van Tassler)*, Dick Gordon *(Arthur Waddington Watts)*, Gertrude Claire *(Ma O'Brien)*, Billy Fletcher *(Pat's buddy)*, Hash *(himself, a dog)*.

Comedy. Patrick O'Brien, a young soldier returning from France, arrives in New York with no money and no prospects. He sets out to walk the 40 miles to his upstate home and, partway there, he gets a ride with Mary Van Tassler, a beautiful and wealthy young woman from his hometown. Patrick returns to a warm welcome but no job. He finally finds work in a garage, where he invents a device to improve carburetion by separating water from gasoline. Patrick begins to see a lot of Mary, much to the annoyance of both her snobbish aunt and the fiancé someone picked out for her. An old Army buddy markets Patrick's invention, and they both become rich as the result. Patrick asks Mary to marry him. She accepts, and they receive the blessing of her family. *Inventors. Mechanics. Veterans. Aunts. Social classes. Smalltown life. Garages. Carburetion. Dogs.*

THE ROMANTIC AGE **F2.4683**

Columbia Pictures. 5 Jun **1927** [c7 Jun 1927; LP24051]. Si; b&w. 35mm. 6 reels, 5,267 ft.

Prod Harry Cohn. *Dir* Robert Florey. *Story-Scen* Dorothy Howell. *Photog* Norbert Brodin.

Cast: Eugene O'Brien *(Stephen Winslow)*, Alberta Vaughn *(Sally Sanborn)*, Stanley Taylor, Bert Woodruff.

Society drama. Stephen Winslow, the bachelor guardian of vivacious young Sally Sanborn, is devoted to the girl and hopes to marry her. He bails her out of jail following a cabaret raid and takes her home after a ruinous canoeing expedition, where she finally accepts his proposal. When Stephen's attractive but worthless younger brother, Tom, unexpectedly returns home, Stephen finds himself neglected by Sally and is led to believe that Tom has won her love. At a dinner, he startles everyone by announcing the engagement of Sally and Tom and abruptly leaves the table to go to save her securities from a fire at the factory; there, when they are trapped in the flames, their misunderstandings are cleared away. Rescued, they return to the dinner, where Stephen announces *their* plans to marry. *Bachelors. Guardians. Brothers. Courtship. Cabarets. Fires.*

ROMANTIC ROGUE **F2.4684**

Harry J. Brown Productions. *Dist* Rayart Pictures. Jun **1927.** Si; b&w. 35mm. 5 reels, 4,800-5,120 ft.

Dir Harry J. Brown. *Scen* Henry R. Symonds. *Photog* Walter Griffen.

Cast: Reed Howes *(Hart Lawson)*, Ena Gregory *(Barbara Warrington)*, James Bradbury *(Uncle Arch Lawson)*, Syd Crossley *(Uncle Reg Lawson)*, Cuyler Supplee *(Harry Lawson)*.

Comedy-drama. Hart Lawson is the pampered scion of an old patent medicine–manufacturing family, whose members are poor advertising for the rejuvenating effects of their own products. Hart's uncles continually insist that he, too, has heart disease, he resolutely insists that he does not, and he eventually proves himself to be in good health. *Uncles. Patent medicines. Heart disease.*

ROMOLA **F2.4685**

Inspiration Pictures. *Dist* Metro-Goldwyn Distributing Corp. 30 Aug **1925** [c1 Dec 1924, 14 Sep 1925; LP21087, LP21859]. Si; b&w. 35mm. 12 reels, 12,974 ft.

Dir Henry King. *Scen* Will M. Ritchey. *Art Dir* Robert M. Haas. *Prod Mgr* Joseph C. Boyle. *Shipbuilder* Tito Neri.

Cast: Lillian Gish *(Romola)*, Dorothy Gish *(Tessa)*, William H. Powell *(Tito Melema)*, Ronald Colman *(Carlo Buccellini)*, Charles Lane *(Baldassarre Calvo)*, Herbert Grimwood *(Savonarola)*, Bonaventure Ibáñez *(Bardo Bardi)*, Frank Puglia *(Adolpo Spini)*, Amelia Summerville *(Brigida)*, Angelo Scatigna *(Bratti)*, Edulilo Mucci *(Nello)*, Tina Rinaldi *(Monna Ghita)*, Alfredo Bertone, Alfredo Martinelli, Ugo Ucellini.

Historical romance. Source: George Eliot, *Romola* (London, 1862). Calvo, a Greek scholar, and his adopted son, Tito, are approaching Italy by boat when they are set upon by pirates. Calvo gives Tito jewels and a ring (Calvo's signet) and instructs him to swim to shore, sell the jewels, and use the money to pay the pirates' ransom. Tito makes his way to Florence, where he forgets all about Calvo and marries Romola, the daughter of a blind scholar. With the assistance of Spini, an adventurer, Tito rises to the position of chief magistrate. Tito becomes unpopular with the people by his bad conduct: he sells Romola's father's sacred books, enters into a mock marriage with Tessa, a peasant girl, and condemns to death the beloved champion of the people, the priest Savonarola. Incited to fury by the cleric's death, a mob goes after Tito, who drowns in the river. Romola finds Tessa and cares for her, eventually finding happiness with Carlo, a sculptor who has remained faithful to her. *Adventurers. Priests. Magistrates. Sculptors. Pirates. Marriage—Fake. The Renaissance. Florence. Girolamo Savonarola.*

THE ROOF TREE **F2.4686**

Fox Film Corp. 25 Dec w*1921* [c2 Dec 1921; LP17462]. Si; b&w. 35mm. 5 reels, 4,409 ft.

Pres by William Fox. *Dir* John Francis Dillon. *Scen* Jules Furthman. *Photog* Sol Polito.

Cast: William Russell *(Ken Thornton)*, Florence Deshon *(Sally McTurk)*, Sylvia Breamer *(Dorothy Harper)*, Robert Daly *(Caleb Harper)*, Arthur Morrison *(Bass Rowlett)*, Al Fremont *(Jim Rowlett)*.

Romantic drama. Source: Charles Neville Buck, *The Roof Tree* (Garden City, New York, 1921). Ken Thornton flees to Kentucky after the slaying of Sam McTurk, his sister's husband, and takes an assumed name. His close resemblance to the Thornton family is seen by Dorothy Harper and her father, Caleb, and they receive him as one of the family and grow to love him. Jealous of the girl's love for Thornton, Bass Rowlett tries to have him killed; Ken is seriously wounded and challenges Bass to a fight when he regains his strength. After revealing his past to Harper, Ken marries Dorothy under the roof tree planted by Ken's pioneer grandfather on the Harper land. Following the ceremony, Bass brings the sheriff and has Thornton arrested for the murder of Sam McTurk; but Thornton's sister confesses to killing Sam in self-defense. Thornton settles his score with Bass, who is disgraced and sent away. *Brother-sister relationship. Murder. Rural life. Disguise. Kentucky.*

ROOKIES **F2.4687**

Metro-Goldwyn-Mayer Pictures. 30 Apr **1927** [c2 May 1927; LP24473]. Si; b&w. 35mm. 7 reels, 6,640 ft.

Dir Sam Wood. *Story-Cont* Byron Morgan. *Titl* Joe Farnham. *Photog* Ira Morgan. *Sets* Cedric Gibbons, David Townsend. *Film Ed* Conrad A. Nervig. *Wardrobe* André-ani. *Titl Illus* Bert Levy.

Cast: Karl Dane *(Sergeant Diggs)*, George K. Arthur *(Greg Lee)*, Marceline Day *(Betty Wayne)*, Louise Lorraine *(Zella Fay)*, Frank Currier *(The Judge)*, E. H. Calvert *(Colonel)*, Tom O'Brien *(Sergeant O'Brien)*, Charles Sullivan *(Corporal Sullivan)*, Lincoln Stedman *(Sleepy)*, Gene Stone *(Smarty)*.

Comedy. Hard-boiled Sergeant Diggs shows open contempt for Greg Lee, a cabaret dancer, while flirting with his partner, Zella Fay. Greg, a simpering dandy, tries to get even with the sergeant, and as a result he is arrested and sent to an Army training camp instead of jail. At camp, his life is made miserable by the constant badgering of Diggs, which he reciprocates in kind. Following a series of comic incidents, Greg, with a full complement of parachutes, rescues Diggs and Betty Wayne, the judge's daughter, from a runaway balloon and thus proves his heroism and fortitude to his rival and opponent. *Dancers. Dandies. Manhood. Parachuting. Balloons. United States Army—Training.*

THE ROOKIE'S RETURN **F2.4688**

Thomas H. Ince Corp. *Dist* Paramount Pictures. 23 Jan **1921** [c20 Dec 1920; LP15967]. Si; b&w. 35mm. 5 reels, 4,123 ft.

Supv Thomas H. Ince. *Dir* Jack Nelson. *Story* Archer McMackin. *Photog* Bert Cann.

Cast: Douglas MacLean *(James Stewart Lee)*, Doris May *(Alicia)*, Frank Currier *(Dad)*, Leo White *(Henri)*, Kathleen Key *(Gloria)*, Elinor Hancock *(Mrs. Radcliffe)*, William Courtright *(Gregg)*, Frank Clark *(Tubbs)*, Aggie Herring *(Mrs. Perkins)*, Wallace Beery *(François Dupont)*.

Comedy. James Lee Stewart, a rookie just returned from the war, vainly tries to sell books for a living until his wealthy aunt dies and leaves him a fortune. A proviso of the will dictates that if any of the servants is fired, he will receive $5,000. Despite their insults, he decides to keep the servants on. He takes his problems to a lawyer, who is, unknown to Jimmy, the father of Alicia, a girl to whom Jimmy is attracted. The father, after settling Jimmy's servant problem, wanting to see the couple get together, makes his daughter believe he has been kidnaped. Jimmy and Alicia get into several adventures, after which all is explained and the lovers are united. *Veterans. Book agents. Domestics. Salesmen. Inheritance. Wills. Kidnaping.*

Note: A sequel to *23 1/2 Hours Leave* (1919).

ROOM AND BOARD **F2.4689**

Realart Pictures. *Dist* Paramount Pictures. 17 Aug **1921** [New York State license application; c8 Aug 1921; LP16865]. Si; b&w. 35mm. 5 reels, 5,107 ft.

Dir Alan Crosland. *Scen* Donnah Darrell. *Story* Charles E. Whittaker. *Photog* George Folsey. *Asst Dir* Lynn Shores.

Cast: Constance Binney *(Lady Noreen)*, Tom Carrigan *(Terrence O'Brien)*, Malcolm Bradley *(Ephraim Roach)*, Arthur Housman *(Desmond Roach)*, Jed Prouty *(Robert Osborne)*, Blanche Craig *(Mary)*, Ben Hendricks, Jr. *(Ryan)*, Ellen Cassidy *(Leila)*, Arthur Barry *(The Earl of Kildoran)*.

Melodrama. The father of Lady Noreen of Kildoran is killed during a fox hunt, and his daughter is left with the debts of the estate and a dilapidated castle. Ephraim Roach, who holds a mortgage on the property, threatens to foreclose unless Noreen marries his son, Desmond; but she rents the castle and the servants to a wealthy young American, Terrence O'Brien, pretending she is only a housemaid. O'Brien sees through her pretence and helps to repair the estate. The arrival of his fiancée, Leila, and her brother, Osborne, leads Noreen to make life uncomfortable for Leila and to break up the engagement. Roach comes to foreclose the mortgage but is thrown out by O'Brien, who announces he has taken over the estate and that Noreen is to be his wife. *Housemaids. Landed gentry. Debt. Mortgages. Ireland.*

ROOSEVELT'S HUNTING GROUNDS *see* **EQUATORIAL AFRICA; ROOSEVELT'S HUNTING GROUNDS**

ROPED BY RADIO **F2.4690**

Art Mix Productions. *Dist* Aywon Film Corp. 23 Nov **1925** [New York State license]. Si; b&w. 35mm. 5 reels, 4,850 ft.

Cast: George Kesterson, Virginia Warwick.

Western melodrama(?). No information about the nature of this film has been found

ROPES *see* **FALSE KISSES**

A ROPIN' RIDIN' FOOL **F2.4691**

William Steiner Productions. c30 Mar **1925** [LU21279]. Si; b&w. 35mm. 5 reels.

Scen Jay Inman Kane, Bob Williamson.

Cast: Pete Morrison *(Jim Warren)*, Martin Turner *(Major, a gentleman of many parts)*.

Western melodrama. Alvin Warren, the weak, younger son of an old Philadelphia banker, goes into debt to Jack Cope, a gambler, and helps him steal a large sum of money from his father's safe. Beth Warren, a ward of the family, discovers them in the act of robbery and gets a good look at Cope. Alvin's brother, Jim, a Texas Ranger on holiday in the East, takes the blame for the crime in order to protect Alvin. A year later, Beth comes west to visit Jim and recognizes Cope, who runs a trading post. Cope kidnaps her with the help of Santo, a halfbreed, and takes her to a cabin. Jim trails them there and mortally wounds Cope, who confesses his guilt in the robbery and returns most of the stolen money. Beth and Jim seem destined for marriage, and the elder Warren uses the money to clear himself of charges of embezzlement that resulted from the original loss of the money. *Bankers. Gamblers. Texas Rangers. Brothers. Traders. Halfcastes. Robbery. Embezzlement. Philadelphia.*

THE ROSARY **F2.4692**

Selig-Rork Productions. *Dist* Associated First National Pictures. 16 Jan **1922** [c19 Jan 1922; LP17474]. Si; b&w. 35mm. 7 reels, 7,045 ft.

Prod William N. Selig, Sam E. Rork. *Dir* Jerome Storm. *Story* Bernard McConville. *Photog* Edwin Linden. *Tech Dir* Gabe Pollock.

Cast: Lewis S. Stone *(Father Brian Kelly)*, Jane Novak *(Vera Mather)*, Wallace Beery *(Kenwood Wright)*, Robert Gordon *(Bruce Wilton)*, Eugenie Besserer *(Widow Kathleen Wilton)*, Dore Davidson *(Isaac Abrahamson)*, Pomeroy Cannon *(Donald MacTavish)*, Bert Woodruff *(Capt. Caleb Mather)*, Mildred June *(Alice Wilton)*, Harold Goodwin *(Skeeters Martin)*.

Melodrama. Source: Edward E. Rose, *The Rosary, a Play in Four Acts* (New York, 1926). Ethelbert Nevin and Robert Cameron Rogers, "The Rosary" (a song; Boston, 1898). Following the death of his uncle, founder of the fishing village of Sandy Bay, Kenwood Wright is cut off with only some marshland while his nephew, Bruce Wilton, inherits the bulk of the estate. Wright is further enraged by the engagement of Vera Mather, whom he loves, to Bruce. Wright joins forces with Donald MacTavish, a pirate captain, and wins the affections of Bruce's sister, Alice, who becomes his victim. Vera, in an attempt to save Alice, becomes involved in the scandal, and Bruce takes back the rosary he has given her to pledge his love. Bruce barely escapes an explosion at the cannery constructed by Wright on his marshlands, and when Wright is named by Father Kelly as a conspirator, the posse sets out to capture him in a storm. He seeks refuge in the church, and when a pistol is drawn against Father Kelly, Bruce's mother receives the fatal bullet; Wright escapes but plunges to his death while crossing an old bridge. *Clergymen. Pirates. Posses. Inheritance. Fishing villages. Churches. Canneries.*

ROSE O' THE SEA **F2.4693**

Anita Stewart Productions. *Dist* Associated First National Pictures. ca2 Jul **1922** [Pittsburgh premiere; c27 Jun 1922; LP18119]. Si; b&w. 35mm. 7 reels, 6,837 ft.

Pres by Louis B. Mayer. *Prod* Louis B. Mayer. *Dir* Fred Niblo. *Scen*

Bess Meredyth, Madge Tyrone. *Photog* Dal Clawson. *Scenic Architect* John Holden. *Asst Dir* Doran Cox.

Cast: Anita Stewart *(Rose Eton)*, Rudolph Cameron *(Elliot Schuyler)*, Thomas Holding *(Peter Schuyler)*, Margaret Landis *(Vivienne Raymond)*, Kate Lester *("Lady Maggie")*, Hallam Cooley *(Roger Walton)*, John P. Lockney *(Daddy Eton)*, Charles Belcher *(George Thornton)*.

Society comedy-drama. Source: Countess Hélène Barcynska, *Rose o' the Sea; a Romance* (New York, 1920). Rose, a waif from the sea, becomes a flower girl in New York on the death of her guardian. Entering into a romance with society roué Elliot Schuyler and his millionaire father, Peter, she becomes involved in gambling and other aristocratic pursuits and eventually marries the father. *Flower girls. Millionaires. Poverty. Gambling. New York City.*

THE ROSE OF KILDARE **F2.4694**

Gotham Productions. *Dist* Lumas Film Corp. 15 Aug **1927** [c22 Aug 1927; LP24329]. Si; b&w. 35mm. 7 reels, 6,875 ft.

Pres by Sam Sax. *Supv* Samuel Bischoff. *Dir* Dallas M. Fitzgerald. *Adapt-Cont* Harold Shumate. *Titl* Garrett Graham. *Photog* Milton Moore.

Cast: Helene Chadwick *(Eileen O'Moore)*, Pat O'Malley *(Barry Nunan)*, Henry B. Walthall *(Bob Avery)*, Lee Moran *("The Kid")*, Edwin J. Brady *(Ed Brady)*, Ena Gregory *(Elsie Avery)*, Carroll Nye *(Larry Nunan)*.

Romantic melodrama. Source: Gerald Beaumont, "The Rose of Kildare," in *Red Book* (40:61–65, Dec 1922). In a region near Kimberly, South Africa, Bob Avery, proprietor of the Eldorado Dancehall, goes to the railroad station to meet Eileen O'Moore, a singer known as the Irish Nightingale, who has been promoted in grand style by her agent, "The Kid." For the 19th time Bob proposes marriage to her, but Eileen sadly declines; in the hotel she reminisces over past days in Kildare when she was betrothed to Barry Nunan, who left to seek his fortune in South Africa and never returned. At her concert she meets Barry but is shocked to find that he is married; consequently, she accepts Bob and becomes his wife. Five years later, Barry has returned to America to become a lawyer, and upon the death of Bob, Eileen sells the Eldorado and goes with her daughter to America, where she opens a roadhouse in which Elsie dances. Nunan, who wants to close the place, is enraged when his son, Larry, falls in love with Elsie but is placated by his own happy reunion with Eileen. *Singers. Booking agents. Courtship. Dancehalls. Roadhouses. South Africa. Ireland.*

THE ROSE OF PARIS (Universal-Jewel) **F2.4695**

Universal Pictures. 1 Oct **1924** [New York showing; released 9 Nov; c28 Jul 1924; LP20423]. Si; b&w. 35mm. 7 reels, 6,362 ft.

Pres by Carl Laemmle. *Dir* Irving Cummings. *Scen* Melville Brown, Edward T. Lowe, Jr. *Adapt* Lenore J. Coffee, Bernard McConville. *Photog* Charles Stumar.

Cast: Mary Philbin *(Mitsi)*, Robert Cain *(Christian)*, John Sainpolis *(André du Vallois)*, Rose Dione *(Madame Bolomoff)*, Dorothy Revier *(Florine du Vallois)*, Gino Corrado *(Paul Maran)*, Doreen Turner *(Yvette)*, Edwin J. Brady *(Jules)*, Charles Puffy *(Victor)*, Carrie Daumery *(Mother Superior)*, Cesare Gravina *(George)*, Alice H. Smith *(governess)*, Frank Currier *(George Der Vroo)*, D. J. Mitsoras *(major domo)*.

Romantic drama. Source: Delly, *Mitsi* (Paris, 1922). Mitsi, an orphan girl, is lured from the cloistered life of a convent to a Paris cafe, where she becomes the victim of a plot to profit by her inheritance. She escapes and becomes a servant in the home of her grandfather, where she falls in love with Christian. After her identity is established they are married. *Orphans. Grandfathers. Inheritance. Convents. Paris.*

ROSE OF THE BOWERY **F2.4696**

David M. Hartford Productions. *Dist* American Cinema Corp. 15 May or 15 Aug **1927.** Si; b&w. 35mm. 6 reels, 5,446 ft.

Dir Bertram Bracken. *Adapt* Bertram Bracken, Walter Griffin. *Photog* Walter Griffin.

Cast: Johnny Walker, Edna Murphy, Mildred Harris.

Crook drama. A satchel—purportedly full of money—is hurriedly passed on by one crook to another. Actually, it contains a baby girl. The "owner" rears the girl as his own daughter in the tenement world of New York's East Side, where years later she is innocently involved in a murder. About to be found guilty, she is recognized as the district attorney's daughter. *A flashback explains how the girl's mother left her husband, hiding the baby in a bag, which was accidentally substituted by a crook for a bag full of money.* Justice and a family reunion ensue. *District attorneys. Foundlings. Murder. New York City—East Side.*

ROSE OF THE DESERT **F2.4697**

Charles R. Seeling Productions. *Dist* Aywon Film Corp. 18 Aug **1925** [New York State license]. Si; b&w. 35mm. 5 reels, 4,900 ft.

Cast: Big Boy Williams.

Western melodrama(?). No information about the nature of this film has been found.

ROSE OF THE GOLDEN WEST **F2.4698**

First National Pictures. 25 Sep **1927** [New York premiere; released 2 Oct; c3 Oct 1927; LP24462]. Si; b&w. 35mm. 7 reels, 6,477 ft.

Pres by Richard A. Rowland. *Dir* George Fitzmaurice. *Adapt-Scen* Bess Meredyth, Philip Bartholomae. *Titl* Mort Blumenstock. *Photog* Lee Garmes. *Cost* Max Ree.

Cast: Mary Astor *(Elena)*, Gilbert Roland *(Juan)*, Gustav von Seyffertitz *(Gómez)*, Montagu Love *(General Vallero)*, Flora Finch *(Señora Comba)*, Harvey Clark *(Thomas Larkin)*, Roel Muriel *(Mother Superior)*, André Cheron *(Russian prince)*, Romaine Fielding *(secretary)*, Thur Fairfax *(orderly)*, William Conklin *(Commander Sloat)*, Christina Montt *(Señorita González)*, Cullen Tate.

Romantic drama. Source: Minna Caroline Smith and Eugenie Woodward, "Rose of the Golden West" (publication undetermined). In 1846, patriots of California join forces to avert a suspected plan of dictator General Vallero to sell out to Russia; by lot, Juan, a handsome youth, is selected to crush the plot, preventing his plan to elope with Elena, a convent novice. General Vallero, actually Elena's father, visits the convent, tells her he is a friend of her dead father, and takes her to Monterey; en route, Juan stops the runaway team, winning the profuse thanks of Vallero, the two remaining unaware of each other's identity. Believing he has been tricked, Juan is about to fulfill his mission during a fiesta when he is seized by soldiers; later he returns to Vallero's home and is recaptured and sentenced to be shot. Elena manages, however, to summon marines from a warship in the bay; Juan is saved from death, and he and Elena are reunited. *Novices. Dictators. Conspiracy. Fatherhood. California—Mexican period. Monterey (California). Russia. United States Marines.*

ROSE OF THE TENEMENTS **F2.4699**

R-C Pictures. *Dist* Film Booking Offices of America. 5 Dec **1926** [c22 Nov 1926; LP23353]. Si; b&w. 35mm. 7 reels, 6,678 ft.

Pres by Joseph P. Kennedy. *Dir* Phil Rosen. *Adapt-Cont* J. Grubb Alexander. *Photog* Lyman Broening. *Asst Dir* Jimmy Dugan.

Cast: Shirley Mason *(Rosie [Rose] Rossetti)*, Johnny Harron *(Danny Lewis)*, Evelyn Selbie *(Sara Kaminsky)*, Sidney Franklin *(Abraham Kaminsky)*, James Gordon *(Tim Galligan)*, Frank McGlynn, Jr. *(Mickey Galligan)*, Scott McKee *(Paddy Flynn)*, Jess Devorska *(Izzie Kohn)*, Mathilde Comont *(Mrs. Kohn)*, Valentina Zimina *(Emma Goldstein)*, Kalla Pasha *(Willofsky)*.

Melodrama. Source: John A. Moroso, *The Stumbling Herd* (New York, 1923). Rose Rossetti, the orphaned daughter of a New York gangster, and Danny Lewis, also an orphan, are reared by the Kaminskys, an elderly Jewish couple who operate an artificial flower factory on the East Side. The Kaminskys die, telling Rose of her parentage, and leave the shop to Danny and Rose. Danny drifts into the clutches of Willofsky, a Bolshevik agitator, and Emma Goldstein, his coworker, to whom Danny is attracted. While agitating against the war with Germany, Willofsky and Emma are attacked by a crowd; and Danny, after assaulting a policeman, prevents Emma from throwing a bomb. Through Galligan, a ward leader, he is exonerated by the police and allowed to enlist, to Rose's joy. After the war, Danny returns and finds that he is in love with Rose. *Flowermakers. Orphans. Jews. Italians. Bolshevists. Agitators. World War I. New York City—East Side.*

ROSE OF THE WORLD **F2.4700**

Warner Brothers Pictures. 21 Nov **1925** [c18 Aug 1925; LP21758]. Si; b&w. 35mm. 8 reels, 7,506 ft. [Copyrighted as 7 reels.]

Dir Harry Beaumont. *Scen* Julien Josephson. *Adapt* Dorothy Farnum. *Photog* David Abel. *Asst Dir* Frank Strayer.

Cast: Patsy Ruth Miller *(Rose Kirby)*, Allan Forrest *(Jack Talbot)*, Pauline Garon *(Edith Rogers)*, Rockliffe Fellowes *(Clyde Bainbridge)*, Barbara Luddy *(Cecilia Kirby)*, Alec Francis *("Gramp" Tallifer)*, Helen Dunbar *(Mrs. John Talbot)*, Lydia Knott *(Mrs. Kirby)*, Edward Peil, Jr. *(The Boy)*, Carrie Clark Ward *(Sally Towsey)*.

Society melodrama. Source: Kathleen Norris, *Rose of the World* (New York, 1926). Wealthy Jack Talbot falls in love with Rose Kirby, a girl living in reduced circumstances, but, through fear of his mother's disapproval, he does not marry her. Rose later marries Clyde Bainbridge, a rotter who knows that, under the terms of a secret contract, Rose will inherit the Talbot ironworks. Rose finds the contract, but, mistrusting her husband, does not make use of it. Talbot marries a vamp, who later dies in childbirth. Clyde is accidentally killed by Rose's demented grandfather. Rose and Talbot then return to each other, finding together a long-delayed happiness. *Vamps. Grandfathers. Lunatics. Marriage. Childbirth. Contracts. Ironworks.*

ROSE-MARIE **F2.4701**

Metro-Goldwyn-Mayer Pictures. 11 Feb **1928** [c11 Feb 1928; LP25288]. Si; b&w. 35mm. 8 reels, 7,745 ft.

Dir-Writ Lucien Hubbard. *Photog* John Arnold. *Set Dsgn* Cedric Gibbons, Richard Day. *Film Ed* Carl L. Pierson. *Mus* Rudolf Friml, Herbert Stothart. *Wardrobe* David Cox.

Cast: Joan Crawford *(Rose-Marie)*, James Murray *(Jim Kenyon)*, House Peters *(Sgt. Terence Malone)*, Creighton Hale *(Étienne Duray)*, Gibson Gowland *(Black Bastien)*, George Cooper *(Fuzzy)*, Lionel Belmore *(Henri Duray)*, William Orlamond *(Émile la Flamme)*, Polly Moran *(Lady Jane)*, Harry Gribbon *(Trooper Gray)*, Gertrude Astor *(Wanda)*, Ralph Yearsley *(Jean)*, Sven Hugo Borg *(Hudson)*.

Romantic melodrama. Source: Otto Harbach, Oscar Hammerstein, II, Rudolf Friml, and Herbert Stothart, *Rose-Marie* (London opening: 20 Mar 1925). Rose-Marie, belle of a Canadian trading post, loves Jim Kenyon, an outlaw trapper wanted for murder by Northwest Mountie Sergeant Malone. To save Kenyon from being exposed by her father, Rose Marie marries Étienne Duray, a Frenchman of means. Kenyon rescues Rose-Marie and Étienne (badly injured) when their canoe capsizes in the river and takes them to a nearby cabin. Malone arrives, still on Kenyon's trail, followed by Black Bastien, Malone's escaped prisoner—another suspect, who murdered an Indian and a town constable. The situation is resolved when Kenyon stabs the evil Black Bastien to prevent him from attacking Rose-Marie, and Étienne dies of a broken back, leaving Rose-Marie and Kenyon to their happiness. *Trappers. Murder. Trading posts. Northwest Mounted Police.*

ROSITA **F2.4702**

Mary Pickford Co. *Dist* United Artists. 3 Sep **1923** [c17 Oct 1923; LP19505]. Si; b&w. 35mm. 9 reels, 8,800 ft.

Dir Ernst Lubitsch. *Adapt-Scen* Edward Knoblock. *Story* Norbert Falk, Hans Kraly. *Photog* Charles Rosher. *Art Dir* William Cameron Menzies. *Set Dsgn* Svend Gade. *Mus Score* Louis F. Gottschalk. *Asst Dir* James Townsend.

Cast: Mary Pickford *(Rosita)*, Holbrook Blinn *(The King)*, Irene Rich *(The Queen)*, George Walsh *(Don Diego)*, Charles Belcher *(The Prime Minister)*, Frank Leigh *(prison commandant)*, Mathilde Comont *(Rosita's mother)*, George Periolat *(Rosita's father)*, Bert Sprotte *(big jailer)*, Snitz Edwards *(little jailer)*, Madame De Bodamere *(The Maid)*, Philippe De Lacey, Donald McAlpin *(Rosita's brothers)*, Doreen Turner *(Rosita's sister)*, Mario Carillo *(majordomo)*, Marian Nixon, Charles Farrell.

Historical romance. Source: Adolphe Philippe Dennery and Philippe François Pinel, *Don César de Bazan* (1844). The King of Spain falls in love with Rosita, a Spanish streetsinger, who in turn loves Don Diego, a penniless nobleman who defends her when the guards arrest her for singing a song lampooning the lusty king. Rosita and Don Diego are imprisoned; Don Diego is sentenced to die; and Rosita is summoned by the king and tempted with gifts of clothing and a luxurious villa. The king arranges a marriage between Rosita and Don Diego—both blindfolded—making Rosita a countess before she is to become a widow. The queen saves Don Diego's life by putting blank cartridges in the executioner's guns. Don Diego, feigning death, is brought to Rosita's villa and jumps up to earn his pardon by saving the king just as the bereaved Rosita raises her knife to stab him. *Royalty. Nobility. Singers. Spain.*

ROUGED LIPS **F2.4703**

Metro Pictures. 20 Aug **1923** [New York premiere; released 17 Sep; c17 Sep 1923; LP19415]. Si; b&w. 35mm. 6 reels, 5,150 ft.

Dir Harold Shaw. *Adapt-Cont* Tom J. Hopkins. *Titl* Clyde Bruckman. *Photog* John Arnold.

Cast: Viola Dana *(Norah MacPherson)*, Tom Moore *(James Patterson III)*, Nola Luxford *(Mamie Dugan)*, Sidney De Gray *(James Patterson II)*, Arline Pretty *(Mariette)*, Francis Powers *(Mr. MacPherson)*, Georgia Woodthorpe *(Mrs. MacPherson)*, Burwell Hamrick *(Billy Dugan)*.

Melodrama. Source: Rita Weiman, "Upstage," in *Cosmopolitan Magazine* (42:35+, Oct 1922). Thrifty orphan Norah MacPherson meets wealthy young James Patterson, who gets her a job as a chorus girl. They fall in love. To put up a good front, she spends all her money on clothes. Patterson doubts her when he sees her wearing a string of (imitation) pearls; he then finds that she hasn't been unfaithful, and they are reconciled. *Orphans. Chorus girls. Thrift.*

ROUGH AND READY (Reissue) **F2.4704**

Fox Film Corp. Jan *w1925*. Si; b&w. 35mm. 5 reels.

Note: A William Farnum western originally released by Fox in 6 reels (24 Mar 1918; c31 Mar 1918; LP12250).

ROUGH AND READY (Blue Streak Western) **F2.4705**

Universal Pictures. 9 Jan **1927** [c2 Oct 1926; LP23183]. Si; b&w. 35mm. 5 reels, 4,409 ft.

Pres by Carl Laemmle. *Dir* Albert Rogell. *Cont* William Lester. *Story* Gardner Bradford. *Photog* William Nobles. *Art Dir* David S. Garber.

Cast: Jack Hoxie *(Ned Raleigh)*, Ena Gregory *(Beth Stone)*, Jack Pratt *("Parson" Smith)*, William A. Steele *(Morris Manning)*, Monte Montague *("Rawhide" Barton)*, Clark Comstock *(John Stone)*, Marin Sais *(Martha Bowman)*, Bert De Marc *(Bill Blake)*, Scout *(himself, a horse)*.

Western melodrama. Ned Raleigh, a cowboy on the Stone Ranch, is laughed at by his pal Rawhide Barton for emulating his chivalrous namesake. Manning, an eastern capitalist, agrees to make Stone a loan to pay off his mortgage if he surrenders 200 head of cattle as security; Manning, after he discovers oil on the property, conspires with Blake, Stone's foreman, to hide the stock, and thus secure the land for himself. Beth, who is in love with Ned, consents to marry Manning to save her father from ruin, but Ned, suspicious of the proceedings, saves Beth from an accident in which Manning is killed; then, with the help of his horse, Scout, Ned brings the rustlers to justice and wins the heart of Beth. *Ranchers. Cowboys. Rustlers. Mortgages. Horses.*

ROUGH AND READY **F2.4706**

William M. Pizor Productions. 14 Mar **1930** [New York State license]. Si; b&w. 35mm. 5 reels, 4,500 ft.

Cast: Montana Bill.

Western melodrama(?). No information about the nature of this film has been found.

THE ROUGH DIAMOND **F2.4707**

Fox Film Corp. 30 Oct **1921** [c30 Oct 1921; LP17235]. Si; b&w. 35mm. 5 reels, 4,458 ft.

Pres by William Fox. *Dir-Scen* Edward Sedgwick. *Titl* Ralph Spence. *Story* Tom Mix, Edward Sedgwick. *Photog* Ben Kline. *Film Ed* Ralph Spence.

Cast: Tom Mix *(Hank Sherman)*, Eva Novak *(Gloria Gómez)*, Hector Sarno *(Emeliano Gómez)*, Edwin J. Brady *(Pedro Sachet)*, Sid Jordan *(Manuel García)*.

Western comedy-melodrama. When he loses his job as ranch hand for singing during work hours, Hank Sherman takes his pet mule and joins a circus. There he meets Gloria Gómez, with whom he had indulged in a mild flirtation, and emerges victorious from a tangle with circus employees. Gloria's father, the ex-president of the Republic of Bargravia, admires Hank's valor and selects him as leader of a counter-revolutionary movement in his country. Gloria forces her fiancé, Pedro, whom she dislikes, to accept Hank, but Pedro becomes jealous and has his rival kidnaped. Hank succeeds in escaping and embarking for Bargravia; there, Pedro attempts to foil Hank's plans but is defeated. After desperate fighting, Gloria's father regains his post and she weds Hank. *Imaginary republics. Circus. Revolutions. Kidnaping. Mules.*

ROUGH GOING **F2.4708**

Independent Pictures. 16 Aug **1925.** Si; b&w. 35mm. 5 reels, 4,800 ft.

Dir Wally Van. *Story* Ruth Stonehouse. *Photog* Allen Siegler.

Cast: Franklyn Farnum *(himself)*, Marion Harlan *(Patricia Burke)*, Vester Pegg *(Jim Benton)*, Dora Baker *(Mother Burke)*, Alys Murrell *("La Rosita")*, Buck Black *(Mickey)*.

Western melodrama(?). No information about the nature of this film has been found.

ROUGH HOUSE ROSIE **F2.4709**

Paramount Famous Lasky Corp. 14 May **1927** [c14 May 1927; LP23959]. Si; b&w. 35mm. 6 reels, 5,952 ft.

Pres by Adolph Zukor, Jesse L. Lasky. *Assoc Prod* B. P. Schulberg. *Dir* Frank Strayer. *Screenplay* Louise Long, Ethel Doherty. *Titl* George Marion, Jr. *Adapt* Max Marcin. *Photog* James Murray, Hal Rosson. *Asst Dir* George Crook.

Cast: Clara Bow *(Rosie O'Reilly)*, Reed Howes *(Joe Hennessey)*, Arthur Housman *(Kid Farrell)*, Doris Hill *(Ruth)*, Douglas Gilmore *(Arthur Russell)*, John Miljan *(Lew McKay)*, Henry Kolker *(W. S. Davids)*.

Society comedy. Source: Nunnally Johnson, "Rough House Rosie," in *Saturday Evening Post* (198:16–17, 12 Jun 1926). On a beach outing, Rosie O'Reilly, her friend Ruth, and her sweetheart, boxer Joe Hennessey, meet Kid Farrell, Joe's trainer; and a fortune-teller predicts Rosie's fame as a dancer. Rosie creates an act and gets it booked for a cabaret. In a misunderstanding over a diamond pin given her by Lew McKay, a cafe habitué, Rosie is jailed for stealing, but Arthur Russell identifies the jewel and rescues her. Impressed by Arthur's wealth and social position, Rosie soon forgets Joe, who then begins to study etiquette, but to no avail. On the night of Joe's big fight, Rosie, losing interest in Arthur's party, goes to the ring, diverts the attention of Joe's opponent, and thus assures Joe's final victory. *Prizefighters. Dancers. Fortune-tellers. Wealth. Etiquette.*

THE ROUGH RIDERS **F2.4710**

Paramount Famous Lasky Corp. 15 Mar **1927** [New York premiere; released 1 Oct; c1 Oct 1927; LP24469]. Si; b&w. 35mm. 13 reels, 12,071 ft. [Release version: 10 reels, 9,443 ft.]

Pres by Adolph Zukor, Jesse L. Lasky. *Assoc Prod* B. P. Schulberg. *Dir* Victor Fleming. *Screenplay* Robert N. Lee, Keene Thompson. *Titl* George Marion, Jr. *Adapt* John F. Goodrich. *Story* Hermann Hagedorn. *Photog* James Howe.

Cast: Noah Beery *(Hell's Bells)*, Charles Farrell *(Stewart Van Brunt)*, George Bancroft *(Happy Joe)*, Charles Emmett Mack *(Bert Henley)*, Mary Astor *(Dolly)*, Frank Hopper *(Theodore Roosevelt)*, Col. Fred Lindsay *(Leonard Wood)*, Fred Kohler *(Sergeant Stanton)*.

Historical melodrama. In 1898, following the destruction of the *Maine* in Cuba, war is declared against Spain by the United States; and Theodore Roosevelt, Assistant Secretary of the Navy, along with Leonard Wood of the Army Medical Corps, are offered the eagles in the first volunteer regiments; but they decline and together assemble the Rough Riders, a motley assortment of volunteers, on the Exposition Grounds at San Antonio. Amidst the regiment are Happy Joe, who skips jail to enlist; his pursuer, a sheriff known as Hell's Bells; Bert Henley, a local boy; Van, a handsome New Yorker; and Dolly, who is the object of Bert's and Van's affections. When the regiment sees action in Cuba, the boys' intense rivalry turns into friendship; and when Bert is wounded, Van carries him back to base in San Juan, where he dies a hero. At the end of the war, Van carries the news to Dolly; later, with the inauguration of Roosevelt as President, Van and Dolly come to the reception with their two children. *War heroes. Friendship. United States—History—War of 1898. Cuba. San Antonio. Theodore Roosevelt. Leonard Wood. United States Army—Cavalry. Rough Riders.*

ROUGH RIDIN' **F2.4711**

Approved Pictures. *Dist* Weiss Brothers Artclass Pictures. 15 Jul **1924** [c1 May 1924; LP20254]. Si; b&w. 35mm. 5 reels, 4,650 ft.

Pres by Lester F. Scott, Jr. *Dir* Richard Thorpe. *Scen* Margaret M. Harris. *Story* Elizabeth Burbridge. *Photog* Ernest Haller.

Cast: Buddy Roosevelt *(Buddy Benson)*, Elsa Benham *(Mary Ross)*, Richard Thorpe *(Dick Ross)*, Joe Rickson *(Jack Wells)*, Frances Beaumont *(Rosalind Nolan)*, Arthur Detlorf *(Tubby)*, Mike Ready *(Nolan)*.

Western melodrama. When an unscrupulous foreman throws suspicion on her brother, Mary Ross is abducted by her sweetheart, Buddy Benson. Meanwhile, he confronts Wells, the foreman, who confesses to rustling and the murder of a ranch hand. With the hero's vindication, Mary consents to be his wife. *Ranch foremen. Brother-sister relationship. Rustling. Abduction. Ranch life.*

ROUGH RIDIN' RED **F2.4712**

FBO Pictures. 4 Nov **1928** [c4 Nov 1928; LP25795]. Si; b&w. 35mm. 5 reels, 4,714 ft.

Dir Louis King. *Story-Cont* Frank Howard Clark. *Titl* Helen Gregg. *Photog* Nick Musuraca. *Asst Dir* Walter Daniels.

Cast: Buzz Barton *(David [Red] Hepner)*, Frank Rice *(Hank Robbins)*, James Welch *(Pap Curtis)*, Bert Moorehouse *(Jerry Martin, the sheriff)*, Ethan Laidlaw *(Cal Rogers)*.

Western melodrama. Red Hepner, an orphan lad, comes to the rescue of Pap Curtis, the owner of a medicine show, after Pap is shot by Rogers. Sometime later, Rogers steals a payroll and shifts the blame for the theft to Pap; Red and Pap's daughter, Sally, then get the wounded Pap into a wagon and race for the state line, closely followed by the sheriff. Little Red captures Rogers and clears Pap of the charges against him; Sally and the sheriff fall in love. *Orphans. Sheriffs. Thieves. Medicine shows.*

ROUGH ROMANCE **F2.4713**

Fox Film Corp. 15 Jun **1930** [c10 May 1930; LP1334]. Sd (Movietone); b&w. 35mm. 6 reels, 4,800 ft.

Pres by William Fox. *Dir* A. F. Erickson. *Scen* Elliott Lester. *Dial* Donald Davis. *Photog* Daniel Clark. *Film Ed* Paul Weatherwax. *Songs: "The Song of the Lumberjack," "Nobody Knows," "She's Somebody's Baby"* George A. Little, John Burke. *Sd Rec* Barney Fredericks. *Asst Dir* Ewing Scott.

Cast: George O'Brien *(Billy West)*, Helen Chandler *(Marna Reynolds)*, Antonio Moreno *(Loup Latour)*, Harry Cording *(Chick Carson)*, David Hartford *(Dad Reynolds)*, Noel Francis *(Flossie)*, Eddie Borden *(Laramie)*, Roy Stewart *(Sheriff Milt Powers)*, Frank Lanning *(Pop Nichols)*.

Action melodrama. Source: Kenneth B. Clarke, "The Girl Who Wasn't Wanted" in *Munsey's Magazine* (93:472–487, Apr 1928). Against the lush backdrop of the Oregon forests, the film depicts the life and death struggle between two men—one a stalwart young lumberjack (Billy West), the other a menacing desperado (Loup Latour)—and the love-inspired bravery of a lonely woodland lass (Marna Reynolds), interspersed with songs. *Lumberjacks. Desperadoes. Dancehall girls. Courtship. Oregon.*

ROUGH SHOD **F2.4714**

Fox Film Corp. 4 Jun **1922** [c4 Jun 1922; LP19157]. Si; b&w. 35mm. 5 reels, 4,486 ft.

Pres by William Fox. *Dir* Reaves Eason. *Scen* Jack Strumwasser. *Photog* Lucien Andriot.

Cast: Charles Jones *("Steel" Brannon)*, Helen Ferguson *(Betty Lawson)*, Ruth Renick *(Josephine Hamilton)*, Maurice B. Flynn *("Satan" Latimer)*, Jack Rollins *(Les Artwell)*, Charles Le Moyne *("Denver")*.

Western melodrama. Source: Charles Alden Seltzer, *West!* (New York, 1922). "Steel" Brannon, Betty Lawson's fiancé, is the foreman on her ranch. He seeks a man who shot and killed his father and suspects "Satan" Latimer. With the help of Josephine Hamilton, a girl from the East who is visiting the ranch, he proves his suspicions and punishes Latimer by pushing him over a cliff. *Ranch foremen. Revenge.*

A ROUGH SHOD FIGHTER **F2.4715**

American Film Co. *Dist* Film Classic Exchange. 18 Feb **1927** [New York State license]. Si; b&w. 35mm. 5 reels, 4,990 ft.

Cast: William Russell, Francelia Billington.

Western melodrama(?). No information about the nature of this film has been found.

Note: May have been produced in 1917; also in distribution in 1921 through Aywon Film Corp.

ROUGH STUFF **F2.4716**

Dell Henderson Productions. *Dist* Rayart Pictures. 16 Sep **1925** [New York State license]. Si; b&w. 35mm. 5 reels, 4,764 ft.

Dir Dell Henderson.

Cast: George Larkin.

Melodrama(?). Source: A. E. Ullman, "Rough Stuff," in *Short Stories Magazine.* No information about the nature of this film has been found.

ROUGH WATERS **F2.4717**

Warner Brothers Pictures. 7 Jun **1930** [c18 May 1930; LP1310]. Sd (Vitaphone); b&w. 35mm. 6 reels, 4,280 ft.

Dir John Daumery. *Story-Adapt* James A. Starr. *Photog* William Rees. *Rec Engr* Robert B. Lee.

Cast: Rin-Tin-Tin *(Rinty)*, Lane Chandler *(Cal Morton)*, Jobyna Ralston *(Mary)*, Edmund Breese *(Captain Thomas)*, Walter Miller *(Morris)*, William Irving *(Bill)*, George Rigon *(Fred)*, Richard Alexander *(Little)*, Skeets Noyes *(Davis)*.

Adventure melodrama. Captain Thomas, a retired sea captain, lives with his daughter, Mary, in an abandoned seacoast town on the Pacific Palisades, confined to a wheelchair. Their only visitors are Cal Morton, a motorcycle patrolman who loves Mary, and his dog, Rinty. Meanwhile, Morris and two fellow gangsters, Little and Davis, rob a payroll car; and posing as government agents, they force their way into the captain's house.

Rinty brings the daily paper to the captain with news of the robbery and murder, and Mary succeeds in dispatching a note to Cal for help. Mail agents Bill and Fred are overtaken by the bandits, and Morris superficially wounds Rinty and Cal on the beach; but Cal and Rinty prevent the fugitives from escaping in a boat, and with Bill's help they are handcuffed. *Sea captains. Invalids. Police. Bandits. Filial relations. Robbery. Pacific Palisades. Dogs.*

THE ROUGHNECK **F2.4718**

Fox Film Corp. 30 Nov **1924** [c30 Nov 1924; LP20928]. Si; b&w. 35mm. 8 reels, 7,619 ft.

Pres by William Fox. *Dir* Jack Conway. *Scen* Charles Kenyon. *Photog* George Schneiderman.

Cast: George O'Brien *(Jerry Delaney)*, Billie Dove *(Felicity Arden)*, Harry T. Morey *(Mad McCara)*, Cleo Madison *(Anne Delaney)*, Charles A. Sellon *(Sam Melden)*, Anne Cornwall *(Zelle)*, Harvey Clark *(fight manager)*, Maryon Aye *(Marrat's girl)*, Edna Eichor *(Zamina)*, Buddy Smith *(Jerry Delaney, at age 3)*.

Adventure melodrama. Source: Robert William Service, *The Roughneck* (New York, 1923). Mad McCara, a brutal sea captain, falsely persuades the Widow Delaney that her son, Jerry, has been killed in an accident and lures her to a South Sea island with the promise of marriage. Years pass: McCara tires of the widow and discards her; Jerry grows to manhood, making his living as a boxer. During a bout at a waterfront athletic club he knocks out an opponent, then, thinking him dead, stows away on a liner bound for the Pacific Islands. On the boat, he meets Felicity Arden, a landscape painter with whom he falls in love without declaring himself for fear of involving her in his disgrace. To avoid repatriation, he jumps ship at the island of Taohing, narrowly being saved from a killer shark by a native girl. On the island, he is reunited with his mother, who is living among the natives, and he saves Felicity from the vile advances of McCara, whom he kills in a savage fight. Jerry returns to San Francisco, intending to give himself up for the death of the fighter, only to discover that the man has recovered from the blows. With the Widow Delaney's consent, Jerry and Felicity are married. *Sea captains. Widows. Boxers. Artists. Stowaways. Filial relations. San Francisco—Barbary Coast. South Sea Islands.*

ROULETTE *see* **WHEEL OF CHANCE**

ROULETTE **F2.4719**

Aetna Pictures. *Dist* Selznick Distributing Corp. 19 Jan **1924** [c20 Jan 1924; LP20002]. Si; b&w. 35mm. 5 reels, 4,850 ft.

Dir S. E. V. Taylor. *Scen-Adapt* Gerald C. Duffy. *Adapt* Lewis Allen Browne. *Story* William Briggs MacHarg.

Cast: Edith Roberts *(Lois Carrington)*, Norman Trevor *(John Tralee)*, Maurice Costello *(Ben Corcoran)*, Mary Carr *(Mrs. Harris)*, Walter Booth *(Peter Marineaux)*, Effie Shannon *(Mrs. Marineaux)*, Montagu Love *(Dan Carrington)*, Henry Hull *(Jimmy Moore)*, Flora Finch *(Mrs. Smith-Jones)*, Jack Raymond *(Hastings)*, Diana Allen *(Mrs. Hastings)*, Dagmar Godowsky *(Rita)*.

Drama. Lois Carrington becomes the ward of gambler John Tralee when her father drops dead during a card game with Tralee. Tralee educates Lois and gives her a home of her own, but he uses her as a decoy in his gambling joint, where she meets Peter Marineaux. When Peter suspects that Lois helped Tralee to cheat him, she offers herself in payment. Tralee objects, but the two men play with both Lois and the money as stakes. Lois controls the roulette wheel to make Peter the winner, and they are married. *Guardians. Gambling.*

ROUNDING UP THE LAW **F2.4720**

Charles R. Seeling Productions. *Dist* Aywon Film Corp. 15 Apr **1922.** Si; b&w. 35mm. 5 reels, 4,500 ft.

Pres by Nathan Hirsh. *Dir* Charles R. Seeling. *Scen* W. H. Allen. *Story* John F. Natteford. *Film Ed* George Martin.

Cast: Big Boy Williams *(Larry Connell)*, Russell Gordon *("Branch" Doughty)*, Chet Ryan *("Bull" Weyman)*, Patricia Palmer *(Doris Hyland)*, William McCall *(Judge Hyland)*.

Western melodrama. Sheriff Bull Weyman and his pal Branch Doughty run their bordertown as they please until cowboy Larry Connell arrives and wins the sheriff's ranch at draw poker. Though Weyman uses his influence with weak Judge Hyland to have Larry declared bankrupt, the hero is determined to fight foul with fair because of his love for Hyland's daughter, Doris. The sale of his cattle is too much for Larry, however. He holds up Doughty, is arrested, and escapes—intending to blow up the sheriff's office. The villains trap Doris in the office, but Larry rescues her just before the explosion. *Sheriffs. Cowboys. Judges. Bankruptcy. Gambling.*

THE ROWDY **F2.4721**

Universal Film Manufacturing Co. 19 Sep **1921** [c26 Aug 1921; LP16897]. Si; b&w. 35mm. 5 reels, 4,974 ft.

Dir David Kirkland. *Scen? (see note)* Doris Schroeder, Jack Cunningham. *Photog* Earl Ellis.

Cast: Rex Roselli *(Capt. Dan Purcell)*, Anna Hernandez *(Mrs. Purcell)*, Gladys Walton *(Kit Purcell)*, C. B. Murphy *(Pete Curry)*, Jack Mower *(Burt Kincaid)*, Frances Hatton *(Mrs. Curry)*, Bert Roach *(Howard Morse)*, Alida B. Jones *(Beatrice Hampton)*, Countess De Cella *(Clarissa Hampton)*.

Melodrama. Source: Hamilton Thompson, "The Ark Angel," in *Saturday Evening Post.* Captain Purcell, a retired New England skipper, finds Kit as a baby in a storm and adopts the child, who grows up to be an adventurous youngster of the docks. One evening, years later, she boards a fishing boat to break up a poker game and extricate the husband of a weeping woman. There she is taken prisoner by Capt. Burt Kincaid, who tries to force his attentions on her, but when she proves her courage he admires and comes to love her. When it is discovered that she is the daughter of the Hamptons, a wealthy family, Kit becomes a woman of fashion but longs for her former life and Captain Burt. It develops, however, that she is not a member of the Hampton family but only a daughter of their former maid, and she joyfully returns to Burt. *Sea captains. Waifs. Parentage. Seafaring life. Docks. Childhood. New England.*

Note: Several sources credit Cunningham with scenario; Universal records show Schroeder.

THE ROYAL AMERICAN **F2.4722**

Harry J. Brown Productions. *Dist* Rayart Pictures. Jul **1927.** Si; b&w. 35mm. 5 reels, 4,800-5,289 ft.

Dir Harry J. Brown. *Scen* George W. Pyper. *Photog* Ross Fisher.

Cast: Reed Howes *(Jack Beaton)*, Nita Martan *(Gail Morton)*, Bill Franey *(Mike)*, David Kirby *(Pat)*, J. P. McGowan *(Captain Burke)*, Hal Salter *(First Mate Dorgan)*, Rosa Gore *(Mother Meg)*, Martin Turner.

Adventure melodrama. "Young officer of the Coast Guard Patrol defends girl from brutal seaman. He is shanghaied and finds the ship contains ammunition and guns for a South American revolution. After desperate fight he gains control and turns the ship and crew over to his Commander." (*Motion Picture News Booking Guide,* 13:39, Oct 1927.) *Seamen. Shanghaiing. Revolutions. Mutiny. Smuggling. Ammunition. Firearms. South America. United States Coast Guard.*

THE ROYAL BOX **F2.4723**

Warner Brothers Pictures. 24 Dec **1929** [New York premiere; released 1930; c6 Oct 1930; LP1629]. Sd (Vitaphone); b&w. 35mm. 9 reels, 8,000 ft.

Dir Bryan Foy. *Screenplay* Murray Roth. *Adapt-Dial* Edmund Joseph, Arthur Hurley. *Translator* Arthur Rundt. *Photog* E. B. Du Par, Ray Foster. *Art Dir* Frank Namczy, Tom Darby. *Mus Score* Harold Levy, *Asst Dir* Phil Quinn.

Cast: Alexander Moissi *(Edmund Kean)*, Camilla Horn *(Alice Doren)*, Lew Hearn *(Salomon)*, Elsa Ersi *(Countess Toeroek)*, William F. Schoeller *(H. R. H. the Prince of Wales)*, Egon Brecher *(Count Toeroek)*, Leni Stengel *(Lady Robert)*, Carlos Zizold *(Lord Melvill)*, Greta Meyer *(Mrs. Barker)*, Siegfried Rumann *(bailiff)*.

Romantic drama. Source: Charles Coghlan, *The Royal Box* (New York opening: 20 Nov 1928). At the height of his popularity and success, Edmund Kean, the English tragedian, falls in love with Helen, Countess Toeroek, wife of the Hungarian Ambassador in London, while she is also pursued by Kean's friend and patron, the Prince of Wales. A wealthy young girl, Alice Doren, being forced into marrying Lord Melvill, becomes sentimentally interested in Kean, and rumor spreads that he has eloped with the girl. But at the ambassador's dinner Kean relates a story about how a famous actor keeps a rendezvous with a married woman during a performance, and Helen takes the hint and visits him from the royal box. Learning that the count has found him out, Kean, during his performance of *Hamlet*, with Alice as Ophelia, denounces the count from the stage in a moment of demented passion. Ten years later, a shabby and bent old man, Kean meets a young actor in Richmond Park; he does not remember the great Kean. *Actors. Nobility. Royalty. Diplomats. Hungarians. Infidelity. Courtship. Theater. England. George Prince of Wales. Edmund Kean. "Hamlet."*

THE ROYAL RIDER **F2.4724**

First National Pictures. 5 May **1929** [c10 May 1929; LP398]. Si; b&w. 35mm. 7 reels, 6,063 ft.

Pres by Charles R. Rogers. *Dir* Harry J. Brown. *Scen* Jacques Jaccard, Sylvia Bernstein Seid. *Titl* Lesley Mason. *Story* Nate Gatzert. *Photog* Ted McCord. *Film Ed* Fred Allen.

Cast: Ken Maynard *(Dick Scott)*, Olive Hasbrouck *(Ruth Elliott)*, Philippe De Lacey *(King Michael XI)*, Theodore Lorch *(prime minister)*, Joseph Burke *(king's tutor)*, Harry Semels *(Parvene)*, William Franey, Frank Rice, Bobby Dunn, Johnny Sinclair, Benny Corbett *(members of the Wild West show)*, Tarzan *(a horse)*.

Western melodrama. Dick Scott takes his Wild West show to the Balkan kingdom of Alvania where the boy king of the country commands the troupe to give a performance. The king is greatly impressed with the American cowboys and makes them his palace guard. The prime minister starts a revolution, and Dick and the Americans put it down. The boy king sanctions a romance between Scott and Ruth Elliott, the royal governess. *Royalty. Cowboys. Governesses. Prime ministers. Revolutions. Imaginary kingdoms. Wild West shows. Balkans. Horses.*

A ROYAL ROMANCE **F2.4725**

Columbia Pictures. 17 Mar **1930** [c2 Apr 1930; LP1198]. Sd (Movietone); b&w. 35mm. 8 reels, 6,359 ft.

Prod Harry Cohn. *Dir* Erle C. Kenton. *Cont-Dial* Norman Houston. *Photog* Ted Tetzlaff. *Art Dir* Harrison Wiley. *Film Ed* Gene Havlick. *Song: "Singing a Song to the Stars"* Howard Johnson, Joseph Meyer. *Song: "Black Minnie's Got the Blues"* Jack Meskill, Cyril Ray. *Ch Sd Engr* John P. Livadary. *Sd Mixing Engr* G. R. Cooper. *Asst Dir* Sam Nelson.

Cast: William Collier, Jr. *(John Hale)*, Pauline Starke *(Countess von Baden)*, Clarence Muse *(Rusty)*, Ann Brody *(Frau Muller)*, Eugenie Besserer *(mother)*, Walter P. Lewis *(Hans)*, Betty Boyd *(Mitzi)*, Ullrich Haupt *(Count von Baden)*, Bert Sprotte *(magistrate)*, Dorothy De Borba *(Gloria)*.

Comedy-drama. John Hale, a struggling American novelist who leads a precarious existence, unexpectedly inherits a small fortune from an uncle and decides to purchase the famous Baden castle in Latavia. He and his faithful Negro valet, Rusty, find the castle allegedly haunted; but in a secret chamber, John discovers its former mistress, Countess von Baden, in hiding to escape detection as the kidnaper of her child, whom the court has awarded to her divorced husband. He befriends her and helps her to escape but is himself detained by the count, who confiscates the aspiring author's entire fortune. Back in his New York boardinghouse, John slaves to produce an exciting novel, but the countess arrives with her father, an American oil king, who reimburses John's loss. John is thus happily reunited with the countess, who assures him of her love. *Novelists. Nobility. Adventuresses. Inheritance. Haunted houses. Imaginary kingdoms. New York City.*

Note: Copyright records indicate that the film was adapted from a story, "Private Property," with no mention of the author's name.

RUBBER HEELS **F2.4726**

Paramount Famous Lasky Corp. 11 Jun **1927** [c11 Jun 1927; LP24076]. Si; b&w. 35mm. 7 reels, 6,303 ft.

Pres by Adolph Zukor, Jesse L. Lasky. *Assoc Prod* William Le Baron. *Dir* Victor Heerman. *Screenplay* J. Clarkson Miller. *Scen* Ray Harris, Sam Mintz, Thomas J. Crizer. *Photog* J. Roy Hunt.

Cast: Ed Wynn *(Homer Thrush)*, Chester Conklin *(Tennyson Hawks)*, Thelma Todd *(Princess Aline)*, Robert Andrews *(Tom Raymond)*, John Harrington *(Grogan)*, Bradley Barker *(Gentleman Joe)*, Armand Cortez *(The Ray)*, Ruth Donnelly *(Fanny Pratt)*, Mario Majeroni *(Prince Zibatchefsky)*, Truly Shattuck *(Mrs. P. Belmont-Fox)*.

Farce. Tennyson Hawks is the leader of a band of thieves who, posing as private detectives, steal jewels and return them for a reward. Homer, who has a degree in amateur detection, is hired by Hawks when he realizes Homer is a sap but is fired when he demands pay. Princess Aline and her uncle arrive in New York to sell the crown jewels of their impoverished country; and with the aid of Tom Raymond, they arrange to have a reception at the home of a socialite. The crooks and Homer arrive, and he manages to retrieve the jewels each time they are stolen. Finding Homer on their trail, they leave for Canada via airplane. Homer lands on an ice floe, gets in the chest, and goes over Niagara Falls; but he recovers the jewels and captures the thieves. *Socialites. Detectives. Thieves. Gangs. Disguise. Royalty. Airplanes. Ice floes. Niagara Falls. Canada. New York City.*

RUBBER TIRES **F2.4727**

De Mille Pictures. *Dist* Producers Distributing Corp. 7 Feb **1927** [c4 Feb 1927; LP23632]. Si; b&w. 35mm. 7 reels, 6,303 ft.

Pres by John C. Flinn. *Supv* A. H. Sebastian. *Dir* Alan Hale. *Adapt* Zelda Sears, Tay Garnett. *Story* Frank Condon. *Photog* Robert Newhard.

Cast: Bessie Love *(Mary Ellen Stack)*, Erwin Connelly *(Pat Stack)*, Junior Coghlan *(Charley Stack)*, May Robson *(Mrs. Stack)*, Harrison Ford *(Bill James)*, John Patrick *(Adolph Messer)*, Clarence Burton *(Mexican)*.

Comedy. Deciding to move to California, Mary Ellen Stack sells the family household goods, buys a dilapidated car, and with her mother, father, and small brother sets out for the West, followed by her sweetheart, Bill. At an auto camp they meet Adolph Messer, a tourist who is attracted to Mary Ellen. Meanwhile, a wealthy automobile manufacturer offers a reward for a car identical to the one owned by the Stacks. Unaware that her father has traded cars with a Mexican, Mary Ellen is victimized by the dealer who wants to cash in on the reward. A wild and humorous race is climaxed by an automobile pile-up, but the Stacks collect the reward and settle down on their California farm, while Bill, having won Mary Ellen, is the happy proprietor of a gas station. *Tourists. Automobiles. Automobile camps. California. Chases.*

THE RUBE **F2.4728**

Aggressive Pictures. 2 Apr *w1925*. Si; b&w. 35mm. 5 reels.

Cast: Sammy Burns.

Comedy(?). No information about the nature of this film has been found.

RUGGED WATER **F2.4729**

Famous Players–Lasky. *Dist* Paramount Pictures. 17 Aug **1925** [c17 Aug 1925; LP21733]. Si; b&w. 35mm. 6 reels, 6,015 ft.

Pres by Adolph Zukor, Jesse L. Lasky. *Dir* Irvin Willat. *Scen* James Shelley Hamilton. *Photog* Alfred Gilks.

Cast: Lois Wilson *(Norma Bartlett)*, Wallace Beery *(Captain Bartlett)*, Warner Baxter *(Calvin Homer)*, Phyllis Haver *(Myra Fuller)*, Dot Farley *(Mrs. Fuller)*, J. P. Lockney *(Superintendent Lockney)*, James Mason *(Wally Oakes)*, Willard Cooley *(Sam Bearse)*, Walter Ackerman *(cook)*, Knute Erickson *(Jarvis)*, Thomas Delmar *(Gammon)*, Jack Byron *(Orrin Hendricks)*, Walter Rodgers *(Bloomer)*, Warren Rodgers *(Josh Phinney)*.

Drama. Source: Joseph Crosby Lincoln, *Rugged Water* (London, 1924). When the captain of the Setuckit Life Saving Station on Cape Cod retires, Calvin Homer, the second in command, expects to be promoted; but the appointment goes instead to Bartlett, a religious fanatic who has been the recipient of a good deal of favorable newspaper publicity. Calvin hands in his resignation, but Norma, Bartlett's daughter, persuades him to stay on. Calvin falls in love with Norma, and Myra Fuller, the village vamp, breaks off her engagement to him. During a big storm, a vessel in distress is sighted, but Bartlett, overcome by cowardice, refuses to send out a rescue team. Calvin takes the men out and effects the rescue. Bartlett is discharged, and Calvin is appointed to replace him. Driven insane by his experiences, Bartlett ventures out in a small boat in rough water, and Calvin rescues him. The old man dies from exposure, and Norma, having realized that Calvin was not responsible for her father's disgrace, seeks refuge in his strong arms. *Vamps. Fanatics. Cowardice. Lifesaving service. Seafaring life. Cape Cod. Storms.*

RUGGLES OF RED GAP **F2.4730**

Famous Players–Lasky. *Dist* Paramount Pictures. 9 Sep **1923** [New York premiere; released 7 Oct; c12 Sep 1923; LP19404]. Si; b&w. 35mm. 8 reels, 7,590 ft.

Pres by Jesse L. Lasky. *Dir* James Cruze. *Scen* Walter Woods, Anthony Coldeway. *Photog* Karl Brown.

Cast: Edward Horton *(Ruggles)*, Ernest Torrence *(Cousin Egbert Floud)*, Lois Wilson *(Kate Kenner)*, Fritzi Ridgeway *(Emily Judson)*, Charles Ogle *(Jeff Tuttle)*, Louise Dresser *(Mrs. Effie Floud)*, Anna Lehr *(Mrs. Belknap-Jackson)*, William Austin *(Mr. Belknap-Jackson)*, Lillian Leighton *(Ma Pettingill)*, Thomas Holding *(Earl of Brinstead)*, Frank Elliott *(Honorable George)*, Kalla Pasha *(Herr Schwitz)*, Sidney Bracey *(Sam Henshaw)*, Milt Brown *(Senator Pettingill)*, Guy Oliver *(Judge Ballard)*, Mister Barker *(himself, a dog)*.

Western comedy. Source: Harry Leon Wilson, *Ruggles of Red Gap* (New York opening: 25 Dec 1915). Newly rich, uncouth Cousin Egbert Floud wins Ruggles, the valet of a British gentleman, in a poker game during a sojourn in Europe with his wife, Effie, and, to his family's chagrin, introduces Ruggles to Red Gap as a colonel. The people of Red Gap treat "Colonel" Ruggles as an honored guest. Ruggles' former employer visits them and falls in love with Kate Kenner, from the other side of the tracks. The chap's brother is summoned to break up the match: he does so by marrying Kate. Meanwhile Ruggles has opened a successful restaurant and married Emily Judson, charming protegée of Kate Kenner. *Valets. Nouveaux riches. English. Poker. Restaurants. Dogs.*

THE RULING PASSION **F2.4731**

Distinctive Productions. *Dist* United Artists. 22 Jan **1922** [New York premiere; released 19 Feb; c13 Feb 1922; LP17554]. Si; b&w. 35mm. 7 reels, 7,000 ft.

Dir Harmon Weight. *Scen* Forrest Halsey. *Photog* Harry A. Fischbeck. *Art Dir* Clark Robinson.

Cast: George Arliss *(James Alden)*, Doris Kenyon *(Angie Alden)*, Edward Burns *("Bill" Merrick)*, Ida Darling *(Mrs. Alden)*, J. W. Johnston *(Peterson)*, Ernest Hilliard *(Carter Andrews)*, Harold Waldridge *("Al")*, Brian Darley *(Dr. Stillings)*.

Comedy-drama. Source: Earl Derr Biggers, "The Ruling Passion," in *Saturday Evening Post* (1922). James Alden—machinist, designer, inventor, and multimillionaire who has given the world the "Alden" automobile engine—is ordered by his doctor to retire. Unable to remain idle on his country estate, Alden goes into partnership with young Merrick, and on the sly he works in a garage they open on a new state highway. Peterson, an unscrupulous business rival, loses trade because of his business methods; Alden and Merrick, on the other hand, attract customers by courtesy and consideration. Angie, Alden's daughter, discovers her father's subterfuge; but Merrick, whom Alden knows as John Grant, is in love with Angie. Her father gives his consent to their marriage and is revived by his "rest cure." *Millionaires. Inventors. Mechanics. Business management. Retirement. Garages.*

THE RUM RUNNERS **F2.4732**

C. B. Hurtt. *Dist* Aywon Film Corp. Jun **1923.** Si; b&w. 35mm. 5 reels, 4,500 ft.

Cast: Leo Maloney.

Western melodrama. "Deals with the troubles of the Mexican border patrol in suppressing the shipment of liquor across the border. Hero brings the lawbreakers to justice and wins the love of a Mexican heiress." (*Motion Picture News Booking Guide*, 5:45, Oct 1923.) *Heiresses. Rumrunners. Border patrol. Mexican border.*

THE RUNAWAY **F2.4733**

Famous Players–Lasky. *Dist* Paramount Pictures. 5 Apr **1926** [c6 Apr 1926; LP22576]. Si; b&w. 35mm. 7 reels, 6,218 ft.

Pres by Adolph Zukor, Jesse L. Lasky. *Dir* William C. De Mille. *Adapt* Albert Shelby Le Vino. *Photog* Charles Boyle.

Cast: Clara Bow *(Cynthia Meade)*, Warner Baxter *(Wade Murrell)*, William Powell *(Jack Harrison)*, George Bancroft *(Lesher Skidmore)*, Edythe Chapman *(Wade's mother)*.

Melodrama. Source: Charles Neville Buck, *The Flight to the Hills* (Garden City, New York, 1926). Cynthia, an ambitious young film actress who seeks advancement through Jack Harrison, flees the movie location in Tennessee when Jack is shot by an accidental pistol discharge, knowing she will be unable to prove her innocence of the act. Wade Murrell, a Kentucky mountaineer, finds her lying in the road and agrees to help her across the state border into Kentucky; she accepts his protection, and he takes her to his home. Lesher Skidmore, leader of a clan opposed to the Murrells, promotes strife against Murrell by announcing the arrival of a "painted woman," but Wade protects her against his enemies. Just as Cynthia, sensing Wade's growing love, decides to leave, Harrison arrives, becomes friends with Wade, and saves his life in a feuding clash. Jack asks the girl to return and marry him; Wade accedes; but at the last minute Cynthia decides in favor of Wade. *Actors. Mountaineers. Motion pictures. Feuds. Courtship. Tennessee. Kentucky.*

THE RUNAWAY BRIDE **F2.4734**

RKO Productions. 4 May **1930** [c4 May 1930; LP1319]. Sd (Photophone); b&w. 35mm. 7 reels, 6,234 ft.

Supv William Sistrom. *Dir* Donald Crisp. *Adapt-Dial* Jane Murfin. *Photog* Leo Tover. *Film Ed* Archie Marshek. *Rec Engr* George Ellis. *Asst Dir* James Anderson.

Cast: Mary Astor *(Mary Gray)*, Lloyd Hughes *(Blaine)*, David Newell *(Dick Mercer)*, Natalie Moorhead *(Clara)*, Maurice Black *("Red" Dugan)*, Paul Hurst *(Daly)*, Edgar Norton *(Williams)*, Francis McDonald *(Barney)*, Harry Tenbrook *(Whitey)*, Phil Brady *(Shorty)*, Theodore Lorch *(Dr. Kent)*.

Melodrama. Source: Lolita Ann Westman and H. H. Van Loan, *Cooking Her Goose* (c1928). Mary Gray and Dick Mercer, who have eloped to Atlantic City, take a hotel room previously occupied by thief "Red" Dugan, who sneaks stolen pearls into Mary's handbag; a policeman appears, and in an ensuing gunbattle both Red and the policeman are mortally wounded. Clara, a chambermaid in league with the thieves, liberates Mary for a price and forces her into reporting to Mr. Blaine as a cook. Meanwhile, her fiancé, along with Clara, is arraigned, but both are released. While Dick makes insinuations about Mary's presence in Blaine's home, Clara retrieves the pearls and Mary is abducted. Blaine rescues Mary from a fake hospital where the gang is holding her captive, and they escape just as the police appear to round up the gangsters. *Thieves. Chambermaids. Cooks. Police. Elopement. Atlantic City.*

THE RUNAWAY EXPRESS (Universal-Jewel) **F2.4735**

Universal Pictures. 10 Oct **1926** [c25 May 1926; LP22782]. Si; b&w. 35mm. 6 reels, 5,865 ft.

Pres by Carl Laemmle. *Dir* Edward Sedgwick. *Scen* Curtis Benton. *Photog* Virgil Miller.

Cast: Jack Daugherty *(Joseph Foley)*, Blanche Mehaffey *(Nora Kelly)*, Tom O'Brien *(Sandy McPherson)*, Charles K. French *(Jim Reed)*, William A. Steele *(Blackie McPherson)*, Harry Todd *(Dad Hamilton)*, Madge Hunt *(Mrs. Foley)*, Sid Taylor *(The Tramp)*.

Melodrama. Source: Frank Hamilton Spearman, "The Nerve of Foley," in *The Nerve of Foley and Other Railroad Stories* (New York, 1900). Joe Foley, charged to deliver a trainload of cattle to his employer, is forced to commandeer the engine when his engineer refuses to continue until he has observed union rest rules. Later, the superintendent offers Joe a job, which he refuses until he sees the superintendent's daughter, Nora. McPherson, the engineer, whose overtures to the girl have been repulsed, becomes jealous, fights Foley, and is beaten. Joe's mother leaves for the West when he writes that he is marrying Nora, and Joe is given the privilege of driving the express on which she is to arrive; but McPherson knocks him unconscious, and his brother, Blackie, puts sleeping powder in Joe's coffee. Nora meets Joe's mother, and they board the express, driven by McPherson. Blackie (thinking Joe is at the engine) dynamites a dam, bringing down the bridge, while McPherson is overcome by the coffee. Joe, hearing of the train's impending doom from a track inspector, rides to the locomotive, stopping it just before the bridge. *Railroad engineers. Cowboys. Railroads. Labor unions. Dams.*

RUNAWAY GIRLS **F2.4736**

Columbia Pictures. 23 Aug **1928** [c18 Oct 1928; LP25739]. Si; b&w. 35mm. 6 reels, 5,725 ft.

Prod Harry Cohn. *Dir* Mark Sandrich. *Cont* Dorothy Howell. *Titl* Morton Blumenstock. *Story* Lillie Hayward. *Photog* Harry Davis. *Art Dir* Harrison Wiley. *Film Ed* Frank Atkinson. *Asst Dir* Joseph Nadel.

Cast: Shirley Mason *(Sue Hartley)*, Arthur Rankin *(Jim Grey)*, Hedda Hopper *(Mrs. Hartley)*, Alice Lake *(Agnes Brady)*, George Irving *(John Hartley)*, Edward Earle *(Varden)*.

Melodrama. When her drunken, irresponsible parents decide to separate, Sue Hartley disgustedly leaves home and gets a job as a manicurist; she is fired the first day, but Varden, a man-about-town, gets her a position as a modiste's model. One evening, Sue is sent to an apartment on the pretext of modeling clothes for a woman customer and finds Varden there, cruelly determined to have his way with her. Sue manages to telephone her sweetheart, Jim, who rushes to the apartment, gun in hand; Varden is shot to death, and Jim is arrested by the police. It soon turns out, however, that the fatal bullet was fired by another man (the father of a girl raped and murdered by Varden), who saw Varden attack Sue from his position on the fire escape. The elder Hartleys are reunited, and Sue and Jim seem likely to follow them into wedlock. *Manicurists. Fashion models. Men-about-town. Rakes. Parenthood. Rape. Murder. Divorce.*

RUNNING WILD **F2.4737**

Paramount Famous Lasky Corp. 11 Jun **1927** [New York premiere; released 20 Aug; c20 Aug 1927; LP24326]. Si; b&w. 35mm. 7 reels, 6,200 ft.

Pres by Adolph Zukor, Jesse L. Lasky. *Dir-Story* Gregory La Cava. *Adapt* Roy Briant. *Photog* Paul Vogel.

Cast: W. C. Fields *(Elmer Finch)*, Mary Brian *(Elizabeth)*, Claud Buchanan *(Jerry Harvey)*, Marie Shotwell *(Mrs. Finch)*, Barney Raskle *(Junior)*, Frederick Burton *(Mr. Harvey)*, J. Moy Bennett *(Mr. Johnson)*,

Frankie Evans *(Amos Barker)*, Ed Roseman *(Arvo, the hypnotist)*, Tom Madden *(truckdriver)*, Rex *(himself)*.

Comedy. Elmer Finch is nervously living in fear of his own shadow, browbeaten by his wife, bothered by her offspring, and awed by his employer, Mr. Harvey. Terrorized at breakfast, and hastened off to work at the urging of his stepson's mastiff, Elmer finds a horseshoe and tosses it over his shoulder—crashing it through the plate-glass window of a local jeweler. The chase by the constabularies is on, and Finch flees into the center of a vaudeville hypnotist's act, which soon entrances him and gives him the courage of a lion. The meek former mouse of a man then goes to work but reverses 20 years of disparaging treatment: he collects an overdue account from notorious skinflint Amos Barker, browbeats the board of directors, and lands a $15,000 contract without half trying. He returns home, has a well-deserved revenge upon his in-laws, and assumes the respect due him as the head of his household. *Businessmen. Hypnotists. Police. In-laws. Family life. Inferiority complex. Superstition. Dogs.*

RUPERT OF HENTZAU **F2.4738**

Selznick Pictures. 15 Jul **1923** [c6 Jul 1923; LP19184]. Si; b&w. 35mm. 9 reels, 9,646 ft.

Pres by Lewis J. Selznick. *Supv* Myron Selznick. *Dir* Victor Heerman. *Scen* Edward J. Montagne. *Photog* Glen MacWilliams, Harry Thorpe.

Cast: Elaine Hammerstein *(Queen Flavia)*, Bert Lytell *(King of Ruritania/ Rudolph Rassendyll)*, Lew Cody *(Rupert of Hentzau)*, Claire Windsor *(Countess Helga)*, Hobart Bosworth *(Colonel Sapt)*, Bryant Washburn *(Count Fritz)*, Marjorie Daw *(Rosa Holf)*, Mitchell Lewis *(Bauer)*, Adolphe Menjou *(Count Rischenheim)*, Elmo Lincoln *(Simon, the king's forester)*, Irving Cummings *(Von Bernenstein)*, Josephine Crowell *(Mother Holf)*, Nigel De Brulier *(Herbert)*, Gertrude Astor *(Paula)*.

Melodrama. Source: Anthony Hope, *Rupert of Hentzau* (1898). Rupert of Hentzau, conspirator against the King of Ruritania who is exiled and thought to be dead, secretly returns to Ruritania. On the road he intercepts a letter from the unhappy Queen Flavia summoning her English lover, Rudolph Rassendyll, who was once able, owing to his striking resemblance to the monarch, to impersonate and rescue the king from conspirators who had vowed to kill him. Rupert kills the king and, intending to use the purloined love letter to establish himself on the throne, threatens Rudolph that he will reveal the contents of the letter unless his terms are met. Rudolph and Rupert fight a duel, and Rupert is slain. Rudolph refuses the offer of the throne and returns to England, where Queen Flavia, having abdicated, soon joins him. *Royalty. Doubles. Imaginary kingdoms. Documentation. Duels.*

Note: A sequel to *The Prisoner of Zenda*.

THE RUSE OF THE RATTLER **F2.4739**

Herald Productions. *Dist* Playgoers Pictures. 4 Dec **1921** [c6 Dec 1921; LU17301]. Si; b&w. 35mm. 5 reels.

Dir J. P. McGowan. *Story-Scen* Anthony Coldewey. *Photog* Ben Bail.

Cast: J. P. McGowan *(The Rattlesnake)*, Lillian Rich *(Helen Sanderson)*, Jean Perry *(Bud Sanderson)*, Gordon McGregor *(Henry Morgan)*, Stanley Fritz *("Squint" Smiley)*, Dorothea Wolbert *(Mrs. Bludgeon)*.

Western melodrama. When Bud Sanderson is arrested for stealing cattle, Henry Morgan advances the money to defend him, in return for securing an option on the Sanderson ranch. Morgan hires "The Rattler" to evict the Sandersons from their ranch, but when he meets Helen Sanderson and discovers the injustice of Morgan's demands, he refuses to carry out his orders. Helen, suspecting Morgan of crooked dealing, follows Bud, who has escaped from jail, to a desperadoes' hangout. The Rattler holds up the gang and forcibly carries Bud off to jail, where he will be safe. Misunderstanding The Rattler's motives, Helen sells the ranch to Morgan, who delivers false money to Helen. The Rattler pursues, and both are caught in a train wreck. Morgan, mortally wounded, clears Bud, and The Rattler, though injured, is urged to recovery by Helen's love. *Ranchers. Swindlers. Gangs. Courtship. Train wrecks.*

THE RUSH HOUR **F2.4740**

De Mille Pictures. *Dist* Pathé Exchange. 12 Dec **1927** [c18 Nov 1927; LP24680]. Si; b&w. 35mm. 6 reels, 5,880 ft.

Pres by John C. Flinn. *Supv* F. McGrew Willis. *Dir* E. Mason Hopper. *Scen* Fred Stanley. *Titl* Lesley Mason. *Adapt* Zelda Sears. *Photog* Dewey Wrigley. *Art Dir* Charles Cadwallader. *Film Ed* Donn Hayes. *Asst Dir* C. C. Coleman.

Cast: Marie Prevost *(Margie Dolan)*, Harrison Ford *(Dan Morley)*, Seena Owen *(Yvonne Dorée)*, David Butler *(William Finch)*, Ward Crane *(Dunrock)*.

Comedy-drama. Source: Frederic Hatton and Fanny Hatton, "The Azure Shore," in *Harper's Bazaar* (Mar 1923). Margie Dolan, a ticket agent in a steamship office, dreams of endless pleasure and adventures abroad, while her sweetheart, Dan Morley, a drugstore owner, is devoted to his business and his eventual marriage to Margie. When the horrors of commuting become unendurable, Margie suggests they take a honeymoon trip to Niagara Falls, but he is shocked at her extravagance; as she boards an ocean liner on a business errand, Margie decides to stowaway, and when discovered she is put to work in the linen room. Dunrock and Yvonne, an unscrupulous pair who plan to relieve Finch, an oil millionaire, of his fortune, hire Margie as a companion to Finch. On the Riviera, Yvonne becomes jealous of Dunrock's attentions to Margie, provoking a riot that culminates in the arrival of Dan, who promises the terrified Margie a fine honeymoon. *Ticket agents. Stowaways. Swindlers. Travel agencies. Drugstores. Courtship. Ocean liners. Riviera.*

RUSSIA THROUGH THE SHADOWS **F2.4741**

Allan S. Broms. *Dist* Friends of Soviet Russia. 7 Dec **1922** [New York State license application]. Si; b&w. 35mm. 7 reels.

Documentary(?). No information about the specific nature of this film has been found. *Russia.*

Note: Country of origin not determined. Also licensed in New York State (1 Sep 1922) as 3 reels.

THE RUSSIAN REVOLUTION **F2.4742**

Dist Collwyn Pictures. 13 Aug **1927** [New York State license]. Si; b&w. 35mm. 6 reels.

Historical documentary. A compilation made from early films (probably newsreels) of events leading up to, during, and after the Russian Revolution of 1917. Includes scenes of Lenin, Trotsky, Kerensky, battles, riots, mass meetings, and destruction. *Russia—History—1917–21 Revolution. Union of Soviet Socialist Republics. Nikolai Lenin. Leon Trotsky. Aleksandr Feodorovich Kerensky.*

THE RUSTLE OF SILK **F2.4743**

Famous Players–Lasky. *Dist* Paramount Pictures. 13 May **1923** [c25 Apr 1923; LP18924]. Si; b&w. 35mm. 7 reels, 6,947 ft.

Pres by Adolph Zukor. *Dir* Herbert Brenon. *Scen* Sada Cowan, Ouida Bergère. *Photog* George R. Meyer. *Adtl Photog* James Van Trees.

Cast: Betty Compson *(Lola De Breze)*, Conway Tearle *(Arthur Fallaray)*, Cyril Chadwick *(Paul Chalfon)*, Anna Q. Nilsson *(Lady Feo)*, Leo White *(Emil)*, Charles Stevenson *(Henry De Breze)*, Tempe Piggot *(Mrs. De Breze)*, Frederick Esmelton *(Blythe)*.

Romantic drama. Source: Cosmo Hamilton, *The Rustle of Silk* (Boston, 1922). A long-time admirer of British M. P. Arthur Fallaray, Lola De Breze takes a position as maid to Arthur's wife, Lady Feo, who prefers a gay life with newspaper owner Paul Chalfon to the political ambitions of her husband. When word comes that Fallaray has been injured in a hunting accident, Lola goes to his side and Lady Feo discovers love letters written—but never mailed—by Lola to Fallaray. On the pretense of forcing Fallaray to allow Feo to divorce him, Chalfon obtains the letters from Lady Feo and publishes them. Feo burns the original letters in anger, while Lola confesses her love to Fallaray and persuades him to continue in politics rather than ruin his career by marrying her. Fallaray becomes prime minister; Lola returns to her father and trusts to the future for her happiness. (In a reception scene there is presented a chauve souris.) *Housemaids. Politics. Chauve souris. Great Britain—Parliament. Documentation.*

THE RUSTLER'S END **F2.4744**

Dist Krelbar Pictures, Collwyn Pictures. 14 Nov **1928** [New York State license]. Si; b&w. 35mm. 5 reels.

Cast: Al Hoxie.

Western melodrama(?). No information about the nature of this film has been found.

Note: May have been produced in 1926 by Anchor Film Distributors.

RUSTLERS OF THE NIGHT **F2.4745**

Westart Pictures. 20 Jun **1921** [Brooklyn showing]. Si; b&w. 35mm.

Dir Leonard Franchon. *Writ* W. M Smith. *Photog* A. H. Vallet.

Cast: Al Hart, Jack Mower, Robert Conville.

Western melodrama. No information about the precise of this film has been found.

RUSTLERS' RANCH (Blue Streak Western) **F2.4746**
Universal Pictures. 11 Apr **1926** [c19 Feb 1926; LP22420]. Si; b&w. 35mm. 5 reels, 5,230 ft.

Dir Clifford S. Smith. *Scen* Harrison Jacobs, E. Richard Schayer. *Story* W. C. Tuttle. *Photog* Eddie Linden.

Cast: Art Acord *(Lee Crush)*, Olive Hasbrouck *(Lois Shawn)*, Duke R. Lee *(Boggs)*, George Chesebro *(Bud Harvey)*, Edith Yorke *(Mary Shawn)*, Matty Kemp *(Clem Allen)*, Stanton Heck *(Bull Dozier)*, Lillian Worth *(Tessie)*, Ned Bassett *(Sheriff Collins)*.

Western melodrama. Lee Crush, an out-of-work cowhand, gets into a fight with Bull Dozier and knocks him through a railing. Thinking he has killed the man, Lee takes to his heels and finds work on the Shawn ranch. Lee prevents Clem Allen from swindling the Widow Shawn and falls in love with her daughter, Mary. Clem is arrested, and Lee learns from the sheriff that Bull Dozier survived the fall. Lee and Mary are wed. *Cowboys. Sheriffs. Widows. Swindlers. Ranchers.*

RUSTLING FOR CUPID **F2.4747**
Fox Film Corp. 11 Apr **1926** [c4 Apr 1926; LP22673]. Si; b&w. 35mm. 5 reels, 4,835 ft.

Pres by William Fox. *Dir* Irving Cummings. *Scen* L. G. Rigby. *Photog* Abe Fried.

Cast: George O'Brien *(Bradley Blatchford)*, Anita Stewart *(Sybil Hamilton)*, Russell Simpson *(Hank Blatchford)*, Edith Yorke *(Mrs. Blatchford)*, Herbert Prior *(Tom Martin)*, Frank McGlynn, Jr. *(Dave Martin)*, Sid Jordan *(Jack Mason)*.

Western melodrama. Source: Peter Bernard Kyne, "Rustling for Cupid," in *Heart's International–Cosmopolitan* (80:68–71, Feb 1926). Bradley Blatchford, returning to his father's ranch from college, meets Sybil Hamilton, who is coming to the ranch town as a schoolteacher. Later, Bradley's father is suspected of rustling cattle, but he denies the charge. As the romance develops between Bradley and Sybil, Bradley comes upon a rustler at work and is about to shoot when he discovers his own father, who claims he is victim of a hereditary taint that he cannot subdue. Some friends, who observe the incident, rustle some of Blatchford's cattle, mark it with Sybil's brand, and accuse her of rustling and hiding some dark secret. She confesses that her brother disgraced the family, and when George learns of it, he is forgiven and is reunited with her. *Rustlers. Schoolteachers. Filial relations. Courtship. Heredity. Ranches.*

S. O. S. PERILS OF THE SEA **F2.4748**
Columbia Pictures. 1 Nov **1925** [c12 Nov 1925; LP21987]. Si; b&w with hand-col sequence. 35mm. 6 reels, 5,303 ft.

Dir James P. Hogan. *Story-Cont* Tom J. Hopkins. *Photog* George Meehan. *Hand Painting* Arnold Hansen.

Cast: Elaine Hammerstein *(Madame La Coeur/Rose La Coeur)*, Robert Ellis *(Ralph Seldon)*, William Franey *(Pete)*, Pat Harmon *(Jim Sheldon?)*, Jean O'Rourke *(Rose, in childhood)*, Frank Alexander *(cook)*, J. C. Fowler *(Andrew Carson)*.

Adventure melodrama. Madame La Coeur and her little daughter, Rose, sail for America aboard a tramp steamer not knowing that Rose's father has died and left a fortune that if not claimed within 10 years will go to charity. The boat is torpedoed, and Madame La Coeur loses her life; but Rose is saved by fishermen Ralph and Jim Seldon, who are brothers. Nine years pass. Ralph and Rose grow fond of each other, but Jim, who also loves Rose, tries to break up their friendship. Jim learns of the inheritance and plots to marry Rose. Circumstances bring the three together on the same ocean liner, where Ralph is an officer. The ship catches fire and sinks after a collision at sea. Jim drowns, and Ralph and Rose are among the few survivors. Rose claims her fortune and marries Ralph. *Brothers. Fishermen. Inheritance. Seafaring life. Ocean liners. Ship fires.*

Note: The shipwreck sequence is hand-colored.

SACKCLOTH AND SCARLET **F2.4749**
Kagor Productions. *Dist* Paramount Pictures. 22 Mar **1925** [c3 Apr 1925; LP21318]. Si; b&w. 35mm. 7 reels, 6,752 ft.

Pres by Robert Kane. *Dir* Henry King. *Scen* Tom Geraghty, Jules Furthman, Julie Herne. *Photog* Robert Kurrle, William Schurr. *Art Dir* Robert M. Haas.

Cast: Alice Terry *(Joan Freeman)*, Orville Caldwell *(Stephen Edwards)*, Dorothy Sebastian *(Polly Freeman)*, Otto Matiesen *(Etienne Fochard)*, Kathleen Kirkham *(Beatrice Selignac)*, John Miljan *(Samuel Curtis)*, Clarissa Selwynne *(Miss Curtis)*, Jack Huff *(Jack)*.

Drama. Source: George Gibbs, *Sackcloth and Scarlet* (London, 1924). Polly Freeman goes to Paradise Valley looking for adventure and finds it in Stephen Edwards, a rugged dry farmer interested in irrigation projects. Polly becomes forward with Stephen, and they spend the night together. Polly later returns home and confesses everything to her sister, Joan. Joan then cancels her own wedding to Sam Curtis and goes with Polly to Paris, where a child is born to the luckless Polly. Sam follows Joan to France and finds her in a small inn, caring for Polly's baby; Sam mistakes it for Joan's child and leaves her. Polly then deserts her child, and Joan returns to Washington, where she is the guest of the Countess Selignac. Joan there meets Stephen, who has been elected to Congress after the success of his desert reclamation projects. Joan and Stephen fall in love, but when Polly shows up, broken in health and spirit, Joan learns that Stephen is the father of Polly's child and insists that Stephen and Polly be married. Before the wedding, Polly dies, freeing Stephen and Joan to find happiness together. *Farmers. Sisters. Land reclamation. Irrigation. Illegitimacy. Paris. Washington (District of Columbia). United States Congress.*

SACRED AND PROFANE LOVE **F2.4750**
Famous Players–Lasky. *Dist* Paramount Pictures. 22 May **1921** [c22 May 1921; LP16573]. Si; b&w. 35mm. 5-6 reels, 4,964 ft.

Dir William D. Taylor. *Scen* Julia Crawford Ivers. *Photog* James Van Trees, T. D. McCord.

Cast: Elsie Ferguson *(Carlotta Peel)*, Conrad Nagel *(Emilie Diaz, a pianist)*, Thomas Holding *(Frank Ispenlove)*, Helen Dunbar *(Constance Peel)*, Winifred Greenwood *(Mary Ispenlove)*, Raymond Brathwayt *(Lord Francis Alcar)*, Clarissa Selwyn *(Mrs. Sardis)*, Howard Gaye *(Albert Vicary)*, Forrest Stanley *(Samson)*, Jane Keckley *(Rebecca)*.

Romantic drama. Source: Arnold Bennett, *Sacred and Profane Love; a Play in Three Acts* (New York, 1920). Carlotta Peel, who though sheltered from the facts of life by her Victorian aunt has acquired some knowledge from indiscriminate reading, meets Diaz, a celebrated pianist, at a concert and spends the evening with him. Later, in London, she acquires fame as a novelist and is followed to France by married publisher Frank Ispenlove, who commits suicide when she spurns him. In Paris, Carlotta finds Diaz a physical wreck from drinking absinthe and devotes herself to his regeneration. Realizing the depth of her love, he is responsive and finds happiness with her. *Novelists. Pianists. Absinthe. Alcoholism. Suicide. London. Paris.*

THE SACRED FLAME **F2.4751**
Warner Brothers Pictures. 24 Nov **1929** [c12 Nov 1929; LP848]. Sd (Vitaphone); b&w. 35mm. 7 reels, 6,051 ft. [Also si.]

Dir Archie L. Mayo. *Scen-Dial* Harvey Thew. *Titl* De Leon Anthony. *Photog* James Van Trees. *Film Ed* James Gribbon. *Song: "The Sacred Flame"* Grant Clarke, Harry Akst.

Cast: Pauline Frederick *(Mrs. Taylor)*, Conrad Nagel *(Col. Maurice Taylor)*, William Courtenay *(Major Liconda)*, Lila Lee *(Stella Elburn)*, Walter Byron *(Colin Taylor)*, Alec B. Francis *(Dr. Harvester)*, Dale Fuller *(Nurse Wayland)*.

Society melodrama. Source: William Somerset Maugham, *The Sacred Flame, a Play in Three Acts* (Garden City, New York, 1928). On the same day that Col. Maurice Taylor of the Royal Flying Corps is married to Stella Elburn, his back is injured in an airplane accident, rendering him an invalid. Three years later, after he has clung to life out of devotion to his wife, his younger brother, Colin, returns from South America and at Maurice's request takes Stella out, resulting in their gradually falling in love. When Maurice dies, Nurse Wayland accuses Colin of murdering him with an overdose of sleeping powder; but Mrs. Taylor, who realized that Stella planned to elope, confesses that she administered the fatal overdose so that her son would never know that his wife left him. *Invalids. Brothers. Motherhood. Marriage. Infidelity. Mercy killing. Murder. Airplane accidents. Great Britain—Royal Flying Corps.*

SADDLE CYCLONE **F2.4752**
Action Pictures. *Dist* Weiss Brothers Artclass Pictures. 13 Nov **1925.** Si; b&w. 35mm. 5 reels, 4,728 ft.

Dir Richard Thorpe. *Scen* Betty Burbridge. *Photog* Ray Ries.

Cast: Buffalo Bill Jr. *(Bill Demming)*, Nell Brantley *(Alice Roland)*, Will Hertford *(Joshua Lowery)*, Norbert Myles *(Frank Lowery)*, Harry Todd *(Andy Simms)*, Bob Fleming *(Regan)*, Lafe McKee *(Burns)*.

Western melodrama. "Regan and Burns intend to foreclose a mortgage on Lowery's ranch. Lowery's foreman, Bill Demming, and his assistant get into a scrap. Bill runs away and is charged with murder. He impersonates Lowery in order to get money from the latter's grandfather to pay off the mortgage, succeeds, but is compelled to marry the old man's niece, Alice. Bill is cleared of the murder charge, Lowery's ranch is saved. Bill and Alice face a happy future together." (*Motion Picture News*, 20 Mar 1926, p1308.) *Ranch foremen. Ranches. Murder. Impersonation. Mortgages.*

THE SADDLE HAWK *see* **THE RIDIN' KID FROM POWDER RIVER**

THE SADDLE HAWK **F2.4753**

Universal Pictures. 8 Mar **1925** [c5 Feb 1925; LP21104]. Si; b&w. 35mm. 6 reels, 4,419 ft.

Dir Edward Sedgwick. *Story-Scen* Edward Sedgwick, Raymond L. Schrock. *Photog* Virgil Miller.

Cast: Hoot Gibson *(Ben Johnson)*, Marion Nixon *(Rena Newhall)*, G. Raymond Nye *(Zach Marlin)*, Josie Sedgwick *(Mercedes)*, Charles French *(Jim Newhall)*, Tote Du Crow *(Vasquez)*, Fred Humes *(Draw Collins)*, William Steele *(Steve Kern)*, Frank Campeau *(Buck Brent)*.

Western melodrama. Ben Johnson, a sheepherder who hates sheep, is instructed by his employer, Vasquez, to escort beautiful Rena Newhall to her father's ranch. On the journey, Rena is abducted by Zach Marlin, who takes her to Buck Brent, an outlaw who has sworn vengeance on Jim Newhall, Rena's father, for sending him to jail years before. Ben later poses as an outlaw, joins Brent's band, and takes a hand in rustling the elder Newhall's cattle. On that raid, Ben contrives to get himself captured and convinces Rena's father both of his own good intentions and of the treachery of Marlin. Ben rejoins Brent's gang, but he is soon exposed as a fraud by Marlin. As Ben is about to be killed, Newhall rides into Brent's camp with a posse and saves him. Brent is wounded, his gang is captured, but Marlin escapes, taking Rena with him. Ben pursues them, captures Marlin, and wins Rena's love. *Sheepherders. Rustlers. Posses. Revenge.*

SADDLE JUMPERS **F2.4754**

Ben Wilson Productions. *Dist* Rayart Pictures. Mar **1927**. Si; b&w. 35mm. 5 reels, 4,482 ft.

Dir Ben Wilson. *Scen* Peggene Olcott. *Photog* Eddie Linden.

Cast: Dick Hatton.

Western melodrama. "Son of wealthy family is disowned by his father. He goes west to the home of a college buddy. He succeeds in defeating bully and his gang intent on defrauding him, and develops romance with pal's sister." (*Motion Picture News Booking Guide*, 13:39, Oct 1927.) *Gangs. Fraud. Brother-sister relationship. Disinheritance.*

THE SADDLE KING **F2.4755**

Anchor Productions. 5 Sep **1929** [New York State license]. Si; b&w. 35mm. 5 reels, 4,900 ft.

Dir Benjamin Franklin Wilson. *Story* Bennett Cohen. *Photog* Robert Cline. *Film Ed* Earl C. Turner.

Cast: Cliff (Tex) Lyons *(Rance Baine)*, Neva Gerber *(Felice Landreau)*, Al Ferguson *(Mort Landreau)*, Glen Cook *(Dr. Harvey Baine)*, Jack Casey *(Sam Winters)*.

Western melodrama. "It is a story of vengeance with the deputy sheriff hero out ... [to] get the gambler who murdered his brother. It calls for a raid into a tough town where the hero plays with the gang as a buddy to get the inside track." (*Film Daily*, 20 Oct 1929, p9.) *Sheriffs. Brothers. Gamblers. Gangs. Murder. Disguise. Revenge.*

SADDLE MATES **F2.4756**

Action Pictures. *Dist* Pathé Exchange. 5 Aug **1928** [c9 Jul 1928; LP25456]. Si; b&w. 35mm. 5 reels, 4,520 ft.

Pres by Lester F. Scott, Jr. *Dir* Richard Thorpe. *Scen* Frank L. Inghram. *Photog* Ray Ries.

Cast: Wally Wales *(John Benson)*, Hank Bell *(Tim Mannick, his pal)*, J. Gordon Russell *(Morgan Shelby, owner of the Lazy B)*, Peggy Montgomery *(Betty Shelby, Morgan's sister)*, Charles Whitaker *(Bob Grice, Shelby's top hand)*, Lafe McKee *(Grouchy Ferris, veteran of the Lazy B)*, Edward Cecil *(George Lemmer, Betty's suitor)*, Lillian Allen *(Mrs. Saunders, the widow)*.

Western melodrama. Source: Harrington Strong, "Saddle Mates," in *Western Story Magazine* (40:3–50, 12 Jan 1924). John Benson and Tim Mannick ride into Marin City in search of Morgan Shelby, a crook who cheated them out of their ranch. Shelby tries to kill them, hiring gunman Bob Grice to do the job, but he is unsuccessful. Shelby is finally exposed and driven out of town while Benson wins Shelby's sister, Betty. *Ranchers. Swindlers. Hired killers. Brother-sister relationship.*

SADIE THOMPSON **F2.4757**

Gloria Swanson Productions. *Dist* United Artists. 7 Jan **1928** [c6 Jan 1928; LP24829]. Si; b&w. 35mm. 9 reels, 8,600 ft.

Dir-Writ Raoul Walsh. *Titl* C. Gardner Sullivan. *Photog* Oliver Marsh, George Barnes, Robert Kurrle. *Art Dir* William Cameron Menzies. *Film Ed* C. Gardner Sullivan. *Asst Dir* William Tummel. *Prod Mgr* Pierre Bedard.

Cast: Gloria Swanson *(Sadie Thompson)*, Lionel Barrymore *(Alfred Atkinson)*, Raoul Walsh *(Sgt. Tim O'Hara)*, Blanche Frederici *(Mrs. Atkinson)*, Charles Lane *(Dr. McPhail)*, Florence Midgley *(Mrs. McPhail)*, James A. Marcus *(Joe Horn, The Trader)*, Sophia Artega *(Ameena)*, Will Stanton *(Quartermaster Bates)*.

Drama. Source: William Somerset Maugham, "Rain," in *The Trembling of a Leaf* (New York, c1921). John Colton and Clemence Randolph, *Rain; a Play in Three Acts* (New York, c1923). Sadie, a girl trying to hide her identity in the South Seas, meets Sergeant O'Hara, a marine, and promises to marry him. Alfred Atkinson, a tyrannical reformer, obsessed with her "immorality," makes life unpleasant for her and threatens to give her up to the police. When she reforms, he seduces her and then commits suicide. She is reunited with her lover, and they leave for Australia. *Reformers. Prostitutes. Religion. Seduction. Suicide. South Seas.*

Note: The Maugham story was originally published in *Smart Set* (Apr 1921) under the title "Miss Thompson."

SAFE GUARDED **F2.4758**

Dist Rayart Pictures. 10 Feb **1924** [New York State license]. Si; b&w. 35mm. 5 reels, 4,800 ft.

Cast: Neal Hart, Eva Novak, George Chesebro, Tommy Ryan, Fred Clark, Milton Stewart.

Melodrama(?). No information about the nature of this film has been found.

SAFETY IN NUMBERS **F2.4759**

Paramount-Publix Corp. 7 Jun **1930** [c6 Jun 1930; LP1346]. Sd (Movietone); b&w. 35mm. 10 reels, 7,074 ft.

Dir Victor Schertzinger. *Scen* Marion Dix. *Titl* George Marion, Jr. *Story* George Marion, Jr., Percy Heath. *Camera* Henry Gerrard. *Film Ed* Robert Bassler. *Songs: "My Future Just Passed," "The Pick Up," "Do You Play Madame?" "I'd Like To Be a Bee in Your Boudoir," "You Appeal to Me," "Business Girl," "Pepola"* George Marion, Jr., Richard A. Whiting. *Dance & Ensemble Dir* David Bennett. *Rec Engr* Eugene Merritt.

Cast: Charles "Buddy" Rogers *(William Butler Reynolds)*, Kathryn Crawford *(Jacqueline)*, Josephine Dunn *(Maxine)*, Carol Lombard *(Pauline)*, Geneva Mitchell *(Cleo Carewe)*, Roscoe Karns *(Bertram Shapiro)*, Francis McDonald *(Phil Kempton)*, Virginia Bruce *(Alma McGregor)*, Raoul Paoli *(Jules)*, Louise Beavers *(Messaline)*, Richard Tucker *(C. Carstairs Reynolds)*.

Musical comedy. William Butler Reynolds, a 20-year-old San Franciscan with a penchant for dancing and song-writing, is about to inherit a sizable fortune. His guardian uncle decides to send him to New York to be educated in the "ways of the world" by three lady friends—Jacqueline, Maxine, and Pauline, Follies girls, who agree not to vamp him though he falls for Jacqueline and is jealous of her admirer, Phil Kempton. Bill's inept attempt to promote a song with a producer results in the firing of all three girls; and when Jacqueline then resists his advances, he picks up Alma, a telephone operator, and becomes attentive to Cleo, a Follies vamp, but the girls save him from her wiles. Luckily, the producer accepts the song and rehires the girls; Jacqueline, realizing the sincerity of the boy's love for her, embarks for Europe with Phil; but Phil realizes the appropriateness of the match and sees to it that the lovers are united. *Showgirls. Guardians. Composers. Telephone operators. Follies. San Francisco. New York City.*

SAFETY LAST **F2.4760**

Hal Roach Studios. *Dist* Pathé Exchange. 1 Apr **1923** [c25 Jan 1923; LU18608]. Si; b&w. 35mm. 7 reels, 6,300 ft.

Pres by Hal Roach. *Dir* Fred Newmeyer, Sam Taylor. *Story* Hal Roach, Sam Taylor, Tim Whelan. *Photog* Walter Lundin. *Art Dir* Fred Guiol. *Prod Asst* C. E. Christensen, John L. Murphy.

Cast: Harold Lloyd *(The Boy)*, Mildred Davis *(The Girl)*, Bill Strother *(The Pal)*, Noah Young *(The Law)*, Westcott B. Clarke *(The Floorwalker)*, Mickey Daniels *(The Kid)*, Anna Townsend *(The Grandma)*.

Comedy. The Boy leaves for the city to seek his fortune, assuring his sweetheart that he will send for her as soon as he has made good. He gets a job as a clerk in a department store but writes home glowing accounts and sends "lavish" gifts. The Girl, thinking he has become wealthy, goes to the city to make sure he does not squander his money. The Boy is surprised to see her and attempts to win $500 for a publicity stunt so he can marry her. He asks his pal, Bill, a "human fly," to climb up the side of a tall building, offering him half of the $1,000 prize. Circumstances force The Boy to scale the 12 stories himself. He achieves this feat, in spite of terrifying obstacles, and finds his sweetheart at the top. *Salesclerks. Department stores. Stunts.*

THE SAGE HEN **F2.4761**

Edgar Lewis. *Dist* Pathé Exchange. Jan **1921** [c22 Dec 1920; LU15948]. Si; b&w. 35mm. 6 reels.

Prod-Dir Edgar Lewis. *Story* Harry Solter. *Photog* Ben Bail.

Cast: Gladys Brockwell *(The Sage Hen)*, Wallace MacDonald *(her son, as a man)*, Richard Headrick *(her son, as a boy)*, Lillian Rich *(Stella Sanson)*, Alfred Allen *(John Rudd)*, James Mason *(Craney)*, Arthur Morrison *(Grote)*, Edgar Lewis.

Western melodrama. Jane Croft is the subject of much malicious gossip in Silver Creek, Arizona, in 1880, and is called "The Sage Hen." The Home Purity League drives her out of town with her son, John. She sends him back to town on a horse when they are attacked by Indians. There he is adopted by the Rudds; and when they move away, Jane loses contact with her son for 20 years. In the meantime, she becomes housekeeper to George Sanson and a "mother" to his daughter, Stella. A gold rush brings John back as a lieutenant of cavalry. He falls in love with Stella, but Craney, a gambler, threatens to expose Jane's past unless she gives Stella to him. The father is killed, but John saves his mother and Stella from further peril. Jane confesses her past to her son and is able to find happiness after years of sorrow. *Reformers. Motherhood. Arizona. United States Army—Cavalry.*

Note: "The peculiar title of this picture is derived from the name which it was customary to give women of doubtful character back in the days when the gold fever hit one Arizona town after another" (*Motion Picture News*, 22 Jan 1921).

SAGEBRUSH GOSPEL **F2.4762**

Wild West Productions. *Dist* Arrow Film Corp. 1 Mar **1924** [c16 Jan 1924; LP19832]. Si; b&w. 35mm. 5 reels, 4,630 ft.

Dir Richard Hatton. *Story-Scen* Carl Coolidge.

Cast: Neva Gerber *(Lucy Sanderson)*, Harry von Meter *(Linyard Lawton)*, Richard Hatton *(Judd Davis)*, Nellie Franzen *(Mrs. Harper)*.

Western melodrama. An evangelist and his pretty daughter, Lucy Sanderson, come to the wild western town of Sagebrush. Finding no church and a dearth of religion, the reverend decides to stay. Dancehall proprietor Linyard Lawton is attracted to Lucy, but she admires happy-go-lucky cowpuncher Judd Davis. Judd wins Lucy by taking the dancehall from Lawton in a card game, and after several complications Lawton and his gang are put behind bars. The dancehall becomes a church on Lucy and Judd's wedding day. *Evangelists. Cowboys. Gambling. Religion. Churches. Dancehalls.*

THE SAGEBRUSH LADY **F2.4763**

H. T. Henderson Productions. *Dist* Chesterfield Motion Picture Corp. 1 Oct **1925**. Si; b&w. 35mm. 5 reels.

Dir? (see note) H. B. Carpenter, Horace Davey. *Scen* Carle Cooly.

Cast: Eileen Sedgwick *(Paula Loring)*, Bernie Corbett *(Doyle's foreman)*, Jack Richardson *(Tom Doyle)*, Eddie Barry *(Harmony Hayden)*, William Steele *(Sheriff Martin)*.

Western melodrama. "Henry Hayden, Government Agent, comes in disguise to check operation of cattle-rustlers around Paula Loring's ranch. His identity is unsuspected by the natives. Tom Doyle, neighboring ranchman schemes to marry Paula. Latter saves Hayden from lynchers, when he is suspected of being a holdup man by telling them he is her fiancé. Tom Doyle's foreman is foiled by Hayden in an attempt to kidnap Paula. Having broken up the gang, Hayden remains as Paula's husband." (*Motion Picture News*, 6 Feb 1926, p702.) *Ranchers. Rustlers. Government agents. Ranch foremen. Lynching.*

Note: Sources disagree in crediting direction.

SAGEBRUSH POLITICS **F2.4764**

Art Mix Productions. *Dist* Hollywood Pictures. 15 May **1930** [New York showing]. Si with talking sequences (Phono Kinema); b&w. 35mm. 5 reels, 4,500 ft.

Dir Victor Adamson.

Cast: Art Mix, Wally Merrill, Lillian Bond, Bill Ryno, Jack Gordon, Jim Campbell, Pee Wee Holmes, Tom Forman.

Western melodrama. Drifters Tom Williams (played by Art Mix?) and Joe Morgan (played by Wally Merrill?) have a chance meeting with the sheriff's daughter (played by Lillian Bond) and learn that her brother is being held captive in Lone Hollow by Wolf, who wants to be the next sheriff. They aid the sheriff in finding the outlaw band and rescue Jim. Tom then decides to stay near the girl. *Sheriffs. Vagabonds. Brother-sister relationship. Politics. Kidnaping.*

THE SAGEBRUSH TRAIL **F2.4765**

Hugh B. Evans, Jr. *Dist* Western Pictures Exploitation Co. May **1922.** Si; b&w. 35mm. 5 reels, 4,471 ft.

Pres by Hugh B. Evans, Jr. *Dir* Robert T. Thornby. *Story-Scen* H. H. Van Loan.

Cast: Roy Stewart *(Larry Reid, Sheriff of Silvertown)*, Marjorie Daw *(Mary Gray)*, Johnny Walker *(Neil, her brother)*, Wallace Beery *(José Fagaro)*.

Western melodrama. Having forbidden the carrying of arms in Silvertown, Sheriff Larry Reid pursues Neil, a stranger whom he has found with a gun after a shooting. Larry ends his chase at the home of the pretty eastern schoolmistress, Mary Gray, notices her evasive answers to his questions, and suspects her of sheltering Neil. When Larry finally captures the fugitive and takes him to Mary's house, the sheriff learns that his prisoner is his sweetheart's brother and arrives in time to save Mary from the unwelcome advances of Mexican bandit José Fagaro, who is bested in a fight and arrested by the sheriff. *Sheriffs. Schoolteachers. Bandits. Brother-sister relationship. Firearms.*

Note: Some reviews and advertising use the working title *Ridin' Wild*, which is also the title of another film released in 1922.

SAILOR IZZY MURPHY **F2.4766**

Warner Brothers Pictures. 8 Oct **1927** [c28 Sep 1927; LP24456]. Si; b&w. 35mm. 7 reels, 6,020 ft.

Dir Henry Lehrman. *Story-Scen* E. T. Lowe, Jr. *Camera* Frank Kesson. *Asst Dir* Frank Shaw.

Cast: George Jessel *(Izzy Goldberg)*, Audrey Ferris *(Marie)*, Warner Oland *(Monsieur Jules de Gondelaurier)*, John Miljan *(Orchid Joe)*, Otto Lederer *(Jake)*, Theodore Lorch *(first mate)*, Clara Horton *(Cecile)*.

Comedy-drama. Izzy, a perfume vendor, is urged by Jake, his partner, to sell Monsieur Jules, a millionaire perfume merchant, their special formula, but the merchant is incensed to see his daughter's picture on Izzy's perfume bottles and gives him the bum's rush. Aboard Jules's palatial yacht, he receives from Orchid Joe notes threatening his life. Joe is a lunatic who hates people who destroy flowers, and he plans to kill Jules with the help of a crew of maniacs on the yacht. Izzy gets aboard by announcing himself as "Muscle-Bound Murphy," along with Jake, and they promise to help the millionaire and his daughter, Marie. When Izzy is assigned to kill Jules, he feigns great joy and induces Jake to stand in for the assassination, but they are captured by the crew. Through his cleverness, Izzy outsmarts the maniacs and attracts a rescue party, thus closing the sale and winning the love of Marie. *Millionaires. Lunatics. Partnerships. Perfume. Yachts.*

A SAILOR-MADE MAN **F2.4767**

Hal Roach Studios. *Dist* Associated Exhibitors. 25 Dec **1921** [c6 Dec 1921; LU17298]. Si; b&w. 35mm. 4 reels, ca4,000 ft.

Pres by Hal Roach. *Dir* Fred Newmeyer. *Titl* H. M. Walker. *Story* Hal Roach, Sam Taylor. *Photog* Walter Lundin.

Cast: Harold Lloyd *(The Boy)*, Mildred Davis *(The Girl)*, Noah Young *(The Rowdy Element)*, Dick Sutherland *(Maharajah of Khairpura-Bhandanna)*.

Slapstick comedy. The Boy is a rich idler and ardent suitor of The Girl, whose father advises him to make a name for himself if he wishes to become his son-in-law. After joining the Navy, he is invited by The Girl to take a cruise on her father's yacht and returns to the recruiting station to cancel his enlistment—but is too late. Stationed on a dreadnought, he reaches Khairpura-Bhandanna where he is granted shore leave and meets The Girl, who has arrived in the same port. The Girl is kidnaped by natives on the island, and after a series of futile attempts to enter the palace of the Maharajah, he daringly rescues her. Called back to duty, he proposes to The Girl, and she accepts. *Sailors. Idle rich. Royalty. Courtship. Battleships. Khairpura-Bhandanna. United States Navy.*

SAILOR'S HOLIDAY F2.4768

Pathé Exchange. 14 Sep **1929** [c24 Sep 1929; LP736]. Sd (Photophone); b&w. 35mm. 6 reels, 5,260 ft. [Also si; 5,299 ft.]

Dir Fred Newmeyer. *Scen-Dial* Joseph Franklin Poland, Ray Harris. *Story* Joseph Franklin Poland. *Photog* Arthur Miller. *Film Ed* Claude Berkeley. *Rec Engr* Ben Winkler, E. A. Holgerson. *Asst Dir* Gordon Cooper.

Cast: Alan Hale *(Adam Pike)*, Sally Eilers *(Molly Jones)*, George Cooper *(Shorty)*, Paul Hurst *(Jimmylegs)*, Mary Carr *(Mrs. Pike)*, Charles Clary *(captain)*, Jack Richardson *(captain)*, Natalie Joyce *(The Fast Worker)*, Phil Sleeman *(her secretary)*.

Comedy. Sailors Pike and Shorty are on leave when a street woman swindles them out of some money by telling them she is looking for her long-lost brother, a sailor. Later Pike and Shorty are accosted by Molly Jones, whose brother, Ethelbert, actually is a missing sailor. Deeming her an impostor, they elude her by slipping into a nearby cafe. Jimmylegs, the bosun's mate, follows, intending to arrest them because the street woman complained when Pike and Shorty reclaimed the money. There Jimmylegs loses his roll of money, and he chases Molly, suspecting her to be a thief. Molly, Pike, and Shorty end up at Ma Pike's chicken farm. Pike and Molly fall in love. Then it is revealed that Jimmylegs is Molly's long-lost brother, Ethelbert, and all ends happily. *Sailors. Swindlers. Prostitutes. Brother-sister relationship. Chickens.*

A SAILOR'S SWEETHEART F2.4769

Warner Brothers Pictures. 24 Sep **1927** [c14 Sep 1927; LP24412]. Si; b&w. 35mm. 6 reels, 5,685 ft.

Dir Lloyd Bacon. *Scen* Harvey Gates. *Story* George Godfrey. *Camera* Frank Kesson. *Asst Dir* Joe Barry.

Cast: Louise Fazenda *(Cynthia Botts)*, Clyde Cook *(Sandy MacTavish)*, Myrna Loy *(Claudette Ralston)*, William Demarest *(detective)*, John Miljan *(Mark Krisel)*, Dorothea Wolbert *(Lena Svenson)*, Tom Ricketts *(Professor Meekham)*.

Farce. Cynthia Botts, an ungainly and awkward spinster who operates a girls' school, inherits the fortune of Doolittle, the school patron, and plans a trip to Hawaii to snare a husband. On the day of her departure, she secretly marries Mark Krisel, supposedly a prominent banker, but whom she discovers to be a bigamist. In a struggle with Krisel she collides with Sandy, a little Scotch sailor, and the two fall into the ocean; they are picked up by rumrunners who are later captured by prohibition officers; though handcuffed together, they manage to escape. At Cynthia's apartment, she dresses Sandy in woman's attire when they are about to be discovered by Professor Meekham; then she introduces him as her husband when Krisel arrives to claim his wife; but Krisel is exposed as Claudette's husband, and Cynthia claims Sandy as her future husband. *Scotch. Spinsters. Revenue agents. Sailors. Rumrunners. Marriage. Bigamy. Inheritance. Female impersonation. Boarding schools.*

SAILORS' WIVES F2.4770

First National Pictures. 22 Jan **1928** [c16 Jan 1928; LP24867]. Si; b&w. 35mm. 6 reels, 5,485 ft.

Prod Henry Hobart. *Dir* Joseph E. Henabery. *Adapt-Cont* Bess Meredyth. *Titl* Dwinelle Benthall, Rufus McCosh. *Photog* Sid Hickox. *Film Ed* Leroy Stone.

Cast: Mary Astor *(Carol Trent)*, Lloyd Hughes *(Don Manning)*, Earle Foxe *(Max Slater)*, Burr McIntosh *(Dr. Bobs)*, Ruth Dwyer *(Pat Scott)*, Jack Mower *(Carey Scott)*, Olive Tell *(Careth Lindsey)*, Robert Schable *(Tom Lindsey)*, Gayne Whitman *(Warren Graves)*, Bess True *("Deuces Wild")*.

Romantic drama. Source: Warner Fabian, *Sailors' Wives* (New York, 1924). Frightened at the impending loss of her eyesight, Carol Trent leaves her fiancé, Don Manning, to have a last fling the year before she goes permanently blind. Rather than reveal her affliction, she leads him to believe that she is fickle. An attempted suicide results in a restoration of both her sight and their romance. *Sailors. Blindness. Suicide.*

ST. ELMO F2.4771

Fox Film Corp. 30 Sep **1923** [c15 Aug 1923; LP19345]. Si; b&w. 35mm. 6 reels, 5,778 ft.

Pres by William Fox. *Dir* Jerome Storm. *Scen* Jules G. Furthman. *Photog* Joe August.

Cast: John Gilbert *(St. Elmo Thornton)*, Barbara La Marr *(Agnes Hunt)*, Bessie Love *(Edna Earle)*, Warner Baxter *(Murray Hammond)*, Nigel De Brulier *(Rev. Alan Hammond)*, Lydia Knott *(Mrs. Thornton)*.

Melodrama. Source: Augusta Jane Evans, *St. Elmo* (New York, 1867). When St. Elmo Thornton finds his fiancée, Agnes, in the arms of his friend Murray Hammond, he shoots Hammond and sets out on a journey around the world, dedicated in his hatred of women. He returns home to find Edna, the blacksmith's daughter, living with his mother. Through Edna's influence Thornton is redeemed, and he marries her after he becomes a minister. *Clergymen. Misogynists. Infidelity. Redemption.*

A SAINTED DEVIL F2.4772

Famous Players–Lasky. *Dist* Paramount Pictures. 17 Nov **1924** [c15 Nov 1924; LP20778]. Si; b&w. 35mm. 9 reels, 8,633 ft.

Pres by Adolph Zukor, Jesse L. Lasky. *Dir* Joseph Henabery. *Adapt* Forrest Halsey. *Photog* Harry Fischbeck. *Art Dir* Lawrence Hitt.

Cast: Rudolph Valentino *(Don Alonzo Castro)*, Nita Naldi *(Carlotta)*, Helen D'Algy *(Julietta)*, Dagmar Godowsky *(Doña Florencia)*, Jean Del Val *(Casimiro)*, Antonio D'Algy *(Don Luis)*, George Siegmann *(El Tigre)*, Rogers Lytton *(Don Baltasar)*, Isabel West *(Doña Encarnación)*, Louise Lagrange *(Carmelita)*, Rafael Bongini *(Congo)*, Frank Montgomery *(Indian spy)*, William Betts *(priest)*, Edward Elkas *(notary)*, A. De Rosa *(jefe político)*, Ann Brody *(duenna)*, Evelyn Axzell *(Guadulupe)*, Marie Diller *(Irala)*.

Melodrama. Source: Rex Beach, "Rope's End," in *Cosmopolitan* (54: 724–736, May 1913). On the night of the wedding of Don Alonzo Castro and Julietta, El Tigre—prompted by Alonzo's former sweetheart, Carlotta—robs the Castro estate and kidnaps Julietta. Alonzo goes to her rescue, sees a woman in Julietta's bridal veil yield to El Tigre's advances, and leaves embittered against all women. Hoping to have revenge on El Tigre, Alonzo haunts a cafe frequented by the bandit and finally is rewarded with his presence. They fight, and El Tigre gets the upper hand but is killed by Don Luis his enemy. Carmelita, a dancer, reveals that Alonzo mistook Carlotta for Julietta, who is safe in a convent. *Bandits. Dancers. Kidnaping. Robbery. Revenge. Weddings. Argentina.*

SAL OF SINGAPORE F2.4773

Pathé Exchange. 4 Jan **1929** [c26 Nov 1928; LP25867]. Talking sequences, sd eff, & mus score (Photophone); b&w. 35mm. 7 reels, 6,389 ft. [Also si, 4 Nov 1928; 6,804 ft.]

Dir Howard Higgin. *Scen* Elliott Clawson. *Dial* Howard Higgin, Pierre Gendron. *Titl* Edwin Justus Mayer. *Photog* John Mescall. *Art Dir* Edward Jewell. *Film Ed* Claude Berkeley. *Mus Score* Josiah Zuro. *Song: "Singapore Sal"* Al Coppell, Billy Stone, Charles Weinberg. *Prod Mgr* R. A. Blaydon.

Cast: Phyllis Haver *(Sal)*, Alan Hale *(Captain Erickson)*, Fred Kohler *(Captain Sunday)*, Noble Johnson *(Erickson's first mate)*, Dan Wolheim *(Erickson's second mate)*, Jules Cowles *(cook)*, Pat Harmon *(Sunday's first mate)*, Harold William Hill *(baby)*.

Melodrama. Source: Dale Collins, *The Sentimentalists* (Boston, 1927). When Captain Lief Erickson finds a baby abandoned in a lifeboat on his ship, he abducts a waterfront prostitute, Singapore Sal, to care for the child; despite her outrage, Sal takes pity on the little tyke and manufactures a bottle for him out of an empty whisky bottle and the finger of a rubber glove. The mate who helped Erickson kidnap Sal becomes obsessed with her, and Erickson knocks him overboard. The baby becomes sick, and Sal and Erickson together fight for his life; his fever breaks as they reach Frisco, and Sal prepares to take the child and go ashore. She becomes suddenly ashamed of her old calling, however, and leaves the baby with Erickson, sailing from port with Captain Sunday, Erickson's arch rival; Erickson sails after them and boards Sunday's ship. He beats Sunday's crew into submission and forces Sunday to marry him to Sal, who is not unwilling. *Sea captains. Prostitutes. Foundlings. Abduction. Waterfront. Singapore. San Francisco.*

SALLY F2.4774

First National Pictures. 29 Mar **1925** [c12 Mar 1925; LP21235]. Si; b&w. 35mm. 9 reels, 8,636 ft.

Dir Alfred E. Green. *Ed Supv–Scen* June Mathis. *Photog* T. D. McCord. *Art Dir* E. J. Shulter. *Film Ed* George McGuire. *Asst Dir* Jack Boland. *Comedy Construc* Mervyn LeRoy.

Cast: Colleen Moore *(Sally)*, Lloyd Hughes *(Blair Farquar)*, Leon Errol *(Duke of Checkergovinia)*, Dan Mason *(Pops Shendorf)*, John T. Murray *(Otis Hooper)*, Eva Novak *(Rosie Lafferty)*, Ray Hallor *(Jimmy Spelvin)*, Carlo Schipa *(Sascha Commuski)*, Myrtle Stedman *(Mrs. Ten Brock)*, Capt. E. H. Calvert *(Richard Farquar)*, Louise Beaudet *(Madame Julie Du Fay)*.

Society comedy. Source: Guy Bolton and Clifford Grey, *Sally; a New Musical Play in Three Acts* (New York, 1921). Sally, an asylum waif, is adopted by Mrs. Du Fay, an old woman who teaches dancing. When the kindly teacher loses all her pupils, Sally goes to work as a dishwasher in a cafe run by Pops Shendorf. There she meets the Duke of Checkergovinia, a European nobleman fallen on hard times who makes his living as a waiter. Sally also meets Blair Farquar, a wealthy young society man to whom she is most attracted. Sally gets a chance to dance at the cafe, and she is an instant hit. A famous Russian dancer disappears, and Sally is hired to impersonate her at a ball given in the Farquar mansion. Sally dances beautifully and finds herself surrounded by adulation, but Pops, who has followed her to the ball, exposes her as a kitchen drudge. Mr. Farquar orders her from his home, and Sally returns to Mrs. Du Fay. The great Ziegfeld, however, was a guest at the Farquar party, and he signs Sally to dance in the Follies. She is soon a great star, and Blair eventually persuades her to marry him. *Dishwashers. Waiters. Nobility. Orphans. Dancers. Dance teachers. Social classes. Impersonation. Adoption. Florenz Ziegfeld.*

Note: Remade in a sound version by First National in 1929.

SALLY **F2.4775**

First National Pictures. 23 Dec **1929** [New York premiere; released 12 Jan 1930; c11 Feb 1930; LP1084]. Sd (Vitaphone); col (Technicolor). 35mm. 12 reels, 9,277 ft. [Also si.]

Dir John Francis Dillon. *Screenplay-Dial* Waldemar Young. *Photog* Dev Jennings, C. Edgar Schoenbaum. *Art Dir* Jack Stone. *Film Ed* LeRoy Stone. *Mus* Leo Forbstein. *Theme Song: "Sally"* Al Dubin, Joe Burke, Jerome Kern. *Songs: "Walking Off Those Balkan Blues," "After Business Hours," "All I Want To Do, Do, Do Is Dance," "If I'm Day-Dreaming Don't Wake Me Up Too Soon," "What Will I Do Without You?"* Al Dubin, Joe Burke. *Song: "Wild Rose"* Clifford Grey, Jerome Kern. *Song: "Look for the Silver Lining"* B. G. De Sylva, Jerome Kern. *Dance Dir* Larry Ceballos. *Cost* Edward Stevenson.

Cast: Marilyn Miller *(Sally)*, Alexander Gray *(Blair Farquar)*, Joe E. Brown *(Connie [The Grand Duke])*, T. Roy Barnes *(Otis Hooper)*, Pert Kelton *(Rosie, his girl friend)*, Ford Sterling *("Pops" Shendorff)*, Maude Turner Gordon *(Mrs. Ten Brock)*, Nora Lane *(Marcia, her daughter)*, E. J. Ratcliffe *(John Farquar, Blair's father)*, Jack Duffy *(The Old Roué)*, Albertina Rasch Ballet.

Musical romance. Source: Guy Bolton, Jerome Kern, Clifford Grey and Pelham Grenville Wodehouse, *Sally* (New York opening: 21 Dec 1920). Sally, a cafe hostess and orphan, aspires to become a dancer; she is loved by Blair Farquar, of an aristocratic family, though his father has arranged a match with Marcia Ten Brock. Forced to leave the cafe when she spills food on the suit of Otis Hooper, a booking agent, she gets a job at the Balkan Tavern, run by "Pops" Shendorff, onetime supporter of a former grand duke who now works as a waiter and is known as Connie. Encouraged to dance for the customers, she is a sensation, and when Hooper engages her to impersonate a Russian dancer who has eloped, she and Connie are lionized at Mrs. Ten Brock's garden party. When Sally learns Farquar is engaged to Marcia, however, she leaves the party in despair. Hooper finds her in a tenement and stars her in his follies; and on her opening night, she is reunited with her lover. Their marriage follows. *Cafe hostesses. Waitresses. Orphans. Dancers. Nobility. Social classes. Courtship. Impersonation. Follies.*

Note: Remake of the 1925 silent film of the same title.

SALLY IN OUR ALLEY **F2.4776**

Columbia Pictures. 3 Sep **1927** [c29 Sep 1927; LP24461]. Si; b&w. 35mm. 6 reels, 5,892 ft.

Prod Harry Cohn. *Dir* Walter Lang. *Cont* Dorothy Howell. *Story* Edward Clark. *Photog* J. O. Taylor. *Art Dir* Robert E. Lee. *Asst Dir* Bert Siebel.

Cast: Shirley Mason *(Sally Williams)*, Richard Arlen *(Jimmie Adams)*, Alec B. Francis *(Sandy Mack)*, Paul Panzer *(Tony Garibaldi)*, William H. Strauss *(Abraham Lapidowitz)*, Kathlyn Williams *(Mrs. Gordon Mansfield)*, Florence Turner *(Mrs. Williams)*, Harry Crocker *(Chester Drake)*.

Romantic comedy. Sally, a girl of the tenements, is adopted by three neighbors—Sandy Mack, Abraham Lapidowitz, and Tony Garibaldi—when her mother dies, and leads a happy home life with her foster fathers. Jimmie Adams, young plumber who loves Sally, visits the house frequently. But the group is broken up when Mrs. Mansfield, Sally's wealthy aunt, takes the girl away to her luxurious home to give her the advantages of social position and introduces her to Chester Drake, a very wealthy young man. When Sally invites her foster fathers and Jimmie to her 18th birthday party, she is embarrassed by their table manners. Mrs. Mansfield tells of Sally's interest in Adams, causing him to leave her, but Sally learns of her aunt's social snobbery and is reunited with Jimmie before he sets sail on a ship. *Orphans. Plumbers. Foster fathers. Aunts. Italians. Jews. Scotch. Social classes. Snobbery. Tenements.*

SALLY, IRENE AND MARY **F2.4777**

Metro-Goldwyn-Mayer Pictures. 27 Dec **1925** [c28 Dec 1925; LP22168]. Si; b&w. 35mm. 6 reels, 5,564 ft.

Scen-Dir Edmund Goulding. *Photog* John Arnold. *Art Dir* Cedric Gibbons, Merrill Pye. *Film Ed* Harold Young. *Asst Film Ed* Arthur Johns.

Cast: Constance Bennett *(Sally)*, Joan Crawford *(Irene)*, Sally O'Neil *(Mary)*, William Haines *(Jimmy Dugan)*, Henry Kolker *(Marcus Morton)*, Douglas Gilmore *(Nester)*, Ray Howard *(college kid)*, Kate Price *(Mrs. Dugan)*, Aggie Herring *(Mrs. O'Brien)*, Sam De Grasse *(Officer O'Dare)*, Lillian Elliott *(Mrs. O'Dare)*, Edna Mae Cooper *(Maggie)*.

Comedy-drama. Source: Edward Dowling and Cyrus Wood, *Sally, Irene and Mary* (New York opening: 4 Sep 1922). Mary, an innocent young Irish girl from the East Side of New York, becomes a chorus girl in a Broadway show, getting to know very well two of the other girls in the show: Sally, who is too wise in the ways of the world; and Irene, lost in dreams of romance. Mary also gets to know Marcus Morton, the wealthy roué who keeps Sally in a luxurious apartment; he falls in love with Mary and asks her to marry him. She at first refuses, but when Jimmy Dugan, her onetime plumber sweetheart, expresses disgust with her new life, she is prompted by anger to accept Morton's offer. Disappointed by a love affair with another millionaire, Irene impulsively marries a college youth, only to be killed shortly afterward in an automobile accident. Greatly sobered by Irene's tragic death, Mary breaks off her engagement with Morton and returns to Jimmy's arms and the simple life on Avenue B. *Chorus girls. Millionaires. Rakes. Mistresses. Plumbers. Theater. New York City—East Side.*

SALLY OF THE SAWDUST **F2.4778**

D. W. Griffith, Inc. *Dist* United Artists. 2 Aug **1925** [c8 Sep 1925; LP21804]. Si; b&w. 35mm. 10 reels, 9,500 ft.

Dir D. W. Griffith. *Adapt* Forrest Halsey. *Photog* Harry Fischbeck. *Adtl Photog* Hal Sintzenich. *Art Dir* Charles M. Kirk. *Film Ed* James Smith.

Cast: Carol Dempster *(Sally)*, W. C. Fields *(Prof. Eustace McGargle)*, Alfred Lunt *(Peyton Lennox)*, Erville Alderson *(Judge Foster)*, Effie Shannon *(Mrs. Foster)*, Charles Hammond *(Lennon, Sr.)*, Roy Applegate *(detective)*, Florence Fair *(Miss Vinton)*, Marie Shotwell *(society woman)*.

Comedy. Source: Dorothy Donnelly, *Poppy* (New York opening: 3 Sep 1923). Sally is in the care of sideshow faker Eustace McGargle, who loves her dearly but isn't above training her to dance and perform as a warm-up for his own act, which includes juggling and other feats of legerdemain. McGargle moves to Green Meadows, where a new carnival job offers the likelihood of a possible reunion with Sally's grandparents Foster, and the two hire on for the afternoon with a local baker, promising to mind his kiln in return for a stake with which to purchase a bit of respectability to take with them to the Foster home. Sally soon meets Peyton Lennox, scion of a leading social clan, and though she is favored by the wistful and daughterless Mrs. Foster, she is jailed by insidious society leverage and accused of the shell game which her mentor, McGargle, has developed into a highly sophisticated con. Eustace falls in with bootleggers but returns in time to prevent Sally's sentencing by the austere judge, who is informed that he very nearly sent his own granddaughter up the river. The Fosters also take the gregarious McGargle under their wing. *Orphans. Confidence men. Jugglers. Bootleggers. Dancers. Judges. Grandfathers. Bakers. Disinheritance. Injustice. Circus. Elephants. Dogs.*

SALLY OF THE SCANDALS **F2.4779**

FBO Pictures. 15 Jul **1928** [c13 Jun 1928; LP25355]. Si; b&w. 35mm. 7 reels, 6,059 ft.

Dir Lynn Shores. *Story-Cont* Enid Hibbard. *Titl* Randolph Bartlett, Jack Conway (of *Variety*). *Photog* Philip Tannura. *Film Ed* Archie Marshek. *Asst Dir* Ken Marr.

Cast: Bessie Love *(Sally Rand)*, Irene Lambert *(Mary)*, Allan Forrest *(Steve Sinclair)*, Margaret Quimby *(Marian Duval)*, Jimmy Phillips *(Kelly)*, Jack Raymond *(Bennie)*, Jerry Miley *(Bill Reilly)*.

Melodrama. Steve Sinclair, backer of a Broadway musical show, and Bill Reilly, a gangleader who masquerades as a businessman, are rivals for chorus girl Sally Rand. Grateful for Reilly's promise to finance an operation for Sally's crippled sister, Mary, Sally agrees to marry him after the opening of her new show. During a cast party, leading lady Marian Duval, insanely jealous of Steve's attentions to Sally, slips a diamond bracelet (a gift from Steve) into Sally's pocket, then accuses her of stealing it. Steve learns of Marian's perfidy and Reilly's true identity in time to save Sally from marrying a thief. All ends happily when Sally is made star of the show. *Chorus girls. Thieves. Theatrical backers. Frameup. Jealousy. Musical revues. New York City—Broadway.*

SALLY'S SHOULDERS **F2.4780**

FBO Pictures. 14 Oct **1928** [c10 Oct 1928; LP25699]. Si; b&w. 35mm. 7 reels, 6,279 ft.

Dir-Cont Lynn Shores. *Titl* Randolph Bartlett. *Photog* Virgil Miller. *Film Ed* Archie F. Marshek, Ann McKnight. *Asst Dir* William Daniels.

Cast: Lois Wilson *(Sally)*, George Hackathorne *(Beau)*, Huntley Gordon *(Hugh Davidson)*, Lucille Williams *(Millie)*, Edythe Chapman *(Emily)*, Ione Holmes *(Mabel)*, Charles O'Malley *(Billy)*, William Marion *(sheriff)*.

Melodrama. Source: Beatrice Burton, *Sally's Shoulders* (New York, 1927). On Sally's slender but capable shoulders fate has placed the burden of caring for her brother, Beau (a wastrel and gambler), her sister, Millie (a flip-witted flapper), and her aged aunt. The banker for whom Beau works informs Sally that the boy has been embezzling, and Sally is forced to go to work for Hugh Davidson, a gambler who advances her enough money to repay the banker. Hugh's nightclub is raided by the police, and Sally puts herself in a compromising position in order to protect Millie's reputation. Millie, however, is overcome by remorse and confesses her indiscretion, thereby taking the first, tentative steps on the road to responsibility. Impressed by Sally's spirit and enterprise, Hugh asks her to be his wife. *Bankers. Gamblers. Flappers. Wastrels. Aunts. Reputation. Embezzlement. Nightclubs.*

SALOME **F2.4781**

Nazimova Productions. *Dist* Allied Producers and Distributors. 31 Dec **1922** [New York premiere; released 15 Feb 1923; c15 Dec 1922; LP18586, LP18655]. Si; b&w. 35mm. 6 reels, 5,595 ft.

Dir Charles Bryant. *Scen* Peter M. Winters. *Photog* Charles Van Enger. *Set Dsgn* Natacha Rambova. *Mus Arr* Ulderico Marcelli. *Cost* Natacha Rambova.

Cast: Nazimova *(Salome)*, Rose Dione *(Herodias)*, Mitchell Lewis *(Herod)*, Nigel De Brulier *(Jokaanan)*, Earl Schenck *(Young Syrian)*, Arthur Jasmine *(page)*, Frederic Peters *(Naaman, the executioner)*, Louis Dumar *(Tigellinus)*.

Tragedy. Source: Oscar Wilde, *Salomé* (1894). Enraged by Jokaanan's refusal of her kiss, Salome dances for Herod in return for Jokaanan's head on a silver platter. Herod grants her request; but he is overcome with disgust at the sight of Salome kissing the head and has her killed. *Dancers. Royalty. Revenge. Judea. Salome. Herod Antipas. John the Baptist. Biblical characters.*

Note: Rambova's sets and costumes were based on designs by Aubrey Beardsley.

SALOME **F2.4782**

Malcolm Strauss Pictures. *Dist* George H. Wiley, Inc. 1 Jan **1923.** Si; b&w. 35mm. 6 reels.

Dir Malcolm Strauss.

Cast: Diana Allen *(Salome)*, Vincent Coleman *(Herod?)*, Christine Winthrop *(Herodias?)*.

Romantic drama. "Egyptian prince visits court of Herod. Herod's wife, Herodias, and his step-daughter Salome fall in love with prince. Herodias spurned by prince has him secretly thrown in dungeon next to The Wanderer. Herod asks Salome to dance for him, promising her anything she will request in return. Salome's intention is to ask for release of prince, who returns her love. Herodias threatens to kill lover if Salome does not ask for death of Wanderer who has aroused Queen's enmity. Salome, fearing for lover, obeys. Later Salome rescues prince and flees with him into desert." (*Motion Picture News Booking Guide,* 4:68, Apr 1923.) *Royalty. Egyptians. Salome. Herod Antipas. Herodias. Biblical characters.*

Note: Also reviewed and advertised as *Strauss' Salome* and *Malcolm Strauss' Salome.*

SALOME OF THE TENEMENTS **F2.4783**

Famous Players–Lasky. *Dist* Paramount Pictures. 23 Feb **1925** [c3 Mar 1925; LP21209]. Si; b&w. 35mm. 7 reels, 7,017 ft.

Pres by Adolph Zukor, Jesse L. Lasky. *Dir* Sidney Olcott. *Scen* Sonya Levien. *Photog* Al Ligouri, David W. Gobbett. *Prod Mgr* John Lynch.

Cast: Jetta Goudal *(Sonya Mendel)*, Godfrey Tearle *(John Manning)*, José Ruben *(Jakey Solomon)*, Lazar Freed *(Jacob Lipkin)*, Irma Lerna *(Gittel Stein)*, Sonia Nodell *(Mrs. Peltz)*, Elihu Tenenholtz *(Banker Ben)*, Mrs. Weintraub *(Mrs. Solomon)*, Nettie Tobias *(widow)*.

Drama. Source: Anzia Yezierska, *Salome of the Tenements* (New York, c1923). Sonya Mendel makes her way through life with a combination of good looks and a wit sharpened on the gutterstone of the East Side. As a reporter for an ethnic newspaper, she is assigned to interview philanthropist John Manning, who is attracted to her and invites her to dinner. She persuades Jakey Solomon, a former sweatshop stitcher who operates a fashionable shop on Fifth Avenue, to provide her with an attractive dress for the evening, and she borrows $1,500 from Banker Ben, a usurer, with the written promise to repay it after she has married Manning. Manning hires her as his secretary and later marries her. Knowing nothing of Sonya's dealings with Banker Ben, Manning attempts to secure an indictment against him. Ben, anticipating that Sonya will try to get back her note, slyly gives her the chance to steal it from his safe, apprehends her, and threatens her with arrest. He then proposes to Manning that he not press charges against Sonya if Manning will refrain from prosecuting him for usury. Manning instead threatens to have Ben jailed for blackmail, forces him into accepting payment on the note, and is reconciled to Sonya. *Reporters. Philanthropists. Couturiers. Secretaries. Usurers. Jews. Blackmail. Newspapers. New York City.*

SALOMY JANE **F2.4784**

Famous Players–Lasky. *Dist* Paramount Pictures. 26 Aug **1923** [c1 Aug 1923; LP19263]. Si; b&w. 35mm. 7 reels, 6,270 ft.

Pres by Jesse L. Lasky. *Dir* George Melford. *Scen* Waldemar Young. *Photog* Bert Glennon.

Cast: Jacqueline Logan *(Salomy Jane)*, George Fawcett *(Yuba Bill)*, Maurice B. Flynn *(The Man)*, William Davidson *(gambler)*, Charles Ogle *(Madison Clay)*, William Quirk *(Colonel Starbottle)*, G. Raymond Nye *(Red Pete)*, Louise Dresser *(Mrs. Pete)*, James Neill *(Larabee)*, Tom Carrigan *(Rufe Waters)*, Clarence Burton *(Baldwin)*, Barbara Brower *(Mary Ann)*, Milton Ross *(Steve Low)*.

Western melodrama. Source: Bret Harte, "Salomy Jane's Kiss." Paul Armstrong, *Salomy Jane* (New York opening: 19 Jan 1907). Vigilantes are about to hang The Stranger for holding up the overland stage when Salomy Jane kisses him and he makes his escape. Meanwhile Larabee, an old enemy of Jane's father, Madison Clay, is killed, and The Stranger is again accused. Madison Clay, thinking that Salomy shot Larabee, takes the blame, but both he and The Stranger are acquitted when the real culprit is found. Salomy marries The Stranger. *Strangers. Vigilantes. Lynching. Stagecoach robberies.*

SALT LAKE TRAIL **F2.4785**

Denver Dixon Productions. *Dist* Aywon Film Corp. 12 Apr **1926** [New York State license]. Si; b&w. 35mm. 5 reels, 4,850 ft.

Cast: George Kesterson, Dorothy Lee.

Western melodrama(?). No information about the nature of this film has been found.

SALTY SAUNDERS **F2.4786**

William Steiner Productions. Apr **1923** [c30 Mar 1923; LU18849]. Si; b&w. 35mm. 5 reels, 4,800 ft.

Dir Neal Hart. *Story* Alvin J. Neitz.

Cast: Neal Hart *(Salty Saunders)*.

Western melodrama. Sam Baxter, chief of the Texas Rangers, learns that Scarface Wheeler has been released from prison and is employed as foreman on the Flying X Ranch. Because Jud Howell, who gave evidence against Scarface, fears revenge from the ex-convict, Baxter sends Salty Saunders to shadow Scarface. Salty gets a job on the Flying X but is fired after saving Betty Hampton from certain death during a roundup. Later, Salty secretly enters the house and overhears Hampton, Betty's supposed uncle, conspire with Scarface to raid Jud Howell's cattle. Salty informs Baxter, who sends deputies after the rustlers, and has several more adventures. The posse returns with Scarface, who turns state's evidence and reveals Hampton as the murderer of Betty's father and of Salty's father. Salty and Betty are united. *Cowboys. Ranch foremen. Texas Rangers. Posses. Rustlers.*

SALUTE F2.4787

Fox Film Corp. 1 Sep **1929** [c20 Aug 1929; LP624]. Sd (Movietone); b&w. 35mm. 9 reels, 7,610 ft.

Pres by William Fox. *Dir* John Ford. *Screenplay-Dial* James K. McGuinness. *Titl* Wilbur Morse, Jr. *Story* Tristram Tupper, John Stone. *Photog* Joseph August. *Film Ed* Alex Troffey. *Sd* W. W. Lindsay. *Asst Dir* Edward O'Fearna, R. L. Hough. *Tech Adv* Schuyler E. Grey.

Cast: George O'Brien *(Cadet John Randall)*, Helen Chandler *(Nancy Wayne)*, Frank Albertson *(Midshipman Albert Edward Price)*, William Janney *(Midshipman Frank Randall)*, Clifford Dempsey *(Major General Somers, U.S.A.)*, Lumsden Hare *(Rear Admiral Randall, U.S.N.)*, Joyce Compton *(Marian Wilson)*, David Butler *(Navy coach)*, Stepin Fetchit *(Smoke Screen)*, Rex Bell *(cadet)*, John Breeden *(midshipman)*, John Wayne, Ward Bond *(football players)*.

Drama. The traditional service rivalry between West Point and Annapolis is typified by two patriarchs, Major General Somers and Rear Admiral Randall, who happen to be the grandfathers of the Randall boys: John, a cadet and ballplayer for the Army, and Paul, who is on his way to the Naval Academy. He arrives at Annapolis and falls prey to the traditional hazing and then some. Midshipman Albert Edward Price adds to his misery, subjecting him to the rigors of initiation, and Paul despondently leaves school, but his desertion is reversed by the pleadings of Helen Chandler, his sweetheart. At the pre-game dance, John pays court to Helen in order to spur his brother to a greater appreciation, and the trickery works only too well; Paul is inspired to get into the game and scores the tying touchdown. *Brothers. Grandfathers. Football. Annapolis (Maryland). United States Military Academy. United States Naval Academy.*

Note: Filmed on location at Annapolis, Maryland.

SALVAGE *see* **GIRL OVERBOARD**

SALVAGE F2.4788

Robertson-Cole Co. 5 Jun **1921** [c5 Jun 1921; LP16658]. Si; b&w. 35mm. 6 reels, 5,745 ft.

Dir Henry King. *Story* Daniel F. Whitcomb. *Photog* J. D. Jennings.

Cast: Pauline Frederick *(Bernice Ridgeway/Kate Martin)*, Ralph Lewis *(Cyrus Ridgeway)*, Milton Sills *(Fred Martin)*, Helen Stone *(Ruth Martin)*, Rose Cade *(Tessie)*, Raymond Hatton *(The Cripple)*, Hobart Kelly *(The Baby)*.

Melodrama. After her wealthy husband informs her of the death of her baby, Bernice Ridgeway leaves him and takes a tenement apartment opposite that of Kate Martin, whose husband is in prison, and becomes acquainted with Kate and her child. When Kate commits suicide, Bernice takes the child and assumes the dead woman's name; and the child's father, Fred Martin, having finished his term, discovers the deception but keeps the secret. At her husband's deathbed, Bernice learns that the child is indeed her own—lame at birth but cured by an operation. Ridgeway dies, leaving his wealth to Bernice, who comes to love Fred Martin. *Children. Cripples. Motherhood. Impersonation. Suicide.*

THE SALVATION HUNTERS F2.4789

Academy Photoplays. *Dist* United Artists. ca7 Feb **1925** [San Francisco premiere; released 15 Feb; c1 Mar 1925; LP21214]. Si; b&w. 35mm. 6 reels, 5,930 ft.

Dir-Story-Scen Josef von Sternberg. *Photog* Edward Gheller. *Prod Asst* George Ruric, Robert Chapman.

Cast: George K. Arthur *(The Boy)*, Georgia Hale *(The Girl)*, Bruce Guerin *(The Child)*, Otto Matiesen *(The Man)*, Nellie Bly Baker *(The Woman)*, Olaf Hytten *(The Brute)*, Stuart Holmes *(The Gentleman)*.

Drama. Three waifs—a boy, a girl, and a child—live aboard a steam dredge owned by a cruel dredgemaster. Unable to tolerate the waterfront conditions and the dredgemaster's foul attentions toward the girl, the three flee to the city where a white slaver attempts to make the girl a prostitute. The white slaver himself makes advances toward the girl, and the boy finds the courage to defend her. The three then go off in search of a better life together. *Waifs. Dredgemasters. White slave traffic. Poverty. Waterfront.*

SALVATION JANE F2.4790

R-C Pictures. *Dist* Film Booking Offices of America. 1 Mar **1927** [c13 Feb 1927; LP23684]. Si; b&w. 35mm. 6 reels, 5,490 ft.

Pres by Joseph P. Kennedy. *Dir* Phil Rosen. *Cont* Doris Schroeder. *Story* Maude Fulton. *Photog* Lyman Broening. *Asst Dir* Ray McCarey.

Cast: Viola Dana *(Salvation Jane)*, J. Parks Jones *(Jerry O'Day)*, Fay Holderness *(Capt. Carrie Brown)*, Erville Alderson *(Gramp)*.

Crook melodrama. Capt. Carrie Brown of the Salvation Army is troubled by Jane, a tenement girl who uses the Army as a cloak for her mischievous deeds. Through Jane's vigilance, Jerry O'Day, a crook, is prevented from robbing a woman; Jerry discovers where she lives and offers to pay her handsomely if she will help him in his "work," but she refuses. Later, she unwillingly agrees to Jerry's proposition to pay her grandfather's medical bills when the doctor threatens to send him to a charity hospital. She makes a haul by stealing from an innocent westerner; but when he tries to kill himself over the loss, Jane restores the money. After she quarrels with Jerry, he promises to go straight; Gramp reveals a money hoard, and Jane is wounded in a scuffle over the money. Jerry is subsequently convinced of her innocence, and they are reconciled. *Grandfathers. Criminals—Rehabilitation. Salvation Army.*

SALVATION NELL F2.4791

Whitman Bennett Productions. *Dist* Associated First National Pictures. Jul **1921** [c28 Jun, 11 Jul 1921; LP16711, LP16749]. Si; b&w. 35mm. 5-7 reels, 6,384 ft.

Supv Whitman Bennett. *Dir* Kenneth Webb. *Adapt* Dorothy Farnum. *Photog* Ernest Haller. *Art Dir* Roy Webb, Al D'Agostino.

Cast: Pauline Starke *(Nell Sanders)*, Joseph King *(Jim Platt)*, Gypsy O'Brien *(Myrtle Hawes)*, Edward Langford *(Major Williams)*, Evelyn C. Carrington *(Hallelujah Maggie)*, Charles McDonald *(Sid McGovern)*, Matthew Betz *(Al McGovern)*, Marie Haynes *(Hash House Sal)*, A. Earl *(Giffen)*, William Nally *(Callahan)*, Lawrence Johnson *(Jimmie)*.

Melodrama. Source: Edward Brewster Sheldon, *Salvation Nell, a Play in Three Acts* (New York, 1908). Nell Sanders, a girl of the lower East Side slums, is compelled to work in the saloon of Sid McGovern as scrubbing woman. Her sweetheart Jim, in rescuing her from the attentions of Al McGovern, kills Al and is sent to prison for 7 years. Meanwhile, Nell is befriended by Maggie, a Salvation Army girl, and after the birth of her child she joins the ranks and becomes a valuable speaker. When Jim is released, he finds Nell being courted by Major Williams; and though she still loves Jim, she refuses to return to their former life. Jim is at last convinced of her sincerity, and he pledges to start a new life with her. *Charwomen. Criminals—Rehabilitation. Slums. Manslaughter. New York City—East Side. Salvation Army.*

SAN FRANCISCO NIGHTS F2.4792

Gotham Productions. *Dist* Lumas Film Corp. May **1928** [c4 Jan 1928; LP24825]. Si; b&w. 35mm. 7 reels, 6,289 ft.

Pres by Sam Sax. *Supv-Adapt* Harold Shumate. *Dir* R. William Neill. *Titl* Maude Fulton. *Photog* James Diamond. *Film Ed* Donn Hayes. *Asst Dir* Donn Diggins. *Prod Mgr* Carrol Sax.

Cast: Percy Marmont *(John Vickery)*, Mae Busch *(Flo)*, Tom O'Brien *("Red")*, George Stone *("Flash" Hoxy)*, Alma Tell *(Ruth)*, Hobart Cavanaugh *(Tommie)*.

Underworld melodrama. Source: Leon De Costa, "The Fruit of Divorce" (publication undetermined). Young lawyer John Vickery is in love with his wife, but he thinks she is in love with another man. He purposely sets up evidence against himself, and she, finding another woman in her apartment, divorces him. He drifts into the night life of the underworld, becoming a desperate alcoholic, and is rescued by Flo, a dancehall girl whom he once befriended. He becomes a lawyer for the underworld and earns the enmity of some hardcore criminals who try to kill him. Flo falls in love with Vickery, but, realizing that she is not the woman for him, she sends for his ex-wife, Ruth. Ruth and Vickery are then reconciled. *Lawyers. Dancehall girls. Alcoholism. Divorce. San Francisco.*

Note: Known also as *The Fruit of Divorce.*

SAND BLIND F2.4793

Ben Wilson Productions. *Dist* Arrow Pictures. 14 Feb **1925** [c14 Mar 1925; LP21254]. Si; b&w. 35mm. 5 reels, 5,110 ft.

Dir Jacques Jaccard. *Story* William E. Wing.

Cast: Ben Wilson.

Western melodrama. "Owners of adjoining ranches are sworn enemies. The villainous one gets a mortgage on the property of the other and holds up an offer from a water company for rights until the date of expiration of the mortgage. Dick attempts to borrow from bank but is refused until his sweetheart arrives with a telegram from the water company making the offer of a huge sum for rights." (*Motion Picture News Booking Guide,* 8: 69, Apr 1925.) *Ranchers. Water rights. Mortgages.*

SANDRA F2.4794

Associated Pictures. *Dist* First National Pictures. Sep **1924** [c27 Oct 1924; LP20692]. Si; b&w. 35mm. 8 reels, 7,794 ft.

Dir Arthur H. Sawyer. *Photog* George Clarke.

Cast: Barbara La Marr *(Sandra Waring)*, Bert Lytell *(David Waring)*, Leila Hyams *(Mait Stanley)*, Augustin Sweeney *(Bob Stanley)*, Maude Hill *(Mrs. Stanley)*, Edgar Nelson *(Mr. Stanley)*, Leon Gordon *(Stephen Winslow)*, Leslie Austin *(Rev. William J. Hapgood)*, Lillian Ten Eyck *(Mimi)*, Morgan Wallace *(François Molyneaux)*, Arthur Edmund Carewe *(Henri La Flamme)*, Helen Gardner *(La Flamme's wife)*, Alice Weaver *(dancer)*.

Society drama. Source: Pearl Doles Bell, *Sandra* (New York, 1924). Torn between her dual personalities of a home-loving wife and a romance-seeking adventuress, Sandra Waring succumbs to the latter influence and makes a bargain with Stephen Winslow to help her husband, David, who faces financial ruin. This arrangement leads Sandra to a glamorous life in European capitals; a sojourn on the Riviera with François Molyneaux, who proves to be a crooked gambler using her as bait; and an affair with banker Henri La Flamme, who is arrested for embezzlement. Disillusionment follows disillusionment, and finally a contrite Sandra returns home believing David to be in love with Mait Stanley and resolved to end her own life. Wandering into a church, she is found by David's friend, the Reverend Hapgood, and is reunited with her forgiving husband. *Adventuresses. Bankers. Gamblers. Clergymen. Dual personality. Marriage. Embezzlement. Infidelity. Riviera.*

SANDY F2.4795

Fox Film Corp. 11 Apr **1926** [c31 Mar 1926; LP22556]. Si; b&w. 35mm. 8 reels, 7,850 ft.

Pres by William Fox. *Dir* Harry Beaumont. *Adapt* Eve Unsell. *Photog* Rudolph Bergquist. *Asst Dir* J. Malcolm Dunn.

Cast: Madge Bellamy *(Sandy McNeil)*, Leslie Fenton *(Douglas Keith)*, Harrison Ford *(Ramon Worth)*, Gloria Hope *(Judith Moore)*, Bardson Bard *(Ben Murillo)*, David Torrence *(Angus McNeil)*, Lillian Leighton *(Isabel McNeil)*, Charles Farrell *(Timmy)*, Charles Coleman *(Bob McNeil)*, Joan Standing *(Alice McNeil)*.

Society melodrama. Source: Elenore Meherin, *"Sandy"* (New York, c1926). Sandy McNeil adopts strictly unconventional jazz ethics and against the wishes of her parents runs with a fast young set. An auto breakdown after a party places her in a compromising situation, and she grudgingly marries a wealthy suitor of her father's choice. When her husband's cruelty results in the death of her child, she leaves him and meets Ramon, an architect with whom she becomes infatuated. The return of his former mistress causes her to seek refuge with her cousin Judith, where she falls in love with Douglas, Judith's sweetheart. As Sandy refuses to return to Ramon, he shoots her and then kills himself. Douglas, taking the blame for her sake, is tried for murder, but Sandy rises from her sickbed and confesses in court; she succumbs after restoring Judith to Douglas. *Architects. Flappers. Jazz life. Marriage. Murder. Suicide.*

THE SANTA FE TRAIL F2.4796

Paramount-Publix Corp. 27 Sep **1930** [c26 Sep 1930; LP1594]. Sd (Movietone); b&w. 35mm. 8 reels, 5,839 ft.

Dir Otto Brower, Edwin H. Knopf. *Screenplay* Sam Mintz. *Dial* Edward E. Paramore, Jr. *Photog* David Abel. *Film Ed* Verna Willis. *Rec Engr* Earl Hayman.

Cast: Richard Arlen *(Stan Hollister)*, Rosita Moreno *(Maria Castinado)*, Eugene Pallette *(Doc Brady)*, Mitzi Green *(Emily)*, Junior Durkin *(Old Timer)*, Hooper L. Atchley *(Marc Coulard)*, Luis Alberni *(Juan Castinado)*, Lee Shumway *(Slaven)*, Chief Standing Bear *(Chief Sutanek)*, Blue Cloud *(Eagle Feather)*, Chief Yowlache *(Brown Beaver)*, Jack Byron *(Webber)*.

Western melodrama. Source: Hal George Evarts, *Spanish Acres* (Boston, 1925). Stan Hollister, Doc Brady, and Old Timer, in charge of moving a vast flock of sheep over range, are deserted by their herders. Discovering that there is pasture and water at Spanish Acres, a grant of land belonging to Juan Castinado, Stan goes to the ranch to make a deal. Castinado is reluctant to allow Indians to be used as sheepherders, as he blames them for his many losses. Meanwhile, Stan falls in love with Rosita, Castinado's daughter, and is about to succeed with her when the barn is burned and Castinado believes Indians are responsible. Hearing that Coulard holds mortagages on the ranch, Stan investigates and finds that Coulard's men constitute the "Indian menace," but Coulard kills Standing Bear and blames Stan; the children—Old Timer and Emily—having seen the killing, tell the Indians, who believe them. Thus, Stan is saved, Spanish Acres is restored, and the Indians are hired as herders. *Sheepherders. Ranchers. Sheep. Mortgages. Children. Frameup.*

SANTA FE PETE F2.4797

Lariat Productions. c12 May **1925** [LP21461]. Si; b&w. 35mm. 5 reels.

Supv-Story Philip H. White. *Dir* Harry S. Webb. *Scen* Ray Walsh.

Cast: Pete Morrison, Lightning *(a horse)*.

Western melodrama. Warren Randolph, known in New Mexico as Santa Fe Pete, visits the Virginia plantation of Col. Henry Morgan, a Kentucky expatriate who has recently lost his fortune. At the sheriff's tax sale, Pete buys the Morgan property, saying nothing about it to the colonel. Pete immediately sends for an oil expert, and he then returns to the Morgan property, where he finds Dan Murray, a crooked oil man, attempting to force his attentions on Lucy in front of her helpless mother. Pete lights into Dan, who makes his escape on the colonel's best horse. Pete finds the old gentleman in the barn, unharmed except for his pride. The sheriff arrives with Pete's oil expert and informs Pete that Murray is notorious criminal. Pete mounts Lightning and goes after him, beating him in a rugged fight. Pete is later forced to tell the colonel that he owns the ranch, and the old fellow is, at first, furious, but when Pete informs him that his father rode with the colonel during the War Between the States, everything is set straight. *Kentucky colonels. Sheriffs. Mortgages. Oil lands. United States—History—Civil War. New Mexico. Virginia. Horses.*

THE SAP F2.4798

Warner Brothers Pictures. 20 Mar **1926** [c20 Mar 1926; LP22513]. Si; b&w. 35mm. 6 reels, 5,519 ft.

Dir Erle Kenton. *Adapt* E. T. Lowe, Jr. *Story* E. T. Lowe, Jr., Philip Klein. *Photog* Ed Du Par. *Asst Camera* Walter Robinson. *Film Ed* Clarence Kolster. *Asst Dir* Al Kelley.

Cast: Kenneth Harlan *(Barry Weston)*, Heinie Conklin *(Wienie Duke)*, Mary McAllister *(Janet)*, David Butler *(Vance)*, Eulalie Jensen *(Mrs. Weston, Barry's mother)*, John Cossar *(Janet's father)*.

Comedy-drama. Source: William A. Grew, *The Sap* (New York opening: 15 Dec 1924). Barry Weston, who has been coddled into cowardice by his mother, goes off to war and out of sheer terror fights splendidly. He is welcomed back to his hometown as a hero, though he himself feels that he does not merit the praise. He is idolized by Janet, his sweetheart, but Vance, the town bully, is jealous of her attentions to Barry and taunts him publicly, daring him to fight. Despite her love for him, Janet gives up on Barry, and even his friend Wienie thinks him an irremediable coward. Barry returns his medals to the War Department and in desperation sets out to conquer all his fears; at last, confident, he determines to even the score with Vance. With his victory over Vance, Barry regains Janet's love and the respect of the town. *Veterans. War heroes. Smalltown life. Cowardice. World War I.*

THE SAP F2.4799

Warner Brothers Pictures. 9 Nov **1929** [c16 Oct 1929; LP773]. Sd (Vitaphone); b&w. 35mm. 9 reels, 7,150 ft. [Also si.]

Dir Archie Mayo. *Screenplay-Dial* Robert Lord. *Titl* De Leon Anthony. *Photog* Dev Jennings. *Film Ed* Desmond O'Brien.

Cast: Edward Everett Horton *(The Sap [Bill Small])*, Alan Hale *(Jim Belden)*, Patsy Ruth Miller *(Betty)*, Russell Simpson *(The Banker)*, Jerry Mandy *(The Wop)*, Edna Murphy *(Jane)*, Louise Carver *(Mrs. Sprague)*, Franklin Pangborn *(Ed Mason)*.

Comedy-drama. Source: William A. Grew, *The Sap* (New York opening: 15 Dec 1924). Bill Small, a smalltown inventor in South Dakota, is full of impractical ideas, though he is defended by his wife, Betty, against her sister Jane and brother-in-law Ed Mason. When Ed confesses that he has been using the bank's funds for speculation, Bill, acting on a hunch, forces cashier Jim Belden to confess that he has been doing the same thing; but Bill is humiliated when his shoe polish ruins the shoes of banker Sprague. Ed and Jim aid him in appropriating $50,000; just as they are on the verge of being discovered, Bill reports that he has played the market and won, and he returns to his wife a hero. *Inventors. Bankers. In-laws. Smalltown life. Speculation. Embezzlement. Shoe polish. South Dakota.*

THE SAP FROM SYRACUSE F2.4800

Paramount-Publix Corp. 26 Jul **1930** [c28 Jul 1930; LP1446]. Sd (Movietone); b&w. 35mm. 7 reels, 6,108 ft.

Dir A. Edward Sutherland. *Screenplay* Gertrude Purcell. *Camera* Larry

Williams. *Songs: "How I Wish I Could Sing a Love Song," "Capitalize That Thing Called It"* E. Y. Harburg, John W. Green, Vernon Duke. *Song: "Aw! What's the Use?"* E. Y. Harburg, John W. Green. *Rec Engr* Edwin Schabbehar, Gordon New.

Cast: Jack Oakie *(Littleton Looney)*, Ginger Rogers *(Ellen Saunders)*, Granville Bates *(Hycross)*, George Barbier *(Senator Powell)*, Sidney Riggs *(Nick Pangolos)*, Betty Starbuck *(Flo Goodrich)*, Vera Teasdale *(Dolly Clark)*, J. Malcolm Dunn *(Captain Barker)*, Bernard Jukes *(Bells)*, Walter Fenner *(Henderson)*, Jack Daly *(Hopkins)*.

Comedy. Source: John Wray, Jack O'Donnell, and John Hayden, "A Sap From Syracuse" (publication undetermined). Littleton Looney, a crane driver and general handyman in Syracuse, is a constant target for local practical jokers. When an unexpected inheritance gives him the chance to travel to Europe, jokesters send word to the ship captain that he is a famous mining engineer, traveling incognito; as a result, he is courted and pursued all over the ship. He meets Ellen Saunders, a mine owner, and two men who are plotting to rob her of her property, and when she seeks his aid, his identity is vouched for by the prominent Senator Powell. Meanwhile, Looney is pursued by two gold diggers, though he is trying to court Ellen. In Europe, a conference of engineers is called to plan a means of transporting machinery to the mine; Looney, learning of a low river bed, suggests damming the stream and using it as a road, an idea hailed by the experts. The plotters are unmasked by Powell, actually the engineer, and Looney wins the girl. *Crane drivers. Gold diggers. Engineers—Mining. Mistaken identity. Inheritance. Ocean liners. Syracuse (New York).*

SARAH AND SON **F2.4801**

Paramount Famous Lasky Corp. 22 Mar **1930** [c22 Mar 1930; LP1169]. Sd (Movietone); b&w. 35mm. 9 reels, 7,740 ft. [Also si.]

Dir Dorothy Arzner. *Adapt-Dial* Zoë Akins. *Camera* Charles Lang. *Film Ed* Verna Willis. *Rec Engr* Earl Hayman.

Cast: Ruth Chatterton *(Sarah Storm)*, Fredric March *(Howard Vanning)*, Fuller Mellish, Jr. *(Jim Gray)*, Gilbert Emery *(John Ashmore)*, Doris Lloyd *(Mrs. Ashmore)*, William Stack *(Cyril Belloc)*, Philippe De Lacy *(Bobby)*.

Society melodrama. Source: Timothy Shea, *Sarah and Son* (New York, 1929). Sarah Storm, a lonely and impoverished singer, marries Jim Gray, with whom she teams up in vaudeville, but he is unable to support her or get a loan from wealthy John Ashmore. Angered by her reproval, he disappears with their baby; she is befriended by Cyril, another singer, with whom she builds a new act. Later, at a hospital where she goes to entertain wounded marines, Sarah discovers Jim; and, dying, he breathes Ashmore's name. Through her lawyer, Howard Vanning, who has fallen in love with her, Sarah finds the Ashmores, and since they deny that Bobby, their 11-year-old boy, is her son, Howard persuades her to continue her vocal studies in Europe. She returns an operatic success but insists on seeing the boy; and the Ashmores substitute a deafmute. She understands the deception; Bobby runs away to join Vanning; but when the Ashmores come to claim him, Sarah realizes he is her child. She and the boy are then victims of a motorboat accident; but Howard rescues them, and they all find happiness together. *Singers. Children. Lawyers. Deafmutes. Motherhood. Marriage. Desertion. Vaudeville. Opera.*

Note: Also produced in a French-language version, *Toute sa vie*, q. v.

SATAN AND THE WOMAN **F2.4802**

Excellent Pictures. 20 Jan **1928** [c21 Jan 1928; LP24899]. Si; b&w. 35mm. 7 reels, 6,300-6,400 ft.

Pres by Samuel Zierler. *Prod* Harry Chandlee. *Dir* Burton King. *Story Supv–Titl* Harry Chandlee. *Adapt* Adrian Johnson. *Photog* Art Reeves. *Film Ed* Harry Chandlee.

Cast: Claire Windsor *(Judith Matheny)*, Cornelius Keefe *(Edward Daingerfield)*, Vera Lewis *(Mrs. Leone Daingerfield)*, Thomas Holding *(Ellison Colby)*, James Mack *(Dallam Colby)*, Edithe Yorke *(Hetty Folinsbee)*, Madge Johnston *(Clementine Atwood)*, Sybil Grove, Lucy Donahue, Blanche Rose *(The Three Graces)*.

Drama. Source: Mary Lanier Magruder, "Courage," in *Young's Magazine*. Leone Daingerfield, a ruthless old woman, tries to crush the romance between her heir, Edward Daingerfield, and her granddaughter, Judith, whose blood relationship she refuses to acknowledge. Judith actually is considered an outcast because of her uncertain parentage. Eventually she inherits Leone Daingerfield's wealth when the old tyrant repents at the last moment. A misunderstanding separates Judith and Edward, and she considers marrying an affectionate lawyer. When she finds that he is after her money, however, she returns to her former lover, Edward. *Grandmothers. Lawyers. Inheritance. Parentage.*

SATAN IN SABLES **F2.4803**

Warner Brothers Pictures. 14 Nov **1925** [c23 Sep 1925; LP21847]. Si; b&w. 35mm. 8 reels, 7,260 ft.

Dir James Flood. *Scen-Adapt* Bradley King. *Photog* John Mescall. *Adtl Photog* Bert Shipman. *Asst Dir* Gordon Hollingshead.

Cast: Lowell Sherman *(Michael Lyev Yervedoff)*, John Harron *(Paul Yervedoff)*, Pauline Garon *(Colette Breton)*, Gertrude Astor *(Dolores Sierra)*, Frank Butler *(Victor)*, Francis McDonald *(Émile)*, Frances Raymond *(Sophia)*, Otto Hoffman *(Sergius)*, Richard Botsford *(Billee)*, Richard Barry, Don Alvarado *(students)*.

Melodrama. During a Mardi Gras celebration, Colette, a girl of Montmartre, meets Grand Duke Michael, a Russian expatriate who lives riotously in Paris. Michael and Colette fall in love. Dolores Sierra, one of the many women loved and then left by Michael, intends to revenge herself on him by vamping his beloved younger brother, Paul. When Paul learns that Dolores has been his brother's mistress, he drives wildly in his car and is killed in an accident. Michael, overcome by grief, repents his past life but finds solace in the promise of future happiness with Colette. *Russians. Brothers. Students. Revenge. Automobile accidents. Mardi Gras. Paris—Montmartre.*

SATAN TOWN **F2.4804**

Charles R. Rogers Productions. *Dist* Pathé Exchange. 15 Aug **1926** [c6 Jul 1926; LU22874]. Si; b&w. 35mm. 6 reels, 5,406 ft.

Pres by Charles R. Rogers. *Dir* Edmund Mortimer. *Scen* Marion Jackson. *Story* Jack Boyle. *Photog* Sol Polito.

Cast: Harry Carey *(Bill Scott)*, Kathleen Collins *(Sue)*, Charles Clary *(John Jerome)*, Trilby Clark *(Sheila Jerome)*, Richard Neill *(Cherokee Charlie)*, Ben Hall *(Crippy Jack)*, Charles Delaney *(Frisco Bob)*, Ben Hendricks *(Malamute)*.

Western melodrama. In Seattle, Bill Scott, who is bound for the gold rush in Alaska, saves an orphan girl from a runaway team, and before his boat sails, he commissions John Jerome, a shady waterfront lawyer, to put the child through boarding school. Twelve years later, Bill returns a millionaire but finds that Jerome has used his capital to promote a town devoted to gambling, dancehalls, and other vices. Intent on vengeance, Bill trails Jerome to Satan Town, where he befriends a cripple and meets Salvation Sue, a beautiful girl devoted to the Salvation Army. In answering a call, Sue is accused of murdering a girl in a fight over a man and is arrested; Cherokee Charlie, Jerome's henchman, incites the crowd to a lynching, but Bill captures Jerome and proves Sue's innocence. The mob sets the town afire, and Sue, recognizing Bill by a tattoo on his hand as her childhood protector, is happily united with him. *Miners. Orphans. Lawyers. Revenge. Gold rushes. Tattoos. Seattle. Alaska. Salvation Army.*

SATAN'S PAWN (Reissue) **F2.4805**

New York Motion Picture Corp. *Dist* W. & H. Productions. 11 Jul **1922** [New York State license application]. Si; b&w. 35mm. 5 reels, 4,900 ft.

Note: An adaptation of the Molnár play starring Bessie Barriscale and originally released by the Mutual Film Corp (1 Apr 1915) as *The Devil;* also reissued by W. & H. as *Satan's Pawn,* May 1918.

THE SATIN GIRL **F2.4806**

Ben Wilson. *Dist* Grand-Asher Distributing Corp. 30 Nov **1923** [New York showing; c19 Nov 1923; LP19627]. Si; b&w. 35mm. 6 reels, 5,591 ft. *Dir* Arthur Rosson. *Adapt* Arthur Statter, George Plympton. *Story* Adam Hull Shirk.

Cast: Mabel Forrest *(Lenore Vance)*, Norman Kerry *(Dr. Richard Taunton)*, Marc MacDermott *(Fargo)*, Clarence Burton *(Moran)*, Florence Lawrence *(Sylvia)*, Kate Lester *(Mrs. Brown-Potter)*, Reed House *(Norton Pless)*, William H. Turner *(Silas Gregg)*, Walter Stevens *(Harg)*.

Crook melodrama. *A girl loses her memory and, falling under the influence of an eccentric master-criminal, is forced to commit robberies. A young doctor falls in love with her and unravels the mystery of her identity.* It develops that the whole story is a novel that Lenore has been reading in which she visualizes herself and Dr. Taunton as the leading characters. *Physicians. Amnesia. Hypnotism. Robbery. Personal identity. Reading.*

THE SATIN WOMAN **F2.4807**

Gotham Productions. *Dist* Lumas Film Corp. 1 Aug **1927** [c5 Jul 1927; LP24149]. Si; b&w. 35mm. 7 reels, 7,000 ft.

Pres by Sam Sax. *Dir-Story-Scen* Walter Lang. *Photog* Ray June. *Film Ed* Edith Wakeling. *Prod Mgr* Cliff Broughton.

Cast: Mrs. Wallace Reid *(Mrs. Jean Taylor)*, Rockliffe Fellowes *(George Taylor)*, Alice White *(Jean Taylor)*, John Miljan *(Maurice)*, Laska Winters *(Maria)*, Charles "Buddy" Post *(Monsieur Francis)*, Ruth Stonehouse *(Claire)*, Gladys Brockwell *(Mae)*, Ethel Wales *("Countess" Debris)*.

Society drama. Jean, the wife of wealthy sportsman George Taylor, indulges her taste for high style and fashion and not only neglects her husband but leaves her young daughter, Jean, to the sole care of her governess. As George drives down Fifth Avenue, he meets Mae, an attractive widow whose apparent loneliness and sympathy for Taylor bring them together. When gossip reaches Jean, she realizes her neglect but is too late to prevent her husband from obtaining a divorce. Five years later, Mrs. Taylor, who has given up fashion in devotion to her child, Jean, saves the girl from the wiles of Maurice, a professional dancer, by becoming a rival against her own daughter; when she is shot by Maria, the dancer's partner, she is reunited with her husband, and Jean learns the true character of Maurice. *Sportsmen. Dancers. Widows. Motherhood. Gossip. Wealth. Fashion. Divorce. New York City.*

SATURDAY NIGHT **F2.4808**

Famous Players–Lasky. *Dist* Paramount Pictures. ca22 Jan **1922** [New York premiere; released 5 Feb; c21 Jan 1922; LP17496]. Si; b&w. 35mm. 9 reels, 8,443 ft.

Pres by Jesse L. Lasky. *Dir* Cecil B. De Mille. *Story-Scen* Jeanie Macpherson. *Photog* Alvin Wyckoff, Karl Struss.

Cast: Leatrice Joy *(Iris Van Suydam, a society girl)*, Conrad Nagel *(Richard Wynbrook Prentiss, her fiancé)*, Edith Roberts *(Shamrock O'Day, a laundress)*, Jack Mower *(Tom McGuire, a chauffeur)*, Julia Faye *(Elsie, Richard's sister)*, Edythe Chapman *(Mrs. Prentiss)*, Theodore Roberts *(Van Suydan)*, John Davidson *(The Count Demitry Scardoff)*, James Neill *(Tompkins, butler)*, Winter Hall *(The Professor)*, Sylvia Ashton *(Mrs. O'Day, a washerwoman)*, Lillian Leighton *(Mrs. Ferguson)*.

Society melodrama. Iris Van Suydam and Richard Wynbrook Prentiss, a wealthy society couple, are engaged. Iris, however, is attracted to her chauffeur, Tom McGuire, who is in love with her; and Richard meets Shamrock O'Day, beautiful daughter of a washerwoman, and falls in love with her. Consequently, they cancel their engagement, and each marries the partner of his choice. Too late, they discover their inability to adjust to another social set: Tom has difficulty in the world of opera, fashionable cabarets, and concerts of Iris; while Shamrock is ill at ease at a formal dinner party and becomes intoxicated. One night, after a party, Tom and Shamrock sneak off to Coney Island where they become stranded on a Ferris wheel; returning home, they find Richard and Iris awaiting them. Tom declares his love for Shamrock, and a fight between Tom and Dick is interrupted by a fire. Following Iris' rescue by Dick, divorces are obtained; Tom marries Shamrock; and Richard, Iris. *Socialites. Chauffeurs. Laundresses. Irish. Social classes. Marriage. Divorce. Ferris wheels. Coney Island.*

THE SATURDAY NIGHT KID **F2.4809**

Paramount Famous Lasky Corp. 26 Oct **1929** [c25 Oct 1929; LP792]. Sd (Movietone); b&w. 35mm. 7 reels, 6,015 ft. [Also si; 6,392 ft.]

Dir Edward Sutherland. *Screenplay* Ethel Doherty. *Dial* Lloyd Corrigan, Edward E. Paramore, Jr. *Titl* Joseph L. Mankiewicz. *Adapt* Lloyd Corrigan. *Story* George Abbott, John V. A. Weaver. *Camera* Harry Fischbeck. *Film Ed* Jane Loring.

Cast: Clara Bow *(Mayme)*, James Hall *(Bill)*, Jean Arthur *(Janie)*, Charles Sellon *(Lem Woodruff)*, Ethel Wales *(Ma Woodruff)*, Frank Ross *(Ken)*, Edna May Oliver *(Miss Streeter)*, Hyman Meyer *(Ginsberg)*, Eddie Dunn *(Jim)*, Leone Lane *(Pearl)*, Jean Harlow *(Hazel)*, Getty Bird *(Riche Ginsberg)*, Alice Adair *(girl)*, Irving Bacon *(McGonigle, sales manager)*, Mary Gordon *(reducing customer)*, Ernie S. Adams *(gambler)*.

Romantic comedy. Mayme, a salesgirl in Ginsberg's department store, is in love with Bill, another clerk; but when he is promoted to floorwalker and Mayme's sister, Janie, is made treasurer of the benefit pageant, Mayme loses Bill to her sister. Janie, however, has been losing racing bets placed with Lem Woodruff, proprietor of the boardinghouse where she and Mayme live; and to make up her losses, she places the pageant money on a winning horse, but inadvertently the bet is placed on another horse. She confesses her predicament to Mayme, who wins back the money by shooting craps with Lem. Janie blames her sister for the loss until Mayme shows up with the money and vents her righteous wrath on her hypocritical sister; Janie finds happiness with Jimmie, a fellow boarder. *Salesclerks. Floorwalkers. Sisters. Gambling. Embezzlement. Horseracing. Department stores. Boardinghouses.*

SATURDAY'S CHILDREN **F2.4810**

Walter Morosco Productions. *Dist* First National Pictures. 14 Apr **1929** [c8 Apr 1929; LP284]. Talking sequences, sd eff, & mus score (Movietone); b&w. 35mm. 8 reels, 7,920 ft. [Also si, 10 Mar 1929; 6,727 ft.]

Pres by Richard A. Rowland. *Dir* Gregory La Cava. *Scen-Dial* Forrest Halsey. *Titl* Paul Perez. *Photog* John Seitz. *Film Ed* Hugh Bennett. *Song: "I Still Believe You"* Grant Clarke, Benny Davis, Harry Akst.

Cast: Corinne Griffith *(Bobby)*, Grant Withers *(Rims)*, Albert Conti *(Mengle)*, Alma Tell *(Florrie)*, Lucien Littlefield *(Willie)*, Charles Lane *(Mr. Halvey)*, Ann Schaeffer *(Mrs. Halvey)*, Marcia Harris *(Mrs. Gorlick)*.

Romantic comedy. Source: Maxwell Anderson, *Saturday's Children; a Comedy in Three Acts* (New York, 1927). Bobby Halvey and Rims O'Neil marry and settle down to love in a cottage. They soon find that married life is more bills than romance, and Bobby leaves Rims, not because she no longer loves him but because she honestly believes that he would be happier without her. She returns to her old job and takes up residence in a boardinghouse. Lonely and hurt, Rims comes to her and asks her to come back to him. She refuses, declaring that she wants a lover, not a husband. Bobby stays in the boardinghouse, and Rims comes to her after dark, sneaking in by the fire escape. *Marriage. Finance—Personal. Boardinghouses.*

THE SAVAGE **F2.4811**

First National Pictures. 18 Jul **1926** [c8 Jul 1926; LP22889]. Si; b&w. 35mm. 5 reels, 6,275 ft. [Copyrighted as 7 reels.]

Supv Earl Hudson. *Dir* Fred Newmeyer. *Scen* Jane Murfin, Charles E. Whittaker. *Titl* Ralph Spence. *Photog* George Folsey. *Art Dir* Milton Menasco. *Film Ed* Arthur Tavares.

Cast: Ben Lyon *(Danny Terry)*, May McAvoy *(Ysabel Atwater)*, Tom Maguire *(Professor Atwater)*, Philo McCullough *(Howard Kipp)*, Sam Hardy *(managing editor)*, Charlotte Walker *(Mrs. Atwater)*.

Comedy. Source: Ernest Pascal, "The Savage" (publication undetermined). Danny Terry, a wild-animal expert for a scientific magazine, goes to the Mariposa Islands and pretends to be a white savage to put over a hoax on a rival magazine's expedition, guided by Professor Atwater. In New York, he is placed on exhibition at a "jungle ball" given by Mrs. Atwater to celebrate the betrothal of her daughter to Howard Kipp. Terry's editor tries to expose the hoax, but Terry has fallen in love with Ysabel and refuses to disgrace her father; meanwhile, Ysabel breaks her engagement upon finding her fiancé with another girl. Though she knows Terry is a fake, she goes away with him, and they declare their mutual love. Terry convinces his pursuers that the "savage" has escaped, and as himself he finds happiness with Ysabel. *Authors. Editors. Courtship. Hoaxes. New York City.*

SAVAGE PASSIONS **F2.4812**

9 Mar **1927** [New York State license]. Si; b&w. 35mm. 5 reels, 4,800 ft.

Cast: Alice Calhoun, Eddie Phillips, Lucy Beaumont.

Drama(?). No information about the nature of this film has been found.

Note: Production and distribution companies not determined. New York State license issued to Merit Film Corp.

SAVAGES OF THE SEA **F2.4813**

Hercules Film Productions. *Dist* Bud Barsky Corp. 17 Feb **1925** [New York State license application]. Si; b&w. 35mm. 5 reels.

Dir Bruce Mitchell. *Scen* William E. Wing.

Cast: Frank Merrill *(Silent Saunders)*, Melbourne MacDowell *(Daniel Rawley)*, Marguerite Snow *(Stella Rawley)*, Danny Hoy *(Ginger)*, Clarence Burton *(Black Brock)*.

Action meldorama. Daniel Rawley's yacht is wrecked during a storm in the South Seas, and Rawley, Stella (Rawley's ward), and Saunders (a stowaway) are rescued by a sailing ship with a brutal captain and a mutinous crew. The captain locks Rawley in a cabin and makes crude advances toward Stella. Saunders takes matters into his own hands and, after a variety of experiences, subdues the captain and the crew. Rawley turns out to be Saunders' father, and Saunders wins Stella for his wife. *Wards. Sailors. Sea captains. Filial relations. Mutiny. Yachts. South Seas.*

SAVED BY RADIO **F2.4814**

Russell Productions. c31 Aug **1922** [LU18248]. Si; b&w. 35mm. 6 reels, ca5,500 ft.

Dir-Story William J. Craft. *Scen* Thomas Berrien. *Photog* Ernest Miller.

Cast: George Larkin *(John Powell)*, William Gould *(Spike Jones)*, Jacqueline Logan *(Mary Stafford)*, Harry Northrup *(Philip Morton)*, Andrew Arbuckle *(Pat)*.

Melodrama. Philip Morton comes to Beauport, a fishing village under the exclusive control of Dr. Stafford, with the secret intention of tricking the doctor into releasing some land. Hoping to marry Mary Stafford, Morton causes the doctor to fire her sweetheart, John Powell. Morton then hires Spike Jones and his gang to kidnap the doctor and force him to sign over the land. John is suspected and jailed, gets out of jail, and scales a cliff to Jones's hideout. The gang escapes but is captured by men John calls for by radio. *Physicians. Gangs. Land rights. Fishing villages. Radio.*

SAWDUST **F2.4815**

Universal Pictures. 25 Jun **1923** [c13 Jun 1923; LP19108]. Si; b&w. 35mm. 5 reels, 4,940 ft.

Dir Jack Conway. *Scen? (see note)* Doris Schroeder, Harvey Gates. *Story* Courtney Ryley Cooper. *Photog* Allan Davey.

Cast: Gladys Walton *(Nita Moore)*, Niles Welch *(Phillip Lessoway)*, Edith Yorke *(Mrs. Nancy Wentworth)*, Herbert Standing *(Ethelbert Wentworth)*, Matthew Betz *(Runner Bayne)*, Frank Brownlee *("Pop" Gifford)*, William Robert Daly *("Speck" Dawson)*, Mattie Peters *(Tressie)*, Mike *(Sawdust, a dog)*.

Melodrama. Nita Moore, a circus performer, is mistreated by the ringmaster and runs away to join an old couple who are persuaded that Nita is their longlost daughter. Phillip Lessoway, the couple's lawyer, falls in love with Nita, but after a quarrel he discovers and reveals to the adoptive parents that Nita is an imposter. Nita attempts suicide but is saved from a watery grave by Lessoway. *Lawyers. Ringmasters. Parentage. Circus. Suicide. Imposture. Dogs.*

Note: Harvey Gates received screen credit for scenario; Universal records have been followed.

THE SAWDUST PARADISE **F2.4816**

Paramount Famous Lasky Corp. 1 Sep **1928** [c4 Sep 1928; LP25594]. Sd eff & mus score (Movietone); b&w. 35mm. 7 reels, 6,165 ft.

Pres by Adolph Zukor, Jesse L. Lasky. *Dir* Luther Reed. *Titl* Julian Johnson. *Adapt* Louise Long. *Story* George Manker Watters. *Photog* Harold Rosson. *Film Ed* Otto Lovering.

Cast: Esther Ralston *(Hallie)*, Reed Howes *(Butch)*, Hobart Bosworth *(Isaiah)*, Tom Maguire *(Danny)*, George French *(Tanner)*, Alan Roscoe *(Ward)*, Mary Alden *(Mother)*, J. W. Johnston *(district attorney)*, Frank Brownlee *(sheriff)*, Helen Hunt *(organist)*.

Drama. Hallie, a shill in a cheap street carnival, falls in love with Butch, a grifter and three-shell artist who works with her. Hallie is arrested for gambling and, when she vows in court to reform, is paroled into the custody of Isaiah, an evangelist whose tent is pitched across the street from the carnival. Hallie quickly comes to respect the kindly old man and uses her carnival skills to make his revival meetings a success. Butch buys a carnival of his own and, seeing the tabernacle as his biggest rival, sets out with his men to put it out of business. Encountering Hallie again, his anger is turned aside, however, and he and his men help her to shill for Isaiah. A rival carnival burns out Butch, and Hallie, convincing Butch that it is for the best, makes plans for a brighter tomorrow with him. *Shills. Confidence men. Evangelists. Reformation. Carnivals. Revivals. Fires.*

THE SAWDUST RING (Reissue) **F2.4817**

Dist Tri-Stone Pictures. **1924.** Si; b&w. 35mm. 5 reels.

Note: A "re-edited and re-titled" Bessie Love film originally released by Triangle Film Corp.

THE SAWDUST TRAIL **F2.4818**

Universal Pictures. 10 Aug **1924** [c25 Jun 1924; LP20343]. Si; b&w. 35mm. 6 reels, 5,509 ft.

Pres by Carl Laemmle. *Dir* Edward Sedgwick. *Scen* E. Richard Schayer. *Adapt* Raymond L. Schrock. *Story* William Dudley Pelley. *Photog* Virgil Miller.

Cast: Hoot Gibson *(Clarence Elwood Butts)*, Josie Sedgwick *("Calamity" Jane Webster)*, David Torrence *(Jonathan Butts)*, Charles K. French *(Square Deal McKenzie)*, Harry Todd *(Quid Jackson)*, G. Raymond Nye *(Gorilla Lawson)*, Pat Harmon *(ranch foreman)*, Taylor Carroll *(Lafe Webster)*, W. T. McCulley *(Red McLaren)*.

Western comedy. Clarence, an eastern college youth masquerading as a mild, inoffensive dandy, joins a Wild West show where he clashes with the leading lady, "Calamity" Jane, a man-hater. Aiding her to flee, he manages to subdue her enmity during a hair-raising automobile ride. *Students. Man-haters. Wild West shows. Chases.*

SAY IT AGAIN **F2.4819**

Famous Players–Lasky. *Dist* Paramount Pictures. 31 May **1926** [c2 Jun 1926; LP22791]. Si; b&w. 35mm. 8 reels, 7,443 ft.

Pres by Adolph Zukor, Jesse L. Lasky. *Dir* Gregory La Cava. *Scen* Ray Harris, Richard M. Friel. *Story* Luther Reed, Ray Harris. *Photog* Edward Cronjager.

Cast: Richard Dix *(Bob Howard)*, Alyce Mills *(Princess Elena)*, Chester Conklin *(Prince Otto V)*, "Gunboat" Smith *(Gunner Jones)*, Bernard Randall *(Baron Ertig)*, Paul Porcasi *(Count Tanza)*, Ida Waterman *(Marguerite)*, William Ricciardi *(Prime Minister Stemmler)*.

Comedy. During the war, Bob Howard and his buddy, Gunner, are patients in a temporary hospital located in the kingdom of Spezonia. Bob and the Princess Elena fall in love, but at the Armistice he is forced to return to the States. Later, when he sets out to find her, he encounters on his steamer Count Tanza and Baron Ertig, Spezonian diplomats. They are returning to Spezonia with the long-lost crown prince, who—upon learning of the death of his ancestors at their coronations—tries to escape from the diplomatic delegation. Bob and his buddy, with whom he is reunited, aid Prince Otto V in subduing the diplomats, and, disguised as the prince's bodyguards, they enter Spezonia. During the coronation, Otto, attempting to escape from anarchists, allows Bob to take his place, and Bob in this impersonation is married to the princess. The inebriated Otto leads a march against the imposter; Bob and Gunner fight off the mob and escape with the princess to America. *Royalty. Veterans. Anarchists. Courtship. Imaginary kingdoms. Hospitals. World War I.*

SAY IT WITH DIAMONDS **F2.4820**

Chadwick Pictures. *Dist* First Division Distributors. 2 Jun **1927** [New York premiere; released 2 Jun 1927]. Si; b&w. 35mm. 7 reels, 6,041-6,700 ft.

Dir Jack Nelson. *Titl* Leon Lee. *Photog* Ernest Miller. *Tech Dir* Earl Sibley. *Film Ed* Gene Milford.

Cast: Betty Compson *(Betty Howard)*, Earle Williams *(Horace Howard)*, Jocelyn Lee *(Fay Demarest)*, Armand Kaliz *(Armand Armour)*, Betty Baker *(secretary)*.

Melodrama. Betty Howard, a young wife, becomes jealous of her husband when a gift intended for her is worn by another young woman, Fay Demarest. Betty arranges an "affair" with a corespondent to permit her husband to divorce her. The misunderstandings are cleared up, however, and she returns home. *Marriage. Jealousy. Fidelity. Divorce.*

SAY IT WITH SABLES **F2.4821**

Columbia Pictures. 13 Jul **1928** [c1 Sep 1928; LP25600]. Si; b&w. 35mm.

Prod Harry Cohn. *Dir* Frank Capra. *Scen* Dorothy Howell. *Story* Frank Capra, Peter Milne. *Photog* Joe Walker. *Art Dir* Harrison Wiley. *Film Ed* Arthur Roberts. *Asst Dir* Joe Nadel.

Cast: Francis X. Bushman *(John Caswell)*, Helene Chadwick *(Helen Caswell)*, Margaret Livingston *(Irene Gordon)*, Arthur Rankin *(Doug Caswell)*, June Nash *(Marie Caswell)*, Alphonz Ethier *(Mitchell)*, Edna Mae Cooper *(maid)*.

Melodrama. John Caswell, a wealthy widower, breaks with gold digger Irene Gordon, his mistress, and takes Helen for his wife. Sometime later, his son, Doug, returns from college with his fiancée, who turns out to be none other than the vengeful Irene. Caswell tells Doug that Irene was his mistress, and Doug, unbelieving, goes to Irene's apartment for confirmation. John follows; and finding Irene dead of a gunshot wound, he arranges her apartment so that her death appears to be a suicide. The following morning, Detective Mitchell from Homicide comes to the Caswell home, and John confesses to the murder. Mitchell has picked up an earring at the scene of the crime, however, and, finding its mate among Helen Caswell's things, he accuses her of Irene's murderer. Helen tells him that the shooting was accidental, and Mitchell officially closes the case, ruling the death a suicide. *Widowers. Detectives. Gold diggers. Mistresses. Filial relations. Murder. Suicide.*

SAY IT WITH SONGS **F2.4822**

Warner Brothers Pictures. 24 Aug **1929** [c2 Aug 1929; LP568]. Sd (Vitaphone); b&w. 35mm. 10 reels, 8,324 ft. [Also si, 19 Oct 1929; 5,699 ft.]

Dir Lloyd Bacon. *Adapt-Dial* Joseph Jackson. *Titl* De Leon Anthony. *Story* Darryl F. Zanuck, Harvey Gates. *Songs: "Little Pal," "I'm in*

Seventh Heaven," "Why Can't You?" "Used to You" Al Jolson, Lew Brown, B. G. De Sylva, Ray Henderson. *Songs: "Back in Your Own Back Yard," "I'm Ka-razy for You"* Al Jolson, Billy Rose, Dave Dreyer. *Song: "One Sweet Kiss"* Al Jolson, Dave Dreyer. *Rec Engr* George R. Groves.

Cast: Al Jolson *(Joe Lane)*, Davey Lee *(Little Pal)*, Marion Nixon *(Katherine Lane)*, Holmes Herbert *(Dr. Robert Merrill)*, Kenneth Thompson *(Arthur Phillips)*, Fred Kohler *(Joe's cellmate)*.

Musical drama. Joe Lane, radio entertainer and songwriter, learns that the manager of the studio, Arthur Phillips, has made improper advances to his wife, Katherine. Infuriated, Lane engages him in a fight, and the encounter results in Phillips' accidental death. Joe goes to prison for a few years, and when he is released he visits his son, Little Pal, at school and is begged by him to run away together. Because Joe earns little money, Little Pal helps by selling papers but is soon struck by a truck, causing the paralysis of his legs and loss of his voice. Joe takes his boy to a specialist named Dr. Merrill, presently married to Joe's former wife, whom Joe divorced while in prison in order to save her good name. After obtaining Joe's promise that he will return Little Pal to his mother, Merrill operates and restores the use of his legs. His voice is regained later when the boy awakens to one of his father's recordings. Keeping his promise, Joe goes on his way with only his melancholy whistling to comfort him. *Composers. Radio announcers. Newsboys. Fatherhood. Manslaughter. Divorce. Paralysis. Prisons.*

SCANDAL **F2.4823**

Universal Pictures. 4 May **1929** [c12 Apr 1929; LP303]. Talking sequences, sd eff, & mus score (Movietone); b&w. 35mm. 7 reels, 6,635 ft. [Also si, 27 Apr 1929; 6,475 ft.]

Prod Harry L. Decker. *Dir* Wesley Ruggles. *Adapt-Cont* Paul Schofield. *Dial* Tom Reed, Walter Anthony. *Titl* Walter Anthony. *Photog* Gilbert Warrenton. *Film Ed* Ray Curtiss, Maurice Pivar.

Cast: Laura La Plante *(Laura Hunt)*, Huntley Gordon *(Burke Innes)*, John Boles *(Maurice)*, Jane Winton *(Vera)*, Julia Swayne Gordon *(Mrs. Grant)*, Eddie Phillips *(Pancho)*, Nancy Dover *(Janet)*.

Melodrama. Source: Adela Rogers St. Johns, "The Haunted Lady," in *Hearst's International Cosmopolitan* (76:38–41, May 1925). When her family meets with financial reverses, socialite Laura Hunt takes up stenography and finds work in a fashionable resort hotel, where she meets up with her former sweetheart, Maurice. Although she still cares for Maurice, Laura marries wealthy Burke Innes instead. In her husband's absence, Maurice calls on Laura late one evening and proposes they renew their affair. While Maurice is with Laura, his wife is murdered, and Maurice gallantly refuses to tell the police where he was at the time of the crime. Maurice is charged with murder and things look bad for him until Laura comes forward and tells the truth. Maurice is set free, and Burke is quickly convinced of his wife's innocence. *Socialites. Stenographers. Murder. Reputation. Resorts. Hotels.*

SCANDAL PROOF **F2.4824**

Fox Film Corp. 24 May **1925** [c17 May 1925; LP21529]. Si; b&w. 35mm. 5 reels.

Pres by William Fox. *Dir* Edmund Mortimer. *Story-Scen* Charles Kenyon.

Cast: Shirley Mason *(Enid Day/Grace Whitney)*, John Roche *(Herbert Wyckoff)*, Freeman Wood *(Monty Brandster)*, Hazel Howell *(Thelma Delores)*, Frances Raymond *(Mrs. Brandster)*, Ruth King *(Lillian Hollister)*, Edward Martindel *(Reed Hollister)*, Joseph Striker *(Dick Thorbeck)*, Billy Fay *(Benny Hollister)*, Clarissa Selwynne *(Miss Wyckoff)*.

Melodrama. Grace Whitney goes to a wild party at the house of Monte Brandster; when he is shot by Thelma Delores, an irate gold digger, Grace is blamed for his murder. Grace is acquitted when Herbert Wyckoff testifies in her favor. After the trial, Grace changes her name to Enid Day and becomes a governess in the Hollister home, which is, by chance, visited by Herbert and his sister. Herbert tells Grace that he probably let his sympathy outweigh his judgment when he testified, and he insists that Grace leave the Hollister home. Mrs. Hollister is having an affair with Dick Thorbeck, and when Mr. Hollister is about to catch his wife and Thorbeck in a bedroom, Grace quickly takes Mrs. Hollister's place—thus compromising herself for the sake of Mrs. Hollister's baby. She is denounced by Hollister, but Herbert still believes in her and asks her to marry him. *Gold diggers. Governesses. Injustice. Infidelity. Murder. Self-sacrifice. Trials.*

SCANDAL STREET **F2.4825**

Arrow Pictures. 9 Jan **1925** [c12 Aug 1925; LP21722]. Si; b&w. 35mm. 7 reels, 6,750 ft.

Dir Whitman Bennett. *Story* Frank R. Adams. *Photog* Edward Paul. *Rec Engr* Eugene Merritt.

Cast: Niles Welch *(Neil Keenly/Harrison Halliday)*, Madge Kennedy *(Sheila Kane)*, Edwin August *(Howard Manning)*, Coit Albertson *(Julian Lewis)*, Louise Carter *(Cora Forman)*, J. Moy Bennett *(Pat O'Malley)*.

Melodrama. During the production of a motion picture, Neil Keenly, the film's star, is killed in an automobile accident. Harrison Halliday, the living image of the dead actor, takes his place, and the film is completed. The deception succeeds, and the public is kept in ignorance of Neil's demise. Harrison falls in love with Sheila Kane, the widow of the late actor, but their happiness is threatened when Cora Forman, a member of the film company at the time of Neil's death, blackmails Harrison. This threat is averted, however, and Harrison gracefully assumes another man's wife and fame. *Actors. Widows. Doubles. Automobile accidents. Motion pictures. Impersonation.*

SCANDALOUS TONGUES **F2.4826**

Playgoers Pictures. *Dist* Associated Exhibitors. 22 Oct **1922.** Si; b&w. 35mm. 5 reels, 4,232 ft.

Dir victor Schertzinger.

Cast: Enid Bennett, Fred Niblo.

Melodrama. "... a bar-room slavey and village outcast who blossoms into the town's pride and joy. The village goes 'dry' and Jim Bradley is forced out of town and into the bootlegging business. Jim's daughter, Nell, has grown up to hate all church folks, but when the new minister happens to come upon their new roadhouse and is given some real hootch for lemonade, there is an hour's heart-to-heart talk and Nell is made to see things in a different light. Nell is given an education. She marries the minister." (*Motion Picture News Booking Guide,* 4:89, Apr 1923.) *Drudges. Clergymen. Bootlegging. Education. Prohibition. Roadhouses.*

THE SCAPULARY *see* **EL RELICARIO**

SCAR HANAN **F2.4827**

Ben Wilson Productions. *Dist* Film Booking Offices of America. 29 Mar **1925** [c29 Mar 1925; LP21283]. Si; b&w. 35mm. 5 reels, 4,684 ft.

Dir Ben Wilson, Eddie Linden, Don Cunliff. *Cont* George W. Pyper. *Story* Yakima Canutt, George W. Pyper. *Photog* Eddie Linden.

Cast: Yakima Canutt *(Scar Hanan)*, Dorothy Woods *(Marion Fleming)*, Helen Bruneau *(Julia Creighton)*, Palmer Morrison *(Dr. Craig Fleming)*, Richard Hatton *(Shorty)*, George Lessey *(Bart Hutchins)*, Francis Ford *(jury foreman)*, Art Walker *(sheriff)*, Frank Baker *(Edward Fitzhugh Carstowe)*, Ben Wilson, Jr. *(Scar, as a child)*.

Western melodrama. Trailing the man who killed his father, Scar Hanan goes to work on the ranch of Bart Hutchins, a mean fellow who takes an instant dislike to Scar and frames him for cattle rustling. During his trial, Scar escapes with the help of Shorty and heads for South America. He gets as far as Los Angeles, where he saves Marion Fleming from a runaway horse and falls in love with her. Marion's father, a surgeon, removes the disfiguring scar from Hanan's face. Hanan then returns to Hutchins' ranch, which, he has discovered from Fleming, is his own property, having been stolen by Hutchins from the elder Hanan. Hutchins attempts to kill Scar and is badly beaten for his pains. The sheriff arrests Hutchins; Scar gets his property and marries Marion. *Cowboys. Ranchers. Surgeons. Revenge. Murder. Rustling. Trials. Plastic surgery. Los Angeles.*

THE SCAR OF SHAME **F2.4828**

Colored Players Film Corp. **1927.** Si; b&w. 35mm. 8 reels, 8,023 ft.

Dir Frank Peregini. *Story* David Starkman. *Photog* Al Ligouri.

Cast: Harry Henderson *(Alvin)*, Lucia Lynn Moses *(Louise)*, Ann Kennedy *(The Landlady)*, Norman Johnstone *(Louise's father)*, William E. Pettus *(Spike)*, Pearl MacCormick *(Miss Hathaway)*, Lawrence Chenault *(Mr. Hathaway)*.

Drama. Louise is beaten by her drunken father, and Alvin, a proper music student, comes to her aid. They fall in love with each other and find a few months of married happiness. Spike, a crony of Louise's father, lusts after Louise and makes plans to destroy her marriage. He sends Alvin a telegram (purportedly from his ailing mother), knowing that Alvin will return home. Louise wants to go with him, but Alvin is ashamed of her low birth and goes without her. Deeply hurt, Louise agrees to run off with Spike. Alvin returns unexpectedly and accidentally wounds Louise in a gun battle with Spike. Alvin is sent to jail, and Louise leaves with Spike, becoming a singer in a cabaret. Alvin breaks out of jail and begins a new life as piano teacher, falling in love with Alice Hathaway, one of his students. Alice's father is having an affair with Louise, and Alvin eventually meets up with her. She asks him to come back, but he refuses. She kills herself, and Alvin explains his past to the Hathaways, who forgive him. *Musicians. Singers. Music teachers. Drunkenness. Suicide. Negro life.*

THE SCARAB RING **F2.4829**

Vitagraph Co. of America. Jun **1921** [c5 May 1921; LP16483]. Si; b&w. 35mm. 6 reels.

Dir Edward José. *Scen* C. Graham Baker. *Photog* Joe Shelderfer.

Cast: Alice Joyce *(Constance Randall)*, Maude Malcolm *(Muriel Randall)*, Joe King *(Ward Locke)*, Edward Phillips *(Burton Temple)*, Fuller Mellish *(John Randall)*, Claude King *(Hugh Martin)*, Joseph Smiley *(James Locke)*, Jack Hopkins *(Mr. Kheres)*, Armand Cortez *(Kennedy)*.

Mystery melodrama. Source: Harriet Gaylord, "The Desperate Heritage" (publication undetermined). Constance Randall learns from her dying father that he has been blackmailed by a cashier in his bank who has knowledge of his part in a crime, and she swears to keep the secret from her younger sister, Muriel. Hugh Martin obtains documentary proof of the crime and threatens to give it to the press unless Constance induces Muriel to marry him. On the day Martin has threatened to reveal the story he is found dead, and a scarab ring, similar to one owned by Constance, is found near the body. She is acquitted of the crime because of insufficient evidence but is later forced to admit to her lover, Ward, that she killed Martin in defense of her honor and has kept the secret. He forgives her, and she accepts his proposal of marriage. *Sisters. Murder. Blackmail. Documentation.*

SCARAMOUCHE **F2.4830**

Metro Pictures. 30 Sep **1923** [New York premiere; released Feb 1924; c10 Oct 1923; LP19477]. Si; b&w. 35mm. 10 reels, 9,850 ft.

Supv-Dir Rex Ingram. *Adapt-Cont* Willis Goldbeck. *Photog* John F. Seitz. *Film Ed* Grant Whytock. *Prod Mgr* Curt Rehfeld. *Cost Dsgn* O'Kane Cornwell, Eve Roth, Van Horn.

Cast: Ramon Novarro *(André-Louis Moreau)*, Alice Terry *(Aline de Kercadiou)*, Lewis Stone *(The Marquis de la Tour d'Azyr)*, Lloyd Ingraham *(Quintin de Kercadiou)*, Julia Swayne Gordon *(The Countess Thérèse de Plougastel)*, William Humphrey *(The Chevalier de Chabrillane)*, Otto Matiesen *(Philippe de Vilmorin)*, George Siegmann *(Georges Jacques Danton)*, Bowditch Turner *(Le Chapelier)*, James Marcus *(Challefau Binet)*, Edith Allen *(Climene Binet)*, Lydia Yeamans Titus *(Madame Binet)*, John George *(Polinchinelle)*, Nelson McDowell *(Rhodomont)*, De Garcia Fuerburg *(Maximilien Robespierre)*, Roy Coulson *(Jean Paul Marat)*, Edwin Argus *(Louis XVI)*, Clotilde Delano *(Marie Antoinette)*, Willard Lee Hall *(The King's Lieutenant)*, Slavko Vorkapitch *(Napoleon Bonaparte, a lieutenant of artillery)*, Lorimer Johnston *(Count Dupuye)*, Edward Connelly *(a minister to the King)*, Howard Gaye *(Viscount d'Albert)*, J. Edwin Brown *(Monsieur Benoît)*, Carrie Clark Ward *(Madame Benoît)*, Edward Coxen *(Jacques)*, William Dyer *(The Gamekeeper)*, Rose Dione *(La Revolte)*, Arthur Jasmine *(a student of Rennes)*, Tom Kennedy *(a dragoon)*, Kalla Pasha *(keeper of the Paris gate)*, B. Hyman *(an extra)*, Louise Carver *(an extra)*.

Historical romance. Source: Rafael Sabatini, *Scaramouche; a Romance of the French Revolution* (Boston, 1921). André-Louis Moreau, a law student, vows to fight against the aristocracy when his friend Philippe is killed in a duel with the Marquis de la Tour. André deserts his guardians and his sweetheart Aline and joins a group of strolling musicians, finding himself in Paris at the outbreak of the Revolution. Caught in a mob determined to destroy the ruling class, André discovers that his father is the much-despised Marquis de la Tour and his mother is a countess. André pleads with the crowds to let his mother's carriage pass out of the city, while his father dies a nobleman's death in the crowds. *Students. Musicians. France—History—Revolution. Paris. Maximilien Robespierre. Jean Paul Marat. Georges Jacques Danton. Louis XVI (France). Marie Antoinette. Napoleon I.*

SCARLET AND GOLD **F2.4831**

J. J. Fleming Productions. *Dist* Davis Distributing Division. 15 Feb **1925** [c14 Jan 1926; LP22264]. Si; b&w. 35mm. 5 reels.

Dir Frank Grandon.

Cast: Al Ferguson *(Mounted Policeman McGee)*, Lucille Du Bois *(Ruth MacLean)*, Frank Granville *(Black Logan)*, Yvonne Pavis *(Indian maid)*.

Northwest melodrama. Dick MacLean, a member of the Northwest Mounted Police, is mortally wounded and, with his dying breath, asks Larry McGee, a friend and fellow Mountie, to take care of Haida, an Indian girl who is bearing Dick's child. Finding her in childbirth, apparently on the point of death, Larry marries her to give the child a name. Haida recovers, however, and a sobered Larry rides after Black Logan, a notorious desperado. Larry brings Logan in, and Haida commits suicide, freeing Larry to marry Ruth MacLean, Dick's sister and his longtime sweetheart. *Northwest Mounted Police. Indians of North America. Illegitimacy.*

Note: J. J. Fleming and Al Ferguson are also credited with the direction.

THE SCARLET CAR **F2.4832**

Universal Pictures. 15 Jan **1923** [c10 Jan 1923; LP18575]. Si; b&w. 35mm. 5 reels, 4,417 ft.

Pres by Carl Laemmle. *Dir* Stuart Paton. *Scen* George Randolph Chester. *Photog* Virgil Miller.

Cast: Herbert Rawlinson *(Billy Winthrop)*, Claire Adams *(Beatrice Forbes)*, Edward Cecil *(Ernest Peabody)*, Norris Johnson *(Violet Gaynor)*, Tom McGuire *(Jim Winthrop)*, Marc Robbins *(Jerry Gaynor)*, Tom O'Brien *(Mitt Deagon)*.

Melodrama. Source: Richard Harding Davis, "Adventures of the Scarlet Car," in *Collier's Weekly* (38:10, 15 Dec 1906; 23, 23 Mar 1907; 39:14, Jun 1907). Billy Winthrop is in love with Beatrice Forbes, who is engaged to Ernest Peabody, a reform candidate for mayor backed by Billy's father. When Billy learns that Peabody has betrayed Violet Gaynor and plans to doublecross Mr. Winthrop, he exposes the candidate with the help of Mitt Deagon and wins Beatrice. *Reformers. Politicians. Mayors.*

THE SCARLET DOVE **F2.4833**

Tiffany-Stahl Productions. 15 Apr **1928** [c23 Apr 1928; LP25181]. Si; b&w. 35mm. 6 reels, 5,102 ft.

Dir-Writ Arthur Gregor. *Scen* John Francis Natteford. *Titl* Harry Braxton, Viola Brothers Shore. *Photog* Ernest Miller. *Art Dir* Hervey Libbert. *Dressings* George Sawley. *Film Ed* Martin G. Cohn. *Asst Dir* M. K. Wilson.

Cast: Lowell Sherman *(Ivan Orloff)*, Robert Frazer *(Alexis Petroff)*, Josephine Borio *(Mara)*, Margaret Livingston *(Olga)*, Shirley Palmer *(Eve)*, Carlos Durand *(Gregory)*, Julia Swayne Gordon *(The Aunt)*.

Romantic drama. A Russian girl (Mara) reared in a convent is engaged to marry a man (Col. Ivan Orloff) she does not love. Mara's aunt has arranged the marriage so as to reinforce her own social position, while Orloff intends to take over the family fortune. On the wedding night Mara runs away with Alexis Petroff, a captain in Ivan's regiment. Ivan, happily enough, believes Mara has died when reports of her overturned sleigh come to him. Later, though, rumors about Mara and Alexis inspire him to have Alexis court-martialed. Alexis is convicted of murdering Mara, but the accusation is dropped when Mara appears in the courtroom. To save himself from humiliation, Ivan suggests a duel with Alexis on the frozen river, hoping, in addition, to regain Mara's fortune. Alexis wins the duel by default when Ivan falls through the ice before the shooting begins, leaving Alexis and Mara to their winter wonderland. *Marriage—Arranged. Murder. Courts-martial. Russia. Duels.*

THE SCARLET HONEYMOON **F2.4834**

Fox Film Corp. 22 Mar **1925** [c22 Feb 1925; LP21197]. Si; b&w. 35mm. 5 reels, 5,080 ft.

Pres by William Fox. *Dir* Alan Hale. *Scen* E. Magnus Ingleton. *Story* Fannie Davis. *Story? (see note)* Edmund Goulding. *Photog* Joseph Valentine.

Cast: Shirley Mason *(Kay Thorpe)*, Pierre Gendron *(Pedro Fernando)*, Allan Sears *(Harrison)*, J. Farrell MacDonald *(Joshua Thorpe)*, Rose Tapley *(Mamie Thorpe)*, Maine Geary *(Elmer Thorpe)*, Eugenie Gilbert *(Stella Thorpe)*, Eric Mayne *(Señor Fernando)*, Eulalie Jensen *(Señora Fernando)*.

Melodrama. Señor Fernando of the Argentine sends his son, Pedro, to New York to work in the American branch of his business. There Pedro meets and falls in love with Kay Thorpe, a stenographer. Kay takes Pedro to meet her family, but, when they discover that he is a $30-a-week clerk, they discourage his interest in Kay. Pedro later returns with a fine car and expensive gifts for Kay's family, and he is received with open arms. Pedro's father learns of the romance and decides to test Kay's loyalty. He arranges with Harrison, his New York manager, to have Pedro framed by some fake detectives on the charge of embezzling. Kay's family again turns against Pedro, but she remains loyal to him, pleading with Harrison to show Pedro leniency. The manager tries to make love to her, but Pedro intervenes and gives him a sound thrashing. Pedro and Kay are married and return to the Argentine. Pedro's father explains everything, and Kay is welcomed by Pedro's family. *Businessmen. Stenographers. Office clerks. Filial relations. Loyalty. Hoaxes. Argentina. New York City.*

Note: Fox records credit Edmund Goulding rather than Fannie Davis with the story.

THE SCARLET LADY **F2.4835**

Columbia Pictures. 1 Aug **1928** [c29 Sep 1928; LP25664]. Mus score (Movietone); b&w. 35mm. 7 reels, 6,443 ft.

Prod Harry Cohn. *Dir* Alan Crosland. *Story* Bess Meredyth. *Photog* James Van Trees. *Art Dir* Harrison Wiley. *Film Ed* Frank Atkinson. *Song: "My Heart Belongs to You"* Lou Herscher. *Asst Dir* Walter Mayo.

Cast: Lya De Putti *(Lya)*, Don Alvarado *(Prince Nicholas)*, Warner Oland *(Zaneriff)*, Otto Matiesen *(valet)*, John Peters *(captain)*, Valentina Zimina *(a revolutionist)*.

Melodrama. Lya, a beautiful Russian revolutionary, seeks refuge in the estate of Prince Nicholas, hiding under his bed from the brutal Cossacks. Nicholas finds her there and allows her to stay on at the palace where she serves as his major-domo. Nicholas and Lya fall in love, but Nicholas learns from his valet that Lya was once the mistress of Zaneriff, a hated Red leader. Denounced by Nicholas, Lya returns to her people and becomes a terrorist. When the Reds seize the palace, Nicholas disguises himself as a servant; Lya recognizes him but does not betray him to his unwitting captors. Nicholas' true identity is eventually discovered, and he is sentenced to be shot; Lya shoots Zaneriff instead and rescues Nicholas, escaping with him to freedom. *Revolutionaries. Aristocrats. Cossacks. Russia—History—1917–21 Revolution.*

THE SCARLET LETTER **F2.4836**

Metro-Goldwyn-Mayer Pictures. 9 Aug **1926** [New York premiere; released 8 Jan 1927; c21 Dec 1926; LP23517]. Si; b&w. 35mm. 9 reels, 8,229 ft.

Dir Victor Seastrom. *Adapt-Scen-Title* Frances Marion. *Photog* Hendrik Sartov. *Sets* Cedric Gibbons, Sidney Ullman. *Film Ed* Hugh Wynn. *Cost* Max Ree.

Cast: Lillian Gish *(Hester Prynne)*, Lars Hanson *(The Reverend Arthur Dimmesdale)*, Henry B. Walthall *(Roger Prynne)*, Karl Dane *(Giles)*, William H. Tooker *(The Governor)*, Marcelle Corday *(Mistress Hibbins)*, Fred Herzog *(The Jailer)*, Jules Cowles *(The Beadle)*, Mary Hawes *(Patience)*, Joyce Coad *(Pearl)*, James A. Marcus *(A Sea Captain)*.

Drama. Source: Nathaniel Hawthorne, *The Scarlet Letter* (1850). Hester, a New England maid of Puritan background, to please her father, marries Roger Prynne, whom she does not love. During her husband's long absence she walks the woodland lanes with her pastor, the Reverend Arthur Dimmesdale, and they soon fall in love. When a child is born to her, she is condemned to wear upon her breast the brand of Adulteress and refuses to divulge the name of the child's father. With patient resignation she faces the jeers and insults of the stern Puritan population and fights to retain her child. Hester is punished in the pillory, and when she is led to the public scaffold, Dimmesdale, who has long been eager yet fearful to share in her public shame, confesses and dies of his anguish in her arms. *Clergymen. Puritanism. Infidelity. New England.*

THE SCARLET LILY **F2.4837**

Preferred Pictures. *Dist* Associated First National Pictures. 15 Jul **1923** [c11 Jun 1923; LP19078]. Si; b&w. 35mm. 6 reels, 6,529 ft.

Pres by B. P. Schulberg. *Dir* Victor Schertzinger. *Adapt* Lois Zellner, Florence Hein. *Story* Fred Sittenham. *Photog* Joseph Brotherton. *Film Ed* Eve Unsell.

Cast: Katherine MacDonald *(Dora Mason)*, Orville Caldwell *(Lawson Dean)*, Stuart Holmes *(Jessup Barnes)*, Edith Lyle *(Mrs. Barnes)*, Adele Farrington *(Trixie Montresse)*, Gordon Russell *(Laurence Peyton)*, Grace Morse *(Beatrice Milo)*, Jane Miskimin *(Little Mollie)*, Lincoln Stedman *(John Rankin)*, Gertrude Quality *(Mrs. Rosetta Bowen)*.

Melodrama. Dora Mason—homeless, jobless, and without funds—accepts the hospitality of Jessup Barnes, a married man, when he gives her the use of his apartment for the care of her dying sister during the month he is absent. Barnes returns unexpectedly with Mrs. Barnes and her private detective "hot on his heels." Dora is named as corespondent and is forced to flee to a country retreat where she meets and falls in love with Lawson Dean, a lawyer recuperating from eyestrain. Following the death of Dora's sister, Dora and Dean marry. Dean is running for district attorney against Barnes, and his chances of winning are nearly ruined when the opposition leaders recognize Dora. Forced to establish her innocence, Dora successfully acquits herself, forces Barnes to withdraw from the campaign, and makes her husband's victory possible. *Sisters. District attorneys. Politics. Reputation.*

SCARLET PAGES **F2.4838**

First National Pictures. 28 Sep **1930** [c22 Sep 1930; LP1582]. Sd (Vitaphone); b&w. 35mm. 9 reels, 5,906 ft.

Dir Ray Enright. *Screenplay* Walter Anthony, *Dial* Maude Fulton. *Rec Engr* Dolph Thomas.

Cast: Elsie Ferguson *(Mary Bancroft)*, John Halliday *(John Remington)*, Marion Nixon *(Nora Mason)*, Grant Withers *(Bob Lawrence)*, Daisy Belmore *(Sister Beatrice)*, De Witt Jennings *(judge)*, William Davidson *(Gregory Jackson)*, Wilbur Mack *(Mr. Mason)*, Charlotte Walker *(Mrs. Mason)*, Helen Ferguson *(Miss Hutchison, secretary)*, Donald MacKenzie *(Callahan)*, Jean Bary *(Carlotta)*, Neely Edwards *(Barnes)*, Fred Kelsey *(judge)*.

Melodrama. Source: Samuel Shipman and John B. Hymer, *Scarlet Pages* (New York opening: 9 Sep 1929). Mary Bancroft, a prominent New York attorney, refuses to marry John Remington, district attorney, for a reason she cannot divulge. At a nightclub, they are entertained by dancer Nora Mason. Nora, on her way to a rendezvous with Bob Lawrence, her sweetheart, learns that her father and Gregory Jackson, a theatrical promoter, are waiting for her; she pleads with Bob to take her away. The next day, Barnes, a friend of Bob's, asks Mary to defend Nora, who is accused of killing her father. Nora then confesses that her father had forced her to submit to Jackson, who promised her a feature role; and Remington, investigating the girl's past, is stunned to find that Mary is the girl's mother. Nora is acquitted of the crime and meets her mother, who is reconciled with Remington. *Lawyers. District attorneys. Dancers. Theatrical producers. Filial relations. Nightclubs. Manslaughter.*

SCARLET SAINT **F2.4839**

First National Pictures. 8 Nov **1925** [c29 Oct 1925; LP21951]. Si; b&w. 35mm. 7 reels, 6,784 ft.

Prod under the supv of Earl Hudson. *Dir* George Archainbaud. *Scen* Eugene Clifford, Jack Jungmeyer. *Titl* John Krafft. *Photog* George Folsey. *Art Dir* Milton Menasco. *Film Ed* Arthur Tavares.

Cast: Mary Astor *(Fidele Tridon)*, Lloyd Hughes *(Philip Collett)*, Frank Morgan *(Baron Badeau)*, Jed Prouty *(Mr. Tridon)*, Jack Raymond *(Josef)*, George Neville *(trainer)*, Frances Grant *(Cynthia)*, J. W. Jenkins *(butler)*.

Melodrama. Source: Gerald Beaumont, "The Lady Who Played Fidele," in *Red Book* (44:31–35, Feb 1925). Betrothed as a child to Baron Badeau, Fidele Tridon, daughter of a wealthy New Orleans importer, finds herself in love with Philip Collett on the day the baron comes to claim her as his bride. The baron refuses to release her, and she plans to elope with Philip. The baron tricks Philip into a duel; Philip wounds him in the arm and is sent to jail. Fidele marries the baron to free Philip but flees to her lover after the ceremony. Finding her gone, the baron is stricken with paralysis, and Fidele returns to nurse her husband. After a year the baron recovers but conceals this fact from his wife lest he lose her. On the night of the Mardi Gras ball he dresses as a jester and is mistaken by Fidele for Philip. She reveals to him that she is aware that her husband is faking; and when the baron's valet enters disguised as his master, she offers the valet a choice of two glasses of water, one of which contains poison. The baron, realizing that he has lost Fidele, gives her her freedom, and Fidele comes into her rightful love. *Nobility. Cripples. Paralysis. Marriage contract. Disguise. Infidelity. Mardi Gras. New Orleans. Duels.*

SCARLET SEAS **F2.4840**

First National Pictures. 12 Jan **1929** [c10 Dec 1928; LP25899]. Sd eff & mus score (Vitaphone); b&w. 35mm. 7 reels, 6,337 ft. [Also si; 6,237 ft.]

Pres by Richard A. Rowland. *Dir* John Francis Dillon. *Screenplay* Bradley King. *Titl* Louis Stevens. *Story* W. Scott Darling. *Photog* Sol Polito. *Film Ed* Edward Schroeder, Jack Gardner.

Cast: Richard Barthelmess *(Donkin)*, Betty Compson *(Rose)*, Loretta Young *(Margaret)*, James Bradbury, Jr. *(Johnson)*, Jack Curtis *(Toomey)*, Knute Erickson *(Captain Barbour)*.

Drama. Steve Donkin, an embittered sailor, anchors his two-masted schooner off Apia and goes ashore for a little fun with Rose, a prostitute plying her trade in a waterfront dive; Rose is ordered to leave the island by the police and persuades Steve to take her to Shanghai. In mid-Pacific,

Steve's schooner sinks, and he, Rose, and a Swedish sailor are cast adrift in a small boat. The sailor tries to kill Steve and is knocked overboard; close to death, Steve and Rose fall in love. They are rescued by a passing ship and fall into the hands of a mutinous crew. Donkin puts down the mutiny and rescues Barbour, the ship's captain. *Sailors. Sea captains. Prostitutes. Swedes. Mutiny. Waterfront. Apia. Samoa. Shipwrecks.*

THE SCARLET WEST **F2.4841**

Frank J. Carroll Productions. *Dist* First National Pictures. 26 Jul **1925** [c2 Jul 1925; LP21625]. Si; b&w. 35mm. 9 reels, 8,390 ft.

Pres by Frank J. Carroll. *Dir* John G. Adolfi. *Scen* Anthony Paul Kelly. *Photog* George Benoit, Benjamin Kline, Victor Shuler, F. L. Hoefler.

Cast: Robert Frazer *(Cardelanche)*, Clara Bow *(Miriam)*, Robert Edeson *(General Kinnard)*, Johnny Walker *(Lieutenant Parkman)*, Walter McGrail *(Lieutenant Harper)*, Gaston Glass *(Captain Howard)*, Helen Ferguson *(Nestina)*, Ruth Stonehouse *(Mrs. Custer)*, Martha Francis *(Harriett Kinnard)*, Florence Crawford *(Mrs. Harper)*.

Western melodrama. Source: A. B. Heath, "The Scarlet West" (publication undetermined). Cardelanche, the son of an Indian chief, has been educated in the East, and he returns to his reservation and encounters the hostility of his people, who believe that he has turned his back on his own race. When Cardelanche saves a detachment of cavalry from a gang of renegade Indians, he is made a captain in the United States Army. He falls in love with Miriam, the daughter of the commandant of Fort Remington, further cutting himself off from his own people. Lieutenant Parkman, who is also in love with Miriam, is demoted to the ranks when he gets into a fight over the girl. Cardelanche's tribe goes on the warpath and slaughters the troops of General Custer. Cardelanche then decides that his true allegiance lies with his own people, and he gives up both Miriam and his commission, returning to the hills where his ancestors once lived and fought. *Indians of North America. George Armstrong Custer. United States Army—Cavalry.*

SCARLET YOUTH **F2.4842**

Circle Pictures. *Dist* Goodart Pictures. Oct **1928.** Si; b&w. 35mm. 7 reels, 6,500 ft.

Dir William Hughes Curran.

Cast: Corliss Palmer, David Findlay, Alphonse Martell, Connie La Mont, Ruth Robinson, Mary Roy, Freeman Wood.

Drama. "Landing in the little town of Galesburg, where he feels safe from the police, he [a crook] meets the unsophisticated daughter of a country boarding house woman. ... Here he makes love to the girl, and with the promise of a life of ease, he persuades her to marry him. He takes her to the city and tries to make her believe that he is looking for work, while he really has gone back to his old habits of traveling around with other women. Thinking that he has really looked for work and is unable to find it, she offers to help, as they must have money to live. He, knowing that she can dance, sends her to a friend who is Manager of a theatre. ... He seems to be impressed and gives her dancing costume. While she is changing into costume, he comes into dressing room and attacks her. She finally succeeds in getting away. Before she reaches home, she finds her husband in conversation with a woman in a car, whom he kisses as he leaves. Realizing the kind of man she has married, she denounces him and starts out to make her way alone. Finding employment as a model, she meets 'Madame Celeste and her Backer' who are very good customers of the dress shop. Madame Celeste, being impressed with the girl's beauty, and learning that she is a dancer, invites her to entertain her guests. She decides to go to Madame Celeste's. ... In the meantime, the husband finds her and borrows money—at another time he returns and pleads with her to take him back. She decides to do this and is to meet him after work to talk things over—but leaving the dress shop she comes upon him unexpectedly with the same woman. This convinces her that she not only must make her own way, but also seek her pleasures, realizing that she was 'young but once.' She then decides to accept the second invitation from Madame Celeste. Persuading her to drink a glass of wine which they tell her is perfectly harmless, she finally becomes intoxicated and is taken to a bedroom by Madame Celeste, where she falls on the bed, apparently unconscious. Almost immediately the door opens and Madame Celeste's 'Backer' enters the room, and locking the door, throws himself on the bed over the prostrate form of the intoxicated girl, kissing her violently on the face and the breast. She regains consciousness sufficiently to try to resist him. There ensues a struggle, when he tears off her clothes, throws her backwards on the bed and throws his body over hers. The following morning, finding some money on the pillow, and realizing what has happened, she makes a protest to Madame Celeste who tells her to 'cut out the innocent bluff' and 'Here's where you stay until you come to my way of thinking.' Meanwhile the husband, having made a 'big haul,' finds a pal who knows a good place to 'drink and dance'—which turns out to be Madame Celeste's, a house of Prostitution, and here he finds his wife, who by this time is an inmate, and with her he finds a male companion on the way upstairs. Attacking the man because of this, a terrible fight ensues—a call is made for the police and the house is raided. Both husband and wife find themselves in the Police Court. The husband, upon examination by the Jail Physician, is told [that he] has Syphilis and must remain for treatment. The history of the wife is brought before the Judge who paroles her in the custody of a Social Worker." (New York State license records.) *Philanderers. Fashion models. Social workers. Marriage. Infidelity. Prostitution. Venereal disease. Whorehouses.*

SCARRED HANDS **F2.4843**

H. B. Productions. *Dist* Madoc Sales. 1 Sep **1923.** Si; b&w. 35mm. 5 reels, 4,700 ft.

Dir Cliff Smith.

Cast: Cliff Smith, Eileen Sedgwick.

Melodrama. "A clash between two factions seeking the control of valuable oil lands introduces a love romance between Tom Stephens, rightful owner of the land, and Jane Wheeler. The villains plot to blow up the oil well, but are prevented by the sudden appearance of Tom who saves the girl and vanquishes his adversaries." *(Motion Picture News Booking Guide,* 6:60, Apr 1924.) *Oil lands. Oil wells.*

Note: Production company may be H. & B. Film Co.

SCARS OF HATE **F2.4844**

Premium Picture Productions. *Dist* Independent Pictures. Nov **1923.** Si; b&w. 35mm. 5 reels, 4,981 ft.

Dir H. G. Moody. *Photog* H. C. Cook.

Cast: Jack Livingston.

Western melodrama. "... a cattle man marries a New York society girl and takes her to his ranch. She finds the pioneer conditions difficult, and a misunderstanding arises which cause [*sic*] him to leave her and become a ranger. Five years later, in carrying out his duty, he comes onto the facts which set matters right." *(Motion Picture News Booking Guide,* 6:60, Apr 1924.) *Rangers. Socialites. Ranch life.*

SCARS OF JEALOUSY **F2.4845**

Thomas H. Ince Corp. *Dist* Associated First National Pictures. 5 Mar **1923** [c19 Mar 1923; LP18790]ÆSi; b&w. 35mm. 7 reels, 6,246 ft.

Pres by Thomas H. Ince. *Pers Supv* Thomas H. Ince. *Dir-Adapt* Lambert Hillyer. *Story* Anthony H. Rudd. *Photog* J. O. Taylor. *Mus* Sol Cohen.

Cast: Frank Keenan *(Colonel Newland)*, Edward Burns *(Jeff Newland)*, Lloyd Hughes *(Coddy Jakes)*, Marguerite De La Motte *(Helen Meanix)*, James Neill *(Colonel Meanix)*, Walter Lynch *(Pere Jakes)*, James Mason *(Zeke Jakes)*, Mattie Peters *(Mandy)*, George Reed *(Mose)*.

Drama. After years of waywardness Jeff Newland is disinherited by his father, Colonel Newland, who goes into the hills to seek a new heir from among the Cajans. He returns with Coddy Jakes, introduces him to Helen Meanix, and educates him. Coddy is suspected of murder, however, and he disappears into the hills, where he encounters Jeff Newland and succeeds in making a man of him. When Coddy is captured and about to be lynched, Helen effects his escape, and they find love together after they are rescued by Jeff and the colonel from a forest fire. *Cajans. Filial relations. Lynching. Alabama. Forest fires.*

THE SCHEMERS **F2.4846**

Reol Productions. c19 Aug **1922** [LU18157]. Si; b&w. 35mm. [Feature length assumed.]

Story Wallace Johnson.

Melodrama. Paul Jackson, a Negro research chemist with a drug company, is close to success in his attempt to develop a chemical substitute for gasoline. Juan Bronson, who is the private secretary of John Davidson, the president of the company, conspires with Miguel Anderson to steal Paul's formula. Believing Paul to be carrying the formula, Bronson and Anderson kidnap him, but the papers are not on his person. Paul manages to call Isobel Benton, his sweetheart, and instructs her to go to his laboratory for the papers. Anderson overhears the conversation and also goes there, but Isobel outwits him and gets away with the formula. Anderson then frames Paul for the theft of some other important formulas, and Paul gives his formula back to Isobel for safekeeping. Anderson abducts Isobel, and Paul rescues her with the help of Davidson and a detective. Isobel proves Paul's innocence, and the detective tells Davidson that Bronson and Anderson are notorious criminals, wanted by a South American government. *Chemists. Secretaries. Detectives. Negro life. Gasoline. Kidnaping. Pharmaceutical houses. Laboratories. Documentation.*

SCHOOL DAYS **F2.4847**

Harry Rapf Productions. *Dist* Warner Brothers Pictures. 1 Dec **1921** [New York premiere; released 25 Dec; c22 Nov 1921; LP17224]. Si; b&w with col titl (Prizma). 35mm. 7-8 reels, 7,000 ft. [Copyrighted as 8 reels.]

Supv Harry Rapf. *Dir-Story-Scen* William Nigh. *Scen* Walter De Leon. *Titl* Hoey Lawlor. *Photog* Jack Brown, Sidney Hickox. *Set Dsgn* Tilford Studios.

Cast: Wesley Barry *(Speck Brown)*, George Lessey *(His Guardian, the Deacon)*, Nellie P. Spaulding *(His Friend's Wife)*, Margaret Seddon *(His Teacher)*, Arline Blackburn *(His Sweetheart)*, Hippy *(His Dog)*, J. H. Gilmore *(The Stranger)*, John Galsworthy *(Mr. Hadley, a new friend)*, Jerome Patrick *(Mr. Wallace, an attorney)*, Evelyn Sherman *(His Sister)*, Arnold Lucy *(The Valet)*.

Rural comedy-drama. Speck Brown, a country boy, is reared by the cruel Deacon Jones, who insists that Speck attend school. Speck is happy with the local boys and his dog, Hippy, as companions and is fond of his kindly schoolteacher, but when she defends the boy against his guardian, the deacon forces her to resign. A stranger comes to town, and through his kindness Speck is able to go to New York City; at a private school he continues his boyish pranks and is snubbed at a party he gives for his wealthy neighbors. He becomes involved in a scheme perpetrated by two friends who turn out to be crooked and plot to rob the house in which he is living. Disgusted with society, and realizing that money cannot buy him happiness, he returns to his boyhood hometown. *Orphans. Churchmen. Schoolteachers. Smalltown life. Boarding schools. New York City. Dogs.*

Note: This film was inspired by a number made famous by Gus Edwards in his vaudeville sketches.

SCHOOL FOR WIVES **F2.4848**

Victory Pictures. *Dist* Vitagraph Co. of America. 5 Apr **1925** [c14 Feb 1925; LP21155]. Si; b&w. 35mm. 7 reels, 6,782 ft.

Dir-Scen Victor Hugo Halperin. *Photog* Joseph Ruttenberg, Jack Zanderbrock. *Sets* Tec-Art Studios.

Cast: Conway Tearle *(Richard Keith)*, Sigrid Holmquist *(Betty Lynch)*, Peggy Kelly *(Lady Atherton)*, Arthur Donaldson *(Jordan B. Lynch)*, Allan Simpson *(Howard Lynch)*, Brian Donlevy *(Ralph)*, Dick Lee *(Tomlinson)*, Dorothy Allen *(Muggins)*, Gerald Oliver Smith *(Ronald Van Stuyvesant)*, Emily Chichester *(Kitty Dawson)*, Alyce Mills *(Mary Wilson)*, Orlando Daly *(Harold Waldehast)*, Jill Lynn *(Dardy Waldehast)*.

Melodrama. Source: Leonard Merrick, *The House of Lynch* (London, 1907). Betty and Howard Lynch, the children of a ruthless New York millionaire, are reared in a life of ease and irresponsibility. Richard Keith, a poor British artist, is hired by Betty's father to paint her portrait, and she and Richard fall in love. Richard, however, refuses to share in her father's fortune and prepares to return to London. Betty arranges passage on the same ship, and they are married on the high seas. They settle down in respectable poverty, and Betty has a child. Howard Lynch is shot and killed by the daughter of a man who was crippled in one of the elder Lynch's factories. Betty's child becomes ill and needs an operation that Richard cannot afford. Her father advances her the money, but the price of the operation is her divorce from Richard. Richard becomes entangled with Lady Atherton, whom he does not love. Betty secretly returns to England, determined to live moderately. Her father dies, and she inherits his fortune—only to give it all to charity. She and Richard are later reunited. *Artists. Millionaires. Fatherhood. Murder. Divorce. Wealth. New York City. London.*

THE SCORCHER **F2.4849**

Harry J. Brown Productions. *Dist* Rayart Pictures. Jan **1927**. Si; b&w. 35mm. 5 reels, 4,529 ft.

Dir Harry J. Brown. *Story* Henry Roberts Symonds. *Photog* William Tuers.

Cast: Reed Howes *(Mike O'Malley)*, Hank Mann, Harry Allen, Ernest Hilliard, George Chapman, Thelma Parr.

Action comedy-drama. "Young mechanic enters a motorcycle race and wins both the contest and the affection of the girl of his heart." (*Motion Picture News Booking Guide*, 12:53, Apr 1927.) *Motorcycle racing. Mechanics.*

SCOTLAND YARD **F2.4850**

Fox Film Corp. 19 Oct **1930** [c24 Sep 1930; LP1615]. Sd (Movietone); b&w. 35mm. 8 reels, 6,750 ft.

Pres by William Fox. *Prod* Ralph Block. *Dir* William K. Howard. *Screenplay-Dial* Garrett Fort. *Photog* George Schneiderman. *Art Dir* Duncan Cramer. *Tech Dir* Gerald L. G. Samson. *Film Ed* Jack Murray. *Sd* Al Protzman. *Asst Dir* R. L. Hough, Ray Flynn. *Cost* Sophie Wachner.

Cast: Edmund Lowe *(Sir John Lasher)*, Edmund Lowe *(Dakin Barrolles)*, Joan Bennett *(Xandra, Lady Lasher)*, Donald Crisp *(Charles Fox)*, Georges Renevant *(Dr. Dean)*, Lumsden Hare *(Sir Clive Heathcote)*, David Torrence *(Captain Graves)*, Barbara Leonard *(Nurse Cecilia)*, Halliwell Hobbes *(Lord St. Arran)*, J. Carrol Naish *(Dr. Remur)*, Arnold Lucy *(McKillop)*.

Melodrama. Source: Denison Clift, *Scotland Yard* (New York opening: 27 Sep 1929). Dakin Barrolles, attempting to elude Scotland Yard detectives, swims to the houseboat of Sir John Lasher, who is forced at gunpoint to shield the thief. Attracted to Lasher's bride, Xandra, Dakin takes a locket containing the couple's bridal photograph; but traced to his hideout, he is forced to join the army to escape. Dakin is badly wounded in action in France, and his face is restored by a plastic surgeon to resemble the features of Lasher on the locket. Xandra, hearing that her husband has been lost in action, takes Dakin to be Sir John, and he returns to England with her and plans, with his former partner, Fox, to rob the Lasher banking concern. His growing love for Xandra, however, dilutes his baser motives; and when he is found out by a Scotland Yard detective, he gives himself up but is placed in the custody of his "wife's" love. *Thieves. Detectives. Criminals—Rehabilitation. Impersonation. Plastic surgery. World War I. London. Scotland Yard. Great Britain—Army.*

SCRAMBLED WIVES **F2.4851**

Marguerite Clark Productions. *Dist* Associated First National Pictures. Mar **1921** [c21 Mar 1921; LP16303]. Si; b&w. 35mm. 7 reels, 6,460 ft.

Prod Adolph Klauber. *Dir* Edward H. Griffith. *Scen* Gardner Hunting. *Photog* William McCoy, Ray June.

Cast: Marguerite Clark *(Mary Lucille Smith)*, Leon P. Gendron *(Larry McLeod)*, Ralph Bunker *(John Chiverick)*, Florence Martin *(Bessie)*, Virginia Lee *(Beatrice Harlow)*, Alice Mann *(Connie Chiverick)*, Frank Badgley *(Dickie Van Arsdale)*, America Chedister *(Mrs. Halsey)*, John Mayer *(Mr. Halsey)*, John Washburn *(Mr. Smith)*, Thomas Braidon *(Martin, the butler)*, Ada Neville *(Mrs. Spencer)*, Emma Wilcox *("Dot")*.

Comedy. Source: Adelaide Matthews and Martha M. Stanley, *The First Mrs. Chiverick, a Play* (New York, 1930). Mary Lucille Smith is expelled from a fashionable boarding school when John Chiverick is found in her room during a midnight party. In desperation she elopes with him, but her father has the marriage annulled. Two years later, Mary returns from Europe, is introduced as Mrs. Lucille Smith, a widow, and falls in love with Larry McLeod. At a houseparty, the efforts of Lucille and Chiverick to keep the latter's new wife and Larry from finding out about their first marriage lead to complications. *Elopement. Marriage—Annulment. Filial relations. Boarding schools.*

SCRAP IRON **F2.4852**

Charles Ray Productions. *Dist* Associated First National Pictures. May **1921** [c12 Jun 1921; LP16756]. Si; b&w. 35mm. 7 reels, 6,747 ft.

Pres by Arthur S. Kane. *Dir* Charles Ray. *Adapt* Finis Fox. *Photog* George Rizard.

Cast: Charles Ray *(John Steel)*, Lydia Knott *(John's mother)*, Vera Steadman *(Midge Flannigan)*, Tom Wilson *(Bill Dugan)*, Tom O'Brien *(Battling Burke)*, Stanton Heck *(Big Tim Riley)*, Charles Wheelock *(Matt Brady)*, Claude Berkeley *(John's chum)*.

Melodrama. Source: Charles E. Van Loan, "Scrap Iron," in *Saturday Evening Post*. John Steel, a mill worker and amateur boxer, gives up boxing at the request of his invalid mother and is called a coward by his fellow workers, who christen him "Scrap Iron." John is in love with Midge Flannigan, but she rejects him when he refuses to fight with professional Battling Burke, and John loses his job when he is late returning from lunch. In order to send his mother to Florida, John accepts the offer of promoter Bill Dugan to be the loser in a fight with Burke in exchange for $200; in the fourth round, however, John fights back, knocks out his opponent, and wins the match. Midge is repentant, but when his mother has a recurrent attack John promises to devote himself to restoring her health. *Invalids. Boxing. Motherhood. Filial relations. Mills.*

THE SCRAPPER (Universal Special) **F2.4853**
Universal Film Manufacturing Co. 6 Feb **1922** [c23 Jan 1922; LP17492]. Si; b&w. 35mm. 5 reels, 4,491 ft.

Pres by Carl Laemmle. *Dir* Hobart Henley. *Scen* E. T. Lowe, Jr. *Photog* Virgil Miller.

Cast: Herbert Rawlinson *(Malloy)*, Gertrude Olmstead *(Eileen McCarthy)*, William Welsh *(Dan McCarthy)*, Frankie Lee *(The Kid)*, Hal Craig *(speed cop)*, George McDaniels *(McGuirk)*, Fred Kohler *(Oleson)*, Edward Jobson *(Riley)*, Al MacQuarrie *(Simms)*, Walter Perry *(Rapport)*.

Romantic drama. Source: Ralph G. Kirk, "Malloy Campeador," in *Saturday Evening Post* (194:3–5, 17 Sep 1921). Malloy, a young Irish construction engineer just out of college, is assigned to a project and immediately falls in love with the contractor's daughter, Eileen. The contractor's secretary, who also loves the girl, hires Oleson, a Swede, to work with Malloy and delay the building sufficiently to arouse the ire of the contractor. Under these conditions, however, Malloy works all the harder, never looking gloomy or restraining his Irish humor until the Swede comes to blows with him over a strike. After thus proving himself, he takes Eileen to the priest, and her resistance is overcome. *Irish. Swedes. Engineers—Civil. Contractors. Secretaries.*

THE SCRAPPIN' KID (Blue Streak Western) **F2.4854**
Universal Pictures. 20 Jun **1926** [c26 Apr 1026; LP22662]. Si; b&w. 35mm. 5 reels, 4,560 ft.

Pres by Carl Laemmle. *Dir* Clifford S. Smith. *Story-Scen* E. Richard Schayer. *Photog* William Nobles.

Cast: Art Acord *(Bill Bradley)*, Velma Connor *(Betty Brent)*, Jimsy Boudwin *(Mike Brent)*, C. E. Anderson *(Hank Prince)*, Jess Deffenbach *(Pete Hendricks)*, Hank Bell *(Slim Hawks)*, Edmund Cobb *(Cliff Barrowes)*, Dudley Hendricks *(Sheriff Bolton)*.

Western melodrama. Bill Bradley, who owns a small house and a one-horse corral in the hills, saves the lives of Betty Brent and her brother Mike from a forest fire in which their mother has perished. He decides to take care of them. When word spreads that Betty is actually 18, a committee of citizens, headed by Cliff Barrowes, whose father holds a mortgage on Bill's property, calls to protest; the sheriff's wife offers the children a home; and soon after, Cliff begins to woo the girl. Bill, meanwhile, is forcibly held by a trio of outlaws about to flee across the border. When Betty arrives, she is kidnaped by the outlaws, and they take her to the cave where their loot is hidden; Bill's dog carries a note to the sheriff, while he overtakes the outlaws and prevents their escape until the arrival of the posse. With the reward Bill pays off the mortgage and marries Betty. *Orphans. Outlaws. Sheriffs. Mortgages. Forest fires. Dogs.*

SCREEN STRUCK *see* **STAGE STRUCK**

SCULPTOR'S DREAM **F2.4855**
Paul Tellegan. 5 Oct **1929** [New York State license]. Si; b&w. 35mm. 5 reels.

Cast: Paul Tellegan.

Drama(?). No information about the nature of this film has been found.

THE SCUTTLERS (Reissue) **F2.4856**
Fox Film Corp. Nov **1924** [New York showing: 29 Jun 1925]. Si; b&w. 35mm.

Note: A William Farnum feature originally released by Fox in 6 reels (Dec 1920; c12 Dec 1920; LP15923).

THE SEA BAT **F2.4857**
Metro-Goldwyn-Mayer Pictures. 5 Jul **1930** [c7 Jul 1930; LP1401]. Sd (Movietone); b&w. 35mm. 8 reels, 6,570 ft. [Also si.]

Dir Wesley Ruggles. *Screenplay-Dial* Bess Meredyth, John Howard Lawson. *Titl* Philip J. Leddy. *Story* Dorothy Yost. *Photog* Ira Morgan. *Art Dir* Cedric Gibbons. *Film Ed* Harry Reynolds, Jerry Thoms. *Song:* "Lo-Lo" Reggie Montgomery, Ed Ward. *Rec Engr* Karl E. Zint, Douglas Shearer.

Cast: Raquel Torres *(Nina)*, Charles Bickford *(Reverend Sims)*, Nils Asther *(Carl)*, George F. Marion *(Antone)*, John Miljan *(Juan)*, Boris Karloff *(Corsican)*, Gibson Gowland *(Limey)*, Edmund Breese *(Maddocks)*, Mathilde Comont *(Mimba)*, Mack Swain *(Dutchy)*.

Melodrama. At an outpost in the Caribbean, Nina, the daughter of Antone, a local sponge fisherman, is in love with Carl, a diver on one of the schooners. On a hunting expedition, Juan, a jealous rival, fouls the air line; and when a monstrous sea bat appears, Juan leaves Carl to drown. In despair, Nina turns to the voodoo rites of the natives and declares she will marry the man who captures the sea bat. Reverend Sims, actually an escaped convict, arrives on a tramp steamer, converts the girl, and in the process falls in love with her. They decide to elope by motorboat, but Juan, who has recognized Sims, succeeds in capturing him with the aid of a friend. The trio are attacked by the sea bat, and all are drowned but Sims, who returns to the waiting Nina. *Fishermen. Divers. Clergymen. Fugitives. Imposture. Religious conversion. Voodoo. Sponges. Caribbean. Sea monsters.*

Note: Filmed on locations off the coast and near Mazatlán, Mexico.

THE SEA BEAST **F2.4858**
Warner Brothers Pictures. 15 Jan **1926** [c12 Dec 1925; LP22137]. Si; b&w. 35mm. 10 reels, 10,250 ft.

Dir Millard Webb. *Adapt* Bess Meredyth. *Photog* Byron Haskins. *Adtl Photog* Frank Kesson. *Asst Dir* George Webster.

Cast: John Barrymore *(Ahab Ceeley)*, Dolores Costello *(Esther Harper)*, George O'Hara *(Derek Ceeley)*, Mike Donlin *(Flask)*, Sam Baker *(Queequeg)*, George Burrell *(Perth)*, Sam Allen *(sea captain)*, Frank Nelson *(Stubbs)*, Mathilde Comont *(Mula)*, James Barrows *(Reverend Harper)*, Vadim Uraneff *(Pip)*, Sojin *(Fedallah)*, Frank Hagney *(Daggoo)*.

Drama. Source: Herman Melville, *Moby Dick, or The Whale* (New York, 1851). Ahab Ceeley and his half brother, Derek, are rivals for the hand of Esther Harper, a minister's beautiful daughter. Because Esther favors his brother, Derek pushes Ahab overboard on a whaling trip; Ahab's leg is chewed off by Moby Dick, a white whale; and he returns to Esther a broken and embittered man. Ahab, believing that Esther no longer loves him, becomes captain of a whaler and obsessively sets out to kill Moby Dick. Ahab learns of Derek's treachery and, after killing the whale, kills Derek. Ahab return to New Bedford and, his obsession gone, settles down with Esther. *Sea captains. Clergymen. Cripples. Whaling. Revenge. New Bedford (Massachusetts).*

SEA CLIFF, LONG ISLAND **F2.4859**
Allen Williams. 14 Jan **1929** [New York State license]. Si; b&w. 35mm. 4 reels.

Travelog. No information about the precise nature of this film has been found. *Long Island.*

SEA FURY **F2.4860**
Tom White. *Dist* H. H. Rosenfield. 16 Oct **1929** [New York State license]. Sd; b&w. 35mm. 6 reels, 5,154 ft.

Pres by Tom White. *Dir* George Melford. *Story* George Melford, Elmer Ellsworth.

Cast: James Hallet, Mildred Harris, George Rigas, Frank Campeau, George Godfrey, Bernard Siegel.

Adventure melodrama. The captain of a ship (played by either George Rigas or Bernard Siegel) carrying contraband from Mexico to the United States is forced by his crew to stop to rescue the sole survivor—a girl (played by Mildred Harris)—of a wrecked ship. The crew mutinies, killing all officers save the new second mate, David Mills (played by James Hallet?), the only navigator left on board. Agreeing to steer the ship if the girl is left unharmed, they are safe for a time, but the crew again grows restless. In the end, they escape the crew and weather a fierce storm with the help of the faithful Negro cook (played by George Godfrey). *Smugglers. Ship crews. Cooks. Mutiny. Shipwrecks. Sea rescue.*

Note: A silent production to which dialog was added (*Motion Picture News*, 7 Dec 1929, p72).

THE SEA GOD **F2.4861**
Paramount-Publix Corp. 13 Sep **1930** [c11 Sep 1930; LP1572]. Sd (Movietone); b&w. 35mm. 9 reels, 8,054 ft.

Dir-Adapt-Dial George Abbott. *Photog* Archie J. Stout. *Rec Engr* Earl Hayman.

Cast: Richard Arlen *(Phillip ["Pink"] Barker)*, Fay Wray *(Daisy)*, Eugene Pallette *(Square Deal McCarthy)*, Robert Gleckler *(Big Schultz)*, Ivan Simpson *(Pearly Nick)*, Maurice Black *(Rudy)*, Robert Perry *(Abe)*, Fred Wallace *(Bill)*, Willie Fung *(Sin Lee)*, Sol K. Gregory *(Duke)*, Mary De Bow *(Mary)*, James Spencer *(Sanaka Joe)*.

Adventure melodrama. Source: John Russell, "The Lost God," in *Where the Pavement Ends* (London, 1921). Trader Phillip Barker and Big Schultz, an unscrupulous rival, both seek the attentions of Daisy, who is forced to accept Schultz's marriage offer to get a job in his general store on a South Seas island. Losing to Schultz in a dice game, Barker bets his ship and cargo on a race to another island; en route, Barker rescues a man in a canoe, permitting Schultz to win. The rescued man gives him some pearls from a treasure trove, and Barker sells them, buys back his ship, and prepares to sail. Hearing of the plan, Schultz's men follow. While Barker is exploring the ocean-bed for pearls, cannibals attack the ship, killing all but Daisy (who has stowed away) and McCarthy, the mate, whom they capture. Mistaken in his diving suit for a god, Barker is able to save the captives. Schultz's men attack them but are routed by a counterattack of the savages; and with the aid of his armor, Barker and his companions are able to escape. *Traders. Adventurers. Cannibals. General stores. Wagers. Pearl diving. Ship racing. South Sea Islands.*

THE SEA GULL *see* **A WOMAN OF THE SEA**

THE SEA HAWK **F2.4862**

Frank Lloyd Productions. *Dist* Associated First National Pictures. 2 Jun **1924** [New York premiere; released 14 Jun; c16 Jun 1924; LP20310]. Si; b&w. 35mm. 12 reels, 11,527-12,045 ft.

Dir Frank Lloyd. *Scen* J. G. Hawks. *Titl* Walter Anthony. *Photog* Norbert F. Brodin. *Art Dir* Stephen Goosson. *Ships dsgnd & executed by* Fred Gabourie. *Film Ed* Edward M. Roskam. *Theme Song: "Sea Hawk"* Modest Altschuler, John LeRoy Johnston. *Cost* Walter J. Israel. *Dir of Research* William J. Reiter.

Cast: Milton Sills *(Sir Oliver Tressilian, later Sakr-el-Bahr, The Sea Hawk)*, Enid Bennett *(Rosamund Godolphin)*, Lloyd Hughes *(Master Lionel Tressilian)*, Wallace MacDonald *(Master Peter Godolphin)*, Marc MacDermott *(Sir John Killigrew)*, Wallace Beery *(Jasper Leigh, a freebooter)*, Frank Currier *(Asad-el-Din, Basha of Algiers)*, Medea Radzina *(Fenzileh, his wife)*, William Collier, Jr. *(Marzak, his son)*, Lionel Belmore *(Justice Baine)*, Fred De Silva *(Ali, Asad's lieutenant)*, Hector V. Sarno *(Tsamanni, Asad's personal aide)*, Albert Prisco *(Yusuf, a Moorish leader)*, George E. Romain *(Spanish commander)*, Robert Bolder *(Ayoub, Fenzileh's servant)*, Christina Montt *(Infanta of Spain)*, Kathleen Key *(Andalusian slave girl)*, Nancy Zann *(Spanish slave girl)*, Louis Morrison *(innkeeper)*, Kate Price *(innkeeper's wife)*, Al Jennings *(Captain of Asad's guards)*, Bert Woodruff *(Nick, Oliver's servant)*, Walter Wilkinson *(Oliver's young son)*, Andrew Johnston *(Sir Walter)*, Henry Barrows *(bishop)*, Edwards Davis *(Chief Justice of England)*, Claire Du Brey *(The Siren)*, Robert Spencer *(boatswain)*, Theodore Lorch *(Turkish merchant)*.

Romantic adventure drama. Source: Rafael Sabatini, *The Sea Hawk* (London, 1915). At the instigation of his half brother, Lionel, Oliver Tressilian, a wealthy baronet, is shanghaied and blamed for the death of Peter Godolphin, brother of Oliver's fiancée, whom actually Lionel has slain. At sea Oliver is captured by Spaniards and made a galley slave, but when he escapes to the Moors he becomes Sakr-el-Bahr, the scourge of Christendom. Learning of Rosamund's marriage to his half brother, he kidnaps both of them, but to avoid sending her to the Basha of Algiers he surrenders to a British ship. Rosamund intercedes to save his life, and following the sacrificial death of Lionel they are married. *Galley slaves. Pirates. Moors. Islam. Seafaring life.*

SEA HORSES **F2.4863**

Famous Players–Lasky. *Dist* Paramount Pictures. 22 Feb **1926** [New York premiere; released 8 Mar; c5 Mar 1926; LP23236]. Si; b&w. 35mm. 7 reels, 6,565 ft.

Pres by Adolph Zukor, Jesse L. Lasky. *Dir* Allan Dwan. *Screenplay* James Shelley Hamilton. *Adapt* Becky Gardiner. *Photog* James Howe.

Cast: Jack Holt *(George Glanville)*, Florence Vidor *(Helen Salvia)*, William Powell *(Lorenzo Salvia)*, George Bancroft *(Cochran)*, Mack Swain *(Bimbo-Bomba)*, Frank Campeau *(Señor Cordoza)*, Allan Simpson *(Harvey)*, George Nichols *(Marx)*, Mary Dow *(Cina Salvia)*, Dick La Reno *(Henry)*, Frank Austin *(Cheadle)*.

Romantic melodrama. Source: Francis Brett Young, *Sea Horses* (London, 1925). Helen Salvia sets sail with her 4-year-old daughter for Panda, an isolated East African port, where she expects to join her Italian husband, Lorenzo, who deserted her a year after their marriage. Cochran, the burly first mate, and Harvey, the youthful third officer, openly vie for her favor, while Captain Glanville remains aloof. In Panda, Helen discovers that her husband has become a drunken derelict and returns to the ship, but Glanville is forced to buy her release from Salvia. Fearful of the implication, Helen returns ashore with her daughter, flees from Lorenzo's attempts to attack her, and is found by Glanville just as a typhoon breaks in all its fury. In regaining possession of the child from Lorenzo, the captain is wounded; and Cochran, covering their retreat, kills Lorenzo. Cochran pays for his daring with his life, and Helen is free to return to England with Glanville. *Ship crews. Italians. Children. Derelicts. Desertion. Portuguese East Africa. Typhoons.*

SEA LEGS **F2.4864**

Paramount-Publix Corp. 7 Nov **1930** [New York premiere; released 29 Nov; c1 Dec 1930; LP1798]. Sd (Movietone); b&w. 35mm. 7 reels, 5,673 ft.

Dir Victor Heerman. *Scen* Marion Dix. *Story* George Marion, Jr. *Photog* Allen Siegler. *Film Ed* Doris Drought. *Song: "It Must Be Illegal"* George Marion, Jr., Ralph Rainger. *Song: "A Daisy Told Me"* George Marion, Jr., W. Franke Harling. *Song: "Ten O'Clock Town"* Arthur Swanstorm, Michael Cleary.

Cast: Jack Oakie *(Searchlight Doyle)*, Lillian Roth *(Asdriene)*, Harry Green *(Gabriel Grabowski)*, Eugene Pallette *(Hyacinth Nitouche)*, Jean Del Val *(Crosetti)*, Albert Conti *(captain)*, André Cheron *(high commissioner)*, Charles Sellon *(Admiral O'Brien)*, Tom Ricketts *(commander)*.

Comedy. Searchlight Doyle, lightweight boxing champion of the United States Navy, is shanghaied into the fleet of Sainte Cassette, an island republic, as a replacement for a wealthy slacker who must serve his country to receive a $2 million inheritance, a scheme concocted by attorney Gabriel Grabowski. All his shipmates, except Hyacinth Nitouche, assume that he is indeed the wastrel he purports to be. Doyle falls in love with Adrienne, the most beautiful of the captain's daughters, and wins her affections by treating his comrades in her teashop. Admiral O'Brien, grandfather of the man Doyle is impersonating, comes to visit, and mistaking him for a civilian, Doyle throws him overboard and to everybody's surprise is complimented on his vigilance. But his real identity is exposed by some American sailors, and he is suspected of killing young O'Brien; he is cleared of suspicion, however, and is reinstated by the admiral, thereby gaining Adrienne's love. *Sailors. Boxers. Impersonation. Inheritance. Courtship. Teashops. Imaginary republics. United States Navy.*

THE SEA LION **F2.4865**

Hobart Bosworth Productions. *Dist* Associated Producers. 5 Dec **1921** [c18 Dec 1921; LP17477]. Si; b&w. 35mm. 5 reels, 4,367 ft.

Dir Rowland V. Lee. *Scen* Joseph Franklin Poland. *Story* Emilie Johnson. *Photog* J. O. Taylor.

Cast: Hobart Bosworth *(Nels Nelson)*, Emory Johnson *(Tom Walton)*, Bessie Love *(Nymph)*, Carol Holloway *(Dolly May)*, Florence Carpenter *(Florence)*, Charles Clary *(Green)*, Jack Curtis *(Bentley)*, Richard Morris *(Billy)*, J. Gordon Russell *(Simmons)*.

Sea melodrama. Nels Nelson, a cruel and embittered captain of a whaling vessel, who has been deserted by his wife 20 years earlier, sails to San Francisco, where he takes aboard young Tom Walton, a spendthrift rejected by his guardian. A shortage of water develops, and Nelson is overpowered by a mutiny. Tom, sent ashore, discovers two castaways—an old man and a beautiful young girl—and he brings them aboard. Nelson, who sees in the girl proof of his wife's unfaithfulness, torments and humiliates her at every opportunity. Tom takes her away in a small boat, and alarmed by storm clouds, Nelson puts out to sea. During the storm, Nelson discovers in the girl's Bible a record of his wife's blameless life, and learning that she is his own daughter he returns to rescue her. *Castaways. Seafaring life. Whaling. Mutiny. Infidelity. San Francisco. Documentation. The Bible.*

SEA PROWLERS *see* **PROWLERS OF THE SEA**

THE SEA TIGER **F2.4866**

First National Pictures. 27 Feb **1927** [c3 Mar 1927; LP23719]. Si; b&w. 35mm. 6 reels, 5,606 ft.

Prod-Scen Carey Wilson. *Dir* John Francis Dillon. *Photog* Charles Van Enger.

Cast: Milton Sills *(Justin Ramos)*, Mary Astor *(Amy)*, Larry Kent *(Charles Ramos)*, Alice White *(Manuella)*, Kate Price *(Bridget)*, Arthur Stone *(Enos)*, Emily Fitzroy *(Mrs. Enos)*, Joe Bonomo *(Sebastiano)*.

Melodrama. Source: Mary Heaton Vorse, "A Runaway Enchantress" (publication undetermined). Following the death of his mother, the departure to Spain of his father with a new bride, and the illness of Charles, his younger brother, Justin Ramos, a stalwart and quick-tempered Canary Island fisherman, swears to protect his brother from harm. He breaks the pledge, however, when Charles boasts that he will make a quick and unworthy conquest of Amy, daughter of Sebastiano Cortissos, an expatriated Spanish nobleman. Justin reprimands his brother but refrains from declaring his love for Amy, who taunts him because he has scorned her; but after he saves his brother during a sea storm, his fiery cousin, Manuella, gives Justin an opportunity to prove his love and expose the unworthiness of Charles. *Fishermen. Brothers. Courtship. Canary Islands.*

THE SEA WOLF **F2.4867**

Ralph W. Ince Corp. *Dist* Producers Distributing Corp. 26 Jul **1926** [c9 Jun 1926; LP22814]. Si; b&w. 35mm. 7 reels, 6,763 ft.

Pres by John C. Flinn. *Dir* Ralph Ince. *Screenplay* J. Grubb Alexander. *Photog* J. O. Taylor. *Art Dir* Harold Grieve. *Asst Dir* Ray Kirkwood, Wilfrid North.

Cast: Ralph Ince *("Wolf" Larsen)*, Claire Adams *(Maud Brewster)*, Theodore von Eltz *(Humphrey Van Weyden)*, Snitz Edwards *(Thomas Mugridge, the cook)*, Mitchell Lewis *(Johansen, the mate)*.

Melodrama. Source: Jack London, *The Sea-Wolf* (New York, 1904). Captain "Wolf" Larsen, the absolute master of a seal schooner, is a mystic and philosopher, though he rules his men with an iron hand. On a ferry going from San Francisco to Oakland, Van Weyden, a critic, and Maud Brewster, a novelist, meet in masquerade costumes and are forced overboard when their boat collides with a steamer. Humphrey, then Maud, are picked up by Larsen's crew. Because of her costume, Maud is taken for a boy and placed in the custody of Mugridge, the cook, who attempts to attack her upon discovering her identity. Larsen takes her under his protection and decides to marry her; but as the ceremony begins, the crew mutinies, and Larsen is stricken with blindness as he faces the rebels. The ship is set afire, and though Humphrey and Maud are rescued by another steamer, Larsen, deserted by his crew, refuses to quit his ship and is enveloped in flames. *Novelists. Critics. Cooks. Ship crews. Seafaring life. Sealing. Disguise. Blindness. San Francisco. Oakland (California). Ship fires. Shipwrecks.*

THE SEA WOLF **F2.4868**

Fox Film Corp. 21 Sep **1930** [c20 Aug 1930; LP1529]. Sd (Movietone); b&w. 35mm. 10 reels, 8,000 ft.

Pres by William Fox. *Dir* Alfred Santell. *Screenplay* Ralph Block. *Dial* S. N. Behrman. *Photog* Glen MacWilliams. *Art Dir* Joseph Wright. *Film Ed* Paul Weatherwax. *Rec Engr* Frank MacKenzie. *Asst Dir* Marty Santell.

Cast: Milton Sills *("Wolf" Larsen)*, Jane Keith *(Lorna Marsh)*, Raymond Hackett *(Allen Rand)*, Mitchell Harris *("Death" Larsen)*, Nat Pendleton *(Smoke)*, John Rogers *(Mugridge)*, Harold Kinney *(Leach)*, Sam Allen *(Neilson)*, Harry Tenbrook *(Johnson)*.

Romantic melodrama. Source: Jack London, *The Sea Wolf* (New York & London, 1904). "Wolf" Larsen, fearsome master of the hellship *Ghost*, attempts in vain to attract Lorna Marsh, a prostitute in a Japanese port of call. Lorna, having first turned down the offer to ship on Larsen's sealer, comes aboard when Allen Rand, with whom she is infatuated, is shanghaied along with two or three sailors who are taken from the crew of a steamer belonging to Wolf's brother, "Death." Scorned by Wolf as a helpless weakling, Rand is made assistant to Mugridge, the cook. Later Larsen promotes Rand to first mate for saving his life when the crew makes an unsuccessful attempt at mutiny. After Wolf has made a particularly large catch of seals off the Aleutians, he determines to seduce Lorna forcibly, knocks out Rand, and is about to succeed when Death overtakes his ship. Lorna and Rand escape in a sealing boat while Mugridge avenges a previous mutilation deliberately caused by Wolf by blinding him with a hot poker. After days adrift, the lovers sight the *Ghost*, ravaged by Death. Wolf, still alive but badly injured, tries to prevent Lorna and Rand from taking supplies and leaving by casting off their boat. But Wolf knows he is dying, and he gives Lorna and Rand directions to the nearest land before he succumbs. *Ship captains. Ship crews. Brothers. Prostitutes. Cooks. Seafaring life. Sealing. Blindness. Mutiny. Japan. Aleutian Islands.*

THE SEA WOMAN *see* **WHY WOMEN LOVE**

SEALED LIPS **F2.4869**

Columbia Pictures. 15 Sep **1925** [c19 Oct 1925; LP21916]. Si; b&w. 35mm. 6 reels, 5,613 ft.

Dir Antonio Gaudio. *Story* Harold Shumate. *Photog* Sam Landers.

Cast: Dorothy Revier *(Margaret Blake)*, Cullen Landis *(Alan Howard)*, Lincoln Stedman *(Jack Warren)*, Scott Turner *(James Blake)*, John Miljan *(George Garnett)*, Barbara Luddy *(Alice Howard)*, Tom Ricketts *(Joseph Howard)*.

Melodrama. Margaret Blake, daughter of notorious gambler "Square Deal" Blake, has not told her sweetheart, Alan Howard, a son of wealth, about her father. College chum Jack Warren takes Alan to Blake's gambling house, and Alan misunderstands Margaret's affection for her dying father and breaks with her without giving her a chance to explain. Margaret inherits the gambling house. George Garnett, Blake's lawyer, who has become friendly with Alan's sister Alice, persuades Howard, Sr., to gamble his wealth ($250,000 in bonds) in a cardgame employing a supposedly stacked deck. He loses and dies of heart failure. Alan accuses Margaret of causing his father's death and refuses her offer to return the bonds. Alice does accept the bonds from her, but Garnett, who plans to flee to South America, has her sign them over to him. He attacks her, and Alice stabs him. Believing she has killed him, Alice flees. Margaret takes the blame, but the police arrest both. Garnett is exposed, and the film ends with Warren and Alice and Alan and Margaret about to celebrate a double wedding. *Gamblers. Swindlers. Lawyers. Filial relations. Courtship.*

THE SECLUDED ROADHOUSE **F2.4870**

Fred Balshofer Productions. 8 Sep **1926** [New York State license]. Si; b&w. 35mm. 5 reels.

Cast: William Barrymore.

Melodrama(?). No information about the precise nature of this film has been found. *Roadhouses.*

SECOND CHOICE **F2.4871**

Warner Brothers Pictures. 4 Jan **1930** [c18 Dec 1929; LP923]. Sd (Vitaphone); b&w. 35mm. 7 reels, 6,150 ft. [Also si.]

Dir Howard Bretherton. *Scen-Dial* Joseph Jackson. *Photog* John Stumar. *Film Ed* Robert Crandall. *Sd Engr* Cal Applegate.

Cast: Dolores Costello *(Vallery Grove)*, Chester Morris *(Don Warren)*, Jack Mulhall *(Owen Mallory)*, Edna Murphy *(Beth Randall)*, Charlotte Merriam *(Madge Harcourt)*, Ethlyne Clair *(Edith Pemberton)*, James Clemmons *(Ned Pemberton)*, Edward Martindel *(Herbert Satterlee)*, Henry Stockbridge *(Mr. Grove)*, Anna Chance *(Mrs. Grove)*.

Society melodrama. Source: Elizabeth Alexander, *Second Choice* (New York, 1928). Though Vallery Grove loves Don Warren, her ambitious mother opposes their match because he has neither money nor social position to offer her. At a party, Madge Harcourt, a spoiled rich girl, flirts with Don, who decides to terminate his engagement to Val. Val is later introduced to Owen Mallory, who has just been jilted by Beth Randall, and learns that Don plans to marry Madge. Later, Owen and Val find comfort in their mutual friendship, and when he proposes to her in a spirit of levity, she accepts and they elope just as Don, realizing he still loves Val, breaks off with Madge. Uncertain of her love for Owen, Val takes in the disillusioned and intoxicated Don while her husband is away on business, and when he challenges Owen, the husband realizes that his wife has remained faithful and loves him rather than Don. *Flirts. Social classes. Marriage. Elopement.*

SECOND FIDDLE **F2.4872**

Film Guild. *Dist* W. W. Hodkinson Corp. 7 Jan **1923.** Si; b&w. 35mm. 6 reels, ca5,800 ft.

Dir Frank Tuttle. *Story* Frank Tuttle, James Ashmore Creelman. *Photog* Fred Waller, Jr.

Cast: Glenn Hunter *(Jim Bradley)*, Mary Astor *(Polly Crawford)*, Townsend Martin *(Herbert Bradley)*, William Nally *(Cragg)*, Leslie Stowe *(George Bradley)*, Mary Foy *(Mrs. Bradley)*, Helenka Adamowska *(Cragg's daughter)*, Otto Lang *(Dr. Crawford)*, Osgood Perkins.

Melodrama. Jim, a boy who has always played second fiddle to his elder brother, Herbert, gets a chance to be a hero when, to protect his mother and sweetheart, Polly, he holds a murderer at bay with an unloaded shotgun. (Herbert took the shells when he went for help.) Eventually Jim faints, and Cragg, the killer, overpowers him. Simultaneously, Herbert returns with help; he takes all the credit and makes Jim look like a coward. Later, Jim proves his courage when he saves Polly and overpowers Cragg, now an escaped convict. Herbert bows to Jim and returns to college. *Brothers. Prison escapees. Murder. Courage.*

THE SECOND FLOOR MYSTERY **F2.4873**

Warner Brothers Pictures. 26 Apr **1930** [c9 Apr 1930; LP1214]. Sd (Vitaphone); b&w. 35mm. 7 reels, 5,628 ft. [Also si.]

Dir Roy Del Ruth. *Scen-Dial* Joseph Jackson. *Sd Engr* Clifford A. Ruberg.

Cast: Grant Withers *(Geoffrey West)*, Loretta Young *(Marian Ferguson)*,

H. B. Warner *(Inspector Bray)*, Claire McDowell *(Aunt Hattie)*, Sidney Bracy *(Alfred)*, Crauford Kent *(Captain Fraser)*, John Loder *(Lieut. Norman Fraser)*, Claude King *(Enright)*, Judith Vosselli *(Mystery Woman)*.

Mystery comedy-melodrama. Source: Earl Derr Biggers, *The Agony Column* (Indianapolis, 1916). Geoffrey West and Marian Ferguson, Americans who see each other in a London hotel, begin a series of epistolary communications through "The Agony Column" in the *Times*, identifying themselves respectively as "the strawberry man" and "the grapefruit lady," denoting their breakfast menus. He is advised that if he publishes a letter for 5 successive days, and if they are sufficiently interesting, she will meet him. He invents a murder in which Captain Fraser and his young brother, Norman, are involved and ends his series of letters by confessing to the crime himself. Marian arrives with the police and has him thrown into a dungeon from which he is rescued by anarchists. He finds her bound and gagged in a perilous situation; but he discovers that the whole affair has been staged by her to give him a taste of his own imagination. *Anarchists. Agony column. Hoaxes. London. "Times" (London).*

SECOND HAND LOVE **F2.4874**

Fox Film Corp. 26 Aug **1923** [c12 Aug 1923; LP19398]. Si; b&w. 35mm. 5 reels, 5,000 ft.

Pres by William Fox. *Dir* William Wellman. *Scen* Charles Kenyon. *Story* Shannon Fife. *Photog* Don Short.

Cast: Charles Jones *(Andy Hanks)*, Ruth Dwyer *(Angela Trent)*, Charles Coleman *("Dugg" [Johnny Walker])*, Harvey Clark *(The Detective, "Scratch")*, Frank Weed *(Deacon Seth Poggins)*, James Quinn *(Dugg's partner)*, Gus Leonard *(The Constable)*.

Melodrama. Tinker Andy Hanks rescues mistreated Angela Trent—first from her bootlegger husband and then from an unwanted suitor, Seth Poggins, the town miser. All ends happily. *Tinkers. Bootleggers. Misers. Marriage.*

SECOND HAND ROSE (Universal-Special) **F2.4875**

Universal Film Manufacturing Co. 8 May **1922** [c1 May 1922; LP17809]. Si; b&w. 35mm. 5 reels, 4,433 ft.

Pres by Carl Laemmle. *Dir* Lloyd Ingraham. *Story-Scen* A. P. Younger. *Photog* Bert Cann.

Cast: Gladys Walton *(Rose O'Grady)*, George B. Williams *(Isaac Rosenstein)*, Eddie Sutherland *(Nat Rosenstein)*, Wade Boteler *(Frankie "Bull" Thompson)*, Max Davidson *(Abe Rosenstein)*, Virginia Adair *(Rebecca Rosenstein)*, Alice Belcher *(Rachel Rosenstein)*, Jack Dougherty *(Terry O'Brien)*, Walter Perry *(Tim McCarthy)*, Bennett Southard *(Hawkins)*, Camilla Clark *(Little Rosie)*, Marion Faducha *(Little Nat)*.

Romantic drama. Source: Grant Clarke and James F. Hanley, "Second Hand Rose" (a song; New York, 5 Jul 1921). Rose, the adopted Irish daughter of the Rosensteins, Second Avenue pawnshop owners, is much sought after by Tim McCarthy, a wealthy Irish contractor many years her senior. Her adopted brother, Nat, is accused of stealing from his firm and is arrested and put in jail; Rosenstein, heartbroken, becomes seriously ill. McCarthy offers to pay Nat's bail provided that Rose will marry him; and although she is in love with Terry O'Brien, Rose consents to the marriage. Shortly afterward, Nat is released and proves his innocence; and McCarthy, realizing that Rose is unhappy with a "second-hand" husband, releases her so that she may marry young O'Brien. *Contractors. Pawnbrokers. Jews. Irish. Courtship. New York City—East Side.*

SECOND HONEYMOON **F2.4876**

Continental Talking Pictures. Sep **1930** [c25 Aug 1930; LP1920]. Mus score & sd eff (Photophone); b&w. 35mm. 6 reels, 5,586 ft. [Also si.]

Dir Phil Rosen. *Scen* Harry O. Hoyt. *Photog* Herbert Kirkpatrick. *Art Dir* Ernest Hickson. *Film Ed* Charles Hunt. *Rec Engr* Neil Jack, C. F. Franklin.

Cast: Josephine Dunn *(Mary Huntley)*, Edward Earle *(Jim Huntley)*, Ernest Hilliard *(Major Ashbrook)*, Bernice Elliott *(Edith)*, Fern Emmett *(maid)*, Harry Allen *(sheriff)*, Henry Roquemore *(deputy)*.

Comedy-drama. Source: Ruby Mildred Ayres, *The Second Honeymoon* (New York, 1921). Mary Huntley, bored with married life, is about to desert her husband, Jim. She turns her affection towards her husband's friend, Major Ashbrook, who devises a scheme to disillusion her about other men, thus hoping to cause her to return to her husband. He persuades Mary to accompany him to a lonely mountain cabin where a fake robbery is to take place. Ashbrook then plans to turn tail and run, leaving Mary to fend for herself until such time as her husband will come to rescue her. The plan fails when some real thugs who have escaped from prison get into the action, but after much confusion and fighting the husband reclaims his wife. *Prison escapees. Infidelity. Marriage. Robbery. Hoaxes.*

SECOND WIFE **F2.4877**

RKO Productions. 9 Feb **1930** [c9 Feb 1930; LP1086]. Sd (Photophone); b&w. 35mm. 7 reels, 6,058 ft.

Dir Russell Mack. *Stgd by* Wallace Fox. *Screenplay* Hugh Herbert, Bert Glennon. *Photog* William Marshall. *Sd Rec* Lambert E. Day. *Asst Dir* Charles Kerr.

Cast: Conrad Nagel *(Walter Fairchild)*, Lila Lee *(Florence Wendell)*, Hugh Huntley *(Gilbert Gaylord)*, Mary Carr *(Mrs. Rhodes)*, Freddie Burke Frederick *(Junior)*.

Domestic drama. Source: Charles Fulton Oursler, *All the King's Men* (a play; publication undetermined). After the death of his first wife, Walter Fairchild, engaged to Florence Wendell, is convinced that he must establish a new home in order that their married life be a success. Following their marriage, Walter's 7-year-old son, Junior, is sent to school in Switzerland. When Florence is expecting her child, Walter receives word that his son is dying and makes preparations to leave; hurt by his lack of consideration for her, Florence tells him he cannot return to her; nevertheless, he goes to the boy, who recovers and returns with his father to be placed in another school. Gaylord, still in love with Florence, finds her receptive to his attentions, and Walter's threats fail to discourage him. Florence is encouraged to leave her husband, but when asked to give up her baby, she relents and is reconciled with Walter and his son. *Children. Stepmothers. Marriage. Family life. Infidelity. Switzerland.*

SECOND YOUTH **F2.4878**

Distinctive Pictures. *Dist* Goldwyn-Cosmopolitan Pictures. 6 Apr **1924** [c12 Mar 1924; LP19977]. Si; b&w. 35mm. 6 reels, 6,169 ft.

Dir Albert Parker. *Adapt* John Lynch. *Photog* J. Roy Hunt. *Art Dir* Clark Robinson. *Prod Mgr* John Lynch.

Cast: Alfred Lunt *(Roland Farwell Francis)*, Dorothy Allen *(Polly, a maid)*, Jobyna Howland *(Mrs. Benson)*, Lynne Fontanne *(Rose Raynor)*, Walter Catlett *(John McNab)*, Herbert Corthell *(George Whiggam)*, Margaret Dale *(Mrs. Twombly)*, Mimi Palmeri *(Ann Winton)*, Winifred Allen *(Phoebe Barney)*, Charles Lane *(Weeks Twombly)*, Lumsden Hare *(James Remmick)*, Mickey Bennett *(Willie, Mrs. Benson's son)*, Faire Binney *(Lucy Remmick)*, Hugh Huntley *(Harley Forbes)*.

Romantic comedy. Source: Allan Eugene Updegraff, *Second Youth; Being, in the Main, Some Account of the Middle Comedy in the Life of a New York Bachelor* (New York, 1917). Roland Farwell Francis, a timid silk salesman, is sought after by the ladies, who think him a likely choice for the altar. Ann Winton, when she is dared by her brother-in-law, Weeks Twombly, invites the salesman to dinner and a night on the town in Greenwich Village. After several entanglements with his pursuers and their boyfriends, Francis finally becomes aggressive, is promoted to assistant buyer, and wins the hand of Ann Winton. *Bachelors. Salesclerks. Buyers. Business management. Silk. New York City—Greenwich Village.*

SECRET CODE (Reissue) **F2.4879**

Triangle Film Corp. *Dist* Tri-Stone Pictures. 27 Mar **1925** [New York State license]. Si; b&w. 35mm. 5 reels.

Note: A Gloria Swanson film originally released by Triangle Film Corp. on 8 Sep 1918.

LE SECRET DU DOCTEUR **F2.4880**

Paramount-Publix Corp. 12 Oct **1930** [Paris premiere]. Sd (Movietone); b&w. 35mm. 7 reels, 5,832 ft.

Dir Charles de Rochefort. *French Adapt* Denis Amiel.

Cast: Marcelle Chantal *(Lillian Garner)*, Leon Bary *(Richard Garner)*, Jean Bradin *(Jean Colman)*, Maxudian *(Dr. Brady)*, Odette Joyeux *(Suzy, the servant)*, Hubert Daix *(Mr. Reading)*, Alice Tissot *(Mrs. Reading)*.

Society melodrama. Source: James Matthew Barrie, "Half an Hour," in *The Plays of J. M. Barrie* (New York, 1929). A French-language version of *The Doctor's Secret*, q. v. *Physicians. Nobility. Social classes. Automobile accidents. England.*

THE SECRET HOUR **F2.4881**

Paramount Famous Lasky Corp. 4 Feb **1928** [c4 Feb 1928; LP24988]. Si; b&w. 35mm. 8 reels, 7,194 ft.

Pres by Adolph Zukor, Jesse L. Lasky. *Dir-Scen* Rowland V. Lee. *Titl* Julian Johnson. *Photog* Harry Fischbeck. *Film Ed* Robert Bassler.

Cast: Pola Negri *(Amy)*, Jean Hersholt *(Tony)*, Kenneth Thomson *(Joe)*, Christian J. Frank *(Sam)*, George Kuwa *(Ah Gee)*, George Periolat *(doctor)*.

Romantic drama. Source: Sidney Howard, *They Knew What They Wanted; a Comedy in Three Acts* (Garden City, New York, 1925). Tiring of bachelorhood, Tony, an elderly fruit grower, sends a photograph of Joe, his foreman, to capture the heart of an attractive waitress named Amy. She falls in love with the photograph, and Tony is left out in the cold when an automobile accident prevents him from meeting her train and he sends Joe instead. Joe and Amy abandon themselves to their magnetism for each other and secretly marry, regretting their action the next morning. Three months later, able to walk again, Tony is planning to marry Amy. They tell him their secret. Furious at first, Tony orders them from the house; later he relents and forgives them, seeing that it was his fault for substituting Joe's photograph. *Bachelors. Waitresses. Fruit culture. Mistaken identity. Marriage. Automobile accidents.*

THE SECRET OF BLACK CANYON **F2.4882**

Arrow Pictures. 12 Jul **1925** [c16 Jun 1925; LP21566]. Si; b&w. 35mm. 5 reels.

Dir Ward Hayes. *Story* William Merrill McCormick, P. G. Şleeman.

Cast: Dick Hatton *(Dick Halsey)*.

Western melodrama. Dick Halsey returns to his hometown in order to sell a herd of cattle and becomes engaged to Dora Markham, his childhood sweetheart. While riding through town, Dick sees clouds of black smoke in the hills and goes to investigate, finding an unwatched still that has exploded. Dick also finds a trickle of oil coming from the earth, indicating that the land, which belongs to Dora's father, Judge Markham, has rich deposits of oil. Dick returns to town with a jug each of moonshine and crude oil and is arrested by the sheriff for moonshining. Alex Carr, who was operating the illegal still, discovers that it has been destroyed, and he also discovers the oil. Carr goes to Judge Markham and offers to buy the land, but the judge is unable to sell it until the following day, when the deed is cleared of a second mortgage. Dick is released from jail in the morning and races Carr to the bank, which holds the mortgage. Carr and Dick fight outside the bank, and Dick subdues him, turning him over to the sheriff as a bootlegger. Dick then secures the title to the judge's land, exchanging this right for a full interest in Dora. *Sheriffs. Judges. Bootleggers. Land rights. Mortgages. Banks. Stills. Oil lands.*

THE SECRET OF THE HILLS **F2.4883**

Vitagraph Co. of America. 25 Sep **1921** [c15 Aug 1921; LP16859]. Si; b&w. 35mm. 5 reels.

Dir Chester Bennett. *Scen* E. Magnus Ingleton. *Photog* Jack MacKenzie.

Cast: Antonio Moreno *(Guy Fenton)*, Lillian Hall *(Marion)*, Kingsley Benedict *(Lincoln Drew)*, George Clair *(Francis Freeland)*, Walter Rodgers *(Benjamin Miltimore)*, Oleta Otis *(Mrs. Miltimore)*, J. Gunnis Davis *(Richards)*, Frank Thorne *(De Vrillefort)*, Arthur Sharpe *(Sidney Coleridge)*.

Mystery melodrama. Source: William Garrett, *The Secret of the Hills; the Romance of a Modern Treasure Hunt* (London, 1920). While in London, American press correspondent Guy Fenton meets Marion Overton through an accidental exchange of coats with her guardian, who is found slain. Some papers are discovered in the coat, and Fenton's friend, Drew, uncovers indications of a lost treasure of King James III of Scotland. Although Fenton is threatened by the Miltimores and made prisoner in their house, he escapes by a secret trapdoor. After a series of adventures, Fenton is rescued by Drew, who pretends to be a chauffeur for the bandits; and they find the treasure. They return to rescue Marion, and in the struggle Miltimore is killed; but he makes a confession clearing Fenton. *Reporters. Treasure. London. Scotland. James III (Scotland). Documentation.*

THE SECRET OF THE PUEBLO **F2.4884**

William Steiner Productions. 15 Feb **1923** [c5 Jan 1923; LU18556]. Si; b&w. 35mm. 5 reels, 4,670 ft.

Dir Neal Hart. *Story* Alvin J. Neitz. *Photog* Jake Badaracco, William Steiner, Jr.

Cast: Neal Hart *(Bob Benson)*, Hazel Deane *(Ruth Bryson)*, Tom Grimes *(Pueblo Charlie)*, Monte Montague.

Western melodrama. "Scenes are laid in Arizona. Story deals with the mystic and weird cliff-dwelling Pueblo Indians. Bob Benson, a young knight of the plains, locates the secret entrance to the Indians' memorial altar room where the heroine is held captive. He rescues her from the hands of the Pueblos. Action of picture embraces hard-riding cowboys, fights and escapes, with a romance running throughout." (*Motion Picture News Booking Guide*, 4:90, Apr 1923.) *Pueblo Indians. Cowboys. Arizona.*

SECRET ORDERS **F2.4885**

R-C Pictures. *Dist* Film Booking Offices of America. 7 Mar **1926** [c7 Mar 1926; LP22541]. Si; b&w. 35mm. 6 reels, 5,486 ft.

Dir Chet Withey. *Scen* J. Grubb Alexander. *Story* Martin Justice. *Photog* Roy Klaffki. *Asst Dir* Doran Cox.

Cast: Harold Goodwin *(Eddie Delano)*, Robert Frazer *(Bruce Corbin)*, Evelyn Brent *(Janet Graham)*, John Gough *(Spike Slavin)*, Marjorie Bonner *(Mary, Janet's friend)*, Brandon Hurst *(butler)*, Frank Leigh *(cook)*.

Spy melodrama. At the outbreak of the World War, Janet Graham, a telegrapher, is persuaded by Eddie Delano, a crook masquerading as a salesman, to marry him. She agrees, but upon discovering his duplicity, she turns him over to the police. Janet enters the U. S. Secret Service and is detailed to uncover the source of a "leak" in the sailing of troop transports; believing that Eddie has been killed in a wreck, she falls in love with Corbin, her superior. Meanwhile, Eddie escapes from prison, joins Slavin, of whose Secret Service affiliation he is unaware, and accepts a job with some German agents in New York. Janet discovers that Louis, Corbin's cook, is a German spy and pretends that she herself is a Hun agent. Complications ensue when Eddie attempts to rob Corbin's safe; she radios for aid from the spy headquarters and is rescued by Corbin, whom she marries after the death of her husband. *Telegraph operators. Secret service. Spies. Cooks. Germans. Troop transports. World War I.*

SECRET SORROW **F2.4886**

Reol Productions. 1 Oct **1921**. Si; b&w. 35mm. 6 reels, 5,544 ft.

Cast: George Edward Brown, Percy Verwayen, Edna Morton, Lawrence Chenault, Inez Clough, Ida Anderson.

Drama. "At the death of her husband, poverty striken, the young widow must part with one of her young children. This boy is adopted by a doctor and educated to become an assistant district attorney. Unknown to anyone but the mother, he prosecutes his own brother for murder. After a verdict of guilty, the mother makes known that the prisoner and attorney are brothers. Later developments prove that the prisoner is innocent." (New York State license application.) *Widows. Physicians. District attorneys. Brothers. Poverty. Adoption. Murder. Trials.*

THE SECRET STUDIO **F2.4887**

Fox Film Corp. 19 Jun **1927** [c26 Jun 1927; LP24151]. Si; b&w. 35mm. 6 reels, 5,870 ft.

Pres by William Fox. *Dir* Victor Schertzinger. *Scen* James Kevin McGuinness. *Photog* Glen MacWilliams. *Asst Dir* William Tummel.

Cast: Olive Borden *(Rosemary Merton)*, Clifford Holland *(Sloan Whitney)*, Noreen Phillips *(Elsie Merton)*, Ben Bard *(Larry Kane)*, Kate Bruce *(Ma Merton)*, Joseph Cawthorn *(Pa Merton)*, Margaret Livingston *(Nina Clark)*, Walter McGrail *(Mr. Kyler)*, Lila Leslie *(Mrs. Kyler)*, Ned Sparks *(The Plumber)*.

Romantic drama. Source: Hazel Livingston, "Rosemary," a serialized novel in *San Francisco Call* (1926). Rosemary Merton, an ambitious girl, agrees to pose in the studio of Larry Kane, a dissolute artist, but she refuses to do so in the nude. Kane, however, makes it appear in the portrait that she posed in that manner, and she is disgraced when local newspapers print the picture with an exposé of her struggle with Kane. She is vindicated by the intervention of Whitney, her wealthy young sweetheart; and Rosemary makes the sacrifice of ambition for love. *Artists. Models. Reputation. Newspapers.*

Note: There is some confusion in credits: although reviews give names and functions stated here, *Film Year Book* and company records suggest that a very different group was once involved with this production.

SECRETS **F2.4888**

Joseph M. Schenck. *Dist* Associated First National Pictures. 24 Mar **1924** [New York premiere; released Mar; c11 Feb 1924; LP19901]. Si; b&w. 35mm. 8 reels, 8,363 ft.

Pres by Joseph M. Schenck. *Dir* Frank Borzage. *Adapt* Frances Marion. *Photog* Tony Gaudio.

Cast—1865: Norma Talmadge *(Mary Marlowe)*, Eugene O'Brien *(John Carlton)*, Patterson Dial *(Susan)*, Emily Fitzroy *(Mrs. Marlowe)*, Claire McDowell *(Elizabeth Channing)*, George Nichols *(William Marlowe)*.

Cast—1870: Norma Talmadge *(Mary Carlton)*, Eugene O'Brien *(John Carlton)*, Harvey Clark *(Bob)*, Charles Ogle *(Dr. McGovern)*.

Cast—1888: Norma Talmadge *(Mary Carlton)*, Eugene O'Brien *(John*

Carlton), Francis Feeney *(John Carlton, Jr.)*, Alice Day *(Blanche Carlton)*, Winston Miller *(Robert Carlton)*, May Giraci *(Audrey Carlton)*, Gertrude Astor *(Mrs. Manwaring)*.

Cast—1923: Norma Talmadge *(Mary Carlton)*, Eugene O'Brien *(John Carlton)*, Winter Hall *(Dr. Arbuthnot)*, Frank Elliott *(Robert Carlton)*, George Cowl *(John Carlton, Jr.)*, Clarissa Selwynne *(Audrey Carlton)*, Florence Wix *(Lady Lessington)*.

Melodrama. Source: Rudolf Besier and May Edginton, *Secrets, a Play in a Prologue, Three Acts and an Epilogue* (New York, c1930). Mary Carlton, an old lady, falls asleep while sitting up with her sick husband, John, and dreams of her girlhood in England, her elopement with John to America, their life on a ranch in the West, their return to England—rich and famous—and her devotion to him when he is unfaithful. She awakens and finds that her husband has passed the crisis. *Old age. Ranch life. Fidelity. England. Dreams.*

THE SECRETS OF PARIS **F2.4889**

Whitman Bennett Productions–H. V. Productions. *Dist* Mastodon Films. 1 Oct **1922** [c1 Nov 1922; LP18359]. Si; b&w. 35mm. 7 reels, 6,481 ft.

Pres by C. C. Burr. *Prod* Whitman Bennett. *Dir* Kenneth Webb. *Adapt* Dorothy Farnum. *Photog* Edward Paul, Harry Stradling. *Art Dir* Elsa Lopez.

Cast: Lew Cody *(King Rudolph)*, Gladys Hulette *(Mayflower)*, Effie Shannon *(Madame Ferrand)*, Montagu Love *(The Schoolmaster)*, Harry Sothern *(Hoppy)*, Rose Coghlan *(Owl)*, William (Buster) Collier, Jr. *(François)*, J. Barney Sherry *(Chancellor)*, Dolores Cassinelli *(Lola)*, Bradley Barker *(The Hindoo)*, Walter James *(The Strangler)*, Jane Thomas *(Margot)*.

Melodrama. Source: Eugène Sue, *Mystères de Paris* (1842–43). King Rudolph, traveling incognito in search of the daughter of his onetime peasant sweetheart, is attracted to Mayflower, whose only friend among the band of thieves with whom she lives is François, son of "The Schoolmaster," leader of the Paris underground. Rudolph puts Mayflower in the care of his former nurse, but she is kidnaped and imprisoned by Owl and her cohorts. François and Rudolph outwit the cutthroats and rescue Mayflower, but François is mortally wounded while releasing the lovers from a flooding dungeon. The king now perceives that Mayflower is the girl whom he has sought. *Royalty. Thieves. Kidnaping. Paris.*

SECRETS OF THE NIGHT (Universal-Jewel) **F2.4890**

Universal Pictures. 15 Feb **1925** [c12 Nov 1924; LP20774]. Si; b&w. 35mm. 7 reels, 6,138 or 6,700 ft.

Pres by Carl Laemmle. *Dir* Herbert Blache. *Adapt-Scen* Edward J. Montagne. *Photog* Gilbert Warrenton.

Cast: James Kirkwood *(Robert Andrews)*, Madge Bellamy *(Anne Maynard)*, Tom Ricketts *(Jerry Hammond)*, Tom S. Guise *(Col. James Constance)*, Arthur Stuart Hull *(Lester Knowles)*, Edward Cecil *(Alfred Austin)*, Frederick Cole *(Teddy Hammond)*, Rosemary Theby *(Mrs. Lester Knowles)*, ZaSu Pitts *(Celia Stebbins)*, Tom Wilson *(Old Tom Jefferson White)*, Joe Singleton *(Charles)*, Bull Montana *(The Killer)*, Tyrone Brereton *(Anne's brother)*, Otto Hoffman *(The Coroner)*, Arthur Thalasso *(Detective Reardon)*, Anton Vaverka *(Joshua Brown)*.

Mystery comedy-drama. Source: Guy Bolton and Max Marcin, *The Nightcap, a Mystery Comedy in Three Acts* (New York, 1929). To keep bank examiner Alfred Austin from examining the records of his bank, Robert Andrews hosts a large party and there stages his own murder. Everyone is suspected—especially young Hammond, who is in love with Andrews' ward, Anne Maynard, and Lester Knowles, who has been suspicious of Andrews' friendship with Mrs. Knowles. The hilarious turmoil that ensues is finally cleared up by the reappearance of Andrews himself and the announcement that Joshua Brown has repaid the large loan that the directors wished to conceal from Austin. Finally, the group learns that Austin has turned to real estate, and Andrews declares his love for Anne. *Bankers. Bank examiners. Banks.*

Note: Working title: *The Night Cap*.

SECRETS OF THE RANGE **F2.4891**

William M. Pizor Productions. **1928** [New York State license: 8 Mar 1928]. Si; b&w. 35mm. 5 reels, 4,250 ft.

Dir-Scen-Titl Robert J. Horner. *Photog* Lauren A. Draper. *Film Ed* Robert J. Horner.

Cast: Montana Bill, Betty Gates, Bud Osborne, Carl Berlin.

Western melodrama(?). No information about the nature of this film has been found.

SEE AMERICA THIRST **F2.4892**

Universal Pictures. 24 Nov **1930** [c19 Nov 1930; LP1745]. Sd (Movietone); b&w. 35mm. 8 reels, 6,256 ft. [Also si.]

Pres by Carl Laemmle. *Dir* William James Craft. *Screenplay-Dial* Henry La Cossitt. *Adapt* C. Jerome Horwin. *Story* Vin Moore, Edward Luddy. *Photog* Arthur Miller, C. Allen Jones. *Film Ed* Harry Lieb. *Mus & Lyr* Lou Handman, Bernie Grossman. *Sd Engr* C. Roy Hunter.

Cast: Harry Langdon *(Wally)*, George "Slim" Summerville *(Slim)*, Bessie Love *(Ellen)*, Mitchell Lewis *(Screwy O'Toole)*, Mathew Betz *(Insect McGann)*, Stanley Fields *(Spumoni)*, Lloyd Whitlock *(O'Toole's henchman)*, Dick Alexander *(McGann's henchman)*, Tom Kennedy *("Shivering" Smith)*, Lew Hearn *(inventor)*, LeRoy Mason *(attorney)*.

Comedy-drama. Two tramps, Slim and Wally, through a misadventure, find themselves embroiled in a bootleggers' war when they are mistaken for the infamous gunmen Shivering Smith and Gunkist Casey, and they are engaged by the Spumoni gang to do away with the McGann faction; McGann, terrified by his opposition, hires them in turn to kill Spumoni. Having accumulated a small fortune, Slim and Wally fall in love with Ellen, a nightclub singer who is actually employed by the district attorney's office, and with her help they plan to doublecross both gangs. They arrange a street battle between the factions, only to be unmasked when the real Shivering Smith shows up, but they finally use tear gas to subdue the gangsters. They are disillusioned to find that Ellen is in love with the district attorney and discover that someone has substituted bombs for their newly acquired wealth. *Tramps. Gangsters. Hired killers. Bootleggers. Singers. District attorneys. Impersonation.*

SEE MY LAWYER **F2.4893**

Christie Film Co. *Dist* Robertson-Cole Distributing Corp. 13 Mar **1921** [c13 Mar 1921; LP16328]. Si; b&w. 35mm. 6 reels.

Dir Al Christie. *Scen* W. Scott Darling. *Photog* Anton Nagy, Alec Phillips.

Cast: T. Roy Barnes *(Robert Gardner)*, Grace Darmond *(Norma Joyce)*, Lloyd Whitlock *(Billy Noble)*, Jean Acker *(Betty Gardner)*, Ogden Crane *(T. Hamilton Brown)*, Tom McGuire *(Leonard D. Robinson)*, J. P. Lockney *(Otto Trueman)*, Lincoln Plumer *(Anson Morse)*, Bert Woodruff *(Dr. Drew)*, Eugenie Ford *(Aunt Kate)*.

Comedy. Source: Max Marcin, *See My Lawyer, a Play* (New York opening: 2 Sep 1915). Robert Gardner and Billy Noble become interested in a machine capable—according to the inventor, Trueman—of producing artificial rubber. A trust is formed, circulars are sent out, and a demonstration is requested. When Billy discovers that the invention is fraudulent and refuses to demonstrate it, the trust lawyer becomes suspicious and notifies postal authorities. Robert feigns insanity, and Trueman accepts an offer of $1 million for the formula, which experts later discover produces an indestructible paving block. *Inventors. Lawyers. Postal inspectors. Rubber. Construction materials. Trusts.*

SEE YOU IN JAIL **F2.4894**

Ray Rockett Productions. *Dist* First National Pictures. 17 Apr **1927** [c11 Apr 1927; LP23842]. Si; b&w. 35mm. 6 reels, 5,800 ft.

Prod Ray Rockett. *Dir* Joseph Henabery. *Scen* Gerald Duffy. *Photog* George Folsey.

Cast: Jack Mulhall *(Jerry Marsden)*, Alice Day *(Ruth Morrisey)*, Mack Swain *(Slossom)*, George Fawcett *(Marsden, Sr.)*, Crauford Kent *(Roger Morrisey)*, John Kolb *(jailer)*, William Orlamond *(inventor)*, Leo White *(valet)*, Carl Stockdale *(attorney)*, Burr McIntosh *(Judge Hauser)*, Charles Clary *(Rollins)*.

Farce. Source: William H. Clifford, "See You in Jail" (publication undetermined). Jerry Marsden, disowned by his wealthy father, agrees to impersonate Roger Morrisey, a noted capitalist, and appears for him before a judge who is handing out jail sentences for speeding. In jail Jerry meets several bona fide millionaires. Meanwhile, he has fallen in love with Morrisey's sister, Ruth, who thinks him a thief but later learns of his innocence. An inventor interests Jerry in an invention, and Jerry persuades the others to form a company in the jail. The infuriated Morrisey exposes Jerry when he is liberated and tries to have him arrested on numerous charges. Ruth saves him by claiming she is the "R. Morrisey" referred to; the two are married, and Jerry's father buys the invention from his son's company. *Millionaires. Inventors. Capitalists. Disinheritance. Reckless driving. Impersonation. Jails.*

SEE YOU LATER **F2.4895**
Sierra Pictures. *Dist* Pizor Productions. Jan **1928.** Si; b&w. 35mm. 5 reels, 4,900 ft.
Cast: Earl Douglas, Barbara Luddy.
Drama(?). No information about the nature of this film has been found.

SEEING'S BELIEVING **F2.4896**
Metro Pictures. 1 May **1922** [c26 Apr 1922; LP17799]. Si; b&w. 35mm. 5 reels, 4,500 ft.
Dir Harry Beaumont. *Adapt* Edith Kennedy. *Story* Rex Taylor. *Photog* John Arnold. *Art-Tech Dir* A. F. Mantz. *Prod Dir* David H. Thompson.
Cast: Viola Dana *(Diana Webster)*, Allan Forrest *(Bruce Terring)*, Gertrude Astor *(Aunt Sue)*, Philo McCullough *(Jimmy Harrison)*, Harold Goodwin *(Hack Webster)*, Edward Connelly *(Henry Scribbins)*, Josephine Crowell *(Martha Scribbins)*, Colin Kenny *(Mr. Reed)*, Grace Morse *(Mrs. Reed)*, J. P. Lockney *(sheriff)*.
Romantic comedy. Diana Webster and her aunt's fiancé, Jimmy Harrison, are caught in a storm and forced to spend the night in a country hotel; there they are seen by Bruce Terring, a friend of Diana's brother, Jack, and Bruce forms his own conclusions. Arriving home, Diana finds Bruce to be her brother's house guest, and as she is unable to convince Bruce of the innocence of her predicament, she plans to prove to him that seeing is not always believing, but the tables are turned on Diana when she engages two crooks. Meanwhile, Bruce learns of her innocence and finds her being blackmailed; in the mixup that follows, the sheriff decides to arrest everyone. But Jimmy arrives, identifies the crooks, and vouches for his friends; and Bruce persuades Diana that he has complete faith in her. *Brother-sister relationship. Circumstantial evidence. Blackmail.*

DIE SEHNSUCHT JEDER FRAU **F2.4897**
Metro-Goldwyn-Mayer Pictures. 16 Dec **1930.** Sd (Movietone); b&w. 35mm. 11 reels, 9,336 ft.
Dir Victor Seastrom. *German Asst* Frank Reicher. *German Dial* Hans Kraly. *Photog* Merritt B. Gerstad. *Art Dir* Cedric Gibbons. *Film Ed* Conrad A. Nervig. *Gowns* Adrian.
Cast: Vilma Banky *(Mizzi)*, Joseph Schildkraut *(Buck)*, Edward G. Robinson *(Tony)*, William Bechtel *(Der Pfarrer)*, Frank Reicher *(Der Doktor)*, Conrad Seidemann *(Der Landbrieftraeger)*, Henry Armetta *(Angelo)*, George Davis *(Georgio)*, Gum Chin *(Ah Gee)*.
Romantic drama. A German-language version of *A Lady To Love,* q. v. *Vineyardists. Waitresses. Italians. Neapolitans. San Franciscans. Marriage. California.*

THE SELF STARTER **F2.4898**
Harry J. Brown Productions. *Dist* Rayart Pictures. 3 May **1926** [New York State license]. Si; b&w. 35mm. 5 reels, 5,194 ft.
Dir Harry J. Brown.
Cast: Reed Howes *(Jerry Neale)*, Mildred Harris, Sheldon Lewis.
Action melodrama. "Returning from war with plans for self-starter for tanks, Jerry Neale is unable to interest manufacturer in his invention. By a 'coup' he is able to sell invention, though he wrecks manufacturer's office in doing so. He realizes love for girl." *(Motion Picture News Booking Guide,* 11:47, Oct 1926.) *Inventors. Veterans. Tanks (armored cars).*

A SELF-MADE FAILURE **F2.4899**
J. K. McDonald Productions. *Dist* Associated First National Pictures. 29 Jun **1924** [c27 Jun 1924; LP20335, LP20483]. Si; b&w. 35mm. 8 reels, 7,345 ft.
Pres by J. K. McDonald. *Dir* William Beaudine. *Scen* Violet Clark, Lex Neal, John Grey. *Adapt* Tamar Lane. *Story* J. K. McDonald. *Photog* Ray June, Barney McGill. *Film Ed* H. P. Bretherton, Beth Matz.
Cast: Ben Alexander *(Sonny)*, Lloyd Hamilton *(Breezy)*, Matt Moore *(John Steele)*, Patsy Ruth Miller *(Alice Neal)*, Mary Carr *(Grandma Neal)*, Sam De Grasse *(Cyrus Cruikshank)*, Chuck Reisner *(Spike Malone)*, Victor Potel *(Pokey Jones)*, Dan Mason *(Dan)*, Harry Todd *(The Constable)*, Alta Allen *(Mrs. Spike Malone)*, Doris Duane *(The Waitress)*, Priscilla Moran *(Alice Neal, aged 4)*, Joel McCrea *(Verman)*, Cameo *(herself, a dog)*.
Comedy. Breezy, a kindly but illiterate tramp, accompanied by a boy, Sonny, and a dog, hops off a freight train in a health resort, and there he is mistaken for a German masseur by a sanitarium proprietor. Breezy discovers that the hotel owner, Cyrus, has stolen the mineral spring from a boardinghouse keeper, and he succeeds in restoring her property to her. *Tramps. Children. Masseurs. Health resorts. Dogs.*

A SELF-MADE MAN **F2.4900**
Fox Film Corp. 25 Jun **1922** [c25 Jun 1922; LP18079]. Si; b&w. 35mm. 5 reels, 4,920 ft.
Pres by William Fox. *Dir* Rowland V. Lee. *Scen* Rowland V. Lee, Monte M. Katterjohn. *Titl* Ralph Spence. *Photog* David Abel. *Film Ed* Ralph Spence.
Cast: William Russell *(Jack Spurlock)*, Renée Adorée *(Anita Gray)*, Mathilde Brundage *(Aunt Lydia)*, James Gordon *(Jonas Spurlock)*, Richard Tucker *(Hugo Bonsall)*, Togo Yamamoto *(Kato)*, Harry Gribbon.
Comedy-drama. Source: George Horace Lorimer, *Jack Spurlock—Prodigal* (New York, 1908). Jack Spurlock, a railroad magnate's indolent son, is estranged from Anita Gray, his fiancée, by his refusal to work. He is brought to his senses when his father disowns him. With Anita's financial aid he is able to save his father from ruin and recover his self-respect. One sequence shows a trained bear in a boxing match. *Railroad magnates. Filial relations. Bears.*

THE SELF-MADE WIFE **F2.4901**
Universal Pictures. 8 Jul **1923** [c27 Jun 1923; LP19161]. Si; b&w. 35mm. 5 reels, 4,960 ft.
Dir Jack Dillon. *Scen* Albert Kenyon. *Photog* William Fildew.
Cast: Ethel Grey Terry *(Corrie Godwin)*, Crauford Kent *(Tim Godwin)*, Virginia Ainsworth *(Dodo Sears)*, Phillips Smalley *(J. D. Sears)*, Dorothy Cumming *(Elena Vincent)*, Maurice Murphy *(Tim Godwin, Jr.)*, Turner Savage *(Jimmy Godwin)*, Honora Beatrice *(The Baby)*, Tom McGuire *(Hotchkiss)*, Laura La Varnie *(Mrs. Satter)*, Mathew Betz *(Bob)*, Frank Butler *(Allerdyce)*.
Melodrama. Source: Elizabeth Alexander, "The Self-Made Wife," in *Saturday Evening Post* (195:3–5, 20–21, 30–34, 28–32, 28 Oct–18 Nov 1922). Impoverished young lawyer Tim Godwin makes money in an oil strike and buys a big house in New York City, to which he moves with his wife, Corrie, and their child. Tim adjusts quickly to city life and his job with a prestigious law firm, but Corrie remains unhappy and burdened with housework. The situation gets worse after Tim hires a former school chum as a social secretary for his wife. Eventually, the secretary is dismissed and a reconciliation is effected. *Lawyers. Nouveaux riches. New York City.*

SELL 'EM COWBOY **F2.4902**
Ben Wilson Productions. *Dist* Arrow Film Corp. 27 Sep **1924** [c14 Aug 1924; LP20511]. Si; b&w. 35mm. 5 reels, 4,821 ft.
Dir Ward Hayes. *Story-Scen* Bennett Cohen.
Cast: Ed Lytell *(Mathewson, Sr.)*, Dick Hatton *(The "& Son")*, Winona Wilkes *(Helen Wharton, Mathewson, Jr.'s, fiancée)*, Martin Turner *(Romeo)*, Ed La Niece *(Sheriff Fowler)*, Yakima Canutt *(Luke Strong)*, Marilyn Mills *(Milly Atwood)*, William McCall *(John Atwood)*.
Western comedy-melodrama. Frank Mathewson, Jr., a would-be cowboy and the son of a Chicago saddle manufacturer, decides to investigate on his own some unexplained competition his father's firm has encountered in Claxton, Arizona. In Claxton, cowboy Luke Strong has been blackmailed by a rival firm to run Mathewson's salesmen out of town and promptly does the same when junior shows up. Frank returns, captures Luke after attempted robbery, and continues his romance with Millie Atwood, daughter of his father's client. *Cowboys. Salesmen. Business competition. Blackmail. Saddles. Arizona.*
Note: The character played by Lytell is referred to as Jimmy in the synopsis in copyright files but as Frank in a review in *Variety* (17 Jun 1925).

SEÑOR AMERICANO **F2.4903**
Ken Maynard Productions. *Dist* Universal Pictures. 10 Nov **1929** [c30 Oct 1929; LP813]. Sd (Movietone); b&w. 35mm. 6 reels, 6,662 ft. [Also si; 5,418 ft.]
Pres by Carl Laemmle. *Dir* Harry J. Brown. *Scen* Bennett Cohen. *Titl-Dial* Lesley Mason. *Story* Helmer Bergman, Henry McCarthy. *Camera* Ted McCord. *Film Ed* Fred Allen.
Cast: Ken Maynard *(Michael Banning)*, Kathryn Crawford *(Carmelita)*, Gino Corrado *(Ramírez)*, J. P. McGowan *(Maddux)*, Frank Yaconelli *(Mañana)*, Frank Beal *(Don Manuel)*, Tarzan *(the horse)*.
Western melodrama. Michael Banning, a U. S. Army lieutenant sent to Southern California to investigate lawless land-grabbing, wins a golden bridle in a riding contest sponsored by Carmelita, daughter of Spanish grandee Don Manuel, thus incurring the enmity of Ramírez, who is in love with her. The Mexican attempts to steal the bridle, and Banning subdues

him. Maddux, leader of a gang who plan to steal Don Manuel's land, sends a spy to follow Banning, who returns from San José with the news that California has been admitted to the Union, but Maddux has him jailed. When Maddux tries to force Don Manuel into surrendering his grants, Ramírez turns against him. Banning, freed by his servant, arrives with a rescue party, and peace is restored. *Spanish. Mexicans. Investigators. Land rights. California.*

SEÑOR DAREDEVIL **F2.4904**

Charles R. Rogers Productions. *Dist* First National Pictures. 1 Aug **1926** [c6 Jul 1926; LP22869]. Si; b&w. 35mm. 7 reels, 6,326 ft.

Pres by Charles R. Rogers. *Dir* Albert Rogell. *Story-Adapt* Marion Jackson. *Photog* Sol Polito. *Prod Mgr* Harry J. Brown.

Cast: Ken Maynard *(Don Luis O'Flagherty)*, Dorothy Devore *(Sally Blake)*, George Nichols *("Tiger" O'Flagherty)*, Josef Swickard *(Juan Estrada)*, J. P. McGowan *(Jesse Wilks)*, Sheldon Lewis *(Ratburn)*, Buck Black *(Pat Muldoon)*, Billy Franey *(The Cook)*, Tarzan *(himself, a horse)*.

Western melodrama. Tiger O'Flagherty, supervisor of a supply-wagon train destined for the miners in Sonora, is repeatedly besieged by bandits headed by Jesse Wilks, who hopes to starve the miners out of their claims. Tiger is wounded, and his servant writes to his wife; the señora sends Don Luis, their son of whose existence Tiger is ignorant, to his aid. Don Luis turns the tables on Wilks in several encounters and falls in love with Tiger's ward, Sally Blake. Despite Wilks's opposition, some investors arrive and are favorably impressed, but they must be assured of wagon-freight service; thus, Don Luis attacks the train and recaptures the wagons in a battle in which Wilks is killed; leaving him free to make arrangements to marry Sally. *Miners. Bandits. Filial relations. Freightage. Wagon trains. Sonora (Mexico). Horses.*

SEÑORITA **F2.4905**

Paramount Famous Lasky Corp. 30 Apr **1927** [c30 Apr 1927; LP23899]. Si; b&w. 35mm. 7 reels, 6,643 ft.

Pres by Adolph Zukor, Jesse L. Lasky. *Assoc Prod* B. P. Schulberg. *Dir* Clarence Badger. *Screenplay* John McDermott, Lloyd Corrigan. *Titl* Robert Hopkins. *Story* John McDermott. *Photog* H. Kinley Martin, William Marshall.

Cast: Bebe Daniels *(Señorita Francesca Hernández)*, James Hall *(Roger Oliveros)*, William Powell *(Ramón Oliveros)*, Josef Swickard *(Don Francisco Hernández)*.

Comedy-drama. At the age of 20, Francesca Hernández is as skillful at riding, shooting, and fencing as any man. At the ancestral Hernández ranch in South America, her grandfather, Don Francisco, is suffering from the depredations of his old enemies, the Oliveros family, and believing his grandchild to be a boy, he calls for "his" aid. Francesca responds, and, when apprised of the situation, dons the costume of a caballero, and through a series of sensational episodes recoups the family fortune. Meanwhile, Roger Oliveros returns from Europe, unaware of his cousin Ramón's scheming and banditry, and falls in love with Francesca (out of disguise). She routs Ramón in a duel and is later forced to fight the man she loves. Ramón leads an attack on the ranch; Roger does not recognize Francesca until he has wounded her, and as a result, the feud is ended. *Tomboys. Caballeros. Disguise. South America. Feuds.*

SENSATION SEEKERS (Universal-Jewel) **F2.4906**

Universal Pictures. 20 Mar **1927** [c22 Dec 1926; LP23466]. Si; b&w. 35mm. 7 reels, 7,015 ft.

Pres by Carl Laemmle. *Dir-Cont* Lois Weber. *Photog* Ben Kline.

Cast: Billie Dove *("Egypt" Hagen)*, Huntley Gordon *(Ray Sturgis)*, Raymond Bloomer *(Reverend Lodge)*, Peggy Montgomery *(Margaret Todd)*, Will Gregory *(Colonel Todd)*, Helen Gilmore *(Mrs. Todd)*, Edith Yorke *(Mrs. Hagen)*, Phillips Smalley *(Mr. Hagen)*, Cora Williams *(Mrs. W. Symme)*, Sidney Arundel *(Deacon W. Symme)*, Clarence Thompson *(Rabbitt Smythe)*, Nora Cecil *(Mrs. Lodge)*, Frances Dale *(Tottie)*, Lillian Lawrence, Fanchon Frankel *(Tibbett sisters)*, Hazel Howell *(guest)*.

Romantic drama. Source: Ernest Pascal, "Egypt" (publication undetermined). Ray Sturgis, leader of the fashionable Long Island jazz set, is engaged to "Egypt" Hagen, an up-to-date girl in every respect. Egypt is arrested at a roadhouse raid, and at her mother's bidding, the Reverend Norman Lodge arranges for her freedom. At a fancy-dress ball, when Ray wears a costume made of newspaper headlines concerning her arrest, Egypt is offended. Seen constantly in the company of Reverend Lodge, her reputation causes church people to take up the matter with the bishop. Leaving the country club, Egypt goes to the Lodge home and hides behind the door when the bishop arrives; Reverend Lodge wants to marry her, and they admit their love; but humiliation causes her to leave with Sturgis that night. Their yacht is wrecked, but Lodge and the bishop follow and rescue Egypt, though Sturgis is drowned. The bishop, realizing the depth of their love, consents to marry them. *Clergymen. Reputation. Jazz life. Long Island. Shipwrecks.*

SENTENCED TO SOFT LABOR *see* **THE BREATHLESS MOMENT**

SENTIMENTAL TOMMY **F2.4907**

Famous Players–Lasky. *Dist* Paramount Pictures. 29 May **1921** [c27 May 1921; LP16592]. Si; b&w. 35mm. 8 reels, 7,575-7,876 ft.

Pres by Adolph Zukor. *Dir* John S. Robertson. *Scen* Josephine Lovett. *Photog* Roy Overbaugh.

Cast: Gareth Hughes *(Tommy Sandys, an author)*, May McAvoy *(Grizel, his sweetheart)*, Mabel Taliaferro *(The Painted Lady)*, George Fawcett *(Dr. McQueen)*, Harry L. Coleman *(Corporal Shiach)*, Leila Frost *(Elspeth Sandys)*, Kempton Greene *(Dr. David Gemmell)*, Virginia Valli *(Lady Alice Pippinworth)*, Kate Davenport *(Gavinia)*, Alfred Kappeler *(The Little Minister)*, Malcolm Bradley *(Dominoe Cathro)*.

Melodrama. Source: James Matthew Barrie, *Sentimental Tommy* (1895). James Matthew Barrie, *Tommy and Grizel* (1900). The people of Thrums ostracize Grizel, a child of 12, and her mother, known as The Painted Lady, until newcomer Tommy Sandys, a highly imaginative boy, comes to the girl's rescue and they become inseparable friends. Six years later Tommy returns from London, where he has achieved success as an author, and finds that Grizel still loves him. In a sentimental gesture he proposes, but she, realizing that he does not love her, rejects him. In London, Tommy is lionized by Lady Pippinworth, and he follows her to Switzerland. Having lost her mother and believing that Tommy needs her, Grizel comes to him but is overcome by grief to see his love for Lady Pippinworth. Remorseful, Tommy returns home, and after his careful nursing Grizel regains her sanity. *Authors. Childhood. Scotland. Switzerland. London.*

SERENADE **F2.4908**

R. A. Walsh Productions. *Dist* Associated First National Pictures. Aug **1921** [c11 Oct 1921; LP17073]. Si; b&w. 35mm. 7 reels, 6,380 ft.

Pres by R. A. Walsh. *Dir* R. A. Walsh. *Scen* James T. O'Donohoe. *Photog* George Peters. *Art Dir* William Cameron Menzies.

Cast: Miriam Cooper *(María del Carmen)*, George Walsh *(Pancho)*, Rosita Marstini *(María's mother)*, James A. Marcus *(Pepuso)*, Josef Swickard *(Domingo Maticas)*, Bertram Grassby *(Ramón Maticas)*, Noble Johnson *(El Capitan Ramírez)*, Adelbert Knott *(Don Fulgencio)*, William Eagle Eye *(Juan)*, Ardita Milano *(The Dancer)*, Peter Venzuela *(Pedro)*, John Eberts *(The Secretary)*, Tom Kennedy *(Zambrano)*.

Romantic drama. Source: José Felín y Codina, *María del Carmen.* In the Spanish town of Magdalena live María and her sweetheart, Pancho, son of the governor. The town is captured by brigands led by Ramírez, the governor is deposed, and Don Domingo Maticas is appointed in his place. Ramón, son of the new governor, becomes infatuated with María. She repulses him, but he is encouraged by her mother. The jealousy of the two young rivals results in a duel in which Ramón is seriously wounded. María promises to marry Ramón on the condition that Pancho's life is spared, but Ramón breaks his promise and has Pancho arrested. A counter revolution occurs, and Pancho escapes and seeks out Ramón; he disarms him in a duel but spares his life. Touched by his rival's generosity, Ramón helps Pancho and María escape to safety and is himself killed. *Bandits. Jealousy. Spain. Duels.*

SERENADE **F2.4909**

Paramount Famous Lasky Corp. 24 Dec **1927** [c31 Dec 1927; LP24821]. Si; b&w. 35mm. 6 reels, 5,209 ft.

Pres by Adolph Zukor, Jesse L. Lasky. *Dir* Harry D'Abbadie D'Arrast. *Auth-Scen* Ernest Vajda. *Photog* Harry Fischbeck.

Cast: Adolphe Menjou *(Franz Rossi)*, Kathryn Carver *(Gretchen)*, Lawrence Grant *(Josef Bruckner)*, Lina Basquette *(The Dancer)*, Martha Franklin *(Gretchen's mother)*.

Romantic drama. Franz Rossi, a Viennese composer, falls in love with Gretchen, a poor but sympathetic girl, and marries her. Later he composes an operetta, which is a tremendous success. He neglects his wife and has an affair with his leading lady; but his wife discovers his infidelity on the eve of the 150th performance of the operetta, and she leaves him. He realizes how much Gretchen means to him, and the next day he follows her to her hotel and effects a reconciliation. *Composers. Singers. Infidelity. Opera. Vienna.*

THE SERVANT IN THE HOUSE **F2.4910**

H. O. Davis. *Dist* Federated Film Exchanges of America, Walgreene Film Corp. ca26 Feb **1921** [Chicago premiere; released Feb; cl Mar 1920; LP14942]. Si; b&w. 35mm. 5 reels, 5,000 ft. [Copyrighted as 9 reels; trade shown in 8 reels.]

Dir (see note) Hugh Ryan Conway, Jack Conway. *Scen* Lanier Bartlett. *Photog* Elgin Lessley.

Cast: Jean Hersholt *(Manson, The Servant in the House)*, Jack Curtis *(Robert Smith, The Drain Man)*, Edward Peil *(William Smythe, The Vicar [Bill Smith])*, Harvey Clark *(The Bishop of Lancashire)*, Clara Horton *(Mary, The Drain Man's Daughter)*, Zenaide Williams *(Martha, The Vicar's Wife)*, Claire Anderson *(Mary Smith, The Drain Man's Wife)*, Jack Gilbert *(Percival)*, Mrs. George Hernandez *(janitress)*.

Religious drama. Source: Charles Rann Kennedy, *The Servant in the House; a Play of the Present Day, in Five Acts* (New York, 1908). Vicar William Smythe, formerly Bill Smith, is expecting a visit from his rich brother, the Bishop of Benares, and hopes to get money from him and his brother-in-law, the Bishop of Lancashire, to rebuild his antiquated church. Benares, however, enters the house in the guise of a servant, Manson, and bears a striking resemblance to the Christ. Robert, the third brother, is rude and uncivilized, but he has sacrificed much for the education of his brothers and has received little but ingratitude from the vicar, who now is taking care of his daughter, Mary. He is also bitter against the Church because the Bishop of Lancashire's neglect caused the death of his wife. After exposing the Bishop of Lancashire and turning him out of the house, Manson through his generous spirit effects a reconciliation among all the members of the family. Robert also becomes less antagonistic toward the Church, and the vicar volunteers metaphorically to go down into the sewers to clean up the material corruption beneath his church. *Clergymen. Religion. The Church. Jesus.*

Note: Apparently this film was scheduled for release in 1920 by Film Booking Office, Inc. However, the Walgreene Film Corp. purchased distribution rights in late October or early November 1920. A month later it arranged to have all its films distributed by the Federated Film Exchanges of America, Inc. Copyright records give the director's name as Jack Conway. Some sources refer to the character of the Vicar as the Curate and the Bishop of Lancashire as the Bishop of Lancaster.

SERVICE FOR LADIES **F2.4911**

Paramount Famous Lasky Corp. 6 Aug **1927** [c6 Aug 1927; LP24277]. Si; b&w. 35mm. 7 reels, 6,170 ft.

Pres by Adolph Zukor, Jesse L. Lasky. *Dir* Harry D'Arrast. *Screenplay* Chandler Sprague. *Story-Supv* Benjamin Glazer. *Titl* George Marion, Jr. *Story* Ernest Vajda. *Photog* Hal Rosson.

Cast: Adolphe Menjou *(Albert Leroux)*, Kathryn Carver *(Elizabeth Foster)*, Charles Lane *(Robert Foster)*, Lawrence Grant *(King Boris)*.

Society comedy. Albert Leroux, headwaiter at an exclusive Paris hotel, falls hopelessly in love with Elizabeth Foster, an American heiress, though he is convinced that she will never admire a waiter. He follows her to a winter resort in the Swiss Alps, where Albert is in constant fear of having his identity revealed; and upon meeting King Boris of Lucania, both admit to traveling incognito. The lovers are brought together in a toboggan spill, and intimacy soon ripens. Winter sports terminate in an ice masquerade, and in his brilliant costume Albert convinces Elizabeth that he is no ordinary mortal. As Albert leaves for Paris, Robert Foster learns of his position. When Elizabeth and Robert come to the hotel, Albert finds himself dismissed but is surprised to receive a controlling interest in the hotel and a managerial appointment from the Fosters. *Waiters. Social classes. Courtship. Hotels. Toboggans. Switzerland. Alps. Paris.*

SERVING TWO MASTERS **F2.4912**

Dist Lee-Bradford Corp. 1 Dec **1921** [New York State release; general release: Jan 1922]. Si; b&w. 35mm. 5 reels, ca4,900 ft.

Cast: Josephine Earle, Dalas Anderson, Pat Somerset, Zoe Palmer.

Domestic drama. Source: Mrs. Alexander Gross, *Break the Walls Down* (a play; c16 May 1914). "A man of wealth refuses to allow his wife to interest herself in his business affairs. He becomes entangled and is on the verge of financial collapse when his wife comes to his rescue with money made in a dressmaking establishment which she had started unknown to her husband and made a success of." (*Variety*, 18 Nov 1921, p42.) *Businesswomen. Dressmakers. Marriage. Finance—Personal.*

Note: "From general appearances it was made in England, or if not it is an antiquated American picture that has long remained on the shelf" (*Variety*, 18 Nov 1921, p42).

SET FREE (Blue Streak Western) **F2.4913**

Universal Pictures. 6 Mar **1927** [c15 Jan 1927; LP23561]. Si; b&w. 35mm. 5 reels, 4,634 ft.

Pres by Carl Laemmle. *Dir* Arthur Rosson. *Story-Scen* Harrison Jacobs. *Photog* Eddie Linden. *Art Dir* David S. Garber.

Cast: Art Acord *("Side Show" Saunders)*, Olive Hasbrouck *(Holly Farrell)*, Claude Payton *(Burke Tanner)*, Robert McKenzie *(Sam Cole)*, Buddy *(a horse)*, Rex *(a dog)*.

Western melodrama. "Side Show" Saunders gains the respect of shopowner Holly Farrell and the townsfolk when he gives up entertaining with his trick horse and dog and goes to work in the general store. Burke Tanner, who has Holly's promise to marry him, schemes to steal funds from the Queen Mine, informs Holly that Saunders is "wanted," and then lures him, by means of a forged note, to a deserted hut. One of Tanner's men discovers a rich vein in the supposedly worthless Farrell mine; and Tanner, abandoning his robbery plans, sets out to marry Holly. Saunders' horse and dog loosen a boulder that crashes into the hut, freeing him; and pursued by the townsmen, he arrives to stop the wedding and produce his credentials as a detective. *Swindlers. Entertainers. Mine claims. Weddings. General stores. Horses. Dogs.*

THE SET-UP (Blue Streak Western) **F2.4914**

Universal Pictures. 16 May **1926** [c10 Apr 1926; LP22595]. Si; b&w. 35mm. 5 reels, 4,600 ft.

Pres by Carl Laemmle. *Dir* Clifford S. Smith. *Scen* Harrison Jacobs. *Photog* Eddie Linden.

Cast: Art Acord *(Deputy Art Stratton)*, Alta Allen *(Thora Barton)*, Albert Schaeffer *(Tub Jones)*, Thomas G. Lingham *(Seth Tolliver)*, Montague Shaw *(Cliff Barton)*, Jack Quinn *(Bert Tolliver)*, William Welsh *(Sheriff Hayes)*.

Western melodrama. Source: L. V. Jefferson, "Horse Sense" (publication undetermined). Cliff Barton, suspicious of the intentions of the local banker, Seth Tolliver, withdraws his money from the bank, hides it, and is later killed by two hirelings of the banker. Deputy Sheriff Art Stratton, who has trained Barton's horse and is in love with his daughter, Thora, is assigned to guard the ranch for the creditors; and Tolliver, who has designs on the property and wants his son to marry Thora, arranges to have the ranch auctioned. The horse leads Art to the empty moneybag; two small boys who have found the money assume him to be the guilty man; the boys restore the money to Thora; and the villains follow. In a showdown, Art traps the leader into a confession and wins the girl. *Bankers. Sheriffs. Robbery. Murder. Auctions. Horses.*

SEVEN CHANCES **F2.4915**

Buster Keaton Productions. *Dist* Metro-Goldwyn Distributing Corp. 16 Mar **1925** [c22 Apr 1925; LP21376]. Si; b&w with col sequences (Technicolor); 35mm. 6 reels, 5,113 ft.

Pres by Joseph M. Schenck. *Dir* Buster Keaton. *Scen* Jean Havez, Clyde Bruckman, Joseph Mitchell. *Photog* Elgin Lessley, Byron Houck. *Art Dir* Fred Gabourie. *Elec Eff* Denver Harmon.

Cast: Buster Keaton *(James Shannon)*, T. Roy Barnes *(his partner)*, Snitz Edwards *(lawyer)*, Ruth Dwyer *(The Girl)*, Frankie Raymond *(her mother)*, Jules Cowles *(hired man)*, Erwin Connelly *(clergyman)*, Loro Bara, Marion Harlan, Hazel Deane, Pauline Toler, Judy King, Eugénie Burkette, Edna Hammon, Barbara Pierce, Jean Arthur, Connie Evans, Rosalind Mooney.

Farce. Source: Roi Cooper Megrue, *Seven Chances; a Comedy in Three Acts* (New York, c1924). On the morning of his 27th birthday, James Shannon, a young lawyer neeeding money to save his partner from jail, is informed that he stands to inherit $7 million if he is married by 7 o'clock that evening. He proposes to his sweetheart, but she rejects him when he offends her by stating that he must marry a girl—any girl—in order to come into a fortune. He then sets out for the country club in the company of his partner and of the lawyer who first informed him of his windfall. The partner picks out seven girls at the club, and Jimmy proposes to each in turn, being refused by all of them. He then goes into town, proposing to everything in skirts, including a Scotsman. Meanwhile, the partner puts a story into the paper detailing Jimmy's predicament and advertising for a bride. Jimmy goes early to the church, falls asleep, and awakens to find the place full of brides. He escapes from them and runs into his sweetheart's

Negro handyman, who has come with a note forgiving him. Jimmy starts out for her house and is soon pursued by the large mob of outraged brides he left at the altar. After a wild chase, Jimmy arrives at his sweetheart's house just in time to be married on the stroke of 7. *Lawyers. Courtship. Inheritance. Weddings. Chases.*

SEVEN DAYS **F2.4916**

Christie Film Co. *Dist* Producers Distributing Corp. 20 Sep **1925** [c6 Aug 1925; LP21706]. Si; b&w. 35mm. 7 reels, 6,974 ft.

Dir Scott Sidney. *Adapt* Frank Roland Conklin. *Photog* Gilbert Warrenton, Alex Phillips.

Cast: Lillian Rich *(Kit Eclair)*, Creighton Hale *(Jim Wilson)*, Lilyan Tashman *(Bella Wilson)*, Mabel Julienne Scott *(Anne Brown)*, William Austin *(Dal Brown)*, Hal Cooley *(Tom Harbison)*, Rosa Gore *(Aunt Selina)*, Tom Wilson *(policeman)*, Eddie Gribbon *(burglar)*, Charles Clary *(seer)*.

Farce. Source: Mary Roberts Rinehart, "Seven Days," in *Lippincott's Magazine* (82:641–712, Dec 1908). Jim and Bella Wilson obtain a divorce, keeping the news from Jim's Aunt Selina, a wealthy woman who does not approve of such things. Because of a smallpox scare, Jim's home is placed under quarantine, and it becomes a madhouse. Trapped inside are: Jim, Bella, Aunt Selina, Kit (a beautiful girl whom Jim has introduced to his aunt as his wife), Tom Harbison (Kit's fiancé), a cop, a burglar, and Mrs. Brown (a frustrated medium). After numerous complications, the quarantine is lifted: Jim decides to remarry Bella, Aunt Selina assures Jim of his inheritance, and Tom and Kit decide to join the Wilsons in matrimony. *Aunts. Police. Burglars. Mediums. Divorce. Impersonation. Inheritance. Quarantine. Smallpox.*

SEVEN DAYS LEAVE **F2.4917**

Paramount Famous Lasky Corp. 25 Jan **1930** [c25 Jan 1930; LP1025]. Sd (Movietone); b&w. 35mm. 9 reels, 7,534 ft. [Also si; 6,507 ft.]

Dir Richard Wallace. *Co-Dir? (see note)* John Cromwell. *Scen-Dial* Dan Totheroh, John Farrow. *Titl* Richard H. Digges, Jr. *Photog* Charles Lang. *Film Ed* George Nichols, Jr. *Mus Adv* Frank Terry. *Rec Engr* Eugene Merritt. *Wardrobe Tech Dir* Bertram Johns, Billy Brighton. *Adv* Col. G. L. McDonell, "Sailor Billy" Vincent.

Cast: Gary Cooper *(Kenneth Dowey)*, Beryl Mercer *(Sarah Ann Dowey)*, Daisy Belmore *(Emma Mickelham)*, Nora Cecil *(Amelia Twymley)*, Tempe Piggott *(Mrs. Haggerty)*, Arthur Hoyt *(Mr. Willings)*, Arthur Metcalfe *(Colonel)*.

War drama. Source: James Matthew Barrie, *The Old Lady Shows Her Medals, a Play in One Act* (New York, 1918). Sarah Ann Dowey, a widowed Scotch charwoman, regrets that she has no son at the front during the war. Reading of the exploits of Kenneth, a young Canadian soldier of the "Black Watch" regiment, she claims he is her son, and when he is wounded and sent to London on a 5-day leave, a Y. M. C. A. worker tells him that he has met his mother. Kenneth chides Sarah for the deception but agrees to let her be his mother during his stay. He gets into a fight with British sailors over his kilts; and cursing the army, he threatens to desert; but touched by his "mother's" patriotism, he returns to the front in good cheer. Later, in Flanders, he is sent on a mission and never returns; his "mother" receives his medals awarded for bravery and marches off to work, her head held high. *Soldiers. Charwomen. Canadians. Scotch. Great Britain—Army. London. World War I. Flanders' Fields.*

Note: Initially reviewed as *Medals*. The *Film Daily Yearbook* credits John Cromwell as codirector.

SEVEN FACES **F2.4918**

Fox Film Corp. 15 Nov **1929** [New York premiere; released 1 Dec; c23 Oct 1929; LP849]. Sd (Movietone); b&w. 35mm. 9 reels, 7,750 ft.

Pres by William Fox. *Assoc Prod* George Middleton. *Dir* Berthold Viertel. *Dial Dir* Lester Lonergan. *Scen-Dial* Dana Burnet. *Photog* Joseph August, Al Brick. *Sets* William S. Darling. *Film Ed* Edwin Robbins. *Sd* Donald Flick. *Asst Dir* J. Edmund Grainger. *Cost* Sophie Wachner.

Cast: Paul Muni *(Papa Chibou/Diablero, the hypnotist/Willie Smith, the costermonger/Franz Schubert/Don Juan/Joe Gans, the prizefighter/Napoleon)*, Marguerite Churchill *(Hélène Berthelot)*, Lester Lonergan *(Judge Berthelot)*, Russell Gleason *(Georges Dufeyel)*, Gustav von Seyffertitz *(Monsieur Pratouchy)*, Eugenie Besserer *(Madame Vallon)*, Walter Rogers *(Henri Vallon)*, Walka Stenermann *(Catherine of Russia [waxworks])*.

Drama. Source: Richard Connell, "A Friend of Napoleon," in *Saturday Evening Post* (195:12–13, 30 Jun 1923). At a waxworks in Paris, youthful lovers Georges, an attorney, and Hélène meet secretly; but Hélène's father, Judge Berthelot, discovers their love and sends Hélène away. When the museum changes ownership and the wax figures are auctioned, Papa Chibou, the caretaker, not having the money to buy the effigy of Napoleon, tries to steal it but is arrested and brought to trial; when Hélène learns of his predicament, she seeks his advice; he then dreams that his various beloved figures come to life, and he questions them about love. Facing her father in court, Hélène and Georges plead successfully for Papa Chibou, causing sentence to be suspended and enough money to be raised to permit him to buy the effigy; and as a result the judge is reconciled to the union of the young lovers. *Hypnotists. Prizefighters. Costermongers. Lawyers. Judges. Museums. Waxworks. Courtship. Napoleon I. Franz Peter Schubert. Catherine the Great. Don Juan. Paris. Dreams.*

SEVEN FOOTPRINTS TO SATAN **F2.4919**

First National Pictures. 17 Feb **1929** [c29 Jan 1929; LP67]. Talking sequences, sd eff, & mus score (Vitaphone); b&w. 35mm. 6 reels, 5,405 ft. [Also si, 27 Jan 1929; 5,237 ft.]

Pres by Richard A. Rowland. *Prod* Wid Gunning. *Dir* Benjamin Christensen. *Screen Vers* Richard Bee. *Titl* William Irish. *Photog* Sol Polito. *Film Ed* Frank Ware.

Cast: Thelma Todd *(Eve)*, Creighton Hale *(Jim)*, Sheldon Lewis *(The Spider)*, William V. Mong *(The Professor)*, Sojin *(himself)*, Laska Winters *(Satan's mistress)*, Ivan Christy *(Jim's valet)*, De Witt Jennings *(Uncle Joe)*, Nora Cecil *(old witch)*, Kalla Pasha *(Professor Von Viede)*, Harry Tenbrook *(Eve's chauffeur)*, Cissy Fitzgerald *(old lady)*, Angelo Rossitto *(The Dwarf)*, Thelma McNeil *(tall girl)*.

Mystery drama. Source: Abraham Merritt, *7 Footprints to Satan* (New York, 1928). Jim Kirkham, a wealthy young chemist and collector of curios, is in love with Eve Martin, the daughter of a gem collector. At a reception in her home, a fabulous gem is exhibited, and as a result the gem is lost in a series of strange occurrences. Jim and Eve set out to notify the police, but after a wild ride they end up at the home of a mysterious stranger known as Satan. They encounter fantastic characters and are befriended by a dwarf. After a masked ball, they are whisked away by minions of Satan who demand the jewel and threaten to torture Eve; the couple are separated but are reunited by a series of adventures that bring them to the brink of insanity. *Chemists. Curio collectors. Witches. Demonology. Gems.*

SEVEN KEYS TO BALDPATE **F2.4920**

Famous Players–Lasky. *Dist* Paramount Pictures. 11 Oct **1925** [Cleveland premiere; released 19 Oct; c26 Oct 1925; LP21947]. Si; b&w. 35mm. 7 reels, 6,648 ft.

Dir Fred Newmeyer. *Screenplay* Frank Griffin, Wade Boteler. *Photog* Jack MacKenzie.

Cast: Douglas MacLean *(William Halowell Magee)*, Edith Roberts *(Mary Norton)*, Anders Randolf *(J. K. Norton)*, Crauford Kent *(Bentley)*, Ned Sparks *(Bland)*, William Orlamond *(The Hermit)*, Wade Boteler *(Cargan)*, Edwin Sturgis *(Lou Max)*, Betty Francisco *(Myra Thornhill)*, Maym Kelso *(Mrs. Rhodes)*, Fred Kelsey *(sheriff)*, John P. Lockney *(Quimby)*, Edithe Yorke *(Mrs. Quimby)*.

Comedy–mystery melodrama. Source: George M. Cohan, *Seven Keys to Baldpate, a Mysterious Melodramatic Farce* (New York, 1914). Earl Derr Biggers, *Seven Keys to Baldpate* (Indianapolis, 1913). Successful author William Halowell Magee is engaged to Mary Norton, his publisher's daughter. The father threatens to break the engagement because Magee has failed to deliver the manuscript of a much publicized novel on time. Magee offers to complete the book within the next 24 hours and is offered the Baldpate Inn, a mountain resort owned by Bentley, his rival for Mary's hand, as a workshop. The caretaker gives him the only key to the inn, and he immediately sets to work. *He is interrupted by Bland, who unlocks the door with his own key and hides $200,000 in the safe. In rapid succession, the hermit, Myra Thornhill, Cargan and Lou Max, and Mary Norton and Mrs. Rhodes enter the inn with their own keys. The crooks are after the money. Mary is there to warn Magee. He believes it all a frameup to prevent his finishing the novel in time. Finally, the sheriff arrives with the seventh key and arrests everyone. Magee escapes by a ruse and returns to his writing.* Magee finishes the book and we realize that the action described is the novel he has just written. Mary arrives, and Magee assures her that they will be married tomorrow. *Novelists. Publishers. Caretakers. Sheriffs. Hotels.*

Note: Remade in 1929 by RKO Productions.

SEVEN KEYS TO BALDPATE **F2.4921**

RKO Productions. 25 Dec **1929** [New York premiere; released 12 Jan 1930; c12 Jan 1930; LP1002]. Sd (Photophone); b&w. 35mm. 8 reels, 6,742 ft.

Dir Reginald Barker. *Adapt-Cont* Jane Murfin. *Photog* Edward Cronjager. *Art Dir* Max Ree. *Rec Engr* Lambert E. Day.

Cast: Richard Dix *(William Magee)*, Miriam Seegar *(Mary Norton)*, Crauford Kent *(Hal Bentley)*, Margaret Livingston *(Myra Thornhill)*, Joseph Allen *(Peters)*, Lucien Littlefield *(Thomas Hayden)*, De Witt Jennings *(Mayor Cargan)*, Carleton Macy *(Kennedy)*, Nella Walker *(Mrs. Rhodes)*, Joe Herbert *(Max)*, Alan Roscoe *(Bland)*, Harvey Clark *(Elijah Quimby)*, Edith Yorke *(Mrs. Quimby)*.

Comedy–mystery melodrama. Source: Earl Derr Biggers, *Seven Keys to Baldpate* (Indianapolis, 1913). A remake of the silent versions of 1917 and 1925, q. v. *Novelists. Publishers. Caretakers. Sheriffs. Hotels.*

SEVEN SINNERS **F2.4922**

Warner Brothers Pictures. 7 Nov **1925** [c17 Sep 1925; LP21830]. Si; b&w. 35mm. 7 reels, 6,826 ft.

Dir Lewis Milestone. *Story-Adapt* Lewis Milestone, Darryl F. Zanuck. *Photog* David Abel. *Adtl Photog* Walter Robinson. *Asst Dir* Frank Richardson.

Cast: Marie Prevost *(Molly Brian)*, Clive Brook *(Jerry Winters)*, John Patrick *(Handsome Joe Hagney)*, Charles Conklin *(Scarlet Fever Saunders)*, Claude Gillingwater *(Pious Joe McDowell)*, Mathilde Brundage *(Mamie McDowell)*, Dan Mason *(doctor)*, Fred Kelsey *(policeman)*.

Comedy. When all the private guards on Long Island go on strike, seven crooks make their separate ways to the deserted Vickers mansion. Molly Brian and Joe Hagney, the first to arrive, immediately loot the safe. As they are about to make their getaway, they are held up by Jerry Winters, a debonair thief who poses as the owner of the house. Just then, two more crooks, the McDowells, arrive, announcing themselves as houseguests; Jerry and Molly then pose as the butler and the maid. Two more crooks show up (one poses as a man of the cloth; the other as a scarlet fever patient), and the house is quarantined. Molly and Jerry, who have fallen in love, decide to go straight and hand themselves over to the police. After serving a short jail term, they are released and go into the burglar alarm business. *Safecrackers. Burglars. Butlers. Housemaids. Clergymen. Police. Criminals—Rehabilitation. Imposture. Quarantine. Scarlet fever. Strikes. Burglar alarms. Long Island.*

SEVEN YEARS BAD LUCK **F2.4923**

Dist Robertson-Cole Distributing Corp. 6 Feb **1921** [c6 Feb 1921; LP16212]. Si; b&w. 35mm. 5 reels.

Prod-Dir-Writ Max Linder. *Photog* Charles J. Van Enger.

Cast: Max Linder *(Max)*, Thelma Percy *(station agent's daughter)*, Alta Allen *(Max's fiancée)*, Betty Peterson *(The Maid)*, Lola Gonzales *(a Hawaiian maid)*, Harry Mann *(The Chef)*, Chance Ward *(a railroad conductor)*, Ralph McCullough *(Max's valet)*, Hugh Saxon *(a station agent)*, Cap Anderson *(a jail bird)*, F. B. Crayne *(a false friend)*, Pudgy *(The Little Dog)*, Joe Martin *(The Monk)*.

Farce. Returning from his last bachelor supper somewhat inebriated, Max goes to bed. In a chase for a kiss, his valet and parlormaid break a cheval glass and try to conceal the loss. When a new glass arrives, Max, afraid he is "seeing things," throws his shoe at the mirror and the bad luck begins: his fiancée abandons him, and his efforts to leave town are thwarted by a mad mishmash of adventures in which policemen, railroad employees, burglars, and wild beasts conspire to make life miserable for him. Finally, matters are adjusted, and Max wins back his sweetheart. *Superstition. Courtship. Railroads. Chases. Dogs.*

THE SEVENTH BANDIT **F2.4924**

Charles R. Rogers Productions. *Dist* Pathé Exchange. 18 Apr **1926** [c6 Mar 1926; LU22461]. Si; b&w. 35mm. 6 reels, 5,353 ft.

Dir Scott R. Dunlap. *Scen* E. Richard Schayer. *Story* Arthur Preston Hankins. *Photog* Sol Polito.

Cast: Harry Carey *(David Scanlon)*, James Morrison *(Paul Scanlon)*, Harriet Hammond *(Dr. Shirley Chalmette)*, John Webb Dillon *(Jim Gresham)*, Trilby Clark *(Ann Drath)*, Walter James *(Ben Goring)*.

Western melodrama. David Scanlon and his brother, Paul, leave their farm and go to California during the gold rush. Paul falls in love with Ann Drath, a dancehall pianist, and is murdered by jealous Ben Goring. David swears revenge and, working on a tip from Ann, poses as an outlaw, joining Goring's bandit band. During a raid on the town bank, David is wounded. Goring abducts Shirley Chalmette, the town doctor, to care for David's head wound, but despite her care David begins to lose his sight. He manages to force Goring to sign a confession, however, and then, although completely blind, kills him in a gunfight. With careful treatment by Dr. Chalmette, his new wife, David recovers full use of his sight. *Outlaws. Physicians. Brothers. Pianists. Murder. Blindness. Kidnaping. Imposture. Gold rushes. California.*

THE SEVENTH DAY **F2.4925**

Inspiration Pictures. *Dist* Associated First National Pictures. 6 Feb **1922** [c30 Jan 1922; LP17529]. Si; b&w. 35mm. 6 reels, 5,335 ft.

Dir Henry King. *Scen* Edmund Goulding. *Story* Porter Emerson Browne. *Photog* Henry Cronjager. *Film Ed* Duncan Mansfield.

Cast: Richard Barthelmess *(John Alden, Jr.)*, Frank Losee *(Uncle Jim Alden)*, Leslie Stowe *(Uncle Ned)*, Tammany Young *(Donald Peabody)*, George Stewart *(Reggie Van Zandt)*, Alfred Schmid *(Monty Pell)*, Grace Barton *(Aunt Abigail)*, Anne Cornwall *(Betty Alden)*, Patterson Dial *(Katinka)*, Teddie Gerard *("Billie" Blair)*, Louise Huff *(Patricia Vane)*.

Society drama. Engine trouble compels a yacht filled with New York society idlers to make port at a New England coastal village, and there Reggie Van Zandt and his fiancée, Patricia Vane, meet John Alden and his sister, Betty. Eager for diversion, Patricia accepts John as her escort during the next 4 days, and Reggie displays an equal interest in Betty. Patricia accepts John's invitation to attend church services, and afterward she becomes remorseful, confessing that she is engaged to Reggie. Heartbroken, John prepares to go to sea, but learning that his sister has been taken aboard the yacht by Reggie, he attacks the society loungers (complacently engaged in "African golf"), knocks down Reggie, and denounces the entire party. Reggie and Patricia are awakened to their error, the former realizing his love for Betty and Patricia her genuine affection for John. *Idlers. Brother-sister relationship. Gambling. Religion. New England.*

7TH HEAVEN **F2.4926**

Fox Film Corp. 6 May **1927** [Los Angeles premiere; released 30 Oct; c19 Jun 1927; LP24098]. Si; b&w. 35mm. 12 reels. [Reduced to 9 reels, 8,500 ft.]

Pres by William Fox. *Dir* Frank Borzage. *Scen* Benjamin Glazer. *Titl* Katherine Hilliker, H. H. Caldwell. *Photog* Ernest Palmer. *Sets* Harry Oliver. *Film Ed* Katherine Hilliker, H. H. Caldwell. *Asst Dir* Lew Borzage.

Cast: Janet Gaynor *(Diane)*, Charles Farrell *(Chico)*, Ben Bard *(Colonel Brissac)*, David Butler *(Gobin)*, Marie Mosquini *(Madame Gobin)*, Albert Gran *(Boul)*, Gladys Brockwell *(Nana)*, Emile Chautard *(Père Chevillon)*, George Stone *(sewer rat)*, Jessie Haslett *(Aunt Valentine)*, Brandon Hurst *(Uncle George)*, Lillian West *(Arlette)*.

Romantic drama. Source: Austin Strong, *Seventh Heaven* (New York, 1922). Chico, a Paris sewer worker, desiring to be elevated to the position of street cleaner, burns prayer candles in the hope that God will give him another chance; he becomes embittered when his prayer for a blonde wife evokes no response. He rescues Diane, who has been victimized by her unscrupulous sister, Nana; and when denounced, Diane is saved from the police by Chico's claim that she is his wife. Their love is finally realized just as war breaks out, but their marriage is interrupted by the call to arms. Diane braves the war as a munitions worker and following the Armistice receives word that Chico is dead. He returns, however, though blinded, to restore the girl's faith and love. *Sisters. Sewer workers. Religion. Courtship. Blindness. World War I. Paris.*

THE SEVENTH SHERIFF **F2.4927**

Wild West Productions. *Dist* Arrow Film Corp. 15 Nov **1923** [c19 Nov 1923; LP19629]. Si; b&w. 35mm. 5 reels, 4,537 ft.

Dir-Writ Richard Hatton.

Cast: Neva Gerber *(Mary Tweedy)*, Richard Hatton *(Jack Rockwell)*.

Western melodrama. "The town of Seely Flats has the reputation of permitting its sheriff to live about a month; the bad men of the town at the expiration of that period removing him by one means or another. Nobody will accept the job until an adventurer seeking excitement volunteers. The gang sets out after him and the adventurer gets all the excitement he wants. He triumphs, however, and is hailed as a hero." (*Motion Picture News Booking Guide*, 6:60, Apr 1924.) *Sheriffs. Gangs.*

SEVENTY FIVE CENTS AN HOUR *see* **SIXTY CENTS AN HOUR**

SEX MADNESS F2.4928

Circle Film Co. *Dist* Public Welfare Pictures. **1929** [New York State license: 12 Sep 1930]. Mus score; b&w. 35mm. 6 reels. [Also si.]

Cast: Jack Richardson, Corliss Palmer.

Drama(?). No information about the nature of this film has been found.

SHACKLED LIGHTNING F2.4929

Hercules Film Productions. *Dist* Bud Barsky Corp. 24 Apr **1925** [New York State license]. Si; b&w. 35mm. 5 reels, 4,900 ft.

Cast: Frank Merrill.

Melodrama(?). No information about the nature of this film has been found.

SHACKLES OF FEAR F2.4930

J. J. Fleming Productions. *Dist* Davis Distributing Division. 15 Nov **1924.** Si; b&w. 35mm. 5 reels, 4,416 ft.

Dir Al Ferguson.

Cast: Al Ferguson *(Richard Dunbar)*, Pauline Curley *(Betty Allison)*, Fred Dayton *(Jim Allison)*, Les Bates *(Bull Hawkins)*, Frank Clark *(Stump Joe)*, Bert De Vore *(detective)*, Paul Emery *(Jack Forbes)*.

Melodrama. Richard Dunbar gets into a fight with a crooked gambler and hits his opponent so hard that the latter falls, apparently dead. Dunbar takes flight and eventually drifts into a lumber camp in Oregon, where he falls in love with Betty Allison and arouses the wrath of one of Betty's suitors, the foreman of the camp. The foreman challenges Dunbar to a fight, but Dunbar remembers the consequences of his last fight and, instead of hitting back at the foreman, leaves the camp in disgrace. Dunbar later learns that the man he thought he had killed is still alive, and he returns to the lumber camp just in time to rescue Betty from death in a house on fire. Dunbar then beats the foreman in a fight and wins Betty for his wife. *Gamblers. Lumber camp foremen. Manslaughter. Lumber camps. Oregon. Fires.*

SHACKLES OF GOLD F2.4931

Fox Film Corp. 30 Apr **1922** [c7 May 1922; LP17858]. Si; b&w. 35mm. 6 reels, 5,957 ft.

Pres by William Fox. *Dir* Herbert Brenon. *Scen* Paul H. Sloane. *Photog* Tom Malloy.

Cast: William Farnum *(John Gibbs, a self-made man)*, Al Loring *(Charles Van Dusen)*, Marie Shotwell *(Mrs. Van Dusen)*, Myrtle Bonillas *(Marie, their daughter)*, Wallace Ray *(Harry, their son)*, C. Elliott Griffin *(Donald Valentine)*, Ellen Cassity *(Elsie Chandler)*, Henry Carvill *(William Hoyt)*.

Society melodrama. Source: Henri Bernstein, *Samson* (1907). John Gibbs, formerly a dock laborer, rises to wealth by shrewd speculation and marries Marie Van Dusen, who consents to the marriage only because her family require his money to maintain their social position. Reestablished in her former social circles, Mrs. Van Dusen continues to enjoy the luxury provided by her daughter's sacrifice. When Gibbs learns Valentine has not only taken Marie to a cabaret but has insulted her, he resolves to seek revenge by breaking Valentine on the market. But in doing so, Gibbs loses his own fortune. After his failure, Mrs. Van Dusen tries to persuade Marie to leave him, but she begins to realize her love for him and decides to remain. *Social classes. Marriage. Speculation. Revenge.*

THE SHADOW F2.4932

Salient Films. *Dist* Forward Films. Mar **1921.** Si; b&w. 35mm. 5 reels.

Dir J. Charles Davis, Jack W. Brown. *Photog* Paul Allen, Allen Davey.

Cast: Muriel Ostriche, Walter Miller, Harold Foshay, Helen Courtenay, Jack Hopkins, Dorothy Blackbourne.

Drama(?). No information about the nature of this film has been found.

Note: Reissued in 1927 (New York State license: 1 Oct 1927).

THE SHADOW F2.4933

Micheaux Pictures. Oct **1921.** Si; b&w. 35mm. 7 reels.

Melodrama(?). No information about the specific nature of this film has been found *Negro life.*

THE SHADOW OF LIGHTNING RIDGE F2.4934

Selig-Rork Productions. *Dist* Aywon Film Corp. 13 Sep **1921** [New York State]. Si; b&w. 35mm. 5 reels, 4,500 ft.

Dir Wilfred Lucas. *Story* Wilfred Lucas, Bess Meredyth.

Cast: Snowy Baker *(The Shadow)*, Wilfred Lucas *(Edward Marriott)*, Brownie Vernon *(Dorothy Harden)*.

Melodrama. Vowing vengeance on Edward Marriott, whom he believes to have dishonored his mother, The Shadow is a highwayman who robs only Marriott. The Shadow attracts the interest of Dorothy Harden, Marriott's fiancée, and finally he captures her. The action includes the kidnaping, by The Shadow's rival, Ben, of Dorothy; The Shadow's capture and escape; and his rescue of Dorothy. All is happily resolved when Dorothy declares her love for The Shadow and Marriott proves to be innocent of injuring The Shadow's mother. *Highwaymen. Revenge. Australia.*

Note: Filmed in Australia.

SHADOW OF THE DESERT *see* **THE SHADOW OF THE EAST**

THE SHADOW OF THE EAST F2.4935

Fox Film Corp. 27 Jan **1924** [c27 Jan 1924; LP19881]. Si; b&w. 35mm. 6 reels, 5,874 ft.

Pres by William Fox. *Dir* George Archainbaud. *Scen* Frederic Hatton, Fanny Hatton. *Photog* Jules Cronjager.

Cast: Frank Mayo *(Barry Craven)*, Mildred Harris *(Gillian Locke)*, Norman Kerry *(Said)*, Bertram Grassby *(Kunwar Singh)*, Evelyn Brent *(Lolaire)*, Edythe Chapman *(Aunt Caroline)*, Joseph Swickard *(John Locke)*, Lorimer Johnson *(Peter Peters)*.

Melodrama. Source: Edith Maude Hull, *The Shadow of the East* (Boston, c1921). Barry Craven meets former sweetheart Gillian Locke, who is visiting India with her father. Craven's love for Gillian is revived, but he already has a wife—Lolaire, a native. In a jealous rage, Lolaire kills herself, freeing Craven, who returns to England and marries Gillian. His Indian servant, Kunwar Singh, casts a spell on Craven, causing him to leave Gillian and to go into the Algerian desert. There he joins Said, an old university friend who is the son of an Algerian sheik. Gillian follows, the servant is killed, and with him dies the spell, "The Shadow of the East." *Suicide. Occult. India. Algeria. Sahara.*

Note: Also reviewed as *Shadow of the Desert.*

THE SHADOW OF THE LAW F2.4936

Associated Exhibitors. 24 Jan **1926** [c22 Jan 1926; LU22286]. Si; b&w. 35mm. 5 reels, 4,526 ft.

Prod Arthur Beck, Leah Baird. *Dir* Wallace Worsley. *Scen* Leah Baird, Grover Jones. *Photog* Ray June.

Cast: Clara Bow *(Mary Brophy)*, Forrest Stanley *(James Reynolds)*, Stuart Holmes *(Carl Lingard)*, Ralph Lewis *(Charles Brophy)*, William V. Mong *("Twist" Egan)*, J. Emmett Beck *(Kid Martin)*, Adele Farrington *(aunt)*, Eddie Lyons *(crook)*, George Cooper *(chauffeur)*.

Melodrama. Source: Harry Chapman Ford, "Two Gates" (publication undetermined). Mary Brophy, who was railroaded into prison for a crime she did not commit, is released from stir and returns to San Francisco, where she falls in love with James Reynolds, a handsome millionaire who knows nothing of her past. Lingard, a sometime nobleman and art connoisseur who framed Mary on a theft charge, tries to make her his mistress and, when she refuses, exposes her "criminal" past at a post reception. One of Lingard's cronies, angered at his treatment of Mary, then exposes him as a thief and murderer, producing a confession that exonerates Mary and clears the way for her future happiness with Reynolds. *Millionaires. Reputation. Frameup. Injustice. San Francisco.*

SHADOW OF THE LAW F2.4937

Paramount-Publix Corp. 6 Jun **1930** [c13 Jun 1930; LP1357]. Sd (Movietone); b&w. 35mm. 9 reels, 6,392 ft.

Dir Louis Gasnier. *Scen-Dial* John Farrow. *Photog* Charles Lang. *Film Ed* Robert Bassler. *Rec Engr* Harold M. McNiff.

Cast: William Powell *(John Nelson/Jim Montgomery)*, Marion Shilling *(Edith Wentworth)*, Natalie Moorhead *(Ethel Barry)*, Regis Toomey *(Tom)*, Paul Hurst *(Pete)*, George Irving *(Colonel Wentworth)*, Frederic Burt *(Mike Kearney)*, James Durkin *(warden)*, Richard Tucker *(Frank)*, Walter James *(guard captain)*.

Melodrama. Source: John A. Moroso, *The Quarry* (Boston, 1913). Max Marcin, *The Quarry* (a play; publication undetermined). A woman being pursued by an intoxicated man breaks into John Nelson's apartment, imploring his help. Nelson, a young engineer, confronts the man, who accidentally topples through a window to his death. Unable to prove the circumstances, Nelson is convicted of murder and sentenced to life imprisonment. With the aid of his cellmate, he escapes and under an assumed name becomes manager of a textile mill in North Carolina. Later, his former cellmate, Pete, is commissioned to find Ethel Barry, the woman who can clear him so that he may marry Edith, the mill owner's daughter;

but Ethel forces his hand through blackmail. Detective Mike Kearney tracks him down, but when Montgomery (Nelson) mutilates his hands in a machine to erase his fingerprint identity, Kearney decides to force Ethel to clear him. *Engineers. Fugitives. Detectives. Circumstantial evidence. Blackmail. Prisons. Textile manufacture. North Carolina.*

THE SHADOW ON THE WALL **F2.4938**

Gotham Productions. *Dist* Lumas Film Corp. Nov **1925** [c16 Nov 1925; LP22010]. Si; b&w. 35mm. 6 reels, 5,800 ft.

Pres by Sam Sax. *Dir* Reeves Eason. *Cont* Elsie Werner. *Adapt* Henry McCarty. *Photog* Ray June.

Cast: Eileen Percy *(Lucia Warring)*, Creighton Hale *(George Walters)*, William V. Mong *(Robert Glaxton)*, Dale Fuller *("The Missus")*, Jack Curtis *("Bleary")*, Hardee Kirkland *(Hode)*, Willis Marks *(George Warring)*.

Mystery-melodrama. Source: John Breckenridge Ellis, *The Picture on the Wall* (Kansas City, 1920). George Walters, with the aid of crooked Uncle Bleary and his associates, passes himself off as the long-lost son of George Warring (Sr.) in order to seize the family fortune. The family becomes convinced of his identity when George's profile casts the same shadow as the bust of the missing son. Bleary presses him for money, and George is about to quit when he is identified by a friend of Warring's daughter as "the polite burglar" who once robbed her. Matters are complicated when George discovers that Glaxton, the family lawyer, is slowly poisoning the father. George decides to stay, unravels the conspiracy, wins a wife, is the means for sending Bleary and Glaxton to jail, and is finally established as the genuine George Warring. *Lawyers. Inheritance. Imposture. Personal identity.*

SHADOW RANCH **F2.4939**

Columbia Pictures. 10 Sep **1930** [c15 Sep 1930; LP1580]. Sd (Movietone); b&w. 35mm. 6 reels, 5,766 ft.

Prod Harry Cohn. *Dir* Louis King. *Cont* Frank Howard Clark. *Dial* Clarke Silvernail. *Photog* Ted McCord. *Art Dir* Edward Jewell. *Tech Dir* Edward Shulter. *Film Ed* James Sweeney. *Ch Sd Engr* John Livadary. *Sd Rec* G. R. Cooper. *Asst Dir* Mack V. Wright.

Cast: Buck Jones *(Sim Baldwin)*, Marguerite De La Motte *(Ruth)*, Kate Price *(Maggie Murphy)*, Ben Wilson *(Tex)*, Al Smith *(Dan Blake)*, Frank Rice *(Williams)*, Ernie Adams *(Joe)*, Slim Whittaker *(Curley)*, Robert McKenzie *(Fatty)*.

Western melodrama. Source: George M. Johnson, unidentified story in *Munsey's Magazine*. Summoned by his friend Ranny Williams, Sim Baldwin, a wanderer, goes to the aid of Ruth Cameron, a rancher under pressure to sell out to Blake, who wants to control a dam on the ranch that is central to the town's water supply. He arrives to find his friend ambushed; and incurring the enmity of Blake, Sim convinces Ruth he is her friend. When Blake begins rustling the cattle on the ranch, Sim lays a trap and captures several of the culprits and marches them, pantsless, into town. Blake threatens him with a showdown unless he leaves town, but Sim engages in a furious gunfight with Blake's gang, saves Ruth from the clutches of the villain, chases him from the town, and fights him to the death. *Wanderers. Ranch foremen. Swindlers. Rustlers. Murder. Water rights. Ranches. Dams.*

SHADOW RANGER **F2.4940**

Denver Dixon Productions. *Dist* Aywon Film Corp. 12 Mar **1926** [New York State license]. Si; b&w. 35mm. 5 reels.

Cast: George Kesterson.

Western melodrama(?). No information about the nature of this film has been found.

SHADOWS **F2.4941**

Preferred Pictures. *Dist* Al Lichtman Corp. 10 Nov **1922** [c7 Oct 1922; LP18347]. Si; b&w. 35mm. 7 reels, 7,040 ft.

Pres by B. P. Schulberg. *Dir* Tom Forman. *Scen* Eve Unsell, Hope Loring. *Photog* Harry Perry.

Cast: Lon Chaney *(Yen Sin, "The Heathen")*, Marguerite De La Motte *(Sympathy Gibbs)*, Harrison Ford *(John Malden)*, John Sainpolis *(Nate Snow)*, Walter Long *(Daniel Gibbs)*, Buddy Messenger *("Mister Bad Boy")*, Priscilla Bonner *(Mary Brent)*, Frances Raymond *(Emsy Nickerson)*.

Melodrama. Source: Wilbur Daniel Steele, "Ching, Ching, Chinaman," in *Pictorial Review* (18:5+, Jun 1917). After Daniel Gibbs is lost at sea, his wife, Sympathy, marries Rev. John Malden. They are supremely happy until John receives a blackmail note falsely indicating that Gibbs is alive. John's dilemma is solved when the Maldens' dying friend, Yen Sin, agrees to become a Christian in exchange for the revelation that Nate Snow sent the note. *Clergymen. Chinese. Blackmail. Religious conversion.*

SHADOWS OF CHINATOWN **F2.4942**

Bud Barsky Corp. 1 Mar **1926.** Si; b&w. 35mm. 5 reels.

Dir Paul Hurst.

Cast: Kenneth McDonald *(Jimmy King)*, Velma Edele *(Velma)*, Elmer Dewey *(The Ace)*, Ben Corbett *(The Weasel)*, Lee Chung *(Wing Lee)*, Frank Chew *(Wo Hop)*.

Action melodrama. "Crooks cloak their operations in Chinatown. Navy Lieutenant is assigned task of exterminating gang. Is aided by friendly Chinese but captured by crooks and faces death with young woman agent disguised as Chinese. They are saved by Police." (*Motion Picture News Booking Guide*, 11:47, Oct 1926.) *Gangs. Chinese. Impersonation. United States Navy. Chinatown.*

SHADOWS OF CONSCIENCE **F2.4943**

Russell Productions. 16 Oct **1921** [trade review; c19 Sep, 25 Nov 1921; LU17075]. Si; b&w. 35mm. 7 reels, 6,322 ft.

Dir John P. McCarthy. *Story-Scen* John P. McCarthy, Francis Powers. *Titl* H. Landers Jackson. *Photog* Victor Milner. *Art Dir* Louis E. Myers. *Film Ed* Fred Allen. *Art Titl* O. A. Kiechle.

Cast: Russell Simpson *(Jim Logan)*, Landers Stevens *(Wade Curry)*, Barbara Tennant *(Alice)*, W. Bradley Ward *(Pedro, the halfbreed)*, Nelson McDowell *(Wesley Coburn)*, Ashley Cooper *(Judson Craft)*, Ida McKenzie *(Winnie Coburn)*, Gertrude Olmstead *(Winifred Coburn)*, Fred Burns *(Sheriff Bowers)*.

Melodrama. In 1882 Jim Logan arrives in a small town in Wyoming to inquire about his sister Alice, whose husband, Wade Curry, a dishonest mine speculator, has deserted her. He finds her ill and learns that her marriage was fraudulent. Curry arrives, and in a fight with Logan he kills Alice. Finding it impossible to convict Curry of his crimes, Logan goes to the Southwest with Winnie, the daughter of Curry's partner. Ten years later, Logan is a successful rancher and Winnie has returned home from a convent school. Discovering the identity of the girl, Curry conspires with a lawyer to get possession of Winnie and have Logan charged with murder. But Logan appeals to an assembly of citizens, and after hearing the whole tale, the judge acquits him. Curry, conscience-stricken, is arrested. *Ranchers. Revenge. Brother-sister relationship. Wyoming.*

SHADOWS OF GLORY *see* **SOMBRAS DE GLORIA**

SHADOWS OF PARIS **F2.4944**

Famous Players–Lasky. *Dist* Paramount Pictures. 11 or 18 Feb **1924** [c27 Feb 1924; LP19949]. Si; b&w. 35mm. 7 reels, 6,549 ft.

Pres by Adolph Zukor, Jesse L. Lasky. *Dir* Herbert Brenon. *Scen* Eve Unsell. *Adapt* Fred Jackson. *Photog* Bert Baldridge.

Cast: Pola Negri *(Claire, Queen of the Apaches)*, Charles De Roche *(Fernand, an Apache)*, Huntley Gordon *(Raoul, Minister of the Interior)*, Adolphe Menjou *(Georges de Croy, his secretary)*, Gareth Hughes *(Émile Boule)*, Vera Reynolds *(Liane)*, Rose Dione *(Madame Boule, cafe owner)*, Rosita Marstini *(Madame Vali, a poetess)*, Edward Kipling *(Pierre, a roué)*, Maurice Cannon *(Robert, a taxi driver)*, Frank Nelson *(Le Bossu, the hunchback)*, George O'Brien *(Louis)*.

Underworld melodrama. Source: André Picard and Francis Carco, *Mon Homme; pièce en 3 actes* (Paris, 1921). At the end of the war, Claire, queen of the Paris underground, finds herself in Paris high society. Believing that her apache lover, Fernand, has been killed in the war, Claire falls in love with Raoul, a French official. De Croy, Raoul's secretary, learns of Claire's past and threatens to expose her unless she yields to him. Fernand returns; Claire realizes that she no longer loves him; and while attempting to steal a diamond necklace, he is killed in a fight with De Croy, who has come to Claire's boudoir to collect his debt. Raoul returns during the fracas, and De Croy keeps Claire's secret by declaring that he has killed a common thief stealing madame's jewels. Claire, however, confesses the truth and is about to leave when Raoul forgives her. *Upper classes. Apaches—Paris. Blackmail. Paris.*

SHADOWS OF THE NIGHT **F2.4945**

Metro-Goldwyn-Mayer Pictures. 26 Oct **1928** [c6 Oct 1928; LP25728]. Si; b&w. 35mm. 7 reels, 5,448 ft.

Dir-Writ D. Ross Lederman. *Titl* Robert Hopkins. *Story* Ted Shane. *Photog* Maximilian Fabian. *Film Ed* Dan Sharits. *Wardrobe* Lucia Coulter.

Cast: Lawrence Gray *(Jimmy Sherwood)*, Louise Lorraine *(Molly)*,

Warner Richmond *(Feagan)*, Tom Dugan *(Connelly)*, Alphonse Ethier *(O'Flaherty)*, Polly Moran *(entertainer)*, Flash *(himself, a dog)*.

Underworld melodrama. "Sergeant O'Flaherty is out to round up the notorious Feagan gang. The inevitable girl pops up, mutual love, and marriage after the hero accomplishes his purpose and saves the girl's honor." ("Motion Picture News Booking Guide," in *Motion Picture News*, 15 Mar 1930, p101.) *Police. Gangs. Dogs.*

SHADOWS OF THE NORTH **F2.4946**

Universal Pictures. 27 Aug **1923** [c28 Jul 1923; LP19255]. Si; b&w. 35mm. 5 reels, 4,943 ft.

Dir Robert F. Hill. *Scen* Paul Schofield. *Photog* Harry Fowler.

Cast: William Desmond *(Ben "Wolf" Darby)*, Virginia Brown Faire *(Beatrice Neilson)*, Fred Kohler *(Ray Brent)*, William Welsh *(Jeffrey Neilson)*, Albert Hart *(Hemingway)*, James O. Barrows *(Ezra "Pancake" Darby)*, Rin-Tin-Tin *(King, the dog)*.

Western melodrama. Source: Edison Marshall, *The Skyline of Spruce* (Boston, 1922). Ben Darby and Pancake, his father, are owners of a mining claim in Northwest Canada. Ben goes to war, leaving Pancake to run the mine. During Ben's absence three claim jumpers take possession of the mine: one of the men is the father of Beatrice, Ben's sweetheart; another, a rival suitor. Pancake is murdered when he and Ben plot to regain the claim. Ben kidnaps Beatrice, resolving to obtain revenge through her. Ben finds that she knew nothing of the stolen claim and that her father was innocent of Pancake's murder. Ben wins back the claim and marries Beatrice. *Claim jumpers. Filial relations. Mines. Kidnaping. Canada. Dogs.*

Note: Working title: *The Skyline of Spruce.*

SHADOWS OF THE SEA **F2.4947**

Selznick Pictures. *Dist* Select Pictures. 10 Jan **1922** [c24 Jan 1922; LP17494]. Si; b&w. 35mm. 5 reels, 4,675 ft.

Pres by Lewis J. Selznick. *Dir* Alan Crosland. *Scen* Lewis Allen Browne. *Story* Frank Dazey. *Photog* Jules Cronjager, Jacob A. Badaracco.

Cast: Conway Tearle *(Capt. Dick Carson)*, Jack Drumier *(Shivering Sam)*, Crauford Kent *(Andrews)*, Arthur Houseman *(Ralph Dean)*, J. Barney Sherry *(Dr. Jordan)*, Doris Kenyon *(Dorothy Jordan)*, Frankie Mann *(Molly)*, Harry J. Lane *("Red")*, William Nally *(Captain Hobbs)*.

Melodrama. After rescuing "Shivering Sam," an old derelict, from a Hong Kong dive, Capt. Dick Carson, a gentleman adventurer, sets sail for the California coast to avoid port authorities who are seeking him for breaking trading and maritime regulations. There, at the residence of Dr. Jordan, he finds Jordan's wife, Dorothy, in the arms of her husband's assistant, Ralph Dean; and wounded by the Coast Guard, Carson seeks refuge with the doctor. Dean attempts to persuade Dorothy to elope but is intercepted by Dr. Jordan; in the struggle, Jordan is killed. To avoid false incrimination, Carson takes both Dean and Dorothy aboard his yacht as prisoners. Although Carson believes her to be an unfaithful woman, he later discovers that Dean is the responsible scoundrel. In a showdown, Carson wins the girl. *Yachtsmen. Physicians. Infidelity. Maritime law. Hong Kong. California. United States Coast Guard.*

SHADOWS OF THE WEST **F2.4948**

Cinema Craft–Motion Picture Producing Co. of America. *Dist* National Exchanges. Aug **1921**. Si; b&w. 35mm. 8 & 5 reels.

Supv Charles Hickman. *Dir* Paul Hurst. *Scen* James Dayton. *Story* Seymour Zeliff.

Cast: Pat O'Brien *(Jim Kern)*, Hedda Nova *(Mary)*, Virginia Dale *(Lucy Norton)*, Seymour Zeliff *(Frank Akuri)*, Pat Corbett.

Western melodrama. California cowpuncher Jim Kern and his pal enlist in the war against Germany and, shortly thereafter, meet Oriental Frank Akuri, who has pledged to colonize the United States for his homeland. While Jim is away, Akuri forces Jim's sweetheart, Mary, to sell her ranch (the "yellows" have pledged not to work for the "whites") and begins his colony. Mary counters by organizing her friends to appeal to Congress. Because it appears that she will be successful, Akuri kidnaps Mary, and he is about to murder her when Jim appears and resolves the situation. Akuri receives his just desserts. *Cowboys. Ranchers. Japanese. Colonization. Yellow peril. Racism. Prejudice. Kidnaping. World War I. United States Congress.*

Note: Reviews in late 1920 (from which the synopsis is taken) label this film as 8 reels in length, produced by Cinema Craft, highly propagandistic, and anti-Japanese. Apparently the Motion Picture Producing Co. of America reduced the film to 5 reels, played down the "yellow peril" menace, and emphasized the western aspects.

THE SHADY LADY **F2.4949**

Pathé Exchange. 20 Jan **1929** [c8 Jan 1929; LP8]. Talking sequences (Photophone); b&w. 35mm. 7 reels, 5,808 ft. [Also si; 6,132 ft.]

Ralph Block Production. *Dir* Edward H. Griffith. *Orig Story–Cont* Jack Jungmeyer. *Dial* Edward H. Griffith. *Titl* Garrett Graham. *Photog* John Mescall. *Film Ed* Doane Harrison. *Asst Dir* E. J. Babille. *Prod Mgr* Harry Poppe.

Cast: Phyllis Haver *(Lola Mantell)*, Robert Armstrong *(Blake)*, Louis Wolheim *(Holbrook)*, Russell Gleason *(Haley)*.

Crime melodrama. Innocent Lola Mantell has been circumstantially involved in a New York murder case and flees to Havana, where she becomes known vaguely as "The Shady Lady." Under threat of exposure, she becomes involved with Holbrook, leader of a gang of gunrunners. She falls in love with Blake and confesses her mission, but he reveals that he has known of this circumstance all along and that he loves her. With the aid of Jimmie Haley, a young American newspaper correspondent, they break up Holbrook's gang and return to New York, where Lola has been cleared of the murder charge. *Reporters. Gunrunners. Murder. Havana. New York City.*

THE SHAKEDOWN (Universal-Jewel) **F2.4950**

Universal Pictures. 10 Mar **1929** [c7 Dec 1928; LP25907]. Talking sequences, sd eff, & mus score (Movietone); b&w. 35mm. 7 reels, 6,613 ft. [Also si; 6,753 ft.]

Dir William Wyler. *Scen* Charles A. Logue, Clarence J. Marks. *Titl-Dial* Albert De Mond. *Story* Charles A. Logue. *Photog* Charles Stumar, Jerome Ash. *Film Ed* Lloyd Nosler, Richard Cahoon. *Mus Score* Joseph Cherniavsky. *Rec Engr* C. Roy Hunter.

Cast: James Murray *(Dave Hall)*, Barbara Kent *(Marjorie)*, George Kotsonaros *(Battling Roff)*, Wheeler Oakman *(manager)*, Jack Hanlon *(Clem)*, Harry Gibbon *(bouncer)*.

Melodrama. Dave Hall arrives in Boonton and finds work in the oil fields, soon falling in love with Marjorie, a waitress. One night in the park Dave gets into a fight with a dancehall bouncer whom he soundly trounces; Dave becomes a local hero and the popular favorite in a match with Battling Roff, a professional fighter who takes on all comers. Dave adopts Clem, an orphan boy, and for the first time in life finds himself in a place that he would like to call home. A traveling salesman comes to town and informs the populace that Dave is a professional patsy who, in town after town, first establishes his reputation as a fighter and then takes a dive. Boonton turns against Dave, but he informs Roff's manager that he is through as a fall guy. Dave wins the fight on guts alone and, redeemed in the eyes of his new friends, prepares to settle down with Clem and Marjorie. *Prizefighters. Bouncers. Orphans. Waitresses. Scapegoats. Traveling salesmen. Oil fields.*

SHAM **F2.4951**

Famous Players–Lasky. *Dist* Paramount Pictures. 26 Jun **1921** [c27 Jun 1921; LP16713]. Si; b&w. 35mm. 5 reels, 4,188 ft.

Dir Thomas N. Heffron. *Adapt* Douglas Doty. *Photog* Charles Edgar Schoenbaum.

Cast: Ethel Clayton *(Katherine Van Riper)*, Clyde Fillmore *(Tom Jaffrey)*, Walter Hiers *(Monte Buck)*, Theodore Roberts *(Jeriamiah Buck)*, Sylvia Ashton *(Aunt Bella)*, Helen Dunbar *(Aunt Louisa)*, Arthur Carewe *(Bolton)*, Thomas Ricketts *(Uncle James)*, Blanche Gray *(Clementine Vickers)*, Eunice Burnham *(Maud Buck)*, Carrie Clark Ward *(Rosie)*.

Society melodrama. Source: Elmer Harris and Geraldine Bonner, *Sham* (New York opening: 27 Mar 1909). Katherine Van Riper, a society girl with extravagant tastes, is left with only a few dollars by her spendthrift father and is unable to pay her creditors. She is refused help by her wealthy aunts, who insist that she marry Monte Buck, son of an oil king. When her situation becomes desperate, Katherine decides to sell the Van Riper pearls. She discovers, however, that her father substituted imitations and sold the real jewels, and in despair she refuses to marry Tom Jaffrey, whom she loves. To keep the family honor intact, the aunts cover her loss with a check, and Katherine then promises to marry Tom. *Socialites. Aunts. Debt. Inheritance.*

SHAME **F2.4952**

Fox Film Corp. 31 Jul **1921** [New York premiere; released 16 Oct; c18 Sep 1921; LP17116]. Si; b&w. 35mm. 8-9 reels, 8,322 ft.

Pres by William Fox. *Dir* Emmett J. Flynn. *Adapt-Scen* Emmett J. Flynn, Bernard McConville. *Photog* Lucien Andriot.

Cast: John Gilbert *(William Fielding/David Fielding, his son)*, Mickey

Moore *(David, at 5)*, Frankie Lee *(David, at 10)*, George Siegmann *(Foo Chang)*, William V. Mong *(Li Clung)*, George Nichols *(Jonathan Fielding)*, Anna May Wong *(The Lotus Blossom)*, Rosemary Theby *(The Weaver of Dreams)*, Doris Pawn *(Winifred Wellington)*, "Red" Kirby *("Once-over" Jake)*.

Melodrama. Source: Max Brand, "Clung," in *All Story Weekly* (109: 1–18, 172–189, 352–371, 518–536; 110:84–102, 260–276; 10 Apr–15 May 1920). William Fielding, who lives in Shanghai with his young son David, is close friends with his secretary, Li Clung, after the death of his wife. Foo Chang, a trader, loves the young woman who cares for young David and kills Fielding when he assumes that she is the boy's mother. Li Clung takes the child to his grandfather in San Francisco, where he grows up and inherits the Fielding estate. Following David's marriage, Foo Chang tries to bribe David to help him bring a cargo of opium into the city, informing him that he is a halfcaste. Without waiting to learn the truth from Li Clung, David takes his infant son and goes to Alaska. He is followed by his wife and his faithful servant Li Clung, who kills Foo Chang and explains that David's mother was not Chinese. Brought to his senses, David returns with them to San Francisco. *Chinese. Halfcastes. Secretaries. Grandfathers. Opium. Shanghai. San Francisco. Alaska.*

SHAMEFUL BEHAVIOR? F2.4953

Preferred Pictures. 1 Oct **1926** [c28 Sep 1926; LP23166]. Si; b&w. 35mm. 6 reels, 5,218 ft.

Pres by J. G. Bachmann. *Dir* Albert Kelley. *Cont* Douglas Bronston. *Adapt* George Scarborough. *Photog* Nicholas Musuraca.

Cast: Edith Roberts *(Daphne Carrol)*, Richard Tucker *(Jack Lee)*, Martha Mattox *(Mrs. Calhoun)*, Harland Tucker *(Custis Lee)*, Grace Carlyle *(Joan Lee)*, Louise Carver *(Sally Long)*, Hayes Robertson *(The Butler)*.

Romantic comedy. Source: Mrs. Belloc Lowndes, "Shameful Behavior?" in *Studies in Wives* (New York, 1910). Daphne Carrol, once a "plain Jane," returns from Paris a "polished" flapper, and finding that her love for Custis Lee, her sister's brother-in-law, is not reciprocated, sets out to win him. His brother, Jack Lee, managing editor of the local newspaper, orders a conspicuous report of Daphne's return, but through an error her picture appears over a news item citing the escape from an insane asylum of Sally Long, bent on revenge on her husband. Daphne gains entrance to Custis' house and poses as Sally, disclaiming him as her husband. Fearful of his life, he humors her until he can engage a nurse to watch her. Daphne enjoys the joke until she discovers that her nurse is actually Sally—and Sally's husband tries to rob the Custis home. In the merry mixup Daphne faints in Custis' arms and is forced to declare that she is his wife; after the complications are resolved, they decide to make the arrangement legal. *Flappers. Editors. Sisters. Courtship. Newspapers. Insanity. Impersonation.*

THE SHAMROCK AND THE ROSE F2.4954

Chadwick Pictures. 15 Apr **1927**. Si; b&w. 35mm. 6-7 reels, 6,700 ft.

Dir Jack Nelson. *Scen* Isadore Bernstein. *Story* James Madison. *Photog* Ernest Miller.

Cast: Mack Swain *(Mr. Kelly)*, Olive Hasbrouck *(Rosie Cohen)*, Edmund Burns *(Tom Kelly)*, Maurice Costello *(Father O'Brien)*, William Strauss *(Mr. Cohen)*, Dot Farley *(Mrs. Kelly)*, Rosa Rosanova *(Mrs. Cohen)*, Leon Holmes *(Sammy Cohen)*, Otto Lederer *(Rabbi Naser)*, Coy Watson, Jr. *(Mickey Kelly)*.

Comedy-drama. Source: Owen Davis, *The Shamrock and the Rose* (a play; publication undetermined). A feud between the "Ice Cream Cohens" (according to their business card) and the Kellys, who have a hot dog stand, cannot prevent the Cohen girl, Rosie, and Kelly boy, Tom, from falling in love. There are sorrows, miniature warfare, and laughs until the two families are finally reconciled by their children's marriage. *Jews. Irish. Feuds. Ice cream. Food stands.*

THE SHAMROCK HANDICAP F2.4955

Fox Film Corp. 2 May **1926** [c26 Apr 1926; LP22716]. Si; b&w. 35mm. 6 reels, 5,685 ft.

Pres by William Fox. *Dir* John Ford. *Scen* John Stone. *Titl* Elizabeth Pickett. *Story* Peter Bernard Kyne. *Photog* George Schneiderman. *Asst Dir* Edward O'Fearna.

Cast: Janet Gaynor *(Sheila Gaffney)*, Leslie Fenton *(Neil Ross)*, J. Farrell MacDonald *(Dennis O'Shea)*, Louis Payne *(Sir Miles Gaffney)*, Claire McDowell *(Molly O'Shea)*, Willard Louis *(Martin Finch)*, Andy Clark *(Chesty Morgan)*, Georgie Harris *(Benny Ginsberg)*, Ely Reynolds *(Puss)*, Thomas Delmar *(Michaels)*, Brandon Hurst *(The Procurer)*.

Romantic drama. Sir Miles Gaffney, an Irishman whose affection for the tenants on his estate leads him to face poverty, is obliged to dispose of part of his stable to a wealthy American, who also takes home with him Neil Ross, a young jockey in love with Sheila, Sir Miles's daughter. When Neil is injured in a race, Sir Miles and Sheila come from Ireland, bringing with them their prize filly, "Dark Rosaleen," which they enter in a steeplechase. When their jockey is injured, Neil takes his place and wins the race; the family fortune is thus recouped, and all return to Ireland, where Neil finds happiness with Sheila. *Irish. Jockeys. Finance—Personal. Steeplechasing. Ireland. Horses.*

Note: Some sources indicate slight variations in character names.

SHAMS OF SOCIETY F2.4956

Walsh-Fielding Productions. *Dist* R-C Pictures. 18 Sep **1921** [c18 Sep 1921; LP17065]. Si; b&w. 35mm. 6 reels, 6,250 ft.

Dir Thomas B. Walsh. *Adapt* Mary Murillo, Kenneth O'Hara. *Photog* John S. Stumar. *Adtl Photog* Charles Stumar.

Cast: Barbara Castleton *(Helen Porter)*, Montague Love *(Herbert Porter)*, Macey Harlam *(Milton Howard)*, Julia Swayne Gordon *(Mrs. Crest)*, Ann Brody *("Mama" Manning)*, Gladys Feldman, Sallie Tysha *(Manning sisters)*, Lucille Lee Stewart *(Lucille Lee)*, Edwards Davis *(Judge Harrington)*, Victor Gilbert *(Reggie Frothingham)*.

Domestic melodrama. Source: Walter McNamara, "Shams" (publication undetermined). Although her husband is well-to-do, Helen Porter is forced into embarrassing situations for lack of ready cash. When she accompanies Mrs. Crest to a gambling hall operated behind the facade of a gown shop, she is forced to borrow money and then to pawn her jewels to Milton Howard in order to pay the debt. At the instigation of Howard, Helen steals a valuable Indian ring at a reception, and when she comes to pawn it he forces a rendezvous with her. Meanwhile, Judge Harrington, who has learned of her troubles, induces Porter to give his wife a check for $5,000. Porter, suspicious, follows her to the meeting with Howard and is about to shoot him when Howard reveals his views on the false values of the society set. Husband and wife reach a mutually happy understanding. *Upper classes. Finance—Personal. Social consciousness. Gambling.*

SHANGHAI BOUND F2.4957

Paramount Famous Lasky Corp. 15 Oct **1927** [c15 Oct 1927; LP24520]. Si; b&w. 35mm. 6 reels, 5,515 ft.

Pres by Adolph Zukor, Jesse L. Lasky. *Dir* Luther Reed. *Screenplay* John Goodrich, Ray Harris. *Titl* Julian Johnson. *Story* E. S. O'Reilly. *Photog* Edward Cronjager.

Cast: Richard Dix *(Jim Bucklin)*, Mary Brian *(Sheila)*, Charles Byer *(Payson)*, George Irving *(Louden)*, Jocelyn Lee *(Shanghai Rose)*, Tom Maguire *(Smith)*, Frank Chew *(Yen)*, Tom Gubbins *(local agent)*, Arthur Hoyt *(Algy)*, Tetsu Komai *(Scarface)*.

Romantic melodrama. Amidst revolution-torn China, Jim Bucklin, captain of the *Fan Tan*, a river freighter, anchors at Chow Luen, a town near Shanghai, and finds the hunger-mad populace in an uprising. In a small cafe he meets Shanghai Rose. During dinner, Louden, owner of the ship, Sheila, his daughter, Payson, his manager, and Algy, an aristocratic Englishman, arrive and demand food. They are attacked by a band of revolutionary bandits, and Jim ushers them aboard his ship and sets out for Shanghai. Scarface and his men, thirsting for vengeance, attack the ship, and Jim, lacking a crew, puts his passengers to work. Sheila realizes her love for Jim when she believes him killed; the Louden party is rescued by a warship; and Sheila is happily reunited with Jim, who is actually a lieutenant-commander in the United States Navy. *Chinese. Ship crews. Revolutionaries. Hunger. Shanghai. United States Navy.*

SHANGHAI LADY F2.4958

Universal Pictures. 17 Nov **1929** [c24 Oct 1929; LP789]. Sd (Movietone); b&w. 35mm. 7 reels, 5,926 ft. [Also si; 5,846 ft.]

Pres by Carl Laemmle. *Dir* John S. Robertson. *Scen-Dial* Houston Branch, Winifred Reeve. *Photog* Hal Mohr. *Film Ed* Milton Carruth. *Song: "I Wonder If It's Really Love"* Bernie Grossman, Arthur Sizemore.

Cast: Mary Nolan *(Cassie Cook)*, James Murray *("Badlands" McKinney)*, Lydia Yeamans Titus *(Polly Voo)*, Wheeler Oakman *(Repen)*, Anders Randolf *(mandarin)*, Yola D'Avril *(Lizzie)*, Mona Rico *(Rose)*, Jimmy Leong *(counsellor)*, Irma Lowe *(Golden Almond)*.

Melodrama. Source: John Colton and Daisy H. Andrews, *Drifting* (New York opening: 21 Dec 1910). Cassie Cook is discharged from Polly Voo's "teashop" because of her disorderly conduct, and she decides to become a "refined lady" for the purpose of gaining the patronage of a Caucasian.

Meanwhile, McKinney, a derelict, is tricked by Repen, a Chinese detective, into admitting he is an escaped convict, but he evades capture with the aid of a Chinese who helps him board a train, where he meets Cassie. Each assumes the other to be respectable, neither having any idea of the other's past. Returning to Shanghai together, their train is attacked by bandits; McKinney bargains to surrender himself to Repen if the latter will remain silent about the past, and Cassie does the same. The detective is recognized by a mandarin as the despoiler of his daughter and is killed in revenge. Cassie and McKinney proclaim their love and unworthiness and plan to start life anew in America. *Fugitives. Detectives. Bandits. Chinese. Personal identity. Teashops. China. Shanghai.*

SHANGHAI ROSE **F2.4959**

Trem Carr Productions. *Dist* Rayart Pictures. 21 Feb or 1 Mar **1929.** Si; b&w. 35mm. 7 reels, 6,416-6,565 ft.

Dir Scott Pembroke. *Story-Scen* Arthur Hoerl. *Photog* Hap Depew. *Film Ed* J. S. Harrington.

Cast: Irene Rich *(Shanghai Rose)*, William Conklin *(Henry West)*, Richard Walling *(Gregor West)*, Ruth Hiatt *(Diane Avery)*, Anthony Merlo *(Ivan Kahn)*, Sid Saylor *(Xavier Doolittle)*, Robert Dudley *(reformer)*, De Sacia Mooers *(Mrs. Doolittle)*.

Underworld melodrama. "Miss Rich has been unjustly accused and driven from home by a jealous husband. She sinks to the depths and finally winds up as 'Shanghai Rose' in a low dive in San Francisco. Reformers demand the district attorney (husband of Rose) close the joint. The D. A. sends his son, a deputy, to investigate. Rose recognizes her son, as does Kahn, the gang leader, who threatens to reveal Rose's true identity to her son. A police raid follows—Rose, fearing Kahn's threatened exposure, shoots the gangster, and goes on trial for murder. Then the story goes into the court room. ... Finally freed, the woman jumps off the ferry dock with a fade-out title, 'come unto me all ye who are heavy laden.' " (*Motion Picture News*, 8 Jun 1929, p1967.) *District attorneys. Gangs. Reformers. Jealousy. Murder. Trials. Suicide. San Francisco.*

SHANGHAIED **F2.4960**

Ralph Ince Productions. *Dist* Film Booking Offices of America. 19 Oct **1927** [c19 Aug 1927; LP24311]. Si; b&w. 35mm. 6 reels, 5,998 ft. [Copyrighted as 7 reels.]

Pres by Joseph P. Kennedy. *Dir* Ralph Ince. *Adapt* J. G. Hawks. *Story* Edward J. Montagne. *Photog* Joe Walker. *Asst Dir* Wallace Fox.

Cast: Ralph Ince *(Hurricane Haley)*, Patsy Ruth Miller *(Polly)*, Alan Brooks *(Crawley)*, Gertrude Astor *(Bessie)*, Walt Robbins *(ship's cook)*, H. J. Jacobson *(Bronson)*.

Melodrama. Hurricane Haley, a sealing captain, drugged and robbed in a waterfront cafe, determines to revenge himself on Polly, his companion. Haley shanghaies Polly aboard his ship, and in a fight over Polly with his mate, Brady, one of Haley's arms is broken; Brady incites the crew to mutiny, but Haley beats him and is himself saved by a collision with a steamer. Haley forces Polly to return to San Francisco and sometime later inquires after her in a Chinese dive. When he upbraids her, she replies by returning to him the sum stolen from him earlier; strained by the confrontation, she faints. Overcome by her gesture, Haley rescues her from the dive, and they are happily united aboard his ship. *Sea captains. Dancers. Sealing. Shanghaiing. Mutiny. Cafes. San Francisco.*

Note: Montagne's original story was entitled "Limehouse Polly."

THE SHANNONS OF BROADWAY **F2.4961**

Universal Pictures. 8 Dec **1929** [c27 Nov 1929; LP876]. Sd (Movietone); b&w. 35mm. 8 reels, 6,155 ft. [Also si; 5,653 ft.]

Pres by Carl Laemmle. *Dir* Emmett J. Flynn. *Scen* Agnes Christine Johnston. *Dial-Titl* James Gleason. *Photog* Jerry Ash. *Film Ed* Byron Robinson. *Song: "Somebody To Love Me"* Ray Klages, Jesse Greer. *Rec Engr* Joseph R. Lapis.

Cast: James Gleason *(Mickey Shannon)*, Lucille Webster Gleason *(Emma Shannon)*, Mary Philbin *(Tessie)*, John Breeden *(Chuck)*, Tom Santschi *(Bradford)*, Harry Tyler *(Eddie Allen)*, Gladys Crolius *(Alice Allen)*, Helen Mehrmann *(Minerva)*, Robert T. Haines *(Albee)*, Slim Summerville *(Newt)*, Tom Kennedy *(Burt)*, Walter Brennan *(Hez)*, Charles Grapewin *(Swanzey)*.

Comedy-drama. Source: James Gleason, *The Shannons of Broadway, a Comedy in Three Acts* (New York, 1928). "The Shannons of Broadway," a vaudeville troupe, are performing in a New England town before an audience including Tessie and Chuck, the young lovers. When Tessie's father, Swanzey, the hotel owner, interrupts the act by taking out his daughter, Mickey Shannon starts a row and Swanzey refuses to give them accommodations at the hotel. Bradford, Chuck's wealthy father, threatens to foreclose the mortgage on Swanzey, causing the Shannons to buy the hotel from him and make extensive alterations. Newt, Bradford's lawyer, tells Emma Shannon that Bradford wants the hotel because of a projected airfield nearby, and she persuades Chuck to buy options for the Shannons near the site. Mickey, hearing that the airfield plan is a hoax, sells to Bradford, while Emma is offered a larger sum by a proper representative; but the drunken Newt confesses to Bradford's conspiracy. The Shannons resell the hotel and return to the stage with a new act. *Theatrical troupes. Vaudeville. Smalltown life. Hotels. Real estate. Airfields. Mortgages. New England.*

SHARE AND SHARE ALIKE **F2.4962**

Whitman Bennett Productions. *Dist* Arrow Film Corp. 15 Dec **1925** [c11 Dec 1925; LP22101]. Si; b&w. 35mm. 6 reels, 5,514 ft.

Dir Whitman Bennett. *Story* Reginald Wright Kauffman.

Cast: Jane Novak *(Marcia Maynard)*, James Rennie *(Sam Jefford)*, Henry Sands *(Titus)*, Cortland Van Deusen *(Benjamin Maynard)*, Frank Conlon *(Duncan)*, Joseph Burke *(Le Blanc)*, Bernard Randall *(Alfonse)*, Mario Majeroni *(sick man)*, Henri Myrial *(Mark, Opie)*.

Melodrama. Seven rising young businessmen enter into a covenant: each of them is to put up $5,000 a year for 25 years and, at the end of 40 years, the money is to be divided equally among the survivors. The 40 years pass; only three of the seven are still alive; and one of the survivors is suffering from typhus. Benjamin Maynard, another of the original seven, is kidnaped, and his daughter, Marcia, sets out to look for him, accompanied by Sam Jefford, a former ace in the American Flying Corps. Sam and Marcia rescue her father, who turns out to be the last surviving member of the seven: one of the others is dead of typhus, and the second is an imposter, having killed the man he is impersonating. The imposter is brought to justice, and Benjamin gives his newly acquired fortune to his daughter on the occasion of her marriage to Sam. *Aviators. Businessmen. Kidnaping. Imposture. Covenants. Typhus.*

THE SHARK MASTER **F2.4963**

Universal Film Manufacturing Co. 5 Sep **1921** [c18 Aug 1921; LP16878]. Si; b&w. 35mm. 5 reels, 4,178 ft.

Dir-Writ Fred Leroy Granville. *Scen* George C. Hull. *Photog* Leland Lancaster.

Cast: Frank Mayo *(McLeod Dean)*, Dorris Deane *(June Marston)*, Herbert Fortier *(Captain Marston)*, Oliver Cross *(Donaldson)*, May Collins *(Flame Flower)*, "Smoke" Turner *(native priest)*, Nick De Ruiz *(native chief)*, Carl Silvera *(Moto)*.

Melodrama. Young McLeod Dean is shipwrecked on Amanu, a South Sea island, where his life is saved by Flame Flower, a white girl who was shipwrecked as a child and reared by the islanders as their queen. She falls desperately in love with Dean, but he rejects her, thinking only of his fiancée in San Francisco. In time, however, he takes Flame Flower as his mate. June Marston, his fiancée, searches the islands for Dean and finally finds him, but she gives him up when she discovers that he and Flame Flower have a child. Flame Flower, however, believing that she has lost him, leaps into the sea, but Dean battles a shark to rescue her. *Polynesians. Suicide. South Sea Islands. Shipwrecks. Sharks.*

SHARP SHOOTERS **F2.4964**

Fox Film Corp. 15 Jan **1928** [c6 Jan 1928; LP24827]. Si; b&w. 35mm. 6 reels, 5,573 ft.

Pres by William Fox. *Dir* J. G. Blystone. *Scen* Marion Orth. *Titl* Malcolm Stuart Boylan. *Story* Randall H. Faye. *Photog* Charles Clarke. *Asst Dir* Jasper Blystone.

Cast: George O'Brien *(George)*, Lois Moran *(Lorette)*, Noah Young *(Tom)*, Tom Dugan *(Jerry)*, William Demarest *("Hi Jack" Murdock)*, Gwen Lee *(Flossy)*, Josef Swickard *(Grandpère)*.

Comedy-drama. George, one of three sailors in a Moroccan port, makes ardent love to Lorette, a French dancing girl, who, unaware that he has a girl in every port, takes his avowals of love seriously. Later, she follows him to the United States, but he studiously avoids her. Out of pity for her, his two friends shanghai him aboard a vessel and force him to marry her. *Sailors. Dancers. French. Shanghaiing. Morocco.*

SHATTERED DREAMS (Universal-Special) **F2.4965**

Universal Film Manufacturing Co. 2 Jan **1922** [c22 Dec 1921; LP17392]. Si; b&w. 35mm. 5 reels, 4,878 ft.

Pres by Carl Laemmle. *Dir* Paul Scardon. *Scen* J. Grubb Alexander. *Photog* Ben Reynolds.

Cast: Miss Du Pont *(Marie Moselle)*, Bertram Grassby *(Théophile Grusant)*, Herbert Heyes *(Louis du Bois)*, Eric Mayne *(The Police Commissioner)*.

Society melodrama. Source: Maude Annesley, *Wind Along the Waste* (New York, 1910). Marie Moselle, an amateur Parisian sculptress, quarrels with her fiancé, Théophile, a society type of the ennuied school, regarding her artistic ambitions, and he is horrified when she selects Louis, a huge apache, as a model. Marie is attracted by his he-manliness but repulsed by his crude advances and retreats to the suave approach of Théophile. When the apache visits her with the intention of carrying her away, she shoots him. Then, driven by remorse to his bedside, she learns that he is a nobleman who turned to the underworld as a result of shell shock, and she comes to love him for his expression of manly courage. *Sculptors. Social classes. Apaches—Paris. Courtship. Shell shock. Paris.*

SHATTERED FAITH **F2.4966**

Jesse J. Ormont Productions. *Dist* Independent Pictures. Dec **1923.** Si; b&w. 35mm. 6 reels.

Dir Jesse J. Ormont.

Cast: Lillian Kemble, Rudolph Cameron, J. Frank Glendon.

Drama. "... in which a husband falsely believes his wife unfaithful. They are separated for fifteen years, he taking the son and she the daughter. At the end of that time, the complications into which their children get result in understanding and forgiveness all around." *(Motion Picture News Booking Guide*, 6:60, Apr 1924.) *Marriage. Parenthood. Infidelity.*

SHATTERED IDOLS **F2.4967**

J. L. Frothingham Productions. *Dist* Associated First National Pictures. 6 Feb **1922** [c7 Dec 1921; LP17488]. Si; b&w. 35mm. 6 reels, 5,850 ft.

Pres by J. L. Frothingham. *Dir* Edward Sloman. *Scen* William V. Mong. *Photog* Tony Gaudio.

Cast: Marguerite De La Motte *(Sarasvati)*, William V. Mong *(Rama Pal)*, James Morrison *(Lieut. Walter Hurst/David Hurst)*, Frankie Lee *(David Hurst, the child)*, Ethel Grey Terry *(Jean Hurst)*, Alfred Allen *(The Judge)*, Louise Lovely *(Diana Chichester)*, Harvey Clark *(Colonel Chichester)*, Josephine Crowell *(Mrs. Chichester)*, Robert Littlefield *(Dick Hathaway)*, Mary Wynn *(Ethel Hathaway)*, George Periolat *(The High Priest)*, Thomas Ricketts *(The Reverend Doctor Romney)*.

Melodrama. Source: Ida Alexa Ross Wylie, *The Daughter of Brahma* (Indianapolis, 1912). Lieut. Walter Hurst, called out with his regiment to quell an uprising against British rule, is killed. His wife has just given birth to a son, David, whose sickly and sensitive nature as he grows up earns him a reputation of cowardice. Upon his return to India after having been educated in England, David learns of his mother's antipathy for him, and, overwrought, he has a vision of his father leading a group of Sikhs and follows him into the jungle to a Brahmin temple, where he witnesses the secret betrothal of Sarasvati to the idol of Siva the Destroyer. He rescues the girl from the temple, and much to his mother's humiliation he marries her and takes her to England, leaving behind Diana, his childhood love. Sarasvati, unable to adjust to English society and customs when her husband is elected to Parliament, is persuaded by one of her countrymen to return to India; David follows and arrives on the eve of a fresh rebellion. Seeking his wife, he evades an attempt on his life, for Sarasvati receives the fatal blow and saves him. *Sikhs. Hinduism. Cowardice. India. Great Britain—Parliament.*

Note: Working title: *Bride of the Gods.*

SHATTERED LIVES **F2.4968**

Gotham Productions. *Dist* Lumas Film Corp. ca8 Jul **1925** [c5 Jun 1925; LP21537]. Si; b&w. 35mm. 6 reels.

Pres by Sam Sax. *Dir-Cont* Henry McCarty. *Story* Victor Gibson. *Photog* Jack MacKenzie.

Cast: Edith Roberts *(Sally Dayton)*, Robert Gordon *(Donald Trent)*, Ethel Wales *(Elizabeth Trent)*, Eddie Phillips *(Red Myers)*, Bernard Randall *(Spencer Foulkes)*, Willis Marks *(John Trent)*, Charles W. Mack *(Enos Dayton)*, Newton House *(Chick Conners)*.

Melodrama. Elizabeth Trent lives alone on a farm with her adopted son, Donald, having been deserted by her husband, John, years earlier when he went to Alaska to make his fortune. When Trent decides to return to his family, a shyster named Spencer Foulkes, who knows that Elizabeth's real son has been lost for year, persuades Red Myers, an unpleasant city youth, to impersonate the missing boy and thus inherit John Trent's fortune. Trent later falls into the hands of Foulkes, and Don saves him from certain death, reuniting him with Elizabeth. It then turns out that Don is in fact the son of the Trents, having been adopted by his own mother! *Lawyers. Adoption. Impersonation. Desertion. Motherhood. Farm life. Alaska.*

SHATTERED REPUTATIONS **F2.4969**

Selznick Pictures. *Dist* Lee-Bradford Corp. 21 Aug **1923** [New York showing; released 1 Oct 1923]. Si; b&w. 35mm. 5 reels, 4,900 ft.

Cast: Johnnie Walker *(Henry Wainright)*, Jackie Saunders *(Sis Hoskins [Mul])*, John Mordaunt *(Dave Hoskins)*, Alfred Lewis *(Joe Hoskins)*, Fred Stonehouse *(Charles Osborne)*, Arthur Bowan *(Stephen Wainright)*, Helen Grant *(Fannie Wainright)*, Torrance Burton *(Vasco da Gama Byles)*.

Crime melodrama. Mul, a loving sister, shields her errant brother, Joe, to protect her father, who worships his only son. Joe's villainous pal is thwarted in his attempts to blackmail Mul by a wealthy young man whom she has mistaken for a chauffeur. *Chauffeurs. Brother-sister relationship. Filial relations. Blackmail. Mistaken identity. Reputation.*

Note: There is some doubt about credit to Selznick Pictures as producer.

SHE COULDN'T SAY NO **F2.4970**

Warner Brothers Pictures. 15 Feb **1930** [c20 Jan 1930; LP1015]. Sd (Vitaphone); b&w. 35mm. 7 reels, 6,413 ft. [Also si.]

Dir Lloyd Bacon. *Scen-Dial* Robert Lord, Arthur Caesar. *Story* Benjamin M. Kaye. *Photog* James Van Trees. *Songs: "Watchin' My Dreams Go By," "That's the Way With a Woman Like Me," "Bouncin' the Baby Around"* Al Dubin, Joe Burke. *Rec Engr* David Forrest.

Cast: Winnie Lightner *(Winnie Harper)*, Chester Morris *(Jerry Casey)*, Louise Beavers *(Cora)*, Sally Eilers *(Iris)*, Johnny Arthur *(Tommy)*, Tully Marshall *(Big John)*.

Melodrama. Winnie Harper, a wisecracking blues singer who can never refuse a favor, is the principal entertainer at the club of racketeer "Big John" and is in love with Jerry, a gang member. Attracted by Winnie's ability, Jerry begins dating her and eventually becomes her manager, hoping thus to go straight. She is successful in a fashionable club, where Jerry meets and becomes romantically involved with Iris, a wealthy society girl; and to keep up with Iris' social set, he joins Big John's gang in another job. Jerry tells Winnie of his love for Iris, but she deems it a mere infatuation; then he is arrested, and Winnie raises the money for his bail, but she is broken-hearted when he returns to Iris. With the help of Tommy, her faithful pianist, she is installed in a revue; then Jerry is mortally wounded in an argument with the gang, and he dies in her arms. Realizing that he has backed her show, Winnie finds strength to go on. *Singers. Racketeers. Socialites. Pianists. Musical revues. Nightclubs. New York City—Broadway.*

SHE GOES TO WAR **F2.4971**

Inspiration Pictures. *Dist* United Artists. 8 Jun **1929** [New York premiere; released 13 Jul; c10 Jun 1929; LP452]. Mus score, sd eff, singing & talking sequences (Movietone); b&w. 35mm. 10 reels, 9,500 ft. [Also si; 8,441 ft.]

Assoc Prod Victor Halperin, Edward R. Halperin. *Dir* Henry King. *Scen* Howard Estabrook. *Dial-Titl* John Monk Saunders. *Adapt* Mme. Fred De Gresac. *Photog* John Fulton, Tony Gaudio. *Art Dir* Al D'Agostino, Robert M. Haas. *Film Ed* Lloyd Nosler. *Songs: "Joan," "There Is a Happy Land"* Harry Akst.

Cast: Eleanor Boardman *(Joan)*, John Holland *(Tom Pike)*, Edmund Burns *(Reggie)*, Alma Rubens *(Rosie)*, Al St. John *(Bill)*, Glen Walters *(Katie)*, Margaret Seddon *(Tom's mother)*, Yola D'Avril *(Yvette)*, Evelyn Hall *(Joan's aunt)*, Augustino Borgato *(major)*, Dina Smirnova *(Joan's maid)*, Yvonne Starke *(major's wife)*, Eulalie Jensen *(matron of canteen)*, Captain H. M. Zier *(major)*, Edward Chandler *(top sergeant)*, Ann Warrington *(lady hostess)*, Gretchen Hartman, Florence Wix *(knitting ladies)*.

War drama. Source: Rupert Hughes, *She Goes to War, and Other Stories* (New York, c1929). Smalltown social leader Joan Morant, who holds herself aloof from the "common people," is thrilled when wartime activity strikes her community, and enlisting the support of her uncle, a congressman, she obtains an assignment overseas. Although she loves Reggie, a wealthy sheik, Joan plays with the affections of Pike, a local garage owner, both of whom she meets in France. Tom Pike, transformed by his war experiences, rebuffs Joan's advances, and she seeks out Reggie, who is living his accustomed life of luxury as a supply sergeant. Joan's female companions, constantly making great sacrifices, impress upon her the seriousness of purpose in her work, and she resolves to do her part.

When Reggie, called to the front, becomes hopelessly drunk, she dons his uniform and replaces him in the ranks, where she experiences a new admiration and love for Tom, her commander. Proving her heroism in battle, she returns to Tom, worthy of his love. *Socialites. Soldiers. Courtship. Snobbery. Smalltown life. Patriotism. Self-sacrifice. Male impersonation. World War I. France.*

SHE GOT WHAT SHE WANTED **F2.4972**

James Cruze Productions. *Dist* Tiffany Productions. 18 Dec **1930** [c19 Dec 1930; LP1844]. Sd (Photophone); b&w. 35mm. 9 reels.

Prod Samuel Zierler. *Dir* James Cruze. *Story-Dial* George Rosener. *Photog* C. Edgar Schoenbaum.

Cast: Betty Compson *(Mahyna)*, Lee Tracy *(Eddie)*, Alan Hale *(Dave)*, Gaston Glass *(Boris)*, Dorothy Christy *(Olga)*, Fred Kelsey *(Dugan)*.

Society comedy. Mahyna, a dissatisfied Russian peasant girl, marries Boris and comes to New York in search of "the soul of love" only to become a drudge in their cheap flat, while Boris, a bookshop keeper, dreams of a prosperous future from the book he is writing. Their boarder, Dave, a partner in a gambling establishment, makes a play for her, and she is tempted to leave with him when Eddie, a former admirer, arrives on the scene and the two get into constant arguments over her. A year later, she is married to Dave; and it is agreed that Boris will live with them. Boris becomes well-to-do with the sale of his book and begins an affair with Olga, the Happiness Girl on radio. A series of complications ensue as the unreliable Eddie returns to renew his suit. Dave is involved in a murder case, and ditched by both men, Mahyna at last finds that Boris is indeed her only true love. *Booksellers. Authors. Gamblers. Russians. Marriage. Ambition. Murder. Radio. New York City.*

SHE STEPS OUT *see* **HARMONY AT HOME**

SHE WOLVES **F2.4973**

Fox Film Corp. 26 Apr **1925** [c26 Apr 1925; LP21429]. Si; b&w. 35mm. 6 reels, 5,783 ft.

Pres by William Fox. *Dir* Maurice Elvey. *Scen* Dorothy Yost.

Cast: Alma Rubens *(Germaine D'Artois)*, Jack Mulhall *(Lucien D'Artois)*, Bertram Grassby *(André Delandal)*, Harry Myers *(Henri de Latour)*, Judy King *(Fox Trot)*, Fred Walton *(valet)*, Diana Miller *(Céleste)*, Josef Swickard *(De Goncourt)*, Helen Dunbar *(Madame De Goncourt)*, Charles Clary *(D'Artois)*.

Drama. Source: Ruth Chatterton, "The Man in Evening Clothes" (adapted from Picard-Mirande; publication undetermined). André Picard and Yves Mirande, *Un Homme en habit; pièce en trois actes* (Paris, 1922). Filled with romantic dreams of youth, Germaine is shocked and disheartened to discover that, for financial reasons, her parents have arranged a marriage for her with Lucien D'Artois, a wealthy man of rough manners who loves dogs more than evening clothes. Germaine makes her distaste known to her new husband, and Lucien goes to Paris in order to make himself over, becoming a regular dandy. Before Lucien can return to Germaine, however, she writes to him, letting him know that she can never be happy. Lucien becomes despondent and dissipates his entire fortune in reckless living. Delandal, an underhanded suitor of the lovely Germaine, leads her falsely to believe that Lucien has been unfaithful, and Germaine goes to Paris to ask Lucien for her freedom, discovering that, although he has been forced by circumstances to take a menial position, he has become a polished gentleman. Germaine belatedly declares her love for Lucien. *Shrews. Dandies. Wealth. Marriage—Arranged. Infidelity. Paris. Dogs.*

SHEEP TRAIL **F2.4974**

Bear Productions. *Dist* Aywon Film Corp. 21 Jan **1926** [New York State license]. Si; b&w. 35mm. 5 reels, 4,850 ft.

Dir Harry L. Fraser.

Cast: Gordon Clifford, Charlotte Pierce.

Western melodrama(?). No information about the nature of this film has been found.

THE SHEIK **F2.4975**

Famous Players–Lasky. *Dist* Paramount Pictures. ca30 Oct **1921** [Los Angeles premiere; released 20 Nov; c25 Oct 1921; LP17131]. Si; b&w. 35mm. 7 reels, 6,579 ft. [Copyrighted as 8 reels.]

Pres by Jesse L. Lasky. *Dir* George Melford. *Scen* Monte M. Katterjohn. *Photog* William Marshall.

Cast: Agnes Ayres *(Diana Mayo)*, Rudolph Valentino *(Sheik Ahmed Ben Hassan)*, Adolphe Menjou *(Raoul de Saint Hubert)*, Walter Long *(Omair)*, Lucien Littlefield *(Gaston)*, George Waggner *(Youssef)*, Patsy Ruth Miller *(slave girl)*, F. R. Butler *(Sir Aubrey Mayo)*.

Melodrama. Source: Edith Maude Hull, *The Sheik* (London, 1919). While traveling through the Sahara, Diana Mayo, a proud and spirited English girl, disguises herself at Biskra as a slave girl and enters a gambling casino where she meets Sheik Ahmed. Later he captures her, but she refuses to surrender to his will; and when she attempts to escape she is recaptured. While Diana and Saint Hubert, a novelist friend of the Sheik's, are riding, they are attacked by Omair's bandits, and Diana is made prisoner. The Sheik summons his tribesmen and attacks Omair's camp just as Diana is about to commit suicide. Omair is slain, but the Sheik is badly wounded; although he is indifferent to her, Diana nurses him to health and declares her love for him. At last he relents, and they embark on their honeymoon. *Sheiks. Novelists. Disguise. Biskra. Sahara.*

THE SHEIK OF ARABY (Reissue) **F2.4976**

Dist R-C Pictures. c15 May **1922** [LP17973]. Si; b&w. 35mm. 5 reels.

Note: A revival of *The Man Who Turned White* (Robertson-Cole, 1919); advertised as reedited and retitled, but essentially the same in length and story line.

THE SHEIK OF MOJAVE **F2.4977**

6 Dec **1928** [New York State license]. Si; b&w. 35mm. 5 reels, 4,500 ft.

Cast: Cheyenne Bill.

Western melodrama(?). No information about the nature of this film has been found.

Note: Production and distribution companies not determined. Released in New York by Industrial Film Co.

SHELL SHOCKED SAMMY **F2.4978**

Sanford Productions. *Dist* Aywon Film Corp. 1 Oct **1923**. Si; b&w. 35mm. 5 reels, 4,800-4,970 ft.

Dir Frank S. Mattison.

Cast: Matty Mattison, Mary Anderson, Vivian Rich, Leonard Clapham, Theodore Lorch.

Melodrama. "... young man who becomes involved in theft of bonds, takes blame, escapes, goes through various thrilling experiences, captures the guilty parties, and in the end proves to be a detective assigned to running down the theft of the bonds, winning the girl in the bargain." (*Motion Picture News Booking Guide*, 6:61, Apr 1924.) *Detectives. Thieves. Shell shock. Disguise.*

SHELTERED DAUGHTERS **F2.4979**

Realart Pictures. May **1921** [c23 Apr 1921; LP16416]. Si; b&w. 35mm. 5 reels, 4,587 ft.

Dir Edward Dillon. *Scen* Clara Beranger. *Story* George Bronson Howard. *Photog* George Folsey. *Art Dir* Robert M. Haas.

Cast: Justine Johnstone *(Jenny Dark)*, Riley Hatch *(Jim Dark, her father)*, Warner Baxter *(Pep Mullins)*, Charles Gerard *(French Pete)*, Helen Ray *(Adele)*, Edna Holland *(Sonia)*, James Laffey *(Cleghorn)*, Jimmie Lapsley *(Pinky Porter)*, Dan E. Charles *(The Ferret)*.

Melodrama. New York policeman Jim Dark determines that his daughter, Jenny, will be shielded from any knowledge of evil, and consequently she lives in a dream world, imagining herself to be a descendant of Jeanne d'Arc. Her school friend Adele, also sheltered, is turned away from home for going out with a young man and gets a job at a fashion shop. Jenny visits her and falls into the hands of a bogus Frenchman, who through her aid collects funds supposedly for war orphans. Jim tracks the criminal to a rendezvous with his daughter, and with the aid of Pep Mullins, who is in love with Jenny, rescues her. *Couturiers. Police. Fatherhood. Good and evil. Adolescence. Jeanne d'Arc.*

THE SHEPHERD KING **F2.4980**

Fox Film Corp. 25 Nov **1923** [c10 Dec 1923; LP19868]. Si; b&w. 35mm. 9 reels, 8,295 or 8,500 ft.

Pres by William Fox. *Dir* J. Gordon Edwards. *Scen* Virginia Tracy. *Photog* Bennie Miggins.

Cast: Violet Mersereau *(Princess Michal)*, Edy Darclea *(Princess Herab)*, Virginia Lucchetti *(Adora, David's adopted sister)*, Nero Bernardi *(David)*, Guido Trento *(Saul)*, Ferrucio Biancini *(Jonathan)*, Alessandro Salvini *(Doeg)*, Mariano Bottino *(Adriel)*, Samuel Balestra *(Goliath)*, Adriano Bocanera *(Samuel)*, Enzo Di Felice *(Ozem)*, Eduardo Balsamo *(Abimelech)*, Amerigo Di Giorgia *(Omah)*, Gordon McEdward *(Egyptian prisoner)*, Ernesto Tranquili *(Jesse, father of David)*, Isabella De Leaso *(his wife)*.

Biblical drama. Source: Wright Lorimer and Arnold Reeves, *The Shepherd King ... a Romantic Drama in Four Acts and Five Scenes* (New York opening: 5 Apr 1904; Mount Vernon, New York, 1903). Saul, King of Israel, prepares to battle the Philistines in spite of the warnings of prophet Samuel, who predicts that Saul will lose his throne and selects David as the new king. Saul's son, Jonathan, makes friends with David and brings him to the court. When David slays Goliath, Saul, believing him to be the man in the prophesy, sends him into a trap against the Philistines. David returns victorious, and he leaves the court after Saul's attempt to kill him. He gathers men; and when the Philistines attack Saul, David conquers them. Saul and Jonathan are killed in battle; David is acclaimed king, and he weds Saul's daughter, Princess Michal. *Royalty. Prophets. Philistines. Israel. Saul. David. Jonathan. Goliath. Biblical characters.*

THE SHEPHERD OF THE HILLS **F2.4981**

First National Pictures. 1 Jan **1928** [c23 Dec 1927; LP24794]. Si; b&w. 35mm. 9 reels, 8,188 ft.

Pres by Richard A. Rowland. *Prod* Charles R. Rogers. *Dir* Albert Rogell. *Adapt-Cont* Marion Jackson. *Titl* Dwinelle Benthall, Rufus McCosh. *Photog* Sol Polito. *Film Ed* Hugh Bennett.

Cast: Alec B. Francis *(David Howitt, The Shepherd)*, Molly O'Day *(Sammy Lane)*, John Boles *(Young Matt)*, Matthew Betz *(Wash Gibbs)*, Romaine Fielding *(Old Matt)*, Otis Harlan *("By Thunder")*, Joseph Bennett *(Ollie)*, Maurice Murphy *(Little Pete)*, Edythe Chapman *(Aunt Mollie)*, Carl Stockdale *(Jim Lane)*, Marian Douglas *(Maggie)*, John Westwood *(The Artist)*.

Rural melodrama. Source: Harold Bell Wright, *The Shepherd of the Hills* (New York, 1907). David Howitt, a stranger, comes among the mountain folk of the Missouri hills and, taken in by an Ozark family, becomes known as The Shepherd because of his gentle and kindly ways. Years earlier, his son betrayed a mountaineer's daughter, and The Shepherd hopes to atone for his error. When a continued drought threatens the people with starvation and ruin, they lose faith in the "miracle man" and mock him, though he begs them to keep the faith. The miraculous coming of the rains restores their faith, and the father of the betrayed girl relents in his thirst for vengeance when The Shepherd confesses his son's guilt. *Shepherds. Fatherhood. Revenge. Mountain life. Arkansas. Ozarks. Drought.*

THE SHERIFF OF GOPHER FLATS *see* **GALLOPING GALLAGHER**

THE SHERIFF OF HOPE ETERNAL **F2.4982**

Ben Wilson Productions. *Dist* Arrow Film Corp. Mar **1921.** Si; b&w. 35mm. 5 reels, 4,380 ft.

Prod-Dir Ben Wilson.

Cast: Jack Hoxie *(Drew Halliday)*, Marin Sais *(Hela Marcale)*, Joseph Girard *("Silk" Lowry)*, William Dyer *(Judge Clayton)*, Bee Monson *(Marybelle Sawyer)*, Theodore Brown *(her father)*, Wilbur McGaugh *(her brother)*.

Western melodrama. Drew Halliday, stage driver, is abashed when the little girl he admires returns from finishing school a beautiful young woman. When a sporty gambler and saloon keeper forces his attentions on the young lady, Drew comes to her defense. Because of his courageous handling of the gambler, Drew is elected sheriff. He acquires more responsibility when he takes Hela for his wife after her father dies. Soon afterward her brother is jailed for a murder that the gambler committed. The gambler again makes advances toward Hela: this time he is caught by his own girl, who in a rage shoots him. Hela is accused of the killing; Drew takes the blame; but when the woman confesses all, the innocent are freed. *Stagecoach drivers. Saloon keepers. Gamblers. Sheriffs. Brother-sister relationship. Murder.*

THE SHERIFF OF SUN-DOG **F2.4983**

Berwilla Film Corp. *Dist* Arrow Film Corp. 5 Dec **1922** [c20 Nov 1922; LP18421]. Si; b&w. 35mm. 5 reels, 4,949 ft.

Dir Supv by Ben Wilson. *Dir? (see note)* Lewis King. *Scen* Daniel F. Whitcomb.

Cast: William Fairbanks *("Silent" Davidson)*, Robert McKenzie *("Harp" Harris)*, Jim Welch *(Scott Martin)*, Florence Gilbert *(Jean Martin)*, Ashton Dearholt *(Pete Kane)*, William White *(Jeff Sedley)*.

Western melodrama. Source: Wilbur C. Tuttle, "The Sheriff of Sun-Dog," in *Adventure Magazine* (31:141–173, 30 Nov 1921). Sheriff "Silent" Davidson tries to protect sheep rancher Scott Martin and his daughter, Jean, from the cattlemen, then is framed for the murder of the old man. He brings his rival, Pete Kane, and Jeff Sedley, Martin's creditor, to justice and wins Jean's heart. *Sheriffs. Ranches. Cattle. Sheep.*

Note: Copyright records credit Lewis King with direction.

THE SHERIFF OF TOMBSTONE *see* **GALLOPING GALLAGHER**

SHERIFF'S GIRL **F2.4984**

Ben Wilson Productions. *Dist* Rayart Pictures. Oct or Nov **1926.** Si; b&w. 35mm. 5 reels, 4,908 ft.

Dir Ben Wilson.

Cast: Ben Wilson, Fang *(a dog)*.

Western melodrama. "Sheriff loves schoolteacher but she wants trip to New York before marrying him. Bank is robbed and hunt is on. Fugitive takes refuge in school house and is aided by girl. He leaves for New York and she follows him. They are discovered together by sheriff but it is disclosed that he is her brother and bank robbery was framed. Sheriff takes girl back to God's country." (*Motion Picture News Booking Guide,* 12:53, Apr 1927.) *Sheriffs. Schoolteachers. Fugitives. Brother-sister relationship. Bank robberies. Frameup. Dogs.*

THE SHERIFF'S LASH **F2.4985**

Anchor Productions. 24 Oct **1929** [New York State license]. Si; b&w. 35mm. 5 reels, 4,500 ft.

Cast: Cliff (Tex) Lyons.

Western melodrama. No information about the precise nature of this film has been found.

THE SHERIFF'S LONE HAND *see* **THE COWBOY AND THE FLAPPER**

SHERLOCK BROWN **F2.4986**

Metro Pictures. 26 Jun **1922** [c21 Jun 1922; LP17986]. Si; b&w. 35mm. 5 reels, 4,800 ft.

Dir-Story Bayard Veiller. *Scen* Lenore J. Coffee. *Photog* Arthur Martinelli. *Art-Tech Dir* A. F. Mantz.

Cast: Bert Lytell *(William Brown)*, Ora Carew *(Barbara Musgrave)*, Sylvia Breamer *(Hilda)*, De Witt Jennings *(J. J. Wallace)*, Theodore von Eltz *(Frank Morton)*, Wilton Taylor *(Chief Bard)*, Hardee Kirkland *(General Bostwick)*, George Barnum *(Henry Stark)*, George Kuwa *(Sato)*.

Comedy-melodrama. William Brown, who wants to become a detective, writes to an agency and receives for $5 a tin badge. At the same time a secret government formula for explosives is stolen from Lieutenant Musgrave, to whom Brown promises his aid. Meanwhile, Musgrave is hospitalized in delirium and utters the name "Wallace" to his sister, Barbara, who discovers that Wallace has hidden the formula in a flowerpot and follows him to his apartment. There, during a struggle, a book on flying alerts Brown. He accidentally discovers the secret formula, and Barbara escapes with the paper but is sidetracked on her way to a government agent. Following numerous complications and a long chase, Sherlock Brown succeeds in tracking down the conspirators, regaining the formula, and winning the heart of Barbara. *Detectives. Government agents. Explosives. Documentation. Chases.*

SHERLOCK HOLMES **F2.4987**

Goldwyn Pictures. 1 May **1922** [New York premiere; released 29 Oct; c3 Apr 1922; LP18273]. Si; b&w. 35mm. 9 reels, 8,200 ft.

Prod F. J. Godsol. *Dir* Albert Parker. *Scen* Marion Fairfax, Earle Browne. *Photog* J. Roy Hunt.

Cast: John Barrymore *(Sherlock Holmes)*, Roland Young *(Dr. Watson)*, Carol Dempster *(Alice Faulkner)*, Gustav von Seyffertitz *(Professor Moriarty)*, Louis Wolheim *(Craigin)*, Percy Knight *(Sid Jones)*, William H. Powell *(Forman Wells)*, Hedda Hopper *(Madge Larrabee)*, Peggy Bayfield *(Rose Faulkner)*, Margaret Kemp *(Therese)*, Anders Randolf *(James Larrabee)*, Robert Schable *(Alf Bassick)*, Reginald Denny *(Prince Alexis)*, David Torrence *(Count Von Stalburg)*, Robert Fischer *(Otto)*, Lumsden Hare *(Dr. Leighton)*, Jerry Devine *(Billy)*, John Willard *(Inspector Gregson)*.

Mystery melodrama. Source: William Gillette, *Sherlock Holmes: A Play; Based on Sir Arthur Conan Doyle's Stories* (Garden City, New York, 1935). Sherlock Holmes is asked by his friend Watson to help Prince Alexis clear himself of charges of a theft he did not commit. He is able to do so, but not until years later does Holmes trap the real culprit, Professor Moriarty, and his agents in their attempts to blackmail Prince Alexis. He also finds love with Alice Faulkner. *Detectives. Physicians. Royalty.*

Blackmail. Theft.
Note: May also be known as *Moriarty*.

SHERLOCK, JR. **F2.4988**
Buster Keaton Productions. *Dist* Metro Pictures. 21 Apr **1924** [c22 Apr 1924; LP20125]. Si; b&w. 35mm. 5 reels, 4,065 ft.
Pres by Joseph M. Schenck. *Dir* Buster Keaton. *Story* Clyde Bruckman, Jean Havez, Joseph Mitchell. *Photog* Byron Houck, Elgin Lessley. *Art Dir* Fred Gabourie. *Cost* Clare West.
Cast: Buster Keaton *(Sherlock, Jr.)*, Kathryn McGuire *(The Girl)*, Ward Crane *(The Rival)*, Joseph Keaton *(The Father)*, Horace Morgan, Jane Connelly, Erwin Connelly, Ford West, George Davis, John Patrick, Ruth Holly.
Comedy. Sherlock, Jr., who is both the cleanup man and the projectionist at a local cinema, becomes an amateur detective through a correspondence course and foils the villain who has stolen his sweetheart and her watch. He dreams of success on the screen and awakens to triumph in his romance. *Detectives. Motion picture theaters. Smalltown life. Correspondence courses.*

SHE'S A SHEIK **F2.4989**
Paramount Famous Lasky Corp. 12 Nov **1927** [c12 Nov 1927; LP24656]. Si; b&w. 35mm. 6 reels, 5,931 or 6,015 ft.
Pres by Adolph Zukor, Jesse L Lasky. *Dir* Clarence Badger. *Screenplay* Lloyd Corrigan, Grover Jones. *Titl* George Marion, Jr. *Story* John McDermott. *Photog* J. Roy Hunt.
Cast: Bebe Daniels *(Zaida)*, Richard Arlen *(Captain Colton)*, William Powell *(Kada)*, Josephine Dunn *(Wanda Fowler)*, James Bradbury, Jr. *(Jerry)*, Billy Franey *(Joe)*, Paul McAllister *(Sheik Yusiff ben Hamad)*, Al Fremont *(The Major)*.
Burlesque. Born of a Spanish mother and an Arabian father, Zaida, granddaughter of Sheik Yusiff ben Hamad, insists that she will have only a Christian husband, and as a result the sheik anticipates trouble from Kada, a desert renegade, who warns that he will have her at all costs. When Kada threatens Jerry and Joe, two American showmen who project movies at desert carnivals, Zaida vanquishes him at the point of a rapier. At a desert garrison where she and her grandfather are guests of the major, Zaida meets Captain Colton and has him abducted; when all her feminine wiles fail to win him, she almost succeeds with jealousy when Kada's tribesmen attack the garrison. Jerry and his pal save the day by projecting a film of attacking Arabs that terrorizes the tribesmen. *Motion picture projectionists. Arabs. Bedouins. Spanish. Sheiks. Grandfathers. Islam. Christianity. Motion pictures.*
Note: Apparently, the novelty film-within-the-film sequence was taken from the same studio's *Beau Sabreur*.

SHE'S MY BABY **F2.4990**
Sterling Pictures. 10 May **1927** [c23 May 1927; LP24002]. Si; b&w. 35mm. 6 reels, 5,249 ft.
Dir Fred Windemere. *Story-Scen* Frances Guihan. *Photog* Herbert Kirkpatrick.
Cast: Robert Agnew *(Bobby Horton)*, Kathleen Myers *(Bernice Wilbur)*, Earle Williams *(John Wilbur)*, Grace Carlyle *(Mary Wilbur)*, Mildred Harris *(Claire Daltour)*, Alphonse Martel *(Alphonze Dabreau)*, Max Asher *(Henry Conrad)*, William Irving *(Chuck Callahan)*.
Farce. After 21 years of marriage, John and Mary Wilbur have reached a bitter stalemate, though they pretend affection for the sake of Bernice, their daughter just home from college. Mrs. Wilbur entertains lavishly and becomes infatuated with Prince Dabreau, while John is beset and vamped by Claire Daltour, an actress who is seeking a divorce from Chuck Callahan, a prizefighter. Bobby Horton, who is infatuated with Claire, thinks Wilbur is his rival until he falls under the spell of Bernice. Mrs. Wilbur sets out to get even with John by going to a jazz rendezvous with Dabreau, and to her surprise she meets her daughter there. In a whirlwind finish with Bernice on Dabreau's yacht and Bobby chasing Dabreau, Mr. and Mrs. Wilbur are reconciled and Bobby and Bernice are married. *Royalty. Vamps. Prizefighters. Actors. Marriage. Divorce. Parenthood. Jazz life. Jealousy.*

SHE'S MY WEAKNESS **F2.4991**
RKO Productions. 1 Aug **1930** [c20 Jun 1930; LP1453]. Sd (Photophone); b&w. 35mm. 8 reels, 6,421 ft.
Prod William Le Baron. *Assoc Prod* Henry Hobart. *Dir* Melville Brown. *Screenplay-Dial* J. Walter Ruben. *Photog* Leo Tover. *Art Dir* Max Ree. *Rec Engr* John Tribby. *Asst Dir* Dewey Starkey.
Cast: Arthur Lake *(Tommy Mills)*, Sue Carol *(Marie Thurber)*, Lucien Littlefield *(Warren Thurber)*, William Collier, Sr. *(David Tuttle)*, Helen Ware *(Mrs. Thurber)*, Alan Bunce *(Bernard Norton)*, Emily Fitzroy *(Mrs. Oberlander)*, Walter Gilbert *(Wilson)*.
Romantic comedy. Source: Howard Lindsay and Bertrand Robinson, *Tommy, a Comedy in Three Acts* (New York, 1928). Tommy Mills and Marie Thurber, sweethearts, plan to marry when Tommy sells some land he has inherited. Marie's parents favor the match, as they prefer Tommy over Bernard Norton, another suitor. Her father, Warren Thurber, however, is in financial straits and plans to sell land to a civic improvement association headed by David Tuttle. When he discovers that Tommy has agreed to sell his land to Mrs. Oberlander, he berates him; but Tommy agrees to boost the price so that Thurber will win out. Tuttle, who favors Bernard as Marie's husband, persuades Tommy that he must endure the displeasure of the Thurbers, and as a result a misunderstanding arises over the sale of the land. But Tuttle's scheme backfires, and Tommy wins the girl after all. *Parenthood. Family life. Courtship. Land speculation.*

THE SHIELD OF HONOR (Universal-Jewel) **F2.4992**
Universal Pictures. 10 Dec **1927** [New York premiere; released 19 Feb 1928; c2 Nov 1927; LP24621]. Si; b&w. 35mm. 6 reels, 6,173 ft.
Pres by Carl Laemmle. *Dir* Emory Johnson. *Adapt-Cont* Leigh Jacobson, Gladys Lehman. *Titl* Viola Brothers Shore. *Story* Emilie Johnson. *Photog* Ross Fisher.
Cast: Neil Hamilton *(Jack MacDowell)*, Dorothy Gulliver *(Gwen O'Day)*, Ralph Lewis *(Dan MacDowell)*, Nigel Barrie *(Robert Chandler)*, Claire McDowell *(Mrs. MacDowell)*, Fred Esmelton *(Howard O'Day)*, Harry Northrup *(A. E. Blair)*, Thelma Todd *(Rose Fisher)*, David Kirby *(Red)*, Joseph Girard *(chief of police)*, William Bakewell *(Jerry MacDowell)*, Hank *(himself, a dog)*.
Melodrama. Veteran policeman Dan MacDowell and his son Jack are being honored at the celebration of the addition of aviation to the police force. Jack, the first flying officer, meets Gwen O'Day, daughter of a wealthy jeweler, when she christens a plane, and they fall in love; later, O'Day asks Jack to assist him in solving numerous jewel robberies of his customers. Dan MacDowell, meanwhile, is retired from the force on his 65th birthday, but O'Day gives him a night watchman's job in his store. With the help of his father, Jack gathers clues on the case, and suspicion soon falls on Robert Chandler, O'Day's business advisor, who is later revealed to be the secret leader of some diamond thieves. Gwen is locked in a vault while the thieves make their getaway, the leader taking to the air. Events culminate in a night air battle in which the villains are subdued. *Police. Thieves. Jewelers. Watchmen. Aviation. Filial relations. Retirement. Dogs.*

THE SHIELD OF SILENCE **F2.4993**
William Steiner Productions. *Dist* Pathé Exchange. c11 Mar **1925** [LU21230]. Si; b&w. 35mm. 5 reels.
Dir Leo Maloney. *Scen* Ford Beebe. *Photog* Jake Badaracco. *Film Ed* Fred Bain.
Cast: Leo Maloney *(Nathan Holden)*, Josephine Hill *(Marjorie Stone)*, Leonard Clapham *(Harry Ramsey)*, Ray Walters, Vester Pegg, Whitehorse.
Western melodrama. Nathan Holden, the top hand on the Lazy-A Ranch, is engaged to Marjorie Stone, the rancher's beautiful daughter. One day, Bob Stone, Marjorie's brother, shows up at the ranch, badly injured and confused by a blow on the head. Nathan hides Bob, who is dressed as a convict, from the sheriff. A stranger named Ramsey then arrives at the ranch and asks for a meal. Ramsey proceeds to steal $3,000 and lays the blame on Nathan, who cannot clear himself of suspicion because Ramsey knows of Bob's presence and threatens to tell the sheriff. Nathan is arrested by the sheriff, and Ramsey rides away; but Nathan has a hunch, escapes, and brings Ramsey to the sheriff for interrogation. Nathan reveals that Ramsey is the escaped convict, responsible for hitting Bob on the head and changing clothes with him. Ramsey is arrested, and Nathan and Marjorie win the affection of the elder Stone for saving Bob. *Prison escapees. Sheriffs. Brother-sister relationship. Amnesia. Theft.*

SHIFTING SANDS **F2.4994**
Luxor Pictures. *Dist* W. W. Hodkinson Corp. 11 Nov **1923**. Si; b&w. 35mm. 6 reels, 5,308 ft.
Dir Fred Leroy Granville. *Photog* Walter Blakely, Silvano Balboni.
Cast: Peggy Hyland *(Barbara Thayer)*, Lewis Willoughby *(Dr. Willard Lindsay)*, Mademoiselle Valia *(Yvonne Lindsay)*, Richard Atwood *(Pierre Moreau)*, Gibson Gowland *(Samuel Thayer)*, Tony Melford *(Leroy*

Lindsay, age 4), Douglas Webster *(Leroy Lindsay, age 14)*.

Melodrama. Willard Lindsay's wife, Yvonne, falls in love with Pierre Moreau while they are in Africa. Taking her son, she follows Moreau to Tripoli and there, after a year, she tires of Moreau. Meanwhile Lindsay has developed an interest in Barbara Thayer, the daughter of his best friend, but at the request of his wife, who would be reunited with him, Lindsay leaves Barbara. The wife dies; her son becomes Barbara's ward; and years later Lindsay is reunited with both. *Physicians. Infidelity. Tripoli.*

SHIFTING SANDS (Reissue) **F2.4995**

Triangle Film Corp. *Dist* Tri-Stone Pictures. 30 Mar **1925** [New York State license]. Si; b&w. 35mm. 5 reels.

Note: A Gloria Swanson film originally released by Triangle Film Corp. on 11 Aug 1918.

THE SHINING ADVENTURE **F2.4996**

Madeline Brandeis Productions. *Dist* Astor Pictures. 7 Aug **1925** [New York State license]. Si; b&w. 35mm. 6 reels, 5,148 ft.

Dir Hugo Ballin. *Adapt* Lawrence Trimble. *Photog* James Diamond.

Cast: Percy Marmont *(Dr. Hugo McLean)*, Mabel Ballin *(Mary)*, Ben Alexander *(Benny)*, B. Wayne Lamont *(Franklin Tribbit)*, Mary Jane Irving *("Lamey")*, Stella De Lanti.

Society melodrama. Source: Dana Burnet, *The Shining Adventure* (New York, 1916). Money intended for charitable purposes is misappropriated. *Embezzlement.*

A SHIP COMES IN **F2.4997**

De Mille Pictures. *Dist* Pathé Exchange. 4 Jun **1928** [c10 May 1928; LP25281]. Si; b&w. 35mm. 7 reels, 6,902 ft.

Dir William K. Howard. *Scen* Sonya Levien. *Titl* John Krafft. *Story-Adapt* Julien Josephson. *Photog* Lucien Andriot. *Art Dir* Anton Grot. *Film Ed* Barbara Hunter. *Asst Dir* Emile De Ruelle. *Cost* Adrian.

Cast: Rudolph Schildkraut *(Peter Plecznik)*, Louise Dresser *(Mrs. Plecznik)*, Milton Holmes *(Eric)*, Linda Landi *(Marthe)*, Fritz Feld *(Sokol)*, Lucien Littlefield *(Dan Casey)*, Robert Edeson *(Judge Gresham)*, Louis Natheaux *(Seymon)*.

Drama. The Hungarian family of Peter Plecznik emigrates to the United States, and there, despite protests from Sokol, one of his radical countrymen, Peter applies for American citizenship. Five years later, assisted by kindly Judge Gresham, Plecznik receives his citizenship papers. His son goes to war. Judge Gresham is seriously wounded and his secretary is killed when a bomb set by Sokol explodes. Plecznik is blamed, convicted, and jailed; he is later freed when Sokol confesses to the crime. Plecznik's son is killed in the war. Despite all this, Plecznik's patriotism never wavers, and he returns to his job as a janitor feeling that he has given all to his country. *Hungarians. Immigrants. Janitors. Judges. Patriotism. Naturalization. Sabotage. World War I.*

THE SHIP FROM SHANGHAI **F2.4998**

Metro-Goldwyn-Mayer Pictures. 31 Jan **1930** [c27 Jan 1930; LP1030]. Sd (Movietone); b&w. 35mm. 8 reels, 6,225 ft. [Also si.]

Dir Charles Brabin. *Screenplay* John Howard Lawson. *Titl* Madeleine Ruthven, Alfred Block. *Photog* Ira Morgan. *Art Dir* Cedric Gibbons. *Film Ed* Grant Whytock. *Rec Engr* Douglas Shearer.

Cast: Conrad Nagel *(Howard Vazey)*, Kay Johnson *(Dorothy Daley)*, Carmel Myers *(Viola Thorpe)*, Holmes Herbert *(Paul Thorpe)*, Zeffie Tilbury *(Lady Daley)*, Louis Wolheim *(Ted)*, Ivan Linow *(Pete)*, Jack McDonald *(Reid)*.

Melodrama. Source: Dale Collins, *Ordeal; a Novel* (New York, 1924). Howard Vazey, an American playboy, becomes reacquainted with Dorothy Daley, an English girl, in Shanghai; and joining up with yacht owners Viola and Paul Thorpe, they decide to cross the Pacific to the United States. Ted, a crazed steward, incites the crew to mutiny following a storm that damages the yacht; and assuming the position of captain, he imprisons the socialites. The crew desert the ship when there is a water shortage; Ted induces Dorothy to come to his cabin, where she persuades him that he is insane, causing him to leap overboard and be devoured by sharks. *Socialites. Yachtsmen. Stewards. English. Yachts. Mutiny. Insanity. Shanghai. Sharks.*

SHIP OF SOULS **F2.4999**

Encore Pictures. *Dist* Associated Exhibitors. 20 Dec **1925** [c30 Dec 1925; LU22203]. Si; b&w. 35mm. 6 reels.

Prod Max O. Miller. *Dir* Charles Miller. *Story* Frank P. Donovan. *Photog* Ed Du Par.

Cast: Bert Lytell *(Langley Barnes)*, Lillian Rich *(Christine Garth)*, Gertrude Astor *(Doris Barnes)*, Earl Metcalf *(Stikeen Harry)*, Russell Simpson *(Angus Garth)*, Ynez Seabury *(Annette Garth)*, Cyril Chadwick *(Churchill)*, Jean Perry *(Hensley)*, Pete Mauer *(Durgin)*, W. J. Miller *(Atlin)*, Jack Irwin *(radio operator)*.

Northwest melodrama. Source: Emerson Hough, *Ship of Souls* (New York, 1925). Deserted by his wife, Langley Barnes goes to the North Country to seek peace, there falling in love with Christine, the daughter of Angus Garth, a factor made mad by the solitudes. Despite the fact that he is not divorced, Langley marries Christine in an illegal ceremony. Captain Churchill arrives to erect a radio transmitter and, returning to the United States, marries Langley's wife, who has in the interim obtained a divorce. Churchill broadcasts news of the divorce to the North Country, and Langley and Christine take steps to be legally married. *Factors. Marriage. Divorce. Bigamy. Insanity. Radio. Canada.*

SHIPS OF THE NIGHT **F2.5000**

Trem Carr Productions. *Dist* Rayart Pictures. 27 Nov **1928.** Si; b&w. 35mm. 6 reels, 5,812 or 5,940 ft.

Dir Duke Worne. *Scen-Titl* Arthur Hoerl. *Story* Frederick Nebel. *Photog* Hap Depew. *Film Ed* John S. Harrington.

Cast: Jacqueline Logan *(Johanna Hearne)*, Sojin *(Yut Sen)*, Jack Mower *(Dan Meloy)*, Andy Clyde *(Alec)*, Arthur Rankin *(Donald Hearne)*, Glen Cavender *(Cransey)*, Thomas A. Curran *(chief of police)*, Frank Lanning *(Moja)*, J. P. McGowan *(Motilla)*, Frank Moran *(first mate)*.

Adventure melodrama. In search of her fugitive brother, who wounded a man who was later murdered, Johanna Hearne encounters pirates, a Chinaman with a harem and criminals as slaves, and love on a desert island for ship captain Dan Meloy. *Sea captains. Fugitives. Pirates. Chinese. Brother-sister relationship. Murder. Slavery. Harems.*

SHIPWRECKED **F2.5001**

Metropolitan Pictures Corp. of California. *Dist* Producers Distributing Corp. 9 May **1926** [c18 May 1926; LP22745]. Si; b&w. 35mm. 6 reels, 5,865 ft. [Copyrighted as 7 reels.]

Pres by John C. Flinn. *Dir* Joseph Henabery. *Scen* Harold Shumate. *Adapt* Finis Fox. *Cinematog* David Kesson. *2d Cinematog* Dewey Wrigley. *Art Dir* Charles Cadwallader. *Asst Dir* Douglas Dawson. *Prod Mgr* George Bertholon. *Asst Prod Mgr* Robert Ross.

Cast: Seena Owen *(Loie Austin)*, Joseph Schildkraut *(Larry O'Neil)*, Matthew Betz *(Captain Klodel)*, Clarence Burton *(Red Gowland)*, Laska Winter *(Zanda)*, Lionel Belmore *(John Beacon)*, Erwin Connelly *(Chumbley)*.

Melodrama. Source: Langdon McCormick, *Shipwrecked* (New York opening: 12 Nov 1924). Loie Austin, an artist's model, is accosted by a ship chandler and shoots him in attempting to escape. She then tries to end her own life in the bay but is rescued by Larry O'Neil, a drifter employed as a cook on a steamer. Loie, with Larry's aid, stows away on his ship, disguised as a boy; but she is discovered by the domineering Captain Klodel, who, when notified of her crime, uses his knowledge of it as a weapon to force his attentions upon her. Larry intercedes in her behalf and thrashes him. A storm wrecks the ship, and Loie and Larry are stranded on an island, where they are befriended by a white trader. Klodel arrives and claims Loie as his prisoner, and believing she loves him, Larry gives way to dissipation; finally, he beats the captain and is reunited with the woman he loves just as the trader learns that her supposed vicitim has recovered after all. *Models. Cooks. Traders. Ship chandlers. Disguise. Seafaring life. Shipwrecks.*

SHIRLEY OF THE CIRCUS **F2.5002**

Fox Film Corp. 12 Nov **1922** [c12 Nov 1922; LP19204]. Si; b&w. 35mm. 5 reels, 4,668 ft.

Pres by William Fox. *Dir* Rowland V. Lee. *Story-Scen* Robert N. Lee. *Photog* G. O. Post.

Cast: Shirley Mason *(Nita)*, George O'Hara *(Pierre)*, Crauford Kent *(James Blackthorne)*, Alan Hale *(Max)*, Lule Warrenton *(Blanquette)*, Maude Wayne *(Susan Van Der Pyle)*, Mathilde Brundage *(Mrs. Van Der Pyle)*.

Melodrama. An American artist in Paris becomes interested in a circus girl's welfare and sends her to school. After 3 years Nita runs away to America and appears at the artist's home, where she is befriended by his fiancée. Nita finds her old friends from the circus performing in the United States and marries her former sweetheart. *Artists. Circus. Education. Paris.*

THE SHOCK (Universal-Jewel) **F2.5003**
Universal Pictures. 10 Jun **1923** [c27 Apr 1923; LP18917]. Si; b&w. 35mm. 7 reels, 6,738 ft.
Dir Lambert Hillyer. *Scen? (see note)* Arthur Statter, Charles Kenyon. *Story* William Dudley Pelley. *Photog* Dwight Warren.
Cast: Lon Chaney *(Wilse Dilling)*, Virginia Valli *(Gertrude Hadley)*, Jack Mower *(Jack Cooper)*, William Welsh *(Mischa Hadley)*, Henry Barrows *(John Cooper, Sr.)*, Christine Mayo *(Anne Vincent ["Queen Anne"])*, Harry Devere *(Olaf Wismer)*, John Beck *(Bill)*, Walter Long *(The Captain)*.
Crook melodrama. Wilse Dilling, a cripple, is sent by his underworld boss, "Queen Anne," to San Francisco to expose banker Mischa Hadley's robbery, for which the gang has been blackmailing him. However, Wilse falls in love with Gertrude Hadley, the daughter of his victim, reforms under her good influence, and destroys the evidence against Hadley. Furious at Wilse's doublecross, "Queen Anne" abducts Gertrude and places her in a Chinese dive to trap Wilse. They are in Anne's power when a great earthquake occurs and allows them to escape. Wilse is cured—possibly by the earthquake itself, possibly by surgery—and marries Gertrude. *Criminals—Rehabilitation. Cripples. Blackmail. Earthquakes. San Francisco—Earthquake 1906.*
Note: Working title: *Bittersweet*. Statter's scenario credit is from Universal records; reviews credit Charles Kenyon.

THE SHOCK PUNCH **F2.5004**
Famous Players–Lasky. *Dist* Paramount Pictures. 25 Feb **1925** [c26 May 1925; LP21501]. Si; b&w. 35mm. 6 reels, 6,151 ft.
Pres by Adolph Zukor, Jesse L. Lasky. *Dir* Paul Sloane. *Screenplay* Luther Reed. *Photog* William Miller. *Art Dir* Ernest Fegte.
Cast: Richard Dix *(Randall Lee Savage)*, Frances Howard *(Dorothy Clark)*, Theodore Babcock *(Dan Savage)*, Percy Moore *(Jim Clark)*, Charles Beyer *(Stanley Pierce)*, Gunboat Smith *(Terrence O'Rourke)*, Jack Scannell *(Mike)*, Walter Long *(Bull Malarkey)*, Paul Panzer *(Giuseppi)*.
Melodrama. Source: John Monk Saunders, "The Shock Punch" (publication undetermined). Randall Savage, who fights with a shock punch, first knocks out Terrence O'Rourke, a championship boxer, and later, at an ironworkers' ball, flattens Bull Malarkey. Randall learns that Dorothy Clark, a girl he greatly admires, will be a daily visitor on the site of a building her father is putting up; and to be near her, he gets a job as a riveter on one of her father's construction crews. Bull Malarkey, who is Clark's foreman, plans to delay completion of the building until after the expiration of a contractual time limit, thereby ruining the elder Clark. Randall learns of the scheme, makes sure that the building is finished on time, and wins Dorothy for his wife. *Boxers. Construction foremen. Riveters. Ironworkers. Contracts. Courtship.*

A SHOCKING NIGHT **F2.5005**
Universal Film Manufacturing Co. ca29 Jan **1921** [St. Louis premiere; released Jan; c30 Dec 1920; LP15991]. Si; b&w. 35mm. 5 reels, 4,695 ft.
Pres by Carl Laemmle. *Dir* Eddie Lyons, Lee Moran. *Scen* C. B. Hoadley. *Story* Edgar Franklin. *Photog* Alfred Gosden.
Cast: Eddie Lyons *(Richard Thayer)*, Lee Moran *(William Harcourt)*, Alta Allen *(Bessie Lane)*, Lillian Hall *(Maude Harcourt)*, Lionel Belmore *(Bill Bradford)*, Clark Comstock *(Jack Lane)*, Florence Mayon *(cook)*, Charles McHugh *(butler)*.
Bedroom farce. William Harcourt loses all his money in a business transaction and is forced to dismiss his servants. Mr. and Mrs. Harcourt are about to entertain Richard Thayer and his fiancée, Bessie Lane, at dinner when there is received a message announcing the arrival of Montana millionaire Bill Bradford, a client of Harcourt's. Anxious to make a good impression, Harcourt and his wife disguise themselves as servants, while Thayer and his fiancée take the part of the Harcourts. Bradford's arrival causes much embarrassment, which is complicated by the arrival of Miss Lane's father. Everything is finally explained, and Bradford takes it all as a joke. He agrees to buy a mine from Harcourt and hires him as his general manager. *Millionaires. Montanans. Disguise. Finance—Personal. Mines.*

SHOOTIN' FOR LOVE **F2.5006**
Universal Pictures. 28 Jun **1923** [New York premiere; released 2 Jul; c9 Jun 1923; LP19100]. Si; b&w. 35mm. 5 reels, 5,160 ft.
Dir Edward Sedgwick. *Scen* Albert Kenyon, Raymond L. Schrock. *Story* Raymond L. Schrock, Edward Sedgwick. *Photog* Virgil Miller.
Cast: Hoot Gibson *(Duke Travis)*, Laura La Plante *(Mary Randolph)*, Alfred Allen *(Jim Travis)*, William Welsh *(Bill Randolph)*, William Steele *(Dan Hobson)*, Arthur Mackley *(Sheriff Bludsoe)*, W. T. McCulley *(Sandy)*, Kansas Moehring *(Tex Carson)*.
Western melodrama. Duke Travis returns from the war suffering from shell shock and an inordinate fear of guns. His father, a ranchowner, refuses to accept Duke's disability and considers him a coward. Duke eventually recovers and ends a bitter feud over water rights between his father and a neighbor, Bill Randolph. *Veterans. Phobias. Shell shock. Cowardice. Water rights. Feuds. Fatherhood.*

SHOOTIN' IRONS **F2.5007**
Paramount Famous Lasky Corp. 8 Oct **1927** [c8 Oct 1927; LP24494]. Si; b&w. 35mm. 6 reels, 5,179 ft.
Pres by Adolph Zukor, Jesse L. Lasky. *Assoc Prod* B. P. Schulberg. *Dir* Richard Rosson. *Screenplay* J. Walter Ruben. *Adapt* J. Walter Ruben, Sam Mintz. *Photog* Henry Gerrard.
Cast: Jack Luden *(Pan Smith)*, Sally Blane *(Lucy Blake)*, Fred Kohler *(Dick Hardman)*, Richard Carlyle *(Jim Blake)*, Loyal Underwood *(Blinky)*, Guy Oliver *(Judge Mathews)*, Scott McGee *(cook)*, Arthur Millett *(sheriff)*.
Western melodrama. Source: Richard Allen Gates, "Shootin' Irons" (publication undetermined). Pan Smith, a young Montana rancher, rescues Jim Blake and his daughter Lucy from a stampede of wild horses and invites the squatters to be his guests. Pan falls in love with Lucy, but rivalry develops soon between him and Dick Hardman, his foreman. At a barn dance, Pan learns from Lucy that her father is being hunted for a bank theft, though she knows him to be innocent; to stall the sheriff, Pan holds up the stage and while hiding the dispatch box, containing incriminating papers, is observed by Dick. Dick informs the sheriff and organizes a posse just as word reaches the judge that Blake is innocent. Dick then proceeds to overtake the posse, his arrival terminates the battle, and Pan is united with Lucy. *Ranchers. Ranch foremen. Fugitives. Squatters. Sheriffs. Posses. Stagecoach robberies. Stampedes. Montana. Documentation.*

SHOOTIN' SQUARE **F2.5008**
Anchor Film Distributors. 15 Nov **1924**. Si; b&w. 35mm. 5 reels, 4,500 ft.
Cast: Jack Perrin, Peggy O'Day.
Western melodrama(?). No information about the nature of this film has been found.

SHOOTING BIG GAME WITH A CAMERA **F2.5009**
Frederick Beck Patterson. c12 Apr **1928** [MU4879]. Si; b&w. 35mm. 8 reels.
Travelog. A pictorial representation of the incidents and hazards encountered on a hunting trip in Africa. *Big game. Africa.*

THE SHOOTING OF DAN MCGREW **F2.5010**
S-L Productions. *Dist* Metro Pictures. 31 Mar **1924** [c9 Apr 1924; LP20126]. Si; b&w. 35mm. 7 reels, 6,318 ft.
Supv Arthur H. Sawyer. *Dir* Clarence Badger. *Scen* Winifred Dunn. *Photog* Rudolph Berquist.
Cast: Barbara La Marr *(Lady Known as Lou)*, Lew Cody *(Dangerous Dan McGrew)*, Mae Busch *(Flo Dupont)*, Percy Marmont *(Jim, Lou's husband)*, Max Ascher *(Isadore Burke)*, Fred Warren *(The Ragtime Kid)*, George Siegmann *(Jake Hubbel)*, Nelson McDowell *(sea captain)*, Bert Sprotte *(beachcomber)*, Ina Anson *(a dancer)*, Philippe De Lacy *(Little Jim)*, Harry Lorraine *(an actor)*, Eagle Eye *(Miguel)*, Milla Davenport *(Madame Resault)*, William Eugene *(pursuer)*.
Melodrama. Source: Robert William Service, *The Spell of the Yukon and Other Verses* (New York, 1907). Although the dance troupe of which she is leading lady is successful in South America, Lou urges her husband, Jim, to seek another environment for the sake of their 2-year-old son. When Dan McGrew offers to put Lou on the New York stage and beats Jim in a fight, she runs away with him to Alaska, where she becomes a decoy in the Malamute saloon. Learning that Lou has been duped by her abductor, Jim follows them to the Klondike and kills McGrew. Husband, wife, and child are then reunited. *Theatrical troupes. Dancers. Infidelity. Alaska. Klondike.*

SHOOTING STRAIGHT **F2.5011**
Independent Pictures. 1 Apr **1927** [New York State license]. Si; b&w. 35mm. 5 reels.
Dir William Wyler. *Story* William Lester.
Cast: Ted Wells *(Jack Roberts)*, Garry O'Dell *(Malpai Joe)*, Buck

Connors *(John Hale)*, Lillian Gilmore *(Bess Hale)*, Joe Bennett *(Tom Hale)*, Wilbur Mack *("Black" Brody)*, Al Ferguson *(sheriff)*.

Western melodrama(?). No information about the nature of this film has been found.

SHOOTING STRAIGHT **F2.5012**

RKO Productions. 20 Jul **1930** [c1 Jun 1930; LP1468]. Sd (Photophone); b&w. 35mm. 8 reels, 5,800 ft.

Supv Louis Sarecky. *Dir* George Archainbaud. *Screenplay-Dial* J. Walter Ruben. *Adapt* Wallace Smith. *Story* Barney A. Sarecky. *Photog* Edward Cronjager. *Art Dir* Max Ree. *Film Ed* Otto Ludwig. *Rec Engr* Lambert E. Day.

Cast: Richard Dix *(Larry Sheldon)*, Mary Lawlor *(Doris Powell)*, James Neill *(Reverend Powell)*, Mathew Betz *(Martin)*, George Cooper *(Chick)*, William Janney *(Tommy Powell)*, Robert E. O'Connor *(Hagen)*, Clarence Wurtz *(Stevens)*, Eddie Sturgis *(Spike)*, Richard Curtis *(Butch)*.

Underworld melodrama. City gambler Larry Sheldon, upon hearing that a pal has been taken for a ride, goes to the hideout of Spot Willis and, to all appearances, wreaks revenge. Sheldon leaves the city with his henchman, Chick, occupying a Pullman section with Mr. Walters, an evangelist; before Sheldon can return Walters' wallet (which Chick has lifted), the train is wrecked. Later, Larry awakes to find himself the guest of the Reverend Powell, who has mistaken him for Walters; he keeps his identity secret, and attracted to Doris, the minister's daughter, he begins to take an interest in the community church and social life. When Doris' brother becomes involved with Martin, a local gambler, Larry covers Martin in a crap game, but Martin, recognizing him, turns him over to the police. After a battle with the police, Larry is subdued, but Martin confesses and reveals that another man is responsible for the murder of Willis. Larry finds happiness with Doris and decides to go straight. *Gangsters. Gamblers. Evangelists. Clergymen. Criminals—Rehabilitation. Informers. Mistaken identity. Revenge. Courtship.*

THE SHOPWORN ANGEL **F2.5013**

Paramount Famous Lasky Corp. 29 Dec **1928** [New York premiere; released 12 Jan 1929; c11 Jan 1929; LP12]. Talking sequences (Movietone); b&w. 35mm. 8 reels, 7,377 ft. [Also si; 7,112 ft.]

Dir Richard Wallace. *Screenplay* Howard Estabrook, Albert Shelby Le Vino. *Titl* Tom Miranda. *Camera* Charles Lang. *Film Ed* Robert Gessler. *Orig mus pieces by* Max Bergunker. *Theme Song: "A Precious Little Thing Called Love"* Lou Davis, J. Fred Coots. *Mus Arr* Andrea Setaro. *Rec Supv* Max Terr.

Cast: Nancy Carroll *(Daisy Heath)*, Gary Cooper *(William Tyler)*, Paul Lukas *(Bailey)*, Roscoe Karns *(dance director)*.

Romantic drama. Source: Dana Burnet, "Private Pettigrew's Girl" (publication undetermined). Daisy, a sophisticated New York chorus girl with a "guardian," falls in love with Bill, a naive army private from Texas who has gone A. W. O. L. to be with her. They decide to marry, but halfway through the ceremony he is arrested and sent off with his regiment to France. She decides to abandon her former life and takes a minor job in the chorus. While rehearsing, she has a vision of Bill's death, but the dance director brings her back to reality and she goes on with her work. *Chorus girls. Texans. Soldiers. Hallucinations. World War I.*

Note: The wedding and the final scene in the theater, in which Nancy Carroll sings the theme song, comprise the talking sequences.

SHORE LEAVE **F2.5014**

Inspiration Pictures. *Dist* First National Pictures. 6 Sep **1925** [c10 Aug 1925; LP21709]. Si; b&w. 35mm. 7 reels, 6,856 ft.

Dir John S. Robertson. *Scen* Josephine Lovett. *Titl* Agnes Smith. *Photog* Roy Overbaugh, Stewart Nelson. *Sets* Tec-Art Studios. *Film Ed* William Hamilton. *Tech Adv* Comdr. Fitzhugh Green. *Art Titl* H. E. R. Studios.

Cast: Richard Barthelmess *("Bilge" Smith)*, Dorothy Mackaill *(Connie Martin)*, Ted McNamara *("Bat" Smith)*, Nick Long *(Capt. Bimby Martin)*, Marie Shotwell *(Mrs. Schuyler-Payne)*, Arthur Metcalfe *(Mr. Schuyler-Payne)*, Warren Cook *(Admiral Smith)*, Samuel Hines *(chief petty officer)*.

Comedy. Source: Hubert Osborne, *Shore Leave; a Sea-goin' Comedy in Three Acts* (New York opening: 8 Aug 1922). The fleet anchors in a small New England port, and while on shore leave "Bilge" Smith, a hardened, easygoing sailor, meets Connie Martin, the village dressmaker. Smith flirts with her, and Connie, who has never had a sweetheart, takes the flirtation seriously. Smith promises to return to her, and in his absence Connie has an old ship, left to her by her father, converted into a tearoom. The fleet returns, and Connie, not knowing Smith's first name, invites all the Smiths in the fleet to a party. Bilge Smith comes and, at first, does not remember Connie. When he realizes how serious she is about him, he proposes, but, learning of her newly found prosperity, he weighs anchor, refusing to live off a rich woman. Connie later writes to Smith and tells him that she has been reduced to poverty. He quickly returns to her and finds that she still owns the ship. Believing himself to have been tricked, Smith is preparing to leave when Connie haltingly tells him that she has put the ship in trust for her first baby, provided that the child's last name is Smith. Smith decides to stay and marry Connie. *Sailors. Dressmakers. Businesswomen. Courtship. Teashops. United States Navy. New England.*

SHORT SKIRTS **F2.5015**

Universal Film Manufacturing Co. Jul **1921** [c29 Jun 1921; LP16728]. Si; b&w. 35mm. 5 reels, 4,330 ft.

Pres by Carl Laemmle. *Dir* Harry B. Harris. *Scen* Doris Schroeder. *Photog* Earl M. Ellis.

Cast: Gladys Walton *(Natalie Smith)*, Ena Gregory *(Stella)*, Jack Mower *(Lance Christie)*, Jean Hathaway *(Mrs. Shirley Smith)*, Scotty MacGregor *(Spike Masters)*, Edward Martindel *(Wallace Brewster)*, Harold Miller *(Billy Gregg)*, William Welsh *(Woodward Christie)*, Howard Ralston *(Douglas Smith)*.

Society melodrama. Source: Alice L. Tildesley, "What Can You Expect?" in *Saturday Evening Post*. Natalie, whose mother is engaged to Wallace Brewster, the reform candidate for mayor, is 17 and resents being treated as a little girl, particularly by her mother's fiancé. When she meets the opposition candidate's son, Lance Christie, he persuades her to secure some papers incriminating Brewster. She does so and sends the papers to his opponent. Soon her conscience bothers her, and she goes to Christie to retrieve the papers and discovers that they were falsified. After receiving Brewster's forgiveness and seeing him win the election, she decides to make him her idol. *Politicians. Mayors. Adolescence. Documentation.*

A SHOT IN THE NIGHT **F2.5016**

Ben Strasser. 24 Mar **1923** [New York State license]. Si; b&w. 35mm. 5 reels.

Cast: Walter Holeby, Walter Long, Ruth Freeman, Tom Amos, Tolliver Brothers, Bobby Smart.

Comedy-drama. "The story tells of a man called 'The Masked Terror' a professional criminal and leader of a gang who kills a financier and steals $500,000. A little boy playing detective finds the gang's den and hides there. He is discovered, tied in a bag and about to be flung into a pond, when he is rescued by the district attorney. The murdered financier's daughter is then abducted by the gang. She is gagged, maltreated then bound and tied to the railroad tracks. She is rescued by the district attorney who catches 'The Masked Terror' and the gang by smoking them out with poisoned gas." (New York State license records.) *Children. Negroes. District attorneys. Gangs. Murder. Abduction.*

Note: Local New York State distribution was handled by American Colored Film Exchange.

SHOULD A GIRL MARRY? **F2.5017**

Trem Carr Productions. *Dist* Rayart Pictures. 22 Oct **1928.** Talking sequences and mus score (Filmtone); b&w. 35mm. 8 reels, 6,795-8,085 ft. [Also si; 6,525 ft.]

Dir Scott Pembroke. *Scen-Dial* Terry Turner. *Story* Arthur Hoerl. *Photog* Hap Depew. *Film Ed* J. S. Harrington. *Disc Orch* Ben Pollak Park Central Orchestra. *Song: "Haunting Memories"* Irving Bibo.

Cast: Helen Foster *(Alice Dunn)*, Donald Keith *(Jerry Blaine)*, William V. Mong *(Andrew Blaine)*, Andy Clyde *(Harry)*, Dot Farley *(Mae Reynolds)*, George Chesebro *(Jarvin)*, Dorothy Vernon *(Aunt Ada)*.

Drama. Acquitted by a jury for shooting her sister's seducer, Alice Dunn seeks a new life in another town, and there she becomes engaged to Jerry Blaine, the son of a wealthy banker. A detective friend of the dead man trails Alice, however, and reveals her past to the elder Blaine, who denounces her and offers her money to leave town. Alice not only refuses but accuses Blaine of robbing his own bank. In the resulting scuffle both the banker and the detective are killed, and Alice is free to marry Jerry. (Apparently, most of the dialog occurs at the end of the film, where a judge expounds on the girl's error in keeping her fiancé ignorant of her past.) *Bankers. Detectives. Murder. Seduction. Embezzlement. Trials. Courtship.*

SHOULD A WIFE WORK? **F2.5018**

J. W. Film Corp. Jan **1922** [c8 Oct, 15 Oct, 12 Nov 1921; LU17209]. Si; b&w. 35mm. 7 reels, 6,850 ft.

Dir Horace G. Plympton. *Story-Scen* Lois Zellner.

Cast: Edith Stockton *(Betty Evans)*, Alice Lowe *(Nina Starr)*, Stuart Robson *(Ed Barnes)*, Louis Kimball *(David Locke)*, Elinor Curtis *(Madame Theodora)*, Walter McEwen *(Jim Paget)*, Harry Mowbray *(Larry Grant)*.

Social melodrama. Two school classmates pursue differing paths: Betty teaches music; Nina marries a lawyer, Ed Barnes, but tiring of domestic life she seeks a career on the stage. Paget, a wealthy and unscrupulous man, seeks to compromise Betty, and she later marries David Locke, then discovers that his income depends on royalties from an invention that Paget controls. Paget again forces himself on Betty; he reduces the royalty, and Betty secretly gets a position as a singer. Paget and David come to blows; David's new invention is destroyed, but he makes a new start at another job. Seeking to reconcile Nina with her husband, Betty innocently provokes her husband's jealousy; however, from Ed, overjoyed at the reunion with his wife, David learns that he owes his success to Betty's efforts. *Music teachers. Inventors. Singers. Lawyers. Marriage. Jealousy.*

THE SHOW **F2.5019**

Metro-Goldwyn-Mayer Pictures. 22 Jan **1927** [c24 Jan 1927; LP23586]. Si; b&w. 35mm. 7 reels, 6,309 ft.

Dir Tod Browning. *Screenplay* Waldemar Young. *Titl* Joe Farnham. *Photog* John Arnold. *Sets* Cedric Gibbons, Richard Day. *Film Ed* Errol Taggart. *Wardrobe* Lucia Coulter.

Cast: John Gilbert *(Cock Robin)*, Renée Adorée *(Salome)*, Lionel Barrymore *(The Greek)*, Edward Connelly *(The Soldier)*, Gertrude Short *(Lena)*, Andy MacLennan *(The Ferret)*.

Melodrama. Source: Charles Tenney Jackson, *The Day of Souls* (Indianapolis, 1910). Among the performers in a Hungarian carnival are Cock Robin, who appears as John the Baptist in the show, and a girl who performs as Salome. Robin is a conceited scalawag of low morals. The Greek, a fiendish villain, conspires to bring about Robin's death during his act but fails. When Robin is pursued by the police, Salome agrees to hide him. She is engaged in writing letters to a blind soldier, purportedly from his son who is imprisoned and condemned to death, and gradually her goodness penetrates the indifference of Robin, who comes to realize his love for her and his own unworthiness. They find happiness after the death of The Greek from the bite of a poisonous lizard intended for Robin. *Actors. Hungarians. Greeks. Carnivals. Good and evil. Salome. John the Baptist.*

SHOW BOAT **F2.5020**

Universal Pictures. 28 Jul **1929** [c27 Apr 1929; LP339]. Talking & singing sequences, sd eff, & mus score (Movietone); b&w. 35mm. 12 reels, 11,650 ft. [Also si; 10,290 ft.]

Pres by Carl Laemmle. *Dir* Harry Pollard. *Adtl Dir* Arch Heath. *Ed Supv* Edward J. Montagne. *Scen* Charles Kenyon. *Dial* Harry Pollard, Tom Reed. *Titl* Tom Reed. *Photog* Gilbert Warrenton. *Spec Eff Photog* Frank H. Booth. *Film Ed* Edward J. Montagne, Maurice Pivar, Daniel Mandell. *Song: "Look Down That Lonesome Road"* Gene Austin, Nathaniel Shilkret. *Song: "Here Comes That Show Boat"* Billy Rose, Maceo Pinkard. *Song: "Love Sings a Song in My Heart"* Joseph Cherniavsky, Clarence J. Marks. *"Ol' Man River"* Joseph Cherniavsky, Oscar Hammerstein, II, Jerome Kern. *Rec Engr* C. Roy Hunter.

Cast—Prolog: Otis Harlan, Helen Morgan, Jules Bledsoe, Aunt Jemima, The Plantation Singers, Carl Laemmle, Florenz Ziegfeld.

Cast: Laura La Plante *(Magnolia)*, Joseph Schildkraut *(Gaylord Ravenal)*, Otis Harlan *(Capt. Andy Hawks)*, Emily Fitzroy *(Parthenia Hawks)*, Alma Rubens *(Julie)*, Elsie Bartlett *(Elly)*, Jack McDonald *(Windy)*, Jane La Verne *(Magnolia as a child/Kim)*, Neely Edwards *(Schultzy)*, Theodore Lorch *(Frank)*, Stepin Fetchit *(Joe)*, Gertrude Howard *(Queenie)*, Ralph Yearsley *(The Killer)*, George Chesebro *(Steve)*, Harry Holden *(Means)*, Max Asher *(utility man)*, Jim Coleman *(stagehand)*, Carl Herlinger *(wheelsman)*.

Musical comedy-drama. Source: Edna Ferber, *Show Boat* (Garden City, New York, 1926). Brought up on a showboat, Magnolia Hawks, the star of her family's river-going revue, marries Gaylord Ravenal, a charming river gambler. Magnolia's father, Captain Andy, is swept overboard in a storm, and Magnolia and Gaylord, harassed by Magnolia's strict, overbearing mother, sell their interest in the showboat to the widow and go to Chicago. Gaylord loses the money at the gambling tables and, following the suggestion of Magnolia's mother, leaves his family, convinced that they would be better off without him. To support herself and her child, Magnolia goes on the variety stage and makes a success singing Negro spirituals. Magnolia's mother dies, and Magnolia returns to the showboat to be reunited with the reformed Gaylord. *Singers. Gamblers. Negroes. Desertion. Spirituals. Showboats. Mississippi River. Chicago.*

Note: For the New York showing, an 18-minute sound prolog was added, including: short speeches by Laemmle and Ziegfeld; and Morgan, Bledsoe, and Aunt Jemima singing numbers from the original New York stage production of *Show Boat*.

SHOW FOLKS **F2.5021**

Pathé Exchange. 21 Oct **1928** [c16 Oct 1928; LP25726]. Talking sequences, sd eff, & mus score (Photophone); b&w. 35mm. 8 reels, 6,466 ft. [Also si; 6,581 ft.]

Prod Ralph Block. *Dir* Paul L. Stein. *Scen* Jack Jungmeyer, George Dromgold. *Titl* John Krafft. *Story* Philip Dunning. *Photog* Peverell Marley, David Abel. *Art Dir* Mitchell Leisen. *Film Ed* Doane Harrison. *Song: "No One But Me"* Al Koppel, Billy Stone, Charles Weinberg. *Asst Dir* Robert Fellows. *Prod Mgr* Harry Poppe.

Cast: Eddie Quillan *(Eddie)*, Lina Basquette *(Rita)*, Carol Lombard *(Cleo)*, Robert Armstrong *(Owens)*, Bessie Barriscale *(Kitty)*.

Comedy-drama. After watching Rita Carey dance with a trained duck, Eddie Kehoe, a two-bit vaudeville hoofer, makes her his dancing partner. Their act is a great success, and Eddie and Rita fall in love. One evening, at the Hotel Metropole, Rita sits with Owens, the manager of a musical revue, and Eddie becomes jealous; they quarrel, and Rita walks out on him, taking a part in Owens' show. Eddie finds himself a new partner, a gold digger named Cleo, but she quits him just before their big opening at Keith's. Rita, who is backstage to wish Eddie luck, takes Cleo's place, and their act is once again the hit of the show. *Dancers. Gold diggers. Theatrical managers. Vaudeville. Musical revues. Ducks.*

THE SHOW GIRL **F2.5022**

Trem Carr Productions. *Dist* Rayart Pictures. Jan **1927** [c21 Jan 1927; LP23629]. Si; b&w. 35mm. 6 reels, 5,201 ft.

Pres by W. Ray Johnston. *Prod* Trem Carr. *Dir* Charles J. Hunt. *Story-Scen* H. H. Van Loan.

Cast: Mildred Harris *(Maizie Udell)*, Gaston Glass *(Billy Barton)*, Mary Carr *(Mrs. Udell)*, Robert McKim *(Edward Hayden)*, Eddie Borden *("Breezy" Ayres)*, William Strauss *(Moe Kenner)*, Sam Sidman *(Heinie)*, Aryel Darma *(Alma Dakin)*.

Melodrama. Owing to the efforts of "Breezy" Ayers, an out-of-work press agent, Heinie's Honky-Tonk Cafe, owned by Maizie Udell and Billy Barton, attracts a new, elite patronage. Kenner, a famous theatrical producer, is attracted by Maizie's talents, but Hayden, a roué, attempts to force his attentions upon her, and when Billy tries to interfere, Hayden has him arrested. Later Billy finds Maizie in Hayden's arms and declares he is finished with her. When Maizie, as the star of a theatrical revue, suffers from stage fright, Billy restores her self-possession by rising in his box and singing, as though he were part of the show. "Breezy" plans to have Maizie kidnaped as a publicity stunt; by a fortunate combination of circumstances, Billy arrives to rescue her. He is accused of killing Hayden, but Alma Dakin, who has been wronged by Hayden, confesses, and Billy is happily reunited with his girl. *Actors. Press agents. Theatrical producers. Rakes. Restaurants. Theater.*

SHOW GIRL **F2.5023**

First National Pictures. 23 Sep **1928** [c24 Sep 1928; LP25645]. Sd eff & mus score (Vitaphone); b&w. 35mm. 7 reels, 6,252 ft. [Also si; 6,113 ft.]

Pres by Richard A. Rowland. *Dir* Alfred Santell. *Scen* James T. O'Donohue. *Titl* George Marion. *Photog* Sol Polito. *Film Ed* LeRoy Stone. *Songs: "Buy, Buy for Baby," "Show Girl"* Bernie Grossman, Ed Ward. *Cost* Max Ree.

Cast: Alice White *(Dixie Dugan)*, Donald Reed *(Álvarez Romano)*, Lee Moran *(Denny)*, Charles Delaney *(Jimmy)*, Richard Tucker *(Milton)*, Gwen Lee *(Nita Dugan)*, James Finlayson *(Mr. Dugan)*, Kate Price *(Mrs. Dugan)*, Hugh Roman *(Eppus)*, Bernard Randall *(Kibbitzer)*.

Comedy-drama. Source: Joseph Patrick McEvoy, *Show Girl* (New York, 1928). Dixie Dugan, a Brooklyn cutie, goes to the offices of theatrical producers Eppus and Kibbitzer and exposes her perfections in a bathing suit. Eppus and Kibbitzer express interest in her future and arrange for her to work in a nightclub act with Álvarez Romano. One evening Dixie accompanies wealthy sugardaddy Jack Milton to his apartment, and Álvarez stalks in and wounds Milton with a knife. Jimmy Doyle, a cynical tabloid reporter in love with Dixie, gets the story for his newspaper's front page. Dixie is then kidnaped by Álvarez, but quickly manages to free herself. Jimmy persuades her to hide low as a publicity stunt and puts the "kidnaping" on page one. Dixie is found by Milton, who, by way of apology for ruining her stunt, finances her in a Broadway show written by Jimmy. The show is a success, and Jimmy and Dixie are married. *Theatrical producers. Reporters. Dancers. Chorus girls. Publicity. Nightclubs. New York City—Brooklyn. New York City—Broadway.*

THE SHOW OF SHOWS **F2.5024**

Warner Brothers Pictures. 20 Nov **1929** [New York premiere; released 28 Dec; c7 Dec 1929; LP903]. Sd (Vitaphone); col (Technicolor). 35mm. 15 reels, 11,692 ft.

Supv Darryl Francis Zanuck. *Dir* John G. Adolfi. *Sp Material* Frank Fay, J. Keirn Brennan. *Photog* Bernard McGill. *Song: "Singing in the Bathtub"* Ned Washington, Herb Magidson, Michael Cleary. *Song: "Lady Luck"* Ray Perkins. *Song: "Motion Picture Pirates"* M. K. Jerome. *Song: "If I Could Learn To Love"* Herman Ruby, M. K. Jerome. *Songs: "Pingo-Pongo," "If Your Best Friends Won't Tell You"* Al Dubin, Joe Burke. *Songs: "The Only Song I Know," "My Sister"* J. Keirn Brennan, Ray Perkins. *Song: Your Mother and Mine"* Joe Goodwin, Gus Edwards. *Song: "You Were Meant for Me"* Arthur Freed, Nacio Herb Brown. *Songs: "Just an Hour of Love," "Li-Po-Li," "Military March"* Al Bryan, Ed Ward. *Song: "Rock-A-Bye Your Baby With a Dixie Melody"* Joe Young, Sam Lewis, Jean Schwartz. *Song: "Jumping Jack"* Bernie Seaman, Herman Ruby, Marvin Smolev, Rube Bloom. *Song: "Your Love Is All I Crave"* Al Dubin, Perry Bradford, Jimmy Johnson. *Dance Dir* Larry Ceballos, Jack Haskell. *Rec Engr* George R. Groves.

Cast—The Principals: Frank Fay *(Master of Ceremonies)*, William Courtenay *(The Minister)*, H. B. Warner *(The Victim)*, Hobart Bosworth *(The Executioner)*, Marian Nixon, Sally O'Neil, Myrna Loy, Alice Day, Patsy Ruth Miller *(Florodora Sextette)*, Ben Turpin *(waiter)*, Heinie Conklin *(ice man)*, Lupino Lane *(street cleaner)*, Lee Moran *(plumber)*, Bert Roach *(father)*, Lloyd Hamilton *(hansom cabby)*, Noah Beery, Tully Marshall, Wheeler Oakman, Bull Montana, Kalla Pasha, Anders Randolf, Philo McCullough, Otto Matiesen, Jack Curtis *(pirates)*, Johnny Arthur *(hero)*, Carmel Myers, Ruth Clifford, Sally Eilers, Viola Dana, Shirley Mason, Ethlyne Clair, Frances Lee, Julanne Johnston *(ladies)*, Douglas Fairbanks, Jr. *(Ambrose)*, Chester Conklin *(traffic cop)*, Grant Withers, William Collier, Jr., Jack Mulhall, Chester Morris, William Bakewell *(boys)*, Lois Wilson, Gertrude Olmstead, Pauline Garon, Edna Murphy, Jacqueline Logan *(girls)*, Monte Blue *(condemned man)*, Albert Gran, Noah Beery, Lloyd Hamilton, Tully Marshall, Kalla Pasha, Lee Moran *(soldiers)*.

Additional Cast Members: Armida, John Barrymore, Richard Barthelmess, Sally Blane, Irene Bordini, Anthony Bushell, Marion Byron, Georges Carpentier, James Clemmons, Betty Compson, Dolores Costello, Helene Costello, Marceline Day, Louise Fazenda, Alexander Gray, Beatrice Lillie, Winnie Lightner, Hariette Lake, Lila Lee, Ted Lewis, Nick Lucas, Molly O'Day, Rin-Tin-Tin, E. J. Radcliffe, Sid Silvers, Sojin, Lola Vendrill, Ada Mae Vaughn, Alberta Vaughn, Ted Williams Adagio Dancers, Alice White, Loretta Young.

Musical revue. Following the introduction of M. C. Frank Fay, a dramatic prolog presents an execution in a medieval setting; the Military Number features Monte Blue and a horde of chorus girls in a dancing routine; Winnie Lightner then sings "Singing in the Bath-Tub" with a male chorus attired as bathing girls, then performs a comedy takeoff with Bull Montana; Georges Carpentier appears as a boulevardier in a number featuring "If I Could Learn To Love," supported by Alice White and Patsy Miller; Irene Bordini appears with 10 composers, each seated at a piano, and sings their successes; in the Florodora Number, the girls sing, then are replaced by the Florodora Boys, demonstrating their occupations in a dance routine; Beatrice Lillie, in a comedy sketch, does "Your Mother and Mine." In the Pirate Number, Ted Lewis appears with an array of leading screen ladies and heavies along with his band on a picturesque pirate ship; Myrna Loy and Nick Lucas appear in an Oriental routine featuring "Li-Po-Li," and an all-star number features eight sets of starlets, each attired in costumes of various countries in "Meet My Sister," with Richard Barthelmess as M. C. A rhythmic ballet number features 75 dancing girls in black and white costumes, highlighted by Louise Fazenda; then Lupino Lane appears in a tramp ballet. John Barrymore, along with Anthony Bushell and E. J. Radcliffe, acts out a scene from *Richard III*. In the Bicycle Built for Two Number, Douglas Fairbanks, Jr., heads a prominent group of stars in a satire of 1900; the Execution Number, laid in the badlands of Mexico, features Monte Blue and some of the screen's leading heavies, headed by Noah Beery. The Lady Luck Finale stars Betty Compson and Alexander Gray along with 15 individual acts, climaxed by a screen image of each of the film's stars singing "Lady Luck." *Pirates. Composers. Men-about-town. Florodora Sextette. Vaudeville. Ballet. Theater. Capital punishment. Mexico. "Richard III".*

THE SHOW OFF **F2.5025**

Famous Players–Lasky. *Dist* Paramount Pictures. 16 Aug **1926** [c16 Aug 1926; LP23027]. Si; b&w. 35mm. 7 reels, 6,196 ft.

Pres by Adolph Zukor, Jesse L. Lasky. *Dir* Malcolm St. Clair. *Screenplay* Pierre Collings. *Photog* Lee Garmes. *Supv Ed* Ralph Block.

Cast: Ford Sterling *(Aubrey Piper)*, Lois Wilson *(Amy Fisher)*, Louise Brooks *(Clara)*, Gregory Kelly *(Joe Fisher)*, C. W. Goodrich *(Pop Fisher)*, Claire McDowell *(Mom Fisher)*, Joseph Smiley *(railroad executive)*.

Comedy. Source: George Edward Kelly, *The Show-Off; a Transcript of Life in Three Acts* (Boston, 1924). Aubrey Piper, a mere clerk at the offices of the Pennsylvania Railroad, poses as an important executive to his sweetheart, Amy Fisher, by blustering, bullying, and showing off continually. Though all the members of her family are contemptuous of Piper, Amy marries him; 3 months later she is fully aware of his faults. To help his son Joe continue work on his invention (a rust-preventing paint), Pop Fisher gives him the money saved for the mortgage and shortly afterward dies of a stroke. Aubrey wins a Ford in a raffle; and while taking it out for a spin, he knocks down a traffic policeman; Joe is forced to pay his fine with the mortgage money. Realizing the tragedy he has brought upon Amy's family, Aubrey visits the directors of a steel company and by bluffing sells them Joe's invention. The *coup* creates a furore in the Fisher household, happy at last that the "show off" has redeemed himself. *Office clerks. Egotists. Inventors. Marriage. Paint. Ford automobiles. Philadelphia. Pennsylvania Railroad Co..*

Note: Exteriors were photographed on locations in Philadelphia.

SHOW PEOPLE **F2.5026**

Metro-Goldwyn-Mayer Pictures. 20 Oct **1928** [c20 Oct 1928; LP25748]. Sd eff & mus score (Movietone); b&w. 35mm. 9 reels, 7,453 ft.

Dir King Vidor. *Cont* Wanda Tuchock. *Titl* Ralph Spence. *Treatment* Agnes Christine Johnston, Laurence Stallings. *Photog* John Arnold. *Sets* Cedric Gibbons. *Film Ed* Hugh Wynn. *Song: "Crossroads"* William Axt, David Mendoza. *Wardrobe* Henrietta Frazer.

Cast: Marion Davies *(Peggy Pepper)*, William Haines *(Billy Boone)*, Dell Henderson *(Colonel Pepper)*, Paul Ralli *(André)*, Tenen Holtz *(casting director)*, Harry Gribbon *(comedy director)*, Sidney Bracy *(dramatic director)*, Polly Moran *(maid)*, Albert Conti *(producer)*, John Gilbert, Mae Murray, Charles Chaplin, Douglas Fairbanks, Elinor Glyn *(themselves)*.

Comedy. Peggy Pepper, a Georgia girl who wants to be a dramatic actress, goes to Hollywood and at first can find work only as a patsy for Billy Boone in slapstick comedies; Billy, however, soon helps Peggy to become both a serious actress and a star. Fame and wealth go to Peggy's head; she becomes vain and snubs Billy in favor of André, her romantic leading man. Peggy eventually comes down to earth, however, and acknowledges her love for the patient Billy. *Actors. Motion picture directors. Georgians. Motion pictures. Hollywood.*

THE SHOWDOWN **F2.5027**

Paramount Famous Lasky Corp. 25 Feb **1928** [c25 Feb 1928; LP25016]. Si; b&w. 35mm. 8 reels, 7,616 ft.

Pres by Adolph Zukor, Jesse L. Lasky. *Dir* Victor Schertzinger. *Adapt-Cont* Hope Loring, Ethel Doherty. *Titl* John Farrow. *Photog* Victor Milner. *Film Ed* George Nichols, Jr.

Cast: George Bancroft *(Cardan)*, Evelyn Brent *(Sibyl Shelton)*, Neil Hamilton *(Wilson Shelton)*, Fred Kohler *(Winter)*, Helen Lynch *(Goldie)*, Arnold Kent *(Hugh Pickerell)*, Leslie Fenton *(Kilgore Shelton)*, George Kuwa *(Willie)*.

Drama. Source: Houston Branch, *Wildcat* (New York opening: 26 Nov 1921). Cardan, a wildcat oil driller, looks after Sibyl Shelton when her husband leaves camp in the Mexican jungle to inspect some oil property. Also remaining behind are three men, all searching for oil and wealth: Kilgore, Sibyl's brother-in-law, considered a weakling and a coward; Winter, a field scout for a big oil company; and Pickerell, a schemer. In Shelton's absence, Sibyl suffers a nervous breakdown caused by the heat, the jungle, the loneliness, and the men, of whose presence she is only too aware. Finally she throws herself at Cardan, the only one of the three who has not tried to seduce her. His love for her makes him step aside when her husband returns. *Oilmen. Neurasthenia. Seduction. Jungles. Self-sacrifice. Mexico.*

SHOWGIRL IN HOLLYWOOD **F2.5028**
First National Pictures. 20 Apr **1930** [c28 Apr 1930; LP1263]. Sd (Vitaphone); b&w with col sequences (Technicolor). 35mm. 9 reels, 7,213 ft.

Prod Robert North. *Dir* Mervyn LeRoy. *Dial* Harvey Thew. *Adapt* Harvey Thew, James A. Starr. *Photog* Sol Polito. *Art Dir* Jack Okey. *Film Ed* Peter Fritch. *Songs: "Hang on to the Rainbow," "I've Got My Eye on You," "There's a Tear for Every Smile in Hollywood"* Bud Green, Sammy Stept. *Mus Cond* Leo Forbstein. *Dance Dir* Jack Haskell. *Asst Dir* Al Alborn.

Cast: Alice White *(Dixie Dugan)*, Jack Mulhall *(Jimmy Doyle)*, Blanche Sweet *(Donna Harris)*, Ford Sterling *(Sam Otis, the producer)*, John Miljan *(Frank Buelow, the director)*, Virginia Sale *(Otis' secretary)*, Lee Shumway *(Kramer)*, Herman Bing *(Bing)*, Spec O'Donnell.

Musical comedy-drama. Source: Joseph Patrick McEvoy, *Hollywood Girl* (New York, 1929). When Jimmy Doyle's Broadway musical is a flop, he takes his rejected star, Dixie Dugan, to a nightclub where she does her number again. Buelow, a Hollywood film director, sees her and persuades her to come to filmland for a part in his new picture. In Hollywood, Dixie meets Donna Harris, a down-and-out actress who is trying to put up a front; and Otis, the producer, is tired of Buelow and fires him. He discovers that Jimmy is the author of the show he is producing and hires him; but when Dixie gets the leading role, she becomes temperamental and conceited, demanding a new director and changes in the story. After Otis fires her and cancels the picture, Donna, also having lost her job, attempts suicide but is saved by Dixie and Jimmy. The film is finished and is a big success, ensuring happiness for all. *Showgirls. Actors. Motion picture directors. Motion picture producers. Motion pictures. Courtship. Suicide. Hollywood. New York City—Broadway.*

THE SHRIEK OF ARABY **F2.5029**
Mack Sennett Productions. *Dist* Allied Producers and Distributors. 5 Mar **1923** [c1 Apr 1923; LP18969]. Si; b&w. 35mm. 5 reels, ca4,250 ft.

Pres by Mack Sennett. *Dir* F. Richard Jones. *Auth* Mack Sennett. *Photog* Homer Scott, Robert Walters. *Film Ed* Allen McNeil.

Cast: Ben Turpin *(a bill poster)*, Kathryn McGuire *(The Girl)*, George Cooper *(Presto, The Magician)*, Charles Stevenson *(Luke Hassen)*, Ray Grey *(The Arab Prince)*, Louis Fronde *(The Chief of Police)*, Dick Sutherland *(The Bandit)*.

Parody. Because he is too handsome, the ballyhoo (Ray Grey) for *The Sheik* loses his job to a bill poster (Ben Turpin). Ben dozes while riding his horse and dreams of desert adventures in which the former ballyhoo is an Arab prince who goes on a vacation and turns his throne over to Ben. The action closely follows that of *The Sheik;* but just as Ben rides away with his bride (Kathryn McGuire), he awakes to find himself in the presence of a traffic cop. *Barkers. Motion pictures. Dreams.*

Note: " ... The picture was made more than a year ago immediately on the heels the tremendous hit Valentino achieved in 'The Sheik'."(*Variety,* 14 Jun 1923, p26.)

SHYLOCK OF WALL STREET *see* **NONE SO BLIND**

SI L'EMPEREUR SAVAIT ÇA! **F2.5030**
Metro-Goldwyn-Mayer Pictures. 4 Nov **1930** [Paris premiere]. Sd (Movietone); b&w. 35mm. 9 reels.

Dir Jacques Feyder. *Screenplay* Yves Mirande. *Photog* William Daniels. *Art Dir* Cedric Gibbons. *Film Ed* Gunther Fritsch. *Rec Engr* Douglas Shearer.

Cast: André Luguet *(Captain Kovacks)*, Françoise Rosay *(The General's Wife)*, Tania Fedor *(The General's Daughter)*, André Berley *(The Gendarme)*, Georges Mauloy *(The General)*, Suzanne Delvé *(A Lady of the Court)*, Marcel André *(The Master of the Horse)*.

Romantic drama. Source: Ferenc Molnár, *Olympia* (Budapest, 1928). A French-language version of *His Glorious Night,* q. v. *Royalty. Social classes. Courtship. Imaginary kingdoms.*

SIAM, THE LAND OF CHANG **F2.5031**
Burton Holmes Lectures. 10 Feb **1929.** Si; b&w. 35mm. 4 reels.

Travelog. No information about the precise nature of this film has been found. *Siam.*

SIBERIA **F2.5032**
Fox Film Corp. 28 Mar **1926** [c28 Mar 1926; LP22611]. Si; b&w. 35mm. 7 reels, 6,950 ft.

Pres by William Fox. *Dir* Victor Schertzinger. *Scen* Eve Unsell. *Adapt* Nicholas A. Dunaev. *1st Camera* Glen MacWilliams. *2d Photog* Robert Martin. *Asst Dir* William Tummel.

Cast: Alma Rubens *(Sonia Vronsky)*, Edmund Lowe *(Leonid Petroff)*, Lou Tellegen *(Egor Kaplan)*, Tom Santschi *(Alexis Vetkin)*, Paul Panzer *(commandant)*, Vadim Uraneff *(Kyrill [Cyril] Vronsky)*, Lilyan Tashman *(beautiful blonde)*, Helen D'Algy *(beautiful brunette)*, James Marcus *(Andrei Vronsky)*, Daniel Makarenko *(governor)*, Harry Gripp *(Ivan the Nameless)*, Samuel Blum *(Feodor)*.

Melodrama. Source: Bartley Campbell, *Siberia, a Picturesque Romantic Drama of Russian Life in Six Acts* (New York, c1911). Petroff, an officer in the Imperial Russian Army, is in love with Sonia, a schoolteacher who casts her lot with revolutionaries. During a wave of cruelty and supression, she is exiled with her brother to Siberia. There Petroff is sent in the discharge of his official duties and secretly renews their romance. When the Bolsheviki overthrow the government, Sonia is freed and aids in the escape of Petroff, who incurs the enmity of Egor, the revolutionary leader, because he is a royalist. Together they escape across the frozen wastes in a sledge, pursued by wolves and Egor, who has used patriotism as a cloak to conceal personal ambitions. *Schoolteachers. Bolshevists. Political refugees. Russia—History—1917–21 Revolution. Saint Petersburg. Siberia.*

THE SIDE SHOW *see* **TWO FLAMING YOUTHS**

THE SIDE SHOW OF LIFE **F2.5033**
Famous Players–Lasky. *Dist* Paramount Pictures. ca20 Jul **1924** [New York premiere; released 1 Sep 1924; c5 Aug 1924; LP20471]. Si; b&w. 35mm. 8 reels, 7,511 ft.

Pres by Adolph Zukor, Jesse L. Lasky. *Prod-Dir* Herbert Brenon. *Scen* Willis Goldbeck, Julie Herne. *Photog* James Howe.

Cast: Ernest Torrence *(Andrew Lackaday)*, Anna Q. Nilsson *(Lady Auriol Dayne)*, Louise Lagrange *(Elodie)*, Maurice Cannon *(Horatio Bakkus)*, Neil Hamilton *(Charles Verity-Stewart)*, William Ricciardi *(Mignon)*, Mrs. Pozzi *(Ernestine)*, Lawrence D'Orsay *(Sir Julius Verity-Stewart)*, Effie Shannon *(Lady Verity-Stewart)*, Katherine Lee *(Evadne)*.

Drama. Source: William John Locke, *The Mountebank* (New York & London, 1921). Ernest Denny, *The Mountebank, a Play.* Andrew Lackaday, an English circus clown brought up in France, rises to the rank of brigadier general during the war. Returning to his old profession as a juggler, he finds that he has lost his skill. He gives up Elodie, his former vaudeville partner, but finds happiness with Lady Auriol. *Clowns. Jugglers. Circus. France. World War I.*

SIDE STREET **F2.5034**
RKO Productions. 8 Sep **1929** [c2 Sep 1929; LP738, LP895] Sd (Photophone); b&w. 35mm. 7 reels, 6,965 ft. [Also si; 6,373 ft.]

Prod William Le Baron. *Dir-Story* Malcolm St. Clair. *Scen* John Russell, Malcolm St. Clair, George O'Hara. *Dial* Eugene Walter. *Titl* George O'Hara. *Photog* William Marshall, Nick Musuraca. *Mus* Oscar Levant. *Lyr* Sidney Clare. *Cost* Max Ree.

Cast: Tom Moore *(Jimmy O'Farrell)*, Matt Moore *(John O'Farrell)*, Owen Moore *(Dennis O'Farrell)*, Kathryn Perry *(Kathleen Doyle)*, Frank Sheridan *(Mr. O'Farrell)*, Emma Dunn *(Mrs. O'Farrell)*, Arthur Housman *("Silk" Ruffo)*, Mildred Harris *(Bunny)*, Charles Byer *(Maxse)*, Edwin August *(Mac)*, Irving Bacon *(Slim)*, Walter McNamara *(Patrick Doyle)*, Al Hill *("Blondie")*, Heinie Conklin *("Drunk")*, Dan Wolheim *("Pinkie")*.

Melodrama. The O'Farrells, who live in a modest flat in Manhattan, have three sons whom they cherish: Jimmy, a policeman; John, an ambulance surgeon; and Dennis, who, unknown to them, is a racketeer. Jimmy gets a promotion and is detailed to work on a murder case involving the Muller gang. Kathleen Doyle, engaged to Jimmy, attends a party at Muller's luxurious home and there learns that "Silk" is a killer hired by Muller. Later, when a man is injured in a brawl, John answers a call and discovers that his brother Dennis is actually the underworld leader, Muller. Jimmy and Kathleen meet, and she tells him of her discovery but is overheard by members of the gang, who then set a trap for the officer. Dennis learns of the rendezvous, rushes to save Jimmy, but is shot down by his own men and dies in his brother's arms; his parents are told he has gone on another long and mysterious trip. *Brothers. Racketeers. Surgeons. Police. Family life. Ambulance service. New York City.*

THE SIDESHOW **F2.5035**

Columbia Pictures. 11 Dec **1928** [c15 Mar 1929; LP221]. Si; b&w. 35mm. 7 reels, 5,879 ft.

Prod Jack Cohn. *Dir* Erle C. Kenton. *Story-Scen* Howard J. Green. *Photog* Joseph Walker. *Art Dir* Harrison Wiley. *Tech Dir* Edward Shulter. *Asst Dir* Buddy Coleman. *Circus Setting* Al G. Barnes Circus.

Cast: Marie Prevost *(Queenie Parker)*, Ralph Graves *(Gentleman Ted Rogers)*, Little Billy *(P. W. Melrose)*, Alan Roscoe *(Ghandi)*, Pat Harmon *(Bowen, the canvas boss)*, Texas Madesen *(tall man)*, Martha McGruger *(fat lady)*, Steve Clemento *(knife thrower)*, Janet Ford *(his aide)*, Paul Dismute *(armless man)*, Bert Price *(tattooed man)*, Chester Morton *(thin man)*, Jacques Ray *(fire eater)*.

Melodrama. Queenie Parker, the junior member of a family trapeze act, is forced to find work in a sideshow when her parents become too old to perform. Assisting a fakir in a basket trick, Queenie is resentful of her lowly status, and the sideshow freaks make her life miserable. A series of accidents befall the sideshow (a trapeze breaks; a pay wagon explodes), and P. W. Melrose, the midget who owns the sideshow, comes to suspect barker Ted Rogers of trying to sabotage the outfit. Queenie, however, discovers that the fakir is the culprit employed by a rival circus to put Melrose out of business. Melrose kills the fakir, and Rogers is cleared. Having fallen in love with Queenie, Melrose must nevertheless stand by—a sad, mute witness to her love for Rogers. *Aerialists. Barkers. Midgets. Fakirs. Murder. Explosions. Circus. Sideshows.*

SIDEWALKS OF NEW YORK **F2.5036**

Lester Park. 6 Aug **1923** [New York premiere]. Si; b&w. 35mm. 6 reels, ca5,500 ft.

Dir Lester Park. *Story-Scen* Willard King Bradley.

Cast: Hanna Lee, Bernard Siegel, Templar Saxe.

Melodrama. Source: James W. Blake and Charles B. Lawlor, "Sidewalks of New York" (a song). A young woman, turned out of her home for refusing to marry the man of her father's choice, takes up prizefighting to save the father from eviction and wins the ladies' world championship in a 3-round bout. *Women athletes. Boxing. Filial relations. New York City.*

SIEGE (Universal-Jewel) **F2.5037**

Universal Pictures. 27 Sep **1925** [c10 Jun 1925; LP21557]. Si; b&w. 35mm. 7 reels, 6,424 ft.

Dir Svend Gade. *Screenplay* Harvey Thew. *Adtl Photog* Charles Stumar.

Cast: Virginia Valli *(Frederika)*, Eugene O'Brien *(Kenyon Ruyland)*, Mary Alden *(Aunt Augusta)*, Marc MacDermott *(Morval Ruyland)*, Harry Lorraine *(Dawley Cole)*, Beatrice Burnham *(Alberta Ruyland)*, Helen Dunbar *(Frederika's mother)*.

Drama. Source: Samuel Hopkins Adams, *Siege* (New York, 1924). Kenyon Ruyland, the son of a wealthy family of New England industrialists, marries Frederika and thereby incurs the wrath of his Aunt Augusta, the elderly and iron-willed head of the Ruyland clan. Aunt Augusta does everything possible to break the spirit of Frederika and finally divides her from Kenyon by making him suspect her of infidelity. Norval Ruyland, a deafmute who has fallen in love with Frederika, commits suicide when he is ridiculed for sending Frederika a box of roses. Norval's will leaves his stock to Frederika, giving her and Kenyon together a controling interest in Ruyland Industries. Frederika attempts to give the stock to Aunt Augusta, but the old woman refuses to accept it and mounts her carriage, lashing her horses in a blind fury. At the risk of her own life, Frederika saves Aunt Augusta's life and finally wins her love and admiration. Frederika and Kenyon are reunited. *Industrialists. Aunts. Deafmutes. Marriage. Suicide. Infidelity. Family life. New England. Horses.*

THE SIGN OF THE CACTUS **F2.5038**

Universal Pictures. 4 Jan **1925** [c19 Dec 1924; LP20934]. Si; b&w. 35mm. 5 reels, 4,938 ft.

Dir Clifford S. Smith. *Scen* Isadore Bernstein. *Story* Norman Wilde. *Story-Cont? (see note)* Charles Logue. *Photog* Harry Neumann.

Cast: Jack Hoxie *(Jack Hayes)*, Helen Holmes *(Belle Henderton)*, J. Gordon Russell *(John Henderton)*, Francis Ford *(Panhandle George)*, Josef Swickard *(Old Man Hayes)*, Frank Newberg *(Earl of Chico)*, Jack Pratt *(sheriff)*, Bobby Gordon *(Jack, as a boy)*, Muriel Frances Dana *(Belle, as a girl)*.

Melodrama. A mysterious rider, known as Whitehorse Cactus, steals from the dishonest water company in order to help ranchers who have been cheated out of their water rights by its crooked agents. This elusive champion is, in actuality, Jack Hayes, whose vendetta began when his father was brutally slain by one of the hired gunmen of John Henderton, the owner of the water company. Riding in the hills one day, Jack stops the runaway horse of Henderton's daughter, Belle, who was his childhood sweetheart. Jack kills one of Henderton's hired gunmen, is tried and convicted, but escapes with the help of Panhandle George. Henderton is shot, and Jack is accused of the murder. Belle captures him, only to be told by the sheriff that she has the wrong man. Belle and Jack are reconciled, and soon they get married. *Ranchers. Water rights. Revenge. Murder.*

Note: Copyright entry credits Charles Logue with both story and continuity.

THE SIGN OF THE CLAW **F2.5039**

Gotham Productions. *Dist* Lumas Film Corp. May **1926** [c28 Jun 1926; LP22859]. Si; b&w. 35mm. 6 reels, 5,925 ft.

Pres by Sam Sax. *Supv* Renaud Hoffman. *Dir* "Breezy" Reeves Eason. *Story-Cont* James Bell Smith. *Photog* Ray June.

Cast: Peter the Great *(himself, a dog)*, Edward Hearn *(Robert Conway)*, Ethel Shannon *(Mildred Bryson)*, Joe Bennett *(Jimmie Bryson)*, Lee Shumway *(Al Stokes)*.

Adventure melodrama. While in pursuit of two bandits with his master, Patrolman Robert Conway, Peter the Great tears away the coatsleeve of Jimmie Bryson, a young bank employee. Jimmie's sister Mildred notices the torn sleeve, and his shady friend Al Stokes makes advances to her. Stokes forces Jimmie to give him the combination of the bank safe, which he plans to rob that night. Meanwhile, Bob, having taken an interest in Mildred, is introduced to Jimmie and becomes suspicious when Peter snarls at the boy, but he declines to arrest him at the pleas of Mildred. Stokes, who is proven to be Peter's former owner, claims the dog and leaves. When Jimmie refuses to go through with the robbery, he is tied up by the crooks, who abduct Mildred; however, Peter frees Jimmie. Bob is trapped by the bandits in the bank, but Jim frees him; and following a thrilling automobile chase, Stokes is killed. *Police. Bank clerks. Brother-sister relationship. Bank robberies. Dogs. Chases.*

THE SIGN OF THE ROSE **F2.5040**

George Beban Productions. *Dist* American Releasing Corp. 3 Sep **1922** [c1 Sep 1922; LP18749]. Si; b&w. 35mm. 6 reels, 6,200 ft. ft.

Pres by Harry Garson. *Supv-Writ* George Beban. *Dir* Harry Garson. *Scen* J. A. Brocklehurst, Carroll Owen. *Titl* Coral Burnette. *Photog* Sam Landers. *Art Dir* Floyd Mueller. *Film Ed* Violet Blair.

Cast: Helene Sullivan *(Lillian Griswold)*, Charles Edler *(William Griswold)*, Jeanne Carpenter *(Dorothy Griswold)*, Gene Cameron *(Philip Griswold)*, Louise Calmenti *(Rosa)*, Stanhope Wheatcroft *(Cecil Robbins)*, Arthur Thalasso *(Detective Lynch)*, George Beban *(Pietro Balletti)*, Dorothy Giraci *(Rosina Balletti)*, M. Solomon *(Moses Erbstein)*.

Melodrama. Source: George Beban and Charles T. Dazey, *The Sign of the Rose* (New York opening: 11 Oct 1911). In need of cash, Philip Griswold kidnaps the daughter of his brother, William, and shifts the blame to Pietro Balletti, who is seen delivering a Christmas tree to the Griswold home. While frantically searching for his child, William kills Pietro's beloved daughter, Rosina, with his automobile. Philip conspires with Cecil Robbins to frame Pietro with the aid of a white rose but finally confesses to the abduction. Pietro receives a substantial gift from the Griswolds and is reunited with his wife, whom he believed to be dead. *Italians. Brothers. Kidnaping. Christmas.*

Note: During the film's pre-released engagements (1921–22), George Beban and three other cast members gave a live stage presentation, elaborated from the original vaudeville sketch upon which the play (and the film?) were based; it was interspersed about reel 4, lasted ca18 minutes as against ca60 minutes of film, and took place in a florist shop set copied from one used in the film. The original play apparently combined film and live action, with the latter dominant. (*Variety*, 10 Mar 1922, p42.)

THE SIGN ON THE DOOR **F2.5041**

Norma Talmadge Productions. *Dist* Associated First National Pictures. May **1921** [c28 Sep 1921; LP17016]. Si; b&w. 35mm. 7 reels, 7,100 ft.

Pres by Joseph M. Schenck. *Dir* Herbert Brenon. *Adapt* Mary Murillo, Herbert Brenon. *Photog* J. Roy Hunt. *Tech Dir* Willard M. Reineck.

Cast: Norma Talmadge *(Ann Hunniwell/Mrs. "Lafe" Regan)*, Charles Richman *("Lafe" Regan)*, Lew Cody *(Frank Devereaux)*, David Proctor *(Colonel Gaunt)*, Augustus Balfour *(Ferguson, Devereaux's valet)*, Mac Barnes *("Kick" Callahan)*, Helen Weir *(Helen Regan)*, Robert Agnew *(Alan Churchill)*, Martinie Burnlay *(Marjorie Blake)*, Paul McAllister

("Rud" Whiting, district attorney), Louis Hendricks *(Inspector Treffy)*, Walter Bussel *(Bates, the Regan butler)*.

Melodrama. Source: Channing Pollock, *The Sign on the Door; a Play and Prologue in Three Acts* (New York, 1924). Ann Hunniwell, innocently accompanying Frank Devereaux, her employer's son, to a questionable New York cafe, is arrested in a raid and is photographed by a newspaperman, although Devereaux manages to obtain the negative. Five years later she is the wife of "Lafe" Regan, a man of high character and social standing; her stepdaughter, Helen, becomes involved with Devereaux, who has had an affair also with the wife of Colonel Gaunt. When the colonel threatens to shoot Devereaux, Regan stalls him, while Ann follows Helen to Frank's apartment; after an oral conflict, Regan shoots Devereaux and leaves a "Not To Be Disturbed" sign on the door. Ann tries to take the blame and shield her family, but the district attorney, having posed as the photographer years before, believes Ann is equally guiltless now and frees her and her husband, stating that no jury would convict Regan on his plea of "Self-Defense." *Stepmothers. District attorneys. Photographers. Reputation.*

SIGNAL FIRES **F2.5042**

Fred Balshofer Productions. 9 Jul **1926** [New York State license]. Si; b&w. 35mm. 5 reels.

Cast: Fred Church.

Western melodrama(?). No information about the nature of this film has been found.

THE SIGNAL TOWER (Universal Super-Jewel) **F2.5043**

Universal Pictures. ca20 Jul **1924** [New York premiere; released 3 Aug; c29 Apr 1924; LP20129]. Si; b&w. 35mm. 7 reels, 6,714 ft.

Pres by Carl Laemmle. *Dir* Clarence L. Brown. *Scen* James O. Spearing. *Photog* Ben Reynolds.

Cast: Virginia Valli *(Sally Tolliver)*, Rockliffe Fellowes *(Dave Tolliver)*, Frankie Darro *(Sonny Tolliver)*, Wallace Beery *(Joe Standish)*, James O. Barrows *(Old Bill)*, J. Farrell MacDonald *(Pete)*, Dot Farley *(Gertie)*, Clarence Brown *(switch man)*, Jitney *(The Dog)*.

Melodrama. Source: Wadsworth Camp, "The Signal Tower," in *Metropolitan* (May 1920, p32). Dave Tolliver, tower signalman on a mountain railroad, takes in his relief man, Joe Standish, as a boarder. During a storm, Standish becomes drunk and makes advances to Dave's wife, Sally. Although warned of his wife's predicament by his son, Dave is compelled to stay on the job when a runaway freight endangers a passenger train. He ditches the runaway and saves the express, while Sally successfully defends herself by shooting Standish. *Signalmen. Drunkenness. Railroads. Dogs.*

Note: Some sources give the surname Taylor to the characters of Sally and Dave Tolliver.

SILENCE **F2.5044**

De Mille Pictures. *Dist* Producers Distributing Corp. 25 Apr **1926** [c19 Apr 1926; LP22697]. Si; b&w. 35mm. 8 reels, 7,518 ft.

Pres by Cecil B. De Mille. *Dir* Rupert Julian. *Prod Ed* Bertram Millhauser. *Adapt* Beulah Marie Dix. *Photog* Peverell Marley. *Art Dir* Max Parker. *Film Ed* Claude Berkeley. *Asst Dir* Leigh R. Smith.

Cast: Vera Reynolds *(Norma Drake/Norma Powers)*, H. B. Warner *(Jim Warren)*, Raymond Hatton *(Harry Silvers)*, Rockliffe Fellowes *(Phil Powers)*, Jack Mulhall *(Arthur Lawrence)*, Virginia Pearson *(Millie Burke)*.

Melodrama. Source: Max Marcin, *Silence, a Melodrama* (New York opening: 12 Nov 1924). Jim Warren is awaiting death by hanging for the murder of Harry Silvers though his attorney, Lawrence, believes he is innocent and is shielding the guilty person. *In a flashback to 1904, Jim recalls the events leading to the present: his new bride, Norma Drake, discovers their marriage is technically invalid and that she is pregnant. Jim decides to reform and legalize his marriage, but Norma is arrested and found with some stolen money. To insure her freedom, he agrees to marry Millie Burke, a saloon owner. Phil, a faithful friend of Norma's, persuades her that Jim has deserted her, and for the child's sake she agrees to marry him. Years later, little Norma has grown up, and on the eve of her wedding, Jim, accompanied by Silvers, a crook, confronts Phil with Norma's letters and suggests blackmail. When Silvers abuses her dead mother, Norma shoots him with Jim's revolver.* As Jim is being led to execution, Norma appears and confesses, but he denounces her; at the last minute Phil corroborates Norma; Jim is then freed, and Norma is absolved by a jury. *Marriage. Blackmail. Parentage. Murder. Capital punishment.*

THE SILENT ACCUSER *see* **THE LOVE PIRATE**

THE SILENT ACCUSER **F2.5045**

Metro-Goldwyn-Mayer Pictures. 17 or 24 Nov **1924** [c10 Nov 1924; LP20746]. Si; b&w. 35mm. 6 reels, 5,883 ft.

Pres by Louis B. Mayer. *Dir* Chester M. Franklin. *Scen* Chester M. Franklin, Frank O'Connor. *Story* Jack Boyle. *Photog* Charles Dreyer. *Film Ed* Lloyd Nezler.

Cast: Eleanor Boardman *(Barbara Jane)*, Raymond McKee *(Jack)*, Earl Metcalfe *(Phil)*, Paul Weigel *(stepfather)*, Edna Tichenor *(The Painted Lady)*, Peter the Great *(himself, a dog)*.

Melodrama. Jack's dog, Peter the Great, is the sole witness to Phil's murder of Barbara Jane's stepfather. Peter fetches his master, and Jack's presence at the scene of the crime results in his being convicted of the murder. With Peter's assistance, however, Jack escapes from jail and goes to Mexico with Barbara Jane. They find Phil, and Peter's ferocity wrings a confession from the culprit. *Murder. Circumstantial evidence. Prison escapes. Mexico. Dogs.*

THE SILENT AVENGER **F2.5046**

Gotham Productions. *Dist* Lumas Film Corp. 5 May **1927** [c2 Aug 1927; LP24264]. Si; b&w. 35mm. 6 reels, 5,690 ft.

Pres by Sam Sax. *Supv-Story* Frank Foster Davis. *Dir* James P. Hogan. *Cont* Herbert C. Clark. *Titl* Delos Sutherland. *Adapt* George Green, Doris Schroeder. *Photog* Ray June. *Film Ed* Fred Burnworth.

Cast: Charles Delaney *(Stanley Gilmore)*, Duane Thompson *(Patsy Wade)*, David Kirby *(Joe Sneed)*, George Chesebro *(Bill Garton)*, Robert E. Homans *(Steven Gilmore)*, Clarence H. Wilson *(Dave Wade)*, Buck Black *(Bud Wade)*, Thunder *(himself, a dog)*.

Melodrama. To atone for a series of wild escapades, young Stanley Gilmore, son of a railroad president, travels to Tennessee to promote the right-of-way for his father's company. With his dog, Thunder, he calls on Dave Wade, who has resisted the encroachments of the railroad, and encounters Patsy, Wade's daughter, with whom he becomes friendly. Stanley's arrival is noted by Joe Sneed, a moonshining henchman of Bill Garton, an engineer for a rival railroad company; and attempting to steal some papers from Stanley, Sneed is chased by the dog, which he reports to the sheriff. Thunder rescues Little Bud Wade from a bear and is thereby saved from Sneed and the sheriff. When Stanley wires his father to come and complete the deal with Wade, he is kidnaped; but Thunder rescues him, flags down a train, and drives the villains to their death. Stanley finds happiness with Patsy, and his father acquires the right-of-way. *Railroad engineers. Railroad magnates. Sheriffs. Moonshiners. Mountain life. Railroads. Tennessee. Documentation. Bears. Dogs.*

THE SILENT CALL **F2.5047**

H. O. Davis. *Dist* Associated First National Pictures. 7 Nov **1921** [c5 Dec 1921; LP17286]. Si; b&w. 35mm. 7 reels, 6,784 ft.

Pres by H. O. Davis. *Dir* Lawrence Trimble. *Adapt* Jane Murfin. *Photog* Charles Dreyer, Glen Gano.

Cast: Strongheart *(Flash)*, John Bowers *(Clark Moran)*, Kathryn McGuire *(Betty Houston)*, William Dyer *(Ash Brent)*, James Mason *(Luther Nash)*, Nelson McDowell *(Dad Kinney)*, Edwin J. Brady *(Jimmy the Dude)*, Robert Bolder *(James Houston)*.

Adventure melodrama. Source: Hal G. Evarts, *The Cross Pull* (New York, 1920). Clark Moran, master of Flash, a crossbreed of gray wolf and sheep dog, is called from his ranch to the city, and Flash, in despair, returns to the wilds. Moran, having developed an interest in Betty Houston as a result of the dog's discovering her camp, follows her to San Francisco. The ranchers, believing Flash to be a sheep killer, capture him and sentence him to be shot. Flash escapes to the mountains and there finds a wolf mate. Betty's father is captured by a gang of rustlers who receive orders from Luther Nash, a rival suitor of Betty's, and she also is kidnaped. Through Flash the gang is trapped by the sheriff and the father is rescued. Flash corners Brent, the leader, in the rapids, and only the dog survives. Betty is reunited with Moran. *Ranchers. Gangs. San Francisco. Sheep. Dogs.*

THE SILENT COMMAND **F2.5048**

Fox Film Corp. 19 Aug **1923** [c20 Aug 1923; LP19411]. Si; b&w. 35mm. 8 reels, 7,809 ft. [Later cut to 6,820 ft.]

Pres by William Fox. *Dir* J. Gordon Edwards. *Scen* Anthony Paul Kelly. *Story* Rufus King. *Photog* George W. Lane. *Coöp* United States Navy.

Cast: Edmund Lowe *(Capt. Richard Decatur)*, Bela Lugosi *(Hisston)*, Carl Harbaugh *(Menchen)*, Martin Faust *(Cordoba)*, Gordon McEdward *(Gridley)*, Byron Douglas *(Admiral Nevins)*, Theodore Babcock *(Admiral Meade)*, George Lessey *(Mr. Collins)*, Warren Cook *(Ambassador Mendizabal)*, Henry Armetta *(Pedro)*, Rogers Keene *(Jack Decatur)*, J. W. Jenkins *(The Butler)*, Alma Tell *(Mrs. Richard Decatur)*, Martha Mansfield *(Peg Williams, the vamp)*, Florence Martin *(her maid)*, Betty Jewel *(Dolores)*, Kate Blancke *(Mrs. Nevins)*, Elizabeth Foley *(Jill Decatur)*.

Melodrama. "This is one of those 'Columbia, the Gem of the Ocean' pictures. Full of the 'Star-Spangled Banner,' patriotic to the nth degree with the navy floating all over the screen. A real hero, a vamp, and a flock of thrills." (*Variety*, 6 Sep 1923, p23.) Foreign agents, determined to destroy the United States Navy's Atlantic Fleet and the Panama Canal, after an unsuccessful attempt to obtain from Capt. Richard Decatur information regarding mine positions in the Canal Zone, hire adventuress Peg Williams to vamp Captain Decatur, thereby putting him at their mercy. Decatur, advised by the Chief of Naval Intelligence, plays along with the spies to gain their confidence. He leaves his wife and is dismissed from the Navy as a result of his association with Miss Williams. Finally, he goes to Panama, thwarts the saboteurs, saves the fleet and the canal, and gains honorable reinstatement and the gratitude of his country for his heroism. *Adventuresses. Spies. Sabotage. Mines (war explosives). Panama Canal. Canal Zone. United States Navy.*

THE SILENT ENEMY **F2.5049**

Burden-Chanler Productions. *Dist* Paramount-Publix Corp. 19 May **1930** [New York premiere; released 2 Aug; c1 Aug 1930; LP1459]. Talking sequence, mus score, & sd eff (Movietone); b&w. 35mm. 9 reels, 7,551 ft.

Prod W. Douglas Burden, William C. Chanler. *Dir* H. P. Carver. *Scen* Richard Carver. *Titl* Julian Johnson. *Ch Camera* Marcel Le Picard. *Adtl Photog* Frank M. Broda, Horace D. Ashton, William Casel, Otto Durkoltz. *Synchronized Mus Score* Massard Kur Zhene. *Song: "Rain Flower"* Sam Coslow, Newell Chase. *Song: "Song of the Waters"* Massard Kur Zhene. *Asst Dir* Earl M. Welch. *Tech* L. A. Bonn.

Cast: Chief Yellow Robe *(Chetoga, tribe leader)*, Chief Long Lance *(Baluk, mighty hunter)*, Chief Akawanush *(Dagwan, medicine man)*, Spotted Elk *(Neewa, Chetoga's daughter)*, Cheeka *(Cheeka, Chetoga's son)*.

Fictional documentary. In a spoken prolog, Chief Yellow Robe introduces the film: "This is the story of my people. Now the White Man has come; his civilization has destroyed my people. ... But now this same civilization has preserved our traditions before it was too late; now you will know us as we really are. Everything that you will see here is real; everything as it always has been. ..." With winter approaching and food scarce, Chetoga, chief of the Ojibwa, calls a council to decide the tribe's course. Baluk, the hunter, wishes to take the hunters south; and in spite of Dagwan's protests, Chetoga agrees to the plan. When winter comes and the hunters return emptyhanded, Baluk decides to move the tribe northward into the path of the migrating caribou, though Dagwan, who is a rival for the chief's daughter, taunts him with cowardice. After days without food, camp is pitched, and Baluk goes forth to a mountain to pray to the Great Spirit and kills a bull moose besieged by timber wolves. But Chetoga dies, leaving Baluk chief of the tribe. After weeks of fruitless travel, Dagwan calls a ritualistic meeting. During his medicine dance, a snow-flurry is taken as a sign of Dagwan's supernatural power, and he tells them the Great Spirit requires the sacrifice of Baluk. Baluk chooses to die by fire, and a funeral pyre is built; but as he mounts it, word reaches the camp of a caribou stampede. Baluk takes charge, great numbers of caribou are slain, and there is feasting. As a result of his treachery, Dagwan is condemned to fare forth without food, water, or weapons, and Baluk takes Neewa for his wife. *Ojibwa Indians. Hunters. Medicine men. Famine. Religion. Canadian Northwest. Temagami Forest Reserve. Ontario. Caribou.*

Note: Filmed largely on the Temagami Forest Reserve in northern Ontario, the film is a by-product of an expedition sponsored by the Museum of Natural History in New York.

THE SILENT GUARDIAN **F2.5050**

Truart Film Corp. c4 Feb **1926** [LP22384]. Si; b&w. 35mm. 5 reels, 4,221 ft.

Dir William Bletcher. *Story* Ewart Adamson. *Photog* Abe Fried.

Cast: Louise Lorraine *(Jessie Stevens)*, Harry Tenbrook *(Job Stevens)*, L. J. O'Connor *(Red Collins)*, Art Acord *(Jim Sullivan)*, Grace Woods *(sheriff's wife)*, Rex *(The Dog)*, Black Beauty *(The Horse)*.

Western melodrama. Red Collins, who is in love with Jessie Stevens, attempts to break up the love affair between her and Jim Sullivan. Red, threatening to expose the involvement of Jessie's father, Job Stevens, in a shady business deal, forces him to order his daughter to marry him. Jim takes to drinking but manages to earn the loyalty of Rex, Red's dog, when he rescues him from a beating by his master. Rex has many opportunities to show his gratitude to Jim in the action following. Jim is left to die by Red, but Rex rescues him; Jim is accused of murder, but Rex helps clear him; and Rex and Jim combine their talents to save Jessie. *Filial relations. Blackmail. Murder. Alcoholism. Dogs. Horses.*

THE SILENT HERO **F2.5051**

Duke Worne Productions. *Dist* Rayart Pictures. Aug **1927**. Si; b&w. 35mm. 6 reels, 5,502 ft.

Pres by W. Ray Johnston. *Dir* Duke Worne. *Scen* George W. Pyper. *Story* H. H. Van Loan. *Photog* Ernest Smith.

Cast: Robert Frazer *(Bud Taylor)*, Edna Murphy *(Mary Stoddard)*, Ernest Hilliard *(Wade Burton)*, Joseph Girard *(John Stoddard)*, Harry Allen *(Blinky)*, Napoleon Bonaparte *("The Phantom," a dog)*.

Northwest melodrama. Hoping to earn enough money to marry Mary Stoddard, Bud Taylor goes north to search for gold. Before he leaves, Bud presents Mary with a German shepherd pup, which later takes an instant dislike to Wade Burton, a rival for Mary's affections. The scene shifts to the frozen North, where Bud has found gold. Burton jumps the claim and steals the gold, but Mary's dog aids Bud in setting things right. *Claim jumpers. Gold mining. Dogs.*

THE SILENT LOVER **F2.5052**

First National Pictures. 21 Nov **1926** [c14 Nov 1926; LP23337]. Si; b&w. 35mm. 7 reels, 6,500 ft.

Dir George Archainbaud. *Scen* Carey Wilson. *Prod Mgr* Carey Wilson.

Cast: Milton Sills *(Count Pierre Tornai)*, Natalie Kingston *(Vera Sherman)*, William Humphrey *(Cornelius Sherman)*, Arthur Edmund Carewe *(Captain Herault)*, William V. Mong *(Kobol)*, Viola Dana *(Scadsza)*, Claude King *(Contarini)*, Charlie Murray *(O'Reilly)*, Arthur Stone *(Greenbaum)*, Alma Bennett *(Haldee)*, Montagu Love *(Ben Achmed)*.

Romantic melodrama. Source: Lajos Biró, *Der Legionër* (a play; c1922). The dissolute Count Pierre Tornai, having dissipated his fortune in Paris, embezzles embassy funds while intoxicated; and after spending his last penny on a dancer, he contemplates suicide but is persuaded to enlist in the Foreign Legion. Reestablished through long and faithful service, Pierre meets Vera, a rich American girl who is touring Africa under the care of Captain Herault, a faithless friend of Pierre's. Herault involves Pierre in a military affair from which he can extricate himself only by blaming Scadsza, a native girl who loves him, hoping thereby to retain Vera's affections. Desert tribesmen attack the outpost, and Herault is forced to released Pierre; amid the raging battle, Pierre and Vera confess their love. Scadsza admits to being the daughter of Ben Achmed, leader of the Bedouins, and in return for his daughter, Ben Achmed agrees to end the slaughter. *Nobility. Bedouins. Embezzlement. Paris. Africa. France—Army—Foreign Legion.*

SILENT PAL **F2.5053**

Gotham Productions. *Dist* Lumas Film Corp. c27 Mar **1925** [LP21278]. Si; b&w. 35mm. 6 reels, 5,452 ft.

Pres by Samuel Sax. *Dir-Cont* Henry McCarty. *Photog* Jack MacKenzie.

Cast: Eddie Phillips *(David Kingston)*, Shannon Day *(Marjorie Winters)*, Colin Kenny *(Randall Phillips)*, Willis Marks *(Daniel Winters)*, Charles Mack *(Lazarus)*, Dorothy Seay *(Betty Winters)*, Thunder *("The Silent Pal")*.

Western melodrama. Source: Frank Foster Davis, "The Silent Pal" (publication undetermined). David Kingston, a university student involved in the study of mine engineering, is falsely accused of theft and expelled from school. David's mother soon dies of grief, and he decides to end it all by jumping in the river. David is deterred from suicide, however, when he adopts a stray pup, which he names "Thunder." The dog later finds a map indicating the location of a gold mine, and David heads west. On the way to the mine, David stops at a sheep ranch, discovering there that the young daughter of the rancher is missing. Thunder soon finds the child, and David rescues her with the help of Randall Phillips, a mining engineer. Phillips later learns of David's map and attempts to kill him. Thunder is then falsely accused of killing sheep, being narrowly saved from the sheriff's posse by the little girl he rescued. David and the dog find the mine and enter its shaft, not knowing that Phillips has sabotaged it with dynamite. Phillips sets off the charge and is himself killed in the exposion; Thunder rescues David. The blast exposes a vein of gold, and David asks the oldest daughter of the sheep rancher, Marjorie, to marry him. *Engineers—Mining. Suicide. Gold mines. Documentation. Dogs. Sheep.*

THE SILENT PARTNER **F2.5054**
Famous Players–Lasky. *Dist* Paramount Pictures. 16 Sep **1923** [c22 Aug 1923; LP19325]. Si; b&w. 35mm. 6 reels, 5,866 ft.

Pres by Jesse L. Lasky. *Dir* Charles Maigne. *Adapt* Sada Cowan. *Photog* Walter Griffin.

Cast: Leatrice Joy *(Lisa Coburn)*, Owen Moore *(George Coburn)*, Robert Edeson *(Ralph Coombes)*, Robert Schable *(Harvey Dredge)*, Patterson Dial *(Cora Dredge)*, E. H. Calvert *(Jim Harker)*, Maude Wayne *(Gertie Page)*, Bess Flowers *(Mrs. Nesbit)*, Laura Anson *(Mrs. Harker)*, Bert Woodruff *(Owens)*, Robert Grey *(Charles Nesbit)*.

Melodrama. Source: Maximilian Foster, "The Silent Partner," in *Harper's Monthly* (116:949, May 1908). Lisa Coburn becomes a "silent partner" for her husband George in his Wall Street financial speculation. Instead of buying jewels and expensive clothes, she saves the money he gives her. When the crash comes and George has gambled away his fortune, Lisa is able to reinstate him with her savings. *Stock market. Finance—Personal. New York City—Wall Street.*

THE SILENT POWER **F2.5055**
Gotham Productions. *Dist* Lumas Film Corp. 1 Nov **1926** [c25 Aug 1926; LP23047]. Si; b&w. 35mm. 6 reels, 5,500 or 5,890 ft.

Pres by Sam Sax. *Supv* Renaud Hoffman. *Dir* Frank O'Connor. *Adapt-Cont* James Bell Smith. *Story* James J. Tynan. *Photog* Ray June. *Prod Mgr* Glenn Belt.

Cast: Ralph Lewis *(John Rollins)*, Ethel Shannon *(Olive Spencer)*, Charles Delaney *(Rob Rollins)*, Vadim Uraneff *(Jerry Spencer)*, Robert E. Homans *(David Webster)*.

Melodrama. John Rollins, an engineer in charge of a hydro-electric plant, welcomes home his son Rob, a brilliant but careless college youth, and persuades Webster, president of the company, to place Rob in charge of a dam construction project. Rob meets Olive Spencer and her brother Jerry; and though Olive is drawn to Rob, she is unhappy to learn that the lake to be created by the dam will flood her old home. Rob's college pals arrive and take him to a party, resulting in his discharge by Webster. Shortly afterward, Webster is found murdered; suspicion falls on Rob, who is arrested and found guilty. At the last moment before the scheduled electrocution, Olive learns that her half-crazed brother, Jerry, killed Webster; and she tries to save Rob. Rollins is obliged to remain on duty and throw the fatal switch. He faints, thinking he has killed his son; but Jerry has atoned by cutting the main prison cable, saving Rob's life but losing his own. *Engineers. Students. Brother-sister relationship. Electricity. Courtship. Murder. Circumstantial evidence. Capital punishment. Self-sacrifice. Insanity. Dams.*

THE SILENT RIDER (Universal-Jewel) **F2.5056**
Universal Pictures. 2 Jan **1927** [c22 Dec 1926; LP23460]. Si; b&w. 35mm. 6 reels, 5,808 ft.

Pres by Carl Laemmle. *Dir* Lynn Reynolds. *Cont* Joseph Franklin Poland. *Photog* Harry Neumann. *Art Dir* David S. Garber.

Cast: Hoot Gibson *(Jerry Alton)*, Blanche Mehaffey *(Marian Faer)*, Ethan Laidlaw *(Red Wender)*, Otis Harlan *(Sourdough Jackson)*, Wendell Phillips Franklin *(Tommy)*, Arthur Morrison *(Green)*, Nora Cecil *(Mrs. Randall)*, Dick La Reno *(sheriff)*, Lon Poff *(Baldy)*, Dick L'Estrange *(Blondy)*.

Western melodrama. Source: Katharine Newlin Burt, "The Red-Headed Husband," in *Cosmopolitan Magazine* (80:50–53, Jan 1926). Cowboy Jerry Alton is content with life on the Bar Z Ranch until Mrs. Randall hires pretty Marian Faer to assist in cooking. Marian explains that she is looking for a redheaded husband. All the men are smitten with her, and several, including Jerry, try to dye their hair red. In partnership with Sourdough Jackson, Jerry purchases a small ranch plot and builds a cabin, in hopes of presenting it to Marian. Then Wender, a man with flaming red hair, applies for work at the ranch, and to Jerry's chagrin, he seems to wield an influence over the girl. Meanwhile, Jerry and Sourdough find a child near their cabin and adopt him. "Red," with his gang, robs a mine and steals the payroll, then claims the boy as his son and later throws suspicion on Jerry. In a fight with Jerry, Red falls to his death, leaving Marian, his former wife, free to marry Jerry. *Cowboys. Cooks. Children. Redheads. Courtship. Robbery. Parentage.*

SILENT SANDERSON **F2.5057**
Hunt Stromberg Corp. *Dist* Producers Distributing Corp. 13 Apr **1925** [cl May 1925; LP21751]. Si; b&w. 35mm. 5 reels, 4,841 ft.

Pres by Hunt Stromberg. *Supv* Hunt Stromberg. *Dir* Scott R. Dunlap. *Adapt* Harvey Gates. *Story* Kate Corbaley. *Photog* Sol Polito. *Art Dir* Edward Withers. *Film Ed* Harry L. Decker.

Cast: Harry Carey *(Joel Parsons/Silent Sanderson)*, Trilby Clark *(Judith Benson)*, John Miljan *(Jim Downing)*, Gardner James *(Art Parsons)*, Edith Yorke *(Mrs. Parsons)*, Stanton Heck *(Silver Smith)*, Sheldon Lewis *(Single Tooth Wilson)*.

Western melodrama. Three ranchers in the Southwest fight over Judith Benson, a beautiful girl whom they all want to marry. She is swept off her feet by Jim Downing, however, and agrees to marry him. Art Parsons is found dead, apparently having killed himself in his grief, and his brother, Joel, sets off for Alaska to assuage his sorrow. Joel later meets Judith in a Yukon dancehall, where—having left her rotten husband—she has become an entertainer. Joel (known now as Silent Sanderson) kidnaps the girl and takes her to his cabin, planning to revenge his brother's death on her. Downing follows them and, stricken with snow blindness, brags to Joel that he will kill him just as he once killed Art. He attacks Judith and, after a fierce fight, Joel throws him to a pack of wolves. Joel and Judith come to an understanding and return together to the cow country. *Ranchers. Brothers. Dancehall girls. Revenge. Murder. Abduction. Snow blindness. Alaska. Yukon. Wolves.*

SILENT SENTINEL **F2.5058**
Chesterfield Motion Picture Corp. 15 May **1929** [New York showing]. Si; b&w. 35mm. 5 reels, 4,700-4,800 ft.

Dir-Story-Scen-Titl Alvin J. Neitz. *Titl? (see note)* Hans Tiesler. *Photog* M. A. Anderson. *Film Ed* Alvin J. Neitz.

Cast: Champion *(himself, the dog)*, Gareth Hughes *(Bob Benton)*, Josephine Hill *(Grace Carlton)*, Walter Maly *(Tom)*, Lew Meehan *(detective)*, Aline Goodwin *(Maizie)*, Alfred Hewston *(Warren Gordon)*, Eddie Brownell *(Joe Carlton)*, Alice Covert *(Mrs. Carlton)*, John Tansey *(convict)*, Edward Cecil *(Chick)*, Jack Knight *(Dick)*, George Morrell *(insurance man)*.

Action melodrama. A banker successfully places the blame for his own embezzling on one of his cashiers (thereby collecting from the bonding company), but he is finally caught in the act by another cashier, the sister of the imprisoned cashier, and Champion, a dog. While Champion keeps the banker busy, the hero goes for the police; and there ensues a long chase, which ends with the capture of the banker, the release of the girl's brother, and her happy embrace of the hero. *Bankers. Brother-sister relationship. Embezzlement. Chases. Dogs.*

Note: A *Film Daily* review attributes titles to Tiesler, but the *Film Year Book* credits Neitz.

SILENT SHELBY (Reissue) **F2.5059**
American Film Co. *Dist* Aywon Film Corp. 30 Mar **1922** [New York State license; trade review 20 May 1922]. Si; b&w. 35mm. 5 reels, 4,600 ft.

Note: Originally titled *Land o' Lizards*, released by Mutual 21 Sep 1916, starring and directed by Frank Borzage.

SILENT SHELDON **F2.5060**
Harry Webb Productions. *Dist* Rayart Pictures. 7 Oct **1925** [New York State license application]. Si; b&w. 35mm. 5 reels, 4,800 ft.

Dir Harry Webb. *Story-Scen* Pierre Couderc. *Photog* William Thornly.

Cast: Jack Perrin *(Jack Sheldon)*, Josephine Hill *(Mary Watkins)*, Martin Turner *(Ivory, his valet)*, Whitehorse *(her father)*, Leonard Clapham *(Bill Fadden)*, Lew Meehan *(Joe Phillips)*, Robert MacFarland *(sheriff)*, Rex *(himself, a dog)*, Starlight *(herself, a horse)*.

Western melodrama. No information about the precise nature of this film has been found. *Dogs. Horses.*

THE SILENT STRANGER **F2.5061**
Monogram Pictures. *Dist* Film Booking Offices of America. 21 Apr **1924** [c11 Apr 1924; LP20066]. Si; b&w. 35mm. 5 reels, 5,040 ft.

Prod Harry J. Brown. *Dir* Albert Rogell. *Scen* Marion Jackson. *Story* Stuart Heisler. *Photog* Ross Fisher.

Cast: Fred Thomson *(Jack Taylor)*, Hazel Keener *(Lillian Warner)*, George Williams *("Dad" Warner, postmaster)*, Richard Headrick *(Laddie Warner)*, Frank Hagney *(Dick Blackwell)*, Horace Carpenter *(Sam Hull, sheriff)*, Bud Osborne *(Law Sleeman, clerk)*, Bob Reeves *("Shorty" Turner, deputy sheriff)*, George Nichols *(Silas Horton, the banker)*, Silver King *(a* *horse).*

Western melodrama. Jack Taylor, supposedly a deafmute, arrives in Valley City at the same time that Postmaster Dad Warner is threatened with the loss of his job because of the many recent mail thefts. Taylor suspects Warner's clerk, Law Sleeman, and is consequently captured by a gang led by local politician Dick Blackwell. He escapes, stops another robbery, rescues Lillian Warner, captures the gang, reveals himself to be a Secret Service agent, and wins Lillian's hand. *Postmasters. Deafmutes. Secret service. Politicians. Mail theft. Horses.*

SILENT TRAIL **F2.5062**

El Dorado Productions. *Dist* Syndicate Pictures. 1 Jul or 15 Aug **1928.** Si; b&w. 35mm. 5 reels, 4,315 ft.

Dir J. P. McGowan. *Story-Scen* Brysis Coleman. *Photog? (see note)* Paul Allen, Hap Depew.

Cast: Bob Custer, Peggy Montgomery, John Lowell, J. P. McGowan, Mack V. Wright, Nancy A. Lee, Jack Ponder, Black Jack *(a horse).*

Western melodrama. A cowboy (played by Bob Custer) in search of adventure comes to the aid of another in a saloon brawl; they both are chased out of town and find refuge with a gang of rustlers. Rescuing a wealthy girl in an automobile accident, Custer brings her to the gang's headquarters and defends her from the leader's advances. Fights and doublecrosses precede a happy ending for the couple. *Cowboys. Gangs. Friendship. Automobile accidents. Horses.*

Note: Sources disagree in crediting photographer.

THE SILENT VOW **F2.5063**

Vitagraph Co. of America. 16 Apr **1922** [c17 Mar 1922; LP17653]. Si; b&w. 35mm. 5 reels, 4,600 ft.

Pres by Albert E. Smith. *Dir* William Duncan. *Scen* Bradley J. Smollen. *Photog* George Robinson.

Cast: William Duncan *(Richard Stratton/"Dick" Stratton),* Edith Johnson *(Anne),* Dorothy Dwan *(Ethel),* Maud Emery *(Elizabeth Stratton),* J. Morris Foster *("Doug" Gorson),* Henry Hebert *("Jim" Gorson),* Fred Burley *("Bill" Gorson),* Jack Curtis *("Sledge" Morton),* Charles Dudley *(The Professor).*

Northwest melodrama. In a prolog, Jim Gorson, a handsome woodcutter, persuades the wife of Richard Stratton to elope with him. Twenty years later, Dick Stratton, Richard's son, a Northwest Mounted Policeman, is ordered to capture Bill and Doug Gorson. Circumstantial evidence points to the Gorsons as murderers of Dick's father, but the Gorsons escape, leaving behind their father wounded by the Mounties. Elizabeth Stratton, who has adopted two orphan children, Anne and Ethel, is abducted by Bill and "Sledge" Morton, a czar of the river district. Meanwhile Dick tracks down Doug Gorson, but he releases him on his pledge to aid in rescuing Ethel and Anne. Following an extended fight with Morton and Bill Gorson, the Gorsons explain that the elder Stratton died of heart failure; the 20-year-feud is ended, and after the death of Elizabeth, Dick and Doug return to civilization with the girls. *Infidelity. Feuds. Murder. Circumstantial evidence. Northwest Mounted Police.*

THE SILENT WATCHER **F2.5064**

Frank Lloyd Productions. *Dist* First National Pictures. 5 Oct **1924** [c1 Oct 1924; LP20615]. Si; b&w. 35mm. 8 reels, 7,575 ft.

Dir Frank Lloyd. *Adapt* J. G. Hawks. *Photog* Norbert F. Brodin. *Settings* John J. Hughes. *Film Ed* Edward M. Roskam. *Wardrobe* Eve Roth.

Cast: Glenn Hunter *(Joe Roberts),* Bessie Love *(Mary, his wife),* Hobart Bosworth *(John Steele, "The Chief"),* Gertrude Astor *(Mrs. Steele),* George Nichols *(Jim Tufts, stage doorman),* Aggie Herring *(Mrs. Tufts),* Lionel Belmore *(Barnes, Steele's campaign manager),* De Witt Jennings *(Stuart, the detective),* Alma Bennett *(Lily Elliott, the soubrette),* Brandon Hurst *(Herrold, the reporter),* Mademoiselle Suzette, David Murray *(solo dancers).*

Domestic drama. Joe Roberts is devoted to his wife, Mary, and fiercely loyal to United States Senate candidate John Steele, by whom he is employed as secretary. Mary does not share her husband's enthusiasm for Steele and believes Joe false to her when actress Lily Elliott dies in an apartment rented in Joe's name. Even under charge of murder and a police "third degree" Joe does not reveal that Lily's affair was with Steele, an unhappily married man; he remains silent in the mistaken belief that Barnes, Steele's campaign manager, has told Mary the truth. When Joe is finally released, Mary is gone, but Steele learns of the situation after he is elected and then reunites the couple. *Secretaries. Police. Actors. Suicide. Politics. Third degree. United States Congress.*

SILENT WIRES **F2.5065**

William Steiner Productions. 15 Sep **1924.** Si; b&w. 35mm. 5 reels.

Cast: Charles Hutchison.

Melodrama(?). No information about the nature of this film has been found.

SILENT YEARS **F2.5066**

R-C Pictures. 27 Nov **1921** [c5 Dec 1921; LP17366]. Si; b&w. 35mm. 6 reels, 6,056 ft.

Dir Louis J. Gasnier. *Scen* Winifred Dunn, Eve Unsell. *Photog* Joseph Dubray.

Cast: Rose Dione *(Mam'selle Jo Morey),* Tully Marshall *(Captain Longville),* George McDaniel *(Henry Langley),* George Siegmann *(Pierre Gavot),* Will Jim Hatton *(Young Tom Gavot),* Jack Mower *(Tom Gavot),* James O. Barrows *(Father Mantelle),* Jack Livingston *(James Norvall),* Ruth King *(Mary Malden),* Kate Toncray *(Marcel Longville),* Lillian Rambeau *(Mrs. Lindsay),* Jean O'Rourke *(Young Donelle),* Ruth Ashby *(Mrs. Norval),* Nick *(The Dog).*

Melodrama. Source: Harriet Theresa Comstock, *Mam'selle Jo* (Garden City, New York, 1918). Jo Morey, who lives in the St. Lawrence River Valley, inherits her father's barren farm and devotes her entire energies to cultivating it and caring for her invalid sister. Henry Langley meets Jo and proposes marriage to her. She asks him to wait until she is free, but Langley refuses and marries Mary Malden. Eight years later Jo has paid off the mortgage to Captain Longville, and one night she finds a baby in her house; it is Langley's, and a note requests that its parentage be kept secret. Donelle is carefully reared by Jo, and the girl is saved from the villagers' insults by Tom Gavot. When Mary Langley returns to claim her daughter, Jo will not receive her. Donelle learns of her parentage in Jo's absence and seeks refuge with Tom, who asks her to marry him. Pierre learns of his son's marriage and goes to Jo's farm; there the village priest, to whom Mary has confessed, explains the girl's parentage, and Jo rejoices in her child's happiness. *Sisters. Invalids. French Canadians. Parentage. Motherhood. Mortgages. Saint Lawrence River. Dogs.*

THE SILK BOUQUET **F2.5067**

Fairmont Productions. *Dist* Hi-Mark Productions. 25 Jun **1926** [New York State license]. Si; b&w. 35mm. 8 reels, 7,700 ft.

Cast: Jimmy Leong, Anna May Wong.

Drama(?). No information about the nature of this film has been found.

Note: Title changed to *The Dragon Horse,* caJan 1927.

SILK LEGS **F2.5068**

Fox Film Corp. 18 Dec **1927** [c7 Dec 1927; LP24731]. Si; b&w. 35mm. 6 reels, 5,446 ft.

Pres by William Fox. *Supv* William Conselman. *Dir* Arthur Rosson. *Scen* Frances Agnew. *Titl* Delos Sutherland. *Story* Frederica Sagor. *Photog* Rudolph Bergquist. *Asst Dir* S. Hanberry.

Cast: Madge Bellamy *(Ruth Stevens),* James Hall *(Phil Barker),* Joseph Cawthorn *(Ezra Fulton),* Maude Fulton *(Mary McGuire),* Margaret Seddon *(Mrs. Fulton).*

Comedy-drama. "Sales agents for rival hosiery concerns try to land an order, the boy for a while succeeding and putting on an exhibition. The girl, however, makes the mannequins use her own brand of hose, flirts with the buyer and wins order away from her rival. They then hear of the consolidation of their firms and themselves consolidate—in marriage." (*Motion Picture News Booking Guide,* [14]:150, 1929.) *Salesmen. Buyers. Fashion models. Hosiery.*

SILK STOCKING SAL **F2.5069**

Gothic Pictures. *Dist* Film Booking Offices of America. 30 Nov **1924** [c30 Nov 1924; LP20927]. Si; b&w. 35mm. 5 reels, 5,367 ft.

Dir Tod Browning. *Story-Scen* E. Richard Schayer. *Photog* Silvano Balboni.

Cast: Evelyn Brent *("Stormy" Martin),* Robert Ellis *(Bob Cooper),* Earl Metcalfe *(Bull Reagan),* Alice Browning *(Bargain Basement Annie),* Virginia Madison *(Mrs. Cooper),* Marylynn Warner *(Miss Cooper),* John Gough *(The "Gopher"),* Louis Fitzroy *(Abner Bingham).*

Melodrama. While she is burgling a palatial townhouse, Silk Stocking Sal is discovered by its owner, Bob Cooper. Intrigued with her poise and daring, he offers to find her an honest job. She accepts his proposition and is hired by Cooper's exporting firm to show antiques to prospective buyers. When Abner Bingham, Bob's partner, is found murdered after an argument with Bob, he is accused of the crime on circumstantial evidence and sentenced to die. To save Bob from the chair, Sal, who suspects Bull Reagen, a mobster, of the murder, goes to his apartment. She plants a microphone in the closet, gets Bull drunk, and, by accusing him of not having the killer instinct, taunts him into boasting of having killed Bingham. The converstion is overheard by the district attorney, who narrowly saves Bob from electrocution and then arrests Bull and his gang. Bob and Silk Stocking Sal are soon married. *Burglars. Exporters. Criminals—Rehabilitation. Murder. Circumstantial evidence. Capital punishment. Antiques.*

SILK STOCKINGS (Universal-Jewel) **F2.5070**

Universal Pictures. 2 Oct **1927** [c16 Aug 1927; LP24324]. Si; b&w. 35mm. 7 reels, 6,166 ft. [Also 6 reels, 5,947 ft.]

Pres by Carl Laemmle. *Dir* Wesley Ruggles. *Scen* Beatrice Van. *Titl* Albert De Mond. *Photog* Ben Reynolds.

Cast: Laura La Plante *(Molly Thornhill)*, John Harron *(Sam Thornhill)*, Otis Harlan *(Judge Foster)*, William Austin *(George Bagnall)*, Marcella Daly *(Helen)*, Heinie Conklin *(watchman)*, Burr McIntosh *(judge)*, Tempe Pigott *(Mrs. Gower)*, Ruth Cherrington *(dowager)*.

Domestic farce. Source: Cyril Harcourt, *A Pair of Silk Stockings* (New York, 1916). Sam and Molly Thornhill, a model married couple very much in love, are nevertheless continually quarreling. On the eve of their wedding anniversary, Sam is detained at the office by his boss to help entertain some buyers, and in his haste to leave he fails to notice a pair of silk stockings slipped into his pocket by a lady. Molly and her friend George Bagnall then hear about the case of another wife who obtained a divorce after finding a silk stocking in *her* husband's clothes. ... Judge Moore, a mutual friend, decides to teach the Thornhills a lesson and suggests a divorce to Molly; she halfheartedly agrees and is granted a quick separation. Both go to the beach to visit friends and are obviously unhappy until the judge suggests that a compromising situation would nullify the divorce. She hurries to what she believes is her husband's bedroom but is confronted there by Bagnall and his fiancée; Sam enters, however, and clasps Molly in his arms. *Judges. Buyers. Wedding anniversaries. Marriage. Divorce.*

SILKEN SHACKLES **F2.5071**

Warner Brothers Pictures. *Dist* Vitagraph Co. of America. 14 May **1926** [c16 Apr 1926; LP22612]. Si; b&w. 35mm. 6 reels, 6,061 ft.

Dir Walter Morosco. *Story-Scen* Walter Morosco, Philip Klein. *Photog* John Mescall. *Asst Camera* Bert Shipman. *Asst Dir* Eddie Sowders.

Cast: Irene Rich *(Denise Lake)*, Huntly Gordon *(Howard Lake)*, Bertram Marburgh *(Lord Fairchild)*, Victor Varconi *(Tade Adrian)*, Evelyn Selbie *(Tade's mother)*, Robert Schable *(Frederic Stanhope)*, Kalla Pasha *(Tade's father)*.

Society melodrama. Howard Lake, an American diplomat on a mission to Buda-Pesth [sic], is distressed when his wife, Denise, becomes entangled in a series of romantic flirtations culminating in the attempted suicide of a youth. He determines to teach her a lesson; and that evening, Denise meets Tade Adrian, a young violinist, in a fashionable restaurant and is captivated by him. Howard conceives a scheme whereby he pays Adrian to make love to his wife, but when Adrian comes to believe that she actually loves him, he abrogates the agreement. Learning about Adrian's boorish peasant family, Howard invites them to the restaurant where Adrian is appearing; and Denise, shocked by their vulgarity, promises never to flirt again and returns home with her husband. *Violinists. Peasants. Flirtation. United States—Diplomatic and consular service. Austria-Hungary. Budapest.*

SILKS AND SADDLES **F2.5072**

Universal Pictures. 20 Jan **1929** [c12 May 1928; LP25262]. Si; b&w. 35mm. 6 reels, 5,809 ft.

Dir Robert F. Hill. *Story Supv* J. G. Hawks. *Cont* Paul Gangelin, Faith Thomas. *Titl* Albert De Mond. *Adapt* Edward Clark, James Gruen. *Story* Gerald Beaumont. *Photog* Joseph Brotherton. *Film Ed* Daniel Mandell.

Cast: Richard Walling *(Johnny Spencer)*, Marion Nixon *(Lucy Calhoun)*, Sam De Grasse *(William Morrissey)*, Montagu Love *(Walter Sinclair)*, Mary Nolan *(Sybil Morrissey)*, Otis Harlan *(Jimmy McKee)*, David Torrence *(Judge Clifford)*, Claire McDowell *(Mrs. Calhoun)*, John Fox, Jr. *(Ellis)*, Hayden Stevenson *(trainer)*.

Drama. Jockey Johnny Spencer loses his job with Mrs. Calhoun for throwing a race. An adventuress named Sybil, who made Johnny hold back Mrs. Calhoun's horse, Lady, leaves him, and he becomes a racetrack bum. Johnny returns to Mrs. Calhoun's stable when the new jockey proves unable to manage Lady. Johnny wins the next race, thereby regaining Mrs. Calhoun's confidence and winning the love of her attractive daughter, Lucy. *Jockeys. Adventuresses. Horseracing. Horses.*

Note: Originally released as *Thoroughbreds.* Working titles: *Thoroughbreds; The Frog.*

THE SILVER CAR **F2.5073**

Vitagraph Co. of America. Jun **1921** [c1 Jun 1921; LP16603]. Si; b&w. 35mm. 6 reels, 5,600 ft.

Dir David Smith. *Story* Wyndham Martin. *Photog* Jack MacKenzie.

Cast: Earle Williams *(Anthony Trent)*, Kathryn Adams *(Daphne Grenvil)*, Geoffrey Webb *(Arthur Grenvil)*, Eric Mayne *(Count Michael Temesvar)*, Emmett King *(Earl of Rosecarrel)*, Mona Lisa *(Pauline)*, John Steppling *(Vicar)*, Max Asher *(Hentzi)*, Walter Rodgers *(Colonel Langley)*.

Crime melodrama. As he departs for Europe, international crook Anthony Trent recognizes "William Smith," a former war comrade (believed to be dead) to whom Trent has confided his true identity. In England Colonel Langley refuses to divulge the man's true identity, and Trent later discovers papers in Langley's safe naming "Smith" as Arthur Grenvil, incriminated in a fraudulent scheme against his uncle, an earl. With the aid of Trent, Daphne, the boy's sister, destroys the evidence. Learning that the earl is being blackmailed by Count Michael Temesvar of Croatia, who threatens to expose a treaty between the two countries, Trent, under every possible handicap, manages to secure the treaty for the earl and is rewarded with an Australian ranch and the hand of Daphne. *Personal identity. Blackmail. Diplomacy. England. Documentation.*

SILVER COMES THROUGH **F2.5074**

R-C Pictures. *Dist* Film Booking Offices of America. 29 May **1927** [c21 May 1927; LP23994]. Si; b&w. 35mm. 6 reels, 5,476 ft.

Pres by Joseph P. Kennedy. *Adapt-Cont-Dir* Lloyd Ingraham. *Story* Frank M. Clifton. *Photog* Mack Stengler.

Cast: Fred Thomson *(Fred)*, Edna Murphy *(Lucindy)*, William Courtright *(Zeke, ranchowner)*, Harry Woods *(Stanton)*, Mathilde Brundage *(Mrs. Bryce-Collins)*, Silver King *(himself, a horse)*.

Melodrama. In a blizzard, Fred rescues Zeke, his employer, and saves the horses and cattle from a hungry puma. Later, a colt, under Fred's care, grows into a magnificent horse. Zeke, who is indebted to Stanton, surrenders several horses, including Silver King, to him, but Zeke decides to keep Silver King when Stanton mistreats the horse. Fred is enamored of Lucindy, Zeke's daughter, and rescues her when Black Eagle, who is being primed for the cross-country race, runs away with her and is injured. Consequently, Zeke enters Silver King in the race. At a party given by Lucindy, Fred is angered by Stanton's attentions to her; and Stanton's men plot to abduct Silver King before the race. Fred pursues and wins a last-minute victory over Stanton's entry. *Ranchers. Horseracing. Courtship. Blizzards. Puma. Horses.*

Note: Some sources render the title as *Silver Comes Thru.* Licensed in New York State as *Silver King Comes Thru.*

SILVER FINGERS **F2.5075**

Dist Capitol Productions. 20 Feb **1926** [New York State license]. Si; b&w. 35mm. 5 reels.

Dir J. P. McGowan.

Cast: George Larkin, Charlotte Morgan, Arthur Morrison, Colin Chase, Mack V. Wright, Olive Kirby.

Action melodrama. In order to protect the Denman diamonds, a clever detective, working in disguise, passes himself off as a suave master criminal. He prevents the real criminals from seizing the jewels and falls in love with Denman's daughter. *Detectives. Thieves. Disguise.*

THE SILVER HORDE **F2.5076**

RKO Radio Pictures. 25 Oct **1930** [c25 Oct 1930; LP1678]. Sd (Photophone); b&w. 35mm. 8 reels, 6,735 ft.

Prod William Le Baron. *Assoc Prod* William Sistrom. *Dir* George Archainbaud. *Screenplay-Dial* Wallace Smith. *Photog* Leo Tover. *Art Dir* Max Ree. *Film Ed* Otto Ludwig. *Rec Engr* Clem Portman. *Asst Dir* Thomas Atkins.

Cast: Evelyn Brent *(Cherry Malotte)*, Louis Wolheim *(George Balt)*, Joel McCrea *(Boyd Emerson)*, Raymond Hatton *(Fraser)*, Jean Arthur *(Mildred Wayland)*, Gavin Gordon *(Fred Marsh)*, Blanche Sweet *(Queenie)*, Purnell Pratt *(Wayne Wayland)*, William Davidson *(Thomas Hilliard)*,

Ivan Linow *(Svenson)*.

Northwest melodrama. Source: Rex Beach, *The Silver Horde* (New York & London, 1909). Boyd Emerson and Fraser drive their dog team into the Alaskan fishing village of Kalvik to find it is dominated by the brutal Balt, whom Boyd thrashes. Cherry Malotte, a notorious dancehall girl, puts an end to the argument and offers them hospitality, telling them of Marsh, a ruthless exploiter, who will permit no outsiders to settle there. Cherry, developing a copper lode, takes Boyd into partnership, having fallen in love with him, and schemes to stake him through Tom Hilliard, a Seattle banker, planning to refinance Balt's fishery and compete with Marsh. Boyd, Fraser, and Balt leave for Seattle, where Boyd calls on Mildred Wayland, his sweetheart, who is promised to Marsh. Boyd secures financial aid, but Marsh stops his credit. Cherry, however, comes to his aid, and with the salmon industry in Salvik in full swing, Boyd comes into conflict with Marsh. Fishing fleets meet in hand-to-hand battle, and Marsh is beaten; he seeks revenge by slandering Cherry, but Boyd counters with Queenie, a discarded old flame. Balt takes revenge on Marsh, strangling him, and Boyd and Mildred are united in love. *Millionaires. Dancehall girls. Bankers. Fishing villages. Copper. Courtship. Alaska. Seattle.*

SILVER KING COMES THRU *see* **SILVER COMES THROUGH**

THE SILVER LINING **F2.5077**

Iroquois Film Corp. *Dist* Metro Pictures. ca29 Jan **1921** [Baltimore premiere; released Jan; c27 Dec 1920; LP15970]. Si; b&w. 35mm. 6 reels.

Pres by Roland West. *Prod-Dir-Writ* Roland West. *Adapt-Scen* D. J. Buchanan, Charles H. Smith. *Motion Photog* Edward Wynard, Frank Zucker. *Sets* Charles O. Seessel.

Cast: Jewel Carmen *("The Angel")*, Leslie Austen *(Robert Ellington)*, Coit Albertson *(George Johnson)*, Virginia Valli *(Evelyn Schofield)*, Julia Swayne Gordon *("Gentle Annie")*, J. Herbert Frank *("Big Joe")*, Edwards Davis *(George Schofield)*, Marie Coverdale *(Mrs. George Schofield)*, Gladden James *(Billy Dean)*, Theodore Babcock *(Eugene Narcom)*, Charles Wellesley *(Burton Hardy)*, Henry Sedley *(Mr. Baxter)*, Jule Powers *(Mrs. Baxter)*, Arthur Donaldson *(friend of the Baxters)*, Paul Everton *(a detective)*, Carl Hyson, Dorothy Dickson *(The Dancers)*.

Crook melodrama. At a reception for Mr. and Mrs. Vance Leighton, three men are discussing the effects of heredity in shaping the careers of children. To prove his contention that the theory of heredity is often demonstrated to be false, John Strong, a secret service agent, tells a true story: *Two orphan sisters are adopted, one by society leaders, the other by a couple of crooks. The latter, known as "The Angel," becomes an expert pickpocket, while the other, Evelyn, becomes a reigning belle. The Angel is caught in the act by Johnson, a confidence man. Together with her adopted parents, they go to Havana, where she meets and falls in love with author Robert Ellington, Evelyn's estranged fiancé. Johnson compels her to help him swindle Ellington out of $25,000. Instead, she confesses to Ellington, and when her sister arrives she stages a love scene with Johnson to break off their relationship. Johnson, realizing that The Angel is in love, reveals to Ellington that he is a Secret Service agent. Ellington goes back to her, and they are married.* To answer a skeptical listener's question whether society accepted the couple, Strong knowingly glances at the Leightons and reveals himself as the "Johnson" of the story. *Sisters. Orphans. Socialites. Pickpockets. Authors. Swindlers. Secret service. Heredity. Adoption. Havana.*

THE SILVER SLAVE **F2.5078**

Warner Brothers Pictures. 12 Nov **1927** [c3 Nov 1927; LP24615]. Si; b&w. 35mm. 7 reels, 6,142 ft.

Dir Howard Bretherton. *Scen* Peter Milne, Anthony Coldewey. *Story* Howard Smith. *Camera* Frank Kesson. *Asst Dir* Gordon Hollingshead.

Cast: Irene Rich *(Bernice Randall)*, Audrey Ferris *(Janet Randall)*, Holmes Herbert *(Tom Richards)*, John Miljan *(Philip Caldwell)*, Carroll Nye *(Larry Martin)*.

Society melodrama. Bernice Randall, who has forsaken the love of her sweetheart, Tom Richards, to marry for wealth, turns down Richards' proposal after the death of her husband, and she is denounced by him as a slave to silver. Lavishing the greater part of her fortune on her daughter, Janet, Bernice determines to give her the advantages she herself lacked. Despite her mother's disapproval, Janet scorns the affection of Larry Martin, a life-long friend, after meeting Philip Caldwell, a wealthy sophisticate. Worried over Janet's growing attachment to Philip, Bernice determines to win Caldwell from her daughter, and in a confrontation involving the girl and Richards, now a millionaire, Janet is disillusioned in her mother and Caldwell. Learning of her mother's sacrifice, Janet forgives her and finds happiness with Larry. *Wealth. Social classes. Courtship. Motherhood.*

SILVER SPURS **F2.5079**

Doubleday Productions. *Dist* Western Pictures Exploitation Co. 1 May **1922**. Si; b&w. 35mm. 5 reels, 4,500 ft.

Supv Charles W. Mack. *Dir* Henry McCarty, Leo Meehan.

Cast: Lester Cuneo.

Western melodrama. "The title comes from a pair of lucky spurs which is given to the hero, a writer of Western stories and general all-round adventurer, by a crowd of his New York club friends. With the spurs as a good luck symbol he goes West in search of romance. In California he meets and falls in love with a Spanish girl, who has been defrauded of her estate by an unscrupulous half-breed. After many fights with the villain and his cohorts, he gets back the girl's property and returns to New York with her as his bride." (*Motion Picture News Booking Guide*, 3:63, Oct 1922.) *Authors. Halfcastes. Spanish. Fraud. Western fiction. California. New York City.*

THE SILVER TREASURE **F2.5080**

Fox Film Corp. 13 or 20 Jun **1926** [c20 Jun 1926; LP22862]. Si; b&w. 35mm. 6 reels, 5,386 ft.

Pres by William Fox. *Dir* Rowland V. Lee. *Scen* Robert N. Lee. *Titl* Elizabeth Pickett. *Photog* G. O. Post. *Asst Dir* Mike Miggins.

Cast: George O'Brien *(Nostromo)*, Jack Rollins *(Ramírez)*, Helena D'Algy *(Linda Viola)*, Joan Renee *(Giselle Viola)*, Evelyn Selbie *(Mother Teresa)*, Lou Tellegen *(Solito, the bandit)*, Otto Matieson *(Martin Decoud)*, Stewart Rome *(Charles Gould)*, Hedda Hopper *(Mrs. Gould)*, Daniel Makarenko *(Giorgio Viola)*, Fred Becker *(Hernández)*, Harvey Clark *(Tito)*, Gilbert Clayton *(Dr. Monygham)*, Sidney De Grey *(Captain Mitchell)*, George Kuwa *(Luis)*.

Melodrama. Source: Joseph Conrad, *Nostromo* (1904). On the island of Sylaco, Nostromo, who is heralded as a brave and good man, is betrothed to Linda, though she actually loves Ramírez, while her cousin Giselle, who slaves in the local inn, deeply loves Nostromo. Gould, an Englishman who owns a silver mine, hires Nostromo to protect his silver train from bandits. In a battle with the thieves, Nostromo transfers the silver to a hay wagon and leads it to safety. His sailing vessel is wrecked in the harbor by the bandits, and torn between his forced bethrothal to Linda and his desire for Giselle, he weakens and hides the silver on an island, hoping to escape with Giselle; however, she rejects him for his dishonesty, and he is redeemed after confessing to Gould. *Bandits. English. Italians. Courtship. Redemption. Imaginary republics. Silver mines.*

SILVER VALLEY **F2.5081**

Fox Film Corp. 2 Oct **1927** [c2 Oct 1927; LP24464]. Si; b&w. 35mm. 5 reels, 5,011 ft.

Pres by William Fox. *Dir* Ben Stoloff. *Scen* Harold B. Lipsitz. *Titl* Malcolm Stuart Boylan. *Story* Harry Sinclair Drago. *Photog* Dan Clark. *Asst Dir* Clay Grahnell.

Cast: Tom Mix *(Tom Tracey)*, Dorothy Dwan *(Sheila Blaine)*, Philo McCullough *(Black Jack Lundy)*, Jocky Hoefli *(Silent Kid)*, Tom Kennedy *(Hayfever Hawkins)*, Lon Poff *(Slim Snitzer)*, Harry Dunkinson *(Mike McCool)*, Clark Comstock *(Wash Taylor)*.

Western melodrama. Cowboy Tom Tracey constructs an airplane, which on its initial flight refuses to fly but rather taxis around the ranch to cause general wreckage including destruction of the automobile of Sheila Blaine, an authoress from the city seeking local color. As a result, Tom loses his job and finds himself appointed sheriff in a town that has been depleted of previous law officers by a gang of desperadoes. He discovers their hideout in the hills near a dormant volcano, and when Sheila is captured by the gang he fights the chief villain; then, with the aid of an airplane, he and Sheila escape from the spewing lava of a volcanic eruption. *Cowboys. Authors. Sheriffs. Gangs. Ranches. Airplanes. Volcanoes.*

SILVER WINGS **F2.5082**

Fox Film Corp. 22 May **1922** [New York premiere; released 27 Aug; c27 Aug 1922; LP19007]. Si; b&w. 35mm. 9 reels, 8,271 ft.

Pres by William Fox. *Dir* Edwin Carewe, Jack Ford. *Scen* Paul H. Sloane. *Photog* Robert Kurrle, Joseph Ruttenberg.

Cast—The Prolog: Mary Carr *(Anna Webb)*, Lynn Hammond *(John Webb, her husband)*, Knox Kincaid *(John)*, Joseph Monahan *(Harry)*, Maybeth Carr *(Ruth)*, Claude Brook *(Uncle Andrews)*, Robert Hazelton

(The Minister), Florence Short *(Widow Martin)*, May Kaiser *(her child)*.

Cast—The Play: Mary Carr *(Anna Webb)*, Claude Brook *(Uncle Andrews)*, Percy Helton *(John)*, Joseph Striker *(Harry)*, Jane Thomas *(Ruth)*, Roy Gordon *(George Mills)*, Florence Haas *(Little Anna)*, Roger Lytton *(bank president)*, Ernest Hilliard *(Jerry Gibbs)*.

Domestic drama. When John Webb dies, his wife, Anna, and his children—John, Harry, and Ruth—are well provided for, thanks to his patent on an improved sewing machine. As time passes, however, Harry mismanages and overspends factory funds, John leaves town accused of stealing the money embezzled by Harry, and Ruth elopes. Anna must sell the business to cover Harry's debts, and, reduced to poverty, she takes a menial factory job. Later, her story appears in a magazine and the family is happily reunited. *Widows. Motherhood. Family life. Factory management. Embezzlement. Sewing machines.*

SIMBA, THE KING OF BEASTS; A SAGA OF THE AFRICA VELDT **F2.5083**

Martin Johnson African Expedition Corp. 25 Jan **1928** [trade review; c14 Jan 1928; MU4642]. Talking prolog & mus score (Brunswick); b&w. 35mm. [Feature length assumed.]

Prod Daniel E. Pomeroy. *Titl-Prolog* Terry Ramsaye. *Story* Martin Johnson. *Camera* Martin Johnson, Osa Johnson.

Travel documentary. The wild animals of Africa are shown in their natural habitat: two lions tear a zebra apart, natives spear lions; crocodiles and rhinoceros cavort in a water hole. Flash pictures of lions drawn to a trap by a zebra bait are introduced as stills to show the beasts bewildered by the flash. There is also the usual African native dance. *Dancers. Jungles. Africa. Lions. Zebras. Crocodiles. Rhinoceros.*

SIMON THE JESTER **F2.5084**

Metropolitan Pictures Corp. of California. *Dist* Producers Distributing Corp. ca24 Oct **1925** [Los Angeles premiere; released 8 Nov; c1 Sep 1925; LP22701]. Si; b&w. 35mm. 7 reels, 6,168 ft.

Dir George Melford. *Adapt* Frances Marion.

Cast: Eugene O'Brien *(Simon de Gex)*, Lillian Rich *(Lola Brandt)*, Edmund Burns *(Dale Kynnersly)*, Henry B. Walthall *(Brandt)*, William Platt *(Midget)*, Sultan *(himself, a horse)*.

Melodrama. Source: William John Locke, *Simon the Jester* (New York, 1910). Simon de Gex, a wealthy young member of Parliament wounded in the World War, has been told that he has only a few months to live. He gives a dinner party where he toasts death and gives up his seat and the larger part of his fortune to his friend, Dale Kynnersly, asking Dale to marry a girl in whom he is interested before he—Simon—dies. Dale, however, is infatuated with Lola Brandt, a circus rider whose husband has disappeared. Dale takes Simon to watch her perform and sees her horse, Sultan, mysteriously shot dead. Lola and her friend Midget, a clown, vow revenge. Simon becomes attracted to Lola and goes to Tangiers to find her husband. In a fight he is injured, and he is operated on and told that he will now live. Lola arrives, and Brandt confronts her and threatens to kill her when Simon interferes. Midget recognizes Brandt as the one who shot Sultan and kills him. A crowd attacks Midget, who is fatally wounded. Simon and Lola start life anew. *Veterans. Clowns. Death. Circus. London. Tangiers. Great Britain—Parliament. Horses.*

THE SIMP **F2.5085**

Reol Productions. **1921.** Si; b&w. 35mm. [Feature length assumed.]

Cast: Sherman H. Dudley, Jr., Inez Clough, Edna Morton, Alex K. Shannon, Percy Verwayen.

Melodrama(?). No information about the precise nature of this film has been found. *Negro life.*

SIMPLE SIS **F2.5086**

Warner Brothers Pictures. 11 Jun **1927** [c1 Jun 1927; LP24033]. Si; b&w. 35mm. 7 reels, 6,218 ft.

Dir Herman C. Raymaker. *Screenplay* Albert Kenyon. *Story* Melville Crossman. *Camera* Frank Kesson. *Asst Dir* John Daumery.

Cast: Louise Fazenda *(Sis)*, Clyde Cook *(Jerry O'Grady)*, Myrna Loy *(Edith Van)*, William Demarest *(Oscar)*, Billy Kent Schaeffer *(Buddy)*, Cathleen Calhoun *(Mrs. Brown, Buddy's mother)*.

Comedy-drama. Sis, a laundry worker who longs for romance, is consistently disheartened by her failure to acquire a boyfriend. Edith, pretty and personable, accidentally conceals a summons from her lover in the pocket of Sis's coat, and Sis is cruelly disappointed by the jeering rebuffs of Edith when she hurries to the trysting place. Jerry, a shy truckdriver, saves Sis from an attempt to steal her purse, and Sis persuades him to take her home. She mistakes his shyness for disinterest until he is induced to kiss her at a company dance. When her neighbor dies, Sis takes care of Buddy, an orphaned child, and consequently loses her job; welfare workers claim Buddy after Sis rescues him from a fire, but she is awarded the child in court when Jerry assures the judge that he can support a family of three. *Laundresses. Truckdrivers. Sisters. Orphans. Social workers. Judges. Courtship. Timidity.*

SIN CARGO **F2.5087**

Tiffany Productions. 15 Nov **1926** [c22 Nov 1926; LP23365]. Si; b&w. 35mm. 7 reels, 6,147 ft.

Dir Louis J. Gasnier. *Cont* John F. Natteford. *Photog* Milton Moore, Mack Stengler. *Art Dir* Edwin B. Willis. *Film Ed* Harold Young.

Cast: Shirley Mason *(Eve Gibson)*, Robert Frazer *(Capt. Matt Russell)*, Earl Metcalfe *(Harry Gibson)*, Lawford Davidson *(Jim Darrell)*, Gertrude Astor *(Mary Wickham)*, Pat Harmon *(Captain Barry)*, William Walling *(customs official)*, Billy Cinders *(Cooper)*, James Mack *(butler)*, K. Nambu *(Charlie Wu)*.

Romantic melodrama. Source: Leete Renick Brown, *Sin Cargo*. Harry Gibson, in extreme financial ruin, keeps the fact from his sister, Eve, and attempts to recover their fortune by a nefarious scheme involving pearl smugglers. As captain of his boat, he hires Matt Russell, who falls in love with Eve, who is also pursued by ungentlemanly Jim Darrell. Matt loses his license and is fined when customs officials find some pearls in an Oriental statue he is delivering for Harry. Darrell, threatening to prosecute Harry for nonpayment of a debt, persuades Eve to come to a yacht party; meanwhile, Matt, having been hired by Darrell, saves Eve from his advances, and the crew starts a mutiny. Captain Barry orders their motorboat run down; and to save Eve, Harry blows up the ship, destroying himself along with the villains. *Smugglers. Brother-sister relationship. Injustice. Mutiny. Courtship. Pearls. Customs (tariff).*

THE SIN FLOOD **F2.5088**

Goldwyn Pictures. 12 Nov **1922** [c31 Dec 1921; LP17423]. Si; b&w. 35mm. 7 reels, 6,500 ft.

Dir Frank Lloyd. *Adapt* J. G. Hawks. *Photog* Norbert Brodin. *Asst Dir* Harry Weil.

Cast: Richard Dix *(Billy Bear)*, Helene Chadwick *(Poppy)*, James Kirkwood *(O'Neil)*, John Steppling *(Swift)*, Ralph Lewis *(Frazer)*, Howard Davies *(Sharpe)*, Will Walling *(Stratton)*, William Orlamond *(Nordling)*, Darwin Karr *(Charlie)*, Otto Hoffman *(Higgins)*, L. H. King *(drunk)*.

Drama. Source: Henning Berger, *Syndafloden*. Frank Allen, *The Deluge, a Drama in Three Acts* (adapted from the Scandinavian of Henning Berger; New York, 1935). Stratton's cafe, a popular spot with the people of Cottonia, a wealthy cotton town on the banks of the Mississippi, installs flood-proof doors as a safeguard against an overflow of the river; when a flood comes, it appears that the entire town will be submerged. Trapped in Stratton's cafe are Billy Bear, a young broker, and Poppy, a chorus girl with whom he has been in love. Also there are a street preacher, a tramp, a stranded Swedish engineer, a poor actor, a corporation lawyer, a grasping stockbroker, the bartender, and Stratton, the proprietor. Protected from the sweeping floodwaters, they are secure until the engineer announces that they will suffocate when the air is exhausted. Facing death, all of the characters reform, and uniting in brotherly love they confess their sins and prepare for death. When they decide to admit the floodwaters, they discover that the crest of the flood has passed, and all then revert to their former selfishness—except Billy and Poppy, who are happily married. *Brokers. Chorus girls. Engineers. Lawyers. Actors. Bartenders. Preachers. Tramps. Redemption. Death. Cafes. Mississippi River. Floods.*

THE SIN OF MARTHA QUEED **F2.5089**

Mayflower Photoplay Corp. *Dist* Associated Exhibitors. 6 Oct **1921** [c15 Oct 1921; LU17094]. Si; b&w. 35mm. 6 reels.

Dir-Writ Allan Dwan. *Photog* Tony Gaudio.

Cast: Mary Thurman *(Martha Queed)*, Joseph J. Dowling *(Marvin Queed)*, Eugenie Besserer *(Alicia Queed)*, Frankie Lee *(Georgie Queed)*, Niles Welch *(Arnold Barry)*, George Hackathorne *(Atlas)*, Frank Campeau *(David Boyd)*, Gertrude Claire *(Grandmother)*.

Melodrama. Martha Queed joins her lover, Arnold Barry, who is vacationing in the mountains, and feigns a sprained ankle in order to see the inside of his cabin. The couple are seen by David Boyd, a drunken ruffian and relative of the Queeds, who informs her domineering and puritanical father; and to save her name, the father forces her to marry

Boyd. When Boyd is found dead the following morning, evidence points to Barry as the murderer. Martha disappears and is found ill and delirious in the swamps by Atlas, a deformed boy; hearing that Barry is to be sentenced, Atlas rushes to the courtroom and confesses to the murder, then commits suicide. While Martha is convalescing, she and Barry are married in the presence of her mother, who has left her cruel husband, Marvin. *Fatherhood. Reputation. Murder. Suicide.*

THE SIN SISTER **F2.5090**

Fox Film Corp. 10 Feb **1929** [c5 Feb 1929; LP91]. Si; b&w. 35mm. 7 reels, 6,072 ft. [Also si; 6,050 ft.]

Dir Charles Klein. *Scen* Harry Behn, Andrew Bennison. *Story* Frederick Hazlitt Brennan, Becky Gardiner. *Camera* Charles Clarke, George Eastman.

Cast: Nancy Carroll *(Pearl)*, Lawrence Gray *(Peter Van Dykeman)*, Josephine Dunn *(Ethelyn Horn)*, Myrtle Stedman *(Sister Burton)*, Anders Randolf *(Joseph Horn)*, Richard Alexander *(Bob Newton)*.

Northwest drama. "Ill-assorted companions marooned at a trading post in the north. A small-time vaudeville dancer invades the frozen spaces and meets the son of wealthy family who has been stranded with bad companions." ("Motion Picture Booking Guide," in *Motion Picture News*, 15 Mar 1930, p102.) *Dancers. Vaudeville. Trading posts.*

SIN TAKES A HOLIDAY **F2.5091**

Pathé Exchange. 10 or 20 Nov **1930** [c10 Nov 1930; LP1804]. Sd (Photophone); b&w. 35mm. 8 reels, 7,304 ft.

Prod E. B. Derr. *Dir* Paul Stein. *Screenplay-Dial* Horace Jackson. *Story* Robert Milton, Dorothy Cairns. *Photog* John Mescall. *Art Dir* Carroll Clark. *Film Ed* Daniel Mandell. *Rec Engr* Charles O'Loughlin, L. A. Carman. *Asst Dir* E. J. Babille. *Cost* Gwen Wakeling.

Cast: Constance Bennett *(Sylvia)*, Kenneth MacKenna *(Gaylord Stanton)*, Basil Rathbone *(Durant)*, Rita La Roy *(Grace)*, Louis John Bartels *(Richards)*, John Roche *(Sheridan)*, ZaSu Pitts *(Anna)*, Kendall Lee *(Miss Munson)*, Murrell Finley *(Ruth)*, Helen Johnson *(Miss Graham)*, Fred Walton *(butler)*.

Domestic drama. Divorce lawyer Gaylord Stanton, who leads a very active social life, has an affair with Grace Lanier, whose third husband is currently suing her for a divorce and has named Gaylord as corespondent. Annoyed at her flippant attitude, Gaylord proposes marriage to his secretary, Sylvia, under an arrangement whereby she is allowed to live wherever she likes. On her trip to Paris, suggested by Gaylord, she meets Durant, who persuades her to live in his villa near Paris and takes her to the beauty and modiste shops of the capital. Meanwhile, Gaylord tells Grace of his marriage, claiming his wife is an invalid confined to a sanitarium. Durant begs Sylvia to get a divorce and marry him; and disconcerted, she returns to Gaylord, whom she loves. Although she comes into conflict with Grace, Sylvia finds that he really does love her. *Secretaries. Lawyers. Marriage. Divorce. Courtship. Ocean liners. Paris.*

SIN TOWN **F2.5092**

De Mille Pictures. *Dist* Pathé Exchange. 20 Jan **1929** [c4 Feb 1929; LP113]. Si; b&w. 35mm. 5 reels, 4,554 ft.

Dir J. Gordon Cooper. *Story-Scen* J. Gordon Cooper, William K. Howard. *Photog* Harold Stein. *Asst Dir* Frank Geraghty.

Cast: Elinor Fair *(Mary Barton)*, Ivan Lebedeff *(Pete Laguerro)*, Hugh Allan *("Silk" Merrick)*, Jack Oakie *("Chicken" O'Toole)*, Robert Perry *("Slippery" Simpson)*.

Western melodrama. After demobilization, Silk Merrick and Chicken O'Toole go west and find work on an Arizona ranch. Fired from their jobs for laziness, they are caught by Mary Barton attempting to steal one of her chickens. Mary's father is killed by Pete Laguerro, the vice lord of Sin Town, and Silk and Chicken are arrested for the crime. Silk escapes from jail and joins a band of ranchers who are determined to burn Sin Town to the ground. Silk frees Chicken from jail and captures Laguerro. The boys then settle down with Mary, punching her cows and helping with odd jobs around the house. *Veterans. Ranchers. Cowboys. Jailbreaks. Arizona. Chickens.*

SINEWS OF STEEL **F2.5093**

Gotham Productions. *Dist* Lumas Film Corp. 4 Apr **1927** [c6 May 1927; LP23934]. Si; b&w. 35mm. 6 reels, 5,765 ft.

Pres by Sam Sax. *Supv* Glenn Belt. *Dir* Frank O'Connor. *Scen* Henry McCarthy. *Titl* Delos Sutherland. *Story* Herbert C. Clark. *Photog* Ray June. *Film Ed* Edith Wakeling.

Cast: Alberta Vaughn *(Helen Blake)*, Gaston Glass *(Robert McNeil, Jr.)*, Anders Randolf *(Robert McNeil, Sr.)*, Paul Weigel *(Jan Van Der Vetter)*, Greta von Rue *(Elsie Graham)*, Nora Hayden *(Martha Jenkins)*, Charles Wellesley *(Douglas Graham)*, John H. Gardener *(Elmer Price)*, Bobby Gordon *(The Office Boy)*.

Drama. Robert McNeil, Sr., the ruthless and efficient head of Consolidated Steel, is temperamentally opposed to his son, leader of a jazz orchestra and full of life. In a stormy interview, McNeil, Sr., tells his son, who objects to his business tactics, that "all is fair in love, war, and the steel business." En route to a lawn party given by Elsie Graham, daughter of one of McNeil's business associates, McNeil, Jr., aids Helen Blake, owner of a rival mill, in quelling an incipient strike and falls in love with her. Unaware of his identity, she offers him a job as superintendent of her plant, arousing the enmity of Price, who has designs on Helen. McNeil, Sr., tries to crush the rival firm. To prove his loyalty, Robert outwits his father in buying Van Der Vetter's steel process and consequently is denounced by his father. McNeil, Sr., relents, however, when the young couple are united, bringing about a combination of interests. *Orchestra conductors. Inventors. Business competition. Steel industry. Filial relations.*

Note: Copyright records incorrectly render Henry McCarthy as McCarty and credit him with the story.

THE SINGAPORE MUTINY **F2.5094**

FBO Pictures. 7 Oct **1928** [c7 Oct 1928; LP25776]. Si; b&w. 35mm. 7 reels, 6,812 ft.

Dir Ralph Ince. *Scen* Fred Myton. *Titl* Ralph Ince, Norman Springer. *Story* Norman Springer. *Photog* J. O. Taylor. *Film Ed* George M. Arthur. *Asst Dir* Thomas Atkins.

Cast: Ralph Ince *(Kelsey)*, Estelle Taylor *(Daisy)*, James Mason *(Borg)*, Gardner James *("The Stiff")*, William Irving *(Huber)*, Harry Allen *(Mrs. Watts)*, Carl Axzelle *(Cockney)*, Martha Mattox *(Mrs. Watts)*, Robert Gaillard *(captain)*, Frank Newberg *(petty officer)*.

Melodrama. Kelsey, chief of the black gang on a tramp steamer, continually insults Daisy Martin, a Broadway jade sailing to find refuge on a Pacific isle. The ship strikes a derelict and sinks; only three of those on board are saved: the stoker, the hooker, and a stowaway. The castaways soon run out of water, and Kelsey drowns himself in order that the other two may survive. *Stokers. Prostitutes. Stowaways. Self-sacrifice. Shipwrecks.*

SINGED **F2.5095**

Fox Film Corp. 9 Jul **1927** [New York premiere; released 23 Aug; c17 Jul 1927; LP24219]. Si; b&w. 35mm. 6 reels, 5,790 ft.

Pres by William Fox. *Dir* John Griffith Wray. *Scen* Gertrude Orr. *Photog* Charles Clarke. *Asst Dir* Buddy Erickson.

Cast: Blanche Sweet *(Dolly Wall)*, Warner Baxter *(Royce Wingate)*, James Wang *(Wong)*, Alfred Allen *(Jim)*, Clark Comstock *(Wes Adams)*, Howard Truesdale *(Indian agent)*, Claude King *(Ben Grimes)*, Ida Darling *(Mrs. Eleanor Cardigan)*, Mary McAllister *(Amy Cardigan)*, Edwards Davis *(Howard Halliday)*, Edgar Norton *(Ernie Whitehead)*.

Society melodrama. Source: Adela Rogers St. Johns, "Love o' Women," in *Hearst's International Cosmopolitan* (80:72–75, Feb 1926). Dolly, a dancehall girl, loves Royce Wingate, an irresponsible chap. To escape their way of life she secretly backs an oil well in which he has an interest, and both become wealthy. In New York, Royce becomes a financial power on Wall Street but is socially frowned upon because of his association with the notorious Dolly. When he plans to marry Amy, a young society belle, Dolly becomes violently jealous and threatens to throw acid in his face; he shoots at the bottle and accidentally hits Dolly, thinking he has killed her. She recovers, however, and they are happily reconciled. *Dancehall girls. Financiers. Wealth. Jealousy. Oil wells.*

SINGED WINGS **F2.5096**

Famous Players–Lasky. *Dist* Paramount Pictures. 26 Nov **1922** [New York and Philadelphia premieres; released 18 Dec 1922; c25 Nov 1922; LP18458]. Si; b&w. 35mm. 8 reels, 7,788 ft.

Pres by Adolph Zukor. *Dir* Penrhyn Stanlaws. *Adapt* Ewart Adamson, Edfrid A. Bingham. *Photog* Paul Perry.

Cast: Bebe Daniels *(Bonita della Guerda)*, Conrad Nagel *(Peter Gordon)*, Adolphe Menjou *(Bliss Gordon)*, Robert Brower *(Don José della Guerda)*, Ernest Torrence *(Emilio, a clown)*, Mabel Trunnelle *(Eve Gordon)*.

Melodrama. Source: Katharine Newlin Burt, "Singed Wings" (publication undetermined). Spanish dancer Bonita della Guerda has a dream in which she is killed by a jester after declaring her love for a prince. Because she fears the dream will come true, she dares not reveal her love for Peter

Gordon, whose uncle, Bliss Gordon, also shows her considerable attention. Bonita's relationship with Bliss is misunderstood by both Peter and her longtime protector, Emilio. In his jealousy the latter shoots Bliss's wife, Eve, who is performing Bonita's dance in hopes of recapturing her husband's love. Bonita no longer fears her dream and is united with Peter. *Dancers. Jealousy. Dreams. Pierrot. Columbine.*

SINGER JIM McKEE **F2.5097**

William S. Hart Co. *Dist* Paramount Pictures. 3 Mar **1924** [c11 Feb 1924; LP19909]. Si; b&w. 35mm. 7 reels, 7,098 ft. [Also 6,900 ft.]

Pres by Adolph Zukor, Jesse L. Lasky. *Dir* Clifford S. Smith. *Scen* J. G. Hawks. *Story* William S. Hart. *Photog* Dwight Warren. *Ed* William Shea.

Cast: William S. Hart *("Singer" Jim McKee)*, Phyllis Haver *(Mary Holden)*, Gordon Russell *(Buck Holden)*, Bert Sprotte *(Dan Gleason)*, Patsy Ruth Miller *(Betty Gleason)*, Edward Coxen *(Hamlin Glass, Jr.)*, William Dyer *(Hamlin Glass)*, George Siegmann *("Brute" Bernstein)*, Baby Turner *(Mary Holden, as a baby)*.

Western melodrama. Unsuccessful miners Jim McKee and Buck Holden disguise themselves as bandits and hold up a stagecoach to provide money for the support of Buck's motherless daughter, Mary. The sheriff kills Buck while McKee escapes with Mary. Fifteen years later McKee dons the bandit's costume again and robs a motor coach to provide new frocks for the 17-year-old Mary, who is ashamed of her old-fashioned clothes. The theft is traced through the serial numbers on the stolen bills, and McKee is caught and sent to jail. On his release from prison, McKee returns to the hills; and there Mary, realizing she loves him, goes to find him. *Miners. Orphans. Criminals—Rehabilitation. Disguise. Stagecoach robberies.*

THE SINGER OF SEVILLE *see* **CALL OF THE FLESH**

THE SINGING FOOL **F2.5098**

Warner Brothers Pictures. 29 Sep **1928** [c19 Sep 1928; LP25677]. Sd (Vitaphone); b&w. 35mm. 11 reels, 9,557 ft. [Also si, 1 Jan 1929; 7,444 ft.]

Dir Lloyd Bacon. *Scen* C. Graham Baker. *Dial-Titl* Joseph Jackson. *Photog* Byron Haskin. *Film Ed* Ralph Dawson, Harold McCord. *Songs: "Sonny Boy," "It All Depends on You," "I'm Sittin' on Top of the World"* Lew Brown, B. G. De Sylva, Ray Henderson. *Songs: "There's a Rainbow Round My Shoulder," "Keep Smiling at Trouble," "Golden Gate," "Spaniard Who Blighted My Life"* Billy Rose, Al Jolson, Dave Dreyer. *Mus Arr* Louis Silvers. *Rec Engr* George R. Groves. *Asst Dir* Frank Shaw.

Cast: Al Jolson *(Al Stone)*, Betty Bronson *(Grace)*, Josephine Dunn *(Molly Winton)*, Arthur Housman *(Blackie Joe)*, Reed Howes *(John Perry)*, Davey Lee *(Sonny Boy)*, Edward Martindel *(Louis Marcus)*, Robert Emmett O'Connor *(cafe manager)*, Helen Lynch.

Musical drama. Source: Leslie S. Barrows, "The Singing Fool" (publication undetermined). Al Stone, a singing waiter at Blackie Joe's cafe, writes a hit song and becomes a Broadway star, marrying Molly Winton, an ambitious, underhanded soubrette. Molly eventually leaves Al and goes off with John Perry, a racketeer, taking their young son with her. Al becomes a derelict and sometime later returns to Blackie Joe's, where Grace, the loyal cigarette girl, inspires him to make a comeback. Al's son dies in a hospital, and Al, going on stage like a trouper, sings the boy's favorite song. The pain caused by his son's death is dulled with the passage of time, and he goes to California with Grace. *Waiters. Singers. Racketeers. Cigarette girls. Fatherhood. New York City—Broadway. California.*

SINGING RIVER **F2.5099**

Fox Film Corp. 21 Aug **1921** [c21 Aug 1921; LP16922]. Si; b&w. 35mm. 5 reels.

Pres by William Fox. *Dir* Charles Giblyn. *Scen* Jules Furthman. *Story* Robert J. Horton. *Photog* George Schneiderman.

Cast: William Russell *(Lang Rush)*, Vola Vale *(Alice Thornton)*, Clark Comstock *(John Thornton)*, Jack Roseleigh *(Lew Bransom)*, Arthur Morrison *(Sam Hemp)*, Jack McDonald *(Bert Condon)*, Jack Hull *(Freud)*, Louis King *(Kane)*, Charles L. King *(Grimes)*.

Western melodrama. Homesteader Lang Rush is threatened with ruin by a drought and fears a mortgage foreclosure on a note held by Ferguson, a banker. Sam Hemp, advising him that Ferguson plans to foreclose, suggests that he rob the bank, and in a gunfight Lang shoots Hemp and his friend Drayton. He flees to the mountains and takes refuge in a deserted shack near Singing River, where he prospects for silver. Condon, a former homesteader who tracks him down for a reward, befriends him instead and helps Lang file his claim when he strikes ore. In the town, Lang rescues Alice Thornton, the sheriff's daughter, from Hemp's gang and thrashes their leader, Bransom. He clears himself of the murder charge and wins Alice. *Prospectors. Homesteaders. Drought. Mortgages. Mine claims.*

SINGLE HANDED **F2.5100**

Universal Pictures. caII Mar **1923** [Cleveland premiere; released 25 Mar; c28 Feb 1923; LP18743]. Si; b&w. 35mm. 5 reels, 4,225 ft.

Dir-Story Edward Sedgwick. *Scen* George C. Hull. *Photog* Virgil Miller.

Cast: Hoot Gibson *(Hector MacKnight)*, Elinor Field *(Ruth Randolph)*, Percy Challenger *(Professor Weighoff)*, William Steele *(Windy Smith)*, Philip Sleeman *(Gypsy Joe)*, Dick La Reno *(Sheriff Simpel)*, Mack V. Wright *(Milo)*, Tom McGuire *(Macklin)*, Gordon McGregor *(The Boss)*, W. T. McCulley *(ringmaster)*, C. B. Murphy *(foreman)*, Bob McKenzie *(manager)*, Sidney De Grey *(rancher)*.

Rural comedy. Hector MacKnight, known to the townspeople as "Goofy" and an irritatingly terrible fiddler, is innocently drawn into a rigged poker game. A general fight brings the sheriff, and a chase ensues. Before the confusion is ended and Hector cleared, he meets Ruth Randolph and becomes involved in a circus while trying to recover the other half of her treasure map. Although the treasure proves to be nothing more than a prehistoric jawbone, Hector receives a reward for capturing the crooks that enables him to marry Ruth. *Violinists. Circus. Gambling. Fossils. Prehistory. Kansas.*

Note: Working title: *Heads Up.*

A SINGLE MAN **F2.5101**

Metro-Goldwyn-Mayer Pictures. 12 Jan **1929** [c12 Jan 1929; LP16]. Si; b&w. 35mm. 7 reels, 5,596 ft.

Dir Harry Beaumont. *Screenplay* F. Hugh Herbert, George O'Hara. *Titl* Joe Farnham, Lucille Newmark. *Photog* André Barlatier. *Sets* Cedric Gibbons. *Film Ed* Ben Lewis. *Gowns* Adrian.

Cast: Lew Cody *(Robin Worthington)*, Aileen Pringle *(Mary Hazeltine)*, Marceline Day *(Maggie)*, Edward Nugent *(Dickie)*, Kathlyn Williams *(Mrs. Cottrell)*, Aileen Manning *(Mrs. Farley)*.

Comedy. Source: Hubert Henry Davies, *A Single Man, New and Original Comedy in Four Acts* (Boston, 1914). Robin Worthington, a middle-aged man attracted by a young woman, at first avoids, then falls for, her. He undergoes a profound change in temperament, but in the end he marries another girl, Mary Hazeltine, his secretary, who had gone away and come back in the best frock creation. This dress so changes her appearance that he cannot believe his eyes. *Secretaries. Bachelors. Middle age. Clothes.*

SINGLE SHOT PARKER (Reissue) **F2.5102**

Dist Exclusive Features. 27 Sep **1923** [New York State license]. Si; b&w. 35mm.

Note: Originally released as *The Heart of Texas Ryan* (Selig, 1917).

THE SINGLE STANDARD **F2.5103**

Metro-Goldwyn-Mayer Pictures. 29 Jul **1929** [c12 Aug, 3 Sep 1929; LP592, LP804]. Mus score & sd eff (Movietone); b&w. 35mm. 8 reels, 6,574 ft. [Also si; 6,474 ft.]

Dir John S. Robertson. *Scen* Josephine Lovett. *Titl* Marian Ainslee. *Photog* Oliver Marsh. *Art Dir* Cedric Gibbons. *Film Ed* Blanche Sewell. *Mus Score* William Axt. *Gowns* Adrian.

Cast: Greta Garbo *(Arden Stuart)*, Nils Asther *(Packy Cannon)*, John Mack Brown *(Tommy Hewlett)*, Dorothy Sebastian *(Mercedes)*, Lane Chandler *(Ding Stuart)*, Robert Castle *(Anthony Kendall)*, Mahlon Hamilton *(Mr. Glendening)*, Kathlyn Williams *(Mrs. Glendenning)*, Zeffie Tilbury *(Mrs. Handley)*.

Romantic drama. Source: Adela Rogers St. Johns, *The Single Standard* (New York, 1928). Arden Stuart maintains that the set of moral principles applying differently to the sexes should be altered in favor of a single standard of conduct applying equally to men and women. She refuses to take seriously the marriage proposal of Tommy Hewlett, of her own social set, and steps out with Kendall, the handsome family chauffeur; but Kendall commits suicide in despair. Then she meets Packy Cannon, an ex-prizefighter turned artist, and takes him on her yacht to the South Seas, where their romance develops over a period of months; but when Packy fears she is interfering with his creativity, she returns home and marries Hewlett. After the birth of their child, Packy returns, realizing that his love for her is stronger than his devotion to his art. Arden plans to leave with him, but her love for the child persuades her to remain with her husband. *Feminists. Artists. Chauffeurs. Double standard. Social classes. Marriage. South Seas.*

THE SINGLE TRACK **F2.5104**

Vitagraph Co. of America. 13 Nov **1921** [c5 Oct 1921; LP17039]. Si; b&w. 35mm. 5 reels.

Dir Webster Campbell. *Scen* C. Graham Baker, Harry Dittmar. *Story* Douglas Grant. *Photog* Charles Davis.

Cast: Corinne Griffith *(Janetta Gildersleeve)*, Richard Travers *(Barney Hoyt)*, Charles Kent *(Andrew Geddes)*, Sidney Herbert *(Peddar)*, Jessie Stevens *(Ma Heaney)*, Edward Norton *(Roland Winfield)*, Matthew Betts *(Mallison)*, Fuller Mellish *(Jud Pettinger)*.

Melodrama. Society heiress Janetta Gildersleeve, who is under the guardianship of her Uncle Andrew, meets financier Roland Winfield, a former enemy of her father, at a dance. Driving to another party, she strikes a tramp on the roadside and is severely lectured by Barney Hoyt, who stops to give assistance. The next day, her uncle informs her that her father's holdings are worthless with the exception of the North Star Copper Mine and that a single-track railroad must be built if the mine is to become productive. Janetta goes to the region and, concealing her identity, takes a job as clerk in the local general store. The Winfields, owners of a rival mine, attempt to frustrate her rights to option, but with the aid of Hoyt, who does not suspect her identity, she finishes the railroad and foils Winfield's plot to dynamite the track bridge. She reveals herself to Hoyt, and they become romantically attached. *Socialites. Financiers. Salesclerks. Mining. Copper. Railroads. Disguise.*

SINGLE WIVES **F2.5105**

Corinne Griffith Productions. *Dist* Associated First National Pictures. 27 Jul **1924** [c21 Jul 1924; LP20403, LP20482]. Si; b&w. 35mm. 8 reels, 7,526 ft.

Supv-Story Earl Hudson. *Dir* George Archainbaud. *Ed Dir* Marion Fairfax. *Scen* Marion Orth. *Photog* James C. Van Trees, Ned Connors. *Architecture* Milton Menasco. *Film Ed* Arthur Tavares.

Cast: Corinne Griffith *(Betty Jordan)*, Milton Sills *(Perry Jordan)*, Kathlyn Williams *(Dorothy Van Clark)*, Phyllis Haver *(Marion Eldridge)*, Phillips Smalley *(Tom Van Clark)*, Jere Austin *(Dr. Walter Lane)*, Lou Tellegen *(Martin Prayle)*, Henry B. Walthall *(Franklin Dexter)*, John Patrick *(Billy Eldridge)*.

Drama. On her first wedding anniversary Betty Jordan perceives her husband's indifference and indulges in a mild flirtation with an old admirer, Martin Prayle. She resolves to divorce her husband, but when he is badly injured their happiness is restored. *Flirtation. Marriage. Wedding anniversaries. Divorce.*

SINNER OR SAINT **F2.5106**

B. B. Productions. *Dist* Selznick Distributing Corp. 2 Jul **1923** [New York State license application; c1 Aug 1923; LP19278]. Si; b&w. 35mm. 6 reels, 5,388 ft.

Dir Lawrence Windom. *Scen* Dorothy Farnum. *Photog* Edward Paul.

Cast: Betty Blythe *(Mademoiselle Iris)*, William P. Carleton *(Paul Reynolds)*, Gypsy O'Brien *(Marguerite Roberts)*, William H. Tooker *(Stephen Roberts)*, Fuller Mellish *(Elijah Homes)*, Richard Neill *(Charles Carter)*, William Collier, Jr. *(young artist)*, Frances Miller Grant, Horace Braham.

Melodrama. Source: Dorothy Farnum, "The Man Who Wouldn't Love" (publication undetermined). Paul Reynolds, a reformer who heads the Welfare Foundation, exposes Mademoiselle Iris, an attractive young fortune-teller of dubious reputation, to the newspapers, thus ruining her business. Carter, her manager, urges her to appeal to Reynolds to retract his statement, but she refuses. Stephen Roberts, a prominent senator of great wealth, reveals to her that she is his long-lost daughter by his first wife, but he is reluctant to take her into his home because she might be a bad influence on his other daughter, Marguerite, who is Reynolds' fiancée. Instead, he offers, and Iris accepts, his protection. Reynolds gets the wrong idea and believes that she has become Roberts' mistress. Carter attacks Iris and is wounded by a gunshot. Reynolds takes the blame, but Roberts bribes Carter to sign a statement that the shooting was accidental. Iris is reunited with her father and half sister and is free to marry Reynolds. *Fortune-tellers. Sisters. Reformers. Fatherhood. Reputation. Newspapers.*

SINNER'S HOLIDAY **F2.5107**

Warner Brothers Pictures. 11 Oct **1930** [c19 Sep 1930; LP1583]. Sd (Vitaphone); b&w. 35mm. 7 reels, 5,536 ft.

Dir John G. Adolfi. *Screenplay-Dial* Harvey Thew. *Photog* Ira Morgan. *Film Ed* James Gribbon.

Cast: Grant Withers *(Angel Harrigan)*, Evelyn Knapp *(Jennie)*, James Cagney *(Harry)*, Lucille La Verne *(Ma Delano)*, Noel Madison *(Buck)*, Otto Hoffman *(George)*, Warren Hymer *(Mitch)*, Ray Gallagher *(Joe)*, Joan Blondell *(Myrtle)*, Hank Mann *(Happy)*, Purnell B. Pratt *(Sykes)*.

Crime melodrama. Source: Marie Baumer, *Penny Arcade* (New York opening: 10 Mar 1930). Ma Delano and her family—Jennie, Joe, and Harry—operate a penny arcade on an amusement pier over which Mitch, a bootlegger doubling as a sideshow operator, wields an influential hand. Angel Harrigan, a barker who works for Mitch, incurs his wrath when he thwarts Mitch's flirtation with Jennie. Harry, the youngest of the family, becomes involved in Mitch's bootlegging operation, and when his superior is picked up on suspicion by the police, Harry takes over the speakeasy business and with Feretti, the bartender, pockets the proceeds. Mitch is unexpectedly released and, discovering Harry's treachery, plans to "get" him, but in their encounter on the darkened pier, Harry shoots him. Harry confesses to his mother, and when she replaces the gun in Angel's valise, suspicion falls on the barker. But Jennie, who witnessed the shooting, breaks down and describes the murder, accusing her brother, who confesses. *Barkers. Bootleggers. Brother-sister relationship. Motherhood. Sideshows. Speakeasies. Amusement parks. Penny arcades.*

Note: Also reviewed as *Women in Love.*

SINNERS IN HEAVEN **F2.5108**

Famous Players–Lasky. *Dist* Paramount Pictures. 15 Sep **1924** [c26 Sep 1924; LP20598]. Si; b&w. 35mm. 7 reels, 6,881 ft.

Pres by Adolph Zukor, Jesse L. Lasky. *Dir* Alan Crosland. *Scen* James Ashmore Creelman. *Photog* Henry Cronjager.

Cast: Bebe Daniels *(Barbara Stockley)*, Richard Dix *(Alan Croft)*, Holmes Herbert *(Hugh Rochedale)*, Florence Billings *(Mrs. Madge Fields)*, Betty Hilburn *(native girl)*, Montagu Love *(native chief)*, Effie Shannon *(Mrs. Stockley)*, Marcia Harris *(Barbara's aunt)*.

Romantic drama. Source: Clive Arden, *Sinners in Heaven* (Indianapolis, 1923). Young aviator Alan Croft and a girl from a strict English background are stranded on a cannibal island when their plane crashes on the way to Australia. The natives worship them, believing them to be gods, until a native girl discovers that the pilot is mortal. Giving up hope of rescue, they marry in the sight of God, but when they are found by a search plane Alan is wounded and left for dead. Barbara is spurned by her friends and family as having sinned, but Alan returns to claim her legally. *Aviators. Cannibals. Religion. South Sea Islands.*

SINNERS IN LOVE **F2.5109**

FBO Pictures. 4 Nov **1928** [c4 Nov 1928; LP25847]. Si; b&w. 35mm. 6 reels, 6,310 ft.

Pres by William Le Baron. *Dir* George Melford. *Scen* J. Clarkson Miller. *Titl* Randolph Bartlett. *Photog* Paul Perry. *Film Ed* Archie Marshek. *Asst Dir* James Dugan. *Cost* Walter Pulunkett.

Cast: Olive Borden *(Ann Hardy)*, Huntley Gordon *(Ted Wells)*, Seena Owen *(Yvonne D'Orsy)*, Ernest Hilliard *(Silk Oliver)*, Daphne Pollard *(Mabel)*, Phillips Smalley *(Spencer)*.

Melodrama. Fleeing the hard, drab life of a sordid mill town, Ann Hardy goes to New York and becomes a hostess in a gambling club run by Ted Wells, where, unknowingly, she comes to play an important part in cheating rich customers at roulette. Ann later discovers that Ted is dishonest and quits her job; Ted quickly finds her and, having fallen in love with the innocent girl, vows to quit gambling if she will marry him. Yvonne D'Orsy, Ted's former mistress, then jealously arranges for Ann to go to the apartment of Silk Oliver, a notorious womanizer; Oliver attacks her, and Ann kills him in self-defense. Tom straightens things out, however, and the two leave the gaudy night life of New York, looking for a fresh start in life. *Gamblers. Mistresses. Nightclub hostesses. Mills. Smalltown life. Manslaughter. New York City.*

SINNERS IN SILK **F2.5110**

Metro-Goldwyn-Mayer Corp. *Dist* Metro-Goldwyn Distributing Corp. 1 Sep **1924** [c16 Sep 1924; LP20688]. Si; b&w. 35mm. 6 reels, 5,750 ft.

Pres by Louis B. Mayer. *Dir* Hobart Henley. *Scen* Carey Wilson. *Story* Benjamin Glazer. *Photog* John Arnold. *Art Dir* Richard Day. *Film Ed* Frank Davis.

Cast: Adolphe Menjou *(Arthur Merrill)*, Eleanor Boardman *(Penelope Stevens)*, Conrad Nagel *(Brock Farley)*, Jean Hersholt *(Dr. Eustace)*, Edward Connelly *(Bates)*, Jerome Patrick *(Jerry Hall)*, John Patrick *(Bowers)*, Hedda Hopper *(Mrs. Stevens)*, Miss Du Pont *(Ynez)*, Virginia Lee Corbin *(flapper)*, Bradley Ward *(Ted)*, Dorothy Dwan *(Rita)*, Frank Elliott *(Sir Donald Ramsey)*, Ann Luther *(Mimi)*, Peggy Elinor *(Estelle)*, Eugenie Gilbert *(Chérie)*, Mary Akin *(Peggy)*, Estelle Clark *(Carmelita)*.

Romantic drama. "This is a contribution to the new school of film play, a picturization of the activities of 'The New Generation' whose hymn is jazz, whose slogan is speed. This feature throws into relief the things for which our flappers and lounge lizards are criticized, even indulging in a discussion of 'free love.'" *(Motion Picture News*, 30 Aug 1924, p1173.) Aging roué Arthur Merrill meets flapper Penelope Stevens on an ocean liner and decides to undergo rejuvenation surgery so that he may enjoy life again. Transformed, he attends a wild jazz party given by Penelope and persuades her to visit his apartment, but he finds that she is a "good girl" and only flirting. After he gives Penelope a scare and a lecture, her old beau, Brock Farley, enters with a letter to Arthur that reveals Brock to be his son. Arthur gladly steps aside, renounces his wild living, and returns to a simple life. *Rakes. Flappers. Surgeons. Jazz life. Free love. Rejuvenation.*

SINNER'S PARADE **F2.5111**

Columbia Pictures. 14 Sep **1928** [c8 Oct 1928; LP25693]. Si; b&w. 35mm. 6 reels, 5,616 ft.

Prod Harry Cohn. *Dir* John G. Adolfi. *Adapt-Cont* Beatrice Van. *Story* David Lewis. *Camera* James Van Trees. *Art Dir* Harrison Wiley. *Film Ed* Ben Pivar. *Asst Dir* Eugene De Rue.

Cast: Victor Varconi *(Al Morton)*, Dorothy Revier *(Mary Tracy)*, John Patrick *(Bill Adams)*, Edna Marion *(Connie Adams)*, Marjorie Bonner *(Sadie)*, Clarissa Selwynne *(Mrs. Adams)*, Jack Mower *(chauffeur)*.

Melodrama. In order to support her sister and her sister's small child, Mary Tracy leads a double life: by day, she works as a schoolteacher; nights, she dances in a cabaret show. Mary becomes interested in Bill Adams, whose mother is prominent in an anti-vice crusade, and therefore attempts to quit her job in the cabaret. Al Morton, the club's owner, holds her to her contract, however, and Mary is caught up in a police raid on the cabaret. The club is shut down, and Mary is fired from her teaching post. Morton threatens to expose Bill (who is running a crime syndicate with money embezzled from his father's bank), and Bill sets out to take Morton for a ride. Finally realizing that she has fallen in love with Morton, Mary calls the cops and saves him from certain death. Bill is arrested, and Mary and Morton decide to get married. *Sisters. Dancers. Schoolteachers. Police. Reformers. Embezzlement. Cabarets.*

SINS OF THE CHILDREN **F2.5112**

Cosmopolitan Productions. *Dist* Metro-Goldwyn-Mayer Distributing Corp. 28 Jun **1930** [c23 Jun 1930; LP1374]. Sd (Movietone); b&w. 35mm. 9 reels, 7,775 ft. [Also si.]

Dir Sam Wood. *Dial* Elliott Nugent, Clara Lipman. *Titl* Leslie F. Wilder. *Adapt* Samuel Ornitz. *Photog* Henry Sharp. *Art Dir* Cedric Gibbons. *Film Ed* Frank Sullivan, Leslie F. Wilder. *Rec Engr* Douglas Shearer. *Wardrobe* David Cox.

Cast: Louis Mann *(Adolf)*, Robert Montgomery *(Nick Higginson)*, Elliott Nugent *(Johnnie)*, Leila Hyams *(Alma)*, Clara Blandick *(Martha Wagenkampf)*, Mary Doran *(Laura)*, Francis X. Bushman, Jr. *(Ludwig)*, Robert McWade *(Joe Higginson)*, Dell Henderson *(Ted Baldwin)*, Henry Armetta *(Tony)*, Jane Reid *(Katherine)*, James Donlan *(Bide Taylor)*, Jeane Wood *(Muriel Stokes)*, Lee Kohlmar *(Dr. Heinrich Schmidt)*.

Drama. Source: J. C. Nugent and Elliott Nugent, "Father's Day" (publication undetermined). Adolf, a German-American barber, is about to invest his savings in a building and loan association in the growing town in which he lives; instead, he sends one of his beloved children, in poor health, to a sanatorium, and his friend Joe Higginson becomes powerful in the growing community, while he remains a barber. As the children grow up, Adolf sacrifices to provide his son, Ludwig, with a medical education and later mortgages the shop to set him up in a local office. Johnnie becomes a collector for an electrical company, and his father gives up the last of his savings to cover a shortage in collections; unable to continue his employment there, Johnnie disappears. Alma falls in love with Higginson's ne'er-do-well son, Nick, who compromises her, then refuses to marry her because of their social inequality. In consequence, Adolf denounces his former friend. On Christmas Eve, having seen the mortgage foreclosed on his shop, he is reunited with all his children, including Johnnie, who finally has met success as an inventor. *Barbers. Social classes. Physicians. Germans. Family life. Sanitariums. Fatherhood. Self-sacrifice. Christmas.*

Note: Originally released and reviewed under the title: *The Richest Man in the World*.

SINS OF THE FATHERS **F2.5113**

Paramount Famous Lasky Corp. 29 Dec **1928** [c28 Dec 1928; LP25953]. Singing sequence, sd eff, & mus score (Movietone); b&w. 35mm. 10 reels, 7,845 ft. [Also si; 7,724 ft.]

Dir Ludwig Berger. *Adapt-Cont* E. Lloyd Sheldon. *Titl* Julian Johnson. *Story* Norman Burnstine. *Photog* Victor Milner. *Film Ed* Frances Marsh. *Mus Score* Hugo Riesenfeld.

Cast: Emil Jannings *(Wilhelm Spengler)*, Ruth Chatterton *(Gretta)*, Barry Norton *(Tom Spengler)*, Jean Arthur *(Mary Spengler)*, Jack Luden *(Otto)*, ZaSu Pitts *(Mother Spengler)*, Matthew Betz *(Gus)*, Harry Cording *(The Hijacker)*, Arthur Housman *(The Count)*, Frank Reicher *(The Eye Specialist)*, Douglas Haig *(Tom, as a boy)*, Dawn O'Day *(Mary, as a girl)*.

Drama. Wilhelm Spengler, a German-American restaurateur, falls for Gretta, an unprincipled adventuress, and Wilhelm's wife, sick from overwork, dies of a broken heart. With the advent of prohibition, Gretta persuades Wilhelm to become a bootlegger, and he amasses a fortune, sending his son, Tom, to the best schools. Upon graduation from college, Tom, who celebrates by getting drunk, goes blind drinking his father's bootleg hootch. Wilhelm is arrested in a raid, and Gretta runs off with his money and another man. His fortune gone, his son blind, and himself serving a prison term, Wilhelm's spirit is broken. He wins an early release for good behavior and becomes a waiter in a beer garden. One day he comes across his son, cured of blindness, and they are happily reunited. *Germans. Restaurateurs. Bootleggers. Adventuresses. Waiters. Fatherhood. Blindness. Infidelity. Beer gardens.*

SIOUX BLOOD **F2.5114**

Metro-Goldwyn-Mayer Pictures. 20 Apr **1929** [c5 Mar 1929; LP185]. Si; b&w. 35mm. 6 reels, 4,811 ft.

Dir John Waters. *Scen* George C. Hull. *Titl* Lucille Newmark. *Adapt* Houston Branch. *Story* Harry Sinclair Drago. *Photog* Arthur Reed. *Film Ed* William Le Vanway. *Wardrobe* Lucia Coulter.

Cast: Tim McCoy *(Flood)*, Robert Frazer *(Lone Eagle)*, Marian Douglas *(Barbara Ingram)*, Clarence Geldert *(Miles Ingram)*, Chief Big Tree *(Crazy Wolf)*, Sidney Bracy *(Cheyenne Jones)*.

Western melodrama. Two brothers are separated during an Indian uprising; one is reared by whites, the other by Indians. Years pass. One of the brothers, Flood, becomes a scout who is known as the scourge of the redskins; the other, known as Lone Eagle, becomes the meanest foe of the white man. Flood befriends Miles Ingram and his daughter, Barbara. Miles is captured by the Indians, and Barbara and Flood give themselves up to the Indians in return for the release of the elder Ingram. Flood fights with Lone Eagle, and they recognize each other. Flood, Lone Eagle, and Barbara then escape from the Indians and make their way back to freedom and the white world. *Brothers. Sioux Indians. Scouts—Frontier. Abduction.*

SIR LUMBERJACK **F2.5115**

R-C Pictures. *Dist* Film Booking Offices of America. 11 Apr **1926** [c25 Feb 1926; LP22533]. Si; b&w. 35mm. 6 reels, 5,146 ft.

Dir Harry Garson. *Story-Scen* Victor Gibson. *Photog* L. William O'Connell. *Asst Dir* Joe O'Brien.

Cast: Lefty Flynn *(William Barlow, Jr.)*, Kathleen Myers *(Bess Calhoun)*, Tom Kennedy *(Bill Blake)*, William Walling *(William Barlow, Sr.)*, Luke Cosgrave *(John Calhoun)*, Bill Nestel *(Lars Hanson)*, Ray Hanford *(Jason Mack)*, Raymond Turner *(colored cook)*.

Melodrama. Bill Barlow, Jr., a wealthy young spendthrift out of favor with his father, sets out to prove himself at his father's lumber camp but is waylaid by tramps who steal his clothes. When he arrives, no one believes his identity, and his father reports that his son has never worked. Rescuing Bess Calhoun from the path of a log, he learns of a plot to gain control of the Calhoun timber through a mortgage and incurs the enmity of Mack, the camp bully. Mack forces Calhoun to an agreement, but Bill borrows the mortgage money and overtakes Mack on a logging engine, pays off the mortgage, sells the property to his father, and wins the hand of Bess. *Lumberjacks. Spendthrifts. Tramps. Filial relations. Lumber camps.*

THE SIREN **F2.5116**

Columbia Pictures. 20 Dec **1927** [c21 Jan 1928; LP24898]. Si; b&w. 35mm. 6 reels, 5,996 ft.

Prod Harry Cohn. *Dir* Byron Haskin. *Adapt* Elmer Harris. *Story*

Harold Shumate. *Photog* Ray June. *Art Dir* Robert E. Lee. *Film Ed* Arthur Roberts. *Asst Dir* Clifford Saum.

Cast: Tom Moore *(Peter Dane)*, Dorothy Revier *(Glenna Marsh)*, Norman Trevor *(Cole Norwood/Felipe Vincenti)*, Jed Prouty *(Geoffrey Fuller)*, Otto Hoffman *(Fleet)*.

Melodrama. Peter Dane meets society girl Glenna Marsh when her car breaks down in a storm near his hunting retreat. Glenna is the unwitting tool of Cole Norwood, a gambler who is using her charm to lure men of wealth to her home for social gatherings that invariably end in a poker game. Dane attends the party at which Glenna discovers that Norwood is a cheat and orders him from her house. Later, Norwood returns and starts a fight by accusing Glenna of being his mistress and business partner. In the struggle, a torn drape ignites, and Glenna shoots Norwood to protect Dane. She is charged with killing Norwood and sentenced to be hanged, but a confession from Norwood's partner (Fleet, Glenna's butler) frees her, revealing that Felipe Vincenti, a South American newsman determined to secure Glenna's conviction, is actually Norwood, who did not die in the fire but was scarred beyond recognition. *Socialites. Gamblers. Journalists. Butlers. Murder. Circumstantial evidence. Disguise. Disfiguration. Capital punishment. Fires.*

THE SIREN CALL **F2.5117**

Famous Players–Lasky. *Dist* Paramount Pictures. ca2 Sep **1922** [Chicago premiere; released 17 Sep; c12 Sep 1922; LP18298]. Si; b&w. 35mm. 6 reels, 5,417 ft.

Pres by Adolph Zukor. *Dir* Irvin Willat. *Scen* J. E. Nash, Philip Hurn. *Adapt* Victor Irvin, Philip Hurn. *Story* J. E. Nash. *Photog* Charles Edgar Schoenbaum.

Cast: Dorothy Dalton *(Charlotte Woods, a dancer)*, David Powell *(Ralph Stevens, a prospector)*, Mitchell Lewis *(Beauregard, a trapper)*, Edward J. Brady *(Edward Brent, a gambler)*, Will Walling *(Gore)*, Leigh Wyant *(Eleanor Du Bois)*, Lucien Littlefield *(Irishman)*, George B. Williams *(Judge Green)*.

Northwest melodrama. Beauregard brings an orphaned baby to Charlotte, a popular dancehall girl, in return for a kiss. When the dancehall is burned down by reformers, she and Edward Brent, to whom she is secretly married, go to the wilderness and open a store. Brent later trades his store and wife to Beauregard for his furs and goes downriver. Charlotte kills the trapper when he makes advances; Ralph Stevens arrives, hears the story, then sets off after Brent. They fight, Brent escapes, Charlotte follows and rescues Ralph from the water, and the two lovers are free to marry when news comes that Brent has been killed by wolves. *Dancehall girls. Prospectors. Gamblers. Trappers. Reformers. Alaska. Wolves.*

THE SIREN OF SEVILLE **F2.5118**

Hunt Stromberg Corp. *Dist* Producers Distributing Corp. 17 Aug **1924** [c1 Sep 1924; LP21572]. Si; b&w. 35mm. 7 reels, 6,724 ft.

Pres by Hunt Stromberg, Charles R. Rogers. *Supv* Hunt Stromberg. *Dir* Jerome Storm, Hunt Stromberg. *Story* H. H. Van Loan. *Photog* Sol Polito.

Cast: Priscilla Dean *(Dolores)*, Allan Forrest *(Gallito)*, Stuart Holmes *(Cavallo)*, Claire De Lorez *(Ardita)*, Bert Woodruff *(Palomino)*, Matthew Betz *(Pedro)*.

Romantic melodrama. On a visit to the Spanish countryside, Pedro Romero, a great matador, meets Dolores, who makes him promise to help Gallito, her childhood sweetheart, who wants nothing more than to fight bulls. When Dolores and Gallito go to Seville, however, Pedro forgets his promise, but Arturo Cavallo, the president of the arena, becomes infatuated with Dolores and gives Gallito a chance to fight. At the bullfight, Pedro's concentration is broken when he sees Ardita, a beautiful dancer whom he loves, sitting with another man, and the bull gores him. Gallito is a great success in his first fight, and the fickle Ardita later lures him into her carriage. Dolores returns home and finds Cavallo, who tries to win her favor by taking her to Ardita's apartment and proving Gallito's infidelity. Dolores becomes a dancer, and Gallito, who has been led to believe that she is Cavallo's mistress, gives him a sound thrashing. Cavallo plots to drug Gallito's wine before a fight, and Dolores, who has overheard the plan, saves his life in the ring as he is about to be fatally gored. *Bullfighters. Dancers. Bullfighting. Jealousy. Spain. Seville.*

SISTERS **F2.5119**

International Film Service. *Dist* American Releasing Corp. 2 Apr **1922** [c29 Mar 1922; LP17702]. Si; b&w. 35mm. 7 reels, 6,785 ft.

Dir Albert Capellani. *Scen* E. Lloyd Sheldon. *Photog* Chester Lyons. *Set Dsgn* Joseph Urban.

Cast: Seena Owen *(Alix Strickland)*, Gladys Leslie *(Cherry Strickland)*, Mildred Arden *(Anna Little)*, Matt Moore *(Peter Joyce)*, Joe King *(Martin Lloyd)*, Tom Guise *(Dr. Strickland)*, Robert Schable *(Justin Little)*, Frances Grant *(colored mammy)*, Fred Miller *(colored servant)*.

Domestic drama. Source: Kathleen Norris, *Sisters* (Garden City, New York, 1919). Cherry, the youngest daughter of Dr. Strickland, marries Martin Lloyd; and Peter, a neighbor who was in love with her, unhappily begins a world tour. Returning home, Peter finds that the doctor has died, leaving the older daughter, Alix, alone; and he marries her out of desperation. Cherry, unhappy with her marriage, leaves her husband and comes to live with her sister and Peter; learning that Peter still loves her, Cherry agrees to run away with him, but they are discovered by his wife and upbraided. Martin is injured in a logging camp accident, and Cherry, realizing that she still loves her husband, goes to him. Peter resolves to free Alix, but she forgives him and they agree to start anew. *Sisters. Physicians. Marriage. Infidelity. Lumber camps.*

SISTERS **F2.5120**

Columbia Pictures. 15 Jun **1930** [c23 Jun 1930; LP1379]. Sd (Movietone); b&w. 35mm. 7 reels, 6,284 ft.

Prod Harry Cohn. *Dir* James Flood. *Scen-Dial* Jo Swerling. *Story* Ralph Graves. *Photog* Ted Tetzlaff. *Art Dir* Harrison Wiley. *Film Ed* Gene Havlick. *Ch Sd Engr* John P. Livadary. *Sd Mix Engr* Russell Malmgren. *Asst Dir* Frank Geraghty.

Cast: Sally O'Neil *(Sally)*, Molly O'Day *(Molly)*, Russell Gleason *(Eddie)*, Jason Robards *(John)*, Morgan Wallace *(Tully)*, John Fee *(Johnson)*, Carl Stockdale *(Jones)*.

Romatic drama. Eddie Collins, a smalltown boy, gets a job as census taker in New York City. On a call he meets Sally Malone, a Fifth Avenue model who is attracted to him because of his conservative demeanor with women. He takes an immediate dislike to William Tully, in whom he senses a basic dishonesty. Molly, Sally's sister, is married to John Shannon, a loving but jobless husband; and consequently Molly calls on her sister to ask for a loan and makes an impression on Tully, who arranges a rendezvous with her. Through a fellow worker Eddie learns that Tully is a former Chicago robber; meanwhile, John blames Sally for Molly's reprehensible behavior, but all ends well as Eddie arrives at Tully's apartment with the police and exposes him. With the reward money, he is able to buy a country newspaper and settle down with Sally. *Census takers. Fashion models. Sisters. Finance—Personal. Newspapers. New York City.*

SISTERS OF EVE (Famous Authors) **F2.5121**

Trem Carr Productions. *Dist* Rayart Pictures. Sep **1928.** Si; b&w. 35mm. 6 reels, 5,553 ft.

Dir Scott Pembroke. *Scen-Titl* Arthur Hoerl. *Photog* Hap Depew. *Film Ed* John S. Harrington.

Cast: Anita Stewart *(Beatrice Franklin)*, Betty Blythe *(Mrs. Wenham Gardner)*, Creighton Hale *(Leonard Tavernake)*, Harold Nelson *(Professor Franklin)*, Francis Ford *(Pritchard)*, Charles L. King *(Wenham Gardner/Jerry Gardner)*.

Drama. Source: Edward Phillips Oppenheim, *The Tempting of Tavernake* (Boston, 1911). "The bad but beautiful wife who cokes up her wealthy husband and gets a giant keeper to squeeze out the checks has too many in-laws. ... Hubby finally thrashes his keeper and holds the knife to his wife just as Tavernake is about to fall from virtue. ... Tavernake gets more ministerial than ever and his real love follows him to a far away isle." (*Variety*, 28 Nov 1928, p20.) "Woman hater meets woman under strange circumstances and feels compelled to take her to his home for care and protection. A strange mixup when a sister is discovered and the girl's past revealed." ("Motion Picture News Booking Guide," in *Motion Picture News*, 15 Mar 1930, p103.) No further information has been found to explain the discrepancy between these two notices. *Sisters. Misogynists. Narcotics. Wealth.*

SITTING BULL AT THE "SPIRIT LAKE MASSACRE" **F2.5122**

Sunset Productions. 15 Jun **1927.** Si; b&w. 35mm. 6 reels, 5,192 ft.

Pres by Anthony J. Xydias. *Dir* Robert North Bradbury. *Adapt* Ben Allah. *Photog* James S. Brown, Jr. *Film Ed* Della M. King.

Cast: Bryant Washburn *(Donald Keefe)*, Ann Schaeffer *(Mame Mulcain)*, Jay Morley *(Pat Mulcain)*, Shirley Palmer *(Ceila Moore)*, Thomas Lingham *(Parson Rogers)*, Chief Yowlache *(Sitting Bull)*, James O'Neil *(Little Bear)*, Bob Bradbury, Jr. *(Bob Keefe)*, Fred Warren *(Happy Hartz)*, Leon

Kent *(John Mulcain)*, Lucille Ballart *(Mary Moore)*.

Historical melodrama. "Details the dream of power [which] came to Sitting Bull, who sets out to do a lot of tomahawking. Usual love story between the young scout and the prairie flower, this time a minister's daughter." (*Variety*, 3 Aug 1927, p19.) *Indians of North America. Sitting Bull. Spirit Lake Massacre.*

Note: Also known as *With Sitting Bull at the Spirit Lake Massacre.*

SIX CYLINDER LOVE F2.5123

Fox Film Corp. 4 Nov **1923** [c4 Nov 1923; LP19678]. Si; b&w. 35mm. 7 reels, 6,659 ft.

Pres by William Fox. *Dir* Elmer Clifton. *Titl* Ralph Spence. *Adapt* Carl Stearns Clancy. *Photog* Alexander G. Penrod. *Film Ed* Ralph Spence.

Cast: Ernest Truex *(Gilbert Sterling)*, Florence Eldridge *(Marilyn Sterling)*, Donald Meek *(Richard Burton)*, Maude Hill *(Geraldine Burton)*, Anne McKittrick *(Phyllis Burton)*, Marjorie Milton *(Marguerite Rogers)*, Thomas Mitchell *(Bertram Rogers)*, Ralph Sipperly *(William Donroy)*, Berton Churchill *(George Stapleton)*, Harold Mann *(Harold Winston)*, Frank Tweed *(Tom Johnson)*, Grace Gordon *(Mary)*.

Comedy-drama. Source: William Anthony McGuire, *Six Cylinder Love, a Comedy* (New York, 1921). The ownership of an expensive automobile nearly wrecks the happiness of two families in turn. When the Burtons and the Sterlings are broke and beginning anew, the janitor of the apartment building buys the car. *Janitors. Finance—Personal. Family life. Automobiles.*

SIX DAYS F2.5124

Goldwyn Pictures. *Dist* Goldwyn-Cosmopolitan Distributing Corp. 9 Sep **1923** [c19 Aug 1923; LP19512]. Si; b&w. 35mm. 9 reels, 8,010 ft.

Dir Charles Brabin. *Adapt* Ouida Bergère. *Photog* John Mescall.

Cast: Corinne Griffith *(Laline Kingston)*, Frank Mayo *(Dion Leslie)*, Myrtle Stedman *(Olive Kingston)*, Claude King *(Lord Charles Chetwyn)*, Maude George *(Clara Leslie [Gilda Lindo])*, Spottiswoode Aitken *(Père Jerome)*, Charles Clary *(Richard Kingston)*, Evelyn Walsh Hall *(Hon. Emily Tarrant-Chetwyn)*, Paul Cazeneuve *(chef)*, Jack Herbert *(guide)*, Robert De Vilbiss *(Dion Leslie, as a child of 6)*.

Melodrama. Source: Elinor Glyn, *Six Days* (Philadelphia, 1923). Laline Kingston, whose mother would like her to marry a wealthy Englishman, meets Dion Leslie, a young sculptor. They visit the grave of Laline's brother, and with a priest acting as their guide, they become trapped in some deserted underground barracks. The priest marries them before he dies in a collapse of the cave, but after a few days they become separated. When Laline extricates herself, her mother takes her to the fiancé's castle. Dion follows and is revealed to be the Englishman's son from a previous marriage. Dion's father gives the young couple his blessing and is himself reunited with his former wife. *Sculptors. Marriage. Courtship. Wealth.*

A SIX SHOOTIN' ROMANCE (Blue Streak Western) F2.5125

Universal Pictures. 7 Mar **1926** [c24 Dec 1925; LP22180]. Si; b&w. 35mm. 5 reels, 4,837 ft.

Dir Clifford S. Smith. *Scen* Alvin J. Neitz. *Photog* William Nobles.

Cast: Jack Hoxie *("Lightning" Jack)*, Olive Hasbrouck *(Donaldeen Travis)*, William A. Steele *(Currier King)*, Carmen Phillips *(Mrs. King)*, Bob McKenzie *(Ricketts)*, Mattie Peters *(Mammy)*, Virginia Bradford *(Muriel Travis)*.

Western melodrama. Source: Ruth Comfort Mitchell, "Dashing" (publication undetermined). Lightning Jack becomes heir to a ranch jointly with Donaldeen Travis, an eastern society girl who evinces an instant dislike to him. Currier King, a neighboring rancher, takes a fancy to Donaldeen and openly courts her despite the fact that he already has a wife. Donaldeen learns that King is married and gives him the cold shoulder, angering him so greatly that he abducts her. Jack and some of his men ride to her rescue, and Donaldeen finally admits to herself that she has come to love Jack truly. *Ranchers. Socialites. Abduction. Infidelity. Inheritance. Courtship.*

THE SIX-FIFTY F2.5126

Universal Pictures. 12 Sep **1923** [New York premiere; released 8 Oct; c17 Sep 1923; LP19424]. Si; b&w. 35mm. 5 reels, 5,100 ft.

Dir Nat Ross. *Scen (see note)* Doris Schroeder, Harvey Gates, Lenore Coffee. *Adapt* Harvey Gates. *Photog* Ben Kline.

Cast: Renée Adorée *(Hester Taylor)*, Orville Caldwell *(Dan Taylor)*, Bert Woodruff *("Gramp")*, Gertrude Astor *(Christine Palmer)*, Niles Welch *(Mark Rutherford)*.

Rural melodrama. Source: Kate L. McLaurin, *The Six-Fifty* (New York opening: 24 Oct 1921). After 2 years of marriage, farmer's wife Hester Taylor tires of her life of hardship and accepts an invitation from Mark Rutherford to visit the city. (The train Mark is riding, the "Six-Fifty," has crashed near her house.) Dan Taylor, sensing the impending loss of his wife, decides to lure her back by becoming a powerful member of his community. He opens a creamery with money given to him as a result of the train crash, and Hester, unable to cope with her hectic city life, returns happily to him. *Marriage. Farming. Rural life. Dairying. Train wrecks.*

Note: Some sources credit Lenore Coffee with scenario instead of Doris Schroeder.

THE SIXTH COMMANDMENT F2.5127

Encore Pictures. *Dist* Associated Exhibitors. 1 Jun **1924** [c28 May 1924; LP20245]. Si; b&w. 35mm. 6 reels, 5,506 ft.

Prod-Dir William Christy Cabanne. *Ed Dir–Titl* Merritt Crawford. *Story* Arthur Hoerl. *Photog* Philip Armand, William Tuers.

Cast: William Faversham *(David Brant)*, Charlotte Walker *(Mrs. Calhoun)*, John Bohn *(John Brant)*, Kathleen Martyn *(Marian Calhoun)*, Neil Hamilton *(Robert Fields)*, Coit Albertson *(Dr. Carvel)*, Sara Wood *(Florence Page)*, Consuelo Flowerton *(Helen Brooks)*, Charles Emmett Mack *(Henry Adams)*, Edmund Breese *(Colonel Saunders)*.

Melodrama. John Brant, a proud minister of the Gospel, secretly in love with Marian Calhoun, conceals his emotions because she is engaged to Robert Fields. Robert seeks the company of other girls, however, and Marian breaks her engagement after John returns blinded from the war and is cured. On being freed from the charge of killing Robert, Marian and John are reunited and married. *Clergymen. Veterans. Blindness. Murder. World War I.*

SIXTY CENTS AN HOUR F2.5128

Famous Players–Lasky. *Dist* Paramount Pictures. 13 May **1923** [c16 May 1923; LP18971]. Si; b&w. 35mm. 6 reels, 5,632 ft.

Pres by Jesse L. Lasky. *Dir* Joseph Henabery. *Scen* Grant Carpenter. *Story* Frank Condon. *Photog* Faxon M. Dean.

Cast: Walter Hiers *(Jimmy Kirk, a soda-jerker)*, Jacqueline Logan *(Mamie Smith, his sweetheart)*, Ricardo Cortez *(William Davis, Jimmy's rival)*, Charles Ogle *(James Smith, a banker)*, Lucille Ward *(Mrs. Smith, Mamie's mother)*, Robert Dudley *(storekeeper)*, Clarence Burton, Guy Oliver, Cullen Tate *(three crooks)*.

Comedy. Although Jimmy Kirk earns only $7.50 a week as a soda jerk, he is ambitious and hopes to marry Mamie Smith, the bank president's daughter. He saves up enough money to rent a car, in which he finds money stolen from the bank. When James Smith tries to keep Jimmy from receiving the reward, Jimmy shrewdly claims that the bank encroaches on his 4-ft. plot of property. Jimmy wins both a financial compromise and Mamie. *Soda clerks. Bankers. Bank robberies. Property rights.*

Note: Working title: *Seventy Five Cents an Hour.*

SKEDADDLE GOLD F2.5129

Action Pictures. *Dist* Pathé Exchange. 31 Jul **1927** [c31 May 1927; LU24028]. Si; b&w. 35mm. 5 reels, 4,562 ft.

Pres by Lester F. Scott, Jr. *Dir* Richard Thorpe. *Scen* Frank L. Inghram. *Story* James French Dorrance. *Photog* Ray Ries.

Cast: Wally Wales *(Kent Blake)*, Betty Baker *(Wanda Preston)*, Robert Burns *(sheriff)*, George F. Marion *(George F.)*, Harry Todd *(Rusty)*, Gordon Standing *(John Martin)*.

Western melodrama. Kent Blake, a deputy sheriff, is about to arrest some claim jumpers when Oakley, the owner, frightens off the villains by causing a landslide, thus uncovering a rich new vein. He tries to persuade Kent to resign his job and take up prospecting with him, but the sheriff sends word for him to arrest dope smugglers on the border, and he foils their efforts. Martin, a lawyer, wins the confidence of Wanda Preston, whom Kent loves, and steals the evidence against the smugglers, forcing Kent to resign. Martin convinces Wanda that she is a potential grand opera star and takes her to the city to study. Kent finds her disillusioned there, thrashes Martin, and takes Wanda home to be his wife. *Sheriffs. Miners. Claim jumpers. Singers. Smugglers. Lawyers. Narcotics. Mexican border. Landslides.*

SKID PROOF F2.5130

Fox Film Corp. 22 Jul **1923** [c1 Aug 1923; LP19471]. Si; b&w. 35mm. 6 reels, 5,565 ft.

Pres by William Fox. *Dir* Scott Dunlap. *Scen* Harvey Gates. *Story* Byron Morgan. *Photog* Don Short.

Cast: Charles Jones *(Jack Darwin)*, Laura Anson *(Nadine)*, Fred Eric *(Dutton Hardmere)*, Jacqueline Gadsden *(Lorraine Hardmere)*, Peggy Shaw *(Marie Hardmere)*, Earl Metcalf *(Rufus Tyler)*, Claude Peyton *(Masters)*, Harry Tracey *(Dancing Joe)*.

Melodrama. Ex-champion racing driver Jack Darwin is invited to participate in a transcontinental automobile race, which he loses when a competitor shoots him from an airplane. Because of his performance in the race, however, Darwin becomes a motion picture actor. He falls in love with Nadine, an actress, and saves her from marrying a scoundrel. He wins the next race and marries Nadine. *Actors. Automobile racing. Motion pictures.*

SKIN DEEP **F2.5131**

Thomas H. Ince Corp. *Dist* Associated First National Pictures. Sep **1922** [c13 Jan, 30 Aug 1922; LP17843, LP18179]. Si; b&w. 35mm. 7 reels, 6,303 ft.

Pres by Thomas H. Ince. *Supv* Thomas H. Ince. *Dir* Lambert Hillyer. *Scen* LeRoy Stone. *Photog* Charles Stumar.

Cast: Milton Sills *(Bud Doyle)*, Florence Vidor *(Ethel Carter)*, Marcia Manon *(Sadie Doyle)*, Charles Clary *(James Carlson)*, Winter Hall *(Dr. Langdon)*, Joe Singleton *(Joe Culver)*, Frank Campeau *(Boss McQuarg)*, Gertrude Astor *(Mrs. Carlson)*, Muriel Dana *(Baby Carlson)*, B. H. De Lay *(The Aviator)*.

Crime melodrama. Source: Marc Edmund Jones, "Lucky Damage" (publication undetermined). Crook Bud Doyle returns from the war intending to go straight but finds it difficult because of his crooklike features. His wife, her newfound companion, Joe Culver, and Boss McQuarg conspire to frame Bud, and he goes to jail. He escapes, has an accident, and is taken to a hospital for plastic surgery. His features transformed, he discovers the plot against him, helps District Attorney Carlson bring the conspirators to justice, and marries his nurse. *Veterans. Criminals—Rehabilitation. Nurses. Plastic surgery.*

Note: Remade in 1929 by Warner Brothers under the same title, q. v.

SKIN DEEP **F2.5132**

Warner Brothers Pictures. 7 Sep **1929** [c11 Aug 1929; LP588]. Sd (Vitaphone); b&w. 35mm. 6 reels, 5,964 ft. [Also si, 2 Nov; 5,035 ft.]

Dir Ray Enright. *Screenplay-Dial* Gordon Rigby. *Titl* De Leon Anthony. *Photog* Barney McGill. *Film Ed* George Marks. *Song: "I Came to You"* Sidney Mitchell, Archie Gottler, Con Conrad. *Rec Engr* Cal Applegate.

Cast: Monte Blue *(Joe Daley)*, Davey Lee *(District Attorney Carlson's son)*, Betty Compson *(Sadie Rogers)*, Alice Day *(Elsa Langdon)*, John Davidson *(Blackie Culver)*, John Bowers *(District Attorney Carlson)*, Georgie Stone *(Dippy)*, Tully Marshall *(Dr. Bruce Landon)*, Robert Perry *(Tim)*.

Crime melodrama. Source: Marc Edmund Jones, "Lucky Damage" (publication undetermined). Joe Daley is the toughened underworld leader of a downtown mob, but he undergoes a reformation when Sadie, a golddigging showgirl, consents to marry him. Her dismay forces her to team with Joe's crosstown rival, Blackie Culver, in framing Joe for the theft of a hundred grand, which he was actually trying to return to District Attorney John Carlson as evidence of his resolution. Joe is sent up for 5 years but, duped by Sadie's solicitous visits, remains unaware of her complicity, deceit, and continuing adultery. She and Blackie further deceive Joe that the D. A. has designs upon Sadie, and she implores him to escape and avenge her "honor." He does so, avoiding the machine-gunning guards, but crashes on a motorcycle and is discovered by Elsa Langdon, who rescues him and has her plastic surgeon father remake his battered visage. Joe returns to the city unrecognized, still bent upon his revenge, but through his disguise is shown Goldie's treachery. She succumbs to a bullet meant for him, and Joe (with his dog, Mugs) returns to Elsa and her innocent pastoral life, to start anew. *Gangsters. Showgirls. District attorneys. Criminals—Rehabilitation. Plastic surgery. Infidelity. Revenge. Theft. Prisons. Prison escapes. Mistaken identity. Dogs.*

Note: Remake of a 1922 Associated First National release of the same title, q. v.

SKINNER STEPS OUT **F2.5133**

Universal Pictures. 24 Nov **1929** [c7 Nov 1929; LP836]. Sd (Movietone); b&w. 35mm. 8 reels, 6,597 ft. [Also si; 6,645 ft.]

Pres by Carl Laemmle. *Dir* William James Craft. *Scen* Matt Taylor. *Dial-Titl* Albert De Mond, Matt Taylor. *Photog* Al Jones. *Film Ed* Harry Lieb. *Mus Score* David Broekman.

Cast: Glenn Tryon *(Skinner)*, Merna Kennedy *("Honey" Skinner)*, E. J. Ratcliffe *(Jackson)*, Burr McIntosh *(McLaughlin)*, Lloyd Whitlock *(Parking)*, William Welsh *(Crosby)*, Katherine Kerrigan *(Mrs. Crosby)*, Frederick Lee *(Gates)*, Jack Lipson *(neighbor)*, Edna Marion *(neighbor's wife)*.

Domestic farce. Source: Henry Irving Dodge, *Skinner's Dress Suit* (Boston & New York, 1916). William Henry Skinner's young wife has great confidence in her husband's abilities and is ambitious for his success. He informs her of his importance at the office; but in reality he is an insignificant employee on a small salary, and when refused a raise, he hasn't the courage to tell his wife. Distressed at her husband's shabby appearance, "Honey" persuades him to buy a dress suit, and at a charity bazaar she pushes him to the front so that he dominates the affair and comes to the attention of the dignitaries. Skinner forces himself upon the attention of his employer and the employer's chief rival, whose admiration he wins when he bluffs him out of a poker pot. In spite of Skinner's efforts to prevent it, the rival companies are consolidated; and impressed by his spirit and enthusiasm, his superiors promote him to sales manager. *Office clerks. Sales managers. Business competition. Marriage. Ambition. Appearances. Bazaars. Clothes.*

Note: Remake of *Skinner's Dress Suit,* 1925.

SKINNER'S BIG IDEA **F2.5134**

FBO Pictures. 24 Apr **1928** [c19 Mar 1928; LP25072]. Si; b&w. 35mm. 7 reels, 5,967 ft.

Dir Lynn Shores. *Cont* Matt Taylor. *Titl* Randolph Bartlett. *Photog* Phil Tannura. *Film Ed* Archie Marshek. *Asst Dir* Joe Nadel.

Cast: Bryant Washburn *(Skinner)*, William Orlamond *(Hemingway)*, James Bradbury, Sr. *(Carlton)*, Robert Dudley *(Gibbs)*, Ole M. Ness *(Perkins)*, Charles Wellesley *(McLaughlin)*, Martha Sleeper *(Dorothy)*, Hugh Trevor *(Jack McLaughlin)*, Ethel Grey Terry *(Mrs. Skinner)*.

Comedy. Source: Henry Irving Dodge, *Skinner's Big Idea* (New York, 1918). McLaughlin and Perkins, partners in a nut-and-bolt concern, take a vacation after promoting Skinner to junior partner and instructing him to fire Hemingway, Gibbs, and Carlton, the company's eldest employees. Instead, Skinner decides to retain and rejuvenate the three by hiring chorus girl Dorothy Cabot to pep up the office; and he also takes a vacation. Soon they are better groomed, show more initiative, and become addicted to golf—a detriment to their office work. However, on the golf course they accidentally win a big contract with Jackson, a customer of the company, thus gaining the respect of McLaughlin and Perkins, who, on their return, decide to retire from the business. *Chorus girls. Old age. Hardware. Business management. Golf.*

SKINNER'S DRESS SUIT (Universal-Jewel) **F2.5135**

Universal Pictures. 18 Apr **1926** [c22 Jan 1926; LP22315]. Si; b&w. 35mm. 7 reels, 6,887 ft.

Dir William A. Seiter. *Scen* Rex Taylor. *Photog* Arthur Todd. *Art Dir* Leo E. Kuter.

Cast: Reginald Denny *(Skinner)*, Laura La Plante *(Honey)*, Ben Hendricks, Jr. *(Perkins)*, E. J. Ratcliffe *(McLaughlin)*, Arthur Lake *(Tommy)*, Hedda Hopper *(Mrs. Colby)*, Lionel Braham *(Jackson)*, Henry Barrows *(Mr. Colby)*, Frona Hale *(Mrs. McLaughlin)*, William H. Strauss *(tailor)*, Betty Morrisey *(Miss Smith)*, Lucille De Nevers *(Mrs. Crawford)*, Lucille Ward *(Mrs. Jackson)*, Lila Leslie *(Mrs. Wilton)*, Broderick O'Farrell *(Mr. Wilton)*.

Comedy. Source: Henry Irving Dodge, *Skinner's Dress Suit* (Boston & New York, 1916). At the urging of his wife, Skinner, a meek and humble clerk, asks his boss for a raise; he is refused, but in order not to disappoint his wife, he tells her that he got it. She immediately buys him a dress suit, and this single purchase puts Skinner on the road to ruin, involving him in so many new social obligations that he is soon faced with bankruptcy. Greatly burdened with debt, Skinner loses his job. Before he can tell his wife, she whisks him off to a society dance at a hotel where one of his most important clients, Jackson, is staying. Jackson's wife wants to go to the dance and persuades her husband to ask Skinner to invite them. By the end of the evening, Skinner has closed a half-a-million-dollar deal, winning a partnership in his old company. *Office clerks. Businessmen. Marriage. Partnerships. Debt. Clothes.*

SKINNING SKINNERS **F2.5136**

Radin Pictures. *Dist* Tyrad Pictures. **1921.** Si; b&w. 35mm. 5 reels.

Dir William Nigh.

Cast: Johnny Dooley.

Melodrama(?). No information about the nature of this film has been found.

SKIRT SHY *see* **LEAP YEAR**

SKIRTS **F2.5137**

Fox Film Corp. 10 Apr **1921** [c10 Apr 1921; LP16425]. Si; b&w. 35mm. 5 reels, 4,950 ft.

Pres by William Fox. *Dir-Writ* Hampton Del Ruth.

Cast: Clyde Cook *(Peter Rocks, Jr.)*, Chester Conklin, Polly Moran, Jack Cooper, Billy Armstrong, Ethel Teare, Glen Cavender, Slim Summerville, Harry McCoy, Bobby Dunn, Tom Kennedy, Ed Kennedy, William Trancy, Harry Booker, Alta Allen, Laura La Varnie, Alice Davenport, Singer Midgets.

Slapstick farce. Following an animated prolog with clay figures representing Adam and Eve in the Garden of Eden, Peter Rocks, Jr., is introduced as a circus handyman whose father is a millionaire separated from his family and whose mother is the sideshow's bearded lady. He attempts to acquire his father's fortune but is outsmarted by the strong man. A circus performance, a tornado, an automobile accident, a rescue by airplane from a speeding train, and a huge banquet scene are prominently featured. *Millionaires. Circus. Biblical characters.*

THE SKY HAWK **F2.5138**

Fox Film Corp. 11 Dec **1929** [New York premiere; released 29 Jan 1930; c21 Nov 1929; LP913]. Sd (Movietone); b&w. 35mm. 7 reels, 6,888 ft. [Also si; 6,966 ft.]

Pres by William Fox. *Dir* John G. Blystone. *Staged by* Campbell Gullan. *Scen-Dial* Llewellyn Hughes. *Photog* Conrad Wells. *Film Ed* Ralph Dietrich. *Song: "Song of Courage"* Edward Lynn, Charles Wakefield Cadman. *Sd* W. W. Lindsay. *Asst Dir* Jasper Blystone. *Tech Adv* Capt. Sterling C. Campbell, Lieut. Peter Ginter. *Mech Eff* Ralph Hammeras.

Cast: Helen Chandler *(Joan Allan)*, John Garrick *(Jack Bardell)*, Gilbert Emery *(Major Nelson)*, Lennox Pawle *(Lord Bardell)*, Lumsden Hare *(Judge Allan)*, Billy Bevan *(Tom Berry)*, Daphne Pollard *(Minnie)*, Joyce Compton *(Peggy)*, Percy Challenger *(butler)*.

War melodrama. Source: Llewellyn Hughes, "Chap Called Bardell," in *Liberty Magazine* (6:7–10, 23 Feb 1929). Jack Bardell, a young English aviator, is accused of having crashed his plane to avoid serving on the French front, and the only people who believe him innocent of the charge are his sweetheart, Joan Allan, and his mechanic, Tom Berry. Although he is paralyzed up to the waist, with the help of Tom he constructs an airplane from wrecked machines; and on the night of a German zeppelin raid, he goes aloft and singlehanded brings the airships down, thus winning the admiration of his colleagues. *Aviators. Mechanics. Paraplegia. Airplanes. Zeppelins. World War I. England.*

SKY HIGH **F2.5139**

Fox Film Corp. 22 Jan **1922** [c15 Jan 1922; LP17480]. Si; b&w. 35mm. 5 reels, 4,546 ft.

Pres by William Fox. *Dir-Story-Scen* Lynn Reynolds. *Photog* Ben Kline. *Asst Dir* George Webster.

Cast: Tom Mix *(Grant Newburg)*, J. Farrell MacDonald *(Jim Halloway)*, Eva Novak *(Estelle, his daughter)*, Sid Jordan *(Bates)*, William Buckley *(Victor Castle)*, Adele Warner *(Marguerite)*, Wynn Mace *(Patterson)*, Pat Chrisman *(Pasquale)*.

Western melodrama. Grant Newburg, an immigration officer, is dispatched to uncover the men behind the smuggling of Chinese across the Mexican border. While Newburg is scouting, he comes upon Estelle, a stranger who has lost her companions in the canyon; he sets up a camp and steals some food for her, but he is captured and bound by Bates, the leader of the smugglers, who knows of his mission. With the aid of Estelle he escapes and returns with assistance; meanwhile, Bates threatens her, unaware that she is the ward of Halloway, his employer. Newburg returns in an airplane, leaps into a stream, and swims to the place where Estelle is being held captive. Estelle is rescued; and though her guardian is arrested for smuggling, Newburg agrees to care for her until his term is served. *Immigration officers. Smugglers. Wards. Chinese. Airplanes. Mexican border.*

SKY HIGH CORRAL (Blue Streak Western) **F2.5140**

Universal Pictures. 28 Feb **1926** [c12 Dec 1925; LP22111]. Si; b&w. 35mm. 5 reels, 4,871 ft.

Dir-Scen Clifford S. Smith. *Story* Ralph Cummins. *Photog* Eddie Linden.

Cast: Art Acord *(Jack McCabe)*, Marguerite Clayton *(Shasta Hayden)*, Duke R. Lee *(Whitey Durk)*, Jack Mower *(Burns)*, Tom Lingham *(Bill Hayden)*, Blackie Thompson *(Gregg)*, Missouri Royer *(Slim)*, Floyd Shackelford *(Sam)*, Raven *(a horse)*.

Western melodrama. When the Government incorporates Bill Hayden's ranch into a Federal game preserve, Jack McCabe, a forest ranger, is sent to serve an eviction notice on Hayden and his daughter, Shasta. Hayden resists the order, and Jack falls in love with Shasta. Whitey Durk steals Hayden's cattle and pins the blame on Jack. The burly ranger later rescues Hayden and Shasta from Duke's men and brings the bandits into court. The law establishing the game preserve is repealed, and Shasta confesses her love for Jack. *Ranchers. Forest rangers. Rustling. Game preserves. Legislation. Horses.*

THE SKY PILOT **F2.5141**

Cathrine Curtis Corp. *Dist* Associated First National Pictures. May **1921** [c14 May 1921; LP16524]. Si; b&w. 35mm. 7 reels, 6,305 ft.

Prod Cathrine Curtis. *Dir* King Vidor. *Scen* John McDermott. *Adapt* Faith Green. *Photog* Gus Peterson.

Cast: John Bowers *(The Sky Pilot)*, Colleen Moore *(Gwen)*, David Butler *(Bill Hendricks)*, Harry Todd *(The Old Timer)*, James Corrigan *(Honorable Ashley)*, Donald MacDonald *(The Duke)*, Kathleen Kirkham *(Lady Charlotte)*.

Melodrama. Source: Ralph Connor, *The Sky Pilot; a Tale of the Foothills* (Chicago, 1899). In the Canadian Northwest a young minister receives a rough reception from cowboys in a cattle settlement. Attempting to hold service in a saloon, he becomes involved in a fight with Bill Hendricks, foreman of the Ashley ranch, who later befriends him and gets him a job at the ranch. There he becomes a favorite and is called "The Sky Pilot." He saves Hendricks' sweetheart, Gwen, from a cattle stampede, but she is injured; and although a plot by her embittered father and some cattle thieves is frustrated, they burn the minister's church. In saving him, however, Gwen regains the use of her limbs. The Sky Pilot brings about the reformation of Gwen's father, and he officiates at her marriage to Hendricks. *Clergymen. Cowboys. Ranch foremen. Canadian Northwest. Stampedes.*

THE SKY PIRATE **F2.5142**

Sun Motion Pictures. *Dist* Aywon Film Corp. 26 Nov **1926** [New York State license]. Si; b&w. 35mm. 5 reels.

Cast: Bryant Washburn, Vola Vale, Charles Delaney, Sheldon Lewis, Sojin.

Melodrama. The leader of a gang with its headquarters in Chinatown attempts to rob the air mail. He is foiled by a dauntless pilot, who brings the gang to justice. *Air pilots. Postal service. Chinatown.*

THE SKY RAIDER **F2.5143**

Encore Pictures. *Dist* Associated Exhibitors. 5 Apr **1925** [c5 Mar 1925; LU21201]. Si; b&w. 35mm. 7 reels, 6,638 ft.

Pres by Gilbert E. Gable. *Dir* T. Hayes Hunter. *Scen* Gerald C. Duffy.

Cast: Capt. Charles Nungesser *(Nungesser)*, Jacqueline Logan *(Lucille Ward)*, Gladys Walton *(Marie)*, Walter Miller *(Paul Willard)*, Lawford Davidson *(Gregg Vanesse)*, Theodore Babcock *(Senator Willard)*, Ida Darling *(Mrs. Willard)*, Wilton Lackaye *(prison commandant)*, Edouard Durand *(Forot)*.

Melodrama. Source: Jack Lait, "The Great Air Mail Robbery" (publication undetermined). Vanesse, a mechanic with the French Air Force, sabotages the plane of Capt. Charles Nungesser, France's Flying Fiend, by placing Paul Willard's flying insignia in Nungesser's intake manifold. Paul is accused of the deed and sentenced to 20 years in a military prison. Six years later, the Willards, a wealthy American family, arrive in France, searching for Paul, who had run away to war. They interview Vanesse, who informs them that Paul died like a hero in the war. The Willards then meet Nungesser, who falls in love with Lucille, Paul's sister, and makes a silent resolution to arrange for Paul's pardon. This he does, and then goes to the United States to find Vanesse and to discover the truth about Paul's case. Nungesser discovers that Vanesse is planning to rob the air mail; with Paul's help, he captures Vanesse and recovers the loot. Vanesse dies from the effects of a plane crash; Paul is cleared of all guilt and marries his former sweetheart, Marie; and Nungesser and Lucille are swept to the heights on the wings of happiness. *Mechanics. Aviators. Injustice. Sabotage. Mail theft. Airplane accidents. France—Air Force. World War I.*

THE SKY RIDER **F2.5144**

Chesterfield Motion Picture Corp. 15 Jun **1928.** Si; b&w. 35mm. 4,900 ft.

Dir-Scen Alvin J. Neitz. *Photog* M. A. Anderson. *Film Ed* Alvin J. Neitz.

Cast: Alfred Heuston, Gareth Hughes, Josephine Hill, J. P. Lockney, John Tansey, Edward Cecil, Lew Meehan, Sheldon Lewis, Champion *(a dog)*.

Melodrama. "Disinherited nephew of aviation magnate plots to get share of uncle's millions. He causes near death of his cousin, when a bomb placed in latter's plane explodes in mid-air. He then hires thugs to abduct uncle, in order to force him to give over part of fortune, but is foiled by arrival of cousin and police." (*Motion Picture News Booking Guide,* [14]: 151, 1929.) *Uncles. Cousins. Millionaires. Abduction. Airplanes. Explosions. Dogs.*

THE SKY SKIDDER **F2.5145**

Universal Pictures. 13 Jan **1929** [c23 Jan 1928; LP24915]. Si; b&w. 35mm. 5 reels, 4,364 ft.

Dir Bruce Mitchell. *Story-Cont* Val Cleveland. *Titl* gardner Bradford. *Photog* William Adams. *Film Ed* Harry Marker.

Cast: Al Wilson *(Al Simpkins)*, Helen Foster *(Stella Hearns)*, Wilbur McGaugh *(Silas Smythe)*, Pee Wee Holmes *(Bert Beatle)*.

Action melodrama. Inventor Al Simpkins develops a new airplane fuel, "Economo," which he claims gets a thousand miles to the pint. During a trial flight he sees his sweetheart, Stella Hearns, motoring with the wealthy and dishonest Silas Smythe. Using a ropeladder, Al rescues Stella when Smythe's automobile goes out of control. Just before the "Economo" demonstration flight, Smythe steals Simpkins' special fuel and refills the tank with gasoline, causing Simpkins to crash land. Stella finances the next venture, a huge monoplane with a full tank of Economo. Smythe steals the formula for Economo and uses this fuel in his airplane. Discovering their loss, Simpkins and Stella chase Smythe in the monoplane. Dropping to Smythe's airplane on a ropeladder, Al retrieves his formula. He returns to his plane, wins the race and, naturally, Stella. *Aviators. Inventors. Aviation. Airplane fuel. Air stunts.*

SKY-HIGH SAUNDERS (Universal Thrill Feature) **F2.5146**

Universal Pictures. 6 Nov **1927** [c20 Jun 1927; LP24118]. Si; b&w. 35mm. 5 reels, 4,393 ft.

Pres by Carl Laemmle. *Dir-Story-Scen* Bruce Mitchell. *Titl* Gardner Bradford. *Photog* William S. Adams.

Cast: Al Wilson *("Sky-High" Saunders/Michael Saunders)*, Elsie Tarron *(Helen Leland)*, Frank Rice *("Whispering" Hicks)*, Bud Osborne *(George Delatour)*.

Action melodrama. While searching for his twin brother, Michael, whom his family believes lost in combat, "Sky-High" Saunders discovers a gang of airplane smugglers. The leader, Delatour, is in love with schoolteacher Helen Leland, whom Sky-High saves from the smuggler's unwelcome attentions, knocking him unconscious in a fight. Mistaking Sky-High for Michael, Delatour seeks to get even but is convinced that he has been "seeing things." On the trail of the smugglers, Sky-High shoots down his brother's plane, and Michael dies in his arms; Sky-High keeps a rendezvous with the gang, disguised as his brother, and with aid from Army planes he dynamites their mountain stronghold while dealing with Delatour on the wings of his plane. *Smugglers. Twins. Brothers. Schoolteachers. Mistaken identity. Airplanes. United States Army—Air Corps.*

SKYFIRE *see* **BLAZING ARROWS**

THE SKYLINE OF SPRUCE *see* **SHADOWS OF THE NORTH**

THE SKYROCKET **F2.5147**

Celebrity Pictures. *Dist* Associated Exhibitors. 14 Feb **1926** [c6 Feb 1926; LU22367]. Si; b&w. 35mm. 8 reels, 7,350 ft.

Dir Marshall Neilan. *Adapt-Cont* Benjamin Glazer. *Photog* David Kesson.

Cast—Prolog: Gladys Brockwell *(Rose Kimm)*, Charles West *(Edward Kimm)*, Muriel McCormac *(Sharon Kimm)*, Junior Coughlan *(Mickey)*.

Cast—Story: Peggy Hopkins Joyce *(Sharon Kimm)*, Owen Moore *(Mickey Reid)*, Gladys Hulette *(Lucia Morgan)*, Paulette Duval *(Mildred Rideout)*, Lilyan Tashman *(Ruby Wright)*, Earle Williams *(William Dvorak)*, Bernard Randall *(Sam Hertzfelt)*, Sammy Cohen *(Morris Pincus)*, Bull Montana *(film comedian)*, Arnold Gregg *(Stanley Craig)*, Ben Hall *(Peter Stanton)*, Nick Dandau *(Vladmir Strogin)*, Eddie Dillon *(comedy director)*, Hank Mann *(comedy producer)*, Joan Standing *(Sharon's secretary)*, Eugenie Besserer *(wardrobe mistress)*.

Romantic drama. Source: Adela Rogers St. Johns, *The Skyrocket* (New York, 1925). In the prolog Sharon Kimm and Mickey Reid are childhood friends in a tenement neighborhood but are separated when Sharon is placed in an orphanage. In the story we see Sharon as a young Hollywood star whose quick rise to fame leaves her self-centered, superficial, and a spendthrift. Ironically, the film that skyrocketed her to fame was written by Mickey. But her success is brief; and when it comes crashing to earth, Mickey is there to pick up the pieces. *Orphans. Actors. Childhood. Hollywood.*

SKY'S THE LIMIT **F2.5148**

Marlborough Productions. *Dist* Aywon Film Corp. 9 Sep **1925** [New York State license]. Si; b&w. 35mm. 5 reels, 4,900 ft.

Dir-Writ (see note) I. W. Irving, Harry L. Fraser. *Photog* Paul Allen. *Asst Dir* Theodore Loos.

Cast: Bruce Gordon *(Detective Robert Bronson)*, Charlotte Pierce *(Edna Hamilton)*, Jack Giddings *(Richard Hamilton)*, Melbourne MacDowell *(Charles Hamilton)*, Mary Jane Irving *(Richard Hamilton's daughter)*, Pat Rooney *(Jusof)*, Frank Earle *(James Kurley)*, Jane Starr *(Sonia Kosloff)*, Alphonse Martell *(Pietro Costello)*.

Melodrama(?). No information about the nature of this film has been found. Although several sources credit Harry L. Fraser as director, screen credits show I. W. Irving.

SKYSCRAPER **F2.5149**

De Mille Pictures. *Dist* Pathé Exchange. 8 Apr **1928** [c2 Apr 1928; LP25114]. Si; b&w. 35mm. 8 reels, 7,040 ft.

Supv Walter Woods. *Assoc Prod* Ralph Block. *Dir* Howard Higgin. *Titl* John Krafft. *Adapt* Elliott Clawson, Tay Garnett. *Story* Dudley Murphy. *Photog* John Boyle. *Art Dir* Stephen Goosson. *Film Ed* Adelaide Cannon. *Asst Dir* Edward Saunders. *Cost* Adrian.

Cast: William Boyd *(Blondy)*, Alan Hale *(Slim)*, Sue Carol *(Sally)*, Alberta Vaughn *(Jane)*.

Drama. Blondy and Slim, buddies, are high steel workers. Blondy falls and is seriously injured while attempting to rescue Slim. As a result of his injury he can no longer work, and he falls into a reclusive depression. Only after his friend pretends to be interested in his sweetheart does he recover his spirit and become well again. *Steeplejacks. Friendship. Neurosis.*

SLANDER THE WOMAN **F2.5150**

Allen Holubar Pictures. *Dist* Associated First National Pictures. 16 Apr **1923** [c24 Apr 1923; LP18889]. Si; b&w. 35mm. 7 reels, 6,400 ft.

Pres by Allen Holubar. *Dir* Allen Holubar. *Scen* Violet Clark. *Photog* Byron Haskin. *Film Ed* Frank Lawrence. *Asst Dir* Harold S. Bucquet.

Cast: Dorothy Phillips *(Yvonne Desmarest)*, Lewis Dayton *(Monsieur Duroacher)*, Robert Anderson *(Dr. Émile Molleur)*, Mayme Kelso *(Nanette)*, George Siegmann *(Scarborough)*, Ynez Seabury *(Indian girl)*, Herbert Fortier *(Father Machette)*, Geno Corrado *(Tetreau, the guide)*, William Orlamond *(The Stranger)*, Robert Schable *(Monsieur Redoux)*, Rosemary Theby *(Madame Redoux)*, Irene Haisman *(Marie Desplanes)*, Cyril Chadwick *(Monsieur Lemond)*.

Melodrama. Source: Jeffrey Deprend, "The White Frontier" (publication undetermined). Through circumstantial evidence Yvonne Desmarest is branded by Judge Duroacher as the "other woman" in a sensational murder case. She retreats to her father's hunting lodge near Hudson Bay, where she meets Scarborough, an Indian girl, and Émile (an old trapper who becomes her protector). Realizing his error, Duroacher follows Yvonne, thus precipitating a series of events in which the judge is suspected of murdering Scarborough and Émile injures Duroacher out of jealousy. Yvonne's name is cleared, as is that of Émile, who has been sought for many years on a murder charge. Yvonne and Duroacher realize their love for each other. *Judges. Trappers. Slander. Murder. Hudson Bay.*

Note: Working title: *The White Frontier.*

THE SLANDERERS **F2.5151**

Universal Pictures. 21 Sep **1924** [c15 Aug 1924; LP20507]. Si; b&w. 35mm. 5 reels, 4,844 ft.

Dir Nat Ross. *Scen* Harvey Gates.

Cast: Johnnie Walker *(Johnny Calkins)*, Gladys Hulette *(Gladys Gray)*, Billy Sullivan *(Larry Calkins)*, George Nichols *(Todd Calkins)*, Edith

Yorke *(Mrs. Calkins)*, Philo McCullough *(Jerome Keefe)*, Margaret Landis *(Ethel Davis)*, Jackie Morgan *(slim kid)*, Turner Savage *(fat kid)*.

Melodrama. Source: Valma Clark, "Judgement of the West" (publication undetermined). "Widow and her two sons are targets for gossips of small town. The slanders continue until the older boy, returning from war a hero, forces the gossips to be quiet and respectful of his mother and his brother. There is a love romance introduced." *(Motion Picture News Booking Guide*, 8:72, Apr 1925.) *War heroes. Smalltown life. Gossip.*

SLAVE OF DESIRE **F2.5152**

Goldwyn Pictures. *Dist* Goldwyn-Cosmopolitan Distributing Corp. 4 Oct **1923** [c14 Oct 1923; LP19511]. Si; b&w. 35mm. 7 reels, 6,673 ft.

Pres by Gilbert E. Gable. *Dir* George D. Baker. *Scen* Charles E. Whittaker. *Adapt* Alice D. G. Miller. *Photog* John Boyle.

Cast: George Walsh *(Raphael Valentin)*, Bessie Love *(Pauline Gaudin)*, Carmel Myers *(Countess Fedora)*, Wally Van *(Restignac)*, Edward Connelly *(The Antiquarian)*, Eulalie Jensen *(Mrs. Gaudin)*, Herbert Prior *(Mr. Gaudin)*, William Orlamond *(Champrose)*, Nicholas De Ruiz *(Tallifer)*, William von Hardenburg *(The General)*, Harmon MacGregor *(Émile)*, George Periolat *(The Duke)*, Harry Lorraine *(Finot)*, Calvert Carter *(The Major Domo)*.

Allegorical melodrama. Source: Honoré de Balzac, "La Peau de Chagrin." Poet Raphael Valentin meets the vampish Russian Countess Fedora, who makes him successful overnight, then rejects him. An antiquarian gives him a piece of magic leather that will grant every wish. The poet becomes rich and famous again, destroys Countess Fedora, and is about to die because he is a "slave of desire" when a girl he once loved but deserted saves him. *Vamps. Poets. Talismans. Russians. Greed.*

Note: Working title: *The Magic Skin.*

A SLAVE OF FASHION **F2.5153**

Metro-Goldwyn-Mayer Pictures. 23 Aug **1925** [c22 Jul 1925; LP21673]. Si; b&w. 35mm. 6 reels, 5,986 ft.

Dir Hobart Henley. *Scen* Bess Meredyth, Jane Murfin. *Story* Samuel Shipman. *Photog* Ben Reynolds. *Art Dir* Cedric Gibbons.

Cast: Norma Shearer *(Katherine Emerson)*, Lew Cody *(Nicholas Wentworth)*, William Haines *(Dick Wayne)*, Mary Carr *(Mother Emerson)*, James Corrigan *(Father Emerson)*, Vivia Ogden *(Aunt Sophie)*, Miss Du Pont *(Madeline)*, Estelle Clark *(Mayme)*, Sidney Bracy *(Hobson)*.

Romantic comedy. Katherine Emerson, an Iowa girl hungry for the good things in life, leaves her small hometown and sets out for New York. En route, she is involved in a train wreck in which another woman is killed. Katherine finds the woman's purse and, among its contents, discovers an invitation for the woman to spend 6 months in an unoccupied luxury apartment in Manhattan. Katherine seizes this opportunity and sets up housekeeping in the elegant suite, living well and dressing in the newest fashions. Her family appears unexpectedly, and Katherine tells them that she is married to Nicholas Wentworth, the apartment's owner. Mother Emerson, disturbed that Nicholas is not living with his "wife," writes to him in Europe and asks him to return. Nicholas arrives unexpectedly and is highly amused at Katherine's predicament, taking every opportunity to make her miserable. Katherine finally decides to tell her family the truth, but she is forestalled when Nicholas, who has decided that she would make a good wife, asks her to marry him. *Motherhood. Imposture. Smalltown life. Iowa. New York City. Train wrecks.*

THE SLAVER **F2.5154**

Morris R. Schlank Productions. *Dist* Anchor Film Distributors. 7 Dec **1927** [New York showing]. Si; b&w. 35mm. 6 reels, 5,500-5,900 ft.

Dir Harry Revier. *Scen* Mabel Z. Carroll. *Story* James Oliver Curwood. *Photog* Dal Clawson.

Cast: Pat O'Malley *(Dick Farnum)*, Carmelita Geraghty *(Natalie Rivers)*, John Miljan *(Cyril Blake)*, J. P. McGowan *("Iron" Larsen)*, Billie Bennett *(Mrs. Rivers)*, William Earle *(Gumbo)*, Leo White, Phil Sleeman.

Melodrama. Sources vary—if not disagree—in describing the action in this film. According to *Film Daily* (20 Nov 1927, p7), "hero shanghaied aboard a disreputable tramp steamer; girl lured aboard nifty yacht and to top it off there's a dirty and wicked sea captain to make life miserable for the pair." *Variety* (14 Dec 1927, p26), on the other hand, describes only "a negro tribal chief on the coast of Africa making a deal with a dissolute white sea captain to buy a white girl. Supposed to be 'squared' by a negro cabin boy sacrificing his life, saving the girl from the black nabob" and "an abundance of fist fighting and hairy-chested sea-going deviltry." *Slavers. Sea captains. Tribal chiefs. Negroes. Shanghaiing. Africa.*

SLAVES OF BEAUTY **F2.5155**

Fox Film Corp. 5 Jun **1927** [c5 Jun 1927; LP24107]. Si; b&w. 35mm. 6 reels, 5,412 ft.

Pres by William Fox. *Dir* J. G. Blystone. *Adapt-Scen* William M. Conselman. *Titl* James K. McGuinness. *Photog* L. William O'Connell. *Film Ed* Margaret V. Clancey. *Asst Dir* Jasper Blystone.

Cast: Olive Tell *(Anastasia Jones)*, Holmes Herbert *(Leonard Jones)*, Earle Foxe *(Paul Perry)*, Margaret Livingston *(Goldie)*, Sue Carol *(Dorothy Jones)*, Richard Walling *(Robert)*, Mary Foy *(Irishwoman)*, Mickey Bennett.

Comedy-drama. Source: Nina Wilcox Putnam, "The Grandflapper," in *Saturday Evening Post* (199:12–13, 23 Oct 1926). When Len Jones develops a beauty clay that brings wealth to his household, his wife, Anastasia, tires of him and falls in love with the beauty shop manager, Paul Terry, a dashing young male vamp. She soon neglects their business and sells the shop to a rival, who turns out to be none other than her husband. Len acquires a new youthfulness by diet and exercise and turns the business into a highly successful enterprise, while Anastasia, learning that Terry is a scoundrel, is reconciled to her husband. *Businesswomen. Rejuvenation. Marriage. Wealth. Infidelity. Business management. Cosmetics. Beauty shops.*

SLAVES OF SCANDAL **F2.5156**

Lee-Bradford Corp. 20 Aug **1924** [New York State license]. Si; b&w. 35mm. 5 reels.

Melodrama(?). No information about the nature of this film has been found.

THE SLEEPWALKER **F2.5157**

Realart Pictures. *Dist* Paramount Pictures. 9 Apr **1922** [c8 Apr 1922; LP17751]. Si; b&w. 35mm. 5 reels, 4,530 ft.

Dir Edward Le Saint. *Scen* Wells Hastings. *Story* Aubrey Stauffer. *Photog* H. Kinley Martin.

Cast: Constance Binney *(Doris Dumond)*, Jack Mulhall *(Phillip Carruthers)*, Edythe Chapman *(Sister Ursula)*, Florence Roberts *(Mrs. Fabian Dumond)*, Bertram Grassby *(Ambrose Hammond)*, Cleo Ridgely *(Mrs. Langley)*, Winifred Edwards *(Mary Langley)*.

Melodrama. Doris Dumond is called home from a convent school by her mother, who has purchased some diamonds and has sold them although she has paid only one instalment of the price. Hammond, the dealer's agent, threatens to have her arrested unless she pays the debt within 24 hours. Doris, who is a somnambulist, enters Hammond's room at night while asleep, and purposely misconstruing her visit, he keeps her there. The house detective, her mother, and her sweetheart, Phillip, gather in the room; and with the exception of Mrs. Dumond, no one believes her story. That night, she again walks in her sleep in response to the cry of a baby who has strayed onto a windowledge in pursuit of pigeons, and she saves the child. With her innocence thus established, Phillip begs her forgiveness, pays for her mother's jewels, and is married to Doris. *Students. Somnambulism. Finance—Personal. Instalment buying.*

SLIDE, KELLY, SLIDE **F2.5158**

Metro-Goldwyn-Mayer Pictures. 12 Mar **1927** [c1 Apr 1927; LP23805]. Si; b&w. 35mm. 8 reels, 7,856 ft.

Dir Edward Sedgwick. *Screenplay* A. P. Younger. *Titl* Joe Farnham. *Photog* Henry Sharp. *Sets* Cedric Gibbons, David Townsend. *Film Ed* Frank Sullivan. *Wardrobe* André-ani. *Tech Adv* Mike Donlin.

Cast: William Haines *(Jim Kelly)*, Sally O'Neil *(Mary Munson)*, Harry Carey *(Tom Munson)*, Junior Coghlan *(Mickey Martin)*, Warner Richmond *(Cliff Macklin)*, Paul Kelly *(Fresbie)*, Karl Dane *(Swede Hansen)*, Guinn Williams *(McLean)*, Mike Donlin, Irish Meusel, Bob Meusel, Tony Lazzeri *(themselves)*.

Sports melodrama. Because of his pitching skill, Jim Kelly, a bush-leaguer, is signed with the New York Yankees, but he soon becomes egotistic and conceited over his victories, with the result that the team fails to give him support and the club begins to fall apart. The team mascot, Mickey Martin, is hurt in an accident when Kelly, who has had a falling out with Macklin, the manager, is pitching his last game in the World Series. Mickey is wheeled to the game from the hospital; and at the last minute Kelly comes through, saves the day with a home run, and wins the heart of Mary Munson. *Baseball. New York Yankees. World Series.*

SLIGHTLY SCARLET **F2.5159**

Paramount Famous Lasky Corp. 22 Feb **1930** [c23 Feb 1930; LP1105]. Sd (Movietone); b&w. 35mm. 7 reels, 6,204 ft. [Also si; 5,234 ft.]

Dir Louis Gasnier, Edwin H. Knopf. *Screenplay* Howard Estabrook, Joseph L. Mankiewicz. *Titl* Gerald Geraghty. *Story* Percy Heath. *Photog* Allen Siegler. *Film Ed* Eda Warren. *Song: "You Still Belong to Me"* Elsie Janis, Jack King.

Cast: Evelyn Brent *(Lucy Stavrin)*, Clive Brook *(Hon. Courtenay Parkes)*, Paul Lukas *(Malatroff)*, Eugene Pallette *(Sylvester Corbett)*, Helen Ware *(his wife)*, Virginia Bruce *(Enid Corbett)*, Henry Wadsworth *(Sandy Weyman)*, Claud Allister *(Albert Hawkins)*, Christiane Yves *(Marie)*, Morgan Farley *(Malatroff's victim)*.

Society melodrama. Lucy Stavrin, living in Paris as the unwilling tool of international jewel thief Malatroff, becomes interested in Parkes, a mysterious Englishman who is her neighbor, but circumstances prevent their meeting. She is assigned to steal a pearl necklace from Sylvester Corbett, a *nouveau riche* American, and posing as a countess, she goes to Nice, where she discovers that Parkes has taken the house next to that of Corbett and his family. A romance develops but is complicated when Corbett's daughter becomes infatuated with Parkes. When Lucy is finally forced to carry out the theft, she comes face to face with Parkes, discovers him to be an accomplished gentleman crook, and therefore tells him about her predicament with Malatroff. Their mutual love is strengthened, and they decide to go straight; Malatroff interrupts their plans, but he is killed as Parkes rescues Lucy from his grasp. *Gentlemen crooks. Socialites. Nouveaux riches. Thieves. English. Courtship. Paris. Nice.*

SLIGHTLY USED **F2.5160**

Warner Brothers Pictures. 3 Sep **1927** [c16 Aug 1927; LP24308]. Si; b&w. 35mm. 7 reels, 6,412 ft.

Dir Archie L. Mayo. *Scen* C. Graham Baker. *Titl* Jack Jarmuth. *Story* Melville Crossman. *Camera* Hal Mohr. *Asst Dir* Frank Shaw.

Cast: May McAvoy *(Cynthia Martin)*, Conrad Nagel *(Maj. John Smith)*, Robert Agnew *(Donald Woodward)*, Audrey Ferris *(Helen Martin)*, Anders Randolf *(Mr. Martin)*, Eugenie Besserer *(Aunt Lydia)*, Arthur Rankin *(Gerald)*, David Mir *(Horace)*, Sally Eilers *(Grace Martin)*, Jack Santoro *(Harold)*.

Farce. Cynthia Martin, taunted by her younger sisters, professes to have married by proxy a Maj. John Smith of Nicaragua, who then, she claims, rejoined his regiment. When she meets handsome Donald Woodward, they are mutually attracted, and in order to "free" herself, Cynthia "kills off" her husband by publishing an account of his death in New York newspapers. Reading his own death notice, the real Major Smith comes to the Martin home, announcing himself as a close friend of Cynthia's late husband. She fearfully plays the part of the bereaved widow until Smith reveals his identity and demands his rights as a husband. Finding that he actually loves her, Cynthia surrenders. *Nicaraguans. Personal identity. Marriage—Proxy. Courtship.*

SLIM FINGERS **F2.5161**

Universal Pictures. 24 Mar **1929** [c22 Aug 1928; LP25562]. Si; b&w. 35mm. 5 reels, 4,232 ft.

Dir Josef Levigard. *Story-Scen* William Lester. *Titl* Val Cleveland. *Photog* Charles Stumar. *Film Ed* Harry Marker.

Cast: Bill Cody *(Al Wellsley)*, Duane Thompson *(Kate)*, Wilbur Mack *(Dan Donovan)*, Monte Montague *(valet)*, Arthur Morrison *(Riley)*, Charles L. King *(Morgan)*.

Crime melodrama. Kate Graham and Dan Donovan steal a valuable painting from a country club, and Kate, making her escape alone, forces clubman Al Wellsley at gunpoint to drive her to her apartment. Al is therefore mistaken for one of the thieves and chased by the police, whom he eludes, returning to Kate for an explanation. Al runs afoul of Donovan, who knocks him out and makes off with Kate and the painting. Al recovers consciousness and gives chase. He captures Donovan, returns the painting to its rightful owner, and prepares to make a repentant Kate his wife. *Criminals—Rehabilitation. Theft. Country clubs.*

SLIM SHOULDERS **F2.5162**

Tilford Cinema Studios. *Dist* W. W. Hodkinson Corp. ca3 Sep **1922** [New York premiere; released 24 Sep 1922]. Si; b&w. 35mm. 6 reels, 6,050 or 6,783 ft.

Dir Alan Crosland. *Scen* Lawrence McCloskey. *Story* Charles K. Harris. *Photog* George Falsey.

Cast: Irene Castle *(Naomi Warren)*, Rod La Rocque *(Richard Langden)*, Anders Randolph *(Edward Langden)*, Warren Cook *(John Clinton Warren)*, Mario Carillo *(Count Giulo Morranni)*, Marie Burke *(Mrs. Warren)*.

Society melodrama. In trying to conceal evidence of her father's forgery, society girl Naomi Warren agrees to marry wealthy promoter Edward Langden, who holds the damning notes; but he dies on the eve of the wedding, and his estate falls to his nephew, Richard. Naomi next makes the acquaintance of a crook who is attempting to steal her jewels, and she persuades him to help her rob Richard's safe. Richard catches Naomi redhanded, but—rather than turn her in—he decides to reform her. Instead, they fall in love, Richard learns Naomi's true purpose in her attempted robbery, and Mr. Warren's forgery is forever secreted with the marriage of Naomi and Richard. *Socialites. Filial relations. Forgery. Inheritance. Robbery. Documentation.*

THE SLINGSHOT KID **F2.5163**

FBO Pictures. 4 Dec **1927** [c4 Dec 1927; LP24723]. Si; b&w. 35mm. 5 reels, 4,486 ft.

Pres by Joseph P. Kennedy. *Dir* Louis King. *Cont* Oliver Drake. *Story* John Twist, Jean Dupont. *Photog* Roy Eslick, William Nobles.

Cast: Buzz Barton *(Red Hepner)*, Frank Rice *(Toby)*, Jeanne Morgan *(Betty)*, Buck Connors *(Clem Windloss)*, Jay Morley *(Santa Fe Sullivan)*, Arnold Gray *(foreman)*.

Western melodrama. Drifters Little Red Hepner and his old pal Toby are pursued by a band of rustlers and escape by riding into Indigo, a haunted town where they meet Clem Windloss, a friend of Toby's. He introduces them to Betty, a young girl whose father has been killed and whose ranch is being plundered by Santa Fe Sullivan and his men. Clem mistakenly hires the Sullivan gang to punch for Betty, and at the roundup they overwhelm the foreman and keep the girl prisoner. Toby and Red don sheets and as ghosts manage to frighten and capture most of the gang with the help of Red's slingshot. Santa Fe escapes with Betty, but Red pursues and ropes the villain. *Wanderers. Ranchers. Rustlers. Ghosts.*

SLIPPY McGEE **F2.5164**

Oliver Morosco Productions. *Dist* Associated First National Pictures. 11 Jun **1923** [New York premiere; c21 Mar 1923; LP18792]. Si; b&w. 35mm. 7 reels, 6,399 ft.

Pres by Oliver Morosco. *Dir* Wesley Ruggles. *Auth* Marie Conway Oemler.

Cast: Wheeler Oakman *(Slippy McGee)*, Colleen Moore *(Mary Virginia)*, Sam De Grasse *(Father De Rance)*, Edmund Stevens *(George Inglesby)*, Edith Yorke *(Madame De Rance)*, Lloyd Whitlock *(Howard Hunter)*, Pat O'Malley *(Lawrence Mayne)*.

Crook melodrama. Severely injured in an attempted getaway, safecracker Slippy McGee is taken in by Father De Rance and nursed back to health by Mary Virginia after his leg is amputated. Under the influence of the kindness shown him, Slippy reforms and falls in love with Mary Virginia, although she intends to marry Lawrence Mayne. When George Inglesby attempts to blackmail Mary Virginia into marrying him, Slippy uses his skill one last time to obtain some incriminating letters from a safe. *Criminals—Rehabilitation. Safecrackers. Amputees. Clergymen. Blackmail. Documentation.*

SLOW AS LIGHTNING **F2.5165**

Sunset Productions. 19 Dec **1923** [New York State license; released 15 Mar 1924]. Si; b&w. 35mm. 5 reels, 4,800 ft.

Pres by Anthony J. Xydias. *Dir* Grover Jones. *Titl* I. J. "Bud" Barsky. *Story* Suzanne Avery. *Photog* Bert Longenecker.

Cast: Kenneth McDonald *(Jimmie March)*, Billy "Red" Jones *(Jimmie March, as a boy)*, Edna Pennington *(Eleanor Philips)*, Gordon Sackville *(E. J. Philips)*, William Malan *(Mortimer Fenton)*, Joe Bonner *(The Italian)*, Max Ascher *(The Hebrew)*, Otto Metzetti *(chief of crooks)*.

Western melodrama(?). No information about the nature of this film has been found.

SLOW DYNAMITE **F2.5166**

Sanford Productions. 1 Jan **1925.** Si; b&w. 35mm. 5 reels, 4,900 ft.

Dir Frank S. Mattison.

Cast: Matty Mattison.

Melodrama. "... dealing with hero who has built up a fortune which everyone around him covets, including his fiancée. A breakdown comes and he is sent out west to a sanitarium, from which he is not to return. He foils them, however, showing up their hypocrisy and marrying his nurse, with whom he has fallen in love." (*Motion Picture News Booking Guide*, 8: 72, Apr 1925.) *Nurses. Mental illness. Sanitariums.*

THE SMALL BACHELOR (Universal-Jewel) **F2.5167**

Universal Pictures. 6 Nov **1927** [c12 Jul 1927; LP24180]. Si; b&w. 35mm. 7 reels, 6,218 ft.

Pres by Carl Laemmle. *Dir* William A. Seiter. *Scen* John Clymer. *Titl* Walter Anthony. *Adapt* Rex Taylor. *Photog* Arthur Todd.

Cast: Barbara Kent *(Molly Waddington)*, André Beranger *(Finch)*, William Austin *(Algernon Chubb)*, Lucien Littlefield *(Mr. Waddington)*, Carmelita Geraghty *(Eulalia)*, Gertrude Astor *(Fanny)*, George Davis *(Garroway)*, Tom Dugan *(Mullelt)*, Vera Lewis *(Mrs. Waddington)*, Ned Sparks *(J. Hamilton Beamish)*.

Comedy. Source: Pelham Grenville Wodehouse, "The Small Bachelor," in *Liberty Magazine* (vol 3, 18 Sep–25 Dec 1926). Finch, a wealthy but bashful artist, falls in love with Molly Waddington and follows her without summoning the courage to speak to her until he retrieves her dog and is invited into her home. There he finds the matronly Mrs. Waddington scolding her husband for reading Wild West novels and imagining himself a cowboy; she sends Finch away finding him an unsuitable match for her daughter, preferring instead Algernon Chubb. Finch prevails upon his friend Beamish to smooth the path for him, and Mrs. Waddington consents to the marriage but immediately plans with Algernon to break it up. On the wedding day, a notorious woman named Fanny claims that Finch is her husband, but Finch reveals the plot and prepares to elope with Molly. In a series of mixups involving a cabaret raid, Mrs. Waddington and Algernon are found in a "compromising situation" and forced to permit the marriage. *Bachelors. Artists. Courtship. Weddings. Cabarets. Western fiction. Reading.*

A SMALL TOWN IDOL **F2.5168**

Mack Sennett Productions. *Dist* Associated Producers. 13 Feb **1921** [c16 Feb 1921; LP16165]. Si; b&w. 35mm. 7 reels.

Pres by Mack Sennett. *Supv-Scen* Mack Sennett. *Dir* Erle Kenton. *Photog* Perry Evans, J. R. Lockwood. *Spec Photog* Fred Jackman.

Cast: Ben Turpin *(Sam Smith [Samuel X. Smythe])*, James Finlayson *(J. Wellington Jones)*, Phyllis Haver *(Mary Brown)*, Bert Roach *(Martin Brown)*, Al Cooke *(Joe Barnum)*, Charles Murray *(Sheriff Sparks)*, Marie Prevost *(Marcelle Mansfield)*, Dot Farley *(Mrs. Smith)*, Eddie Gribbon *(bandit chief)*, Kalla Pasha *(bandit chief's rival)*, Billy Bevan *(director)*, George O'Hara *(cameraman)*.

Farce. Sam Smith is engaged to the village belle until he is accused of stealing by J. Wellington Jones and is driven from town. Chance leads him to a film studio in Los Angeles, where, in desperation, he stands in for an actor who declines to jump off a bridge. Becoming a success as a result, he returns to the town rich and famous but finds himself jailed and threatened with lynching. A confession by the heroine's father finally frees him, and he becomes the "small town idol." *Actors. Motion pictures. Smalltown life. Hollywood.*

THE SMART SET **F2.5169**

Metro-Goldwyn-Mayer Pictures. 25 Feb or 10 Mar **1928** [c25 Feb 1928; LP25326]. Si; b&w. 35mm. 7 reels, 6,476 ft.

Dir Jack Conway. *Scen* Byron Morgan, Ann Price. *Titl* Robert Hopkins. *Story* Byron Morgan. *Photog* Oliver Marsh. *Sets* Cedric Gibbons, Merrill Pye. *Film Ed* Sam S. Zimbalist. *Wardrobe* David Cox.

Cast: William Haines *(Tommy)*, Jack Holt *(Nelson)*, Alice Day *(Polly)*, Hobart Bosworth *(Durant)*, Coy Watson, Jr. *(Sammy)*, Constance Howard *(Cynthia)*, Paul Nicholson *(Mr. Van Buren)*, Julia Swayne Gordon *(Mrs. Van Buren)*.

Society comedy-drama. Tommy Van Buren, star player on a polo team, is thrown off the team for lack of teamwork, disowned by his father, and dispossessed of his horse, Pronto. In an important match with Great Britain, the American team fares badly. Team captain Nelson, his rival for Polly, drops out of the game injured. Tommy is restored to the team in time to win the match. Incidentally, he also wins Polly. *Smart set. Polo. Sportsmanship. Horses.*

THE SMART SEX **F2.5170**

Universal Film Manufacturing Co. Mar **1921** [c16 Mar 1921; LP16296]. Si; b&w. 35mm. 5 reels, 4,800 ft.

Pres by Carl Laemmle. *Dir* Fred Leroy Granville. *Scen* Doris Schroeder. *Story* Emma Bell Clifton. *Photog* Leland Lancaster.

Cast: Eva Novak *(Rose)*, Frank Braidwood *(Guy)*, Geoffrey Webb *(Fred)*, Mayre Hall *(Edith)*, C. Norman Hammond *(Mr. Vaughn)*, Dorothy Hagan *(Mrs. Vaughn)*, Calvert Carter *(Mr. Haskins)*, Margaret Mann *(Mrs. Haskins)*, Jim O'Neill *(Danny)*, Evelyn McCoy *(Dorothy)*.

Rural comedy-melodrama. Rose, a stranded showgirl, participates in a local amateur show and wins the prize. After the performance she meets a wealthy young man who buys her supper, gets her an accommodation on a farm adjoining his father's estate, and turns farmhand to win her love. His family objects to the girl, and when a jewel robbery occurs during a party Rose is suspected. She uncovers the thief, however, and soon the wedding day is set. *Actors. Theater—Amateur. Farming. Robbery.*

Note: Working title: *The Girl and the Goose.*

SMASHED BACK **F2.5171**

Hollywood Producers Finance Association. *Dist* Hi-Mark Productions. 19 Dec **1927** [New York State license]. Si; b&w. 35mm. 5 reels, ca4,500 ft.

Western melodrama(?). No information about the nature of this film has been found.

SMASHING BARRIERS **F2.5172**

Vitagraph Co. of America. 17 Jun **1923** [c13 Jul 1923; LP19242]. Si; b&w. 35mm. 6 reels, 5,906 ft.

Dir William Duncan. *Scen* Graham Baker, R. Cecil Smith, Harvey Gates. *Story* Albert E. Smith, Cyrus Townsend Brady.

Cast: William Duncan *(Dan Stevens)*, Edith Johnson *(Helen Cole)*, Joe Ryan *("Wirenail" Hedges)*, Walter Rogers *("Slicker" Williams)*, George Stanley *(John Stevens)*, Frederick Darnton *(Benjamin Cole)*, Slim Cole *("Long Tom" Brown)*, William McCall *(Henry Marlin)*.

Western melodrama. A compact arrangement of the most exciting episodes in the 15-chapter serial formerly bearing this title, its hero is Dan Stevens, a young man who goes out west, gets a job in a logging camp, falls in love with the owner's daughter, and rescues both from the camp's foreman and his gang when they try to take ownership of the camp. *Gangs. Lumbering.*

Note: Edited from the serial, of the same title, released in 15 chapters in 1919. The names of the characters, however, have been changed.

SMILE, BROTHER, SMILE **F2.5173**

Charles R. Rogers Productions. *Dist* First National Pictures. 27 Aug **1927** [New York premiere; released 11 Sep; c1 Aug 1927; LP24251]. Si; b&w. 35mm. 7 reels, 6,669 ft.

Prod Charles R. Rogers. *Dir* John Francis Dillon. *Titl* Dwinelle Benthall, Rufus McCosh. *Adapt* Rex Taylor. *Story* Al Boasberg. *Camera* Charles Van Enger.

Cast: Jack Mulhall *(Jack Lowery)*, Dorothy Mackaill *(Mildred Marvin)*, Philo McCullough *(Harvey Renrod)*, E. J. Ratcliffe *(Fred Bowers)*, Harry Dunkinson *(Mr. Potter)*, Ernest Hilliard *(Mr. Saunders)*, Charles Clary *(Mr. Markel)*, Jack Dillon *(Mr. Kline)*, Yola D'Avril *(Daisy)*, Hank Mann *(The Collector)*, T. Roy Barnes, Jed Prouty, Sam Blum *(three high-powered salesmen)*.

Comedy-drama. Jack Lowrey, of the Bonfillia Cosmetic Co., who is engaged to Mildred Marvin (a secretary), is given an opportunity as a salesman by Mr. Bowers, the company president. While lunching at a fashionable cafe, they see Renrod, the sales manager, with the manager of the Florodora, a rival concern, and Mildred overhears talk that suggests Renrod is in the pay of the rival company. On Jack's first trip, Renrod deliberately tries to thwart his success; but Mildred intercepts the messages, with the result that Jack proves himself. When Jack reports that a wholesaler has placed his order with Saunders, Mildred "sends" a model for a beauty demonstration; and after a "transformation" the model emerges as a ravishing creature who is actually Mildred. Renrod's dishonesty is exposed, and Jack wins his position for his good work. *Salesmen. Secretaries. Demonstrators—Commercial products. Cosmetics. Business competition.*

SMILES ARE TRUMPS **F2.5174**

Fox Film Corp. 5 Feb **1922** [c5 Feb 1922; LP17600]. Si; b&w. 35mm. 5 reels, 4,049 ft.

Pres by William Fox. *Dir* George E. Marshall. *Scen* Delbert F. Davenport. *Photog* Frank B. Good.

Cast: Maurice B. Flynn *(Jimmy Carson)*, Ora Carew *(Marjorie Manning)*, Myles McCarthy *(John Slevin)*, Herschel Mayall *(James Manning)*, Kirke Lucas *(Enrico)*, C. Norman Hammond *(Martino)*.

Melodrama. Source: Frank L. Packard, "The Iron Rider," in *All-Story Magazine* (vol 55–56, 11 Mar–8 Apr 1916). Jimmy Carson, assistant paymaster of a railroad company, discovers that Slevin, his superior, is cheating the company. Out of fear, Slevin instructs his foreman, Martino, to thrash Carson. Following the assault, Carson resigns and engages in a fight with Slevin, whom he knocks unconscious. Believing he has killed him, Carson starts for the county seat to surrender. He happens to board the special train of James Manning, the company's vice president, who—accompanied by his daughter Marjorie—is on an inspection tour. Meanwhile, Slevin, having stolen from the company and framed Carson for the theft, joins Martino; and the two capture the official's locomotive and escape with Marjorie. Carson, now on the track of Slevin's gang, pursues in a locomotive chase and routs the gang. *Paymasters. Railroad magnates. Railroads. Theft. Chases.*

SMILIN' AT TROUBLE **F2.5175**

Harry Garson Productions. *Dist* Film Booking Offices of America. 6 Dec **1925** [c6 Dec 1925; LP22086]. Si; b&w. 35mm. 6 reels, 5,175 ft.

Dir Harry Garson. *Screen Adapt–Cont* Gertrude Orr, A. B. Barringer. *Story* Rob Wagner. *Camera* Gilbert Warrenton.

Cast: Maurice B. Flynn *(Jerry Foster)*, Helen Lynch *(Alice Arnold)*, Ray Ripley *(Lafayette Van Renselaer)*, Lee Shumway *(Swazey)*, Charles McHugh *(Clancey O'Toole)*, Hal Wilson *(Michael Arnold)*, Kathleen Myers *(Kathleen O'Toole)*, Raymond Turner *(colored boy)*, Joe O'Brien *(Tom)*.

Melodrama. Wealthy contractor Michael Arnold hires civil engineer Jerry Foster to work on a dam he is constructing in the West. He has ambitions to make his mark in society and encourages his daughter, Alice, to marry Lafayette Van Renselaer, a blueblooded young dandy. Alice is attracted to Jerry but mistakes his friendship with Kathleen O'Toole for love. Meanwhile, Van Renselaer has been having an affair with Kathleen but drops her when he has an opportunity to wed Alice. He imputes that Jerry has been trifling with Kathleen's affections. Jerry finally uncovers the conspiracy and in a showdown beats up and fires Swazey, the bullying foreman, who then runs amok, releasing the water in the reservoir and causing a flood. Van Renselaer drowns, but Jerry saves Alice and wins her hand. *Contractors. Engineers—Civil. Construction foremen. Dandies. Dams. Social Classes. Floods.*

Note: Copyright title: *Smiling at Trouble.*

SMILIN' GUNS (Universal–Jewel) **F2.5176**

Universal Pictures. 31 Mar **1929** [c22 Aug 1928; LP25560]. Si; b&w. 35mm. 6 reels, 5,270 ft.

Dir Henry MacRae. *Scen* George Morgan. *Titl* Harold Tarshis. *Story* Shannon Fife. *Photog* Harry Neumann. *Film Ed* Gilmore Walker.

Cast: Hoot Gibson *(Jack Purvin)*, Blanche Mehaffey *(Helen Van Smythe)*, Virginia Pearson *(Mrs. Van Smythe)*, Robert Graves *(Durkin)*, Leo White *(Count Baretti)*, Walter Brennan *(ranch foreman)*, Jack Wise *(professor)*, James Bradbury, Jr. *(barber)*, Dad Gibson *(stationmaster)*.

Western melodrama. "Dirty Neck" Jack Purvin sees a newspaper picture of beautiful Helen Van Smythe, an eastern socialite who has come west to summer on a dude ranch; falling in love with her at first sight, he visits a San Francisco specialist who promises to make him a Galahad in 2 weeks. Jack returns from San Francisco with some new and somewhat unusual manners and becomes the foreman of the dude ranch, where he saves Helen from the continental villainy of phony Count Baretti and protects her mother's jewelry from Durkin, a low bandit. Recognizing Jack's good nature despite his rough manner, Helen declares her love for him. *Socialites. Ranch foremen. Newspapers. Dude ranches. San Francisco.*

SMILIN' ON **F2.5177**

Sanford Productions. 15 Apr or 1 Jul **1923.** Si; b&w. 35mm. 5 reels, 4,166 ft.

Dir William J. Craft.

Cast: Pete Morrison, Gene Crosby.

Western comedy-drama. "Bashful cowboy in love with the village belle, captures the mysterious masked rider, a bandit, who proves to be his rival for the girl's hand." (*Motion Picture News Booking Guide,* 5:49, Oct 1923.) *Cowboys. Bandits.*

SMILIN' THROUGH **F2.5178**

Norma Talmadge Productions. *Dist* Associated First National Pictures. 13 Feb **1922** [c7 May 1922; LP18047]. Si; b&w. 35mm. 8 reels, 8,000 ft.

Pres by Joseph M. Schenck. *Supv* Joe Aller. *Dir* Sidney A. Franklin. *Adapt* Sidney A. Franklin, James Ashmore Creelman. *Photog* Charles Rosher, Roy Hunt.

Cast: Norma Talmadge *(Kathleen/Moonyeen)*, Wyndham Standing *(John Carteret)*, Harrison Ford *(Kenneth Wayne/Jeremiah Wayne)*, Alec B. Francis *(Dr. Owen)*, Glenn Hunter *(Willie Ainsley)*, Grace Griswold *(Ellen)*, Miriam Battista *(Little Mary, Moonyeen's sister)*, Eugene Lockhart *(village rector)*.

Romantic drama. Source: Allan Langdon Martin, *"Smilin' Through"; a Romantic Comedy in Three Acts* (New York, c1924). On the very day that John Carteret is to wed Moonyeen, Jeremiah Wayne, one of Moonyeen's rejected suitors, inadvertently kills her while attempting to shoot John. Twenty years later, John's niece, Kathleen, announces to his shock that she is going to marry Jeremiah Wayne's son, Kenneth. John bitterly opposes the match and orders Kathleen never to see Kenneth again. The World War breaks out, and Kenneth goes to France, where he is badly wounded. Returning to the United States, he allows Kathleen (who has waited patiently for him to return) to believe that he has come to love another. Kathleen is heartbroken, and John, feeling her sorrow keenly, arranges for her to be united with Kenneth. With the young lovers together again, John quietly dies, joining the spirit of Moonyeen in the Great Beyond. *Uncles. Murder. World War I. Supernatural.*

Note: Copyright title: *Smiling Through.*

SMILING ALL THE WAY **F2.5179**

D. N. Schwab Productions. *Dist* Jans Productions. Feb **1921** [c19 Jul 1920; LU15364]. Si; b&w. 35mm. 5 reels, 4,979 ft.

Dir Fred J. Butler. *Co-Dir* Hugh McClung. *Scen* Paul Schofield. *Photog* Robert Martin. *Art Dir* Danny Hall. *Art Titl* Frank Currier.

Cast: David Butler *(Hannibal Pillsbury)*, Leatrice Joy *(Alice Drydan)*, Frances Raymond *(Alice's Aunt Ellen)*, J. Parker McConnell *(Andrew Cadman)*, Rhea Haines *(Minerva Finch)*, Helen Scott *(Teddy McCall)*, Charles Smiley *(Professor Kingsbury)*, Arthur Reddin *(Mickey)*, P. D. Tabler, Harry Duffield, Charles McHugh *(The "Big Three")*, Jack Cosgrave *(The Chef)*, Lydia Yeamans Titus *(Mrs. Webster)*, Peggy Blackwood *(Mary Green-Brown)*.

Comedy-drama. Source: Henry Payson Dowst, "Alice in Underland" (publication undetermined). Hannibal Pillsbury, a shy country boy who was star cook in a Maine lumber camp famous for his flapjacks, and snobbish society girl Alice Drydan take over the Purple Guinea Pig Restaurant in Greenwich Village and make it prosper. Alice's Aunt Ellen, anxious for her to marry a wealthy suitor, has her kidnaped aboard lumberman Andrew Cadman's yacht. Hannibal rescues her, however, and they return to the Purple Guinea Pig after a visit to the minister. *Cooks. Lumber camps. Restaurants. New York City—Greenwich Village.*

SMILING BILLY **F2.5180**

Duke Worne Productions. *Dist* Rayart Pictures. Jan **1927.** Si; b&w. 35mm. 5 reels, 4,434 ft.

Dir Duke Worne. *Photog* Ernest Smith.

Cast: Billy Sullivan.

Melodrama. "U. S. gob learns of lunatic's contraption meant for the destruction of the U. S. fleet. When his girl is captured by lunatic, fellow gobs help hero defeat madman's henchmen and rescue heroine." (*Motion Picture News Booking Guide,* 12:54, Apr 1927.) *Sailors. Lunatics. Sabotage. Abduction. United States Navy.*

SMILING AT TROUBLE *see* **SMILIN' AT TROUBLE**

SMILING IRISH EYES **F2.5181**

First National Pictures. 28 Jul **1929** [c18 Sep 1929; LP740]. Sd (Vitaphone); b&w. 35mm. 8 reels, 8,550 ft. [Also si, 22 Sep 1929; 7,932 ft.]

Prod John McCormick. *Dir* William A. Seiter. *Story-Screenplay-Titl-Dial* Tom J. Geraghty. *Photog* Sid Hickox, Henry Freulich. *Set Dsgn* Anton Grot. *Film Ed* Al Hall. *Mus* Louis Silvers. *Songs: "A Wee Bit of Love," "Then I'll Ride Home With You," "Old Killarney Fair"* Norman Spencer, Herman Ruby. *Song: "Smiling Irish Eyes"* Ray Perkins. *Choreog* Larry Ceballos, Walter Wills, Carl McBride. *Asst Dir* James Dunne. *Wardrobe* Edward Stevenson.

Cast: Colleen Moore *(Kathleen O'Connor)*, James Hall *(Rory O'More)*, Robert Homans *(Shamus O'Connor)*, Claude Gillingwater *(Michael O'Connor)*, Tom O'Brien *("Black Barney" O'Toole)*, Robert E. O'Connor *(Sir Timothy Tyrone)*, Aggie Herring *(Grandmother O'More)*, Betty Francisco *(Frankie West)*, Julanne Johnston *(Goldie De Vere)*, Edward Earle *(George Prescott)*, Fred Kelsey *(county fair manager)*, Barney Gilmore, Charles McHugh *(his assistants)*, Madame Bosocki *(fortune-teller)*, George Hayes *(taxi driver)*, Anne Schaefer *(landlady)*, John Beck *(Sir Timothy's butler)*, Oscar Apfel *(Max North)*, Otto Lederer *(Izzy Levi)*, William Strauss *(Moe Levi)*, Dave Thursby *(Scotch barker)*, Dan Crimmins *(The Trouble-maker)*.

Comedy-drama. Rory O'More, a musician who works in an Irish peat bog, comes to the United States, leaving his sweetheart, Kathleen, behind.

He promises to send for her as soon as he makes good. Although he writes letters daily to Kathleen, he does not post them, determined to hold them until he has good news to go with them. Finally he gets a job playing the violin in a theatrical production. Despondent at not hearing from him, Kathleen borrows money to go to America and to bring Rory back to Ireland. She returns to Ireland in a huff when she sees Rory on stage playing their song, "Darlin' My Darlin'," while a blonde girl kisses him. They are reconciled when Rory appears in Ireland and explains everything to Kathleen's satisfaction, and the whole family emigrates to the States. *Immigrants. Irish. Musicians. Violinists. Theater. Peat bogs.*

SMILING JIM F2.5182

Phil Goldstone Productions. 1 Apr **1922.** Si; b&w. 35mm. 5 reels.

Dir Joseph Franz. *Story-Cont* Hal C. Norfleet. *Photog* Edgar Lyons.

Cast: Franklyn Farnum *(Smiling Jim/Frank Harmon)*, Alma Bennett *(Louise Briggs)*, Percy Challenger *(Judd Briggs)*, Al Ferguson *(Sheriff Thomas)*.

Western melodrama. Smiling Jim, a young stranger in town, has to leave hurriedly to escape the sheriff, who mistakes him for a wanted bandit, but Jim finds refuge on the outskirts of town with Louise Briggs. Shortly thereafter, Frank Harmon, another stranger—this one elegant and bearing a strong resemblance to Smiling Jim—arrives by train. After some complications Smiling Jim is cleared, and Frank is revealed to be Jim's brother. *Sheriffs. Bandits. Brothers. Mistaken identity.*

THE SMILING TERROR F2.5183

Universal Pictures. 30 Jun **1929** [c16 Nov 1928; LP25837]. Si; b&w. 35mm. 5 reels, 4,525 ft.

Supv William Lord Wright. *Dir* Josef Levigard. *Scen* George Plympton. *Titl* Val Cleveland. *Story* William Lester. *Photog* William Adams. *Film Ed* Gene Havlick.

Cast: Ted Wells *(Ted Wayne)*, Derelys Perdue *(Mabel)*, Al Ferguson *(Hank Sims)*, Bud Osborne *(Ned)*.

Western melodrama. Ted Wayne, a smiling, dangerous cowboy, rescues Mabel and her father from a runaway team and later advises the old man against buying a mine from Hank Sims, an unsavory character. The old man buys the mine anyway, and Ted must rescue Mabel when she falls down a shaft. Mabel's father discovers a rich vein of ore, and Sims kidnaps Mabel in an attempt to get the mine back. Ted rescues Mabel for the third time and puts the unscrupulous Sims out of business. *Cowboys. Prospectors. Kidnaping. Mines.*

SMILING THROUGH *see* **SMILIN' THROUHGH**

SMOKE BELLEW F2.5184

Big 4 Productions. *Dist* First Division Distributors. 25 Jan **1929** [New York showing]. Si; b&w. 35mm. 7 reels, 6,605 ft.

Supv David Thomas. *Dir* Scott Dunlap. *Scen-Titl* Fred Myton. *Photog* J. O. Taylor, Joseph Walters. *Film Ed* Charles Hunt.

Cast: Conway Tearle *(Kit "Smoke" Bellew)*, Barbara Bedford *(Joy Gastrell)*, Mark Hamilton *(Shorty)*, Alphonse Ethier *(Harry Sprague)*, William Scott *(Stine)*, Alaska Jack, J. P. Lockney.

Northwest melodrama. Source: Jack London, *Smoke Bellew* (London, 1912). "A romance of the Klondike. During the gold rush of 1897 there is great rivalry between the 'Sourdoughs,' who were the old timers, and the 'Chekakos,' the new comers. A girl and her father after many heartbreaking experiences finally stake their claim through the aid of a man [Kit "Smoke" Bellew] who comes to the Klondike to forget his past. Romance enters his life when he meets the girl whose loyalty and heroism have brought her father and her through many hardships." (*National Board of Review Magazine,* Oct 1928, p8.) *Prospectors. Sourdoughs. Cheechakos. Gold rushes. Mine claims. Klondike.*

THE SMOKE EATERS F2.5185

Trem Carr Productions. *Dist* Rayart Pictures. 5 Nov **1926** [New York State license]. Si; b&w. 35mm. 6 reels, 5,716 ft.

Dir? (see note) Charles Hunt, Charles Hutchison. *Story-Scen* Arthur Hoerl. *Photog* William Tuers.

Cast: Cullen Landis *(Ed)*, Wanda Hawley *(Jacqueline)*, Edward Cecil *(Edmund Kane)*, Aryel Darma *(his wife)*, Broderick O'Farrell *(Roscoe Wingate)*, Mae Prestelle *(Marie Wingate)*, Harold Austin *(Kenneth Wingate)*, Baby Moncur *(Junior Wingate)*.

Society melodrama. "Society people lose two-year old son in ship-fire and fireman, finding child, adopts him. Society people get baby girl. Both children grow up, meet in later years but girl has affair with rich profligate. Boy has become fireman and through his instrumentality girl is saved from death in fire. She gives up rich youth and marries firefighter." (*Motion Picture News Booking Guide,* 12:54, Apr 1927.) *Firemen. Adoption. Fires. Ship fires.*

Note: Sources disagree in crediting direction.

SMOKING GUNS F2.5186

Bud Barsky Productions. *Dist* Wild West Pictures. Apr **1927.** Si; b&w. 35mm. 5 reels, 4,500-4,900 ft.

Cast: Al Hoxie, Buddy Roosevelt *(see note)*.

Western melodrama(?). No information about the nature of this film has been found.

Note: A New York State duplicate license application lists Buddy Roosevelt as the star of this film.

THE SMOKING TRAIL F2.5187

Frank D. Hutter Productions. *Dist* Madoc Sales. 22 Sep **1924** [New York State license]. Si; b&w. 35mm. 5 reels, 4,500 ft.

Dir William Bertram.

Cast: Bill Patton, William Bertram, Jack House, Tom Ross, Alma Rayford, Adrian Rayford, Maine Geary.

Western melodrama. "... with a plot concerning the capture of cattle rustlers by a Ranger who makes his investigations while working as a cowboy. His disclosure of the crooks comes opportunely for Barton, ranch owner, who has been forced to borrow money from Lathrop, the head of the rustlers gang. The ranger's reward is the love of the beautiful daughter of Barton." (*Motion Picture News Booking Guide,* 8:73, Apr 1925.) *Cowboys. Texas Rangers. Ranchers. Rustlers. Debt.*

SMOOTH AS SATIN F2.5188

R-C Pictures. *Dist* Film Booking Offices of America. 14 Jun **1925** [c14 Jun 1925; LP21597]. Si; b&w. 35mm. 6 reels, 6,003 ft.

Dir Ralph Ince. *Adapt-Cont* Fred Kennedy Myton. *Photog* Silvano Balboni. *Asst Dir* Pan Berman.

Cast: Evelyn Brent *(Gertie Jones)*, Bruce Gordon *(Jimmy Hartigan)*, Fred Kelsey *(Kersey)*, Fred Esmelton *(Bill Munson)*, Mabel Van Buren *(Mrs. Manson)*, John Gough *(Henderson)*.

Melodrama. Source: Bayard Veiller, "The Chatterbox" (publication undetermined). Gertie Jones, a female raffles posing as a maid in a fancy home in order to rifle the safe, suprises Jimmy Hartigan in the act of robbing that very safe. She offers to split the take 50-50, a proposition to which he is about to agree when the police arrive. Jim takes full responsibility for the crime, protecting Gertie from arrest. Gertie helps Jim escape from jail, and they take refuge in the country, where they are married by an overeager magistrate who believes them to be an eloping couple. Jim and Gertie decide to go straight and return to the city, investing $10,000 in stolen cash with Bill Munson, who runs off with it. Jim is rearrested by a detective, and Gertie goes after Munson, recovering the money. Jim is being returned by rail to the penitentiary when Gertie boards the train, offering the money to the detective in return for Jim's freedom. The detective refuses until Jim and Gertie save his life when the train is caught in a tunnel collapse. The detective then promises to return the money, letting Jim go to begin a new life with Gertie. *Housemaids. Detectives. Justices of the peace. Safecrackers. Jailbreaks. Tunnels. Train wrecks.*

SMOULDERING FIRES F2.5189

Dist Universal Pictures. 18 Jan **1925** [c25 Nov 1924; LP20842]. Si; b&w. 35mm. 8 reels, 7,356 ft.

Dir Clarence Brown. *Screenplay* Sada Cowan, Howard Higgin, Melville Brown. *Titl* Dwinelle Benthall. *Story* Margaret Deland, Sada Cowan, Howard Higgin. *Photog* Jackson Rose. *Art Dir (see note)* Leo E. Kuter, E. E. Sheeley. *Film Ed* Edward Schroeder. *Asst Dir* Charles Dorian.

Cast: Pauline Frederick *(Jane Vale)*, Laura La Plante *(Dorothy)*, Malcolm McGregor *(Robert Elliott)*, Tully Marshall *(Scotty)*, Wanda Hawley *(Lucy)*, Helen Lynch *(Kate Brown)*, George Cooper *(Mugsy)*, Bert Roach, Billy Gould, Rolfe Sedan, Jack McDonald, William Orlamond, Robert Mack, Frank Newberg *(members of the committee)*.

Drama. At 40, Jane Vale, a domineering and successful businesswoman, falls in love with Robert Elliott, a young man employed in the factory she manages. She makes him her private secretary, and he soon asks her to marry him, both out of gratitude and to defend her reputation against the ugly gossip of his fellow workers. Before the wedding, Jane's younger sister, Dorothy, returns from college, and she and Robert fall in love, but they lack the courage to tell Jane. Robert and Jane are married, and he tries to make her happy, but everything conspires to make her feel the difference in their ages: she is worn out and worried, unsuccessfully trying to look young and unable to mingle easily with Robert's young friends. When Jane finally realizes that Robert, though he is faithful and attentive to her, is really in love with Dorothy, she pretends that she no longer loves him and asks for a divorce. Robert and Dorothy, alike in age and inclination, are thus free to find the happiness that has eluded Jane. *Businesswomen. Secretaries. Sisters. Self-sacrifice. Divorce. Factory management. Yosemite National Park.*

Note: Some exteriors were shot in Yosemite National Park. At least one source credits Kuter as art director.

SMUDGE **F2.5190**

Charles Ray Productions. *Dist* First National Exhibitors Circuit. Jul **1922** [c11 Jul 1922; LP18048]. Si; b&w. 35mm. 5 reels, 4,830 ft. [Copyrighted as 6 reels.]

Pres by Arthur S. Kane. *Dir* Charles Ray. *Story-Scen* Rob Wagner. *Titl* Edward Withers. *Photog* George Rizard. *Asst Photog* Ellsworth H. Rumer. *Art Dir* Alfred W. Alley. *Film Ed* Harry Decker. *Asst Dir* Al Ray, Charles Van Deroef.

Cast: Charles Ray *(Stephen Stanton)*, Charles K. French *(John Stanton)*, Florence Oberle *(Mrs. Clement)*, Ora Carew *(Marie Clement)*, J. P. Lockney *(Purdy)*, Blanche Rose *(Mrs. Purdy)*, Lloyd Bacon *(McGuire)*, Ralph McCullough *(Regan)*.

Comedy-drama. Returning from college to take over his father's newspaper, Stephen Stanton changes its editorial policy and comes out against the use of smudge pots to fight frost in the local orange groves. His father, the local politicians, and the rival newspaper conspire against him. After a kidnaping and a daring automobile escape, he unveils a device to eliminate the need for smudge pots, thus winning the day. *Editors. Newspapers. Kidnaping. Agriculture. Fruit culture.*

THE SNARL OF HATE **F2.5191**

Bischoff Productions. 15 Mar **1927** [New York showing]. Si; b&w. 35mm. 6 reels, 5,300 ft.

Pres by Sam Bischoff. *Dir* Noel Mason Smith. *Scen* Ben Allah. *Story* Edward Curtiss, Noel Mason Smith. *Photog* James Brown.

Cast: Johnnie Walker *(Charles Taylor/Robert Taylor)*, Mildred June *(Laura Warren)*, Jack Richardson *(William Reynolds)*, Wheeler Oakman *(Boyd* [*Maxson*]*)*, Silverstreak *(a dog)*.

Melodrama. "Johnnie Walker is two people in this picture. The odd man is his bearded brother, killed early by a human vulture [William Reynolds] who preys on luckless prospectors .... Scene switches to the city, where the smooth-shaven twin tracks down the murderers through the discovery of a mating glove by Silverstreak in the home of the gal's guardian. Walker stages a night club scrap with Wheeler Oakman, assistant villain." (*Variety*, 16 Mar 1927, p19.) *Twins. Brothers. Guardians. Prospectors. Murder. Nightclubs. Dogs.*

THE SNITCHING HOUR **F2.5192**

Houseman Comedies. *Dist* Clark-Cornelius Corp. 1 Jul or 11 Aug **1922.** Si; b&w. 35mm. 5 reels, 4,850 ft.

Pres by Herbert L. Steiner. *Dir* Alan Crosland. *Story-Scen* Lewis Allen Browne. *Titl* Joseph W. Farnham.

Cast: Arthur Houseman *(Bunny)*, Gladys Leslie *(Lois Dickerson)*, Frank Currier *(Mr. Dickerson)*, Nita Naldi *(The "Countess")*, George Lessey *(Larry)*, Mario Carillo.

Comedy. A valuable ruby in Mr. Dickerson's possession and hidden in his wine cellar attracts a pair of crooks, who pose as a count and countess. Mr. Dickerson and his daughter, Lois, give a weekend party, during which the "countess" uses her wiles to learn the gem's whereabouts. Mr. Dickerson suspects nothing, but Lois' suitor, Bunny, foils the crooks' scheme when he industriously samples the contents of the cellar and there finds and absentmindedly pockets the ruby. Firmly established in Mr. Dickerson's good graces, Bunny wins Lois with his promise to reform. *Imposture. Drunkenness.*

THE SNOB **F2.5193**

Realart Pictures. Jan **1921** [c27 Dec 1920; LP15981]. Si; b&w. 35mm. 5 reels, 4,015 ft.

Dir Sam Wood. *Scen* Alice Eyton. *Photog* Alfred Gilks.

Cast: Wanda Hawley *(Kathryn Haynes)*, Edwin Stevens *(Jim Haynes)*, Walter Hiers *(Pud Welland)*, Sylvia Ashton *(Mrs. Haynes)*, William E. Lawrence *(Capt. Bill Putnam)*, Julia Faye *(Betty Welland)*, Richard Wayne *("Pep" Kennedy)*.

Comedy-drama. Source: William J. Neidig, "The Snob," in *Saturday Evening Post* (28 Sep 1918). Kathryn Haynes, daughter of Jimmie Haynes, ex-sheepherder turned oil millionaire, is snobbish as a result of her parents' social ambitions. Home from college, she meets Bill Putnam, a football hero. At a college dance, Kathryn strikes his name from her dance card when she finds out that he is working his way through college by waiting on tables. His wealthy friends teach her a lesson by telling her they are waiters too. Kathryn leaves the party in a rage and spends the next days observing the behavior of others, concluding that work and service are commendable virtues; and to atone for her previous scorn for such things, she works as a waitress in a restaurant where Bill's friends spy her. When Bill is told of the new Kathryn, he rushes to her and proposes. After the wedding, Mr. Haynes puts Bill in charge of his oil interests. *Sheepherders. Millionaires. Waiters. Waitresses. Snobbery. Football. Oil business.*

THE SNOB **F2.5194**

Metro-Goldwyn-Mayer Pictures. 3 or 10 Nov **1924** [c10 Nov 1924; LP20768]. Si; b&w. 35mm. 7 reels, 6,495 ft.

Pres by Louis B. Mayer. *Dir-Scen* Monta Bell. *Photog* André Barlatier. *Film Ed* Ralph Lawson. *Cost* Sophie Wachner. *Set Dsgn* Cedric Gibbons.

Cast: John Gilbert *(Eugene Curry)*, Norma Shearer *(Nancy Claxton)*, Conrad Nagel *(Herrick Appleton)*, Phyllis Haver *(Dorothy Rensheimer)*, Hedda Hopper *(Mrs. Leiter)*, Margaret Seddon *(Mrs. Curry)*, Aileen Manning *(Lottie)*, Hazel Kennedy *(Florence)*, Gordon Sackville *(Sherwood Claxton)*, Roy Laidlaw *(doctor)*, Nellie Bly Baker *(maid)*.

Drama. Source: Helen Reimensnyder Martin, *The Snob; the Story of a Marriage* (New York, 1924). Nancy Claxton disappears when her wealthy father is involved in a scandal and becomes a teacher in a small Pennsylvania town. There she meets Eugene Curry, also a teacher. He is determined to climb the ladder of wealthy society, shuns his Mennonite family, and fawns on anyone of prominence. Eugene marries Nancy but continues his affair with wealthy Dorothy Rensheimer; and Eugene's friend Herrick Appleton recognizes Nancy as his childhood sweetheart. Nancy gives birth to a stillborn child, blames the tragedy on her awareness of a letter to Dorothy from Eugene, and reveals to him that she is an heiress. Suddenly contrite, Eugene tries to regain his wife's love, but Nancy announces her intention to divorce him so as to marry Herrick. *Schoolteachers. Mennonites. Social climbers. Social classes. Snobbery. Wealth. Infidelity. Marriage. Pennsylvania.*

THE SNOB BUSTER **F2.5195**

Harry J. Brown Productions. *Dist* Rayart Pictures. 19 May **1925** [New York State license application]. Si; b&w. 35mm. 5 reels, 4,970 ft.

Pres by W. Ray Johnston. *Dir* Albert Rogell. *Scen* Forrest Sheldon. *Photog* Ross Fisher.

Cast: Reed Howes *(Ted Pendergast)*, Wilfred Lucas *(John Pendergast)*, George French *(Uncle Tobias)*, David Kirby *(Butch McGuire)*, Gloria Grey *(Molly McGuire)*, Ray Johnston *(Kid Lowry)*, Max Asher *(Schultz)*.

Action melodrama. When he goes to war, Theodore Pendergast is a snob. When he returns from the trenches of France, he is a democrat whose best friend is Butch McGuire, an ex-prizefighter and regular guy. Ted (as he is now called) takes Butch home with him to meet his father, and the old gentleman immediately has Ted committed to a sanitarium. Ted escapes and goes to live with Butch, whose sister, Molly, runs a beanery in a rough section of town. Ted is accepted by all of Butch's friends except Kid Lowry, a prizefighter who finally goads Ted into a grudge match. Before the fight takes place, however, the elder Pendergast has Ted kidnaped and placed in a padded cell. Ted again escapes and arrives in time for his match with Lowry. Ted is losing the fight when Molly appears and urges him on. The police raid the place, and Ted escapes with Lowry, whom he trounces after they have eluded the cops. Ted proposes to Molly, insuring a marriage that pleases the elder Pendergast, who has belatedly come to appreciate the loyalty that Molly and Butch have shown his son. *Veterans. Prizefighters. Millionaires. Snobbery. Social classes. Restaurants. Sanitariums. World War I.*

THE SNOW BRIDE **F2.5196**

Famous Players–Lasky. *Dist* Paramount Pictures. 29 Apr **1923** [c24 Apr 1923; LP18892]. Si; b&w. 35mm. 6 reels.

Pres by Adolph Zukor. *Dir* Henry Kolker. *Scen* Sonya Levien. *Story* Sonya Levien, Julie Herne. *Photog* George Webber.

Cast: Alice Brady *(Annette Leroux)*, Maurice B. Flynn *(André Porel)*, Mario Majeroni *(Gaston Leroux)*, Nick Thompson *(Indian Charlie)*, Jack

Baston *(Paul Gerard)*, Stephen Gratton *(Padre)*, William Cavanaugh *(Pierre)*, Margaret Morgan *(Leonia)*, Jean *(a dog)*.

Melodrama. Annette Leroux is in love with Sheriff André Porel; but her father, Gaston Leroux, promises her to Paul Gerard when Gerard sees Gaston kill Indian Charlie. In despair, Annette contemplates suicide, but Gerard drinks the poison by mistake. Annette is convicted of murder and is being led to her execution by André when an avalanche buries the gallows and Gaston. The villagers take this as a sign of Annette's innocence; she is released and marries André. *Trappers. Murder. Capital punishment. Suicide. Canadian Northwest. Avalanches. Dogs.*

SNOWBLIND **F2.5197**

Goldwyn Pictures. **1921** [c16 May 1921; LP16547]. Si; b&w. 35mm. 6 reels.

Dir Reginald Barker. *Scen* J. G. Hawks. *Photog* Percy Hilburn. *Asst Dir* Charles Stallings.

Cast: Russell Simpson *(Hugh Garth)*, Mary Alden *(Bella)*, Cullen Landis *(Pete Garth)*, Pauline Starke *(Sylvia Dooner)*.

Melodrama. Source: Katharine Newlin Burt, "Snowblind," in *Redbook* (36:27–32, 54–58, 73–77, Dec 1920–Feb 1921). Hugh Garth, fleeing a murder charge in England, makes his home in the Canadian Northwest with his younger brother, Pete, and Bella, a girl devoted to Hugh despite his brutal ways. One day, he finds Sylvia, member of a strolling theatrical group, blinded by glare from the snowdrifts, and she falls in love with him. However, recovering her sight and discovering the truth about Hugh, she conceals her recovery and when caught in a blizzard with Pete reveals her love for him instead. Realizing Sylvia does not love him, Hugh departs with Bella down the rapids, leaving the lovers together. *Brothers. Actors. Murder. Blindness. Canadian Northwest.*

SNOWBOUND **F2.5198**

Tiffany Productions. 1 May **1927** [c12 Jul 1927; LP24174]. Si; b&w. 35mm. 6 reels, 5,182 ft.

Dir Phil Stone. *Story-Scen* Douglas Bronston. *Photog* Joseph Dubray, Earl Walker, Elwood Bredel. *Art Dir* George E. Sawley. *Film Ed* Leroy O. Lodwig.

Cast: Betty Blythe *(Julia Barry)*, Lillian Rich *(Alice Blake)*, Robert Agnew *(Peter Foley)*, George Fawcett *(Uncle Tim Foley)*, Martha Mattox *(Aunt Amelia Foley)*, Harold Goodwin *(Joe Baird)*, Guinn Williams *(Bull Morgan)*, Pat Harmon *(Mr. Parker)*, William A. Carroll *(Judge Watkins)*, Dorothea Wolbert *(maid)*.

Farce. Peter Foley passes a fraudulent check, thinking he is marrying a wealthy girl; and to save him from jail, Julia Barry poses as his wife. Peter is actually in love with Alice Blake, and he encounters complications with Bull, a motorcycle cop who is engaged to Julia. Alice and a false friend add to the mixup; and through various chases and complications they are all snowbound together in a mountain lodge. After numerous attempts to catch or elude one another, all ends well. *Police. Fraud. Wealth. Chases.*

SNOWDRIFT **F2.5199**

Fox Film Corp. 22 or 29 Apr **1923** [c23 Apr 1923; LP19127]. Si; b&w. 35mm. 5 reels, 4,617 ft.

Pres by William Fox. *Dir* Scott Dunlap. *Scen* Jack Strumwasser. *Story* James B. Hendryx. *Photog* George Schneiderman.

Cast—Prolog: Bert Sprotte *(Jean McLaire)*, Gertrude Ryan *(Margot McFarlane)*, Colin Chase *(Murdo McFarlane)*, Evelyn Selbie *(Wananebish)*, Annette Jean *(Little Margot)*.

Cast—Story: Charles Jones *(Carter Brent)*, Irene Rich *(Kitty)*, G. Raymond Nye *(Johnnie Claw)*, Dorothy Manners *(Snowdrift)*, Lalo Encinas *(Joe Pete)*, Lee Shumway *(John Reeves)*, Charles Anderson.

Melodrama. Source: James B. Hendryx, *Snowdrift* (New York, 1922). Renegade mining engineer Carter Brent loses his money at gambling in the Yukon. He falls in love with Snowdrift, a girl believed to be a halfbreed who is actually an orphan of white parents though reared by an Indian squaw. Brent is regenerated through his association with Snowdrift and eventually rescues her from a dancehall manager who has made her a prisoner. *Engineers—Mining. Halfcastes. Orphans. Gambling. Yukon.*

THE SNOWSHOE TRAIL **F2.5200**

Chester Bennett Productions. *Dist* Film Booking Offices of America. 17 Sep **1922** [c6 Sep 1922; LP18196]. Si; b&w. 35mm. 6 reels, 5,382 ft.

Dir Chester Bennett. *Scen* Marion Fairfax. *Photog* Jack MacKenzie.

Cast: Jane Novak *(Virginia Tremont)*, Roy Stewart *(Bill Bronson)*, Lloyd Whitlock *(Harold Lounsbury)*, Herbert Prior *(Kenly Lounsbury)*, Kate Toncray *(Mrs. Bronson)*, Spottiswoode Aitken *(Herbert Lounsbury)*, Chai Hung *(Mah Lung)*.

Northwest melodrama. Source: Edison Marshall, *The Snowshoe Trail* (Boston, 1921). Virginia Tremont, her guardian Kenly Lounsbury, and their guide Bill Bronson set out for the Northwest in search of her fiancé, Harold Lounsbury. After being left by Kenly without horses, Virginia and Bill find Harold living as a squaw man. Her affections are transferred to Bill when he twice rescues her from danger and when Harold is revealed to be worthless. *Guardians. Guides. Squaw men. Indians of North America. Miscegenation. Pacific Northwest.*

SO BIG **F2.5201**

First National Pictures. 28 Dec **1924** [c5 Dec 1924, 5 Jan 1925; LP20982, LP21125]. Si; b&w. 35mm. 9 reels, 8,562 ft.

Supv Earl Hudson. *Dir* Charles Brabin. *Ed Dir* Marion Fairfax. *Scen* Adelaide Heilbron. *Adapt* Earl Hudson. *Photog* T. D. McCord. *Art Dir* Milton Menasco. *Film Ed* Arthur Tavares.

Cast: Colleen Moore *(Selina Peake)*, Joseph De Grasse *(Simeon Peake)*, John Bowers *(Pervus DeJong)*, Ben Lyon *(Dirk DeJong)*, Wallace Beery *(Klass Poole)*, Gladys Brockwell *(Maartje Poole)*, Jean Hersholt *(Aug Hempel)*, Charlotte Merriam *(Julie Hempel)*, Dot Farley *(Widow Paarlenburg)*, Ford Sterling *(Jacob Hoogenduck)*, Frankie Darrow *(Dirk DeJong as boy)*, Henry Herbert *(William Storm)*, Dorothy Brock *(Dirk DeJong as baby)*, Rosemary Theby *(Paula Storm)*, Phyllis Haver *(Dallas O'Meara)*.

Drama. Source: Edna Ferber, *So Big* (Garden City, New York, 1924). After graduating from a fashionable finishing school and touring Europe with her father, Selina Peake returns to the United States, where her father is accidentally killed after losing his fortune in a gambling den. Selina is reduced to teaching in a high school in the Dutch community at High Prarie near Chicago. She boards in the farmhouse of Klass Poole, a dull-witted market gardener, and finally marries Pervus DeJong, a poor and backward farmer. She shares the drudgery of her husband's futile life and finds happiness only in their small son, Dirk, whom she calls "So-Big." Pervus dies from the strain of hard work, and Selina is reduced to abject poverty, eking out a marginal existence selling the few vegetables she can raise. When she meets Julie Hempel, an old school friend, Julie's father lends her enough money to begin to farm her land successfully. After 18 years of stinting and hard work, Selina sees Dirk educated as an architect, but Dirk's promising career is then threatened by scandal. William Storm, the husband of the woman with whom Dirk has been having an affair, threatens to name him as corespondent in a divorce suit. Selina appeals to Storm not to ruin her son's life, and Storm relents. Dirk returns to his true love, Dallas, and Selina looks forward to a serene old age. *Dutch. Schoolteachers. Farmers. Truck farmers. Architects. Motherhood. Chicago. Illinois.*

SO LONG LETTY **F2.5202**

Warner Brothers Pictures. 16 Oct **1929** [c4 Nov 1929; LP820]. Sd (Vitaphone); b&w. 35mm. 6 reels, 5,865 ft. [Also si.]

Dir Lloyd Bacon. *Adapt-Dial* Robert Lord, Arthur Caesar. *Titl* De Leon Anthony. *Camera* James Van Trees. *Film Ed* Jack Killifer. *Songs: "One Little Sweet Yes," "Beauty Shop," "Am I Blue," "Let Me Have My Dreams," "My Strongest Weakness Is You"* Grant Clarke, Harry Akst. *Song: "So Long Letty"* Earl Caroll. *Song: "Down Among the Sugar Cane"* Grant Clark, Charles Tobias.

Cast: Charlotte Greenwood *(Letty Robbins)*, Claude Gillingwater *(Claude Davis)*, Grant Withers *(Harry Miller)*, Patsy Ruth Miller *(Grace Miller)*, Bert Roach *(Tommy Robbins)*, Marion Byron *(Ruth Davis)*, Helen Foster *(Sally Davis)*, Hallam Cooley *(Clarence De Brie)*, Harry Gribbon *(Joe Casey)*, Lloyd Ingraham *(judge)*, Jack Grey *(police sergeant)*.

Musical comedy. Source: Elmer Harris, Earl Carroll, and Oliver Morosco, *So Long Letty* (New York opening: 23 Oct 1916). Uncle Claude, an eccentric millionaire, brings his flapper granddaughters, Ruth and Sally, to a fashionable beach hotel, where he is accosted by Letty Robbins, a beauty parlor solicitor. Infuriated by her tactics, he calls upon the "personality man," Harry Miller, a would-be singer who charms the girls; Claude rushes into the adjoining suite to find Clarence De Brie, a composer, who tries to induce him to produce his new opera; and back in his own suite, he encounters Joe Casey, who wants to give him swimming lessons; thus he resolves to escape to the beauty salon. Later, Letty and Tom decide to swap partners with their neighbors Harry and Grace; complications ensue when Claude, who is Harry's uncle, arrives with his granddaughters; and when they are all booked in a raid on their "wild party," the judge straightens out matters. *Millionaires. Grandfathers. Uncles. Composers. Flappers. Marriage. Beauty shops. Resorts. Opera.*

SO THIS IS ARIZONA **F2.5203**

William M. Smith Productions. *Dist* Merit Film Corp. Jan **1922** [New York State license]. Si; b&w. 35mm. 6 reels.

Dir Francis Ford. *Photog* Reginald Lyons.

Cast: Franklyn Farnum *(Norman Russell)*, Francis Ford *(Ned Kendall)*, "Shorty" Hamilton *(Art Pulvers)*, Al Hart *(Buck Saunders)*, Genevieve Bert *(Peggy Newton)*, Art Phillips *(Bob Thompson)*.

Western melodrama. Source: Marie Schrader and C. C. Wadde, "So This Is Arizona," in *Argosy Magazine* (135:145–163, 313–330, 461–477, 678–689, 808–818, 2–30 Jul 1921; 136:122–133, 6 Aug 1921). "Norman Russell picks up a purse which a young woman has dropped while riding horseback but is unable to return it to her before she has left for Arizona. He follows. Art Pulvers, a policeman, sees him and decides that he is a crook, notifying thereupon the sheriff in Lone Rock, for which Russell is bound. Through some mistake the sheriff believes that the purse contains a diamond necklace, and Russell is afraid to return it [the purse] for fear he will be arrested for stealing a necklace which he has never seen. He is framed by some crooks and is accused of a murder. He rides away, is followed, and hides in a mine underground. Meanwhile the girl has gathered together some rescuers headed by the sheriff and arrives in time to save him, while the two real culprits are exposed." (*Moving Picture World*, 22 Apr 1922, p878.) *Police. Sheriffs. Theft. Murder. Arizona.*

SO THIS IS COLLEGE **F2.5204**

Metro-Goldwyn-Mayer Pictures. 8 Nov **1929** [c1 Nov 1929; LP838]. Sd (Movietone); b&w. 35mm. 11 reels, 9,143 ft. [Also si; 6,104 ft.]

Dir Sam Wood. *Screenplay* Al Boasberg, Delmer Daves. *Dial* Joe Farnham, Al Boasberg. *Titl* Joe Farnham. *Photog* Leonard Smith. *Art Dir* Cedric Gibbons. *Film Ed* Frank Sullivan, Leslie F. Wilder. *Mus* Martin Broones. *Song: "Sophomore Prom"* Jesse Greer. *Songs: "College Days," "Campus Capers"* Martin Broones. *Song: "I Don't Want Your Kisses"* Fred Fisher, Martin Broones. *Mus Cond* Arthur Lange. *Interpolations* Fred Fisher, Jesse Greer, Raymond Klages, Charlotte Greenwood, Al Boasberg. *Rec Engr* Douglas Shearer. *Wardrobe* Henrietta Frazer.

Cast: Elliott Nugent *(Eddie)*, Robert Montgomery *(Biff)*, Cliff Edwards *(Windy)*, Sally Starr *(Babs)*, Phyllis Crane *(Betty)*, Dorothy Dehn *(Jane)*, Max Davidson *(Moe)*, Ann Brody *(Momma)*, Oscar Rudolph *(Freshie)*, Gene Stone *(Stupid)*, Polly Moran *(Polly)*, Lee Shumway *(Coach)*.

Comedy-drama. Biff and Eddie, two college classmates at the University of Southern California, are life-long friends, fraternity brothers, and members of the football team, and they share for each other a great affection and admiration until it comes to the matter of courtship, that being a case of "all's fair in love." They both fall for Babs, a scheming co-ed, who keeps one out on a late auto ride, thus causing a breach between the boys, but both are reconciled at the USC-Stanford game where her duplicity is discovered. The boys vow that no woman will ever come between them again. *Students. College life. Football. Courtship. Friendship. Fraternities. University of Southern California. Stanford University.*

Note: Stock footage from the 1928 USC-Stanford football game is used in this film.

SO THIS IS FLORIDA **F2.5205**

Burton Holmes Lectures. 21 Mar **1926.** Si; b&w. 35mm. 5 reels.

Travelog. No information about the specific nature of this film has been found. *Florida.*

SO THIS IS LONDON **F2.5206**

Fox Film Corp. 23 May **1930** [New York premiere; released 6 Jun; c6 May 1930; LP1328]. Sd (Movietone); b&w. 35mm. 10 reels, 8,300 ft.

Pres by William Fox. *Dir* John Blystone. *Scen* Sonya Levien. *Adapt-Dial* Owen Davis. *Camera* Charles G. Clarke. *Sets* Jack Schulze. *Film Ed* Jack Dennis. *Mus & Lyr* James F. Hanley, Joseph McCarthy. *Sd Engr* Frank MacKenzie. *Asst Dir* Jasper Blystone. *Cost* Sophie Wachner.

Cast: Will Rogers *(Hiram Draper)*, Irene Rich *(Mrs. Hiram Draper)*, Frank Albertson *(Junior Draper)*, Maureen O'Sullivan *(Elinor Worthing)*, Lumsden Hare *(Lord Percy Worthing)*, Mary Forbes *(Lady Worthing)*, Bramwell Fletcher *(Alfred Honeycutt)*, Dorothy Christy *(Lady Amy Ducksworth)*, Ellen Woodston *(nurse)*, Martha Lee Sparks *(little girl)*.

Comedy. Source: Arthur Frederick Goodrich, *So This Is London* (New York, 1926). Hiram Draper, a cotton mill owner and a chauvinistic American who dislikes anything British, leaves Texas for London on a business trip with his wife and son. En route, his son, Junior, meets and falls in love with Elinor, an English girl, and determines to marry her even though his parents disapprove. In London, he conspires to have his parents meet Lord and Lady Worthing at a party; and to prove that his son's judgment is askew, Hiram lives up to the English conception of the uncouth, uncivilized American on a shooting match with Lord Worthing and in his humorous dabbling in international politics. But when Hiram meets Elinor, he instinctively senses that he has been wrong and smooths out matters. *Businessmen. Texans. Nobility. English. Courtship. Anglophobia. Chauvinism. Cotton mills. London.*

SO THIS IS LOVE **F2.5207**

Columbia Pictures. 6 Feb **1928** [c9 Mar 1928; LP25044]. Si; b&w. 35mm. 6 reels, 5,611 ft.

Prod Harry Cohn. *Dir* Frank Capra. *Cont* Rex Taylor. *Adapt* Elmer Harris. *Story* Norman Springer. *Photog* Ray June. *Art Dir* Robert E. Lee. *Film Ed* Arthur Roberts. *Asst Dir* Eugene De Rue.

Cast: Shirley Mason *(Hilda Jensen)*, William Collier, Jr. *(Jerry McGuire)*, Johnnie Walker *("Spike" Mullins)*, Ernie Adams *("Flash" Tracy)*, Carl Gerard *(Otto)*, William H. Strauss *("Maison" Katz)*, Jean Laverty *(Mary Malone)*.

Comedy. Jerry McGuire, a dress designer, and "Spike" Mullins, a boxer, vie for the attentions of Hilda Jensen, a flaxen-haired counter girl, until Jerry takes boxing lessons and wins both a match and Hilda. *Couturiers. Shopgirls. Boxing.*

SO THIS IS MARRIAGE **F2.5208**

Metro-Goldwyn Pictures. 24 Nov **1924** [c12 Dec 1924; LP20908]. Si; b&w with col sequence (Technicolor). 35mm. 7 reels, 6,300 ft.

Pres by Louis B. Mayer. *Supv* Harry Rapf. *Dir* Hobart Henley. *Scen* John Lynch, Alice D. G. Miller. *Story* Carey Wilson. *Photog* John Arnold. *Art Dir* Cedric Gibbons. *Asst Dir* Arthur Smith.

Cast: Conrad Nagel *(Peter Marsh)*, Eleanor Boardman *(Beth Marsh)*, Lew Cody *(Daniel Rankin)*, Clyde Cook *(Mr. Brown)*, Edward Connelly *(Nathan)*, John Boles *(Uriah)*, Warner Oland *(King David)*, Mabel Julienne Scott *(Bath-Sheba)*, Miss Du Pont *(Vera Kellogg)*, John Patrick *(Augustus Sharp)*, Claire De Lorez *(Mrs. Stuyvesant Lane)*, Shannon Day *(Mollie O'Brien)*, Jack Edwards *(Bobbie)*, Estelle Clark *(maid)*, Thelma Morgan *(Theress)*, Francis McDonald *(Smith)*, Eugenie Gilbert *(Dorothy Pringle)*, Sidney Bracey *(Hawkins)*, Tom O'Brien *(Riley)*, Philip Sleeman *(Donald Gibson)*, Gloria Heller *(Daisy de Belle)*.

Comedy-drama. After 5 years of marriage, Beth and Peter Marsh's life together is a series of rows and reconciliations. Beth is frivolous and extravagant; Peter is domineering and ambitious and has difficulty in meeting the bills. Daniel Rankin, who lives in the same apartment building, becomes attracted to Beth and arranges with the Marsh chauffeur to have her car break down, allowing him to offer assistance and gracefully introduce himself; Rankin later invites her to a dance. Resenting Rankin's attentions to his wife, Peter forbids her to go; she goes to spite him, and Rankin proposes that she divorce Peter and become his wife instead. After she returns home, Beth has a bitter fight with Peter, walks out of the apartment, and goes to see Rankin. Rankin repeats his proposal, but, suspecting that the tearful Beth truly loves her husband, he reads her the story of David and Bathsheba from the Bible. This account of the severe consequences of illicit love prompts her to return to Peter, with whom she is soon reconciled. *Marriage. Infidelity. David. Bathsheba. Biblical characters.*

SO THIS IS PARIS **F2.5209**

Warner Brothers Pictures. 31 Jul **1926** [c2 Jul 1926; LP22890]. Si; b&w. 35mm. 7 reels, 6,135 ft.

Dir Ernst Lubitsch. *Adapt* Hans Kraly. *Photog* John Mescall. *Asst Camera* Bert Shipman. *Asst Dir* George Hippard.

Cast: Monte Blue *(Dr. Eisenstein)*, Patsy Ruth Miller *(Rosalind Eisenstein)*, Lilyan Tashman *(Adela, a dancer)*, André Beranger *(Alfred, her husband)*, Myrna Loy *(maid)*, Sidney D'Albrook *(cop)*.

Domestic comedy. Source: Henri Meilhac and Ludovic Halévy, *Le Réveillon; comédie en trois actes* (1872). To relieve the boredom of their marriage, Alfred and Adela, a young dancing team, are constantly on the alert for a new flirtation. One morning Dr. Eisenstein comes to their apartment with the intent of thrashing Alfred with his cane for entrancing his wife, Rosalind, by practicing in front of the open window, but his temper quickly cools as he recognizes Adela as a former sweetheart, and he tells Rosalind a fantastic story to cover his flirtation with Adela.

Alfred, however, returns the doctor's cane, begins a counter flirtation with Rosalind, and tells her about her husband's philandering. Driving to meet Adela, Eisenstein is arrested for speeding; meanwhile, Alfred visits Rosalind, but when officers come to take the doctor to jail, Alfred declares he is Eisenstein to save Rosalind's reputation. Rosalind hears on the radio that Adela and Eisenstein have won a Charleston contest at the ball, where she finds the doctor intoxicated. After a number of amusing tiffs, Adela finds a new admirer and the couple are reconciled. *Dancers. Physicians. Marriage. Flirtation. Automobile driving. Charleston (dance).*

A SOCIAL CELEBRITY **F2.5210**
Famous Players–Lasky. *Dist* Paramount Pictures. 29 Mar **1926** [c31 Mar 1926; LP22559]. Si; b&w. 35mm. 6 reels, 6,025 ft.
Pres by Adolph Zukor, Jesse L. Lasky. *Dir* Malcolm St. Clair. *Scen* Pierre Collings. *Story* Monte M. Katterjohn. *Photog* Lee Garmes.
Cast: Adolphe Menjou *(Max Haber)*, Louise Brooks *(Kitty Laverne)*, Elsie Lawson *(April King)*, Roger Davis *(Tenny)*, Hugh Huntley *(Forrest Abbott)*, Chester Conklin *(Johann Haber)*, Freeman Wood *(Gifford Jones)*, Josephine Drake *(Mrs. Jackson-Greer)*, Ida Waterman *(Mrs. Winifred King)*.
Comedy-drama. Max Haber, a smalltown barber, is the pride of his father, Johann, who owns an antiquated barbershop. Max adores Kitty Laverne, the manicurist, who loves him but aspires to be a dancer and leaves for New York, hoping that he will follow in pursuit of better things. Mrs. Jackson-Greer, a New York society matron, has occasion to note Max fashioning the hair of a town girl and induces him to come to New York and pose as a French count. There he meets April, Mrs. King's niece, and loses his heart to her, as well as to Kitty, now a showgirl. At the theater where Kitty is appearing Max is the best-dressed man in April's party, but later at a nightclub Kitty exposes him, and he is deserted by his society friends. Disillusioned, Max returns home at the request of his father. Kitty follows, realizing that he needs her. *Barbers. Manicurists. Showgirls. Social classes. Imposture. Smalltown life. New York City.*

THE SOCIAL CODE **F2.5211**
Metro Pictures. Oct **1923** [c16 Oct 1923; LP19499]. Si; b&w. 35mm. 5 reels, 4,843 ft.
Dir Oscar Apfel. *Scen* Rex Taylor. *Photog* John Arnold.
Cast: Viola Dana *(Babs Van Buren)*, Malcolm McGregor *(Dean Cardigan)*, Edna Flugrath *(Connie Grant)*, Huntly Gordon *(Judge Evans Grant)*, Cyril Chadwick *(Colby Dickinson)*, William Humphrey *(district attorney)*, John Sainpolis *(attorney for the defense)*.
Mystery drama. Source: Rita Weiman, "To Whom It May Concern," in *Cosmopolitan* (72:19–23, Feb 1922). A young girl saves her lover from the electric chair and at the same time extricates her older sister from a trying situation. *Sisters. Murder. Blackmail. Capital punishment.*

THE SOCIAL EXILE *see* **DÉCLASSÉE**

THE SOCIAL HIGHWAYMAN **F2.5212**
Warner Brothers Pictures. 15 May **1926** [c15 May 1926; LP22736]. Si; b&w. 35mm. 7 reels, 6,107 ft.
Dir William Beaudine. *Adapt* Edward T. Lowe, Jr., Philip Klein. *Story* Darryl Francis Zanuck. *Photog* John Mescall. *Asst Camera* Bert Shipman. *Asst Dir* George Webster.
Cast: John Patrick *(Jay Walker, reporter)*, Dorothy Devore *(Elsie Van Tyler)*, Montagu Love *(Ducket Nelson)*, Russell Simpson *(The Mayor's partner)*, George Pearce *(Old Van Tyler)*, Lynn Cowan *(Bobbie)*, James Gordon *(editor)*, Frank Brownlee *(Simpson, the convict)*, Fred Kelsey *(chief of police)*, Charles Hill Mailes *(The Mayor)*.
Comedy-drama. Cub newsreporter Jay Walker is assigned to investigate the activities of Ducket Nelson, a notorious bandit. Driving in the country, Jay is held up by Nelson, disguised as an old Gypsy woman, and he is so severely ridiculed by the newspaper staff that the owner orders him not to return until he has captured Nelson. Jay meets Dr. Runyon, a traveling medicine man (actually Nelson), but Jay poses as "the social highwayman" himself and holds up a flivver in which Elsie Van Tyler (who also claims to be a female crook) is riding. Through an escaped convict, Jay learns the doctor's true identity but is himself denounced by Runyon as the criminal he purports to be. Jay accidentally rescues a child from a bank safe, then pursues Nelson and the convict aboard a moving freight train, which ironically takes them into a prison yard. *Bandits. Reporters. Medicine men. Prison escapees. Disguise.*

THE SOCIAL LION **F2.5213**
Paramount-Publix Corp. 21 Jun **1930** [c20 Jun 1930; LP1372]. Sd (Movietone); b&w. 35mm. 7 reels, 5,403 ft.
Dir A. Edward Sutherland. *Dial Dir* Perry Ivins. *Scen* Agnes Brand Leahy. *Adapt-Dial* Joseph L. Mankiewicz. *Photog* Allen Siegler. *Film Ed* Otto Levering. *Sd* R. H. Quick.
Cast: Jack Oakie *(Marco Perkins)*, Mary Brian *(Cynthia Brown)*, Skeets Gallagher *(Chick Hathaway)*, Olive Borden *(Gloria Staunton)*, Charles Sellon *(Jim Perkins)*, Cyril Ring *(Ralph Williams)*, E. H. Calvert *(Henderson)*, James Gibson *(Howard)*, Henry Roquemore *(Smith)*, William Bechtel *(Schultz)*, Richard Cummings *(McGinnis)*, Jack Byron *("Knockout" Johnson)*.
Comedy. Source: Octavus Roy Cohen, "Marco Himself," in *Hearst's International Cosmopolitan* (87:78–81, Sep 1929). Marco Perkins, a ham prizefighter, after an inglorious defeat is taken home by his wise-cracking manager, Chick, and meets Cynthia, who secretly adores him. But Marco's eye is set on Gloria, a selfish society girl of the country club set who leads him on for laughs; however, when they learn that Marco is an ace polo player, he and Chick are welcomed to the club as members. Cynthia, the hatcheck girl, sadly watches as Marco becomes madly infatuated with Gloria and his new self-image, but when Gloria jokingly encourages him to propose to her, he is deeply hurt. Cynthia, who has overhead the joke, takes Gloria to task, and Marco, after winning the polo game for the club, gives Gloria and her society friends a piece of his mind. Realizing that Cynthia loves him, Marco returns to the ring to win the championship. *Prizefighters. Fight managers. Socialites. Checkgirls. Social classes. Country clubs. Polo.*

SOCIAL SECRETARY (Reissue) **F2.5214**
Fine Arts Pictures. *Dist* Tri-Stone Pictures. c8 Dec **1924** [LP23370]. Si; b&w. 35mm. 5 reels.
Note: A "re-edited and re-titled" Norma Talmadge film originally released by Triangle Film Corp. on 10 Sep 1916.

A SOCIETY SCANDAL **F2.5215**
Famous Players–Lasky. *Dist* Paramount Pictures. 24 Mar **1924** [c19 Mar 1924; LP20003]. Si; b&w. 35mm. 7 reels, 6,857 ft.
Pres by Adolph Zukor, Jesse L. Lasky. *Prod-Dir* Allan Dwan. *Scen* Forrest Halsey. *Photog* Hal Rosson.
Cast: Gloria Swanson *(Marjorie Colbert)*, Rod La Rocque *(Daniel Farr)*, Ricardo Cortez *(Harrison Peters)*, Allan Simpson *(Hector Colbert)*, Ida Waterman *(Mrs. Maturin Colbert)*, Thelma Converse *(Mrs. Hamilton Pennfield)*, Fraser Coalter *(Schuyler Burr)*, Catherine Proctor *(Mrs. Burr)*, Wilfred Donovan *(Hamilton Pennfield)*, Yvonne Hughes *(Patricia De Voe)*, Catherine Coleburn, Marie Shelton, Dorothy Stokes, Cornelius Keefe *(friends of Marjorie)*.
Society drama. Source: Alfred Sutro, *The Laughing Lady; a Comedy in Three Acts* (London, 1922). Hector Colbert sues his wife Marjorie for a divorce after Peters, an admirer of Marjorie, deliberately compromises her. Colbert's lawyer, Daniel Farr, believing that Marjorie's behavior was wrong, gets the divorce, but he ruins the reputation of a fun-loving woman who was simply bored with her husband. Later, she and Farr meet; she plots a revenge against the lawyer but confesses her fabrication when she realizes that she loves him. *Lawyers. Divorce. Revenge. Reputation.*

SOCIETY SECRETS **F2.5216**
Universal Film Manufacturing Co. Feb **1921** [c18 Feb 1921; LP16166]. Si; b&w. 35mm. 5 reels, 4,795 ft.
Pres by Carl Laemmle. *Dir* Leo McCarey. *Scen* Douglas Z. Doty. *Story* Helen Christine Bennett. *Photog* William Fildew.
Cast: Eva Novak *(Louise)*, Gertrude Claire *(Mrs. Kerran)*, George Verrell *(Amos Kerran)*, Clarissa Selwynne *(Aunt)*, William Buckley *(Arthur)*, Ethel Ritchie *(Maybelle)*, L. C. Shumway *(George)*, Carl Stockdale *(squire)*, Lucy Donohue *(squire's wife)*.
Satire. Amos Kerran and his wife live a traditional, old-fashioned life on a Connecticut farm, while their son and daughter, Arthur and Maybelle, are successes in New York society. The children want to invite their parents to the city at Christmastime but are ashamed of their unrefined appearance. Louise, Arthur's fashionable sweetheart, visits the older Kerrans, gains their confidence, and sends them to a finishing school. In consequence, their New York debut is a big success. *Family life. Social classes. Farming. Connecticut. New York City.*

SOCIETY SNOBS F2.5217

Selznick Pictures. *Dist* Select Pictures. Feb **1921** [c4 Feb 1921; LP16083]. Si; b&w. 35mm. 5 reels, 4,234 ft.

Pres by Lewis J. Selznick. *Dir* Hobart Henley. *Scen* Lewis Allen Browne. *Story* Conway Tearle. *Photog* Jack Brown.

Cast: Conway Tearle *(Lorenzo Carilo/Duke d'Amunzi)*, Vivian Forrester *(Martha Mansfield)*, Ida Darling *(Mrs. Forrester)*, Jack McLean *(Ned Forrester)*, Huntley Gordon *(Duane Thornton)*.

Society melodrama. Italian American Lorenzo Carilo, failing at clerical work, becomes a waiter and falls under the charms of Vivian Forrester, a society girl contemptuous of her social inferiors. She rejects the suit of wealthy Duane Thornton, and in retaliation he presents Carilo to Vivian as the Duke d'Amunzi. Abetted by her ambitious mother, she responds to Carilo's advances. On their wedding night he confesses the deception, and Vivian promptly leaves him to make arrangements to have the marriage annulled. She does forgive him, however, and they are reunited. *Italians. Waiters. Imposture. Social classes. Marriage. Snobbery.*

SODA WATER COWBOY F2.5218

Action Pictures. *Dist* Pathé Exchange. 25 Sep **1927** [c17 Sep 1927; LU24418]. Si; b&w. 35mm. 5 reels, 4,546 ft.

Pres by Lester F. Scott, Jr. *Dir* Richard Thorpe. *Scen* Betty Burbridge. *Story* Tommy Gray. *Photog* Ray Ries.

Cast: Wally Wales *(Wally)*, Beryl Roberts *(Mademoiselle Zalla)*, J. P. Lockney *(Professor Beerbum)*, Charles Whitaker *(Ross)*, Al Taylor *(Joe)*.

Western melodrama. Wally, a soda jerk who longs for an adventurous life, is fired by his employer for reading western stories on the job and hops a freight bound west. He is thrown off near the camp of Prof. Hector Beerbum, who with his daughter, Zalla, operates a medicine show. He saves them from some crooks and is rewarded by being made deputy sheriff. Wally is lured to Zalla's tent by Ross, who forces his attentions on the girl; Wally is knocked cold while the gang spring their confederate from jail. Zalla discovers the identity of the criminals while Wally sets out alone to vindicate himself. He succeeds singlehandedly in capturing Ross and wins the heart of the girl. *Soda clerks. Robbers. Sheriffs. Medicine shows. Jailbreaks. Reading. Western fiction.*

SOFT BOILED F2.5219

Fox Film Corp. 26 Aug **1923** [c18 Aug 1923; LP19378]. Si; b&w. 35mm. 8 reels, 7,054 ft.

Pres by William Fox. *Dir-Scen* J. G. Blystone. *Story* J. G. Blystone, Edward Moran. *Photog* Don Clark.

Cast: Tom Mix *(Tom Steele)*, Joseph Girard *(The Ranch Owner)*, Billie Dove *(The Girl)*, L. C. Shumway *(The Road House Manager)*, Tom Wilson *(The Colored Butler)*, Frank Beal *(John Steele)*, Jack Curtis *(The Ranch Foreman)*, Charles Hill Mailes *(The Lawyer)*, Harry Dunkinson *(The Storekeeper)*, Wilson Hummell *(The Reformer)*, Tony *(himself, a horse)*.

Western comedy. Cowboy Tom Steele has a temper that he finally learns to control. His uncle, John Steele, who is similarly afflicted, decides to test Tom to determine if the boy really has mastered the family frailty. Tom comes out on top after the required 30 days' moratorium, but then he destroys everything in sight to avenge the insults made to his sweetheart. They begin their honeymoon on the family yacht, and Uncle John, who was thought to be dead, appears, alive. *Cowboys. Uncles. Personality. Honeymoons. Horses.*

Note: Working title: *Tempered Steel.*

SOFT CUSHIONS F2.5220

Paramount Famous Lasky Corp. 27 Aug **1927** [c27 Aug 1927; LP24341]. Si; b&w. 35mm. 7 reels, 6,838 ft.

Pres by Adolph Zukor, Jesse L. Lasky. *Dir* Edward F. Cline. *Screenplay* Wade Boteler, Frederic Chapin. *Story* George Randolph Chester. *Photog* Jack MacKenzie. *Sets* Ben Carré.

Cast: Douglas MacLean *(The Young Thief)*, Sue Carol *(The Girl)*, Richard Carle *(The Slave Dealer)*, Russell Powell *(The Fat Thief)*, Frank Leigh *(The Lean Thief)*, Wade Boteler *(The Police Judge)*, Nigel De Brulier *(The Notary)*, Albert Prisco *(The Wazir)*, Boris Karloff *(The Chief Conspirator)*, Albert Gran *(The Sultan)*, Fred Kelsey *(The Police)*, Harry Jones *(The Citizen)*, Noble Johnson *(The Captain of the Guard)*.

Arabian Nights comedy. A young thief, spying a beautiful slave girl, penetrates the harem in which she is imprisoned and, when apprehended, announces that he wants to buy her. Though she dreams of winning the favor of the sultan, she is attracted to the thief. He robs his partners, a fat and a lean thief, to raise the money; but just as he is about to marry the girl, the partners expose his fraud. The police judge takes a look at the girl, confiscates her and the plunder, and orders the young thief's decapitation. But the notary remembers that the thief has promised to pull the sultan's whiskers, thus automatically moving the case to the wazir's court; the wazir also falls for the girl and orders an execution. The thief escapes, and disguised as the wazir, he saves the life of the sultan, winning forgiveness for his sins; and as wazir he purchases the slave girl for his wife. *Thieves. Royalty. Slavery. Capital punishment. Harems. Trials.*

SOFT LIVING F2.5221

Fox Film Corp. 5 Feb **1928** [c2 Feb 1928; LP24939]. Si; b&w. 35mm. 6 reels, 5,629 ft.

Pres by William Fox. *Dir* James Tinling. *Scen* Frances Agnew. *Titl* Malcolm S. Boylan. *Story* Grace Mack. *Photog* Joseph August. *Film Ed* J. Edwin Robbins. *Asst Dir* Leslie Selander.

Cast: Madge Bellamy *(Nancy Woods)*, John Mack Brown *(Stockney Webb)*, Mary Duncan *(Lorna Estabrook)*, Joyce Compton *(Billie Wilson)*, Thomas Jefferson *(Philip Estabrook)*, Henry Kolker *(Rodney S. Bowen)*, Olive Tell *(Mrs. Rodney S. Bowen)*, Maine Geary *(office boy)*, Tom Dugan *(hired man)*, David Wengren *(Swede)*.

Domestic comedy. Intrigued by the idea of collecting alimony payments, Nancy Woods, secretary to a divorce lawyer, marries Stockney Webb with the intention of fleecing him after the honeymoon. Realizing that he has been duped, Webb determines to teach Nancy—whom he truly loves—a lesson in humility and wifely behavior by taking her to his cabin in the wilderness. The story finishes happily. *Secretaries. Lawyers. Marriage. Divorce. Alimony.*

SOFT SHOES F2.5222

Stellar Productions. *Dist* Producers Distributing Corp. 1 Jan **1925** [c10 Jun 1925; LP21547]. Si; b&w. 35mm. 6 reels, 5,527 ft.

Pres by Hunt Stromberg. *Supv* Hunt Stromberg. *Dir* Lloyd Ingraham. *Screenplay* Hunt Stromberg, Harvey Gates. *Story* Harry Carey. *Photog* Sol Polito. *Art Dir* Edward Withers. *Film Ed* Harry L. Decker.

Cast: Harry Carey *(Pat Halahan)*, Lillian Rich *(Faith O'Day)*, Paul Weigel *(Dummy O'Day)*, Francis Ford *(Quig Mundy)*, Stanton Heck *(Bradley)*, Harriet Hammond *(Mrs. Bradley)*, Jimmie Quinn *(Majel)*, Sojin *(Yet Tzu)*, Majel Coleman *(Mabel Packer)*, John Steppling *(Markham)*.

Western melodrama. Pat Halahan, the sheriff of a western town, receives a legacy and goes to see the sights in San Francisco, where he captures a pretty burglar, Faith O'Day, when she attempts to rob his room. Pat talks to Faith, and she agrees to give up her life of crime. Pat then takes it upon himself to return a brooch Faith has stolen that same evening. He is detected while putting it back in a jewelry case in a woman's boudoir, and detectives follow him back to the hotel. Faith pretends that she is his wife, telling the detectives that they have been together the entire evening. Faith later escapes from Pat, and he follows her to her home, where he meets Quig Mundy, a gangster. In order to ingratiate himself with Mundy, Pat impersonates The Chicago Kid, a gangster, and joins Mundy's gang. Pat tips off the police, but when the real Chicago Kid shows up, Pat is beaten and locked in a cellar. The police free Pat, and he goes to Faith's house, where he saves her from Mundy, who is shot by a mysterious Chinese undercover agent working for the San Francisco police. *Sheriffs. Burglars. Detectives. Gangsters. Criminals—Rehabilitation. Chinese. San Francisco.*

SOILED F2.5223

Phil Goldstone Productions. *Dist* Truart Film Corp. 1 Nov **1924**. Si; b&w. 35mm. 7 reels, 6,800 ft.

Phil Goldstone Production. *Dir* Fred Windemere. *Scen* J. F. Natteford. *Photog* Bert Baldridge. *Adtl Photog* Edgar Lyons.

Cast: Kenneth Harlan *(Jimmie York)*, Vivian Martin *(Mary Brown)*, Mildred Harris *(Pet Darling)*, Johnny Walker *(Wilbur Brown)*, Mary Alden *(Mrs. Brown)*, Robert Cain *(John Duane)*, Wyndham Standing *(James P. Munson)*, Maude George *(Bess Duane)*, Alec B. Francis *(Rollo Tetheridge)*, John T. Mack.

Melodrama. Source: Jack Boyle, "Debt of Dishonor," in *Red Book.* Wilbur Brown steals $2,500 from his employer and is threatened with jail. His sister, a chorus girl named Mary, then borrows $2,500 from John Duane, a married man with a weakness for young girls. Jimmie York, who is in love with Mary, writes Duane a check for the total amount of Mary's debt, although he has only a couple of hundred in the bank. Jimmie plans on winning an important automobile race to make the check good, but he loses instead, and Mary can repay Duane only by submitting to his embraces. Jimmie gets the money, however, and arrives in time to save

Mary from Duane's lecherous advances. *Chorus girls. Theft. Debt. Lechery. Automobile racing.*

SOLACE OF THE WOODS *see* **DIAMOND CARLISLE**

SOLD FOR CASH *see* **ON THE STROKE OF THREE**

SOLDIERS AND WOMEN **F2.5224**

Columbia Pictures. 30 Apr **1930** [c24 May 1930; LP1330]. Sd (Movietone); b&w. 35mm. 7 reels, 6,671 ft.

Prod Harry Cohn. *Dir* Edward Sloman. *Cont-Dial* Dorothy Howell. *Camera* Ted Tetzlaff. *Art Dir* Harrison Wiley. *Film Ed* Leonard Wheeler. *Ch Sd Engr* John Livadary. *Asst Dir* Buddy Coleman.

Cast: Aileen Pringle *(Brenda)*, Grant Withers *(Capt. Clive Branch)*, Helen Johnson *(Helen)*, Walter McGrail *(Captain Arnold)*, Emmett Corrigan *(General Mitchell)*, Blanche Frederici *(Martha)*, Wade Boteler *(Sergeant Conlon)*, Ray Largay *(Colonel Ritchie)*, William Colvin *(doctor)*, Sam Nelson *(Private Delehanty)*.

Melodrama. Source: Paul Hervey Fox and George Tilton, *The Soul Kiss* (New York opening: 28 Jan 1908). At a Marine Corps post in Haiti, Brenda, daughter of General Mitchell and wife of Colonel Ritchie, becomes bored with her uneventful life. Having in the past taken a fancy to Capt. Clive Branch, she persuades her father to have him transferred to Haiti. Unaware of her interest, Branch falls in love with Helen Arnold, whose husband is a brutal and indifferent captain; jealous of their relationship, Brenda plans to force Branch into making love to her, but her efforts are repulsed. Arnold learns of his wife's affair with the captain and warns his wife against a divorce, but he is murdered. During the investigation, Brenda reveals the affair between Branch and Helen, hoping to throw suspicion on him, but when she is proved guilty of the crime, Brenda shoots herself. *Marriage. Infidelity. Jealousy. Murder. Suicide. Haiti. United States Marines.*

A SOLDIER'S PLAYTHING **F2.5225**

Warner Brothers Pictures. 1 Nov **1930** [c8 Oct 1930; LP1630]. Sd (Vitaphone); b&w. 35mm. 6 reels, 5,166 ft.

Dir Michael Curtiz. *Screenplay-Dial* Perry Vekroff. *Story* Viña Delmar. *Photog* J. O. Taylor. *Film Ed* Jack Killifer. *Rec Engr* Clifford A. Ruberg.

Cast: Lotti Loder *(Gretchen Rittner)*, Harry Langdon *(Tim)*, Ben Lyon *(Georgie)*, Jean Hersholt *(Grandfather Rittner)*, Noah Beery *(Captain Plover)*, Fred Kohler *(Hank)*, Lee Moran *(Corporal Brown)*, Otto Matieson *(Herman)*, Marie Astaire *(Lola)*, Frank Campeau *(Dave)*.

Comedy-drama. At the beginning of the war, Georgie Wilson, an irresponsible but likable citizen having no sympathy with the conflict, decides to stick to his all-night poker sessions, but his bashful friend, Tim, joins the Army. After a game, Georgie goes to Lola's apartment to pay a debt he owes her brother, and her sweetheart, Hank, accuses him of flirting and cheating. Georgie pushes him from a balcony and assumes that he killed him. To elude Hank's friends, Georgie and Tim enlist in the Army. His easy manner wins him many friends, and after the war, while with the Army of Occupation, Georgie falls in love with Gretchen, daughter of a cafe proprietor in Koblenz; but he decides to return to the States and clear his name before marrying her. He discovers, to his delight, that Hank is alive and also in the Army, and he promises to return to Gretchen as soon as he is discharged. *Soldiers. Friendship. Courtship. Military occupation. World War I. France. Koblenz. United States Army.*

SOLOMON IN SOCIETY **F2.5226**

Cardinal Pictures. *Dist* American Releasing Corp. ca25 Dec **1922** [New York premiere; released 31 Dec 1922 or 28 Jan 1923]. Si; b&w. 35mm. 6 reels, 5,600 ft.

Pres by Carl Krusada. *Dir* Lawrence C. Windom. *Story-Scen* Val Cleveland. *Photog* Edward Paul.

Cast: William H. Strauss *(I. Solomon)*, Brenda Moore *(Rosie Solomon)*, Nancy Deaver *(Mary Bell)*, Charles Delaney *(Frank Wilson)*, Fred T. Jones *(Orlando Kolin)*, Lillian Herlein *(Mrs. Levy)*, Charles Brook *(The Butler)*.

Domestic drama. I. Solomon, a humble tailor on New York's East Side, dreams of being a designer with a shop on Fifth Avenue, but he makes no headway until a dress that he designs for Mary Bell, a laundress who suddenly becomes a movie star, attracts attention and becomes popular. Three years later Solomon has a successful Fifth Avenue shop, but his prosperity is too much for his wife, Rosie, who succumbs to a scheming Greenwich Village pianist, Orlando Kolin. Resigned to giving Rosie her freedom, Solomon, with Mary's help, stages evidence to give Rosie a reason for divorce. Fortunately, Rosie realizes her mistake in time and falls into Solomon's arms; Mary resumes her romance with Solomon's lawyer. *Jews. Tailors. Couturiers. Laundresses. Actors. Pianists. Lawyers. Divorce. Motion pictures. New York City—East Side. New York City—Fifth Avenue.*

Note: Pre-release advertising used the working title *House of Solomon.*

SOMBRAS DE GLORIA **F2.5227**

Sono-Art Productions. 1 Feb **1930** [c4 Apr 1930; LP1216]. Sd (in Spanish); b&w. 35mm. 11 reels, ca9,500 ft.

Pres by O. E. Goebel, George W. Weeks. *Pers Supv* O. E. Goebel, George W. Weeks. *Dir* Andrew L. Stone. *Spanish version* Fernando C. Tamayo. *Photog* Arthur Martinelli. *Tech Dir* Charles Cadwallader. *Film Ed* Arthur Tavares. *Songs: "Bienvenidos," "Arrullo Militar," "Oh Paris," "Si la vida te sonrie," "Canoe-dle-oodle Along," "Roja rosa de amor"* James F. Hanley, Fernando C. Tamayo, José Bohr, José C. Barros, Charles Tobias. *Mus Arr* Robert A. Shepherd. *Mus Dir* Loren Powell. *Choreog* Don Summers. *Sd* Ben Harper, J. G. Greger. *Prod Mgr* J. R. Crone.

Cast: José Bohr *(Eddie Williams)*, Mona Rico *(Helen Williams)*, Francisco Maran *(Dr. Castelli, defense counsel)*, César Vanoni *(district attorney)*, Ricardo Cayol *(Jean)*, Demetrius Alexis *(Carl Hummel)*, Juan Torena *(Jack)*, Enrique Acosta *(judge)*, Tito Davison, Roberto Saa Silva, Federico Godoy.

Drama. Source: Thomas Alexander Boyd, "The Long Shot," in *Points of Honor* (New York, 1925). A Spanish-language version of *Blaze o' Glory;* the synopsis is given under that title. *Actors. Lawyers. Germans. Gas warfare. Infidelity. Murder. Trials. Unemployment. World War I.*

SOME MOTHER'S BOY (Imperial Photoplays) **F2.5228**

Trem Carr Productions. *Dist* Rayart Pictures. 29 Jan or 15 Feb **1929.** Si; b&w. 35mm. 6 reels, 5,768-6,092 ft.

Dir Duke Worne. *Scen* Arthur Hoerl. *Story* Bennett Cohen. *Photog* Hap Depew. *Film Ed* J. S. Harrington.

Cast: Mary Carr *(The Mother)*, Jason Robards *(The Boy)*, Jobyna Ralston *(The Girl)*, M. A. Dickinson *(The Son)*, Henry Barrows *(The Salesman)*.

Drama. Fleeing from the scene of a crime, one of two young crooks is shot; the other escapes, assumes the identity of his partner, and visits the latter's mother. She recognizes the boy to be the son from whom she has been separated for 15 years. He decides to go straight—with the help of a girl, with whom he falls in love—and the reappearance of the other son fails to dampen anyone's spirits. *Criminals—Rehabilitation. Brothers. Motherhood. Impersonation.*

SOME PUN'KINS **F2.5229**

Chadwick Pictures. 29 Sep **1925** [New York showing; released 1 Nov; c31 Oct 1925; LP21957]. Si; b&w. 35mm. 6 or 7 reels, 5,900 or 6,500 ft.

Pres by I. E. Chadwick. *Dir* Jerome Storm. *Writ* Bert Woodruff, Charles E. Banks. *Cinematog* Phillip Tannura, James Brown.

Cast: Charles Ray *(Lem Blossom)*, George Fawcett *(Pa Blossom)*, Fanny Midgley *(Ma Blossom)*, Duane Thompson *(Mary Griggs)*, Bert Woodruff *(Josh Griggs)*, Hallam Cooley *(Tom Perkins)*, William Courtright *(constable)*, Ida Lewis *(gossip)*.

Rural comedy-drama. Lem Blossom—inventor, fire chief of Mosville, and son of a pumpkin farmer—falls in love with unsophisticated country girl Mary Griggs. His rival for her hand is the worldly Tom Perkins, who is conspiring with her father, Joshua, to corner the pumpkin market. When Lem fails to sell his father's pumpkins, Pa Blossom in desperation turns bootlegger. Lem learns that the pumpkin crop up north has been destroyed by frost and attempts to corner the market in the county by offering a $1,000 prize for the largest pumpkin. The Griggs home catches fire, and Lem saves the father and daughter with the aid of his water pump and folding ladder, both his own inventions. Joshua Griggs helps Lem corner the pumpkin market and blesses the union of Lem and Mary. *Farmers. Inventors. Firemen. Bootleggers. Pumpkins. Monopoly. Contests. Rural life.*

SOMEBODY'S MOTHER **F2.5230**

Gerson Pictures. *Dist* Rayart Pictures. 17 Mar **1926** [New York State license]. Si; b&w. 35mm. 5 reels, 4,619 ft.

Dir-Writ Oscar Apfel.

Cast: Mary Carr *(Matches Mary)*, Rex Lease *(her adopted son)*, Mickey McBan *(her lost son)*, Kathryn McGuire, Sidney Franklin, Edward Martindel, Robert Graves.

Murder mystery. A banker has his son taken away from the boy's mother on the grounds that she is not fit to rear him. The woman becomes a peddler and, known as Matches Mary, roams the streets looking for the boy. Unknown to her, the boy, now grown to manhood, has married a young girl and goes to the banker (whom he supposes to be his uncle) and asks him to recognize his new wife. Believing the girl to be a gold digger, the banker refuses; when the banker is murdered sometime later, the youth is accused of the crime on circumstantial evidence. The boy's mother comes forward at the trial and confesses to the murder, but before she can be incriminated by her story, a detective tells the court that two yegg men have confessed to the crime. Mary is reunited with her son. *Bankers. Peddlers. Murder. Fatherhood. Motherhood. Circumstantial evidence. Trials.*

SOMEONE TO LOVE **F2.5231**

Paramount Famous Lasky Corp. 1 Dec **1928** [c4 Dec 1928; LP25890]. Si; b&w. 35mm. 7 reels, 6,323 ft.

Dir F. Richard Jones. *Screenplay* Keene Thompson, Monte Brice. *Titl* George Marion. *Adapt* Ray Harris. *Photog* Allen Siegler.

Cast: Charles (Buddy) Rogers *(William Shelby)*, Mary Brian *(Joan Kendricks)*, William Austin *(Aubrey Weems)*, Jack Oakie *(Michael Casey)*, James Kirkwood *(Mr. Kendricks)*, Mary Alden *(Harriet Newton)*, Frank Reicher *(Simmons)*.

Romantic comedy. Source: Alice Duer Miller, *The Charm School* (New York, 1919). William Shelby, a music store clerk, becomes engaged to wealthy Joan Kendricks and greatly impresses her father by affirming that he will not marry Joan until he is in a position to support her comfortably. Through a misunderstanding, Joan comes to believe that William is a fortune hunter, and the engagement is broken off. William loses his job and becomes the director of an exclusive girls' school in the country. Joan eventually learns that she has misjudged William, and they again receive her father's blessing to be married. *Salesclerks. Socialites. Fortune hunters. Courtship. Boarding schools. Music stores.*

SOMETHING ALWAYS HAPPENS **F2.5232**

Paramount Famous Lasky Corp. 24 Mar **1928** [c24 Mar 1928; LP25102]. Si; b&w. 35mm. 5 reels, 4,792 ft.

Pres by Adolph Zukor, Jesse L. Lasky. *Dir-Writ* Frank Tuttle. *Screenplay* Florence Ryerson, Raymond Cannon. *Titl* Herman J. Mankiewicz. *Adapt* Florence Ryerson. *Photog* J. Roy Hunt. *Film Ed* Verna Willis.

Cast: Esther Ralston *(Diana)*, Neil Hamilton *(Roderick)*, Sojin *(Chang-Tzo)*, Charles Sellon *(Perkins)*, Roscoe Karns *(George)*, Lawrence Grant *(The Earl of Rochester)*, Mischa Auer *(Clark)*, Noble Johnson *(The Thing)*.

Melodramatic farce. While a guest of her fiancé's parents at their English country home, Diana, a thrill-seeking American girl, is taught a lesson by Roderick, her fiancé, who takes her to a "haunted house" for some excitement. However, they are both surprised to meet there Chang-Tzo, a notorious Chinese outlaw who is bent on stealing the family's famous Rochester ruby. After more excitement than either bargained for the couple finally escape with their jewel. *Chinese. Thieves. Haunted houses. Gems. Thrill-seeking. England.*

SOMEWHERE IN SONORA **F2.5233**

Charles R. Rogers Productions. *Dist* First National Pictures. 3 Apr **1927** [c23 Feb 1927; LP23691]. Si; b&w. 35mm. 6 reels, 5,718 ft.

Pres by Charles R. Rogers. *Supv* Harry J. Brown. *Dir* Albert Rogell. *Adapt* Marion Jackson. *Photog* Sol Polito.

Cast: Ken Maynard *(Bob Bishop)*, Kathleen Collins *(Mary Burton)*, Frank Leigh *(Monte Black)*, Joe Bennett *(Bart Leadley)*, Charles Hill Mailes *(Mexicali Burton)*, Carl Stockdale *(Bob Leadley)*, Yvonne Howell *(Patsy)*, Richard Neill *(Ramón Bistula)*, Ben Corbett *("Sockeye" Kelly)*, Monte Montague *("Kettle Belly" Simpson)*, Tarzan *(himself, a horse)*.

Western melodrama. Source: Will Levington Comfort, *Somewhere South in Sonora* (Boston, 1925). Bob Bishop, expert horseman and cowboy, goes to Sonora to seek the wayward son of a rancher who has joined Monte Black's bandit gang. En route, Bob encounters Mary Burton and her two chums. The daughter of a railroad man, Mary is seeking her father. The gang tries to capture the girls but is thwarted. Bob falls in love with Mary and finds Bart, the missing boy, but both Bob and Bart are captured and ordered to be shot. They escape only to be caught in quicksand, but Bob's horse, Tarzan, brings aid. They are rescued, the gang is captured, and Mary and Bob plight their troth. *Cowboys. Bandits. Courtship. Quicksand. Sonora (Mexico). Horses.*

SON OF A GUN **F2.5234**

Bud Barsky Productions. 15 Nov **1926.** Si; b&w. 35mm. 5 reels, 4,500 ft.

Dir Paul Hurst.

Cast: Al Hoxie.

Western melodrama. "Arriving on the border scornful of tales of the wild west, hero is forced to submit to changing clothes with bandit for whom he is afterwards mistaken by sheriff and posse. He finally captures real bandit and holds him for sheriff, and then devotes his time to mistress of post office store." (*Motion Picture News Booking Guide*, 12:54, Apr 1927.) *Sheriffs. Bandits. Postmistresses. Mistaken identity.*

A SON OF HIS FATHER **F2.5235**

Famous Players–Lasky. *Dist* Paramount Pictures. ca15 Aug **1925** [San Francisco premiere; released 21 Sep; c13 Oct 1925; LP21903]. Si; b&w. 35mm. 7 reels, 6,925 ft.

Pres by Adolph Zukor, Jesse L. Lasky. *Dir* Victor Fleming. *Screenplay* Anthony Coldeway. *Photog* C. Edgar Schoenbaum.

Cast: Bessie Love *(Nora)*, Warner Baxter *("Big Boy" Morgan)*, Raymond Hatton *(Charlie Grey)*, Walter McGrail *(Holdbrook)*, Carl Stockdale *(Zobester)*, Billy Eugene *(Larry)*, James Farley *(Indian Pete)*, Charles Stevens *(Pablo)*, Valentina Zimina *(Dolores)*, George Kuwa *(Wing)*.

Western melodrama. Source: Harold Bell Wright, *A Son of His Father* (New York, 1925). "Big Boy" Morgan, a "real westerner" like his father, has lost a controlling interest in his ranch to Holdbrook, who has come under the influence of a gang of gamblers and smugglers led by Zobester. They wish to take over the property for illicit purposes. Nora O'Shea, fresh from Ireland, shows up at the Morgan ranch looking for her brother, Larry, who has been lured into becoming a member of the gang. Morgan keeps the truth from her, but she eventually learns it from Holdbrook and goes to her brother. The gang kidnaps her, but Morgan, with the aid of the U. S. Cavalry, comes to her rescue. The gang is broken up, Holdbrook gives Nora his share in the ranch, Nora and Morgan marry, and Larry is put on probation. *Ranchers. Irish. Smugglers. Gangs. Brother-sister relationship. Gambling. United States Army—Cavalry.*

A SON OF SATAN **F2.5236**

Micheaux Film Corp. 18 Sep **1924** [New York State license application]. Si; b&w. 35mm. 6 or 7 reels.

Cast: Andrew S. Bishop, Ida Anderson.

Melodrama. Depiction of the experiences of an ordinary Negro going to a haunted house to stay all night as the result of an argument. "This picture is filled with scenes of drinking, carousing and shows masked men becoming intoxicated. It shows the playing of crap for money, a man [Captain Tolston] killing his wife by choking her, the killing of the leader of the hooded organization and the killing of a cat by throwing a stone at it." (New York State license records.) *Negro life. Superstition. Drunkenness. Haunted houses. Cats.*

THE SON OF SONTAG **F2.5237**

Ermine Productions. *Dist* Goodwill Distributing Corp. c3 Mar, 5 Mar, 17 Mar **1925** [LU21249]. Si; b&w. 35mm. 5 reels.

Supv Bernard D. Russell. *Dir* Paul Hurst. *Story* Cynthia Penn.

Cast: Jack Meehan.

Western melodrama. No information about the precise nature of this film has been found.

SON OF TARZAN *see* **JUNGLE TRAIL OF THE SON OF TARZAN**

A SON OF THE DESERT **F2.5238**

F. W. Kraemer. *Dist* American Releasing Corp. 11 Feb **1928.** Si; b&w. 35mm. 5 reels, 4,144 ft.

Dir-Writ William Merrill McCormick.

Cast: William Merrill McCormick *(Sheik Hammid Zayad)*, Marin Sais *(Helen Dobson)*, Robert Burns *(Steve Kinard)*, Faith Hope *(Zuebida)*, James Welsh *(Colonel Dobson)*.

Melodrama. Helen Dobson, an art student traveling in Arabia with her father, wishes to paint the portrait of Sheik Hammid Zayad, but the Arab explains that the custom of his country does not permit it. Against the advice of her father and Steve Kinard, a Texas cowboy employed to buy horses, Helen accepts the sheik's invitation to visit his camp, where he promises to show her treasures to satisfy her interest in the picturesque. Helen's horse returns riderless. Suspecting that the sheik is holding her against her will, Steve and Mr. Dobson, after several adventures, rescue Helen. *Artists. Cowboys. Sheiks. Texans. Abduction. Arabia. Horses.*

SON OF THE GODS **F2.5239**

First National Pictures. 9 Mar **1930** [c17 Mar 1930; LP1218]. Sd (Vitaphone); b&w with col sequences (Technicolor). 35mm. 9 reels, 8,344 ft. [Also si.]

Dir Frank Lloyd. *Scen-Dial-Titl* Bradley King. *Photog* Ernest Haller. *Song: "Pretty Little You"* Ben Ryan, Sol Violinsky.

Cast: Richard Barthelmess *(Sam Lee)*, Constance Bennett *(Allana)*, Dorothy Mathews *(Alice Hart)*, Barbara Leonard *(Mabel)*, James Eagle *(Spud)*, Frank Albertson *(Kicker)*, Mildred Van Dorn *(Eileen)*, King Hoo Chang *(Moy)*, Geneva Mitchell *(Connie)*, E. Alyn Warren *(Lee Ying)*, Ivan Christie *(cafe manager)*, Anders Randolf *(Wagner)*, George Irving *(attorney)*, Claude King *(Bathurst)*, Dickey Moore *(boy)*, Robert Homans *(Dugan)*.

Romantic melodrama. Source: Rex Beach, "Son of the Gods," in *Hearst's International Cosmopolitan* (85:24–31, 46–49, 60–63, Oct–Dec 1928; 86:66–69, 80–83, 72–75, Jan–Mar 1929). Sam Lee, reared by a wealthy Chinese merchant in San Francisco's Chinatown, is tolerated in college only because of his money. He determines to prove himself and works his way to the Riviera, where he is befriended by Bathurst, a novelist, who introduces him to Allana, a sophisticated American girl. She falls hopelessly in love with him and refuses to hear anything of his past or background; but upon discovering he is Chinese, she denounces him and lashes the boy with her riding crop. Sam returns home, heartbroken, to see his dying father, and through Eileen, his dearest friend, he learns that he was orphaned by white parents; the repentant Allana returns to the United States, and the lovers are happily reunited. *Students. Chinese. Novelists. Courtship. Racial prejudice. Flagellation. San Francisco—Chinatown. Riviera.*

SON OF THE GOLDEN WEST **F2.5240**

FBO Pictures. 1 Oct **1928** [c1 Oct 1928; LP25777]. Si; b&w. 35mm. 6 reels, 6,037 ft.

Dir Eugene Forde. *Story-Cont* George W. Pyper. *Titl* Randolph Bartlett. *Photog* Norman Devol. *Film Ed* Henry Weber. *Asst Dir* Charles Kerr.

Cast: Tom Mix *(Tom Hardy)*, Sharon Lynn *(Alice Calhoun)*, Tom Lingham *(Jim Calhoun)*, Duke R. Lee *(Slade)*, Lee Shumway *(Tennessee)*, Fritzi Ridgeway *(Rita)*, Joie Ray *(Keller)*, Mark Hamilton *(Kane)*, Wynn Mace *(Slade's henchman)*, Tony *(himself, a horse)*.

Western melodrama. Tom Hardy, a pony express rider, escapes from a bandit attack by the Slade gang and rescues Alice Calhoun, the daughter of the telegraph survey chief, from a runaway stage. Tom then rides to Echo with a sealed request from Calhoun for government troops to put down the Slade bunch. With Tom gone, Slade's men attack the telegraph workers and kidnap Alice; Tom returns and rescues Alice, and the Cavalry comes and rounds up the Slade gang. *Bandits. Telegraph. Pony Express. United States Army—Cavalry. Horses.*

A SON OF THE SAHARA **F2.5241**

Edwin Carewe Productions. *Dist* Associated First National Pictures. 13 Apr **1924** [c24 Apr 1924; LP20118]. Si; b&w. 35mm. 8 reels, 7,603 ft.

Pres by Edwin Carewe. *Dir* Edwin Carewe. *Co-Dir* René Plaisetty. *Scen* Adelaide Heilbron. *Photog* Robert Kurrle. *Asst Photog* Al M. Greene. *Art Dir* John D. Schulze. *Film Ed* Robert De Lacy. *Asst Dir* Wallace Fox. *Laboratory Technician* J. L. Courcier.

Cast: Claire Windsor *(Barbara Barbier)*, Bert Lytell *(Raoul Le Breton [Cassim Ammeh])*, Walter McGrail *(Capt. Jean Duval)*, Rosemary Theby *(Rayma)*, Marise Dorval *(Annette Le Breton)*, Montagu Love *(Sultan Cassim Ammeh/Colonel Barbier)*, Paul Panzer *(Cassim Sr.'s lieutenant/Cassim Jr.'s lieutenant/auctioneer)*, Georges Chebat *(Raoul, as a boy)*, Madame De Castilo.

Romantic drama. Source: Louise Gerard, *A Son of the Sahara* (New York, 1922). As a boy, Raoul is reared by an Arab tribe. Years later, as a refined Europeanized gentleman, he falls in love with Barbara, an officer's daughter, who rejects him when she discovers his background. Affecting a raid, he captures her and then secretly buys her at a slave auction. When she is rescued by French troops, however, his ancestry is established and they find happiness together. *Arabs. Slavery. France—Army—Foreign Legion. Sahara.*

THE SON OF THE SHEIK **F2.5242**

Feature Productions. *Dist* United Artists. 9 Jul **1926** [Los Angeles premiere; released 5 Sep; c24 Aug 1926; LP23046]. Si; b&w. 35mm. 7 reels, 6,685 ft.

Prod John W. Considine, Jr. *Dir* George Fitzmaurice. *Titl* George Marion, Jr. *Adapt* Frances Marion, Fred De Gresac. *Photog* George Barnes. *Art Dir* William Cameron Menzies.

Cast: Rudolph Valentino *(Ahmed/The Sheik)*, Vilma Banky *(Yasmin)*, George Fawcett *(André)*, Montague Love *(Ghabah)*, Karl Dane *(Ramadan)*, Bull Montana *(Ali)*, B. Hyman *(Pincher)*, Agnes Ayres *(Diana)*, Charles Requa, William Donovan, Erwin Connelly.

Melodrama. Source: Edith Maude Hull, *The Sons of the Sheik* (Boston, c1925). Ahmed, The Son of the Sheik, falls in love with Yasmin, a dancer and the daughter of a renegade Frenchman who leads a troupe of mountebanks and thieves. When Ahmed is captured by Yasmin's father and held for ransom, he is led to believe that she has tricked him; and when freed he abducts her, taking her to a desert camp. He is about to force her to submit to him when his father, the sheik, barges into the tent and frees the girl. Later, Ahmed learns that it was not she but rather her jealous admirer who betrayed him. He follows Yasmin to a dancehall, where a bitter fight with knives takes place, Ahmed emerges victorious, unscathed and with the girl in his arms. *Sheiks. Thieves. Charlatans. Dancers. Jealousy. Abduction. Ransom. Deserts. Arabia.*

THE SON OF THE WOLF **F2.5243**

R-C Pictures. 11 Jun **1922** [c11 Jun 1922; LP17957]. Si; b&w. 35mm. 5 reels, 4,970 ft.

Dir Norman Dawn. *Scen* W. Heywood.

Cast: Wheeler Oakman *(Scruff Mackenzie)*, Edith Roberts *(Chook-Ra)*, Sam Allen *(Father Roubeau)*, Ashley Cooper *(Ben Harrington)*, Fred Kohler *(Malemute Kid)*, Thomas Jefferson *(Chief Thling Tinner)*, Fred Stanton *(The Bear)*, Arthur Jasmine *(The Fox)*, William Eagle Eye *(Shaman)*.

Melodrama. Source: Jack London, "The Son of the Wolf," in *Tales of the Far North* (New York, 1900). Scruff Mackenzie, arriving at his quarters in the Yukon, announces his intentions of seeking a wife. Later, he meets Father Roubeau and his Indian ward, Chook-Ra, whom Scruff comes to love, but the priest forbids their marriage until the arrival of her father, Chief Tinner. When Scruff goes to a nearby town to buy gifts for Chook-Ra, he becomes infatuated with a dancehall girl. Chook-Ra follows and, determined to win him, takes some dancing lessons and surprises him at the local ball. Chief Tinner arrives, however, and forces Chook-Ra to return to her own people. Scruff follows to the Indian camp and after much bargaining wins the girl, but the minor chiefs decree that he must first fight The Bear, who also is her suitor. The latter is killed in the ensuing conflict, and the couple depart for civilization. *Dancehall girls. Clergymen. Indians of North America. Courtship. Yukon.*

THE SON OF WALLINGFORD **F2.5244**

Vitagraph Co. of America. 30 Oct **1921** [c20 Sep 1921; LP16976]. Si; b&w. 35mm. 8 reels, 7,851 ft.

Dir-Story-Scen George Randolph Chester, Mrs. George Randolph Chester. *Photog* Stephen Smith, Jr.

Cast: Wilfrid North *(J. Rufus Wallingford)*, Tom Gallery *(Jimmy Wallingford)*, George Webb *(Blackie Daw)*, Antrim Short *("Toad" Edward Jessup)*, Van Dyke Brooke *(Henry Beegoode)*, Sidney D'Albrook *(Bertram Beegoode)*, Andrew Arbuckle *(Talbot Curtis)*, Bobby Mack *(O. O. Jones ["Onion"])*, Walter Rodgers *("Petrograd" Pete)*, Priscilla Bonner *(Mary Curtis)*, Florence Hart *(Fannie [Mrs. Wallingford])*, Lila Leslie *(Violet Bonnie Daw)*, Margaret Cullington *(Caroline Beegoode)*, Martha Mattox.

Comedy-drama. When his parents become convinced that he has inherited criminal tendencies, Jimmy Wallingford leaves home with his adopted brother, "Toad." In a nearby town, Toad discovers signs of oil on the Curtis farm, where Mary, Jimmy's new girl friend, lives, but their investments come to nothing. Suddenly, J. Rufus arrives in town disguised as an East Indian, making great promises to the people. He and Blackie purchase some land, "strike" oil (pumped from tank cars), and sell oil stock to the populace; but Henry Beegoode denies having sold land to Wallingford, and the third copy of the bill of sale is stolen. During an oil fire that traps Jimmy and his friends, Wallingford admits that the well is a fake—a scheme to expose Beegoode. The bill of sale is regained from Beegoode, and Jimmy has an authentic strike. *Brothers. Swindlers. Heredity. Oil wells. Documentation. Fires.*

THE SONG AND DANCE MAN F2.5245

Famous Players–Lasky. *Dist* Paramount Pictures. 8 Feb **1926** [c11 Feb 1926; LP22393]. Si; b&w. 35mm. 7 reels, 6,997 ft.

Pres by Adolph Zukor, Jesse L. Lasky. *Dir* Herbert Brenon. *Screenplay* Paul Schofield. *Photog* James Howe. *Art Dir* Julian Boone Fleming.

Cast: Tom Moore *(Happy Farrell)*, Bessie Love *(Leola Lane)*, Harrison Ford *(Joseph Murdock)*, Norman Trevor *(Charles Nelson)*, Bobby Watson *(Fred Carroll)*, Josephine Drake *(Jane Rosemond)*, George Nash *(Inspector Craig)*, William B. Mack *(Tom Crosby)*, Helen Lindroth *(Marsha Lane)*, Jane Jennings *(Ma Carroll)*.

Comedy-drama. Source: George M. Cohan, *The Song and Dance Man* (New York opening: 31 Dec 1923). Happy Farrell is caught trying to hold up two men—Charles Nelson, theatrical producer, and Joseph Murdock, a rich artist. He exonerates himself by relating his tribulations as a song-and-dance man and how he gave his last penny to an old woman and her daughter, Leola, also a dancer. Nelson agrees to give both Happy and Leola a chance on Broadway. Leola is a success, but Happy fails and goes west to try his luck. When he returns successful, he finds that Leola, now engaged to Murdock, has become a star. Happy yearns to return to the song and dance circuit and does so. *Artists. Criminals—Rehabilitation. Theatrical producers. Song-and-dance men. New York City—Broadway.*

SONG O' MY HEART F2.5246

Fox Film Corp. 11 Mar **1930** [New York premiere; released 7 Sep; c11 Feb 1930; LP1136]. Sd (Movietone); b&w. 35mm and 70mm (Grandeur). 9 reels, 7,740 ft.

Pres by William Fox. *Dir* Frank Borzage. *Cont* Sonya Levien. *Story-Dial* Tom Barry. *Photog* Chester Lyons, Al Brick. *Grandeur Camera* J. O. Taylor. *Art Dir* Harry Oliver. *Film Ed* Margaret V. Clancey. *Songs: "I Feel You Near Me," "A Pair of Blue Eyes," "Song o' My Heart"* Charles Glover, William Kernell, James Hanley. *Song: "Paddy, Me Lad"* Albert Malotte. *Song: "Rose of Tralee"* Charles Glover, C. Mordaunt Spencer. *Rec Engr* George P. Costello. *Asst Dir* Lew Borzage. *Cost* Sophie Wachner.

Cast: John McCormack *(Sean O'Carolan)*, Alice Joyce *(Mary O'Brien)*, Maureen O'Sullivan *(Eileen O'Brien)*, Tom Clifford *(Tad O'Brien)*, J. M. Kerrigan *(Peter Conlon)*, John Garrick *(Fergus O'Donnell)*, Edwin Schneider *(Vincent Glennon)*, J. Farrell MacDonald *(Joe Rafferty)*, Effie Ellsler *(Mona)*, Emily Fitzroy *(Elizabeth)*, Andres De Segurola *(Guido)*, Edward Martindel *(Fullerton)*.

Musical drama. "John McCormack brings his attractive personality and marvelous voice to the screen in a tale full of tender pathos, fine humor delivered in rich brogue, and delightful settings. The outstanding moments in the film are those in which he sings, of course, and his voice loses none of its richness and charm in the recording. The story, laid principally in a lovely little Irish village, is a simple one telling of a talented singer who years before had given up his career when the woman he loves was forced to marry a wealthy man. He finds happiness in being able to help her children when their father deserts them." (*National Board of Review Magazine,* Apr 1930, p20.) *Singers. Children. Motherhood. Ireland.*

Note: McCormack sings the following songs: "Then You'll Remember Me," "A Fairy Story by the Fireside," "Just for Today," "Kitty, My Love," "Luoghi Sereni e Cari," "Little Boy Blue," "Ireland, Mother Ireland," "I Hear You Calling Me."

A SONG OF KENTUCKY F2.5247

Fox Film Corp. 10 Nov **1929** [c31 Oct 1929; LP802]. Sd (Movietone); b&w. 35mm. 9 reels, 7,125 ft.

Pres by William Fox. *Assoc Prod* Chandler Sprague. *Dir* Lewis Seiler. *Staged by* Frank Merlin. *Scen-Dial* Frederick Hazlitt Brennan. *Photog* Charles G. Clarke. *Art Dir* William Darling. *Film Ed* Carl Carruth. *Songs: "Sitting by the Window," "A Night of Happiness"* Con Conrad, Sidney Mitchell, Archie Gottler. *Sd* Frank MacKenzie. *Asst Dir* Horace Hough. *Cost* Sophie Wachner.

Cast: Joseph Wagstaff *(Jerry Reavis)*, Lois Moran *(Lee Coleman)*, Dorothy Burgess *(Nancy Morgan)*, Douglas Gilmore *(Kane Pitcairn)*, Herman Bing *(Jake Kleinschmidt)*, Hedda Hopper *(Mrs. Coleman)*, Edwards Davis *(Mr. Coleman)*, Bert Woodruff *(Steve)*.

Romantic drama. "Jerry, a young song writer, falls in love with Lee Coleman, a wealthy Southern girl. She is being forced into marriage with a fortune hunter who upon learning of her infatuation pays a former vaudeville partner of Jerry's to frame him. Stunned by what she believes to be the truth, Lee goes back to Kentucky and there she makes a wager with her would-be fiancé that if her horse does not win the Derby she will marry him. She loses her wager and on the eve of her wedding she slips away to attend a concert where Jerry directs his own symphony. At the close of the concert the girl who had caused the trouble confesses and so Lee and Jerry are happy." (*National Board of Review Magazine,* Nov 1929, p20.) *Composers. Southerners. Vaudevillians. Fortune hunters. Horseracing. Wagers. Courtship. Kentucky. Kentucky Derby.*

Note: Some sources indicate the film was based on an original story by Frederick Brennan, rather than the book by Conrad, Mitchell, and Gottler.

THE SONG OF LIFE F2.5248

Louis B. Mayer Productions. *Dist* Associated First National Pictures. 2 Jan **1922** [c29 Dec 1921; LP17410]. Si; b&w. 35mm. 7 reels, 6,920 ft.

Pres by Louis B. Mayer. *Dir* John M. Stahl. *Scen* Bess Meredyth. *Story* Frances Irene Reels. *Photog* Ernest Palmer.

Cast: Gaston Glass *(David Tilden)*, Grace Darmond *(Aline Tilden)*, Georgia Woodthorpe *(Mary Tilden)*, Richard Headrick *(neighbor's boy)*, Arthur Stuart Hull *(district attorney)*, Wedgewood Nowell *(Richard Henderson)*, Edward Peil *(Amos Tilden)*, Fred Kelsey *(police inspector)*, Claude Payton *(central office man)*.

Society melodrama. Mary Tilden, finding life unbearable in the desert as housewife to a railroad foreman, runs away from her husband and child. Twenty-five years later she is still washing dishes in the city, and worn and tired of her fruitless struggles she attempts suicide but is saved by David Tilden, a young writer, who takes her into his home to relieve his wife, Aline, from the drudgery of housework, enabling Aline to return to singing in a music store. Aline meets Henderson, an attractive young publisher; David visits Henderson's office, sees his wife's picture on the desk, and returns later with the intention of killing Henderson. Meanwhile, Mary discovers that David is her son but remains silent until she tries to take the blame for Henderson's murder and divulges the relationship. David tries to confess but is believed to be shielding his mother. Both are saved by the news that the shot was not fatal, and there is a happy reunion of husband, mother, and wife. *Authors. Singers. Marriage. Drudgery. Motherhood. Jealousy. Music stores.*

THE SONG OF LOVE F2.5249

Norma Talmadge Productions. *Dist* Associated First National Pictures. 24 Dec **1923** [c13 Dec 1923; LP19710]. Si; b&w. 35mm. 8 reels, 8,000 ft.

Pres by Joseph M. Schenck. *Dir* Chester Franklin, Frances Marion. *Adapt* Frances Marion. *Photog* Antonio Gaudio.

Cast: Norma Talmadge *(Noorma-hal)*, Joseph Schildkraut *(Raymon Valverde)*, Arthur Edmund Carew *(Ramlika)*, Laurence Wheat *(Dick Jones)*, Maude Wayne *(Maureen Desmard)*, Earl Schenck *(Commissionnaire Desmard)*, Hector V. Sarno *(Chandra-lal)*, Albert Prisco *(Chamba)*, Mario Carillo *(Captain Fregonne)*, James Cooley *(Dr. Humbert)*.

Romantic melodrama. Source: Margaret Peterson, *Dust of Desire* (New York, 1922). Ramlika, an Arab chief in Algeria, has plans to drive out the French and crown himself king of North Africa. Noorma-hal, a dancing girl whom he would like to marry, detests Ramlika but is instructed by her uncle, Chandra-lal, to lead him on. The French sense trouble among the Arabs and send for famous spy Raymon Valverde to learn the Arabs' plans. Arriving incognito, Valverde charms Noorma-hal, causing her to disclose the plans for the rebellion. When Ramlika leads the attack on the French garrison, Valverde, who is prepared for the attack but has no troops, fights singlehanded until Noorma-hal arrives and offers to sacrifice her life if Ramlika frees Valverde. Then, rather than go with Ramlika, Noorma-hal shoots herself. Fortunately, French troops arrive and kill Ramlika. Noorma-hal recovers. *French. Arabs. Dancers. Spies. Colonialism. Revolts. Algeria.*

THE SONG OF LOVE F2.5250

Edward Small Productions. *Dist* Columbia Pictures. 25 Nov **1929** [c27 Dec 1929; LP944]. Sd (Movietone); b&w. 35mm. 9 reels, 7,720 ft. [Also si.]

Supv Harry Cohn. *Dir* Erle C. Kenton. *Story-Scen* Howard Green, Henry McCarthy, Dorothy Howell. *Dial* Dorothy Howell, Norman Houston. *Photog* Joe Walker. *Film Ed* Gene Havlick. *Song: "I'm Somebody's Baby Now"* Mack Gordon, Max Rich. *Song: "I'm Walking With the Moonbeams (Talking to the Stars)"* Mack Gordon, Max Rich, Maurice Abrahams. *Song: "I'll Still Go On Wanting You"* Bernie Grossman. *Song: "White Way Blues"* Mack Gordon, Max Rich, George Weist. *Ch Sd Engr* John Livadary. *Sd Mixing Engr* Harry Blanchard, E. L. Bernds. *Asst Dir* Sam Nelson.

Cast: Belle Baker *(Anna Gibson)*, Ralph Graves *(Tom Gibson)*, David Durand *(Buddy Gibson)*, Eunice Quedens *(Mazie)*, Arthur Housman *(acrobat)*, Charles Wilson *(traveling salesman)*.

Domestic drama. Tom and Anna Gibson, along with their little boy, Buddy, form a successful vaudeville song-and-dance act and a happy family. Anna, however, is worried about her son's future when she finds him playing ball, forgetting a performance; she determines to retire from the stage temporarily to give Buddy a proper home environment. Tom, a hardened trouper, is not in sympathy with her plans, and when Mazie, a flirtatious blonde, applies to take Anna's place, Tom accepts her. Tom finally confesses to Anna that he is in love with Mazie; she moves away and supports Buddy as a cafe entertainer, soon placing him in a military school. Learning of the rift between his parents, Buddy persuades his father to leave Mazie, and they are all unexpectedly reunited in a rendition of their old stage act. *Entertainers. Theatrical troupes. Children. Family life. Vaudeville. Infidelity. Motherhood. Military schools.*

SONG OF THE CABALLERO **F2.5251**

Ken Maynard Productions. *Dist* Universal Pictures. 29 Jun **1930** [c20 Jun 1930; LP1377]. Sd (Movietone); b&w. 35mm. 7 reels, 6,524 ft.

Pres by Carl Laemmle. *Dir* Harry J. Brown. *Dial* Lesley Mason. *Adapt* Bennett Cohen. *Story* Kenneth C. Beaton, Norman Sper. *Photog* Ted McCord. *Film Ed* Fred Allen. *Rec Engr* C. Roy Hunter.

Cast: Ken Maynard *(Juan)*, Doris Hill *(Anita)*, Francis Ford *(Don Pedro Madera)*, Gino Corrado *(Don José)*, Evelyn Sherman *(Doña Luisa)*, Josef Swickard *(Manuel)*, Frank Rice *(Andrea)*, William Irving *(Bernardo)*, Joyzelle *(Conchita)*, Tarzan *(himself, a horse)*.

Western melodrama. Accompanied by two followers, Juan becomes known as a bandit who preys only on the Madera family, because of ill treatment accorded his mother by Pedro Madero. He robs Don José at a tavern celebration while his father is away escorting the beautiful Anita, betrothed to José. Juan meets the party and as a reward for saving Anita's life is invited to the rancho for the fiesta. The guests are alarmed to hear that Juan is actually the bandit enemy of the family; Anita, attracted to Juan, resents her coming marriage all the more when she surprises José in the arms of a former sweetheart. Juan fights a desperate sword battle until Don Pedro learns he is his nephew; they are reconciled, José is discredited, and Anita is betrothed to Juan. *Bandits. Filial relations. Revenge. Courtship. Ranches. Baja California. Horses.*

SONG OF THE FLAME **F2.5252**

First National Pictures. ca6 May **1930** [New York premiere; released 25 May; c12 Jun 1930; LP1353]. Sd (Vitaphone); col (Technicolor). 35mm. 9 reels, 6,501 ft.

Dir Alan Crosland. *Screen Vers–Dial* Gordon Rigby. *Photog* Lee Garmes. *Set Dsgn* Anton Grot. *Film Ed* Al Hall. *Songs: "Liberty Song," "The Goose Hangs High," "Petrograd," "Passing Fancy," "One Little Drink"* Grant Clarke, Harry Akst, Eddie Ward. *Song: "When Love Calls"* Ed Ward. *Mus Cond* Leo Forbstein. *Chorus Dir* Ernest Grooney, Norman Spencer. *Dance Dir* Jack Haskell. *Rec Engr* George R. Groves. *Asst Dir* Ben Silvey. *Cost Dsgn* Edward Stevenson.

Cast: Alexander Gray *(Prince Volodya)*, Bernice Claire *(Anuita, the Flame)*, Noah Beery *(Konstantin)*, Alice Gentle *(Natasha)*, Bert Roach *(Count Boris)*, Inez Courtney *(Grusha)*, Shep Camp *(officer)*, Ivan Linow *(Konstantin's pal)*.

Operetta. Source: Oscar Hammerstein, II, Otto Harbach, George Gershwin, and Herbert Stothart, *Song of the Flame* (New York opening: 30 Dec 1925). Before the downfall of the Czar of Russia, Anuita, "The Flame," sings to incite the people to revolt, eluding Prince Voloyda, who tries to capture her with his Cossack troop. Her fellow conspirator, Konstantin, watches her covetously, though he is pledged to Natasha, who is jealous of the younger girl. The conspirators overthrow the czar and plunge the country into chaotic revolt, but Anuita, disgusted with Konstantin's brutality, goes south to her native Polish village where she meets the prince at the Festival of the Harvest, and they fall in love. Konstantin and his troops intercede and arrest the prince, who is to be executed, but Anuita buys his liberty by promising to be Konstantin's mistress. She is imprisoned, and the prince is captured when he comes in disguise to her aid; but Natasha kills Konstantin and the lovers safely escape. *Peasants. Royalty. Courtship. Cossacks. Disguise. Russia—History—1917–21 Revolution. Poland.*

SONG OF THE WEST **F2.5253**

Warner Brothers Pictures. 27 Feb **1930** [New York premiere; released 15 Mar; c1 Mar 1930; LP1114]. Sd (Vitaphone); col (Technicolor). 35mm. 9 reels, 7,185 ft.

Dir Ray Enright. *Scen-Dial* Harvey Thew. *Photog* Dev Jennings. *Film Ed* George Marks. *Songs: "The Bride Was Dressed in White," "Hay-Straw"* Vincent Youmans, Oscar Hammerstein, II. *Song: "Come Back to Me"* Grant Clarke, Harry Akst. *Sd Engr* Glenn E. Rominger.

Cast: John Boles *(Stanton)*, Vivienne Segal *(Virginia)*, Joe E. Brown *(Hasty)*, Marie Wells *(Lotta)*, Sam Hardy *(Davolo)*, Marion Byron *(Penny)*, Eddie Gribbon *(Sergeant Major)*, Edward Martindel *(Colonel)*, Rudolph Cameron *(Singleton)*.

Western romantic drama. Source: Laurence Stallings and Oscar Hammerstein, II, *Rainbow* (New York opening: 21 Nov 1928). At Fort Independence, Kansas, Lieutenant Singleton, a rival for the colonel's daughter, Virginia, recognizes Stanton, a young scout who previously was involved in a scandal and a row with Davolo (his own rival) over a woman named Lotta. In a quarrel with Davolo, Stanton shoots him and is held on a murder charge at the fort; but on the morning of the departure of a wagon train for California, Stanton escapes and, disguised in a minister's garb, joins the train and soon falls in love with Virginia, who reciprocates. Secretly, they go to San Francisco and open a gambling hall, but Stanton is shamed by his former military associates and decides to leave Virginia; after being involved in a mining camp incident, he is offered the choice of either reenlisting as a private or of being deported. Stanton gladly reenlists and finds that Virginia still loves him. *Scouts—Frontier. Clergymen. Murder. Courtship. Gambling. Wagon trains. California. San Francisco. Kansas. United States Army—Desertion.*

SONIA **F2.5254**

Dist Film Distributing Co. 1 Dec **1928.** Mus score & sd eff (Aurafone); b&w. 35mm. 5 reels, 4,900 ft.

Dir Hector V. Sarno. *Photog* William Thompson. *Film Ed* Abe Heller.

Cast: Rosa Rosanova, Evelyn Pierce, Hector V. Sarno.

Melodrama(?). No information about the nature of this film has been found.

SONNY **F2.5255**

Inspiration Pictures. *Dist* Associated First National Pictures. May **1922** [c12 Jun, 16 Jun 1922; LP17974, LP18156]. Si; b&w. 35mm. 7 reels, 6,968 ft.

Pres by Charles H. Duell. *Dir* Henry King. *Adapt* Frances Marion, Henry King. *Photog* Henry Cronjager. *Art Dir* Charles Osborne Seessel. *Film Ed* Duncan Mansfield.

Cast: Richard Barthelmess *(Sonny [Charles Crosby]/Joe)*, Margaret Seddon *(Mrs. Crosby)*, Pauline Garon *(Florence Crosby)*, Lucy Fox *(Madge Craig)*, Herbert Grimwood *(Harper Craig)*, Patterson Dial *(Alicia)*, Fred Nicholls *(Summers)*, James Terbell *(James)*, Margaret Elizabeth Falconer, Virginia Magee *(Crosby twins)*.

Drama. Source: George V. Hobart and Raymond Hubbell, *Sonny* (New York opening: 16 Aug 1921). Two look-alikes—Joe, a poolroom-owner, and Sonny, son of a wealthy, blind mother—go to war at the same time. They meet and become buddies. Sonny is wounded, and, before dying, he makes Joe promise to take his place in order to spare his mother grief. Joe carries on the deception, even though he falls in love with Sonny's sister. He is finally exposed in a dream through which the mother realizes her son is dead, but nevertheless he is warmly accepted by her. *Doubles. Filial relations. Blindness. Impersonation. Billiard parlors. World War I. Dreams.*

SONNY BOY **F2.5256**

Warner Brothers Pictures. 27 Feb **1929** [New York premiere; released 18 Apr; c13 Apr 1929; LP767]. Sd (Vitaphone); b&w. 35mm. 7 reels, 6,010 ft. [Also si.]

Dir Archie Mayo. *Scen* C. Graham Baker. *Titl-Dial* James A. Starr. *Story* Leon Zuardo. *Photog* Ben Reynolds. *Film Ed* Owen Marks. *Mus Arr* Louis Silvers.

Cast: Davey Lee *(Sonny Boy)*, Betty Bronson *(Winifred Canfield)*, Edward Everett Horton *(Crandall Thorpe, Attorney)*, Gertrude Olmstead *(Mary)*, John T. Murray *(Hamilton)*, Tommy Dugan *(Mulcahy)*, Lucy Beaumont *(Mother Thorpe)*, Edmund Breese *(Thorpe, Sr.)*, Jed Prouty *(Phil)*.

Domestic melodrama. Mary and Hamilton, Sonny Boy's parents, quarrel, and Hamilton plans to take the boy to Europe while Mary telegraphs her sister, Winifred, to help her retain custody of the child. Pretending to be the maid, Winifred sends Sonny Boy out in a clothes basket, carried by a detective hired by Hamilton. At the railway station, Winifred learns that Lawyer Thorpe's apartment is vacant, and pretending to be Thorpe's wife, she and the boy gain entrance. Thorpe's parents arrive unexpectedly, and she keeps up the pretense, even when Hamilton and Thorpe arrive, followed by Mary. Hamilton attacks the attorney, thinking his wife has planned a rendezvous, but the appearance of Winifred and Sonny Boy clears the air. The parents are reconciled, and Thorpe is united with Winifred. *Children. Detectives. Sisters. Lawyers. Marriage. Disguise.*

THE SONORA KID **F2.5257**

R-C Pictures. *Dist* Film Booking Offices of America. 13 Mar **1927** [c26 Feb 1927; LP23702]. Si; b&w. 35mm. 5 reels, 4,565 ft.

Pres by Joseph P. Kennedy. *Dir* Robert De Lacy. *Cont* Percy Heath. *Scen* J. G. Hawks. *Camera* Nick Musuraca. *Asst Dir* William Cody.

Cast: Tom Tyler *(Tom MacReady)*, Peggy Montgomery *(Phyllis Butterworth)*, Billie Bennett *(Aunt Marie)*, Mark Hamilton *(Chuck Saunders)*, Jack Richardson *(Arthur Butterworth)*, Ethan Laidlaw *(Tough Ryder)*, Bruce Gordon *(James Poindexter)*, Barney Furey *(Doc Knight)*, Vic Allen *(sheriff)*, Beans *(himself, a dog)*.

Western melodrama. Source: William Wallace Cook, "A Knight of the Range" (publication undetermined). Tom, the new foreman of the Butterworth ranch, takes an interest in Phyllis, the boss's daughter, but Butterworth, who brings in a prospective son-in-law, orders Tom off the ranch. Tom, however, plans secretly to elope with Phyllis. Meanwhile, Poindexter arranges with Tough Ryder, an outlaw, to kidnap Phyllis so that he (Poindexter) may "rescue" her. Ryder holds up Knight, an itinerant patent-medicine man, and his assistant, a colored boy dressed in a suit of armor; and disguising himself with the armor, Ryder manages to evade the sheriff. Tom, learning of the kidnaping, arrives at Ryder's secret cabin in time to rescue Phyllis from the forced attentions of Poindexter; and as a result, he is accepted by her father as a son-in-law. *Ranch foremen. Outlaws. Peddlers. Courtship. Kidnaping. Dogs.*

SONS OF THE SADDLE **F2.5258**

Ken Maynard Productions. *Dist* Universal Pictures. 3 Aug **1930** [c31 Jul 1930; LP1451]. Sd (Movietone); b&w. 35mm. 8 reels, 6,872 ft. [Also si.]

Pres by Carl Laemmle. *Dir* Harry J. Brown. *Story-Scen* Bennett Cohen. *Dial* Leslie Mason. *Photog* Ted McCord. *Film Ed* Fred Allen. *Song: "Down the Home Trail With You"* Bernie Grossman, Lou Handman. *Rec Engr* C. Roy Hunter.

Cast: Ken Maynard *(Jim Brandon)*, Doris Hill *(Ronnie Stavnow)*, Joseph Girard *(Martin Stavnow)*, Carroll Nye *(Harvey)*, Francis Ford *("Red" Slade)*, Harry Todd *("Pop" Higgins)*, Tarzan *(himself, the horse)*.

Western melodrama. Jim Brandon, foreman of the Wind River Ranch, owned by Martin Stavnow, is in love with Ronnie, the rancher's daughter, though he is unaware that Harvey, a youthful cowhand, also loves her. Thus, Jim asks the boy, whom he protects like a brother, to speak for him. When he is spurned by Ronnie, Harvey decides to join Red Slade's gang, who are plotting a raid on the Wind River herd. As Jim forcibly attempts to separate him from the gang, Harvey is killed; and through the aid of his horse, Tarzan, Jim foils Slade's attempt to stampede the herd. Slade takes refuge in a wagon where Ronnie is hiding; Jim rescues Ronnie from the wagon just before the runaway team plunges over a cliff with Slade riding to his doom. *Ranch foremen. Rustlers. Courtship. Horses.*

SONS OF THE WEST **F2.5259**

Dist Aywon Film Corp. Jul **1922**. Si; b&w. 35mm. 5 reels.

Western melodrama. Deals "with man who goes west to forget faithless wife, whom he has divorced. He falls in love with young girl, and, despite efforts of former sweetheart, marries her. Former wife appears and in his absence, tells girl she is still his wife. The girl, heart-broken, leaves. The man returns and denounces divorced wife. Brings his real wife back. She falls ill, and, unable to find work, he goes west. He receives word that $100 must be forthcoming for an operation. Desperate, he robs stagecoach, but in mailsack finds letter for him with money. Repents and returns loot. He is freed, his wife recovers, and all ends happily." (*Motion Picture News Booking Guide*, 3:66, Oct 1922.) *Marriage. Divorce. Infidelity. Stagecoach robberies.*

SOPHIE SEMENOFF *see* **MAKING THE GRADE**

THE SOPHOMORE **F2.5260**

Pathé Exchange. 24 Aug **1929** [c16 Sep 1929; LP691]. Sd (Photophone); b&w. 35mm. 8 reels, 6,526 ft. [Also si; 5,799 ft.]

Supv William Conselman. *Dir* Leo McCarey. *Dial Dir* Anthony Brown. *Dial* Earl Baldwin, Walter De Leon. *Adapt* Joseph Franklin Poland. *Story* Corey Ford, T. H. Wenning. *Photog* John J. Mescall. *Film Ed* Doane Harrison. *Song: "Little by Little"* Bobby Dolan, Walter O'Keefe. *Sd Engr* Charles O'Loughlin, Ben Winkler. *Asst Dir* E. J. Babille. *Prod Mgr* Richard Blaydon.

Cast: Eddie Quillan *(Joe Collins)*, Sally O'Neil *(Margie Callahan)*, Stanley Smith *(Tom Week)*, Jeanette Loff *(Barbara Lange)*, Russell Gleason *(Dutch)*, Sarah Padden *(Mrs. Collins)*, Brooks Benedict *(Armstrong)*, Spec O'Donnell *(Joe Collins' nephew)*, Walter O'Keefe *(radio announcer)*.

Comedy-drama. Joe Collins arrives at Hanford College to begin his second year with $200 to pay his tuition, is enticed into a craps game, and loses all. He takes a job in a soda fountain where Margie Callahan, who worships him, also works. When he loses his job, Margie pays the tuition. Joe discovers that Margie is his benefactor halfway through a football game: running off the field, he catches her before her train departs, and they embrace. *Students. Soda clerks. College life. Football. Gambling.*

SORRELL AND SON **F2.5261**

Feature Productions. *Dist* United Artists. 12 Nov **1927** [New York premiere; released 2 Dec; c22 Dec 1927; LP24781]. Si; b&w. 35mm. 10 reels, 9,000 ft.

Pres by Joseph M. Schenck. *Dir-Scen* Herbert Brenon. *Adapt* Elizabeth Meehan. *Photog* James Wong Howe. *Art Dir* William Cameron Menzies. *Set Dsgn* Julian Boone Fleming. *Film Ed* Marie Halvey. *Asst Dir* Ray Lissner. *Makeup* Fred C. Ryle.

Cast: H. B. Warner *(Stephen Sorrell)*, Anna Q. Nilsson *(Dora Sorrell)*, Mickey McBan *(Kit Sorrell, as a child)*, Carmel Myers *(Flo Palfrey)*, Lionel Belmore *(John Palfrey)*, Norman Trevor *(Thomas Roland)*, Betsy Ann Hisle *(Molly Roland, as a child)*, Louis Wolheim *(Buck)*, Paul McAllister *(Dr. Orange)*, Alice Joyce *(Fanny Garland)*, Nils Asther *(Kit Sorrell, as a man)*, Mary Nolan *(Molly Roland, as a grown woman)*.

Drama. Source: George Warwick Deeping, *Sorrell and Son* (New York, 1925). Captain Stephen Sorrell returns to postwar London with the Military Cross, only to find his pleasure-seeking wife, Dora, packing off with another man to avoid enduring Sorrell's reduced status: he is without health, work, and riches. He then begins a life-long battle to endure the privations that have been thrust upon him and his infant son, Kit, striving to retain honor and grace through it all. He is humiliated and vamped by coarse innkeeper Flo Palfrey, who delights in the irony of his debasement; but Sorrell walks out on her temptations and is fired. Destitute, he maintains his integrity, taking a job as porter in yet another inn. Trouble with his supervisor further degrades the august captain, but he endures all for his son's sake, finally obtaining for him an appointment to a genteel boarding school. Kit grows up determined to emulate the surgeon who saved the life of his childhood sweetheart, Molly, and while in college is rediscovered by the errant and predatory Dora, who, married to money, tries to buy with London flappers and promises of wealth the place in his heart she rejected years before. Kit dismisses her as a sad and pathetic creature, and returns to his father's patronage, increasing his own reputation as a surgeon and their mutual admiration. Sorrell has found a gentle woman to comfort him and, dying, has Kit dispatch him at the last, completing an affair of intense devotion and filial love. *War heroes. Surgeons. Innkeepers. Porters. Flappers. Boarding schools. Desertion. Inns. Filial relations. Mercy killing. London.*

Note: Filmed in part on location in England.

THE SORROWS OF SATAN **F2.5262**

Famous Players–Lasky. *Dist* Paramount Pictures. 12 Oct **1926** [New York premiere; released 5 Feb 1927; c7 Feb 1927; LP23647]. Si; b&w. 35mm. 9 reels, 8,691 ft.

Pres by Adolph Zukor, Jesse L. Lasky. *Dir* D. W. Griffith. *Screenplay* Forrest Halsey. *Titl* Julian Johnson. *Adapt* John Russell, George Hull. *Photog* Harry Fischbeck, Arthur De Titta. *Art Dir* Charles Kirk. *Film Ed* Julian Johnson. *Miniatures* Fred Waller, Jr.

Cast: Adolphe Menjou *(Prince Lucio de Rimanez)*, Ricardo Cortez *(Geoffrey Tempest)*, Lya De Putti *(Princess Olga)*, Carol Dempster *(Mavis Claire)*, Ivan Lebedeff *(Amiel)*, Marcia Harris *(The Landlady)*, Lawrence D'Orsay *(Lord Elton)*, Nellie Savage *(dancing girl)*, Dorothy Hughes *(Mavis' chum)*, Josephine Dunn, Dorothy Nourse, Jeanne Morgan.

Allegorical melodrama. Source: Marie Corelli, *The Sorrows of Satan; or The Strange Experience of One Geoffrey Tempest, Millionaire* (New York, 1895). After completing a novel in his London garret, Geoffrey Tempest meets Mavis Claire, another struggling writer, and they drink to the success of his novel, in which he rails at God and fate. When his publisher rejects his supernatural theme, Tempest meets Rimanez, a mysterious nobleman, who takes him to a sumptuous hotel, where he is transfixed by the lovely Princess Olga. Informing Geoffrey that he has been made heir to a fortune, Rimanez arranges for his marriage to Olga; and following a successful courtship, there is a spectacular wedding. Married life, however, proves a failure for Geoffrey, and while dining with wealthy friends he sees Mavis, forlorn and poorly clad; when he rises to follow, Rimanez reveals his identity as Satan and threatens to strip him of his riches. Morning finds Geoffrey in his garret, reconciled with Mavis. *Novelists. Courtship. Wealth. The Devil. London.*

SO'S YOUR OLD MAN **F2.5263**

Famous Players–Lasky. *Dist* Paramount Pictures. 25 Oct **1926** [c22 Oct 1926; LP23265]. Si; b&w. 35mm. 7 reels, 6,347 ft.

Pres by Adolph Zukor, Jesse L. Lasky. *Dir* Gregory La Cava. *Screenplay* J. Clarkson Miller. *Prod Ed* Ralph Block. *Titl* Julian Johnson. *Adapt* Howard Emmett Rogers. *Photog* George Webber. *Art Sets* John Held, Jr. *Film Ed* Julian Johnson.

Cast: W. C. Fields *(Samuel Bisbee)*, Alice Joyce *(Princess Lescaboura)*, Charles Rogers *(Kenneth Murchison)*, Kittens Reichert *(Alice Bisbee)*, Marcia Harris *(Mrs. Bisbee)*, Julia Ralph *(Mrs. Murchison)*, Frank Montgomery *(Jeff)*, Jerry Sinclair *(Al)*.

Farce. Source: Julian Leonard Street, *Mr. Bisbee's Princess and Other Stories* (Garden City, New York, 1925). Waukegus, New Jersey, is a small town where Samuel Bisbee lives in a state of confused but devilish dilapidation. His daughter, Alice, is being courted by Kenneth Murchison, and on the afternoon that Mrs. Murchison comes to meet the apple of her son's eye, Old Sam stumbles in from his shop in the back, having partaken of sarsaparilla and spirits with some amiable cronies, and horrifies the orotund social heiress. He assures all that their tune will change when his newest invention—an unbreakable auto glass—is snapped up by a group of automen who are meeting in Washington and have asked Sam for a demonstration. He parks his flivver in front of the hotel, but his auto is displaced. Soon the committee follows him out, and Sam proceeds to bombard what he thinks is his chariot with bricks. Much to his chagrin, the glass in the car shatters into a jigsaw. Sam grabs a train for home; he contemplates suicide, but his vial of poison is broken. He then is jostled into the compartment of the lovely Spanish princess Lescaboura, and upon spying a bottle of iodine, reads his own thwarted intentions onto the princess and tries to salvage her spirits. Sam is spied on the train by some gossips and so slandered that he returns from his 3-day binge searching for the fortitude to face the Missus. He is wending his way home, having purchased a pony as a peace offering, when the town's elite and the princess overtake him, and she shows them his affectionate place in her heart. Sam is given the honor of blasting the first ball at the new country club opening, and when his glass is proven impervious, he wins a million-dollar contract. *Inventors. Glaziers. Royalty. Golf. Smalltown life. Social classes. Gossip. Automobiles. Country clubs. Horses.*

SOUL AND BODY **F2.5264**

Peacock Productions. *Dist* Rialto Productions. 5 Nov **1921** [trade review]. Si; b&w. 35mm. 6 reels.

Dir Frank Beal. *Story* Samuel N. London.

Cast: Ann Luther *(Katinka Vechez)*, William Garland *(Jan Drakachu)*, Frank Brownlee *(Victor Dravitche)*.

Melodrama(?). Apparently concerned with white slavery, containing scenes of a slave market and a volcanic eruption. *White slave traffic. Volcanoes.*

THE SOUL HARVEST *see* **SOULS IN BONDAGE**

THE SOUL KISS *see* **A LADY'S MORALS**

SOUL MATES **F2.5265**

Metro-Goldwyn-Mayer Pictures. 20 Dec **1925** [c11 Jan 1926; LP22257]. Si; b&w. 35mm. 6 reels, 5,590 ft.

Dir Jack Conway. *Scen* Carey Wilson. *Titl* Joe Farnham. *Photog* Oliver Marsh. *Sets* Cedric Gibbons, James Basevi. *Film Ed* James McKay. *Wardrobe* Clement André-ani.

Cast: Aileen Pringle *(Velma)*, Edmund Lowe *(Lord Tancred)*, Phillips Smalley *(Markrute)*, Antonio D'Algy *(Velma's brother)*, Edythe Chapman *(Tancred's mother)*, Mary Hawes *(Velma's maid)*, Catherine Bennett *(Dolly)*, Lucien Littlefield *(Stevens)*, Ned Sparks *(Tancred's chauffeur)*.

Drama. Source: Elinor Glyn, *The Reason Why* (London, 1911). Markrute, who holds the mortgage on the estate of Lord Tancred, insists that his niece, Velma, marry Tancred in order to improve his own social standing. Velma refuses and cuts all financial ties with her uncle. She later meets Tancred and, not knowing who he is, falls madly in love with him. Velma's brother is charged with embezzlement, and her uncle offers to make good the boy's accounts if she marries Tancred. She finds out then that her lover and her prospective husband are one and the same man and, feeling bitter and tricked, marries him. The marriage remains one in name only until Tancred, frustrated and disappointed, threatens to get a divorce. Velma then realizes the depth of her love for Tancred, a love that increases when she learns that he had paid off the mortgage before they were married, attesting that he married her for love alone. *Nobility. Uncles. Brother-sister relationship. Mortgages. Marriage. Embezzlement. England.*

THE SOUL OF A WOMAN **F2.5266**

Dist Associated Photoplays. **1922.** Si; b&w. 35mm. [Feature length assumed.]

Cast: Jane Novak.

Melodrama(?). No information about the nature of this film has been found.

Note: Date indicated is approximate.

THE SOUL OF BRONZE **F2.5267**

Houdini Picture Corp. c19 Nov **1921** [LU17369]. Si; b&w. 35mm. [Length undetermined.]

Adapt Henry Roussell.

Cast: Harry Houdini.

Melodrama. Source: Georges Le Faure, "The Soul of Bronze" (publication undetermined). Losing his fiancée, Nanette, to Capt. Duval Van Jean of the French Army, Jacques, an engineer in a large gun factory, cannot contain his jealousy. In the same factory the officer is overseeing the construction of a cannon of his own invention, and on the day of its casting Jacques secretly causes him to fall into the molten bronze. War breaks out on the next day, Jacques enters the service of his country, and he survives many bloody battles. Finally, alone and badly wounded during a German assault, a vision leads Jacques to a cannon—Duval's cannon—and he turns the tide of the battle just as he collapses. The spirit of Duval places the French flag over Jacques' body. *Engineers. Jealousy. Revenge. Murder. Visions. Ordnance. Bronze. World War I. France. France—Army.*

THE SOUL OF MAN **F2.5268**

Feature Pictures. *Dist* Producers Security Corp. Jun **1921.** Si; b&w. 35mm. 6 reels.

Dir William Nigh.

Drama. "A rich, arrogant man, in his desire to gain the whole world and be a power god, almost loses all when his own flesh and blood double-crosses him. But a grandson, who refuses to permit greed of gold to destroy his ideals, and a sweet blind girl, one of God's innocent children, show the old man and his unscrupulous kin that the greatest possession is love." (*Motion Picture News Booking Guide*, 1:104, Dec 1921.) *Grandfathers. Wealth. Greed. Blindness. Mammon.*

SOUL OF THE BEAST **F2.5269**

Thomas H. Ince Corp. *Dist* Metro Pictures. 7 May **1923** [c18 Jun 1923; LP19153]. Si; b&w. 35mm. 5 reels, 5,020 ft.

Pres by Thomas H. Ince. *Pers Supv* Thomas H. Ince. *Dir* John Griffith Wray. *Scen* Ralph H. Dixon. *Story* C. Gardner Sullivan. *Photog* Henry Sharp.

Cast: Madge Bellamy *(Ruth Lorrimore)*, Oscar *(himself, an elephant)*, Cullen Landis *(Paul Nadeau)*, Noah Beery *(Caesar Durand)*, Vola Vale *(Jacqueline)*, Bert Sprotte *(Silas Hamm)*, Harry Rattenberry *(Père Boussut)*, Carrie Clark Ward *(Mrs. Boussut)*, Lincoln Stedman *(Henri)*, Larry Steers *(policeman)*, Vernon Dent *(The Boob)*.

Melodrama. "Ruth Lorrimore is abused by her stepfather, the owner of a circus, and, aided by Oscar, the elephant, escapes to the Canadian woods, meeting Paul Nadeau, a crippled boy musician, who has incurred the wrath of the town bully, Caesare[*sic*]. After proving himself a hero many times, the elephant rescues Ruth from Caesare. Paul and Ruth marry and Oscar willingly rocks the cradle." (*Moving Picture World*, 5 May 1923.) *Stepfathers. Musicians. Cripples. Circus. Canada. Elephants.*

SOUL-FIRE **F2.5270**

Inspiration Pictures. *Dist* First National Pictures. 31 May **1925** [c7 May 1925; LP21428]. Si; b&w. 35mm. 9 reels, 8,262 ft.

Dir John S. Robertson. *Scen* Josephine Lovett. *Titl* Agnes Smith. *Photog* Roy Overbaugh. *Art Dir* Everett Shinn. *Sets* Tec-Art Studios. *Film Ed* William Hamilton. *Art Titles* H. E. R. Studios.

Cast: Richard Barthelmess *(Eric Fane)*, Bessie Love *(Teita)*, Percy Ames, Charles Esdale *(critics)*, Lee Baker *(Howard Fane)*, Carlotta Monterey *(Princess Rhea)*, Helen Ware *(San Francisco Sal)*, Walter Long *(Herbert Jones)*, Harriet Sterling *(Ruau)*, Richard Harlan *(Nuku)*, Arthur Metcalfe *(Dr. Travers, of Leper Island)*.

Drama. Source: Martin Brown, *Great Music* (New York opening: 4 Oct 1924). In order to study music, Eric Fane goes to Paris, where he becomes infatuated with a Russian princess. Eric writes popular songs, earning enough money from several successes to lead a wild and rich night life. Eric soon tires of the superficiality of his music and turns to serious composition—living a life of poverty which the princess refuses to share. Eric eventually drifts into Port Said, where he plays the piano in a low dancehall; he gets into a fight with a drunken sailor, shooting him and assuming his identity. He sails to the South Seas, where he jumps ship and is found by Teita, a beautiful young English girl whose parents have died. Eric and Teita find love and happiness, but the night before they are to be married in a native ceremony, Eric finds a mark on her shoulder that he believes to indicate leprosy. He sends for a Christian doctor, and, while he is waiting, composes a great concerto. The doctor arrives and informs the couple that the girl suffers only from a minor ailment. Eric's music is later performed in London, where it is received enthusiastically by the people and the critics. *Composers. Pianists. Physicians. Nobility. Russians. English. Sailors. Leprosy. South Sea Islands. Paris. London. Port Said.*

SOULS AFLAME **F2.5271**

Furst Wells Productions. *Dist* First Division Distributors. 10 Mar or 5 Jul **1928**. Si; b&w. 35mm. 7 reels, 6,200 ft. [Also 6 reels, 5,799 ft.]

Prod James Ormont. *Dir-Scen* Raymond Wells. *Titl* Jack Kelly. *Photog* Jack Fuqua. *Film Ed* Earl Turner.

Cast: Gardner James, Grace Lord, Buddy Barton, Raymond Wells, Edward Lackey, Gael Kelton.

Drama. Shortly after the Civil War a feud between the Bucks and the Lillys begins over the murder of a Lilly by five Buck boys, who are acquitted by a jury in deference to the judge, a kin of the Bucks. Years later the dead Lilly's son becomes a preacher, tries to bring peace to the mountains, and falls in love with a Buck girl. He is abused for "enticing" the girl to church, and his mother insists on eradicating the Bucks once and for all. There is a bloody battle in which all of the Bucks are killed except the girl, who refuses to carry on the feud and marries the preacher. *Clergymen. Judges. Murder. Feuds. Mountain life. Trials. Ozarks.*

Note: Filmed partly in the Ozarks.

SOULS FOR SABLES **F2.5272**

Tiffany Productions. 14 Sep **1925** [New York showing; cl Sep 1925; LP21788]. Si; b&w. 35mm. 7 reels, 6,500 ft.

Pers Supv A. P. Younger. *Dir* James C. McKay. *Titl* Philbin Stoneman. *Adapt* A. P. Younger. *Photog* Paul Perry. *Art Dir* Edwin B. Willis. *Tech Dir* Edward Wiese. *Film Ed* F. Haddon Ware.

Cast: Claire Windsor *(Alice Garlan)*, Eugene O'Brien *(Fred Garlan)*, Claire Adams *(Helen Ralston)*, Edith Yorke *(Mrs. Kendall)*, George Fawcett *(Mr. Nelson)*, Eileen Percy *(Esther Hamilton)*, Anders Randolf *(Harrison Morrill)*, Robert Ober *(Jim Hamilton)*.

Melodrama. Source: David Graham Phillips, "Garlan & Co." (publication undetermined). Fred Garlan, a prosperous maufacturer, neglects his wife, Alice, in favor of business; she, in turn, neglects him in favor of fine clothes and fast company. Becoming good friends with Esther Hamilton, Alice gets to know Harrison Morrill, a scoundrel who has bought Esther's body with a sable coat. Morrill becomes infatuated with Alice and arranges for her to win enough money at poker to buy a fur coat of her own. Fred believes that she has been unfaithful to him and leaves her. Alice decides to accompany Morrill to Paris, but when she reads in the paper that Jim Hamilton has killed both Esther and himself, she has a change of heart. Returning home, she finds Fred waiting for her with forgiveness and open arms. *Manufacturers. Infidelity. Suicide. Murder. Marriage. Gambling. Clothes.*

SOULS FOR SALE **F2.5273**

Goldwyn Pictures. 27 Mar **1923** [New York premiere; released 22 Apr; c12 Apr 1923; LP18869]. Si; b&w. 35mm. 8 reels, 7,864 ft.

Prod-Dir-Adapt Rupert Hughes. *Photog* John Mescall.

Cast—The Story: Eleanor Boardman *(Remember Steddon)*, Mae Busch *(Robina Teele)*, Barbara La Marr *(Leva Lemaire)*, Richard Dix *(Frank Claymore)*, Frank Mayo *(Tom Holby)*, Lew Cody *(Owen Scudder)*, Arthur Hoyt *(Jimmy Leland)*, David Imboden *(Caxton)*, Roy Atwell *(Arthur Tirrey)*, William Orlamond *(Lord Fryingham)*, Forrest Robinson *(Rev. John Steddon)*, Edith Yorke *(Mrs. Steddon)*, Dale Fuller *(Abigail Tweedy)*, Snitz Edwards *(Hank Kale)*, Jack Richardson *(motion picture heavy)*, Aileen Pringle *(Lady Jane)*, Eve Southern *(Velma Slade)*, May Milloy *(Mrs. Sturges)*, Sylvia Ashton *(Mrs. Kale)*, Margaret Bourne *(Leva Lemaire's mother)*, Fred Kelsey *(Quinn)*, Jed Prouty *(Magnus)*, Yale Boss *(prop man)*, William Haines *(Pinkey)*, George Morgan *(Spofford)*, Auld Thomas *(assistant cameraman)*, Leo Willis *(electrician)*, Walter Perry *(grip)*, Sam Damen *(violin player)*, R. H. Johnson *(melodeon player)*, Rush Hughes *(2d cameraman)*, L. J. O'Connor *(Doyle)*, Charles Murphy *(boss canvasman)*.

Cast—Celebrities: Hugo Ballin, Mabel Ballin, T. Roy Barnes, Barbara Bedford, Hobart Bosworth, Charles Chaplin, Chester Conklin, William H. Crane, Elliott Dexter, Robert Edeson, Claude Gillingwater, Dagmar Godowsky, Raymond Griffith, Elaine Hammerstein, Jean Haskell, K. C. B., Alice Lake, Bessie Love, June Mathis, Patsy Ruth Miller, Marshall Neilan, Fred Niblo, Anna Q. Nilsson, ZaSu Pitts, John Sainpolis, Milton Sills, Anita Stewart, Erich von Stroheim, Blanche Sweet, Florence Vidor, King Vidor, Johnny Walker, George Walsh, Kathlyn Williams, Claire Windsor.

Comedy-drama. Source: Rupert Hughes, *Souls for Sale* (New York, 1922). Remember Steddon, the daughter of a smalltown minister, marries Owen Scudder but has second thoughts while their train crosses the desert on their wedding night, and she leaves the train when it stops for water. A movie company on location finds her in poor condition and takes her to Hollywood. Because she has heard bad things about movie people, Mem at first rejects the urgings of director Frank Claymore and star Tom Holby to work in motion pictures, but she eventually makes the rounds of the studios (Famous Players–Lasky, Metro, Fox, Robertson-Cole, Pickford-Fairbanks, Goldwyn) in search of a job and sees many well-known directors and actors at work, including Stroheim (*Greed*), Fred Niblo (*The Famous Mrs. Fair*), and Charles Chaplin. Mem finally gets her chance from Frank Claymore, works hard, and steadily rises to fame. Claymore and Holby become friendly rivals for Mem's affections, while Scudder continues his habit of marrying unsuspecting girls, insuring them, and murdering them. Scudder comes to Hollywood to assert his marital claim on Mem, thus precipitating the climax in which there is an enormous fire, Scudder is killed by the wind machine he has aimed at Claymore, and Mem chooses Claymore over Tom Holby—to the delight of Robina Teele. *Actors. Motion picture directors. Motion pictures. Insurance. Murder. Hollywood. Fires.*

SOULS IN BONDAGE (Sanford Special) **F2.5274**

Sanford Productions. Sep **1923** [c24 Jul 1923; LU19227]. Si; b&w. 35mm. 7 reels, 6,800 ft.

Dir-Story William H. Clifford. *Photog* Lynn Darling. *Art Sets* Ferdinand P. Earle.

Cast: Pat O'Malley *(The Peacock)*, Cleo Madison *(The Chameleon)*, Otto Lederer *(Peter, the Healer)*, Eugenia Gilbert *(Helen De Lacy)*, Frank Hayes, Gene Crosby, Peter Howard, Leon Artigue.

Crook melodrama. The Peacock (Harlan Brooks), a member of Anthony Farone's gang of crooks, is the son of wealthy parents and is known for his stylish clothes. Farone gives him jewels, stolen from socialite Louise De Lacey, to hide. After doing so he has an encounter with a policeman in which he is struck on the head and loses his memory. In desperation, Farone accedes to the pleas of the Chameleon (the gang's only female member), who loves the Peacock, and sends him to Peter, the Healer. His gang accompany him disguised as cripples. A cure is effected by an accident, but Farone is not told. The Peacock becomes attracted to Mrs. De Lacey's daughter, Helen, who is a regular visitor to Peter's camp, and returns the jewels to her. The Chameleon, jealous of the Peacock's attentions to Helen, tells Farone that the Peacock is faking. The arrival of the police prevents Farone from blinding the Peacock. Helen persuades her mother to drop the robbery charges against the gang, the Peacock and the Chameleon are reconciled, and through Peter's efforts Farone and his gang are reformed. *Criminals—Rehabilitation. Socialites. Faith healers. Gangs. Amnesia. Robbery. Clothes.*

Note: Reviewed but apparently not released under the title: *The Soul Harvest.*

SOULS OF MEN **F2.5275**

P. & J. Co. 17 Jun **1921** [trade review]. Si; b&w. 35mm. [Feature length assumed.]

Cast: William Jeffries.

Melodrama. "A sea captain returns home unexpectedly after a long voyage and finds his wife in the arms of another man, a pearl trader. Husband and lover exchange shots, both being wounded and husband tells wife she is free to go off with his rival, but he will 'get them' elsewhere where the law will not interfere with his vengeance. Thereupon the husband takes up his stand on a South Sea island where the pearl trader sooner or later is bound to appear. ... The pearl trader does appear, accompanied by the faithless wife, and the story goes through endless complications. ..." (*Variety,* 17 Jun 1921, p34.) *Sea captains. Pearl traders. Infidelity. Revenge. South Sea Islands.*

SOUP TO NUTS **F2.5276**

Fox Film Corp. 28 Sep **1930** [c16 Aug 1930; LP1548]. Sd; b&w. 35mm. 7 reels, 6,340 ft.

Dir Benjamin Stoloff. *Scen* Rube Goldberg, Howard J. Green. *Story-Dial* Rube Goldberg. *Photog* Joseph Valentine. *Film Ed* Clyde Carruth. *Sd* Al Bruzlin.

Cast: Ted Healy *(Ted)*, Frances McCoy *(Queenie)*, Stanley Smith *(Carlson)*, Lucille Brown *(Louise)*, Charles Winninger *(Schmidt)*, Hallam Cooley *(Throckmorton)*, George Bickel *(Klein)*, William H. Tooker *(Ferguson)*.

Comedy. "A hilarious jumble of nonsense about a crazy inventor and a lackadaisical fire company ending up in a comic fire." (*National Board of Review Magazine,* 5:7:17, Sep 1930). *Inventors. Fire departments. Fires.*

SOUTH OF NORTHERN LIGHTS **F2.5277**

William Steiner Productions. Nov **1922** [c22 Sep 1922; LU18231]. Si; b&w. 35mm. 5 reels.

Dir-Story-Adapt Neal Hart. *Photog* William Steiner, Jr., Jacob A. Badaracco.

Cast: Neal Hart *(Jack Hampton)*, James McLaughlin *(Corporal McAllister)*, Ben Corbett *(Chick Rawlins)*, Hazel Deane *(Jane Wilson)*.

Northwest melodrama. Falsely accused of murder by a gang that wants to obtain possession of his ranch (on which gold has been discovered) northwestern rancher Jack Hampton flees across the border into Canada pursued by the Northwest Mounted Police and an American sheriff. Chick Rawlins, the gang's leader, runs a place at a trading post, and the Canadian authorities have sent Jane Wilson into the camp to get evidence against him. Captured by the crooks, she has been imprisoned in the mountains. Her escape develops into a long chase by the crooks, Hampton, and his pursuers. The hero battles with Rawlins, who falls on his knife and confesses the frameup. Jack falls in love with the rescued heroine. *Ranchers. Sheriffs. Frameup. Trading posts. Canada. Northwest Mounted Police.*

SOUTH OF PANAMA **F2.5278**

Chesterfield Motion Picture Corp. 15 Nov **1928** [or 1 Jun 1929]. Si; b&w. 35mm. 7 reels.

Supv-Story Lon Young. *Dir (see note)* Charles J. Hunt, Bernard F. McEveety. *Scen* Arthur Hoerl. *Titl* Charles J. Hunt, Lon Young. *Photog* M. A. Anderson. *Film Ed* Charles J. Hunt.

Cast: Carmelita Geraghty *(Carmelita)*, Edouard Raquello *(Emilio Cervantes)*, Lewis Sargent *(Dick Lewis)*, Philo McCullough *("Ace" Carney)*, Marie Messinger *("Patsy")*, Henry Arras *("Red" Hearn)*, Carlton King *(Presidente Laredon)*, Joseph Burke *(García)*, Fred Walton *(captain of guard)*.

Melodrama. To bolster his faltering gunrunning business, an American profiteer sends his assistant to a Latin American republic south of Panama to foment a war. The assistant falls in love with the president's daughter and reverses his alliance by aiding the republic. *Profiteers. Presidents. Revolutions. Gunrunners. Latin America.*

Note: Sources disagree; credit for direction has not been determined.

SOUTH OF SANTA FE **F2.5279**

Art Mix Productions. *Dist* Aywon Film Corp. 3 Sep **1924** [New York State license]. Si; b&w. 35mm. 5 reels.

Cast: Art Mix.

Western melodrama. No information about the precise nature of this film has been found.

SOUTH OF SONORA **F2.5280**

West Coast Studios. *Dist* Industrial Pictures. 8 Nov **1930** [New York State license]. Sd; b&w. 35mm. 5 reels, 4,500 ft.

Cast: Buffalo Bill Jr. *(Bill Tracy)*, Betty Joy *(Betty)*, Fred Church, Lew Meehan, H. B. Carpenter, Gene Schuler, Jack Walker, Frank Allen, James Merrill.

Western melodrama. Hired by the Cattlemen's Protective Association and on his way to clean up Sonora, a town dominated by pistol-slinging rustlers, Bill Tracy performs a gallantry for Betty Carter, but her father—believing Blackie's suggestion that Bill is a rustler—later warns her against seeing him. Bill and Heine Schmaltz rescue each other from assorted ambushes, discover Blackie (Carter's foreman) to be the gang leader, and rescue Betty from Blackie's clutches. *Investigators. Ranch foremen. Rustlers. Cattlemen. Abduction. Protective associations.*

SOUTH OF SUVA **F2.5281**

Realart Pictures. *Dist* Paramount Pictures. ca18 Jun **1922** [New York premiere; released 16 Jul; c24 May 1922; LP17920]. Si; b&w. 35mm. 5 reels, 4,639 ft.

Dir Frank Urson. *Scen* Fred Myton. *Story* Ewart Adamson. *Photog* Allen Davey.

Cast: Mary Miles Minter *(Phyllis Latimer)*, Winifred Bryson *(Pauline Leonard)*, Walter Long *(Sydney Latimer)*, John Bowers *(John Webster)*, Roy Atwell *(Marmaduke Grubb)*, Fred Kelsey *(Karl Swartz)*, Lawrence Steers *(Alfred Bowman)*.

Adventure melodrama. Phyllis Latimer goes to Fiji to rejoin her husband of 3 years and finds him in a state of drunken degeneracy, incapable of reform. Fleeing his advances, she escapes to a nearby island; and there she impersonates Pauline Leonard, ward of John Webster. When Latimer incites a native uprising against Webster, who hires Hindu laborers, he finds Phyllis on the island, drags her home with him, and in a frenzy gives her to the natives for a human sacrifice. Webster and the government police arrive in time to save Phyllis, and Latimer is killed in the riot. Phyllis and Webster reveal their mutual love. *Degeneracy. Alcoholism. Impersonation. Human sacrifice. Fiji Islands.*

SOUTH OF THE EQUATOR **F2.5282**

Bud Barsky Corp. 10 Oct **1924** [New York State license]. Si; b&w. 35mm. 5 reels, 4,800 ft.

Dir William James Craft. *Scen* Robert Dillon.

Cast: Kenneth McDonald, Eugene Corey, Robert Barnes, Virginia Warwick.

Comedy-melodrama. The daughter of the president of a South American republic arrives in the United States for the express purpose of purchasing arms and ammunition for loyal citizens and supporters of her country's government. The leader of the revolutionary forces that threaten the peace and stability of her government follows her to New York and attempts to prevent her from completing her mission; but a courageous American comes to her aid, and she succeeds. The American, who is an adventurer at heart, then returns with her to South America and takes command of her father's subjects. The revolutionists are defeated, the president is restored to power, and the American wins the president's daughter for his wife. *Adventurers. Revolutions. Firearms. Ammunition. South America.*

SOUTH SEA LOVE **F2.5283**

Fox Film Corp. 25 Nov **1923** [c25 Nov 1923; LP19815]. Si; b&w. 35mm. 5 reels, 4,168 ft.

Pres by William Fox. *Dir* David Soloman. *Scen* Harrison Josephs.

Cast: Shirley Mason *(Dolores Medina)*, J. Frank Glendon *(Gerald Wilton)*, Francis McDonald *(Manuel Salarno)*, Lillian Nicholson *(Maria)*, Charles A. Sellon *(captain)*, Fred Lancaster *(innkeeper)*, Robert Conville *(Stubbs)*.

Melodrama. Source: Frederick Hatton and Fanny Hatton, "With the Tide," in *Young's Magazine* (45:3–36, Mar 1923). Dolores Medina's father, a ship's captain, dies, leaving her in the care of Gerald Wilton, an English trader. Dolores falls in love with Wilton, but she suffers disillusionment on learning that he is already married and becomes a dancer in a tropical cafe. She escapes the owner's lustful advances and rescues Wilton from a group of sailors who want to horsewhip him. His wife's death leaves Dolores and Wilton free to continue their romance. *Dancers. Sailors. Traders. English. South Seas.*

SOUTH SEA LOVE **F2.5284**

R-C Pictures. *Dist* Film Booking Offices of America. 10 Dec **1927** [c3 Nov 1927; LP24636]. Si; b&w. 35mm. 7 reels, 6,388 ft.

Pres by Joseph P. Kennedy. *Dir* Ralph Ince. *Cont* Enid Hibbard. *Titl* George M. Arthur. *Camera* Nick Musuraca. *Film Ed* George M. Arthur.

Cast: Patsy Ruth Miller *(Charlotte Guest)*, Lee Shumway *(Fred Stewart)*,

Alan Brooks *(Tom Malloy)*, Harry Crocker *(Bob Bernard)*, Barney Gilmore *(George Billways)*, Gertrude Howard *(Moana)*, Albert Conti *(Max Weber)*, Everett Brown *(Nahalo)*, Harry Wallace *(Jake Streeter)*.

Romantic melodrama. Source: Georges Surdez, "A Game in the Bush," in *Adventure Magazine.* Fred Stewart slaves for 2 years on the isolated island of Lamu Vita to send Charlotte Guest, a chorus girl, money for their future together. Meanwhile, Charlotte is approaching stardom through the efforts of her manager, Tom Malloy, and by means of Stewart's hard-earned money—while at the same time keeping reckless young Bob Bernard on the string. When she tells Bob she is already married to a beachcomber in the Western Carolines, Bob dramatically announces he will hunt Stewart down and kill him unless he agrees to a divorce. Stewart, shocked by her infidelity, decides to remain on the island and drink away his memories. Bob arrives and, when stricken with fever, is cared for by Stewart. Together they plan revenge on the girl, whom they entice to the island; both, however, are intermittently swayed by her charms, and when they fight, she attempts to drown herself. Stewart rescues her, and following Bob's departure, they find happiness together. *Chorus girls. Beachcombers. Theatrical managers. Jealousy. Alcoholism. Suicide. South Sea Islands. Caroline Islands.*

SOUTH SEA ROSE **F2.5285**

Fox Film Corp. 8 Dec **1929** [c24 Oct 1929; LP864]. Sd (Movietone); b&w. 35mm. 9 reels, 6,500 ft.

Pres by William Fox. *Dir* Allan Dwan. *Scen* Sonya Levien. *Dial* Elliott Lester. *Camera* Harold Rosson. *Sets* William S. Darling. *Film Ed* Harold Schuster. *Songs: "South Sea Rose," "If You Believed in Me"* L. Wolfe Gilbert, Abel Baer. *Sd* Willard W. Starr. *Asst Dir* William Tummel. *Cost* Sophie Wachner.

Cast: Lenore Ulric *(Rosalie Dumay)*, Charles Bickford *(Captain Briggs)*, Kenneth MacKenna *(Dr. Tom Winston)*, Farrell MacDonald *(Hackett)*, Elizabeth Patterson *(Sarah)*, Tom Patricola *(Willie Gump)*, Ilka Chase *(maid)*, George MacFarlane *(tavern keeper and trader)*, Ben Hall *(cabin boy)*, Daphne Pollard *(Mrs. Nott)*, Roscoe Ates *(ship's cook)*, Charlotte Walker *(mother superior)*, Emile Chautard *(Rosalie's uncle)*.

Romantic drama. Source: Tom Cushing, *La Gringa, a Play in Six Scenes and an Epilogue* (c1928). On the South Sea island of Tongawarra lives Rosalie Dumay, an orphaned French girl who previously lived on her father's trading ship. It is understood that she is an heiress and that her father left her a fortune in care of an uncle in France. A young trader, Captain Briggs, decides to marry her for her money and tricks her into the ceremony. Later, however, he finds that he genuinely loves the girl but has almost lost her; when she realizes his love for her is true, Rosalie responds promptly. ... *Orphans. Traders. French. Inheritance. South Sea Islands. Courtship. Marriage.*

SOUTH SEAS **F2.5286**

Gifford Pinchot–Mrs. Gifford Pinchot. *Dist* Talking Picture Epics. 23 May **1930** [New York showing; released 1 Sep 1930]. Sd b&w. 35mm. 5,538 ft. [Also si.]

Photog Howard Cleaves.

Travelog. On an expedition sponsored by the National Museum (Washington, D. C.) and the Philadelphia Academy of Natural Sciences, the Pichots journey in their schooner, the *Mary Pinchot*, from New York, southward through the Panama Canal, and across to the Galápagos Islands and the Marquesas. Highlights of their trip include scenes of pearl diving, the San Blas Indians, and animals—especially a porpoise and a large turtle. *Pearl diving. San Blas Indians. Panama Canal. South Seas. Galápagos Islands. Marquesas Islands. Turtles. Porpoises.*

Note: Also known as *In the South Seas With Mr. and Mrs. Pinchot* and *To the South Seas.*

SOWING THE WIND **F2.5287**

Anita Stewart Productions. *Dist* Associated First National Pictures. Apr **1921** [c15 Sep 1921; LP16140]. Si; b&w. 35mm. 9 reels. [Also 6 reels.]

Pres by Louis B. Mayer. *Dir* John M. Stahl. *Photog* René Guissart.

Cast: Anita Stewart *(Rosamond Athelstane)*, James Morrison *(Ned Brabazon)*, Myrtle Stedman *(Baby Brabant)*, Ralph Lewis *(Brabazon)*, William V. Mong *(Watkins)*, Josef Swickard *(Petworth)*, Ben Deely *(Cursitor)*, Harry Northrup, Margaret Landis, William Clifford.

Melodrama. Source: Sydney Grundy, *Sowing the Wind* (New York, 1901). When Rosamond, a convent girl, discovers that her mother is Baby Brabant, a notorious queen of Petworth's gambling house, her ideals are shattered and she denounces her mother's life. Following her daughter's departure, Baby leaves the gambler and resorts to opium in her remorse. Rosamond becomes a successful actress and falls in love with Ned, the foster son of a wealthy man, Brabazon, who advises Ned to treat her as a plaything, but he refuses to drop her. Brabazon then learns that Baby Brabant is his former wife and that Rosamond is his own daughter. Ned and Rosamond are united after her mother dies. *Actors. Motherhood. Fatherhood. Gambling. Opium.*

SPANGLES (Universal-Jewel) **F2.5288**

Universal Pictures. 7 Nov **1926** [c25 Aug 1926; LP23055]. Si; b&w. 35mm. 6 reels, 5,633 ft.

Pres by Carl Laemmle. *Dir* Frank O'Connor. *Scen* Leah Baird. *Titl* Walter Anthony. *Adapt* Hugh Hoffman. *Story* Nellie Revell. *Photog* André Barlatier.

Cast: Marian Nixon *("Spangles" Delancy)*, Pat O'Malley *(Dick Radley)*, Hobart Bosworth *("Big Bill" Bowman)*, Gladys Brockwell *(Mademoiselle Dazie)*, Jay Emmett *(Vincent)*, James Conly *(Zip, the halfwit)*, Grace Gordon *(bearded lady)*, Paul Howard *(armless man)*, Tiny Ward *(giant)*, Charles Becker *(dwarf)*, Nelle B. Lane *(fat woman)*, Clarence Wertz *(Rawlins)*, Harry Schultz *(strong man)*, Herbert Shelly *(skeleton)*.

Melodrama. Spangles, the star bareback rider of the Bowman Circus, is engaged to the owner though she does not love him. Dick Radley, who is being sought by the police in a murder case, conceals himself in her berth on the circus train; and believing that he is innocent, Spangles helps him to evade capture. Bowman agrees to hire him as a driver in the chariot race, though his open attentions to Spangles arouse the jealousy of Bowman and the rival chariot racer, who fouls Dick in the race. Identifying Dick as the fugitive, Bowman threatens to inform on Dick unless Spangles relinquishes her plan to marry him. Later, Bowman is found dead; and though Dick is suspected, he is found to have already surrendered to the police. Dick is cleared but is attacked by the circus mob; Zip, a halfwit, reveals that the elephant Sultana killed Bowman when he abused the animal. Dick and Spangles are happily united. *Roman riders. Fugitives. Halfwits. Circus. Murder. Elephants.*

THE SPANIARD **F2.5289**

Famous Players–Lasky. *Dist* Paramount Pictures. 4 May **1925** [c17 Apr 1925; LP21366]. Si; b&w. 35mm. 7 reels, 6,635 ft.

Pres by Adolph Zukor, Jesse L. Lasky. *Dir* Raoul Walsh. *Scen* James T. O'Donohue. *Photog* Victor Milner.

Cast: Ricardo Cortez *(Don Pedro de Barrego)*, Jetta Goudal *(Dolores Annesley)*, Noah Beery *(Gômez)*, Mathilda Brundage *(Señora de la Carta)*, Renzo De Gardi *(Count de Albaveque)*, Emily Fitzroy *(María)*, Bernard Seigel *(Manuel)*, Florence Renart *(Consuelo)*.

Romantic melodrama. Source: Juanita Savage, *The Spaniard* (New York, 1924). Don Pedro de Barrego, a Spanish grandee, visits England and falls in love with Dolores Annesley, a beautiful young English girl who refuses his advances. Barrego returns home and resumes his profession as a bullfighter; Dolores journeys to Seville, where she watches Barrego at work in the ring. Dolores is later forced by a storm to seek refuge in the mountain castle owned by Barrego, and there he holds her against her will. She attempts to escape with the help of Gómez, Barrego's valet, but Barrego discovers her plans and dismisses Gómez. Dolores later escapes alone on horseback, and Barrego gives chase, but his horse falls, badly injuring him. Gómez then seizes Dolores, but Barrego, despite his injuries, rescues her. Dolores, at last, freely admits that she loves the Spaniard and makes plans to become his wife. *Bullfighters. Valets. Spanish. English. Abduction. England. Seville.*

THE SPANISH DANCER **F2.5290**

Famous Players–Lasky. *Dist* Paramount Pictures. 7 Oct **1923** [New York premiere; released 4 Nov; c17 Oct 1923; LP19503]. Si; b&w. 35mm. 9 reels, 8,434 ft.

Pres by Adolph Zukor. *Prod-Dir* Herbert Brenon. *Adapt* June Mathis, Beulah Marie Dix. *Photog* James Howe.

Cast: Pola Negri *(Maritana, a Gypsy dancer)*, Antonio Moreno *(Don César de Bazan)*, Wallace Beery *(King Philip IV)*, Kathlyn Williams *(Queen Isabel of Bourbon)*, Gareth Hughes *(Lazarillo, a prisoner)*, Adolphe Menjou *(Don Salluste, a courtier)*, Edward Kipling *(Marquis de Rotundo)*, Dawn O'Day *(Don Balthazar Carlos)*, Charles A. Stevenson *(cardinal's ambassador)*, Robert Agnew *(Juan, a thief)*.

Historical romance. Source: Adolphe Philippe Dennery and Philippe François Pinel, *Don César de Bazan* (1844). A costume drama based on the adventures of Maritana, a Gypsy dancer, who is in love with Don

César de Bazan, a penniless nobleman. Don César is arrested for dueling and sentenced to die when he intercedes on behalf of Lazarillo, a lad who was cruelly beaten by the captain of the guards. Maritana implores Queen Isabel to save her lover's life, and the queen induces the king to pardon him. Maritana and Don César are married. However, the king is attracted to Maritana and lures her to a hunting lodge, where Don César, who escapes jail, arrives in time to save her from his advances. The queen arrives, stirred by jealousy, just as the king and Don César engage in combat. Maritana's quick wit saves the king from disgrace, and as a reward he restores Don César's estates to him. *Dancers. Gypsies. Royalty. Nobility. Spain—History. Philip IV (Spain). Isabel of Bourbon.*

THE SPANISH JADE **F2.5291**

Famous Players–Lasky. *Dist* Paramount Pictures. 30 Apr **1922** [c25 Apr 1922; LP17782]. Si; b&w. 35mm. 5 reels, 5,111 ft.

Pres by Adolph Zukor. *Supv* Tom J. Geraghty. *Dir* John S. Robertson. *Scen* Josephine Lovett. *Photog* Roy Overbaugh.

Cast: David Powell *(Gil Pérez)*, Marc MacDermott *(Don Luis Ramônez de Alavia)*, Charles de Rochefort *(Esteban)*, Evelyn Brent *(Mañuela)*, Lionel D'Aragon *(Mañuela's stepfather)*, Frank Stanmore *(Tormillo, Don Luis' servant)*, Roy Byford *(Esteban's spy and confidant)*, Harry Ham *(Oswald Manvers)*.

Melodrama. Source: Maurice Henry Hewlett, *The Spanish Jade* (New York, 1908). Louis Joseph Vance, *The Spanish Jade; a Play in 4 Acts* (c12 Jan 1909). Mañuela, who is made the subject of a wager by her stepfather and thus falls into the power of Esteban, a gambler, is warned by Gil Pérez, a romantic adventurer, and she runs away. Esteban pursues them, and Oswald Manvers, a young American, rescues Mañuela from a band of ruffians outside the city; in a struggle with Esteban, Mañuela prevents him from killing Manvers, and falling on his knife he dies while the girl escapes. Don Luis, Esteban's father, hires an assassin to slay Manvers and revenge his son's death, but he succeeds only in wounding him. Mañuela gives herself up for the slaying of Esteban and is sentenced to life imprisonment; but Spanish law allows her release if a man is willing to wed her, and Manvers agrees. Mañuela offers her own life to Don Luis if he will spare Manvers; but Pérez, whom Mañuela really loves, intervenes, and Don Luis frees Mañuela from her pledge. *Wagers. Murder. Revenge. Spain.*

Note: Filmed on location in Spain.

SPARKS OF FLINT *see* **TWO-FISTED JEFFERSON**

SPARKS OF FLINT **F2.5292**

Ben Wilson Productions. *Dist* Arrow Film Corp. 10 Dec **1921** [c3 Jan 1922; LP17426]. Si; b&w. 35mm. 5 reels, 4,732 ft.

Dir-Story Roy Clements.

Cast: Jack Hoxie.

Western melodrama. Jack Stokes, a young ranchman, and Elizabeth Welsh, eldest daughter of an old miner who owns land rich in gold, are sweethearts. Elizabeth, tired of ranch life, goes east to finish her education. Blane Flint, a man-about-town, realizing the value of the land the Welsh girls stand to inherit, endeavors to marry Phoebe, the younger sister. Jack rescues Phoebe from Flint's carefully laid plans, and Flint goes east in search of Elizabeth. Elizabeth, having become indifferent to Jack and unaware of Flint's true character, consents to his marriage proposal. The news of her marriage breaks Jack's heart; and Phoebe, who secretly admires him, soon finds that Jack is not entirely indifferent to her. In the meantime, Flint plots with Hamby, a crooked attorney, to take the mineral rights to the land. Jack thwarts the scheme, sending Flint to jail for fraud. Jack and Phoebe marry, and the sisters are reconciled. *Ranchers. Sisters. Men-about-town. Inheritance. Gold. Fraud. Mineral rights.*

SPARROWS **F2.5293**

Pickford Corp. *Dist* United Artists. ca19 Sep **1926** [New York premiere; c30 Apr 1926; LP22664]. Si; b&w. 35mm. 9 reels, 7,763 ft. [Also 6-7 reels.]

Dir William Beaudine. *Collaborators* Tom McNamara, Carl Harbaugh, Earle Browne. *Titl* George Marion, Jr. *Adapt* C. Gardner Sullivan. *Story* Winifred Dunn. *Photog* Charles Rosher, Karl Struss, Hal Mohr. *Art Dir* Harry Oliver. *Elec Eff* William S. Johnson.

Cast: Mary Pickford *(Mama Mollie)*, Gustav von Seyffertitz *(Grimes)*, Roy Stewart *(Richard Wayne)*, Mary Louise Miller *(Doris Wayne)*, Charlotte Mineau *(Mrs. Grimes)*, Spec O'Donnell *(Ambrose Grimes)*, Lloyd Whitlock *(Bailey)*, A. L. Schaeffer *(his confederate)*, Mark Hamilton *(hog buyer)*, Monty O'Grady *(Splutters)*, Muriel McCormac, Billy "Red" Jones, Cammilla Johnson, Mary McLane, Billy Butts, Jack Lavine, Florence Rogan, Seesel Ann Johnson, Sylvia Bernard *(The Sparrows)*.

Melodrama. In a corner of the southern swamplands, Grimes and his sullen, halfwitted wife and brutal son, Ambrose, maintain a farm for unwanted children, who are mistreated, nearly starved, and virtually imprisoned by their evil guardians. Mama Mollie, the oldest of the children, protects the others as best she can and bolsters their courage by having them believe that God will care for them as He does for the sparrows. A child (Doris) is kidnaped from the city, and Grimes tells his son to throw her into the swamp to keep the police off his trail; Mollie rescues her from Ambrose and battles Grimes with a pitchfork, then plans an escape with her band of "sparrows." After miles of dangers through the alligator-ridden swamp, the children find the police trailing Grimes; his wife and son are arrested, but the kidnapers escape and are pursued by motorboat and end in watery deaths. Mollie finds happiness at last when her entire brood is adopted by a millionaire. *Children. Halfwits. Religion. Child care. Child labor. Children's homes. Kidnaping. Swamps. United States—South.*

SPAWN OF THE DESERT **F2.5294**

Berwilla Film Corp. *Dist* Arrow Film Corp. 10 Jan **1923** [c23 Jan 1923; LP18614]. Si; b&w. 35mm. 5 reels, 4,979 ft.

Prod Ben Wilson. *Dir? (see note)* Ben Wilson, Lewis King. *Scen* Daniel F. Whitcomb.

Cast: William Fairbanks *(Duke Steele)*, Florence Gilbert *(Nola "Luck" Sleed)*, Dempsey Tabler *(Silver Sleed)*, Al Hart *(Sam Le Saint)*.

Western melodrama. Source: W. C. Tuttle, "Spawn of the Desert," in *Short Stories* (99:105–126, 10 May 1922). Desert guide Duke Steele makes a friend of Le Saint, a mysterious hermit who is in search of a man who destroyed his home years ago. Duke meets Silver Sleed, the town rascal, falls in love with his daughter, "Luck," then learns that Sleed is Le Saint's enemy. Sam kills Sleed, and Luck proves to be Sam's long-lost daughter. *Guides. Hermits. Fatherhood. Deserts.*

Note: Various sources give either Ben Wilson or Lewis King as director, but not both.

SPEAKEASY **F2.5295**

Fox Film Corp. 24 Mar **1929** [c29 Mar 1929; LP261]. Sd (Movietone); b&w. 35mm. 7 reels, 5,775 ft.

Pres by William Fox. *Dir* Benjamin Stoloff. *Scen* Frederick Hazlitt Brennan, Edwin Burke. *Dial* Edwin Burke. *Photog* Joseph A. Valentine. *Film Ed* J. Edwin Robbins. *Sd* W. W. Lindsay. *Asst Dir* R. L. Hough. *Wardrobe* Sophie Wachner.

Cast: Lola Lane *(Alice Woods)*, Paul Page *(Paul Martin)*, Sharon Lynn *(Mazie)*, Warren Hymer *(Cannon Delmont)*, Helen Ware *(Min)*, Henry B. Walthall *(Fuzzy)*, Stuart Erwin *(Cy Williams)*, James Guilfoyle *(Davey)*, Erville Alderson *(city editor)*, Joseph Cawthorn *(yokel)*, Ivan Linow *(wrestler)*, Marjorie Beebe, Sailor Vincent, Helen Lynch *(speakeasy hangers-on)*.

Melodrama. Source: Edward Knoblock and George Rosener, "Speakeasy" (publication undetermined). Alice Woods, a New York newspaper reporter, is assigned to write a story on Martin, a middleweight fighter who has just lost the championship. Martin refuses to see her in his dressing room, and Alice must later force her way into the speakeasy that is his hangout. Martin refuses to speak with her, and she fabricates a story, writing that Martin is planning to make a comeback. Alice soon falls for the ex-champ and uses her ingenuity to prove that he has been sold down the river by his crooked manager, Cannon Delmont. Martin goes back into the ring on his own and, with Alice's encouragement, regains the middleweight crown. *Prizefighters. Reporters. Fight managers. Speakeasies. New York City.*

SPECIAL DELIVERY **F2.5296**

Famous Players–Lasky. *Dist* Paramount Pictures. 6 May **1927** [c26 Mar 1927; LP23886]. Si; b&w. 35mm. 6 reels, 5,524 ft.

Pres by Adolph Zukor, Jesse L. Lasky. *Assoc Prod* B. P. Schulberg. *Dir* William Goodrich. *Cont* John Goodrich. *Titl* George Marion, Jr. *Story* Eddie Cantor. *Photog* Henry Hallenberger.

Cast: Eddie Cantor *(Eddie, The Mail Carrier)*, Jobyna Ralston *(Madge, The Girl)*, William Powell *(Harold Jones, a get-rich-quick artist)*, Donald Keith *(Harrigan, The Fireman)*, Jack Dougherty *(Flannigan, a cop on the beat)*, Victor Potel *(Nip, a detective)*, Paul Kelly *(Tuck, another detective)*, Mary Carr *(The Mother)*.

Comedy. Eddie, a conscientious if blundering mail carrier, is in love with

Madge, a waitress, who is equally admired by Officer Flannigan and Harrigan, a fireman. The persistent efforts of Harold Jones, a promoter, to win Madge as his secretary unite the three rivals against Jones. They toss a coin to determine who will escort Madge to the postal ball, and Eddie wins; meanwhile, two detectives, undergoing tests to qualify them as postal inspectors, concentrate on Eddie. Madge accepts Jones's offer when the cafe owner tries to force his attentions on her. At the ball, Eddie, who does not dance, leaves Madge to his rivals, but during a black bottom contest, a piece of ice falls into his collar; and his wild gyrations win him the prize cup. Eddie is disillusioned to learn that Madge is engaged to Jones, but in delivering a package to the Jones home, he discovers that Jones is a swindler and with the aid of the detectives rushes to save Madge. ... *Mail carriers. Waitresses. Firemen. Police. Detectives. Postal inspectors. Postal service. Courtship. Black bottom (dance).*

LE SPECTRE VERT **F2.5297**

Metro-Goldwyn-Mayer Pictures. 7 May **1930** [Paris premiere]. Sd (Movietone); b&w. 35mm. 10 reels.

Dir Jacques Feyder. *Scen-Dial* Yves Mirande. *Photog* William Daniels. *Art Dir* Cedric Gibbons. *Rec Engr* Douglas Shearer.

Cast: André Luguet *(Lord Montague)*, Jetta Goudal *(Lady Efra)*, Pauline Garon *(Lady Vi)*, Georges Renevant *(Dr. Ballou)*, Jules Rancourt *(Sir James Ramsay)*.

Mystery melodrama. French-language version of *The Unholy Night*, q. v. *Detectives. Heirs. Murder. Great Britain—Army. Scotland Yard. London.*

SPEED **F2.5298**

Banner Productions. 26 Apr **1925** [c6 Mar 1925; LP21210]. Si; b&w. 35mm. 6 reels, 5,800 ft.

Ben Verschleiser Production. *Dir* Edward J. Le Saint. *Adapt* Lois Zellner. *Photog* King Grey, Orin Jackson.

Cast: Betty Blythe *(Mary Whipple)*, Pauline Garon *(Wiletta Whipple)*, William V. Mong *(Sam Whipple)*, Arthur Rankin *(Dick Whipple)*, Alfred Allen *(Nat Armstrong)*, Robert Ellis *(Nat Armstrong, Jr.)*, Eddie Phillips *(Jack Cartwright)*, Fred Becker *(Señor Querino)*, Stella De Lanti *(Señora Querino)*.

Melodrama. Source: Grace Sartwell Mason, "Speed," in *Saturday Evening Post* (197:5–7, 30–34, 18 Oct, 25 Oct 1924). Wiletta and Dick Whipple are jazz-mad children who follow the pursuit of pleasure recklessly: Wiletta is attracted by Jack Cartwright, a lounge lizard, and gives the cold shoulder to Nat Armstrong, a worthy fellow who loves her; Dick drinks too much. Their parents, Sam and Mary, go on a trip and return with a new car and new clothes. On a trip, the elder Whipples have become involved with the Querinos, Spanish crooks, who soon kidnap Wiletta. Nat and Sam give chase to the Querinos' car. Nat snatches Wiletta from the bandits' machine, and her father then runs it with its occupants over a cliff. Mutual reconciliation follows. *Spanish. Jazz life. Alcoholism. Kidnaping.*

THE SPEED CLASSIC **F2.5299**

Excellent Pictures. *Dist* First Division Pictures. 31 Jul **1928** [c11 Aug 1928; LP25521]. Si; b&w. 35mm. 5 reels, 4,700 ft.

Pres by Samuel Zierler. *Dir* Bruce Mitchell. *Titl* Al Martin. *Photog* Max Dupont, William Underhill. *Film Ed* Bertha A. Montaigen.

Cast: Rex Lease *(Jerry Thornton)*, Mitchell Lewis *(Mr. Thornton)*, Mildred Harris *(Sheila Van Hauten)*, James Mason *(Pedro de Malpa)*, Garry O'Dell *(Jonah, a racing mechanic)*, Helen Jerome Eddy *(Keziah Stubbs)*, Jack Richardson *(speed cop)*, Otis Harlan *(The Thirsty One)*.

Melodrama. Source: Arthur Hoerl, "They're Off" Jerry Thornton, a wealthy young fellow with a mania for fast cars, is shown the door by Sheila Van Hauten, his timid fiancée, when he insists on racing against professional drivers in the Speed Classic. Brokenhearted, Jerry goes on a binge, ending up in Tijuana, Mexico, where, through the machinations of a rival driver, he is thrown into jail. Sheila learns of his incarceration and, relenting of her former hardheartedness, sends Jerry's mechanic, Jonah, to Mexico to bail out her sometime sweetheart. Jerry and Jonah make it back to the States in time for Jerry to enter the Speed Classic; Jerry wins and, after taking care of the driver who framed him in Mexico, is reunited with Sheila. *Mechanics. Automobile racing. Frameup. Tijuana (Mexico).*

SPEED COP **F2.5300**

Duke Worne Productions. *Dist* Rayart Pictures. Nov **1926.** Si; b&w. 35mm. 5 reels, 4,972 ft.

Dir Duke Worne. *Story-Scen* Grover Jones. *Photog* Ernest Smith.

Cast: Billy Sullivan, Rose Blossom, Francis Ford.

Action melodrama. A motorcycle cop (played by Billy Sullivan) falls in love with a pretty girl (played by Rose Blossom) when he gives her a speeding ticket, and she realizes that she loves him at the dinner she stages, with the help of her uncle, a judge, as a joke on the policeman. Instead of being disgraced, Billy recognizes a silk thief (played by Francis Ford) among the guests and arrests him. *Police. Judges. Thieves. Automobile driving.*

SPEED CRAZED **F2.5301**

Duke Worne Productions. *Dist* Rayart Pictures. 3 Nov **1926** [New York State license; New York showing 20 May 1927]. Si; b&w. 35mm. 5 reels, 5,241 ft.

Pres by W. Ray Johnston. *Dir* Duke Worne. *Scen* Grover Jones. *Story* Suzanne Avery. *Photog* King Grey.

Cast: Billy Sullivan *(Billy Meeks)*, Andrée Tourneur *(Eloise Harfer)*, Joseph W. Girard *(Maclyn Harfer)*, Harry Maynard *(Mr. Payton)*, Albert J. Smith *(Dave Marker)*.

Action melodrama. Billy is kidnaped by a gang of criminals and forced to drive a getaway car. The gangleader escapes, while Billy is arrested along with two of the holdup men. Billy escapes and rides the rods to another town, where he becomes acquainted with Harfer, the owner of a racing car, who is being hoodwinked by the car's driver. The driver is fired, and Billy is hired to drive the car in an important race. The gangleader who kidnaped Billy is determined to prevent Harfer from winning the race and arranges for Billy to be kidnaped again, but Billy escapes from his abductors and arrives at the racetrack in time to win the race. The gangleader is arrested by the police, and Billy wins the love of Harfer's daughter, Eloise. *Mechanics. Gangs. Automobile racing. Kidnaping.*

THE SPEED DEMON **F2.5302**

Bud Barsky Productions. 25 Jun **1925** [New York State license]. Si; b&w. 35mm. 5 reels, 5,500 ft.

Dir Robert N. Bradbury. *Story-Scen* Samuel M. Pyke. *Titl* Robert Hopkins. *Film Ed* Della M. King. *Asst Dir* Hal Davitt.

Cast: Kenneth McDonald *(Speed Sherman)*, Peggy Montgomery *(Enid Warren)*, B. Wayne Lamont *(Joe Blake)*, Art Manning *(Ed Norton)*, Clark Comstock *(Colonel Warren)*, Jack Pierce *(Pickles Rankin)*, Frank Rice *(Colonel Warren's butler)*, Barney Oldfield *(himself)*.

Action melodrama. In order to obtain the prize filly of Warren, a hospitable and unsuspecting Kentucky colonel, a New York racetrack shark wins the old man's confidence and is invited by him to stay in the family mansion. The plans of the tout are spoiled by Speed Sherman, a Yankee racing driver, who protects the colonel's filly and marries his daughter, Enid. *Kentucky colonels. Touts. Horseracing. Kentucky. Horses.*

THE SPEED GIRL **F2.5303**

Realart Pictures. *Dist* Paramount Pictures. Nov **1921** [c19 Sep 1921; LP17031]. Si; b&w. 35mm. 5 reels, 5,792 ft.

Dir Maurice Campbell. *Scen* Douglas Doty. *Story* Elmer Harris. *Photog* H. Kinley Martin.

Cast: Bebe Daniels *(Betty Lee)*, Theodore von Eltz *(Tom Manley)*, Frank Elliott *(Carl D'Arcy)*, Walter Hiers *(Soapy Taylor)*, Norris Johnson *(Hilda)*, Truly Shattuck *(Mrs. Lee)*, William Courtright *(Judge Ketcham)*, Barbara Maier *(little girl)*.

Comedy. At 20, Betty Lee has become famous for movie stunts with airplanes and highpower roadsters. While horseback riding, she allows Ensign Tom Manley to believe that he has saved her from a runaway; then at the studio he meets her suitor, Carl D'Arcy. Betty evades Carl's marriage proposal and accepts Tom's luncheon invitation. Through a trick, she delays him in meeting his ship, and at the last minute, Betty, along with Tom and her press agent, Soapy Taylor, burn up the road to San Diego. Through Carl's plotting, the police arrest Betty for speeding and sentence her to 10 days in jail, although she manages to deliver Tom on time. Carl, trailed by revenue officers, shifts blame to Hilda, a chambermaid whom he has deceived, and she meets Betty in jail. Soapy plans a jail wedding for Carl and Betty as a publicity stunt, but Tom exposes Carl and wins the hand of Betty. *Press agents. Motion pictures. Automobiles. Airplanes. Hollywood. San Diego. Stunts.*

SPEED KING **F2.5304**

Phil Goldstone. Jan **1923.** Si; b&w. 35mm. 5 reels.

Dir Grover Jones. *Photog* Arthur Todd.

Cast: Richard Talmadge *(Jimmy Martin/King Charles)*, Virginia Warwick *(Princess Margaret)*, Mark Fenton *(General Mendell)*, Harry

Van Meter *(Rodolph D'Henri)*.

Comedy-drama. Jimmy Martin, king of the motorcycle speedsters, visits the Kingdom of Mandavia for a race. There he is persuaded to impersonate the king by a traitor, Rodolph D'Henri, who intends to annex part of Mandavia for neighboring Selmarnia. The real king is in jail. D'Henri's plot is successful until Martin falls in love with Princess Margaret of Alvernia. Then he discloses his true identity, releases the real king, exposes the traitor, earns knighthood, and marries Margaret. *Royalty. Traitors. Motorcyclists. Imaginary kingdoms. Impersonation.*

THE SPEED LIMIT **F2.5305**

Gotham Productions. *Dist* Lumas Film Corp. Mar **1926** [c11 Feb 1926; LP22394]. Si; b&w. 35mm. 6 reels, 5,675 ft.

Supv Renaud Hoffman. *Dir* Frank O'Connor. *Story* James J. Tynan.

Cast: Raymond McKee *(Tom Milburn)*, Ethel Shannon *(Bess Stanton)*, Bruce Gordon *(Claude Roswell)*, George Chapman *(Henry Berger)*, James Conley *(Eightball Jackson)*, Edward W. Borman *(Biff Garrison)*, Rona Lee *(Muriel Hodge)*, Paul Weigel *(Mr. Charles Benson)*, Lucille Thorndyke *(Mrs. Charles Benson)*.

Romantic comedy. Tom Milburn, racing enthusiast experimenting with a new tire process, wants to marry Bess Stanton. However, her head is turned by a young man, Claude Roswell, driving a Rolls-Royce. The two men engage in a series of pranks culminating in Roswell's framing Tom for car theft. Tom's name is cleared, and so he is able to drive in the big race and test his experimental tires. The tires prove to be successful, and he wins the race, a manufacturer's royalty contract, and Bess. *Frameup. Automobile racing. Automobile tires. Rolls-Royce automobiles.*

SPEED MAD **F2.5306**

Perfection Pictures. *Dist* Columbia Pictures. 15 Jul **1925** [c4 Aug 1925; LP21694]. Si; b&w. 35mm. 5 reels, 4,442 ft.

Dir Jay Marchant. *Titl* Malcolm Stuart Boylan. *Story* Dorothy Howell. *Photog* George Meehan. *Film Ed* Charles J. Hunt. *Prod Mgr* Harry Cohn.

Cast: William Fairbanks *(Bill Sanford)*, Edith Roberts *(Betty Hampton)*, Lloyd Whitlock *(Alan Lawton)*, Melbourne MacDowell *(John Sanford)*, John Fox, Jr. *(Freckles Smithers)*, Florence Lee *(Grandma Smithers)*, Charles K. French *(Charles Hampton)*, Buddy *(a dog)*.

Action melodrama. Bill Sanford, a young daredevil, frequently races his speedster on country roads, his happiness dampened only by cops, courts, and crashes. After an argument with his father, Bill leaves home with $5 for a stake and begins sleeping in haystacks. He discovers that there is a race with a prize of $5,000 and hocks his car to put up the entrance fee. Allan Lawton, a mortgage broker who is about to foreclose on the property of Charles Hampton, the father of Bill's girl, abducts Bill before the race. Bill escapes from the freight car where he is tied up and gets to the track in time to drive his car to victory. He pays off the Hampton mortgage and exposes Lawton's perfidy. *Brokers. Filial relations. Abduction. Mortgages. Reckless driving. Automobile racing. Dogs.*

SPEED MADNESS **F2.5307**

Hercules Film Productions. c3 Oct **1925** [LP21870]. Si; b&w. 35mm. 5 reels, 4,597 ft.

Pres by Peter Kanellos. *Dir* Bruce Mitchell. *Story* William E. Wing.

Cast: Frank Merrill, Clara Horton, Evelyn Sherman, Garry O'Dell, Joe Girard, Jimmy Quinn, Geno Corrado, Jack *(a dog)*.

Action melodrama. Ted Bromley devotes his considerable energies to perfecting a radical valve design for automobile engines. Taking his car for a test drive, Ted meets Alice Carey, whose mother owns property in which Ted's father is highly interested. Julien Riccardo, the husband of the elder Bromley's secretary, plots to marry Alice, thereby obtaining possession of her property and selling it at a great profit to Ted's father. Ted learns of the scheme and prevents the marriage. Ted later gets a large check for his invention and uses it to pay off the mortgage on the Carey property, winning Alice's permanent gratitude and love. *Inventors. Secretaries. Bigamy. Property rights. Automobiles. Mortgages. Dogs.*

THE SPEED SPOOK **F2.5308**

East Coast Films. 30 Aug **1924** [c20 Aug 1924; LP20523]. Si; b&w. 35mm. 7 reels, 6,750 ft.

Dir Charles Hines. *Scen* Raymond S. Harris. *Titl* Ralph Spence. *Story* William Wallace Cook. *Photog* Charles E. Gilson, John Geisel.

Cast: Johnny Hines *("Blue Streak" Billings)*, Faire Binney *(Betty West)*, Edmund Breese *("Chuck")*, Warner Richmond *(Jud Skerrit)*, Frank Losee *(Sheriff West)*, Henry West *(Hiram Smith)*.

Comedy-melodrama. "Blue Streak" Billings returns to his hometown to prove the qualities of the Comet brand of automobile sold by his girl, Betty West, whose trade has suffered through the schemings of a wealthier competitor. While exploiting his "driverless" car, he learns that his rival is faking the ballots for the sheriff's election, exposes him, and identifies himself as the mysterious driver of the car. *Salesmen. Sheriffs. Automobile manufacture. Political corruption.*

SPEED WILD **F2.5309**

Harry Garson Productions. *Dist* Film Booking Offices of America. 10 May **1925** [c10 May 1925; LP21521]. Si; b&w. 35mm. 5 reels, 4,700 ft.

Dir Harry Garson. *Scen* Frank S. Beresford. *Story* H. H. Van Loan. *Photog* William Tuers.

Cast: Lefty Flynn *(Jack Ames)*, Ethel Shannon *(Mary Bryant)*, Frank Elliott *(Wendell Martin)*, Ralph McCullough *(Charles Bryant)*, Raymond Turner *(Ulysses)*, Fred Burns *(Red Dugan)*, Charles Clary *(Herbert Barron)*.

Melodrama. For the sake of adventure, Jack Ames joins the police department as a motorcycle cop and is immediately assigned to the vice squad, which is investigating the smuggling of Chinese picture brides into the United States. When he rescues Mary Bryant after an automobile accident, Jack falls in love with her and soon promises to help straighten out her brother, Charles, who has become involved with the gang of smugglers. Jack goes to Chinatown, where he finds Charles, whom he is forced to knock out when the boneheaded boy won't leave of his own accord. Wendell Martin, the smugglers' leader, is in love with Mary and lures her aboard a yacht by telling her that Charles is held prisoner below deck. Jack learns of Mary's peril and gives chase, fighting with Martin and his gang until the police arrive. The gang is captured, and Jack wins Mary. *Police. Smugglers. Chinese. Brother-sister relationship. Yachts. San Francisco—Chinatown.*

SPEEDING HOOFS **F2.5310**

Ben Wilson Productions. *Dist* Rayart Pictures. Jan **1927.** Si; b&w. 35mm. 5 reels, 4,621 ft.

Dir Louis Chaudet. *Photog* Eddie Linden.

Cast: Dick Hatton.

Western melodrama. "Treasure concealed on ranch is hunted by rightful owner and her boy friend and a gang of thieves, who spread rumor ranch is haunted. Owner continues search helped by the boy. Thieves plan attack but learning plans girl and boy ward off the gang. They find treasure and marry." *(Motion Picture News Booking Guide,* 12:56, Apr 1927.) *Thieves. Haunted houses. Ranches. Treasure.*

SPEEDING THROUGH **F2.5311**

Ellbee Pictures. 15 Sep **1926.** Si; b&w. 35mm. 6 reels, 5,259 ft.

Dir Bertram Bracken. *Photog* William Tuers.

Cast: Creighton Hale, Judy King, Helen Lynch.

Melodrama(?). No information about the nature of this film has been found.

THE SPEEDING VENUS **F2.5312**

Metropolitan Pictures Corp. of California. *Dist* Producers Distributing Corp. 13 Sep **1926** [c28 Jun 1926; LP22857]. Si; b&w. 35mm. 6 reels, 5,560 ft.

Dir Robert Thornby. *Adapt* Finis Fox. *Photog* Georges Benoit.

Cast: Priscilla Dean *(Emily Dale)*, Robert Frazer *(John Steele)*, Dale Fuller *(Midge Rooney)*, Johnny Fox *(Speck O'Donnell)*, Ray Ripley *(Chet Higgins)*, Charles Sellon *(Jed Morgan)*.

Melodrama. Source: Welford Beaton, "Behind the Wheel" (publication undetermined). Jed Morgan, a Detroit automobile manufacturer, calls in John Steele, a mechanical genius, and Chet Higgins, a promoter, and offers a half interest in profits to the first man to perfect his gearless motor invention. Emily Dale, Morgan's confidential adviser, prefers Steele and urges him to win, while Higgins calls to his aid a renegade mechanic. Steele places his car on a train, and Higgins plans to wreck it so as to be the first to claim the prize; his plan succeeds, but Morgan is taken ill, giving Steele and Emily time to recondition the car. Emily obtains right-of-way over main roads and permission to speed on a record-breaking trip to California. In spite of attempts to stall her, Emily wins the race, though forced to drive her car through a show window. Steele is rewarded by Morgan with the money and the love of Emily. *Mechanics. Automobile manufacturers. Automobile racing. Inventions. Detroit. California. Train wrecks.*

SPEEDWAY F2.5313

Metro-Goldwyn-Mayer Pictures. 7 Sep **1929** [c9 Sep 1929; LP664]. Mus score & sd eff (Movietone); b&w. 35mm. 8 reels, 6,962 or 7,075 ft. [Also si.]

Dir Harry Beaumont. *Titl* Joe Farnham. *Adapt* Alfred Block, Ann Price, Byron Morgan. *Story* Byron Morgan. *Photog* Henry Sharp. *Art Dir* Cedric Gibbons. *Film Ed* George Hively. *Wardrobe* David Cox. *Coöp* Indianapolis Speedway Association.

Cast: William Haines *(Bill Whipple)*, Anita Page *(Patricia)*, Ernest Torrence *(Jim MacDonald)*, Karl Dane *(Dugan)*, John Miljan *(Lee Renny)*, Eugenie Besserer *(Mrs. MacDonald)*, Polly Moran *(waitress)*.

Action melodrama. Racecar driver Bill Whipple has an argument with his foster father, Jim MacDonald, also a racer, before the Indianapolis 500 Race, and deserts him to drive another car. MacDonald is barred from the race because of a weak heart; simultaneously, Whipple is ditched by the owner of the other car. He returns to race with MacDonald, and toward the end Whipple lets him take the wheel for the winning finish. *Foster fathers. Automobile racing. Filial relations. Heart disease. Indianapolis 500.*

SPEEDY F2.5314

Harold Lloyd Corp. *Dist* Paramount Famous Lasky Corp. 7 Apr **1928** [c7 Apr 1928; LP25135]. Si; b&w. 35mm. 8 reels, 7,690 ft.

Dir Ted Wilde. *Titl* Albert De Mond. *Story* John Grey, Lex Neal, Howard Emmett Rogers, Jay Howe. *Photog* Walter Lundin. *Song:* *"Speedy Boy"* Ray Klages, Jesse Greer. *Prod Mgr* John L. Murphy.

Cast: Harold Lloyd *(Harold "Speedy" Swift)*, Ann Christy *(Jane Dillon)*, Bert Woodruff *(Pop Dillon)*, Brooks Benedict *(Steven Carter)*, King Tut *(himself, a dog)*, Dan Wolheim, Babe Ruth, Hank Knight.

Comedy. "Speedy," who is unable to hold a job, comes to the rescue when his girl's grandfather nearly loses his horsecar franchise. A gang of men steal the car and hide it on the riverfront, but "Speedy" finds it, drives it furiously through the crowded streets, and gets it back on the track in time to make the daily run. *Grandfathers. Gangs. Horsecars. Dogs.*

SPEEDY SMITH F2.5315

Duke Worne Productions. *Dist* Rayart Pictures. Jun **1927.** Si; b&w. 35mm. 5 reels, 5,005 ft.

Dir Duke Worne. *Story-Scen* Suzanne Avery. *Photog* Ernest Smith.

Cast: Billy Sullivan *(Billy Smith)*, Hazel Deane *(Tena Lucian)*, Harry Tenbrook *(Slugger Sampson)*, Virginia True Boardman *(Widow Lucian)*, George Periolat *(Charles C. Smith)*, Arthur Thalasso *(James Mortimer Dorfee)*.

Melodrama. Seeking adventure, Billy Smith, a wealthy ne'er-do-well, joins a tent show and meets aspiring novelist Tena Lucian in a small town. Her blind mother, Widow Lucian, requires an operation, and the youth fights the bully, Slugger Sampson, for the necessary money. *Ne'er-do-wells. Novelists. Bullies. Filial relations. Blindness. Tent shows.*

SPEEDY SPURS F2.5316

Action Pictures. *Dist* Weiss Brothers Artclass Pictures. 1 Jun **1926.** Si; b&w. 35mm. 5 reels, 4,396 ft.

Dir Richard Thorpe. *Story-Cont* Frank L. Inghram.

Cast: Buffalo Bill Jr. *(Bill Clark)*, Charles Whittaker, Jr. *(Buttons, the orphaned child)*, James Welch *(Luke Tuttle, sheriff, grocer, fire-chief, and general politician)*, Alma Rayford *(Marie Tuttle, his daughter)*, Frank Ellis *(Mr. Wells, a bully)*, Clyde McClary, William Ryno, Charles Colby *(The Three City Fathers)*, Charles Whittaker *(The Convict)*, Harry Belmour *(The Doctor)*, Emily Barrye *(The Witch)*.

Western comedy. "Hero, knocked out by villain, imagines himself in Heaven and Hell (where the comedy occurs) until he comes to. In the end he defeats the bad man and wins the girl." (*Motion Picture News Booking Guide,* 11:49, Oct 1926.) *Orphans. Sheriffs. Politicians. Hell. Heaven. Good and evil.*

THE SPENDERS F2.5317

Great Authors Pictures. *Dist* W. W. Hodkinson Corp. Jan **1921.** Si; b&w. 35mm. 5-6 reels, 5,693 ft.

Prod Benjamin B. Hampton. *Dir* Jack Conway. *Scen* E. Richard Schayer. *Photog* E. J. Vallejo.

Cast: Claire Adams *(Avice Milbrey)*, Robert McKim *(Rulon Shepler)*, Joseph J. Dowling *(Uncle Peter Bines)*, Niles Welch *(P. Percival Bines)*, Betty Brice *(Psyche Bines)*, Adele Farrington *(Mrs. Bines)*, Virginia Harris *(Mrs. Athelstane)*, Tom Ricketts *(Mr. Milbrey)*, Otto Lederer *(Abe Trummel)*, Harold Holland *(Lord Mauburn)*.

Comedy-melodrama. Source: Harry Leon Wilson, *The Spenders; A Tale of the Third Generation* (Boston, 1902). Full of youthful enthusiasm and dreams of conquering Wall Street, P. Percival, Psyche, and Mrs. Bines go to New York—against the wishes of Uncle Peter Bines, who wants his family to remain in the West, the home of his financial interests. They find more than they bargained for from Rulon Shepler and other Wall Street "wolves"; but Uncle Peter comes to their rescue by operating exactly contrary to Hoyle, Percival wins Avice Milbrey from Shepler, and Psyche finds true love with Lord Mauburn. *Financiers. Uncles. Nobility. English. New York City—Wall Street.*

Note: Also reviewed as *The Respondent.*

THE SPICE OF LIFE *see* **SPORTING YOUTH**

THE SPIDER AND THE ROSE F2.5318

B. F. Zeidman Productions. *Dist* Principal Pictures. 15 Feb **1923** [c19 Nov 1923; LP19620]. Si; b&w. 35mm. 7 reels, 6,800 ft.

Dir John McDermott. *Story* Gerald C. Duffy. *Photog* Charles Richardson, Glen MacWilliams.

Cast: Alice Lake *(Paula)*, Richard Headrick *(Don Marcello, as a child)*, Gaston Glass *(Don Marcello)*, Joseph J. Dowling *(The Governor)*, Robert McKim *(Mendozza)*, Noah Beery *(Maître Renaud)*, Otis Harlan *(The Secretary)*, Frank Campeau *(Don Fernando)*, Andrew Arbuckle *(The Priest)*, Alec Francis *(Good Padre)*, Edwin Stevens *(Bishop Oliveros)*, Louise Fazenda *(Dolores)*.

Action melodrama. The story is set in southern California during the Mexican regime. Don Marcello, son of the governor of the territory, returns home to find that Mendozza, his father's secretary, has taken over and has aroused the anger of the revolutionary faction. Don Marcello affiliates himself with the revolutionists, who rid the community of Mendozza and reinstate the governor. *Revolutions. California—Mexican period.*

SPIDER WEBS F2.5319

Artlee Pictures. 1 May **1927.** Si; b&w. 35mm. 6 reels, 4,768-5,900 ft.

Dir Wilfred Noy. *Adapt* Charles Horan. *Camera* Roy Hunt, Alvin Wyckoff.

Cast: Niles Welch *(Bert Grantland)*, Alice Lake *(Flora Benham)*, J. Barney Sherry *(Chester Sanfrew)*, Martin Faust *(Joe Dickson)*, Bert Harvey *(Nick Sinclair)*, Maurice Costello *(Jeffrey Stanton)*, Edna Richmond *(Mrs. Stanton)*.

Society drama. Source: H. G. Logalton, "The Fast Pace" (publication undetermined). In New York City, an innocent young girl falls victim to blackmailers, who use her to retrieve a married woman's incriminating letters. She is arrested for the murder of a man, but the hero solves the mystery, and the real murderer is captured. *Blackmail. Murder. New York City. Documentation.*

THE SPIDER'S WEB F2.5320

Micheaux Film Corp. 3 Jan **1927** [New York State license]. Si; b&w. 35mm. 7 reels, 6,913 ft.

Oscar Micheaux Production.

Cast: Lorenzo McLane, Evelyn Preer *(Norma Shepard)*, Edward Thompson, Grace Smythe, Marshall Rodgers, Henrietta Loveless, Billy Gulfport.

Melodrama. On a visit to her aunt in a small Mississippi delta town, Norma Shepard, a young Negro girl, is accosted on the street by Ballinger, the lecherous son of a white planter. Ballinger later comes to the home of Norma's aunt and attempts to force his attentions on the young girl. Elmer Harris, an investigator for the Justice Deparment who is in Mississippi looking into conditions of peonage there, then arrests Ballinger. Norma and her aunt return to Harlem, where the old lady loses every penny she possesses playing the numbers. When she finally picks the winning number, she goes to the office of Martinez for the payoff and finds him dead. She takes the amount of her winnings from his safe and is later arrested for his murder. Elmer Harris, working undercover, discovers that Madame Boley, a wealthy woman from Oklahoma, killed Martinez in a fit of passion. Norma's aunt is freed, and Elmer wins Norma. *Planters. Negro life. Oklahomans. Government agents. Lechery. Race relations. Numbers racket. Murder. Gambling. Mississippi. New York City—Harlem.*

Note: This film is based on the story "The Policy Player," the authorship of which has not been determined.

THE SPIELER F2.5321

Ralph Block Productions. *Dist* Pathé Exchange. 20 Dec **1928** [c3 Dec 1928; LP25886]. Talking sequences, sd eff, & mus score (Photophone); b&w. 35mm. 7 reels, 5,606 ft.

Dir Tay Garnett. *Titl* John Krafft. *Adapt-Dial* Hal Conklin, Tay Garnett. *Story* Hal Conklin. *Photog* Arthur Miller. *Film Ed* Doane Harrison. *Mus Dir* Josiah Zuro. *Asst Dir* Robert Fellows. *Prod Mgr* Harry H. Poppe. *Prop* Walter Bradford.

Cast: Alan Hale *(Flash)*, Clyde Cook *(Luke)*, Renée Adorée *(Cleo)*, Fred Kohler *(Red Moon)*, Fred Warren *(The Barker)*, Jimmy Quinn *(The Rabbit)*, Kewpie Morgan *(Butch)*, Billie Latimer *(bearded lady)*.

Melodrama. Cleo inherits a carnival and announces in the newspapers that her show will be operated free of all grifters, dips, three-shell men, confidence artists, and hookers. Flash and Luke, a couple of dips, see in this policy their big chance and, passing themselves off as honest men, find work in Cleo's show. Flash is greatly attracted to Cleo, but she rebuffs him when he tries to cultivate her friendship too fast. Red Moon, the carnival's concession manager, robs the office safe and lays the blame on Flash. Red later kills Luke, and Flash goes after Red in a rage, breaking his neck; Flash is reinstated in Cleo's good graces and finds solace for the loss of his friend in her love. *Pickpockets. Confidence men. Murder. Carnivals.*

SPINNER O' DREAMS F2.5322

Buffalo Motion Picture Co. *Dist* Rollo Sales Corp. Apr **1922** [New York State]. Si; b&w. 35mm. 5 reels.

Cast: Mr. Livesey, Miss Clifford.

Society drama. No information about the precise nature of this film has been found.

THE SPIRIT OF '76 (Reissue) F2.5323

Dist All-American Film Co. 6 Aug **1921** [trade review]. Si; b&w. 35mm.

Note: Originally produced by Continental Producing Co., 1917.

THE SPIRIT OF THE U. S. A. F2.5324

Emory Johnson Productions. *Dist* Film Booking Offices of America. 18 May **1924** [c12 May 1924; LP20290]. Si; b&w. 35mm. 9 reels, 8,312 ft.

Dir Emory Johnson. *Story-Scen* Emilie Johnson. *Photog* Ross Fisher, Leon Eycke. *Asst Dir* Jerry Callahan.

Cast: Johnnie Walker *(Johnnie Gains)*, Mary Carr *(Mary Gains)*, Carl Stockdale *(Thomas Gains)*, Dave Kirby *(Jim Fuller)*, Mark Fenton *(John J. Burrows)*, Rosemary Cooper *(Zelda Burrows)*, William S. Hooser *(Otto Schultz)*, Gloria Grey *(Gretchen Schultz)*, Cuyler Supplee *(Silas Gains)*, Dicky Brandon *(Little Johnnie)*, Newton House *(Little Silas)*, Richard Morris.

Melodrama. Johnnie Gains, son of a farming couple, is industrious and imbued with a spirit of sacrifice. Rejected for military service because of an eye injury, he enlists in the Salvation Army. His indolent brother marries but is goaded into enlisting and dies on the battlefield. The parents are evicted from their home by the dead son's widow, but Johnnie returns and restores the homestead to them. *Brothers. Family life. World War I. Salvation Army.*

Note: Working title: *Swords and Plowshares*.

THE SPIRIT OF YOUTH F2.5325

Tiffany-Stahl Productions. 15 or 20 Feb **1929** [c28 Jan 1929; LP73]. Si; b&w. 35mm. 7 reels, 6,216 ft.

Dir Walter Lang. *Story-Cont* Eve Unsell, Elmer Harris. *Titl* Frederic Hatton, Fanny Hatton. *Photog* John Boyle. *Film Ed* Desmond O'Brien.

Cast: Dorothy Sebastian *(Betty Grant)*, Larry Kent *(Jim Kenney)*, Betty Francisco *(Claire Ewing)*, Maurice Murphy *(Ted Ewing)*, Anita Fremault *(Toodles Ewing)*, Donald Hall *(Mr. Ewing)*, Douglas Gilmore *(Hal Loring)*, Charles Sullivan *(prizefighter)*, Sidney D'Albrook *(fight promoter)*.

Comedy. Jim Kenney, the fleet middleweight boxing champion, is enamored of Betty Grant, the village librarian, and promises to write to her from every port. Meanwhile, he falls in love with Claire Ewing, a rich heiress who lives in the city and who knows Betty. Claire prevails upon Jim to stage an exhibition bout before retiring, but he is blinded from contact with resin on his opponent's glove and is knocked out. The heiress is disillusioned, but Betty's faith in Larry reunites them. *Librarians. Sailors. Heiresses. Prizefighting. Blindness.*

SPITE MARRIAGE F2.5326

Joseph M. Schenck Productions. *Dist* Metro-Goldwyn-Mayer Distributing Corp. 6 Apr **1929** [c22 Apr 1929; LP329]. Si; b&w. 35mm. 9 reels, 7,047 ft.

Supv Larry Weingarten. *Dir* Edward Sedgwick. *Cont* Richard Schayer. *Titl* Robert Hopkins. *Adapt* Ernest S. Pagano. *Story* Lew Lipton. *Photog* Reggie Lanning. *Art Dir* Cedric Gibbons. *Film Ed* Frank Sullivan. *Wardrobe* David Cox.

Cast: Buster Keaton *(Elmer)*, Dorothy Sebastian *(Trilby Drew)*, Edward Earle *(Lionel Denmore)*, Leila Hyams *(Ethyle Norcrosse)*, William Bechtel *(Nussbaum)*, John Byron *(Giovanni Scarzi)*, Hank Mann.

Comedy. Elmer, a pants-presser, falls in love with Trilby Drew, the star of a legitimate show, and attends every performance. Trilby is then jilted by her leading man, Lionel Denmore, and marries Elmer out of spite. She becomes intoxicated on their wedding night, and Elmer, realizing the reason for the marriage, leaves her and finds work as a sailor on a rumrunner's boat. Elmer later transfers at sea to a yacht on which Trilby is a passenger and proves his love and courage during a series of disasters. Trilby at last comes to realize her love for Elmer. *Pants-pressers. Sailors. Rumrunners. Actors. Theater. Marriage. Yachts.*

SPITFIRE F2.5327

Reol Productions. c24 Jul **1922** [LU18085]. Si; b&w. 35mm. [Length undetermined.]

Copyright Auth Osborne Williams.

Cast: Edna Morton.

Melodrama. Guy Rogers, the son of a well-known publisher, sets out to prove his father's racist critics wrong by putting Booker T. Washington's philosophy into practice. He goes to a little Maryland Hills town where through his efforts a school and a library are built. He falls in love with Ruth Hill, whose recently widowered father, an ex-schoolteacher, is killed after being involved in horsethievery. "Buck" Bradley, the local dealer in hay and feed, who put Ruth's father up to the crime, has been made her guardian, and he beats up Guy when he tries to defend her. She nurses Guy back to health, love blooms, and they marry. *Negroes. Schoolteachers. Publishers. Horsethieves. Racism. Fodder. Libraries. Maryland. Booker Taliaferro Washington.*

Note: Apparently an all-Negro cast.

THE SPITFIRE F2.5328

Murray W. Garsson Productions. *Dist* Associated Exhibitors. 4 May **1924** [c6 May 1924; LU20156]. Si; b&w. 35mm. 7 reels, 6,109 ft.

Pres by Murray W. Garsson. *Dir* William Christy Cabanne. *Scen* Raymond S. Harris. *Photog* Walter Arthur, Jack Brown.

Cast: Betty Blythe *(Jean Bronson)*, Lowell Sherman *(Horace Fleming)*, Elliott Dexter *(Douglas Kenyon)*, Robert Warwick *(Oliver Blair)*, Pauline Garon *(Marcia Walsh)*, Burr McIntosh *(Joshua Carrington)*, Jack Donovan *(Abel Carrington)*, Ray Allen *(Henry Hammil)*.

Society melodrama. Source: Frederic Arnold Kummer, *Plaster Saints* (New York, 1922). Following a scandalous poker party, Douglas Kenyon acts as escort to Marcia Walsh, a showgirl whom he "wins" in a game. When it is discovered that she has spent the night in his apartment, though innocently, he is discharged from the bank where he works. He then is separated from his sweetheart, Jean Bronson, who becomes an actress when he plans to prosecute her grandfather. After many complications, including the heroine's rescue from an unscrupulous theatrical producer, the lovers are reunited. *Shopgirls. Actors. Theatrical producers. Gambling. Theater. Poker.*

THE SPLENDID CRIME F2.5329

Famous Players–Lasky. *Dist* Paramount Pictures. 4 Jan **1926** [c5 Jan 1926; LP22228]. Si; b&w. 35mm. 6 reels, 6,069 ft.

Pres by Adolph Zukor, Jesse L. Lasky. *Dir-Story* William C. De Mille. *Scen* Violet Clark. *Photog* L. Guy Wilky.

Cast: Bebe Daniels *(Jenny)*, Neil Hamilton *(Bob Van Dyke)*, Anne Cornwall *(Beth Van Dyke)*, Anthony Jowitt *(John Norton)*, Fred Walton *(Dugan)*, Lloyd Corrigan *(Kelly)*, Mickey McBan *(The Kid)*, Josephine Crowell *(Mary)*, Marcelle Corday *(Madame Denise)*.

Comedy-drama. Jenny, a pretty thief, is discovered by Bob Van Dyke, a young millionaire, when she is about to burgle his safe. He lectures her on the evils of crime and, to test her decency, leaves her alone with a large roll of bills. Jenny decides to go straight and leaves the money alone. She then gets a job as a dressmaker and is later called to the Van Dyke home to do some work for Bob's sister, and Jenny discovers that, faced with financial ruin in the stock market, Bob is about to steal $20,000 from his housekeeper. To forestall him, Jenny arranges for her old confederates to steal the money first, taking the blame for the crime herself. Inspired by Jenny's example, Bob accepts his bankruptcy with grace, becomes a golf pro, and marries Jenny, who, in the meantime, has returned the money and settled her score with the law. *Criminals—Rehabilitation. Millionaires. Housekeepers. Brother-sister relationship. Theft. Bankruptcy. Stock market. Golf.*

THE SPLENDID LIE **F2.5330**

J. G. Pictures. *Dist* Arrow Film Corp. 3 Jan **1922** [c6 Feb 1922; LP17526]. Si; b&w. 35mm. 6 reels, 5,500 ft.

Dir-Story-Scen Charles Horan.

Cast: Grace Davison *(Dorris Delafield)*, Jack Drumier *(David Delafield)*, Noel Tearle *(Crafton Wolcott)*, J. Thornton Baston *(Dean De Witt)*, Mabel Baudine *(Goldie)*, Jere Austin *(James Holden)*, Emily Fitzroy *(Mrs. Wolcott Delafield)*.

Society melodrama. Dorris Delafield, who supports herself and her aged grandfather as a private secretary, is given a vacation in Hot Springs by her employer. There she meets Dean De Witt, who, posing as an unmarried man, wins her affections and proposes to her; his wife discovers the deception, and after confronting the couple, she causes Dorris and her grandfather to be evicted from the hotel. Returning home, Dorris is turned out of her house and loses her position as a result of the scandal, but she finds a friend in banker's son James Holden, who gives her a position as secretary to his mother. Suspicion is again cast upon her when Mrs. De Witt recognizes her at a party, but she eventually establishes her innocence and finds happiness as James's wife. *Secretaries. Grandfathers. Divorce. Scandal. Hot Springs.*

THE SPLENDID ROAD **F2.5331**

Frank Lloyd Productions. *Dist* First National Pictures. 6 Dec **1925** [c23 Nov 1925; LP22024]. Si; b&w. 35mm. 8 reels, 7,646 ft.

Pres by Frank Lloyd. *Pers Dir* Frank Lloyd. *Adapt* J. G. Hawks. *Photog* Norbert F. Brodin.

Cast: Anna Q. Nilsson *(Sandra De Hault)*, Robert Frazer *(Stanton Halliday)*, Lionel Barrymore *(Dan Clehollis)*, Edwards Davis *(Banker John Grey)*, Roy Laidlaw *(Captain Sutter)*, De Witt Jennings *(Captain Bashford)*, Russell Simpson *(Captain Lightfoot)*, George Bancroft *(Buck Lockwell)*, Gladys Brockwell *(Satan's sister)*, Pauline Garon *(Angel Allie)*, Marceline Day *(Lilian Grey)*, Mary Jane Irving *(Hester Gephart)*, Mickey McBan *(Billy Gephart)*, Edward Earle *(Doctor Bidwell)*.

Western melodrama. Source: Vingie E. Roe, *The Splendid Road* (New York, 1925). Sandra De Hault, a fair "soldier of fortune," arrives in Sacramento during the Gold Rush of 1849, after a sea voyage in which she adopted three children when their mother died. She is saved from a drunk by Stanton Halliday, an agent of eastern capitalist John Grey. They are attracted to each other, but believing that Grey's daughter, Lilian, is in love with Halliday and not wanting to ruin his career, Sandra gives Halliday up. She goes to Reading Flat and becomes a squatter. Halliday is sent to evict her but ends up rescuing her from the attentions of Dan Clehollis, a gambler. He is shot in the scuffle. Eventually, Halliday recovers and returns to rescue Sandra and her family from a flood. *Squatters. Gamblers. Adoption. Seafaring life. Gold rushes. Sacramento. California. Floods.*

SPLITTING THE BREEZE **F2.5332**

R-C Pictures. *Dist* Film Booking Offices of America. 29 May **1927** [c29 Jun 1927; LP24230]. Si; b&w. 35mm. 5 reels, 4,930 ft.

Pres by Joseph P. Kennedy. *Dir* Robert De Lacey. *Story-Cont* Frank Howard Clark. *Ch Camera* Nick Musuraca. *Asst Dir* William Cody.

Cast: Tom Tyler *(Death Valley Drake)*, Harry Woods *(Dave Matlock)*, Barney Furey *(Rev. Otis Briggs)*, Tom Lingham *(Tom Rand)*, Peggy Montgomery *(Janet Rand)*, Red Lennox *(Red)*, Alfred Heuston *(Hank Robbins)*, Barbara Starr *(Lois Cortez)*.

Western melodrama. A reign of terror is created in the town of Boulder Gulch by Dave Matlock, a saloon owner, who sends death warnings to his victims. Rev. Otis Briggs, a friend of Death Valley Drake, warns him that Matlock wants to frame him, but Drake refuses to leave, having taken an interest in Janet, the sheriff's daughter. When the sheriff is shot, Drake is accused by Matlock and is arrested; but he escapes jail and goes to join Matlock's gang. He draws a lot with the death sign on it, pretends to shoot the parson, but is exposed by the villain, who plots to escape with Janet. Lois, Matlock's woman, helps Drake escape, and he forces Matlock over a cliff in a showdown. *Cowboys. Clergymen. Sheriffs. Saloon keepers. Gangs. Terrorism. Frameup.*

THE SPOILERS (Reissue) **F2.5333**

Selig Polyscope Co. *Dist* Film Market. **1921.** Si; b&w. 35mm. 9 reels.

Note: The first film version of Rex Beach's novel, originally released Apr 1914; c14 Apr; LP2509.

THE SPOILERS **F2.5334**

Jesse D. Hampton Productions. *Dist* Goldwyn Distributing Corp. 5 Aug **1923** [New York premiere; released 26 Aug; c19 Jul 1923; LP19225]. Si; b&w. 35mm. 8 reels, 8,020 ft.

Dir Lambert Hillyer. *Adapt? (see note)* Fred Kennedy Myton, Elliott Clawson, Hope Loring. *Photog* John S. Stumar, Dwight Warren.

Cast: Milton Sills *(Roy Glennister)*, Anna Q. Nilsson *(Cherry Malotte)*, Barbara Bedford *(Helen Chester)*, Robert Edeson *(Joe Dextry)*, Ford Sterling *("Slapjack" Simms)*, Wallace MacDonald *(Broncho Kid)*, Noah Beery *(Alex McNamara)*, Mitchell Lewis *(Marshall Voorhees)*, John Elliott *(Bill Wheaton, Attorney)*, Robert McKim *(Struve)*, Tom McGuire *(Captain Stevens)*, Kate Price *(The Landlady)*, Rockliffe Fellowes *(Matthews)*, Gordon Russell *(Burke)*, Louise Fazenda *(Tilly Nelson)*, Sam De Grasse *(Judge Stillman)*, Albert Roscoe *(Mexico Mullins)*, Jack Curtis *(Bill Nolan)*.

Action melodrama. Source: Rex Beach, *The Spoilers* (New York, 1906). Rex Beach and James MacArthur, *The Spoilers, a Play in Four Acts* (New York, 1906). "Roy Glennister and his partner are victimized by a crooked political plot which involves the possession of gold-mines in Alaska. Alex McNamara [Nome's political boss] and Judge Stillman unite in robbing the owners by jumping their claims. Roy has befriended Helen Chester, Stillman's niece, but believes she is an accomplice. He saves Stillman from hanging, however, but Helen now suspicious of her uncle investigates. She is saved from a compromising situation by her brother and McNamara gets his full dues from the fists of Glennister." (*Moving Picture World,* 7 Jul 1923, p64.) *Uncles. Brother-sister relationship. Political corruption. Gold mines. Mine claims. Alaska. Nome.*

Note: *Moving Picture World* credits Clawson and Loring with the adaptation in addition to Myton.

THE SPOILERS **F2.5335**

Paramount-Publix Corp. 20 Sep **1930** [c19 Sep 1930; LP1591]. Sd (Movietone); b&w. 35mm. 11 reels, 8,128 ft.

Dir Edwin Carewe. *Screenplay* Agnes Brand Leahy. *Adapt-Dial* Bartlett Cormack. *Photog* Harry Fischbeck. *Film Ed* William Shea. *Rec Engr* Harry M. Lindgren.

Cast: Gary Cooper *(Roy Glenister)*, Kay Johnson *(Helen Chester)*, Betty Compson *(Cherry Malotte)*, William Boyd *(Alec McNamara)*, Harry Green *(Herman)*, James Kirkwood *(Joe Dextry)*, Slim Summerville *(Slapjack Simms)*, Lloyd Ingraham *(Judge Stillman)*, Oscar Apfel *(Struve)*, Edward Coxen *(lawyer)*, Jack Trent *(Bronco Kid)*, Edward Hearn *(lieutenant)*, Hal David *(Bill Wheaton)*, Knute Erickson *(Captain Stevens)*, John Beck *(Hansen)*, Jack N. Holmes *(Voorhees)*.

Melodrama. Source: Rex Beach, *The Spoilers* (New York, 1906). On a voyage to Nome, Roy Glenister, one of the several owners of a rich mine, The Midas, is captivated by Helen Chester, while he both fascinates and disquiets her by his primitive nature. He arrives to find his partners, Slapjack Simms and Joe Dextry, befuddled by a trio of no-gooders: Voorhees, the U. S. marshal, Judge Stillman, and McNamara, a politician. Their racket is to cloud title to the various mine claims, eject the miners, and make McNamara owner of the disputed properties. The Midas falls prey to their plotting, and McNamara also steals the personal cache of Glenister, Dextry, and Slapjack, blocking all possibility of their enlisting legal aid from the States. Finally Dextry and Glenister plan a vigilante action, and McNamara calls for a detail of soldiers to protect "his property." The final chase ends with Glenister taking the vengeance that he has been denied by legal process, whipping the tar out of McNamara, and winning the hand of Helen. *Miners. United States marshals. Judges. Politicians. Receivership. Fraud. Injustice. Mines. Alaska. Documentation.*

SPOILERS OF THE WEST **F2.5336**

Metro-Goldwyn-Mayer Pictures. 10 Dec **1927** [c22 Nov 1927; LP24745]. Si; b&w. 35mm. 6 reels, 4,784 ft.

Dir W. S. Van Dyke. *Scen* Madeleine Ruthven, Ross B. Wills. *Titl* Joe Farnham. *Story* John Thomas Neville. *Photog* Clyde De Vinna. *Film Ed* Dan Sharits. *Wardrobe* Lucia Coulter.

Cast: Tim McCoy *(Lieutenant Lang)*, Marjorie Daw *(The Girl)*, William Fairbanks *(The Girl's Brother)*, Chief Big Tree *(Red Cloud)*, Charles Thurston.

Western melodrama. Supported by a handful of Indian Police, an Army lieutenant is assigned, under threat of war from the Indians, to clear out the trappers and white squatters from some Indian land. The settlers are all driven off except for a young girl who owns a trading post. The girl realizes her foolishness, moves from the land, and later weds the lieutenant. Generals Sherman and Custer are depicted. *Indians of North America. Indian Police. Trappers. Squatters. George Armstrong Custer. William Tecumseh Sherman. United States Army—Cavalry.*

SPOOK RANCH (Universal-Jewel) **F2.5337**

Universal Pictures. 20 Sep **1925** [c3 Jun 1925; LP21531]. Si; b&w. 35mm. 6 reels, 5,147 ft.

Dir Edward Laemmle. *Scen* Raymond L. Schrock. *Story* Edward Sedgwick, Raymond L. Schrock. *Photog* Harry Neumann.

Cast: Hoot Gibson *(Bill Bangs)*, Ed Cowles *(George Washington Black)*, Tote Du Crow *(Navarro)*, Helen Ferguson *(Elvira)*, Robert McKim *(Don Ramies)*, Frank Rice *(sheriff)*.

Western melodrama. Bill Bangs and his Negro valet, George Washington Black, stray into a mining town and are arrested when they attempt to steal something to eat. The sheriff promises them their freedom if they solve the mystery of a haunted house near the town. Bill agrees, the sheriff makes him a deputy, and he and George go to the house, quickly discovering that it is being used as the hideout for a gang of outlaws, led by Don Ramies, who are trying to find the location of a ranchowner's gold mine. Bill foils the plans of the outlaws, brings Ramies to justice, and wins the love of the rancher's daughter. *Sheriffs. Ranchers. Valets. Gangs. Theft. Gold mines. Haunted houses. Mining towns.*

THE SPORT OF THE GODS **F2.5338**

Reol Productions. ca23 Apr **1921** [Washington showing]. Si; b&w. 35mm. 7 reels.

Pers Supv Robert Levy. *Dir* Henry Vernot.

Cast: Elizabeth Boyer *(Kitty Hamilton)*, Edward R. Abrams *(Jim Skaggs)*, George Edward Brown *(Joe Hamilton)*, Leon Williams *(Berry Hamilton)*, Lucille Brown *(Fannie Hamilton)*, Lindsay J. Hall *(Maurice Oakley)*, Jean Armour *(Julia Oakley)*, Stanley Walpole *(Francis Oakley)*, Walter Thomas *(Thomas)*, Lawrence Chenault *("Sadness")*, Ruby Mason *(Mrs. Jones)*, Edna Morton Wilson *(Hattie Sterling)*, Jim Burris *(manager)*, Dink Stewart.

Melodrama. Source: Paul Lawrence Dunbar, *The Sport of the Gods* (New York, 1902). When a Negro Virginian is unjustly sent to prison, his family moves to New York to escape the scorn and gossip of their neighbors. The son falls in with evil companions, and the daughter becomes a singer in an underworld cabaret. The man is released from jail and follows his family to New York, only to discover that his wife, convinced that a penitentiary sentence is the same as a divorce, has remarried. After numerous complications, all ends well. *Virginians. Singers. Reputation. Bigamy. Injustice. Negro life. Cabarets. New York City.*

THE SPORTING AGE **F2.5339**

Columbia Pictures. 2 Mar **1928** [c23 Mar 1928; LP25099]. Si; b&w. 35mm. 6 reels, 5,464 ft.

Prod Harry Cohn. *Dir* Erle C. Kenton. *Cont* Peter Milne. *Adapt* Elmer Harris. *Story* Armand Kaliz. *Photog* Ray June. *Art Dir* Robert E. Lee. *Film Ed* Arthur Roberts. *Asst Dir* Charles Huber.

Cast: Belle Bennett *(Miriam Driscoll)*, Holmes Herbert *(James Driscoll)*, Carroll Nye *(Phillip Kingston)*, Josephine Borio *(Nancy Driscoll)*, Edwards Davis *(The Doctor)*.

Melodrama. James Driscoll's wife, Miriam, thinks he is more interested in his horses than in her. She falls in love with Phillip Kingston, her husband's young secretary, and their love affair develops unhindered by the husband, who is temporarily blinded in a train accident. Gradually Driscoll regains his sight and, unknown to Miriam, he witnesses her efforts to recapture romance with Phillip. He invites to his home his niece, Nancy, who, he hopes, will attract Phillip from his wife. The scheme works, and Driscoll and his wife are reconciled. *Horsemen. Secretaries. Marriage. Infidelity. Blindness.*

THE SPORTING CHANCE **F2.5340**

Tiffany Productions. *Dist* Truart Film Corp. ca21 Jun **1925** [New York showing; c7 Jul 1925; LP21634]. Si; b&w. 35mm. 7 reels, 6,696 ft.

Dir Oscar Apfel. *Adapt* John P. Bernard. *Story* Jack Boyle.

Cast: Lou Tellegen *(Darrell Thornton)*, Dorothy Phillips *(Patricia Winthrop)*, George Fawcett *(Caleb Winthrop)*, Theodore von Eltz *(Robert Selby)*, Sheldon Lewis *(Michael Collins)*, Andrew Clark *(jockey)*, Kentucky Boy *(a horse)*.

Melodrama. Pat Winthrop becomes engaged to Bob Shelby, a southerner who owns Kentucky Boy, a horse entered in the Nassau Handicap. To save her father from going to jail, Pat later breaks her engagement to Bob and accepts the proposal of Darrell Thornton, a smooth bounder insincere in racing as in love. Bob owes Thornton money, and, the night before the handicap, Thornton attaches Kentucky Boy. Bob steals the horse from his stall, and Bob's jockey rides him to victory. The purse saves Pat's father from jail and allows Bob to repay Thornton. Pat and Bob are married. *Southerners. Jockeys. Debt. Horseracing. Nassau Handicap. Horses.*

SPORTING GOODS **F2.5341**

Paramount Famous Lasky Corp. 11 Feb **1928** [c11 Feb 1928; LP24989]. Si; b&w. 35mm. 6 reels, 5,951 ft.

Dir Malcolm St. Clair. *Story-Scen* Ray Harris, Tom Crizer. *Titl* George Marion. *Photog* Edward Cronjager. *Film Ed* Otto Levering.

Cast: Richard Dix *(Richard Shelby)*, Ford Sterling *(Mr. Jordan)*, Gertrude Olmstead *(Alice Eliott)*, Philip Strange *(Henry Thorpe)*, Myrtle Stedman *(Mrs. Elliott)*, Wade Boteler *(Regan)*, Claude King *(Timothy Stanfield)*, Maude Turner Gordon *(Mrs. Stanfield)*.

Comedy. Socialite Alice Eliott mistakes Richard Shelby, a traveling salesman of sporting goods and inventor of a new type of golf suit, for millionaire Timothy Stanfield. Having fallen in love with her, Shelby, afraid to disabuse Alice of the notion that he is wealthy, allows himself to be installed in an expensive California hotel. Following a "get-rich-quick" inspiration, Shelby induces Jordan, head of a department store and a keen golfer, to wear his golf suit made of "elasto-tweed" on the golf course, in hopes that Jordan will buy a great quantity of them. It begins to rain, causing the suit to stretch to the ground. Jordan cancels his order, leaving Shelby with an exorbitant hotel bill. Shelby is caught trying to sneak out of the hotel wearing one of Stanfield's suits. Simultaneously, Jordan returns and doubles his order for the golf suits, having heard that they are the rage in the East; and Stanfield, owner of the company that makes the suits, promotes Shelby to sales manager, thus providing Shelby with enough money to marry Alice Eliott. *Socialites. Traveling salesmen. Millionaires. Golf. Clothes. Clothing manufacture. Mistaken identity.*

SPORTING LIFE (Universal-Jewel) **F2.5342**

Universal Pictures. 29 Nov **1925** [c16 Oct 1925; LP21919]. Si; b&w. 35mm. 7 reels, 6,709 ft.

Pres by Carl Laemmle. *Dir* Maurice Tourneur. *Adapt-Cont* Curtis Benton. *Photog* Arthur Todd. *Art Dir* Leo E. Kuter.

Cast: Bert Lytell *(Lord Woodstock)*, Marian Nixon *(Norah Cavanaugh)*, Paulette Duval *(Olive Carteret)*, Cyril Chadwick *(Phillips)*, Charles Delaney *(Joe Lee)*, George Siegmann *(Dan Crippen)*, Oliver Eckhardt *(Cavanaugh)*, Ena Gregory, Kathleen Clifford *(chorus girls)*, Frank Finch Smiles, Ted "Kid" Lewis *(boxers)*.

Melodrama. Source: Cecil Raleigh and Seymour Hicks, *Sporting Life* (a play; c12 Jan 1898). Lord Woodstock loses money in a musical revue that starred dancer Olive Carteret. He will be ruined unless his horse, Lady Luck, runs in the Derby, and he cannot afford to run the horse unless his protégé, Joe Lee, wins a forthcoming fight. He incurs Olive's enmity by falling in love with Norah Cavanaugh, daughter of his horsetrainer. Olive conspires with Phillips, a gambler, to drug Lee, but Woodstock takes his place in the ring and wins the fight. Lee overhears Olive and Phillips plot to kidnap Norah and thus force Woodstock to withdraw Lady Luck from the Derby. He kills Olive but is too late to prevent Phillips from abducting Norah. Lee and Woodstock are imprisoned when they attempt to rescue Norah. Lee is killed, but Woodstock escapes, Lady Luck wins the race, Phillips is arrested for murder, and Norah and Woodstock are free to marry. *Prizefighters. Gamblers. Dancers. Horseracing. Kidnaping. Horses.*

THE SPORTING LOVER **F2.5343**

Faultless Pictures. *Dist* First National Pictures. 17 Jun **1926** [c2 Jun 1926; LP22792]. Si; b&w. 35mm. 7 reels, 6,642 ft.

Pres by E. M. Asher, Edward Small. *Dir* Alan Hale. *Titl* Malcolm Stuart Boylan. *Adapt* Carey Wilson. *Photog* Faxon M. Dean, Robert Newhard. *Art Dir* Horace Jackson. *Film Ed* Edward M. Roskam. *Prod Mgr* Ben Verschleiser.

Cast: Conway Tearle *(Capt. Terance Connaughton)*, Barbara Bedford

(Lady Gwendolyn Cavens), Ward Crane *(Capt. Sir Phillip Barton)*, Arthur Rankin *(Algernon Cavens)*, Charles McHugh *(Paddy, Connaughton's servant)*, John Fox, Jr. *(Aloysius Patrick O'Brien, his son)*, Bodil Rosing *(Nora O'Brien)*, George Ovey *(jockey)*, "Good Luck", "Bad Luck" *(The Horses)*.

Romantic drama. Source: Seymour Hicks and Ian Hay, *Good Luck* (London production: 1923). During the war, Capt. Terance Connaughton loses his prize horses in a card game with Algernon Cavens and Sir Phillip Barton. Shortly afterward, he is wounded and sent to a field hospital where he meets Gwendolyn, Cavens' sister, who nurses him, and they fall in love. During an air raid Gwen and Terance are buried beneath a pile of debris and when found are evacuated to different hospitals. With the Armistice, Terance returns home broken in spirit and poverty-stricken; and learning that Gwen is about to marry Barton, he declines to see her. Gwen tries to postpone the wedding and finally agrees with Barton that if "Good Luck" wins in a race, she may decide the wedding arrangement, and if "Bad Luck" wins, Barton reserves the right to do so. When "Bad Luck" wins, Paddy and Aloysius, Terance's servants, reveal that the horses have been switched by Barton; Lady Gwen denounces him and resumes her abandoned romance with Terance. *Nurses. Gambling. Horseracing. Poverty. Aerial bombardment. World War I. England. Horses.*

THE SPORTING VENUS **F2.5344**

Metro-Goldwyn Pictures. 13 Apr **1925** [c21 May 1925; LP21515]. Si; b&w. 35mm. 7 reels, 5,938 ft.

Pres by Louis B. Mayer. *Dir* Marshall Neilan. *Scen* Thomas J. Geraghty. *Photog* David Kesson. *Art Dir* Cedric Gibbons. *Film Ed* Blanche Sewell. *Asst Dir* Thomas Held. *Wardrobe* Ethel P. Chaffin.

Cast: Blanche Sweet *(Lady Gwendolyn)*, Ronald Colman *(Donald MacAllan)*, Lew Cody *(Prince Carlos)*, Josephine Crowell *(Countess Van Alstyne)*, Edward Martindel *(Sir Alfred Grayle)*, Kate Price *(housekeeper)*, Hank Mann *(Carlos' valet)*, Arthur Hoyt *(detective)*, George Fawcett *(Father)*.

Romantic drama. Source: Gerald Beaumont, "The Sporting Venus," in *Red Book* (43:58–61, Jun 1924). Lady Gwen, the last of the sporting Grayles, falls in love with Donald MacAllan, a bright young medical student far below her station. Gwen's father, who opposes the match, introduces her to Prince Carlos, who wishes to marry her in order to pay off his creditors. Donald enlists during the World War, and Carlos continues his courtship. When Donald returns from the fighting, Carlos tells him that he is engaged to Gwen, and Donald therefore makes no attempt to see her. Gwen mistakes Donald's seeming indifference for contempt and seeks to forget him by living riotously in several European capitals. Having exhausted her fortune and ruined her health, Gwen returns to Scotland and goes to live in the same cottage where Donald used to study. She becomes ill and in delirium calls for Donald. Her old nurse goes to fetch him at the Grayle estate, which, having become wealthy, he has just bought. Donald rescues Gwen (who has wandered out in a storm) and nurses her back to health. *Students. Physicians. Sportswomen. Nobility. Royalty. Debt. Dissipation. World War I. Scotland. Storms.*

SPORTING WEST **F2.5345**

Roberts & Cole. *Dist* Aywon Film Corp. 13 Apr **1925** [New York State license]. Si; b&w. 35mm. 5 reels, 4,850 ft.

Story Scott Darling.

Cast: Big Boy Williams, Peggy O'Day.

Western melodrama(?). No information about the nature of this film has been found.

SPORTING YOUTH (Universal-Jewel) **F2.5346**

Universal Pictures. 4 Feb **1924** [c16 Jan 1924; LP19829]. Si; b&w. 35mm. 7 reels, 6,712 ft.

Dir Harry A. Pollard. *Scen* Harvey Thew. *Story* Byron Morgan. *Photog* Clyde De Vinna.

Cast: Reginald Denny *(Jimmy Wood)*, Laura La Plante *(Betty Rockford)*, Hallam Cooley *(Walter Berg)*, Frederick Vroom *(John K. Walker)*, Lucille Ward *(Mrs. Rockford)*, Malcolm Denny *("Splinters" Wood)*, Leo White *("The Souse")*, Henry Barrows *(William Rockford)*, Rolfe Sedan *(valet)*, L. J. O'Connor *(The Cop)*, C. L. Sherwood, William A. Carroll *(detectives)*.

Comedy-drama. Jimmy Wood, a chauffeur, is mistaken for famous racing driver "Splinters" Wood. Because he is deeply in debt, he enters a race on the advice of Betty Rockford, daughter of a wealthy automobile manufacturer. Secretly, she helps Wood win the race. *Chauffeurs. Automobile manufacturers. Automobile racing. Impersonation. Mistaken identity. Debt.*

Note: Working titles: *There He Goes, The Spice of Life.*

THE SPOTLIGHT **F2.5347**

Paramount Famous Lasky Corp. 19 Nov **1927** [c19 Nov 1927; LP24674]. Si; b&w. 35mm. 5 reels, 4,866 ft.

Pres by Adolph Zukor, Jesse L. Lasky. *Dir* Frank Tuttle. *Titl* Herman Mankiewicz. *Adapt* Hope Loring. *Photog* Victor Milner. *Film Ed* Louis D. Lighton.

Cast: Esther Ralston *(Lizzie Stokes/Olga Rostova)*, Neil Hamilton *(Norman Brooke)*, Nicholas Soussanin *(Daniel Hoffman)*, Arlette Marchal *(Maggie Courtney)*, Arthur Housman *(Ebbetts)*.

Romantic drama. Source: Rita Weiman, "Footlights," in *Saturday Evening Post* (191:53–54, 17 May 1919). Lizzie Stokes, an obscure and colorless actress, is elevated to stardom through publicity and better coaching from Daniel Hoffman, a theatrical producer. As Olga Rostova, an exotic Russian, she meets Norman Brooke, whose infatuation turns to love. Hoffman suggests that Norman could never care for Lizzie and proves his point. Heartbroken, Lizzie decides to see no more of him. On closing night, when he proposes to her in her dressing room and she refuses, Norman declares he must believe all the lurid details of her past; in desperation, she bares her true identity, only to find it is not her glamorous image but rather her real self that he loves. *Actors. Theatrical producers. Impersonation. Personal identity.*

SPRING FEVER **F2.5348**

Metro-Goldwyn-Mayer Pictures. 22 Oct **1927** [c14 Sep 1927; LP24401]. Si; b&w. 35mm. 7 reels, 6,705 ft.

Dir Edward Sedgwick. *Screenplay* Albert Lewin, Frank Davis. *Titl* Ralph Spence. *Photog* Ira Morgan. *Sets* Cedric Gibbons, David Townsend. *Film Ed* Frank Sullivan. *Wardrobe* David Cox.

Cast: William Haines *(Jack Kelly)*, Joan Crawford *(Allie Monte)*, George K. Arthur *(Eustace Tewksbury)*, George Fawcett *(Mr. Waters)*, Eileen Percy *(Martha Lomsdom)*, Edward Earle *(Johnson)*, Bert Woodruff *(Pop Kelly)*, Lee Moran *(Oscar)*.

Romantic comedy. Source: Vincent Lawrence, *Spring Fever* (New York opening: 3 Aug 1925). "Jack Kelly, wise-cracking shipping clerk, secures a card to an exclusive country club, and meets Allie Monte, who after some wooing reciprocates his love. Through a series of disillusionments Kelly maintains his balance, alternately playing the rich guy, and finally, his rivals vanquished, he succeeds in winning the girl, who proves to be wealthy in her own right." (*Moving Picture World,* 10 Dec 1927, p42.) *Shipping clerks. Wealth. Country clubs.*

SPRING IS HERE **F2.5349**

First National Pictures. 13 Apr **1930** [c28 Apr 1930; LP12611]. Sd (Vitaphone); b&w. 35mm. 8 reels, 6,386 ft.

Dir John Francis Dillon. *Adapt* James A. Starr. *Photog* Lee Garmes. *Songs: "Spring Is Here in Person," "Yours Sincerely," "Rich Man, Poor Man," "Baby's Awake Now," "With a Song in My Heart"* Lorenz Hart, Richard Rodgers. *Songs: "Cryin' for the Carolines," "Have a Little Faith in Me," "Bad Baby," "How Shall I Tell?"* Sam Lewis, Joe Young, Harry Warren.

Cast: Lawrence Gray *(Steve Alden)*, Alexander Gray *(Terry Clayton)*, Bernice Claire *(Betty Braley)*, Ford Sterling *(Peter Braley)*, Louise Fazenda *(Emily Braley)*, Inez Courtney *(Mary Jane Braley)*, Natalie Moorhead *(Rita Clayton)*, Frank Albertson *(Stacy Hayden)*, Gretchen Thomas *(Maude Osgood)*, The Brox Sisters.

Romantic musical drama. Source: Owen Davis, Lorenz Hart, and Richard Rogers, *Spring Is Here* (New York opening: 11 Mar 1929). Peter Braley, the blustering father of Betty, disapproves of her affection for Steve Alden, whom Betty favors in preference to Terry Clayton, another suitor, and he loses all patience with her on discovering she has returned home at 5 a. m. with Steve. Discouraged, Terry is advised by Mary Jane, Betty's 18-year-old sister, to make Betty jealous; and on the first opportune occasion, he reveals unsuspected ability in capturing the attention of susceptible women, making sure that Betty is aware of it. Although Betty's jealousy is aroused, she carries through, but when her father banishes Alden from his house and he returns to elope with Betty, Terry intervenes and carries her off himself. *Sisters. Fatherhood. Courtship. Jealousy.*

SPUDS **F2.5350**

Larry Semon Productions. *Dist* Pathé Exchange. 10 Apr **1927** [c4 Feb 1927; LU23635]. Si; b&w. 35mm. 5 reels, 4,930 ft.

Pres by John Adams. *Dir-Writ* Larry Semon. *Photog* H. F. Koenekamp, James Brown.

Cast: Larry Semon *("Spuds")*, Dorothy Dwan *(Madelon)*, Edward Hearn *(captain [Arthur])*, Kewpie Morgan *(sergeant)*, Robert Graves *(general)*, Hazel Howell *(Bertha)*, Hugh Fay *(spy)*.

Farce. Spuds, an American private in France, assigned to KP duty, meets his buddy, Arthur McLaughlin, a Boston banker, in a dugout. He learns that Arthur will be court-martialed unless he recovers a pay car containing $250,000 that was stolen while in his care, and that two spies in the neighborhood are believed to be the source of the trouble. In Mayonnaise, Spuds meets and falls in love with Madelon, a French waitress, but the doughboy is forced to flee for his life. By accident he discovers the whereabouts of the pay car and brings it back across a battlefield, through attacks from all sides. He arrives to save the captain from being shot and is fittingly rewarded. *Waitresses. Germans. Spies. Courts-martial. World War I. France. United States Army.*

SPURS **F2.5351**

Hoot Gibson Productions. *Dist* Universal Pictures. 24 Aug **1930** [c11 Aug 1930; LP1482]. Sd (Movietone); b&w. 35mm. 6 reels, 5,303 ft. [Also si.]

Pres by Carl Laemmle. *Dir-Story-Dial* Reaves Eason. *Photog* Harry Neumann. *Rec Engr* C. Roy Hunter.

Cast: Hoot Gibson *(Bob Merrill)*, Helen Wright *(Peggy Bradley)*, Robert Homans *(Pop Merrill)*, Frank Clark *(Charles Bradley)*, Buddy Hunter *(Buddy Hazlet)*, Gilbert Holmes *(Shorty)*, William Bertram *(Indian Joe)*, Philo McCullough *(Tom Marsden)*, Cap Anderson *(Pecos)*, Pete Morrison *(Blackie)*, Artie Ortega *(Eagle-claw)*.

Western melodrama. Seeking Indian Joe, suspected of murdering the father of 12-year-old Buddy Hazlet, Bob Merrill and his friend Shorty secretly enter the stronghold of the Pecos gang. They learn that the actual killer is Tom Marsden, foreman of the Merrill ranch and also a gang member. At a riding contest in which members of the gang are pitted against Bob, he is told by Peggy, his sweetheart, that his friends Shorty and Buddy have been captured and taken to the gang's stronghold. Descending from a precipice, Bob frees his friends; and when the gang returns, he fires on them with their own machineguns. They are captured, Marsden confesses to the Hazlet murder, and Bob wins the love of the girl. *Ranch foremen. Gangs. Indians of North America. Murder. Horsemanship.*

SPURS AND SADDLES (Blue Streak Western) **F2.5352**

Universal Pictures. 17 Jul w*1927* [c4 Jun 1927; LP24044]. Si; b&w. 35mm. 5 reels, 4,867 ft.

Pres by Carl Laemmle. *Dir* Clifford S. Smith. *Adapt-Scen* Harrison Jacobs. *Story* Paul M. Bryan. *Photog* Eddie Linden. *Art Dir* David S. Garber.

Cast: Art Acord *(Jack Marley)*, Fay Wray *(Mildred Orth)*, Bill Dyer *(Bud Bailey)*, J. Gordon Russell *("Blaze" Holton)*, C. E. Anderson *("Hawk")*, Monte Montague *(stage driver)*, Raven *(himself, a horse)*.

Western melodrama. Jack Marley, seeking adventure in the frontier West, finds a Pony Express rider mortally wounded and delivers his mailbag to Caspar. En route, he stops a runaway stage and gains the admiration of Mildred Orth from the East, who is searching for her father, Norman, lost since her childhood. The local boss and owner of the dancehall, "Hawk" Kent, covets the girl and orders Blaze Holton to frame her. She is compelled to work out her board in the dancehall. Jack auctions his horse to help her, then aids her escape. Blaze offers his aid against Kent, and before dying he tells Mildred he is her father and leaves his money to her. *Frontier and pioneer life. Dancehalls. Fatherhood. Pony Express. Horses.*

THE SQUALL **F2.5353**

First National Pictures. 9 May **1929** [New York premiere; released May; c10 Jun 1929; LP445]. Sd (Vitaphone); b&w. 35mm. 11 reels, 9,456 ft. [Also si, 23 Jun; 7,085 ft.]

Pres by Richard A. Rowland, Richard A. Rowland. *Dir* Alexander Korda, Alexander Korda. *Screenplay-Dial* Bradley King. *Titl* Paul Perez. *Photog* John Seitz. *Film Ed* Edward Schroeder. *Mus Synchronization & Score* Leo Forbstein. *Song: "Gypsy Charmer"* Grant Clarke, Harry Akst.

Cast: Myrna Loy *(Nubi)*, Richard Tucker *(Josef Lajos)*, Alice Joyce *(Maria, his wife)*, Carroll Nye *(Paul)*, Loretta Young *(Irma)*, Harry Cording *(Peter)*, ZaSu Pitts *(Lena)*, Nicholas Soussanin *(El Moro)*, Knute Erickson *(Uncle Dani)*, George Hackathorne *(Niki)*.

Melodrama. Source: Jean Bart, *The Squall, a Drama in Three Acts* (New York, 1932). The serene love of farmer Josef Lajos and his wife, Maria, the youthful romance of their son, Paul, with Irma, and the betrothal of their servants, Peter and Lena, are suddenly interrupted by a "squall" and the arrival of a Gypsy camp near the farm. The squall is in the person of Nubi, an exotic, amoral beauty who finds sanctuary with the Lajos family under the pretense that she is actually a Christian by birth. Peter is the first to succumb to her charms, and he recklessly spends his savings on trinkets for her—and hours in the field with her. Then she turns to Paul, a college student, who soon loses interest in his studies and in Irma. Peter is fired when Nubi convinces Lajos that he has forced himself on her. Then, Lajos himself submits to her charm. When a veritable storm threatens, El Moro enters the house, declaring that he has been married to Nubi for 4 years and that she is the daughter of a chieftan. As Nubi and her mocking laughter subside, the sun breaks through the clouds, and all is sweet and serene again. *Farmers. Gypsies. Family life. Courtship. Infidelity. Revenge. Hungary. Squalls.*

SQUARE CROOKS **F2.5354**

Fox Film Corp. 4 Mar **1928** [c22 Feb 1928; LP25008]. Si; b&w. 35mm. 6 reels, 5,397 ft.

Pres by William Fox. *Prod* Philip Klein. *Dir* Lewis Seiler. *Scen* Becky Gardiner. *Titl* Malcolm S. Boylan. *Photog* Rudolph Bergquist. *Film Ed* Jack Dennis. *Asst Dir* Horace Hough.

Cast: Robert Armstrong *(Eddie Ellison)*, John Mack Brown *(Larry Scott)*, Dorothy Dwan *(Jane Brown)*, Dorothy Appleby *(Kay Ellison)*, Eddie Sturgis *(Mike Ross)*, Clarence Burton *(Harry Welsh)*, Jackie Coombs *(Phillip Carson)*, Lydia Dickson *(Slavey)*.

Crook melodrama. Source: James P. Judge, *Square Crooks; a Comedy-Mystery Play* (New York, 1927). "Two young crooks decide to lead honest life, but one wavers and takes charge of jewelry swiped by member of old gang. His pal returns this in time to avert arrest. Both decide an honest life is the best and get jobs as chauffeurs, one marrying telephone operator of a big hotel." (*Motion Picture News Booking Guide,* [14]:285, 1929.) *Criminals—Rehabilitation. Chauffeurs. Telephone operators.*

SQUARE JOE **F2.5355**

E. S. & L. Colored Feature Productions. **1921.** Si; b&w. 35mm. [Feature length assumed.

Cast: Joe Jeanette, John Lester Johnson, Marion Moore, Bob Slater.

Melodrama(?). No information about the precise nature of this film has been found. *Negro life.*

SQUARE SHOULDERS **F2.5356**

Pathé Exchange. 10 Mar **1929** [c18 Mar 1929; LP216]. Talking sequences (Photophone); b&w. 35mm. 7 reels, 5,438 ft. [Also si; 5,477 ft.]

Supv Paul Bern. *Dir* E. Mason Hopper. *Titl* John Krafft. *Adapt* Peggy Prior. *Story* George Dromgold, Houston Branch. *Photog* David Abel. *Film Ed* Barbara Hunter. *Asst Dir* Lonnie D'Orsa. *Prod Mgr* Richard Blaydon. Robert McCrellis.

Cast: Louis Wolheim *(Slag)*, Junior Coughlan *(Tad)*, Philippe De Lacy *(Eddie)*, Anita Louise *(Mary Jane)*, Montague Shaw *(Cartwright)*, Johnny Morris *(Hook)*, Kewpie Morgan *(Delicate Don)*, Clarence Geldert *(commandant)*, Erich von Stroheim, Jr., Chuck Reisner, Jr..

Melodrama. A hero in the Great War, Slag has become a hobo, living by his wits and a little theft. Together with two partners in crime, Slag returns to his hometown and finds that his wife has died, leaving no one to care for his son, Tad. Slag takes pity on the boy and steals enough to send him to military school. Slag himself finds work there as a stableboy and teaches Tad to ride and to blow the bugle. Slag's former partners in crime show up and force him to help them rob the academy. Tad walks in on the three as they are dividing the spoils, and Slag is killed by a bullet meant for the boy. Tad plays taps over his grave, never having known that Slag was his own father. *War heroes. Tramps. Orphans. Stableboys. Buglers. Murder. Fatherhood. Robbery. Military schools. World War I.*

THE SQUEALER **F2.5357**

Columbia Pictures. 20 Aug **1930** [c3 Sep 1930; LP1536]. Sd (Movietone); b&w. 35mm. 7 reels, 6,358 ft. [Also si.]

Prod Harry Cohn. *Dir* Harry J. Brown. *Screenplay* Dorothy Howell. *Cont* Casey Robinson. *Dial* Jo Swerling. *Photog* Ted Tetzlaff. *Art Dir* Edward Jewell. *Tech Dir* edward Shult er. *Film Ed* Leonard Wheeler. *Sd*

Rec Engr Edward Bernds.

Cast: Jack Holt *(Charles Hart)*, Dorothy Revier *(Margaret Hart)*, Davey Lee *(Bunny Hart)*, Matt Moore *(John Sheridan)*, ZaSu Pitts *(Bella)*, Robert Ellis *(Valletti)*, Mathew Betz *(Red Majors)*, Arthur Housman *(Mitter Davis)*, Louis Natheaux *(Edwards)*, Eddie Kane *(Whisper)*, Eddie Sturgis *(The Killer)*, Elmer Ballard *(Pimply-face)*.

Underworld melodrama. Source: Mark Linder, *The Squealer* (New York opening: 12 Nov 1928). Charlie Hart, ostensibly in real estate, operates an undercover bootlegging trade and is an underworld power, with no mercy for his opponents. When Ratface Edwards tips off Valletti—Hart's business rival and enemy—he is quickly eliminated by Mitter Davis, Hart's right-hand man. His business is the source of many quarrels between Hart and his wife, Margaret, who is secretly loved by John Sheridan, Hart's lawyer and best friend. Hart goes to see Valletti, who plans to get revenge on Davis, but violence is avoided; later, Valletti is found dead and Hart flees to a resort; but Valletti's men learn of his whereabouts from his young son, Bunny. Hart is caught and sentenced to a 7-year prison term. Following a prison break, he seeks revenge on Margaret and Sheridan, but realizing his son will be better off in the care of the lawyer, Hart disguises himself as Sheridan and walks into the trap he has prepared for him. *Bootleggers. Lawyers. Gangsters. Informers. Speakeasies. Prison escapes.*

SQUIRE PHIN **F2.5358**

San Antonio Pictures. *Dist* Producers Security Corp. Apr or 10 Oct **1921.** Si; b&w. 35mm. 5 reels, 5,100 ft.

Dir Leopold Wharton, Robert H. Townley. *Scen* Lee Royal. *Photog* John K. Holbrook.

Cast: Maclyn Arbuckle *(Phineas Look, "Squire Phin")*.

Rural comedy-drama. Source: Holman Francis Day, *Squire Phin* (New York, 1905). Squire Phin endears himself to the residents of Palermo for his ability to settle all disputes; while his brother, Hiram, who returns after 10 years' absence, is well remembered and disliked for being the town bully. Hiram learns that Judge Willard is using the town treasury for his own ends and seeks to defeat him in an election. Meanwhile, Squire Phin, who loves Willard's sister, campaigns for the judge. Hiram is appeased when Squire Phin persuades Judge Willard to return the money, and the peacemaker receives the judge's permission to marry his sister. *Brothers. Peacemakers. Bullies. Judges. Embezzlement. Elections.*

STACKED CARDS **F2.5359**

Circle Productions. 27 May **1926** [New York State license]. Si; b&w. 35mm. 5 reels.

Pres by Fred J. Balshofer. *Dir* Robert Eddy. *Scen* Guy C. Cleveland. *Story* William D. Geiger. *Photog* Ernest Haller.

Cast: Fred Church *(Steve Spencer)*, Kathryn McGuire *(Fay Hall)*, Robert Thurston *(Zack Miller)*, John Watson *("Dad" Hall)*, Art Ortega *("Poker Face" Pete)*.

Western melodrama(?). No information about the nature of this film has been found.

STAGE COACH DRIVER (Reissue) **F2.5360**

Dist Aywon Film Corp. Oct **1924** [scheduled release]. Si; b&w. 35mm. 5 reels, 5,480 ft.

Note: Originally released by Selig Polyscope Co., ca1916, in 2 or 3 reels, starring Tom Mix.

STAGE KISSES **F2.5361**

Columbia Pictures. 2 Nov **1927** [c3 Dec 1927; LP24720]. Si; b&w. 35mm. 6 reels, 5,435 ft.

Prod Harry Cohn. *Dir* Albert Kelly. *Adapt-Cont* Dorothy Howell. *Photog* Joseph Walker. *Art Dir* Robert E. Lee. *Asst Dir* Clifford Saum.

Cast: Kenneth Harlan *(Donald Hampton)*, Helene Chadwick *(Fay Leslie)*, John Patrick *(Keith Carlin)*, Phillips Smalley *(John Clarke)*, Ethel Wales *(Mrs. John Clarke)*, Frances Raymond *(Mrs. Hampton)*.

Society melodrama. Fay Leslie, a chorus girl, marries Donald Hampton, scion of an aristocratic New York family, and his mother disinherits him. Donald is reduced to financial straits, and Fay calls on Keith Carlin, an unsuccessful suitor, who agrees to reinstitute for her a former theatrical booking. Donald's uncle, John Clarke, uses this incident to instill suspicion in the mind of Donald. While Donald is at his club, Keith calls upon Fay, and when he tries to force his attentions upon her, she horsewhips him out of her apartment; he vengefully provokes a compromising situation for Donald's benefit. Clarke refuses to assist her; and to teach him a lesson, she skillfully creates a similar situation in his own home, obliging him to defend her cause. Donald forces a confession from Keith, and the Hampton family receives Fay with open arms. *Aristocrats. Chorus girls. Uncles. Marriage. Wealth. Infidelity. Revenge. Disinheritance. Flagellation.*

STAGE MADNESS **F2.5362**

Fox Film Corp. 9 Jan **1927** [c9 Jan 1927; LP23570]. Si; b&w. 35mm. 6 reels, 5,620 ft.

Pres by William Fox. *Dir* Victor Schertzinger. *Scen* Randall H. Faye. *Story* Polan Banks. *Photog* Glen MacWilliams. *Asst Dir* William Tummel.

Cast: Virginia Valli *(Madame Lamphier)*, Tullio Carminati *(Andrew Marlowe)*, Virginia Bradford *(Dora Anderson)*, Lou Tellegen *(Pierre Doumier)*, Richard Walling *(Jimmy Mason)*, Tyler Brooke *(H. H. Bragg)*, Lillian Knight *(French maid)*, Bodil Rosing *(maid)*.

Melodrama. Madame Lamphier, a ballet dancer, tires of domestic life after the birth of her daughter, Dora, and returns to the stage. Her husband, Andrew, however, disappears with her daughter. Years later, Madame Lamphier is injured by a fall, and when a younger girl threatens to take her place, Lamphier in a jealous rage shoots the manager, Pierre, and frames the girl for murder. When she discovers that the girl is her own long-lost daughter, she herself dies. *Dancers. Desertion. Motherhood. Ballet. Murder.*

A STAGE ROMANCE **F2.5363**

Fox Film Corp. 5 Mar **1922** [c5 Mar 1922; LP17741]. Si; b&w. 35mm. 7 reels, 6,416 ft.

Pres by William Fox. *Dir* Herbert Brenon. *Scen* Paul H. Sloane. *Photog* Tom Malloy.

Cast: William Farnum *(Kean)*, Peggy Shaw *(Anna Damby)*, Holmes Herbert *(Prince of Wales)*, Mario Carillo *(Lord Melville)*, Paul McAllister *(Count Koefeld)*, Etienne Gerardot *(Salomon)*, Bernard Seigel *(Mr. Sleeker)*, Hal De Forrest *(Old Bob)*, Edward Kipling *(Darious [hairdresser])*, Harry Grippe *(John [prizefighter])*, Augustus Balfour *(stage manager)*, Jack Collins *(Bardolph)*, Cuyler Supplee *(Tom)*, Edward Boring *(Needles [spy])*, Myrtle Bonillas *(Countess Koefeld)*, Paula Shay *(Amy, Countess of Goswill)*, Viva Verome *(Gidsa)*, Florence Ashbrook *(Mrs. Bob)*, America Chedister *(Lady Anne Boyle)*, Ruth D. Goodwin *(Little Emily)*.

Biographical melodrama. Source: Alexandre Dumas, père, *Kean, ou désordre et génie* (1836). Edmund Kean, the great Shakespearean actor at the zenith of his popularity in London, is inspired by the Countess Koefeld. Among his devoted admirers is Anna Damby, whose guardian plans to force a marriage with Lord Melville, a roué. When Anna seeks Kean's aid, Melville's spy reports that she has eloped. Kean refutes the rumor at a reception given by the Koefelds and announces a benefit performance for a crippled child. Meanwhile, Melville lures Anna to an inn, but her kidnapers are thrashed by Kean, who happens on the scene. At the benefit performance, Kean—believing the Prince of Wales to be a rival for the countess' affections—begs the prince not to appear in the Koefeld box, but he ignores the request. Seeing the prince, a fit of madness overtakes Kean; he denounces the prince from the stage and is taken fainting to his dressing room, where he explains complications regarding the countess' presence in his chamber and apologizes to the prince. Ultimately he and Anna are united. *Actors. Nobility. Theater. London. George Prince of Wales. Edmund Kean.*

STAGE STRUCK **F2.5364**

Famous Players–Lasky. *Dist* Paramount Pictures. 16 Nov **1925** [c16 Nov 1925; LP22007]. Si; b&w with col sequences (Technicolor). 35mm. 7 reels, 6,691 ft.

Dir Allan Dwan. *Screenplay* Forrest Halsey. *Adapt* Sylvia La Varre. *Story* Frank R. Adams. *Photog* George Webber. *Art Dir* Van Nest Polglase.

Cast: Gloria Swanson *(Jennie Hagen)*, Lawrence Gray *(Orme Wilson)*, Gertrude Astor *(Lillian Lyons)*, Marguerite Evans *(Hilda Wagner)*, Ford Sterling *(Waldo Buck)*, Carrie Scott *(Mrs. Wagner)*, Emil Hoch *(Mr. Wagner)*, Margery Whittington *(soubrette)*.

Comedy. Jennie Hagen, a stagestruck waitress in a diner, is in love with the cook, Orme Wilson, who has a weakness for actresses. The *Water Queen*, a showboat, arrives, and Orme falls for the leading lady, Lillian Lyons. Jennie tries to win him back by taking a correspondence course in acting. Buck, the manager of the show, gives her a chance, billing her as "The Masked Marvel" in a boxing fight with Lillian. The exhibition disgusts Orme; and Jennie, in despair, jumps overboard. Orme comes to her rescue; they are reconciled and later open up their own diner. *Actors. Cooks. Waitresses. Correspondence courses. Showboats. Diners* *(restaurants).*

Note: Working title: *Screen Struck.* The opening sequence, where Jennie dreams of herself as a famous actress, and the closing sequence, with Jennie and Orme in their diner, are in color.

STAIRS OF SAND **F2.5365**

Paramount Famous Lasky Corp. 8 Jun **1929** [c7 Jun 1929; LP466]. Si; b&w. 35mm. 6 reels, 5,020 ft.

Dir Otto Brower. *Titl* Ben Grauman Kohn. *Adapt* Agnes Brand Leahy, Sam Mintz, J. Walter Ruben. *Photog* Rex Wimpy. *Film Ed* Frances Marsh.

Cast: Wallace Beery *(Guerd Larey)*, Jean Arthur *(Ruth Hutt)*, Phillips R. Holmes *(Adam Wansfell)*, Fred Kohler *(Boss Stone)*, Chester Conklin *(Tim)*, Guy Oliver *(Sheriff Collishaw)*, Lillian Worth *(Babe)*, Frank Rice *(stage driver)*, Clarence L. Sherwood *(waiter).*

Romantic western drama. Source: Zane Grey, *Stairs of Sand* (New York, 1943). Guerd Larey holds up a stagecoach and takes the money with which Ruth Hunt had hoped to leave the town of Lost Lake forever; as a result, she is forced to take a dancing job in Boss Stone's dancehall. Guerd derides Sheriff Collishaw and Stone's attempts to capture the bandit. Boss Stone tries to win Ruth's love, and in order to escape, she steals Guerd's wallet. Though he catches her, he is sympathetic upon discovering that it was she whose money he stole. He becomes a boarder at her cabin and begins to fall in love with her. Meanwhile, the sheriff suspects Adam Wansfell, a stranger from the East, but Guerd saves him by claiming he is his nephew. Ruth falls in love with the young stranger, and they plan to elope; but Guerd, wounded in a robbery attempt, returns to the cabin. Adam claims he is the bandit, hoping to save Guerd; but Guerd, realizing his loyalty, leaves proof of his own guilt, and Ruth frees Adam in time to prevent his hanging. *Bandits. Sheriffs. Courtship. Dancehalls. Stagecoach robberies.*

THE STAMPEDE **F2.5366**

Victor Kremer Film Features. Oct **1921** [New York State]. Si; b&w. 35mm. 5 reels.

Dir Francis Ford. *Adapt* Kingsley Benedict. *Story* Eugenie Kremer. *Rec Engr* Harold C. Lewis.

Cast: Texas Guinan *(Tex Henderson)*, Francis Ford *(Robert Wagner)*, Frederick Moore *(Jim Henderson, Tex's father)*, Jean Carpenter *(Mary, Robert Wagner's little motherless daughter)*, Vale Rio *(Pancho, Snowflake's trainer)*, Fred Kohler *(Steve Norton)*, Cecil McLean *(Sylvia Dean, Tex's cousin)*, Kingsley Benedict *(Beauty Anders)*, Snowflake *(a horse).*

Western melodrama(?). No information about the precise nature of this film has been found. *Stampedes. Horses.*

STAMPEDE THUNDER **F2.5367**

Lariat Productions. *Dist* Vitagraph Co. of America. c21 Nov **1925** [LP22047]. Si; b&w. 35mm. 5 reels, 4,820 ft.

Dir Tom Gibson. *Story-Cont* Victor Roberts.

Cast: Pete Morrison, Betty Goodwin, Lightning *(himself, a horse).*

Western melodrama. A band of rustlers, after a pitched battle with honest cattlemen, drive off hundreds of cattle. The leader of the cattlemen (played by Pete Morrison) follows but is captured. His horse, Lightning, escapes and leads a sheriff's posse to the bandits' lair. Pete is saved, but the outlaw chief escapes. Pete follows, with the heroine (played by Betty Goodwin) trailing behind. In the end, the gang leader and the remnants of his band are defeated. *Rustlers. Ranchers. Posses. Horses.*

STAMPEDIN' TROUBLE **F2.5368**

B. A. Goodman Productions. Nov w*1925*. Si; b&w. 35mm. 5 reels.

Dir Forrest Sheldon.

Cast: Bruce Gordon.

Western melodrama. "Easterner incurs enmity of crooked ranch foreman, jealous because rancher's daughter prefers Ted, and whose plotting leads to youth's arrest for murder. Lynching is attempted but Ted escapes, exposes the villains and marries the girl." ("Motion Picture News Booking Guide," in *Motion Picture News*, 8 May 1926, p44.) *Ranch foremen. Murder. Lynching.*

STAND AND DELIVER **F2.5369**

De Mille Pictures. *Dist* Pathé Exchange. 19 Feb **1928** [c24 Jan 1928; LP24910]. Si; b&w. 35mm. 6 reels, 5,423 ft.

Assoc Prod Ralph Block. *Dir* Donald Crisp. *Scen* Sada Cowan. *Titl* John Krafft. *Photog* David Abel. *Art Dir* Anton Grot. *Asst Dir* Emile De Ruelle. *Prod Mgr* Richard Donaldson. *Cost* Adrian.

Cast: Rod La Rocque *(Roger Norman)*, Lupe Velez *(Jania)*, Warner Oland *(Chika)*, Louis Natheaux *(Captain Dargis)*, James Dime *(Patch Eye)*, A. Palasthy *(Muja)*, Frank Lanning *(Pietro)*, Bernard Siegel *(blind operator)*, Clarence Burton *(commanding officer)*, Charles Stevens *(Krim).*

Romantic drama. Roger Norman, a British veteran of World War I, enlists in the Greek Army. As a lieutenant, he meets Jania, a local girl whom he rescues from a burning house. To show her appreciation, Jania goes to the army camp to give Roger a bottle of wine. Roger's commanding officer attacks her and then dies accidentally in a fight with Roger. They escape and are captured by bandits who force Roger to cooperate with them. Eventually Roger is reinstated in the military service for thwarting a bandit attack and capturing their leader, Chika. Roger and Jania find they have fallen in love. *British. Veterans. Bandits. Military life. Greco-Turkish War (1921–22). Greece—Army.*

THE STAR DUST TRAIL **F2.5370**

Fox Film Corp. 28 Dec **1924** [c18 Jan 1925; LP21057]. Si; b&w. 35mm. 5 reels, 4,800 ft.

Pres by William Fox. *Dir* Edmund Mortimer. *Scen* Dorothy Yost. *Story* Frederick Hatton, Fanny Hatton. *Photog* Joseph Valentine.

Cast: Shirley Mason *(Sylvia Joy)*, Bryant Washburn *(John Warding)*, Thomas R. Mills *(Horace Gibbs)*, Richard Tucker *(John Benton)*, Merta Sterling *(The Maid)*, Shannon Day *(Nan Hartley).*

Domestic drama. Sylvia Joy, a popular and beautiful cabaret dancer, refuses the suit of an influential theatrical producer, John Benton, and marries instead John Warding, a promising young actor. Benton hopes to break up the marriage and secretly spreads false rumors about Sylvia's fidelity that cause Warding to become jealous and inattentive to his work. As a result of his poor performances, Warding's show fails, and he finds it impossible to find work. Refusing to live off her earnings, Warding leaves Sylvia. Living in a cheap boardinghouse, Warding becomes friends with Nan Hartley, and Benton informs Sylvia that John has been unfaithful to her. Feeling himself a failure, John is on his way to ask Sylvia for a divorce when he is run down by a taxi. Nan is a witness to the accident, and she goes for Sylvia, who she finds is about to consent to Benton's offer of marriage. Sylvia rushes to Warding's bedside, and they are reconciled. *Actors. Dancers. Theatrical producers. Divorce. Theater. Boardinghouses.*

THE STAR REPORTER **F2.5371**

Berwilla Film Corp. *Dist* Arrow Film Corp. Apr **1921**. Si; b&w. 35mm. 6 reels, 5,622 ft.

Dir Duke Worne.

Cast: Billie Rhodes *(Nan Lambert)*, Truman Van Dyke *(Anthony Trent)*, William Horne *(Conington Warren).*

Mystery drama. Source: Wyndham Martin, *The Mysterious Mr. Garland* (London, 1922). Determined to learn the cause of her father's confinement to a sanitarium, Nan Lambert gets involved in a series of hectic experiences, in which she frequently meets Anthony Trent, a daring young man who alway helps her without revealing his purpose. Nan and Trent finally deliver to the district attorney evidence that Conington Warren (whose watch contains the combination to the safe containing the evidence) schemed with his associates to kidnap Nan's father and place him in the sanitarium. Trent reveals that he is a newspaper reporter, who has just been promoted to managing editor, and proposes to Nan. *Reporters. Filial relations. District attorneys. Sanitariums. Documentation.*

STARDUST **F2.5372**

Hobart Henley Productions. *Dist* Associated First National Pictures. 21 Nov **1921** [c6 Dec 1921; LP17296]. Si; b&w. 35mm. 6 reels, 5,800 ft.

Dir Hobart Henley. *Adapt* Anthony Paul Kelly. *Photog* Alfred Ortlieb.

Cast: Hope Hampton, Edna Ross *(Lily Becker)*, Thomas Maguire *(Henry Becker)*, Mary Foy *(Mrs. Becker)*, Charles Mussett *(Jethro Penny)*, Vivia Ogden *(Mrs. Penny)*, Ashley Buck, Noel Tearle *(Albert Penny)*, George Humbert *(Antonio Marvelli)*, Gladys Wilson *(Daisy Cameron)*, Charles Wellesley *(Bruce Visigoth)*, James Rennie *(Thomas Clemons).*

Society melodrama. Source: Fannie Hurst, *Stardust* (New York, 1919). Lily Becker, daughter of middle-class parents in Iowa, has always aspired to be a musician but receives little sympathy from her environment. She is forced into an unhappy marriage with Albert Penny, son of wealthy parents, whose brutality proves unbearable; fleeing to New York, she is saved from starvation by a friendly chorus girl and gives birth to a child, which dies. On the point of suicide, she meets young composer Tom Clemons in Central Park, and their friendship ripens into love. In a restaurant, Lily is discovered by Antonio Marvelli, a vocal instructor, who recognizes her talent and offers to teach her for nothing. After a year of hard work, Lily is fitted for an operatic career and makes her debut in *Thaïs*. At the same time, she is freed from her husband by his death in a railroad accident and finds happiness and success with Tom. *Singers. Chorus girs. Composers. Vocal instructors. Opera. New York City. Iowa. "Thaïs".*

Note: Copyright title: *Star Dust*.

STARK LOVE **F2.5373**

Paramount Famous Lasky Corp. 28 Feb **1927** [New York premiere; released 17 Sep; c17 Sep 1927; LP24429]. Si; b&w. 35mm. 7 reels, 6,203 ft. *Pres by* Adolph Zukor, Jesse L. Lasky. *Prod-Dir-Writ* Karl Brown *Assoc Prod* William Le Baron. *Adapt* Walter Woods. *Photog* James Murray.

Cast: Helen Munday *(Barbara Allen)*, Forrest James *(Rob Warwick)*, Silas Miracle *(Jason Warwick)*, Reb Grogan *(Quill Allen)*.

Drama. Amidst the primitive mountain culture of the Carolina hills lives young Rob Warwick. He, unlike his fellowmen, has learned to read and entertains ambitions of another life. He learns of another world, where woman is looked up to by man, who builds a home for her and protects and supports her, as opposed to the position of drudge that she maintains in his society. Fired with ambition to attend school, he tells young Barbara, whose parents are his nearest neighbors, of his plans. When the itinerant minister arrives to perform the yearly marriage and burial services, Rob goes with him to the settlement, sells his horse, pays the tuition for schooling, but enrolls Barbara in his place. He returns to find that his mother has died and that his father, left with a brood to care for, has selected Barbara to be his wife. Rob pleads with his father but is beaten; the girl is aroused to threaten Warwick with an ax, and she escapes with the boy, floating down the swollen stream to the settlement and freedom. *Clergymen. Mountain life. Education. Courtship. Great Smoky Mountains. North Carolina.*

Note: The film was photographed on location in the Great Smoky Mountains of North Carolina, employing a nonprofessional local cast.

STARK MAD **F2.5374**

Warner Brothers Pictures. 2 Feb **1929** [c21 Jan 1929; LP44]. Sd (Vitaphone); b&w. 35mm. 7 reels, 6,681 ft. [Also si, 2 Mar 1929; 4,917 ft.]

Dir Lloyd Bacon. *Scen-Dial* Harvey Gates. *Titl* Francis Powers. *Story* Jerome Kingston. *Camera* Barney McGill. *Asst Dir* Frank Shaw.

Cast: H. B. Warner *(Professor Dangerfield)*, Louise Fazenda *(Mrs. Fleming)*, Jacqueline Logan *(Irene)*, Henry B. Walthall *(Captain Rhodes)*, Claude Gillingwater *(James Rutherford)*, John Miljan *(Dr. Milo)*, André Beranger *(Simpson, the guide)*, Warner Richmond *(first mate)*, Floyd Shackelford *(Sam, the cook)*, Lionel Belmore *(Amos Sewald)*.

Mystery thriller. James Rutherford has organized an expedition to the jungles of Central America to find his missing son, Bob, and his guide, Simpson. Professor Dangerfield intercepts the party, bringing with him Simpson, whose jungle experience has made him a raving maniac. They go ashore and decide to spend a night at a Mayan temple. Irene, Bob's fiancée, disappears; they come across a gigantic ape chained to the floor, and Captain Rhodes, commander of the yacht, is abducted by a strange monster with great hairy talons. Messages are found warning the party to leave. Sewald, an explorer, is mysteriously killed by an arrow. Simpson's reason returns, and he saves the party, revealing that the demented hermit, whom he has just killed, and who formerly occupied the ruins, murdered Bob 2 months before. *Guides. Explorers. Lunatics. Monsters. Insanity. Jungles. Central America. Apes.*

STARLIGHT, THE UNTAMED **F2.5375**

Harry Webb Productions. *Dist* Rayart Pictures. 2 Sep **1925** [New York State license]. Si; b&w. 35mm. 5 reels, 4,800 ft.

Dir Harry Webb.

Cast: Jack Perrin, Starlight *(a horse)*.

Western melodrama(?). No information about the nature of this film has been found. *Horses.*

STARLIGHT'S REVENGE **F2.5376**

Harry Webb Productions. *Dist* Rayart Pictures. 21 May **1926** [New York State license]. Si; b&w. 35mm. 5 reels.

Dir Harry Webb.

Cast: Jack Perrin, Starlight *(a horse)*.

Western melodrama. No information about the precise nature of this film has been found. *Horses.*

STATE STREET SADIE **F2.5377**

Warner Brothers Pictures. 25 Aug **1928** [c16 Jul 1928; LP25471]. Mus score & talking sequences (Vitaphone); b&w. 35mm. 7 reels, 6,313 or 7,169 ft. [Also si; 9 reels.]

Dir Archie Mayo. *Adapt-Scen-Dial* E. T. Lowe, Jr. *Titl* E. T. Lowe, Jr., Joe Jackson. *Story* Melville Crossman. *Photog* Barney McGill. *Film Ed* George Marks.

Cast: Conrad Nagel *(Ralph Blake)*, Myrna Loy *(Isobel/State Street Sadie)*, William Russell *("The Bat")*, Georgie Stone *(Slinkey)*, Pat Hartigan *("The Bull")*.

Crook melodrama. Framed for the murder of a policeman, gangster Joe Blake commmits suicide. "The Bat," a gang leader, is the real murderer. Joe's twin brother, Ralph, joins the gang to get revenge and clear Joe's name. There he meets the daughter of the murdered policeman, Isobel, posing as "State Street Sadie" to get her own revenge. The two become involved in a net of intrigue culminating in the capture of the gang by police. The Bat, trapped on a roof, leaps to his death while Ralph and Isobel contemplate marriage. *Gangsters. Police. Twins. Brothers. Filial relations. Suicide. Revenge. Murder.*

STATION CONTENT (Reissue) **F2.5378**

Triangle Film Corp. *Dist* Tri-Stone Pictures. 25 Mar **1925** [New York State license]. Si; b&w. 35mm. 5 reels.

Note: A Gloria Swanson film originally released by Triangle Film Corp. on 16 Jun 1918.

STAY HOME *see* **I CAN EXPLAIN**

THE STEADFAST HEART **F2.5379**

Distinctive Pictures. *Dist* Goldwyn-Cosmopolitan Distributing Corp. 7 Oct **1923** [c13 Sep 1923; LP19388]. Si; b&w. 35mm. 7 reels, 7,012 ft.

Dir Sheridan Hall. *Adapt* Philip Lonergan.

Cast: Marguerite Courtot *(Lydia Canfield)*, Miriam Battista *(Lydia Canfield, as a child)*, Joseph Striker *(Angus Burke)*, Joseph Depew *(Angus Burke, as a child)*, Hugh Huntley *(Malcolm Crane)*, Jerry Devine *(Malcolm Crane, as a child)*, William B. Mack *(Crane)*, Sherry Tansey *(Biswang)*, Mary Alden *(Mrs. Burke)*, William Black *(Henry Woodhouse)*, Mario Majeroni *(David Wilkins)*, Harlan Knight *(Jake Bicknell)*, Walter Lewis *(Titus Burke)*, Louis Pierce *(Trueman)*, Mildred Ardin *(Mary)*, Helen Strickland *(Mrs. Canfield)*, Leslie Hunt *(Craig Browning)*.

Rural melodrama. Source: Clarence Budington Kelland, *The Steadfast Heart* (New York, 1924). Young Angus Burke accidently shoots the sheriff, who is leading a posse to get the boy's father, a thief. Angus' mother dies, and he is taken to trial alone. Found not guilty, he is given a job with the local newspaper office. He leaves when several citizens object to his presence—to return several years later. He takes over the newspaper and saves the townspeople from a gang of crooks. *Thieves. Sheriffs. Gangs. Filial relations. Newspapers. Trials.*

STEAMBOAT BILL, JR. **F2.5380**

Buster Keaton Productions. *Dist* United Artists. 12 May **1928** [c2 Jun 1928; LP25362]. Si; b&w. 35mm. 7 reels, 6,400 ft.

Pres by Joseph M. Schenck. *Dir* Charles F. Reisner. *Story-Scen-Titl* Carl Harbaugh. *Photog* Dev Jennings, Bert Haines. *Tech Dir* Fred Gabourie. *Film Ed* Sherman Kell. *Asst Dir* Sandy Roth.

Cast: Buster Keaton *(Steamboat Bill, Jr.)*, Ernest Torrence *(Steamboat Bill)*, Tom Lewis *(Tom Carter, his first mate)*, Tom McGuire *(John James King, his rival)*, Marion Byron *(Mary King, his daughter)*.

Comedy. William Canfield, known as Steamboat Bill, once River Junction's leading citizen, owns the riverboat *Stonewall Jackson*. His rival, J. J. King, the town banker, storekeeper, hotelkeeper, and wealthiest citizen, is attempting to cause Bill's financial ruin with his new river packet named *King*, after himself. Bill happily anticipates the arrival of his son, whom he has not seen since babyhood, and goes to the station to meet him. Anticipating that he will have a husky partner in his struggle with King, Bill and his mate are dismayed to find that Willie is a shrimp who wears college clothes, plays a ukelele, and sports a mustache. He hustles Willie off to the local haberdasher, and there Willie meets a girl with whom he falls in love—King's daughter, naturally. After several quarrels with King, Bill lands in jail, his boat condemned. Willie tries, unsuccessfully, to spring his father and ends up in the hospital just as a cyclone hits River Junction. The film concludes with Willie saving the *Stonewall Jackson*, his sweetheart, his father (floating down the river in the jailhouse), King, and, finally, a preacher. *Businessmen. Bankers. Fatherhood. Riverboats. Smalltown life. Cyclones.*

STEEL PREFERRED **F2.5381**

Metropolitan Pictures. *Dist* Producers Distributing Corp. 3 Jan **1926** [c14 Dec 1925; LP22132]. Si; b&w. 35mm. 7 reels, 6,680 ft.

Dir James P. Hogan. *Adapt* Elliott J. Clawson. *Photog* Dev Jennings. *Art Dir* Charles Cadwallader. *Asst Dir* Douglas Dawson. *Prod Mgr* George Bertholon.

Cast: Vera Reynolds *(Amy Creeth)*, William Boyd *(Wally Gay)*, Hobart Bosworth *(James Creeth)*, Charlie Murray *(Dicker)*, Walter Long *(Redface)*, William V. Mong *(Nicker)*, Nigel Barrie *(Waldron)*, Helene Sullivan *(Mrs. Creeth)*, Ben Turpin *(bartender)*.

Melodrama. Source: Herschel S. Hall, *Steel Preferred* (New York, 1920). Wally Gay, a young engineer employed in the Creeth steel works, is demoted by superintendent Waldron, who is jealous of Amy Creeth's interest in Wally. While working as a puddler, Wally conceives a radical design for a new furnace and interests Amy's father in it. The design is implemented, but Waldron leads the men out on strike in protest. Wally bests Waldron in a fight and convinces the workers to return to their jobs. When a ladle full of molten steel is upset, Wally saves Amy's life, thereby winning her heart. The elder Creeth, having fully realized Wally's good character and abilities, recognizes him as both son-in-law and successor. *Inventors. Engineers. Steelworkers. Puddlers. Jealousy. Strikes. Furnaces.*

STEELE OF THE ROYAL MOUNTED **F2.5382**

Vitagraph Co. of America. 15 Jun **1925** [c4 Jul 1925; LP21638]. Si; b&w. 35mm. 6 reels, 5,700 ft.

Pres by Albert E. Smith. *Dir* David Smith. *Scen* Jay Pilcher. *Photog* Stephen Smith, Jr.

Cast: Bert Lytell *(Philip Steele)*, Stuart Holmes *(Bucky Nome)*, Charlotte Merriam *(Isobel Becker)*, Sidney De Grey *(Colonel Becker)*, John Toughey *(Colonel MacGregor)*.

Northwest melodrama. Source: James Oliver Curwood, *Steele of the Royal Mounted; a Story of the Great Canadian Northwest* (New York, 1911). In order to arouse the jealousy of Philip Steele, a wealthy young man who is infatuated with her, Isobel Becker introduces her father to him as her husband. Steele is bitterly disappointed and before Isobel can explain her little joke, he leaves and joins the Northwest Mounted Police, in which he soon distinguishes himself. He is assigned to bring in Bucky Nome, a notorious gambler and lecher who is wanted for murder. Colonel Becker, Isobel's wealthy father, is interested in the fur business and goes to Canada, taking her with him. Bucky wrecks the pleasure train on which they are riding and kidnaps Isobel. Steele eventually catches up with Bucky, bringing him to justice and rescuing Isobel. The subdued girl explains her joke, and Steele resigns from the force, again taking his place in polite society. *Jealousy. Kidnaping. Murder. Fur industry. Railroads. Canada. Northwest Mounted Police. Train wrecks.*

STEELHEART **F2.5383**

Vitagraph Co. of America. 6 Nov **1921** [c20 Aug 1921; LP16885]. Si; b&w. 35mm. 6 reels.

Dir William Duncan. *Scen* Bradley J. Smollen. *Photog* George Robinson.

Cast: William Duncan *(Frank Worthing)*, Edith Johnson *(Ethel Kendall)*, Jack Curtis *("Butch" Dorgan)*, Walter Rodgers *(Steve)*, Euna Luckey *(Mrs. Freeman)*, Ardeta Malino *(Vera)*, Earl Crain *(Dick Colter)*, Charles Dudley *("Old Tom" Shelley)*.

Western melodrama. Ethel Kendall arrives at a mining town in search of her husband and is rescued from Dorgan's disreputable cabaret by Frank Worthing, a declared woman-hater, and delivered to a respectable lodging. Worthing promises to see Ethel to her destination safely and makes an enemy of Dorgan. In a neighboring town, Ethel and Frank visit an engineer friend, and while examining a mine shaft they are trapped by a slide instigated by Dorgan's men. With death before them, Ethel and Frank confess their love; then, believing her husband to be dead, she marries him after they are saved. Dorgan and Colter, the latter an alias for Ethel's first husband, are killed in a gun battle, and all ends happily. *Misogynists. Engineers—Mining. Mines. Bigamy. Desertion.*

STELLA DALLAS **F2.5384**

Samuel Goldwyn, Inc. *Dist* United Artists. 16 Nov **1925** [New York premiere; c24 Feb 1926; LP22421]. Si; b&w. 35mm. 11 reels, 10,157 ft.

Pres by Samuel Goldwyn. *Dir* Henry King. *Adapt* Frances Marion. *Photog* Arthur Edeson. *Film Ed* Stuart Heisler.

Cast: Ronald Colman *(Stephen Dallas)*, Belle Bennett *(Stella Dallas)*, Alice Joyce *(Helen Morrison)*, Jean Hersholt *(Ed Munn)*, Beatrix Pryor *(Mrs. Grovesnor)*, Lois Moran *(Laurel Dallas)*, Douglas Fairbanks, Jr. *(Richard Grovesnor)*, Vera Lewis *(Miss Tibbets)*, Maurice Murphy, Jack Murphy, Newton Hall *(Morrison children)*, Charles Hatten, Robert Gillette, Winston Miller *(Morrison children 10 years later)*.

Drama. Source: Olive Higgins Prouty, *Stella Dallas* (Boston, 1923). Upon the suicide of his father, socialite Stephen Dallas leaves his opulent home and goes to live in a small town where he marries Stella, a woman far below his social station. The marriage is a failure, and Stephen soon separates from Stella, returning to New York and leaving Stella to care for Laurel, their little girl. Years pass. Laurel grows to young womanhood, and Stella, realizing that she cannot properly provide for her tender, sensitive daughter, agrees at last to divorce Stephen so that he can marry Helen Morrison and thereby provide a good home for Laurel. Laurel at first refuses to leave her mother, but Stella marries a drunkard and Laurel is forced to live with her father. Laurel later marries Richard Grovesnor, a society lad of considerable charm and promise, and Stella, standing in the rain outside, watches the ceremony through a window of the Morrison home. *Socialites. Widows. Social classes. Suicide. Divorce. Marriage. Motherhood. Smalltown life. New York City.*

STELLA MARIS **F2.5385**

Universal Pictures. 13 Dec **1925** [c28 Dec 1925; LP22220]. Si; b&w. 35mm. 7 reels, 5,786 ft.

Dir Charles J. Brabin. *Scen* Charles J. Brabin, Mary Alice Scully. *Photog* Milton Moore.

Cast: Mary Philbin *(Stella Maris/Unity Blake)*, Elliott Dexter *(John Risca)*, Gladys Brockwell *(Louisa Risca)*, Jason Robards *(Walter Herold)*, Phillips Smalley *(Sir Oliver Blount)*, Lillian Lawrence *(Lady Blount)*, Robert Bolder *(Dr. Haynes)*, Aileen Manning *(Mary Heaton)*.

Drama. Source: William John Locke, *Stella Maris* (New York, 1912). Stella Maris, the crippled daughter of an aristocratic couple, is brought up in tender solicitude, living in a castle amidst gardens and rustic walks. Her constant companions are Walter Herold and John Risca, who provide Stella with a daily round of make-believe and fancy. John Risca, who is separated from his wife, assumes the care of a slavey named Unity Blake when his wife is sent to jail for 3 years for torturing the girl. Stella is cured by a great physician, and John declares his love for her. John's wife, released from jail, learns of his devotion to Stella and tells her that John is not free to love her. Unity, who has become devoted to John, kills his wife and then takes her own life. John comes to realize that Stella loves Herold and gives his blessing to their marriage. *Cripples. Drudges. Physicians. Aristocrats. Torture. Murder. Suicide.*

STEP ON IT! **F2.5386**

Universal Film Manufacturing Co. 29 May **1922** [c19 May 1922; LP17906]. Si; b&w. 35mm. 5 reels, 4,225 ft.

Pres by Carl Laemmle. *Dir* Jack Conway. *Scen* Arthur F. Statter. *Photog* Charles Kaufman.

Cast: Hoot Gibson *(Vic Collins)*, Edith Yorke *(Mrs. Collins)*, Frank Lanning *(Pidge Walters)*, Barbara Bedford *(Lorraine Leighton)*, Vic Potel *(Noisy Johnson)*, Gloria Davenport *(Letty Mather)*, Joe Girard *(Lafe Brownell)*, L. C. Shumway *(Bowman)*.

Western melodrama. Source: Courtney Ryley Cooper, "The Land of the Lost" (publication undetermined). Cowpuncher Vic Collins, who is suffering tremendous losses at the hand of cattle rustlers, falls in love with Lorraine Leighton from Kansas City. The rustlers hide their tracks, but Lorraine is suspected of being their leader. Vic, however, will not believe the rumor even though she hits him on the head with a gun butt while he is fighting a rustler. Ultimately, Lorraine discloses that she is trying to capture the gang for sending her brother to jail, and with the help of Lafe Brownell they capture the horsethieves. *Cowboys. Ranchers. Horsethieves. Brother-sister relationship. Kansas City.*

STEPHEN STEPS OUT **F2.5387**

Famous Players–Lasky. *Dist* Paramount Pictures. 25 Nov **1923** [c24 Nov 1923; LP19641]. Si; b&w. 35mm. 6 reels, 5,652 ft.

Pres by Jesse L. Lasky, William Elliott. *Dir* Joseph Henabery. *Scen* Edfrid Bingham. *Photog* Faxon Dean.

Cast: Douglas Fairbanks, Jr. *(Stephen Harlow, Jr.)*, Theodore Roberts *(Stephen Harlow, Sr.)*, Noah Beery *(Muley Pasha)*, Harry Myers *(Harry Stetson)*, Frank Currier *(Dr. Lyman Black)*, James O. Barrows *(Professor Gilman)*, Fannie Midgley *(Mrs. Gilman)*, Bertram Johns *(Virgil Smythe)*,

George Field *(Osman)*, Maurice Freeman *(Rustem)*, Fred Warren *(The Sultan)*, Pat Moore *(The Sultan's Son)*, Jack Herbert *(secretary)*, Frank Nelson *(hotel proprietor)*.

Comedy. Source: Richard Harding Davis, "The Grand Cross of the Desert," in *From "Gallegher" to "The Deserter"* (New York, 1927). When Stephen Harlow, Jr., fails his course in Turkish history, his father, a founder of the school, sends him to Turkey to learn his lessons and fires Gilman, the history teacher, whom he could not bully into passing his underachieving son. Stephen, Jr., to make amends, has Gilman reinstated, and, after a thrilling adventure in Turkey in which he rescues the sultan's son and is given a coveted medal, returns to school and presents the medal to Gilman. *Schoolteachers. Students. Royalty. History. Turkey.*

STEPPIN' OUT **F2.5388**

Columbia Pictures. 15 Oct **1925** [c15 Sep 1925; LP21818]. Si; b&w. 35mm. 6 reels, 5,221 ft.

Dir Frank Strayer. *Story* Bernard Vorhaus. *Photog* Dewey Wrigley.

Cast: Dorothy Revier *(Daisy Moran)*, Ford Sterling *(John Durant)*, Robert Agnew *(Henry Brodman, Jr.)*, Cissy Fitzgerald *(Mrs. John Durant)*, Ethel Wales *(Mrs. Henry Brodman)*, Tom Ricketts *(Henry Brodman)*, Harry Lorraine *(Sergeant)*.

Comedy. Henry Brodman refuses to meet the girl with whom his son, Henry, Jr., has eloped. Mrs. Brodman leaves for a visit to her mother, and John Durant, whom Brodman has never met, arrives in town on business. Henry arranges for his secretary, Daisy, to pose as Mrs. Brodman and allows her to wear his wife's pearl necklace. Henry, Daisy, and the Durants go out to dinner; Mrs. Brodman returns home unexpectedly, finds her necklace missing, and calls the cops. The cafe where Henry and his guests are dining is raided by the dry agents. They are all arrested, and Daisy is charged with stealing the necklace. Everything is soon explained satisfactorily, and Daisy turns out to be young Henry's bride. *Secretaries. Police. Revenue agents. Filial relations. Elopement. Impersonation.*

STEPPING ALONG **F2.5389**

B & H Enterprises. *Dist* First National Pictures. 14 Nov **1926** [c14 Nov 1926; LP23338]. Si; b&w. 35mm. 7 reels, 7,038 ft.

Pres by C. C. Burr. *Dir* Charles Hines. *Photog* George Peters, Albert Wetzel, Albert Wilson.

Cast: Johnny Hines *(Johnny Rooney)*, Mary Brian *(Molly Taylor)*, William Gaxton *(Frank Moreland)*, Ruth Dwyer *(Fay Allen)*, Edmund Breese *(Prince Ferdinand Darowitsky)*, Dan Mason *(Mike)*, Lee Beggs *(Boss O'Brien)*.

Comedy-drama. Source: Matt Taylor, "The Knickerbocker Kid" (publication undetermined). In the City Hall section of New York City, Johnny Rooney sells newspapers and dreams of a future with Molly, who has ambitions for a Broadway career, while Johnny hopes to become a successful politician. Boss O'Brien, of the Sugar Lane district, invites Johnny to a political outing at an amusement park and informs the young man that he is going to run him for assemblyman against Frank Moreland. Meanwhile, Moreland fosters Molly's footlight career, which ends in disaster. Heartbroken, she leaves the district. With election night growing near, Moreland steals Johnny's birth certificate and tries to prove him ineligible for candidacy; Johnny pursues the rival in a fire chief's car, unwittingly kidnaping a foreign prince. The plot against Johnny is revealed, and he is elected and happily united with Molly. *Newsboys. Politicians. Actors. Courtship. Elections. State legislatures. New York City. Documentation.*

STEPPING FAST **F2.5390**

Fox Film Corp. 13 May **1923** [c13 May 1923; LP19146]. Si; b&w. 35mm. 5 reels, 4,608 ft.

Pres by William Fox. *Dir* Joseph J. Franz. *Story-Scen* Bernard McConville. *Photog* Dan Clark.

Cast: Tom Mix *(Grant Malvern)*, Claire Adams *(Helen Durant)*, Donald MacDonald *(Fabian)*, Hector Sarno *(Martinez)*, Edward Peil *(Sun Yat)*, George Siegmann *("Red" Pollock)*, Tom S. Guise *(Quentin Durant)*, Edward Jobson *(Commodore Simpson)*, Ethel Wales *(Miss Higgins)*, Minna Redman *(Mrs. Malvern)*, Tony *(himself, a horse)*.

Western melodrama. "A young ranchman is captured by criminals because he possesses the secret of the location of a gold mine in the Arizona desert. After being thrown into San Francisco Bay, he is picked up by a tramp steamer and forced to work his way to China, where he again meets the gang. With the aid of some American sailors, Mix and the daughter of the scientist who discovered the mine fight their way out of a Chinese den and start back to the States, where they succeed in getting the treasure." *(Moving Picture World,* 26 May 1923, p325.) *Ranchers. Gold mines. China. San Francisco. Arizona. Horses.*

Note: Working title: *A Modern Monte Cristo.*

STEPPING LIVELY **F2.5391**

Carlos Productions. *For* Truart Film Corp. *Dist* Film Booking Offices of America. 28 Sep **1924** [c28 Sep 1924; LP20617]. Si; b&w. 35mm. 6 reels, 5,317 ft.

Dir James W. Horne. *Story-Scen* Frank Howard Clark. *Photog* William Marshall, Jack Stevens. *Asst Dir* Arthur Flaven.

Cast: Richard Talmadge *(Dave Allen, the boy, private secretary to a banker)*, Mildred Harris *(Evelyn Pendroy, the girl, the banker's daughter)*, Norval MacGregor *(James Pendroy, her father, a wealthy banker)*, Brinsley Shaw *(Robbins, butler in the banker's home)*, Fred Kelsey *(Artemus Doolittle, bank's private detective)*, Mario Carillo *(Josef Le Baron, a gentleman of means)*, William Clifford *(Black Mike, a vagabond of the underworld)*, John Dillon *(Dan Carter, Central Office detective)*, Victor Metzetti *(Chicago Red, leader of a tough gang of crooks)*.

Mystery melodrama. "Here is another one of those Richard Talmadge stunt pictures in which this athletic star does his usual stuff of knocking a whole row of yeggs into oblivion, jumping all over the inside and outside of houses, catching the villain after a merry chase which takes hero and bad man over the top of a moving freight and gives him opportunity to jump from the top of a water tank to the moving train as well as stage a fight with the villain on the locomotive which he has detached from the cars. Accused of the theft of some bonds from his employer, Dave Allen, who is in love with the banker's daughter, starts in to round up the real culprits. He disguises himself as a thug and gets the aid of a band of thieves. They find the real thief, a bogus nobleman, but he escapes in a fight that ensues when the gang discovers that Dave has been masquerading. After a chase Dave catches the slippery count and wins the daughter." *(Motion Picture News,* 1 Nov 1924, p2234.) *Secretaries. Gangs. Bankers. Imposture. Theft. Stunts. Chases.*

STICK TO YOUR STORY **F2.5392**

Harry J. Brown Productions. *Dist* Rayart Pictures. 16 Dec **1926** [New York State license]. Si; b&w. 35mm. 5 reels, 4,761 ft.

Dir Harry J. Brown. *Scen* Henry Roberts Symonds. *Titl* Arthur Q. Hagerman. *Story* Ralph O. Murphy.

Cast: Billy Sullivan *(Scoop Martin)*, Estelle Bradley *(Peggy Miles)*, Melbourne MacDowell *(Colonel Miles)*, Bruce Gordon *(Whipple)*, Jack McHugh *(Copy O'Hara)*, Barney Furey *(Number Seven)*, Harry Semels *(fanatic)*, Richard Lewis *(Reverend Brown)*.

Action melodrama. "Cub reporter with weakness for passing up assignments in favor of seemingly better stories, is nearly fired but is given another chance through intercession of editor's daughter. In the end he proves his worth, landing scoop for his paper and marrying girl after saving her father from bomb." *(Motion Picture News Booking Guide,* 11:49–50, Oct 1926.) *Reporters. Editors. Newspapers. Bombs.*

THE STILL ALARM (Universal-Jewel) **F2.5393**

Universal Pictures. 2 May **1926** [c8 Feb 1926; LP22389]. Si; b&w. 35mm. 7 reels, 7,207 ft.

Dir Edward Laemmle. *Scen* Charles Kenyon. *Adapt* Harvey J. O'Higgins.

Cast: Helene Chadwick *(Lucy Fay)*, William Russell *(Richard Fay)*, Richard C. Travers *(Perry Dunn)*, Edna Marion *(Drina Fay)*, Andy Todd *(John T. Murray)*, Edward Hearn *(Tom Brand)*, Erin La Bissoniere *(Masie Mush)*, Dot Farley *(Mrs. Maloney)*, Jacques D'Auray *(manager, modiste shop)*.

Melodrama. Source: Joseph Arthur and A. C. Wheeler, *The Still Alarm* (London opening: 2 Aug 1888). Lucy Fay leaves her husband, Richard, a fireman, for a suave politician, Perry Dunn. Richard compensates for the loss by adopting Drina, a baby girl whose mother perished in a fire. Drina develops into a beautiful young lady and becomes a model at a modiste shop owned by Dunn and managed by Lucy. Dunn is attracted to Drina and plots to get her alone by giving her a drugged drink. An untimely fire interferes with his plans, leaving Drina drugged and trapped by flames in Dunn's room, where she is sleeping. Later, Lucy reassures Richard that Drina has not been harmed and concludes that Dunn is unscrupulous. Richard forgives Lucy, and the two become reconciled. *Fashion models. Modistes. Firemen. Politicians. Infidelity. Adoption. Fires.*

THE STING OF THE LASH **F2.5394**

Robertson-Cole Co. *Dist* R-C Pictures. 11 Sep **1921** [c1 Sep 1921; LP16924]. Si; b&w. 35mm. 6 reels, 5,485 ft.

Dir Henry King. *Scen* H. Tipton Steck. *Story* Harvey Gates. *Photog* Dev Jennings.

Cast: Pauline Frederick *(Dorothy Keith)*, Clyde Fillmore *(Joel Gant)*, Lawson Butt *(Rhodes)*, Lionel Belmore *(Ben Ames)*, Jack Richardson *(Seeley)*, Edwin Stevens *(Daniel Keith)*, Betty Hall *(Crissy, aged 6)*, Evelyn McCoy *(Crissy, aged 10)*, Percy Challenger *(Rorke)*.

Drama. After her father, Daniel, is killed in an automobile accident on a western ranch, Dorothy Keith falls in love with young miner Joel Gant and marries him. Gant's claim is seized by her cousin, Ben, on behalf of a development company, and the couple go through years of poverty and hardship. Gant resorts to bootlegging and drinking, while Dorothy does washing to support herself and Gant's niece, Crissy. Rhodes, a lawyer for the mining company who is interested in Dorothy, offers Gant a job, which he refuses; when Gant threatens to strike Crissy with a whip, Dorothy has him secured and lashes him severely. Gant is arrested for bootlegging, and Dorothy gets a position with the mining company through Rhodes and refuses to live with her husband after his release. Later, however, he reforms, and they are reunited. *Poverty. Marriage. Bootlegging. Alcoholism. Mining. Flagellation.*

THE STING OF THE SCORPION **F2.5395**

Ashton Dearholt Productions. *Dist* Arrow Film Corp. 1 Oct **1923** [c9 Oct 1923; LP19485]. Si; b&w. 35mm. 5 reels, 4,629 ft.

Dir Richard Hatton. *Story-Scen* Daniel F. Whitcomb.

Cast: Edmund Cobb, Ashton Dearholt, Helene Rosson, Joseph Girard, Arthur Morrison, Harry Dunkinson.

Western melodrama. "Young rancher befriends Indian who has found valuable gold mine. Saloon keeper, coveting the mine and rancher's sweetheart, plots against both. Hero is accused of killing Indian but girl aids him to clear himself, and the Indian makes them a present of the mine." (*Motion Picture News Booking Guide*, 6:65, Apr 1924.) *Ranchers. Saloon keepers. Indians of North America. Gold mines.*

STOCKS AND BLONDES **F2.5396**

FBO Pictures. 9 Sep **1928** [c28 Aug 1928; LP25572]. Si; b&w. 35mm. 6 reels, 5,493 ft.

Supv Louis Sarecky. *Story-Scen-Dir* Dudley Murphy. *Titl* Jack Conway, Randolph Bartlett. *Photog* Virgil Miller. *Film Ed* Pandro S. Berman. *Asst Dir* Ray McCarey.

Cast: Gertrude Astor *(Goldie)*, Jacqueline Logan *(Patsy)*, Richard "Skeets" Gallagher *(Tom Greene)*, Albert Conti *(Powers)*.

Comedy-drama. Tom Greene, a swaggering broker's messenger, is fired from his job just as he and his sweetheart, Patsy, put the first down payment on what is to be their honeymoon cottage. Patsy, a dancer at the Kit Kat Club, is introduced that evening to Powers, Tom's former boss, and gets some inside information on a stock deal. The following day, Tom gets a note from a law firm authorizing him on behalf of an unknown client (Patsy) to buy and sell a certain stock at a certain price. Tom does so and makes a killing; other deals follow, and Tom becomes arrogant and vain. He later finds Patsy and Powers together, and suspecting the worst, he spurns her and turns to drink and dames for consolation. Patsy tells Tom that she herself has been his client and then has Powers ruin him in the market. Greatly chastened, Tom returns to Patsy, and they prepare to live together on love and dreams. *Messengers. Brokers. Dancers. Courtship. New York City—Wall Street.*

THE STOLEN BRIDE **F2.5397**

First National Pictures. 14 Aug **1927** [c27 Jul 1927; LP24238]. Si; b&w. 35mm. 8 reels, 7,179 ft.

Pres by Richard A. Rowland. *Prod-Writ* Carey Wilson. *Dir* Alexander Korda. *Photog* Robert Kurrle. *Cost* Max Ree.

Cast: Billie Dove *(Sari, Countess Thurzo)*, Lloyd Hughes *(Franz Pless)*, Armand Kaliz *(Captain, The Baron von Heimberg)*, Frank Beal *(Count Thurzo)*, Lilyan Tashman *(Ilona Taznadi)*, Cleve Moore *(Lieutenant Kiss)*, Otto Hoffman *(Papa Pless)*, Charles Wellesley *(The Regiment Pater)*, Bert Sprotte *(The Sergeant)*.

Romantic melodrama. Franz Pless, son of a Hungarian peasant, goes to New York to become an architect and while there meets Sari, Countess Thurzo, whom he knew as a child. A romance develops but is cut short as Sari must return to Hungary with her father. Franz follows her to Europe, but to his dismay he learns he must serve 3 years' compulsory military service; gaining leave to visit his grandfather, he quarrels with Baron von Heimberg, captain of his regiment, who makes him his orderly. In secret meetings Sari promises to wait for Franz, but her father announces at a formal banquet the engagement of his daughter and Heimberg without consulting her. Franz assaults the captain and is pursued by soldiers; Sari conceals him, but he is discovered and offered his freedom provided that he leave the country. Ilona, the captain's mistress, conceals herself in Sari's wedding gown while she meets Franz; Ilona then forces the captain to go through with the wedding. *Nobility. Architects. Mistresses. Courtship. Weddings. Hungary.*

THE STOLEN CHILD **F2.5398**

15 Apr **1923** [scheduled release]. Si; b&w. 35mm. 5 reels.

Cast: Matty Roubert.

Drama(?). No information about the nature of this film has been found. *Children.*

Note: Production and distribution companies have not been identified; New York State local distribution handled by Anthony Moratto.

STOLEN KISSES **F2.5399**

Warner Brothers Pictures. 23 Feb **1929** [c11 Feb 1929; LP106]. Talking sequences, sd eff, & mus score (Vitaphone); b&w. 35mm. 7 reels, 6,273 ft. [Also si, 13 Apr 1929; 5,658 ft.]

Dir Ray Enright. *Titl-Dial* James A. Starr. *Adapt* Edward T. Lowe, Jr. *Story* Franz Suppe. *Photog* Ben Reynolds. *Film Ed* George Marks.

Cast: May McAvoy *(May Lambert)*, Hallam Cooley *(Hal Lambert)*, Reed Howes *(Jack Harding)*, Claude Gillingwater *(H. A. Lambert, Sr.)*, Edna Murphy *(Fanchon La Vere)*, Arthur Hoyt *(Hoyt)*, Agnes Franey *(Nanette)*, Phyllis Crane *(Margot)*.

Farce. Hal Lambert, the meek son of the irascible publisher of a Detroit daily, believes his wife, May, to be in the family way and tells all the neighbors. He is mistaken, however, and May forces him to take her on a trip to Paris. They are accompanied by Hal's father, who hires Jack Harding, a Paris divorce lawyer, to bring the bickering Hal and May closer together. To accomplish the rapprochement, Harding decides to make them jealous of each other: he personally courts May and fixes Jack up with a hot French number. After many complications and misunderstandings, Hal and May are reconciled. *Publishers. Lawyers. Pregnancy. Jealousy. Newspapers. Paris. Detroit.*

STOLEN LOVE **F2.5400**

FBO Pictures. 2 Dec **1928** [c2 Dec 1928; LP25884]. Si; b&w. 35mm. 7 reels, 6,223 ft.

Dir Lynn Shores. *Scen* Winifred Day. *Titl* Helen Gregg. *Story* Hazel Livingston. *Photog* Ted Pahle. *Film Ed* Ann McKnight. *Asst Dir* Walter Daniels.

Cast: Marceline Day *(Joan Hastings)*, Rex Lease *(Bill)*, Owen Moore *(Curtis Barstow)*, Helen Lynch *(Ruth)*, Blanche Frederici *(Aunt Evvie)*, Joy Winthrop *(Aunt Babe)*, Betty Blythe *(modiste)*.

Melodrama. Young Joan Hastings, shut off from the excitement of courtship by two strict maiden aunts, plans to elope with Bill, but before Bill can get in over the garden wall, he is arrested by police. Thinking she has been jilted, Joan goes to the city and finds work in Barstow's dress shop; she goes out with Barstow, and they run into Bill at a party. Bill insults Joan, and she spitefully asks Barstow to take her home; Barstow takes her to his apartment instead and makes a pass at her. As Joan is struggling to free herself, Bill shows up and after a bone-crushing fight subdues Barstow and proves to Joan that his love has not weakened. *Aunts. Spinsters. Modistes. Police. Elopement.*

STOLEN PLEASURES **F2.5401**

Columbia Pictures. 5 Jan **1927** [c15 Jan 1927; LP23544]. Si; b&w. 35mm. 6 reels, 5,064 ft.

Supv Harry Cohn. *Dir* Philip E. Rosen. *Story-Cont* Leah Baird. *Photog* J. O. Taylor.

Cast: Helene Chadwick *(Doris Manning)*, Gayne Whitman *(John Manning)*, Dorothy Revier *(Clara Bradley)*, Ray Ripley *(Herbert Bradley)*, Harlan Tucker *(Guy Summers)*.

Domestic drama. Each of two married couples—John and Doris Manning and Herbert and Clara Bradley—separate as the result of arguments. Bradley meets Doris and offers to take her to the city, but they are caught by a storm and forced to seek shelter in a roadhouse. Guy Summers, a lounge lizard, calls on Clara Bradley and induces her to attend a party with him, but he takes her to the same roadhouse. There, in a private room, he tries to seduce her, but she escapes when the roadhouse catches fire. Manning denounces his wife for going there and accuses Bradley of cheating with his wife. But Mrs. Bradley stops the battle by explaining that she was present that night and that their visit was entirely innocent. *Marriage. Jealousy. Seduction. Roadhouses. Fires.*

THE STOLEN RANCH (Blue Streak Western) **F2.5402**

Universal Pictures. 26 Dec **1926** [c1 Nov 1926; LP23295]. Si; b&w. 35mm. 5 reels, 4,578 ft.

Pres by Carl Laemmle. *Dir* William Wyler. *Scen* George H. Plympton. *Story* Robert F. Hill. *Photog* Al Jones.

Cast: Fred Humes *("Breezy" Hart)*, Louise Lorraine *(Mary Jane)*, William Norton Bailey *(Sam Hardy)*, Ralph McCullough *(Frank Wilcox)*, Nita Cavalier *(June Marston)*, Edward Cecil *(Silas Marston)*, Howard Truesdell *(Tom Marston)*, Slim Whittaker *(Hank)*, Jack Kirk *(Slim)*.

Western melodrama. Breezy Hart and his war buddy, Frank Wilcox, a victim of shell shock, return home, and Breezy finds that his dead uncle's ranch is now claimed by Sam Hardy, though Frank has good reason to believe himself to be the rightful owner. Breezy gets a kitchen job at the ranch and supports Frank in his hideout. Frank becomes friendly with June Marston, daughter of a neighboring rancher, and Breezy falls in love with Mary Jane, his kitchen pal. Hardy, learning of Frank's return, determines to do away with him, but Breezy overhears the plot and rescues the deed to the ranch and saves Frank from a battle with Hardy's henchmen. The sheriff arrests the conspirators, and Frank, cured of his illness, is united with June. *Veterans. Sheriffs. Ranchers. Shell shock. Inheritance. Documentation.*

STOLEN SECRETS **F2.5403**

Universal Pictures. 10 Mar **1924** [c21 Feb 1924; LP19946]. Si; b&w. 35mm. 5 reels, 4,742 ft.

Dir Irving Cummings. *Scen* Rex Taylor. *Story* Richard Goodall. *Photog* Charles Stumar.

Cast: Herbert Rawlinson *(The Eel, Miles Manning)*, Kathleen Myers *(Cordelia Norton)*, Edwards Davis *(John Norton)*, Henry Herbert *(Brooks Waters)*, Arthur Stuart Hull *(Sterling Mann)*, William Conklin *(Chapman Hoggins)*, George Siegmann *(Nat Fox)*, Joseph North *(Cruthers)*, Alfred Allen *(Judge Wright)*, William A. Carroll *(Arthur Welch)*, Edwin J. Brady *(Smith)*, Joseph W. Girard *(police chief)*, R. M. Batten *(Jimmy)*, George Magrill *(Tom)*.

Mystery melodrama. Noted criminologist Miles Manning captures a gang of crooks by posing as a super criminal—a mysterious man called "The Eel"—when the mayor's daughter, Cordelia, believing that he really is a crook, enlists his assistance in ridding the city of its criminals. Romance develops between Cordelia and Manning. *Criminologists. Mayors. Reformers. Gangs. Disguise.*

THE STOOL PIGEON *see* **THE TIP-OFF**

STOOL PIGEON **F2.5404**

Columbia Pictures. 25 Oct **1928** [c27 Nov 1928; LP25871]. Si; b&w. 35mm. 6 reels, 5,592 ft.

Prod Jack Cohn. *Dir* Renaud Hoffman. *Adapt-Cont* Stuart Anthony. *Titl* Morton Blumenstock. *Story* Edward Meagher. *Photog* Teddy Tetzlaff. *Art Dir* Harrison Wiley. *Film Ed* Arthur Roberts. *Asst Dir* Glenn Belt.

Cast: Olive Borden *(Goldie)*, Charles Delaney *(Jimmy Wells)*, Lucy Beaumont *(Mrs. Wells)*, Louis Natheaux *(Butch)*, Ernie Adams *(Dropper)*, Al Hill *(Red)*, Robert Wilber *(Augie)*, Clarence Burton *(Mike Shields)*.

Underworld melodrama. Jimmy Wells, the apple of his mother's eye, joins a criminal gang in order to provide his mother with gifts and a better life. He falls in love with Goldie, the gun moll of Butch, the gang leader, and arouses Butch's enmity. The police are tipped off about a factory robbery, and Butch believes that Jimmy squealed on the gang; Butch orders Jimmy shot, but a cigarette case stops the bullet, saving his life. Goldie then turns stool pigeon in revenge, and Detective Shields sets a trap for the gang. Butch is killed, and Shields allows Jimmy to go west with his mother for a fresh start. *Detectives. Informers. Molls. Criminals—Rehabilitation.*

STOP AT NOTHING **F2.5405**

Charles R. Seeling Productions. *Dist* Aywon Film Corp. Feb **1924.** Si; b&w. 35mm. 5 reels, ca4,800 ft.

Dir Charles R. Seeling.

Cast: George Larkin.

Melodrama. "Burley Walters and 'Shadow' Brice, rival crook leaders are after the Denman diamonds. 'Shadow' wins the confidence of Daphne Denman, but Walters beats him to it and gets the diamonds as they are being transported on a San Francisco ferry boat. After a furious fight 'Shadow' wrests the gems from Walters and then reveals himself to the girl as a secret service man." (*Motion Picture News Booking Guide,* 6:65, Apr 1924.) *Diamonds. Theft. Secret service. Ferryboats. San Francisco.*

STOP FLIRTING **F2.5406**

Christie Film Co. *Dist* Producers Distributing Corp. 30 Mar **1925** [23 Apr 1925; LP21393]. Si; b&w. 35mm. 6 reels, 5,161 ft.

Pres by Al Christie, Charles Christie. *Dir* Scott Sidney. *Adapt* Joseph W. Farnham. *Photog* Georges Benoit.

Cast: John T. Murray *(Perry Reynolds)*, Wanda Hawley *(Vivian Marsden)*, Hallam Cooley *(Geoffrey Dangerfield)*, Ethel Shannon *(Marjorie Deeds)*, Vera Steadman *(Suzanne)*, Jimmie Adams *(Count Spinagio)*, Jack Duffy *(butler)*, Jimmy Harrison *(Teddy)*, David James *(Bobby Anderson)*.

Farce. Source: Fred Jackson, *Stop Flirting* (London opening: 30 May 1923). Perry and Vivian Reynolds are on their honeymoon when Vivian finds Perry with a girl in his arms; he explains that he merely caught her when she slipped, and Vivian is satisfied about his fidelity. Shortly thereafter, Vivian finds Perry with a girl sitting on his lap and quickly decides to teach him a lesson, flirting with everything in pants, including a Scotsman. Perry is enraged and, on the advice of his friend, Geoffrey, boards a small plan bound for Hawaii. Geoffrey follows the plane in a boat, and Perry jumps out, returning to land and hiding in his own boathouse. The plane on which Perry was riding crashes, and Vivian is disconsolate. She later discovers that Perry is alive, and she resumes her mad flirting. A policeman reports that there is a lunatic on the loose, and Perry, disguising himself as the Hunchback of Notre Dame, crashes one of Vivian's wild parties. After some confusion, Perry and Vivian are reconciled. *Flirts. Scotch. Marriage. Honeymoons. Infidelity. Disguise. Airplane accidents. Hawaii.*

STOP, LOOK, AND LISTEN **F2.5407**

Larry Semon Productions. *Dist* Pathé Exchange. 1 Jan **1926** [c1 Feb 1926; LU22348]. Si; b&w. 35mm. 6 reels, 5,305 ft.

Pres by John Adams. *Dir* Larry Semon. *Scen* Harry B. Smith, Larry Semon. *Photog* H. F. Koenekamp, James Brown. *Asst Dir* Earl Montgomery, Oliver Hardy.

Cast: Larry Semon *(Luther Meek)*, Dorothy Dwan *(Dorothy)*, Mary Carr *(Mother)*, William Gillespie *(Bill)*, Lionel Belmore *(sheriff)*, Bull Montana *(strong man)*, Babe Hardy *(show manager)*, Curtis McHenry *(porter)*, Joseph Swickard *(old actor)*.

Comedy-melodrama. Source: Harry B. Smith and Irving Berlin, *Stop, Look, and Listen* (New York opening: 25 Dec 1915). Luther Meek, a subdued and frugal young man, is in love with a schoolteacher, Dorothy, who wants to try her luck at becoming a stage actress before saying "yes" to marriage. Luther's stepbrother, Bill, and Dorothy successfully scheme to get Luther to finance a waning musical comedy troupe in return for giving Dorothy the starring part. However, Bill and the show manager doublecross them and run off with the box office receipts, shifting the blame to Luther. The town engages in a mad chase to catch Luther while Bill and the manager make their getaway. But Luther manages to escape from his pursuers and catches the thieves. Having had her fill of stage life, Dorothy marries Luther. *Schoolteachers. Theatrical backers. Theatrical managers. Brothers. Theater. Theft. Chases.*

STOP THAT MAN (Universal-Jewel) **F2.5408**

Universal Pictures. 11 Mar **1928** [c31 Jan 1928; LP24944]. Si; b&w. 35mm. 6 reels, 5,389 ft.

Dir Nat Ross. *Story Supv* Joseph Franklin Poland. *Cont* Harry O. Hoyt. *Titl* Tom Reed. *Adapt* Dick Smith. *Story* George V. Hobart. *Photog* George Robinson. *Film Ed* Robert Jahns.

Cast: Arthur Lake *(Tommy O'Brien)*, Barbara Kent *(Muriel Crawford)*, Eddie Gribbon *(Bill O'Brien)*, Warner Richmond *(Jim O'Brien)*, Walter McGrail *("Slippery Dick" Sylvaine)*, George Siegmann *("Butch" Barker)*, Joseph W. Girard *(Captain Ryan)*.

Farce. Tommy O'Brien appears in public wearing his brother's police uniform to impress his sweetheart, Muriel, and he unwittingly admits "Slippery Dick" Sylvaine, a notorious crook, into a house. Tommy's brother is blamed when his policeman's badge is found in the burglarized house, but Tommy explains everything at the police station. Despondent because he no longer has a place to live and because Muriel has left him,

Tommy decides to commit suicide. He hires "Butch" Barker to kill him for $10; then later, when his brother relents and Muriel returns, he tries to escape being killed. Seeking shelter in a streetcar barn, Tommy captures Sylvaine and is forgiven by everyone. Barker returns the $10, saying he recently has got religion. *Brothers. Police. Burglary. Suicide. Impersonation.*

THE STORM (Universal-Jewel) **F2.5409**

Universal Film Manufacturing Co. 18 Jun **1922** [New York premiere; released 4 Sep; c1 Aug 1922; LP18101]. Si; b&w. 35mm. 8 reels, 7,400 ft.

Pres by Carl Laemmle. *Dir* Reginald Barker. *Scen* J. G. Hawks. *Photog* Percy Hilburn.

Cast: Matt Moore *(Dave Stewart)*, House Peters *(Burr Winton)*, Josef Swickard *(Jacques Fachard)*, Virginia Valli *(Manette Fachard)*, Frank Lanning *(Manteeka)*, Gordon McGee *(N. W. M. Police sergeant)*.

Melodrama. Source: Langdon McCormick, *The Storm* (New York opening: 2 Oct 1919). War buddies Burr Winton and Dave Stewart retreat to Burr's cabin in the Canadian Northwest after Dave helps Burr pay a gambling debt. During the winter months, Jacques Fachard, a French trapper, and his daughter Manette, who have eluded the Mounted Police, seek refuge in their cabin. Fachard dies of a bullet wound, after having persuaded the men to care for his daughter. Both fall in love with Manette; Burr, deeply in love for the first time and eager to marry her, is furiously jealous and threatens Dave. Food shortage makes it necessary for Burr to seek aid. Manette, after having been defended by Burr, starts after him in the storm; but Dave stops her and brings his friends back and leaves them to their happiness. *Trappers. Friendship. Jealousy. Canadian Northwest. Northwest Mounted Police. Storms.*

Note: Remade in 1930 under the same title, q. v.

THE STORM **F2.5410**

Universal Pictures. 18 Aug **1930** [c7 Aug 1930; LP1467]. Sd (Movietone); b&w. 35mm. 9 reels, 7,203 ft.

Pres by Carl Laemmle. *Dir* William Wyler. *Screenplay* Wells Root. *Dial* Tom Reed. *Adapt* Charles A. Logue. *Photog* Alvin Wyckoff. *Rec Engr* Joseph P. Lapis, C. Roy Hunter.

Cast: Lupe Velez *(Manette Fachard)*, Paul Cavanagh *(Dave Steuart)*, William Boyd *(Burr Winton)*, Alphonse Ethier *(Jacques Fachard)*, Ernest Adams *(Johnny)*, Tom London, Nick Thompson, Erin La Bissoniere.

Melodrama. Source: Langdon McCormick, *The Storm* (New York opening: 2 Oct 1919). Remake of the 1922 film, q. v. *Trappers. Friendship. Jealousy. Canadian Northwest. Northwest Mounted Police. Storms.*

THE STORM BREAKER (Universal-Jewel) **F2.5411**

Universal Pictures. 25 Oct **1925** [c23 Sep 1925; LP21850]. Si; b&w. 35mm. 7 reels, 6,064 ft.

Dir Edward Sloman. *Adapt* E. T. Lowe, Jr. *Photog* Jackson Rose.

Cast: House Peters *(John Strong)*, Ruth Clifford *(Lysette DeJon)*, Nina Romano *(Judith Nyte)*, Ray Hallor *(Neil Strong)*, Jere Austin *(Tom North)*, Lionel Belmore *(parson)*, Gertrude Claire *(Elspeth Strong)*, Mark Fenton *(Malcolm)*.

Drama. Source: Charles Guernon, *Titans* (New York, 1922). John Strong, a fearless and boasting Nova Scotia sea captain, weds Lysette DeJon, a refined and dreamy young woman. During his long absences at sea, Lysette becomes increasingly attached to John's younger and more poetic brother, Neil. Judith Nyte, a dark-browed village girl, sees Neil and Lysette in an embrace and tells John of his wife's love for his brother. John hardens his heart against both of them. During a storm at sea, Neil is imperiled, and John, at Lysette's pleading, rescues him. John promises Lysette her freedom and sets sail, intending to return, in time, for Judith. *Sea captains. Brothers. Marriage. Divorce. Seafaring life. Nova Scotia. Storms.*

THE STORM DAUGHTER (Universal-Jewel) **F2.5412**

Universal Pictures. 23 Mar **1924** [c28 Feb 1924; LP19953]. Si; b&w. 35mm. 6 reels, 5,303 ft.

Dir George Archainbaud. *Scen* Edward J. Montagne. *Story* Leete Renick Brown. *Photog* Jules Cronjager.

Cast: Priscilla Dean *(Kate Masterson)*, Tom Santschi *("Brute" Morgan)*, William B. Davidson *(Rennert)*, J. Farrell MacDonald *(Con Mullaney)*, Cyril Chadwick *(The Duke)*, Bert Roach *(Olaf Swensen)*, Alfred Fisher *(Hoskins)*, George Kuwa *(Ah Sin)*, Harry Mann *(Izzy)*.

Melodrama. "Brute" Morgan, a skipper with a "terrible reputation," runs down Kate Masterson's sailboat, imprisons her and her crew, and forces them to hard work. In a mutiny led by Rennert, Morgan is overpowered and put in irons, but he is released to command the ship during a terrific storm. The ship sinks; and Morgan and Kate, the only survivors, reach a deserted island. The experience has softened Morgan, and the two have fallen in love. *Sea captains. Seafaring life. Mutiny. Shipwrecks.*

Note: Working title: *The Storm's Daughter.*

STORM GIRL **F2.5413**

New Era Productions. *Dist* Anchor Film Distributors. 1 Nov **1922.** Si; b&w. 35mm. 5 reels, 5,090 ft.

Pres by Morris R. Schlank. *Dir* Francis Ford. *Story-Scen* Elsie Van Name.

Cast: Peggy O'Day *(Patsy)*, Francis Ford *(Dr. Blake)*, Phil Ford *(Lewis Lester)*.

Melodrama. Patsy joins the chorus of a burlesque show. One night she encounters Dr. Blake, with whom she falls in love. Lewis Lester, a crook, when his own sweetheart's beauty is marred by a fire, diverts his attention to Patsy. Lewis persuades her to believe that the doctor has cast her off. Developments prove the contrary, and, repentant and disillusioned, Patsy seeks forgetfulness in the country, where Dr. Blake follows. Lewis, pursued by the police, also appears, and further complications eventually work out with happiness for Dr. Blake and Patsy. *Physicians. Singers. Burlesque. Disfiguration.*

THE STORM'S DAUGHTER *see* **THE STORM DAUGHTER**

STORMSWEPT **F2.5414**

Robert Thornby Productions. *Dist* Film Booking Offices of America. 18 Feb **1923** [c18 Feb 1923; LP18692]. Si; b&w. 35mm. 5 reels, 5,000 ft.

Dir Robert Thornby. *Scen* Winifred Dunn. *Story* H. H. Van Loan. *Photog* Ben Reynolds.

Cast: Wallace Beery *(William McCabe)*, Noah Beery *(Shark Moran)*, Virginia Browne Faire *(Ann Reynolds)*, Arline Pretty *(Helda McCabe)*, Jack Carlyle *(Snape)*.

Drama. Despondent over the infidelity of his wife, William McCabe wanders on the waterfront considering suicide, but instead he saves the life of Shark Moran. Moran gives McCabe a job on his lightship, where McCabe enjoys the solitude and falls in love with Ann Reynolds, the daughter of the captain of the supply ship. One day Moran rescues a woman in a storm and makes advances toward her. When McCabe discovers the woman to be his own wife, there is a violent quarrel between the two men. But their friendship prevails, Moran apologizes, and Helda McCabe reveals that William is free to marry Ann. *Suicide. Friendship. Infidelity. Lightships.*

Note: Working title: *Wreckage.*

STORMY SEAS **F2.5415**

Continental Pictures. *Dist* Associated Exhibitors. 1 Jul **1923** [c6 Jun 1923; LU19043]. Si; b&w. 35mm. 5 reels, 4,893 ft.

Dir J. P. McGowan. *Story* Arthur W. Donaldson.

Cast: J. P. McGowan *(Captain Morgan)*, Helen Holmes *(Mary Weems)*, Leslie Casey *(George Tracey)*, Harry Dalroy *(Angus McBride)*, Francis Seymour *("Storm" Weems)*, Gordon Knapp *("Shorty," the steward)*.

Melodrama. Captain Morgan promises his sweetheart, Mary Weems, whose father owns the ship, that he will not touch a drink while on an important cruise. He breaks his word and wrecks the ship. Years later Morgan is rescued from a Central American port by George Tracey, a seaman and rival for Mary. George determines to make a man of Morgan and takes him aboard. Morgan realizes his worthlessness and gives up Mary to George. *Sea captains. Seamen. Seafaring life. Alcoholism. Central America. Shipwrecks.*

STORMY WATERS **F2.5416**

Tiffany-Stahl Productions. 1 Jun **1928** [c26 May 1928; LP25338]. Si; b&w. 35mm. 6 reels, 5,735 ft.

Supv Roy Fitzroy. *Dir* Edgar Lewis. *Adapt-Cont* Harry Dittmar. *Titl* Leslie Mason. *Photog* Ernest Miller. *Art Dir* Hervey Libbert. *Set Dsgn* George Sawley. *Film Ed* Martin G. Cohn.

Cast: Eve Southern *(Lola)*, Malcolm McGregor *(David Steele)*, Roy Stewart *(Capt. Angus Steele)*, Shirley Palmer *(Mary)*, Olin Francis *(bos'n)*, Norbert Myles *(first mate)*, Bert Apling *(second mate)*.

Melodrama. Source: Jack London, "Yellow Handkerchief," in *Brown Wolf, and Other Jack London Stories,* as chosen by Franklin K. Mathiews

(New York, 1920). Angus, the elder of seafaring brothers, is captain of the *Condon*, while David is a crewman. Although David has a fiancée in New York, he succumbs to the temptations of Lola, a barfly, while in Buenos Aires. Angus reluctantly allows her to make the trip to New York when Lola insists that she and David are married. Bored with the drudgery of housekeeping, Lola plans to run away with a boxer named Jimmy Cardigan until Angus prevents it. Taking her and David, delirious with fever and anguish, on board, Angus returns to Buenos Aires, sets Lola adrift in a small boat, and brings David back to his fiancée. *Sailors. Sea captains. Boxers. Prostitutes. Seafaring life. Infidelity. Marriage—Fake. New York City. Buenos Aires.*

Note: Working title: *The Captain of the Hurricane.*

THE STORY WITHOUT A NAME **F2.5417**

Famous Players–Lasky. *Dist* Paramount Pictures. 5 Oct **1924** [New York premiere; released 27 Oct; c7 Oct 1924; LP20645]. Si; b&w. 35mm. 6 reels, 5,912 ft.

Pres by Adolph Zukor, Jesse L. Lasky. *Dir* Irvin Willat. *Screenplay* Victor Irvin. *Photog* Hal Rosson.

Cast: Agnes Ayres *(Mary Walsworth)*, Antonio Moreno *(Alan Holt)*, [Frederick] Tyrone Power *(Drakma)*, Louis Wolheim *(Kurder)*, Dagmar Godowsky *(Claire)*, Jack Lionel Bohn *(Don Powell)*, Maurice Costello *(The Cripple)*, Frank Currier *(Admiral Walsworth)*, Ivan Linow.

Action melodrama. Source: Arthur Stringer, *The Story Without a Name* (New York, 1924). "This is certainly an action-melodrama, with the hero and heroine undergoing enough perils ... to supply a number of episodes of a serial. A few of these include the overpowering of the hero by the spy's gang, his being spirited away in an aeroplane, his fight with the pilot and leap into the sea, ... the rush of a warship to their rescue, the sinking of the spy's yacht by a bomb from an aeroplane launched from the deck of the warship, the rescue, and the arrival of another plane filled with U. S. marines." (*Moving Picture World,* 18 Oct 1924, p1625.) Drakma, an international spy, seeks the possession of the triangulator (a device emitting electronic death rays), which radio expert Alan Holt invented for the United States Government. Mary Walsworth manages to smash the machine before Drakma can get it; therefore, the villain captures Alan and Mary, puts Mary on a rumrunner, and leaves Alan on an island to build another triangulator—under pain of Mary's death. Instead, Alan builds a radio and broadcasts an SOS, which is answered by Admiral Walsworth, Mary's father; gets to the rumrunner on a raft; and holds off the crew until the sailors arrive to the rescue. *Radio. Espionage. Rumrunners. Airplanes. United States Navy. United States Marines. War matériel.*

Note: May also be known as *Without Warning.*

STRAIGHT FROM PARIS **F2.5418**

Equity Pictures. ca16 Apr **1921** [New York premiere; released May; c15 Mar 1921; LP17242]. Si; b&w. 35mm. 6 reels.

Dir Harry Garson. *Scen* Sada Cowan.

Cast: Clara Kimball Young *(Lucette Grenier)*, Bertram Grassby *(Robert Van Austen)*, William P. Carleton *(John Van Austen)*, Betty Francisco *(Doris Charming)*, Thomas Jefferson *(Henri Trevel)*, Gerard Alexander *(Mrs. Stevenson)*, Clarissa Selwynne *(Mrs. Van Austen)*.

Society melodrama. On her way to Paris, Lucette Grenier, owner of a smart Fifth Avenue millinery shop, meets and falls in love with Robert Van Austen; they become engaged, but Robert, because of his former affair with Doris Charming, and knowing that his mother does not approve of working girls, persuades her to keep her occupation a secret. At a dinner given by Mrs. Van Austen, Lucette is recognized by Mrs. Stevenson, one of her customers, and consequently she is snubbed by Mrs. Van Austen, although John, Robert's uncle, is charmed by her. When Doris visits her shop and charges expensive articles to Robert, Lucette decides to break the engagement; John Van Austen then pleads his own suit and is accepted. *Uncles. Milliners. Upper classes. Courtship. Paris. New York City.*

STRAIGHT FROM THE SHOULDER **F2.5419**

Fox Film Corp. 19 Jun **1921** [c19 Jun 1921; LP16701]. Si; b&w. 35mm. 6 reels, 5,527 ft.

Pres by William Fox. *Dir* Bernard Durning. *Scen* John Montague. *Story* Roy Norton. *Photog* Frank B. Good.

Cast: Buck Jones *(The Mediator)*, Helen Ferguson *(Maggie, The Waitress)*, Norman Selby *(Bill Higgins)*, Frances Hatton *(Mrs. Bill Higgins)*, Herschel Mayall *(Joseph Martin)*, Yvette Mitchell *(Gladys Martin)*, G. Raymond Nye *(Big Ben Williams)*, Glen Cavender *(Pete)*, Dan Crimmins *(hotel owner)*, Albert Knott *(The Parson)*, Lewis King *(Rogers)*.

Western comedy-melodrama. Bill Higgins disturbs the peace of a little western mining town and causes Buck to wound him in a fight. Nursing Bill back to health, Buck learns that he lives in Peaceful Valley and has been banished from home by his wife for drinking. Buck arrives there in time to reprimand Williams, a crooked mine superintendent; and the owner, Joseph Martin, replaces Williams with Buck, "The Mediator." Williams induces the workers to strike and threatens to blow up the mine. Buck helps to avert the strike, thwarts a gold theft, and is rewarded with Maggie's promise to marry him. With peace declared in his household, Bill returns to town. *Mining. Strikes. Marriage. Alcoholism. Mining towns.*

STRAIGHT IS THE WAY **F2.5420**

Cosmopolitan Productions. *Dist* Paramount Pictures. ca20 Feb **1921** [New York showing; released 6 Mar; c5 Mar 1921; LP16220]. Si; b&w. 35mm. 5 or 6 reels.

Dir Robert G. Vignola. *Scen* Frances Marion. *Photog* Al Ligouri. *Asst Dir* Phil Carle.

Cast: Matt Moore *("Cat" Carter)*, Mabel Bert *(Aunt Mehitabel)*, Gladys Leslie *(Dorcas, her orphan niece)*, George Parsons *("Loot" Follett)*, Henry Sedley *(Jonathan Squoggs)*, Van Dyke Brooks *(Constable Whipple)*, Emily Fitzroy *(Mrs. Crabtree)*, Peggy Parr *(Bobby)*.

Comedy-melodrama. Source: Ethel Watts Mumford, "The Manifestations of Henry Ort" (publication undetermined). Two thieves, "Cat" Carter and "Loot" Follett, locate themselves in the unused part of the home of Aunt Mehitabel and her niece Dorcas. Loan shark Jonathan Squoggs presses Mehitabel for payment of the mortgage, and the two crooks decide to help the ladies when they consult their Ouija board to find a buried treasure. After capturing an intruder who turns out to be Squoggs, the two "detectives" reform and Follett marries Dorcas. *Thieves. Aunts. Spiritualism. Mental telepathy.*

STRAIGHT SHOOTIN' (Blue Streak Western) **F2.5421**

Universal Pictures. 16 Oct **1927** [c24 Aug 1927; LP24332]. Si; b&w. 35mm. 5 reels, 4,202 ft.

Pres by Carl Laemmle. *Dir* William Wyler. *Story-Scen* William Lester. *Titl* Gardner Bradford. *Photog* Milton Bridenbecker. *Art Dir* David S. Garber.

Cast: Ted Wells *(Jack Roberts)*, Garry O'Dell *(Malpai Joe)*, Lillian Gilmore *(Bess Hale)*, Joe Bennett *(Tom Hale)*, Wilbur Mack *(Black Brody)*, George Connors *(John Hale)*, Al Ferguson *(Stephen Clemens?)*.

Western melodrama. Jack Roberts and his sidekick, Malpai Joe, see John Hale and his nephew, Tom, attempting to run a bandit blockade with supplies for their mine; John is wounded by the outlaws, and Tom makes his getaway. Jack rescues John, whom he carries to safety in the hills while Black Brody and his men, who are plotting to flush the miners from their claims, loot the wagon. Bess Hale, infuriated with her cousin's cowardice, begs Jack to stay and aid them. Tom angrily goes to join the gang in order to get his share of the mine and contacts Stephen Clemens, the gang leader. Jack and his friend are captured by the gang and locked in a room with Tom, while John is forced at gunpoint to sign over the claim. But the prisoners escape in time to overcome the bandits in a galloping battle. *Cousins. Miners. Bandits. Cowardice.*

Note: Also reviewed as *Range Riders.*

STRAIGHT THROUGH **F2.5422**

Universal Pictures. 5 Apr **1925** [c14 Jan 1925; LP21030]. Si; b&w. 35mm. 5 reels.

Pres by Carl Laemmle. *Dir* Arthur Rosson. *Story-Cont* Charles Logue. *Photog* Jackson Rose.

Cast: William Desmond *(Good Deed O'Day)*, Marguerite Clayton *(Denver Nell)*, Albert J. Smith *(Granger)*, Ruth Stonehouse *(Mary Snowden)*, Frank Brownlee *(Bill Higgins)*, Bill Gillis *(sheriff)*, George F. Marion *(Parson Sanderson)*.

Western melodrama. God Damn O'Day, the terror of Red Gulch, wins the entire stake of a gambler named Granger in a poker game but gives it all to Denver Nell, a dancehall girl, when she tells him her sad story. O'Day later discovers that she has returned the money to Granger, and he decides to reform. He goes to another town, where (now known as Good Deed O'Day) he meets an old friend, Eric Snowden, a wealthy rancher with whose sister, Mary, he is in love. Snowden takes a trip to Denver and returns with Nell, whom he has married. O'Day meets her alone and promises to say nothing of her shady past if she will play square with Snowden. She gives him her word to be faithful but deliberately violates it by meeting Granger on the sly. Seeing O'Day with Nell, Snowden believes him to be philandering and beats him in a fight. When Nell and Granger are packing, before absconding with Snowden's money, Snowden discovers them and is shot by the gambler. O'Day is accused of the murder but clears himself by capturing Granger and forcing him to confess. *Dancehall girls. Ranchers. Gambling. Murder. Denver.*

Note: Also reviewed as *Ridin' Through.*

STRANDED **F2.5423**

Sterling Pictures. 15 Aug **1927** [c14 Sep 1927; LP24406]. Si; b&w. 35mm. 6 reels, 5,443 ft.

Supv Joe Rock. *Dir* Phil Rosen. *Cont* Frances Guihan. *Titl* Wyndham Gittens. *Story* Anita Loos. *Photog* Herbert Kirkpatrick. *Film Ed* Leotta Whytock.

Cast: Shirley Mason *(Sally Simpson)*, William Collier, Jr. *(Johnny Nash)*, John Miljan *(Grant Payne)*, Florence Turner *(Mrs. Simpson)*, Gale Henry *(Lucille Lareaux)*, Shannon Day *(Betty)*, Lucy Beaumont *(Grandmother)*, Rosa Gore *(landlady)*.

Romantic melodrama. Sally Simpson, a smalltown girl, is helped by her sacrificing mother and grandmother in her ambition to embark on a Hollywood career, although her fiancé, Johnny Nash, tries to dissuade her. In Hollywood, Sally finds hard realities but luckily gets an extra part and makes friends with Lucille Lareaux, a friendly old trouper. While her mother is working to make ends meet, Sally, though jobless, sends home letters about her success. Through the influence of a friend she meets Grant Payne, who spends his money on innocent Hollywood girls, and he intimates that he will do something for her, "provided ... ." When Sally fails miserably at an acting job, she gets work in a beanery. Her mother needs money for an operation, and Sally is prepared to sacrifice herself to Grant just as Johnny arrives, summoned by Lucille, and overcomes Payne in a fight. Sally gives up her career ambitions for Johnny. *Actors. Motherhood. Smalltown life. Restaurants. Motion pictures. Hollywood.*

STRANDED IN PARIS **F2.5424**

Famous Players–Lasky. *Dist* Paramount Pictures. 13 Dec **1926** [c14 Dec 1926; LP23429]. Si; b&w. 35mm. 7 reels, 6,106 ft.

Pres by Adolph Zukor, Jesse L. Lasky. *Dir* Arthur Rosson. *Screenplay* Ethel Doherty, Louise Long. *Titl* George Marion, Jr. *Adapt* Herman J. Mankiewicz, John McDermott. *Photog* William Marshall.

Cast: Bebe Daniels *(Julie McFadden)*, James Hall *(Robert Van Wye)*, Ford Sterling *(Count Pasada)*, Iris Stuart *(Theresa Halstead)*, Mabel Julienne Scott *(Countess Pasada)*, Tom Ricketts *(Herr Rederson)*, Helen Dunbar *(Mrs. Van Wye)*, Ida Darling *(Mrs. Halstead)*, George Grandee *(Pettipan)*, André Lanoy *(Schwab)*.

Romantic comedy. Source: Hans Bachwitz and Fritz Jakobstetter, *Jennys Bummel; Humoreske in vier Akten* (Berlin, 1926). Julie McFadden, an American shopgirl, wins a free passage to Paris; en route she meets Robert Van Wye, who has to kiss her when she loses a sack race. In Paris, Julie finds her proposed residence destroyed, and while waiting for Bob her purse is snatched; in the ensuing chase she gets lost and enters a modiste's shop, where the two owners are in dire need of an English-speaking girl to deliver some gowns. Accidentally she is given entree to the apartment of Countess Pasada and is shown to her rooms; the count is in his pajamas when she emerges from her bath, and she locks him in the bathroom. Later, attempting to escape, she runs into Bob's arms and is forced to hide from the countess in a perambulator. Following a series of whirlwind escapades, Julie extricates herself and is happily united with Bob. *Salesclerks. Modistes. Nobility. Paris.*

STRANGE CARGO **F2.5425**

Pathé Exchange. 31 Mar **1929** [c26 Mar 1929; LP243]. Sd (Photophone); b&w. 35mm. 7 reels, 7,045 ft. [Also si; 6,134 ft.]

Supv–Sd Dir Benjamin Glazer. *Dir of Si Sequences* Arthur Gregor. *Screenplay* Horace Jackson. *Dial* Benjamin Glazer. *Titl* John Krafft. *Story* Benjamin Glazer, Melchior Lengyel. *Photog* Arthur Miller. *Film Ed* Paul Weatherwax, Jack Ogilvie. *Rec Engr* George Ellis.

Cast: Lee Patrick *(Diana Foster)*, June Nash *(Ruth)*, George Barraud *(Bruce Lloyd)*, Cosmo Kyrle Bellew *(Barclay)*, Russell Gleason *(Hungerford)*, Frank Reicher *(Dr. Stecker)*, Claude King *(captain)*, Ned Sparks *(first mate)*, Josephine Brown *(Mrs. Townsend)*, Charles Hamilton *(boatswain)*, André Beranger *(first stranger)*, Otto Matiesen *(second stranger)*, Harry Allen *(Short)*, Warner Richmond *(Neil Stoker)*.

Mystery melodrama. Sir Richard Barclay is murdered on his yacht, and the captain holds an inquest. Suspicion falls primarily on two people: Bruce Lloyd, who had once threatened to kill Barclay for tampering with his fiancée, Diana Foster; and Dr. Stecker, a known criminal wanted by the London police. Bruce is kidnaped by a stowaway and placed in a locker; he is later rescued. A Yogi is found on board and claims to know nothing of the murder, having been in a trance at the time. The Yogi later confesses to the crime, however, and is arrested by the captain. Diana asks Bruce to forgive her for doubting his sincerity. *Physicians. Yogis. Stowaways. Murder. Yachts.*

STRANGE IDOLS **F2.5426**

Fox Film Corp. 28 May **1922** [c28 May 1922; LP18016]. Si; b&w. 35mm. 5 reels, 4,300 ft.

Pres by William Fox. *Dir* Bernard J. Durning. *Scen* Jules Furthman. *Story* Emil Forst. *Photog* Don Short.

Cast: Dustin Farnum *(Angus MacDonald)*, Doris Pawn *(Ruth Mayo)*, Philo McCullough *(Ted Raymond)*, Richard Tucker *(Malcolm Sinclair)*.

Society drama. While visiting in New York, lumberman Angus MacDonald is introduced to Ruth Mayo, a cabaret dancer, by his friend Sinclair. Their romance culminates in marriage, and soon MacDonald takes his bride back to the Northwest. Ruth grows tired of the Northwest, and MacDonald returns with her to New York, where their child is born; but his business does not permit him to remain. One night Ruth returns to the cafe, dances with her old partner, and accepts an agent's offer of a European tour. Six years later, MacDonald learns that his daughter is dancing at the same cafe, and through her a reconciliation is effected between husband and wife. *Dancers. Lumbermen. Marriage. New York City—Broadway.*

Note: Working title: *Vows That May Be Broken.*

THE STRANGE RIDER **F2.5427**

Arrow Pictures. 26 Jul **1925** [c16 Jun 1925; LP21564]. Si; b&w. 35mm. 5 reels.

Dir Ward Hayes. *Story* Perry N. Vekroff.

Cast: Yakima Canutt.

Western melodrama. Jim Weston saves Mary Drake's life and gets a job on her father's ranch, where he soon becomes well liked for his quick humor and hard riding. Some of Drake's cattle are stolen, and Hank Bennett, foreman of the ranch, accuses Jim. Mary then challenges Jim to prove his innocence, and he rides after the rustlers, capturing three of them. Tying up his prisoners, Jim rides on and finds a shack, which he suspects is the hideout of the gang. Mary, who has followed Jim, appears and tells him of her pride in him. He hears men coming, and she hides behind some barrels. Jim then meets Slavin, the leader of the gang, and beats him in a fight, later capturing two more of his men. Drake arrives, and Jim, who has cleared himself of all suspicion of crime, flashes a badge and reveals himself to be a lawman. *Cowboys. Sheriffs. Ranch foremen. Gangs. Rustling.*

THE STRANGER **F2.5428**

Famous Players–Lasky. *Dist* Paramount Pictures. ca27 Jan **1924** [New York showing; released 11 or 25 Feb; c19 Feb 1924; LP19922]. Si; b&w. 35mm. 7 reels, 6,515 or 6,660 ft.

Pres by Adolph Zukor, Jesse L. Lasky. *Dir* Joseph Henabery. *Adapt* Edfrid Bingham. *Photog* Faxon M. Dean, L. Guy Wilky. *Tech Dir* A. Moresby White.

Cast: Betty Compson *(Peggy Bowlin)*, Richard Dix *(Larry Darrant)*, Lewis Stone *(Keith Darrant)*, Tully Marshall *(The Stranger)*, Robert Schable *(Jim Walenn)*, Mary Jane Irving *(Maizie Darrant)*, Frank Nelson *(Jackal, or Bill Cutts)*, Marian Skinner *(landlady)*.

Melodrama. Source: John Galsworthy, *The First and the Last* (London, 1920). "The Stranger," a poor nameless scrubman in a London pub, takes the blame for Larry Darrant's killing of Jim Walenn, an ex-convict who attacked Larry's fiancée, Peggy Bowlin, on the eve of their wedding. The Stranger, whom Peggy befriended, goes on trial, refuses to talk, and is sentenced to death by hanging. He has a heart attack on the scaffold and dies naturally just as Darrant is about to come forward to confess. Thus, Darrant's family name is saved from scandal, and the two lovers face a happy future. *Scrubmen. Scapegoats. Strangers. Trials. Capital punishment. Injustice. London.*

THE STRANGER IN CANYON VALLEY **F2.5429**

Dist Arrow Film Corp. Apr **1921.** Si; b&w. 35mm. 5 reels, 4,625 ft.

Dir Cliff Smith.

Cast: Edith Sterling.

Western melodrama. "About a maid who roamed the bad lands of a section in Arizona, a sort of woman Robin Hood, of whom never a glimpse was caught except at night. Some years before, with an oath of vengeance on those who had murdered her father and burned her home, she determined to live lonely and secluded. She knew a man who professed love for her had murdered her father. A young prospector comes along and is unwelcomed by the girl until circumstances bring her to admire his courage and in time respond to his proffered love." (*Motion Picture News Booking Guide*, 1:106, Dec 1921.) *Recluses. Prospectors. Bandits. Revenge. Arizona.*

THE STRANGER OF THE HILLS **F2.5430**

Farra Feature Productions. *Dist* Anchor Film Distributors. 1 Nov **1922.** Si; b&w. 35mm. 5 reels, 3,930 or 4,900 ft.

Dir Bruce Mitchell.

Cast: Edward Coxen, Ethel Ritchie, Charles Farra.

Western melodrama. "Western drama of the great outdoors, which features a girl falling in love with The Stranger, who is accused by a rival of being 'The Killer,' upon whom there is a heavy price for his capture, dead or alive. The Sheriff arrests The Stranger, but his release is effected by the girl. Eventually the rival proves to be 'The Killer' and The Stranger is identified as a Captain of the Rangers. He finds romance and happiness with the girl." (*Motion Picture News Booking Guide*, 4:95, Apr 1923.) *Strangers. Sheriffs. Texas Rangers.*

STRANGER THAN FICTION **F2.5431**

Katherine MacDonald Pictures. *Dist* Associated First National Pictures. Jun **1921** [c12 Jul, 2 Sep 1921; LP16757, LP17266]. Si; b&w. 35mm. 6 reels, 6,388 ft.

Pres by B. P. Schulberg. *Dir* J. A. Barry. *Titl* Ralph Spence. *Story* Charles Richman, Albert Shelby Le Vino. *Photog* Joseph Brotherton. *Art Dir* A. Douda. *Film Ed* Ralph Spence.

Cast: Katherine MacDonald *(Diane Drexel)*, Dave Winter *(Dick Mason)*, Wesley Barry *(Freckles)*, Wade Boteler *(The Black Heart)*, Jean Dumont *(The Shadow)*, Harry O'Connor *(The Croaker)*, Evelyn Burns *(Diane's aunt)*, Tom McGuire *(police commissioner)*.

Underworld melodrama. Society girl Diane Drexel invites her friends to see a screening of *Carmen* in which they have acted. She then tells the projectionist to show her original film, *Stranger Than Fiction*. This film then unfolds the following action: *When the lights are turned up the guests find they have been robbed by the "Black Heart," head of a notorious gang, who have left their familiar mark. Diane declares that she will not marry her indolent fiancé until he has tracked down the robbers. In the slums, Diane meets The Shadow and through him learns that Dick is endangered; with his help she joins the gang. Following a series of escapes, climaxed by an airplane stunt in which the "Black Heart" is forced to his death,* the lights flash on and Diane informs the guests that this is her idea of how motion pictures ought to be made. *Socialites. Motion pictures. Robbery. Air stunts. "Carmen".*

Note: The film originally included only the "fictional" story, the framework of a film-within-the-film being added later.

THE STRANGER'S BANQUET **F2.5432**

Marshall Neilan Productions. *Dist* Goldwyn Distributing Corp. 31 Dec **1922** [c31 Dec 1922; LP18551]. Si; b&w. 35mm. 9 reels, 8,800 ft. [Later cut to 7 reels, 6,842 ft.]

Pres by Marshall Neilan. *Dir* Marshall Neilan. *Cont* Frank Urson, Marshall Neilan. *Photog* David Kesson, Max Fabian. *Asst Dir* Thomas Held.

Cast: Hobart Bosworth *(Shane Keogh)*, Claire Windsor *(Derith Keogh)*, Rockliffe Fellowes *(Angus Campbell)*, Ford Sterling *(Al Norton)*, Eleanor Boardman *(Jean McPherson)*, Thomas Holding *(John Trevelyan)*, Eugenie Besserer *(Mrs. McPherson)*, Nigel Barrie *(John Keogh)*, Stuart Holmes *(Prince)*, Claude Gillingwater *(Uncle Sam)*, Margaret Loomis *(bride)*, Tom Guise *(bride's father)*, Lillian Langdon *(bride's mother)*, William Humphrey *(groom's friend)*, Edward McWade *(Harriman)*, Lorimer Johnson *(Ross)*, James Marcus *(Braithwaite)*, Edward W. Borman *(Dolan)*, Jack Curtis *(McKinstry)*, Brinsley Shaw *(Krischenko)*, Arthur Hoyt *(Morel)*, Aileen Pringle *(Mrs. Schuyler-Peabody)*, Virginia Ruggles *(Olive Stockton)*, Cyril Chadwick *(Bond)*, Philo McCullough *(Britton)*, Jean Hersholt *(fiend)*, Lucille Ricksen *(flapper)*, Dagmar Godowsky *(Spanish señorita)*, Hayford Hobbs *(toreador)*, Violet Joy *(cabaret girl)*.

Melodrama. Source: Brian Oswald Donn-Byrne, *The Stranger's Banquet* (New York, 1919). In managing the shipyard inherited from her father, Derith Keogh has considerable labor problems and accedes to the unreasonable demands of John Trevelyan, anarchist labor agitator. Derith's brother, John, is off in pursuit of an adventuress, and Angus Campbell, her superintendent, resigns in exasperation. Angus returns, however, to help Derith persuade Trevelyan to settle a strike, which Trevelyan accomplishes in spite of being shot by one of his own men. *Businesswomen. Anarchists. Labor agitators. Shipyards. Labor. Strikes.*

STRANGERS OF THE NIGHT **F2.5433**

Louis B. Mayer Productions. *Dist* Metro Pictures. 10 Sep **1923** [c5 Sep 1923; LP19402]. Si; b&w. 35mm. 8 reels, 7,792 ft.

Pres by Louis B. Mayer. *Prod-Dir* Fred Niblo. *Scen* Bess Meredyth. *Titl* Renaud. *Adapt* C. Gardner Sullivan. *Photog* Alvin Wyckoff. *Scenic Architecture* Robert Ellis. *Film Ed* Lloyd Nosler.

Cast: Matt Moore *(Ambrose Applejohn)*, Enid Bennett *(Poppy Faire)*, Barbara La Marr *(Anna Valeska)*, Robert McKim *(Borolsky)*, Mathilde Brundage *(Mrs. Whatacombe)*, Emily Fitzroy *(Mrs. Pengard)*, Otto Hoffman *(Horace Pengard)*, Thomas Ricketts *(Lush)*.

Mystery-comedy. Source: Walter Hackett, *Captain Applejack; an Arabian Night's Adventure, in Three Acts* (New York, 1925). Ambrose Applejohn, a typical English country gentleman, seeks adventure and finds it when thieves come to steal a treasure secreted by his pirate ancestor, Captain Applejack. Temporarily thwarting them, he falls asleep dreaming of Applejack's conquests. Instilled with courage, Applejohn awakens to secure the booty, then finds romance with Poppy Faire, his aunt's ward. *Pirates. Treasure. England. Dreams.*

Note: Working title: *Captain Applejack*.

STRAUSS' SALOME *see* **SALOME**

A STREAK OF LUCK **F2.5434**

Action Pictures. *Dist* Weiss Brothers Artclass Pictures. 23 Dec **1925.** Si; b&w. 35mm. 5 reels, 4,767 ft.

Dir Richard Thorpe. *Scen* Frank L. Inghram. *Story* Philip Hubbard.

Cast: Buffalo Bill Jr. *(Billy Burton)*, Dorothy Wood *(Francie Oliver)*, Nelson McDowell *(Big Ben Tuttle)*, Bertram Marburgh *(Mr. Burton)*, Charles Whittaker *(Black Pete)*, Fred Holmes *(Burton's valet)*, George Y. Harvey *(The Police Officer)*, Edward Klein *(Burton's secretary)*, Jack O'Brien *(Jack Hurst)*, Norbert Myles *(Sam Kellman)*, Ronald Rondell.

Western melodrama. "... with hero disowned by father after night club escapade. He goes west, is robbed, rescues heroine, becomes involved in all sorts of adventurous scrapes and ultimately triumphs." ("Motion Picture News Booking Guide," in *Motion Picture News*, 8 May 1926, p45.) *Nightclubs. Robbery. Filial relations.*

STREET ANGEL **F2.5435**

Fox Film Corp. 9 Apr **1928** [New York premiere; released 19 Aug; c3 Apr 1928; LP25115]. Talking sequences, mus score, and sd eff (Movietone); b&w. 35mm. 10 reels, 9,221 ft. [Also si.]

Pres by William Fox. *Dir* Frank Borzage. *Scen* Marion Orth. *Titl* Katherine Hilliker, H. H. Caldwell. *Adapt* Philip Klein, Henry Roberts Symonds. *Photog* Ernest Palmer. *Film Ed* Barney Wolf. *Asst Dir* Lew Borzage.

Cast: Janet Gaynor *(Angela)*, Charles Farrell *(Gino)*, Alberto Rabagliati, Gino Conti *(policemen)*, Guido Trento *(Neri, police sergeant)*, Henry Armetta *(Mascetto)*, Louis Liggett *(Beppo)*, Milton Dickinson *(Bimbo)*, Helena Herman *(Andrea)*, Natalie Kingston *(Lisetta)*, David Kashner *(The Strong Man)*, Jennie Bruno *(landlady)*.

Drama. Source: Monckton Hoffe, *Cristilinda* (New York, 1926). Angela, a poor Neapolitan girl, desperate to acquire medication for her sick mother, comes into conflict with the police and finds refuge with a traveling circus. She meets Gino, a painter, who has her pose for a Madonna portrait; but the authorities track her down, and she is forced to serve a prison term, while Gino, who loves her, becomes despondent and loses interest in his work. Released from prison, Angela recognizes her portrait in a church and encounters Gino; they are reunited when she convinces him she is still worthy of having posed for a Madonna. *Artists. Filial relations. Circus. Prisons. Naples.*

Note: Some sources list Miss Gaynor as *Maria*, Mr. Farrell as *Angelo*, Guido Trento as *Rio*, and Natalie Kingston as *Nina*.

STREET GIRL **F2.5436**

RKO Productions. 30 Jul **1929** [New York premiere; released 21 Aug; c29 Jul 1929; LP612, LP894]. Sd (Photophone); b&w. 35mm. 9 reels, 8,200 ft.

Supv William Le Baron. *Assoc Prod* Luther Reed, Louis Sarecky. *Dir* Wesley Ruggles. *Adapt-Dial* Jane Murfin. *Photog* Leo Tover. *Mus Dir* Victor Baravalle. *Songs: "Huggable and Sweet," "My Dream Melody," "Broken Up Tune"* Oscar Levant, Sidney Clare. *Dances* Pearl Eaton. *Cost* Max Ree.

Cast: Betty Compson *(Freddie Joyzelle)*, John Harron *(Mike Fall)*, Ned Sparks *(Happy Winter)*, Jack Oakie *(Joe Spring)*, Guy Buccola *(Pete Summer)*, Joseph Cawthorn *(Keppel)*, Ivan Lebedeff *(Prince Nicholaus)*, Eddie Kane *(club manager)*, Doris Eaton and the Radio Pictures Beauty Chorus, Raymond Maurel and the Cimini Male Chorus, Gus Arnheim and His Cocoanut Grove Ambassadors.

Romantic drama. Source: William Carey Wonderly, "The Viennese Charmer" (publication undetermined). The Four Seasons (Mike, Joe, Pete, and Guy) make a meager living playing jazz at a shabby East Side restaurant. On their way home one night, Mike saves a little blonde from a drunken masher. Freddie Joyzelle, as she calls herself, is a destitute Hungarian violinist, and Mike persuades his partners to let her stay with them. She inspires the boys to ask for a raise, and when they are fired she finds them a better place at a little Hungarian restaurant, joining them as violinist. Prince Nicholaus of Aragon visits the cafe one night and kisses the girl when she plays a song for him, arousing Mike's jealousy; as a result of the prince's patronage, the cafe becomes famous and the musicians the toast of the town. Keppel manages to keep them by planning a new nightclub; but Mike's jealousy causes him to leave the group. The prince, however, reunites the lovers, and at the club opening all ends happily. *Violinists. Royalty. Nightclubs. Jazz. Hungarians. New York City—East Side.*

Note: Initially reviewed as *Barber John's Boy.*

STREET OF CHANCE F2.5437

Paramount Famous Lasky Corp. 8 Feb **1930** [c7 Feb 1930; LP1055]. Sd (Movietone); b&w. 35mm. 9 reels, 7,023 ft. [Also si; 5,962 ft.]

Dir John Cromwell. *Dial* Lenore J. Coffee. *Titl* Gerald Geraghty. *Adapt* Howard Estabrook. *Story* Oliver H. P. Garrett. *Photog* Charles Lang. *Film Ed* Otto Levering. *Rec Engr* Harry D. Mills.

Cast: William Powell *(John B. Marsden ["Natural" Davis])*, Jean Arthur *(Judith Marsden)*, Kay Francis *(Alma Marsden)*, Regis Toomey *("Babe" Marsden)*, Stanley Fields *(Dorgan)*, Brooks Benedict *(Al Mastick)*, Betty Francisco *(Mrs. Mastick)*, John Risso *(Tony)*, Joan Standing *(Miss Abrams)*, Maurice Black *(Nick)*, Irving Bacon *(Harry)*, John Cromwell *(Imbrie)*.

Melodrama. John Marsden, a powerful New York gambler, is devoted to his wife, Alma, and his younger brother, "Babe," to whom he sends a wedding gift of $10,000, which Babe may keep on the condition that he does not indulge in gambling. Alma, dismayed by John's ruthless tactics and his obsession with gambling, threatens to leave him unless he takes his winnings and leaves the city with her. He agrees, but that evening Babe insists on playing, and he wins remarkably. John decides to break the gambler's code and cheat in order to teach his brother a lesson, but he is caught by Dorgan and later is mortally wounded, in spite of his wife's attempts to save him. *Gamblers. Brothers. Cheating. New York City.*

THE STREET OF FORGOTTEN MEN F2.5438

Famous Players–Lasky. *Dist* Paramount Pictures. 24 Aug **1925** [c22 Aug 1925; LP21769]. Si; b&w. 35mm. 7 reels, 6,366 ft.

Pres by Adolph Zukor, Jesse L. Lasky. *Dir* Herbert Brenon. *Screenplay* Paul Schofield. *Adapt* John Russell. *Photog* Hal Rosson. *Art Dir* Frederick A. Foord.

Cast: Percy Marmont *(Easy Money Charlie)*, Mary Brian *(Fancy Vanhern)*, Neil Hamilton *(Philip Peyton)*, John Harrington *(Bridgeport White-Eye)*, Juliet Brenon *(Portland Fancy)*, Josephine Deffry *(Dutch Molly)*, Riley Hatch *(Diamond Mike)*, Agostino Borgato *(Adolphe)*, Albert Roccardi *(Adolphe's assistant)*, Dorothy Walters *(Widow McKee)*.

Melodrama. Source: George Kibbe Turner, "Street of the Forgotten Men," in *Liberty Magazine* (1:17–19, 14 Feb 1925). Easy Money Charlie is a whole man who disguises himself as a cripple and makes his living as a professional beggar. When Portland Fancy dies, Charlie takes her child and sends the little girl to the country, providing her with a proper education and upbringing. Years later, the girl, known as Fancy Vanhern, meets and captures the heart of Philip Peyton, a young lawyer whose name is prominent in the social register. In order to secure Fancy's future happiness, Charlie feigns death in an ocean accident; Fancy then prepares to marry Philip. Bridgeport White-Eye, a beggar who affects blindness, discovers Charlie's secret and tries to blackmail Philip. White-Eye and Charlie fight, and White-Eye is indeed blinded. Philip marries Fancy, and Charlie takes over the care of White-Eye. *Beggars. Cripples. Lawyers. Blindness. Imposture. Social classes.*

THE STREET OF ILLUSION F2.5439

Columbia Pictures. 3 Sep **1928** [c1 Nov 1928; LP25798]. Si; b&w. 35mm. 7 reels, 5,988 ft.

Prod Harry Cohn. *Dir* Erle C. Kenton. *Cont* Dorothy Howell. *Titl* Morton Blumenstock. *Adapt* Harvey Thew. *Photog* Joseph Walker. *Art Dir* Harrison Wiley. *Film Ed* Frank Atkinson. *Asst Dir* Joseph Nadel.

Cast: Virginia Valli *(Sylvia Thurston)*, Ian Keith *(Edwin Booth Benton)*, Harry Myers *(Lew Fielding)*, Kenneth Thomson *(Curtis Drake)*.

Drama. Source: Channing Pollock, "The Street of Illusion" (publication undetermined). Edwin Booth Benton, an impecunious, egotisitical, and embittered actor who is given a small part in a Broadway production, secures for Sylvia Thurston, a beautiful young actress of his acquaintance, the feminine lead in the play. Sylvia falls in love with Curtis Drake, the play's leading man, and Benton's jealousy is greatly aroused; when Drake and Sylvia announce their engagement, Benton is overcome with rage and substitutes real bullets for the blanks in the prop pistol used to shoot Drake in the third act. The following day, Drake is injured in a fall just after the second act, and Benton (Drake's understudy) must go on in his place; mortally wounded, Drake confesses all and dies with the audience's applause still sounding in his ears. *Actors. Theater. Jealousy. New York City—Broadway.*

THE STREET OF SIN F2.5440

Paramount Famous Lasky Corp. 26 May **1928** [c26 May 1928; LP25298]. Si; b&w. 35mm. 7 reels, 6,218 ft.

Pres by Adolph Zukor, Jesse L. Lasky. *Assoc Prod* B. P. Schulberg, Benjamin Glazer. *Dir* Mauritz Stiller. *Scen* Chandler Sprague. *Titl* Julian Johnson. *Story* Josef von Sternberg, Benjamin Glazer. *Photog* Bert Glennon. *Photog? (see note)* Harry Fischbeck, Victor Milner. *Set Dsgn* Hans Dreier. *Film Ed* George Nichols, Jr.

Cast: Emil Jannings *("Basher Bill")*, Fay Wray *(Elizabeth)*, Olga Baclanova *(Annie)*, Ernest W. Johnson *(Mr. Smith)*, George Kotsonaros *("Iron Mike")*, John Gough, Johnnie Morris *(cronies of "Basher Bill")*, John Burdette *(proprietor of pub)*.

Crime melodrama. "Basher Bill," a retired prizefighter turned criminal, pretends to reform by joining a Salvation Army shelter in London run by a pious wraith named Elizabeth. Attracted to Elizabeth (although he is engaged to a street girl named Annie), Bill confesses to a bank robbery, has a spiritual revelation, and decides to go straight. His cast-off sweetheart reports him to the police; then, contrite, she warns Bill of the impending danger. Bill is captured immediately, but he escapes and sacrifices his life to save Elizabeth and the Salvation Army nursery when the rest of the gang use them as a human barricade against the police. *Prizefighters. Criminals—Rehabilitation. Prostitutes. Piety. Self-sacrifice. Salvation Army. London.*

Note: Indication from some sources that Harry Fischbeck and Victor Milner were the photographers has not been verified.

THE STREET OF TEARS F2.5441

Rayart Pictures. 1 Oct **1924**. Si; b&w. 35mm. 5 reels, 4,748 ft.

Dir Travers Vale. *Photog* Travers Vale.

Cast: Tom Santschi *(Jim Carlson)*, Marguerite Clayton *(Betty Blair)*, Gordon Griffith *(Ted Weller)*, Barbara Tennant *(Mary Weller)*, George MacQuarrie *(Dan Weller)*, Charlotte Morgan *(Mamie Ryan)*.

Melodrama. "... of poor family in which father is framed into penitentiary by crooks. The boy, as a messenger, meets famous actress. The crooks attempt to frame the boy, but are foiled by kind hearted policeman. Father is released and becomes involved with gang leader. Mother despairs of overcoming bad environment, when actress solves problem by sending family to her Vermont farm." (*Motion Picture News Booking Guide*, 8:75, Apr 1925.) *Actors. Police. Motherhood. Gangs. Vermont.*

THE STREET OF THE FLYING DRAGON *see* **FIVE DAYS TO LIVE**

THE STREETS OF NEW YORK F2.5442

State Pictures. *Dist* Arrow Film Corp. 30 Oct **1922** [Jersey City premiere; released 15 Nov; c10 Nov 1922; LP18388]. Si; b&w. 35mm. 7 reels, 6,541 ft.

Dir Burton King. *Photog* Alfred Ortlieb.

Cast: Anders Randolf *(Gideon Bloodgood)*, Leslie King *(Badger)*, Barbara Castleton *(Lucy Bloodgood)*, Edward Earle *(Paul Fairweather)*, Dorothy Mackaill *(Sally Ann)*, Kate Blanke *(Jennie)*.

Society melodrama. Source: Leota Morgan, *The Streets of New York* (a play; publication undetermined). Paul Fairweather, whose father was robbed by Gideon Bloodgood, is crippled by an accident for which Lucy Bloodgood is unknowingly responsible. Badger, a clerk who has blackmailed Bloodgood for many years, identifies Paul and becomes jealous of the latter's love for Lucy. He arranges a meeting between Paul, now healthy, and Bloodgood to eliminate both of them. There ensue a fight and a storm during which Badger and Bloodgood fall to their deaths; Lucy is rescued by Paul. *Cripples. Blackmail. Murder. New York City. Storms.*

STREETS OF SHANGHAI **F2.5443**

Tiffany-Stahl Productions. 15 Dec **1927** [c4 Jan 1928; LP24824]. Si; b&w. 35mm. 6 reels, 5,276 ft.

Dir Louis Gasnier. *Titl* Viola Brothers Shore, Harry Braxton. *Story-Cont* John Francis Natteford. *Photog* Max Dupont, Earl Walker. *Set Dsgn* George E. Sawley. *Film Ed* Martin G. Cohn.

Cast: Pauline Starke *(Mary Sanger)*, Kenneth Harlan *(Sergeant Lee)*, Eddie Gribbon *(Swede)*, Margaret Livingston *(Sadie)*, Jason Robards *(Eugene Fong)*, Mathilde Comont *(Buttercup, Mary's companion)*, Sojin *(Fong Kiang)*, Anna May Wong *(Su Quan)*, Tetsu Komai *(Chang Ho)*, Toshyie Ichioka *(Girl Wife)*, Media Ichioka *(F'aien Shi, the Chinese girl)*.

Melodrama. Mary Sanger, an American missionary in Shanghai, angers Fong Kiang, a Chinese vice overlord, when she rescues a little Chinese girl from a bawdy house. His son, Eugene Fong, is in love with Mary, who in turn competes with Sadie, a reformed prostitute, for the love of Lee, a marine. Fong Kiang stages an attack on the mission and accidentally has his own son killed. During the attack Mary declares her love for Lee, and they embrace just as the mission is penetrated. They are saved, however, when the little Chinese girl goes for help and returns with a small army of marines. *Missionaries. Prostitution. Shanghai. United States Marines.*

STRENGTH OF THE PINES **F2.5444**

Fox Film Corp. 5 Feb **1922** [c5 Feb 1922; LP17601]. Si; b&w. 35mm. 5 reels, 4,382 ft.

Pres by William Fox. *Dir* Edgar Lewis. *Adapt* Louise Lewis. *Photog* Don Short, Sol Polito.

Cast: William Russell *(Bruce Duncan)*, Irene Rich *(Linda)*, Lule Warrenton *(Elmira Ross)*, Arthur Morrison *(Bill Turner)*, Les Bates *(Simon Turner)*.

Melodrama. Source: Edison Marshall, *The Strength of the Pines* (Boston, 1921). Shortly after graduating from college, Bruce Duncan receives word that Linda, supposedly his sister, is in danger; he goes west and discovers that an estate owned by the girl's father has been seized by the Turners, who forged a deed before Linda's return from the orphanage where she and Bruce were reared. Bruce further discovers that she is not actually his sister but was put in the orphanage to escape Turner's abuse. Of those who witnessed the forgery, only one person is living; and with Linda's assistance Bruce obtains the testimony of that person. After the property is restored to its rightful owner, Bruce wins Linda. *Orphans. Property rights. Forgery.*

STRICTLY MODERN **F2.5445**

First National Pictures. 2 Mar **1930** [c17 Mar 1930; LP1158]. Sd (Vitaphone); b&w. 35mm. 6 reels, 5,632 ft.

Dir William A. Seiter. *Story-Scen-Dial* Ray Harris, Gene Towne. *Photog* Sid Hickox. *Rec Engr* Robert B. Lee.

Cast: Dorothy Mackaill *(Kate)*, Sidney Blackmer *(Heath Desmond)*, Julanne Johnston *(Amy Spencer)*, Warner Richmond *(Judge Bartlett)*, Mickey Bennett *(Bobby)*, Katherine Clare Ward *(Ma Spencer)*, Lottie Williams.

Comedy. Source: Hubert Henry Davies, *Cousin Kate, a Comedy in Three Acts* (Boston, 1910). Following the advice of Judge Bartlett, novelist Amy Spencer tells her prospective husband, Heath Desmond, that there will be no painting of nudes on Sunday and no passion in their marriage; consequently, he leaves her at the altar and disappears. As the judge is consoling Amy (though actually he disapproves of her cynical writings on love), her mother announces that Cousin Kate is arriving for the wedding. Meanwhile, Kate meets Heath on the train, and they enter into a mutual courtship; but when Kate learns that he is Amy's fiancé, she pretends that she was only flirting. When, however, she perceives that the judge and Amy are in love, she gives the judge a drug just before Amy's marriage to Heath is to be solemnized. With this development, Amy declares her love for the judge, and Heath and Kate decide on an early marriage. *Novelists. Artists. Judges. Cousins. Courtship. Weddings.*

STRICTLY UNCONVENTIONAL **F2.5446**

Metro-Goldwyn-Mayer Pictures. 19 Apr or 3 May **1930** [c28 Apr 1930; LP1259]. Sd (Movietone); b&w. 35mm. 6 reels, 4,970 ft.

Dir David Burton. *Screenplay* Sylvia Thalberg, Frank Butler. *Photog* Oliver Marsh, William Daniels. *Art Dir* Cedric Gibbons. *Film Ed* Margaret Booth. *Rec Engr* G. A. Burns, Douglas Shearer. *Wardrobe* David Cox.

Cast: Catherine Dale Owen *(Elizabeth)*, Paul Cavanagh *(Ted)*, Tyrrell Davis *(Arnold Champion-Cheney, M. P.)*, Lewis Stone *(Clive Champion-Cheney)*, Ernest Torrence *(Lord Porteous)*, Alison Skipworth *(Lady Catherine Champion-Cheney)*, Mary Forbes *(Mrs. Anna Shenstone)*, Wilfred Noy *(butler)*, William O'Brien *(footman)*.

Society-domestic drama. Source: William Somerset Maugham, *The Circle, a Comedy in Three Acts* (London, 1921). Elizabeth, the wife of ambitious and foppish Clive Champion-Cheney, finds her marriage a bitter disappointment because of her husband's puritanical ideas; and she falls in love with Ted, a young Canadian who is visiting them. Clive's mother, Lady Catherine, who ran away from her husband 30 years before with a lover, pays them a visit, and when Elizabeth connives to leave with Ted, her mother-in-law warns her against it, citing her own life as an example of the consequences. Clive, learning of his wife's intentions and advised by his divorced father, tries to regain his wife's affections; she agrees to stay with him, but when Ted takes matters in his own hands Elizabeth returns to her young lover. *Marriage. Infidelity. Aristocrats. Canadians. England. Great Britain—Parliament.*

Note: Initially reviewed as *The Circle*, this film is a remake of the 1925 film of that title, q. v.

STRIVING FOR FORTUNE **F2.5447**

Excellent Pictures. 20 Dec **1926** [c24 Dec 1926; LP23476]. Si; b&w. 35mm. 6 reels, 5,300 ft.

Pres by Samuel Zierler. *Dir* Nat Ross. *Story* Merle Johnson.

Cast: George Walsh *(Tom Sheridan)*, Beryl Roberts *(Hope Loring)*, Tefft Johnson, Joseph Burke, Louise Carter, Dexter McReynolds.

Melodrama. Tom Sheridan, a son of a family of shipbuilders in Newport News, is completing the construction of a new vessel to meet a scheduled deadline. Pete Lardner, the hull boss, conspires with a rival firm and promises to delay the progress of his work to assure the rival a large contract. While Lardner is showing President Harrington and his daughter, Gerry, the drydocks, Reggie, an idle-rich suitor, is endangered, and Tom comes to his rescue. Dad Loring has invented a launching trigger for the company, but Harrington rejects his offer because he once loved Loring's wife, but through the intervention of Hope, Loring's daughter, he is persuaded. In spite of sabotage attempts, Tom uncovers Lardner's perfidy and succeeds in launching the ship. He is finally united with his sweetheart, Hope. *Shipbuilding. Sabotage. Newport News (Virginia).*

STRONG BOY **F2.5448**

Fox Film Corp. 3 Mar **1929** [c15 Feb 1929; LP120]. Sd eff and mus score (Movietone); b&w. 35mm. 6 reels, 5,567 ft. [Also si; 5,526 ft.]

Pres by William Fox. *Dir* John Ford. *Scen* James Kevin McGuinness, Andrew Bennison, John McLain. *Titl* Malcolm Stuart Boylan. *Story* Frederick Hazlitt Brennan. *Photog* Joseph August.

Cast: Victor McLaglen *(Strong Boy)*, Leatrice Joy *(Mary McGregor)*, Farrell MacDonald *(Angus McGregor)*, Clyde Cook *(Pete)*, Kent Sanderson *(Wilbur Watkins)*, Douglas Scott *(Wobby)*, Slim Summerville *(Slim)*, Tom Wilson *(baggage master)*, Eulalie Jensen *(Queen of Lisonia)*, David Torrence *(president of the railroad)*, Dolores Johnson *(prima donna)*, Robert Ryan, Jack Pennick *(baggage men)*.

Comedy-melodrama. Strong Boy, a baggage handler in a railroad station, saves the child of a railroad vice president from being crushed by a trunk and is promoted to the head of the lost-and-found department. Mary McGregor, his sweetheart, becomes disgusted and walks out on him. Strong Boy later returns a pearl necklace to a movie star and is again promoted, this time to the position of fireman on the locomotive of which Mary's father is the engineer. Strong Boy prevents a holdup and is forgiven by Mary, whom he marries. *Porters. Railroad firemen. Railroad engineers. Actors. Train robberies.*

THE STRONG MAN **F2.5449**

Harry Langdon Corp. *Dist* First National Pictures. 19 Sep **1926** [c31 Aug 1926; LP23063]. Si; b&w. 35mm. 7 reels, 6,882 ft.

Dir Frank Capra. *Story* Arthur Ripley. *Photog* Elgin Lessley, Glenn Kershner. *Comedy Construc* Clarence Hennecke.

Cast: Harry Langdon *(Paul Bergot)*, Priscilla Bonner *(Mary Brown)*, Gertrude Astor *(Gold Tooth)*, William V. Mong *(Parson Brown)*, Robert McKim *(Roy McDevitt)*, Arthur Thalasso *(Zandow the Great)*.

Comedy. As part of the war effort, Mary Brown, an American, writes letters to Paul Bergot, a Belgian soldier fighting on the German front. Paul is captured by the Germans, however, and loses track of Mary. After the war, he emigrates to the United States in the company of Zandow the Great, a professional German weightlifter he has met during his captivity in Germany. Paul looks everywhere for Mary and finally finds her in a small town. They declare their love for each other, but Mary's father, Parson Brown, objects to Paul because he works in the music hall. Paul is instrumental in running a gang of bootleggers out of town, however, and Mary's father relents, giving her his permission to marry Paul. *Belgians. Germans. Bootleggers. Clergymen. Weightlifters. Prisoners of war. Music halls. World War I.*

THE STRONGER WILL **F2.5450**

Excellent Pictures. 20 Feb **1928** [c28 Feb 1928; LP25014]. Si; b&w. 35mm. 7 reels, 6,600-6,723 ft.

Pres by Samuel Zierler. *Prod-Story-Titl* Harry Chandlee. *Dir* Bernard McEveety. *Scen* Adrian Johnson. *Photog* Art Reeves. *Film Ed* Harry Chandlee.

Cast: Percy Marmont *(Clive Morton)*, Rita Carewe *(Estelle Marsh)*, Howard Truesdell *(Stephen Marsh)*, Merle Ferris *(Marguerite Marsh)*, William Norton Bailey *(Ralph Walker)*, Erin La Bissoniere *(Muriel Cassano)*.

Drama. Clive Morton, Wall Street financier, is engaged to marry Estelle Marsh, but the wedding is postponed when business takes him to Mexico. While he is gone Estelle announces her engagement to rival suitor Ralph Walker. Morton returns and forces Estelle to marry him, informing her that the business trip was to save her father's fortune and threatening that unless she marries him her father will be ruined. They marry but live in separate suites, and Estelle continues an affair with Walker. They are reconciled when Morton proves that Walker has been interested only in effecting his financial ruin. *Financiers. Marriage. Infidelity. Mexico. New York City—Wall Street.*

THE STRUGGLE **F2.5451**

William N. Selig Productions. *Dist* Canyon Pictures. May **1921** [c28 Dec 1920; LP15971]. Si; b&w. 35mm. 5 reels.

Dir Otto Lederer. *Story* William E. Wing.

Cast: Franklyn Farnum *(Dick Storm)*, Genevieve Bert *(Norma Day)*, Edwin Wallock *(Hayes Storm)*, Karl Formes *(Dr. Beer)*, Vester Pegg *(Diamond Joe)*, Bud Osborne *(sheriff)*, George Washington Jones *(Pumpkins)*.

Melodrama. "Spirited story of West, which begins after hero has spent four years overseas and has left the army so much of a fighting devil that he becomes embroiled in a mix-up. Learning that his antagonist has died from wounds is the reason for the hero going West, when he meets a tramp who is on his way to join a gang of outlaws and who invites ex-soldier to join. There is a girl who lives near the gang headquarters, and meeting her changes hero's perspective." (*Motion Picture News Booking Guide*, 1:106, Dec 1921.) *Veterans. Tramps. Outlaws.*

THE STUDENT PRINCE IN OLD HEIDELBERG **F2.5452**

Metro-Goldwyn-Mayer Pictures. 21 Sep **1927** [New York premiere; released 30 Jan 1928; c30 Jan 1928; LP25374]. Si; b&w. 35mm. 10 reels, 9,435 ft.

Dir Ernst Lubitsch. *Scen* Hans Kraly. *Titl* Marian Ainslee, Ruth Cummings. *Photog* John Mescall. *Sets* Cedric Gibbons, Richard Day. *Film Ed* Andrew Marton. *Mus Score* David Mendoza, William Axt. *Wardrobe* Ali Hubert, Eric Locke.

Cast: Ramon Novarro *(Prince Karl Heinrich)*, Norma Shearer *(Kathi)*, Jean Hersholt *(Dr. Juttner)*, Gustav von Seyffertitz *(King Karl VII)*, Philippe De Lacy *(Heir Apparent)*, Edgar Norton *(Lutz)*, Bobby Mack *(Kellerman)*, Edward Connelly *(court marshal)*, Otis Harlan *(Old Ruder)*, John S. Peters, George K. Arthur *(students)*, Edythe Chapman, Lionel Belmore, Lincoln Steadman.

Romantic drama. Source: Wilhelm Meyer-Förster, *Alt Heidelberg. Schauspiel in fünf Aufzügen* (New York, 1902). Dorothy Donnelly and Sigmund Romberg, *The Student Prince* (New York opening: 2 Dec 1924). Crown Prince Karl Heinrich, nephew of the king of a small domain, has a joyless existence in the pretentious formalism of the moribund court until his tutor, Dr. Juttner, arrives. After several years, Juttner takes Karl Heinrich to Heidelberg to study at the university. Here the prince falls in love with Kathi, the niece of the owner of an inn where the tutor and the prince have taken rooms. Karl Heinrich's happiness is shattered when the king dies and he must return to take the throne. Lonely and still in love with Kathi, although he is betrothed to an unattractive princess, Karl Heinrich returns to Heidelberg and finds that everything has changed: the students who were once his comrades salute him stiffly; his tutor has died; and only Kathi welcomes him as of old. After brief reunion they part again, for the Princess Ilse and he are celebrating their betrothal. *Royalty. Students. Innkeepers. Tutors. Imaginary kingdoms. Heidelberg.*

THE STUDIO MURDER MYSTERY **F2.5453**

Paramount Famous Lasky Corp. 1 Jun **1929** [c31 May 1929; LP436]. Sd (Movietone); b&w. 35mm. 8 reels, 6,070 ft. [Also si; 5,020 ft.]

Dir Frank Tuttle. *Photog* Victor Milner. *Film Ed* Merrill White.

Cast: Doris Hill *(Helen MacDonald)*, Neil Hamilton *(Tony White)*, Fredric March *(Dick Hardell)*, Warner Oland *(Borka)*, Guy Oliver *(MacDonald)*, Florence Eldridge *(Blanche Hardell)*, Chester Conklin *(George)*, Donald MacKenzie *(Captain Coffin)*, Eugene Pallette *(Lieutenant Dirk)*, Jack Luden *(Bob)*, Gardner James *(Ted MacDonald)*, E. H. Calvert *(Goff)*, Lane Chandler *(Bill Martin)*, Lawford Davidson *(Al Hemming)*, Mary Foy *(Miss O'Brien)*.

Mystery melodrama. Source: A. Channing Edington and Carmen Ballen Edington, *The Studio Murder Mystery* (Chicago, 1929). Richard Hardell, a debonair young man who wins a magazine contest sponsored by a motion picture studio, comes to Hollywood. When he is found murdered on a deserted sound stage, the police learn that five people had ample motives and opportunities to commit the crime: Rupert Borka, who was directing Hardell in his first picture, while knowing he was engaged in a flirtation with his own wife; Blanche, Rupert's wife, who discovered his affair with the studio watchman's daughter; Helen MacDonald, the watchman's daughter, who threatened to make him suffer for his false promises of marriage; Ted MacDonald, Helen's brother, who knew of his sister's secret trysts with Hardell; and Helen's father. MacDonald admits knowledge of the guilty party but dies before he can make the disclosure. Helen is convicted on circumstantial evidence; then studio gagman Tony White, who loves Helen, stumbles on a clue, and Borka is revealed as the actual killer. *Actors. Gagmen. Motion picture directors. Watchmen. Motion pictures. Contests. Infidelity. Murder. Circumstantial evidence. Hollywood.*

SUBMARINE **F2.5454**

Columbia Pictures. 12 Nov **1928** [c15 Nov 1928; LP25833]. Si; b&w. 35mm. 9 reels, 8,374 ft. [Also si; 8,192 ft.]

Irvin Willat Production. *Prod* Harry Cohn. *Dir* Frank R. Capra. *Scen* Dorothy Howell. *Story* Norman Springer. *Photog* Joe Walker. *Art Dir* Harrison Wiley. *Film Ed* Arthur Roberts. *Song: "Pals, Just Pals"* Herman Ruby, Dave Dreyer. *Asst Dir* Buddy Coleman.

Cast: Jack Holt *(Jack Dorgan)*, Dorothy Revier *(Bessie)*, Ralph Graves *(Bob Mason)*, Clarence Burton *(submarine commander)*, Arthur Rankin *(The Boy)*.

Melodrama. Jack Dorgan, the finest deep-sea diver in the Navy, marries Bessie, a dancehall girl, and, shortly thereafter, is ordered out into the Pacific to work on a wreck. While Jack is at sea, Bob Mason, a fellow petty officer and Jack's best friend, comes into Oakland and meets Bessie, who has returned to the dancehall. The two begin a passionate affair, and Bessie never tells Bob that she is married; Jack returns to port and, discovering them in each other's arms, accuses Bob of forcing his unwanted attentions on Bessie. Bob's submarine later sinks to the bottom, and the crew is trapped inside; Jack is the only diver in the fleet good enough to reach the men, but he is still too dispirited to care. Bessie at last confesses that she and not Bob was to blame for the affair, and Jack, regaining his composure, rescues the trapped men. *Divers. Dancehall girls. Infidelity. Submarines. Oakland (California). United States Navy.*

THE SUBSTITUTE WIFE **F2.5455**

Arrow Pictures. 15 Oct **1925** [c23 Sep 1925; LP21843]. Si; b&w. 35mm. 6 reels, 6,580 ft.

Dir Wilfred May. *Story* Katherine Smith. *Photog* Harry Stradling.

Cast: Jane Novak *(Hilda Nevers)*, Niles Welch *(Lawrence Sinton)*, Coit Albertson *(Victor Bronson)*, Louise Carter *(Evelyn Wentworth)*, Gordon Standing *(Dr. Kitchell)*, Mario Majeroni *(Dr. De Longe)*.

Melodrama. On his wedding night, Lawrence Sinton is accidentally blinded. His wife, Evelyn, who is in love with Dr. Kitchell, discovers that Hilda Nevers, a nurse, has a voice identical to her own. Dr. Kitchell and Evelyn run off together, hiring Hilda to substitute as Lawrence's wife. Hilda falls in love with Lawrence, and an operation restores his sight. Lawrence learns the true identity of his "wife," divorces Evelyn, and marries Hilda. *Physicians. Nurses. Impersonation. Blindness.*

THE SUBURBAN HANDICAP *see* **THE KENTUCKY DERBY**

SUBWAY SADIE **F2.5456**

Al Rockett Productions. *Dist* First National Pictures. 12 Sep **1926** [c18 Aug 1926; LP23036]. Si; b&w. 35mm. 7 reels, 6,727 ft.

Dir Alfred Santell. *Scen* Adele Commandini, Paul Schofield. *Photog* Arthur Edeson. *Film Ed* Hugh Bennett. *Prod Mgr* Al Rockett.

Cast: Dorothy Mackaill *(Sadie Hermann)*, Jack Mulhall *(Herb McCarthy)*, Charles Murray *(Driver)*, Peggy Shaw *(Ethel)*, Gaston Glass *(Fred Perry)*, Bernard Randall *(Brown)*.

Comedy-drama. Source: Mildred Cram, "Sadie of the Desert," in *Red Book* (45:85–89, Oct 1925). Sadie Hermann, saleslady in a New York fur establishment, cherishes one ambition—to go to Paris. One day while on her way to work, Sadie is extricated from the crowded subway by Herb McCarthy, a subway guard, and strikes up a friendly conversation; Herb makes a date to meet her beneath Cleopatra's Needle in Central Park the following Sunday. Soon the couple are engaged; and Sadie, promoted to the position of buyer for her firm, is told she is to sail for Paris. Sadie is thus obliged to cancel their wedding date, and Herb is disheartened. On the day she is to depart, Sadie receives a wire from Herb saying that he is in the hospital as the result of an accident. Sadie goes to him, and they decide on matrimony instead of Paris and the buying job; then Herb reveals that his father is president of the subway company. *Salesclerks. Buyers. Subway guards. Courtship. Fur industry. Subways. New York City. Paris.*

SUCCESS **F2.5457**

Murray W. Garsson. *Dist* Metro Pictures. 26 Mar **1923** [c29 Mar 1923; LP18830]. Si; b&w. 35mm. 7 reels, 6,800 ft.

Pres by Murray W. Garsson. *Dir* Ralph Ince. *Titl* George V. Hobart. *Adapt* Theodore A. Liebler, Jr., Adeline Leitzbach. *Photog* William J. Black. *Sets* Tec-Art Studios. *Prod Mgr* H. L. Atkins, George M. Arthur.

Cast: Brandon Tynan *(Barry Carleton)*, Naomi Childers *(Jane Randolph)*, Mary Astor *(Rose Randolph)*, Dore Davidson *(Sam Lewis)*, Lionel Adams *(Willis Potter)*, Stanley Ridges *(Gilbert Gordon)*, Robert Lee Keeling *(Henry Briggs)*, Billy Quirk *(Nick Walker)*, Helen Macks *(Ruth)*, Gaylord Pendleton *(Joe)*, John Woodford *(Treadwell, the peasant)*.

Drama. Source: Adeline Leitzbach and Theodore A. Liebler, *Success* (New York opening: 28 Jan 1918). Famous Shakespearian actor Barry Carleton is unable to cope with his success, falls into drunkenness, and causes his wife to leave him and then to bring up their daughter, Rose, in the belief that her father is dead. Years later, when applying to play again the role of Lear, he is assigned to be dresser for Gilbert Gordon and learns that the production's backer seeks Rose's favor by casting her as Cordelia. On opening night Gilbert, who knows the truth, gets drunk; and Barry goes on in his place. The performance is a great success, Barry is reunited with his wife, and Rose is engaged to Gilbert. *Actors. Fatherhood. Alcoholism. Theater. "King Lear".*

SUCH A LITTLE QUEEN **F2.5458**

Realart Pictures. Jul **1921** [c1 Jun 1921; LP16602]. Si; b&w. 35mm. 5 reels, 4,942 ft.

Dir George Fawcett. *Scen* J. Clarkson Miller, Lawrence McCloskey. *Photog* Ernest Haller.

Cast: Constance Binney *(Anne Victoria of Gzbfernigambia)*, Vincent Coleman *(Stephen of Hetland)*, J. H. Gilmour *(Baron Cosaco)*, Roy Fernandez *(Bob Trainor)*, Frank Losee *(Adolph Lawton)*, Betty Carpenter *(Elizabeth Lawton)*, Jessie Ralph *(Mary)*, Henry Leone *(Boris)*.

Romantic comedy. Source: Channing Pollock, *Such a Little Queen; a Comedy in Four Acts* (New York, 1920). Queen Anne of Gzbfernigambia, who is betrothed to King Stephen of Hetland, flees to the United States with the Baron Cosaco when revolution breaks out in her country. In New York they are befriended by breezy young Bob Trainor, office manager for wealthy meatpacker Adolph Lawton, who finds them a flat on the East Side. Although Lawton is eager to marry his daughter, Elizabeth, to royalty, she is in love with Bob and becomes jealous of the exiled queen. The arrival of Stephen revives the royal courtship, however, and after Lawton lends the monarchs money to pay their national debts and unite the two kingdoms Elizabeth and Bob become engaged. *Royalty. Imaginary kingdoms. Courtship. Business management. Meatpacking. Debt—Public. New York City—East Side.*

SUCH MEN ARE DANGEROUS **F2.5459**

Fox Film Corp. 9 Mar **1930** [c25 Jan 1930; LP1074]. Sd (Movietone); b&w. 35mm. 8 reels, 7,400 ft. [Also si.]

Pres by William Fox. *Assoc Prod* Al Rockett. *Dir* Kenneth Hawks. *Stgd by* Melville Burke. *Adapt-Dial* Ernest Vajda. *Story* Elinor Glyn. *Photog* L. William O'Connell, George Eastman. *Art Dir* Stephen Goosson. *Film Ed* Harold Schuster. *Mus* Dave Stamper. *Song: "Bridal Hymn"* Albert Malotte, George Gramlich. *Song: "Cinderella by the Fire"* Dave Stamper. *Orch* Will Vodery. *Ballet Dir* Danny Dare. *Sd* Arthur L. von Kirbach. *Asst Dir* Max Gold. *Cost* Sophie Wachner.

Cast: Warner Baxter *(Ludwic Kranz)*, Catherine Dale Owen *(Elinor)*, Albert Conti *(Paul Strohm)*, Hedda Hopper *(Muriel Wyndham)*, Claude Allister *(Frederick Wyndham)*, Bela Lugosi *(Dr. Erdmann)*.

Melodrama. Belgian financier Ludwic Kranz, who believes that wealth can buy him anything, marries Elinor, a beautiful young girl who is virtually forced into the marriage for financial reasons. She deserts him, repulsed by his disfigured face, and he sails for Germany, leaving the impression that he has committed suicide. There his face is transformed under the care of a plastic surgeon, and he returns to revenge himself on his wife; but when this woman who has despised him actually falls in love with him, he relents and is willing to forget the past. *Financiers. Belgians. Marriage. Disfiguration. Plastic surgery. Revenge.*

Note: Initially reviewed as *The Mask of Love.*

SUMMER BACHELORS **F2.5460**

Fox Film Corp. 18 Dec **1926** [c5 Dec 1926; LP23436]. Si; b&w. 35mm. 7 reels, 6,727 ft. [Also 6 reels, 5,500 ft.]

Pres by William Fox. *Dir* Allan Dwan. *Scen* James Shelley Hamilton. *Photog* Joseph Ruttenberg. *Art Dir* Sam Corso. *Scenic Dir* Al Panci. *Interior Decorator* Miss S. Baxter. *Asst Dir* Barton Adams. *Cost* Emery J. Herrett. *Draperies* J. G. Horton.

Cast: Madge Bellamy *(Derry Thomas)*, Allan Forrest *(Tony Landor)*, Matt Moore *(Walter Blakely)*, Hale Hamilton *(Beverly Greenway)*, Leila Hyams *(Willowdean French)*, Charles Winninger *(Preston Smith)*, Clifford Holland *(Martin Cole)*, Olive Tell *(Mrs. Preston Smith)*, Walter Catlett *(Bachelor No. 1)*, James F. Cullen *(Bachelor No. 2)*, Cosmo Kyrle Bellew *(Bachelor No. 3)*, Charles Esdale *(Bachelor No. 4)*.

Romantic comedy. Source: Warner Fabian, *Summer Widowers* (New York, 1926). Derry Thomas, a secretary who is averse to marriage because of the unfortunate experience of her sisters with men, organizes a club for summer bachelors—flirtatious husbands who step out with single girls while their wives are away for the summer. A department store flirtation leads her to invite Tony Landor, whom she believes to be married, to the club meeting; and she falls madly in love with him. After learning he is still single, she hesitates. A professor puts her in a trance with a hypnotizing crystal; and when she confesses her love for Tony, a judge who is a club member marries them. Though at first displeased, Derry is finally reconciled to her fate. *Secretaries. Sisters. Flirts. Bachelors. Judges. Courtship. Hypnotism. Department stores.*

SUN DOG TRAILS **F2.5461**

Ben Wilson Productions. *Dist* Arrow Film Corp. 15 Jun **1923** [c26 May 1923; LP19005]. Si; b&w. 35mm. 5 reels, 4,586 ft.

Dir Lewis King. *Scen* Daniel Whitcomb. *Story* W. C. Tuttle.

Cast: William Fairbanks.

Western melodrama. Coming into the town of Sun-Dog, the stage is held up, and Dave Richards and his pal, Silent Slade, find a note in the empty coach that implicates Scott Martin, the driver. Richards loves Jean, Martin's daughter, and, suspecting a frameup, he decides not to report his discovery to the sheriff. The gang's leader, Zell Mohr, later throws suspicion on Richards, and when things get too hot for him, he escapes into the hills. Meanwhile, Jean wrings the truth from her father: the note was left by the gang to repay Martin for refusing to join in with them; Jean, Richards, and Slade capture the gang, and the sheriff takes them off to jail while Richards takes Jean in his arms. *Stagecoach drivers. Sheriffs. Gangs. Stagecoach robberies. Frameup. Blackmail.*

SUN-UP F2.5462

Metro-Goldwyn-Mayer Corp. 20 Sep **1925** [c10 Aug 1925; LP21714]. Si; b&w. 35mm. 6 reels, 5,819 ft.

Dir-Adapt Edmund Goulding. *Cont* Arthur Statter. *Titl* Joseph W. Farnham. *Photog* John Arnold. *Film Ed* Harold Young.

Cast: Pauline Starke *(Emmy)*, Conrad Nagel *(Rufe)*, Lucille La Verne *(mother)*, Sam De Grasse *(Sheriff Weeks)*, George K. Arthur *(stranger)*, Arthur Rankin *(Bud)*, Edward Connelly *(Pap Todd)*, Bainard Beckwith *(Bob)*.

Melodrama. Source: Lulu Vollmer, *Sun-Up; a Play in Three Acts* (New York, 1924). Having lived in the hills of Kentucky all her life, Ma Cagle has an intense hatred for revenue agents, one of whom, Zeb Turner, killed both her husband and her father. Her son Rufus, who is drafted during the World War, is reported killed in action, and, in an act of defiance, Ma shelters an Army deserter for more than a year. When Rufus unexpectedly returns, he informs his mother that the deserter, whom she has come to love like a son, is the son of Zeb Turner. Ma demands that Rufus kill the boy, but, softened by his experiences outside of the hill country, Rufus refuses and lets him go. Rufus' new attitude is put to a severe test when Emmy Todd, the girl he loves, is attacked by the sheriff. Rufus goes after the sheriff in a homicidal rage, but instead of killing him, he brings him back to his own jail to stand trial. Rufus is appointed the new sheriff and brings law and order to the backwoods. *Revenue agents. Soldiers. Sheriffs. Revenge. Motherhood. World War I. Kentucky. United States Army—Desertion.*

SUNDOWN F2.5463

First National Pictures. Jun or 23 Nov **1924** [c2 Oct 1924; LP20616]. Si; b&w. 35mm. 9 reels, 8,640 ft. [Copyrighted as 8 reels.]

Pers Supv Earl Hudson. *Dir* Laurence Trimble, Harry O. Hoyt. *Ed Supv* Marion Fairfax. *Scen* Frances Marion, Kenneth B. Clarke. *Story* Earl Hudson. *Photog* David Thompson. *Art Dir* Milton Menasco. *Film Ed* Cyril Gardner. *Art Title Studies* Paul Grenbeaux.

Cast: Bessie Love *(Ellen Crawley)*, Roy Stewart *(Hugh Brent)*, Hobart Bosworth *(John Brent)*, Arthur Hoyt *(Henry Crawley)*, Charles Murray *(Pat Meech)*, Jere Austin *(John Burke)*, Charles Crockett *(Joe Patton)*, E. J. Radcliffe *(President [Theodore] Roosevelt)*, Margaret McWade *(Mrs. Brent)*, Bernard Randall *(William Dickson)*, Charles Sellon *(ranchman)*.

Western epic. Threatened with financial ruin by the growing numbers of homesteaders who fence in the range for farmland, John Brent and his son, Hugh, go east to seek monetary aid. They fail, and upon their return, the ranchers decide to make one last, great cattledrive to Mexico and reestablish themselves there. The move begins, and a stampede wipes out the homestead of Henry Crawley and his children (one of whom, Ellen, Hugh Brent met on the train from the East). Hugh persuades the cattlemen to admit the Crawleys, and Ellen gradually wins their friendship with her helpfulness. After many hardships, the drive reaches Mexico, the ranchers take up a collection for the Crawleys, and Hugh promises to marry Ellen. *Cattlemen. Homesteaders. Finance—Personal. Stampedes. Mexico. Theodore Roosevelt.*

SUNKEN ROCKS F2.5464

Burr Nickle. Apr **1923** [scheduled release]. Si; b&w. 35mm. 5 reels.

Cast: Alma Taylor.

Drama(?). No information about the nature of this film has been found.

SUNNY F2.5465

First National Pictures. 9 Nov **1930** [c19 Nov 1930; LP1803]. Sd (Vitaphone); b&w. 35mm. 9 reels, 7,256 ft.

Dir William Seiter. *Dial* Humphrey Pearson. *Adapt* Humphrey Pearson, Henry McCarty. *Photog* Ernest Haller. *Film Ed* LeRoy Stone. *Songs: "Sunny," "Who?" "D'Ya Love Me?" "Two Little Love Birds," "I Was Alone"* Otto Harbach, Oscar Hammerstein, II, Jerome Kern. *Mus Dir* Erno Rapee. *Dir Ballet Scenes* Theodore Kosloff.

Cast: Marilyn Miller *(Sunny)*, Lawrence Gray *(Tom Warren)*, Joe Donahue *(Jim Deming)*, Mackenzie Ward *(Wendell-Wendell)*, O. P. Heggie *(Peters)*, Inez Courtney *(Weenie)*, Barbara Bedford *(Marcia Manners)*, Judith Vosselli *(Sue)*, Clyde Cook *(Sam)*, Harry Allen *(barker)*, William Davidson *(first officer)*, Ben Hendricks, Jr. *(second officer)*.

Romantic musical drama. Source: Otto Harbach, Oscar Hammerstein, II, and Jerome Kern, *Sunny* (New York opening: 22 Sep 1925). Sunny, a circus performer pledged by her father to marry an Englishman (Wendell-Wendell) she does not love, becomes a stowaway on an ocean liner to America, along with her father, Peters. Sunny is obliged to act as dancer and entertainer to pay her passage, while her father is put to swabbing decks. Aboard is Tom Warren, the man she loves; but he is engaged to Marcia Manners. In order to be near him and to enter the United States without a passport, she marries his best friend, Jim Deming, in name only, planning to divorce him soon after landing. Meanwhile Jim establishes a popular gymnasium resort but is put in a difficult position when his former fiancée, Weenie, and Wendell-Wendell arrive from England. When Marcia hears Sunny tell Tom that she knows he loves her, Marcia declares that their engagement will be announced at the hunt ball that very night. At the ball, Sunny announces her plans to return to England, but Tom proposes just as she is about to leave. ... *Stowaways. Courtship. Divorce. Circus. Ocean liners. Resorts. England.*

SUNNY SIDE UP F2.5466

De Mille Pictures. *Dist* Producers Distributing Corp. 2 Aug **1926** [c28 Jun 1926; LP22858]. Si; b&w. 35mm. 6 reels, 5,994 ft.

Supv Elmer Harris. *Dir* Donald Crisp. *Adapt* Beulah Marie Dix, Elmer Harris. *Photog* Peverell Marley. *Art Dir* Max Parker. *Asst Dir* Emile De Ruelle.

Cast: Vera Reynolds *(Sunny Ducrow)*, Edmund Burns *(Stanley Dobrington)*, George K. Arthur *(Bert Jackson)*, ZaSu Pitts *(Evelyn)*, Ethel Clayton *(Cissy Cason)*, Louis Natheaux *(Stanley's assistant)*, Sally Rand *(a dancer)*, Jocelyn Lee, Majel Coleman *(showgirls)*.

Comedy-drama. Source: Henry St. John Cooper, *Sunny Ducrow* (New York, 1920). Sunny, a girl with a bright disposition, sings in the streets to obtain funds for a country outing for Bert, a gloomy lad. Stanley Dobrington, a theater owner, is leaving just as a policeman routs Sunny and Bert on a Saturday night; he hears her story, takes an interest, and promises her a part in his new revue in which she makes her debut as Little Bopeep in a Louis XIV tableau. Sunny forgets her lines but her improvisation is a hit, and Dobrington takes Sunny and Bert on a fishing trip to the country. As Sunny and Dobrington reach the point of proposals, the estranged Mrs. Dobrington suddenly appears, whereupon Sunny declines his offer and decides to marry Bert. She then learns that Bert is secretly married to Tessie, the wardrobe assistant. A false fire alarm sets off a panic in the theater, but Sunny manages to calm the audience. Mrs. Dobrington, returning to the theater for her jewels, is killed by an automobile, leaving Sunny and Dobrington free to marry. *Singers. Theater. Infidelity. Fires.*

SUNNY SIDE UP F2.5467

Fox Film Corp. 3 Oct **1929** [New York premiere; released 29 Dec; c8 Oct 1929; LP748]. Sd (Movietone); b&w with col sequences (Multicolor). 35mm. 13 reels, 12,000 ft.

Pres by William Fox. *Dir-Adapt* David Butler. *Story-Dial* Buddy De Sylva, Ray Henderson, Lew Brown. *Photog* Ernest Palmer, John Schmitz. *Art Dir* Harry Oliver. *Film Ed* Irene Morra. *Mus Dir* Howard Jackson, Arthur Kay. *Songs: "I'm a Dreamer, Aren't We All," "If I Had a Talking Picture of You," "Turn on the Heat," "Sunny Side Up," "You've Got Me Picking Petals Off o' Daisies"* Buddy De Sylva, Lew Brown, Ray Henderson. *Dances staged by* Seymour Felix. *Rec Engr* Joseph Aiken. *Asst Dir* Ad Schaumer. *Cost* Sophie Wachner.

Cast: Janet Gaynor *(Molly Carr)*, Charles Farrell *(Jack Cromwell)*, El Brendel *(Eric Swenson)*, Marjorie White *(Bee Nichols)*, Frank Richardson *(Eddie Rafferty)*, Sharon Lynn *(Jane Worth)*, Mary Forbes *(Mrs. Cromwell)*, Joe Brown *(Joe Vitto)*, Alan Paull *(Raoul)*, Peter Cawthorne *(Lake)*.

Musical comedy-drama. Young society man John Cromwell is summering at the fashionable resort of Southampton, while department store worker Molly Carr lives in an East Side tenement. Each locale is introduced at a Fourth of July party. Molly tries to make Cromwell's flapper girl friend jealous, and her plan works. Cromwell realizes at length that he loves Molly—all of which provides opportunities for singing and dancing numbers. *Socialites. Salesclerks. Social classes. Resorts. Fourth of July. Long Island. New York City—East Side.*

SUNNY SKIES F2.5468

Tiffany Productions. 12 May **1930** [c1 May 1930; LP1266]. Sd (Photophone); b&w. 35mm. 8 reels, 6,994 ft.

Dir Norman Taurog. *Adtl Dir* Ralph De Lacy. *Scen* Earl Snell. *Dial* George Cleveland. *Story* A. P. Younger. *Photog* Arthur Reeves. *Film Ed* Clarence Kolster. *Rec Engr* John Buddy Myers.

Cast: Benny Rubin *(Benny Krantz)*, Marceline Day *(Mary Norris)*, Rex Lease *(Jim Grant)*, Marjorie "Babe" Kane *(Doris)*, Greta Granstedt *(college widow)*, Wesley Barry *(Sturrle)*, Robert Randall *(Dave)*, James

Wilcox *(Smith)*.

Musical comedy. Jim Grant, a smartly dressed athletic type among the freshmen at Standtech, takes an interest in modest Mary Norris, who has scholastic ambitions but is claimed by Dave, her hometown sweetheart. Jim's roommate is Benny Krantz, a shy, blundering son of a delicatessen keeper. Jim promises Benny's father, Isadore, that he will take care of his son; and Doris, a co-ed friend of Mary's, teaches Benny what "It" is all about. Mary becomes infatuated with Jim until she discovers him intoxicated with a "fast" girl, and he is disqualified from the football team for failing in his studies. Jim tries to win Mary back, bringing on a fight with Dave, whose arm Jim breaks. Benny tries to emulate Jim, and Mary achieves a reputation for dating; when Benny is critically injured during a spree, Jim saves his life with a transfusion and, called back on the team, he scores the winning touchdown. *Students. Jews. College life. Courtship. Football. Blood transfusion.*

SUNRISE—A SONG OF TWO HUMANS **F2.5469**

Fox Film Corp. 23 Sep **1927** [New York premiere; released 4 Nov 1928; c12 Jun 1927; LP24070]. Sd eff & mus score (Movietone); b&w. 35mm. 10-11 reels. [Reduced to 9 reels, 8,729 ft; also si.]

Pres by William Fox. *Dir* F. W. Murnau. *Scen* Carl Mayer. *Titl* Katherine Hilliker, H. H. Caldwell. *Photog* Charles Rosher, Karl Struss. *Asst Photog* Hal Carney, Stuart Thompson. *Prod Dsgn* Rochus Gliese. *Asst Art Dir* Edgar G. Ulmer, Alfred Metscher. *Film Ed* Katherine Hilliker, H. H. Caldwell. *Synchronized Score* Hugo Riesenfeld. *Asst Dir* Herman Bing.

Cast: George O'Brien *(The Man)*, Janet Gaynor *(The Wife)*, Bodil Rosing *(maid)*, Margaret Livingston *(woman from the city)*, J. Farrell MacDonald *(photographer)*, Ralph Sipperly *(barber)*, Jane Winton *(manicure girl)*, Arthur Housman *(The Obtrusive Gentleman)*, Eddie Arnold *(The Obliging Gentleman)*, Sally Eilers, Gino Corrado, Barry Norton, Robert Kortman.

Romantic drama. Source: Hermann Sudermann, *Die Reise nach Tilsit* (Berlin, 1917). At a rural summer retreat, a vacationing lady from the city engages the interest of a young farmer, and soon he is enslaved to her. She persuades him to murder his wife, sell his farm, and join her in the city. He finally makes an attempt to drown his wife but, conscience-stricken, cannot carry it through. The man and his wife ride into the city on a trolley, she in terror, he in contrition; soon love overpowers her fear, and they renew their vows in a church while watching a wedding. They spend a joyous day in an amusement park and that evening return home; a storm overtakes them, and he gives her the rushes that were to provide his own protection while he swims ashore. Later the fishermen search for her during the night and finally give up hope; he searches out the city woman and is about to strangle her when word comes that his wife has been found alive. At her bedside, he watches the sunrise. *Vamps. Farmers. Fishermen. Rural life. Marriage. Infidelity. Murder. Amusement parks. Streetcars.*

THE SUNSET DERBY **F2.5470**

First National Pictures. 5 Jun **1927** [c17 May 1927; LP23964]. Si; b&w. 35mm. 6 reels.

Prod Charles R. Rogers. *Dir* Albert Rogell. *Scen* Curtis Benton. *Titl* Mort Blumenstock. *Photog* Ross Fisher.

Cast: Mary Astor *(Molly Gibson)*, William Collier, Jr. *(Jimmy Burke)*, Ralph Lewis *(Sam Gibson)*, David Kirby *(Mike Donovan)*, Lionel Belmore *(Jock McTeague)*, Burt Ross *(Bobby McTeague)*, Henry Barrows *("Lucky" Davis)*, Bobby Doyle *(Skeeter Donohue)*, Michael Visaroff *(peddler)*.

Melodrama. Source: William Dudley Pelley, "The Sunset Derby," in *American Magazine* (101:12–15, Jan 1926). Sam Gibson and Jock McTeague, former partners in a livery stable, have a falling out when McTeague opens a service station and insists that his son, Bobby, keep away from the horses. Queen, a racehorse owned by Gibson, breaks loose on the street and is rescued by Jimmy Burke, a famous jockey, who agrees to ride Queen in a race to please Mollie, Gibson's daughter. During the race, Queen falls, injuring Jimmy, and though he recovers they are forced to sell the horse to defray hospital expenses. Jimmy prevents a peddler, the new owner, from beating the horse at a fair and makes him resell the horse to Sam. Jimmy secretly trains young Bobby to ride, but when the boy is unable to ride in a race, Jimmy, regaining his courage, wins the race and the heart of Millie. *Jockeys. Peddlers. Horseracing. Automobile servicing. Fairs.*

SUNSET JONES **F2.5471**

American Film Co. *Dist* Pathé Exchange. Jan **1921** [c14 Feb 1921; LP16138]. Si; b&w. 35mm. 5 reels.

Dir George L. Cox. *Scen* Daniel F. Whitcomb.

Cast: Charles Clary *(Sunset Jones)*, James Gordon *(David Rand)*, Irene Rich *(Marion Rand)*, Kathleen O'Connor *(Molly Forbes)*.

Western melodrama. David Rand, a discharged railroad employee, leads a gang of holdup men who terrorize the trains in Shoshone Basin. Sunset Jones is hired by the railroad officials to capture the bandits, and he discovers his former fiancée, Marion, married to Rand. When the sheriff is killed by Rand, Sunset tracks him down in time to save Marion; Rand is killed in the showdown. *Bandits. Sheriffs. Railroads. Train robberies.*

THE SUNSET LEGION **F2.5472**

Paramount Famous Lasky Corp. 21 Apr **1928** [c21 Apr 1928; LP25187]. Si; b&w. 35mm. 7 reels, 6,763 ft.

Dir Lloyd Ingraham, Alfred L. Werker. *Story-Scen* Frank M. Clifton. *Titl* Garrett Graham. *Photog* Mack Stengler. *Asst Photog* Jack Greenhalgh. *Film Ed* Duncan Mansfield.

Cast: Fred Thomson *(Black-robed Stranger/Whittling Cowboy)*, William Courtright *(Old Bill)*, Edna Murphy *(Susan)*, Harry Woods *(Honest John)*, Silver King *(himself, a horse; see note)*.

Western melodrama. A Texas Ranger assumes the dual disguise of a masked stranger and an itinerant gun salesman to round up a gang of outlaws. As the easy-going gun salesman, he meets Susan, the daughter of gold miner Old Bill, while collecting evidence against saloon keeper Honest John (whom he suspects to be the leader of the gang). As the masked Stranger, he captures Honest John and the gang. Revealing his true identity, the ranger saves Old Bill's life, thereby earning the admiration of Susan, with whom he has fallen in love. *Texas Rangers. Strangers. Traveling salesmen. Gold miners. Saloon keepers. Disguise. Horses.*

Note: The horse, Silver King, also plays a dual role: when Thomson's part calls for a black horse, Silver King appears in a tailor-made suit of black cloth.

SUNSET PASS **F2.5473**

Paramount Famous Lasky Corp. 9 Feb **1929** [c11 Feb 1929; LP117]. Si; b&w. 35mm. 6 reels, 5,862 ft.

Dir Otto Brower. *Adapt-Scen* J. Walter Ruben, Ray Harris. *Titl* Ray Harris. *Photog* Roy Clark. *Film Ed* Jane Loring.

Cast: Jack Holt *(Jack Rock)*, Nora Lane *(Leatrice Preston)*, John Loder *(Ashleigh Preston)*, Christian J. Frank *(Chuck)*, Pee Wee Holmes *(Shorty)*, Chester Conklin *(Windy)*, Pat Harmon *(Clink Peeples)*, Alfred Allen *(Amos Dabb)*, Guy Oliver *(Clark)*.

Western melodrama. Source: Zane Grey, *Sunset Pass* (New York, 1931). Looking for a gang of cattle rustlers, Marshal Jack Rock takes a job punching cows for Ashleigh Preston, an English rancher whom he suspects of leading a double life. Jack falls in love with Preston's sister, Leatrice, and, discovering that Ashleigh is a rustler, gives the Englishman a chance to go straight. Ashleigh refuses, and Jack kills him. *Cowboys. Ranchers. United States marshals. Brother-sister relationship. Rustling. Arizona.*

Note: Filmed on location near Tiba City and Flagstaff, Arizona.

THE SUNSET TRAIL **F2.5474**

Universal Pictures. 2 Nov **1924** [c5 Sep 1924; LP20558]. Si; b&w. 35mm. 5 reels, 4,920 ft.

Dir Ernst Laemmle. *Cont* Wyndham Gittens. *Adapt* Isadore Bernstein. *Photog* Jackson Rose.

Cast: William Desmond *(Happy Hobo)*, Gareth Hughes *(Collie King)*, Lucille Hutton *(Louise Lacharme)*, S. E. Jennings *(Silent Saunders)*, Clark Comstock *(Constable Hicks)*, Albert J. Smith *(Dick Fenlow)*, William A. Steele *(Brand Williams)*.

Western comedy-melodrama. Source: Henry Herbert Knibbs, *Overland Red, a Romance of the Moonstone Cañon Trail* (Boston & New York, 1914). On a passenger train passing through the desert, Louise offers to pay the fares of Happy Hobo and Collie. The boy Collie accepts, but Happy continues on foot and finds on a dying man a map to a gold mine and a photograph of his daughter, who is none other than Louise. A constable tries to take the map from Happy, but he escapes, meets Louise and the boy again, and files the claim for her. After many adventures, he finds the mine and marries the girl. *Children. Tramps. Mines. Documentation.*

SUNSHINE HARBOR **F2.5475**

Playgoers Pictures. 2 Apr **1922** [c25 Mar 1922; LU17679]. Si; b&w. 35mm. 5 reels, 4,300 ft.

Dir Edward L. Hemmer. *Story* Jerome N. Wilson. *Photog* William Tuers.

Cast: Margaret Beecher *(Betty Hopkins)*, Howard Hall *(Dr. Hopkins)*, Coit Albertson *(Hamilton Graves)*, Ralf Harolde *(Billy Saunders)*, Julian Greer *(Editor MacSorley)*, Daniel Jarrett *(Dugan)*.

Society melodrama. Betty Hopkins, a hoydenish daughter of a southern eye specialist, refuses to marry Graves, her father's choice, and goes motor-boating with Billy Saunders, a city newspaper reporter; when the engine fails, they are forced to spend the night on the lake, and her indignant father assumes that the worst has occurred. Betty runs away to New York. There she achieves fame as a newswriter, but while covering a spectacular chemical fire she is blinded by an explosion. Billy Saunders, returning from Havana, finds her in the hospital and proposes, but Betty declines because of her blindness; her father, however, performs a successful operation to restore her sight. Following a reconciliation between father and daughter, Hopkins consents to her marriage to Saunders. *Reporters. Filial relations. Eye surgery. Blindness. New York City. Fires.*

SUNSHINE OF PARADISE ALLEY **F2.5476**

Chadwick Pictures. 15 Dec **1926.** Si; b&w. 35mm. 7 reels, 6,850 ft.

Supv Jesse J. Goldburg. *Dir* Jack Nelson. *Adapt-Cont* Josephine Quirk. *Titl* Rick Todd. *Photog* Ted Tetzlaff, Ernest Miller. *Set Dsgn* Earl Sibley.

Cast: Barbara Bedford *(Sunshine O'Day)*, Kenneth McDonald *(Jerry Sullivan)*, Max Davidson *(Solomon Levy)*, Nigel Barrie *(Stanley Douglas)*, Gayne Whitman *(Glen Wathershoon)*, Lucille Lee Stewart *(Gladys Waldroon)*, Tui Lorraine *(Queenie May)*, J. Parks Jones *(Chet Hawkins)*, Bobby Nelson *("Bum")*, Frank Weed *(Daddy O'Day)*, Max Ascher, Lydia Yeamans Titus, Evelyn Sherman, Leon Holmes, Monty O'Grady.

Melodrama. Source: Denman Thompson and George W. Ryer, *The Sunshine of Paradise Alley; a Domestic Drama in Four Acts* (c1895). "In New York's 'East Side' lives Sunshine, admired by iceman sweetheart—Jerry. She saves her tenement home from the razers by appearing at its owner's social function. Accused of robbery, both Sunshine and Jerry escape the talons of the law through the machinations of a friendly monkey and the timely confession of a rogue." (*Motion Picture News Booking Guide*, 12: 57, Apr 1927.) *Icemen. Social classes. Tenements. Monkeys. New York City—East Side.*

THE SUNSHINE TRAIL **F2.5477**

Thomas H. Ince Corp. *Dist* Associated First National Pictures. 23 Apr **1923** [c25 Apr 1923; LP18896]. Si; b&w. 35mm. 5 reels, 4,509 ft.

Pres by Thomas H. Ince. *Dir* James W. Horne. *Adapt* Bradley King. *Story* William Wallace Cook. *Photog* Henry Sharp.

Cast: Douglas MacLean *(James Henry MacTavish)*, Edith Roberts *(June Carpenter)*, Muriel Frances Dana *(Algernon Aloysius Fitzmaurice Bangs)*, Rex Cherryman *(Willis Duckworth)*, Josephine Sedgwick *(woman crook)*, Albert Hart *(Colonel Duckworth)*, Barney Furey *(man crook)*, William Courtright *(mystery man)*.

Western comedy-drama. Jimmy MacTavish decides to return to his hometown and see his childhood sweetheart, June Carpenter. He intends to spread sunshine along the way, but he soon finds himself robbed of his clothes and money, accused of kidnaping, and jailed as an imposter. Finally, word comes that Jimmy was not killed in the war, as the citizens believed, and he is freed, celebrated as a hero, awarded his rightful inheritance, and reunited with June. *War heroes. Kidnaping. Robbery. Inheritance.*

SUPER SPEED **F2.5478**

Harry J. Brown Productions. *Dist* Rayart Pictures. 2 Apr **1925** [New York premiere]. Si; b&w. 35mm. 5 reels, 5,227 ft.

Dir Albert Rogell. *Story* J. W. Grey, Henry Roberts Symonds.

Cast: Reed Howes *(Pat O'Farrell)*, Mildred Harris *(Claire Knight)*, Charles Clary *(Warner Knight)*, Sheldon Lewis *(Stanton Wade)*, Martin Turner *(Pat's valet)*, George Williams *(Dad Perkins)*.

Comedy-melodrama. Pat O'Farrell, a wealthy young man who works as a truckdriver for his uncle's milk company, saves Claire Knight from thugs and falls instantly in love with her. Pat then discovers that Stanton Wade, a crooked attorney, is planning to steal a newly perfected supercharger from its inventor, Dad Perkins. Pat manfully manages to prevent Wade's henchmen from obtaining it. Claire later confides to Pat that her father, who manufactures Night-Hawk racing cars, is deeply in debt to Wade. Pat decides to enter an important automobile race using a Night-Hawk racer equipped with the revolutionary supercharger. Wade's thugs kidnap Pat, but he frees himself by racetime and, despite dirty work by Wade, wins the race. The winner's share is enough to pay off the elder Knight's debt to Wade, and, to the delight of everyone, Claire and Pat become engaged. *Truckdrivers. Milkmen. Lawyers. Inventors. Automobile manufacture. Automobile racing. Abduction. Combustion.*

THE SUPER-SEX **F2.5479**

Frank R. Adams Productions. *Dist* American Releasing Corp. 19 Nov **1922** [c15 Nov 1922; LP18807]. Si; b&w. 35mm. 6 reels, 5,749 ft.

Prod P. H. Burke. *Dir-Adapt-Scen* Lambert Hillyer. *Photog* John S. Stumar.

Cast: Robert Gordon *(Miles Brewster Higgins)*, Charlotte Pierce *(Irene Hayes)*, Tully Marshall *(Mr. Higgins)*, Lydia Knott *(Mrs. Higgins)*, Gertrude Claire *(Grandma Brewster)*, Albert MacQuarrie *(Cousin Roy)*, Louis Natheaux *(J. Gordon Davis)*, George Bunny *(Mr. Hayes)*, Evelyn Burns *(Mrs. Hayes)*.

Comedy. Source: Frank R. Adams, "Miles Brewster and the Super Sex," in *Cosmopolitan* (71:35–39, Jul 1921). Miles Brewster Higgins, a self-conscious smalltown youth, endures his jealousy in silence when a flashy automobile salesman appears and captures the attention of his sweetheart, Irene Hayes. On the insistence of Cousin Roy, Miles invests in Baby Blue oil stock, which quickly earns a fortune. It is his intention to become engaged to Irene, then jilt her, but the rumor that his money was actually invested in another company—and therefore accruing no profit—spoils his plans. Miles "faces the music" and learns that Grandma Brewster has spread the news about the false investment to test him. Miles has his fortune and his girl. *Grandmothers. Salesmen. Smalltown life. Jealousy. Speculation.*

SUPERSTITION *see* **OUT OF LUCK**

SUPERSTITION **F2.5480**

Dwan Film Corp. *Dist* Lee-Bradford Corp. 22 Nov **1922.** Si; b&w. 35mm. 5 reels, 4,480 ft.

Dir Allan Dwan.

Cast: Jack Devereaux, Veta Searl, Stafford Windsor.

Comedy-drama. "Will Clayton is superstitious clean through. He is ridiculed for his superstitions—fired because of them—becomes involved in a murder mystery—is seized by bandits—scorned by the girl—but clings to his amulets and his horseshoe. Finally, when the girl agrees to marry him if he will throw away his silly amulets and horseshoe, he seizes her in his arms, throws a horseshoe out of the window and it knocks the gun from his rival's hand just as he is about to fire." (*Motion Picture News Booking Guide*, 4:96, Apr 1923.) *Superstition. Murder. Talismans.*

THE SUPREME PASSION **F2.5481**

Robert W. Priest. *Dist* Film Market, Playgoers Pictures. c10 May **1921** [LU16563; adtl c17 Feb 1923; LU18688 (see note)]. Si; b&w. 35mm. 6 reels.

Dir Samuel Bradley. *Story* Robert McLaughlin, Charles T. Dazey. *Photog* Ben Reynolds.

Cast: Robert Adams *(Jerry Burke)*, William Mortimer *(Judge Burke)*, Daniel Kelly *(Dan Manning)*, Mrs. Charles Willard *(Mrs. Manning)*, George Fox *(Gardner)*, Cecil Owen *(James Lacey)*, Florence Dixon *(Mary Manning)*, Madelyn Clare *(Clara)*, Selmer Jackson *(Clara's beau)*, Edward Keane *(Dr. Jennings)*.

Melodrama. Inspired by: Thomas Moore, "Believe Me If All Those Endearing Young Charms." Jerry Burke is engaged to marry Mary Manning, daughter of a wealthy old Irishman, but his father opposes the match and disowns him. Meanwhile, Lacey, a successful but crooked politician, returns to Ireland and persuades the retired Manning to emigrate with Mary to the United States. Jerry follows and finds a position on a newspaper, but he is disheartened to hear that Mary plans to marry Lacey. While she is preparing for the ceremony, her veil catches on fire and a doctor announces that her beauty is impaired, whereupon Lacey withdraws his suit. Returning to Ireland, she meets Jerry and reveals that the fire was a pretext to prevent her marriage to Lacey, and the lovers are reunited. *Irish. Immigrants. Politicians. Reporters. Marriage. Ireland.*

Note: Although the 1923 copyright (and distribution) were by Playgoers Pictures, there appears to have been no change in length or story.

THE SUPREME TEST **F2.5482**

Cosmosart Production Co. 1 Dec **1923** [scheduled release]. Si; b&w. 35mm. 6 reels.

J. E. Bowen Production. *Dir-Writ* W. P. MacNamara.

Cast: Johnny Harron, Gloria Grey, Minna Redman, Eugene Beaudino, Dorothy Revier, Ernest Shields, Geraldine Powell, Gene Walsh.

Melodrama. " ... dealing with the workings of a couple of crooks and their female accomplices, of the attempt of one of the men to pin the guilt of a theft on another lad, followed by the eventual capture of the crook and the subsequent happiness of the innocent hero with the little blind girl whose sight is restored for the finale." (*Film Daily*, 23 Dec 1923, p12.) *Thieves. Frameup. Blindness.*

SURE FIRE **F2.5483**

Universal Film Manufacturing Co. 7 Nov **1921** [c22 Oct 1921; LP17122]. Si; b&w. 35mm. 5 reels, 4,481 ft.

Dir Jack Ford. *Scen* George C. Hull. *Story* Eugene Manlove Rhodes. *Photog* Virgil Miller.

Cast: Hoot Gibson *(Jeff Bransford)*, Molly Malone *(Marian Hoffman)*, Breezy Eason, Jr. *(Sonny)*, Harry Carter *(Rufus Coulter)*, Fritzi Brunette *(Elinor Parker)*, Murdock MacQuarrie *(Major Parker)*, George Fisher *(Burt Rawlings)*, Charles Newton *(Leo Ballinger)*, Jack Woods *(Brazos Bart)*, Jack Walters *(Overland Kid)*, Joe Harris *(Romero)*, Steve Clements *(Gomez)*.

Western melodrama. Jeff Bransford, a vagabond cowpuncher, returns home to find his sweetheart, Marian, hardened against him because he lacks ambition. He learns that Elinor, Marian's married sister, is about to elope with a young easterner and prevents it; but in turn he is blamed for the disappearance of $5,000 belonging to the sister's husband, Major Parker. Rather than expose Elinor's intrigue, Jeff escapes to an abandoned cabin, while the easterner absconds with the money and is killed by bandits, who also capture Marian. Jeff rescues Marian and returns with the money and the bandits. The husband remains in complaisant ignorance, and Marian rewards Jeff by agreeing to their engagement. *Cowboys. Vagabonds. Sisters. Bandits. Ambition.*

SURE FIRE FLINT **F2.5484**

Mastodon Films. 25 Aug **1922** [c1 Nov 1922; LP18362]. Si; b&w. 35mm. 7 reels, 6,423 ft.

Pres by C. C. Burr. *Prod* C. C. Burr. *Dir* Dell Henderson. *Scen* Gerald C. Duffy. *Titl* Ralph Spence. *Photog* Billy Bitzer, Charles Gibson, Neil Sullivan.

Cast: Johnny Hines *(Sure Fire Flint)*, Edmund Breese *(Johnny Jetts)*, Robert Edeson *(Anthony De Lanni)*, Effie Shannon *(Mrs. De Lanni)*, Barney Sherry *(The Proud Father)*, Doris Kenyon *(June De Lanni)*, Charles Gerard *(Dipley Poole)*.

Comedy-melodrama. Source: Gerald C. Duffy, "Sure Fire Flint," in *Ace High Magazine* (8:40–47, Nov 1922). Sure Fire Flint, an energetic chap just returned from wartime military service, meets June De Lanni, the girl of his dreams, while working as a cabdriver and busboy. Her father gives Flint a job in his factory, but Dipley Poole, who hoped to marry June, becomes jealous of Flint's success and attempts to rob the company safe. June is trapped in the safe, but Flint, after a series of adventures, arrives in time to rescue her. *Veterans. Taxi drivers. Robbery. Factories.*

SURGING SEAS **F2.5485**

Hurricane Film Corp. *Dist* New-Cal Film Corp. 1 May **1924** [c10 Apr 1924; LU20065]. Si; b&w. 35mm. 5 reels, ca4,750 ft.

Pres by William Steiner. *Prod* William Steiner. *Dir* James Chapin. *Scen* J. F. Natteford. *Story-Scen? (see note)* Louis Weadock. *Photog* Ernest Miller. *Tech Dir* James Chapin.

Cast: Charles Hutchison *(Bob Sinclair)*, Edith Thornton *(Edith Stafford)*, George Hackathorne *(Charles Stafford)*, David Torrence *(Lionel Sinclair)*, Earl Metcalfe *(Edwin Sinclair)*, Charles Force *(Captain Regan)*, Pat Harmon *(Mate Hansen)*.

Melodrama. Bob Sinclair, black sheep of his wealthy family, returns home after making his fortune and soon finds himself accused of embezzlement and of the attempted murder of his father, Lionel Sinclair. He also finds that his sweetheart, Edith Stafford, is being courted by his brother, Edwin. Bob escapes by stowing away on a ship on which Edwin and Edith are passengers. In a series of thrilling adventures Bob is able to produce evidence to clear his name and reveal that Edwin forced Edith's brother, Charles, to embezzle funds and to strike Mr. Sinclair. *Brothers. Brother-sister relationship. Filial relations. Stowaways. Embezzlement.*

Note: One source credits Louis Weadock with story and scenario.

SURRENDER (Universal-Jewel) **F2.5486**

Universal Pictures. 3 Nov **1927** [New York premiere; released 4 Mar; c15 Jul 1927; LP24200]. Si; b&w. 35mm. 8 reels, 8,249 ft.

Pres by Carl Laemmle. *Dir* Edward Sloman. *Scen* Charles Kenyon, Edward J. Montagne. *Titl* Albert De Mond. *Photog* Gilbert Warrenton. *Film Ed* Edward Cahn.

Cast: Mary Philbin *(Lea Lyon)*, Ivan Mosjukine *(Constantine)*, Otto Matieson *(Joshua)*, Nigel De Brulier *(Rabbi Mendel)*, Otto Fries *(Tarras)*, Daniel Makarenko *(Russian general)*.

Romantic drama. Source: Alexander Brody, *Lea Lyon* (a play; c1915). Lea Lyon, daughter of Rabbi Mendel, spiritual advisor of a Galician town near the Russian border, is playing by a stream when she meets Constantine, a Russian prince in peasant's garb. Objecting to the attentions paid his daughter, the rabbi insults the prince. Later, war is declared, and the Russians under Constantine occupy the town; the prince invites himself to the rabbi's home, demanding Lea, but finds her betrothed to Joshua. He threatens Joshua, who pleads with Lea to surrender to the prince, but she refuses. When Constantine threatens to burn the town and its inhabitants, Lea yields to the entreaties of the crowd. Impressed by her character, the prince discovers he loves her and spares the town and the girl; she hides him from the Austrian guard, and sent from her home, she is stoned by her people; the rabbi is killed, but the prince escapes. After the war, he returns to Lea. *Rabbis. Royalty. Jews. Russians. Self-sacrifice. World War I. Galicia. Austria.*

SUSPICIOUS WIVES **F2.5487**

Trojan Pictures. *Dist* World Film Corp. 1 Sep **1921** [New York State release]. Si; b&w. 35mm. 6 reels, 6,240 ft.

Dir John M. Stahl. *Scen* Paul Bern. *Titl* William B. Laub, Harry Chandlee. *Story* Robert F. Roden. *Photog* Harry Fischbeck.

Cast: H. J. Herbert *(James Brunton, Jr.)*, Mollie King *(Molly Fairfax)*, Ethel Grey Terry *(Helen Warren)*, Rod La Rocque *(Bob Standing)*, Gertrude Berkeley *(The Old Woman)*, Frank De Camp *(The Old Man)*, Warren Cook *(James Brunton, Sr.)*.

Domestic drama. "James Brunton's wife, Molly, believing she has found her husband to be unfaithful, leaves him without asking an explanation. The 'other woman,' however, is Brunton's sister-in-law, whom he is supporting. In his search for his wife Brunton is hurt and temporarily blinded in an automobile accident. He is carried to the very house in which his wife has secreted herself. She nurses him back to health without his recognizing her until, when his sight is restored the sister-in-law appears on the scene, an explanation is made, and Brunton and his wife are reconciled." (*Moving Picture World*, 14 Jan 1922, p204.) *Sisters. Infidelity. Blindness. Automobiles. Automobile accidents.*

SUZANNA **F2.5488**

Mack Sennett Productions. *Dist* Allied Producers and Distributors. ca24 Dec **1922** [Los Angeles premiere; released 15 Feb 1923; c4 Jan 1923; LP18621]. Si; b&w. 35mm. 8 reels, 6,500 ft.

Pres by Mack Sennett. *Supv-Adapt* Mack Sennett. *Dir* F. Richard Jones. *Photog* Homer Scott, Fred W. Jackman, Robert Walters. *Lighting Expert* Paul Guerin. *Art Dir* Sanford D. Barnes. *Film Ed* Allen McNeil. *Asst Dir* Ray Grey. *Cost* Madame Violet.

Cast: Mabel Normand *(Suzanna)*, George Nichols *(Don Fernando)*, Walter McGrail *(Ramón)*, Evelyn Sherman *(Doña Isabella)*, Leon Bary *(Pancho)*, Eric Mayne *(Don Diego)*, Winifred Bryson *(Dolores)*, Carl Stockdale *(Ruiz)*, Lon Poff *(Álvarez)*, George Cooper *(Miguel)*, Indian Minnie *(herself)*, Black Hawk *(himself)*.

Romantic comedy-drama. Source: Linton Wells, "Suzanna" (publication undetermined). Hoping to consolidate their adjoining ranches, Don Fernando and Don Diego betroth their children, Ramón and Dolores, although Ramón is in love with Suzanna, the daughter of a peon on his father's ranch, and Dolores is interested in Pancho, a toreador. When Suzanna learns that she was kidnaped in infancy and is really Don Diego's daughter, she keeps silent; but Ramón finally rebels and steals Suzanna from the altar as she is about to marry Pancho. There are explanations, Ramón marries Suzanna, and Dolores marries Pancho. *Ranchers. Peons. Bullfighters. Parentage. California.*

THE SWAMP **F2.5489**

Hayakawa Feature Play Co. *Dist* R-C Pictures. 30 Oct **1921** [c30 Oct 1921; LP17174]. Si; b&w. 35mm. 6 reels, 5,560 ft.

Dir Colin Campbell. *Scen* J. Grubb Alexander. *Story* Sessue Hayakawa. *Photog* Frank D. Williams. *Art Dir* W. L. Heywood.

Cast: Sessue Hayakawa *(Wang)*, Bessie Love *(Mary)*, Janice Wilson *(Norma)*, Frankie Lee *(Buster)*, Lillian Langdon *(Mrs. Biddle)*, Harland Tucker *(Spencer Wellington)*, Ralph McCullough *(Johnnie Rand)*.

Melodrama. In "The Swamp," the slum quarter of a great city, live Mary, a deserted wife, and her small son Buster, struggling for an existence. They meet Wang, a Chinese vegetable peddler, when the peddler gets a black eye defending the boy. When Mary and Buster are about to be evicted, Wang saves them by peddling his horse, Bimbo; and he then becomes a fortune-teller, assisted by Buster. Rand, the new rent collector, proves to be Mary's childhood sweetheart. Through one of Wang's clients, she obtains a letter revealing that her husband, Spencer Wellington, is about to remarry. Wang, who is engaged to entertain at Norma's wedding reception, there reveals Spencer's past, thus breaking the engagement. Mary divorces Spencer and goes with Rand, while Wang, after redeeming his horse, returns to the home of his ancestors where a girl awaits him. *Chinese. Peddlers. Fortune-tellers. Divorce. Motherhood. Slums. Horses.*

THE SWAN **F2.5490**

Famous Players–Lasky. *Dist* Paramount Pictures. 16 Feb **1925** [c17 Feb 1925; LP21173]. Si; b&w. 35mm. 6 reels, 5,889 ft.

Pres by Adolph Zukor, Jesse L. Lasky. *Dir-Screenplay* Dimitri Buchowetzki. *Photog* Alvin Wyckoff.

Cast: Frances Howard *(Alexandra, The Swan)*, Adolphe Menjou *(H. R. H. Albert of Kersten-Rodenfels)*, Ricardo Cortez *(Dr. Walter, the tutor)*, Ida Waterman *(Princess Beatrice)*, Helen Lindroth *(Amphirosa)*, Helen Lee Worthing *(Wanda von Gluck)*, Joseph Depew *(Prince George)*, George Walcott *(Prince Arsene)*, Michael Visaroff *(Father Hyacinth)*, Mikhael Vavitch *(Colonel Wunderlich)*, Nicholas Soussanin *(Lutzow)*, Arthur Donaldson *(Franz, the court chamberlain)*, General Lodijensky *(Master of the Hunt)*, Clare Eames *(Princess Dominica)*.

Romantic comedy. Source: Ferenc Molnár, *Â Hattyú Vigjáték Hârom Felvonâsbarn* (Budapest, 1921; trans. by Melville C. Baker as *The Swan*, New York, 1922). For reasons of state, a marriage is arranged between Prince Albert and Princess Alexandra. The prince, who delights in wine and women, is uninterested in the haughty princess and initiates an intrigue with Wanda von Gluck, a beautiful lady-in-waiting. Alexandra's mother suggests that her daughter should flirt with Dr. Walter, a tutor employed at the castle, in order to excite the prince's jealousy. The princess arranges a picnic and is kind to Walter, who expresses his love. During a storm, she takes shelter with him in a hut, where they are discovered by Albert. At a drinking bout in the castle later that evening, Albert insults Walter, and the men begin to duel. Walter disarms Albert but is wounded by Albert's aide, Wunderlich. Alexandra rushes to Walter and confesses her love for him before the entire court. Albert releases her from her troth, and Alexandra's mother finally reconciles herself to a marriage between her daughter and a commoner. *Royalty. Tutors. Flirts. Motherhood. Marriage of convenience. Imaginary kingdoms. Duels.*

SWEDEN TODAY **F2.5491**

Amandus Johnson. 21 Apr **1928** [New York State license]. Si; b&w. 35mm. 8 reels.

Travelog. No information about the precise nature of this film has been found. *Sweden.*

Note: Country of origin undetermined.

SWEEPING AGAINST THE WINDS **F2.5492**

Victor Adamson Productions. 20 Jun **1930** [New York State license]. Mus score; b&w. 35mm. 5 reels, 4,800 ft. [Also si.]

Cast: Theodore von Eltz.

Drama(?). No information about the nature of this film has been found.

SWEET ADELINE **F2.5493**

Chadwick Pictures. 14 Jan **1926** [New York premiere; c31 Dec 1925; LP22237]. Si; b&w. 35mm. 7 reels.

Dir Jerome Storm. *Story-Cont* Charles E. Banks. *Photog* Philip Tannura.

Cast: Charles Ray *(Ben Wilson)*, Gertrude Olmstead *(Adeline)*, Jack Clifford *(Bill Wilson)*, John P. Lockney *(Pa Wilson)*, Sibyl Johnston *(fat lady)*, Gertrude Short *(cabaret dancer)*, Ida Lewis *(Ma Wilson)*.

Comedy-drama. Suggested by the song by: Richard H. Gerrard and Harry Armstrong, "Sweet Adeline" (1903). Ben Wilson, a simple country boy, is constantly bullied and belittled by his older brother, Bill, a halfhearted, inferior fellow who becomes Bill's rival for the affections of Adeline, a new girl in town. Possessed of a good tenor voice, Ben makes a hit singing a new song called "Sweet Adeline." Given a chance to go to Chicago to sing in a cabaret, Ben changes his singing style and dresses in a suit. He is an instant flop. Backstage, he takes off his collar, screws up his courage, and returns onstage to sing "Sweet Adeline" in the country style. He becomes a great success and wins Adeline's love for life. *Singers. Brothers. Cabarets. Smalltown life. Chicago.*

SWEET DADDIES **F2.5494**

First National Pictures. 13 Jun **1926** [c12 May 1926; LP22715]. Si; b&w. 35mm. 7 reels, 6,562 ft.

Pres by M. C. Levee. *Dir* Alfred Santell. *Titl* George Marion, Jr. *Adapt* W. C. Clifford. *Photog* Arthur Edeson. *Art Dir* Jack Okey. *Film Ed* Frank Lawrence. *Asst Dir* James F. O'Shea.

Cast: George Sidney *(Abie Finklebaum)*, Charlie Murray *(Patrick O'Brien)*, Vera Gordon *(Rosie Finklebaum)*, Jobyna Ralston *(Mariam Finklebaum)*, Jack Mulhall *(Jimmy O'Brien)*, Gaston Glass *(Sam Berkowitz)*, Aggie Herring.

Comedy-drama. Noted stage comedian Pat O'Brien prematurely celebrates his son's graduation from college and is fired from his act for being intoxicated; later, at a cafe where father and son continue their celebration, Jimmy sees Mariam Finklebaum, whom he has met at a school prom. Abie (her father) and Pat become friends and enter into a business arrangement to import a mysterious product from the Bahamas, and they are arrested on a rumrunning charge after Berkowitz, Mariam's jealous suitor, tips off prohibition officers. Jimmy meets their ship in a hydroplane and is also arrested. They are all released when it is learned that they are importing molasses; and Mariam's plans to marry Berkowitz are canceled when it is learned that he is a leading Florida bootlegger. All ends happily with Jimmy engaged to Mariam. *Actors. Bootleggers. Jews. Irish. Filial relations. Partnerships. Drunkenness. Molasses. Hydroplanes. Florida.*

SWEET KITTY BELLAIRS **F2.5495**

Warner Brothers Pictures. 9 Aug **1930** [c31 Jul 1930; LP1449]. Sd (Vitaphone); col (Technicolor). 35mm. 9 reels, 5,772 ft.

Dir Alfred E. Green. *Screenplay-Dial* J. Grubb Alexander. *Adapt* Herman Harrison. *Photog* Watkins McDonald. *Songs, including: "You—O-O, I Love But You"* Bobby Dolan, Walter O'Keefe. *Rec Engr* George R. Groves.

Cast: Claudia Dell *(Sweet Kitty Bellairs)*, Ernest Torrence *(Sir Jasper Standish)*, Walter Pidgeon *(Lord Verney)*, Perry Askam *(Captain O'Hara)*, June Collyer *(Julia Standish)*, Lionel Belmore *(Colonel Villiers)*, Arthur Carew *(Captain Spicer)*, Flora Finch *(gossip)*, Douglas Gerrard *(Tom Stafford)*, Christiane Yves *(Lydia)*.

Musical costume drama. Source: David Belasco, *Sweet Kitty Bellairs* (New York opening: 9 Dec 1903). Agnes Castle and Egerton Castle, *The Bath Comedy* (New York, 1900). In 18th-century England, a coach bound for Bath carries gouty Lord Verney, a maid named Lydia, and the famous flirt known as Sweet Kitty Bellairs, en route to visit her sister Julia, wife of Sir Jasper Standish. They are all robbed by a highwayman who returns Kitty's valuables, along with kisses and embraces. Kitty enchants the people of Bath; receiving a burning poem from the shy Lord Verney and a pledge from the highwayman, she causes Standish to think his wife has been unfaithful and that Verney is the culprit. ... Later, Standish mistrusts everyone except Verney, whom he discovers with Kitty in a compromising situation; thus Verney claims she is to be his wife. The following night, the highwayman kidnaps Kitty and reveals himself as Captain O'Hara; he fights with a masked stranger (Verney), who wins and claims Kitty. *Highwaymen. Flirts. Sisters. Nobility. Kidnaping. Bath (England). Duels.*

SWEET MAMA **F2.5496**

First National Pictures. 6 Jul **1930** [c14 Jul 1930; LP1421]. Sd (Vitaphone); b&w. 35mm. 7 reels, 5,012 ft.

Dir Edward Cline. *Screenplay-Dial* Earl Baldwin, Frederick Hazlitt Brennan. *Photog* Sid Hickox. *Film Ed* Frederick Y. Smith, Edward Schroeder. *Rec Engr* Cal Applegate.

Cast: Alice White *(Goldie)*, David Manners *(Jimmy)*, Kenneth Thomson *(Joe Palmer)*, Rita Flynn *(Lulu)*, Lee Moran *(Al Hadrick)*, Richard Cramer *(Elmer)*, Robert Elliott *(Mack)*, Lew Harvey *(gangster)*.

Crime melodrama. While stranded in a tank town with her burlesque troupe, Goldie receives a message from her roommate Lulu, in the city, that her sweetheart, Jimmy, has been arrested. Desperate and penniless, she stows away on a train and bumps into Mack, a city detective, who learns of her plight and pays her fare. It develops that Jimmy has been released through the intercession of cafe owner and racketeer Joe Palmer, who also has given him a job. Mack persuades Goldie to take a dancing job with Palmer so as to secure evidence against him. When she tips off the police about a planned bank robbery, Jimmy is suspected of the betrayal, but Goldie convinces Palmer of his innocence. Later, to save Goldie, Jimmy tells Palmer that he did divulge the information; and as he is about to be pushed from a skyscraper, Goldie brings the police to the rescue. *Showgirls. Racketeers. Detectives. Burlesque. Bank robberies.*

SWEET ROSIE O'GRADY **F2.5497**

Columbia Pictures. 17 Sep **1926** [trade showing; released 5 Oct; c22 Nov 1926; LP23366]. Si; b&w. 35mm. 7 reels, 6,108 ft.

Supv Harry Cohn. *Dir* Frank R. Strayer. *Scen* Harry O. Hoyt. *Photog* J. O. Taylor.

Cast: Shirley Mason *(Rosie O'Grady)*, Cullen Landis *(Victor McQuade)*, E. Alyn Warren *(Uncle Ben Shapiro)*, William Conklin *(James Brady)*, Lester Bernard *(kibitzer)*, Otto Lederer *(friend)*.

Comedy-drama. Suggested by: Maude Nugent, "Sweet Rosie O'Grady" (a song; 1896). Rosie, an orphan, grows to womanhood under the care of Uncle Ben, a genial pawnbroker, and Brady, an Irish policeman. One day Rosie rescues Victor McQuade, a youth of the fashionable set, from some ruffians, and tends his wounds in the pawnshop. The next day, Victor, in a uniform borrowed from his chauffeur, calls to take Rosie for a ride; at his home she is detained by his sister, Muriel, who is giving a "poverty party." Rosie accidentally gets shoved in among the guests and wins first prize for having the most comical costume. Angry and mortified, she flees from Victor to Uncle Ben, who consents to her going to live with Brady in his comfortable home. Victor, intent on marrying Rosie, abducts her from Brady's home, and when they are stopped by a policeman, they have him perform the marriage ceremony. *Police. Orphans. Pawnbrokers. Jews. Irish. Social classes. Poverty. Wealth.*

SWEET SIXTEEN (Imperial Photoplays) **F2.5498**

Trem Carr Productions. *Dist* Rayart Pictures. Aug **1928.** Si; b&w. 35mm. 6 reels, 5,831 or 5,991 ft.

Dir Scott Pembroke. *Scen* Arthur Hoerl. *Story* Phyllis Duganne. *Photog* Walter Griffin. *Film Ed* J. S. Harrington.

Cast: Helen Foster *(Cynthia Perry)*, Gertrude Olmstead *(Patricia Perry)*, Gladden James *(Howard De Hart)*, Lydia Yeamans Titus *(Grandma Perry)*, Reginald Sheffield *(Tommy Lowell)*, William H. Tooker *(Patrick Perry)*, Harry Allen, Carolynne Snowden.

Drama. Cynthia Perry falls prey to the romancing of rounder Howard De Hart despite repeated warnings from her older sister, Patricia. The latter, finally taking it upon herself to separate the couple, risks her own reputation in the man's apartment and almost loses her sweetheart in the process. *Sisters. Philanderers. Adolescence. Reputation.*

SWEETHEARTS AND WIVES **F2.5499**

First National Pictures. 15 Jun **1930** [c11 Jun 1930; LP1350]. Sd (Vitaphone). b&w. 35mm. 9 reels, 7,003 ft.

Dir Clarence Badger. *Scen-Dial* Forrest Halsey. *Photog* John Seitz. *Film Ed* Jack Rollins. *Sd Tech* Glenn E. Rominger.

Cast: Billie Dove *(femme de chambre)*, Clive Brook *(Reginald De Brett)*, Sidney Blackmer *(Anthony Peel)*, Crauford Kent *(Sir John Deptford)*, Leila Hyams *(Angela Worthing)*, John Loder *(Sam Worthing)*, Fletcher Norton *(maître d'hôtel)*, Albert Gran *(police inspector)*, Alphonse Martell *(gendarme)*, Rolfe Sedan *(waiter)*.

Mystery melodrama. Source: Walter Hackett, *Other Men's Wives* (New York opening: 29 Nov 1929). On a stormy night, Anthony Peel and Angela Worthing are forced to seek shelter at a secluded inn. There they find the maître d'hôtel, a waiter, and a maid in earnest conference. Angela is hesitant about staying overnight because of a possible scandal; and the maid, pretending to understand only French, is curious about the young lovers. Screams from an adjoining room bring the police and detective Reginald De Brett in search of a stolen diamond necklace; a murder is discovered, and all are detained overnight. Anthony learns that the maid is the sister of the woman who owned the missing jewels and discovers a button near the location of the murder, proving ultimately that De Brett is actually the killer. *Chambermaids. Waiters. Maîtres d'hôtel. Detectives. Murder. France.*

SWEETHEARTS ON PARADE **F2.5500**

Christie Film Co. *Dist* Columbia Pictures. 15 Aug **1930** [c13 Sep 1930; LP1564]. Sd (Movietone); b&w. 35mm. 7 reels, 6,247 ft.

Prod Al Christie. *Dir* Marshall Neilan. *Cont-Dial* Colin Clements. *Story* Al Cohn, James A. Starr. *Photog* Gus Peterson. *Film Ed* Sidney Walsh. *Song: "Sweethearts on Parade"* Charles Newman, Carmen Lombardo. *Song: "Dream of Me"* Henry Cohen, Irving Bibo. *Song: "Yearning Just for You"* Benny Davis, Joe Burke. *Song: "Misstep"* Irving Bibo. *Sd Engr* Alfred M. Granich, Ted Murray.

Cast: Alice White *(Helen)*, Lloyd Hughes *(Bill)*, Marie Prevost *(Nita)*, Kenneth Thomson *(Hendricks)*, Ray Cooke *(Hank)*, Wilbur Mack *(Parker)*, Ernest Wood *(Denham)*, Max Asher *(store manager)*.

Romantic comedy-drama. Helen, a pretty country girl, comes to the city in search of a millionaire and meets Nita, a city girl with whom she decides to team up. Helen flirts with Hank, a sailor on shore leave, and when he leaves to get some ice cream, Bill, a marine, makes friends with her. The girls are engaged as window demonstrators in a department store, attracting large crowds, including Hank and Bill, who fight over Helen. On the last night of shore leave, they take the girls to a dancehall, where Harrison Hendricks and a party of millionaire friends try to date the girls, causing a free-for-all. Helen, who has come to care for Bill, agrees to await his return from sea duty, but Hendricks' attentions turn her head in Bill's absence. At a dinner party, Bill unexpectedly returns, and Helen, angered by his attitude, accepts Hendricks' marriage proposal. Nita becomes suspicious and accompanied by Hank and Bill goes to the millionaire's yacht. Meanwhile, Helen decides she does not want to marry a millionaire and agrees to overlook Bill's penchant for fighting. *Sailors. Demonstrators—Commercial products. Millionaires. Socialites. Courtship.*

SWEETIE **F2.5501**

Paramount Famous Lasky Corp. 25 Oct **1929** [New York premiere; released 2 Nov; c1 Nov 1929; LP816]. Sd (Movietone); b&w. 35mm. 12 reels, 8,969 ft. [Also si; 6,303 ft.]

Dir Frank Tuttle. *Story-Scen-Dial* George Marion, Jr., Lloyd Corrigan. *Titl* George Marion, Jr. *Photog* Alfred Gilks. *Film Ed* Verna Willis. *Songs: "Sweeter Than Sweet," "Alma Mammy," "The Prep Step," "I Think You'll Like It," "Bear Down Pelham"* Richard A. Whiting, George Marion, Jr. *Dance Dir* Earl Lindsay. *Rec Engr* Eugene Merritt.

Cast: Nancy Carroll *(Barbara Pell)*, Helen Kane *(Helen Fry)*, Stanley Smith *(Biff Bentley)*, Jack Oakie *(Tap-Tap Thompson)*, William Austin *(Percy [Pussy] Willow)*, Stuart Erwin *(Axel Bronstrup)*, Wallace MacDonald *(Bill Barrington)*, Charles Sellon *(Dr. Oglethorpe)*, Aileen Manning *(Miss Twill)*.

Romantic musical comedy. Axel Bronstrup, a lazy student at Pelham, is induced by Helen Fry of Miss Twill's School for Girls to play football, while Barbara Pell, a chorus girl, wants Biff Bentley to marry her and go into show business. She is aided in her elopement plans by Tap-Tap Thompson, but Biff is persuaded to stay in school by the football coach. Embittered, Nancy goes to New York, only to find she has inherited property, including the school; and Thompson, liking school life, enrolls at Pelham and falls for Helen. The school stages a welcome for Barbara, the new owner, and Thompson sings "Alma Mammy"; but she orders an English exam and rules that athletes who flunk will be barred from the forthcoming game. Biff fails but is given another chance, and he and Axel are the heroes for the victorious Pelham. *Students. Chorus girls. Athletic coaches. College life. Football. Boarding schools.*

Note: Studio press materials indicate there were 10 songs written for the film, though inclusive titles are not listed.

THE SWELL-HEAD **F2.5502**

Columbia Pictures. 5 Aug **1927** [c6 Sep 1927; LP24358]. Si; b&w. 35mm. 6 reels, 5,484 ft.

Prod Harry Cohn. *Dir* Ralph Graves. *Screenplay* Robert Lord. *Photog* Conrad Wells.

Cast: Ralph Graves *(Lefty Malone)*, Johnnie Walker *(Bill O'Rourke)*, Eugenia Gilbert *(Molly O'Rourke)*, Mildred Harris *(Kitty)*, Mary Carr *(Mother Malone)*, Tom Dugan.

Melodrama. Bill O'Rourke and Lefty Malone, partners in a moving business, live in adjoining flats in an East Side tenement. Bill's younger sister, Molly, keeps house for her brother and assists Mrs. Malone, Lefty's invalid mother. When the boys mistake the belongings of a "Mrs. Murphy" for those of Spug Murphy, a heavyweight fighter, Lefty proves his fistic ability; and in order to raise money for his mother's operation, he accepts the offer of a fight manager. He proves successful in the ring, but quick success turns his head and he becomes infatuated with Kitty. In a bout with Murphy, Lefty is overconfident and loses the fight, but the excitement cures his mother. Realizing the error of conceit, he is reunited with Sally. *Movers. Prizefighters. Invalids. Fight managers. Partnerships. Filial relations. Brother-sister relationship. New York City—East Side.*

THE SWELLHEAD **F2.5503**

Tiffany Productions. 20 Mar **1930** [c22 Mar 1930; LP1172]. Sd (Photophone); b&w. 35mm. 7 reels, 7,040 ft. [Also si.]

Dir James Flood. *Scen* Richard Cahoon, Adele Buffington. *Dial* Adele Buffington, James Gleason. *Photog* Jackson Rose, Art Reeves. *Film Ed* Richard Cahoon. *Rec Engr* Dean Daily.

Cast: James Gleason *(Johnny Trump)*, Johnny Walker *(Bill "Cyclone" Hickey)*, Marion Shilling *(Mamie Judd)*, Natalie Kingston *(Barbara Larkin)*, Paul Hurst *(Mugsy)*, Freeman Wood *(Clive Warren)*, Lillian Elliott *(Mrs. Callahan)*.

Melodrama. Source: A. P. Younger, "Cyclone Hickey" (publication undetermined). Cyclone Hickey, a ham prizefighter who lives in an East Side tenement, is a joke to the public, a pest to matchmakers, and a hero to little Mamie Judd, the factory girl who lives across the hall from him in Maggie Callahan's boardinghouse. Mamie induces sportswriter Johnny Trump to take her savings and manage Cyclone, but when Cyclone becomes overconfident and insults Johnny and Mrs. Callahan, they give up on him and he fails to win matches. Mrs. Callahan, ill in bed, hears a radio account of a losing bout and implores Johnny to go to the ring and advise him; Cyclone wins the day and is happily united with Mamie. *Prizefighters. Landladies. Sportswriters. Fight managers. Boardinghouses. New York City—East Side.*

THE SWIFT SHADOW **F2.5504**

FBO Pictures. 11 Dec **1927** [c11 Dec 1927; LP24767]. Si; b&w. 35mm. 5 reels, 4,892 ft.

Dir Jerome Storm. *Story-Cont* Ethel Hill. *Photog* Robert De Grasse. *Asst Dir* Jack Merton.

Cast: Ranger *(The Swift Shadow, a dog)*, Josephine Borio *(Helen Todd* [*see note*]*)*, William Bertram *(Joseph Todd, Helen's father)*, Sam Nelson *(Jim)*, Al Smith *(Butch Kemp)*, Lorraine Eason *(see note)*, Milburn Morante *(Sheriff Miller)*.

Melodrama. The Swift Shadow, a dog trained to be a vicious killer, is captured by police after his master, Butch Kemp, commits a murder and flees. The dog is about to be put to death when Jim, the son of the murdered man, suggests that the criminal be tracked down with his own dog. The trail leads them to a ranch where Kemp attacks Jim and orders The Swift Shadow to finish him. The dog's gratitude for Jim's kindness prevents him from following Kemp's order, and in a frenzy of hate he kills his former master. *Filial relations. Murder. Dogs.*

Note: One source gives Lorraine Eason in the part of *Helen Todd* and Josephine Borio in an unidentified role.

SWIM, GIRL, SWIM **F2.5505**

Paramount Famous Lasky Corp. 3 Sep **1927** [New York premiere; released 17 Sep; c17 Sep 1927; LP24428]. Si; b&w. 35mm. 7 reels, 6,124 ft.

Pres by Adolph Zukor, Jesse L. Lasky. *Assoc Prod* B. P. Schulberg. *Dir* Clarence Badger. *Story-Screenplay* Lloyd Corrigan. *Titl* George Marion, Jr. *Photog* J. Roy Hunt.

Cast: Bebe Daniels *(Alice Smith)*, James Hall *(Jerry Marvin)*, Gertrude Ederle *(herself)*, Josephine Dunn *(Helen Tracey)*, William Austin *(Mr. Spangle, Ph. D.)*, James Mack *(Professor Twinkle)*.

Farce. Alice Smith, a plain and serious university co-ed, is wholly engrossed, it would appear, in chasing butterflies and rare insects under the guidance of her friend, Mr. Spangle, Ph. D., though she secretly yearns to be an athlete and thus win the admiration of Jerry Marvin, a popular schoolmate. She takes up swimming, making herself the campus joke because of her ideas on the subject, which result from the malicious influence of Helen Tracey. She is persuaded to enter a channel swim, but en route she is relieved by Spangle's boat; through a heavy fog, Spangle maneuvers the boat unwittingly in the direction of the finish line; and when they collide with a fishing boat, Alice is thrown into the water and is acclaimed the winner. Jerry begins to fall for her as a result and introduces her to Gertrude Ederle, who trains Alice in swimming; learning of the previous deception, Jerry rejects her, then relents when she enters another race and wins on her own merits. *College life. Entomology. Swimming. English Channel.*

SWING HIGH **F2.5506**

Pathé Exchange. 18 May **1930** [c19 May 1930; LP1311]. Sd (Photophone); b&w. 35mm. 10 reels, 8,311 ft.

Prod E. B. Derr. *Dir* Joseph Santley. *Cont* Ray McCarey. *Adapt-Dial* James Seymour. *Story* Joseph Santley, James Seymour. *Camera* David Abel. *Art Dir* Carroll Clark. *Set Dresser* Ted Dickson. *Film Ed* Daniel Mandell. *Songs: "Do You Think I Could Grow on You?" "It Must Be Love," "With My Guitar and You," "Shoo the Hoodoo Away"* Mack Gordon, Abner Silver, Ted Snyder. *Mus Dir* Josiah Zuro. *Rec Engr* Homer Ackerman, Charles O'Loughlin, Ben Winkler. *Asst Dir* Ray McCarey, Bert Gilroy. *Cost Dsgn* Gwen Wakeling. *Script Clerk* Eleanor Donahue. *Prop Man* Mel Wolfe.

Cast: Helen Twelvetrees *(Maryan)*, Fred Scott *(Garry)*, Dorothy Burgess *(Trixie)*, John Sheehan *(Doc May)*, Daphne Pollard *(Mrs. May)*, George Fawcett *(Pop Garner)*, Bryant Washburn *(Ringmaster Joe)*, Nick Stuart *(Billy)*, Sally Starr *(Ruth)*, Little Billy *(Major Tiny)*, William Langan *(Babe)*, Stepin Fetchit *(Sam)*, Chester Conklin *(sheriff)*, Ben Turpin *(bartender)*, Robert Edeson *(doctor)*, Mickey Bennett *(Mickey)*.

Melodrama. To avoid hostilities, Maryan, the ward of Doc May, a medicine show owner, induces Pop Garner, a circus owner, to join forces with her guardian. Doc May and Daphne, his wife, work as clowns; and Garry, a singing soldier of fortune, sings along with Maryan's act. Ruth, Maryan's partner, quits to get married; and Joe, who is jealous of Garry, replaces her with Trixie, his former assistant. When Garry announces his engagement to Maryan, Trixie persuades him to join a strip poker game in a drunken state and "compromises" him in the presence of his fiancée. Grief-stricken, Maryan falls during her act, and Garry, robbed of circus funds, is arrested. In spite of her injuries, Maryan, learning of Trixie's treachery, performs the act with her and forces a confession by threatening to drop her; Garry is released and is welcomed back to the show. *Trapezists. Clowns. Ringmasters. Soldiers of fortune. Thieves. Courtship. Jealousy. Circus. Medicine shows.*

THE SWORD OF VALOR **F2.5507**

Phil Goldstone Productions. 6 May **1924** [New York showing]. Si; b&w. 35mm. 5 reels, 4,800 ft.

Dir Duke Worne. *Scen* Jefferson Moffitt. *Story* Julio Sabello. *Photog* Roland Price.

Cast: Rex (Snowy) Baker, Dorothy Revier, Percy Challenger, Eloise Hess, Stella De Lanti, Otto Lederer, Fred Kavens, Armando Pasquali, Edward Cecil.

Melodrama. "The story concerns the fair Ynez, the daughter of a Spanish Don living quietly in the ancient hacienda. Her father, Don Guzman de Ruis y Montejo (Otto Lederer), determines upon a rich marriage for the girl. A chance meeting with an American, Captain Crooks, develops into love at first sight. Papa, not knowing, takes his daughter to the Riviera, where Ismid Matrouli (Edwin [*sic*] Cecil), a Levantine of mongrel origin, but wealthy, falls in love and asks dad for her hand. The captain appears upon the scene in time to rescue Ynez from a watery death. ... Matrouli sicks a professional swordsman on the cap, but the latter socks him in the jaw instead of arranging a duel. ... The inevitable duel follows. ... A gypsy lover of Ynez takes a pot shot at the cap during the duel, but hits his opponent. The latter then kidnaps Ynez and carries her away to a mountain stronghold, where the captain corners him ... ." (*Variety,* 14 May 1924, p28.) *Levantines. Nobility. Spain. Riviera. Duels.*

SWORDS AND PLOWSHARES *see* **THE SPIRIT OF THE U. S. A.**

SYMBOL OF THE UNCONQUERED **F2.5508**

Micheaux Film Corp. caJan **1921.** Si; b&w. 35mm. 7 reels.

Cast: Lawrence Chenault, Walker Thompson, Iris Hall, E. G. Tatum, Jim Burris, Mattie Wilkes, Lee Whipper.

Western melodrama. After the death of her grandfather, Evon Mason, a beautiful Negress, comes west to identify the mine claim she has been willed. Thrown out of the only hotel in town, she is cared for by Van Allen, a prospector whose life she later saves. *Prospectors. Racial prejudice. Negro life. Mine claims. Hotels.*

Note: Known also as *The Wilderness Trail.*

THE SYMPHONY *see* **JAZZ MAD**

SYNCOPATING SUE **F2.5509**

Corinne Griffith Productions. *Dist* First National Pictures. 31 Oct **1926** [c20 Oct 1926; LP23230]. Si; b&w. 35mm. 7 reels, 6,770 ft.

Pres by Asher-Small-Rogers. *Dir* Richard Wallace. *Screenplay* Adelaide Heilbron, Jack Wagner. *Photog* Harold Wenstrom.

Cast: Corinne Griffith *(Susan Adams)*, Tom Moore *(Eddie Murphy)*, Rockliffe Fellowes *(Arthur Bennett)*, Lee Moran *(Joe Horn)*, Joyce Compton *(Marge Adams)*, Sunshine Hart *(landlady)*, Marjorie Rambeau *(herself)*.

Romantic comedy. Source: Reginald Butler Goode, *Syncopating Sue* (a play; publication undetermined). Susan Adams, who is employed as a pianist in a Broadway music shop, entertains ambitions for a stage career. Arthur Bennett, famous theatrical producer and successful star-maker, summons her to his office to complain about her noisy piano below him, and she haughtily responds that she will stop if he gives her a chance on the stage. Susan mistakes Eddie Murphy, recently arrived in town, for a flirtatious masher, until she finds him living in her boardinghouse; and their friendship grows when she learns he is a friend of Joe Horn, a saxophonist. Eddie, who plays drums in a cabaret, is disillusioned at seeing Susan with Bennett. When Bennett seeks to ensnare Susan's sister, Marge, Susan proves her acting abilities at his apartment; but learning that Eddie has left for Europe, she confesses her love for him, and they are happily united. *Sisters. Pianists. Theatrical producers. Drummers. Saxophonists. Courtship. Theater. New York City—Broadway.*

Note: Working title: *Broadway Blues.*

SYNCOPATION **F2.5510**

RKO Productions. 24 Mar **1929** [cl Mar 1929; LP248]. Sd (Photophone); b&w. 35mm. 8 reels, 7,626 ft.

Supv Robert Kane. *Dir* Bert Glennon. *Sd Dir* Tommy Cumming. *Dial Dir* Bertram Harrison, James Seymour. *Dial* Gene Markey. *Titl* Paul S. Haschke. *Adapt* Frances Agnew. *Photog* Dal Clawson, George Webber, Frank Landi. *Film Ed* Edward Pfitzenmeier. *Song: "Jericho"* Leo Robin, Richard Myers. *Song: "Mine Alone"* Herman Ruby, Richard Myers. *Song: "I'll Always Be in Love With You"* Bud Green, Sammy Stept. *Asst Dir* Basil Smith, Fred Uttal.

Cast: Barbara Bennett *(Flo)*, Bobby Watson *(Benny)*, Ian Hunter *(Winston)*, Morton Downey *(Lew)*, Osgood Perkins *(Hummel)*, Mackenzie Ward *(Henry)*, Vera Teasdale *(Rita)*, Dorothy Lee, Fred Waring and his Pennsylvanians.

Musical comedy-drama. Source: Gene Markey, *Stepping High* (Garden City, New York, 1929). Benny and Flo, a husband-and-wife vaudeville act who form the dancing team of Sloane and Darrel, reach the Broadway big time in a revue that folds under them. They are signed up for a nightclub, however, and become a sensation. Winston, a society playboy, takes a fancy to Flo, and she soon becomes discontented with the unsophisticated Benny and his Broadway buddies. Flo divorces Benny and breaks up the act, finding a new dancing partner for a revue backed by Winston. The act is a flop, and Winston offers Flo a trip to Europe without benefit of clergy. Coming to her senses at last, Flo returns to Benny, and they go on the road again with their old act. *Dancers. Divorce. Social classes. Vaudeville. Nightclubs. New York City—Broadway.*

SYNTHETIC SIN **F2.5511**

First National Pictures. 6 Jan **1929** [c11 Dec 1928; LP25913]. Mus score (Vitaphone); b&w. 35mm. 7 reels, 7,035 ft. [Also si; 6,724 ft.]

Pres by John McCormick. *Dir* William A. Seiter. *Cont* Tom J. Geraghty. *Titl* Tom Reed. *Photog* Sidney Hickox. *Film Ed* Terry Morse, Al Hall. *Song: "Betty"* Harold Christy, Nathaniel Shilkret.

Cast: Colleen Moore *(Betty)*, Antonio Moreno *(Donald)*, Edythe Chapman *(Mrs. Fairfax)*, Kathryn McGuire *(Margery)*, Gertrude Howard *(Cassie)*, Gertrude Astor *(Sheila)*, Raymond Turner *(Sam)*, Montague Love *(Brandy)*, Ben Hendricks, Jr. *(Frank)*, Phil Sleeman *(Tony)*, Jack Byron *(Tony's henchman)*, Fred Warren, Jay Eaton, Stanley Blystone, Art Rowlands, Dick Gordon, Julanne Johnston, Hazel Howell *(Frank's gang)*.

Comedy. Source: Frederick Hatton and Fanny Hatton, *Synthetic Sin* (New York opening: 10 Oct 1927). Donald Anthony, foremost playwright of the United States, returns to his home in Magnolia Gap, Virginia, and proposes to Betty Fairfax, a pretty and talented local girl. She accepts and makes him promise to give her the lead in his next play. The play flops, and Donald tells her that she is too unsophisticated for the role. Betty then decides to remain in New York and be wicked. She moves into an apartment next to four gangsters; Donald comes to visit, and they throw him out. There is a gunfight, and a gangster is killed. In the excitement Donald rescues Betty, after which they are all arrested in a police raid. Betty retires from the stage and devotes herself to Donald. *Playwrights. Gangsters. Actors. Police. Theater. Virginia. New York City.*

THE SYRIAN IMMIGRANT **F2.5512**

Eastern Star Film Co. Sep **1921** [New York State]. Si; b&w. 35mm. 8 reels.

Cast: Nicholas S. Haber, Estella Mackintosh.

Documentary. An educational picture showing the historical points of Syria, Palestine, and Egypt, and a story of the Syrian progress in the United States. *Immigrants. Syrians. Syria. Palestine. Egypt.*

Note: Country of origin not determined.

T. N. T. (THE NAKED TRUTH) **F2.5513**

Public Welfare Pictures. c25 Aug **1924** [LP20573]. Si; b&w. 35mm. 7 reels.

Prod Samuel Cummins. *Orig Story* George D. Walters.

Cast: Jack Mulhall *(Bob)*, Helene Chadwick *(Mary)*, Leo Pierson *(Bob's playmate)*, Charles Spere *(another playmate)*, Irene Davis *(Isobel)*, Emmett King *(Dr. Brown)*.

Sociological drama. The story of three youths, only one of whom has had proper training in social hygiene. Bob, who has had proper sex education, leads a clean life, becomes a lawyer, and marries. The second youth, whose father believed that "Youth should have its fling," becomes infected with veneral disease. He goes to a legitimate doctor but refuses the necessary longterm treatment; instead, he consults a "quack" doctor who produces a quick but phony cure. He is about to be married when the real doctor stops the wedding. The third youth also gets infected and goes directly to a quack. He marries, and the disease soon affects his brain. He goes insane and kills his wife. At his trial, Bob is able to free him on a plea of insanity. The Sanity Commission concludes that youths whose parents neglect them are prey to social diseases. *Physicians. Quacks. Lawyers. Insanity. Venereal disease. Sex instruction.*

Note: Also released as *The Naked Truth.*

TABLE TOP RANCH **F2.5514**

William Steiner Productions. Jul **1922** [c24 Apr 1922; LU17770]. Si; b&w. 35mm. 5 reels, 4,590 ft.

Prod William Steiner. *Story-Scen-Dir* Paul Hurst. *Photog* Jacob A. Badaracco.

Cast: Neal Hart *(John Marvin)*, William Quinn *(Palque Powell)*, Hazel Maye *(Kate Bowers)*.

Western melodrama. Kate Bowers, owner of a sheep ranch, is opposed by neighboring cattle ranchers who file a complaint that, despite an agreement made with her father, sheep have encroached upon their land. John Marvin intervenes on her behalf and incurs the enmity of Palque Powell, a bully who pretends to be enamored of Kate. Powell sets a dynamite trap in Marvin's path, but the latter manages to evade injury and regains consciousness in time to rescue Kate from the marauding ranchers. After rounding up the offenders, Marvin wins her love. *Ranchers. Sheep. Cattle.*

A TAILOR MADE MAN **F2.5515**

Charles Ray Productions. *Dist* United Artists. ca5 Aug **1922** [Los Angeles premiere; released 15 Oct; cl Oct 1922; LP18418]. Si; b&w. 35mm. 9 reels, 8,469 ft.

Pres by Arthur S. Kane. *Dir* Joseph De Grasse. *Adapt-Scen* Albert Ray. *Photog* George Rizard, George Meehan. *Art Dir* Robert Ellis. *Film Ed* Harry L. Decker. *Art Titl* Edward Withers.

Cast: Charles Ray *(John Paul Bart)*, Thomas Ricketts *(Anton Huber)*, Ethel Grandin *(Tanya Huber)*, Victor Potel *(Peter)*, Stanton Heck *(Abraham Nathan)*, Edythe Chapman *(Mrs. Nathan)*, Irene Lentz *(Miss Nathan)*, Frederick Thompson *(Mr. Stanlaw)*, Kate Lester *(Mrs. Stanlaw)*, Jacqueline Logan *(Corinne Stanlaw)*, Frank Butler *(Theodore Jellicot)*, Douglas Gerrard *(Gustavus Sonntag)*, Nellie Peck Saunders *(Kitty Dupuy)*, Charlotte Pierce *(Bessie Dupuy)*, Thomas Jefferson *(Gerald Whitcomb)*, Henry Barrows *(Hobart Sears)*, Eddie Gribbon *(Russell)*, Michael Dark *(Cecil Armstrong)*, Isabelle Vernon *(Mrs. Fitzmorris)*, Aileen Manning *(Miss Shayn)*, John McCallum *(butler)*, William Parke *(Rowlands)*, Frederick Vroom *(Harvey Benton)*, Harold Howard *(Arthur Arbuthnot)*, S. J. Bingham *(Cain)*, Fred Sullivan *(Flynn)*.

Comedy-drama. Source: Harry James Smith, *A Tailor Made Man; a Comedy in Four Acts* (New York, 1917). John Paul Bart, a presser who has high respect for the favorable impression created by expensive clothes, "borrows" a suit to wear to an exclusive reception. There he attracts the attention of shipping magnate Abraham Nathan, who hires John Paul to handle his company's labor problems. Against great odds and despite Gustavus Sonntag's scheming, John Paul is successful, but he returns to

Anton Huber's shop when he is exposed by Sonntag. Nathan, however, finds him and gives him a permanent position, and John Paul then marries Tanya Huber. *Pants-pressers. Business management. Labor. Clothes. Shipping companies.*

TAINTED MONEY **F2.5516**

Perfection Pictures. *Dist* C. B. C. Film Sales. 15 Dec **1924** [c23 Jan 1925; LP21066]. Si; b&w. 35mm. 5 reels, 4,906 ft.

Dir Henry MacRae. *Story* Stuart Payton. *Photog* Allen Thompson.

Cast: William Fairbanks *(Chester Carlton)*, Eva Novak *(Adams' daughter)*, Bruce Gordon *(Marston)*, Edwards Davis *(John Carlton)*, Carl Stockdale, Paul Weigel, Frank Clark.

Melodrama. A feud of long standing between Carlton and Adams, two lumber magnates, prevents them from cooperating with each other during an industry crisis. Carlton has contracts and no lumber; Adams has lumber, but Carlton has forbidden him to use the only road by which he can bring it to market. Disgusted by his father's spite, Chester Carlton leaves home and supports himself by driving a taxi. Chester later rescues Adams' daughter from a runaway horse and obtains a job, under an assumed name, as a chauffeur for her grateful father. Steele, Adams' general manager, later attempts to dynamite John and Chester Carlton, but Miss Adams saves them, earning the elder Carlton's gratitude and putting an end to the feud. *Taxi drivers. Chauffeurs. Feuds. Filial relations. Lumber industry. Business management. Business competition.*

TAKE IT FROM ME (Universal-Jewel) **F2.5517**

Universal Pictures. 10 Oct **1926** [c27 Sep 1926; LP23175]. Si; b&w. 35mm. 7 reels, 6,649 ft.

Pres by Carl Laemmle. *Dir* William A. Seiter. *Scen* Harvey Thew. *Photog* Arthur Todd.

Cast: Reginald Denny *(Tom Eggett)*, Blanche Mehaffey *(Grace Gordon)*, Ben Hendricks, Jr. *(Dick)*, Lee Moran *(Van)*, Lucien Littlefield *(Cyrus Crabb)*, Ethel Wales *(Miss Abbott)*, Bertram Johns *(Percy)*, Jean Tolley *(Gwen Forsythe)*, Tom O'Brien *(taxi driver)*, Vera Lewis *(Mrs. Forsythe)*.

Comedy-drama. Source: William B. Johnstone and Will R. Anderson, *Take It From Me* (vocal score; New York, 1919). Tom Eggett, with the help of his pals, Dick and Van, loses the last cent of his inheritance, is evicted from his apartment, and is rejected by Gwen, his fiancée. A codicil to his uncle's will, however, stipulates that he shall inherit the Eggett department store provided that he operate it for 3 months at a profit. Cyrus Crabb, manager of the store, is determined to gain possession of the business and arranges for the company's credit to be canceled during Tom's management, though Grace Gordon, a stenographer, has evidence of his perfidy. Tom takes a liking to Grace and hires her as his secretary though Gwen warns her that he is her fiancé. When the business suffers great losses, Tom decides to induce bankruptcy by extravagant expenditures such as a million-dollar fashion show. His tactics boomerang, but when a man returns merchandise stolen by his daughter, the store shows a profit and Tom wins Grace. *Secretaries. Inheritance. Business management. Courtship. Bankruptcy. Kleptomania. Department stores. Wills.*

TAKE ME HOME **F2.5518**

Paramount Famous Lasky Corp. 13 Oct **1928** [c15 Oct 1928; LP25714]. Si; b&w. 35mm. 6 reels, 5,614 ft.

Dir Marshall Neilan. *Screenplay* Ethel Doherty. *Titl* Herman Mankiewicz. *Story (see note)* Grover Jones, Tom Crizer, Harlan Thompson. *Photog* J. Roy Hunt. *Film Ed* Otto Lovering.

Cast: Bebe Daniels *(Peggy Lane)*, Neil Hamilton *(David North)*, Lilyan Tashman *(Derelys Devore)*, Doris Hill *(Alice Moore)*, Joe E. Brown *(Bunny)*, Ernie Wood *(Al Marks)*, Marcia Harris *(landlady)*, Yvonne Howell *(Elsie)*, Janet MacLeod *(Betty)*, J. W. Johnston *(The Producer)*.

Comedy-drama. Peggy Lane, a chorus girl, finds a small part in a new show for David North, a stagestruck country boy. At rehearsal, David meets Delerys Devore, the show's star, and she quickly offers him a larger part in her act. Quite taken with David, Delerys invites him to her home on the pretext that Peggy will be there; when Peggy does not show up, David leaves, infuriating his hostess. Derelys has Peggy fired the next day, and in reprisal Peggy goads her into a Carmenesque fight backstage just before the show. Derelys is unable to go on stage, and Peggy takes her place, becoming the hit of the show. Peggy and David are later married and give up show business, deciding to live on a farm. *Chorus girls. Entertainers. Theater. Farming. New York City—Broadway.*

Note: Sources disagree in crediting story.

TAKE THE HEIR **F2.5519**

Screen Story Syndicate. John R. Freuler–C. A. Stimson. *Dist* Big 4 Film Corp. 15 Jan **1930**. Talking sequences & mus score (Photophone); b&w. 35mm. 6 reels, 5,700 ft. [Also si.]

Dir Lloyd Ingraham. *Scen-Cont* Beatrice Van. *Photog* Allen Siegler. *Mus Score and Synchronization* J. M. Coopersmith.

Cast: Edward Everett Horton *(Smithers)*, Dorothy Devore *(Susan)*, Frank Elliott *(Lord Tweedham)*, Edythe Chapman *(Lady Tweedham)*, Otis Harlan *(John Walker)*, Kay Deslys *(Muriel Walker)*, Margaret Campbell *(Mrs. Smythe-Bellingham)*.

Comedy. Lord Tweedham, a tipsy Englishman, falls heir to his deceased uncle's estate in the United States; and upon his arrival there, his valet, Smithers, is forced to impersonate Tweedham because of his master's drunken state. At the home of the uncle's executor, John Walker, Smithers falls in love with the maid, Susan, though he is pursued by the executor's fat daughter, Muriel. After numerous complications, Smithers admits his identity and marries Susan, while Lord Tweedham falls victim to the wiles of Muriel. *Nobility. English. Valets. Housemaids. Inheritance. Impersonation. Drunkenness.*

TAKING A CHANCE **F2.5520**

Fox Film Corp. 18 Nov **1928** [c18 Nov 1928; LP25920]. Si; b&w. 35mm. 5 reels, 4,876 ft.

Pres by William Fox. *Dir* Norman Z. McLeod. *Scen* A. H. Halprin. *Photog* Sol Halprin. *Film Ed* J. Logan Pearson. *Asst Dir* Horace Hough.

Cast: Rex Bell *(Joe Courtney)*, Lola Todd *(Jessie Smith)*, Richard Carlyle *(Dan Carson)*, Billy Butts *(Little Billy)*, Jack Byron *(Pete)*, Martin Cichy *(Luke)*, Jack Henderson *(Jake)*.

Western melodrama. Source: Bret Harte, "The Saint of Calamity Gulch," in *Hutchinson's Magazine* (Jul 1925). "Gun fights, romance, adventure and all the other accessories of a wild west drama form basis of story woven about the exploits of Joe Courtney." ("Motion Picture News Booking Guide," in *Motion Picture News,* 15 Mar 1930, p105.)

TAKING CHANCES **F2.5521**

Phil Goldstone Productions. Mar **1922** [New York State]. Si; b&w. 35mm. 5 reels, 4,800 ft.

Dir Grover Jones. *Photog* Harry Fowler.

Cast: Richard Talmadge *(himself)*, Zella Gray *(Mildred Arlington)*, Elmer Dewey *(José Borquez)*, Percy Challenger *(James Arlington)*.

Comedy-drama. "Richard Talmadge, a book salesman, not only sells James Arlington, a capitalist, a volume of his firm's latest novel, but also talks himself into a position as private secretary to the millionaire. He falls in love with his daughter, whose hand is sought by Jose Borquez. The latter is scheming with a number of financiers to gain control of a corporation headed by Arlington. He plans a cruise and invites Arlington and his daughter to go along as his guests. At a ball prior to the departure of the party, Dick overhears a conspiracy in which Borquez plays a leading part. It is planned to keep Arlington away from New York so that the 'bulls' can wash him out financially. Richard is kidnapped, but after a series of adventures he not only overtakes the party but subjects Borquez to a severe punishment and wins the hand of Miss Arlington." *(Moving Picture World,* 18 Feb 1922, p756.) *Secretaries. Salesmen. Millionaires. Publishers. Stock market.*

Note: From a story, "Vim, Vigor and Vitality", the authorship and publication of which have not been determined.

A TALE OF TWO WORLDS (Eminent Authors) **F2.5522**

Goldwyn Pictures. Mar **1921** [c17 Mar 1921; LP16286]. Si; b&w. 35mm. 6 reels, 5,649 ft.

Dir Frank Lloyd. *Scen* J. E. Nash. *Story* Gouverneur Morris. *Photog* Norbert Brodin. *Asst Dir* Harry Weil.

Cast: J. Frank Glendon *(Newcombe)*, Leatrice Joy *(Sui Sen)*, Wallace Beery *(Ling Jo)*, E. A. Warren *(Ah Wing)*, Margaret McWade *(attendant)*, Togo Yamamoto *(One Eye)*, Jack Abbe *(The Worm)*, Louie Cheung *(Chinaman)*, Chow Young *(slave girl)*, Etta Lee *(Ah Fah)*, Ah Wing *(servant spy)*, Goro Kino *(windlass man)*, Arthur Soames *(Dr. Newcombe)*, Edythe Chapman *(Mrs. Newcombe)*, Dwight Crittenden *(Mr. Carmichael)*, Irene Rich *(Mrs. Carmichael)*.

Melodrama. Carmichael, an American dealer in antiques who gains possession of the priceless Ming scepter, is slain, with his wife, by Boxers in China, but their infant daughter is saved by a servant, Ah Wing. Years later, the girl, brought up by Ah Wing as his daughter, is known as Sui Sen in San Francisco's Chinatown. Though loved by Ah Wing's assistant, the

Worm, she is coveted by Ling Jo, a Boxer leader, who obtains the Ming scepter as a condition for their betrothal. However, Sui Sen falls in love with Newcombe, a wealthy young American. Newcombe rescues her from Ling Jo, who dies in a windlass trap actually prepared for his rival. *Parentage. China—History—Boxer Rebellion. San Francisco—Chinatown.*

Note: Working title: *The Water Lily.*

THE TALK OF HOLLYWOOD **F2.5523**

Prudence Pictures. *Dist* Sono Art–World Wide Pictures. 9 Dec **1929** [c20 Dec 1930; LP1863]. Sd; b&w. 35mm. 7 reels, 6,586 ft.

Pres by Samuel Zierler, Harry H. Thomas. *Dir* Mark Sandrich. *Dial* Darby Aaronson. *Story* Mark Sandrich, Nat Carr. *Photog* Walter Strenge. *Film Ed* Russell Shields. *Rec Engr* George Osthmann, John Dolan.

Cast: Nat Carr *(J. Pierpont Ginsburg)*, Fay Marbé *(Adore Renée)*, Hope Sutherland *(Ruth)*, Sherline Oliver *(John Applegate)*, Edward Le Saint *(Edward Hamilton)*, Gilbert Marbe *(Reginald Whitlock)*, John Troughton *(Butler)*, Al Goodman and His Orchestra, Leonidoff Ballet.

Comedy-drama. J. Pierpont Ginsburg, a successful producer of silent films, finds he is unable to raise the money to produce an all-talking production. He wants the picture to be a success for the sake of his daughter, Ruth, who is in love with John Applegate, his lawyer. At the studio, Ginsburg finds that Adore Renée, his high-priced star, has not shown up; his casting director has cast the characters wrong; and an expensive chorus and ballet are earning money waiting for shooting to begin. After he puts them all through their paces at rehearsal, his first day's work goes well until he discovers that the microphone is not recording properly. Applegate nevertheless saves the picture by staking all his money on it. When the picture is completed, Ginsburg arranges a projection for distributors, but a drunken operator mixes the reels so that they all leave in disgust. Ginsburg is thoroughly disheartened, but Applegate brings in a contract from a buyer who interpreted the results as an attempt at burlesque and ordered more. *Motion picture producers. Actors. Motion pictures. Fatherhood.*

THE TALKER **F2.5524**

First National Pictures. 24 May **1925** [c11 May 1925; LP21446]. Si; b&w. 35mm. 8 reels, 7,861 ft.

Pres by Sam E. Rork. *Dir* Alfred E. Green. *Adapt* Marion Fairfax. *Photog* Arthur Edeson. *Sets* Jack Okey. *Film Ed* LeRoy Stone. *Asst Dir* Jack Boland.

Cast: Anna Q. Nilsson *(Kate Lennox)*, Lewis S. Stone *(Harry Lennox)*, Shirley Mason *(Ruth Lennox)*, Ian Keith *(Ned Hollister)*, Tully Marshall *(Henry Fells)*, Barbara Bedford *(Barbara Farley)*, Harold Goodwin *(Lonnie Whinston)*, Gertrude Short *(Maud Fells)*, Lydia Yeamans Titus *(Mrs. Fells)*, Cecille Evans *(stenographer)*, Charles West *(detective)*, E. H. Calvert *(Mr. Grayson)*.

Drama. Source: Marion Fairfax, *The Talker* (New York opening: 8 Jan 1912). Kate Lennox, the beautiful wife of a modestly affluent suburbanite, considers life a matter of one dirty dish after another and, like a canary in a narrow cage, longs for the life of the sparrow. She preaches the doctrine of woman's freedom and rights, greatly to the displeasure of her husband, Harry, and to the delight of Ruth Lennox, Harry's young and impressionable sister. Ruth eventually decides to test Kate's theories and elopes with a married man; she soon leaves the man, however, and disappears, greatly disillusioned by his criminal life and rough manner. Harry blames Kate for Ruth's misfortunes and leaves her, instituting divorce proceedings. Ruth returns before the final decree, however, and reunites Kate and Harry, regaining for herself the affection of a goodhearted youth named Lonnie, who has always loved her. *Brother-sister relationship. Elopement. Infidelity. Divorce. Women's rights.*

THE TAME CAT **F2.5525**

Dramafilms. *Dist* Arrow Film Corp. Jul **1921.** Si; b&w. 35mm. 5 reels, 4,943 ft.

Dir William Bradley.

Cast: Ray Irwin, Marion Harding.

Melodrama. Source: Robert Louis Stevenson, "The Rajah's Diamond." "The gem is supposedly a creation of a Hindu magician, with a power of producing in the minds of all those who gaze upon it an overpowering desire to secure it, regardless of price." (*Motion Picture News Booking Guide,* 1:107, Dec 1921.) *Hindus. Magic.*

Note: Country of origin undetermined.

TAMING OF THE SHREW **F2.5526**

Pickford Corp.–Elton Corp. *Dist* United Artists. 26 Oct **1929** [c1 Nov 1929; LP825]. Sd (Movietone); b&w. 35mm. 8 reels, 6,116 ft.

Dir-Adapt Sam Taylor. *Photog* Karl Struss. *Art Dir* William Cameron Menzies, Laurence Irving. *Film Ed* Allen McNeil. *Sd* David Forrest. *Prod Asst* Earle Browne, Lucky Humberstone, Walter Mayo, Constance Collier, John Craig.

Cast: Mary Pickford *(Katherine)*, Douglas Fairbanks *(Petruchio)*, Edwin Maxwell *(Baptista)*, Joseph Cawthorn *(Gremio)*, Clyde Cook *(Grumio)*, Geoffrey Wardwell *(Hortensio)*, Dorothy Jordan *(Bianca)*.

Farce. Source: William Shakespeare, *The Taming of the Shrew.* Baptista, a wealthy merchant of Padua, announces he will not sanction the marriage of his youngest daughter, Bianca, until her sister Katherine is wed, though the latter is shunned by young men of her set because of her shrewish demeanor. Then the swaggering Petruchio arrives from Verona, accompanied by his servant Grumio; and from Hortensio he learns of the fiery Katherine and her magnificent dowry; boasting of his prowess as a lover, he gains permission to seek her hand; and though his wooing is met with scorn, he sets a wedding date. Petruchio arrives late and dressed as a beggar; and although mortified, she capitulates. At his country home, he bewilders her with inconsiderate acts and protests of love, and she is defiant until she sees that his actions are tricks to subdue her will; later, at a wedding feast, he invites the guests to observe the obedience of the shrew, but after her famous speech, she gives the women an understanding wink. *Shrews. Courtship. Marriage. Padua. Verona.*

THE TAMING OF THE WEST **F2.5527**

Universal Pictures. 1 Mar **1925** [c8 Apr 1925; LP21347]. Si; b&w. 35mm. 6 reels, 5,304 ft.

Dir Arthur Rosson. *Cont* Raymond L. Schrock. *Photog* Harry Neumann.

Cast: Hoot Gibson *(John Carleton)*, Marceline Day *(Beryl)*, Morgan Brown *(Terrence Weaver)*, Edwin Booth Tilton *(John P. Carleton)*, Herbert Prior *(Old Man King)*, Louise Hippe *(Perry Potter)*, Albert J. Smith *(Lafe Conners)*, Francis Ford *(Frosty Miller)*, Frona Hale *(Aunt Lodenna)*.

Western melodrama. Source: Bertha Sinclair Muzzy, *The Range Dwellers* (New York, 1906). John Carleton, a wild eastern youth, is sent west by his father in an effort to make a man of him. The cowhands at first mock John because of his foppish golf suit, but when he rides a mean bucking bronco he wins their friendship and respect. John falls in love with Beryl King, the daughter of a longtime enemy of his father, and is strictly forbidden to visit her. John defies this prohibition and rides to the King ranch, fighting off a number of unkindly disposed ranch hands; he later dances with Beryl at a village party and persuades her to run away with him and be married. On the way to the wedding, John stops at the King spread long enough to invite Beryl's irate father to see his daughter married. Carleton, Senior, turns up later, and the old enemies are finally reconciled. *Dudes. Broncobusters. Ranch life. Manhood. Fatherhood. Feuds.*

TANGLED HERDS **F2.5528**

Action Pictures. *Dist* Weiss Brothers Artclass Pictures. 8 Mar **1926.** Si; b&w. 35mm. 5 reels, 4,840 ft.

Dir William Bertram.

Cast: Buddy Roosevelt.

Western melodrama. "Owner of gold mine from which pay dust is stolen sets out to apprehend robber and effects his capture, though in danger of arrest as a cattle rustler." (*Motion Picture News Booking Guide,* 11:51, Oct 1926.) *Robbers. Rustlers. Gold mines.*

TANGLED TRAILS **F2.5529**

Neal Hart Productions. *Dist* William Steiner Productions. Dec **1921** [c12 Dec 1921; LU17355]. Si; b&w. 35mm. 5 reels, 4,902 ft.

Dir-Story Charles Bartlett. *Photog* Jacob A. Badaracco.

Cast: Neal Hart *(Cpl. Jack Borden)*, Violet Palmer *(Milly)*, Gladys Hampton *(Blanche Hall)*, Jean Bary *(Mrs. Hall)*, Jules Cowles *(The Stranger)*, Ed Roseman *(Phil Lawson)*.

Melodrama. Lawson, an unscrupulous promoter selling stock in a worthless mine, is sought by Jack Borden, of the Northwest Mounted, for the murder of his partner. The trail leads to New York, where a fight occurs in a skyscraper and another in a Bowery den. Lawson escapes and returns to the Northwest, and following a number of adventures he is eventually captured by Borden. Borden learns that a stranger in the snow country is the husband of a woman whom he has met in New York and that the two girls to whom he has been attracted—Blanche Hall in the city, and Milly in the Northwest—are sisters. He brings about a reconciliation among the members of the family, then returns to his duty. *Sisters. Murder. Canadian Northwest. New York City. Northwest Mounted Police.*

TANGO CAVALIER **F2.5530**

Charles R. Seeling. *Dist* Aywon Film Corp. Sep **1923.** Si; b&w. 35mm. 5 reels, ca4,700 ft.

Dir Charles R. Seeling.

Cast: George Larkin *(Don Armingo)*, Frank Whitson *(Colonel Pomeroy)*, Doris Dare *(Doris)*, Ollie Kirby *(Carmelita)*, Billy Quinn *(Brute Morgan)*, Michael Tellegen *(Strongarm)*.

Melodrama. Don Armingo, a member of the Secret Service, is inspired while dancing the tango to join a group of smugglers at the Mexican border. As he is about to make the arrest, they take flight, kidnaping Don's sweetheart. Following in his airplane, he circles above the getaway car and plucks the girl from the tonneau cover just as it speeds over an embankment. *Smugglers. Secret service. Tango. Kidnaping. Mexican border. Air stunts.*

TANNED LEGS **F2.5531**

RKO Productions. 10 Nov **1929** [c10 Nov 1929; LP922]. Sd (Photophone); b&w. 35mm. 7 reels, 6,377 ft.

Supv Louis Sarecky. *Dir* Marshall Neilan. *Photog* Leo Tover, George Hull. *Art Dir* Max Ree. *Film Ed* Archie Marshek. *Songs: "With You, With Me," "You're Responsible"* Oscar Levant, Sidney Clare. *Asst Dir* Ray McCarey.

Cast: June Clyde *(Peggy Reynolds)*, Arthur Lake *(Bill)*, Sally Blane *(Janet Reynolds)*, Allen Kearns *(Roger)*, Albert Gran *(Mr. Reynods)*, Edmund Burns *(Clinton Darrow)*, Dorothy Revier *(Mrs. Lyons-King)*, Ann Pennington *(Tootie)*, Lincoln Stedman *(Pudgy)*, Lloyd Hamilton *(detective)*.

Comedy-melodrama. At a fashionable beach resort, Mr. Reynolds is having an affair with Mrs. Lyons-King, whom his daughter Peggy suspects to be an adventuress; Mrs. Reynolds is fascinated with Roger, a boyfriend of another youngster; and Janet, Peggy's sister, is enamored of Clinton Darrow. Mr. Reynolds is about to be persuaded to buy some worthless stock, and Darrow has possession of some indiscreet letters from Janet. Janet enters Darrow's room in a vain effort to retrieve them and, without her knowledge, is seen by Bill and Peggy. Threatened with extortion, Janet plans to kill Darrow but, instead, she accidentally wounds Peggy. Roger, a friend of Peggy's, obtains the letters during a fake robbery, and Peggy is reconciled with Bill. *Swindlers. Adventuresses. Resorts. Flirtation. Speculation. Extortion. Documentation.*

DER TANZ GEHT WEITER **F2.5532**

Warner Brothers Pictures. 14 Nov **1930** [Berlin premiere]. Sd (Vitaphone); b&w. 35mm. 7 reels.

Dir Wilhelm Dieterle. *Scen* Heinrich Fraenkel. *Photog* Sidney Hickox. *Film Ed* Edward Schroeder. *Mus Arr* Erno Rapee. *Prod Mgr* Heinz Blanke.

Cast: Wilhelm Dieterle, Lissi Aran, Anton Pontner, Carla Bartheel, Werner Klinger, Lothar Mayring, John Reinhardt, Paul Panzer, Adolph Millar.

Underworld melodrama. Source: George Kibbe Turner, "Those Who Dance" (publication undetermined). A German-language version of *Those Who Dance* (1930), q. v. *Gangsters. Molls. Detectives. State governors. Brother-sister relationship. Imposture. Frameup. Dictographs.*

TARNISH **F2.5533**

Goldwyn Pictures. *Dist* Associated First National Pictures. Aug **1924** [c9 Sep 1924; LP20551]. Si; b&w. 35mm. 7 reels, 6,831 ft.

Pres by Samuel Goldwyn. *Dir* George Fitzmaurice. *Scen* Frances Marion. *Photog* William Tuers, Arthur Miller. *Tech Dir* Ben Carré. *Film Ed* Stuart Heisler.

Cast: May McAvoy *(Letitia Tevis)*, Ronald Colman *(Emmet Carr)*, Marie Prevost *(Nettie Dark)*, Albert Gran *(Adolf Tevis)*, Mrs. Russ Whytall *(Josephine Tevis)*, Priscilla Bonner *(Aggie)*, Harry Myers *(The Barber)*, Kay Deslys *(Mrs. Stutts)*, Lydia Yeamans Titus *(Mrs. Healy)*, William Boyd *(Bill)*, Snitz Edwards *(Mr. Stutts)*.

Drama. Source: Gilbert Emery, *Tarnish, a Play in 3 Acts* (New York, 1924). Letitia Tevis has to support her parents owing to her father's profligate self-indulgence with other women, and she works with Emmet Carr, who is in love with her. When her father is victimized by manicurist Nettie Dark, Letitia demands a return of his money. She is disillusioned by Emmet's presence in the girl's apartment, but eventually she realizes his innocence and finds happiness with him. *Manicurists. Filial relations. Infidelity. Extortion.*

TARZAN AND THE GOLDEN LION **F2.5534**

R-C Pictures. *Dist* Film Booking Offices of America. 2 Jan **1927** [c2 Jan 1927; LP23748]. Si; b&w. 35mm. 6 reels, 5,807 ft.

Pres by Joseph P. Kennedy. *Dir* J. P. McGowan. *Adapt-Cont* William E. Wing. *Photog* Joe Walker. *Tech Dir* Maj. F. J. Franklin. *Asst Dir* Mack V. Wright.

Cast: James Pierce *(Tarzan, Lord Greystoke)*, Frederic Peters *(Esteban Miranda)*, Edna Murphy *(Ruth Porter)*, Harold Goodwin *(Burton Bradney)*, Liu Yu-Ching *(Cadj, High Priest)*, Dorothy Dunbar *(Lady Greystoke)*, D'Arcy Corrigan *(Weesimbo)*, Boris Karloff *(Owaza)*, Robert Bolder *(John Peebles)*, Jad-Bal-Ja *(himself, the Golden Lion)*.

Adventure melodrama. Source: Edgar Rice Burroughs, *Tarzan and the Golden Lion* (Chicago, 1923). Tarzan, Lord Greystoke, at his estate in the heart of Africa, awaits the arrival of a company including his wife, her niece (Ruth Porter), Bradney (the overseer), and Ruth's fiancé. Weesimbo tells Tarzan of a mysterious city of diamonds from which he has escaped, and Tarzan, going to meet the caravan, arrives in time to drive off an attack by Esteban, an unscrupulous trader. When Tarzan goes on a hunting trip, Esteban and his men attack the unprotected estate, capture Weesimbo, and make a hostage of Ruth. Tarzan embarks on their trail with Jad-Bal-Ja, a pet lion. Cadj, High Priest of the Palace of Diamonds, is warned of the arrival and captures Ruth for sacrifice to Numa, lion-god. Weesimbo reveals to Tarzan the secret passage to the city; he rescues Ruth and after killing Numa is acclaimed as a new god. Esteban is killed by the lion, and all ends happily. *Nobility. Traders. Priests. Human sacrifice. Diamonds. Jungles. Africa. Lions.*

THE TAXI DANCER **F2.5535**

Metro-Goldwyn-Mayer Pictures. 5 Feb **1927** [c2 Mar 1927; LP23715]. Si; b&w. 35mm. 7 reels, 6,203 or 6,289 ft.

Dir Harry Millarde. *Screenplay* A. P. Younger. *Titl* Ralph Spence. *Photog* Ira Morgan. *Sets* Cedric Gibbons, David Townsend. *Film Ed* George Hively. *Wardrobe* André-ani.

Cast: Joan Crawford *(Joslyn Poe)*, Owen Moore *(Lee Rogers)*, Marc MacDermott *(Henry Brierhalter)*, Gertrude Astor *(Kitty Lane)*, Rockliffe Fellowes *(Stephen Bates)*, Douglas Gilmore *(James Kelvin)*, William Orlamond *(Doc Ganz)*, Claire McDowell *(Aunt Mary)*, Bert Roach *(Charlie Cook)*.

Comedy-melodrama. Source: Robert Terry Shannon, *The Taxi Dancer* (New York, 1931). "Joslyn, unable to get a job as a stage dancer, goes to work in a dancing academy and is befriended by Lee, a gambler. She becomes infatuated with Kelvin, a professional dancer, who is a cad, and when he kills a rounder, she hides him. To save him she agrees to sacrifice herself to Brierhalter, a millionaire, but Kelvin is killed trying to escape the police and Joslyn finds happiness with Lee, who has reformed." (*Moving Picture World,* 12 Mar 1927, p133.) *Taxi dancers. Gamblers. Millionaires. Seduction. New York City.*

THE TAXI MYSTERY **F2.5536**

Banner Productions. *Dist* Henry Ginsberg Distributing Corp. 10 Apr **1926** [c22 Mar 1926; LP22510]. Si; b&w. 35mm. 6 reels, 5,052 ft.

Dir Fred Windermere. *Story* Tom J. Hopkins.

Cast: Edith Roberts *(Nancy Cornell/Vera Norris)*, Robert Agnew *(Harry Canby)*, Virginia Pearson *(Mrs. Blaine Jameson)*, Phillips Smalley *(Willoughby Thomson)*, Bertram Grassby *(Fred Norris)*.

Mystery melodrama. Young millionaire Harry Canby, returning from a cruise, finds a taxi without a driver on the docks and helps a young girl escape some ruffians who are pursuing her. She disappears, but Harry identifies her as Nancy Cornell from an inscribed cigarette case and finds the driver, who then is killed before he can reveal her whereabouts. Harry is suspected of the crime, but his guardian, Willoughby Thomson, vouches for him. At a society party given by Mrs. Jameson, Harry learns that the girl is a musical comedy star, but when he confronts her she denies knowledge of the taxi incident. Following a series of complications, Harry learns that Nancy is Thomson's daughter. Vera Norris, a jealous rival of Nancy's, with the aid of her husband, Fred, tries to take Nancy's place and steal Thomson's money, but the plot is foiled. *Actors. Taxi drivers. Millionaires. Mistaken identity.*

TAXI! TAXI! (Universal-Jewel) F2.5537

Universal Pictures. 24 Apr **1927** [c14 Oct 1926; LP23237]. Si; b&w. 35mm. 7 reels, 7,173 ft.

Pres by Carl Laemmle. *Dir-Cont* Melville W. Brown. *Adapt* Raymond Cannon. *Photog* Gilbert Warrenton.

Cast: Edward Everett Horton *(Peter Whitby)*, Marian Nixon *(Rose Zimmerman)*, Burr McIntosh *(Grant Zimmerman)*, Edward Martindel *(David Parmalee)*, William V. Mong *(Nosey Ricketts)*, Lucien Littlefield *(Billy Wallace)*, Freeman Wood *(Jersey)*.

Farce. Source: George Weston, "Taxi! Taxi!" in *Saturday Evening Post* (198:3–5, 22–23, 26–30, 25 Jul–8 Aug 1925). Peter Whitby, a lowly draftsman in the service of a distinguished architectural firm, is sent to the railway station to meet the president's niece and makes a very favorable impression on Rose. At Rose's request, Peter is sent shopping with her. He takes her to a notorious roadhouse to which her uncle has forbidden her to go; and discovering Zimmerman (her uncle) there with Parmalee, a wealthy contractor, they leave, arousing the suspicions of the house detective. Unable to find a cab, Peter *buys* one, not knowing it is the notorious "white taxi" in which a robbery and murder have been committed. Zimmerman threatens to send Rose home and discharges Peter, who drives his taxi to meet her. En route to the justice of the peace, they are chased by the police, Zimmerman, and Parmalee; they manage, however, to complete the marriage ceremony in time, and the real crooks are arrested. *Draftsmen. Architects. Taxicabs. Roadhouses. Chases.*

TAXI 13 F2.5538

FBO Pictures. 18 Nov **1928** [c2 Sep 1928; LP25651]. Talking sequences, sd eff, & mus score (Photophone); b&w. 35mm. 7 reels, 5,760 ft.

Dir Marshall Neilan. *Story-Cont* W. Scott Darling. *Dial* George Le Maire. *Titl* Randolph Bartlett, Garrett Graham, Mildred Richter. *Photog* Phil Tannura. *Film Ed* Pandro S. Berman. *Asst Dir* James Graham.

Cast: Chester Conklin *(Angus Mactavish)*, Ethel Wales *(Mrs. Mactavish)*, Martha Sleeper *(Flora Mactavish)*, Hugh Trevor *(Dan Regan)*, Lee Moran *(Dennis Moran)*, Jerry Miley *(Mason)*, Charles Byer *(Berger)*.

Comedy-drama. Angus Mactavish, who supports his careworn wife and 10 children on the small profits from a wornout old taxi, is doing his best to earn $100 for the down payment on a new vehicle. Berger and Mason, two crooks, hire Angus' cab and have it wait outside the Addison mansion while they blow the safe. Officer Dan Regan surprises the men at work, and they make a run for it, using Angus' taxi for their getaway. Regan pursues them in another taxi, and the men, hiding a pearl necklace in the upholstery of Angus's vehicle, flee on foot. Angus' daughter meets up with Mason and learns the whereabouts of the pearls; the necklace is recovered, and Angus receives a $5,000 reward with which he buys a new taxi. *Taxi drivers. Police. Safecrackers. Robbery.*

TEA FOR THREE F2.5539

Metro-Goldwyn-Mayer Pictures. 29 Oct **1927** [New York premiere; released 10 Dec; c22 Nov 1927; LP24746]. Si; b&w. 35mm. 7 reels, 6,273 ft.

Dir Robert Z. Leonard. *Scen* F. Hugh Herbert. *Titl* Garrett Graham, Lucille Newmark. *Adapt* Roi Cooper Megrue. *Photog* André Barlatier. *Set Dsgn* Cedric Gibbons, Richard Day. *Film Ed* William Le Vanway. *Wardrobe* Gilbert Clark.

Cast: Lew Cody *(Carter Langford)*, Aileen Pringle *(Doris Langford)*, Owen Moore *(Philip Collamore)*, Phillips Smalley *(Harrington)*, Dorothy Sebastian *(Annette)*, Edward Thomas *(Austin, the butler)*.

Domestic comedy. Source: Karl Sloboda, *Am Teetisch, Lustspiel in drei Akten* (Vienna, 1915). Businessman Carter Langford is violently jealous of his wife's attentions to other men, particularly young bachelor Philip Collamore. When Doris hears a funny story from Collamore that her husband has already told her, she laughs at his rendition rather than that of her husband. Ultimately, Langford is willing to cut cards for the heart of Doris, the loser to exit via the suicide route. But when they all end up aboard an ocean liner, Doris brings her husband to his senses and cures him of his jealousy. ... *Businessmen. Bachelors. Suicide. Marriage. Jealousy. Ocean liners.*

TEARIN' INTO TROUBLE F2.5540

Action Pictures. *Dist* Pathé Exchange. 20 Mar **1927** [c4 Feb 1927; LU23633]. Si; b&w. 35mm. 5 reels, 4,483 ft.

Pres by Lester F. Scott, Jr. *Dir* Richard Thorpe. *Scen* Betty Burbridge. *Story* John Harold Hamlin. *Photog* Ray Reis.

Cast: Wally Wales *(Wally Tilland)*, Olive Hasbrouck *(Ruth Martin)*, Walter Brennan *(Billy Martin)*, Tom Bay *(Johnnie)*, Nita Cavalier *(Maisie)*.

Western melodrama. Two bandits hold up a party at a roadhouse and force Wally Tilland, a society idler, to drive them west in their getaway car. Billy Martin, who has stolen a horse, meets Wally, knocks him unconscious, and steals his car and clothes. Dressed in Billy's clothes, Wally is mistaken for the thief by Billy's sister, Ruth. He is arrested on the testimony of the two bandits. Ruth finds Billy dying from a wound received during his escape; he confesses to the horse stealing and bank robbery. Ruth arrives with the money during Wally's trial, the bandits are arrested, and Ruth and Wally find happiness together. *Socialites. Bandits. Horsethieves. Brother-sister relationship. Mistaken identity.*

TEARIN' LOOSE F2.5541

Action Pictures. *Dist* Weiss Brothers Artclass Pictures. 4 Sep **1925.** Si; b&w. 35mm. 5 reels, 4,900 ft.

Pres by Lester F. Scott, Jr. *Dir* Richard Thorpe. *Scen* Frank L. Inghram. *Photog* William Marshall.

Cast: Wally Wales *(Wally Blake)*, Jean Arthur *(Sally Harris)*, Charles Whitaker *(Matt Harris)*, Alfred Hewston *(Dad Burns)*, Polly Vann *(Nora)*, Harry Belmour *(Stubb Green)*, Bill Ryno *(The Philosopher)*, Vester Pegg *(Jim, a tramp)*, Frank Ellis *(The Law)*.

Western melodrama. Dad Burns, an aging rancher, writes to his nephew, Wally Blake, whom he has never seen, requesting that he take over the management of his large cattle ranch. On the way there, Wally is framed for a crime and sent to jail; Matt Harris, using Burns's letter to Wally as proof of his identity, takes Wally's place and, accompanied by his sister, Sally, goes to the Burns ranch, passing himself off as Burns's nephew. Wally eventually arrives at the ranch and catches Harris robbing the safe; Harris manages to pin the blame on Wally. Dad Burns is jumped by Jim, and the wily oldtimer kills the tramp. Wally is also blamed for this crime. Wally and Harris fight it out on the edge of a precipice, and Wally sends the imposter to his doom. Wally establishes his true identity and wins the affection of both his uncle and Harris' sister. *Ranchers. Tramps. Uncles. Brother-sister relationship. Ranch management. Impersonation. Robbery. Injustice. Documentation.*

TEARING THROUGH F2.5542

Richard Talmadge Productions. *Dist* Film Booking Offices of America. 12 Apr **1925** [c17 Apr 1925; LP21361]. Si; b&w. 35mm. 5 reels, 4,714 ft.

Pres by A. Carlos. *Dir* Arthur Rosson. *Cont* Frederick Stowers. *Photog* William Marshall.

Cast: Richard Talmadge *(Richard Jones)*, Kathryn McGuire *(Constance Madison)*, Herbert Prior *(district attorney)*, Frank Elliott *(Mr. Greer)*, Arthur Rankin *(Bob Madison)*, Marcella Daly *(Polly)*, Dave Morris *(Chester)*.

Action melodrama. When District Attorney Johnson is seemingly unable to break up a gang of dope smugglers, his assistant, Richard Jones, sets out on his own to investigate the lawbreakers. In the course of his snooping, he discovers that Bob Madison, his sweetheart's brother, is a drug addict, caught in the clutches of a gang. Richard is responsible for Bob's regeneration, and together they find that Greer, who is Richard's rival for the affections of Constance Madison, is, in fact, the proprietor of an opium den in Chinatown. Constance is kidnaped by Greer, and Richard rescues her from a narcotics hellhole. Richard proves that the D. A. is being bribed by the drug peddlers, and, as a reward for his good work, Richard is appointed the new district attorney. *Smugglers. District attorneys. Drug addicts. Brother-sister relationship. Opium. Chinatown.*

THE TEASER (Universal-Jewel) F2.5543

Universal Pictures. 6 Sep **1925** [c2 Jun 1925; LP21532]. Si; b&w. 35mm. 7 reels, 6,800 ft.

Dir William A. Seiter. *Scen* Edward T. Lowe, Jr. *Adapt* Lewis Milestone. *Photog* George Barnes. *Art Dir* Leo E. Kuter.

Cast: Laura La Plante *(Ann Barton)*, Pat O'Malley *(James McDonald)*, Hedda Hopper *(Margaret Wyndham)*, Walter McGrail *(Roderick Caswell)*, Byron Munson *(Perry Grayle)*, Vivian Oakland *(Lois Caswell)*, Wyndham Standing *(Jeffry Loring)*, Margaret Quimby *(Janet Comstock)*, Frank Finch Smiles *(Jenkins)*.

Comedy-drama. Source: Martha M. Stanley and Adelaide Matthews, *The Teaser* (New York opening: 27 Jul 1921). Ann Barton, the daughter of a once-wealthy family, is forced to clerk at the cigar counter of a village hotel, where she meets James McDonald, a breezy, handsome salesman. Ann is adopted by an aristocratic aunt, who disapproves of James's manners and breaks up Ann's relationship with him. Ann soon revenges herself on her aunt by placing both her aunt and herself in compromising positions. James sets out to learn to be a gentleman and soon wins Ann back with his acquired good manners and dignified bearing. *Aunts. Salesclerks. Traveling salesmen. Village life. Manners. Adoption. Cigarstores. Hotels.*

TEA—WITH A KICK **F2.5544**

Victor H. Halperin Productions. *Dist* Associated Exhibitors. 26 Aug **1923** [c11 Aug 1923; LU19296]. Si; b&w. 35mm. 6 reels, 5,950 ft. [Also 5,747 ft.]

Gen Supv–Story Victor Hugo Halperin. *Dir* Erle C. Kenton. *Photog* William Marshall, Philip Rand.

Cast: Doris May *(Bonnie Day)*, Creighton Hale *(Art Binger)*, Ralph Lewis *(Jim Day)*, Rosemary Theby *(Aunt Pearl)*, Stuart Holmes *(Napoleon Dobbings)*, ZaSu Pitts *("Brainy" Jones)*, Irene D'Annelle *(Irene, danseuse)*, Gale Henry *(Hesperis McGowan)*, Dot Farley *(Mrs. Juniper)*, Louise Fazenda *(Birdie Puddleford)*, Dale Fuller *(Kittie Wiggle, reformer)*, Edward Jobson *(Editor Octavius Juniper)*, Spike Rankin *(Mrs. Bump, reformer)*, Harry Lorraine *(Rev. Harry White)*, Sidney D'Albrook *(Pietro)*, Tiny Ward *(King Kick)*, Earl Montgomery *(Convict Dooley)*, Hazel Keener *(Hazel)*, Julanne Johnston *(Gwen Van Peebles)*, William De Vaull *(Napoleon)*, Hank Mann *(Sam Spindle)*, Chester Conklin *(Jiggs, taxi driver)*, Snitz Edwards *(Oscar Puddleford)*, William Dyer *(a businessman)*, Harry Todd *(Chris Kringle)*, Billy Franey *(Convict Hooney)*, Victor Potel *(Bellboy 13)*.

Comedy-melodrama. To help raise funds needed to appeal her father's case, Bonnie Day opens a tearoom featuring a group of stranded choristers performing a cabaret revue. The father is in prison because of a trumped-up charge made by some stock swindlers. Aunt Pearl would like Bonnie to marry smalltown capitalist Napoleon Dobbings, but Bonnie is in love with young lawyer Art Binger. Binger eventually effects a release from prison for Mr. Day just at the height of Bonnie's business career. *Swindlers. Lawyers. Entertainers. Capitalists. Aunts. Filial relations. Injustice. Smalltown life. Teashops.*

TEETH **F2.5545**

Fox Film Corp. 2 Nov **1924** [c3 Nov 1924; LP20749]. Si; b&w. 35mm. 7 reels, 6,190 ft.

Pres by William Fox. *Dir* John Blystone. *Scen* Donald W. Lee.

Cast: Tom Mix *(Dave Deering)*, Lucy Fox *(Paula Grayson)*, George Bancroft *(Dan Angus)*, Edward Piel *(sheriff)*, Lucien Littlefield *(under sheriff)*, Tony *(himself, a horse)*, Duke *(Teeth, a dog)*.

Western melodrama. Source: Clinton H. Stagg, "Teeth," in *People's Magazine* (22:1–74, Feb 1917). Virginia Hudson Brightman, *Sonny* (New York, 1923). Baggagemaster Dan Angus tosses Paula Grayson's dog, Teeth, off a moving train, and prospector Dave Deering finds the injured animal and cares for it. Dan is fired, gets off at a small town, kills the postmaster, and frames Dave for the murder. With Teeth's aid, Dave escapes to the woods and is followed by Paula, who, in turn, is pursued by Dan. The villain attacks Paula, puts her in a cabin, and accidentally starts a forest fire. Teeth brings Dave to rescue Paula; Dan confesses his crime; and dispute over the ownership of Teeth ends with a declaration of love between Paula and Dave. *Prospectors. Baggagemasters. Postmasters. Murder. Forest fires. Horses. Dogs.*

THE TELEPHONE GIRL **F2.5546**

Famous Players–Lasky. 26 Mar **1927** [c26 Mar 1927; LP23792]. Si; b&w. 35mm. 5,455 ft.

Pres by Adolph Zukor, Jesse L. Lasky. *Prod-Dir* Herbert Brenon. *Scen* Elizabeth Meehan. *Camera* Leo Tover.

Cast: Madge Bellamy *(Kitty O'Brien)*, Holbrook Blinn *(Jim Blake)*, Warner Baxter *(Matthew Standish)*, May Allison *(Grace Robinson)*, Lawrence Gray *(Tom Blake)*, Hale Hamilton *(Mark)*, Hamilton Revelle *(Van Dyke)*, W. E. Shay *(detective)*, Karen Hansen *(Mrs. Standish)*.

Melodrama. Source: William Churchill De Mille, *The Woman* (New York opening: 19 Sep 1911). Jim Blake, political boss, supports his son-in-law, Mark Robinson, for governor. They discover that Robinson's opponent registered in a hotel as "Matthew Standish and wife" 3 years before his marriage. Blake traps Standish into attempting to warn the girl in question of this discovery, but Kitty, a telephone operator important to their scheme, refuses to cooperate. Eventually the facts are sorted out, and Kitty marries Blake's son, Tom. *Telephone operators. Political bosses. State governors. Political campaigns. Muckraking.*

TELL IT TO SWEENEY **F2.5547**

Paramount Famous Lasky Corp. 24 Sep **1927** [c24 Sep 1927; LP24450]. Si; b&w. 35mm. 6 reels, 6,006 ft.

Pres by Adolph Zukor, Jesse L. Lasky. *Assoc Prod* B. P. Schulberg. *Dir* Gregory La Cava. *Screenplay* Percy Heath, Kerry Clarke. *Titl* George Marion, Jr. *Story* Percy Heath, Monte Brice. *Photog* H. Kinley Martin.

Cast: Chester Conklin *(Luke Beamish)*, George Bancroft *(Cannonball Casey)*, Jack Luden *(Jack Sweeney)*, Doris Hill *(Doris Beamish)*, Franklin Bond *(Superintendent Dugan)*, William H. Tooker *(Old Man Sweeney)*.

Farce. Luke Beamish is the engineer of the *Isobel*, an old iron steed, and Cannonball Casey handles the throttle of the *Mogul*, a modern locomotive. Cannonball falls in love with Doris, Luke's daughter, who is greatly admired by Jack Sweeney, the railroad president's son. Doris rejects Casey's affections, considering him a bully, and consequently Casey challenges Jack to a wrestling match at the picnic. Superintendent Dugan, hearing of the match, plots to save young Sweeney from destruction; Luke learns the secret of defeating Casey, while Luden is lured away by Dugan; but the boy returns in time to knock out his rival. When Doris elopes with Jack, his father gives chase in a locomotive. Casey, relenting in favor of Jack, restrains Sweeney until the marriage has been legalized. *Railroad engineers. Railroad magnates. Railroads. Locomotives. Wrestling. Chases.*

TELL IT TO THE MARINES **F2.5548**

Metro-Goldwyn-Mayer Pictures. 23 Dec **1926** [New York premiere; released 29 Jan 1927; c21 Dec 1926; LP23475]. Si; b&w. 35mm. 9 reels, 8,800 ft. [Copyrighted as 10 reels.]

Dir George Hill. *Story-Scen* E. Richard Schayer. *Titl* Joe Farnham. *Photog* Ira Morgan. *Sets* Cedric Gibbons, Arnold Gillespie. *Film Ed* Blanche Sewell.

Cast: Lon Chaney *(Sergeant O'Hara)*, William Haines *(Private "Skeet" Burns)*, Eleanor Boardman *(Norma Dale)*, Eddie Gribbon *(Corporal Madden)*, Carmel Myers *(Zaya)*, Warner Oland *(Chinese bandit leader)*, Mitchell Lewis *(native)*, Frank Currier *(General Wilcox)*, Maurice E. Kains *(Harry)*.

Melodrama. Skeet Burns goes to San Diego on the pretext of joining the Marines, then skips to Tia Juana on arrival. Later, he returns, penniless and hungry, and under Sergeant O'Hara's care he joins the Leathernecks. Skeet becomes enamored of Norma Dale, a commissioned Navy nurse, but on tour duty in the Philippines he is taken with Zaya, a native girl, and incurs the wrath of her friends. Hearing of the affair, Norma breaks off with Skeet, and the latter blames his misfortune on O'Hara. Norma is ordered to Hangchow, and when news arrives that her party is endangered by Chinese bandits, the Marines rescue the beleaguered whites; O'Hara is wounded in the fighting but is happy because he has at last made a man of Skeet. After his hitch, Skeet leaves the service and his friend O'Hara behind, promising Norma that he will wait for her. *Nurses. Bandits. Chinese. Philippines. Hangchow. San Diego. Tia Juana (California). United States Marines.*

TELLING THE WORLD **F2.5549**

Metro-Goldwyn-Mayer Pictures. 30 Jun **1928** [c23 Jun 1928; LP25397]. Si; b&w. 35mm. 8 reels, 7,184 ft.

Dir Sam Wood. *Scen* Raymond L. Schrock. *Titl* Joe Farnham. *Story* Dale Van Every. *Photog* William Daniels. *Sets* Cedric Gibbons. *Film Ed* Margaret Booth, John Colton. *Wardrobe* Gilbert Clark.

Cast: William Haines *(Don Davis)*, Anita Page *(Chrystal Malone)*, Eileen Percy *(Mazie)*, Frank Currier *(Don's father)*, Polly Moran *(landlady)*, Bert Roach *(Lane)*, William V. Mong *(city editor)*, Matthew Betz *(The Killer)*.

Comedy-drama. Don Davis becomes a newspaper reporter when his wealthy father disowns him. His first assignment is to interview his father. Later, while he is working the night shift, a prankster colleague sends him to a cafe to cover a "murder." While he is there a murder does occur in a telephone booth, and Don holds the killer at bay until the police arrive. In the cafe he meets chorus girl Chrystal Malone, falls in love with her, and follows her to China when her troupe goes to entertain American servicemen there. When she is falsely accused of assassinating the governor, and is sentenced to be beheaded, Don signals an American rescue party to save her. *Reporters. Chorus girls. Theatrical troupes. Filial relations. Murder. Assassination. Capital punishment. China.*

TEMPERED STEEL *see* **SOFT BOILED**

TEMPEST F2.5550

Joseph M. Schenck Productions. *Dist* United Artists. 11 Aug **1928** [c11 Oct 1927; LP25492]. Si; b&w. 35mm. 10 reels, 9,300 ft. [Copyrighted as 11 reels.]

Prod John W. Considine, Jr. *Dir* Sam Taylor. *Story-Adapt* C. Gardner Sullivan. *Photog* Charles Rosher. *Art Dir* William Cameron Menzies. *Mus Score* Hugo Riesenfeld. *Cost* Alice O'Neill.

Cast: John Barrymore *(Sgt. Ivan Markov)*, Camilla Horn *(Princess Tamara)*, Louis Wolheim *(Sergeant Bulba)*, Boris De Fas *(peddler)*, George Fawcett *(general)*, Ullrich Haupt *(captain)*, Michael Visaroff *(guard)*, Lena Malena, Albert Conti *(see note)*.

Romantic drama. Markov, a peasant soldier, becomes an officer in the Russian Army before the Revolution. He loves Princess Tamara, who scorns him for his common origins and has him stripped of his rank and thrown into prison. During the Revolution, Markov, an important Red official, saves Tamara from execution, kills his Bolshevik leader, and makes his escape to new lands with her as his wife. *Soldiers. Royalty. Bolshevists. Russia—History—1917–21 Revolution.*

Note: Unconfirmed sources indicate that Lena Malena and Albert Conti are in the cast.

THE TEMPLE OF VENUS F2.5551

Fox Film Corp. 29 Oct **1923** [New York opening; released 11 Nov; c11 Nov 1923; LP19690]. Si; b&w. 35mm. 7 reels, 6,695 ft.

Pres by William Fox. *Dir* Henry Otto. *Story-Scen* Henry Otto, Catherine Carr. *Photog* Joe August.

Cast: William Walling *(Dennis Dean)*, Mary Philbin *(Moira)*, Mickey McBan *(Mickey)*, Alice Day *(Peggy)*, David Butler *(Nat Harper)*, William Boyd *(Stanley Dale)*, Phyllis Haver *(Constance Lane)*, Leon Barry *(Phil Greyson)*, Celeste Lee *(Venus)*, Señorita Consuella *(Thetis)*, Robert Klein *(Neptune)*, Marilyn Boyd *(Juno)*, Frank Keller *(Jupiter)*, Lorraine Eason *(Echo)*, Helen Vigil *(Diana)*.

Allegorical fantasy. Venus sends Cupid to earth to find if romance still exists there. He finds Moira and Peggy, a fisherman's daughters, who become entangled in the amorous pursuits of an artist and a fisherman. Cupid returns to Venus with his report. *Artists. Sisters. Fishermen. Venus. Cupid. Mythological characters.*

TEMPLE TOWER F2.5552

Fox Film Corp. 13 Apr **1930** [c16 Mar 1930; LP1196]. Sd (Movietone); b&w. 35mm. 7 reels, 5,200 ft. [Also si.]

Pres by William Fox. *Dir* Donald Gallaher. *Screenplay-Dial* Llewellyn Hughes. *Photog* Charles G. Clarke. *Film Ed* Clyde Carruth. *Sd Rec* Frank MacKenzie. *Asst Dir* Horace Hough.

Cast: Kenneth MacKenna *(Capt. Hugh Drummond)*, Marceline Day *(Patricia Verney)*, Henry B. Walthall *(Blackton)*, Cyril Chadwick *(Peter Darrell)*, Peter Gawthorne *(Matthews)*, Ivan Linow *(Gaspard)*, Frank Lanning *(The Nightingale)*, Yorke Sherwood *(constable)*.

Mystery melodrama. Source: Herman Cyril McNeile, *Temple Tower* (Garden City, New York, 1929). Bulldog Drummond discovers that a gang of thieves are stationed in a house located in his part of town, and he determines to capture them. Headed by Blackton, they have doublecrossed their previous companions in crime, one of whom is known as The Masked Strangler. Patricia Verney takes a position as secretary to Backton, who killed her uncle and robbed him of some emeralds. Though Blackton employs various fiendish ruses to safeguard the jewels, Drummond and his men from Scotland Yard unmask the strangler and bring the criminals to justice. *Detectives. Thieves. Gangs. Personal identity. Scotland Yard. England.*

TEMPORARY MARRIAGE F2.5553

Sacramento Pictures. *Dist* Principal Pictures. 30 Jun **1923** [c2 Nov 1923; LP19558]. Si; b&w. 35mm. 7 reels, 6,500 ft.

Dir Lambert Hillyer. *Scen* Lambert Hillyer. *Adapt* Gilbert Patten. *Photog* John Stumar.

Cast: Kenneth Harlan *(Robert Belmar)*, Mildred Davis *(Hazel Manners)*, Myrtle Stedman *(Mrs. Hugh Manners)*, Tully Marshall *(Hugh Manners, lawyer)*, Maude George *(Olga Kazanoff, an adventuress)*, Stuart Holmes *(Preston Ducayne, gambler)*, Edward Coxen *(prosecuting attorney)*.

Domestic melodrama. Mrs. Hugh Manners tires of her husband, a stodgy lawyer, and arranges to divorce him. She gives a party to celebrate her freedom and becomes involved with Preston Ducayne, a gambler, and Olga Kazanoff, an adventuress. Ducayne is killed and suspicion points to Mrs. Manners until her husband establishes her innocence. *Lawyers. Gamblers. Adventuresses. Divorce. Marriage. Murder.*

TEMPORARY SHERIFF F2.5554

Ben Wilson Productions. *Dist* Rayart Pictures. Sep **1926.** Si; b&w. 35mm. 5 reels, 4,358 ft.

Dir Dick Hatton. *Photog* Joseph Walker.

Cast: Dick Hatton.

Western melodrama. "Rich youth, drunk, is put on freight train for the West. Reaches a small town simultaneously with the robbery of the express office. Through his efforts money is returned and, having become interested in girl in the town decides to spend the rest of his life there, an idea to which she is not averse." (*Motion Picture News Booking Guide*, 12: 59, Apr 1927.) *Sheriffs. Drunkenness. Robbery. Express service.*

TEMPTATION F2.5555

Dist C. B. C. Film Sales. 1 Mar **1923** [c10 Apr 1923; LP18856]. Si; b&w. 35mm. 7 reels, 6,500 ft.

Dir-Scen Edward J. Le Saint. *Story* Lenore Coffee. *Photog* King Gray.

Cast: Bryant Washburn *(Jack Baldwin)*, Eva Novak *(Marjorie Baldwin)*, June Elvidge *(Mrs. Martin)*, Phillips Smalley *(Frederick Arnold)*, Vernon Steele *(John Hope)*.

Domestic melodrama. To prove his belief that any woman can be corrupted by wealth, stockbroker Frederick Arnold secretly causes Jack Baldwin to achieve sudden financial success. Jack's wife, Marjorie, does begin to spend profusely and to run around with a fast crowd, while ignoring Jack's objections. Frederick falls in love with Marjorie, but his efforts to ruin Jack fail and Jack soon follows Marjorie's example. When a police raid on a bootleg roadhouse finds Jack and Marjorie with different companions, they escape together and are brought to their senses. *Stockbrokers. Wealth. Marriage. Prohibition.*

TEMPTATIONS OF A SHOP GIRL F2.5556

Chadwick Pictures. *Dist* First Division Pictures. 1 Nov **1927.** Si; b&w. 35mm. 6 reels, 5,461-5,700 ft.

Pres by I. E. Chadwick. *Dir* Tom Terriss. *Story-Scen* L. V. Jefferson. *Titl* Jean Le'Ple. *Photog* George Benoit, Ted Tetzlaff.

Cast: Betty Compson *(Ruth Harrington)*, Pauline Garon *(Betty Harrington)*, Armand Kaliz *(André Le Croix)*, Raymond Glenn *(Jerry Horton)*, William Humphreys *(John Horton)*, Cora Williams *(Mrs. Harrington)*, Gladden James *(Bud Conway)*, John Francis Dillon *(Jim Butler)*.

Drama. Department store salesgirl Ruth Harrington goes to jail in place of her younger sister, Betty, also a salesgirl, who has fallen in with bad company (Bud Conway and others) and committed theft at the bidding of gentleman crook André Le Croix. Released with a suspended sentence, the heroine tips off the police, who round up the gang, and finds that she has not lost the love of her sweetheart, Jerry Horton, the store owner's son. *Shopgirls. Gentlemen crooks. Sisters. Theft. Department stores.*

THE TEMPTRESS F2.5557

Cosmopolitan Productions. *Dist* Metro-Goldwyn-Mayer Distributing Corp. 3 Oct **1926** [c18 Oct 1926; LP23282]. Si; b&w. 35mm. 9 reels, 8,221 ft.

Dir Fred Niblo. *Adtl Dir (see note)* Mauritz Stiller. *Titl* Marian Ainslee. *Adapt* Dorothy Farnum. *Photog* Gaetano Gaudio, William Daniels. *Sets* Cedric Gibbons, James Basevi. *Film Ed* Lloyd Nosler. *Asst Dir* Bruce Humberstone. *Wardrobe* André-ani, Max Ree.

Cast: Greta Garbo *(Elena)*, Antonio Moreno *(Robledo)*, Roy D'Arcy *(Manos Duros)*, Marc MacDermott *(Monsieur Fontenoy)*, Lionel Barrymore *(Canterac)*, Virginia Brown Faire *(Celinda)*, Armand Kaliz *(Torre De Bianca)*, Alys Murrell *(Josephine)*, Robert Anderson *(Pirovani)*, Francis McDonald *(Timoteo)*, Hector V. Sarno *(Rojas)*, Inez Gomez *(Sebastiana)*, Steve Clemento *(Salvadore)*, Roy Coulson *(Trinidad)*.

Romantic tragedy. Source: Vicente Blasco-Ibáñez, *La Tierra de Todos* (trans. by Leo Ongley as *The Temptress;* New York, 1923). At an amateur circus given by banker Fontenoy for his guests, Elena, his mistress and the wife of the Marquis Torre De Bianca, meets Robledo, her husband's boyhood friend, who has just arrived in Paris from the Argentine. Fontenoy is insanely jealous of Robledo and upbraids Elena for flirting with him; yet, she leaves Fontenoy upon discovering his financial ruin, and he commits suicide. Bianca, humiliated by the scandal, retires to the Argentine with Robledo, who is supervising the building of a dam, and takes Elena with him. Although Robledo resents Elena's presence, he fights Duros, a local outlaw who is enamored of her and who tries to kidnap her; and a quarrel over her erupts into murder. Duros dynamites the dam, and the villagers flee from the resulting flood. Robledo swears to kill Elena, but passion overcomes his wrath; realizing her defeat, Elena leaves him and returns to Paris, where she sinks to drunkenness and degradation. *Mistresses. Bankers. Suicide. Flirtation. Murder. Drunkenness. Jealousy. Circus. Dams. Paris. Argentina. Floods.*

Note: Stiller was replaced by Niblo during filming, and Niblo received sole screen credit.

THE TEN COMMANDMENTS **F2.5558**

Famous Players–Lasky. *Dist* Paramount Pictures. 21 Dec **1923** [New York premiere; c21 Dec 1923; LP19766]. Si; b&w with Technicolor prolog. 35mm. 13 reels, 12,397 ft. [Later changed to 10 reels, 9,946 ft.]

Pres by Adolph Zukor, Jesse L. Lasky. *Dir* Cecil B. De Mille. *Story-Scen* Jeanie Macpherson. *Photog* Bert Glennon, Peverell Marley, Archibald Stout, J. F. Westerberg. *Art Dir* Paul Iribe. *Tech Dir* Roy Pomeroy. *Cutter* Anne Bauchens. *Asst Dir* Cullen Tate.

Cast—Prolog: Theodore Roberts *(Moses)*, Charles De Roche *(Ramses, the Pharaoh)*, Estelle Taylor *(Miriam)*, Julia Faye *(Pharaoh's wife)*, Terrence Moore *(Pharaoh's son)*, James Neill *(Aaron)*, Lawson Butt *(Dathan)*, Clarence Burton *(The Taskmaster)*, Noble Johnson *(The Bronze Man)*.

Cast—Part 2: Edythe Chapman *(Mrs. McTavish)*, Richard Dix *(John McTavish)*, Rod La Rocque *(Dan McTavish)*, Leatrice Joy *(Mary Leigh)*, Nita Naldi *(Sally Lung)*, Robert Edeson *(Redding, an inspector)*, Charles Ogle *(The Doctor)*, Agnes Ayres *(The Outcast)*, Viscount Glerawly.

Spectacular melodrama. A prolog depicts the Biblical stories from *Exodus:* the ill-treatment of the Jews by the Egyptians; their escape across the parted water of the Red Sea; the presentation to Moses of the Ten Commandments; Moses finding the Israelites worshipping the golden calf; and his breaking of the tablets. *Main Story:* The remainder of the film takes place in modern-day San Francisco. Two brothers, John and Dan McTavish, love Mary Leigh. She chooses Dan, who becomes a wealthy building contractor by using inferior materials and bribing the building inspector, Redding. This is the beginning of his downfall, ending in his death when he is crushed on the rocks in a motorboat accident. Before his death, Dan kills Sally Lung, his Oriental mistress, while trying to obtain bribe money and then discovers that he may have contracted leprosy from her. Drunk and panicstricken, Dan takes the fatal boatride. Mary weds John. *Israelites. Brothers. Contractors. Mistresses. Orientals. Bribery. Leprosy. Egypt. San Francisco. Moses.*

TEN DAYS **F2.5559**

Paul Gerson Pictures. 5 Jan **1925**. Si; b&w. 35mm. 5 reels.

Pres by B. Berger. *Dir* Duke Worne. *Scen* Arthur Hoerl.

Cast: Richard Holt *(Dick Van Buren)*, Hazel Keener *(Fay Whitney)*, Victor Potel *(constable)*, Joseph Girard *(Ezra Van Buren)*, Hal Stephens *(Bill Bradley)*, Lloyd Potter *(Jimmy Dunn)*, W. Mollenhauer *(judge)*, Carmelita Tellos.

Comedy. Dick Van Buren, a wealthy young man with a penchant for breaking traffic laws, is arrested for speeding and sentenced to 10 days in jail. He is given the option to work out his sentence and becomes a lifeguard at a public beach, where he rescues a mysterious woman from several perils. The woman, with whom he begins a romance, turns out to be a famous film actress caught up in the frenetic antics of a publicity campaign. *Actors. Lifeguards. Motion pictures. Reckless driving. Publicity.*

THE TEN DOLLAR RAISE **F2.5560**

J. L. Frothingham. *Dist* Associated Producers. 26 Jun **1921** [c7 Jun 1921; LP16653]. Si; b&w. 35mm. 6 reels, 5,726 ft.

Prod J. L. Frothingham. *Dir* Edward Sloman. *Screen Vers* Albert S. Le Vino. *Photog* Tony Gaudio.

Cast: William V. Mong *(Wilkins)*, Marguerite De La Motte *(Dorothy)*, Pat O'Malley *(Jimmy)*, Helen Jerome Eddy *(Emily)*, Hal Cooley *(Don)*, Lincoln Plumer *(Bates)*, Charles Hill Mailes *(Stryker)*.

Society melodrama. Source: Peter Bernard Kyne, "The Ten Dollar Raise," in *Saturday Evening Post* (182:18, 4 Dec 1909). Wilkins, a bookkeeper in the employ of Bates & Stryker for 20 years, has long expected a raise, promised annually by President Bates, which would enable him to marry Emily, a stenographer. Stryker sympathetically tries to intervene on his behalf but succeeds only in hiring Jimmy, a hungry boy seeking work, as Wilkins' assistant. His senior employer's son, Don, who is desperately in debt, pawns off on Wilkins some property that proves to be under water; Wilkins strikes oil, however, buys out Bates's stock in the company, and decides to retain Bates as general manager. Wilkins and Emily then get married, as do Jimmy and Stryker's daughter, Dorothy. *Bookkeepers. Stenographers. Speculation. Business management.*

TEN MODERN COMMANDMENTS **F2.5561**

Paramount Famous Lasky Corp. 2 Jul **1927** [c2 Jul 1927; LP24148]. Si; b&w. 35mm. 7 reels, 6,497 ft.

Pres by Adolph Zukor, Jesse L. Lasky. *Dir* Dorothy Arzner. *Screenplay* Doris Anderson, Paul Gangelin. *Titl* George Marion, Jr. *Story* Jack Lait. *Photog* Alfred Gilks. *Asst Dir* Otto Brower.

Cast: Esther Ralston *(Kitten O'Day)*, Neil Hamilton *(Tod Gilbert)*, Maude Truax *(Aunt Ruby)*, Romaine Fielding *(Zeno)*, El Brendel *(Speeding Shapiro)*, Rose Burdick *(Belle)*, Jocelyn Lee *(Sharon Lee)*, Arthur Hoyt *(Disbrow)*, Roscoe Karns *(Benny)*.

Comedy-drama. Kitten O'Day, who works as maid in a theatrical boardinghouse, firmly refuses a stage career, though she is the daughter of a theater family. When song-writer Tod Gilbert takes up residence in the house, Kitten falls in love. Tod poses as a success, intimating that he is to write songs for Sharon Lee, a Broadway prima donna; Kitten learns, however, that he is unable to get to Disbrow, Sharon's manager, and decides to help. Thus, Kitten takes a chorus job, arousing Sharon's animosity through her efforts to promote Tod's song; but when Tod assaults the manager, Kitten is forced to lock Disbrow in the bathroom while she tries to persuade Sharon to sing the song. In a stunning manner, Kitten presents the song herself, winning over Disbrow and assuring her happiness with Tod. *Actors. Housemaids. Composers. Singers. Theatrical managers. Theater. Boardinghouses.*

TEN NIGHTS IN A BAR ROOM **F2.5562**

Blazed Trail Productions. *Dist* Arrow Film Corp. 11 Dec **1921** [c23 Sep 1921; LP16984]. Si; b&w. 35mm. 8 reels. [Copyrighted as 9 reels.]

Dir Oscar Apfel. *Adapt* L. Case Russell. *Photog* Joseph Settle.

Cast: Baby Ivy Ward *(Little Mary Morgan)*, John Lowell *(Joe Morgan)*, Nell Clarke Keller *(Fanny Morgan)*, Charles Mackay *(Simon Slade)*, James Phillips *(Frank Slade)*, Ethel Dwyer *(Dora Slade)*, Charles Beyer *(Harvey Green)*, John Woodford *(Judge Hammond)*, Kempton Greene *(Willie Hammond)*, Mrs. Thomas Ward *(his aunt)*, Harry Fisher *(Sample Switchel)*, Lillian Kemble *(Mehitabel)*, J. Norman Wells *(Hank Smith)*, Leatta Miller *(Mrs. Hank Smith)*, Thomas Vill *(Judge Lyman)*, Richard Carlyle *(The Village Doctor)*, Robert Hamilton *(foreman of the mill)*.

Rural melodrama. Source: Timothy Shay Arthur, Ten Nights in a Bar Room (Philadelphia, 1854). William W. Pratt, *Ten Nights in a Bar Room, a Drama in 5 Acts* (New York, 1890). Joe Morgan, worker in a northern logging camp, falls under the influence of alcohol when a new saloon opens in the town. Eventually he becomes useless as a worker and neglects his wife and child, Little Mary. When his child comes to the saloon to urge her father to return home, a thrown beer tumbler strikes her; she is taken home and later dies. Joe, at least realizing the evil of drink, sets about seeking revenge for his daughter's death. Following a series of thrilling incidents, including a spectacular fire and logging jam, Joe abandons his pursuit of revenge and is reunited with his wife. *Children. Alcoholism. Revenge. Family life. Lumber camps. Saloons. Fires.*

TEN NIGHTS IN A BARROOM *see* **FOLKS FROM WAY DOWN EAST**

TEN NIGHTS IN A BARROOM **F2.5563**

Colored Players Film Corp. 27 Dec **1926** [New York State license]. Si; b&w. 35mm. 7 reels, 6,700 ft.

Cast: Charles Gilpin, Myra Burwell, Lawrence Chenault, Harry Henderson, William A. Clayton, Jr., Ethel Smith, Arline Mickey, Edward Moore, William Johnson, Florence Kennedy, William Milton, Sam Sadler, Roxanna Mickelby.

Melodrama. No information about the precise nature of this film has been found. *Negro life. Drunkenness.*

THE TENDER HOUR **F2.5564**

John McCormick Productions. *Dist* First National Pictures. 1 May **1927** [c21 Apr 1927; LP23880]. Si; b&w. 35mm. 8 reels, 7,400 ft.

Pres by John McCormick. *Dir* George Fitzmaurice. *Scen* Winifred Dunn. *Story* Carey Wilson. *Photog* Robert Kurrle.

Cast: Billie Dove *(Marcia Kane)*, Ben Lyon *(Wally McKenzie)*, Montagu Love *(Grand Duke Sergei)*, Alec B. Francis *(Francis Chinilly)*, Constantine

Romanoff *(Gorki)*, Laska Winter *(Tana)*, T. Roy Barnes *(Tough-House Higgins)*, George Kotsonaros *(The Wrestler)*, Charles A. Post *(Pussy-Finger)*, Anders Randolph *(leader of pageant)*, Frank Elliott, Lionel Belmore, Lon Poff *(guests at party)*, August Tollaire *(prefect of police)*, Yola D'Avril *(cabaret girl)*.

Romantic melodrama. Marcia Kane, daughter of an American capitalist, is persuaded by her father to marry the expatriated Russian Grand Duke Sergei, and believing Wally, her real love, to be dead, she consents. Discovering after the ceremony that her father has tricked her, Marcia vows to be the duke's wife in name only, though she refuses Wally's proposal that she go away with him. Sergei persuades Chinilly, who is fond of his wife, to present a pageant in her honor, and in Paris Chinilly finds Wally along with some crooks and reunites the lovers. The suspicious Sergei threatens to kill Wally, but Marcia bargains with her brutal husband. Gathering his underworld friends, Wally breaks into the duke's villa and saves her at the last minute. Sergei is forced to consent to a divorce, and Chinilly takes the lovers to his home on the Riviera. *Russians. Nobility. Marriage. Divorce. Fatherhood. Paris. Riviera.*

TENDERFEET **F2.5565**

Midnight Productions. **1928.** Si; b&w. 35mm. [Feature length assumed.]

Cast: Spencer Bell, Mildred Washington, Flora Washington, James Robinson, Spencer Williams.

Melodrama(?). No information about the precise nature of this film has been found. *Negro life.*

TENDERLOIN **F2.5566**

Warner Brothers Pictures. 14 Mar **1928** [New York premiere; released 28 Apr 1928; c22 Mar 1928; LP25089]. Talking sequences (Vitaphone); b&w. 35mm. 8 reels, 7,340-7,782 ft. [Also si.]

Dir Michael Curtiz. *Adapt-Scen* Edward T. Lowe, Jr. *Titl-Dial* Joseph Jackson, Edward T. Lowe, Jr. *Titl* Joseph Jackson. *Story* Melville Crossman. *Photog* Hal Mohr. *Film Ed* Ralph Dawson. *Asst Dir* John Daumery.

Cast: Dolores Costello *(Rose Shannon)*, Conrad Nagel *(Chuck White)*, Georgie Stone *("Sparrow")*, Mitchell Lewis *(The Professor)*, Dan Wolheim *("Lefty")*, Pat Hartigan *("The Mug")*, Fred Kelsey *(Detective Simpson)*, G. Raymond Nye *(Cowles)*, Evelyn Pierce *(Bobbie)*, Dorothy Vernon *(Aunt Molly)*, John Miljan *(bank teller)*.

Crook melodrama. The film's title refers to the district of a city so identified. Rose Shannon, a cabaret dancer, falls in love with Chuck, a hardened criminal. When some of Chuck's cronies pull a bank job, Chuck suspects Rose of having hidden the money for them. He pretends to care for her, but finally he realizes that she knows nothing at all about the robbery. By then, however, he has genuinely fallen in love with her, she has persuaded him to reform, and they have decided to get married. *Criminals—Rehabilitation. Dancers. Robbery.*

Note: In the first week of its premiere run, two of the four talking sequences were eliminated.

TENTACLES OF THE NORTH **F2.5567**

Ben Wilson Productions. *Dist* Rayart Pictures. Nov **1926.** Si; b&w. 35mm. 6 reels, 5,998 ft.

Pres by W. Ray Johnston. *Dir* Louis Chaudet. *Adapt* Leslie Curtis. *Photog* Joseph Walker.

Cast: Gaston Glass, Alice Calhoun, Al Roscoe, Al Ferguson, Joseph Girard, T. Hohai *(a native of Iceland)*.

Drama. Source: James Oliver Curwood, "In the Tentacles of the North," in *Blue Book* (20:510–527, Jan 1915). "Ice in North seas ties up two vessels; one with boy mate and other with daughter of seaman left alone through death of crew. Boy leaves his ship and discovers girl. He is chased by his crew but outwits them and escapes both them and the Arctic wastes. He brings girl back to civilization. *(Motion Picture News Booking Guide,* 12: 59, Apr 1927.) *Ship crews. Arctic regions.*

TENTH AVENUE **F2.5568**

De Mille Studio Productions. *Dist* Pathé Exchange. 6 Aug **1928** [c11 Jul 1928; LP25442]. Si; b&w. 35mm. 7 reels, 6,370 ft.

Dir William C. De Mille. *Scen* Douglas Z. Doty. *Titl* John Krafft. *Photog* David Abel. *Art Dir* Stephen Goosson. *Film Ed* Adelaide Cannon. *Asst Dir* William Scully. *Prod Mgr* Richard Donaldson.

Cast: Phyllis Haver *(Lyla Mason)*, Victor Varconi *(Bob Peters)*, Joseph Schildkraut *(Joe Ross)*, Louis Natheaux *(Fink)*, Robert Edeson *(Ed Burton, a detective)*, Ethel Wales *(Ma Mason)*, Casson Ferguson *(Curley)*, Ernie S. Adams *(Benny)*.

Melodrama. Source: John McGowan and Lloyd Griscom, *Tenth Avenue* (New York opening: 15 Aug 1927). Joe, a weakling gangster, and Bob, an ex-gambler, compete for Lyla Mason, a working girl who also runs a 10th Avenue roominghouse in New York city. Bob's desire to show Lyla he can support her leads him back to the gambling table when past-due rent threatens her with eviction. Bob and Joe are both suspected when Fink, a bootlegger, is found murdered in his room. It is revealed that Joe killed and robbed Fink to help Lyla pay the rent. Bob agrees to help Joe escape if he will promise to leave Lyla alone, but Joe doublecrosses Bob, allowing him to be caught with the evidence. Her suspicions aroused, Lyla wrings a confession from Joe while hidden detectives listen. He is caught attempting a getaway, is shot, and dies in Lyla's arms. Lyla and Bob face a happy future. *Gangsters. Gamblers. Landladies. Bootleggers. Boardinghouses. New York City.*

THE TENTH WOMAN **F2.5569**

Warner Brothers Pictures. 25 Aug **1924** [c10 Sep 1924; LP20563]. Si; b&w. 35mm. 7 reels, 6,900 ft.

Dir James Flood. *Scen* Julian Josephson. *Photog* John Mescall.

Cast: Beverly Bayne *(Willa Brookes)*, John Roche *(Barry Compton)*, June Marlowe *(Rose Ann Brainherd)*, Raymond McKee *(Billy Brainherd)*, Charles "Buddy" Post *(Donaldson)*, Gilbert Holmes *(Shorty)*, Alec Francis *(Mr. Brainherd)*, Edith Yorke *(Mrs. Brainherd)*.

Melodrama. Source: Harriet Theresa Comstock, *The Tenth Woman* (Garden City, New York, 1923). Barry Compton, a young rancher, saves Willa Brookes from a suicide attempt, and as his housekeeper she becomes secretly infatuated with him. Visiting in the East, he renews acquaintance with a married flapper, Rose Ann, who deserts her husband after they quarrel and comes to the ranch. Willa believes Barry is in love with the married woman and runs away, but she is rescued from an accident just as Rose Ann's husband arrives to take his wife home. *Ranchers. Flappers. Housekeepers. Suicide. Infidelity.*

THE TENTS OF ALLAH **F2.5570**

Encore Pictures. *Dist* Associated Exhibitors. 4 Mar **1923** [c17 Feb 1923; LU18687]. Si; b&w. 35mm. 7 reels, 6,357 ft.

Pres by Edward A. MacManus. *Dir-Story* Charles A. Logue. *Photog* Abe Fried, Eugene O'Donnell.

Cast: Monte Blue *(Chiddar Ben-Ek)*, Mary Alden *(Oulaid)*, Frank Currier *(Abou Ben-Ek/American Consul)*, Mary Thurman *(Elaine Calvert)*, Amalia Rivera *(Chala)*, Martin Faust *(Ahleef)*, Macey Harlam *(The Sultan)*, Charles Lane *(Commander Millgrate)*, Sally Crute *(Cynthia Wheeler)*.

Melodrama. While visiting her uncle, the American consul in Tangiers, Elaine Calvert inadvertently incurs the wrath of the sultan and is kidnaped by Abou Ben-Ek and his men, who hope to gain favor with the sultan. At the request of the consul, Commander Millgrate leads a group of marines into the desert to rescue Elaine, who is now in the protective custody of Chiddar Ben-Ek. Millgrate pursues the sheik with the permission of the sultan, who knows the commander, to Chiddar's father and captures him. At the sight of Chiddar's mother Millgrate realizes Chiddar's identity, releases his son, and resigns his commission. Chiddar refuses Millgrate's friendship but later rescues him and Oulaid (Chiddar's mother) when they are captured by the sultan. Millgrate dies from torture; Chiddar and Oulaid return to the desert with Elaine's promise of future happiness. *Royalty. Sheiks. Berbers. Deserts. United States—Diplomatic and consular service. United States Marines. Tangiers.*

Note: In the copyright synopsis Millgrate does not die but accompanies Chiddar and Oulaid.

TERROR *see* **MOCKERY**

THE TERROR (Blue Streak Western) **F2.5571**

Universal Pictures. 25 Jul **1926** [c12 May 1926; LP22724]. Si; b&w. 35mm. 5 reels, 4,862 ft.

Pres by Carl Laemmle. *Dir* Clifford S. Smith. *Story-Scen* E. Richard Schayer. *Photog* Eddie Linden.

Cast: Art Acord *(Art Downs)*, Velma Connor *(Molly Morton)*, Dudley Hendricks *(Pop Morton)*, C. E. Anderson *(Blair Hatley)*, Edmund Cobb *(Jim Hatley)*, Jess Deffenbach *(Steve)*, Hank Bell *(sheriff)*.

Western melodrama. While Pop Morton, a rancher, is being sworn in as deputy sheriff, his daughter Molly, to escape the unwelcome attentions of usurer Blair Hatley (who holds the mortgage on their ranch), meets Art

Downs. Art is mistaken by Steve Baird, one of Hatley's henchmen, for "The Terror," a notorious Arizona bandit, and uses this mistake as an excuse to invade their stronghold, where he finds Molly—kidnaped by the rustlers. Art rescues the girl, makes a getaway, but is again accosted by Hatley's brother; later, he arrives at the Morton ranch with a posse, rescues Pop Morton and Molly from the rustlers, and—disclosing his true identity as a Texas Ranger—wins the girl. *Rustlers. Sheriffs. Brothers. Posses. Usurers. Texas Rangers. Mistaken identity.*

TERROR **F2.5572**

FBO Pictures. 19 Aug **1928** [c14 Aug 1928; LP25529]. Si; b&w. 35mm. 5 reels, 4,884 ft.

Dir Louis King. *Cont* Frank Howard Clark. *Titl* Helen Gregg. *Story* Wyndham Gittens. *Ch Camera* Nick Musuraca. *Film Ed* Della M. King. *Asst Dir* William Cody.

Cast: Tom Tyler *(Tom Tyler)*, Jane Reid *(Lucille Roberts)*, Al Ferguson *(Luke Thorne)*, Jules Cowles *(Jed Burke)*, Frankie Darro *(Buddy Roberts)*.

Western melodrama. Buddy Roberts, who lives alone with his sister, Lucille, in a deserted house on top of a mountain, begins to receive threatening letters and to see apparitions. With no family to turn to, he writes to cowboy star Tom Tyler in Hollywood and asks him for assistance. Tom is about to leave for a vacation and gladly comes to help out his desperate young fan. Tom defeats the outlaw gang threatening Buddy and Lucille, restores a large sum of money (hidden by their late uncle) to the children, and promises to bring them to Hollywood to stay with him. *Orphans. Brother-sister relationship. Actors. Gangs. Motion pictures. Ghosts.*

THE TERROR **F2.5573**

Warner Brothers Pictures. 6 Sep **1928** [c22 Aug 1928; LP25563]. Sd (Vitaphone) b&w. 35mm. 9 reels, 7,654 ft. [Also si, 20 Oct 1928; 5,443 ft.]

Dir Roy Del Ruth. *Scen-Dial* Harvey Gates. *Titl* Joseph Jackson. *Photog* Chick McGill. *Film Ed* Thomas Pratt, Jack Killifer.

Cast: May McAvoy *(Olga Redmayne)*, Louise Fazenda *(Mrs. Elvery)*, Edward Everett Horton *(Ferdinand Fane)*, Alec B. Francis *(Dr. Redmayne)*, Matthew Betz *(Joe Connors)*, Holmes Herbert *(Goodman)*, Otto Hoffman *(Soapy Marks)*, Joseph W. Girard *(Superintendent Hallick)*, John Miljan *(Alfred Katman)*, Frank Austin *(Cotton)*.

Mystery melodrama. Source: Edgar Wallace, *The Terror* (London, 1929). The Terror, a maniacal killer whose identity is unknown, makes his headquarters in an old English country house that has been converted into an inn. With mysterious organ recitals and strange noises, The Terror frightens the guests, who include Mrs. Elvery, a spiritualist; Ferdinand Fane, a Scotland Yard detective who is not so stupid as he seems; and Joe Connors and Soapy Marks, a couple of criminals just released from jail who have sworn revenge on The Terror. After a night of murder and mayhem, the identity of The Terror is revealed. *Lunatics. Organists. Detectives. Spiritualists. Murder. Inns. England. Scotland Yard.*

THE TERROR OF BAR X **F2.5574**

Bob Custer Productions. *Dist* Film Booking Offices of America. 20 Mar **1927** [c16 Feb 1927; LP23672]. Si; b&w. 35mm. 5 reels, 4,982 ft.

Pres by Joseph P. Kennedy. *Dir* Scott Pembroke. *Cont* George M. Merrick. *Titl* Ruth Todd. *Photog* Ernest Miller.

Cast: Bob Custer *(Bob Willis)*, Ruby Blaine *(Dorothy Hunter)*, William Rhine *(Ross Hunter)*, Jack Castle *(Reginald Brooks)*, Duke R. Lee *(Jim Ashland)*, Walter Maly *(Hoke Channing)*, Roy Bassett *(sheriff)*.

Western melodrama. Source: George M. Johnson, "Stan Willis, Cowboy" (publication undetermined). By borrowing money from a wealthy Indian friend, Bob Willis, foreman of the Bar X Ranch, comes to the assistance of Ross Hunter, the invalid owner of the ranch, when Ross is pressed for payment of a note. Ashland, a gambler who holds the note, has designs on Dorothy Hunter; and seeing in Willis a dangerous rival, he directs the sheriff's suspicions toward Willis as a bandit and has Channing, one of his henchmen, plant stolen currency in Willis' bunk. Willis is arrested, and Dorothy goes to Ashland to seek his release; she learns of Ashland's complicity, and he pursues her to the ranch. Willis observes the chase from the jail, and by a ruse, escapes. The sheriff follows and learns the identity of the true culprit. ... Willis finds happiness with the girl. *Ranchers. Invalids. Ranch foremen. Gamblers. Frameup. Jailbreaks. Debt.*

THE TERROR OF PUEBLO **F2.5575**

Art Mix Productions. *Dist* Aywon Film Corp. 26 Nov **1924** [New York State license]. Si; b&w. 35mm. 5 reels, 4,850 ft.

Cast: Art Mix.

Western melodrama(?). No information about the nature of this film has been found.

TESS OF THE D'URBERVILLES **F2.5576**

Metro-Goldwyn Pictures. 27 Jul **1924** [New York premiere; released 11 Aug 1924; c27 Aug 1924; LP20527]. Si; b&w. 35mm. 8 reels, 7,500 ft.

Pres by Louis B. Mayer. *Dir* Marshall Neilan. *Adapt* Dorothy Farnum. *Photog* David Kesson.

Cast: Blanche Sweet *(Tess)*, Conrad Nagel *(Angel Clare)*, Stuart Holmes *(Alec D'Urberville)*, George Fawcett *(John Durbeyfield)*, Victory Bateman *(Joan Durbeyfield)*, Courtenay Foote *(Dick)*, Joseph J. Dowling *(The Priest)*.

Drama. Source: Thomas Hardy, *Tess of the D'Urbervilles, a Pure Woman Faithfully Presented* (New York, 1892). When John Durbeyfield learns that he is a descendant of the rich D'Urbervilles, he sends his daughter Tess to Alec, who employs her as a maid. Betrayed by him, she leaves, and tragedy stalks her life. Tess loses her baby, but she finds happiness with Angel, though he leaves her upon learning her history. To free herself from the influence of Alec, she is forced to kill him and is executed for the crime. *Housemaids. Filial relations. Murder. Capital punishment. Class conflict. Wessex.*

TESS OF THE STORM COUNTRY **F2.5577**

Mary Pickford Co. *Dist* United Artists. 12 Nov **1922** [c1 Dec 1922; LP18587]. Si; b&w. 35mm. 10 reels, 9,639 ft.

Dir John S. Robertson. *Adapt* Elmer Harris. *Photog* Charles Rosher. *Trick Photog* Paul Eagler. *Art Dir* Frank Ormston. *Asst Dir* Shaw Lovett.

Cast: Mary Pickford *(Tessibel Skinner)*, Lloyd Hughes *(Frederick Graves)*, Gloria Hope *(Teola Graves)*, David Torrence *(Elias Graves)*, Forrest Robinson *(Daddy Skinner)*, Jean Hersholt *(Ben Letts)*, Danny Hoy *(Ezra Longman)*, Robert Russell *(Dan Jordan)*, Gus Saville *(Old Man Longman)*, Madame De Bodamere *(Mrs. Longman)*.

Melodrama. Source: Grace Miller White, *Tess of the Storm Country* (New York, 1909). Wealthy Elias Graves buys a house on a hill and tries to remove the squatters who live below. Harsh measures are urged on Graves by Dan Jordan, for whose murder Daddy Skinner is unjustly convicted. In leading the squatters' struggle for survival, Skinner's daughter, Tess, wins the sympathy and love of Graves's son, Frederick, but she loses him when Frederick discovers her with a child. Tess is reunited with her father and Frederick when Ben Letts is revealed as Jordan's murderer and when Frederick's sister, Teola, claims the baby as her own. Graves is reconciled with the squatters. *Squatters. Injustice. Brother-sister relationship. Filial relations. Poverty. Murder.*

TESSIE **F2.5578**

Arrow Pictures. 18 Sep **1925** [New York showing; c23 Sep 1925; LP21842]. Si; b&w. 35mm. 7 reels, 6,221 ft.

Dir Dallas M. Fitzgerald. *Photog* Merritt Gerstad.

Cast: May McAvoy *(Tessie)*, Bobby Agnew *(Roddy Wells)*, Lee Moran *(Barney Taylor)*, Myrtle Stedman *(Mrs. Wells)*, Gertrude Short *(Mame McQuire)*, Mary Gordon *(Aunt Maggie)*, Frank Perry *(Uncle Dan)*.

Comedy-drama. Source: Sewell Ford, "Tessie and the Little Sap," in *Saturday Evening Post* (196:20–21, 28 Mar 1925). Tessie, who is in charge of the cigar and candy counter in a large hotel, is engaged to Barney Taylor, an automobile mechanic. At Tessie's urging, Barney sells a car to Roddy Wells, the son of a wealthy widow. Mrs. Wells becomes attached to Barney, and out of spite Tessie accepts Roddy's attentions. Mrs. Wells goes to Tessie and tries to pay her to stop seeing Roddy. Tessie refuses. Barney shows up and, when Tessie will not forgive him, tries to get rough with her. Roddy also arrives, thrashes Barney, and carries Tessie off to a preacher. *Widows. Mechanics. Salesclerks. Social classes. Courtship. Cigarstores. Hotels.*

THE TEST OF DONALD NORTON **F2.5579**

Chadwick Pictures. 1 Mar **1926** [c26 Mar 1926; LP22534]. Si; b&w. 35mm. 7 reels, 6,600 ft. [Copyrighted as 8 reels.]

Dir B. Reeves Eason. *Scen* Adele Buffington. *Photog* Art Reeves.

Cast: George Walsh *(Wen-dah-ben, known as Donald Norton)*, [Frederick] Tyrone Power *(John Corrigal)*, Robert Graves *(Dale Millington)*, Eugenie Gilbert *(Lorraine)*, Evelyn Selbie *(Nee-tah-wee-gan)*, Mickey Moore, Virginia True Boardman, Jack Dillon, Virginia Marshall.

Melodrama. Source: Robert E. Pinkerton, *The Test of Donald Norton* (Chicago, 1924). Wen-dah-ben, halfbreed son of Nee-tah-wee-gan, becomes a protégé of the Layards, who rename him Donald Norton. He grows to manhood under their care and with the companionship of their little girl, Janet, who comes to love him. He becomes manager of a fur-trading post for the Hudson's Bay Company. After a year, he goes to be reassigned, but the new district manager, John Corrigal, though he likes Indians, dislikes Donald. It is only by Layard's plea that Corrigal allows Donald to return to his old post, though under the supervision of another post manager, Dale Millington, who loves Janet. Donald becomes seriously ill that winter, and Millington takes advantage of his absence to impugn Donald's loyalty. Donald is fired by Corrigal, but in the confrontation he becomes convinced that Corrigal is his father. He becomes district manager of a rival concern, causing a decline in the profits of the Hudson's Bay Co. Hearing that his mother has nearly been choked to death, he and Corrigal rush to her side, but she dies before she can clear up the mystery. Millington abducts Janet, but Donald overtakes them and brings them back to the post. Millington tells the story Nee-tah-wee-gan told him—that she had set fire to and burned Corrigal's house and taken his son, John Corrigal, Jr. Corrigal embraces his son and Janet, his daughter-in-law to be. *Fur traders. Indians of North America. Halfcastes. Parentage. Trading posts. Hudson's Bay Co.*.

TEX **F2.5580**

Ward Lascelle Productions. 3 Dec **1926** [New York State license]. Si; b&w. 35mm. 6 reels.

Dir Tom Gibson.

Cast: Ruth Mix, Robert McKim, Gladden James, Francelia Billington.

Western melodrama. No information about the precise nature of this film has been found.

THE TEXAN **F2.5581**

Paramount-Publix Corp. 10 May **1930** [c10 May 1930; LP1293]. Sd (Movietone); b&w. 35mm. 9 reels, 7,142 ft.

Dir John Cromwell. *Screenplay* Daniel Nathan Rubin. *Adapt* Oliver H. P. Garrett. *Photog* Victor Milner. *Film Ed* Verna Willis. *Songs: "Chico," "To Hold You"* L. Wolfe Gilbert, Abel Baer. *Rec Engr* Harry M. Lindgren.

Cast: Gary Cooper *(Enrique ["Quico," The Llano Kid])*, Fay Wray *(Conseulo)*, Emma Dunn *(Señora Ibarra)*, Oscar Apfel *(Thacker)*, James Marcus *(John Brown)*, Donald Reed *(Nick Ibarra)*, Solidad Jiminez *(duenna)*, Veda Buckland *(Mary [nurse])*, César Vanoni *(Pasquale)*, Edwin J. Brady *(Henry)*, Enrique Acosta *(Sixto)*, Romualdo Tirado *(cabman)*.

Western drama. Source: O. Henry, "The Double-dyed Deceiver," in *Everybody's Magazine* (13:814, Dec 1905). The Llano Kid, a young bandit with a price on his head, stops at the smithy of John Brown, a scripture-quoting sheriff, gets into a poker game with a young gambler whom he catches cheating, and is forced to kill him in self-defense. Aboard a train, he meets the unscrupulous Thacker, by whom he is induced to pose as the son of a wealthy South American widow, Señora Ibarra, whose own child disappeared at the age of 10. At the family hacienda in a little seaport town, he easily passes himself off as Enrique, with the intention of helping Thacker steal the widow's gold. But when he falls in love with Consuelo, his niece, and realizes that the old lady's son was the very man he shot in the saloon brawl, The Kid calls off the deal. Thacker organizes a gang to steal the gold, and The Kid is tracked down by Sheriff Brown, who, however, is persuaded to wait until nightfall to arrest him. In the attack, The Kid is wounded, and Thacker is killed. The sheriff agrees to keep his identity secret and reports Thacker's death as that of The Llano Kid. *Bandits. Fugitives. Widows. Sheriffs. Impersonation. Motherhood. South America. Texans.*

A TEXAN'S HONOR **F2.5582**

J. Charles Davis Productions. 20 Dec **1929.** Sd; b&w. 35mm. 5 reels.

Cast: Yakima Canutt *(Bob Morgan)*.

Western melodrama. Robbed of the cash from the sale of his employer's cattle, Bob Morgan accepts Sam Anthony's offer of employment and soon finds himself in deep trouble. The Anthony ranch, which has ample water, is surrounded by another ranch owned by Monica Valdez, who innocently supports her foreman's underhanded efforts to remove Anthony. When Sam is shot, his daughter, Betty, suspects Bob, whom she has seen in Monica's flirtatious company; Monica assures the sheriff of Bob's guilt; and Bob is forced to take action. Rescuing Betty and Sam from the villain, Bob elicits a confession from the foreman's henchman. *Texans. Ranchers. Ranch foremen. Sheriffs. Water rights.*

TEXAS **F2.5583**

Phil Goldstone Productions. 1 Jun **1922.** Si; b&w. 35mm. 5 reels.

Dir William Bertram.

Cast: Franklyn Farnum.

Western melodrama. "Hero owns ranch which [railroad] purchasing agent wants for valuable coal deposits. Hero refuses to sell ranch. Railroad president arrives, and hero falls in love with daughter. They block hero's effort to pay mortgage, then steal money. They then attempt to blacken him in eyes of president's daughter, with aid of local girl, but girl repents and reveals plot. They attempt to waylay hero, and, failing, incite mob to lynch him. Girl saves him. Hero fights president in streets, wins, then saves him from mob." (*Motion Picture News Booking Guide,* 3:68, Oct 1922.) *Ranchers. Railroads. Coal. Mortgages. Lynching. Reputation.*

THE TEXAS BEARCAT **F2.5584**

R-C Pictures. *Dist* Film Booking Offices of America. 31 May **1925** [c31 May 1925; LP21554]. Si; b&w. 35mm. 5 reels, 4,770 ft.

Pres by Jesse J. Goldburg. *Dir* B. Reeves Eason. *Cont* George Plympton. *Story* F. J. Rhetore. *Photog* Lauren A. Draper.

Cast: Bob Custer *(Dave Sethman)*, Sally Rand *(Jean Crawford)*, Harry von Meter *(John Crawford)*, Jack Richardson *(Watson)*, Carlton King *(Sethman)*, Lee Shumway *(Murdock)*.

Western melodrama. Dave Sethman has been brought up to believe that he is the halfbreed son of Sethman, a tough rancher who opposes the plans of John Crawford, an eastern industrialist, to buy up a group of ranches. Crawford comes west with his daughter, Jean, and attempts to break the elder Sethman's opposition. Dave saves Jean from a runaway horse and later protects her when Murdock, Crawford's unprincipled assistant, makes unwanted advances. Sethman plans to rustle Crawford's cattle and is mortally wounded by him, telling Dave, as he lies dying, that Crawford is Dave's real father from whom he was stolen as an infant. Dave and Crawford are reconciled, and Crawford, whom Dave has shot in the hand, tells the boy that Jean is his adopted daughter, leaving the way free for a romance between the young people. *Ranchers. Texans. Industrialists. Halfcastes. Parentage. Adoption. Rustling.*

A TEXAS COWBOY **F2.5585**

Big Productions Film Corp. *Dist* Syndicate Pictures. 26 Dec **1929** [New York State license]. Si; b&w. 35mm. 5 reels.

Cast: Bob Steele.

Western melodrama(?). "Dick returns and finds his mother married to Brute Kettle who is trying to obtain control of her property. Dick succeeds in trouncing and obtaining evidence against him. Brute is killed in attempting to escape." ("Motion Picture News Booking Guide," in *Motion Picture News,* 15 Mar 1930, p105.) *Property rights. Filial relations.*

TEXAS FLASH **F2.5586**

Associated Independent Producers. 28 Nov **1928** [New York State license]. Si; b&w. 35mm. 5 reels, 4,450 ft.

Dir-Scen Robert J. Horner. *Titl* Bert Ames. *Photog* Jack Draper. *Film Ed* William Austin.

Cast: Pawnee Bill Jr., Ione Reed, Bud Osborne, Bill Nestel.

Western melodrama. No information about the precise nature of this film has been found.

A TEXAS RANGER *see* **PURE GRIT**

A TEXAS STEER (Reissue) **F2.5587**

23 Dec **1927** [New York State license]. Si; b&w. 35mm. 5 reels, 5000 ft.

Note: Originally released in 1915 by Selig Polyscope Co.

A TEXAS STEER **F2.5588**

Sam E. Rork Productions. *Dist* First National Pictures. 4 Dec **1927** [c28 Nov 1927; LP24702]. Si; b&w. 35mm. 8 reels, 7,418 ft.

Pres by Sam E. Rork. *Dir* Richard Wallace. *Screenplay* Bernard McConville. *Titl* Will Rogers, Garrett Graham. *Adapt* Paul Schofield. *Photog* Jack MacKenzie. *Film Ed* Frank Lawrence. *Asst Dir* James F. O'Shea. *Prod Mgr* Ben Singer. *Comedy Construction* Jack Wagner.

Cast: Will Rogers *(Maverick Brander)*, Louise Fazenda *(Mrs. Ma Brander)*, Sam Hardy *(Brassy Gall)*, Ann Rork *(Bossy Brander)*, Douglas Fairbanks, Jr. *(Fairleigh Bright)*, Lilyan Tashman *(Dixie Style)*, George Marion, Sr. *(Fishback)*, Bud Jamieson *(Othello)*, Arthur Hoyt *(Knott Innitt)*, Mack Swain *(Bragg)*, William Orlamond *(Blow)*, Lucien Littlefield *(Yell)*.

Farce. Source: Charles Hale Hoyt, *A Texas Steer, a Musical Farce in Four Acts* (c1899). Easygoing but lucre-laden Texas rancher Maverick Brander is out on the range while his social lioness of a wife and his romance-ridden daughter, Bossy (along with Texas political bosses Bragg, Blow, and Yell), secure his election to Congress in order to ensure passage of the Eagle Rock Dam Bill. Opponents of the bill—Brassy Gall and his yellow rose, Dixie Style—have gone to Washington to scuttle the very same proposal and to try intimidating Brander with blackmail pictures, finally locking him up without even a hankie for modesty in a roominghouse outside of town. Maverick escapes, picking up a nightgown along the way, and returns to "the biggest circus in the world" in time to expose his opponents' treacherous trickery and force a successful re-vote on the bill. Bossy gets Fairleigh Bright in the bargain though Ma Brander is left holding Maverick's pants in the ensuing celebration. *Ranchers. Legislation. Water rights. Kidnaping. Blackmail. Dams. United States Congress. Washington (District of Columbia). Texas.*

THE TEXAS STREAK (Universal-Jewel) **F2.5589**

Universal Pictures. 26 Sep **1926** [c13 Sep 1926; LP23115]. Si; b&w. 35mm. 7 reels, 6,259 ft.

Pres by Carl Laemmle. *Dir-Story-Scen* Lynn Reynolds. *Photog* Edward Newman.

Cast: Hoot Gibson *(Chad Pennington)*, Blanche Mehaffey *(Amy Hollis)*, Alan Roscoe *(Jefferson Powell)*, James Marcus *(Colonel Hollis)*, Jack Curtis *("Jiggs" Cassidy)*, George "Slim" Summerville *("Swede" Sonberg)*, Les Bates *("Pat" Casey)*, Jack Murphy *(Jimmy Hollis)*, William H. Turner *(Charles Logan)*.

Western comedy-drama. Chad Pennington and his pals "Jiggs" and "Swede" are extras on a film location in Arizona. Stranded when they lose their railroad fares, Chad stages a stunt and gets hired as a guard for surveyors involved in a dispute over water power. He attends a masked country dance, quarrels with Powell—a rancher who is leading the fight—and while fleeing his pursuers, is wounded. He is found by Amy Hollis, who feeds and nurses him. Later, he returns to the Hollis ranch, frees his pals who have been captured by the ranchers, prevents another attack on the surveyors, and establishes his innocence in the shooting of Jimmy, Amy's brother. Colonel Hollis is finally convinced that the water company plans to deal fairly with him, and Chad's assistant director reports that the company plans to "star" him in westerns. *Actors. Motion picture extras. Ranchers. Surveyors. Waterpower. Motion pictures. Arizona.*

THE TEXAS TERROR **F2.5590**

Anchor Film Distributors. 28 Oct **1926** [New York State license]. Si; b&w. 35mm. 5 reels, 4,500 ft.

Cast: Al Hoxie.

Western melodrama(?). No information about the nature of this film has been found.

TEXAS TOMMY **F2.5591**

El Dorado Productions. *Dist* Syndicate Pictures. Dec **1928** [or 15 Mar 1929]. Si; b&w. 35mm. 5 reels, 4,271 or 4,546 ft.

Prod J. Charles Davis. *Dir* J. P. McGowan. *Story-Scen* Sally Winters. *Photog* Paul Allen. *Film Ed* Philip Schuyler.

Cast: Bob Custer *(Texas Cooper)*, Lynn Anderson, Bud Osborne, Mary Mayberry, H. B. Carpenter, Frank Ellis, J. P. McGowan.

Western melodrama. Mistaken for gunman Texas Tommy, who is en route to join Segrue's gang and rustle Hardacre's cattle, Texas Cooper takes charge of Hardacre's ranch, prevents the invalid from being victimized by the gang, and rescues Sally Hardacre from abduction. *Ranchers. Invalids. Outlaws. Gangs. Rustling. Abduction. Mistaken identity.*

THE TEXAS TORNADO **F2.5592**

FBO Pictures. 24 Jun **1928** [c1 Feb 1928; LP24935]. Si; b&w. 35mm. 5 reels, 4,793 ft.

Dir-Story-Scen Frank Howard Clark. *Titl* Randolph Bartlett. *Photog* E. T. McManigal. *Film Ed* Pandro S. Berman.

Cast: Tom Tyler *(Tom King)*, Frankie Darro *(Bud Martin)*, Nora Lane *(Ellen Briscoe)*, Jack Anthony *(Bill Latimer)*, Frank Whitson *(Tim Briscoe)*, Beans *(himself, a dog)*.

Western melodrama. Bill Latimer, a dishonest rancher, is attempting to obtain possession of a valuable oil lease held by neighbors Ellen Briscoe and her father by preventing them from renewing before expiration. On the day the renewal must be made, Latimer detains them at the door of their home. A half hour before forfeiture time, a mysterious stranger rides by, notes the predicament, and helps by secretly accepting the lease and taking it to the bank. There, after a fistfight with Latimer's men, he has it renewed on the stroke of three. The stranger, who is actually Tom King, uncle of Bud Martin, an orphaned boy in the Briscoe household, returns to the Briscoes, still keeping secret his identity, and begins to develop the oil prospects. Possessed by greed when he sees that there is oil on the land, Latimer shoots Briscoe and blames King; but Briscoe recovers and names Latimer as his assailant. Tom, having escaped from jail, rescues his nephew from Latimer, who has kidnaped the boy, and takes Latimer prisoner. All ends happily for King, his nephew, and the Briscoes. *Ranchers. Orphans. Strangers. Texans. Oil lands. Kidnaping. Documentation. Dogs.*

THE TEXAS TRAIL **F2.5593**

Hunt Stromberg Corp. *Dist* Producers Distributing Corp. 1 Jun **1925**. Si; b&w. 35mm. 5 reels, 4,720 ft.

Dir Scott R. Dunlap. *Photog* George Benoit.

Cast: Harry Carey *(Pete Grainger)*, Ethel Shannon *(Betty Foster)*, Charles K. French *(Ring 'Em Foster)*, Claude Payton *(Dan Merrill)*, Sidney Franklin *(Ike Collander)*.

Western melodrama. Source: Guy Morton, *Rangy Pete* (Boston, 1922). Betty Foster comes west to visit her uncle and witnesses a robbery in which $10,000 of her uncle's money is stolen. Appalled by the lack of heroics on the part of her uncle's foreman, Pete Grainger, Betty accidentally learns the probable location of the stolen money and, turning bandit, steals a box of apples in which she suspects the money to be hidden. The box turns out to be the wrong one, but Pete soon recovers the money and kills Merrill, the man who held him up. Pete wins Betty's heart with his heroics and a new suit of clothes. *Uncles. Ranch foremen. Bandits. Texas.*

THANK YOU **F2.5594**

Fox Film Corp. 1 Nov **1925** [c23 Aug 1925; LP21783]. Si; b&w. 35mm. 7 reels, 6,900 ft.

Prod John Golden. *Dir* John Ford. *Scen* Frances Marion. *Photog* George Schneiderman.

Cast: Alec B. Francis *(David Lee)*, Jacqueline Logan *(Diane Lee)*, George O'Brien *(Kenneth Jamieson)*, J. Farrell MacDonald *(Andy)*, George Fawcett *(Cornelius Jamieson)*, Cyril Chadwick *(Mr. Jones)*, Edith Bostwick *(Mrs. Jones)*, Marion Harlan *(Milly Jones)*, Vivian Ogden *(Miss Blodgett)*, James Neill *(Dr. Cobb)*, Billy Rinaldi *(Sweet, Jr.)*, Aileen Manning *(Hannah)*, Maurice Murphy *(Willie Jones)*, Robert Milasch *(Sweet, Sr.)*, Ida Moore, Frankie Bailey *(gossips)*.

Comedy-drama. Source: Winchell Smith and Tom Cushing, *Thank You, a Play in Three Acts* (New York, 1922). After a series of wild escapades, Kenneth Jamieson is sent by his irate millionaire father to stay on a chicken farm in the little village of Dedham. On the same day, Diane, the niece of the Reverend David Lee, arrives from Paris, sporting French manners and the latest Parisian clothes. A few days later, Kenneth gets drunk and makes a fool of himself, but David speaks to him and shows him the error of his ways. Grossly underpaid, David asks the vestrymen for a raise. They refuse it to him, claiming that he is deserving of nothing until he sends Diane away. Kenneth's father learns of his son's infatuation with Diane and comes to Dedham, expecting to find a gold digger. He is quickly won over by the girl, particularly after she nurses Kenneth back to health when he becomes ill. The elder Jamieson, angered by the hypocrisy of the vestrymen, gives them a piece of his mind. David receives his deserved raise, and Kenneth and Diane become engaged. *Millionaires. Clergymen. Vestrymen. Filial relations. Village life. Drunkenness. Hypocrisy. Chickens.*

THANKS FOR THE BUGGY RIDE (Universal-Jewel) **F2.5595**

Universal Pictures. 21 Jan **1928** [New York premiere; released 1 Apr; c29 Nov 1927; LP24716]. Si; b&w. 35mm. 6 reels, 6,179 ft.

Pres by Carl Laemmle. *Dir* William A. Seiter. *Ed Supv* Joseph Franklin Poland. *Scen* Beatrice Van. *Titl* Tom Reed. *Story* Byron Morgan. *Photog* Arthur Todd. *Film Ed* Edward McDermott.

Cast: Laura La Plante *(Jenny)*, Glenn Tryon *(Joe Hall)*, Richard Tucker *(Mr. McBride)*, Lee Moran *(Bill Barton)*, David Rollins *(Harold McBride)*, Kate Price *(Mrs. Crogan, landlady)*, Jack Raymond *(Mr. Belkoff, dancing master)*, Trixie Friganza *(actress)*.

Comedy-drama. Jenny, a dance instructor, accidentally meets Joe Hall, a song promoter, who escorts her home; she gives him a song idea by calling "Thanks for the Buggy Ride." At a picnic they fall desperately in love, and during a rainstorm they take refuge in a house for sale. When Jenny goes to a cafe to give a private dance lesson to Harold McBride, she incurs the enmity of his father, a song publisher, by repulsing his advances.

When McBride refuses to hear Joe's song, Jenny dons blackface and successfully introduces the song at a music salon. Joe forgives her; and after claiming the rights for his song, they are married and buy the home that previously sheltered them. *Dance teachers. Composers. Publishers.*

THAT CERTAIN THING **F2.5596**

Columbia Pictures. 1 Jan **1928** [c2 Feb 1928; LP24942]. Si; b&w. 35mm. 7 reels, 6,047 ft.

Prod Harry Cohn. *Dir* Frank Capra. *Story-Adapt* Elmer Harris. *Titl* Al Boasberg. *Photog* Joe Walker. *Art Dir* Robert E. Lee. *Film Ed* Arthur Roberts. *Asst Dir* Eugene De Rue.

Cast: Viola Dana *(Molly Kelly)*, Ralph Graves *(Andy B. Charles, Jr.)*, Burr McIntosh *(A. B. Charles, Sr.)*, Aggie Herring *(Mrs. Kelly)*, Carl Gerard *(Secretary Brooks)*, Syd Crossley *(valet)*.

Comedy-drama. Molly Kelly, a cigarstand drudge who supports her family, marries Andy B. Charles, Jr., idle son of wealthy A. B. Charles, Sr., a restaurateur. Papa cuts off his son without a cent when he hears of the marriage, forcing junior to work as a day laborer. Eating a box lunch prepared by Molly gives him an inspiration to open an eatery—the "Molly Box Lunch Company." When Andy's father, the owner of a nearby restaurant whose business is falling off, visits the upstart entrepreneurs, he is so pleased to see that his son is a success that he gives the young couple money to expand their business and welcomes them back into the family. *Restaurateurs. Fatherhood. Disinheritance. Wealth. Business management. Cigarstores.*

THAT DEVIL QUEMADO **F2.5597**

R-C Pictures. *Dist* Film Booking Offices of America. 5 Apr **1925** [c5 Apr 1925; LP21556]. Si; b&w. 35mm. 5 reels, 4,768 ft.

Dir Del Andrews. *Story* Marvin Wilhite. *Photog* Ross Fisher. *Asst Dir* Al Werker.

Cast: Fred Thomson *(Quemado)*, Albert Priscoe *(José Ramériz)*, Nola Luxford *(Conchita Ramériz)*, Byron Douglas *(John Thatcher)*, Joseph Bell *(Ned Thatcher)*, Gloria Hope *(Joanna Thatcher)*, Alan Roscoe *(Gretorix)*, Robert Cantiero *(Juan Gonzales)*.

Western melodrama. A former Yale student returns to the land where his Spanish forefathers once reigned supreme and lives in the Mexican hills, occasionally riding into border towns, where he takes the law into his own hands and protects the weak from crooked elements. Known as Quemado, he prevents the marriage of a girl to a notorious desperado and meets Joanna Thatcher, an eastern girl to whom he makes the promise that she will someday come to love him. Joan becomes engaged to Gretorix, unwilling to admit to herself that she has become infatuated with the daring horseman. On Joan's wedding day, Quemado kidnaps her, forces her to admit that she loves him, and arranges to be wed by a parson on horseback as they ride furiously into the hills to avoid the pursuit of the angry Gretorix. *Reformers. Bandits. Clergymen. Abduction. Weddings. Mexico. Mexican border. Yale University.*

THAT FRENCH LADY **F2.5598**

Fox Film Corp. 17 Aug **1924** [c6 Aug 1924; LP20473]. Si; b&w. 35mm. 6 reels, 5,470 ft.

Pres by William Fox. *Dir* Edmund Mortimer. *Scen* Charles Kenyon. *Story* William Hurlbut. *Photog* G. O. Post.

Cast: Shirley Mason *(Inez de Pierrefond)*, Theodore von Eltz *(John Hemingway)*, Harold Goodwin *(Charlie Abbey)*, Charles Coleman *(Uncle Walter)*.

Romantic drama. John Hemingway, while in Paris studying architecture, falls in love with Inez de Pierrefond, an author who believes in marriage free of state and church laws. He brings her to his home in Iowa, where she is scorned by the villagers until she threatens to reveal their own hypocrisy. Ultimately her faith in marriage is restored. *Architects. Authors. Free love. Marriage. Paris. Iowa.*

THAT GIRL MONTANA **F2.5599**

Jesse D. Hampton. *Dist* Pathé Exchange. Jan **1921** [c22 Dec 1920; LU15951]. Si; b&w. 35mm. 5 reels.

Pres by Jesse D. Hampton. *Dir* Robert Thornby. *Scen* George H. Plympton. *Photog* Lucien Andriot.

Cast: Blanche Sweet *(Montana Rivers)*, Mahlon Hamilton *(Dan Overton)*, Frank Lanning *(Jim Harris)*, Edward Peil *(Lee Holly)*, Charles Edler *(Akkomi)*, Claire Du Brey *(Lottie)*, Kate Price *(Mrs. Huzzard)*, Jack Roseleigh *(Max Lyster)*.

Western melodrama. Source: Marah Ellis Ryan, *That Girl Montana* (New York, 1901). Lee Holly, a cardsharp, has brought up his daughter, Monte, in boys' clothing, She escapes to an Indian village when Holly is chased out of town and remains there 2 years with her friend Akkomi, resuming feminine attire and taking the name Tana. Dan Overton, a young prospector, becomes interested in her and takes her to live with white people in a boardinghouse. She is introduced by Dan to his mining partner Harris as Montana Rivers, the daughter of a partner of his, but Harris recognizes her as "Lee Holly's brat" and denounces her. Dan defends her, and after Harris suffers a paralyzing stroke he relents and makes her a partner in their mine. Holly comes to their camp after they strike gold and is killed by Harris, who learns that Tana is the daughter stolen from him. Dan's unfaithful wife is killed by a jealous lover, freeing him to marry Tana. *Cardsharps. Indians of North America. Fatherhood.*

THAT GIRL OKLAHOMA **F2.5600**

Ward Lascelle Productions. 28 Aug **1926** [New York State license]. Si; b&w. 35mm. 6 reels.

Cast: Ruth Mix, Bryant Washburn.

Western melodrama. No information about the precise nature of this film has been found.

THAT LASS O' LOWRIE'S *see* **THE FLAME OF LIFE**

THAT MAN JACK! **F2.5601**

Independent Pictures. *Dist* Film Booking Offices of America. 23 Aug **1925** [c18 Aug 1925; LP21727]. Si; b&w. 35mm. 5 reels, 5,032 ft.

Pres by Jesse J. Goldburg. *Dir* William J. Craft. *Cont* Adele S. Buffington. *Story* George Paul Bauer. *Photog* Arthur Reeves. *Adtl Photog* William Reis. *Asst Dir* Joe Murphy.

Cast: Bob Custer *(Jack)*, Mary Beth Milford *(Anita Leland)*, Monte Collins *(Joe Leland)*, Hayford Hobbs *(Sammy Sills)*, Buck Moulton *(Bill Stearns)*.

Western melodrama. Jack Burton saves Anita from a runaway horse and then saves Sam Sills from a beating at the hands of Bill Stearns. Jack goes into partnership with Sam, who is later murdered by Bill. Jack, blamed for the murder on circumstantial evidence, is arrested by the sheriff. He escapes and finds Bill just in time to save Anita from his foul advances. Bill is arrested by the sheriff, and Jack and Anita anticipate a happy future together. *Cowboys. Sheriffs. Murder. Partnerships. Circumstantial evidence.*

THAT MODEL FROM PARIS **F2.5602**

Tiffany Productions. 15 Oct **1926** [c7 Sep 1926; LP23091]. Si; b&w. 35mm. 7 reels, 6,200 ft.

Dir Louis J. Gasnier. *Scen* Frederica Sagor. *Photog* Milton Moore, Mack Stengler.

Cast: Marceline Day *(Jane Miller)*, Bert Lytell *(Robert Richmond)*, Eileen Percy *(Mamie)*, Ward Crane *(Morgan Grant)*, Miss Du Pont *(Lila)*, Crauford Kent *(Henry Marsh)*, Otto Lederer *(Mr. Katz)*, Nellie Bly Baker *(masseuse)*, Leon Holmes, Sabel Johnson, George Kuwa.

Comedy-drama. Source: Gouverneur Morris, "The Right To Live" (publication undetermined). Jane Miller, a cashier for Katz & Katz, is a plain, retiring girl who does not know how to dress. When her girl friend persuades her to borrow a gown from Mr. Katz for the theater, she is seen by her employer there and loses her job. Morgan Grant, her friend's sweetheart, then gets her a position with a modiste. When a famous French model is scheduled to appear in a fashion show and fails to appear, Jane is forced to substitute for her and to cover her ignorance of French by responding *Non* to all questions. Robert Richmond, son of the owner, becomes infatuated with her, but to no avail, and Grant also makes advances to her. Richmond discovers her imposture, but after explanations he becomes convinced of her worth. *Cashiers. Fashion models. Modistes. Impersonation.*

THAT OLD GANG OF MINE **F2.5603**

Kerman Films. 18 Dec **1925** [New York State license]. Si; b&w. 35mm. 5 reels.

Dir-Writ May Tully.

Cast: Maclyn Arbuckle *(Senator Jim Walton)*, Brooke Johns *(musician)*, Tommy Brown *(Tom Pierce)*.

Comedy-drama. Suggested by the song by: Billy Rose, Ray Henderson and Mort Dixon, "That Old Gang of Mine" (1923). Just before an important primary, Senator Jim Walton and Tom Pierce, friends since boyhood, become engaged in a bitter rivalry that threatens to disrupt their party. During a political meeting, a speech by Walton so aggravates Pierce that the two men appear likely to come to blows. A musician then sings "That Old Gang of Mine," and, as memories come flooding back of a shared childhood on the East Side, Tom and Jim put aside all animosity. They later return to their old neighborhood and recall for each other the joys and sorrows of a Manhattan childhood. Their friendship is renewed, and they decide to join forces and present a united front to the opposition party. *Politicians. Childhood. New York City—East Side. United States Congress.*

"THAT ROYLE GIRL" **F2.5604**

Famous Players–Lasky. *Dist* Paramount Pictures. 7 Dec **1925** [c8 Dec 1925; LP22094]. Si; b&w. 35mm. 10 reels, 10,253 ft.

Pres by Adolph Zukor, Jesse L. Lasky. *Dir* D. W. Griffith. *Screenplay* Paul Schofield. *Photog* Harry Fischbeck, Hal Sintzenich. *Art Dir* Charles M. Kirk. *Film Ed* James Smith.

Cast: Carol Dempster *(Joan Daisy Royle [The Royle Girl])*, W. C. Fields *(her father)*, James Kirkwood *(Calvin Clarke [deputy district attorney])*, Harrison Ford *(Fred Ketlar [King of Jazz])*, Marie Chambers *(Adele Ketlar)*, Paul Everton *(George Baretta)*, George Rigas *(his henchman)*, Florence Auer *(Baretta's "girl")*, Ida Waterman *(Mrs. Clarke)*, Alice Laidley *(Clarke's fiancée)*, Dorothea Love *(Lola Neeson)*, Dore Davidson *(Elman)*, Frank Allworth *(Oliver)*, Bobby Watson *(Hofer)*.

Underworld melodrama. Source: Edwin Balmer, *That Royle Girl* (New York, 1925). Joan Daisy Royle is the daughter of a drunken confidence man and a sickly mother dependent upon drugs. A frail type, she has grown up innocent of the world's evils and finds inspiration in a statue of her ideal, Lincoln. She becomes a model, gets involved with a jazz set, and falls in love with Fred Ketlar, famous leader of a Chicago dancehall orchestra separated from his wife, Adele. Adele is killed, and Ketlar is arrested. Straitlaced Deputy District Attorney Calvin Clarke becomes strangely attracted to Daisy, though she is a witness for the defense. Ketlar is convicted, and as the day of his execution nears, Daisy works frantically to save him. Learning that gangster George Baretta is the real culprit, she attracts his attention, thus arousing the jealousy of his girl. In the resulting quarrel, Baretta confesses, but Daisy is discovered and imprisoned in a cellar. A cyclone wrecks the building; the gangsters are killed, but Daisy is safe. Clarke finds her and they marry, while Ketlar is freed and marries a chorus girl. *Fashion models. Confidence men. District attorneys. Gangsters. Swindlers. Narcotics. Capital punishment. Chicago. Abraham Lincoln. Cyclones.*

Note: Title also rendered: *D. W. Griffith's "That Royle Girl."*

THAT SOMETHING **F2.5605**

Hermann Film Corp. *Dist* Celebrated Players Film Corp. 8 Apr **1921** [trade review]. Si; b&w. 35mm. 5 reels.

Dir? (see note) Margery Wilson, Lawrence Underwood. *Photog* E. W. Willat.

Cast: Charles Meredith *(Edwin Drake)*, Margery Wilson *(Sarah Holmes)*, Nigel De Brulier, Eugenia Drake, John Hooper, Helen Wright, Carl Ulman, Gordon Griffith, James Farley, John Cossar.

Melodrama. Source: William Witherspoon Woodbridge, *That Something* (Tacoma, Washington, 1914). Edwin Drake, disowned by his wealthy father for lack of self-sufficiency, is unable to get a job and becomes a tramp. But after a prophetic vision he discovers his better self, and his regeneration begins. He obtains a job, quickly progressing to a key position. At the same time, Sarah Holmes is being taught to think positively by her friend, The Professor. Quite by accident, she meets Mrs. Drake, who takes a liking to her and treats her as her own daughter. One day Mrs. Drake is lamenting about her estranged son, showing Sarah a picture of Edwin. Sarah recognizes him as the young man who lives in her boardinghouse. She arranges for Mrs. Drake to be reunited with her now successful son, and eventually she becomes Mrs. Drake's daughter-in-law. *Tramps. Regeneration. Filial relations. Positivity. Visions.*

Note: Sources disagree in crediting direction.

THAT WILD WEST **F2.5606**

Phil Goldstone Productions. 15 Oct **1924**. Si; b&w. 35mm. 5 reels.

Dir Alvin J. Neitz. *Scen* J. F. Natteford. *Photog* Roland Price.

Cast: William Fairbanks, Dorothy Revier, Jack Richardson, Milton Ross, Margaret Cullington, Andrew Waldron *(sheriff)*.

Western melodrama. Source: J. F. Natteford, "The Bar-T Mystery" (publication undetermined). A society girl goes west to take over the management of her ranch, which has been going to ruin. She hires a cowhand as her foreman, but when the postmaster is killed, the foreman is accused of the murder on circumstantial evidence. A mob sets out to lynch the foreman, and he heads for the hills. The killer then kidnaps the girl and takes her to the camp of his outlaw gang. The foreman comes upon the camp in his travels and takes on the entire gang. As he is about to be killed, men from the ranch show up and subdue the outlaws. The killer is brought to justice, and the foreman and the girl realize their love for each other. *Socialites. Ranch foremen. Postmasters. Outlaws. Murder. Kidnaping. Lynching. Circumstantial evidence.*

THAT WOMAN **F2.5607**

F. C. Mims Productions. *Dist* American Releasing Corp. 31 Dec **1922**. Si; b&w. 35mm. 6 reels, 5,840 ft.

Dir Harry O. Hoyt. *Scen* Wallace Clifton. *Story* Sabin Wood.

Cast: Catherine Calvert *(Adora Winstanley)*, Joseph Bruelle *(William Arnold Kelvin)*, William Black *(William Kelvin)*, George Pauncefort *(Somerton Randall)*, William Ricciardi *(Morris Eltman)*, Jack Newton *(Hilary Weston)*, Norbert Wicki *(Mishu)*, Grace Field, Guy Coombes, Ralph Bunker.

Society drama. Adora Winstanley, Broadway's newest idol, receives the adoration of many wealthy men, but Billy Kelvin wins her heart. They are married—to the great displeasure of Billy's father, a leader in New York society, who offers money to Adora in exchange for Billy's freedom. She refuses, and Mr. Kelvin desperately hatches a plot in which a young man lures Adora to his yacht; she (Kelvin assumes) compromises herself, and Billy witnesses his wife's disgrace. Adora proves faithful, however, and the elder Kelvin finally concedes her worthiness. *Actors. Social classes. Marriage. Wealth. New York City—Broadway.*

THAT'S A BAD GIRL *see* **WHY BE GOOD?**

THAT'S MY BABY **F2.5608**

Famous Players–Lasky. *Dist* Paramount Pictures. call Apr **1926** [New York premiere; released 19 Apr; c20 Apr 1926; LP22627]. Si; b&w. 35mm. 7 reels, 6,805 ft.

Dir William Beaudine. *Adapt* Joseph Franklin Poland. *Story* George J. Crone, Wade Boteler. *Photog* Jack MacKenzie.

Cast: Douglas MacLean *(Alan Boyd)*, Margaret Morris *(Helen Raynor)*, Claude Gillingwater *(John Raynor)*, Eugenie Forde *(Mrs. John Raynor)*, Wade Boteler *(Dave Barton)*, Richard Tucker *(Schuyler Van Loon)*, Fred Kelsey *(Murphy)*, Harry Earles *(The Baby)*, William Orlamond *(drug clerk)*.

Farce. While rehearsing for his wedding, businessman Alan Boyd receives a telegram announcing the elopment of his prospective bride with another man, and he swears he is finished with women. An hour later he meets another girl, Helen Raynor, who admires him and is incidentally the daughter of a business rival; however, her mother takes an instant dislike to him. Schuyler Van Loon, a rival suitor, adds insult to injury by presenting him with a strange baby and insisting that Alan is the child's father; his efforts to rid himself of the baby are curtailed by a detective. When Mr. Raynor develops a headache, Alan gives him a medicine he later discovers to be poison. In his pursuit to warn Raynor, Alan and the baby become involved in numerous hilarious adventures. *Businessmen. Infants. Weddings. Courtship.*

THAT'S MY DADDY (Universal-Jewel) **F2.5609**

Universal Pictures. 5 Feb **1928** [c11 Nov 1927; LP24655]. Si; b&w. 35mm. 6 reels, 6,073 ft.

Pres by Carl Laemmle. *Dir* Fred Newmeyer. *Cont* Earl Snell. *Titl* Albert De Mond. *Adapt* Faith Thomas, Pierre Couderc. *Story* Reginald Denny. *Photog* Arthur Todd.

Cast: Reginald Denny *(Jimmy Norton)*, Barbara Kent *(Nora Moran)*, Lillian Rich *(Sylvia Van Tassel)*, Tom O'Brien *(Pat)*, Armand Kaliz *(Francis)*, Jane La Verne *(Pudge)*, Mathilde Brundage *(Mrs. Van Tassel)*, Wilson Benge *(Perkins)*, Rosa Gore, Charles Coleman, Arthur Currier.

Romantic comedy. Jimmy Norton, a wealthy, handsome young bachelor, is trapped into an engagement to Sylvia Van Tassel, a society girl, whom he does not love. When, en route to her house, he is stopped by a policeman for speeding, he explains that he is on his way to the Children's Hospital to see his injured child. The officer accompanies him, and there, by chance, Pudge, a runaway orphan, believes that Jimmy is actually her father. To avoid embarrassment Jimmy takes the child home, along with her nurse, Nora, and is forced to hide them from the Van Tassels. But the wedding is spoiled when Pudge climbs aboard Jimmy's yacht and calls him "Daddy" in front of the wedding guests. Greatly relieved, Jimmy decides to adopt the child, and Nora, who realizes his virtues, finds happiness in his arms. *Orphans. Nurses. Children. Police. Adoption. Hospitals. Weddings.*

THEIR HOUR **F2.5610**

Tiffany-Stahl Productions. 1 Mar **1928** [c26 Mar 1928; LP25103]. Si; b&w. 35mm. 6 reels, 5,652 ft.

Dir Alfred Raboch. *Titl* Viola Brothers Shore, Harry Braxton. *Story* Albert Shelby Le Vino. *Art Dir* Hervey Libbert. *Film Ed* Martin G. Cohn.

Cast: John Harron *(Jerry)*, Dorothy Sebastian *(Cora)*, June Marlowe *(Peggy)*, John Roche *(Bob)*, Huntley Gordon *(Mr. Shaw)*, Myrtle Stedman *(Peggy's mother)*, John Steppling *(Peggy's father)*, Holmes Herbert *(Cora's father)*.

Bedroom comedy. Jerry, a simple clerk, is lured away from Peggy, his sweetheart, by Cora, a pampered daughter of wealth. She takes him for a ride in her private plane and conveniently gets stranded near a rural inn, where during the night she seduces him. When Cora's fiancé arrives on the scene, Jerry comes to his senses and returns to Peggy, who forgives him. *Clerks. Seduction. Airplanes.*

THEIR OWN DESIRE **F2.5611**

Metro-Goldwyn-Mayer Pictures. 27 Dec **1929** [c6 Jan 1930; LP974]. Sd (Movietone); b&w. 35mm. 7 reels, 5,927 ft. [Also si.]

Dir E. Mason Hopper. *Adtl Dir–Dial* James Grant Forbes. *Screenplay* Frances Marion. *Photog* William Daniels. *Art Dir* Cedric Gibbons. *Film Ed* Harry Reynolds. *Mus Score* Fred Fisher, Reggie Montgomery, George Ward. *Song: "Blue Is the Night"* Fred Fisher. *Rec Engr* J. K. Brock, Douglas Shearer. *Gowns* Adrian.

Cast: Norma Shearer *(Lally)*, Belle Bennett *(Harriet)*, Lewis Stone *(Marlett)*, Robert Montgomery *(Jack)*, Helene Millard *(Beth)*, Cecil Cunningham *(Aunt Caroline)*, Henry Hebert *(Uncle Nate)*, Mary Doran *(Susan)*, June Nash *(Mildred)*.

Romantic drama. Source: Sarita Fuller, "Their Own Desire" (publication undetermined). When she discovers that her father is having a clandestine affair with another woman, Lally takes her mother, Harriet, to a resort, meets there a young man named Jack, and falls in love with him. After promising to marry him, she discovers that his mother is her father's mistress; and they decide to part. On a farewell boat ride they are caught in a storm, and the following morning they are reported missing. In their frantic search for them, Marlett and Beth (Lally's father and Jack's mother) realize the serious consequences of their affair, and reunion with their children brings about a return to their respective spouses. *Mistresses. Infidelity. Parenthood. Resorts. Storms.*

THELMA **F2.5612**

Chester Bennett Productions. *Dist* Film Booking Offices of America. 26 Nov **1922** [c25 Nov 1922; LP18430]. Si; b&w. 35mm. 6 reels, 6,497 ft.

Dir Chester Bennett. *Adapt* Thomas Dixon, Jr. *Camera* Jack MacKenzie. *Art Titl* Renaud.

Cast: Jane Novak *(Thelma Guildmar)*, Barbara Tennant *(Britta)*, Gordon Mullen *(Lovissa)*, Bert Sprotte *(Olaf Guildmar)*, Vernon Steel *(Sir Phillip Errington)*, Peter Burke *(Lorimer)*, Jack Rollens *(Sigurd)*, Harvey Clark *(Dyceworthy)*, June Elvidge *(Lady Clara Winsleigh)*, Wedgewood Nowell *(Lennox)*, Virginia Novak *(Little Thelma)*, Harry Lonsdale *(Neville)*.

Melodrama. Source: Marie Corelli, *Thelma, a Norwegian Princess* (London, 1887). Though loved by many in her Norwegian village home, Thelma herself does not know love until she meets Sir Phillip Errington. They are married and go to London, where she is well received except by Phillip's jealous "friends." Lady Clara and Lennox plot to make Phillip appear to be unfaithful, and Thelma returns to Norway. Phillip, however, pursues her and proves his innocence. *Social classes. Marriage. Infidelity. Norway. London.*

THEN CAME THE WOMAN **F2.5613**

David Hartford Productions. *Dist* American Cinema Association. 1 Aug **1926** [c5 Jun 1926; LP22799]. Si; b&w. 35mm. 7 reels, 6,805 ft.

Prod-Dir-Writ David Hartford. *Photog* Walter Griffin.

Cast: Frank Mayo *(John Hobart)*, Cullen Landis *(Bob Morris)*, Mildred Ryan *(Mary)*, Blanche Craig *(Mrs. McCann)*, Tom Maguire *(Mr. McCann)*.

Northwest drama. Bob Morris is given an opportunity in his father's factory after being expelled from college but loses his position because of his ungovernable temper. He is arrested by mistake while tramping through the Northwest, but John Hobart, a wealthy lumberman, has him released into his custody. After quelling Bob's fiery temper in a fight, Hobart becomes fast friends with the boy, who learns self-control and assumes many of Hobart's responsibilities. Bob persuades Hobart to marry the young widow of a college friend, but when Mary arrives, Bob falls in love with her against his will. Hobart resigns himself to their youthful romance, and when they are trapped by a raging forest fire, he heroically saves them and sacrifices his feelings for their happiness. *Lumbermen. Widows. Friendship. Self-sacrifice. Lumber camps. Forest fires.*

THERE ARE NO VILLAINS **F2.5614**

Metro Pictures. ca23 Oct **1921** [Atlanta premiere; released 14 Nov; c20 Jan 1922; LP17485]. Si; b&w. 35mm. 5 reels, 4,410 ft.

Prod-Dir Bayard Veiller. *Adapt* Mary O'Hara. *Photog* John Arnold. *Art Dir* A. F. Mantz.

Cast: Viola Dana *(Rosa Moreland)*, Gaston Glass *(John King)*, Edward Cecil *(George Sala)*, De Witt Jennings *(Detective Flint)*, Fred Kelsey *(Dugall)*, Jack Cosgrave *(Reverend Stiles)*.

Crook melodrama. Source: Frank Ramsay Adams, "There Are No Villains" (publication undetermined). Her failure to obtain evidence to convict George Sala of opium smuggling sends Rosa Moreland of the Secret Service on the trail of John King, an ex-soldier and cripple whom Rosa has met in Sala's office. By a ruse, Rosa gains access to King's apartment, and he provides a home for her. For the sake of helping Rosa, King joins the gang; and they move to an expensive apartment and soon fall in love. Rosa reports that King is above suspicion; nevertheless, Chief Flint suspects her and has her trailed. King agrees to give up his connection with Sala if Rosa will marry him, and realizing that she cannot testify against her husband, Rosa agrees. The wedding ceremony is interrupted by the arrival of Sala, who has discovered Rosa's identity; and when Flint arrives to arrest King, the latter is revealed to be a Secret Service man himself. *Veterans. Cripples. Secret service. Smugglers. Opium.*

THERE HE GOES *see* **SPORTING YOUTH**

THERE YOU ARE! **F2.5615**

Metro-Goldwyn-Mayer Pictures. 28 Nov **1926** [c21 Dec 1926; LP23584]. Si; b&w. 35mm. 6 reels, 5,652 ft.

Supv Harry Cohn. *Adapt-Cont* F. Hugh Herbert. *Titl* Ralph Spence. *Photog* Benjamin F. Reynolds. *Sets* Cedric Gibbons, Arnold Gillespie. *Film Ed* Arthur Johns. *Wardrobe* Kathleen Kay, Maude Marsh.

Cast: Conrad Nagel *(George Fenwick)*, Edith Roberts *(Joan Randolph)*, George Fawcett *(William Randolph)*, Gwen Lee *(Anita Grant)*, Eddie Gribbon *(Eddie Gibbs)*, Phillips Smalley *(J. Bertram Peters)*, Gertrude Bennett *(Mrs. Gibbs)*.

Farce. Source: F. Hugh Herbert, *There You Are* (New York, 1925). "Good natured but dull hero working in office loves employer's daughter. Through accident he captures bandit, becoming a hero and girl promises to marry him. There is a merry mix-up before the act is accomplished." (*Motion Picture News Booking Guide*, 12:59, Apr 1927.) *Office clerks. Bandits.*

THEY ALL WANT SOMETHING *see* **WHAT A MAN**

THEY HAD TO SEE PARIS **F2.5616**

Fox Film Corp. 8 Sep **1929** [c11 Sep 1929; LP675]. Sd (Movietone); b&w. 35mm. 9 reels, 8,602 ft. [Also si.]

Pres by William Fox. *Dir* Frank Borzage. *Stgd by* Bernard Steele. *Scen* Sonya Levien. *Dial* Owen Davis. *Titl* Wilbur Morse, Jr. *Photog* Chester Lyons, Al Brick. *Art Dir* Harry Oliver. *Film Ed* Margaret V. Clancey. *Song: "I Could Do It for You"* Sidney Mitchell, Archie Gottler, Con Conrad. *Sd* George P. Costello. *Asst Dir* Lew Borzage. *Cost* Sophie Wachner.

Cast: Will Rogers *(Pike Peters)*, Irene Rich *(Mrs. Peters)*, Owen Davis, Jr. *(Ross Peters)*, Marguerite Churchill *(Opal Peters)*, Fifi Dorsay *(Claudine)*, Rex Bell *(Clark McCurdy)*, Ivan Lebedeff *(Marquis de Brissac)*, Edgar Kennedy *(Ed Eggers)*, Bob Kerr *(Tupper)*, Christiane Yves *(Fleuril)*, Marcelle Corday *(Marquise de Brissac)*, Theodore Lodi *(Grand Duke Makiall)*, Marcia Manon *(Miss Mason)*, André Cheron *(valet)*, Gregory Gaye *(Prince Ordinsky)*.

Comedy-drama. Source: Homer Croy, *They Had To See Paris* (New York, 1926). Pike Peters, an Oklahoma garage owner, strikes it rich in oil. His wife insists on going to Paris, and there she tries to marry her daughter, Opal, to a mercenary count, Marquis de Brissac. A millstone around his wife's neck as far as her social aspirations are concerned, Peters tries to persuade her to return to Oklahoma. Peters finally induces her to return home by pretending he is having an affair with a chanteuse named Claudine. *Nouveaux riches. Garage-keepers. Singers. Social climbers. Nobility. Oil wells. Paris. Oklahoma.*

THEY LEARNED ABOUT WOMEN **F2.5617**

Metro-Goldwyn-Mayer Pictures. 31 Jan or 14 Feb **1930** [c3 Mar 1930; LP1117]. Sd (Movietone); b&w. 35mm. 11 reels. [Also si.]

Dir Jack Conway, Sam Wood. *Scen* Sarah Y. Mason. *Dial* Arthur "Bugs" Baer. *Titl* Alfred Block. *Story* A. P. Younger. *Photog* Leonard Smith. *Art Dir* Cedric Gibbons. *Film Ed* James McKay, Thomas Held. *Song: "Dougherty Is the Name"* Joseph T. Schenck, Gus Van. *Songs: "Harlem Madness," "He's That Kind of a Pal," "Ain't You Baby?" "A Man of My Own," "Does My Baby Love?" "There'll Never Be Another Mary," "Ten Sweet Mammas"* Jack Yellen, Milton Ager. *Dance Dir* Sammy Lee. *Rec Engr* Robert Shirley, Douglas Shearer. *Wardrobe* David Cox.

Cast: Joseph T. Schenck *(Jack)*, Gus Van *(Jerry)*, Bessie Love *(Mary)*, Mary Doran *(Daisy)*, J. C. Nugent *(Stafford)*, Benny Rubin *(Sam)*, Tom Dugan *(Tim)*, Eddie Gribbon *(Brennan)*, Francis X. Bushman, Jr. *(Haskins)*.

Musical-sports drama. Jack and Jerry, two major league baseball stars, entertain vocal ambitions; and after the World Series, the boys become a success in vaudeville. They fall in love with Mary, a dancer, but a vamp enters to break up the team and the boys return to play in another World Series. Ultimately, Mary and Jack are reunited. *Singers. Dancers. Vamps. Baseball. Vaudeville. World Series.*

THEY LIKE 'EM ROUGH **F2.5618**

Metro Pictures. 12 Jun **1922** [c12 Jun 1922; LP17962]. Si; b&w. 35mm. 5 reels, 4,700 ft.

Dir Harry Beaumont. *Story-Scen* Rex Taylor, Irma Whepley Taylor. *Photog* John Arnold. *Art–Tech Dir* A. F. Mantz.

Cast: Viola Dana *(Katherine)*, William E. Lawrence *(Richard Wells, Jr.)*, Hardee Kirkland *(Richard Wells, Sr.)*, Myrtle Richell *(Mrs. Wells)*, Colin Kenny *(Waddie)*, Steve Murphy *(Grogan)*, Walter Rodgers *(Kelly)*, Burton Law *(La Grande)*, W. Bradley Ward *(Pete)*, Knute Erickson *(Dr. Curtis)*, Elsa Lorimer *(Mrs. Curtis)*.

Comedy-drama. Katherine Trowbridge, a rebellious young orphan, lives with her aunt and uncle, the Curtises, who desire a match between Katherine and Weathersbee but pretend to oppose the union, knowing she will be the more likely to accept it. Accidentally discovering their trickery, she leaves home and determines to marry the first man who will have her. Consequently she offers herself to a bearded lumberjack (actually Dick Wells, a former suitor in disguise), and he accepts her. She is forced to go to a logging camp and there to cook and otherwise make herself useful. Kelly, a camp agitator, captures Katherine when she tries to escape from her husband, but Dick trails them and rescues her after a savage fight. When the doctor removes Dick's beard to dress a wound, Katherine recognizes him and finds that she has learned to love him. *Orphans. Lumberjacks. Courtship. Marriage. Disguise. Lumber camps.*

THEY SHALL PAY **F2.5619**

Playgoers Pictures. *Dist* Associated Exhibitors. 17 Aug **1921** [c19 Jul 1921; LU16774]. Si; b&w. 35mm. 6 reels, 5,200 ft.

Dir-Scen Martin Justine. *Photog* William O'Connell.

Cast: Lottie Pickford *(Margaret Seldon)*, Allan Forrest *(Allan Forbes)*, Paul Weigel *(Henry Seldon)*, Lloyd Whitlock *(Courtland Wells)*, George Periolat *(Amos Colby)*, Katherine Griffith *(Mrs. Yates)*.

Melodrama. Margaret Seldon's father, who has been victimized by three business associates and sent to prison, calls his daughter to him in his dying moments and asks her to avenge him. Through a detective agency she locates Amos Colby and Courtland Wells; and learning that the third man is dead, she adds his son, Allan Forbes, to the list. She foils Colby's attempt to ruin two financiers by gaining a position aboard his yacht. Disguised as a Spanish dancer, she appears at a reception given by Wells's fiancée, traps him into making love to her, and then exposes him. But she meets Forbes, Greenwich Village architect, and falls in love with him before learning his identity; stifling her feelings, she leaves him, but finding no satisfaction in pursuing her revenge, she returns. *Architects. Filial relations. Injustice. Revenge. New York City—Greenwich Village.*

THEY'RE OFF *see* **THE MARRIED FLAPPER**

THEY'RE OFF *see* **THE KENTUCKY DERBY**

THEY'RE OFF **F2.5620**

New Era Productions. *Dist* Anchor Film Distributors. 1 Oct **1922**. Si; b&w. 35mm. 5 reels, 4,381 ft.

Dir-Writ Francis Ford. *Titl* Marion C. Hatch. *Photog* O. G. Hill.

Cast: Peggy O'Day *(Slats/Mrs. Frank Blake [Peggy])*, Francis Ford *(Colonel Blake)*, Martin Turner *("Cellar," the colonel's servant)*, Frederick Moore *(Jim Blake, his half brother)*, Phil Ford.

Melodrama. Slats, a happy, harum-scarum girl of the mountains, and Peggy Blake, the unhappy, genteel wife of Colonel Blake, are twin sisters separated in infancy. Seeking excitement, Peggy goes to the hills, accidentally meets Slats, and persuades Slats to take her place while she pursues a theatrical career. Slats enjoys her role until the colonel's half brother, Jim, discovers the deception and tries to doublecross Blake with the information. On the day of the big horserace, Jim attacks Blake and disables his jockey, but Slats—facing arrest for the assault on Blake—escapes and rides the colonel's horse to victory. Learning of Slats's sacrifices and Peggy's death in a theater fire, Colonel Blake gladly accepts his "wife" as the real thing. *Sisters. Brothers. Twins. Jockeys. Impersonation. Horseracing. Theater. Mountain life.*

THICKER THAN WATER *see* **RAILROADED**

A THIEF IN PARADISE **F2.5621**

George Fitzmaurice Productions. *Dist* First National Pictures. 18 Jan **1925** [29 Dec 1924; LP20957]. Si; b&w. 35mm. 8 reels, 7,355 ft.

Pres by Samuel Goldwyn. *Dir* George Fitzmaurice. *Adapt* Frances Marion. *Photog* Arthur Miller.

Cast: Doris Kenyon *(Helen Saville)*, Ronald Colman *(Maurice Blake)*, Aileen Pringle *(Rosa Carmino)*, Claude Gillingwater *(Noel Jardine)*, Alec Francis *(Bishop Saville)*, John Patrick *(Ned Whalen)*, Charles Youree *(Philip Jardine)*, Etta Lee *(Rosa's maid)*, Lon Poff *(Jardine's secretary)*.

Society melodrama. Source: Leonard Merrick, *The Worldlings* (New York, 1900). Years of failure and bad luck have made Maurice Blake a beachcomber on an island in the Samoas, earning a precarious living by diving for pearls with Philip Jardine, the disinherited son of a San Francisco millionaire. When Philip is killed by a shark, his halfcaste common-law wife, Rosa, informs Maurice that Philip had been forgiven by his father, and she persuades him to assume Philip's identity and return to the States. Maurice's impersonation is successful: he is taken to heart by the elder Jardine and falls in love with Helen Saville, Philip's childhood sweetheart. After Maurice reluctantly declares his love, he and Helen are married, but before the contrite Maurice can explain his deception Rosa spitefully tells Helen of his masquerade. Helen leaves him, and he attempts to commit suicide. He is nursed back to health by Helen, who has forgiven him, and is later reconciled to the elder Jardine, who expresses the intention of adopting him. Rosa returns to paradise. *Halfcastes. Millionaires. Filial relations. Marriage—Common law. Pearl diving. Impersonation. Suicide. Samoa. Sharks.*

A THIEF IN THE DARK **F2.5622**

Fox Film Corp. 20 May **1928** [c13 Apr 1928; LP25172]. Si; b&w. 35mm. 6 reels, 5,937 ft.

Pres by William Fox. *Dir* Albert Ray. *Scen* C. Graham Baker. *Titl* William Kernell. *Story (see note)* Albert Ray, Kenneth Hawks, Andrew Bennison. *Photog* Arthur Edeson. *Film Ed* Jack Dennis. *Asst Dir* Horace Hough.

Cast: George Meeker *(Ernest)*, Doris Hill *(Elise)*, Gwen Lee *(Flo)*, Marjorie Beebe *(Jeanne)*, Michael Vavitch *(Professor Xeno)*, Noah Young *(Monk)*, Charles Belcher *(Duke)*, Raymond Turner *(Beauregard)*, Erville Alderson *(Armstrong)*, James Mason, Yorke Sherwood, Frank Rice, Tom McGuire.

Mystery-drama. A troupe of fake spiritualists traveling with a carnival are crooks on the side. Professor Xeno, a mystic, kills a "rich old bunny" for a case of jewels, while Ernest, the newest recruit, falls for Elise, the granddaughter. Ernest relents after his first job and turns hero by exposing Xeno as the murderer. Xeno meets his end when the jewel case, wired for burglars, blows up in his face when he opens it. *Thieves. Spiritualism. Murder. Carnivals.*

Note: Some sources credit Albert Ray and Andrew Bennison as coauthors of the story, while others credit Albert Ray and Kenneth Hawks.

THE THIEF OF BAGDAD **F2.5623**

Douglas Fairbanks Pictures. *Dist* United Artists. 18 Mar **1924** [New York premiere; released 1 Jan 1925; c23 Mar 1924; LP20112]. Si; b&w.

35mm. 14 reels, 12,933 ft. [Release length: 12 reels, 11,230 ft.]

Dir Raoul Walsh. *Scen Ed* Lotta Woods. *Story* Elton Thomas. *Photog* Arthur Edeson. *Asst Photog* P. H. Whitman, Kenneth MacLean. *Art Dir* William Cameron Menzies. *Consulting Art Dir* Irvin J. Martin. *Tech Dir* Robert Fairbanks. *Film Ed* William Nolan. *Mus Comp* Mortimer Wilson. *Asst Dir* James T. O'Donohoe. *Prod Mgr* Theodore Reed. *Cost Dir* Mitchell Leisen. *Master of Wardrobe & Prop* Paul Burns. *Dir Mech Eff* Hampton Del Ruth. *Consultant* Edward Knoblock. *Research Dir* Arthur Woods. *Assoc Artist* Anton Grot, Paul Youngblood, H. R. Hopps, Harold Grieve, Park French, William Utwich, Edward M. Langley. *Master Electrn* Albert Wayne. *Tech* Howard MacChesney, Clinton Newman, Walter Pallman, J. C. Watson. *Still Photog* Charles Warrington.

Cast: Douglas Fairbanks *(The Thief of Bagdad)*, Snitz Edwards *(His Evil Associate)*, Charles Belcher *(The Holy Man)*, Julanne Johnston *(The Princess)*, Anna May Wong *(The Mongol Slave)*, Winter-Blossom *(The Slave of the Lute)*, Etta Lee *(The Slave of the Sand Board)*, Brandon Hurst *(The Caliph)*, Tote Du Crow *(The Soothsayer)*, Sojin *(The Mongol Prince)*, K. Nambu *(His Counselor)*, Sadakichi Hartmann *(His Court Magician)*, Noble Johnson *(The Indian Prince)*, Mathilde Comont *(The Persian Prince)*, Charles Stevens *(His Awaker)*, Sam Baker *(The Sworder)*, Jess Weldon, Scotty Mattraw, Charles Sylvester *(eunuchs)*.

Adventure fantasy. Until he encounters the Princess, the Thief of Bagdad flouts religious teachings. Pretending to be a prince, he wins her love. After suffering humility and confessing the truth to the Holy Man, he is sent on a quest for a magic chest to earn his happiness. Overcoming tremendous obstacles, he wins the reward and rescues Bagdad and the Princess from the Mongols. *Thieves. Religion. Magic. Bagdad. Mongols.*

THINGS MEN DO **F2.5624**

Cyrus J. Williams. *Dist* M. B. Schlesinger. caApr **1921** [c12 Mar 1921; LU16265]. Si; b&w. 35mm. 5 reels, 5,000 ft.

Dir-Writ Robert North Bradbury. *Photog* L. W. McManigal.

Cast: Patricia Palmer *(The Girl)*, Edward Hearn *(The Boy)*, William Lion West *(Pixley)*, Gertrude Claire *(The Boy's Mother)*, William Moran *(The Spider)*, Dorothy Ketchum *(His Accomplice)*.

Melodrama. Source: Cyrus J. Williams, "Into the Light" (publication undetermined). A simple country girl, brutally mistreated by her stepfather, awakens first the sympathy and then the love of The Boy. The Spider, who lusts after The Girl, makes a bargain with the stepfather and takes her to the city, where, kept prisoner, she is soon broken in health and spirit. Cast out and near death, she is taken in by The Boy. Following the demise of The Spider, The Boy takes her to church, where he prays; and after many hours she is restored to health. *Stepfathers. Religion. Good and evil. Redemption.*

THINGS WIVES TELL **F2.5625**

Macfadden True Story Pictures. c23 Mar, 6 Apr **1926** [LU22550, LP22579]. Si; b&w. 35mm. 7 reels.

Dir Hugh Dierker. *Adapt* Lewis Allen Browne.

Crook melodrama. Disappointed by the refusal of his son, Carl, to join him in his shipbuilding business, Colonel Burgess seeks the help of his friend Judge Langhorne in diverting Carl from his hobby—criminology. Langhorne engages reformed crook Spike Hennessey to stage sufficient criminal activity to satisfy Carl's curiosity, and Spike further plans with Ben Felton and Kerrigan to plant Elaine Mackay in Carl's apartment. However, Ben and Red decide to play their blackmail threat for real; Carl marries Elaine, who, reforming, declines further connection with the conspiracy. Finally, coerced by Ben and Red, Elaine leaves Carl, who follows her and discovers the truth of the situation. Rescuing Elaine, Carl declares his intention to keep her as his wife; he receives his family's approval when it is learned that Elaine is the granddaughter of Langhorne's sister, and Burgess happily welcomes Carl into his business. *Criminals—Rehabilitation. Social classes. Judges. Criminology. Blackmail. Reputation. Shipbuilding.*

THE THIRD ALARM **F2.5626**

Emory Johnson Productions. *Dist* Film Booking Offices of America. ca24 Dec **1922** [Cleveland premiere; released 7 Jan 1923; c31 Dec 1922; LP18553]. Si; b&w. 35mm. 7 reels, 6,700 ft.

Pres by P. A. Powers. *Prod-Dir* Emory Johnson. *Story* Emilie Johnson. *Camera* Henry Sharp. *Asst Dir* Charles Watt.

Cast: Ralph Lewis *(Dan McDowell)*, Johnnie Walker *(Johnny McDowell)*, Ella Hall *(June Rutherford)*, Virginia True Boardman *(Mother McDowell)*, Richard Morris *(Dr. Rutherford)*, Josephine Adair *(Alice McDowell)*, Frankie Lee *(Little Jimmie)*, Bullet *(a horse)*.

Melodrama. Because Dan McDowell is unable to operate the new mechanized fire equipment, he is retired with a small pension; his son, Johnny, quits school to work in the fire department; and his old horse, Bullet, is sold to a dirt-hauler. Dan is charged with stealing Bullet and is jailed, but he is cleared in time to give valuable aid in a fire that traps Johnny's sweetheart, June Rutherford. *Filial relations. Fire departments. Retirement. Fires. Horses.*

THE THIRD ALARM **F2.5627**

Tiffany Productions. 17 Nov **1930** [c28 Nov 1930; LP1775]. Sd (Photophone); b&w. 35mm. 7 reels, 6,300 ft.

Dir Emory Johnson. *Cont-Dial* Frances Hyland, John F. Natteford. *Story* Emilie Johnson. *Photog* Max Dupont. *Art Dir* George Sawley. *Set Dsgn* Ralph De Lacy. *Sd Engr* Buddy Myers.

Cast: Anita Louise *(Milly Morton)*, James Hall *(Dan)*, Paul Hurst *(Beauty)*, Jean Hersholt *(Dad Morton)*, Hobart Bosworth *(captain)*, Mary Doran *(Neeta)*, Dot Farley *(woman barber)*, Nita Martan *(Mamie)*, George Billings *(Jimmy)*, Walter Perry *(uncle)*, Aileen Manning *(matron)*.

Melodrama. When fireman Dad Morton is killed on duty, leaving his two motherless children, Milly and Jimmy, orphans, two firemen, Dan and Beauty, propose to take the children into their care but are rejected because of their single status. Each, unknown to the other, decides to solve the problem by getting married. Dan proposes to Neeta, and she accepts. Milly is heart-broken over the news of their engagement, and Neeta notes her adoration of Dan; but Dan is arrested on the orphanage matron's charge of contributing to the delinquency of minors. Later, after his release, he realizes his feelings for Milly, prompted by Neeta. A fire breaks out in the orphanage, and the children are trapped. After the third alarm, Dan, though suspended, joins the firemen and rescues the children, including Milly, his bride-to-be. *Firemen. Orphans. Children. Brother-sister relationship. Marriage. Motherhood. Fires.*

THE THIRD DEGREE **F2.5628**

Warner Brothers Pictures. 25 Dec **1926** [c25 Dec 1926; LP23505]. Si; b&w. 35mm. 8 reels, 7,647 ft.

Dir Michael Curtiz. *Adapt* Graham Baker. *Camera* Hal Mohr. *Asst Camera* Edward Ulman. *Film Ed* Clarence Kolster. *Asst Dir* Henry Blanke.

Cast: Dolores Costello *(Annie Daly)*, Louise Dresser *(Alicia Daly)*, Rockliffe Fellowes *(Underwood)*, Jason Robards *(Howard Jeffries, Jr.)*, Kate Price *(Mrs. Chubb)*, Tom Santschi *("Daredevil Daly")*, Harry Todd *(Mr. Chubb)*, Mary Louise Miller *(Annie as a baby)*, Michael Vavitch *(Clinton, chief of detectives)*, David Torrence *(Howard Jeffries, Sr.)*, Fred Kelsey *(asst. chief of detectives)*.

Melodrama. Source: Charles Klein, *The Third Degree, a Play in Four Acts* (New York, 1908). Alicia, a circus artist, deserts her husband and child to elope with Underwood, her handsome lover. Fifteen years later, Annie Martin, Alicia's deserted daughter, is a trapeze performer in a sideshow at Coney Island, operated by Mr. and Mrs. Chubb, and has married Howard Jeffries in spite of opposition by his wealthy parents. Jeffries, Sr., hires a man (Underwood) to separate the young couple. Underwood convinces the newlyweds that each is being unfaithful to the other, and consequently he is threatened by Howard. Driven to fury by Underwood's insatiable demands, Alicia shoots him in a quarrel and makes her escape just as Howard enters; despite his innocence, Howard confesses to the crime when subjected to the third degree. Annie, realizing her mother's guilt, claims to be guilty, but Alicia then confesses. Annie is saved from suicide by Howard, and they are united by love. *Trapezists. Circus. Infidelity. Murder. Third degree. Coney Island.*

THIRST *see* **DESERT NIGHTS**

13 WASHINGTON SQUARE (Universal-Jewel) **F2.5629**

Universal Pictures. ca28 Jan **1928** [New York premiere; released 8 Apr; c11 Jan 1928; LP24861]. Si; b&w. 35mm. 6 reels, 6,274 ft.

Pres by Carl Laemmle. *Dir* Melville W. Brown. *Adapt-Cont* Harry O. Hoyt. *Titl* Walter Anthony. *Photog* John Stumar. *Film Ed* Ray Curtiss.

Cast: Jean Hersholt *("Deacon" Pyecroft)*, Alice Joyce *(Mrs. De Peyster)*, George Lewis *(Jack De Peyster)*, ZaSu Pitts *(Mathilde)*, Helen Foster *(Mary Morgan)*, Helen Jerome Eddy *(Olivetta)*, Julia Swayne Gordon *(Mrs. Allistair)*, Jack McDonald *(Mayfair)*, Jerry Gamble *(Sparks)*.

Comedy. Source: Leroy Scott, *No. 13 Washington Square* (Boston, 1914). In an attempt to break up the engagement of her son, Jack, to Mary, a grocer's daughter, aristocratic Mrs. De Peyster plans to take him to Europe. When he fails to appear at the steamer, Mrs. De Peyster sets out to foil their plan to elope. Exchanging clothes with her cousin, she and her maid go to the cousin's boardinghouse. There she meets art thief "Deacon" Pyecroft and learns that he plans to pilfer her house. So warned, she quickly returns home. Meanwhile, Jack and Mary have stopped off at the De Peyster home to get some of Jack's clothing. While all three are there, Pyecroft arrives, thinking the coast is clear. Finally, the police and reporters come, and, wishing to avoid scandal, Mrs. De Peyster gives her blessing to the young couple and introduces Pyecroft as her personal art critic! *Thieves. Motherhood. Social classes. Impersonation. Elopement. Art.*

THE THIRTEENTH CHAIR **F2.5630**

Metro-Goldwyn-Mayer Pictures. 19 Oct **1929** [c28 Oct 1929; LP794]. Sd (Movietone); b&w. 35mm. 8 reels, 6,571 ft. [Also si; 5,543 ft.]

Dir Tod Browning. *Scen-Dial* Elliott Clawson. *Titl* Joe Farnham. *Photog* Merritt B. Gerstad. *Art Dir* Cedric Gibbons. *Film Ed* Harry Reynolds. *Rec Engr* Paul Neal, Douglas Shearer. *Gowns* Adrian.

Cast: Conrad Nagel *(Richard Crosby)*, Leila Hyams *(Helen O'Neill)*, Margaret Wycherly *(Madame Rosalie La Grange)*, Helene Millard *(Mary Eastwood)*, Holmes Herbert *(Sir Roscoe Crosby)*, Mary Forbes *(Lady Crosby)*, Bela Lugosi *(Inspector Delzante)*, John Davidson *(Edward Wales)*, Charles Quartermaine *(Dr. Philip Mason)*, Moon Carroll *(Helen Trent)*, Cyril Chadwick *(Brandon Trent)*, Bertram Johns *(Howard Standish)*, Gretchen Holland *(Grace Standish)*, Frank Leigh *(Professor Feringeea)*, Clarence Geldert *(Commissioner Grimshaw)*, Lal Chand Mehra *(Chotee)*.

Mystery melodrama. Source: Bayard Veiller, *The Thirteenth Chair, a Play in Three Acts* (New York, 1922). The mysterious killing of writer Spencer Lee in Calcutta prompts authorities to consult Madame Rosalie La Grange, a reputedly successful medium. At a seance, Wales, Lee's best friend, is killed at the very moment he is about to reveal the murderer's identity; but through a reconstruction of the seance, the killer is frightened into a confession. Ample use is made of sounds emerging from a blackened screen to provide the proper effects. *Mediums. Authors. Murder. Spiritualism. Calcutta.*

THE THIRTEENTH HOUR **F2.5631**

Metro-Goldwyn-Mayer Pictures. 13 Oct **1927** [c24 Oct 1927; LP24548]. Si; b&w. 35mm. 6 reels, 5,252 ft.

Dir Chester Franklin. *Story-Screenplay* Douglas Furber, Chester Franklin. *Cont* Edward T. Lowe, Jr. *Titl* Wellyn Totman. *Photog* Maximilian Fabian. *Sets* Eugene Hornbostel. *Film Ed* Dan Sharits.

Cast: Lionel Barrymore *(Professor Leroy)*, Jacquelin Gadsdon *(Mary Lyle)*, Charles Delaney *(Matt Gray)*, Fred Kelsey *(Detective Shaw)*, Napoleon *(The Dog)*, Polly Moran *(Polly)*.

Mystery melodrama. "Professor Leroy, a noted Criminologist, is discovered by Detective Matt Gray, to be a criminal wanted for many murders. Closing in on him at the professor's home, Gray with the help of his dog, rescues a girl held captive, and the dog finally brings Leroy to retribution when the latter falls to death from a roof in a battle with the animal." (*Moving Picture World,* 3 Dec 1927, p26.) *Professors. Criminologists. Detectives. Murder. Dogs.*

THE THIRTEENTH JUROR (Universal-Jewel) **F2.5632**

Universal Pictures. 13 Nov **1927** [c3 Sep 1927; LP24380]. Si; b&w. 35mm. 6 reels, 5,598 ft.

Pres by Carl Laemmle. *Dir* Edward Laemmle. *Screenplay* Charles A. Logue. *Titl* Walter Anthony. *Photog* Ben Reynolds.

Cast: Anna Q. Nilsson *(Helen Marsden)*, Francis X. Bushman *(Henry Desmond)*, Walter Pidgeon *(Richard Marsden)*, Martha Mattox *(The Housekeeper)*, Sidney Bracy *(The Butler)*, Sailor Sharkey *(The Prisoner)*, Lloyd Whitlock *(The District Attorney)*, George Siegmann *(The Politician [George Quinn])*, Fred Kelsey *(The Detective)*.

Mystery melodrama. Source: Henry Irving Dodge, *Counsel for the Defense* (a play). Richard Marsden, married to Helen Fraine, is a long-time friend of Henry Desmond, a powerful and successful attorney. The district attorney and the political machine plan to break Desmond by having George Quinn infer that Marsden's wife is having an affair with the lawyer. An argument ensues between Quinn and Desmond; and in the struggle, Quinn is killed. Finding that Marsden has been arrested for the crime, Desmond, despite Helen's pleading, refuses to defend him because of a guilty conscience and his hope to win Helen's love for himself. At the climax of the trial, as Marsden is found guilty, Desmond confesses his guilt but is unable to convince the officials. Ultimately, Desmond produces evidence to prove his guilt, but he is released on a plea of self-defense, and the Marsdens are reaffirmed in their love. *Lawyers. Political corruption. Manslaughter. Friendship. Circumstantial evidence. Trials. Documentation.*

30 BELOW ZERO **F2.5633**

Fox Film Corp. 31 Oct **1926** [c7 Nov 1926; LP23335]. Si; b&w. 35mm. 5 reels, 4,691 ft.

Pres by William Fox. *Dir* Robert P. Kerr, Lambert Hillyer. *Story-Scen* John Stone. *Photog* Reginald Lyons. *Asst Dir* Daniel Keefe.

Cast: Buck Jones *(Don Hathaway, Jr.)*, Eva Novak *(Ann Ralston)*, E. J. Ratcliffe *(Don Hathaway, Sr.)*, Frank Butler *(Prof. Amos Hopkins)*, Paul Panzer *(Fighting Bill Ralston)*, Harry Woods *(Cavender)*, Fred Walton *(butler)*, Henry Murdock *(halfbreed Indian)*, Howard Vincent *(bootlegger)*.

Northwest melodrama. "Hero goes to Alaska to escape Follies girl and meets with accident. Girl helps him and takes him to her home where jealous rival accuses him of being a bootlegger, when he is the culprit himself. Hero proves innocence and defeats rival for affection of girl." (*Motion Picture News Booking Guide,* 12:59, Apr 1927.) *Chorus girls. Bootleggers. Courtship. Alaska.*

THIRTY DAYS **F2.5634**

Famous Players–Lasky. *Dist* Paramount Pictures. 10 Dec **1922** [New York premiere; released 8 Jan 1923; c14 Nov 1922; LP18525]. Si; b&w. 35mm. 5 reels, 4,930 ft.

Pres by Jesse L. Lasky. *Dir* James Cruze. *Adapt* Walter Woods. *Photog* Karl Brown.

Cast: Wallace Reid *(John Floyd)*, Wanda Hawley *(Lucille Ledyard)*, Charles Ogle *(Judge Hooker)*, Cyril Chadwick *(Huntley Palmer)*, Herschel Mayall *(Giacomo Polenta)*, Helen Dunbar *(Mrs. Floyd)*, Carmen Phillips *(Carlotta)*, Kalla Pasha *(warden)*, Robert Brower *(Professor Huxley)*.

Farce. Source: A. E. Thomas and Clayton Hamilton, *Thirty Days; a Farce in Three Acts* (New York, 1923). After being innocently friendly with an Italian woman, John Floyd tries to escape the wrath of Giacomo, her jealous husband, by having himself sentenced to jail for 30 days. But Giacomo also is sent to jail, and both are released at the same time. John explains matters to his fiancée, Lucille, and Giacomo is put on a ship before he can harm John. *Italians. Jealousy. Jails.*

THIRTY YEARS BETWEEN **F2.5635**

Dist Aywon Film Corp. **1921.** Si; b&w. 35mm. [Feature length assumed.]

Cast: Vera Stewart.

Melodrama(?). No information about the nature of this film has been found.

Note: Date indicated is approximate.

THIRTY YEARS LATER **F2.5636**

Micheaux Pictures. c25 Feb **1928** [LU25007]. Si; b&w. 35mm. 7 reels.

Dir-Writ Oscar Micheaux.

Cast: William Edmonson *(George Eldridge Van Paul)*, A. B. de Comatheire *(Habisham Strutt)*, Mabel Kelly *(Hester Morgan)*, Ardella Dabney *(Clara Booker)*, Gertrude Snelson *(Mrs. Van Paul)*.

Melodrama. Source: Henry Francis Downing, "The Tangle" (publication undetermined). George Eldridge Van Paul, the son of a white father and a Negro mother, is brought up to believe that he is completely white. He falls in love with Hester Morgan, a Negro girl, but when she learns that he is white, she refuses to see him. George is later told by his mother of his Negro heritage, and he becomes proud of his race. Hester then accepts his proposal of marriage. *Mulattoes. Negro life. Miscegenation.*

THIS IS HEAVEN **F2.5637**

Samuel Goldwyn, Inc. *Dist* United Artists. 22 Jun **1929** [c15 Jun 1929; LP505]. Talking sequences, mus score, & sd eff (Movietone); b&w. 35mm. 8 reels, 7,948 ft. [Also si; 7,859 ft.]

Pres by Samuel Goldwyn. *Dir* Alfred Santell. *Screenplay* Hope Loring. *Dial-Titl* George Marion, Jr. *Story* Arthur Mantell. *Photog* George Barnes, Gregg Toland. *Film Ed* Viola Lawrence. *Mus Score* Hugo Riesenfeld. *Song: "This Is Heaven"* Jack Yellen, Harry Akst.

Cast: Vilma Banky *(Eva Petrie)*, James Hall *(James Stackpoole)*, Fritzi Ridgeway *(Mamie Chase)*, Lucien Littlefield *(Frank Chase)*, Richard Tucker *(E. D. Wallace)*.

Romantic comedy. At Ellis Island in New York, Eva Petrie, a Hungarian immigrant, meets her uncle, Frank Chase, a subway motorman, and his daughter, Mamie, with whom she will reside in the Bronx. Mamie gets Eva a job as a cook and waitress at Child's Restaurant on Fifth Avenue and tries, unsuccessfully, to interest her in wealthy men. Eva spots Jimmy on the subway one morning wearing a chauffeur's cap, though he is actually a millionaire. Later, she is sent to preside over a griddle at a charity bazaar where she becomes reacquainted with Jimmy—pretending to be an exiled Russian princess. He realizes the deception and pretends to be a chauffeur. Eva and Jimmy, following a romantic courtship, are married, and she insists he go into the taxi business. Uncle Frank, however, gambles their last payment on a taxi and Eva is forced to borrow money from Mamie's wealthy lover; then Jimmy drops the pretense, revealing his true position in life, and Eva realizes "this ees Heaven!" *Hungarians. Immigrants. Cooks. Chauffeurs. Uncles. Subway motormen. Millionaires. Personal identity. Courtship. Bazaars. Restaurants. New York City. Ellis Island. Childs Restaurants.*

THIS MAD WORLD **F2.5638**

Metro-Goldwyn-Mayer Pictures. 12 Apr **1930** [c21 Apr 1930; LP1235]. Sd (Movietone); b&w. 35mm. 8 reels, 5,446 or 6,100 ft. [Also si.]

Dir William De Mille. *Dial* Clara Beranger, Arthur Caesar. *Titl* Madeleine Ruthven. *Adapt* Clara Beranger. *Photog* Peverell Marley, Hal Rosson. *Art Dir* Cedric Gibbons. *Film Ed* Anne Bauchens. *Sd Engr* J. K. Brock, Douglas Shearer. *Gowns* Adrian.

Cast: Kay Johnson *(Victoria)*, Basil Rathbone *(Paul)*, Louise Dresser *(Pauline)*, Veda Buckland *(Anna)*, Louis Natheaux *(Émile)*.

War melodrama. Source: François Curel, *Terre inhumaine, drame en trois actes* (Paris, 1923). Paul, a French secret agent, impelled by a mission and a desire to visit his mother, Pauline, lands behind German lines in Alsace-Lorraine and makes his way to her inn. He is recognized by Victoria, the wife of a German general who is there to keep a rendezvous with her husband. Her attempt to have him arrested is circumvented by their mutual attraction, not daunted by the fact that Paul has caused the death of her nephew. Later, in anguish over his confession, she tries to bring about his arrest and finally commits suicide over having betrayed her lover. When the Germans investigate her death, Pauline disclaims any knowledge of her son's identity in order to carry out herself his mission. Paul is executed by a firing squad. *Spies. French. Germans. Motherhood. Suicide. Capital punishment. World War I. Alsace-Lorraine.*

THIS THING CALLED LOVE **F2.5639**

Pathé Exchange. 13 Dec **1929** [c14 Dec 1929; LP921]. Sd (Photophone); b&w with col sequence (Technicolor). 35mm. 8 reels, 6,697 ft. [Also si; 6,687 ft.]

Assoc Prod Ralph Block. *Dir* Paul L. Stein. *Adapt-Dial* Horace Jackson. *Photog* Norbert Brodin. *Art Dir* Edward Jewell. *Film Ed* Doane Harrison. *Rec Engr* Charles O'Loughlin, Ben Winkler. *Asst Dir* E. J. Babille. *Cost* Gwen Wakeling. *Prop Man* Syd Fogel.

Cast: Edmund Lowe *(Robert Collings)*, Constance Bennett *(Ann Marvin)*, Roscoe Karns *(Harry Bertrand)*, ZaSu Pitts *(Clara Bertrand)*, Carmelita Geraghty *(Álvarez Guerra)*, John Roche *(De Witt)*, Stuart Erwin *(Fred)*, Ruth Taylor *(Dolly)*, Wilson Benge *(Dumary)*, Adele Watson *(secretary)*.

Romantic comedy. Source: Edwin Burke, *This Thing Called Love, a Comedy in Three Acts* (New York, 1929). Ann Marvin, who is thoroughly disillusioned about marital bliss because of the turbulence in her sister Clara's marriage, meets Robert Collings, a millionaire gold miner, while visiting her brother-in-law Bertrand's law office. Bertrand invites Collings to dinner, and before his arrival, Clara stages a battle royal over Bertrand's buying a dress for Álvarez Guerra, who is also invited to dinner, and the two women ultimately come to blows. When Collings proposes marriage to Ann, she compromises by offering to work as housewife for a salary ($25,000 a year); he accepts, agreeing that each will be free to consort with his own friends. When she remains indifferent to him, Collings arouses her jealousy by flirting with Miss Guerra; she responds by romancing De Witt. The reconciliation of the Bertrands, however, causes the Collingses to realize a genuine feeling for each other. *Sisters. Secretaries. Lawyers. Millionaires. Marriage of convenience. Gold mines.*

THIS WOMAN **F2.5640**

Warner Brothers Pictures. ca18 Oct **1924** [New York premiere; released 2 Nov; c30 Sep 1924; LP20619]. Si; b&w. 35mm. 7 reels, 6,842 ft.

Dir Phil Rosen. *Screenplay* Hope Loring, Louis Duryea Lighton. *Photog* Lyman Broening.

Cast: Irene Rich *(Carol Drayton)*, Ricardo Cortez *(Whitney Duane)*, Louise Fazenda *(Rose)*, Frank Elliott *(Gordon Duane)*, Creighton Hale *(Bobby Bleeker)*, Marc MacDermott *(Stratini)*, Helen Dunbar *(Mrs. Sturdevant)*, Clara Bow *(Aline Sturdevant)*, Otto Hoffman *(Judson)*.

Drama. Source: Howard Rockey, *This Woman* (New York, 1924). Facing poverty, Carol Drayton is prevented from suicide by Rose, a woman of the streets, who buys Carol a meal in a cafe of questionable reputation. The cafe is raided, and Carol is arrested and jailed on the false testimony of wealthy Gordon Duane. When she is released, Carol is again penniless until intoxicated Bobby Bleeker pays her to sing beneath the window of his sweetheart, Aline Sturdevant, where she is discovered by Stratini, a famous impresario. While studying with Stratini, Carol is blackmailed by the butler. Whitney Duane (Gordon's brother) falls in love with her but doubts her because of the gossip, and Carol incurs Aline's wrath by borrowing money from Bobby for Rose. Carol finally realizes her love for Stratini, who has remained loyal to her, and they are married. *Singers. Prostitutes. Brothers. Impresari. Blackmail. Suicide.*

THORNS AND ORANGE BLOSSOMS **F2.5641**

Preferred Pictures. *Dist* Al Lichtman Corp. 10 Dec **1922** [c11 Nov 1922; LP18588]. Si; b&w. 35mm. 7 reels, 6,971 ft.

Pres by B. P. Schulberg. *Dir* Louis J. Gasnier. *Adapt* Hope Loring. *Photog* Karl Struss. *Film Ed* Eve Unsell.

Cast: Estelle Taylor *(Rosita Mendez)*, Kenneth Harlan *(Alan Randolph)*, Arthur Hull *(Barnes Ramsey)*, Edith Roberts *(Violet Beaton)*, Carl Stockdale *(Colonel Beaton)*, John Cossar *(Pio Guerra, Rosita's manager)*, Evelyn Selbie *(Fallie, Rosita's maid)*.

Romantic drama. Source: Bertha M. Clay, *Thorns and Orange Blossoms* (New York, ca1883). On a trip to Spain, New Orleans businessman Alan Randolph and opera star Rosita Mendez fall in love, but Alan hastens home when he is reminded of his fiancée, Violet Beaton. Rosita follows him, but Alan, though his infatuation with Rosita is still strong, secretly marries Violet. In her jealousy Rosita tries to kill Alan but is herself wounded and accuses Alan, who is sentenced to prison. Rosita relents when she visits Violet and her baby, confesses to her perjury, and returns to Spain. *Businessmen. Singers. Perjury. Jealousy. New Orleans. Spain.*

THOROBRED **F2.5642**

Dist Clark-Cornelius Corp. 1 Aug **1922.** Si; b&w. 35mm. 5 reels, 4,204 ft.

Dir-Writ George Halligan.

Cast: Helen Gibson *(Helen)*, Robert Burns *(Ben Grey)*, Otto Nelson *(Pop Martin)*, Jack Ganzhorn *(Blackie Wells)*.

Western melodrama. "Helen Martin takes her father's place when he is too ill to carry out his duties as Sheriff, and followed by Jim Grey, tracks down Blackie Wells, notorious 'bad man,' who has shot up a town. The trail leads over prairie and woodland, ending when Helen assumes the part of a dancing girl in the Last Chance saloon and learns the hiding place of Blackie and his associates." (*Motion Picture News*, 21 Oct 1922, p2041.) *Sheriffs. Outlaws. Dancehall girls. Saloons.*

THE THOROUGHBRED **F2.5643**

Phil Goldstone Productions. *Dist* Truart Film Corp. 14 Jul **1925** [New York State license]. Si; b&w. 35mm. 6 reels, 5,481 ft.

Dir Oscar Apfel. *Scen* Leete Renick Brown. *Photog* Roland Price.

Cast: Maclyn Arbuckle *(Peter Bemis)*, Theodore von Eltz *(Robert Bemis)*, Gladys Hulette *(Mitzi Callahan)*, Hallam Cooley *(Dan Drummond)*, Virginia Brown Faire *(Gwen Vandermere)*, Carter De Haven, Thomas Jefferson, Robert Brower, Edith Yorke, Lillian Langdon.

Comedy-melodrama. Wealthy Peter Bemis insists that his nephew, Robert Bemis, break into high society. Robert makes a manful try but only succeeds in falling in love with Mitzi Callahan, a beautiful and goodhearted chorus girl. Robert then buys an old racehorse from Mitzi's father and later thrashes a man who makes improper advances to the girl. Robert is arrested on the false charge of giving a bad check, and the horse, entered in the big race, loses badly. Peter is cleared of the suspicion of guilt, and he and Mitzi are wed with his uncle's blessing. *Chorus girls. Upper classes. Horseracing. Horses.*

THE THOROUGHBRED **F2.5644**

Tiffany Productions. 10 Aug **1930** [c11 Aug 1930; LP1502]. Sd (Photophone); b&w. 35mm. 7 reels, 5,425 ft.

Dir Richard Thorpe. *Screenplay* John Francis Natteford. *Photog* Max Dupont. *Sets* Ralph De Lacy. *Film Ed* Clarence Kolster. *Rec Engr* Dean Daily.

Cast: Wesley Barry *(Tod Taylor)*, Nancy Dover *(Colleen Riley)*, Pauline Garon *(Margie)*, Larry Steers *(Drake)*, Robert Homans *(Riley)*, Walter Perry *(Donovan)*, Onest Conly *(Ham)*, Mildred Washington *(Purple)*, Madame Sul-Te-Wan *(Sacharine)*.

Melodrama. Riley and Donovan, racehorse owners and trainers who have been rivals and enemies for years, seek to befriend Tod Taylor, a jockey, and Ham, a retainer. Tod elects to work for Riley, incurring the enmity of rival jockeys. Riley's daughter, Colleen, sympathizes with Tod and cares for his bruises. Trying to befriend Donovan, Tod wins a match between Riley's colt, Reckless, and Donovan's best horse; and many more victories bolster his confidence. His head is turned by Margie, a come-on girl for Drake, a gambler. She precipitates his dissipation, and Tod is induced to throw the race to avoid a jail sentence. Nevertheless, Tod wins the race, and when he is arrested, Riley, learning of the circumstances, makes good the boy's debts and he is released. *Jockeys. Horsetrainers. Gamblers. Horseracing. Courtship.*

THOROUGHBREDS *see* **SILKS AND SADDLES**

THOSE THREE FRENCH GIRLS **F2.5645**

Metro-Goldwyn-Mayer Pictures. 11 Oct **1930** [c23 Oct 1930; LP1670]. Sd (Movietone); b&w. 35mm. 8 reels, 6,760 ft.

Dir Harry Beaumont. *Adapt-Cont* Sylvia Thalberg, Frank Butler. *Dial* Pelham Grenville Wodehouse. *Story* Dale Van Every, Arthur Freed. *Photog* Merritt B. Gerstad. *Art Dir* Cedric Gibbons. *Film Ed* George Hively. *Songs: "You're Simply Delish," "Six Poor Mortals"* Joseph Meyer, Arthur Freed. *Dance Dir* Sammy Lee. *Rec Engr* Douglas Shearer. *Wardrobe* René Hubert.

Cast: Fifi D'Orsay *(Charmaine)*, Reginald Denny *(Larry)*, Cliff Edwards *(Owly)*, Yola D'Avril *(Diane)*, George Grossmith *(Earl of Ippleton)*, Edward Brophy *(Yank)*, Peter Gawthorne *(Parker)*.

Comedy. Larry, an Englishman of noble birth, comes to the aid of three French modistes—Charmaine, Madelon, and Diane— when their landlord is about to evict them for not paying the rent; but a misunderstanding arises, and they are all sent to jail. There Larry meets Owly and Yank, two American ex-servicemen who have remained in France after the war. Together, they manage to escape and go to Larry's estate where the Earl of Ippleton, Larry's uncle, becomes infatuated with Charmaine and, thinking that Larry has been untrue to her, plans to marry her. But it develops that the earl has used Larry's name to cover his own indiscretions, and Larry claims Charmaine as his own. *Veterans. Nobility. Modistes. Landlords. Uncles. French. English. Jailbreaks. France.*

THOSE WHO DANCE **F2.5646**

Thomas H. Ince Productions. *Dist* Associated First National Pictures. 27 Apr **1924** [c21 May 1924; LP20228]. Si; b&w. 35mm. 8 reels, 7,312 ft.

Pres by Thomas H. Ince. *Pers Supv* Thomas H. Ince. *Dir* Lambert Hillyer. *Adapt* Lambert Hillyer, Arthur Statter. *Story* George Kibbe Turner.

Cast—Original Version: Blanche Sweet *(Rose Carney)*, Bessie Love *(Vida)*, Warner Baxter *(Bob Kane)*, Robert Agnew *(Matt Carney)*, John Sainpolis *(Monahan)*, Lucille Ricksen *(Ruth Kane)*, Matthew Betz *(Joe the Greek)*, Lydia Knott *(Mrs. Carney)*, Charles Delaney *(Tom Andrus)*, W. S. McDonough *(Bob Kane's father)*, Jack Perrin *(Frank Church)*, Frank Campeau *("Slip" Blaney)*.

Cast—Revised: Blanche Sweet *(Ruth Jordan)*, Bessie Love *(Veda Carney)*, Warner Baxter *(Robert Kane)*, Matthew Betz *("Red" Carney)*, John Sainpolis *(Chief Monahan)*, Lucille Ricksen *(Mary Kane)*, Lydia Knott *(Mrs. Jordan)*, Robert Agnew *(Matt Jordan)*, Frank Campeau *(Blaney)*.

Melodrama. Bootleg liquor causes an automobile wreck that blinds a young driver, Bob Kane, and kills his sister. Declaring war on moonshiners, Kane helps Rose Carney (Ruth Jordan) save her brother, Matt, who works for a rumrunner, when he is framed for killing a dry agent. *Government agents. Bootlegging. Murder. Frameup. Blindness. Automobile accidents. Prohibition.*

Note: The "revised" cast was listed in *Motion Picture News* and was referred to in other trade reviews. Remade in 1930 by Warner Brothers under the same title, q. v.

THOSE WHO DANCE **F2.5647**

Warner Brothers Pictures. 19 Apr **1930** [c7 Apr 1930; LP1215]. Sd (Vitaphone); b&w. 35mm. 7 reels, 6,876 ft. [Also si.]

Dir William Beaudine. *Scen-Dial* Joseph Jackson. *Story* George Kibbe Turner. *Photog* Sid Hickox. *Film Ed* George Amy. *Rec Engr* Clare A. Riggs.

Cast: Monte Blue *(Dan Hogan)*, Lila Lee *(Nora Brady)*, William Boyd *("Diamond Joe" Jennings)*, Betty Compson *(Kitty)*, William Janney *(Tim Brady)*, Wilfred Lucas *("Big Ben" Benson)*, Cornelius Keefe *(Pat Hogan)*, De Witt Jennings *(Captain O'Brien)*, Gino Corrado *(Tony)*, Bob Perry *(bartender)*, Charles McAvoy *(prison guard)*, Kernan Cripps *(detective)*, Richard Cramer *(Steve Daley)*, Harry Semels, Nick Thompson, Frank Mills, Lew Meehan *(hoods)*.

Underworld melodrama. Detective Benson, secretly allied with a gang of thieves, arrests young Tim Brady, who is framed for a murder and sentenced to die, though Diamond Joe Jennings promises Tim's sister that through his influence with the governor he will endeavor to free Tim. Nora Brady takes refuge with Joe and his moll, Kitty, who tells her Joe wants Tim to die so as to cover the crime. Nora informs the police, who assign Dan Hogan, brother of Pat, the murder victim, to aid her; under the alias of "Scar" Sherman, he is introduced to Joe, and with the aid of a dictograph he learns of Tim's innocence. At a dance, the gangsters expose him as an imposter, but Benson shoots Joe to protect himself just as the police, who have been called by Kitty, arrive. Dan arrests Benson, the execution is stayed, and Dan and Nora find happiness together. *Gangsters. Molls. Detectives. State governors. Brother-sister relationship. Imposture. Frameup. Dictographs.*

Note: Remake of a 1924 Associated First National Film of the same title. Also produced in French and German versions: *Contre-Enquête, Der Tanz Geht Weiter,* q. v.

THOSE WHO DARE **F2.5648**

Creative Pictures. 15 Nov **1924.** Si; b&w. 35mm. 6 reels.

Dir John B. O'Brien. *Adapt* Frank Beresford. *Story* I. W. Irving. *Photog* Devereaux Jenkins.

Cast: John Bowers *(Captain Manning)*, Marguerite De La Motte *(Marjorie)*, Joseph Dowling *(David Rollins)*, Claire McDowell *(Mrs. Rollins)*, Martha Marshall *(Cecelia Thorne)*, Edward Burns *(Harry Rollins)*, Spottiswoode Aitken *(Thorne Wetherell)*, Sheldon Lewis *(Serpent Smith)*, Cesare Gravina *(Panka)*.

Melodrama. Captain Manning, a seasoned salt, is ordered to remove his battered ship, the *Swallow,* from the town's harbor because of a superstition connected with it. The captain, who lives alone, then goes to the Mariner's Home and there relates the story of how he came into possession of the schooner. *Manning was the first mate on the yacht of a wealthy man when it encountered the* Swallow *at sea. Manning went on board, accompanied by the drug-addicted son of his employer, and discovered a mutinous crew and a disabled captain fighting for control of the ship. Manning took charge and brought the ship safely to port, after successfully putting down the mutineers by humiliating their leader, who had kept them in fear by practicing voodoo in the ship's hold. Manning later married the daughter of the* Swallow's *captain.* Now he controls the ship. *Sea captains. Drug addicts. Mutiny. Voodoo. Schooners. Yachts.*

Note: Jenkins (Photog) may be a misspelling of Dev Jennings.

THOSE WHO JUDGE **F2.5649**

Banner Productions. 15 Oct **1924** [c17 Nov 1924; LP20780]. Si; b&w. 35mm. 6 reels, 5,700 ft.

Dir Burton King. *Adapt* Harry Chandlee.

Cast: Patsy Ruth Miller *(Angelique Dean)*, Lou Tellegen *(John Dawson)*, Mary Thurman *(Kitty Drexel)*, Flora Le Breton *(Shirley Norton)*, Edmund Breese *(Henry Dawson)*, Walter Miller *(Bob Dawson)*, Coit Albertson *(Chapman Griswold)*, Cornelius Keefe *(Tom Eustace)*, John Henry *(Major Twilling)*.

Society melodrama. Source: Margery Land May, *Such As Sit in Judgement* (London, 1923). In spite of Angelique Dean's seeming friendship for Chapman Griswold, a society bum, John Dawson falls in love with her and asks the charming and mysterious "widow" to marry him. John then learns from Griswold that Angelique has never been married. When John breaks off the engagement, Angelique is forced to accept Griswold's proposal of marriage, fearing that he will expose the fact that she had been inveigled into a mock marriage with Major Twilling, a British officer. When John, however, learns that Angelique had sacrificed her reputation in order to protect Twilling from scandal, he prevents her marriage to Griswold and marries her himself. *English. Courtship. Marriage of convenience. Reputation.*

THOU SHALT NOT LOVE **F2.5650**

Eiko Film Co. *Dist* Graphic Film Corp. 1 Feb **1922.** Si; b&w. 35mm. 6 reels.

Cast: Vivian Le Picard.

Drama. "A hindoo maid, according to East India's religious custom, when 12 years old marries a boy of the same age. Boy is drowned soon after the ceremony. The girl vows never to love another. Later meets Parisian artist and realizes she loves him. They are separated, but meet again and acknowledge their love. but the vow comes between them. Finally, she renounces her superstitious faith and they are happy." (*Motion Picture News Booking Guide*, 2:75, Apr 1922.) *Artists. Parisians. Hinduism. India.*

Note: Country of origin not determined.

THREE AGES **F2.5651**

Buster Keaton Productions. *Dist* Metro Pictures. 24 Sep **1923** [c25 Jul 1923; LP19231]. Si; b&w. 35mm. 6 reels, 5,251 ft.

Prod Joseph M. Schenck. *Dir* Buster Keaton, Eddie Cline. *Story-Titl* Clyde Bruckman, Joseph Mitchell, Jean Havez. *Photog* William McGann, Elgin Lessley. *Art Dir* Fred Gabourie.

Cast: Buster Keaton *(The Hero)*, Margaret Leahy *(The Girl)*, Wallace Beery *(The Villain)*, Joe Roberts *(The Father)*, Horace Morgan *(The Emperor)*, Lillian Lawrence *(The Mother)*.

Comedy. "The hero faces the problem of the lover with a formidable rival in three ages. In the stone age he and his rival throw giant pebbles at each other and eventually he drags off the girl by the hair. In the Roman age a chariot race settles the competition and in the modern age he has to combat with the most popular asset of the suitor of today—wealth. Just as the girl is about to wed the moneyed suitor, the hero makes a bold play for her, however, and wins." (*Moving Picture World*, 8 Sep 1923, p155.) *Courtship. Prehistory. Rome—History—Empire.*

THREE AT THE TABLE *see* **THE UNKNOWN WIFE**

THREE BAD MEN **F2.5652**

Fox Film Corp. 13 Aug **1926** [trade showing; released 28 Aug; c22 Aug 1926; LP23044]. Si; b&w. 35mm. 9 reels, 8,710 ft.

Pres by William Fox. *Dir* John Ford. *Adapt-Scen* John Stone. *Titl* Ralph Spence, Malcolm Stuart Boylan. *Photog* George Schneiderman. *Asst Dir* Edward O'Fearna.

Cast: George O'Brien *(Dan O'Malley)*, Olive Borden *(Lee Carlton)*, Lou Tellegen *(Layne Hunter)*, J. Farrell MacDonald *(Mike Costigan)*, Tom Santschi *(Bull Stanley)*, Frank Campeau *(Spade Allen)*, George Harris *(Joe Minsk)*, Jay Hunt *(old prospector)*, Priscilla Bonner *(Millie Stanley)*, Otis Harlan *(Zack Leslie)*, Walter Perry *(Pat Monahan)*, Grace Gordon *(Millie's pal)*, Alec B. Francis *(Rev. Calvin Benson)*, George Irving *(General Neville)*, Phyllis Haver *(Prairie Beauty)*, Vester Pegg, Bud Osborne.

Western melodrama. Source: Herman Whitaker, *Over the Border; a Novel* (New York, 1917). In the 1870's when the lands of the Dakota Indians are finally opened to settlers and prospectors, three outlaws—Mike Costigan, Bull Stanley, and Spade Allen—wanted from Mexico to Canada, join the rush. Though they are horsethieves, they decide not to rob Lee Carlton, a southern girl, of her thoroughbreds when her father's wagon is attacked and he is killed by a rival gang. The trio band together to protect the girl and her sweetheart, Dan O'Malley. They guard the trail up a mountain as Lee and Dan are pursued by the gang of Layne Hunter, a crooked sheriff, to stake out a valuable claim. One by one the three men are dropped by the villain's gunman, though Hunter is himself killed in the gunplay. *Dakota Indians. Outlaws. Horsethieves. Sheriffs. Mine claims. Land rushes.*

Note: Filmed on location in Jackson Hole, Wyoming, and in the Mojave Desert.

THE THREE BUCKAROOS **F2.5653**

Balshofer Productions. *Dist* American Releasing Corp. 16 Apr **1922.** Si; b&w. 35mm. 5 reels, 4,599 ft.

Dir-Story-Scen Fred J. Balshofer.

Cast: Buck Humes *(Dartigan)*, Peggy O'Dare *(Constance Kingsley)*, Monty Montague *(Athor)*, "Tex" Keith *(Forthor)*, "Silent Bill" Conant *(Aramor)*, Allan Garcia *("Card" Ritchie)*, Cleo Childers *(Flores)*.

Western melodrama. Dartigan, an adventure-seeking Nebraskan with a broken-down horse, seeks the famous Three Buckaroos and receives their challenges to three individual pistol duels when he stumbles onto them. En route to these appointments he meets and falls in love with Constance Kingsley, and he valiantly assists the Buckaroos in repulsing an attack by cattle rustlers at the rendezvous. Thus, Dartigan is allowed to take the oath of The Three Buckaroos, which forbids him to declare his love to Constance. Led by Dartigan, the Buckaroos engage in many valorous exploits and finally round up the rustlers—freeing Dartigan to tell Constance what she has been waiting to hear. *Cowboys. Nebraskans. Rustlers. Duels.*

THREE DAYS *see* **HOW TO HANDLE WOMEN**

THREE DAYS TO LIVE **F2.5654**

Paul Gerson Pictures. *Dist* Renown Pictures. 22 Apr **1924** [New York showing]. Si; b&w. 35mm. 5 reels.

Dir-Writ Tom Gibson.

Cast: Ora Carew *(Grace Harmon)*, Jay Morley *(Bob Raymond)*, Dick La Reno *(Wolf Raymond)*, Hal Stephens *(Rajah)*, Helen Lowell *(Hadj)*, James Lono *(Hakim)*.

Melodrama. Rajah comes to America in search of three men who humiliated him in his own kingdom by forcing him to kiss the dust after severely beating a slave. Seeking revenge he has two of the men killed and warns the third that he has only 3 days to live. Grace intercedes and saves the man's life. *Royalty. Revenge. Reputation.*

THREE FACES EAST **F2.5655**

Cinema Corp. of America. *Dist* Producers Distributing Corp. 3 Feb **1926** [New York showing; c14 Dec 1925; LP22130]. Si; b&w. 35mm. 7 reels, 7,419 ft.

Pres by Cecil B. De Mille. *Dir* Rupert Julian. *Adapt* C. Gardner Sullivan, Monte Katterjohn. *Photog* Peverell Marley. *Film Ed* Claude Berkeley. *Rec Engr* Clifford A. Ruberg.

Cast: Jetta Goudal *(Miss Hawtree/Fräulein Marks)*, Robert Ames *(Frank Bennett)*, Henry Walthall *(George Bennett)*, Clive Brook *(Valdar)*, Edythe Chapman *(Mrs. Bennett)*, Clarence Burton *(John Ames)*, Ed Brady *(Firking)*.

Melodrama. Source: Anthony Paul Kelly, *Three Faces East; a Drama in a Prologue and Three Acts* (New York, 1935). While a prisoner of war in Germany, Frank Bennett is attended by Fräulein Marks, a German nurse to whom he is greatly attracted. Fräulein Marks is captured in a British raid and turns out to be Miss Hawtree of the British Secret Service. She is sent to the home of George Bennett, the head of the War Office, with instructions to run to ground a German spy named Boelke. At Bennett's home, Miss Hawtree gives the appearance of falling in love with Valdar, a servant who has been wounded in the war. Valdar turns out to be Boelke in disguise, and Miss Hawtree is responsible for his death. After the war, Frank looks forward to a happy future with Miss Hawtree. *Prisoners of war. Nurses. Domestics. Spies. Secret service. World War I. Great Britain—War Office. Germany.*

THREE FACES EAST **F2.5656**

Warner Brothers Pictures. 26 Aug **1930** [c11 Jul 1930; LP1412]. Sd (Vitaphone); b&w. 35mm. 9 reels, 6,120 ft.

Dir Roy Del Ruth. *Screenplay-Dial* Oliver H. P. Garrett, Arthur Caesar. *Camera* Bernard McGill. *Film Ed* William Holmes. *Rec Engr* Harry D. Mills.

Cast: Constance Bennett *(Frances Hawtree)*, Erich von Stroheim *(Valdar)*, Anthony Bushell *(Arthur Chamberlain)*, William Courtenay *(Mr. Yates)*, Crauford Kent *(General Hewlett)*, Charlotte Walker *(Lady Chamberlain)*, William Holden *(Sir Winston Chamberlain)*.

Spy melodrama. Source: Anthony Paul Kelly, *Three Faces East* (1918). The plot is similar to that of the 1925 silent version. *Nobility. English. Valets. Housemaids. Inheritance. Impersonation. Drunkenness.*

THREE HOURS **F2.5657**

Corinne Griffith Productions. *Dist* First National Pictures. 5 Mar **1927** [New York premiere; released 3 Apr; c23 Feb 1927; LP23693]. Si; b&w. 35mm. 6 reels, 5,774 ft. [Copyrighted as 7 reels.]

Pres by Asher-Small-Rogers. *Prod* E. M. Asher. *Dir* James Flood. *Screenplay* Paul Bern. *Photog* Harry Jackson.

Cast: Corinne Griffith *(Madeline Durkin)*, John Bowers *(James Finlay)*, Hobart Bosworth *(Jonathan Durkin)*, Paul Ellis *(Gilbert Wainwright)*, Anne Schaefer *(The Governess)*, Mary Louise Miller *(Baby Durkin)*.

Melodrama. Source: May Edginton, "Purple and Fine Linen," in *Bedside Book of Famous British Stories* (New York, 1940). Madeline Durkin, formerly married to one of San Francisco's wealthiest men, is reduced to poverty and longs to see her baby. She resorts to begging on the street. Young James Finlay is about to give her some money when a distraction enables her to steal his wallet and escape. He traces her to a shop where she arrays herself in fine attire, but Finlay takes her in a taxi to the police station; she begs for 3 hours' reprieve, and he agrees. She goes with him to his apartment, and in flashback her story is revealed: *She has been accused of having an affair with a man named Wainwright, and in a divorce action she loses custody of her child; she is permitted to see the child once, this very evening.* Finlay goes with her to the home of her husband, where she finds the child dead. She finds consolation in the love of Finlay. *Pickpockets. Children. Motherhood. Divorce. Poverty. San Francisco.*

THREE IN EXILE **F2.5658**

Truart Film Corp. 30 Oct **1925** [c24 Jul 1925; LP21672]. Si; b&w. 35mm. 5 reels, 4,474 ft.

Dir Fred Windemere. *Story* George Hively.

Cast: Louise Lorraine *(Lorraine Estes)*, Art Acord *(Art Flanders)*, Tom London *(Jed Hawkins)*, Rex *(a dog)*, Black Beauty *(a horse)*.

Western melodrama. Following a fight, Art Flanders is forced to leave town and wanders into the desert, where he meets a dog and a horse. The three stick together, and just as they are about to die of thirst, they chance upon the house of Lorraine Estes. Lorraine takes care of the trio, and, out of gratitude and growing love, Art begins to do the manual labor necessary to keep her mine going. Jed Hawkins, who wants to gain possession of Lorraine's land, sends several of his men to dynamite the mine, but Art and Black Beauty run them off. Hawkins is punished, and Art marries Lorraine. *Miners. Mines. Deserts. Thirst. Dogs. Horses.*

THREE JUMPS AHEAD **F2.5659**

Fox Film Corp. 25 Mar **1923** [c25 Mar 1923; LP19147]. Si; b&w. 35mm. 5 reels, 4,854 ft.

Pres by William Fox. *Dir-Writ* Jack Ford. *Photog* Dan Clark.

Announced Cast: Tom Mix *(Steve McLean)*, Alma Bennett *(Ann Darrell)*, Edward Piel *(Buck Taggitt)*, Joe Girard *(John Darrell)*, Virginia True Boardman *(Mrs. Darrell)*, Margaret Joslin *(Alicia)*, Frank Forde *(Ben McLean)*, Harry Todd *(Lige McLean)*.

Alternate Cast: Tom Mix *(Steve Clancy)*, Alma Bennett *(Annie Darrell)*, Virginia True Boardman *(Mrs. Darrell)*, Edward Piel *(Taggitt)*, Joe Girard *(Annie's father)*, Francis Ford *(Virgil)*, Margaret Joslin *(Juliet)*, Harry Todd *(Cicero)*, Buster Gardner *(Brutus)*.

Western melodrama. Steve McLean and his uncle are captured by outlaws and taken to a hideout where they meet John Darrell, who has been a captive for 2 years. Darrell escapes, and the gang leader promises McLean his freedom if he will bring Darrell back. McLean agrees and meets Ann, with whom he falls in love. He captures Darrell and returns him to the outlaws. He then learns that Darrell is Ann's father, and he sets out to rescue him. *Gangs. Hostages. Fatherhood.*

Note: Working title: *The Hostage.* The alternate cast is listed in Peter Bogdanovich's *John Ford* (Berkeley, 1968). (Possibly, Frank Forde is intended to be Francis Ford.) The character played by Tom Mix is also rendered as Boone McLean, Alma Bennett's as Anna Darrell, and Edward Piel's as Burk Taggert.

THREE KEYS **F2.5660**

Banner Productions. 1 Jan **1925** [10 Dec 1924; LP20903]. Si; b&w. 35mm. 6 reels, 5,800 ft.

Ben Verschleiser Production. *Dir* Edward J. Le Saint. *Scen* Robert Dillon. *Photog* Ernest Haller.

Cast: Edith Roberts *(Clarita Ortega)*, Jack Mulhall *(Jack Millington)*, Gaston Glass *(George Lathrop)*, Virginia Lee Corbin *(Edna Trevor)*, Miss Du Pont *(Alice Trevor)*, Charles Clary *(John Trevor)*, Stuart Holmes *(Fenwick Chapman)*, Joseph W. Girard *(Sam Millington)*.

Society melodrama. Source: Frederic V. R. Dey, *Three Keys* (New York, 1909). When John Trevor is about to go broke on Wall Street, George Lathrop, who is engaged to Trevor's daughter, Alice, promises to lend him $100,000. Since he has squandered his own inheritance, George obtains the sum by the theft of some negotiable securities from wealthy Sam Millington, whose son, Jack, has entrusted him with the keys to the family safe. Alice finds out that George is frequently visited by Clarita Ortega at his apartment, and, suspecting him of infidelity, she breaks the engagement. Jack Millington, discovering both the theft and the reason for it, decides to clear George: he lends Trevor the necessary capital, buys back the stolen securities, and, by faking an automobile accident, convinces his father that the securities have been in his possession the whole time. George realizes that he loves Clarita, who is his ward, and who turns out to be the long-lost daughter of John Trevor. Alice marries an Italian count. *Theft. Parentage. Finance—Personal. New York City—Wall Street.*

THREE LIVE GHOSTS **F2.5661**

Famous Players–Lasky. *Dist* Paramount Pictures. ca1 Jan **1922** [New York premiere; released 29 Jan; c25 Jan 1922; LP17508]. Si; b&w. 35mm. 6 reels, 5,784 ft.

Pres by Adolph Zukor. *Dir* George Fitzmaurice. *Scen* Ouida Bergère. *Photog* Arthur Miller.

Cast: Anna Q. Nilsson *(Ivis)*, Norman Kerry *(Billy Foster)*, Cyril Chadwick *(Spoofy)*, Edmund Goulding *(Jimmy Gubbins)*, John Miltern *(Peter Larne)*, Claire Greet *(Mrs. Gubbins)*, Annette Benson *(Miss Woofers)*, Dorothy Fane *(The Duchess)*, Windham Guise *(Briggs)*.

Comedy-melodrama. Source: Frederic Stewart Isham and Max Marcin, *Three Live Ghosts* (a play; New York, 1922). Three men who have escaped from a German prison camp and are reported missing return to England as stowaways on the night of the Armistice celebration: Jimmy Gubbins, Cockney; Billy Foster, an American; and "Spoofy," who is absentminded as the result of shell shock. Ivis Ayers, an American girl entertaining wounded soldiers at her London home, is recognized by Billy, who discovers her with Peter Larne, for whose defalcations Billy is wanted by the police. Larne offers him a bribe to leave the country and remain dead; in a struggle Larne is shot and Billy escapes. Mrs. Gubbins discovers that there is a reward for Billy's return and telephones Scotland Yard; meanwhile, Spoofy finds new clothes in a nearby residence and departs with money and a baby in a perambulator. Arrival of the detectives restores him to sanity, Ivis clears Billy of the accusations against him, and Spoofy—when his wife recognizes him—discovers that he has robbed his own home. *Stowaways. Prisoners of war. Robbers. Shell shock. World War I. London. Scotland Yard.*

THREE LIVE GHOSTS **F2.5662**

Joseph M. Schenck Productions. *Dist* United Artists. 15 Sep **1929** [c1 Sep 1929; LP701]. Sd (Movietone); b&w. 35mm. 9 reels, 7,486 ft.

Prod-Adapt-Dial Max Marcin. *Dir* Thornton Freeland. *Scen* Helen Hallett. *Story* Sally Winters. *Photog* Robert H. Planck. *Film Ed* Robert Kern.

Cast: Beryl Mercer *(Mrs. Gubbins)*, Hilda Vaughn *(Peggy Woofers)*, Harry Stubbs *(Bolton)*, Joan Bennett *(Rose Gordon)*, Nancy Price *(Alice)*, Charles McNaughton *(Jimmie Gubbins)*, Robert Montgomery *(William Foster)*, Claud Allister *("Spoofy")*, Arthur Clayton *(paymaster)*, Tenen Holtz *(crockery man)*, Shayle Gardner *(Briggs)*, Jack Cooper *(Benson)*, Jocelyn Lee *(Lady Leicester)*.

Comedy-melodrama. Source: Frederic Stewart Isham and Max Marcin, *Three Live Ghosts; a Comedy in Three Acts* (New York, c1922). Three war veterans, "Spoofy," a shell-shocked English officer who is suffering from amnesia; Jimmy Gubbins, a Cockney; and William Foster, an American wanted for embezzling funds from his father's business—escape from a German prison camp and return to London after the Armistice to find themselves listed among the dead. Gubbins' mother, who runs a boardinghouse, sees a chance to collect a reward offered for Foster, and she calls Scotland Yard; however, she wishes Gubbins would "stay dead" until the last death insurance payment has arrived. Police officers arrive to arrest Foster, and instead they solve a burglary and kidnaping committed the previous night: driven temporarily insane by amnesia, Spoofy broke into the house, stole some jewels, and kidnaped a baby. Knocked unconscious when he resists arrest, Spoofy suddenly recovers his memory. He discovers that he is Lord Leicester and that he robbed his own house and kidnaped his own child. Foster's situation is resolved when an American detective informs him that he is heir to his deceased father's fortune and that the embezzlement charges are being dropped. Foster and Rose, a girl he met on the boat from the United States, return to the United States to marry, while Gubbins marries his sweetheart, Peggy Woofers. *Veterans. Prisoners of war. Embezzlement. Burglary. Kidnaping. Amnesia. Shell shock. World War I. London.*

THREE MILES OUT **F2.5663**

Kenma Corp. *Dist* Associated Exhibitors. 10 Feb **1924** [c20 Feb 1924; LU19928]. Si; b&w. 35mm. 5,700 ft.

Dir Irvin Willat. *Scen* John Emerson, Anita Loos. *Story* Neysa McMein. *Photog* Henry Cronjager.

Cast: Madge Kennedy *(Molly Townsend)*, Harrison Ford *(John Locke)*, Marc MacDermott *(Luis Riccardi)*, Ivan Linow *("Bull" Jordan)*, Walter Lewis *("Smoothy" Smith)*, M. W. Rale *("Highbrow" Higgins)*, Joseph Henderson *(Dandy)*, Edna Morton *(Susie)*, Marie Burke *(Mrs. Ormsby Townsend)*.

Melodrama. Molly Townsend, engaged to Luis Riccardi, learns from

Capt. John Locke half an hour before the wedding that Riccardi is a thief and a smuggler. Locke, Riccardi's rival for Molly, persuades Molly to sail away with him in his boat bound for South America. He is thrown overboard by the cutthroat crew, and crewleader Jordan nearly makes her his victim before Locke, who has saved himself, rescues her. Riccardi and Jordan, who murdered a man in the Townsend home and stole a diamond necklace, are both jailed. *Smugglers. Thieves. Murder. Seafaring life. South America.*

THREE MILES UP (Universal Thrill Feature) **F2.5664**

Universal Pictures. 4 Sep **1927** [c20 Jun 1927; LP24119]. Si; b&w. 35mm. 5 reels, 4,041 or 4,136 ft.

Pres by Carl Laemmle. *Dir-Story* Bruce Mitchell. *Scen* Carl Krusada. *Titl* Gardner Bradford. *Photog* William Adams.

Cast: Al Wilson *("Ace" Morgan [Dick])*, William Malan *(John Worthing)*, Ethlyne Clair *(Nadine Worthing)*, William Clifford *(Boss Scanlon)*, Frank Rice *(Professor)*, Billy "Red" Jones *(Kid)*, Joe Bennett *(Garret)*, Art Goebel.

Action melodrama. Dick Morgan, formerly a professional crook, returns from the war as the "Ace" of his squadron and is met by his buddy, Dr. Worthing. Dick falls in love with Worthing's daughter, Nadine, and is determined to break his former criminal ties. Threatened with exposure by the gang, Dick helps them in a jewel robbery; but by feigning death in an accident and undergoing an operation to remove an identifying scar, he is able to return to the crooks' rendezvous and take back the stolen money unrecognized. In a climactic air battle, the gang are forced down with the money, and Dick overtakes the leader when he attempts to escape in a car with Nadine. *Veterans. Aviators. Criminals—Rehabilitation. Thieves. Physicians. Plastic surgery. Airplanes.*

THE THREE MUSKETEERS **F2.5665**

Douglas Fairbanks Pictures. *Dist* United Artists. 28 Aug **1921** [New York premiere; c13 Sep 1921; LP16959]. Si; b&w. 35mm. 12 reels, 11,700 ft.

Pres by Douglas Fairbanks. *Dir* Fred Niblo. *Scen Ed* Lotta Woods. *Adapt* Edward Knoblock. *Photog* Arthur Edeson. *Art Dir* Edward M. Langley. *Tech Dir* Frank England. *Film Ed* Nellie Mason. *Mus Score* Louis F. Gottschalk. *Asst Dir* Doran Cox. *Master of Cost* Paul Burns. *Elec* Albert Wayne. *Master of Properties* Harry Edwards.

Cast: Douglas Fairbanks *(D'Artagnan)*, Leon Barry *(Athos)*, George Siegmann *(Porthos)*, Eugene Pallette *(Aramis)*, Boyd Irwin *(De Rocheford)*, Thomas Holding *(George Villiers, Duke of Buckingham)*, Sidney Franklin *(Bonacieux)*, Charles Stevens *(Planchet, D'Artagnan's lackey)*, Nigel De Brulier *(Cardinal Richelieu)*, Willis Robards *(Captain de Treville)*, Lon Poff *(Father Joseph)*, Mary MacLaren *(Queen [Anne of Austria])*, Marguerite De La Motte *(Constance Bonacieux)*, Barbara La Marr *(Milady de Winter)*, Walt Whitman *(D'Artagnan's father)*, Adolphe Menjou *(Louis XIII, King of France)*, Charles Belcher *(Bernajoux)*.

Historical romance. Source: Alexandre Dumas, père, *Les Trois mousquetaires.* Cardinal Richelieu, engaged in intrigue at the court of Louis XIII, attempts to rule by threatening the queen, who is secretly in love with the Duke of Buckingham. From Gascony comes D'Artagnan to join the King's Musketeers in his quest for adventure. He wins the right to membership by proving his prowess with the sword and forms an eternal alliance with Athos, Porthos, and Aramis, the Three Musketeers. After many adventures, he embarks on a dangerous mission to England to recover a diamond brooch, a gift of the king, which the queen has given to Buckingham as a token of affection. He recovers it and returns in time to save the queen from the wrath of Louis, defeat the cardinal's intrigue, and win Constance, the queen's seamstress. *Royalty. Adventurers. Musketeers. Blackmail. Infidelity. Loyalty. France—History—Bourbons. Cardinal Richelieu. Louis XIII (France). Anne of Austria.*

THE THREE MUST-GET-THERES **F2.5666**

Max Linder Productions. *Dist* Allied Producers and Distributors. 27 Aug **1922** [c1 Sep 1922; LP18419]. Si; b&w. 35mm. 5 reels, 4,900 ft.

Dir-Writ Max Linder. *Titl* Tom Miranda. *Photog* Harry Vallejo, Max Dupont. *Asst Dir* Fred Cavens.

Cast: Max Linder *(Dart-In-Again)*, Bull Montana *(Duke of Rich-Lou)*, Frank Cooke *(King Louis XIII)*, Catherine Rankin *(The Queen, see note)*, Jobyna Ralston *(Connie)*, Jack Richardson *(Walrus)*, Charles Metzetti *(Octopus)*, Clarence Werpz *(Porpoise)*, Fred Cavens *(Bernajoux)*, Harry Mann *(Bunkumin)*, Jazbo *(a donkey)*.

Burlesque. On his way to Paris, Dart-In-Again loses a duel to the Man of Meung, challenges each of the Three Must-Get-Theres, then joins the trio in routing the Duke of Rich-Lou's soldiers. Asked by Connie, the queen's seamstress, to recover from the queen's lover, Bunkumin, a brooch given to her by the king, Dart-In-Again travels to England and has many adventures while accomplishing his task. The king rewards him for "finding" the brooch by making him a full member of the Three Must-Get-Theres, giving him permission to marry Connie, and allowing Dart-In-Again to give a "present" to the Duke of Rich-Lou. *Seamstresses. Royalty. Musketeers. Paris. Louis XIII (France). Donkeys.*

Note: Catherine Rankin, as credited in all sources, should probably read Caroline Rankin.

THREE O'CLOCK IN THE MORNING **F2.5667**

C. C. Burr Pictures. 1 Dec **1923** [c4 Dec 1923; LP19672]. Si; b&w. 35mm. 6-7 reels, 6,293 ft.

Pres by C. C. Burr. *Dir* Kenneth Webb. *Scen* Gerald C. Duffy. *Story* Mann Page. *Photog* Jack Brown, William McCoy, Neil Sullivan.

Cast: Constance Binney *(Elizabeth Winthrop)*, Edmund Breese *(Mr. Winthrop)*, Richard Thorpe *(Clayton Webster)*, Mary Carr *(Mrs. Winthrop)*, William Bailey *(Hugo von Strohm)*, Edna May Oliver *(Hetty)*, Russell Griffin *(Mickey Flynn)*.

Melodrama. Elizabeth Winthrop, a headstrong flapper, rebels against her parents and moves to New York after breaking with her fiancé, Clayton Webster. Hugo von Strohm, a wealthy playboy, procures Elizabeth a job as a chorus dancer and secretly pays her salary. After he tries to seduce her, Elizabeth sees through his kindnesses and returns to her parents and Clayton. *Flappers. Dancers. Family life. Filial relations. Seduction. New York City.*

Note: Copyrighted by Mastodon Films.

THE THREE OUTCASTS **F2.5668**

Waca Productions. *Dist* Bell Pictures, J. Charles Davis Productions. 14 Feb or 1 Mar **1929.** Si; b&w. 35mm. 5 reels, 4,800-4,950 ft.

Dir Clifford Smith. *Scen* Enos Edwards, Robert Walker. *Titl* Gardner Bradford. *Story* Enos Edwards. *Photog* Harry McGuire.

Cast: Yakima Canutt *(Dick Marsh)*, Pete Morrison *(Bruce Slavin)*, Gertrude Short *(June)*, Lew Short *(Rance Slavin)*, Frank Jennings *(sheriff)*, Maurice Murphy *(Dick Marsh, as a boy)*, Florence Midgely *(Mrs. Slavin)*, Whitehorse *(Nels Nolan)*.

Western melodrama. No information about the nature of this film has been found.

THREE PALS **F2.5669**

Davis Distributing Division. c5 Jan **1926** [LP22227]. Si; b&w. 35mm. 5 reels, 4,987 ft.

Dir Wilbur McGaugh. *Story* L. V. Jefferson. *Photog* Robert De Grasse.

Cast: Marilyn Mills *(Betty Girard)*, Josef Swickard *(Colonel Girard)*, William H. Turner *(Major Wingate)*, Martin Turner *(Uncle Lude)*, Walter Emerson *(Larry Wingate)*, James McLaughlin *(Wingate's secretary)*.

Romantic melodrama. Colonel Girard and Major Wingate, two old southern gentlemen, are the best of friends until Wingate's secretary does not acknowledge payment of a promissory note by Colonel Girard to the major. Girard goes to Wingate for an explanation and, while he is there, Major Wingate is murdered by an unknown assailant. Colonel Girard is arrested for the crime, and his daughter, Betty, returning from finishing school abroad, sets out to prove her father's innocence. With the help of Larry Wingate, Major Wingate's son with whom she is in love, she proves that Wingate was murdered by his secretary, intended to use the note to blackmail Betty into marriage. Betty's horse wins $10,000 in a race, and she and Larry prepare to be married. *Secretaries. Filial relations. Murder. Injustice. Blackmail. Horseracing. Documentation.*

THREE SEVENS **F2.5670**

Vitagraph Co. of America. Jan **1921** [c25 Feb 1921; LP16198]. Si; b&w. 35mm. 5 reels.

Pres by Albert E. Smith. *Dir* Chester Bennett. *Scen* Calder Johnstone. *Photog* Jack MacKenzie.

Cast: Antonio Moreno *(Daniel Craig)*, Jean Calhoun *(Joan Gracie)*, Emmett King *(Maj. Jerome Gracie)*, Geoffrey Webb *(Gary Lee)*, De Witt Jennings *(Samuel Green)*, Starke Patterson *(Brewster Green)*, Beatrice Burnham *(Amy Green)*.

Drama. Source: Perley Poore Sheehan, *Three Sevens; a Detective Story* (New York, c1927). Found guilty of manslaughter and sentenced on the strength of circumstantial evidence, Daniel Craig (Convict 777) and other prisoners overpower the guards and force the cruel warden, Samuel Green, to sign a document admitting his misdeeds. Joan Gracie, daughter of the newly appointed warden, arrives, and the major, who believes in prison reform, urges Craig to persuade the convicts to surrender. It transpires that the ex-warden's son has committed the crime for which Craig was sentenced, and Craig is cleared. *Prison wardens. Prison revolts. Prison reform. Manslaughter. Circumstantial evidence.*

THREE SINNERS F2.5671

Paramount Famous Lasky Corp. 14 Apr **1928** [c14 Apr 1928; LP25157]. Si; b&w. 35mm. 8 reels, 7,092 ft.

Dir Rowland V. Lee. *Titl* Julian Johnson. *Adapt* Doris Anderson, Jean De Limur. *Photog* Victor Milner. *Film Ed* Robert Brassler.

Cast: Pola Negri *(Baroness Gerda Wallentin)*, Warner Baxter *(James Harris)*, Paul Lukas *(Count Dietrich Wallentin)*, Anders Randolph *(Count Hellemuth Wallentin)*, Tullio Carminati *(Raoul Stanislav)*, Anton Vaverka *(valet to Dietrich)*, Ivy Harris *(Countess Lilli)*, William von Hardenburg *(Prince von Scherson)*, Olga Baclanova *(Baroness Hilda Brings)*.

Drama. Source: Bernauer Österreicher, *Das zweite Leben* (unpublished play). Perceiving that her husband no longer loves her, Gerda, Countess Wallentin, agrees to go to Vienna to visit relatives, leaving the count in Germany to pursue his political ambitions with Baroness Brings, a close friend. En route, Gerda is seduced by Raoul Stanislav, a famous musician. She leaves the train for a brief time, and it departs without her; later she finds that the train crashed, killing everyone aboard. Guilty because of her affair, Gerda fails to notify her husband of her survival. Later, as hostess in a fashionable Viennese gambling den, she sees her husband, who is strangely attracted to her because of what seems to be a remarkable resemblance to his wife. Gerda discloses her identity and returns to her husband. Later, seeing that he does not really love her, she takes their child and sails to America with a wealthy patron of the gambling house. *Politicians. Musicians. Nobility. Seduction. Infidelity. Gambling. Germany. Vienna. Train wrecks.*

THE 3 SISTERS F2.5672

Fox Film Corp. 20 Apr **1930** [c18 Feb 1930; LP1181]. Sd (Movietone); b&w. 35mm. 7 reels, 6,442 ft. [Also si.]

Pres by William Fox. *Dir* Paul Sloane. *Screenplay-Dial* James K. McGuinness, George Brooks. *Story* George Brooks, Marion Orth. *Photog* L. William O'Connell. *Song: "Italian Kisses"* L. Wolfe Gilbert, Abel Baer. *Songs: "Lonely Feet," "Hand in Hand," "Keep Smiling," "Won't Dance," "Roll on Rolling Road," "What Good Are Words," "You Are Doing Very Well"* Jerome Kern, Oscar Hammerstein, II. *Rec Engr* Harold Hobson. *Asst Dir* Sam Wurtzel.

Cast: Louise Dresser *(Marta)*, Tom Patricola *(Tony)*, Kenneth MacKenna *(Count D'Amati)*, Joyce Compton *(Carlotta)*, June Collyer *(Elena)*, Addie McPhail *(Antonia)*, Clifford Saum *(Pasquale)*, Sidney De Grey *(Tito)*, Paul Porcasi *(Rinaldi)*, John St. Polis *(judge)*, Herman Bing *(Von Kosch)*.

Melodrama. Marta, an Italian mother, has three daughters. On the night of her wedding, Carlotta stabs the village banker, and aided by Rinaldi, a friend of the family, she escapes with Antonia, who has returned from her musical studies for the nuptials. Elena, the third daughter, marries Count D'Amati the same night; but when the son-in-law goes to war, Elena dies in childbirth; later, D'Amati is killed, leaving the grandmother with only the child for comfort. Marta goes to Rome and is befriended by Rinaldi, but the child reverts to his ducal grandparents by court order. Left penniless by misfortune, Marta finds employment as a dishwasher in a restaurant, but she is rescued from her poverty and loneliness by her two daughters, who have become prosperous in the United States. *Sisters. Dishwashers. Motherhood. Murder. Poverty. World War I. Italy. Rome. New York City.*

THREE WEEK-ENDS F2.5673

Paramount Famous Lasky Corp. 8 Dec **1928** [c7 Dec 1928; LP25909]. Si; b&w. 35mm. 6 reels, 5,962 ft.

Dir Clarence Badger. *Screenplay* Louise Long, Percy Heath, Sam Mintz. *Titl* Paul Perez, Herman Mankiewicz. *Adapt* John Farrow. *Story* Elinor Glyn. *Photog* Harold Rosson. *Film Ed* Tay Malarkey. *Dance numbers stgd by* Fanchon & Marco.

Cast: Clara Bow *(Gladys O'Brien)*, Neil Hamilton *(James Gordon)*, Harrison Ford *(Turner)*, Lucille Powers *(Miss Witherspoon)*, Julia Swayne Gordon *(Mrs. Witherspoon)*, Jack Raymond *(Turner's secretary)*, Edythe Chapman *(Ma O'Brien)*, Guy Oliver *(Pa O'Brien)*, William Holden *(Carter)*.

Comedy-drama. Chorus girl Gladys O'Brien falls hard for apparently wealthy James Gordon, an insurance salesman who is trying hard to sell a policy to Turner, a Broadway playboy. Turner invites Gladys to a weekend party at his country house, and she accepts, hoping to persuade Turner to sign James's policy. James crashes the affair and punches Turner in the nose. He and Gladys start back to the city together, and James tells her that, in reality, he is as poor as a churchmouse. To add to his financial woes, James loses his job for hitting Turner. Gladys uses her charms to have him rehired and then genteelly blackmails Turner into signing the insurance policy written up by James. James sees them together and suspects the worst. He and Gladys are soon reconciled, however, and make plans to be married. *Insurance agents. Playboys. Chorus girls. Blackmail. Insurance. New York City.*

THREE WEEKS F2.5674

Goldwyn Pictures. *Dist* Goldwyn-Cosmopolitan Distributing Corp. 10 Feb **1924** [c12 Mar 1924; LP19980]. Si; b&w. 35mm. 8 reels, 7,468 or 7,540 ft.

Dir Alan Crosland. *Ed Dir* June Mathis. *Scen* Elinor Glyn. *Adapt* Carey Wilson. *Photog* John J. Mescall. *Sets* Cedric Gibbons. *Cost* Sophie Wachner.

Cast: Aileen Pringle *(The Queen)*, Conrad Nagel *(Paul Verdayne)*, John Sainpolis *(King Constantine)*, H. Reeves Smith *(Sir Charles Verdayne)*, Stuart Holmes *(Petrovich)*, Mitchell Lewis *(Vassili)*, Robert Cain *(Verchoff)*, Nigel De Brulier *(Dmitry)*, Claire De Lorez *(Mitze)*, Dale Fuller *(Anna)*, Helen Dunbar *(Lady Henrietta)*, Alan Crosland, Jr. *(The Young King of Sardalia)*, Joan Standing *(Isabella)*, William Haines *(curate)*, George Tustain *(captain of the guards)*, Dane Rudhyar *(Peter)*.

Romantic drama. Source: Elinor Glyn, *Three Weeks* (New York, 1907). The Queen of Sardalia, a small European principality, becomes disgusted with the king's debauchery and retires to Switzerland. There she falls in love with Paul Verdayne, a young, aristocratic Briton. They vacation in Venice but separate when Paul's life is threatened by the king's henchmen. Their passion remains strong, and 3 years later the queen sends for Paul. The king discovers this meeting and kills her in a fit of jealousy. Later, Paul returns to Sardalia to see his son crowned king and remembers his great love for the queen. *Royalty. English. Infidelity. Jealousy. Murder. Imaginary kingdoms. Switzerland. Venice.*

THREE WEEKS IN PARIS F2.5675

Warner Brothers Pictures. 5 Dec **1925** [c19 Aug 1925; LP21756]. Si; b&w. 35mm. 6 reels.

Dir Roy Del Ruth. *Scen* Darryl Francis Zanuck. *Story* Gregory Rogers. *Photog* David Abel. *Adtl Photog* Walter Robinson. *Film Ed* Clarence Kolster. *Asst Dir* Ross Lederman.

Cast: Matt Moore *(Oswald Bates)*, Dorothy Devore *(Mary Brown)*, Willard Louis *(Gus Billikins)*, Helen Lynch *(Dolly Withers)*, Gayne Whitman *(Duke Laporte)*, John Patrick *(Bruce Gordon)*, Frank Bond *(Alex Darrows)*, Rosa Gore *(Mrs. Brown)*.

Comedy. In spite of dire predictions from her mother, Mary Brown marries Oswald Bates, an energetic young businessman. *He then is forced to go to Paris alone on their wedding night. Haunted by thoughts of his neglected bride, Oswald seeks to drown his sorrow in Parisian night life. Flirting with Dolly Withers, an American, Oswald is challenged to a duel by Duke Laporte. Through the ineptness of his friend, Gus Billikins, he is jailed; the steamer on which he was to have returned home sinks in mid-Atlantic; and he is declared dead. Posing as a count (with Dolly Withers as his countess), Oswald returns to the United States and obtains a position as a cook for Mary's mother. When he learns that Mary is to marry Bruce Gordon, Oswald reveals his true identity. He and Mary are reconciled, and Dolly discovers that Bruce is her long-lost husband.* It all turns out to have been a daydream, however, for Mary and Oswald actually are uneventfully wed. *Businessmen. Brides. Cooks. Flirtation. Imposture. Weddings. Paris. Shipwrecks. Dreams. Duels.*

THREE WHO PAID F2.5676

Fox Film Corp. 7 Jan **1923** [c7 Jan 1923; LP19155]. Si; b&w. 35mm. 5 reels, 4,859 ft.

Pres by William Fox. *Dir* Colin Campbell. *Scen* Joseph Franklin Poland. *Photog* Don Short.

Cast: Dustin Farnum *(Riley Sinclair)*, Fred Kohler *(Jim Quade)*, Bessie Love *(John Caspar/Virginia Cartright)*, Frank Campeau *(Edward Sanderson)*, Robert Daly *(Sam Lowrie)*, William Conklin *(Jude Cartright)*, Robert Agnew *(Hal Sinclair)*.

Western melodrama. Source: George Owen Baxter, "Three Who Paid," in *Western Story Magazine* (8 Apr–27 May 1922). Determined to avenge the death of his brother Hal, Riley Sinclair sets out to kill the three men who left Hal to die on the desert. One of them commits suicide, another is killed by the hero in self-defense, and the third is killed in a gunfight by someone else. A young "schoolmaster," who is actually a woman trying to escape her cruel husband, is accused of murder; but Sinclair establishes her innocence and wins her love. *Brothers. Schoolteachers. Revenge. Suicide. Murder. Disguise.*

THREE WISE CROOKS **F2.5677**

Gothic Productions. *Dist* Film Booking Offices of America. 6 Sep **1925** [premiere?; released 20 Sep 1925; c6 Sep 1925; LP21892]. Si; b&w. 35mm. 6 reels, 6,074 ft.

Dir F. Harmon Weight. *Story-Scen* John C. Brownell, Fred Kennedy Myton. *Camera* Roy Klaffki. *Asst Dir* Charles Kerr. *Propertyman* Gene Rossi.

Cast: Evelyn Brent *(Molly [Dolly?])*, Fannie Midgley *(Ma Dickenson)*, John Gough *(Spug Casey)*, Bruce Gordon *(Dan Pelton)*, William Humphrey *(Grogan)*, Carroll Nye *(Don Gray)*, Dodo Newton *(Betsy)*.

Crook melodrama. After robbing a diamond merchant, Dolly seeks refuge at the country home of "Ma" Dickenson, an elderly lady whom she recently befriended in the city. Discovering that Wetherby, the local banker, and Wadsworth, an oil promoter, are planning to steal the townspeople's savings (including "Ma" Dickenson's), Dolly sends for her two cohorts in crime, Spug and Dan, so as to beat Wetherby to the money and return it to the people. Their plan succeeds, and, while robbing the bank, Dan picks up evidence that will incriminate Wetherby. Consequently, when Detective Grogan finds Dolly and the money, he believes her story and lets them all go scot-free. Dan and Dolly, also Spug and a local girl with whom he has fallen in love, begin a new life in the country. *Bankers. Oilmen. Criminals—Rehabilitation. Robbery. Rural life.*

THREE WISE FOOLS **F2.5678**

Goldwyn Pictures. 19 Aug **1923** [c5 Jul 1923; LP19173]. Si; b&w. 35mm. 7 reels, 6,946 ft.

Dir-Writ King Vidor. *Screenplay* June Mathis. *Adapt* John McDermott, James O'Hanlon. *Photog* Charles Van Enger.

Cast: Claude Gillingwater *(Theodore Findley)*, Eleanor Boardman *(Rena Fairchild/Sydney Fairchild)*, William H. Crane *(Hon. James Trumbull)*, Alec B. Francis *(Dr. Richard Gaunt)*, John Sainpolis *(John Crawshay)*, Brinsley Shaw *(Benny, the Duck)*, Fred Esmelton *(Gray)*, William Haines *(Gordon Schuyler)*, Lucien Littlefield *(Douglas)*, ZaSu Pitts *(Mickey)*, Martha Mattox *(Saunders)*, Fred J. Butler *(Poole)*, Charles Hickman *(Clancy)*, Craig Biddle, Jr. *(Young Findley)*, Creighton Hale *(Young Trumbull)*, Raymond Hatton *(Young Gaunt)*.

Comedy-melodrama. Source: Austin Strong and Winchell Smith, *Three Wise Fools, a Play In Three Acts* (Ottawa, 1919). Sydney Fairchild, the daughter of a woman who was once loved by three bachelors, surprises the men with a visit. Findley, Trumbull, and Gaunt honor their former sweetheart's last request by becoming Sydney's guardians. The arrangement works well until Sydney is suspected of assisting a criminal who breaks into the house. She is arrested, but Findley's nephew saves her and everything is explained. *Bachelors. Guardians.*

THREE WOMEN **F2.5679**

Warner Brothers Pictures. 18 Aug **1924** [c9 Aug 1924; LP20479]. Si; b&w. 35mm. 8 reels, 7,400-8,200 ft.

Dir Ernst Lubitsch. *Scen* Hans Kraly. *Story* Ernst Lubitsch, Hans Kraly. *Photog* Charles J. Van Enger. *Art Dir* Svend Gade. *Asst Dir* James Flood, Henry Blanke.

Cast: May McAvoy *(Jeanne Wilton)*, Pauline Frederick *(Mabel Wilton)*, Marie Prevost *(Harriet)*, Lew Cody *(Edmund Lamont)*, Willard Louis *(Harvey Craig)*, Pierre Gendron *(Fred Armstrong)*, Mary Carr *(his mother)*, Raymond McKee *(Fred's friend)*.

Society drama. Beseiged by creditors, Edmund Lamont presses an affair with wealthy widow Mabel Wilton but transfers his affections to her daughter, Jeanne. After marrying Jeanne, Lamont continues an affair with Harriet, a flapper. Meanwhile, Jeanne is in love with young doctor Fred Armstrong, and when Lamont refuses her a divorce her mother kills him and is acquitted, leaving Jeanne free to seek happiness with Fred. *Widows. Flappers. Physicians. Debt. Wealth. Marriage. Infidelity.*

THREE WORD BRAND **F2.5680**

William S. Hart Co. *Dist* Paramount Pictures. ca25 Sep **1921** [New York premiere; released 16 Oct; c16 Oct 1921; LP17783]. Si; b&w. 35mm. 7 reels, 6,638 ft.

Prod William S. Hart. *Adapt-Dir* Lambert Hillyer. *Story* Will Reynolds. *Photog* Joseph August.

Cast: William S. Hart *(Three Word Brand/Governor Marsden/Ben Trego)*, Jane Novak *(Ethel Barton)*, S. J. Bingham *(George Barton)*, Gordon Russell *(Bull Yeates)*, Ivor McFadden *(Solly)*, Herschel Mayall *(Carrol)*, Colette Forbes *(Jean)*, George C. Pearce *(John Murray)*, Leo Willis *(McCabe)*.

Western melodrama. Ben Trego, a pioneer ambushed by Indians, sends his twin boys to safety and kills himself rather than fall into the hands of his attackers. The twins grow to manhood in separate parts of Utah: Marsden is governor of the state, and the other, known as "Three Word" Brand because of his economy of speech, is a rancher. Brand's partner, George Barton, is framed for murder by the owners of an adjoining ranch, since he and Brand are opposed to a bill that would give control of water rights to politicians. The governor, who is urged to sign the act, resolves to investigate the matter himself; when Brand notices their strong resemblance, he goes to the capital, impersonates the governor (having Marsden detained), vetoes the water rights act, and signs a pardon for Barton. Meanwhile, he returns to find that Marsden, mistaken by his enemies for Brand, has been wounded. Brand then evens the score with them, learns of his brother's identity, and wins the hand of Ethel, his partner's sister. *Brothers. Twins. Ranchers. State governors. Water rights. Political corruption. Impersonation. Utah.*

THREE-RING MARRIAGE **F2.5681**

First National Pictures. 10 June **1928** [c28 May 1928; LP25306]. Si; b&w. 35mm. 6 reels, 5,834 ft.

Prod Henry Hobart. *Dir* Marshall Neilan. *Adapt-Cont* Harvey Thew. *Titl* Tom Geraghty. *Story* Dixie Willson. *Photog* David Kesson. *Art Dir* Edward Shulter. *Film Ed* Stuart Heisler.

Cast: Mary Astor *(Anna)*, Lloyd Hughes *(Cal)*, Lawford Davidson *(Souvane)*, Yola D'Avril *(Minnie)*, Alice White *(trapeze performer)*, Harry Earles *(Cubby Snodd)*, Tiny Earles *(Mrs. Cubby Snodd)*, George Reed *(valet)*, R. E. Madsen *(giant)*, Anna MacGruder *(fat woman)*, James Neill *(Hutch)*, Del Henderson, Rudy Cameron, Skeets Gallagher, Jay Eaton, Art Rollins *(gangsters)*.

Melodrama. Source: Dixie Willson, "Help Yourself to Hay," in *Hearst's International/Cosmopolitan* (82:90–93, May 1929). Anna runs away from her wealthy father's ranch and becomes a trick rider in a circus to be with her sweetheart, Cal Coney, a circus cowboy, when her father disapproves the match. There she achieves fame as "Anna Montana," but she remains unhappy because Cal refuses to admit that he loves her. Meanwhile, Rawl Souvane, manager of the circus, plans to woo and marry Anna when he preceives that she is wealthy. Cal discovers the plot in time to save Anna from an unhappy marriage, and Anna's father relents and invites her and her husband, Cal, to return home. *Cowboys. Ranchers. Equestrians. Circus.*

THREE'S A CROWD **F2.5682**

Harry Langdon Corp. *Dist* First National Pictures. 28 Aug **1927** [c17 Aug 1927; LP24303]. Si; b&w. 35mm. 6 reels, 5,668 ft.

Dir Harry Langdon. *Adapt* James Langdon, Robert Eddy. *Story* Arthur Ripley. *Photog* Elgin Lessley, Frank Evans. *Song: "Body and Soul"* John W. Green.

Cast: Harry Langdon *(The Odd Fellow)*, Gladys McConnell *(The Girl)*, Cornelius Keefe *(The Man)*, Henry Barrows, Frances Raymond, Agnes Steele, Brooks Benedict, Bobby Young, Julia Brown, Joe Butterworth, Fred Warren, John Kolb, Arthur Thalasso.

Comedy-melodrama. Harry, The Odd Fellow, is a tenement worker who lives alone in a shack alongside a warehouse and longs for the companionship of a wife and children like other men. One day he spies a pretty girl in his telescope and sends her by carrier pigeon a note that, alas, is received by the wrong party. The Girl marries and, poverty-striken, leaves her husband during a snowstorm. Harry takes her in, and minutes later her child is born. He works like a slave for the mother and child, pretending they are his own. Meanwhile, the husband finds her and comes to the shack on Christmas Eve as Harry is preparing to play Santa Claus. Not realizing the unhappiness she is causing him, The Girl thanks him profusely and leaves with her husband. Overcome, Harry sits overnight on the doorstep and the next morning is found frozen stiff except for his eyes—with amusing results. *Poverty. Motherhood. Tenements. Christmas. Storms. Pigeons.*

THE THRILL CHASER **F2.5683**

Universal Pictures. 26 Nov **1923** [c29 Oct 1923; LP19549]. Si; b&w. 35mm. 6 reels, 5,196 ft.

Dir Edward Sedgwick. *Scen* E. Richard Schayer. *Story* Edward Sedgwick, Raymond L. Schrock. *Photog* Virgil Miller.

Cast: Hoot Gibson *(Omar K. Jenkins)*, James Neill *(Sheik Ussan)*, Billie Dove *(Olala Ussan)*, William E. Lawrence *(Prince Ahmed)*, Bob Reeves *(Lem Bixley)*, Gino Gerrado *(Rudolph Bigeddo)*, Lloyd Whitlock *(Abdul Bey)*, Mary Philbin, Norman Kerry, Reginald Denny, Hobart Henley, King Baggot, Edward Sedgwick, Laura La Plante.

Action melodrama. Omar K. Jenkins, a simple westerner working as a motion picture extra, impresses Sheik Ussan, a visiting Arab prince, with his fistic ability. Engaged to go to Arabia, he becomes involved in war between rival principalities and falls in love with Olala, a princess who is promised. Omar is taken prisoner and readied for the chopping block when Sheik Ussan intervenes. *Royalty. Sheiks. Cowboys. Motion pictures. Capital punishment. Arabia.*

THE THRILL CHASER **F2.5684**

Dist Associated Independent Producers. 3 Oct **1928** [New York State license]. Si; b&w. 35mm. 5 reels, 4,280 ft.

Dir-Scen Robert J. Horner. *Titl* Harold Cummings. *Photog* Jack Draper. *Film Ed* William Austin.

Cast: Pawnee Bill Jr., Boris Bullock, Bill Nestel, Bud Osborne.

Western melodrama(?). No information about the nature of this film has been found.

THE THRILL GIRL *see* **EXCITEMENT**

THE THRILL HUNTER **F2.5685**

Waldorf Pictures. *Dist* Columbia Pictures. 1 Feb **1926** [c19 Feb 1926; LP22414]. Si; b&w. 35mm. 6 reels, 5,520 ft.

Dir Eugene De Rue. *Dir? (see note)* Frank R. Strayer. *Adapt* Janet Crothers. *Story* Douglas Bronston. *Photog* Kenneth MacLean.

Cast: William Haines *(Peter J. Smith)*, Kathryn McGuire *(Alice Maynard)*, Alma Bennett *(Princess Zola)*, E. J. Ratcliffe *(T. B. Maynard)*, Bobby Dunn *(Ferdie)*, Frankie Darrow *(boy prince)*.

Comedy. Author Peter J. Smith, who works for Maynard, a large publisher, falls in love with Maynard's daughter, Alice. Maynard publishes a book about the downfall of Grecovia, and the Grecovians, who believe that Maynard knows the whereabouts of their missing king, seek revenge. Mistaking Peter for the missing heir, the Grecovians kidnap him and attempt to force him to marry Princess Zola. Peter escapes, and the Grecovians blow themselves up with dynamite. Peter finally settles down with Alice. *Authors. Publishers. Royalty. Kidnaping. Thrill-seeking. Imaginary kingdoms.*

Note: Strayer also has been credited with the direction.

THE THRILL SEEKERS **F2.5686**

H. V. Productions. *Dist* Hi-Mark Film Co. Sep **1927.** Si; b&w. 35mm. 6 reels, 5,275 ft.

Dir Harry Revier. *Scen* Mabel Z. Carroll. *Photog* Jerry Fairbanks, Harry Vallet.

Cast: Jimmy Fulton *(Gerald Kenworth)*, Ruth Clifford *(Adrean Wainwright)*, Gloria Grey *(mystery girl)*, Sally Long *(Marie St. Claire)*, Lee Moran *(Lester, the valet)*, Robert McKim *(Hal Walker)*, Raymond Wells *(Jack Newman)*, Harold Austin *(Jimmy, the chauffeur)*, Max Wagner *(a hood)*.

Melodrama. "A young lumberjack comes to the big city and aids a lady in distress. His enemy later kidnaps both him and the girl, but the lumberjack succeeds in getting aboard the launch on which she is kept captive with the result that the girl is set free, the villain overpowered and romance developed between the man and girl." (*Motion Picture News Booking Guide*, [14]:289, 1929.) *Lumberjacks. Thrill-seeking. Kidnaping.*

THRILLING YOUTH **F2.5687**

Billy West Productions. *Dist* Rayart Pictures. 3 Aug **1926** [New York State license]. Si; b&w. 35mm. 5 reels, 4,319 ft.

Dir-Scen Grover Jones. *Photog* George Crocker.

Cast: Billy West *(Billy Davis)*, Gloria Grey *(Mary Bryson)*, George Bunny *(Billy's father)*, Charles Clary *(Thomas Bryson)*, John J. Richardson *(Bryson's secretary)*, Span Kennedy *(detective)*, Joseph Smith *(Vallman)*.

Comedy-drama. Billy Davis discovers that his father's bakery business is in serious financial trouble and leaves college in order to help his family. He goes to work as a baker and soon falls in love with Mary Bryson, whose father is Davis' biggest rival in the bread business. When Bryson's secretary bribes the Davis foreman to put cement in the bread, Mary learns of the plot and warns Billy. The concrete loaves have been delivered, so Billy is forced to rent a plane and tell his customers of the trick by means of a sky-written message. The elder Bryson berates his foreman for underhanded dealing, and Billy later beats the foreman in a fight. *Bakers. Business management. Filial relations. Bakeries. Airplanes. Skywriting.*

THROUGH A GLASS WINDOW **F2.5688**

Realart Pictures. *Dist* Paramount Pictures. 2 Apr **1922** [c10 Apr 1922; LP17750]. Si; b&w. 35mm. 5 reels, 4,490 ft.

Dir Maurice Campbell. *Story-Scen* Olga Printzlau. *Photog* Hal Rosson.

Cast: May McAvoy *(Jenny Martin)*, Fanny Midgley *(Mrs. Martin)*, Burwell Hamrick *(Dan Martin)*, Raymond McKee *(Tomasso Barilio)*, Fred Turner *(Matt Clancy)*, Carrie Clark Ward *(Molly Clancy)*, Frank Butterworth *(Jimmy)*, Wade Boteler *(Hartigan)*, Russ Powell *("Coffee Pete")*.

Romantic drama. Mrs. Martin lives in New York's East Side with her son, Dan, who sells papers, and her daughter, Jenny, who works in a local doughnut shop. During the summer, Mrs. Martin becomes ill, and a trip away from the city is recommended; unable to finance such an undertaking, Jenny converts the backyard into a blooming garden, and in the outdoor activity thus provided her mother recovers. During the winter, Dan suffers from the cold, and when Pete drops a $5 bill in the shop, Jenny uses it to buy him a coat; Pete later threatens her with arrest, and she promises to return the money, which Dan obtains by robbing another store. Brother Dan is caught and sent to a reformatory; when Mrs. Martin goes blind, Jenny tells her that Dan has obtained a job in South America. Meanwhile, Jenny opens a rival doughnut shop, which is a success; and after her brother's return, she accepts the proposal of Tomasso, her suitor. *Filial relations. Brother-sister relationship. Newsvendors. Poverty. Blindness. Gardening. Bakeries. New York City—East Side.*

THROUGH DARKEST AFRICA; IN SEARCH OF WHITE RHINOCEROS **F2.5689**

Harry K. Eustace. 21 Mar **1927** [New York showing]. Si; b&w. 35mm. 7 reels, 6,820 ft.

Photog Harry K. Eustace.

Participants: Harry K. Eustace, Mrs. Harry K. Eustace.

Travelog. A typical animal hunt film, in which are seen groups of animals grazing, playing, and resting—interspersed with frequent titles and candid shots of the hunters in pursuit of one exotic beast or another. Highlights include an animal burial ground, some native comic relief, hippopotami, and, of course, the white rhinoceros. *Africa. Hippopotami. Rhinoceros.*

Note: Distribution company not determined; released in New York by Big Three Film Exchange.

THROUGH THE BACK DOOR **F2.5690**

Mary Pickford Co. *Dist* United Artists. 17 May **1921** [c21 Jun 1921; LP16691]. Si; b&w. 35mm. 6-7 reels.

Dir Alfred E. Green, Jack Pickford. *Scen* Marion Fairfax. *Photog* Charles Rosher. *Lighting Eff* William S. Johnson.

Cast: Mary Pickford *(Jeanne Bodamere)*, Gertrude Astor *(Hortense Reeves)*, Wilfred Lucas *(Elton Reeves)*, Helen Raymond *(Marie)*, C. Norman Hammond *(Jacques Lanvain)*, Elinor Fair *(Margaret Brewster)*, Adolphe Menjou *(James Brewster)*, Peaches Jackson *(Conrad)*, Doreen Turner *(Constant)*, John Harron *(Billy Boy)*, George Dromgold *(chauffeur)*.

Comedy-melodrama. When Hortense Bodamere, a Belgian widow, marries wealthy New Yorker Elton Reeves, she is persuaded to leave her daughter Jeanne behind in the care of her nurse, Marie. Five years later Mrs. Reeves sends for Jeanne, but Marie, who has married a farmer and brought up Jeanne as her own daughter, tells Hortense that the child is dead. With the outbreak of war, Marie sends Jeanne with two orphan boys to New York to the Reeves home. Jeanne is unable to reveal her identity and is given a job as maid. When she discovers that her stepfather is about to be victimized by the wiles of Margaret Brewster, however, Jeanne reveals herself; and Reeves, having recognized his error, becomes reconciled with his wife. *Widows. Nursemaids. Refugees. Housemaids. Orphans. Personal identity. World War I. Belgium.*

THROUGH THE BREAKERS **F2.5691**

Gotham Productions. *Dist* Lumas Film Corp. 28 Sep **1928** [New York State license; c18 Oct 1928; LP25746]. Si; b&w. 35mm. 6 reels, 5,035 ft.

Pres by Sam Sax. *Assoc Prod–Scen* Harold Shumate. *Dir* Joseph C. Boyle. *Titl* John Steele. *Photog* Ray June. *Film Ed* Ray Snyder. *Prod Mgr* Donn Diggins.

Cast: Holmes Herbert *(Eustis Hobbs)*, Margaret Livingston *(Diane Garrett)*, Clyde Cook *(John Lancaster)*, Natalie Joyce *(Taya)*, Frank Hagney *(Gamboa)*.

Melodrama. Source: Owen Davis, *Through the Breakers; a Melodrama* (c1898). Diane Garrett, a beautiful London socialite, promises John Lancaster that she will join him in a year's time to be married on the South Seas island where he is to be a plantation manager for the British Trading Co. Time passes, and Diane refuses to leave the gay life; she embarks on an ocean voyage, however, and the liner on which she is traveling is wrecked off John's island. Diane is washed ashore on a spar and is soon using her feminine wiles to make John forgive her for not coming to him of her own volition. Taya, an island girl who loves John, is killed by her native lover, who then places her body in a canoe and paddles out to his own death in the open sea. Sobered by this example of *Liebestod,* Diane decides that her proper place in life is in John's arms. *Socialites. Plantation managers. Marriage. Murder. Suicide. Ocean liners. South Sea Islands. Shipwrecks.*

THROUGH THE DARK **F2.5692**

Cosmopolitan Corp. *Dist* Goldwyn-Cosmopolitan Distributing Corp. 6 Jan **1924** [c6 Jan 1924; LP19917]. Si; b&w. 35mm. 8 reels, 7,999 ft.

Dir George Hill. *Scen* Frances Marion. *Photog* L. William O'Connell, Allen Siegler. *Sets* Joseph Urban. *Art Titl* Oscar C. Buchheister.

Cast: Colleen Moore *(Mary McGinn)*, Forrest Stanley *(Boston Blackie)*, Margaret Seddon *(Mother McGinn)*, Hobart Bosworth *(warden)*, George Cooper *("Travel")*, Edward Phillips *(The "Glad Rags" Kid)*, Wade Boteler *(Detective O'Leary)*, Tom Bates *(Sandy)*, Carmelita Geraghty *(Ethel Grayson)*.

Crook drama. Source: Jack Boyle, "The Daughter of Mother McGinn" (publication undetermined). Mother McGinn, whose home is a refuge for criminals, has concealed from her daughter, Mary, the fact that her father died in prison. Mary is a pupil in a fashionable girls' school. A riot in San Quentin provides an opportunity for Boston Blackie to escape. On his way to Mother McGinn's, Mary unknowingly assists him in evading the police, and she is expelled from school when detectives inform school administrators the truth about her father. Returning home, Mary finds Blackie, whom she has grown to love. Her attempts to reform him are frustrated at first; but eventually, he goes straight (to jail) with the promise that he will marry her when he is released. *Criminals—Rehabilitation. Prison escapees. Boarding schools. San Quentin.*

THROUGH THE STORM **F2.5693**

Irving Ross. *Dist* Playgoers Pictures. 13 Aug **1922** [c9 Aug 1922; LU18124]. Si; b&w. 35mm. 6 reels, 5,905 ft.

Dir Horace G. Plympton. *Photog* Lawrence L. Fowler.

Cast: Edith Stockton *(Helen Stone)*, Louis Kimball *(Dr. Ernest Bruce)*, Mary Worth *(Lillian Atterbury)*, Leonard Mudie *(Jeremiah)*, Gladys Stockton *(Sally)*, Regan Stewart *(Jack Henderson)*, James Cooley *(Samuel Drake)*.

Melodrama. During a violent thunderstorm Helen Stone takes refuge in a building with her traveling companion, who is killed when lightning strikes the building. Helen, a forger's daughter who has never been able to find her way in the world, then assumes the dead girl's identity and goes to the home of the girl's aunt, where she is accepted as one of the family. Her true identity is later discovered by an architect, who attempts to force her into marriage and causes the aunt to have a paralytic stroke. Overcome by remorse, Helen confesses her deception and is forgiven everything by one and all; and she soon finds herself making preparations to marry Ernest Bruce, a young surgeon with whom she is in love. *Surgeons. Architects. Aunts. Impersonation. Blackmail. Storms.*

THROUGH THICK AND THIN **F2.5694**

Camera Pictures. *Dist* Lumas Film Corp. 27 Sep **1927** [c16 Jul 1926; LP22916]. Si; b&w. 35mm. 5 reels, 5,000 ft.

Dir (see note) "Breezy" Reeves Eason, Jack Nelson. *Story-Cont* Edward J. Meagher. *Photog* Ray June. *Film Ed* Fred Burnworth. *Asst Dir* Bert Clark. *Prod Mgr* Glenn Belt.

Cast: William Fairbanks *(Don Davis)*, Ethel Shannon *(Ruth Morris)*, Jack Curtis *("Red" Grimley)*, George Periolat *(James Morris)*, Ina Anson *(Rita)*, Eddie Chandler *("Bull")*, Fred Behrle *(Mike)*.

Crime melodrama. Don Davis, a United States Secret Service agent, is detailed to follow a gang of opium smugglers. Disguised as a gangster, he visits the Green Dragon Cafe, where he learns from Rita, a dancer, that "Red" Grimley is expecting Morris, with whom he has some nefarious business. Morris arrives and makes arrangements to purchase an opium shipment. At the same time, Morris' daughter, Ruth, is saved by Don from a gangster who requests a dance, and Don is consequently hired as bouncer. At the Morris home, Don improves his relationship with Ruth; then, uncovering the details of Morris' transaction, he finds the cache of opium at the cafe and overhears the gang's plans. Don is overcome by the crooks, and, accusing Morris of a doublecross, they rob him and kidnap Ruth. After an automobile chase Don and several detectives capture the gang, Morris also is revealed to be a Secret Service man, and Ruth and Don are united. *Bouncers. Dancers. Smugglers. Secret service. Disguise. Kidnaping. Opium. Chases.*

Note: Sources disagree in crediting direction.

THROWING LEAD **F2.5695**

William M. Pizor Productions. **1928.** Si; b&w. 35mm. 5 reels, 4,350 ft.

Dir Robert J. Horner. *Scen* L. V. Jefferson. *Titl* Jack Kelly. *Photog* Lauren A. Draper. *Film Ed* William Austin.

Cast: Al Hoxie.

Western melodrama(?). No information about the nature of this film has been found.

THRU DIFFERENT EYES **F2.5696**

Fox Film Corp. 14 Apr **1929** [c16 Apr 1929; LP313]. Sd (Movietone); b&w. 35mm. 6 reels, 5,166 ft.

Pres by William Fox. *Dir* John Blystone. *Dial Dir* A. H. Van Buren. *Dial* Tom Barry, Milton Herbert Gropper. *Story* Milton Herbert Gropper, Edna Sherry. *Photog* Ernest Palmer, Al Brick. *Film Ed* Louis Loeffler. *Song: "I'm Saving All My Loving"* William Kernell, Dave Stamper. *Sd* Edmund H. Hansen. *Asst Dir* Jasper Blystone. *Cost* Sophie Wachner.

Cast: Mary Duncan *(Viola Manning)*, Edmund Lowe *(Harvey Manning)*, Warner Baxter *(Jack Winfield)*, Natalie Moorhead *(Frances Thornton)*, Earle Foxe *(Howard Thornton)*, Donald Gallagher *(Spencer)*, Florence Lake *(Myrtle)*, Sylvia Sidney *(Valerie Briand)*, Purnell Pratt *(Marston)*, Selmer Jackson *(King, defense attorney)*, Dolores Johnson *(Anna)*, Nigel De Brulier *(Maynard)*, Lola Salvi *(maid)*, Stepin Fetchit *(janitor)*, De Witt Jennings *(Paducah)*, Arthur Stone *(Crane)*, George Lamont *(Traynor)*, Natalie Warfield *(Aline Craig)*, Jack Jordan, Marian Spitzer, Stanley Blystone, Stuart Erwin *(reporters)*.

Crime melodrama. Harvey Manning is placed on trial for the murder of Jack Winfield, his closest friend, whose body was found in the Manning home. During the trial, the prosecuting and the defense attorneys put forward sharply different versions of the character of Manning and his wife, Viola, and of the events leading up to the murder. The jury returns a verdict of guilty, but a young girl then comes forward and confesses that she killed Winfield for having wronged her. *Lawyers. Murder. Friendship. Injustice. Seduction. Trials.*

Note: Known also as *Guilty* and *Public Opinion.*

THRU THE FLAMES **F2.5697**

Phil Goldstone Productions. May **1923** [scheduled release]. Si; b&w. 35mm. 5 reels.

Dir Jack Nelson. *Scen* George Plympton.

Cast: Richard Talmadge *(Dan Merrill)*, Charlotte Pierce *(Mary Fenton)*, Maine Geary *(Jim Hanley)*, S. J. Bingham *(Captain Strong)*, Taylor Graves *(Jerry Fenton)*, Ruth Langston *(Marjory Arnold)*, Fred Kohler *("Red" Burke)*, Edith Yorke *(Dan's mother)*, George Sherwood *(Howard Morton)*, C. H. Hailes *(Bertram Arnold)*, Pal *(Sparks, the dog)*.

Comedy-drama. "Dan Merrill is discharged from the fire department where he has distinguished himself because he is physically unable to stay in a smoking room. His enemies tell his girl, Mary Fenton, that he is a coward. But he proves his efficiency by trailing a gang of crooks who have been responsible for robberies in which they covered their tracks by starting fires. Once more a hero, he squares himself with the company and with the girl." (*Moving Picture World,* 30 Jun 1923, p786.) *Firemen. Robbery. Cowardice. Incendiarism. Dogs.*

THUMBS DOWN F2.5698

Banner Productions. *Dist* Sterling Pictures Distributing Corp. 15 Jun **1927** [c5 Jul 1927; LP24146]. Si; b&w. 35mm. 5 reels, 4,723 ft.

Dir Phil Rosen. *Scen* Frances Guihan. *Story* Gladys E. Johnson. *Photog* Herbert Kirkpatrick.

Cast: Creighton Hale *(Richard Hale)*, Lois Boyd *(Helen Stanton)*, Wyndham Standing *(James Breen)*, Helen Lee Worthing *(Marion Ames)*, Vera Lewis *(Mrs. Hale)*, Scott Seaton *(Mr. Stanton)*.

Domestic melodrama. Though typist Helen Stanton loves wealthy Richard Hale, she refuses to marry him. Mrs. Hale prefers that he marry Marion Ames, her ward and a society girl, and solicits the aid of Jim Breen, her cousin, in convicing Richard. Helen unwillingly elopes with Richard, but she is received coldly by the family; Mrs. Dale persuades Richard that Helen and Breen are unduly intimate and hires a detective to watch her. Dick accuses Helen; she pleads with him; but he goes in a rage to Breen. Breen overpowers him and informs him that Helen's father has been wrongfully jailed and that she wishes to keep this fact a secret. Dick repents, Helen's father is freed through Breen, and they are all reunited. *Typists. Socialites. Wards. Cousins. Marriage. Injustice. Social classes.*

THUNDER F2.5699

Metro-Goldwyn-Mayer Pictures. 20 Jul **1929** [c29 Jul 1929; LP558]. Mus score & sd eff (Movietone); b&w. 35mm. 9 reels, 7,783 ft. [Also si.]

Supv Hunt Stromberg. *Dir* William Nigh. *Scen* Byron Morgan, Ann Price. *Titl* Joe Farnham. *Story* Byron Morgan. *Photog* Henry Sharp. *Film Ed* Ben Lewis. *Dance Dir* George Cunningham.

Cast: Lon Chaney *(Grumpy Anderson)*, Phyllis Haver *(Zella)*, George Duryea *(Jim)*, James Murray *(Tommy)*, Frances Norris *(Molly)*, Wally Albright, Jr. *(Davey)*.

Melodrama. Twenty-nine minutes late into Chicago, engineer Anderson, nicknamed Grumpy because of his single-minded devotion to timetables and railroad protocol, plows through heavy snowdrifts to make up lost time. His sons have followed into the railroading business, but they are gradually embittered by his apparent callousness. One of them was worked to exhaustion as the fireman of the Chicago run through the snow but gained sympathy from Zella, a nightclub singer whose private car Anderson had refused to tow, forcing her to jump into the cab and ride. His stubborn inflexibility eventually alienates his in-laws, causes the death of one of his sons, and provokes a wreck on the train on which the body was being carried by scuffling with his other son over his culpability for the death. Relegated to the railroad machine shop, he is called to service during the crisis of the Mississippi floods, and he ends up, along with his estranged son, at the throttle of a relief train that blasts through the flooded area on track often submerged as much as 4 feet to save the widow of his son and Zella, who are stranded in the flood area. *Singers. Railroad engineers. Railroad firemen. Filial relations. Railroads. Floods. Storms. Mississippi Delta.*

THUNDER ISLAND F2.5700

Universal Film Manufacturing Co. Jun **1921** [c7 Jun 1921; LP16662]. Si; b&w. 35mm. 5 reels, 4,279 ft.

Dir Norman Dawn. *Scen* Wallace Clifton. *Photog* Thomas Rae.

Cast: Edith Roberts *(Isola Garcia/Juan Garcia)*, Fred De Silva *(Pio Mendoza)*, Jack O'Brien *(Paul Corbin)*, Arthur Jasmine *(Sanchez the Loco)*, Fred Kohler *(Barney the Mate)*.

Melodrama. Source: Beatrice Grimshaw, *My Lady of the Island* (Chicago, 1916). Isola Garcia falls in love with Paul Corbin, young American sea captain, after he rescues her from Mexican sheep bandits. Then she suddenly discovers she is the wife of Mendoza, a ranch owner who married her when he appeared to be dying, but who is reported to have recovered. The rancher's agent, learning that the owner actually has died, escorts the girl to Thunder Island as Mendoza. Disguising herself, the girl flees to the security of the American captain's ship, and when the gang attack the schooner the ship's officers quell a mutiny and Isola learns she is free to marry Corbin. *Sea captains. Ranchers. Bandits. Ship crews. Mutiny. Disguise. Male impersonation. Mexico.*

THUNDER MOUNTAIN F2.5701

Fox Film Corp. 11 Oct **1925** [c4 Oct 1925; LP21954]. Si; b&w. 35mm. 8 reels, 7,537 ft.

Pres by William Fox. *Dir* Victor Schertzinger. *Scen* Eve Unsell. *Photog* Glen MacWilliams.

Cast: Madge Bellamy *(Azalea)*, Leslie Fenton *(Sam Martin)*, Alec B. Francis *(preacher)*, Paul Panzer *(Morgan)*, Arthur Houseman *(Joe Givens)*, ZaSu Pitts *(Mandy Coulter)*, Emily Fitzroy *(Ma MacBirney)*, Dan Mason *(Pa MacBirney)*, Otis Harlan *(Jeff Coulter)*, Russell Simpson *(Si Pace)*, Natalie Warfield *(Mrs. Coulter)*.

Rural melodrama. Source: Pearl Franklin, *Thunder* or *Howdy Folks* (a play, based on a story by Elia W. Peattie; publication undetermined). Thunder Mountain is the home of illiterate folk where only the moneylender, Si Pace, has "book larnin'," and there is a long-standing feud between the Martins and Givenses. Sam Martin is persuaded by the preacher to leave and acquire an education. He returns after 3 years determined to build a schoolhouse, but Pace refuses to lend him the money. Azalea, a circus performer, flees from the show and its owner, Morgan. Sam befriends her against the wishes of his people. She dances for Pace in tights and spangles in a vain attempt to raise the funds. Discovered and doubted by Sam, she determines to elope with Joe Givens. Just before they elope, Givens robs and murders Pace, and the townspeople fix the blame on Sam. They proceed to the mountain to hang Sam when the preacher, as a sign of God's wrath, ignites a charge of dynamite he planted in the mountain. Givens, in his fear, confesses to the crime; Sam builds his school and marries Azalea. *Moneylenders. Education. Murder. Robbery. Feuds. Circus. Mountain life.*

THUNDER RIDERS F2.5702

Universal Pictures. 8 Apr **1928** [c31 Oct 1927; LP24620]. Si; b&w. 35mm. 5 reels, 4,363 ft.

Pres by Carl Laemmle. *Dir* William Wyler. *Scen* Carl Krusada. *Titl* Gardner Bradford. *Story* Basil Dickey. *Photog* Milton Bridenbecker. *Art Dir* David S. Garber. *Film Ed* Harry Marker.

Cast: Ted Wells *(Jack Duncan)*, Charlotte Stevens *(Betty Barton)*, William A. Steele *(Lem Dawson)*, Bill Dyer *(Lon Seeright)*, Leo White *(Prof. Wilfred Winkle)*, Julia Griffith *(Cynthia Straight)*, Bob Burns *(sheriff)*, Pee Wee Holmes, Dick L'Estrange *(riders)*.

Western melodrama. Betty Barton comes west to claim the ranch and fortune left her by her father—in trust with his old friend, Lon Seeright. He and his foreman, Jack, plan a reception calculated to measure up to the easterner's ideas of the wild and wooly West. When Betty arrives with her Aunt Cynthia Straight, the trip is interrupted by an Indian attack, planned by Seeright, which frightens her companions but delights Betty. Thus, when Jack plans to "kidnap" Betty from a masked ball, local gambler Lem Dawson sees his chance to get his hands on her; and Jack is captured by Dawson's gang, while Dawson takes Betty to the hills; Jack escapes and arrives just in time to save her from a forced marriage. *Ranch foremen. Aunts. Inheritance. Kidnaping. Disguise. Ranches.*

THUNDERBOLT F2.5703

Paramount Famous Lasky Corp. 22 Jun **1929** [c20 Jun 1929; LP487]. Sd (Movietone); b&w. 35mm. 8 reels, 8,571 ft. [Also si; 7,311 ft.]

Assoc Prod B. P. Fineman. *Dir* Josef von Sternberg. *Screenplay* Jules Furthman. *Dial* Herman J. Mankiewicz. *Titl* Joseph Mankiewicz. *Story* Charles Furthman, Jules Furthman. *Photog* Henry Gerrard. *Sets* Hans Dreier. *Film Ed* Helen Lewis. *Song: "Thinkin' About My Baby"* Sam Coslow. *Rec Engr* M. M. Paggi.

Cast: George Bancroft *(Thunderbolt Jim Lang)*, Fay Wray *("Ritzy")*, Richard Arlen *(Bob Morgan)*, Tully Marshall *(warden)*, Eugenie Besserer *(Mrs. Morgan)*, James Spottswood *(Snapper O'Shea)*, Fred Kohler *(Bad Al Frieberg)*, Robert Elliott *(prison chaplain)*, E. H. Calvert *(District Attorney McKay)*, George Irving *(Mr. Corwin)*, Mike Donlin *(Kentucky Sampson)*, S. S. Stewart *(Negro convict)*, William L. Thorne *(police inspector)*.

Underworld melodrama. Thunderbolt Jim Lang, wanted on robbery and murder charges, ventures out with his girl, "Ritzy," to a Harlem nightclub, where she informs him that she is going straight. During a raid on the club, Thunderbolt escapes. His gang shadows Ritzy and reports that she is living with Mrs. Morgan, whose son, Bob, a bank clerk, is in love with Ritzy. Fearing for Bob's safety, Ritzy engineers a police trap for Thunderbolt; he escapes but is later captured, tried, and sentenced to be executed at Sing Sing. From the death house he plots to frame Bob in a bank robbery and killing. Bob is placed in the facing cell, and guards frustrate Thunderbolt's attempts to get to his rival. When Ritzy marries Bob in the death house, Thunderbolt is affected and pretends repentance, confessing his part in Bob's conviction. He plots to kill the boy on the night of his execution, but instead his hand falls on his shoulder in a gesture of friendship. *Gangsters. Bank clerks. Criminals—Rehabilitation. Capital punishment. Prisons. Sing Sing. New York City—Harlem.*

THE THUNDERBOLT STRIKES **F2.5704**

Harry Webb Productions. *Dist* Rayart Pictures. 29 Jan **1926** [New York State license]. Si; b&w. 35mm. 5 reels, 4,800 ft.

Cast: Jack Perrin.

Western melodrama(?). No information about the nature of this film has been found.

THUNDERBOLT'S TRACKS **F2.5705**

Morris R. Schlank Productions. *Dist* Rayart Pictures. Apr **1927.** Si; b&w. 35mm. 5 reels, 4,846 ft.

Dir? J. P. McGowan, Bennett Cohn. *Scen* Bennett Cohn. *Photog* William Hyer.

Cast: Jack Perrin *(Sgt. Larry Donovan)*, Pauline Curley *(Alice Hayden)*, Jack Henderson *(Pop Hayden)*, Billy Lamar *(Red)*, Harry Tenbrook *(Cpl. Biff Flannagan)*, Ethan Laidlaw *(Buck Moulton)*, Ruth Royce *(Speedy)*, Starlight *(a horse)*.

Western melodrama. "Two Marines searching for family of a mate killed in France, find the family in Mexico. They have been duped by town bad man, who sells them worthless ranch. The Marines right matters after a fight." (*Motion Picture News Booking Guide*, 13:43, Oct 1927.) *Fraud. World War I. United States Marines. Mexico.*

Note: Although screen credit is given to McGowan, *Film Year Book* and *Motion Picture News Booking Guide* credit Bennett Cohn with direction.

THUNDERCLAP **F2.5706**

Fox Film Corp. Aug **1921** [c25 Aug 1921; LP17004]. Si; b&w. 35mm. 7 reels, 6,745 ft.

Pres by William Fox. *Dir* Richard Stanton. *Story-Scen* Paul H. Sloane. *Photog* George W. Lane.

Cast: Mary Carr *(Mrs. Jamieson)*, J. Barney Sherry *(Lionel Jamieson)*, Paul Willis *(Tommy)*, Violet Mersereau *(Betty, The Girl)*, Carol Chase *(Betty, The Baby)*, John Daly Murphy *(Wah Leong)*, Walter McEwen *(Foster)*, Maude Hill *(Marian Audrey)*, Thomas McCann *(Gunga Din)*.

Melodrama. Lionel Jamieson, a gambling house proprietor whose brutality has rendered his wife paralytic, takes his young stepdaughter from a convent and proposes to use her as a lure for customers. Tommy, an employee of Jamieson's who sympathizes with the mother and daughter, falls in love with Betty; with the assistance of Gunga Din, an old stablehand, he is training his horse Thunderclap for a racing event. When Jamieson is caught cheating by a client, his victim threatens to kill him unless he repays his loss of $40,000; and the gambler's friend, Foster, agrees to help provided that his horse wins against Thunderclap. Jamieson plots to blow up a bridge and destroy Tommy's horse, but Gunga Din, suspecting foul play, takes the horse safely to the track. Tommy rescues Betty from abduction by Chinese, returns to the track, and rides Thunderclap to victory. Jamieson is killed by his victim, and the shock restores his wife to health. *Gamblers. Stepfathers. Chinese. Invalids. Horseracing. Abduction.*

THUNDERGATE **F2.5707**

Associated First National Pictures. 15 Oct **1923** [c17 Oct 1923; LP19498]. Si; b&w. 35mm. 7 reels, 6,565 ft.

Dir Joseph De Grasse. *Scen* Perry N. Vekroff. *Story* Sydney Herschel Small. *Photog* Sam Landers, Robert De Grasse.

Cast: Owen Moore *(Robert Wells [Kong Sue])*, Virginia Brown Faire *(Ellen Ainsmith [Jen Jue])*, Edwin Booth Tilton *(James Sanderson, Bob's uncle)*, Sylvia Breamer *(Alberta Hayward)*, Robert McKim *(Ray Williams)*, Richard Cummings *(Jim Davis)*, W. E. Dyer *(Mike)*, Tully Marshall *(Suen Tung [Lord of Thundergate])*, Tote Du Crow *(Yuen Kai)*, Ynez Seabury *(Mey Wang)*.

Melodrama. Robert Wells, an American youth who was reared in China, goes abroad for his uncle, James Sanderson, to assist in the construction of a bridge for the Chinese Government. Ray Williams, construction manager secretly employed by Chinese imperialists whose aim is to impede construction, introduces Wells to a narcotic that when taken causes him to neglect his work. Wells is in a dissolute stupor when the wayward son of the Lord of Thundergate meets him by chance and, noting the striking resemblance between them, exchanges identities with Wells, who as a result becomes involved in a daring conspiracy culminating in romance with a Chinese-reared white girl and in his own physical rehabilitation. *Engineers—Civil. Narcotics. Impersonation. Bridges. China.*

THUNDERGOD **F2.5708**

Morris R. Schlank Productions. *Dist* Anchor Film Distributors. 15 Jun **1928.** Si; b&w. 35mm. 6 reels, 5,917 ft.

Dir Charles J. Hunt. *Scen* Arthur Hoerl. *Photog* Robert E. Cline. *Film Ed* William Holmes.

Cast: Cornelius Keefe *(Roland Hale)*, Lila Lee *(Enid Bryant)*, Walter Long *(Bruce Drossler)*, Helen Lynch *(Alyce)*, Ray Hallor *(Ollie Sanderson)*, Jules Cowles *(Clinky)*.

Northwest melodrama. Source: James Oliver Curwood, unidentified story. Trying to forget the sweetheart who jilted him, Roland Hale comes from the city to a lumber camp, which is managed by Enid Bryant. Her superintendent tries mightily to prevent the heroine from getting her logs down the river in time, but right prevails, and the villain is killed by a bolt of lightning from Thundergod Mountain—thus carrying out its old Indian legend of vengeance. *Lumber camps. Lumbering. Lightning. Revenge.*

THUNDERING DAWN (Universal-Jewel) **F2.5709**

Universal Pictures. 5 Nov **1923** [c24 Sep 1923; LP19449]. Si; b&w. 35mm. 7 reels, 6,600 ft.

Prod-Dir Harry Garson. *Scen* Lenore Coffee, John Goodrich. *Titl* Sada Cowan. *Adapt* Raymond L. Schrock. *Story* John Blackwood. *Photog* Charles Richardson, Louis Physioc, Elmer Ellsworth.

Cast: Winter Hall *(The Elder Standish)*, J. Warren Kerrigan *(Jack Standish)*, Anna Q. Nilsson *(Mary Rogers)*, Tom Santschi *(Gordon Van Brock)*, Charles Clary *(Lawyer Sprott)*, Georgia Woodthorpe *(Mrs. Standish)*, Richard Kean *(The Hotel Keeper)*, Edward Burns *(Michael Carmichael)*, Winifred Bryson *(Lullaby Lou)*, Anna May Wong *(The Honky Tonk Girl)*.

Melodrama. Jack Standish feels responsible for the failure of the partnership with his father and goes to the South Seas where he falls prey to alcohol, is seduced by Lullaby Lou, a vamp, and tricked by a brutal plantation owner, Gordon Van Brock. Mary Rogers, Standish's fiancée, finds him in Java and nurses him back to health. They return to the States. *Vamps. Planters. Filial relations. Alcoholism. South Sea Islands. Java.*

Note: Universal records credit Leonore Coffee and John Goodrich with story; Raymond L. Schrock with adaptation; and Sada Cowan with titles. Working titles: *Havoc; The Bond of the Ring.*

THE THUNDERING HERD **F2.5710**

Famous Players–Lasky. *Dist* Paramount Pictures. 7 Mar **1925** [c23 Feb 1925; LP21180]. Si; b&w. 35mm. 7 reels, 7,187 ft.

Pres by Adolph Zukor, Jesse L. Lasky. *Dir* William K. Howard. *Scen* Lucien Hubbard. *Photog* Lucien Andriot.

Cast: Jack Holt *(Tom Doan)*, Lois Wilson *(Milly Fayre)*, Noah Beery *(Randall Jett)*, Raymond Hatton *(Jude Pilchuk)*, Charles Ogle *(Clark Hudnall)*, Col. T. J. McCoy *(Burn Hudnall)*, Lillian Leighton *(Mrs. Clark Hudnall)*, Eulalie Jensen *(Mrs. Randall Jett)*, Stephen Carr *(Ory Tacks)*, Maxine Elliott Hicks *(Sally Hudnall)*, Edward J. Brady *(Pruitt)*, Pat Hartigan *(Catlett)*, Fred Kohler *(Follansbee)*, Robert Perry *(Joe Dunn)*.

Western melodrama. Source: Zane Grey, *The Thundering Herd* (New York, c1925). In 1876, a band of buffalo hunters assembles at Sprague's Trading Post and is joined by Tom Doan, fresh from a Kansas farm. At the post, Tom meets, and falls in love with, Milly Fayre, the stepdaughter of Randall Jett, the leader of a gang of notorious outlaws who make a brutal living robbing buffalo hunters. Milly and Tom are separated, and there is an Indian uprising sparked by the irresponsible slaughtering of the buffalo herds by white adventurers. Jett is killed by his own men, and Milly escapes, attempting to make her way back to civilization. She is chased by a party of hostile Indians and falls in front of a herd of stampeding buffalo. Tom rescues her. The buffalo hunters subdue the Indians, and Tom and Milly head back to civilization. *Kansans. Stepfathers. Bandits. Indians of North America. Buffalo.*

THUNDERING HOOFS **F2.5711**

New Era Productions. *Dist* Anchor Film Distributors. Sep or 1 Oct **1922.** Si; b&w. 35mm. 5 reels, 4,514 ft.

Dir Francis Ford. *Photog* O. G. Hill.

Cast: Peggy O'Day *(The Girl)*, Francis Ford *(Jimmy)*, Florence Murth *(His Sister)*, Phil Ford *(Her Son)*, Harry Kelly *(Bill)*.

Melodrama. "Race-track drama which treats of southern girl who returns to Kentucky after a long absence in a boarding school. She arrives just in time to keep an important entry in the Kentucky Derby from being forfeited through the evil intentions of a woman plotter. The girl mounts the horse with the discarded colors and wins the race. She also wins the contest in a race for a husband." (*Motion Picture News Booking Guide*, 4: 100, Apr 1923.) *Horseracing. Kentucky Derby.*

THUNDERING HOOFS F2.5712

Monogram Pictures. *Dist* Film Booking Offices of America. 26 Oct **1924** [c21 Sep 1924; LP20751]. Si; b&w. 35mm. 5 reels, 5,033 ft.

Dir Albert Rogell. *Story-Cont* Marion Jackson. *Photog* Ross Fisher.

Cast: Fred Thomson *(Dave Marshall)*, Fred Huntley *(John Marshall)*, Charles Mailes *(Don Juan Estrada)*, Charles De Revenna *(Don Carlos)*, Ann May *(Carmelita)*, Carrie Clark Ward *(duenna)*, William Lowery *(Luke Severn)*, Silver King *(himself, a horse)*.

Western melodrama. Dave Marshall takes many dangerous chances in his efforts to visit his sweetheart, Carmelita, as a result of bandit Luke Severn's success in making Carmelita's father, Don Juan Estrada, believe that Dave is an outlaw. When Don Estrada takes his daughter back to Mexico, Severn finally has Dave jailed on trumped-up charges; but Dave escapes in time to save his horse, Silver King, from being gored in a bullring; and the pair proceed to bulldog the bull—American style. The audience is enthusiastic in its praise, Don Estrada consents to the marriage of Carmelita and Dave, and the sheriff arrives for Severn. *Cowboys. Bandits. Bullfighting. Bulldogging. Horses. Mexico.*

THUNDERING ROMANCE F2.5713

Action Pictures. *Dist* Weiss Brothers Artclass Pictures. 15 Dec **1924** [c7 Feb 1925; LU21110]. Si; b&w. 35mm. 5 reels, 4,750 ft.

Pres by Lester F. Scott, Jr., W. T. Lackey. *Dir* Richard Thorpe. *Story* Ned Nye. *Photog* Ray Ries.

Cast: Buffalo Bill Jr. *("Lightning" Bill)*, Jean Arthur *(Mary Watkins)*, René Picot *(Lew Simons)*, Harry Todd *(Davey Jones)*, Lew Meehan *(Hank Callahan)*, J. P. Lockney *(Mark Jennings)*, George A. Williams *(The Oil Representative)*, Lafe McKee *(The Sheriff)*.

Western melodrama. Davey Jones, an old sailor looking for treasure buried in the desert, is forced into a fight with Hank Callahan, the town bully and brother-in-law of the sheriff. Bill intervenes in the fight, floors Hank, and, when Hank draws on him, shoots him in the shoulder. Bill then rides quickly out of town, followed closely by the posse, which he eludes by jumping his horse across a wide gorge. Bill is later mistaken by Mary Watkins for her long-lost brother. Bill continues with the impersonation in order to save Mary's ranch from the oil company, which has given her just 3 days to pay off a lien on her land. Bill decides to sell Mary's cattle to raise the necessary money, but his plan is overheard, and the cattle are stampeded over the edge of a deep gorge by the hired guns of a crooked attorney. Bill collects the money for the dead cattle from the attorney at the point of the gun, pays off the lien, reveals his true identity, and asks Mary to marry him. Davey Jones finds the buried treasure. *Sailors. Lawyers. Posses. Impersonation. Oil business. Land rights. Ranches. Treasure. Stampedes.*

THUNDERING SPEED F2.5714

Chesterfield Motion Pictures. May or 15 Aug **1926.** Si; b&w. 35mm. 5 reels, 4,510 ft.

Prod H. T. Henderson. *Dir* Alvin J. Neitz. *Photog* Bert Baldridge.

Cast: Eileen Sedgwick.

Western melodrama. "Girl is involved in legal tangle over water rights through villain's scheming. With the assistance of U. S. Marshal the girl regains her property." (*Motion Picture News Booking Guide,* 11:51, Oct 1926.) *United States marshals. Water rights.*

THUNDERING THOMPSON F2.5715

Morris R. Schlank Productions. *Dist* Anchor Film Distributors. 8 Oct **1929** [New York showing]. Si; b&w. 35mm. 5 reels, 4,600 ft.

Dir Benjamin Franklin Wilson. *Story* Robert Dillon. *Photog* Robert Cline. *Film Ed* Earl C. Turner.

Cast: Cheyenne Bill, Neva Gerber, Al Ferguson, Ed La Niece.

Western melodrama. "The hero is appointed a deputy sheriff to oust the girl and her father from certain grazing lands that the heavy claims belong to him. So the deputy sheriff takes a beating from the hands of the gang, but comes back strong in the finish fight and outwits the gang leader and saves the land and the gal and everything." (*Film Daily,* 27 Oct 1929, p12.) *Sheriffs. Ranchers. Homesteaders. Gangs. Land rights.*

THUNDERING THROUGH F2.5716

Action Pictures. *Dist* Weiss Brothers Artclass Pictures. 13 Dec **1925.** Si; b&w. 35mm. 5 reels, 4,527 ft.

Dir Fred Bain. *Scen* Barr Cross.

Cast: Buddy Roosevelt *(Bud Lawson)*, Jean Arthur *(Ruth Burroughs)*, Charles Colby *(Blaze Burroughs)*, Lew Meehan *(Rufe Gorman)*, Frederick Lee *(Aaron Austin)*, L. J. O'Connor *(Ezra Hendrix)*, Lawrence Underwood *(John Richmond)*.

Western melodrama. Bud Lawson becomes a partner with John Richmond, the owner of a large ranch; Bud then falls in love with Ruth Burroughs, the daughter of Blaze Burroughs, a neighboring rancher. Aaron Austin, the town banker, knows that the new railroad will pass through the spreads of both Burroughs and Lawson and tries to gain control of the land with the help of the Gorman gang. Bud fights off the intruders, brings them to justice, and wins Ruth. *Ranchers. Bankers. Land rights. Railroads.*

THY NAME IS WOMAN F2.5717

Louis B. Mayer Productions. *Dist* Metro Pictures. 4 Feb **1924** [c20 Feb 1924; LP19940]. Si; b&w. 35mm. 9 reels, 9,087 ft.

Pres by Louis B. Mayer. *Dir* Fred Niblo. *Adapt-Cont* Bess Meredyth. *Photog* Victor Milner. *Art Dir* Ben Carré. *Film Ed* Lloyd Nosler.

Cast: Ramon Novarro *(Juan Ricardo)*, Barbara La Marr *(Guerita)*, William V. Mong *(Pedro the Fox, her husband)*, Wallace MacDonald *(Captain Roderigo de Castelar)*, Robert Edeson *(The Comandante)*, Edith Roberts *(Dolores, his daughter)*, Claire McDowell *(Juan's mother)*.

Romantic tragedy. Source: C. Schöner, *Thy Name Is Woman* (trans. by Benjamin Floyer Glazer; New York opening: 15 Nov 1920). Juan Ricardo, a soldier in the Spanish Army, is promised a promotion to the rank of sergeant if he will make love with Guerita, the wife of Pedro, a known smuggler, so that she will disclose the location of her husband's illicit booty. He genuinely falls in love with her and, realizing that he will be dishonored if he fails to fulfill his mission, he decides to run away with Guerita. Pedro sees what is happening, kills Guerita, then himself dies of heart disease. Dolores, daughter of the *comandante,* saves Juan from court-martial by pleading for him. *Soldiers. Smugglers. Military life. Spain.*

TIDE OF EMPIRE F2.5718

Cosmopolitan Productions. *Dist* Metro-Goldwyn-Mayer Distributing Corp. 23 Mar **1929** [c5 Mar 1929; LP181]. Mus score & sd eff (Movietone); b&w. 35mm. 8 reels, 6,552 ft.

Dir Allan Dwan. *Cont* Waldemar Young. *Titl* Joseph Farnham. *Photog* Merritt B. Gerstad. *Set Dsgn* Cedric Gibbons. *Film Ed* Blanche Sewell. *Song: "Josephine"* Ray Klages, Jesse Greer. *Wardrobe* David Cox.

Cast: Renée Adorée *(Josephita)*, George Duryea *(Dermod D'Arcy)*, George Fawcett *(Don José)*, William Collier, Jr. *(Romauldo)*, Fred Kohler *(Cannon)*, James Bradbury, Sr. *(Bejabbers)*, Harry Gribbon *(O'Shea)*, Paul Hurst *(Poppy)*.

Western melodrama. Source: Peter Bernard Kyne, *Tide of Empire* (New York, 1928). "Hero wins ranch of girl's father but falls in love with her and gives her the deed. He leaves to hunt for gold. Girl's father commits suicide and girl seeks hero. Town is attacked by outlaws but repulsed by people of the town. Heroine's brother is wounded and sentenced to hang for forced part in attack but rescued by hero. They return to the ranch where he marries the girl." ("Motion Picture News Booking Guide," in *Motion Picture News,* 15 Mar 1930, p106) *Outlaws. Brother-sister relationship. Suicide. Injustice. Property rights. Capital punishment.*

TIDES OF PASSION F2.5719

Vitagraph Co. of America. 26 Apr **1925** [c6 Apr 1925; LP21344]. Si; b&w. 35mm. 7 reels, 6,279 ft.

Dir J. Stuart Blackton. *Adapt* Marian Constance. *Photog* William S. Adams.

Cast: Mae Marsh *(Charity)*, Ben Hendricks *(William Pennland)*, Laska Winter *(Hagar)*, Earl Schenck *(Jonas)*, Ivor McFadden *(Alick)*, Thomas Mills *(Michael)*.

Melodrama. Source: Basil King, *In the Garden of Charity* (New York, 1903). In a small Nova Scotia fishing village, Charity Byfleet marries William Pennland, a romantic soldier of fortune, just before he starts the long voyage home on a small ship bound for Canada. The irrepressible Pennland, however, soon begins a flirtation with the captain's wife and is thrown overboard. He manages to swim to shore, landing on a rough and isolated stretch of the Nova Scotia coast, where he is found half dead and nursed back to health by Hagar, a beautiful girl of mixed blood. Pennland stays with Hagar until he is well and gallantly marries her so as to quiet village gossip; he tells her later of his intention to return to Charity, and Hagar abandons him on a barren island off the coast, relenting only when he is about to expire from exposure and starvation. Charity learns of Pennland's whereabouts and arrives in time to be with him when he dies. Charity takes Hagar into her home, and Hagar soon gives birth to a child, who greatly delights Charity. Hagar, repenting of her deeds, tries to commit suicide, but Charity prevents her, and both women eventually find in new loves a solace for wounded hearts. *Soldiers of fortune. Halfcastes. Bigamy. Fishing villages. Nova Scotia. India.*

THE TIE THAT BINDS **F2.5720**

Jacob Wilk. *Dist* Warner Brothers Pictures. 15 Mar **1923** [scheduled release]. Si; b&w. 35mm. 7 reels.

Prod? (see note) Ben Goetz. *Dir* Joseph Levering. *Adapt* Pearl Keating. *Photog* George Robinson.

Cast: Walter Miller *(David Winthrop)*, Barbara Bedford *(Mary Ellen Gray)*, Raymond Hatton *(Hiram Foster)*, William P. Carleton *(Daniel Kenyon)*, Robert Edeson *(Charles Dodge)*, Julia Swayne Gordon *(Leila Brant)*, Marian Swayne *(Flora Foster)*, Effie Shannon *(Mrs. Mills)*.

Melodrama. Source: Peter Bernard Kyne, "The Tie That Binds" (publication undetermined). Mary Gray, a secretary, chooses to marry David Winthrop, an employee in the firm where Dan Kenyon, who also loves her, is a partner. Winthrop is fired, the marriage fails, and Mary returns to work as Kenyon's secretary. Kenyon continues his unwelcome suit, and Mary is suspected of killing Kenyon when he is found dead. So as to shield Mary, whom he believes to be guilty, Winthrop confesses. Both are exonerated when Hiram Foster, the night watchman whose daughter Kenyon wronged, confesses to the crime and then commits suicide. *Secretaries. Watchmen. Marriage. Murder. Suicide.*

Note: Some sources indicate that the film was manufactured by Ben Goetz of the Erbograph Co.

TIES OF BLOOD **F2.5721**

Reol Productions. **1921.** Si; b&w. 35mm. [Feature length assumed.]

Cast: Inez Clough, Arthur Ray, Harry Pleasant.

Melodrama(?). No information about the precise nature of this film has been found. *Negro life.*

TIGER LOVE **F2.5722**

Famous Players–Lasky. *Dist* Paramount Pictures. 30 Jun **1924** [c25 Jun 1924; LP20344]. Si; b&w. 35mm. 6 reels, 5,325 ft.

Pres by Adolph Zukor, Jesse L. Lasky. *Dir* George Melford. *Scen* Howard Hawks. *Adapt* Julie Herne. *Photog* Charles G. Clarke.

Cast: Antonio Moreno *(The Wildcat)*, Estelle Taylor *(Marcheta)*, G. Raymond Nye *(El Pezuño)*, Manuel Camero *(Don Ramón)*, Edgar Norton *(Don Victoriano Fuentes)*, David Torrence *(Don Miguel Castelar)*, Snitz Edwards *(The Hunchback)*, Monte Collins *(Father Zaspard)*.

Romantic drama. Source: Manuel Peñella, *El Gato Montes* (light opera; New York opening [as "The Wildcat"]: Feb 1922). The Wildcat, a Robin Hood of the Spanish hills and son of an aristocrat, falls in love with Marcheta, who is pledged to marry Don Ramón to save the family fortune. On her wedding day The Wildcat abducts her and reveals his aristocratic identity. *Aristocrats. Bandits. Impersonation. Abduction. Spain.*

TIGER ROSE **F2.5723**

Warner Brothers Pictures. 28 Nov **1923** [Baltimore showing; released 9 Dec; c22 Nov 1923; LP19639]. Si; b&w. 35mm. 8 reels, 7,400 ft.

Pres by David Belasco. *Dir* Sidney A. Franklin. *Adapt* Edmund Goulding, Millard Webb. *Photog* Charles Rosher.

Cast: Lenore Ulric *("Tiger Rose," Rose Bocion)*, Forrest Stanley *(Michael Devlin)*, Joseph Dowling *(Father Thibault)*, André de Beranger *(Pierre)*, Sam De Grasse *(Dr. Cusick)*, Theodore von Eltz *(Bruce Norton)*, Claude Gillingwater *(Hector McCollins)*.

Melodrama. Source: Willard Mack, *Tiger Rose, a Melodrama of the Great Northwest, in 3 Acts* (New York opening: 3 Oct 1917; New York, Belasco Play Bureau, 1917). Royal Northwest Mounted Policeman Michael Devlin saves Rose Bocion from drowning and subsequently falls in love with her. However, she is attracted to engineer Bruce Norton and aids him to escape when he kills the man who seduced his sister. Later, Norton turns himself in to Devlin, serves a short jail sentence, and marries Rose. *Engineers. Seduction. Murder. Northwest Mounted Police.*

Note: Remade in 1929 under the same title, q. v.

TIGER ROSE **F2.5724**

Warner Brothers Pictures. 21 Dec **1929** [c3 Dec 1929; LP882]. Sd (Vitaphone); b&w. 35mm. 6 reels, 5,509 ft. [Also si.]

Dir George Fitzmaurice. *Scen-Dial* Harvey Thew, Gordon Rigby. *Titl* De Leon Anthony. *Photog* Tony Gaudio. *Film Ed* Thomas Pratt. *Song: "The Day You Fall In Love"* Ned Washington, Herb Magidson, Michael Cleary.

Cast: Monte Blue *(Devlin)*, Lupe Velez *(Rose)*, H. B. Warner *(Dr. Cusick)*, Tully Marshall *(Hector McCollins)*, Grant Withers *(Bruce)*, Gaston Glass *(Pierre)*, Bull Montana *(Joe)*, Rin-Tin-Tin *(Scotty)*, Slim Summerville *(Heine)*, Louis Mercier *(Frenchie)*, Gordon Magee *(Hainey)*, Heinie Conklin *(Gus)*, Leslie Sketchley *(Mounted Police Officer)*.

Northwest melodrama. Source: Willard Mack, *Tiger Rose, a Melodrama of the Great Northwest, in 3 Acts* (New York opening: 3 Oct 1917; New York, Belasco Play Bureau, 1917). Rose, the tempestuous French Canadian ward of Hector McCollins of the Hudson's Bay Co., is courted by Devlin, a Mountie, and Joe, an Irishman, among others. But she falls in love with Bruce, a young railroad engineer, while Dr. Cusick, an erratic physician, keeps a fanatically protective eye on her and resents the intrusion of the railroad. Rose keeps a secret engagement with her lover, and Cusick, spying, learns of their plan to elope, intercepts Bruce, and tries to kill him. In the ensuing struggle, the maddened doctor is killed. After many escapes from the posse, Bruce and Rose start down the river in a canoe but discover that Devlin, hidden under a blanket, is accompanying them. Devlin, however, convinced of their love, returns to the settlement with the news that they have "gone over the rapids." *Railroad engineers. Physicians. French Canadians. Railroads. Hudson's Bay Co.. Dogs.*

Note: Remake of a 1923 film of the same title, q. v.

TIGER THOMPSON **F2.5725**

Stellar Productions. *Dist* W. W. Hodkinson Corp. 13 Jul **1924** [c13 Jul 1924; LP20414]. Si; b&w. 35mm. 6 reels, 4,920 ft.

Pres by Hunt Stromberg. *Supv* Hunt Stromberg. *Dir* B. Reeves Eason. *Story-Scen* Buckleigh Fritz Oxford. *Photog* Henry Sharp. *Film Ed* Harry Marker.

Cast: Harry Carey *(Tiger Thompson)*, Marguerite Clayton *(Ethel Brannon)*, John Dillon *(Jim Morley)*, Jack Richardson *(Bull Dorgan)*, George Ring *(Charlie Wong)*.

Western melodrama. Embittered because he has been dispossessed of a claim, Tiger Thompson finds a dying bandit from whom he learns about a hidden cache of plunder. He sets out to obtain a map from the bandit's daughter, but instead he falls in love with the girl and foils the efforts of another gang also seeking the loot. *Bandits. Treasure.*

TIGER TRUE **F2.5726**

Universal Film Manufacturing Co. Jan **1921** [c8 Jan 1921; LP16004]. Si; b&w. 35mm. 5 reels, 4,689 ft.

Dir J. P. McGowan. *Adapt* George C. Hull. *Photog* Jack Brown. *Film Ed* Frank Lawrence, Edward Schroeder.

Cast: Frank Mayo *(Jack Lodge)*, Fritzi Brunette *(Mary Dover)*, Eleanor Hancock *(Mrs. Lodge)*, Al Kaufman *(Larry Boynton)*, Walter Long *(Old Whitey/The Baboon)*, Charles Brinley *(McGuire)*, Herbert Bethew *(Sanford)*, Henry A. Barrows *(Mr. Lodge)*.

Mystery melodrama. Source: Max Brand, "Tiger," in *Argosy All-Story Weekly* (129:289–306, 460–474; 130:62–78, 214–227, 367–382, 552–565; 8 Jan–12 Feb 1921). Tiring of hunting big game in the jungle, Jack Lodge, son of a wealthy man, seeks adventure in the underworld district of a big city. With his companion, Sanford, he visits a saloon, where Jack soundly beats the bouncer. As a reward, Mary Dover, the owner, hires him; and all goes well until The Baboon, a jealous intruder, orders Jack to leave the establishment within an hour. After consulting with Old Whitey, Mary bids him leave, but Jack discovers that Old Whitey and The Baboon are not only one and the same but also Mary's half-brother. Jack wins the girl and takes her to his home. *Bouncers. Brother-sister relationship. Saloons. Big game.*

THE TIGER'S CLAW **F2.5727**

Famous Players–Lasky. *Dist* Paramount Pictures. ca18 Mar **1923** [New York premiere; released 22 Apr; c13 Mar 1923; LP18854]. Si; b&w. 35mm. 6 reels, 5,297 ft.

Pres by Jesse L. Lasky. *Dir* Joseph Henabery. *Story-Scen* Jack Cunningham. *Photog* Faxon M. Dean.

Cast: Jack Holt *(Sam Sandell)*, Eva Novak *(Harriet Halehurst)*, George Periolat *(Henry Frazer Halehurst)*, Bertram Grassby *(Raj Singh)*, Aileen Pringle *(Chameli Brentwood, a halfcaste)*, Carl Stockdale *(Sathoo Ram, a Thug chief)*, Frank Butler *(George Malvin, an inspector)*, George Field *(Prince)*, Evelyn Selbie *(Azun, Chameli's mother)*, Frederick Vroom *(Colonel Byng)*, Lucien Littlefield *(Goyrem)*, Robert Cain *(Sothern)*, Robert Dudley, Robin Hood *(a horse)*.

Melodrama. Sam Sandell, an American engineer working in India, is attacked by a tiger but rescued and nursed back to health by Chameli

Brentwood, a halfcaste. Sam's subsequent marriage to Chameli angers her uncle, Sathoo Ram, and Raj Singh, a former suitor, and results in a plot to destroy Sam and his dam. Sam's onetime English sweetheart, Harriet Halehurst, on the other hand, takes the marriage well and even accepts Chameli into society. Chameli proves to be faithless and is killed by a bullet meant for Sam, who has again been saved from a tiger—this time by Harriet. Sathoo, Singh, and their fellow Thugs succeed in breaking the dam; Sam is reunited with Harriet after rescuing her from the flood. *Engineers—Civil. Thugs. Halfcastes. English. Dams. India. Floods. Tigers. Horses.*

THE TIGRESS **F2.5728**

Columbia Pictures. 21 Oct **1927** [c23 Nov 1927; LP24687]. Si; b&w. 35mm. 6 reels, 5,357 ft.

Prod Harry Cohn. *Dir* George B. Seitz. *Scen* Harold Shumate. *Photog* Joseph Walker. *Art Dir* Robert E. Lee. *Film Ed* Ben Pivar. *Asst Dir* Clifford Saum.

Cast: Jack Holt *(Winston Graham, Earl of Eddington)*, Dorothy Revier *(Mona, "The Tigress")*, Frank Leigh *(Pietro the Bold)*, Philippe De Lacy *(Pippa)*, Howard Truesdell *(Tser)*, Frank Nelson *(Wibble)*.

Romantic melodrama. Mona, daughter of the Gypsy chieftain Tser, is coveted by Pietro the Bold, who resents taking orders from Tser. He organizes a poaching expedition to the estate of Doerlou Castle, and the Earl of Eddington is fired at during their early morning excursion; Pietro returns to camp with the body of Tser, and Mona swears vengeance upon her father's slayer. She is injured on Eddington's grounds and remains there during her convalescence. Posing as a servant, Eddington falls in love with her; later, incensed by Pietro, she confronts Eddington with his deception and performs the tribal "Dance of Death"; but love conquers her hate. Pietro orders Eddington seized, but Pippa, a mute boy, informs her that it was Pietro who killed Tser; the Gypsies pursue Pietro, and he is slain by Mona, who thereafter is united with Eddington. *Gypsies. Dancers. Mutes. Murder. Revenge. Impersonation. Poaching. Spain.*

TILL WE MEET AGAIN **F2.5729**

Dependable Pictures. *Dist* Associated Exhibitors. 15 Oct **1922** [c11 Oct 1922; LU18303]. Si; b&w. 35mm. 6 reels, 5,822 ft.

Dir-Story William Christy Cabanne. *Scen* Edmund Goulding. *Photog* William Tuers, Philip Armond. *Art Dir* Joseph Clement.

Cast: Julia Swayne Gordon *(Mrs. Whitney Carter)*, Mae Marsh *(Marion Bates)*, J. Barney Sherry *(Arthur Montrose)*, Walter Miller *(Jim Brennan)*, Norman Kerry *(Robert Carter)*, Martha Mansfield *(Henrietta Carter)*, Tammany Young *(Sam McGuire)*, Danny Hayes *(Pete Morrison)*, Dick Lee *(Clarence De Vere)*, Cyril Chadwick *(one of the gang)*.

Melodrama. Marion Bates, tricked by Arthur Montrose into becoming an inmate of an insane asylum, escapes and falls in with a gang of crooks. She agrees to cook for them and is befriended by their leader, Jim Brennan. Marion runs away from the gang and collapses at the home of her friends, the Carters. The Carters realize that Montrose has swindled Marion and them out of their money, and Robert Carter, who has fallen in love with Marion, steals some incriminating papers from Montrose's home. Robert reveals the evidence to Montrose, who hires Jim and his gang to recover the papers. In the melee that ensues Jim sees Marion and realizes Montrose's purposes, recognizes Robert as the wartime commanding officer who saved his life, summons the police by radio, and is killed. Montrose dies, and Robert comforts Marion. *Gangs. Swindlers. Insanity. Documentation.*

TILLIE **F2.5730**

Realart Pictures. *Dist* Paramount Pictures. 29 Jan **1922** [c1 Feb 1922; LP17513]. Si; b&w. 35mm. 5 reels.

Dir Frank Urson. *Scen* Alice Eyton. *Photog* Allen Davey.

Cast: Mary Miles Minter *(Tillie Getz)*, Noah Beery *(Jacob Getz)*, Allan Forrest *(Jack Fairchild)*, Lucien Littlefield *(Doc Weaver)*, Lillian Leighton *(Sarah Oberholtzer)*, Marie Treboul *(Sallie Getz)*, Virginia Adair *(Louisa)*, Robert Anderson *(Absalom Puntz)*, Ashley Cooper *(lawyer)*.

Rural drama. Source: Helen Reimensnyder Martin, *Tillie, a Mennonite Maid* (New York, 1904). Frank Howe, Jr., *Tillie, a Mennonite Maid* (Washington, D.C., production: Dec 1918). Tillie, daughter of a stern Pennsylvania Dutch farmer, Jake Getz, is treated as a farm chattel by her father, the trustee of the will of Sarah Oberholtzer, who leaves an inheritance to Tillie on the condition that she become a Mennonite before her 18th birthday. Doc Weaver takes an oath never to tell Tillie of this bequest, but the lawyer who draws up the will accepts a promissory note from young Absalom, whom he informs of the contents of the will. Absalom asks Jake for the hand of Tillie, promising him a stake in her inheritance. Frightened at the prospect of marrying Absalom, Tillie attempts suicide but is saved by Doc and Jack Fairchild, a stranger who learns about the will. Tillie then becomes a Mennonite, and to escape her father's tyranny she runs away. Tillie and Jack are married, and although she is turned from the church, Jack, who is Sarah Oberholtzer's nephew, assures her of her rights. *Farmers. Mennonites. Pennsylvania Dutch. Inheritance. Wills.*

Note: Copyright and working title: *Tillie, a Mennonite Maid.*

TILLIE, A MENNONITE MAID *see* **TILLIE**

TILLIE THE TOILER **F2.5731**

Cosmopolitan Productions. *Dist* Metro-Goldwyn-Mayer Distributing Corp. 21 May **1927** [c23 May 1927; LP24004]. Si; b&w. 35mm. 7 reels, 6,160 ft.

Dir Hobart Henley. *Screenplay* A. P. Younger. *Titl* Ralph Spence. *Story* Agnes Christine Johnston, Edward T. Lowe, Jr. *Photog* William Daniels. *Art Dir* Cedric Gibbons, David Townsend. *Film Ed* Daniel J. Gray. *Wardrobe* André-ani.

Cast: Marion Davies *(Tillie Jones)*, Matt Moore *(Mac)*, Harry Crocker *(Pennington Fish)*, George Fawcett *(Mr. Simpkins)*, George K. Arthur *(Mr. Whipple)*, Estelle Clark *(Sadie)*, Bert Roach *(Bill)*, Gertrude Short *(Bubbles)*, Claire McDowell *(Maude Jones)*, Arthur Hoyt *(Mr. Smythe)*.

Comedy-drama. Suggested by: Russ Westover, "Tillie the Toiler" (King Feature Syndicate). Tillie Jones, a beautiful but dumb stenographer, captures millionaire Pennington Fish and decides to go through with the marriage for the sake of her mother, though she loves Mac, a simple office worker. At the 11th hour she decides to accept Mac, who at last rebels over his underling's job and is promoted to general manager of the company, replacing the four-flushing Mr. Whipple. *Stenographers. Office clerks. Millionaires. Courtship. Filial relations.*

TILLIE'S PUNCTURED ROMANCE **F2.5732**

Christie Film Co. *Dist* Paramount Famous Lasky Corp. 3 Mar **1928** [c18 Feb 1928; LP25031]. Si; b&w. 35mm. 6 reels, 5,733 ft.

Pres by Al Christie. *Dir* Edward Sutherland. *Scen* Monte Brice, Keene Thompson. *Photog* Charles Boyle, William Wheeler. *Film Ed* Arthur Huffsmith.

Cast: W. C. Fields *(Ringmaster)*, Chester Conklin *(Horatio Q. Frisbee)*, Louise Fazenda *(Tillie)*, Mack Swain *(Tillie's Old Man/General Pilsner)*, Doris Hill *(The Girl Trapezist)*, Grant Withers *(The Boy Trapezist/wireless operator)*, Tom Kennedy *(The Villain)*, Babe London *(The Strong Woman)*, Kalla Pasha *(The Axe Thrower)*, William Platt *(The Midget)*, Mickey Bennett *(The Bad Boy)*, Mike Rafetto *(The Lion Tamer)*, Baron von Dobeneck *(German officer)*.

Burlesque. Tillie leaves home for the lure of the lion tamer in Frisbee's Colossal Circus, an enterprise sporting all the accouterments: cream-puff-stuffed lions, a skullduggerous ringmaster, the blossoming apple of whose eye is an amorous amazon of a strong woman, a "girl with a voice of gold and an arm of iron." The circus picks up stakes and goes "over there" to entertain the boys in the French trenches, but Tillie, Frisbee, and his ringmaster get caught in a draft that blows them into the German Army where, as privates, they find themselves facing the Allies. *Orphans. Ringmasters. Circus. World War I. France. Germany—Army.*

TIMBER WOLF **F2.5733**

Fox Film Corp. 20 Sep **1925** [c6 Aug 1925; LP21705]. Si; b&w. 35mm. 5 reels, 4,809 ft.

Pres by William Fox. *Dir* William S. Van Dyke. *Scen* John Stone. *Story* Jackson Gregory. *Photog* Allan Davey. *Asst Dir* Leslie Selander.

Cast: Buck Jones *(Bruce Standing)*, Elinor Fair *(Reenee Brooks)*, David Dyas *(Babe Deveril)*, Sam Allen *(Joe Terry)*, William Walling *(sheriff)*, Jack Craig *(The Boy)*, Robert Mack *(Billy Winch)*.

Western melodrama. Bruce Standing, known as The Timber Wolf, puts up a grubstake for Joe Terry, an old prospector in search of gold. Joe finds a rich lode, and Babe Deveril, a scoundrel who wants Joe's claim, has him jailed and beaten by the sheriff in an attempt to discover the mine's location. When Joe won't talk, Deveril orders his release from jail and forces Reenee Brooks to use her feminine wiles in another attempt to learn the mine's location. Bruce discovers this plot; after thrashing Deveril, he abducts Reenee and takes her to his cabin. Reenee gradually comes to love and respect Bruce, and he breaks up the Deveril gang. *Prospectors. Sheriffs. Injustice. Gold mines.*

TIME, THE COMEDIAN F2.5734

Metro-Goldwyn-Mayer Pictures. 8 Nov **1925** [c7 Dec 1925; LP22122]. Si; b&w. 35mm. 5 reels, 4,757 ft.

Dir Robert Z. Leonard. *Adapt* Frederick Hatton, Fanny Hatton. *Photog* Oliver Marsh.

Cast: Mae Busch *(Nora Dakon)*, Lew Cody *(Larry Brundage)*, Gertrude Olmsted *(Ruth Dakon)*, Rae Ethelyn *(Ruth Dakon, as a child)*, Roy Stewart *(Michael Lawler)*, Paulette Duval *(Mrs. St. Germaine)*, Creighton Hale *(Tom Cautley)*, Nellie Parker Spaulding *(Aunt Abbey)*, Robert Ober *(Anthony Dakon)*, David Mir *(Count de Brissac)*, Templar Saxe *(Prince Strotoff)*, Mildred Vincent *(Swedish maid)*.

Drama. Source: Kate Jordan, *Time, the Comedian* (New York, 1905). Nora Dakon, bored with the dullness of her life in a small New Jersey town, leaves her husband and small daughter and runs off with Larry Brundage, a wealthy New York sportsman. Nora's husband kills himself, and, to avoid scandal, Brundage walks out on Nora. She returns to her child and, as the years pass, becomes a noted singer. She goes to live in Paris and, at a party to celebrate the Armistice, again meets Brundage, who falls madly in love with her daughter, Ruth. To break up a proposed marriage, Nora is forced to tell Ruth of her tragic relationship with Brundage years before. Ruth leaves Brundage and soon finds consolation in the love of Tom Cautley, a young art student. *Sportsmen. Singers. Students. Smalltown life. Infidelity. Marriage. Suicide. World War I. New Jersey. New York City. Paris.*

THE TIME, THE PLACE, AND THE GIRL F2.5735

Warner Brothers Pictures. 8 Jul **1929** [c28 May 1929; LP416]. Sd (Vitaphone); b&w. 35mm. 7 reels, 6,339 ft. [Also si; 5,200 ft.]

Dir Howard Bretherton. *Screenplay-Dial* Robert Lord. *Titl* De Leon Anthony. *Photog* John Stumar. *Film Ed* Jack Killifer. *Song: "How Many Times"* Irving Berlin. *Song: "I Wonder Who's Kissing Her Now"* Frank Adams, Will Hough, Joseph E. Howard. *Song: "Collegiate"* Moe Jaffe, Nat Bonx. *Song: "Collegiana"* Dorothy Fields, Jimmy McHugh. *Song: "Doin' the Raccoon"* Ray Klages, J. Fred Coots, Herb Magidson. *Song: "Fashionette"* Robert King, Jack Glogau. *Song: "Jack and Jill"* Larry Spier, Sam Coslow. *Song: "Everything I Do I Do for You"* Al Sherman. *Song: "If You Could Care"* E. Ray Goetz, Arthur Wimperis, Herman Darewski.

Cast: Grant Withers *(Jim Crane)*, Betty Compson *(Doris Ward)*, Gertrude Olmstead *(Mae Ellis)*, James Kirkwood *(professor)*, Vivian Oakland *(Mrs. Davis)*, Gretchen Hartman *(Mrs. Winter)*, Irene Haisman *(Mrs. Parks)*, John Davidson *(Ward)*, Gerald King *(radio announcer)*, Bert Roach *(butter & egg man)*.

Musical comedy-drama. Source: Frank R. Adams, Joseph E. Howard, and Will Hough, *The Time, the Place, and the Girl* (New York opening: 5 Aug 1907). Jim Crane, football hero at Stanton, has too high an opinion of himself. Unknown to him, classmate Mae Ellis is desperately in love with him as the result of helping him with his studies. During a particularly crucial game, Jim scores a spectacular victory, and falling under the influence of a group of lionizing New Yorkers, he meets Doris Ward and her wealthy husband, Peter, of Wall Street, who urge him to sell bonds after graduation—which he does. Later, Ward encounters Mae, now a hotel telegrapher, and offers her a job in his office. Upon finding that Jim works there, she accepts. Jim is a failure as a bond salesman, antagonizing everyone he meets. However, at a Long Island party, Ward gets the idea of having him sell fraudulent stock to women, but with Mae's help he extricates himself from amusing complications. *Bond salesmen. Students. Telegraph operators. College life. Football. New York City. Long Island.*

TIME TO LOVE F2.5736

Paramount Famous Lasky Corp. 18 Jun **1927** [c18 Jun 1927; LP24102]. Si; b&w. 35mm. 5 reels, 4,926 ft.

Pres by Adolph Zukor, Jesse L. Lasky. *Assoc Prod* B. P. Schulberg. *Dir* Frank Tuttle. *Screenplay* Pierre Collings. *Story* Alfred Savoir. *Photog* William Marshall.

Cast: Raymond Griffith *(Alfred Sava-Goiu)*, William Powell *(Prince Alado)*, Vera Voronina *(Countess Elvire)*, Josef Swickard *(Elvire's father)*, Mario Carillo *(first duelist)*, Pierre De Ramey *(second duelist)*, Helene Giere *(Elvire's guardian)*, Alfred Sabato *(Hindu mystic)*.

Farce. Alfred, a young Frenchman disillusioned in love, attempts suicide by jumping off a bridge and lands unhurt in the boat of Countess Elvire, with whom he immediately falls in love. Elvire's father, on the advice of a spiritualist, gives his daughter in marriage to Prince Alado, a former acquaintance of Alfred's. Alfred challenges Alado to a duel; but thinking that Elvire loves Alado, Alfred feigns death and plans to sail for the United States, though she professes her love for him. Alfred returns disguised as a spirit, is exposed by the prince, but escapes. Alfred abducts Elvire from the wedding altar, and they escape in balloons that are to be used as practice targets for antiaircraft guns. After narrow escapes, their balloon is pulled through a tunnel by a train, and they parachute into Elvire's home. There they are married by a nearsighted minister. *Nobility. Disguise. Spiritualism. Balloons. Suicide. Abduction. France. Duels.*

TIMES HAVE CHANGED F2.5737

Fox Film Corp. 7 Oct **1923** [c7 Sep 1923; LP19447]. Si; b&w. 35mm. 5 reels, 5,082 ft.

Pres by William Fox. *Dir* James Flood. *Scen* Jack Strumwasser. *Photog* Joseph Brotherton.

Cast: William Russell *(Mark O'Rell)*, Mabel Julienne Scott *(Marjorie)*, Charles West *(Al Keeley)*, Martha Mattox *(Aunt Cordelia)*, Edwin B. Tilton *(Uncle Hinton)*, George Atkinson *(Cousin Felix)*, Allene Ray *(Irene Laird)*, Dick La Reno *(Jim Feener)*, Gus Leonard *(Gabe Gooch)*, Jack Curtis *(Dirty Dan)*.

Comedy-drama. Source: Elmer Holmes Davis, *Times Have Changed* (New York, 1923). Mark O'Rell is sent to New York by his wife's Aunt Cordelia to recover a valuable quilt. In the city he finds the quilt, discovers that it conceals stolen jewels, and in consequence is pursued by both police and thieves. Police catch the thieves, Mark gets the quilt, and he returns home safely. *Aunts. Thieves. Quilts. New York City.*

TIMES SQUARE F2.5738

Gotham Productions. *Dist* Lumas Film Corp. Sep **1929** [c9 Nov 1928; LP25809]. Talking sequences b&w. 35mm. 6 reels.

Pres by Sam Sax. *Supv* Harold Shumate. *Dir* Joseph C. Boyle. *Screenplay* Adele Buffington. *Dial* Harold Shumate. *Titl* Casey Robinson. *Story* Norman Houston. *Photog* Ray June. *Film Ed* Donn Hayes. *Prod Mgr* Donn Diggins.

Cast: Alice Day *(Elaine Smith)*, Arthur Lubin *(Russ Glover/Benjamin Lederwitski)*, Emil Chautard *(David Lederwitski)*, Ann Brady *(Sarah Lederwitski)*, John Miljan *(Dick Barclay)*, Arthur Housman *(Lon Roberts)*, Joseph Swickard *(Professor Carrillo)*, Natalie Joyce *(Lida)*, Eddie Kane *(Nat Ross)*.

Drama. Benny Lederwitski, the latest of a long line of serious composers and musicians, breaks with his family and gets a job plugging songs for a music publisher in Tin-pan Alley. Benny changes his name to Russ Glover and falls in love with Elaine Smith, a secretary, for whom he writes a song. Lon Roberts, an underhanded songwriter, steals the song and then accuses Benny of plagiarism. Benny loses his job and is reduced to banging a piano in a slum cafe. Tormented by despair and remorse, he absentmindedly composes a masterpiece on the back of a menu. The kindly cafe violinist takes the composition to a publisher of serious music, and David Lederwitski, Benny's father, soon becomes interested in its enchanting harmonies and goes to the cafe, where he is tearfully renited with his son. *Composers. Pianists. Song promoters. Secretaries. Publishers. Violinists. Plagiarism. Cafes. New York City—Tin-pan Alley.*

THE TIMID TERROR F2.5739

R-C Pictures. *Dist* Film Booking Offices of America. 7 Nov **1926** [c8 Nov 1926; LP23309]. Si; b&w. 35mm. 5 reels, 4,782 or 4,892 ft.

Pres by Joseph P. Kennedy. *Dir* Del Andrews. *Screenplay* Gerald C. Duffy. *Camera* Al Siegler. *Asst Dir* Charles Kerr.

Cast: George O'Hara *(Talbot Trent)*, Edith Yorke *(Mrs. Trent)*, Doris Hill *(Dorothy Marvin)*, Rex Lease *(Howard Cramm)*, George Nichols *(Amos Milliken)*, Dot Farley *(Mrs. Milliken)*.

Comedy-drama. Source: Walter A. Sinclair, "Hi, Taxi" (publication undetermined). Talbot Trent and Howard Cramm, office workers, both love Dorothy Marvin, secretary to the president of the firm; but Trent, a bashful, unassuming type, feels inferior because he does not own a roadster. Like Cramm, Trent aspires to be an out-of-town manager, but when the latter approaches the president, Amos Milliken, he is gruffly told that he is not energetic enough for the job. A friend of Trent's, knowing his desire for a car, gives him a taxicab, but Dorothy is displeased with the use of the taxi as a private car. Trent approaches Milliken again about the promotion and is fired; reckless and defiant, he decides to bully Milliken, and during a wild and furious taxi ride, he convinces him that he has both energy and initiative; as a result, he wins the position *and* Dorothy. *Office clerks. Business management. Timidity. Ambition. Courtship. Automobiles. Taxicabs.*

TIMOTHY'S QUEST F2.5740

Dirigo Films. *Dist* American Releasing Corp. 17 Sep **1922** [c15 Sep 1922; LP18806]. Si; b&w. 35mm. 7 reels, 6,377 ft.

Dir Sidney Olcott. *Scen* Katherine Stuart. *Photog* Al Ligouri, Eugene French. *Sets* Tec-Art Studios. *Prod Mgr* Charles M. Seay.

Cast: Joseph Depew *(Timothy)*, Baby Helen Rowland *("Lady Gay")*, Marie Day *(Miss Avilda Cummins)*, Margaret Seddon *(Samantha Ann Ripley)*, Bertram Marburgh *(Jabe Slocum)*, Vivia Ogden *(Hitty Tarbox)*, Gladys Leslie *(Miss Dora)*, William F. Haddock *(Dave Milliken)*, Rags *(himself, a dog)*.

Rural drama. Source: Kate Douglas Wiggin, *Timothy's Quest* (1890). Timothy, an orphan of the slums, and "Lady Gay," the little girl he protects, strike out for the country rather than go to an asylum. They select the home of Miss Avilda Cummins and ask to be adopted. She and her "help," Samantha Ann Ripley (also a spinster), take a harsh attitude toward the children but take them in for the night and eventually soften. When Timothy overhears Avilda's plan to adopt Lady Gay and send him to an asylum, he decides to move on; but he lingers to tell Samantha of a man living in a lonely house who calls out "Samanthy." Samantha recognizes him as a former suitor and goes to him; Avilda regrets her harshness toward her sister, who had "followed the primrose path and died in sin"; Timothy is retrieved and adopted. *Orphans. Spinsters. Sisters. Adoption. Dogs.*

TIN GODS F2.5741

Famous Players–Lasky. *Dist* Paramount Pictures. 6 Sep **1926** [c10 Sep 1926; LP23096]. Si; b&w. 35mm. 9 reels, 8,568 ft.

Pres by Adolph Zukor, Jesse L. Lasky. *Assoc Prod* William Le Baron. *Dir* Allan Dwan. *Screenplay* James Shelley Hamilton. *Adapt* Paul Dickey, Howard Emmett Rogers. *Photog* Alvin Wyckoff.

Cast: Thomas Meighan *(Roger Drake)*, Renée Adorée *(Carita)*, Aileen Pringle *(Janet Stone)*, William Powell *(Tony Santelli)*, Hale Hamilton *(Dr. McCoy)*, John Harrington *(Dougherty)*, Joe King *(first foreman)*, Robert E. O'Connor *(second foreman)*, Delbert Emory Whitten, Jr. *(Billy)*.

Domestic melodrama. Source: William Anthony McGuire, *Tin Gods* (a play; c7 Aug 1923). In a mountain village in South America, Dr. McCoy and the padre watch Roger Drake enter a small chapel near a towering bridge, and McCoy recounts the story of Drake's life: *As a rising engineer, he marries Janet Stone, the ambitious daughter of a wealthy family, and neglects his career while Janet becomes a candidate for the State Assembly. Drake comes into conflict with her political friends, and when their baby falls from its nursery window, the couple remorsefully decide to separate. Drake, degenerated by drink, goes to South America to construct a bridge; there he is stricken by fever and is redeemed by the love and care of Carita, a dancer. Carita, however, learns of Janet's political defeat and her attempt to effect a reconciliation with Drake; thinking he still loves his wife, she leaps from the bridge.* Drake returns each year to the chapel he has errected in her memory. *Engineers. Dancers. Women in politics. Physicians. Clergymen. Marriage. Alcoholism. Redemption. State legislatures. South America.*

TIN HATS F2.5742

Metro-Goldwyn-Mayer Pictures. 28 Nov **1926** [c21 Dec 1926; LP23516]. Si; b&w. 35mm. 7 reels, 6,598 ft.

Dir-Story Edward Sedgwick. *Cont* Albert Lewin. *Titl* Ralph Spence. *Adapt* Lew Lipton, Donald W. Lee. *Photog* Ben Reynolds. *Sets* Cedric Gibbons, Frederic Hope. *Film Ed* Frank Davis. *Wardrobe* André-ani.

Cast: Conrad Nagel *(Jack Benson)*, Claire Windsor *(Elsa von Bergen)*, George Cooper *("Lefty" Mooney)*, Bert Roach *("Dutch" Krausmeyer)*, Tom O'Brien *(Sergeant McGurk)*, Eileen Sedgwick *(Freida)*.

Farce. At Armistice time, three members of the A. E. F. become separated from their regiment attempting to retrieve some souvenirs. Looking for their company, they cycle into a Rhenish village and are accepted by the burgomaster as the new overlords. Jack Benson takes an interest in Elsa von Bergen, a wealthy aristocrat; and another personable girl becomes enamored of hard-boiled Lefty Mooney. With his friends, Jack invades Elsa's castle with the intention of "rescuing" her from some danger. She arranges a welcome with mysterious doors, traps, and other surprises, culminating in a battle with a ghost in ancestral armor. The trio are arrested, but through Elsa's influence they are released and the couples are happily married. *Mayors. Aristocrats. Ghosts. World War I. Germany.*

THE TIP-OFF F2.5743

Universal Pictures. 2 Jun **1929** [c15 May 1929; LP379]. Si; b&w. 35mm. 5 reels, 4,109 ft.

Prod William Lord Wright. *Dir* Leigh Jason. *Story-Cont* Basil Dickey. *Titl* Val Cleveland. *Photog* Charles Stumar. *Film Ed* Frank Atkinson.

Cast: Bill Cody *(Jimmy Lamar)*, George Hackathorne *("Shrimp" Riley)*, Duane Thompson *("Crystal Annie")*, L. J. O'Connor *(Captain McHugh)*, Jack Singleton *(confidence man)*, Robert Bolder *(Duke)*, Monte Montague *(Negro)*, Walter Shumway *(stock salesman)*.

Crook melodrama. Crook "Shrimp" Riley and his wounded pal, Jimmy Lamar, hide out at the home of fortune-teller Crystal Annie, Shrimp's girl. Although Shrimp's friends warn him that he will lose Annie to Jimmy, he scoffs at the idea. When the inevitable happens, Shrimp begins to plan his revenge by arranging a frameup for Jimmy. He persuades Jimmy to join a robbery, although Jimmy has promised Annie to go straight, and tips off the police, intending himself to escape. Annie sees the danger in her crystal ball, hastens to the scene of the crime, and helps Jimmy escape. Shrimp realizes the futility of his actions and allows the couple to escape while he dies ensuring their getaway. *Seers. Fortune-tellers. Informers. Frameup. Self-sacrifice.*

Note: Copyrighted as *The Stool Pigeon*, 25 Jul 1928; LP25488.

TIPPED OFF F2.5744

Harry A. McKenzie. *Dist* Playgoers Pictures. 14 Aug **1923** [New York premiere; released Aug; c2 Aug 1923; LU19273]. Si; b&w. 35mm. 5 reels, 4,284 ft.

Prod William Matthews. *Dir* Finis Fox. *Story* Frederick Reel, Jr. *Photog* Harry Fowler.

Cast: Arline Pretty *(Mildred Garson)*, Harold Miller *(Anthony Moore)*, Tom Santschi *("The Fox," Dan Grogan)*, Noah Beery *(Chang Wo)*, Stuart Holmes *(Sidney Matthews, confidence man)*, Zella Gray *(Rita Garson, Mildred's sister)*, Tom O'Brien *(Jim "Pug" Murphy, Mildred's brother)*, Bessie Wong *(Chinese maid)*, James Alamo *(Chuck Morrison, henchman)*, Jimmie Truax *(Baldy Bates, henchman)*, Si Wilcox *(The Detective Sergeant)*, James Wang *(Chang Wo's major-domo)*, Scotty MacGregor *(The Stage Director)*.

Melodrama. Mildred Garson, secretary and fiancée of playwright Anthony Moore, would like to play the leading role in his new play, a crook drama. Jim, her brother, and Rita, her sister, arrange to stage a fake robbery at Moore's home so that Mildred can demonstrate her ability. Real thieves appear and kidnap Mildred, but the thieves are caught and everything is cleared up. *Playwrights. Actors. Secretaries. Robbery. Imposture.*

THE TIRED BUSINESS MAN F2.5745

Tiffany Productions. 30 Jun **1927** [c16 Aug 1927; LP24295]. Si; b&w. 35mm. 6 reels, 5,607 ft.

Dir Allen Dale. *Story-Scen* John Francis Natteford. *Photog* Roy Klaffki, Earl Walker. *Art Dir* George Sawley. *Film Ed* John Rowlins.

Cast: Raymond Hitchcock *(Alderman McGinnis)*, Dot Farley *(Mrs. McGinnis)*, Mack Swain *(Mike Murphy)*, Margaret Quimby *(Rita)*, Charles Delaney *(Larry Riley)*, Lincoln Plummer *(Pat Riley)*, Blanche Mehaffey *(Violet Clark)*, Gibson Gowland *(Ole Swanson)*, James Farley *(Sergeant)*.

Farce. Paving contractors Murphy and Riley, on the verge of ruin, are desperate to get a contract with Alderman McGinnis. Rita, a party girl, announces herself to have been hired as their stenographer by the alderman the night before, while Violet Clark, followed by Larry, Riley's son, arrives from an employment agency. When the landlord demands the rent, they urge McGinnis to sign the contract, but he insists on seeing their latest project. Murphy buys a hat for the alderman, loses it, steals the mayor's hat, and is chased by a police sergeant. At a stag dinner, the alderman becomes excited over a dancer and the party is raided. Later, Rita is offered as the alderman's secretary, and complications ensue, involving his wife, who catches him in an embarrassing situation. Rita signs the contract for McGinnis, and all ends happily. *Businessmen. Contractors. Aldermen. Mayors. Secretaries. Police. Dancers. Paving. Business management. Infidelity.*

TO A FINISH F2.5746

Fox Film Corp. 21 Aug **1921** [c21 Aug 1921; LP16921]. Si; b&w. 35mm. 5 reels.

Pres by William Fox. *Dir* Bernard J. Durning. *Story-Scen* Jack Strumwasser. *Photog* Frank B. Good.

Cast: Buck Jones *(Jim Blake)*, Helen Ferguson *(Doris Lane)*, G.

Raymond Nye *(Bill Terry)*, Norman Selby *(Wolf Gary)*, Herschel Mayall *(Joe Blake)*.

Western melodrama. Bill Terry, the virtual owner of the town of Half-Way, wants to gain possession of Joe Blake's ranch. He "plants" calves among Blake's cattle and then accuses him of rustling and orders the town clerk not to serve Blake. Doris Lane, the sheriff's daughter, who has been promised to Terry, loses faith in him when she hears his gang plotting against Joe Blake's son, Jim, the rival suitor. When Jim is wounded in a fight with Terry's men, Doris hides him; Terry and his gang leader, Wolf Gray, abduct Doris; but Jim defeats them in a gun battle and wins the girl he loves. *Ranchers. Town clerks. Rustling.*

TO HAVE AND TO HOLD **F2.5747**

Famous Players–Lasky. *Dist* Paramount Pictures. 29 Oct **1922** [c18 Oct 1922; LP18364]. Si; b&w. 35mm. 8 reels, 7,518 ft.

Pres by Adolph Zukor. *Dir* George Fitzmaurice. *Adapt-Scen* Ouida Bergère. *Photog* Arthur Miller.

Cast: Betty Compson *(Lady Jocelyn Leigh, the king's ward)*, Bert Lytell *(Capt. Ralph Percy, a Virginia adventurer)*, Theodore Kosloff *(Lord Carnal, a court gallant)*, W. J. Ferguson *(Jeremy Sparrow, Percy's servant)*, Raymond Hatton *(King James I, a dissolute monarch)*, Claire Du Brey *(Patience Worth, Jocelyn's maid)*, Walter Long *(Red Gill, a pirate)*, Anne Cornwall *(Lady Jane Carr)*, Fred Huntley *(Paradise)*, Arthur Rankin *(Lord Cecil, Jocelyn's brother)*, Lucien Littlefield *(Duke of Buckingham)*.

Historical romance. Source: Mary Johnston, *To Have and To Hold* (Boston, 1900). To escape enforced marriage to the hateful Lord Carnal, Jocelyn Leigh joins her maid on a "bride ship" bound for the American colonies. She is dismayed by the conditions she finds in Virginia, and, for her protection, she marries Capt. Ralph Percy, whom she comes to love. Meanwhile, Carnal finds Jocelyn and has Percy imprisoned. Percy escapes and rescues Jocelyn from Carnal's departing ship but takes Carnal along in their small boat. The three run into a violent storm and are driven to a pirates' camp. Through Percy's courage they escape but are taken to England, where Carnal again causes Percy's imprisonment and is promised Jocelyn's hand. Percy escapes with the help of Lord Buckingham, defeats Carnal in a duel, and is reunited with Jocelyn. *Colonists. Pirates. Jamestown. James I (England). Great Britain—History—Stuarts. United States—History—Colonial period.*

TO THE LADIES **F2.5748**

Famous Players–Lasky. *Dist* Paramount Pictures. 25 Nov **1923** [New York premiere; released 9 Dec; c9 Dec 1923; LP19707]. Si; b&w. 35mm. 6 reels, 6,268 ft.

Pres by Jesse L. Lasky. *Dir* James Cruze. *Scen* Walter Woods. *Photog* Karl Brown.

Cast: Edward Horton *(Leonard Beebe, a clerk)*, Theodore Roberts *(John Kincaid, a piano manufacturer)*, Helen Jerome Eddy *(Elsie Beebe, a clever wife)*, Louise Dresser *(Mrs. Kincaid, her husband's boss)*, Z. Wall Covington *(Chester Mullin, a visionary clerk)*, Arthur Hoyt *(Tom Baker, an efficiency man)*, Jack Gardner *(Bob Cutter, a salesman)*.

Farce. Source: Marc Connelly and George S. Kaufman, *To the Ladies, a Comedy in Three Acts* (New York, c1923). Beebe, Baker, and Mullin, three clerks in a piano-manufacturing concern, vie for the position of factory manager. Baker, aware that the president's wife, Mrs. Kincaid, makes all the important decisions, becomes first choice by currying favor. Later, however, Mrs. Kincaid, impressed with Beebe's wife's intelligence, chooses Beebe. *Clerks. Factory management. Pianos.*

TO THE LAST MAN **F2.5749**

Famous Players–Lasky. *Dist* Paramount Pictures. 23 Sep **1923** [c29 Aug 1923; LP19380]. Si; b&w. 35mm. 7 reels, 6,965 ft.

Pres by Jesse L. Lasky. *Dir* Victor Fleming. *Adapt* Doris Schroeder. *Photog* James Howe, Bert Baldridge.

Cast: Richard Dix *(Jean Isbel)*, Lois Wilson *(Ellen Jorth)*, Noah Beery *(Colter)*, Robert Edeson *(Gaston Isbel)*, Frank Campeau *(Blue)*, Fred Huntley *(Lee Jorth)*, Edward Brady *(Daggs)*, Eugene Pallette *(Simm Bruce)*, Leonard Clapham *(Guy)*, Guy Oliver *(Bill)*, Winifred Greenwood *(Mrs. Guy)*.

Western. Source: Zane Grey, *To the Last Man* (New York, 1921). Jean and Ellen are members of two feuding families—the Isbels, who are cattle ranchers; and the Jorths, who are sheepraisers. Jean's father, Gaston Isbel, accuses his enemy, Lee Jorth, of stealing cattle. Jorth, the sheepraiser, who lives with his daughter Ellen, denies the charge. Ellen sees that her father is a thief when Jean visits her and insists that a horse in her possession belongs to him. This accusation sparks renewed conflict between the families, which, when ended, leaves only Jean and Ellen surviving. *Ranchers. Feuds. Arizona. Cattle. Sheep.*

TO THE SOUTH SEAS *see* **SOUTH SEAS**

TODAY **F2.5750**

Majestic Pictures. 1 Nov **1930** [c7 Nov 1930; LP1709]. Sd (Photophone); b&w. 35mm. 8 reels, 6,660 ft.

Pres by Harry Sherman, Jack D. Trop. *Supv* Harry Sherman. *Dir* William Nigh. *Scen* Seton I. Miller. *Photog* James Howe. *Art Dir* Al D'Agostino. *Rec Engr* Lester E. Tope. *Asst Dir* Melville Shyer. *Prod Mgr* Walter Ford Tilford. *Prod Asst* Leonard Ross.

Cast: Conrad Nagel *(Fred Warner)*, Catherine Dale Owen *(Eve Warner)*, Sarah Padden *(Emma Warner)*, John Maurice Sullivan *(Henry Warner)*, Judith Vosselli *(Marian Garland)*, Julia Swayne Gordon *(Mrs. Farringdon)*, William Bailey *(Gregory)*, Edna Marion *(Gloria Vernon)*, Robert Thornby *(Telka)*, Drew Demarest *(Pierre)*.

Society drama. Source: Abraham Schomer and George H. Broadhurst, *Today* (New York opening: 6 Oct 1913). Although he is ruined financially, Fred Warner is confident that his wife, Eve, whom he loves dearly, will help him in his struggle to start a new life. Eve, however, addicted to a life of luxury, is terror-stricken at the prospect of poverty. Fred takes a position as a salesman of secondhand automobiles, and Eve becomes fretful in the drudgery of housework. When she goes shopping with Marian Garland, she meets Mrs. Farringdon, unaware that she operates a house of ill repute. Later, Eve incurs her husband's scorn by running up a big bill at the dressmaker's; but when she finds that Pierre is "understanding" with beautiful women, her bill is marked "Paid." Fred takes a new job as rental agent for apartments owned by Mr. Telka; and while waiting for Mrs. Farringdon to sign the lease on her apartment, he sees his wife's picture, and, in despair, makes an appointment to meet her there. Realizing the trick, she declares she no longer loves him, and Fred, driven to frenzy by her scoffing, kills her, then calls the police. *Dressmakers. Marriage. Finance—Personal. Poverty. Luxury. Prostitution. Murder. Whorehouses.*

Note: An alternative "happy ending" was also provided in which Eve awakens to find that she has had a nightmare; giving Fred her jewels, she tells him he can have everything as long as she has him.

THE TOILERS **F2.5751**

Tiffany-Stahl Productions. 1 Oct **1928** [c18 Jul 1928; LP25469]. Mus score & sd eff (Photophone); b&w. 35mm. 8 reels, 7,256 ft. [Also si; 9 reels.]

Dir Reginald Barker. *Story-Scen* L. G. Rigby. *Titl* Harry Braxton. *Photog* Ernest Miller. *Art Dir* Hervey Libbert. *Set Dsgn* George Sawley. *Film Ed* Robert J. Kern. *Mus Arr* Hugo Riesenfeld.

Cast: Douglas Fairbanks, Jr. *(Steve)*, Jobyna Ralston *(Mary)*, Harvey Clark *(Joe)*, Wade Boteler *(Toby)*, Robert Ryan.

Melodrama. Toby, Steve, and Joe, three coal miners who live together, have their happy home broken up when Steve brings Mary, an orphan, home after rescuing her in a snowstorm on Christmas Eve. She and Steve fall in love and plan to marry. The day after Christmas, disaster strikes the coal mines. Steve, Joe, and 10 other miners become trapped in a remote shaft behind a barricade while fires rage throughout the mine. After three days of searching, the rescue party gives up hope of finding them. Rescuers hear a tapped message, however, while Mary, anxiously waiting at the mine entrance, is convinced by a dream that Steve is still alive. The rescuers resume their efforts, drill down into the shaft, and reach the miners just as the fire threatens to destroy the barricade. *Coal miners. Orphans. Mining towns. Mine disasters. Christmas. Fires.*

TOILERS OF THE SEA (United States/Italy) **F2.5752**

Community International Corp. *Dist* Selznick Distributing Corp. 19 Nov **1923** [New York premiere; released 21 Jul; c28 Jul 1923; LP19268]. Si; b&w. 35mm. 6 reels, 5,128 ft.

Prod-Dir R. William Neill. *Photog* Carl Corwin, G. Ventimiglia.

Cast: Lucy Fox *(Hélène)*, Holmes Herbert *(Sandro)*, Horace Tesseron *(Captain Jean)*, Dell Cawley *(Captain André)*, Lucius Henderson *(The Priest)*.

Melodrama. Source: Victor Hugo, *Les Travailleurs de la mer* (1866). Captain Jean and his daughter, Hélène, live in a Sicilian fishing hamlet. Captain André persuades him to induce the villagers to invest all their savings in a project to buy new ships to meet the growing business with the mainland. Instead of investing it, André steals the money and retreats to

Etna. Sandro, Hélène's sweetheart, pursues the culprit and returns the money to Captain Jean after André is killed in a battle between the two—fought while Etna erupts. *Embezzlement. Volcanoes. Fishing villages. Sicily. Etna.*

Note: Filmed in Italy; only the leading players are Americans.

TOL'ABLE DAVID **F2.5753**

Inspiration Pictures. *Dist* Associated First National Pictures. 21 Nov **1921** [c14 Dec 1921; LP17357]. Si; b&w. 35mm. 7 reels, 7,118 ft.

Pres by Charles H. Duell. *Dir* Henry King. *Scen* Edmund Goulding, Henry King. *Photog* Henry Cronjager. *Film Ed* Duncan Mansfield.

Cast: Richard Barthelmess *(David Kinemon)*, Gladys Hulette *(Esther Hatburn)*, Walter P. Lewis *(Iscah Hatburn)*, Ernest Torrence *(Luke Hatburn)*, Ralph Yearsley *(Luke's brother)*, Forrest Robinson *(Grandpa Hatburn)*, Laurence Eddinger *(Senator Gault)*, Edmund Gurney *(David's father)*, Warner Richmond *(David's brother, Allen)*, Marion Abbott *(David's mother)*, Henry Hallam *(The Doctor)*, Patterson Dial *(Rose, Allen's wife)*, Lassie *(The Dog)*.

Rural drama. Source: Joseph Hergesheimer, "Tol'able David," in *The Happy Life* (New York, 1919). Allen Kinemon, driver of the stagecoach carrying the U. S. mail in the Virginia mountains, is the hero of his young romantic brother, David, who dreams of emulating him. Into their quiet community come the three Hatburns, fugitives from justice, who impose themselves upon the unwilling hospitality of Esther Hatburn's grandfather. When Allen sees the Hatburns attack his brother's dog, he warns them that he will avenge it, and Iscah Hatburn strikes him with a large rock that cripples him for life. David's father suffers a fatal stroke, and the boy is forced to accept the duties of heading the household; because of his mother's fear, he foregoes revenge for his brother and is branded a coward by the villagers. Forced by circumstances to deliver the mail, David encounters Hatburn, whom he engages in an unequal fight, but David proves to be a worthy successor to his brother and wins the heart of Esther. *Brothers. Fugitives. Cripples. Feuds. Postal service. Mountain life. Revenge. West Virginia. Dogs.*

Note: The original adaptation was begun by D. W. Griffith and was partially used in the final scenario. Copyright records show Ralph Yearsley, an Australian actor, as Ralph Bausfield.

TOL'ABLE DAVID **F2.5754**

Columbia Pictures. 15 Nov **1930** [c26 Nov 1939; LP1766]. Sd (Movietone); b&w. 35mm. 8 reels, 7,350 ft.

Prod Harry Cohn. *Dir* John G. Blystone. *Dial Dir* Perry Ivins. *Treatment-Cont-Dial* Benjamin Glazer. *Photog* Ted Tetzlaff. *Art Dir* Edward Jewell. *Tech Dir* Edward Shulter. *Film Ed* Glenn Wheeler. *Sd Engr* G. R. Cooper. *Asst Dir* Jasper Blystone.

Cast: Richard Cromwell *(David Kinemon)*, Noah Beery *(Luke)*, Joan Peers *(Esther Hatburn)*, Henry B. Walthall *(Amos Hatburn)*, George Duryea *(Alan Kinemon)*, Edmund Breese *(Hunter Kinemon)*, Barbara Bedford *(Rose Kinemon)*, Helen Ware *(Mrs. Kinemon)*, Harlan Knight *(Iska)*, Peter Richmond *(Buzzard)*, James Bradbury, Sr. *(Galt)*, Richard Carlyle *(doctor)*.

Rural melodrama. Source: Joseph Hergesheimer, "Tol'able David," in *The Happy Life* (New York, 1919). The story follows the same general plot as the earlier 1921 version, with the exception that the climactic encounter between David and the Hatburns is staged as a gun battle in which he dispatches the villains. *Brothers. Fugitives. Cripples. Feuds. Postal service. Mountain life. Revenge. West Virginia. Dogs.*

THE TOLL OF THE SEA **F2.5755**

Technicolor Motion Picture Co. *Dist* Metro Pictures. ca26 Nov **1922** [New York premiere; released 22 Jan 1923; c5 Dec 1922; LP18473]. Si; col (Technicolor). 35mm. 5 reels, 4,600 ft.

Dir Chester M. Franklin. *Story* Frances Marion. *Dir Photog* J. A. Ball.

Cast: Anna May Wong *(Lotus Flower)*, Kenneth Harlan *(Allen Carver)*, Beatrice Bentley *(Barbara Carver)*, Baby Marion *(Little Allen)*, Etta Lee, Ming Young *(gossips)*.

Romantic drama. Lotus Flower finds a man (Allen Carver, an American) washed up on the seashore and, although an old man reminds her of the Chinese legend that the sea takes in pain and sorrow twice the amount of joy it gives, she rescues him. They fall in love and marry, but he returns to the United States without her. A son is born to Lotus Flower, and when Allen does return he is accompanied by his American wife. Overcome with grief, Lotus Flower persuades the Carvers to take little Allen, then gives herself up to the sea. *Bigamy. Infidelity. Suicide. The Sea. China.*

TOM AND HIS PALS **F2.5756**

R-C Pictures. *Dist* Film Booking Offices of America. 7 Sep or 7 Nov **1926** [c7 Sep 1926; LP23199]. Si; b&w. 35mm. 5 reels, 4,346 ft.

Pres by Joseph P. Kennedy. *Dir* Robert De Lacy. *Cont* F. A. E. Pine. *Story* Frederick Arthur Mindlin. *Photog (see note)* John Leezer, Gilbert Warrenton.

Cast: Tom Tyler *(Tom Duffy)*, Doris Hill *(Mary Smith)*, Frankie Darro *(Frankie Smith)*, Dicky Brandon *(Junior Carroll)*, LeRoy Mason *(Courtney)*, Helen Lynch *(Pandora Golden)*, Beans *(a dog)*, Sitting Bull.

Romantic western drama. Tom Duffy, whose father is half-owner of the Flying-V ranch, admires movie actress Pandora Golden and is delighted to learn that she and her company are arriving on location at the ranch. Mary Smith, his father's ward, is less enthusiastic, but Courtney, the leading man, learns of Mary's financial prospects and connives with Pandora to keep Tom busy while he persuades Mary to elope with him. Tom overcomes a bear that attacks Junior, Miss Golden's child; and in gratitude, the actress tells Tom about Courtney's scheme. Tom pursues them after they catch a train; and after forcing a confession from Courtney, he is happily reunited with Mary. *Ranchers. Cowboys. Actors. Children. Courtship. Motion pictures. Bears.*

Note: The movie actress is not identified in sources consulted.

TOM MIX IN ARABIA *see* **ARABIA**

TOM SAWYER **F2.5757**

Paramount-Publix Corp. 15 Nov **1930** [c17 Nov 1930; LP1736]. Sd (Movietone); b&w. 35mm. 9 reels, 7,648 ft.

Dir John Cromwell. *Screenplay* Sam Mintz, Grover Jones, William Slavens McNutt. *Photog* Charles Lang. *Film Ed* Alyson Shaffer. *Rec Engr* Harold C. Lewis.

Cast: Jackie Coogan *(Tom Sawyer)*, Junior Durkin *(Huckleberry Finn)*, Mitzi Green *(Becky Thatcher)*, Lucien Littlefield *(teacher)*, Tully Marshall *(Muff Potter)*, Clara Blandick *(Aunt Polly)*, Mary Jane Irving *(Mary)*, Ethel Wales *(Mrs. Harper)*, Jackie Searle *(Sid)*, Dick Winslow *(Joe Harper)*, Jane Darwell *(Widow Douglass)*, Charles Stevens *(Injun Joe)*, Charles Sellon *(minister)*, Lon Poff *(Judge Thatcher)*.

Juvenile comedy-drama. Source: Mark Twain, *The Adventures of Tom Sawyer* (1896). Tom Sawyer has a falling out with Becky Thatcher, his sweetheart, and seeks comfort in the forbidden company of Huck Finn, town ragamuffin, who tells him of a mysterious cure for warts that requires them to visit the town graveyard at midnight. There they see Injun Joe, a treacherous halfbreed, murder one of his companions. Muff Potter, also there, but in a drunken state, is made to believe he committed the crime. Tom and Huck swear a blood-oath that they will not divulge what they have seen. Wrongfully rebuked by his Aunt Polly, Tom runs away from home, joining Huck and Joe Harper on an expedition to an island on the Mississippi where they live for 3 days in carefree abandon. Getting homesick, Tom returns to find he is thought drowned; and the boys attend their own obsequies at the church. Tom confesses the truth about the murder at Muff Potter's trial, but Injun Joe eludes a posse. At the school picnic near a cavern, Tom and Becky get lost and stumble on Injun Joe unearthing a chest of gold; he pursues them but falls into a crevasse to his death. Huck finds Tom and Becky and leads them to safety from the cave, retrieving the chest of gold. ... *Children. Halfcastes. Ragamuffins. Aunts Courtship. Murder. Smalltown life. Treasure. Funerals. Missouri. Mississippi River.*

THE TOMBOY **F2.5758**

Fox Film Corp. Apr **1921** [c10 Apr 1921; LP16426]. Si; b&w. 35mm. 5 reels, 4,630 ft.

Pres by William Fox. *Dir-Story-Scen* Carl Harbaugh. *Photog* Otto Brautigan.

Cast: Eileen Percy *(Minnie Ann Thomas)*, Hal Cooley *(The Stranger)*, Richard Cummings *(Uncle Jake)*, Paul Kamp *(Ferdinand Judd, The Boob)*, Byron Munson *(J. Houston Pike, Jr.)*, Harry Dunkinson *(The Circus Manager)*, James McElhern *(Daniel Thomas)*, Leo Sulky *(The Ex-Bartender)*, Grace McClean *(Ann Phillips)*, Walter Wilkinson *(Buster)*, Virginia Stern *(Sister)*, Wilson Hummel *(The Police Force)*, Ethel Teare *(The Village Belle)*.

Comedy-melodrama. Minnie, the village tomboy, meets a handsome Stranger after playing ball one afternoon. She invites him to see a bridge model her father has designed; but finding her intoxicated father in the act of destroying the model, she swears vengeance on the local bootleggers and joins a newspaper as sportswriter so as to expose their activities. Pike, the station agent, leader of the bootleggers, spreads a scandal about Minnie when she rejects him, but through the help of the Stranger everything is cleared up. *Tomboys. Strangers. Bootleggers. Engineers. Reporters. Alcoholism. Filial relations.*

THE TOMBOY **F2.5759**

Chadwick Pictures. 26 Dec **1924** [New York State license]. Si; b&w. 35mm. 6 reels.

Dir David Kirkland. *Story* Frank Dazey. *Photog* Milton Moore.

Cast: Herbert Rawlinson *(Aldon Farwell)*, Dorothy Devore *(Tommy Smith)*, James Barrows *(Henry Smith)*, Lee Moran *(Hiram, the sheriff)*, Helen Lynch *(Sweetie Higgins)*, Lottie Williams *(Mrs. Higgins)*, Harry Gribbon *(Rugby Blood)*, Virginia True Boardman *(Mrs. Smith)*.

Melodrama. Tommy Smith, a tomboy who runs a boardinghouse in a small rustic village, falls in love with Aldon Farwell, a stranger from the city. Tommy then finds out that Aldon is a revenue agent assigned to track down local smugglers. The sheriff is killed, and Tommy's father is accused of the crime, an accusation that is further substantiated when a supply of contraband liquor is found in a truck in the barn. The bootleggers steal the truck, and Tommy and Aldon chase and capture them. The gang leader turns out to be Rugby Blood, who has been posing as an invalid. Tommy's father reveals himself as a revenue agent, and Aldon reaffirms his love for the pretty tomboy. *Tomboys. Revenue agents. Smugglers. Sheriffs. Smalltown life. Murder. Boardinghouses.*

TOMORROW'S LOVE **F2.5760**

Famous Players–Lasky. *Dist* Paramount Pictures. 5 Jan **1925** [c9 Jan 1925; LP20985]. Si; b&w. 35mm. 6 reels, 5,842 ft.

Pres by Adolph Zukor, Jesse L. Lasky. *Dir* Paul Bern. *Screenplay* Howard Higgin. *Photog* Bert Glennon.

Cast: Agnes Ayres *(Judith Stanley)*, Pat O'Malley *(Robert Stanley)*, Raymond Hatton *(Brown)*, Jane Winton *(Bess Carlysle)*, Ruby Lafayette *(grandmother)*, Dale Fuller *(maid)*.

Comedy-drama. Source: Charles William Brackett, "Interlocutory," in *Saturday Evening Post* (196:16–17, 15 Mar 1924). Judith marries Robert Stanley and for a time her dreams of happiness are all realized. As the months go by, however, she is increasingly disturbed by his stubborn adherence to annoying habits, wrong beliefs, and small faults: he leaves the windows open when he is cold and drives out in an open car in the rain when he feels ill. On one of these aquatic trips, Robert's car breaks down; and he is picked up by Bess Carlysle, an old girl friend, who insists that he return with her to her apartment to dry his clothes. He is dancing with Bess, after a whisky and a hot bath for his feet, when Judith walks in on them. She suspects the worst, and Robert is too stubborn to explain. Judith secures an interlocutory divorce and goes to Europe; Robert becomes engaged to Bess, more out of pique than love. Judith decides at the 11th hour that she does not want the divorce to become final and returns to the United States. After a frantic trip by car and boat, she arrives just in time to prevent Tom's remarriage; she and Tom are later reconciled. *Marriage. Divorce.*

TOM'S GANG **F2.5761**

R-C Pictures. *Dist* Film Booking Offices of America. 10 Jul **1927** [c10 Jul 1927; LP24218]. Si; b&w. 35mm. 5 reels, 4,954 ft.

Pres by Joseph P. Kennedy. *Dir* Robert De Lacy. *Story-Cont* Frank Howard Clark. *Ch Camera* Nick Musuraca. *Asst Dir* William Cody.

Cast: Tom Tyler *(Dave Collins)*, Sharon Lynn *(Lucille Rogers)*, Frankie Darro *(Spuds)*, Beans *(Sitting Bull, a dog)*, Harry Woods *(Bart Haywood)*, Frank Rice *(Andy Barker)*, Barney Furey *(Ray Foster)*, Tom Lingham *(George Daggett)*, Jack Anthony *(Bill Grimshaw)*.

Western melodrama. The ranch of Elias Barnet is bequeathed to his granddaughter, Lucille Rogers, and Dave Collins on the condition that they marry. Dave arrives at the ranch with his pal, Spuds, an orphan, and finds Ray Foster, a nephew of Barnet's attorney, posing as Dave Collins. Lucille, however, falls in love with Dave, and Foster hires Bart Haywood to kill Dave; by accident Foster is wounded and Dave is tied to a handcar in the path of an approaching train; but Spuds and his dog, Sitting Bull, save him from collision. Meanwhile, Daggett tells Lucille that Foster is mortally wounded and induces her to agree to marry him so as to inherit the ranch, but Dave arrives in time to prevent the wedding. Elias, to everyone's surprise, appears—still alive—gives rout to Daggett and Foster, and presents the ranch to Dave and Lucille. *Grandfathers. Ranchers. Imposture. Inheritance. Wills. Courtship. Dogs.*

TONGUES OF FLAME **F2.5762**

Famous Players–Lasky. *Dist* Paramount Pictures. 15 Dec **1924** [c17 Dec 1924; LP20920]. Si; b&w. 35mm. 7 reels, 6,763 ft.

Pres by Adolph Zukor, Jesse L. Lasky. *Dir* Joseph Henabery. *Screenplay* Townsend Martin. *Photog* Faxon M. Dean.

Cast: Thomas Meighan *(Henry Harrington)*, Bessie Love *(Lahleet)*, Eileen Percy *(Billie Boland)*, Berton Churchill *(Boland)*, John Miltern *(Scanlon)*, Leslie Stowe *(Hornblower)*, Nick Thompson *(Adam John)*, Jerry Devine *(Mickey)*, Kate Mayhew *(Mrs. Vickers)*, Cyril Ring *(Clayton)*.

Melodrama. Source: Peter Clark MacFarlane, *Tongues of Flame* (New York, 1924). The town of Edgewater, built on land formerly belonging to "Siwash" Indians, owes its prosperity to its wealthy developer, Boland. When he attempts to buy the remainder of the Siwash Reservation, the Indians, led by Lahleet, their beautiful schoolteacher, are distrustful, and Boland refers them to Henry Harrington, a respected young lawyer under whose command some of their number served in the Great War. Harrington advises them to accept Boland's generous offer and draws up the necessary papers. After the sale, Boland sinks oil wells on the land; angered at this duplicity and fraud, Harrington exposes him as a common swindler. Boland then has Harrington jailed on a false charge of robbery. Meanwhile, an action instituted by Hornblower, a shyster, on the Indians' behalf results in a court decision awarding the tribe the entire town of Edgewater, owing to irregularities in Boland's original surveys. The townspeople, angered at Boland, set fire to his properties. Released from jail when the fires burn out of control, Harrington organizes the Indians and saves the town. The Indians get back their reservation and return Edgewater to its grateful citizens. Harrington declares his love for Lahleet. *Indians of North America. Oil wells. Land rights. Fires.*

TONGUES OF SCANDAL **F2.5763**

Sterling Pictures. 3 Jan **1927** [c10 Jan 1927; LP23518]. Si; b&w. 35mm. 6 reels, 5,253 ft.

Dir Roy Clements. *Adapt* George L. Sargent. *Story* Adele De Vore. *Photog* Leon Shamroy. *Film Ed* D. E. Rothchild.

Cast: Mae Busch *(Helen Hanby)*, William Desmond *(Gov. John Rhodes)*, Ray Hallor *(Jimmy Rhodes, his brother)*, Mathilde Brundage *(Mrs. Rhodes, their mother)*, Lloyd Carleton *(Mr. Plunkett)*, Wilfrid North *(Mr. Collett)*, James Gordon *(O'Rourke)*, Jerome La Grasse *(Colvin)*, De Sacia Mooers *(Peggy Shaw)*.

Society drama. Jimmy Rhodes, younger brother of Gov. John Rhodes, falls in love with an American girl abroad, and because of his mother's intervention she commits suicide, causing a scandal in the Rhodes family. On the governor's wedding day, his bride, Helen Hanby, recognizes the portrait of her dead sister, and believing her husband to be the moral slayer and betrayer of her sister, she determines to do everything in her power to ruin his chances for reelection. She allows Colvin, a young bounder secretly in league with the governor's political opponents, to accompany her to disreputable roadhouses, and at a charity benefit she auctions off her clothes to raise money. Learning of her scheming, Jimmy confesses that he, not his brother, abandoned her sister; and reaffirming her love for John, she is forgiven by him. *Brothers. Cads. State governors. Suicide. Marriage. Politics. Revenge.*

TONIGHT AT TWELVE **F2.5764**

Universal Pictures. 29 Sep **1929** [c20 Sep 1929; LP705]. Sd (Movietone); b&w. 35mm. 7 reels, 6,884 ft. [Also si; 5,176 ft.]

Dir Harry A. Pollard. *Scen* Matt Taylor. *Adapt-Dial* Harry A. Pollard, Matt Taylor. *Titl* Owen Davis. *Photog* Jerome Ash. *Film Ed* Maurice Pivar.

Cast: Madge Bellamy *(Jane Eldredge)*, Robert Ellis *(Jack Keith)*, Margaret Livingston *(Nan Stoddard)*, Vera Reynolds *(Barbara Warren)*, Norman Trevor *(Professor Eldredge)*, Hallam Cooley *(Bill Warren)*, Mary Doran *(Mary)*, George Lewis *(Tony Keith)*, Madeline Seymour *(Alice Keith)*, Josephine Brown *(Dora Eldredge)*, Donald Douglas *(Tom Stoddard)*, Louise Carver *(Ellen)*, Nick Thompson *(Joe)*.

Drama. Source: Owen Davis, *Tonight at 12* (New York opening: 15 Nov 1928). Alice Keith, a suspicious wife, believes that her husband is running after his old sweetheart, Dora Eldredge, and two other married women in her circle. Making her accusation during a dinner party at which the women and their husbands are present, Alice exhibits a rendezvous note she found in her husband's pocket, reading "Tonight at 12." To protect his father and his future mother-in-law, Jack Keith, who is engaged to marry Jane Eldredge, admits to having an affair with Mary, the maid in the Eldredge household, and to being the recipient of the love note. Mary sees an opportunity to force Jack, whom she loves, to marry her, and she begins to make plans when Jane breaks her engagement with him. Eventually, Mrs. Eldredge confesses her affair with Keith to restore her daughter's happiness. Mary returns to her hometown, aware of the social differences between Jack and herself. *Housemaids. Infidelity. Social classes. Filial relations.*

TONIO, SON OF THE SIERRAS **F2.5765**

Davis Distributing Division. 19 Dec **1925** [trade review]. Si; b&w. 35mm. 5 reels.

Dir Ben Wilson. *Photog* Alfred Gosden.

Cast: Ben Wilson *(Lieutenant Richard Harris)*, Neva Gerber *(Evelyn Archer)*, Chief Yowlache *(Tonio)*, Jim Welch *(Colonel Archer)*, Bob Walker *(Lieutenant Willett)*, Ruth Royce *(Mrs. Bennett)*, Fay Adams *(Captain Stannard)*.

Western melodrama. Source: Gen. Charles King, *Tonio, Son of the Sierras; a Story of the Apache War* (New York, 1906). "Tonio, U. S. Indian scout at Fort Almy, disappears when Tontos go on warpath. Lieutenant Harris wounded while saving Lucille, married daughter of Post Commandant during an attack. He and Lieutenant Willett are rivals for the love of Evelyn, Lucille's sister. Willett accuses Tonio of treachery. Harris defends missing man. Willett is shot, Harris arrested, but allowed to lead his men later and defeats enemy. Tonio returns wounded. It develops that Willett was killed by a man whose sister he wronged. Harris and Evelyn are united." *(Motion Picture News*, 19 Dec 1925, p3042.) *Tonto Indians. Scouts—Frontier. Injustice. Murder. Forts. Sierras. United States Army—Cavalry.*

TONY RUNS WILD **F2.5766**

Fox Film Corp. 18 Apr **1926** [c11 Apr 1926; LP22615]. Si; b&w. 35mm. 6 reels, 5,477 ft.

Pres by William Fox. *Dir* Thomas Buckingham. *Scen* Edfrid Bingham, Robert Lord. *Story* Henry Herbert Knibbs. *Photog* Daniel Clark. *Asst Dir* Wynn Mace.

Cast: Tom Mix *(Tom Trent)*, Tony *(himself, a horse)*, Jacqueline Logan *(Grace Percival)*, Lawford Davidson *(Slade)*, Duke Lee *(Bender)*, Vivian Oakland *(Mrs. Johnson [Johnston?])*, Edward Martindel *(Mr. Johnson [Johnston?])*, Marion Harlan *(Ethel Johnson [Johnston?])*, Raymond Wells *(sheriff)*, Richard Carter *(ranch foreman)*, Arthur Morrison *(auto stage driver)*, Lucien Littlefield *(Red)*, Jack Padjan *(deputy sheriff)*.

Western melodrama. Tony, an intelligent and beautiful wild horse, the leader of a pack of wild horses, eludes capture. He is being pursued by Slade when Grace Percival, daughter of a wealthy mineowner, wrecks her car in the path of the oncoming horses. Tom Trent risks his own life to rescue her, and a friendship develops. Grace spurs a rivalry between Tom and Slade to see which one can capture Tony first. Tom wins and after 2 weeks captures and tames Tony and brings him to Grace; he overhears her making light of the affair, however, and frees Tony. Tom then leaves, his feelings wounded. Slade tries to kiss Grace but is rebuffed. He then frames Tom as responsible for a stage holdup. Tom is arrested, and Slade takes advantage of the opportunity to abduct Grace. Tom overhears the plans and eludes his captors. He faces Slade and his men in an unequal standoff, but Tony comes to the rescue with his herd of wild horses. Tom proposes marriage to Grace. *Cowboys. Frameup. Stagecoach robberies. Kidnaping. Horses.*

TOO MANY CROOKS **F2.5767**

Famous Players–Lasky. *Dist* Paramount Pictures. 2 Apr **1927** [c2 Apr 1927; LP23821]. Si; b&w. 35mm. 6 reels, 5,399 ft.

Pres by Adolph Zukor, Jesse L. Lasky. *Dir* Fred Newmeyer. *Screenplay* Rex Taylor. *Photog* Harry Jackson.

Cast: Mildred Davis *(Celia Mason)*, Lloyd Hughes *(John Barton)*, George Bancroft *(Bert the Boxman)*, El Brendel *(Botts)*, William V. Mong *(Coxey the Con-man)*, John St. Polis *(Erastus Mason)*, Otto Matiesen *(Fast Hands Foster)*, Betty Francisco *(Frisco Flora)*, Gayne Whitman *(Marshall Stone)*, Tom Ricketts *(butler)*, Cleve Moore *(Freddie Smythe)*, Ruth Cherrington *(Mrs. Smythe)*, Pat Hartigan *("Big Dan" Boyd)*.

Farce. Source: E. J. Rath, *Too Many Crooks* (New York, 1918). Celia Mason, the only daughter of a retired banker, discusses with Marshall Stone, the family lawyer, a crook drama she has just seen and maintains she can write a better one herself. Stone puts her in touch with John Barton (actually the author of the play), who supplies bad men on demand. Celia asks him to invite a group of crooks as guests at her house party. Within 24 hours, Fast Hands Foster has stolen 3 suitcases of jewelry; Frisco Flora has vamped 15 millionaires and obtained material for an equal number of blackmail suits; and Coxey the Con-man has sold most of the neighboring homes to "fall guys." Celia is amazed to learn they believe her to be an accomplice, but Barton removes the loot from her safe before the crooks abscond with it. Learning Barton's true calling, Celia is relieved. *Playwrights. Actors. Lawyers. Confidence men. Thieves. Blackmail.*

TOO MANY KISSES **F2.5768**

Famous Players–Lasky. *Dist* Paramount Pictures. 11 Jan **1925** [c2 Mar 1925; LP21208]. Si; b&w. 35mm. 6 reels, 5,759 ft.

Pres by Adolph Zukor, Jesse L. Lasky. *Dir* Paul Sloane. *Scen* Gerald Duffy. *Photog* Hal Rosson.

Cast: Richard Dix *(Richard Gaylord, Jr.)*, Frances Howard *(Yvonne Hurja)*, William Powell *(Julio)*, Frank Currier *(Richard Gaylord, Sr.)*, Joseph Burke *(Mr. Simmons)*, Albert Tavernier *(Manuel Hurja)*, Arthur Ludwig *(Miguel)*, Alyce Mills *(flapper)*, Paul Panzer *(Pedro)*, Harpo Marx *(The Village Peter Pan)*.

Romantic comedy. Source: John Monk Saunders, "A Maker of Gestures," in *Cosmopolitan Magazine* (64:97–101, Apr 1923). Richard Gaylord always puts pleasure before business, so when his father learns that Basque women will not marry outside of their race, he sends him to Spain to keep him away from his numerous feminine admirers. In a Basque village, Richard meets and falls in love with Yvonne Hurja, whose affections are claimed by Julio, a captain in the Civil Guard. Julio challenges Richard to a duel, but Yvonne secures the American's promise not to fight. Richard is later kidnaped by Julio's men and taken to the mountains; Julio then goes to claim Yvonne's hand in marriage, but Richard escapes and confronts him at a festival. Julio throws a knife at Richard but misses; Richard then trounces him in a fight. At that moment, Richard's father appears and is greatly pleased with his son's grit. He approves of Richard's love for Yvonne and gives him a half interest in the family business. *Basques. Civil guard. Playboys. Kidnaping. Fatherhood. Spain.*

TOO MANY WIVES **F2.5769**

21 Sep **1927** [New York State license]. Si; b&w. 35mm. 5 reels, 4,600 ft.

Cast: Norma Shearer.

Drama(?). No information about the nature of this film has been found. It is probably a reissue with a changed title. Production and distribution companies not determined; released in New York by Unique Fotofilm. Possibly made in 1921.

TOO MUCH BUSINESS **F2.5770**

Vitagraph Co. of America. 9 Apr **1922** [c25 Mar 1922; LP17667]. Si; b&w. 35mm. 7 reels, 6,100 ft.

Pres by Albert E. Smith. *Dir* Jess Robbins. *Scen* Ford I. Beebe. *Photog* Irving Reis.

Cast: Edward Horton *(John Henry Jackson)*, Ethel Grey Terry *(Myra Dalton)*, Tully Marshall *(Amos Comby)*, John Steppling *(Simon Stecker)*, Carl Gerard *(Ray Gorham)*, Elsa Lorimer *(Mrs. Comby)*, Helen Gilmore *(The Head Nurse)*, Mark Fenton *(Robert Gray)*, Tom Murray *(Officer 16)*.

Comedy. Source: Earl Derr Biggers, "John Henry and the Restless Sex," in *Saturday Evening Post* (193:10, 5 Mar 1921). John Henry Jackson is in love with Myra Dalton, private secretary to his employer, Amos Comby. He induces her to sign a 30-day option agreeing to marry him if he doubles his salary within that time. Learning of the agreement, Comby, determined not to lose his secretary, discharges Jackson. A month later, Jackson is the proprietor of "Hotellerie des Enfants—a parking place for children of busy mothers" and ready to claim Myra. At the same time a large firm proposes a consolidation with Comby on the condition that John Henry be made general manager. Comby is refused when he offers to buy out Jackson's business, and Gorham induces his nurses to strike, allowing the children to escape and causing wild confusion. John Henry comes to Comby in a rage and is appointed general manager of the consolidation. Myra is only too happy to have the option taken up. *Secretaries. Business management. Marriage. Child care—Day nurseries.*

TOO MUCH MARRIED **F2.5771**

Associated Photoplays. 23 Nov **1921** [New York State]. Si; b&w. 35mm. 5 reels.

Dir Scott Dunlap. *Scen* John W. Grey. *Story* Florence Bolles. *Photog* Steve Norton.

Cast: Mary Anderson *(Betty Colford)*, Roscoe Karns *(Bob Holiday)*, Jack Connolly *(William Trevor)*, Mathilde Brundage *(Mrs. De Courcey)*, Ben Lewis *(detective)*, Carmen Phillips *(Mrs. William Trevor)*, Lillian

Elliott *(Mrs. Peter Gulp)*, Bert Woodruff *(Peter Gulp)*.

Farce. "Betty and Bob, guests at the brilliant De Courcey–Varnay wedding, suddenly decide to elope. Bob slips away to make accommodations at a nearby Inn, where they plan to spend a honeymoon. Betty prepares to join him, but is halted by a detective who demands to know the contents of her bag. She refuses, but is told by the sleuth that a necklace belonging to the bride had been stolen. She opens the bag, but Billy Trevor, standing nearby, stoops to help the young woman, dropping a handkerchief into the bag. He offers to accompany Betty to the station. The detective allows Betty to go, but holds Billy, who escapes and arrives at the Inn before the girl and Bob, who had figured in an automobile accident and [had been] taken to the hospital. Developments show that Billy had dropped the necklace in the bag and tries in vain to regain it, these efforts resulting in a series of complications. Finally Bob arrives and the bride is saved from further humiliation and embarrassment, while Billy makes a confession that exonerates everybody." *(Moving Picture World,* 18 Feb 1922, p755.) *Detectives. Elopement. Robbery.*

TOO MUCH MONEY **F2.5772**

First National Pictures. 3 Jan **1926** [c7 Jan 1926; LP22233]. Si; b&w. 35mm. 7 reels, 7,600 ft.

Supv Earl Hudson. *Dir* John Francis Dillon. *Scen* Joseph Poland, Jack Jungmeyer. *Titl* Ralph Spence. *Photog* George Folsey. *Art Dir* Milton Menasco. *Film Ed* Arthur Tavares.

Cast: Lewis Stone *(Robert Broadley)*, Anna Q. Nilsson *(Annabel Broadley)*, Robert Cain *(Dana Stuart)*, Derek Glynne *(Duke Masters)*, Edward Elkas *(Rabinowitz)*, Ann Brody *(Mrs. Rabinowitz)*.

Farce. Source: Israel Zangwill, *Too Much Money; a Farcial Comedy in Three Acts* (London, 1924). Unhappy millionaire Robert Broadley finds that his wife, Annabel, has no time left over from her social obligations to spend with him. At the urging of his friend, Dana Stuart, Robert puts all of his money in safekeeping with Stuart and declares himself bankrupt. He moves with Annabel to the Lower East Side and, with her love and encouragement, finds work first as a janitor and later as a clerk in a delicatessen. Stuart converts all of Broadley's money into negotiable securities and goes to Annabel, begging her to leave with him immediately for Europe. Annabel pretends to agree, leaving word for Robert where he can find her. Aboard ship, Annabel gains possession of the securities, and she and Robert prepare to go to Europe on their second honeymoon. *Millionaires. Janitors. Salesclerks. Marriage. Bankruptcy. Delicatessens. New York City—Lower East Side.*

TOO MUCH SPEED **F2.5773**

Famous Players–Lasky. *Dist* Paramount Pictures. 10 Jul **1921** [c9 Jul 1921; LP16743]. Si; b&w. 35mm. 5 reels, 4,629 ft.

Pres by Jesse L. Lasky. *Dir* Frank Urson. *Scen* Byron Morgan. *Photog* Charles E. Schoenbaum.

Cast: Wallace Reid *(Dusty Rhoades)*, Agnes Ayres *(Virginia MacMurran)*, Theodore Roberts *(Pat MacMurran)*, Jack Richardson *(Tyler Hellis)*, Lucien Littlefield *(Jimmy Rodman)*, Guy Oliver *("Howdy" Zeeker)*, Henry Johnson *(Billy Dawson)*, Jack Herbert *(Hawks)*.

Action melodrama. Source: Byron Morgan, "Too Much Speed," in *Saturday Evening Post* (193:5–7, 28 May 1921). Dusty Rhoades, who is engaged to Virginia, daughter of Pat MacMurran, manufacturer of Pakro automobiles, retires from racing to please his future father-in-law. Hellis, of the Ronado Car Co., who is trying to secure an order from a South American dealer, ditches Dusty in a road challenge, and MacMurran cancels the wedding; but Dusty elopes with Virginia in a racing car. Pursued by her father, they are both arrested for speeding, and Dusty spends 2 days in jail. Later, he purchases a Pakro car and enters the automobile race. Dusty and his mechanic, Jimmy Rodman, defeat the Ronado entry and win the South American contract, and Dusty and Virginia are reconciled to MacMurran. *Automobile manufacture. Automobile racing.*

TOO MUCH WIFE **F2.5774**

Realart Pictures. *Dist* Paramount Pictures. 1 Jan **1922** [c1 Jan 1922; LP17461]. Si; b&w. 35mm. 5 reels, 4,900 ft.

Supv Elmer Harris. *Dir* Thomas N. Heffron. *Scen* Percy Heath. *Story* Lorna Moon. *Photog* William E. Collins. *Asst Dir* Maynard Laswell.

Cast: Wanda Hawley *(Myra Morgan)*, T. Roy Barnes *(Jack Morgan)*, Arthur Hoyt *(John Coningsby)*, Lillian Langdon *(Mrs. Coningsby)*, Leigh Wyant *(Jane Cunningham)*, Willard Louis *(Tom Hare)*, Bertram Johns *(Jim Walker)*, John Fox *(office boy)*.

Comedy-drama. Myra Coningsby, who is engaged to marry Jack Morgan, has been accustomed to seeing her father dominated by her mother and is determined not to follow the example of her parents. Despite Myra's good resolves, following her marriage she insists on going wherever Jack goes, whether following sports or playing cards; moreover, she takes an embarrassing interest in his business affairs and becomes his private secretary against his will. At last, driven by despair, Jack schemes to obtain freedom for a fishing trip with his friends Tom and Jim; during a storm his boat capsizes, and though his friends believe he has drowned, Jane, his former secretary, rescues him. Myra, in remorse for her suspicions of infidelity, forms a mourning party but spies Jack and Jane together on an island. After mutual explanations, Myra awakens to the folly of her conduct and comes to an understanding with her husband. *Marriage. Manhood.*

TOO MUCH YOUTH **F2.5775**

Paul Gerson Pictures. 7 May **1925** [New York premiere]. Si; b&w. 35mm. 5 reels.

Pres by B. Berger. *Dir* Duke Worne. *Scen* Grover Jones. *Photog* Roland Price.

Cast: Richard Holt *(Jimmy Kenton)*, Sylvia Breamer *(Marguerite)*, Eric Mayne *(George Crandall)*, Charles K. French *(Mark Kenton)*, Walter Leroy *(Casey)*, Harris Gordon *(Ned Crandall)*, Walter Perry *(Pat Casey)*, Joseph Belmont *(Francetti)*.

Comedy-melodrama. Jimmy Kenton, a rake who plays the "bright lights" route, is smitten with sudden love for Marguerite Crandall when she sneers at his sporty antics at a health resort. Jimmy then gets into a fight with her escort and is thrown into jail. Deciding to reform, he is bailed out by his father, who sends him to San Francisco to close an important real estate deal with Marguerite's father. Jimmy vows not to sleep until he has transacted the business, and his father decides to make him regret that rash promise. He arranges with the elder Crandall to delay closing the deal as long as possible and sends Pat Casey with Jimmy to make sure that he stays awake. Crandall delays the closing until Jimmy rescues his daughter from a forest fire. Crandall then closes the deal and gives his blessing to the marriage of his daughter to Jimmy. *Businessmen. Rakes. Real estate business. Health resorts. San Francisco. Forest fires.*

Note: Exteriors shot in San Francisco Bay area.

TOO WISE WIVES **F2.5776**

Famous Players–Lasky. *Dist* Paramount Pictures. 22 May **1921** [c22 May 1921; LP16588]. Si; b&w. 35mm. 6 reels, 5,164 ft.

Dir-Scen Lois Weber. *Story* Lois Weber, Marion Orth. *Photog* William C. Foster.

Cast: Louis Calhern *(David Graham)*, Claire Windsor *(Marie, his wife)*, Phillips Smalley *(John Daly)*, Mona Lisa *(Sara, his wife)*.

Domestic drama. Marie, wife of David Graham, is so devoted to her husband that he wearies of her constant attempts to please him and criticizes her. Sara, a former sweetheart of David's who has selfishly married for wealth, secretly determines to lure him from Marie. When forced to keep an overnight business engagement, Daly invites the Grahams to keep his wife company, and Sara writes David begging him to see her alone—but her letter is intercepted by Marie. When the Grahams accept the invitation, Marie confronts Sara with the unopened evidence. Discovering the plot, David denounces Mrs. Daly and reaffirms his love for Marie. *Businessmen. Marriage. Infidelity. Documentation.*

TOP HAND **F2.5777**

Goodwill Pictures. 5 Oct **1925** [New York State license]. Si; b&w. 35mm. 5 reels.

Cast: Bill Bailey.

Melodrama(?). No information about the nature of this film has been found.

THE TOP O' THE MORNING **F2.5778**

Universal Film Manufacturing Co. 4 Sep **1922** [c18 Aug 1922; LP18169]. Si; b&w. 35mm. 5 reels, 4,627 ft.

Pres by Carl Laemmle. *Dir* Edward Laemmle. *Scen* George Randolph Chester, Wallace Clifton. *Story* Anne Caldwell. *Photog* Charles Stumar.

Cast: Gladys Walton *("Jerry" O'Donnell)*, Harry Myers *(John Garland)*, Doreen Turner *(Dot Garland)*, Florence D. Lee *(Jerry's aunt)*, William Welsh *(Dermott O'Donnell)*, Don Bailey *(Mulrooney)*, Dick Cummings *(Father Quinn)*, Margaret Campbell *(Mrs. O'Donnell)*, Ralph McCullough *(Eugene O'Donnell)*, Ethel Shannon *(Katherine Vincent)*, Harry Carter *(Blakely Stone)*, William Moran *(Thomas Wilson)*, Sally Russell *(Katie*

McDougal), Martha Mattox *(Miss Murdock)*.

Romantic drama. Source: Anne Caldwell, *Top o' the Mornin'; a Comedy in Three Acts* (c1913). An Irish girl, Jerry, comes to her father in America. But finding life unpleasant with her stepmother, Jerry leaves home and encounters John Garland, a millionaire, now a widower, whom she knew in Ireland. Garland hires her to be governess to his daughter. Jerry's brother, Eugene, a cashier in Garland's bank, is implicated in a robbery of his employer; and Jerry is also involved, apprehended, and jailed. Garland, however, clears the O'Donnells and declares his love for Jerry. *Irish. Stepmothers. Governesses. Widowers. Millionaires. Bank clerks. Brother-sister relationship. Robbery.*

THE TOP OF NEW YORK **F2.5779**

Realart Pictures. *Dist* Paramount Pictures. 18 Jun **1922** [New York premiere; released 21 Aug; c14 Mar 1922; LP18044]. Si; b&w. 35mm. 5 reels, 5,148 ft.

Pres by Jesse L. Lasky. *Dir* William D. Taylor. *Adapt* George Hopkins. *Story* Sonya Levien. *Photog* James Van Trees.

Cast: May McAvoy *(Hilda O'Shaunnessey)*, Walter McGrail *(Emery Gray)*, Pat Moore *(Micky O'Shaunnessey)*, Edward Cecil *(Gregory Stearns)*, Charles Bennett *(Mr. Isaacson)*, Mary Jane Irving *(Susan Gray)*, Carrie Clark Ward *(Mrs. Brady)*, Arthur Hoyt *(Mr. Brady)*.

Melodrama. Shopgirl Hilda O'Shaunnessey accepts an expensive gift from her employer and pawns it to raise money to send her crippled brother to a hospital, then decides to commit suicide. Emery Gray, a neighbor, prevents her and exposes her employer, Gregory Stearns, as the one who stole his wife. Hilda and Emery marry; the brother is cured; and the affair ends happily. *Shopgirls. Cripples. Suicide. Brother-sister relationship.*

THE TOP OF THE WORLD **F2.5780**

Famous Players–Lasky. *Dist* Paramount Pictures. 9 Feb **1925** [c31 Dec 1924; LP20967]. Si; b&w. 35mm. 7 reels, 7,167 ft.

Pres by Adolph Zukor, Jesse L. Lasky. *Dir* George Melford. *Screenplay* Jack Cunningham. *Photog* Charles G. Clarke.

Cast: James Kirkwood *(Guy Ranger/Burke Ranger)*, Anna Q. Nilsson *(Sylvia Ingleton)*, Joseph Kilgour *(Sylvia's father)*, Mary Mersch *(her stepmother)*, Raymond Hatton *(Captain Preston)*, Sheldon Lewis *("Doctor" Kieff)*, Charles A. Post *(Hans)*, Mabel Van Buren *(Mary Ann)*, Frank Jonasson *(Joe)*, Lorimer Johnston *(Vreiboom)*.

Melodrama. Source: Ethel May Dell, *The Top of the World* (London & New York, 1920). To avoid a marriage arranged by her stepmother, Sylvia Ingleton follows Guy Ranger to South Africa, and there she discovers that he has become addicted to alcohol and drugs. Sylvia is unable to find shelter, until Burke Ranger, Guy's cousin, takes her in, and, to avoid malicious gossip, enters into a companionate marriage with her. Guy becomes despondent and attempts suicide. He is nursed back to health by "Doctor" Kieff, a narcotics peddler. When Burke is called away to help a sick neighbor, Guy steals the money from Burke's strongbox and goes to a nearby city to spend it in debauchery. Attempting to recover the money, which was entrusted to her, Sylvia follows him and is seen by Burke, who believes her unfaithful. The three of them return to Burke's home, which is soon threatened by floods. Burke sends Guy and Sylvia off on the only horse, but she returns, wanting only to be with him. After being caught in the raging waters, Sylvia and Burke find safety and a new beginning on a high plateau called "the top of the world." *Cousins. Alcoholism. Narcotics. Theft. Marriage—Companionate. Suicide. South Africa. Floods.*

TOP SERGEANT MULLIGAN **F2.5781**

Morris R. Schlank Productions. *Dist* Anchor Film Distributors. 15 Jan **1928.** Si; b&w. 35mm. 6 reels, 5,836 ft.

Dir James P. Hogan. *Story-Scen* Francis Fenton. *Titl* De Leon Anthony. *Photog* Robert Cline. *Film Ed* De Leon Anthony.

Cast: Donald Keith *(Osborne Wellington Pratt)*, Lila Lee *(The Girl)*, Wesley Barry *(Mickey Neilan)*, Gareth Hughes *(Lieut. Fritz von Lang)*, Wheeler Oakman *(The Captain)*, Wade Boteler *(Top Sergeant Mulligan)*, Arthur Thalasso, Sid Smith, Sheldon Lewis *(The Spy)*.

Comedy. "Mickey Neilan is himself enlisted for service while out helping the recruiting officers with his vaude partner, Lila Lee. At the training camp he encounters top-kick Mulligan who proceeds to make life miserable for the rookie. On top of that the sergeant, Y. M. C. A. worker and the captain make a play for his girl. In France Mulligan and Neilan are sent spy hunting and are captured with a labor unit after putting on cork. Taken to Berlin they get their man and bring him back after the war is over and get the bird from their buddies. Meantime the girl the rookie has left behind with an entertainment outfit gets hitched to the 'Y' worker." (*Variety*, 2 May 1928, p26.) *Soldiers. Spies. World War I. United States Army—Training. United States Army—Recruiting. United States Army—Negro troops. France. Berlin. Young Men's Christian Association.*

TOP SPEED **F2.5782**

First National Pictures. 24 Aug **1930** [c6 Sep 1930; LP1552]. Sd (Movietone); b&w. 35mm. 8 reels, 7,200 ft.

Dir Mervyn LeRoy. *Screenplay-Dial* Humphrey Pearson, Henry McCarty. *Photog* Sid Hickox. *Film Ed* Harold Young. *Songs: "Goodness Gracious," "I'll Know and She'll Know," "Keep Your Undershirt On," "What Would I Care?" "Sweeter Than You"* Bert Kalmar, Harry Ruby. *Song: "As Long As I Have You and You Have Me"* Al Dubin, Joe Burke. *Rec Engr* Earl Sitar.

Cast: Joe E. Brown *(Elmer Peters)*, Bernice Claire *(Virginia Rollins)*, Jack Whiting *(Jerry Brooks)*, Frank McHugh *(Tad Jordan)*, Laura Lee *(Babs Green)*, Rita Flynn *(Daisy)*, Edwin Maxwell *(J. W. Rollins)*, Wade Boteler *(sheriff)*, Edmund Breese *(Spencer Colgate)*, Cyril Ring *(Vincent Colgate)*, Billy Bletcher *(Ipps)*, Al Hill *(Briggs)*.

Comedy. Source: Bert Kalmar, Harry Ruby, and Guy Bolton, *Top Speed* (New York opening: 25 Dec 1929). At the fashionable Lackawanna Lodge, where they are spending the last day of their vacation, bond clerks Jerry and Elmer decide to stay for another day to watch the speedboat race. At the last minute, Rollins, a boat owner, fires his pilot and induces Jerry to substitute and throw the race. Jerry then plans to accept half the payoff which Elmer, having boasted of being a millionaire, bets on Rollins' boat. Jerry wins the race but is confronted by a sheriff who claims that he and Elmer are wanted for the theft of a bond; but Elmer, who finds the missing certificate, turns it over to the sheriff. Then, with sighs of relief, both boys embrace their girls. ... *Bond clerks. Courtship. Boat racing. Resorts.*

TOPSY AND EVA **F2.5783**

Feature Productions. *Dist* United Artists. 16 Jun **1927** [Los Angeles premiere; released Aug; c13 Jul 1927; LP24175]. Si; b&w. 35mm. 8 reels, 7,456 ft.

Prod Consult Myron Selznick. *Dir* Del Lord. *Cont* Scott Darling. *Titl* Dudley Early. *Adapt* Lois Weber. *Photog* John W. Boyle.

Cast: Rosetta Duncan *(Topsy)*, Vivian Duncan *(Eva)*, Gibson Gowland *(Simon Legree)*, Noble Johnson *(Uncle Tom)*, Marjorie Daw *(Marietta)*, Myrtle Ferguson *(Aunt Ophelia)*, Nils Asther *(George Shelby)*, Henry Victor *(St. Claire)*.

Burlesque. Source: Catherine Chisholm Cushing, *Topsy and Eva* (New York opening: 23 Dec 1924). Topsy, a little black imp, is offered for sale at an auction on the Shelby estate by Simon Legree; when no one bids, Eva St. Claire gets her for a nickel, and in company with Uncle Tom and other slaves she is turned over to Aunt Ophelia for correction and cleaning. When St. Claire is unable to pay his debt to Legree, the latter reclaims his property; but Topsy escapes from Legree while Legree and Shelby engage in a furious battle. Struggling against great drifts of snow, she finds a pair of skis and later a horse equipped with snowshoes, and she reaches the river before Legree and his dogs and finds a graveyard where runaway slaves have sought refuge; later, learning that Eva is gravely ill, she prays for her recovery. Eva revives, and the two friends are happily reunited. *Children. Negroes. Slavery. Miracles. "Uncle Tom's Cabin".*

TORMENT **F2.5784**

Maurice Tourneur Productions. *Dist* Associated First National Pictures. 25 Feb **1924** [c21 Feb 1924; LP19939]. Si; b&w. 35mm. 6 reels, 5,442 ft.

Pres by M. C. Levee. *Dir* Maurice Tourneur. *Scen* Fred Myton. *Titl* Marion Fairfax. *Photog* Arthur L. Todd. *Set Dsgn* Jack Okey. *Film Ed* Frank Lawrence. *Asst Dir* Scott R. Beal.

Cast: Owen Moore *(Hansen)*, Bessie Love *(Marie)*, Jean Hersholt *(Boris)*, Joseph Kilgour *(Charles G. Hammond)*, Maude George *(Mrs. Hammond)*, Morgan Wallace *(Jules Carstock)*, George Cooper *(Chick Fogarty)*.

Crook melodrama. Source: William Dudley Pelley, "Torment" (publication undetermined). Count Boris escapes from Russia during the Revolution with the crown jewels, intending to use them to aid his starving countrymen. Three international crooks—Carstock, Hansen, and Fogarty—plan to steal the jewels, but Hansen meets Marie en route to Yokohama and decides to go straight. They are all engulfed, including Boris, by an earthquake and trapped in a bank vault. Boris is slain. Hansen gets the jewels, which he promises to use helping the poor. He and Marie are rescued, and they plan to marry. *Nobility. Thieves. Charity. Russia—History—1917–21 Revolution. Yokohama. Earthquakes.*

THE TORNADO (Universal-Jewel) **F2.5785**

Universal Pictures. ca13 Dec **1924** [New York premiere; released 4 Jan 1925; c31 Oct 1924; LP20733]. Si; b&w. 35mm. 7 reels, 6,375 ft.

Pres by Carl Laemmle. *Dir* King Baggot. *Adapt* Grant Carpenter. *Photog* John Stumar.

Cast: House Peters *(Tornado)*, Ruth Clifford *(Ruth Travers)*, Richard Tucker *(Ross Travers)*, Snitz Edwards *("Pewee")*, Dick Sutherland *("Gorilla")*, Jackie Morgan *("Hurricane")*, Kate Price *(Emily)*, Charlotte Stevens *(Molly Jones)*, Fred Gamble *(Pa Jones)*, Caroline Irwin *(Ma Jones)*, James Welsh *("Drunk")*.

Melodrama. Source: Lincoln J. Carter, *The Tornado; a Spectacular Comedy Drama in Five Acts* (c26 Oct 1891). A lumber camp foreman, known as Tornado, encounters Ruth, his former sweetheart, and Ross Travers, whom Tornado thought to be his best friend. He learns that Ross tricked Ruth into marrying him with the story of Tornado's death in the war and that their marriage is an unhappy one for Ruth. Threatened with his just deserts if he should further mistreat Ruth, Ross leaves with his wife on a train, which is tossed from a bridge by a tornado. The hero arrives in time to rescue Ruth from the swirling water, but his efforts to save Ross are in vain. *Veterans. Lumberjacks. Friendship. Train wrecks. Tornadoes.*

THE TORRENT **F2.5786**

Universal Film Manufacturing Co. ca22 Jan **1921** [San Francisco premiere; released Jan; c23 Dec 1920; LP15964]. Si; b&w. 35mm. 5 reels, 4,855 ft.

Pres by Carl Laemmle. *Dir* Stuart Paton. *Adapt* Philip Hurn, Wallace Clifton. *Photog* Bert Glennon, Roland Price.

Cast: Eva Novak *(Velma Patton)*, Oleta Ottis *(Anne Mayhew)*, Jack Perrin *(Lieut. Paul Mack)*, L. C. Shumway *(Sam Patton)*, Jack Curtis *(Red Galvin)*, Harry Carter *(Jud Rossen)*, Bert Alpino *(first mate)*.

Melodrama. Source: George Rix, "Out of the Sunset," in *Telling Tales* (4:1–24, May 1920). Velma is unhappily married to Sam Patton, a millionaire roué. Aboard his yacht bound for the South Seas, Sam pays more attention to his guests than to his wife, and she flees when he attempts to force liquor on her. A sudden paralytic stroke renders him helpless, and she believes him dead. A storm comes up, and Velma is washed ashore on a desert isle. She is later joined by Lieut. Paul Mack, whose hydroplane has run out of fuel. They fall in love, but their idyll is broken when they are captured by a band of moonshiners. After suffering torture, they escape and go to Velma's home in California, where they find Sam alive but a hopeless cripple. Velma feels obligated to her husband and refuses to see Paul again. Realizing the wrong he has done his wife, Sam violates his doctor's orders by taking an overdose of whisky, and he dies. Velma is free to marry Paul, and together they take an airplane trip back to the scene of their first meeting. *Moonshiners. Millionaires. Suicide. Hydroplanes. South Sea Islands. Shipwrecks.*

THE TORRENT **F2.5787**

Phil Goldstone Productions. *Dist* Truart Film Corp. 1 Aug **1924.** Si; b&w. 35mm. 6 reels.

Dir A. P. Younger, William Doner. *Scen* A. P. Younger. *Photog* Roland Price, Edgar Lyons, Paul Allen.

Cast: William Fairbanks *(Hale Garrison)*, Ora Carew *(Gloria Manner)*, Frank Elliott *(Ernest Leeds)*, Joseph Kilgour *(Leed's friend)*, Gertrude Astor *(The Cast-off)*, June Elvidge *(The Friend)*, Fontaine La Rue *(dancing girl)*, Ashley Cooper *(butler)*, Robert McKim *(detective)*, Charles French *(captain)*.

Melodrama. Source: Langdon McCormick, "The Torrent" (publication undetermined). Hale Garrison, a big game hunter returning from safari in Africa, meets Gloria Manner on shipboard and falls in love with her. Influenced by the atmosphere of revelry and gin on the high seas, they undergo a mock marriage ceremony performed by the ship's captain. Gloria is met at the dock by a suitor whom she still plans to marry, but Hale, insisting that he and Gloria are legitimately married, "kidnaps" her. He takes her to a mountain lodge, and her former fiancé hires a thug to kill him. The thug throws Hale into a raging river, from which he is rescued by an Indian guide. The thug is later killed when the car in which he is abducting Gloria crashes near the river. Hale and Gloria are reunited and decide to remain together, having learned to love each other. *Hunters. Indians of North America. Kidnaping. Automobile accidents. Ocean liners.*

THE TORRENT **F2.5788**

Cosmopolitan Pictures. *Dist* Metro-Goldwyn-Mayer Distributing Corp. 8 Feb **1926** [c1 Mar 1926; LP22444]. Si; b&w. 35mm. 7 reels, 6,769 ft.

Dir Monta Bell. *Titl* Katherine Hilliker, H. H. Caldwell. *Adapt* Dorothy Farnum. *Photog* William Daniels. *Set Dsgn* Cedric Gibbons, Merrill Pye. *Film Ed* Frank Sullivan. *Wardrobe* Kathleen Kay, Maude Marsh, André-ani, Max Ree.

Cast: Ricardo Cortez *(Don Rafael Brull)*, Greta Garbo *(Leonora)*, Gertrude Olmsted *(Remedios)*, Edward Connelly *(Pedro Moreno)*, Lucien Littlefield *(Cupido)*, Martha Mattox *(Doña Bernarda Brull)*, Lucy Beaumont *(Doña Pepa)*, Tully Marshall *(Don Andreas)*, Mack Swain *(Don Mattias)*, Arthur Edmund Carew *(Salvatti)*, Lillian Leighton *(Isabella)*, Mario Carillo *(King of Spain)*.

Romantic drama. Source: Vicente Blasco-Ibáñez, *Entre Naranjos* (Valencia, 1900?). Don Rafael Brull, the son of landed Spanish aristocrats, falls in love with Leonora, the daughter of one of his family's tenants. Doña Bernada, who is ambitious for her son, breaks up the romance by dispossessing Leonora's family. Leonora goes to Paris, where she becomes an opera singer; Rafael stays at home and runs for public office, becoming engaged to Remedios. Leonora returns home for a visit, and Rafael saves her life during a flash flood. Their passion reawakens, but Doña Bernada persuades Rafael to renounce his love. Years pass. Rafael and Leonora meet only once again, each having made his own life: Leonora is a world-famous opera singer, and Rafael is prominent in public office. *Landed gentry. Singers. Filial relations. Opera. Spain. Paris. Floods.*

Note: Known also as *Ibáñez' Torrent*.

THE TOTEM POLE BEGGAR *see* **EYES OF THE TOTEM**

THE TOUGH GUY **F2.5789**

Film Booking Offices of America. 1 Feb **1926** [c31 Jan 1926; LP22469]. Si; b&w. 35mm. 6 reels, 5,455 ft.

Dir David Kirkland. *Scen* Buckleigh Fritz Oxford. *Story* Frank M. Clifton. *Photog* Ross Fisher. *Asst Dir* Al Werker.

Cast: Fred Thomson *(Fred Saunders)*, Lola Todd *(June Hardy)*, Robert McKim *(Con Carney)*, William Courtwright *(minister)*, Billy Butts *(Buddy Hardy)*, Leo Willis *(Sam Jacks)*, Silver King *(a horse)*.

Western melodrama. Fred Saunders rides into a wild town and aids the minister in recovering money stolen from the collection plate, thereby winning the love of the minister's daughter, June. Fred prevents Buddy, an orphan boy, from being trampled by a runaway horse and later "kidnaps" Buddy from an orphanage. Carney and his gang kidnap the boy in earnest, and Fred rescues him. Buddy turns out to be June's long-lost brother, and Fred and June are married by her father. *Clergymen. Orphans. Brother-sister relationship. Theft. Kidnaping. Horses.*

TOUTE SA VIE **F2.5790**

Paramount-Publix Corp. 9 Nov **1930** [Paris premiere]. Sd (Movietone); b&w. 35mm. 9 reels.

Dir Alberto Cavalcanti. *Scen-Dial* Jean Aragny.

Cast: Marcelle Chantal *(Suzanne Valmond)*, Fernand Fabré *(Jim Grey)*, Émilie Vautier *(Mrs. Asmore)*, Paul Guide *(Mrs. Asmore)*, Richard William *(Stanley Vanning)*, Jean Mercanton *(Bobby)*.

Drama. Source: Timothy Shea, *Sarah and Son* (New York, 1929). A French-language version of *Sarah and Son,* q. v. *Singers. Children. Lawyers. Motherhood. Marriage. Desertion. Vaudeville. Opera.*

THE TOWER OF LIES **F2.5791**

Metro-Goldwyn-Mayer Pictures. 11 Oct **1925** [c11 Sep 1925; LP21882]. Si; b&w. 35mm. 7 reels, 6,849 ft.

Dir Victor Seastrom. *Scen* Agnes Christine Johnston, Max Marcin. *Titl* Marian Ainslee, Ruth Cummings. *Photog* Percy Hilburn. *Sets* Cedric Gibbons, James Basevi.

Cast: Norma Shearer *(Glory)*, Lon Chaney *(Jan)*, Ian Keith *(Lars)*, Claire McDowell *(Katrina)*, William Haines *(August)*, David Torrence *(Eric)*.

Drama. Source: Selma Ottiliana Lovisa Lagerlöf, *Kejsarn av Portugallien; en Värmlandsberättelse* (Stockholm, 1914). Jan, a sober and industrious Swedish farmer, works long hours tilling the soil, knowing neither joy nor sorrow. A daughter, Glory, is born to him, and the drudgery of his life turns to happiness. Years later, the landlord of the estate is accidentally killed, and his son withdraws credit from the farmers, demanding payment of all notes immediately. To prevent their eviction, Glory goes to the city to find work. She is followed by Lars, the new landlord, and money arrives in time to allow Jan to keep his land. Glory does not return, and Lars loses his sanity, playing at lords and ladies with the neighborhood children. Time passes, and Glory finally comes home, dressed in finery. Suspected of being a fallen woman, she is driven away by the neighbors and boards a boat for the mainland. Lars is a passenger on the boat and accidentally falls to his death; Jan tries to follow Glory but falls from the dock and drowns. Glory one day returns and marries her childhood sweetheart. *Farmers. Landlords. Prostitution. Filial relations. Insanity. Sweden.*

THE TOWN SCANDAL **F2.5792**

Universal Pictures. 16 Apr **1923** [c29 Mar 1923; LP18832]. Si; b&w. 35mm. 5 reels, 4,704 ft.

Dir King Baggot. *Scen* Hugh Hoffman. *Photog* Victor Milner.

Cast: Gladys Walton *(Jean Crosby)*, Edward Hearne *(Toby Caswell)*, Edward McWade *(Avery Crawford)*, Charles Hill Mailes *(Bill Ramsey)*, William Welsh *(Samuel Grimes)*, William Franey *(Lysander Sprowl)*, Anna Hernandez *(Mrs. Crawford)*, Virginia Boardman *(Mrs. Sprowl)*, Rosa Gore *(Effie Strong)*, Nadine Beresford *(Mrs. Grimes)*, Louise Reming Barnes *(Mrs. Ramsey)*, Margaret Morris *(Trixie)*.

Comedy-drama. Source: Frederic Arnold Kummer, "The Town Scandal" (publication undetermined). Broadway chorus girl Jean Crosby visits her sister in Murphysburg and finds that not only has her brother-in-law, Lysander Sprowl, squandered all the money she has sent, but the leading male citizens—all members of the Purity League—who were so friendly to her in New York will not now give her a second glance. With the help of newspaperman Toby Caswell, however, she anonymously publishes her life story in the town newspaper, thus frightening the men into offering Jean "hush money." Jean refuses their bribery, but before she and Toby leave town they get the gentlemen's promises to end their push for blue laws. *Chorus girls. Sisters. Reporters. Newspapers. Smalltown life. Blue laws.*

Note: Working titles: *The Chicken; The Chicken That Came Home To Roost.*

THE TOWN THAT FORGOT GOD **F2.5793**

Fox Film Corp. 30 Oct **1922** [New York premiere; released 11 Feb 1923; c11 Feb 1922; LP19158]. Si; b&w. 35mm. 9 reels, ca8,500 ft.

Pres by William Fox. *Dir* Harry Millarde. *Story-Scen* Paul H. Sloane. *Photog* Joseph Ruttenberg, Albert Wilson. *Film Ed* Hettie Grey Baker.

Cast: Bunny Grauer *(David, as a boy)*, Warren Krech *(Eben, the carpenter)*, Jane Thomas *(Betty Gibbs, the teacher)*, Harry Benham *(Harry Adams, the surveyor)*, Edward Denison *(The Squire)*, Grace Barton *(his wife)*, Raymond Bloomer *(David, as a man)*, Nina Casavant *(David's wife)*.

Rural melodrama. A village schoolteacher, unaware that Eben, the village carpenter, is in love with her, marries a surveyor and has a son, David. Eben, distraught at losing her, goes away, and he returns years later to find that David, now an orphan, is running away from his cruel foster father, the squire. Eben befriends David, and when the town is destroyed by a storm the two escape harm. An epilog shows David 25 years later as a successful businessman, happily married, helping to rebuild the town. *Schoolteachers. Orphans. Carpenters. Surveyors. Foster fathers. Village life. Religion.*

TRACKED **F2.5794**

FBO Pictures. 4 Nov **1928** [c4 Nov 1928; LP25981]. Si; b&w. 35mm. 5 reels, 4,957 ft.

Dir Jerome Storm. *Scen* Frank Howard Clark. *Titl* Helen Gregg. *Story* John Stuart Twist. *Photog* Robert De Grasse. *Film Ed* Tod Cheesman.

Cast: Ranger *(The Dog)*, Sam Nelson *(Jed Springer)*, Caryl Lincoln *(Molly Butterfield)*, Al Smith *(Lem Hardy)*, Jack Henderson *(The Rustler)*, Art Robbins *(The Herder)*, Clark Comstock *(Nathan Butterfield)*.

Western melodrama. Ranger, a sheep dog belonging to Jed Springer, is accused of being a killer, and local sheepherders attempt to drown the animal. Jed saves Ranger, and they go to a cave in the hills, fugitives from the crude injustice of the sheepmen. Jed later rescues Molly when a team runs away with her rig. Evidence then comes to light that proves Ranger not to be a killer, and Molly and Jed find themselves in each other's arms. *Sheepherders. Injustice. Dogs.*

TRACKED BY THE POLICE **F2.5795**

Warner Brothers Pictures. 7 May **1927** [c30 Apr 1927; LP23900]. Si; b&w. 35mm. 6 reels, 5,813 ft.

Dir Ray Enright. *Scen* John Grey. *Story* Gregory Rogers. *Camera* Ed Du Par. *Asst Dir* Eddie Sowders.

Cast: Rin-Tin-Tin *(Rinty)*, Jason Robards *(Bob Owen)*, Virginia Browne Faire *(Marcella Bradley)*, Tom Santschi *(Sandy Sturgeon)*, Dave Morris *(Wyoming Willie)*, Theodore Lorch *(Bull Storm)*, Nanette *(Princess)*, Ben Walker *(crook)*, Wilfred North *(Tom Bradley)*.

Action melodrama. Rinty, owned by society girl Marcella Bradley, escapes from the city with Princess, a white police dog. Bob Owen, assigned by Marcella's father to an irrigation project in the Arizona desert, is saved from a rockslide by the warning of Rinty. Storm, the foreman, who is in the hire of a rival camp, stirs the workers into rebellion against Bob; but Rinty frees him, and they flee to Bradley's home. Wyoming Willie is secretly dispatched for the sheriff when the drunken Sandy arrives at the house where Marcella is alone with her injured father; angered by her repulses, he abducts her. Rinty saves her from the brute, who falls into the river. ... Marcella and Bob are happily united. *Socialites. Irrigation. Abduction. Dams. Arizona. Dogs. Police dogs.*

TRACKED IN THE SNOW COUNTRY **F2.5796**

Warner Brothers Pictures. 13 Jul **1925** [c23 Apr 1925; LP21386]. Si; b&w. 35mm. 7 reels, 7,159 ft.

Dir Herman C. Raymaker. *Story-Cont* Herman C. Raymaker, Edward J. Meagher. *Photog* Ray June.

Cast: Rin-Tin-Tin *(himself)*, June Marlowe *(Joan Hardy)*, David Butler *(Terry Moulton)*, Mitchell Lewis *(Jules Renault)*, Charles Sellon *(Silent Hardy)*, Princess Lea *(Wah-Wah)*.

Northwest melodrama. Silent Hardy and his daughter, Joan, journey to the North Country, where the old man discovers a rich vein of gold and is murdered by Jules Renault, who wants Hardy's map that gives the location of the mine. His dog, Rin-Tin-Tin, who did his best to save Silent Hardy, is blamed for the crime and forced to flee to the woods. Renault later returns to the Hardy cabin looking for the map and is seen by Joan's sweetheart, Terry Moulton, who follows him to the mine. There Terry sees a fight between Rin-Tin-Tin and Renault and hears Renault threaten to kill the dog in the same way that he killed his master. Terry makes his presence known and is overpowered by Renault. Rin-Tin-Tin pursues Renault over a frozen lake, and the man falls through the ice and drowns. Rin-Tin-Tin is reinstated in Joan's affections and mates with a she-wolf that presents him with a fine litter of pups. *Gold mines. Murder. Documentation. Dogs.*

TRACKED TO EARTH (Universal Special) **F2.5797**

Universal Film Manufacturing Co. 6 Mar **1922** [c11 Feb 1922; LP17549]. Si; b&w. 35mm. 5 reels, 4,477 ft.

Pres by Carl Laemmle. *Dir* William Worthington. *Scen* Wallace Clifton. *Photog* Leland Lancaster.

Cast: Frank Mayo *(Charles Cranner)*, Virginia Valli *(Anna Jones)*, Harold Goodwin *(Dick Jones)*, Duke R. Lee *(Stub Lou Tate)*, Buck Connors *(Shorty Fuller)*, Arthur Millett *("Big Bill" Angus)*, Lon Poff *(Meenie Wade)*, Percy Challenger *(Zed White)*.

Western melodrama. Source: William J. Neidig, "Tracked to Earth," in *Saturday Evening Post.* Cranner, a railroad agent in search of train robbers, is caught riding a branded horse and is arrested as a horsethief. He escapes, however, by tunneling through the wall of the building in which he is confined and hides by burying himself in the desert sand. Anna Jones's dog discovers him, but loath to deliver him to the posse, Anna provides him with a horse. Hoping to see her again, Cranner returns and is almost captured by the posse, but the sheriff arrests the real horsethieves and reveals Cranner's true identity. *Railroad agents. Horsethieves. Sheriffs. Posses. Train robberies. Dogs.*

TRACKS **F2.5798**

Western Pictures. *Dist* Playgoers Pictures. 7 May **1922** [c27 Apr 1922; LU17787]. Si; b&w. 35mm. 6 reels, 5,466 ft.

Dir Joseph Franz. *Scen* L. V. Jefferson. *Story* Mark Noble. *Photog* George Barney.

Cast: Bill Patton *(Norman Draper)*, George Berrell *(Phillip Carlson)*, François Dumas *(Marcos Valverde)*, Beatrice Burnham *(Elicia)*, Noble Johnson *(Leon Serrano)*, J. Farrell MacDonald *(Jack Bess)*.

Western melodrama. Norman Draper, a Texas Ranger sent to round up a band of cattle rustlers, finds Phillip Carlson at the deathbed of his wife and assists him in burying her. Meanwhile, cow thieves are plaguing Marcos Valverde and his daughter Elicia; and Leon Serrano, the local deputy sheriff (actually the leader of the rustlers), realizing the community will demand a victim, arrests Carlson, who has innocently bought a stolen horse from the thieves. Draper rescues him from a lynching party and learns the whereabouts of the rustlers. Leon Serrano is unmasked as the culprit and then is arrested by Draper, who gives his reward to Carlson and is himself rewarded by the love of Elicia. *Texas Rangers. Rustlers. Sheriffs. Lynching.*

TRACY THE OUTLAW **F2.5799**

Foto Art Productions. *Dist* New-Cal Film Corp., Artistic Pictures. Mar **1928.** Si; b&w. 35mm. 6 reels, 6,400 ft.

Dir Otis B. Thayer. *Titl* Merritt Crawford.

Cast: Jack Hoey, Rose Chadwick, Dave Marrell, Jane La Rue, Howard Chandler.

Western biographical drama. Source: Pierce Kingsley, *Tracy the Outlaw* (a play; publication undetermined). "[Harry] Tracy [1870–1902] was one of the west's bad men during the days when it was young. ... As we see him he was more sinned against than sinning. Marked with the stigma of crime after he had escaped from a Texas gambling hall, he is everywhere sought as a dangerous man. He is forced to flee from state to state, the hunted of posses. There are brief spans of restfullness or security, but these are always broken by impending sounds of pursuit as the net is drawn closer. The outlaw can never relax; he must always be ready to fight back. Finally they corner him and he, but one cartridge left him, turns it on himself." (*Motion Picture News,* 31 Mar 1928, p1041.) *Outlaws. Posses. Fugitives. Suicide. Texas. Harry Tracy.*

THE TRAFFIC COP **F2.5800**

R-C Pictures. *Dist* Film Booking Offices of America. 17 Jan **1926** [c17 Jan 1926; LP22339]. Si; b&w. 35mm. 5 reels, 5,175 ft.

Dir Harry Garson. *Scen* James Gruen, John Grey. *Story* Gerald Beaumont. *Photog* Gilbert Warrenton.

Cast: Lefty Flynn *(Joe Regan)*, Kathleen Myers *(Alicia Davidson)*, James Marcus *(Radcliffe Davidson)*, Adele Farrington *(Mrs. Davidson)*, Ray Ripley *(Marmalade Laidlaw)*, Nigel Barrie *(Harvey Phillips)*, Raymond Turner *(Tapioca)*, Jerry Murphy *(Jerry Murphy)*.

Melodrama. Joe Regan, a kindly traffic cop, comes home with presents for Jerry Murphy, his young ward, and discovers that the boy has been hit by a car. The doctors advise a sea cure, and Joe takes Jerry to a seaside resort, where they meet Alicia Davidson. Joe falls in love with the girl, but her mother opposes the romance, disapproving of Joe's low social station. Joe later saves the entire Davidson family from certain death when the brakes of their car fail on a mountain road, and Mrs. Davidson then gives her grateful consent to a match between Joe and Alicia. *Police. Orphans. Automobile accidents. Resorts. Social classes.*

TRAFFIC IN HEARTS **F2.5801**

Columbia Pictures. *Dist* C. B. C. Film Sales. 23 May **1924** [c1 Jun 1924; LP20274]. Si; b&w. 35mm. 6 reels, 5,549 ft.

Dir Scott Dunlap. *Scen* Jack Stone. *Story* Dorothy Yost. *Photog* Lucien Andriot.

Cast: Robert Frazer *(Lawrence Hallor)*, Mildred Harris *(Alice Hamilton)*, Don Marion *(Shrimp)*, Charles Wellesley *(John Hamilton)*, John Herdman *(Dad Clark)*, Betty Morrisey *(Jerry)*.

Melodrama. Lawrence Hallor's plans to build model tenements for the poor are wrecked by his sweetheart's father, John Hamilton, a tyrannical political boss. He revives his plan under another identity, and Hamilton orders him crushed; but when Alice reveals his true identity, Hamilton revokes his order and sanctions the housing plan as well as his daughter's marriage. *Political bosses. Housing. Tenements. Poverty.*

THE TRAGEDY OF YOUTH **F2.5802**

Tiffany-Stahl Productions. 15 Jan or 1 Mar **1928** [c10 Feb 1928; LP24973]. Si; b&w. 35mm. 7 reels, 6,273 or 6,361 ft.

Dir George Archainbaud. *Cont* Olga Printzlau. *Titl* Frederick Hatton, Fanny Hatton. *Story* Albert Shelby Le Vino. *Photog* Faxon Dean. *Set Dsgn* Burgess Beall. *Film Ed* Robert J. Kern.

Cast: Patsy Ruth Miller *(Paula Wayne)*, Warner Baxter *(Frank Gordon)*, William Collier, Jr. *(Dick Wayne)*, Claire McDowell *(Mother)*, Harvey Clarke *(Father)*, Margaret Quimby *(Diana)*, Billie Bennett *(landlady)*, Stepin Fetchit *(porter)*.

Romantic drama. Young newlywed Paula Wayne turns to Frank Gordon when her husband, Dick, neglects her to practice bowling. Their affair ends when Dick pretends an attempt at suicide, and out of fear Paula consents to a reconciliation. Frank departs on an ocean voyage that ends in disaster, but he returns alive and the lovers are reunited. *Marriage. Infidelity. Suicide. Bowling. Shipwrecks.*

TRAIL DUST **F2.5803**

Dist Rayart Pictures. 1 Nov **1924.** Si; b&w. 35mm. 6 reels.

Prod K. Lee Williams. *Dir* Gordon Hines.

Cast: David Dunbar.

Western melodrama. "... of Oklahoma in the Seventies, dealing with the hardships and adventures of the homeseekers. The heroine is a minister's daughter. Hero is the town capitalist of Purgatory. The story concerns the efforts on the part of the villain to discredit the hero and win the heroine, which finally involve the entire community and a band of unfriendly Indians. In the end, the girl's faith wins out. (*Motion Picture News Booking Guide,* 8:79, Apr 1925.) *Indians of North America. Homesteaders. Oklahoma.*

THE TRAIL OF COURAGE **F2.5804**

FBO Pictures. 8 Jul **1928** [c8 Jul 1928; LP25590]. Si; b&w. 35mm. 6 reels, 4,758 ft.

Dir Wallace W. Fox. *Screenplay* Frank Howard Clark. *Titl* Helen Gregg. *Photog* Roy Eslick. *Film Ed* Della M. King.

Cast: Bob Steele *(Tex Reevers)*, Marjorie Bonner *(Ruth Tobin)*, Tom Lingham *(Jack Tobin)*, Jay Morley *(Chili Burns)*.

Western melodrama. Source: Kenneth Perkins, "Better Than a Rodeo" (publication undetermined). Tex Reevers, a young trailhand, loses his job for spending more time romancing Ruth Tobin, the rancher's daughter, than punching cows. Tex heads for California and, months later, meets up with the Tobin clan, which is headed west to do some prospecting. Fearing for their safety, Tex rides on ahead and is captured by Chili Burns, an old enemy, who ties him up in close proximity to a killer horse. Tex frees himself from his bonds, tames the horse, and saves the Tobin family from Burns and his cutthroat cohorts. The killer horse kills Burns, and Tex continues west with the Tobins. *Cowboys. Ranchers. Prospectors. Horses.*

TRAIL OF HATE **F2.5805**

Frederick Herbst Productions. *Dist* Di Lorenzo, Inc. Oct **1922.** Si; b&w. 35mm. 5 reels.

Dir W. Hughes Curran. *Story-Scen* John Anthony Miles. *Photog* Charles Stumar.

Cast: Guinn "Big Boy" Williams *(Silent Kerry)*, Molly Malone *(Mary Stockdale)*, Gordon Russell *(Jack Beecker)*, Andrée Tourneur *("Sunny" Kerry)*, Sydney Harris *(Stockdale)*, Maurine Chadwick *(Carmencita)*, William A. Hackett *(sheriff)*.

Western melodrama. Cowboy Silent Kerry falls in love with Mary Stockdale during his sojourn in the East and later rescues her from two drunks when she visits the West. It develops that Mary's father is an unwitting dupe of a gang of rustlers, and Carmencita, a dancehall girl, leads Mary to believe that she is secretly married to Kerry. Kerry and his fellow townsmen decide to rid themselves of the rustlers, whose leader, Jack Beecker, kidnaps Mary and Kerry's sister; thrilling action brings the gang to justice; Beecker falls over a cliff in a fight with Kerry. *Cowboys. Rustlers. Dancehall girls. Brother-sister relationship. Kidnaping.*

THE TRAIL OF '98 **F2.5806**

Metro-Goldwyn-Mayer Pictures. 5 Jan **1929** [c29 Jul 1929; LP551]. Mus score & sd eff (Movietone); b&w. 35mm. 10 reels, 8,799 ft. [Also si.]

Dir Clarence Brown. *Cont* Benjamin Glazer, Waldemar Young. *Titl* Joe Farnham. *Adapt* Benjamin Glazer. *Photog* John Seitz. *Art Dir* Cedric Gibbons, Merrill Pye. *Film Ed* George Hively. *Mus Score* David Mendoza, William Axt. *Song: "I Found Gold When I Found You"* Hazel Mooney, Evelyn Lyn, William Axt. *Asst Dir* Charles Dorian. *Wardrobe* Lucia Coulter.

Cast: Dolores Del Rio *(Berna)*, Ralph Forbes *(Larry)*, Karl Dane *(Lars Petersen)*, Harry Carey *(Jack Locasto)*, Tully Marshall *(Salvation Jim)*, George Cooper *(Samuel Foote, The Worm)*, Russell Simpson *(Old Swede)*, Emily Fitzroy *(Mrs. Bulkey)*, Tenen Holtz *(Mr. Bulkey)*, Cesare Gravina *(Berna's grandfather)*, E. Alyn Warren *(engineer)*, John Down *(mother's boy)*, Ray Gallagher, Doris Lloyd.

Northwest drama. Source: Robert William Service, *The Trail of '98; a Northland Romance* (New York, 1911). The gold fever hits San Francisco and then the nation as men pick up roots and head for Alaska. Family man

Samuel Foote, known as The Worm, forsakes his home; Lars Petersen, an outsized Michigan lumberman, leaves his wife; Salvation Jim leaves the Nevada desert; and the Bulkeys, with a poor relation, Berna, and her blind grandfather, plan to move their restaurant to the Klondike. Berna's grandfather is among the many who die during the months of travel from Dawson City across the Alaskan wastes. They arrive to find evil men like Jack Locasto enforcing a cutthroat existence, which drives the Bulkeys back to the States but strengthens the love between Berna and young adventurer Larry. She convinces him to return, but he prevails to try once more. Lars, Larry, Jim, and The Worm finally hit a vein, and Larry and The Worm stay on guard while the others return to record the claim. Left to die by his friend, Larry survives only when The Worm's attempt to steal the last matches backfires and he is eaten by wolves. Larry returns to find Berna a fallen woman, and only after burning Locasto to death in a saloon brawl can Larry and Berna, with the only other survivors, Lars Petersen and Jim, salvage the remains of their greed-gutted lives. *Adventurers. Lumbermen. Miners. Gold rushes. Greed. Family life. Saloons. San Francisco. Alaska. Klondike. Fires.*

THE TRAIL OF THE AXE **F2.5807**

Dustin Farnum Productions. *Dist* American Releasing Corp. 23 Jul or 21 Aug **1922**. Si; b&w. 35mm. 5 reels, 4,320 ft.

Dir Ernest C. Warde. *Story* Ridgwell Cullum. *Photog* Robert Newhard.

Cast: Dustin Farnum *(Dave Malkern)*, Winifred Kingston *(Betty Somers)*, George Fisher *(Jim Malkern)*, Joseph J. Dowling *(Doctor Somers)*.

Melodrama. Lumber foreman Dave Malkern is not only hard-pressed to meet his contract deadline but also concerned for his drunken and unreliable brother, Jim. Dave strongly advises Jim to reform for the sake of his sweetheart, Betty Somers, whom Dave secretly loves, but Dave is finally forced to dismiss his brother. Seeking revenge, Jim dynamites the sawmill—nearly killing Dave, but Dave cannot bring himself to release his brother to the angry lumbermen and allows Jim to escape. Dave finds consolation in Betty, who now realizes where her true love lies. *Brothers. Lumbering. Drunkenness. Revenge.*

THE TRAIL OF THE HORSE THIEVES **F2.5808**

FBO Pictures. *Dist* RKO Productions. 13 Jan **1929** [c7 Jan 1929; LP25974]. Si; b&w. 35mm. 5 reels, 4,823 ft.

Dir Robert De Lacy. *Titl* Helen Gregg. *Adapt-Cont* Frank Howard Clark. *Camera* Nick Musuraca. *Film Ed* Jack Kitchen. *Asst Dir* John Burch.

Cast: Tom Tyler *(Vic Stanley)*, Bee Amann *(Amy Taggart)*, Harry O'Connor *(Clint Taggart)*, Frankie Darro *(Buddy)*, Barney Furey *("The Eagle")*, Bill Nestel *(Babcock)*, Vic Allen *(sheriff)*, Ray Childs *(rustler)*, Leo Willett *(Curtis)*.

Western melodrama. Source: William E. Wing, "Desert Madness" (publication undetermined). Vic Stanley, a wandering cowboy, is found by Clint Taggart and his daughter, Amy, after he has escaped from a band of rustlers. Upon recovering his sight from a desert sandstorm, he sees and falls in love with Amy and becomes resolute in his decision to uncover the identity of the rustlers and particularly their leader, "The Eagle." Though blind during his capture, he nevertheless recognizes the voice of The Eagle in McElroy, a leading banker. After another escape from the gang, Vic manages to save Taggart and Amy from The Eagle's sticky clutches, exposes their operation, and proceeds on course with Amy. *Cowboys. Rustlers. Horsethieves. Bankers. Disguise. Blindness. Deserts. Sandstorms.*

TRAIL OF THE LAW **F2.5809**

Oscar Apfel. *Dist* Producers Security Corp. 25 Jan **1924** [New York showing; released Dec 1923]. Si; b&w. 35mm. 5 reels.

Dir Oscar Apfel. *Scen* Marion Brooks. *Photog* Alfred Gondolfi.

Cast: Wilfred Lytell, Norma Shearer, John Morse, George Stevens, actor, Richard Neill, Charles Beyer.

Melodrama. "A girl who, because of the dangerous community [Maine woods settlement], masquerades as a boy during the day, only to become herself again when safely ensconced in her own home at night. Years before, her mother had been murdered by a renegade, and her father has sworn to get the villain. It develops that a nasty neighbor is the party wanted. Her father gives him what's coming to him and is only prevented from homicide by Lytell, as the young man from the City who has fallen in love with the daughter." (*Variety*, 31 Jan 1924, p23.) *Disguise. Revenge. Male impersonation. Murder. Maine.*

THE TRAIL OF THE LONESOME PINE **F2.5810**

Famous Players–Lasky. *Dist* Paramount Pictures. ca18 Mar **1923** [New York premiere; released 15 Apr; c27 Mar 1923; LP18853]. Si; b&w. 35mm. 6 reels, 5,500-5,695 ft.

Pres by Adolph Zukor. *Dir* Charles Maigne. *Adapt-Scen* Will M. Ritchey. *Photog* James Howe.

Cast: Mary Miles Minter *(June Tolliver)*, Antonio Moreno *(John Hale)*, Ernest Torrence *("Devil" Jud Tolliver)*, Edwin J. Brady *("Bad" Rufe Tolliver)*, Frances Warner *(Ann)*, J. S. Stembridge *(Buck Falin)*, Cullen Tate *(Dave Tolliver)*.

Drama. Source: John William Fox, *The Trail of the Lonesome Pine* (New York, 1908). Eugene Walter, *The Trail of the Lonesome Pine* (New York opening: 29 Jan 1912). June Tolliver, whose family has long feuded with the Falins, falls in love with engineer John Hale when he comes to their mountain town. John sends her to the city to be educated with the promise of marriage when she returns. Because John is appointed deputy he tries to remain neutral, but he finds the Falins supporting him when June's Uncle Rufe is accused of murder. June is called to testify during his trial but does not perjure herself for Rufe's sake. To prevent a Tolliver from being hanged, Jud Tolliver has Rufe shot. John is also injured, but June's pleading finally brings an end to the feud. *Engineers. Feuds. Murder. Capital punishment. Education. Tennessee.*

THE TRAIL OF VENGEANCE **F2.5811**

J. J. Fleming Productions. *Dist* Davis Distributing Division. 15 Dec **1924**. Si; b&w. 35mm. 6 reels, 5,404 ft.

Dir Al Ferguson.

Cast: Al Ferguson, Pauline Curley.

Northwest melodrama. "Hero [a Mountie] swears to avenge death of pal, and follows murderer into far North. Meets and falls in love with prospector's daughter, but circumstances lead him to believe prospector is guilty party. As he is about to arrest him, matters are cleared up. The real villain is arrested and hero and girl find happiness." (*Motion Picture News Booking Guide*, 8:79, Apr 1925.) *Prospectors. Revenge. Murder. Northwest Mounted Police.*

THE TRAIL RIDER **F2.5812**

Fox Film Corp. 22 Feb **1925** [c8 Feb 1925; LP21119]. Si; b&w. 35mm. 5 reels, 4,752 ft.

Pres by William Fox. *Dir* William S. Van Dyke. *Scen* Thomas Dixon, Jr. *Photog* Reginald Lyons.

Cast: Buck Jones *(Tex Hartwell)*, Nancy Deaver *(Sally McCoy)*, Lucy Fox *(Fanny Goodnight)*, Carl Stockdale *(Jim Mackey)*, Jack McDonald *(Dee Winch)*, George Berrell *(Uncle Boley)*, Jacques Rollens *(Barber Ollie)*, Will Walling *(Malcolm Duncan)*.

Western melodrama. Source: George Washington Ogden, *The Trail Rider; a Romance of the Kansas Range* (New York, 1924). Tex Hartwell comes to the aid of an old cobbler by protecting him from the blows and insults of Jim Mackey, a skinflint banker. Mackey orders his hired guns to get Tex, but Tex is too quick for them. On the strength of his fast draw, Tex is hired as a trail rider by Dee Winch, being given the job of keeping diseased cattle off Winch's grasslands. Mackey's men later stampede a herd of infected cattle onto Winch's land, and Tex is fired in disgrace. Fanny Goodnight informs Tex that Mackey is the leader of the cattle runners, and Tex forces him to sign a confession to that effect. The old cobbler later kills Mackey, Tex is cleared with the cattlemen, and he and Fanny decide to ride a trail of their own together. *Trail riders. Skinflints. Bankers. Cobblers. Murder. Cattle—Diseases. Stampedes.*

TRAIL RIDERS **F2.5813**

Trem Carr Productions. *Dist* Rayart Pictures. Apr **1928**. Si; b&w. 35mm. 5 reels, 4,627 ft.

Dir-Scen J. P. McGowan. *Story* Milton Angle. *Photog* Bob Cline. *Film Ed* Mac V. Wright.

Cast: Buddy Roosevelt, Lafe McKee, Betty Baker, Pee Wee Holmes, Paul Malvern, Leon De La Mothe, Tommy Bay.

Western melodrama. "Adjacent ranch owners become involved in a question of water rights. The newcomers, headed by girl, are induced by an unscrupulous cattle rustler to enter upon a deal which they do not know is crooked. The rustler is shown up by young rancher as the stolen cattle are returned. Girl and rancher realize they are in love." (*Motion Picture News Booking Guide*, [14]:290, 1929.) *Ranchers. Rustlers. Water rights. Fraud.*

THE TRAIL TO RED DOG F2.5814

Westart Pictures. 19 Jul **1921** [New York showing]. Si; b&w. 35mm. *Dir* Leonard Franchon. *Writ* W. M. Smith. *Photog* A. H. Vallet.

Cast: Al Hart, Jack Mower, Robert Conville.

Western melodrama. No information about the precise nature of this film has been found.

Note: Originally advertised as *Cold Steel.*

TRAILIN' F2.5815

Fox Film Corp. 11 Dec **1921** [c11 Dec 1921; LP17417]. Si; b&w. 35mm. 5 reels, 4,355 ft.

Pres by William Fox. *Dir-Adapt* Lynn F. Reynolds. *Photog* Ben Kline.

Cast—Prolog: Jay Morley *(William Drew)*, Cecil Van Auker *(John Bard)*, J. Farrell MacDonald *(Piotto)*, Carol Holloway *(Joan)*.

Cast—The Story: Tom Mix *(Anthony Woodbury)*, Eva Novak *(Sally Fortune)*, Bert Sprotte *(John Woodbury [John Bard])*, James Gordon *(William Drew)*, Sid Jordan *(Steve Nash)*, William Duvall *(Deputy Glendon)*, Duke Lee *(Butch Conklin)*, Harry Dunkinson *(Sandy Ferguson)*, Al Fremont *(Lawlor)*, Bert Handley *(Dr. Young)*, Carol Holloway *(Joan)*.

Mystery melodrama. Source: Max Brand, *Trailin'* (New York, 1920). When Piotto, a notorious bandit chief, and his daughter, Joan, take William Drew to their hiding place, Drew falls in love with Joan, who is also loved by his partner, John Bard. They toss a coin for the girl, and although Drew wins, Bard later steals his infant son and takes him to an eastern city. As Woodbury, Bard becomes a man of wealth and culture, and he remains evasive in responding to the questions of his son, Anthony, about his mother. Drew finds Woodbury, and in a duel John is killed. Swearing to avenge his father, Anthony finds a picture that enables him to identify his old home in Idaho, where he finds the grave of his mother and, nearby, the ranch of Drew. Following a series of exciting incidents, Drew reveals the secret of Anthony's parentage, and Anthony marries Sally Fortune, a hotel waitress. *Personal identity. Parentage. Kidnaping. Revenge. Idaho.*

TRAILIN' BACK F2.5816

Trem Carr Productions. *Dist* Rayart Pictures. Mar **1928.** Si; b&w. 35mm. 5 reels, 4,308 or 4,652 ft.

Dir-Scen J. P. McGowan. *Titl* Arthur Hoerl. *Story* Victor Rousseau. *Photog* Bob Cline. *Film Ed* Mac V. Wright.

Cast: Buddy Roosevelt, Betty Baker, Lafe McKee, Leon De La Mothe, Tommy Bay, Bert Sanderson, Al Bertram.

Western melodrama. In pursuit of a bandit and his gang, a sheriff (played by Buddy Roosevelt) suspects the hideout to be the ranch belonging to the heroine (played by Betty Baker) and her father. One of the posse is actually a member of the gang, and he several times thwarts the sheriff's success, but justice finally triumphs with the aid of the hero's amazing hunches. *Ranchers. Sheriffs. Bandits. Gangs. Posses.*

TRAILIN' TROUBLE F2.5817

Universal Pictures. 23 Mar **1930** [c14 Mar 1930; LP1150]. Sd (Movietone); b&w. 35mm. 6 reels, 5,198 ft. [Also si; 5,336 ft.]

Pres by Carl Laemmle. *Dir-Writ* Arthur Rosson. *Dial-Titl* Harold Tarshis. *Photog* Harry Neumann. *Film Ed* Gilmore Walker. *Rec Engr* C. Roy Hunter.

Cast: Hoot Gibson *(Ed King)*, Margaret Quimby *(Molly)*, Pete Morrison *(Buck Saunders)*, Olive Young *(Ming Toy)*, William McCall *(Father)*, Bob Perry.

Western comedy-drama. Ed King is in love with Molly, daughter of the rancher for whom he works; and when he takes a shipment of horses to Kansas City, Buck Moran, his rival, plots to have Ed robbed of the sale money and thereby discredit him in the eyes of Molly and her father. Ed saves Ming Toy, a Chinese girl, from some ruffians; but in bidding him an affectionate farewell, she robs him of his money. Ed misses the train and steals a ride in an airplane. Molly's father accuses him of theft, but Ming Toy returns the money and denounces Buck as the conspirator. Ed captures the villain and turns him over to the authorities, then is reunited with Molly. *Cowboys. Chinese. Gangs. Robbery. Kansas City. Horses.*

TRAILING AFRICAN WILD ANIMALS F2.5818

Martin Johnson African Films. *Dist* Metro Pictures. 15 Apr **1923** [Baltimore showing; released 23 Apr; c24 Oct 1923; LP19529]. Si; b&w. 35mm. 7 reels, 6,500 ft.

Titl Terry Ramsaye. *Photog* Martin Johnson. *Film Ed* Martin Johnson, Terry Ramsaye.

Cast: Martin Johnson, Osa Johnson; Jerramini, Ferraragi *(themselves, gunbearers and heads of labor)*; Kalowatt *(himself, Mrs. Johnson's pet monkey)*.

Travel documentary. This film is about a 2-year excursion made by Mr. and Mrs. Martin Johnson across British East Africa to the "lost" Lake Paradise. Accompanied by guides, porters, gunbearers, and more than 100 natives, Mr. and Mrs. Johnson begin the safari in Nairobi, pass Mt. Kenya, and continue through hundreds of miles of jungle and swampland and across deserts and plains. The party encounters many types of wild animals, including some in danger of becoming extinct. It shoots antelope, buffalo, seven lions, four black rhinoceros, and one African elephant, but, according to the press sheet, kills "only when it was necessary." The film climaxes with an elephant hunt in which one beast rushes headlong into the camera to be stopped within 6 feet by a well-placed bullet from Mrs. Johnson's Winchester. *Safaris. Exploration. Africa. British East Africa. Lake Paradise. Monkeys. Lions. Buffalo. Elephants. Rhinoceros. Antelope.*

THE TRAIL'S END *see* **THE MAN GETTER**

TRAIL'S END F2.5819

William M. Smith Productions. *Dist* Merit Film Corp. 25 Jul **1922** [New York premiere; released 1 Sep 1922]. Si; b&w. 35mm. 5 reels, 4,700 ft.

Dir francis Ford. *Story* Arthur Somers R oche.

Cast: Franklyn Farnum *(Wilder Armstrong)*, Peggy O'Day *(Edith Kilgallen)*, George Reehm *(Frayne)*, Al Hart *(Stanley)*, Shorty Hamilton *(Cahoots)*, Genevieve Bert *(Molly)*.

Western melodrama. Despite Stanley's explanation that a fortune awaits Frayne, rancher Wilder Armstrong refuses to reveal his friend's whereabouts. Shortly thereafter, Edith Kilgallen, also an heir to the fortune, seeks Frayne; and Armstrong decides that he should find Frayne, who has disappeared. Stanley arrives first and tries to trap Edith, but Armstrong comes to the rescue. Explanations follow: Stanley's purpose was to frame Frayne for a crime, thus disqualifying him from the inheritance. "Frayne" is actually Frayne's half brother, who, accused of a crime, was sent from his uncle's home, then later killed Frayne in self-defense and assumed his identity. Edith and Wilder are united. *Brothers. Ranchers. Impersonation. Inheritance.*

Note: May also be known as *The Man Getter.*

TRAILS OF DANGER *see* **TRAILS OF PERIL**

TRAILS OF DESTINY F2.5820

Lee-Bradford Corp. 8 Jun **1926** [New York State license]. Si; b&w. 35mm. 5 reels.

No information about the nature of this film has been found.

TRAILS OF PERIL F2.5821

National Players. *Dist* Big 4 Film Corp. 30 Sep **1930.** Sd; b&w. 35mm. 6 reels, 5,800 ft.

Dir-Scen-Dial Alvin J. Neitz. *Story* Henry Taylor. *Photog* William Nobles. *Film Ed* Ethel Davey. *Sd* James Lowrie.

Cast: Wally Wales *(Bob Bartlett)*, Virginia Browne Faire *(Mary Martin)*, Frank Ellis *(Butch Coleson)*, Lew Meehan *(Joe Fenton)*, Jack Perrin *(Sheriff Johnson)*, Joe Rickson *(U. S. Marshal Bartlett)*, Buck Connors *(John Martin)*, Bobby Dunn *(Shorty)*, Pete Morrison *(Tom Weld)*, Hank Bell *(Hank)*.

Western melodrama. During a rescue of Mary Martin and her father, Bob Bartlett finds a good horse, which later causes him to be mistaken for Butch Coleson, a wanted outlaw. Wounded by a posse, Bob heads for Poker Flats hoping to capture Coleson for the reward; Butch gets the same idea about Bob; and the sheriff chases the gang to Martin's ranch, where Mary is held captive. The gang is rounded up, and Bob is exonerated. *Outlaws. Bounty hunters. Sheriffs. Posses. Gangs. Horses.*

Note: Working title: *Trails of Danger.*

TRAILS OF TREACHERY F2.5822

William M. Pizor Productions. 17 Nov **1928** [New York State license]. Si; b&w. 35mm. 5 reels, 4,300 ft.

Dir-Scen-Titl Robert J. Horner. *Photog* Lauren A. Draper. *Film Ed* Robert J. Horner.

Cast: Montana Bill.

Western melodrama(?). No information about the nature of this film has been found.

THE TRAIN WRECKERS **F2.5823**

Morris R. Schlank Productions. *Dist* Anchor Film Distributors. 1 Dec **1925** [New York State license]. Si; b&w. 35mm. 5 reels.

Dir J. P. McGowan.

Cast: Helen Holmes.

Melodrama. No information about the precise nature of this film has been found. *Train wrecks.*

TRAMP, TRAMP, TRAMP **F2.5824**

Harry Langdon Corp. *Dist* First National Pictures. 21 Mar **1926** [c7 Mar 1926; LP22515]. Si; b&w. 35mm. 6 reels, 5,831 ft.

Dir Harry Edwards. *Story* Frank Capra, Tim Whelan, Hal Conklin, J. Frank Holliday, Gerald Duffy, Murray Roth. *Photog* Elgin Lessley.

Cast: Harry Langdon *(Harry)*, Joan Crawford *(Betty Burton)*, Edwards Davis *(John Burton)*, Carlton Griffin *(Roger Caldwell)*, Alec B. Francis *(Harry's father)*, Brooks Benedict *(taxi driver)*, Tom Murray *(The Argentine)*.

Comedy. Harry, a young hobo, chances upon a barbecue given by Burton, a shoe manufacturer, and falls for Burton's daughter, Betty. Burton is the sponsor of a transcontinental walking contest, which Harry eagerly enters, erroneously believing that, if he wins the contest, Betty will marry him. Harry starts on his hike and soon wins the adoration of a sunbonneted miss riding on the tailboard of a westbound wagon. Harry wins the race only to discover that Betty is engaged to another. He again comes across his friend with the sunbonnet and joins her on the tailboard of her wagon. *Tramps. Manufacturers. Shoes. Walking contests.*

THE TRANS-CONTINENTAL RAILROAD *see* **THE IRON HORSE**

TRANSCONTINENTAL LIMITED **F2.5825**

Chadwick Pictures. c4 Feb **1926** [LP22184]. Si; b&w. 35mm. 7 reels, 6,400 ft.

Dir Nat Ross. *Adapt* Hampton Del Ruth. *Photog* Stephen Smith, Jr.

Cast: Johnnie Walker *(Johnnie Lane)*, Eugenia Gilbert *(Mary Reynolds)*, Alec B. Francis *(Jerry Reynolds)*, Edith Yorke *(Sara Reynolds)*, Bruce Gordon *(Joe Slavin)*, Edward Gillace *(Slim)*, George Ovey *(Pudge)*, Eric Mayne *(doctor)*, James Hamel *(Bob Harrison)*.

Melodrama. Johnnie Lane returns from the trenches in France and discovers that Joe Slavin has been wooing Mary Reynolds, who has been waiting patiently for Johnnie to come back home. Slavin, who is the fireman for Mary's father on the Transcontinental Limited, knows that the elder Reynold's sight is failing and attempts to blackmail the old man into agreeing to his marrying Mary. Money is desperately needed for an operation on Mary's mother, and two of Johnnie's war buddies steal it from the station safe. Slavin attempts to pin the theft on Johnnie, but the two buddies return the money and Johnnie is cleared of any suspicion. Johnnie threatens Slavin, saves the Transcontinental Limited from being wrecked, and marries Mary. *Veterans. Railroad engineers. Railroad firemen. Theft. Blackmail. Blindness. Train wrecks.*

THE TRAP (Universal-Jewel) **F2.5826**

Universal Film Manufacturing Co. ca6 May **1922** [New York premiere; released 22 May; c9 May 1922; LP17860]. Si; b&w. 35mm. 6 reels, 5,481 ft.

Dir Robert Thornby. *Story-Scen* George C. Hull. *Photog* Virgil Miller.

Cast: Lon Chaney *(Gaspard)*, Alan Hale *(Benson)*, Dagmar Godowsky *(Thalie)*, Stanley Goethals *(The Boy)*, Irene Rich *(The Teacher)*, Spottiswoode Aitken *(The Factor)*, Herbert Standing *(The Priest)*, Frank Campeau *(The Police Sergeant)*.

Northwest melodrama. Gaspard, a French-Canadian trapper, is betrayed when his sweetheart, Thalie, weds Benson, an adventurer who has previously tricked Gaspard out of a mine claim, and he waits 7 years for revenge. Benson begins to drink when his mine is ruined by a landslide and Thalie is taken ill. Influenced by Gaspard, Pierre forces a fight on Benson, who shoots him, and Gaspard refuses to testify that Benson shot in self-defense. After Benson is imprisoned, Gaspard takes in his child and sends it to the village school. Upon the father's release, Gaspard, fearing to lose the child, captures a half-starved wolf, which he conceals as a trap for Benson. By chance the child arrives first, and Gaspard, after a fight with the wolf, is reconciled with Benson and to the relinquishment of the child. *Trappers. Children. Revenge. Canadian Northwest. Wolves.*

TRAPPED **F2.5827**

Denver Dixon Productions. 1 Aug **1925.** Si; b&w. 35mm. 5 reels, 4,700 ft.

Cast: Carl Miller, Elinor Fair.

Melodrama(?). No information about the nature of this film has been found.

TRAPPED IN THE AIR **F2.5828**

Doubleday Productions. *Dist* Western Pictures Exploitation Co. Jul **1922.** Si; b&w. 35mm. 5 reels, 4,750 ft.

Dir Henry McCarthy, Leo Meehan.

Cast: Lester Cuneo.

Melodrama. "Aerial melodrama, dealing with operations of air bandits who prey on U. S. Air Mail Service. Hero, mail flier, is shot down by bandits, but heroine rescues him. Heroine is kidnapped by bandits. Hero sends call for help on bandit's radio. Heroine has hidden mailpouch with $100,000, and bandits threaten her. Hero learns of her capture, and sets out to rescue her. He is outnumbered, but at the crucial moment girl's father arrives with rescuing posse. Hero gives up flying to marry." (*Motion picture News Booking Guide*, 3:72, Oct 1922.) *Bandits. Air pilots. Airplanes. Postal service. Kidnaping. Radio.*

TRAVELIN' FAST **F2.5829**

Anchor Film Distributors. 30 Dec **1924.** Si; b&w. 35mm. 5 reels.

Cast: Jack Perrin *(Jack Foster)*, Jean Arthur *(Betty Conway)*, Peggy O'Day *(Ora Perdue)*, Lew Meehan *(Red Sampson)*, John Pringle *(William Conway)*, Horace B. Carpenter *(Sheriff Ted Clark)*.

Western melodrama. Evil Red Sampson and his band of rustlers shoot up Mineral Point, the ranch of William Conway, owner of a gold mine. Shot and dying, Conway reveals the location of his mine at Boulder Creek in a note. Ranger Jack Foster comes on the scene disguised as an outlaw, Doc Hargis, and liberates Ora Perdue, Conway's enforced bandit queen, who is known as a widowed restaurant keeper to the rest of the town. Red and his cronies revengefully attack the town, but Foster leads the citizens in a successful rebuff and wins the late Conway's daughter, Betty, for his heroics. *Rangers. Widows. Rustlers. Restaurateurs. Murder. Disguise. Gold mines.*

TRAVELIN' ON **F2.5830**

William S. Hart Co. *Dist* Paramount Pictures. 5 Mar **1922** [c24 Feb 1921; LP16193]. Si; b&w. 35mm. 7 reels, 6,267 ft.

Dir-Adapt Lambert Hillyer. *Story* William S. Hart. *Photog* Joe August. *Art Dir* J. C. Hoffner. *Paintings* Harry Barndollar.

Cast: William S. Hart *(J. B., The Stranger)*, James Farley *(Dandy Dan McGee)*, Ethel Grey Terry *(Susan Morton)*, Brinsley Shaw *(Hi Morton)*, Mary Jane Irving *(Mary Jane Morton)*, Robert Kortman *(Gila)*, Willis Marks *("Know-It-All" Haskins)*, Jacko the Monk *(himself)*.

Western melodrama. Hi Morton, a reformed crook, brings his wife, Susan, and his daughter to a southwestern town to build a new church. A mysterious Stranger also arrives, and after rescuing Susan from the attentions of Dandy Dan McGee he tells her that he covets her himself. But she appeals to his better nature so effectively that when Hi holds up a stage to get money for his church The Stranger rescues Hi from a lynching, takes the blame himself, then rides off. *Criminals—Rehabilitation. Strangers. Robbery. Lynching. Churches. Monkeys.*

THE TRAVELING SALESMAN **F2.5831**

Famous Players–Lasky. *Dist* Paramount Pictures. 5 Jun **1921** [c2 Jun 1921; LP16604]. Si; b&w. 35mm. 5 reels, 4,514 ft.

Dir Joseph Henabery. *Scen* Walter Woods. *Photog* Karl Brown.

Cast: Roscoe Arbuckle *(Bob Blake)*, Betty Ross Clark *(Beth Elliott)*, Frank Holland *(Franklin Royce)*, Wilton Taylor *(Martin Drury)*, Lucille Ward *(Mrs. Babbitt)*, Jim Blackwell *(Julius)*, Richard Wayne *(Ted Watts)*, George Pearce *(John Kimball)*, Robert Dudley *(Pierce Gill)*, Gordon Rogers *(Bill Crabb)*.

Farce. Source: James Grant Forbes, *The Traveling Salesman: A Comedy in Four Acts* (New York, 1908). Traveling salesman Bob Blake finds himself at a railroad junction instead of his intended destination through a practical joke played on him by two drummer friends, and he spends the night in an unoccupied house up for sale. In Grand River he falls in love with its owner, Beth Elliott. Politician Martin Drury conspires with her suitor, Franklin, to buy the property cheaply, knowing it is wanted by the railroad, but Bob beats him to the sale and pays the taxes. Beth, thinking Bob has deceived her, accepts their offer, but when he learns that a wife's signature is invalid without the assent of her husband they get married, thus checkmating the schemers. *Traveling salesmen. Politicians. Real estate. Railroads.*

TREASURE CANYON **F2.5832**

Sunset Productions. *Dist* Aywon Film Corp. Jan **1924.** Si; b&w. 35mm. 5 reels, 4,900 ft.

Cast: J. B. Warner, Marie Walcamp.

Western melodrama. Plot concerns the struggle to regain possession of a map to a silver mine. *Mine claims. Silver mines.*

Note: One source indicates release may have been Jan 1925.

TRENT'S LAST CASE **F2.5833**

Fox Film Corp. 31 Mar **1929** [c30 Mar 1929; LP256]. Sd eff & mus score (Movietone); b&w. 35mm. 6 reels, 5,834 ft. [Also si; 5,809 ft.]

Pres by William Fox. *Supv* Bertram Millhauser. *Dir* Howard Hawks. *Scen* Scott Darling. *Titl* Malcolm S. Boylan. *Adapt* Beulah Marie Dix. *Photog* Harold Rosson. *Asst Dir* E. D. Leshin.

Cast: Donald Crisp *(Sigsbee Manderson)*, Raymond Griffith *(Philip Trent)*, Raymond Hatton *(Joshua Cupples)*, Marceline Day *(Evelyn Manderson)*, Lawrence Gray *(Jack Marlowe)*, Nicholas Soussanin *(Martin)*, Anita Garvin *(Ottilie Dunois)*, Ed Kennedy *(Inspector Murch)*.

Mystery melodrama. Source: Edmund Clerihew Bentley, *Trent's Last Case* (London, 1913). Sigsbee Manderson is apparently murdered, and Inspector Murch lines up the suspects for interrogation: Manderson's wife, Evelyn; his secretary, who is in love with Evelyn; Manderson's uncle; the butler; and the maid. Murch suspects the secretary but Trent proves that Manderson committed suicide, killing himself in such a way as to cast suspicion on his innocent secretary. *Detectives. Police. Butlers. Secretaries. Housemaids. Suicide.*

THE TRESPASSER **F2.5834**

Gloria Productions. *Dist* United Artists. 5 Oct **1929** [c29 Jul 1929; LP796]. Sd (Photophone); b&w. 35mm. 10 reels, 8,223 ft.

Pres by Joseph P. Kennedy. *Story-Dial-Dir* Edmund Goulding. *Photog* George Barnes, Gregg Toland. *Art Dir* Stephen Goosson. *Film Ed* Cyril Gardner. *Mus* Josiah Zoro. *Song: "Love Your Magic Spell Is Everywhere"* Edmund Goulding, Elsie Janis. *Sd Tech* Earl A. Wolcott. *Wardrobe* Ann Morgan, Judge Johnson.

Cast: Gloria Swanson *(Marion Donnell)*, Robert Ames *(Jack Merrick)*, Purnell Pratt *(Hector Ferguson)*, Henry B. Walthall *(Fuller)*, Wally Albright, Jr. *(Jackie)*, William Holden *(John Merrick, Sr.)*, Blanche Frederici *(Miss Potter)*, Kay Hammond *(Catherine "Flip" Merrick)*, Mary Forbes *(Mrs. Ferguson)*, Marcelle Corday *(Blanche)*.

Society drama. Marion Donnell, stenographer to Hector Ferguson, Chicago corporation lawyer, elopes with Jack Merrick, scion of a wealthy family; and in the midst of their honeymoon, Jack's father induces him to annul the marriage and arrange a proper society wedding, causing the enraged Marion to leave him. Over a year later she lives in a tenement with her child and returns to the law office. Suffering a breakdown as a result of her financial straits, she is aided by her employer, who furnishes her with a luxury apartment. When Ferguson dies, he bequeaths Marion half a million dollars, and to protect her child, she sends for Jack, who is married to an invalid; but Merrick, Sr., realizing that there is a male heir by his son's first wife, threatens to acquire custody of the child. She surrenders him willingly, however, when Jack's wife offers to divorce him. Later, after the wife's death, Marion and Jack are reconciled. *Stenographers. Lawyers. Millionaires. Children. Elopement. Marriage—Annulment. Chicago.*

TRIAL MARRIAGE **F2.5835**

Imperial Productions. *Dist* States Cinema Corp. caJul **1928.** Si; b&w. 35mm. 6 reels, 5,317 ft.

Dir William Curran.

Cast: Jack Richardson, Corliss Palmer, Paul Power, Ruth Robinson, Marcella Arnold, Evelyn Burns.

Melodrama. "Marion, a child adopted from a foundling asylum by Mrs. Payson, a wealthy member of society, is caught in a gambling raid and brought to the police station. Her foster brother Billy, son of Mrs. Payson, leaves her to the mercy of the police, who inform Mrs. Payson of arrest and send Marion home. After the upbraiding by Mrs. Payson, Billy, who has concealed himself in Marion's bedroom, proposes a 'companionate marriage, retaining their freedom to do as they wish, not bound by conventions.' The following morning, Mrs. Payson discovers Billy in Marion's room and Marion in bed—scene which shows plainly that they have spent the night together. Marion tells Mrs. Payson that she and Billy have entered into a companionate marriage. Billy lays full blame upon Marion and Mrs. Payson turns her out. The following reels show the efforts of Marion to obtain a position, always hounded by Billy. In desperation she attempts to commit suicide, but is rescued by Madame Ethel—Mrs. Gray of yesterday—who conducts a house of prostitution, and brings her there. There are numerous scenes of girls plying their trade and Marion among them. Lawrence Gray is shown visiting said house, where he is attracted to Marion and finally forces her to go upstairs to room with him and attacks her. In struggle on stairs between Marion and Gray, her dress is torn off and a birthmark on her shoulder is revealed to Madame Ethel. She realizes with horror that the girl is her own daughter and that Gray, whom she previously has recognized as the husband who deserted her years ago, taking the baby with him, is the father of the girl whom he is forcibly taking to a room for his own wicked purposes. In an attempt to rescue the girl, Madame Ethel shoots Gray and herself. Marion is accused of the crime and returned to the police court, where, through the Judge, she is reconciled to Mrs. Payson and Billy, who offers to make amends by marrying her." (New York State license records.) *Foundlings. Marriage—Companionate. Adoption. Prostitution. Motherhood. Incest. Murder. Whorehouses. Birthmarks.*

Note: Also known as *About Trial Marriage.*

TRIAL MARRIAGE **F2.5836**

Columbia Pictures. 10 Mar **1929** [15 May 1929; LP380]. Mus score & sd eff (Movietone); b&w. 35mm. 7 reels, 6,639 ft. [Also si; 6,506 ft.]

Prod Harry Cohn. *Dir* Erle C. Kenton. *Story-Scen* Sonya Levien. *Photog* Joe Walker. *Art Dir* Harrison Wiley. *Film Ed* William Hamilton, Pandro S. Berman. *Asst Dir* Charles C. Coleman.

Cast: Norman Kerry *(Oliver Mowbray)*, Sally Eilers *(Constance Bannister)*, Jason Robards *(Thorvald Ware)*, Thelma Todd *(Grace)*, Charles Clary *(George Bannister)*, Naomi Childers *(Mrs. George Bannister, 1st)*, Rosemary Theby *(Mrs. George Bannister, 4th)*, Gertrude Short *(Prudence)*.

Drama. Constance Bannister enters into a trial marriage contract with Dr. Thorvald Ware and finds happiness with him. She defies his wishes by dancing at a charity ball in a revealing costume, however, and he dissolves the contract, not knowing that she is with child. A year passes. Constance marries Oliver Mowbray, and Thorvald marries Constance's sister, Grace. Both couples are quite unhappy and later obtain divorces. Oliver and Grace go to Europe, and Constance and Thorvald are married in a civil ceremony, united by their love both for each other and for their child. *Physicians. Marriage—Trial. Divorce. Parenthood.*

THE TRIAL OF MARY DUGAN **F2.5837**

Metro-Goldwyn-Mayer Pictures. 8 Jun **1929** [c20 May 1929; LP386]. Sd (Movietone); b&w. 35mm. 12 reels, 10,621 ft. [Also si.]

Dir-Dial Bayard Veiller. *Cont* Becky Gardiner. *Photog* William Daniels. *Art Dir* Cedric Gibbons. *Film Ed* Blanche Sewell. *Rec Engr* J. K. Brock, Douglas Shearer. *Wardrobe* Adrian.

Cast: Norma Shearer *(Mary Dugan)*, Lewis Stone *(Edward West)*, H. B. Warner *(District Attorney Galway)*, Raymond Hackett *(Jimmy Dugan)*, Lilyan Tashman *(Dagmar Lorne)*, Olive Tell *(Mrs. Edgar Rice)*, Adrienne D'Ambricourt *(Marie Ducrot)*, De Witt Jennings *(Police Inspector Hunt)*, Wilfred North *(Judge Nash)*, Landers Stevens *(Dr. Welcome)*, Mary Doran *(Pauline Agguerro)*, Westcott B. Clarke *(Police Captain Price)*, Charles Moore *(James Madison)*, Claud Allister *(Henry Plaisted)*, Myra Hampton *(May Harris)*.

Courtroom drama. Source: Bayard Veiller, *The Trial of Mary Dugan; a Melodrama of New York Life, in Three Acts* (New York, 1928). Pretty Mary Dugan is placed on trial for the murder of her sugardaddy, who was found shot to death in the apartment he kept for her. Edward West, Mary's attorney, deliberately restrains himself in his cross-examination of the witnesses for the prosecution, and Mary's brother, Jimmy, who is a fledgling lawyer, strongly protests. West withdraws from the case, and Jimmy takes over his sister's defense. Jimmy puts Mary on the stand, and her subsequent testimony reveals that she had been the mistress of four successive men in order to earn enough money to put Jimmy through law school. Jimmy brings about Mary's acquittal by proving that Edward West was the man who murdered Mary's benefactor. *Mistresses. Lawyers. District attorneys. Brother-sister relationship. Finance—Personal. Murder. Trials.*

Note: Also made in a German-language version.

A TRICK OF HEARTS (Universal Jewel) **F2.5838**

Universal Pictures. 18 Mar **1928** [c17 Jan 1928; LP24883]. Si; b&w. 35mm. 6 reels, 5,495 ft.

Dir Reeves Eason. *Cont* Arthur Statter. *Titl* Tom Reed. *Story* Henry

Irving Dodge. *Photog* Harry Neumann. *Film Ed* M. C. Dewar.

Cast: Hoot Gibson *(Ben Tully)*, Georgia Hale *(The Girl)*, Heinie Conklin *(The Crook)*.

Western melodrama. The women of a western town elect a woman sheriff whose niece is loved by Ben Tully. Hoping to restore the sheriff's office to masculine control, he stages a series of fake holdups designed to terrify the sheriff. A notorious crook carries off the niece; but Ben gives chase, saves the girl, and frees other captives from the bandit's gang. *Sheriffs. Women in public office.*

Note: Working titles: *The Horse Trader; Western Suffragettes.* According to Universal records, Arthur Statter received credit for original story although "his idea was from Henry Irving Dodge's story."

TRICKS **F2.5839**

Marilyn Mills. *Dist* Davis Distributing Division. 16 Nov **1925** [New York State license application; c4 Dec 1925; LP22075]. Si; b&w. 35mm. 5 reels, 5,000 ft.

Pres by J. Charles Davis, 2d. *Dir* Bruce Mitchell. *Story* Mary C. Bruning. *Photog* William S. Adams.

Cast: Marilyn Mills *(Angelica "Trix" Varden)*, J. Frank Glendon *(The New Foreman)*, Gladys Moore *(Aunt Angelica)*, Myles McCarthy *(William Varden)*, Dorothy Vernon *(housekeeper)*, William Lowery *(Buck Barlow)*, Harry Valeur *(Red)*, Beverly, Star *(themselves, horses)*.

Western comedy-drama. Collegian Angelica "Trix" Varden, willful daughter of William Varden, after a midnight spread of lobster and ice cream, has a dream about an adventure on her father's ranch involving her horse Beverly, one Jack Norton, and Buck Barlow's gang of rustlers. She is expelled from school and returns home to find a handsome new foreman, who is none other than Jack Norton. Trix's curiosity is aroused by her dream, and she finds evidence of rustlers. Barlow shows up, and she locks herself in a cabin and sends Jack's horse, Star, for help. Jack finally defeats Barlow in a fight, and the two horses "realize" that they now have both a master and a mistress. *Students. Ranch foremen. Ranchers. Rustlers. Dreams. Horses.*

THE TRIFLERS **F2.5840**

B. P. Schulberg Productions. 15 Dec **1924.** Si; b&w. 35mm. 7 reels, 6,626 ft.

Dir Louis Gasnier. *Adapt* Eve Unsell, John Goodrich. *Photog* William Tuers.

Cast: Mae Busch *(Marjorie Stockton)*, Elliott Dexter *(Peter Noyes)*, Frank Mayo *(Monte Covington)*, Walter Hiers *(Chick Warren)*, Eva Novak *(Beatrice Noyes)*, Lloyd Whitlock *(Teddy Hamilotn)*.

Society drama. Source: Frederick Orin Bartlett, *The Triflers* (Boston, 1917). Wealthy Marjorie Stockton marries Monte Covington in order to protect herself from several overeager suitors. Monte treats the marriage lightly, but Marjorie quickly falls in love with her new husband. Peter Noyes, a sometime pursuer of Marjorie, is blinded, and Marjorie takes pity on him. Monte mistakes Marjorie's treatment of Peter for love and decides to leave her. Marjorie quickly declares her love for Monte, however, and Peter, who has also mistaken her affection for love, shoots them both in a jealous rage. Their wounds are fortunately slight, and Marjorie and Monte look forward to the future with confidence and love in their hearts. *Marriage. Blindness. Jealousy.*

TRIFLING WITH HONOR (Universal-Jewel) **F2.5841**

Universal Pictures. 28 May **1923** [New York premiere; released 4 Jun; c24 Apr 1923; LP18898]. Si; b&w. 35mm. 8 reels, 7,785 ft.

Dir Harry A. Pollard. *Scen* Frank Beresford, Raymond L. Schrock. *Adapt* Raymond L. Schrock. *Photog* Jack Brown.

Cast: Rockliffe Fellowes *(Gas-Pipe Kid/Bat Shugrue)*, Fritzi Ridgeway *(Ida Hunt)*, Buddy Messinger *(Jimmy Hunt)*, Hayden Stevenson *(Kelsey Lewis)*, Emmett King *(Judge Drury)*, William Welsh *(warden)*, Frederick Stanton *(Lute Clotz)*, William Robert Daly *(The Kid's father)*, Jim Farley *(Murray Jessop)*, Sidney De Grey *(Dud Adams)*, John Hatton *(Jimmy, at 8 years)*, Mike Gaffner *(landlord)*.

Drama. Source: William Slavens McNutt, "His Good Name," in *Colliers* (70:3–4, 22 Jul 1922). Released from prison on parole, the "Gas-Pipe Kid" returns to his home in the slums to find his mother dead and his father evicted. He is arrested for beating up the landlord but escapes with the help of Ida Hunt, his sweetheart. Years later he is a baseball star known as Bat Shugrue and is widely idolized by boys who read about his clean living. When Shugrue realizes his influence, he refuses to "throw" a game for blackmailers who threaten to reveal his past, and he goes to Judge Drury to tell the whole truth. The judge decides that Shugrue is more valuable free than in jail; the star is reunited with Ida. *Criminals—Rehabilitation. Judges. Landlords. Baseball. Blackmail. Slums.*

Note: Working titles: *Your Good Name, His Good Name.*

TRIFLING WOMEN **F2.5842**

Metro Pictures. ca1 Oct **1922** [New York premiere; released 6 Nov; c13 Nov 1922; LP18406]. Si; b&w. 35mm. 9 reels, 8,800 ft.

Dir-Story Rex Ingram. *Photog* John F. Seitz. *Art Dir* Leo E. Kuter. *Prod Mgr* Starret Ford.

Cast: Barbara La Marr *(Jacqueline de Séverac/Zareda)*, Ramon Novarro *(Henri/Ivan de Maupin)*, Pomeroy Cannon *(Léon de Séverac)*, Edward Connelly *(Baron François de Maupin)*, Lewis Stone *(The Marquis Ferroni)*, Hughie Mack *(Père Alphonse Bidondeau)*, Gene Pouyet *(Colonel Roybet)*, John George *(Achmet)*, Jess Weldon *(Caesar)*, B. Hyman *(Hassan)*, Joe Martin *(Hatim-Tai, a chimpanzee)*.

Romantic drama. To teach his capricious daughter, Jacqueline, the dangers of faithlessness, novelist Léon de Séverac reads her his latest story: *In maneuvering for the favors of Zareda, a captivating Parisian adventuress, Baron de Maupin sends his son, Ivan, to war and takes the poison he intended for the Marquis Ferroni. Zareda marries the marquis, but she causes him to duel with Ivan, her true love, when Ivan returns. Ferroni is vanquished but lives long enough to imprison Zareda and kill Ivan.* Jacqueline is impressed by this story and accepts her faithful suitor, Henri. *Novelists. Fatherhood. Infidelity. Paris. Chimpanzees.*

TRIGGER FINGER **F2.5843**

Independent Pictures. *Dist* Film Booking Offices of America. 2 or 9 Nov **1924** [c9 Nov 1924; LP20766]. Si; b&w. 35mm. 5 reels, 4,775 ft.

Jesse J. Goldburg Production. *Dir* "Breezy" Reeves Eason. *Story-Scen* William Lester. *Photog* Walter Griffin.

Cast: Bob Custer *(Sergeant Steele)*, George Field *(Dr. Deering)*, Margaret Landis *(Ruth Deering)*, Bill Dyer *(Sheriff Mackhart)*, Max Asher *(Mackhart's deputy)*, Joe Bennett *(Bob Murtison)*, Fontaine La Rue *(Wetona)*.

Western melodrama. Promised a promotion if he brings in "The Black Hawk," a bandit terrorizing the countryside, Sergeant Steele disguises himself as an outlaw and goes after his man. Steele is successful at the end of a series of thrilling fights and chases. The Hawk gets the drop on the hero in the climax, but he is killed by Wetona, an Indian girl. Steele discovers The Hawk to be Dr. Deering, the father of Ruth Deering, whose love he has won. *Outlaws. Texas Rangers. Physicians. Indians of North America. Disguise. Chases.*

TRIGGER TRICKS **F2.5844**

Hoot Gibson Productions. *Dist* Universal Pictures. 1 Jun **1930** [c22 May 1930; LP1324]. Sd (Movietone); b&w. 35mm. 6 reels, 5,462 ft.

Pres by Carl Laemmle. *Dir-Story-Scen* Reaves Eason. *Photog* Harry Neumann. *Film Ed* Gilmore Walker. *Rec Engr* C. Roy Hunter.

Cast: Hoot Gibson *(Tim Brennon)*, Sally Eilers *(Betty Dawley)*, Robert Homans *(Thomas Kingston)*, Jack Richardson *(Joe Dixon)*, Monty Montague *(Nick Dalgus)*, Neal Hart *(sheriff)*, Walter Perry *(Ike)*, Max Asher *(Mike)*.

Western melodrama. Tim Brennan rides onto Betty Dawley's sheep ranch to avenge the killing of his brother, Betty's former foreman, and she persuades him to intervene in the feud with Tom Kingston, a neighboring cattleman. He hires out to Kingston and rounds up Kingston's gang by a ruse involving a Victrola. Meanwhile, he lures Kingston to a narrow pass near the hideouts, and he is forced into a confession before the sheriff. Just as Kingston's men discover the trick, Tim and Betty arrive with the villain under the protection of the law. Betty and Tim decide to make their alliance permanent. *Ranchers. Rustlers. Revenge. Phonographs. Cattle. Sheep.*

TRILBY **F2.5845**

Richard Walton Tully Productions. *Dist* Associated First National Pictures. 29 Jul **1923** [c17 Jul 1923; LP19206]. Si; b&w. 35mm. 8 reels, 7,321 ft.

Pres by Richard Walton Tully. *Dir* James Young. *Scen* Richard Walton Tully. *Photog* Georges Benoit.

Cast: Andrée Lafayette *(Trilby)*, Creighton Hale *(Little Billee)*, Arthur Edmund Carew *(Svengali)*, Philo McCullough *(Taffy)*, Wilfred Lucas *(The Laird)*, Maurice Cannon *(Zouzou)*, Gordon Mullen *(Durien)*, Martha Franklin *(Madame Vinard)*, Gilbert Clayton *(Reverend Bagot)*, Edward

Kimball *(impresario)*, Francis McDonald *(Geko)*, Max Constant *(Dodor)*, Gertrude Olmstead *(Miss Bagot)*, Evelyn Sherman *(Mrs. Bagot)*, Rose Dione *(laundress)*, Robert De Vilbiss *(Jeannot)*.

Melodrama. Source: George Du Maurier, *Trilby* (1894). Trilby, an artist's model and habituée of the Latin Quarter, meets Little Billee, an English art student, who falls in love with her. On the night of their engagement, Svengali, a wild musician with hypnotic powers, hypnotizes Trilby and takes her away, presenting her as a concert singer. Months later, Billee, who has abandoned his search for Trilby, attends a theater where "Madame Svengali" is billed. Trilby appears and triumphs in her first number; then Svengali has a heart attack and Trilby sings without his influence—ruining her reputation. Trilby is reunited with Billee, but the strain of her career has exhausted her and she dies. *Models. Students. Musicians. Singers. Hypnotism. Bohemianism. Paris—Quartier Latin.*

Note: A happy ending was also filmed.

TRIMMED F2.5846

Universal Film Manufacturing Co. 3 Jul **1922** [c28 Jun 1922; LP18023]. Si; b&w. 35mm. 5 reels, 4,583 ft.

Dir Harry Pollard. *Scen* Arthur F. Statter, Wallace Clifton. *Photog* Sol Polito.

Cast: Hoot Gibson *(Dale Garland)*, Patsy Ruth Miller *(Alice Millard)*, Alfred Hollingsworth *(John Millard)*, Fred Kohler *(Young Bill Young)*, Otto Hoffman *(Nebo Slayter)*, Dick La Reno *(Judge William Dandridge)*, R. Hugh Sutherland *(Lem Fyfer)*.

Western comedy-drama. Source: Hapsburg Liebe, "Trimmed and Burning," in *Collier's* (68:12–13, Sep 1921). Returning from service in the A. E. F., Dale Garland is given a rousing reception by his townsmen. County political boss Nebo Slayter persuades the community to nominate Dale for sheriff—thinking he can be easily manipulated—against John Millard, the incumbent, who refuses political compromises. Dale easily wins and pledges to give the citizens an honest deal. Millard's daughter, Alice, who is Dale's childhood sweetheart, learns of Slayter's dishonest schemes and sees his men murder a moonshiner for whom they had been furnishing protection. She informs Dale, who tracks down the slayers and arrests them after a battle. Meanwhile, the deputies arrest the slain man's accomplices, who implicate the political ring, and Dale jails them all. His honesty wins Alice's love. *Veterans. Sheriffs. Political bosses. Moonshiners. Murder.*

TRIMMED IN SCARLET F2.5847

Universal Pictures. cal Apr **1923** [Cleveland premiere; released 9 Apr; c16 Mar 1923; LP18783]. Si; b&w. 35mm. 5 reels, 4,765 ft.

Dir Jack Conway. *Scen* Edward T. Lowe, Jr. *Story* William Hurlbut. *Photog* Charles Kaufman.

Cast: Kathlyn Williams *(Cordelia Ebbing/Madame de la Fleur)*, Roy Stewart *(Revere Wayne)*, Lucille Rickson *(Faith Ebbing)*, Robert Agnew *(David Peirce)*, David Torrence *(Charles Knight)*, Phillips Smalley *(Peter Ebbing)*, Eve Southern *(Fifi Barclay)*, Bert Sprotte *(Duroc)*, Grace Carlyle *(Molly Todd)*, Gerrard Grassby *(Ruth Kipp)*, Raymond Hatton *(Mr. Kipp)*, Philo McCullough *(Count De Signeur)*.

Society melodrama. Source: William Hurlbut, *Trimmed in Scarlet* (New York opening: 2 Feb 1920). Disapproving of the loose woman her father has married, Faith Ebbing leaves home and goes to work, but she later steals $5,000 in Liberty Bonds to pay off Duroc, a blackmailer threatening her mother, Cordelia Ebbing. Cordelia, who left her husband many years earlier and has been touring the Continent, compromises herself to replace the money Faith stole. Eventually there are explanations, and Cordelia is reunited with Revere Wayne, a former admirer. *Filial relations. Blackmail. Theft.*

A TRIP THROUGH SYRIA F2.5848

Fares and Debs. 12 Feb **1922** [New York State]. Si; b&w. 35mm. 5 reels.

Scenic documentary(?). No information about the nature of this film has been found. *Syria.*

Note: Country of origin not determined.

A TRIP TO CHINATOWN F2.5849

Fox Film Corp. 6 Jun **1926** [c6 Jun 1926; LP22832]. Si; b&w. 35mm. 6 reels, 5,594 ft.

Pres by William Fox. *Supv* George E. Marshall. *Dir* Robert P. Kerr. *Scen* Beatrice Van. *Photog* Barney McGill. *Asst Dir* Horace Hough.

Cast: Margaret Livingston *(Alicia Cuyer)*, Earle Foxe *(Welland Strong)*, J. Farrell MacDonald *(Benjamin Strong)*, Anna May Wong *(Ohtai)*, Harry Woods *(Norman Blood)*, Marie Astaire *(Rose Blood)*, Gladys McConnell *(Marion Haste)*, Charles Farrell *(Gayne Wilder)*, Hazel Howell *(Henrietta Lott)*, Wilson Benge *(Slavin)*, George Kuwa *(Tulung)*.

Farce. Source: Charles Hale Hoyt, "A Trip to Chinatown," in *The Dramatic Works of Charles H. Hoyt. Printed in Conformity With the Provisions of His Last Will and Testament and Under the Direction of His Executors* ([New York, 1901?]). Millionaire and hypochondriac Welland Strong is given only 6 months to live and decides to take a trip. Aboard a pullman he runs afoul of a jealous bridegroom who mistakenly believes that Strong has been making love to his wife. John then arrives in San Francisco's Chinatown. There he meets a charming widow, and the excitement of pursuing her cures him. In the end, he wins the widow. *Hypochondriacs. Millionaires. Widows. Bridegrooms. Jealousy. San Francisco—Chinatown.*

A TRIP TO PARADISE F2.5850

Metro Pictures. 5 Sep **1921** [c25 Aug 1921; LP16906]. Si; b&w. 35mm. 6 reels, 5,800 ft.

Dir Maxwell Karger. *Scen* June Mathis. *Adapt* Benjamin F. Glazer. *Photog* Arthur Martinelli. *Art Dir* Julian Garnsey.

Cast: Bert Lytell *("Curley" Flynn)*, Virginia Valli *(Nora O'Brien)*, Brinsley Shaw *(Meek)*, Unice Vin Moore *(Widow Boland)*, Victory Bateman *(Mrs. Smiley)*, Eva Gordon *(Mary)*.

Drama. Source: Ferenc Molnár, *Liliom, a Legend in Seven Scenes and a Prologue* (English text by Benjamin F. Glazer; New York, 1921). Curley Flynn is a successful barker at Coney Island near the entrance to the Widow Boland's "Trip to Paradise" concession. Nora O'Brien, whose aunt operates a photograph gallery, captures Curley's heart, and he loses his job when the widow learns she has a rival. When Curley and Nora are out late one evening, she accepts his offer of marriage rather than return home. Mrs. Smiley makes him her partner, but the business does not thrive, and he is about to accept the widow's offer to leave his wife and return to his former job when he learns his wife is with child. Desperate for money, he is shot while helping to rob a house; in the hospital he has a vision of heaven, where his case is tried: he is sent back to earth to live for his wife and child. *Widows. Barkers. Photographers. Visions. Robbery. Amusement parks. Coney Island.*

TRIPLE ACTION (Blue Streak Western) F2.5851

Universal Pictures. 20 Dec **1925** [c20 Nov 1925; LP22034]. Si; b&w. 35mm. 5 reels, 4,800 ft.

Dir-Story-Cont Tom Gibson. *Photog* William Thornley.

Cast: Pete Morrison *(Dave Mannion)*, Trilby Clark *(Doris Clayton)*, Dolores Gardner *(Donna Méndez)*, Harry von Meter *(Eric Prang)*, Lafayette McKee *(Don Pío Méndez)*, Harry Belmour *(Pancho)*, Floyd Ames *(servant)*, Les Bates *(Blackie Braxton)*, Leon Kent, Walter Patterson *(bandits)*, Milburn Morante *(Scaby MacGonigal? Squinty McGee?)*, Fred Burns *(chief of rangers)*, Ted Oliver *(assistant chief)*, Charles L. King *(Dick Clayton)*, Charles Banton *(deputy ranger)*, Art Acord *(see note)*.

Western melodrama. Ranger Dave Mannion is deprived of his badge for allowing the notorious Braxton gang to drive diseased cattle past his border patrol. He suspects Eric Prang to be a spy for the gang and sets out to prove it. He comes upon a herd of diseased cattle but is shot by Blackie Braxton. The latter sends the cattle and his men to a hacienda run by unsuspecting Don Pío Méndez. Donna Méndez, his daughter, finds Dave, who sends her for the rangers. Prang lures Doris Clayton, Dave's sweetheart, to the hacienda, and there she is held captive. With the aid of Doris' brother, Dick (an aviator in the ranger service), Dave parachutes into the hacienda and singlehandedly defeats the gang and regains his badge. *Rangers. Aviators. Gangs. Border patrol. Cattle—Diseases. Parachuting. Mexican border.*

Note: Pre-release advertising announced the star to be Art Acord.

TRIPLE PASS F2.5852

Balshofer Productions. *Dist* Biltmore Pictures. 1 Jun **1928** [New York State license]. Si; b&w. 35mm. 5 reels, 4,800 ft.

Cast: William Barrymore.

Melodrama(?). No information about the precise nature of this film has been found. *Football.*

TRIUMPH F2.5853

Famous Players–Lasky. *Dist* Paramount Pictures. 28 Apr **1924** [c14 May 1924; LP20203]. Si; b&w. 35mm. 8 reels, 8,288 ft.

Pres by Adolph Zukor, Jesse L. Lasky. *Prod-Dir* Cecil B. De Mille. *Adapt* Jeanie Macpherson. *Photog* Bert Glennon.

Cast: Leatrice Joy *(Ann Land)*, Rod La Rocque *(King Garnet)*, Victor Varconi *(William Silver)*, Charles Ogle *(James Martin)*, Theodore Kosloff *(Varinoff)*, Robert Edeson *(Samuel Overton)*, Julia Faye *(Countess Rika)*, George Fawcett *(David Garnet)*, Spottiswoode Aitken *(Torrini)*, ZaSu Pitts *(a factory girl)*, Raymond Hatton *(a tramp)*, Alma Bennett *(The Flower Girl)*, Jimmie Adams *(a painter)*.

Society drama. Source: May Edginton, *Triumph* (New York, 1924). King Garnet, a wealthy young wastrel, fails to make good according to a prescription in his father's will and thus loses his estate to his half brother, who is his rival for the hand of Ann Land. She chooses the wealth of the new owner, who soon falls into adversity, but she finds her place with King when he works his way to the top of the factory by his own efforts. *Brothers. Wastrels. Inheritance. Business management. Factories. "Romeo and Juliet".*

Note: The film contains a scene from Shakespeare's *Romeo and Juliet.*

TROOPER O'NEIL **F2.5854**

Fox Film Corp. 16 Jul **1922** [c16 Jul 1922; LP19104]. Si; b&w. 35mm. 5 reels, 4,862 ft.

Pres by William Fox. *Dir* Scott Dunlap, C. R. Wallace. *Scen* William K. Howard. *Photog* Lucien Andriot.

Cast: Charles Jones *(Trooper O'Neil)*, Beatrice Burnham *(Marie)*, Francis McDonald *(Pierre)*, Claude Payton *(Black Flood)*, Sidney Jordan *(Rodd)*, Jack Rollins *(Paul)*, Karl Formes *(Jules Lestrange)*.

Melodrama. Source: George Goodchild, *Trooper O'Neil* (London, 1921). Northwest Mountie Trooper O'Neil is sent to apprehend the murderer of Jacob Dell, found dead in his cabin. He meets Marie Lestrange, whose sister—treated badly by Dell—has died. O'Neil suspects Pierre, the dead girl's suitor, but evidence points to Marie. O'Neil dutifully arrests the girl, though he has fallen in love with her. Pierre attempts to rescue Marie, falls after a fight with O'Neil, and, dying, confesses that he shot Dell. *Sisters. Murder. Northwest Mounted Police.*

TROOPERS THREE **F2.5855**

Tiffany Productions. 15 Feb **1930** [c23 Feb 1930; LP1107]. Sd (Photophone); b&w. 35mm. 9 reels, 7,239 ft. [Also si.]

Dir Norman Taurog, Reeves Eason. *Screenplay-Dial* John F. Natteford. *Story* Arthur Guy Empey. *Photog* Ernest Miller, Benjamin Kline, Jackson Rose. *Film Ed* Clarence Kolster. *Song: "As Long As You Love Me"* George Waggner, Abner Silver. *Rec Engr* Dean Daily.

Cast: Rex Lease *(Eddie Haskins)*, Dorothy Gulliver *(Dorothy Clark)*, Roscoe Karns *(Bugs)*, Slim Summerville *(Sunny)*, Tom London *(Hank Darby)*, Joseph Girard *(Captain Harris)*, Walter Perry *(Halligan)*.

Comedy-drama. Eddie, Bugs, and Sunny, three ham actors, find themselves in a misfortune and decide to join the CMTC and acquire free food and lodging. At a recruiting station, Eddie mistakes Corporal Halligan of the Cavalry for a civilian representing the CMTC, and as a result they are all enlisted in the Army for 3 years. At the post, the three rookies try to impress the troopers with their own importance, and Eddie starts a flirtation with Dorothy Clark, a sergeant's daughter, incurring the wrath of Darby, her escort; but later he is rescued by Dorothy and sings a song he has written for her. Darby, however, thrashes the winsome recruit; and though Eddie claims to have been thrown from a horse, Darby admits his guilt and is punished. Eddie is cold-shouldered by everyone but proves his courage in battle maneuvers; he rescues Darby from a stable fire; and, before he dies, Darby asks Eddie to take care of Dorothy. Thus, Eddie wins back the respect of his fellows and the girl. *Soldiers. Actors. Courtship. Citizens Military Training Camps. United States Army—Cavalry. Fires.*

TROPIC MADNESS **F2.5856**

FBO Pictures. 19 Dec **1928** [c3 Dec 1928; LP25883]. Si; b&w. 35mm. 7 reels, 6,217 ft.

Dir Robert Vignola. *Cont* Wyndham Gittens. *Titl* Randolph Bartlett. *Story* Ramon Romero. *Photog* Nick Musuraca. *Film Ed* Jack Kitchen. *Asst Dir* Phil Carle.

Cast: Leatrice Joy *(Juanita)*, Lena Malena *(Koki)*, George Barraud *(Henderson)*, Henry Sedley *(Johnson)*, Albert Valentino *(Lennox)*, David Durand *(Frankie)*.

Melodrama. Driven into bankruptcy by his wife's extravagance, Herbert Pomeroy sends his young son, Frankie, to live with Henderson, a South Seas trader, and then kills himself. After 6 years of frantic searching for her child, Juanita Pomeroy gives up hope and embarks on a world cruise with wealthy Jules Lennox. Lennox's yacht lands on Henderson's island, and Juanita persuades Henderson to let her be Frankie's governess. Johnson, a destitute doctor, falls in love with Juanita, and Koki, Johnson's common-law native wife, vengefully persuades the witch doctor to sacrifice Frankie to propitiate the angry volcano when it errupts. Henderson saves mother and child, declaring his love for them both. *Traders. Physicians. Witch doctors. Motherhood. Marriage—Common law. Bankruptcy. South Sea Islands.*

TROPICAL LOVE **F2.5857**

Playgoers Pictures–Porto Rico Photoplays. *Dist* Associated Exhibitors. 23 Oct **1921** [c12 Oct 1921; LU17086]. Si; b&w. 35mm. 5 reels.

Dir Ralph Ince. *Scen* Reginald Denny. *Photog* William J. Black.

Cast: Ruth Clifford *(Rosario)*, Fred Turner *(The Seeker)*, Reginald Denny *(The Drifter)*, Huntley Gordon *(Clifford Fayne)*, Ernest Hilliard *(Carlos Blasco)*, Carl Axzelle *(Miguel)*, Margaret Fitzroy *(Mercedita)*, Paul Doucet *(Pedro)*.

Melodrama. Source: Guy M. McConnell, "Peaks of Gold" (publication undetermined). In San Juan, The Drifter, young and educated, and The Seeker, old and feebleminded, meet and form a partnership. The Seeker meets Rosario, unaware that she is his daughter, left there 20 years previously when his mind was affected by a tropical storm that killed his wife and wrecked his home. Rosario is deeded land belonging to her father and is about to sell it to Clifford Fayne when The Seeker discovers gold there and urges her to desist. Fayne lures her to a cabin and tries to force her to sign the bill of sale; The Drifter and her father rescue her; the father is mortally wounded but lives long enough to learn that Rosario is his daughter and that she will be happy with The Drifter. *Wanderers. Amnesia. Parentage. San Juan (Puerto Rico).*

TROPICAL NIGHTS **F2.5858**

Tiffany-Stahl Productions. 10 Dec **1928** [c22 Nov 1928; LP25856]. Si; b&w. 35mm. 6 reels, 5,449 ft.

Dir Elmer Clifton. *Story-Cont* Bennett Cohen. *Titl* Harry Carr. *Photog* John Boyle, Ernest Miller. *Film Ed* Desmond O'Brien.

Cast: Patsy Ruth Miller *(Mary Hale)*, Malcolm McGregor *(Jim)*, Ray Hallor *(Harvey)*, Wallace MacDonald *(Stavnow)*, Russell Simpson *(Singapore Joe)*.

Melodrama. Source: Jack London, "A Raid on the Oyster Pirates," in *Tales of the Fish Patrol* (New York, 1905). On a South Sea island, Harvey and his brother, Jim, operate a pearl diving barge in partnership with Stavnow. Harvey becomes fresh with Mary Hale, a stranded opera singer working in a waterfront dive, and she knocks him cold. Stavnow sees the fight and robs Harvey of his pearls. Harvey regains consciousness, and Stavnow kills him with a stone jar. Mary, who believes herself responsible, takes refuge with Jim, and they fall in love. He asks her to marry him, but she refuses. While diving, Stavnow's foot is caught in a giant clam; and before he dies, he signals to Jim that he killed Harvey. Jim and Mary are united. *Brothers. Singers. Pearl diving. Murder. Clams. South Sea Islands.*

TROUBLE **F2.5859**

Jackie Coogan Productions. *Dist* Associated First National Pictures. ca27 May **1922** [New York and Los Angeles premieres; released 7 Aug; c28 May 1922; LP18097]. Si; b&w. 35mm. 5 reels, 4,912 ft.

Pres by Sol Lesser. *Prod* Jack Coogan, Sr. *Dir* Albert Austin. *Titl* Max Abramson. *Photog* Glen MacWilliams, Robert Martin. *Film Ed* Irene Morra.

Cast: Jackie Coogan *(Danny, the kid)*, Wallace Beery *(Ed Lee, the plumber)*, Gloria Hope *(Mrs. Lee, the plumber's wife)*, Queenie *(the dog)*.

Comedy-drama. Danny, a ragamuffin orphan, is adopted by a brutal plumber and his frail wife. His fear of hunger, resulting from his foster father's indifference, at one point leads him to substitute for the plumber in repairing a leak, but he causes a flood. Later, Danny is instrumental in saving a policeman's life and in sending the plumber to jail. He finds new happiness with his foster mother on her parents' farm. *Orphans. Plumbers. Childhood. Adoption. Dogs.*

THE TROUBLE BUSTER **F2.5860**

William Steiner Productions. c17 Jan **1925** [LU21034]. Si; b&w. 35mm. 5 reels, 5,000 ft.

Dir Leo Maloney. *Scen* Ford Beebe.

Cast: Leo Maloney *(Harvey Martin)*, Josephine Hill *(Helen Williams)*, Whitehorse *(Rawhide Williams)*, Evelyn Thatcher *(Mrs. Williams)*, Leonard Clapham *(Larry Simons)*, Bud Osborne *(Slim Yates)*, Grace Rouch

(Dorothy Willis), Barney Furey *(Robert Willis)*, Baby Charlotte Johnson *(Dot)*, Ray Walters, William Stratton *(cowpunchers)*, Bullet *(a dog)*.

Western comedy. Harvey Martin and Helen Williams are in love and want to be married, but Helen's mother disapproves of Harvey and opposes the marriage. Larry Simons, Harvey's rival for Helen's affections, tries to discredit Harvey, and Harvey gets the better of him in a fight. Dorothy Willis, fleeing from her husband with her baby, takes refuge in Harvey's ranchhouse during his absence. She is discovered there by Mrs. Williams, who charges Harvey with intentions of becoming a bigamist. As Helen and her mother are about to leave, two thugs hired by Robert Willis, Dorothy's estranged husband, break into the house and demand the baby. Harvey fights them off while the three women attempt to escape. Dorothy is apprehended by her irate husband outside the house, and the estranged pair fight savagely for possession of the baby. This brutal action angers Mrs. Williams, and she berates Dorothy and Robert for their stupidity. Brought to their senses Dorothy and Robert are reconciled; and Mrs. Williams, impressed by Harvey's honesty and resolve, decides to allow him to marry Helen. *Ranchers. Infants. Ranch life. Motherhood. Courtship. Marriage. Bigamy. Dogs.*

TROUBLE CHASER **F2.5861**

Dist Rayart Pictures. 16 Dec **1926** [New York State license]. Si; b&w. 35mm. 5 reels.

No information about the nature of this film has been found.

THE TROUBLE SHOOTER **F2.5862**

Fox Film Corp. 4 May **1924** [c6 May 1924; LP20160]. Si; b&w. 35mm. 6 reels, 5,702 ft.

Pres by William Fox. *Dir* Jack Conway. *Story-Scen* Frederic Hatton, Fanny Hatton. *Photog* Daniel Clark.

Cast: Tom Mix *(Tom Steele)*, Kathleen Key *(Nancy Brewster)*, Frank Currier *(Benjamin Brewster)*, J. Gunnis Davis *(Pete Highley/Francis Earle)*, Mike Donlin *(Chet Conners)*, Dolores Rousse *(Chiquita)*, Charles McHugh *(Scotty McTavish)*, Al Fremont *(Stephen Kirby)*.

Western melodrama. Tom Steele, lineman for a power company, meets Nancy Brewster, daughter of a rival capitalist. Both companies want rights to a strip of land, the ownership of which is to be claimed by the first to stake it off. Against tremendous odds, and with help of Nancy, whom he rescues from a storm in the mountains, Tom beats Brewster and wins his daughter. *Linemen. Land rights. Courtship. Power companies.*

TROUBLE TRAIL **F2.5863**

Wild West Productions. *Dist* Arrow Film Corp. 15 Jan **1924** [c21 Dec 1923; LP19743]. Si; b&w. 35mm. 5 reels, 4,676 ft.

Dir George Holt. *Story-Scen* George Elwood Jenks.

Cast: Neva Gerber *(Cora Atwood)*, Richard Hatton *(Cal Frazer)*.

Western melodrama. Cora Atwood, an easterner, visits her uncle's ranch in Wyoming and there meets Cal Frazer. He kidnaps her when he discovers that she is deliberately toying with his affections, and inadvertently he plays into the hands of bandits. After Cal and Cora are rescued by a posse, Cora finds herself in love. *Bandits. Posses. Kidnaping. Ranches. Wyoming.*

THE TROUBLE WITH WIVES **F2.5864**

Famous Players–Lasky. *Dist* Paramount Pictures. 28 Sep **1925** [c30 Sep 1925; LP21862]. Si; b&w. 35mm. 7 reels, 6,489 ft.

Pres by Adolph Zukor, Jesse L. Lasky. *Dir* Malcolm St. Clair. *Story-Scen* Sada Cowan, Howard Higgin. *Photog* L. Guy Wilky.

Cast: Florence Vidor *(Grace Hyatt)*, Tom Moore *(William Hyatt)*, Esther Ralston *(Dagmar)*, Ford Sterling *(Al Hennessey)*, Lucy Beaumont *(Grace's mother)*, Edward Kennedy *(detective)*, Etta Lee *(maid)*, William Courtright *(butler)*.

Comedy. William Hyatt, the proprietor of an exclusive bootery, has a contented and unruffled marriage until his best friend, Al Hennessey, blunderingly informs Will's wife, Grace, that Will has been dining out with Dagmar, a pretty Parisian designer. William temporarily squares himself with Grace, but his troubles begin anew when Hennessey tells Grace that he and Will have been visitors at Dagmar's apartment. Although the visit was in the interest of business, Grace believes Will to have been unfaithful and makes his life unbearable. Will eventually leaves home and goes to a summer hotel. Spurred on by fury and suspicion, Grace follows him and finds Dagmar in the same hotel. To her surprise and relief, however, Grace discovers that Dagmar is there as a bride, having just married Hennessey. Grace and Will are quickly reconciled. *Couturiers. Businessmen. Marriage. Hotels. Shoeshops.*

TROUBLES OF A BRIDE **F2.5865**

Fox Film Corp. 30 Nov **1924** [c7 Dec 1924; LP20914]. Si; b&w. 35mm. 5 reels, 4,915 ft.

Pres by William Fox. *Dir* Thomas Buckingham. *Story-Scen* John Stone, Thomas Buckingham.

Cast: Robert Agnew *(Robert Wallace)*, Mildred June *(Mildred Patterson)*, Alan Hale *(Gordon Blake)*, Bruce Covington *(Colonel Patterson)*, Dolores Rousse *(Vera)*, Charles Conklin *(Jeff)*, Lew Harvey *(chauffeur)*, Bud Jamieson *(architect)*.

Comedy. Escaping from the police, The Baron, a gentleman crook, learns that Colonel Patterson, a wealthy banker, is remodeling his house as a surprise for his daughter, Mildred, who is about to be married to Robert Wallace. The Baron goes to the house, and, by impersonating the architect, discovers the location of the safe and also gains the confidence of Mildred, who is angry at Robert for kissing a vamp. Mildred arranges with The Baron to feign a kidnaping in order to test Robert's loyalty; but she soon regrets the deception, for The Baron, having burgled the Patterson safe, really does abduct her. Trapped on a runaway train, she is rescued by Robert just as it crashes into a deep river. Mildred forgives Robert for his indiscretion with the vamp, and The Baron is apprehended. *Gentlemen crooks. Bankers. Brides. Vamps. Thieves. Abduction. Impersonation. Train wrecks.*

THE TROUPER **F2.5866**

Universal Film Manufacturing Co. ca17 Jul **1922** [New York premiere; released 23 Jul; c8 Jul 1922; LP18038]. Si; b&w. 35mm. 5 reels, 4,480 ft.

Dir Harry B. Harris. *Story-Scen* A. P. Younger. *Photog* Earl Ellis.

Cast: Gladys Walton *(Mamie Judd)*, Jack Perrin *(Herman Jenks)*, Thomas Holding *(Frank Kramer)*, Kathleen O'Connor *(Irene La Rue)*, Roscoe Karns *(Neal Selden)*, Mary Philbin *(Mary Lee)*, Mary True *(Minnie Brown)*, Tom S. Guise *(Warren Selden)*, Florence D. Lee *(Mrs. Selden)*.

Comedy-drama. Mamie Judd, a young wardrobe girl in a cheap traveling stock company, secretly loves Jenks, the leading man, who hardly pays attention to her. She saves Neal Selden, son of a smalltown banker, from being accused of robbery and murder, acts committed by the company's manager and leading lady. In the end, although Jenks comes to realize his love for her, she becomes engaged to Selden. *Wardrobe mistresses. Actors. Theatrical troupes. Robbery. Murder.*

TROUPING WITH ELLEN **F2.5867**

Eastern Productions. *Dist* Producers Distributing Corp. 5 Oct **1924** [c5 Oct 1924; LP20905]. Si; b&w. 35mm. 7 reels, 6,452 ft.

Dir T. Hayes Hunter. *Screen Dramatization* Gerald C. Duffy. *Photog* J. Roy Hunt.

Cast: Helene Chadwick *(Ellen Llewellyn)*, Mary Thurman *(Lil)*, Gaston Glass *(Andy Owens)*, Basil Rathbone *(Tony Winterslip)*, Riley Hatch *("The Old Man")*, Zena Keefe *(Mabel Llewellyn)*, Kate Blanke *(Mrs. Llewellyn)*, [Frederick] Tyrone Power *(Mr. Llewellyn)*, John Tansey *(Dave Llewellyn)*, Charles McDonald *(Dan)*, Ernest Hilliard *(Jack Prentice)*, Jane Jennings *(Tony's mother)*, Estar Banks *(Tony's grandmother)*.

Romantic comedy. Source: Earl Derr Biggers, "Trouping With Ellen," in *Saturday Evening Post* (194:5–7, 8 Apr 1922). After visiting her mother for Sunday dinner, Ellen Llewellyn, a chorus girl, is late for the rehearsal of a Boston musical, but she is spared the wrath of the stage manager when the orchestra leader, Andy Owens, diverts his attention until she is in place. Andy has often proposed to Ellen but is always refused, for she feels that marriage to him would mean an uncertain and marginal existence. Ellen meets aristocratic, wealthy Tony Winterslip, who soon proposes to her; she turns him down also, knowing him to be unambitious and dependent upon his name and fortune. When Ellen catches pneumonia, Tony provides her with a nurse and then persuades her to convalesce at the family mansion. Ellen is bored by the dull routine of life in the Winterslip home, and Tony's grandmother, realizing that Ellen would never be happy with Tony, reunites her with Andy. They are now married, on the promise of a rewarding career for Andy, who has just sold a musical to Broadway. *Chorus girls. Composers. Grandmothers. Upper classes. Theater. Pneumonia. Boston.*

THE TRUANT HUSBAND **F2.5868**

Rockett Film Corp. *Dist* W. W. Hodkinson Corp. Jan **1921.** Si; b&w. 35mm. 5 reels, 5,000 ft.

Dir Thomas N. Heffron. *Story* Albert Payson Terhune. *Photog* Allen Siegler.

Cast: Mahlon Hamilton *(Billy Sayre)*, Betty Blythe *(Vera Delauney)*, Francelia Billington *(Sybil Sayre)*, Edward Ryan *(Bram Woller)*.

Comedy-drama. "Husband happily married. Wife gives in to his every whim. Indeed humors and watches over him with great affection. One day a romance from the past comes to haunt him. He will live over the memories again, so fibbing to his wife about an intended trip, he takes a sentimental journey with an erstwhile sweetheart only to be convinced at the end that memories should remain memories. Comedy drama of present day married life." (*Motion Picture News Booking Guide*, 1:111, Dec 1921.) *Marriage. Infidelity. Memory.*

TRUCKER'S TOP HAND **F2.5869**

William Steiner Productions. *Dist* New-Cal Film Corp. 26 Apr **1924** [c12 Apr 1924; LU20067]. Si; b&w. 35mm. 5 reels, 4,500 ft.

Pres by William Steiner. *Dir-Adapt* Neal Hart. *Story* Romaine H. Lowdermilk. *Photog* Al Siegler. *Film Ed* Fred Burnworth.

Cast: Neal Hart *(Barry Huston)*.

Western melodrama. Because John Tucker is laid up after a calf-roping accident, he can offer no resistance when his creditor, Jake Stoldt, and Bobitt decide to take over his ranch. Top hand Barry Huston endeavors to round up and sell the cattle so that Tucker can pay his debt, but Stoldt frames him for the murder of a deputy. Bobitt finally turns against Stoldt and helps Tucker clear Barry. The cattle are sold, Tucker's ranch is saved, and Barry is rewarded with a share in the ranch and the love of Miss Miles, Tucker's nurse. *Ranchers. Cowboys. Nurses. Murder. Frameup. Debt.*

Note: Story and character names, derived from shooting script in copyright files, may differ from the final film.

TRUE AS STEEL **F2.5870**

Goldwyn Pictures. *Dist* Metro-Goldwyn Distributing Corp. 20 Apr **1924** [c1 Apr 1924; LP20046]. Si; b&w. 35mm. 7 reels, ca6,400 ft.

Dir-Story-Scen Rupert Hughes. *Photog* John J. Mescall.

Cast: Aileen Pringle *(Mrs. Eva Boutelle)*, Huntley Gordon *(Frank Parry)*, Cleo Madison *(Mrs. Parry)*, Eleanor Boardman *(Ethel Parry)*, Norman Kerry *(Harry Boutelle)*, William Haines *(Gilbert Morse)*, Louise Fazenda *(Miss Leeds, stenographer)*, Louis Payne *(Jake Leighton)*, William H. Crane *(Commodore Fairfield)*, Raymond Hatton *(Great Grandfather)*, Lucien Littlefield *(Mr. Foote, secretary)*.

Drama. Source: Rupert Hughes, "True as Steel," in *Cosmopolitan* (74: 24–29, Dec 1923). Successful middle-aged manufacturer Frank Parry takes a business trip to New York, where he becomes infatuated with Eva Boutelle, manager of the Swansea Cotton Mills. For a time, their affair develops, but Eva remains true to her husband and rejects Frank's suggestion that they divorce their spouses and marry each other. Frank returns home; receives his wife's forgiveness; and finds that his daughter, Ethel, is determined to enter the business world. *Manufacturers. Businesswomen. Fidelity. Cotton mills.*

TRUE HEAVEN **F2.5871**

Fox Film Corp. 13 or 20 Jan **1929** [c22 Jan 1929; LP50]. Sd eff (Movietone); b&w. 35mm. 6 reels, 5,531 ft. [Also si; 5,563 ft.]

Pres by William Fox. *Supv* Kenneth Hawks. *Dir* James Tinling. *Titl* Malcolm Stuart Boylan. *Adapt* Dwight Cummins. *Photog* Conrad Wells. *Asst Dir* Leslie Selander.

Cast: George O'Brien *(Lieut. Philip Gresson)*, Lois Moran *(Judith)*, Phillips Smalley *(British Colonel Mason)*, Oscar Apfel *(German general)*, Duke Martin *(British sergeant major)*, André Cheron *(British spy)*, Donald MacKenzie *(British colonel)*, Hedwig Reicher *(Madame Grenot)*, Will Stanton *(Gresson's chauffeur)*.

War melodrama. Source: Charles Edward Montague, "Judith," in *Action, and Other Stories* (Garden City, New York, 1929). Lieut. Philip Gresson, a British soldier in Belgium, falls in love with Judith, a cafe entertainer, who later saves his life. Sent to spy behind the German lines disguised as a German officer, he discovers that she is an enemy agent. Torn between love and duty, she turns him in. He is saved by the Armistice from being shot. *Spies. Entertainers. Disguise. World War I. Belgium. Great Britain—Army.*

Note: Working title: *False Colors.*

THE TRUE NORTH *see* **ALASKAN ADVENTURES**

THE TRUE NORTH **F2.5872**

Dist Robertson-Young. 18 Oct **1925** [trade review]. Si; b&w. 35mm. 7 reels.

Dir Capt. Jack Robertson. *Photog* Wylie Wells Kelly.

Personages: Capt. Jack Robertson, Arthur H. Young.

Travelog. A trip through Alaska to Siberia and back, which includes such highlights as caribou and bear; Young killing and skinning a moose, then making a canoe of its hide; Mount McKinley; the Yukon River rapids and the breaking up of 2,000 miles of ice; the Bering Sea; Eskimos; the midnight sun; Mount Kalmai; kodiac; and spawning salmon. *Eskimos. Alaska. Siberia. Mount McKinley. Mount Kalmai. Bering Sea. Yukon River. Caribou. Moose. Kodiak bears.*

TRUE TO THE NAVY **F2.5873**

Paramount-Publix Corp. 31 May **1930** [c29 May 1930; LP1337]. Sd (Movietone); b&w. 35mm. 8 reels, 6,393 ft.

Dir Frank Tuttle. *Screenplay* Keene Thompson, Doris Anderson. *Dial* Herman J. Mankiewicz. *Photog* Victor Milner. *Film Ed* Doris Drought. *Songs: "Believe It or Not, I Lost My Man," "There's Only One What Matters for Me"* L. Wolfe Gilbert, Abel Baer. *Rec Engr* M. M. Paggi.

Cast: Clara Bow *(Ruby Nolan)*, Fredric March *(Gunner McCoy)*, Harry Green *(Solomon Bimberg)*, Rex Bell *(Eddie)*, Eddie Fetherston *(Michael)*, Eddie Dunn *(Albert)*, Ray Cooke *(Peewee)*, Harry Sweet *(Artie)*, Adele Windsor *(Maizie)*, Sam Hardy *(Grogan)*, Jed Prouty *(dancehall manager)*.

Romantic comedy. Ruby Nolan, a soda jerk in Solomon Bimberg's San Diego drugstore, has a boyfriend on every ship, precipitating a melee among competing factions. In revenge, they try to persuade the ace gunner (McCoy) on the *Mississippi* to fall for her; he refuses, but they accidentally meet and the inevitable happens. At a dancehall in Tia Juana, Ruby gives $100 to the manager to be offered as a prize to any couple who will be married on the dancehall floor, but when her rejected suitors appear, Gunner McCoy thinks she is playing him for his money. Solomon places a bet with some crooked gamblers on Gunner in a shooting match; swallowing her pride, Ruby induces Gunner to desist from drinking, and he wins the target practice. When he sees that Ruby is sincere, they are happily united. *Soda clerks. Sailors. Courtship. Drugstores. Dancehalls. San Diego. Tia Juana (California).*

TRUMPIN' TROUBLE **F2.5874**

Action Pictures. *Dist* Weiss Brothers Artclass Pictures. 1 Feb **1926.** Si; b&w. 35mm. 5 reels, 4,446 ft.

Dir Richard Thorpe. *Scen* Betty Burbridge, Sergey Sergeyeff.

Cast: Buffalo Bill Jr. *(Bill Lawson)*, Bob Fleming *(John Lawson)*, Alma Rayford *(Molly Rankin)*, Charles Whitaker *("Red Star" Dorgan)*, Mark Hamilton *(Cal Libby)*, Dick Winslow *(Jimmie Dyson)*, Cora Shannon *(Mrs. Perkins)*.

Western melodrama. "... with hero accused of murdering father after discovery of rich mine. Dance hall entertainer aids his escape when lynching is threatened. After many hazardous situations, hero is cleared and villains routed. Hero marries girl." ("Motion Picture News Booking Guide," in *Motion Picture News*, 8 May 1926, p47.) *Dancehall girls. Mining. Patricide.*

THE TRUNK MYSTERY **F2.5875**

Pathé Exchange. 12 Jun **1927** [c24 & 26 Sep 1925, 7 Jun 1927; LP21855, LU24052]. Si; b&w. 35mm. 5 reels, 4,338 ft.

Dir Frank Hall Crane. *Scen* Frederic Chapin. *Story* Forrest Sheldon. *Photog* Leon Shamroy.

Cast: Charles Hutchison *(Jim Manning)*, Alice Calhoun *(Marion Hampton)*, Richard Neill *(Joe Fawcett)*, Ben Walker *(Turner)*, Ford Sterling *(Jeff)*, Otto Lederer *(Stevanov)*, Charles Mack *(John Hampton)*.

Crook melodrama. Jim Manning, recently retired from the Secret Service, buys a trunk at a police auction of stolen and unclaimed goods. That night his house is broken into by Fawcett and Turner, two crooks, and by Margaret Hampton; the men escape, but she takes him into her confidence by explaining that her father, John Hampton, had been a trusted employee of Olaff Stevanov, a jewel merchant; although guiltless, Hampton is accused of absconding with a valuable necklace and has been given a prison sentence. Manning shares her suspicions of Fawcett and Turner, who return to steal the trunk but are unable to find the jewels inside. Manning, by swift action and cunning, catches them as well as Stevanov, their master, and produces the pearls, which he had removed from the trunk. *Thieves. Detectives. Secret service. Jewelers. Filial relations. Auctions.*

TRUST YOUR WIFE F2.5876

Katherine MacDonald Pictures. *Dist* Associated First National Pictures. Mar **1921** [c23 Mar 1921; LP16306]. Si; b&w. 35mm. 5 or 6 reels.

Dir J. A. Barry. *Screenplay* J. A. Barry, Gerald C. Duffy. *Photog* Joseph Brotherton. *Art Dir* Arthur Rouda. *Asst Dir* James Dugan.

Cast: Katherine MacDonald *(Margot Hastings)*, Dave Winter *(Dick Hastings)*, Charles Richman *(Slater T. Holcomb)*, Mary Alden *(Claire Bodai)*.

Melodrama. Source: H. S. Sheldon, *Conscience, a Play* (publication undetermined). Margot Hastings, the lovely wife of a handsome but needy inventor, Dick, is the latest prey of lothario financier, Slater T. Holcomb who may be persuaded to produce some of her husband's inventions. Holcomb promises Margot jewels and riches if she will be agreeable. She manages to keep her distance until he invites her aboard his yacht, where she makes him realize how comtemptible she regards his behavior. Claire Bodai, the financier's girl, jealous of the young wife, goes to Dick, informing him that his wife has been unfaithful. But the contrite financier reassures Dick that his wife not only is faithful but has made him, Holcomb, see the foolishness of his ways. Dick then receives financial backing. *Rakes. Inventors. Financiers. Fidelity. Jealousy. Yachts.*

TRUTH ABOUT MEN F2.5877

Macfadden True Story Pictures. c30 Apr, 12 May **1926** [LP22690, LU22718]. Si; b&w. 35mm. 7 reels.

Dir Elmer Clifton. *Adapt* Lewis Allen Browne.

Domestic melodrama. Dominated and restricted by a selfish mother, Elsie Hastings finds it hard to resist the attentions of handsome Jimmie Scott, a stranger in town, and she is soon sneaking out to meet him for trips to hotels in various nearby towns. About the time that Elsie discovers "her condition," Jimmie disappears. Determined to take poison, Elsie meets an elderly woman who invites Elsie to tea and gradually reveals that she is searching for her son, Jimmie Scott. Elsie's friend Sam finds a sullen Jimmie, Elsie and Jimmie marry, and Elsie lives with Mrs. Scott while Jimmie goes off to war. In the months that pass, a son is born to Elsie, and Jimmie returns. But it is not the Jimmie Scott Elsie married, and Mrs. Scott is heartbroken at the news. Elsie's husband later turns up, however (the baby died in the meantime), and demands his wife, who refuses him out of love for the other Jimmie. There is a scuffle, in which the husband wounds Jimmie, but Sam—now a state policeman—pursues and kills the husband. *Police. Motherhood. Filial relations. Marriage. Seduction. Courtship. Mistaken identity.*

THE TRUTH ABOUT WIVES F2.5878

B. B. Productions. *Dist* American Releasing Corp. 3 Feb **1923** [c28 Feb 1923; LP18755]. Si; b&w. 35mm. 6 reels, 5,973 ft.

Dir Lawrence Windom. *Scen* Val Cleveland. *Story* E. C. Holland. *Photog* Edward Paul.

Cast: Betty Blythe *(Helen Frazer)*, [Frederick] Tyrone Power *(Howard Hendricks)*, William P. Carleton *(Alfred Emerson)*, Ann Luther *(Letty Lorraine)*, Fred C. Jones *(Harold Lawton)*, John Daly Murphy *(Col. Bob Alton)*, Marcia Harris *(maid)*, Nellie Parker Spaulding *(Mrs. Anthony Frazer)*, Frankie Evans *(baby)*.

Melodrama. Helen Frazer marries Harold Lawton to please her domineering grandmother. Harold does not break off his dalliance with chorus girl Letty Lorraine, however, and embezzles from Howard Hendricks' firm to support her luxurious taste. To protect her son, Helen enters into a financial agreement with Hendricks, a former—but still hopeful—suitor. A year later Lawton has squandered this money, and he kills Hendricks. Helen is found guilty of murder just as Lawton confesses and commits suicide, leaving Helen to find happiness with loyal Alfred Emerson. *Grandmothers. Chorus girls. Motherhood. Infidelity. Embezzlement. Murder. Suicide.*

THE TRUTH ABOUT WOMEN F2.5879

Banner Productions. 1 Jul **1924** [c10 Jul 1924; LP20395]. Si; b&w. 35mm. 6 reels, 6,000 ft.

Dir Burton King. *Cont* William B. Laub. *Story* Leota Morgan. *Photog* Edward Paul, Charles Davis.

Cast: Hope Hampton *(Hilda Carr)*, Lowell Sherman *(Warren Carr)*, David Powell *(Howard Bronson)*, Mary Thurman *(Nona Boyd)*, Dainty Lee *(Blossom Carr)*, Louise Carter *(Bronson's mother)*, Charles Craig *(Smead)*, Rosella Ray *(Molly)*, Warren Cook *(Jack)*, Charles Edwards *(Fred)*, Augusta Carey *(Florence)*.

Melodrama. Young artist Warren Carr abandons his wife, Hilda, and their child for the worldly Nona Boyd. Hilda then becomes a cabaret sensation under the tutelage of novelist Howard Bronson. The death of the child causes Warren to attempt a reconciliation, but Hilda chooses to remain with Bronson. *Entertainers. Novelists. Artists. Marriage.*

THE TRUTH ABOUT YOUTH F2.5880

First National Pictures. 19 Oct or 3 Nov **1930** [c15 Nov 1930; LP1727]. Sd (Vitaphone); b&w. 35mm. 7 reels, 6,235 ft.

Dir William Seiter. *Adapt–Adtl Dial* Harrison Orkow. *Photog* Arthur Miller. *Film Ed* Frederick Y. Smith. *Rec Engr* Robert B. Lee.

Cast: Loretta Young *(Phyllis Ericson)*, David Manners *(Richard Dane, The Imp)*, Conway Tearle *(Richard Carewe)*, J. Farrell MacDonald *(Colonel Graham)*, Harry Stubbs *(Horace Palmer)*, Myrtle Stedman *(Mrs. Ericson)*, Myrna Loy *(Kara, The Firefly)*, Ray Hallor *(Hal)*, Dorothy Mathews *(Cherry)*, Yola D'Avril *(Babette)*.

Romantic society drama. Source: Henry V. Esmond, *When We Were Twenty-One* (New York opening: 5 Feb 1900). Richard Carewe, the guardian of Richard Dane, plans for him to marry Phyllis Ericson, the daughter of Carewe's housekeeper; Dick, however, falls for Kara, a nightclub entertainer. Mrs. Ericson finds a note implicating Dick, The Imp, with The Firefly and shows it to Phyllis, who in turn, shows it to Carewe. Not wanting the note to destroy his plans for Phyllis and The Imp, Carewe claims the note as his and offers Kara $5,000 to simulate being in love with him, unaware that she has married The Imp the day before. But when gambler Jim Green wins enough money to claim Kara again, she dismisses young Dick. Kara returns the $5,000, and all parties agree on a divorce in 6 months. The Imp confesses his escapade to Phyllis and decides to go west, leaving Phyllis free to declare her love for Carewe, whom she has long loved. *Wards. Guardians. Entertainers. Gamblers. Courtship. Bribery. Marriage. Divorce. Nightclubs.*

THE TRUTHFUL LIAR F2.5881

Realart Pictures. *Dist* Paramount Pictures. 23 Apr **1922** [c18 Apr 1922; LP17768]. Si; b&w. 35mm. 6 reels, 5,243 ft.

Dir Thomas N. Heffron. *Scen* Percy Heath. *Story* Will J. Payne. *Photog* William E. Collins.

Cast: Wanda Hawley *(Tess Haggard)*, Edward Hearn *(David Haggard)*, Charles Stevenson *(Harvey Mattison)*, Casson Ferguson *(Arthur Sinclair)*, Lloyd Whitlock *(Larry Steffens)*, George Siegmann *(Mark Potts)*, E. A. Warren *(Peter Vanetti)*, Charles K. French *(Police Commissioner Rogers)*.

Mystery melodrama. Tess, who has a taste for society life, is neglected by her hard-working husband, David. She goes with an ex-suitor, Arthur Sinclair, to a notorious gambling establishment; while there, a raid is staged by the henchmen of Potts, Arthur is wounded, and Tess's rings are stolen. She lies to David but is exposed when the police show the jewels for identification; David then becomes infuriated with Sinclair. A letter written to Sinclair by Tess, discrediting her husband, falls into the hands of a housemaid, who sells it to Potts. The latter offers to return it for $15,000; Tess tries to buy it for a smaller sum and is refused. When detectives arrive to arrest Potts, he is found murdered; at the inquiry the fateful letter falls into the hands of David, but the murderer proves to be Vanetti, an enemy of Potts. David is reunited with Tess after destroying the letter, unread. *Marriage. Blackmail. Mendacity. Murder. Documentation.*

THE TRUTHFUL SEX F2.5882

Columbia Pictures. 20 Nov **1926** [c20 Dec 1926; LP23452]. Si; b&w. 35mm. 6 reels, 5,831 ft.

Supv by Harry Cohn. *Dir* Richard Thomas. *Photog* H. Lyman Broening, Herman Schoop.

Cast: Mae Busch *(Sally Carey)*, Huntley Gordon *(Robert Mapes)*, Ian Keith *(Tom Barnes)*, Leo White, Billy Kent Schaeffer, John Roche, Rosemary Theby, Richard Travers, Joan Meredith.

Domestic comedy-drama. Source: Albert Shelby Le Vino, "Husbands Preferred" (publication undetermined). After an ecstatic period of marital bliss, Sally Carey and Robert Mapes begin to drift apart, though the birth of a son brings them temporarily together again. Their estrangement widens, however, as Robert, Jr., becomes Sally's center of interest. Sally is flattered by Paul Gregg, and, despite her husband's warnings, continues her affair with Paul, leading to a bitter quarrel. Jennie, the governess, soon becomes a source of consolation for Robert, Jr., and she becomes friendly with Tom Barnes, a shrewd thief who visits the house as an electrician. Sally agrees to leave with Paul, but Barnes steals her jewels, then Jennie forces Barnes to surrender them. Realizing her folly, Sally decides to return to homelife and her husband and child. *Governesses. Thieves. Electricians. Children. Marriage. Infidelity.*

TRUTHFUL TULLIVER (Reissue) **F2.5883**

Kay-Bee Pictures. *Dist* Film Distributors League. **1921.** Si; b&w. 35mm. 5 reels.

Note: A William S. Hart film originally released by Triangle Film Corp. on 7 Jan 1917.

TRUXTON KING **F2.5884**

Fox Film Corp. 18 Feb **1923** [c18 Feb 1923; LP18990]. Si; b&w. 35mm. 6 reels, 5,613 ft.

Pres by William Fox. *Dir* Jerome Storm. *Scen* Paul Schofield. *Photog* Joe August.

Cast: John Gilbert *(Truxton King)*, Ruth Clifford *(Lorraine)*, Frank Leigh *(Count Marlaux)*, Mickey Moore *(Prince Robin)*, Otis Harlan *(Hobbs)*, Henry Miller, Jr. *(Count Carlos Von Enge)*, Richard Wayne *(John Tullis)*, Willis Marks *(William Spanz)*, Winifred Bryson *(Olga Platanova)*, Mark Fenton *(Baron Dangloss)*.

Melodrama. Source: George Barr McCutcheon, *Truxton King; a Story of Graustark* (New York, 1909). Truxton King, an American seeking adventure in Graustark, strikes up an acquaintance with 6-year-old Prince Robin and his Aunt Lorraine. The next day Truxton overhears a plot against the prince, is taken prisoner, then escapes to rescue both Prince Robin and Lorraine and to prevent an attack on the castle. Truxton's love for Lorraine leads to marriage when she reveals that she, too, is American. *Royalty. Imaginary kingdoms.*

TRY AND GET IT **F2.5885**

Samuel V. Grand. *Dist* Producers Distributing Corp. 9 Mar **1924.** Si; b&w. 35mm. 6 reels, 5,607-5,707 ft.

Dir Cullen Tate. *Adapt* Jules Furthman.

Cast: Bryant Washburn *(Joseph Merrill)*, Billie Dove *(Rhoda Perrin)*, Edward Horton *(Glenn Collins)*, Joseph Kilgour *(Larry Donovan)*, Lionel Belmore *(Timothy Perrin)*, Rose Dione *(Madame Florio)*, Hazel Deane *(telephone operator)*, Carl Stockdale *(bookkeeper)*.

Comedy-drama. Source: Eugene P. Lyle, Jr., "The Ringtailed Galliwampus," in *Saturday Evening Post* (195:12–13, 15 Jul 1922). Two young bill collectors, Joseph Merrill and Glenn Collins, must collect a debt owed by Timothy Perrin, cement manufacturer and backer of a modiste's shop, or lose their jobs. Both are rebuffed, but Merrill's persistence wins him both Perrin's daughter and the payment of the bill. *Bill collectors. Modistes. Debt. Cement.*

TUMBLEWEEDS **F2.5886**

William S. Hart Co. *Dist* United Artists. 20 Dec **1925** [New York premiere; released 27 Dec; c11 Nov 1925; LP21988]. Si; b&w. 35mm. 7 reels, 7,254 ft.

Dir King Baggot. *Adapt for the screen by* C. Gardner Sullivan. *Story* Hal G. Evarts. *Photog* Joseph August.

Cast: William S. Hart *(Don Carver)*, Barbara Bedford *(Molly Lassiter)*, Lucien Littlefield *(Kentucky Rose)*, J. Gordon Russell *(Noll Lassiter)*, Richard R. Neill *(Bill Freel)*, Jack Murphy *(Bart Lassiter)*, Lillian Leighton *(Mrs. Riley)*, Gertrude Claire *(old woman)*, George F. Marion *(old man)*, Capt. T. E. Duncan *(major of cavalry)*, James Gordon *(Hinman, of Box K Ranch)*, Fred Gamble *(hotel proprietor)*, Turner Savage *(Riley boy)*, Monte Collins *(Hicks)*.

Western epic. In 1889 the Cherokee Strip is opened to homesteaders, and Don Carver, one of the self-styled "tumbleweeds" and range boss of the Box K Ranch, finds himself out of a job. He meets and falls in love with Molly Lassiter, who belongs to one of the many families of homesteaders who have gathered in Caldwell, Kansas, for the big land rush. Don decides to sign up for a piece of land and hopes to claim the site of the Box K ranchhouse, which controls the water for the strip. Molly's evil half-brother, Noll, and Bill Freel, Don's rival for Molly's hand, conspire to have Don arrested as a "sooner" when he tries to round up some stray cattle in the Strip. Don breaks out of the stockade to join the rush, but he finds Noll and Freel already at the ranchhouse when he arrives. Don evicts them, and troopers arrive and arrest the two as "sooners." Molly finally consents to be Don's wife. *Sooners. Homesteaders. Brother-sister relationship. Cherokee Strip. Kansas. Oklahoma.*

Note: Hart is said to have codirected with Baggot.

TUMBLING RIVER **F2.5887**

Fox Film Corp. 21 Aug **1927** [c14 Aug 1927; LP24288]. Si; b&w. 35mm. 5 reels, 4,675 ft.

Pres by William Fox. *Dir* Lewis Seiler. *Scen* Jack Jungmeyer. *Photog* Dan Clark. *Asst Dir* Wynn Mace.

Cast: Tom Mix *(Tom Gier)*, Dorothy Dwan *(Edna Barton)*, William Conklin *(Jim Barton)*, Stella Essex *(Eileen Barton)*, Elmo Billings *(Kit Mason)*, Edward Peil, Sr. *(Roan Tibbets)*, Wallace MacDonald *(Keechie)*, Buster Gardner *(Cory)*, Harry Gripp *(Titus)*, Tony *(The Wonder Horse)*, Buster *(another horse)*.

Western melodrama. Source: Jesse Edward Grinstead, *The Scourge of the Little C* (New York, 1925). "While Tom is away, rustlers steal his horses and in trailing them he saves Edna from a runaway. The rustlers try to trap him but he escapes and when they raid her father's stock he gives chase, saves the girl from the rapids and breaks up the gang." (*Moving Picture World,* 27 Aug 1927, p612.) *Ranchers. Rustlers. Cowboys. Horses.*

THE TUNNEY-GREB BOXING MATCH **F2.5888**

J. C. Clark Productions. Jun **1922.** Si; b&w. 35mm. 4 reels.

Boxing film. Gene Tunney loses his American light heavyweight title to Harry Greb by a decision after 15 rounds of boxing. (Madison Square Garden, 23 May 1922.) *Boxing. Gene Tunney. Harry Greb. Madison Square Garden.*

TURKISH DELIGHT **F2.5889**

De Mille Pictures. *Dist* Pathé Exchange. 11 Nov **1927** [c3 Nov 1927; LP24612]. Si; b&w. 35mm. 6 reels, 5,397 ft.

Supv C. Gardner Sullivan. *Dir* Paul Sloane. *Scen* Tay Garnett. *Titl* John Krafft. *Adapt* Albert Shelby Le Vino. *Story* Irvin S. Cobb. *Photog* Jacob A. Badaracco. *Art Dir* Max Parker. *Film Ed* Margaret Darrell. *Asst Dir* William J. Scully.

Cast: Julia Faye *(Zelma)*, Rudolph Schildkraut *(Abdul Hassan)*, Kenneth Thomson *(Donald Sims)*, Louis Natheaux *(Achmet Ali)*, May Robson *(Tsakran)*, Harry Allen *(Scotty)*, Toby Claude *(Nassarah)*.

Comedy. Abdul Hassan, a pompous Turkish rug dealer in New York, disdains all womanhood, excepting his American-born niece Zelma, to whom he turns for counsel. Meanwhile, in Tamboustan, the sultan dies, and his violent and officious widow rules, for the seven male heirs have met violent deaths. Villainous Achmet Ali brings her news of Abdul, now rightful heir, and she orders him brought for her inspection as a mate. Aboard their ocean liner, Zelma meets and falls in love with Donald Sims, a wealthy American adventurer, and despite Abdul's protests, Donald follows them to Tamboustan. Achmet has Donald captured, and while Abdul courts a member of the harem, Zelma plans to rescue Donald, instigating a revolt in the harem and thwarting the sultana's henchmen, who are after Abdul. The quartet escape and return to the United States, where all is well. *Misogynists. Widows. Adventurers. Turks. Royalty. Courtship. Harems. Rugs. Imaginary kingdoms. New York City.*

THE TURMOIL (Universal-Jewel) **F2.5890**

Universal Pictures. 14 Sep **1924** [c20 Mar 1924; LP20218]. Si; b&w. 35mm. 7 reels, 6,741 ft.

Pres by Carl Laemmle. *Dir* Hobart Henley. *Scen* E. T. Lowe, Jr. *Photog* Charles Stumar. *Film Ed* Daniel Mandell.

Cast: Emmett Corrigan *(James Sheridan, Sr.)*, George Hackathorne *(Bibbs Sheridan)*, Edward Hearn *(Roscoe Sheridan)*, Theodore von Eltz *(James Sheridan, Jr.)*, Eileen Percy *(Mrs. Roscoe Sheridan)*, Pauline Garon *(Edith Sheridan)*, Eleanor Boardman *(Mary Vertrees)*, Winter Hall *(Henry Vertrees)*, Kitty Bradbury *(Mrs. Henry Vertrees)*, Kenneth Gibson *(Bobby Lamhorn)*, Victory Bateman *(Mrs. James Sheridan)*.

Domestic drama. Source: Booth Tarkington, *The Turmoil* (New York, 1915). Industrialist James Sheridan, Sr., once a laborer, insists on moulding the careers of his three sons; however, he loses James, Jr., in a flood disaster, and Roscoe suffers a mental breakdown. Realizing his mistake, he begins to insure the happiness of the third son, Bibbs, by bringing him together with Mary, the girl he loves. *Industrialists. Family life. Fatherhood. Mental illness. Floods.*

TURN BACK THE HOURS **F2.5891**

Gotham Productions. *Dist* Lumas Film Corp. 12 Mar **1928** [c9 Mar 1928; LP25049]. Si; b&w. 35mm. 6 reels, 6,500 ft.

Pres by Sam Sax. *Supv* Harold Shumate. *Dir* Howard Bretherton. *Scen* Jack Jungmeyer. *Titl* Casey Robinson. *Photog* Norbert Brodin. *Film Ed* Donn Hayes.

Cast: Myrna Loy *(Tiza Torreon)*, Walter Pidgeon *(Phillip Drake)*, Sam Hardy *("Ace" Kearney)*, George Stone *("Limey" Stokes)*, Sheldon Lewis *("Breed")*, Josef Swickard *(Colonel Torreon)*, Ann Brody *(Maria)*, Nanette Villon *(a dancer)*, Joyzelle Joyner *(a cantina girl)*.

Romantic drama. Source: Edward E. Rose, *Turn Back the Hours* (Hoboken, N. J., opening: Oct 1917). Nursed back to health by young Tiza, discharged Navy Lieut. Phillip Drake proves to be a coward when she needs his help. When her father is hounded by a band of criminals and her own safety is threatened, Drake awakens to her danger and courageously fights off the bandits until the U. S. Navy sends help. *Gangs. Cowardice. United States Navy.*

TURN TO THE RIGHT **F2.5892**

Metro Pictures. ca12 Feb **1922** [Milwaukee premiere; released 27 Feb; c27 Feb 1922; LP17686]. Si; b&w. 35mm. 8 reels, 7,703 ft.

Dir Rex Ingram. *Scen* June Mathis, Mary O'Hara. *Photog* John F. Seitz.

Cast: Alice Terry *(Elsie Tillinger)*, Jack Mulhall *(Joe Bascom)*, Harry Myers *(Gilly)*, George Cooper *(Mugsy)*, Edward Connelly *(Deacon Tillinger)*, Lydia Knott *(Mrs. Bascom)*, Betty Allen *(Betty Bascom)*, Margaret Loomis *(Jessie Strong)*, William Bletcher *(Sammy Martin)*, Eric Mayne *(Mr. Morgan)*, Ray Ripley *(Lester Morgan)*.

Comedy-melodrama. Source: Winchell Smith and Jack E. Hazzard, *Turn to the Right, a Comedy in a Prologue and Three Acts* (New York, 1916). Joe Bascom, only son of a widow, lives in a Connecticut village. He loves Elsie Tillinger, daughter of the deacon, the wealthiest man in town; but the deacon forbids Joe to speak to her. Joe leaves home to make his way in the world, but his employer, Mr. Morgan, a wealthy racehorse owner, accuses him unjustly of stealing. Actually, Morgan's son, Lester, is guilty of the crime, but Joe is sentenced to a prison term; there he becomes acquainted with Mugsy and Gilly, two crooks. Meanwhile, though courted by young Morgan, Elsie remains faithful to Joe. Mrs. Bascom, who makes superlative peach jam from her orchard, is in debt to the Deacon Tillinger, and he intends to buy her orchard and make Lester head of a jam industry. But Joe arrives with his crook friends, outwits the deacon, and takes over the peach orchard. Mugsy and Gilly are reformed by the goodness of Joe's mother and fall in love with Betty and Jessie; and after exposing Lester Morgan's deceit, Joe marries Elsie. *Village life. Theft. Injustice. Prisons. Orchards. Jam. Connecticut.*

TURNED UP **F2.5893**

William Steiner Productions. *Dist* Hurricane Film Corp. 1 Nov **1924** [c20 Sep 1924; LU20593]. Si; b&w. 35mm. 5 reels, 4,990 ft.

Prod William Steiner. *Dir* James Chapin. *Story-Scen* Frederic Chapin. *Photog* Ernest Miller.

Cast: Charles Hutchison *(Bruce Pomroy)*, Mary Beth Milford *(Betty Browne)*, Crauford Kent *(Paul Gilmore)*, Otto Lederer *(John Creighton)*, Betty Morrisey *(Lola)*, Charles Cruz *(Joe Turner)*, Charles Force *(Tom Martin)*.

Crook melodrama. Paul Gilmore, a respected bank president, who is in league with a gang of bond thieves headed by Creighton, attempts to frame Bruce Pomroy, a young teller. When he is arrested, Bruce escapes and becomes part of Creighton's gang. In a robbery attempt, he rescues his girl, Betty, from the villains and reveals himself as an agent of the Department of Justice. *Government agents. Bankers. Bank clerks. Gangs. Robbery. United States—Justice Department.*

TWELVE MILES OUT **F2.5894**

Metro-Goldwyn-Mayer Pictures. 9 Jul **1927** [c8 Aug 1927; LP24279]. Si; b&w. 35mm. 8 reels, 7,899 ft.

Dir Jack Conway. *Screenplay* A. P. Younger. *Titl* Joe Farnham. *Photog* Ira Morgan. *Sets* Cedric Gibbons, Eugene Hornbostel. *Film Ed* Basil Wrangell. *Wardrobe* René Hubert.

Cast: John Gilbert *(Jerry Fay)*, Ernest Torrence *(Red McCue)*, Joan Crawford *(Jane)*, Eileen Percy *(Maizie)*, Paulette Duval *(Trini)*, Dorothy Sebastian *(Chiquita)*, Gwen Lee *(Hulda)*, Edward Earle *(John Burton)*, Bert Roach *(Luke)*, Tom O'Brien *(Irish)*.

Melodrama. Source: William Anthony McGuire, *Twelve Miles Out* (New York opening: 16 Nov 1925). Jerry Fay and Red McCue, friendly rivals, after encounters in various parts of the world, meet in New York as rival bootleggers. Jerry, being pursued by the Coast Guard, finds refuge in a seashore house, and when Jane and her fiancé threaten to inform the authorities, he takes them aboard his boat. Red, posing as a revenue agent, hijacks the boat with his gang and makes advances to Jane. Following a drinking match, there is a fight between Jerry and Red over the girl. Jerry ultimately surrenders the boat to the Coast Guard in order to protect Jane; and when wounded, he finds solace in her arms. *Bootleggers. Hijackers. Friendship. Business competition. New York City. United States Coast Guard.*

TWENTY DOLLARS *see* **FOOLS AND RICHES**

$20 A WEEK **F2.5895**

Distinctive Pictures. *Dist* Selznick Distributing Corp. 12 Apr **1924** [c29 Mar 1924; LP20205]. Si; b&w. 35mm. 6 reels, 5,990 ft.

Dir Harmon Weight. *Scen* Forrest Halsey. *Photog* Harry A. Fischbeck.

Cast: George Arliss *(John Reeves)*, Taylor Holmes *(William Hart)*, Edith Roberts *(Muriel Hart)*, Walter Howe *(Henry Sloane)*, Redfield Clarke *(George Blair)*, Ronald Colman *(Chester Reeves)*, Ivan Simpson *(James Pettison)*, Joseph Donohue *(Little Arthur)*, William Sellery *(Clancy, restaurant keeper)*, George Henry *(butler at Hart's)*.

Comedy. Source: Edgar Franklin, "The Adopted Father" (publication undetermined). On his son's wager that he cannot live on $20 a week, John Reeves takes a job in William Hart's steel plant, where he is soon befriended by the boss. By uncovering a schemer, he saves the company from financial destruction and gains a partnership, while his son wins Hart's sister as a wife. *Filial relations. Steel industry. Business ethics. Wagers.*

TWENTY-ONE **F2.5896**

Inspiration Pictures. *Dist* Associated First National Pictures. 17 Dec **1923** [c12 Dec 1923; LP19699]. Si; b&w. 35mm. 7 reels, 6,560 or 6,620 ft.

Pres by Charles H. Duell. *Dir* John S. Robertson. *Scen* Josephine Lovett. *Photog* George Folsey.

Cast: Richard Barthelmess *(Julian McCullough)*, Joe King *(Mr. McCullough)*, Dorothy Cumming *(Mrs. McCullough)*, Dorothy Mackaill *(Lynnie Willis)*, Elsie Lawson *(Paula)*, Bradley Barker *(Peter Straski)*, Ivan Simpson *(Mr. Willis)*, Nellie P. Spaulding *(Mrs. Willis)*, Helen Tracy *(Mrs. Jordan)*.

Romantic drama. Julian McCullough, child of divorced parents, waits until his 21st birthday to marry his sweetheart, Lynnie. *Divorce. Family life.*

TWIN BEDS **F2.5897**

First National Pictures. 14 Jul **1929** [c23 Sep 1929; LP715]. Sd (Movietone); b&w. 35mm. 8 reels, 7,266 ft. [Also si, 4 Aug 1929; 5,902 ft.]

Pres by Richard A. Rowland. *Dir* Alfred Santell. *Scen-Dial-Titl* F. McGrew Willis. *Photog* Sol Polito. *Film Ed* LeRoy Stone.

Cast: Jack Mulhall *(Danny)*, Patsy Ruth Miller *(Elsie Dolan)*, Edythe Chapman *(Ma Dolan)*, Knute Erickson *(Pa Dolan)*, Jocelyn Lee *(Maizie Dolan)*, Nita Martan *(Bobby Dolan)*, ZaSu Pitts *(Tillie)*, Armand Kaliz *(Monty Solari)*, Gertrude Astor *(Mrs. Solari)*, Carl Levinus *(Jason Treejohn)*, Alice Lake *(Mrs. Treejohn)*, Ben Hendricks, Jr. *(Pete)*, Eddie Gribbon *(Red)*, Bert Roach *(Edward J. Small)*.

Farce. Source: Margaret Mayo and Edward Salisbury Field, *Twin Beds; A Farce in Three Acts* (New York, 1931). Elsie Dolan, a telephone operator, by chance meets Danny Brown, a show doctor and song composer. They fall in love and are married. They rent an apartment, but their first night together is interrupted when Danny must go to the theater and rehearse an understudy to go on for Monty Solari, the show's intoxicated star. Danny leaves the door open, and Solari, who lives in the same building, wanders drunkenly into the apartment, puts on Danny's pajamas, and climbs into Danny's twin bed. Danny comes home, and Solari is discovered. Everything is explained satisfactorily, however, and the Browns go to Europe for the rest of their honeymoon. *Telephone operators. Composers. Show doctors. Actors. Theater. Honeymoons.*

TWIN FLAPPERS **F2.5898**

Classplay Pictures. *Dist* Aywon Film Corp. 26 Sep **1927** [New York State license]. Si; b&w. 35mm. 5 reels.

Cast: Harry Morey, Muriel Kingston, Marguerite Clayton, James Morrison, Mary Alden.

Comedy(?). No information about the precise nature of this film has been found. *Flappers.*

TWIN SIX O'BRIEN **F2.5899**

Robert J. Horner Productions. *Dist* Aywon Film Corp. 19 Feb **1926** [New York State license]. Si; b&w. 35mm. 5 reels.

Dir Robert J. Horner. *Photog* Lauren A. Draper.

Cast: Kit Carson, Pauline Curley.

Western melodrama. "'Twin Six' O'Brien, ace in the saddle and champion broncho buster of Arizona, is so named because of his ability to shoot straight. He is smitten by beauty of a prairie lass. Fixer for irrigation company sets out to get 'Twin Six' as a menace to his plans. The tables are turned." ("Motion Picture News Booking Guide," in *Motion Picture News*, 15 Mar 1930, p107.) *Broncobusters. Irrigation. Arizona.*

TWIN TRIGGERS **F2.5900**

Action Pictures. *Dist* Weiss Brothers Artclass Pictures. 13 Apr **1926.** Si; b&w. 35mm. 5 reels, 4,368 ft.

Pres by Lester F. Scott, Jr. *Dir* Richard Thorpe. *Scen* Betty Burbridge. *Story* Jack Townley.

Cast: Buddy Roosevelt *(Bud Trigger/Kenneth Trigger)*, Nita Cavalier *(Gwen, Kenneth's fiancée)*, Frederick Lee *(Dan Wallace, Gwen's uncle)*, Laura Lockhart *(Muriel Trigger, the twins' mother)*, Lafe McKee *(Silas Trigger, Muriel's ex-husband)*, Charles Whitaker *(Kelly, the garage proprietor)*, Clyde McClary *(Bugs, the radio nut)*, Togo Frye *(The Cook)*, Hank Bell *(The Law)*.

Western melodrama. "Twin brothers are pitted against each other as one is engaged in smuggling Chinese and other is out to stop practice. The law and order chap accomplishes his task and also wins brother's girl." (*Motion Picture News Booking Guide*, 11:52, Oct 1926.) *Twins. Brothers. Chinese. Smuggling.*

TWINKLETOES **F2.5901**

John McCormick Productions. *Dist* First National Pictures. 28 Nov **1926** [c2 Dec 1926; LP23387]. Si; b&w. 35mm. 8 reels, 7,833 ft.

Pres by John McCormick. *Dir* Charles Brabin. *Scen* Winifred Dunn. *Photog* James C. Van Trees. *Comedy Construc* Mervyn LeRoy.

Cast: Colleen Moore *(Twinkletoes)*, Kenneth Harlan *(Chuck Lightfoot)*, Tully Marshall *(Dad Minasi)*, Gladys Brockwell *(Cissie)*, Lucien Littlefield *(Hank)*, Warner Oland *(Roseleaf)*, John Philip Kolb *(Bill Carsides)*, Julanne Johnston *(Lilac)*, William McDonald *(Inspector Territon)*.

Melodrama. Source: Thomas Burke, *Twinkletoes, a Tale of Chinatown* (London, 1917). By dancing for the people, Twinkletoes, a child of the London Limehouse district, saves a crowd from abuse by the police, and she meets Chuck Lightfoot, a champion fighter whose wife, Cissie, started the brawl. Twink tries to resist loving Chuck, but when he saves her from an attack one night, her feelings are confirmed. At the head of the "Quayside Kids," Twink scores a success in a local music hall under the management of Roseleaf. Jealous Cissie, learning that Twink's dad is a burglar, exposes him to the police. At the pub where Twink goes in search of him she learns the truth about her father and faints—Roseleaf takes her to his apartment, but she manages to escape his clutches. Cissie is killed in an accident, and, in despair, Twink throws herself into the river. She is rescued by Chuck and in his arms finds something to live for. *Boxers. Burglars. Filial relations. Suicide. Music halls. London—Limehouse.*

TWISTED TRIGGERS **F2.5902**

Action Pictures. *Dist* Associated Exhibitors. 11 Jul **1926** [c22 Jul 1926; LU22940]. Si; b&w. 35mm. 5 reels, 4,470 ft.

Pres by Lester F. Scott, Jr. *Dir* Richard Thorpe. *Cont* Betty Burbridge. *Story* Tommy Gray. *Photog* Ray Reis.

Cast: Wally Wales *(Wally Weston)*, Jean Arthur *(Ruth Regan)*, Al Richmond *(Norris)*, Art Winkler *("Angel-Face")*, J. P. Lockney *(Hiram Weston)*, William Bertram *(Jim Regan)*, Harry Belmour *(cook)*, Lawrence Underwood *(sheriff)*.

Western melodrama. Upon his release from prison, Jim Regan, who had been framed for theft by Dan Norris, is jailed again for attempting to shoot Norris. His friend Wally, seeking work at the Bar X ranch, is held up by "Angel-Face," a member of Denver Dan's gang; realizing his victim is faint from hunger, he shares his food with him and the two decide to become partners and get work together at the ranch. Regan is released on the understanding he will not leave town and goes to the Weston ranch to see Wally. Hiram, Wally's father, sends him away, but when Regan is found dead near the ranch, Hiram is arrested for the murder. Overhearing Norris admit to the crime, Angel-Face informs Wally but is himself shot by the culprit, who then escapes. Wally follows and captures him. Angel-Face recovers, Hiram is released, and Wally marries Ruth, the daughter of Regan. *Ranchers. Gangs. Injustice. Murder.*

TWO ARABIAN KNIGHTS **F2.5903**

Caddo Co. *Dist* United Artists. ca22 Oct **1927** [New York premiere; released 23 Sep; c14 Sep 1927; LP24407]. Si; b&w. 35mm. 9 reels, 8,250 ft.

Pres by Howard Hughes, John W. Considine, Jr. *Supv* John W. Considine, Jr. *Dir* Lewis Milestone. *Screenplay* James T. O'Donohue, Wallace Smith. *Titl* George Marion, Jr. *Photog* Antonio Gaudio, Joseph August. *Art Dir* William Cameron Menzies. *Tech Dir* Ned Mann. *Asst Dir* Nate Watt. *Prod Mgr* Walter Mayo, Leeds Baster.

Cast: William Boyd *(Pvt. W. Daingerfield Phelps)*, Mary Astor *(Anis Bin Adham [Mirza])*, Louis Wolheim *(Sgt. Peter McGaffney)*, Michael Vavitch *(Emir of Jaffa)*, Ian Keith *(Shevket)*, De Witt Jennings *(American consul)*, Michael Visaroff *(ship captain)*, Boris Karloff *(purser)*.

Romantic comedy. Source: Donald McGibney, "Two Arabian Knights," in *McClure's Magazine.* Private Phelps and Sergeant McGaffney, who are constantly scrapping until they meet a common foe, are taken prisoners by Germans during the war, and failing many attempts to escape, they succeed in slipping out in Arab disguise. Finding themselves on a steamer bound for Jaffa, McGaffney, Phelps, and the ship's captain discover themselves rivals for Mirza, an Arab girl of rank. Young Phelps makes progress with her by sign language, even to the point of making her remove her veil. In Jaffa, a spying servant informs Shevket, her fiancé, of her acquaintance with the American, and her father, the emir, plots to imprison them, but they are saved by the American consul. The emir makes the soldiers knights so that Phelps can fight a duel with Shevket; but in a series of escapades, the boys foil their enemies and abscond with the girl. *Soldiers. Prisoners of war. Sea captains. Royalty. Arabs. World War I. Jaffa (Palestine). Germany.*

TWO CAN PLAY **F2.5904**

Encore Pictures. *Dist* Associated Exhibitors. 21 Feb **1926** [c22 Jan 1926; LU22288]. Si; b&w. 35mm. 6 reels, 5,465 ft.

Dir Nat Ross. *Scen* Reginald G. Fogwell. *Photog* André Barlatier. *Film Ed* Gene Milford.

Cast: George Fawcett *(John Hammis)*, Allan Forrest *(James Radley)*, Clara Bow *(Dorothy Hammis)*, Wallace MacDonald *(Robert MacWorth)*, Vola Vale *(Mimi)*.

Society melodrama. Source: Gerald Mygatt, "Two Can Play," in *Saturday Evening Post* (194:20–21, 20–21; 25 Feb–4 Mar 1922). John Hammis, a wealthy financier, disapproves of James Radley, his daughter Dorothy's choice for a fiancé, and hires Robert MacWorth, an ex-aviator, to try to find something in Radley's past or present conduct that will discredit him in her eyes. MacWorth suspects Radley of larcenous intentions and places some valuable pearls within his easy reach, believing that he can catch Radley in the act of stealing them. This plan fails, and MacWorth arranges for Dorothy, Radley, and himself to be stranded together on a desert isle. There, contrary to all expectations, Radley proves himself to be the better man, overcoming both the forces of nature and MacWorth. Dorothy and Radley are then wed. *Financiers. Aviators.*

TWO FISTED BUCKAROO **F2.5905**

Fred Balshofer Productions. 24 Dec **1926.** Si; b&w. 35mm. 5 reels.

Cast: Fred Church.

Western melodrama(?). No information about the nature of this film has been found.

TWO FISTED JUSTICE **F2.5906**

Ben Wilson Productions. *Dist* Arrow Film Corp. 30 Aug **1924** [c12 Jun 1924; LP20295]. Si; b&w. 35mm. 5 reels, 4,626 ft.

Dir Dick Hatton. *Story* Bennett Cohen.

Cast: Dick Hatton *(Rance Raine)*, Marilyn Mills *(Mort Landeau's wife)*.

Western melodrama. Rance Raine, seeking to avenge the death of his brother Harvey, a doctor, unknowingly stops at the same ranch house where the killer, Mort Landeau, and his wife are staying. Rance and the wife become enamored of each other, and she reveals that her husband is the murderer. Meantime, "Red" Oldham has become infatuated with the wife and has his gang hold Rance captive. A fight ensues between Oldham and Landeau in which the latter is killed. Rance is freed by his horse, Star; Rance then defeats Oldham in a fight and marries Mrs. Landeau. *Brothers. Revenge. Murder. Ranches. Horses.*

Note: Copyright title: *Two-Fisted Justice.*

A TWO FISTED TENDERFOOT **F2.5907**

Independent Pictures. 13 Feb **1924.** Si; b&w. 35mm. 5 reels, 4,300-5,000 ft.

Pres by Jesse J. Goldburg. *Dir* J. P. McGowan. *Story (see note)* James Ormont. *Photog* Walter Griffin.

Cast: Franklyn Farnum.

Western melodrama. "... dealing with rival packing plants. Crooked head of one attempts to prevent large shipment of cattle reaching other firm. Son of other firm, a waster, is ousted from home and goes west. Here he saves his father's interests and outwits enemies." (*Motion Picture News Booking Guide,* 6:69, Apr 1924.) *Wastrels. Cattle. Meatpacking.*

Note: There is some doubt about the credit to Ormont for the story.

TWO FISTED THOMPSON **F2.5908**

Ward Lascelle Productions. 23 Jan **1925** [New York State license]. Si; b&w. 35mm. 5 reels, 4,800 ft.

Cast: Lester Cuneo.

Western melodrama. No information about the nature of this film has been found.

TWO FLAMING YOUTHS **F2.5909**

Paramount Famous Lasky Corp. 17 Dec **1927** [c17 Dec 1927; LP24772]. Si; b&w. 35mm. 6 reels, 5,319 ft.

Pres by Adolph Zukor, Jesse L. Lasky. *Dir* John Waters. *Supv Fields-Conklin Unit* Louis D. Lighton. *Screenplay* Percy Heath, Donald Davis. *Titl* Jack Conway (of *Variety*), Herman J. Mankiewicz. *Story* Percy Heath. *Photog* H. Kinley Martin.

Cast—The Story: W. C. Fields *(Gabby Gilfoil)*, Chester Conklin *(Sheriff Ben Holden)*, Mary Brian *(Mary Gilfoil)*, Jack Luden *(Tony Holden)*, George Irving *(Simeon Trott)*, Cissy Fitzgerald *(Madge Malarkey)*, Jimmy Quinn *(Slippery Sawtelle)*.

Cast—Comedy Teams: Beery & Hatton, Clark & McCullough, Duncan Sisters, Kolb & Dill, Moran & Mack, Weber & Fields, Savoy & Brennan [Brennan & Rogers], Baker & Silvers, Benny & McNulty, Pearl & Bard.

Cast—Pit Show Attractions: John Aasen *(The Giant)*, Anna Magruder *(The Fat Lady)*, William Platt *(The Dwarf)*, Chester Moorten *(The Human Pin Cushion)*, Lee W. Parker *(The Tattooed Man)*, John Seresheff *(The Strong Man)*, Jack Delaney *(himself, a boxing kangaroo)*.

Comedy. Circus owner Gabby Gilfoil finds himself at odds with the county sheriff, Ben Holden, because of bad debts, and the sheriff is deluded into thinking the good-hearted carney to be one and the same as the notorious Slippery Sawtelle, whose mug is gracing $1,500 "wanted" posters all over the county. Gilfoil could use a like amount to help pretty Miss Malarkey out of a financial debt to Simeon Trott, but he must elude the persistent sheriff. Holden finally nails the real Sawtelle. *Sheriffs. Jugglers. Hotelkeepers. Confidence men. Circus. Carnivals. Debt.*

Note: Working title: *The Side Show.*

2 GIRLS WANTED **F2.5910**

Fox Film Corp. 11 Sep **1927** [c11 Sep 1927; LP24399]. Si; b&w. 35mm. 7 reels, 6,293 ft.

Pres by William Fox. *Dir* Alfred E. Green. *Scen* Seton I. Miller, Randall H. Raye. *Titl* Malcolm Stuart Boylan. *Story* Gladys Unger. *Photog* George Schneiderman. *Asst Dir* Jack Boland.

Cast: Janet Gaynor *(Marianna Miller)*, Glenn Tryon *(Dexter Wright)*, Ben Bard *(Jack Terry)*, Marie Mosquini *(Sarah Miller)*, Joseph Cawthorn *(Philip Hancock)*, Doris Lloyd *(Miss Timoney)*, Alyce Mills *(Edna Delafield)*, William Tooker *(William Moody)*, Pauline Neff *(Mrs. Delafield)*, William Bletcher *(Johnny)*, C. L. Sherwood *(Michael)*.

Comedy-drama. Marianna Miller, dressing as a boy to seek employment in the city, becomes involved with a gang of ruffians; and when she hits Dexter Wright, a young businessman, with a tomato, he detects her disguise and helps her obtain a secretarial position with his competitor. Misunderstanding his interests in her girl friend, Edna, Marianna and her pal answer an advertisement for two girls wanted—a maid and a cook—and end up as servants in the country house of Dexter's uncle. Marianna learns of a plan to swindle Dexter's uncle, and in the process, she and Dexter fall in love. ... *Businessmen. Secretaries. Housemaids. Cooks. Swindlers. Male impersonation. Employment—Women.*

TWO GUN MURPHY **F2.5911**

Dist Krelbar Pictures, Collwyn Pictures. 20 Sep **1928** [New York State license]. Si; b&w. 35mm. 5 reels.

Cast: Al Hoxie.

Western melodrama(?). No information about the nature of this film has been found.

TWO GUN O'BRIEN **F2.5912**

Dist Exhibitors Film Corp. **1928.** Si; b&w. 35mm. 5 reels, 4,300 ft. *Dir* Robert J. Horner.

Cast: Art Acord.

Western melodrama(?). No information about the nature of this film has been found.

TWO GUN SAP **F2.5913**

Independent Pictures. 2 Oct **1925** [New York State license]. Si; b&w. 35mm. 5 reels, 4,800 ft.

Cast: Franklyn Farnum.

Western melodrama(?). No information about the nature of this film has been found.

TWO KINDS OF WOMEN **F2.5914**

R-C Pictures. 22 Jan **1922** [c22 Jan 1922; LP17515]. Si; b&w. 35mm. 6 reels, 6,000 ft.

Dir Colin Campbell. *Scen* Winifred Dunn. *Photog* Dev Jennings. *Asst Dir* George Bertholon.

Cast: Pauline Frederick *(Judith Sanford)*, Tom Santschi *(Bud Lee)*, Charles Clary *(Bayne Trevor)*, Dave Winter *(Pollock Hampton)*, Eugene Pallette *(Old Carson)*, Billy Elmer *(Poker Face)*, Jack Curtis *(Chris Quinnion)*, Jim Barley *(Benny)*, Sam Appel *(Crowdy)*, Clarissa Selwynne *(Mrs. Grimley)*, Otis Harlan *(Major Langworthy)*, Jean Calhoun *(Marcia Langworthy)*, Tom Bates *(José)*, Lydia Yeamans Titus *(Mrs. Simpson)*, Frank Clark *(Dr. Tripp)*, Bud Sterling *(Tommy Burkitt)*, Elise Collins *(maid)*, Joe Singleton *(Charles Miller)*, Stanhope Wheatcroft *(Ferris)*.

Western melodrama. Source: Jackson Gregory, *Judith of Blue Lake Ranch* (New York, 1919). Judith Sanford, daughter of a wealthy ranchowner, returns from the East when her father dies so as to take charge of his ranch. She finds Bayne Trevor, the ranch manager, in league with a rival concern, and she fires him after she buys out a third partner. Trevor has the payroll stolen, tries to corrupt her men, breeds discontent, and tries to obstruct her cattle business. With the assistance of Bud Lee, her foreman who remains loyal, she wins out and in the process falls in love with him. Pollock Hampton, one of Judith's partners, becomes Trevor's dupe but realizes his mistake when Judith is kidnaped; he then assists Bud in rescuing her. *Ranch managers. Ranch foremen. Ranches. Partnerships.*

TWO LOVERS **F2.5915**

Samuel Goldwyn, Inc. *Dist* United Artists. 23 Mar **1928** [New York premiere; released Sep; c22 Mar 1928; LP25472]. Mus score & sd eff (Movietone); b&w. 35mm. 9 reels, 8,817 ft. [Also si; 8,706 ft.]

Dir Fred Niblo. *Titl* John Colton. *Adapt* Alice D. G. Miller. *Photog* George Barnes. *Film Ed* Viola Lawrence. *Mus Score* Hugo Riesenfeld. *Song: "Grieving"* Wayland Axtell. *Song: "Leonora"* Abner Silver. *Asst Dir* H. B. Humberstone.

Cast: Ronald Colman *(Mark Van Rycke)*, Vilma Banky *(Donna Leonora de Vargas)*, Noah Beery *(The Duke of Azar)*, Nigel De Brulier *(The Prince of Orange)*, Virginia Bradford *(Grete)*, Helen Jerome Eddy *(Inez)*, Eugenie Besserer *(Madame Van Rycke)*, Paul Lukas *(Ramón de Linea)*, Fred Esmelton *(Meinherr Van Rycke, Bailiff of Ghent)*, Harry Allen *(Jean)*, Marcella Daly *(Marda)*, Scotty Mattraw *(Dandermonde innkeeper)*, Lydia Yeamans Titus *(innkeeper's wife)*.

Historical romance. Source: Emmuska Orczy, *Leatherface: A Tale of Old Flanders* (New York, 1916). Donna Leonora, a Spanish girl of nobility, is forced by her cruel uncle, the Duke of Azar, to marry Mark Van Rycke, the son of the Burgomaster of Ghent, ostensibly to cement relations between the conquered and the conqueror, but in reality to ferret out the secrets of William of Orange, silent leader of the Flemish in their attempt to throw off the yoke of Spanish rule. Leonora becomes a spy after having been persuaded by her uncle to forget her Spanish sweetheart, Don Ramón de Linea, commander of the Spanish forces in Ghent. Leonora's hatred for the Dutch is intensified when her sweetheart is killed by Leatherface (Mark), bodyguard and advisor to William of Orange, but eventually she realizes that the Dutch cause is just. She makes a heroic ride to Ghent, saves the lives of a group of conspirators, helps the Flemish take a fortress guarding Ghent, and is happily reunited with her estranged husband. *Nobility. Spanish. Flemings. Marriage—Arranged. Netherlands. Ghent. William the Silent.*

TWO MEN AND A MAID **F2.5916**

Tiffany-Stahl Productions. 10 or 15 Jun **1929** [c11 Jun 1929; LP463]. Talking sequences, mus score, & sd eff (Photophone); b&w. 35mm. 7 reels,

6,539 ft. [Also si; 6,532 ft.]

Dir George Archainbaud. *Cont* Frances Hyland. *Dial-Titl* Frederic Hatton, Fanny Hatton. *Story* John Francis Natteford. *Photog* Harry Jackson. *Film Ed* Desmond O'Brien. *Mus Score* Hugo Riesenfeld. *Song: "Love Will Find You"* L. Wolfe Gilbert, Abel Baer. *Tech Adv* Louis Van Den Ecker.

Cast: William Collier, Jr. *(Jim Oxford)*, Alma Bennett *(Rose)*, Eddie Gribbon *(Adjutant)*, George E. Stone *(Shorty)*, Margaret Quimby *(Margaret)*.

Romantic melodrama. Englishman Jim Oxford mistakenly assumes that his bride previously had a lover, and his idealistic nature is so offended that he enlists in the French Foreign Legion to hide his shame. In an Algerian village, where he rejects women, he nevertheless is attracted to Rose, though he knows she is the brutal adjutant's sweetheart. On the eve of breaking camp, Jim recklessly disobeys orders and keeps a rendezvous with Rose. Just as they are about to be discovered by the wrathful adjutant, a gun discharges, wounding the girl; but she paves the way for Jim's escape, then dies in the adjutant's arms, asking him to spare the deserter. Jim is captured for a reward, and the adjutant, telling him the circumstances of the girl's death, shows mercy. Later, Jim returns home find that Margaret, his bride, is blameless and still loves him. *English. Soldiers. Jealousy. France—Army—Foreign Legion. Algeria.*

TWO MINUTES TO GO **F2.5917**

Charles Ray Productions. *Dist* Associated First National Pictures. 17 Oct **1921** [c22 Nov 1921; LP17225]. Si; b&w. 35mm. 6 reels, 5,920 ft.

Pres by Arthur S. Kane. *Dir* Charles Ray. *Story* Richard Andres. *Photog* George Rizard. *Asst Photog* Ellsworth H. Rumer.

Cast: Charles Ray *(Chester Burnett)*, Mary Anderson *(Ruth Turner)*, Lionel Belmore *(her father)*, Lincoln Stedman *("Fatty")*, Truman Van Dyke *("Angel")*, Gus Leonard *(butler)*, Tom Wilson *(football coach)*, Bert Woodruff *(janitor)*, François Dumas *(Dean of Baker University)*, Phillip Dunham *(Professor of Spanish)*.

Comedy-drama. When his father suffers business reverses, Chester Burnett, star of the college football team, is compelled to work as a milk deliveryman during the early morning hours. Afraid of embarrassing his sweetheart, Ruth Turner, Chester keeps his job a secret, although it forces him to forfeit his place on the school team. "Angel" (the yell leader) learns his secret, and Ruth, while motoring one morning, discovers him delivering milk and upbraids him for being ashamed of his work. Finally Chester resolves to play in the game of the year, but he plays poorly until he receives from his father a telegram announcing his financial recovery and from Ruth a note of forgiveness. He then leads his team to victory. *Milkmen. Filial relations. College life. Football.*

TWO O'CLOCK IN THE MORNING **F2.5918**

Dist Bell Pictures. 6 Nov **1929** [New York State license]. Sd; b&w. 35mm. 8 reels, 6,800 ft.

Dir Andrew Marton.

Cast: Edith Roberts, Noah Beery, Margaret Livingston.

Mystery melodrama. On the day she is married to Paul, Mary is handed a deed to a house from Robert Wheeler, who later is revealed to be her father. A former menace, Marc Read, reenters Mary's life and is murdered, and Mary hides his body with the help of her housekeeper, Nancy. Mary is tried for the murder and is saved at the last minute when Wheeler rushes in and forces Nancy to confess to the murder. *Housekeepers. Filial relations. Murder.*

THE TWO ORPHANS *see* **ORPHANS OF THE STORM**

THE TWO OUTLAWS **F2.5919**

Universal Pictures. 18 Nov **1928** [c31 Jan 1928; LP24945]. Si; b&w. 35mm. 5 reels, 4,616 ft.

Dir-Story Henry MacRae. *Adapt-Cont* George Morgan. *Titl* Gardner Bradford. *Photog* Virgil Miller. *Film Ed* Thomas Malloy.

Cast: Jack Perrin *(Phil Manners/The Lone Rider)*, Rex *(himself, a horse)*, Starlight *(herself, a horse)*, Kathleen Collins *(Mary Ransome)*, J. P. McGowan *(Abner Whitcomb)*, Cuyler Supplee *(other man)*.

Western melodrama. Phil Manners assumes the disguise of a masked stranger to capture a band of horsethieves led, he suspects, by Abner Whitcomb, guardian of his sweetheart, Mary Ransome. Rex, leader of a herd of wild horses whose permanent loyalty Manners has earned, helps him round up the outlaws and goes for the sheriff when Manners gets in a jam. *Strangers. Horsethieves. Horses.*

TWO SHALL BE BORN **F2.5920**

Twin Pictures. *Dist* Vitagraph Co. of America. 7 Dec **1924** [c13 Nov 1924; LP29811]. Si; b&w. 35mm. 6 reels, 5,443 ft.

Dir Whitman Bennett. *Story* Marie Conway Oemler. *Photog* Edward Paul.

Cast: Jane Novak *(Countess Mayra Zuleska)*, Kenneth Harlan *(Brian Kelly)*, Sigrid Holmquist *(Janet Van Wyck)*, Frank Sheridan *(Dominick Kelly)*, Herman Lieb *(Baron von Rittenheim)*, Fuller Mellish *(Count Florian)*, Joseph Burke *(Wenceslaus)*, Blanche Craig *(Aunt Honora Kelly)*, Joseffa De Bok *(Franciska)*, Catharine Evans *(Widow Callaghan)*, Walter James *(Hund)*.

Melodrama. Inspired by: Susan Marr Spaulding, "Two Shall Be Born," in *An American Anthology, 1787–1900* (Boston, c1900). As he lies dying, Count Florian Zuleski of Poland, the head of a committee working for perpetual peace among European nations, entrusts his daughter, Mayra, with the dangerous mission of delivering some important documents to New York. Arriving in the United States, Mayra is unable to establish contact with the Polish representative and goes to live with her aunt. She soon meets Brian Kelly, who is working as a traffic cop after being disinherited by his irate millionaire father for not entering into a marriage of convenience with patrician Janet Van Wyck. Brian and Mayra are secretly married, and she is finally able to deliver the papers, but she is immediately kidnaped by the Polish traitor, Baron von Rittenheim, who takes her to a deserted house in the slums. Mayra is severely beaten but refuses to divulge the whereabouts of the vital documents. She is rescued by Brian, von Rittenheim is turned over to the police, and Brian is reconciled with his father. *Poles. Police. Peace. Disinheritance. Abduction. New York City. Documentation.*

TWO SISTERS (Famous Authors) **F2.5921**

Trem Carr Productions. *Dist* Rayart Pictures. 23 Mar or 15 Apr **1929.** Si; b&w. 35mm. 6 reels, 4,998 or 5,161 ft. [Also with synchronized mus score.]

Dir Scott Pembroke. *Scen* Arthur Hoerl. *Photog* Hap Depew.

Cast: Viola Dana *(Jean/Jane)*, Rex Lease *(Allan Rhodes)*, Claire Du Brey *(Rose)*, Tom Lingham *(Jackson)*, Irving Bacon *(Chumley)*, Tom Curran *(Judge Rhodes)*, Boris Karloff *(Cecil)*, Adalyn Asbury *(Mrs. Rhodes)*.

Drama. Source: Virginia Terhune Vandewater, *The Two Sisters* (New York, 1914). Twin department store clerks Jean and Jane resemble each other only in looks—one is nice, sweet, and honest, but the other is a bobbed-hair thief. The nice one tries to protect the other, who uses their similarity to cover herself; and even the former's fiancé takes the wrong sister to meet his mother—and empty her wall safe! Developments eventually solve the dilemma for the police, however. *Salesclerks. Twins. Sisters. Thieves. Department stores.*

THE TWO SOULED WOMAN *see* **THE UNTAMEABLE**

TWO WEEKS OFF **F2.5922**

First National Pictures. 12 May **1929** [c14 May 1929; LP400]. Talking sequences (Vitaphone); b&w. 35mm. 7 reels, 8,081 ft. [Also si; 6,701 ft.]

Pres by Richard A. Rowland. *Dir* William Beaudine. *Scen* F. McGrew Willis, Joseph Poland. *Dial* Richard Weil. *Photog* Sidney Hickox. *Film Ed* Ralph Holt. *Song: "Love Thrills"* Al Bryan, George W. Meyer.

Cast: Dorothy Mackaill *(Frances Weaver)*, Jack Mulhall *(Dave Brown)*, Gertrude Astor *(Agnes)*, Jimmy Finlayson *(Pa Weaver)*, Kate Price *(Ma Weaver)*, Jed Prouty *(Harry)*, Eddie Gribbon *(Sid Winters)*, Dixie Gay *(Maizie Loomis)*, Gertrude Messinger *(Tessie McCann)*.

Romantic comedy. Source: Kenyon Nicholson and Thomas Barrows, *Two Weeks Off, a Summertime Comedy* (New York, 1927). Shopgirl Frances Weaver plans her vacation at the beach while she sells bathing suits and eludes the vigilance of a sour floorwalker; Agnes, sales manager of her department, is to go with her, and Maizie, another shopgirl, gives her a list of telephone numbers collected at the beach. Dave Brown, a young plumber, arrives to repair her bathroom faucet just she is preparing to leave home. A series of a rainy days at the beach prove disappointing to Frances until Sid, a lifeguard, turns up and breaks the monotony. Then Dave Brown arrives, being mistaken for a cinematic celebrity and so introduced to Frances; Dave incurs Sid's enmity, and Maizie, seeking revenge, exposes Dave as a plumber. Humiliated, Frances gives Dave the air and goes home to Ma and Pa; her father secretly summons Dave to the house, and Frances, who has begun to miss him, is happily reconciled with him. *Shopgirls. Lifeguards. Actors. Courtship. Mistaken identity. Resorts. Bathing suits.*

TWO WEEKS WITH PAY **F2.5923**

Realart Pictures. May **1921** [c1 May 1921; LP16460]. Si; b&w. 35mm. 5 reels, 4,136 ft.

Dir Maurice Campbell. *Adapt-Scen* Alice Eyton. *Photog* H. Kinley Martin.

Cast: Bebe Daniels *(Pansy O'Donnell/Marie La Tour)*, Jack Mulhall *(J. Livingston Smith)*, James Mason *(Montague Fox)*, George Periolat *(Ginsberg)*, Frances Raymond *(Mrs. Wainsworth)*, Polly Moran *(chambermaid)*, Walter Hiers *(hotel clerk)*.

Comedy. Source: Nina Wilcox Putnam, "Two Weeks With Pay," in *Saturday Evening Post* (193:20–21, 9 Oct 1920). Salesgirl Pansy O'Donnell is given a 2-week vacation at a summer resort, where she advertises clothing made by her company. The hotel clerk mistakes her for movie actress Marie La Tour, and gossip spreads that she is staying incognita. She carries out the deception, appearing at a charity performance, but when compelled to make a high dive as an advertising stunt she is saved by J. Livingston Smith, an acquaintance. Smith proposes marriage and is rejected because Pansy believes him to be an "aristocrat," but she accepts him after he convinces her of his true circumstances. *Actors. Impersonation. Advertising. Clothing manufacture. Resorts.*

TWO-FISTED JEFFERSON **F2.5924**

Ben Wilson Productions. *Dist* Arrow Film Corp. 14 Jan **1922** [c24 Jan 1922; LP17497]. Si; b&w. 35mm. 5 reels.

Dir-Scen Roy Clements.

Cast: Jack Hoxie, Evelyn Nelson, Claude Payton, Bill White, Steve Clements, James Welch, Ed La Niece.

Western melodrama. Sheriff Jefferson Mosby, of the Kentucky Mosbys, is assigned by the district inspector of Arid, a small town in Nevada, to investigate a dangerous region known as Cactus Flats, which is infested by outlaws bent on driving out the homesteaders. In Cactus Flats, he meets Molly Miller and Danny Duggan, the last of the homesteaders, and learns of the cruel way Buck Connor, the mayor, orders them to vacate every now and then. By means of disguise, Mosby infiltrates Connor's gang and catches Connor with the goods; then, with the aid of Molly and Danny, he arrests the culprits. In the end, in spite of the inspector's advice not to trust a woman, he decides to take orders from Molly for the rest of his life. *Kentuckians. Homesteaders. Mayors. Gangs. Disguise. Nevada.*

Note: Copyright title: *Two Fisted Jefferson*. Working titles: *Sparks of Flint, Flints of Steel,* and *Under Orders.*

TWO-FISTED JONES (Blue Streak Western) **F2.5925**

Universal Pictures. 6 Dec **1925** [c23 Sep 1925; LP21851]. Si; b&w. 35mm. 5 reels, 4,555 ft.

Dir Edward Sedgwick. *Scen* W. Scott Darling. *Story* Sarah Saddoris. *Photog* Harry Neumann.

Cast: Jack Hoxie *(Jack Wilbur)*, Kathryn McGuire *(Mary Mortimer)*, William Steele *(Hank Gage)*, Harry Todd *(Bart Wilson)*, Frank Rice *(Old Bill)*, Paul Grimes *(traitor)*, William Welsh *(Henry Mortimer)*, Frederick Cole *(Paul Jones)*, Byron Douglas *(John Wilbur, Sr.)*, Ed Burns *(sheriff)*, Art Ortega *(Buck Oxford)*.

Western melodrama. While hunting for a missing man out west, Jack Wilbur falls in love with Mary Mortimer, a beautiful girl whose ranch is in danger of being seized by Bart Wilson, a crooked moneylender. Wilson hires a gang of rustlers to run off Mary's cattle. Old Bill, a hermit, identifies the man whom Jack has been hunting. Jack spoils the rustler's raid, gets his man, and marries Mary. *Ranchers. Rustlers. Moneylenders. Hermits. Property rights.*

A TWO-FISTED SHERIFF **F2.5926**

Ben Wilson Productions. *Dist* Arrow Pictures. 12 Apr **1925** [c8 May 1925; LP21440]. Si; b&w. 35mm. 5 reels, 4,149 ft.

Dir Ben Wilson, Ward Hayes. *Story* George W. Pyper.

Cast: Yakima Canutt *(Jerry O'Connell)*, Ruth Stonehouse *(Midge Blair)*, Art Walker, Cliff Davidson, Jack Woods *(three strangers)*, Joe Rickson *(George Rivers)*.

Western melodrama. Jerry O'Connell, a two-fisted sheriff, rescues Midge Blair from a runaway stage and falls in love with her. They return to town together, and Jerry is entrusted by George Rivers with a valuable shipment of platinum, which Jerry secures in his office. Three strangers, hired by Rivers, steal the platinum from the office after knocking Jerry out in a rough fight, during which the telephone receiver is detached from its hook. Midge, who has become the town switchboard operator, hears the bandits discussing their hiding place and, after they have gone, goes to Jerry's office. She revives him and informs him of the bandit's plans. Jerry starts off in pursuit and, after some hard riding and fighting, brings the bandits to justice. Jerry collects a $10,000 reward and marries Midge. *Telephone operators. Sheriffs. Telephones. Platinum.*

THE TWO-GUN MAN **F2.5927**

R-C Pictures. *Dist* Film Booking Offices of America. 13 Jun **1926** [c3 Jul 1926; LP22875]. Si; b&w. 35mm. 6 reels, 5,139 ft.

Pres by Joseph P. Kennedy. *Dir* David Kirkland. *Scen* William E. Wing. *Story* Stewart Edward White. *Photog* Ross Fisher. *Asst Camera* Jack Greenhalgh.

Cast: Fred Thomson *(Dean Randall)*, Joseph Dowling, Spottiswoode Aitken *(Dad Randall; see note)*, Sheldon Lewis *(Ivor Johnson)*, Frank Hagney *(Bowie Bill)*, Ivor McFadden *(Texas Pete)*, Olive Hasbrouck *(Grace Stickley)*, William Courtwright *(Dad Stickley)*, Billy Butts *(Billy Stickley)*, Arthur Millett *(Sheriff Dalton)*, Willie Fung *(Quong)*, Silver King *(himself, a horse)*.

Western melodrama. Dad Randall is forced to mortgage his cattle to pay a debt to Ivor Johnson, who has bought them after stealing the receipts for the money Randall actually has paid. His son, Dean, returns home from action in the trenches and saves John Stickley, his daughter Grace, and a child from the grasping tactics of Texas Pete, a Johnson hireling who is charging for use of the waterhole. Meanwhile, Dad Randall is being forced to sign over the ranch, but Dean arrives and disposes of the villains just before Dad's death. When Johnson's cattle are rustled, Dean goes to work for him to track down the rustlers; returning the stolen cattle, Dean is tricked by Johnson, but with the aid of Grace and his horse, Silver King, he escapes. By a pulley stunt, Dean leads his pursuers into the sheriff's trap, and following a final showdown with Johnson, Dean and Grace are united. *Veterans. Rustlers. Debt. Revenge. Water rights. Horses.*

Note: Copyright records credit Dowling with the role of Randall, but trade reviews give Aitken.

TWO-GUN OF THE TUMBLEWEED **F2.5928**

Leo Maloney Productions. *Dist* Pathé Exchange. 17 Jul **1927** [c6 May 1927; LU23933]. Si; b&w. 35mm. 6 reels, 5,670 ft.

Dir Leo Maloney. *Story-Scen* Ford I. Beebe. *Photog* Ben White.

Cast: Leo Maloney *("Two-Gun" Calder)*, Peggy Montgomery *(Doris Gibson)*, Josephine Hill *(Nan Brunelle)*, Frederick Dana *(Brunelle)*, Joe Rickson *(Darrel)*, Whitehorse Miles, Bud Osborne, Robert Burns.

Western melodrama. "Two-Gun helps Doris run her ranch but they quarrel because he champions a nester who is hiding from Darrel, a rival rancher. Two-Gun is captured by Darrel's men, but escapes, rescues Doris by beating Darrel in a gun duel and takes her in his arms." (*Moving Picture World,* 23 Jul 1927, p275.) *Cowboys. Ranchers. Homesteaders. Rustlers.*

TYPHOON LOVE **F2.5929**

Norman Dawn Productions. *Dist* Lee-Bradford Corp. Feb **1926.** Si; b&w. 35mm. 6 reels, 5,600 ft.

Dir Norman Dawn.

Cast: Mitchell Lewis, Ruth Clifford.

Melodrama. "Two young adventurers work an opal mine, coveted by sea captain. His man is in their employ, but double dealing is discovered. Typhoon causes death of captain, freeing daughter who is in love with one of the adventurers." ("Motion Picture News Booking Guide," in *Motion Picture News,* 8 May 1926, p47.) *Sea captains. Opal mines. South Seas. Typhoons.*

TYRANT OF RED GULCH **F2.5930**

FBO Pictures. 25 Nov **1928** [c25 Nov 1928; LP20]. Si; b&w. 35mm. 5 reels, 4,778 ft.

Dir Robert De Lacy. *Story-Cont* Oliver Drake. *Titl* Randolph Bartlett. *Camera* Nick Musuraca. *Film Ed* Jay Joiner.

Cast: Tom Tyler *(Tom Masters)*, Frankie Darro *("Tip")*, Josephine Borio *(Mitza)*, Harry Woods *(Ivan Petrovitch)*, Serge Temoff *(Boris Kosloff)*, Barney Furey *(Anton)*.

Melodrama. While looking for an old friend, Tom and his pal, Tip, come upon a little mining settlement under the despotic rule of a Russian, Ivan Petrovitch, and save Mitza and her little brother from his cruelty. Later, they are ambushed, and when Tom is separated from the party, Mitza and her brother are recaptured. Tom and Tip follow Petrovitch into a cave;

the Russian escapes, leaving a halfwit to dynamite the cave; but Tip overpowers him, and Tom arrives at the mine to lead the inmates against the guards. Tom finds a friend among the prisoners, and they overtake Petrovitch, who has escaped with Mitza. *Despots. Halfwits. Russians. Mining camps. Friendship.*

THE UNBEATABLE GAME **F2.5931**

Rev. Robert R. Jones. c15 May **1925** [LP21467]. Si; b&w. 35mm. 9 reels.

Supv-Dir J. Law Siple.

Lecturer: Rev. Robert R. Jones.

Drama. The Reverend Jones addresses a congregation of 4,000 people in a tabernacle, preaching a sermon entitled "Be Sure Your Sins Will Find You Out." Jones relates several true incidents and experiences from his own life. He speaks of a wealthy libertine who sinned without consequence until his own son was denied the right to practice as a doctor because of his father's iniquities; of a society woman seeking spiritual help for her sins; and of a college girl and her unfortunate marriage. After the sermon, the converted come to the pulpit to receive the blessing of Jones. *Evangelists. Good and evil. Religious conversion.*

UNBLAZED TRAIL **F2.5932**

Sanford Productions. 18 Sep **1923** [New York showing]. Si; b&w. 35mm. 5 reels.

Dir Richard Hatton.

Cast: Richard Hatton, Vivian Rich, Donald McCollum.

Melodrama. "The faithful secretary [played by Richard Hatton] of the wealthy John Miller, power in the financial field, is accused of a theft committed by his employer's worthless son, and the circumstantial evidence being strong, he is sent to jail. His wife dies and his baby girl is sent to a home. Three years later Miller's son is killed in an auto wreck, but before he dies he clears La Grange. Miller and his daughter Doris adopt the baby and set out for the west to find the secretary, who has buried himself in seclusion to live down the stain of the stripes. Doris gets off the train for a moment as it stops in the great unblazed regions and in her hurry to catch it as it starts, [she] slips and plunges over a cliff into the water below. LaGrange rescues her, and finally, she and her father and LaGrange and his daughter are all united." (*Variety,* 21 Sep 1923, p37.) *Secretaries. Financiers. Theft. Circumstantial evidence. Injustice. Adoption. Fatherhood. Automobile accidents.*

UNCHARTED SEAS **F2.5933**

Metro Pictures. 25 Apr **1921** [c26 Apr 1921; LP16431]. Si; b&w. 35mm. 6 reels.

Dir Wesley Ruggles. *Scen* George Elwood Jenks. *Photog* John F. Seitz. *Art Dir* John Holden.

Cast: Alice Lake *(Lucretia Eastman),* Carl Gerard *(Tom Eastman),* Rudolph Valentino *(Frank Underwood),* Robert Alden *(Fred Turner),* Charles Mailes *(Old Jim Eastman),* Rhea Haines *(Ruby Lawton).*

Romantic melodrama. Source: John Fleming Wilson, "The Uncharted Sea," in *Munsey's Magazine* (70:607–621, Sep 1920). Persuaded by her father-in-law to give her negligent and drunken husband one more chance, Lucretia Eastman accompanies him on an expedition to the Arctic Circle, but Eastman turns back out of fear. Another ship, commanded by Frank Underwood, who loves Lucretia, arrives on the same mission, and she joins it. While Eastman denounces his wife and obtains a divorce, she and her lover are imprisoned for months in the icebound ship. After a trek across the frozen waste, they are rescued. *Infidelity. Cowardice. Arctic regions.*

Note: Copyright title: *The Uncharted Sea.*

THE UNCHASTENED WOMAN (Chadwick Special Production) **F2.5934**

Chadwick Pictures. ca4–11 Oct **1925** [Houston premiere; released 15 Nov; c16 Nov 1925; LP22004]. Si; b&w. 35mm. 7 reels, 6,800 ft.

Dir James Young. *Scen* Douglas Doty. *Photog* William O'Connell.

Cast: Theda Bara *(Caroline Knollys),* Wyndham Standing *(Hubert Knollys),* Dale Fuller *(Hildegarde Sanbury),* John Miljan *(Lawrence Sanbury),* Harry Northrup *(Michael Krellin),* Eileen Percy *(Emily Madden),* Mayme Kelso *(Susan Ambie).*

Society melodrama. Source: Louis Kaufman Anspacher, *The Unchastened Woman; a Modern Comedy in Three Acts* (New York, 1916). Caroline Knollys is about to tell her husband, Hubert, that she is pregnant when she discovers him in the arms of his secretary, Emily Madden. Determined to teach him a lesson, she does not tell him of her condition but goes off to Europe and leaves Hubert in the care of Emily. She has the baby, but this does not prevent her from becoming the most discussed woman on the Continent. Hubert becomes jealous, especially when she returns home in the company of young architect Lawrence Sanbury, whom she is sponsoring. Tired of Emily, Hubert repents, but Caroline is obdurate. He pays Caroline an unexpected visit, hoping to discover evidence for a divorce. Instead, he is presented with his son, and the couple are reconciled. *Secretaries. Architects. Marriage. Infidelity. Pregnancy.*

UNCLE JACK *see* **PIED PIPER MALONE**

UNCLE JASPER'S WILL **F2.5935**

Micheaux Film Corp. **1922.** Si; b&w. 35mm. 6 reels.

Cast: William E. Fountaine, Shingzie Howard.

Melodrama(?). No information about the precise nature of this film has been found. *Negro life. Wills.*

Note: Known also as *Jasper Landry's Will.*

UNCLE TOM'S CABIN **F2.5936**

Universal Pictures. 4 Nov **1927** [New York premiere; released 2 Sep 1928; c10 Nov 1927; LP24673]. Mus score (Movietone); b&w. 35mm. 13 reels, 13,000 ft. [Also si.]

Pres by Carl Laemmle. *Supv* Edward J. Montagne, Julius Bernheim. *Dir* Harry Pollard. *Scen* Harvey Thew, Harry Pollard. *Titl* Walter Anthony. *Photog* Charles Stumar, Jacob Kull. *Film Ed* Gilmore Walker, Daniel Mandell, Byron Robinson. *Mus Score* Hugo Riesenfeld. *Tech Adv* Col. George L. Bryam.

Cast: James Lowe *(Uncle Tom),* Virginia Grey *(Eva St. Clare),* George Siegmann *(Simon Legree),* Margarita Fisher *(Eliza),* Eulalie Jensen *(Cassie),* Arthur Edmund Carew *(George Harris, a slave),* Adolph Milar *(Haley),* Jack Mower *(Mr. Shelby),* Vivian Oakland *(Mrs. Shelby),* J. Gordon Russell *(Tom Loker),* Skipper Zeliff *(Edward Harris, a slaveowner),* Lassie Lou Ahern *(Little Harris),* Mona Ray *(Topsy),* Aileen Manning *(Miss Ophelia),* John Roche *(St. Clare),* Lucien Littlefield *(Lawyer Marks),* Gertrude Astor *(Mrs. St. Clare),* Gertrude Howard *(Uncle Tom's wife),* Geoffrey Grace *(The Doctor),* Rolfe Sedan *(Adolph),* Marie Foster *(Mammy in St. Clare house),* Francis Ford *(lieutenant),* Martha Franklin *(landlady),* Nelson McDowell *(Phineas Fletcher),* Grace Carlisle *(Mrs. Fletcher),* C. E. Anderson *(Johnson),* Dick Sutherland *(Sambo),* Tom Amardares *(Quimbo),* Bill Dyer *(auctioneer).*

Melodrama. Source: Harriet Beecher Stowe, *Uncle Tom's Cabin* (1852). The favorite and "beloved slaves" of neighboring Kentucky plantation owners, mulattoes George Harris and Eliza, are about to be married when plans are scotched by Edward Harris, George's master. Over the next 5 years, the Shelbys (Eliza's kindly masters) incur a deepening debt to a blackguard named Haley, forcing them to surrender Tom and Harry (Eliza's young son). Eliza, overhearing the plans, escapes with Harry across the border but is pursued by Lawyer Marks and his companion, Loker, and though harbored by Quaker Phineas Fletcher, is extradited by dint of the new Dred Scott Decision. They are returning on a riverboat with Haley (with Tom in service) and George (who had escaped from Harris' clutches and obtained work as a stoker), and Haley's presence forces George into a watery escape and Marks and Loker into a stealthy evasion until they can finally sell Harry to yet another slaveowner, while Eliza's grief drives her to near self-destruction. White northerner Augustus St. Claire and his young daughter, Eva, intervene on Tom's behalf and buy him, leaving Eliza to be sold downriver at a New Orleans slave auction. A deep friendship develops between Eva and Topsy, a scurvy little black imp who inevitably becomes her servant, but the little white girl dies, soon followed by her father; and thus follows Tom's sale to Simon Legree, a villainous northerner who also buys Eliza. He brings her into his home, usurping the place of Cassie, an older mulatto slave, who jealously confides to Tom her bitter and tortuous history at the hands of Legree. The story reveals her to be Eliza's mother, and they, reunited, try to escape, ending up in Legree's attic. Though Tom is beaten to death, their whereabouts are concealed until Legree happens upon them, and a fight ensues, in which Legree, drunk and hysterical, and tormented by visions of the goodly Tom, falls from the attic to his death. A band of refugees passing by the house includes George, who has found and claimed little Harry, and the long sought reunion follows. *Slaves—Runaway. Mulattoes. Planters. Lawyers. Slavery. Drunkenness. Filial relations. Extradition. Marriage. Riverboats. Plantations. New Orleans. Kentucky. Society of Friends. Dred Scott Decision.*

UNCLE TOM'S CABIN (Reissue) F2.5937

Thanhouser Film Corp. *Dist* Cosmos Film Co. 7 Mar **1928** [New York State license]. Si; b&w. 35mm.

Note: Originally released in 1914 by the World Film Corp.

UNCONQUERED *see* **FREEDOM OF THE PRESS**

UNCONQUERED WOMAN F2.5938

Pasha Film Corp. *Dist* Lee-Bradford Corp. May **1922.** Si; b&w. 35mm. 4,611 ft.

Dir Marcel Perez. *Story-Scen* John Clymer. *Photog* William Cooper.

Cast: Rubye De Remer *(Helen Chapelle)*, Walter Miller *(Bruce Devereux)*, Fred C. Jones *(Serge Ronoff)*, Frankie Mann *(Millicent)*, Nick Thompson *(Antonio)*.

Melodrama. Helen offers herself in marriage to the winner of a poker game in order to obtain money to replace what her brother has stolen. Antonio, a halfbreed, is the winner, but Helen is saved from fulfilling her bet by Bruce Devereux when he doubles the stakes and wins the girl. She marries Bruce but leaves for New York when she finds the marriage to be a fake one. There she marries her previous music teacher, but he proves to be faithless, leaving her with a small son. Bruce returns and assures her he had not arranged for a fake marriage. Her present husband, not able to cope with the pressures of his many affairs, kills himself, leaving Helen free to remarry Bruce. *Halfcastes. Music teachers. Brother-sister relationship. Poker. Theft. Debt. Marriage—Fake. Suicide. Infidelity.*

UNDER A TEXAS MOON F2.5939

Warner Brothers Pictures. 1 Apr **1930** [c19 Mar 1930; LP1161]. Sd (Vitaphone); col (Technicolor). 35mm. 8 reels, 7,498 ft.

Dir Michael Curtiz. *Screenplay* Gordon Rigby. *Photog* William Rees. *Film Ed* Ralph Dawson. *Song: "Under a Texas Moon"* Ray Perkins. *Sd* Hal Shaw.

Cast: Frank Fay *(Don Carlos)*, Raquel Torres *(Raquella)*, Myrna Loy *(Lolita Romero)*, Armida *(Dolores)*, Noah Beery *(Jed Parker)*, Georgie Stone *(Pedro)*, George Cooper *(Philipe)*, Fred Kohler *(Bad Man of Pool)*, Betty Boyd *(Girl of the Pool)*, Charles Sellon *(José Romero)*, Jack Curtis *(Buck Johnson)*, Sam Appel *(Pancho Gonzales)*, Tully Marshall *(Aldrich)*, Mona Maris *(Lolita Roberto)*, Francisco Maran *(Antonio)*, Tom Dix *(Tom)*, Jerry Barrett *(Jerry)*, Inez Gomez *(Mother)*, Edythe Kramera *(Moza)*, Bruce Covington *(Don Roberto)*.

Romantic western drama. Source: Edward Stewart White, "Two-Gun Man," in *Famous Story Magazine* (1:103-109, Oct 1925). Don Carlos, a dashing Mexican adventurer, and his guitar-strumming friends, Pedro and Philipe, ride into the Lazy Y Ranch on the Texas border and become enamored of the beautiful sisters Dolores and Raquella. Gus Aldrich offers a reward for the capture of rustlers who have been stealing his cattle, and the trio embark on their mission; but Don Carlos dallies over a pretty girl at an inn and runs into trouble with her bullfighting brother, Antonio. At the hacienda of Don Roberto, he encounters Lolita, who tries to persuade him to kill Gonzales, her fiancé, whom she is being forced to marry; but he escapes and, locating the stolen cattle, drives them back to the ranch. The Bad Man, Antonio, and Gonzales arrive bent on vengeance; Don Carlos accepts the reward and drives the adversaries into a food cooler; after evading the clutches of the quarreling señoritas, Don Carlos kidnaps the innkeeper's daughter and rides into Mexico. *Adventurers. Ranch foremen. Rustlers. Bullfighters. Mexicans. Ranches. Courtship. Mexican border. Texas.*

UNDER FIRE F2.5940

Clifford S. Elfelt Productions. *Dist* Davis Distributing Division. c1 Jan **1926** [LP22255]. Si; b&w. 35mm. 5 reels.

Prod Albert I. Smith. *Dir* Clifford S. Elfelt. *Adapt* Frank Howard Clark.

Cast: Bill Patton, Jean Arthur, Cathleen Calhoun, Norbert Myles, William Bertram, Harry Moody, W. Cassel, H. Renard.

Western melodrama. Source: Capt. Charles King, *Under Fire* (Philadelphia, 1895). Lieutenant Tom Brennan is cashiered from the 7th Cavalry on two charges, both unjust: that of deserting his men in the face of a cruel Indian attack, and of entertaining a married woman in his quarters after hours. Tom wanders into the desert and is picked up half dead by Yuba Bill, a prospector with whom he goes into partnership. The Indians go on the warpath, and Tom rides to the fort and warns the colonel. Tom's innocence is established by the confession of an enlisted man, and Tom is reinstated to the service with full honors, renewing his engagement with Margaret Cranston. *Indians of North America. Prospectors. Infidelity. Courts-martial. Forts. United States Army—Cavalry.*

UNDER MONTANA SKIES F2.5941

Tiffany Productions. 10 Sep **1930** [c6 Sep 1930; LP1543]. Sd (Photophone); b&w. 35mm. 6 reels, 5,273 ft.

Dir Richard Thorpe. *Screenplay-Dial* Bennett Cohen, James A. Aubrey. *Story* James A. Aubrey. *Photog* Harry Zech. *Sets* Ralph De Lacy. *Film Ed* Carl Himm. *Rec Engr* J. Stransky, Jr.

Cast: Kenneth Harlan *(Clay Conning)*, Slim Summerville *(Sunshine)*, Dorothy Gulliver *(Mary)*, Nita Martan *(Blondie)*, Christian Frank *(Frank Blake)*, Harry Todd *(Abner Jenkins)*, Ethel Wales *(Martha Jenkins)*, Lafe McKee *(Pinky)*.

Western comedy-drama. Cowboy Clay Conning rescues a theatrical troupe stranded in the little town of Red Rock by using the lead dancer, Blondie, to threaten to compromise the hotel owner, Abner Jenkins. Clay pays their hotel bill and induces the townsmen to pay their rent in advance. But Martha Jenkins, whose husband owns the opera house, intervenes, whereupon Clay, who has fallen in love with Mary, the leading lady, begins courting Mrs. Jenkins to win her consent. The show goes on as they are riding and romancing, but Frank Blake, a cattle rustler convicted by Clay's testimony and just released from jail, holds up the box office and captures Clay. He escapes, captures the villain, and wins Mary. *Cowboys. Rustlers. Theatrical troupes. Courtship. Robbery. Montana.*

Note: Songs in the film include "Sweetest Man I Ever Had," "Under Montana Skies," "Cryin' Blues," "How Could Anyone Help Lovin' a Man Like You," and "Harlem Hop."

UNDER OATH F2.5942

Selznick Pictures. *Dist* Select Pictures. 6 Aug **1922** [c2 Aug 1922; LP18103]. Si; b&w. 35mm. 5 reels, 5,100 ft.

Pres by Lewis J. Selznick. *Dir* George Archainbaud. *Story-Scen* Edward J. Montagne. *Photog* Merritt Gerstad.

Cast: Elaine Hammerstein *(Shirley Marvin)*, Mahlon Hamilton *(Jim Powers)*, Niles Welch *(Hartley Peters)*, Carl Gerard *(Steve Powers)*, Dwight Chittenden *(Chester Marvin)*, Wallace MacDonald *(Ralph Marvin)*,

Drama. Shirley Marvin agrees to marry the degenerate brother of her father's business rival, Jim Powers, but when the brother gives evidence against Jim to the district attorney and is murdered, Jim is arrested. He is saved by Shirley's testimony, and in the end Jim and Shirley marry. *Brothers. Business ethics. Murder.*

UNDER ORDERS *see* **TWO-FISTED JEFFERSON**

UNDER TEXAS SKIES F2.5943

W. Ray Johnston. *Dist* Syndicate Pictures. 15 Nov **1930.** Sd; b&w. 35mm. 6 reels, 5,119 or 5,800 ft.

Dir J. P. McGowan. *Story-Cont-Dial* G. A. Durlam. *Ch Camera* Otto Himm. *Film Ed* Alfred Brook.

Cast: Bob Custer *(Rankin)*, Natalie Kingston *(Joan Prescott)*, Bill Cody *(agent)*, Tom London *(Hartford)*, Lane Chandler *(Martin)*, Bob Roper *(Dummy)*, William McCall *(Marshal Walsh)*, Joseph Marba *(sheriff)*.

Western melodrama. Trying to make ends meet, Joan Prescott contracts to sell her horses to the Army, for which Captain Hartford is acting as agent. During the negotiations he casts suspicion of working with below-border revolutionists on Tom Rankin, ostensibly a wrangler; but after Rankin recovers the stolen horses he exposes Hartford and a Secret Service agent as rustlers and his own identity as the real Captain Hartford. *Cowboys. Secret service. Rustlers. Wranglers. United States Army—Cavalry. Texas. Horses.*

UNDER THE BLACK EAGLE F2.5944

Metro-Goldwyn-Mayer Pictures. 24 Mar **1928** [c24 Mar 1928; LP25175]. Si; b&w. 35mm. 6 reels, 5,901 ft.

Dir W. S. Van Dyke. *Cont* Bradley King. *Titl* Madeleine Ruthven. *Story* Norman Houston. *Photog* Hendrik Sartov. *Film Ed* Ben Lewis. *Wardrobe* Lucia Coulter.

Cast: Ralph Forbes *(Karl von Zorn)*, Marceline Day *(Margareta)*, Bert Roach *(Hans Schmidt)*, William Fairbanks *(Ulrich Muller)*, Marc MacDermott *(Colonel Luden)*, Flash *(Prinz, a dog)*.

War drama. Young German artist Karl von Zorn, a pacifist, is drafted to serve "under the Black Eagle," and sadly leaves his dog (Prinz) and sweetheart behind. Prinz finds Karl at the battlefront, wounded in an attempt to seek revenge for the death of his comrade by blowing up the enemy's machine gun nest. Prinz also is wounded; but they recover, and Karl returns to his sweetheart. *Artists. Pacifists. World War I. Germany—Army. Dogs.*

UNDER THE LASH F2.5945

Famous Players–Lasky. *Dist* Paramount Pictures. 16 Oct **1921** [New York premiere; released 18 Dec; c26 Oct 1921; LP17132]. Si; b&w. 35mm. 6 reels, 5,675 ft.

Pres by Jesse L. Lasky. *Dir* Sam Wood. *Scen* J. E. Nash. *Photog* Al Gilks. *Asst Dir* A. R. Hamm.

Cast: Gloria Swanson *(Deborah Krillet)*, Mahlon Hamilton *(Robert Waring)*, Russell Simpson *(Simeon Krillet)*, Lillian Leighton *(Tant Anna Vanderberg)*, Lincoln Stedman *(Jan Vanderberg)*, Thena Jasper *(Memke)*, Clarence Ford *(Kaffir boy)*.

Melodrama. Source: Alice Askew and Claude Askew, *The Shulamite* (New York, 1907). Claude Askew and Edward Knoblock, *The Shulamite* (New York production: 29 Oct 1906). Deborah Krillet is the young wife of Simeon Krillet, a Boer farmer and religious fanatic. She falls in love with young Englishman Robert Waring, who comes to the farm as overseer. Krillet threatens to beat her for reading Shakespeare's *Romeo and Juliet* but relents when she falsely states that she is pregnant; later she confesses the lie to Waring and records it in her diary. Discovering the deception, Krillet tells Deborah he must kill her, and Waring, summoned by a servant during a storm, shoots Krillet to save Deborah. Krillet is reported to have been killed in the storm, but the farmer's sister, Anna, discovers the truth. To silence her, Deborah surrenders the farm and her husband's money. Waring discovers that his wife has been granted a divorce, and the lovers are united. *Boers. Farmers. Fanatics. Kaffirs. South Africa. "Romeo and Juliet".*

UNDER THE RED ROBE F2.5946

Cosmopolitan Corp. *Dist* Goldwyn-Cosmopolitan Distributing Corp. ca24 Nov **1923** [New York premiere; released 13 Jan; c13 Jan 1924; LP19918]. Si; b&w. 35mm. 10 reels, 9,062 ft. [Also 12,000 ft.]

Dir Alan Crosland. *Scen* Bayard Veiller. *Photog* Harold Wenstrom, Gilbert Warrenton. *Sets* Joseph Urban. *Mus Score* William Frederick Peters. *Cost* Gretl Urban. *Art Titl* Oscar C. Buchheister Art Title Co.

Cast: Robert B. Mantell *(Cardinal Richelieu)*, John Charles Thomas *(Gil de Bérault)*, Alma Rubens *(Renée de Cocheforet)*, Otto Kruger *(Henri de Cocheforet)*, William H. Powell *(Duke of Orléans)*, Ian MacLaren *(King Louis XIII)*, Genevieve Hamper *(Duchess de Chevreuse)*, Mary MacLaren *(Anne of Austria)*, Rose Coghlan *(Marie de Medici)*, Gustav von Seyffertitz *(Clon)*, Sidney Herbert *(Father Joseph)*, Arthur Houseman *(Captain La Rolle)*, Paul Panzer *(lieutenant in the French Army)*, Charles Judels *(Antoine)*, George Nash *(Jules, innkeeper)*, Evelyn Gosnell *(Madame de Cocheforet)*.

Historical costume drama. Source: Stanley J. Weyman, *Under the Red Robe* (New York, 1894). Gil de Bérault engages in a duel despite the orders of Cardinal Richelieu, Prime Minister of France under King Louis XIII. To save his life, Bérault must capture Henri de Cocheforet, a suspected leader in a plot to overthrow the monarch, and bring him to the palace. Bérault captures Cocheforet but becomes a captive of the wiles of Renée, Cocheforet's beautiful sister. He abandons his purpose and returns to the palace emptyhanded. In the meantime, the king's brother, the Duke of Orléans, a conspirator against Richelieu, persuades the king to dismiss Richelieu. Bérault reveals Orléans's treachery; Richelieu is returned to favor, and Bérault is praised for his loyalty. *Duels. Conspiracy. France—History—Bourbons. Cardinal Richelieu. Gaston Orléans. Louis XIII (France). Anne of Austria. Marie de Medicis.*

UNDER THE ROUGE F2.5947

Encore Pictures. *Dist* Associated Exhibitors. 18 Oct **1925** [c20 Jul 1925; LU21664]. Si; b&w. 35mm. 6 reels, 6,055 ft.

Dir Lewis H. Moomaw. *Story-Scen* A. P. Younger. *Photog* King Gray, Herbert H. Brownell, John La Mond.

Cast: Eileen Percy *(Kitty)*, Tom Moore *(Whitey)*, Eddie Phillips *(Skeeter)*, James Mason *(Mal)*, Claire De Lorez *(Daisy)*, William V. Mong *(Doc Haskell)*, Chester Conklin *(Mr. Fleck)*, Aileen Manning *(Mrs. Fleck)*, Stanley Blystone *(Jim Condon)*, Peggy Prevost *(Maybelle)*, Frank Clark *(Simmons)*, Mary Alden *(Martha Maynard)*, Bruce Guerin *(Little Tommy)*, Carmelita Geraghty *(Evelyn)*, Tom Gallery *(Fred Morton)*.

Melodrama. Several years after the war, during which they were decorated, Whitey and Skeeter are blowing safes for a living. While pulling off a job, Skeeter is surprised by the police and killed. Taken into custody, Whitey learns that a lounge lizzard named Mal, who hangs around on the edge of the underworld, is the police informer responsible for Skeeter's death. Whitey is held as a material witness, but, through the good offices of an old Army buddy, he is released. Looking for Kitty, his underworld sweetheart, who has gone to the country to find peace and quiet, Whitey finds her in a small town and, believing her to be in love with Fred Morton, a bank clerk, pretends that he has found another girl. Mal arrives in town as the advance man for a confidence agent who poses as an evangelist, and he persuades Evelyn, the daughter of Skeeter's mother, with whom she is living, to elope with him. Kitty learns of this and, in order to expose Mal, tells the story of her own criminal past. Fred drops her, and Kitty tries to drown herself in the river. Whitey saves her life, and exposes Fred as an embezzler. *Veterans. Safecrackers. Evangelists. Bank clerks. Informers. Police. Confidence men. Embezzlement. Suicide.*

UNDER THE SOUTHERN CROSS *see* **THE DEVIL'S PIT**

UNDER THE TONTO RIM F2.5948

Paramount Famous Lasky Corp. 4 Feb **1928** [c4 Feb 1928; LP24951]. Si; b&w. 35mm. 6 reels, 5,947 ft.

Pres by Adolph Zukor, Jesse L. Lasky. *Assoc Prod* B. P. Schulberg. *Dir* Herman C. Raymaker. *Screenplay* J. Walter Ruben. *Titl* Alfred Hustwick. *Photog* C. Edgar Schoenbaum. *Film Ed* William Shea.

Cast: Richard Arlen *(Edd Denmeade)*, Alfred Allen *(Dad Denmeade)*, Mary Brian *(Lucy Watson)*, Jack Luden *(Bud Watson)*, Harry T. Morey *(Sam Spralls)*, William Franey *("One Punch")*, Harry Todd *(Bert)*, Bruce Gordon *(Killer Higgins)*, Jack Byron *(Middleton)*.

Western melodrama. Source: Zane Grey, *Under the Tonto Rim* (New York, 1926). Gold miner Edd Denmeade loves Lucy Watson, the sister of the official mining claim recorder. Denmeade suspects Watson of killing his father, who after a poker game was shot by a gambler "who shuffles with one hand." The real murderer, Sam Spralls, has convinced Watson that he killed Denmeade and threatens to expose him unless Watson assigns him all the gold claims. Spralls assembles a band of killers to jump the claims when Watson complies. Eventually, Denmeade learns the identity of the killer when he sees Spralls shuffle a deck of cards. He forms a vigilante party and rids the community of Spralls and his gang. *Recorders. Gamblers. Claim jumpers. Vigilantes. Gold mining. Blackmail. Murder. Arizona.*

UNDER TWO FLAGS F2.5949

Universal Film Manufacturing Co. ca24 Sep **1922** [New York–Chicago premiere; released 6 Nov; c21 Sep 1922; LP18229]. Si; b&w. 35mm. 8 reels, 7,407 ft.

Pres by Carl Laemmle. *Dir* Tod Browning. *Scen* Edward T. Lowe, Jr., Elliott Clawson. *Adapt* Tod Browning, Edward T. Lowe, Jr. *Photog* William Fildew.

Cast: Priscilla Dean *(Cigarette)*, James Kirkwood *(Corporal Victor)*, John Davidson *(Sheik Ben Ali Hammed)*, Stuart Holmes *(Marquis de Chateauroy)*, Ethel Grey Terry *(Princess Corona)*, Robert Mack *(rake)*, Burton Law *(The Sheik's Aide)*, Albert Pollet *(Captain Tollaire)*, W. H. Bainbridge *(The Colonel)*.

Melodrama. Source: Ouida, *Under Two Flags* (Philadelphia, 1867). An English nobleman, known only as Victor, arrives in Algiers and joins the French Foreign Legion as a private without revealing his true identity. He attracts and is loved by Cigarette, a French-Arab girl and "daughter of the regiment," but does not return her attentions. She is at first furious, and when she learns Victor's past and the name of his true love she goes to the Princess Corona with the intention of killing her. But Cigarette's hate turns to admiration, and she reveals Victor's identity to the princess. Learning of Sheik Ben Ali Hammed's plots against Victor and Algiers, she gives evidence that clears him of treason, makes a wild ride ahead of the Arabs to warn the troops, and dies in Victor's arms after shielding him from the executioner's bullet. *Royalty. Nobility. Arabs. English. Algiers. France—Army—Foreign Legion.*

UNDER WESTERN SKIES F2.5950

Dist Aycie Pictures **1921.** Si; b&w. 35mm. 5 reels.

Dir George Martin. *Photog* Bud Young.

Cast: Wallace Ray, Grace Lloyd.

Western melodrama(?). No information about the nature of this film has been found.

UNDER WESTERN SKIES (Universal-Jewel) **F2.5951**

Universal Pictures. 7 Feb **1926** [c12 Jan 1926; LP22261]. Si; b&w. 35mm. 7 reels, 6,452 ft.

Dir-Story Edward Sedgwick. *Scen* Charles E. Whittaker. *Photog* Virgil Miller.

Cast: Norman Kerry *(Robert Erskine)*, Anne Cornwall *(Ella Parkhurst)*, Ward Crane *(Otto Stern)*, George Fawcett *(James Erskine)*, Kathleen Key *(Milly Lewis)*, Eddie Gribbon *(Reed)*, Harry Todd *(Payne)*, Charles K. French *(Sam Parkhurst)*, William A. Steele *(Fleming)*, John S. Peters *(Count Andriani)*, Art Artego *(Indian cook)*.

Western melodrama. Bob Erskine, the son of a wealthy New York banker, falls in love with Ella Parkhurst, the daughter of an Oregon rancher. Bob goes to work as a fieldhand for the elder Parkhurst and discovers that the Oregon crops may fail because eastern bankers, led by Bob's father, refuse to advance the farmers credit. Bob intercedes with his father, who promises to help the ranchers if Bob wins the steeplechase in the Pendleton rodeo. Bob rides in the race and wins it handily, saving the crops and assuring himself of Ella's devotion. *Bankers. Ranchers. Farming. Credit. Rodeos. Steeplechasing. Pendleton (Oregon).*

Note: Scenes for this film were photographed at the Pendleton, Oregon, Roundup of 1925.

THE UNDERSTANDING HEART **F2.5952**

Cosmopolitan Productions. *Dist* Metro-Goldwyn-Mayer Distributing Corp. 26 Feb **1927** [c28 Mar 1927; LP23794]. Si; b&w. 35mm. 7 reels, 6,657 ft.

Dir Jack Conway. *Adapt-Screenplay* Edward T. Lowe, Jr. *Titl* Joe Farnham. *Photog* John Arnold. *Sets* Cedric Gibbons, B. H. Martin. *Film Ed* John W. English. *Wardrobe* André-ani.

Cast: Joan Crawford *(Monica Dale)*, Rockliffe Fellowes *(Bob Mason)*, Francis X. Bushman, Jr. *(Tony Garland)*, Carmel Myers *(Kelcey Dale)*, Richard Carle *(Sheriff Bentley)*, Jerry Miley *(Bardwell)*, Harvey Clark *(Uncle Charley)*.

Adventure melodrama. Source: Peter Bernard Kyne, *The Understanding Heart* (New York, 1926). Forest ranger Bob Mason is forced to kill Bardwell in self-defense; but Kelcey Dale, to whom Bob is attracted, commits perjury and causes him to be convicted for murder. Bob escapes and is sheltered by Monica, Kelcey's sister, who is loved by Tony Garland, another ranger. A forest fire breaks out, and Tony rides for aid; when the party is trapped, Kelcey confesses the truth. An airplane brings parachutes by which the wife and her child are saved by jumping off a cliff, and a rainfall saves the others. Monica finds happiness with Tony. *Forest rangers. Sisters. Infidelity. Perjury. Parachuting. Forest fires.*

THE UNDERSTUDY **F2.5953**

R-C Pictures. *Dist* Film Booking Offices of America. 25 Jun **1922** [c25 Jun 1922; LP18033]. Si; b&w. 35mm. 5 reels, 4,537 ft.

Dir William A. Seiter. *Scen* Beatrice Van. *Story* Ethel M. Hadden. *Photog* Joseph Dubray.

Cast: Doris May *(Mary Neil)*, Wallace MacDonald *(Tom Manning)*, Christine Mayo *(Grace Lorimer)*, Otis Harlan *(Martha Manning)*, Arthur Hoyt *(Cathbert Vane)*.

Comedy. Tom Manning's father (*see note, below*) objects to the intense involvement of his son with Grace Lorimer, an actress. He sends Tom out west and notifies Grace that he is willing to pay any sum if she will give up claim to his heir. Unable to appear in person to claim the check, Grace persuades Mary Neil, a stagestruck girl, to impersonate her and to visit the elder Manning. Tom's father discovers through a photograph that she is not Grace, but he invites her to remain temporarily with the family. Tom is struck by Mary's beauty, and the family soon becomes attached to her. Before Grace can arrive to create a disturbance, Tom, with the consent of his father, marries Mary. *Actors. Impersonation. Filial relations.*

Note: Although Otis Harlan portrays the father, most sources incorrectly render his character name as "Martha Manning."

UNDERTOW **F2.5954**

Universal Pictures. 16 Feb **1930** [c10 Feb 1930; LP1063]. Sd (Movietone); b&w. 35mm. 6 reels, 5,085 ft. [Also si; 6,338 ft.]

Pres by Carl Laemmle. *Dir* Harry Pollard. *Adapt-Dial* Winifred Reeve, Edward T. Lowe, Jr. *Photog* Jerome Ash. *Film Ed* Daniel Mandell. *Rec Engr* C. Roy Hunter.

Cast: Mary Nolan *(Sally Blake)*, Robert Ellis *(Jim Paine)*, Johnny Mack Brown *(Paul Whalen)*, Churchill Ross *(Lindy)*, Audrey Ferris *(Kitty)*.

Romantic melodrama. Source: Wilbur Daniel Steele, "Ropes," in *Harper's Monthly* (142:193–208, Jan 1921). Sally Blake and her finacé, Jim Paine, a lighthouse inspector, are strolling on the beach when they see Paul Whalen, a lifeguard, rescue a drowning child; Sally expresses her attraction for him, provoking a quarrel with Jim, and as a result breaks off their engagement. She soon meets Paul and marries him. Paul is assigned to an offshore lighthouse as keeper, and he and Sally live there for 5 years, during which their child is born. Paul loses his eyesight just before Jim arrives to inspect the lighthouse; weary of the loneliness, Sally is induced to go ashore to parties and dances with Jim, but, conscience-stricken, she returns to her husband. Paul recovers his sight to find Jim attempting to kiss his wife and gives him a beating; realizing, however, that Sally acted under compulsion, Paul is reconciled with her. *Lifeguards. Marriage. Blindness. Lighthouses.*

UNDERWORLD **F2.5955**

Paramount Famous Lasky Corp. 20 Aug **1927** [New York premiere; released 29 Oct; c29 Oct 1927; LP24601]. Si; b&w. 35mm. 8 reels, 7,643 ft.

Pres by Adolph Zukor, Jesse L. Lasky. *Prod* Hector Turnbull. *Dir* Josef von Sternberg. *Screenplay* Robert N. Lee. *Titl* George Marion, Jr. *Adapt* Charles Furthman. *Story* Ben Hecht. *Photog* Bert Glennon. *Set Dsgn* Hans Dreier.

Cast: George Bancroft *("Bull" Weed)*, Clive Brook *("Rolls Royce")*, Evelyn Brent *("Feathers")*, Larry Semon *("Slippy" Lewis)*, Fred Kohler *("Buck" Mulligan)*, Helen Lynch *(Mulligan's girl)*, Jerry Mandy *(Paloma)*, Karl Morse *("High Collar" Sam)*.

Crime melodrama. "Bull" Weed, the uncrowned king of the underworld, during a getaway from a bank robbery, meets a bum on the streetcorner whom he later adopts as "Rolls Royce," a member of the gang, and whose gentility is a source of pride to Bull. Rolls Royce soon becomes the brains behind the gang's nocturnal maneuvers and holds the key to its hideaway; "Feathers," Bull's girl, takes an interest in Rolls, and though their love grows, it is restrained by respect for their leader. On the night of a gangland ball, Buck Mulligan, a rival for Feathers, tries to force his attentions on the girl; and pursued by Bull, he is killed. Bull is caught, tried, and sentenced to be hanged; and on the eve of the execution, Rolls's scheme to free him goes afoul. Believing he has been doublecrossed by the man who has stolen his girl, Bull effects his escape to get revenge. In a gang battle with the police, Rolls is fatally wounded, and Bull, realizing their loyalty to him and the purity of their love, surrenders in peace. *Gangsters. Friendship. Loyalty. Murder. Revenge. Prison escapes. Capital punishment.*

UNDISPUTED EVIDENCE **F2.5956**

Cotton Blossom Film Corp. **1922.** Si; b&w. 35mm. [Feature length assumed.]

Melodrama(?). No information about the precise nature of this film has been found. *Negro life.*

UNDRESSED **F2.5957**

Sterling Pictures. c18 Jul **1928** [LP25468]. Si; b&w. 35mm. 6 reels, 5,300 ft.

Dir Philip Rosen. *Cont* Frances Guihan. *Titl* Terrence Daugherty. *Story* John Leeds. *Photog* Herbert Kirkpatrick. *Film Ed* Robert Carlisle.

Cast: David Torrence *(Martin Stanley)*, Hedda Hopper *(Mrs. Stanley)*, Virginia Brown Faire *(Diana Stanley)*, Buddy Messenger *(Bobby Arnold)*, Bryant Washburn *(Paul Howard)*, Virginia Vance *(Marjorie Stanley)*.

Drama. The miserliness of Martin Stanley, a man of considerable wealth, reduces his wife, Louise, and his daughters, Diana and Marjorie, to desperate measures. Diana poses for painter Paul Howard, thereby incurring the jealousy of her sister, who is in love with the artist, and the wrath of her mother, who sells some clothes to repay Diana's wages to Paul. To further complicate matters, Paul tries to break up Diana's happy romance with Bobby Arnold by altering his painting of Diana to suggest that she posed indecorously. Learning of Paul's designs, Marjorie attacks him, resulting in Paul's apparent death and Bobby's knowledge of the painting. Stanley finally realizes the consequences of his penury, Diana's danger of arrest for Paul's murder passes when the artist revives, and the family's happiness is increased by the reconciliation of Bobby and Diana. *Artists. Sisters. Misers. Jealousy. Nudity. Murder.*

UNEASY PAYMENTS **F2.5958**

R-C Pictures. *Dist* Film Booking Offices of America. 19 Jan or Feb **1927** [c19 Jan 1927; LP23575]. Si; b&w. 35mm. 5 reels, 4,770 ft.

Pres by Joseph P. Kennedy. *Dir* David Kirkland. *Cont* Dorothy Yost.

Story Walter A. Sinclair. *Photog* Charles Boyle. *Asst Dir* Bill Dagwell.

Cast: Alberta Vaughn *(Bee Haven)*, Jack Luden *(Tom Gatesby)*, Gino Corrado *(Bozoni)*, Gene Stone *(Charlie Ross)*, Victor Potel *(press agent)*, Betty Francisco *(Marie Valentia)*, Amber Norman *(Lily)*.

Farce. Bee Haven, a little country girl from Missouri, wins a Charleston contest and goes to New York to pursue a theatrical career, accompanied by Charlie Ross, a bucolic sheik. Her country attire merely amuses the stage managers, but Tom Gatesby, a backer, persuades Bozoni, a cabaret owner, to give her a job. She innocently accepts money from Bozoni to furnish a luxury apartment; and when disillusioned Bozoni cancels the payments for her furniture and new clothes, Bee tries to avoid the gown-collectors, but they retrieve her gown and fur coat. In desperation, she joins a revue chorus, doing a lingerie number that results in a fight with Valentia, the star of the show. Tom rescues Bee from her precarious position, and all ends happily. *Chorus girls. Missourians. Dance contests. Instalment buying. Charleston (dance). Cabarets. New York City.*

AN UNEXPECTED WIFE *see* **YOUTH MUST HAVE LOVE**

THE UNFAIR SEX **F2.5959**

Diamant Film Co. of America. *Dist* Associated Exhibitors. 17 Apr **1926** [c5 May 1926; LU22676]. Si; b&w. 35mm. 5 reels, 5,016 ft.

Dir Henri Diamant-Berger. *Titl* Arthur Hoerl. *Story* Eugene Walter. *Photog* Alfred Ortlieb.

Cast: Hope Hampton *(Shirley Chamberlain)*, Holbrook Blinn *(Don Calvert)*, Nita Naldi *(Blanchita D'Acosta)*, Walter Miller *(William Emerson)*.

Society melodrama. On the night that Shirley Chamberlain's father announces her engagement to Billy Emerson, her childhood sweetheart, Don Calvert, a stranger from the city, is present. Learning that Billy is to spend a year establishing himself before the marriage, Calvert invites him to New York; and following a tearful farewell he sets out. Calvert arranges for Billy to become infatuated with Blanchita D'Acosta, a revue star, then summons Shirley to the city; but when Calvert undertakes a flirtation with Shirley, Blanchita becomes violently jealous. At a nightclub with Calvert, Shirley pretends to be gay and frivolous, shocking Billy and provoking his wrath. Drugged by Calvert, she is taken to his apartment; Billy arrives to find her defying him for stealing her jewels, rescues her, and takes her home. *Actors. Courtship. Jealousy. Lechery. Narcotics. New York City.*

THE UNFOLDMENT **F2.5960**

Producers Pictures. *Dist* Associated Exhibitors. 1 Jan **1922** [c31 Dec 1921; LU17413]. Si; b&w. 35mm. 6 reels, 5,795 ft.

Dir George Kern, Murdock MacQuarrie. *Story-Scen* James Couldwell, Reed Heustis. *Photog* Hal Mohr, Edward Gheller.

Cast: Florence Lawrence *(Katherine Nevin)*, Barbara Bedford *(Martha Osborne)*, Charles French *(James Osborne)*, William Conklin *(Charles MacLaughlin)*, Albert Prisco *(Angus)*, Lydia Knott *(Mrs. MacLaughlin)*, Raymond Cannon *(Jack Nevin)*, Murdock MacQuarrie *(Mayor of Avenue A)*, Wade Boteler *(Ted Packham)*.

Melodrama. Katherine Nevin and her brother Jack are given positions on the newspaper of James Osborne following their father's death. Osborne's city editor, Charles MacLaughlin, who is hated and feared by his business associates, is strongly attracted to Katherine, who accepts his mother's invitation to dinner. In spite of his ruthless manner Katherine tries to change the atheistic views of "Mac" and his embittered crippled brother, Angus. Jack, who loves Osborne's daughter, Martha, discovers a case of graft involving the Mayor of Avenue A, who has been ruined by Osborne. The publisher becomes infuriated at Jack's attentions to Martha, and when Martha intervenes she is crippled by a fall and declared an invalid. Katherine is assigned by Osborne to make a film showing him as a philanthropic political candidate; the picture, called "The Unfoldment," shows, however, the characters as they are in real life. Osborne, stunned by the revelation and Martha's miraculous recovery, asks the "mayor's" forgiveness, and Angus kneels by his mother in prayer. *Editors. Brothers. Cripples. Brother-sister relationship. Newspapers. Graft. Miracles. Motion pictures. Religious conversion. Atheism.*

UNGUARDED GIRLS **F2.5961**

Circle Films. *Dist* Public Welfare Pictures. 31 Aug **1929** [New York showing; New York State license: 25 Apr 1930]. Mus score; b&w. 35mm. 7 reels. [Also si.]

Dir William Curran. *Story* Jack Townley.

Cast: Paddy O'Flynn, Marcella Arnold, Alphonse Martell, Jean Porter, Jack Hopkins, Merle Ferris, Tom Gentry, Ida May.

Melodrama. "Mary, the daughter of a wealthy attorney for the underworld, getting caught in the snare of the roadhouse that her father owns. Of course there is her upstanding chauffeur, who is in love with Mary and who comes to the rescue just in time. The 'big' sex scene shows Mary under the influence of knockout drops in a room of the roadhouse, where the manager has himself flashlighted alongside the unconscious gal partially disrobed. ... Then the old blackmail gag." (*Film Daily*, 8 Sep 1929, p8.) *Lawyers. Chauffeurs. White slave traffic. Blackmail. Roadhouses.*

THE UNGUARDED HOUR **F2.5962**

First National Pictures. 22 Nov **1925** [c20 Nov 1925; LP22022]. Si; b&w. 35mm. 7 reels, 6,613 ft.

Prod under supv of Earl Hudson. *Dir* Lambert Hillyer. *Scen* Joseph Poland. *Titl* John Krafft. *Story* Margaretta Tuttle. *Photog* Roy Carpenter. *Art Dir* Milton Menasco. *Film Ed* Arthur Tavares.

Cast: Milton Sills *(Andrea)*, Doris Kenyon *(Virginia Gilbert)*, Claude King *(Bryce Gilbert)*, Dolores Cassinelli *(Duchess Bianca)*, Cornelius Keefe *(Russell Van Alstyne)*, Jed Prouty *(Gus O'Rorick, a yeggman)*, Tammany Young *(another yeggman)*, Charles Beyer *(Stelio)*, Lorna Duveen *(Elena)*, Vivia Ogden *(Annie, the maid)*, J. Moy Bennett *(butler)*.

Society comedy-drama. Bryce Gilbert convinces his daughter, Virginia, that she should not elope with a casual boyfriend and sends her to Italy to stay with his fiancée, Duchess Bianca. Bianca's nephew, Duke Andrea d'Arona, is indifferent to women and devotes his time to experiments with ether waves. Virginia arrives in an airplane, which crashes into Andrea's radio tower. Eventually, he succumbs to Virginia's charms. Elena, Andrea's sister, has been indiscreet in her love for Count Stelio Danieli, and he refuses to marry her. She asks Virginia to plead with Stelio. Virginia invites Stelio to her room, and there he makes advances to her. Andrea and Bianca come into the room and find the two in a compromising situation. Virginia refuses to explain, hoping to protect Elena. Elena kills herself, leaving a note explaining her unrequited love. Andrea attempts to kill Stelio, and a fight ensues in which Stelio falls to his death. The tragedy brings Virginia and Andrea to a deeper understanding of their love. *Nobility. Fatherhood. Seduction. Suicide. Radio. Airplane accidents. Italy.*

UNGUARDED WOMEN **F2.5963**

Famous Players–Lasky. *Dist* Paramount Pictures. 22 Jun **1924** [New York showing; released 17 Aug; c9 Jul 1924; LP20383]. Si; b&w. 35mm. 6 reels, 6,500 ft.

Pres by Adolph Zukor, Jesse L. Lasky. *Dir* Alan Crosland. *Scen* James Ashmore Creelman. *Photog* Henry Cronjager.

Cast: Bebe Daniels *(Breta Banning)*, Richard Dix *(Douglas Albright)*, Mary Astor *(Helen Castle)*, Walter McGrail *(Larry Trent)*, Frank Losee *(George Castle)*, Helen Lindroth *(Aunt Louise)*, Harry Mestayer *(Sing Woo)*, Donald Hall *(James Craig)*, Joe King *(Capt. Robert Banning)*.

Melodrama. Source: Lucy Stone Terrill, "Face," in *Saturday Evening Post* (196:8–9, 26 Jan 1924). Douglas Albright, a hero just returned from the war, is conscience-striken over allowing his buddy to die. Taking charge of his future father-in-law's business, he goes to China to gain self-control. There he meets his friend's widow and offers to give up Helen, his fiancée, for her; however, the widow's suicide frees him from this obligation, and he finds happiness with Helen. *War heroes. Veterans. Suicide. World War I. China.*

THE UNHOLY NIGHT *see* **LE SPECTRE VERT**

THE UNHOLY NIGHT **F2.5964**

Metro-Goldwyn-Mayer Pictures. 14 Sep **1929** [c23 Sep 1929; LP703]. Sd (Movietone); b&w. 35mm. 10 reels, 8,498 ft.

Dir Lionel Barrymore. *Screenplay* Edwin Justus Mayer. *Titl* Joe Farnham. *Adapt* Dorothy Farnum. *Story* Ben Hecht. *Photog* Ira Morgan. *Art Dir* Cedric Gibbons. *Film Ed* Grant Whytock. *Rec Engr* Paul Neal, Douglas Shearer. *Gowns* Adrian.

Cast—In Lord Montague's Home: Ernest Torrence *(Dr. Ballou)*, Roland Young *(Lord Montague)*, Dorothy Sebastian *(Lady Efra)*, Natalie Moorhead *(Lady Vi)*, Sidney Jarvis *(butler)*, Polly Moran *(maid)*, George Cooper *(orderly)*, Sojin *(mystic)*, Boris Karloff *(Abdoul)*.

Cast—In Scotland Yard: Claude Fleming *(Sir James Ramsey [Rumsey?])*, Clarence Geldert *(Inspector Lewis)*.

Cast—In the Doomed Regiment: John Miljan *(Major Mallory)*, Richard Tucker *(Colonel Davidson)*, John Loder *(Captain Dorchester)*, Philip Strange *(Lieutenant Williams)*, John Roche *(Lieutenant Savor)*, Lionel Belmore *(Major Endicott)*, Gerald Barry *(Captain Bradley)*, Richard

Travers *(Major McDougal)*.

Mystery melodrama. Perceiving a pattern in the mysterious deaths of four members of an English regiment, Sir James Ramsey of Scotland Yard calls together the surviving members of the regiment in the hope of solving the murders. While they are assembled at the Montague mansion, Lady Efra, the daughter of the late Marquis of Cavendar, who was thrown out of the regiment for misconduct, arrives with her father's will. Dividing his vast fortune among Efra and the members of the regiment, and making them guardians of his daughter, Cavendar hopes to harvest his lifelong hatred by causing the regiment to fight over his money and his daughter. Each officer is suspected of being the murderer until Ramsey discovers, through a fake seance, that Efra and Mallory, one of the officers, plan to murder the whole regiment and take possession of the fortune. *Detectives. Heirs. Murder. Spiritualism. Wills. Great Britain—Army. Scotland Yard. London.*

THE UNHOLY THREE **F2.5965**

Metro-Goldwyn-Mayer Pictures. 16 Aug **1925** [c24 Jun 1925; LP21593]. Si; b&w. 35mm. 7 reels, 6,948 ft.

Pres by Louis B. Mayer. *Dir* Tod Browning. *Screenplay* Waldemar Young. *Photog* David Kesson. *Sets* Cedric Gibbons, Joseph Wright. *Film Ed* Daniel J. Gray. *Rec Engr* Anstruther MacDonald.

Cast: Lon Chaney *(Echo)*, Mae Busch *(Rosie O'Grady)*, Matt Moore *(Hector McDonald)*, Victor McLaglen *(Hercules)*, Harry Earles *(Tweedledee)*, Harry Betz *(Regan)*, Edward Connelly *(judge)*, William Humphreys *(attorney)*, A. E. Warren *(prosecuting attorney)*, John Merkyl *(jeweler)*, Charles Wellesley *(John Arlington)*.

Melodrama. Source: Clarence Aaron Robbins, *The Unholy Three* (New York, 1917). Three dime museum freaks—Hercules (a strongman), Professor Echo (a ventriloquist), and Tweedledee, a dwarf—perform in a sideshow, while Rosie O'Grady, who is in league with them, goes through the crowd picking pockets. Seeking larger stakes, the three men hit upon a plan to make themselves rich. They open a store stocked with parrots that will not talk, and Echo, disguised as an old woman, works in the store, making the birds seem to talk by ventriloquism. After the birds are sold, if there are any complaints by dissatisfied customers, Echo goes to the customer's house, pushing Tweedledee, disguised as a baby, in a baby carriage. The two men then look over the customer's house, while Echo makes the bird talk again, silencing the customer's complaint. They later return and rob the likely houses. They hire Hector, a gentle clerk, and Rosie falls in love with him. Hercules and Tweedledee kill someone while on a job, and Hector is blamed for the crime. Rosie and "The Unholy Three" take to the hills, and Rosie promises to stay with Echo if he will save Hector; Echo returns to the city and has Hector acquitted by testifying for him—sitting on the witness stand mumbling the Lord's Prayer. Echo later allows Rosie to go to Hector, and a gorilla kills Hercules and Tweedledee. *Strongmen. Dwarfs. Pickpockets. Salesclerks. Ventriloquism. Murder. Trials. Sideshows. Museums. Female impersonation. Parrots. Apes.*

Note: Remade in 1930 under the same title, q. v.

THE UNHOLY THREE **F2.5966**

Metro-Goldwyn-Mayer Pictures. 4 Jul **1930** [New York premiere; released 12 Jul; c2 Jul 1930; LP1391]. Sd (Movietone); b&w. 35mm. 8 reels, 6,300 ft.

Dir Jack Conway. *Cont-Dial* J. C. Nugent, Elliott Nugent. *Photog* Percy Hilburn. *Art Dir* Cedric Gibbons. *Film Ed* Frank Sullivan. *Rec Engr* Anstruther MacDonald, Douglas Shearer. *Wardrobe* David Cox.

Cast: Lon Chaney *(Echo)*, Lila Lee *(Rosie)*, Elliott Nugent *(Hector)*, Harry Earles *(Midget)*, John Miljan *(prosecuting attorney)*, Ivan Linow *(Hercules)*, Clarence Burton *(Regan)*, Crauford Kent *(defense attorney)*.

Melodrama. Source: Clarence Aaron Robbins, *The Unholy Three* (New York, 1917). The story line is essentially the same as that of the 1925 silent version, enhanced by Chaney's ability at vocal impersonation. *Strongmen. Dwarfs. Pickpockets. Salesclerks. Ventriloquism. Murder. Trials. Sideshows. Museums. Female impersonation. Parrots. Apes.*

THE UNINVITED GUEST **F2.5967**

Submarine Film Corp. *Dist* Metro Pictures. 11 Feb **1924** [c26 Feb 1924; LP19962]. Si; b&w with col sequence (Technicolor). 35mm. 7 reels, 6,145 ft.

Pres by J. Ernest Williamson. *Dir* Ralph Ince. *Story-Scen* Curtis Benton. *Photog* J. O. Taylor. *Studio Sets* Tec-Art Studios. *Tech Asst* Gordon Mayer.

Cast: Maurice B. Flynn *(Paul "Gin" Patterson)*, Jean Tolley *(Olive Granger)*, Mary MacLaren *(Irene Carlton)*, William Bailey *(Fred Morgan)*, Louis Wolheim *(Jan Boomer)*.

Melodrama. Heiress Olive Granger survives a shipwreck in the South Seas and is washed ashore an island along with international crooks Irene Carlton and Fred Morgan, who steal her credentials and escape to America, where Irene poses as Olive. Paul Patterson and Jan Boomer, divers, find Olive abandoned in a cave and fight through the jungle in competition for the girl. While diving for pearls, the treacherous Boomer dies in the clutching coils of a giant octopus. Olive and Paul arrive in New York, expose the imposters, and get married. *Heiresses. Divers. Thieves. Imposture. South Sea Islands. New York City. Shipwrecks. Octopi.*

Note: Natural color scenes by the Technicolor Motion Picture Corp. utilized underwater camera patents of the Williamson Submarine Corp.

UNITED STATES SMITH **F2.5968**

Gotham Productions. *Dist* Lumas Film Corp. 15 Jun **1928** [c21 Jul 1928; LP25480]. Si; b&w. 35mm. 7 reels, 7,022 ft.

Pres by Sam Sax. *Prod* Harold Shumate. *Dir* Joseph Henabery. *Screenplay* Curtis Benton. *Scen* Louis Stevens. *Story* Gerald Beaumont. *Photog* Ray June.

Cast: Eddie Gribbon *(Sgt. Steve Riley)*, Lila Lee *(Molly Malone)*, Mickey Bennett *(Ugo [U. S. Smith])*, Kenneth Harlan *(Cpl. Jim Sharkey)*, Earle Marsh *(Danny)*.

Melodrama. Sgt. Steve Riley, a Marine, is returning to the States to box Army Cpl. Jim Sharkey for the championship. Aboard ship, Steve meets a poor Russian boy named Ugo who has no family, and Steve takes him into the service as a sort of mascot, calling him U. S. Smith. After Ugo saves Steve's life, the sergeant decides to give him a good education and agrees to throw the fight to obtain the money for his plan. Ugo begs him not to do so, and Steve, after seeing Sharkey wearing his girl friend Molly's charm (which Ugo has placed on him purposely in order to rile Steve), wins the fight out of anger. Everything is worked out, however, and all ends happily. *Russians. Orphans. Boxing. Jealousy. United States Army. United States Marines.*

THE UNKNOWN **F2.5969**

Phil Goldstone Productions. 25 Dec **1921** [New York State]. Si; b&w. 35mm. 5 reels.

Dir Grover Jones. *Photog* Harry Fowler.

Cast: Richard Talmadge *(Dick Talmadge/The Unknown)*, Andrée Tourneur *(Sylvia Sweet)*, Mark Fenton *(Parker Talmadge)*, J. W. Early *(J. Malcolm Sweet)*.

Stunt melodrama. In the days of hard times Dick Talmadge leads a double life: he is the indolent son of Parker Talmadge, the controlling power in the flour market; and he masquerades as The Unknown, a champion of the people and leader of the fight against high prices. Mr. Talmadge and sugar baron J. Malcolm Sweet agree that Dick should marry Sylvia Sweet, but Sylvia disapproves of Dick's worthlessness and considers The Unknown the man of her dreams. A raid on the profiteer's stored goods causes a panic among the financiers, who unsuccessfully set detectives on The Unknown's trail, then stage a grand reception as a trap for their enemy. The plot fails, but Dick is unmasked in a fight. Sylvia changes her mind about the young man, and all ends happily. *Financiers. Profiteers. Dual lives. Price control. Sugar. Flour.*

THE UNKNOWN **F2.5970**

Metro-Goldwyn-Mayer Pictures. 4 Jun **1927** [c27 Jun 1927; LP24123]. Si; b&w. 35mm. 6 reels, 5,517 ft. [Copyrighted as 7 reels.]

Dir-Story Tod Browning. *Scen* Waldemar Young. *Titl* Joe Farnham. *Photog* Merritt Gerstad. *Art Dir* Cedric Gibbons, Richard Day. *Film Ed* Harry Reynolds, Errol Taggart. *Wardrobe* Lucia Coulter.

Cast: Lon Chaney *(Alonzo)*, Norman Kerry *(Malabar)*, Joan Crawford *(Estrellita)*, Nick De Ruiz *(Zanzi)*, John George *(Cojo)*, Frank Lanning *(Costra)*.

Melodrama. To escape the police, Alonzo, who has two thumbs on one hand, poses in a sideshow as an armless wonder. He falls in love with Estrellita, and when detected by her father, he kills him. Then, discovering that the girl abhors the touch of a man's hand, he has both his arms amputated. Returning, he finds to his dismay that she has fallen in love with Malabar and is to marry him; Alonzo seeks revenge on Malabar, but loses his own life. *Freaks. Revenge. Self-sacrifice. Frigidity. Amputation. Circus.*

THE UNKNOWN CAVALIER F2.5971

Charles R. Rogers Productions. *Dist* First National Pictures. 14 Nov **1926** [c27 Sep 1926; LP23156]. Si; b&w. 35mm. 7 reels, 6,595 ft.

Pres by Charles R. Rogers. *Dir* Albert Rogell. *Titl* Don Ryan. *Adapt* Marion Jackson. *Photog* Sol Polito. *Prod Mgr* Harry J. Brown.

Cast: Ken Maynard *(Tom Drury)*, Kathleen Collins *(Ruth Gaunt)*, David Torrence *(Peter Gaunt)*, T. Roy Barnes *(Clout Pettingill)*, James Mason *(Henry Suggs)*, Otis Harlan *(Judge Blowfly Jones)*, Joseph Swickard *(Lingo)*, Bruce Gordon *(Bob Webb)*, Fred Burns *(sheriff)*, Jimsy Boudwin *(Billy Gaunt)*, Pat Harmon, Frank Lackteen, Raymond Wells *(The Three Bad Men)*, Tarzan *(himself, a horse)*.

Western melodrama. Source: Kenneth Perkins, *Ride Him Cowboy* (New York, 1923). Henry Suggs, by daytime a vigilante and leading citizen of the town of Cattelo, is by night a marauder who terrorizes the countryside; his true identity is known only by Tarzan, a horse whose master is killed by the desperado. Suggs succeeds in having the horse condemned to death because of his supposed wickedness, but Ruth Gaunt, daughter of the murdered man, persuades Tom Drury, an itinerant cowboy, to find a way to save Tarzan. A permanent friendship springs up between Tom and the horse, while Tom and Suggs become rivals for the hand of Ruth. After a number of narrow escapes, Tom and Tarzan unmask the villain and ride triumphantly home with their prisoner. *Cowboys. Vigilantes. Bandits. Duplicity. Murder. Horses.*

UNKNOWN DANGERS F2.5972

Hercules Film Productions. 15 Apr **1926** [c15 May 1926; LP22726]. Si; b&w. 35mm. 5 reels, 4,900 ft.

Pres by Peter Kanellos. *Dir-Writ* Grover Jones.

Cast: Frank Merrill *(Frank Carter)*, Gloria Grey *(Corliss McHenry)*, Eddie Boland *(David Parker?)*, Marcin Asher, Emily Gerdes, Theodore Lorch.

Comedy-drama. Theatrical producer David Parker and his stage manager, Joe Greve, are dismayed to find that critic Frank Carter has panned their latest play as being untrue to life. At the same time they learn that Red Wilson, an ex-convict, has kidnaped Corliss, the daughter of Judge McHenry; and Parker has members of the company disguise themselves as members of the Wilson gang, while Flossie Martini, the leading lady, pretends to be Corliss for Carter's benefit. Although wise to their hoax, Carter goes through with the act and is directed to the Ghost House, where the actual gang is headquartered. Realizing they are not play-acting, Carter is wounded in aiding Corliss; the acting troupe arrives, and all are imprisoned by Wilson's gang. Parker and Greve bring in the police; the gang is arrested, and Corliss and Carter admit their love; and Parker triumphs in thus proving the strangeness of reality. *Theatrical producers. Stage managers. Actors. Critics. Theatrical troupes. Gangs. Kidnaping. Hoaxes.*

THE UNKNOWN LOVER F2.5973

Victory Pictures. *Dist* Vitagraph Co. of America. 30 Oct **1925** [New York showing; c11 Jul 1925; LP21647]. Si; b&w. 35mm. 7 reels, 6,895 ft.

Dir-Writ Victor Hugo Halperin.

Cast: Frank Mayo *(Kenneth Billings)*, Elsie Ferguson *(Elaine Kent)*, Mildred Harris *(Gale Norman)*, Peggy Kelly *(Gladys)*, Leslie Austin *(Fred Wagner)*.

Drama. Upon the death of her father, a research chemist, Elaine Kent marries Kenneth Billings, the charming, irresponsible young son of a wealthy family. Kenneth is immediately disinherited by his father and, using a dye formula developed by Elaine's father, goes into business for himself, becoming extremely successful and devoting himself to work at the expense of his health. When Kenneth appears to be on the verge of a nervous breakdown, Elaine deliberately sets out to ruin his business by changing the bid on an all-important contract; Kenneth's creditors then quickly foreclose. When he discovers that Elaine was responsible for his bankruptcy, Kenneth accuses her of being in league with Fred Wagner, one of her former suitors and his biggest rival in the dye business. Kenneth, who then disappears for a year, returns from a sea voyage in the best of health and asks Elaine to forgive him for neglecting her. She then discloses that, at the time she changed the bid, she secretly went into business with Fred. Kenneth and Elaine are reunited, and he makes plans to resume his business career in partnership with Fred. *Chemists. Businesswomen. Disinheritance. Bankruptcy. Neurosis. Contracts. Business management. Partnerships. Dye.*

THE UNKNOWN PURPLE F2.5974

Carlos Productions. *Dist* Truart Film Corp. Oct **1923** [c8 Dec 1923; LP19682]. Si; b&w. 35mm. 7 reels, 6,950-7,800 ft.

Dir Roland West. *Titl* Alfred A. Cohn. *Adapt* Roland West, Paul Schofield. *Photog* Oliver T. Marsh. *Set Dsgn* Horace Jackson. *Film Ed* Alfred A. Cohn.

Cast: Henry B. Walthall *(Peter Marchmont/Victor Cromport)*, Alice Lake *(Jewel Marchmont)*, Stuart Holmes *(James Dawson)*, Helen Ferguson *(Ruth Marsh)*, Frankie Lee *(Bobbie)*, Ethel Grey Terry *(Mrs. Freddie Goodlittle)*, James Morrison *(Leslie Bradbury)*, Johnny Arthur *(Freddie Goodlittle)*, Richard Wayne *(George Allison)*, Brinsley Shaw *(Hawkins)*, Mike Donlin *(Burton)*.

Mystery melodrama. Source: Roland West and Carlyle Moore, *The Unknown Purple* (New York opening: 14 Sep 1918). Inventor Peter Marchmont has discovered a purple light that renders the user invisible. On his release from prison, Marchmont, disguised as Victor Cromport, uses the light to revenge himself against his former wife, Jewel, and her partner, James Dawson, who framed him for theft. Making himself invisible, Marchmont gradually ruins Dawson. He so wins Jewel's confidence and love that she is willing to kill Dawson at Marchmont's request. Finally, Marchmont leaves the scheming couple to their own misery and marries Jewel's sister, Ruth Marsh. *Inventors. Sisters. Frameup. Revenge. Disguise. Invisibility.*

THE UNKNOWN RIDER F2.5975

Robert J. Horner Productions. *Dist* Associated Independent Producers. 1 Jun **1929**. Si; b&w. 35mm. 5 reels, 4,564 ft.

Dir A. R. Meals. *Scen* Fred Church. *Titl* H. B. Otis. *Photog* John Jenkins.

Cast: Fred Church, Frank Lanning, Mary Lou Winn, Jack Kruger.

Western melodrama(?). No information about the nature of this film has been found.

THE UNKNOWN SOLDIER F2.5976

Renaud Hoffman Productions. *Dist* Producers Distributing Corp. 30 May **1926** [c10 May 1926; LP22725]. Si; b&w. 35mm. 8 reels, 7,979 ft.

Pres by Charles R. Rogers. *Prod-Dir* Renaud Hoffman. *Scen* E. Richard Schayer. *Adapt* James J. Tynan. *Theme suggested by* Dorothy Farnum. *Photog* Ray June.

Cast: Charles Emmett Mack *(Fred Williams)*, Marguerite De La Motte *(Mary Phillips)*, Henry B. Walthall *(Mr. Phillips)*, Claire McDowell *(Mrs. Phillips)*, George Cooper *(Corporal Fogarty)*, Syd Crossley *(Peaceful Perkins)*, Jess Devorska *(Mike Ginsberg)*, Willis Marks *(Reverend Doctor Mortimer)*.

War drama. When the United States declares war on Germany in 1917, Fred Williams, a millworker in the little town of Homewood, leaves his sweetheart, Mary Phillips, enlists, and goes to France. At a variety show, Fred recognizes one of the dancers as Mary, who has joined the Entertainment Division; and she agrees to marry him the day before a troop advance. Too late to convey the fact to Fred she learns that the marriage ceremony was performed by a deserter who had disguised himself as a chaplain. At the front, Fred receives a letter from Mary telling him all, adding that she is with child and awaits his return at Loure; in desperation, he volunteers to contact American troops cut off between a farmhouse and Loure; he is successful but is wounded by a shell on his return and is assumed lost. When peace comes, Mary returns home with her child and is turned away by her father; at the burial of the unknown soldier in Arlington, however, Fred, a victim of shell shock, is reunited with Mary, and the parents are reconciled to the young couple. *Illegitimacy. Courtship. Disguise. Shell shock. Smalltown life. World War I. France. The Unknown Soldier.*

UNKNOWN TREASURES F2.5977

Sterling Pictures. 1 Sep **1926** [c10 Sep 1926; LP23089]. Si; b&w. 35mm. 6 reels, 5,643 ft.

Dir Archie Mayo. *Adapt-Cont* Charles A. Logue. *Photog* Harry Davis.

Cast: Gladys Hulette *(Mary Hamilton)*, Robert Agnew *(Bob Ramsey)*, John Miljan *(Ralph Cheney)*, Bertram Marburgh *(Cyrus Hamilton)*, Jed Prouty *(Remus)*, Gustav von Seyffertitz *(Simmons)*.

Mystery-melodrama. Source: Mary Spain Vigus, "The House Behind the Hedge" (publication undetermined). Bob Ramsey, who loves Mary, niece of banker Cyrus Hamilton, declines to propose to her because of his poverty and devotes himself to uncovering missing securities belonging to his uncle, though he operates a public garage with the assistance of Remus, a devoted Negro. Receiving notice from his uncle's lawyers, Bob is advised to search his uncle's deserted house for the securities; his cousin Ralph, who also loves Mary, also sets out, secretly, to find the treasure. Mary conspires with her uncle to plant bonds in the house, hoping to facilitate an engagement. Bob discovers Cheney, Mary, and her uncle, when Cheney, trying to hide, takes refuge in the very closet that conceals Mary and Hamilton; he locks up Cheney. Later, Cheney is found strangled; and by trailing an ape, Bob discovers that Simmons, the caretaker, has stolen the securities found by his cousin. The ape attacks Bob but then revolts and kills Simmons. Bob and Mary are happily united. *Bankers. Uncles. Caretakers. Courtship. Murder. Treasure. Garages. Documentation. Apes.*

THE UNKNOWN WIFE **F2.5978**

Universal Film Manufacturing Co. 14 Mar **1921** [c7 Mar 1921; LP16260]. Si; b&w. 35mm. 5 reels, 4,854 ft.

Dir William Worthington. *Scen* Wallace Clifton. *Story* Bennett Cohen. *Photog* William Edmonds.

Cast: Edith Roberts *(Helen Wilburton)*, Spottiswoode Aitken *(Henry Wilburton)*, Casson Ferguson *(Donald Grant)*, Joe Quinn *("Lefty" Mayes)*, Joe Neary *("Slim" Curry)*, Augustus Phillips *(John Mayberry)*, Bertram Frank *(Thomas Gregory)*, Mathilde Brundage *(Mrs. Stanwood Kent)*, Jessie Pratt *(Mrs. Dalton)*, Edith Stayart *(Doris Dalton)*, Hal Wilson *(Brooks)*.

Melodrama. Donald Grant, after serving a prison term, obtains a job in a smalltown factory where he meets Helen Wilburton, who invites him to board with her and her father. He marries her, and on the first night of their honeymoon a burglary is traced to one of Donald's former cohorts. Though he himself is shadowed by detectives, Helen is faithful and helpful when he loses his job. The deathbed confession of the burglar clears his name, and his job is restored to him. *Criminals—Rehabilitation. Burglary. Factories.*

Note: Working title: *Three at the Table.*

THE UNMARRIED BRIDE *see* **LUXURY**

UNMARRIED WIVES **F2.5979**

Gotham Productions. *Dist* Lumas Film Corp. 1 Aug **1924** [c19 Aug 1924; LP20524]. Si; b&w. 35mm. 6 reels.

Pres by Samuel Sax. *Prod-Dir* James P. Hogan. *Story-Adapt* Dorothy Howell. *Photog* Jack MacKenzie.

Cast: Mildred Harris *(Princess Sonya [Maggie])*, Gladys Brockwell *(Mrs. Gregory)*, Lloyd Whitlock *(Tom Gregory)*, Bernard Randall *(Morris Sands)*, George Cooper *(Joe Dugan)*, Mrs. Davenport *("Ma" Casey)*, Majel Coleman *(Mrs. Lowell)*.

Society drama. Maggie Casey, who through the efforts of her press agent has become famous in a New York revue as Princess Sonya, spends much time with Tom Gregory, whose wife learns of their affair and is herself the victim of a publicity-kidnaping case. Meanwhile, the theater manager tries to attack Maggie but is thwarted by a fire from which she is rescued by her sweetheart, Joe. The Gregorys are reconciled, and all ends happily. *Actors. Theater. Kidnaping. Infidelity.*

UNMASKED **F2.5980**

Weiss Brothers Artclass Pictures. 15 Dec **1929**. Sd (De Forest Phonofilm); b&w. 35mm. 6 reels, 5,559 ft.

Dir Edgar Lewis. *Scen* Albert Cowles. *Dial* Bert Ennis, Edward Clark. *Story* Arthur B. Reeve. *Photog* Thomas Malloy, Buddy Harris, Irving Browning. *Film Ed* Martin G. Cohn.

Cast: Robert Warwick *(Craig Kennedy)*, Milton Krims *(Prince Hamid)*, Sam Ash *(Billy Mathews)*, Charles Slattery *(Inspector Collins)*, Susan Conroy *(Mary Wayne)*, Lyons Wickland *(Larry Jamieson)*, William Corbett *(Franklin Ward)*, Roy Byron *(Cafferty)*, Marie Burke *(Mrs. Brookfield)*, Kate Roemer *(Madam Ramon)*, Helen Mitchell *(Mrs. Ward)*, Waldo Edwards *(Gordon Hayes)*, Clyde Dillson *(imposter)*.

Mystery drama. At a society gathering in the home of Mrs. Brookfield, detective Craig Kennedy tells the story of one of his unsolved cases (in flashback)—the mysterious poison murder of Mrs. Franklin Ward. Although Kennedy had discovered that the suspect, Mary Wayne (later, Kennedy's fiancée), had administered the poison under the hypnotic influence of Prince Hamid, that East Indian mystic slipped out of the hands of the police and is still at large. It soon becomes apparent that Kennedy's story is part of a strategem to expose and capture Prince Hamid, who is at the party in the guise of Count Sebastian Domingo de Navarre, and whose forearm scar provides proof of Kennedy's identification. (Also in flashback Kennedy relates how he exposed a seance rigged by Hamid for the benefit of Franklin Ward, who sought contact with his deceased son.) *Detectives. Mystics. Socialites. East Indians. Hypnotism. Spiritualism. Murder. Disguise.*

THE UNNAMED WOMAN **F2.5981**

Embassy Pictures. *Dist* Arrow Pictures. 24 Oct **1925** [c19 Oct 1925; LU21924]. Si; b&w. 35mm. 6 reels, 6,300 ft.

Prod Arthur F. Beck. *Dir* Harry O. Hoyt. *Writ* Charles E. Blaney. *Story* Leah Baird.

Cast: Katherine MacDonald *(Flora Brookes)*, Herbert Rawlinson *(Donald Brookes)*, Wanda Hawley *(Doris Gray)*, Leah Baird *(Billie Norton)*, John Miljan *(Archie Wesson)*, Mike Donlin *(chauffeur)*, Grace Gordon, J. Emmett Beck.

Melodrama. Hounded by creditors, Doris Gray decides to marry a rich husband. With the aid of a friend, Billie Norton, she weds idler and spender Archie Wesson while he is drunk, only to find out that he, too, is broke. Unhappy in their marriage, they invite Flora Brookes to stay the night while her husband is out of town. James, Archie's ex-chauffeur, attempts to rob the house and frightens Flora, who summons Archie to her room. Doris and Billie discover them in a compromising situation, and Doris sues for divorce. For a sum of money, she promises Flora not to name her as corespondent. Doris hires Flora's husband, Donald, as her attorney but unwittingly blurts out Flora's name as "The Unnamed Woman." In a rage, Donald demands that Flora explain; she tells him about the intruder, but he does not believe her. He then whips Archie in a fight, but the chauffeur arrives and confesses. Flora and Donald are reunited, and Doris and Archie decide to make a fresh start. *Fortune hunters. Idlers. Lawyers. Burglars. Drunkenness. Debt. Marriage. Divorce. Blackmail.*

UNRESTRAINED YOUTH **F2.5982**

Lee-Bradford Corp. 25 May **1925** [New York State premiere]. Si; b&w. 35mm. 6 reels, 5,800 ft.

Dir Joseph Levering.

Cast: Brandon Tynan *(John Powers)*, Gardner James *(Jamie Powers)*, Mildred Arden *(Mary Powers)*, Blanche Davenport *(Mrs. Powers, Sr.)*, John Hopkins *(Fred Whitney)*, Deek Reynolds *(Arthur Blake)*, Alice Mann *(Betty Brown)*, Helen Lindroth *(Mrs. Brown)*, C. H. Keefe *(Jerry Powers)*, Charles McDonald *(Stewart Ransom)*, Thomas Brooks *(Randolph Smith)*.

Melodrama. Fred Whitney, a boy with a venemous temper, injures young Jamie Powers so severely that the child is brain-damaged for life. Whitney grows into a villainous manhood and attempts to implicate Jamie in an embezzlement scandal. Jamie's brother, John, then has no choice but to go to prison for 20 years in order to shield Jamie. *Brothers. Mental illness. Brain damage. Embezzlement. Temperament.*

UNSEEING EYES **F2.5983**

Cosmopolitan Productions. *Dist* Goldwyn-Cosmopolitan Distributing Corp. 21 Oct **1923** [New York premiere; released 18 Nov; c25 Nov 1923; LP19774]. Si; b&w. 35mm. 9 reels, 8,150 ft.

Dir E. H. Griffith. *Adapt* Bayard Veiller. *Photog* Al Siegler, John La Mond. *Set Dsgn* Joseph Urban. *Asst Dir* Bert Siebel.

Cast: Lionel Barrymore *(Conrad Dean)*, Seena Owen *(Miriam Helston)*, Louis Wolheim *(Laird)*, Gustav von Seyffertitz *(Father Paquette)*, Walter Miller *(Dick Helston)*, Charles Beyer *(Arkwright)*, Helen Lindroth *(Mrs. Arkwright)*, Jack Johnston *(Trapper)*, Louis Deer *(Eagle Blanket)*, Frances Red Eagle *(Singing Pine)*, Paul Panzer, Dan Red Eagle *(halfbreeds)*.

Northwest melodrama. Source: Arthur Stringer, "Snowblind," in *Hearst's International Magazine* (39:13–15, Mar 1921). Miriam Helston flies with ace pilot Conrad Dean to her brother's silver mine in the Canadian Rocky Mountains to help him take possession from illegal operators "Frozen Face" Laird and a crew of cutthroat halfbreeds. Miriam has been summoned by Laird's squaw, Singing Pine, who is protecting the wounded brother, Dick. En route, pilot Dean is forced to make an emergency landing in the snow. He becomes separated from Miriam, who, lost and blinded by the snow, ends up in Laird's clutches. Dean rescues Miriam from Laird after he (Dean) and Dick are saved by Singing Pine. Laird is shot by Singing Pine's father. Dean and Miriam marry. *Air pilots. Indians of North America. Halfcastes. Brother-sister relationship. Silver mines. Snow blindness. Canada.*

UNSEEN ENEMIES **F2.5984**

Morris R. Schlank Productions. *Dist* Anchor Film Distributors. 2 Apr **1926** [New York State license]. Si; b&w. 35mm. 5 reels, ca4,500 ft.

Dir J. P. McGowan.
Cast: Al Hoxie.
Western melodrama(?). No information about the nature of this film has been found.

UNSEEN HANDS **F2.5985**
Encore Pictures. *Dist* Associated Exhibitors. 25 May **1924** [c12 May 1924; LU20192]. Si; b&w. 35mm. 6 reels, 5,382 ft.
Prod-Writ Walker Coleman Graves, Jr. *Dir* Jacques Jaccard.
Cast: Wallace Beery *(Jean Scholast)*, Joseph J. Dowling *(Georges Le Quintrec)*, Fontaine La Rue *(Madame Le Quintrec)*, Jack Rollins *(Armand Le Quintrec)*, Cleo Madison *(Matoaka)*, Jim Corey *(Wapita)*, Jamie Gray *(Nola)*.
Melodrama. At the insistence of his wife, Le Quintrec, a wealthy mineowner, hires wandering adventurer Jean Scholast as a reward for gallantry. When Quintrec dies as a result of Jean's plotting, she marries Jean, giving him power of attorney. Jean sells her property and flees to Arizona, where he marries an Indian squaw. Pursued by Armand, Le Quintrec's son, Jean dies of heart failure when Le Quintrec's spirit appears. *Indians of North America. Miners. Vagabonds. Ghosts. Bigamy. Miscegenation. Land rights. Wills. Arizona.*

THE UNTAMEABLE **F2.5986**
Universal Pictures. 10 Sep **1923** [c4 Aug 1923; LP19290]. Si; b&w. 35mm. 5 reels, 4,776 ft.
Dir Herbert Blache. *Cont* Hugh Hoffman. *Photog* Howard Oswald, Ben Kline.
Cast: Gladys Walton *(Edna Fielding/Joy Fielding)*, Malcolm McGregor *(Chester Castle)*, John Sainpolis *(Dr. Copin)*, Etta Lee *(Ah Moy)*.
Drama. Source: Gelette Burgess, *The White Cat* (Indianapolis, 1907). Chester Castle's fiancée, Joy Fielding, develops a split personality, thinking at times that she is cruel and vampish Edna Fielding. Castle discovers that Copin, Joy's physician, is hypnotizing her because he is interested in her money. Hoping to break the spell, Castle insists that they marry immediately. Copin, not to be discouraged, enters the house at night and hypnotizes Joy. Copin and Castle struggle; Copin is accidentally killed, and Joy is relieved of her split personality. *Physicians. Hypnotism. Split personality.*
Note: Known also as *The White Cat* and *The Two Souled Woman.*

UNTAMED **F2.5987**
Metro-Goldwyn-Mayer Pictures. 23 Nov **1929** [c7 Apr 1930; LP1209]. Sd (Movietone); b&w. 35mm. 9 reels, 7,911 ft. [Also si; 5,348 ft.]
Dir Jack Conway. *Adapt-Cont* Sylvia Thalberg, Frank Butler. *Dial* Willard Mack. *Titl* Lucille Newmark. *Photog* Oliver Marsh. *Art Dir* Cedric Gibbons, Van Nest Polglase. *Film Ed* William S. Gray, Charles Hockberg. *Song: "That Wonderful Something Is Love"* Joe Goodwin, Louis Alter. *Song: "Chant of the Jungle"* Nacio Herb Brown, Arthur Freed. *Rec Engr* Fred R. Morgan, Douglas Shearer. *Gowns* Adrian.
Cast: Joan Crawford *(Bingo)*, Robert Montgomery *(Andy)*, Ernest Torrence *(Ben Murchison)*, Holmes Herbert *(Howard Presley)*, John Miljan *(Bennock)*, Gwen Lee *(Marjory)*, Edward Nugent *(Paul)*, Don Terry *(Gregg)*, Gertrude Astor *(Mrs. Mason)*, Milton Fahrney *(Jollop)*, Lloyd Ingraham *(Dowling)*, Grace Cunard *(Billie)*, Wilson Benge *(Billcombe)*.
Musical comedy-drama. Source: Charles E. Scoggins, unidentified story. Bingo, an American girl, is reared in the uninhibited atmosphere of the jungle tropics by her father. Upon his death, she falls heir to his fortune accrued through oil investments. Her father's friend Ben Murchison takes her to New York, and en route she falls for Andy, an American, and decides to marry him; but her guardian, who has considerable difficulty in civilizing his young ward, induces her to wait. After a year in New York she becomes a lovely, cultured young lady, but Andy refuses to live on her fortune. Bingo finally takes matters into her own hands by having Murchison offer Andy a job in South America, ensuring their future happiness. *Guardians. Inheritance. Jungles. Oil business. South America. New York City.*

UNTAMED JUSTICE **F2.5988**
Biltmore Productions. 22 Jan **1929** [New York showing]. Si; b&w. 35mm. 7 reels, 5,700 ft.
Dir Harry Webb. *Story-Scen* John Francis Natteford. *Photog* Arthur Reeves.
Cast: Gaston Glass *(Norman Bard)*, Virginia Browne Faire *(Louise Hill)*, David Torrence *(George Morrow)*, Philo McCullough *(Herbert Winslow)*, Alice Lake *(Ann)*, Tom London, Sheldon Lewis *(The Sheriff)*, Arab *(himself)*, Muro *(himself)*.
Melodrama. Suspected of stealing her employer's bonds, Louise Hill escapes to her brother's Nevada ranch, where she meets an airmail pilot. The real crooks show up and trick the pilot into landing so that they can rob him, but instead the bandits are rounded up with the help of a horse and a dog. *Air pilots. Mail theft. Postal service. Nevada. Horses. Dogs.*

THE UNTAMED LADY **F2.5989**
Famous Players–Lasky. *Dist* Paramount Pictures. ca14 Mar **1926** [New York premiere; released 22 Mar; c22 Mar 1926; LP22508]. Si; b&w. 35mm. 7 reels, 6,132 ft.
Pres by Adolph Zukor, Jesse L. Lasky. *Dir* Frank Tuttle. *Scen* James Ashmore Creelman. *Photog* George Webber.
Cast: Gloria Swanson *(St. Clair Van Tassel)*, Lawrence Gray *(Larry Gastlen)*, Joseph Smiley *(Uncle George)*, Charles Graham *(Shorty)*.
Society melodrama. Source: Fannie Hurst, "The Untamed Lady" (publication undetermined). St. Clair Van Tassel, a wealthy society girl with an ungovernable temper, has broken numerous engagements because of her disposition and decides to retire to the country. On the way, she stalls her car in a stream and is aided by Larry Gastlen. Their friendship soon develops into love. Larry sails for Cuba on his yacht, having refused to allow St. Clair to accompany him; and when she is discovered to be a stowaway, he turns back to New York. She contrives to throw the yacht off course, and when they encounter a gale, the boat is battered and St. Clair is forced to substitute for an injured stoker. Reaching port, St. Clair departs for her hunting lodge in the Catskills, where Larry follows. Trying to catch her, Larry is hurt in a fall from his horse. At the hospital, St. Clair realizes that love has at last conquered her temper. *Yachtsmen. Stowaways. Stokers. Upper classes. Temperament. Courtship. Yachts. Catskill Mountains.*

UNTAMED YOUTH **F2.5990**
R-C Pictures. *Dist* Film Booking Offices of America. 5 May **1924** [c18 Apr 1924; LP20105]. Si; b&w. 35mm. 5 reels, 4,558 ft. [Copyrighted as 6 reels.]
Dir Emile Chautard. *Scen* Charles Stillson, Charles Beahan. *Photog* Joseph A. Dubray, Pierre Collings.
Cast—Release Version: Derelys Perdue *(Marcheta)*, Lloyd Hughes *(Robert Ardis)*, Ralph Lewis *(Joe Ardis)*, Emily Fitzroy *(Emily Ardis)*, Josef Swickard *(Pietro)*, Joseph J. Dowling *(Reverend Loranger)*, Tom O'Brien *(Jim Larson)*, Mickey McBan *(Ralph)*.
Cast—Copyright Version: Derelys Perdue *(Lila)*, Lloyd Hughes *(François)*, Ralph Lewis *(Antoine)*, Max Davidson *(Pierre)*, Mickey McBan *(Raoul)*, Josef Swickard *(Gorgio)*, Emily Fitzroy *(Manon)*, Caroline Rankin *(Madame Guernette)*.
Melodrama. Source: G. Marion Burton, *Born of the Cyclone* (a play; publication undetermined). Robert Ardis, a smalltown youth studying for the ministry, encounters a visiting Gypsy, Marcheta, and is displeased by her pagan conduct. When she saves the life of his younger brother, however, Robert becomes fascinated with her. Though scorning his religion, she saves his life during a storm by praying for a miracle, and in rescuing him she comes to believe in God. *Ministerial students. Gypsies. Brothers. Religion. Miracles. Paganism. Youth.*
Note: In the release version the story and the characters were altered to introduce the idea of religious conversion. Working title: *Beware the Woman.*

AN UNWILLING HERO **F2.5991**
Goldwyn Pictures. May **1921** [c28 Apr 1921; LP16433]. Si; b&w. 35mm. 5 reels, 4,759 ft.
Dir Clarence G. Badger. *Scen* Arthur F. Statter. *Photog* Marcel Le Picard. *Art Dir* Cedric Gibbons.
Cast: Will Rogers *(Dick)*, Molly Malone *(Nadine)*, John Bowers *(Hunter)*, Darrel Foss *(Richmond)*, Jack Curtis *(Boston Harry)*, George Kunkel, Dick Johnson, Larry Fisher, Leo Willis *(hoboes)*, Nick Cogley *(Negro servant)*, Edward Kimball *(Lovejoy)*.
Comedy-drama. Source: O. Henry, "Whistling Dick's Christmas Stocking," in *Roads of Destiny* (New York, 1909). Whistling Dick, a tramp fond of whistling classical tunes, arrives in New Orleans to discover that fellow hoboes plan to rob a plantation on Christmas night. They are aided by Richmond, a guest and suitor of Nadine, daughter of the house, who loves the overseer, Hunter. Dick refuses to join them, and on the road he meets Nadine and Hunter, who offer him a ride and give him a package

containing by error a pair of stockings. Dick warns the house of the robbers and is welcomed as a guest, given new clothes, and offered a job; but the next morning he resumes his wandering. *Tramps. Robbery. Plantations. Christmas. New Orleans.*

THE UNWRITTEN LAW **F2.5992**

Columbia Pictures. 1 Aug **1925** [c15 Aug 1925; LP21732]. Si; b&w. 35mm. 7 reels.

Supv Harry Cohn. *Dir* Edward J. Le Saint. *Story-Cont* Tom J. Hopkins. *Photog* Frank B. Good.

Cast: Elaine Hammerstein, Forrest Stanley, William V. Mong, Mary Alden, Charles Clary, John Fox, Jr., William Carroll.

Melodrama. Helen Merritt, the private secretary of John Randall, falls in love with Jack Wayne, one of Randall's employees. Having himself fallen in love with Helen, Randall sends Jack to Mexico, later faking reports that he has been killed in a saloon brawl. Randall then gets her father, an impoverished southern colonel, into his power by paying off some of the colonel's debts. Randall invites the Merritts to be his guests at his Long Island estate and persuades the brokenhearted Helen to marry him for the sake of her father's comfort. Jack returns from Mexico and arrives at Randall's estate in time to be the first to congratulate Helen on her marriage. Randall confesses his plot, but Helen decides to stay married to him rather than cause scandal. Randall is mysteriously murdered, and, despite Jack's false and noble confession, Helen is arrested. Miss Grant, Randall's housekeeper, confesses to the crime, however, telling the sheriff that Randall went back on his promise to give her child a name. *Secretaries. Housekeepers. Murder. Debt. Marriage. Illegitimacy. Long Island.*

UP AND AT 'EM **F2.5993**

R-C Pictures. *Dist* Film Booking Offices of America. 6 Aug **1922** [c6 Aug 1922; LP18188]. Si; b&w. 35mm. 5 reels, 4,580 ft.

Dir William A. Seiter. *Scen* Eve Unsell. *Story* William A. Seiter, Lewis Milestone. *Photog* Joseph A. Dubray.

Cast: Doris May *(Barbara Jackson)*, Hallam Cooley *(Bob Everett)*, J. Herbert Frank *(Carlos Casinelli)*, Otis Harlan *(William Jackson)*, Clarissa Selwynne *(Jane Jackson)*, John Gough, Harry Carter *(crooks)*.

Romantic comedy. Barbara Jackson, disguised as her father's chauffeur, falls in with crooks and is forced to accompany them while they rob the home of art collector Bob Everett, her father's collecting and business rival. She reveals her identity, recovers the portrait, and marries Everett. *Art collectors. Business competition. Robbery. Disguise.*

UP AND GOING **F2.5994**

Fox Film Corp. 2 Apr **1922** [c2 Apr 1922; LP17857]. Si; b&w. 35mm. 5 reels, 4,350 ft.

Pres by William Fox. *Dir-Scen* Lynn Reynolds. *Story* Tom Mix, Lynn Reynolds. *Photog* Ben Kline, Dan Clark.

Cast—Prolog: Cecil Van Auker *(Albert Brandon)*, Carol Holloway *(Marie Brandon)*, Helen Field *(Jacquette McNabb)*, Marion Feducha *(David Brandon)*.

Cast—The Play: Tom Mix *(David Brandon)*, Eva Novak *(Jackie McNabb)*, William Conklin *(Basil Du Bois)*, Sidney Jordan *(Louis Patie)*, Tom O'Brien *(Sergeant Langley)*, Pat Chrisman *(Sandy McNabb)*, Paul Weigel *(Father Le Claire)*.

Melodrama. David Brandon, born in the Canadian Northwest, is taken to England when his father, Albert, inherits a title and a fortune. Later, as a youth, when he fails to win the girl he loves, David returns to Canada. Joining the Mounted Police, he aids in tracking some bootleggers. Jackie, his childhood sweetheart, warning him of an attempt to frame him, is kidnaped and held prisoner. David learns of her plight through an old woman (actually his mother, whom he had previously thought dead) who befriends him. Following a long chase and an undersea fight, he rescues Jackie and discovers the identity of the woman his father had deserted years before. *Bootleggers. Parentage. Kidnaping. Primogeniture. London. Canadian Northwest. Northwest Mounted Police.*

UP IN MABEL'S ROOM **F2.5995**

Christie Film Co. *Dist* Producers Distributing Corp. 20 Jun **1926** [c29 May 1926; LP22783]. Si; b&w. 35mm. 7 reels, 6,345 ft.

Prod Al Christie. *Dir* E. Mason Hopper. *Adapt* F. McGrew Willis. *Photog* Hal Rosson, Alex Phillips. *Film Ed* James Morley.

Cast: Marie Prevost *(Mabel Ainsworth)*, Harrison Ford *(Garry Ainsworth, her ex-husband)*, Phyllis Haver *(Sylvia Wells, a blonde)*, Harry Myers *(Jimmy Larchmont, a young businessman)*, Sylvia Breamer *(Alicia, his wife)*, Paul Nicholson *(Leonard Mason, a gay bachelor)*, Carl Gerard *(Arthur Walters, a man-about-town)*, Maude Truax *(Henrietta, his spinster sister)*, William Orlamond *(Hawkins, Garry's valet)*, Arthur Hoyt *(Simpson, Garry's office assistant)*.

Farce. Source: Otto Harbach, *Up in Mabel's Room, a Frivolous Farce of Feminine Foibles in Three Acts* (New York opening: 15 Jan 1919). Wilson Collison, "Oh Chemise" (publication undetermined). When Mabel Ainsworth finds her husband, Garry, buying lingerie that he will not explain, she obtains a Paris divorce. Later, she learns that the purchase was to have been an anniversary present, embroidered with her name, and she follows him back to the States, there finding him posing as a single man. While being pursued by Leonard Mason, she determines to win Garry back. At a party given by Jimmy Larchmont, Mabel pretends not to recognize Garry, who is now being vamped by Sylvia Wells; Mabel plants evidence to arouse the suspicions of her rival and thus put Garry on the spot. Sylvia finds Mabel's chemise, which Hawkins, the butler, has stolen, in Garry's pocket; she faints and is taken to Mabel's room, where Garry is hiding under the bed. Following a series of mixups and misunderstandings, Mabel retrieves her chemise, and finding that their divorce has not been validated, Mabel and Garry decide to remain married. *Divorce. Jealousy. Lingerie. Paris. New York City.*

UP IN THE AIR ABOUT MARY **F2.5996**

William Watson. *Dist* Associated Exhibitors. 25 Jun **1922** [c22 Jun 1922; LU17985]. Si; b&w. 35mm. 5 reels, 4,627 ft.

Prod William Watson.

Cast: Louise Lorraine *(Mary)*, Joe Moore *(Joe)*, Laura La Varnie *(Mary's mother)*, Robert Anderson *(Algernon Emptihead)*.

Burlesque. Mary's mother, who is eager to advance socially, chooses Algernon Emptihead as a fiancé for her daughter, Mary. On her wedding day, Mary flees to the farm of a friend, and there she meets Joe, who fulfills in every way her ideal of a proper lover. Mary's mother discovers her refuge and captures the truant. Mary then accompanies her mother to a seaside resort, and Joe joins the party disguised as a chauffeur. Algernon stages a fake rescue in a successful attempt to win Mary's affections, but Joe foils his plan by abducting Mary in an airplane. Upon learning that Joe is a millionaire, Mary's mother declares her satisfaction with her daughter's choice in suitors. *Social climbers. Millionaires. Chauffeurs. Courtship. Abduction. Airplanes.*

UP THE CONGO **F2.5997**

Alice M. O'Brien. *Dist* Sono Art–World Wide Pictures. 15 Dec **1929** [or 1 Jan 1930]. Sd; b&w. 35mm. 6 reels, 5,474 ft.

Pres by Alice M. O'Brien. *Dir* Alice M. O'Brien. *Scen* Harry Chandlee. *Story* Grace Flandreau. *Photog* Charles Bell.

Personages: Alice M. O'Brien, Grace Flandreau, Ben Burbridge.

Travelog. Alice O'Brien and Grace Flandreau begin their African journey by traveling up the Congo River to Stanleyville. Wishing to visit the Mangbetous on the other side of the Iture forest, they continue by automobile through the jungle, then by foot safari. Later they join safaris with the veteran explorer Ben Burbridge and head for elephant country, where special notice is taken of an experiment by the Belgian Government in domesticating elephants for farming. Returning to the Congo River via the Aruwimi River, the boats capsize, but the party persists on foot across East Africa to Lake Tanganyika and Mombasa (Kenya). *Explorers. Safaris. Africa. Stanleyville. Congo. Aruwimi River. Congo River. Lake Tanganyika. Mombasa. Kenya.*

Note: Synchronized lectures available in English, Spanish, German, French, and Italian.

UP THE LADDER (Universal-Jewel) **F2.5998**

Universal Pictures. 3 May **1925** [c30 Jan 1925; LP21088]. Si; b&w. 35mm. 7 reels, 5,922 ft.

Dir Edward Sloman. *Scen* Tom McNamara. *Adapt* Grant Carpenter. *Photog* Jackson Rose.

Cast: Virginia Valli *(Jane Cornwall)*, Forrest Stanley *(James Van Clinton)*, Margaret Livingston *(Helen Newhall)*, Holmes Herbert *(Robert Newhall)*, George Fawcett *(Judge Seymore)*, Priscilla Moran *(Peggy)*, Olive Ann Alcorn *(dancer)*, Lydia Yeamans Titus *(housekeeper)*.

Melodrama. Source: Owen Davis, *Up the Ladder* (New York opening: 6 Mar 1922). Jane Cornwall, a young heiress, is in love with James Van Clinton and sacrifices her fortune to enable him to perfect an invention he calls "Tele-vision-scope." Jim's invention is successful and he and Jane are married. After 5 years of domestic life, Jim begins to neglect both his business and his wife, directing his attentions toward Helen Newhall, Jane's best friend. Jane learns of Jim's infidelity but does not confront him with her knowledge of it. Jim finds himself in serious financial trouble and again needs Jane's assistance. Jane walks out on him, and he is forced to assume a subordinate position in his own business. Jim then settles down to hard work and is promoted to the head of the firm. He and Jane are later reconciled. *Businessmen. Heiresses. Inventors. Marriage. Infidelity. Television.*

UP THE RIVER *see* **THE MAN WHO FOUND HIMSELF**

UP THE RIVER **F2.5999**

Fox Film Corp. 12 Oct **1930** [c16 Sep 1930; LP1598]. Sd (Movietone); b&w. 35mm. 10 reels, 8,280 ft.

Pres by William Fox. *Dir* John Ford. *Stgd by* William Collier, Jr. *Story-Scen-Dial* Maurine Watkins. *Photog* Joseph August. *Set Dsgn* Duncan Cramer. *Film Ed* Frank E. Hull. *Mus & Lyr* Joseph McCarthy, James F. Hanley. *Sd Engr* W. W. Lindsay. *Asst Dir* Edward O'Fearna, Wingate Smith. *Wardrobe* Sophie Wachner.

Cast: Spencer Tracy *(St. Louis)*, Warren Hymer *(Dannemora Dan)*, Humphrey Bogart *(Steve)*, Claire Luce *(Judy)*, Joan Lawes *(Jean)*, Sharon Lynn *(Edith La Verne)*, George MacFarlane *(Jessup)*, Gaylord Pendleton *(Morris)*, William Collier, Sr., Robert E. O'Connor *(guard)*, Louise MacIntosh *(Mrs. Massey)*, Edythe Chapman *(Mrs. Jordan)*, Johnny Walker *(Happy)*, Noel Francis *(Sophie)*, Mildred Vincent *(Annie)*, Wilbur Mack *(Whitelay)*, Goodee Montgomery *(Kit)*, Althea Henly *(Cynthia)*, Carol Wines *(Daisy Elmore)*, Adele Windsor *(Minnie)*, Richard Keene *(Dick)*, Elizabeth Keating *(May)*, Helen Keating *(June)*, Robert Burns *(Slim)*, John Swor *(Clem)*, Pat Somerset *(Beauchamp)*, Joe Brown *(deputy warden)*, Harvey Clark *(Nash)*, Black and Blue *(Slim and Clem)*, Morgan Wallace *(Frosby)*, Robert Parrish.

Comedy. Two convicts, St. Louis and Dannemora Dan, break out of prison and split up when the former doublecrosses Dan and makes his getaway. Dan undergoes a brief religious conversion and joins the Brotherhood of Man, but upon seeing St. Louis around town with two pretty girls, he vents his wrath and both are sent back to jail. Judy, convicted on a bogus charge, falls for Steve; when paroled, he promises to wait for her. Meanwhile, Frosby, her former flame, learns of the love match and follows Steve to his New England home, threatening to expose him unless he cooperates in a swindle. Using the annual prison show as an excuse, St. Louis and Dan escape and arrive in New England to appropriate the bonds Steve's mother had turned over to Frosby, and they return in time to win the prison's annual baseball game. *Convicts. Swindlers. Prison escapes. Theater—Amateur. New England.*

THE UPLAND RIDER **F2.6000**

First National Pictures. 3 Jun **1928** [c10 Apr 1928; LP25140]. Si; b&w. 35mm. 6 reels, 5,731 ft.

Pres by Charles R. Rogers. *Supv* Harry J. Brown. *Dir* Albert Rogell. *Titl* Ford Beebe. *Story* Marion Jackson. *Photog* Ted McCord. *Film Ed* Fred Allen.

Cast: Ken Maynard *(Dan Dailey)*, Marian Douglas *(Sally Graham)*, Lafe McKee *(John Graham)*, Sidney Jarvis *(Ross Cheswick)*, Robert Walker *(Bent)*, Bobby Dunn *(Shorty)*, David Kirby *(Red)*, Robert Milash *(Slim)*, Tarzan *(himself, a palomino)*.

Western melodrama. John Graham, well-known breeder of palomino broncos, challenges Cheswick, an easterner who raises thoroughbreds, to a race, the winner of which gets an important government contract. Dan Dailey, riding the bronco entry, Tarzan, proves the superiority of his horse in spite of serious obstacles placed by the crooked Cheswick; and, in addition, he wins his employer's daughter. *Horsebreeders. Horseracing. Horses.*

UPSIDE DOWN *see* **THE CLEAN UP**

UPSTAGE **F2.6001**

Metro-Goldwyn-Mayer Pictures. 7 Nov **1926** [c8 Nov 1926; LP23307]. Si; b&w. 35mm. 7 reels, 6,048 ft.

Dir Monta Bell. *Story-Scen* Lorna Moon. *Titl* Joe Farnham. *Camera* Gaetano Gaudio. *Sets* Cedric Gibbons, Arnold Gillespie. *Film Ed* Frank Sullivan. *Asst Film Ed* Nick Grinde. *Wardrobe* Kathleen Kay, Maude Marsh, André-ani.

Cast: Norma Shearer *(Dolly Haven)*, Oscar Shaw *(Johnny Storm)*, Tenen Holtz *(Sam Davis)*, Gwen Lee *(Dixie Mason)*, Dorothy Phillips *(Miss Weaver)*, J. Frank Glendon *(Mr. Weston)*, Ward Crane *(Wallace King)*, Charles Meakin *(stage manager)*.

Romantic drama. Dolly, a smalltown girl with theatrical ambitions, arrives in New York and applies for a stenographic position at the theatrical agency of Sam Davis. She mistakes actor Johnny Storm for Davis; and struck by her freshness and innocence, Johnny decides to sign Dolly for his act. Through Johnny's efforts the act is a success, but Dolly takes all the credit herself and is persuaded by another actor to join his act; her conceit is soon exposed, and meanwhile, Johnny signs Dixie Mason. Later, as a chorus girl, Dolly is booked into a theater with Johnny. During the performance—a knife-throwing act—the child of Miss Weaver and Mr. Weston dies as the result of a fall, and Dolly insists upon taking the mother's place in the act. Johnny, terrified, but filled with love and pride, rushes to her as the curtain falls and promises never to leave her. *Stenographers. Actors. Theatrical agents. Conceit. Theater. New York City.*

UPSTREAM **F2.6002**

Fox Film Corp. 30 Jan **1927** [c23 Jan 1927; LP23638]. Si; b&w. 35mm. 6 reels, 5,510 ft.

Pres by William Fox. *Dir* John Ford. *Scen* Randall H. Faye. *Photog* Charles G. Clarke. *Asst Dir* Edward O'Fearna.

Cast: Nancy Nash *(Gertie Ryan)*, Earle Foxe *(Eric Brasingham)*, Grant Withers *(Jack La Velle)*, Lydia Yeamans Titus *(Miss Hattie Breckenbridge)*, Raymond Hitchcock *(star boarder)*, Emile Chautard *(Campbell Mandare)*, Ted McNamara, Sammy Cohen *(Callahan and Callahan)*, Judy King, Lillian Worth *(sister team)*, Jane Winton *(soubrette)*, Harry Bailey *(Gus Hoffman)*, Francis Ford *(juggler)*, Ely Reynolds *(Deerfoot)*.

Comedy-drama. Source: Wallace Smith, "The Snake's Wife," in *Hearst's International Cosmopolitan* (80:100–102, May 1926). In a boardinghouse for vaudeville actors, the wealthy young Brasingham, suffering from extreme egotism, is chosen for a West End revival of *Hamlet* and makes good. His sweetheart, Gertie King, is also sought after by Jack La Velle, her partner in a knife-throwing act. Failing to credit his success to the coaching of former Shakespearean actor Mandare Campbell, Brasingham becomes a victim of his own conceit. When he comes home to the wedding party of Gertie and her partner, he assumes it to be a reception for himself and is kicked out; he manages, however, to regain his composure for the photographers. *Actors. Dancers. Jugglers. Egotists. Boardinghouses. Vaudeville. Weddings. London. "Hamlet".*

THE UTAH KID **F2.6003**

Tiffany Productions. 27 Oct **1930** [c24 Oct 1930; LP1689]. Sd (Photophone); b&w. 35mm. 6 reels, 4,408 ft.

Dir Richard Thorpe. *Story-Scen* Frank Howard Clark. *Photog* Arthur Reed. *Film Ed* Billy Bolen. *Rec Engr* Carson J. Jowett.

Cast: Rex Lease *(Cal Reynolds)*, Dorothy Sebastian *(Jennie)*, Tom Santschi *(Butch)*, Mary Carr *(Aunt Ada)*, Walter Miller *(Sheriff Bentley)*, Lafe McKee *(Parson Joe)*, Boris Karloff *(Baxter)*, Bud Osborne *(deputy)*.

Western melodrama. Cal Reynolds, a hunted outlaw, after eluding the sheriff and his posse, finds Butch, leader of his gang, making advances to Jennie Lee, a young school teacher, in the local saloon. Seeing that she is not there of her own choice, Cal is forced into an immediate marriage ceremony, though she is already engaged to Sheriff Bentley. Discovering that Jennie is legally his wife, Cal plans to reform, but the members of his gang think he is doublecrossing them when the sheriff and his posse arrive at their hideout. Thus, to prove his loyalty, Cal fights the sheriff and posse and wounds Bentley, but he saves his life, realizing that Jennie loves him. Butch is killed in a duel with Cal, and Jennie then decides that Cal, not Bentley, is her man. *Outlaws. Schoolteachers. Sheriffs. Marriage.*

THE VAGABOND CUB **F2.6004**

FBO Pictures. *Dist* RKO Productions. 10 Feb **1929** [c10 Feb 1929; LP146]. Si; b&w. 35mm. 6 reels, 4,717 ft.

Dir Louis King. *Story-Cont* Oliver Drake. *Titl* Helen Gregg. *Photog* Virgil Miller. *Film Ed* Jack Kitchen. *Asst Dir* Walter Daniels.

Cast: Buzz Barton *(David [Red] Hepner)*, Frank Rice *(Hank Robbins)*, Sam Nelson *(Bob McDonald)*, Al Ferguson *(James Sykes)*, Bill Patton *(Pete Hogan)*, Milburn Morante *(Dan Morgan)*, Ione Holmes *(June Morgan)*.

Western melodrama. After 3 years, veteran prospector Hank Robbins and his freckled protégé, Red Hepner, return to their old haunts at Boulder Gulch. Hank is accused by Bob McDonald of the murder of his father, Joe McDonald, and put in jail. Red finds the true murderer and sees to his arrest. Hank is freed, and he and Red mosey along. *Prospectors. Murder. Injustice.*

THE VAGABOND KING **F2.6005**

Paramount Famous Lasky Corp. 18 Feb **1930** [New York premiere; released 19 Apr; c23 Apr 1930; LP1265]. Sd (Movietone); Col (Technicolor). 35mm. 12 reels, 9,413 ft.

Dir Ludwig Berger. *Adapt-Dial* Herman J. Mankiewicz. *Photog* Henry Gerrard, Ray Rennahan. *Col Cons* Natalie Kalmus. *Art Dir* Hans Dreier. *Film Ed* Merrill White. *Songs: "Huguette Waltz," "Love for Sale," "Love Me Tonight," "Only a Rose," "Some Day" "Song of the Vagabonds"* Brian Hooker, Rudolf Friml. *Songs: "If I Were King," "King Louie," "Mary Queen of Heaven"* Leo Robin, Sam Coslow, Newell Chase. *Ch Rec Engr* Franklin Hansen. *Wardrobe* Travis Banton.

Cast: Dennis King *(François Villon)*, Jeanette MacDonald *(Katherine)*, O. P. Heggie *(Louis XI)*, Lillian Roth *(Huguette)*, Warner Oland *(Thibault)*, Lawford Davidson *(Tristan)*, Arthur Stone *(Olivier)*, Thomas Ricketts *(astrologer)*.

Romantic operetta. Source: William H. Post, Brian Hooker, and Rudolf Friml, *The Vagabond King* (New York opening: 21 Sep 1925). Justin Huntly McCarthy, *If I Were King, a Romantic Drama in Five Acts* (New York, 1901). In 1463 when Paris is beseiged by the Burgundians, the people are in revolt against the weak King Louis XI, who fails to defend the city. His Grand Marshal, Thibault, secretly in league with the Burgundians, plots the murder of the king and his royal niece, Katherine, but she is saved by François Villon, leader of the vagabonds, who falls in love with her. The king's astrologer tells him that a vagabond will redeem Paris; he goes in disguise to the tavern of the vagabonds, hears François mocking him in song, and orders him arrested, along with Huguette, a girl who loves him. François accepts the offer of being temporary monarch for a week, followed by death; meanwhile, Thibault leads the vagabonds to free him, hoping to kill the king, and Huguette is accidentally killed. François leads a successful attack against the Burgundians; and when Katherine offers her life in exchange for his, Louis relents before the crowd, granting the lovers their freedom. *Vagabonds. Royalty. Astrologers. Burgundians. Courtship. Disguise. Paris. Louis XI (France). François Villon.*

THE VAGABOND LOVER **F2.6006**

RKO Productions. 1 Dec **1929** [c25 Nov 1929; LP970]. Sd (Photophone); b&w. 35mm. 8 reels, 6,217 ft. [Also si.]

Prod-Story-Scen-Dial James Ashmore Creelman. *Dir* Marshall Neilan. *Photog* Leo Tover. *Art Dir* Max Ree. *Songs: "A Little Kiss Each Morning," "Heigh-Ho Everybody"* Harry M. Woods. *Song: "Piccolo Pete"* Phil Baxter. *Song: "I Love You Believe Me I Love You"* Ruby Cowen, Philip Bartholomae, Phil Boutelje. *Asst Dir* Wallace Fox.

Cast: Rudy Vallee *(Rudy Bronson)*, Sally Blane *(Jean)*, Marie Dressler *(Mrs. Whitehall)*, Charles Sellon *(Officer Tuttle)*, Norman Peck *(Swiftie)*, Danny O'Shea *(Sam)*, Eddie Nugent *(Sport)*, Nella Walker *(Mrs. Tod Hunter)*, Malcolm Waite *(Ted Grant)*, Alan Roscoe *(manager)*, The Connecticut Yankees.

Comedy-drama. Members of a college senior class, led by Rudy Bronson, form an orchestra and embark on a search for Ted Grant, an impresario with whom Rudy has studied by mail. They invade his fashionable Long Island home to play for him; and Mrs. Whitehall and her niece, Jean, notify Officer Tuttle. Whereupon, Rudy claims to be Grant, who is away; as a result Mrs. Whitehall engages his orchestra for a musicale, and Rudy falls in love with Jean. On the evening of the benefit, however, Jean discovers the impersonation and denounces Rudy; but the band is a sensational hit, and Grant arrives in time to prevent an arrest. Rudy is hailed as a great discovery, thus winning both success and the girl. *Students. Band leaders. Musicians. Impresari. Impersonation. Correspondence courses. Long Island.*

THE VAGABOND TRAIL **F2.6007**

Fox Film Corp. 9 Mar **1924** [c9 Mar 1924; LP20035]. Si; b&w. 35mm. 5 reels, 4,302 ft.

Dir William A. Wellman. *Scen* Doty Hobart. *Photog* Joe August.

Cast: Charles Jones *(Donnegan)*, Marian Nixon *(Lou Macon)*, Charles Coleman *(Aces)*, L. C. Shumway *(Lord Nick)*, Virginia Warwick *(Nellie LeBrun)*, Harry Lonsdale *(Colonel Macon)*, Frank Nelson *(Slippy)*, George Reed *(George)*, George Romain.

Western melodrama. Source: George Owen Baxter, *Donnegan* (New York, 1923). Traveling as a hobo in hopes of finding his long-lost brother, Donnegan is thrown off a freight train and is found injured by Colonel Macon and his daughter, Lou. Once recovered, Donnegan discovers that Lord Nick, Lou's unfaithful fiancé and Macon's dishonest mining partner, is the man he has been seeking. Lord Nick gives up Lou to Donnegan and makes restitution to her father. *Tramps. Migratory workers. Brothers.*

VALENCIA **F2.6008**

Metro-Goldwyn-Mayer Pictures. 18 Dec **1926** [c21 Dec 1926; LP23619]. Si; b&w. 35mm. 6 reels, 5,680 ft.

Dir Dimitri Buchowetzki. *Adapt* Alice D. G. Miller. *Story* Dimitri Buchowetzki, Alice D. G. Miller. *Photog* Percy Hilburn. *Sets* Cedric Gibbons, Arnold Gillespie. *Film Ed* Hugh Wynn. *Wardrobe* André-ani.

Cast: Mae Murray *(Valencia)*, Lloyd Hughes *(Felipe)*, Roy D'Arcy *(Don Fernando)*, Max Barwyn *(Don Alvarado)*, Michael Vavitch *(captain)*, Michael Visaroff *(cafe owner)*.

Romantic drama. "Felipe, a sailor falls madly in love with Valencia, a Spanish dancing girl, who is sought after by Don Fernando, the governor. When Felipe deserts his ship, the Don throws him in prison, but Valencia obtains his release and shares his disgrace and exile." (*Moving Picture World*, 8 Jan 1927, p144.) *Sailors. Dancers. Exile. Spain.*

THE VALIANT **F2.6009**

Fox Film Corp. 19 May **1929** [c14 May 1929; LP366]. Talking sequences (Movietone); b&w. 35mm. 6 reels, 5,537 ft.

Pres by William Fox. *Dir* William K. Howard. *Dial-Scen* John Hunter Booth, Tom Barry. *Photog* Lucien Andriot, Glen MacWilliams. *Film Ed* Jack Dennis. *Sd* Frank MacKenzie. *Rec Engr, Spanish-language vers* Eugene Grossman. *Asst Dir* Gordon Cooper.

Cast: Paul Muni *(James Dyke)*, John Mack Brown *(Robert Ward)*, Edith Yorke *(Mrs. Douglas)*, Richard Carlyle *(chaplain)*, Marguerite Churchill *(Mary Douglas)*, De Witt Jennings *(warden)*, Clifford Dempsey *(police lieutenant)*, Henry Kolker *(judge)*, Don Terry, George Pearce.

Melodrama. Source: Holworthy Hall and Robert M. Middlemass, *The Valiant, a Play in One Act* (Summit, New Jersey, 1924). James Dyke kills a man in a squalid tenement and then gives himself up to the police. Refusing to give his rightful name, he is quickly tried and sentenced to be executed. His aged mother sees a poorly reproduced picture of James in an Ohio newspaper and, thinking it might be of her missing son, sends her daughter, Mary, east to see James in prison. James convinces Mary that he is not her brother, however, telling her that her brother died a hero in the World War. James then goes resignedly to his death. *War heroes. Brother-sister relationship. Murder. Motherhood. Personal identity. Capital punishment. Trials. Ohio.*

Note: A spanish-language version of this film was produced in 1930.

THE VALLEY OF BRAVERY **F2.6010**

Independent Pictures. *Dist* Film Booking Offices of America. 16 May **1926** [c8 May 1926; LP22703]. Si; b&w. 35mm. 5 reels, 5,021 ft.

Prod Jesse J. Goldburg. *Dir* Jack Nelson. *Scen* Carl Krusada, James Ormont. *Story* E. Lanning Masters. *Photog?* Ernest Miller.

Cast: Bob Custer *(Steve Tucker)*, Tom Bay *(Jim Saunders)*, Eugenia Gilbert *(Helen Coburn)*, William Gillespie *(Percy Winthrop)*, Ernie Adams *(valet)*, Art Artego *(Joe)*, Nelson McDowell *(Missouri)*.

Western melodrama. Steve Tucker, who has been badly wounded in the war, goes with his pal Jim Saunders to the Montana ranch of Helen Coburn, Steve's wartime nurse. There Steve lives with Bobby, an adopted French war orphan. Jim and Helen go to Helen's mine to get a shipment of gold bullion, while Percy Winthrop, a crook masquerading as a society man, comes to the ranch with his valet and plots with Joe to waylay the shipment. Bobby overhears the plot, and after alerting a deputy, Steve heads for the mine. The bandits, after wounding Jim, flee with Helen and the bullion to a secluded cabin. Meanwhile, Steve forces Percy to write a note recommending him as a former pal, but the bandits mistrust him and a fracas ensues. The cabin is set afire, and Helen is trapped; but Steve overcomes his foes and rescues her. *Veterans. Nurses. War victims. Orphans. Ranchers. Bandits. Adoption. Gold mines. Montana. Fires.*

THE VALLEY OF HATE **F2.6011**

Russell Productions. 20 Jun **1924.** Si; b&w. 35mm. 5 reels.

Dir Russell Allen. *Cont* George Hively. *Story* Harry Farnsworth MacPherson. *Photog* Ernest Miller.

Cast: Raymond McKee *(Harvey Swope)*, Helen Ferguson *(Milly Hendricks)*, Earl Metcalf *(Lem Darley)*, Wilfred Lucas *(Old Jim Darley)*, Ralph Yearsley *(Bob Darley)*, Helen Lynch *(Maurine Foster)*, Frank Whitson.

Melodrama. A wealthy young man in South Carolina inherits property in a valley he has never seen. He goes there to inspect his new holdings and is mistaken for a revenue officer by the native population, which supports itself by circumventing the Volstead Act. The young man falls in love with the ward of one of the moonshiners, and he eventually must fight another man to win her hand in marriage. *Moonshiners. Wards. Revenue agents. Prohibition. Inheritance. South Carolina.*

THE VALLEY OF HELL **F2.6012**

Metro-Goldwyn-Mayer Pictures. 19 Feb **1927** [c2 Mar 1927; LP23714]. Si; b&w. 35mm. 5 reels, 4,070 ft.

Pres by The Big Horn Ranch. *Dir* Clifford S. Smith. *Story* Isadore Bernstein. *Photog* George Stevens, Jack Roach. *Film Ed* Richard Currier.

Cast: Francis McDonald *(Creighton Steele)*, Edna Murphy *(Mary Calvert)*, William Steele *(James Brady)*, Anita Garvin, Joe Bennett.

Western melodrama. "Forced to protect ranch interests college youth travels West and meets girl searching for lost brother. He befriends her and finds brother who is in with evil companions. Villain attempts seduction of girl but the collegian saves her and himself, as villain is also author of his misfortunes." (*Motion Picture News Booking Guide*, 12:62, Apr 1927.) *Bandits. Brother-sister relationship. Courtship. Ranches.*

THE VALLEY OF HUNTED MEN **F2.6013**

Action Pictures. *Dist* Pathé Exchange. 19 Feb **1928** [c2 Feb 1928; LP24937]. Si; b&w. 35mm. 5 reels, 4,520 ft.

Dir Richard Thorpe. *Scen-Titl* Frank L. Inghram. *Story* Harrington Strong. *Photog* Ray Ries.

Cast: Buffalo Bill Jr. *(Tom Mallory)*, Oscar Apfel *(Dan Phillips)*, Kathleen Collins *(Betty Phillips)*, Jack Ganzhorn *("Frenchy" Durant)*, Alma Rayford *(Valita)*, Frank Griffith *("Yucca" Jake)*, Frank Ellis, Beryl Roberts.

Action melodrama. Revenue agent Tom Mallory, newly stationed at the U. S.–Mexican border, wagers that he can bring a gang of rum and gun runners into U. S. territory. Disguised, he arrives in a Mexican village, the rendezvous of the cutthroats, and leads them across the border into his trap by provoking each desperado into angry pursuit after him. *Revenue agents. Rumrunners. Gunrunners. Wagers. Mexican border.*

THE VALLEY OF LOST SOULS **F2.6014**

Iroquois Productions. *Dist* Independent Pictures. 1 May **1923.** Si; b&w. 35mm. 5 reels, 4,700-4,817 ft.

Dir Caryl S. Fleming. *Scen* George Dubois Proctor. *Story* J. Seton Drummond. *Photog* Frank Perugini.

Cast: Muriel Kingston *(Julie Lebeau)*, Victor Sutherland *(Sergeant MacKenzie)*, Anne Hamilton *(Wahneta)*, Edward Roseman *(Anton Lebeau)*, Luis Alberni *(Jacques)*, Stanley Walpole *(Constable Frazier)*.

Northwest melodrama. Northwest Mountie Sergeant MacKenzie visits a Canadian valley to investigate some "ghost" killings. He meets Julie Lebeau, who has recently rejected a suitor, a halfbreed named Jacques. Jacques, who proves to be the mysterious killer, offers to serve as a guide to the stranger. In fear and jealousy (MacKenzie and Julie have fallen in love), he dynamites a hut where MacKenzie has sought shelter. MacKenzie escapes the blast but is knocked unconscious in the ensuing fight. Jacques returns to the trading post to kidnap Julie. The arrival of MacKenzie and his aide brings Jacques to justice. *Guides. Halfcastes. Murder. Northwest Mounted Police.*

THE VALLEY OF SILENT MEN **F2.6015**

Cosmopolitan Productions. *Dist* Paramount Pictures. 10 Sep **1922** [c6 Sep 1922; LP18253]. Si; b&w. 35mm. 7 reels, ca6,500 ft.

Dir Frank Borzage. *Scen* John Lynch. *Photog* Chester Lyons. *Prod Mgr* John Lynch.

Cast: Alma Rubens *(Marette Radison, a Canadian girl)*, Lew Cody *(Cpl. James Kent of the Royal Northwest Mounted)*, Joseph King *("Buck" O'Connor)*, Mario Majeroni *(Pierre Radison, the father)*, George Nash *(Inspector Kedsty, of the Mounted)*, J. W. Johnston *(Jacques Radison, the brother)*.

Northwest melodrama. Source: James Oliver Curwood, *The Valley of Silent Men; a Story of the Three River Country* (New York, 1920). Seriously wounded in an ambush and believing himself to be near death, Corporal Kent assumes the guilt for a murder apparently committed by his friend, Jacques Radison. Nevertheless, Jacques is arrested. Marette Radison hears of his plight and helps him escape to her home in the Valley of Silent Men. Closely pursued by Mounties, they all arrive just in time to hear her dying father confess to three murders. *Filial relations. Friendship. Murder. Northwest Mounted Police.*

THE VALLEY OF THE GIANTS **F2.6016**

First National Pictures. 4 Dec **1927** [New York premiere; released 11 Dec; c12 Dec 1927; LP24752]. Si; b&w. 35mm. 7 reels, 6,600 ft.

Pres by Richard A. Rowland. *Prod* Wid Gunning. *Dir* Charles J. Brabin. *Scen* L. G. Rigby. *Photog* T. D. McCord.

Cast: Milton Sills *(Bryce Cardigan)*, Doris Kenyon *(Shirley Pennington)*, Arthur Stone *(Buck Ogilvy)*, George Fawcett *(John Cardigan)*, Paul Hurst *(Randeau)*, Charles Sellon *(Pennington)*, Yola D'Avril *(Felice)*, Phil Brady *(Big Boy)*.

Melodrama. Source: Peter Bernard Kyne, *The Valley of the Giants* (Garden City, New York, 1918). Bryce Cardigan, son of northwestern pioneer lumber baron John Cardigan, returns home after several years of travel. Shirley Pennington, daughter of a rival lumber baron, arrives on the same train and meets Bryce. At home, Bryce finds his father blind and the business in danger. Because Pennington denies their company the use of the local railway line, Bryce decides to build his own railroad, borrows money to finance it, and hires a buddy, Buck, to build it. Buck gets the city council, controlled by Pennington, to grant a franchise; he then faces the problem of secretly crossing the Pennington line. Pennington, discovering the plans, assembles his men for battle. But Shirley, siding against her father, warns Bryce of the impending attack. After a bitter struggle, Pennington's forces are routed and the crossing is made. John Cardigan gives Bryce and Shirley, who have fallen in love, his blessing and tells them to carry on the work he began. *Business management. Lumbering. Railroads. Blindness. Filial relations.*

THE VALLEY OF VANISHING MEN **F2.6017**

Dist New-Cal Film Corp. **1924** [c10 Nov 1924; LU20742]. Si; b&w. 35mm. 5 reels, 4,652 ft.

Pres by William Steiner. *Dir* Neal Hart. *Story* Alvin J. Neitz.

Cast: Neal Hart.

Western melodrama. Explaining that he cannot stand watch over his own father, Dick Benton quits his job as prison guard so that he may find his mother and the man who framed his father (William Benton) into a life sentence. Dick doesn't take long to be reunited with his mother and to fall in love with Dorris, but his encounter with Wolf presents more trouble. Captured by Wolf, Dick and Dorris are sent in chains to labor in a gold mine; but Dick eventually manages an escape with the aid of an Indian chief, learns that Wolf is responsible for his father's imprisonment, and leads the culprit off to the authorities—thus freeing William for a reunion with his family. *Prison guards. Indians of North America. Filial relations. Frameup. Prisons. Gold mines.*

VAMOOSE *see* **WEST OF CHICAGO**

VAMPING VENUS **F2.6018**

First National Pictures. 13 May **1928** [c19 Apr 1928; LP25165]. Si; b&w. 35mm. 7 reels, 6,021 ft.

Pres by Richard A. Rowland. *Dir* Eddie Cline. *Titl* Ralph Spence. *Adapt* Howard J. Green. *Story* Bernard McConville. *Photog* Dev Jennings. *Film Ed* Paul Weatherwax.

Cast: Charlie Murray *(Michael Cassidy/King Cassidy of Ireland)*, Louise Fazenda *(Maggie Cassidy/Circe)*, Thelma Todd *(Madame Vanezlos, the dancer/Venus)*, Russ Powell *(Pete Papaglos/Bacchus)*, Joe Bonomo *(Simonides, the strongman/Hercules)*, Big Boy Williams *(Mars)*, Spec O'Donnell *(Western Union boy/Mercury)*, Fred O'Beck *(Vulcan)*, Gustav von Seyffertitz *(Jupiter)*, Gus Partos *(shopkeeper)*, Janet MacLeod *(Juno)*, Yola D'Avril *(stenographer)*.

Comedy-drama. Irish American Michael Cassidy sneaks out one evening to join his buddies at their annual dinner at the Silver Spoon Night Club. There he is knocked unconscious by Simonides, strongman in a troupe of performers, who resents Cassidy's flirting with Madame Vanezlos, another member of the troupe. *Cassidy dreams of himself as King of Ireland cavorting in ancient Greece among the gods and goddesses: Venus, actually Madame Vanezlos; Circe, in real life his wife; and Hercules (Simonides). In time he becomes ruler of the country by introducing many marvels of modern machinery. Then a rebellion is started against Cassidy and his buzzers, telephones, tanks, and machine guns. In the midst of the battle Cassidy sees Hercules abducting Venus, and, with the aid of his troops, he rescues her.* Cassidy regains consciousness and realizes it was all a dream. *Strongmen. Irish. Theatrical troupes. Technology. Greece—Ancient. Dreams. Mythological characters.*

THE VANISHING AMERICAN **F2.6019**

Famous Players–Lasky. *Dist* Paramount Pictures. 15 Oct **1925** [New York premiere; released 15 Feb 1926; c16 Feb 1926; LP22402]. Si; b&w. 35mm. 10 reels, 9,916 ft.

Pres by Adolph Zukor, Jesse L. Lasky. *Dir* George B. Seitz. *Screenplay* Ethel Doherty. *Adapt* Lucien Hubbard. *Photog* C. Edgar Schoenbaum, Harry Perry. *Tech Adv* Louisa Wetherill.

Cast: Richard Dix *(Nophaie)*, Lois Wilson *(Marion Warner)*, Noah Beery *(Booker)*, Malcolm McGregor *(Earl Ramsdale)*, Nocki *(Indian boy)*, Shannon Day *(Gekin Yashi)*, Charles Crockett *(Amos Halliday)*, Bert Woodruff *(Bart Wilson)*, Bernard Siegel *(Do Etin)*, Guy Oliver *(Kit Carson)*, Joe Ryan *(Jay Lord)*, Charles Stevens *(Shoie)*, Bruce Gordon *(Rhur)*, Richard Howard *(Glendon)*, John Webb Dillon *(Naylor)*.

Western epic. Source: Zane Grey, *The Vanishing American* (New York, 1925). After a prolog unfolding the history of the Navajo in the West, the story is told of Nophaie, a strong, righteous Indian, who thrashes Booker, an evil Indian agent, for attempting to force his attentions on Marion Warner, the white schoolteacher with whom Nophaie is in love. Nophaie flees into the hills in order to escape Booker's vengeance and returns only to persuade his people to give over their horses to Earl Ramsdale, an Army procurement agent needing horses for the war. Nophaie enlists and saves Ramsdale's life during the fighting, learning then that Ramsdale is in love with Marion. After the war Nophaie returns to his people and finds that they are living in squalor. The Indians go on the warpath, and Nophaie rides to warn the whites. Nophaie and Booker die in the fighting, and his only comfort is to die in the arms of Marion. *Indians of North America. Navajo Indians. Indian agents. Schoolteachers. United States Army—Cavalry.*

VANISHING HOOFS **F2.6020**

Action Pictures. *Dist* Weiss Brothers Artclass Pictures. 28 Mar **1926.** Si; b&w. 35mm. 5 reels, 4,900 ft.

Dir John P. McCarthy. *Scen* Betty Burbridge. *Story* L. V. Jefferson.

Cast: Wally Wales *(Wally Marsh)*, Alma Rayford *(Lucy Bowers)*, William Ryno *(Colonel Bowers)*, Hazel Keener *(Edith Marsh)*, Frank Ellis *(Jack Warren)*, William Dunn *(Jack Slade)*, Jane Sherman *(Kate)*, Charles Whittaker *(The Doctor)*, W. J. Willett *(The Sheriff)*.

Western melodrama. "Star in role of shell-shocked victim, is used by villain for own schemes. Regains mental balance and rounds up villain's rustler gang and saves friend from lynching. Fully recovered, he seeks girl for his wife." (*Motion Picture News Booking Guide*, 11:54, Oct 1926.) *Lynching. Shell shock. Friendship.*

THE VANISHING PIONEER **F2.6021**

Paramount Famous Lasky Corp. 23 Jun **1928** [c23 Jun 1928; LP25399]. Si; b&w. 35mm. 6 reels, 5,834 ft.

Dir John Waters. *Scen* J. Walter Ruben. *Titl* Julian Johnson. *Adapt* John Goodrich, Ray Harris. *Story* Zane Grey. *Photog* C. Edgar Schoenbaum. *Film Ed* Doris Drought.

Cast: Jack Holt *(Anthony Ballard/John Ballard)*, Sally Blane *(June Shelby)*, William Powell *(John Murdock)*, Fred Kohler *(Sheriff Murdock)*, Guy Oliver *(Mr. Shelby)*, Roscoe Karns *(Ray Hearn)*, Tim Holt *(John Ballard, age 7)*, Marcia Manon *(The Apron Woman)*.

Western melodrama. A western settlement of pioneer descendants is threatened with the loss of its water supply through the encroachments of nearby townspeople. Rancher John Ballard leads the settlers in their fight against a self-appointed committee consisting of corrupt politician John Murdock and his brother, a crooked sheriff, who are determined to acquire the water rights by force. Arrested when a rancher shot by Murdock dies, Ballard is temporarily banished. He returns, extracts a confession from Murdock, then shoots him when he tries to escape. After the ranchers have won back their water rights, a well-meaning mayor convinces them of the town's needs, offering to pay for the land. The ranchers sacrifice their homes and move on by covered-wagon train. *Pioneers. Politicians. Sheriffs. Ranchers. Water rights. Wagon trains.*

VANITY **F2.6022**

De Mille Pictures. *Dist* Producers Distributing Corp. 9 May **1927** [c30 Apr 1927; LP23897]. Si; b&w. 35mm. 6 reels, 5,923 ft.

Supv C. Gardner Sullivan. *Dir* Donald Crisp. *Adapt-Cont* Douglas Doty. *Titl* John Krafft. *Photog* Arthur Miller. *Art Dir* Anton Grot. *Film Ed* Barbara Hunter. *Asst Dir* Emile De Ruelle. *Cost* Adrian.

Cast: Leatrice Joy *(Barbara Fiske)*, Charles Ray *(Lloyd Van Courtland)*, Alan Hale *(Dan Morgan)*, Mayme Kelso *(Mrs. Fiske)*, Noble Johnson *(The Ship's Cook)*, Helen Lee Worthing *(Tess Ramsay)*, Louis Payne *(butler)*.

Society melodrama. Fastidious society girl Barbara Fiske, who has made the acquaintance of Dan Morgan, an audacious bully, is invited to his tramp steamer on the day before her marriage to Lloyd Van Courtland. She declines, but the boredom of an evening alone in her luxurious home overwhelms her. Aboard the yacht, Barbara is the victim of a seduction attempt by Dan and is terror-stricken by the hideous figure of the ship's cook, a monstrous, tattooed man. Resenting his steady leer at Barbara, Dan attacks him, and in the ensuing struggle, Barbara shoots the cook, who has killed Dan. Chastened by her experience, Barbara is glad to find peace and happiness in marriage to Van Courtland. *Socialites. Bullies. Cooks. Seduction. Lechery. Yachts.*

VANITY FAIR **F2.6023**

Hugo Ballin Productions. *Dist* Goldwyn Distributing Corp. 25 Mar **1923** [c27 Mar 1923; LP18821]. Si; b&w. 35mm. 8 reels, 7,668 ft.

Dir-Scen Hugo Ballin. *Photog* James R. Diamond.

Cast: Mabel Ballin *(Becky Sharp)*, Hobart Bosworth *(Marquis of Steyne)*, George Walsh *(Rawdon Crawley)*, Harrison Ford *(George Osborne)*, Earle Foxe *(Captain Dobbin)*, Eleanor Boardman *(Amelia Sedley)*, Willard Louis *(Joseph Sedley)*, Robert Mack *(Sir Pitt Crawley)*, William Humphreys *(Mr. Sedley)*, Dorcas Matthews *(Lady Jane)*, Laura La Varnie *(Miss Crawley)*, James A. Marcus *(Old Osborne)*, Eugene Acker *(Max)*, Leo White *(Isadore)*, Tempe Pigott *(Mrs. Sedley)*, Sadie Gordon *(Miss Firkins)*, Georgia Sherart *(Miss Briggs)*, Frank Hayes *(Mr. Wenham)*, John MacKinnon *(Captain Machmurdo)*, Les Bates *(Mr. Sharp)*, Pat Calhoun *(Mr. Quill)*, Laura Pollard *(Mrs. Tinker)*, Kathleen Chambers *(Mrs. Sharp)*, Otto Lederer *(Mr. Bloom)*, Mrs. A. Newton *(Miss Pinkerton)*, Rosa Gore *(Jemina Pinkerton)*, Edward Jones *(Fritz)*, B. Hyman *(Mr. Moss)*, Otto Matiesen *(Napoleon)*.

Drama. Source: William Makepeace Thackeray, *Vanity Fair* (1847–48). Adventuress Becky Sharp lives by her wits and charm in an effort to ascend from humble backgrounds into society. She fails to lure Joseph Sedley, the brother of her chum Amelia, into marriage but succeeds with Rawdon Crawley, the son of her employer. However, his family's displeasure keeps Becky from living in wealth, as she had hoped to do. Ever the flirt, Becky has affairs with George Osborne soon after he marries Amelia and with Lord Steyne while Rawdon is away at war with Napoleon. Her adventures come to an end, however; neither Rawdon nor Steyne will have her, and Becky is reduced to touring the Continent under an assumed name. Her lesson learned, Becky brings together Amelia and her faithful suitor, Captain Dobbin, after George is killed in battle; and finally she returns to London to live a quiet life. *Adventuresses. Social classes. Vanity. Napoleonic Wars. London. Napoleon I.*

VANITY'S PRICE **F2.6024**

Gothic Pictures. *Dist* Film Booking Offices of America. 7 Sep **1924** [c7 Sep 1924; LP20647]. Si; b&w. 35mm. 6 reels, 6,124 ft.

Dir R. William Neill. *Story-Scen* Paul Bern. *Photog* Hal Mohr. *Asst Dir* Josef von Sternberg.

Cast: Anna Q. Nilsson *(Vanna Du Maurier)*, Stuart Holmes *(Henri De Greve)*, Wyndham Standing *(Richard Dowling)*, Arthur Rankin *(Teddy, Vanna's son)*, Lucille Rickson *(Sylvia, Teddy's fiancée)*, Robert Bolder *(Bill Connors, theatrical manager)*, Cissy Fitzgerald *(Mrs. Connors)*, Dot Farley *(Katherine, Vanna's maid)*, Charles Newton *(butler)*.

Society melodrama. Successful actress Vanna Du Maurier ignores her friends' advice and overworks herself toward her goal of having her own theater. She is introduced to Henri De Greve, a millionaire who might help her, but she recognizes him to be her former husband, the father of her son, Teddy, and a throughgoing cad, and therefore refuses to have anything to do with him. The shock of seeing De Greve is hard on Vanna, however, and—fearing the loss of her youthful beauty—she visits a physician in Vienna to be rejuvenated. Vanna returns thoroughly changed and even invites the attentions of De Greve when she realizes his interest in Sylvia Grayson, Teddy's sweetheart. Teddy turns against his mother, Sylvia attempts to drown herself, and Vanna lures De Greve to her boudoir, where she discloses his past and gives him a beating with a riding crop. Sylvia and Teddy are reunited and forgive Vanna, who now recognizes the folly of vanity and accepts the proposal of long-time admirer Richard Dowling. *Actors. Millionaires. Filial relations. Theater. Rejuvenation. Flagellation. Vanity.*

VARSITY **F2.6025**

Paramount Famous Lasky Corp. 27 Oct **1928** [c29 Oct 1928; LP25771]. Talking sequences, sd eff, & mus score (Movietone); b&w. 35mm. 8 reels, 6,348 ft. [Also si; 6,063 ft.]

Dir Frank Tuttle. *Screenplay* Howard Estabrook. *Titl* George Marion. *Story-Dial* Wells Root. *Photog* A. J. Stout. *Film Ed* Verna Willis. *Song: "My Varsity Girl, I'll Cling to You"* Al Bryan, W. Franke Harling.

Cast: Charles (Buddy) Rogers *(Jimmy Duffy)*, Mary Brian *(Fay)*, Chester Conklin *(Pop Conlan)*, Phillips R. Holmes *(Middlebrook)*, Robert Ellis *(Rod Luke)*, John Westwood *(The Senior)*.

Romantic comedy-drama. Pop Conlan, the whimsical, alcoholic dean of janitors at Princeton University, arranges for Jimmy Duffy, an orphan, to be enrolled in the freshman class and thereafter keeps a close eye on him, helping him to become an honor student. During his sophomore year, Jimmy gets in with a fast crowd and meets a showgirl named Fay at a drunken carnival in Trenton; later, after a quarrel with Fay, Jimmy gets drunk and is accused of losing the class funds at the gambling tables. Pop helps Jimmy out of this jam and sees him through the rest of his college career. Upon graduation, Jimmy marries Fay, never learning that Pop is his real father, who, years earlier, placed him in an orphanage in an effort to break the family curse of alcoholism. *Orphans. Showgirls. Janitors. Students. Alcoholism. College life. Princeton University. Trenton (New Jersey).*

Note: Filmed on location at Princeton University.

THE VEILED WOMAN **F2.6026**

Renco Film Co. *Dist* W. W. Hodkinson Corp. 3 Sep **1922.** Si; b&w. 35mm. 6 reels, 5,300 ft.

Prod H. J. Reynolds. *Dir* Lloyd Ingraham. *Scen* David Kirkland. *Photog* Ross Fisher.

Cast: Marguerite Snow *(Elvina Grey)*, Edward Coxen *(The Piper)*, Landers Stevens *(The Doctor)*, Lottie Williams *(Aunt Hitty)*, Ralph McCullough *(The Doctor's Son)*, Charlotte Pierce *(Araminta Lee)*.

Drama. Source: Myrtle Reed, *A Spinner in the Sun* (New York, 1906). Sweethearts Elvina Grey and Dr. Dexter are injured in a laboratory explosion, and the physician leaves the small town when he is told that Elvina's face will be scarred for life. Twenty-five years later Elvina and the doctor return—she with a heavy veil over her face, and he a widower with a son, also a physician. When Dexter hears that Elvina is lonely, he wants to atone for his youthful folly and proposes marriage. Elvina not only refuses: she also lifts her veil to reveal a beautiful, unmarked face. Filled with remorse, the doctor commits suicide. It seems assured that Elvina will find happiness with a kindly gardener (The Piper), and the doctor's son receives man-hating Aunt Hittie's permission to marry Araminta Lee. (There is a sequence intended to propagandize against vivisection.) *Physicians. Gardeners. Man-haters. Aunts. Disfiguration. Suicide. Vivisection. Explosions. Dogs.*

THE VEILED WOMAN **F2.6027**

Fox Film Corp. 14 Apr **1929** [c15 Apr 1929; LP298]. Sd (Movietone); b&w. 35mm. 6 reels, 5,192 ft. [Also si; 6 reels, 5,185 ft.]

Pres by William Fox. *Dir* Emmett Flynn. *Scen* Douglas Z. Doty. *Story* Julio De Moraes, Lia Tora. *Photog* Charles Clarke. *Asst Dir* Ray Flynn.

Cast: Lia Tora *(Nanon)*, Paul Vincenti *(Pierre)*, Walter McGrail *(diplomatic attaché)*, Josef Swickard *(Colonel De Selincourt)*, Kenneth Thomson *(Dr. Donald Ross)*, André Cheron *(Count De Bracchi)*, Ivan Lebedeff *(Capt. Paul Fevier)*, Maude George *(Countess De Bracchi)*, Lupita Tovar *(young girl)*.

Melodrama. Following the rescue of a young girl from a notorious rake, Nanon tells her the story of the men in her own life: *A seducer, who just pulled the same line on the innocent girl; Pierre, owner of a gambling joint, who meant well and gave her a job as a roulette wheel shill; an Englishman on the make, whom Nanon killed in defending herself from his advances; and the man she married, who gave her the air when he learned of her past.* Nanon hails a cab for the girl, discovers the driver to be Pierre, learns that he sacrificed everything to cover up for the shooting she committed, and finally finds happiness with him. (Locale: Paris.) *Rakes. Gamblers. Taxi drivers. Seduction. Marriage. Desertion. Murder. Self-sacrifice. Paris.*

VENGEANCE **F2.6028**

Columbia Pictures. 22 Feb **1930** [c7 Mar 1930; LP1139]. Sd (Movietone); b&w. 35mm. 7 reels, 6,160 ft. [Also si.]

Prod Harry Cohn. *Dir* Archie Mayo. *Cont-Dial* F. Hugh Herbert. *Story* Ralph Graves. *Camera* Ben Reynolds. *Art Dir* Harrison Wiley. *Film Ed* Gene Milford. *Ch Sd Engr* John P. Livadary. *Asst Dir* David Selman.

Cast: Jack Holt *(John Meadham)*, Dorothy Revier *(Margaret Summers)*, Philip Strange *(Charles Summers)*, George Pearce *(The Doctor)*, Hayden Stevenson *(The Ambassador)*, Irma Harrison *(Nidia)*, Onest Conly.

Melodrama. Charles Summers and his young wife, Margaret, arrive at a British West African trading post on the upper Congo, to take over the duties of Meadham, who is tiring of life in the jungle. Meadham is indignant that Summers should expose a young girl to such an environment and does not take kindly to Summers' constant criticism of the operations. Summers offends the natives, moreover, and when he whips a young boy, Meadham, whom the natives respect, narrowly prevents an uprising. Margaret becomes ill and confesses to being mistreated by her husband, who has taken to drinking; but when Meadham appeals to him, Summers only retorts with insinuations about his interests in Margaret. Meadham secretly arranges to take Margaret away, but Summers kills his messenger boy, arousing the natives against him; Meadham comes to Summers' rescue, but he expires from a poisoned dart. Margaret leaves for the coast, assured that Meadham will join her soon. *Trading posts. Marriage. Alcoholism. Revenge. Uprisings. Jungles. British West Africa. Congo River.*

THE VENGEANCE OF PIERRE **F2.6029**

Dist Western Pictures Exploitation Co. 3 Jan **1923** [New York State license]. Si; b&w. 35mm. 5 reels, 4,800 ft.

Cast: Lester Cuneo.

Western melodrama(?). No information about the precise nature of this film has been found. *Revenge.*

Note: Other Cuneo features of about this period were produced by Doubleday Productions, but production credits for this film have not been found.

VENGEANCE OF THE DEEP **F2.6030**

A. B. Barringer. *Dist* American Releasing Corp. 13 Apr **1923** [New York trade showing; released 18 Apr 1923]. Si; b&w. 35mm. 5 reels, 4,753 or 4,840 ft.

Dir A. B. Barringer. *Scen* Julian La Mothe, Agnes Parsons. *Photog* Paul Ivano, William McGann, Homer Scott.

Cast: Ralph Lewis *(Captain Musgrove)*, Virginia Brown Faire *(Ethel Musgrove)*, Van Mattimore *(Jean)*, Harmon MacGregor *(Frederico)*, William Anderson *(Tagu)*, "Smoke" Turner *(native chief)*, Maida Vale *(Kiliki)*.

Melodrama. Captain Musgrove, brutal lord of a South Sea island and controller of the pearl diving industry, catches Tagu, son of the native chief, in the act of poaching. Tagu revenges himself by attempting to kill Frederico, Musgrove's chief diver. Frederico and Jean, a beachcomber, are rivals for the affection of Musgrove's daughter, Ethel. During an experimental dive, Jean and Frederico discover a treasure chest and decide to conceal their find from Musgrove. Returning, Frederico abandons Jean when he is trapped by a giant clam, but Jean extricates himself and wins Ethel. Musgrove reforms and puts Jean in charge of the diving. *Beachcombers. Pearl diving. Poaching. Treasure. South Sea Islands. Clams.*

THE VENGEANCE TRAIL **F2.6031**

Charles R. Seeling Productions. *Dist* Aywon Film Corp. 15 Oct **1921.** Si; b&w. 35mm. 5 reels, ca4,500 ft.

Dir Charles R. Seeling. *Story* Guinn Williams.

Cast: Big Boy Williams *(Big Boy Bronson)*, Maryon Aye *(Grace Winwood)*, Charles Arling *(Lady Killer Larson)*, Bert Apling *(Broncho Powell)*, Will Rogers, Jr. *(Buddy Hicks)*.

Western melodrama. Big Boy Bronson's tendency to stray from the straight and narrow path brings him into conflict with his father, and ranch hands Lady Killer Larson and Broncho Powell take every opportunity to make Big Boy appear in a bad light. As a result, Big Boy must prove to his father that he is guilty of neither the cattle rustling carried on by Larson and Powell nor the bank robbery into which they lure him. The hero sees considerable action in rounding up the rustlers (with an airplane) and rescuing his sweetheart, Grace, and young Buddy Hicks from the clutches of the villains. *Cowboys. Filial relations. Rustling. Bank robberies. Airplanes.*

VENICE **F2.6032**

Burton Holmes Lectures. 6 Jan **1930** [New York State license]. Si(?); b&w. 35mm. 4 reels.

Travelog. No information about the precise nature of this film has been found. *Venice.*

VENUS OF THE SOUTH SEAS F2.6033

Dist Lee-Bradford Corp. Feb **1924.** Si; b&w. 35mm. 5 reels.

Dir James R. Sullivan.

Cast: Annette Kellerman.

Melodrama. "Story of South Sea adventure. Girl raised on lonely isle meets and falls in love with wealthy young man. He goes away, but decides to return. When her father, a pearl diver, dies, she sets out for civilization, but meets with obstacles, which the return of her lover solves." (*Motion Picture News Booking Guide,* 6:70, Apr 1924.) *Pearl diving. South Sea Islands.*

VENUS OF VENICE F2.6034

Constance Talmadge Productions. *Dist* First National Pictures. 20 Mar **1927** [c8 Mar 1927; LP23739]. Si; b&w. 35mm. 7 reels, 6,324 ft.

Pres by Joseph M. Schenck. *Dir* Marshall Neilan. *Story-Scen* Wallace Smith. *Titl* George Marion, Jr. *Photog* George Barnes.

Cast: Constance Talmadge *(Carlotta)*, Antonio Moreno *(Kenneth)*, Julanne Johnston *(Jean)*, Edward Martindel *(journalist)*, Michael Vavitch *(Marco)*, Arthur Thalasso *(Ludvico)*, André Lanoy *(Giuseppe)*, Carmelita Geraghty *(bride)*, Mario Carillo *(bridegroom)*, Tom Ricketts *(bride's father)*, Hedda Hopper *(Jean's mother)*.

Romantic comedy. At a fashionable wedding in Venice, Carlotta and Marco, presumably a blind beggar, rob the bridegroom and the bride's father during the confusion that ensues when Carlotta feigns a swoon. Trying to evade the police, Carlotta lands in the gondola of Kenneth Wilson, an American artist. Feeling that Carlotta is reformable, Kenneth advertises for the canal Gypsy, and she calls, but under the domination of Marco. They plot to rob Kenneth of his valuables but are thwarted when discovered by him. Carlotta and Kenneth encounter Jean, the artist's fiancée, who arrives on a surprise visit; a journalist who fancies himself a great lover makes advances to Carlotta, which she avoids by jumping into the canal; and she outwits her pursuers by disguising herself in "borrowed" finery. During the Venetian Carnival, Carlotta and Marco are identified and searched when Jean's pearls are stolen. Later, Carlotta identifies Marco as the thief; and Kenneth, who has been rejected by his fiancée, wins Carlotta's love. *Beggars. Artists. Robbery. Courtship. Venice.*

THE VERDICT F2.6035

Phil Goldstone Productions. *Dist* Truart Film Corp. 16 Apr **1925** [New York State license]. Si; b&w. 35mm. 7 reels, 6,150 ft.

Dir Fred Windemere. *Scen* John F. Natteford. *Photog* Roland Price.

Cast: Lou Tellegen *(Victor Ronsard)*, Louise Lorraine *(Carol Kingsley)*, William Collier, Jr. *(Jimmy Mason)*, Gertrude Astor *(Mrs. Ronsard)*, Joseph Swickard *(Pierre Ronsard)*, Paul Weigel *(butler)*, Taylor Holmes *(valet)*, Stanton Heck *(detective)*, Elliott Dexter *(lawyer)*, George Fawcett *(judge)*, Gaston Glass *(district attorney)*, Walter Long *(convict)*.

Mystery melodrama. Carol Kingsley and Jimmy Mason, who are both employed in a fashion emporium run by Pierre Ronsard, fall in love and are married. Victor Ronsard, the son of the owner, falls in love with Carol and designs to break up the Mason marriage. He falsely informs Carol that Jimmy, who is the Ronsard bookkeeper, is short in his accounts and that, if she will have dinner with him, he will give her the incriminating papers. Carol reluctantly goes to dinner, and Ronsard is felled by a shot fired by an unknown intruder. Jimmy is later proven to have been in the vicinity at the time of the crime; he is arrested, tried, and sentenced to death in the electric chair. At the last minute, Jimmy is granted a temporary reprieve and given a new trial. Carol seeks to sacrifice herself for Jimmy by confessing that she committed the crime, but Ronsard's butler comes forward and informs the jury that he killed Ronsard in self-defense when Ronsard attacked him. *Bookkeepers. Couturiers. Butlers. Trials. Capital punishment. Murder. Documentation.*

THE VERDICT OF THE DESERT F2.6036

William Steiner Productions. *Dist* Ambassador Pictures. 15 Jan **1925** [c5 Sep 1924; LU20544]. Si; b&w. 35mm. 5 reels, 4,745 ft.

Pres by William Steiner. *Dir* Neal Hart. *Story* Arthur Henry Gooden.

Cast: Neal Hart *(Jack Dawson)*.

Western melodrama. "Poker" Gibbs and his gang run the booming mining town of Nugget. Jack Dawson comes to town after finding gold but decides to return to the desert after attempts by Gibbs's gang to cheat him at cards and to steal the map to his mine. (It is revealed that Gibbs fathered the illegitimate child of Jack's sister and that Jack had forced Gibbs to marry her; also, that Gibbs and Tom Davis, Gibbs's longtime associate, later killed Jack's father while rustling his cattle and let the blame fall on Jack.) Gibbs, Tom, and a halfbreed Indian pursue Jack, using "Roulette" Rose, Gibbs's mistress, as a decoy. They, in turn, are followed by Laura, Tom's sister, who has been searching for Tom for several years. Gibbs abandons Tom and the Indian after a dispute over water. Laura finds her dying brother, shot by the Indian, and he reveals Jack's innocence of the murder. She goes on to find Jack. The next morning, after a heavy rainstorm, Gibbs falls from a cliff during a fight with Jack. Jack and Laura later marry, and Rose reforms. *Gangs. Halfcastes. Mistresses. Indians of North America. Brother-sister relationship. Rustling. Illegitimacy. Deserts. Mining towns.*

Note: Character names and story are from shooting script in copyright records and may differ from the final film.

THE VERMILION PENCIL F2.6037

R-C Pictures. 19 Mar **1922** [c19 Mar 1922; LP17664]. Si; b&w. 35mm. 5 reels, 4,900 ft.

Dir Norman Dawn. *Scen* Edwin Warren Juyol, Alice Catlin. *Story* Homer Lea. *Photog* Joseph Dubray. *Art Dir* W. L. Heywood. *Asst Dir* George Woolstenhulme.

Cast: Sessue Hayakawa *(Tse Chan/The Unknown/Li Chan)*, Ann May *(his wife)*, Misao Seki *(Pai Wang)*, Bessie Love *(Hyacinth)*, Sidney Franklin *(Fu Wong)*, Thomas Jefferson *(Ho Ling)*, Tote Du Crow *(The Jackal)*, Omar Whitehead *(Ma Shue)*.

Oriental melodrama. Tse Chan, a Chinese viceroy, believing his wife to be unfaithful, sentences her to death; learning of her innocence too late, he sends his son, Li Chan, to America and goes into seclusion. Li Chan returns to the fatherland as a successful engineer and falls in love with Hyacinth, daughter of a poor basket-weaver. She is kidnaped by the viceroy, and thinking she has deserted him, Li Chan goes to the city and becomes famous as a teacher. Engaged to give private lessons to the niece of Ho Ling, he soon learns that his pupil is none other than Hyacinth, and he plans an escape for her. They seek refuge in the caverns of "The Sleeping Dragon," an active volcano; but overcome by fumes, they are forced to surrender and are sentenced to the torture of Ling Chee by the lifting of the "Vermilion Pencil." During an eruption of the volcano, the lovers escape and flee from the city. *Engineers. Tutors. Infidelity. Torture. Volcanoes. China.*

VERY CONFIDENTIAL F2.6038

Fox Film Corp. 6 Nov **1927** [c1 Nov 1927; LP24594]. Si; b&w. 35mm. 6 reels, 5,620 ft.

Pres by William Fox. *Dir* James Tinling. *Scen* Randall H. Faye. *Story* James Kevin McGuinness, Randall H. Faye. *Photog* Joseph August.

Cast: Madge Bellamy *(Madge Murphy)*, Patrick Cunning *(Roger Allen)*, Mary Duncan *(Priscilla Travers)*, Joseph Cawthorn *(Donald Allen)*, Marjorie Beebe *(Stella)*, Isabelle Keith *(Adelaide Melbourne)*, Carl von Haartmann *(chauffeur)*.

Romantic comedy. Madge Murphy, a fashion model in a sporting goods store, learning that Adelaide Melbourne, "a famous sportswoman, is to spend the Summer in Alaska ... conceives the idea of impersonating her at another resort in the hope of winning Roger Allen, who does not know, but greatly admires Miss Melbourne. She puts the deception over, but it involves her in a number of scrapes, trying to live up to her assumed reputation, including the handling of a speed boat and an auto race up a mountain trail, but she comes through triumphant and wins Roger in her proper person against the machinations of Priscilla Travers." (*Moving Picture World,* 3 Dec 1927, p27.) *Fashion models. Sportswomen. Impersonation. Speedboats. Automobile racing. Sporting goods. Resorts. Alaska.*

THE VERY IDEA F2.6039

RKO Productions. 15 Sep **1929** [c15 Sep 1929; LP896]. Sd (Photophone); b&w. 35mm. 7 reels, 6,139-6,150 ft. [Also si.]

Supv Myles Connolly. *Dir* Richard Rosson. *Dial Dir* Frank Craven. *Story-Scen-Dial* William Le Baron. *Photog* Leo Tover. *Art Dir* Max Ree. *Film Ed* Ann McKnight, George Marsh.

Cast: Sally Blane *(Nora)*, Jeanne De Bard *(Dorothy Green)*, Allen Kearns *(Gilbert Goodhue)*, Doris Eaton *(Edith Goodhue)*, Theodore von Eltz *(George Green)*, Olive Tell *(Marion Green)*, Hugh Trevor *(Joe Garvin)*, Frank Craven *(Alan Camp)*, Adele Watson *(Miss Duncan)*.

Comedy. Alan Camp, author of a book on eugenics, urges his sister, Edith Goodhue, who has no children, to let him produce a eugenic child for her and her husband, Gilbert, and they agree. Alan chooses Joe, his chauffeur, and Nora, the Goodhue maid, as the parents, offering the sweethearts $15,000 if they deliver a child within a year. The Goodhues depart for California and return a year later to find their home converted into a nursery but with no child; after much confusion, Joe and Nora appear with their baby and refuse to surrender it, as they have been married. In desperation, Alan dispatches Joe to the orphanage to obtain another baby, but the baby chosen is totally unsuited to the Goodhues; Alan is about to have the nursery removed when Mrs. Goodhue reveals that she and Gilbert are to have a child of their own. *Authors. Chauffeurs. Housemaids. Infants. Marriage. Eugenics. Parenthood.*

VERY TRULY YOURS **F2.6040**

Fox Film Corp. 30 Apr **1922** [c30 Apr 1922; LP17855]. Si; b&w. 35mm. 5 reels, 5,000 ft.

Pres by William Fox. *Dir* Harry Beaumont. *Scen* Paul Schofield. *Story* Hannah Hinsdale. *Photog* John Arnold.

Cast: Shirley Mason *(Marie Tyree)*, Allan Forrest *(Bert Woodmansee)*, Charles Clary *(A. L. Woodmansee)*, Otto Hoffman *(Jim Watson)*, Harold Miller *(Archie Small)*, Helen Raymond *(Mrs. Evelyn Grenfall)*, Hardee Kirkland *(Dr. Maddox)*.

Romantic drama. Marie Tyree, a hotel stenographer, falls in love with Archie Small but is disillusioned when he is lured away by a wealthy widow and resolves to trap for herself a wealthy spouse. At a business convention, she makes the acquaintance of Bert Woodmansee, reputedly worth millions, and captures him after a brief courtship. Later she is dismayed to find that he is merely the nephew of Woodmansee, the millionaire lumberman. The uncle discovers her indiscretion, and when Marie leaves her husband, he finds her. She wins his heart completely and through his kindness is happily reunited with her husband. *Stenographers. Millionaires. Lumbermen. Courtship. Hotels.*

VIA FAST FREIGHT *see* **THE FAST FREIGHT**

VIC DYSON PAYS **F2.6041**

Ben Wilson Productions. *Dist* Arrow Film Corp. 3 Jan **1925** [c4 Jan 1925; LP21026]. Si; b&w. 35mm. 5 reels, 5,067 ft.

Dir Jacques Jaccard. *Story* William E. Wing.

Cast: Ben Wilson *("Mad" Vic Dyson)*, Archie Ricks *("Skip")*, Neva Gerber *(Neva)*, Vic Allen *(Madden)*, Merrill McCormick *(Albert Stacey, Neva's fiancé)*, Joseph Girard *(Dayton Keever, Vic's enemy)*, Dad Learned *(Dr. Crandall, Vic's only friend)*.

Western melodrama. Vic Dyson owns a ranch, through which, unknown to him, a railroad is forced to route its right-of-way. Dayton Keever, a local cattle baron who speculates in real estate, hires the Madden gang to drive Dyson off the land. Madden's men stampede Dyson's cattle and cut off his water supply, but he holds firm. Dyson is then responsible for an accident to Keever's secretary, Neva, that leaves her blind, and he takes the girl in when she is deserted by her fiancé. Bitten by remorse for the girl's blindness, Dyson sells his cattle to Keever and deeds his ranch to Neva, with whom he has fallen in love. He then rides off to a showdown with Keever, killing several of Madden's men on the way. He fights Keever and throws him from a bridge into a swift river. Neva, who has recovered from her blindness, rides up and begs Dyson to save Keever's life. After Dyson pulls the cattle baron from the water, Neva tells him that the railroad has offered $50,000 for his former land and offers to share her good fortune with him on a permanent basis. *Ranchers. Real estate. Railroads. Cattle. Land rights. Blindness.*

THE VICTIM (Reissue) **F2.6042**

Goebel Productions. *Dist* C. B. C. Film Sales. **1921.** Si; b&w. 35mm. 6 reels.

Melodrama. "... concerning the murder of a man and the evidence imprisoning an innocent suspect the lover of the murdered man's daughter. She finally secures evidence to clear him but a terrific electric storm destroys all methods of communication, so she attempts to reach the prison in a roadster in time." (*Motion Picture News Booking Guide,* 1:114, Dec 1921.) *Murder. Capital punishment. Injustice. Storms.*

Note: Cut down from a 9-reel production by the Catholic Art Association (c6 Dec 1917), for which O. E. Goebel wrote the adaptation. The re-release date indicated is a reflection of the information in the *Booking Guide.*

THE VICTIM (Reissue) **F2.6043**

21 Apr **1922** [New York State license]. Si; b&w. 35mm.

Note: Stars Mae Marsh and Robert Harron; produced under the same title by Majestic, 1914.

THE VICTOR **F2.6044**

Universal Pictures. 22 or 30 Jul **1923** [c5 Jul 1923; LP19183]. Si; b&w. 35mm. 5 reels, 4,880 ft.

Dir Edward Laemmle. *Scen* E. Richard Schayer. *Photog* Clyde De Vinna.

Cast: Herbert Rawlinson *(Hon. Cecil Fitzhugh Waring)*, Dorothy Manners *(Teddy Walters)*, Frank Currier *(Lord Waring)*, Otis Harlan *(J. P. Jones)*, Esther Ralston *(Chiquita Jones)*, Eddie Gribbon *(Porky Schaup)*, Tom McGuire *(Jacky Williams)*.

Romantic comedy. Source: Gerald Beaumont, "Two Bells for Pegasus," in *Redbook Magazine* (38:41, Feb 1922). The Honorable Fitzhugh Waring, eldest son of Lord Waring, comes to America on his father's advice to marry Chiquita Jones, the daughter of J. P. Jones, a rich chewing gum king, and save the family estate. Almost starving because he is too proud to carry out his original plan, Fitzhugh meets Teddy, a poor but pretty actress, who shares her meal of doughnuts with him. Fitzhugh becomes a prizefighter to earn some money and is so successful that he wins the British middleweight crown. The money saves Lord Waring's finances, and Fitzhugh gets the old man's approval of his marriage to Teddy. *Actors. Boxers. English. Finance—Personal. Chewing gum.*

THE VIENNESE MEDLEY *see* **THE GREATER GLORY**

VIENNESE NIGHTS **F2.6045**

Warner Brothers Pictures. 26 Nov **1930** [New York premiere; released 1931; c4 Aug 1930; LP1463]. Sd (Vitaphone); col (Technicolor). 35mm. 11 reels, 9,007 ft.

Dir Alan Crosland. *Screenplay* Oscar Hammerstein, II. *Photog* James Van Trees. *Film Ed* Hal McLaren. *Mus* Sigmund Romberg. *Songs: "I Bring a Love Song," "I'm Lonely," "Will You Remember Vienna?" "Here We Are," "Regimental March," "Yes, Yes, Yes," "Viennese Nights," "Goodbye My Love"* Oscar Hammerstein, II, Sigmund Romberg. *Mus Cond* Louis Silvers. *Dance Dir* Jack Haskell. *Rec Engr* George R. Groves.

Cast: Alexander Gray *(Otto)*, Vivienne Segal *(Elsa)*, Bert Roach *(Gus)*, Milton Douglas *(Bill Jones)*, Jean Hersholt *(Hochter)*, June Purcell *(Mary)*, Walter Pidgeon *(Franz)*, Louise Fazenda *(Gretl)*, Lothar Mayring *(Baron)*, Alice Day *(Barbara)*.

Operetta. Three young men—Franz, Otto, and Gus—friends from childhood, leave their homes to take their places in the Austrian Army. Franz becomes a lieutenant, and military discipline ends his friendship with Otto and Gus. Otto falls in love with Elsa, a cobbler's daughter, and he and Gus take her to a cafe; there Franz falls in love with Elsa and takes her from Otto, who is helpless before an officer, and persuades her to marry him. Heartbroken, Otto goes to America with Gus; 11 years later he is playing the violin in a theater orchestra, struggling to support a child by his wife, Emma. When he again sees Elsa at the theater and learns she is unhappy, they determine to defy conventions, but learning of his child, she sacrifices her happiness and returns to Franz. Forty years later, Elsa expects her granddaughter, Barbara, to marry wealth and revive the family fortune, but the girl elopes with an American composer, who, Elsa discovers, is Otto's grandson. Renewing the romance of her youth, Elsa dreams that Otto comes and sings to her, comforting her in old age. ... *Violinists. Soldiers. Composers. Courtship. Vienna. New York City. Austria—Army.*

THE VIKING **F2.6046**

Metro-Goldwyn-Mayer Pictures. 2 Nov **1929** [c29 Jul 1929; LP553]. Mus score & sd eff (Movietone); col (Technicolor). 35mm. 9 reels, 8,394 ft.

Dir R. William Neill. *Scen* Jack Cunningham. *Titl* Randolph Bartlett. *Photog* George Cave. *Film Ed* Aubrey Scott.

Cast: Donald Crisp *(Leif Ericsson)*, Pauline Starke *(Helga)*, LeRoy Mason *(Alwin)*, Anders Randolph *(Eric the Red)*, Richard Alexander *(Siguard)*, Harry Woods *(Egil)*, Albert MacQuarrie *(Kark)*, Roy Stewart *(King Olaf)*, Torben Meyer *(Odd)*, Claire McDowell *(Lady Editha)*, Julia Swayne Gordon *(Thorhild)*.

Historical melodrama. Source: Ottilia Adelina Liljencrantz, *The Thrall of Leif the Lucky; a Story of Viking Days* (Chicago, 1902). Leif Ericsson and his merry crew sail from Norway to what later came to be known as Rhode Island along a stream of wild adventures. Helga is the beauty of the group and attracts her share of constant admirers. An incident of attempted mutiny, several battle scenes, and Ericsson's climactic conversion to Christianity all contribute action to this "historic" tale. *Norsemen.*

Christianity. Mutiny. America—Discovery and exploration. Leif Ericsson. Eric the Red. Olaf II (Norway).

THE VILLAGE BLACKSMITH **F2.6047**

Fox Film Corp. 2 Nov **1922** [New York premiere; released 1 Jan 1923; c31 Dec 1922; LP19092]. Si; b&w. 35mm. 8 reels, 7,540 ft.

Pres by William Fox. *Dir* Jack Ford. *Adapt* Paul H. Sloane. *Photog* George Schneiderman.

Cast: William Walling *(John Hammond, The Village Blacksmith)*, Virginia True Boardman *(his wife)*, Virginia Valli *(Alice, his daughter)*, Ida McKenzie *(Alice as a child)*, David Butler *(Bill, his son)*, Gordon Griffith *(Bill as a child)*, George Hackathorne *(Johnnie, another son)*, Pat Moore *(Johnnie as a child)*, Tully Marshall *(Ezra Brigham, The Squire)*, Ralph Yearsley *(Anson, his son)*, Henri De La Garrique *(Anson as a child)*, Francis Ford *(Asa Martin)*, Bessie Love *(Rosemary, his daughter)*, Helen Field *(Rosemary as a child)*, Lon Poff *(Gideon Crane)*, Mark Fenton *(Dr. Brewster)*, Cordelia Callahan *(Aunt Hattie)*, Caroline Rankin *(squire's wife)*, Eddie Gribbon *(The Village Gossip)*, Lucille Hutton *(flapper)*.

Rural melodrama. Inspired by: Henry Wadsworth Longfellow, "The Village Blacksmith." In a prolog, Johnnie, one of the village blacksmith's two sons, falls from a tree that Anson Brigham, the squire's son, had dared him to climb and is crippled. The squire is an enemy of the blacksmith, who married the woman the squire loved. The main story shows the children grown up. Bill, the other son, has become a doctor, and Alice, the daughter, is having an affair with the squire's son, who has just returned from college. Bill is injured in a train accident, and Alice, accused of stealing some money belonging to the church, tries to commit suicide. The blacksmith rescues Alice; the elder brother recovers and successfully operates on Johnnie's legs, and the film ends happily. *Blacksmiths. Brothers. Invalids. Physicians. Theft. Family life. Village life.*

THE VIRGIN **F2.6048**

Phil Goldstone Productions. *Dist* Truart Film Corp. 1 Aug **1924.** Si; b&w. 35mm. 6 reels.

Dir Alvin J. Neitz. *Adapt* J. F. Natteford. *Photog* Edgar Lyons. *Adtl Photog* Roland Price, Paul Allen.

Cast: Kenneth Harlan *(David Kent)*, Dorothy Revier *(María Valdez)*, Sam De Grasse *(Ricardo Ruiz)*, Frank Lackteen *(his valet)*, Rosa Rosanova *(The Widow Montez)*, Alice Lake *(Rosa, her daughter)*, Walter Hiers *(Sam Hawkins)*, Nell Clarke Keller *(The Duenna)*, Lois Scott *(The Maid)*, J. P. Lockney *(major domo)*.

Melodrama. Source: Julio Sabello, "The Virgin of San Blas" (publication undetermined). María Valdez, known as the Virgin of San Blas because of her charitable acts and great beauty, falls in love with David Kent, an American who is in Spain to investigate the death of his father years earlier. María and Kent set the date for a wedding, but Ricardo Ruiz, an excellent duelist and rake who desires to marry María to recoup his fortunes, informs the girl that her father was killed by Kent's father in the distant past. María then decides to avenge the family honor and immediately enters into a companionate marriage with Ricardo. Kent goes to María seeking an explanation for her sudden change of heart, and Ricardo finds them together. He challenges the American to a duel, instructing his valet to shoot Kent if he seems to be gaining the advantage. But in the course of the duel, Kent extinguishes the candles, and the valet inadvertently kills Ricardo. María and Kent are reconciled and make plans to be married. *Rakes. Valets. Marriage—Companionate. Spain. Duels.*

VIRGIN LIPS **F2.6049**

Columbia Pictures. 25 Jul **1928** [c21 Aug 1928; LP25599]. Si; b&w. 35mm. 6 reels, 6,048 ft.

Prod Harry Cohn. *Dir* Elmer Clifton. *Scen* Dorothy Howell. *Story* Charles Beahan. *Photog* Joe Walker. *Asst Dir* Joe Nadel.

Cast: Olive Borden *(Norma)*, John Boles *(Barry)*, Marshall Ruth *(Slim)*, Alexander Gill *(García)*, Richard Alexander *(Carta)*, Erne Veo *(Nick)*, Harry Semels *(patron)*, Arline Pretty *(Madge)*, William Tooker *(presidente)*.

Melodrama. American oil and mining concerns in Central America hire Barry Blake, an American aviator, to protect their interests against the raids of the bandit leader Carta. Blake's plane crashes in the jungle and, accompanied by García (one of Carta's spies), Blake takes refuge in a cafe, where he falls in love with Norma Stewart, an American dancer lured there by false promises. Carta's men arrive at the cafe, and, with Norma's help, Blake sends for the government soldiers and helps them to subdue Carta. Blake and Norma become engaged. *Aviators. Dancers. Spies. Bandits. Oil business. Mining. Cafes. Central America.*

THE VIRGIN OF SEMINOLE **F2.6050**

Micheaux Film Corp. 15 Apr **1923** [scheduled release]. Si; b&w. 35mm. 6 reels, 5,400 ft.

Cast: William E. Fontaine, Shingzie Howard.

Melodrama(?). No information about the nature of this film has been found.

A VIRGIN PARADISE **F2.6051**

Fox Film Corp. 4 Sep **1921** [c25 Aug 1921; LP17003]. Si; b&w. 35mm. 8 reels.

Pres by William Fox. *Dir* J. Searle Dawley. *Story* Hiram Percy Maxim. *Photog* Joseph Ruttenberg, Bert Dawley.

Cast: Pearl White *(Gratia Latham)*, Robert Elliott *(Bob Alan)*, J. Thornton Baston *(Slim)*, Alan Edwards *(Bernard Holt)*, Henrietta Floyd *(Mrs. Holt)*, Grace Beaumont *(Constance Holt)*, Mary Beth Barnelle *(Ruth Hastings)*, Lynn Pratt *(The Attorney)*, Lewis Seeley *(Peter Latham)*, Charles Sutton *(Captain Mulhall)*, Hal Clarendon *(John Latham)*.

Comedy-melodrama. The parents of Gratia Latham are killed by a volcanic eruption on a South Sea island, the only survivors being the little girl and her native servant. Gratia survives and grows up with only the beasts as her companions. Her cousin comes to fetch her when her wealthy uncle dies and other relatives plan to claim the estate. On the homebound ship, Bob Alan, an "ex-college graduate," and his chum, Slim, rescue Gratia from a forced marriage to her cousin Bernard, and in New York the three swim ashore to a deserted house on Long Island that happens to be Gratia's property. Bernard notifies the police that they are thieves, but Gratia establishes her identity and is brought into society, where her unconventional manners cause a sensation. She burns the house; and when Bernard tries to coerce her again into marriage, she soundly thrashes him and weds Bob. *Inheritance. Naturalism. Social customs. Manners. Volcanoes. South Sea Islands. Long Island.*

THE VIRGIN WIFE **F2.6052**

Macfadden True Story Pictures. c12 May **1926** [LU22717]. Si; b&w. 35mm. [Feature length assumed.]

Society melodrama. Wishing to make contact with his deceased first wife, wealthy Henry Lattimer permits the frequent visits of bogus medium Earl Van Dorn; Henry's son, Tom, loves Lattimer's secretary, Mary Jordan; and Mrs. Lattimer hopes to achieve a place in society through the marriage of Tom and her friend, Virginia Jamieson. Immediately following a secret wedding of Mary and Tom, Mary misunderstands Virginia's advances toward Tom and angrily leaves the house; and Tom believes from evidence he finds that Mary has perished in a pool of quicksand. While Tom is under increasing pressure to marry Virginia, Mary becomes the unconscious dupe of Van Dorn and a Dr. Everett Webb. Action comes fast and furious when Webb steals Lattimer's jewels, Tom chases Van Dorn, and Mary is incriminated. But the truth is revealed, and Mary is reunited with Tom. *Mediums. Secretaries. Social classes. Theft. Courtship. Marriage. Quicksand. Seances.*

A VIRGINIA COURTSHIP **F2.6053**

Realart Pictures. *Dist* Paramount Pictures. Dec **1921** [c17 Oct 1921; LP17104]. Si; b&w. 35mm. 5 reels, 4,415 ft.

Dir Frank O'Connor. *Scen* Edfrid A. Bingham. *Photog* Hal Rosson.

Cast: May McAvoy *(Prudence Fairfax)*, Alec B. Francis *(Colonel Fairfax)*, Jane Keckley *(Betty Fairfax)*, L. M. Wells *(Squire Fenwick)*, Casson Ferguson *(Tom Fairfax)*, Kathlyn Williams *(Constance Llewellyn)*, Richard Tucker *(Dwight Neville)*, Guy Oliver *(Buck Lawton)*, Verne Winter *(Zeb)*.

Melodrama. Colonel Fairfax, who lives on a Virginia plantation with his adopted daughter, Prudence, has remained faithful to the memory of his former fiancée, Constance Llewellyn, with whom he had a misunderstanding 20 years earlier. Constance, now a widow, returns home to the adjoining plantation, and the colonel, to avoid an embarrassing situation, decides to move; but Prue sets out to reconcile the couple. Meanwhile, Tom, the colonel's nephew, arrives and strikes up a romance with Prue, and neighbor Neville falls in with counterfeiters in an attempt to buy the colonel's estate. Prue discovers the plot and brings about Neville's arrest when she is held captive in his home. The colonel and the widow are reunited, and Tom wins Prue. *Widows. Counterfeiters. Adoption. Courtship. Plantations. Virginia.*

THE VIRGINIAN **F2.6054**

B. P. Schulberg Productions. *Dist* Preferred Pictures. 30 Sep **1923** [c15 Oct 1923; LP19494]. Si; b&w. 35mm. 8 reels, 8,010 ft.

Pres by B. P. Schulberg. *Dir* Tom Forman. *Scen* Hope Loring, Louis D. Lighton. *Photog* Harry Perry.

Cast: Kenneth Harlan *(The Virginian)*, Florence Vidor *(Molly Woods)*, Russell Simpson *(Trampas)*, Pat O'Malley *(Steve)*, Raymond Hatton *(Shorty)*, Milton Ross *(Judge Henry)*, Sam Allen *(Uncle Hughey)*, Bert Hadley *(Spanish Ed)*, Fred Gambold *(fat drummer)*.

Western melodrama. Source: Owen Wister and Kirk La Shelle, *The Virginian; a Play in Four Acts* (1923). Owen Wister, *The Virginian; a Horseman of the Plains* (New York, 1902). A cowboy from Virginia falls in love with a schoolteacher from New England. He alienates her affection by leading a posse against cattle rustlers and hanging his childhood friend, Steve, who joined the rustlers. Later, when he is wounded, she rescues him and they are married. *Cowboys. Schoolteachers. Virginians. New Englanders. Posses. Rustlers. Courtship. Friendship. Wyoming.*

THE VIRGINIAN **F2.6055**

Paramount Famous Lasky Corp. 9 Nov **1929** [c8 Nov 1929; LP835]. Sd (Movietone); b&w. 35mm. 9 reels, 8,717 ft. [Also si; 7,407 ft; copyrighted as 12 reels.]

Dir Victor Fleming. *Dial* Edward E. Paramore, Jr. *Adapt* Howard Estabrook. *Photog* J. Roy Hunt. *Rec Engr* M. M. Paggi.

Cast: Gary Cooper *(The Virginian)*, Walter Huston *(Trampas)*, Richard Arlen *(Steve)*, Mary Brian *(Molly Wood)*, Chester Conklin *(Uncle Hughey)*, Eugene Pallette *(Honey Wiggin)*, E. H. Calvert *(Judge Henry)*, Helen Ware *(Ma Taylor)*, Victor Potel *(Nebraskey)*, Tex Young *(Shorty)*, Charles Stevens *(Pedro)*.

Western melodrama. Source: Owen Wister and Kirk La Shelle, *The Virginian; a Play in Four Acts* (1923). The Virginian, foreman of the Box H Ranch, near Medicine Bow, Wyoming, meets Steve, an old friend, and gives him a job; and they both encounter Molly Wood, the new schoolteacher just arrived from Vermont. In a saloon the Virginian and Trampas quarrel over a dancer, but the foreman forces him down. At a christening party the foreman and Steve play a prank—for which Steve is blamed—on some sleeping babies, leaving the Virginian free to walk Molly home. Soon their friendship grows into love, but Molly declines marriage. Steve joins up with Trampas and his gang of rustlers; and when he is captured by a posse, the Virginian is forced to supervise his hanging, causing Molly to spurn the Virginian. When he is wounded, however, she nurses him, and they plan to marry. Trampas orders him to leave town, and though the girl resists, the Virginian shoots Trampas in a duel. *Ranch foremen. Schoolteachers. Rustlers. Virginians. Vermonters. Lynching. Wyoming. Duels.*

VIRGINIAN OUTCAST **F2.6056**

Robert J. Horner Productions. *Dist* Aywon Film Corp. Feb **1924**. Si; b&w. 35mm. 5 reels, 4,600 ft.

Dir Robert J. Horner.

Cast: Jack Perrin, Marjorie Daw.

Melodrama. "Melodrama of the Tennessee hills. A stranger, unwelcome in the small town, is 'framed' as a counterfeiter because he finds favor with the best looking girl in the village. Several attempts to kill him are frustrated and finally the stranger triumphs by proving his own innocence and exposing the crook, the bully of the town." (*Motion Picture News Booking Guide*, 6:70, Apr 1924.) *Strangers. Virginians. Counterfeiters. Bullies. Mountain life. Frameup. Tennessee.*

A VIRGIN'S SACRIFICE **F2.6057**

Vitagraph Co. of America. 21 May **1922** [c20 Apr 1922; LP17767]. Si; b&w. 35mm. 5 reels, 4,867 ft.

Pres by Albert E. Smith. *Dir* Webster Campbell. *Story-Scen* William B. Courtney. *Photog* Arthur Ross.

Cast: Corinne Griffith *(Althea Sherrill)*, Curtis Cooksey *(Tom Merwin)*, David Torrence *(David Sherrill)*, Louise Cussing *(Mrs. Sherrill)*, Nick Thompson *(Jacques)*, Miss Eagle *(Nokomis)*, George MacQuarrie *(Sam Bellows)*, Charles Henderson *(Batielle)*.

Northwest melodrama. Tom Merwin meets Althea Sherrill treking in the Northwoods, and she accepts his hospitality for the night; a warm friendship develops, and Tom, sensing that she is troubled, promises to protect her and pose as her husband accompanying her home. There Althea reveals that her child's father, Sam Bellows, has followed from Montreal and threatens to turn over an affidavit of the child's birth to her father unless she pays his price: marriage. She is abducted by Bellows, but Tom learns of her predicament and trails them with a score of woodsmen and dogs. Althea's faithful dogs attack and kill Bellows, and the papers proving that Althea's mother is the mother of the illegitimate child are destroyed by Merwin, who is thereafter united with Althea. *Illegitimacy. Abduction. Canadian Northwest. Documentation.*

Note: Also shown (after release) as *A Woman's Sacrifice.*

VIRTUE'S REVOLT **F2.6058**

William Steiner Productions. 11 Oct **1924** [New York State license application; c9 Sep 1924; LU20547]. Si; b&w. 35mm. 6 reels, 5,175 ft.

Prod William Steiner. *Dir* James Chapin. *Story-Scen* Frederic Chapin. *Photog* Ernest Miller.

Cast: Edith Thornton *(Streisa Cane)*, Crauford Kent *(Bertram Winthrope)*, Betty Morrisey *(Ruth Cane)*, Charles Cruz *(Tom Powers)*, Florence Lee *(Mrs. Cane)*, Edward Phillips *(Elton Marbridge)*, Melbourne MacDowell *(family lawyer)*, Niles Welch *(Steve Marbridge)*.

Melodrama. Actress Streisa Cane comes to New York to get a break on the stage but refuses to make personal concessions to Winthrope, a successful manager. Evicted from her room when she is unable to pay the rent, she seeks refuge in the home of Elton Marbridge, where Steve Marbridge at first denounces, then proposes to, her. Surrendering to Winthrope's bargain, she becomes a success but is saved from fulfilling her obligation by the manager's death and is free to marry Steve. *Actors. Theater. Virtue. New York City.*

VIRTUOUS LIARS **F2.6059**

Whitman Bennett Productions. *Dist* Vitagraph Co. of America. 30 Mar or 18 May **1924**. Si; b&w. 35mm. 6 reels, 5,624 or 5,800 ft.

Dir Whitman Bennett. *Scen* Eve Stuyvesant. *Story* E. C. Holland. *Photog* Edward Paul.

Cast: David Powell *(Norman Wright)*, Maurice Costello *(Josiah Wright)*, Edith Allen *(Edith Banton)*, Ralph Kellard *(Jack Banton)*, Naomi Childers *(Julia Livingston)*, Burr McIntosh *(Livingston)*, Dagmar Godowsky *(Juanita)*.

Melodrama. Jack Banton deserts his wife, Edith, and their child, goes to Havana, and there falls in love with Juanita. Edith studies art, backed by Josiah Wright, a wealthy man whose nephew, Dr. Norman Wright, is engaged to Julia Livingston. Josiah dies, leaving his money to Edith, who has fallen in love with Norman. Banton returns, blackmails his wife, and kidnaps the child. Juanita follows Banton and causes his death when a rejected lover kills him. Julia breaks her engagement with Norman; he and Edith marry. *Students. Family life. Desertion. Wealth. Blackmail. Havana.*

THE VIRTUOUS SIN **F2.6060**

Paramount-Publix Corp. 24 Oct **1930** [New York premiere; released 1 Nov; c31 Oct 1930; LP1705]. Sd (Movietone); b&w. 35mm. 9 reels, 7,238 ft.

Dir George Cukor, Louis Gasnier. *Screenplay* Martin Brown. *Scen* Louise Long. *Photog* David Abel. *Film Ed* Otto Levering. *Rec Engr* Harold M. McNiff.

Cast: Walter Huston *(Gen. Gregori Platoff)*, Kay Francis *(Marya Ivanovna)*, Kenneth MacKenna *(Lieut. Victor Sablin)*, Jobyna Howland *(Alexandra Stroganov)*, Paul Cavanagh *(Captain Orloff)*, Eric Kalkurst *(Lieutenant Glinka)*, Oscar Apfel *(Major Ivanoff)*, Gordon McCleod *(Colonel Nikitin)*, Youcca Troubetzkoy *(Captain Sobakin)*, Victor Potel *(sentry)*.

Romantic drama. Source: Lajos Zilahy, *A Tábornok* (Budapest, 1928). Marya Ivanovna, a wealthy and beautiful Russian girl, agrees to marry Lieut. Victor Sablin, a young medical student, though she is unconvinced of his love. When war is declared, Sablin, a reserve officer, is taken from his bacteriological research, and Marya goes to Platoff, a stern and unyielding general, to plead for his exemption, but this favor is curtly refused. Sablin proves a poor soldier in the accepted sense, and maddened by Platoff's sarcasm, he berates the general for refusing him a transfer to the medical corps. Later, General Platoff has him arrested and sentenced to death for sedition. Hoping to sway the general, Marya bribes her way into a brothel, there causing him to fall in love with her, but he harshly refuses her request that he spare her husband. Later, however, he pardons Sablin and restores him to duty. Learning how his life has been "bought," Sablin plots to kill the general, who, for a second time, saves his life in action. Realizing that Marya sincerely loves the general, Sablin returns to St. Petersburg and gives her her liberty. She is reunited with Platoff.

Bacteriologists. Students. Infidelity. Military life. Suicide. Whorehouses. Saint Petersburg. Russia—Army.

VISIT TO SOVIET RUSSIA **F2.6061**

Argus Film Co. Oct **1929.** Si; b&w. 35mm. 9 reels, ca8,500 ft.

Travelog. No information about the specific nature of this film has been found. *Russia. Union of Soviet Socialist Republics.*

THE VOICE FROM THE MINARET **F2.6062**

Norma Talmadge Productions. *Dist* Associated First National Pictures. ca28 Jan **1923** [Cleveland premiere; released Jan or 11 Mar; c22 Jan 1923; LP18603]. Si; b&w. 35mm. 7 reels, 6,685 ft.

Pres by Joseph M. Schenck. *Pers Dir* Frank Lloyd. *Adapt* Frances Marion. *Photog* Tony Gaudio, Norbert Brodin.

Cast: Norma Talmadge *(Lady Adrienne Carlyle)*, Eugene O'Brien *(Andrew Fabian)*, Edwin Stevens *(Lord Leslie Carlyle)*, Winter Hall *(Bishop Ellsworth)*, Carl Gerard *(Secretary Barry)*, Claire Du Brey *(Countess La Fontaine)*, Lillian Lawrence *(Lady Gilbert)*, Albert Prisco *(Seleim)*.

Romantic drama. Source: Robert Smythe Hichens, *The Voice From the Minaret* (London opening: Sep 1919). Adrienne leaves Bombay, where her husband is governor, to return to England, and on the boat meets Andrew Fabian, who is studying to become a minister. Andrew persuades her to join his pilgrimage to the Holy Land. They fall in love, but Adrienne returns to her husband when she hears of his ill health and when a voice from a minaret urges the faithful to keep their vows. Later, in England, they meet again. A suspicious Lord Carlyle tricks them into confessing their love for each other, then suddenly dies, leaving the lovers to their happiness. *Clergymen. Islam. Infidelity. The Holy Land. Bombay. England.*

A VOICE IN THE DARK **F2.6063**

Goldwyn Pictures. ca26 Mar **1921** [c1 Dec 1920; LP16000]. Si; b&w. 35mm. 5 reels, 4,256 ft.

Dir Frank Lloyd. *Scen* Arthur F. Statter. *Story* Ralph E. Dyar.

Cast: Ramsey Wallace *(Harlan Day)*, Irene Rich *(Blanche Walton [Warren?])*, Alec Francis *(Joseph Crampton)*, Alan Hale *(Dr. Hugh Sainsbury)*, Ora Carew *(Adele Walton [Warren?])*, William Scott *(Chester Thomas)*, Richard Tucker *(Lieut. Patrick Cloyd)*, Alice Hollister *(Amelia Ellingham)*, Gertrude Norman *(Mrs. Lydiard)*, James Neill *(Edward Small, superintendent)*.

Mystery melodrama. Source: Ralph E. Dyar, *A Voice in the Dark* (New York opening: 28 Jul 1919). Two sisters become engaged on the same day: Adele Walton to Dr. Hugh Sainsbury, and Blanche, the elder, to Assistant District Attorney Harlan Day. Both girls are suspected of murder when Sainsbury is found shot. Blanche has a motive: Sainsbury nearly dishonored her, and she would prevent his marriage to her sister. With the testimony of two witnesses, one deaf and the other blind, who reside at the sanitarium where Sainsbury worked, the mystery is solved and the murderer is revealed to be Amelia Ellingham, a nurse at the sanitarium, whom Sainsbury had seduced and failed to marry. *Sisters. Physicians. Lawyers. Nurses. Murder. Blindness. Deafness. Seduction. Sanitariums.*

VOICE OF THE CITY **F2.6064**

Metro-Goldwyn-Mayer Pictures. 13 Apr **1929** [c1 Apr, 9 Sep 1929; LP263, LP662]. Si; b&w. 35mm. 9 reels, 7,427 ft. [Also si; 5,319 ft.]

Dir-Story-Scen-Dial Willard Mack. *Titl* Joe Farnham. *Photog* Maximilian Fabian. *Art Dir* Cedric Gibbons. *Film Ed* William S. Gray, Basil Wrangell. *Rec Engr* Douglas Shearer.

Cast: Robert Ames *(Bobby Doyle)*, Willard Mack *(Biff)*, Sylvia Field *(Beebe)*, James Farley *(Wilmot)*, John Miljan *(Wilkes)*, Clark Marshall *(Johnny)*, Duane Thompson *(Mary)*, Tom McGuire *(Kelly)*, Alice Moe *(Martha)*, Beatrice Banyard *(Betsy)*.

Melodrama. Bobby Doyle is framed for murder and sent up the river for 20 years. He escapes with the help of hophead Johnny and remains in hiding in Johnny's attic. Wilkes, the gangster responsible for framing Bobby, wants to put him permanently out of the way and makes a play for Bobby's girl, Beebe, in an effort to flush Bobby out of hiding. Bobby confronts Wilkes, and Biff Myers, a hardboiled detective, kills Wilkes to save Bobby's life. A note in Wilkes's possession clears Bobby of the charge of murder, freeing him to find happiness with Beebe. *Detectives. Gangsters. Drug addicts. Murder. Frameup. Prison escapes.*

THE VOICE OF THE STORM **F2.6065**

FBO Pictures. 13 Jan **1929** [c12 May 1929; LP611]. Si; b&w. 35mm. 7 reels, 6,036 ft.

Dir Lynn Shores. *Screenplay* Walter Woods. *Titl* Randolph Bartlett. *Story* Fred Myton, Harold Shumate. *Photog* Robert Martin. *Film Ed* Archie Marshek.

Cast: Karl Dane *(Spike)*, Martha Sleeper *(Ruth)*, Hugh Allan *(Tom Powers)*, Theodore von Eltz *(Franklin Wells)*, Brandon Hurst *(Dr. Isaacs)*, Warner Richmond *(Dobbs)*, Lydia Yeamans Titus *(Mrs. Parkin)*.

Melodrama. Tom Powers, a telephone lineman, is accused of murdering aged inventor Dr. Isaacs, but his buddy Spike and detective novelist Franklyn Wells believe differently. They set out to find the true criminal and in an underworld resort discover Dobbs, the Isaacs' butler, who confesses to the killing. After a grueling journey through a storm, Spike repairs a telephone line and thus is able to inform the governor of Dobb's confession minutes before Tom's scheduled execution. *Linemen. Inventors. Novelists. Butlers. Murder. Capital punishment.*

THE VOICE WITHIN **F2.6066**

Tiffany Productions. 15 Apr **1929.** Talking sequences (Photophone); b&w. 35mm. [Feature length assumed.]

Dir George Archainbaud. *Story-Scen* Frances Hyland. *Photog* Harry Jackson.

Cast: Eve Southern, Walter Pidgeon, Montagu Love, J. Barney Sherry.

Melodrama(?). No information about the nature of this film has been found.

VOICES OF THE CITY *see* **THE NIGHT ROSE**

VOLCANO **F2.6067**

Famous Players–Lasky. *Dist* Paramount Pictures. 12 or 28 Jun **1926** [c19 Jul 1926; LP22930]. Si; b&w. 35mm. 6 reels, 5,462 ft.

Pres by Adolph Zukor, Jesse L. Lasky. *Dir* William K. Howard. *Scen* Bernard McConville. *Photog* Lucien Andriot.

Cast: Bebe Daniels *(Zabette de Chauvalons)*, Ricardo Cortez *(Stéphane Séquineau)*, Wallace Beery *(Quembo)*, Arthur Edmund Carew *(Maurice Séquineau)*, Dale Fuller *(Cédrien)*, Eulalie Jensen *(Madame de Chauvalons)*, Brandon Hurst *(André de Chauvalons)*, Marjorie Gay *(Marie de Chauvalons)*, Robert Perry *(Père Bénédict)*, Snitz Edwards *(auctioneer)*, Emily Barrye *(Azaline)*, Bowditch Turner *(cafe manager)*, Edith Yorke *(Mother Superior)*, Mathilde Comont *(Madame Timbuctoo)*.

Melodrama. Source: Laurence Eyre, *Martinique* (New York opening: 26 Apr 1920). Zabette de Chauvalons leaves a convent in Brussels to join her father on the island of Martinique, escorted by Père Bénédict. In St. Pierre she finds that her father has died; his widow, who rules the island's French society, believes Zabette to be the child of a beautiful quadroon with whom Zabette's father left for France; when Zabette is sent to the mulatto quarter, Stéphane Séquineau is present and takes an interest in her. Destitute, Zabette is forced to auction off her Paris fashions, and though Quembo, a cunning quadroon, is the highest bidder, Stéphane outbids him at the last minute and professes his love, which she accepts, believing herself to be *une fille de couleur;* however, his older brother, Maurice, insinuating that a mixed marriage would ruin him, persuades her to desist. On the night of Stéphane's marriage to another girl, Mont Pelée errupts and Stéphane rescues Zabette. Learning of her pure French parentage, Zabette and her lover are happily united. *French. Quadroons. Racism. Parentage. Volcanoes. Mount Pelée. Martinique.*

THE VOLGA BOATMAN **F2.6068**

De Mille Pictures. *Dist* Producers Distributing Corp. 4 Apr **1926** [c18 Apr 1926; LP22696]. Si; b&w. 35mm. 11 reels, 10,660 ft.

Dir Cecil B. De Mille. *Adapt* Lenore J. Coffee. *Photog* Arthur Miller, Peverell Marley, Fred Westerberg. *Art Dir* Max Parker, Mitchell Leisen, Anton Grot. *Film Ed* Anne Bauchens. *Asst Dir* Frank Urson. *Cost* Adrian.

Cast: William Boyd *(Feodor, a Volga Boatman)*, Elinor Fair *(Vera, a Princess of Russia)*, Robert Edeson *(Prince Nikita, her father)*, Victor Varconi *(Prince Dimitri, an officer in the White Army)*, Julia Faye *(Mariusha, a Tartar camp-follower)*, Theodore Kosloff *(Stephan, a mute blacksmith)*, Arthur Rankin *(Vasili, a boatman)*.

Romantic drama. Source: Konrad Bercovici, *The Volga Boatman* (New York, 1926). Princess Vera, while riding along the Volga River with her betrothed, Prince Dimitri, meets Feodor, a sturdy young peasant and boatman. With the rumblings of revolution, the castle of Prince Nikita is stormed, and a revolutionary is killed by a servant. Feodor, their commander, demands a life in exchange, and Vera is seized; but finding himself alone with her, Feodor lacks the courage to kill her, and she simulates death as the mob returns. Her life is spared when Feodor declares her to be his wife. When the White Army arrives, Vera is captured and Feodor escapes, but he is soon captured and held for punishment; Vera is presented for the officers' entertainment, but Dimitri orders her executed with Feodor. When the Reds take the town, they are saved; and the aristocrats are forced to pull a boat under the lash of peasants. Feodor takes Vera and Dimitri to the border and gives them their freedom, but Vera breaks from Dimitri and hurries after Feodor through a snowstorm. *Boatmen. Nobility. Peasants. Russia—History—1917–21 Revolution. Volga River.*

THE VOW OF VENGEANCE **F2.6069**

Premium Picture Productions. *Dist* Independent Pictures. Oct **1923**. Si; b&w. 35mm. 5 reels, ca4,800 ft.

Dir H. G. Moody.

Cast: Jack Livingston.

Northwest melodrama. "... hero swears to avenge murder of his 'pal.' The trail takes him to the Mexican border. He wrongly suspects father of girl he has fallen in love with, but the real murderer turns up at the head of gang of cattle rustlers, and hero captures him." (*Motion Picture News Booking Guide,* 4:71, Apr 1923.) *Rustlers. Revenge. Mexican border.*

VOWS THAT MAY BE BROKEN *see* **STRANGE IDOLS**

WAGES FOR WIVES (John Golden Unit of Clean American Plays) **F2.6070**

Fox Film Corp. 13 Dec **1925** [c29 Nov 1925; LP22056]. Si; b&w. 35mm. 7 reels, 6,650 ft.

Pres by William Fox. *Dir* Frank Borzage. *Scen* Kenneth B. Clarke. *Photog* Ernest G. Palmer. *Asst Dir* Bunny Dunn.

Cast: Jacqueline Logan *(Nell Bailey)*, Creighton Hale *(Danny Kester)*, Earle Foxe *(Hughie Logan)*, ZaSu Pitts *(Luella Logan)*, Claude Gillingwater *(Jim Bailey)*, David Butler *(Chester Logan)*, Margaret Seddon *(Annie Bailey)*, Margaret Livingston *(Carol Bixby)*, Dan Mason *(Mr. Tevis)*, Tom Ricketts *(Judge McLean)*.

Domestic comedy. Source: Guy Bolton and Winchell Smith, *Chicken Feed; or Wages for Wives; a Comedy in Three Acts* (New York, 1924). Nell Bailey, taking a lesson from the married lives of her sister, Luella Logan, and her mother, agrees to marry Danny Kester provided that he will split his paycheck 50-50 with her. When, after marriage, he refuses to honor the agreement, she goes on strike, getting her sister and mother to join in. The three deserted husbands have a difficult time but hate to give in. A vamp complicates matters, but everything is straightened out in the end with each side meeting the other halfway. *Sisters. Marriage. Women's rights. Finance—Personal.*

WAGES OF CONSCIENCE **F2.6071**

Superlative Pictures. *Dist* Hi-Mark Film Co. 24 Dec **1927** [New York showing; released Jan 1928]. Si; b&w. 35mm. 5 reels, 5,427 ft.

Dir John Ince. *Story-Scen-Titl* Mrs. George Hall. *Photog* Bert Baldridge. *Film Ed* Mrs. George Hall.

Cast: Herbert Rawlinson *(Henry McWade)*, Grace Darmond *(Lillian Bradley/Mary Knowles)*, John Ince *(Frank Knowles)*, Henri La Garde *(Dr. Covington)*, Margaret Campbell *(Lillian's aunt)*, Jasmine *(Mifa, the servant)*.

Drama. "Drama of man's unhappiness caused by his conscience. When young, he contrived to have rival for girl convicted of murder. His wife dies in childbirth, and he is haunted by his crime. The man whom he framed escapes from prison, but he [the escapee] does not attempt the life of his enemy, because he sees the ruin wrought on him by an aroused conscience." (*Motion Picture News Booking Guide,* [14]:292, 1929.) *Prison escapees. Murder. Frameup. Conscience. Childbirth.*

THE WAGES OF SIN **F2.6072**

Dist Art & Science Photoplays. 2 Feb **1922** [New York State license application]. Si; b&w. 35mm. 7 reels, ca6,500 ft.

Cast: Jean Gabriel, Arline Pretty, Pearl Shepard.

Drama. No information about the nature of this film has been found.

Note: The New York State license for this film, which may also have been known as *God's Pay Day,* was "abandoned."

WAGES OF VIRTUE **F2.6073**

Famous Players–Lasky. *Dist* Paramount Pictures. 10 Nov **1924** [c14 Nov 1924; LP20775]. Si; b&w. 35mm. 7 reels, 7,093 ft.

Pres by Adolph Zukor, Jesse L. Lasky. Allan Dwan Production. *Scen* Forrest Halsey. *Photog* George Webber.

Cast: Gloria Swanson *(Carmelita)*, Ben Lyon *(Marvin)*, Norman Trevor *(John Boule)*, Ivan Linow *(Luigi)*, Armand Cortez *(Giuseppe)*, Adrienne D'Ambricourt *(Madame La Cantinière)*, Paul Panzer *(Sergeant Le Gros)*, Joe Moore *(Le Bro-way)*.

Romance. Source: Percival Christopher Wren, *Wages of Virtue* (New York, 1917). Luigi, a traveling-show strongman, saves Carmelita from drowning and persuades her to join him. When Luigi kills his assistant, Giuseppe, in a jealous rage, they flee to Algiers, where Luigi joins the Foreign Legion and installs Carmelita as proprietress of a cafe. Marvin, an American legionnaire, falls in love with Carmelita, who has become a favorite of the regiment, but she remains loyal to Luigi out of gratitude. Luigi frames Marvin, who is punished by the authorities. In the ensuing fight between Marvin and Luigi, the strongman is getting the better of the American when Carmelita, who has learned of Luigi's intent to marry Madame La Cantinière, stabs her benefactor. The legionnaires decide to attribute Luigi's death to an Arab; Marvin and Carmelita are united. *Strongmen. Sutlers. Italians. Jealousy. Murder. Loyalty. Virtue. Algiers. France—Army—Foreign Legion.*

THE WAGON MASTER (Universal-Jewel) **F2.6074**

Ken Maynard Productions. *Dist* Universal Pictures. 8 Sep **1929** [c25 Jun 1929; LP498]. Talking sequences & mus score (Movietone); b&w. 35mm. 6 reels, 6,335 ft. [Also si; 5,679 ft.]

Pres by Carl Laemmle. *Dir* Harry J. Brown. *Story-Scen* Marion Jackson. *Dial-Titl* Leslie Mason. *Photog* Ted McCord. *Film Ed* Fred Allen. *Sd Rec* C. Roy Hunter.

Cast: Ken Maynard *(The Rambler)*, Edith Roberts *(Sue Smith)*, Frederick Dana *(Bill Hollister)*, Tom Santschi *(Jake Lynch)*, Al Ferguson *(Jacques Frazelle)*, Jack Hanlon *(Billie Hollister)*, Billie Dunn *(Buckeye Pete)*, Whitehorse *(Stuttering Sam)*, Frank Rice *(Grasshopper)*.

Western melodrama. A wagon train is organized by Bill Hollister to break the unfair monopoly acquired by Jake Lynch on food prices in numerous mining communities. The Rambler joins the train when it leaves for Gold Hill; he rescues Sue Smith from a runaway horse and takes command of the wagon train when Hollister is killed from ambush by Lynch's henchmen. Jacques Frazelle, formerly Hollister's second, schemes to displace the Rambler and to win Sue. At a waterhole, The Rambler outwits Lynch's men, and Frazelle schemes with Lynch to disrupt the wagon train. The Rambler vanquishes Frazelle in a whip fight at a dancehall; then he and his men make their way to Gold Hill in time to prevent the miners from signing an exorbitant contract with Lynch. *Wagon masters. Price control. Courtship. Mining camps. Wagon trains.*

THE WAGON SHOW **F2.6075**

First National Pictures. 19 Feb **1928** [c23 Dec 1927; LP24796]. Si; b&w. 35mm. 7 reels, 6,212 ft.

Pres by Charles R. Rogers. *Dir* Harry J. Brown. *Scen* Ford I. Beebe. *Titl* Don Ryan. *Photog* George Benoit. *Akeley Camera Eff* William Sickner. *Film Ed* Fred Allen. *Bus Mgr* Sid Rogell.

Cast: Ken Maynard *(Bob Mason)*, Marian Douglas *(Sally Beldan)*, Maurice Costello *(Colonel Beldan)*, Fred Malatesta *(Vicarino)*, George Davis *("Hank")*, May Boley *(The Strong Woman)*, Paul Weigel *(Joey)*, Henry Roquemore *(The Barker)*, Sidney Jarvis *(Sayre)*, Tarzan *(himself, a horse)*.

Western melodrama. When two rival circuses attempt to operate in the same territory, one of the circus owners uses unscrupulous means to drive the other out of business. Bob Mason, a cowboy, is guiding the circus of the honest owner, and when the star rider leaves to join the rival circus Mason takes his place. The rival circus steals several of the wagons, and the show is delayed for lack of equipment; but Mason recovers the missing wagons in time to satisfy the impatient audience. *Cowboys. Circus. Wagon shows. Horses.*

THE WAKEFIELD CASE **F2.6076**

Weber-World. *Dist* World Film Corp. ca21 May **1921** [Detroit premiere]. Si; b&w. 35mm. 6 reels.

Dir George Irving. *Scen* Shannon Fife. *Story* Mrs. L. Case Russell. *Photog (see note)* William S. Adams, Walter Young.

Cast: Herbert Rawlinson *(Wakefield, Jr.)*, John P. Wade *(Wakefield, Sr.)*, J. H. Gilmore *(Gregg)*, Charles Dalton *(Richard Krogan)*, Joseph Burke *(James Krogan)*, Jerry Austin *(Bryson)*, W. W. Black *(Blaine)*, H. L. Dewey *(Briggs)*, Florence Billings *(Ruth Gregg [the Breen girl])*.

Mystery melodrama. A playwright, Wakefield, Jr., turns detective when his father is killed after nearly capturing two brothers in possession of four rubies belonging to the British Museum. An investigation suggests that "the Breen girl" is responsible for Wakefield's death, and the younger Wakefield pursues her across the ocean to the United States. The true identity of several characters, including the robbers and the girl, is in constant question, but Wakefield finally gets to the culprits; solves his case; and learns that Ruth Gregg, with whom he has fallen in love, is not only "the Breen girl," but actually was posing as a gang member for the Secret Service. *Playwrights. Detectives. Gangs. Secret service. Theft. Murder. Mistaken identity. British Museum.*

Note: Sources disagree on the photography credit; actual responsibility has not been determined.

WAKING UP THE TOWN F2.6077

Mary Pickford Co. *Dist* United Artists. 14 Apr **1925** [c1 Mar 1925; LP21213]. Si; b&w. 35mm. 6 reels, 5,800 ft.

Dir James Cruze. *Story* James Cruze, Frank Condon. *Photog* Arthur Edeson, Paul Perry.

Cast: Jack Pickford *(Jack Joyce)*, Claire McDowell *(Mrs. Joyce)*, Alec B. Francis *(Abner Hope)*, Norma Shearer *(Mary Ellen Hope)*, Herbert Pryor *(Curt Horndyke)*, Ann May *(Helen Horndyke)*, George Dromgold *(Joe Lakin)*.

Comedy. Jack Joyce, a rural Edison who works on his inventions in old Abner Hope's garage, develops a plan for a power project to utilize local water resources, but he cannot interest Horndyke, the town banker, in the scheme. Mary Ellen Hope comes to stay with her grandmother, and she and Jack fall in love. Abner Hope, an astrologer, predicts the end of the world and gives all his money to Jack with the express instruction to spend it. Jack buys a car and a house and impresses Horndyke, who lends him the necessary capital to finance the power project. Jack and Mary later separate over a misunderstanding, and Jack's house is struck by lightning, injuring him slightly. Jack then imagines that the world is coming to an end but wakes up to find Mary at his side. *Bankers. Inventors. Astrologers. Power projects. Doomsday.*

WALKING BACK F2.6078

De Mille Pictures. *Dist* Pathé Exchange. 21 May **1928** [c7 May 1928; LP25225]. Si; b&w. 35mm. 6 reels, 5,035 ft.

Dir Rupert Julian. *Scen* Monte Katterjohn. *Photog* John Mescall. *Art Dir* Anton Grot. *Film Ed* Claude Berkeley. *Asst Dir* Fred Tyler. *Unit Prod Mgr* John Rohlfs. *Cost* Adrian.

Cast: Sue Carol *(Patsy Schuyler)*, Richard Walling *(Smoke Thatcher)*, Ivan Lebedeff *(Beaut Thibaut)*, Robert Edeson *(Mr. Thatcher, Sr.)*, Jane Keckley *(Mrs. Thatcher)*, Florence Turner *(Mrs. Schuyler)*, James Bradbury, Sr. *(Gyp)*, Arthur Rankin *(Pet Masters)*, Billy Sullivan, George Stone *(crooks)*.

Drama. Source: George Kibbe Turner, "A Ride in the Country," in *Liberty Magazine* (vol 4, 6 Aug–8 Oct 1927). Jazz age youngster Smoke Thatcher "borrows" a neighbor's car to take Patsy, his sweetheart, to a dance after his father refuses to lend him his car. A car-fight with a rival results in the borrowed automobile's being so wrecked that Smoke cannot return it. The garage to which he and Patsy take the car for repair turns out to be actually a gang's hideaway and a place where stolen cars are brought and later fenced. The gangsters compel Smoke, accompanied by Patsy, to drive a getaway car, promising enough money to replace the neighbor's car. The gang robs the bank where Smoke's father is employed, and they shoot Thatcher in making their getaway. Forced to leave his father wounded in the street, Smoke makes a wild drive through the city, ending up at the police station. He is rewarded for "capturing" the crooks. *Gangs. Bankers. Jazz life. Filial relations. Automobile accidents. Bank robberies.*

THE WALL FLOWER F2.6079

Goldwyn Pictures. May **1922** [c29 Jun 1922; LP18020]. Si; b&w. 35mm. 6 reels, 5,228 ft.

Dir-Writ Rupert Hughes. *Photog* John J. Mescall.

Cast: Colleen Moore *(Idalene Nobbin)*, Richard Dix *(Walt Breen)*, Gertrude Astor *(Pamela Shiel)*, Laura La Plante *(Prue Nickerson)*, Tom Gallery *(Roy Duncan)*, Rush Hughes *(Phin Larrabee)*, Dana Todd *(Allen Lansing)*, Fanny Stockbridge *(Mrs. Nobbin)*, Emily Rait *(Mrs. Nickerson)*.

Romantic drama. Idalene Nobbin, who is accustomed to being treated as a hopeless wallflower by her mother and her brothers, attends a dance given by Prue Nickerson and is greatly surprised when Roy Duncan, a football star, asks her to dance. Later, however, she is the victim of an unkind jest, which so mortifies her that she throws herself in front of a speeding auto; with both legs broken, she is picked up by wealthy society girl Pamela Shiel and her guest Walter Breen and taken to Pamela's home. Idalene tells Pamela she wished to die because no man would ever want to marry her. Pamela surrounds Idalene with luxuries and teaches her to walk gracefully and wear stylish clothes; and soon her blooming charm attracts Breen. At a party Pamela gives in her honor her former critics pay her homage. Idalene refuses Breen's proposal of marriage when she learns that Pamela also loves him; but Pamela suppresses her feelings in favor of Idalene, and the lovers are happily united. *Social customs. Inferiority complex. Personality.*

Note: Copyright title: *The Wallflower.*

WALL STREET F2.6080

Columbia Pictures. 23 Nov **1929** [New York premiere; released 1 Dec; c8 Jan 1930; LP996]. Sd (Movietone); b&w. 35mm. 7 reels, 6,336 ft. [Also si; 6,004 ft.]

Prod Harry Cohn. *Dir* R. William Neill. *Dial Dir* James Seymour. *Cont-Dial* Norman Houston. *Story* Paul Gangelin, Jack Kirkland. *Camera* Ted Tetzlaff. *Art Dir* Harrison Wiley. *Film Ed* Ray Snyder. *Ch Sd Engr* John Livadary. *Sd Mix Engr* Edward Bernds. *Asst Dir* Sam Nelson.

Cast: Ralph Ince *(Roller McCray)*, Aileen Pringle *(Ann Tabor)*, Philip Strange *(Walter Tabor)*, Freddie Burke Frederick *(Richard Tabor)*, Sam De Grasse *(John Willard)*, Ernest Hilliard *(Savage)*, Jimmy Finlayson *(Andy)*, George MacFarlane *(Ed Foster)*, Camille Rovelle *(Miss Woods)*, Grace Wallace *(Bonnie Tucker)*, Hugh McCormack *(Jim Tucker)*, Marshall Ruth *(Billy)*, Ben Hall *(Cliff)*, Billy Colvin *(Hoffman)*, Frederick Graham *(Baring)*, Louise Beavers *(Magnolia)*.

Melodrama. Roller McCray, a former steelworker, becomes a ruthlessly powerful man in the financial world. He crushes his rival, Walter Tabor; and when Roller refuses to relent, Tabor kills himself, leaving Anne, his wife, and a child, Richard. Roller tries to make amends for his actions, and believing she can practice his own philosophy and ruin him, Anne accepts his attentions, while plotting with John Willard, her husband's former partner. A strong friendship develops between Roller and little Richard, resulting in the child's unwittingly divulging financial information that Willard uses to destroy Roller. At a picnic Anne realizes her admiration for Roller and regrets having caused his downfall; ultimately, they are united because of the child's influence. *Financiers. Children. Speculation. Steel industry. Suicide. Revenge. New York City—Wall Street.*

THE WALL STREET WHIZ F2.6081

Richard Talmadge Productions. *Dist* Film Booking Offices of America. 27 Sep **1925** [c3 Oct 1925; LP21869]. Si; b&w. 35mm. 5 reels, 5,452 ft.

Pres by A. Carlos. *Dir* Jack Nelson. *Story-Cont* James Bell Smith. *Photog* William Marshall. *Adtl Photog* Jack Stevens. *Asst Dir* Alfred Metzetti.

Cast: Richard Talmadge *(Richard Butler)*, Marceline Day *(Peggy McCooey)*, Lillian Langdon *(Mrs. McCooey)*, Carl Miller *(Clayton)*, Billie Bennett *(Aunty Jones)*, Dan Mason *(Mr. McCooey)*.

Action melodrama. During a raid on a gambling house, Dick Butler, who leads a double life (as a wealthy bounder and as the Wall Street Whiz), dodges the police and leaps into a car driven by Mrs. McCooey. Immediately taken with the poise and beauty of Mrs. McCooey's daughter, Peggy, Dick proclaims himself to be a "Butler." The old lady misunderstands, and Dick soon finds himself employed as the butler in the McCooey home. He foils the attempts of John Clayton, a crooked stockbroker, to ruin Mr. McCooey in the market and protects the elderly gentleman's money from a couple of yeggs hired by Clayton. Dick's identity is eventually disclosed, and he and Peggy wed. *Brokers. Butlers. Police. Impersonation. Stock market. New York City—Wall Street.*

WALLFLOWERS F2.6082

FBO Pictures. 16 Feb **1928** [c1 Feb 1928; LP24936]. Si; b&w. 35mm. 7 reels, 6,339 ft.

Dir Leo Meehan. *Scen* Dorothy Yost. *Photog* Allen Siegler. *Film Ed* Edward Schroeder. *Asst Dir* Charles Kerr.

Cast: Hugh Trevor *(Rufus)*, Mabel Julienne Scott *(Sherry, Rufus' stepmother)*, Charles Stevenson *(Mr. Fisk)*, Jean Arthur *(Sandra)*, Lola Todd *(Theodora)*, Tempe Pigott *(Mrs. Claybourne)*, Crauford Kent *(Maulsby)*, Reginald Simpson *(Markham)*.

Society drama. Source: Temple Bailey, *Wallflowers* (Philadelphia, 1927). Sandra and her sister Dody (Theodora) leave the Virginia countryside to join Washington's social set. Dody determines to marry wealth, while

Sandra wants romance. Both girls' fortunes are reversed when Sandra falls in love with wealthy Rufus Fisk, whose stepmother threatens to cut him off if he marries her. Dody loves Gale Markham, an ex-soldier, once wealthy, in whom Stephanie Moore, a recognized beauty, also takes an interest. Gale returns Dody's affection, but he is reluctant to propose marriage because of his depleted finances. Both girls find happiness when Rufus sacrifices his wealth for Sandra, and Dody her desire to marry money for Gale. *Sisters. Socialites. Stepmothers. Wealth. Courtship. Virginia. Washington (District of Columbia).*

THE WALLOP **F2.6083**

Universal Film Manufacturing Co. 9 May **1921** [c25 Apr 1921; LP16439]. Si; b&w. 35mm. 5 reels, 4,539 ft.

Dir Jack Ford. *Scen* George C. Hull. *Photog* Harry Fowler.

Cast: Harry Carey *(John Wesley Pringle)*, Mignonne Golden *(Stella Vorhis)*, William Gettinger *(Christopher Foy)*, Charles Le Moyne *(Matt Lisner)*, Joe Harris *(Barela)*, C. E. Anderson *(Applegate)*, J. Farrell MacDonald *(Neuces River)*, Mark Fenton *(Major Vorhis)*, Noble Johnson *(Espinol)*.

Western melodrama. Source: Eugene Manlove Rhodes, "The Girl He Left Behind Him" (publication undetermined). John Wesley Pringle, adventurer at large, returns home after making his strike and finds his old girl friend, Stella, engaged to Christopher Foy, who is running for sheriff. Pringle foils an attempt by incumbent sheriff Matt Lisner to kill Foy, but when Foy is accused of a murder, Pringle, in a clever ruse, captures Foy, holds the posse at gunpoint, and then releases him, explaining his motive. Lisner is summarily dealt with, and Pringle returns to his mine. *Miners. Sheriffs. Murder.*

Note: Working title: *The Homeward Trail.*

WALLOPING KID **F2.6084**

Robert J. Horner Productions. *Dist* Aywon Film Corp. 5 Jan **1926** [New York State license]. Si; b&w. 35mm. 5 reels, 4,900 ft.

Dir-Writ Robert J. Horner. *Photog* Bert Baldridge.

Cast: Kit Carson *(The Walloping Kid)*, Jack Richardson *(Don Dawson, foreman of Hampton's ranch)*, Dorothy Ward *(Sally Carter)*, Frank Whitson *(her father, a prospector)*, Al Kaufman *(Wild Cat McKee, whom Hampton fights)*, Jack Herrick *(Battling Lewis, another fighter)*, Pauline Curley.

Western melodrama. "Young pugilist, born a fighter but always a gentleman, is sent west to take possession of his dad's ranch, with condition that he give up the prize ring. He joins a gang of rustlers to break up the intrigue threatening the ranch." ("Motion Picture News Booking Guide," in *Motion Picture News,* 15 Mar 1930, p108.) *Ranchers. Rustlers. Prizefighters. Filial relations.*

WALLOPING WALLACE **F2.6085**

Approved Pictures. *Dist* Weiss Brothers Artclass Pictures. 15 Oct **1924** [c31 Oct 1924; LU20715]. Si; b&w. 35mm. 5 reels, 4,830 ft.

Prod Lester F. Scott, Jr. *Dir? (see note)* Richard Thorpe. *Dir-Writ* Norbert Myles.

Cast: Buddy Roosevelt *(Buddy Wallace, foreman of the Lazy-B)*, Violet La Plante *(Carol Grey, owner of the Lazy-B)*, Lew Meehan *(Squinty Burnt, a Lazy-B hand)*, N. E. Hendrix *(Shorty, another Lazy-B hand)*, Lillian Gale *(Ma Fagin, just a squatter)*, Terry Myles *(Spud, Ma Fagin's child)*, Olin Francis *(sheriff)*, Dick Bodkins *(cattle buyer)*.

Western melodrama. Source: Robert J. Horton, "A Man of Action" (publication undetermined). Buddy Wallace, foreman of Carol Grey's Lazy B Ranch, fires Squinty Burnt for shirking his work while loading a shipment of cattle and gets the best of Squinty in the resulting fight. To get even, Squinty forges Carol's name on a bill of sale, abducts her, and hides her in a squatter's cabin. Buddy sets off in pursuit; gets involved in a series of fights, stunts, and horseraces while escaping from the sheriff, who arrested Buddy for kidnaping Carol; and succeeds in rescuing Carol and saving the cattle. Buddy is rewarded with Carol's promise to marry him. *Cowboys. Ranch foremen. Squatters. Cattle. Kidnaping. Documentation.*

Note: Copyright records credit Richard Thorpe as director.

THE WANDERER **F2.6086**

Famous Players–Lasky. *Dist* Paramount Pictures. 1 Feb **1926** [c4 Feb 1926; LP22355]. Si; b&w. 35mm. 9 reels, 8,173 ft.

Pres by Adolph Zukor, Jesse L. Lasky. *Dir* Raoul Walsh. *Scen* James T. O'Donohoe. *Camera* Victor Milner.

Cast: Greta Nissen *(Tisha)*, William Collier, Jr. *(Jether)*, Ernest Torrence *(Tola)*, Wallace Beery *(Pharis)*, [Frederick] Tyrone Power *(Jesse)*, Kathryn Hill *(Naomi)*, Kathlyn Williams *(Huldah)*, George Rigas *(Gaal)*, Holmes Herbert *(prophet)*, Snitz Edwards *(jeweler)*.

Religious drama. Source: Maurice V. Samuels, *The Wanderer* (New York opening: 1 Feb 1917). Wilhelm August Schmidtbonn, *Der verlorene Sohn, ein Legendenspiel* (Berlin, 1912). Jether, a shepherd, is lured from his home by Tisha, priestess of the goddess Ishtar. He journeys to the city of Babylon where he lavishes Tisha with gifts and spends his share of his father's wealth on riotous living. Having expended his gold, Tisha turns Jether out. A prophet's prediction of the city's destruction is fulfilled during a banquet honoring Ishtar, but Jether is saved, for he has neither denied God nor worshipped Ishtar. His return home is celebrated by his father with the Feast of the Fatted Calf. *Shepherds. Jews. Ishtar. Babylon.*

WANDERER OF THE WASTELAND **F2.6087**

Famous Players–Lasky. *Dist* Paramount Pictures. 21 Jun **1924** [Los Angeles premiere; released 10 Aug; c1 Jul 1924; LP20362]. Si; col (Technicolor). 35mm. 6 reels, 5,775 ft.

Pres by Adolph Zukor, Jesse L. Lasky. *Supv* Lucien Hubbard. *Dir* Irvin Willat. *Scen* George C. Hull, Victor Irvin. *Photog* Arthur Ball. *Art Titl* Oscar C. Buchheister.

Cast: Jack Holt *(Adam Larey)*, Noah Beery *(Dismukes)*, George Irving *(Mr. Virey)*, Kathlyn Williams *(Magdalene Virey)*, Billie Dove *(Ruth Virey)*, James Mason *(Guerd Larey)*, Richard R. Neill *(Collishaw)*, James Gordon *(Alex MacKay)*, William Carroll *(Merryvale)*, Willard Cooley *(camp doctor)*.

Western melodrama. Source: Zane Grey, *Wanderer of the Wasteland* (New York, 1923). When Adam Larey, a young mining engineer, shoots his brother Guerd in a quarrel and wounds the sheriff in escaping from town, he seeks refuge in the desert and is saved by Dismukes, an old prospector. After severe hardships, he stumbles on the home of the Vireys, the parents of his sweetheart, Ruth. Virey, who believes his wife is unfaithful, starts an avalanche which destroys both himself and his wife. Adam informs Ruth of the tragedy, and she urges him to return to atone for his past. He finds his brother has sustained only a minor injury, and thus he is free to marry Ruth. *Brothers. Prospectors. Deserts. Avalanches.*

WANDERER OF THE WEST **F2.6088**

Trem Carr Productions. *Dist* Rayart Pictures. Nov or Dec **1927.** Si; b&w. 35mm. 5 reels, 4,200 ft.

Dir? (see note) R. E. Williamson, Joseph E. Zivelli. *Scen* Arthur Hoerl. *Adapt* Victor Rousseau. *Story* W. Ray Johnston. *Photog* Ernest Depew.

Cast: Tex Maynard, Betty Caldwell, Frank Clark, Walter Shumway, Tom Brooker, Roy Watson, Al Rogers, M. A. Dickinson.

Western melodrama. "Rancher plans to get hold of Lazy Y ranch which controls water rights of region. Rancher's aide plays up to daughter of Lazy Y's owner. Girl is kidnapped but rescued by father's foreman. Rancher's gang is run out of town, and girl realizes that foreman would make a very good husband." (*Motion Picture News Booking Guide,* [14]: 293, 1929.) *Ranchers. Ranch foremen. Gangs. Water rights. Kidnaping.*

Note: Sources disagree in crediting direction.

WANDERING DAUGHTERS **F2.6089**

Sam E. Rork. *Dist* Associated First National Pictures. 1 Jul **1923** [c25 May 1923; LP18986]. Si; b&w. 35mm. 6 reels, 5,547 ft.

Pres by Sam E. Rork. *Dir-Scen* James Young. *Titl* Lenore J. Coffee. *Photog* Georges Benoit. *Asst Dir* James Ewens, Clifford Saum.

Cast: Marguerite De La Motte *(Bessie Bowden)*, William V. Mong *(Will Bowden, her father)*, Mabel Van Buren *(Annie Bowden, her mother)*, Marjorie Daw *(Geraldine Horton)*, Noah Beery *(Charles Horton, her father)*, Pat O'Malley *(John Hargraves)*, Allan Forrest *(Austin Trull)*, Alice Howell *(servant in the Bowden home)*.

Comedy-drama. Source: Dana Burnet, "Wandering Daughters," in *Hearst's International Magazine* (42:26, Jul 1922). The daughter of straightlaced parents, Bessie Bowden is attracted to the social life of the fast set and finds Austin Trull, lounge lizard and sometime artist, more interesting than hard-working John Hargraves. Mr. Bowden and John try to compete with Bessie's new friends and spend all the family savings on making the Bowden home appear wealthy and a part of the social whirl. Bessie and Geraldine Horton finally catch Trull at his doubledealing, and Bessie wisely returns to home and Hargraves. *Artists. Filial relations. Jazz life. Family life.*

WANDERING FIRES F2.6090

Maurice Campbell. *Dist* Arrow Pictures. 15 Sep or 1 Oct **1925** [c23 Nov 1925; LP22043]. Si; b&w. 35mm. 6 reels, 5,866 ft.

Prod-Dir Maurice Campbell. *Story* Warner Fabian. *Photog* Harry Stradling.

Cast: Constance Bennett *(Guerda Anthony)*, George Hackathorne *(Raymond Carroll)*, Wallace MacDonald *(Norman Yuell)*, Effie Shannon *(Mrs. Satorius)*, Henrietta Crosman *(Mrs. Carroll)*.

Melodrama. Guerda Anthony sacrifices her reputation to protect the name of her fiancé, Raymond Carroll, supposedly killed in the war. Norman Yuell, a youth with puritanical ideas, falls in love with her and proposes marriage. She agrees but insists that he first learn all the details of the scandal. They marry, but Norman is haunted by increasing doubts of Guerda's love for him. Raymond shows up, a victim of amnesia from shell shock. Familiar surroundings gradually restore his memory, and he absolves Guerda from any wrongdoing. Guerda and Norman, at last, find happiness. *Veterans. Scandal. Marriage. Amnesia. Shell shock.*

WANDERING FOOTSTEPS F2.6091

Banner Productions. *Dist* Henry Ginsberg Distributing Corp. 23 Oct **1925** [New York showing; released Oct; c19 Oct 1925; LP21922]. Si; b&w. 35mm. 6 reels, 5,060 ft.

Dir Phil Rosen. *Cont* Hope Loring, Louis Duryea Lighton. *Photog* Lyman Broening. *Sets* Earl Sibley. *Descriptive Filmusic Guide* Michael Hoffman.

Cast: Alec B. Francis *(Timothy Payne)*, Estelle Taylor *(Helen Maynard)*, Bryant Washburn *(Hal Whitney)*, Eugenie Besserer *(Elizabeth Stuyvesant Whitney)*, Ethel Wales *(Matilda)*, Phillips Smalley *(Mr. Maynard)*, Sidney Bracey *(Dobbins)*, Frankie Darro *(Billy)*.

Melodrama. Source: Charles Sherman, *A Wise Son* (Indianapolis, 1914). Hal Whitney, a young, foolish, yet lovable millionaire, likes his booze a bit too much. While drunk, he befriends Timothy Payne, once a gentleman, now a bum thanks to tipping his elbow too often. Hal "adopts" Timothy as his father, but Hal's sweetheart, Helen Maynard, believes that Timothy will be a bad influence. Timothy understands, and the friends part. Hal finds Timothy in a breadline in front of a rescue mission in which Helen is interested and takes him into his household despite Helen's objections. Timothy straightens Hal out; Hal regains Helen's affections; and Timothy marries Hal's mother, his former sweetheart. *Millionaires. Alcoholism. Adoption. Friendship. Missions. Social service.*

WANDERING GIRLS F2.6092

Columbia Pictures. 20 Jan **1927** [c25 Jan 1927; LP23578]. Si; b&w. 35mm. 6 reels, 5,426 ft.

Supv Harry Cohn. *Dir* Ralph Ince. *Adapt* Harry O. Hoyt. *Story* Dorothy Howell. *Photog* J. O. Taylor.

Cast: Dorothy Revier *(Peggy Marston)*, Eugenie Besserer *(Peggy's mother)*, Frances Raymond *(Mrs. Arnold)*, Robert Agnew *(Jerry Arnold)*, William Welsh *(James Marston)*, Armand Kaliz *(Maurice Dumond)*, Mildred Harris *(Maxine)*.

Society melodrama. Peggy Marston, a jazz-mad smalltown girl, when forbidden to go dancing by her stern parents, slips out to a ball with wealthy young Jerry Arnold. There she meets Maurice Dumond and Maxine, entertainers and society thieves, and she is flattered by Maurice's superb dancing. When she leaves home after a disagreement with her parents, Peggy is victimized by Maxine, who exchanges suitcases with her, thus causing her to be arrested for possession of stolen jewels. While Jerry goes to arrange her bail, a lawyer friend of Maurice's frees her, and she is engaged by Maurice as a dance teacher. In a quarrel Maxine shoots Maurice, but before dying in an automobile crash Maxine confesses to the theft and murder, clearing Peggy, who is then reunited with Jerry and her sick father. *Entertainers. Thieves. Jazz life. Filial relations. Smalltown life. Murder. Automobile accidents.*

WANDERING HUSBANDS F2.6093

Regal Pictures. *Dist* W. W. Hodkinson Corp. 20 Apr **1924** [c1 Apr 1924; LP20132]. Si; b&w. 35mm. 7 reels, 6,306 ft.

Dir William Beaudine. *Story-Scen* C. Gardner Sullivan. *Photog* Ray June.

Cast: James Kirkwood *(George Moreland)*, Lila Lee *(Diana Moreland)*, Margaret Livingston *(Marilyn Foster)*, Eugene Pallette *(Percy)*, Muriel Frances Dana *(Rosemary Moreland)*, Turner Savage *(Jim)*, George Pearce *(Bates)*, George French *(butler)*.

Society drama. Diana Moreland, aware of her husband's attentions to Marilyn Foster, surprises the pair dining at a roadhouse and invites Marilyn to her home. On a boat ride, Diana arranges to have the boat sink. Threatened with drowning, Moreland's affection for Diana is renewed as they swim ashore together, while Marilyn is saved by another boat and retires defeated. *Marriage. Infidelity.*

THE WANING SEX F2.6094

Metro-Goldwyn-Mayer Pictures. 5 Sep **1926** [c30 Aug 1926; LP23067]. Si; b&w. 35mm. 7 reels, 6,039 ft.

Dir Robert Z. Leonard. *Adapt-Cont* F. Hugh Herbert. *Titl* Joe Farnham. *Photog* Ben Reynolds. *Sets* Cedric Gibbons, Paul Youngblood. *Film Ed* William Le Vanway. *Wardrobe* Kathleen Kay, Maude Marsh, André-ani.

Cast: Norma Shearer *(Nina Duane)*, Conrad Nagel *(Philip Barry)*, George K. Arthur *(Hamilton Day)*, Mary McAllister *(Mary Booth)*, Charles McHugh *(J. J. Flannigan)*, Tiny Ward *(J. J. Murphy)*, Martha Mattox *(Ellen B. Armstrong)*.

Romantic comedy. Source: Raymond Hatton and Fanny Hatton, *The Waning Sex* (a play; c13 Aug 1923). Nina Duane, a pretty young criminal lawyer, is resented professionally by Philip Barry, a district attorney, but he invites her to a dinner party. Mary Booth, a simpering young widow, makes a play for Philip, much to Nina's amusement; and later, at his summer house, Nina imitates Mary's tricks for Philip and answers his declaration that if he wins the case in which they are opposed, he may dictate his own marriage terms. Nina wins the case, but Mary insists on inviting Philip to dinner; out of curiosity, Nina strolls over to watch the proceedings. Spilling coffee on Philip's pants, Mary insists on cleaning them; he tries to escape but Mary "faints" to delay him. Finally, he locks her in and escapes in the pants of her younger brother, as Nina has hidden his own. Nina exposes Mary's scheming and saves her younger brother from a compromising situation. Philip forgives Nina, and they are happily united. *Lawyers. District attorneys. Widows. Brother-sister relationship. Courtship.*

WANTED, A HOME *see* **THE DARLING OF NEW YORK**

WANTED BY THE LAW F2.6095

Sunset Productions. 15 Mar **1924.** Si; b&w. 35mm. 5 reels, 4,800 or 5,010 ft.

Dir-Writ Robert N. Bradbury.

Cast: J. B. Warner *(Jim Lorraine)*, Dorothy Woods.

Western melodrama. Jim Lorraine assumes the blame for a shooting to save his brother, a scapegrace, and goes to Montana. There he finds that a map to a rich claim owned by his sweetheart's uncle has been stolen. He recovers the map but is arrested for the previous murder. After it is revealed that the brother confessed to his crime before dying, Jim is exonerated. He then marries his sweetheart. *Brothers. Self-sacrifice. Mine claims. Montana. Documentation.*

WANTED FOR MURDER, OR BRIDE OF HATE (Reissue) F2.6096

Dist Tri-Stone Pictures. 10 Nov **1922** [New York State license]. Si; b&w. 35mm. 5 reels.

Note: Released by Triangle Film Corp. (1917) and copyrighted by Tri-Stone Pictures 12 Jun 1924 (LP20306) under the title *Bride of Hate.*

WANTED—A COWARD F2.6097

Banner Productions. *Dist* Sterling Pictures Distributing Corp. 15 Feb **1927** [c14 May 1927; LP23963]. Si; b&w. 35mm. 6 reels, 5,348 ft.

Prod-Dir Roy Clements. *Story-Scen* Vincent Starrett.

Cast: Lillian Rich *(Isabell Purviance)*, Robert Frazer *(Rupert Garland)*, Frank Brownlee *(Adrian Purviance)*, James Gordon *(Bull Harper)*, Frank Cooley *(Bates)*, Harry S. Northrup *(Ortegas)*, Fred O'Beck *(Stamboff)*, William Bertram *(Slim Ellis)*.

Comedy-drama. Rupert Garland, a handsome soldier, adventurer, and traveler, announces to the press that all men are cowards, including himself. One of his fellow clubmembers, desiring to test the efficacy of his statement, advertises for a coward to call at his home, and Garland, taking on the offer, bets he will prove himself to be a coward. At the house prepared for him, Garland meets Isabell, the old man's niece, and a gang headed by Purviance, an ex-actor: he is chased by a dog, climbs a tree, and scales the wall into the yard to avoid a sniper. Garland becomes a rival of Colonel Ortegas for the love of Isabell and wins a fight with Bull Harper, the chief henchman. The conspirators are arrested, and Garland and Isabell find happiness. *Adventurers. Actors. Cowardice. Clubs.*

THE WANTERS **F2.6098**

Louis B. Mayer Productions. *Dist* Associated First National Pictures. 26 Nov **1923** [c26 Nov 1923; LP19653]. Si; b&w. 35mm. 7 reels, 6,800 ft.

Dir John M. Stahl. *Scen* J. G. Hawks, Paul Bern. *Story* Leila Burton Wells. *Photog* Ernest G. Palmer.

Cast: Marie Prevost *(Myra Hastings)*, Robert Ellis *(Elliot Worthington)*, Norma Shearer *(Marjorie)*, Gertrude Astor *(Mrs. Van Pelt)*, Huntley Gordon *(Theodore Van Pelt)*, Lincoln Stedman *(Bobby)*, Lillian Langdon *(Mrs. Worthington)*, Louise Fazenda *(Mary)*, Hank Mann *(The Star Boarder)*, Lydia Yeamans Titus *(The Landlady)*, Vernon Steele *(Tom Armstrong)*, Harold Goodwin *(chauffeur)*, William Buckley *(butler)*.

Society melodrama. Elliot Worthington falls in love with Myra, the maid in his sister's household. Myra is dismissed; Elliot finds her, proposes marriage, and returns home with his new bride. She is snubbed by his relatives and shocked by the hypocrisy of his wealthy friends. Disillusioned, she runs away: Elliot follows and saves her from being hit by a train when her foot gets caught in a switch. *Housemaids. Social classes. Brother-sister relationship. Wealth. Snobbery. Hypocrisy.*

WANTON KISSES *see* **FREE KISSES**

THE WAR HORSE **F2.6099**

Fox Film Corp. 6 Feb **1927** [c6 Feb 1927; LP23637]. Si; b&w. 35mm. 5 reels, 4,953 ft.

Pres by William Fox. *Dir-Scen* Lambert Hillyer. *Story* Buck Jones, Lambert Hillyer. *Photog* Reginald Lyons. *Asst Dir* Virgil Hart.

Cast: Buck Jones *(Buck Thomas)*, Lola Todd *(Audrey Evans)*, Lloyd Whitlock *(Captain Collins)*, Stanley Taylor *(Lieutenant Caldwell)*, Yola D'Avril *(Yvonne)*, James Gordon *(General Evans)*.

War melodrama. When his horse is conscripted by the government for service in France, Buck Thomas enlists and becomes the orderly to the captain entrusted with the horse. Buck falls in love with Audrey Evans, a beautiful ambulance driver, and when he is cited for his heroism in saving a detachment of American soldiers from an ambuscade, he wins her lasting affection. *Orderlies. Ambulance drivers. War heroes. World War I. France. Horses.*

WAR NURSE **F2.6100**

Metro-Goldwyn-Mayer Pictures. 22 Oct **1930** [New York premiere; released 22 Nov; c13 Nov 1930; LP1724]. Sd (Movietone); b&w. 35mm. 9 reels, 7,333 ft.

Dir Edgar Selwyn. *Scen* Becky Gardiner. *Adtl Dial* Joe Farnham. *Photog* Charles Rosher. *Art Dir* Cedric Gibbons. *Film Ed* William Le Vanway. *Rec Engr* Douglas Shearer. *Wardrobe* René Hubert.

Cast: Robert Montgomery *(Wally)*, Anita Page *(Joy)*, June Walker *(Babs)*, Robert Ames *(Robin)*, ZaSu Pitts *(Cushie)*, Marie Prevost *(Rosalie)*, Helen Jerome Eddy *(Kansas)*, Hedda Hopper *(matron)*, Edward Nugent *(Frank)*, Martha Sleeper *(Helen)*, Michael Vavitch *(doctor)*.

War drama. The film opens with the title: "This is the story of a group of girls, who, at the outbreak of the World War, volunteered for nursing duty in France, untrained, unorganized, unrelated to the vast army of nurses sent out by government authorities or under the banner of the Red Cross, yet they rendered valiant service." Among these are Babs, head nurse, who becomes the focus of attention for Wally, an American aviator in the French Army; Joy, a pampered and convent-trained daughter of a rich American who experiences great difficulty in adjusting to her environment; and Kansas, a studious and naive country girl who is constantly amazed at the horrors of war and the actions of the nurses in the emergency hospital. Joy falls in love with Robin, whom she later discovers to be already married, and when ordered home returns to the front-line hospital. There she dies after giving birth to her child during a bombardment. ... *Nurses. Aviators. Illegitimacy. Hospitals. World War I. France.*

Note: Based on the anonymous work, *War Nurse: The True Story of a Woman Who Lived, Loved and Suffered on the Western Front* (New York, 1930).

WAR PAINT **F2.6101**

Metro-Goldwyn-Mayer Pictures. 10 Oct **1926** [c18 Oct 1926; LP23231]. Si; b&w. 35mm. 6 reels, 5,034 ft.

Dir W. S. Van Dyke. *Cont* Charles Maigne. *Titl* Joe Farnham. *Story* Peter B. Kyne. *Photog* Clyde De Vinna.

Cast: Tim McCoy *(Lieut. Tim Marshall)*, Pauline Starke *(Polly Hopkins)*, Charles French *(Major Hopkins)*, Chief Yowlache *(Iron Eyes)*, Chief Whitehorse *(White Hawk)*, Karl Dane *(Petersen)*.

Western melodrama. Iron Eyes, a medicine man, foments discontent among his people during the early 1880's, and young Lieut. Tim Marshall arrests him after a knife duel in which both are wounded and from which Tim is saved by Chief Fearless Eagle (White Hawk?), a friend of the whites. Tim meets Polly, daughter of Major Hopkins, picking flowers outside the fort, and he forces her to return to safety. Meanwhile, Iron Eyes escapes from the guardhouse and vows vengeance on the whites. At a dance, where Tim declares his love for Polly, a wounded messenger arrives telling of his escape from Iron Eyes; and the major delivers an ultimatum to Fearless Eagle that unless Iron Eyes is delivered up in 24 hours, American troops will destroy his tribe. Iron Eyes stages an attack on the fort, but Tim escapes and persuades Fearless Eagle to rout the attackers and save the women and children of the garrison. *Arapahoe Indians. Medicine men. Frontier and pioneer life. Forts. United States Army.*

WARMING UP **F2.6102**

Paramount Famous Lasky Corp. 4 Aug **1928** [c4 Aug 1928; LP25507]. Mus score & sd eff (Movietone); b&w. 35mm. 8 reels, 6,509 ft.

Pres by Adolph Zukor, Jesse L. Lasky. *Dir* Fred Newmeyer. *Adapt-Screenplay* Ray Harris. *Titl* George Marion. *Story* Sam Mintz. *Photog* Edward Cronjager. *Film Ed* Otto Lovering. *Song: "Out of the Dawn"* Walter Donaldson.

Cast: Richard Dix *(Bert Tulliver)*, Jean Arthur *(Mary Post)*, Claude King *(Mr. Post)*, Philo McCullough *(McRae)*, Billy Kent Schaefer *(Edsel)*, Roscoe Karns *(Hippo)*, James Dugan *(Brill)*, Mike Donlin *(veteran)*, Mike Ready, Chet Thomas, Joe Pirrone, Wally Hood, Bob Murray, Truck Hannah *(themselves)*.

Comedy-drama. Bert Tulliver, the star pitcher of a smalltown baseball team, gets a chance to try out for the Green Sox and immediately arouses the animosity of McRae, the league's home-run king. Bert falls in love with Mary Post, the daughter of the club's owner, and further angers McRae, who considers Mary to be his girl. McRae is hired by another major league team and does not meet Bert again until the World Series, when they are on opposing teams. In the first game, Bert, who has come to believe that McRae has the jinx on him, walks McRae and is pulled from the game. In the final and deciding game of the series, Bert must face McRae again and, bolstered by Mary's love, he strikes him out, winning the series for the Green Sox and assuring himself of Mary's love. *Baseball. World Series.*

THE WARNING **F2.6103**

Columbia Pictures. 26 Nov **1927** [c31 Dec 1927; LP24815]. Si; b&w. 35mm. 6 reels, 5,791 ft.

Prod Harry Cohn. *Dir-Writ* George B. Seitz. *Story* Lillian Ducey, H. Milner Kitchin. *Photog* Ray June. *Art Dir* Robert E. Lee. *Asst Dir* Max Cohn.

Cast: Jack Holt *(Tom Fellows/Col. Robert Wellsley)*, Dorothy Revier *(Mary Blake)*, Frank Lackteen *(Tso Lin)*, Pat Harmon *(London Charlie)*, Eugene Strong *(No. 24)*, George Kuwa *(Ah Sung)*, Norman Trevor *(Sir James Gordon)*.

Underworld melodrama. While in Shanghai, Tom Fellows, captain of an opium-smuggling tramp steamer, finds Mary Blake, Secret Service Agent No. 63, held captive in a waterfront opium den by the notorious "London Charlie." After a struggle with the gang leader, Fellows rescues the girl, takes her to his room, and sets her free. Agent Blake immediately leads a raiding party on the opium den and is once again captured. About to be put to death, the girl is once more rescued by Fellows, and the gang is rounded up. Mary then learns that Fellows is actually Col. Robert Wellsley, Chief of the British Intelligence Service in China. The way to romance is clear. *Secret service. Opium. China. Shanghai. Great Britain—Intelligence service.*

THE WARNING SIGNAL **F2.6104**

Ellbee Pictures. 14 Jul **1926** [New York State license]. Si; b&w. 35mm. 5 reels, 4,998 ft.

Dir Charles Hunt. *Story-Scen* A. B. Barringer. *Photog* William Tuers.

Cast: Gladys Hulette, Kent Mead, Lincoln Stedman, Clarence Burton, Martha Mattox, William H. Turner, Joseph Girard.

Melodrama. The son of a wealthy railroad magnate, wishing to succeed independently, conceals his identity and takes a menial job on his father's line. He quickly proves himself to be extremely competent and arouses the enmity of a superintendent. The two men fight over a girl, and the boy is transferred to a remote signal shack. The superintendent tampers with the warning signal at the boy's shack, and the president's special thunders through, headed for a collision with another train. The boy uses a radio device of his invention and alerts the engineer to the danger, preventing a disaster. The boy's father learns of his son's heroism and appoints him to the presidency of the railroad. *Signalmen. Railroad magnates. Filial relations. Inventions. Railroads. Radio.*

THE WARRENS OF VIRGINIA **F2.6105**

Fox Film Corp. 12 Oct **1924** [c8 Sep 1924; LP20592]. Si; b&w. 35mm. 7 reels, 6,536 ft.

Pres by William Fox. *Dir* Elmer Clifton. *Scen* William C. De Mille.

Cast: George Backus *(General Warren)*, Rosemary Hill *(Betty Warren)*, Martha Mansfield *(Agatha Warren)*, Robert Andrews *(Arthur Warren)*, Wilfred Lytell *(Lieutenant Burton)*, Harlan Knight *("Pap")*, James Turfler *("Danny")*, Helen Ray Kyle *("The Little Reb")*, Lieut. Wilbur J. Fox *(General Grant)*, J. Barney Sherry *(General Lee)*, Frank Andrews *(General Griffin)*.

Historical romance. Source: William C. De Mille, "The Warrens of Virginia," in John Ben Russak, ed., *Monte Cristo ... and Other Plays* (Princeton, 1941). Union officer Burton is assigned to be captured by Confederates in his sweetheart's home so that they may obtain false dispatches. Burton sacrifices his love and is almost hanged as a spy when Betty misinterprets his motives. As he is about to be executed, word arrives of Lee's surrender, and Betty rescues him. After the war, misunderstandings are cleared up and their romance is revived. *Espionage. United States—History—Civil War. Virginia. Robert Edward Lee. Ulysses Simpson Grant.*

WARRIOR GAP **F2.6106**

Davis Distributing Division. *Dist* Vital Exchanges. 4 Dec **1925** [New York State license]. Si; b&w. 35mm. 5 reels, 4,900 ft.

Dir Alvin J. Neitz. *Scen* George W. Pyper. *Photog* Alfred Gosden.

Cast: Ben Wilson *(Captain Deane)*, Neva Gerber *(Elinor Folsom)*, Robert Walker *(Major Burleigh)*, Jim Welch *(Colonel Stevens)*, Aline Goodwin *(Mrs. Hal Folsom)*, Lafe McKee *(John Folsom)*, Dick Hatton *(Hal Folsom)*, Alfred Hewston *(Sergeant Casey)*, Ruth Royce *(Mrs. Fletcher)*, Len Haynes *(Chief Red Cloud)*, William Patten *(courier)*.

Western melodrama. Source: Capt. Charles King, *Warrior Gap, a Story of the Sioux Outbreak of '68* (New York, c1897). Captain Deane and Major Burleigh are returning with their troops from a frontier post when they are attacked by hostile Indians. The men have been ordered to avoid a direct military confrontation, but Major Burleigh, prompted by military vainglory, insists on counterattacking. Deane refuses and parts company with the major and his men, later defending Elinor Folsom from an Indian attack on her isolated ranch. Deane is arrested for insubordination and cowardice, but he is cleared of these charges, is released, and whips Burleigh in a fight. Deane is then ordered to convey a military payroll, and Burleigh incites a band of Indians to intercept him. Elinor learns of this plot and rides to warn Deane, and the two are soon compelled to fight for their lives. They are rescued by the cavalry, and Burleigh is shot. Elinor and the captain are wed. *Indians of North America. Sioux Indians. United States Army—Cavalry. Red Cloud.*

WAR'S WOMEN (Reissue) **F2.6107**

Dist Tri-Stone Pictures. **1923.** Si; b&w. 35mm. 5 reels.

Note: A "re-edited and re-titled" Frank Keenan film originally released by Triangle Film Corp. (c19 Dec 1915; LP11949).

WAS HE GUILTY? (Reissue) **F2.6108**

Sierra Pictures. *Dist* Pizor Productions. 13 Sep **1927** [New York State license]. Si; b&w. 35mm. 5 reels.

Note: When this film about drug addiction was originally released in 1919, William Boyd was featured in a supporting role. It was later reissued to capitalize on his stardom.

WAS IT BIGAMY? **F2.6109**

William Steiner Productions. 27 Sep **1925** [c2 Mar, 3 Mar 1925; LU21193]. Si; b&w. 35mm. 5 reels.

Dir Charles Hutchinson. *Scen* John Francis Natteford. *Story* Forrest Sheldon. *Photog* Ernest Miller.

Cast: Edith Thornton *(Ruth Steele)*, Earle Williams *(Carleton)*, Thomas Ricketts *(Judge Gaynor)*, Charles Cruz *(Harvey Gaynor)*, Wilfred Lucas *(attorney)*, Natalie Warfield.

Melodrama. Ruth Steele is a bigamist: she marries once for love and once to help her beloved guardian out of financial difficulties. She then sets about obtaining a divorce from the man she loves by making him think that she is a bold, bad girl. The action moves to Central America, where the wicked husband is put out of the way by a jealous native rival. Ruth and her first husband are happily reunited. *Bigamy. Divorce. Murder. Good and evil. Central America.*

WASTED LIVES **F2.6110**

Mission Film Corp. *Dist* Second National Film Corp. 10 Jan **1923** [c27 Mar 1923; LP18843]. Si; b&w. 35mm. 5 reels, 4,874 ft.

Dir Clarence Geldert. *Titl* William B. Laub.

Cast: Richard Wayne *(Randolph Adams)*, Catherine Murphy *(Dorothy Richards)*, Winter Hall *(Dr. Wentworth)*, Lillian Leighton *(Mrs. Jonathan Adams)*, Margaret Loomis *(Madge Richards)*, Arthur Osborne *(Ned Hastings)*, Walt Whitman *(Noah Redstone)*, Philippe De Lacy *(Bobby Adams)*, Fannie Midgley *(Mrs. Hastings)*.

Society drama. Rich, idle Randolph Adams leaves his medical studies, but an incident with an injured child causes him to return to medicine and devote his life to a children's hospital. He marries Madge Richards, who is also loved by his friend Ned Hastings, and shortly thereafter he goes to war. Randy is reported killed, and in her bitterness his mother withdraws her support of the hospital. Ned asks Madge to marry him, and she is almost persuaded when Mrs. Adams is seriously injured in an accident. Then, Randy suddenly reappears, saves his mother's life with a "vibrameter," a machine of his own invention, and returns to his family and work. *Physicians. Inventors. Motherhood. Friendship. Hospitals. World War I.*

WASTED LIVES **F2.6111**

Banner Productions. *Dist* Ginsberg Distributing Corp. c7 Apr **1925** [LP21341]. Si; b&w. 35mm. 6 reels.

Prod George H. Davis, Samuel J. Briskin. *Dir* John Gorman. *Scen* Van A. James. *Adapt* Maude P. Kelso.

Cast: Elliott Dexter, Cullen Landis, Edith Roberts, Betty Francisco, Henry Hull.

Melodrama. After the death of her brother, "Tommy" Carlton makes the acquaintance of a neighbor, Harold Graypon, who invites her to a party. Tommy, who is a bit of a hoyden, attends the party in overalls and shocks the guests. Tommy is later ejected from her home and takes refuge in a shack in the mountains, where shé makes rustic furniture for a living. Despite the interference of Grace, Tommy and Harold finds happiness with each other. *Tomboys. Cottage industries. Furniture.*

THE WASTER **F2.6112**

Paul Gerson Pictures. *Dist* Aywon Film Corp. 9 Sept **1926** [New York State license]. Si; b&w. 35mm. 5 reels.

Melodrama(?). No information about the nature of this film has been found.

WATCH HIM STEP **F2.6113**

Phil Goldstone Productions. Feb or 1 Mar **1922.** Si; b&w. 35mm. 5 reels, 4,800 ft.

Dir Jack Nelson. *Story-Scen* W. Scott Darling. *Photog* Hal Mohr.

Cast: Richard Talmadge *(Dick Underwood)*, Ethel Shannon *(Dorothy Travers)*, Al Filson *(John Travers)*, Nellie Peck Saunders *(Mrs. John Travers)*, Colin Kenny *(Jack Allen)*, Hugh Saxon *(The Uncle)*.

Comedy-drama. Dick Underwood's desire to marry Dorothy Travers receives strong opposition from her father, and the couple decide to elope. Their escape is thwarted by an accident, however, and John Travers takes his daughter home, where she is courted by Jack Allen, a crooked stock promoter. Dick and Dorothy's second attempt to elope is fouled by Allen, and Dick lands in jail. He escapes, and a fight with Allen leaves Dick as sole contender for Dorothy. Allen is caught for misusing the mails, and Dick receives John Travers' blessing. The hero's athletic stunts are featured. *Stock promoters. Fatherhood. Mail fraud. Elopement. Stunts.*

WATCH YOUR STEP **F2.6114**

Goldwyn Pictures. Feb **1922** [c11 Feb 1922; LP17544]. Si; b&w. 35mm. 5 reels, 4,713 ft.

Dir William Beaudine. *Story-Scen* Julien Josephson. *Photog* John J. Mescall.

Cast: Cullen Landis *(Elmer Slocum)*, Patsy Ruth Miller *(Margaret Andrews)*, Bert Woodruff *(Russ Weaver)*, George Pierce *(Lark Andrews)*, Raymond Cannon *(Lon Kimball)*, Gus Leonard *(Jennifer Kimball)*, Henry Rattenbury *(Constable)*, Joel Day *(Ky Wilson)*, L. J. O'Connor *(Detective Ryan)*, John Cossar *(Henry Slocum)*, Lillian Sylvester *(Mrs. Spivey)*, L. H.

King *(Lote Spivey)*, Cordelia Callahan *(Mrs. Andrews)*, Alberta Lee *(Mrs. Weaver)*.

Comedy-melodrama. Elmer Slocum has just served a jail sentence for speeding. On his first day of liberty he encounters a physician whose car has broken down and offers to take him to his patient; he is pursued by motorcops for speeding, wrecks his car in a closed street, and knocks down and believes he has killed a policeman. Elmer boards a freight train and makes his way to a small town in Iowa, where he meets Margaret Andrews, daughter of the town's richest citizen and is given a job by storekeeper Russ Weaver. Margaret's father and her suitor, Lon Kimball, are suspicious of him; and when a detective hired by his father finds him, Lon is overjoyed at the removal of his rival. Elmer learns, however, that the policeman is alive and that he is free to accept the attentions of Margaret. *Physicians. Detectives. Police. Automobile driving. Iowa.*

WATCH YOUR WIFE (Universal-Jewel) **F2.6115**

Universal Pictures. 4 Apr **1926** [c24 Feb 1926; LP22425]. Si; b&w. 35mm. 7 reels, 6,974 ft.

Dir Svend Gade. *Scen* Charles E. Whittaker, Svend Gade. *Photog* Arthur L. Todd.

Cast: Virginia Valli *(Claudia Langham)*, Pat O'Malley *(James Langham)*, Nat Carr *(Benjamin Harris)*, Helen Lee Worthing *(Gladys Moon)*, Albert Conti *(Alphonse Marsac)*, Aggie Herring *(Madame Buff)*, Nora Hayden *(maid)*.

Comedy-drama. Source: Gösta Segercrantz, "Watch Your Wife" (publication undetermined). Writer James Langham and his wealthy wife, Claudia, quarrel and are divorced. Claudia moves into a posh hotel and renews her acquaintance with Alphonse Marsac, an old European friend with an eye on her fortune. Alone in the family mansion, James goes to an agency and rents a "wife" to be his daytime companion and housekeeper. Claudia finds them together one evening, and, suspecting the worst of an innocent relationship, impulsively informs Alphonse that she will marry him. James goes after her, sweeps her from a moving train, and marries her for the second time. *Authors. Fortune hunters. Hired companions. Housekeepers. Marriage. Divorce.*

WATCHING EYES **F2.6116**

Frazer Productions. *Dist* Arrow Film Corp. 4 Oct or 12 Nov **1921.** Si; b&w. 35mm. 5 reels, 4,577 ft.

Story-Scen Robert Blaine.

Cast: Kiki *(herself, a dog)*, Edna Beaumont *(Evelyn Selby)*, Geoffrey H. Mallins *(Adam Dewey)*, John Wickens *(Clayton Miles)*.

Melodrama. "'Kiki' is the pet Pomeranian belonging to Evelyn Selby, who is engaged to Adam Dewey. Evelyn is waning in her affection for Adam, due to the interference of Clayton Miles, keeper of the horses, with whom she believes herself infatuated. Kiki leads Adam to a seat in the garden one night where he finds Clayton making love to Evelyn. Clayton senses that Kiki is an enemy and tries to drown her, but the dog is too smart for that. Later Evelyn and Clayton try to elope, but Kiki delays the event by hiding herself so that her mistress can't find her until Adam appears. Adam proves to the girl that he is the man for her and she gives up Clayton." (*Moving Picture World,* 20 May 1922, p343.) *Courtship. Dogs. Horses.*

THE WATER HOLE **F2.6117**

Paramount Famous Lasky Corp. 25 Aug **1928** [c25 Aug 1928; LP25567]. Si; b&w with col sequences (Technicolor). 35mm. 7 reels, 6,319 ft.

Pres by Adolph Zukor, Jesse L. Lasky. *Dir* F. Richard Jones. *Titl* Herman J. Mankiewicz. *Photog* C. Edgar Schoenbaum. *Film Ed* Jane Loring, Albert S. Le Vino.

Cast: Jack Holt *(Philip Randolph)*, Nancy Carroll *(Judith Endicott)*, John Boles *(Bert Durland)*, Montague Shaw *(Mr. Endicott)*, Ann Christy *(Dolores)*, Lydia Yeamans Titus *("Ma" Bennett)*, Jack Perrin *(Ray)*, Jack Mower *(Mojave)*, Paul Ralli *(Diego)*, Tex Young *(Shorty)*, Bob Miles *(Joe)*, Greg Whitespear *(Indian)*.

Western melodrama. Source: Zane Grey, "The Water Hole," in *Collier's* (8 Oct–24 Dec 1927). Judith Endicott, the daughter of a wealthy eastern banker, vamps Philip Randolph, an Arizonan, when he comes east to talk business with her father. Philip proposes and discovers that Judith has only been kidding him along. He returns angrily to Arizona, and the elder Endicott, accompanied by his daughter, follows him west. With her father's permission, Richard "kidnaps" Judith and takes her to a deserted Indian cliff dwelling, where she must cook and care for him. Bert Durland, Judith's fiancé, follows after her, and his Indian guide steals all of the horses. Judith and Bert and Philip start back to civilization across the desert, and Bert goes berserk from the heat. They are rescued by cowboys, and Judith returns east, "kidnaping" Philip and taking him with her. *Cowboys. Bankers. Indians of North America. Vamps. Abduction. Deserts. Heatstroke. Arizona.*

THE WATER LILY *see* **A TALE OF TWO WORLDS**

WATERED STOCK *see* **BEWARE OF THE LAW**

WATERFRONT **F2.6118**

First National Pictures. 16 Sep **1928** [c17 Sep 1928; LP25619]. Mus score & sd eff (Vitaphone); b&w. 35mm. 7 reels, 6,368 ft. [Also si; 6,142 ft.]

Prod Ned Marin. *Dir* William A. Seiter. *Cont* Tom Geraghty. *Titl* Gene Towne, Casey Robinson. *Story* Will Chappell, Gertrude Orr. *Photog* Lee Garmes. *Film Ed* John Rawlins.

Cast: Dorothy Mackaill *(Peggy Ann Andrews)*, Jack Mulhall *(Jack Dowling)*, James Bradbury, Sr. *(Peter Seastrom)*, Knute Erickson *(Capt. John Andrews)*, Ben Hendricks, Jr. *(Oilcan Olson)*, William Norton Bailey *(Brute Mullin)*, Pat Harmon *(an oiler)*.

Comedy-drama. Jack Dowling, an oiler on a tramp steamer, falls in love with Peggy Ann Andrews and thereby angers her father, a San Francisco tugboat skipper. Jack asks Peggy if she will marry him and go to live in the country, but she turns him down, wanting no part of farm life. When Peggy's father learns that Jack wants to be a farmer, he changes his mind about him, and the two men are soon conspiring to make Peggy give up waterfront life: they shanghai Peggy and put her to work peeling potatoes on a docked freighter. Peggy is at first resentful but soon comes to realize that she truly loves Jack and prepares to be a country housewife. *Oilers. Sea captains. Farming. Courtship. Waterfront. Tugboats. San Francisco.*

WATERFRONT WOLVES **F2.6119**

Gerson Pictures. *Dist* Renown Pictures. 26 Feb **1924** [New York showing; released 15 Jan]. Si; b&w. 35mm.

Dir-Writ Tom Gibson.

Cast: Ora Carew, Jay Morley, Hal Stephens, Dick La Reno.

Melodrama. Some valuable pearls are stolen in China and transported to America. The plot deals with the efforts of Ora Carew, as the heroine, to return the pearls, stolen by her father, to their owner. She is assisted by a Chinaman whose life was once saved by the girl's mother and the ubiquitous young hero who climaxes the film in a fistic encounter with the father aboard a schooner. *Chinese. Filial relations. Pearls.*

WAY FOR A SAILOR **F2.6120**

Metro-Goldwyn-Mayer Pictures. 11 Oct or 1 Nov **1930** [c6 Nov 1930; LP1698]. Sd (Movietone); b&w. 35mm. 9 reels, 7,967 ft.

Dir Sam Wood. *Scen-Dial* Laurence Stallings, W. L. River. *Adtl Dial* Charles MacArthur, Al Boasberg. *Photog* Percy Hilburn. *Art Dir* Cedric Gibbons. *Film Ed* Frank Sullivan. *Rec Engr* Robert Shirley, Douglas Shearer. *Wardrobe* Vivian Beer.

Cast: John Gilbert *(Jack)*, Wallace Beery *(Tripod)*, Jim Tully *(Ginger)*, Leila Hyams *(Joan)*, Polly Moran *(Polly)*, Doris Lloyd *(Flossy)*.

Romantic melodrama. Source: Albert Richard Wetjen, *Way of a Sailor* (New York, 1928). Jack, a sailor, along with his buddies Tripod and Ginger, feels himself an indomitable force until he falls for Joan, who repeatedly repels his advances every time he comes into port, and only after a number of years is he able to see her alone. Finally he wins her and they are married, but Joan, learning he plans to return to the sea, leaves him. Later, having become a quartermaster on an ocean liner, he finds her still unforgiving; then a storm wrecks the ship on which all are traveling, and to her grief he is lost with Tripod and Ginger, but the trio is rescued by a whaling vessel and returned to port. After receiving Jack's message, Joan, having realized her true feelings, is reunited with him. *Sailors. Quartermasters. Courtship. Ocean liners. Whaling ships.*

THE WAY MEN LOVE *see* **BY DIVINE RIGHT**

THE WAY OF A GIRL **F2.6121**

Metro-Goldwyn Pictures. 6 Apr **1925** [c31 Mar 1925; LP21286]. Si; b&w. 35mm. 6 reels, 5,025 ft.

Pres by Louis B. Mayer. *Dir* Robert G. Vignola. *Scen* Albert Shelby Le Vino. *Photog* John Arnold. *Art Dir* Cedric Gibbons. *Asst Dir* Phil Carle.

Cast: Eleanor Boardman *(Rosamond)*, Matt Moore *(George)*, William

Russell *(Brand)*, Mathew Betz *(Matt)*, Charles K. French *(police judge)*, Floyd Johnson, Jack Herrick *(prizefighters)*, Leo Willis *(traffic cop)*, Kate Price *(woman in jail)*.

Society melodrama. Source: Katharine Newlin Burt, "Summoned," in *Ainslee's* (50:2–57, Feb 1923). Rosamond, a pampered society girl who craves excitement, becomes annoyed with her very proper fiancé, George, when he avoids trouble at a prizefight. To compensate for the staid evening, she races her car through the streets of the city until she is arrested by a traffic cop and summoned before a judge. The judge recognizes her as a habitual offender and agrees to release her only under the condition that George assume responsibility for her conduct. Rosamond at first refuses to be released under George's supervision, but after spending a night in jail with a drunk, she changes her mind and accepts the probation. George and Rosamond later attend an artists' ball which becomes rowdy, and George insists that Rosamond leave with him. She refuses and, greatly angered, jumps in her car, returning at great speed to the city. The car goes off the road and plunges down an embankment; Rosamond is not hurt, but she is captured by two convicts. For 2 weeks she lives as a captive in a cave. One of the convicts falls in love with her and helps her escape, losing his life for this kindness. Rosamond is chased by the other convict, but George arrives in time to capture the criminal and turn him over to the police. Rosamond repents of her wild life and seeks refuge in George's conventional arms. *Socialites. Police. Convicts. Prizefighters. Judges. Artists. Alcoholism. Probation. Automobile accidents.*

THE WAY OF A MAID **F2.6122**

Selznick Pictures. *Dist* Select Pictures. 30 Nov **1921** [c5 Nov 1921; LP17281]. Si; b&w. 35mm. 5 reels, 4,800 ft.

Pres by Lewis J. Selznick. *Dir* William P. S. Earle. *Scen* Lewis Allen Browne. *Story* Rex Taylor. *Photog* William Wagner.

Cast: Elaine Hammerstein *(Naida Castleton)*, Niles Welch *(Thomas Lawlor)*, Diana Allen *(Dorothy Graham)*, Charles D. Brown *(Gordon Witherspoon)*, George Fawcett *(David Lawlor)*, Arthur Housman *(Jimmy Van Trent)*, Helen Lindroth *(Mrs. Lawlor)*.

Society comedy-drama. Returning to a friend's apartment after a masquerade ball where she has won first prize as a lady's maid, society girl Naida Castleton is mistaken for the housemaid by Thomas Lawlor. He is struck by her beauty, however, and in a spirit of mischief she keeps up the deception. Naida suffers a financial misfortune, and she is obliged to sell her city property and lease her summer home, which is acquired by Tom's socially ambitious mother; Naida then continues in the role of secretary to Mr. Lawlor, who does not suspect her deception. While shopping, Naida is discovered by her friends and taken to her home, where she serves them cocktails. Mrs. Lawlor arrives and, realizing the situation, pretends to be a guest. Before Tom discovers the truth, he proposes to her, and after revealing her true identity, she accepts. *Socialites. Secretaries. Upper classes. Impersonation. Courtship.*

THE WAY OF ALL FLESH **F2.6123**

Paramount Famous Lasky Corp. 25 Jun **1927** [New York premiere; released 1 Oct; c1 Oct 1927; LP24471]. Si; b&w. 35mm. 9 reels, 8,486 ft.

Pres by Adolph Zukor, Jesse L. Lasky. *Dir* Victor Fleming. *Screenplay* Jules Furthman. *Titl* Julian Johnson. *Adapt* Lajos Biró. *Photog* Victor Milner.

Cast: Emil Jannings *(August Schiller)*, Belle Bennett *(Mrs. Schiller)*, Phyllis Haver *(Mayme)*, Donald Keith *(August, Junior)*, Fred Kohler *(The Tough)*, Philippe De Lacey *(August, as a child)*, Mickey McBan *(Evald)*, Betsy Ann Lisle *(Charlotte)*, Carmencita Johnson *(Elizabeth)*, Gordon Thorpe *(Karl)*, Jackie Coombs *(Heinrich)*, Dean Harrell, Anne Sheridan, Dorothy Kitchen.

Drama. Source: Perley Poore Sheehan, "The Way of All Flesh" (publication undetermined). The world of bank cashier August Schiller centers chiefly around his patient wife and six children, and he prides himself on being an ideal father, a faithful worker, and a loyal husband. For the first time since his honeymoon, August leaves Milwaukee to deliver some bonds in Chicago, and on the train he innocently becomes involved with Mayme, an adventuress, who seduces him and during a drunken revel steals his bonds; her lover, The Tough, and his gang beat him and attempt to take his watch, but August in his fury grapples with The Tough, who is killed by a passing train. August changes clothing with The Tough and is reported as having died a hero's death defending his employer's trust. Years later, a broken derelict, he learns that his oldest son has become a famous violinist, and he hoards to buy a gallery seat at a concert; he follows the boy home on Christmas Day, catching furtive glimpses of his happy family, who fail to recognize him. *Bankers. Adventuresses. Germans. Derelicts. Violinists. Fatherhood. Robbery. Seduction. Family life. Christmas. Milwaukee. Chicago.*

THE WAY OF ALL MEN **F2.6124**

First National Pictures. 7 Sep **1930** [c21 Jul 1930; LP1447]. Sd (Vitaphone); b&w. 35mm. 7 reels, 6,032 ft.

Dir Frank Lloyd. *Screenplay-Dial* Bradley King. *Film Ed* Ray Curtiss.

Cast: Douglas Fairbanks, Jr. *(Billy Bear)*, Dorothy Revier *(Poppy)*, Robert Edeson *(Swift)*, Anders Randolf *(Frazer)*, Ivan Simpson *(Higgins)*, William Orlamond *(Nordling)*, Henry Kolker *(Sharp)*, Louis King *(Levee Louie)*, William Courtenay *(Preacher)*, Noah Beery *(Stratton)*, Wade Boteler *(Charlie)*, Dorothy Mathews *(Edna)*, Pat Cummings *(Dick)*, Alona Marlowe *(Gwen)*, Eddie Clayton *(Jack)*.

Melodrama. Source: Henning Berger, "Syndaloden" (publication undetermined). The plot is similar to that of the 1926 silent version, *The Sin Flood*, also directed by Frank Lloyd. *Brokers. Chorus girls. Engineers. Lawyers. Actors. Bartenders. Preachers. Tramps. Redemption. Death.*

THE WAY OF THE STRONG **F2.6125**

Columbia Pictures. 19 Jun **1928** [c7 Aug 1928; LP25517]. Si; b&w. 35mm. 6 reels, 5,752 ft.

Prod Harry Cohn. *Dir* Frank Capra. *Scen* Peter Milne. *Story* William Conselman. *Photog* Ben Reynolds.

Cast: Mitchell Lewis *(Handsome Williams)*, Alice Day *(Nora)*, Margaret Livingston *(Marie)*, Theodore von Eltz *(Dan)*, William Norton Bailey *(Tiger Louie)*.

Melodrama. Handsome Williams, the king of the bootleggers, falls in love with Nora, a beautiful blind violinist, and gives her a job in his cafe. Handsome (who is an extremely ugly man) convinces the girl that he is a man of great good looks, and she begins to return his affection. Tiger Louie, a bootlegger out to get Handsome, kidnaps the girl and forces Handsome to let his booze trucks into the city unmolested. Handsome leads a raid on Louie's place and, with the help of Dan, the piano player, gets Nora to safety. Running from the police, Handsome finally recognizes the love that has been developing between Dan and Nora; letting them out of the car, he sacrifices his life to give them enough time to find safety and a new life. *Violinists. Pianists. Bootleggers. Hijackers. Kidnaping. Self-sacrifice. Cafes. Mississippi River. Floods.*

THE WAY OF THE TRANSGRESSOR **F2.6126**

Premium Picture Productions. *Dist* Independent Pictures. Dec **1923.** Si; b&w. 35mm. 5 reels, 4,900 ft.

Dir William J. Craft.

Cast: George Larkin *("Silk" Raymond)*, Ruth Stonehouse *(Alma Barclay)*, Frank Whitson *("Moose" McKay)*, Al Ferguson *(Jim Finley)*, Laura Anson *(Olive Stark)*, Carl Silvera *(Charlie Wong)*, William Vaughn Moody *("Spider")*.

Crook melodrama. Silk Raymond, a reformed safecracker, is railroaded to jail by Moose McKay, a mastermind criminal who masquerades as a society man. While in jail Silk meets society girl Alma Barclay, also the object of McKay's affections. Silk's attempts to prove his innocence when he is released from jail are thwarted by McKay, and he is forced to rejoin the gang for a livelihood. Finally McKay loses his life when a Chinese servant stabs him. Silk goes straight and marries Alma. *Socialites. Safecrackers. Chinese. Criminals—Rehabilitation. Gangs. Imposture.*

WAY OUT WEST **F2.6127**

Metro-Goldwyn-Mayer Pictures. 2 Aug **1930** [c1 Dec 1930; LP1773]. Sd (Movietone); b&w. 35mm. 8 reels, 6,407 ft. [Also si.]

Dir Fred Niblo. *Story-Cont* Byron Morgan, Alfred Block. *Dial* Joe Farnham, Alfred Block, Ralph Spence. *Photog* Henry Sharp. *Art Dir* Cedric Gibbons. *Film Ed* William S. Gray, Jerry Thoms. *Song: "Singing a Song to the Stars"* Howard Johnson, Joseph Meyer. *Rec Engr* Douglas Shearer. *Wardrobe* David Cox.

Cast: William Haines *(Windy)*, Leila Hyams *(Molly)*, Polly Moran *(Pansy)*, Cliff Edwards *(Trilby)*, Francis X. Bushman, Jr. *(Steve)*, Vera Marsh *(La Belle Rosa)*, Charles Middleton *(Buck)*, Jack Pennick *(Pete)*, Buddy Roosevelt *(Tex)*, Jay Wilsey *(Hank)*.

Western comedy-drama. Windy, a sideshow barker playing a small western town, swindles some cowboys with a rigged roulette wheel, and they decide to hang him for his perfidy; but he is saved by the intervention of a ranch foreman, who suggests that he work on the ranch and pay back the money he swindled. At the ranch, where Windy is forced to do menial tasks, he falls in love with the ranch owner, Molly; however, he is beaten in a fight with Steve, Molly's suitor. He decides to make his getaway during the roundup, but he saves Molly when she is bitten by a rattlesnake by taking her to an Indian medicine man. Returning, they are caught in a sandstorm, and she is retrieved by Buck, her brother. Thinking Molly has been kidnaped, the cowboys corner Windy in a deserted Indian village, and this time he defeats Steve; cleared by Buck, Windy is declared a hero and is reunited with Molly. *Barkers. Cowboys. Medicine men. Ranchers. Swindlers. Courtship. Snakes.*

WE AMERICANS (Universal-Jewel) **F2.6128**

Universal Pictures. 25 Mar or 6 May **1928** [c20 Mar 1928; LP25092]. Si; b&w. 35mm. 9 reels, 8,700 ft.

Supv Carl Laemmle, Jr. *Dir-Cont* Edward Sloman. *Adapt-Cont* Alfred A. Cohn. *Photog* Jackson J. Rose. *Film Ed* Robert Jahns.

Cast: George Sidney *(Mr. Levine)*, Patsy Ruth Miller *(Beth Levine)*, George Lewis *(Phil Levine)*, Eddie Phillips *(Pete Albertini)*, Beryl Mercer *(Mrs. Levine)*, John Boles *(Hugh Bradleigh)*, Albert Gran *(Mr. Schmidt)*, Michael Visaroff *(Mr. Albertini)*, Kathlyn Williams *(Mrs. Bradleigh)*, Edward Martindel *(Mr. Bradleigh)*, Josephine Dunn *(Helen Bradleigh)*, Daisy Belmore *(Mrs. Schmidt)*, Rosita Marstini *(Mrs. Albertini)*, Andy Devine *(Pat O'Dougal)*, Flora Bramley *(Sara Schmidt)*, Jake Bleifer *(Korn)*.

Society drama. Source: Milton Herbert Gropper and Max Siegel, *We Americans: A New Play* (New York, 1928). Hugh Bradleigh, the son of a socially prominent family, falls in love with Beth Levine, whose parents are Russian-Jewish immigrants. Pete Albertini, the son of an Italian-American family, is affianced to Sara Schmidt, whose parents are German immigrants. When war with Germany breaks out, Hugh, Pete, and Beth's brother Phil all enlist. Overseas, Phil loses his life in order to save Hugh's, and Pete loses a leg. Returning from Europe, Pete marries Sara, and when Hugh announces his engagement to Beth his parents object. All objections are dropped, however, when the Bradleighs meet Beth's parents and learn of Phil's sacrifice for Hugh. *Immigrants. Veterans. Russians. Jews. Italians. Germans. Social classes. World War I.*

WE MODERNS **F2.6129**

John McCormick Productions. *Dist* First National Pictures. 15 Nov **1925** [c3 Nov 1925; LP21963]. Si; b&w. 35mm. 7 reels, 6,656 ft.

Pres by John McCormick. *Dir* John Francis Dillon. *Ed Dir–Writ for the screen by* June Mathis. *Photog* T. D. McCord. *Art Dir* Edward Shulter. *Film Ed* Edwin Robbins. *Comedy Construc* Mervyn LeRoy.

Cast: Colleen Moore *(Mary Sundale)*, Jack Mulhall *(John Ashler)*, Carl Miller *(Oscar Pleat)*, Claude Gillingwater *(Sir Robert Sundale)*, Clarissa Selwyn *(Lady Kitty Sundale)*, Cleve Morison *(Dick Sundale)*, Marcelle Corday *(Theodosia)*, Tom McGuire *(Beamish)*, Blanche Payson *(Johanna)*, Dorothy Seastrom *(Dolly Wimple)*, Louis Payne *(Sir William Wimple)*.

Comedy. Source: Israel Zangwill, *We Moderns; a Post-War Comedy in Three Movements (Allegro, Andante, Adagio)* (New York, 1926). Mary Sundale is a member of a gay London set who call themselves "We Moderns" and scorns the Victorianism of her parents. They, in turn, have nothing but contempt for the ways of the younger generation. Mary is courted by John Ashler, a sane young civil engineer, but she fancies herself in love with a poetic humbug named Oscar Pleat ("God's Gift to Women"), a married man. In the course of a treasure hunt, Mary enters Pleat's rooms but is saved by John. However, she continues to associate with Pleat. During a jazz party aboard a zeppelin, Pleat tries to force his attentions on her; but Mary escapes after a plane crashes into the airship. Mary is glad to fall into John's arms and admits that her parents were right. *Engineers—Civil. Filial relations. Jazz life. Parenthood. Victorianism. Dirigibles. Airplanes. Airplane accidents. London.*

Note: Copyright records indicate some doubt whether Dorothy Seastrom and Louis Payne are in the final film.

WEALTH **F2.6130**

Famous Players–Lasky. *Dist* Paramount Pictures. 21 Aug **1921** [c20 Aug 1921; LP16884]. Si; b&w. 35mm. 5 reels, 5,131 ft.

Pres by Jesse L. Lasky. *Dir* William D. Taylor. *Scen* Julia Crawford Ivers. *Story* Cosmo Hamilton. *Photog* James C. Van Trees.

Cast: Ethel Clayton *(Mary McLeod)*, Herbert Rawlinson *(Phillip Dominick)*, J. M. Dumont *(Gordon Townsend)*, Lawrence Steers *(Oliver Marshall)*, George Periolat *(Irving Seaton)*, Claire McDowell *(Mrs. Dominick)*, Jean Acker *(Estelle Rolland)*, Richard Wayne *(Dr. Howard)*.

Society drama. Artist Mary McLeod, while returning to New York, discovers she has lost her train ticket; young Phillip Dominick, a millionaire playboy, offers her his drawing room, posing as her brother, and their friendship in time develops into love. They are married, and Phillip takes his bride to his wealthy mother, on whom he is financially dependent. Mrs. Dominick, however, has plans to separate the couple and marry Phillip to a society girl, and though Mary begs him to take her away, she agrees to remain until the birth of her baby. The grandmother assumes full charge of the child, but despite careful nursing the child dies, and a subsequent misunderstanding causes Mary to leave. Phillip finds her and promises to start a new life in their own home on his own resources. *Millionaires. Mothers-in-law. Artists. Motherhood. Wealth. Self-reliance. New York City.*

WEARY RIVER **F2.6131**

First National Pictures. 10 Feb **1929** [c14 Mar 1929; LP229]. Talking sequences, sd eff, & mus score (Vitaphone); b&w. 35mm. 8 reels, 7,978 ft. [Also si, 7 Apr 1929; 7,565 ft.]

Pres by Richard A. Rowland. *Dir* Frank Lloyd. *Screenplay* Bradley King. *Dial* Tom J. Geraghty. *Story* Courtney Ryley Cooper. *Photog* Ernest Hallor. *Art Dir* John J. Hughes. *Film Ed* Edward Schroeder, Paul Perez. *Song: "Weary River"* Louis Silvers, Grant Clarke. *Wardrobe* Max Ree.

Cast: Richard Barthelmess *(Jerry)*, Betty Compson *(Alice)*, William Holden *(warden)*, Louis Natheaux *(Spadoni)*, George Stone *(Blackie)*, Raymond Turner *(elevator boy)*, Gladden James *(manager)*.

Drama. Bootlegger Jerry Larrabee is framed by a rival gangster and is sent to prison, where he comes under the kindly influence of the warden. Jerry turns to music and forms a prison band, broadcasting over the radio. Radio listeners are deeply moved by his singing, and Jerry wins an early parole. He goes into vaudeville and quickly flops; he then moves from job to job, haunted by the past. Forced at last to return to his old gang, Jerry takes up with his former sweetheart, Alice. She gets in touch with the warden, who arrives on the scene in time to keep Jerry on the straight and narrow path. Jerry eventually becomes a radio star and marries Alice. *Bootleggers. Prison wardens. Singers. Criminals—Rehabilitation. Parole. Vaudeville. Radio. Prisons.*

WEB OF FATE **F2.6132**

Dallas M. Fitzgerald Productions. *Dist* Peerless Pictures. 7 Nov **1927**. Si; b&w. 35mm. 6 reels, 5,800 ft.

Dir Dallas M. Fitzgerald. *Titl* Gardner Bradford. *Adapt* Gladys Gordon, Ada McQuillan. *Story* Willard King Bradley. *Photog* Milton Moore. *Film Ed* Desmond O'Brien.

Cast: Lillian Rich *(Gloria Gunther/Beverly Townsend)*, Henry Sedley *(Linton)*, Eugene Strong *(Don Eddington)*, John Cossar *(Carlton Townsend)*, Frances Raymond *(Mrs. Townsend)*, Edwin Coxen.

Society melodrama. "Scheming financier meets young millionaire, whom he tricks. Financier spends money on stage star. Later, through accident, she is badly scarred and another girl substitutes. Financier proposes to latter, threatening ruin if she refuses. He is killed and millionaire and girl charged with murder. Former stage star confesses, and girl and millionaire are freed." *(Motion Picture News Booking Guide*, [14]:294, 1929.) *Financiers. Millionaires. Actors. Disfiguration. Murder. Blackmail. Injustice.*

THE WEB OF THE LAW **F2.6133**

Gibson-Dyer Ranger Productions. *Dist* American Releasing Corp. 25 Feb **1923**. Si; b&w. 35mm. 5 reels, 4,900 or 5,065 ft.

Dir Tom Gibson. *Story* Victor Gibson. *Photog* Elmer G. Dyer.

Cast: Ranger Bill Miller *(Bill Barton)*, Patricia Palmer *(Mollie Barbee)*, George Sherwood *("Wolf" Blake)*, Harry Belmour *(Buck Barbee)*, Alfred Heuston *(Jasper Leveen)*, Jean Walsh *("Slim" Easton)*, Barry Jackson *("Sundown" Brown)*, Frank Cutter *("Squint" Castile)*.

Western melodrama. Cattle rancher Buck Barbee suspects his neighbor, Jasper Leveen, to whom he owes money, of stealing his cattle. Texas Ranger Bill Barton believes that "Wolf" Blake, Barbee's foreman, is changing brands and crediting the cattle to Leveen. Barton goes to work for Barbee and falls in love with Mollie, the ranchowner's daughter. Barbee dies after a fall from his horse when Blake tampers with his saddle. Barton discovers Blake's hiding place for the stolen cattle just as Blake and his men (with Mollie as a hostage) are driving the cattle to the Mexican border. Barton rescues Mollie and arrests the rustlers. *Texas Rangers. Ranchers. Ranch foremen. Rustlers.*

Note: "Ranger Bill" Miller was actually a Texas Ranger.

WEBS OF STEEL **F2.6134**

Morris R. Schlank Productions. *Dist* Anchor Film Distributors. 24 Oct **1925** [New York State license]. Si; b&w. 35mm. 5 reels.

Dir J. P. McGowan.

Cast: Helen Holmes.

Melodrama. No information about the precise nature of this film has been found. *Railroads.*

WEDDING BELLS **F2.6135**

Constance Talmadge Productions. *Dist* Associated First National Pictures. Jun **1921** [c16 Jun 1921; LP16678]. Si; b&w. 35mm. 6 reels, 6,000 ft.

Pres by Joseph M. Schenck. *Dir* Chet Withey. *Adapt* Zelda Crosby. *Photog* Oliver Marsh.

Cast: Constance Talmadge *(Rosalie Wayne)*, Harrison Ford *(Reginald Carter)*, Emily Chichester *(Marcia Hunter)*, Ida Darling *(Mrs. Hunter)*, James Harrison *(Douglas Ordway)*, William Roselle *(Spencer Wells)*, Polly Vann *(Hooper)*, Dallas Welford *(Jackson)*, Frank Honda *(Fuzisaki)*.

Comedy. Source: Edward Salisbury Field, *Wedding Bells; a Comedy in Three Acts* (New York, 1923). Rosalie and Reginald become acquainted while they are guests at a Palm Beach hotel, and later they are married. Misunderstandings, aggravated by a case of measles, send the young wife to Reno for a divorce. A year later she finds her ex-husband engaged to Marcia Hunter—a match promoted by Mrs. Hunter with an eye for Carter's wealth and social position—and, regretting her hasty divorce, she almost succeeds in winning him back until the Hunters, a poet, and a rejected suitor interfere with her plan. Nevertheless, Rosalie stops the wedding by sending a note to the bishop, telling him Reggie is divorced; and returning to Reggie, she becomes Mrs. Carter again. *Poets. Divorce. Weddings. Measles. Reno. Palm Beach.*

WEDDING BILL$ **F2.6136**

Paramount Famous Lasky Corp. 7 May **1927** [c7 May 1927; LP23948]. Si; b&w. 35mm. 6 reels, 5,869 ft.

Pres by Adolph Zukor, Jesse L. Lasky. *Assoc Prod* B. P. Schulberg. *Dir* Erle Kenton. *Story-Screenplay* Grover Jones, Keene Thompson, Lloyd Corrigan. *Titl* George Marion, Jr. *Photog* William Marshall.

Cast: Raymond Griffith *(Algernon Schuyler Van Twidder)*, Anne Sheridan *(Miss Bruce)*, Hallam Cooley *(Tom Milbank)*, Iris Stuart *(Miss Markham)*, Vivian Oakland *(Mademoiselle Mimi de Lyle)*, Tom S. Guise *(Mr. Markham)*, Louis Stern *(Judson, valet)*, Edgar Kennedy *(detective)*, John Steppling *(district attorney)*.

Farce. Much sought after as best man at weddings, Van Twidder goes to sleep during a ceremony, mixes up the rings, and kisses the minister instead of the bride. He swears that he is through with weddings when Tom, his best friend, becomes involved with Mimi, a blonde vamp who threatens to expose him with compromising letters and ruin his romance. Van Twidder and Tom plan to borrow a necklace she wants, then steal it back from her, but in the jewelry store Van Twidder is distracted by a pretty girl and loses her in the traffic only to see her again at the wedding rehearsal. Mimi absconds with the gems; Van Twidder retrieves them but finds them missing at the wedding; and in a riotous climactic chase after a pigeon, ending at the jewelry shop, Van Twidder finds himself engaged to Miss Bruce, the pretty secretary. *Secretaries. Vamps. Blackmail. Courtship. Weddings. Chases. Pigeons.*

THE WEDDING MARCH **F2.6137**

Paramount Famous Lasky Corp. 6 Oct **1928** [c8 Oct 1928; LP25696]. Mus score & sd eff (Movietone); b&w with col sequences (Technicolor). Stroheim, Erich von Prince Nicki, their son 10,721 ft. [Also si; 10,659 ft.]

Pres by Adolph Zukor, Jesse L. Lasky. *Prod* P. A. Powers. *Dir* Erich von Stroheim. *Screenplay* Erich von Stroheim, Harry Carr. *Photog* Hal Mohr, B. Sorenson, Ben Reynolds. *Art Dir* Richard Day, Erich von Stroheim. *Orig Mus Synchronization* J. S. Zamecnik. *Song: "Paradise"* Harry D. Kerr, J. S. Zamecnik. *Asst Dir* Eddie Sowders, Louis Germonprez, Richard Day. *Cost* Max Ree.

Cast: George Fawcett *(Prince von Wildeliebe-Rauffenburg)*, Maude George *(Princess von Wildeliebe-Rauffenburg)*, George Nichols *(Fortunat Schweisser)*, ZaSu Pitts *(Cecelia Schweisser)*, Hughie Mack *(wine-garden proprietor)*, Mathew Betz *(Schani Eberle)*, Cesare Gravina *(Martin Schrammell)*, Dale Fuller *(Mrs. Schrammell)*, Fay Wray *(Mitzi Schrammell)*, Sidney Bracey *(Navratil)*, Anton Vaverka *(Franz Joseph I)*.

Melodrama. The setting is Vienna in 1914 before the outbreak of war. The aristocratic and somewhat jaded Prince Nicki, pursued by all the ladies, begins a flirtation with Mitzi, a crippled harpist who works in a suburban wine-garden, and who is in turn idolized by Schani, an uncouth and violently jealous butcher. Their first encounter significantly takes place in front of St. Stephen's Cathedral on Corpus Christi day, with Nicki among the emperor's cavalry regiment. Later, in the refracted light of falling apple blossoms in the wine-garden—scenes of a distilled, ethereal beauty—Nicki gradually wins her faith and love. Meanwhile, amidst the sumptuous and corrupt milieu of the family palace, Nicki is drawn into complicity against his will, as his unscrupulous mother informs him he must marry Cecelia, the daughter of a wealthy commoner, in order to revive the family fortune. Mitzi has a vision of The Iron Man (a symbol of the declining power and position of the Hapsburg dynasty) and falls before the crucifix in fear; but her love remains steadfast, and she protests her faith though abused by her mother and Schani. Infuriated by her rejection, Schani threatens to kill Nicki on his wedding day unless Mitzi agrees to marry him. Following the processional splendor of the cathedral wedding, Schani appears to carry out his threat, but Mitzi arrives in time to stop him; and through the downpouring rain Nicki sadly gazes on his true love in the crowd as he drives away with his bride. *Harpists. Butchers. Royalty. Weddings. Franz Josef. Vienna.*

Note: Stroheim had in mind a two-part work, the first half of which was *The Wedding March.* This film was completed as planned, but during the filming of Part Two, the producer, Pat Powers, alarmed by the rising expenditures incurred by the production, ceased filming, and the material was edited together as *The Honeymoon* and given a very limited European release.

THE WEDDING ON THE VOLGA **F2.6138**

Dist Hollywood Pictures. 10 Dec **1929** [New York State license]. Sd; b&w. 35mm. 6 reels, 5,139 ft.

Cast: Mark Schweid, Mary Fowler.

Drama. In gratitude for saving his life, Piotr offers the brutish Zhuck the hand of his daughter, Olga, who loves Alexis, a sailor home on leave. However, Borrah, an old chemist, tosses a tear bomb during the wedding ceremony, and Alexis escapes with Olga to a shack belonging to Darya, Zhuck's rejected sweetheart. Accusing Piotr of doublecross, Zhuck hears the other fishermen reveal his hesitation during his rescue of Piotr, so that the latter might sign a will beneficial to him. Amid a happy celebration Alexis and Olga marry with Piotr's blessing. *Sailors. Fishermen. Chemists. Weddings. Russia. Volga River.*

Note: Country of origin undetermined. Songs: "The Volga Boatman," "The Sun Rises and Sets."

WEDDING RINGS **F2.6139**

First National Pictures. 29 Dec **1929** [c24 Jan 1930; LP1021]. Sd (Vitaphone); b&w. 35mm. 7 reels, 6,621 ft. [Also si.]

Dir William Beaudine. *Scen-Dial-Titl* Ray Harris. *Photog* Ernest Haller. *Song: "Love Will Last Forever If It's True"* Al Bryan, Ed Ward.

Cast: H. B. Warner *(Lewis Dike)*, Lois Wilson *(Cornelia Quinn)*, Olive Borden *(Eve Quinn)*, Hallam Cooley *(Wilfred Meadows)*, James Ford *(Tom Hazelton)*, Kathlyn Williams *(Agatha)*, Aileen Manning *(Esther Quinn)*.

Society drama. Source: Ernest Pascal, *The Dark Swan* (New York, 1924). Eve Quinn, a shallow but attractive debutante, makes a practice of leading men on, then cooly casting them aside for new conquests. She openly boasts that she would find pleasure in taking a man from her sister, Cornelia, who is an art student. When Cornelia falls in love with wealthy clubman Lewis Dike, Eve succeeds in vamping and capturing him; broken-hearted when they marry, Cornelia deliberately introduces Eve to Wilfred Meadows, a playboy with whom she begins a flirtation. Dike soon tires of the modernistic furnishings of their home and the jazz-mad parasites who frequent his drawing room, and he is refreshed by visits to Cornelia. When Dike accidentally learns of Eve's liaison with Wilfred, he realizes his error and is reunited with Cornelia. *Sisters. Vamps. Students. Jazz life. Marriage.*

THE WEDDING SONG **F2.6140**

Cinema Corp. of America. *Dist* Producers Distributing Corp. 29 Nov **1925** [c16 Nov 1925; LP22008]. Si; b&w. 35mm. 7 reels, 7,373 ft.

Pres by Cecil B. De Mille. *Supv* Cecil B. De Mille. *Dir* Alan Hale. *Adapt* Charles E. Whittaker, Douglas Doty. *Titl* George Marion, Jr.

Cast: Leatrice Joy *(Beatrice Glynn)*, Robert Ames *(Hayes Hallan)*, Charles Gerard *(Paul Glynn, a crook)*, Ruby Lafayette *("Mother," another crook)*, Rosa Rudami *(Ethea)*, Jack Curtis *(Captain Saltus [George*

Pappadoulos?]), Clarence Burton *(Captain Saltus?),* Gertrude Claire *(Grandma),* Ethel Wales *(Auntie),* Gladden James *(Jeffrey King),* Casson Ferguson *(Madison Melliah).*

Crook melodrama. Source: Ethel Watts Mumford, *The Wedding Song* (Garden City, New York, 1924). Hayes Hallan leaves the Pacific island where he was born for San Francisco to dispose of a fortune in pearls he has accumulated. He is befriended by confidence man Paul Glynn, who, learning about the pearls, arranges for his "family" to meet them in San Francisco. Following Glynn's plans, Hayes falls in love with and marries Glynn's sister, Beatrice. The newlyweds and the bogus family go to the island, where Beatrice has a change in heart and refuses to go along with the scheme. Glynn, however, makes her open Hayes's safe. Hayes appears and forces them at gunpoint to leave the island. Beatrice learns that a bomb has been planted under Hayes's house, retrieves it, and throws it off a cliff. The explosion creates a landslide, which sinks the crooks' ship. Beatrice and Hayes are reunited. *Confidence men. Pearls. Imposture. South Sea Islands. San Francisco. Landslides.*

Note: The press sheet credits Jack Curtis with the role of Captain Saltus, though at least one other source credits him as playing George Pappadoulos. Several other sources credit Clarence Burton with the role of Captain Saltus and do not list Jack Curtis.

WEEK END HUSBANDS **F2.6141**

Daniel Carson Goodman Corp. *Dist* Equity Pictures. 10 Feb **1924.** Si; b&w. 35mm. 7 reels, ca6,500 ft.

Dir E. H. Griffith. *Story-Scen* Daniel Carson Goodman.

Cast: H. J. Herbert *(William Randall),* Alma Rubens *(Barbara Belden),* Montague Love *(Thomas Mowry),* Maurice Costello *(John Keane),* Sally Cruze *(Mrs. Dawn),* Charles Byer *(Robert Stover),* Paul Panzer *(Monsieur La Rue),* Margaret Dale *(Mrs. Sarah Belden).*

Domestic melodrama. William Randall becomes a bootlegger to provide his wife with the luxuries she demands. As a consequence, he is free only on weekends while Barbara is influenced by a jazz set and spends most of her time at fashionable resorts. Although Barbara remains faithful to her husband, gossipers at the resort cause him to leave her. She goes to Paris while Federal agents arrest Randall and release him under bail. Meanwhile Barbara, left alone, sends for her husband, who, instead of replying, catches the first plane to Paris. Barbara has already taken poison, but she recovers when Randall arrives and they return to America together. *Bootleggers. Jazz life. Suicide. Paris.*

WELCOME CHILDREN **F2.6142**

Drascena Productions. *Dist* National Exchanges. Jul **1921.** Si; b&w. 35mm. 5-6 reels.

Dir Harry C. Mathews.

Cast: Elsie Albert *(Mary Ellen Martin),* Graham Griffiths *(Joey Martin),* Doughboy *(Doughboy Martin),* Dumplings *(Dumplings Martin),* Sidney Franklin *(Isaac Cohen),* Orpha Alba *(Rebecca Cohen),* George Sherwood *(Dr. Randall).*

Domestic drama. The death of her mother leaves 18-year-old Mary Ellen Martin alone to care for her eight brothers and sisters. Leaving the farm for the city, Mary Ellen finds that no landlord will have children. She finally uses deception and gets the children into an apartment through a dumbwaiter, thereby attracting the sympathetic attention of young Dr. Randall. It develops that the building houses a number of underworld types; but the children, who by now have been discovered by the landlady, are suspected of a series of burglaries. Luckily, the Martin brood is instrumental in capturing the culprits, the landlady changes her opinion of children, and Mary Ellen marries Dr. Randall. *Orphans. Landladies. Physicians. Children. Brother-sister relationship. Burglary. Prejudice.*

WELCOME DANGER **F2.6143**

Harold Lloyd Corp. *Dist* Paramount Famous Lasky Corp. 12 Oct **1929** [c20 Oct 1929; LP777]. Sd (Movietone); b&w. 35mm. 10 reels, 9,955 ft. [Copyrighted as 12 reels. Also si; 10,796 ft.]

Dir Clyde Bruckman. *Dial* Paul Gerard Smith. *Story* Clyde Bruckman, Lex Neal, Felix Adler. *Photog* Walter Lundin, Henry Kohler. *Song: "Billie"* Lynn Cowan. *Song: "When You Are Mine"* Paul Titsworth. *Rec Engr* George Ellis.

Cast: Harold Lloyd *(Harold Bledsoe),* Barbara Kent *(Billy Lee),* Noah Young *(Clancy),* Charles Middleton *(John Thorne),* William Walling *(Captain Walton),* James Wang *(Doctor Gow),* Douglas Haig *(Roy).*

Comedy melodrama. Harold Bledsoe, the son of a former Chief of Police in San Francisco, is called to the city to quell the flourishing crime among Oriental and American gangsters. En route, Harold, a meek botanist, stops to examine some flowers and misses his train, but he gets a ride with Billy Lee and her young crippled brother, who are going to San Francisco for an operation on the boy's leg. Dr. Gow, a kindly physician, complains of the evil of narcotics to Captain Walton, as does John Thorne, a supposed reformer but actually an underworld leader. Harold promises action and, disguised as a Chinaman, he enters a flower shop where he rescues the doctor from the villains, though they escape. By matching a set of fingerprints, Harold proves Thorne's guilt and forces a confession from him. *Botanists. Gangsters. Police. Cripples. Physicians. Chinese. Narcotics. San Francisco.*

WELCOME HOME **F2.6144**

Famous Players–Lasky. *Dist* Paramount Pictures. 17 May **1925** [c15 May 1925; LP21466]. Si; b&w. 35mm. 6 reels, 5,909 ft.

Pres by Adolph Zukor, Jesse L. Lasky. *Dir* James Cruze. *Screenplay* Walter Woods, F. McGrew Willis. *Photog* Karl Brown.

Cast: Luke Cosgrave *(Old Man Prouty),* Warner Baxter *(Fred Prouty),* Lois Wilson *(Nettie Prouty),* Ben Hendricks *(Jim Corey),* Margaret Morris *(Lil Corey),* Josephine Crowell *(Miss Pringle),* Adele Watson *(Annie).*

Domestic comedy-drama. Source: George S. Kaufman and Edna Ferber, *Minick; a Play Based on the Short Story "Old Man Minick"* (publication undetermined). Old man Prouty arrives unexpectedly at the small apartment occupied by his son and daughter-in-law and announces that he has come to stay. Fred and Nettie do their best to make him happy and comfortable; but his presence seriously interferes with their way of life, and he soon becomes a source of constant irritation in the household. Nettie arranges a luncheon for a few of her friends, and the old man and his friends make a mess of the apartment and eat all the sandwiches; he later breaks up the luncheon with his constant interruptions. This is the last straw for Nettie, and she tells Fred that either his father goes or she goes. The old man then visits his cronies at the old folks' home and likes it well enough to plan to live there. Fred and Nettie dissuade him for a while, but when he discovers that Nettie is pregnant, he moves out for good, realizing that the old must give way to the young. *Fathers-in-law. Family life. Old age. Old age homes. Pregnancy.*

WELCOME STRANGER **F2.6145**

Belasco Productions. *Dist* Producers Distributing Corp. 24 Aug **1924** [c24 Aug 1924; LP20575]. Si; b&w. 35mm. 7 reels, 6,618 ft.

Dir James Young. *Titl* Katherine Hilliker, H. H. Caldwell. *Adapt* James Young, Willard Mack. *Photog* George Benoit.

Cast: Dore Davidson *(Isadore Solomon),* Florence Vidor *(Mary Clark),* Virginia Brown Faire *(Essie Solomon),* Noah Beery *(Icabod Whitson),* Lloyd Hughes *(Ned Tyler),* Robert Edeson *(Eb Hooker),* William V. Mong *(Clem Beemis),* Otis Harlan *(Seth Trimble),* Fred J. Butler *(Gideon Tyler),* Pat Hartigan *(detective).*

Comedy-drama. Source: Aaron Hoffman, *Welcome Stranger, a Play* (New York, 1926). Isadore Solomon, a Jew, is driven from the small New England town of Valley Falls by the mayor and some leading citizens when he arrives to open a general store. Clem Beemis, a handyman at the hotel, befriends Solomon and Mary Clark, another newcomer to Valley Falls, and persuades them to invest in an electric light plant which would provide illumination for the whole town. Banker's son Ned Tyler, who falls in love with Mary, gets a bank's assistance for the project while the mayor and his henchmen attempt to thwart it. Eventually the power plant is erected, and the townspeople honor Clem, Solomon, and Mary at a great celebration. *Jews. Mayors. Prejudice. Smalltown life. Electric power. New England.*

WELCOME TO OUR CITY **F2.6146**

San Antonio Pictures. *Dist* Producers Security Corp. 1 Feb **1922.** Si; b&w. 35mm. 5 reels, 5,100 ft.

Dir Robert H. Townley. *Scen* Basil Dickey.

Cast: Maclyn Arbuckle *(Jim Scott),* Bessie Emerick *(Geraldine),* Fred Dalton *(Luigi),* Bessie Wharton *(Agnes Scott),* Jack Crosby *(Richard Scott),* Gertrude Robinson *(Eleanor Scott),* Charles Holleman *(Bert Scott),* Joyce Fair *(Dolly),* Gene Baker *(The Maid).*

Farce. Source: George V. Hobart, *Welcome to Our City* (New York opening: 12 Sep 1910). "Jim Scott on a visit to New York with his wife, steals out one evening for a little adventure and meets a young lady who is weeping. His efforts to assist her result in the arrest of both, and a number of embarrassing complications that threaten Jim's marital happiness. It turns out that the whole experience was a 'frame up'—an effort on the part of Jim's son to force Jim to consent to his marrying a chorus girl."

(*Moving Picture World,* 18 Feb 1922, p756.) *Chorus girls. Marriage. Hoaxes. New York City.*

WE'RE ALL GAMBLERS **F2.6147**

Paramount Famous Lasky Corp. 3 Sep **1927** [c3 Sep 1927; LP24356]. Si; b&w. 35mm. 7 reels, 5,935 ft.

Pres by Adolph Zukor, Jesse L. Lasky. *Supv* Lucien Hubbard. *Dir* James Cruze. *Screenplay* Hope Loring. *Titl* Jack Conway (of *Variety*). *Photog* Bert Glennon.

Cast: Thomas Meighan *(Lucky Sam McCarver),* Marietta Millner *(Carlotta Asche),* Cullen Landis *(Georgie McCarver),* Philo McCullough *(Monty Garside),* Gertrude Claire *(Mrs. McCarver),* Gunboat Smith *(Gunboat),* Spec O'Donnell *(Spec).*

Society melodrama. Source: Sidney Howard, *Lucky Sam McCarver, Four Episodes in the Life of a New Yorker* (New York, 1926). As an orphaned child, Sam is reared by the McCarvers on New York's Lower East Side. Later, as a contender for the heavyweight boxing championship, he is cheered by the crowds and admired by a wealthy society woman, Carlotta Asche, at the gymnasium. While escorting his aging stepmother across the street, Sam is struck by Carlotta's automobile, and at the hospital he again wins her admiration by refusing a money settlement. As a nightclub proprietor in New York's Roaring Forties, Sam tries to conceal his affection for Carlotta, and she does likewise because of her aristocratic training. During the New Year festivities, Georgie McCarver, drunk, is repulsed by Carlotta; and Sam refuses to honor any more checks from Monty, Carlotta's friend. When she is implicated in Monty's shooting, Sam takes the blame; and when the death is found to be suicide, Sam and Carlotta acknowledge their mutual love. *Orphans. Prizefighters. Stepmothers. Socialites. Social classes. Drunkenness. Suicide. Automobile accidents. Nightclubs. New Year's Eve. New York City—Lower East Side.*

WE'RE IN THE NAVY NOW **F2.6148**

Famous Players–Lasky. *Dist* Paramount Pictures. 6 Nov **1926** [New York premiere; released 22 Nov; c27 Nov 1926; LP23392]. Si; b&w. 35mm. 6 reels, 5,519 ft.

Pres by Adolph Zukor, Jesse L. Lasky. *Assoc Prod* B. P. Schulberg. *Dir* Edward Sutherland. *Screenplay* John McDermott. *Titl* George Marion, Jr. *Story* Monty Brice. *Photog* Charles Boyle.

Cast: Wallace Beery *(Knockout Hansen),* Raymond Hatton *(Stinky Smith),* Chester Conklin *(Captain Smithers),* Tom Kennedy *(Sailor Percival Scruggs),* Donald Keith *(Radio Officer),* Lorraine Eason *(Madelyn Phillips),* Joseph W. Girard *(U. S. Admiral),* Max Asher *(Admiral Puckerlip).*

Farce. At the outbreak of war, Knockout Hansen, under the egis of manager Stinky Smith, is knocked out by Sailor Percival Scruggs. Stinky absconds with the funds from the fight; Hansen apprehends him near a naval recruiting station during a parade; and both unintentionally are drafted into the Navy. For annoying Captain Smithers, they are thrown into the brig, only to find that Sailor Scruggs is master-at-arms. As their ship enters a mine zone, Madelyn Phillips induces them to take her over the side in a rowboat. She miraculously disappears, and their boat is run down by a French dreadnaught; after their rescue, the convoy is attacked, but the ship is accidentally saved by the pair. After the war, Madelyn is awarded a medal for her service. Mustered out of the Navy, Knockout bests Scruggs in a match. *Prizefighters. Fight managers. World War I. United States Navy. France—Navy.*

WEST IS EAST *see* **WEST VS. EAST**

WEST OF ARIZONA **F2.6149**

Lariat Productions. *Dist* Vitagraph Co. of America. cl Aug **1925** [LP21696]. Si; b&w. 35mm. 5 reels.

Dir Tom Gibson. *Adapt* Victor Roberts. *Story* Barr Cross.

Cast: Pete Morrison, Betty Goodwin, Lightning *(a horse).*

Western melodrama. A beautiful young woman riding on the westbound stage is greatly endangered when the driver is shot and the horses run wild. The stage careens wildly down a mountain trail, and a brave and honest westerner, seeing the young woman's peril, spurs his horse into a gallop and pulls the girl to safety. The outlaws then capture the westerner and the girl, riding Lightning, his horse, goes to the shack where he is being held and holds up the outlaws. The pair escape, and the outlaws are captured. *Cowboys. Outlaws. Horses.*

WEST OF BROADWAY **F2.6150**

Metropolitan Pictures Corp. of California. *Dist* Producers Distributing Corp. 18 Oct **1926** [c5 Oct 1926; LP23185]. Si; b&w. 35mm. 6 reels, 5,186 ft.

Pres by John C. Flinn. *Dir* Robert Thornby. *Adapt* Harold Shumate. *Photog* Georges Benoit. *Ed Supv* Jack Cunningham.

Cast: Priscilla Dean *(Freddy Hayden),* Arnold Gray *(Bruce Elwood),* Majel Coleman *(Muriel Styles),* Walter Long *(Bad Willie),* George Hall *(Cherokee Charlie),* William Austin *(Mortimer Allison).*

Western romantic comedy. Source: Wallace Smith, "New York West," in *Blue Book Magazine* (43:7–16, Aug 1926). Bruce Elwood, a Wyoming rancher and confessed woman-hater, converts a part of his ranch into a golf course, greatly to the discomfort of Mrs. Snodgrass, who declares it to be highly improper. Elwood hires from New York a golf instructor named Freddy Hayden, who proves to be a sportswoman, though she is at first mistaken for a boy. Freddy creates a sensation by appearing in a fashionable gown at a banquet, and Mortimer, keeper of a haberdashery, defends her against Elwood's objections; she creates a stampede of Elwood's herd, and takes advantage of the excitement to invite a dozen women to the club's first ladies' night. Meanwhile, Blodgett, a rustler, plans to kidnap Freddy and rustle the cattle; Elwood, jealous of Mortimer, tries to kiss Freddy, who punches him in the jaw. Elwood disguises himself as Blodgett, but Freddy saves his life in a battle with the real gang, and they are united. *Ranchers. Sportswomen. Rustlers. Misogynists. Courtship. Mannishness. Haberdasheries. Golf. Wyoming.*

WEST OF CHICAGO **F2.6151**

Fox Film Corp. 17 Aug **1922** [New York premiere; released 3 Sep; c3 Sep 1922; LP19304]. Si; b&w. 35mm. 5 reels, 4,694 ft.

Pres by William Fox. *Dir* Scott Dunlap, C. R. Wallace. *Scen* Paul Schofield. *Story* George Scarborough. *Photog* Lucien Andriot. *Asst Dir* Ray Flynn.

Cast: Charles Jones *(Conroy Daly),* Renée Adorée *(Della Moore),* Philo McCullough *(John Hampton),* Sidney D'Albrook *(English Kid),* Charles French *(Judson Malone),* Marcella Daly *(Patricia Daly),* Kathleen Key *(Señorita Gonzales).*

Western melodrama. Responding to the request of his uncle, Conroy Daly returns to the elder Daly's ranch to help in its management. When he arrives, Con is told by foreman John Hampton that his uncle has been killed and that he (Hampton) is in charge. Con conceals his identity but agrees with Hampton to "pose" as Conroy Daly while Della Moore, the sister of Daly's accused murderer, acts as Conroy's wife. Con eventually exposes Hampton, discovers that his uncle is alive, and asks Della to be a real Mrs. Daly. *Uncles. Ranch foremen. Ranches. Imposture.*

Note: Working title: *Vamoose.*

WEST OF MOJAVE **F2.6152**

Bear Productions. *Dist* Aywon Film Corp. 11 Nov **1925** [New York State license]. Si; b&w. 35mm. 5 reels, 4,800 ft.

Dir Harry L. Fraser.

Cast: Gordon Clifford.

Western melodrama(?). No information about the nature of this film has been found.

WEST OF PARADISE **F2.6153**

Dist Anchor Film Distributors. 20 Sep **1928** [New York State license]. Si; b&w. 35mm. 5 reels, 4,500 ft.

Cast: Cheyenne Bill.

Western melodrama(?). No information about the nature of this film has been found.

WEST OF SANTA FE **F2.6154**

El Dorado Productions. *Dist* Syndicate Pictures. Sep or 1 Oct **1928.** Si; b&w. 35mm. 5 reels, 4,341 or 4,421 ft.

Dir J. P. McGowan. *Scen* Mack V. Wright. *Story* Brysis Coleman. *Photog* Paul Allen.

Cast: Bob Custer *(Jack),* Peggy Montgomery *(Helen),* Mack V. Wright, J. P. McGowan, Bud Osborne.

Western melodrama. A Major Seabury, who is negotiating the purchase of maverick horses for the Army, stops at Helen's ranch, where considerable action and danger lead to the disclosure of a plot to cheat the government. Jack, a neighboring rancher, discovers the real major in the custody of the confederates of Helen's foreman, Bull, who planned to cash the vouchers for the horses. *Ranchers. Ranch foremen. Fraud. United States Army—Cavalry. Horses.*

WEST OF THE LAW **F2.6155**
Ben Wilson Productions. *Dist* Rayart Pictures. Dec **1926.** Si; b&w. 35mm. 5 reels, ca4,500 ft.
Dir Ben Wilson.
Cast: Ben Wilson *(John Adams)*, Neva Gerber *(Alice Armstrong)*, Ashton Dearholt *(Frank Armstrong)*, Hal Walters *(Dick Walton)*, Cliff Lyons *(sheriff)*, Lafe McKee *(Jim Armstrong)*, Al Ferguson *(Surly Dorgan)*, Myrna Thompson *(Phyllis Parker)*, Fang *(a dog)*.
Western melodrama. Ranch foreman John Adams rescues Alice, headstrong niece of crippled rancher Jim Armstrong, from death—for which she promises to marry him—and covers a check forged by Alice's weakling brother, Frank, who is in debt to Surly Dorgan. When John realizes that Dorgan is responsible for the recent rustling on the ranch, and that Alice, who is much younger than he, has fallen in love with young easterner Dick Walton, he rounds up the bad guys (with Fang's help), clears Frank, and gives up the girl. *Ranch foremen. Rustlers. Brother-sister relationship. Forgery. Dogs.*

WEST OF THE PECOS **F2.6156**
William Steiner Productions. Jun **1922** [c12 Apr 1922; LU17753]. Si; b&w. 35mm. 5 reels, 4,300 ft.
Prod William Steiner. *Dir-Story-Scen* Neal Hart. *Photog* Jacob A. Badaracco.
Cast: Neal Hart *(Jack Laramie)*, William Quinn *(Chuck Wallace)*, Max Wessel *(Joe Madison)*, Sarah Bindley *(Mrs. Osborne)*, Hazel Maye *(Irene Osborne)*, Ben Corbett *(Wolf Bradley)*.
Western melodrama. A United States marshal in the Southwest learns of a Mrs. Osborne, whose son and husband have been killed by raiders and whose daughter, June, has been taken captive. He orders Jack Laramie, his best man, to investigate the affair and arrest the guilty parties at any cost. Jack arrives at the local cafe and learns the identity of the outlaw gang and June's whereabouts. Meanwhile, Jack has rescued a child whose parents have been killed while crossing the prairie to stake out a homestead. Laramie rescues June from her captor's hideout, shoots him, and brings about the arrest of the other outlaws. He claims June for his bride, and they adopt the little orphaned girl. *United States marshals. Homesteaders. Orphans. Outlaws. Kidnaping. Rio Pecos.*

WEST OF THE RAINBOW'S END **F2.6157**
George Blaisdell Productions. *Dist* Rayart Pictures. 13 Aug **1926** [New York State license; released Oct]. Si; b&w. 35mm. 5 reels, 4,829 ft.
Harry Webb Production. *Dir* Bennett Cohn. *Scen* Daisy Kent. *Story* Victor Rousseau. *Photog* William Thornley.
Cast: Jack Perrin *(Don Brandon)*, Pauline Curley *(Daisy Kent)*, Billy Lamar *(Red)*, Tom London *(Harry Palmer)*, James Welch *(Abe Brandon)*, Milburn Morante *(Tim)*, Whitehorse *(Tom Palmer)*, Starlight *(a horse)*, Rex *(a dog)*.
Western melodrama. While Brandon is in France in the World War, Palmer kills his father and appropriates the family ranch. Returning from the war, Brandon regains his ranch, overcomes Palmer, and wins the girl. *Veterans. Property rights. Ranches. World War I.*

WEST OF THE RIO GRANDE **F2.6158**
Bert Lubin Pictures. Oct **1921** [New York State]. Si; b&w. 35mm. 5 reels.
Dir-Scen Robert H. Townley. *Story* "Tex" O'Reilly.
Cast: Harry McLaughlin *(Tom Norton)*, Allene Ray *(Eileen Nawn)*, John Hagin *("Handy" Adams)*, "Tex" O'Reilly *("Pecos Bill" Sinto)*, Marguerite Davis *(Wanda)*, George Cravy *(Tom Sadler)*, Sam White *("Shorty")*, Roberta Bellinger *(Mrs. Nawn)*, Charles Holleman *(Charles Nawn)*.
Western melodrama. A portrayal of the conflict between the pioneer cattle ranchers and the newcomer farming homesteaders in the Big Bend region of Texas: The problems for both sides are heightened by cattle rustlers who take advantage of downed fences. While struggling to maintain law and order, Texas Ranger Tom Norton falls in love with New Yorker Eileen Nawn, and the way is cleared for their romance when Tom rounds up the culprits. *Ranchers. Homesteaders. Texas Rangers. New Yorkers. Rustling. Texas.*

WEST OF THE ROCKIES **F2.6159**
J. Charles Davis Productions. 15 Dec **1929.** Sd; b&w. 35mm. 6 reels.
Dir H. B. Carpenter. *Story* Philip Schuyler.
Cast: Art Mix *(Bob Strong)*, H. B. Carpenter *(Hair-Trigger Strong)*, George Edward Brown *(George)*, Cliff Lyons *(Snakey Rogers)*, Bud Osborne *(Juan Escobar)*, Fontaine La Rue *(Celia de la Costa)*, Inez Gomez *(Rosita)*, Ione Reed *(Beth Lee)*, Alfred Hewston *(Tex)*, Pete Crawford *(sheriff)*, Antone Sanchez *(Pedro)*.
Western melodrama. While trying to discover who is rustling horses from his father's ranch, Bob Strong meets and falls in love with Celia de la Costa, the daughter of Hair-Trigger Strong's long-time enemy, who was apparently killed by the elder Strong. Bob goes in pursuit of Juan Escobar, whom he suspects to be the rustler chief, and gets in trouble; Celia warns Strong of Bob's danger; and Strong fetches the sheriff to go after Bob. When the dust settles and justice is served, Strong finally consents to a union between Bob and Celia. *Ranchers. Rustlers.*

WEST OF THE WATER TOWER **F2.6160**
Famous Players–Lasky. *Dist* Paramount Pictures. 6 Jan **1924** [c9 Jan 1924; LP19800]. Si; b&w. 35mm. 8 reels, 7,432 ft.
Pres by Adolph Zukor. *Dir* Rollin Sturgeon. *Scen* Doris Schroeder. *Adapt* Lucien Hubbard. *Photog* Harry B. Harris.
Cast: Glenn Hunter *(Guy Plummer)*, May McAvoy *(Bee Chew)*, Ernest Torrence *(Adrian Plummer)*, George Fawcett *(Charles Chew)*, ZaSu Pitts *(Dessie Arnhalt)*, Charles Abbe *(R. N. Arnhalt)*, Anne Schaefer *(Mrs. Plummer)*, Riley Hatch *(Cod Dugan)*, Allen Baker *(Ed Hoecker)*, Jack Terry *(Harlan Thompson)*, Edward Elkas *(Wolfe, the druggist)*, Joseph Burke *(town drunk)*, Gladys Feldman *(Tootsie)*, Alice Mann *(Pal)*.
Melodrama. Source: Homer Croy, *West of the Water Tower* (New York, 1923). Guy and Bee, believing themselves married, later suspect that the ceremony was illegal. Bee becomes pregnant. They are ostracized by the townspeople and are temporarily separated. Finally, the squire who performed the marriage ceremony sees an account in a newspaper of Guy's predicament; he delivers the missing marriage certificate, thereby acquitting Guy and Bee—and the baby—of any wrongdoing. *Marriage. Illegitimacy. Documentation.*

WEST OF ZANZIBAR **F2.6161**
Metro-Goldwyn-Mayer Pictures. 24 Nov **1928** [c24 Nov 1928; LP25865]. Sd eff & mus score (Movietone); b&w. 35mm. 7 reels, 6,150 ft. [Also si.]
Dir Tod Browning. *Scen* Elliott Clawson, Waldemar Young. *Titl* Joe Farnham. *Story* Chester De Vonde, Kilbourne Gordon. *Photog* Percy Hilburn. *Sets* Cedric Gibbons. *Film Ed* Harry Reynolds. *Wardrobe* David Cox.
Cast: Lon Chaney *(Flint)*, Lionel Barrymore *(Crane)*, Mary Nolan *(Maizie)*, Warner Baxter *(Doc)*, Jacquelin Gadsdon *(Anna)*, Roscoe Ward *(Tiny)*, Kalla Pasha *(Babe)*, Curtis Nero *(Bumbo)*.
Melodrama. Flint, a Limehouse magician, loses the use of his legs as the result of a fight with Crane, an ivory trader who has taken an interest in Flint's wife. Several months later, Mrs. Flint dies, leaving behind a daughter, Maizie, whom the magician believes to be Crane's child rather than his own. Flint takes the child and goes to Africa. Years later, Flint, still believing Maizie to be Crane's daughter, arranges for her to become a prostitute in one of the native fleshpots. Crane shows up and convinces Flint that Maizie is indeed Flint's own child. Crane is killed by the natives, and Flint sacrifices his life so that Maizie can escape from the tropics with a regenerated white doctor. *Magicians. Physicians. Prostitutes. Traders. Cripples. Ivory. London—Limehouse. Africa.*

WEST POINT **F2.6162**
Metro-Goldwyn-Mayer Pictures. 31 Dec **1927** [New York premiere; released 7 or 21 Jan 1928; c7 Jan 1928; LP25328]. Si; b&w. 35mm. 9 reels, 8,090 or 8,134 ft.
Dir Edward Sedgwick. *Story-Cont* Raymond L. Schrock. *Titl* Joe Farnham. *Photog* Ira Morgan. *Film Ed* Frank Sullivan. *Asst Dir* Edward Brophy. *Wardrobe* Gilbert Clark. *Adv* Maj. Raymond G. Moses. *Coöp* United States Military Academy. *Prod with permission of* United States Department of War.
Cast: William Haines *(Brice Wayne)*, Joan Crawford *(Betty Channing)*, William Bakewell *("Tex" McNeil)*, Neil Neely *(Bob Sperry)*, Ralph Emerson *(Bob Chase)*, Leon Kellar *(Captain Munson)*, Maj. Raymond G. Moses *(Coach Towers)*.
Comedy-drama. Arrogant and impudent Brice Wayne, a West Point cadet who is a star player on the football team, painfully learns the error

of his ways when, after a year, he realizes that he hasn't acquired the proper school spirit. Dismissed from the football team shortly before the Army-Navy match, Brice resigns from the Military Academy, then retracts when his friends Tex McNeil and Betty Channing encourage him to stay. Restored to the team, Brice scores the decisive goal in the game with Navy. *Braggarts. Cadets. Athletic coaches. Football. United States Military Academy. United States Naval Academy.*

WEST VS. EAST **F2.6163**

Sanford Productions. *Dist* Arrow Film Corp. 15 Oct **1922.** Si; b&w. 35mm. 5 reels.

Dir Marcel Perez.

Cast: Pete Morrison *(Harry Atterridge)*, Dorothy Wood *(Betsy Macon)*, Gene Crosby *(Mrs. De Wyle Jenkins)*, Renée Danti *(Jennie)*, Robert Grey *(Murray Brierson)*, Bessie De Litch *(Frances)*, Lorenz Gillette *(Sato)*.

Western melodrama. Harry Atterridge will lose his ranch unless he develops the mineral on his land within a certain time. He is unaware of this condition, and Brierson, his attorney, plots to get a small fortune for himself; his accomplice, Mrs. De Wyle Jenkins, plans to have her daughter, Jennie, marry Atterridge. Instead, Atterridge falls in love with the governess who goes to live with his sister. Brierson and the sister's servant kidnap the governess when they discover that she has the real claim on the property. Atterridge arrives in time to save her and the property. *Ranchers. Lawyers. Governesses. Brother-sister relationship. Property rights.*

Note: Reviewed in one source as *West Is East.*

WESTBOUND **F2.6164**

Sunset Productions. *Dist* Aywon Film Corp. Jan **1924.** Si; b&w. 35mm. 5 reels, 4,700 ft.

Cast: J. B. Warner, J. B. Warner *(Bob Lanier)*, Molly Malone *(Evelyn Vaughn)*, Mathilde Brundage *(Aunt Abigail)*, Theodore Lorch, Luis Barnes, Harry Fraser.

Western melodrama. Bob Lanier fakes a hold-up and kidnaping in an attempt to excite a a New York girl and her aunt. Bob's scheme fails when the aunt is abducted by real kidnapers. *Aunts. Kidnaping.*

THE WESTBOUND LIMITED **F2.6165**

Emory Johnson Productions. *Dist* Film Booking Offices of America. 15 Apr **1923** [c15 Apr 1923; LP18949]. Si; b&w. 35mm. 7 reels, 6,100 ft.

Pres by P. A. Powers. *Dir* Emory Johnson. *Story-Scen* Emilie Johnson. *Photog* Ross Fisher.

Cast: Ralph Lewis *(Bill Buckley)*, Claire McDowell *(Mrs. Buckley)*, Ella Hall *(Esther Miller)*, Johnny Harron *(Johnny Buckley)*, Taylor Graves *(Henry)*, Wedgewood Nowell *(Raymond McKim)*, David Dirby *(Jack Smith)*, Richard Morris *(Bernard Miller)*, Jane Morgan *(Mrs. Miller)*.

Melodrama. Railroad engineer Bill Buckley narrowly averts injury to Esther Miller, the daughter of the president of the company, when she falls on the tracks in front of his speeding train. In receiving a reward from Mr. Miller, Bill becomes involved in the villainous schemes of Raymond McKim, Mr. Miller's personal secretary, who makes it appear that Mrs. Buckley has been unfaithful to Bill and attempts to force Esther to marry him (McKim). Bill's son, Johnny, interferes on Esther's behalf; McKim receives his just deserts; and all ends happily. *Railroad engineers. Railroad magnates. Secretaries. Blackmail.*

A WESTERN ADVENTURER **F2.6166**

Western Star Productions. *Dist* Pioneer Film Corp. 4 Jun **1921** [trade review]. Si; b&w. 35mm. 5 reels.

Cast: William Fairbanks.

Western comedy-melodrama. "The hero has inherited the Bar-U ranch near the town of Ord. On the way to Ord he meets a charming girl who invites him to ride in her automobile. ... Bill meets the half brother of his traveling companion and a parson. They announce that they are oil promoters and have discovered that his ranch is the center of the oil region. Bill has his suspicions, but tells them to go ahead. They sell stock to the town folks. When the two crooks are about to make their getaway, Bill steps in. He has some thrilling experiences, ... with the help of the girl the money is saved. ... The indignant citizens chase the promoters out of town. Bill and the girl have a private meeting at the church, where the knot is tied." (*Moving Picture World,* 4 Jun 1921, p540.) *Stock promoters. Swindlers. Clergymen. Oil lands. Inheritance.*

WESTERN BLOOD **F2.6167**

Sanford Productions. 1 Jun **1923** [scheduled release]. Si; b&w. 35mm. 5 reels, 4,427 ft.

Dir Robert Hunter.

Cast: Pete Morrison.

Western melodrama. "Foreman on cattle ranch aids girl in fight against his employer when he learns the man is a crook trying to cheat her out of the property left by her uncle" (*Motion Picture News Booking Guide,* 5:56, Oct 1923.) *Ranchers. Ranch foremen. Inheritance.*

WESTERN COURAGE **F2.6168**

Ben Wilson Productions. *Dist* Rayart Pictures. Apr **1927.** Si; b&w. 35mm. 5 reels, 4,319 ft.

Dir Ben Wilson. *Scen* Leslie Curtis. *Photog* Eddie Linden.

Cast: Dick Hatton, Elsa Benham, Robert Walker, Ed La Niece, Al Ferguson.

Western melodrama. "Girl [played by Elas Benham] becomes infatuated with man [played by Robert Walker], who plans to defraud her. She is ignorant of his real intention, but the man who really loves her [played by Dick Hatton], after much conflict with band of crooks, shows up the villain in his true colors." (*Motion Picture News Booking Guide,* 13:45, Oct 1927.) *Ranchers. Swindlers.*

A WESTERN DEMON **F2.6169**

Western Feature Productions. May **1922** [New York State]. Si; b&w. 35mm. 5 reels, 4,725 ft.

Dir Robert McKenzie. *Photog* Edgar Lyons.

Cast: William Fairbanks *(Ned Underwood)*, Marilyn Mills *(Rose Dale)*, Monte Montague *(Joe Dalton)*, Murray Miller *(The Bandit)*, Billy Franey *(The Cook)*.

Western melodrama. Impressed by cowboy Ned Underwood's rescue of a drowning child, Rose Dale is pleased to find herself on the same westward-bound train with Ned. She relates her purpose of investigating reports of rustling at her ranch, and he offers to take a dishwashing job on her ranch and find out who is responsible. Rose's foreman, who wants her ranch for himself, tries to scare her away, then takes more drastic measures. To rescue Rose, who has been locked in a cabin with a bear, Ned wrestles with the animal, lassoes an airplane, climbs up the rope, and tosses the villain out of the airplane. *Cowboys. Ranch foremen. Rustling. Air stunts. Bears.*

A WESTERN ENGAGEMENT **F2.6170**

Arrow Pictures. 26 Apr **1925** [c12 May 1925; LP21454]. Si; b&w. 35mm. 5 reels.

Dir Paul Hurst.

Cast: Dick Hatton.

Western comedy. Dick Rawlins, a cowpoke on the Jackson ranch, is in love with Inez, the beautiful daughter of the ranchowner; planning to ask Inez to marry him, Dick goes to town to buy her an engagement ring, eventually going into hock to Bob for $500. When Dick returns to the ranch, he learns that he has been fired as the result of a mysterious stranger's testimony. Dick goes to the bunkhouse and sacks out; *while asleep, he dreams that at Bob's request he has faked a suicide in order to avoid paying his debts. Bob then knocks him unconscious and orders Dismal David, the town lunatic, to feed him to the crows; Dick escapes from Dismal David and rides to the minister's house, tangling himself in a sheet on the way. He finds that Inez is being married to Bob and starts to fight everyone present.* Dick wakes up in a terrible sweat and finds out that Bob was pulling his leg when he told him that he had been fired. Bob also tells Dick that the stranger has brought him a check for $10,000, one month's option for oil rights on a piece of land that Dick owns. Dick embraces Inez and tells her how they will spend the cash. *Cowboys. Debt. Suicide. Oil lands. Dreams.*

WESTERN FATE **F2.6171**

Wild West Productions. *Dist* Arrow Film Corp. 1 Apr **1924** [c18 Feb 1924; LP19915]. Si; b&w. 35mm. 5 reels, 4,937 ft.

Dir George Holt. *Story-Scen* George H. Plympton.

Cast: Dick Hatton, Neva Gerber.

Western melodrama. "An eastern girl, seeking to avenge her brother, who was murdered, goes west, the scene of the crime. In her search for the criminals she is aided by a handsome cowboy. Many stirring adventures befall them before the guilty man is found, and these serve to increase their love for each other." (*Motion Picture News Booking Guide*, [7]:56, Oct 1924.) *Cowboys. Brother-sister relationship. Murder. Revenge.*

WESTERN FEUDS **F2.6172**

Ashton Dearholt Productions. *Dist* Arrow Film Corp. 1 Feb **1924** [c26 Dec 1923; LP19770]. Si; b&w. 35mm. 5 reels, 4,908 ft.

Dir Francis Ford. *Story-Scen* Isabel Blodgett, Ashton Dearholt.

Cast: Edmund Cobb *(Ed Jones)*, Florence Gilbert *(Sally Warner)*, Al McCormick *(Black Pete)*, Kathleen Calhoun *(Bonita)*, William White *(Bill Warner)*, Ashton Dearholt *(Joe)*, Francis Ford *(J. P. Hartley)*.

Western melodrama. Posing as a ranch hand, Ed Jones attempts to discover the source of the enmity between the local cattle and sheep ranchers. He falls in love with Sally Warner, the daughter of the leading sheepman, and several times rescues her from the unwelcome attentions of Black Pete, an outlaw posing as a sheepman to cover his operations. The arrival of eastern ranchowner J. P. Hartley precipitates fights, a kidnaping, and danger to the principals; but in the end the outlaws are taken care of, and the feud is ended by the marriage of Sally and Ed, who is revealed to be Hartley's son. *Outlaws. Feuds. Ranches. Disguise. Kidnaping. Cattle. Sheep.*

WESTERN FIREBRANDS **F2.6173**

Charles R. Seeling Productions. *Dist* Aywon Film Corp. Nov **1921** [New York State]. Si; b&w. 35mm. 5 reels.

Dir Charles R. Seeling.

Cast: Big Boy Williams *(Billy Fargo)*, Virginia Adair *(Mildred Stanton)*, J. Conrad Needham *(Tom Fargo)*, William Horne *(Richard Stanton)*, Jack Pitcairn *(Victor Lanning)*, Bert Apling *(Pete Carson)*, Helen Yoder *(Red Feather)*.

Western melodrama. Victor Lanning, employed by eastern capitalist Richard Stanton to buy the Shasta Lumber Co., conspires with Pete Carson to start forest fires in order to make his own profit from the sale. En route to investigate the fires that have killed his cattle, Billy Fargo rescues Stanton and his daughter, Mildred, from a train wreck. Mildred's attentions to Billy at dinner that evening enrage Lanning, who plans a fake kidnaping. The actual abductors are serious, however, and Billy rescues her (with the help of Red Feather, an Indian girl with whom Lanning has flirted) in the midst of a raging storm. *Capitalists. Indians of North America. Lumbering. Kidnaping. Train wrecks. Storms. Forest fires.*

WESTERN GRIT **F2.6174**

Ward Lascelle Productions. 21 May **1924** [New York State license application; c1 Jun 1924; LP20308]. Si; b&w. 35mm. 5 reels, 4,500 ft.

Dir-Writ Ad Cook.

Cast: Lester Cuneo *(Walt Powers)*, Alma Deer *(Alma Grayson)*, Joe Bonner *(Mickey)*, Raye Hampton *(Minnie Smith)*, Lafayette McKee *(Jed Black)*, Newton Campbell *(Jim Grayson)*, "Slim" Padgett *(Jed Black's stage driver)*, Slim Allen *(Slim Burrows)*, Pietro Sosso *(government official)*, "Slim" Chambers *(John Grayson's stage driver)*.

Western melodrama. Two stagelines, one representing the "trust" headed by Jed Black and the other an "independent" owned by John Grayson, are competing for the award of a government mail contract. Grayson's employees (with the exception of ranch foreman Walt Powers) and his weakling son Jim are in league with Black to cause his downfall. The government official finally decides to base the award on the outcome of a race. Walt finds that Grayson's driver is in Black's pay and takes his place. The abduction by Black, during the race, of Grayson's daughter, Alma, causes Jim to repent his actions. She is rescued by Walt, who goes on to win the race, getting the contract for Grayson and Alma for himself. *Filial relations. Business competition. Postal service. Stagelines.*

WESTERN HEARTS **F2.6175**

Cliff Smith Productions. *Dist* Associated Photoplays. **1921** [c23 Sep 1921; LP16987]. Si; b&w. 35mm. 5 reels, 4,711 ft.

Dir Cliff Smith. *Story-Cont* Cliff Smith, Alvin J. Neitz. *Photog* Frank Cotner.

Cast: Josie Sedgwick *(Edith Caldwell)*, Art Straton *(Jack Manning)*, Floyd Taliaferro *(Pete Marcel)*, Hazel Hart *(Grace Adams)*, Edward Moncrief *(George Adams)*, Bert Wilson *(Robert Caldwell)*.

Western melodrama. While out west, easterner Edith Caldwell is admired by Jack Manning, a cowboy employed on the Adams ranch, of which her father is to take possession in one year. Grace Adams, the present owner's daughter, is infatuated with Jack, although another ranch hand, Pete, has vainly sought her love. Grace arranges with Pete to intercept all letters exchanged between Jack and Edith, and Jack, believing that Edith no longer loves him, leaves the ranch. Pete then induces Grace to marry him. When Edith and her father return to the ranch, there is evidence of cattle rustling, and Jack is detailed to apprehend the culprits. He is unable to make Edith believe that he has not eloped with Grace, until he has rounded up Pete and his gang of rustlers. *Cowboys. Ranchers. Rustlers. Courtship. Documentation.*

WESTERN HONOR *see* **THE MAN FROM NOWHERE**

WESTERN JUSTICE **F2.6177**

A. B. Maescher Productions. *Dist* Arrow Film Corp. 1 Mar **1923** [c15 Nov 1922; LP18408]. Si; b&w. 35mm. 5 reels.

Dir-Writ Fred Caldwell.

Cast: Josephine Hill.

Melodrama. A certain lawless woman, known to her intimates as Lady Lucifer or the Bandit Queen, hides under the cloak of respectability to promote the operations of a fake company. To generate interest in her project, she hires respected mining engineer Tom Taylor, who is unaware of her nefarious plans. She sends Taylor out of town with all the company funds. He is abducted by the Bandit Queen's gang, and a warrant is issued for his arrest. However, the faith of Taylor's fiancée, Grace, is unshaken, and she begins an investigation. The Bandit Queen and her weak-willed brother decide to make a getaway, but first they kidnap Grace to get her out of the way. Meanwhile, Taylor escapes and rescues Grace. The Bandit Queen, conscience-stricken, confesses, clearing the way for the happiness of the two lovers. *Engineers—Mining. Brother-sister relationship. Kidnaping. Fraud.*

Note: Copyright records indicate that this film is a "William Fairbanks Subject," but no verification of this fact has been found.

WESTERN LUCK **F2.6178**

Fox Film Corp. 22 Jun **1924** [c22 May 1924; LP20263]. Si; b&w. 35mm. 5 reels, 5,020 ft.

Pres by William Fox. *Dir* George André Beranger. *Story-Scen* Robert N. Lee. *Photog* Joseph Brotherton.

Cast: Charles Jones *(Larry Campbell)*, Beatrice Burnham *(Betty Gray)*, Pat Hartigan *(James Evart)*, Tom Lingham *(Lem Pearson)*, J. Farrell MacDonald *("Chuck" Campbell)*, Edith Kennick *(Mrs. Pearson)*, Bruce Gordon *(Leonard Pearson)*.

Western melodrama. Two brothers are separated in infancy—one being reared by a rancher as his son, the other remaining with his father, a Wall Street banker. Leonard, the easterner, conspires to steal property from a rancher, but Larry discovers the plot, prevents its execution, and brings about a reunion with his brother. *Bankers. Ranchers. Brothers. Theft. New York City—Wall Street.*

WESTERN METHODS **F2.6179**

Robert J. Horner Productions. *Dist* Bell Pictures. 10 Dec **1929** [New York State license]. Si; b&w. 35mm. 5 reels, 4,500 ft.

Cast: Fred Church.

Western melodrama(?). No information about the nature of this film has been found.

THE WESTERN MUSKETEER **F2.6180**

Long Beach Motion Pictures. *Dist* Truart Film Corp. 24 Dec **1922** [New York State]. Si; b&w. 35mm. 5 reels.

Dir-Writ William Bertram.

Cast: Leo Maloney *(Ranger)*, Dixie Lamont, Gus Suvall *(Tom Wilkes)*.

Western melodrama. "The usual ranger played by Maloney, and he has the usual old mother that he takes care of. The girl is the daughter of the impoverished and aged prospector, who still holds faith in a hole in the ground that he has dug. The bold, bad heavy is the general storekeeper, whose advances have been repulsed by the girl. To get even he first tries to blow up the old man and fasten a murder on the favored suitor, who is the ranger. There is the regulation stuff that has its horse features, its automobiles ... and the heroine making her way down a log chute to be in at the death. ... At the finish is the usual fadeout with the hero clasping the heroine to his manly bosom." (*Variety*, 1 Feb 1923, p41.) *Rangers. Prospectors. Storekeepers. Filial relations.*

WESTERN PLUCK (Blue Streak Western) **F2.6181**
Universal Pictures. 24 Jan **1926** [c14 Nov 1925; LP22001]. Si; b&w. 35mm. 5 reels, 4,207 ft.
Pres by Carl Laemmle. *Dir* Travers Vale. *Scen* Wyndham Gittens. *Story* W. C. Tuttle. *Photog* Eddie Linden, Harry Neumann.
Cast: Art Acord *("Arizona [Art]" Allen)*, Marceline Day *(Clare Dyer)*, Ray Ripley *(Gale Collins)*, Robert Rose *("Rowdy [Johnny]" Dyer)*, William Welsh *("Dynamite [Dan]" Dyer)*, Helen Cobb *(Molly)*, S. E. Jennings *(Buck Zaney)*, Charles Newton *(Sheriff [Dan] Wayne)*, Helen Cobb *(Molly, The Dance Hall Girl)*, Darkie *(Art's horse)*.
Western melodrama. Rowdy Dyer, the weak but tough-acting son of wealthy rancher Dynamite Dyer, greets the stage in which his sister Clare is arriving by disguising himself as a bandit. He fires a shot that causes the horses to bolt. Cowpuncher Arizona Allen stops the horses but is shot at by passenger Dale Collins, the bank manager. Dynamite hires Arizona, and Clare asks him to look after Rowdy. Arizona saves Rowdy from being fleeced by gambler Buck Zaney, thus incurring Zaney's enmity. A stage is held up, and Arizona, then Rowdy, are implicated. Arizona fights for Rowdy, but the latter, for the first time, stands up like a man. Arizona and Rowdy are proved innocent, and Dynamite congratulates Arizona as his future son-in-law. *Ranchers. Cowboys. Bandits. Manhood. Stagecoach robberies. Horses.*

WESTERN PROMISE **F2.6182**
Ward Lascelle Productions. 17 Feb **1925** [New York State license]. Si; b&w. 35mm. 5 reels, 4,800 ft.
Cast: Lester Cuneo.
Western melodrama(?). No information about the nature of this film has been found.

THE WESTERN ROVER (Blue Streak Western) **F2.6183**
Universal Pictures. 5 Jun **1927** [c3 May 1927; LP23925]. Si; b&w. 35mm. 5 reels, 4,404 ft.
Pres by Carl Laemmle. *Dir* Albert Rogell. *Story-Scen* George C. Hively. *Photog* Edwin Linden. *Art Dir* David S. Garber.
Cast: Art Acord *(Art Hayes)*, Ena Gregory *(Millie Donlin)*, Charles Avery *(Hinkey Hall)*, William Welch *(Alexander Seaton)*, Raven *(himself, a horse)*, Rex *(himself, a dog)*.
Western melodrama. Art leaves his father's ranch over an argument and becomes a circus performer. When the circus folds, he is forced to return to ranching and gets a job through the efforts of Millie Donlin, who introduces him to Barstry (Hall?), foreman of the ranch adjoining that of Seaton. Learning that Barstry is rustling his father's cattle, Art, who is none other than Seaton's long-missing son, rounds up the cattle at night, sends them to Chicago, and saves his father from bankruptcy. Seaton arrives at the ranch and finds that his son is acting as foreman during Barstry's sojourn in jail and has won the love of Millie. *Ranch foremen. Rustlers. Cowboys. Ranches. Circus. Bankruptcy. Horses. Dogs.*

WESTERN SPEED **F2.6184**
Fox Film Corp. 23 Apr **1922** [c23 Apr 1922; LP17853]. Si; b&w. 35mm. 5 reels, 5,002 ft.
Pres by William Fox. *Dir* Scott Dunlap, C. R. Wallace. *Scen* Scott Dunlap. *Photog* George Schneiderman.
Cast: Charles Jones *("Red" Kane)*, Eileen Percy *("Dot" Lorimer)*, Jack McDonald *(Brad Usher)*, J. P. Lockney *(Ben Lorimer)*, Jack Curtis *("Spunk" Lemm)*, Milton Ross *(Kansas Casey)*, Walt Robbins *("Shorty")*, Charles Newton *(express agent)*.
Western melodrama. Source: William Patterson White, *Lynch Lawyers* (Boston, 1920). Ben Lorimer and his daughter, Dot, are received with suspicion in a western town; when "Red" Kane rescues Dot, however, he wins her confidence and learns that Lorimer has adopted a new name and is wanted for a crime in Colorado for which he is not guilty. Trying to protect them from the sheriff and his posse, Red is wounded, but Dot nurses him. "Spunk" Lemm circulates rumors that Red is hiding behind a woman's skirts; Red engages in a fight with Spunk and, thinking he has killed him, returns to the hills; there he discovers the men who robbed the express office and gets a confession that clears Lorimer of the crime in Colorado. After resolving his difficulties, Red claims Dot as his future wife. *Fugitives. Cowboys. Robbers. Disguise. Express service.*

WESTERN SUFFRAGETTES *see* **A TRICK OF HEARTS**

A WESTERN THOROUGHBRED **F2.6185**
Horizon Pictures. 12 Sep **1922** [New York State license]. Si; b&w. 35mm. 5 reels, 4,500 ft.
Pres by Franklyn E. Backer.
Cast: Harry McCabe.
Western melodrama. No information about the precise nature of this film has been found.

WESTERN TRAILS **F2.6186**
Sierra Pictures. *Dist* Chesterfield Motion Picture Corp. Apr or 15 May **1926.** Si; b&w. 35mm. 5 reels, 4,580 ft.
Dir H. B. Carpenter. *Photog* Paul Allen.
Cast: Bill Patton.
Western melodrama. "Father and daughter are persecuted by chief of cattle rustlers but they beat him at his own game with the aid of deputy sheriff, who falls in love with daughter." (*Motion Picture News Booking Guide*, 11:54, Oct 1926.) *Rustlers. Sheriffs. Ranchers.*

WESTERN VENGEANCE **F2.6187**
Independent Pictures. 20 Jul **1924.** Si; b&w. 35mm. 5 reels.
Pres by Jesse J. Goldburg. *Dir* J. P. McGowan. *Story* James Ormont. *Photog* Walter Griffin.
Cast: Franklyn Farnum *(Jack Caldwell)*, Doreen Turner *(Helen Caldwell)*, Marie Walcamp *(Mary Sterling)*, Jim Corey *(Santag)*, Martin Turner *(Luke Mosby)*, Mack V. Wright *(Dick Sterling)*, Pete *(himself, a dog)*.
Melodrama. Dick Sterling, secret leader of a gang of outlaws, leads them to loot Jack Caldwell's mine when gold is discovered on his ranch. Caldwell loves Sterling's sister, Mary, but he vows vengeance upon the gang when an explosion in the shaft kills Jack's little sister, Helen. Capturing a runaway outlaw, Jack is horrified to recognize Mary's brother. Mary pleads for the boy's life, but Dick's death by suicide paves the way for the loving couple's happiness. *Outlaws. Brother-sister relationship. Gold mines. Suicide. Dogs.*

THE WESTERN WALLOP **F2.6188**
Universal Pictures. 10 Oct **1924** [New York premiere; released 2 Nov or 14 Dec; c23 Sep 1924; LP20603]. Si; b&w. 35mm. 5 reels, 4,611 or 4,662 ft.
Dir Clifford Smith. *Screenplay* Wyndham Gittens. *Adapt* Isadore Bernstein. *Photog* Harry Neumann.
Cast: Jack Hoxie *(Bart Tullison)*, Margaret Landis *(Anita Stillwell)*, James Gordon Russell *(Jefferson Bradshaw)*, Charles Brinley *(Sheriff Malloy)*, Duke R. Lee *(The Bandit)*, Fred Burns *(Marshall Malloy)*, Jack Pratt *(convict leader)*, Herbert Fortier *(Jim Stillwell)*, Joseph W. Girard *(prison warden)*, William Welsh *(Italian convict)*.
Western melodrama. Source: Adolph Bannauer, "On Parole" (publication undetermined). Parolee Bart Tullison becomes foreman of Anita Stillwell's ranch near the Nevada border. While Anita considers Bart a coward because he will not pursue cattle rustlers across the border, Jefferson Bradshaw learns of Bart's past and resolves to use it to end the growing affection between Anita and Bart. Bradshaw kidnaps Anita and takes her into Nevada, and Bart follows and rescues her. While Bradshaw is taking a beating, the sheriff arrives with a pardon for Bart and the news of the confession of the true perpetrator of the crime for which Bart was convicted on circumstantial evidence. *Ranch foremen. Cowboys. Rustling. Circumstantial evidence. Parole. Prisons. Nevada.*
Note: Working title: *On Parole.*

THE WESTERN WHIRLWIND (Blue Streak Western) **F2.6189**
Universal Pictures. 20 Feb **1927** [c19 Oct 1926; LP23262]. Si; b&w. 35mm. 5 reels, 4,967 ft.
Pres by Carl Laemmle. *Dir-Story* Albert Rogell. *Scen* Harrison Jacobs. *Photog* William Nobles. *Art Dir* David S. Garber.
Cast: Jack Hoxie *(Jack Howard)*, Margaret Quimby *(Molly Turner)*,

Claude Payton *(Jeff Taylor)*, Billy Engle *("Beans" Baker)*, Edith Yorke *(Mrs. Martha Howard)*, Jack Pratt *(Jim Blake)*, Scout *(a horse)*.

Western melodrama. Jack Howard, returning from the war, learns that his father, Sheriff Howard, has been killed by an unknown assailant, and he induces the mayor of Gold Strike to swear him in as sheriff. Jack resolves to avenge his father, though he is scoffed at by local heavies, headed by Jeff Taylor, who spread a tale of Jack's cowardice in the war. Mrs. Howard pleads with Jack not to endanger himself, and he refrains from interfering with the gang's depredations and robberies until Taylor tries to frame a robbery on him and tricks Jack's girl, Molly, into going to a mountain retreat. Jack pursues the bandits, forces a confession of Taylor's guilt in the murder of his father, and rescues Molly from Taylor. *Veterans. Sheriffs. Robbers. Motherhood. Courtship. Revenge. Murder.*

WESTERN YESTERDAYS **F2.6190**

Ashton Dearholt. *Dist* Arrow Film Corp. 1 May **1924** [24 Mar 1924; LP19975]. Si; b&w. 35mm. 5 reels, 5,050 ft.

Dir-Adapt Francis Ford. *Story* E. R. Hickson, Ashton Dearholt. *Mus Synop* James C. Bradford.

Cast: Florence Gilbert *(Rose Silver)*, Edmund Cobb *(Jim Blake, deputy)*, William White *(Bill Hickson, sheriff)*, Ashton Dearholt *(Pinto Pete)*, Helen Broneau *(Juanita)*, Joe De La Cruz *(Rude Reverence)*, Francis Ford *("Twitchie")*, Clark Coffey *(Clarence)*, Slim Hamilton *("Blackstone")*.

Western melodrama. "Rose, only daughter of 'Old Man' Silver is left an orphan when shot is fired across gaming table. In love with Sheriff Blake she suspects him of being untrue, leaves him and wanders into outlaw camp of Pinto Pete, who attracted by her, gives her a horse and sends her back home. The peculiar manner in which the horse is shod reveals Pinto Pete as the instigator of many crimes. He is captured by Blake who in turn weds the girl." (*Motion Picture News Booking Guide*, [7]:57, Oct 1924.) *Orphans. Outlaws. Sheriffs. Horses.*

WESTWARD BOUND **F2.6191**

Webb-Douglas Productions. *Dist* Syndicate Pictures. 1 Dec **1930**. Sd (Cinephone); b&w. 35mm. 6 reels, 5,800 ft.

Dir Harry S. Webb. *Story-Cont-Dial* Carl Krusada. *Photog* William Nobles. *Film Ed* Fred Bain. *Sd Engr* Ralph M. Like.

Cast: Buffalo Bill Jr. *(Bob Lansing)*, Allene Ray *(Marge Holt)*, Buddy Roosevelt *(Frank)*, Fern Emmett *(Emma)*, Ben Corbett *(Ben)*, Yakima Canutt *(Jim)*, Tom Langdon *(Dick)*, Robert Walker *(Steve)*, Pete Morrison.

Western melodrama. After Bob Lansing is peripherally involved in a nightclub scrape (at which he meets Montana rancher Marge Holt), Bob's father sends him west with his chauffeur, Ben. They are mistaken for rustlers Dick and Jim and again meet up with Marge, who recognizes Bob but wishes to make his life difficult. Nevertheless, Bob, deciding to help Marge end the rustling of her cattle, infiltrates the gang, brings the rustlers to justice, and hears Marge ask him to remain. *Rustlers. Ranchers. Chauffeurs. Gangs. Scandal. Personal identity. Nightclubs. Montana.*

WET GOLD **F2.6192**

Submarine Film Corp. *Dist* Goldwyn Distributing Corp. Jun **1921** [c23 Apr 1921; LP16413]. Si; b&w. 35mm. 6 reels.

Prod-Story J. Ernest Williamson. *Dir* Ralph Ince. *Photog* William J. Black, Jay Rescher.

Cast: Ralph Ince *(John Cromwell)*, Aleen Burr *(Grace Hamilton)*, Alicia Turner *(Susan)*, Harry McNaughton *('Arry)*, Thomas Megraine *(Colonel Hamilton)*, John Butler *(Chubby Madison)*, Charles McNaughton *(James Chipman)*.

Melodrama. John Cromwell escapes from a gang of "pirates" to Havana, where he meets Kentucky Colonel Hamilton and his daughter Grace. Though threatened by his former captors, Cromwell has a chart showing the whereabouts of a sunken treasure ship, which they set out to find. When he is accosted in his diving gear and the Hamilton party is marooned by pirates headed by Chipman, Cromwell escapes, boards their submarine, and, after the villains are killed in an explosion, rescues the party. *Kentucky colonels. Pirates. Diving. Treasure. Submarines. Caribbean. Havana.*

WET PAINT **F2.6193**

Famous Players–Lasky. *Dist* Paramount Pictures. 3 May **1926** [c18 May 1926; LP22743]. Si; b&w. 35mm. 6 reels, 5,109 ft.

Pres by Adolph Zukor, Jesse L. Lasky. *Dir* Arthur Rosson. *Scen* Lloyd Corrigan. *Story* Reginald Morris. *Photog* William Marshall.

Cast: Raymond Griffith *(He)*, Helene Costello *(She)*, Bryant Washburn *(Her Brother)*, Natalie Kingston *(A Beautiful Woman)*, Henry Kolker *(A Husband)*.

Farce. He, a wealthy bachelor, is in love with She, a beautiful rich girl, but on the night He proposes She calls in a crowd of friends who have been hiding and asks them to pay their betting debts. Deeply hurt, He announces He is through with She and will marry the first girl He meets. He pursues exciting experiences with a number of women. Returning home one morning, He finds that his key will not fit the lock and asks a policeman to help him through the window; discovering himself in a strange house with a married woman whom He has met earlier, He and this woman spend considerable time trying to escape each other and her mean, muscular husband. Following a wild ride in a driverless automobile, He and She, his former sweetheart, are permanently united. *Bachelors. Wagers. Courtship.*

WHAT A GIRL CAN DO **F2.6194**

Edward Stuart. *Dist* International Education Board. c13 Nov **1924** [MP2875]. Si; b&w. 35mm. 7 reels.

Scen Edward Stuart.

Educational documentary. The death of her father leaves 15-year-old Mary Martin with a semi-invalid mother and a farm she does not know how to work. Her friend Mildred introduces her to 4-H Club work, however, and Mary is soon involved in vegetable gardening. From that she successfully advances to canning, poultry raising, home improvement, and sewing. Entering a canning contest, she is awarded a scholarship for a short course at the State Agricultural College. "She thus rounds out three stages in her career, first creating earning capacity, second, increasing the comfort of her surroundings and improving her own appearance, and third, culture." (Copyright records.) *Farming. Self-reliance. Four-H Clubs.*

Note: Subtitle: "Girls' Club Work Film."

WHAT A MAN **F2.6195**

Sono-Art Productions. 1 Apr or 1 Jun **1930** [c3 Apr 1930; LP1217]. Sd; b&w. 35mm. 7 or 9 reels.

Dir George J. Crone. *Dial* A. A. Kline. *Adapt* Harvey Gates. *Photog* Arthur Todd. *Tech Dir (see note)* Charles Cadwallader. *Film Ed* Harry Chandlee. *Sd Engr (see note)* J. G. Greger.

Cast: Reginald Denny *(Wade Rawlins)*, Miriam Seegar *(Eileen Kilbourne)*, Harvey Clark *(Mr. Kilbourne)*, Lucille Ward *(Mrs. Kilbourne)*, Carlyle Moore *(Kane Kilbourne)*, Anita Louise *(Marion Kilbourne)*, Norma Drew *(Elsie Thayer)*, Christiane Yves *(Marquise de la Fresne)*, Charles Coleman *(William, English butler)*, Greta Granstedt *(Hanna, the maid)*.

Comedy. Source: E. J. Rath, *The Dark Chapter* (New York, 1924). Courtenay Savage, *They All Want Something; a Comedy in a Prologue and Three Acts* (New York, 1927). Overhearing a train conductor describe wealthy Mrs. Kilbourne's penchant for taking in hoboes, Wade Rawlins maneuvers her into hiring him as a chauffeur. The other members of the Kilbourne family object, and their butler, William, is particularly suspicious, but Wade wins them over one by one—especially elder daughter Eileen, who falls in love with him. William is the last to relent—when he recognizes Wade as a former British Army officer—and the chauffeur reveals his past experiences as a well-bred English gentleman and Canadian bootlegger. *Hoboes. Chauffeurs. Butlers. Bootleggers. English. Canadians.*

Note: Also advertised and reviewed as *His Dark Chapter* and *They All Want Something*. A Spanish version is entitled *Así es la vida*, q. v.; its technical director, Charles Cadwallader, and its sound engineer, J. G. Greger, may also have worked on this film.

WHAT A NIGHT! **F2.6196**

Paramount Famous Lasky Corp. 22 Dec **1928** [c22 Dec 1928; LP25938]. Si; b&w. 35mm. 6 reels, 5,378 ft.

Dir Edward Sutherland. *Screenplay* Louise Long. *Titl* Herman J. Mankiewicz. *Story* Grover Jones, Lloyd Corrigan. *Photog* Edward Cronjager. *Film Ed* Doris Drought.

Cast: Bebe Daniels *(Dorothy Winston)*, Neil Hamilton *(Joe Madison)*, William Austin *(Percy Penfield)*, Wheeler Oakman *(Mike Corney)*, Charles Sellon *(Editor Madison)*, Charles Hill Mailes *(Patterson)*, Ernie Adams *(Snarky)*.

Comedy-melodrama. When Dorothy Winston, the daughter of an industrialist, arranges to work on a newspaper in which her father places a substantial amount of advertising, Joe Madison, the reporter son of the paper's editor, offers to show her the ropes. A gunman employed by Mike Corney lands in jail, and Dorothy succeeds in interviewing him, getting him to divulge the whereabouts of a canceled check that will link Corney to Patterson, a corrupt political boss. Dorothy and Joe get the check, and Joe telephones his father to urge him to print an exposé of Patterson. Corney recovers the check, however, and Patterson institutes a ruinous libel suit against the paper. Dorothy gets the check back and obtains photographic evidence to further incriminate Patterson and Corney. Dorothy and Joe decide to write the story of their life with each another. *Reporters. Editors. Industrialists. Political bosses. Newspapers. Documentation.*

Note: Working title: *Number Please.*

WHAT A WIDOW! **F2.6197**

Gloria Productions. *Dist* United Artists. 13 Sep **1930** [c4 Sep 1930; LP1586]. Sd (Movietone); b&w. 35mm. 10 reels, 8,128 ft.

Pres by Joseph P. Kennedy. *Dir* Allan Dwan. *Adapt-Dial* James Gleason, James Seymour. *Story* Josephine Lovett. *Photog* George Barnes. *Art Dir* Paul Nelson. *Film Ed* Viola Lawrence. *Mus Dir* Josiah Zuro. *Song Numbers: "Love, Thy Magic Spell Is Everywhere," "Love Is Like a Song," "Say Oui Chérie," "You're the One"* Vincent Youmans. *Sp Orchestrations* Hugo Felix. *Rec Engr* Earl A. Wolcott, D. A. Cutler.

Cast: Gloria Swanson *(Tamarind)*, Owen Moore *(Gerry)*, Lew Cody *(Victor)*, Margaret Livingston *(Valli)*, William Holden *(Mr. Lodge)*, Herbert Braggiotti *(José Alvarado)*, Gregory Gaye *(Bastikoff)*, Adrienne D'Ambricourt *(Paulette)*, Nella Walker *(marquise)*, Daphne Pollard *(masseuse)*.

Romantic comedy. Tamarind Brooks, widowed for a year, sails for Paris in search of romance and adventure. Aboard ship she meets many socialites—among them, Gerry Morgan, a successful young lawyer; Victor, an alcoholic nightclub dancer; and his partner and wife, Valli, who plans to divorce him in Paris to marry Ivan Bastikoff, a Russian violinist. Although Tam encourages many men, it is Gerry who falls in love and proposes marriage; however, she rejects him. In Paris, Tam leases the modernistic town house of the Marquise de la Fousbouget, who arranges for her to meet *tout Paris,* including José, a Spanish baritone with whom she has a fling while arranging for Valli's divorce. Tam and Gerry separate as the result of an argument and cause a fight between Bastikoff and José. After a spree with Victor, Tam passes out; and the next morning, assuming they have had sexual intercourse, she agrees to marry him; then, realizing her error, she joins Gerry aboard a Dornier D-OX bound for New York, and they are married as the plane flies over the Statue of Liberty and Broadway. *Widows. Lawyers. Dancers. Violinists. Singers. Flirtation. Alcoholism. Weddings. Ocean liners. Dornier airplanes. Paris. New York City.*

WHAT A WIFE LEARNED **F2.6198**

Thomas H. Ince Productions. *Dist* Associated First National Pictures. ca4 Feb **1923** [Des Moines and Omaha premieres; released 28 Jan; c26 Jan 1923; LP18616]. Si; b&w. 35mm. 7 reels, 6,228 ft.

Pres by Thomas H. Ince. *Pers Supv* Thomas H. Ince. *Dir* John Griffith Wray. *Story* Bradley King. *Photog* Henry Sharp.

Cast: John Bowers *(Jim Russell)*, Milton Sills *(Rudolph Martin)*, Marguerite De La Motte *(Sheila Dorne)*, Evelyn McCoy *(Esther Russell)*, Harry Todd *(Tracy McGrath)*, Aggie Herring *(Maggie McGrath)*, Francelia Billington *(Lillian Martin)*, Bertram Johns *(Percy)*, Ernest Butterworth *(Terry)*, John Steppling *(Maxfield)*.

Melodrama. Sheila Dorne marries rancher Jim Russell when he assures her that he will never interfere with her literary career. The success of Sheila's novel and its subsequent dramatization take her to New York and new friends, including Rudolph Martin. Jim unhappily throws himself into the construction of a large dam, which is completed just as Sheila comes home accompanied by Rudolph. The dam breaks, and Jim, assuming Sheila loves Rudolph, rescues him. It becomes obvious, however, that Sheila prefers her husband. *Novelists. Ranchers. Marriage. Theater. Dams.*

WHAT DO MEN WANT? **F2.6199**

Lois Weber Productions. *Dist* Wid Gunning, Inc. ca13 Nov **1921** [New York premiere; released Nov; c1 Dec 1921; LP17262]. Si; b&w. 35mm. 7 reels, 6,141 ft.

Prod-Dir-Writ Lois Weber. *Photog* Dal Clawson.

Cast: Claire Windsor *(Hallie [The Girl])*, J. Frank Glendon *(Frank [The Youth])*, George Hackathorne *(Arthur [His Brother])*, Hallam Cooley *(Yost [The Evil Influence])*, Edith Kessler *(Bertha [The Unfortunate])*.

Domestic melodrama. Frank Boyd, a restless but energetic youth, has his heart set on Hallie, the village belle, and invents an automobile attachment that brings him a fortune. Marriage, fatherhood, and homelife all prove irksome to him, and his fancy leads him to neglect his family. His brother Arthur develops an intrigue with Bertha, a poor seamstress whom he deserts, and later returns to find she has drowned herself. Frank, unable to derive any satisfaction from life, finds diversion in artificial gaiety, but when he suspects Yost, a young man-about-town, of being his wife's lover, his jealousy is aroused. Discovering that he is in error, he realizes his shameful neglect of Hallie and turns over a new leaf to the happiness of all. *Inventors. Brothers. Seamstresses. Men-about-town. Marriage. Fatherhood. Suicide.*

WHAT EVERY GIRL SHOULD KNOW **F2.6200**

Warner Brothers Pictures. 12 Mar **1927** [c1 Mar 1927; LP23720]. Si; b&w. 35mm. 7 reels, 6,281 ft.

Dir Charles F. Reisner. *Screenplay* Lois Jackson. *Story* Jack Wagner. *Camera* David Abel. *Asst Dir* Sandy Roth.

Cast: Patsy Ruth Miller *(Mary Sullivan)*, Ian Keith *(Arthur Graham)*, Carroll Nye *(Dave Sullivan)*, Mickey McBan *(Bobby Sullivan)*, Lillian Langdon *(Mrs. Randolph)*, Hazel Howell *(Estelle Randolph)*, Carmelita Geraghty *(Madame Le Fleur)*.

Romantic drama. Mary Sullivan, age 17, and Bobby, her little brother, who are both dependent upon their elder brother, Dave, are sent to an orphanage when Dave—though innocent—is convicted of transporting illicit liquor and sentenced to prison. As they are housed in separate buildings, Mary disguises herself in boy's clothing in an effort to see Bobby, but she is discovered by the matron and taken to the superintendent. Touched by Mary's story, director Arthur Graham, a wealthy young philanthropist, adopts the two orphans; and they find happiness together. Owing to the insinuations of Mrs. Randolph, Mary and Bobby run away, and Graham is unable to find them. Mary achieves prominence as a tennis player, and Graham is reunited with her at a match with Madame Le Fleur. Overruling her objections, he plans a speedy wedding, and as a wedding gift he uses his influence to obtain Dave's freedom. *Orphans. Millionaires. Philanthropists. Brother-sister relationship. Bootlegging. Tennis. Injustice.*

WHAT EVERY WOMAN KNOWS **F2.6201**

Famous Players–Lasky. *Dist* Paramount Pictures. 12 Mar **1921** [New York premiere; released 24 Apr; c24 Apr 1921; LP16412]. Si; b&w. 35mm. 7 reels, 6,772 ft.

Dir William C. De Mille. *Scen* Olga Printzlau. *Photog* L. Guy Wilky.

Cast: Lois Wilson *(Maggie Wylie)*, Conrad Nagel *(John Shand)*, Charles Ogle *(Alick Wylie)*, Fred Huntly *(David Wylie)*, Guy Oliver *(James Wylie)*, Winter Hall *(Charles Venables)*, Lillian Tucker *(Sybil Tenterden)*, Claire McDowell *(Comtesse de la Brière)*, Robert Brower *(Scotch lawyer)*.

Comedy-drama. Source: James Matthew Barrie, *What Every Woman Knows* (1908). When railroad porter John Shand is caught reading in the Wylies' library, Alick offers to pay for Shand's education on the condition that he marry Maggie within 5 years. At the end of the period he is a Member of Commons and Maggie is his wife. Though it is Maggie's wit and judgment, typed into his speeches, which marks his fame, Shand falls in love with Lady Sybil. Unaware of the infatuation, Maggie arranges for them to visit a country estate. Shand prepares an unimpressive speech for a cabinet minister, but as rewritten by Maggie the speech is a success, and he realizes her devotion and the degree to which he owes her his position. *Politicians. Porters. Education. Great Britain—Parliament.*

WHAT FOOLS MEN **F2.6202**

First National Pictures. 13 Sep **1925** [c2 Sep 1925; LP21789]. Si; b&w. 35mm. 8 reels, 7,349 ft.

Dir George Archainbaud. *Ed Dir* June Mathis. *Scen* Eve Unsell. *Photog* Norbert Brodin. *Art Dir* E. J. Shulter. *Film Ed* Bert Moore.

Cast: Lewis Stone *(Joseph Greer)*, Shirley Mason *(Beatrice Greer)*, Ethel Grey Terry *(Violet Williamson)*, Barbara Bedford *(Jenny McFarlan)*, John Patrick *(Lancing Ware)*, Hugh Allan *(Burns)*, David Torrence *(Williamson)*, Lewis Dayton *(Henry Craven)*, Joyce Compton *(Dorothy)*.

Melodrama. Source: Henry Kitchell Webster, *Joseph Greer and His Daughter* (Indianapolis, 1922). Separated from his wife for many years, Joseph Greer learns that he is the father of a grown daughter, Beatrice. The girl comes to live with him, and he does not know what to do with her. Thinking that she should become a member of fashionable society, Greer sells an invention for the manufacture of linen to a group of dishonest financiers, hoping thereby to advance his position in society. Vi Williamson, the socialite wife of one of the crooked bankers, flirts with Greer, and he spurns her. Deeply offended, Vi convinces her husband that he should ruin Greer. Beatrice elopes with the chauffeur, and Greer is injured in an automobile accident. Broken in health and wealth, Greer goes to live in a poor quarter of the city, drinking himself into oblivion. The chauffeur remains loyal, however, and takes the old man into his home, offering him a place to continue his experiments. With renewed energy and confidence, Greer sets out to regain the high place he once held in the world of commerce. *Inventors. Bankers. Chauffeurs. Socialites. Fatherhood. Elopement. Automobile accidents. Alcoholism. Linen.*

WHAT FOOLS MEN ARE **F2.6203**

Pyramid Pictures. *Dist* American Releasing Corp. 29 Oct **1922** [c15 Dec 1922; LP18747]. Si; b&w. 35mm. 6 reels, 6,087 ft.

Dir George Terwilliger. *Scen* Peter Milne. *Photog* Rudolph Mariner. *Art Dir* Ben Carré. *Mus Cues* J. Ernest Zivelli.

Cast: Faire Binney *(Peggy Kendricks)*, Lucy Fox *(Ola)*, Joseph Striker *(Ralph Demarest)*, Huntley Gordon *(Bartley Claybourne)*, Florence Billings *(Kate Claybourne)*, J. Barney Sherry *(Horace Demarest)*, Templar Saxe *(Bayard Thomas)*, Harry Clay Blaney *(Steve O'Malley)*.

Society drama. Source: Eugene Walter, *The Flapper; an American Drama in Three Acts* (c15 Apr 1922). Kate Claybourne is too busy with her literary career to notice that her husband, Bartley, is providing the finery for her flapper sister, Peggy Kendricks. When she does find out, she seeks a divorce, with the understanding that Bartley will marry Peggy. But Peggy, who toys with many men's hearts, marries Ralph Demarest, thereby cutting off Ralph from his disapproving father's fortune. Peggy accepts money from Horace Demarest to leave Ralph but then flings it in Ralph's face and urges him to make a man of himself. Peggy stands by Ralph, wins Horace's affection, and reunites the Claybournes. *Sisters. Flappers. Authors. Divorce. Manhood.*

WHAT HAPPENED TO FATHER **F2.6204**

Warner Brothers Pictures. 25 Jun **1927** [c18 Jun 1927; LP24106]. Si; b&w. 35mm. 6 reels, 5,567 ft.

Dir John G. Adolfi. *Scen* Charles R. Condon. *Photog* Willard Van Enger. *Asst Dir* Eddie Sowders.

Cast: Warner Oland *(W. Bradberry, father)*, Flobelle Fairbanks *(Betty Bradberry)*, William Demarest *(Dibbin, detective)*, Vera Lewis *(Mrs. Bradberry, mother)*, John Miljan *(Victor Smith)*, Hugh Allan *(Tommy Dawson)*, Cathleen Calhoun *(Violet)*, Jean Lefferty *(Gloria)*.

Farce. Source: Mary Roberts Rinehart, "What Happened to Father," in *Lippincott's Magazine* (84:329, Sep 1909). Bradberry, an absentminded student of Egyptian lore, is cowed by an ambitious wife who plans her daughter's marriage to Victor Smith, a man of wealth and social standing, while Betty actually loves Tommy Dawson. Secretly, father becomes successful as the author of a musical comedy under a *nom de plume*. On the day before the wedding, Bradberry is summoned by the producer of his latest play to the dress rehearsal; unused to society, he is confused and dazzled by the backstage glamour and is vamped by Gloria, a fast-stepping dancer. At her mother's insistence, Betty has a detective put on the case who poses as a waiter. Father discovers that the backer, Smith, is his daughter's fiancé and returns home in time to assert his authority by marrying Betty to Dawson. *Social climbers. Theatrical backers. Dancers. Detectives. Playwrights. Family life. Fatherhood. Theater.*

WHAT HAPPENED TO JONES (Universal-Jewel) **F2.6205**

Universal Pictures. 31 Jan **1926** [c9 Dec 1925; LP22098]. Si; b&w. 35mm. 7 reels, 6,726 ft.

Pres by Carl Laemmle. *Dir* William A. Seiter. *Adapt-Cont* Melville W. Brown. *Photog* Arthur Todd. *Art Dir* Leo E. Kuter.

Cast: Reginald Denny *(Tom Jones)*, Marian Nixon *(Lucille Bigbee)*, Melbourne MacDowell *(Mr. Bigbee)*, Frances Raymond *(Mrs. Bigbee)*, Otis Harlan *(Ebenezer Goodly)*, Emily Fitzroy *(Mrs. Goodly)*, Margaret Quimby *(Marjorie Goodly)*, Ben Hendricks, Jr. *(Richard)*, William Austin *(Henry Fuller)*, Nina Romano *(Minerva Starlight)*, ZaSu Pitts *(Hilda)*, John Elliott *(The Bishop)*, Edward Cecil *(Smith)*, Broderick O'Farrell *(Rector)*.

Farce. Source: George H. Broadhurst, *What Happened to Jones; an Original Farce in Three Acts* (New York, 1910). Tom Jones, a young man of wealth and irreproachable character, is inveigled on the eve of his wedding to attend a poker party given by his henpecked friend Ebenezer Goodly. The party is raided, but Tom and Ebenezer escape the police by ducking into a ladies' turkish bath. The police are called, and the two exit in the guise of female clients. The police find Tom's wallet and look for him at his fiancée's home. The two make their way to Ebenezer's house, and Tom dons the clothes of Ebenezer's brother, a bishop, who is expected to arrive soon. Complications arise when the bishop does arrive to officiate at the wedding. In the end, Tom is finally married by the bishop in a speeding automobile while being pursued by the police. *Police. Poker. Impersonation. Weddings. Turkish baths. Chases.*

WHAT HAPPENED TO ROSA? **F2.6206**

Goldwyn Pictures. 23 Apr **1921** [trade review; c22 Nov 1920; LP15839]. Si; b&w. 35mm. 5 reels.

Dir Victor Schertzinger. *Scen* Gerald C. Duffy. *Story* Pearl Lenore Curran. *Photog* George F. Webber.

Cast: Mabel Normand *(Mayme Ladd)*, Hugh Thompson *(Dr. Drew)*, Doris Pawn *(Gwendolyn)*, Tully Marshall *(Peacock)*, Eugenie Besserer *(Madame O'Donnelly)*, Buster Trow *(Jim)*.

Farce. Mayme Ladd, a shopgirl whose mother was a Spanish dancer, is told by a fortune-teller that she is the reincarnation of a noble Spanish maiden. Mayme meets handsome Dr. Drew in the store and learns he will be attending a masquerade on a steamboat. She goes to the ball dressed as a highborn Spanish maiden; there is a row over her; and rather than reveal her identity, Mayme discards her costume and swims ashore. When her clothes are found by the doctor, she is thought to have drowned. After having been hit by a pushcart, she is taken to Dr. Drew's, where she washes up and sneaks back into her own Spanish togs that she finds there. When the doctor enters he is delighted to find his Spanish charmer alive, radiant, and anxious to become his bride! *Physicians. Shopgirls. Dancers. Fortune-tellers. Spanish. Reincarnation. Disguise. Steamboats.*

WHAT LOVE WILL DO **F2.6207**

Fox Film Corp. 11 Sep **1921** [c11 Sep 1921; LP17001]. Si; b&w. 35mm. 5 reels, 4,252 ft.

Pres by William Fox. *Dir* William K. Howard. *Scen* Jack Strumwasser. *Story* L. G. Rigby. *Photog* Victor Milner.

Cast: Edna Murphy *(Mary Douglas)*, Johnnie Walker *(Johnny Rowan)*, Glen Cavender *(Abner Rowan)*, Barbara Tennant *(Goldie Rowan)*, Richard Tucker *(Herbert Dawson)*, Edwin B. Tilton *(Reverend Douglas)*.

Melodrama. Herbert Dawson entices Goldie Rowan to elope with him, leaving her husband and 3-year-old son, Johnny. Later, hearing her husband has died, she marries Dawson but is soon deserted by him. Johnny, growing up, gets a job in a grocery store, falls in love with the minister's daughter, Mary Douglas, and joins the church. When a traveling evangelist comes to town, Johnny is delegated to act as treasurer of his funds, but the evangelist—none other than Dawson—is a swindler who plans to have Johnny beaten and robbed. Seeing the wife he deserted in his congregation, Dawson tries to alter his plan to seize the funds but is killed by his cohorts. Goldie is reunited with her lost son and nurses him back to health. *Evangelists. Swindlers. Churchmen. Infidelity. Desertion. Motherhood. Religion.*

WHAT LOVE WILL DO **F2.6208**

Sunset Productions. 1 Oct **1923.** Si; b&w. 35mm. 5 reels, ca4,800 ft.

Dir Robert North Bradbury. *Photog* Victor Milner.

Cast: Kenneth McDonald, Marguerite Clayton.

Comedy-drama. "Hoodooed Dale Pemberton, reporter, fails on many jobs and locates on farm with Gregory family. Amos Gregory is accused of murdering three scheming bankers who have disappeared. Dale clears up the mystery after many thrilling experiences and marries Gregory's daughter." (*Motion Picture News Booking Guide,* 6:72, Apr 1924.) *Reporters. Bankers. Farm life. Murder.*

WHAT MEN WANT **F2.6209**

Universal Pictures. 13 Jul **1930** [c8 Jul 1930; LP1414]. Sd (Movietone); b&w. 35mm. 7 reels, 6,041 ft.

Pres by Carl Laemmle. *Dir* Ernst Laemmle. *Adapt-Dial* John B. Clymer, Dorothy Yost. *Story* Warner Fabian. *Photog* Roy Overbaugh. *Rec Engr* C. Roy Hunter.

Cast: Pauline Starke *(Lee)*, Ben Lyon *(Kendall Phillips)*, Robert Ellis *(Howard)*, Barbara Kent *(Betty)*, Hallam Cooley *(Bunch)*, Carmelita Geraghty *(Mabel)*.

Society drama. Lee, a seductive young girl, is the mistress of Howard, debonair man-about-town, but she declares to him that she wishes to marry Kendall Phillips, and he gracefully bows out, wishing her luck. Then Lee's naive but attractive young sister, Betty, arrives, and Phillips becomes infatuated with her. In spite of Lee's attempts to separate them and win back his affections, Phillips and Betty become engaged, and in a jealous rage, Lee tells Betty that she has been his mistress. Heartbroken, Betty announces Lee's engagement to Phillips at a party, and the next morning he bursts into Lee's apartment, demanding an explanation; she confesses and sends him to Betty, then telephones Howard, with whom she has previously planned a European trip. *Socialites. Sisters. Mistresses. Jealousy. Courtship.*

WHAT NO MAN KNOWS **F2.6210**

Harry Garson Productions. *Dist* Equity Pictures. 1 Nov **1921** [c29 Sep 1921; LP17032]. Si; b&w. 35mm. 6 reels, 6,200 ft.

Dir Harry Garson. *Story-Scen* Sada Cowan. *Photog* Sam Landers.

Cast: Clara Kimball Young *(Norma Harvey)*, Lowell Sherman *(Craig Dunlap)*, Dorothy Wallace *(Bertha Dunlap?)*, William P. Carleton *(Drake Blackly?)*, Jeanne Carpenter *(Mazie)*, Dulcie Cooper.

Melodrama. Norma Harvey, a newspaperwoman who devotes much of her time to relieving the sufferings of slum children, still loves her childhood sweetheart, Craig Dunlap, a lawyer who tries to cover up his wife's kleptomania by bribing a witness at her trial. Dunlap, however, is exposed and disbarred. While working in the slums, Norma encounters him in a disreputable dive and takes him to her home along with little Mazie, a blind orphan. Two gossipy neighbors declare her morally unfit, and the child is removed from her custody. On Norma's advice, Dunlap decides to give his wife another chance, but he demands a divorce when he finds her rough-housing with friends. She refuses, but when he threatens to allow her to be arrested for the theft of a fur, she consents. After proving her worthiness, Norma regains the child and finds happiness with Craig. *Journalists. Lawyers. Orphans. Social service. Marriage. Kleptomania. Blindness. Slums.*

WHAT PRICE BEAUTY **F2.6211**

S. George Ullman. *Dist* Pathé Exchange. 22 Jan **1928** [c18 Jan 1928; LP24880]. Si; b&w. 35mm. 5 reels, 4,000 ft.

Dir Thomas Buckingham. *Story-Scen* Natacha Rambova. *Titl* Malcolm Stuart Boylan. *Photog* J. D. Jennings.

Cast: Nita Naldi *(Rita Rinaldi)*, Pierre Gendron *(John Clay)*, Virginia Pearson *(Mary)*, Dolores Johnson, Myrna Loy, Sally Winters, La Supervia, Marilyn Newkirk, Victor Potel, Spike Rankin, Templar Saxe, Leo White.

Melodrama. A vamp competes with Mary, a country girl, for the attention of John Clay, a handsome young manager of a beauty parlor. He wavers between the two attractions but at last succumbs to the lure of the country girl's natural beauty. *Vamps. Beauty shops.*

WHAT PRICE FAME **F2.6212**

Ridek Film Co. *Dist* Abram Curt. 14 Nov **1928** [New York State license]. Si; b&w. 35mm. 7 reels.

Drama(?). No information about the nature of this film has been found.

Note: Country of origin undetermined.

WHAT PRICE GLORY **F2.6213**

Fox Film Corp. 23 Nov **1926** [New York premiere; released 28 Aug 1927; c4 Dec 1926; LP23393]. Si; b&w. 35mm. 12 reels, 11,400 ft. [Also 11,109 ft.]

Pres by William Fox. *Dir* Raoul Walsh. *Scen* James T. O'Donohoe. *Titl* Malcolm Stuart Boylan. *Photog* Barney McGill, John Marta, John Smith. *Mus Score* Erno Rapee. *Asst Dir* Daniel Keefe.

Cast: Victor McLaglen *(Captain Flagg)*, Edmund Lowe *(Sergeant Quirk)*, Dolores Del Rio *(Charmaine)*, William V. Mong *(Cognac Pete)*, Phyllis Haver *(Hilda of China)*, Elena Jurado *(Carmen)*, Leslie Fenton *(Lieutenant Moore)*, August Tollaire *(French Mayor)*, Barry Norton *(Private Lewisohn)*, Sammy Cohen *(Private Lipinsky)*, Ted McNamara *(Private Kiper)*, Mathilde Comont *(Camille, the cook)*, Pat Rooney *(Mulcahy)*.

War drama. Source: Laurence Stallings and Maxwell Anderson, *What Price Glory* (New York, 1934). Captain Flagg and Sergeant Quirk, two hard-boiled U. S. Marines, are fierce rivals in China and the Philippines, particularly in regard to women. In a small French village, the two marines encounter the fiery Charmaine, who gives her love freely to both men. Flagg wins her in a gamble but, learning that she actually prefers Quirk, relents out of respect. Twice the rival comrades return from the trenches; and on their third call to the front, Flagg, though on leave, starts with the company, and Quirk, wounded, calls out to his friend. Charmaine sadly reflects that though they have come back twice, they will not return again. *World War I. Philippines. China. France. United States Marines.*

WHAT PRICE LOVE **F2.6214**

Morris R. Schlank Productions. *Dist* Anchor Film Distributors. 30 Aug **1927** [New York State license]. Si; b&w. 35mm. 6 reels, 5,520 ft.

Dir Harry Revier. *Story* Mabel Z. Carroll. *Photog* Dal Clawson.

Cast: Jane Novak *(Ruth Randall)*, Charles Clary *(Gordon Randall)*, Mahlon Hamilton *(Bruce Barton)*, George Nordelli *(Baron Ferroni)*, Dorothy Dunbar *(Alice George)*, William Earle.

Crook melodrama. "The old Russian jewels do the disappearing act again. ... The idea of a disappointed lover [Bruce Barton] retrieving the stolen jewel so that the woman [Ruth Randall] he loved, and who had elected to marry another, can be happy with her husband [Gordon Randall]." (*Film Daily*, 23 Oct 1927, p7.) *Theft. Marriage.*

WHAT SHALL I DO? **F2.6215**

Dist W. W. Hodkinson Corp. 11 May **1924** [c11 May 1924; LP20296]. Si; b&w. 35mm. 6 reels, 6,111 ft.

Supv-Story Frank Woods. *Dir* John G. Adolfi. *Photog* Joseph Walker. *Art Dir* Edward M. Langley. *Film Ed* Frank Woods. *Theme Song (see note)* Irving Berlin.

Cast: Dorothy Mackaill *(Jeanie Andrews)*, John Harron *(Jack Nelson)*, Louise Dresser *(Mrs. McLean)*, William V. Mong *(Henry McLean)*, Betty Morrissey *(Dolly McLean)*, Ann May *(Mary Conway)*, Ralph McCullough *(Tom Conway)*, Joan Standing *(Lizzie)*, Tom O'Brien *(Big Jim Brown)*, Danny Hoy *(Joe, a bus boy)*.

Drama. Under the name of Jack Nelson, Don McLean goes to work in his father's factory. He meets a restaurant cashier, Jeanie; they are married and have a child. Stricken by amnesia as a result of an accident, Jack forgets his family and returns to his former life. Eventually his memory is restored, and he is reunited with his wife and child. *Cashiers. Family life. Amnesia. Factories.*

Note: Irving Berlin's "What'll I Do?" was advertised as being the theme song for this film.

WHAT THREE MEN WANTED **F2.6216**

Independent Pictures. Feb **1924.** Si; b&w. 35mm. 5 reels, 4,600-5,200 ft.

Dir Paul Burns.

Cast: Miss Du Pont, Jack Livingston, Catherine Murphy, Otto Lederer, J. Parks Jones, Frank Jonasson, Albert MacQuarrie, Robert Bolder.

Mystery melodrama. "... dealing with extravagant young girl whose attorney warns her that her money is running low. She depends on arrival of uncle from England. Several bogus 'uncles' appear, and there is general confusion until the arrival of the real uncle with explanations all around. A love story is interwoven." (*Motion Picture News Booking Guide*, 6:72, Apr 1924.) *Uncles. Spendthrifts. Impersonation.*

WHAT WIVES WANT **F2.6217**

Universal Pictures. 6 May **1923** [c20 Apr 1923; LP18890]. Si; b&w. 35mm. 5 reels, 4,745 ft.

Dir Jack Conway. *Scen* Edward T. Lowe, Jr., Perry N. Vekroff. *Story* Edward T. Lowe, Jr. *Photog* Charles Kaufman.

Cast: Ethel Grey Terry *(Claire Howard)*, Vernon Steele *(Austin Howard)*, Ramsey Wallace *(John Reeves)*, Niles Welsh *(David Loring)*, Margaret Landis *(Alice Loring)*, Lila Leslie *(Mrs. Van Dusen)*, Harry A. Burrows *(Newhart)*.

Domestic drama. Claire Howard, neglected by her husband, Austin, succumbs to the attentions of Austin's business partner, John Reeves, to the dismay of Alice Loring, her sister. When Claire ignores Alice's advice to end the affair, Alice goes to Reeves hoping to reason with him. Austin and Alice's husband, David, discover Alice and Claire with Reeves, but Alice takes the blame—causing David to ask for a divorce. Claire confesses to Austin, who resolves to mend his ways, and Alice is reunited with David. *Sisters. Marriage. Divorce.*

Note: Writing credits are based on Universal records. All reviews credit Lowe and Vekroff with story, Lowe with scenario.

WHAT WOMEN WILL DO **F2.6218**

Associated Exhibitors. *Dist* Pathé Exchange. Feb **1921** [c28 Jan 1921; LU16056]. Si; b&w. 35mm. 6 reels.

Dir Edward José. *Scen* Charles E. Whittaker. *Story* Charles A. Logue. *Photog* J. Roy Hunt.

Cast: Anna Q. Nilsson *(Lily Gibbs)*, Earl Metcalfe *(Jim Coring)*, Allan Forrest *(Arthur Brent)*, George Majeroni *(Dr. Joe)*, Jane Jennings *(Mrs. Wade)*, Riley Hatch *(Stryker)*.

Melodrama. Lily Gibbs gets involved with two crooks—Jim Corling, her lover, and Dr. Joe Parmenter. They pass the girl off as the daughter-in-law of wealthy Mrs. Wade, whose son is dead. At a seance Mrs. Wade is made to believe that Lily is the girl her son married, and Mrs. Wade takes her into her home and lavishes riches upon her. Lily then falls in love with Arthur Brent, who treats her with a kindness she has never known. Experiencing this new emotion, she wishes to break with her criminal crowd and does so when she discovers that Dr. Joe killed Mrs. Wade's son. When both Dr. Joe and Corling meet their deaths, and after receiving Mrs. Wade's forgiveness for her deception, Lily marries Brent. *Criminals—Rehabilitation. Physicians. Motherhood. Spiritualism. Murder. Imposture.*

WHATEVER SHE WANTS **F2.6219**

Fox Film Corp. 11 Dec **1921** [c11 Dec 1921; LP17418]. Si; b&w. 35mm. 5 reels, 4,616 ft.

Pres by William Fox. *Dir* C. R. Wallace. *Photog* Otto Brautigan.

Cast: Eileen Percy *(Enid North)*, Herbert Fortier *(Henry North)*, Richard Wayne *(John Barr)*, Otto Hoffman *(Amos Lott)*.

Comedy-drama. Source: Edgar Franklin, "Whatever She Wants," in *Argosy All-Story Weekly* (134:577–579, 746–761; 135:77–99, 240–257; 11 Jun–9 Jul 1921). Enid North, who is engaged to manufacturer John Barr, secretly takes a business course and gets a position in Barr's offices, without his knowledge. (The general manager has been instructed to give her anything she wants.) Attracting the attentions of the office men, she is threatened with dismissal by Barr, and she returns her engagement ring. She suspects John of being unfaithful when she sees him comforting a cafe performer. Enid visits a roadhouse with Amos Lott, who unknown to her is married and has a brood of children; they barely escape detectives who mistake them for criminals; and at Lott's home Enid is berated by his wife. She discovers that Barr has been following her, and confessing her folly she begs his forgiveness. *Businesswomen. Manufacturers. Courtship.*

WHAT'S A WIFE WORTH? **F2.6220**

Robertson-Cole Co. *Dist* R-C Pictures. 27 Mar **1921** [c2 Aug 1921; LP16832]. Si; b&w. 35mm. 6 reels, 5,700 ft.

Dir-Writ William Christy Cabanne. *Photog* Georges Benoit.

Cast: Casson Ferguson *(Bruce Morrison)*, Ruth Renick *(Rose Kendall)*, Cora Drew *(her aunt)*, Virginia Caldwell *(Jane Penfield)*, Alec Francis *(James Morrison)*, Howard Gaye *(Henry Burton)*, Lillian Langdon *(Mrs. Penfield)*, Maxfield Stanley *(Murray Penfield)*, Charles Wyngate *(Dr. Durant)*, Helen Lynch *(Girl in the Retrospect)*.

Society melodrama. Following his marriage to Rose Kendall, Bruce Morrison is notified that his father is ill and is advised not to inform him of his marriage because the father has selected Jane Penfield to be his son's bride. Murray Penfield learns about Rose, demands money to keep the secret, and turns her against her husband in his sister's interest. Rose returns to her mother, and Penfield arranges a divorce for Bruce, who then marries Jane. Rose and Jane both become mothers, but Jane's baby dies and the family physician substitutes Rose's baby for the dead child. Bruce gradually becomes disillusioned with Jane, who neglects her home for social aspirations, and when Rose calls to see her child Bruce learns the truth and wins Rose back. *Brother-sister relationship. Filial relations. Blackmail. Marriage. Divorce. Motherhood.*

WHAT'S WORTH WHILE? **F2.6221**

Lois Weber Productions. *For* Famous Players–Lasky. *Dist* Paramount Pictures. 27 Feb **1921** [c8 Feb 1921; LP16122]. Si; b&w. 35mm. 6 reels, 5,623 ft.

Prod-Dir-Writ Lois Weber. *Photog* William C. Foster.

Cast: Claire Windsor *(Phoebe Jay Morrison)*, Arthur Stuart Hull *(Mr. Morrison)*, Mona Lisa *(Sophia)*, Louis Calhern *("Squire" Elton)*, Edwin Stevens *(Rowan)*.

Society melodrama. Southern aristocrat Phoebe Morrison falls in love with her father's handsome young business partner after seeing a snapshot of him. When she arrives in the West, although she finds his rough manners repulsive, her infatuation grows, and he agrees to spend 2 years abroad in refined society. She is delighted with the result, and they are married; but after returning to the Elton ranch she tires of his gentlemanly ways. Realizing her discontent, he successfully blends his natural and acquired virtues. *Aristocrats. Southerners. Manners. Photographs. Ranches.*

WHAT'S WRONG WITH THE WOMEN? **F2.6222**

Daniel Carson Goodman Corp. *Dist* Equity Pictures. 12 Sep **1922** [c15 Aug 1922; LP18152]. Si; b&w. 35mm. 7 reels, 7,254 ft.

Pres by Daniel Carson Goodman. *Dir* R. William Neill. *Story-Adapt* Daniel Carson Goodman. *Photog* George Folsey. *Sets* Tilford Cinema Studios.

Cast: Wilton Lackaye *(James Bascom)*, Montague Love *(Arthur Belden)*, Rod La Rocque *(Jack Lee)*, Huntley Gordon *(Lloyd Watson)*, Paul McAllister *(John Mathews)*, Julia Swayne Gordon *(Mrs. Bascom)*, Constance Bennett *(Elise Bascom)*, Barbara Castleton *(Janet Lee)*, Helen Rowland *(Baby Helen Lee)*, Hedda Hopper *(Mrs. Neer)*, Mrs. Oscar Hammerstein *(a friend)*.

Domestic drama. When Janet Lee finds new, wealthy friends, she insists that her husband get a raise to support the jazz way of life she now enjoys. Instead, he loses his job. They become more and more estranged when Janet strikes up an acquaintance with millionaire Arthur Belden. But a serious injury to her baby and the urging of old friends bring Janet to her senses and back to her family. *Wealth. Jazz life. Millionaires. Motherhood.*

WHAT'S YOUR DAUGHTER DOING *see* **DAUGHTERS OF TODAY**

WHAT'S YOUR REPUTATION WORTH? **F2.6223**

Vitagraph Co. of America. Mar **1921** [c11 Apr 1921; LP16380]. Si; b&w. 35mm. 6 reels.

Dir Webster Campbell. *Scen* C. Graham Baker, Harry Dittmar. *Story* Heliodore Tenno. *Photog* Arthur Ross.

Cast: Corinne Griffith *(Cara Deene)*, Percy Marmont *(Anthony Blake)*, Leslie Roycroft *(Wallace Trant)*, George Howard *(Kent Jerrold)*, Robert Gaillard *(Mr. Pettus)*, Jane Jennings *(Mrs. Pettus)*, Louise Prussing *(Mrs. Blake)*.

Melodrama. When Anthony Blake plans to provide his discontented wife with evidence for a divorce, his secretary, Cara Deene, who secretly loves him, consents to become his corespondent. All goes well until Mrs. Blake accuses Cara of acting for money and of being in love with her husband. Believing Blake and his wife to be reconciled, Cara leaves; but later, in financial straits, she seeks his aid. When her loyalty is recognized, she is united with Blake. *Secretaries. Divorce.*

THE WHEEL **F2.6224**

Fox Film Corp. 20 Sep **1925** [c9 Aug 1925; LP21715]. Si; b&w. 35mm. 8 reels, 7,264 ft.

Pres by William Fox. *Dir* Victor Schertzinger. *Scen* Edfrid Bingham. *Photog* Glen MacWilliams. *Asst Dir* William Tummel.

Cast: Margaret Livingston *(Elsie Dixon)*, Harrison Ford *(Ted Morton)*, Claire Adams *(Kate O'Hara)*, Mahlon Hamilton *(Edward Baker)*, David Torrence *(Theodore Morton, Sr.)*, Julia Swayne Gordon *(Mrs. Morton)*, Clara Horton *(Nora Malone)*, Georgie Harris *(Sammy)*, Erin La Bissoniere *(Rhea Weinstein)*, Russ Powell *(Dan Satterly)*, Hazel Howell *(Clara)*.

Drama. Source: Winchell Smith, *The Wheel* (New York opening: 29 Aug 1921). Ted Morton, the son of a wealthy banker, loses heavily at roulette and, urged to settle down by his gravely concerned parents, informs them that he is engaged to Kate O'Hara, a milliner. His parents object to the match, but Ted nevertheless marries Kate. The elder Morton then disinherits Ted, who finds work as an automobile salesman. Eddie Baker, a gambler with a grudge against Ted, lures him back to the wheel, and Ted loses $2,000 of company funds. He desperately tries to raise the money, but Kate loses another large sum betting on a horse. Baker regrets his malice and makes Ted's losses good, writing a check and giving it to Kate. Ted sees them together and, misunderstanding, takes a shot at Baker, slightly wounding Kate. She quickly forgives him, and the young couple soon wins acceptance at the Morton hearthside, completely in the good graces of Ted's family. *Bankers. Gamblers. Salesmen. Milliners. Filial relations. Disinheritance. Gambling. Parenthood.*

WHEEL OF CHANCE **F2.6225**

First National Pictures. 17 Jun **1928** [c4 Jun 1928; LP25341]. Si; b&w. 35mm. 7 reels, 6,813-6,895 ft.

Pres by Richard A. Rowland. *Dir* Alfred Santell. *Adapt-Cont* Gerald C. Duffy. *Titl* Garrett Graham. *Photog* Ernest Haller. *Film Ed* Cyril Gardner.

Cast: Richard Barthelmess *(Nickolai Turkeltaub/Jacob Talinef* [*born Schmulka Turkeltaub*]*)*, Bodil Rosing *(Sara Turkeltaub)*, Warner Oland *(Mosher Turkeltaub)*, Ann Schaeffer *(Hanscha Talinef)*, Lina Basquette *(Ada Berkowitz)*, Margaret Livingston *(Josie Drew)*, Sidney Franklin *(Pa Berkowitz)*, Martha Franklin *(Ma Berkowitz)*.

Melodrama. Source: Fannie Hurst, "Roulette," in *The Vertical City* (New York & London, 1922). The Turkeltaub family leaves Russia for the

United States during the czarist regime, saddened by the apparent death of little Schmulka, fraternal twin of the other son, Nickolai. In America the Turkeltaubs prosper; Nickolai becomes a prominent district attorney, and he is engaged to marry Ada Berkowitz. Schmulka, known as Jacob Talinef, is revealed to have survived his childhood, having been nursed back to health by Hanscha Talinef, a midwife who brought him as a youth to New York. A young gangster and a drunkard, Jacob accidentally kills Josie Drew, a promiscuous girl who once had a relationship with Nickolai. Nickolai, as prosecuting attorney, is influenced by his mother, who is drawn to the redheaded boy, to ask for leniency. After serving a short jail sentence Jacob is finally reunited with his family. *Russians. Immigrants. Twins. Brothers. Criminals—Rehabilitation. District attorneys. Midwives. Alcoholism.*

Note: Working title of film may have been *Roulette*.

THE WHEEL OF DESTINY **F2.6226**

Duke Worne Productions. *Dist* Rayart Pictures. Oct **1927.** Si; b&w. 35mm. 6 reels, 5,746 or 5,869 ft.

Dir Duke Worne. *Scen* George W. Pyper. *Photog* Walter Griffen.

Cast: Forrest Stanley, Georgia Hale, Percy Challenger, Miss Du Pont, Ernest Hilliard, Sammy Blum, B. Hyman, Jack Herrick.

Drama. Source: Joseph Anthony, "The Man Without a Past," in *Farm and Fireside*. Walking in a daze after being snubbed by a society girl (played by Miss Du Pont), a young man (played by Forrest Stanley) falls and loses his memory. He wanders into an amusement park, where he is befriended by a sideshow girl (played by Georgia Hale), and he joins a show. With her help he regains his memory, is welcomed by his hometown as the discoverer of a serum, and marries his new love in preference to the snob. *Showgirls. Amnesia. Snobbery. Amusement parks. Sideshows. Serums.*

THE WHEEL OF LIFE **F2.6227**

Paramount Famous Lasky Corp. 15 Jun **1929** [c14 Jun 1929; LP471]. Sd (Movietone); b&w. 35mm. 6 reels, 5,153 ft. [Also si; 5,305 ft.]

Dir Victor Schertzinger. *Dial-Titl* Julian Johnson. *Adapt* John Farrow. *Camera* Edward Cronjager. *Film Ed* Otto Lovering. *Song: "I Wonder Why You Love Me"* Victor Schertzinger.

Cast: Richard Dix *(Capt. Leslie Yeullat)*, Esther Ralston *(Ruth Dangan)*, O. P. Heggie *(Col. John Dangan)*, Arthur Hoyt *(George Faraker)*, Myrtle Stedman *(Mrs. Faraker)*, Larry Steers *(major)*, Regis Toomey *(Lieutenant MacLaren)*, Nigel De Brulier *(Tsering Lama)*.

Romantic melodrama. Source: James Bernard Fagan, *The Wheel of Life, a Play in Three Acts* (New York, 1923). Captain Yeullat, a young British officer, on furlough in London from duty in India, prevents a young woman, Ruth Dangan, from drowning herself in the Thames, but she disappears before he learns her identity. Later, with his regiment in India, he meets her as the wife of Colonel Dangan, his commanding officer, and they fall in love. Finding himself in an impossible position, Yeulla has himself transferred to another regiment. Later, at a lonely outpost, he receives word that British travelers have been besieged by natives at a Buddhist monastery and leads his men to the rescue; there he finds Ruth and her party trying to defend the building, and during the battle they pledge their love, expecting to die together. But Dangan arrives with reinforcements and saves them; circumstantially, he is killed by a sniper, clearing the way for the marriage of Ruth and the captain. *Suicide. Courtship. Monasteries. India. London. Great Britain—Army.*

WHEN A DOG LOVES **F2.6228**

R-C Pictures. *Dist* Film Booking Offices of America. 1 Mar **1927** [c27 Feb 1927; LP23830]. Si; b&w. 35mm. 5 reels, 4,390 ft.

Pres by Joseph P. Kennedy. *Dir* J. P. McGowan. *Cont* F. A. E. Pine. *Story* John A. Moroso. *Camera* Philip Tannura. *Asst Dir* Jack Wright.

Cast: Ranger *(himself, a dog)*, Harold Goodwin *(James Alston)*, Helen Foster *(Agnes Flanagan)*, Mickey McBan *(Mickey Flanagan)*, Frank McGlynn, Jr. *(Bert Morton)*, Irvin Renard *(Bernard Howe)*, Dorothy Dunbar *(Letty Carroll)*, Jack Ryan *(detective)*.

Melodrama. Ranger, a dog owned by wealthy young Jimmy Alston, is entrusted with a valuable diamond necklace intended for Letty Carroll, Jimmy's girl. But Letty proves untrue; and on his way home, Jimmy swerves to avoid hitting little Mickey Flanagan, and Ranger is thrown out of the car. The boy takes the dog to his tenement home, where he lives with his sister, Agnes. Bert, a would-be suitor of Agnes', tries to steal the necklace but is prevented by Ranger. Alston recognizes the necklace on Agnes and becomes acquainted with her. Bert, after kidnaping Ranger, attacks Agnes, but Ranger escapes and corners the villain until Alston and the police arrive. *Children. Wealth. Tenements. Diamonds. Dogs.*

WHEN A GIRL LOVES **F2.6229**

Halperin Productions. *Dist* Associated Exhibitors. 20 Apr **1924** [c20 Mar 1924; LP20010]. Si; b&w. 35mm. 6 reels, 5,876 ft.

Dir-Writ Victor Hugo Halperin. *Photog* Alvin Wyckoff.

Cast: Agnes Ayres *(Sasha Boroff)*, Percy Marmont *(Count Michael)*, Robert McKim *(Dr. Godfrey Luke)*, Kathlyn Williams *(Helen, Michael's wife)*, John George *(Grishka)*, Mary Alden *(The Czarina)*, George Siegmann *(Rogojin)*, Ynez Seabury *(Fania)*, William Orlamond *(Alexis)*, Rosa Rosanova *(Ferdova)*, Leo White *(Yussoff)*.

Romantic drama. The revolution causes Sasha Boroff's wealthy family to lose its fortune; and her lover, Count Michael, is sentenced to death by Rogojin, the Boroffs' former coachman. Rogojin's sudden death saves Sasha from marriage to the despot, and the Boroffs escape to the United States, where she marries Dr. Godfrey Luke to please her family. Later Sasha discovers that Michael is alive and married to an American. Michael's wife has a love affair with Dr. Luke, Sasha is wounded in a duel between Michael and Luke, the shock prostrates Michael, and Grishka cures him with a radio-vibration device. At the end, Sasha and Michael are still happily married to their respective spouses. *Physicians. Russia—History—1917–21 Revolution. Duels.*

WHEN A MAN LOVES **F2.6230**

Warner Brothers Pictures. 3 Feb **1927** [New York premiere; released 21 Aug; c26 Dec 1926; LP23485]. Si; b&w. 35mm. 10 reels, 10,049 ft.

Dir Alan Crosland. *Adapt* Bess Meredyth. *Camera* Byron Haskins. *Asst Camera* Frank Kesson. *Ed in Ch* Harold McCord.

Cast: John Barrymore *(Chevalier Fabien des Grieux)*, Dolores Costello *(Manon Lescaut)*, Warner Oland *(André Lescaut)*, Sam De Grasse *(Comte Guillot de Morfontaine)*, Holmes Herbert *(Jean Tiberge)*, Stuart Holmes *(Louis XV, King of France)*, Bertram Grassby *(Le Duc de Richelieu)*, Tom Santschi *(captain of the convict boat)*, Marcelle Corday *(Marie)*, Charles Clary *(a lay brother)*, Templar Saxe *(Baron Chevral)*, Eugenie Besserer *(The Landlady)*, Rose Dione *(Nana)*, Noble Johnson *(an apache)*, Tom Wilson *(a convict aboard the boat)*.

Romantic costume drama. Source: Abbé Prévost, *Histoire du Chevalier des Grieux et de Manon Lescaut* (1731). Chevalier Fabien des Grieux, who has forsworn the world for the church, falls passionately in love with young Manon Lescaut when he encounters her en route to a convent with her brother, André. The lustful Comte Guillot de Morfontaine offers André a tempting sum for Manon, and learning of their bargain, Fabien takes her to Paris, where they spend an idyllic week in a garret. André finds her, persuades her to leave Fabien, and tries to force her into an alliance with Morfontaine—then rescues Manon from the advances of a brutal apache. Fabien, crushed to believe that Manon has become Morfontaine's mistress, is about to take his vows but is deterred by her love for him. King Louis sees Manon in Richelieu's drawing room and wins her. The rejected Morfontaine orders her arrest and deportation, but he is killed by Fabien, who joins Manon on a convict ship bound for America. After inciting the convicts to mutiny, he escapes with her in a small boat. *Cavaliers. Brother-sister relationship. Apaches—Paris. Mutiny. France. Louis XV (France). Duc de Richelieu, Louis François Armand de Vignerot du Plessis.*

WHEN A MAN'S A MAN **F2.6231**

Principal Pictures. *Dist* Associated First National Pictures. 3 Feb **1924** [New York premiere; released Feb; c12 Feb 1924; LP19903]. Si; b&w. 35mm. 7 reels, 6,910 ft.

Pres by Sol Lesser. *Dir* Edward F. Cline. *Adapt* Walter Anthony, Harry Carr. *Photog* Harold Janes, Ned Van Buren.

Cast: John Bowers *(Lawrence Knight, "Patches")*, Marguerite De La Motte *(Helen Wakefield)*, Robert Frazer *(Phil Acton)*, June Marlowe *(Kitty Reid)*, Forrest Robinson *(The Dean)*, Elizabeth Rhodes *(Stella)*, Fred Stanton *(Nick Cambert)*, George Hackathorne *(Yapavai Joe)*, Edward Hearne *(Stanford Manning)*, John Fox, Jr. *(Little Billy)*, Arthur Hoyt *(Professor Parkhill)*, Ray Thompson *(Curley Elson)*, Charles Mailes *(Jim Reid)*.

Western melodrama. Source: Harold Bell Wright, *When a Man's a Man* (New York, 1916). Helen Wakefield refuses the marriage proposal of Lawrence Knight, a rich lounge lizard, and advises him to improve himself by developing manly traits. He goes out west, changes his name to "Patches," and gets together some cattle rustlers. He is accused of being an outlaw and of shooting a fellow cowpuncher, falls in love with a ranch girl, leaves her, and then accidentally meets Helen Wakefield in a pasture where he is trying to rope a ferocious bull and she is drawing water. The bull makes for her; Knight lassos it, saving the woman from death; and they recognize each other. During his absence Helen has married and come to the West accompanied by her surveyor husband. Knight's old love flashes up, but having recently developed manly traits, he sets his jaw and departs for another section of the country. *Rustlers. Cowboys. Surveyors. Manhood. Ranches.*

WHEN BEARCAT WENT DRY (Reissue) **F2.6232**

20 Apr **1928** [New York State license]. Si; b&w. 35mm. 6 reels.

Note: A 1919 film produced by C. R. McCauley Photoplays and starring Lon Chaney.

WHEN DANGER CALLS **F2.6233**

Camera Pictures. *Dist* Lumas Film Corp. c23 Sep **1927** [LP24439]. Si; b&w. 35mm. 5 reels.

Pres by Sam Sax. *Supv* Sam Bischoff. *Dir* Charles Hutchison. *Story-Cont* Ben Allah. *Photog* William Reis. *Prod Mgr* Carrol Sax.

Cast: William Fairbanks *(Ralph Spencer)*, Eileen Sedgwick *(June Weldon)*, Ethan Laidlaw *(James Gwyn)*, Sally Long *(Eva Gwyn)*, Donald MacDonald *(George Marsden)*, Hank Mann *(Tommy Shultz)*.

Melodrama. A tenement fire brings about an investigation by Ralph Spencer, fire inspector, who condemns the Marsden buildings despite political opposition. Without knowing of the condemnation, wealthy welfare worker June Weldon buys the buildings from Marsden, converting one into a mission. A fight ensues when Ralph goes to inspect the buildings, and Ralph tells June of Marsden's scheming. Marsden plots to frame Ralph by planting money on him in a nightclub; the money is thought to be a bribe, and Ralph is dismissed as a result. Spurlin, a club owner, becomes suspicious of Marsden's relations with his wife, and in a confrontation a fire breaks out; Ralph rescues June from the burning building, and Marsden dies in the conflagration. Ralph is reinstated and happily reunited with June. *Fire inspectors. Politicians. Tenements. Nightclubs. Missions. Fires.*

WHEN DANGER SMILES **F2.6234**

Vitagraph Co. of America. 3 Oct **1922** [c14 Oct 1922; LP18325]. Si; b&w. 35mm. 5 reels, 4,928 ft.

Pres by Albert E. Smith. *Dir* William Duncan. *Scen* Bradley J. Smollen. *Story* John B. Clymer. *Photog* George Robinson.

Cast: William Duncan *(Ray Chapman)*, Edith Johnson *(Frania Caravalle)*, James Farley *(Jacob Holnar)*, Henry Hebert *(Francisco Caravalle)*, Charles Dudley *(Jim Barker)*, William McCall *(Marshall)*.

Western melodrama. Ray Chapman becomes intrigued with veiled Frania Caravalle at a dance, but he is unable to learn her name. Soon afterward he attempts to help a robbery victim, is injured, and is taken to the Caravalle home, where he is nursed by Frania. In his dazed condition he neither recognizes Frania nor remembers their encounter; therefore, when Ray agrees with Francisco Caravalle to become betrothed to his daughter, he still does not recognize Frania. She is infuriated and plots with her hated former suitor, Jacob Holnar, to kill Ray. Instead, Ray's friend, Jim Barker, is killed, and Ray is suspected of that murder. Just as he is about to be lynched his horse drags him away, but Frania, who now understands the situation, arrives to save him. Holnar confesses, and the lovers are united. *Samaritanism. Murder. Lynching.*

WHEN DESTINY WILLS **F2.6235**

Redwood Pictures. 16 Sep **1921** [trade review]. Si; b&w. 35mm. [Feature length assumed.]

Dir R. C. Baker. *Story* A. L. Brunton, A. Rotheim.

Cast: Grace Davison.

Melodrama. "Girl and man she loves are caught in a storm, taking refuge in a cabin. The inevitable, with the man losing trace of the girl who feels he has deserted her. She becomes poverty stricken and tries to earn a living in a factory for herself and child, but is discharged, attempts suicide, is rescued and befriended by a rich lumber man. She marries him and makes her home in the west. He dies leaving her his sole heir. The child's father is also in the lumber business and comes in contact with her when a big deal is pulled off. This brings about an explanation and the customary ending." *(Variety,* 16 Sep 1921, p35.) *Factory workers. Lumbermen. Illegitimacy. Poverty. Suicide. Storms.*

WHEN DREAMS COME TRUE (Imperial Photoplays) **F2.6236**

Trem Carr Productions. *Dist* Rayart Pictures. 15 Jan **1929.** Si; b&w. 35mm. 6 reels, 6,082 or 6,242 ft.

Dir Duke Worne. *Scen* Arthur Hoerl. *Photog* Hap Depew. *Film Ed* J. S. Harrington.

Cast: Helene Costello *(Caroline Swayne)*, Rex Lease *(Ben Shelby)*, Claire McDowell *(Martha Shelby)*, Danny Hoy *(Jack Boyle)*, Ernest Hilliard *(Jim Leeson)*, Buddy Brown *(Billy Shelby)*, George Periolat *(Robert Swayne)*, Emmett King *(Judge Clayburn)*, Ranger *(Dream Lad, a horse)*, Rags *(himself, a dog)*.

Melodrama. Source: Victor Rousseau, "Sunburst Valley" (publication undetermined). Ben Shelby, a poor blacksmith, falls in love with Caroline Swayne; but her wealthy father, Robert Swayne, opposes the match and raises some question about the legitimacy of Ben's birth. Shortly after Ben attacks Swayne in response to the latter's remarks, Swayne is found murdered, and Ben is charged and jailed. He escapes, overhears Jim Leeson (Swayne's former horsebreeding partner) plot to sabotage Swayne's entry in a horserace, and wrings a confession to Swayne's murder out of Leeson's accomplice. The Swayne horse wins, and Caroline is set straight on the identity of Ben's father. *Blacksmiths. Horseracing. Murder. Jailbreaks. Illegitimacy. Horses. Dogs.*

WHEN EAST COMES WEST **F2.6237**

Phil Goldstone Productions. ca6 Apr **1922** [New York State license]. Si; b&w. 35mm. 5 reels, 4,450 ft.

Dir B. Reeves Eason. *Scen* Anthony Coldeway.

Cast: Franklyn Farnum, Andrew Waldron.

Western melodrama. "Jones arrives in a notorious Western town and volunteers to be sheriff. On meeting Mary Brennan, a ranchowner, he arranges for a Chinese friend of his to be her cook. Jones discovers that Mary's foreman is the leader of the gunrunners in town. After leading them to believe he is on their side, Jones captures the gang, aided by the Chinaman and later reveals to Mary that he and the Chinaman are United States marshals in disguise." *(National Film Archive Catalogue, Part III, Silent Fiction Films, 1895–1930;* The British Film Institute, London, 1966, p249.) *Sheriffs. Ranchers. Cooks. Gunrunners. Ranch foremen. Chinese.*

WHEN HUSBANDS DECEIVE **F2.6238**

Arthur F. Beck. *Dist* Associated Exhibitors. 20 Aug **1922** [c9 Aug 1922; LU18126]. Si; b&w. 35mm. 6 reels, 5,708 ft.

Pres by Arthur F. Beck. *Supv* Arthur F. Beck. *Dir* Wallace Worsley. *Story-Scen* Leah Baird. *Photog* Charles J. Stumar.

Cast: Leah Baird *(Viola Baxter)*, William Conklin *(Marshall Walsh)*, Jack Mower *(Richard Fletcher)*, Eulalie Jensen *(Lulu Singleton)*, John Cossar *(Andrew Singleton)*, Teddy *(himself, a dog)*, Darwin *(himself, a monkey)*.

Domestic melodrama. Viola Baxter is deceived into a hasty marriage with her guardian, Marshall Welch, who is after her money and has framed her fiancé, Dick Fletcher, for theft. She discovers and exposes her husband's perfidy. Humiliated, Welch decides to take his wife's life along with his own, but she is saved by her Great Dane. *Guardians. Marriage. Suicide. Frameup. Dogs. Monkeys.*

WHEN HUSBANDS FLIRT **F2.6239**

Columbia Pictures. 15 Oct or 1 Nov **1925** [c23 Nov 1925; LP22046]. Si; b&w. 35mm. 6 reels, 5,625 ft.

Prod Harry Cohn. *Dir* William Wellman. *Story-Cont* Paul Gangelin, Dorothy Arzner. *Photog* Sam Landers.

Cast: Dorothy Revier *(Violet Gilbert)*, Forrest Stanley *(Henry Gilbert)*, Tom Ricketts *(Wilbur Belcher)*, Ethel Wales *(Mrs. Wilbur Belcher)*, Maude Wayne *(Charlotte Germaine)*, Frank Weed *(Percy Snodgrass)*, Erwin Connelly *(Joe McCormick)*.

Domestic comedy. Newlywed lawyer Henry Gilbert lends his car to his partner, Wilbur Belcher, while he works late one night on a case for Percy Snodgrass' Purity League. Wilbur, a gay old blade, goes joyriding with Charlotte Germaine, an old sweetheart. The next day, Henry's wife, Violet, finds incriminating evidence and, with Mrs. Belcher's aid, plans a divorce. After various complications, Charlotte explains matters to Violet, and Henry is cleared. *Lawyers. Reformers. Flirts. Infidelity. Divorce.*

WHEN JOHNNY COMES MARCHING HOME *see* **RIDERS UP**

WHEN KNIGHTHOOD WAS IN FLOWER **F2.6240**

Cosmopolitan Productions. *Dist* Paramount Pictures. 14 Sep **1922** [New York premiere; released 4 Feb 1923; c20 Sep 1922; LP18748]. Si; b&w. 35mm. 12 reels, 11,618 ft.

Dir Robert G. Vignola. *Adapt* Luther Reed. *Photog* Ira Morgan, Harold Wenstrom. *Set Dsgn* Joseph Urban. *Mus* William Frederick Peters. *Asst Dir* Philip Carle. *Cost* Gretl Urban Thurlow. *Armor Adv* Bashford Dean. *Fencing Supv* James Murray.

Cast: Marion Davies *(Princess Mary Tudor)*, Forrest Stanley *(Charles Brandon)*, Lyn Harding *(King Henry VIII)*, Theresa Maxwell Conover *(Queen Catherine)*, Pedro De Cordoba *(Duke of Buckingham)*, Ruth Shepley *(Lady Jane Bolingbroke)*, Ernest Glendenning *(Sir Edwin Caskoden)*, Arthur Forrest *(Cardinal Wolsey)*, Johnny Dooley *(Will Somers)*, William Kent *(The King's Tailor)*, Charles Gerrard *(Sir Adam Judson)*, Arthur Donaldson *(Sir Henry Brandon)*, Downing Clarke *(Lord Chamberlain)*, William Norris *(Louis XII of France)*, Macey Harlam *(Duc de Longueville)*, William H. Powell *(Francis I)*, George Nash *(Captain Bradhurst)*, Gustav von Seyffertitz *(Grammont)*, Paul Panzer *(Captain of the Guard)*, Guy Coombes *(follower of Buckingham)*, Mortimer Snow, George Ogle, Flora Finch *(French countess)*, Red Wing, Black Diamond, Winchester *(themselves, horses)*.

Spectacular romantic drama. Source: Charles Major, *When Knighthood Was in Flower* (Indianapolis, 1898). For political reasons King Henry VIII is determined that his sister, Mary Tudor, will marry King Louis XII of France, even though she wishes to be the wife of commoner Charles Brandon. The lovers run away but are captured, and Mary agrees to the king's demands provided that she may choose her second husband. Louis dies shortly after the wedding, and, although King Francis I connives to make her his, Mary finally marries Brandon with Henry's blessing. *Knighthood. Great Britain—History—Tudors. Mary Tudor. Henry VIII (England). Louis XII (France). Francis I (France). Thomas Wolsey. Catherine of Aragon. Horses.*

WHEN LAW COMES TO HADES **F2.6241**

Sanford Productions. Sep **1923** [scheduled release]. Si; b&w. 35mm. 5 reels.

Cast: Noah Beery, Eileen Sedgwick, Edward W. Borman.

Comedy-drama(?). No information about the nature of this film has been found.

WHEN LIGHTS ARE LOW *see* **WHERE LIGHTS ARE LOW**

WHEN LOVE COMES **F2.6242**

Ray Carroll Productions. *Dist* Film Booking Offices of America. 10 Dec **1922** [c9 Dec 1922; LP18478]. Si; b&w. 35mm. 6 reels, 4,800 ft.

Pres by Ray Carroll. *Dir* William A. Seiter. *Scen* Winifred Dunn. *Story* Ray Carroll. *Camera* Lucien Andriot.

Cast: Helen Jerome Eddy *(Jane Coleridge)*, Harrison Ford *(Peter Jamison)*, Fannie Midgley *(Aunt Susie Coleridge)*, Claire Du Brey *(Marie Jamison)*, Joseph Bell *(Jim Matthews)*, Gilbert Clayton *(Rufus Terrence)*, Buddy Messenger, Molly Gordon *(Coleridge twins)*, James Barrows *(David Coleridge)*, Fay McKenzie *(Ruth)*.

Melodrama. When his design for a new dam is rejected, Peter Jamison prepares to leave town and proposes to Jane Coleridge, but her father's sudden death prevents Jane from meeting Peter. Five years pass, and Peter returns with his daughter and the explanation that his wife, Marie, deserted him. Peter and Jane's love grows anew, then Marie reappears and causes trouble for Jane. Marie dies in a dam burst. *Engineers—Civil. Desertion. Dams.*

WHEN LOVE GROWS COLD **F2.6243**

R-C Pictures. *Dist* Film Booking Offices of America. 31 Jan **1925** [c31 Jan 1926; LP22340]. Si; b&w. 35mm. 7 reels, 6,500 ft.

Supv Daniel Carson Goodman. *Dir-Cont* Harry O. Hoyt. *Photog* William Miller. *Adtl Photog* Alfred Ortlieb.

Cast: Natacha Rambova *(Margaret Benson)*, Clive Brook *(Jerry Benson)*, Sam Hardy *(William Graves)*, Kathryn Hill *(Gloria Trevor)*, John Gough *(Alec Clark)*, Kathleen Martyn *(Vera Clark)*.

Melodrama. Source: Laura Jean Libbey, "When Love Grows Cold" (publication undetermined). Margaret gives up her stage career to wed Jerry Benson, a dreamy inventor who fails to promote an invention when he appears before the board of a large oil company. Margaret, however, goes before the board and quickly and easily persuades its members to accept her husband's plans. The Bensons become wealthy, and Jerry is made an official of the firm. William Graves, the president, becomes interested in Margaret and attempts to break up the Benson marriage by introducing Jerry to Gloria Trevor, a scheming vamp; Graves then ruins him in the stock market. When Jerry learns of Graves's perfidy, he goes after him with a gun, but Graves pleads for his life and promises to make good the financial losses incurred by Jerry. Jerry then returns to Margaret, a sadder but wiser man, well aware that the damage done to his marriage by Graves will be difficult to repair. *Actors. Inventors. Vamps. Marriage. Stock market. Oil business.*

WHEN LOVE IS YOUNG **F2.6244**

Victor Kremer Film Features. *Dist* Arista Film Corp. 1 Feb **1922.** Si; b&w. 35mm. 5 reels, 3,656 ft.

Cast: Russell Simpson, Zena Keefe.

Rural comedy-drama. No information about the nature of this film has been found.

WHEN ODDS ARE EVEN **F2.6245**

Fox Film Corp. 25 Nov **1923** [c5 Nov 1923; LP19580]. Si; b&w. 35mm. 5 reels, 4,284 ft.

Pres by William Fox. *Dir* James Flood. *Story-Scen* Dorothy Yost. *Photog* Joseph Brotherton.

Cast: William Russell *(Jack Arnold)*, Dorothy Devore *(Caroline Peyton)*, Lloyd Whitlock *(Neal Travis)*, Frank Beal *(Clive Langdon)*, Allan Cavan *(British consul)*.

Melodrama. Jack Arnold is competing with Clive Langdon for interests in an opal mine in Pago Tai. Accompanying Langdon on the steamer bound for the small island are his niece, Caroline Peyton, and her fiancé, Neal Travis. Jack and Caroline fall in love. In spite of attempts by Langdon and Travis to sabotage him, Jack wins the friendship of the mine-owner, thereby gaining the option to the mine. *Uncles. Opal mines. Pago Tai.*

WHEN ROMANCE RIDES **F2.6246**

Benjamin B. Hampton. *Dist* Goldwyn Pictures. ca2 Apr **1922** [New York premiere; c20 Apr 1922; LP17842]. Si; b&w. 35mm. 5 reels, 5,003 ft.

Prod-Adapt Benjamin B. Hampton. *Dir* Eliot Howe, Charles O. Rush, Jean Hersholt. *Photog* Gus Peterson, William Edmonds.

Cast: Claire Adams *(Lucy Bostil)*, Carl Gantvoort *(Lin Slone)*, Jean Hersholt *(Joel Creech)*, Harry Van Meter *(Bill Cordts)*, Charles Arling *(Bostil)*, Tod Sloan *(Holley)*, Frank Hayes *(Dr. Binks)*, Mary Jane Irving *("Bostie" Bostil)*, Audrey Chapman, Helen Howard *(Lucy's chums)*, Stanley Bingham *(Dick Sears)*, Walter Perkins *(Thomas Brackton)*, Babe London *(Sally Brackton)*, John Beck *(Van)*.

Melodrama. Source: Zane Grey, *Wildfire* (New York, 1916). Lucy Bostil, daughter of a Colorado ranchowner, is led by a dog to his master, Lin Slone, who is exhausted from a struggle to capture a wild horse; she revives Lin and they christen the horse "Wildfire." The Bostils have entered Sage King in a race, but Lucy agrees to tame and train the wild horse, since Buckles, her favorite colt, has been stolen. When Joel Creech, a halfwitted stablehand, is discharged, he becomes a tool of the Cordtses—who also have entered a horse (Buckles) in the race—in drugging Sage King. Lin and Lucy enter Wildfire under the Bostil colors, and she rides him to victory, When Cordts is disgraced and discovered to be a horsethief, he persuades Joel to abduct Lucy. Joel does so, but first he kills Cordts. Warned by his dog of Lucy's danger, Lin pursues and rescues the girl. *Ranchers. Horsethieves. Horseracing. Colorado. Horses. Dogs.*

WHEN SECONDS COUNT **F2.6247**

Duke Worne Productions. *Dist* Rayart Pictures. Apr **1927**. Si; b&w. 35mm. 5 reels, 4,803 ft.

Dir Oscar Apfel. *Scen* Suzanne Avery. *Photog* Ernest Smith.

Cast: Billy Sullivan *(Billy Mathewson)*, Mildred June *(Elinor)*, Rose Kimman *(Mimi, the dancer)*, Jerome La Grasse *(George Milburn)*, Marie Messenger *(Toots Sweet)*, James Aubrey *(Dizzy Durby)*, Earl Wayland Bowman *(Dave Streater)*, Joseph Girard *(James Mathewson)*.

Society melodrama. Incurring his father's wrath for bringing home a hard-boiled cabaret dancer as a prospective bride, young Broadway wastrel Billy Mathewson escapes with a friend, Dizzy Durby, to make good in a small town where his father is building a dam. A crooked foreman is engaged in making himself rich at the expense of his employer and the villagers, but Billy spots the villain, exposes him, and wins Elinor, the daughter of a prominent local resident. *Dancers. Construction foremen. Dams. Fraud. Filial relations. Smalltown life.*

WHEN THE CLOCK STRUCK NINE **F2.6248**
c20 Apr **1921** [LU16408]. Si; b&w. 35mm. [Feature length assumed.] *Writ* Lillian Howarth.

Melodrama. Lower New York City's Kelly's Corners is the home of Jim Grady, who loves Maggie Murphy, the beauty and belle of the Corners, and good-natured Tony Morrillo, with whom Maggie indulges in a light flirtation. Over her mother's objections, Maggie accepts a bracelet from Tony on the night of the big Kelly Club dance, but she discards it for a necklace from Jim. *The events of the evening turn topsy-turvy the lives of all three: the necklace turns out to be stolen, Detective Jarvis catches Tony with the necklace in his possession, and Maggie's unwillingness to incriminate Jim results in a 3-year prison term for Tony. By the time Tony is released, Maggie has married Jim and left him for wealthy gambler Dick Martin, and Jim has become a barroom lounger. Seeing an opportunity for revenge, Tony maneuvers Jim into burglarizing Martin's house, where he is shot by Martin. Maggie falls to Jim's side and* ... awakens from a bad dream. Arriving to escort Maggie to the dance, Jim assures her that the bracelet presents no problem and slips a ring on her finger. *Detectives. Gamblers. Irish. Italians. Revenge. Robbery. Courtship. Perjury. New York City. Dreams.*

Note: Production and distribution companies not determined.

WHEN THE DESERT CALLS **F2.6249**
Pyramid Pictures. *Dist* American Releasing Corp. 8 Oct **1922** [c25 Nov 1922; LP18628]. Si; b&w. 35mm. 6 reels, 6,159 ft.

Dir Ray C. Smallwood. *Adapt* Peter Milne, Georgette Duchesne. *Photog* Michael Joyce. *Art Dir* Ben Carré. *Film Ed* George McGuire. *Asst Dir* George McGuire.

Cast: Violet Heming *(Louise Caldwell)*, Robert Frazer *(Eldred Caldwell/ George Stevenson)*, Sheldon Lewis *(Richard Manners)*, Huntley Gordon *(Dr. Thorpe)*, J. Barney Sherry *(Lieutenant Colonel Potter)*, David Wall *(Frank Warren, U. S. Consul)*, Julia Swayne Gordon *("The White Angel")*, Nick Thompson *(Nazim)*, Tammany Young *(British Tommy)*.

Melodrama. Source: Donald McGibney, "When the Desert Calls," in *Ladies Home Journal* (37:22–24, May 1920). Bank cashier Eldred Caldwell and his wife, Louise, happily live on the edge of the desert until Richard Manners reappears. He discredits Caldwell, who apparently commits suicide, and pursues Louise into the desert. Manners dies, but Louise finds shelter with a sheik's widow. Years pass, and the end of the World War sees England in search of Sheik El-Din (in reality, Eldred Caldwell) to reward him for his bravery. He faints on receiving the decoration, and while recuperating he recognizes a nurse as Louise. Though about to marry a doctor, she is reunited with her husband. *Bank clerks. Sheiks. Nurses. Disguise. Deserts. World War I.*

WHEN THE DEVIL DRIVES **F2.6250**
Leah Baird Productions. *Dist* Associated Exhibitors. 4 Jun **1922** [c29 May 1922; LU17926]. Si; b&w. 35mm. 5 reels, 4,687 ft.

Prod Arthur F. Beck. *Dir* Paul Scardon. *Story-Scen* Leah Baird. *Photog* Charles Stumar.

Cast: Leah Baird *(Blanche Mansfield)*, Arline Pretty *(Grace Eldridge)*, Richard Tucker *(John Graham)*, Vernon Steel *(Robert Taylor)*, Katherine Lewis *(Nanette Henley)*.

Society melodrama. When Blanche Mansfield learns that Robert Taylor, her lover, is casting her aside to marry Grace Eldridge, she wounds him with a knife. Disillusioned, Grace breaks her engagement and seeks seclusion in anonymity. Blanche also moves and changes her name. Later, the two women meet and become friends, neither aware that the other has been her rival; upon discovering the truth, Grace shoots Blanche but does not kill her. During her convalescence Blanche comes to understand the situation and to forgive Grace and Robert, who are happily reunited. Blanche then marries Graham, whom she has always loved. *Friendship. Infidelity. Jealousy.*

WHEN THE DOOR OPENED **F2.6251**
Fox Film Corp. 6 Dec **1925** [c15 Nov 1925; LP22142]. Si; b&w. 35mm. 7 reels, 6,515 ft.

Pres by William Fox. *Dir* Reginald Barker. *Scen* Bradley King. *Photog* Ernest G. Palmer. *Asst Dir* Harry Schenck.

Cast: Jacqueline Logan *(Teresa de Fontenac)*, Walter McGrail *(Clive Grenfal)*, Margaret Livingston *(Mrs. Grenfal)*, Robert Cain *(Henry Morgan)*, Frank Keenan *(Grandfather de Fontenac)*, Roy Laidlaw *(O'Flaherty)*, Diana Miller *(siren)*, Walter Chung *(Oh My)*.

Northwest melodrama. Source: James Oliver Curwood, "When the Door Opened," in *Leslie's Weekly* (131:613, 13 Nov 1920). Clive Grenfal returns home unexpectedly and discovers his wife in the arms of Henry Morgan; he takes a shot at Morgan and, believing him to be dead, runs for cover, becoming a hermit in the Canadian north woods. During his travels, Clive meets up with de Fontenac, a courtly old man who lives in a castle with his beautiful granddaughter, Teresa. She falls in love with Clive, and Clive comes to love her in return but does nothing to indicate this feeling, thinking himself a wanted man. Henry Morgan shows up and turns his lustful advances toward Teresa; Clive protects the girl and, knowing now that Morgan is alive (and married to Clive's former wife, who has obtained a divorce in his absence), for the first time feels free to open his heart to the expectant Teresa. *Hermits. Infidelity. Divorce. Canada.*

WHEN THE LAD CAME HOME **F2.6252**
Dist Arrow Pictures. 3 Mar **1922** [New York State license]. Si; b&w. 35mm. 5 reels, 4,200 ft.

Cast: Harry Myers, Ali Raby.

Comedy-drama. No information about the nature of this film has been found.

WHEN THE LAW RIDES **F2.6253**
FBO Pictures. 26 Feb **1928** [c16 May 1928; LP25259]. Si; b&w. 35mm. 5 reels, 4,898 ft.

Dir Robert De Lacy. *Story-Cont* Oliver Drake. *Titl* Randolph Bartlett. *Photog* Nick Musuraca. *Film Ed* Jay Joiner. *Asst Dir* William Cody.

Cast: Tom Tyler *(Tom O'Malley)*, Jane Reid *(Becky Ross)*, Frankie Darro *(Frankie Ross)*, Harry O'Connor *(Henry Blaine)*, Harry Woods *(The Raven)*, Charles Thurston *(Joshua Ross)*, Bill Nestel *(Snake Arnold)*, Barney Furey *(The Little Man)*.

Western melodrama. Young Federal agent Tom O'Malley, assigned to clean up a gang of outlaws, masquerades as "The Raven," an outlaw whom he finds dead, to gain the confidence of the crooks. Instead, he incurs the wrath of local crime leaders Arnold and Blaine by inviting a parson to conduct services in the local tavern. Arnold and Blaine accuse O'Malley when the local bank is robbed, but he outwits them by sending for his deputies. Waiting outside the town, the deputies capture Arnold, Blaine, and the gang. O'Malley reveals his identity and his intentions—to the minister's daughter. *Government agents. Clergymen. Outlaws. Disguise. Robbery.*

WHEN THE WIFE'S AWAY **F2.6254**
Columbia Pictures. 20 Oct **1926** [c29 Nov 1926; LP23403]. Si; b&w. 35mm. 6 reels, 5,330 ft.

Supv Harry Cohn. *Dir* Frank R. Strayer. *Story-Scen* Douglas Bronston.

Cast: George K. Arthur *(Billy Winthrop)*, Dorothy Revier *(Ethel Winthrop)*, Bobby Dunn, Ned Sparks, Harry Depp, Lincoln Plummer, Tom Ricketts, Ina Rorke.

Domestic comedy. Billy Winthrop and his wife, Ethel, who lead a meager existence on Billy's salary, suddenly learn that they will inherit the estate of Billy's grandfather, provided that Billy has "made good." Billy and Ethel rent a fashionable apartment for a few days to deceive Uncle Hiram, who visits them, with a show of luxury. They are unaware, however, that the woman who signed the lease is "Slim Pretty," alias Joe Carter, a notorious crook and female impersonator, who, with his partner, Chicago Dan, plans to rob the apartment. Billy impersonates the butler, and failing to impress his uncle, he more successfully impersonates a Miss Smith, with whom Uncle Hiram becomes infatuated. Complications ensue, and Billy mistakes Chicago Dan for the owner of the apartment; then the owner and the police arrive. ... Billy and Ethel threaten to reveal the uncle's flirtation, and he finally agrees to surrender the inheritance. *Uncles. Inheritance. Female impersonation. Robbery. Blackmail.*

WHEN WE WERE TWENTY-ONE **F2.6255**
Jesse D. Hampton. *Dist* Pathé Exchange. ca22 Jan **1921** [Cleveland premiere; released Jan; c22 Dec 1920; LU15949]. Si; b&w. 35mm.

Pres by Jesse D. Hampton. *Dir* Henry King. *Photog* Victor Milner.

Cast: H. B. Warner *(Richard Carewe)*, Claire Anderson *(Phyllis)*, James Morrison *(Richard Audaine)*, Christine Mayo *(Kara Glynesk)*, Claude Payton *(Dave Hirsch)*, Minna Grey *(Mrs. Ericson)*.

Comedy-drama. Source: Henry V. Esmond, *When We Were Twenty-one, a Comedy in Four Acts* (New York, 1901). Dick Audaine, known affectionately as the Imp, is engaged to Phyllis Ericson, who really loves Dick's guardian, Richard Carewe. Dick falls in love with Kara Glynesk, who is only after his money. Phyllis intercepts a letter from Kara, believes it to be intended for Carewe, and is hurt. Carewe, trying to protect the Imp, does not deny that he is the intended recipient. Carewe and the "Trinity"—three life-long friends and self-appointed coguardians of the Imp—try, in vain, to stop the Imp's marriage to Kara. When Kara finds her husband to be penniless, she runs away with another man. The Imp realizes his folly, and Phyllis marries Carewe. *Guardians. Fortune hunters. Wealth.*

WHEN WINTER WENT **F2.6256**

Independent Pictures. M. P. Waite. caFeb **1925**. Si; b&w. 35mm. 5 reels.

Dir Reginald Morris.

Cast: Raymond Griffith, Charlotte Merriam.

Farce. "... burlesquing the favorite story of the Southern colonel whose homestead is staked on his favorite horse in the racing classic. The opening shows a bookworm facing death from freezing in an unheated room of a country hotel. He reads the story of the South, hoping thus to cheat death from the wintry blasts. The burlesque is a picturization of the novel he reads." (*Motion Picture News Booking Guide,* 8:83, Apr 1925.) *Hotels. Horseracing. Winter. United States—South. Bookworms.*

WHERE EAST IS EAST **F2.6257**

Metro-Goldwyn-Mayer Pictures. 4 May **1929** [c15 May 1929; LP362]. Si; b&w. 35mm. 7 reels, 6,683 ft.

Dir Tod Browning. *Scen* Richard Schayer. *Titl* Joe Farnham. *Adapt* Waldemar Young. *Story* Tod Browning, Harry Sinclair Drago. *Photog* Henry Sharp. *Art Dir* Cedric Gibbons. *Film Ed* Harry Reynolds. *Wardrobe* David Cox.

Cast: Lon Chaney *(Tiger Haynes),* Lupe Velez *(Toyo),* Estelle Taylor *(Madame de Sylva),* Lloyd Hughes *(Bobby Bailey),* Louis Stern *(Father Angelo),* Mrs. Wong Wing *(Ming).*

Melodrama. Tiger Haynes, a wild-animal trapper in Indochina, bears the scars of many a mauling and cares for only one thing in life: his beloved daughter, Toyo. Bobby Bailey, the son of an American circus owner, falls in love with Toyo, and Tiger reluctantly gives them his blessing after Bobby saves the girl from a tiger. Toyo's mother, Madame de Sylva, arrives unexpectedly and uses all her feminine wiles to lure Bobby away from Toyo. Tiger seeks to eliminate her and sets loose a killer gorilla. Toyo begs him to save Madame de Sylva, and Tiger is badly mauled in a futile attempt to do his daughter's bidding. Madame de Sylva is killed, and Tiger lives only long enough to see Bobby and Toyo wed by Father Angelo. *Trappers. Priests. Fatherhood. Indochina. Circus. Tigers. Apes.*

WHERE IS MY WANDERING BOY TONIGHT? **F2.6258**

B. F. Zeidman Productions. *Dist* Equity Pictures. 5 Feb **1922** [c5 Feb 1922; LP17565]. Si; b&w. 35mm. 7 reels.

Prod B. F. Zeidman. *Dir* James P. Hogan, Millard Webb. *Story-Scen* Gerald C. Duffy. *Photog* David Abel. *Art Dir* Henry Scott Ramsey.

Cast: Cullen Landis *(Garry Beecher),* Carl Stockdale *(Silas Rudge),* Virginia True Boardman *(Martha Beecher),* Patsy Ruth Miller *(Lorna Owens),* Kathleen Key *(Veronica Tyler),* Ben Beeley *(Stewart Kilmer),* Clarence Badger, Jr. *(R. Sylvester Jones).*

Melodrama. Suggested by: Robert Lowry, "Where is My Wandering Boy Tonight?" (a song; 1877). Garry Beecher, forgetting his mother and sweetheart, Lorna, falls in love with Veronica, a chorus girl, and heads for the city; finding her with a millionaire, he returns home and robs his former employer, then returns to Veronica and begins a career of reckless spending. When he is unable to pay for a diamond necklace, Garry is threatened with arrest and is betrayed by Veronica; he is convicted of grand larceny and sentenced to 10 years' imprisonment. To assuage the broken heart of Garry's mother, Lorna sends her letters ostensibly written by him. In prison, Garry saves the warden from an attack by one of the prisoners, but when a wholesale break is perpetrated, Garry follows the prisoners aboard a speeding locomotive and rescues the warden just as a freight train is sighted coming in the opposite direction. As a result, the grateful warden secures a pardon for Garry, who returns home to his mother and sweetheart. *Chorus girls. Prison wardens. Filial relations. Motherhood. Larceny. Prisons. New York City.*

WHERE IS THIS WEST? **F2.6259**

Universal Pictures. 17 Sep **1923** [c7 Aug 1923; LP19308]. Si; b&w. 35mm. 5 reels, 4,532 ft.

Pres by Carl Laemmle. *Dir* George E. Marshall. *Scen* George C. Hively. *Story* George C. Hull. *Photog* Clyde De Vinna, Ray Ramsey.

Cast: Jack Hoxie *(John Harley),* Mary Philbin *(Sallie Summers),* Bob McKenzie *(Bimbo McGuire),* Sid Jordan *(Buck Osborne),* Slim Cole *(Wild Honey),* Joseph Girard *(Lawyer Browns),* Bernard Siegel *(Indian servant).*

Western comedy-melodrama. John Harley leaves his milkman job to take possession of half of a cattle ranch while waitress Sallie Summers goes west on a similar mission to take her half of their shared inheritance. Together, Harley and Sallie fight for ownership of the ranch with foreman Buck Osborne and his gang, who, to scare off the new owners, stage fake holdups, Indian battles, and gunfights. Harley beats the gang at its game and marries Sallie after rescuing her from a kidnaping. *Milkmen. Waitresses. Ranch foremen. Gangs. Inheritance. Ranches.*

WHERE LIGHTS ARE LOW **F2.6260**

Hayakawa Feature Play Co. *Dist* R-C Pictures. 4 Sep **1921** [c7 Dec 1920; LU15855]. Si; b&w. 35mm. 6 reels.

Dir Colin Campbell. *Adapt* Jack Cunningham. *Photog* Frank D. Williams.

Cast: Sessue Hayakawa *(T'Su Wong Shih),* Togo Yamamoto *(Chang Bong Lo),* Goro Kino *(Tuang Fang),* Gloria Payton *(Quan Yin),* Kiyosho Satow *(Lang See Bow),* Misao Seki *(Chung Wo Ho Kee),* Toyo Fujita *(Wung),* Jay Eaton *("Spud" Malone),* Harold Holland *(Sergeant McConigle).*

Oriental melodrama. Source: Lloyd Osbourne, "East is East," in *Metropolitan Magazine* (51:11, Apr 1920). T'Su Wong Shih, a Chinese prince, loves Quan Yin, a gardener's daughter, though his uncle plans to marry him into a wealthy mandarin family; and before leaving for America to obtain an education, he promises the girl that he will join her soon. Following graduation from college, while visiting a slave auction in San Francisco's Chinatown, he recognizes his beloved one and bids $5,000 for her; he wins but is unable to raise the required sum. The auctioneer agrees to give him a 3-year extension on the payment, and T'Su Wong Shih goes to work at various sorts of jobs but meets with little success until he wins a lottery prize. Threats from an Oriental gangster induce the auctioneer to yield his captive, but T'Su Wong Shih engages in a fight with the gangster, rescues Quan Yin, and claims her for his wife. *Chinese. Gangsters. Slavery. Lotteries. San Francisco—Chinatown.*

Note: Also reviewed under the title *When Lights Are Low.*

WHERE MEN ARE MEN **F2.6261**

Vitagraph Co. of America. 1 Sep **1921** [c14 Jul 1921; LP16760]. Si; b&w. 35mm. 5 reels.

Dir William Duncan. *Scen* Thomas Dixon, Jr. *Photog* George Robinson.

Cast: William Duncan *(Vic Foster),* Edith Johnson *(Eileen, "Princess"),* George Stanley *(Frank Valone),* Tom Wilson *("Dutch" Monahan),* Gertrude Wilson *(Laura Valone),* Harry Lonsdale *(R. C. Cavendish),* George Kunkel *(Sheriff Grimes),* William McCall *(Mike Regan),* Charles Dudley *(Monty Green).*

Western melodrama. Source: Ralph Cummins, "The Princess of the Desert Dream" (publication undetermined). Penniless and discouraged, Vic Foster comes out of Death Valley and enters the Desert Dream Dance Hall. There he meets a singer known as "Princess," who inquires if he ever knew a man named Waldron, whereupon he is drugged by the proprietor and robbed of a deed to the Pink Lead Mine. Monty Green advises Vic to leave town, for the sheriff has evidence that he killed Jerry Wright, his partner. On the way to his mine, he meets his engineer friend Frank Valone, who invites him to the city. Receiving a telegram from Valone that he is being followed by the sheriff, Foster returns to clear his name and finds a letter addressed to Ruth Waldron, which he delivers to "Princess," the dead partner's daughter. The letter gives the location of the lost mine and proves Foster innocent. With the mystery solved, he and "Princess" become partners. *Entertainers. Engineers. Mine claims. Death Valley. Documentation.*

WHERE ROMANCE RIDES **F2.6262**

Ben Wilson Productions. *Dist* Arrow Pictures. c28 Apr **1925** [LP21409]. Si; b&w. 35mm. 5 reels, 4,301 ft.

Dir Ward Hayes.

Cast: Dick Hatton *(Dick Manners),* Marilyn Mills *(Muriel Thompson),* Roy Laidlaw *(Andrew J. Thompson),* Jack Richardson *(Dave Colton),* Gerry O'Dell *(Thomas Lapsley),* Arthur Johnson *("Walrus" McNutt),* Archie Ricks *("Dunk" Gresham),* Clara Morris *(Imogene Harris).*

Western melodrama. Andrew J. Thompson, a wealthy New York banker, goes to the Pine View Lodge, a western resort, accompanied by his daughter, Muriel, and some of her young friends. Dave Colton, the foreman of the guides at the lodge, recognizes Imogene Harris, a gold digger who is vamping the banker, as one of his former accomplices. Muriel falls in love with Dick Manners, one of the cowboy guides, and every day the two ride out together. Colton sends one of his men to ambush Dick, who is saved from certain death by Beverly, his horse. Imogene and Colton plot to compromise Muriel, and Dick comes to her rescue, ordering Colton from the country. Muriel and Dick come to the conclusion that life together is meant for them. *Cowboys. Bankers. New Yorkers. Guides. Resorts. Horses.*

WHERE THE NORTH BEGINS **F2.6263**

Warner Brothers Pictures. 1 Jul **1923** [c28 Jul 1923; LP19256]. Si; b&w. 35mm. 6 reels, 6,200 ft.

Harry Rapf Production. *Dir* Chester M. Franklin. *Scen* Fred Myton, Chester M. Franklin. *Story* Fred Myton, Millard Webb.

Cast: Claire Adams *(Felice McTavish)*, Walter McGrail *(Gabriel Dupré)*, Pat Hartigan *(Shad Galloway)*, Myrtle Owen *(Marie)*, Charles Stevens *(The Fox)*, Fred Huntley *(Scotty McTavish)*, Rin-Tin-Tin *(The Wolf-Dog)*.

Melodrama. Rin-Tin-Tin, a German shepherd puppy, is lost while being transported across Alaska and is adopted by a wolf pack. As a grown "wolf-dog," Rin-Tin-Tin rescues Gabriel Dupré, a young French Canadian, when Dupré is attacked while carrying furs across Canada and abandoned for dead. Dupré and Rin-Tin-Tin become fast friends: the dog proves himself to be a staunch defender, eventually saving Dupré's sweetheart when her life is endangered. *French Canadians. Fur industry. Canada. Alaska. Dogs. Wolves.*

WHERE THE NORTH HOLDS SWAY **F2.6264**

Morris R. Schlank Productions. *Dist* Rayart Pictures. Jan **1927**. Si; b&w. 35mm. 5 reels, 4,859 ft.

Dir Bennett Cohn. *Photog* William Hyer.

Cast: Jack Perrin, Starlight *(a horse)*.

Northwest melodrama. "Northwest Mounted man's brother is murdered by gambler, and brother, leaving service, seeks revenge. Through accident becomes charge of gambler and his wife, to whom he is unknown. Discovers truth and in fight kills gambler. Falls in love with wife and they marry." (*Motion Picture News Booking Guide*, 12:64, Apr 1927.) *Brothers. Gamblers. Murder. Revenge. Northwest Mounted Police. Horses.*

WHERE THE PAVEMENT ENDS **F2.6265**

Metro Pictures. 19 Mar **1923** [c27 Mar 1923; LP18829]. Si; b&w. 35mm. 8 reels, 7,706 ft.

Exec Prod Morton Spring. *Dir-Adapt* Rex Ingram. *Photog* John F. Seitz. *Tech Dir* Gordon Mayer. *Film Ed* Grant Whytock.

Cast: Edward Connelly *(Pastor Spener)*, Alice Terry *(Miss Matilda, his daughter)*, Ramon Novarro *(Motauri)*, Harry T. Morey *(Capt. Hull Gregson)*, John George *(Napuka Joe, his servant)*.

Melodrama. Source: John Russell, "The Passion Vine," in *The Red Mark, and Other Stories* (New York, 1919). Pastor Spener, dedicated to the conversion of the natives of Wallis Islands, is in constant contention with Hull Gregson, an unscrupulous trader who operates a saloon—to the detriment of the people. Because Gregson wishes to marry Matilda, the pastor's daughter, he makes Spener believe that he has reformed. Matilda, however, loves Motauri, a young native chief, and runs away with him despite the enormous obstacles to their union. In a violent storm they are forced to take refuge in Gregson's shack. Motauri overpowers Gregson, takes Matilda to his hut, leaves her after she faints, and jumps over a waterfall. (In the copyright synopsis Motauri turns out to be a white man and happily returns to New England with Matilda.) *Clergymen. Missionaries. Traders. South Sea Islands. Wallis Islands.*

WHERE THE TRAILS BEGIN *see* **WHERE TRAILS BEGIN**

WHERE THE WEST BEGINS **F2.6266**

Dist Associated Independent Producers. 13 Aug **1928** [New York State license]. Si; b&w. 35mm. 5 reels, 4,800 ft.

Dir-Scen Robert J. Horner. *Titl* Joe O'Hara. *Photog* Jack Draper. *Film Ed* William Austin.

Cast: Pawnee Bill Jr., Boris Bullock, Bud Osborne.

Western melodrama(?). No information about the nature of this film has been found.

WHERE THE WORST BEGINS **F2.6267**

Co-Artists Productions. *Dist* Truart Film Corp. Nov **1925** [c11 Nov 1925; LP22103]. Si; b&w. 35mm. 6 reels, 6,139 ft.

Dir John McDermott. *Adapt* Joseph Anthony Roach. *Photog* Byron Haskins. *Film Ed* Edward McDermott. *Asst Dir* Edward Bernoudy. *Tech Dir* Edward Hass.

Cast: Ruth Roland *(Jane Brower)*, Alec B. Francis *(August Van Dorn)*, Matt Moore *(Donald Van Dorn)*, Grace Darmond *(Annice Van Dorn)*, Roy Stewart *(Cliff Ranger)*, Derelys Perdue *(Annice's friend)*, Theodore Lorch, Ernie Adams, J. P. Lockney, Robert Burns, Floyd Shackelford.

Western comedy. Source: George Frank Worts, "Out Where the Worst Begins," in *Argosy–All Story Weekly* (vol 57, 5 Jan–2 Feb 1924). Jane Brower wants nothing more in life than to leave the West behind and go to live in New York. When she comes across a party being given in a private railroad car by August Van Dorn, she kidnaps Van Dorn's son, Donald, and holds him for ransom. While Jane is negotiating with the elder Van Dorn, two bandits kidnap Donald. He soon escapes and comes looking for Jane, with whom he has fallen in love. The bandits kidnap Jane, and Donald rescues her. Donald and Jane make plans to be married, intending to spend their honeymoon in Manhattan. *Capitalists. Bandits. Kidnaping. Ransom. New York City.*

WHERE TRAILS BEGIN **F2.6268**

Bischoff Productions. May **1927**. Si; b&w. 35mm. 6 reels, 5,700 ft.

Dir Noel Mason Smith. *Scen* Ben Allah. *Story* Samuel Bischoff. *Photog* Harry Cooper, James Brown.

Cast: Johnnie Walker *(Gordon Ramsey)*, Silverstreak *(a dog)*, Charlotte Stevens *(Lucille Bennett)*, Albert J. Smith *(Bruce Hodges)*, Hughie Mack *("Heftie" McNutt)*, Arthur Taylor *(Rufus Bennett)*.

Northwest melodrama. "Silverstreak has his lost innings but when the score is counted he comes through the victor with villain all nicely tucked under an avalanche, the dog's family safe in the home of the chap who befriended him and the sailing all smooth and pretty" (*Film Daily*, 3 Jul 1927, p9). *Avalanches. Dogs.*

Note: May also be known as *Where the Trails Begin.*

WHERE WAS I? (Universal-Jewel) **F2.6269**

Universal Pictures. 15 Nov **1925** [c21 Aug 1925; LP21766]. Si; b&w. 35mm. 7 reels, 6,630 ft.

Dir William A. Seiter. *Scen* Rex Taylor, Melville Brown. *Photog* Charles Stumar.

Cast: Reginald Denny *(Thomas S. Berford)*, Marion Nixon *(Alicia Stone)*, Pauline Garon *(Claire)*, Lee Moran *(Henry)*, [Frederick] Tyrone Power *(George Stone)*, Otis Harlan *(Bennett)*, Chester Conklin *(Elmer)*, William H. Turner *(Jones)*, Tom Lingham *(McPherson)*, Arthur Lake *(Jimmy)*.

Farce. Source: Edgar Franklin, "Where Was I?" in *Argosy Allstory Weekly* (164:161–185, 363–387, 545–569, 761–785, 1–22 Nov 1924). Thomas S. Berford, a successful young businessman, becomes engaged to Alicia Stone, the daughter of his primary business rival. George Stone, who loathes Tom, sets out to ruin him in love and commerce, hiring Claire to proclaim publicly that she and Tom have been married for several years. Tom cannot disprove her statement, and Claire moves into his house, establishing herself as his wife. After numerous complications, Claire repents of her duplicity and exposes Stone's plot. Tom then marries Alicia. *Businessmen. Courtship. Duplicity. Business competition. Courtship.*

WHICH SHALL IT BE? **F2.6270**

Renaud Hoffman Productions. *Dist* W. W. Hodkinson Corp. 15 Jun **1924** [c12 Jun 1924; LP20300]. Si; b&w. 35mm. 5 reels, 4,600 ft.

Madeline Brandeis Production. *Dir-Adapt* Renaud Hoffman. *Photog* Renaud Hoffman.

Cast: Willis Marks *(John Moore)*, Ethel Wales *(Mrs. Moore)*, David Torrence *(Robert Moore)*, Paul Weigel *(musicmaster)*, Mary McLane, Billy Bondwin, Newton House, Miriam Ballah, Dick Winslow, Buck Black, Thayer Strain *(The Children)*.

Domestic drama. Source: Ethel Lynn Beers, "Not One To Spare," or "Which Shall It Be?" (publication undetermined). A Vermont family with seven children is presented with an offer from a wealthy relative of an estate and an allowance in return for one child, which he wishes to adopt to brighten his lonely life. After much speculation, they decide on the oldest girl, whose musical interests cannot be furthered by their limited means. She no sooner leaves than the mother suffers remorse, and the father, equally unable to surrender his child, brings her back to the farm. *Musicians. Family life. Adoption. Vermont.*

Note: Also released under its copyright title, *Not One To Spare.*

WHILE JUSTICE WAITS F2.6271

Fox Film Corp. 19 Nov **1922** [c19 Nov 1922; LP19128]. Si; b&w. 35mm. 5 reels, 4,762 ft.

Pres by William Fox. *Dir* Bernard J. Durning. *Scen* Edwin B. Tilton, Jack Strumwasser. *Story* Charles A. Short, Don Short. *Photog* Don Short.

Cast: Dustin Farnum *(Dan Hunt)*, Irene Rich *(Nell Hunt)*, Earl Metcalf *(George Carter)*, Junior Delameter *(Hunt, Jr.)*, Frankie Lee *(Joe)*, Hector Sarno *(a man)*, Peaches Jackson *(a man's daughter)*, Gretchen Hartman *(Mollie Adams)*.

Western melodrama. Dan Hunt makes money in an Alaskan gold mine venture and returns home to find his wife, Nell, and his son gone. He joins a band of criminals to find the man who stole his wife and meets a boy seeking his lost mother. Together they continue the search. Eventually Dan finds his wife in a small mining town, and he shoots it out with the interloper. After Nell explains that she was kidnaped and that the boy is her son, the family starts anew. *Miners. Waifs. Gangs. Kidnaping.*

Note: Working title: *As a Man Thinketh.*

WHILE LONDON SLEEPS F2.6272

Warner Brothers Pictures. 27 Nov **1926** [c29 Nov 1926; LP23394]. Si; b&w. 35mm. 6 reels, 5,810 ft.

Dir H. P. Bretherton. *Story-Scen* Walter Morosco. *Camera* Frank Kesson. *Asst Camera* Fred West. *Asst Dir* William Cannon.

Cast: Rin-Tin-Tin *(Rinty)*, Helene Costello *(Dale Burke)*, Walter Merrill *(Thomas Hallard)*, John Patrick *(Foster)*, Otto Matieson *(London Letter)*, George Kotsonaros *(The Monk)*, De Witt Jennings *(Inspector Burke)*, Carl Stockdale *(Stokes)*, Les Bates *(Long Tom)*.

Crook melodrama. Inspector Burke of Scotland Yard concentrates all his forces on the capture of London Letter, a notorious criminal leader in the Limehouse district who possesses both Rinty, a splendid dog, and a man-beast monster that ravages and kills at his master's command. Burke almost apprehends the gang in the midst of an attempted theft, but Rinty's uncanny perceptions foil Burke's coup, and Foster is killed for betraying the gang. When Rinty loses in a fight against another dog, Burke's daughter, Dale, rescues Rinty from London Letter's abuse, and he becomes devoted to his new mistress. At the criminal's order, the monster kidnaps Dale and imprisons her. Burke and his men wound London Letter while on his trail, and Rinty finds him dying. In a ferocious battle Rinty kills the monster. *Gangs. Monsters. London—Limehouse. Scotland Yard. Dogs.*

Note: A number of sources credit Walter Morosco with direction.

WHILE PARIS SLEEPS F2.6273

Maurice Tourneur Productions. *Dist* W. W. Hodkinson Corp. 21 Jan **1923.** Si; b&w. 35mm. 6 reels, 4,850 ft.

Dir Maurice Tourneur. *Photog* René Guissart.

Cast: Lon Chaney *(Henri Santodos)*, Mildred Manning *(Bebe Larvache)*, Jack Gilbert *(Dennis O'Keefe)*, Hardee Kirkland *(his father)*, Jack McDonald *(Father Marionette)*, J. Farrell MacDonald *(Georges Morier)*.

Melodrama. Source: "Pan," *The Glory of Love* (London, 1919). "A sculptor in the Latin Quarter of Paris harbors an unrequited passion for his model. The latter meets young American tourist and they become infatuated. The youth's father pleads with girl to give him up and she agrees if she may be permitted to have one evening of happiness during the Mardi Gras festival. The jealous sculptor enlists the aid of half-crazed keeper of wax museum to dispose of American youth. The boy is kidnapped and tortured, but rescued in the nick of time. The young people finally receive the father's blessing." (*Motion Picture News Booking Guide,* 4: 108, April 1923.) *Sculptors. Models. Waxworks. Kidnaping. Mardi Gras. Paris—Quartier Latin.*

Note: Produced in 1920 by Tourneur as *The Glory of Love;* not released until 1923.

WHILE SATAN SLEEPS F2.6274

Famous Players–Lasky. *Dist* Paramount Pictures. ca25 Jun **1922** [New York, Chicago, and Los Angeles premieres; released 18 Sep; c21 Jun 1922; LP18050]. Si; b&w. 35mm. 7 reels, 6,069 ft.

Pres by Jesse L. Lasky. *Dir* Joseph Henabery. *Scen* Albert S. Le Vino. *Photog* Faxon M. Dean.

Cast: Jack Holt *(Phil)*, Wade Boteler *(Red Barton)*, Mabel Van Buren *(Sunflower Sadie)*, Fritzi Brunette *(Salome Deming)*, Will R. Walling *(Bud Deming)*, J. P. Lockney *(Chuckkawalla Bill)*, Fred Huntley *(Absolom Randall)*, Bobby Mack *(Bones)*, Sylvia Ashton *(Mrs. Bones)*, Herbert Standing *(Bishop)*.

Western melodrama. Source: Peter Bernard Kyne, "The Parson of Panamint," in *The Parson of Panamint, and Other Stories* (New York, 1929). Phil Webster, alias "Slick Phil," the son of a minister, escapes from prison with his pal Red Barton and disguises himself as a minister. He accepts an invitation to become the parson of the mining town of Panamint, intent on using his position to rob the bank. He is welcomed by all the congregation except saloon owner Bud Deming and his daughter Salome. His activities as a fighting parson and the growing love of Salome cause him to reform, and when Red Barton carries out the planned robbery alone, Phil recovers the money and confesses his past to the congregation. The bishop arrives to investigate the new minister and discovers him to be his long-lost son. Phil returns to jail to serve out his sentence. Upon his release, he finds Salome and his father waiting for him. *Clergymen. Criminals—Rehabilitation. Imposture. Filial relations. Robbery.*

WHILE THE CITY SLEEPS F2.6275

Metro-Goldwyn-Mayer Pictures. 15 Sep **1928** [c29 Sep 1928; LP25705]. Sd eff & mus score (Movietone); b&w. 35mm. 9 reels, 7,231 ft.

Dir Jack Conway. *Story-Scen* A. P. Younger. *Titl* Joseph Farnham. *Photog* Henry Sharp. *Sets* Cedric Gibbons. *Film Ed* Sam S. Zimbalist. *Wardrobe* Gilbert Clark.

Cast: Lon Chaney *(Dan)*, Anita Page *(Myrtle)*, Carroll Nye *(Marty)*, Wheeler Oakman *(Skeeter)*, Mae Busch *(Bessie)*, Polly Moran *(Mrs. McGinnis)*, Lydia Yeamans Titus *(Mrs. Sullivan)*, William Orlamond *(Dwiggins)*, Richard Carle *(Wally)*.

Underworld melodrama. Myrtle, a silly, innocent flapper, falls in love with Marty, a dapper gangster, and learns too much for her own good about Skeeter, the gang leader. Skeeter threatens to rub her out, and Myrtle appeals for help to Dan Callahan, a veteran detective with flat feet and a tough disposition. Dan puts her up in his boardinghouse and against his better judgment soon falls in love with her; he asks her to marry him, and out of gratitute she agrees. Dan eventually learns that Myrtle is in love with Marty, and he reunites them, meantime helping Marty to take his first, tentative steps on the straight and narrow path. *Flappers. Gangsters. Detectives. Criminals—Rehabilitation. Boardinghouses.*

WHILE THE DEVIL LAUGHS F2.6276

Fox Film Corp. 13 Feb **1921** [c13 Feb 1921; LP16184]. Si; b&w. 35mm. 5 reels, 4,200 ft.

Pres by William Fox. *Dir-Story-Scen* George W. Hill. *Photog* Friend Baker.

Cast: Louise Lovely *(Mary Franklin)*, William Scott *(Billy Anderson)*, G. Raymond Nye *("Fence" McGee)*, Edwin Booth Tilton *(Mr. Foreman)*, Wilson Hummell *(Joe Franklin)*, Molly Shafer *(Mother Franklin)*, Oleta Ottis *(Pearl De La Marr)*, Coy Watson, Jr. *(Gus Franklin)*, Helen Field *(Gertie Franklin)*.

Underworld melodrama. Mary Franklin supports her family, as a hostess in "Fence" McGee's cafe, by lifting jewelry from her dancing partners. Her boyfriend, Billy Anderson, who has invented a washing machine, inspires her to go straight. Billy is framed by McGee, however, and McGee's wife suggests that Mary has been untrue. McGee explains everything in a last-minute confession, and the lovers are reunited after escaping from a burning building. *Cafe hostesses. Thieves. Inventors. Criminals—Rehabilitation.*

THE WHIP F2.6277

First National Pictures. 30 Sep **1928** [c27 Aug 1928; LP25565]. Mus score & sd eff (Vitaphone); b&w. 35mm. 7 reels, 6,056 ft. [Also si; 6,058 ft.]

Pres by Richard A. Rowland. *Dir* Charles J. Brabin. *Cont* Bernard McConville, J. L. Campbell. *Titl* Dwinelle Benthall, Rufus McCosh. *Photog* James Van Trees. *Film Ed* George McGuire.

Cast: Dorothy Mackaill *(Lady Diana)*, Ralph Forbes *(Lord Brancaster)*, Anna Q. Nilsson *(Iris d'Aquila)*, Lowell Sherman *(Greville Sartoris)*, Albert Gran *(Sam Kelley)*, Marc MacDermott *(Lord Beverly)*, Lou Payne *(Lambert)*, Arthur Clayton *(Richard Haslam)*.

Melodrama. Source: Cecil Raleigh and Henry Hamilton, *The Whip* (New York opening: 22 Nov 1912). Lord Brancaster loses his memory after an automobile accident and is cared for by Lord Beverly, outside of whose estate his car has wrecked. Brancaster falls in love with Beverly's daughter, Diana, and they become engaged, planning the formal announcement for the hunt ball. Iris d'Aquila (to whom Brancaster had been engaged before finding out she loved him for his title alone) learns of his amnesia and forges a certificate of marriage with the help of Sartoris, presenting herself at the hunt ball as Lady Brancaster. Diana's horse, The

Whip, is to run at Ascot, and Sartoris, having heavily bet on another horse and fearing The Whip might win, attempts to kill him. Brancaster saves the horse, however, which goes on to win the Ascot. Iris' deception comes to light, and Brancaster (his title and fortune restored) prepares to marry Diana. *Fortune hunters. Aristocrats. Amnesia. Fox hunts. Horseracing. Ascot.*

THE WHIP WOMAN **F2.6278**

First National Pictures. 5 Feb **1928** [c23 Jan 1928]. Si; b&w. 35mm. 6 reels, 5,087 ft.

Pres by Robert Kane. Allan Dwan Production. *Dir* Joseph C. Boyle. *Cont* Earle Roebuck. *Titl* Edwin Justus Mayer. *Story* Forrest Halsey, Leland Hayward. *Photog* Ernest Haller. *Film Ed* Terrell Morse.

Cast: Estelle Taylor *(Sari)*, Antonio Moreno *(Count Michael Ferenzi)*, Lowell Sherman *(The Baron)*, Hedda Hopper *(Countess Ferenzi)*, Julanne Johnston *(Miss Haldane)*, Loretta Young *(The Girl)*, Jack Ackroyd *(see note)*.

Society drama. Sari, a whip-wielding Hungarian peasant, and Ferenzi, a dissolute nobleman whom she saved from suicide, fall in love. On their wedding day Countess Ferenzi, his mother, intervenes and persuades the girl to cancel the ceremony. After a while they drift together and marry in spite of the obstacles. *Peasants. Nobility. Suicide. Whips. Hungary.*

Note: Jack Ackroyd may have been a member of the cast.

THE WHIPPING BOSS **F2.6279**

Monogram Pictures. 22 May **1924** [New York State license application]. Si; b&w. 35mm. 6 reels, 5,800 ft.

Dir J. P. McGowan. *Scen* P. J. Hurn. *Story* Jack Boyle, P. J. Caldeway. *Photog* Walter Griffin.

Cast: Wade Boteler *(The Whipping Boss)*, Eddie Phillips *(Jim)*, J. P. McGowan *(Livingston)*, Lloyd Hughes *(Dick Forrest)*, Barbara Bedford *(Grace Woodward)*, Billy Elmer *(Spike)*, Andrew Waldron *(Timkins)*, George Cummings *(Brady)*, Lydia Knott *(Jim's mother)*, Clarence Geldert *(Jackknife Woodward)*.

Melodrama. Under a system whereby convicts are leased by the State of Oregon to individual private companies, Jim is sent to work for a lumber company and forced to toil in a cypress swamp. He soon becomes ill and, unable to work, is cruelly whipped by the company's whipping boss. Jim's mother learns of his plight and comes to Oregon, enlisting the aid of Dick Forrest, the head of the local post of the American Legion. Forrest obtains an order for Jim's release, and Livingston, the owner of the lumber camp, seeking to destroy the evidence of wrongdoing, orders the whipping boss to set fire to the stockade in which the prisoners are chained. Forrest and members of the American Legion arrive in time to save the convicts, and Livingston and the whipping boss are themselves sent to prison. Jim is freed, and Forrest becomes engaged to Grace Woodward, the daughter of the president of the logging company. The elder Woodward vows to eliminate the inhumane conditions in the lumber camps. *Convicts. Whipping bosses. Prisons. Lumber camps. Oregon. American Legion.*

THE WHIRLWIND OF YOUTH **F2.6280**

Paramount Famous Lasky Corp. 30 Apr **1927** [c30 Apr 1927; LP23898]. Si; b&w. 35mm. 6 reels, 5,866 ft.

Pres by Adolph Zukor, Jesse L. Lasky. *Assoc Prod* B. P. Schulberg. *Dir* Rowland V. Lee. *Screenplay* Julien Josephson. *Photog* G. O. Post.

Cast: Lois Moran *(Nancy Hawthorne)*, Vera Voronina *(Heloise)*, Donald Keith *(Bob Whittaker)*, Alyce Mills *(Cornelia Evans)*, Larry Kent *(Lloyd Evans)*, Gareth Hughes *(Curley)*, Charles Lane *(Jim Hawthorne)*.

Romantic drama. Source: Arthur Hamilton Gibbs, *Soundings* (Boston, 1925). Nancy Hawthorne, an unsophisticated English girl reared in seclusion by her artist father, goes to Paris to pursue her studies and there meets Cornelia Evans, a worldly-wise American art student, who invites her to a party given for her brother, Lloyd, and his chum, Bob Whittaker, both from Oxford. Nancy finds Bob to be the boy of her dreams; and they spend a weekend together at a beach, where their mutual feeling gains in intensity during a storm. Feeling himself unworthy of Nancy, Bob contrives to be discovered in an affectionate pose with Heloise. Nancy, her illusions demolished, returns to England. At the outbreak of war, Nancy enlists as an ambulance driver and is reunited with Bob on the battlefields of France. They are married before the regiment leaves for the front. *Ambulance drivers. Students. Courtship. World War I. England. Paris. Oxford University.*

THE WHIRLWIND RANGER **F2.6281**

Wild West Productions. *Dist* Arrow Film Corp. 1 May **1924** [c20 Mar 1924; LP20018]. Si; b&w. 35mm. 5 reels, 4,585 ft.

Dir Richard Hatton. *Story* Robert McKenzie.

Cast: Richard Hatton, Neva Gerber.

Western melodrama. Ranger Jamie O'Hara, known as the "Whirlwind," assists Sheriff Bill Jarvis in tracking down Mickey Walker, wanted in connection with the killing of a prominent citizen. O'Hara encounters Mickey's sister, Berenda; she unwittingly leads him to Mickey's hideout; and he rescues her and Mickey from a band of outlaws. At Mickey's trial the jury returns a verdict of justified homicide and he is acquitted; O'Hara and Berenda then plan to marry. *Rangers. Outlaws. Sheriffs. Brother-sister relationship. Murder. Trials.*

Note: Character names (with the exception of O'Hara) and some plot details are derived from shooting script in copyright files and may differ from the final film.

THE WHISPERED NAME **F2.6282**

Universal Pictures. 21 Jan **1924** [c10 Dec 1923; LP19701]. Si; b&w. 35mm. 5 reels, 5,196 ft.

Dir King Baggot. *Scen* Lois Zellner. *Scen? (see note)* Raymond L. Schrock. *Photog* Jackson Rose.

Cast: Ruth Clifford *(Anne Gray)*, Charles Clary *(Lagdon Van Kreel)*, William E. Lawrence *(Robert Gordon)*, May Mersch *(Marcia Van Kreel)*, John Merkyl *(Craig Stephenson)*, Niles Welch *(John Manning)*, Hayden Stevenson *(Fred Galvin)*, Buddy Messinger *(The Office Boy)*, Herbert Fortier *(Judge James Morrell)*, Joseph North *(Mahoney, detective)*, Emily Fitzroy *(Amanda Stone)*, Jane Starr *(Mrs. Billy Shotwell)*, Carl Stockdale *(Z. Todd)*.

Comedy-drama. Source: Rita Weiman and Alice Leal Pollock, *The Co-respondent* (New York opening: 10 Apr 1916). Anne Gray is saved from a fake marriage to scapegrace Robert Gordon by the arrival of millionaire Lagdon Van Kreel. Later, as a reporter, sent to cover a sensational society divorce, she finds that Van Kreel's wife intends to sue him, naming her (Anne) as corespondent. John Manning, managing editor of the paper, saves Anne and silences the wife. *Reporters. Editors. Millionaires. Divorce. Newspapers.*

Note: Working titles: *Blackmail; The Co-respondent.* Some sources credit Raymond L. Schrock with scenario. According to company records, Lois Zellner should have been credited instead.

WHISPERING CANYON **F2.6283**

Banner Productions. *Dist* Ginsberg-Kann Distributing Corp. 10 May **1926** [c27 Apr 1926; LP22640]. Si; b&w. 35mm. 6 reels, 5,652 ft.

Dir Tom Forman. *Adapt-Cont* Mary Alice Scully. *Photog* Harry Davis, William Tuers.

Cast: Jane Novak *(Antonia Lee)*, Robert Ellis *(Bob Cameron)*, Lee Shumway *(Lew Selby)*, Josef Swickard *(Eben Beauregard)*, Eugene Pallette *(Harvey Hawes [Hinky Dink])*, James Mason *(Medbrook)*, Edward Brady *(Gonzales)*.

Melodrama. Source: John Mersereau, *The Whispering Canyon* (New York, 1926). Returning from the war to his father's California sawmill, Bob Cameron takes up with Hinky Dink, a cocky Englishman and man of the road. Ignoring a "no trespassing" sign on Cameron's property, Hinky is caught in a steel trap; Cameron, seeking aid, is threatened by Eben Beauregard, an old southerner, but the appearance of Antonia ("Tony") Lee, Bob's childhood friend, quells his temper. Bob learns that Lew Selby, an unscrupulous timber baron, is trying to buy Tony's land and that his father has been murdered. At the suggestion of Hinky (who has innocently fallen asleep on the riverbank), Bob and Tony pool their interests against Selby; he attempts to prevent their passage through land belonging to Medbrook, an eccentric; and Gonzales, Selby's henchman, kidnaps Tony. Medbrook blows up the dam, and Selby tries to buy out the couple; but the plot is thwarted by the timely intervention of Hinky Dink. *Veterans. Lumbermen. Timberlands. Sawmills. Business competition. Murder. California.*

WHISPERING PALMS **F2.6284**

Charles Granlich Feature Photoplays. *Dist* Fidelity Pictures. 9 Aug **1923** [New York State license]. Si; b&w. 35mm. 5 reels.

Cast: Val Cleary, Gladys Hulette.

Melodrama(?). No information about the nature of this film has been found.

WHISPERING SAGE **F2.6285**

Fox Film Corp. 20 Mar **1927** [c13 Mar 1927; LP23781]. Si; b&w. 35mm. 5 reels, 4,783 ft.

Pres by William Fox. *Dir* Scott R. Dunlap. *Scen* Harold Shumate. *Photog* Reginald Lyons. *Asst Dir* Ted Brooks.

Cast: Buck Jones *(Buck Kildare)*, Natalie Joyce *(Mercedes)*, Emile Chautard *(José Arastrade)*, Carl Miller *(Esteban Bengoa)*, Albert J. Smith *(Ed Fallows)*, Joseph Girard *(Hugh Acklin)*, William A. Steele *(Tom Kildare)*, Ellen Winston *(Mrs. Kildare)*, Hazel Keener *(Mercedes' friend)*, Enrique Acosta *(Old Pedro)*, Joseph Rickson.

Western melodrama. Source: Harry Sinclair Drago and Joseph Noel, *Whispering Sage* (New York, 1922). Buck Kildare, searching for a killer, encounters a colony of Basques in the desert and saves them from the henchmen of Hugh Acklin, owner of an adjoining ranch who wants to take over the immigrants' land. Discovering Acklin's duplicity, Buck soon becomes an ally of the Basques and falls in love with Mercedes, daughter of their leader. In a showdown between the factions, Buck discovers that Acklin's foreman murdered his brother, Tom. Government forces save the Basques at the last minute, and Buck is happily united with the girl. *Ranchers. Basques. Desperadoes. Land rights. Courtship.*

WHISPERING SMITH **F2.6286**

Metropolitan Pictures. *Dist* Producers Distributing Corp. 28 Mar **1926** [c20 Mar 1926; LP22506]. Si; b&w. 35mm. 7 reels, 6,155 or 6,187 ft.

Pres by John C. Flinn. *Dir* George Melford. *Adapt* Elliott J. Clawson, Will M. Ritchey. *Cinematog* Charles G. Clarke. *2d Cinematog* Joe La Shelle. *Art Dir* Charles Cadwallader. *Asst Dir* Edward Bernoudy. *Prod Mgr* George Bertholon. *Asst Prod Mgr* Robert Ross.

Cast: H. B. Warner *("Whispering Smith")*, Lillian Rich *(Dicksie Dunning)*, John Bowers *(McCloud)*, Lilyan Tashman *(Marion Sinclair)*, Eugene Pallette *(Bill Dancing)*, Richard Neill *(Lance Dunning)*, James Mason *(Du Sang)*, Warren Rodgers *(Karg)*, Nelson McDowell *(Seagrue)*, Robert Edeson *(J. S. Bucks)*.

Western melodrama. Source: Frank Hamilton Spearman, *Whispering Smith* (New York, 1906). Railroad foreman Murray Sinclair is ousted by George McCloud, division superintendent, for looting wrecks. With his henchmen, Sinclair retires to his ranch and forays against the railroad. "Whispering Smith," engaged by the railroad to restore order, is hesitant in dealing with Sinclair when he falls in love with Marion, Sinclair's wife, who is separated from her husband and operates a small shop in Medicine Bend. Dicksie, McCloud's sweetheart, overhears Sinclair threaten McCloud, and she rides through a storm to warn him; Smith, with the aid of Bill Dancing, tracks down Sinclair and his men, and Bill kills the villain. Dicksie and McCloud marry and take Marion under their protection. Marion realizes her love for Smith, who before parting promises to return to her. *Detectives. Railroads. Looting. Train wrecks.*

WHISPERING WINDS **F2.6287**

Tiffany-Stahl Productions. 1 May or 5 Sep **1929** [c9 Sep 1929; LP688]. Talking & singing sequences (Photophone); b&w. 35mm. 7 reels, 5,881 ft. [Also si; 5,652 ft.]

Dir James Flood. *Story-Cont* Jean Plannette. *Dial* Charles Logue. *Photog* Harry Jackson, Jack MacKenzie. *Film Ed* James Morley. *Mus Score* Erno Rapee. *Mus Cond* Joseph Littau.

Cast: Patsy Ruth Miller *(Dora)*, Malcolm McGregor *(Jim)*, Eve Southern *(Eve Benton)*, Eugenie Besserer *(Jim's mother)*, James Marcus *(Pappy)*.

Domestic melodrama. Jim, a Maine fisherman who lives with his widowed mother, marries a neighborhood girl, Dora, when his sweetheart, Eve, goes to New York to become a pop singer. Dora is unsure of Jim's love for her until Eve, visiting them a year later, shows herself as aloof and jaded. Dora learns that Eve purposely assumed this attitude to make Jim forget her and to assure Dora's happiness. *Fishermen. Singers. Filial relations. Fishing villages. Maine.*

Note: Theme song: "When I Think of You."

WHISPERING WIRES **F2.6288**

Fox Film Corp. 24 Oct **1926** [c24 Oct 1926; LP23284]. Si; b&w. 35mm. 6 reels, 5,906 ft.

Pres by William Fox. *Dir* Albert Ray. *Scen* L. G. Rigby. *Titl* William Conselman. *Adapt* Henry Leverage. *Photog* George Schneiderman. *Asst Dir* Horace Hough.

Cast: Anita Stewart *(Doris Stockbridge)*, Edmund Burns *(Barry McGill)*, Charles Clary *(Montgomery Stockbridge)*, Otto Matieson *(Bert Norton)*, Mack Swain *(Cassidy)*, Arthur Housman *(McCarthy)*, Charles Conklin *(Jasper, the butler)*, Frank Campeau *(Andrew Murphy)*, Scott Welsh *(Triggy Drew)*, Mayme Kelso *(Ann Cartwright)*, Charles Sellon *(Tracy Bennett)*, Cecille Evans.

Mystery melodrama. Source: Kate L. McLaurin, *Whispering Wires: a Play in Three Acts* (Boston, 1934). Henry Leverage, *Whispering Wires* (New York, 1918). A whispering voice over the telephone foretells a murder to occur at a specified time. Another occurs on schedule. The heroine, Doris Stockbridge, is then threatened, but she is saved through the ingenuity of her sweetheart, Barry, who, with the help of Cassidy and McCarthy, two boob detectives, uncovers the diabolical scheming of an ex-convict and his inventor pal, both of whom are seeking revenge. A bloodhound is called in, and the villains are tracked down with alternately thrilling and comic sequences. *Detectives. Inventors. Murder. Revenge.*

WHISPERING WOMEN **F2.6289**

James Keane. *Dist* Clark-Cornelius Corp. 25 Dec **1921** [New York premiere; released 1 Apr 1922]. Si; b&w. 35mm. 5 reels, 4,800 ft.

Dir James Keane.

Cast: Walter Davis *(David Hartley)*, Esther Welty *(Florence Hartley)*, Clara Heller *(Dolly)*, Everett Moran *(Bobby)*, George C. Welsh *("Blackie" Devoe)*, Brindle *(A Fourth Hartley)*.

Rural melodrama. "Dave Hartley operates the largest lumber camp in his section of the Northwest. He has a loveable wife and charming little daughter who is loved by little Bobbie. Dave is called to his camp. While at camp a mysterious stranger visits the community and the babbling tongues of idle gossipers charge Mrs. Hartley with undue intimacy with him. This gossip reaches Hartley, who sets out to learn of his wife's disloyalty for himself. Hartley is exhausted in the dense woods and is forced to hide. The wolf pack arrives. Meanwhile little Bobbie and Dolly are lost in the forest and spy Hartley. Dolly's faithful dog, Brindle, sensing danger, ... arrives ... just as the wolves are about to make a final plunge for the three. He fights off the wolves, killing one. Later Hartley learns ... that the mysterious stranger was none other than her [Florence's] brother, who, having committed a crime, comes to his sister, Mrs. Hartley, for help." (*Moving Picture World*, 28 Jan 1922, p431.) *Brother-sister relationship. Strangers. Children. Lumbering. Gossip. Dogs. Wolves.*

THE WHISTLE **F2.6290**

William S. Hart Productions. *For* Famous Players–Lasky. *Dist* Paramount Pictures. Apr **1921** [c4 Feb 1921; LP16123]. Si; b&w. 35mm. 6 reels, 5,302 ft.

Dir-Adapt Lambert Hillyer. *Story* May Wilmoth, Olin Lyman. *Photog* Joe August. *Art Dir* J. C. Hoffner. *Paintings* Harry Barndollar.

Cast: William S. Hart *(Robert Evans)*, Frank Brownlee *(Henry Chapple)*, Myrtle Stedman *(Mrs. Chapple)*, Georgie Stone *(Georgie)*, Will Jim Hatton *(Danny)*, Richard Headrick *(Baby)*.

Drama. Robert Evans, who works in the mills of Henry Chapple, urges the owner to make necessary repairs to avoid accidents, but Chapple refuses. That day, his son, Danny, is caught in an unprotected belt and dies. Evans, stricken with grief, rescues the infant son of Chapple from an automobile when it plunges into a river, then kidnaps the baby and claims it as an adopted son. Chapple befriends Evans, however, and when the worker sees that restoration of the child is important to Mrs. Chapple's welfare, he confesses his actions and surrenders the child. *Mills. Accidents—Prevention. Kidnaping.*

WHISTLING JIM **F2.6291**

Roberts & Cole. *Dist* Aywon Film Corp. 19 Jun **1925** [New York State license]. Si; b&w. 35mm. 5 reels, 4,750 ft.

Dir Wilbur McGaugh. *Story* Peggy O'Day. *Photog* J. P. Whalen.

Cast: Big Boy Williams, Peggy O'Day, Dan Peterson.

Western melodrama. Whistling Jim, an itinerant cowboy who is given to whistling at difficult moments, rides in mining country, where in a deserted saloon he meets an outlaw leader named Dan Lee. The men strike up a conversation, and Dan soon offers Jim a job as payroll guard at the mine of his brother, Jack Lee; Jim quickly realizes, however, that Dan is using him to find out the time and place of the gold shipments, which Dan and his gang have been robbing. With the help of Peggy, Jack Lee's daughter, Jim sets a trap for Dan by simultaneously notifying Dan and the sheriff of the time of the next shipment. Dan's gang stampedes the pack train, and the sheriff and his posse round up the gang members. *Cowboys. Sheriffs. Brothers. Gangs. Posses. Robbery. Mines. Whistling.*

WHITE AND UNMARRIED **F2.6292**

Famous Players–Lasky. *Dist* Paramount Pictures. 12 Jun **1921** [c14 Jun 1921; LP16673]. Si; b&w. 35mm. 5 reels, 4,458 ft.

Pres by Jesse L. Lasky. *Dir* Tom Forman. *Scen* Will M. Ritchey. *Photog* Harry Perry.

Cast: Thomas Meighan *(Billy Kane)*, Jacqueline Logan *(Andrée Duphot)*, Grace Darmond *(Dorothea Welter)*, Walter Long *(Chicoq)*, Lloyd Whitlock *(Marechal)*, Fred Vroom *(Mr. Welter)*, Marian Skinner *(Mrs. Welter)*, Georgie Stone *(Victor)*, Jack Herbert *(Jacques)*.

Comedy-melodrama. Source: John D. Swain, "Billy Kane, White and Unmarried" (publication undetermined). When burglarizing the home of millionaire Welter, Billy Kane is captivated by a photograph he finds of Welter's daughter, Dorothea. Later, after receiving an inheritance and reforming, Billy meets the Welters in Paris. In a cafe, he finds favor with a dancer, Andrée, and Dorothea dances with young Marechal; but Chicoq, a jealous apache, attacks Billy and kidnaps Andrée. Dorothea weds Marechal, then is deserted when he is not financed by her father; and with her aid Billy discovers the hideout of the two men, shoots the gang, and rescues Andrée. *Criminals—Rehabilitation. Dancers. Millionaires. Burglars. Apaches—Paris. Inheritance. Photographs. Paris.*

WHITE ASHES *see* **THE LURE OF YOUTH**

THE WHITE BLACK SHEEP **F2.6293**

Inspiration Pictures. *Dist* First National Pictures. 12 Dec **1926** [c29 Nov 1926; LP23374]. Si; b&w. 35mm. 7 reels, 6,798 ft.

Dir Sidney Olcott. *Adapt* Jerome N. Wilson, Agnes Pat McKenna. *Story* Violet E. Powell. *Photog* David W. Gobbett.

Cast: Richard Barthelmess *(Robert Kincairn)*, Patsy Ruth Miller *(Zelie)*, Constance Howard *(Enid Gower)*, Erville Alderson *(Yasuf)*, William H. Tooker *(Colonel Kincairn)*, Gino Corrado *(El Rahib)*, Albert Prisco *(Kadir)*, Sam Appel *(Dimos)*, Col. G. L. McDonell *(Colonel Nicholson)*, Templar Saxe *(Stanley Fielding)*.

Romantic melodrama. Robert Kincairn, son of Colonel Kincairn of the British Army, assumes guilt for a theft for which his fiancée is responsible; and renounced by his father, he joins the British forces in Palestine. While defending Zelie, a Greek dancer, from the unwelcome advances of El Rahib, a traitorous desert chieftain in the service of the British, Robert is in turn saved by Zelie, who revives his health. In the guise of a mute beggar, he enters El Rahib's camp and learns of his plans to attack the British; he is discovered and tortured, but he escapes and reveals El Rahib's treachery to his father. When the tribesmen are subdued, the colonel discloses that Enid has confessed her part in the theft, thus absolving Robert, who finds happiness with Zelie. *Traitors. Dancers. Greeks. Filial relations. Disguise. Palestine. Great Britain—Army.*

THE WHITE CAT *see* **THE UNTAMEABLE**

THE WHITE DESERT **F2.6294**

Metro-Goldwyn Pictures. 4 May **1925** [c22 Jul 1925; LP21668]. Si; b&w. 35mm. 7 reels, 6,464 ft.

Pres by Louis B. Mayer. *Dir* Reginald Barker. *Scen* L. G. Rigby. *Adapt* Monte M. Katterjohn. *Comedy Relief* Lew Lipton. *Photog* Percy Hilburn.

Cast: Claire Windsor *(Robinette)*, Pat O'Malley *(Barry)*, Robert Frazer *(Keith)*, Frank Currier *(Saul MacFarlane)*, William Eugene *(Foster)*, Roy Laidlaw *(engineer)*, Sojin *(Chinese cook)*, Priscilla Bonner *(Mrs. Foster)*, Snitz Edwards *(Runt)*, Milton Ross *(Dr. Carter)*, Matthew Betz *(Buck Carson)*.

Melodrama. Source: Courtney Ryley Cooper, *The White Desert* (New York 1922). Barry Houston, the superintendent of a gang building a railroad tunnel through a Colorado mountain, warns John Keith, the project engineer, that he is doing too much blasting, thereby placing the crew in danger from avalanches. Attempting to set a record, Keith ignores Barry's advice, and, as a result of continued blasting, there is an avalanche that destroys the line camp, knocking out telegraph lines and the commissary. John and Barry go for help, returning with food and medical aid. Buck Carson, half-crazed by hunger and despair, attacks Robinette, and she throws boiling water in his face; Buck then blindly chases her toward a precipice. Barry saves her from Buck, and she confesses her love for the burly superintendent. *Engineers—Civil. Construction foremen. Railroads. Tunnels. Colorado. Avalanches.*

WHITE FANG **F2.6295**

R-C Pictures. *Dist* Film Booking Offices of America. 24 May **1925** [c24 May 1925; LP21555]. Si; b&w. 35mm. 6 reels, 5,800 ft.

Dir Lawrence Trimble. *Adapt-Scen* Jane Murfin. *Photog* John Leezer, King Gray, Glen Gano. *Asst Dir* George Betherton.

Cast: Theodore von Eltz *(Weadon Scott)*, Ruth Dwyer *(Mollie Holland)*, Matthew Betz *(Frank Wilde)*, Walter Perry *(Joe Holland)*, Charles Murray *(Judson Black)*, Tom O'Brien *(Matt)*, Steve Murphy *("Beauty" Smith)*, John Burch *(Bill Morry)*, Margaret McWade *(Mrs. Black)*, Silver *(a wolf)*, Strongheart *(White Fang, a dog)*.

Western melodrama. Source: Jack London, *White Fang* (New York, 1905). Joe Holland, the superintendent of a gold mine, saves his invalid friend, Weadon Scott, from a pack of wolves. Frank Wilde, an executive engaged to Holland's daughter, Mollie, buys White Fang, a man-eating dog, from an Indian and matches him with a bulldog in a pit fight. Scott rescues the dog and tames him. After Mollie Holland marries Wilde, she discovers that he is robbing the mine. Mollie tells Scott of Wilde's perfidy, but Wilde escapes, blackjacking Scott and killing Holland. Orphaned, Mollie goes to the home of Judson Black, the owner of the mine. Wilde attempts to spirit her away and is killed by White Fang. Scott and Mollie eventually find happiness together. *Mine superintendents. Invalids. Orphans. Indians of North America. Murder. Theft. Gold mines. Dogs. Wolves.*

WHITE FLAME **F2.6296**

I. H. Adam. *Dist* Biltmore Pictures. 20 Mar **1928** [New York State license]. Si; b&w. 35mm. 6 reels, 5,800 ft.

Cast: Mahlon Hamilton, William V. Mong, Eileen Sedgwick.

Society drama(?). No information about the nature of this film has been found.

WHITE FLANNELS **F2.6297**

Warner Brothers Pictures. 19 Mar **1927** [c5 Mar 1927; LP23472]. Si; b&w. 35mm. 7 reels, 6,820 ft.

Dir Lloyd Bacon. *Scen* C. Graham Baker. *Photog* Ed Du Par. *Asst Dir* Ted Stevens.

Cast: Louise Dresser *(Mrs. Jacob Politz)*, Jason Robards *(Frank Politz)*, Virginia Brown Faire *(Anne)*, Warner Richmond *(Ed)*, George Nichols *(Jacob Politz)*, Brooks Benedict *(Paul)*, Rose Blossom *(Berenice Nolden)*, Rosemary Cooper *(Paul's sister)*.

Domestic melodrama. Source: Lucian Cary, "White Flannels," in *Saturday Evening Post* (197:20–21, 27 Jun 1925). Mrs. Jacob Politz, whose son and husband are coal miners, saves for years to send her son, Frank, to college and implores Anne, a girl to whom he becomes engaged, not to stand in the way of his college career. At college Frank's athletic prowess wins him a place on the football team, and he is lionized by the wealthy college set, which spreads the rumor that he is a foreign nobleman. Mrs. Politz and Frank's friend Ed, eager to see Frank play, come to the college town, unknown to each other; and Mrs. Politz obtains work as a waitress in the local cafe. After Frank leads the team to victory, a dinner in his honor is given at the cafe, and when his mother's identity is revealed, Frank's friends turn against him. Returning to the mining town, he saves Ed from a mining disaster, and Anne, who has been betrothed to Ed, is released by him and happily reunited with Frank. *Students. Miners. Mining towns. Family life. College life. Football. Motherhood. Snobbery.*

THE WHITE FLOWER **F2.6298**

Famous Players–Lasky. *Dist* Paramount Pictures. 25 Feb **1923** [New York premiere; released 4 Mar; c21 Feb 1923; LP18722]. Si; b&w. 35mm. 6 reels, 5,731 ft.

Pres by Adolph Zukor. *Dir-Story-Adapt* Julia Crawford Ivers. *Photog* James Van Trees.

Cast: Betty Compson *(Konia Markham)*, Edmund Lowe *(Bob Rutherford)*, Edward Martindel *(John Markham)*, Arline Pretty *(Ethel Granville)*, Sylvia Ashton *(Mrs. Gregory Bolton)*, Arthur Hoyt *(Gregory Bolton)*, Leon Barry *(David Panuahi)*, Lily Philips *(Bernice Martin)*, Reginald Carter *(Edward Graeme)*, Maui Kaito *(kahuna)*.

Melodrama. Konia Markham, the daughter of an American father and a Hawaiian mother, is told by a sorceress that the man who presents her with a perfect white flower will be her true love. When Bob Rutherford offers a gardenia to Konia at a banquet, David Panuahi, a rejected suitor, becomes even more jealous and persuades Konia to have the *kahuna* put a death curse on Bob's fiancée, Ethel Granville. Bob's devotion to a failing Ethel softens Konia, however, and she has the curse removed. She is about to jump into a volcano when Bob—now released by Ethel from their engagement—finds her and declares his love. *Sorcerers. Curses. Volcanoes. Hawaii.*

THE WHITE FRONTIER *see* **SLANDER THE WOMAN**

WHITE GOLD **F2.6299**

De Mille Pictures. *Dist* Producers Distributing Corp. 24 Feb **1927** [New York premiere; released 14 Mar; c8 Mar 1927; LP23762]. Si; b&w. 35mm. 7 reels, 6,108 ft.

Supv C. Gardner Sullivan. *Dir* William K. Howard. *Titl* John Krafft, John Farrow. *Adapt* Garrett Fort, Marion Orth, Tay Garnett. *Photog* Lucien Andriot. *Art Dir* Anton Grot. *Film Ed* Jack Dennis.

Cast: Jetta Goudal *(Dolores Carson)*, Kenneth Thomson *(Alec Carson)*, George Bancroft *(Sam Randall)*, George Nichols *(Carson, Alec's father)*, Robert Perry *(Bucky O'Neil)*, Clyde Cook *(Homer)*.

Drama. Source: J. Palmer Parsons, *White Gold* (New York opening: 2 Nov 1925). Alec Carson, son of an embittered old Arizona sheepherder, marries Dolores, a Mexican dancehall girl, and takes her to the ranch, which is suffering from a drought. Carson strongly resents the girl's intrusion and tries to make his son doubt her fidelity; soon her nerves become strained between the old man's insults and her husband's failure to stand up for her. Sam Randall, a nomadic sheepherder, comes to the ranch looking for work, and Carson hires him when he notes Randall's inclination to flirt with Dolores. Alec, made suspicious by his father, quarrels with his wife, and they part in anger, Alec sleeping in the bunkhouse. That night, Randall sneaks into the girl's bedroom; the following morning Carson declares he caught the guilty couple and killed Randall; Dolores refuses Alec an explanation because of his lack of faith in her. Destroying the evidence of her innocence, she throws the gun with which she shot Randall into a mud hole and walks away to freedom. *Dancehall girls. Ranchers. Sheepherders. Mexicans. Filial relations. Marriage. Jealousy. Drought. Arizona.*

WHITE HANDS **F2.6300**

Graf Productions. *Dist* Wid Gunning, Inc. 9 Jan **1922** [c31 Dec 1922; LP18272]. Si; b&w. 35mm. 6 reels, 5,654 ft.

Prod Max Graf. *Dir-Writ* Lambert Hillyer. *Story* C. Gardner Sullivan. *Asst Dir* Stephen Roberts.

Cast: Hobart Bosworth *("Hurricane" Hardy)*, Robert McKim *(Leon Roche)*, Freeman Wood *(Ralph Alden)*, Al Kaufman *("Grouch" Murphy)*, Muriel Frances Dana *(Peroxide)*, Elinor Fair *(Helen Maitland)*, George O'Brien *(sailor)*.

Melodrama. Sea captain "Hurricane" Hardy goes searching for treasure in the Sahara and encounters Helen Maitland, the last remaining member of a missionary group. Although his intentions are evil, he offers her protection, and they travel towards the coast. While pausing at a hotel Hardy decides to attack Helen, but the touch of the white hands of a child stops him. Hardy is reformed and adopts the child, leaving Helen free to rehabilitate her new love, Ralph Alden, temporary victim of drugs and drinking. *Sea captains. Missionaries. Treasure. Alcoholism. Narcotics. Sahara. San Francisco.*

Note: Exteriors were filmed at Coyote Point, San Francisco Bay, and San Francisco Beach.

WHITE HELL **F2.6301**

Charles E. Bartlett Productions. *Dist* Aywon Film Corp. 1 Sep **1922.** Si; b&w. 35mm. 5 reels, 4,750 ft.

Dir Bernard Feikel. *Story* Leota Morgan.

Cast: Richard Travers *(Dave Manley)*, Muriel Kingston *(Helen Allen)*, J. Thornton Baston *(Hart Kelly)*, Ruth La Marr *(Wauna)*, Charles Graham *(Henry Allen)*, Harry Foulds *(Jim)*.

Northwest melodrama. A village in the "White Hell" region of northern Canada includes among its inhabitants Dave Manley, the upstanding protector of Jim, whose mother was betrayed by evil Hart Kelly; Henry Allen and his beautiful daughter, Helen; and a mysterious Indian squaw with a nearly-white daughter (Wauna). Kelly threatens Allen with the exposure of his fathering of Wauna unless he arranges for the villain's marriage to Helen, who prefers Dave. Kelly further plans to disgrace Dave in Helen's eyes, but in the action that follows crimes are revealed, lovers united, and evil punished. (In another version, which was reviewed closer to the release date, Allen's brother is the father of Wauna.) *Halfcastes. Indians of North America. Perfidy. Canada.*

WHITE MAN **F2.6302**

B. P. Schulberg Productions. 1 Nov **1924.** Si; b&w. 35mm. 7 reels, 6,337 ft.

Dir Louis Gasnier. *Scen* Olga Printzlau, Eve Unsell. *Photog* Karl Struss.

Cast: Kenneth Harlan *(White Man)*, Alice Joyce *(Lady Andrea Pellor)*, Walter Long *(The River Thief)*, Clark Gable *(Lady Andrea's brother)*, Stanton Heck *(Mark Hammer)*.

Melodrama. Source: George Agnew Chamberlain, *The White Man* (Idianapolis, c1919). Lady Andrea, consenting to a loveless marriage with Mark Hammer in order to preserve the ancestral estate of her impoverished family, journeys to South Africa, where her prospective husband owns a diamond mine. On the evening she is to be married, Andrea takes a walk along a deserted beach and meets an aviator, whom she begs to help her get away. He flies her to his camp in the jungle, and there they are stranded when he breaks his propeller during a rough landing. Lady Andrea falls in love with the aviator, who is known as "White Man" and worshipped by the natives as a god. She is later kidnaped by a renegade river thief who attempts to return her to Hammer. The aviator goes in pursuit and kills the river thief. Lady Andrea and the aviator return to London, and she consents to marry him when she discovers that he is an old and trusted friend of her brother. *Aristocrats. Landed gentry. Aviators. Kidnaping. Religion. Diamond mines. South Africa. London.*

THE WHITE MASKS **F2.6303**

William M. Smith Productions. *Dist* Merit Film Corp. Nov **1921** [New York State]. Si; b&w. 35mm. 5 reels.

Dir George Holt. *Scen* Marian Hatch. *Photog* Reginald Lyons.

Cast: Franklyn Farnum *(Jack Bray)*, Al Hart *(Jim Dougherty)*, Virginia Lee *(Olga Swenson)*, Shorty Hamilton *(Battling Rush)*.

Western melodrama. Source: Ett Corr, unidentified story. "Jack Bray is a wanderer in the wilderness of a Western town, governed principally by a band known as the 'six-o-one,' a gang of masked riders. While their original purpose was protection and not disturbance, they are temporarily under the direction of a degenerate, Jim Dougherty, keeper of the saloon. Jim is the unwelcome suitor of Olga Swenson, the pianist in the cafe. Jack falls in love with her and incurs the enmity of Jim. Jack manages Battling Rush in a prize fight which is the event of the season, and in spite of his big opponent and the crooked work of the gang, he wins. Jack finds he has to fight for Olga, but he gets her." (*Moving Picture World*, 1 Jul 1922, p58.) *Wanderers. Pianists. Vigilantes. Saloon keepers. Prizefighting.*

WHITE MICE **F2.6304**

Pinellas Films. *Dist* Associated Exhibitors. 31 Jan **1926** [c22 Jan 1926; LU22289]. Si; b&w. 35mm. 6 reels, 5,412 ft.

Prod Royal W. Wetherald. *Dir* Edward H. Griffith. *Adapt* Randolph Bartlett. *Photog* Marcel Le Picard.

Cast: Jacqueline Logan *(Inez Rojas)*, William Powell *(Roddy Forrester)*, Ernest Hilliard *(Colonel Vega)*, Bigelow Cooper *(R. B. Forrester)*, Lucius Henderson *(General Rojas)*, Marie Burke *(Señora Rojas)*, Harlan Knight *(MacKildrick)*, Reginald Sheffield *(Peter de Peyster)*, F. Vaux Wilson *(Dr. Vicenti)*, William Wadsworth *(Sylvanus Codman)*, Richard Lee *(Manuel)*, George De Richelevie *(El Comandante)*, Vivian Vernon *(La Borrachita)*.

Melodrama. Source: Richard Harding Davis, *White Mice* (New York, 1909). Roddy Forrester, a charter member of the White Mice Club (dedicated to aiding people in distress), is sent by his father to a Latin American republic, where he falls in love with Inez Rojas, the daughter of General Rojas, a former and greatly beloved president of the republic. When Roddy learns that Inez's father is slowly dying in a prison cell, he vows to get him out. Roddy keeps his word: He frees Rojas, winning Inez's love as the result. *Presidents. Filial relations. Prisons. Latin America.*

THE WHITE MONKEY **F2.6305**

Associated Pictures. *Dist* First National Pictures. 7 Jun **1925** [c26 May 1925; LP21492]. Si; b&w. 35mm. 7 reels, 6,121 ft.

Supv Arthur H. Sawyer. *Dir* Phil Rosen. *Titl* Louis Sherwin. *Adapt* Arthur Hoerl. *Photog* Rudolph Bergquist. *Art Dir* M. P. Staulcup. *Film Ed* Teddy Hanscom. *Asst Dir* Al Hall. *Prod Mgr* Barney Lubin.

Cast: Barbara La Marr *(Fleur Forsyte)*, Thomas Holding *(Michael Mont)*, Henry Victor *(Wilfrid Desert)*, George F. Marion *(Soames Forsyte)*, Colin Campbell *(Ethelbert Danby)*, Charles Mack *(Tony Bicket)*, Flora Le Breton *(Victorine)*, Tammany Young *(Bill Hawks)*.

Drama. Source: John Galsworthy, *The White Monkey* (London, 1924). Fleur Forsyte marries Michael Mont, whose best friend, Wilfrid Desert, soon falls in love with her—a love she does nothing to discourage. Wilfrid tells Michael of his love for Fleur, indicating that he will do everything possible in the future to take her away from him. Michael confronts Fleur with Wilfrid's statement, and she professes to be ignorant of any wrongdoing. Michael fires Bicket, one of his shipping clerks, who was caught stealing books. When Bicket is reduced to selling balloons on the streets, his wife, Victorine, goes to Michael for help, and he sends her to Wilfrid, for whom she poses in the nude. Bicket learns about this situation and goes to Michael in a rage; together, the two men go to Wilfrid's studio, where Michael unexpectedly finds Fleur. She quickly assures Bicket that his wife has been faithful to him, for she herself was present each time Victorine posed for Wilfrid. But Michael believes that Fleur herself has been unfaithful, and he leaves her to Wilfrid. Fleur soon realizes that she loves only Michael and goes to him, asking to be taken back. Michael consents, but when Fleur tells him that she is pregnant, he is suspicious of the parentage until Fleur shows him a letter from Wilfrid that proves her fidelity. *Models. Shipping clerks. Peddlers. Artists. Friendship. Pregnancy. Infidelity. Marriage. Nudity. England.*

THE WHITE MOTH **F2.6306**

Maurice Tourneur Productions. *Dist* Associated First National Pictures. 11 May **1924** [c7 May 1924; LP20157]. Si; b&w. 35mm. 7 reels, 6,571 ft.

Prod M. C. Levee. *Dir* Maurice Tourneur. *Scen* Izola Forrester. *Adapt* Albert Shelby Le Vino. *Photog* Arthur L. Todd. *Art Dir* Jack Okey. *Film Ed* Frank Lawrence. *Asst Dir* Scott R. Beal.

Cast: Barbara La Marr *(The White Moth)*, Conway Tearle *(Robert Vantine)*, Charles De Roche *(Gonzalo Montrez)*, Ben Lyon *(Douglas Vantine)*, Edna Murphy *(Gwen)*, Josie Sedgwick *(Ninon)*, Kathleen Kirkham *(Mrs. Delancey)*, William Orlamond *(Tothnes)*.

Melodrama. Robert Vantine, to prevent his brother from marrying The White Moth, a dancer, takes her from Paris to New York and marries her himself. When her former dance partner, Montrez, begins to court her, Vantine discovers his genuine love for her, and they are reconciled after the partner's death. *Dancers. Brothers. Paris. New York City.*

WHITE OAK **F2.6307**

William S. Hart Co. *Dist* Paramount Pictures. 18 Dec **1921** [c15 Aug 1921; LP16860]. Si; b&w. 35mm. 7 reels, 6,208 ft.

Dir Lambert Hillyer. *Adapt* Bennet Musson. *Story* William S. Hart. *Photog* Joe August.

Cast: William S. Hart *(Oak Miller, a gamblin' man)*, Vola Vale *(Barbara, his sweetheart)*, Alexander Gaden *(Mark Granger, a crook)*, Robert Walker *(Harry, Barbara's brother)*, Bert Sprotte *(Eliphalet Moss, a banker)*, Helen Holly *(Rose Miller, Oak's sister)*, Chief Standing Bear *(Long Knife, an Indian chief)*.

Western melodrama. Oak Miller, a card dealer at the Red Front Saloon, is obsessed with desire to punish the man who deceived his sister, Rose, with a promise of marriage. Granger, the man for whom Oak is searching, arrives in disguise, attempts to capture Barbara, Oak's sweetheart and guardian of his sick sister, and plots with Chief Long Knife to attack an emigrant train. After Rose's death, Moss, Barbara's stepfather, is shot by Harry, her brother; and to save her from suspicion, Oak robs Moss's bank. The wagon train on which Barbara and her brother leave town is ambushed by Indians, but a dog brings Miller to the rescue. The Indians are dispersed and the chief is captured, Granger's identity is discovered, and the chief kills him for betraying his daughter. *Gamblers. Settlers. Indians of North America. Brother-sister relationship. Revenge. Breach of promise. Wagon trains. Dogs.*

THE WHITE OUTLAW (Blue Streak Western) **F2.6308**

Universal Pictures. 6 Sep **1925** [c10 Jun 1925; LP21558]. Si; b&w. 35mm. 5 reels, 4,830 ft.

Dir Clifford Smith. *Story* Isadore Bernstein. *Photog* William Nobles.

Cast: Jack Hoxie *(Jack Lupton)*, Marceline Day *(Mary Gale)*, William Welsh *(Malcolm Gale)*, Duke Lee *(James Hill)*, Floyd Shackelford *(cook)*, Charles Brinley *(sheriff)*, Scout *(a horse)*.

Western melodrama. Jack Lupton captures and tames a wild horse known as The White Outlaw, teaching him to do tricks and untie knots. Another cowboy mistreats the horse, and it runs away into the open country. Jack meets with reverses and goes to live with his dog in a line shack. When horses begin to disappear, James Hill, the ranch foreman, who is jealous of Jack's love for Mary Gale, accuses Jack of stealing them. Jack proves his innocence when he demonstrates that The White Outlaw is unlocking barns with his teeth, thereby freeing horses from human servitude. Jack then promises to capture the horse and bring back the missing herd. He finds the herd and returns to inform the local ranchers of its whereabouts. Hill then rides out, intending to drive the herd across the border into Mexico. The cook at the ranch warns the sheriff, and Mary, riding hard to warn Jack, is caught in a stampede. Jack saves Mary, and the sheriff rounds up Hill and his men. *Cowboys. Sheriffs. Ranch foremen. Cooks. Stampedes. Horses. Dogs.*

THE WHITE OUTLAW **F2.6309**

J. Charles Davis Productions. *Dist* Exhibitors Film Corp. 7 Jan **1929.** Si; b&w. 35mm. 5 reels, 4,478 ft.

Dir Robert J. Horner. *Story* Bob McKenzie. *Photog* Ernest Laszlo. *Film Ed* William Austin.

Cast: Art Acord *(Johnny Douglas, White Outlaw)*, Lew Meehan *(Jed Izbell)*, Walter Maly *(his deputy, Bud Mason)*, Howard Davies *(Colonel Holbrook)*, Vivian May *(Janice Holbrook)*, Bill Patton *(Ted Williams)*, Art Hoxie *(Sheriff Ralston of Grant Pass)*, Slim Mathews *(Joe Walton)*, Dick Nores *(Chet Wagner)*, Betty Carter *(her sister, Mary)*.

Western melodrama. No information about the precise nature of this film has been found.

THE WHITE PANTHER **F2.6310**

Phil Goldstone Productions. 22 Jan **1924** [New York showing]. Si; b&w. 35mm. 5 reels, 4,600 ft.

Dir Alvin J. Neitz. *Story* John F. Natteford.

Cast: Rex (Snowy) Baker *(Bruce Wainright)*, Gertrude McConnell *(Irene)*, Phil Burke *(Tommy)*, Lois Scott *(Yasmiri)*, Frank Whitson *(Shere Ali)*, W. H. Bainbridge *(Sir Arthur Fallington)*.

Melodrama. Yasmiri, the daughter of a chieftan of Persian hillsmen, falls in love with Tommy Farrell, an English officer stationed at the Khyber Pass. Yasmiri's family deplores her infatuation and seeks revenge against the British when Tommy dishonors her. They capture Irene, the governor's daughter whom Tommy loves, and plan to sacrifice her. "The White Panther," Bruce Wainright—actually another British officer and champion of victims of the desert bandits—rescues Irene and holds the angry natives at bay until the cavalry arrives. Tommy meets his death in a feud, and Irene and Wainright marry. *Persians. Seduction. Revenge. Colonial administration. Great Britain—Army. Khyber Pass. India. Afghanistan.*

WHITE PANTS WILLIE **F2.6311**

B & H Enterprises. *Dist* First National Pictures. 24 Jul **1927** [c18 Jul 1927; LP24194]. Si; b&w. 35mm. 7 reels, 6,350 ft.

Pres by C. C. Burr. *Dir* Charles Hines. *Adapt* Howard J. Green. *Photog* James Diamond.

Cast: Johnny Hines *(Willie Bascom)*, Leila Hyams *(Helen Charters)*, Henry Barrows *(Philip Charters)*, Ruth Dwyer *(Judy)*, Walter Long *(Mock Epply)*, Margaret Seddon *(Winifred Barnes)*, George Kuwa *(Wong Lee)*, Bozo *(Peaches, an educated goose)*.

Farce. Source: Elmer Holmes Davis, *White Pants Willie* (Indianapolis, 1932). Even though he works in a garage and is bullied by his boss, Mock Epply, Willie Bascom sports a pair of fashionable white trousers that get him into considerable difficulty. Willie meets Helen Charters, daughter of an automobile manufacturer, when they stop on their way to a summer resort. Charters takes an interest in a magnetic bumper device invented by Willie, who gets an opportunity to repair a car and deliver it to the resort, dressed in his white pants and with Wong, a Chinese laundryman, as his chauffeur. Willie is mistaken for a crack polo player, and by bluffing he manages to win a polo game, the admiration of Helen, and Charters' support in promoting his invention. *Inventors. Garagemen. Chinese. Laundrymen. Chauffeurs. Automobile manufacturers. Fashion. Polo. Geese.*

WHITE PEBBLES **F2.6312**

Action Pictures. *Dist* Pathé Exchange. 7 Aug **1927** [c8 Jul 1927; LU24155]. Si; b&w. 35mm. 5 reels, 4,485 ft.

Pres by Lester F. Scott, Jr. *Dir* Richard Thorpe. *Scen* Betty Burbridge. *Story* Reginald C. Barker. *Photog* Ray Ries.

Cast: Wally Wales *(Zip Wallace)*, Olive Hasbrouck *(Bess Allison)*, Walter Maly *(Sam Harvey)*, Tom Bay *(Happy Bill)*, Harry Todd *(Tim)*, K. Nambu *(Ah Wung)*.

Western melodrama. Cattle rustling and the mysterious deaths of hired help cause Bess Allison to write an old friend of her father's for help. The friend's son, Zip Wallace, posing as a tenderfoot, comes instead. Two ranch hands are found dead, each with two white pebbles beneath his head, and it is assumed that the killer and the rustler are the same man. Sam Harvey, the foreman, suspects Zip and sends him to the postmaster, from whom he learns that Harvey had formerly been associated with Bess's father and the sheriff. Harvey tries to frame Zip for another murder, but Ah Wung, the Chinese cook, realizing that Bess loves Zip, confesses to both murders, revealing that Harvey and the victims were stealing her stock; Harvey shoots Ah Wung and is caught by Zip trying to escape. *Cooks. Ranch foremen. Sheriffs. Postmasters. Chinese. Rustling. Murder. Ranch life.*

THE WHITE ROSE **F2.6313**

D. W. Griffith, Inc. *Dist* United Artists. 22 May **1923** [New York premiere; c26 Jul 1923; LP19240]. Si; b&w. 35mm. 12 reels, 12,000 ft. [Released 19 Aug 1923; 10 reels, 9,800 ft.]

Pres by D. W. Griffith. *Dir* D. W. Griffith. *Story-Scen* Irene Sinclair. *Photog* G. W. Bitzer, Hendrik Sartov, Hal Sintzenich. *Set Dsgn* Charles M. Kirk. *Mus Sets* Joseph Carl Breil. *Asst Dir* Herbert Sutch. *Sp Eff* Edward Scholl.

Cast: Mae Marsh *(Bessie Williams, known as "Teazie")*, Carol Dempster *(Marie Carrington)*, Ivor Novello *(Joseph Beaugarde)*, Neil Hamilton *(John White)*, Lucille La Verne *("Auntie" Easter)*, Porter Strong *(Apollo, a servant)*, Jane Thomas *(a cigarstand girl)*, Kate Bruce *(an aunt)*, Erville Alderson *(a man of the world)*, Herbert Sutch *(The Bishop)*, Joseph Burke *(The Landlord)*, Mary Foy *(The Landlady)*, Charles Emmett Mack *(guest at inn)*, Uncle Tom Jenkins *(an old Negro)*.

Melodrama. Joseph Beaugarde, a young, aristocratic southerner studying for the ministry, meets and seduces Bessie Williams, a cigarstand girl who is in love with him. Beaugarde returns to his plantation to prepare for his ordination and his forthcoming marriage to Marie Carrington, a girl of his own social standing. Bessie bears his child and loses her job because of the baby, and some Negro servants give her shelter in a log cabin when she inadvertently wanders near Beaugarde's plantation in search of a resting place. Thinking that she is dying, they call for Beaugarde. Beaugarde repents when he sees Bessie; he marries her immediately and severs his ties with the church. His erstwhile fiancée transfers her affections to another admirer. *Clergymen. Social classes. Negroes. Seduction. United States—South.*

WHITE SHADOWS IN THE SOUTH SEAS **F2.6314**

Cosmopolitan Productions. *Dist* Metro-Goldwyn-Mayer Distributing Corp. 10 Nov **1928** [c17 Nov 1928; LP25845]. Talking sequences, mus score, & sd eff (Movietone); b&w. 35mm. 9 reels, 7,968 ft.

Dir W. S. Van Dyke. *Adtl Dir* Robert Flaherty. *Scen* Jack Cunningham. *Dial-Titl* John Colton. *Adapt* Ray Doyle. *Photog* Clyde De Vinna, George Nagle, Bob Roberts. *Film Ed* Ben Lewis. *Song: "Flower of Love"* William Axt, David Mendoza.

Cast: Monte Blue *(Lloyd)*, Raquel Torres *(Faraway)*, Robert Anderson *(Sebastian)*.

Drama. Source: Frederick O'Brien, *White Shadows in the South Seas* (New York, 1919). Lloyd, a drunken, demoralized white doctor who defends a tribe of Marquesan natives against the greed of Sebastian, an unscrupulous trader, is unjustly accused of a crime and tied to the wheel of a plagued ship that is set adrift. The vessel is wrecked in a typhoon, and Lloyd is washed ashore on an island where the natives, who have never seen a white man before, revere him as a god. Sebastian's trading schooner anchors offshore, and Lloyd pleads with the natives to keep Sebastian and his men off the island; the natives do not heed his advice, however, and Lloyd is shot to death by one of Sebastian's crew. With Lloyd out of the way, Sebastian is free to set up a trading post, cheating the natives and ruining their lives with bad whiskey. *Physicians. Traders. Alcoholism. Plague. South Seas. Marquesas Islands. Typhoons. Shipwrecks.*

Note: Photographed on location in the Marquesas Islands.

THE WHITE SHEEP **F2.6315**

Hal Roach Productions. *Dist* Pathé Exchange. 14 Dec **1924** [c3 Dec 1924; LU20829]. Si; b&w. 35mm. 6 reels, 6,091 ft.

Story-Dir Hal Roach. *Photog* Fred Jackman, George Stevens.

Cast: Glenn Tryon *(Tobias Tyler)*, Blanche Mehaffey *(Patience Matthews)*, Jack Gavin *(Nelse Tyler)*, Robert Kortman *(Milt Tyler)*, Leo Willis *(Mose Tyler)*, Richard Daniels *(Al Morton)*, Chris Lynton *(Judge Matthews)*, J. J. Clayton *(Tom Calvert)*, Dick Gilbert *(Newt Randall)*.

Comedy-melodrama. Mayor Nelse Tyler, who runs a small town by force, has three sons: Milt and Mose, who like nothing better than knocking heads, and Tobias, who is a quiet, thoughtful soul. All three court Patience Matthews, but she favors Tobias, much to the disgust of his roughneck brothers. Tom Calvert tries to displace Nelse as mayor and, failing at that, has him framed for the murder of Newt Randall, who has disappeared without leaving a trace. Nelse is convicted and sentenced to be executed. At the last minute, Tobias discovers where Newt Randall is hiding and brings him back to town in time to save his father's life. *Mayors. Brothers. Filial relations. Murder. Frameup. Capital punishment.*

WHITE SHOULDERS **F2.6316**

Preferred Pictures. *Dist* Associated First National Pictures. Oct **1922** [c6 Sep 1922; LP18200]. Si; b&w. 35mm. 6 reels, 5,966 ft.

Pres by B. P. Schulberg. *Dir* Tom Forman. *Adapt* Lois Zellner. *Story* George Kibbe Turner. *Photog* Joseph Brotherton.

Cast: Katherine MacDonald *(Virginia Pitman)*, Lillian Lawrence *(Mrs. Pitman, her mother)*, Tom Forman *(Robert Lee Pitman, her brother)*, Bryant Washburn *(Cole Hawkins)*, Nigel Barrie *(Clayborne Gordon)*, Charles K. French *(Col. Jim Singleton)*, James O. Barrows *(Judge Blakelock)*, Richard Headrick *(Little Jimmie Blakelock)*, Fred Malatesta *(Maurice, a modiste)*, Lincoln Stedman *("Cupid" Calvert)*, William De Vaull *(Uncle Enoch)*.

Melodrama. Mrs. Pitman seeks a wealthy husband for her daughter, Virginia. The first prospect, Colonel Singleton, insults Virginia and is shot by her brother. They move, assume another name, and find a new suitor, Clayborne Gordon, who changes his mind when he learns of Virginia's past. She then tells her story to poor racing-driver Cole Hawkins, whom actually she loves. He not only accepts her but reveals himself to be one of the wealthiest men in the area. *Fortune hunters. Motherhood. Brother-sister relationship.*

THE WHITE SIN **F2.6317**

Palmer Photoplay Corp. *Dist* Film Booking Offices of America. 24 Feb **1924** [c18 Feb 1924; LP19919]. Si; b&w. 35mm. 6 reels, 6,237 ft.

Dir William Seiter. *Adapt* Del Andrews, Julian La Mothe. *Story* Harold Shumate. *Photog* Max Dupont.

Cast: Madge Bellamy *(Hattie Lou Harkness)*, John Bowers *(Grant Van Gore)*, Francelia Billington *(Grace Van Gore)*, Hal Cooley *(Spencer Van Gore)*, James Corrigan *(Peter Van Gore)*, Billy Bevan *(Travers Dale)*, Norris Johnson *(Grace's aunt)*, Ethel Wales *(Aunt Cynthia)*, Otis Harlan *(Judge Langley)*, Myrtle Vane *(Mrs. Van Gore)*, Arthur Millett *(The Doctor)*, James Gordon *(yacht captain)*.

Melodrama. Smalltown girl Hattie Lou Harkness takes a position as a maid with the Van Gores, a wealthy family bound for the South Seas on their yacht. On board she falls in love with Spencer Van Gore, who "marries" her in a mock wedding with the captain officiating. Learning of the trick, Hattie Lou leaves for New York. Two years later, destitute in the city, Hattie Lou seeks help from the elder Van Gores, who take her and her baby in. She meets Grant Van Gore, a war invalid. Spencer arrives and tells Hattie Lou that the marriage was legal, but he dies when the Van Gore home burns. Grant and Hattie Lou then marry. *Housemaids. Wealth. Marriage—Fake. Yachts. South Seas. New York City.*

THE WHITE SISTER **F2.6318**

Inspiration Pictures. *Dist* Metro Pictures. 5 Sep **1923** [New York premiere; c21 Sep 1923, 12 Jan 1924; LU19430, LP19852]. Si; b&w. 35mm. 13 reels, 13,147 ft. [Released Feb 1924. 10 reels, 10,055 ft. Later, ca17 Apr 1924, cut to 9,361 ft.]

Pres by Charles H. Duell. *Dir* Henry King. *Scen* George V. Hobart, Charles E. Whittaker. *Titl* Will M. Ritchey, Don Bartlett. *Photog* Roy Overbaugh. *Asst Photog* William Schurr, Fernando Risi. *Art Dir* Robert M. Haas. *Film Ed* Duncan Mansfield. *Prod Mgr* Joseph C. Boyle.

Cast: Lillian Gish *(Angela Chiaromonte)*, Ronald Colman *(Capt. Giovanni Severini)*, Gail Kane *(Marchesa di Mola)*, J. Barney Sherry *(Monsignor Saracinesca)*, Charles Lane *(Prince Chiaromonte)*, Juliette La Violette *(Madame Bernard)*, Signor Serena *(Professor Ugo Severini)*, Alfredo Bertone *(Filmore Durand)*, Ramón Ibáñez *(Count del Ferice)*, Alfredo Martinelli *(Alfredo del Ferice)*, Carloni Talli *(mother superior)*, Giovanni Viccola *(General Mazzini)*, Antonio Barda *(Alfredo's tutor)*, Giacomo D'Attino *(solicitor to the prince)*, Michele Gualdi *(solicitor to the count)*, Giuseppe Pavoni *(The Archbishop)*, Francesco Socinus *(Professor Torricelli)*, Sheik Mahomet *(The Bedouin Chief)*, James Abbe *(Lieutenant Rossini)*, Duncan Mansfield *(Commander Donato)*.

Romantic drama. Source: Francis Marion Crawford, *The White Sister* (New York, 1909). Angela Chiaromonte, heir to a vast Italian estate, is left penniless and homeless when her father dies and her half-sister, the

Marchesa di Mola, destroys the will dividing the property between the two daughters. Angela's fiancé, Giovanni Severini, goes to war in Africa, promising marriage on his return. When reports of his death arrive, Angela joins a convent. Severini, taken prisoner, escapes to Italy and there meets Angela, whom he tries to persuade to renounce her vows. Angela rejects him, unable to leave the order. Severini dies helping the townspeople escape the erupting Vesuvius. *Sisters. Nuns. Inheritance. Convents. Religious orders. Italy. Vesuvius.*

THE WHITE SLAVE **F2.6319**

Wolfe Productions. *Dist* Top-Notch Film Exchange. 15 Nov **1929** [New York State license]. Si; b&w. 35mm. 6 reels.

Cast: Charles Vanel, Lucille Barns.

Drama(?). No information about the precise nature of this film has been found. *White slave traffic.*

Note: Country of origin undetermined.

WHITE THUNDER **F2.6320**

Ben Wilson Productions. *Dist* Film Booking Offices of America. 24 May **1925** [24 May 1925; LP21553]. Si; b&w. 35mm. 5 reels, 4,550 ft.

Pres by Ben Wilson. *Dir* Ben Wilson. *Story-Scen* Kingsley Benedict. *Photog* Al Siegler.

Cast: Yakima Canutt *(Chick Richards)*, William H. Turner *(Charles Evans)*, Lew Meehan *(Black Morgan)*, George Lessey *(Sheriff Richards)*, Nell Brantley *(Alice Norris)*, Kingsley Benedict *(Reverend Norris)*.

Western melodrama. During a feud between sheepmen and cattle ranchers, Sheriff Richards is murdered by a man with the ace of spades tattooed on his arm. When he learns of his father's death, Chick Richards returns from college but seems to do nothing to avenge the murder, appearing in public as a sissy dude. Soon after Chick's return, a mysterious white-robed rider appears in town, fighting for the rights of the oppressed sheepmen. Black Morgan, the leader of the cattlemen, attacks Alice Norris, Chick's onetime sweetheart, and The White Rider appears, besting Morgan in a rough fight. The White Rider then removes his robe, reveals himself to be Chick, and arrests Morgan, who has the ace of clubs tattooed on his arm, for the murder of his father. Alice marries Chick. *Dudes. Sheriffs. Sheepmen. Ranchers. Filial relations. Feuds. Murder. Disguise. Tattoos.*

WHITE TIGER (Universal-Jewel) **F2.6321**

Universal Pictures. 17 Dec **1923** [c13 Nov 1923; LP19608]. Si; b&w. 35mm. 7 reels, 7,177 ft.

Dir-Story Tod Browning. *Scen* Tod Browning, Charles Kenyon. *Photog* William Fildew.

Cast: Priscilla Dean *(Sylvia Donovan)*, Matt Moore *(Dick Longworth)*, Raymond Griffith *(Roy Donovan)*, Wallace Beery *("Count Donelli" [Hawkes])*.

Crook mystery-melodrama. Sylvia Donovan, Roy Donovan, and "Count Donelli" are three international crooks who come to America. Sylvia and Roy are unaware that they are brother and sister. The three cooperate to rob wealthy homes by using a gimmick known as a chessplaying machine. Eventually, Sylvia and Roy learn that they are brother and sister and that "Count Donelli," alias Hawkes, killed their father. The detective and Sylvia fall in love. *Detectives. Brother-sister relationship. Robbery. Personal identity. Chess.*

WHO AM I? **F2.6322**

Selznick Pictures. *Dist* Select Pictures. Jul **1921** [c6 Jun 1921; LP16692]. Si; b&w. 35mm. 5 reels, 4,943 ft.

Pres by Lewis J. Selznick. *Dir* Henry Kolker. *Scen* Katherine Reed. *Photog* Max Dupont.

Cast: Claire Anderson *(Ruth Burns)*, Gertrude Astor *(Victoria Danforth)*, Niles Welch *(Jimmy Weaver)*, George Periolat *(John Collins)*, Josef Swickard *(Jacques Marbot)*, Otto Hoffman *(William Zoltz)*.

Melodrama. Source: Max Brand, "Who Am I?" in *Argosy All-Story Weekly* (vols 81–82, Feb–Mar 1918). Ruth Burns is not aware that her father is a professional gambler until she receives a notification of his death and comes to New York. She inherits his gambling palace, and Jimmy Weaver, one of his associates, instructs her in its operation. Informed of her father's debt to John Collins, she gambles to pay off the debt until one of her victims tries to commit suicide and she realizes the wrong she is doing. In a final game she loses her winnings, and Collins not only is unmasked by Jimmy as a cheater but is killed by a woman he deserted. Ruth discovers the debt to have been pure invention and decides to marry Jimmy. *Gamblers. Debt. Suicide.*

WHO ARE MY PARENTS? **F2.6323**

Fox Film Corp. Sep **1922** [Boston premiere; released 26 Nov; c26 Nov 1922; LP19031]. Si; b&w. 35mm. 9 reels, 8,361 ft.

Pres by William Fox. *Dir* J. Searle Dawley. *Scen* Paul H. Sloane. *Photog* Bert Dawley.

Cast: Roger Lytton *(Colonel Lewis)*, Peggy Shaw *(Betty Lewis)*, Florence Billings *(Barbara Draper)*, Ernest Hilliard *(Frank Draper)*, Robert Agnew *(Bob Hale)*, Adelaide Prince *(Mrs. Tyler)*, Niles Welch *(Ken, her son)*, Marie Reichardt *(Hannah)*, Florence Haas, Jimmie Lapsley *(orphan children)*.

Domestic melodrama. Source: Merle Johnson, "The Divine Gift" (publication undetermined). When Colonel Lewis refuses to allow his younger daughter, Betty, to marry Bob Hale, the two elope. Bob is killed in an automobile accident, and when the colonel discovers Betty's pregnancy he takes her away, puts the baby, when it is born, in an orphanage, and tells Betty that the baby died. Betty later marries Ken Tyler, keeping secret (at the colonel's request) her previous marriage. One day while visiting an orphanage with her sister, Barbara, who wants to adopt a child, she finds her own daughter, takes her home, and admits to her husband that she is the child's mother. Ken at first denounces her and threatens to leave; then, persuaded by his own mother, Ken relents and accepts the child. *Orphans. Sisters. Parentage. Motherhood. Marriage. Adoption.*

Note: Known also as *A Little Child Shall Lead Them.*

WHO CARES **F2.6324**

Columbia Pictures. 1 Feb **1925** [c2 Mar 1925; LP21192]. Si; b&w. 35mm. 6 reels, 5,600 ft.

Dir David Kirkland. *Cont* Douglas Doty. *Titl* Walter Anthony. *Photog* Allen Thompson.

Cast: Dorothy Devore *(Joan Ludlow)*, William Haines *(Martin Grey)*, Lloyd Whitlock *(Gilbert Palgrave)*, Beverly Bayne *(Mrs. Hosack)*, Wanda Hawley *(Irene)*, Vola Vale *(Tootles)*, Charlie Murray *(Greaves)*, Vera Lewis *(Grandmother Ludlow)*, Ralph Lewis *(Grandfather Ludlow)*, William Austin *(Dr. Harry Oldershaw)*, Carrie Clark Ward *(housekeeper)*.

Society drama. Source: Cosmo Hamilton, *Who Cares? A Story of Adolescence* (Boston, 1919). Martin Grey offers Joan Ludlow the protection of his name in a companionate marriage; and their life together is a round of dances and dinners. Joan tells Martin, in answer to an unspoken plea in his eyes, that she is still just a kid. At the home of Mrs. Hosack, a social freelancer, Joan meets Gilbert Palgrave, a man whose lack of morals is well covered by his perfect manners. Joan and Palgrave become constant if platonic companions, and Martin spends a few innocent days at home with some friends. Joan returns home with Palgrave to find another woman in her living room, and she suspects the innocent Martin of the worst. Martin goes to his club, and Palgrave attacks Joan. Martin returns and rescues her from a fate worse than death, and Joan tells Martin that all is well between them and that she loves him only. *Socialites. Adolescence. Marriage—Companionate. Lechery.*

THE WHOLE DAMN WAR *see* **THE WHOLE DARN WAR**

THE WHOLE DARN WAR **F2.6325**

Sam Citron. 23 Apr **1928** [New York State license]. Si; b&w. 35mm. 5 reels.

Comedy(?). No information about the precise nature of this film has been found. *World War I.*

Note: May also have been known as *The Whole Damn War.*

THE WHOLE TOWN'S TALKING (Universal-Jewel) **F2.6326**

Universal Pictures. 14 Aug or 26 Dec **1926** [c21 Jul 1926; LP22943]. Si; b&w. 35mm. 7 reels, 6,662 ft.

Pres by Carl Laemmle. *Dir* Edward Laemmle. *Scen* Raymond Cannon. *Photog* Charles Stumar.

Cast: Edward Everett Horton *(Chester Binney)*, Virginia Lee Corbin *(Ethel Simmons)*, Trixie Friganza *(Mrs. Simmons)*, Otis Harlan *(Mr. Simmons)*, Robert Ober *(Donald Mont-Allen)*, Aileen Manning *(Mrs. Van Loon)*, Hayden Stevenson *(Tom Murphy)*, Margaret Quimby *(Sadie Wise)*, Dolores Del Rio *(Rita Renault)*, Malcolm Waite *(Jack Shields)*.

Farce. Source: John Emerson and Anita Loos, *The Whole Town's Talking, a Farce in Three Acts* (New York, 1925). Chester Binney, a wounded war veteran, erroneously believes he is carrying a silver plate in his head and must avoid all excitement. He returns to his hometown, and there his former employer, George Simmons, attempts to arrange a match between Chester (who is to inherit a fortune) and his daughter Ethel. Ethel, however, finds Chester unexciting as a lover; and to enliven the affair, the father invents a lurid past for the boy by displaying a signed photograph of Rita Renault, a famous movie star. Rita, accompanied by her jealous husband, Jack Shields, arrives in the town for a personal appearance. By chance, Jack discovers the photograph of Rita, presumably the property of Chester, and when he sees his wife kissing Chester, a running fight ensues. When Chester discovers he is not ill, he knocks out both Shields and Mont-Allen, another suitor of Ethel's; and he thus wins Ethel. *Veterans. Actors. Smalltown life. Courtship. Jealousy. Motion pictures.*

WHOM SHALL I MARRY **F2.6327**

Sun Motion Pictures. *Dist* Aywon Film Corp. 26 Nov **1926** [New York State license]. Si; b&w. 35mm. 6 reels.

Cast: Wanda Hawley, Elmo Lincoln, Mary Carr.

Melodrama(?). No information about the nature of this film has been found.

Note: May have been "manufactured" in 1920.

WHOOPEE! **F2.6328**

Samuel Goldwyn, Inc. *Dist* United Artists. 7 Sep **1930** [cl Sep 1930; LP1584]. Sd (Movietone); col (Technicolor). 35mm. 12 reels, 8,393 ft.

Pres by Samuel Goldwyn, Florenz Ziegfeld. *Dir* Thornton Freeland. *Scen* William Conselman. *Photog* Lee Garmes, Ray Rennahan, Gregg Toland. *Art Dir* Richard Day. *Film Ed* Stuart Heisler. *Mus Dir* Alfred Newman. *Songs: "Making Whoopee," "Stetson," "My Baby Just Cares for Me," "A Girl Friend of a Boy Friend of Mine"* Gus Kahn, Walter Donaldson. *Song: "I'll Still Belong to You"* Edward Eliscu, Nacio Herb Brown. *Music by* George Olsen and his Orchestra. *Dance Dir* Busby Berkeley. *Sd Engr* Oscar Lagerstrom. *Asst Dir* H. B. Humberstone. *Cost Dsgn* John Harkrider.

Cast: Eddie Cantor *(Henry Williams)*, Eleanor Hunt *(Sally Morgan)*, Paul Gregory *(Wanenis)*, John Rutherford *(Sheriff Bob Wells)*, Ethel Shutta *(Mary Custer)*, Spencer Charters *(Jerome Underwood)*, Chief Caupolican *(Black Eagle)*, Albert Hackett *(Chester Underwood)*, William H. Philbrick *(Andy McNabb)*, Walter Law *(Judd Morgan)*, Marilyn Morgan *(Harriett Underwood)*, Jeanne Morgan, Virginia Bruce, Muriel Finley, Ernestine Mahoney, Christine Maple, Jane Keithley, Mary Ashcraft, Georgia Lerch, Betty Stockton *(showgirls)*.

Musical comedy. Source: Walter Donaldson, Gus Kahn, and William Anthony McGuire, *Whoopee!* (New York opening: 4 Dec 1928). Owen Davis, *The Nervous Wreck* (a play; 1923). Though Sally Morgan has long been in love with Wanenis, an Indian boy who lives near her father's ranch, she is obliged to become engaged to the sheriff while Wanenis is away being educated to the white man's ways. Unwilling to go through with the marriage, Sally prevails upon Henry Williams, an invalid living on the ranch, to take her away in his ramshackle Ford. With her father and the sheriff in pursuit, Sally and Henry run out of gas, but they steal gasoline from a car belonging to a family to whose ranch they later go for food. When the family arrives, Henry, now the cook, disguises himself in blackface. Later they narrowly escape the sheriff and take refuge in an Indian reservation. Wanenis, believing that his race makes his love for Sally impossible, has abandoned white civilization, and Sally is about to be carried off by her father when it is discovered that Wanenis is a white, abandoned at birth; Sally's father now consents to the marriage. *Indians of North America. Invalids. Sheriffs. Cooks. Courtship. Elopement. Racial prejudice. Ranches. Ford automobiles.*

WHO'S CHEATING? **F2.6329**

Dist Lee-Bradford Corp. 7 Apr or 1 Aug **1924.** Si; b&w. 35mm. 5 reels, 4,800 ft.

Dir Joseph Levering. *Story* Dorothy Chappell.

Cast: Dorothy Chappell *(June Waugh)*, Ralph Kellard *(Larry Fields)*, Zena Keefe *(Myrtle Meers)*, Montague Love *(Harrison Fields)*, Marie Burke *(Mrs. Fields)*, William H. Tooker *(John Rogers)*, Frank Montgomery *(Alexander Waugh)*, Edward Roseman *(Steve Bowman)*, Marcia Harris *(Mrs. Freeman)*.

Melodrama. Myrtle Meers breaks her engagement with Larry Fields when he proves to be a coward. Fields goes to work in his father's Pennsylvania coal mines to find his manhood. There he thwarts a plan to control the mines, rescues June Waugh, the girl he loves, and wins self-respect. *Filial relations. Coal mines. Manhood. Pennsylvania.*

WHO'S YOUR FRIEND **F2.6330**

Goodwill Pictures. 16 Dec **1925** [New York State license]. Si; b&w. 35mm. 5 reels, 4,725 ft.

Prod Otto K. Schreier. *Dir-Writ* Forrest K. Sheldon. *Cont* Tay Garnett. *Titl* Garrett Graham. *Photog* Roland Price. *Film Ed* Della M. King.

Cast: Francis X. Bushman, Jr. *(Ken Lanning)*, Jimmy Aubrey *(his valet, Bilkins)*, Patricia Palmer *(Alice Stanton)*, Hal Thompson *(Mr. Stanton)*, Erwin Renard *(Gregory)*, Laura La Verne *(Aunty)*, Hazel Howell *(Yvette)*, William Moran *(Reverend Jenkins)*.

Comedy. The wedding rehearsal for Ken Lanning and Alice Stanton is cut short when the bride-to-be's parents discover another woman in Ken's apartment. The vamp, Yvette, was placed there by Gregory, a jealous suitor who is preferred by Alice's parents. Convinced Ken is a two-timer, Alice decides to marry Gregory. Ken intercepts Gregory en route to the ceremony, knocks him out, and persuades the minister to accompany him to Alice's, where they climb through her window. Alice decides Ken is the one she loves, and the ceremony begins only to be interrupted by the police, who arrest them for housebreaking. They elude the police and again start the wedding when Alice's parents rush in and take the bride away—with Ken and the minister in pursuit. Ken transfers Alice to his car during the chase. They run to a construction job, jump on a hoist, and are married high above the city's street and safely out of reach of further interference. *Vamps. Police. Clergymen. Filial relations. Weddings. Chases.*

WHY ANNOUNCE YOUR MARRIAGE? **F2.6331**

Selznick Pictures. *Dist* Select Pictures. 20 Jan **1922** [c15 Jan 1922; LP17510]. Si; b&w. 35mm. 5 reels, 5,200 ft.

Pres by Lewis J. Selznick. *Dir* Alan Crosland. *Story-Scen* Lewis Allen Browne, Alan Crosland. *Photog* William Wagner.

Cast: Elaine Hammerstein *(Arline Mayfair)*, Niles Welch *(Jimmy Winthrop)*, Frank Currier *(David Mayfair)*, Arthur Housman *(Teddy Filbert)*, James Harrison *(Bobby Kingsley)*, Florence Billings *(Widow Gushing)*, Marie Burke *(Mrs. Jerome)*, Huntley Gordon *(Mr. Walton)*, Elizabeth Woodmere *(Gladys Jerome)*.

Comedy-drama. Arline Mayfair, a successful illustrator, though in love with Jimmy Winthrop, fears that marriage would impair her career. While aiding another young couple to elope, however, Arline and Jimmy decide to marry secretly. When some of Jimmy's garments are found in Arline's studio by visitors, a scandal develops and friends go to Jimmy with the intention of warning him, only to find some incriminating lingerie in his bedroom. Arline decides to leave for the country, and Jimmy follows to her cottage. A burglar from a nearby hotel is chased by an intoxicated guest to Arline's house, and the pursuing crowd find Arline and Jim *en deshabille;* the embarrassing situation is cleared up when the intoxicated gentleman discovers their marriage license. *Careerwomen. Artists. Marriage. Scandal.*

Note: Working title: *The Deceivers.*

WHY BE GOOD? **F2.6332**

First National Pictures. 12 Mar **1929** [c28 Feb 1929; LP168]. Mus score (Movietone); b&w. 35mm. 8 reels, 7,507 ft. [Also si, 3 Mar; 7,067 ft.]

Pres by John McCormick. *Dir* William A. Seiter. *Story-Scen* Carey Wilson. *Titl* Paul Perez. *Photog* Sidney Hickox. *Film Ed* Terry Morse. *Song: "I'm Thirsty for Kisses"* Lou Davis, J. Fred Coots.

Cast: Colleen Moore *(Pert)*, Neil Hamilton *(Peabody, Jr.)*, Bodil Rosing *(Ma Kelly)*, John Sainpolis *(Pa Kelly)*, Edward Martindel *(Peabody, Sr.)*, Eddie Clayton *(Tom)*, Lincoln Stedman *(Jerry)*, Louis Natheaux *(Jimmy)*, Collette Merton *(Julie)*, Dixie Gay *(Susie)*.

Comedy. Pert Kelly, a wild but virtuous young girl, meets Peabody, Jr., at a roadhouse, and they make a date for the following evening. The next day Pert is late for work and is called in to see the personnel manager, who turns out to be her acquaintance of the night before. At the insistence of Peabody, Sr., who owns the store, Pert is fired; Peabody, Jr., however, is still taken with the girl and invites her to one of his parents' swank parties. The elder Peabody remarks to his son that he does not think that Pert is quite nice, and Junior decides to test her virtue. He takes her to a disreputable roadhouse, and she protests long and loud. They are married that same night, and Peabody, Jr., assures his father that Pert is all right. *Salesclerks. Personnel managers. Reputation. Roadhouses.*

Note: Originally scheduled for release as *That's a Bad Girl.*

WHY BRING THAT UP? **F2.6333**

Paramount Famous Lasky Corp. 4 Oct **1929** [New York premiere; released 12 Oct; c14 Sep 1929; LP766]. Sd (Movietone); b&w. 35mm. 10

reels, 7,882 ft. [Also si; 6,036 ft.]

Dir George Abbott. *Dial* George Abbott. *Titl* George Marion, Jr. *Adapt* Hector Turnbull, George Abbott. *Story* Octavus Roy Cohen. *Photog* J. Roy Hunt. *Film Ed* William Shea. *Song: "Do I Know What I'm Doing While I'm in Love"* Leo Robin, Richard Whiting. *Song: "Shoo Shoo Boogie Boo"* Sam Coslow, Richard Whiting. *Rec Engr* Harry D. Mills.

Cast: Charles E. Mack *(Charlie)*, George Moran *(George)*, Evelyn Brent *(Betty)*, Harry Green *(Irving)*, Bert Swor *(Bert)*, Freeman Wood *(Powell)*, Lawrence Leslie *(Casey)*, Helen Lynch *(Marie)*, Selmer Jackson *(Eddie)*, Jack Luden *(treasurer)*, Monte Collins, Jr. *(Skeets)*, George Thompson *(doorman)*, Eddie Kane *(manager)*, Charles Hall *(tough)*.

Comedy-drama. George's partner in vaudeville quits their act, claiming that Betty has broken his heart. George then teams up with Charlie, a stranded trouper, and Irving becomes their manager. Later, in New York, the "Two Black Crows" are starred in their own revue and save to build their own theater on Broadway. Betty comes to the theater with her lover, who poses as a cousin and induces George to hire her. He showers her with jewels and money. She tries to persuade George to invest in oil stock her lover is selling, and though their act is a success, Charlie fires Betty. When Charlie and Betty's lover quarrel, Charlie is injured. Realizing that he has been duped, George is called to the hospital, and in desperation he does bits of the act for Charlie, who, as a result, regains consciousness. *Singers. Chorus girls. Vaudeville. Musical revues. New York City—Broadway.*

WHY GIRLS GO BACK HOME **F2.6334**

Warner Brothers Pictures. 27 Mar **1926** [c3 Apr 1926; LP22564]. Si; b&w. 35mm. 6 reels, 5,262 ft.

Dir James Flood. *Scen* Sonya Hovey. *Adapt* Walter Morosco. *Story* Catherine Brody. *Photog* Charles Van Enger. *Asst Camera* Frank Kesson. *Asst Dir* Ross Lederman.

Cast: Patsy Ruth Miller *(Marie Downey)*, Clive Brook *(Clifford Dudley)*, Jane Winton *(A Model)*, Myrna Loy *(Sally Short)*, George O'Hara *(John Ross)*, Joseph Dowling *(Joe Downey)*, Herbert Pryor, Virginia Ainsworth, Brooks Benedict *(three in the badger game)*.

Comedy-drama. Smalltown girl Marie Downey becomes infatuated with New York actor Clifford Dudley when he visits her town with a road company. Although he encourages Marie's flirtation, he is astonished to learn—as she follows him to New York—that she considers herself engaged to him. Sally Short, his leading lady, tries to comfort the disillusioned girl and gets her a chorus job. When Sally overhears derogatory remarks about Dudley, she defends him, declaring she is his fiancée; as a result she becomes notorious, receives a promotion in the show, and has a success rivaling Dudley's. When her smalltown sweetheart, John, comes to the city, Marie realizes that it is John, not Dudley, she loves; and she returns home. Though received with suspicion by the townsfolk, she is accepted when she contributes money for a new church. *Flirts. Chorus girls. Actors. Smalltown life. Churches. New York City—Broadway.*

WHY GIRLS LEAVE HOME **F2.6335**

Harry Rapf Productions. *Dist* Warner Brothers Pictures. Jul **1921** [c20 Sep 1921; LP16977]. Si; b&w. 35mm. 7-8 reels, 7,000 ft.

Prod Harry Rapf. *Dir-Writ* William Nigh. *Photog* Jack Brown. *Sets* Tilford Studios.

Cast: Anna Q. Nilsson *(Anna Hedder)*, Maurine Powers *(Madeline Wallace)*, Julia Swayne Gordon *(Mrs. Wallace)*, Corinne Barker *(Ethel—Gold Digger)*, Mrs. Owen Moore *(Edith—Gold Digger)*, Kate Blanke *(Mrs. Hedder)*, Claude King *(Mr. Wallace)*, Coit Albertson *(Mr. Reynolds)*, George Lessey *(Mr. Hedder)*, Jack O'Brien *(Joseph)*, Dan Mason *(Dodo)*, Arthur Gordini *(Mr. Jackson)*.

Society drama. Because her father has strict ideas about what clothing his daughter wears and with whom she associates, Anna Hedder leaves home and takes up residence with two girl friends. She meets Madeline Wallace, whose father is extremely lenient, but he soon discovers that she is becoming too indiscriminate in her associates; Madeline rebels, and she is enticed to Anna's apartment by Reynolds, an old roué, while the girls are out. Anna and her friends return in time to save Madeline's reputation; Madeline, having learned her lesson, returns to her father, and Anna's father, having softened his attitude, persuades her also to return home. *Family life. Fatherhood. Reputation.*

WHY LEAVE HOME? **F2.6336**

Fox Film Corp. 25 Aug **1929** [c22 Aug 1929; LP626]. Sd (Movietone); b&w. 35mm. 7 reels, 6,388 ft.

Pres by William Fox. *Assoc Prod* Malcolm Stuart Boylan. *Dir* Raymond Cannon. *Dial* Walter Catlett. *Adapt* Robert S. Carr. *Photog* Daniel Clark. *Film Ed* Jack Murray. *Songs: "Doing the Boom-Boom," "Look What You've Done to Me," "Bonita," "Old Soldiers Never Die"* Sidney Mitchell, Archie Gottler, Con Conrad. *Sd* Frank MacKenzie. *Asst Dir* Clark Murray.

Cast: Sue Carol *(Mary)*, Nick Stuart *(Dick)*, Dixie Lee *(Billie)*, Jean Bary *(Jackie)*, Richard Keene *(José)*, David Rollins *(Oscar)*, Jed Prouty *(George)*, Walter Catlett *(Elmer)*, Gordon De Main *(Roy)*, Ilka Chase *(Ethel)*, Dot Farley *(Susan)*, Laura Hamilton *(Maude)*.

Musical comedy-drama. Source: Russell G. Medcraft and Norma Mitchell, *Cradle Snatchers, a Farce-Comedy in Three Acts* (New York, c1931). Billie, Jackie, and Mary are coquettish chorus girls who happen by the frat house of José, Oscar, and Dick, and they emerge from the encounter with dates for the evening, although they were previously committed to Roy, George, and Elmer, three devious devils who have used duck hunting as the deception for their wives, Ethel, Susan, and Maude. The ladies, feeling themselves somewhat deserted, engage three young bucks at $200 apiece for the soirée, and not only do the three escorts turn out to be none other than José, Oscar, and Dick, but Dame Fortune sends the delirious dozen to the same roadhouse. All the couples eventually get sorted out as Mary happily serenades Dick with "Look What You've Done to Me." *Chorus girls. Flirts. Students. Infidelity. Jealousy. Marriage. Roadhouses. Fraternities.*

Note: Remake of *The Cradle Snatchers*, 1927.

WHY MEN LEAVE HOME **F2.6337**

Louis B. Mayer Productions. *Dist* Associated First National Pictures. 3 Mar **1924** [c12 Mar 1924; LP19986; LP20057]. Si; b&w. 35mm. 8 reels, 8,002 ft.

Pres by Louis B. Mayer. *Dir* John M. Stahl. *Adapt* A. P. Younger. *Photog* Sol Polito. *Art Dir* Jack Holden. *Film Ed* Robert Kern, Margaret Booth. *Asst Dir* Sidney Algier.

Cast: Lewis Stone *(John Emerson)*, Helene Chadwick *(Irene Emerson)*, Mary Carr *(Grandma Sutton)*, William V. Mong *(Grandpa Sutton)*, Alma Bennett *(Jean Ralston)*, Hedda Hopper *(Nina Neilson)*, Sidney Bracey *(Sam Neilson)*, Lila Leslie *(Betty Phillips)*, E. H. Calvert *(Arthur Phillips)*, Howard Truesdell *(Dr. Bailey)*.

Comedy-drama. Source: Avery Hopwood, *Why Men Leave Home* (New York opening: 12 Sep 1922). John and Irene Emerson's marriage begins well enough, but it is not long before John becomes less attentive. Feeling neglected, Irene spends more time with her girl friends, and John, consequently, falls prey to the vamping wiles of his secretary, Jean Ralston. When John comes home from the theater smelling of Jean's perfume, Irene procures a divorce; John then marries Jean. Grandma Sutton cleverly maneuvers John and Irene into her house and has it quarantined. They realize they love each other; John divorces Jean, remarries Irene, and takes her on a second honeymoon. *Secretaries. Marriage. Divorce. Infidelity.*

WHY NOT MARRY? **F2.6338**

Brownie Comedies. *Dist* National Exchanges. Mar **1922.** Si; b&w. 35mm. 5 reels, 4,800 ft.

Pres by Walter L. Johnson. *Dir* John S. Lopez.

Cast: Albert Edward, Margery Wilson, Fred C. Jones, George A. Wright, Ralph Yearsley, Alice Christie, Albert Roccardi, Harold Foshay, Agnes Neilsen.

Comedy-drama. No information about the precise nature of this film has been found.

WHY SAILORS GO WRONG **F2.6339**

Fox Film Corp. 25 Mar **1928** [c16 Mar 1928; LP25087]. Si; b&w. 35mm. 6 reels, 5,112 ft.

Pres by William Fox. *Dir* Henry Lehrman. *Scen* Randall H. Faye. *Titl* Delos Sutherland. *Story* William Conselman, Frank O'Connor. *Photog* Sidney Wagner. *Film Ed* Ralph Dietrich.

Cast: Sammy Cohen *(himself)*, Ted McNamara *(Mac)*, Sally Phipps *(Doris Martin)*, Carl Miller *(John Hastings)*, Nick Stuart *(James Collier)*, Jules Cowles, Noble Johnson *(natives)*, E. H. Calvert *(Cyrus Martin)*, Jack Pennick *(first mate)*.

Farce. In an attempt to win her back, would-be suitor John Hastings invites Doris Martin and her father to take a yacht cruise with him. Her fiancé, James Collier, tries to stowaway and hires two taxicab drivers, Cohen and Mac, to get work on the ship and help him get aboard. When Hastings sees Collier on deck, however, he orders Cohen and Mac to lock him up. Cohen and Mac wake the next morning on the shores of Pago Pago. They wrestle with lions, alligators, and monkeys and are about to be slain by the natives when they are saved by the crew of an American warship. *Sailors. Taxi drivers. Samoa. Pago Pago. San Diego. Lions. Alligators. Monkeys.*

Note: Filmed in Balboa Park, San Diego, and at Laguna Beach and Point Loma. Character names are derived from documentary sources; the final version of the film differs in character names as follows: Cohen, *Sammy Beezeroff;* Phipps, *Betty Green;* Miller, *John Dunning;* McNamara, *Angus McAxle;* Stuart, *Jimmy Collier;* Calvert, *Cyrus Green.*

WHY TRUST YOUR HUSBAND? **F2.6340**

Fox Film Corp. 16 Jan **1921** [c16 Jan 1921; LP16064]. Si; b&w. 35mm. 5 reels.

Pres by William Fox. *Dir* George E. Marshall. *Scen* William M. Conselman. *Story* George E. Marshall, Paul Cazeneuve. *Photog* Lucien Andriot.

Cast: Eileen Percy *(Eunice Day)*, Harry Myers *(Elmer Day)*, Ray Ripley *(Joe Perry)*, Harry Dunkinson *(Uncle Horace)*, Milla Davenport *(Aunt Miranda)*, Jane Miller *(Maud Stone)*, Hayward Mack *(Gilbert Stone)*, Bess True *(Marie, phone girl)*.

Farce. Elmer Day and his wife, Eunice, are visiting Gilbert and Maud Stone, and the two husbands, wishing to attend a masquerade, plead business engagements to escape from their wives. But the wives, discovering the invitation, also attend, and matters are complicated by changes and substitutions of costumes and the appearance of Mrs. Day's aunt and uncle. After a police raid there are general explanations and reconciliations at the police court. *Businessmen. Police. Marriage. Disguise.*

WHY WOMEN LOVE **F2.6341**

Edwin Carewe Productions. *Dist* First National Pictures. 18 Oct **1925** [c15 Oct 1925; LP21909]. Si; b&w. 35mm. 7 reels, 6,723 ft.

Pres by Edwin Carewe. *Pers Dir* Edwin Carewe. *Adapt-Scen* Lois Leeson. *Titl* Ralph Spence. *Ch Photog* Robert B. Kurrle. *2d Photog* Al M. Green. *Art Dir* John D. Schulze. *Film Ed* Edward McDermott. *Asst Dir* Wallace Fox. *Lab Tech* Victor E. Presbrey.

Cast: Blanche Sweet *(Molla Hansen)*, Bert Sprotte *(Olaf Hansen, her father)*, Robert Frazer *(Rodney O'Malley, The Captain)*, Charles Murray *(Josiah Scott* [*Jerry*]*)*, Russell Simpson *(Silas Martin, lighthouse keeper)*, Dorothy Sebastion *(Pearl, his daughter)*, Alan Roscoe *(Charley Watts)*, Fred Warren *(Johnny Hickey)*, Edward Earle *(Ira Meers, the engineer)*.

Melodrama. Source: Willard Robertson, *The Sea Woman* (New York opening: 24 Aug 1925). An oil tanker burns at sea, and Molla Hansen, the captain's daughter, is the only survivor. She is rescued by lighthouse-keeper Silas Martin, who suffers fatal burns. He makes Molla promise to look after his orphan daughter, Pearl. Meanwhile, Molla's grief-stricken fiancé, Capt. Rodney O'Malley, departs on a long cruise. Two years pass. Pearl is seduced by rumrunner Charley Watts, and Molla learns of her pregnancy. Pearl implicates engineer Ira Meers as the man responsible, and Molla holds him at gunpoint at the lighthouse. Pearl then learns that Watts is already married and locks him in the lighthouse tower, fills it with gas, and hurls a lighted lantern at him. Pearl and Watts are killed, but Ira recovers. The explosion signals Rod's ship, and he and Molla are reunited. *Orphans. Rumrunners. Marine engineers. Smugglers. Seduction. Sea rescue. Lighthouses. Ship fires.*

Note: Also released as *The Sea Woman.* Working title: *Barriers Aflame.*

WHY WOMEN REMARRY **F2.6342**

John Gorman Productions. *Dist* Associated Photoplays. 30 Oct **1923** [New York premiere; c27 Mar 1923; LP18822]. Si; b&w. 35mm. 5 reels.

Dir John Gorman. *Story* Van A. James.

Cast: Milton Sills *(Dan Hannon)*, Ethel Grey Terry *(Mary Talbot)*, William Lowery *(Martin Talbot)*, Marion Feducha *(Jimmy Talbot)*, Jeanne Carpenter *(Mildred Talbot)*, Wilfred Lucas *(Mr. Compton)*, Clarissa Selwynne *(Mrs. Compton)*, James Barton *(Don Compton)*, Anita Simons *(Mrs. McKinnon)*, George Hayes *(Tuck McKinnon)*, Thomas McGuire *(Robert Milton)*, Maine Geary *(Billy)*, Carol Holloway *(Dan Hannon's sister)*, W. B. Clarke *(Dan Hannon's sister's first husband)*, Robert Walker *(Dan Hannon's sister's second husband)*.

Domestic crook drama. Martin Talbot, a gambler who mistreats and neglects his family for his own comfort, is killed by Tuck McKinnon, but the blame falls on Don Compton, whose mother was insulted by Talbot, when he is found with the murder weapon. Policeman Dan Hannon, who has taken an interest in Mary Talbot and her children, eventually solves the crime. The wives involved in the case all find new husbands: Mary Talbot marries Dan; Mrs. Compton realizes that Robert Milton, the sweetheart of her youth, is more understanding of her settlement work; jazz-crazed Mrs. McKinnon finds Billy, a musician, more to her liking; and Dan's sister seeks happiness with a new mate. *Widows. Police. Settlement workers. Marriage. Murder.*

WHY WORRY? **F2.6343**

Hal E. Roach Studios. *Dist* Pathé Exchange. 16 Sep **1923** [c11 Aug 1923; LU19294]. Si; b&w. 35mm. 6 reels, 5,500 ft.

Pres by Hal Roach. *Dir* Fred Newmeyer, Sam Taylor. *Story* Sam Taylor. *Photog* Walter Lundin.

Cast: Harold Lloyd *(Harold Van Pelham)*, Jobyna Ralston *(The Nurse)*, John Aasen *(Colosso)*, Leo White *(Herculeo)*, James Mason *(Jim Blake)*, Wallace Howe *(Mr. Pipps)*.

Farce. Wealthy young hypochondriac Harold Van Pelham visits a South American "island of paradise" and encounters a revolution which he believes is staged for his entertainment. Van Pelham enlists the help of Colosso, a giant bodyguard, when he sees that the revolt is genuine; and together they defend themselves against the revolutionaries. After quelling the revolution and receiving the ministration of his charming nurse, Van Pelham discovers he has exchanged his imaginary illnesses for a real sweetheart. *Nurses. Hypochondriacs. Revolutions. South America.*

WICKEDNESS PREFERRED **F2.6344**

Metro-Goldwyn-Mayer Pictures. 28 Jan **1928** [c28 Jan 1928; LP25216]. Si; b&w. 35mm. 6 reels, 5,011 ft.

Dir Hobart Henley. *Scen* Florence Ryerson, Colin Clements. *Titl* Robert Hopkins. *Photog* Clyde De Vinna. *Set Dsgn* Cedric Gibbons, Richard Day. *Film Ed* William Hamilton. *Wardrobe* Gilbert Clark.

Cast: Lew Cody *(Anthony Dare)*, Aileen Pringle *(Kitty Dare)*, Mary McAllister *(Babs Burton)*, Bert Roach *(Homer Burton)*, George K. Arthur *(Leslie)*.

Farce. According to titler Robert Hopkins, "Marriage is like a cafeteria. You take the first thing that looks good ... and pay for it later." Babs Burton loves author Anthony Dare, whom she believes to be a real he-man. Mrs. Dare, knowing that her husband is a fourflusher, lets him elope with Babs, then, with Mr. Burton, follows them to their love nest. Burton, naturally, falls for the deserted wife. The two couples are finally reconciled. *Authors. Marriage. Infidelity.*

Note: Indication in copyright records that the film has sound has not been verified.

THE BLUE MOUNTAIN MYSTERY **F2.6345**

Dist Wid Gunning, Inc. May **1922** [c1 Sep 1922; LP18601]. Si; b&w. 35mm. 5 reels.

Dir-Scen Raymond Longford, Lottie Lyell. *Photog* Arthur Higgins.

Cast: John Faulkner *(Henry Tracey)*, Marjorie Osborne *(Hilda Gordon)*, Bernice Ware *(Pauline Tracey)*, Billy Williams *(Dick Maxon)*.

Mystery melodrama. Source: Harrison Owen, "The Mount Marunga Mystery" (publication undetermined). At the height of a society ball Henry Tracey is found dead, and an inquest reveals that Henry and his daughter, Pauline, had a quarrel earlier that evening and that Hector Blunt, once spurned by Pauline, saw her walking from her father's room with a smoking pistol in her hand. Dick Maxon, Pauline's sweetheart, finds the missing revolver behind a grate in Blunt's room, but Blunt insists that he hid it to protect Pauline. Blunt and Pauline both stand trial; Pauline testifies she remembers nothing that happened on the night of the murder; Blunt is acquitted; Pauline is convicted and sentenced to death. Dick Maxon continues his investigation, with no success. Then, one day, Henry Tracey reappears. "He holds the solution [to the mystery], and the key unlocks the door of Pauline's cell and places her in the arms of those who love her" (copyright synopsis). *Patricide. Capital punishment.*

WIDE OPEN **F2.6346**

Sharlin Productions. *Dist* Sunset Productions. 14 Jan **1927** [New York showing]. Si; b&w. 35mm. 5 reels.

Dir-Scen John Wesley Grey.

Cast: Dick Grace, Grace Darmond, Lionel Belmore, Ernest Hilliard.

Action melodrama. Two men quarrel about the design of an aircraft engine and go their separate ways, each attempting to prove the other wrong by winning an aircraft race with his own version of the design. The son of one of the men, who has been serving in the Air Mail Service, goes to work for his father's rival and falls in love with the rival's daughter. The children together design an engine incorporating elements from both of the rival designs and enter it in the air race, easily winning. The children's love and accomplishments reunite their parents. *Aviation. Airplanes. Airplane racing. Postal service.*

Note: Based apparently on a story, "Out to Win," the authorship of which has not been determined.

WIDE OPEN **F2.6347**

Warner Brothers Pictures. 1 Feb **1930** [c13 Jan 1930; LP992]. Sd (Vitaphone); b&w. 35mm. 7 reels, 6,341 ft. [Also si.]

Dir Archie Mayo. *Scen-Dial* James A. Starr, Arthur Caesar. *Rec Engr* Alex Hurdley.

Cast: Edward Everett Horton *(Simon Haldane)*, Patsy Ruth Miller *(Julia Faulkner/Doris)*, Louise Fazenda *(Agatha Hathaway)*, Vera Lewis *(Agatha's mother)*, T. Roy Barnes *(Bob Wyeth)*, E. J. Ratcliffe *(Trundle)*, Louise Beavers *(Easter)*, Edna Murphy *(Nell Martin)*, Frank Beal *(Faulkner)*, Vincent Barnett *(Dvorak)*, Lloyd Ingraham *(doctor)*, Bobby Gordon *(office boy)*, B. B. B. *(Richards)*, Fred Kelsey *(detective)*, Robert Dudley *(office worker)*.

Farce. Source: Edwin Bateman Morris, *The Narrow Street* (Philadelphia, 1924). Simon Haldane, a timid bachelor, lives alone with his cat and works as bookkeeper for the Faulkner Phonograph Co., and though he offers many improvements, everyone—from Easter, his maid, to Bob Wyeth, the star salesman—treats him shabbily. He resents the attentions of women, particularly those of Agatha, a stenographer with an eye for romance whose marriage proposal is accidentally recorded. But Doris, a stranger, finds his address and comes with her mother to demand that he marry her; when he refuses, she promptly faints and is allowed to stay overnight. Doris gives Simon confidence in his ideas; he is promoted by Trundle, the general manager; and he gives Wyeth a drubbing when he offends one of the ladies. Then Faulkner introduces his daughter, Julia, whom Simon recognizes as Doris; Simon proposes; and they live happily together as man and wife. *Bachelors. Bookkeepers. Stenographers. Inferiority complex. Phonographs. Cats.*

A WIDE-OPEN TOWN **F2.6348**

Selznick Pictures. *Dist* Select Pictures. ca19 Feb **1922** [Indianapolis premiere; released 4 Mar; c10 Feb 1922; LP17564]. Si; b&w. 35mm. 5 reels, 4,650 ft.

Pres by Lewis J. Selznick. *Dir* Ralph Ince. *Scen* Edward J. Montagne. *Story* Earle Mitchell. *Photog* William Wagner.

Cast: Conway Tearle *(Billy Clifford)*, Faire Binney *(Helen Morely)*, James Seeley *(Mayor Morely)*, Harry Tighe *(Tug Wilson)*, Claude Brooks *(Fred Tatum)*, Ned Sparks *(Si Ryan)*, Danny Hayes *(Rufe Nimbo)*, John P. Wade *(Governor Talbot)*, Alice May *(Mrs. Tatum)*, Bobby Connelly *(Governor Talbot as a boy)*, Jerry Devine *(Billy Clifford as a boy)*.

Underworld melodrama. Billy Clifford, who has served a sentence in reform school for a devoted friend, Talbot, later in life becomes a successful gambler. He meets and falls in love with Helen Morely, daughter of the mayor. His partner—advised that the mayor intends to raid his establishment—kidnaps Helen and holds her prisoner as security against the raid. Clifford rescues her as the police arrive but is forced to shoot his partner. Helen's reputation is saved, but Clifford is arrested and sentenced to life imprisonment on a murder charge. An interested friend, however, visits the governor, who intervenes in Clifford's behalf, and following their mutual recognition as childhood friends, Clifford is pardoned by Governor Talbot and wins the love of Helen. *Gamblers. State governors. Mayors. Kidnaping. Murder. Friendship.*

THE WIDOW FROM CHICAGO **F2.6349**

First National Pictures. 23 Nov **1930** [c29 Nov 1930; LP1778]. Sd (Vitaphone); b&w. 35mm. 7 reels, 5,773 ft.

Dir Edward Cline. *Screenplay-Dial* Earl Baldwin. *Story* Earl Baldwin. *Photog* Sol Polito. *Film Ed* Edward Schroeder. *Rec Engr* Clifford A. Ruberg.

Cast: Alice White *(Polly)*, Neil Hamilton *("Swifty" Dorgan)*, Edward G. Robinson *(Dominic)*, Frank McHugh *(Slug)*, Lee Shumway *(Johnston)*, Brooks Benedict *(Mullins)*, John Elliott *(Lieutenant Finnegan)*, Dorothy Mathews *(Cora)*, Anne Cornwall *(Mazie)*, E. H. Calvert *(Captain)*, Betty Francisco *(Helen)*, Harold Goodwin *(Jimmy)*.

Underworld melodrama. Lieutenant Finnegan of the New York Police Department and Jimmy Henderson, youngest detective on the force, board an inbound train trailing "Swifty" Dorgan, a Chicago gangster en route to work for Dominic, a local underworld figure; Dorgan leaps from the train at a bridge crossing and is thought to be killed. Planting a newspaper story that Dorgan escaped from the police, Jimmy assumes the gangster's identity and joins Dominic's gang; but he is shot down by the mob. Determined to avenge her brother's death, Polly poses as Swifty Dorgan's widow and gets work in Dominic's nightclub. When Dorgan actually returns, Polly persuades him to acquiese to her scheme, and he considers reforming. During an attempted holdup, Polly shoots a detective to protect Dorgan and later unwittingly gets a confession from Dominic that he killed her brother; cornered by police, he uses Polly as a shield, but Dominic and Dorgan shoot it out until Dominic is forced to surrender. *Detectives. Gangsters. Revenge. Personal identity. Murder. Impersonation. Nightclubs. New York City. Chicago.*

WIFE AGAINST WIFE **F2.6350**

Whitman Bennett Productions. *Dist* Associated First National Pictures. 12 Sep **1921** [c29 Aug, 28 Sep 1921; LP16919, LP17015]. Si; b&w. 35mm. 6 reels, 5,864 ft.

Pres by Whitman Bennett. *Dir* Whitman Bennett. *Scen* Dorothy Farnum. *Photog* Ernest Haller.

Cast: Pauline Starke *(Gabrielle Gautier)*, Percy Marmont *(Stannard Dole)*, Edward Langford *(Dr. Ethan Bristol)*, Emily Fitzroy *(Mrs. Dole)*, Ottola Nesmith *(Florence Bromley)*.

Melodrama. Source: George H. Broadhurst, *The Price, a Drama* (Philadelphia, 1911). Stannard Dole, an American sculptor, falls in love with model Gabrielle Gautier while vacationing in Paris. He leaves before completing a statue for which she modeled. Later, in New York, Gabrielle discovers that he is married. Although Mrs. Dole refuses him a divorce, he persuades Gabrielle to remain until he can finish the statue; and he places her in the care of a friend, Dr. Ethan Bristol. Dole, who is ill, dies, though not before triumphantly completing his work and learning that Bristol proposes to marry Gabrielle. Dole's wife, in distress, is given a position in the Bristols' home and tries to separate the couple by exposing Gabrielle's former liaison, but their child holds them together. *Sculptors. Models. Physicians. Marriage. Infidelity. Parenthood. Paris. New York City.*

THE WIFE HUNTERS **F2.6351**

Lone Star Motion Picture Co. **1922.** Si; b&w. 35mm. [Feature length assumed.]

Dir Bob White. *Photog* D. Teycer.

Melodrama(?). No information about the precise nature of this film has been found. *Negro life.*

WIFE IN NAME ONLY **F2.6352**

Pyramid Pictures. *Dist* Selznick Distributing Corp. 25 Aug **1923** [c23 Aug 1923; LP19343]. Si; b&w. 35mm. 5 reels, 4,868 ft.

Dir George W. Terwilliger. *Adapt* Adeline Hendricks. *Photog* A. L. Martiner.

Cast: Mary Thurman *(Philippa L'Estrange)*, Arthur Housman *(Victor Harwood)*, Edmund Lowe *(Norman Arleigh)*, William Tucker *(John Dean)*, Florence Dixon *(Madeline Dornham)*, Edna May Oliver *(Mrs. Dornham)*, [Frederick] Tyrone Power *(Dornham)*.

Melodrama. Source: Bertha M. Clay, "Wife in Name Only" (publication undetermined). Wealthy orphan Philippa L'Estrange loves handsome Norman Arleigh and is confident of marrying him until he discloses that he has only brotherly affection for her. Determined to have revenge, Philippa introduces Arleigh to Madeline Dornham and reveals on their wedding day that Madeline, his bride, is the daughter of the man who killed his mother. In the end it is learned that Madeline is Mrs. Dornham's daughter from a previous marriage, not the daughter of a criminal. *Marriage. Murder. Parentage. Revenge.*

WIFE OF THE CENTAUR **F2.6353**

Metro-Goldwyn Pictures. 1 Dec **1924** [c12 Dec 1924; LP20909]. Si; b&w. 35mm. 7 reels, 6,586 ft.

Pres by Louis B. Mayer. *Dir* King Vidor. *Adapt* Douglas Z. Doty. *Photog* John Arnold. *Art Dir* Cedric Gibbons. *Film Ed* Hugh Wynn. *Asst Dir* David Howard. *Cost* Sophie Wachner.

Cast: Eleanor Boardman *(Joan Converse)*, John Gilbert *(Jeffrey Dwyer)*, Aileen Pringle *(Inez Martin)*, Kate Lester *(Mrs. Converse)*, William Haines *(Edward Converse)*, Kate Price *(Mattie)*, Jacquelin Gadsdon *(Hope Larrimore)*, Bruce Covington *(Mr. Larrimore)*, Philo McCullough *(Harry*

Todd), Lincoln Stedman *(Chuck)*, William Orlamond *(Uncle Roger)*.

Domestic drama. Source: Cyril Hume, *Wife of the Centaur* (New York, c1923). Jeffrey Dwyer, a gifted but neurotic novelist, is attracted to Joan Converse, a young and innocent girl, but neglects her when he meets the voluptuous Inez Martin. After a short, passionate affair, Inez discards Jeffrey in favor of Harry Todd, whom she marries; Jeffrey turns to drink and debauchery and no longer writes. When he realizes the waste and futility of his life, he marries Joan, rents a lodge in the mountains, and writes a second and successful novel. He and Joan are happy until Inez, whose marriage has failed, decides that she wants to resume her relationship with him. She rents a lodge near his, and Jeffrey, after a sharp conflict between the idealistic and the sensual in his nature, leaves a letter for Joan, telling her that he is deserting her, and goes to Inez. Quickly realizing, however, that his infatuation with Inez is over, he returns to Joan, who forgives him and gladly welcomes him home again. *Novelists. Marriage. Infidelity. Alcoholism.*

WIFE SAVERS **F2.6354**

Paramount Famous Lasky Corp. 7 Jan **1928** [c7 Jan 1928; LP24839]. Si; b&w. 35mm. 6 reels, 5,434 ft.

Pres by Adolph Zukor, Jesse L. Lasky. *Prod* James Cruze. *Assoc Prod* B. P. Schulberg. *Dir* Ralph Cedar. *Screenplay* Tom J. Geraghty, Grover Jones. *Titl* George Marion, Jr. *Photog* Alfred Gilks, H. Kinley Martin. *Film Ed* George Nichols, Jr.

Cast: Wallace Beery *(Louis Hozenozzle)*, Raymond Hatton *(Rodney Ramsbottom)*, ZaSu Pitts *(Germaine)*, Sally Blane *(Colette)*, Tom Kennedy *(General Lavoris)*, Ford Sterling *(The Tavern Keeper)*, George Y. Harvey *(The Major)*, August Tollaire *(The Mayor)*.

Farce. Source: Paul Frank Wilhelm, Julius Wilhelm and Arthur Wimperis, *Louie the Fourteenth* (adaptation by Wimperis; New York opening: 3 Mar 1925). Louis Hozenozzle and 2d Lieut. Rodney Ramsbottom, two American soldiers, are stationed in Switzerland after World War I. Ramsbottom is in love with Colette, a pretty Swiss girl, and when he receives orders to leave Switzerland he orders Hozenozzle to remain there to protect Colette. General Lavoris, a Swiss, also desires Colette, but she spurns him. Returning home, he has a fake order issued stating that all unmarried women must immediately take husbands. At her request, Hozenozzle marries Colette. Ramsbottom then receives a letter from General Lavoris telling him that he has been doublecrossed, and the lieutenant immediately returns to Switzerland and challenges Hozenozzle to a duel. Colette intercedes, explaining that she married only to save herself from Lavoris. The mayor grants Colette a divorce from Hozenozzle, but all the suitors lose her to a handsome young major. *Courtship. Divorce. World War I. Switzerland. United States Army. Duels.*

THE WIFE WHO WASN'T WANTED **F2.6355**

Warner Brothers Pictures. 12 Sep **1925** [c14 Jul 1925; LP21650]. Si; b&w. 35mm. 7 reels, 6,858 ft.

Dir James Flood. *Scen* Bess Meredyth. *Photog* John Mescall. *Adtl Photog* Bert Shipman. *Asst Dir* James Townsend.

Cast: Irene Rich *(Mrs. John Mannering)*, Huntly Gordon *(John Mannering)*, John Harron *(Bob Mannering)*, Gayne Whitman *(Jerome Wallace)*, June Marlowe *(Mary Paterson)*, Don Alvarado *(Theo)*, Edward Piel *("Slick" Jennings)*, George Kuwa *(Japanese servant)*, Jimmie Quinn *(Simi)*, Wilfred Lucas *(Judge Bledsoe)*, Gertrude Astor *(Greta)*, George Pearce *(editor)*, Elinor Fair *(Diane)*.

Melodrama. Source: Gertie Wentworth-James, *The Wife Who Wasn't Wanted* (London, 1923). Bob Mannering, the son of the district attorney, is a passenger in a car that is involved in a fatal accident, and he assumes the blame for it in order to protect Diane Graham. John Mannering, Bob's father, refuses to intercede on his son's behalf, and Bob's mother, frantic with worry as she sees her son led off to prison, arranges with Jerome Wallace, a candidate for her husband's position, to create a scandal that will prevent her husband's reelection. Mannering finds his wife with Wallace, and they separate. At a country hotel, Diane admits her responsibility for the accident to Mrs. Mannering, and, after narrowly escaping death in a forest fire and a flood, the women return to the city. Diane confesses to the police, Bob is freed, and the Mannerings are reconciled. *District attorneys. Automobile accidents. Elections. Filial relations. Marriage. Scandal. Hotels. Floods. Forest fires.*

A WIFE'S AWAKENING **F2.6356**

Robertson-Cole Co. *Dist* R-C Pictures. 25 Sep **1921** [c16 Sep 1921; LP16963]. Si; b&w. 35mm. 6 reels, 5,800 ft.

Dir Louis Gasnier. *Scen* Joseph Dubray. *Story* Jack Cunningham. *Photog* Joseph A. Dubray.

Cast: William P. Carleton *(Howard)*, Fritzi Brunette *(Florence Otis)*, Sam De Grasse *(George Otis)*, Beverly Travers *(Grace)*, Edythe Chapman *(Mrs. Kelcey)*.

Domestic drama. George Otis, a dishonest promoter who uses his wife to forward his schemes, finds himself in danger of arrest for embezzlement and seeks to cover himself by borrowing from John Howard, his wife's former suitor. Failing, he sends his wife to visit Howard and obtain the loan, but the unhappy wife goes to her mother instead for the money. Caught by a second financial disaster, Otis tries again to persuade his wife to borrow from her former lover. Realizing at last his weakness and deceptiveness, she arraigns him for his liaison with Grace, a society girl, and he threatens to blackmail Howard; but Howard's denunciation renders him helpless, and Florence leaves him for a happier life. *Finance—Personal. Embezzlement. Blackmail. Marriage.*

THE WIFE'S RELATIONS **F2.6357**

Columbia Pictures. 13 Jan **1928** [c14 Feb 1928; LP24991]. Si; b&w. 35mm. 6 reels, 5,508 ft.

Prod Harry Cohn. *Dir* Maurice Marshall. *Adapt* Stephen Cooper. *Story* Adolph Unger. *Photog* Ray June. *Art Dir* Robert E. Lee. *Film Ed* Arthur Roberts. *Asst Dir* Max Cohn.

Cast: Shirley Mason *(Patricia Dodd)*, Gaston Glass *(Tom Powers)*, Ben Turpin *(Rodney St. Clair)*, Armand Kaliz *(Clifford Rathburn)*, Flora Finch *(Mrs. Cyrus Dodd)*, Arthur Rankin *(Bud)*, Maurice Ryan *(Tubby)*, James Harrison *(Jimmy)*, Lionel Belmore *(Cyrus Dodd)*.

Comedy. Aspiring inventor Tom Powers gets a position as caretaker of the Clifford Rathburn estate and invites his impoverished friends to visit him while his employer is away. Rathburn has gone to Palm Beach to visit Cyrus Dodd, millionaire automobile manufacturer whose daughter, Patricia, Rathburn would like to marry. Disliking Rathburn, Patricia slips away to New York, becomes an elevator operator, and meets Powers. They marry and honeymoon at the Rathburn estate. Patricia takes an interest in Tom's invention and persuades her parents to visit them in hopes of securing financial backing for the invention, a new type of automobile paint. Tom's friends pretend to be his servants, making a big impression on the Dodds. Clifford Rathburn arrives home. The friends tie him up in an upstairs bathroom. Freeing himself, he breaks a pipe: water floods through the ceiling and into the dining room just as Dodd is signing a sizable check. The ceiling caves in; Clifford denounces the couple; Mrs. Dodd threatens to have the marriage annulled; but Cyrus Dodd, recognizing the importance of his son-in-law's invention, is happy with his daughter's choice and makes Powers a business partner. *Caretakers. Inventors. Elevator operators. Automobile manufacturers. In-laws. Paint. New York City. Palm Beach.*

A WIFE'S ROMANCE **F2.6358**

Harry Garson Productions. *Dist* Metro Pictures. 17–19 Sep **1923** [New York premiere; released Dec; c9 Oct 1923; LP19488]. Si; b&w. 35mm. 6 reels, 5,169 ft.

Prod Samuel Zierler. *Dir* Thomas N. Heffron. *Scen* Frank Beresford. *Photog* Charles Richardson.

Cast: Clara Kimball Young *(Joyce Addison)*, Lewis Dayton *(John Addison)*, Louise Bates Mortimer *(Isabel de Castellar)*, Albert Roscoe *(Ramón)*, Lillian Adrian *(Joseffa)*, Wedgewood Nowell *(Marquis de Castellar)*, Arthur Hull *(Evan Denbigh)*, Robert Cauterio *(Pablo)*.

Melodrama. Source: H. W. Roberts, "La Rubia" (publication undetermined). Artist-housewife Joyce Addison becomes attracted to Ramón, a Spanish crook whose portrait she is painting, when her diplomat husband neglects her. She sees the futility of her liason with Ramón and calls it off before her marriage is damaged. Her husband, who overhears their parting, determines to reform. *Artists. Diplomats. Infidelity. Spain. Madrid.*

WILD BEAUTY (Universal-Jewel) **F2.6359**

Universal Pictures. 27 Nov **1927** [c30 Jun 1927; LP24136]. Si; b&w. 35mm. 6 reels, 5,192 ft.

Pres by Carl Laemmle. *Dir* Henry MacRae. *Scen* Edward Meagher. *Titl* Tom Reed. *Story* Sylvia Bernstein Seid. *Photog* John Stumar.

Cast: June Marlowe *(Nancy Cunningham)*, Hugh Allan *(Art Hemming)*, Scott Seaton *(Colonel Cunningham)*, Hayes Robinson *(Tom)*, William Bailey *(Jim [Bull] Kennedy)*, J. Gordon Russell *(Davis)*, Jack Pratt *(Jeff Davison)*, Rex *(Thunderhoof, a horse)*, Valerie *(his mate)*.

Melodrama. Art Hemming, a young American soldier, brings a filly that he has saved from shellfire back to his California ranch. He falls in love with Nancy Cunningham, whose father maintains a racing stable; and though in financial difficulty, he hopes to retrieve his fortune in a forthcoming race. Bull Kennedy, hearing of Thunderhoof, a wild horse, plans to capture him and defeat the colonel; he tricks the colonel into a bet, then has his men capture the horse. Thunderhoof escapes and tries to lure the filly, Valerie, away; and the colonel's horse is incapacitated by Thunderhoof in a fight. Kennedy recaptures Thunderhoof, and Art rides Valerie against him as the Cunningham entry; Art wins the race and Nancy, and the colonel pays off the mortage. *Veterans. Horsemen. Horseracing. Mortgages. California. Horses.*

WILD BILL HICKOK **F2.6360**

Famous Players–Lasky. *Dist* Paramount Pictures. 18 Nov **1923** [New York showing; released 2 Dec; c1 Dec 1923; LP19724]. Si; b&w. 35mm. 7 reels, 6,893 ft.

Pres by Adolph Zukor. *Prod-Writ* William S. Hart. *Dir* Clifford S. Smith. *Scen* J. G. Hawks. *Photog* Dwight Warren, Arthur Reeves.

Cast: William S. Hart *(Wild Bill Hickok)*, Ethel Grey Terry *(Calmity Jane)*, Kathleen O'Connor *(Elaine Hamilton)*, James Farley *(Jack McQueen)*, Jack Gardner *(Bat Masterson)*, Carl Gerard *(Clayton Hamilton)*, William Dyer *(Col. Horatio Higginbotham)*, Bert Sprotte *(Bob wright)*, Leo Willis *(Joe McCord)*, Naida Carle *(Fanny Kate)*, Herschel Mayall *(gambler)*.

Western historical drama. The initial scenes, in Washington, depict important political and military persons of the Civil War period. In the aftermath, renowned gunfighter Wild Bill Hickok retires to Dodge City, where he puts aside his weapons and becomes a card dealer. Hickok comes forward when the local lawmen ask him to help rid Dodge City of its lawless elements; he visits General Custer to retrieve his sword, thus symbolizing his return to active life; but McQueen, the gang's leader, escapes. Hickok hunts him down and shoots him, then leaves Dodge City with a broken heart—he fell in love with a woman already married. *United States marshals. Dodge City. Abraham Lincoln. Philip Henry Sheridan. George Armstrong Custer. James Butler Hickok. William Barclay Masterson. Martha Jane Burke.*

WILD BLOOD **F2.6361**

Universal Pictures. 10 Feb **1929** [c1 Mar 1928; LP25032]. Si; b&w. 35mm. 5 reels, 4,497 ft.

Dir Henry MacRae. *Story-Cont* George Morgan. *Titl* Gardner Bradford. *Photog* George Robinson. *Film Ed* Thomas Malloy.

Cast: Rex *(himself, a horse)*, Jack Perrin *(Jack Crosby)*, Ethlyne Clair *(Mary Ellis)*, Theodore Lorch *(Luke Conner)*, Nelson McDowell *(John Ellis)*, Starlight *(herself, a horse)*.

Western melodrama. Luke Conner, saloon keeper and leader of a gang of horsethieves in the little mining town of Red Gulch, attempts to blackmail Jack Crosby, a gambler who has kept his real identity secret from Mary Ellis, daughter of a gold miner. Conner would like to own Mary's pet horse, Rex. His blackmail plot having failed, Crosby attempts to steal Rex and then force his attentions on Mary. Jack Crosby saves Mary while Rex leads Connor over a cliff to fall to his death. Mary allows Jack to explain the reason for his deception, and all is forgiven. *Saloon keepers. Horsethieves. Rustlers. Miners. Blackmail. Horses.*

WILD BORN **F2.6362**

Trem Carr Productions. *Dist* Rayart Pictures. Dec **1927.** Si; b&w. 35mm. 5 reels, 4,367-4,490 ft.

Dir Edward R. Gordon. *Adapt* Arthur Hoerl. *Story* Tom Roan. *Photog* Ernest Depew.

Cast: Tex Maynard, Ruby Blaine, Charles Schaeffer, Jack Anthony, Arthur Witting, Edward Heim, Marshall Ruth, Patsy Page.

Western melodrama. "Young sheriff in love with judge's daughter is framed by crook and serves year in jail for robbery he did not commit. He leaves prison swearing vengeance and learns father has been arrested for murder of his partner. A witness clears older man and ex-sheriff brings man who framed him and murderer to justice aided by girl." (*Motion Picture News Booking Guide,* [14]:295, 1929.) *Sheriffs. Revenge. Murder. Frameup. Prisons.*

THE WILD BULL'S LAIR **F2.6363**

R-C Pictures. *Dist* Film Booking Offices of America. 28 Jun **1925** [c28 Jun 1925; LP21661]. Si; b&w. 35mm. 6 reels, 5,280 ft.

Dir Del Andrews. *Scen* Marion Jackson. *Photog* Ross Fisher. *Asst Dir* Al Werker.

Cast: Fred Thomson *(Dan Allen)*, Catherine Bennett *(Eleanor Harbison)*, Herbert Prior *(James Harbison)*, Tom Carr *(Henry Harbison)*, Frank Hagney *(Eagle Eye)*, Frank Abbott *(Yuma)*, Silver King *(himself)*.

Western melodrama. Source: Frank M. Clifton, "The Wild Bull's Lair" (publication undetermined). Eagle Eye, an embittered Indian college graduate, disguises himself as a white man and persuades James Harbison to create a new breed of cattle by crossing cows with bison. The first of the strain, a wild bull called Diablo, escapes from Harbison's ranch and goes to Skull Mountain, headquarters of a band of savage Indians led by Eagle Eye and dedicated to the destruction of the white man. Eagle Eye trains the bull to lead away the rancher's cattle and to gore anyone who attempts to stop him. Dan Allen is sent by the government to investigate and goes to the Harbison ranch, where he falls in love with Eleanor, the rancher's pretty daughter. Eagle Eye lures Harbison and his daughter to Skull Mountain and sets Diablo loose on them; Dan arrives and overcomes the bull. The Indians are subdued, and Dan marries Eleanor. *Indians of North America. Cattle. Ranches. Bison. Bulls. Horses.*

WILD COMPANY **F2.6364**

Fox Film Corp. 5 Jul **1930** [c16 Jun 1930; LP1382]. Sd (Movietone); b&w. 35mm. 8 reels, 6,666 ft.

Pres by William Fox. *Assoc Prod* Al Rockett. *Dir* Leo McCarey. *Adapt-Dial* Bradley King. *Story* John Stone, Bradley King. *Photog* L. William O'Connell. *Art Dir* Stephen Goosson. *Film Ed* Clyde Carruth. *Mus & Lyr* Jimmy Monaco, Jack Meskill, Cliff Friend, Con Conrad. *Rec Engr* Alfred Bruzlin. *Asst Dir* Virgil Hart. *Cost* Sophie Wachner.

Cast: H. B. Warner *(Henry Grayson)*, Frank Albertson *(Larry Grayson)*, Sharon Lynn *(Sally)*, Joyce Compton *(Anita)*, Claire McDowell *(Mrs. Grayson)*, Mildred Van Dorn *(Natalie)*, Richard Keene *(Dick)*, Frances McCoy *(Cora)*, Kenneth Thomson *(Joe Hardy)*, Bela Lugosi *(Felix Brown)*, Bobby Callahan *(Eddie)*, George Fawcett *(judge)*.

Society melodrama. Source: Philip Hurn, "Soft Shoulders" (publication undetermined). While influential citizen Henry Grayson is celebrating the election of a "reform" mayor, his children, Larry and Anita, are partying at a beachclub. Larry becomes intoxicated; and abandoned by Natalie, his sweetheart, he pays a visit to a speakeasy, where he meets a singer named Sally. Her boyfriend, Joe Hardy, a racketeer, advises her to make a play for Larry so that his father's influence might be invoked in the future. The boy becomes infatuated and showers Sally with costly gifts at his father's expense; angered at his father's reproval, he leaves home and is implicated by Hardy in the robbing of a roadhouse safe. Grayson, Sr., forces a confession from his son, implicating Sally and Hardy, then turns the trio over to the police. Although Larry is convicted of manslaughter, the sentence is suspended and he is paroled in the custody of his father for 5 years. ... *Politicians. Mayors. Racketeers. Singers. Fatherhood. Speakeasies. Robbery. Manslaughter. Parole.*

Note: Songs sung by Sharon Lynn include: "Joe" and "That's What I Like About You."

WILD GEESE **F2.6365**

Tiffany-Stahl Productions. 15 Nov **1927** [c26 Nov 1927; LP24698]. Si; b&w. 35mm. 7 reels, 6,448 ft.

Prod Supv L. L. Ostrow. *Dir* Phil Stone. *Screenplay* A. P. Younger. *Photog* Max Dupont, Earl Walker, Joseph Dubray. *Art Dir* George E. Sawley. *Film Ed* Martin G. Cohn.

Cast: Belle Bennett *(Amelia Gare)*, Russell Simpson *(Caleb Gare)*, Eve Southern *(Judith Gare)*, Donald Keith *(Sven Sandbo)*, Jason Robards *(Mark Jordan)*, Anita Stewart *(Lind Archer)*, Wesley Barry *(Martin Gare)*, Rada Rae *(Ellen Gare)*, Austin Jewel *(Charlie Gare)*, Evelyn Selbie *(Mrs. Klovatz)*, D'Arcy Corrigan *(Mr. Klovatz)*, Jack Gardner *(Skuli)*, James Mack *(Parson)*, Bert Sprotte *(Marshal)*, Bodil Rosing *(Mrs. Sandbo)*, Bert Starkey.

Melodrama. Source: Martha Ostenso, *Wild Geese* (New York, 1925). Twenty-five years ago, before her marriage to Minnesota farmer Caleb Gare, Amelia, then engaged to Mark Jordan, bore Mark's child out of wedlock when he was accidentally killed. Now, Caleb, with his merciless intolerance, uses this knowledge to dominate her as well as her other children: Martin, a soft-eyed youth of 21; Judith, a spirited girl of 19; Ellen, a stupid, nearsighted girl of 16; and young Charlie, a hell-raising imp. Lind Archer, a young schoolteacher, comes to live with the family and becomes friends with Judith, though she abhors the tyranny of Caleb and soon falls in love with Mark Jordan, who works at the Klovatz farm and is actually Amelia's illegitimate son. Judith, who loves Sven Sandbo, longs to be freed of her oppressive yoke and rebels against Caleb, causing her mother at last to show open defiance. To expose her, Caleb summons Mark Jordan to the house; but on the night of the meeting, Caleb falls into quicksand, and they are all liberated by his death. *Farmers. Schoolteachers. Marriage. Family life. Bigotry. Illegitimacy. Quicksand. Minnesota.*

THE WILD GIRL **F2.6366**

Truart Film Corp. 10 Oct **1925** [New York State license]. Si; b&w. 35mm. 5 reels, 4,514 ft.

Dir William Bletcher.

Cast: Louise Lorraine *(Pattie)*, Art Acord *(Billy Woodruff)*, Andrew Waldron *(Grandpapa Toto)*, Rex *(The Dog)*, Black Beauty *(The Horse)*.

Melodrama. While roaming through the woods and taking photographs, Billy Woodruff accidentally encounters Pattie, a wild girl of the forest, who lives in a cabin with her grandfather and her pet dog, Rex. Billy and Pattie are strongly attracted to each other. Lige Blew, a mountaineer, asks Pattie to be his wife, but she will have nothing to do with him. Lige then has Pattie's grandfather framed for murder and sent to jail, leaving Pattie in his power. Rex goes to fetch Billy, and he returns in time to protect Pattie from Lige's overpowering advances. The grandfather is released from jail, and Pattie becomes betrothed to Billy. *Grandfathers. Mountain life. Photography. Murder. Frameup. Horses. Dogs.*

THE WILD GOOSE **F2.6367**

Cosmopolitan Productions. *For* Famous Players–Lasky. *Dist* Paramount Pictures. 5 Jun **1921** [c2 Jun 1921; LP16600]. Si; b&w. 35mm. 7 reels, 6,497 ft.

Dir Albert Capellani. *Story* Gouverneur Morris. *Photog* Harold Wenstrom.

Cast: Mary MacLaren *(Diana Manners)*, Holmes E. Herbert *(Frank Manners)*, Dorothy Bernard *(Mrs. Hastings)*, Joseph Smiley *(Mr. Hastings)*, Norman Kerry *(Ogden Fenn)*, Rita Rogan *(Tam Manners)*, Lucia Backus Seger *(Nou Nou)*.

Melodrama. Source: Gouverneur Morris, "The Wild Goose," in *Hearst's* (vols.34–36, Sep 1918–Aug 1919). Ogden Fenn, a visitor in New York, is attracted to Diana Manners, wife of Frank Manners, an architect who is away on business in San Francisco, and they become involved. The husband returns unexpectedly and learns that his wife loves Fenn. When Diana and Fenn go to the latter's cabin near New York, Mrs. Hastings, who though married loves Frank, persuades him not to interfere because of the effects on his child. Mr. Hastings, learning of his wife's own infidelity, motors to the cabin, forces Fenn into his car, and drives the vehicle over a steep embankment. Mrs. Hastings then brings Manners and Diana back together. *Architects. Marriage. Infidelity. Suicide.*

THE WILD HEART OF AFRICA **F2.6368**

Kenneth R. Walker–Cub Walker. *Dist* Parthenon Pictures, General Pictures. 25 May **1929.** Si; b&w. 35mm. 6 reels, 5,600-5,750 ft.

Dir Cub Walker. *Titl* Charles M. Glouner. *Photog* Kenneth R. Walker. *Film Ed* Charles M. Glouner.

Exploration documentary. A record of the Walker-Arbuthnot African expedition beginning in Egypt and continuing into the jungle. Notably pictured are ancient Egyptian monuments, a trip down the Nile, numerous landscapes, an elephant hunt, and tribal dancing. *Exploration. Jungles. Walker-Arbuthnot African Expedition. Africa. Egypt. Nile River. Thomas S. Arbuthnot. Elephants.*

WILD HONEY (Universal-Jewel) **F2.6369**

Universal Film Manufacturing Co. 6 Mar **1922** [c24 Feb 1922; LP17575]. Si; b&w. 35mm. 7 reels, 6,422 ft.

Pres by Carl Laemmle. *Dir* Wesley Ruggles. *Scen* Lucien Hubbard. *Photog* Harry Thorpe.

Cast: Priscilla Dean *(Lady Vivienne)*, Noah Beery *(Henry Porthen)*, Lloyd Whitlock *("Freddy" Sutherland)*, Raymond Blathwayt *(Sir Hugh)*, Percy Challenger *(Ebenezer Leamish)*, Helen Raymond *(Joan Rudd)*, Landers Stevens *(Wolf Montague)*, Robert Ellis *(Kerry Burgess)*, Wallace Beery *("Buck" Roper)*, Carl Stockdale *(Liverpool Blondie)*, Christian J. Frank *(Repington)*, Harry De Roy *(Koos)*.

Melodrama. Source: Cynthia Stockley, *Wild Honey; Stories of South Africa* (New York, 1914). When Lady Vivienne refuses to marry Henry Porthen, a man of wealth but of poor social bearing, Porthen entices her to his country home with Freddy Sutherland, a spineless young aristocrat of her acquaintance, and, isolating her, places her at Freddy's mercy. Lady Vivienne faints, and on awakening she finds Porthen dead—shot by a jealous secretary. Freddy disappears, fearing implication in the crime. Some years later, while investigating her property in the Transvaal, Vivienne is saved from bandits by Kerry Burgess, a homesteader with whom she falls in love; but she is conscience-stricken (until he confesses his cowardice) upon discovering Freddy in a degenerate state. Wolf Montague, an unscrupulous politician who has been rejected by Vivienne, plots to flood a river valley; Vivienne races against time to warn the settlers and is rescued from the torrent by her lover, Kerry. *Homesteaders. Politicians. Bandits. Murder. England. South Africa—Transvaal. Floods.*

WILD HONEY (Reissue) **F2.6370**

25 May **1922** [New York State license]. Si; b&w. 35mm. 5 reels, 5,675 ft.

Note: Originally released 23 Dec 1918, starring Doris Kenyon.

WILD HORSE MESA **F2.6371**

Famous Players–Lasky. *Dist* Paramount Pictures. 14 Sep **1925** [c15 Sep 1925; LP21823]. Si; b&w. 35mm. 8 reels, 7,164 ft.

Pres by Adolph Zukor, Jesse L. Lasky. *Dir* George B. Seitz. *Screenplay* Lucien Hubbard. *Photog* Bert Glennon.

Cast: Jack Holt *(Chane Weymer)*, Noah Beery *(Bud McPherson)*, Billie Dove *(Sue Melberne)*, Douglas Fairbanks, Jr. *(Chess Weymer)*, George Magrill *(Bert Manerube)*, George Irving *(Lige Melberne)*, Edith Yorke *(Grandma Melberne)*, Bernard Siegel *(Toddy Nokin)*, Margaret Morris *(Sosie)*.

Western melodrama. Source: Zane Grey, *Wild Horse Mesa* (New York, 1928). Bert Manerube interests Lige Melberne in a scheme to capture a herd of wild horses by running them into a barbwire corral. Chane Weymer, a trail rider, realizes that this procedure will maim or kill most of the horses and convinces Melberne to change his plans. Manerube then joins up with the McPherson gang and persuades them to uses the barbwire trap. The men stampede the wild horses toward the wire, and Chane rides out in front of them, leading the horses away from the corral. McPherson is killed by an Indian seeking revenge for the death of his daughter. Chane weds Sue. *Trail riders. Indians of North America. Outlaws. Barbwire. Stampedes. Horses.*

THE WILD HORSE STAMPEDE (Blue Streak Western) **F2.6372**

Universal Pictures. 5 Sep **1926** [c18 Jun 1926; LP22835]. Si; b&w. 35mm. 5 reels, 4,776 ft.

Pres by Carl Laemmle. *Dir* Albert Rogell. *Scen* Doris Malloy. *Photog* William Nobles.

Cast: Jack Hoxie *(Jack Tanner [Parker?])*, Fay Wray *(Jessie Hayden)*, William Steele *(Charlie Champion [Compton?])*, Marin Sais *(Grace Connor)*, Clark Comstock *(Cross Hayden)*, Jack Pratt, George Kesterson, Bert De Marc, Monte Montague *(henchmen)*, Scout *(himself, a horse)*, Bunk *(himself, a dog)*.

Western melodrama. Source: W. C. Tuttle, "Blind Trails" (publication undetermined). Young rancher Jack Tanner, who is in love with Jessie Hayden, offers to corral a herd of wild horses that have been spoiling the neighboring cattle ranges, stopping Champion, who wants to shoot them. Meanwhile, a strange woman (Grace Connor?) meets Jack on the range, and he gives her shelter while he searches futilely for the herd; at length, his horse Scout and dog Bunk corral the horses. Jack wants to propose to Jessie, but when she sees the strange woman, she spurns him and goes to Champion, whose proposal she has rejected; and Champion's men set out to steal the herd. While she and Champion ride to town in a buckboard, the herd is freed and begins to stampede, and Jack, learning that the strange woman is Champion's wife, rides after the endangered buckboard; Champion is flung from the wagon and killed, and Jessie is rescued by Jack. A posse arrests the gang, and the lovers are reunited. *Ranchers. Stampedes. Horses. Dogs.*

WILD JUSTICE **F2.6373**

United Picture Artists. *Dist* United Artists. 6 Jul **1925** [c15 Aug 1925; LP21806]. Si; b&w. 35mm. 6 reels.

Pres by John W. Considine, Jr. *Dir* Chester Franklin. *Story* C. Gardner Sullivan. *Photog* Ray Binger. *Art Dir* Fred Gabourie. *Film Ed* Hal C. Kern.

Cast: Peter the Great *(Arno, a dog)*, George Sherwood *(Dr. Dave Wright)*, Frank Hagney *(Bob Blake)*, Frances Teague *(Polly Ann Hadley)*.

Melodrama. Arno's master is murdered by an unknown assailant, and Bob Blake, a brutal ruffian, takes possession both of the dog and of the late owner's cabin. Arno despises Blake and runs off, seeking protection with Dave Wright, a kindly doctor. Polly Ann Hadley, the dead man's niece, arrives on a visit to her uncle and goes to the cabin now occupied by Blake. Blake seeks to defile her, but Arno comes to her aid, keeping the lecher at bay until Dr. Wright appears. Blake is proven to have killed Arno's master, and Dr. Wright woos and wins Polly Ann. *Physicians. Uncles. Murder. Rape. Dogs.*

WILD MEN AND BEASTS OF BORNEO **F2.6374**

29 Apr **1925** [trade review]. Si; b&w. 35mm. 5 reels.

Photog Lou Hutt.

Travelog. Lou Hutt and his party land in Hong Kong and meet the Sultan of Perak. They then move up river into the interior of Malaya. The leader of a herd of white elephants is trapped in a pit. Hutt and his party visit a Pygmy village. Leopards and a 40-foot python are trapped. *Pygmies. Hong Kong. Malaya. Perak. Borneo. Elephants. Leopards. Snakes.*

WILD MEN OF KALAHARI **F2.6375**

C. Ernest Cadle. *Dist* Talking Picture Epics. 21 Nov **1930**. Si; b&w. 35mm. 5 reels, 4,485 ft.

Dir C. Ernest Cadle. *Film Ed* Paul F. Maschke.

Travelog. An introduction regarding the history of man in Africa precedes the beginning of Dr. Cadle's Denver African Expedition at Cape Town, South Africa. There are visits to Zulu warriors, Bushmen, diamond mines, coconut groves, and Victoria Falls. *Zulus. Bushmen. Diamond mines. Africa. South Africa. Kalahari Desert. Victoria Falls.*

WILD OATS LANE **F2.6376**

Marshall Neilan Productions. *Dist* Producers Distributing Corp. 28 Feb **1926** [c15 Mar 1926; LP22498]. Si; b&w. 35mm. 7 reels, 6,900 ft.

Dir Marshall Neilan. *Adapt* Benjamin Glazer. *Photog* David Kesson, Donald Keyes. *Art Dir* Harold Grieve. *Film Ed* Helen Warne. *Asst Dir* Thomas Held.

Cast: Viola Dana *(The Girl [Marie])*, Robert Agnew *(The Boy)*, John MacSweeney *(The Priest)*, Margaret Seddon *(The Mother)*, George Barnum *(The Father)*, Jerry Miley *(The Dude)*, Scott Welch *(The Detective)*, Robert Brower *(The Kleptomaniac)*, Eddie James *(The Gangster)*, Mitchell Lewis *(The Bum)*.

Melodrama. Source: George H. Broadhurst, *Wild Oats Lane* (New York opening: 6 Sep 1922). Leaving Sing Sing after serving time for theft, The Boy drifts into a small Pennsylvania town and falls in love with Marie, an innocent local girl. The Boy leaves for New York, first obtaining Marie's promise to follow him in a week to become his wife. The Boy runs into some of his former associates in crime, however, and they hold him prisoner until they can pull off a big job. Meanwhile, Marie arrives in the city, and there is no one to meet her. Ashamed to return home, Marie supports herself by prostitution until she is reformed by a kindly priest, who, unknown to her, is also attempting to help The Boy, who has become a dope fiend. The Boy and Marie finally meet and are reconciled. The priest then sends for her parents, and Marie and The Boy are married. *Criminals—Rehabilitation. Drug addicts. Prostitutes. Priests. Pennsylvania. New York City. Sing Sing.*

WILD ORANGES **F2.6377**

Goldwyn Pictures. *Dist* Goldwyn-Cosmopolitan Distributing Corp. 20 Jan **1924** [c15 Jan 1924; LP19826]. Si; b&w. 35mm. 7 reels, 6,837 ft.

Dir-Adapt King Vidor. *Photog* John W. Boyle.

Cast: Virginia Valli *(Nellie Stope)*, Frank Mayo *(John Woolfolk)*, Ford Sterling *(Paul Halvard)*, Nigel De Brulier *(Lichfield Stope)*, Charles A. Post *(Iscah Nicholas)*.

Melodrama. Source: Joseph Hergesheimer, *Wild Oranges* (New York, 1919). Despondent because his new bride has been killed in a carriage accident, John Woolfolk seeks solace cruising in his sailing boat with his cook and only companion, Paul Halvard. The sight of a dilapidated mansion and the odor of oleander and wild orange trees lure him to an island off the Georgia coast to seek fresh water. There he meets unsophisticated Nellie Stope and her fear-crazed grandfather, Lichfield Stope, who are being held in terror by homicidal maniac Iscah Nicholas. While attempting to help the pair escape Nicholas' wrath, Woolfolk falls in love with Nellie. Rowing ashore to rescue her, he finds that Nicholas has killed the old man and has tied Nellie to a bed. After a terrific fight, Woolfolk subdues the madman and escapes to the yacht with Nellie. Following them to the water's edge, Nicholas fires a gun at the boat, injuring Paul Halvard, and is finally killed when a fierce dog that has broken its leash buries its teeth into Nicholas' throat. *Widowers. Yachtsmen. Cooks. Grandfathers. Murder. Insanity. Yachts. Georgia.*

WILD ORCHIDS **F2.6378**

Metro-Goldwyn-Mayer Pictures. 23 Feb **1929** [c28 Jan 1929; LP58]. Mus score & sd eff (Movietone); b&w. 35mm. 11 reels, 9,235 ft. [Also si.]

Dir Sidney Franklin. *Cont* Hans Kraly, Richard Schayer. *Titl* Marian Ainslee, Ruth Cummings. *Adapt* Willis Goldbeck. *Story* John Colton. *Photog* William Daniels. *Art Dir* Cedric Gibbons. *Film Ed* Conrad A. Nervig. *Gowns* Adrian.

Cast: Greta Garbo *(Lili Sterling)*, Lewis Stone *(John Sterling)*, Nils Asther *(Prince De Gace)*.

Romantic drama. John and Lili Sterling embark on a second honeymoon combined with a business trip, to Java. On their liner they meet Prince De Gace, a dashing and amorous fellow, who also owns a Java tea plantation. Unaware that the prince has made advances to his wife, John accepts an invitation to be his guest at the estate. On an inspection of the plantations, they are caught in a rainstorm, and the prince agrees to remain at a native hut and protect Mrs. Sterling. John, returning, sees the shadow of a couple embracing and suspects his wife of infidelity. On a tiger hunt, arranged by the prince, his suspicions are confirmed when Lili runs to the side of the wounded prince; he prepares to leave her, but her love for him is ultimately reaffirmed. *Royalty. Planters. Marriage. Infidelity. Big game. Tea. Ocean liners. Java. Tigers.*

THE WILD PARTY **F2.6379**

Universal Pictures. 9 Oct **1923** [New York premiere; released 22 Oct; c22 Sep 1923; LP19433]. Si; b&w. 35mm. 5 reels, 5,034 ft.

Dir Herbert Blache. *Scen* Hugh Hoffman. *Story* Marion Orth. *Photog* Clyde De Vinna.

Cast: Gladys Walton *(Leslie Adams)*, Robert Ellis *(Basil Wingate/ Stuart Furth)*, Freeman Wood *(Jack Cummings)*, Dorothy Revier *(Blanche Cartwright)*, Sidney De Grey *(Paul Cartwright)*, Lewis Sargent *("Scissors" Hogan)*, Esther Ralston *(Bess Furth)*, Kate Lester *(Mrs. Furth)*, Joseph W. Girard *(Mr. Furth)*, Sidney Bracey *(Jasper Johnston)*, William Robert Daly *(city editor)*.

Comedy-drama. Leslie Adams, secretary to the city editor of a newspaper, persuades him to let her write up a society affair. Her efforts result in a libel suit against the paper, and Leslie is told to prove her story or join the ranks of the unemployed. She fails to prove that she was right, but she wins the love of Stuart Furth, the man who threatened the libel suit. Incidentally, she adjusts the marital affairs of several "misunderstood" couples. *Secretaries. Editors. Reporters. Newspapers. Marriage counsel. Libel.*

Note: Working title: *Notoriety*.

THE WILD PARTY **F2.6380**

Paramount Famous Lasky Corp. 6 Apr **1929** [c5 Apr 1929; LP279]. Sd (Movietone); b&w. 35mm. 7 reels, 7,167 ft. [Also si; 6,036 ft.]

Dir Dorothy Arzner. *Screenplay* E. Lloyd Sheldon. *Dial* E. Lloyd Sheldon, John V. A. Weaver. *Titl* E. Lloyd Sheldon, George Marion, Jr. *Story* Warner Fabian. *Photog* Victor Milner. *Film Ed* Otto Lovering. *Theme Song: "My Wild Party Girl"* Leo Robin, Richard Whiting. *Rec Engr* Earl Hayman. *Wardrobe* Travis Banton.

Cast: Clara Bow *(Stella Ames)*, Fredric March *(Gil Gilmore)*, Shirley O'Hara *(Helen Owens)*, Marceline Day *(Faith Morgan)*, Joyce Compton *(Eva Tutt)*, Adrienne Dore *(Babs)*, Virginia Thomas *(Tess)*, Jean Lorraine *(Ann)*, Kay Bryant *(Thelma)*, Alice Adair *(Maisie)*, Renée Whitney *(Janice)*, Amo Ingram *(Jean)*, Marguerite Cramer *(Gwen)*, Jack Oakie *(Al)*, Phillips R. Holmes *(Phil)*, Ben Hendricks, Jr. *(Ed)*, Jack Luden *(George)*, Jack Raymond *(Balaam)*.

Comedy-drama. Stella Ames, a flapper at an exclusive girls' college, falls in love with Gil Gilmore, the new anthropology professor. Gil rescues Stella from a masher at a roadhouse and falls in love with her as well. Stella's roommate is involved in a minor scandal, and Stella takes the blame, resigning from school. Knowing her innocence, Gil resigns his post and goes to find her. *Flappers. Professors. Reputation. Anthropology. College life. Roadhouses.*

WILD TO GO **F2.6381**

R-C Pictures. *Dist* Film Booking Offices of America. 18 Apr **1926** [c14 Apr 1926; LP22610]. Si; b&w. 35mm. 5 reels, 4,570 ft.

Dir Robert De Lacey. *Story-Adapt* F. A. E. Pine. *Photog* John Leezer. *Asst Dir* John Burch.

Cast: Tom Tyler *(Tom Blake)*, Frankie Darrow *(Frankie Blake)*, Fred Burns *(Simon Purdy)*, Ethan Laidlaw *(Jake Trumbull)*, Earl Haley *("Baldy," a henchman)*, Eugenie Gilbert *(Marjorie Felton)*, Sitting Bull *(himself, a dog)*.

Western melodrama. Tom Blake, en route to the bank to draw money to pay off the mortgage for Felton, his boss, is intercepted by Trumbull, acting for Purdy (who holds the mortgage). Blake escapes and swims ashore to a private school for girls. There he meets Marjorie, Felton's daughter, and on their way to the ranch they are kidnaped by Trumbull and taken to a deserted cabin. There the bandits force Blake to admit that the check obtained from the bank was left in his hat at the time of the holdup; but Frankie, his little brother, delivers the check to Felton just as Purdy is demanding payment. Meanwhile, Blake frees himself from his captors and rescues Marjorie from the clutches of Purdy. *Brothers. Bandits. Mortgages. Kidnaping.*

WILD WEST ROMANCE **F2.6382**

Fox Film Corp. 10 Jun **1928** [c31 May 1928; LP25307]. Si; b&w. 35mm. 5 reels, 4,921 ft.

Pres by William Fox. *Dir* R. Lee Hough. *Scen* Jack Cunningham. *Titl* Delos Sutherland. *Story* John Stone. *Photog* Sol Halperin. *Film Ed* Barney Wolf, J. Logan Pearson. *Asst Dir* David Todd.

Cast: Rex Bell *(Phil O'Malley)*, Caryl Lincoln *(Ruth Thorndyke)*, Neil Neely *(Brake Martin)*, Billy Butts *(The Kid)*, Jack Walters *(sheriff)*, Fred Parke *(Beef Strickland)*, Albert Baffert *(blacksmith)*, George Pearce *(Rev. William Thorndyke)*, Ellen Woodston *(Mrs. Breeze)*.

Western melodrama. "Cowpuncher is in love with minister's beautiful daughter and has as a rival the local bad man, whom he knows is chief of a gang of bandits. When the latter pulls another robbery, the cowboy gets the goods on him and proves to the sheriff and the girl that he is no good." *(Motion Picture News Booking Guide*, [14]:295, 1929.) *Clergymen. Cowboys. Bandits.*

THE WILD WEST SHOW (Universal-Jewel) **F2.6383**

Universal Pictures. 20 May **1928** [c5 Jan 1928; LP24835]. Si; b&w. 35mm. 6 reels, 5,254 ft.

Dir Del Andrews. *Cont* John B. Clymer. *Titl* Garrett Graham. *Adapt* Isadore Bernstein. *Story* Del Andrews, St. Elmo Boyce. *Photog* Harry Neumann. *Art Dir* David S. Garber. *Film Ed* Harry Marker.

Cast: Hoot Gibson *(Rodeo Bill)*, Dorothy Gulliver *(Ruth Henson)*, Allan Forrest *(Alexander)*, Gale Henry *(Zella)*, Monte Montague *(The Goof)*, Roy Laidlaw *(Joe Henson)*, John Hall *(sheriff)*.

Western melodrama. A cowboy goes to work for his girl's father, a circus owner. His rival for the girl stages a holdup and frames the cowboy, who, informed by the girl, joins the sheriff to catch the bandit. *Cowboys. Circus. Wild West shows. Frameup.*

Note: Working title: *Hey Rube!*

WILD, WILD SUSAN **F2.6384**

Famous Players–Lasky. *Dist* Paramount Pictures. 7 Sep **1925** [c9 Sep 1925; LP21803]. Si; b&w. 35mm. 6 reels, 5,774 ft.

Pres by Adolph Zukor, Jesse L. Lasky. *Dir* Edward Sutherland. *Scen* Tom J. Geraghty. *Photog* J. Roy Hunt. *Art Dir* Ernest Fegte.

Cast: Bebe Daniels *(Susan Van Dusen)*, Rod La Rocque *(Tod Waterbury)*, Henry Stephenson *(Peter Van Dusen)*, Jack Kane *(Edgar)*, Helen Holcombe *(Emily Dutton)*, Osgood Perkins *(M. Crawford Dutton)*, Ivan Simpson *(Malcolm)*, Russell G. Medcraft *(Eustace Waterbury)*, Warren Cook *(Chauncey Ames Waterbury)*, Joseph Smiley *(Parker)*, Mildred Ryan *(Edgar's sweetheart)*.

Comedy. Source: Steuart M. Emery, "The Wild, Wild Child," in *Liberty Magazine* (1:13–19, 31 Jan 1925). Susan Van Dusen, an affluent New York girl in search of thrills and laughter, leaves home and finds work with a private detective agency. She meets Tod Waterbury, who, under another name, is working as a cab driver (in search of story material for a novel), and the two fall in love. Tod offers the detective agency a reward to find himself and arranges for Susan to be assigned to the case; since they are constantly together, Susan hasn't a chance in the world of finding him. Susan is assigned to another case and follows a gang of crooks to a dark and deserted house. After a series of harrowing adventures in the house, she comes to realize that the whole affair has been fabricated by Tod and her family to cure her of her lust for adventure. Susan marries Tod, greatly to her own and her father's delight. *Detectives. Taxi drivers. Novelists. Thrill-seeking. Hoaxes.*

THE WILDCAT **F2.6385**

Independent Pictures. 1 Feb **1924**. Si; b&w. 35mm. 5 reels, 4,800 ft.

Cast: Robert Gordon.

Western melodrama. "... dealing with husky young hero who, after fight with stockyards bully, thinking he has killed him, hides in small town. Here he falls in love, incurs the enmity of a local judge and is about to be arrested for murder. The bully turns up and the girl rescues hero." *(Motion Picture News Booking Guide*, 6:74, Apr 1924.) *Judges. Stockyards. Murder.*

THE WILDCAT **F2.6386**

Bear Productions. *Dist* Aywon Film Corp. 24 Mar **1926**. Si; b&w. 35mm. 5 reels.

Dir Harry L. Fraser.

Cast: Gordon Clifford.

Western melodrama(?). No information about the nature of this film has been found.

WILDCAT JORDAN **F2.6387**

Phil Goldstone Productions. 1 Jul **1922**. Si; b&w. 35mm. 5 reels, 4,800 ft.

Dir Al Santell. *Photog* Harry Fowler.

Cast: Richard Talmadge *(Dick Jordan)*, Eugenia Gilbert *(Sylvia Grant)*, Harry Van Meter *(Roger Gale)*, Jack Waltemeyer *(Billy Talbot)*.

Society comedy-drama. Roger Gale invites young westerner Dick Jordan, who has refused Gale's offering price for his ranch, to his eastern home in the belief that sufficient entertaining and excitement will change Jordan's mind. However, Jordan falls in love with society belle Sylvia Grant. Gale recruits Sylvia to his plot and stages her kidnaping; but Jordan turns the tables, finds excitement aplenty, and decides to live on his ranch with Sylvia as his wife. *Socialites. Ranchers. Kidnaping.*

THE WILDERNESS TRAIL *see* **SYMBOL OF THE UNCONQUERED**

THE WILDERNESS WOMAN **F2.6388**

Robert Kane Productions. *Dist* First National Pictures. 9 May **1926** [New York premiere; released 16 May; c29 Apr 1926; LP22656]. Si; b&w. 35mm. 8 reels, 7,533 ft.

Pres by Robert T. Kane. *Dir* Howard Higgin. *Titl* Don Bartlett. *Photog* Ernest Haller. *Art Dir* Robert M. Haas. *Film Ed* Paul F. Maschke. *Prod Mgr* Joseph C. Boyle.

Cast: Aileen Pringle *(Juneau [Junie] MacLean)*, Lowell Sherman *(Alan Burkett)*, Chester Conklin *(Kadiak MacLean)*, Henry Vibart *(The Colonel)*, Robert Cain *(his confederate)*, Harriet Sterling *(squaw)*, Burr McIntosh *(The Judge)*.

Comedy. Source: Arthur Stringer, "The Wilderness Woman," in *Saturday Evening Post* (198:3–5, 20–21, 22–23, 16–30 Jan 1926). Kadiak MacLean, an Alaskan miner, strikes gold, sells his mine for a million dollars, and sets out with his daughter, Junie, for New York. En route, they encounter two confidence men—The Colonel and Robert, his son—who, noticing Kadiak's bankroll, ingratiate themselves. In New York they are met by Alan Burkett, the engineer who appraised their mine; and Skeemo, Junie's pet bear, creates a riot in the hotel lobby. Junie discards her outlandish clothes and blossoms in Fifth Avenue fashions, attracting the attentions of Robert. Meanwhile, Kadiak, having professed a marvelous interest in the subway, is being offered a subway station, with its nickle-turnstile privileges, "at a bargain" by The Colonel, but Kadiak refuses to believe that the trains run under the river. Robert tries to get fresh with Juneau, but she knocks him out before Burkett arrives. All ends happily. *Miners. Confidence men. Engineers—Mining. Nouveaux riches. Subways. New York City. Alaska. Bears.*

WILDFIRE **F2.6389**

Distinctive Pictures. *Dist* Vitagraph Co. of America. 7 Jun **1925** [New York premiere; c2 May 1925; LP21420]. Si; b&w. 35mm. 7 reels, 6,550 ft.

Pers Supv Albert E. Smith. *Dir* T. Hayes Hunter. *Photog* J. Roy Hunt.

Cast: Aileen Pringle *(Claire Barrington)*, Edna Murphy *(Myrtl Barrington)*, Holmes Herbert *(Garrison)*, Edmund Breese *(Senator Woodhurst)*, Antrim Short *(Ralph Woodhurst)*, Tom Blake *(Matt Donovan)*, Lawford Davidson *(John Duffy)*, Arthur Bryson *(Chappie Raster)*, Will Archie *(Bud)*, Edna Morton *(Hortense)*, Robert Billoupe *(valet)*.

Melodrama. Source: George V. Hobart and George H. Broadhurst, *Wildfire* (New York opening: 7 Sep 1908). Claire Barrington, who owns the Duffy racing stables, hopes that her sister, Myrtl, will marry Ralph Woodhurst, whose father is violently opposed to horseracing; in order not to jeopardize the match, Claire lets no one know of her ownership of the establishment. John Duffy, who holds the mortgage on the stable, attempts to use it to force Claire to marry him, but she refuses, citing her love for Garrison, who has been gone for 5 years. Garrison returns just before the big race and, recalling that Duffy persecuted him in the Army, sets out to bankrupt the Duffy stables, not knowing that he is working against the woman he loves. Garrison buys Jackdaw, the only racehorse fast enough to beat Wildfire, the prize Duffy filly. Duffy then sets the Duffy stables on fire in order to discredit Garrison, who is blamed for the fire, and to ruin Claire by killing Wildfire; the horse is saved, however. Duffy hires a jockey named Chappie Raster to ride Wildfire, plotting with him to throw the race. Claire outwits Duffy, however, and Wildfire wins by a nose. Claire and Garrison clear things up between them, and Duffy is left out in the cold. *Veterans. Sisters. Mortgages. Horseracing. Fires.*

WILDNESS OF YOUTH **F2.6390**

Graphic Film Corp. 29 Sep **1922** [c4 Aug 1922; LU18118]. Si; b&w. 35mm. 8 reels, 7,370 ft.

Dir Ivan Abramson. *Story-Scen* Ivan Abramson, Don Dundas. *Photog* Marcel Le Picard. *Set Dsgn* Tri-Art Studios.

Cast: Virginia Pearson *(Louise Wesley)*, Harry T. Morey *(James Surbrun)*, Mary Anderson *(Jule Grayton)*, Joseph Striker *(Andrew Kane)*, Thurston Hall *(Edward Grayton)*, Julia Swayne Gordon *(Mrs. Martha Kane)*, Bobby Connelly *(Teddy Wesley)*, Harry Southard *(Dr. Carlyle Preston)*, Madeline La Varre *(Señora Gonzalez)*, George J. Williams *(Roger Moore)*.

Society melodrama. Andrew Kane, the spoiled and wayward son of once wealthy parents, vies with stockbroker James Surbrun for the hand of Jule Grayton, the wild and willful daughter of a philanthropist. Accused of murdering his rival, Kane is convicted but later cleared of the charge. The "wild" couple settle down and find happiness in reconciliation. *Philanthropists. Stockbrokers. Courtship. Filial relations. Murder.*

WILFUL YOUTH **F2.6391**

Dallas M. Fitzgerald Productions. *Dist* Peerless Pictures. 19 Dec **1927**. Si; b&w. 35mm. 6 reels, 5,644-5,900 ft.

Dir Dallas M. Fitzgerald. *Cont* Ada McQuillan, Gladys Gordon. *Titl* Gardner Bradford. *Photog* Milton Moore. *Film Ed* Desmond O'Brien.

Cast: Edna Murphy *(Edna Tavernay)*, Kenneth Harlan *(Jack Compton)*, Jack Richardson *(Edward Compton)*, Walter Perry *(Terrance Clang)*, James Aubrey *(Steve Daley)*, James Florey *(Bull Thompson)*, Eugenie Forde *(Mrs. Claudia Tavernay)*, Arthur Morrison *(sheriff)*, Barbara Luddy.

Melodrama. Source: Edith Sessions Tupper, "Whispering Pines" (publication undetermined). Jack Compton, the younger brother of a lumber king, is suspected of causing the death of a tragically wronged girl; but his fiancée loyally proves that the guilt rightly belongs to the elder brother, who thereupon commits suicide. *Brothers. Lumbermen. Suicide.*

WILLIAM FOX MOVIETONE FOLLIES OF 1929 *see* **FOX MOVIETONE FOLLIES OF 1929**

WIN, LOSE OR DRAW (Western Gem) **F2.6392**

Maloford Productions. *Dist* Weiss Brothers Clarion Photoplays. 12 Sep **1925** [New York State license]. Si; b&w. 35 um. 5 reels, 4,988 ft.

Dir Leo Maloney. *Story* Ford Beebe.

Cast: Leo Maloney *(Ward Austin/Ben Austin)*, Roy Watson *(U. S. Marshal)*, Whitehorse *(Pierre Fayette)*, Josephine Hill *(Heloise)*, Leonard Clapham *(Fred Holt)*, Bud Osborne *(Barney Sims)*, Bullet *(thd dog)*, Senator *(the horse)*.

Western melodrama. No information about the precise nature of this film has been found. *United States marshals. Indians of North America. Dogs. Horses.*

WIN THAT GIRL **F2.6393**

Fox Film Corp. 16 Sep **1928** [c11 Sep 1928; LP25613]. Sd eff & mus score (Movietone); b&w. 35mm. 6 reels, 5,337 ft.

Pres by William Fox. *Dir* David Butler. *Scen* John Stone. *Titl* Dudley Early. *Photog* Glen MacWilliams. *Film Ed* Irene Morra. *Asst Dir* Leslie Selander.

Cast: David Rollins *(Johnny Norton, 3d)*, Sue Carol *(Gloria Havens)*, Tom Elliott *(Larry Brawn, 3d)*, Roscoe Karns *(Johnny Norton, 2d)*, Olin Francis *(Larry Brawn, 2d)*, Mack Fluker *(Johnny Norton, 1st)*, Sidney Bracey *(Larry Brawn, 1st)*, Janet MacLeod *(Clara Gentle)*, Maxine Shelly *(1880 girl)*, Betty Recklaw *(1905 girl)*.

Comedy. Source: James Hopper, "Father and Son," in *Saturday Evening Post* (25 Oct 1924). A gridiron rivalry between two colleges is entering its third generation, and the Norton family (father and grandfather were members of teams defeated by rival squads captained by members of the Brawn family) rears Johnny Norton, 3d, to be a star football player. The lad is underweight, however, and initially shows a talent only for drop kicking. During the big game, Johnny is substituted for another player and leads his team to victory, winning for himself the love of Gloria Havens. *College life. Football.*

THE WIND **F2.6394**

Metro-Goldwyn-Mayer Corp. 23 Nov **1928** [c10 Nov 1928; LP25816]. Talking sequences & sd eff (Movietone); b&w. 35mm. 8 reels, 6,721 ft. [Also si.]

Dir Victor Seastrom. *Scen* Frances Marion. *Titl* John Colton. *Camera* John Arnold. *Set Dsgn* Cedric Gibbons, Edward Withers. *Film Ed* Conrad A. Nervig. *Theme Song: "Love Brought the Sunshine"* Herman Ruby, William Axt, Dave Dreyer, David Mendoza. *Asst Dir* Harold S. Bucquet. *Wardrobe* André-ani.

Cast: Lillian Gish *(Letty)*, Lars Hanson *(Lige)*, Montagu Love *(Roddy)*, Dorothy Cumming *(Cora)*, Edward Earle *(Beverly)*, William Orlamond *(Sourdough)*, Laon Ramon, Carmencita Johnson, Billy Kent Schaefer *(Cora's children)*.

Melodrama. Source: Dorothy Scarborough, *The Wind* (New York & London, 1925). Letty, a girl from Virginia, trainbound for her cousin's ranch in the western prairies, meets Roddy, who hints at a marriage proposal. At the ranch, Cora's children and husband become too fond of Letty, and she is forced to leave. With nowhere to go, she decides to accept Roddy's implied invitation to become his wife. When she discovers him already married, she hastily marries Lige, a roughhewn son of the soil at whom she had previously scoffed. While Lige is away for a round-up of wild horses during a particularly fierce windstorm, Roddy forces his way into Lige's home and stays the night with Letty, urging her to go with him in the morning. She refuses, shoots him when he becomes insistent, laboriously drags his body outside, and buries it in the shifting sand. Letty spends a day of terror that approaches madness; but Lige returns, and Letty decides that she no longer wishes to return to Virginia—they will face the wind together. *Drudges. Cousins. Virginians. Seduction. Wind.*

Note: Originally, the film's ending followed the novel's: Letty, driven insane, wanders off into the desert. Studio officials required a happy ending, however, before the film's release.

THE WINDING STAIR **F2.6395**

Fox Film Corp. 25 Oct **1925** [c18 Oct 1925; LP21926]. Si; b&w. 35mm. 6 reels, ca6,100 ft.

Pres by William Fox. *Dir* John Griffith Wray. *Scen* Julian La Mothe. *Photog* Karl Struss.

Cast: Alma Rubens *(Marguerite)*, Edmund Lowe *(Paul)*, Warner Oland *(Petras)*, Mahlon Hamilton *(Gerard)*, Emily Fitzroy *(Madame Muller)*, Chester Conklin *(Onery)*, Frank Leigh *(Andrea)*.

Romantic drama. Source: Alfred Edward Woodley Mason, *The Winding Stair* (New York, 1923). Paul Ravenal, an officer in the French Foreign Legion, falls in love with Marguerite Lambert, who through unfortunate circumstances is a dancer in the notorious Iris Cafe in Morocco. He is ordered to quell an uprising among the Riffs but learns that the uprising is a ruse to enable the natives to precipitate a massacre in the city. His superiors will not listen to him, and he returns to town, disguised as a native, and saves his sweetheart and the Europeans. Cast out as a deserter, he organizes a regiment of natives when the World War breaks out and under an assumed name offers them to France. His heroism on Flanders' Fields restores his honors and citizenship. Wounded, he is rejoined by Marguerite, who is serving as a Red Cross nurse, and she becomes his wife. *Riffs. Dancers. Nurses. World War I. Flanders' Fields. Morocco. France—Army—Foreign Legion.*

THE WINDING TRAIL **F2.6396**

Victor Kremer Film Features. 5 Feb **1921** [trade review]. Si; b&w. 35mm. 5 reels.

Dir George Martin. *Film Ed* J. N. Haron.

Cast: Marjorie Clifford *(Alene Hamlin)*, Buck Manning *("Laughing Larry")*, William V. Mong.

Western melodrama. "'Laughing Larry' proposes to Alene Hamlin and is accepted by her. The girl had several suitors, one of whom takes his defeat with a smile, although he is nearly lynched, the villagers accusing him of having cowardly shot Larry when the latter is bit by a rattlesnake. Larry, however, is saved by Indians and recovers in time to save his friend. Later Alene's father, pressed for money, is tempted to rob the savings of his men. The theft is discovered by Larry, who shoots him, but on seeing it is Hamlin he hides him. Suspicion turns to him. Repentant, the old man resolves to right what wrong he has done, but this he finally does with the help of Larry, who advances the money to the boys, while Hamlin re-establishes himself and saves the ranch. Finally he makes a confession and all hands are made happy, but not until after a series of thrilling happenings in which the happy-go-lucky hero is almost hanged." (*Exhibitor's Trade Review,* 5 Feb 1921, p978.) *Ranchers. Indians of North America. Embezzlement. Courtship.*

THE WINDJAMMER **F2.6397**

Harry J. Brown Productions. *Dist* Rayart Pictures. 10 Jun **1926** [New York State license]. Si; b&w. 35mm. 5 reels, 5,016 ft.

Dir Harry J. Brown. *Scen* Grover Jones.

Cast: Billy Sullivan.

Action melodrama. "Plot concerns young milksop who in spite of his fearful attitude towards things physical, triumphs over prize-ring champion winner, gets admiration of girl whom he loves and saves fortunes of her father." (*Motion Picture News Booking Guide,* 11:55, Oct 1926.) *Prizefighting. Courage.*

WINDS OF CHANCE **F2.6398**

First National Pictures. ca16 Aug **1925** [New York premiere; c20 Aug 1925; LP21736]. Si; b&w. 35mm. 10 reels, 9,554 ft.

Dir Frank Lloyd. *Adapt* J. G. Hawks. *Photog* Norbert Brodin.

Cast: Anna Q. Nilsson *(Countess Courteau),* Ben Lyon *(Pierce Phillips),* Viola Dana *(Rouletta Kirby),* Hobart Bosworth *(Sam Kirby),* Dorothy Sebastian *(Laura),* Larry Fisher *(Frank McCaskey),* Fred Kohler *(Joe McCaskey),* Claude Gillingwater *(Tom Linton),* Charles Crockett *(Jerry),* J. Gunnis Davis *(Danny Royal),* Fred Warren *(Kid Bridges),* Tom London *(Sergeant Rock),* William Conklin *(inspector),* J. W. Johnston *(Mountie),* Anne M. Wilson *(dancer),* Victor McLaglen *(Poleon Doret),* Wade Boteler *(Jack McCaskey),* Fred Sullivan *(Morris Best),* John T. Murray *(Lucky Broad),* Charles Anderson *(Fred Miller),* Barney Furey *(corporal),* Philo McCullough *(Count Courteau),* James O'Malley *(Mountie).*

Northwest melodrama. Source: Rex Beach, *The Winds of Chance* (New York & London, 1918). Pierce Phillips joins the Alaska gold rush and is trimmed clean by the operator of a shell game. He gets a job packing luggage for the Countess Courteau, and a mutual love develops. When she finally admits that she is still entangled in the bonds of matrimony, Pierce brokenheartedly returns to Dawson and gets a job as a gold weigher in a dancehall. He is framed for robbery by Count Courteau and a piqued vamp called Laura, but the countess obtains evidence to clear him. Count Courteau is killed, and Pierce is blamed unjustly for his death. The Mounties find the real killer, and Pierce is free to find happiness with the countess. *Nobility. Prospectors. Vamps. Assayers. Gold rushes. Murder. Robbery. Gambling. Alaska. Northwest Mounted Police.*

WINDS OF THE PAMPAS **F2.6399**

Cloninger Productions. *Dist* Hi-Mark Productions. Oct **1927.** Si; b&w. 35mm. 6 reels, 5,436 ft.

Dir-Scen-Titl Arthur Varney. *Photog* David W. Gobbett. *Sets* Tec-Art Studios. *Film Ed* Arthur Varney.

Cast: Ralph Cloninger *(Don Rafael Casandos),* Harry Holden *(Don José Casandos),* Vesey O'Davoren *(Eusabio),* Edwards Davis *(Don Escamillo Casandos),* Claire McDowell *(Doña María Casandos),* Anne Drew *(Mariquita),* Lucille McMurrin *(Mercedes),* Vincent Padule *(Emilio).*

Drama. Source: Elynor Ewing, "Winds of the Pampas" (publication undetermined). Argentinean rancher Don José Casandos is the recipient of an annual "gift of hate" from his foster brother, Don Escamillo Casandos, as evidence of a long-standing grudge. His nerves frazzled as the time for the gift grows near, Don José sends his son, Don Rafael, who has just returned from his studies abroad, to spy on Don Escamillo. As a guest on Don Escamillo's ranch, Rafael falls in love with his host's younger daughter, Mariquita, while the rest of the family encourages his interest in the willing elder daughter, Mercedes. Don Escamillo discovers Rafael's identity and has him punished, but the families are finally reconciled through the efforts of Rafael and Mariquita. *Ranchers. Foster brothers. Sisters. Gauchos. Feuds. Ranches. Argentina.*

WINE (Universal-Jewel) **F2.6400**

Universal Pictures. 31 Aug **1924** [c31 Jul 1924; LP20450]. Si; b&w. 35mm. 7 reels, 6,220 ft.

Pres by Carl Laemmle. *Dir* Louis J. Gasnier. *Scen* Philip Lonergan, Eve Unsell. *Adapt* Raymond L. Schrock. *Photog* John Stumar.

Cast: Clara Bow *(Angela Warriner),* Forrest Stanley *(Carl Graham),* Huntley Gordon *(John Warriner),* Myrtle Stedman *(Mrs. Warriner),* Robert Agnew *(Harry Van Alstyne),* Walter Long *(Benedict [Count Montebello]),* Arthur Thalasso *(Amoti),* Walter Shumway *(revenue officer),* Grace Carlisle *(Mrs. Bruce Corwin),* Leo White *(The Duke).*

Melodrama. Source: William Briggs MacHarg, "Wine," in *Hearst's International* (41:8–10, Mar 1922). John Warriner, facing financial ruin, accepts the proposal of a bootlegger, Benedict, to underwrite the business of illegal wine-selling. His daughter, Angela, takes up with the jazz set and is caught in a raid, at a cafe owned by Benedict. Her former sweetheart, Carl Graham, comes to the rescue and saves her from notoriety, while the family struggles back to its former respectability following Warriner's prison term. *Fatherhood. Prohibition. Jazz life. Bootlegging. Reputation.*

WINE OF YOUTH **F2.6401**

Metro-Goldwyn Pictures. 10 Aug **1924** [New York premiere; released 15 Sep; c20 Aug 1924; LP20526]. Si; b&w. 35mm. 7 reels, 6,600 ft.

Pres by Louis B. Mayer. *Prod-Dir* King Vidor. *Scen* Carey Wilson. *Photog* John J. Mescall. *Art Dir* Charles L. Cadwallader. *Asst Dir* David Howard.

Cast—Episode of 1870: Eleanor Boardman *(Mary),* James Morrison *(Clinton),* Johnnie Walker *(William).*

Cast—Episode of 1897: Eleanor Boardman *(Mary),* Niles Welch *(Robert),* Creighton Hale *(Richard).*

Cast—The Modern Story: Eleanor Boardman *(Mary),* Ben Lyon *(Lynn),* William Haines *(Hal),* William Collier, Jr. *(Max),* Pauline Garon *(Tish),* Eulalie Jensen *(Mother),* E. J. Ratcliffe *(Father),* Gertrude Claire *(Granny),* Robert Agnew *(Bobby),* Lucille Hutton *(Anne),* Virginia Lee Corbin, Gloria Heller *(flappers),* Sidney De Grey *(doctor).*

Comedy-drama. Source: Rachel Crothers, *Mary the Third: a Comedy in Prologue and Three Acts* (Boston, c1923). Unlike earlier generations of Marys who used every wile to obtain husbands, Mary the Third questions the validity of marriage in her search for adventure. Unable to decide between quiet, considerate Lynn and aggressive Hal, she follows her suitors, along with sweethearts Max and Tish, on an outing, but an attempted seduction sends her home, where she becomes disillusioned by the quarreling of her parents. When they are reconciled, however, she regains her ideals and accepts Lynn. *Marriage. Family life. Parenthood. Seduction.*

WING TOY **F2.6402**

Fox Film Corp. 30 Jan **1921** [c30 Jan 1921; LP16112]. Si; b&w. 35mm. 5-6 reels.

Pres by William Fox. *Dir* Howard M. Mitchell. *Scen* Thomas Dixon, Jr. *Story* Pearl Doles Bell. *Photog* Glen MacWilliams. *Asst Dir* Edward Dodds.

Cast: Shirley Mason *(Wing Toy),* Raymond McKee *(Bob Harris),* Edward McWade *(Wong),* Harry S. Northrup *(Yen Low),* Betty Schade *(White Lily),* Scott McKee *(The Mole).*

Melodrama. In her 16th year Wing Toy learns how as an infant she was brought to Wong, a Chinese laundryman, by a former convict known as The Mole and that her father was Chinese and her mother American. Later, to give her a better home, Wong pledged her in marriage to Yen Low, a powerful and unscrupulous underworld figure, when she would come of age. Yen Low plans to divorce his American wife, White Lily, and marry Wing Toy. The intervention of reporter Bob Harris leads to the release of Wing Toy; Yen Low is killed by White Lily; and Wing Toy's engagement to the reporter becomes possible when it is revealed that she is the daughter of the district attorney. *Reporters. Laundrymen. Chinese. Waifs. Marriage—Arranged. Miscegenation. New York City—Chinatown.*

THE WINGED HORSEMAN (Universal-Jewel) **F2.6403**

Universal Pictures. 24 May **1929** [New York showing; c1 May 1929; LP351]. Si; b&w. 35mm. 6 reels, 5,540 ft.

Dir? (see note) Arthur Rosson, Reeves Eason. *Story-Cont* Raymond L. Schrock. *Titl* Harold Tarshis. *Photog* Harry Neumann. *Film Ed* Gilmore Walker.

Cast: Hoot Gibson *(Skyball Smith),* Mary Elder *(Joby Hobson),* Charles Schaeffer *(Colonel Hobson),* Allan Forrest *(Curly Davis),* Herbert Prior

(Eben Matthews).

Western melodrama. Colonel Hobson's ranch is bombed by a mysterious plane, and Texas Ranger Skyball Smith is sent to investigate. Arriving at the ranch on a motorcycle, Skyball is taken for a dude, but he wins the respect of the cowboys when he heads off a stampede by using his motorcycle. Skyball discovers that Davis, the ranch foreman, is behind the bombing, and Davis kidnaps Joby, the rancher's beautiful daughter, taking her off in an airplane; Skyball follows in another airplane. Skyball's machine catches fire, and he parachutes to earth. Joby wrests the controls of the other airplane from Davis, and they too must jump. Skyball captures Davis and wins Joby's love. *Texas Rangers. Dudes. Ranch foremen. Stampedes. Aerial bombardment. Airplane accidents. Parachuting.*

Note: Sources disagree in crediting direction.

WINGS **F2.6404**

Paramount Famous Lasky Corp. 5 Jan **1929** [c5 Jan 1929; LP25985]. Sd eff & mus score (Movietone); b&w. 35mm. 13 reels, 12,267 ft. [Also si.]

Prod Lucien Hubbard. *Dir* William A. Wellman. *Screenplay* Hope Loring, Louis D. Lighton. *Titl* Julian Johnson. *Story* John Monk Saunders. *Photog* Harry Perry. *Adtl Photog* E. Burton Steene, Cliff Blackston, Russell Harland, Bert Baldridge, Frank Cotner, Faxon M. Dean, Ray Olsen, Herman Schoop, L. Guy Wilky, Al Williams. *Film Ed* Lucien Hubbard. *Mus Score* J. S. Zamecnik. *Song: "Wings"* J. S. Zamecnik, Ballard MacDonald. *Asst Dir* Norman Z. McLeod. *Supv Flying Sequences* S. C. Campbell, Ted Parson, Carl von Hartmann, James A. Healy. *Stills Photog* Otto Dyar.

Cast: Clara Bow *(Mary Preston)*, Charles (Buddy) Rogers *(Jack Powell)*, Richard Arlen *(David Armstrong)*, Jobyna Ralston *(Sylvia Lewis)*, Gary Cooper *(Cadet White)*, Arlette Marchal *(Celeste)*, El Brendel *(Patrick O'Brien)*, Gunboat Smith *(The Sergeant)*, Richard Tucker *(air commander)*, Julia Swayne Gordon *(Mrs. Armstrong)*, Henry B. Walthall *(Mr. Armstrong)*, George Irving *(Mr. Powell)*, Hedda Hopper *(Mrs. Powell)*, Nigel De Brulier *(peasant)*, Dick Grace, Rod Rogers *(aviators)*.

War drama. During the Great War, Jack Powell and David Armstrong, two boys in love with the same girl, Sylvia Lewis, enlist in the Army Air Corps and are sent to basic training together. Their acrimonious rivalry soon turns to mutual respect, and they become the best of friends. At the front in France, they help to bring down a German fighter plane and are rewarded with leave in Paris, where they encounter Mary Preston, a vivacious young girl from their hometown who is in France as an ambulance driver. As the result of a tactical emergency, all leaves are canceled, and since Jack is too drunk to return to his unit, Mary sees that he gets back safely but must compromise her reputation to do so. David is shot down in enemy territory and reported dead. Jack goes into the air to avenge his death and shoots down a plane with German markings, later discovering to his horrow that the plane was piloted by David, who had survived the German manhunt and stolen it from an airfield. Jack returns home a reluctant hero and marries Mary. *Aviators. Ambulance drivers. World War I. France. Paris.*

Note: The re-creation of the battle of St. Mihiel was shot on location near San Antonio, Texas. Portions of this film were projected in Magnascope.

WINGS OF ADVENTURE **F2.6405**

Tiffany Productions. 1 Aug **1930** [c17 Jul 1930; LP1442]. Sd (Photophone); b&w. 35mm. 6 reels, 5,050 ft.

Dir Richard Thorpe. *Story-Scen* Harry Frazer. *Dial* Zella Young. *Photog* Arthur Reeves. *Film Ed* Clarence Kolster. *Rec Engr* j. Stransky, Jr.

Cast: Rex Lease *(Dave Kent)*, Armida *(María)*, Clyde Cook *(Skeets Smith)*, Fred Malatesta *(La Panthera)*, Nick De Ruiz *(Manuel)*, Eddie Boland *(Viva)*.

Adventure melodrama. Dave Kent, a commercial aviator, and his mechanic, Skeets Smith, are forced to make an emergency landing in Mexico and find themselves in the hands of La Panthera, a notorious bandit who wishes to overthrow the government and become president of a new republic. Manuel, his chief henchman, obliges them to collect the booty in a robbery, but Kent manages to meet María Valdez, a prisoner—held for marriage to the insurgent leader—who implores his aid. Kent and Skeets are arrested for the robbery and sentenced to death, but Manuel, believing it is La Panthera who has been captured, arrives with the *rurales* diverted from the execution. Kent returns to rescue Maria, and after a hair-raising pursuit, all dash to the border and safety. *Aviators. Mechanics. Bandits. Revolutionaries. Rurales. Mexico. Chases.*

WINGS OF THE STORM **F2.6406**

Fox Film Corp. 28 Nov **1926** [c28 Nov 1926; LP23396]. Si; b&w. 35mm. 6 reels, 5,374 ft.

Pres by William Fox. *Dir* J. G. Blystone. *Scen* Dorothy Yost, L. G. Rigby. *Titl* Elizabeth Pickett. *Photog* Robert Kurrle. *Asst Dir* Jasper Blystone.

Cast: Thunder *(himself, a dog)*, Virginia Brown Faire *(Anita Baker)*, Reed Howes *(Allen Gregory)*, William Russell *(Bill Martin)*, Hank Mann *(Red Jones)*.

Northwest melodrama. Source: Lawrence William Pedrose, "On the Wings of the Storm," in *Sunset Magazine* (56:20–22, Feb 1926). Thunder, a police dog, born the weakling of his brood, gains the reputation of cowardice and runs away from his mistress, Anita Baker, who operates a lumber camp in the northwest woods. Thunder is adopted by Allen Gregory, a forest ranger. Bill Martin, the rascally and brutal camp superintendent, who covets the heroine's property, attacks her, but Thunder, coming to the rescue, proves his mettle by warding off the villain and thus redeems himself. *Forest rangers. Cowardice. Lumber camps. Police dogs.*

WINGS OF YOUTH **F2.6407**

Fox Film Corp. 21 May **1925** [c19 Apr 1925; LP21427]. Si; b&w. 35mm. 6 reels, 5,340 ft.

Pres by William Fox. *Dir* Emmett Flynn. *Scen* Bernard McConville. *Photog* Ernest G. Palmer.

Cast: Ethel Clayton *(Katherine Manners)*, Madge Bellamy *(Madelyne Manners/Angela Du Bois)*, Charles Farrell *(Ted Spaulding)*, Freeman Wood *(Lucien Angoola)*, Robert Cain *(Pierre Du Bois/Marcus Jones)*, Katherine Perry *(Gwen Manners)*, Marion Harlan *(Betty Manners)*, George Stewart *(Jimmie Dale)*, Douglas Gerard *(Grantland Dobbs)*.

Melodrama. Source: Harold P. Montayne, "Sisters of Jezebel," in *Real Life Stories* (Jan–Apr 1924). Katherine Manners discovers that her three daughters are running wild: Betty and Madelyne are having love affairs with unworthy men, and Gwen, a studious girl with an independent mind, is planning to marry Grantland Dobbs as soon as he obtains a divorce. All the girls have money of their own, and Mrs. Manners is forced to extreme measures to bring them back to their senses. She goes abroad and returns with a husband much younger than herself; she takes a swell apartment and begins to lead a wild life, giving herself up to drunkenness and reckless pleasures. Madelyne finally berates her mother for her unbecoming behavior, and Mrs. Manners then reveals that her drunkenness and frivolity have been feigned in order to show the three girls the errors of their ways. Mrs. Manners then introduces her "husband" as the girls' British cousin, and the girls return to normal ways and pleasures. *Jazz life. Divorce. Reformation. Family life. Motherhood.*

THE WINNER **F2.6408**

Harry J. Brown Productions. *Dist* Rayart Pictures. 28 Oct **1926** [New York State license]. Si; b&w. 35mm. 5 reels, 5,168 ft.

Dir Harry J. Brown.

Cast: Billy Sullivan *(Scotty MacTavish)*, Lucille Hutton *(Patsy Thorne)*, Tom O'Brien *(Slugger Martin)*, Ben Walker *(Ben Reader)*, George Williams *(Archer Thorne)*.

Melodrama. "Through sudden infatuation with girl, wealthy young idler obtains position in locomotive works, where he saves her from death and conquers bully foreman in slugging contest. He wins girl and saves her father from disgrace." (*Motion Picture News Booking Guide*, 11:55, Oct 1926.) *Idlers. Shop foremen. Railroads. Locomotives.*

WINNER TAKE ALL **F2.6409**

Fox Film Corp. 12 Oct **1924** [c5 Oct 1924; LP20640]. Si; b&w. 35mm. 6 reels, 5,949 ft.

Pres by William Fox. *Dir* William S. Van Dyke. *Scen* Ewart Adamson. *Photog* Joseph Brotherton, E. D. Van Dyke.

Cast: Buck Jones *(Perry Blair)*, Peggy Shaw *(Cecil Manners)*, Edward Hearn *(Jack Hamilton)*, Lilyan Tashman *(Felicity Brown)*, William Norton Bailey *(Jim Devereaux)*, Ben Deeley *(Charles Dunham)*, Tom O'Brien *(Dynamite Galloway)*.

Melodrama. Source: Larry Evans, *Winner Take All* (New York, c1920). When Perry Blair's foreman fires him for fighting, fight promoter Charles Dunham hires him and takes him east to enter the boxing ring. Perry becomes a star boxer but breaks his contract and returns home when he is ordered to fight a crooked match. Sometime later Dunham again comes west and engages Perry to fight one more contest on a winner-take-all basis. He wins the fight and Cecil Manners, who has believed him to be a coward. *Cowboys. Fight promoters. Prizefighting.*

WINNERS OF THE WILDERNESS F2.6410

Metro-Goldwyn-Mayer Pictures. 15 Jan **1927** [c24 Jan 1927; LP23585]. Si; b&w with col sequences (Technicolor). 35mm. 7 reels, 6,343 ft.

Dir W. S. Van Dyke. *Cont* Josephine Chippo. *Titl* Marian Ainslee. *Photog* Clyde De Vinna. *Sets* David Townsend. *Film Ed* Conrad A. Nervig. *Wardrobe* Lucia Coulter.

Cast: Tim McCoy *(Colonel O'Hara)*, Joan Crawford *(Renée Contrecoeur)*, Edward Connelly *(General Contrecoeur)*, Roy D'Arcy *(Captain Dumas)*, Louise Lorraine *(Mimi)*, Edward Hearn *(George Washington)*, Tom O'Brien *(Timothy)*, Will R. Walling *(General Braddock)*, Frank Currier *(Governor de Vaudreuil)*, Lionel Belmore *(Governor Dinwiddie)*, Chief Big Tree *(Pontiac)*.

Historical melodrama. Colonel O'Hara, "dashing young officer of Braddock's staff is aided to escape from the French by daughter of commandant whom he worships. When the positions are reversed and she is his prisoner of war she willingly consents to become his prisoner for life." (*Motion Picture News Booking Guide*, 12:65, Apr 1927.) "The costumes of the period offer a pleasing contrast to the interesting sequences ... in which are seen such historical figures as Washington and Braddock. The latter's disastrous defeat is the film's highlight and it is carried out with realism." (*Motion Picture News*, 8 Apr 1927, p1276.) *French and Indian War. Edward Braddock. George Washington. Robert Dinwiddie. Pontiac.*

WINNING A CONTINENT F2.6411

Arrow Pictures. c22 Dec **1924** [LP20938]. Si; b&w. 35mm. 6 reels.

Dir-Adapt Harold Shaw.

Cast: Percy Marmont, Edna Flugrath, Harold Shaw.

Historical drama. In 1837, the Dutch settlers in Cape Colony decide to establish a Free Dutch Republic in Natal. Among the settlers who prepare to make the journey are Jan Faber, a Boer youth, and Sabuzu, a Zulu warrior converted to Christianity. An advance party, led by Piet Retief, the newly designated President of the Dutch Republic, goes to the kraal of the Zulu chief, Dingaan, in an attempt to make a treaty, but they have been preceded by two renegade traders, Jenke and Janos, who have turned the black leader against them. Dingaan sends out a band of warriors, who attack the settlers, only to be turned back by the superior firepower of the Boer rifles. Sabuzu kills Dingaan, and the settlers are free to realize their dream of a new nation. *Dutch. Boers. Traders. South Africa. Zululand. Natal. Cape Colony. Piet Retief.*

Note: Filmed in South Africa.

WINNING A WOMAN F2.6412

Dist Rayart Pictures. caApr **1925**. Si; b&w. 35mm. 5 reels, 4,865 ft.

Cast: Jack Perrin, Josephine Hill.

Western melodrama(?). No information about the nature of this film has been found.

THE WINNING OAR F2.6413

Excellent Pictures. 1 May **1927** [c13 Jun 1927; LP24078]. Si; b&w. 35mm. 6 reels, 5,750 ft.

Pres by Samuel Zierler. *Dir* Bernard McEveety. *Story-Cont* Arthur Hoerl. *Photog* Marcel Le Picard.

Cast: George Walsh *(Ted Scott)*, Dorothy Hall *(Gloria Brooks)*, William Cain *(Fred Blake)*, Arthur Donaldson *(Robert Brooks)*, Harry Southard *(Stanley Wharton)*, Gladys Frazin *(Valerie)*.

Romantic melodrama. Ted Scott, a noted scholar and college athlete, is informally engaged to Gloria Brooks, but she is unable to marry him; instead, Gloria consents to make herself the pawn in obtaining her dad's release from a man who has the power to destroy him financially. Both Gloria and Ted are heartbroken; she tries to be a good wife to her neglectful husband, while Ted embarks on a legal career that ultimately makes him district attorney. At a party, Gloria's husband openly encourages other men to flirt with her, and she leaves in shame and disgust; he pursues her home, and while they quarrel he is suddenly shot. All evidence points to Gloria as the murderer. One of the jurors holds out for acquittal and confesses to being the murderer, seeking revenge for the early seduction of his daughter by the villain. Gloria is acquitted and happily reunited with Ted. *Athletes. Lawyers. District attorneys. Juries. College life. Marriage. Murder. Trials.*

THE WINNING OF BARBARA WORTH F2.6414

Samuel Goldwyn, Inc. *Dist* United Artists. 14 Oct **1926** [Los Angeles premiere; released Dec; c2 Dec 1926; LP23391]. Si; b&w. 35mm. 9 reels, 8,757 ft.

Pres by Samuel Goldwyn. *Dir* Henry King. *Adapt* Frances Marion. *Photog* George Barnes. *Art Dir* Karl Oscar Borg.

Cast: Ronald Colman *(Willard Holmes)*, Vilma Banky *(Barbara Worth)*, Charles Lane *(Jefferson Worth)*, Paul McAllister *(The Seer)*, E. J. Ratcliffe *(James Greenfield)*, Gary Cooper *(Abe Lee)*, Clyde Cook *(Tex)*, Erwin Connelly *(Pat)*, Sam Blum *(Blanton)*.

Western romantic drama. Source: Harold Bell Wright, *The Winning of Barbara Worth* (Chicago, 1911). Willard Holmes, an eastern engineer, comes west to assist his unscrupulous stepfather in the execution of a vast desert irrigation project, and he meets Barbara Worth, adopted daughter of banker Jefferson Worth, who originated the reclamation plan. Holmes's stepfather, Greenfield, builds a cheap and dangerous intake at the river to fleece the settlers of their money; Worth moves away to form another city, offering the settlers free land and water. The avaricious Greenfield shuts off Worth's credit and breeds discontent among his workers. To bring money, Holmes and Abe Lee make a desperate ride across the mountains and succeed, though Lee is wounded. Greenfield's dam overflows and floods his town, but Holmes succeeds in building a new dam and marries Barbara. *Bandits. Capitalists. Engineers. Settlers. Stepfathers. Irrigation. Land reclamation. Deserts. Dams.*

WINNING OF THE WEST F2.6415

Dist Aywon Film Corp. Aug **1922**. Si; b&w. 35mm. 5 reels.

Western melodrama. "Tom Sherman and his family live in a stockade home in the west. When only the two children are at home, the stockade is attacked by a band of whiskey-maddened Indians. The children explode a can of powder, driving the Indians off. Years later, the boy is in the army and the girl has a daughter of her own, whose dearest playmate is an Indian girl whom they have nursed back to health. The daughter is kidnaped by the Indians and the Indian girl rescues her. A fight follows between whites and Indians, with the brother's troop riding to the rescue." (*Motion Picture News Booking Guide*, 3:79, Oct 1922.) *Indians of North America. Children. Kidnaping. United States Army—Cavalry.*

WINNING THE FUTURITY F2.6416

Chadwick Pictures. 15 Mar or 15 Apr **1926** [c8 May 1926; LP22689]. Si; b&w. 35mm. 6 reels, ca5,500 ft.

Pres by I. E. Chadwick. *Dir* Scott Dunlap. *Adapt* Finis Fox. *Story* Hunt Stromberg.

Cast: Cullen Landis, Clara Horton, Henry Kolker, Pat Harmon, Otis Harlan.

Melodrama. Chet Kildare, a war profiteer, seeks the hand of Colonel Barkley's daughter, Nelle, though she looks with disfavor upon his undiplomatic advances. Instead, she becomes attracted to Luke Allen, a carefree mountain boy whose strength and spirit impress her. Luke, with the connivance of Uncle Mose, faithful retainer of the Barkleys, saves a baby colt owned by the colonel from being shot, intending to raise it to contend in the Kentucky Futurity. A year passes. Kildare wins the Barkley estate from the colonel in a poker game while the colonel is drunk. The next morning, Nelle finds her father dead—leaving a document in which Kildare agrees to return the estate upon payment of $100,000 within 18 months. Another year passes, and Luke's horse, Firefly, is a contender in the Futurity. Kildare, who also has an entry, tries unsuccessfully to dope Firefly. Firefly wins the race, however, and Luke wins not only the $100,000 needed to regain the estate but also Nelle's hand. *Profiteers. Kentucky colonels. Horseracing. Gambling. Courtship. Kentucky Derby. Horses.*

THE WINNING WALLOP F2.6417

Gotham Productions. *Dist* Lumas Film Corp. 8 Oct? **1926** [c12 Oct 1926; LP23210]. Si; b&w. 35mm. 5 reels, 5,000 ft.

Pres by Sam Sax. *Dir* Charles Hutchinson. *Photog* James Brown. *Asst Dir* Bernard Ray.

Cast: William Fairbanks *(Rex Barton)*, Shirley Palmer *(Marion Wayne)*, Charles K. French *(Peter Wayne)*, Melvin McDowell *(Cyrus Barton)*, Melbourne MacDowell *(see note)*, Crauford Kent *(Lawrence Duncan)*, Jimmy Aubrey *(fight manager)*, Frank Hagney *("Pug" Brennan)*.

Comedy-melodrama. Source: L. V. Jefferson, *The Winning Wallop* (publication undetermined). Rex Barton, the easygoing son of wealthy Cyrus Barton, accomplishes little at college except winning the amateur boxing title. Pretending to quarrel with his father, he leaves home and takes a job as physical instructor in a ladies' gymnasium owned by his sweetheart, Marion Wayne. One of the jealous ladies informs Peter Wayne that his daughter is flirting with Rex, and he orders him fired. Duncan, a local broker, offers to set up a championship match but makes a deal with Brennan, a champion boxer; and when Wayne stands to lose financially from the match, he agrees on Rex as an entry. Duncan then tries to make it appear that Rex has murdered Wayne; after exciting complications, Rex evades the police and wins the girl by defeating Brennan. *Physical instructors. Brokers. Filial relations. Boxing. Gymnasiums.*

Note: One source lists Melbourne MacDowell as playing the part of Cyrus Barton.

WINNING WITH WITS (Twentieth Century Series) **F2.6418**

Fox Film Corp. 8 Jan **1922** [c8 Jan 1922; LP17463]. Si; b&w. 35mm. 5 reels, 4,435 ft.

Pres by William Fox. *Dir* Howard M. Mitchell. *Scen* Jack Strumwasser, Dorothy Yost. *Photog* Max Dupont.

Cast: Barbara Bedford *(Mary Sudan/Mary Wyatt)*, William Scott *(King)*, Harry S. Northrup *(Corday)*, Edwin B. Tilton *(Sudan, Mary's father)*, Wilson Hummel *(stage manager)*.

Melodrama. Source: H. H. Van Loan, "The Girl Who Dared" (publication undetermined). Simultaneously with Mary Sudan's first chance to play a leading theatrical role comes the news that her father has been sent to prison on a false charge of theft. Determined to find the culprit and bring him to justice, she visits her father's company, posing as a wealthy widow seeking investment securities. She is given a partnership in the firm and cultivates the acquaintance of the president, Corday, whom she invites to a staged sêance; he becomes so frightened at her apparent possession of facts regarding his guilt that he confesses his part in the crime. Later, Mary sees Corday enter the office safe to steal valuable securities; however, the vice president, with the aid of Mary's evidence and two detectives, forces a confession from him. Mary and King, the young vice president, decide to spend their honeymoon with her father, who is cleared of the charge. *Actors. Filial relations. Theft. Injustice. Imposture. Spiritualism.*

WISCONSIN UNDER FIRE **F2.6419**

Dist Pictorial Sales Bureau. c14 Apr **1924** [MU2491]. Si; b&w. 35mm. 8 reels.

Documentary. "The story of the Wisconsin troops in the World War ... opens with the training of these troops at Camp McArthur, Waco, Texas, follows them aboard the transports, conducts them through the submarine area to the several landing ports in France and England. They are shown at work in the Service of Supplies and in the 10th Training Area. This is followed by battle action in the following sectors. Alsace, Chatteau Thierry, Junigny and the Meuse Argonne. Along with the battle scenes their activities in the rest areas and drilling sectors are also shown. Following the close of the Meuse Argonne battle and the Armistice, movements of the Wisconsin troops into Germany are depicted with the final review held in Germany and the sailing from France for the U. S. A." (Copyright records.) *United States Army. United States Army—Training. World War I. Submarines. England. France. Germany. Wisconsin. Waco (Texas). Camp McArthur.*

WISE BABY *see* **FUGITIVES**

A WISE FOOL **F2.6420**

Famous Players–Lasky. *Dist* Paramount Pictures. 26 Jun **1921** [c27 Jun 1921; LP16714]. Si; b&w. 35mm.

Dir George Melford. *Adapt* Gilbert Parker. *Photog* William Marshall.

Cast: James Kirkwood *(Jean Jacques Barbille)*, Alice Hollister *(Carmen Dolores)*, Ann Forrest *(Zoe Barbille)*, Alan Hale *(George Masson)*, Fred Huntley *(Sebastian Dolores)*, William Boyd *(Gerard Fynes)*, Truly Shattuck *(Virginia Poucette)*, Harry Duffield *(Fille)*, Charles Ogle *(Judge Carcasson)*, John Herdman *(The Curate)*, Mabel Van Buren *(Madame Langlois)*.

Domestic melodrama. Source: Gilbert Parker, *The Money Master* (New York, 1915). After visiting Paris, wealthy egotist Jean Jacques Barbille, on his voyage homeward to Quebec, falls in love with Carmen Dolores, traveling with her father, Sebastian, a Spanish adventurer, and they are married. As their daughter, Zoe, grows up, Barbille unintentionally neglects Carmen, and she is about to elope with George Masson when he discovers their plan. He spares Masson, realizing that he himself is partly to blame; and Carmen leaves for Montreal where she becomes a chorus girl. Zoe, against her father's will, marries Gerard Fynes and goes west with him. Barbille is ruined by a fire in his mill, but later he is happily reunited with his wife and child in Montreal. *Chorus girls. Egotists. Infidelity. Fatherhood. Quebec. Montreal.*

WISE GIRLS **F2.6421**

Metro-Goldwyn-Mayer Pictures. 21 Sep **1929** [c30 Sep 1929; LP729]. Sd (Movietone); b&w. 35mm. 11 reels, 8,818 ft. [Also si.]

Dir E. Mason Hopper. *Titl* Margaret Booth. *Adapt–Stage Dir–Dial* J. C. Nugent, Elliott Nugent. *Photog* William Daniels. *Art Dir* Cedric Gibbons. *Film Ed* Margaret Booth. *Song: "I Love You Truly"* Carrie Jacobs Bond. *Rec Engr* Douglas Shearer, Karl E. Zint. *Wardrobe* David Cox.

Cast: Elliott Nugent *(Kempy)*, Norma Lee *(Kate)*, Roland Young *(Duke Merrill)*, J. C. Nugent *(Dad)*, Clara Blandick *(Ma)*, Marion Shilling *(Ruth Bence)*, Leora Spellman *(Jane Wade)*, James Donlan *(Ben Wade)*.

Comedy-drama. Source: J. C. Nugent and Elliott Nugent, *Kempy* (New York opening: 15 May 1922). Kempy, a plumber who aspires to be an architect, is repairing a pipe in the Bence household when Kate, the artistic and independent eldest daughter, persuades him to marry her to prove something to Duke Merrill, the man she really loves. Bence, an irascible old man, attempts to throw Kempy out of the house when Kate and he arrive married, but Duke, a lawyer, helps to turn the tables by selling Kempy the deed to Bence's house. Again assisted by Duke, Kempy gets an annulment from his shrewish wife when he discovers he has fallen in love with Ruth, the youngest daughter, and all ends happily. *Plumbers. Architects. Shrews. Artists. Sisters. Lawyers. Marriage—Annulment.*

Note: Also known as *Kempy*.

THE WISE GUY **F2.6422**

Frank Lloyd Productions. *Dist* First National Pictures. 23 May **1926** [c18 May 1926; LP22746]. Si; b&w. 35mm. 8 reels, 7,775 ft.

Pres by Frank Lloyd. *Dir* Frank Lloyd. *Scen* Ada McQuillin. *Titl* George Marion, Jr. *Adapt* Adela Rogers St. Johns. *Story* Jules Furthman. *Photog* Norbert Brodin.

Cast: Mary Astor *(Mary)*, James Kirkwood *(Guy Watson)*, Betty Compson *(Hula Kate)*, George F. Marion *(Horace Palmer)*, Mary Carr *(Ma Palmer)*, George Cooper *(The Bozo)*.

Crook melodrama. Guy Watson, because of his magnetic personality, is able to persuade people to purchase fake medicines while his cohorts—Bozo, Hula Kate, and Ma—pick the onlookers' pockets; later, posing as a minister, he delivers a sermon at a country funeral. The decedent's daughter, Mary, joins the traveling mission, convinced by Guy's preaching although she incurs the jealousy of Hula Kate. Guy soon attains a great hold on the public, but gradually Ma and her husband, the professor, get "hooked" on religion, and Bozo leaves the group when he is reunited with his long-lost mother. Later, he is shot by a policeman who mistakes him for a burglar. When Ma dies in spite of Guy's prayers, he confesses to his congregation that he is a fraud and hypocrite, and they forgive him. Mary is discovered to be a crook, and though she and Guy are sent to separate prisons, they await eventual happiness together. *Swindlers. Pickpockets. Evangelists. Religious conversion. Hypocrisy.*

Note: The film was considerably shortened for release in New York State to meet licensing requirements.

WISE HUSBANDS **F2.6423**

Pioneer Film Corp. 21 Aug **1921** [trade review]. Si; b&w. 35mm. 6 reels.

Pres by Lester Park, Edward Whiteside. *Dir* Frank Reicher. *Adapt* J. Clarkson Miller. *Story* Charles D. Isaacson.

Cast: Gail Kane, J. Herbert Frank, Gladden James, Arthur Donaldson, Lillian Worth.

Society drama. "A young man [played by Gladden James] with no other apparent occupation than to be a constant attendant at his club is in love with a girl [played by Gail Kane] who devotes herself to Red Cross work. His mother [played by Lillian Worth] thinks the girl isn't good enough for him, and his father [played by Arthur Donaldson] believes she is too good for the son. The father confides in a friend—an artist [played by J. Herbert Frank]—and they conspire to break down the opposition of the mother by having the artist, who is a libertine, lure the mother into becoming interested and compromised in and with the artist. By this means the mother, realizing the girl isn't so wicked, consents to the girl becoming her daughter-in-law." (*Variety,* 12 Aug 1921, p34.) *Socialites. Artists. Rakes. Parenthood. Courtship. Reputation. Red Cross.*

THE WISE KID (Universal Special) **F2.6424**

Universal Film Manufacturing Co. ca4 Mar **1922** [St. Louis premiere; released 13 Mar; c22 Feb 1922; LP17577]. Si; b&w. 35mm. 5 reels, 4,606 ft.

Pres by Carl Laemmle. *Dir* Tod Browning. *Scen* Wallace Clifton. *Story* William Slavens McNutt. *Photog* William Fildew.

Cast: Gladys Walton *(Rosie Cooper)*, David Butler *(Freddie Smith)*, Hallam Cooley *(Harry)*, Hector Sarno *(Tony Rossi)*, Henry A. Barrows *(Jefferson Southwick)*, C. Norman Hammond *(Mr. Haverty)*.

Romantic comedy-drama. "Rosie Cooper is cashier in a cheap restaurant and among those she favors is ... Smith, the bakery boy. Rose is a 'wise kid' all right, but it takes her some time to see through a shiny young thin model gent ... . The girl entertains his advances because he means romance to her. But he proves his shallow character and Rosie is glad to turn to Jimmy, the bakery youth." (*Motion Picture News Booking Guide*, 3:79, Oct 1922.) *Cashiers. Bakers. Courtship. Restaurants.*

THE WISE VIRGIN **F2.6425**

Peninsula Studios. *Dist* Producers Distributing Corp. 10 Aug **1924** [c15 Aug 1924; LP20698]. Si; b&w. 35mm. 6 reels, 5,951 ft.

Supv-Writ Elmer Harris. *Dir* Lloyd Ingraham. *Photog* Joseph Walker. *Art Dir* Una Hopkins. *Tech Dir* Earl Sibley.

Cast: Patsy Ruth Miller *("Billie" Farrington)*, Edythe Chapman *(Mrs. John Farrington, her aunt)*, Lucy Fox *(Effie Green, a friend)*, Matt Moore *(Bob Hanford, manager of Mrs. Farrington's ranch)*, Leon Bary *(Count Ricardo Venino)*, Charles A. Stevenson *(Thomas Green, Effie's husband)*.

Drama. Although Billie Farrington's aunt, Mrs. Farrington, wishes her to marry Farrington ranch foreman Bob Hanford, Billie refuses to be interested in anyone but Count Venino, a fake nobleman. Mrs. Farrington becomes seriously ill, and Billie weds Bob to please her aunt but treats him with chilly reserve. When Mrs. Farrington learns of Venino's masquerade and his halfcaste birth, she gives a reception to which she invites Venino's Burmese mother. Billie runs away, is kidnaped by Venino, and then is rescued by Bob, whose rugged honesty Billie finally appreciates. *Ranch foremen. Halfcastes. Burmese. Nobility. Ranches. Miscegenation.*

THE WISE WIFE **F2.6426**

De Mille Pictures. *Dist* Pathé Exchange. 24 Oct **1927** [c11 Oct 1927; LP24498]. Si; b&w. 35mm. 6 reels, 5,610 ft.

Supv William De Mille. *Dir* E. Mason Hopper. *Adapt-Cont* Zelda Sears, Tay Garnett. *Titl* John Krafft. *Photog* Frank Good. *Art Dir* Mitchell Leisen. *Film Ed* Adelaide Cannon. *Asst Dir* E. J. Babille. *Prod Mgr* Richard Donaldson. *Cost* Adrian.

Cast: Phyllis Haver *(Helen Blaisdell)*, Tom Moore *(John Blaisdell)*, Fred Walton *(Helen's father)*, Jacqueline Logan *(Jenny Lou)*, Joseph Striker *(Carter Fairfax)*, Robert Bolder *(Jason, the butler)*.

Domestic farce. Source: Arthur Somers Roche, *The Wise Wife* (New York, 1928). John Blaisdell, a stolid businessman married for 10 years, concludes that romantic love is a thing of the past for him. His wife, Helen, a very domestic and conservative woman, invites Jenny Lou, a young southern girl, as her houseguest, and the girl flirts with John; she is conspicuously unsuccessful until she pretends to faint on the golf course and the unsuspecting victim finds her in his arms. Local gossips inform Helen, she feigns ignorance of the matter, but later she insists that Jenny do the housework to prove her merits as a housewife, an arrangement to which Jenny reluctantly agrees. Meanwhile, Helen has her hair bobbed, buys a new wardrobe, and attracts Fairfax, Jenny's southern fiancé, provoking jealous reactions by both Jenny and John. Ultimately John realizes his wife's worth, and all ends happily. *Businessmen. Flirts. Southerners. Marriage. Jealousy. Golf.*

THE WITCHING EYES **F2.6427**

Ernest Stern. c26 Nov **1929** [LU871]. Si; b&w. 35mm. [Feature length assumed.]

Written by Ernest Stern.

Melodrama. Haitian Val Napolo, possessed of a witching hand and the evil eye, is persuaded by his friend Cortex to go to the United States and pose as a leader of his people. Napolo meets with great success and gets to know Sylvia Smith, the daughter of a recently deceased Negro leader. Napolo develops a burning desire for Sylvia, but she favors Ralph Irving, a gentle poet. Napolo puts a curse on them and breaks up their love affair. When Sylvia still refuses him, Napolo kidnaps her. Ralph learns of the abduction and rescues Sylvia, discrediting Napolo in the eyes of his people. *Negroes. Poets. Kidnaping. Voodoo. Haiti.*

THE WITCHING HOUR **F2.6428**

Famous Players–Lasky. *Dist* Paramount Pictures. 10 Apr **1921** [c9 Feb 1921: LP16139]. Si; b&w. 35mm. 7 reels, 6,734 ft.

Pres by Jesse L. Lasky. *Dir* William D. Taylor. *Scen* Julia Crawford Ivers. *Photog* James Van Trees. *Asst Dir* Frank O'Connor.

Cast: Elliott Dexter *(Jack Brookfield)*, Winter Hall *(Judge Prentice)*, Ruth Renick *(Viola Campbell)*, Robert Cain *(Frank Hardmuth)*, Edward Sutherland *(Clay Whipple)*, Mary Alden *(Helen Whipple)*, Fred Turner *(Lew Ellinger)*, Genevieve Blinn *(Mrs. Campbell)*, Charles West *(Tom Denning)*, L. M. Wells *(Judge Henderson)*, Clarence Geldert *(Colonel Bailey)*, Jim Blackwell *(Harvey)*.

Mystery melodrama. Source: Augustus Thomas, *The Witching Hour* (1907). While Jack Brookfield is entertaining guests at his gambling house in Louisville, young Clay Whipple, who is obsessed by a fear of cat's-eye jewels, is taunted by Tom Denning with a scarfpin and kills him. Clay, who loves Viola, Brookfield's niece, is then tried and sentenced to death. Brookfield visits Judge Prentice and convinces him that Clay is entitled to a retrial; and he exposes Hardmuth, an attorney seeking the gubernatorial nomination, as involved in the governor-elect's murder. Hardmuth tries to shoot Brookfield, but the latter, through mental suggestion, thwarts him, and in the second trial Clay is acquitted. He is later reunited with the woman he loves. *Politicians. Gambling. Superstition. Murder. Mental telepathy. Trials. Capital punishment.*

THE WITCH'S LURE **F2.6429**

Capital Film Co. *Dist* Aywon Film Corp. Apr **1921**. Si; b&w. 35mm. 5 reels.

Cast: Davide.

Melodrama. "A man is imprisoned upon the top of a derrick, which is set aflame by the villain and all escape is blocked. Heroine climbs up a long rope to the rescue, but after she gets to the top the rope burns through. Aeroplane catches their cries of distress, and, recognizing their predicament, sails over top of derrick trailing a rope, to which heroine clings, carrying unconscious victim with her." (*Motion Picture News Booking Guide*, 1:123, Dec 1921.) *Oil wells. Airplanes. Fires.*

WITH BUFFALO BILL ON THE U. P. TRAIL *see* **BUFFALO BILL ON THE U. P. TRAIL**

WITH BYRD AT THE SOUTH POLE **F2.6430**

Paramount-Publix Corp. 19 Jun **1930** [New York premiere; released 28 Jun; c12 Jun 1930; LP1418]. Mus & narr (Movietone); b&w. 35mm. 8 reels, 7,411 ft.

Synchronized Narration Floyd Gibbons. *Titl* Julian Johnson. *Photog* Joseph Rucker, Willard Van der Veer. *Film Ed* Emanuel Cohen. *Mus Score* Manny Baer. *Song: "Back Home"* Irving Kahal, Sammy Fain, Pierre Norman.

Persons: Rear Adm. Richard E. Byrd *(Expedition Commander)*, Clair D. Alexander *(Supply Officer)*, Bernt Balchen *(Aviation Pilot)*, George H. Black *(Seaman and Tractor Man)*, Quin A. Blackburn *(Topographer)*, Kennard F. Bubier *(Aviation Mechanic)*, Christopher Braathen *(Seaman, Ski Man)*, Jacob Bursey *(Seaman, Dog Driver)*, Arnold H. Clark *(Fireman)*, Dr. Francis D. Coman *(Medical Officer)*, Frederick E. Crockett *(Dog Driver)*, Victor H. Czegka *(Machinist)*, Frank T. Davies *(Physicist)*, Joe De Ganahl *(Mate)*, E. J. Demas *(Aviation Mechanic)*, James A. Feury *(Fireman)*, Edward E. Goodale *(Dog Driver)*, Charles F. Gould *(Carpenter)*, Dr. Lawrence M. Gould *(Geologist and Geographer/2d Comm.)*, William C. Haines *(Meteorologist)*, Malcolm P. Hanson *(Radio Operator)*, Henry R. Harrison, Jr. *(Aerologist)*, Harold I. June *(Aviation Pilot)*, Charles E. Lofgren *(Personnel Officer)*, Howard F. Mason *(Radio Operator)*, Capt. Ashley C. McKinley *(Aerial Photographer)*, Thomas B. Mulroy *(Chief Engineer)*, John S. O'Brien *(Surveyor)*, Russell Owen *(Newspaper Correspondent)*, Capt. Alton U. Parker *(Aviation Pilot)*, Carl O. Peterson *(Radio Operator)*, Martin Ronne *(Sailmaker)*, Benjamin Roth *(Aviation Mechanic)*, Paul A. Siple *(Boy Scout)*, Dean Smith *(Aviation Pilot)*, Sverre Stron *(Second Officer)*, George W. Tennant *(Cook)*, George A. Thorne, Jr. *(Seaman, Ski Man, Surveyor)*, Norman D. Vaughn *(Dog Driver)*, Arthur T. Walden *(In Charge of Dogs)*.

Documentary. Rear Admiral Byrd introduces the film with scenes of the expedition leaving New York, escorted by the *Leviathan*, and this introduction is followed by a storm at sea and a battle with the Antarctic icepack. On Christmas Day port is sighted, and while Byrd inspects unusual ice formations, penguins inspect the visitors, at Ross Barrier. With Little America achieved, the airplane *City of New York* leaves under

Gould; but the plane is wrecked in a fierce blizzard and Byrd heads a rescue party. During the long winter night of 6 months, the men equip themselves with new clothes and make preparations for the Polar flight; in the spring, with the first glimpse of the returning sun, Byrd raises the flags of Britain and Norway in memory of Scott and Amundsen. Gould leaves on an emergency base-laying trek by dogsled, while the *Floyd Bennett* is assembled; but the Gould party like Byrd's Polar flight is delayed 7 days by a blizzard. Finally, they are off; Byrd tries an unknown pass and reaches the Pole; through the trapdoor, he drops the Stars and Stripes. After a hazardous return flight, they are welcomed at Little America and prepare for the voyage homeward. *Explorers. Ships. Aviation. Navigation. Antarctic regions. Little America. South Pole. Byrd Polar Explorations.*

WITH CAR AND CAMERA AROUND THE WORLD **F2.6431**

Aloha Wanderwell. 11 Nov **1929** [New York showing; released 14 Dec 1929]. Si(?); b&w. 35mm. 6 reels, 5,500 ft.

Photog Walter Wanderwell.

Personages: Aloha Wanderwell, Walter Wanderwell.

Travelog. Starting from Paris in 1922, Mr. and Mrs. Walter Wanderwell take 7 years to make their way around the world, visiting such countries as Spain, Italy, Germany, Poland, Arabia, India, China, Manchuria, United States, Cuba, parts of Africa, and Portugal. Highlights include scenes of the Taj Mahal, Mecca, African natives, cremation pyres at Benares, the Great Wall of China, a visit to Douglas Fairbanks and Mary Pickford in Hollywood, and Miami after the hurricane of 1926. *Arabia. China. Cuba. Germany. India. Italy. Manchuria. Poland. Portugal. Spain.*

Note: *Motion Picture News* (21 Dec 1929, p40) quotes these credits: "Author, God, for He created the earth and its people. Scenario by All Peoples."

WITH DAVY CROCKETT AT THE FALL OF THE ALAMO *see* **DAVY CROCKETT AT THE FALL OF THE ALAMO**

WITH EUSTACE IN AFRICA **F2.6432**

Harry K. Eustace. *Dist* African Jungle Films. 19 Aug **1922** [New York State license]. Si; b&w. 35mm. 6 reels, ca5,500 ft.

Travel documentary. "A film showing the life of Mr. Harry K. Eustace and Mrs. Eustace in the jungles of Africa. A natural history study of animals in their own wild nature habitat." (New York State license records.) *Jungles. Natural history. Africa.*

Note: Filmed between 1914 and 1918.

WITH GENERAL CUSTER AT LITTLE BIG HORN *see* **GENERAL CUSTER AT LITTLE BIG HORN**

WITH KIT CARSON OVER THE GREAT DIVIDE *see* **KIT CARSON OVER THE GREAT DIVIDE**

WITH NAKED FISTS **F2.6433**

Norca Film Corp. 9 May **1923** [New York State license]. Si; b&w. 35mm. 5 reels.

Cast: Tom Kennedy, Leonard Clapham.

Western melodrama. No information about the precise nature of this film has been found.

WITH SITTING BULL AT THE SPIRIT LAKE MASSACRE *see* **SITTING BULL AT THE "SPIRIT LAKE MASSACRE"**

WITH THIS RING **F2.6434**

B. P. Schulberg Productions. 5 Sep **1925.** Si; b&w. 35mm. 6 reels, 5,333 ft.

Dir Fred Windermere. *Photog* A. Fried.

Cast: Alyce Mills *(Cecilie Vaughn)*, Forrest Stanley *(John Wendell)*, Lou Tellegen *(Rufus Van Buren)*, Donald Keith *(Donald Van Buren)*, Dick Sutherland *(The Portuguese)*, Martha Mattox *(Luella Van Buren)*, Joan Standing *(Cecilie's maid)*, Eulalie Jensen *(Tabitha Van Buren)*.

Melodrama. Source: Fanny Heaslip Lea. *With This Ring* (New York, 1925). Stranded on a desert isle, Donald and Cecilie become man and wife in the eyes of God. Donald is attacked by a mad Portuguese and is knocked unconscious; Cecilie mistakes him for dead and leaves him behind on the island when a rescue party arrives. She returns to the United States and goes to see Donald's wealthy family. They not only refuse to recognize her as Donald's wife but also refuse to recognize her baby as Donald's child. Donald's brother offers to take her as his mistress, however; when she refuses, he attempts to bribe her into giving up all claims on the Van Buren name. John Wendell, the family lawyer, takes pity on Cecilie and offers her the protection of his name in marriage; she accepts, with the provision that it be in name only. Donald having been rescued, however, he and Cecilie are joyfully reunited. *Castaways. Lawyers. Portuguese. Social classes. Marriage—Common law.*

WITH WINGS OUTSPREAD **F2.6435**

Camus Productions. *Dist* Aywon Film Corp. Jun **1922.** Si; b&w. 35mm. 5 reels, 4,862 ft.

Cast: Fred Terry, Walter Franklin, Madeline Cassinelli.

Adventure melodrama. "A daring gang of bandits outside of Havana becomes so bold that the government sends two aviators borrowed from the U. S. Army after them. Flying over the camp, the mechanic is wounded and they land, hiding the plane. A girl nurses the mechanic back to health. The aviator is captured by the bandits but wins their confidence and escapes. Learning that the bandit chief covets the girl, the mechanic hides her in a cave, where they are joined by the aviator. They are attacked by the bandits, but manage to escape in the hidden plane, and happiness follows." (*Motion Picture News Booking Guide,* 3:79, Oct 1922.) *Bandits. Air pilots. Mechanics. Airplanes. United States Army. Cuba.*

WITHIN PRISON WALLS *see* **THE RIGHT WAY**

WITHIN THE LAW *see* **PAID**

WITHIN THE LAW **F2.6436**

Joseph M. Schenck Productions. *Dist* Associated First National Pictures. ca29 Apr **1923** [New York premiere; released 30 Apr; c18 Apr 1923; LP18875]. Si; b&w. 35mm. 8 reels, 8,034 ft.

Pres by Joseph M. Schenck. *Personally dir by* Frank Lloyd. *Adapt* Frances Marion. *Photog* Tony Gaudio.

Cast: Norma Talmadge *(Mary Turner)*, Lew Cody *(Joe Garson)*, Jack Mulhall *(Dick Gilder)*, Eileen Percy *(Aggie Lynch)*, Joseph Kilgour *(Edward Gilder)*, Arthur S. Hull *(Demarest)*, Helen Ferguson *(Helen Morris)*, Lincoln Plummer *(Cassidy)*, Thomas Ricketts *(General Hastings)*, Ward Crane *(English Eddie)*, Catherine Murphy *(Gilder's secretary)*, De Witt Jennings *(Burke)*, Lionel Belmore *(Irwin)*, Eddie Boland *(Darcy)*.

Crook melodrama. Source: Bayard Veiller, *Within the Law; a Melodrama in Four Acts* (New York, 1917). Unjustly convicted of theft, shopgirl Mary Turner is determined to have revenge on Edward Gilder, her employer and prosecutor. When her term is completed and she finds no job open to her, Mary joins Aggie Lynch in blackmailing wealthy men with threats of breach-of-promise suits. Eventually Dick Gilder, her enemy's son, falls victim to Mary's designs, and though she falls in love with him she is determined to carry out her plans. Dick is nearly framed for a murder committed by Joe Garson; Helen Morris confesses to the theft for which Mary was imprisoned; and Mary finally admits her love for Dick. *Shopgirls. Blackmail. Theft. Murder. Injustice. Breach of promise.*

WITHOUT BENEFIT OF CLERGY **F2.6437**

Robert Brunton Productions. *Dist* Pathé Exchange. Jul **1921** [c2 Jun 1921; LU16677]. Si; b&w. 35mm. 6 reels, 5,200 ft.

Dir James Young. *Adapt* Randolph C. Lewis. *Photog* Jack Okey. *Prod Dsgn* Rudyard Kipling.

Cast: Virginia Brown Faire *(Ameera)*, Thomas Holding *(John Holden)*, Evelyn Selbie *(Ameera's mother)*, Otto Lederer *(Ahghan, moneylender)*, Boris Karloff *(Ahmed Khan)*, Nigel De Brulier *(Pir Khan)*, Herbert Prior *(Hugh Sanders)*, Ruth Sinclair *(Alice Sanders)*, E. G. Miller *(Michael Devenish)*, Philippe De Lacey *(Tota, at 5)*.

Drama. Source: Rudyard Kipling, *Without Benefit of Clergy* (New York, 1899). In Lahore, English engineer John Holden rescues Ameera from an unwelcome suitor. Charmed by the girl, he offers a generous dowry for her, and an elaborate native ceremony takes place. A son is born to them, and they are very happy until the boy dies and Holden is forced to go away on a construction project. When cholera breaks out in Lahore, Holden returns, but Ameera is stricken by the plague and dies. *Engineers. Marriage—Mixed. Plague. Cholera. Lahore.*

Note: Kipling himself made the sketches for the scenes and properties used in this production.

WITHOUT COMPROMISE **F2.6438**

Fox Film Corp. 29 Oct **1922** [c29 Oct 1922; LP19135]. Si; b&w. 35mm. 6 reels, 5,173 ft.

Pres by William Fox. *Dir* Emmett J. Flynn. *Scen* Bernard McConville. *Photog* Dev Jennings.

Cast: William Farnum *(Dick Leighton)*, Lois Wilson *(Jean Ainsworth)*, Robert McKim *(David Ainsworth)*, Tully Marshall *(Samuel McAllister)*, Hardee Kirkland *(Judge Gordon Randolph)*, Otis Harlan *(Dr. Evans)*, Will Walling *(Bill Murray)*, Alma Bennett *(Nora Foster)*, Eugene Pallette *(Tommy Ainsworth)*, Fred Kohler *(Cass Blake)*, Jack Dillon *(Jackson)*.

Western melodrama. Source: Lillian Bennett-Thompson and George Hubbard, *Without Compromise* (New York, 1922). When the ability of Leighton, sheriff of Randolph, Oregon, to enforce law and order is tested by the leader of the political opposition, he stands his ground and overpowers the unruly element. *Sheriffs. Politics. Oregon.*

WITHOUT FEAR F2.6439

Fox Film Corp. 16 Apr **1922** [c16 Apr 1922; LP17825]. Si; b&w. 35mm. 5 reels, 4,406 ft.

Pres by William Fox. *Dir* Kenneth Webb. *Scen* Paul H. Sloane. *Photog* Tom Malloy.

Cast: Pearl White *(Ruth Hamilton)*, Robert Elliott *(John Miles [Martin?])*, Charles Mackay *(Warren Hamilton)*, Marie Burke *(Mrs. Hamilton)*, Robert Agnew *(Walter Hamilton)*, Macey Harlam *(Bill Barton)*.

Society melodrama. Ruth Hamilton, from a wealthy aristocratic family, cares little for society or its conventions and refuses the proposal of William Barton, a socialite of her parents' choice. While giving some poor children an outing on a beach, Ruth meets John Martin (Miles?), a young *nouveau riche* with no social standing who is snubbed by the aristocratic circles, and begins to visit him secretly. When Ruth visits John to show off a new costume, her father arrives to seek his financial aid. Ruth escapes, but she is observed by Barton, who informs her father. Hamilton insists that Martin marry his daughter, but Ruth refuses to be compromised by her father. Later, however, she consents to marry John, discovering that he really loves her. *Socialites. Nouveaux riches. Upper classes. Filial relations.*

WITHOUT LIMIT F2.6440

S-L Pictures. *Dist* Metro Pictures. 28 Feb **1921** [c2 Mar 1921; LP16211]. Si; b&w. 35mm. 7 reels.

Pres by Arthur H. Sawyer, Herbert Lubin. *Dir-Writ* George D. Baker. *Photog* André Barlatier. *Set Dsgn* M. P. Staulcup.

Cast: Anna Q. Nilsson *(Ember Edwards)*, Robert Frazer *(David Marlowe)*, Frank Currier *(The Reverend Marlowe)*, Kate Blancke *(Mrs. Marlowe)*, Charles Lane *(Clement Palter)*, Robert Schable *(Bunny Fish)*, Thomas W. Ross *(Charley)*, Nellie Anderson *(The Landlady)*.

Society melodrama. Source: Calvin Johnston, "Temple Dusk," in *Saturday Evening Post* (193:3–5, 16 Oct 1920). David Marlowe, son of a clergyman, falls in with fast company and, at the persuasion of man-about-town Bunny Fish, marries Ember Edwards while he is intoxicated. The party goes to Clement Palter's gambling house, where David, after losing all his money on a loan from Bunny, seeks the aid of the owner. Hearing their story, Palter sympathetically calls in David's father, whereupon the boy makes his restitution by serving in the Army. Later he is happily reunited with his wife. *Clergymen. Gambling. Drunkenness.*

WITHOUT MERCY F2.6441

Metropolitan Pictures. *Dist* Producers Distributing Corp. 4 Oct **1925** [c15 Aug 1925; LP21734]. Si; b&w. 35mm. 7 reels.

Dir George Melford. *Adapt* Monte Katterjohn. *Photog* Charles G. Clarke.

Cast: Dorothy Phillips *(Mrs. Enid Garth)*, Rockliffe Fellowes *(Sir Melmoth Craven)*, Vera Reynolds *(Margaret Garth)*, Robert Ames *(John Orme, M. P.)*, Lionel Belmore *(Horace Massingham)*, Patricia Palmer *(Natalie)*, Fred Malatesta *(Ducrow)*, Sidney D'Albrook *(Sugden)*, Eugene Pallette *(Link)*, Tempe Piggott *(Madame Gordon)*.

Melodrama. Source: John Goodwin, *Without Mercy* (New York, 1920). In the Argentine, when Enid Garth's family discovers a valuable mine, Enid is kidnaped by Melmoth Craven, who whips her into insensibility to discover the mine's location. Years later, Enid has become the head of a great London banking house from which Craven borrows money to finance his campaign for a seat in Parliament. Enid revengefully calls back the loan without warning, and the desperate Craven kidnaps her daughter, Margaret. The girl is rescued by John Orme, and Enid sets a trap for Craven. The police arrest Craven, and Margaret and John are married. *Bankers. Kidnaping. Flagellation. Political campaigns. Mines. Argentina. London. Great Britain—Parliament.*

WITHOUT ORDERS F2.6442

Maloford Productions. *Dist* Weiss Brothers Clarion Photoplays. 21 Jun **1926.** Si; b&w. 35mm. 5 reels, 5,100 ft.

Dir Leo Maloney. *Scen* Ford I. Beebe.

Cast: Leo Maloney *(Dale Monroe)*, Josephine Hill *(Martha Wells)*, Whitehorse *(Harvey Wells)*, Bud Osborne *(a ranger)*, Fred Burns *(Uncle "Jody" Miller)*, Frank Ellis *(Taylor Beal)*, Ben Corbett *("Squinty" Moore)*, Bullet *(himself, a dog)*, Monte Cristo *(himself, a horse)*.

Western melodrama. "... of cattle rustlers and their defeat by young ranger called in to stop depredations by cattle owners. Develops romance with ranchman's daughter." (*Motion Picture News Booking Guide*, 11:55, Oct 1926.) *Ranchers. Rustlers. Rangers. Dogs. Horses.*

WITHOUT WARNING *see* **THE STORY WITHOUT A NAME**

WIVES AT AUCTION F2.6443

Macfadden True Story Pictures. c10 Apr, 17 Apr **1926** [LP22591, LU22635]. Si; b&w. 35mm. 6 reels, 5,874 ft.

Story-Dir Elmer Clifton. *Adapt* Lewis Allen Browne. *Photog* A. G. Penrod.

Cast: Edna Murphy, Gaston Glass.

Society melodrama. Violet Kingston is attacked by tramps, and Mark Cameron, a wealthy socialite, comes to her rescue. Sylvester Hatch, the rich landlord of the building in which the Kingston family is forced to live in reduced circumstances, gives Mark and Violet a ride home and later does everything in his power to further a romance between them, hoping thereby to gain acceptance to high society. Mark soon asks Violet to marry him, but she refuses. Hatch learns of this eventuality and insists that Violet marry him instead. On the day of the wedding, Mark learns that Violet is being railroaded into this repugnant marriage by her avaricious stepmother and kidnaps her, taking her to a justice of the peace to be married. Hatch is found murdered, and Mark is arrested for the crime. The real murderer is quickly discovered, however, and Mark is set free to begin a belated honeymoon. *Tramps. Socialites. Landlords. Social classes. Murder. Injustice.*

THE WIVES OF THE PROPHET F2.6444

J. A. Fitzgerald Productions. *Dist* Lee-Bradford Corp. Jan **1926.** Si; b&w. 35mm. 7 reels, 6,560 ft.

Dir J. A. Fitzgerald. *Photog* Larry Williams.

Cast: Orville Caldwell *(Howard Brice)*, Alice Lake *(Judith)*, Violet Mersereau *(Alma)*, Harlan Knight *(The Patriarch)*, Ruth Stonehouse *(Rachael)*, Warner Richmond *(Ben Blake)*, Maurice Costello *(William Neil)*, Ed Roseman *(Boyle)*, Mary Thurman *(Laura Neil)*.

Romantic drama. Source: Opie Percival Read, *The Wives of the Prophet* (Chicago, 1894). Expecting the arrival of a prophet, a religious sect in the mountains of Virginia every year selects five beautiful girls to be his wives. A young lawyer, Howard Brice, happens along and admires the face of Judith, one of the brides-to-be. He is mistaken for the prophet (because of a tattooed portrait of Judith on his chest), becomes involved in religious ceremonies, and finally escapes with his life—and Judith. *Lawyers. Prophets. Polygamy. Religious sects. Rites and ceremonies. Tattoos. Virginia.*

Note: Filmed in the Shenandoah Valley of Virginia.

THE WIZARD F2.6445

Fox Film Corp. 11 Dec **1927** [c1 Dec 1927; LP24711]. Si; b&w. 35mm. 6 reels, 5,629 ft.

Pres by William Fox. *Dir* Richard Rosson. *Scen* Harry O. Hoyt, Andrew Bennison. *Titl* Malcolm Stuart Boylan. *Photog* Frank Good. *Asst Dir* Park Frame.

Cast: Edmund Lowe *(Stanley Gordon)*, Leila Hyams *(Anne Webster)*, Gustav von Seyffertitz *(Dr. Paul Coriolos)*, E. H. Calvert *(Edwin Palmer)*, Barry Norton *(Reginald Van Lear)*, Oscar Smith *(Sam)*, Perle Marshall *(Detective Murphy)*, Norman Trevor *(Judge Webster)*, George Kotsonaros *(The Ape)*, Maude Turner Gordon *(Mrs. Van Lear)*.

Mystery melodrama. Source: Gaston Leroux, *Balaoo* (Paris, 1912). "Dr. Coriolos, whose son was tried, convicted and electrocuted for murder, obtains an ape and trains it to overpower those whom its master seeks to destroy. Stanley Gordon, newspaper reporter, seeking a new angle on the murder of Palmer, stumbles onto the secret of Dr. Coriolos and saves two intended victims, Judge Webster and the latter's daughter, with whom Stanley is in love." (*Moving Picture World*, 3 Dec 1927, p26.) *Sorcerers. Reporters. Judges. Murder. Insanity. Capital punishment. Apes.*

THE WIZARD OF OZ F2.6446

Chadwick Pictures. ca12 Apr **1925** [New York showing; c27 Jun 1925; LP21623]. Si; b&w. 35mm. 7 reels, 6,300 ft.

Dir Larry Semon. *Scen* Larry Semon, L. Frank Baum, Jr., Leon Lee. *Titl* Leon Lee. *Photog* H. F. Koenekamp, Frank Good, Leonard Smith. *Art Dir* Robert Stevens. *Film Ed* Sam S. Zimbalist. *Asst Dir* William King.

Cast: Larry Semon *(Scarecrow)*, Bryant Washburn *(Prince Kynde)*, Dorothy Dwan *(Dorothy)*, Virginia Pearson *(Countess Vishuss)*, Charles Murray *(the Wizard)*, Oliver Hardy *(The Tin Woodsman)*, Josef Swickard *(The Prime Minister)*, Mary Carr *(Dorothy's mother)*, G. Howe Black *(Rastus)*.

Fantasy. Source: Lyman Frank Baum, *The Wonderful Wizard of Oz* (New York & Chicago, 1900). Nearing her 18th birthday, Dorothy learns from her "aunt" that she is a foundling, left on the doorstep as an infant. The aunt then produces a letter, found with the baby, that is to be opened when she becomes 18. *Before they can read the letter, a cyclone descends and sweeps Dorothy, her uncle, and two hired men into the Kingdom of Oz. Dorothy's letter proves that she is the Queen of the Realm, and Prince Kynde and his followers duly hail her as such. Prime Minister Kruel asks the wizard to put a spell on Dorothy's followers, but the wizard, who has no real magical powers, is unable to do so. The two hired men obligingly disguise themselves, changing into a scarecrow and a tin woodsman. They are put in jail but manage to escape, only to encounter a lion in his den. The men climb a high tower, and the scarecrow seizes a ladder hanging from an airplane. The ladder breaks, and the scarecrow tumbles.* ... The whole adventure turns out to have been a child's dream. *Foundlings. Scarecrows. Woodsmen. Sorcerers. Royalty. Prime ministers. Imaginary kingdoms. Disguise. Airplanes. Lions. Cyclones. Dreams. Documentation.*

WIZARD OF THE SADDLE F2.6447

FBO Pictures. 22 Jan **1928** [c22 Jan 1928; LP24979]. Si; b&w. 35mm. 5 reels, 4,805 ft.

Dir-Writ Frank Howard Clark. *Titl* Randolph Bartlett. *Photog* Roy Eslick.

Cast: Buzz Barton *(Red Hepner)*, Milburn Morante *(Hank Robbins)*, James Ford *(Tom Ellis)*, Duane Thompson *(Jenny Adams)*, James Welch *("Pop" Adams)*, Bert Apling *(Kirk McGrew)*.

Western melodrama. While they are searching for Red's father in the High Sierras, Red Hepner and his pal, Hank Robbins, become involved in the lives of "Pop" Adams, an old prospector, and his granddaughter, Jenny. Red finds a gold nugget, decides to file a claim, and finds that the property has already been assigned to Adams. Three desperadoes, Kirk McGrew and his two henchmen, are anxious to drive Jenny and Pop away from their cabin. There the gang has hidden a machine that manufactures counterfeit money. Red and Hank, backed by Tom Ellis, a government agent disguised as a surveyor, repel the villains. McGrew and his men return when Pop is alone. Knocking him unconscious, they rip up the floorboards and find, instead of the printing press, several sacks of gold Pop has stashed away. This leads them to try to claim the mine when Pop's claim (by coincidence) expires; but Red, Hank, and Tom join efforts to prevent this disaster. Tom has enough evidence to arrest McGrew and his gang. Red and Hank resume their search, while Tom and Jenny go into the final clinch. *Surveyors. Government agents. Counterfeiters. Prospectors. Sierras.*

WOLF BLOOD F2.6448

Ryan Brothers Productions. *Dist* Lee-Bradford Corp. 16 Dec **1925** [New York State license]. Si; b&w. 35mm. 6 reels, 5,800 ft.

Dir George Chesebro, George Mitchell. *Scen* C. A. Hill.

Cast: Marguerite Clayton *(Edith Ford)*, George Chesebro *(Dick Bannister)*, Ray Hanford *(Dr. Eugene Horton)*, Roy Watson *(Jules Deveroux)*, Milburn Morante *(Jacques Lebeq)*, Frank Clark *(Pop Hadley)*.

Melodrama. Dick Bannister, the foreman of the Ford Logging Co., sends for a doctor when several of his men are hurt in a fight with employees of a rival lumber company. Edith Ford, the owner of the company, comes to Bannister's aid, bringing with her Dr. Horton, one of her ardent admirers; Edith and Dick soon fall in love. Dick is later injured, and Dr. Horton is forced to use the blood of a wolf in a transfusion for him. Dick is haunted by the fear that he is becoming half beast and attempts to commit suicide by jumping off a cliff. Edith saves him, he recovers, and they are married. *Lumber camp foremen. Physicians. Lumbering. Blood transfusion. Suicide. Wolves.*

WOLF FANGS F2.6449

Fox Film Corp. 27 Nov **1927** [c17 Nov 1927; LP24676]. Si; b&w. 35mm. 6 reels, 5,331 ft.

Pres by William Fox. *Dir* Lewis Seiler. *Scen* Seton I. Miller. *Titl* Elizabeth Pickett. *Story* Seton I. Miller, Elizabeth Pickett. *Photog* L. William O'Connell. *Asst Dir* Virgil Hart.

Cast: Thunder *(himself, a dog)*, Caryl Lincoln *(Ellen)*, Charles Morton *(Neal Barrett)*, Frank Rice *(Pete)*, James Gordon *(Bill Garside)*, White Fawn *(herself, a dog)*, Zimbo *(himself, a dog [villain])*, Oswald *(himself, a mutt dog)*.

Action melodrama. Thunder, a dog raised by Ellen, a sheepherder's daughter, is driven to the wilderness by the brutal treatment of her father, Bill Garside, and becomes an outlaw; when grown, he takes command of a wolfdog pack. Later, Ellen, driven from her home by the same brutal herder, seeks refuge at the cabin of Neal Barrett, the forest ranger; she is pursued by the hungry pack and is stranded on a rocky cliff where Thunder once again encounters his former mistress. He challenges the pack in her defense, provoking a battle between himself and a rival for his command. Later, Thunder rescues Ellen from her brutal father. *Sheepherders. Forest rangers. Fatherhood. Oregon. Dogs.*

Note: Filmed on locations in Oregon.

THE WOLF HUNTERS F2.6450

Ben Wilson Productions. *Dist* Rayart Pictures. 20 Jul **1926** [New York State license]. Si; b&w. 35mm. 6 reels, 5,976 ft.

Dir Stuart Paton.

Cast: Robert McKim, Virginia Browne Faire, Alan Roscoe, Mildred Harris, David Torrence, Al Ferguson.

Melodrama. Source: James Oliver Curwood, "The Wolf Hunters" (publication undetermined). "Mounted policeman loves girl in whom three others are interested. One is killed and girl is accused. Policeman is ordered to bring her in and, broken hearted, he carries out his orders only to find that she has been wrongfully accused. They decide to face life together." (*Motion Picture News Booking Guide*, 12:66, Apr 1927.) *Murder. Injustice. Northwest Mounted Police.*

WOLF LAW F2.6451

Universal Film Manufacturing Co. 23 Oct **1922** [c3 Oct 1922; LP18297]. Si; b&w. 35mm. 5 reels, 4,463 ft.

Pres by Carl Laemmle. *Dir* Stuart Paton. *Scen* Charles Sarver. *Photog* Benjamin Kline.

Cast: Frank Mayo *(Jefferson De Croteau)*, Sylvia Breamer *(Francine Redney)*, Tom Guise *(Etienne De Croteau)*, Dick Cummings *(Enoch Lascar)*, William Quinn *(Simon Santey)*, Nick De Ruiz *(Samson Bender)*, Harry Carter *("Dandy" Dawson)*, Paul Wismer *(nountaineer)*.

Melodrama. Source: Hugh Pendexter, "Wolf Law," in *Adventure* (31: 3–103, 30 Oct 1921). Hotheaded Jeff De Croteau wins a horserace, shoots a poor loser who has insulted him, and escapes across the state line. He falls in with a gang of rough men who are victimizing an old judge and his daughter. Jeff escapes with the judge and the girl and returns to his hometown to find that his enemy did not die. But he must—and does—prove himself innocent of a theft before declaring his love for the girl. *Gangs. Judges. Horseracing.*

THE WOLF MAN F2.6452

Fox Film Corp. 17 Feb **1924** [c17 Jan 1924; LP19869]. Si; b&w. 35mm. 6 reels, 5,145 ft.

Pres by William Fox. *Dir* Edmund Mortimer. *Scen* Frederick Hatton, Fanny Hatton. *Story* Reed Heustis. *Photog* Don Short, Michael Farley.

Cast: John Gilbert *(Gerald Stanley)*, Norma Shearer *(Elizabeth Gordon)*, Alma Francis *(Beatrice Joyce)*, George Barraud *(Lord Rothstein)*, Eugene Pallette *(Pierre)*, Edgar Norton *(Sir Reginald Stackpoole)*, Thomas R. Mills *(Caulkins)*, Max Montisole *(Phil Joyce)*, Charles Wellesley *(Sam Gordon)*, Richard Blaydon *(Lieutenant Esmond)*, D. R. O. Hatswell *(Lord St. Cleve)*, Mary Warren *(English barmaid)*, Ebba Moną *(ballet girl)*.

Melodrama. Convinced by his own brother that he has killed his fiancée's brother while drunk, Gerald Stanley, a gentleman when sober and a beast when drunk, leaves England for Canada to avoid incrimination. There he does not drink until news arrives that his brother has married Beatrice, his former fiancée. In his desperation, he kidnaps Elizabeth Gordon, a tourist, and takes her to his shack. Pursued by Elizabeth's father, Gerald attempts to escape with her by canoe. Caught in rapids, the canoe overturns; Gerald saves Elizabeth from drowning and asks her forgiveness. Finally, exonerated of the murder of Beatrice's brother and

saved by Elizabeth from being lynched, he faces a happy future together with her. *Brothers. Alcoholism. Kidnaping. England. Canada. Rapids.*
Note: Working title: *The Beast.*

WOLF MAN **F2.6453**
Sunset Productions. Oct **1924** [scheduled release]. Si; b&w. 35mm. 5 reels, 4,750 ft.
Cast: J. B. Warner.
Western melodrama(?). No information about the nature of this film has been found.

THE WOLF OF WALL STREET **F2.6454**
Paramount Famous Lasky Corp. 9 Feb **1929** [c9 Feb 1929; LP108]. Sd (Movietone); b&w. 35mm. 8 reels, 6,810 ft. [Also si; 6,396 ft.]
Dir Rowland V. Lee. *Story-Screenplay-Dial* Doris Anderson. *Titl* Julian Johnson. *Photog* Victor Milner. *Film Ed* Robert Bassler. *Song: "Love Take My Heart"* Harold Cristy, Joseph Meyer. *Ch Rec Engr* Franklin Hansen.
Cast: George Bancroft *(The Wolf)*, Baclanova *(Olga, his wife)*, Paul Lukas *(David Tyler)*, Nancy Carroll *(Gert, the maid)*, Arthur Rankin *(Frank)*, Brandon Hurst *(Sturgess)*, Paul Guertzman *(office boy)*, Crauford Kent *(Jessup)*.
Melodrama. The Wolf of Wall Street corners the market in copper and then sells short, making a fortune and ruining the fiancé of his maid, Gert. Out of spite, Gert then tells The Wolf that his wife has been cheating on him with his partner, Tyler. To revenge himself, The Wolf deliberately ruins himself and Tyler in the market and then walks out on his wife. *Stockbrokers. Housemaids. Infidelity. Copper. Revenge. New York City—Wall Street.*

WOLF PACK **F2.6455**
World Film Corp. *Dist* Rialto Productions. 16 Mar **1922** [New York State license]. Si; b&w. 35mm. 5 reels.
Dir-Writ William J. Craft.
Cast: Joe Moore *(Joe Hammond)*, Eileen Sedgwick *(Jeanne Lamont)*, S. W. Williams *(Henry Lamont/Stephen Lamont)*, Robert Kortman *(The Wolf)*.
Northwest melodrama. "Henry Lamont, a wealthy miner, is mysteriously murdered. Trooper Joe Hammond, in the neighborhood, hears the shot and comes to the aid of Jeanne Lamont, who is at loss to explain the fatal attack on her father. The girl goes to live with her uncle, who has already been visited by a bogus trooper, who imparts the information that one of the Northwest Police is suspected of being 'the lone wolf,' a desperate criminal. Trooper Hammond, too, seeks 'the wolf.' Developments disclose ... that the bogus trooper was 'the wolf,' but not until the latter tries to file claim on a gold vein is he detected by the girl." (*Moving Picture World,* 15 Apr 1922, p763.) *Uncles. Impersonation. Mine claims. Murder. Northwest Mounted Police.*

WOLF SONG **F2.6456**
Paramount Famous Lasky Corp. 30 Mar **1929** [c29 Mar 1929; LP254]. Singing sequences, sd eff, & mus score (Movietone); b&w. 35mm. 8 reels, 6,769 ft. [Also si; 6,060 ft.]
Dir Victor Fleming. *Screenplay* John Farrow, Keene Thompson. *Titl* Julian Johnson. *Photog* Allen Siegler. *Film Ed* Eda Warren. *Mus Dir* Irvin Talbot. *Songs: "Mi Amado," "Yo Te Amo Means I Love You"* Richard Whiting, Al Bryan. *Supv Mus Rec* Max Terr.
Cast: Gary Cooper *(Sam Lash)*, Lupe Velez *(Lola Salazar)*, Louis Wolheim *(Gullion)*, Constantine Romanoff *(Rube Thatcher)*, Michael Vavitch *(Don Solomon Salazar)*, Ann Brody *(duenna)*, Russ Colombo *(Ambrosia Guiterrez)*, Augustina Lopez *(Louisa)*, George Rigas *(Black Wolf)*.
Western melodrama. Source: Harvey Ferguson, "Wolf Song," in *Red Book* (49:39–47, 52–59, Jul–Aug 1927). Lola Salazar, the daughter of a haughty California don, elopes with Sam Lash, an unkempt Kentucky trapper of no particular means. They live together in a settlement in the mountains until Sam decides that he is sick of civilization and rejoins his former companions in the Canadian wilderness; Lola returns to her family. Sam soon finds the nights too long and lonely and heads home only to be shot by a couple of braves. He drags himself to Lola's hacienda, however, and they are reunited. *Trappers. Spanish. Kentuckians. Indians of North America. Elopement. Sierras. California. Canada.*
Note: Filmed on location in the California Sierras.

WOLFHEART'S REVENGE **F2.6457**
Charles R. Seeling Productions. *Dist* Aywon Film Corp. 4 Mar **1925** [New York State license]. Si; b&w. 35mm. 5 reels, 4,800 ft.
Cast: Big Boy Williams, Wolfheart *(a dog)*.
Western melodrama(?). No information about the nature of this film has been found. *Dogs.*

WOLF'S CLOTHING **F2.6458**
Warner Brothers Pictures. 15 Jan **1927** [c12 Jan 1927; LP23527]. Si; b&w. 35mm. 8 reels, 7,068 ft.
Dir Roy Del Ruth. *Screenplay* Darryl Francis Zanuck. *Camera* Byron Haskins. *Asst Camera* Willard Van Enger. *Asst Dir* Edward Sowders.
Cast: Monte Blue *(Barry Baline)*, Patsy Ruth Miller *(Minnie Humphrey)*, John Miljan *(Johnson Craigie)*, Douglas Gerrard *(Herbert Candish)*, Lew Harvey *(Vanelli)*, Ethan Laidlaw *(Vanelli's pal)*, J. C. Fowler *(hotel manager)*, Walter Rodgers *(hotel doctor)*, Arthur Millett *(hotel detective)*, John Webb Dillon *(crook "doctor")*, Lee Moran *(millionaire)*, Paul Panzer, Charles Haefeli, Jack Cooper *(three toughs)*, Kalla Pasha *(ship captain)*, Jack Curtis, Edwin Sturgis *(two sailors)*.
Mystery melodrama. Source: Arthur Somers Roche, "Wolf's Clothing," in *Heart's International Cosmopolitan* (vol 80–81, May–Oct 1926). Barry Baline, a New York subway guard, is knocked unconscious by the speeding automobile of Johnson Craigie, who has just escaped from an insane asylum. *While unconscious Barry imagines himself exchanging places with Craigie, the millionaire; he attends a New Year's Eve ball and is drugged, is mistaken for Craigie by two blackmailers, and along with Minnie, a lady's maid, is taken to a dive on the East River waterfront. Minnie is held for hostage while Barry is sent to get ransom money. After numerous exciting events, he obtains the money from Craigie, succeeds in cornering the gang on a barge, escapes from the police, and saves the passengers of a runaway subway train from the demented Craigie.* Awakening in the hospital, Barry finds that the girl of his dreams, Minnie, is his nurse. *Subway guards. Millionaires. Nurses. Insanity. New Year's Eve. Dreams.*

THE WOLF'S FANGS **F2.6459**
Apfel Productions. *Dist* Producers Security Corp. 15 May **1922.** Si; b&w. 35mm. 5 reels.
Dir Oscar Apfel.
Cast: Wilfred Lytell, Nancy Deaver, Manilla Martans.
Melodrama. "North woods melodrama centering about a brutal trapper known as 'The Wolf.' He is in love with the daughter of the French factor, but is opposed by her sweetheart. The two suitors fight and the Wolf is defeated. He vows revenge, and later captures his rival, threatening to kill him unless the girl consents to marry himself. To save her lover's life, she agrees. But the Wolf had reckoned without a girl whom he had betrayed and discarded, and when he returns to his cabin, finds her. He struggles with her, but is shot and killed by the girl's sweetheart, leaving the lovers free to marry." (*Motion Picture News Booking Guide,* 3:80, Oct 1922.) *Trappers. Factors. French Canadians. Revenge.*

WOLF'S TRACKS **F2.6460**
Sunset Productions. Apr **1923** [scheduled release]. Si; b&w. 35mm. 5 reels, 4,818 ft.
Cast: Jack Hoxie.
Western melodrama. No information about the precise nature of this film has been found.
Note: Reissued Dec 1929.

WOLF'S TRAIL (Universal Thrill Feature) **F2.6461**
Universal Pictures. 2 Oct **1927** [c20 Jun 1927; LP24120]. Si; b&w. 35mm. 5 reels, 4,167 ft.
Pres by Carl Laemmle. *Dir* Francis Ford. *Story-Cont* Basil Dickey. *Titl* Gardner Bradford. *Photog* Jerry Ash.
Cast: Edmund Cobb *(Capt. Tom Grant)*, Dixie Lamont *(Jane Drew)*, Edwin Terry *(Simeon Kraft)*, Joe Bennett *(Bert Farrel)*, Dynamite *(himself, the dog)*.
Action melodrama. Tom Grant, a Texas Ranger detailed to investigate contraband activities on the border, captures "One Shot" Morgan on his way to find Simeon Kraft, a smuggler. Learning that Kraft is not acquainted with Morgan, he impersonates the outlaw, and en route he rescues the smuggler's ward, Jane Drew, from a runaway horse. Farrel, Kraft's chief aide, receives Tom with suspicion, while Kraft also suspects him and sends for information about his confederate. Kraft, who is deathly afraid of a stray police dog, traps the dog and is about to kill him when

Tom interferes. Tom is exposed as an imposter and overpowered by the gang, but the dog, remembering Tom's kindness, enables him to escape. The gang makes a break for the border, but Tom and the dog upset their plans, and the rangers arrive in time to arrest them. *Texas Rangers. Smugglers. Wards. Impersonation. Mexican border. Police dogs.*

THE WOLVERINE **F2.6462**

Spencer Productions. *Dist* Associated Photoplays. c23 Sep **1921** [LP16986]. Si; b&w. 35mm. 5 reels.

Dir William Bertram. *Adapt* Helen Van Upp. *Photog* Steve Norton.

Cast: Helen Gibson *(Billy Louise)*, Jack Connolly *(Ward Warren)*, Leo Maloney *(Charlie Fox)*, Ivor McFadden *(Buck Olney)*, Anne Schaefer *(Martha Meilke)*, Gus Saville *(Jase Meilke)*.

Western melodrama. Source: B. M. Bower, *The Ranch at the Wolverine* (Boston, 1914). Ward Warren, who has served a prison term for the crimes of Buck Olney, returns home and settles on the Wolverine Ranch, operated by Billy Louise, a girl of 18, since the death of her parents. Buck meets up with Charlie Fox, scapegrace nephew of Martha and Jase, an elderly couple, and deciding to team up as rustlers, they find work with the relatives on a ranch nearby. When cattle are reported missing from the Wolverine, Warren tracks down Olney and threatens him; later Charlie and Olney engage in a fight that results in Olney's death. The rustlers try to throw suspicion on Warren, and he disappears on a scouting trip, being thrown from his horse and stranded with a broken leg. Worried by rumors of his guilt, Billy Louise rides to his cabin, where she remains until he is fully recovered and declared innocent. *Rustlers. Ranches. Injustice.*

WOLVES OF THE AIR **F2.6463**

Sterling Pictures. 22 Jan **1927** [or 25 Nov 1926; c10 Jan 1927; LP23522]. Si; b&w. 35mm. 6 reels, 5,414 ft.

Dir Francis Ford. *Adapt-Cont* James Bell Smith. *Story* J. Francis O'Fearna. *Photog* Herbert Kirkpatrick.

Cast: Johnnie Walker *(Bob Warne)*, Lois Boyd *(Peggy Tanner)*, Maurice Costello *(Bob's father)*, Mildred Harris *(Marceline Manning)*, Gayne Whitman *(Evan Steele)*, William Boyd *(Jerry Tanner)*, Billy Bletcher *("Big Boy" Durkey)*, Bud Jamieson *("Short-Cut" McGee)*.

Action melodrama. Bob Warne returns from the war to find that his father's airplane factory has been taken over by Evan Steele, his former assistant, and that Steele has married Marceline Manning, Bob's sweetheart. His father's friend, Jerry Tanner, now operates a machine shop and gives Bob and his friends jobs. Bob soon falls in love with Peggy, Tanner's daughter, who persuades him to enter an air race in order to win a government contract. Steele sends his men to destroy Bob's plane; and though the plan is thwarted, the shop is destroyed by fire and a man is wounded. Bob enters the race; and in spite of numerous attempts at sabotage and foul play, he wins the race and the love of Peggy. *Veterans. Aviators. Airplane racing. Airplane factories. Machine shops. Sabotage. Fires.*

WOLVES OF THE BORDER **F2.6464**

Phil Goldstone. 15 Jan **1923.** Si; b&w. 35mm. 5 reels.

Dir Alvin J. Neitz. *Photog* William Nobles.

Cast: Franklyn Farnum, William Dyer, William Lester, Andrew Waldron, Margaret Cullington, Violet Schram.

Western comedy-drama. "In the Western cow country a mysterious band of men were harassing the ranchers. Their leader, known only as 'The Wolf,' was secure in the confidence of the countryside, posing as a well-to-do rancher. Only one ranch in the district refused to pay tribute to 'The Wolf' and his pack, the El Fanita Rancho, owned by Dick Donaldson. The arrival of Dick's Aunt Martha and a friend, Mary Wagner, makes Dick more determined than ever to catch 'The Wolf.' Then follows a series of fights between Dick and his men and 'The Wolf's' gang. Dick finally triumphs and delivers the man to the Sheriff." (*Motion Picture News Booking Guide,* 4:111, Apr 1923.) *Ranchers. Aunts. Gangs.*

WOLVES OF THE CITY **F2.6465**

Universal Pictures. 24 Feb **1929** [c19 Sep 1928; LP25633]. Si; b&w. 35mm. 5 reels, 4,160 ft.

Supv William Lord Wright. *Dir* Leigh Jason. *Titl* Val Cleveland. *Story-Cont* Val Cleveland, Vin Moore. *Photog* Charles Stumar. *Film Ed* Harry Marker.

Cast: Bill Cody *(Jack Flynn)*, Sally Blane *(Helen Marsh)*, Al Ferguson *(Mike)*, Monty Montague *(Roscoe Jones)*, Louise Carver *(Mother Machin)*, Charles Clary *(Frank Marsh)*.

Melodrama. Jack Flynn rescues Helen Marsh when her horse runs away with her in the park, later going to work for her wealthy father, an art collector who has been robbed of a valuable oriental jade. Jack recovers the jade only to see Helen kidnaped by the same crooks who took the jade. Jack rescues Helen and turns the crooks over to the police. *Collectors. Kidnaping. Jade.*

WOLVES OF THE DESERT **F2.6466**

Ben Wilson Productions. *Dist* Rayart Pictures. Nov **1926.** Si; b&w. 35mm. 5 reels, 4,168 ft.

Dir Ben Wilson.

Cast: Ben Wilson.

Western melodrama. "Adventures of newcomer to Arizona who through his efforts in defending heroine and her kin from malignant foes is finally rewarded with promise of her hand in marriage." (*Motion Picture News Booking Guide,* 12:66, Apr 1927.) *Arizona.*

WOLVES OF THE NIGHT (Reissue) **F2.6467**

c14 Aug **1924** [LP20485]. Si; b&w. 35mm. 6 reels.

Note: A reissue of a 1919 Fox film directed by J. Gordon Edwards.

WOLVES OF THE NORTH **F2.6468**

Universal Film Manufacturing Co. 16 Apr **1921** [c29 Apr 1921; LP16459]. Si; b&w. 35mm. 5 reels, 4,404 ft.

Story-Dir Norman Dawn. *Scen* Wallace Clifton. *Photog* Thomas Rae.

Cast: Herbert Heyes *("Wiki" Jack Horn)*, Percy Challenger *(Professor Norris)*, Eva Novak *(Aurora Norris)*, Starke Patterson *(David Waters)*, Barbara Tennant *(Jenfau Jen)*, William Eagle Eye *(Massakee)*, Clyde Tracy *(Lech)*, Millie Impolito *(Rose of Spain)*.

Melodrama. Aurora, daughter of Professor Norris, a student of Eskimo culture in the region of Unalik, is devoted to David, a youth of weak character who has been reared in the family, and she is aloof to other men. "Wiki" Jack, primitive and passionate, sets out to win her despite her unconcealed disdain for him. After David's death in an avalanche, Aurora begins to admire Wiki's steadfast courage and submits to his overpowering love. *Eskimos. Alaska. Avalanches.*

Note: Working title: *The Evil Half.*

WOLVES OF THE RANGE **F2.6469**

Harmony Film Co. *Dist* Sunnywest Films. c13 May **1921** [LU16502]. Si; b&w. 35mm. 5 reels.

Copyright author Constance L. Brinsley.

Cast: Jack Livingston.

Western melodrama. In financial difficulty because of helping his father with bad oil investments, Jim Hudson must mortgage his ranch and ride a man-killing bucking horse in the rodeo. Meanwhile, Arthur Blake, the guardian of Jim's fiancée, Cora, tries to discredit Jim so that he may have a chance to marry Cora himself, thereby concealing his misappropriation of her fortune. There is some more double-dealing when Jim's father strikes oil, and Blake "encourages" Cora to see his point of view by kidnaping her; but Jim finds Blake's hideaway cabin, rescues Cora, and supervises Blake's arrest. *Ranchers. Guardians. Kidnaping. Duplicity. Oil. Mortgages. Rodeos.*

WOLVES OF THE ROAD **F2.6470**

Arrow Pictures. 17 May **1925** [c5 Jun 1925; LP21535]. Si; b&w. 35mm. 5 reels, 4,357 ft.

Dir Ward Hayes. *Story* George W. Pyper.

Cast: Yakima Canutt.

Western melodrama. The sheriff is unable to prevent a band of robbers from holding up the stagecoach and stealing the gold dust from the Golden Rod Mine. He telephones his daughter, Marta, about the robbery and gives her a description of the gang leader. A stranger in town, calling himself the Pronto Kid, answers to the description of the outlaw, and Marta attempts to arrest him; but when he tells her the sad story of his life, she lets him go. Marta soon finds the stranger holding a gun on her two brothers, and she interferes, freeing her brothers and again holding the stranger at gunpoint. The stranger again escapes, and, when the sheriff returns, he and Marta pursue him. The stranger, however, captures the outlaws and hands them over to the sheriff when he arrives. As it turns out, the stranger and the sheriff are old friends; and the astonished Marta quickly realizes that the outlaw leader is a dead ringer for the stranger. Her father then explains that the stranger is the owner of the Golden Rod Mine, while the prisoner is a desperate character, having long been wanted by the law. *Sheriffs. Strangers. Outlaws. Brothers. Brother-sister relationship. Stagecoach robberies. Gold mines. Doubles.*

A WOMAN AGAINST THE WORLD **F2.6471**

Tiffany-Stahl Productions. 1 Jan **1928** [c25 Jan 1928; LP24912]. Si; b&w. 35mm. 6 reels, 5,283 ft.

Dir George Archainbaud. *Cont* Gertrude Orr. *Titl* Frederic Hatton, Fanny Hatton. *Story* Albert Shelby Le Vino. *Photog* Chester Lyons. *Set Dsgn* Burgess Beall. *Film Ed* Desmond O'Brien.

Cast: Harrison Ford *(Schuyler Van Loan)*, Georgia Hale *(Carol Hill)*, Lee Moran *(Bob Yates)*, Harvey Clark *(city editor)*, Walter Hiers *(reporter)*, Gertrude Olmstead *(Bernice Crane, bride)*, William Tooker *(bride's father, Mortimer Crane)*, Ida Darling *(bride's mother, Mrs. Crane)*, Wade Boteler *(Jim Barnes, chauffeur)*, Charles Clary *(warden)*, Sally Rand *(Maysie Bell)*, Rosemary Theby *(housekeeper)*, Jim Farley *(detective)*.

Melodrama. Newspaperwoman Carol Hill loves Schuyler Van Loan, a man convicted of killing chorus girl Maysie Bell and sentenced to die in the electric chair. While her editor thinks Van Loan is guilty, Carol proves that he is innocent by extracting a confession from the dead chorus girl's chauffeur, thereby saving her lover in the nick of time. *Reporters. Chorus girls. Editors. Murder. Injustice. Capital punishment.*

THE WOMAN BREED **F2.6472**

R-C Pictures. *Dist* Film Booking Offices of America. Jun **1922.** Si; b&w. 35mm. 6 reels.

Cast: Pauline Frederick.

Melodrama(?). No information about the nature of this film has been found.

Note: Because it is unusual to find no information on an FBO or Pauline Frederick film (all facts here are from the *Film Year Book*, 1923), it can be concluded that this film was also known by another title.

THE WOMAN CONQUERS **F2.6473**

Preferred Pictures. *Dist* Associated First National Pictures. Dec **1922** [c19 Oct 1922; LP18330]. Si; b&w. 35mm. 5-6 reels, 5,102 ft.

Pres by B. P. Schulberg. *Prod* B. P. Schulberg. *Dir* Tom Forman. *Story* Violet Clark. *Photog* Joseph Brotherton.

Cast: Katherine MacDonald *(Ninon Le Compte)*, Bryant Washburn *(Frederick Van Court, III)*, Mitchell Lewis *(Lazar)*, June Elvidge *(Flora O'Hare)*, Clarissa Selwynne *(Jeanette Duval)*, Boris Karloff *(Raoul Maris)*, Francis McDonald *(Lawatha [loyal Indian guide])*.

Northwest melodrama. Bored with her friends and her life as a society leader, Ninon Le Compte goes north to the Hudson Bay area to inspect trapping holdings inherited from her uncle. Frederick Van Court, who frequently proposes to her, and Flora O'Hare accompany her. Lazar, the Canadian manager of the post, openly desires both the company and Ninon for himself and sets fire to the warehouse when Ninon sends him away. When Ninon, Frederick, and Lawatha catch up with Lazar, he makes advances to Ninon; Frederick defends her and is seriously hurt. Lazar and Lawatha kill each other, and Ninon and Frederick survive the difficult return journey to find a happy future. *Socialites. Trappers. Indians of North America. Incendiarism. Hudson Bay.*

THE WOMAN DISPUTED **F2.6474**

United Artists. Sep **1928** [c17 Oct 1928; LP25736]. Mus score & sd eff (Movietone); b&w. 35mm. 9 reels, 8,129 ft. [Also si; 8,051 ft.]

Pres by Joseph M. Schenck. *Dir* Henry King, Sam Taylor. *Scen-Titl* C. Gardner Sullivan. *Photog* Oliver Marsh. *Set Dsgn* William Cameron Menzies. *Film Ed* Hal Kern. *Mus Score* Hugo Riesenfeld. *Song: "Woman Disputed I Love You"* Bernie Grossman, Eddie Ward.

Cast: Norma Talmadge *(Mary Ann Wagner)*, Gilbert Roland *(Paul Hartman)*, Arnold Kent *(Nika Turgenov)*, Boris De Fas *(The Passer-by)*, Michael Vavitch *(Father Roche)*, Gustav von Seyffertitz *(Otto Krueger)*, Gladys Brockwell *(The Countess)*, Nicholas Soussanin *(The Count)*.

Drama. Source: Denison Clift, *The Woman Disputed* (New York opening: 28 Sep 1926). Guy de Maupassant, "Boule de Suif." Paul Hartman, an affable Austrian officer, and his devoted friend, Nika Turgenov, a proud Russian lieutenant on furlough in Lemberg [Lvov], Austria, together bring about the regeneration of Mary Ann Wagner, a prostitute with a noble heart. War is declared between Russia and Austria, and both men are ordered to report to their regiments; Mary promises to marry Paul, and Nika swears revenge. A Russian Army unit led by Nika later occupies Lemberg, and Mary finds that she must submit to his embraces in order to obtain the freedom of a captured spy. The following day, the Austrian Army, guided by the spy's intelligence report, retakes Lemberg, and Paul learns of Mary's sacrifice. He at first refuses to forgive her, but when 10,000 men kneel at her feet in thanks, Paul gratefully joins them. *Prostitutes. Spies. Russians. Self-sacrifice. Austria. World War I. Lvov.*

THE WOMAN FROM HELL **F2.6475**

Fox Film Corp. 21 Apr **1929** [c16 Apr 1929; LP315]. Si; b&w. 35mm. 6 reels, 5,442 ft.

Pres by William Fox. *Supv* James K. McGuinness. *Dir* A. F. Erickson. *Screenplay* Ray Doyle, Charles Kenyon. *Titl* Malcolm Stuart Boylan. *Adapt* George Scarborough, Annette West Bay Scarborough. *Story* Lois Leeson, Jaime Del Rio. *Photog* Conrad Wells. *Art Dir* Ben Carré. *Asst Dir* Ewing Scott.

Cast: Mary Astor *(Bee)*, Robert Armstrong *(Alf)*, Dean Jagger *(Jim)*, Roy D'Arcy *(Slick Glicks)*, May Boley *(Mother Price)*, James Bradbury, Sr. *(Pat)*.

Melodrama. Jim, the son of a New England lighthouse keeper, marries Bee, a girl playing the "Devil" in an amusement concession at a beach resort, and takes her with him to his home on an island off the rockbound coast. Jim and Bee later return to the concession, and Slick Glicks, the barker, attempts to persuade Bee to come back to work, making Jim jealous. Jim and Bee quarrel and return to the lighthouse. Jim's irrational jealousy of the barker continues, and he goes to the mainland to have it out with Slick Glicks. Glicks sees him coming, however, and sneaks out to the lighthouse, attempting to persuade Bee to elope to Havana with him. Jim returns, and the two men Jim eventually comes to realize the innate goodness and loyalty of Bee, and everything turns out all right. *Barkers. Jealousy. Resorts. Lighthouses. New England.*

THE WOMAN FROM MOSCOW **F2.6476**

Paramount Famous Lasky Corp. 3 Nov **1928** [c3 Nov 1928; LP25791]. Sd eff & mus score (Movietone); b&w. 35mm. 7 reels, 6,938 ft.

Dir Ludwig Berger. *Screenplay-Titl* John Farrow. *Photog* Victor Milner. *Film Ed* Frances Marsh, E. Lloyd Sheldon.

Cast: Pola Negri *(Princess Fedora)*, Norman Kerry *(Loris Ipanoff)*, Paul Lukas *(Vladimir)*, Otto Matiesen *(Gretch Milner)*, Lawrence Grant *(The General)*, Maude George *(Olga Andreavitshka)*, Bodil Rosing *(Nadia)*, Jack Luden *(Ipanoff's brother)*, Martha Franklin *(Ipanoff's mother)*, Mirra Rayo *(Ipanoff's sister)*, Tetsu Komai *(groom)*.

Romantic drama. Source: Victorien Sardou, *Fedora, comédie en quatre actes* (Paris, 1908). When Princess Fedora's fiancé, Vladimir, is found murdered in a deserted summer house on his father's estate, Fedora sets out to find Loris Ipanoff, a nihilist whom she suspects of having killed Vladimir. She meets Loris and, not knowing who he is, falls in love with him. Discovering his true identity, she comes to believe him innocent of the murder. He later confesses to it, however, and Fedora betrays him to Vladimir's father; she then discovers that Loris killed Vladimir (who had violated his sister) in self-defense, and she protects him against the assassins hired by Vladimir's father. Loris' family is ordered to Siberia, and his brother is slain resisting arrest; Loris turns against Fedora, and she takes poison. Contrite, Loris returns to Fedora in time to hold her in his arms as she breathes her last. *Aristocrats. Nihilists. Murder. Russia. Siberia.*

THE WOMAN GOD CHANGED **F2.6477**

Cosmopolitan Productions. *Dist* Paramount Pictures. 3 Jul **1921** [c5 Jul 1921; LP16734]. Si; b&w. 35mm. 7 reels, 6,306 or 6,502 ft.

Dir Robert G. Vignola. *Scen* Doty Hobart. *Photog* Al Ligouri. *Set Dsgn* Joseph Urban.

Cast: Seena Owen *(Anna Janssen)*, E. K. Lincoln *(Thomas McCarthy)*, Henry Sedley *(Alastair De Vries)*, Lillian Walker *(Lilly)*, H. Cooper Cliffe *(Donogan)*, Paul Nicholson *(district attorney)*, Joseph Smiley *(police commissioner)*, Templar Saxe *(French commissionaire)*.

Melodrama. Source: Brian Oswald Donn-Byrne, "The Woman God Changed," in *Hearst's* (39:15–17, 44–46, 34–35, Feb–Apr 1921). Dancer Anna Janssen, common-law wife of Alastair De Vries, shoots him in a cafe for dallying with a chorus girl. The story opens with Anna's trial 5 years later, and detective Thomas McCarthy narrates his version of the case. *He is sent to Tahiti where he finds and arrests her; when their ship sinks at sea, only the detective and his prisoner are saved, being cast up on a deserted island. After 2 years together, they realize the strong attachment that has developed, and Anna is regenerated by her free, natural existence. As hope of rescue dims, they take marriage vows, but when a ship is sighted,* *she insists, against his wishes, that she return to face trial.* Anna is sentenced by the judge to be released in the custody of her husband for her natural life. *Dancers. Detectives. Regeneration. Infidelity. Murder. Trials. Tahiti. Shipwrecks.*

THE WOMAN HATER (Warner Brothers Pictures) **F2.6478**
6 Aug **1925** [c12 May 1925; LP21456]. Si; b&w. 35mm. 7 reels, 6,591 ft.

Dir James Flood. *Scen* Hope Loring, Louis D. Lighton. *Adapt* Ruby Mildred Ayres. *Photog* John Mescall.

Cast: Helene Chadwick *(Marie Lamont)*, Clive Brook *(Miles)*, John Harron *(Philip Tranter)*, Helen Dunbar *(Mrs. Tranter)*, Dale Fuller *(secretary)*.

Melodrama. Source: Dorothy Day, *The Eleventh Virgin* (New York, 1924). Miles believes that Marie Lamont has been untrue to him and leaves her. Years pass, and she becomes a famous actress. Young Philip Tranter becomes infatuated with her, and his mother goes to Miles and asks him to disillusion the lad. Miles, who still loves Marie despite his distrust, sets out to court her in the sight of Philip. When Marie breaks several engagements with Philip, he becomes furiously jealous and goes to Miles's apartment with a gun, finding Miles and Marie in each other's arms. He threatens to shoot Miles, and Marie, in order to save his life, tells Miles that she was only toying with his emotions. Miles leaves in dejection and prepares to sail for Europe. But Philip, realizing the depth of Marie's love for Miles, tells her that he will not stand in her way. Marie hurries to the pier, arriving in time to sail with Miles to a European honeymoon. *Actors. Misogynists. Motherhood. Jealousy.*

THE WOMAN HE LOVED **F2.6479**
J. L. Frothingham. *Dist* American Releasing Corp. 1 Oct **1922.** Si; b&w. 35mm. 5 reels, 5,200 ft.

Dir Edward Sloman. *Story-Scen* William V. Mong. *Photog* Antonio Gaudio.

Cast: William V. Mong *(Nathan Levinsky)*, Marcia Manon *(Esther Levinsky)*, Eddie Sutherland *(Jimmy Danvers)*, Mary Wynn *(Helen Comstock)*, Charles French *(John Comstock)*, Fred Malatesta *(Max Levy)*, Harvey Clark *(John Danvers)*, Bruce Guerin *(David Levinsky, as a child)*, Lucille Ward *(Rosie Romansky)*.

Drama. Suffering persecution, Russian Jews Nathan Levinsky, his wife, Esther, and his son, David, escape their homeland for the United States, where Nathan ekes out a feeble existence as a peddler. Esther despairs of her life and leaves Nathan for Max Levy, but reverses cause her to allow David to be adopted by the wealthy Danvers family. Some years later, Nathan prospers on a small California ranch, which adjoins the larger ranch of John Comstock. Comstock makes no secret of his dislike for Jews, yet he unknowingly approves when his daughter, Helen, falls in love with the Danvers' adopted son, Jimmy, whom Nathan secretly recognizes as David. Nathan loses everything in a fire, goes to San Francisco to begin anew, and is reunited with a contrite Esther. Jimmy learns the truth about his parentage and goes to San Francisco to search for Nathan; Helen and Comstock follow, and Helen disappears. Nathan saves Helen from disgrace at the hands of Max Levy, and gratitude prompts Comstock to sanction Helen's marriage to Jimmy. *Jews. Immigrants. Peddlers. Prejudice. Parentage. Adoption. Ghettos. Marriage—Mixed. California. San Francisco.*

THE WOMAN HE MARRIED **F2.6480**
Anita Stewart Productions. *Dist* Associated First National Pictures. ca2 Apr **1922** [New York premiere; released May; c29 Mar 1922; LP17695]. Si; b&w. 35mm. 7 reels, 6,562 ft.

Pres by Louis B. Mayer. *Dir* Fred Niblo. *Scen* Bess Meredyth. *Story* Herbert Bashford. *Photog* Dal Clawson.

Cast: Anita Stewart *(Natalie Lane)*, Darrel Foss *(Roderick Warren)*, Donald MacDonald *(Byrne Travers)*, William Conklin *(Andrew Warren)*, Shannon Day *(Mimi)*, Charlotte Pierce *(Muriel Warren)*, Charles Belcher *(Richard Steel)*, Frank Tokawaja *(Yosi)*.

Domestic drama. Natalie Lane, an artist's model, marries Roddy Warren, son of a steel magnate, who has been a persistent suitor and idler; but because she is considered an unsuitable match by his family, Roddy is disinherited. The couple are thus forced to give up their luxurious apartment for a cheap furnished room, and Roddy, inexperienced and totally unfitted for any kind of work, tries his hand, unsuccessfully, at writing plays. To help the domestic finances, Natalie, who has previously resisted the advances of Byrne Travers, a famous artist, agrees to pose for him. Roddy is unaware of this arrangement, but the elder Warren learns of Natalie's clandestine visits to the artist and informs his son; they discover Travers murdered in his apartment. Suspicion first rests on Natalie, but Mimi, a French model, jealous of Travers' attentions to Muriel, Roddy's sister, confesses that she shot him. Natalie, learning of Travers' scheming, protects Muriel. Roddy's father is convinced of Natalie's innocence and is reconciled to his son, who acquires a job with a theatrical agency. *Models. Artists. Playwrights. Filial relations. Marriage. Inheritance. Theater. Murder.*

THE WOMAN I LOVE **F2.6481**
FBO Pictures. 1 May **1929** [c1 May 1929; LP427]. Si; b&w. 35mm. 7 reels, 6,199 ft.

Dir George Melford. *Screenplay* Gordon Rigby. *Titl* Randolph Bartlett. *Photog* Virgil Miller. *Film Ed* Jack Kitchen.

Cast: Margaret Morris *(Edna Reed)*, Robert Frazer *(John Reed)*, Leota Lorraine *(Lois Parker)*, Norman Kerry *(Kenneth Hamilton)*, Bert Moorehouse *(Lois' boyfriend)*.

Society melodrama. Source: Irma Stormquist, "The Woman I Love" (publication undetermined). Edna Reed, wife of a petty salesclerk, is denied the pleasures of a holiday celebration because of their limited income. Mrs. Parker, who lives in an adjoining apartment and is the lover of Kenneth Hamilton, asks Edna to join a companion of Hamilton's for tea at a Russian cafe; during the outing, Hamilton becomes fascinated with Edna. The following day, he induces Edna to come to his apartment, but Mrs. Parker on a surprise visit discovers them and becomes violently jealous. Edna's husband, John, receives a promotion and rejects Hamilton's gift of flowers. But Hamilton inadvertently reveals his liaison with Edna to John on a business trip. John enters Mrs. Parker's apartment, accuses Hamilton of intimacy with his wife, and apparently kills Hamilton. At the trial, Edna confesses to being intimate with Hamilton, but the prosecuting attorney brings out the truth and Mrs. Parker confesses to the murder. *Salesclerks. Marriage. Infidelity. Luxury. Jealousy. Murder. Trials.*

THE WOMAN IN CHAINS **F2.6482**
Amalgamated Producing Corp. 20 Feb **1923** [New York showing; released Dec 1923]. Si; b&w. 35mm. 7 reels.

Supv Harry Grossman. *Dir* William P. Burt.

Cast: E. K. Lincoln *(Paul Marceau)*, William H. Tooker *(Governor Coudret)*, Mrs. Rodolph Valentino *(Felicia Coudret)*, Martha Mansfield *(Claudia Marvelle)*, Joseph Striker *(Jacques Despard)*, Coit Albertson *(Gene)*.

Underworld melodrama. Source: Edward Owings Towne, "The Madonna in Chains" (publication undetermined). A faithless wife deserts her husband and child to become a cabaret dancer. Her lover goes to jail to protect her. In his absence she marries an artist whom she deserts when her lover is released from prison. Aware of the futility of awaiting her return, the second husband returns to his birthplace, Martinique, and to his childhood sweetheart. *Dancers. Artists. Desertion. Cabarets. Martinique.*

Note: Also known as *The Women in Chains.*

A WOMAN OF AFFAIRS **F2.6483**
Metro-Goldwyn-Mayer Pictures. 15 Dec **1928** [c10 Dec 1928; LP25980]. Sd eff & mus score (Movietone); b&w. 35mm. 8,319 ft. [Also si.]

Dir Clarence Brown. *Cont* Bess Meredyth. *Titl* Marian Ainslee, Ruth Cummings. *Photog* William Daniels. *Art Dir* Cedric Gibbons. *Film Ed* Hugh Wynn. *Song: "Love's First Kiss"* William Axt, David Mendoza. *Asst Dir* Charles Dorian. *Gowns* Adrian.

Cast: Greta Garbo *(Diana)*, John Gilbert *(Neville)*, Lewis Stone *(Hugh)*, John Mack Brown *(David)*, Douglas Fairbanks, Jr. *(Jeffrey)*, Hobart Bosworth *(Sir Morton)*, Dorothy Sebastian *(Constance)*.

Drama. Source: Michael Arlen, *The Green Hat* (New York, c1924). Sleek, elegant Diana Merrick falls in love with aristocratic Neville Holderness, but owing to his father's disapproval of her family's way of life, she and Neville are forbidden to marry. Living with a reckless enthusiasm, Diana finally marries her brother's friend, David Furness, unaware that he is a thief. On their honeymoon in France, learning that the police are after him, David kills himself, and Diana sets out to repay the victims of her husband's crimes. Returning after some years to England, she is too late to save her brother from his fatal alcoholism; and when Neville attempts to return to her, Diana turns him away, influenced by his father's attitude and the fact that he is married. Diana then drives her car into the tree beneath which she and Neville first declared their love, and dies. *Aristocrats. Thieves. Social classes. Filial relations. Brother-sister relationship. Suicide. England. France.*

THE WOMAN OF BRONZE F2.6484

Samuel Zierler Photoplay Corp. *Dist* Metro Pictures. ca18 Feb **1923** [San Francisco premiere; released 26 Feb; c24 Apr 1923; LP18900]. Si; b&w. 35mm. 6 reels, 5,643 ft.

Harry Garson Production. *Dir* King Vidor. *Adapt-Scen* Hope Loring, Louis Duryea Lighton. *Photog* William O'Connell. *Art Dir* Joseph Wright.

Cast: Clara Kimball Young *(Vivian Hunt)*, John Bowers *(Paddy Miles)*, Kathryn McGuire *(Sylvia Morton)*, Edwin Stevens *(Reggie Morton)*, Lloyd Whitlock *(Leonard Hunt)*, Edward Kimball *(Papa Bonelli)*.

Drama. Source: Henry Kistemaeckers, *Woman of Bronze* (trans. by Paul Kester; Chicago opening: Jan 1920). Struggling sculptor Leonard Hunt wins a large sum of money and the commission for a war memorial. He uses Sylvia Morton as his model for "Victory" and soon falls in love with her, but Leonard is dissatisfied with his work, feeling that the figure "lacks a soul." When Vivian Hunt finally confronts her husband, Leonard smashes the statue in grief and rage, then leaves. Some months later, Leonard returns to find the statue restored, and he now perceives in Vivian's face the subtle quality that eluded him in the sculpture. Vivian does not welcome him but announces her departure for Italy. Leonard works at a fever pitch to finish the work, then joins Vivian. *Sculptors. Models. Marriage. Italy.*

A WOMAN OF FLESH F2.6485

3 Nov **1927** [New York State license application]. Si; b&w. 35mm. 6 reels, 5,800 ft.

Cast: Charles Richardson, Edith Hampton.

Note: Production and distribution companies and country of origin not determined. Released in New York by Unique Fotofilm.

A WOMAN OF PARIS F2.6486

United Artists. 1 Oct **1923** [c17 Oct 1923; LP19504]. Si; b&w. 35mm. 8 reels, ca7,500 ft.

Prod-Dir-Writ Charles Chaplin. *Photog* Rollie Totheroh, Jack Wilson. *Art Dir* Arthur Stibolt. *Ed Dir* Monta Bell. *Asst Dir* Eddie Sutherland. *Research* Jean De Limur, Harry D'Arrast. *Bus Mgr* Alfred Reeves.

Cast: Edna Purviance *(Marie St. Clair)*, Adolphe Menjou *(Pierre Revel)*, Carl Miller *(Jean Millet)*, Lydia Knott *(his mother)*, Charles French *(his father)*, Clarence Geldert *(Marie's father)*, Betty Morrissey *(Fifi, Marie's friend)*, Malvina Polo *(Paulette, Marie's friend)*, Karl Gutman *(The Orchestra Conductor)*, Nellie Bly Baker *(masseuse)*, Henry Bergman *(maître d'hôtel)*, Harry Northrup *(valet)*, Charles Chaplin *(station porter)*.

Romantic drama. Marie St. Clair, a French country girl, and her lover, Jean Millet, an art student, plan to elope to Paris when her father locks her out of the house and his parents object to Marie's presence in their home. Marie waits at the railway station while Jean returns home to collect his belongings. His father dies while he is there, and Marie, through a misunderstanding, goes to Paris alone. She becomes wealthy playboy Pierre Revel's mistress, and a year later she accidently meets Jean, who has come to Paris with his mother to study art. Marie commissions the poor artist to paint her portrait, leading to a renewal of their love affair. She accepts his marriage proposal and decides to sever her relationship with Pierre, who has become engaged to a wealthy socialite; later Marie reneges, believing that Jean proposed in a weak moment. The next evening Jean follows Marie and Pierre to a cabaret, sees her for the last time, and commits suicide. Marie and Jean's mother go to the country to care for orphaned children. She never sees Pierre again, but they pass on the road—Pierre in an automobile; Marie riding a haycart—and do not recognize each other. (This symbolic ending was apparently made for American audiences. In an alternative ending made for European audiences, Marie returns to Pierre after her fiancé's suicide.) *Artists. Mistresses. Socialites. Suicide. Paris.*

Note: Working titles: *Public Opinion; Destiny.*

A WOMAN OF THE SEA F2.6487

Charles Chaplin. **1926** [premiered but not released; see note]. Si; b&w. 35mm.

Dir-Writ Josef von Sternberg. *Adtl Dir (see note)* Charles Chaplin. *Photog* Paul Ivano. *Set Dsgn* Danny Hall.

Cast: Edna Purviance, Eve Southern, Gayne Whitman.

Drama. The sea motif is employed as a device counterpointing a psychologically dramatic though simple love story. *The Sea. Monterey (California).*

Note: The story for this film is variously attributed to Chaplin and Sternberg, but Sternberg was definitely contracted to direct the film, intended as the screen comeback of Edna Purviance. Filmed as *The Sea Gull*, it was found lacking by Chaplin, who directed some additional scenes and inserted them into the version finally premiered as *A Woman of the Sea* at a Beverly Hills theater. It was screened only once, then withdrawn into Chaplin's vaults. Filmed largely on the coast near Monterey.

A WOMAN OF THE WORLD F2.6488

Famous Players–Lasky. *Dist* Paramount Pictures. 28 Dec **1925** [c25 Jan 1926; LP22324]. Si; b&w. 35mm. 7 reels, 6,353 ft.

Pres by Adolph Zukor, Jesse L. Lasky. *Dir* Malcolm St. Clair. *Scen* Pierre Collings. *Photog* Bert Glennon.

Cast: Pola Negri *(Countess Elnora)*, Charles Emmett Mack *(Gareth Johns)*, Holmes Herbert *(Richard Granger)*, Blanche Mehaffey *(Lennie Porter)*, Chester Conklin *(Sam Poore)*, Lucille Ward *(Lou Poore)*, Guy Oliver *(Judge Porter)*, Dot Farley *(Mrs. Baerbauer)*, May Foster *(Mrs. Fox)*, Dorothea Wolbert *(Annie)*.

Comedy-drama. Source: Carl Van Vechten, *The Tattooed Countess; a Romantic Novel With a Happy Ending* (New York, 1924). The Countess Elnora, disappointed in love, leaves the decadent European playgrounds and comes to the United States to stay with her cousin, Sam Poore, who lives in a small midwestern town. Her extraordinary appearance and exotic manner set off the town gossips, and various slanders soon reach the ears of Richard Granger, the reforming and virtuous district attorney. He orders her out of town, and she refuses. At a church bazaar, Granger castigates the countess, and she horsewhips him. Granger takes the lashes in good grace, and the countess realizes that he must be in love with her. She drops the whip, and they are quickly in each other's arms, exchanging proposals and acceptances. *District attorneys. Nobility. Reformers. Gossip. Flagellation.*

THE WOMAN ON THE JURY F2.6489

Associated First National Pictures. 20 Apr **1924** [c24 Apr 1924; LP20117]. Si; b&w. 35mm. 7 reels, 7,408 ft.

Pers Supv Earl Hudson. *Dir* Harry O. Hoyt. *Ed Dir* Marion Fairfax. *Adapt* Mary O'Hara. *Photog* James C. Van Trees. *Architecture* Milton Menasco. *Film Ed* LeRoy Stone.

Cast—The Story: Sylvia Breamer *(Betty Brown)*, Frank Mayo *(Fred Masters)*, Lew Cody *(George Montgomery/George Wayne)*, Bessie Love *(Grace Pierce)*, Mary Carr *(Mrs. Pierce)*, Hobart Bosworth *(Judge Davis)*, Myrtle Stedman *(Marion Masters)*, Henry B. Walthall *(prosecuting attorney)*, Roy Stewart *(defense attorney)*.

Cast—Jurymen: Jean Hersholt, Ford Sterling, Arthur Lubin, Stanton Heck, Fred Warren, Edwards Davis, Arthur S. Hull, Kewpie King, Leo White.

Melodrama. Source: Bernard K. Burns, *Woman on the Jury* (New York production: 1923). Betty and her husband, Fred, are called to serve on a jury to try Grace Pierce for the murder of George Montgomery. Finding that Grace's case parallels her own, that they have been both betrayed by the same man, Betty finally confesses her own similar experiences, changing the jury's verdict to acquittal. Realizing her sacrifice, her husband forgives her for the past. *Murder. Trials. Juries.*

Note: Remade by First National in 1929 as *The Love Racket*.

THE WOMAN ON TRIAL F2.6490

Paramount Famous Lasky Corp. 25 Sep **1927** [New York premiere; released 29 Oct; c29 Oct 1927; LP24602]. Si; b&w. 35mm. 6 reels, 5,960 ft.

Pres by Adolph Zukor, Jesse L. Lasky. *Assoc Prod* B. P. Schulberg. *Dir* Mauritz Stiller. *Screenplay* Elsie von Koczain. *Titl* Julian Johnson. *Adapt* Hope Loring. *Photog* Bert Glennon.

Cast: Pola Negri *(Julie)*, Einar Hanson *(Pierre Bouton)*, Arnold Kent *(Gaston Napier)*, André Sarti *(John Morland)*, Baby Dorothy Brock *(Paul)*, Valentina Zimina *(Henrietta)*, Sidney Bracy *(Brideaux)*, Bertram Marburgh *(Morland's lawyer)*, Gayne Whitman *(Julie's lawyer)*.

Melodrama. Source: Ernö Vajda, *Confession* (a play). Julie Morland, on trial for the murder of Gaston Napier, recalls the events of her life 6 years earlier: *She is in love with Pierre Bouton, an artist striken with a serious illness, and during a party at Gaston's studio she prevents his suicide. At an art dealer's Julie meets John Morland, a wealthy suitor who again makes her a marriage offer; and she accepts, thinking that she can thus obtain money to care for Pierre. Five years later, her husband's jealousy drives her to seek consolation in her only child, Paul. Morland finds a letter from Pierre, who is at a sanitarium; and learning that she has visited Pierre, Morland forbids her to see her child. She then kidnaps the boy, and a divorce* *results in Paul's remaining with his mother. Morland forces Gaston, who owes him money, to arrange a compromising situation in his studio, and realizing his cruel trickery, Julie shoots Gaston.* After an acquittal, Julie goes to a beach resort with Paul, and ultimately she finds happiness with Pierre. *Artists. Invalids. Children. Marriage. Murder. Jealousy. Trials. Paris—Quartier Latin.*

THE WOMAN RACKET **F2.6491**

Metro-Goldwyn-Mayer Pictures. 24 Jan **1930** [c20 Jan, 21 Apr 1930; LP1005, LP1234]. Sd (Movietone); b&w. 35mm. 8 reels. [Also si.]

Dir Robert Ober, Albert Kelley. *Scen-Dial* Albert Shelby Le Vino. *Titl* Fred Niblo, Jr. *Photog* Peverell Marley. *Art Dir* Cedric Gibbons. *Film Ed (sd version)* Basil Wrangell. *Film Ed (si version)* Anson Stevenson. *Dance Dir* Sammy Lee. *Rec Engr* Russell Franks, Douglas Shearer. *Wardrobe* David Cox.

Cast: Tom Moore *(Tom)*, Blanche Sweet *(Julia)*, Sally Starr *(Buddy)*, Bobby Agnew *(Rags)*, John Miljan *(Chris)*, Tenen Holtz *(Ben)*, Lew Kelly *(Tish)*, Tom London *(Hennessy)*, Eugene Borden *(Lefty)*, John Byron *(Duke)*, Nita Martan *(Rita)*, Richard Travers *(Wardell)*.

Society drama. Source: Philip Dunning and Frances Dunning, *The Night Hostess* (New York, 1928). During a police raid on a nightclub, hostess Julia Barnes meets Tom, a policeman; they fall in love and are married, but soon Julia tires of domestic life and decides to leave him and return to her old job as a singer and entertainer with her former partner, Chris. But when she becomes involved in a gang killing, Tom comes to her aid and they are reconciled. *Nightclub hostesses. Police. Entertainers. Marriage.*

WOMAN TRAP **F2.6492**

Paramount Famous Lasky Corp. 30 Aug or 28 Sep **1929** [c27 Sep 1929; LP724]. Sd (Movietone); b&w. 35mm. 7 reels, 6,168 ft. [Also si; 6,384 ft.]

Dir William A. Wellman. *Screenplay-Dial* Bartlett Cormack. *Scen* Louise Long. *Photog* Henry Gerrard. *Film Ed* Alyson Shaffer. *Rec Engr* Earl Hayman.

Cast: Hal Skelly *(Dan Malone)*, Chester Morris *(Ray Malone)*, Evelyn Brent *(Kitty Evans)*, William B. Davidson *(Watts)*, Effie Ellsler *(Mrs. Malone)*, Guy Oliver *(Mr. Evans)*, Leslie Fenton *(Eddie Evans)*, Charles Giblyn *(Smith)*, Joseph Mankiewicz *(reporter)*, Wilson Hummell *(detective captain)*, "Sailor Billy" Vincent *(himself, a boxer)*, Virginia Bruce *(nurse)*.

Crook melodrama. Source: Edwin Burke, *Brothers* (a play; publication undetermined). Dan, a tough police captain, and Ray, a hardened criminal, are estranged brothers. When Ray faces capture, Kitty, the sister of Ray's ex-partner (whom Dan helped to convict), offers to help him escape because she sees an opportunity for revenge against Dan. She notifies the police and Dan of Ray's whereabouts, regretting her actions too late to prevent their capture. To avert arrest by his brother, Ray commits suicide. Kitty consoles Dan in his grief, and they come to an understanding over Ray's body. *Police. Brothers. Fugitives. Revenge. Suicide.*

WOMAN, WAKE UP! **F2.6493**

Florence Vidor Productions. *Dist* Associated Exhibitors. 5 Mar **1922** [c21 Feb 1922; LU17568]. Si; b&w. 35mm. 6 reels, 5,241 ft.

Dir Marcus Harrison. *Scen* C. B. Manly. *Story* Ben Moore Clay. *Photog* George Barnes.

Cast: Florence Vidor *(Anne)*, Charles Meredith *(Henry Mortimer)*, Louis Calhern *(Monte Collins)*.

Society comedy-drama. Married after a brief courtship, Monte Collins finds that his wife Anne's concern for domestic duties and a simple life are incompatible with his preference for a fast society life. Seeing that it is impossible to convert him to her way of thinking, Anne decides to meet him halfway. She learns the latest dance steps, dresses in luxurious gowns, and (using her husband's friend, Henry Mortimer, as an escort) visits various gay establishments. At length, Monte awakens to the fact that Anne is drifting from him and becomes wildly jealous, threatening his friend, Henry. Anne convinces him that her love is unchanged, and Monte happily settles for his wife's domestic charm. *Socialites. Marriage. Jealousy.*

THE WOMAN WHO BELIEVED **F2.6494**

Artclass Pictures. *Dist* Weiss Brothers Artclass Pictures. Aug or Nov **1922.** Si; b&w. 35mm. 6 reels.

Dir John Harvey. *Photog* John K. Holbrook.

Cast: Walter Miller, Ann Luther.

Melodrama. "Wild animal drama dealing with the havoc wrought by a jealous mind while three people, forming the eternal triangle, battle for existence in the wilds of the African jungle. The building of a railroad through the jungle, the conflict between the beasts of prey and the little band of explorers, and the dynamiting of a great bridge are a few of the high spots of the story. An aggregation of lions, elephants, leopards, tigers and monkeys, play a prominent part in the unfolding of the plot." (*Motion Picture News Booking Guide*, 3:82, Oct 1922.) *Explorers. Jungles. Courtship. Railroads. Lions. Elephants. Leopards. Tigers. Monkeys.*

THE WOMAN WHO DID NOT CARE **F2.6495**

Gotham Productions. *Dist* Lumas Film Corp. 5 Jul **1927** [c16 Aug 1927; LP24296]. Si; b&w. 35mm. 6 reels, 5,996 ft.

Pres by Sam Sax. *Supv* Carrol Sax, Sam Bischoff. *Dir* Phil Rosen. *Adapt-Cont* Marion Orth. *Photog* Ray June.

Cast: Lilyan Tashman *(Iris Carroll)*, Edward Martindel *(Franklin Payne)*, Arthur Rankin *(Jeffrey Payne)*, Philo McCullough *(Gregory Payne)*, Olive Hasbrouck *(Diana Payne)*, Sarah Padden *(Mrs. Carroll)*, Guinn Williams *(Lars)*.

Society drama. Source: Rida Johnson Young, "The Woman Who Did Not Care" (publication undetermined). Through the faults of her father, Iris Carroll and her mother are reduced to operating a boardinghouse near a railroad. Iris, who has absorbed her mother's hatred of men, and especially her hatred of her own drab surroundings, closes the house upon her mother's death, and with her remaining money determines to use men to further her career. At a fashionable hotel, she meets young Jeff Payne, scion of a wealthy family; the youth becomes infatuated, and Iris quickly accepts his proposal. Franklin Payne, Jeff's father, invites her to the family estate, and falling under her charms, he tries to persuade Iris to marry him rather than his son. In despair at the wreck Iris is making of their home, Diana Payne turns for aid to her Uncle Gregory, a sea captain and a pronounced woman-hater. Intrigued by his indifference, Iris tries unsuccessfully to arouse *his* admiration. By a ruse, he lures her to his boat where they realize their mutual love. *Man-haters. Misogynists. Social classes. Poverty. Boardinghouses.*

THE WOMAN WHO FOOLED HERSELF **F2.6496**

Edward A. MacManus. *Dist* Associated Exhibitors. 29 Oct **1922** [c27 Sep 1922; LU18244]. Si; b&w. 35mm. 6 reels, 5,401 ft.

Pres by Edward A. MacManus. *Dir* Charles A. Logue, Robert Ellis. *Story* Charles A. Logue. *Photog* A. Fried, Eugene O'Donnell.

Cast: May Allison *(Eva Lee)*, Robert Ellis *(Fernando Pennington)*, Frank Currier *(Don Fernando Casablanca)*, Bessie Wharton *(Doña Marie Pennington)*, Robert Schable *(Cameron Camden)*, Louis Dean *(Eban Burnham)*, Rafael Arcos *(The Padre)*.

Melodrama. Desperate for a job, New York showgirl Eva Lee accepts an offer from Cameron Camden and Eban Burnham to go to South America to dance and capture the heart of Fernando Pennington so as to get an option on his Grandfather Casablanca's land. Eva succeeds in snaring Fernando but also falls in love with him. Persuading Camden to surrender the papers, she takes them to the Casablanca residence, only to find it being attacked by Burnham. Fernando repulses the attackers, kills Burnham, and finds happiness with Eva. *Dancers. Land rights. South America. Documentation.*

THE WOMAN WHO NEEDED KILLING *see* **A DANGEROUS WOMAN**

A WOMAN WHO SINNED **F2.6497**

R-C Pictures. *Dist* Film Booking Offices of America. 7 Jul **1924** [c20 Jun 1924; LP20326]. Si; b&w. 35mm. 7 reels, 6,078 ft.

Dir-Writ Finis Fox. *Photog* Hal Mohr, Jean Smith.

Cast: Morgan Wallace *(George Ransdell)*, Irene Rich *(Mrs. Ransdell)*, Lucien Littlefield *(Reverend Hillburn)*, Mae Busch *(Mrs. Hillburn)*, Dicky Brandon *(her son, as a boy)*, Rex Lease *(her son, grown)*, Ethel Teare *(Mitzi)*, Cissy Fitzgerald *(burlesque queen)*, Hank Mann *(Tattu)*, Snitz Edwards *(Grabini)*, Bobby Mack *(sailor)*, Carlos and Jeanette *(apache dancers)*.

Domestic melodrama. A minister's wife leaves her husband and child because of the disgrace of being compromised by George Ransdell, a Wall Street operator, aboard his yacht. Fifteen years later, after having been his mistress, she has him arrested for fraud and imprisoned. Ultimately, she is redeemed by her son, who has become an evangelist, and following Ransdell's death she is reunited with her family. *Clergymen. Evangelists. Mistresses. Infidelity.*

THE WOMAN WHO WALKED ALONE F2.6498

Famous Players–Lasky. *Dist* Paramount Pictures. 11 Jun **1922** [c7 Jun 1922; LP17948]. Si; b&w. 35mm. 6 reels, 5,947 ft.

Pres by Jesse L. Lasky. *Supv?* Penrhyn Stanlaws, Thompson Buchanan. *Dir* George Melford. *Scen* Will M. Ritchey. *Photog* Bert Glennon.

Cast: Dorothy Dalton *(The Honorable Iris Champneys)*, Milton Sills *(Clement Gaunt)*, E. J. Radcliffe *(Earl of Lemister)*, Wanda Hawley *(Muriel Champneys)*, Frederick Vroom *(Marquis [of] Champneys)*, Maym Kelso *(Marchioness [of] Champneys)*, John Davidson *(Otis Yeardley)*, Harris Gordon *(Sir Basil Deere)*, Charles Ogle *(Schriemann)*, Mabel Van Buren *(Hannah Schriemann)*, Maurice B. Flynn *(Jock MacKinney)*, Cecil Holland *(Mombo)*, John MacKinnon *(Lemister's butler)*.

Melodrama. Source: John Colton, "The Cat That Walked Alone" (publication undetermined). Iris Champneys, forced into a marriage of convenience with the Earl of Lemister, attempts to recover some compromising letters for her sister Muriel, who has been seduced by a social parasite. Iris is thus caught by Lemister in a delicate situation, and he demands a divorce. Clement Gaunt, formerly employed by Lemister and in love with Iris, has become a ranch foreman in South Africa. He becomes entangled with Hannah, the rancher's wife, who shoots her husband, then places the blame on Clem when he refuses to run away with her. Seven years later, Gaunt—trying to escape the police—meets Iris, who is operating a tavern on the African caravan road. Iris, learning of his predicament, rides to Hannah Schriemann, telling her that Clem has been executed for her crime. When the police bring Clem to the house, Hannah—frightened by his "ghost"—confesses, and Iris and Clem find a way to happiness. *Sisters. Nobility. Marriage of convenience. Seduction. Divorce. Murder. Blackmail. London. South Africa. Documentation.*

THE WOMAN WHO WAS FORGOTTEN F2.6499

Woman Who Was Forgotten, Inc. *Dist* States Cinema Corp. 1 Jan **1930.** Si; b&w. 35mm. 8 reels, 7,650-7,800 ft.

Prod Charles Goetz. *Dir* Richard Thomas. *Scen* Bert Levino.

Cast: LeRoy Mason *(Richard Atwell)*, Belle Bennett *(Miss Miller)*, Jack Mower *(Andrew Hamilton)*, Gladys McConnell *(Sally)*, William Walling *(Mr. Riggs)*, Jack Trent *(Percy)*.

Drama. Source: Bess Streeter Aldrich, "The Woman Who Was Forgotten," in *American Magazine* (101:50–52, Jun 1926). Miss Miller, a dedicated teacher beloved by her students, loses her job when she protects a favorite pupil, Richard Atwell, who is accused of embezzling from Mr. Riggs's bank. Years later, Richard organizes a banquet as a testimonial to Miss Miller's inspiration throughout 40 years of service, at which is presented a confession to that long-ago crime (possibly committed by Percy Riggs), an apology from Mr. Riggs, and the promise of a principalship of a new school. *Schoolteachers. Students. Bankers. Embezzlement.*

WOMAN WISE F2.6500

Fox Film Corp. 8 Jan **1928** [c3 Jan 1928; LP24817]. Si; b&w. 35mm. 6 reels, 5,050 ft.

Dir Albert Ray. *Scen* Randall H. Faye. *Titl* Malcolm Boylan. *Adapt* Andrew Bennison. *Story* Donald McGibney, James Kevin McGuinness. *Photog* Sidney Wagner. *Film Ed* Ralph Dixon. *Asst Dir* Horace Hough.

Cast: William Russell *(Ne'er-Do-Well)*, June Collyer *(Millie Baxter)*, Walter Pidgeon *(The U. S. Consul)*, Theodore Kosloff *(Abdul Mustapha)*, Ernie Shields *(valet)*, Raoul Paoli *(Khurd chief)*, Duke Kahanamoku *(guard)*, Josephine Borio, Carmen Castillo *(native girls)*.

Comedy-drama. "The American consul in the capital of Persia, his demure and attractive secretary, an American friend with strong inclinations to gallivant after women, and various Oriental personages are the characters who parade through this concoction of comedy pieced together with snatches of drama and fistic brawls" (Raymond Ganley in *Motion Picture News*, 10 Mar 1928, p825). An American consul is forced to shield a rakish American friend who has incurred the enmity of a ruling pasha. Both the consul and his friend are attracted to Millie Baxter, the consul's pretty secretary, but the two forget they are rivals when the pasha attempts to steal the girl. In the end the girl marries the consul. *Ne'er-do-wells. Diplomats. Rakes. Secretaries. Persia. United States—Diplomatic and consular service.*

THE WOMAN WITH FOUR FACES F2.6501

Famous Players–Lasky. *Dist* Paramount Pictures. 24 Jun **1923** [c27 Jun 1923; LP19166]. Si; b&w. 35mm. 6 reels, 5,700 ft.

Pres by Jesse L. Lasky. *Dir* Herbert Brenon. *Adapt* George Hopkins. *Photog* Jimmie Howe.

Cast: Betty Compson *(Elizabeth West)*, Richard Dix *(Richard Templer)*, George Fawcett *(Judge Westcott)*, Theodore von Eltz *(Jim Hartigan)*, Joseph Kilgour *(Judson Osgood)*, James Farley *(Morton)*, Guy Oliver *(Warden Cassidy)*, Charles A. Stevenson *(Ralph Dobson)*, Gladden James *(The Boy)*, Eulalie Jensen *(The Mother)*.

Underworld melodrama. Source: Bayard Veiller, *The Woman With Four Faces* (a play; publication undetermined). Elizabeth West, a reformed crook, works in cooperation with District Attorney Richard Templer to convict a gang of criminals suspected of running a dope ring. Miss West catches the criminals and finds that she has fallen in love with the district attorney. *District attorneys. Criminals—Rehabilitation. Gangs. Narcotics.*

WOMAN-PROOF F2.6502

Famous Players–Lasky. *Dist* Paramount Pictures. 28 Oct **1923** [c6 Nov 1923; LP19569]. Si; b&w. 35mm. 8 reels, 7,687 ft.

Pres by Adolph Zukor. *Dir* Alfred E. Green. *Scen* Tom Geraghty. *Story* George Ade. *Photog* Ernest Hallor.

Cast: Thomas Meighan *(Tom Rockwood, an engineer)*, Lila Lee *(Louise Halliday, his fiancée)*, John Sainpolis *(Milo Bleech, a lawyer)*, Louise Dresser *(Wilma Rockwood)*, Robert Agnew *(Dick Rockwood)*, Mary Astor *(Violet Lynwood)*, Edgar Norton *(Cecil Updyke)*, Charles A. Sellon *(Uncle Joe Gloomer)*, George O'Brien *(Bill Burleigh)*, Vera Reynolds *(Celeste Rockwood)*, Hardee Kirkland *(Colonel Lynwood)*, Martha Mattox *(wistful wooer)*, William Gonder *(Isaac Dirge)*, Mike Donlin *(foreman)*.

Comedy. Tom Rockwood's brother and two sisters attempt to induce him to marry so that they may inherit money left to them by their father. Rockwood, a civil engineer, rescues Louise Halliday, a family friend and ward of Bleech, the Rockwood family lawyer, from a blasting site, and he is so attracted to the girl that he determines to marry her. Bleech attempts to break up the couple because he has nefarious plans for the money, but he fails, and Tom and Louise marry on the last day alloted to them by the will, thereby saving the family fortune. *Engineers. Lawyers. Brother-sister relationship. Inheritance. Marriage.*

Note: Working title: *All Must Marry.*

WOMANHANDLED F2.6503

Famous Players–Lasky. *Dist* Paramount Pictures. 28 Dec **1925** [c21 Dec 1925; LP22163]. Si; b&w. 35mm. 7 reels, 6,765 ft.

Pres by Adolph Zukor, Jesse L. Lasky. *Dir* Gregory La Cava. *Adapt* Luther Reed. *Photog* Edward Cronjager. *Art Dir* Ernest Fegte.

Cast: Richard Dix *(Bill Dana)*, Esther Ralston *(Mollie)*, Cora Williams *(Aunt Abby)*, Olive Tell *(Gwen)*, Eli Nadel *(The Kid)*, Edmund Breese *(Uncle Les)*, Margaret Morris *(Lucille)*, Ivan Simpson *(butler)*, Edgar Nelson *(Pinky)*.

Farce. Source: Arthur Stringer, "Woman-handled," in *Saturday Evening Post* (197:10–11, 2 May 1925). Bill Dana, a society playboy, jumps into the lake in Central Park and rescues a little boy, winning the gratitude of the boy's beautiful cousin, Mollie. She is at first impressed with Bill, but when she discovers that he is one of the "womanhandled" eastern men she despises, Mollie gives him the cold shoulder. In order to become the kind of strong, silent fellow she wants him to be, Bill heads for the West to make a man of himself, quickly discovering that all the real cowboys have gone to Hollywood and that, for the rest, there is nothing left but dudes and tennis players. Mollie comes west, and Bill bribes some local types to act like real cowboys. Mollie sees through the deception and starts for home. A herd of cattle stampedes, and Bill pulls Molly from under their sharp hooves. Having proven his love and manhood at last, Bill wins Mollie's love. *Playboys. Courtship. Stampedes. New York City—Central Park.*

WOMANPOWER F2.6504

Fox Film Corp. 19 Sep **1926** [c5 Sep 1926; LP23074]. Si; b&w. 35mm. 7 reels, 6,240 ft.

Pres by William Fox. *Dir* Harry Beaumont. *Scen* Kenneth B. Clarke. *Photog* Rudolph Bergquist. *Asst Dir* James Dunne.

Cast: Ralph Graves *(Johnny White Bromley)*, Kathryn Perry *(Jenny Killian)*, Margaret Livingston *(Dot)*, Ralph Sipperly *(Gimp Conway)*, William Walling *(Jake Killian)*, David Butler *(Mallory, the Trainer)*, Lou Tellegen *(The Broker)*, Anders Randolf *(Bromley, Sr.)*, Robert Ryan *(Sands)*, Frankie Grandetta *(Sheik)*.

Comedy-drama. Source: Harold MacGrath, "You Can't Always Tell," in *Red Book Magazine* (46:84–90, Dec 1925). Johnny Bromley, a rich young idler, goaded by the sneering laughter of Dot, a vamp, and by his father's open contempt, retires to a prizefighters' training camp for rehabilitation. There he meets Jenny Killian, daughter of the camp owner, and with her encouragement and love he overcomes the unpleasant memories of Dot's accusations of cowardice. When at last he is a success, he wins the hand of Jenny in marriage and his parent's forgiveness; upon meeting his former rival (The Broker) with Dot, he surprises him with a swift punch in the jaw. *Idlers. Filial relations. Cowardice. Vamps. Courtship. Physical training. Prizefighting.*

A WOMAN'S FAITH (Universal-Jewel) **F2.6505**

Universal Pictures. 17 May **1925** [c13 May 1925; LP21464]. Si; b&w. 35mm. 7 reels, 6,023 ft.

Dir Edward Laemmle. *Adapt* E. T. Lowe, Jr., C. R. Wallace. *Photog* John Stumar.

Cast: Alma Rubens *(Nerée Caron)*, Percy Marmont *(Donovan Steele)*, Jean Hersholt *(Cluny)*, ZaSu Pitts *(Blanche)*, Hughie Mack *(François)*, Cesare Gravina *(Odilion Turcott)*, William H. Turner *(Xavier Caron)*, André Beranger *(Leandre Turcott)*, Rosa Rosanova *(Delima Turcott)*.

Melodrama. Source: Clarence Budington Kelland, *Miracle* (New York, 1925). Donovan Steele returns to Quebec to be married and finds his fiancée in the arms of another man. This shatters his faith in God and woman alike, and he takes to the wilderness, becoming known as 'the man who denies God." Visiting a small town, he renews his acquaintance with Nerée Caron, whom he met on a train and who, it happens, is unjustly wanted by the law for the murder of her brother. When Nerée's uncle comes looking for her, Donovan throws him off Nerée's track; Donovan, however, is not clever enough to fool Cluny, her uncle's secretary, who finds Nerée and attempts to force her first to the shrine of St. Anne de Beaupré, where, on the Sacred Stairway, she prays for guidance. She then learns that her uncle has confessed to the murder of her brother, and she and Donovan are wed in the chapel. *Atheists. Fugitives. Hermits. Miracles. Injustice. Quebec.*

A WOMAN'S HEART **F2.6506**

Sterling Pictures. 15 Sep **1926** [c10 Sep 1926; LP23088]. Si; b&w. 35mm. 6 reels, 5,800 ft.

Dir Phil Rosen. *Adapt* Lucille De Nevers.

Cast: Enid Bennett *(Eve Waring)*, Gayne Whitman *(John Waring)*, Edward Earle *(Ralph Deane)*, Mabel Julienne Scott *(Vixen)*, Lois Boyd *(Patsy Allen)*, Louis Payne *(lawyer)*.

Domestic melodrama. Source: Ruth D'Agostino, *The Revelations of a Woman's Heart* (a novel; publication undetermined). Eve marries John Waring for his money though she is infatuated with Ralph Deane and has informed John of the fact. From Ralph she accepts a dinner engagement, which, she insists, will be their farewell; but he conquers her resistance, and John, though he loves her, arranges for a divorce. Though her sister, Patsy, proves that Ralph is a rotter, Eve refuses to be convinced. John confronts Ralph when he tries to seduce Patsy. Vixen, Ralph's jealous mistress, shoots him; and when, following the discovery of Vixen's suicide, John is cleared, he and Eve are happily reconciled. *Sisters. Mistresses. Marriage. Infidelity. Lechery. Murder. Jealousy. Seduction. Suicide.*

WOMAN'S LAW **F2.6507**

Dallas M. Fitzgerald Productions. *Dist* Peerless Pictures. 15 Aug **1927.** Si; b&w. 35mm. 6 reels, 5,955 ft.

Dir Dallas M. Fitzgerald. *Story-Scen* H. Tipton Steck. *Photog* Milton Moore. *Film Ed* Desmond O'Brien.

Cast: Pat O'Malley *(Trooper Bucky O'Hare)*, Lillian Rich *(Helene)*, Ernest Wood *(Vaughan Neil)*, John Cossar *(John Collon)*, Harold Miller *(Philip Harley)*, Edward Cecil *(Inspector Steele)*, Audrey Ferris *(Rose La Pierre)*, Sam Allen *(Jules La Pierre)*, Bert Starkey, James Florey, Charles Stevens.

Northwest melodrama. Helene is forced into marrying blackmailer Vaughan Neil, who holds incriminating evidence of a scandal involving her father. In a struggle with the girl the villain is killed, and she is suspected. But eventually she is cleared and finds happiness with the Mountie assigned to the case. *Blackmail. Scandal. Northwest Mounted Police.*

A WOMAN'S MAN (Reissue) **F2.6508**

8 May **1930** [New York State license]. Si; b&w. 35mm. 5 reels, 4,700 ft.

Note: Originally released by Arrow Film Corp. in 1920.

WOMAN'S PLACE **F2.6509**

Joseph M. Schenck Productions. *Dist* Associated First National Pictures. 17 Oct **1921** [c6 Oct 1921; LP17059]. Si; b&w. 35mm. 6 reels, 5,645 or 5,900 ft.

Pres by Joseph M. Schenck. *Dir* Victor Fleming. *Story* John Emerson, Anita Loos. *Photog* Oliver Marsh, J. Roy Hunt.

Cast: Constance Talmadge *(Josephine Gerson)*, Kenneth Harlan *(Jim Bradley)*, Hassard Short *(Freddy Bleeker)*, Florence Short *(Amy Bleeker)*, Ina Rorke *(Mrs. Margaret Belknap)*, Marguerite Linden *(Miss Jane Wilson)*, Jack Connolly *(Dan Dowd)*.

Comedy. The Women's Political League in a midwestern city selects Josephine Gerson as its candidate for mayor because of her stylishness and good looks. Her fiancé, Jim Bradley, a political leader, backs his friend Freddy Bleeker as the opposition candidate. When Josephine overhears Freddy promising certain appointments, she breaks her engagement and in a notable speech wins the men of the town to her side, but the women vote against her and Freddie wins by a narrow margin. Jim Bradley splits with the gang, and the new appointments are all filled by women; converted to honest politics, he is reunited with Josephine, who accepts her "defeat" with grace. *Mayors. Women in politics. Politics. Elections.*

A WOMAN'S SACRIFICE *see* **A VIRGIN'S SACRIFICE**

THE WOMAN'S SIDE **F2.6510**

Preferred Pictures. *Dist* Associated First National Pictures. Mar **1922** [c28 Dec 1921; LP17616]. Si; b&w. 35mm. 6 reels, 5,366 ft.

Pres by B. P. Schulberg. *Dir-Writ* J. A. Barry. *Scen* Elliott Clawson. *Photog* Joseph Brotherton.

Cast: Katherine MacDonald *(Mary Gray)*, Edward Burns *(Theodore Van Ness, Jr.)*, Henry Barrows *(Theodore Van Ness, Sr.)*, Dwight Crittenden *(Judge Gray)*, Ora Devereaux *(The ex Mrs. Judge Gray)*, Wade Boteler *("Big Bob" Masters)*.

Melodrama. Judge Gray, who is running for governor, is supported by Theodore Van Ness, Sr., prominent newspaper publisher, with the understanding that he has a clean record. His opponent, Bob Masters, is attorney for Mrs. Gray in securing a "framed" divorce from the judge on the grounds of desertion and mental cruelty. The judge's daughter, Mary, meets Theodore, Jr., and falls in love with him, though he is unaware of her identity until his father threatens, at the behest of Masters, to publish the story of Gray's divorce. Overhearing a conversation between Gray and Masters, Mary, unable to secure help from her mother, goes to Masters' office and threatens suicide unless he retracts the story. Gray forces Masters, at gunpoint, to have the story retracted, and the ex Mrs. Gray, in a jealous rage, shoots at Masters and wounds Mary. Masters is beaten in the election; Mary recovers and is engaged to Van Ness, Jr. *Judges. State governors. Publishers. Lawyers. Politics. Divorce. Elections. Newspapers.*

A WOMAN'S WAY **F2.6511**

Columbia Pictures. 18 Feb **1928** [c15 Mar 1928; LP25066]. Si; b&w. 35mm. 6 reels, 5,472 ft.

Prod Harry Cohn. *Dir* Edmund Mortimer. *Cont* Will M. Ritchie. *Adapt* Elmer Harris. *Story* Izola Forrester. *Photog* Ray June. *Art Dir* Robert E. Lee. *Film Ed* Arthur Roberts. *Asst Dir* Eugene De Rue.

Cast: Margaret Livingston *(Liane)*, Warner Baxter *(Tony)*, Armand Kaliz *(Jean)*, Mathilde Comont *(Mother Suzy)*, Ernie Adams *(Pedro)*, John St. Polis *(Mouvet)*.

Melodrama. Liane, a Parisian dancer aspiring to join the company of the Opéra, falls in love with Tony, a wealthy American who helps her become *première danseuse*. When Jean, a criminal whom she once shielded, escapes from prison and seeks her out, she assists the police in his capture and frees herself of the only blight on her otherwise happy life. *Dancers. Prison escapes. Opera. Ballet. Paris.*

A WOMAN'S WOMAN **F2.6512**

Albion Productions. *Dist* Allied Producers and Distributors. 24 Sep **1922** [c12 Jun 1922; LP17961]. Si; b&w. 35mm. 8 reels, 7,900 ft.

Dir Charles Giblyn. *Scen* Raymond Schrock. *Photog* Jacques Bizeul. *Art Dir* Joseph Clement.

Cast: Mary Alden *(Densie Plummer)*, Louise Lee *(Harriet Plummer)*, Dorothy Mackaill *(Sally Plummer)*, Holmes E. Herbert *(John Plummer)*, Albert Hackett *(Kenneth Plummer)*, Rod La Rocque *(Dean Laddbarry)*, Horace James *(Sam Hippler)*, Cleo Madison *(Iris Starr)*, Donald Hall *(Rex Humberstone)*, J. Barney Sherry *(Senator James Gleason)*.

Domestic melodrama. Source: Nalbro Isadorah Bartley, *A Woman's Woman* (Boston, 1919). After 20 years of married life, Densie Plummer comes to the realization that the only pride her family take in her is in her cooking. In fact, Kenneth, her youngest son, is the only family member on whom she can rely. As John, her husband, is facing financial difficulties, Denise opens a tearoom, prospers, and soon becomes prominent in club circles. When John begins a flirtation with a young widow and asks for a divorce, Densie agrees; but with a market crash, John loses the widow along with his money. Sally, the youngest daughter, is refused marriage by an unsavory suitor, and she attempts suicide; Kenneth goes to avenge his sister and is killed by the man. His tragic death brings the family to its senses, and Mrs. Plummer leaves her business to establish a new home for them all. *Businesswomen. Marriage. Family life. Motherhood. Suicide. Teashops.*

WOMEN AND GOLD **F2.6513**

Gotham Productions. *Dist* Lumas Film Corp. 18 Jan **1925** [7 Feb 1925; LP21106]. Si; b&w. 35mm. 6 reels, 5,400 ft.

Dir-Story James P. Hogan. *Scen* Betty Grace Hartford. *Photog* William Daniels.

Cast: Frank Mayo *(Dan Barclay)*, Sylvia Breamer *(Myra Barclay)*, William Davidson *(Señor Ortego)*, Frankie Darrow *(Dan Barclay, Jr.)*, Ina Anson *(Carmelita)*, Tote Du Crow *(Ricardo)*, James Olivio *(Humpy)*, John T. Prince *(Doc Silver)*.

Melodrama. Dan and Myra Barclay, on vacation in Monte Carlo, are forced to cut short their European visit when Dan is ordered by his company to take charge of a gold mine in South America. Having once experienced the sweet life, Myra can no longer tolerate the rough monotony of life in the mining country, and she runs off with Señor Ortego, the owner of the mine. Myra soon realizes that Ortego's intentions are dishonorable and she decides to return to Dan, but on the way home she is in an accident and loses her memory. Myra is taken to a country rest home and Dan is later jailed for the attempted murder of Ortego. Dan escapes from prison with Ricardo, a fellow convict who also has a grudge against Ortego. Dan and Ricardo go to Ortego's home, and Ricardo forestalls Dan by killing Ortego with a knife. Dan later finds Myra, and the shock of seeing him again restores her memory and they are happily reunited. *Infidelity. Amnesia. Murder. Prison escapes. Gold mines. Monte Carlo. South America.*

WOMEN EVERYWHERE **F2.6514**

Fox Film Corp. 1 Jun **1930** [c9 May 1930; LP1316]. Sd (Movietone); b&w. 35mm. 8 reels, 7,500 ft.

Pres by William Fox. *Assoc Prod* Ned Marin. *Dir* Alexander Korda. *Scen-Dial* Harlan Thompson, Lajos Biró. *Story* George Grossmith, Zoltan Korda. *Photog* Ernest Palmer. *Sets* William Darling. *Film Ed* Harold Schuster. *Songs: "Women Everywhere," "Beware of Love," "One Day," "Good Time Fifi," "Bon Jour," "Marching Song"* William Kernell. *Song: "All the Family"* William Kernell, George Grossmith. *Song: "Smile, Legionnaire"* William Kernell, Charles Wakefield Cadman. *Rec Engr* Arthur L. von Kirbach. *Asst Dir* Edwin Marin. *Wardrobe* Sophie Wachner.

Cast: J. Harold Murray *(Charlie Jackson)*, Fifi Dorsay *(Lili La Fleur)*, George Grossmith *(Aristide Brown)*, Clyde Cook *(Sam Jones)*, Ralph Kellard *(Michel Kopulos)*, Rose Dione *(Zephyrine)*, Walter McGrail *(Lieutenant of Legionnaires)*.

Romantic drama. Charlie Jackson, a gunrunner in Morocco, becomes infatuated with cabaret singer Lili La Fleur, favorite of the Legionnaires, and proposes marriage to her, but he is captured by a French destroyer through information supplied by Michel. While being escorted through Casablanca, Charlie escapes from the police and takes refuge in Lili's dressing room; she disguises him as a singer and later helps to plan his escape; however, he is caught in a Legionnaire's uniform and is sent into the desert to fight the Arabs. He returns later and wins the admiration and affections of Lili. *Gunrunners. Singers. Courtship. Cabarets. France—Army—Foreign Legion. Morocco. Casablanca.*

Note: Working title: *Hell's Belles.*

WOMEN FIRST **F2.6515**

Perfection Pictures. *Dist* Columbia Pictures. 1 Nov **1924** [c17 Nov 1924; LP20779]. Si; b&w. 35mm. 5 reels, 4,875 ft.

Dir Reeves Eason. *Story* Wilfred Lucas. *Photog* Allen Thompson.

Cast: William Fairbanks *(Billy Decker)*, Eva Novak *(Jennie Doon)*, Lydia Knott *(Mrs. Abigail Doon)*, Bob Rhodes *(Johnny Doon)*, Lloyd Whitlock *(Harvey Boyd)*, Andy Waldron *(Judge Weatherfax)*, Dan Crimmins *(Amos Snivens)*, William Dyer *(sheriff)*, Max Ascher *(H. L. S. J. Lee)*, Merta Sterling *(Mandy, his wife)*, Jack Richardson *(Madden)*, William Carroll *(stableman)*.

Melodrama. En route to apply for a job as horsetrainer for Colonel Doon, ex-jockey Billy Decker rescues a girl on a runaway horse and discovers that she is Jennie Doon, the late colonel's daughter and manager of the stables. Jennie hires Billy to train Moonstone for the Kentucky Derby and approves of her brother, Johnny, as jockey. While the Doons work with Moonstone, Harvey Boyd places his hopes on his horse, Bluebell, the derby favorite, so that he may satisfy the demand of Amos Snivens that he repay certain loans. Boyd unsuccessfully offers to buy Moonstone and attempts to bribe Billy. While Billy and Johnny guard the stable, Boyd's men drug them and set fire to the building. Moonstone is rescued, Johnny is injured, and Jennie herself dons the family silks and arrives at the track in time to ride to victory. Boyd must answer to the sheriff for his tactics. *Horsetrainers. Jockeys. Moneylenders. Brother-sister relationship. Horseracing. Arson. Bribery. Kentucky Derby.*

THE WOMEN IN CHAINS *see* **THE WOMAN IN CHAINS**

WOMEN IN LOVE *see* **SINNER'S HOLIDAY**

WOMEN LOVE DIAMONDS **F2.6516**

Metro-Goldwyn-Mayer Pictures. 12 Feb **1927** [c2 Mar 1927; LP23716]. Si; b&w. 35mm. 7 reels, 6,365 ft.

Dir-Story Edmund Goulding. *Scen* Lorna Moon, Waldemar Young. *Titl* Edwin Justus Mayer. *Photog* Ray Binger. *Sets* Cedric Gibbons, Arnold Gillespie. *Film Ed* Hugh Wynn. *Wardrobe* André-ani.

Cast: Pauline Starke *(Mavis Ray)*, Owen Moore *(Patrick Michael Regan)*, Lionel Barrymore *(Hugo Harlan)*, Cissy Fitzgerald *(Mrs. Ray)*, Gwen Lee *(Roberta Klein)*, Douglas Fairbanks, Jr. *(Jerry Croker-Kelley)*, Pauline Neff *(Mrs. Croker-Kelley)*, Constance Howard *(Dorothy Croker-Kelley)*, George Cooper *(Snub Flaherty)*, Dorothy Phillips *(Mrs. Flaherty)*.

Society melodrama. Mavis Ray, supported by Hugo Harlan, whom she believes to be her uncle, is attracted to young society man Jerry Croker-Kelley, and they plan to elope unless the "uncle" consents to their marriage. Harlan informs Jerry of the "unholy secret" of Mavis' parentage, and both he and the girl are disillusioned. Later, taking a liking to her chauffeur, Patrick Regan, Mavis is drawn to him by witnessing the death of his wife(?) when they are injured in an automobile accident. She cares for his children but considers herself unworthy of him. In a hysterical outburst, Mavis severs her ties to Harlan. Later, having become a taxicab driver, Regan finds her working as a hospital nurse, and they are happily reconciled. *Chauffeurs. Nurses. Taxi drivers. Illegitimacy. Parentage. Courtship.*

WOMEN MEN LIKE **F2.6517**

Plaza Pictures. 23 May **1928** [New York State license]. Si; b&w. 35mm. 6 reels, 5,800 ft.

Cast: Alice Lake.

Melodrama(?). No information about the nature of this film has been found.

Note: Entitled *Any Woman's Man* previous to New York State licensing.

WOMEN MEN LOVE **F2.6518**

Bradley Feature Film Corp. 29 Jan **1921** [Trade review]. Si; b&w. 35mm. 6 reels.

Dir Samuel R. Bradley. *Scen* Charles T. Dazey, Frank Dazey. *Photog* Harry Gersted.

Cast: William Desmond *(David Hunter)*, Marguerite Marsh *(Evelyn Hunter)*, Martha Mansfield *(Ruth Gibson)*, Charlotte Naulting *(Baby Dora)*, Evan Burrows Fontaine *(Moira Lamson)*, Denton Vane *(Stephen Dabney)*, Pauline Dempsey *(Mammy Chloe)*.

Domestic melodrama. Source: Charles T. Dazey, "Women Men Love" (publication undetermined). David Hunter, a successful architect, lives with his wife, Evelyn (who loves gambling and admiration), small daughter Dora, and sister-in-law Ruth. When Evelyn tells her husband she owes $10,000 in bridge losses, she promises not to gamble or see her lover, Stephen Dabney, again if he will pay the debt. Stephen's friend, Moira Lamson, however, entices her to the country club for one last game. David and Ruth, worried by her prolonged absence, go to the club where they find her in Stephen's arms. Evelyn accuses her sister of spying on her and demands a divorce from her husband. Ruth, weary of her sister's frailties, moves out of the household and takes up nursing. Evelyn's health suffers from the strain, and now with David and Ruth gone, she is ill and alone.

David and Ruth take pity on her and return. Now wiser, Evelyn is reconciled with David. *Architects. Nurses. Sisters. Gambling. Infidelity. Country clubs. Bridge.*

WOMEN MEN MARRY **F2.6519**

Edward Dillon Productions. *Dist* Truart Film Corp. 2 Dec **1922** [New York premiere; released Dec; c27 Dec 1922; LP18531]. Si; b&w. 35mm. 6 reels, ca5,600 ft.

Prod-Dir Edward Dillon. *Story-Scen* Adelaide Heilbron. *Photog* Roy Overbaugh.

Cast: E. K. Lincoln *(Dick Clark)*, Florence Dixon *(Emerie Rogers)*, Charles Hammond *(Montgomery Rogers)*, Hedda Hopper *(Eleanor Carter)*, Cyril Chadwick *(Lord Brooks Fitzroy)*, Margaret Seddon *(Hetty Page)*, Richard Carlyle *(Adam Page)*, Julia Swayne Gordon *(Aunt Gertrude)*, Maude Turner Gordon *(Lady Mowbray)*, James Harrison *(Warren Mortimer)*, Tammany Young.

Society drama. Reared by Montgomery Rogers as his own child, Emerie Rogers seeks to marry a titled Englishman, as instructed by Aunt Gertrude. On an ocean liner she meets Dick Clark and later turns to him when Rogers' death reveals her to be the daughter of servants and leaves her penniless. Emerie returns to her parents, the Pages, and her happiness is complete when Rogers' second will leaves the bulk of his estate to her. *Aunts. Parentage. Inheritance. Adoption. Ocean liners.*

Note: "The picture is probably an old one that has waited for release a long time. All the dresses of the women are a foot and a half from the ground, in the fashion of nearly two years ago." (*Variety*, 5 Jan 1923.)

WOMEN THEY TALK ABOUT **F2.6520**

Warner Brothers Pictures. 11 Aug **1928** [c30 Jul 1928; LP25502]. Talking sequences & mus score (Vitaphone); b&w. 35mm. 6 reels, 5,527 ft. [Also si, 8 Sep 1928; 5,275 ft.]

Dir Lloyd Bacon. *Scen-Dial* Robert Lord. *Titl* Joseph Jackson. *Story* Anthony Coldeway. *Photog* Frank Kesson. *Film Ed* Tommy Pratt.

Cast: Irene Rich *(Irene Mervin Hughes)*, Audrey Ferris *(Audrey Hughes)*, William Collier, Jr. *(Steve Harrison)*, Anders Randolph *(John Harrison)*, Claude Gillingwater *(Grandfather Mervin)*, Jack Santoro *(frameup man)*, John Miljan *(officer)*.

Comedy-drama. Mervin, a banker in a small town, successfully forbids his daughter, Irene, to marry John Harrison, the office boy in his bank. Years pass; John becomes the mayor, and Irene marries another, going abroad to live. After the death of her husband, she returns to her hometown, accompanied by her flapper daughter, Audrey. Audrey immediately falls in love with Harrison's son, Steve, and Irene, not liking the way Harrison is running the town, decides to run for mayor herself. Harrison instructs his police force to find something with which to discredit Irene, and unable to find anything, they discredit Audrey instead. Harrison straightens out the scandal, and Irene decides that she would rather be a mayor's wife than a mayor. *Bankers. Mayors. Police. Flappers. Scandal. Frameup. Smalltown life.*

WOMEN WHO DARE **F2.6521**

Excellent Pictures. 31 Mar **1928** [c10 Apr 1928; LP25146]. Si; b&w. 35mm. 7 reels, ca6,600 ft.

Pres by Samuel Zierler. *Dir* Burton King. *Ed Supv* Harry Chandlee. *Adapt* Adrian Johnson. *Story* Langdon McCormick. *Photog* Art Reeves. *Film Ed* Harry Chandlee.

Cast: Helene Chadwick *(Stella Mowbray)*, Charles Delaney *(Ralph Miles)*, Frank Beal *(Edgar Mowbray)*, Jack Richardson *(Frank Lawson)*, Henry A. Barrows *(Dr. Alden)*, James Quinn *(Benny, the Spider)*, James Fitzgerald *(Spike Carson)*, Grace Elliott *(Satin Maggie)*, Margaret McWade *(Mrs. Kelly)*.

Society melodrama. Stella Mowbray, daughter of a wealthy and prestigious family owning extensive property in the slums, becomes a nurse in a slum hospital. Deeply affected by her experiences, Stella begins to write newspaper articles attacking slum conditions. By accident, Stella meets young rounder Ralph Miles, nurses him back to health when he falls ill, influences him to change his bachelor ways, and persuades him and her father to adopt humanitarian ideals. *Nurses. Humanitarianism. Wealth. Poverty. Slums.*

Note: Some sources give Stella's surname as Vance.

WOMEN WHO GIVE **F2.6522**

Louis B. Mayer Productions. *Dist* Metro-Goldwyn Distributing Corp. 3 Mar **1924** [c7 Mar 1924; LP20032]. Si; b&w. 35mm. 8 reels, 7,500 ft.

Pres by Louis B. Mayer. *Dir* Reginald Barker. *Scen* A. P. Younger. *Adapt-Cont* Bernard McConville, J. G. Hawks. *Photog* Percy Hilburn. *Art Dir* Jack Holden.

Cast: Barbara Bedford *(Emily Swift)*, Frank Keenan *(Jonathan Swift)*, Renée Adorée *(Becky Keeler)*, Robert Frazer *(Capt. Joe Cradlebow)*, Joseph Dowling *(Capt. Bijonah Keeler)*, Margaret Seddon *(Ma Keeler)*, Joan Standing *(Sophia Higginbottom)*, Victor Potel *(Ephraim Doolittle)*, Eddie Phillips *(Noah Swift)*, William Eugene *(Ezra Keeler)*.

Drama. Source: Sarah P. McLean Greene, *Cape Cod Folks* (Boston, 1881). Jonathan Swift, stern Cape Cod businessman, has ambitions for his children, Emily and Noah, which are thwarted when they take romantic interests in Capt. Joe Cradlebow and Becky Keeler, respectively. Not realizing that Becky expects a child and has been promised marriage, Swift has Noah shanghaied, while Becky stows away on Cradlebow's vessel. There is a terrific storm; but Cradlebow rescues Noah, and the fleet returns safely to shore—thanks to lighthouse keeper Bijonah Keeler, Becky's father, who sets his house afire to give the sailors light. Swift relents, and his children marry whom they please. *Stowaways. Social classes. Fishing industry. Shanghaiing. Seafaring life. Lighthouses. Cape Cod.*

WOMEN WHO WAIT *see* **FORBIDDEN LOVE**

WOMEN'S WARES **F2.6523**

Tiffany Productions. 1 Oct **1927** [c14 Oct 1927; LP24513]. Si; b&w. 35mm. 6 reels, 5,614 ft.

Dir Arthur Gregor. *Scen* Frances Hyland. *Story* E. Morton Hough. *Photog* Chester Lyons. *Sets* Burgess Beall. *Film Ed* Desmond O'Brien.

Cast: Evelyn Brent *(Dolly Morton)*, Bert Lytell *(Robert Crane)*, Larry Kent *(Jimmie Hayes)*, Gertrude Short *(Maisie Duncan)*, Myrtle Stedman *(Mrs. James Crane)*, Richard Tucker *(Frank Stanton)*, Cissy Fitzgerald *(Mrs. Frank Stanton)*, Sylvia Ashton *(patron)*, Stanhope Wheatcroft *(floorwalker)*, Gino Corrado *(modiste)*, Robert Bolder *(boarder)*, James Mack *(patron)*.

Romantic drama. Dolly Morton, a salesgirl in a New York department store, like her sophisticated roommate Maisie Duncan, maintains high ideals regarding men; and among her many admirers she prefers Jimmie Hayes for his clean-cut and engaging manner. His persistence pays off when she accepts a dinner invitation, and after a movie he takes her to her boardinghouse; the presence of a gossipy boarder forces her to admit Jimmie to her room, where his feeling overcomes his judgment, and she denounces him. At the insistence of Maisie, Dolly determines to use men to her advantage and accepts an expensive Park Avenue apartment from millionaire Frank Stanton. Dolly begins to cultivate the attentions of young Robert Crane, an aristocratic gentleman, while working as a mannequin, but he loses all respect for her upon finding her in a luxury flat; realizing the distastefulness of her position, Dolly finds happiness with Jimmie, whom she loves. *Salesclerks. Fashion models. Millionaires. Wealth. Department stores. Boardinghouses. New York City.*

WON IN THE CLOUDS (Universal Thrill Feature) **F2.6524**

Universal Pictures. 22 Apr **1928** [c24 Oct 1927; LP24585]. Si; b&w. 35mm. 5 reels, 4,348 ft.

Pres by Carl Laemmle. *Dir* Bruce Mitchell. *Adapt-Cont* Carl Krusada. *Titl* Gardner Bradford. *Photog* William Adams. *Film Ed* Lee Anthony. *Tech Adv* Al Johnson.

Cast: Al Wilson *(Art Blake)*, Helen Foster *(Grace James)*, Frank Rice *(Percy Hogan)*, George French *(Dr. Cecil James)*, Joe Bennett *(Portuguese Jack Woods)*, Albert Prisco *(Bangula)*, Myrtis Crinley *(Mira)*, Frank Tomick, Roy Wilson, Evan Unger, Red Sly *(henchmen)*, Art Goebel *(Sam Highflyer)*.

Adventure melodrama. Dr. Cecil James and his daughter, Grace, accompanied by her maid, Mira, journey to Africa to investigate Jack Woods, manager of the Consolidated Diamond Mining Co., who has used the excuse of a native plague to close the mine and hold up shipments. Being advised by his men of the doctor's visit, he has the party waylaid by Swahili; the two girls flee and Jack "rescues" them, taking them to the mine dwelling. Fearing for their safety, Sir Henry Blake sends his son, Art, after them, and he succeeds in eluding the gang at the mine. Art sneaks into the Swahili village and frees the doctor but is himself captured and thrown in a lions' den, from which, however, he escapes. Jack forces Grace to accompany him in a getaway by air. Art pursues in another plane and in an air battle subdues the villain, who falls to his death. *Physicians. Swahili. Aviation. Diamond mines. Plague. Africa. Lions.*

WONDER OF WOMEN **F2.6525**

Metro-Goldwyn-Mayer Pictures. 13 Jul **1929** [c5 Sep 1929; LP658]. Talking sequences (Movietone); b&w. 35mm. 11 reels, 8,347 ft. [Also si; 8,796 ft.]

Dir Clarence Brown. *Cont-Dial* Bess Meredyth. *Titl* Marian Ainslee. *Photog* Merritt B. Gerstad. *Art Dir* Cedric Gibbons. *Film Ed* William Le Vanway. *Song: "Ich Liebe Dich"* Fred Fisher, Martin Broones. *Song: "At Close of Day"* Ray Klages, Jesse Greer, Martin Broones. *Rec Engr* Ralph Shugart, Douglas Shearer. *Asst Dir* Charles Dorian. *Wardrobe* David Cox.

Cast: Lewis Stone *(Stephen Tromholt)*, Leila Hyams *(Karen)*, Peggy Wood *(Brigitte)*, Harry Myers *(Bruno Heim)*, Sarah Padden *(Anna)*, George Fawcett *(Doctor)*, Blanche Frederici *(Stephen Tromholt's housekeeper)*, Wally Albright, Jr *(Wulle-Wulle)*, Carmencita Johnson *(Lottie)*, Anita Fremault *(Lottie)*, Dietrich Haupt *(Kurt)*, Ullrich Haupt *(Kurt)*.

Drama. Source: Hermann Sudermann, *Die Frau des Steffen Tromholt* (Stuttgart, 1927). Stephen Tromholt is a German concert pianist whose artistic temperament leads him around and about the creation of his "masterpiece." With a constant eye for the feminine flare, he meets Brigitte (a widow with three children and a strong sense of responsibility) on a train, wines and dines her, and has her engaged to be married that very evening as the train whizzes by the concert stop for the night. As they set up a home by the sea, Stephen is often struck by the wanderlust and though unfaithful on several occasions, most ardently with his former lover, Karen, he eventually comes to realize, at his wife's deathbed, the true measure and worth of her unflagging devotion. *Pianists. Germans. Widows. Marriage. Infidelity.*

THE WONDERFUL THING **F2.6526**

Norma Talmadge Productions. *Dist* Associated First National Pictures. 7 Nov **1921** [c20 Oct 1921; LP17112]. Si; b&w. 35mm. 7 reels, 6,880 ft.

Pres by Joseph M. Schenck. *Dir* Herbert Brenon. *Scen* Clara Beranger, Herbert Brenon. *Photog* J. Roy Hunt. *Set Dsgn* Ben Carré.

Cast: Norma Talmadge *(Jacqueline Laurentine Boggs)*, Harrison Ford *(Donald Mannerby)*, Julia Hoyte *(Catherine Mannerby)*, Howard Truesdale *(James Sheridan Boggs)*, Robert Agnew *(Laurence Mannerby)*, Ethel Fleming *(Dulcie Mannerby Fosdick)*, Mabel Bert *(Lady Sophia Alexandria Mannerby)*, Fanny Burke *(Angelica Mannerby)*, Walter McEwen *("Smooth Bill" Carser)*, Charles Craig *(General Lancaster)*.

Melodrama. Source: Lillian Trimble Bradley and Forrest Halsey, *The Wonderful Thing* (New York opening: 17 Feb 1920). Laurence, younger son of the Mannerbys, while intoxicated, forges his mother's name to a £50 check to pay off "Smooth Bill" Carser, a gambler. Jacqueline Boggs, a young American visiting the Mannerbys, falls in love with Donald, who marries her in an effort to solve the family's financial difficulties; but his sense of honor prevents his using her money. Donald partially reimburses Carser, however, under an agreement whereby Laurence will not leave the jurisdiction of British courts. Determined to reform Laurence, Jacqueline persuades him to go to her father's American ranch, whereupon Carser tells Jacqueline that Donald married her for her wealth and receives a payment for the breach of the agreement. In America, Donald becomes a strong admirer of Mr. Boggs, and through the latter's effort husband and wife are happily reunited. *Gamblers. Forgery. Wealth. Marriage. Blackmail.*

A WONDERFUL WIFE (Universal Special) **F2.6527**

Universal Film Manufacturing Co. 24 Apr **1922** [c16 Apr 1922; LP17759]. Si; b&w. 35mm. 5 reels, 4,668 ft.

Pres by Carl Laemmle. *Dir* Paul Scardon. *Scen* Arthur F. Statter. *Photog* Ben Reynolds.

Cast: Miss Du Pont *(Chum)*, Vernon Steele *(Alaric Lewin)*, Landers Stevens *(Gregory)*, Charles Arling *(Halton)*, Ethel Ritchie *(Diana)*, Harris Gordon *(Nugent)*, Nick De Ruiz *(native groom)*.

Domestic melodrama. Source: Dolf Wyllarde, *The Rat Trap* (New York, 1904). Capt. Alaric Lewin and his bride, Chum, are sent to Key Island, off the coast of Africa, where he has been commissioned as assistant to Gregory of the British Service. Chum determines to vamp the commissioner and thereby win a better post for her husband, and her husband finds favor in the eyes of Diana Churton, whose husband is away on an expedition. Instead of carrying out orders to send Lewin to Malta, Gregory puts him in charge of a dangerous jungle expedition; but Chum, learning of his treachery, forces him at gunpoint to organize a search party. Alaric is found delirious from fever, the party is attacked by natives, and Gregory is killed. Alaric, reunited with his wife, is given his orders to Malta. *Vamps. Jungles. Great Britain—Diplomatic and consular service. Key Island. Africa.*

WONDERS OF THE SEA **F2.6528**

Williamson's Undersea Wonders. *Dist* Film Booking Offices of America. Oct **1922** [New York showing; released 29 Apr 1923; c15 Oct 1922, 29 Apr 1923; LP18799, LP18915]. Si; b&w. 35mm. 4-5 reels, 3,600-5,500 ft.

Prod-Dir-Writ J. Ernest Williamson. *Photog* Jay Rescher.

Cast: J. Ernest Williamson *(The Oceanographer)*, Richard Ross *(The Stowaway)*, Asa Cassidy *(The Artist)*, Lulu McGrath *(The Girl)*, Jack Gardner *(The Diver)*, Jay Rescher *(The Cameraman)*.

Exploration documentary. The ocean depths are explored with the aid of a submarine chamber of Williamson's invention and a few hardy souls. The construction of the device is examined; but most of the footage is given to plant and animal life, a girl swimming among the coral growths, and two divers who encounter a moray and an octopus. *Oceanographers. Stowaways. Artists. Divers. Motion picture cameramen. Nassau. The Sea. Octopi. Eels.*

Note: Filmed near Nassau.

WONDERS OF THE WILD **F2.6529**

Burr Nickle Pictures. ca30 Mar **1925** [New York premiere]. Si; b&w. 35mm. 7 reels.

Travelog. The picture depicts Burr Nickle's travels in several strange and exotic lands. Starting from Mexico City, Nickle journeys into the interior of Mexico and visits the Yaqui Indians. From there, he goes to the west coast of Mexico and embarks on a visit to the islands off the coast of Baja California, where he fishes and visits a herd of sea lions. Nickle then goes to Yokohama and on to Borneo. He ends his trip in Singapore, where he attends the annual Hindu worship in the Mamman Temple. *Yaqui Indians. Hinduism. Mexico City. Yokohama. Borneo. Singapore. Seals.*

THE WOODROW WILSON FILM MEMORIAL **F2.6530**

Woodrow Wilson Memorial Society. Jun **1924** [c9 May 1927; MP4007]. Si; b&w. 35mm. 6 reels.

Prod H. F. Drugan. *Compiler* H. F. Drugan.

Documentary film. Woodrow Wilson's public and private lives are shown as he travels in the United States, England, France, Belgium, Italy, and on the sea, including his notification of his election to the presidency, his inaugurations, life in the White House, outdoor recreation, events leading up to the declaration of war, drafting of soldiers, scenes of fighting, the Armistice celebration, making of the peace treaty, return of our soldiers from France. There are scenes of the President's collapse, the relinquishment of the office and the inauguration of President Harding, tribute to the Unknown Soldier, death of President Harding, inauguration of President Coolidge, last public appearances of Wilson, and his funeral. *World War I. England. France. Belgium. Italy. Thomas Woodrow Wilson. Warren Gamaliel Harding. John Calvin Coolidge. The White House. The Unknown Soldier.*

WORDS AND MUSIC **F2.6531**

Fox Film Corp. 18 Aug **1929** [c15 Aug 1929; LP600]. Sd (Movietone); b&w. 35mm. 7 reels, 6,500 ft. [Also si; 5,745 ft.]

Pres by William Fox. *Prod Executive* Chandler Sprague. *Dir* James Tinling. *Stgd by* Frank Merlin. *Dial* Andrew Bennison. *Story* Frederick Hazlitt Brennan, Jack McEdwards. *Photog* Charles G. Clarke, Charles Van Enger, Don Anderson. *Film Ed* Ralph Dixon. *Song: "Stepping Along"* William Kernell. *Song: "Too Wonderful for Words"* Dave Stamper, William Kernell, Edmund Joseph, Paul Gerard Smith. *Song: "Shadows"* Sidney Mitchell, Archie Gottler, Con Conrad. *Mus Dir* Arthur Kay. *Ensembles Dir* Edward Royce. *Sd* Donald Flick, Joseph Aiken. *Asst Dir* William Tinling. *Cost* Sophie Wachner.

Cast: Lois Moran *(Mary Brown)*, David Percy *(Phil Denning)*, Helen Twelvetrees *(Dorothy Bracey)*, William Orlamond *(Pop Evans)*, Elizabeth Patterson *(Dean Crockett)*, Duke Morrison *(Pete Donahue)*, Ward Bond *(Ward)*, Richard Keene *(singer in "Stepping Along")*, Frank Albertson *(Skeet Mulroy)*, Tom Patricola *(Hannibal)*, Bubbles Crowell *(Bubbles)*, Eddie Bush, Paul Gibbons, Bill Seckler, Ches Kirkpatrick *(Biltmore Quartet)*, Dorothy Ward *(girl)*, Collier Sisters *(dancers)*, Muriel Gardner, Dorothy Jordan, Lois Moran, Helen Parrish, David Percy, Jack Wade *(song and dance principals)*, Vina Gale, Arthur Springer *(adagio dancers)*, Harriet Griffith, John Griffith *(adagio dancers)*, Helen Hunt, Charles Huff *(adagio dancers)*, Sugar Adair, Iris Ashton, Lita Chevret, Marie Cooper, Blanche Fisher, Katherine Irving, Lucile Jacques, Jean Lorraine, Marion

Mills, Sue Rainey, Betty Recklaw *(showgirls)*, Bubbles Crowell, Muriel Gardner, Dorothy Jordan, Lois Moran, Tom Patricola, Jack Wade *(specialty dancers)*, Harry Albers, Sayre Dearing, Carl Dial, Tom Gentry, Kenneth Gibson, Dick Gordon, Earl Hughes, Earl McCarthy, William Miller, Paul Power, Maurice Salvage, John Sylvester, M. Troubetsky *(chorus men)*, Darline Addison, Julie Blake, Raymonda Brown, Adele Cutler, Diana Dare, Dot Darling, Lucille Day, June Glory, Charlotte Hagaler, Kathryne Hankin, Billy Kittridge, Paula Langlen, Mildred Laube, Mildred Livingston, Helen Louise, Mae Madison, Peggy Malloy, Mavis May, Emily Renard, Bobby Renee, Thelma Roberts, Bernice Snell, Darleen Ver Jean, Marion Waldon, Wilma Wray *(young ladies of the ensemble)*.

Musical revue. Fraternity brothers Phil Denning and Pete Donahue are competing to have campus sweetheart Mary Brown lead their musical numbers in the college's annual revue. Phil wins out, but Mary gets involved in a practical joke directed toward the straitlaced dean of women and is about to be exposed by Dorothy Blake, who sets as the price of her silence the leading part in Tom's number. A good sport, Mary joins Pete's skit and helps make it a success; then, when she hears about Dorothy's ruse, Mary boldly confesses to Dean Crockett that she is responsible for the practical joke, replaces Dorothy in Phil's number, and wins the contest for him. *Students. College life. Fraternities. Theater—Amateur.*

THE WORLD AT HER FEET **F2.6532**

Paramount Famous Lasky Corp. 14 May **1927** [c14 May 1927; LP23987]. Si; b&w. 35mm. 6 reels, 5,691 ft.

Pres by Adolph Zukor, Jesse L. Lasky. *Assoc Prod* B. P. Schulberg. *Dir* Luther Reed. *Screenplay* Louise Long. *Titl* George Marion, Jr. *Adapt* Doris Anderson. *Photog* Harry Fischbeck.

Cast: Florence Vidor *(Jane Randall)*, Arnold Kent *(Richard Randall)*, Margaret Quimby *(Alma Pauls)*, Richard Tucker *(Dr. H. G. Pauls)*, William Austin *(Detective Hall)*, David Torrence *(client)*.

Bedroom farce. Source: Georges Berr and Louis Verneuil, *Maître Bolbec et son mari; comèdie en trois actes* (Paris, c1927). Richard Randall withdraws from his wife's law office when he becomes independently wealthy, and Jane then becomes neglectful of her husband. Convinced that the only means of regaining her attention is as a client, he deliberately collides with Alma Pauls's automobile. Alma also is being neglected by her mate, Dr. Pauls. Jane agrees to act as his attorney, while Alma and Richard agree to help each other win back their partners. Alma's husband becomes suspicious and asks for a divorce when he finds Randall in her boudoir, and he seeks the counsel of Jane. Randall finds them in a seemingly intimate relationship, and after explanations, Jane and Pauls agree to devote less time to their work. *Lawyers. Physicians. Marriage. Infidelity. Women in public office.*

THE WORLD STRUGGLE FOR OIL **F2.6533**

United States Bureau of Mines of the Department of the Interior–Sinclair Consolidated Oil Corp. *Dist* Selznick Distributing Corp. 15 Aug **1924** [c23 Aug 1923; MP2313]. Si; b&w. 35mm. 7 reels, 6,321 ft. [Also 5 reels, 4,480 ft.]

Prod-Dir Capt. Hank E. Butler.

Educational film. Source: Isaac Frederick Marcosson, "The World Struggle for Oil," in *Saturday Evening Post* (vol 196, 22 Dec 1923–26 Jan 1924). "Early history of petroleum demonstrated by extracts from feature films including the defense of Babylon from *Intolerance*; early drilling endeavours by Col. E. L. Drake; the effect of petroleum on industry and transport; uses in World War I; world consumption and production, chiefly illustrated by maps and diagrams." *(National Film Archive Catalogue, Part II, Silent Non-Fiction Films, 1895-1934;* The British Film Institute, London, 1960, p142.) *Oil. World War I. Edwin Laurentine Drake. "Intolerance".*

THE WORLD WAR **F2.6534**

George F. Zimmer. *Dist* American Legion Film Service. 23 Dec **1926** [New York State license]. Si; b&w. 35mm. 9 reels, 8,900 ft.

Documentary. This film is a historical record composed entirely of official war films. *World War I.*

WORLDLY GOODS **F2.6535**

Famous Players–Lasky. *Dist* Paramount Pictures. ca2 Nov **1924** [New York premiere; released 24 Nov; c4 Nov 1924; LP20736]. Si; b&w. 35mm. 6 reels, 6,055 ft.

Pres by Adolph Zukor, Jesse L. Lasky. *Dir* Paul Bern. *Screenplay* A. P. Younger. *Photog* Bert Glennon.

Cast: Agnes Ayres *(Eleanor Lawson)*, Pat O'Malley *(Fred Hopper)*, Victor Varconi *(Clifford Ramsay)*, Edythe Chapman *(Mrs. Lawson)*, Bert Woodruff *(Mr. Lawson)*, Maude George *(Letitia Calhoun)*, Cecille Evans *(Vivian Steel)*, Otto Lederer *(Sol Shipik)*.

Domestic comedy-drama. Source: Sophie Kerr, "Worldly Goods," in *Ladies Home Journal* (40:6–8; 41:20–21, 24–26, 34–35; Dec 1923–Mar 1924). Eleanor Lawson refuses the marriage proposal of wealthy Clifford Ramsay but accepts that of Fred Hopper, a breezy, fast-talking automobile salesman with big ideas and grand schemes. Early in their marriage Eleanor realizes that Fred is more talk than industry, and mounting bills force her to get a job. Even Fred is about to take that drastic step when he overhears Ramsay's plans to build on a certain site and buys the property with a loan from Letitia Calhoun. Fred makes a large profit, but Eleanor is jealous of his relations with Letitia and seeks a divorce. She is dissuaded by Fred, who promises to mend his ways. *Salesmen. Courtship. Marriage. Real estate. Finance—Personal.*

WORLDLY GOODS **F2.6536**

Trem Carr Productions. *Dist* Continental Talking Pictures. 1 Aug **1930** [c15 Jul 1930; LP1679]. Sd; b&w. 35mm. 7 reels, 6,065 ft.

Prod Trem Carr. *Dir* Phil Rosen. *Adapt-Dial* John Grey, Scott Littleton. *Story* Andrew Soutar. *Photog* Herbert Kirkpatrick. *Film Ed* Carl Himm. *Sd* Neil Jack.

Cast: James Kirkwood *(John C. Tullock)*, Merna Kennedy *(Mary Thurston)*, Shannon Day *(Cassie)*, Ferdinand Schumann-Heink *(Jeff)*, Eddie Featherstone *(Jimmy)*, Thomas Curran *(secretary)*.

Melodrama. Blinded by an airplane crash in France, Jeff swears vengeance on John C. Tullock, a profiteering manufacturer, who produces faulty planes for government contracts. Not wanting to inflict his disability on others, he has his pal Jimmy tell Mary, his sweetheart, that he was killed and buried at sea. Jeff and Jimmy become mechanics in a Tullock plant, and when Tullock finds Jeff working on his own plane and learns the circumstances of his affliction, he pays the cost of an operation to restore his sight, meanwhile keeping his identity a secret. At a party given by Tullock, Mary, at the insistence of her fellow chorus girl, Cassie, meets the manufacturer, who takes an interest in her ambitions to be a singer; as a result of his affection for Mary, he becomes a philanthropist, and they are married. Recovering his sight, Jeff resigns himself to the state of affairs, though he still loves Mary. While on a flight with Jeff, however, the industrialist, realizing his wife loves Jeff, leaps out of the plane to his death. *Aviators. Mechanics. Chorus girls. Manufacturers. Marriage. Blindness. Philanthropy. Suicide. World War I.*

THE WORLDLY MADONNA **F2.6537**

Harry Garson Productions. *Dist* Equity Pictures. 15 Apr or 1 May **1922.** Si; b&w. 35mm. 6 reels, ca5,500 ft.

Pres by Harry Garson. *Dir* Harry Garson. *Story* Sada Cowan. *Photog* Arthur Edeson.

Cast: Clara Kimball Young *(Lucy Trevor, the dancer/Janet Trevor, the nun)*, William P. Carleton *(John McBride)*, Richard Tucker *(Alan Graves)*, George Hackathorne *(Ramez)*, Jean De Limur *(Toni Lorenz)*, William Marion *(Dr. Krell)*, Milla Davenport *(jail matron)*.

Melodrama. Janet Trevor, a convent novitiate, agrees to exchange places with her twin, cabaret dancer Lucy Trevor, who believes that she has killed politician John McBride. With her gentle manner, Janet achieves some success as a performer and falls in love with McBride when he recovers from his wound. Restaurateur Alan Graves tries to implicate McBride and Janet in the murder of Toni Lorenz (to which Ramez, a hunchback, confesses) and forces a confession of narcotics addiction out of Lucy, but it is revealed that Graves bribed Lorenz to leave the country. Janet finds happiness with McBride, and Lucy finds peace as a nun. *Nuns. Dancers. Twins. Sisters. Politicians. Hunchbacks. Restaurateurs. Narcotics. Murder.*

THE WORLD'S A STAGE **F2.6538**

Principal Pictures. 1 Nov **1922.** Si; b&w. 35mm. 6 reels, 5,700 ft.

Dir Colin Campbell. *Scen* Colin Campbell, George Bertholon. *Story* Elinor Glyn. *Photog* Dal Clawson, Byron Haskins.

Cast: Dorothy Phillips *(Jo Bishop)*, Bruce McRae *(John Brand)*, Kenneth Harlan *(Wallace Foster)*, Otis Harlan *(Richard Manseld Bishop)*, Jack McDonald *(property man)*.

Romantic drama. A screen star chooses to marry a salesman rather than an older admirer and sees her mistake when her husband becomes a shiftless alcoholic. Brand, the former suitor, tries to straighten out the husband and comfort the star. The accidental death by drowning of the husband gives Brand the chance to marry her. *Actors. Salesmen. Motion pictures. Marriage. Alcoholism.*

WORLDS APART **F2.6539**

Selznick Pictures. *Dist* Select Pictures. Jan **1921** [c30 Jan 1921; LP16078]. Si; b&w. 35mm. 5-6 reels, 5,780 ft.

Pres by Lewis J. Selznick. *Dir* Alan Crosland. *Scen* R. Cecil Smith. *Story* John Lynch. *Photog* Jules Cronjager.

Cast: Eugene O'Brien *(Hugh Ledyard)*, Olive Tell *(Elinor Ashe)*, William H. Tooker *(Peter Lester)*, Florence Billings *(Marcia Marshall)*, Arthur Housman *(Harley Marshall)*, Louise Prussing *(Phyllis Leigh)*, Warren Cook *(Ten Eyck)*.

Mystery melodrama. Hugh, having been rejected by Phyllis Leigh in favor of Peter Lester, a wealthier suitor, prevents Elinor Ashe from drowning herself. Recklessly he marries Elinor, but they occupy different wings of his house. Lester and Phyllis arrive as guests, and a new manservant, favored by Elinor, is hired. When Lester is murdered, the servant is charged with the crime, and Elinor admits to Hugh that he is indeed her father, recently released from prison. While in the company of Marcia Marshall, Hugh discovers her husband, Harley, dying in a Chinese opium den. He confesses that, victimized by Lester, he killed him. Elinor's father is released, and she is reconciled with Hugh. *Filial relations. Marriage. Suicide. Murder. Opium.*

THE WORLD'S APPLAUSE **F2.6540**

Famous Players–Lasky. *Dist* Paramount Pictures. ca14 Jan **1923** [Chicago premiere; released 29 Jan; c3 Jan 1923; LP18562]. Si; b&w. 35mm. 8 reels, 6,526 ft.

Pres by Adolph Zukor. *Dir* William De Mille. *Story-Scen* Clara Beranger. *Photog* Guy Wilky. *Set Dsgn* Paul Iribe. *Cost* Paul Iribe.

Cast: Bebe Daniels *(Corinne d'Alys)*, Lewis Stone *(John Elliott)*, Kathlyn Williams *(Elsa Townsend)*, Adolphe Menjou *(Robert Townsend)*, Brandon Hurst *(James Crane)*, Bernice Frank *(maid to Corinne)*, Mayme Kelso *(secretary to Corinne)*, George Kuwa *(valet to Townsend)*, James Neill *(valet to Elliott)*.

Drama. Broadway star Corinne d'Alys turns a deaf ear to producer John Elliott's admonitions to be more cautious in her craving for the world's applause. She accepts the attentions of artist Robert Townsend, who is married to John's sister. Elsa Townsend accidentally stabs her husband in her anger but doesn't confess to the crime until John is about to be arrested and Corrinne has gained much notoriety. With their names cleared Corinne and John find happiness. *Actors. Artists. Theatrical producers. Theater. New York City—Broadway.*

THE WORLD'S CHAMPION **F2.6541**

Famous Players–Lasky. *Dist* Paramount Pictures. ca25 Feb **1922** [New York premiere; released 12 Mar; c8 Mar 1922; LP17624]. Si; b&w. 35mm. 5 reels, 5,030 ft.

Pres by Jesse L. Lasky. *Supv by* Thompson Buchanan. *Dir* Philip E. Rosen. *Adapt* J. E. Nash, Albert Shelby Le Vino. *Photog* Charles Edgar Schoenbaum.

Cast: Wallace Reid *(William Burroughs)*, Lois Wilson *(Lady Elizabeth)*, Lionel Belmore *(John Burroughs)*, Henry Miller, Jr. *(George Burroughs)*, Helen Dunbar *(Mrs. Burroughs)*, Leslie Casey *(Rev. David Burroughs)*, Stanley J. Sandford *(Lord Brockington)*, W. J. Ferguson *(butler)*, Guy Oliver *(Mooney)*.

Society comedy. Source: Thomas Louden and A. E. Thomas, *The Champion, a Comedy in Three Acts* (New York, 1922). William Burroughs, son of a prosperous Briton, aspires to associate with nobility, but when he approaches Lady Elizabeth Galton, he is thrashed by her cousin, Lord Brockington, and disowned by his father. Emigrating to America, he enters the ring and becomes a middleweight champion. Seven years later he returns home to find that Lady Galton, in poor circumstances, has become his father's social secretary. Burroughs, at first horrified to hear of his son's profession, relents when newspapers exploit his fame and he is visited by nobility, but Lady Galton spurns him because of his fighting reputation, though she also refuses to marry Lord Brockington. Challenging William to a fight, Brockington is badly beaten, but when William renounces the ring to become an attorney, Elizabeth announces she is willing to go to America with him as his wife. *Immigrants. Prizefighters. Social classes. Nobility. Lawyers. Secretaries. England.*

THE WORLD'S HEAVYWEIGHT CHAMPIONSHIP CONTEST BETWEEN JACK DEMPSEY AND GEORGES CARPENTIER **F2.6542**

Fred C. Quimby, Inc. c4 Jul **1921** [MP1989]. Si; b&w. 35mm. 5 reels.

Pres by G. L. (Tex) Rickard.

Sports actuality. An account of Georges Carpentier's unsuccessful challenge of Jack Dempsey's heavyweight boxing championship in an open-air arena in Jersey City, New Jersey, 3 July 1921. Preliminary material includes Carpentier's arrival, inspection of the arena by various officials, Dempsey and Carpentier in training, and pre-bout excitement. The fight itself is ended by Dempsey's fourth-round knockout of Carpentier. *Prizefighting. Jersey City. Jack Dempsey. Georges Carpentier.*

THE WRECK **F2.6543**

Columbia Pictures. 5 Feb **1927** [c7 Feb 1927; LP23645]. Si; b&w. 35mm. 6 reels, 5,631 ft.

Supv Harry Cohn. *Dir* William J. Craft. *Story* Dorothy Howell. *Photog* William Fildew.

Cast: Shirley Mason *(Ann)*, Malcolm McGregor, Francis McDonald, James Bradbury, Jr., Barbara Tennant, Frances Raymond.

Crook melodrama. Ann unknowingly goes through a bogus marriage ceremony with Joe, a thief, and she is held as an accomplice to his crimes by the police. On her way to the prison, there is a train wreck, and when Ann is rescued she is mistaken for Dorothy (Mrs. Robert) Brooks, a prison matron, and is taken to the home of Robert's mother; charmed by Ann, he begs her to continue to pose as his wife at least until she is well. Joe, who has escaped from the police, plots with his friend, Pete, to get her back and to steal the Brooks jewels. Ann is abducted, and when she realizes that Robert is following them, she causes the car to plunge over a cliff. Though Ann is unhurt, Joe is killed; but Pete, still alive, confesses to the fake marriage, and Ann is united with Robert. *Prison matrons. Thieves. Marriage—Fake. Mistaken identity. Train wrecks.*

THE WRECK OF THE HESPERUS **F2.6544**

De Mille Pictures. *Dist* Pathé Exchange. 31 Oct **1927** [c27 Oct 1927 LP24577]. Si; b&w. 35mm. 7 reels, 6,447 ft.

Supv-Screenplay Harry Carr. *Dir* Elmer Clifton. *Titl* John Krafft. *Story* John Farrow. *Photog* John Mescall. *Art Dir* Stephen Goosson. *Film Ed* Eleanor Hall. *Asst Dir* Leigh Smith. *Prod Mgr* Harry Poppe. *Cost* Adrian.

Cast: Sam De Grasse *(Capt. David Slocum)*, Virginia Bradford *(Gale Slocum)*, Francis Ford *(John Hazzard)*, Frank Marion *(John Hazzard, Jr.)*, Alan Hale *(Singapore Jack)*, Ethel Wales *(Deborah Slocum)*, Josephine Norman *(The Bride)*, Milton Holmes *(Zeke)*, James Aldine *(cabin boy)*, Budd Fine *(first mate)*.

Romantic drama. Suggested by: Henry Wadsworth Longfellow, "The Wreck of the Hesperus," in *Ballads and Other Poems* (1841). Captain Slocum of the *Hesperus* arrives on shore in a New England village to find that the girl he loves has been tricked into marrying John Hazzard in his absence. Heartbroken and bitter, the captain, with his daughter, Gale, and second mate, Singapore Jack, returns to sea. He rescues from a burning vessel John Hazzard, Jr., son of his rival, and though he tries to keep the boy from Gale, a romance develops. To separate the lovers, he puts his daughter ashore with her aunt. Discovering the captain's treachery, the boy swims to shore and joins her; the captain retrieves her and puts to sea in the face of storm warnings. When the storm breaks in all its fury, the captain lashes Gale to the mast, which then is washed overboard; but young Hazzard rescues her, and they find happiness together. *Sea captains. Seafaring life. Village life. Revenge. Ships. New England. Shipwrecks.*

WRECKAGE *see* **STORMSWEPT**

WRECKAGE **F2.6545**

Banner Productions. *Dist* Henry Ginsberg Distributing Corp. 12 Sep **1925** [New York showing; c15 Sep 1925; LP21821]. Si; b&w. 35mm. 6 reels.

Ben Verschleiser Production. *Dir* Scott R. Dunlap. *Titl* Frederick Hatton, Fanny Hatton. *Adapt* Agnes Parsons. *Photog* King Gray, A. Fried.

Cast: May Allison *(Rene)*, Holmes Herbert *(Stuart Ames)*, John Miljan *(Maurice Dysart)*, Rosemary Theby *(Margot)*, James Morrison *(Grant Demarest)*.

Melodrama. Source: Izola Forrester, "Salvage," in *Ainslee's* (vol 54,

Sep–Dec 1924). In order to protect Grant Demarest from a siren named Margot, Stuart Ames attempts to disillusion him about the girl. Margot threatens to kill herself; Grant reaches for the gun and is accidentally shot. Blaming himself for his friend's death, Stuart books passage on a liner, where he meets Rene, the daughter of a dishonest dealer in gems. They are shipwrecked, and Rene returns to the United States, becoming the guest of Margot, her childhood friend. Rene is later lured to a wilderness cabin by Dysart (an accomplice of Rene's father who is disguised as a count); he attempts to assault her, and Ames, who has followed them, knocks him over a cliff. Ames and Rene make plans to be married. *Murder. Suicide. Impersonation. Shipwrecks.*

THE WRIGHT IDEA **F2.6546**

C. C. Burr Pictures. *Dist* First National Pictures. 5 Aug **1928** [c26 Jul 1928; LP25493]. Si; b&w. 35mm. 7 reels, 6,225-6,300 ft.

Dir Charles Hines. *Story-Scen* Jack Townley. *Titl* Paul Perez. *Photog* William J. Miller, Al Wilson. *Film Ed* George Amy.

Cast: Johnny Hines *(Johnny Wright)*, Louise Lorraine *(Helen)*, Edmund Breese *(Mr. Filbert)*, Walter James *(Captain Sandy)*, Fred Kelsey *(M. T. Flatt)*, Henry Barrows *(Mr. Smoot)*, Henry Hebert *(Mr. Stein)*, Charles Giblyn *(Mr. Carter)*, Jack McHugh *(Spec)*, J. Barney Sherry *(O. J. Gude)*, Charles Gerrard *(Mr. Roberts)*, Betty Egan *(Betty)*, Blanche Craig *(Mrs. O'Toole)*, Richard Maitland *(Mr. Saunders)*, George Irving *(see note)*.

Comedy. Johnny Wright has invented luminous, blotterless ink. Having been presented with a yacht by an escaped lunatic, Johnny invites a number of business prospects for an afternoon on the yacht. The captain and crew use the yacht as a rumrunner, taking all the passengers as prisoners, while the real owner of the yacht is on another boat pursuing them. Realizing the dangerous predicament of all aboard, Johnny slides down to the side of the yacht and letters a plea for help on the hull in his new ink. This action helps the real owner rescue the yacht, and he is so impressed with Johnny's ingenuity that he offers him a job in his advertising firm. *Inventors. Lunatics. Rumrunners. Businessmen. Yachts. Ink. Advertising.*

Note: An unconfirmed source lists George Irving as playing O. J. Gude.

THE WRONG MR. WRIGHT (Universal-Jewel) **F2.6547**

Universal Pictures. 27 Feb **1927** [c15 Jan 1927; LP23560]. Si; b&w. 35mm. 7 reels, 6,459 ft.

Pres by Carl Laemmle. *Dir* Scott Sidney. *Scen* Harold Shumate. *Titl* James Madison. *Photog* George Robinson.

Cast: Jean Hersholt *(Seymour White)*, Enid Bennett *(Henrietta)*, Dorothy Devore *(Teddy)*, Edgar Kennedy *(Trayguard)*, Walter Hiers *(Bond)*, Robert Anderson *(Wright)*, Jay Belasco, Mathilde Comont.

Farce. Source: George H. Broadhurst, *The Wrong Mr. Wright* (a play; New York, c1938). Seymour White, vice president of the White Corset Co., an outmoded business, has never married because of a childhood sweetheart who jilted him 15 years before. On the same day that Fred Bond, John Wright, and Teddy, Wright's daughter, conspire to use advertising money to promote a new line of lingerie, Seymour is summoned to Atlantic City by his lost sweetheart, and a group of detectives are dispatched to track down Wright. Finding his erstwhile love grown fat and ugly, Seymour denies he is White and takes the name of Wright, thus misleading the detectives. Meanwhile, "Wright" and his daughter are successful with their new fashion designs. Seymour gets out of his engagement by disguising himself as a seedy oaf, and Henrietta, a lady detective, falls in love with him herself. *Detectives. Corsets. Lingerie. Courtship. Disguise. Fashion. Business management. Atlantic City.*

THE WRONGDOERS **F2.6548**

Astor Pictures. 3 Sep **1925** [New York State license application]. Si; b&w. 35mm. 7 reels, 6,230 ft.

Bernarr Macfadden Production. *Dir* Hugh Dierker. *Scen* Lewis Allen Browne. *Photog* John K. Holbrook, Fred Chaston.

Cast: Lionel Barrymore *(Daniel Abbott)*, Anne Cornwall *(Helen Warren)*, Henry Hull *(Jimmy Nolan)*, Henry Sedley *(Sylvester Doane)*, Blanche Craig *(Honora)*, Flora Finch *(society woman)*, William Calhoun *(butler)*, Harry Lee *(solemn man)*, Tammany Young *(crook)*, Tom Brown *(Little Jimmy)*.

Melodrama. Daniel Abbott, a philanthropical druggist who occasionally robs the rich to take care of the poor, goes to court with his young ward, Jimmy Nolan. In the courtroom Daniel meets Mrs. Warren, who, despondent over her inability to care for a newborn baby, has been charged with attempted suicide. Daniel takes mother and daughter under his wing, watching with pride as the girl, Helen, and his ward, Jimmy, grow to a tender adolescence. Sylvester Doane, a tenement owner, falls in love with Helen, and Daniel makes plans to rob him. Jimmy learns with shock of the plans and goes to Doane's apartment to prevent the robbery. Jimmy takes the gems to forestall his father, but he is found with them in his possession and put in jail. Daniel kills Doane and is himself shot. Jimmy is released from jail, and he and Helen are married. *Philanthropists. Pharmacists. Wards. Children. Motherhood. Suicide. Robbery.*

WRONGS RIGHTED **F2.6549**

Sanford Productions. 17 May **1924** [New York State license]. Si; b&w. 35mm. 5 reels, 4,700 ft.

Cast: Tom Gallery, Clara Horton.

Melodrama. No information about the nature of this film has been found.

WU LI CHANG **F2.6550**

Metro-Goldwyn-Mayer Pictures. 18 Dec **1930** [New York State license]. Sd (Movietone); b&w. 35mm. 7 reels.

Dir Nick Grinde. *Cont* Salvador De Alberich. *Scen* Frances Marion. *Adapt* Madeleine Ruthven. *Photog* Leonard Smith. *Art Dir* Cedric Gibbons. *Film Ed* George Baemler. *Rec Engr* Douglas Shearer.

Cast: Ernesto Vilches *(Mister Wu)*, José Crespo *(Alfredo Gregory)*, Angelita Benítez *(Nag Ping)*, Marcela Nivón *(Mrs. Gregory)*, José Soriano Viosca *(Mister Gregory)*, Ura Mita *(Al Wong)*, Mara Del Sobral *(Hilda Gregory)*, Martín Carralaga *(Mister Holman)*.

Melodrama. Source: Maurice Vernon and Harold Owen, *Mr. Wu* (New York opening: 14 Oct 1914). A Spanish-language version of *Mr. Wu* (1927); the synopsis is entered under that title. *Chinese. Seduction. Revenge. Courtship.*

WYOMING **F2.6551**

Metro-Goldwyn-Mayer Pictures. 24 Mar **1928** [c24 Mar 1928; LP25190]. Si; b&w. 35mm. 5 reels, 4,435 ft.

Dir-Writ W. S. Van Dyke. *Scen* Madeleine Ruthven, Ross B. Wills. *Titl* Ruth Cummings. *Photog* Clyde De Vinna. *Film Ed* William Le Vanway. *Wardrobe* Lucia Coulter.

Cast: Tim McCoy *(Lieut. Jack Colton)*, Dorothy Sebastian *(Samantha Jerusha Farrell)*, Charles Bell *(Chief Big Cloud)*, William Fairbanks *(Buffalo Bill)*, Chief Big Tree *(an Indian)*, Goes in the Lodge *(Chief Chapulti)*, Blue Washington *(Mose)*, Bert Henderson *(Oswald)*.

Western melodrama. Big Cloud, an Indian boy, and Jack Colton, son of a pioneer, are united as children by a pledge of friendship but are enemies as adults. The son of Chief Chapulti, Big Cloud insists on fighting for what he believes is Indian territory. Violating a treaty, Big Cloud raids a wagon train. Colton, a lieutenant of Cavalry who is leading the party across the prairie, has a romantic interest in Samantha Farrell, a headstrong woman who would rather hasten west to stake her claim instead of stopping to fight Indians. The raiding party attacks, is repelled by the Cavalry, and is defeated when Chapulti, to stop the killing, shoots his own son. The romance between Colton and Samantha continues. *Indians of North America. Murder. Frontier and pioneer life. Wagon trains. William Frederick Cody. United States Army—Cavalry.*

Note: Indication in copyright records that the film has sound has not been verified.

WYOMING TORNADO **F2.6552**

J. Charles Davis Productions. 1 Jul **1929.** Si; b&w. 35mm. 5 reels.

Cast: Art Acord.

Western melodrama(?). No information about the nature of this film has been found.

THE WYOMING WILDCAT **F2.6553**

R-C Pictures. *Dist* Film Booking Offices of America. 1 Nov **1925** [c1 Nov 1925: LP22016]. Si; b&w. 35mm. 5 reels, 5,156 ft.

Dir Robert De Lacey. *Story* Percy Heath. *Camera* John Leezer. *Asst Dir* Edward Sullivan.

Cast: Tom Tyler *(Phil Stone)*, Billie Bennett *(Blendy Betts)*, G. Clayton *(Jeff Kopp, see note)*, Ethan Laidlaw *(Rudy Kopp)*, Virginia Southern *(Isabel Hastings)*, Alfred Heuston *(Dan Slade)*, Thomas Delmar *(Cyclops)*, Frankie Darro *(Barney Finn)*.

Western melodrama. Cowboy Phil Stone gets work as a foreman on a ranch owned by Isabel Hastings. He learns that Jeff Kopp, a coldblooded old rancher, has some kind of claim on the Hastings ranch; later it is revealed that if Isabel dies before she is 21, unmarried, Kopp will inherit the ranch. Isabel rejects the marriage proposals of his son Rudy, so Kopp decides to kill her. He hires "Cyclops," a notorious one-eyed killer, to do the job. Cyclops kidnaps her and throws her off a cliff into a river; Phil leaps off the cliff with his horse to rescue her. Cyclops and Kopp get their just deserts, while Isabel and Phil get married. *Cowboys. Ranch foremen. Ranchers. Land claims. Inheritance.*

Note: G. Clayton is possibly Gilbert Clayton.

THE YANKEE CLIPPER **F2.6554**

De Mille Pictures. *Dist* Producers Distributing Corp. 23 Mar **1927** [Los Angeles premiere; released 7 May; c11 Feb 1927; LP23654]. Si; b&w. 35mm. 8 reels, 7,920 ft. [Copyrighted as 9 reels.]

Supv C. Gardner Sullivan. *Dir* Rupert Julian. *Titl* John Krafft. *Adapt* Garrett Fort, Garnett Weston. *Story* Denison Clift. *Photog* John Mescall. *Art Dir* John Hughes. *Cutter* Claude Berkeley. *Asst Dir* Fred Tyler. *Unit Mgr* Leigh Smith.

Cast: William Boyd *(Hal Winslow)*, Elinor Fair *(Jocelyn Huntington)*, Junior Coghlan *(Mickey)*, John Miljan *(Richard)*, Walter Long *(Portuguese Joe)*, Louis Payne *(Huntington)*, Burr McIntosh *(Mr. Winslow)*, George Ovey *(Alf)*, Zack Williams *(Ham)*, William Blaisdell *(Ike)*, Clarence Burton *(Captain McIntosh)*, Stanton Heck *(American mate)*, Julia Faye *(Queen Victoria)*, Harry Holden *(Zachary Taylor)*, W. Sousania *(Prince Consort)*, James Wang *(Chinese merchant)*.

Epic melodrama. Thomas Winslow, a Boston shipbuilder, failing to interest the Government in his revolutionary clipper ship, invests his own money in the *Yankee Clipper,* which his son, Hal, takes on her maiden voyage. In England, a design similar to that of Winslow's produces the *Lord of the Isles,* and the two vessels meet in Foochow Harbor, China, each in quest of a cargo of tea. Aboard the English ship is Huntington and his daughter Jocelyn, betrothed to Richard. A wealthy Chinese merchant invites Captain Winslow and Sir Anthony to dinner, and Winslow rescues Jocelyn from a mob of rioting beggars; Winslow, attracted to her, knows of her fiancé's infidelity but says nothing. A race is set, the first ship to arrive in Boston to win the tea trade in its entirety for its nation. Winslow sails with Jocelyn and Richard aboard; Richard proves himself a traitor and coward; Winslow wins the race and the love of Jocelyn. *Clipper ships. Shipbuilding. Ship racing. Tea. China. Foochow. Boston. Queen Victoria. Zachary Taylor. Prince Albert.*

THE YANKEE CONSUL **F2.6555**

Douglas MacLean Productions. *Dist* Associated Exhibitors. 10 Feb **1924** [New York premiere; released 24 Feb; c26 Jan 1924; LU19865]. Si; b&w. 35mm. 6 reels, 6,135 or 6,148 ft.

Dir James W. Horne. *Scen* Raymond Cannon. *Adapt* Raymond Griffith, Lewis Milestone. *Photog* Max Dupont. *Ed* George J. Crone.

Cast: Arthur Stuart Hull *(Jack Morrell)*, Douglas MacLean *(Dudley Ainsworth)*, Patsy Ruth Miller *(Margarita)*, Stanhope Wheatcroft *(Leopoldo)*, Eulalie Jensen *(Donna Theresa)*, L. C. Shumway *(purser of S. S. President)*, Fred Kelsey *(John J. Doyle, secret service agent)*, George Periolat *(Don Rafael Deschado)*, Eric Mayne *(Admiral Rutledge, U. S. N.)*, Bert Hadley *(servant)*.

Farce. Suggested by: Henry Martyn Blossom and Alfred G. Robyn, *The Yankee Consul; a Musical Comedy* (New York opening: 22 Feb 1904; vocal score c1903). Last-minute confusion forces travel agent Dudley Ainsworth to pose as Abijah Boos, American consul to a South American country. On a passenger ship bound for Rio, he meets Margarita Carrosa and becomes involved in a conspiracy involving Margarita and some thieves intent upon stealing a chest of gold from the consulate in Rio. Landing in Rio, Ainsworth notifies the U. S. Navy, then rushes to a castle outside the city where Margarita is being held captive. He rescues Margarita, captures the thieves, greets the summoned Admiral, who arrives accompanied by the real Yankee consul, and then finds that the adventure was all a joke devised by Ainsworth's friends. *Travel agents. Diplomats. Impersonation. Hoaxes. United States—Diplomatic and consular service. Brazil. Rio de Janeiro. United States Navy.*

YANKEE DOODLE, JR. **F2.6556**

Cineart. *Dist* M. J. Burnside. 1 Apr **1922.** Si; b&w with col sequences (Hambschlegel). 35mm. 5 reels, 5,450 ft.

Dir Jack Pratt. *Titl* Ralph Spence. *Photog* William Beckly.

Cast: J. Frank Glendon *(John Arnold, Jr.)*, Zelma Morgan *(Señorita Zorra Gamorra)*, Edward M. Kimball *(John Arnold, Sr.)*, Victor Sarno *(The President)*, Sidney D'Albrook *(The Secret)*, Teddy Whack *(a dog)*.

Romantic comedy-drama. Sent by his fireworks manufacturer father to South America to peddle the pyrotechnics, John Arnold, Jr., has his last chance to make good. He finds in Santa Maria a just-completed revolution, the celebration for which provides a ready market for his products. Adventure beckons him further, however, when John falls in love with Zorra Gamorra, the daughter of the deposed president. With the aid of his fireworks John engineers another revolution that reinstalls Zorra's father in the presidency. The celebration which follows requires a large order of fireworks from Arnold, Sr.—thus reinstating Arnold, Jr., in his father's good graces. *Presidents. Filial relations. Imaginary republics. Revolutions. Fireworks. South America. Dogs.*

Note: A 10-minute fireworks display in the Hambschlegel color process climaxes the film.

A YANKEE GO-GETTER **F2.6557**

Berwilla Film Corp. *Dist* Arrow Film Corp. Jul **1921** [c27 Jul 1921; LP16797]. Si; b&w. 35mm. 5 reels.

Prod Ben Wilson. *Dir* Duke Worne. *Story* Clifford Howard, Burke Jenkins. *Photog* King Gray.

Cast: Neva Gerber *(Lucia Robilant/Vera Robilant)*, James Morrison *(Barry West)*, Joseph Girard *(Nicholas Lanza)*, Ashton Dearholt *("Tronto")*.

Melodrama. Struggling young author Barry West's typewriter is stolen, and he is evicted from his room. Setting out in search of adventure, he finds a pocketbook, which is claimed by two almost identical women. Unable to decide which is its owner, he loses touch with both of them. In applying to Nicholas Lanza for a job, which involves marriage to Lanza's niece, Lucia Robilant, Barry is startled to recognize her as one of the claimants. Unknown to Barry and Lucia, Nicholas, in league with Vera Robilant, a political plotter, plans that they will marry so as to secure Lucia's legacy. Vera succeeds in having her henchmen kidnap Lucia and installs herself in the Lanza home. Barry discovers a secret passage and uncovers the plot after marrying Vera. Then, following the gang's arrest, he is reunited with Lucia, his true love. *Doubles. Authors. Gangs. Politicians. Kidnaping.*

YANKEE MADNESS **F2.6558**

Charles R. Seeling Productions. *Dist* Film Booking Offices of America. 31 Mar **1924** [c31 Mar 1924; LP20036]. Si; b&w. 35mm. 5 reels, 4,680 ft.

Dir-Story Charles R. Seeling. *Scen* George Plympton. *Photog* Pliny Goodfriend.

Cast: George Larkin *(Richard Morton)*, Billie Dove *(Dolores)*, Walter Long *(Pablo del Gardo)*, Earl Schenck *(Rodolfo Emanon)*, Manuel Camere *(Estaban)*, Ollie Kirby *(Theresa)*, Arthur Millett *(Robert Morton)*, J. L. Powell *(President Dominguez)*, Jean Goulven *(Castro)*, Annette Perry *(duenna)*.

Melodrama. En route to Sevilla, Central America, Richard Morton rescues a beautiful girl, whom he knows only as Dolores, from bandits and learns that she also is en route to Sevilla. Arriving, he finds his father under attack by Sevilla revolutionists. Intending to manage his father's ranch, Richard instead gets involved in the revolution; saves President Dominguez from his enemy, Rodolfo Emanon; and learns that Dolores, who has consented to be his wife, is the president's daughter. *Filial relations. Revolutions. Central America.*

THE YANKEE SEÑOR **F2.6559**

Fox Film Corp. 10 Jan **1926** [c27 Dec 1925; LP22167]. Si; b&w. 35mm. 5 reels, 4,902 ft.

Pres by William Fox. *Dir* Emmett Flynn. *Scen* Eve Unsell. *Photog* Daniel Clark. *Asst Dir* Ray Flynn.

Cast: Tom Mix *(Paul Wharton)*, Olive Borden *(Manuelita)*, Tom Kennedy *(Luke Martin)*, Francis McDonald *(Juan Gutiérrez)*, Margaret Livingston *(Flora)*, Alec B. Francis *(Don Fernando)*, Kathryn Hill *(Doris Mayne)*, Martha Mattox *(Aunt Abagail)*, Raymond Wells *(ranch foreman)*, Tony *(Paul's horse)*.

Western melodrama. Source: Katharine Fullerton Gerould, *Conquistador* (New York, 1923). Don Fernando Gutiérrez, an aging Spanish rancher, has for many years searched in vain for his missing grandson, born to a daughter he rashly disinherited when she married an American adventurer. Paul Wharton arrives at Don Fernando's ranch and identifies himself as the missing relative. Fernando's adopted son, Juan, resents Paul's presence and attempts to put him out of the way by tying him on the back of a wild horse. Paul escapes with the help of his own horse, Tony, and returns to the ranch, where he finds his fiancée just arrived from Boston. Don Fernando dies and, through a misunderstanding, Paul's fiancée breaks off the engagement and returns home. Paul gives Juan a sound thrashing and marries Manuelita, a distant relative of Don Fernando's. *Ranchers. Spanish. Bostonians. Grandfathers. Disinheritance.*

YANKEE SPEED **F2.6560**

Sunset Productions. *Dist* Aywon Film Corp. 1 Jul **1924.** Si; b&w. 35mm. 6 reels, 5,200 ft.

Pres by Anthony J. Xydias. *Dir-Scen* Robert N. Bradbury. *Photog* L. W. McManigal.

Cast: Kenneth McDonald *(Dick Vegas)*, Jay Hunt *(Don Verdugo)*, Richard Lewis *(Pedro Ramírez)*, Milton Fahrney *(José T. Vegas)*, John Henry *(Ramón García)*, Viola Yorga *(Marquita Fernández)*, Virginia Ainsworth *(Inez La Velle)*.

Western melodrama. A wealthy oil man, José Vegas, orders his son, Richard, shipped west in a boxcar after the boy shows considerably more interest in athletics than in business. Richard arrives in Arizona, where he is put to work in the oil fields by his father's foreman. At a nearby hacienda, Don Manuel feigns death in order to discover what his heirs will do. Dick eventually brings to justice one of Don Manuel's heirs, García, after that evil Mexican attempts to discover the location of the family fortune by force and cunning. Richard wins the love of Don Manuel's niece, Marquita. *Athletes. Mexicans. Fatherhood. Inheritance. Oil fields. Arizona.*

THE YELLOW BACK (Blue Streak Western) **F2.6561**

Universal Pictures. 3 Oct **1926** [c26 Jun 1926; LP22853]. Si; b&w. 35mm. 5 reels, 4,766 ft.

Pres by Carl Laemmle. *Dir-Writ* Del Andrews. *Photog* Al Jones.

Cast: Fred Humes *(Andy Hubbard)*, Lotus Thompson *(Anne Pendleton)*, Claude Payton *(Bruce Condon)*, Buck Connors *(John Pendleton)*, Willie Fung *(Chinese)*.

Western melodrama. Andy Hubbard, a hired hand on the Circle Bar Ranch, is fired by Condon, the owner, because of his inherent fear of horses, but he is hired by Pendleton, a neighboring rancher whose daughter, Anne, captures his fancy. Andy does not dare reveal his terror of horses when she urges him to ride, and her father assumes him to be a good rider. Condon fences off a spring used by both ranches when Pendleton refuses Condon's suit for the hand of Anne, and she suggests entering her horse in a prize race to pay for a well. Andy, deciding to hide the horse until after the race, learns that the ranch will be lost by default and admits his cowardice to Anne; but her love and encouragement spur him on to ride in and win the race, thereby saving the ranch. *Ranchers. Cowardice. Water rights. Horseracing. Horses.*

YELLOW CONTRABAND **F2.6562**

Pathé Exchange. 28 Oct **1928** [c9 Nov 1928; LP25818]. Si; b&w. 35mm. 6 reels, 5,686 ft.

Dir Leo Maloney. *Story-Scen* Ford I Beebe. *Photog* Edward A. Kull. *Film Ed* Joseph Kane. *Prod Mgr* Don F. Osborne.

Cast: Leo Maloney *(Leo McMahon/Blackie Harris)*, Greta Yoltz *(Mazie)*, Noble Johnson *(Li Wong Foo)*, Tom London *(Drag Conners)*, Joseph Rickson *(Pierre Dufresne)*, Robert Burns *(sheriff)*, Vester Pegg *(Dude McClain)*, Walter Patterson *(Ice-house Joe)*, Bill Patton *(Rawhide)*, Bud Osborne, Frank Ellis, Tom Forman *(dope runners)*.

Melodrama. When Leo McMahon, an Internal Revenue agent who closely resembles Blackie Harris, a notorious Chicago gangster, learns that Blackie is coming west to transport a shipment of heroin across the Canadian border, he disguises himself as Blackie in an attempt to intercept the narcotics. Blackie outwits Leo, however, and returns to Chicago with the dope. Blackie is killed, and Leo recovers the heroin with the help of Mazie, a policewoman disguised as a gun moll. *Government agents. Policewomen. Gangsters. Heroin. Disguise. Internal Revenue Service. Chicago. Canada.*

YELLOW FINGERS **F2.6563**

Fox Film Corp. 21 Mar **1926** [c21 Mar 1926; LP22555]. Si; b&w. 35mm. 6 reels, 5,594 ft.

Pres by William Fox. *Dir* Emmett Flynn. *Scen* Eve Unsell. *Photog* Ernest G. Palmer, Paul Ivano. *Asst Dir* Ray Flynn.

Cast: Olive Borden *(Saina)*, Ralph Ince *(Brute Shane)*, Claire Adams *(Nona Deering)*, Edward Piel *(Kwong Li)*, Otto Matieson *(Kario)*, Nigel De Brulier *(Rajah Jagore)*, Armand Kaliz *(De Vries)*, Josephine Crowell *(Mrs. Van Kronk)*, May Foster *(Toinette)*, John Wallace *(Pegleg LaForge)*, Charles Newton *(Higgins)*.

Melodrama. Source: Gene Wright, *Yellow Fingers* (Philadelphia, 1925). Saina, who has been reared as a white girl by Captain Shane, a trader, falls in love with him and dreams of marrying him. On a trip to Bangkok, two of Shane's sailors resue Nona, an English girl, and she stows away on Shane's ship to escape Kwong Li, a Chinaman who desires her. Saina becomes jealous of the captain's attentions to Nona, and accidentally learning of her own halfcaste parentage, she conspires to deliver the English girl to Kwong Li. It develops that Saina is, in fact, a rajah's granddaughter and an inheritor of a throne. Eventually, she relents and leads Shane to the girl's rescue; he marries Nona, leaving Saina to her fate. *Traders. Sea captains. Chinese. English. Halfcastes. Royalty. Inheritance. Malaysia.*

THE YELLOW LILY **F2.6564**

First National Pictures. 20 May **1928** [c7 May 1928; LP25223]. Si; b&w. 35mm. 8 reels, 7,187 ft.

Pres by Richard A. Rowland. *Prod* Ned Marin. *Dir* Alexander Korda. *Cont* Bess Meredyth. *Titl* Garrett Graham. *Story-Adapt* Lajos Biró. *Photog* Lee Garmes. *Art Dir* Max Parker. *Film Ed* Harold Young. *Cost* Max Ree.

Cast: Billie Dove *(Judith Peredy)*, Clive Brook *(Archduke Alexander)*, Gustav von Seyffertitz *(Kinkeline)*, Marc MacDermott *(Archduke Peter)*, Nicholas Soussanin *(Eugene Peredy)*, Eugenie Besserer *(The Archduchess)*, Jane Winton *(Mademoiselle Julie)*, Charles Puffy *(The Mayor)*.

Romantic drama. Rakish Archduke Alexander falls in love with Judith Peredy, sister of the doctor who practices in a Hungarian village near Alexander's hunting lodge. Although Judith loves Alexander, she outwardly spurns him, having been warned by her brother, Eugene. Not one to suffer denial lightly, the archduke comes to Judith's room during Eugene's absence from home and makes violent love to her. Eugene arrives and is saved from the archduke's sword when Judith shoots the man she loves. She and her brother are imprisoned in Budapest at the command of the archduke's father, who does not want his son to marry beneath himself. When Judith is sure of her love for Alexander, she convinces his father and mother of her sincerity. By special dispensation from the emperor the marriage is allowed. *Rakes. Physicians. Nobility. Brother-sister relationship. Social classes. Hungary. Budapest.*

YELLOW MEN AND GOLD **F2.6565**

Goldwyn Pictures. ca20 May **1922** [Chicago and Des Moines premieres; c1 Jun 1922; LP17936]. Si; b&w. 35mm. 6 reels, 5,224 ft.

Dir Irvin V. Willat. *Scen* Irvin V. Willat, L. V. Jefferson. *Photog* Clyde De Vinna. *Art Dir* Cedric Gibbons. *Film Ed* Clayton Hamilton.

Cast: Richard Dix *(Parrish)*, Helene Chadwick *(Bessie)*, Henry Barrows *(Carroll)*, Rosemary Theby *(Carmen)*, Richard Tucker *(Lynch)*, Fred Kohler *(Craven)*, Henry Hebert *(Todd)*, William Moran *(Cunningham)*, Goro Kino *(Chang)*, George King *(Jili)*, William Carroll *(John)*, R. T. Frazier *(Abraham)*.

Adventure melodrama. Source: Gouverneur Morris, *Yellow Men and Gold* (New York, 1911). Parrish, a young author, leaves his study during a storm to answer a call for help. *He discovers a dying man and is rewarded with a treasure map, which he shows to Carroll, a retired sea captain. They plan a quest for the treasure; but before Carroll's ship sails, Parrish is drugged, relieved of the map, and thrown from the dock. Bessie, a girl aboard the* Shantung, *rescues Parrish. Parrish has concealed a copy of the treasure map; and learning that Carroll has tricked him, he embarks on the* Shantung *and arrives at the site of the treasure before Carroll's armed gang interrupt. Bessie is imprisoned on Carroll's ship but is rescued by Parrish, who burns that ship and returns to the* Shantung. *After many adventures together, Parrish and Bessie discover their mutual love.* At this point, it transpires that the young author, in his study, has recounted the story from one of his own manuscripts. *Authors. Sea captains. Treasure. Ships.*

THE YELLOW STAIN **F2.6566**

Fox Film Corp. 21 May **1922** [c21 May 1922; LP18015]. Si; b&w. 35mm. 5 reels, 5,006 ft.

Pres by William Fox. *Dir* Jack Dillon. *Story-Scen* Jules Furthman. *Photog* Don Short.

Cast: John Gilbert *(Donald Keith)*, Claire Anderson *(Thora Erickson)*, John P. Lockney *(Quartus Hembly)*, Mark Fenton *(Olaf Erickson)*, Herschel Mayall *(Dr. Brown)*, Robert Daly *(Daniel Kersten)*, Mace Robinson *(Lyman Rochester)*, James McElhern *(clerk)*, Frank Hemphill *(Pete Borg)*, May Alexander *(Mrs. Borg)*.

Melodrama. Donald Keith, a young lawyer who takes up residence in the small town of Owasco, Michigan, finds himself opposed by lumber king Quartus Hembly, feared by all the townspeople. Keith takes up the case of Daniel Kersten against Hembly, who has cheated him out of his property, and during his investigation he discovers that the father of Thora Erickson, whom he loves, conspired with Hembly against Kersten, and at length he obtains a deathbed confession from Erickson. Hembly has Keith wounded on the night before the trial and bribes the jury, but Keith appears, stirs up the town in rebellion against Hembly in spite of his weakened condition, and wins his case. *Lawyers. Lumbermen. Smalltown life. Michigan.*

A YELLOW STREAK **F2.6567**

Ben Wilson Productions. *Dist* Rayart Pictures. Feb **1927.** Si; b&w. 35mm. 5 reels, 4,929 ft.

Dir Ben Wilson.

Cast: Ben Wilson, Neva Gerber.

Western melodrama. "Hero, forced to give up ranch, is also accused of murder of new owner. His sister loves hero, but they are estranged when she learns he killed her brother. Trouble is ironed out when bandit, dying, confesses to brother's murder." (*Motion Picture News Booking Guide,* 12: 67, Apr 1927.) *Ranchers. Bandits. Murder. Brother-sister relationship.*

THE YELLOWBACK **F2.6568**

FBO Pictures. *Dist* RKO Productions. 20 Jan **1929** [c20 Jan 1929; LP257]. Si; b&w. 35mm. 7 reels, 5,957 ft.

Dir Jerome Storm. *Cont* John Twist. *Titl* Randolph Bartlett. *Story* James Oliver Curwood. *Photog* Phil Tannura. *Film Ed* Jack Kitchen. *Asst Dir* Sam Nelson.

Cast: Tom Moore *(O'Mara),* Irma Harrison *(Elsie Loisel),* Tom Santschi *(Jules Breton),* William Martin *(Poleon),* Lionel Belmore *(McDougal).*

Northwest melodrama. Jules Breton, a giant trapper, kills a man in a barroom fight, and O'Mara, a Mounted Policeman, is detailed to bring him in. O'Mara finds Breton with Elsie Loisel, Breton's fiancée, and the men fight. Elsie knocks O'Mara cold with a pair of metal tongs, and Breton escapes; the following day, Elsie shows the unsuspecting Mountie the wrong trail. Breton kills Elsie's father, however, and she then helps O'Mara (with whom she falls in love) to bring Breton before the bar of justice. *Trappers. Murder. Canada. Northwest Mounted Police.*

YESTERDAY'S WIFE **F2.6569**

Columbia Pictures. *Dist* C. B. C. Film Sales. 15 Aug **1923** [c10 Jan 1924; LP19820]. Si; b&w. 35mm. 6 reels, 5,800 ft.

Dir Edward J. Le Saint.

Cast: Irene Rich *(Megan Daye),* Eileen Percy *(Viola Armes),* Lottie Williams *(Sophia),* Josephine Crowell *(Mrs. Harbours),* Lewis Dayton *(Gilbert Armes),* Philo McCullough *(Victor Fleming),* William Scott *(Jeo Coombs).*

Romantic drama. Source: Evelyn Campbell, "Yesterday's Wife," in *Snappy Stories* (50:3–26, 1 May 1920). Megan Daye and Gilbert Armes expect to be happily married forever, but a quarrel over an incidental thing makes a divorce inevitable. Gilbert marries Viola, a pretty switchboard operator, and Megan gets a job as a companion to a rich old lady. They meet at a resort and effect a reconciliation soon after Viola's accidental boating death. *Telephone operators. Marriage. Divorce. Resorts.*

THE YIDDISH MAMA *see* **MY YIDDISHE MAMA**

YOLANDA **F2.6570**

Cosmopolitan Pictures. *Dist* Metro-Goldwyn Distributing Corp. 19 Feb **1924** [New York premiere; released 15 Sep; c30 Jul 1924; LP20448]. Si; b&w. 35mm. 11 reels, 10,700 ft.

Dir Robert G. Vignola. *Scen* Luther Reed. *Photog* Ira H. Morgan, George Barnes. *Set Dsgn* Joseph Urban. *Cost* Gretl Urban.

Cast: Marion Davies *(Princess Mary of Burgundy),* Lyn Harding *(Charles the Bold, Duke of Burgundy),* Holbrook Blinn *(King Louis XI),* Maclyn Arbuckle *(Bishop La Balue),* Johnny Dooley *(The Dauphin, Charles, Duke of Paris),* Ralph Graves *(Maximillian of Styria),* Ian MacLaren *(Campt-Basso),* Gustav von Seyffertitz *(Olivier de Daim),* Theresa Maxwell Conover *(Queen Margaret),* Paul McAllister *(Count Jules d'Humbercourt),* Leon Errol *(innkeeper),* Mary Kennedy *(Antoinette Castleman),* Thomas Findlay *(Castleman),* Arthur Donaldson *(Lord Bishop),* Roy Applegate *(Sir Karl de Pitti),* Martin Faust *(Count Calli).*

Historical romance. Source: Charles Major, *Yolanda* (New York, 1905). Traveling under the name of Yolanda, Princess Mary of Burgundy falls in love with Maximillian, disguised as a knight, at a silk fair. Later he is imprisoned by conspirators but is saved from execution by the princess. Threatened by war with the Swiss, her father, the duke, cancels her matrimonial plans and betroths her to the half-witted Dauphin of France. Maximillian rescues her from the French court and following the duke's death leads the Burgundians to victory in battle; the wedding of Maximillian and Mary is then announced. *Royalty. Nobility. Swiss. Disguise. Burgundy. France—History—House of Valois. Charles the Bold. Louis XI (France).*

THE YOSEMITE TRAIL **F2.6571**

Fox Film Corp. 24 Sep **1922** [c24 Sep 1922; LP19171]. Si; b&w. 35mm. 5 reels, 4,735 ft.

Pres by William Fox. *Dir* Bernard J. Durning. *Scen* Jack Strumwasser. *Photog* Don Short.

Cast: Dustin Farnum *(Jim Thorpe),* Irene Rich *(Eve Marsham),* Walter McGrail *(Ned Henderson),* Frank Campeau *(Jerry Smallbones),* W. J. Ferguson *(Peter Blunt),* Charles French *(The Sheriff).*

Melodrama. Source: Ridgwell Cullum, *The One Way Trail* (London, 1911). Jim Thorpe and his Cousin Ned both love Eve Marsham, but their friendship comes to an end when Ned wins Eve. Jim goes off to South America and on returning home finds that Ned has become a criminal and is mistreating his wife. Eventually Ned is shot and killed, and Eve realizes that she loves Jim. *Marriage. Friendship. South America.*

YOU ARE GUILTY **F2.6572**

Mastodon Films. c21 May **1923** [LP18980]. Si; b&w. 35mm. 5 reels, ca5,000 ft.

Pres by C. C. Burr. *Dir* Edgar Lewis. *Titl* Gerald C. Duffy. *Story* Roy Middleton. *Photog* Edward C. Earle.

Cast: James Kirkwood *(Stephen Martin),* Doris Kenyon *(Alice Farrell),* Robert Edeson *(Theodore Tennent),* Mary Carr *(Mrs. Grantwood),* Russell Griffin *("Buddy" Tennent),* Edmund Breese *(Judge Elkins),* Carleton Brickert *(Joseph D. Grantwood),* William Riley Hatch *(Murphy).*

Drama. Stephen Martin takes the blame for the misappropriation of funds by Joe Grantwood, his half brother, to spare Mrs. Grantwood shame. While Steve wanders aimlessly around the world, Alice Farrell, his former sweetheart, marries Theodore Tennent, who dies after they have a son, Buddy. Steve returns, refuses a bribe offered by Joe, then is accused of Joe's murder. His trial is interrupted by Buddy, who reveals that Steve was rescuing Buddy from a fire at the time of the murder. A free man, Steve is reunited with Alice. *Brothers. Self-sacrifice. Embezzlement. Injustice. Trials. Bribery. Fires.*

YOU ARE IN DANGER *see* **THE LITTLE GIRL NEXT DOOR**

YOU CAN'T BEAT THE LAW **F2.6573**

Trem Carr Productions. *Dist* Rayart Pictures. Feb **1928.** Si; b&w. 35mm. 6 reels, 5,260 ft.

Dir Charles J. Hunt. *Adapt-Scen* Arthur Hoerl. *Story* H. H. Van Loan. *Photog* Ernest Depew.

Cast: Lila Lee *(Patricia Berry),* Cornelius Keefe *(Jerry Judd),* Warner Richmond *(Bowery Blackie),* Betty Francisco *(Bessie),* Charles L. King *(Red),* Bert Starkey *(Canada),* Frank Clark *(Lieutenant O'Connor).*

Crook drama. On the trail of the gang of crooks responsible for a series of jewelry store stickups, a young policeman, Jerry Judd, falls in love with Patricia Berry, whose brother, Bowery Blackie, leads the gang. The gang tries to frame Jerry so as to discredit him in Patricia's eyes, but the trick only tips off Jerry to their hideout. Both Patricia and Jerry are torn between love and duty: she pleads for her brother, he decides he must do his job. Patricia warns Blackie, who is killed in the fray, and Jerry reports to his superior that Blackie was killed defending his sister. *Police. Gangs. Brother-sister relationship. Robbery. Frameup.*

YOU CAN'T FOOL YOUR WIFE **F2.6574**

Famous Players–Lasky. *Dist* Paramount Pictures. ca22 Apr **1923** [New York premiere; released 29 Apr; c19 Apr 1923; LP18888]. Si; b&w. 35mm. 6 reels, 5,703 ft.

Pres by Jesse L. Lasky. *Dir* George Melford. *Story-Scen* Waldemar Young. *Photog* Bert Glennon.

Cast: Leatrice Joy *(Edith McBride),* Nita Naldi *(Ardrita Saneck),* Lewis Stone *(Garth McBride),* Pauline Garon *(Vera Redell),* Paul McAllister *(Dr. Konrad Saneck),* John Daly Murphy *(Jackson Redell),* Julia Swayne Gordon *(Lillian Redell),* Tom Carrigan *(Russell Fenton),* Dan Pennell *(John Yates),* Brownie Roberts, "Beach Pete" Morris.

Society melodrama. Wealthy stockbroker Garth McBride and his wife,

Edith, accept an invitation to visit friends in Florida. A flirtation between Garth and Ardrita Saneck, the wife of a famous surgeon, develops into a more serious relationship, and they decide to take an airplane ride to Nassau. When they miss their return trip and must remain overnight in Nassau, Edith returns to New York alone and finds work as a nurse. Later, Garth is seriously injured by a business rival (Russell Fenton) and is taken to Dr. Saneck, who is made aware that his patient is his wife's lover. When Dr. Saneck realizes, however, that Garth is also the husband of the attending nurse (Edith), he saves him. Apologies and explanations are exchanged, and both couples are reconciled. *Surgeons. Stockbrokers. Nurses. Infidelity. Airplanes. Florida. Nassau.*

YOU CAN'T GET AWAY WITH IT **F2.6575**

Fox Film Corp. 18 Nov or 9 Dec **1923** [c3 Dec 1923; LP19677]. Si; b&w. 35mm. 6 reels, 6,152 or 6,019 ft.

Pres by William Fox. *Dir* Rowland V. Lee. *Scen* Robert N. Lee. *Photog* G. O. Post.

Cast: Percy Marmont *(Charles Hemingway)*, Malcolm McGregor *(Henry Adams)*, Betty Bouton *(Jill Mackie)*, Barbara Tennant *(Jane Mackie)*, Grace Morse *(May Mackie)*, Clarissa Selwyn *(Mrs. Hemingway)*, Charles Cruz *(Charles Hemingway, Jr.)*.

Romantic drama. Source: Gouverneur Morris, "You Can't Get Away With It," in *Incandescent Lily, and Other Stories* (New York, 1914). Poverty forces Jill Mackie to work in a department store, and there she falls in love with its owner, Charles Hemingway. They form an illicit alliance when Mrs. Hemingway refuses to grant Charles a divorce. Eventually, Hemingway becomes ill and dies, leaving Jill a sum of money. She leaves the country, falls in love with a young man to whom she confides her past, but breaks with him when he suggests they make a similar arrangement. *Infidelity. Poverty. Department stores.*

YOU CAN'T KEEP A GOOD MAN DOWN **F2.6576**

Lone Star Motion Picture Co. **1922.** Si; b&w. 35mm. 6 reels.

Melodrama(?). No information about the precise nature of this film has been found. *Negro life.*

YOU FIND IT EVERYWHERE **F2.6577**

Outlook Photoplays. *Dist* Jans Film Service. Jul **1921.** Si; b&w. 35mm. 5 reels.

Dir Charles Horan. *Photog* Harry Fischbeck.

Cast: Catherine Calvert *(Nora Gorodna)*, Herbert Rawlinson *(Andrew Gibson)*, Macey Harlam *(José Ferra)*, Riley Hatch *(Dan Carter)*, Nathaniel Sacks *(Wurtzel Pantz)*, Arnold Lucy *(Charles Simpson)*, Robert Ayerton *(Ignatius Riley)*, Jack Drumier *(Harvey Hill)*, Norbert Wicki *(Salvatore)*, Peggy Worth *(Lila Normand)*, Dora Mills Adams *(Mrs. Normand)*, Hattie Delaro *(Mrs. Simpson)*.

Comedy-drama. Source: Booth Tarkington and Harry Leon Wilson, *The Gibson Upright* (Garden City, New York, 1919). Andrew Gibson inherits problems when his father dies and leaves shares of his piano manufacturing business to his workmen. To add to his troubles, Andrew's girl, Nora Gorodna, is being pursued by José Ferra, one of the workmen; and Lila Normand, a society girl, tricks Andrew into proposing. José finds out about the proposal and informs Nora. Andrew tries to solve the factory difficulties by turning the plant over to the workmen. No longer having a job, Andrew is rejected by Lila, and Nora has accepted José. Andrew goes to the Maine woods for a rest, while José hires thugs and begins to destroy the factory. Andrew returns in time to head off José's plans and to convince Nora he loves her. She willingly forsakes José. *Factory management. Pianos. Maine.*

YOU NEVER KNOW **F2.6578**

Vitagraph Co. of America. 10 Dec **1922** [c22 Oct 1922; LP18351]. Si; b&w. 35mm. 5 reels, 4,867 ft.

Dir Robert Ensminger. *Scen* J. Raleigh Davies. *Story* Harry Dittmar. *Story-Scen? (see note)* C. Graham Baker. *Photog* Ernest Smith.

Cast: Earle Williams *(Eddie Manning)*, Gertrude Astor *(Miriam Folansbee)*, George Field *(Carlos Medina)*, Claire Du Brey *(Inez)*, Coy Watson, Jr. *(Muggsy)*, James Conway *(Jasper Folansbee)*, Louis Dumar *(José De Silva)*, Leonard Trainor *(Miguel)*.

Melodrama. Carlos Medina, leader of a Latin American revolution, is visiting Jasper Folansbee, a backer of the revolutionists, and is wooing Folansbee's daughter, Miriam. As a result of striking Muggsy, a street urchin, with her automobile, Miriam meets Eddie Manning, a mysterious American who frequents a Spanish bar, and offers him employment as her chauffeur. Eddie has learned from Inez, a Spanish dancer, that Medina has only his own gain in mind; he stations Muggsy to watch Medina's yacht and is imprisoned in the bar. Rescued by Muggsy in time to pursue the fleeing Medina, Eddie reveals himself to be a Secret Service agent, exposes the South American as a swindler of both his people and Folansbee, and rescues a grateful Miriam. *Children. Secret service. Revolutions. Latin America.*

Note: Some sources give release date as Nov 1922 and attribute story and scenario to C. Graham Baker.

YOU NEVER KNOW WOMEN **F2.6579**

Famous Players–Lasky. *Dist* Paramount Pictures. 20 Sep **1926** [c22 Sep 1926; LP23135]. Si; b&w. 35mm. 6 reels, 6,064 ft.

Pres by Adolph Zukor, Jesse L. Lasky. *Dir* William Wellman. *Screenplay* Benjamin Glazer. *Story* Ernest Vajda. *Photog* Victor Milner.

Cast: Florence Vidor *(Vera)*, Lowell Sherman *(Eugene Foster)*, Clive Brook *(Norodin)*, El Brendel *(Toberchik)*, Roy Stewart *(Dimitri)*, Joe Bonomo *(The Strong Man)*, Irma Kornelia *(Olga)*, Sidney Bracy *(manager)*.

Melodrama. On her way to the theater, Vera, star of a Russian vaudeville troupe, is rescued from a falling girder by Eugene Foster, a wealthy broker who persists in his efforts to win the girl. Foster engages the troupe to perform at his home, and Vera, stunned by a fall, awakens to find Foster pleading his love, while Norodin, her partner who loves her, sees them embrace. Norodin, who performs an underwater stunt, asks Vera not to be present for his act and causes her to believe him dead; heartbroken, Vera tells Foster of her mistake; and enraged, he attempts to seize her. The magician appears, pins Foster to the wall with knives, and advises him to leave before the last blade is thrown. Vera and Norodin are thus happily reunited. *Brokers. Russians. Magicians. Vaudeville. Jealousy.*

YOU'D BE SURPRISED **F2.6580**

Famous Players–Lasky. *Dist* Paramount Pictures. 25 Sep **1926** [New York premiere; released 4 Oct; c1 Nov 1926; LP23279]. Si; b&w. 35mm. 6 reels, 5,994 ft.

Pres by Adolph Zukor, Jesse L. Lasky. *Assoc Prod* B. P. Schulberg. *Dir* Arthur Rosson. *Story-Screenplay* Jules Furthman. *Photog* William Marshall.

Cast: Raymond Griffith *(The Coroner)*, Dorothy Sebastian *(Ruth Whitman)*, Earle Williams *(Deputy District Attorney)*, Edward Martindel *(District Attorney)*.

Comedy-mystery. At a houseparty given by the district attorney, the lights are extinguished following the theft of a valuable diamond, and he is later found murdered. The coroner arrives to investigate and discovers Ruth Whitman, the district attorney's ward, hidden in a large clock, clutching the missing gem. She claims that she was pushed in; and as he prepares to take everyone's fingerprints, the lights are again turned off. The coroner is attacked by an armored figure, who is revealed to be the dead man's deaf and dumb valet. He then apparently confesses to the crime but is later himself found murdered. The coroner accuses the girl but by accident discovers the real killer—the deputy assistant attorney. *Thieves. Valets. District attorneys. Coroners. Deafmutes. Murder.*

YOUNG AMERICA **F2.6581**

Essanay Film Manufacturing Co. *Dist* Elk Photo Plays. c6 May **1922** [LP17846]. Si; b&w. 35mm. 5 reels.

Dir Arthur Berthelet.

Cast: Charles Frohman Everett *("Art" Simpson)*, Jasper *(himself, a dog)*, Madelyn Clare *(Edith Doray)*, Howard I. Smith *(Jack Doray)*, Wilson Reynolds *(Officer Reuter)*, Marlow Bowles *(Nutty Bremer)*, William Wadsworth *(Joe, the Grouch)*, Leona Ball *(Mrs. Grouch)*, Florence Barr *(Mrs. McGuire)*, Evelyn Ward *(Mary Blount, Art's sweetheart)*, Frances Raymond *(Mrs. Blount)*.

Melodrama. Source: Frederick Ballard, *Young America; a Play in Three Acts ... (Suggested by Pearl Franklin's "Mrs. Doray" Stories)* ... (New York, 1917). Art and Jasper, a poor American boy and his faithful dog, have only each other in the face of a cruel world, which constantly imperils their liberty. Art's efforts to raise $2 for Jasper's tax brings him into conflict with the law, but he eventually proves his good intentions and finds a loving home with the Dorays. *Children. Police. Taxes. Friendship. Dogs.*

Note: "This picture was started by Essanay some years ago, but only completed late last fall. ... Elk Photo Plays ... aver it is not a reissue." (*Variety*, 7 Jul 1922, p60.)

YOUNG APRIL F2.6582

De Mille Pictures. *Dist* Producers Distributing Corp. 11 Oct **1926** [c16 Aug 1926; LP23031]. Si; b&w. 35mm. 7 reels, 6,858 ft.

Supv William Sistrom. *Dir* Donald Crisp. *Adapt* Jeanie Macpherson, Douglas Doty. *Photog* Peverell Marley. *Art Dir* Anton Grot. *Asst Dir* Fred Tyler. *Prod Mgr* Emile De Ruelle. *Cost* Adrian.

Cast: Joseph Schildkraut *(Prince Caryl)*, Rudolph Schildkraut *(King Stefan)*, Bessie Love *(Victoria)*, Bryant Washburn *(Prince Michael)*, Clarence Geldert *(Krutchki)*, Alan Brooks *(Jerry Lanningan)*, Dot Farley *(Maggie)*, Carrie Daumery *(Countess Morne)*, Baldy Belmont *(Hans [Ivan?])*.

Romantic comedy-drama. Source: Egerton Castle, *"Young April"* (New York, 1899). Youthful Crown Prince Caryl is told he must marry the Archduchess of Saxheim; and when his father, King Stefan, refuses him a last fling in Paris, he "borrows" the crown, skips off to Paris, and pawns it. Meanwhile, at an American finishing school for girls, Archduchess Victoria is informed that she must return to Europe to marry Prince Caryl and decides to have one last week in Paris; there, on a shopping spree, she buys Caryl's crown from a jeweler. One evening she sees Caryl in a famous gambling club and falls in love with him. Prince Michael, next in succession to the throne, comes to inform the prince of the possible political complications resulting from his scandalous behavior. Discovering that Victoria has his crown, Caryl falls in love with her; she learns of his identity; but her note, revealing her own identity, is intercepted by Michael. Caryl abdicates in order to marry his American sweetheart; then, perceiving the plot, he returns to Paris, heartbroken. Following the abdication of Stefan, however, Caryl abducts Victoria, and they escape via carriage, automobile, and airplane. *Royalty. Abdication. Abduction. Imaginary kingdoms. Paris.*

YOUNG DESIRE F2.6583

Universal Pictures. 8 Jun **1930** [c3 Jun 1930; LP1345]. Sd (Movietone); b&w. 35mm. 7 reels, 6,529 ft. [Also si; 6,110 ft.]

Pres by Carl Laemmle. *Dir* Lew Collins. *Adapt-Dial* Winifred Reeve, Matt Taylor. *Photog* Roy Overbaugh. *Rec Engr* C. Roy Hunter.

Cast: Mary Nolan *(Helen Herbert)*, William Janney *(Bobby Spencer)*, Ralf Harolde *(Blackie)*, Mae Busch *(May)*, George Irving *(Mr. Spencer)*, Claire McDowell *(Mrs. Spencer)*, Alice Lake, Gretchen Thomas.

Romantic drama. Source: William R. Doyle, *Carnival* (New York opening: 24 Apr 1924). Helen Herbert, a dancer in a carnival sideshow, wearying of her drab life, leaves the show and falls in love with young Bobby Spencer, who insists on helping her. She hesitates to marry him, however, because of her past, but he insists. Realizing that their marriage would alienate Bobby's family and jeopardize his future, Helen returns to the carnival, and though Bobby follows, Helen's companions keep her concealed from him. After a talk with his father, Helen resolves the dilemma by volunteering for a balloon ascension and leaps to her death. *Dancers. Social classes. Balloons. Suicide. Carnivals. Sideshows.*

THE YOUNG DIANA F2.6584

Cosmopolitan Productions. *Dist* Paramount Pictures. 7 Aug **1922** [c28 Jun 1922; LP18021]. Si; b&w. 35mm. 7 reels, 6,744 ft.

Dir Albert Capellani, Robert G. Vignola. *Scen* Luther Reed. *Photog* Harold Wenstrom. *Set Dsgn* Joseph Urban.

Cast: Marion Davies *(Diana May)*, Maclyn Arbuckle *(James P. May)*, Forrest Stanley *(Commander Cleeve)*, Gypsy O'Brien *(Lady Anne)*, Pedro De Cordoba *(Dr. Dimitrius)*.

Melodrama. Source: Marie Corelli, *The Young Diana; an Experiment of the Future, a Romance* (New York, c1918). *The father of young Diana May wishes to marry her to British nobility although she is in love with Richard Cleeve, a sailor, and is pursued by Dr. Dimitrius, a scientist in search of the "elixir of youth." Dimitrius informs Diana that Richard is eloping with Lady Anne, and she believes the false accusation. Twenty years later, as an embittered spinster, she goes to Switzerland in answer to a scientist's advertisement for an experimental subject. Leaving indications of her suicide, she finds Dimitrius, who restores Diana's youth and beauty. Amid the social whirl of Europe, she meets Cleeve, now married, whom she spurns though he offers to desert his wife.* Diana awakens to find she has only been dreaming. Cleeve returns, explaining he had received sudden orders for departure, now revoked, and that he was escorting Lady Anne to her new husband. The picture fades out on the wedding of Diana and Cleeve. *Spinsters. Scientists. Sailors. Rejuvenation. Weddings. Switzerland. Dreams.*

YOUNG EAGLES F2.6585

Paramount Famous Lasky Corp. 21 Mar **1930** [New York premiere; released 5 Apr; c5 Apr 1930; LP1202]. Sd (Movietone); b&w. 35mm. 8 reels, 6,406 ft. [Also si; 6,710 ft.]

Dir William A. Wellman. *Scen-Dial* Grover Jones, William Slavens McNutt. *Photog* A. J. Stout. *Film Ed* Allyson Shaffer. *Song: "Love Here Is My Heart"* Ross Adrian, Leo Silesu. *Song: "The Sunrise and You"* Arthur A. Penn. *Rec Engr* Eugene Merritt. *Asst Dir* Charles Barton.

Cast: Charles Rogers *(Lieut. Robert Banks)*, Jean Arthur *(Mary Gordon)*, Paul Lukas *(Von Baden)*, Stuart Erwin *("Pudge" Higgins)*, Virginia Bruce *(Florence Welford)*, Gordon De Main *(Major Lewis)*, James Finlayson *(Scotty)*, Frank Ross *(Lieutenant Graham)*, Jack Luden *(Lieutenant Barker)*, Freeman Wood *(Lieutenant Mason)*, George Irving *(Colonel Wilder)*, Stanley Blystone *(Captain Deming)*, Newell Chase, Lloyd Whitlock.

War melodrama. Source: Elliott White Springs, "The One Who Was Clever," in *Red Book* (53:74–79, Aug 1929). Elliott White Springs, "Sky-High," in *Red Book* (53:50–54, Jul 1929). Lieut. Robert Banks, an American aviator on leave in Paris, meets Mary Gordon, a young American who lives abroad, but their romance is cut short by his return to the front. In an air battle, Robert brings down and captures the Grey Eagle, Baden, and takes him to American Intelligence in Paris. Mary, ostensibly a spy for the Germans, drugs Robert, who awakens to find that his uniform has been stolen by Baden. Later, in an exciting air conflict, Baden is wounded but shoots down Robert's plane. The German rescues him, however, and takes him to an Allied hospital, assuring him of Mary's love; his faith in her is restored when he learns that she is actually a spy for U. S. Intelligence. *Spies. Aviators. Germans. World War I. Paris. American Expeditionary Force.*

YOUNG IDEAS F2.6586

Universal Pictures. 7 Jul **1924** [c17 Jun 1924; LP20313]. Si; b&w. 35mm. 5 reels, 4,095 ft.

Dir Robert F. Hill. *Scen* Hugh Hoffman. *Photog* Jackson Rose.

Cast: Laura La Plante *(Octavia Lowden)*, T. Roy Barnes *(Pritchett Spence)*, Lucille Ricksen *(Eloise Lowden)*, James O. Barrows *(Uncle Eph)*, Lydia Yeamans Titus *(Aunt Minnie)*, Jennie Lee *(Grandma)*, Rolfe Sedan *(Bertie Loomis)*, Buddy Messinger *(Bob Lowden)*, Brownie *(himself)*.

Comedy. Source: Sophie Kerr, "Relative Values," in *Saturday Evening Post* (195:5–7, 27 Jan 1923). Octavia Lowden supports her aunt, uncle, sister, kid brother, and grandmother, all of whom, except the last, claim ailments to avoid work. When Pritchett Spence, her employer and admirer, calls and discovers the imposition, he lures Octavia away and has her quarantined, thus creating a situation that compels the family to go to work and offers her time for a romantic attachment. *Parasites. Family life. Courtship. Quarantine.*

Note: Working title: *Relativity.*

YOUNG MAN OF MANHATTAN F2.6587

Paramount-Publix Corp. 17 May **1930** [c17 May 1930; LP1307]. Sd (Movietone); b&w. 35mm. 8 reels, 7,306 ft.

Dir Monta Bell. *Dial* Daniel Reed. *Adapt* Robert Presnell. *Photog* Larry Williams. *Film Ed* Emma Hill. *Songs: "Good 'n' Plenty," "I've Got It," "I'd Fall in Love All Over Again," "I'll Bob Up With the Bob-O-Link"* Irving Kahal, Pierre Norman, Sammy Fain. *Sd Rec* Ernest F. Zatorsky.

Cast: Claudette Colbert *(Ann Vaughn)*, Norman Foster *(Toby McLean)*, Ginger Rogers *(Puff Randolph)*, Charles Ruggles *(Shorty Ross)*, Leslie Austin *(Dwight Knowles)*, H. Dudley Hawley *(doctor)*, Four Aalbu Sisters *(Sherman Sisters)*.

Domestic drama. Source: Katherine Brush, *Young Man of Manhattan* (New York, 1930). Toby McLean, New York sportswriter, meets movie columnist Ann Vaughn while covering the Dempsey-Tunney fight in Philadelphia, and their subsequent romance leads to marriage. They begin life modestly in a New York apartment, but shortly afterward he is sent to St. Louis to cover the World Series and is introduced to Puffy Randolph, a dizzy young socialite, though he is too engrossed with Ann to notice her. Soon he becomes jealous of his wife's success and earnings and goes on the town with Puffy; they again meet at the bicycle races, and returning home drunk, he is ordered from the house by his wife. They separate, but when Ann is temporarily blinded by tainted liquor, Toby realizes she still loves him and plunges into his work; with the aid of his fellow reporter, Shorty Ross, he regains his self-esteem and is reunited with Ann. *Sportswriters. Motion picture columnists. Socialites. Marriage. Jack Dempsey. Gene Tunney. World Series. Philadelphia. Saint Louis (Missouri).*

YOUNG NOWHERES F2.6588

First National Pictures. 1 Oct **1929** [New York premiere; released 20 Oct; c12 Dec 1929; LP914]. Sd (Vitaphone); b&w. 35mm. 7 reels, 7,850 ft. [Also si; 5,256 ft.]

Dir Frank Lloyd. *Scen-Dial* Bradley King Wray. *Titl* Bradley Barker. *Photog* Ernest Haller. *Film Ed* Ray Curtiss.

Cast: Richard Barthelmess *(Albert Whalen [Binky])*, Marion Nixon *(Annie Jackson)*, Bert Roach *(Mr. Jesse)*, Anders Randolf *(Cleaver)*, Raymond Turner *(George)*, Jocelyn Lee *(brunette)*.

Romantic drama. Source: Ida Alexa Ross Wylie, "Young Nowheres," in *Saturday Evening Post* (199:18–19, 16 Apr 1927). Albert Whalen, known as "Binky," is a lonely, sentimental youth who operates an elevator in an apartment house owned by Cleaver. His employer leaves for California for the Christmas holiday, and Binky's sweetheart, Annie Jackson, a poor orphan, visits him; they go to Coney Island to loll on the beach, and there they talk about the future and fall asleep. Toward dawn they are awakened by the tide and return home, wet and cold. When Annie develops pneumonia and is taken to the hospital, Binky spends his last penny to buy her a cheap coat. He takes her to Cleaver's luxurious apartment to recuperate, and Cleaver surprises them by returning unexpectedly on Christmas Eve. Binky tells this story to a judge in night court; he dismisses the case, putting Cleaver to shame for spoiling the couple's happiness; and Mr. Jesse, who befriends them, sees to their future. *Elevator operators. Orphans. Judges. Landlords. Courtship. Christmas. New York City. Coney Island.*

THE YOUNG RAJAH F2.6589

Famous Players–Lasky. *Dist* Paramount Pictures. 12 Nov **1922** [c25 Oct 1922; LP18343]. Si; b&w. 35mm. 8 reels, 7,705 ft.

Pres by Jesse L. Lasky. *Dir* Philip Rosen. *Adapt-Scen* June Mathis. *Photog* James C. Van Trees.

Cast: Rodolph Valentino *(Amos Judd)*, Wanda Hawley *(Molly Cabot)*, Pat Moore *(Amos Judd as a boy)*, Charles Ogle *(Joshua Judd)*, Fanny Midgley *(Sarah Judd)*, Robert Ober *(Horace Bennett)*, Jack Giddings *(Slade)*, Edward Jobson *(John Cabot)*, Josef Swickard *(Narada)*, Bertram Grassby *(Maharajah)*, J. Farrell MacDonald *(Tehjunder Roy)*, George Periolat *(General Gadi)*, George Field *(Prince Musnud)*, Maude Wayne *(Miss Van Kovert)*, William Boyd *(Stephen Van Kovert)*, Joseph Harrington *(Dr. Fettiplace)*, Spottiswoode Aitken *(Caleb)*.

Romantic drama. Source: John Ames Mitchell, *Amos Judd* (New York, 1895). Alethea Luce, *Amos Judd, a Play in a Prologue and Four Acts* (c26 Jul 1919). A young rajah, believed to be descended from Arjuna, the mortal brother of the god Krishna, is brought to America for safety and raised as Amos Judd. He becomes a star athlete and popular student at Harvard, falls in love with Molly Cabot, and discovers his ability to see the future in dreams. Because on the day before his wedding to Molly he dreams that an attack will be made upon his life, Amos goes into a sanatorium for protection. Even so, he is attacked but is rescued and told that he is needed by his people. Amos realizes his duty and leaves Molly to return to India—sadly, yet with optimism, for he has dreamt of a Hindu wedding with Molly as his bride. *Royalty. Hinduism. Divination. Sanitariums. India. Harvard University.*

YOUNG WHIRLWIND F2.6590

FBO Pictures. 16 Sep **1928** [c28 Aug 1928; LP25573]. Si; b&w. 35mm. 5 reels, 4,764 ft.

Prod William Le Baron. *Dir* Louis King. *Screenplay* Ethel Hill. *Titl* Helen Gregg. *Story* H. C. Schmidt. *Photog* Virgil Miller. *Film Ed* George Marsh. *Asst Dir* Charles Kerr.

Cast: Buzz Barton *(David "Red" Hepner)*, Edmund Cobb *(Jack)*, Frank Rice *(Hank)*, Alma Rayford *(Molly)*, Tom Lingham *(sheriff)*, Eddie Chandler *(Johnson)*, Bill Patton *(Bart)*, Tex Phelps *(bandit)*.

Western melodrama. Four desperate men sabotage the plane of Jack Merrill, a young air mail pilot, and it crashes in the desert. The bandits then attempt to steal the moneybags, but Jack, with the help of Jeff Johnson and Red Hepner, fights them off. The bandit leader, Bart, later abducts Red (a young boy) and forces Jeff to steal the moneybags in exchange for Red's release. Jeff is jailed by the sheriff, and little Red follows Bart back to the outlaw camp. He knocks out two of the bandits with his slingshot and leads the other two right into the sheriff's posse. Jeff is paroled in Red's custody. *Aviators. Bandits. Sheriffs. Hostages. Postal service. Airplane accidents.*

THE YOUNGER GENERATION F2.6591

Columbia Pictures. 4 Mar **1929** [c18 Mar 1929; LP227]. Talking sequences (Movietone); b&w. 35mm. 8 reels, 7,866 ft. [Also si; 7,246 ft.]

Prod Jack Cohn. *Dir* Frank R. Capra. *Scen* Sonya Levien. *Dial* Howard J. Green. *Story* Fannie Hurst. *Photog* Teddy Tetzlaff. *Art Dir* Harrison Wiley. *Tech Dir* Edward Shulter. *Film Ed* Arthur Roberts. *Asst Dir* Tenny Wright. *Prod Mgr* Joe Cook.

Cast: Jean Hersholt *(Julius Goldfish)*, Lina Basquette *(Birdie Goldfish)*, Rosa Rosanova *(Tildie Goldfish)*, Ricardo Cortez *(Morris)*, Rex Lease *(Eddie Lesser)*, Martha Franklin *(Mrs. Lesser)*, Julia Swayne Gordon *(Mrs. Striker)*, Julanne Johnston *(Irma Striker)*, Jack Raymond *(Pinsky)*, Syd Crossley *(butler)*, Otto Fries *(tradesman)*.

Drama. Morris Goldfish, the son of a Jewish emigrant family living on Delancey Street, becomes a successful Fifth Avenue antique dealer and, changing his name to Fish, takes his parents out of the East Side and installs them in his swank apartment. His father becomes ill, longing for the old neighborhood. Birdie marries her childhood sweetheart; Birdie's husband is sent to jail, and Morris kicks her out of his apartment. The elder Goldfish dies, and his wife returns to Delancey Street to be with Birdie, whose husband is soon released from jail. *Jews. Antique dealers. Family life. Wealth. New York City—Fifth Avenue. New York City—Lower East Side.*

YOUR BEST FRIEND F2.6592

Harry Rapf Productions. *Dist* Warner Brothers Pictures. 26 Mar **1922** [c20 Apr 1922; LP17766]. Si; b&w. 35mm. 7 reels, 6,650 ft.

Prod Harry Rapf. *Story-Scen-Dir* William Nigh. *Photog* James Diamond, Jack Brown, Sidney Hickox.

Cast: Vera Gordon *(Mrs. Esther Meyers)*, Harry Benham *(Robert Meyers)*, Stanley Price *(Harry Meyers)*, Belle Bennett *(Aida)*, Beth Mason *(Aida's mother)*, Dore Davidson *(Morris)*.

Society melodrama. Mrs. Esther Meyers, a wealthy widow who bestows every care on her two sons, Robert and Harry, is disappointed when Robert elopes with Aida, a society girl who has a frivolous and socially ambitious mother. To satisfy her son and his mother-in-law, Mrs. Meyers moves from her modest home to a fashionable residence in New York's West Side. Harry, to meet debts, misappropriates funds from the bank where he is employed; Mrs. Meyers persuades him to confess and then appeals to Robert, destined for district attorneyship, who in turn accuses Harry of jeopardizing his (Robert's) future. After selling her jewels to make good the loss, Mrs. Meyers castigates Robert, Aida, and her mother and returns with Harry to her old home. Later, she is visited by the repentant wife and her mother, who are forced to remain through a quarantine imposed because of a smallpox epidemic; Aida becomes gradually domesticated and an inseparable friend of her mother-in-law. *Mothers-in-law. Motherhood. Family life. Smallpox. New York City.*

YOUR FRIEND AND MINE (Metro-SL Special Production) F2.6593

S-L Pictures. *Dist* Metro Pictures. 5 Mar **1923** [c21 Mar 1923; LP18798]. Si; b&w. 35mm. 6 reels, 5,750 ft.

Prod Arthur H. Sawyer, Herbert Lubin. *Dir* Clarence G. Badger. *Scen* Winifred Dunn. *Photog* Rudolph Bergquist.

Cast: Enid Bennett *(Patricia Stanton)*, Huntly Gordon *(Hugh Stanton)*, Willard Mack *(Ted Mason)*, Rosemary Theby *(Mrs. Beatrice Mason)*, J. Herbert Frank *(Victor Reymier)*, Otto Lederer *(Andrea Mertens)*, Allene Ray *(Marie Mertens)*.

Society melodrama. Source: Willard Mack, *Your Friend and Mine* (a play; publication undetermined). Finding her husband more interested in his oil dealings than in her, Patricia Stanton is susceptible to the wooings of a bogus artist (who is supposedly painting her portrait while a real artist works behind a screen) and is lured to his island retreat. The Ted Masons hear of it and rush to the rescue. Ted reads his new play, which is so closely related to Patricia's actions that she sees the point and returns with the Masons to her enlightened husband. *Playwrights. Artists. Marriage. Oil business.*

YOUR GOOD NAME *see* **TRIFLING WITH HONOR**

YOUR WIFE AND MINE F2.6594

Excellent Pictures. 1 Aug **1927** [c30 Aug 1927; LP24339]. Si; b&w. 35mm. 6 reels, 5,867 ft.

Pres by Samuel Zierler. *Dir* Frank O'Connor. *Titl* Marc Edmund Jones. *Photog* André Barlatier.

Cast: Phyllis Haver *(Phyliss Warren)*, Stuart Holmes *(Charlie Martin)*,

Wallace MacDonald *(Robert Warren)*, Barbara Tennant *(prisoner)*, Katherine Lewis *(Winifred Martin)*, Blanche Upright *(Mrs. Coy)*, June Lufboro *(Tabitha Tubbs)*, Jay Emmett *(Antonio Tubbs)*.

Farce. Among the guests at a garden party are a newly married couple, the husband being attorney to the host. The host informs him that he has arranged for the prison escape of a girl, who is to return to him a considerable sum of money, and enlists the lawyer's aid. The girl is concealed in the host's mansion, causing considerable agitation among the guests. In order to get to the city to collect the money, both men are forced to lie to their wives and thus arouse their suspicion. The pair of wives go to the hotel where they know their husbands are to be found and themselves become innocently involved in the intrigue. A marital mixup grows into a major turmoil, which is finally settled in a common police court. *Prison escapees. Lawyers. Marriage. Blackmail.*

YOU'RE FIRED **F2.6595**

Goodwill Pictures. 8 Dec **1925** [New York State license]. Si; b&w. 35mm. 5 reels, 4,800 ft.

Cast: Bill Bailey.

Comedy(?). No information about the nature of this film has been found.

YOURS TO COMMAND **F2.6596**

R-C Pictures. *Dist* Film Booking Offices of America. 1 May **1927** [c29 Mar 1927; LP23803]. Si; b&w. 35mm. 5 reels, 4,734 ft.

Pres by Joseph P. Kennedy. *Dir* David Kirkland. *Cont* Scott Darling, Ewart Adamson. *Story* Basil Dickey, Harry Haven. *Photog* Jules Cronjager. *Asst Dir* Bill Dagwell.

Cast: George O'Hara *(Robert Duane)*, Shirley Palmer *(Colleen O'Brien)*, William Burress *(Pa O'Brien)*, Dot Farley *(Ma O'Brien)*, Jack Luden *(Ted Hanson)*, William Humphrey *(Parsons)*.

Romantic comedy. While driving through Oklahoma, Robert Duane, a wealthy New York youth, meets Colleen O'Brien, a schoolteacher who believes him to be the Duane chauffeur. Subsequently, Colleen's father strikes oil and comes to New York, bent on social conquest. When the O'Briens come to rent Duane's Long Island home, he continues to pose as the chauffeur and has the agent agree to rent the estate with the condition that he remain to drive their car. Ted Hanson, a society crook, persuades the family to give a dinner and invite his friends, and he induces O'Brien to buy a priceless tiara, which he plans to steal. Duane, realizing Hanson's duplicity, twice saves the jewelry. The ensuing struggle of Duane and O'Brien against the gang is ended by the police, and the lovers are happily united. *Chauffeurs. Schoolteachers. Thieves. Mistaken identity. Oklahoma. New York City. Long Island.*

YOUTH AND ADVENTURE **F2.6597**

Richard Talmadge Productions. *Dist* Film Booking Offices of America. 4 Jan **1925** [c15 Jan 1925; LP21036]. Si; b&w. 35mm. 6 reels, 5,525 ft.

Pres by A. Carlos. *Dir* James W. Horne. *Story-Cont* Frank Howard Clark. *Photog* William Marshall. *Film Ed* Doane Harrison. *Athletic stunts conceived and personally executed by* Richard Talmadge.

Cast: Richard Talmadge *(Reggie Dillingham)*, Pete Gordon *(Joe Potts)*, Joseph Girard *(Clint Taggart)*, Margaret Landis *(Mary Ryan)*, Fred Kelsey *(Red Mullin)*, Katherine Lewis *(Phyllis)*.

Comedy. Reggie Dillingham, a society clubman who has squandered all but $70,000 of his million-dollar inheritance from his father, is upbraided by his attorney, who bets Reggie that he cannot support himself for 6 months. Reggie hands over the remaining money to the attorney for investment and sets out to find a job. He fails at being a book agent and a motorcycle cop. When, however, he snaps a compromising picture of Clint Taggart, a political boss who likes chorus girls, Taggart makes Reggie the managing editor of a city newspaper to keep him quiet. Reggie immediately liberalizes the policy of the paper and falls in love with Mary Ryan, Taggart's secretary, with whose help he discovers that Taggart is mixed up with bootlegging. Reggie uses Taggart's own paper to expose this fact, and Taggart orders Reggie to resign. Reggie refuses, Taggart brings in a gang of thugs to throw him out, and Reggie resists with the help of the loyal staff of the paper. Reggie obtains documentary evidence of Taggart's criminal activities and holds him for the police. Mary and Reggie make plans to continue their relationship, and Reggie is informed by his lawyer that his money has been doubled by fortunate investments. *Wastrels. Editors. Secretaries. Lawyers. Police. Book agents. Newspapers. Bootlegging. Inheritance. Wagers.*

YOUTH FOR SALE **F2.6598**

C. C. Burr Pictures. 1 Aug **1924** [c14 Jul 1924; LP20305]. Si; b&w. 35mm. 6 reels, 6,000 ft.

Dir William Christy Cabanne. *Scen-Titl* Raymond S. Harris. *Scen? (see note)* Gerald C. Duffy. *Photog* Jack Brown.

Cast: May Allison *(Molly Malloy)*, Sigrid Holmquist *(Connie Sutton)*, Richard Bennett *(Montgomery Breck)*, Charles Emmett Mack *(Tom Powers)*, Alice Chapin *(Mrs. Malloy)*, Tom Blake *(Bill Brophy)*, Dorothy Allen *(Pansy Mears)*, Charles Beyer *(George Archibald)*, Harold Foshay *(Edward Higgins)*.

Society drama. Source: Izola Forrester, "The Gray Path," in *Ainslee's* (50:1-50, Sep 1922). Molly and her boyfriend, Tom, are persuaded by Connie to attend a party, where Molly is temporarily blinded by her first drink of alcohol. To obtain funds to save Molly's sight, Connie agrees to marry a wealthy man of the theater, but this stratagem becomes unnecessary when Molly and Tom go to Vienna on their honeymoon and have her sight restored by a famous surgeon. *Surgeons. Blindness. Prohibition. Vienna.*

Note: Advertising before release gives the title as *Youth To Sell* and the scenarist as Gerald C. Duffy.

YOUTH MUST HAVE LOVE **F2.6599**

Fox Film Corp. 1 Oct **1922** [c10 Oct 1922; LP19090]. Si; b&w. 35mm. 5 reels, 4,368 ft.

Pres by William Fox. *Dir* Joseph Franz. *Story-Scen* Dorothy Yost. *Photog* George Schneiderman.

Cast: Shirley Mason *(Della Marvin)*, Cecil Van Auker *(Marvin)*, Wallace MacDonald *(Earl Stannard)*, Landers Stevens *(Frank Hibbard)*, Wilson Hummel *(Austin Hibbard)*.

Western melodrama. Earl Stannard, accused of murder, is arrested and sent to jail. He escapes and finds that he was framed by the murderer and his sweetheart's father, Marvin, who lied to protect himself and his friend. Eventually, the old man clears Stannard and reveals his friend as the culprit. *Murder. Frameup. Prison escapes.*

Note: Working title: *An Unexpected Wife.*

YOUTH TO SELL *see* **YOUTH FOR SALE**

YOUTH TO YOUTH **F2.6600**

Metro Pictures. 16 Oct **1922** [c10 Oct 1922; LP18308]. Si; b&w. 35mm. 6 reels, 6,900 ft.

Prod-Dir Emile Chautard. *Adapt-Scen* Edith Kennedy. *Story* Hulbert Footner. *Photog* Arthur Martinelli. *Art Dir* J. J. Hughes.

Cast: Billie Dove *(Eve Allinson)*, Edythe Chapman *(Mrs. Cora Knittson)*, Hardee Kirkland *(Taylor)*, Sylvia Ashton *(Mrs. Jolley)*, Jack Gardner *(Maurice Gibbon)*, Cullen Landis *(Page Brookins)*, Mabel Van Buren *(Mrs. Brookins)*, Tom O'Brien *(Ralph Horry)*, Paul Jeffrey *(Everett Clough)*, Carl Gerard *(Howe Snedecor)*, ZaSu Pitts *(Emily)*, Lincoln Stedman *(Orlando Jolley)*, Gertrude Short *(Luella)*, Noah Beery *(Brutus Tawney)*.

Melodrama. Eve Allinson, a country girl come to Broadway, becomes a star overnight but slips away to join a touring group when she realizes she is rumored to be the mistress of her middle-aged backer, Brutus Tawney. Page Brookins, a farmer, sees Eve perform; falls in love with her; and writes to a friend in New York, hoping to further her career. Tawney sets out to fetch her, and when Page hears about her reputation he assumes the rumor to be true and breaks their engagement. Left with no alternative, Eve leaves with Tawney on his yacht, but Page reconsiders and rows out after them. Tawney gives Eve and Page his blessing. *Actors. Farmers. Theatrical troupes. Reputation. New York City—Broadway.*

YOUTHFUL CHEATERS **F2.6601**

Film Guild. *Dist* W. W. Hodkinson Corp. 6 May **1923** [c7 May 1923; LP19111]. Si; b&w. 35mm. 6 reels, 5,700 ft.

Dir Frank Tuttle. *Story* Townsend Martin. *Photog* Fred Waller, Jr. *Tech Dir* Fred Waller, Jr. *Mus Cue* E. Jessup Smith.

Cast: William Calhoun *(Edmund MacDonald)*, Glenn Hunter *(Ted MacDonald)*, Martha Mansfield *(Lois Brooke)*, Marie Burke *(Mrs. H. Clifton Brooke)*, Nona Marden *(Marie Choisuil)*, Dwight Wiman *(Dexter French)*.

Romantic drama. Ted MacDonald deserts his father and their sailing ship after meeting Lois Brooke and succumbs to an easy life, disregarding his father's order to continue their relief work among cholera victims in the South Sea Islands. Captain MacDonald visits Lois' home and persuades

Ted and Lois to return to the ship. *Filial relations. Social service. Cholera. South Sea Islands.*

YOUTH'S GAMBLE **F2.6602**

Harry J. Brown Productions. *Dist* Rayart Pictures. 7 Jul **1925** [New York premiere]. Si; b&w. 35mm. 5 reels, 5,264 ft.

Pres by W. Ray Johnston. *Supv* Harry J. Brown. *Dir* Albert Rogell. *Story-Cont* Henry Roberts Symonds, John Wesley Grey. *Photog* Ross Fisher.

Cast: Reed Howes *(William Ignatius Newton)*, James Thompson *(Addison Simms)*, Margaret Morris *(Hazel Dawn)*, Wilfred Lucas *(Harry Blaine)*, Gale Henry *(Winifred Elaine Thomas)*, William Buckley *(Tombstone Reilly)*, David Kirby *(Obituary Blake)*.

Action melodrama. A charmingly worthless young man inherits a car, a dime, and a valet from his millionaire father and sets out to learn about life. *Millionaires. Valets. Playboys. Inheritance.*

ZANDER THE GREAT **F2.6603**

Cosmopolitan Pictures. *Dist* Metro-Goldwyn Distributing Corp. 4 May **1925** [c20 May 1925; LP21491]. Si; b&w. 35mm. 8 reels, 6,844 ft.

Dir George Hill. *Adapt* Frances Marion. *Photog* George Barnes, Harold Wenstrom. *Sets* Joseph Urban. *Film Ed* James McKay. *Asst Dir* James O'Neil. *Cost* Gretl Urban.

Cast: Marion Davies *(Mamie Smith)*, Holbrook Blinn *(Juan Fernández)*, Harrison Ford *(Dan Murchison)*, Harry Watson *(Good News)*, Harry Myers *(Texas)*, George Siegmann *(Black Bart)*, Emily Fitzroy *(The Matron)*, Hobart Bosworth *(The Sheriff)*, Richard Carle *(Mr. Pepper)*, Hedda Hopper *(Mrs. Caldwell)*, Master Jack Huff *(Zander)*, Olin Howland *(Elmer Lovejoy)*.

Western melodrama. Source: Edward Salisbury Field, *Zander the Great; a Comedy in Prologue and Three Acts* (New York, 1923). Mamie Smith is rescued from an orphanage by Mrs. Caldwell, the mother of a small child whom Mamie calls Zander. Mrs. Caldwell dies, and Mamie takes Zander west in search of the boy's missing father. In Arizona she meets Dan Murchison, a liquor smuggler who pretends to be Caldwell in order to avoid the sheriff. Mamie falls in love with Dan but learns of his illegal activities and threatens to inform on him. Dan locks her up and send Zander to his friend Juan for safekeeping. Mamie escapes and is captured by Black Bart's gang, who tie her to a tree. She frees herself and goes to Juan's men, arriving in time to round up the gang members. Dan tells Mamie that he is not Caldwell, and she and Dan are married. *Orphans. Sheriffs. Gangs. Smugglers. Impersonation. Arizona.*

ZAZA **F2.6604**

Famous Players–Lasky. *Dist* Paramount Pictures. 16 Sep **1923** [New York premiere; released 21 Oct; c9 Oct 1923; LP19484]. Si; b&w. 35mm. 7 reels, 7,076 ft.

Pres by Adolph Zukor. *Dir* Allan Dwan. *Scen* Albert Shelby Le Vino. *Photog* Hal Rosson.

Cast: Gloria Swanson *(Zaza, an actress)*, H. B. Warner *(Bernard Dufresne, a diplomat)*, Ferdinand Gottschalk *(Duke de Brissac)*, Lucille La Verne *(Aunt Rosa)*, Mary Thurman *(Florianne, a soubrette)*, Yvonne Hughes *(Nathalie, Zaza's maid)*, Riley Hatch *(Rigault, a theater manager)*, Roger Lytton *(stage manager)*, Ivan Linow *(The Apache)*.

Melodrama. Source: Pierre François Samuel Berton and Charles Simon, *Zaza, pièce en cinq actes* (Paris, 1904). Zaza, a Parisian music hall soubrette, falls in love with Bernard Dufresne, a French diplomat, whom she believes to be unmarried. When she learns the truth from Florianne, a jealous colleague, she releases Dufresne despite his offers to divorce his wife. Years later Zaza is reunited with Dufresne after his wife has died. *Diplomats. Entertainers. Infidelity. Music halls. Paris.*

THE ZEPPELIN'S LAST RAID (Reissue) **F2.6605**

6 Jun **1930** [New York State license]. Si; b&w. 35mm. 5 reels, 4,900 ft.

Note: Thomas H. Ince's companion to *Civilization*; originally released by U. S. Exhibitors' Booking Corp. in 1918.

THE ZERO HOUR **F2.6606**

Dist Principal Pictures. 6 Mar **1923** [New York State license]. Si; b&w. 35mm. 5 reels.

Cast: Lester Cuneo.

Melodrama(?). No information about the nature of this film has been found.

Note: Production company not determined.